THE
SOURCEBOOK

To Public Record Information

The Comprehensive Guide to County, State, & Federal Public Records Sources

Second Edition

BRB Publications, Inc.
www.brbpub.com

Dedicated to the Searching & Understanding of Public Records

Public Record Research Library

THE
SOURCEBOOK
To Public Record Information - Second Edition

Edited by: Michael L. Sankey, James R. Flowers Jr., and Peter J. Weber

©2001 By BRB Publications, Inc.
1971 East Fifth Street, Suite 101
Tempe, AZ 85281
800-929-3811   Fax 800-929-3810

www.brbpub.com

ISBN 1-879792-60-5

The sourcebook to public record information : the
    comprehensive guide to county, state, and federal public
    records sources / [edited by : Michael L. Sankey, James R.
    Flowers Jr. and Peter J. Weber]. -- 2nd ed.
        p. cm.
        ISBN: 1-879792-60-5

        1. Public records--United States--States--Information
Services--Directories. 2. Courts--United States--States
--Directories. 3. Public records--United States--States
--Computer network resources.   I. Sankey, Michael L.,
1949- II. Flowers, James R. (James Robert), 1973-
Weber, Peter J. (Peter Julius), 1952-

    JK468.P76S68 2000   352.3'87
                          QBI00-700980

The Sourcebook combines elements of *The Sourcebook of State Public Records,*
The Sourcebook of County Court Records, Federal Court Records,
County Asset and Lien Records, and *The County Locator*

Contents

Introduction 1

How This Book is Organized 3

Section I: Public Record Primer 6

Public Records Unveiled 7

Definition of Public Records 7
Public vs. Private vs. Personal 7
How Personal Information Enters the Public Domain 8
Where Public Records are Held 8
The Common Methods Used to Access Public Records 9

Public Record & Public Information Categories 11

Business Records 11
Lien and Security Interest Records 12
Important Individual Records 13
Additional Public Information Records Worth Mentioning 16

Searching for State Public Records 19

Additional State Offices 19
State Restrictions Table 19
State Agency Public Record Restrictions Table 20

Searching State Occupational Licensing Boards 23

The Privacy Question 23
Using the Licensing Section 23
Search Fees 24
Search Tip--Distinguish the Type of Agency 24
Other Forms of Licensing & Registration 25
Other Information Available 26

Searching Federal Court Records 27

Federal Court Structure 27
How Federal Trial Courts are Organized 28
Electronic Access to Federal Courts 30
A Few Searching Hints 32
Federal Records Centers and the National Archives 33

Searching Other Federal Government Records Online 35

EDGAR 35
Aviation Records 36
Military Records 36
Online Sources Used by the Experts 37
Best Gateways to Government Records 37
Best Online Government Resources 39
State & Regional Resources 41

Searching County Court Records 43

The County Court Records Sections 43
Reading the State Charts 44
Reading the Court Profiles 44
Some Court Basics 46
Types of Litigation in Trial Courts 46
State Court Structure 45
How Courts Maintain Records 46

Performing a Search at the County Level 49

Ways to Obtain Records 49
Fees, Charges & Usage 50
A Few Words About Searching Public Records Online 50

Searching Recording Office Records 51

The Lowdown on Recorded Documents 51
How the Recording Offices Section is Organized 52
General Searching Rules 52
Special Categories of Collateral 52
More Details About UCC Records 53
The UCC Locator Chart 55

Using the County Locator Section 57

Using ZIP Codes When Searching for Public Records 57

Using a Public Record Vendor 59

Hiring Someone to Obtain the Record 59
Which Type of Vendor is Right for You? 60
10 Questions to Ask an Online Vendor 61

Section II: Public Records by State 65

57 State Chapters 67 and forward

Each State Chapter is Organized as Follows
State Agencies
State Licensing Boards
Federal Courts
County Courts
Recording Offices
County Locator

Introduction

Complex and Mysterious?

The words "Public Records" often convey a complex, almost mysterious source of information that is perceived as difficult to access, hard to decipher and likely to be of interest only to private investigators and reporters. This view could not be further from the truth!

Indeed, the use of current public records is one of the fundamental pillars of our democratic society.

The Information Trail

Have you ever—

- paid property taxes?
- purchased a home?
- registered to vote?
- owned a business?
- been married?

If so, YOU have become part of the "public record information paper trail!"

Modern society has become extremely dependent on information. Information is, indeed, the life load of most business and personal interaction. Government and private industry require record keeping to regulate, license and hire/fire. Individuals need public information for managing personal affairs and meeting one's responsibilities as citizens. Nearly all individuals and entities create a **trail of information** that is a **history of daily life**.

You could say that the trail starts with a birth certificate, a Social Security Number or articles of incorporation. The trail extends past the death certificate or record of dissolution into, virtually, infinite time. These many records—some accessible, some accessible with restrictions, and some inaccessible—create and embellish an identity.

Your Access to Over 20,000 Government Agencies

Herein, we will examine these paper trails that begin or maintained at the federal, state, county, and in certain instances, the city and town level. This *Sourcebook* is especially useful for these applications:

Background Searching and Investigation

Pre-Employment and Tenant Screening

Locating People

Locating Assets

Legal Research

This *Sourcebook* reveals where records are kept, outlines the access requirements and gives searching hints, tells which agencies are online. Over 20,000 government agencies are profiled so you can explore the depths of the public record industry.

Public records are meant to be used for the benefit of society. As a member of the public, you or someone in authority is entitled to review the public records held and established by government agencies. Whether you are a business owner, a reporter, an investigator, or even a father trying to check on your daughter's first date, you can access public records to meet your needs.

Equipped with the information contained in these pages, you can find the facts, gain access to the information you need and even track your own "information trail!"

Special Note From the Editors

The Sourcebook to Public Record Information represents thousands of hours of research, right up to the day of printing.

For those of you who need to know more or need to have this information constantly updated, we recommend two expanded versions of this product. ***The Public Records Research System*** (PRRS) is available on CD-ROM updated semi-annually, and on the Internet at www.publicrecordsources.com. BRB Publications is 100% devoted to the understanding of public records.

How This Book is Organized

General Layout

The Sourcebook is organized into two Sections--

♦   Public Record Primer

♦   Individual State Chapters

The Public Record Primer

The purpose of this section is to assist the reader in knowing *how to search* and *where categories of records can be found.* An important part of this section is the discussion of privacy issues including public information vs. personal information and how records enter the public domain.

The Primer contains many searching hints and is an excellent overall source of information that will especially help those not familiar with searching government records.

The **Finding Federal Records Online** chapter is highlighted by an excellent article contributed by Alan Schlein, author of *Find it Online!* (Facts on Demand Press). Mr. Schlein presents a unique dissertation about the best federal government Internet sites for finding usual information quickly and efficiently.

Another important chapter is **Using a Vendor to Obtain Public Records.** This chapter contains a wealth of information about commercial vendors, especially those who offer online access to records.

The State Chapters

The individual state chapters in the *Sourcebook* have been compiled into an easy to use format. Six sub-chapters or sections are presented in this order:

1. State Public Record Agencies
2. State Licensing and Regulatory Boards
3. Federal Courts (US District and Bankruptcy)
4. County Courts
5. County Recorder Offices
6. City/County Cross Reference and ZIP Code/City Cross Reference

Information Found in the Agency Profiles

What separates this *Sourcebook* from a typical address and phone listing reference book, is the depth of knowledge presented about each agency. The beginning of each state and/or county sub-chapter has an overall discussion of the public records policies, with important characteristics and searching hints. The following details are have been researched and presented (when applicable) within each profile:

Agency Facts: office hours; time zone; web sites

Record Access: methods of access; restrictions (to whom); indexing; search requirements; when records available online; when free public access terminals are at the counter; turnaround times, how far back (years) records are kept.

Fees: access fees, copy fees; certification fees; expedited fees, if credit cards accepted; what types of checks accepted; to whom to make the check to

Misc: how to purchase databases or customized lists; if the more than one agency must be visited in the county to get all records

Section I

Public Record Primer

Public Records Unveiled

Definition of Public Records

The strict **definition** of **public records** is—

> *"Those records maintained by government agencies*
> *that are open without restriction to public inspection,*
> *either by statute or by tradition."*

If access to a record that is held by a government agency is restricted in some way, then it is not a public record.

Accessibility Paradox

Adding to the mystique of government records is the accessibility paradox. For example, in some states a specific category of records is severely restricted, and therefore those records are not "public," while the very same category of records may be 100% open in other states. Among these categories are criminal histories, vehicle ownership records and worker's compensation records.

At times, you will see the following box printed on pages throughout this Sourcebook. We are not trying to fill up space. As your public record searching takes you from state-to-state, this is the one important adage to keep in mind.

> "Just because records are maintained in a certain way in your state or county, do not assume that any other county or state does things the same way you are used to."

Public vs. Private vs. Personal

Before reading further, let's define types of records held by government or by private industry. Of course, not all information about a company or individual is public. The boundaries between public and private information are not well understood, and continually undergo intense scrutiny. The following is an introduction to the subject from a viewpoint of a professional record searcher.

Public Record

Public records are records of **incidents** or **actions** filed or recorded with a government agency for the purpose of notifying others about the matter—the "public." The **deed** to your house recorded at the county recorder's office is a public record—it is a legal requirement that you record it with the county recorder. Anyone requiring details about your property may review or copy the documents.

Public Information

Your **telephone listing** in the phone book is public information; that is, you freely furnished the information to ease the flow of commercial and private communications.

Personal Information

Any information about a person or business that the person or business might consider private and confidential in nature, such as your **Social Security Number**, is personal information. Such information will remain private to a limited extent unless it is disclosed to some outside entity that could make it public. **Personal information may be found in either public records or in public information.**

How Personal Information Enters the Public Domain

Many people confuse the three categories above, lump them into one and wonder how "big brother" accumulated so much information about them. Therefore, these distinctions are important. The reality is that **much of this information is given willingly**.

Actually, there are two ways that personal information can enter the public domain—statutory and voluntary. In a **voluntary** transaction, you **share** personal information of your own free will. In a **statutory** transaction, you **disclose** personal information because the law requires you to.

The confusion of terms used today feeds the increasing conflict between privacy advocates and commercial interests. This, in turn, is driving legislation towards more and more **restrictions** on the **dissemination of personal information**—the same personal information which, in fact, is willingly shared by most people and companies in order to participate in our market economy.

Where Public Records are Held

There are two places you can find public records—

    at a government agency

    within the database of a private company

Government agencies keep or maintain records in a variety of ways. While many state agencies and highly populated county agencies are computerized, many others use microfiche, microfilm, and paper to store of files and indexes. Agencies that have converted to computer will not necessarily place complete file records on their system; they are more apt to include only an index, pointer or summary data to the files.

Private enterprises develop their databases in one of two ways: they buy the records in bulk from government agencies; or they send personnel to the agencies and compile this information by using a copy machine or keying information into a laptop computer. The database is then available for internal use or for resale purposes. An example of such a company is *Superior Information* (800 848-0489). Superior maintains a very comprehensive database of civil judgments, tax liens, Uniform Commercial Code filings and bankruptcy data for the Mid-Atlantic States.

The Common Methods Used to Access Public Records

The following is a look at the various methods available to access public records.

Visit in Person

This is easy if you live close by. Many courthouses and recorders offices have free access terminals open to the public. Certain records, such as corporate or UCC records are generally found at the Secretary of State, can be viewed or pulled for free, but will incur a fee for copies. A signed release is a common requirement for accessing motor vehicle and criminal records.

Mail, Fax, or Telephone

Although some agencies permit phone or fax requests, the majority of agencies prefer mail requests. Some agencies consider fax requesting an expedited service that incurs higher fees. Agencies that permit telephone requests may merely answer "Yes" or "No" to questions such as "Does John Doe have a boat registered in his name?" We have indicated when telephone and fax requesting is available, as well as the extent of the service.

Online and the Internet

There is a definite trend of certain agencies posting public record data on the Internet for free. Three examples are the Secretary of State offices (whose records include corporation, UCC and tax liens) the county/city tax assessor offices (whose records reveal property ownership) and the federal court systems (whose case includes bankruptcy, civil and criminal proceedings). Usually this information is limited to name indexes and summary data, rather than complete file information. In addition, there are a growing number of occupational licensing agencies posting their membership lists on the net (although addresses and phone numbers of the licensed individuals typically are not listed).

Also, the Internet is a good place to find *general* information about government agencies. Many web sites enable one to download, read and/or print current forms, policies and regulations.

The Internet may serve as the dial-up means, or there may be a restricted dial-up site to the commercial accounts described above. Commercial online access of public records is much more prevalent at the state level compared to the county level. Many agencies, such as DMVs, make the information available to pre-approved, high volume, ongoing accounts. Typically these commercial accounts involve fees and a specified, minimum amount of usage.

Hire Someone Else

As mentioned above, one place to access public records is from a private company. The companies must comply with state and federal laws, so if the government agency will not a release a record, chances are a private company will not either. There are a variety of types of companies that can be hired to perform record searches. An excellent, quick source to find the right vendor for a particular need is www.publicrecordsources.com.

Bulk or Database Purchases

Many agencies offer programs to purchase all or parts of their database for statistical or commercial purposes. The restrictions vary widely from state to state even within the same record type or category. Typically, records are available (to those who qualify) in the following media types; magnetic tape, disk, paper printouts, labels, disks, microfiche and/or microfilm. Throughout the state chapters, we have indicated where these bulk purchases are available, to whom, and for what purposes as well as the costs involved.

Using the Freedom of Information Act and Other Acts

The Federal Freedom of Information Act has bearing on state, county or local government agencies. These agencies are subject to that state's individual act. The record categories profiled in this book virtually have no need for the use of such an act. However, if you are trying to obtain records from agencies beyond the scope of this book, there are many useful Internet sites that will give you the information you need to complete such a request. We can recommend these sites:

www.epic.org/open_gov/rights.html

http://spj.org/foia

Public Record & Public Information Categories

The following descriptions of the record categories fall into our definitions of either "public records" or "public information."

In considering these definitions, keep the following points in mind:

♦ Very little government record information is truly open to the public. Even presumably harmless information is subject to restrictions somewhere in the US. Likewise items that you believe should be highly confidential are probably considered "public information" in one or more states.

♦ Just because your state or county has certain rules, regulations and practices regarding the accessibility and content of public records does not mean that any other state or county follows the same rules.

Business Records

Corporation Records (found at the state level)

Checking to see if a corporation is incorporated is considered a **"status check."** The information that results from a status check typically includes the date of incorporation, status, type, registered agent and, sometimes, officers or directors. This is a good way to find the start of a paper trail and/or to find affiliates of the subject of your search. Some states permit status checks over the telephone.

If available, articles of incorporation (or amendments to them) as well as copies of annual reports may also provide useful information about a business or business owner. However, corporate records may *not* be a good source for a business address because most states allow corporations to use a registered agent as their address for service of process.

Partnership Records (found at the state level)

Some state statutes require registration of certain kinds of partnerships at the state level. Sometimes, these partner names and addresses may be available from the same office that handles corporation records. Some states have a department created specifically to administer limited partnerships and the records associated with them. These filings provide a wealth of information about other partners. Such information can be used to uncover other businesses that may be registered as well.

Limited Liability Companies (found at state level)

A newer form of business entity, that looks like a corporation but has the favorable tax characteristics of a partnership, is known as the Limited Liability Company (LLC). An LLC is legal in most every state. An offspring of this, which many states now permit, is the Limited Liability Partnership (LLP).

Trademark & Trade Name (found at state and county levels)

States will not let two entities use the same (or close to the same) name or trademark, as such they must be registered. Furthermore, "trade names" and "trademarks" are relative terms. A trademark may be known as a "service mark." Trade names may be referred to as "fictitious names," "assumed names," or "DBAs."

Typically, the agency that oversees corporation records usually maintains the files for trademarks and/or trade names. Most states will allow verbal status checks of names or worded marks. Some states will administer "fictitious names" at the state level while county agencies administer "trade names," or vice versa.

Sales Tax Registrations (found at state level)

Any individual or firm that sells applicable goods or services to the end user of the product or service, is required to register with the appropriate state agency. Such registration is necessary to collect applicable sales tax on the goods and services, and to ensure remittance of those taxes to the state.

45 states collect some sort of sales tax on a variety of goods and services. Of these, 38 will at the very least confirm that a tax permit exists. Each sales tax registrant is given a special state tax permit number, which may be called by various names, including tax ID number or seller's permit number. These numbers are not to be confused with the federal employer identification number.

SEC & Other Financial Data

The Securities and Exchange Commission is the public repository for information about publicly held companies, which are required to share their material facts with existing and prospective stockholders.

Private companies, on the other hand, are not subject to public scrutiny, so their financial information is public information only to the extent that the company itself decides to disclose information.

Lien and Security Interest Records

Uniform Commercial Code (found at state and county or city levels)

All 50 states and the District of Columbia have passed a version of the model Uniform Commercial Code (UCC). Article 9 of this code covers security interests in personal property. As such, UCC filings are used in financing transactions such as equipment loans, leases, inventory loans, and accounts receivable financing. The Code allows other possible lenders to be notified that certain assets belonging to a debtor are being used to secure a loan or lease. *Therefore, examining UCC filings is one way to find bank accounts, security interests, financiers, and assets.*

Of the 7.5 million new UCC financing statements filed annually, 2.5 million are filed at the state level; 5 million are filed at the local level within the states. Although there are significant variations among state statutes, the state level is usually a good starting place to uncover liens filed against an individual or business.

Tax Liens (found at state and county or city levels)

The federal government and every state have some sort of taxes, such as those associated with sales, income, withholding, unemployment, and/or personal property. When these taxes go unpaid, the appropriate state agency can file a lien on the real or personal property of the subject. *Normally, the state agency that maintains UCC records also maintains tax liens.*

Individuals vs. Businesses

Tax liens filed against individuals are frequently maintained at separate locations from those liens filed against businesses. For example, a large number of states require liens filed against businesses to be filed at a central state location (i.e., Secretary of State's office) and liens against individuals to be filed at the county level (i.e., Recorder, Register of Deeds, Clerk of Court, etc.).

State vs. Federal Liens

Liens for a company may not all be filed in the same location. A federal tax lien will not necessarily be recorded at the same location/jurisdiction as a lien filed by the state.. This holds true for both individual liens and as well as business liens filed against personal property. Typically, state tax liens on personal property will be found where UCCs are filed. *Tax liens on real property will be found where real property deeds are recorded*, with few exceptions. Unsatisfied state and federal tax liens may be renewed if prescribed by individual state statutes. However, once satisfied, the time the record will remain in the repository before removal varies by jurisdiction.

Real Estate and Tax Assessor (found at county and local levels)

Traditionally, real estate records are public so that everyone can know who owns what property. Liens on real estate must be public so a buyer knows all the facts. The county (or parish) recorder's office is the source. However, many private companies purchase entire county record databases and create their own database for commercial purposes.

This category of public record is perhaps the fastest growing in regards to becoming free over the Internet. We have indicated all the recorder offices that offer **name queries;** many more offer location searches (using maps and parcel numbers to locate an address).

Bankruptcies (found at federal court level)

This entails case information about people and businesses that have filed for protection under the bankruptcy laws of the United States. Only federal courts handle bankruptcy cases. Some private companies compile databases with names and dates. Many types of financial records maintained by government agencies are considered public records; bankruptcy records, unlike some other court records, are in this class of fully open court records.

Important Individual Records

Criminal Records (found at state level, county courts, and federal courts)

Every state has a central repository of major misdemeanor, felony arrest records and convictions. States submit criminal record activity to the National Crime Information Center (which is not open to the public). Of those states that *will* release records to the public, many require fingerprints or signed release forms. The information that *could be* disclosed on the report includes the arrest record, criminal charges, fines, sentencing and incarceration information.

Not all states open their criminal records to the public. In this case, the best places to search for criminal record activity is at the city or county level with the county or district court clerk. Many of these searches can be done with a phone call.

Litigation & Civil Judgments (found at county, local, and federal courts)

Actions under federal laws are found at US District Courts. Actions under state laws are found within the state court system at the county level. Municipalities also have courts. Litigation and judgment information is often collected by commercial database vendors. For more information, please refer to the **County Court Records** chapter.

Motor Vehicle Records

Driver History Records (found at state level, but, on occasion, accessible at county level)

The retrieval industry often refers to driving records as "MVRs." Typical information on an MVR might include full name, address, Social Security Number, physical description and date of birth as well as the actual driving history. Also, the license type, restrictions and/or endorsements can provide background data on an individual.

In recent years there have been major changes regarding the release of motor vehicle data to the public. This is the result of the Driver's Privacy Protection Act (DPPA). States differentiate between permissible users (14 are designated in DPPA) casual requesters to determine who may receive a record and/or how much personal information is reported on the record. Effective June 2000 (see below), if a state chooses to sell records to casual requesters, the record can contain no personal information (address, etc.) without the consent of the subject.

Ironically, as states are moving towards making data readily available electronically, they are also closing the door to many users. Pay particular attention to the restriction requirements mentioned in this category throughout this publication. Also, we strongly urge those interested in further information about either driver or vehicle records to obtain BRB Publication's *The MVR Book*.

Vehicle & Vessel Ownership, Registration, VINs, Titles, & Liens
(found at state and, on occasion, at county level)

State repositories of vehicle/vessel registration and ownership records encompass a wide range of publicly accessible data. Generally, you submit a name to uncover vehicle(s) owned, or you submit vehicle information to learn a name and address.

Some states do not issue titles (only registrations), others require a title if a vessel is a certain length or propelled by a certain size motor or by sail. All states require some form of registration.

The original language of DPPA requires the states to offer an "opt out" option to drivers and vehicle owners, if they (the states) sell marketing lists or individual records to casual requesters (those requesters not specifically mentioned in DPPA). Public Law 106-69 reverses this. Effective June 1, 2000, it instructs the states to automatically opt out all individuals, unless the individual specifically asks to be included (opt-in). Nearly all states have this "opt in" procedure in place. (Some states have extra time to comply, since their state legislatures do not convene until after the deadline.)

Compliance with 106-69 essentially does away with:

◆ The sale of marketing lists;

◆ Sales of records with addresses to "casual" requesters;

◆ And sales of bulk or database formats to information vendors and database compilers.

Accident Reports (found at state level or local level)

The State Police or Department of Public Safety usually maintains accident reports. For the purposes of this publication, "accident records" are those that are prepared by the investigating officer. Copies of a *citizen's* accident report are not usually available to the public and are not mentioned here. Typical information found on a state accident report includes drivers' addresses and license numbers as well as a description of the incident. Accidents investigated by local officials and accidents where the damage does not exceed the state reporting limit, are not available from state agencies.

Occupational Licensing & Business Registration (found at state boards)

Occupational licenses and business registrations contain a plethora of information readily available from various state agencies. A common reason to call these agencies is to corroborate professional or industry credentials. Often, a telephone call to the agency may secure an address and phone number.

GED Records (found at state level)

By contacting the state offices that oversee GED Records, one can verify whether someone truly received GED certificate for the high school education equivalency. These records are useful for pre-employment screening or background checking purposes. Most states will verify over the phone the existence of a GED certificate. Many even offer copies of transcripts free-of-charge. When doing a record search, you must know the name of the student at the time of the test and a general idea of the year and test location. GED Records are *not* very useful when trying to locate an individual.

Hunting & Fishing Licenses (found at state, county & local levels)

We have singled out one type of state license that merits a closer look. When trying to locate an individual, state hunting and fishing license information can be very informative. Currently 37 states maintain a central repository of fishing and/or hunting license records that may be accessed in some capacity by the public. Although some of these record repositories are literally "in boxes in the basement," more and more are becoming computerized.

Effects of Cooperative State-Federal Program on Hunting/Fishing License Databases

In 1992, the US Fish and Wildlife Service implemented a Migratory Bird Harvest Information Program which will change state hunting licensing procedures. Under this cooperative program, which will help biologists better manage the Nation's migratory bird populations, hunters will provide their names and addresses when buying state licenses to hunt migratory birds. The states must provide the name and address information to the US Fish and Wildlife Service on a timely basis. In 1997, 23 states participated in the program. All states except Hawaii are scheduled to participate in 1998. Each state will have several options for how they provide the US Fish and Wildlife Service with the names and address of their hunters.

The policy of the Service is to use the names and addresses only for conducting hunter surveys. All records of hunters' names and addresses will be deleted after the surveys, and no permanent record would be maintained.

However, since the states collect these names and addresses under state authority, the state may decide not to delete the information. Therefore, as more states begin to maintain new automated record repositories, the possible release of these records, by the states, for investigative or search purposes will depend on individual "state sunshine laws." For more information about the program, contact the Office of Migratory Bird Management in Laurel, MD at 301-497-5980.

Workers' Compensation Records (found at state level)

Researching at state workers' compensation boards is generally limited to determining if an employee has filed a claim and/or obtaining copies of the claim records themselves. With the passage of the Americans with Disabilities Act (ADA) in the early 1990s, pre-employment screening using information from workers' compensation boards has been virtually eliminated. However, *a review of workers' compensation histories may be conducted after a conditional job offer has been made* and when medical information is reviewed. The legality of performing this review is subject to individual state statutes, which vary widely.

Voter Registration (found at state & county levels)

Every state has a central election agency or commission, and most have a central repository of voter information. The degree or level of accessibility to these records varies widely from state to state. Over half of the states will sell portions of the registered voter database, but only ten states permit individual searching by name. Most states only allow access for political purposes such as "Get Out the Vote" campaigns or compilation of campaign contribution lists.

Voting Registration Records are a good place to find addresses and voting history. Nearly every state blocks the release of Social Security Numbers and telephone numbers found on these records.

Vital Records: Birth, Death, Marriage, & Divorce Records
(found at state & county levels)

Copies of vital record certificates are needed for a variety of reasons—social security, jobs, passports, family history, litigation, lost heir searching, proof of identity, etc. Most states understand the urgency of these requests, and many offer an expedited service. *A number of states will even take requests over the phone if you use a credit card.* Searchers must also be aware that in many instances certain vital records are *not* kept at the state level. The searcher must then turn to city and county record repositories to find the information needed.

Most states offer expedited fax ordering, requiring the use of a credit card, through the services of an outside vendor known as VitalChek. This independent company maintains individual fax lines at each state office they service. Whether it is behind the scenes or not, ordering vital records by fax typically involves VitalChek in some manner.

Older vital records may be found in the state archives. Another source of historical vital record information is The Family History Library of the Mormon Church (located at 35 North West Temple, Salt Lake City 84150). They have millions of microfilmed records from church and civil registers from all over the world.

Additional Public Information Records Worth Mentioning

State Legislation & Regulations

Telephone numbers, costs and procedures for obtaining copies of passed and pending bills are listed under the heading "Legislation." Most states offer free Internet access (all www addresses are listed) to the text of bills. Notwithstanding federal guidelines, the state legislatures and legislators control the policies and provisions for the release of state held information. Every year there is a multitude of bills introduced in state legislatures that would, if passed, create major changes in the access and retrieval of records and personal information.

Education & Employment

Information about an individual's schooling, training, education, and jobs is important to any employer. Learning institutions maintain their own records of attendance, completion and degree/certification granted. Employers will confirm certain information about former employees. This is an example of private information that becomes public by voluntary disclosure. As part of your credit record, this information would be considered restricted. If, however, you disclose this information to Who's Who, or to a credit card company, it becomes public information.

Environmental

Information about hazards to the environment is critical. There is little tradition and less law regarding how open or restricted information is at the state and local (recorder's office) levels. Most information on hazardous materials, soil composition, even OSHA inspection reports is public record.

Medical

Medical record Information about an individual's medical status and history are summarized in various repositories that are accessible only to authorized insurance and other private company employees. Medical information is neither public information nor closed record. Like credit information, it is not meant to be shared with anyone, unless you give authorization.

Military

Each branch maintains its own records. Much of this, such as years of service and rank, is open public record. However, some details in the file of an individual may be subject to restrictions on access—approval by the subject may be required.

Social Security Numbers

There is a persistent myth that a Social Security Number is private information. The truth is individuals gave up the privacy of that number by writing it on a voter registration form, using it a driver's license number, or any of a myriad of other voluntary disclosures made over the years. It is probable that a good researcher can find the Social Security Number of anyone (along with at least an approximate birth date) with ease.

Addresses & Phone Numbers

This is basic locator information about a person or organization and is a category of information that may be obtained from both government and private sources. Even though you have an unlisted telephone number, anyone can still find you if you have listed your number on, for example, a voter registration card or magazine subscription form. The most elementary of public information categories, addresses and telephone numbers are no longer considered unrestricted information by some people.

Credit Information

These are records derived from financial transactions of people or businesses. **Private companies maintain this information; government only regulates access.** Certain credit information about individuals is restricted by law, such as the Fair Credit Reporting Act, at the federal level and by even more restrictive laws in many states. Credit information about businesses is not restricted by law and is fully open to anyone who requests (pays for) it.

Searching For State Public Records

The previous chapter includes a wealth of knowledge about the various types of public records found at the state level. The introduction to the State Agencies in the body of this *Sourcebook* is a good place to start, if you have questions not answered in the individual profiles.

We have included some general information here and chosen not to be redundant and repeat what is printed elsewhere, but offer further suggestions and information.

Additional State Offices

Each state chapter begins with a list of important state offices that may be helpful to your record searching needs.

Governor's Office

The office of the Governor is a good place to start if you are looking for an obscure agency, phone number or address. We have found that typically the person who answers the phone will point you in the right direction if he or she cannot answer your question.

Attorney General's Office

If you are looking for a non-profit organization, the Attorney General's Office may be able to help you out.

State Archives

The state archives contain an abundance of historical documents and records, especially useful to those interested in genealogy.

State Court Administrator

The court administrator oversees the state court system, which is also known as the county court system. This office can inform you of the structure of that system (i.e. the courts of general and limited jurisdiction and the types of cases they handle). The state judicial web site is a good place to find opinions of state supreme court and appeals court opinions.

In some states, the state court administration offices that oversee a statewide online access system to court records. These are commercial systems and fees are involved.

State Restrictions Table

The next two pages present a helpful State Public Record Restrictions Table. This quick guide indicates if records are truly open, and if not, the level of restriction.

The Table also indicates if special forms are needed prior to doing a search.

State Agency Public Record Restrictions Table

Codes
O   Open to Public
R   Some Access Restrictions (Requesters Screened)
N/A   Not Available to the Public
F   Special Form Needed
S   Severe Access Restrictions (Signed Authorization, etc.)
L   Available only at Local Level

State	Criminal Records	UCC Records	Worker's Comp	Driver Records [2]	Vehicle Records [2]	Vessel Records	Voter Reg. [3]
Alabama	S	O,F	S	S	S	O	L
Alaska	R	O,F	R	S	R	S	O
Arizona	S	O,F	S	S	S	R	L
Arkansas	S	O,F	O	S	R	O	L
California	N/A,L	O,F	R	S	S	S	L
Colorado	R	O,F	S	S	S	R	O
Connecticut	O	O,F	S	S	S	R	L
Delaware	S	O,F	S	S	S	S	O
Dist. of Columbia	S,F	O,F	S	S	S	N/A	O
Florida	O	O,F	S	S	S	R	L
Georgia	S	L,F₁	S	S	S	O	O
Hawaii	O	O,F	S	S	N/A	R	L
Idaho	R	O,F	S	S	S	S	L
Illinois	S,F	O,F	O	S	S	O	L
Indiana	S,F	O,F	S	S	R	R	L
Iowa	O	O,F	O	S	S	L	O
Kansas	R,F	O,F	R	S	S	R	L
Kentucky	S	O	R	S	S	O	O
Louisiana	S	L,F₁	R	S	S	O	L
Maine	O	O,F	R	S	S	O	L
Maryland	S	O,F	O	S	S	O	L
Massachusetts	R	O,F	R	S	S	O	L
Michigan	O	O,F	R	S	S	S	L
Minnesota	R	O,F	S	S	S	O	L
Mississippi	N/A,L	O,F	R	S	S	O	L

State	Criminal Records	UCC Records	Worker's Comp	Driver Records [2]	Vehicle Records [2]	Vessel Records	Voter Reg. [3]
Missouri	O	O,F	R	S	S	R	L
Montana	O	O,F	S	S	R	R,F	O
Nebraska	O	O,F	O	S	S	S	L
Nevada	S	O,F	S	S	S	O	L
New Hampshire	S	O,F	S	S	S	S	L
New Jersey	S,F	O,F	O,F	S	S	S	L
New Mexico	S	O	S	S	S	S	L
New York	L	O,F	S	S	S	S	L
North Carolina	N/A,L	O,F	S	S	S	O	L
North Dakota	S	O,F	S	S	S	O	L
Ohio	S,F	O	O	S	S	O	O&L
Oklahoma	O	O,F	O	S	S	S	O&L
Oregon	O	O,F	S	S	S	O	L
Pennsylvania	R,F	O,F	S	S	S	N/A	L
Rhode Island	S,L	O,F	S	S	S	R	L
South Carolina	O	O,F	S	S	S	O	O
South Dakota	S,F	O,F	S	S	S	R	L
Tennessee	N/A,L	O,F	S	S	S	O	L
Texas	O	O,F	S,F	S	S	R	L
Utah	N/A,L	O,F	S	S	S	R	L,R
Vermont	N/A,L	O,F	S	S	S	S	L
Virginia	S,F	O,F	S	S	S	R	L
Washington	O	O,F	S	S	S	S	L
West Virginia	S,F	O,F	S	S	S	R	L
Wisconsin	O	O,F	S	S	S	O	L
Wyoming	S,F	O,F	S	S	S	O	L

1 =   Georgia and Louisiana UCCs are filed locally, but a state central index is available.

2 =   These categories -- Driver and Vehicle -- indicate restriction codes based on the assumption that the **requester** is "**the general public**." In general, these records are open ("O") to employers, their agents, the insurance industry and other permissible users as defined by DPPA. See the next page for a list of these 14 permissible uses.

3 =   This category, Voter Registration, indicates most record searching requires going to the local county or municipality. However, many state election agencies will sell customized voter lists statewide or for multiple counties.

The 14 Permissible Uses (From the DPPA)

The Driver's Privacy Protection Act Title XXXI—Protection of Privacy of Information in State Motor Vehicle Records, was attached as an amendment to the Violent Crime Control Act of 1994 and was signed by President Clinton late in the summer of that year. The intent of the DPPA is to protect the personal privacy of persons licensed to drive, by prohibiting certain disclosures of information maintained by the states. States were given three years to comply. The bill prohibits disclosure of **personal information** from the driver history, vehicle registration, title files held by state DMVs, **except for 14 specific "permissible uses."**

The permissible uses do, in general, permit ongoing, legitimate businesses and individuals to obtain full record data, but with added compliance procedures. The following text, taken directly from the Act, details these 14 Permissible Uses—

"§2721. Prohibition on release and use of certain personal information from State motor vehicle records

"(a) IN GENERAL.--Except as provided in subsection (b), a State department of motor vehicles, and any officer, employee, or contractor, thereof, shall not knowingly disclose or otherwise make available to any person or entity personal information about any individual obtained by the department in connection with a motor vehicle record.

"(b) PERMISSIBLE USES.--Personal information referred to in subsection (a) shall be disclosed for use in connection with matters of motor vehicle or driver safety and theft, motor vehicle emissions, motor vehicle product alterations, recalls, or advisories, performance monitoring of motor vehicles and dealers by motor vehicle manufacturers, and removal of non-owners records from the original owner records of motor vehicle manufacturers to carry out the purposes of the Automobile Information Disclosure Act, the Motor Vehicle Information and Cost Saving Act, the National Traffic and Motor Vehicle Safety Act of 1966, the Anti-Car Theft Act of 1992, and the Clean Air Act, and may be disclosed as follows:

"(1) For use by **any government agency**, including any court or law enforcement agency, in carrying out its functions, or any private person or entity acting on behalf of a Federal, State, or local agency in carrying out its functions.

"(2) For use in connection with matters of motor vehicle or **driver safety** and **theft**; motor vehicle emissions; motor vehicle product alterations, recalls, or advisories; performance monitoring of motor vehicles, motor vehicle parts and dealers; motor vehicle **market research** activities, including survey research; and removal of non-owner records from the original owner records of motor vehicle manufacturers.

"(3) For use in the normal course of business by a legitimate business or its agents, employees, or contractors, but only--

"(A) to **verify the accuracy of personal information submitted** by the individual to the business or its agents, employees, or contractors; and

"(B) if such information as so submitted is not correct or is no longer correct, to obtain the correct information, but only for the purposes of preventing fraud by, **pursuing legal remedies** against, or **recovering on a debt** or security interest against, the individual.

"(4) For use in connection with any civil, criminal, administrative, or arbitral proceeding in any Federal, State, or local court or agency or before any self-regulatory body, including the service of process, **investigation in anticipation of litigation**, and the execution or enforcement of judgments and orders, or pursuant to an order of a Federal, State, or local court.

"(5) For use in **research activities**, and for use in producing statistical reports, so long as the personal information is not published, redisclosed, or used to contact individuals.

"(6) For use by **any insurer or insurance support organization**, or by a self-insured entity, or its agents, employees, or contractors, in connection with claims investigation activities, antifraud activities, rating or underwriting.

"(7) For use in providing notice to the owners of towed or impounded vehicles.

"(8) For use by any **licensed private investigative agency** or licensed security service for any purpose permitted under this subsection.

"(9) For use by an employer or its agent or insurer to obtain or verify information relating to a holder of a commercial driver's license that is required under the Commercial Motor Vehicle Safety Act of 1986 (49 U.S.C. App. 2710 et seq.)

"(10) For use in connection with the operation of private toll transportation facilities.

"(11) For any other use in response to requests for individual motor vehicle records if the motor vehicle department has provided in a clear and conspicuous manner on forms for issuance or renewal of operator's permits, titles, registrations, or identification cards, notice that personal information collected by the department may be disclosed to any business or individual, and has provided in a clear and conspicuous manner on such forms an opportunity to prohibit such disclosures.

"(12) For bulk distribution for surveys, marketing or solicitations if the motor vehicle department has implemented methods and procedures to ensure that--

"(A) individuals are provided an opportunity, in a clear and conspicuous manner, to prohibit such uses; and

"(B) the information will be used, rented, or sold solely for bulk distribution for surveys, marketing, and solicitations, and that surveys, marketing, and solicitations will not be directed at those individuals who have requested in a timely fashion that they not be directed at them.

"(13) For use by any requester, if the requester demonstrates it has obtained the written consent of the individual to whom the information pertains.

"(14) For any other use specifically authorized under the law of the State that holds the record, if such use is related to the operation of a motor vehicle or public safety.

Searching State Occupational Licensing Boards

The Privacy Question

While some agencies consider this information private and confidential, most agencies freely release at least some basic data over the phone or by mail.

Our research indicates that many agencies appear to make their own judgments regarding what specifically is private and confidential in their files. For example, although most agencies will not release an SSN, 8% do. On the other side, 45% of the agencies indicate that they will disclose adverse information about a registrant, and many others will only disclose selected portions of the information.

In any event, the basic rule to follow when you contact a licensing agency is to **ask for the specific kinds of information available.**

What Information May Be Available

An agency may be willing to release part or all of the following—

- ◆ Field of Certification
- ◆ Status of License/Certificate
- ◆ Date License/Certificate Issued
- ◆ Date License/Certificate Expires
- ◆ Current or Most Recent Employer
- ◆ Social Security Number
- ◆ Address of Subject
- ◆ Complaints, Violations or Disciplinary Actions

Using the Licensing Section

Each state *State License* section is separated into three parts—

1. Licenses Searchable Online
2. Licensing Quick Finder
3. Licensing Agency Information

A "Key Number" ties the sections together.

The License Searchable Online List

This is a list of boards and their corresponding URLs that offer **free Internet access** to their records. This means that you can do a name search or query from this web site.

Using the Quick Finder

The place to start a verification search is in the **Licensing Quick Finder.** Here you will find, licenses, registrations or occupations listed in alphabetical order.

Although we reflect the official name used in a state for most items, names of some of the major license types have been standardized to make them easier to locate. For example, some states use the word "Physician" rather than "Medical Doctor." We have chosen to use the latter.

Agency Information

This section gives the address and telephone number of the agency or board where the records are maintained.

Use the "Key Number"

The **Key Number** is the *identifying number* for the agency that maintains information about this license. By matching the Key Number found in the Quick Finder to the profile in the Agency Information, you will have the address and other details about how this agency operates. The key number follows the "#" sign in the Quick Finder Section.

An Example of How to Use the Sections

Let's say the following appears in the *Quick Finder Section*:

Beautician #03   216-123-4536

As stated above, the Key Number, which follows the # sign, leads you to the Agency Information Section, where you will find the Agency or Board's address and phone number. For example, "#3" refers to the following:

(3) Department of Health & Social Services, Division of Public Health, 123 Sesame Street, Mapletown, OH 44414, 216-123-4536

Search Fees

Several trends are observed when verifying search fees of the various licensing agencies. They are—

1. There is no charge to verify if a particular person is licensed; this can usually be done by phone.

2. The fee for copies or faxes ranges from $.25 to $2.00.

3. A fee of $5 to $20 usually applies to written requests. This is due to the fact that written certifications give more information than verbal inquiries, i.e. disciplinary action, exam scores.

4. A fee that is $25 or more is typically for a list of licensed professionals. For example, a hospital might need a roster of registered nurses in a certain geographic area.

Searching Tip—Distinguish the Type of Agency

Within the agency category listings, it is important to note that there are five general types of agencies. When you are verifying credentials, you should be aware of what distinguishes each type, which in turn could alter the questions you ask.

Private Certification

Private Licensing and Certification—requires a proven level of minimum competence before license is granted. These professional licenses separate the true "professions" from the third category below. In many of these professions, the certification body, such as the American Institute of Certified Public Accountants, is a private association whereas the licensing body, such as the New York State Education Department, is the licensing agency. Also, many professions may provide additional certifications in specialty areas.

State Certification

State Licensing & Certification—requires certification through an *examination* and/or other *requirements supervised* directly *by the state* rather than by a private association.

By Individual

Individual Registration—required if an individual intends to offer specified products or services in the designated area, but does not require certification that the person has met minimum requirements. An everyday example would be registering a handgun in a state that does not require passing a gun safety course.

By Business

Business Registration—required if a business intends to do business or offer specified products or services in a designated area, such as registering a liquor license. Some business license agencies require testing or a background check. Others merely charge a fee after a cursory review of the application.

Special Permits

Permits—give the grantee specific permission to do something, whether it is to sell hot-dogs on the corner or to put up a three story sign. Permits are usually granted at the local level rather than the state level of government.

Other Forms of Licensing & Registration

Although the state level is where much of the licensing and registration occurs, you should be aware of other places you may want to search.

Local Government Agencies

Local government agencies at both the **county** and **municipal levels** require a myriad of business registrations and permits in order to do business (construction, signage, etc.) within their borders. Even where you think a business or person, such as a remodeling contractor, should have local registrations you want to check out, it is still best to start at the state level.

County Recording Office and City Hall

If you decide to check on local registrations and permits, call the offices at both the county—try the **county recording office**—and municipal level—try **city hall**—to find out what type of registrations may be required for the person or business you are checking out.

Like the state level, you should expect that receiving basic information will only involve a phone call and that you will not be charged for obtaining a status summary.

Professional Associations

As mentioned above, many professional licenses are based on completion of the requirements of professional associations. In addition, there are *many professional designations* from such associations that *are not recognized as official licenses by government*. Other designations are basic certifications in fields that are so specialized that they are not of interest to the states, but rather only to the professionals within an industry. For example, if your company needs to hire an investigator to check out a potential fraud against you, you might want to hire a CFE—Certified Fraud Examiner— who has meet the minimum requirements for that title from the Association of Certified Fraud Examiners.

Other Information Available

Mail Lists & Databases

Many agencies make their lists available in reprinted or computer form, and a few maintain online access to their files. If you are interested in the availability of licensing agency information in bulk (e.g. mailing lists, magnetic tapes, disks) or online, call the agency and ask about formats that are available.

Online Searching & CD-ROMS

A number of private vendors also compile lists from these agencies and make them available online or on CD-ROM. We do not suggest these databases for credential searching because they may not be complete, may not be up to date and may not contain all the information you can obtain directly from the licensing agency. However, these databases are extremely valuable as a general source of background information on an individual or company that you wish to do business with.

Searching Federal Court Records

First published in May 1993, BRB's Publication The Sourcebook of Federal Courts *provided the first truly complete coverage of where and how to search for case records in the United States Federal Courts. Now, this book has been fully revised and integrated into* The Sourcebook.

In addition to updating the Federal Court information, another objective of this publication is to show searchers how the Federal Court system has evolved during the past few years. One problem searchers encounter is that older records may be in a different form or in a different location from newer records. For example, a searcher can go astray trying to find bankruptcy cases in Ohio unless they know about changes in Dayton.

One development that continues to change the fundamental nature of Federal Courts case record access is, of course, computerization. Now, every Federal Court in the United States has converted to a computerized index. As a result of this computerization, three major trends have developed that affect the availability of information from Federal Courts:

Federal Court Structure

The Federal Court system includes three levels of courts, plus some special courts, described as follows—

Supreme Court of the United States

The Supreme Court of the United States is the court of last resort in the United States. It is located in Washington, DC, where it hears appeals from the United States Courts of Appeals and from the highest courts of each state.

United States Court of Appeals

The United States Court of Appeals consists of thirteen appellate courts that hear appeals of verdicts from the courts of general jurisdiction. They are designated as follows:

The Federal Circuit Court of Appeals hears appeals from the US Claims Court and the US Court of International Trade. It is located in Washington, DC.

The District of Columbia Circuit Court of Appeals hears appeals from the district courts in Washington, DC as well as from the Tax Court.

Eleven geographic **Courts of Appeals**—each of these appeal courts covers a designated number of states and territories. The chart on the pages 33-34 lists the circuit numbers (1 through 11) and location of the Court of Appeals for each state.

United States District Courts

The United States District Courts are the courts of general jurisdiction, or trial courts, and are subdivided into two categories—

The District Courts are courts of general jurisdiction, or trial courts, for federal matters, excluding bankruptcy. Essentially, this means they hear cases involving federal law and cases where there is diversity of citizenship. Both **civil** and **criminal** cases come before these courts.

The Bankruptcy Courts generally follow the same geographic boundaries as the US District Courts. There is at least one bankruptcy court for each state; within a state there may be one or more judicial districts and within a judicial district there may be more than one location (division) where the courts hear cases. While civil lawsuits may be filed in either state or federal courts depending upon the applicable law, all bankruptcy actions are filed with the US Bankruptcy Courts.

Special Courts/Separate Courts

The Special Courts/Separate Courts have been created to hear cases or appeals for certain areas of litigation demanding special expertise. Examples include the US Tax Court, the Court of International Trade and the US Claims Court.

How Federal Trial Courts are Organized

At the federal level, all cases involve federal or US constitutional law or interstate commerce. The task of locating the right court is seemingly simplified by the nature of the federal system—

♦   All court locations are based upon the plaintiff's county of domicile.

♦   All civil and criminal cases go to the US District Courts.

♦   All bankruptcy cases go to the US Bankruptcy Courts.

However, a plaintiff or defendant may have cases in any of the 500 court locations, so it is really not all that simple to find them.

There is at least one District and one Bankruptcy Court in each state. In many states there is more than one court, often divided further into judicial districts—e.g., the State of New York consists of four judicial districts, the Northern, Southern, Eastern and Western. Further, many judicial districts contain more than one court location (usually called a division).

The Bankruptcy Courts generally use the same hearing locations as the District Courts. If court locations differ, the usual variance is to have fewer Bankruptcy Court locations.

Case Numbering

When a case is filed with a federal court, a case number is assigned. This is the primary indexing method. Therefore, in searching for case records, you will need to know or find the applicable case number. If you have the number in good form already, your search should be fast and reasonably inexpensive.

You should be aware that case numbering procedures are not consistent throughout the Federal Court system: one judicial district may assign numbers by district while another may assign numbers by location (division) within the judicial district or by judge. Remember that case numbers appearing in legal text citations may not be adequate for searching unless they appear in the proper form for the particular court.

All the basic civil case information that is entered onto docket sheets, and into computerized systems like PACER (see next page), starts with standard form JS-44, the Civil Cover Sheet, or the equivalent.

Docket Sheet

As in the state court system, information from cover sheets, and from documents filed as a case goes forward, is recorded on the **docket sheet**, which then contains the case history from initial filing to its current status. While docket sheets differ somewhat in format, the basic information contained on a docket sheet is consistent from court to court. As noted earlier in the state court section, all docket sheets contain:

♦ Name of court, including location (division) and the judge assigned;

♦ Case number and case name;

♦ Names of all plaintiffs and defendants/debtors;

♦ Names and addresses of attorneys for the plaintiff or debtor;

♦ Nature and cause (e.g., US civil statute) of action;

♦ Listing of documents filed in the case, including docket entry number, the date and a short description (e.g., 12-2-92, #1, Complaint).

Assignment of Cases

Traditionally, cases were assigned within a district by county. Although this is still true in most states, the introduction of computer systems to track dockets has led to a more flexible approach to case assignment, as is the case in Minnesota and Connecticut. Rather than blindly assigning all cases from a county to one judge, their districts are using random numbers and other logical methods to balance caseloads among their judges.

This trend may appear to confuse the case search process. Actually, the only problem that the searcher may face is to figure out where the case records themselves are located. Finding cases has become significantly easier with the wide availability of PACER from remote access and on-site terminals in each court location with the same district-wide information base.

Computerization

Traditionally, cases were assigned within a district by county. Although this is still true in most states, the introduction of computer systems to track dockets has led to a more flexible approach to case assignment, as is the case in Minnesota and Connecticut. Rather than blindly assigning all cases from a county to one judge, their districts are using random numbers and other logical methods to balance caseloads among their judges.

This trend may appear to confuse the case search process. Actually, the only problem that the searcher may face is to figure out where the case records themselves are located. Finding cases has become significantly easier with the wide availability of PACER from remote access and on-site terminals in each court location with the same district-wide information base.

Computerized Indexes are Available

Computerized courts generally index each case record by the names of some or all the parties to the case—the plaintiffs and defendants (debtors and creditors in Bankruptcy Court) as well as by case number. Therefore, when you search by name you will first receive a listing of all cases in which the name appears, both as plaintiff and defendant.

Electronic Access to Federal Courts

Numerous programs have been developed for electronic access to Federal Court records. In recent years the Administrative Office of the United States Courts in Washington, DC has developed three innovative public access programs: VCIS, PACER, and ABBS. The most useful program for online searching is PACER.

PACER

PACER, the acronym for **P**ublic **A**ccess to **E**lectronic **C**ourt **R**ecords, provides docket information online for open cases at **all US Bankruptcy courts** and **most US District courts**. Cases for the US Court of Federal Claims are also available. The user fee is $.60 per minute. Each court controls its own computer system and case information database; therefore, there are some variations among jurisdictions as to the information offered.

A continuing problem with PACER is that each court determines when records will be purged and how records will be indexed, leaving you to guess how a name is spelled or abbreviated and how much information about closed cases your search will uncover. A PACER search for anything but open cases **cannot** take the place of a full seven-year search of the federal court records available by written request from the court itself or through a local document retrieval company. Many districts report that they have closed records back a number of years, but at the same time indicate they purge docket items every six months.

Sign-up and technical support is handled at the PACER Service Center in San Antonio, Texas (800) 676-6856. You can sign up for all or multiple districts at once. In many judicial districts, when you sign up for PACER access, you will receive a PACER Primer that has been customized for each district. The primer contains a summary of how to access PACER, how to select cases, how to read case numbers and docket sheets, some searching tips, who to call for problem resolution, and district specific program variations.

The most impressive change in Federal Courts record access is the expansion of the PACER System. It covers all 190 Bankruptcy Court Districts and all but 8 of the 300 Civil/Criminal Court Districts.

Before Accessing PACER, Search the "National" US Party/Case Index

It is no longer necessary to call each court in every state and district to determine where a debtor has filed bankruptcy, or if someone is a defendant in Federal litigation. National and regional searches of district and bankruptcy filings can be made with one call (via modem) to the US Party/Case Index.

The **US Party/Case Index** is a national index for U.S. district, bankruptcy, and appellate courts. This index allows searches to determine whether or not a party is involved in federal litigation almost anywhere in the nation.

The US Party/Case Index provides the capability to perform national or regional searches on party name and Social Security Number in the bankruptcy index, party name and nature of suit in the civil index, and party name in the criminal and appellate indices.

The search will provide a list of case numbers, filing locations and filing dates for those cases matching the search criteria. If you need more information about the case, you must obtain it from the court directly or through that court's individual PACER system.

You may access the US Party/Case Index by dialup connection or via the Internet. The Internet site for the US Party/Case Index is http://pacer.uspci.uscourts.gov. The toll-free dial-up number for the US Party/Case Index is 800-974-8896. For more information, call the PACER service center at 800-676-6856.

In accordance with Judicial Conference policy, most courts charge a $.60 per minute access fee for this service. Persons desiring to use this service must first register with the PACER Service Center at 1-800-676-6856. For more information on the U.S. Party/Case Index, please contact the PACER Service Center at 1-800-676-6856.

ECF

Electronic Case Files (ECF) is a prototype system that focuses on the filing of cases electronically. This service initially introduced in January 1996 enables participating attorneys and litigants to electronically submit pleadings and corresponding docket entries to the court via the Internet thereby eliminating substantial paper handling and processing time. ECF permits any interested parties to instantaneously access the entire official case docket and documents on the Internet of selective civil and bankruptcy cases within these jurisdictions.

It is important to note, that when you search ECF you are ONLY searching cases that have been filed electronically. You must still conduct a search using PACER if you want to know if a case exists.

The following courts utilize ECF, see their profiles for more information:

Arizona (Bankruptcy)	California (Bankruptcy – Southern)
Georgia (Bankruptcy – Northern)	Missouri (District – Western)
New York (Bankruptcy – Southern)	New York (District – Eastern)
Ohio (District – Northern)	Oregon (District)
Virginia (Bankruptcy – Eastern)	

Although, all of the above courts offer filing electronically, not all of them offer searching of those same files. Arizona does not allow searching at this time. In addition, both California and Virginia have additional systems in place.

RACER

RACER stands for Remote Access to Court Electronic Records. Accessed through the Internet, RACER offers access to the same records as PACER. At present, searching RACER is free, but there are plans to make it a fee-based system. The following courts offer RACER access (for more information see the profiles for the individual courts):

Idaho (Bankruptcy)	Idaho (District)
Nevada (Bankruptcy)	

webPACER

webPACER is a system that has replaced the traditional PACER system for the Central District of California. At this time, it is only being offered for that district. According to court employees, there are plans to make webPACER more widespread, and possibly, the dominant online system.

One must have a PACER ID and password to use the system, and the .60 per minute charge applies.

Although, webPACER includes "web" in its name, it is still very much a dial-up system. One must have special software (in addition to a compatible Internet browser application), and one must use access numbers. For access information, see the profiles for the courts in the Central District of California.

Miscellaneous Online Systems

Many courts have developed their own online systems. The Bankruptcy Courts for the Eastern District of Virginia have an elaborate system accessible for free and available on their web site. In addition to RACER, Idaho's Bankruptcy and District Courts have additional searching options available on their web site. Likewise, the Southern District Court of New York offers CourtWeb, which provides information to the public on selected recent rulings of those judges who have elected to make information available in electronic form.

VCIS

Another system worth mentioning is **VCIS** (Voice Case Information System). Nearly all of the US Bankruptcy Court judicial districts provide **VCIS**, a means of accessing information regarding open bankruptcy cases by merely using a touch-tone telephone. There is no charge. Individual names are entered last name first with as much of the first name as you wish to include. For example, Carl R. Ernst could be entered as ERNSTC or ERNSTCARL. Do not enter the middle initial. Business names are entered as they are written, without blanks. BRB Publications has books available with all the VCIS numbers listed (800-929-3811).

The VCIS System, like the PACER System, has become pervasive and now covers open cases for all but a few US Bankruptcy Court locations.

A Few Searching Hints

VCIS should *only* be used to locate information about open cases. Do not attempt to use VCIS as a substitute for a PACER search.

Since this publication includes the counties of jurisdiction for each court, the list of counties in each Court's profile is a good starting point for determining where case records may or may not be found.

Before performing a general PACER search to determine whether cases exist under a particular plaintiff, debtor, or defendant name, first be certain to review that Court's profile, which will show the earliest dates of case records available on the PACER. Also, searchers need to be sure that the Court's case index includes all cases, open and closed, for that particular period. Be aware that some courts purge older, closed cases after a period of time, making such a PACER search incomplete. (Wherever known, this publication indicates within the court profiles the purge timeframe for PACER records. Times vary from court to court and state to state.)

Experience shows that court personnel are typically not aware of — nor concerned about — the types of searches this publication's readers do. Court personnel often focus on only open cases, whereas a searcher may want to know as much about closed cases as open ones. Thus, court personnel are sometimes fuzzy in answering questions about how far back case records go on PACER, and whether closed cases have been purged. If you are looking for cases older than a year or two, there is no substitute for a real, on-site search performed by the court itself or by a local search expert (if the court allows full access to its indexes).

Courts are more willing to give out information by telephone because most courts have converted from the old card index system to fully computerized indexes, which are easily accessible, while on the phone.

Federal Records Centers and the National Archives

After a federal case is closed, the documents are held by Federal Courts themselves for a number of years, then stored at a designated Federal Records Center (FRC). After 20 to 30 years, the records are then transferred from the FRC to the regional archives offices of the National Archives and Records Administration (NARA). The length of time between a case being closed and its being moved to an FRC varies widely by district. Each court has its own transfer cycle and determines access procedures to its case records, even after they have been sent to the FRC.

When case records are sent to an FRC, the boxes of records are assigned accession, location and box numbers. These numbers, which are called case locator information, **must be obtained from the originating court in order to retrieve documents from the FRC.** Some courts will provide such information over the telephone, but others require a written request. This information is now available on PACER in certain judicial districts. The Federal Records Center for each state is listed as follows:

State	Circuit	Appeals Court	Federal Records Center
AK	9	San Francisco, CA	Anchorage (Some temporary storage in Seattle)
AL	11	Atlanta, GA	Atlanta
AR	8	St. Louis, MO	Fort Worth
AZ	9	San Francisco, CA	Los Angeles
CA	9	San Francisco, CA	Los Angeles (Central & Southern) San Francisco (Eastern & Northern)
CO	10	Denver, CO	Denver
CT	2	New York, NY	Boston
DC		Washington, DC	Washington, DC
DE	3	Philadelphia, PA	Philadelphia
FL	11	Atlanta, GA	Atlanta
GA	11	Atlanta, GA	Atlanta
GU	9	San Francisco, CA	San Francisco
HI	9	San Francisco, CA	San Francisco
IA	8	St. Louis, MO	Kansas City, MO
ID	9	San Francisco, CA	Seattle
IL	7	Chicago, IL	Chicago
IN	7	Chicago, IL	Chicago
KS	10	Denver, CO	Kansas City, MO
KY	6	Cincinnati, OH	Atlanta
LA	5	New Orleans, LA	Fort Worth
MA	1	Boston, MA	Boston
MD	4	Richmond, VA	Philadelphia
ME	1	Boston, MA	Boston
MI	6	Cincinnati, OH	Chicago
MN	8	St. Louis, MO	Chicago
MO	8	St. Louis, MO	Kansas City, MO
MS	5	New Orleans, LA	Atlanta
MT	9	San Francisco, CA	Denver
NC	4	Richmond, VA	Atlanta
ND	8	St. Louis, MO	Denver
NE	8	St. Louis, MO	Kansas City, MO
NH	1	Boston, MA	Boston
NJ	3	Philadelphia, PA	New York
NM	10	Denver, CO	Denver
NV	9	San Francisco, CA	Los Angeles (Clark County) San Francisco (Other counties)
NY	2	New York, NY	New York

State	Circuit	Appeals Court	Federal Records Center
OH	6	Cincinnati, OH	Chicago, Dayton (Some bankruptcy)
OK	10	Denver, CO	Fort Worth
OR	9	San Francisco, CA	Seattle
PA	3	Philadelphia, PA	Philadelphia
PR	1	Boston, MA	New York
RI	1	Boston, MA	Boston
SC	4	Richmond, VA	Atlanta
SD	8	St. Louis, MO	Denver
TN	6	Cincinnati, OH	Atlanta
TX	5	New Orleans, LA	Fort Worth
UT	10	Denver, CO	Denver
VA	4	Richmond, VA	Philadelphia
VI	3	Philadelphia, PA	New York
VT	2	New York, NY	Boston
WA	9	San Francisco, CA	Seattle
WI	7	Chicago, IL	Chicago
WV	4	Richmond, VA	Philadelphia
WY	10	Denver, CO	Denver

GU is Guam, PR is Puerto Rico, and VI is the Virgin Islands.

According to some odd logic, the following Federal Records Centers are located somewhere else:

Atlanta—East Point, GA; Boston—Waltham, MA; Los Angeles—Laguna Niguel, CA;

New York—Bayonne, NJ; San Francisco—San Bruno, CA

Searching Other Federal Records Online

EDGAR

EDGAR, the Electronic Data Gathering Analysis, and Retrieval system was established by the Securities and exchange Commission (SEC) to allow companies to make required filing to the SEC by direct transmission. As of May 6, 1996, all public domestic companies are required to make their filings on EDGAR, except for filings made to the Commission's regional offices and those filings made on paper due to a hardship exemption.

EDGAR is an extensive repository of US corporation information and it is available online.

What is Found on EDGAR?

Companies must file the following reports with the SEC:

♦   10-K, an annual financial report, which includes audited year-end financial statements.

♦   10-Q, a quarterly report, unaudited.

♦   8K - a report detailing significant or unscheduled corporate changes or events.

♦   Securities offering and trading registrations and the final prospectus.

The list above is not conclusive. There are other miscellaneous reports filed, including those dealing with security holdings by institutions and insiders. Access to these documents provides a wealth on information.

How to Access EDGAR Online

EDGAR is searchable online at: www.sec.gov/edgarhp.htm. LEXIS/NEXIS acts as the data wholesaler or distributor on behalf of the government. LEXIS/NEXIS sells data to information retailers, including it's own NEXIS service.

Aviation Records

The Federal Aviation Association (FAA) is the US government agency with the responsibility of all matters related to the safety of civil aviation. The FAA, among other functions, provides the system that registers aircraft, and documents showing title or interest in aircraft. Their web site, at www.faa.gov, is the ultimate source of aviation records, airports and facilities, safety regulations, and civil research and engineering.

The Aircraft Owners and Pilots Association is the largest organization of its kind with a 340,000 members. Their web site is www.aopa.org and is an excellent source of information regarding the aviation industry.

Two other excellent sources are *Jane's World Airlines* at www.janes.com and the Insured Aircraft Title Service at 800-654-4882 or its web site at www.insured.aircraft.com

Military Records

This topic is so broad that there can be a book written about it, and in fact there is! *The Armed Forces Locator Directory* from MIE Publishing (800-937-2133) is an excellent source. The book, now in its 8th edition, covers every conceivable topic regarding military records.

The Privacy Act of 1974 (5 U.S.C. 552a) and the Department of Defense directives require a written request, signed and dated, to access military personnel records. For further details, visit the NPRC site listed below.

Military Internet Sources

There are a number of great Internet sites that provide valuable information on obtaining military and military personnel records as follows:

www.nara.gov/regional/mpr.html This is the National Personnel Records Center (NPRC), maintained by the National Archives and Records Administration. This site is full of useful information and links.

www.army.mil	The official site of the US Army
www.af.mil	The official site of the US Air Force
www.navy.mil	The official site of the US Navy
www.usmc.mil	The official site of the US Marine Corps
www.ngb.dtic.mil	The official site of the National Guard
www.uscg.mil	The official site of the US Coast Guard

Online Sources Used by the Experts

The remainder of this chapter was written and contributed by online pioneer and award-winning journalist Alan M. Schlein, author of Find It Online.

We sincerely thank Alan for permitting the use of his material in this Sourcebook. Alan can be reached at his www.deadlineonline.com. It's a great web site with lots of useful sources and URLs!

Almost every federal government agency is online. There's a nationwide network of depository libraries, including the enormous resources of the National Archives (www.nara.gov), the twelve presidential libraries, and four national libraries (the Library of Congress, the National Agricultural Library, the National Library of Education and the National Library of Medicine). A 1997 government survey counted 4,300 web sites and 215 computer bulletin boards at 42 departments and agencies, and those numbers keep growing. State and city government web sites are mushrooming, too. While the material is easily accessible, finding it sometimes requires professional researching skills. In response, the government has been developing government resource gateways and finding aids. Many of them are quite good. Among them:

Commonly Requested Federal Services

www.whitehouse.gov/WH/services

This is the White House's collection of top federal government sites.

Fedstats

www.fedstats.gov

A terrific collection of statistical sites from the federal government.

Healthfinder

www.healthfinder.gov

This is a great starting point for health-related government information

Best Gateways to Government Records

In addition, there are hundreds of web sites, called government gateways, that organize and link government sites. Some are simply collections of links. Others provide access to bulletin boards of specific government agencies so that you find and contact employees with specific knowledge. Guides are becoming increasingly important in light of the growing number of reports and publications that aren't printed any more, but simply posted online.

Here are some of the best government gateway sites:

Documents Center

www.lib.umich.edu/libhome/Documents.center/index.html

Documents Center is a clearinghouse for local, state, federal, foreign, and international government information. It is one of the more comprehensive online searching aids for all kinds of government information on the Internet. It's especially useful as a meta-site of meta-sites.

FedLaw

http://fedlaw.gsa.gov

FedLaw is an extremely broad resource for federal legal and regulatory research containing 1600+ links to law-related information. It has very good topical and title indexes that group web links into hundreds of subjects. It is operated by the General Services Administration (GSA).

FedWorld Information Network

www.fedworld.gov

FedWorld is a massive collection of 14,000 files and databases of government sites, including bulletin boards that can help you identify government employees with expertise in a broad range of subjects. A surprising number of these experts will take the time to discuss questions from the general public.

US Federal Government Agencies Directory

www.lib.lsu.edu/gov/fedgov.html

This directory of federal agencies is maintained by Louisiana State University and links to hundreds of federal government Internet sites. It's divided by branch and agency and is very thorough, but focus on your target because it's easy to lose your way or become overwhelmed en route.

GOVBOT – Government Search Engine

http://eden.cs.umass.edu/Govbot

Developed by the Center For Intelligent Information Retrieval, GOVBOT's searchable keyword index of government web sites is limited to sites with a top-level domain name ending in .gov or .mil.

US Government Information

www-libraries.colorado.edu/ps/gov/us/federal.htm

This is a gem of a site and a good starting point. From the University of Colorado, it's not as thorough as the LSU site above, but still very valuable.

INFOMINE: Scholarly Internet Resource Collections

http://lib-www.ucr.edu

INFOMINE provides collections of scholarly Internet resources, best for academics. Its government portion — Government INFOMINE — is easily searchable by subject. It has detailed headings and its resource listings are very specific. Since it's run by a university, some of its references are to limited to student use only.

YAHOO! Government

www.yahoo.com/Government

Yahoo is one of the best known and most frequently-used general Internet engines. Its' subject approach is especially good for subjects like government. It is substantial, frequently updated, broad in scope and has sections for all levels of government.

Federal Web Locator

www.law.vill.edu

This web locator is really two sites in one: a federal government web site and a separate site that tracks federal courts – both of which are browsable by category or by keywords. Together they provide links to thousands of government agencies and departments. In addition, this site has an excellent **State Web Locator** at www.infoctr.edu/swl and a **State Court Locator** at www.law.vill.edu/Locator/statecourt/index.htm. All four are top-notch resources.

Best Online Government Resources

Your tax dollars are put to good and visible use here. A few of the government's web pages are excellent. Some can be used in lieu of commercial tools, but only if you have the time to invest.

A few of the top government sites – the Census and the Securities and Exchange Commission – are models of content and presentation. They are very deep, very thorough and easy to use. If only the rest of the federal government would follow suit. Unfortunately, the best of the federal government is just that: *the best*. Not all agencies maintain such detailed and relevant resources.

Following are the crown jewels of the government's collection, in ranked order:

US Census Bureau

www.census.gov

Without question, this is the US government's top site. It's saturated with information and census publications – at times overwhelmingly so – but worth every minute of your time. A few hours spent here is a worthwhile investment for almost anyone seeking to background a community, learn about business or find any kind of demographic information. You can search several ways: alphabetically by subject, by word, by location, and by geographic map. The only problem is the sheer volume of data.

One feature, the **Thematic Mapping System**, allows users to extract data from Census CD-ROMs and display them in maps by state or county. You can create maps on all kinds of subjects – for example, tracking violent crime to farm income by region.

The site also features the **Statistical Abstract of the US** in full text, with a searchable version at www.census.gov:80/stat_abstract.

The potential uses of census data are infinite. Marketers use it to find community information. Reporters search out trends by block, neighborhood or region. Educators conduct research. Businesses evaluate new business prospects. Genealogists trace family trees though full census data isn't available for 72 years from the date the census was taken. You can even use it to identify ideal communities in which to raise a family. The *San Jose Mercury News*' Jennifer LaFleur used it to find eligible bachelors in specific areas of San Jose for an article on which she was working.

US Securities & Exchange Commission (SEC)

www.sec.gov

This SEC site, which is first-rate and surpassed only by the Census site, is a must-stop place for information shopping on US companies. Its **EDGAR** database search site www.sec.gov/edaux/searches.htm is easy to use and provides access to documents that companies and corporations are required to file under regulatory laws.

The SEC site is a great starting point for information about specific companies and industry trends. The SEC requires all publicly held corporations and some large privately held corporations to disclose detailed financial information about their activities, plans, holdings, executives' salaries and stakes, legal problems and so forth.

Library of Congress (LOC)

www.loc.gov

An extraordinary collection of documents. **Thomas**, the Library's Congressional online center site (http://thomas.loc.gov/home/thomas2.html) provides an exhaustive collection of congressional documents, including bill summaries, voting records and the full Congressional Record, which is the official record of Congressional action. This LOC site also links to many international, federal, state and local government sites. You can also access the library's 4.8 million records online, some versions in full-text and some in abstract form. Though the Library's entire 27 million-item collection is not yet available online, the amount increases daily. In addition to books and papers, it includes an extensive images collection ranging from Frank Lloyd Wright's designs to the Dead Sea Scrolls to the world's largest online collection of baseball cards.

Superintendent of Documents Home Page (GPO)

www.access.gpo.gov/su_docs

The GPO is the federal government's primary information printer and distributor. All federally funded information from every agency is sent here, which makes the GPO's holdings priceless. Luckily, the GPO site is well-constructed and easy to use. For example, it has the full-text of the Federal Register, which lists all federal regulations and proposals, and full-text access to the Congressional Record. The GPO also produces an online version of the Congressional Directory, providing details on every congressional district, profiles of members, staff profiles, maps of every district and historical documents about Congress. EFOIA required all federal government resources to be computerized and available online by the end of 1999. This site will continue to expand over the next few years, as the number of materials go out of print and online.

National Technical Information Service (NTIS)

www.ntis.gov

The best place to find federal government reports related to technology and science. NTIS is the nation's clearinghouse for unclassified technical reports of government-sponsored research. NTIS collects, indexes, abstracts and sells US and foreign research – mostly in science and technology – as well as behavioral and social science data.

IGnet: Internet. . . . for the Federal IG Community

www.ignet.gov

This is a truly marvelous collection of reports and information from the Inspector Generals of about sixty federal agency departments. Well worth checking when starting research on government-related matters.

White House

www.whitehouse.gov

This site wouldn't make this list if not for two features. One, a terrific list of federal government links called **Commonly Requested Federal Services** and two, a transcript of every official action the US President takes. Unfortunately, as with many government sites, its primary focus is in promoting itself.

Defense LINK – US Department of Defense (DOD)

www.defenselink.mil

This is the brand-name site for Pentagon-related information. There's a tremendous amount of data here, categorized by branch of service – including US troop deployments worldwide. But the really valuable information is on the DTIC site below.

Defense Technical Information Center (DTIC)

www.dtic.mil

The DTIC site is loaded with links and defense information – everything from contractors to weapon systems. It even includes recently de-classified information about the Gulf War. It is the best place to start for defense information. You can even find a list of all military-related contracts, including beneficiary communities and the kinds of contracts awarded.

Bureau of Transportation Statistics

www.bts.gov

The US Department of Transportation's enormous collection of information about every facet of transportation. There's a lot of valuable material here including the Transportation Statistics Annual Report. It also holds financial data for airlines and searchable databases containing information about fatal accidents and on-time statistics for airlines, which can be narrowed to your local airport.

National Archives & Records Administration

www.nara.gov

A breathtaking collection of research online. The National Archives has descriptions of more than 170,000 documents related to the Kennedy assassination, for example. It also contains a world-class database holding descriptions of more than 95,000 records held by the Still Picture and Motion Picture, Sound and Video Branches. This site also links to the twelve Presidential Archives with their records of every person ever mentioned in Executive Branch correspondence. You can view an image of the original document.

State & Regional Resources

The federal government isn't the only government entity with valuable information online. Each of the fifty state governments and the US territories have a web presence. Some are top quality, like Texas and Florida. Others aren't as good. Here are some of the better regional compilation sites:

NASIRE - National Association of State Information Resource Executives

www.nasire.org

This site provides state-specific information on state-government innovations and is a companion to the NASIRE State Search site mentioned by Greg Notess in his book *Government Information on the Internet*.

Government Information Sharing Project

http://govinfo.kerr.orst.edu

This site, from the Oregon State University Library, is a great collection of online databases about everything from economics to demographics. It's particularly valuable because it has regional information on the economy and demographic breakdowns all the way down to the county level. Its content is sometimes outdated. Still, it's worthwhile for finding how federal money trickles down to localities and where state and local agencies spend tax dollars.

USADATA

www.usadata.com/usadata/market

This is an innovative site for finding information about a particular region or part of the country. Data is not only sorted by region, but also by twenty subjects within each region.

Global Computing

www.globalcomputing.com/states.html

A solid collection of links on a variety of topics. This site is especially strong on state and local government topics.

Searching County Court Records

The County Court Records Sections

The purpose of the County Court Records Sections is to provide quick yet detailed access information on the more than 6,400 major courts that have jurisdiction over significant criminal and civil cases under state law.

Included in *The Sourcebook* are all state felony courts, larger claim civil courts, and probate courts in the United States. Since most courts have jurisdiction over a number of categories of cases, we also include many of the courts that hear misdemeanor, eviction, and small claims court cases. In addition, each County Court Records Section begins with an introduction that summarizes where other major categories of court cases—DUI, preliminary hearings, and juvenile cases—can be found.

The term "County Courts," as used in this publication, refers to those courts of original jurisdiction (trial courts) within each state's court system that handle...

- **Felonies**   -- Generally defined as crimes punishable by one year or more of jail time
- **Civil Actions**   -- For money damages usually greater than $3,000
- **Probate**   -- Estate matters
- **Misdemeanors**   -- Generally defined as minor infractions with a fine or minimal jail time
- **Evictions**   -- Landlord/tenant actions
- **Small Claims**   -- Actions for minor money damages, generally under $3,000

Useful Applications

The County Court Record Sections are especially useful for four kinds of applications—

General litigation searching/background searching... Combined with the *Federal Court section*, you have complete coverage of all important courts in the United States.

Employment background checking... Included is full coverage of local criminal courts at the felony level, and many misdemeanor courts as well.

Tenant background checking... Courts where landlord/tenant cases are filed are included in the state introduction charts, and most of the courts handling such cases are profiled.

Asset searching... The probate courts have records of wills and estate matters that can be used to determine assets, related parties, and useful addresses.

Reading the State Charts

On the first page of each County Court Records Section are three charts. Together, they present that state's court structure.

When searching for case records, keep in mind that many higher level courts also handle appeals from lower courts.

The First Chart

The chart at the top of the page summarizes the structure of the court system, listing the court of general jurisdiction, followed underneath by the courts of limited, municipal, and special jurisdiction. Court types with an asterisk (*) after their names are profiled in *The Sourcebook*.

The number of case record locations is indicated for each court. Where two classifications of courts are combined into one location and only one entry appears in the profiles, the number of combined courts is noted. The number of locations for courts not profiled in *The Sourcebook* are estimates.

Where useful, the number and type of organization of each of the classifications of court are indicated under the "How Organized" column.

The Civil and Criminal Charts

The other two charts consolidate information about what types of cases each court hears, i.e. the "jurisdiction" of the type of court.

Where more than one court has jurisdiction for a particular kind of civil case, the minimum and maximum claim fields clarify whether there is overlapping jurisdiction in the state. In most states, the lower and upper court civil claim limits dovetail nicely between the court levels, so you can readily tell which court has the type of civil case you are concerned about.

Although these charts oversimplify complex sets of state statues, their purpose is to provide you with a practical starting point to help you decide where to search for case records.

Beyond the Charts

When you cannot make a determination to your satisfaction where to search, we suggest you contact that state's administrator of courts by telephone or visit their Internet site.

The address, telephone number, and Internet address of the administrative office in each state are listed under the heading "Administration."

Reading the Court Profiles

Basic Information

The 3,139 US counties (and where applicable—parishes, towns, cities, etc.) are listed in alphabetical order, within each state. When a county has more than one court profiled, the courts appear in order beginning with the court of general jurisdiction, then proceeding down to more limited jurisdictions. If a level of court has divisions, civil courts are listed before criminal courts. Where more than one court of the same type is located in a county, they are listed in alphabetical order by the name of the city where they are located.

All city/ZIP Code combinations have been verified against our most in-depth versions of *The County Locator* database for accuracy. In addition to the address and telephone number, the time zone is indicated (see below for an explanation of the abbreviations used). Fax numbers are given for most courts.

Additional information for each court includes whether the court accepts searches by phone, whether the office's records are accessible by modem, also the payee for checks, certification fees, and turnaround times for mailed-in requests. When a county has multiple offices, general information helps determine which office to search in, depending upon the subject's address.

Furthermore, to maximize your search possibilities, online system availability for each state, if any, is summarized in the state introductions.

Major Variations

Do not assume that the structure of the court system in another state is anything like your own. In one state, the Circuit Court may be the highest trial court whereas in another it is a limited jurisdiction court. Examples are: (1) New York, where the Supreme Court is not very "supreme," and the downstate court structure varies from upstate; and (2) Tennessee, where circuit courts are in districts.

Access

The number of courts that no longer conduct name searches has risen. For these courts, you must hire a local retriever, directly or through a search company, to search for you. It should be noted that usually these courts still take specific document copy requests by mail. Because of long mail turnaround times and court fees, local retrievers are frequently used even when the court will honor a request by mail. A court's entry indicates if it is one of the many to offer a public access terminal, free of charge, to view case documents or indexes.

Note: in many instances two types of courts (e.g., circuit and district) are combined. When phoning or writing these courts, we recommend that your request specifically state in your request that you want both courts included in the search.

Index & Record Systems

Most profiles of the civil courts indicate whether the plaintiffs as well as the defendants are indexed. A plaintiff search is useful, for example, to determine if someone is especially litigious.

During the past 12 years, thousands of courts have installed computerized indexing systems. The year when computer indexing started in each of these courts is indicated in the profile of most of the automated courts. Computerized systems are considerably faster and easier to search, allowing for more indexing capability than the microfilm and card indexes that preceded them.

Search Requirements

There is a strong tendency for courts to overstate their search requirements. For civil cases, the usual reasonable requirement is a defendant (or plaintiff) name—full name if it is a common name—and the time frame to search—e.g., 1987-1996. For criminal cases, the court may require more identification, such as date of birth (DOB), to ascertain the correct individual. Other information "required" by courts— such as Social Security Number (SSN)—is often just "helpful" to narrow the search on a common name. Further, we have indicated when certain pieces of information may be helpful but are not required.

Restricted Records

Most courts have a number of types of case records, such as juvenile and adoptions, which are not released without a court order. These types are indicated in each profile.

Fees & Other Requirements

Search, copy, and certification fees are given for most courts, as well as fax fees if known. Where specified, we indicate whether the court requires a self-addressed stamped envelope (SASE) to accompany a written search request. Even where it is not indicated, we recommend including a SASE to make sure the results are returned to you.

Special Notes

Where two or more courts divide jurisdiction of a county, a profile for each court is given. Often a city is specified to help you determine which court to access.

Some Court Basics

Before trudging into a courthouse and demanding to view a document, you should first be aware of some basic court procedures. Whether the case is filed in a state, municipal, or federal court, each case follows a similar process.

A **civil case** usually commences when a plaintiff files a complaint with a court against defendants. The defendants respond to the complaint with an answer. After this initial round, there may be literally hundreds of activities before the court issues a judgment. These activities can include revised complaints and their answers, motions of various kinds, discovery proceedings (including depositions) to establish the documentation and facts involved in the case. All of these activities are listed on a **docket sheet**, which may be a piece of paper or a computerized index.

Once the court issues a judgment, either party may appeal the ruling to an appellate division or court. In the case of a money judgment, the winning side can usually file it as a judgment lien with the county recorder. Appellate divisions usually deal only with legal issues and not the facts of the case.

In a **criminal case**, the plaintiff is a government jurisdiction. The Government brings the action against the defendant for violation of one or more of its statutes.

In a **bankruptcy case,** which can be heard only in federal courts, there is neither defendant nor plaintiff. Instead, the debtor files voluntarily for bankruptcy protection against creditors, or the creditors file against the debtor in order to force the debtor into involuntary bankruptcy.

Types of Litigation in Trial Courts

Criminal

Criminal cases are categorized as *felonies* or *misdemeanors*. A general rule, used in this publication, makes this distinction: usually a felony involves a jail term of one year or more, whereas a misdemeanor may only involve a monetary *fine*.

Civil

Civil cases are categorized as *tort*, *contract*, and *real property* rights. Torts can include *automobile accidents*, *medical malpractice*, and *product liability* cases. Actions for small money damages, typically under $3,000, are known as *small claims*.

Other

Other types of cases that frequently are handled by separate courts or specialized divisions of courts include *juvenile*, *probate* (wills and estates), and *domestic relations*.

State Court Structure

The secret to determining where a state court case is located is to understand how the court system is structured in that particular state. The general structure of all state court systems has four parts:

Appellate courts	Limited jurisdiction trial courts
Intermediate appellate courts	General jurisdiction trial courts

The two highest levels, appellate and intermediate appellate courts, only hear cases on appeal from the trial courts. Opinions of these appellate courts are of interest primarily to attorneys seeking legal precedents for new cases.

General jurisdiction trial courts usually handle a full range of civil and criminal litigation. These courts usually handle felonies and larger civil cases.

Limited jurisdiction trial courts come in two varieties. First, many limited jurisdiction courts handle smaller civil claims (usually $10,000 or less), misdemeanors, and pretrial hearing for felonies. Second, some of these courts, sometimes called special jurisdiction courts, are limited to one type of litigation, for example the Court of Claims in New York, which only handles liability cases against the state.

Some states, for instance Iowa, have consolidated their general and limited jurisdiction court structure into one combined court system. In other states there may be a further distinction between state-supported courts and municipal courts. In New York, for example, nearly 1,300 Justice Courts handle local ordinance and traffic violations, including DWI.

Generalizations should not be made about where specific types of cases are handled in the various states. Misdemeanors, probate, landlord/tenant (eviction), domestic relations, and juvenile cases may be handled in either or both the general and limited jurisdiction courts. To help you locate the correct court to perform your search in, this publication specifically lists the types of cases handled by each court.

How Courts Maintain Records

Case Numbering

When a case is filed, it is assigned a case number. This is the primary indexing method in every court. Therefore, in searching for case records, you will need to know—or find—the applicable case number. If you have the number in good form already, your search should be fast and reasonably inexpensive.

You should be aware that case numbering procedures are not consistent throughout a state court system. One district may assign numbers by district while another may assign numbers by location (division) within the district, or by judge. Remember: case numbers appearing in legal text citations may not be adequate for searching unless they appear in the proper form for the particular court in which you are searching.

All basic civil case information is entered onto docket sheets.

Docket Sheet

Information from cover sheets and from documents filed as a case goes forward is recorded on the docket sheet. The docket sheet then contains an outline of the case history from initial filing to its current status. While docket sheets differ somewhat in format, the basic information contained on a docket sheet is consistent from court to court. All docket sheets contain:

♦ Name of court, including location (division) and the judge assigned;

♦ Case number and case name;

♦ Names of all plaintiffs and defendants/debtors;

♦ Names and addresses of attorneys for the plaintiff or debtor;

♦ Nature and cause (e.g., statute) of action.

Computerization

Most courts are computerized, which means that the docket sheet data is entered into a computer system. Within a state or judicial district, the courts *may* be linked together via a single computer system.

Docket sheets from cases closed before the advent of computerization may not be in the computer system. For pre-computer cases, most courts keep summary case information on microfilm, microfiche, or index cards.

Case documents are not generally available on computer because courts are still experimenting with and developing electronic filing and imaging of court documents. Generally, documents are only available to be copied by contacting the court where the case records are located.

Performing a Search at the County Level

How you search depends on what information you have, what you are looking for, and the time frame you are dealing with. Whichever access method you decide to use, before you begin, you must gather as much of the required, essential information as you can, and be prepared to be as specific as possible in your search request.

Ways to Obtain Records

Here are five ways you can access information from government agencies and courts: Please note this chapter is applicable for both **court records** and **recorder office records**.

Telephone

While the amount of information agencies and courts will release over the telephone varies, this is an inexpensive way to begin a search. Today's widespread computerization of records allows agency/court personnel nearly immediate access to more readily available data. This book contains the phone numbers for every court profiled. However, the trend is towards fewer courts providing information via telephone.

Mail

Many courts and state agencies will conduct a search based upon a written request. Generally, you can call first to see if the agency has the record you are seeking and what the fee will be. Always be sure to be specific in your written request, and include a self-addressed stamped envelope for quicker service.

In Person

If you are near the court or agency where you want to search, you can visit the location yourself. Personnel are usually available to assist you. Many courts now have public access computer terminals for viewing case information within their districts. We recommend that you take the opportunity to visit the nearest court or recorder's office for another reason: by seeing how the office is physically organized and by chatting with personnel, you will get "a feel" for what is involved in searching a similar agency elsewhere.

Online

You will find online access is more readily available at the federal court level and certain state agencies than can be found at the county court level. We have indicated in the State Introductions where online access is available statewide. In the court profiles, we indicate if online access is available for that particular court. Keep in mind, many are primarily commercial fee-based systems.

The trend to access information on the Internet is slowing coming to the state court systems. Internet site addresses are indicated for those courts that have a site with some substance. There are 3 states that have a free statewide access URL (CT, NM, and WI).

Provider or Retriever Firm

Hiring a service company that knows the local court(s) in its area is frequently the only way to access remote locations effectively. Among these are national companies that cover all courts, and local companies that cover courts in their geographic vicinity.

Fees, Charges, and Usage

Public records are not necessarily free of charge, certainly not if they are maintained by private industry. Remember that **public records are records of incidents or transactions**. These incidents can be civil or criminal court actions, recordings, filings or occurrences such as speeding tickets or accidents. **It costs money** (time, salaries, supplies, etc.) **to record and track these events**. Common charges found at the government level include copy fees (to make copies of the document), search fees (for clerical personnel to search for the record), and certification fees (to certify that a document as being accurate and coming from the particular agency). Fees can vary from $.10 per page for copies to a $15.00 search fee for court personnel to do the actual look-up. Some government agencies will allow you to walk in and view records at no charge. Fewer will release information over the phone for no fee.

If a private enterprise is in the business of maintaining a public records database, it generally does so to offer these records for resale. Typical clients include financial institutions, the legal industry, the insurance industry, and pre-employment screening firms among others. Usually, records are sold via online access or on a CD-ROM.

Also, there are a number of public record search firms—companies that will do a name search—for a fee. These companies do not warehouse the records, but search on demand for a specific name.

Private companies usually offer different price levels based on volume of usage, while government agencies have one price per category, regardless of the amount of requests.

A Few Words About Searching Public Records Online

No, you will not find an abundance of public records on the Internet. The availability of online public records is not as widespread as one might think. According to studies conducted by the *Public Record Research Library*, only *20% of public records can be found online*. Nonetheless, more than 200 private companies offer online access to proprietary database(s) of public record information.

A key to purchasing public records online direct from a government agency is the frequency of usage. Many agencies require a minimum amount of requests per month or per session. Certainly, it does not make economic sense to spend a lot of money for programming and set-up fees if you will be ordering fewer than five records a month. You would be better off to do the search by more conventional methods—in-person, via mail, fax, or by hiring a vendor. Going online direct to the source is not always the least expensive way to go!

Searching Recording Office Records

Combined, the Recording Offices section for each state section contains 4,265 local recording offices where Uniform Commercial Code and real estate records are maintained.

The Lowdown on Recorded Documents

Documents filed and record at local county, parish, city or town offices represent some of the best opportunities to gain access to open public records. If you are lucky enough to live in close proximity, you can visit your local office and, for free, view records. Recorded documents are also one of the most available types of public records that can be viewed or obtain via online and through the Internet.

Real Estate

As mentioned previously, real estate records are public so that everyone can know who owns what property. Liens on real estate must be public so a buyer knows all the facts. The county (or parish or city) recorder's office is the source. Also, access is also available form many private companies that purchase entire county record databases and create their own database for commercial purposes.

Uniform Commercial Code (UCC)

UCC filings are to personal property what mortgages are to real estate property. UCCs are in the category of financial records that must be fully open to public scrutiny so that other potential lenders are on notice about which assets of the borrower have been pledged as collateral.

As with tax liens, UCC recordings are filed, according to state law, either at the state or county level. Some companies require dual filing (must file at BOTH locations, thus records can be searched at BOTH locations). As with real estate records, there are a number of private companies who have created their own databases for commercial resale.

A Great Source of Information

Although recorded documents are a necessity to making an informed business-related decision, they are also a virtual treasure trove of data. UCC filing documents will you the names and addresses of creditors and debtors, describe the asset offered for collateral, the date of the filing, and whether or note the loan has been satisfied. This information contained on the statements can lead an experience investigator to other roads done the information trail. For example, if the collateral is a plane or a boat, this will lead to registration records or if the debtor is a business, other names on the filing may lead to other traceable business partners or ventures.

EDITOR'S NOTE: An excellent book that gives great insight on how to use these and other public records to find information about any person or business in Dennis King's *Get the Facts on Anyone* published by MacMillan.

How the Recording Offices Section is Organized

General Organization

The mailing address, telephone, time zone and fax number are listed for each office. If online access is available from the agencies, a detailed profile is provided. Included are other categories of information offered online from this or a related agency, such as tax assessor information and vital records, licenses, etc.

An introduction to each state Recording Offices section contains a summary of the facts about where and how real estate records are maintained, as well as indicating information about Uniform Commercial Code and tax lien filings. It mentions any unusual conditions pertaining to real estate, tax lien and UCC searching in that state. A list of some of the other liens that are filed at the local level is also included.

General Searching Rules

The general rules for background searching of UCC records are as follows:

Except in local filing states, a search at the state level is adequate to locate all UCC records on a subject.

Mortgage record searches will include any real estate related UCC filings.

- See the sections below for discussions of special collateral rules.

- Due diligence searching, however, usually demands searching the local records in dual filing states as well.

Special Categories of Collateral

Real Estate Related UCC Collateral

A specific purpose of lien statutes under both the UCC and real estate laws is to put a buyer or potential secured creditor on notice that someone has a prior security interest in real or personal property. UCC financing statements are to personal property what mortgages or deeds of trust are to real property.

One problem addressed by the UCC is that certain types of property have the characteristics of both real and personal property. In those instances, it is necessary to have a way to provide lien notice to two different categories of interested parties: those who deal with the real estate aspect of the property and those who deal with the "personal" aspect of the property.

In general, our definition of real estate related UCC collateral is any property that in one form is attached to land, but that in another form is not attached. For the sake of simplicity, we can define the characteristics of two broad types of property that meet this definition:

Property that is initially attached to real property, but then is separated. Three specific types of collateral have this characteristic: *minerals* (including oil and gas), *timber*, and *crops*. These things are grown on or extracted from land. While they are on or in the ground they are thought of as real property, but once they are harvested or extracted they become personal property. Some states have a separate central filing system for crops.

> *Property that is initially personal property, but then is attached to land, generally called **fixtures**.*
> Equipment such as telephone systems or heavy industrial equipment permanently affixed to a building are examples of fixtures. It is important to realize that what is a fixture, like beauty, is in the eye of the beholder, since it is a vague concept at best.

UCC financing statements applicable to real estate related collateral must be filed where the real estate and mortgage records are kept, which is generally at the county level—except in Connecticut, Rhode Island and Vermont, where the Town/City Clerk maintains these records. The chart gives the titles of the local official who maintains these records.

Consumer Goods

Among the state-to-state variations, some states require filing where real estate is filed for certain consumer goods.

Equipment Used in Farming Operations

33 states require only local filing for equipment used in farming operations.

Searching Note

If you are looking for information on subjects that might have these types of filings against them, a search of county records may be revealing even if you would normally search only at the state level.

More Details About UCC Records

Uniform Commercial Code financing statements and changes to them may be filed at two or three government agencies in each state, depending upon the type of collateral involved in the transaction. Each state's UCC statute contains variations on a nationally recommended Model Act. Each variation is explained below. The charts appear at the end of this chapter.

33 Central Filing States

Central filing states are those where most types of personal property collateral require filing of a UCC financing statement only at a central filing location within that state.

5 Statewide Database States

Minnesota and **Wisconsin** are central filing states with a difference: UCC financing statements filed at the county level are also entered into a statewide database. In **North Dakota** UCC financing statements may be filed at either the state or county level, and all filings are entered into a statewide database. In **Louisiana**, **Nebraska**, and **Georgia**, UCC financing statements may be filed with **any** county (parish). In each of these six states the records are entered into a central, statewide database that is available (except in Georgia) for searching in each county, as well as at the state agency (no state agency in Louisiana or Georgia).

8 Dual Filing States

The usual definition of a dual filing state is one in which financing statements containing collateral such as inventory, equipment or receivables *must* be filed in *both* a central filing office, usually with the Secretary of State, and in a local (county) office where the collateral or business is located. The three states below are also dual filing states, with a difference.

3 Triple Filing States

The systems in three states, MA, NH, and PA, can be described as triple filing because the real estate portion of the filings goes to an office separate from the UCC filing office. In Massachusetts and New Hampshire, UCC filings go to the town/city while real estate filings go to the county. In Pennsylvania, county government is separated into the Prothonotary for UCC filings and the Recorder for real estate filings.

Some counties in other states do have separate addresses for real estate recording, but this is usually just a matter of local departmentalization.

2 Local Filing States

Kentucky and Wyoming are the only *local filing only* states as of January 1, 2000. In both these states a few filings are also found at the state level. In both states, filings for out of state debtors go to the Secretary of State, and in Wyoming, filings for Wyoming debtor accounts receivable and farm products require dual filing.

The UCC Locator Chart

This handy chart will tell you at a glance where UCC and real estate records are filed on a state-by-state basis.

State	Most Personal Property Central Filing Office	Local Filing Office	All Real Property Filing Office
AK	Department of Natural Resources		District Recorder
AL	Secretary of State		Judge of Probate
AR	Secretary of State	and Circuit Clerk	Circuit Clerk
AZ	Secretary of State		County Recorder
CA	Secretary of State		County Recorder
CO	Secretary of State	or any County Recorder (as of July 1, 1996)	County Clerk & Recorder
CT	Secretary of State		Town/City Clerk
DC	County Recorder		County Recorder
DE	Secretary of State		County Recorder
FL	Secretary of State		Clerk of Circuit Court
GA	None	Clerk Superior Court	Clerk of Superior Court
HI	Bureau of Conveyances		Bureau of Conveyances
IA	Secretary of State		County Recorder
ID	Secretary of State		County Recorder
IL	Secretary of State		County Recorder
IN	Secretary of State		County Recorder
KS	Secretary of State		Register
KY	Secretary of State (Out of state only)	County Clerk	County Clerk
LA	None	Clerk of Court	Clerk of Court
MA	Secretary of the Commonwealth	and Town/City Clerk	Register of Deeds
MD	Department of Assessments & Taxation	and Clerk of Circuit Court (until 7/1/95)	Clerk of Circuit Court
ME	Secretary of State		County Register
MI	Secretary of State		County Register
MN	Secretary of State or Recorder		County Recorder
MO	Secretary of State	and County Recorder	County Recorder
MS	Secretary of State	and Chancery Clerk	Chancery Clerk

| State | Most Personal Property | | All Real Property |
	Central Filing Office	Local Filing Office	Filing Office
MT	Secretary of State		Clerk & Recorder
NC	Secretary of State	and Register of Deeds	Register of Deeds
ND	Secretary of State or County Register		County Register
NE	Secretary of State (Out of state only)	County Clerk	County Register
NH	Secretary of State	and Town/City Clerk	County Register
NJ	Secretary of State		County Clerk/Register
NM	Secretary of State		County Clerk
NV	Secretary of State		County Recorder
NY	Secretary of State	and County Clerk (Register)	County Clerk (Register)
OH	Secretary of State	and County Recorder	County Recorder
OK	Oklahoma County Clerk		County Clerk
OR	Secretary of State		County Clerk
PA	Department of State	and Prothonotary	County Recorder
RI	Secretary of State		County Clerk & Recorder
SC	Secretary of State		County Register/Clerk
SD	Secretary of State		County Register
TN	Secretary of State		County Register
TX	Secretary of State		County Clerk
UT	Division of Corporations & Commercial Code		County Recorder
VA	Corporation Commission	and Clerk of Circuit Court	Clerk of Circuit Court
VT	Secretary of State	and Town/City Clerk (until 7/1/95)	Town/City Clerk
WA	Department of Licensing		County Auditor
WI	Dept. of Financial Institutions		County Register
WV	Secretary of State		County Clerk
WY	Secretary of State (Out of state and A/R only)	County Clerk	County Clerk

Using the County Locator Section

A list at the end of each state section cross references place names to counties. Comprised of every official US Postal Service place name, the city/county cross references contain more that 40,000 entries. This information is summarized from the BRB publication The County Locator.

The cross references contain a special feature that identifies ZIP Codes that cross county lines.

Using ZIP Codes When Searching For Public Records

A place name (capitalized type) may be listed more than once in the city/county cross references. For example,

> LOS GATOS (95030) Santa Clara (88), Santa Cruz (12)
> LOS GATOS Santa Clara

This duplicate listing indicates that the bulk of LOS GATOS addresses is in Santa Clara county, but those addresses with the ZIP Code 95030 may be in Santa Cruz county. Specifically, ZIP Code 95030 is approximately 88% in Santa Clara and 12% in Santa Cruz.

Note: county names are listed in upper and lower case type, and place names are always capitalized.

10,000 Problems Pointed Out

Multiple county ZIP Codes always appear, as in the above example, before the main entry for a place name. The percentages may not always add up to 100% because of rounding off. Counties that represent less than 1% of the addresses in a ZIP Code have also been eliminated. In all, there are almost 10,000 ZIP Codes shown in this *Sourcebook* that cross county lines.

Using Multiple County Information

The special multiple county entries put you on notice that addresses within a ZIP Code may not be in the county usually associated with that place name. This information can be crucial to finding public records, including court cases that are filed based on the location of property or residence. Remember, if you search in the wrong county, then you may get a false "no hit" response.

Non-Geographic Zip Codes

When trying to locate public records based upon place names and ZIP Codes, be aware that 10,000 ZIP Codes are useless in determining county of residence because they are assigned exclusively to post office boxes or rural routes. Anyone can have a post office box in any county. Never use an address containing one of these non-geographic ZIP Codes to determine where to search.

For More Extensive Information

BRB's Public Record Research System CD-ROM contains an additional 40,000 place names, as well as information about the characteristics of each ZIP Code, for example, whether the ZIP Code only contains post office boxes. An even more complete source, with over 95,000 place names, is BRB's publication *The County Locator*.

Using a Public Record Vendor

Using a Public Record Vendor

Hiring Someone to Obtain the Record

There are five main categories of public record professionals: distributors and gateways; search firms; local document retrievers; investigative firms; and information brokers.

Distributors and Gateways (Proprietary Database Vendors)

Distributors are automated public record firms who combine public sources of bulk data and/or online access to develop their own database product(s). Primary Distributors include companies that collect or buy public record information from its original source and reformat the information in some useful way. They tend to focus on one or a limited number of types of information, although a few firms have branched into multiple information categories.

Gateways are companies that either compile data from or provide an automated gateway to Primary Distributors. Gateways thus provide "one-stop shopping" for multiple geographic areas and/or categories of information.

Companies can be both Primary Distributors and Gateways. For example, a number of online database companies are both primary distributors of corporate information and also gateways to real estate information from other Primary Distributors

Search Firms

Search firms are companies that furnish public record search and document retrieval services through outside online services and/or through a network of specialists, including their own employees or correspondents (see Retrievers below). There are three types of Search Firms.

Search Generalists offer a full range of search capabilities in many public record categories over a wide geographic region. They may rely on gateways, primary distributors and/or networks of retrievers. They combine online proficiency with document retrieval expertise.

Search Specialists focus either on one geographic region—like Ohio—or on one specific type of public record information—like driver/vehicle records.

Application Specialists focus on one or two types of services geared to specific needs. In this category are pre-employment screening firms and tenant screening firms. Like investigators, they search many of the public record categories in order to prepare an overall report about a person or business.

Local Document Retrievers

Local document retrievers use their own personnel to search specific requested categories of public records usually in order to obtain documentation for legal compliance (e.g., incorporations), for lending, and for litigation. They do not usually review or interpret the results or issue reports in the sense that investigators do, but rather return documents with the results of searches. They tend to be localized, but there are companies that offer a national network of retrievers and/or correspondents. The retriever or his/her personnel goes directly to the agency to look up the information. A retriever may be relied upon for strong knowledge in a local area, whereas a search generalist has a breadth of knowledge and experience in a wider geographic range.

The 725+ members of the **Public Record Retriever Network (PRRN)** can be found, by state and counties served, at <u>www.brbpub.com</u>. This organization has set industry standards for the retrieval of public record documents and operates under a Code of Professional Conduct. Using one of these record retrievers is an excellent way to access records in those jurisdictions that do not offer online access.

Private Investigation Firms

Investigators use public records as tools rather than as ends in themselves, in order to create an overall, comprehensive "picture" of an individual or company for a particular purpose. They interpret the information they have gathered in order to identify further investigation tracks. They summarize their results in a report compiled from all the sources used.

Many investigators also act as Search Firms, especially as tenant or pre-employment screeners, but this is a different role from the role of Investigator per se, and screening firms act very much like investigators in their approach to a project. In addition, an investigator may be licensed, and may perform the types of services traditionally thought of as detective work, such as surveillance.

Information Brokers

There is one additional type of firm that occasionally utilizes public records. **Information Brokers** (IB) gather information that will help their clients make informed business decisions. Their work is usually done on a custom basis with each project being unique. IBs are extremely knowledgeable in online research of full text databases and most specialize in a particular subject area, such as patent searching or competitive intelligence. The Association of Independent Information Professionals (AIIP), at www.aiip.org, has over 750 experienced professional information specialist members from 21 countries.

Which Type of Vendor is Right for You?

With all the variations of vendors and the categories of information, the obvious question is; "How do I find the right vendor to go to for the public record information I need?" Before you start calling every interesting online vendor that catches your eye, you need to narrow your search to the **type** of vendor for your needs. To do this, ask yourself the following questions—

What is the Frequency of Usage?

If you have on-going, recurring requests for a particular type of information, it is probably best to choose a different vendor then if you have infrequent requests. Setting up an account with a primary distributor, such as Metromail, will give you an inexpensive per search fee, but the monthly minimum requirements will be prohibitive to the casual requester, who would be better off finding a vendor who accesses or is a gateway to Metromail. **EDITOR'S NOTE**: Check out Metromail and similar vendors at www.publicrecordsources.com.

What is the Complexity of the Search?

The importance of hiring a vendor who understands and can interpret the information in the final format increase with the complexity of the search. Pulling a corporation record in Maryland is not difficult, but doing an online criminal record search in Maryland, when only a portion of the felony records are online, is not so easy.

Thus, part of the answer to determining which vendor or type of vendor to use is to become conversant with what is (and is not) available from government agencies. Without knowing what is available (and what restrictions apply), you cannot guide the search process effectively. Once you are comfortable knowing the kinds of information available in the public record, you are in a position to find the best method to access needed information.

What are the Geographic Boundaries of the Search?

A search of local records close to you may require little assistance, but a search of records nationally or in a state 2,000 miles away will require seeking a vendor who covers the area you need to search. Many national primary distributors and gateways combine various local and state databases into one large comprehensive system available for searching. However, if your record searching is narrowed by a region or locality, an online source that specializes in a specific geographic region, like Superior Information Services in NJ, may be an alternative to a national vendor. Keep in mind that many national firms allow you to order a search online, even though results cannot be delivered immediately and some hands-on local searching is required.

Of course, you may want to use the government agency online system if available for the kind of information you need.

10 Questions to Ask a Public Records Vendor

(Or a Vendor Who Uses Online Sources)

The following discussion focuses specifically on automated sources of information because many valuable types of public records have been entered into a computer and, therefore, require a computer search to obtain reliable results. The original version of this article was authored by **Mr. Leroy Cook**, Director of ION and The Investigators Anywhere Resource Line (www.investigatorsanywhere.com). Mr. Cook has graciously allowed us to edit the article and reprint it for our readers.

1. Where does he or she get the information?

You may feel awkward asking a vendor where he or she obtained the information you are purchasing. The fake Rolex watch is a reminder that even buying physical things based on looks alone—without knowing where they come from—is dangerous.

Reliable information vendors *will* provide verification material such as the name of the database or service accessed, when it was last updated, and how complete it is.

It is important that you know the gathering process in order to better judge the reliability of the information being purchased. There *are* certain investigative sources that a vendor will not be willing to disclose to you. However, that type of source should not be confused with the information that is being sold item by item. Information technology has changed so rapidly that some information vendors may still confuse "items of information" with "investigative reports." Items of information sold as units are *not* investigative reports. The professional reputation of an information vendor is a guaranty of sorts. Still, because information as a commodity is so new, there is little in the way of an implied warranty of fitness.

2. How long does it take for the new information or changes to get into the system?

Any answer *except* a clear, concise date and time or the vendor's personal knowledge of an ongoing system's methods of maintaining information currency is a reason to keep probing. In view of the preceding question, this one might seem repetitive, but it *really* is a different issue. Microfiche or a database of records may have been updated last week at a courthouse or a DMV, but the department's computer section may also be working with a three-month backlog. In this case, a critical incident occurring one month ago would *not* show up in the information updated last week. The importance of timeliness is a variable to be determined by you, but to be truly informed you need to know how "fresh" the information is. Ideally, the mechanism by which you purchase items of information *should* include an update or statement of accuracy—as a part of the reply—*without* having to ask.

3. What are the searchable fields? Which fields are mandatory?

If your knowledge of "fields" and "records" is limited to the places where cattle graze and those flat, round things that play music, you *could* have a problem telling a good database from a bad one. An MVR vendor, for example, should be able to tell you that a subject's middle initial is critical when pulling an Arizona driving record. You don't have to become a programmer to use a computer and you needn't know a database management language to benefit from databases, *but* it is very helpful to understand how databases are constructed and (*at the least*) what fields, records, and indexing procedures are used.

As a general rule, the computerized, public-record information world is not standardized from county to county or from state to state; in the same way, there is little standardization within or between information vendors. Look at the system documentation from the vendor. The manual should include this sort of information.

4. How much latitude is there for error (misspellings or inappropriate punctuation) in a data request?

If the vendor's requirements for search data appear to be concise and meticulous, then you're probably on the right track. Some computer systems will tell (or "flag") an operator when they make a mistake such as omitting important punctuation or using an unnecessary comma. Other systems allow you to make inquiries by whatever means or in whatever format you like—and then tell you the requested information has *not* been found. In this instance, the desired information may *actually* be there, but the computer didn't understand the question because of the way in which it was asked. It is easy to misinterpret "no record found" as "there is no record." Please take note that the meanings of these two phrases are quite different.

5. What method is used to place the information in the repository and what error control or edit process is used?

In some databases, information may be scanned in or may be entered by a single operator as it is received and, in others, information may be entered *twice* to allow the computer to catch input errors by searching for non-duplicate entries. You don't have to know *everything* about all record options, but the vendor selling information in quantity *should*.

6. How many different databases or sources does the vendor access *and* how often?

The chance of obtaining an accurate search of a database increases with the frequency of access and the vendor's/searcher's level of knowledge. If he or she only makes inquiries once a month—and the results are important—you may need to find someone who sells data at higher volume. The point here is that it is better to find someone who specializes in the type of information you are seeking than it is to utilize a vendor who *can* get the information, but actually specializes in another type of data.

7. Does the price include assistance in interpreting the data received?

A report that includes coding and ambiguous abbreviations may look impressive in your file, but may not be too meaningful. For all reports, except those you deal with regularly, interpretation assistance can be *very* important. Some information vendors offer searches for information they really don't know much about through sources that they only use occasionally. Professional pride sometimes prohibits them from disclosing their limitations—until *you* ask the right questions.

8. Do vendors "keep track" of requesters and the information they seek (usage records)?

This may not seem like a serious concern when you are requesting information you're legally entitled to; however, there *is* a possibility that your usage records could be made available to a competitor. Most probably, the information itself is *already* being (or will be) sold to someone else, but you may not necessarily want *everyone* to know what you are requesting and how often. If the vendor keeps records of who-asks-what, the confidentiality of that information should be addressed in your agreement with the vendor.

9. Will the subject of the inquiry be notified of the request?

If your inquiry is sub rosa or if the subject's discovery of the search could lead to embarrassment, double check! There are laws that mandate the notification of subjects when certain types of inquires are made into their files. If notification is required, the way it is accomplished could be critical.

10. Is the turnaround time and cost of the search made clear at the outset?

You should be crystal clear about what you expect and/or need; the vendor should be succinct when conveying exactly what will be provided and how much it will cost. Failure to address these issues can lead to disputes and hard feelings.

These are excellent questions and concepts to keep in mind when searching for the right public record vendor to meet your needs.

Section II

Public Records by State

Alabama

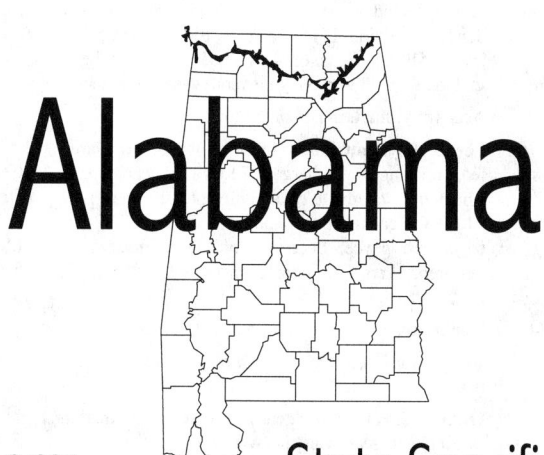

General Help Numbers:

Governor's Office
600 Dexter Ave, #N-104   334-242-7100
Montgomery, AL 36130   Fax 334-242-0937
www.governor.state.al.us   8AM-5PM

Attorney General's Office
State House   334-242-7300
11 S. Union Street, 3rd Fl   Fax 334-242-7458
Montgomery, AL 36130   8AM-5PM
www.ago.state.al.us

State Court Administrator
300 Dexter Ave   334-242-0300
Montgomery, AL 36104-3741   Fax 334-242-2099
www.alacourt.org   8AM-5PM

State Archives
Archives & History Department   334-242-4435
Reference Room, PO Box 300100   Fax 334-240-3433
Montgomery, AL 36130-0100
www.archives.state.al.us   8AM-5PM T-F, 9AM-5PM SA

State Specifics:

Capital:	Montgomery Montgomery County
Time Zone:	CST
Number of Counties:	67
Population:	4,369,862
Web Site:	www.state.al.us

State Agencies

Criminal Records

Alabama Department of Public Safety, A.B.I., Identification Unit, PO Box 1511, Montgomery, AL 36102-1511 (Courier: 502 Washington St, Montgomery, AL 36104); 334-242-4244, 334-242-4270 (Fax), 8AM-5PM.

Indexing & Storage: Records are available from 1942 on.

Searching: Must have notarized release from subject. The request must be on a state form (call to have copy sent). They will release records of arrests without dispositions. Include the following in your request-date of birth, Social Security

Number, full name, race, sex. The following data is not released: juvenile records.

Access by: mail, in person, online.

Fee & Payment: Prepayment required. Fee payee: Alabama Bureau of Investigation. Cashier checks and money orders accepted. No credit cards accepted.

Mail search: Turnaround time: 7 days. No self addressed stamped envelope is required. Search costs $25.00 per applicant.

In person search: You may bring in the required release and request form, but record is returned by mail.

Online search: The State Court Administration provides records over its State Judicial Online System (SJIS) at www.alacourt.org. SJIS contains criminal records from all county courthouses. Access to the state system, which is used by the courts as well as the public, requires a $150 setup fee plus a $50 per month for unlimited access. The system is open 24 hours daily. Fees at the commercial web site are slightly higher, but the site itself is more user friendly. Call Cheryl Lenoir at 334-242-0300 for more information.

Corporation Records
Limited Partnership Records
Limited Liability Company Records
Limited Liability Partnerships
Trade Names
Trademarks/Servicemarks

Secretary of State, Corporations Division, PO Box 5616, Montgomery, AL 36103-5616 (Courier: 11 S Union St, Ste 207, Montgomery, AL 36104); 334-242-5324, 334-242-5325 (Trademarks), 334-240-3138 (Fax), 8AM-5PM.

www.sos.state.al.us

Note: The office for trademarks, trade names, and service marks is located in Room 208.

Indexing & Storage: Records are available for all corporations, active or inactive. All information here on file is considered public information. Formal registration of trademarks and service marks was codified in 1981, and trade name registration in 1989. It takes 1 month before new records are available for inquiry. Records are indexed on microfiche, inhouse computer.

Searching: Include the following in your request- full name of business. In addition to the articles of incorporation, corporation records include the following information: Annual Reports, Officers, Directors, Prior (Merged) names, Inactive and Reserved names.

Access by: mail, phone, in person, online.

Fee & Payment: Prepayment required. Fee payee: Secretary of State. The agency will invoice members of the AL state bar. Personal checks accepted. No credit cards accepted.

Mail search: Turnaround time: 1 week. A self addressed stamped envelope is requested. No fee for mail request. Copies cost $1.00 per page.

Phone search: There is a limit of 3 inquiries per call.

In person search: No fee for request. Copies cost $1.00 per page. Call first for page amount before going to their office.

Online search: 2 systems. The commercial online system is called STARPAS. It functions 24 hours a day, 7 days a week. The initial set-up fee is $36 and access costs $.30 per minute. Call 602-542-0685 for a sign-up package. The web site has free searches of corporate and UCC records. Search individual files for Active Names at http://arc-sos.state.al.us/CGI/SOSCRP01.MBR/INPUT.

Expedited service: Expedited service is available for mail and phone searches. Turnaround time: 24-48 hours. Add $100.00 per package. Expedited service ends at 2PM each day.

Uniform Commercial Code
Federal Tax Liens
State Tax Liens

UCC Division, Secretary of State, PO Box 5616, Montgomery, AL 36103-5616 (Courier: 11 South Union St, Suite 207, Montgomery, AL 36104); 334-242-5231, 8AM-5PM.

www.sos.state.al.us/sosinfo/inquiry.cfm

Indexing & Storage: Records are indexed on inhouse computer.

Searching: Use search request form UCC-11. The search includes tax liens. Federal and state tax liens on individuals may also be filed at the county level. All tax liens on businesses are filed here. Include the following in your request-debtor name.

Access by: mail, in person, online.

Fee & Payment: In addition to the $5.00 search fee, this agency charges $1.00 for each page (financing statement or assignment) searched plus $1.00 for each listing. The copy fee is $1.00 per page. Fee payee: Secretary of State. Prepayment required. Personal checks accepted. No credit cards accepted.

Mail search: Turnaround time: 1-2 weeks.

In person search: Searching is available in person.

Online search: The agency has UCC information available to search at the web address, there is no fee. Corporation data is also available.

Sales Tax Registrations
Access to Records is Restricted

Alabama Department of Revenue, Sales, Use and Business Tax Division, 4303 Gordon Persons Bldg, 50 N Ripley St, Montgomery, AL 36104; 334-242-1490, 334-242-8916 (Fax), 8AM-5PM.

www.ador.state.al.us

Note: According to state law 40-2A-10, Code of Alabama 1975, this agency is unable to release any information about tax registrations.

Birth Certificates

Center for Health Statistics, Record Services Division, PO Box 5625, Montgomery, AL 36103-5625 (Courier: RSA Tower Suite 1150, 201 Monroe St, Montgomery, AL 36104); 334-206-5418, 334-262-9563 (Fax), 8AM-5PM.

www.alapubhealth.org

Note: Certificates can, also, be delivered in any County Health Department for any vital record event occurring in AL. Delivery time is usually 15-30 minutes.

Indexing & Storage: Records are available from 1908-present. New records are available for inquiry immediately. Records are indexed on microfiche, inhouse computer.

Searching: Requester must be immediate family for births less than 125 years old. Include the following in your request-full name, names of parents, mother's maiden name, date of birth, county, reason for information request. Include a daytime phone number and a signature.

Access by: mail, phone, fax, in person.

Fee & Payment: Fee is $12.00, add $4.00 per name for each additional copy. Additional expedite fee is $10.00, use of credit card is $5.00. Fee payee: Alabama State Vital Records. Prepayment required. Credit cards accepted for phone, fax and expedited requests only. Personal checks accepted. Credit cards accepted: Mastercard, Visa, AmEx, Discover.

Mail search: Turnaround time: 2-3 weeks. No self addressed stamped envelope is required.

Phone search: Telephone requests allowed using a credit card, see expedited service.

Fax search: Same criteria as phone searching.

In person search: Also, go to the nearest County Health Department.

Expedited service: Expedited service is available for mail, phone and fax searches. Turnaround time: 1 day. The total fee of $37.50 per record includes use of credit card and overnight shipping.

Death Records

Center for Health Statistics, Record Services Division, PO Box 5625, Montgomery, AL 36103-5625 (Courier: RSA Tower Suite 1150, 201 Monroe St, Montgomery, AL 36104); 334-206-5418, 334-262-9563 (Fax), 8AM-5PM.

www.alapubhealth.org

Indexing & Storage: Records are available from 1908 on. New records are available for inquiry immediately. Records are indexed on microfiche, inhouse computer.

Searching: Must be immediate family for ordering death records less than 25 years old. Include the following in your request-full name, date of death, names of parents, county, reason for information request. Include a daytime phone number.

Access by: mail, phone, fax, in person.

Fee & Payment: Fee is $12.00, add $4.00 per copy for each additional copy. Additional expedite fee is $10.00, use of credit card is $5.00. Fee payee: Alabama State Vital Records. Prepayment required. Personal checks accepted. Credit cards accepted: Mastercard, Visa, AmEx, Discover.

Mail search: Turnaround time: 2-3 weeks. No self addressed stamped envelope is required.

Phone search: Telephone requests allowed using a credit card, see expedited service.

Fax search: Same criteria as phone searching.

In person search: Also, you can go to the nearest County Health Department.

Other access: Records are available on microfilm for $40.00 per roll. There are 6 rolls of records for 1908 through 1959.

Expedited service: Expedited service is available for mail, phone and fax searches. The total including overnight shipping is $37.50.

Marriage Certificates

Center for Health Statistics, Record Services Division, PO Box 5625, Montgomery, AL 36103-5625 (Courier: RSA Tower Suite 1150, 201 Monroe St, Montgomery, AL 36104); 334-206-5418, 334-262-9563 (Fax), 8AM-5PM.

www.alapubhealth.org

Indexing & Storage: Records are available from 1936-present. New records are available for inquiry immediately. Records are indexed on microfiche, inhouse computer.

Searching: Include the following in your request- names of husband and wife, date of marriage, county of license issue. Include a daytime phone number.

Access by: mail, phone, fax, in person.

Fee & Payment: Fee is $12.00, add $4.00 per copy for additional copies. Additional expedite fee is $10.00, the credit card fee is $5.00. Fee payee: Alabama State Vital Records. Prepayment required. Personal checks accepted. Credit cards accepted: Mastercard, Visa, AmEx, Discover.

Mail search: Turnaround time: 2-3 weeks. No self addressed stamped envelope is required.

Phone search: Telephone requests allowed using a credit card, see expedited service.

Fax search: Same criteria as phone searches.

In person search: Also, you can go to the nearest County Health Department.

Other access: Microfilm rolls are available for purchase at $40.00 each. There are 11 rolls available which includes records from 1936-1969.

Expedited service: Expedited service is available for mail, phone and fax searches. Turnaround time: 1-2 days. The total fee of $37.50 also includes overnight delivery.

Divorce Records

Center for Health Statistics, Record Services Division, PO Box 5625, Montgomery, AL 36103-5625 (Courier: RSA Tower Suite 1150, 201 Monroe St, Montgomery, AL 36104); 334-206-5418, 334-206-2659 (Fax), 8AM-5PM.

www.alapubhealth.org

Indexing & Storage: Records are available from 1950-present. New records are available for inquiry immediately. Records are indexed on inhouse computer, microfiche.

Searching: Include the following in your request-names of husband and wife, date of divorce, county. Include a daytime phone number.

Access by: mail, phone, fax, in person.

Fee & Payment: Fee is $12.00, add $4.00 per copy for additional copies. Additional expedite fee is $10.00, the credit card fee is $5.00. Fee payee: Alabama State Vital Records. Prepayment required. Personal checks accepted. Credit cards accepted: Mastercard, Visa, AmEx, Discover.

Mail search: Turnaround time: 2-3 weeks. No self addressed stamped envelope is required.

Phone search: Telephone requests allowed using a credit card, see expedited service.

Fax search: Same criteria as phone searches.

In person search: Also, you can go to the nearest County Health Department.

Other access: There is one microfilm roll of records for 1950-59 available for $40.00.

Expedited service: Expedited service is available for mail, phone and fax searches. Turnaround time: 1-2 days. The total fee of $37.50 includes overnight shipping.

Workers' Compensation Records

Department of Industrial Relations, Disclosure Unit, 649 Monroe Street, Rm. 276, Montgomery, AL 36131; 334-242-8980, 334-261-2304 (Fax), 8AM-4:30PM.

Indexing & Storage: Records are available from 1986 on computer (index). Actual file copies are placed on microfilm after 6 months. Older records (pre 1986) are on microfiche and must be searched by SSN.

Searching: Must have a written, notarized release from claimant. Include the following in your request-claimant name, Social Security Number.

Access by: mail, in person.

Fee & Payment: The fee is $8.00 per record. Fee payee: Department of Industrial Relations, Workers Compensation. Prepayment required.

Personal checks accepted. No credit cards accepted.

Mail search: Turnaround time: 1 week. No self addressed stamped envelope is required.

In person search: A notarized release form is required.

Driver Records

Department of Public Safety, Driver Records-License Division, PO Box 1471, Montgomery, AL 36102-1471 (Courier: 500 Dexter Ave, Montgomery, AL 36104); 334-242-4400, 334-242-4639 (Fax), 8AM-5PM.

www.ador.state.al.us/motorvehicle/MVD_MAIN.html

Note: Ticket information must be secured at the local level.

Indexing & Storage: Records are available for convictions in last five years for moving violations, surrendered licenses, DWI and suspensions. It takes 2 weeks before new records are available for inquiry.

Searching: Some juvenile records are considered confidential and are not released. Need full name, DOB and license number to obtain a record. Use Form MV-DPPA1 if you are a permissible user.

Access by: mail, in person, online.

Fee & Payment: The fee is $5.75 per record for all access modes. Fee payee: Alabama DPS, Drivers License Division. Prepayment required. No credit cards accepted.

Mail search: Turnaround time: 3-5 days. Providing a self-addressed return envelope usually means quicker service.

In person search: Walk-in requesters are not charged for a no record found report.

Online search: Alabama offers real time batch processing access via the AAMVAnet 3270 Terminal Connection. There is a minimum order requirement of 500 requests per month. Fee is $5.75 per record. Requesters must provide their own connection device and terminal emulation software. Generally, requests are available 30 minutes after request transmission.

Vehicle Ownership
Vehicle Identification

Motor Vehicle Division, Title Section, PO Box 327640, Montgomery, AL 36132-7640 (Courier: 50 North Ripley St, Montgomery, AL 36140); 334-242-9000, 334-242-0312 (Fax), 8AM-5PM.

www.ador.state.al.us/motorvehicle/MVD_MAIN.html

Indexing & Storage: Records are available from 1975 for title records and 10 years for registration records. It takes 2 weeks before new records are available for inquiry.

Searching: The restrictions specified under the DPPA (Driver's Privacy Protection Act) apply. Access is restricted to permissible users who must use Form MV-DPPA1. An opt-out provision is in place. The address of the title or registration holder must be included as part of the request. The following data is not released: bulk information or lists for commercial purposes.

Access by: mail.

Fee & Payment: Fees are $3.00 per record per year for registration records and $15.00 for title

searches (includes lien data). Fee payee: Alabama Department of Revenue. Prepayment required. Only certified funds are accepted. No credit cards accepted.

Mail search: Turnaround time: 3-4 weeks. No self addressed stamped envelope is required.

Other access: Records of those drivers who have opted-in are available for marketing purposes.

Accident Reports

Alabama Department of Public Safety, Accident Records, PO Box 1471, Montgomery, AL 36102-1471 (Courier: 502 Washington Ave, Montgomery, AL 36104); 334-242-4241, 8AM-5PM.

Indexing & Storage: Records are available for a minimum of 10 years. After 2 years, they put reports on microfiche. It takes 2 weeks before new records are available for inquiry.

Searching: Include the following in your request-date of accident, location of accident, county. Also, submit names of drivers.

Access by: mail, phone, in person.

Fee & Payment: Prepayment required. Fee payee: Alabama DPS, Accident Reports. Only certified funds or cash is accepted. No credit cards accepted.

Mail search: Turnaround time: within 2 weeks. A self addressed stamped envelope is requested. Search costs $5.00 per record.

Phone search: No fee for telephone request. They will search to see if a report exists, but will not give any information over the phone.

In person search: Search costs $5.00 per record. Turnaround time is while you wait.

Boat & Vessel Ownership
Boat & Vessel Registration

Dept of Conservation & Natural Resources, Marine Police Div. Boat Reg. Records, PO Box 301451, Montgomery, AL 36130 (Courier: 64 N Union St, Montgomery, AL 36104); 334-242-3673, 334-242-0336 (Fax), 8AM-5PM.

www.dcnr.state.al.us

Indexing & Storage: Records are available from 1985-the present. Records are indexed on computer. All mechanically propelled, sail or rental boats must be registered. It takes 2 months before new records are available for inquiry.

Searching: Vessels that have been commercially documented by the Coast Guard are not required to register with Alabama. Liens are not recorded here, but at the central state locations for UCC filings. To search, at least one of the following is required: owner's name, hull id #, current decal #, or registration #. For purged records, the registration # is required to search.

Access by: mail, phone, fax, in person.

Fee & Payment: There is no search fee, except for bulk searches (see below) or lengthy lists ($1.00 per record). Fee payee: Department of Conservation. Prepayment required. No credit cards accepted.

Mail search: Turnaround time: 1-2 days. No self addressed stamped envelope is required.

Phone search: Searching is available by phone.

Fax search: Turnaround time is within 1 day.

In person search: Searching is available in person.

Other access: The state accepts e-mail requests for records at rthornell@dcnr.state.al.us. The state will sell all or parts of its database. Fees start at $100.00 for the first 2,500 records.

Legislation-Current/Pending
Legislation-Passed

Alabama Legislature, State House, 11 S Union St, Montgomery, AL 36130-4600; 334-242-7826 (Senate), 334-242-7637 (House), 334-242-8819 (Fax), 8:30AM-4:30PM.

www.legislature.state.al.us

Note: Use Room 716 for the Senate, Room 512 for the House.

Indexing & Storage: Records are available from 1995-present on computer and from 1819 in journal books. Records are indexed on inhouse computer, books (volumes).

Searching: Include the following in your request- bill number. You may also request bills by subject or sponsor.

Access by: mail, phone, fax, in person, online.

Fee & Payment: The search fee is $1.00 per page with a $25.00 maximum. Computer printouts are $1.00 per page. The state will charge postage for large print runs. Fee payee: Either to the Senate or the House. Prepayment required. Personal checks accepted. No credit cards accepted.

Mail search: Turnaround time: 1 day. No self addressed stamped envelope is required.

Phone search: Searching is available by phone.

Fax search: The fax fee is $5.00.

In person search: You may make copies at $.25 per page. This is the preferred request method.

Online search: Their commercial online access system is called "ALIS" and provides state code, bill text, bill status, voting history, statutory retrieval, and boards/commission information. The initial fee is $400 plus $100 per month. You must sign up for 12 months. The fees entitle you to unlimited usage per month. The system is open 24 hours a day, 7 days a week. For details, call Angela Sayers at 334-242-7482. Current session and the Code of Alabama is available from the web site.

Voter Registration
Access to Records is Restricted

Alabama State House, Voter Registration, 11 S Union, Rm 236, Montgomery, AL 36130; 334-242-4337, 334-242-2940 (Fax), 8AM-5PM.

Note: Individual name requests must be done at the county level, there are no restrictions. The SSN is not released. Bulk requests can be ordered from this office for data from 55 of 69 counties. Call for fees and breakdowns of customized requests.

GED Certificates

State Dept of Education, GED Testing Office, PO Box 302101, Montgomery, AL 36130-2101 (Courier: Gordon Persons Bldg Rm 5345, 50 N Ripley St, Montgomery, AL 36104); 334-242-8181 (Main Number), 334-242-2236 (Fax), 8AM-5PM.

www.alsbe.edu

Searching: Only the name is needed to verify. All of the following is required for a transcript: a signed release, name, year of test, date of birth, Social Security Number, and city of testing.

Access by: mail, phone, fax, in person.

Fee & Payment: There is no search fee, but there is a $5.00 certification fee. If transcript is needed, fee is $5.00 plus $5.00 for certification. Fee payee: GED Testing. Only cashier's checks and money orders are accepted. No credit cards accepted.

Mail search: Turnaround time is 1-2 days. No self addressed stamped envelope is required.

Phone search: Verification only.

Fax search: Turnaround time is same day. Results will be called or faxed.

In person search: No fee for request. Turnaround time is a few minutes.

Hunting License Information
Fishing License Information
Access to Records is Restricted

Conservation & Natural Resources Department, Game & Fish Division, 64 N Union Street, Room 559, Montgomery, AL 36130; 334-242-3829, 334-242-3032 (Fax), 8AM-5PM.

Note: They do not have a central database. They only track the number of licenses issued to the issuing agent, not to the individual.

Licenses Searchable Online

Architect #08.. www.alarchbd.state.al.us/rostersearch/rostersearch.asp
Attorney #03 .... www.alabar.org/Database_search/dirSearch.cfm
Forester #26.. http://home.earthlink.net/~pbsears/foresters.html
Home Inspector #42 .... www.sos.state.al.us/sosinfo/inquiry.cfm
Insurance Agent #39 .... www.aldoi.org/Agents/dirSearch.cfm
Insurance Company #39.. www.aldoi.org/examiners/dirSearch.cfm
Medical Doctor #19 .... www.mindspring.com/~bmedixon
Notary Public #42.. www.sos.state.al.us/sosinfo/inquiry.cfm
Nursing Home Administrator #22 .... www.alboenha.state.al.us/logon.html
Optometrist #20 .... www.arbo.org/nodb2000/licsearch.asp
Real Estate Broker #02 .... www.arec.state.al.us/search/search.asp
Real Estate Salesperson #02 .... www.arec.state.al.us/search/search.asp

Licensing Quick Finder

Abortion Center #31 933-424-0350
Aircraft Personnel #51 205-731-1557
Ambulatory Surgery Center #31...........933-424-0350
Anesthesiologist Assistant #19 334-242-4116
Architect #08......................................334-242-4179
Assisted Living Unit (Assisted Living Facilities) #31
....933-424-0350
Attorney #03 334-269-1515
Auctioneer #09 334-269-9990
Bank #05 334-242-3452
Bar Pilot #45 334-479-9247
Beauty Shop #11 334-242-1918
Beauty Shop/Booth Rental #11 334-242-1918
Birthing Center #31 334-240-3500
Boxer #52 334-242-1380
Broker Dealer Agent #48 334-242-2984
Chiropractor #10 205-755-8000
Clinical Nurse Specialist #21 334-242-0767
Consumer Finance Company #05.........334-242-3452
Cosmetic Studio #11 334-242-1918
Cosmetologist & Cosmetology Instructor #11
....334-242-1918
Cosmetologist Student/Apprentice #11 .334-242-1918
Cosmetologist/Pending Exam #11 334-242-1918
Cosmetology School #11......................334-242-1918
Counselor #15 205-458-8716
Dental Scholarship Award #13..............205-934-4384
Dentist/Dental Hygienist #12...............256-533-4638
Dietitian/Nutritionist #33......................334-242-4505
Education Administrator #49.................334-242-9977
Electrical Contractor #14 334-269-9990
Elementary Teacher #49 334-242-9977
Embalmer #17 334-242-4049
Emergency Medical Technician #50......334-206-5383
Endstage Renal Disease & Treatment Center #31
....334-240-3500
Engineer #27 334-242-5568
Engineer-In-Training #27 334-242-5568
Esthetician #11 334-242-1918
Esthetician Apprentice #11 334-242-1918
Esthetician Salon #11 334-242-1918
Esthetician/Pending Exam #11 334-242-1918
Firefighter #36.....................................205-391-3776
Forester #26 334-240-9368
Funeral Director #17............................334-242-4049
Gas Fitter #46 205-945-4857
General Contractor #07 334-242-2839
Geologist #37......................................334-264-0730
Hearing Instrument Dealer #35 334-242-1925
Heating & Air Conditioning Contractor #38
....334-242-5550

Home Builder #53 334-242-2230
Home Inspector #42 334-242-7205
Hospice #31 334-240-3500
Hospital #31 334-206-5175
Independent Clinical/Physiological Lab #31
....334-240-3500
Instructor-Cosmetology/Esthetician/Manicurist #11
....334-242-1918
Insurance Adjuster #39........................334-241-4126
Insurance Agent #39 334-241-4126
Insurance Broker #39 334-241-4126
Insurance Company #39 334-241-4126
Insurance Corporation/Partnership #39..334-241-4126
Interior Designer #54...........................205-669-0542
Investment Advisor #48 334-242-2984
Investment Advisor Representative #48
....334-242-2984
Journeyman Electrician #14..................334-269-9990
Landscape Architect #18 334-262-1351
Landscape Planter #55........................334-240-7171
Law Enforcement Personnel #44 334-242-4047
Legal/Dental Service Representative #39
....334-241-4126
Livestock Market Operator #30............334-240-7208
Managing Cosmetologist/Esthetician/Manicurist #11
....334-242-1918
Managing Cosmetologist #11 334-242-1918
Manicurist #11 334-242-1918
Manicurist Apprentice #11 334-242-1918
Manicurist Salon #11 334-242-1918
Manicurist School #11 334-242-1918
Manicurist/Pending Exam #11 334-242-1918
Massage Therapist #56.......................334-263-3407
Master Cosmetologist/Esthetician/Manicurist #11
....334-242-1918
Maternity Home #31 334-240-3500
Medical Doctor #19 334-242-4116
Medical Gas #46 205-945-4857
Mine Personnel #34 205-254-1275
Mine Safety and Inspection #32...........205-254-1275
Mobile Home Manufacturer #41............334-242-4036
Motor Club Representative #39 334-241-4126
Notary Public #42................................334-242-7205
Nurse #21 334-242-0767
Nurse Anesthetist #21 334-242-0767
Nurse Midwife #21 334-242-0767
Nurse-LPN #21 334-242-0767
Nurse-RN #21 334-242-0767
Nursing Home #31 334-240-3500
Nursing Home Administrator #22 334-271-6214
Occupational Therapist #57 334-353-4466

Occupational Therapist Assistant #57 ...334-353-4466
Optometrist #20 256-538-9903
Osteopathic Physician #19 334-242-4116
Pawn Shop #05....................................334-242-3452
Pest Control #30 334-240-7241
Pesticide Applicator #30 334-240-7239
Pesticide Dealer #30 334-240-7239
Pharmacist #23....................................205-967-0130
Physical Therapist #24 334-242-4064
Physical Therapist Assistant #24 334-242-4064
Physician Assistant #19.......................334-242-4116
Pilot #45 334-479-9247
Plumber #46 205-945-4857
Podiatrist #04 205-995-8537
Polygraph Examiner #47 334-260-1182
Propane Gas Broker #40 334-242-5649
Psychological Technician #16...............334-242-4127
Psychologist #16 334-242-4127
Public Accountant-CPA #25.................334-242-5700
Real Estate Appraiser #43 334-242-8747
Real Estate Broker #02 334-242-5544
Real Estate Salesperson #02 334-242-5544
Real Estate Time-Share Seller #43 334-242-8747
Rehabilitation Center #31 334-240-3500
Reinsurance Intermediary #39 334-241-4126
Restricted Managing Cosmetologist #11
....334-242-1918
Rural Primary Care Hospital #31...........334-240-3500
School Bus Driver #49..........................334-242-9730
School Counselor #49 334-242-9977
School for Esthetician #11 334-242-1918
Securities Broker/Dealer #48 334-242-2984
Shampoo Assistant #11........................334-242-1918
Social Worker #58 334-242-5860
Soil Classifier #01 334-242-2620
Speech Pathologist/Audiologist #28.......334-269-1434
Student Esthetician/Manicurist #11 334-242-1918
Sub Contractor #07 334-242-2839
Surface Mining #32 334-242-8265
Surgeon Assistant #19 334-242-4116
Surplus Lines Broker #39 334-241-4126
Surveyor #27 334-242-5568
Teacher #49...334-242-9977
Timeshare Seller #02 334-242-5544
Tree Surgeon #55 334-240-7171
Veterinarian #29..................................256-353-3544
Veterinary Premise Permit #29 256-353-3544
Veterinary Technician #29 256-353-3544
Water Transportation Personnel #45.....334-479-9247
Wrestler #52 334-242-1380

Licensing Agency Information

01 Soil and Water Conservation Committee, 100 N Union St #334, Montgomery, AL 36104-3702; 334-242-2620, Fax: 334-242-0551.

02 Real Estate Commission, 1201 Carmichael Way, Montgomery, AL 36106; 334-242-2620, Fax: 334-242-0551. www.arec.state.al.us

03 Alabama State Bar Association, PO Box 671 (415 Dexter Ave (36104)), Montgomery, AL 36106; 334-242-5544, Fax: 334-270-9118. www.alabar.org

04 Board of Podiatry, 13 Innisbrook Ln, Birmingham, AL 35242; 205-995-8537, Fax: 205-995-8537. www.alabamapodiatryboard.org

05 Banking Department, 401 Adams St, #680, Montgomery, AL 36130; 334-242-3452, Fax: 334-353-5961.

06 Bear Creek Development Authority, PO Box 670 (PO Box 670), Russelville, AL 35653; 256-332-4392, Fax: 256-332-4372.

www.getaway.net/bcda

07 Board for General Contractors, 400 S Union St, #235, Montgomery, AL 36130; 334-242-2839, Fax: 334-240-3424.

http://agencies.state.al.us/gencontrbd

08 Board for Registration of Architects, 770 Washington Ave, Montgomery, AL 36130-4450; 334-242-4179, Fax: 334-242-4531. www.alarchbd.state.al.us

09 Board of Auctioneers, 660 Adams Ave #254, Montgomery, AL 36104; 334-269-9990, Fax: 334-263-6115.

10 Board of Chiropractic Examiners, 737 Logan Road, Clanton, AL 35056; 205-755-8000, Fax: 205-755-0081.

http://chiro.state.al.us

11 Board of Cosmetology, PO Box 301750, RSA Union Bldg #320, Montgomery, AL 36130-1750; 334-242-1918, Fax: 334-242-1926.

www.aboc.state.al.us

12 Board of Dental Examiners, 2327-B Pansy St, Huntsville, AL 35801; 256-533-4638, Fax: 256-533-4690.

13 Board of Dental Scholarship Awards, 1600 University, Volker P115, Birmingham, AL 35294; 205-934-4384, Fax: 205-975-6066.

14 Board of Electrical Contractors, 660 Adams Ave #301, Montgomery, AL 36104; 334-269-9990, Fax: 334-263-6115. www.aecb@state.al.us

15 Board of Examiners in Counseling, PO Box 550397 (950 22nd St N. #670), Birmingham, AL 35203; 205-458-8716, Fax: 205-458-8718.

16 Board of Examiners in Psychology, 660 Adams Ave, #360, Mongomery, AL 36104; 334-242-4127. www.psychology.state.al.us

17 Board of Funeral Service, 11 State House Station, Montgomery, AL 36104; 334-242-4049, Fax: 334-353-7988.

18 Board of Landscape Architects, 908 S Hull St, Montgomery, AL 36104; 334-262-1351, Fax: 334-262-1351.

19 Board of Medical Examiners, 848 Washington Ave, Montgomery, AL 36104; 334-242-4116, Fax: 334-242-4155.

www.mindspring.com/~bmedixon You cannot actually search online. However, you can download ASCII and dbf files of currently licensed physicians for offline viewing.

20 Board of Optometry, PO Box 448, Attalla, AL 35954; 256-538-9903, Fax: 256-538-9904. www.al-optometry.com

21 Board of Nursing, PO Box 303900 (PO Box 303900), Montgomery, AL 36130-3900; 334-242-4060, Fax: 334-242-4360. www.abn.state.al.us

22 Board of Nursing Home Administrators, 4156 Carmichael Road, Montgomery, AL 36130; 334-271-6214, Fax: 334-244-6509. www.alboenha.state.al.us

23 Board of Pharmacy, 1 Perimeter Park S, #425, Birmingham, AL 35243; 205-967-0130, Fax: 205-967-1009. www.albop.com

24 Board of Physical Therapy, 100 N Union St, #627, Montgomery, AL 36130-5040; 334-242-4064, Fax: 334-240-3288.

25 Board of Public Accounting, 770 Washington Ave, #236, Montgomery, AL 36130; 334-242-5700, Fax: 334-240-2711.

26 Board of Registration for Foresters, 513 Madison Ave, Montgomery, AL 36130; 334-353-3640, Fax: 334-353-3641.

http://home.earthlink.net/~pbsears

27 Board of Registration for Professional Engineers & Land Surveyors, PO Box 304451 (PO Box 304451), Montgomery, AL 36130-4451; 334-242-5568, Fax: 334-242-5105.

28 Board of Examiners for Speech-Language Pathology & Audiology, PO Box 143 (PO Box 304760 (400 S Union St #225)), Montgomery, AL 36130-4760; 334-269-1434, Fax: 334-269-6379.

www.mindspring.net/~abespa

29 Board of Veterinary Medical Examiners, PO Box 1968 (PO Box 1968), Decatur, AL 35602; 256-353-3544, Fax: 256-350-5629.

30 Department of Agriculture & Industries, 1445 Federal Dr, Montgomery, AL 36107; 205-240-7100, Fax: 205-240-7193.

31 Department of Health, Division of Licensing, 434 Monroe St, Montgomery, AL 36130-3017; 334-206-5100, Fax: 334-240-3147.

32 Department of Industrial Relations, State Programs Division, 649 Monroe St, Rm 2211, Montgomery, AL 36131-5200; 334-242-8265, Fax: 334-242-8403. http://dir.state.al.us/sp.htm

33 Dietetic/Nutrition Examiners Board, 400 S Union St #445, Montgomery, AL 36104; 334-242-4505, Fax: 334-834-6398.

34 Examiners of Mine Personnel, PO Box 10444 (PO Box 10444), Birmingham, AL 35202; 205-254-1275, Fax: 205-254-1278.

35 Hearing Aid Dealers, Executive Secretary, 400 S Union St, #445, Montgomery, AL 36130-3010; 334-242-1925, Fax: 334-834-6389.

36 Fire College & Personnel Standards Commission, 2501 Phoenix Dr, Tuscaloosa, AL 35405; 205-391-3776, Fax: 205-391-3747.

www.alabamafirecollege.cc.al.us

37 Geological Survey, PO Box 869999 (PO Box 175), Montgomery, AL 36104; 334-264-0730, Fax: 334-263-6115. www.algeobd.com

38 Heating & Air Conditioning Contractors Board, 100 N Union St, #627, Montgomery, AL 36130; 205-349-2852, Fax: 205-349-2861.

39 Department of Insurance, Agent Licensing Division, 201 Monroe St #1700, Mongomery, AL 36130-3351; 334-241-4126, Fax: 334-240-3282.

www.aldoi.org

40 Liquefied Petroleum Gas Board, 820 S Quincy, Montgomery, AL 36130; 334-242-5649, Fax: 334-240-3255.

41 Manufactured Housing Commission, 350 S Decatur St, Montgomery, AL 36104; 334-242-4036, Fax: 334-240-3178.

42 Office of the Secretary of State, PO Box 5616 (PO Box 5616), Montgomery, AL 36104; 334-242-7205, Fax: 334-242-4993. www.sos.state.al.us

43 Office of the Secretary of State, Real Estate Appraisers Licensing, 100 North Union Street #370, RSA Bldg, Montgomery, AL 36103-5616; 334-242-8747, Fax: 334-242-8749.

http://agencies.state.al.us/reab

44 Peace Officers Standards & Training Commission, PO Box 300075 (100 Union St, RSA Union Bldg, #600), Montgomery, AL 36130-0075; 334-242-4045, Fax: 334-242-4633.

45 Pilotage Commission, PO Box 273 (PO Box 273), Mobile, AL 36601; 334-432-2639, Fax: 334-432-9964.

46 Plumbers & Gas Fitters Examining Board, 11 W Oxmoor, #104, Birmingham, AL 35209; 205-945-4857, Fax: 205-945-9915.

47 Polygraph Examiners Board, 2720-A W Gunter Park Dr, Montgomery, AL 36109; 344-260-1182, Fax: 344-260-8788.

48 Securities Division, 770 Washington Ave, #570, Montgomery, AL 36130; 334-260-2984, Fax: 334-242-0240.

49 Department of Education, 50 N Ripley St, Montgomery, AL 36104; 334-242-9977, Fax: 334-242-2818. www.alsde.edu

50 Department of Health, Emergency Medical Services Division, PO Box 303017 (PO Box 303017), Birmingham, AL 36130-3017; 334-206-5383, Fax: 334-206-5260.

www.alapubhealth.org/ems

51 Department of Transportation, Flight Standards District Office, 6500 43rd Ave N, Birmingham, AL 35206; 205-731-1557.

52 Department of Revenue, Athletic Commission, 50 N Ripley St Rm 4131, Montgomery, AL 36132; 334-242-1380.

53 Home Builders Licensure Board, 400 S Union St #195, Montgomery, AL 36130; 334-242-2230.

54 Board of Registration for Interior Designers, PO Box 1965, Columbiana, AL 35051; 205-669-0542.

55 Department of Agriculture & Industries, Plant Protection & Pesticide Management Division, PO Box 3336 - Beard Building, Montgomery, AL 36109-0336; 334-240-7171.

56 Board of Massage Therapy, PO Box 56, Montgomery, AL 36101-0056; 334-263-3407.

57 Board of Occupational Therapy, 64 N Union St #734, PO Box 4510, Montgomery, AL 36130-4510; 334-353-4466.

58 Board of Social Work Examiners, 64 N Union St #129, Montgomery, AL 36130; 334-242-5860.

The following list indicates the district and division name for each county in the state. If the district or division name of the bankruptcy court is different from the civil/criminal court, it appears in parentheses.

County/Court Cross Reference

County	District	Division
Autauga	Middle	Montgomery
Baldwin	Southern	Mobile
Barbour	Middle	Montgomery
Bibb	Northern	Birmingham (Tuscaloosa)
Blount	Northern	Birmingham
Bullock	Middle	Montgomery
Butler	Middle	Montgomery
Calhoun	Northern	Birmingham (Anniston)
Chambers	Middle	Opelika (Montgomery)
Cherokee	Northern	Gadsden (Anniston)
Chilton	Middle	Montgomery
Choctaw	Southern	Mobile
Clarke	Southern	Mobile
Clay	Northern	Birmingham (Anniston)
Cleburne	Northern	Birmingham (Anniston)
Coffee	Middle	Dothan (Montgomery)
Colbert	Northern	Florence (Decatur)
Conecuh	Southern	Mobile
Coosa	Middle	Montgomery
Covington	Middle	Montgomery
Crenshaw	Middle	Montgomery
Cullman	Northern	Huntsville (Decatur)
Dale	Middle	Dothan (Montgomery)
Dallas	Southern	Selma (Mobile)
De Kalb	Northern	Gadsden (Anniston)
Elmore	Middle	Montgomery
Escambia	Southern	Mobile
Etowah	Northern	Gadsden (Anniston)
Fayette	Northern	Jasper (Tuscaloosa)
Franklin	Northern	Florence (Decatur)
Geneva	Middle	Dothan (Montgomery)
Greene	Northern	Birmingham (Tuscaloosa)
Hale	Southern	Selma (Mobile)
Henry	Middle	Dothan (Montgomery)
Houston	Middle	Dothan (Montgomery)
Jackson	Northern	Huntsville (Decatur)
Jefferson	Northern	Birmingham
Lamar	Northern	Jasper (Tuscaloosa)
Lauderdale	Northern	Florence (Decatur)
Lawrence	Northern	Huntsville (Decatur)
Lee	Middle	Opelika (Montgomery)
Limestone	Northern	Huntsville (Decatur)
Lowndes	Middle	Montgomery
Macon	Middle	Opelika (Montgomery)
Madison	Northern	Huntsville (Decatur)
Marengo	Southern	Selma (Mobile)
Marion	Northern	Jasper (Tuscaloosa)
Marshall	Northern	Gadsden (Anniston)
Mobile	Southern	Mobile
Monroe	Southern	Mobile
Montgomery	Middle	Montgomery
Morgan	Northern	Huntsville (Decatur)
Perry	Southern	Selma (Mobile)
Pickens	Northern	Birmingham (Tuscaloosa)
Pike	Middle	Montgomery
Randolph	Middle	Opelika (Montgomery)
Russell	Middle	Opelika (Montgomery)
Shelby	Northern	Birmingham
St. Clair	Northern	Gadsden (Anniston)
Sumter	Northern	Birmingham (Tuscaloosa)
Talladega	Northern	Birmingham (Anniston)
Tallapoosa	Middle	Opelika (Montgomery)
Tuscaloosa	Northern	Birmingham (Tuscaloosa)
Walker	Northern	Jasper (Tuscaloosa)
Washington	Southern	Mobile
Wilcox	Southern	Selma (Mobile)
Winston	Northern	Jasper (Tuscaloosa)

US District Court

Middle District of Alabama

Dothan Division c/o Montgomery Division, PO Box 711, Montgomery, AL 36101 (Courier Address: 15 Lee St, Montgomery, AL 36104), 334-223-7308.

www.almd.uscourts.gov

Counties: Coffee, Dale, Geneva, Henry, Houston.

Indexing & Storage: Cases are indexed by defendant and plaintiff as well as by case number. New cases are available in the index immediately after filing date. A computer index is maintained. Open records are located at the Division.

Fee & Payment: The fee is $15.00 per item (one party name or case number). Payment may be made by money order, cashier check. Business checks are not accepted. Personal checks are not accepted.

Phone Search: An automated voice case information service (VCIS) is not available.

In Person Search: In person searching is available.

PACER: Sign-up number is 800-676-6856. Access fee is $.60 per minute. Case records are available back to 1994. New records are available online after 1 day.

Montgomery Division Records Search, PO Box 711, Montgomery, AL 36101-0711 (Courier Address: 15 Lee St, Montgomery, AL 36104), 334-223-7308.

www.almd.uscourts.gov

Counties: Autauga, Barbour, Bullock, Butler, Chilton, Coosa, Covington, Crenshaw, Elmore, Lowndes, Montgomery, Pike.

Indexing & Storage: Cases are indexed by defendant and plaintiff as well as by case number. New cases are available in the index immediately after filing date. Both computer and card indexes are maintained. Records are also indexed on microfiche. Open records are located at this court.

Fee & Payment: The fee is $15.00 per item (one party name or case number). Payment may be made by money order, cashier check, business check. Personal checks are not accepted. Prepayment is required. Payee: Clerk, US District Court. Certification fee: $5.00 per document. Copy fee: $.50 per page.

Phone Search: Searching is not available by phone.

Mail Search: Always enclose a stamped self addressed envelope.

In Person Search: In person searching is available.

PACER: Sign-up number is 800-676-6856. Access fee is $.60 per minute. Case records are available back to 1994. New records are available online after 1 day.

Opelika Division c/o Montgomery Division, PO Box 711, Montgomery, AL 36101 (Courier Address: 15 Lee St, Montgomery, AL 36104), 334-223-7308.

www.almd.uscourts.gov

Counties: Chambers, Lee, Macon, Randolph, Russell, Tallapoosa.

Indexing & Storage: Cases are indexed by defendant and plaintiff as well as by case number. New cases are available in the index immediately after filing date. A computer index is maintained. Open records are located at the Division.

Fee & Payment: The fee is $15.00 per item (one party name or case number). Payment may be made by money order, cashier check. Business checks are not accepted. Personal checks are not accepted.

Phone Search: An automated voice case information service (VCIS) is not available.

Mail Search: A stamped self addressed envelope is not required.

In Person Search: In person searching is available.

PACER: Sign-up number is 800-676-6856. Access fee is $.60 per minute. Case records are available back to 1994. New records are available online after 1 day.

US Bankruptcy Court

Middle District of Alabama

Montgomery Division PO Box 1248, Montgomery, AL 36102-1248 (Courier Address: Suite 127, 1 Court Square, Montgomery, AL 36104), 334-206-6300, Fax: 334-206-6374.

www.almb.uscourts.gov

Counties: Autauga, Barbour, Bullock, Butler, Chambers, Chilton, Coffee, Coosa, Covington, Crenshaw, Dale, Elmore, Geneva, Henry, Houston, Lee, Lowndes, Macon, Montgomery, Pike, Randolph, Russell, Tallapoosa.

Indexing & Storage: Cases are indexed by debtor as well as by case number. New cases are available in the index within 3 days after filing date. A computer index is maintained. Open records are located at this court.

Fee & Payment: The fee is $15.00 per item (one party name or case number). Payment may be made by money order, cashier check, business check. Personal checks are not accepted. Court may bill on request. Payee: Clerk of Court. Certification fee: $5.00 per document. Copy fee: $.50 per page.

Phone Search: Docket information is available by phone. An automated voice case information service (VCIS) is not available.

Fax Search: The fee is $1.50 per page to fax back.

Mail Search: Always enclose a stamped self addressed envelope.

In Person Search: In person searching is available.

PACER: Sign-up number is 800-676-6856. Access fee is $.60 per minute. Toll-free access: 888-247-9272. Local access: 334-223-7486,. NIBS court. Use of PC Anywhere V4.0 recommended. Case records are available back to case 89-02000. Records are purged every 6 months. New civil records are available online after 2-3 days.

US District Court

Northern District of Alabama

Birmingham Division Room 104, US Courthouse, 1729 5th Ave N, Birmingham, AL 35203, 205-278-1700.

www.alnd.uscourts.gov

Counties: Bibb, Blount, Calhoun, Clay, Cleburne, Greene, Jefferson, Pickens, Shelby, Sumter, Talladega, Tuscaloosa.

Indexing & Storage: Cases are indexed by defendant and plaintiff as well as by case number. New cases are available in the index 2-3 days after filing date. A computer index is maintained.

Records are also indexed on microfiche. Open records are located at this court.

Fee & Payment: The fee is $15.00 per item (one party name or case number). Payment may be made by money order, cashier check, personal check. Prepayment is required. Payee: Clerk of Court. Certification fee: $5.00 per document. Copy fee: $.50 per page. You are allowed to make your own copies. These copies cost Not Applicable per page.

Phone Search: All public information will be released over the phone. An automated voice case information service (VCIS) is not available.

Mail Search: Always enclose a stamped self addressed envelope.

In Person Search: In person searching is available.

PACER: Sign-up number is 800-676-6856. Access fee is $.60 per minute. Case records are available back to 1994. Records are purged every 18 months. New records are available online after 1 day. PACER is available on the Internet at http://pacer.alnd.uscourts.gov.

Florence Division PO Box 776, Florence, AL 35630 (Courier Address: 210 Court St, Florence, AL 35631), 205-760-5815, Fax: 205-760-5727.

www.alnd.uscourts.gov

Counties: Colbert, Franklin, Lauderdale.

Indexing & Storage: Cases are indexed by defendant and plaintiff as well as by case number. New cases are available in the index 2-3 days after filing date. A computer index is maintained. Records are also indexed on microfiche. Open records are located at this court. Some case files may be held in Birmingham if a Birmingham judge is assigned.

Fee & Payment: The fee is $15.00 per item (one party name or case number). Payment may be made by money order, cashier check, personal check. Prepayment is required. Payee: US District Court. Certification fee: $5.00 per document. Copy fee: $.50 per page.

Phone Search: Only docket information is available by phone. An automated voice case information service (VCIS) is not available.

Mail Search: A stamped self addressed envelope is not required.

In Person Search: In person searching is available.

PACER: Sign-up number is 800-676-6856. Access fee is $.60 per minute. Case records are available back to 1994. Records are purged every 18 months. New records are available online after 1 day. PACER is available on the Internet at http://pacer.alnd.uscourts.gov.

Gadsden Division c/o Birmingham Division, Room 140, US Courthouse, 1729 5th Ave N, Birmingham, AL 35203, 205-278-1700.

www.alnd.uscourts.gov

Counties: Cherokee, De Kalb, Etowah, Marshall, St. Clair.

Indexing & Storage: Cases are indexed by defendant and plaintiff as well as by case number. New cases are available in the index 2-3 days after filing date. A computer index is maintained. Open records are located at the Division.

Fee & Payment: The fee is $15.00 per item (one party name or case number). Payment may be made by money order, cashier check. Business

checks are not accepted. Personal checks are not accepted.

Phone Search: An automated voice case information service (VCIS) is not available.

In Person Search: In person searching is available.

PACER: Sign-up number is 800-676-6856. Access fee is $.60 per minute. Case records are available back to 1994. Records are purged every 18 months. New records are available online after 1 day. PACER is available on the Internet at http://pacer.alnd.uscourts.gov.

Huntsville Division Clerk's Office, US Post Office & Courthouse, 101 Holmes Ave NE, Huntsville, AL 35801, 205-534-6495.

www.alnd.uscourts.gov

Counties: Cullman, Jackson, Lawrence, Limestone, Madison, Morgan.

Indexing & Storage: Cases are indexed by defendant and plaintiff as well as by case number. New cases are available in the index 2 days after filing date. A computer index is maintained. Records are also indexed on microfiche. Open records are located at this court.

Fee & Payment: The fee is $15.00 per item (one party name or case number). Payment may be made by money order, cashier check, personal check. Prepayment is required. Payee: US District Court Clerk. Certification fee: $5.00 per document. Copy fee: $.50 per page.

Phone Search: All public information will be released over the phone. An automated voice case information service (VCIS) is not available.

Mail Search: All requests for criminal searches will be sent to Birmingham. Always enclose a stamped self addressed envelope.

In Person Search: In person searching is available.

PACER: Sign-up number is 800-676-6856. Access fee is $.60 per minute. Case records are available back to 1994. Records are purged every 18 months. New records are available online after 1 day. PACER is available on the Internet at http://pacer.alnd.uscourts.gov.

Jasper Division c/o Birmingham Division, Room 140, US Courthouse, 1729 5th Ave N, Birmingham, AL 35203, 205-278-1700.

www.alnd.uscourts.gov

Counties: Fayette, Lamar, Marion, Walker, Winston.

Indexing & Storage: Cases are indexed by defendant and plaintiff as well as by case number. New cases are available in the index 2-3 days after filing date. A computer index is maintained. Open records are located at the Division. Some case records may be held in Florence, depending upon the judge assigned.

Fee & Payment: The fee is no charge per item (one party name or case number). Payment may be made by money order, cashier check. Business checks are not accepted. Personal checks are not accepted.

Phone Search: An automated voice case information service (VCIS) is not available.

In Person Search: In person searching is available.

PACER: Sign-up number is 800-676-6856. Access fee is $.60 per minute. Case records are available back to 1994. Records are purged every 18 months. New records are available online after

1 day. PACER is available on the Internet at http://pacer.alnd.uscourts.gov.

US Bankruptcy Court

Northern District of Alabama

Anniston Division 914 Noble St, Anniston, AL 36201, 256-741-1500, Fax: 256-741-1503.

www.alnb.uscourts.gov

Counties: Calhoun, Cherokee, Clay, Cleburne, De Kalb, Etowah, Marshall, St. Clair, Talladega.

Indexing & Storage: Cases are indexed by debtor as well as by case number. New cases are available in the index immediately after filing date. A computer index is maintained. Open records are located at this court.

Fee & Payment: The fee is $15.00 per item (one party name or case number). Payment may be made by money order, cashier check, personal check. Prepayment is required. Payee: Clerk, US Bankruptcy Court, Northern District. Certification fee: $5.00 per document. Copy fee: $.50 per page.

Phone Search: Only docket information available by phone. An automated voice case information service (VCIS) is not available.

Mail Search: Always enclose a stamped self addressed envelope.

In Person Search: In person searching is available.

PACER: Sign-up number is 800-676-6856. Access fee is $.60 per minute. Toll-free access: 800-689-7645. Local access: 256-238-0456,. Use of PC Anywhere v4.0 suggested. Case records are available back to October 31, 1976. New civil records are available online after 1 day.

Birmingham Division Room 120, 1800 5th Ave N, Birmingham, AL 35203, 205-714-4000.

www.alnb.uscourts.gov

Counties: Blount, Jefferson, Shelby.

Indexing & Storage: Cases are indexed by debtor as well as by case number. New cases are available in the index immediately after filing date. Along with the debtor's name and the case number, the searcher must provide the year the case was closed and the location where the case was filed. A computer index is maintained. Open records are located at this court.

Fee & Payment: The fee is $15.00 per item (one party name or case number). Payment may be made by money order, cashier check, personal check. Prepayment is required. Payee: Clerk, US Bankruptcy Court. Certification fee: $5.00 per document. Copy fee: $.50 per page.

Phone Search: Only docket information is available by phone. An automated voice case information service (VCIS) is not available.

Mail Search: Always enclose a stamped self addressed envelope.

In Person Search: In person searching is available.

PACER: Sign-up number is 800-676-6856. Access fee is $.60 per minute. Toll-free access: 800-689-7621. Local access: 205-731-3746, 205-731-3749, 205-731-3750. Use of PC Anywhere v4.0 suggested. Case records are available back to 1992. Records are purged every six months. New civil records are available online after 1 day.

Decatur Division PO Box 1289, Decatur, AL 35602 (Courier Address: Room 220, 400 Well St, Decatur, AL 35601), 256-353-2817, Fax: 256-350-7334.

www.alnb.uscourts.gov

Counties: Colbert, Cullman, Franklin, Jackson, Lauderdale, Lawrence, Limestone, Madison, Morgan. The part of Winston County North of Double Springs is handled by this division.

Indexing & Storage: Cases are indexed by debtor as well as by case number. New cases are available in the index immediately after filing date. Along with the debtor's name and the case number, the searcher must provide the year the case was closed and the location where the case was filed. A computer index is maintained. Open records are located at this court.

Fee & Payment: The fee is $15.00 per item (one party name or case number). Payment may be made by money order, cashier check, personal check. Prepayment is required. Payee: Clerk, US Bankruptcy Court. Certification fee: $5.00 per document. Copy fee: $.50 per page.

Phone Search: If a searcher calls, the court will indicate charges but not release information.

Mail Search: Always enclose a stamped self addressed envelope.

In Person Search: In person searching is available.

PACER: Sign-up number is 800-676-6856. Access fee is $.60 per minute. Toll-free access: 800-362-9279. Local access: 256-355-2349,. Use of PC Anywhere v4.0 suggested. Case records are available back to 1992. Records are purged every six months. New civil records are available online after 1 day.

Tuscaloosa Division PO Box 3226, Tuscaloosa, AL 35403 (Courier Address: 1118 Greensboro Ave, Tuscaloosa, AL 35401), 205-752-0426, Fax: 205-752-6468.

www.alnb.uscourts.gov

Counties: Bibb, Fayette, Greene, Lamar, Marion, Pickens, Sumter, Tuscaloosa, Walker, Winston. The part of Winston County North of Double Springs is handled by Decatur Division.

Indexing & Storage: Cases are indexed by debtor as well as by case number. New cases are available in the index 2 days after filing date. Both computer and card indexes are maintained. Card indexes are maintained on cases filed prior to October 1, 1979. Computer indexes only on cases filed commencing October 1, 1979. Open records are located at this court.

Fee & Payment: The fee is $15.00 per item (one party name or case number). Payment may be made by money order, cashier check, business check. Personal checks are not accepted. Prepayment is required. Payee: Clerk, US Bankruptcy Court. Certification fee: $5.00 per document. Copy fee: $.50 per page.

Phone Search: Searching is not available by phone.

Mail Search: Always enclose a stamped self addressed envelope.

In Person Search: In person searching is available.

PACER: Sign-up number is 800-676-6856. Access fee is $.60 per minute. Toll-free access: 800-686-5824. Local access: 205-758-1309,. Use of PC Anywhere v4.0 suggested. Case records are

available back to 1990. Records are never purged. New civil records are available online after 1 day.

US District Court

Southern District of Alabama

Mobile Division Clerk, 113 St Joseph St, Mobile, AL 36602, 334-690-2371.

www.als.uscourts.gov

Counties: Baldwin, Choctaw, Clarke, Conecuh, Escambia, Mobile, Monroe, Washington.

Indexing & Storage: Cases are indexed by defendant and plaintiff as well as by case number. New cases are available in the index immediately after filing date. A computer index is maintained. Open records are located at this court.

Fee & Payment: The fee is $15.00 per item (one party name or case number). Payment may be made by money order, cashier check, personal check. Prepayment is required. Payee: Clerk, US District Court. Certification fee: $5.00 per document. Copy fee: $.50 per page. You are allowed to make your own copies. These copies cost $.25 per page.

Phone Search: Will only check docket information for a case number over the phone. An automated voice case information service (VCIS) is not available.

Mail Search: Always enclose a stamped self addressed envelope.

In Person Search: In person searching is available.

PACER: Sign-up number is 800-676-6856. Access fee is $.60 per minute. Toll-free access: 800-622-9392. Local access: 334-694-4672,. Case records are available back to 1993. New records are available online after 1 day. PACER is available on the Internet at http://pacer.alsd.uscourts.gov.

Selma Division c/o Mobile Division, 113 St Joseph St, Mobile, AL 36602, 334-690-2371.

www.als.uscourts.gov

Counties: Dallas, Hale, Marengo, Perry, Wilcox.

Indexing & Storage: Cases are indexed by defendant and plaintiff as well as by case number. New cases are available in the index immediately after filing date. A computer index is maintained. Open records are located at the Division.

Fee & Payment: The fee is $15.00 per item (one party name or case number). Payment may be made by money order, cashier check. Business checks are not accepted. Personal checks are not accepted.

Phone Search: An automated voice case information service (VCIS) is not available.

In Person Search: In person searching is available.

PACER: Sign-up number is 800-676-6856. Access fee is $.60 per minute. Toll-free access: 800-622-9392. Local access: 334-694-4672,. Case records are available back to 1993. New records are available online after 1 day. PACER is available on the Internet at http://pacer.alsd.uscourts.gov.

US Bankruptcy Court

Southern District of Alabama

Mobile Division Clerk, 201 St. Louis St, Mobile, AL 36602, 334-441-5391, Fax: 334-441-6286.

www.alsb.uscourts.gov

Counties: Baldwin, Choctaw, Clarke, Conecuh, Dallas, Escambia, Hale, Marengo, Mobile, Monroe, Perry, Washington, Wilcox.

Indexing & Storage: Cases are indexed by debtor as well as by case number. New cases are available in the index immediately after filing date. Both computer and card indexes are maintained. Open records are located at this court. District wide computer searches are available for information from 1985 for this court.

Fee & Payment: The fee is $15.00 per item (one party name or case number). Payment may be made by money order, cashier check, business check. Personal checks are not accepted. Prepayment is required. Payee: Clerk, US Bankruptcy Court. Certification fee: $5.00 per document. Copy fee: $.50 per page. You are allowed to make your own copies. These copies cost $.25 per page.

Phone Search: Only the name and case number is released over the phone. An automated voice case information service (VCIS) is available.

Mail Search: A stamped self addressed envelope is not required.

In Person Search: In person searching is available.

PACER: Sign-up number is 800-676-6856. Access fee is $.60 per minute. Toll-free access: 800-622-9392. Local access: 334-441-5638,. Case records are available back to 1993. New civil records are available online after 1 day.

Court	Jurisdiction	No. of Courts	How Organized
Circuit Courts*	General	17	40 Circuits
District Courts*	Limited	15	67 Districts
Combined Courts*		61	
Municipal Courts	Municipal	253	
Probate Courts*	Probate	68	

* Profiled in this Sourcebook.

	CIVIL								
Court	Tort	Contract	Real Estate	Min. Claim	Max. Claim	Small Claims	Estate	Eviction	Domestic Relations
Circuit Courts*	X	X	X	$3000	No Max				X
District Courts*	X	X	X	$3000	$10,000	$3000		X	
Municipal Courts									
Probate Courts*							X		

	CRIMINAL				
Court	Felony	Misdemeanor	DWI/DUI	Preliminary Hearing	Juvenile
Circuit Courts*	X				
District Courts*		X	X	X	X
Municipal Courts		X	X		
Probate Courts*					

ADMINISTRATION

Director of Courts, 300 Dexter Ave, Montgomery, AL, 36104; 334-242-0300, Fax: 334-242-2099. www.alacourt.org

COURT STRUCTURE

The Circuit are the courts of general jurisdiction and the District Courts have limited jurisdiction in civil matters. These courts are combined in all but eight larger counties. Barbour, Coffee, Jefferson, St. Clair, Talladega, and Tallapoosa Counties have two court locations within the county.

Jefferson County (Birmingham), Madison (Huntsville), Marshall, and Tuscaloosa Counties have separate criminal divisions for Circuit and/or District Courts. Misdemeanors committed with felonies are tried with the felony. The Circuit Courts are appeals courts for misdemeanors.

District Courts can receive guilty pleas in felony cases.

All counties have separate probate courts. Probate court telephone numbers are generally included with the Circuit or District Court entry although the court location may be different.

ONLINE ACCESS

A commercial online system is available over the Internet or through the Remote Access system of the State Judicial Information System (SJIS). Access is designed to provide "off-site" users with a means to retrieve basic case information and to allow a user access to any criminal, civil, or traffic record in the state. The system is available 24 hours per day. There is a $150 setup fee, and the monthly charge is $50 for unlimited access Call Cheryl Lenoir at 334-242-0300 for add'l information. The Alabama legal information web site offers commercial access to appellate opinions. For information, go to www.alacourt.org.

ADDITIONAL INFORMATION

Although in most counties Circuit and District courts are combined, each index may be separate. Therefore, when you request a search of both courts, be sure to state that the search is to cover "both the Circuit and District Court records." Several offices do not perform searches. Some offices do not have public access computer terminals.

📖📖📖📖📖📖📖

Autauga County

Circuit & District Court 134 N Court St, #114, Prattville, AL 36067-3049; 334-361-3737. Hours: 8AM-5PM (CST). *Felony, Misdemeanor, Civil, Eviction, Small Claims.*

Civil Records: Access: Phone, mail, online, in person. Both court and visitors may perform in person searches. No search fee. Required to search: name, years to search. Civil cases indexed by defendant, plaintiff. Civil records on computer since April 1994 and in books from 1978. Online access available through SJIS. See state introduction. **Criminal Records:** Access: Phone, mail, remote online, in person. Both court and visitors may perform in person searches. No search fee. Required to search: name, years to search; also helpful-DOB, SSN. Criminal records on computer since April 1994 and in books from 1978. Online access available through SJIS. See state introduction. **General Information:** No sealed, adoptions, youthful offenders or juvenile records released. Turnaround time 1-2 weeks. Copy fee: $.25 per page. Certification fee: $1.00. Fee payee: Circuit Court. Only cashiers checks and money orders accepted. Prepayment is required. Public access terminal is available.

Probate Court 176 W 5th, Prattville, AL 36067; 334-361-3725; Fax: 334-361-3740. Hours: 8:30AM-5PM (CST). *Probate.*

Baldwin County

Circuit & District Court PO Box 1149, Bay Minette, AL 36507; 334-937-0370; Civil phone:334-937-0277; Criminal phone:334-937-0277. Hours: 8AM-4:30PM (CST). *Felony, Misdemeanor, Civil, Eviction, Small Claims.*

Civil Records: Access: online, in person. Court does not conduct in person searches; visitors must perform searches for themselves. Search fee: No civil searches performed by court. Required to search: name, years to search. Civil cases indexed by defendant, plaintiff. Civil records indexed on computer from 1977, index books by case # to early 1900s. Online access available through SJIS. See state introduction. **Criminal Records:** Access: Remote online, in person. Court does not conduct in person searches; visitors must perform searches for themselves. Search fee: No criminal searches performed by court. Required to search: name, years to search, DOB. Criminal records indexed on computer from 1977, index books by case # to early 1900s. Online access available through SJIS. See state introduction. **General Information:** No sealed, adoptions, youthful offenders or juvenile records released. Certification fee: $1.00. Fee payee: Circuit Court Clerk. Only cashiers checks and money orders accepted. Prepayment is required. Public access terminal is available.

Probate Court PO Box 1258, Bay Minette, AL 36507; 334-937-9561. Hours: 8AM-4:30PM (CST). *Probate.*

Barbour County

Circuit & District Court-Clayton Division PO Box 219, Clayton, AL 36016; 334-775-8366; Probate phone:334-775-8371; Fax: 334-775-1125. Hours: 8AM-5PM (CST). *Felony, Misdemeanor, Civil, Eviction, Small Claims, Probate.*

Note: Probate court is separate from this court, and can be contacted at the telephone number above

Civil Records: Access: Mail, online, in person. Both court and visitors may perform in person searches. Search fee: $5.00 per name. Fee is per division. Required to search: name, years to search. Civil cases indexed by defendant. Civil records on computer from 1989, books from 1977. Online access available through SJIS. See state introduction. **Criminal Records:** Access: Mail, remote online, in person. Both court and visitors may perform in person searches. Search fee: $5.00 per name. $5.00 per division. Required to search: name, years to search, DOB; also helpful-SSN. Criminal records on computer from 1977. Online access available through SJIS. See state introduction. **General Information:** No sealed, adoptions, youthful offenders records released. SASE required. Turnaround time 2-3 days. Copy fee: $.50 per page. Certification fee: $2.00. Fee payee: David S Nix. Business checks accepted.

Circuit & District Court-Eufaula Division 303 E Broad St, Rm 201, Eufaula, AL 36027; 334-687-1513/1516; Probate phone:334-687-1530; Fax: 334-687-1599. Hours: 8AM-4:30PM (CST). *Misdemeanor, Civil, Eviction, Small Claims, Probate.*

Note: Probate court is separate from this court, and can be contacted at the telephone number above

Civil Records: Access: online, in person. Court does not conduct in person searches; visitors must perform searches for themselves. Search fee: No civil searches performed by court. Required to search: name, years to search. Civil cases indexed by defendant, plaintiff. Civil records on computer from 1993. Index from 1977 to present, records are easily searched, prior to 1977 more difficult to search. Online access available through SJIS. See state introduction. **Criminal Records:** Access: Remote online, in person. Court does not conduct in person searches; visitors must perform searches

for themselves. Search fee: No criminal searches performed by court. Required to search: name, years to search; also helpful-DOB, SSN. Criminal records on computer from 1993. Index from 1977 to present, records are easily searched, prior to 1977 more difficult to search. Online access available through SJIS. See state introduction. **General Information:** No sealed, adoptions, youthful offenders or juvenile records released. Copy fee: $.25 per page. Certification fee: $3.00. Fee payee: Clerk of Courts. Personal checks accepted. Prepayment is required. Public access terminal is available.

Bibb County

Circuit & District Court Bibb County Courthouse, PO Box 185, Centreville, AL 35042; 205-926-3103 Civil (Circuit); Civil phone:205-926-3100 (Dist); Criminal phone:205-926-3100 (Dist); Probate phone:205-926-3108; Fax: 205-926-3132. Hours: 8AM-5PM (CST). *Felony, Misdemeanor, Civil, Eviction, Small Claims, Probate.*

Note: Probate court is separate from this court, and can be contacted at the telephone number above.

Civil Records: Access: Mail, online, in person. Both court and visitors may perform in person searches. No search fee. Required to search: name, years to search. Civil cases indexed by defendant. Civil records on index book back to 1940s. Online access available through SJIS. See state introduction. **Criminal Records:** Access: Mail, remote online, in person. Both court and visitors may perform in person searches. No search fee. Required to search: name, years to search, DOB; also helpful-SSN. Criminal records on computer from 1988, on index books back to 1940s. Online access available through SJIS. See state introduction. **General Information:** No sealed, adoptions, youthful offenders or juvenile records released. SASE required. Turnaround time 3-4 days. Copy fee: $.25 per page. Certification fee: $1.25. Fee payee: John H Stacy, Clerk. Business checks accepted. Prepayment is required. Public access terminal is available.

Blount County

Circuit & District Court 220 2nd Ave East Room 208, Oneonta, AL 35121; 205-625-4153. Hours: 8AM-5PM (CST). *Felony, Misdemeanor, Civil, Eviction, Small Claims.*

Civil Records: Access: Mail, online, in person. Both court and visitors may perform in person searches. Search fee: $10.00 per name. Required to search: name, years to search. Civil cases indexed by defendant, plaintiff. Civil records on computer from March 1994, on index books from 1977. Online access available through SJIS. See state introduction. **Criminal Records:** Access: Mail, remote online, in person. Both court and visitors may perform in person searches. Search fee: $10.00 per name. Required to search: name, years to search, DOB; also helpful-SSN. Criminal records on computer from March 1994, on index books from 1977. Online access available through SJIS. See state introduction. **General Information:** No sealed, adoptions, youthful offenders or juvenile records released. SASE required. Turnaround time up to 1 month. Copy fee: $.25 per page. Certification fee: $1.25. Fee payee: Mike Chriswell. No personal checks accepted. Prepayment is required. Public access terminal is available.

Probate Court 220 2nd Ave E, Oneonta, AL 35121; 205-625-4191; Fax: 205-625-4206. Hours:

8AM-4PM M,T,W,F 8AM-Noon Th,Sat (CST). *Probate.*

Bullock County

Circuit & District Court PO Box 230, Union Springs, AL 36089; 334-738-2280; Probate phone:334-738-2250; Fax: 334-738-2282. Hours: 8AM-4:30PM (CST). *Felony, Misdemeanor, Civil, Eviction, Small Claims, Probate.*

Note: Probate court is separate from this court, and can be contacted at the telephone number above

Civil Records: Access: Phone, fax, mail, online, in person. Both court and visitors may perform in person searches. No search fee. Required to search: name, years to search. Civil cases indexed by defendant, plaintiff. Civil records on index books back to 1930s. Online access available through SJIS. See state introduction. **Criminal Records:** Access: Phone, fax, mail, remote online, in person. Both court and visitors may perform in person searches. No search fee. Required to search: name, years to search, DOB; also helpful-SSN. Criminal records on index books back to 1930s. Online access available through SJIS. See state introduction. **General Information:** No sealed, adoptions, youthful offenders or juvenile records released. SASE required. Turnaround time depends on clerk availability. Fax notes: No fee to fax results.

Butler County

Circuit & District Court PO Box 236, Greenville, AL 36037; 334-382-3521; Probate phone:334-382-3512. Hours: 8AM-4PM (CST). *Felony, Misdemeanor, Civil, Eviction, Small Claims, Probate.*

Note: Probate court is separate from this court, and can be contacted at the telephone number above

Civil Records: Access: Mail, online, in person. Both court and visitors may perform in person searches. Search fee: $5.00 per name. Fee is for first 2-3 years. Required to search: name, years to search. Civil cases indexed by defendant, plaintiff. Civil records on computer from 1992, books to 1979. Online access available through SJIS. See state introduction. **Criminal Records:** Access: Mail, remote online, in person. Both court and visitors may perform in person searches. Search fee: $5.00 per name. Fee for first 2-3 years. Required to search: name, years to search, DOB; also helpful-SSN. Criminal records on computer from 1992, books to 1979. Online access available through SJIS. See state introduction. **General Information:** No sealed, adoptions, youthful offenders or juvenile records released. SASE requested. Turnaround time 1-2 weeks. Copy fee: $.50 per page. Certification fee: $1.50 per page. Fee payee: Butler County District Court. Business checks accepted. Prepayment is required.

Calhoun County

Circuit Court 25 W 11th St, Box 4, Anniston, AL 36201; 256-231-1750; Fax: 256-231-1826. Hours: 8AM-4:30PM (CST). *Felony, Civil Actions Over $10,000.*

Civil Records: Access: online, in person. Court does not conduct in person searches; visitors must perform searches for themselves. Search fee: No civil searches performed by court. Required to search: name, years to search. Civil cases indexed by defendant. Civil records indexed on computer from 1970s, books go back indefinitely. Online access available through SJIS. See state introduction. **Criminal Records:** Access: Remote online, in person. Court does not conduct in person searches; visitors must perform searches for themselves. Search fee: No criminal searches performed by court. Required to search: name, years to search, DOB; also helpful-SSN. Criminal records indexed on computer from 1970s, books go back indefinitely. Online access available through SJIS. See state introduction. **General Information:** No sealed, adoptions, youthful offenders or juvenile records released. Copy fee: $.25 per page. Certification fee: $1.25. Personal checks accepted. Prepayment is required. Public access terminal is available.

District Court 25 W 11th St, Box 9, Anniston, AL 36201; 256-231-1850; Fax: 256-231-1826. Hours: 8AM-4:30PM (CST). *Misdemeanor, Civil Actions Under $10,000, Eviction, Small Claims.*

Civil Records: Access: online, in person. Court does not conduct in person searches; visitors must perform searches for themselves. Search fee: No civil searches performed by court. Required to search: name, years to search. Civil cases indexed by defendant, plaintiff. Civil records on computer from 1989, books from 1977 to 1989. Online access available through SJIS. See state introduction. **Criminal Records:** Access: Remote online, in person. Court does not conduct in person searches; visitors must perform searches for themselves. Search fee: No criminal searches performed by court. Required to search: name, years to search; also helpful-SSN. Criminal records on computer from 1989, books from 1977 to 1989. Online access available through SJIS. See state introduction. **General Information:** No sealed, adoptions, youthful offenders or juvenile records released. Copy fee: $.25 per page. Certification fee: $1.25. Fee payee: District Court. Personal checks accepted. Prepayment is required. Public access terminal is available.

Probate Court 1702 Noble St, #102, Anniston, AL 36201; 256-236-8231. *Probate.*

Chambers County

Circuit & District Court Chambers County Courthouse, Lafayette, AL 36862; 334-864-4348; Probate phone:334-864-4372. Hours: 8AM-4:30PM (CST). *Felony, Misdemeanor, Civil, Eviction, Small Claims, Probate.*

Note: Probate court is separate from this court, and can be contacted at the telephone number above

Civil Records: Access: Mail, online, in person. Both court and visitors may perform in person searches. No search fee. Required to search: name, years to search. Civil cases indexed by defendant, plaintiff. Civil records on computer from 4/93, on index books to early 1900s. Online access available through SJIS. See state introduction. **Criminal Records:** Access: Mail, remote online, in person. Both court and visitors may perform in person searches. No search fee. Required to search: name, years to search; also helpful-DOB, SSN. Criminal records are computerized since 1993. Online access available through SJIS. See state introduction. **General Information:** No sealed, adoptions, youthful offenders or juvenile records released. Turnaround time 1 week. Copy fee: $.25 per page. Certification fee: $1.00. Fee payee: Charles Story. Business checks accepted.

Cherokee County

Circuit & District Court 100 Main St, Rm 203, Centre, AL 35960-1532; 256-927-3340. Hours: 8AM-4:30PM (CST). *Felony, Misdemeanor, Civil, Eviction, Small Claims.*

Civil Records: Access: Mail, online, in person. Both court and visitors may perform in person

searches. No search fee. Required to search: name, years to search. Civil cases indexed by defendant, plaintiff. Civil records on books from 1977. Online access available through SJIS. See state introduction. **Criminal Records:** Access: Mail, remote online, in person. Both court and visitors may perform in person searches. No search fee. Required to search: name, years to search; also helpful-DOB, SSN. Criminal records on books from 1977. Online access available through SJIS. See state introduction. **General Information:** No sealed, adoptions, youthful offenders or juvenile records released. Turnaround time up to 2 wks. Copy fee: $.25 per page. Certification fee: $1.00. Fee payee: Circuit Clerk. Business checks accepted. Prepayment is required. Public access terminal is available.

Probate Court 100 Main St, Rm 204, Centre, AL 35960; 256-927-3363; Fax: 256-927-6949. Hours: 8AM-4PM M-F, 8AM-Noon Sat (CST). *Probate.*

Chilton County

Circuit & District Court PO Box 1946, Clanton, AL 35046; 205-755-4275; Probate phone:205-755-1555. Hours: 8AM-5PM (CST). *Felony, Misdemeanor, Civil, Eviction, Small Claims, Probate.*

Note: Probate court is separate from this court, and can be contacted at the telephone number above

Civil Records: Access: online, in person. Court does not conduct in person searches; visitors must perform searches for themselves. Search fee: No civil searches performed by court. Required to search: name, years to search. Civil cases indexed by defendant, plaintiff. Civil records on computer from 9/93, on books from 1950s. Online access available through SJIS. See state introduction. **Criminal Records:** Access: Remote online, in person. Court does not conduct in person searches; visitors must perform searches for themselves. Search fee: No criminal searches performed by court. Required to search: name, years to search; also helpful-DOB, SSN. Criminal records on computer since 1977. Online access available through SJIS. See state introduction. **General Information:** No sealed, adoptions, youthful offenders or juvenile records released. Copy fee: $.25 per page. Certification fee: $1.00. Fee payee: Clerk. Business checks accepted. Prepayment is required. Public access terminal is available.

Choctaw County

Circuit & District Court Choctaw County Courthouse, Ste 10, Butler, AL 36904; 205-459-2155; Probate phone:205-459-2417. Hours: 8AM-4:30PM (CST). *Felony, Misdemeanor, Civil, Eviction, Small Claims, Probate.*

Note: Probate court is separate from this court, and can be contacted at the telephone number above

Civil Records: Access: Mail, online, in person. Both court and visitors may perform in person searches. No search fee. Required to search: name, years to search. Civil cases indexed by defendant, plaintiff. Civil records on index books from 1940. Putting records on computer starting September 1994. Online access available through SJIS. See state introduction. **Criminal Records:** Access: Mail, remote online, in person. Both court and visitors may perform in person searches. No search fee. Required to search: name, years to search; also helpful-DOB, SSN. Criminal records on index books from 1940. Putting records on computer starting September 1994. Online access available through SJIS. See state introduction. **General**

Information: No sealed, adoptions, youthful offenders or juvenile records released. Copy fee: $.25 per page. Certification fee: $1.00. Fee payee: Circuit Clerk. Business checks accepted. Prepayment is required. Public access terminal is available.

Clarke County

Circuit & District Court PO Box 921, Grove Hill, AL 36451; 334-275-3363; Probate phone:334-275-3251. Hours: 8AM-5PM (CST). *Felony, Misdemeanor, Civil, Eviction, Small Claims, Probate.*

Note: Probate court is separate from this court, and can be contacted at the telephone number above

Civil Records: Access: Mail, online, in person. Both court and visitors may perform in person searches. Search fee: $5.00 per name. Required to search: name, years to search. Civil cases indexed by defendant, plaintiff. Civil records on index cards from 1977. Online access available through SJIS. See state introduction. **Criminal Records:** Access: Mail, remote online, in person. Both court and visitors may perform in person searches. Search fee: $5.00 per name. Required to search: name, years to search; also helpful-DOB, SSN. Criminal records on index cards from 1977. Online access available through SJIS. See state introduction. **General Information:** No sealed, adoptions, youthful offenders or juvenile records released. Turnaround time 1 week. Copy fee: $.40 per page. Certification fee: $2.50. Fee payee: Circuit Clerk. Business checks accepted.

Clay County

Circuit & District Court PO Box 816, Ashland, AL 36251; 256-354-7926; Probate phone:256-354-2198. Hours: 8AM-4:30PM (CST). *Felony, Misdemeanor, Civil, Eviction, Small Claims, Probate.*

Note: Probate court is separate from this court, and can be reached at the telephone number given above.

Civil Records: Access: online, in person. Court does not conduct in person searches; visitors must perform searches for themselves. Search fee: No civil searches performed by court. Required to search: name, years to search. Civil cases indexed by defendant, plaintiff. Civil records on log books from early 1900s, civil records being entered on computer when filing fees received. Online access available through SJIS. See state introduction. **Criminal Records:** Access: Remote online, in person. Court does not conduct in person searches; visitors must perform searches for themselves. Search fee: No criminal searches performed by court. Required to search: name, years to search; also helpful-SSN. Criminal records entered on computer back to 1994. Online access available through SJIS. See state introduction. **General Information:** No sealed, adoptions, youthful offenders or juvenile records released. Copy fee: $.25 per page. Certification fee: $1.25. Fee payee: Circuit Clerk. Business checks accepted. Public access terminal is available.

Cleburne County

Circuit & District Court 120 Vickery St Room 202, Heflin, AL 36264; 256-463-2651; Probate phone:256-463-5655; Fax: 256-463-2257. Hours: 8AM-4:30PM (CST). *Felony, Misdemeanor, Civil, Eviction, Small Claims, Probate.*

Note: Probate court is separate from this court, and can be contacted at the telephone number above

Civil Records: Access: Phone, mail, online, in person. Both court and visitors may perform in person searches. No search fee. Required to search: name, years to search. Civil cases indexed by defendant, plaintiff. Civil records on computer from 1994, on books and cards from 1977. Online access available through SJIS. See state introduction. **Criminal Records:** Access: Phone, mail, remote online, in person. Both court and visitors may perform in person searches. No search fee. Required to search: name, years to search, DOB; also helpful-SSN. Criminal records on computer from 1994, on books and cards from 1977. Online access available through SJIS. See state introduction. **General Information:** No sealed, adoptions, youthful offenders or juvenile records released. SASE required. Turnaround time 1-2 days. Copy fee: $.25 per page. Certification fee: $1.00. Fee payee: Clerk. Only cashiers checks and money orders accepted.

Coffee County

Circuit & District Court-Elba Division

230 M Court Ave, Elba, AL 36323; 334-897-2954. Hours: 8AM-4:30PM (CST). *Felony, Misdemeanor, Civil, Eviction, Small Claims, Probate.*

Civil Records: Access: Mail, online, in person. Both court and visitors may perform in person searches. No search fee. Required to search: name, years to search. Civil cases indexed by defendant. Civil records on index books from 1950s, on computer since August 1993. Online access available through SJIS. See state introduction. **Criminal Records:** Access: Mail, remote online, in person. Both court and visitors may perform in person searches. No search fee. Required to search: name, years to search; also helpful-DOB. Criminal records on index books from 1950s, on computer since August 1993. Online access available through SJIS. See state introduction. **General Information:** No sealed, adoptions, youthful offenders or juvenile records released. SASE required. Turnaround time 3-4 days. Copy fee: $.25 per page. Certification fee: $1.25. Fee payee: Jim Ellis, Circuit Clerk. Business checks accepted. Public access terminal is available.

Circuit & District Court-Enterprise Division

PO Box 1294, Enterprise, AL 36331; 334-347-2519. Hours: 8AM-4:30PM (CST). *Felony, Misdemeanor, Civil, Eviction, Small Claims.*

Civil Records: Access: Mail, fax, online, in person. Both court and visitors may perform in person searches. No search fee. Required to search: name, years to search. Civil cases indexed by defendant, plaintiff. Civil records on books from 1920s, on computer since August 1993. Online access available through SJIS. See state introduction. **Criminal Records:** Access: Mail, fax, remote online, in person. Both court and visitors may perform in person searches. No search fee. Required to search: name, years to search, DOB; also helpful-SSN. Criminal records on books from 1920s, on computer since August 1993. Online access available through SJIS. See state introduction. **General Information:** No sealed, adoptions, youthful offenders or juvenile records released. Turnaround time up to 1 week. Copy fee: $.25 per page. Certification fee: $1.25. Fee payee: Clerk of Courts. Only cashiers checks and money orders accepted. Prepayment is required.

Enterprise Division-Probate

PO Box 311247, Enterprise, AL 36331; 334-347-2688;

Fax: 334-347-2095. Hours: 8AM-4:30PM (CST). *Probate.*

Colbert County

Circuit Court

Colbert County Courthouse, 201 N main Street, Tuscumbia, AL 35674; 256-386-8512; Probate phone:256-386-8542. Hours: 8AM-4:30PM (CST). *Felony, Civil Actions Over $10,000, Probate.*

Note: Probate court is separate from this court, and can be contacted at the telephone number above

Civil Records: Access: online, in person. Court does not conduct in person searches; visitors must perform searches for themselves. Search fee: No civil searches performed by court. Required to search: name, years to search. Civil cases indexed by defendant, plaintiff. Civil records on computer from 1993, books from 1959. Online access available through SJIS. See state introduction. **Criminal Records:** Access: Remote online, in person. Court does not conduct in person searches; visitors must perform searches for themselves. Search fee: No criminal searches performed by court. Required to search: name, years to search; also helpful-DOB, SSN. Criminal records on computer from 1993, books prior. Online access available through SJIS. See state introduction. **General Information:** No sealed, youthful offenders or juvenile records released. Copy fee: $.25 per page. Certification fee: $1.00. Fee payee: Circuit Court Clerk. Business checks accepted. Prepayment is required.

District Court

Colbert County Courthouse, 201 N Main Street, Tuscumbia, AL 35674; 256-386-8518. Hours: 7:30AM-4:30PM (CST). *Misdemeanor, Civil Actions Under $10,000, Eviction, Small Claims.*

Civil Records: Access: online, in person. Court does not conduct in person searches; visitors must perform searches for themselves. Search fee: No civil searches performed by court. Required to search: name, years to search. Civil cases indexed by defendant, plaintiff. Civil records on computer from 1993, prior on books. Online access available through SJIS. See state introduction. **Criminal Records:** Access: Remote online, in person. Court does not conduct in person searches; visitors must perform searches for themselves. Search fee: No criminal searches performed by court. Required to search: name, years to search; also helpful-SSN. Criminal records on computer from 1993, prior on books. Online access available through SJIS. See state introduction. **General Information:** No sealed, adoptions, youthful offenders or juvenile records released. Copy fee: $.25 per page. Certification fee: $1.00. Fee payee: Circuit Clerk. Only cashiers checks and money orders accepted. Prepayment is required. Public access terminal is available.

Conecuh County

Circuit & District Court

PO Box 107, Evergreen, AL 36401; 334-578-2066; Probate phone:334-578-1221. Hours: 8AM-4:30PM (CST). *Felony, Misdemeanor, Civil, Eviction, Small Claims, Probate.*

Note: Probate court is separate from this court, and can be contacted at the telephone number above

Civil Records: Access: Phone, mail, online, in person. Both court and visitors may perform in person searches. No search fee. Required to search: name, years to search. Civil cases indexed by defendant, plaintiff. Civil records on index cards from 1977, entering on computer starting 1994. Online access available through SJIS. See

state introduction. **Criminal Records:** Access: Phone, mail, remote online, in person. Both court and visitors may perform in person searches. No search fee. Required to search: name, years to search; also helpful-DOB, SSN. Criminal records on index cards from 1977, entering on computer starting 1994. Online access available through SJIS. See state introduction. **General Information:** No sealed, adoptions, youthful offenders or juvenile records released. Turnaround time 1 week. Copy fee: $.50 per page. Certification fee: $2.50. Fee payee: Circuit Clerk, George Hendrix. Business checks accepted. Prepayment is required. Public access terminal is available.

Coosa County

Circuit & District Court

PO Box 98, Rockford, AL 35136; 256-377-4988; Probate phone:256-377-4919. Hours: 8AM-4:30PM (CST). *Felony, Misdemeanor, Civil, Eviction, Small Claims, Probate.*

Note: Probate court is separate from this court, and can be contacted at the telephone number above

Civil Records: Access: online, in person. Court does not conduct in person searches; visitors must perform searches for themselves. Search fee: No civil searches performed by court. Required to search: name, years to search. Civil cases indexed by plaintiff. Civil records on books from the late 1800s, on computer since July 1994. Online access available through SJIS. See state introduction. **Criminal Records:** Access: Remote online, in person. Court does not conduct in person searches; visitors must perform searches for themselves. Search fee: No criminal searches performed by court. Required to search: name, years to search; also helpful-DOB, SSN. Criminal records on books from the late 1800s, on computer since July 1994. Online access available through SJIS. See state introduction. **General Information:** No sealed, adoptions, youthful offenders or juvenile records released. Copy fee: $.25 per page. Certification fee: $1.00. Fee payee: Clerk of Court. Business checks accepted.

Covington County

Circuit & District Court

Covington County Courthouse, Andalusia, AL 36420; 334-428-2520; Probate phone:334-428-2510. Hours: 8AM-5PM (CST). *Felony, Misdemeanor, Civil, Eviction, Small Claims, Probate.*

Note: Probate court is separate from this court, and can be contacted at the telephone number above

Civil Records: Access: online, in person. Only the court conducts in person searches; visitors may not. Search fee: No civil searches performed by court. Required to search: name, years to search. Civil cases indexed by defendant, plaintiff. Civil records on computer from 3/94. Online access available through SJIS. See state introduction. **Criminal Records:** Access: Remote online, in person. Only the court conducts in person searches; visitors may not. Search fee: No criminal searches performed by court. Required to search: name, years to search, DOB; also helpful-SSN. Criminal records on computer from 3/94. Online access available through SJIS. See state introduction. **General Information:** No sealed, adoptions, youthful offenders or juvenile records released. Copy fee: $.25 per page. Certification fee: $1.00. Fee payee: Circuit Clerk. Business checks accepted.

Crenshaw County

Circuit & District Court PO Box 167, Luverne, AL 36049; 334-335-6575; Probate phone:334-335-6568; Fax: 334-335-2076. Hours: 8AM-4:30PM (CST). *Felony, Misdemeanor, Civil, Eviction, Small Claims, Probate.*

Note: Probate court is separate from this court, and can be contacted at the telephone number above

Civil Records: Access: Mail, online, in person. Both court and visitors may perform in person searches. No search fee. Required to search: name, years to search. Civil cases indexed by defendant, plaintiff. Civil records on computer from 1993, on book from 1977. Online access available through SJIS. See state introduction. **Criminal Records:** Access: Mail, remote online, in person. Both court and visitors may perform in person searches. No search fee. Required to search: name, years to search, DOB; also helpful-SSN. Criminal records on computer from 1993, on book from 1977. Online access available through SJIS. See state introduction. **General Information:** No sealed, adoptions, youthful offenders or juvenile records released. SASE requested. Turnaround time 2-3 days. Copy fee: $.50 per page. Certification fee: no charge. Fee payee: Ann W Tate. Only cashiers checks and money orders accepted. Prepayment is required. Public access terminal is available.

Cullman County

Circuit Court Cullman County Courthouse, Rm 303, 500 2nd Ave SW, Cullman, AL 35055; 256-775-4654; Probate phone:256-775-4652. Hours: 8AM-4:30PM (CST). *Felony, Civil Actions Over $10,000, Probate.*

Civil Records: Access: Mail, online, in person. Both court and visitors may perform in person searches. No search fee. Required to search: name, years to search. Civil cases indexed by defendant, plaintiff. Civil records on computer from 1977, books from 1900. Online access available through SJIS. See state introduction. **Criminal Records:** Access: Mail, remote online, in person. Both court and visitors may perform in person searches. No search fee. Required to search: name, DOB; also helpful-years to search, SSN. Criminal records on computer since 1977. Online access available through SJIS. See state introduction. **General Information:** No sealed, adoptions, youthful offenders or juvenile records released. SASE not required. Turnaround time 10 days. Copy fee: $.25 per page. Add postage costs if by mail. Certification fee: $1.00. Fee payee: Robert Bates, Circuit Clerk. Business checks accepted. Prepayment is required. Public access terminal is available.

District Court 500 2nd Ave SW, Courthouse Rm 211, Cullman, AL 35055-4197; 256-775-4660. Hours: 8AM-4:30PM (CST). *Misdemeanor, Civil Actions Under $10,000, Eviction, Small Claims.*

Civil Records: Access: Mail, online, in person. Both court and visitors may perform in person searches. Search fee: No civil searches performed by court. Required to search: name, years to search. Civil cases indexed by defendant. Civil records on computer from 11/92, on books 10 yrs back. Online access available through SJIS. See state introduction. **Criminal Records:** Access: Mail, remote online, in person. Both court and visitors may perform in person searches. Search fee: No criminal searches performed by court. Required to search: name, years to search, DOB; also helpful-SSN. Criminal records on computer from 11/92, on books 10 yrs back. Online access available through SJIS. See state introduction.

General Information: No sealed, adoptions, youthful offenders or juvenile records released. SASE required. Turnaround time 1 week. Copy fee: $.25 per page. Certification fee: $1.25. Fee payee: District Clerk. Only cashiers checks and money orders accepted. Prepayment is required. Public access terminal is available.

Dale County

Circuit & District Court PO Box 1350, Ozark, AL 36361; 334-774-5003; Probate phone:334-774-2754. Hours: 8AM-4:30PM (CST). *Felony, Misdemeanor, Civil, Eviction, Small Claims, Probate.*

Note: Probate court is separate from this court, and can be contacted at the telephone number above

Civil Records: Access: online, in person. Court does not conduct in person searches; visitors must perform searches for themselves. Search fee: No civil searches performed by court. Required to search: name, years to search. Civil cases indexed by defendant, plaintiff. Civil records on computer from 8/92, on books and index cards from the 1920s. Online access available through SJIS. See state introduction. **Criminal Records:** Access: Remote online, in person. Court does not conduct in person searches; visitors must perform searches for themselves. Search fee: No criminal searches performed by court. Required to search: name, years to search, DOB; also helpful-SSN. Criminal records on computer from 8/92, on books and index cards from the 1920s. Online access available through SJIS. See state introduction. **General Information:** No sealed, adoptions, youthful offenders or juvenile records released. Copy fee: $.25 per page. Certification fee: $1.00. Fee payee: Dale County Circuit Clerk. Only cashiers checks and money orders accepted. Public access terminal is available.

Dallas County

Circuit Court PO Box 1148, Selma, AL 36702; 334-874-2523; Probate phone:334-874-2597. Hours: 8AM-5PM (CST). *Felony, Civil Actions Over $10,000, Probate.*

Note: Probate court is separate from this court, and can be contacted at the telephone number above

Civil Records: Access: Mail, online, in person. Both court and visitors may perform in person searches. No search fee. Required to search: name, years to search. Civil cases indexed by defendant, plaintiff. Civil records on computer from 1980, on microfiche from the late 1800s, index books prior. Online access available through SJIS. See state introduction. **Criminal Records:** Access: Phone, mail, remote online, in person. Both court and visitors may perform in person searches. No search fee. Required to search: name, years to search, DOB; also helpful-SSN. Criminal records on computer from 1980, on microfiche from the late 1800s, index books prior. Online access available through SJIS. See state introduction. **General Information:** No sealed, adoptions, youthful offenders or juvenile records released. SASE required. Turnaround time less than 1 week for civil cases. Copy fee: $.25 per page. Certification fee: $1.00. Fee payee: Dallas County Circuit Court. Personal checks accepted. Prepayment is required. Public access terminal is available.

District Court PO Box 1148, Selma, AL 36702; 334-874-2526. Hours: 8AM-5PM (CST). *Misdemeanor, Civil Actions Under $10,000, Eviction, Small Claims.*

Civil Records: Access: online, in person. Court does not conduct in person searches; visitors must

perform searches for themselves. Search fee: No civil searches performed by court. Required to search: name, years to search. Civil cases indexed by defendant. Civil records on books from 1967, on computer since 1993. Online access available through SJIS. See state introduction. **Criminal Records:** Access: Remote online, in person. Court does not conduct in person searches; visitors must perform searches for themselves. Search fee: No criminal searches performed by court. Required to search: name, years to search; also helpful-DOB, SSN. Criminal records on books from 1967, on computer since 1993. Online access available through SJIS. See state introduction. **General Information:** No sealed, adoptions, youthful offenders or juvenile records released. Copy fee: $.25 per page. Certification fee: $1.00. Fee payee: W A Kynard, Clerk. Personal checks accepted. Prepayment is required. Public access terminal is available.

De Kalb County

Circuit & District Court PO Box 681149, Fort Payne, AL 35968; 256-845-8525; Probate phone:256-845-8510. Hours: 8AM-4PM (CST). *Felony, Misdemeanor, Civil, Eviction, Small Claims, Probate.*

Note: Probate court is separate from this court, and can be contacted at the telephone number above

Civil Records: Access: Mail, online, in person. Both court and visitors may perform in person searches. No search fee. Required to search: name, years to search. Civil cases indexed by defendant. Civil records on computer from August 1991, on books from 1959. Online access available through SJIS. See state introduction. **Criminal Records:** Access: Mail, remote online, in person. Both court and visitors may perform in person searches. No search fee. Required to search: name, years to search; also helpful-DOB, SSN. Criminal records on computer from August 1991, on books from 1959. Online access available through SJIS. See state introduction. **General Information:** No sealed, adoptions, youthful offenders or juvenile records released. Turnaround time 1 week. Copy fee: $.25 per page. Certification fee: $1.25. Fee payee: Jimmy Lindsey. Business checks accepted. Prepayment is required. Public access terminal is available.

Elmore County

Circuit & District Court-Civil Division PO Box 310, Wetumpka, AL 36092; 334-567-1123; Probate phone:334-567-1139; Fax: 334-567-5957. Hours: 8AM-4:30PM (CST). *Civil, Probate.*

Note: Probate court is separate from this court, and can be contacted at the telephone number above

Civil Records: Access: online, in person. Court does not conduct in person searches; visitors must perform searches for themselves. Search fee: No civil searches performed by court. Required to search: name, years to search. Civil cases indexed by defendant, plaintiff. Civil records on computer from 1983, books from 1930. Online access available through SJIS. See state introduction. **General Information:** No sealed, adoptions, youthful offenders or juvenile records released. Copy fee: $.25 per page. Certification fee: $1.25. Fee payee: Circuit Court Clerk. Business checks accepted. Prepayment is required. Public access terminal is available.

Criminal Circuit Court PO Box 310, 8935 US Hwy 233, Wetumpka, AL 36092; 334-567-1123; Fax: 334-567-5957. Hours: 8AM-4:30PM (CST). *Felony, Misdemeanor.* **Criminal**

Records: Access: Remote online, in person. Court does not conduct in person searches; visitors must perform searches for themselves. Search fee: No criminal searches performed by court. Required to search: name, years to search, DOB, SSN. Criminal records on computer from mid 1991, books from 1960-1992. Online access available through SJIS. See state introduction. **General Information:** No sealed, adoptions, youthful offenders or juvenile records released. Copy fee: $.25 per page. Certification fee: $1.25. Fee payee: Circuit Court Clerk. Only cashiers checks and money orders accepted. Prepayment is required. Public access terminal is available.

Escambia County

Circuit & District Court PO Box 856, Brewton, AL 36427; 334-867-0305; Probate phone:334-867-0201; Fax: 334-867-0275. Hours: 8AM-4:30PM (CST). *Felony, Misdemeanor, Civil, Eviction, Small Claims, Probate.*

Note: Probate court is separate from this court, and can be contacted at the telephone number above

Civil Records: Access: Mail, online, in person. Both court and visitors may perform in person searches. No search fee. Required to search: name, years to search. Civil cases indexed by defendant, plaintiff. Civil records on computer from 10/93, books and cards back 5 yrs. Online access available through SJIS. See state introduction. **Criminal Records:** Access: Mail, remote online, in person. Both court and visitors may perform in person searches. No search fee. Required to search: name, years to search, DOB. Criminal records on computer from 10/93, books and cards back 5 yrs. Online access available through SJIS. See state introduction. **General Information:** No sealed, adoptions, youthful offenders or juvenile records released. SASE required. Turnaround time 2-3 days. Copy fee: $.25 per page. Certification fee: $1.00. Fee payee: James K Taylor. Business checks accepted.

Etowah County

Circuit & District Court PO Box 798, Gadsden, AL 35902; 256-549-5437/5430; Probate phone:256-549-8135. Hours: 8AM-5PM (CST). *Felony, Misdemeanor, Civil, Eviction, Small Claims, Probate.*

Note: Probate court is separate from this court, and can be contacted at the telephone number above

Civil Records: Access: Mail, online, in person. Both court and visitors may perform in person searches. No search fee. Required to search: name, years to search. Civil cases indexed by defendant. Civil records on computer from 1984, index on computer since 1977, books prior to 1977. Online access available through SJIS. See state introduction. **Criminal Records:** Access: Mail, remote online, in person. Both court and visitors may perform in person searches. No search fee. Required to search: name, years to search; also helpful-DOB, SSN. Criminal records on computer from 1984, index on computer since 1977, books prior to 1977. Online access available through SJIS. See state introduction. **General Information:** No sealed, adoptions, youthful offenders or juvenile records released. SASE requested. Turnaround time 4-6 weeks. Copy fee: $.25 per page. Certification fee: $1.25. Fee payee: Clerk of Court. Only cashiers checks and money orders accepted. Public access terminal is available.

Fayette County

Circuit & District Court PO Box 206, Fayette, AL 35555; 205-932-4617; Probate phone:205-932-4519. Hours: 8AM-4:30PM (CST). *Felony, Misdemeanor, Civil, Eviction, Small Claims, Probate.*

Note: Probate court is separate from this court, and can be contacted at the telephone number above

Civil Records: Access: online, in person. Court does not conduct in person searches; visitors must perform searches for themselves. Search fee: No civil searches performed by court. Required to search: name, years to search. Civil cases indexed by defendant. Civil records on computer from 3/94, on books and cards from 1977. Online access available through SJIS. See state introduction. **Criminal Records:** Access: Remote online, in person. Court does not conduct in person searches; visitors must perform searches for themselves. Search fee: No criminal searches performed by court. Required to search: name, years to search, DOB; also helpful-SSN. Criminal records on computer from 3/94, on books and cards from 1977. Online access available through SJIS. See state introduction. **General Information:** No sealed, adoptions, youthful offenders or juvenile records released. Copy fee: $.25 per page. Certification fee: $1.00. Fee payee: Circuit Clerk. Business checks accepted.

Franklin County

Circuit & District Court PO Box 160, Russellville, AL 35653; 256-332-8861; Probate phone:256-332-8801. Hours: 8AM-4:30PM (CST). *Felony, Misdemeanor, Civil, Eviction, Small Claims, Probate.*

Civil Records: Access: Mail, online, in person. Both court and visitors may perform in person searches. Search fee: Search fee is $5.00 per five years searched per name. Required to search: name, years to search; also helpful-address. Civil cases indexed by defendant, plaintiff. Civil records on computer from 1993, on index books prior. SSN and DOB helpful, but records are not indexed by SSN. Online access available through SJIS. See state introduction. **Criminal Records:** Access: Mail, remote online, in person. Both court and visitors may perform in person searches. Search fee: $5.00 per five years searched per name. Required to search: name, years to search, DOB; also helpful-SSN. Criminal records on computer from 1993, on index books prior. SSN and DOB helpful, but records are not indexed by SSN. Online access available through SJIS. See state introduction. **General Information:** No sealed, youthful offenders or juvenile released released. SASE required. Turnaround time 3-4 days. Copy fee: $.25 per page. Certification fee: $1.00. Fee payee: Circuit Court Clerk. Business checks accepted. Prepayment is required. Public access terminal is available.

Geneva County

Circuit & District Court PO Box 86, Geneva, AL 36340; 334-684-5620; Probate phone:334-684-2276; Fax: 334-684-5605. Hours: 8AM-5PM (CST). *Felony, Misdemeanor, Civil, Eviction, Small Claims, Probate.*

Note: Probate court is separate from this court, and can be contacted at the telephone number above

Civil Records: Access: Mail, online, in person. Both court and visitors may perform in person searches. Search fee: $5.00 per name. Required to search: name, years to search; also helpful-address. Civil cases indexed by defendant, plaintiff. Civil

records on computer from 1992, index cards from the 1950s. Online access available through SJIS. See state introduction. **Criminal Records:** Access: Mail, remote online, in person. Both court and visitors may perform in person searches. Search fee: $5.00 per name. Required to search: name, years to search, DOB; also helpful-SSN. Criminal records on computer from 1992, index cards from the 1950s. Online access available through SJIS. See state introduction. **General Information:** No sealed, adoptions, youthful offenders or juvenile records released. Turnaround time 1 week. Copy fee: $.25 per page. Certification fee: $1.50. Fee payee: Circuit Clerk Valerie Thomley. Business checks accepted. Out of state personal checks not accepted. Prepayment is required. Public access terminal is available.

Greene County

Circuit & District Court PO Box 307, Eutaw, AL 35462; 205-372-3598; Probate phone:205-372-3340. Hours: 8AM-4PM (CST). *Felony, Misdemeanor, Civil, Eviction, Small Claims, Probate.*

Note: Probate court is separate from this court, and can be contacted at the telephone number above

Civil Records: Access: Mail, online, in person. Both court and visitors may perform in person searches. No search fee. Required to search: name, years to search. Civil cases indexed by defendant, plaintiff. Civil records on books from 1984. Online access available through SJIS. See state introduction. **Criminal Records:** Access: Mail, remote online, in person. Both court and visitors may perform in person searches. No search fee. Required to search: name, years to search, DOB; also helpful-SSN. Criminal records on books from 1984. Online access available through SJIS. See state introduction. **General Information:** No sealed, adoptions, youthful offenders or juvenile records released. SASE required. Turnaround time 1 week. Copy fee: $.25 per page. Certification fee: $1.25. Fee payee: Circuit Clerk. Business checks accepted. Prepayment is required. Public access terminal is available.

Hale County

Circuit & District Court Hale County Courthouse, Rm 8, PO Drawer 99, Greensboro, AL 36744; 334-624-4334; Probate phone:334-624-7391. Hours: 8AM-5PM (CST). *Felony, Misdemeanor, Civil, Eviction, Small Claims, Probate.*

Note: Probate court is separate from this court, and can be contacted at the telephone number above

Civil Records: Access: Mail, online, in person. Both court and visitors may perform in person searches. No search fee. Required to search: name, years to search. Civil cases indexed by defendant, plaintiff. Civil records on books from 1985. Online access available through SJIS. See state introduction. **Criminal Records:** Access: Mail, remote online, in person. Both court and visitors may perform in person searches. No search fee. Required to search: name, years to search; also helpful-DOB, SSN. Criminal records on books from 1985. Online access available through SJIS. See state introduction. **General Information:** No sealed, adoptions, youthful offenders or juvenile records released. Turnaround time 1 week. Copy fee: $.25 per page. Certification fee: $1.00. Fee payee: Clerk of the Court. Business checks accepted. In state personal checks accepted. Prepayment is required. Public access terminal is available.

Henry County

Circuit & District Court 101 W Court St, Suite J, Abbeville, AL 36310-2135; 334-585-2753; Probate phone:334-585-3257; Fax: 334-585-5006. Hours: 8AM-4:30PM (CST). *Felony, Misdemeanor, Civil, Eviction, Small Claims, Probate.*

Note: Probate court is separate from this court, and can be contacted at the telephone number above

Civil Records: Access: Mail, online, in person. Both court and visitors may perform in person searches. Search fee: $3.00 per name. Required to search: name, years to search. Civil cases indexed by defendant. Civil records on computer from 1994, index cards 10 yrs back. Online access available through SJIS. See state introduction. **Criminal Records:** Access: Mail, remote online, in person. Both court and visitors may perform in person searches. Search fee: $3.00 per name. Required to search: name, years to search, DOB; also helpful-SSN. Criminal records on computer from 5/93, index cards 10 yrs back. Online access available through SJIS. See state introduction. **General Information:** No sealed, adoptions, youthful offenders or juvenile records released. SASE required. Turnaround time 2-3 day. Copy fee: $.25 per page. Certification fee: $1.00. Fee payee: Circuit Clerk. Personal checks accepted. Prepayment is required.

Houston County

Circuit & District Court PO Drawer 6406, Dothan, AL 36302; 334-677-4800/4872; Probate phone:334-677-4719. Hours: 7:30AM-4:30PM (CST). *Felony, Misdemeanor, Civil, Eviction, Small Claims, Probate.*

Note: Probate court is separate from this court, and can be contacted at the telephone number above

Civil Records: Access: Mail, online, in person. Both court and visitors may perform in person searches. No search fee. Required to search: name, years to search. Civil cases indexed by defendant. Civil records on computer from 1977, index books from 1950s. Online access available through SJIS. See state introduction. **Criminal Records:** Access: Mail, remote online, in person. Both court and visitors may perform in person searches. No search fee. Required to search: name, years to search; also helpful-DOB, SSN. Criminal records on computer from 1977, index books from 1950s. Online access available through SJIS. See state introduction. **General Information:** No sealed, adoptions, youthful offenders or juvenile records released. Turnaround time 1 week. Copy fee: $.25 per page. Certification fee: $1.00. Fee payee: Judy Byrd. Business checks accepted. Prepayment is required. Public access terminal is available.

Jackson County

Circuit & District Court PO Box 397, Scottsboro, AL 35768; 256-574-9320; Civil phone:256-574-9320; Criminal phone:256-574-9320; Probate phone:256-574-9290; Fax: 256-574-6575. Hours: 8AM-4:30PM (CST). *Felony, Misdemeanor, Civil, Eviction, Small Claims, Probate.*

Note: Probate court is separate from this court, and can be contacted at the telephone number above

Civil Records: Access: Mail, online, in person. Both court and visitors may perform in person searches. No search fee. Required to search: name, years to search. Civil cases indexed by defendant. Civil records on computer from May 1993, on cards from 1977. Online access available through SJIS. See state introduction. **Criminal Records:** Access: Mail, remote online, in person. Both court and visitors may perform in person searches. No search fee. Required to search: name, years to search, DOB; also helpful-SSN. Criminal records on computer from May 1993, on cards from 1977. Online access available through SJIS. See state introduction. **General Information:** No sealed, adoptions, youthful offenders or juvenile records released. SASE required. Turnaround time 1-2 days. Copy fee: $.25 per page. Certification fee: $2.00. Fee payee: Circuit Court Clerk. Only cashiers checks and money orders accepted. Prepayment is required. Public access terminal is available.

Jefferson County

Bessemer Division-Circuit Court Rm 606, Courthouse Annex, Bessemer, AL 35020; 205-481-4165. Hours: 8AM-5PM (CST). *Felony, Civil Actions Over $10,000.*

Civil Records: Access: online, in person. Court does not conduct in person searches; visitors must perform searches for themselves. Search fee: No civil searches performed by court. Required to search: name, years to search. Civil cases indexed by defendant, plaintiff. Civil records on computer from 1988, on index books from 1930s to 1977. Online access available through SJIS. See state introduction. **Criminal Records:** Access: Remote online, in person. Court does not conduct in person searches; visitors must perform searches for themselves. Search fee: No criminal searches performed by court. Required to search: name, years to search, DOB; also helpful-SSN. Criminal records on computer from 1988, on index books from 1930s to 1977. Online access available through SJIS. See state introduction. **General Information:** No sealed, adoptions, youthful offenders or juvenile records released. Copy fee: $.25 per page. Certification fee: $1.25. Fee payee: Clerk of Circuit Court. Business checks accepted. Prepayment is required. Public access terminal is available.

Bessemer Division-District Court Rm 506, Courthouse Annex, Bessemer, AL 35020; 205-481-4187. Hours: 8AM-5PM (CST). *Misdemeanor, Civil Actions Under $10,000, Eviction, Small Claims.*

Civil Records: Access: online, in person. Court does not conduct in person searches; visitors must perform searches for themselves. Search fee: No civil searches performed by court. Required to search: name, years to search. Civil cases indexed by defendant, plaintiff. Civil records on computer from 1986, on index cards from 1977, prior on docket books. Online access available through SJIS. See state introduction. **Criminal Records:** Access: Remote online, in person. Court does not conduct in person searches; visitors must perform searches for themselves. Search fee: No criminal searches performed by court. Required to search: name, years to search, DOB; also helpful-SSN. Criminal records on computer from 1986, on index cards from 1977, prior on docket books. Online access available through SJIS. See state introduction. **General Information:** No sealed, adoptions, youthful offenders or juvenile records released. Copy fee: $.25 per page. Certification fee: $1.25. Fee payee: Bessemer District Court. Business checks accepted. Prepayment is required. Public access terminal is available.

Birmingham Division-Civil Circuit Court 716 N 21st St, Rm 400, Birmingham, AL 35263; 205-325-5355. Hours: 8AM-5PM (CST). *Civil Actions Over $10,000 (Over $5,000 if jury trial).*

Civil Records: Access: Phone, mail, online, in person. Both court and visitors may perform in person searches. No search fee. Required to search: name, years to search. Civil cases indexed by defendant, plaintiff. Civil records on computer from 1976, on index books from 1976 to 1986, prior to 1976 archived. Online access available through SJIS. See state introduction. **General Information:** No sealed, adoptions, youthful offenders or juvenile records released. Turnaround time 1-2 weeks. Copy fee: $.25 per page. Certification fee: $1.25. Fee payee: Clerk of Circuit Court. Business checks accepted. Prepayment is required. Under $10.00 need not prepay. Public access terminal is available.

Birmingham Division-Criminal Circuit Court 801 N 21st St, Rm 506, Birmingham, AL 35263; 205-325-5285. Hours: 8AM-4:55PM (CST). *Felony.* **Criminal Records:** Access: Remote online, in person. Court does not conduct in person searches; visitors must perform searches for themselves. Search fee: No criminal searches performed by court. Required to search: name, years to search, DOB, signed release; also helpful-address, SSN. Criminal records on computer from 1960s, index books prior. Online access available through SJIS. See state introduction. **General Information:** No sealed, adoptions, youthful offenders, sex offender cases or juvenile records released. Copy fee: $.25 per page. Certification fee: $1.00. Fee payee: Clerk of Court. Only cashiers checks and money orders accepted. Prepayment is required. Public access terminal is available.

Birmingham Division-Civil District Court 716 Richard Arrington BLVD N, Birmingham, AL 35263; 205-325-5331. Hours: 8AM-5PM (CST). *Civil Actions Under $10,000, Eviction, Small Claims.*

Civil Records: Access: Phone, mail, online, in person. Both court and visitors may perform in person searches. No search fee. Required to search: name, years to search. Civil cases indexed by defendant, plaintiff. Civil records on computer from 1977, index books stored in warehouse. Online access available through SJIS. See state introduction. **General Information:** No sealed, adoptions, youthful offenders or juvenile records released. SASE required. Turnaround time 1-2 days. Copy fee: $.25 per page. Certification fee: $1.00. Fee payee: District Court. Only cashiers checks and money orders accepted. Prepayment is required. Public access terminal is available.

Birmingham Division-Criminal District Court 801 21st St, Rm 207, Birmingham, AL 35263; 205-325-5309. Hours: 8AM-5PM (CST). *Misdemeanor.* **Criminal Records:** Access: Mail, remote online, in person. Both court and visitors may perform in person searches. No search fee. Required to search: name, DOB; also helpful-years to search, SSN. Criminal records on computer from 1987. To search for records prior to 1987, require arrest date. Online access available through SJIS. See state introduction. **General Information:** No sealed, sexual abuse, adoptions, youthful offenders or juvenile records released. Turnaround time 5-10 days. Copy fee: $.25 per page. Certification fee: $1.25. Fee payee: District Court. Only cashiers checks and money orders accepted. Prepayment is required. Public access terminal is available.

Zip	City	Zip	City	Zip	City	Zip	City
35459-35459	EMELLE	35650-35650	MOULTON	36005-36005	BANKS	36272-36272	PIEDMONT
35460-35460	EPES	35651-35651	MOUNT HOPE	36006-36006	BILLINGSLEY	36273-36273	RANBURNE
35461-35461	ETHELSVILLE	35652-35652	ROGERSVILLE	36008-36008	BOOTH	36274-36274	ROANOKE
35462-35462	EUTAW	35653-35654	RUSSELLVILLE	36009-36009	BRANTLEY	36275-36275	SPRING GARDEN
35463-35463	FOSTERS	35660-35660	SHEFFIELD	36010-36010	BRUNDIDGE	36276-36276	WADLEY
35464-35464	GAINESVILLE	35661-35662	MUSCLE SHOALS	36013-36013	CECIL	36277-36277	WEAVER
35466-35466	GORDO	35670-35670	SOMERVILLE	36015-36015	CHAPMAN	36278-36278	WEDOWEE
35468-35468	KELLERMAN	35671-35671	TANNER	36016-36016	CLAYTON	36279-36279	WELLINGTON
35469-35469	KNOXVILLE	35672-35672	TOWN CREEK	36017-36017	CLIO	36280-36280	WOODLAND
35470-35470	LIVINGSTON	35673-35673	TRINITY	36020-36020	COOSADA	36301-36305	DOTHAN
35471-35471	MC SHAN	35674-35674	TUSCUMBIA	36022-36022	DEATSVILLE	36310-36310	ABBEVILLE
35473-35473	NORTHPORT	35677-35677	WATERLOO	36023-36023	EAST TALLASSEE	36311-36311	ARITON
35474-35474	MOUNDVILLE	35699-35699	DECATUR	36024-36024	ECLECTIC	36312-36312	ASHFORD
35475-35476	NORTHPORT	35739-35739	ARDMORE	36025-36025	ELMORE	36313-36313	BELLWOOD
35477-35477	PANOLA	35740-35740	BRIDGEPORT	36026-36026	EQUALITY	36314-36314	BLACK
35478-35478	PETERSON	35741-35741	BROWNSBORO	36027-36027	EUFAULA	36316-36316	CHANCELLOR
35480-35480	RALPH	35742-35742	CAPSHAW	36028-36028	DOZIER	36317-36317	CLOPTON
35481-35481	REFORM	35744-35744	DUTTON	36029-36029	FITZPATRICK	36318-36318	COFFEE SPRINGS
35482-35482	SAMANTHA	35745-35745	ESTILLFORK	36030-36030	FOREST HOME	36319-36319	COLUMBIA
35485-35487	TUSCALOOSA	35746-35746	FACKLER	36031-36031	FORT DAVIS	36320-36320	COTTONWOOD
35490-35490	VANCE	35747-35747	GRANT	36032-36032	FORT DEPOSIT	36321-36321	COWARTS
35491-35491	WEST GREENE	35748-35748	GURLEY	36033-36033	GEORGIANA	36322-36322	DALEVILLE
35501-35504	JASPER	35749-35749	HARVEST	36034-36034	GLENWOOD	36323-36323	ELBA
35540-35540	ADDISON	35750-35750	HAZEL GREEN	36035-36035	GOSHEN	36330-36331	ENTERPRISE
35541-35541	ARLEY	35751-35751	HOLLYTREE	36036-36036	GRADY	36340-36340	GENEVA
35542-35542	BANKSTON	35752-35752	HOLLYWOOD	36037-36037	GREENVILLE	36343-36343	GORDON
35543-35543	BEAR CREEK	35754-35754	LACEYS SPRING	36038-36038	GANTT	36344-36344	HARTFORD
35544-35544	BEAVERTON	35755-35755	LANGSTON	36039-36039	HARDAWAY	36345-36345	HEADLAND
35545-35545	BELK	35756-35758	MADISON	36040-36040	HAYNEVILLE	36346-36346	JACK
35546-35546	BERRY	35759-35759	MERIDIANVILLE	36041-36041	HIGHLAND HOME	36349-36349	MALVERN
35548-35548	BRILLIANT	35760-35760	NEW HOPE	36042-36042	HONORAVILLE	36350-36350	MIDLAND CITY
35549-35549	CARBON HILL	35761-35761	NEW MARKET	36043-36043	HOPE HULL	36351-36351	NEW BROCKTON
35550-35550	CORDOVA	35762-35762	NORMAL	36045-36045	KENT	36352-36352	NEWTON
35551-35551	DELMAR	35763-35763	OWENS CROSS ROADS	36046-36046	LAPINE	36353-36353	NEWVILLE
35552-35552	DETROIT	35764-35764	PAINT ROCK	36047-36047	LETOHATCHEE	36360-36361	OZARK
35553-35553	DOUBLE SPRINGS	35765-35765	PISGAH	36048-36048	LOUISVILLE	36362-36362	FORT RUCKER
35554-35554	ELDRIDGE	35766-35766	PRINCETON	36049-36049	LUVERNE	36370-36370	PANSEY
35555-35555	FAYETTE	35767-35767	RYLAND	36051-36051	MARBURY	36371-36371	PINCKARD
35559-35559	GLEN ALLEN	35768-35769	SCOTTSBORO	36052-36052	MATHEWS	36373-36373	SHORTERVILLE
35560-35560	GOODSPRINGS	35771-35771	SECTION	36053-36053	MIDWAY	36374-36374	SKIPPERVILLE
35563-35563	GUIN	35772-35772	STEVENSON	36054-36054	MILLBROOK	36375-36375	SLOCOMB
35564-35564	HACKLEBURG	35773-35773	TONEY	36057-36057	MOUNT MEIGS	36376-36376	WEBB
35565-35565	HALEYVILLE	35774-35774	TRENTON	36061-36061	PEROTE	36401-36401	EVERGREEN
35570-35570	HAMILTON	35775-35775	VALHERMOSO SPRINGS	36062-36062	PETREY	36419-36419	ALLEN
35571-35571	HODGES	35776-35776	WOODVILLE	36064-36064	PIKE ROAD	36420-36420	ANDALUSIA
35572-35572	HOUSTON	35801-35899	HUNTSVILLE	36065-36065	PINE LEVEL	36425-36425	BEATRICE
35573-35573	KANSAS	35901-35905	GADSDEN	36066-36068	PRATTVILLE	36426-36427	BREWTON
35574-35574	KENNEDY	35906-35906	RAINBOW CITY	36069-36069	RAMER	36429-36429	BROOKLYN
35575-35575	LYNN	35907-35907	GADSDEN	36071-36071	RUTLEDGE	36431-36431	BURNT CORN
35576-35576	MILLPORT	35950-35951	ALBERTVILLE	36072-36072	EUFAULA	36432-36432	CASTLEBERRY
35577-35577	NATURAL BRIDGE	35952-35952	ALTOONA	36075-36075	SHORTER	36435-36435	COY
35578-35578	NAUVOO	35953-35953	ASHVILLE	36078-36078	TALLASSEE	36436-36436	DICKINSON
35579-35579	OAKMAN	35954-35954	ATTALLA	36079-36079	TROY	36439-36439	EXCEL
35580-35580	PARRISH	35956-35957	BOAZ	36080-36080	TITUS	36441-36441	FLOMATON
35581-35581	PHIL CAMPBELL	35958-35958	BRYANT	36081-36082	TROY	36442-36442	FLORALA
35582-35582	RED BAY	35959-35959	CEDAR BLUFF	36083-36083	TUSKEGEE	36444-36444	FRANKLIN
35584-35584	SIPSEY	35960-35960	CENTRE	36087-36088	TUSKEGEE INSTITUTE	36445-36445	FRISCO CITY
35585-35585	SPRUCE PINE	35961-35961	COLLINSVILLE	36089-36089	UNION SPRINGS	36446-36446	FULTON
35586-35586	SULLIGENT	35962-35962	CROSSVILLE	36091-36091	VERBENA	36449-36449	GOODWAY
35587-35587	TOWNLEY	35963-35963	DAWSON	36092-36093	WETUMPKA	36451-36451	GROVE HILL
35592-35592	VERNON	35964-35964	DOUGLAS	36101-36191	MONTGOMERY	36453-36453	KINSTON
35593-35593	VINA	35966-35966	FLAT ROCK	36201-36207	ANNISTON	36454-36454	LENOX
35594-35594	WINFIELD	35967-35968	FORT PAYNE	36250-36250	ALEXANDRIA	36455-36455	LOCKHART
35601-35609	DECATUR	35971-35971	FYFFE	36251-36251	ASHLAND	36456-36456	MC KENZIE
35610-35610	ANDERSON	35972-35972	GALLANT	36253-36253	BYNUM	36457-36457	MEGARGEL
35611-35614	ATHENS	35973-35973	GAYLESVILLE	36254-36254	CHOCCOLOCCO	36458-36458	MEXIA
35615-35615	BELLE MINA	35974-35974	GERALDINE	36255-36255	CRAGFORD	36460-36462	MONROEVILLE
35616-35616	CHEROKEE	35975-35975	GROVEOAK	36256-36256	DAVISTON	36467-36467	OPP
35617-35617	CLOVERDALE	35976-35976	GUNTERSVILLE	36257-36257	DE ARMANVILLE	36470-36470	PERDUE HILL
35618-35618	COURTLAND	35978-35978	HENAGAR	36258-36258	DELTA	36471-36471	PETERMAN
35619-35619	DANVILLE	35979-35979	HIGDON	36260-36260	EASTABOGA	36473-36473	RANGE
35620-35620	ELKMONT	35980-35980	HORTON	36261-36261	EDWARDSVILLE	36474-36474	RED LEVEL
35621-35621	EVA	35981-35981	IDER	36262-36262	FRUITHURST	36475-36475	REPTON
35622-35622	FALKVILLE	35983-35983	LEESBURG	36263-36263	GRAHAM	36476-36476	RIVER FALLS
35630-35634	FLORENCE	35984-35984	MENTONE	36264-36264	HEFLIN	36477-36477	SAMSON
35640-35640	HARTSELLE	35986-35986	RAINSVILLE	36265-36265	JACKSONVILLE	36480-36480	URIAH
35643-35643	HILLSBORO	35987-35987	STEELE	36266-36266	LINEVILLE	36481-36481	VREDENBURGH
35645-35645	KILLEN	35988-35988	SYLVANIA	36267-36267	MILLERVILLE	36482-36482	WHATLEY
35646-35646	LEIGHTON	35989-35989	VALLEY HEAD	36268-36268	MUNFORD	36483-36483	WING
35647-35647	LESTER	35990-35990	WALNUT GROVE	36269-36269	MUSCADINE	36501-36501	ALMA
35648-35648	LEXINGTON	35999-35999	GADSDEN	36270-36270	NEWELL	36502-36504	ATMORE
35649-35649	MOORESVILLE	36003-36003	AUTAUGAVILLE	36271-36271	OHATCHEE	36505-36505	AXIS

36507-36507 BAY MINETTE	36564-36564 POINT CLEAR	36744-36744 GREENSBORO	36852-36852 CUSSETA
36509-36509 BAYOU LA BATRE	36567-36567 ROBERTSDALE	36745-36745 JEFFERSON	36853-36853 DADEVILLE
36511-36511 BON SECOUR	36568-36568 SAINT ELMO	36748-36748 LINDEN	36854-36854 VALLEY
36512-36512 BUCKS	36569-36569 SAINT STEPHENS	36749-36749 JONES	36855-36855 FIVE POINTS
36513-36513 CALVERT	36570-36570 SALITPA	36750-36750 MAPLESVILLE	36856-36856 FORT MITCHELL
36515-36515 CARLTON	36571-36571 SARALAND	36751-36751 LOWER PEACH TREE	36858-36858 HATCHECHUBBEE
36518-36518 CHATOM	36572-36572 SATSUMA	36752-36752 LOWNDESBORO	36859-36859 HOLY TRINITY
36521-36521 CHUNCHULA	36574-36574 SEMINOLE	36753-36753 MC WILLIAMS	36860-36860 HURTSBORO
36522-36522 CITRONELLE	36575-36575 SEMMES	36754-36754 MAGNOLIA	36861-36861 JACKSONS GAP
36523-36523 CODEN	36576-36576 SILVERHILL	36756-36756 MARION	36862-36862 LAFAYETTE
36524-36524 COFFEEVILLE	36577-36577 SPANISH FORT	36758-36758 PLANTERSVILLE	36863-36863 LANETT
36525-36525 CREOLA	36578-36578 STAPLETON	36759-36759 MARION JUNCTION	36865-36865 LOACHAPOKA
36526-36526 DAPHNE	36579-36579 STOCKTON	36760-36760 MILLERS FERRY	36866-36866 NOTASULGA
36527-36527 SPANISH FORT	36580-36580 SUMMERDALE	36761-36761 MINTER	36867-36870 PHENIX CITY
36528-36528 DAUPHIN ISLAND	36581-36581 SUNFLOWER	36762-36762 MORVIN	36871-36871 PITTSVIEW
36529-36529 DEER PARK	36582-36582 THEODORE	36763-36763 MYRTLEWOOD	36872-36872 VALLEY
36530-36530 ELBERTA	36583-36583 TIBBIE	36764-36764 NANAFALIA	36874-36874 SALEM
36532-36533 FAIRHOPE	36584-36584 VINEGAR BEND	36765-36765 NEWBERN	36875-36875 SEALE
36535-36536 FOLEY	36585-36585 WAGARVILLE	36766-36766 OAK HILL	36877-36877 SMITHS
36538-36538 FRANKVILLE	36586-36586 WALKER SPRINGS	36767-36767 ORRVILLE	36879-36879 WAVERLY
36539-36539 FRUITDALE	36587-36587 WILMER	36768-36768 PINE APPLE	36901-36901 BELLAMY
36540-36540 GAINESTOWN	36590-36590 THEODORE	36769-36769 PINE HILL	36904-36904 BUTLER
36541-36541 GRAND BAY	36601-36612 MOBILE	36773-36773 SAFFORD	36906-36906 CROMWELL
36542-36542 GULF SHORES	36613-36613 EIGHT MILE	36775-36775 SARDIS	36907-36907 CUBA
36543-36543 HUXFORD	36614-36695 MOBILE	36776-36776 SAWYERVILLE	36908-36908 GILBERTOWN
36544-36544 IRVINGTON	36701-36703 SELMA	36778-36778 SNOW HILL	36910-36910 JACHIN
36545-36545 JACKSON	36720-36720 ALBERTA	36779-36779 SPROTT	36912-36912 LISMAN
36547-36547 GULF SHORES	36721-36721 ANNEMANIE	36782-36782 SWEET WATER	36913-36913 MELVIN
36548-36548 LEROY	36722-36722 ARLINGTON	36783-36783 THOMASTON	36915-36915 NEEDHAM
36549-36549 LILLIAN	36723-36723 BOYKIN	36784-36784 THOMASVILLE	36916-36916 PENNINGTON
36550-36550 LITTLE RIVER	36726-36726 CAMDEN	36785-36785 TYLER	36919-36919 SILAS
36551-36551 LOXLEY	36727-36727 CAMPBELL	36786-36786 UNIONTOWN	36921-36921 TOXEY
36553-36553 MC INTOSH	36728-36728 CATHERINE	36790-36790 STANTON	36922-36922 WARD
36555-36555 MAGNOLIA SPRINGS	36731-36731 DAYTON	36792-36792 RANDOLPH	36925-36925 YORK
36556-36556 MALCOLM	36732-36732 DEMOPOLIS	36793-36793 LAWLEY	
36558-36558 MILLRY	36736-36736 DIXONS MILLS	36801-36804 OPELIKA	
36559-36559 MONTROSE	36738-36738 FAUNSDALE	36830-36832 AUBURN	
36560-36560 MOUNT VERNON	36740-36740 FORKLAND	36849-36849 AUBURN UNIVERSITY	
36561-36561 ORANGE BEACH	36741-36741 FURMAN	36850-36850 CAMP HILL	
36562-36562 PERDIDO	36742-36742 GALLION	36851-36851 COTTONTON	

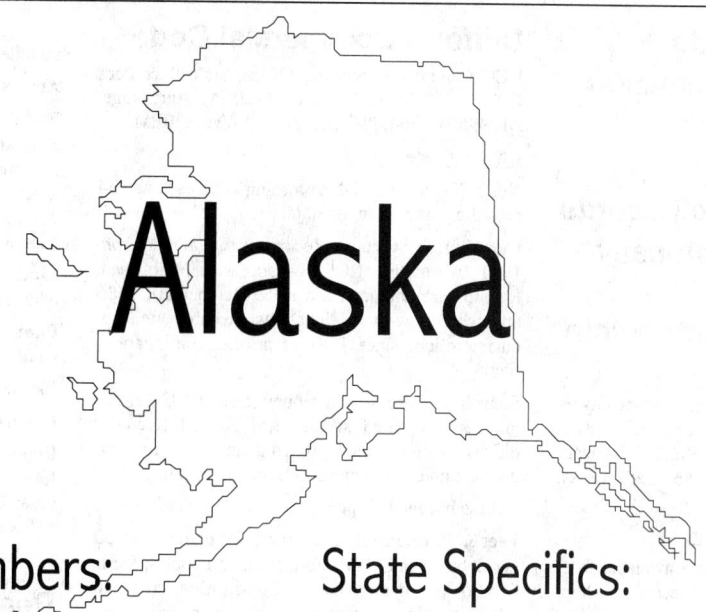

Alaska

General Help Numbers:

Governor's Office
PO Box 110001   907-465-3500
Juneau, AK 99811-0001   Fax 907-465-3532
www.gov.state.ak.us   8AM-5PM

Attorney General's Office
Law Department   907-465-3600
PO Box 110300   Fax 907-465-2075
Juneau, AK 99811-0300   8AM-4:30PM
www.law.state.ak.us

State Court Administrator
303 K St   907-264-0547
Anchorage, AK 99501   Fax 907-264-0881
www.alaska.net/~akctlib/homepage.htm   8AM-4:30PM

State Archives
Alaska State Archives   907-465-2270
141 Willoughby Ave   Fax 907-465-2465
Juneau, AK 99801-1720   9AM-5PM
www.archives.state.ak.us

State Specifics:

Capital: Juneau
Juneau Borough

Time Zone: AK (Alaska Standard Time)*
* Alaska's Aleutian Islands are HT (Hawaii Standard Time)

Number of Counties: 23

Population: 609,311

Web Site: www.state.ak.us

State Agencies

Criminal Records

Department of Public Safety, Records and Identification, 5700 E Tudor Rd, Anchorage, AK 99507; 907-269-5765, 907-269-5091 (Fax), 8AM-4:30PM.

Note: If authorized, a requester may also request a national check by the FBI for an additional $24.00.

Indexing & Storage: Records are available for 10 years from the unconditional discharge date of the incident.

Searching: "Interested Party" reports are processed for employment purposes. "Any Person" reports can be processed for those who have a proper letter of explanation (and fingerprints). "Full Criminal History Report" is only available for criminal justice agencies. Include the following in your request-set of fingerprints, full name. Requester must provide verification of status as an "interested party." Interested party is defined a person who employs, appoints or permits the subject with or without compensation with supervisory power over others. The following data is not released: sealed records.

Access by: mail, in person.

Fee & Payment: The fee is $35.00 per search. Fee payee: State of Alaska. Prepayment required. No credit cards accepted.

Mail search: Results of search are also sent to the subject.

In person search: Searching is available in person.

Corporation Records
Trademarks/Servicemarks
Fictitious Name
Assumed Name
Limited Partnership Records
Limited Liability Company Records
Limited Liability Partnership Records

Corporation Section, Department of Community & Econ Dev, PO Box 110808, Juneau, AK 99811-0808 (Courier: 150 Third Street Rm 217, Juneau, AK 99801); 907-465-2530, 907-465-3257 (Fax), 8AM-5PM.

www.dced.state.ak.us/bsc/corps.htm

Indexing & Storage: Records are available from early 1900's on. Prior to 1960, the records are kept at the State Archives. You must go through this office in order to get records. New records are available for inquiry immediately. Records are indexed on microfiche, inhouse computer.

Searching: All information contained is considered public record. Include the following in your request-full name of business. In addition to the articles of incorporation, corporation records include the following information: Annual Reports, Officers, Directors, DBAs, Prior (Merged) names, Inactive and Reserved names.

Access by: mail, phone, fax, in person, online.

Fee & Payment: Fees are $10.00 for articles and amendments and $30.00 for everything on file. The fee is $5.00-certify a document and $10.00 for a good standing. A copy of a one page document is $1.00 and a print of a computer screen is $1.00. Fee payee: State of Alaska. Prepayment required. Personal checks accepted. Credit cards accepted: Mastercard, Visa.

Mail search: Turnaround time: 2 weeks.

Phone search: You can make a search request only if you are local and you plan to pick-up.

Fax search: Typical fax searches involve credit cards and are considered expedited service, unless otherwise specified.

In person search: All results are mailed unless request is being processed using expedited service. The agency will call the requester when his/her request has been processed and is ready for pick-up, if it is a local call.

Online search: At the web site, one can access status information on corps, LLCs, LLP, LP (all both foreign and domestic), registered and reserved names, as well as trademark information. There is no fee.

Other access: For bulk purchase, the requester must use a third party. Call 907-465-2530 for more information.

Expedited service: Expedited service is available for mail, phone and in person searches. Turnaround time: 48 hours. Add $35.00 per business name. Cash, check, and credit cards are allowed. It is $150.00-expedite a filing.

Uniform Commercial Code

UCC Central File Systems Office, State Recorder's Office, 550 West 7th Ave #1200A, Anchorage, AK 99501-3564; 907-269-8873, 8AM-3:30PM.

www.dnr.state.ak.us

Note: There are 14 recording offices and 34 recording districts in the state.

Indexing & Storage: Records are available from 1961 when the UCC system was established. Records are computerized since October 20, 1986 or earlier if with continuations. Records are kept on microfiche since 1981 or prior if continuations filed.

Searching: Use search request form UCC-11. All tax liens are filed at the local District Recorder offices. Include the following in your request-debtor name. All requests must be in writing.

Access by: mail, in person.

Fee & Payment: Fee to search by name is $5.00 per debtor name. For information and copies, fee is $15.00 per debtor name. Certification costs an additional $5.00. Single page copies are $2.00 each. Fee payee: Alaska Department of Revenue. Prepayment required. Personal checks accepted. Credit cards accepted: Mastercard, Visa.

Mail search: Turnaround time: 1-2 days. No self addressed stamped envelope is required.

In person search: A public access terminal is available. State UCC personnel will not perform official record searches for in-person requests.

Other access: Bulk file tapes of the entire UCC database can be purchased from the State Recorder's Office (907-269-8881). Also, a private vendor offers online service. Call Motznik Computer Services at 907-344-6254 for more information.

Federal Tax Liens
State Tax Liens
Records not maintained by a state level agency.

Note: All tax liens are filed at local District Recorder Offices.

Sales Tax Registrations
State does not impose sales tax.

Birth Certificates

Department of Health & Social Services, Bureau of Vital Statistics, PO Box 110675, Juneau, AK 99811-0675 (Courier: 350 Main, Room 114, Juneau, AK 99811); 907-465-3392, 907-465-3618 (Fax), 8AM-4:30PM.

www.hss.state.ak.us/dph/bvs/bvs_home.htm

Indexing & Storage: Records are available from 1913-present. New records are available for inquiry immediately. Records are indexed on microfiche, inhouse computer.

Searching: Person requesting must be a parent or guardian or give a justifying reason for request. No adoption information will be given except according to statute. Records are public after 100 years. Include the following in your request-full name, names of parents, mother's maiden name, date of birth, place of birth, reason for information

request, relationship to person of record. Also, include a day time phone number.

Access by: mail, phone, fax, in person.

Fee & Payment: The $10.00 search fee includes a 3 year search; add $1.00 per year for each additional year searched. Fee payee: Bureau of Vital Statistics. Prepayment required. Personal checks accepted. Credit cards accepted: Mastercard, Visa, AmEx, Discover.

Mail search: Turnaround time: 2 weeks. No self addressed stamped envelope is required.

Phone search: Credit card requests require an additional $10.00.

Fax search: Same criteria as phone searching.

In person search: Turnaround time 10 minutes.

Expedited service: Expedited service is available for mail, phone and fax searches. Turnaround time: 2 days. Add $10.00 if using a credit card and $15.50 for Fed Ex or $11.75 for Express Mail.

Death Records

Department of Health & Social Services, Bureau of Vital Statistics, PO Box 110675, Juneau, AK 99811-0675 (Courier: 350 Main, Room 114, Juneau, AK 99811); 907-465-3392, 907-465-3618 (Fax), 8AM-4:30PM.

www.hss.state.ak.us/dph/bvs/bvs_home.htm

Indexing & Storage: Records are available from 1913-present. New records are available for inquiry immediately. Records are indexed on microfiche, inhouse computer.

Searching: You must be next of kin or have a notarized release statement from immediate family. Records are public after 50 years. Include the following in your request-full name, date of death, place of death, names of parents, reason for information request, relationship to person of record. Also, include a daytime phone number.

Access by: mail, phone, fax, in person.

Fee & Payment: The $10.00 search fee includes a 3 year search. Add $1.00 per year searched for each year over 3 years. Fee payee: Bureau of Vital Statistics. Prepayment required. Personal checks accepted. Credit cards accepted: Mastercard, Visa, AmEx, Discover.

Mail search: Turnaround time: 2 weeks.

Phone search: Add $10.00 for using a credit card.

Fax search: Same criteria as phone searching.

In person search: Turnaround time 10 minutes.

Expedited service: Expedited service is available for mail, phone and fax searches. Turnaround time: 2 days. Add $10.00 if using a credit card and add $15.50 for Fed Ex or $11.75 for Express Mail.

Marriage Certificates

Department of Health & Social Services, Bureau of Vital Statistics, PO Box 110675, Juneau, AK 99811-0675 (Courier: 350 Main, Room 114, Juneau, AK 99811); 907-465-3392, 907-465-3618 (Fax), 8AM-4:30PM.

www.hss.state.ak.us/dph/bvs/bvs_home.htm

Indexing & Storage: Records are available from 1913-present. New records are available for inquiry immediately. Records are indexed on microfiche, inhouse computer.

Searching: Person requesting must be one of the registrants or an attorney representing one of them.

Records are public after 50 years. Include the following in your request-names of husband and wife, date of marriage, place or county of marriage. Include wife's maiden name and a daytime phone number.

Access by: mail, phone, fax, in person.

Fee & Payment: The $10.00 search fee includes a 3 year search. Add $1.00 per year searched for each year over 3 years. Fee payee: Bureau of Vital Statistics. Prepayment required. Personal checks accepted. Credit cards accepted: Mastercard, Visa.

Mail search: Turnaround time: 2 weeks.

Phone search: Add $10.00 for using a credit card.

Fax search: Same criteria as phone searches.

In person search: Turnaround time 10 minutes.

Expedited service: Expedited service is available for mail, phone and fax searches. Turnaround time: 2 days. Add $10.00 if using a credit card and add $15.50 for Fed Ex or $11.75 for Express Mail.

Divorce Records

Department of Health & Social Services, Bureau of Vital Statistics, PO Box 110675, Juneau, AK 99811-0675 (Courier: 350 Main, Room 114, Juneau, AK 99811); 907-465-3392, 907-465-3618 (Fax), 8AM-4:30PM.

www.hss.state.ak.us/dph/bvs/bvs_home.htm

Indexing & Storage: Records are available from 1950-present. New records are available for inquiry immediately. Records are indexed on microfiche, inhouse computer.

Searching: Person requesting must be one of the registrants or an attorney representing a registrant. Records are public after 50 years. Include the following in your request-names of husband and wife, date of divorce, place of divorce. Also, include a daytime phone number.

Access by: mail, phone, fax, in person.

Fee & Payment: The $10.00 search fee includes a 3 year search. Add $1.00 per year searched for each year over 3 years. Fee payee: Bureau of Vital Statistics. Prepayment required. Personal checks accepted. Credit cards accepted: Mastercard, Visa, AmEx, Discover.

Mail search: Turnaround time: 2 weeks. No self addressed stamped envelope is required.

Phone search: Add $10.00 for use of a credit card.

Fax search: Same criteria as phone searches.

In person search: Turnaround time 10 minutes.

Expedited service: Expedited service is available for mail, phone and fax searches. Turnaround time: 2 days. Add $10.00 if using a credit card and add $15.50 for Fed Ex or $11.75 for Express Mail.

Workers' Compensation Records

Workers' Compensation, PO Box 25512, Juneau, AK 99802 (Courier: 1111 W Eighth St, Room 307, Juneau, AK 99802); 907-465-2790, 907-465-2797 (Fax), 8AM-4:30PM.

www.labor.state.ak.us/wc/wc.htm

Indexing & Storage: Records are available from 1982 on the computer and prior to 1982 the records are on microfilm and/or microfiche to the 1960s. New records are available for inquiry immediately.

Searching: All requests must be in writing. To receive a copy of a file, a signed medical release from claimant is required. Include the following in your request-claimant name, Social Security Number, date of accident.

Access by: mail, fax, in person, online.

Fee & Payment: Copies cost $.35 per page for active files and $.75 per page for microfilmed files. A computer printout costs $.50 per screen. There is no search fee. Fee payee: State of Alaska. Large orders require prepayment. Personal checks accepted. No credit cards accepted.

Mail search: Turnaround time: 2-3 weeks. No self addressed stamped envelope is required.

Fax search: Fax searching available.

In person search: Searching is available in person.

Online search: Online access is available for pre-approved accounts. Request in writing to the Director.

Other access: This agency sells its entire database. Call for information and fees.

Driver Records

Division of Motor Vehicles, Driver's Records, PO Box 20020, Juneau, AK 99802-0020 (Courier: 450 Whitter St, Room 105, Juneau, AK 99801); 907-465-4361 (Motor Vehicle Reports Desk), 907-463-5860 (Fax), 8AM-5PM.

www.state.ak.us/dmv

Note: Copies of tickets are only released, in writing, to the participant, legal representative, or insurance representative.

Indexing & Storage: Records are available for minor moving violations and suspensions for three years, major moving violations for five years. Convictions are automatically purged from public record by conviction date. Accidents are reported only if action is taken.

Searching: Any private company or individual must have a signed release from the licensee or a subpoena. High volume requesters may maintain these forms rather than send in with requests. Include the following in your request-name, driver's license number, date of birth. Driver's residence and mailing address are included as part of the search report.

Access by: mail, in person, online.

Fee & Payment: Prepayment required. Fee payee: State of Alaska. Personal checks accepted. No credit cards accepted.

Mail search: Turnaround time: 3-4 working days. No self addressed stamped envelope is required. Search costs $5.00 per record.

In person search: Search costs $5.00 per record. Turnaround time is while you wait.

Online search: Online access costs $5.00 per record. Inquiries may be made at any time, 24 hours a day. Batch inquiries may call back within thirty minutes for responses. Search by the first four letters of driver's name, license number and date of birth. At present, there is only one phone line available for users; you may experience a busy signal.

Vehicle Ownership
Vehicle Identification
Boat & Vessel Registration

Division of Motor Vehicles, Research, 2150 E Dowling Rd, Anchorage, AK 99507; 907-269-5551, 8AM-5PM.

www.state.ak.us/dmv

Indexing & Storage: Records are available for 7 years to present.

Searching: Record requests are honored for employment, insurance, court or impound purposes. Otherwise, a signed release is required. Service is generally slower in the summer months.

Access by: mail, in person.

Fee & Payment: The fee is $5.00 per record. Fee payee: State of Alaska. Prepayment required. No credit cards accepted.

Mail search: Turnaround time: 2-3 weeks. No self addressed stamped envelope is required.

In person search: Turnaround time depends on workload and complexity of request. Typically, requests are processed within 5-10 days, but can extend to 5 weeks or more.

Other access: The entire master tape file of registration information is available at a cost of approximately $50 per 1,000 records. Call the Director's Office (907-269-5551) for more information.

Accident Reports

Department of Public Safety, Driver Services, PO Box 20020, Juneau, AK 99802-0020 (Courier: 450 Whittier, Room 105, Juneau, AK 99801); 907-465-4361, 907-463-5509 (Fax), 8AM-5PM.

www.state.ak.us/dmv

Indexing & Storage: Records are available from seven years.

Searching: Only legal representatives and insurance agents of the participants, or the participant him/herself may obtain copies. The lawyer or legal representative must have a notarized request, an insurance agent a signed request with reason. Items required for search include names, date of incident, city, physical location of the accident.

Access by: mail, in person.

Fee & Payment: The cost of obtaining an accident report is $1.00 for the first page and $.25 for each additional page. Fee payee: State of Alaska, Department of Public Safety. Prepayment required. Personal checks accepted. No credit cards accepted.

Mail search: Turnaround time: 1-2 weeks. No self addressed stamped envelope is required.

In person search: Turnaround time is while you wait.

Boat & Vessel Ownership

Records not maintained by a state level agency.

Note: Alaska is not a title state. Until Jan. 1, 2000, all boat registrations were done through the US Coast Guard (970-463-2294). As of Jan. 1, 2000 they are at the DMV. Liens are filed with the Department of Natural Resources at 907-269-8882.

Legislation-Current/Pending Legislation-Passed

Alaska State Legislative Affairs Agency, Legislative Information Office, 120 4th St #111, Juneau, AK 99801-1182; 907-465-4648, 907-465-2864 (Fax), 8AM-5PM.

www.legis.state.ak.us

Indexing & Storage: Records are available from 1982-present. Records are indexed on inhouse computer.

Searching: Include the following in your request-bill number, year.

Access by: mail, phone, in person, online.

Fee & Payment: There is no search fee nor is there a fee for one copy of a bill. Copy fees vary; therefore, call for fees, if you need more than one copy. Fee payee: State of Alaska. Prepayment required. Personal checks accepted. No credit cards accepted.

Mail search: Turnaround time: 1 day. No self addressed stamped envelope is required.

Phone search: You may call for copies.

In person search: Turnaround time is while you wait.

Online search: All information, including statutes, is available on the Internet. At the main web site, click on "Bills."

Voter Registration

Division of Elections, PO Box 110017, Juneau, AK 99811-0017 (Courier: Court Plaza Building, 4th Floor, 240 Main Street, Juneau, AK 99801); 907-465-4611, 8AM-4:30PM.

www.elections.state.ak.us

Note: There are four regional Elections Offices, each has access to the election records database.

Indexing & Storage: Records are available from 1983. It takes 1 day before new records are available for inquiry.

Searching: Searching by name is permitted. The following data is not released: Social Security Numbers or date of birth.

Access by: mail, phone, fax, in person.

Fee & Payment: There is no fee.

Mail search: Turnaround time: 1 day.

Phone search: Searching is available by phone.

Fax search: Fax searching available.

In person search: Turnaround time is immediate unless extensive lists or requests for older records are presented.

Other access: The agency offers the complete record database on tape or cartridge for $165. Individual districts (there are 40) can be purchased on disk for $20.00 each.

GED Certificates

Department of Labor, Employment Security Division, PO Box 25509, Juneau, AK 99802-5509 (Courier: 111 8th Street #210, Juneau, AK 99802); 907-465-4685, 907-465-8753 (Fax), 8:30AM-5PM.

www.educ.state.ak.us/TLS/AVE/ged.html

Searching: Include the full name, DOB, SSN, year of test and city of test. Fax requesters must include a signed release.

Access by: mail, fax, in person.

Fee & Payment: There is no fee for a verification or a transcript copy. There is a $10.00 for a copy of a diploma.

Mail search: Turnaround time: 1-2 weeks. No self addressed stamped envelope is required.

Fax search: A written release form is required.

In person search: Searching is available in person.

Hunting License Information Fishing License Information

Department of Fish & Game, Licensing Section, PO Box 25525, Juneau, AK 99802-5525 (Courier: 1255 W 8th St, Juneau, AK 99802); 907-465-2376, 907-465-2440 (Fax), 8AM-5PM.

www.state.ak.us/local/akpages/FISH.GAME/adfghome.htm

Indexing & Storage: Records are available from 10 years to present. Records since 1994 are computerized, older records are on microfiche. It takes 4 weeks before new records are available for inquiry.

Searching: Information used to search includes SSN, DOB, address, driver's license number, or year license issued. The following data is not released: Social Security Numbers or telephone numbers.

Access by: mail, phone, fax, in person.

Fee & Payment: No fee unless you request a large list. For certified copies the turnaround time is 6 weeks. Fee payee: State of Alaska. Prepayment required. Personal checks accepted. Credit cards accepted.

Mail search: Turnaround time: within 3 weeks. No self addressed stamped envelope is required.

Phone search: Limited number of requests given over the phone.

Fax search: Same criteria as phone searches.

In person search: Large lists will not be processed immediately.

Other access: The vendor file is available for $25 on paper or disk. The entire license file is available for $350 on CD-ROM.

Licenses Searchable Online

Acupuncturist #14	www.dced.state.ak.us/occ/search3.htm
Architect #14	www.dced.state.ak.us/occ/search3.htm
Audiologist/Hearing Aid Dealer #14	www.dced.state.ak.us/occ/search3.htm
Barber #14	www.dced.state.ak.us/occ/search3.htm
Boxing & Wrestling Related Occupation #14	www.dced.state.ak.us/occ/search3.htm
Chiropractor #14	www.dced.state.ak.us/occ/search3.htm
Collection Agency/Operator #14	www.dced.state.ak.us/occ/search3.htm
Concert Promoter #14	www.dced.state.ak.us/occ/search3.htm
Construction Contractor #14	www.dced.state.ak.us/occ/search3.htm
Dental Hygienist #14	www.dced.state.ak.us/occ/search3.htm
Dentist #14	www.dced.state.ak.us/occ/search3.htm
Electrical Administrator #14	www.dced.state.ak.us/occ/search3.htm
Engineer #14	www.dced.state.ak.us/occ/search3.htm
Examining Physician, Boxing #14	www.dced.state.ak.us/occ/search3.htm
Geologist #14	www.dced.state.ak.us/occ/search3.htm
Guide Outfitter (Hunting) #14	www.dced.state.ak.us/occ/search3.htm
Hairdresser & Cosmetologist #14	www.dced.state.ak.us/occ/search3.htm
Hearing Aid Dealer #14	www.dced.state.ak.us/occ/search3.htm
Lobbyist #09	www.state.ak.us/local/akpages/ADMIN/apoc/lobcov.htm
Marine Pilot #14	www.dced.state.ak.us/occ/search3.htm
Mechanical Administrator #14	www.dced.state.ak.us/occ/search3.htm
Medical Doctor/Surgeon #14	www.dced.state.ak.us/occ/search3.htm
Mortician-Embalmer #14	www.dced.state.ak.us/occ/search3.htm
Naturopathic Physician (Naturopathic Doctor) #14	www.dced.state.ak.us/occ/search3.htm
Nurse #14	www.dced.state.ak.us/occ/search3.htm
Nurse (RN & LPN)-Nurse Anesthetist #14	www.dced.state.ak.us/occ/search3.htm
Nurses' Aide #14	www.dced.state.ak.us/occ/search3.htm
Nursing Home Administrator #14	www.dced.state.ak.us/occ/search3.htm
Occupational Therapist/Assistant #14	www.dced.state.ak.us/occ/search3.htm
Optician #14	www.dced.state.ak.us/occ/search3.htm
Optometrist #14	www.dced.state.ak.us/occ/search3.htm
Osteopathic Physician #14	www.dced.state.ak.us/occ/search3.htm
Paramedic #14	www.dced.state.ak.us/occ/search3.htm
Pharmacist #14	www.dced.state.ak.us/occ/search3.htm
Physical Therapist/Assistant #14	www.dced.state.ak.us/occ/search3.htm
Physician Assistant #14	www.dced.state.ak.us/occ/search3.htm
Podiatrist #14	www.dced.state.ak.us/occ/search3.htm
Psychologist & Psychological Assistant #14	www.dced.state.ak.us/occ/search3.htm
Real Estate Agent & Broker #14	www.dced.state.ak.us/occ/search3.htm
Real Estate Appraiser #14	www.dced.state.ak.us/occ/search3.htm
Residential Contractor #14	www.dced.state.ak.us/occ/search3.htm
Surveyor #14	www.dced.state.ak.us/occ/search3.htm
Underground Storage Tank Worker & Contractor #14	www.dced.state.ak.us/occ/search3.htm
Veterinarian #14	www.dced.state.ak.us/occ/search3.htm
Veterinary Technician #14	www.dced.state.ak.us/occ/search3.htm

Licensing Quick Finder

Acupuncturist #14	907-465-2695
Aircraft Related Occupation #18	907-271-2000
Alocohol Server #21	907-269-0350
Architect #14	907-465-2540
Asbestos Removal Worker #22	907-269-4925
Attorney #11	907-272-7469
Audiologist/Hearing Aid Dealer #14	907-465-2695
Barber #14	907-465-2547
Boiler Operator #22	907-269-4925
Bondsman #13	907-465-2515
Boxing & Wrestling Related Occupation #14	907-465-2695
Broker-Dealer #12	907-465-2521
Child Care Provider (Home & Center) #16	907-465-3207
Chiropractor #14	907-465-2589
Collection Agency/Operator #14	907-465-2695

Commercial Fishing Operator #08	907-260-4882
Concert Promoter #14	907-465-2695
Construction Contractor #14	907-465-2546
Crewmember (Fishing Boat) #04	907-465-2376
Defibillator Technician #17	907-465-3029
Dental Hygienist #14	907-465-2542
Dentist #14	907-465-2542
Electrical Administrator #14	907-465-2589
Electrician #07	907-269-4925
Emergency Medical Technician #17	907-465-3029
Employment Agency Operator #05	907-269-8160
Engineer #14	907-465-2540
Examining Physician, Boxing #14	907-465-2695
Explosives Handler #22	907-269-4925
Geologist #14	907-465-2695
Guide (Sport Fishing) #08	907-260-4882
Guide Outfitter (Hunting) #14	907-465-2543

Hairdresser & Cosmetologist #14	907-465-2547
Hearing Aid Dealer #14	907-465-2695
Hunting Guide #20	907-465-2543
Independent Adjuster #13	907-465-2515
Insurance Occupation #13	907-465-2515
Insurance Producer #13	907-465-2515
Investment Advisor #12	907-465-2521
Investment Broker-Dealer & Related Occupation #12	907-465-2521
Lobbyist #09	907-465-4864
Managing General Agent #13	907-465-2515
Marine Pilot #14	907-465-2548
Marital & Family Therapist #20	907-465-2551
Mechanical Administrator #14	907-465-2589
Medical Doctor/Surgeon #14	907-465-2541
Midwife #20	907-465-2580
Mobile Home Dealer #20	907-465-2547

Mortician-Embalmer #14 607-465-2695
Naturopathic Physician (Naturopathic Doctor) #14
....907-465-2695
Notary Public #19..............................907-465-3509
Nurse #14..907-465-2544
Nurse (RN & LPN)-Nurse Anesthetist #14
....907-465-2544
Nurses' Aide #14................................907-269-8169
Nursing Home Administrator #14 907-465-2695
Occupational Therapist/Assistant #14 ...907-465-2580
Optician #14.......................................907-465-5470
Optometrist #14 907-465-2580
Osteopathic Physician #14 907-465-2541
Painter #07 907-269-4925
Paramedic #14....................................907-465-2541
Pesticide Applicator #02 907-745-3236

Pharmacist #14...................................907-465-2589
Physical Therapist/Assistant #14 907-465-2580
Physician Assistant #14.......................907-269-8163
Plumber #07 907-269-4925
Podiatrist #14.....................................907-465-2541
Process Server #10.............................907-269-0392
Professional Counselor #20..................907-465-2551
Psychologist & Psychological Assistant #14
....907-465-3811
Public Accountant-CPA #20..................907-465-2580
Real Estate Agent & Broker #14 907-269-8162
Real Estate Appraiser #14....................907-465-2542
Reinsurance Intermediary Broker #13 ...907-465-2515
Reinsurance Intermediary Manager #13
....907-465-2515
Residential Contractor #14 907-465-2546

Securities Agent #12 907-465-2521
Security Guard #10 907-269-0393
Social Worker #20...............................907-465-2551
Surplus Line Broker #13 907-465-2515
Surveyor #14 907-465-2540
Taxidermist #04 907-465-2376
Teacher #01..907-465-2831
Underground Storage Tank Worker & Contractor #14
....907-465-5470
Veterinarian #14..................................907-465-5470
Veterinary Technician #14 907-465-5470
Waste Water System Operator #03.......907-465-5140

Licensing Agency Information

01 Department of Education & Early Development, Teacher Education & Certification, 801 W 10th St, #200, Juneau, AK 99801-1894; 907-465-2831, Fax: 907-465-2441.

www.eed.state.ak.us

02 Department of Environmental Conservation, Division of Environmental Health, 500 S Alaska St, Palmer, AK 99645; 907-745-3236, Fax: 907-745-8125.

www.state.ak.us/dec

03 Department of Environmental Conservation, Facility Construction & Operation, 410 Willoughby Ave, Juneau, AK 99801-1795; 907-465-5140, Fax: 907-465-5177.

04 Department of Fish & Game, Licensing Section, PO Box 25525 (PO Box 25525), Juneau, AK 99802-5525; 907-465-2376, Fax: 907-265-2440.

www.state.ak.us/local/akpages/FISH.GAME/admin/license/crew.htm

05 Department of Labor, Department of Commerce, 33601 C St, #722, Anchorage, AK 99503; 907-269-8160, Fax: 907-261-8156.

07 Department of Labor, Labor Standards & Safety, Mechanical Inspection Section, PO Box 107020 (PO Box 107020), Anchorage, AK 99510; 907-269-4925, Fax: 907-269-4932.

08 Department of Natural Resources, Division of Parks & Outdoor Recreation, 514 Funny River Rd, Soldotna, AK 99669; 907-260-4882, Fax: 907-260-5992.

09 Public Offices Commission, PO Box 110222 (PO Box 110222), Juneau, AK 99811-0222; 907-465-4864, Fax: 907-465-4832.

www.state.ak.us/local/akpages/ADMIN/apoc/lobcov.htm

Direct URL to search licenses: www.state.ak.us/local/akpages/ADMIN/apoc/lobcov.htm By visiting the web site, you can download directories of licensed lobbyists. There is no actual searching online; however, once you've downloaded the file for the appropriate year, you can begin your search.

10 Alaska State Troopers, Permits & Licensing Unit, 5700 E Tudor Rd, Anchorage, AK 99507-1225; 907-269-0391, Fax: 907-269-0394.

www.dps.state.ak.us

11 Alaska Bar Association, Board of Governors, PO Box 100279 (PO Box 100279), Anchorage, AK 99510-0279; 907-272-7469, Fax: 907-272-2932.

www.alaskabar.org

12 Department of Commerce & Economic Development,, Division of Banking; Securities & Corporations, PO Box 110807 (PO Box 110807), Juneau, AK 99811-0807; 907-465-2521, Fax: 907-465-1230.

www.dced.state.ak.us/bsc/secur.htm

13 Department of Community & Economic Development, Division of Insurance, PO Box 110805 (PO Box 110805), Juneau, AK 99811-0805; 907-465-2515, Fax: 907-465-3422.

www.commerce.state.ak.us/insurance

14 Department of Commerce & Economic Development, Division of Occupational Licensing, PO Box 110806 (PO Box 110806), Juneau, AK 99811-0806; 907-465-2538, Fax: 907-465-2974.

www.dced.state.ak.us/occ

Direct URL to search licenses: www.dced.state.ak.us/occ/search3.htm You can search online using board, license type, license #, name, or city

16 Department of Health & Social Services, Division of Family & Youth Services, PO Box 110630 (PO Box 110630), Juneau, AK 99811-0630; 907-465-3207, Fax: 907-465-3397.

17 Department of Health & Social Services, Division of Public Health/Section of Community Health and EMS, PO Box 110616 (PO Box 110616), Juneau, AK 99811-0616; 907-465-3027, Fax: 907-465-4101.

www.chems.alaska.gov

Direct URL to search licenses: http://chems.alaska.gov/emsdata/ You can search online using Last name, SSN, Certificate #.

18 Federal Aviation Administration, Flight Standards Regional Office, 222 W 7th Ave, AAL 200, #14, Anchorage, AK 99513-7587; 907-271-5514, Fax: 907-271-1665.

19 Office of Lieutenant Governor, PO Box 110015 (State Capitol), Juneau, AK 99811; 907-465-3520, Fax: 907-465-5400.

20 Department of Commerce & Economic Development, PO Box 110806, Juneau, AK 99811-0806.

21 Department of Revenue, Alcholic Beverage Control Board, 550 W 7th Ave #350, Anchorage, AK 99501-3510; 907-269-0350.

22 Department Labor & Workforce Development, Labor Standards & Safety - Mech Insp Section, PO Box 107020, Anchorage, AK 99510; 907-269-4925.

The following list indicates the district and division name for each county in the state. If the district or division name of the bankruptcy court is different from the civil/criminal court, it appears in parentheses.

County/Court Cross Reference

Aleutian Islands, East.. Anchorage
Aleutian Islands, West... Anchorage
Anchorage Borough Borough .... Anchorage
Bethel... Fairbanks (Anchorage)
Bristol Bay Borough Borough... Anchorage
Fairbanks North Star Borough Borough.............. Fairbanks (Anchorage)
Haines. Borough Borough .... Juneau (Anchorage)
Juneau Borough Borough................................... Juneau (Anchorage)
Kenai Peninsula Borough Borough .... Anchorage
Ketchikan Gateway Borough Borough................ Ketchikan (Anchorage)
Kodiak Island Borough Borough.................................... Anchorage
Matanuska-Susitna Borough Borough............................ Anchorage

Nome.. Nome (Anchorage)
North Slope Borough Borough.......................... Fairbanks (Anchorage)
Northwest Arctic Borough................................. Fairbanks (Anchorage)
Prince of Wales-Outer Ketchikan .... Juneau (Anchorage)
Sitka Borough Borough...................................... Juneau (Anchorage)
Southeast Fairbanks.. Fairbanks (Anchorage)
Valdez-Cordova.. Anchorage
Wade Hampton... Fairbanks (Anchorage)
Wrangell-Petersburg.. Juneau (Anchorage)
Yakutat... Juneau (Anchorage)
Yukon-Koyukuk.. Fairbanks (Anchorage)

US District Court

District of Alaska

Anchorage Division Box 4, 222 W 7th Ave, Anchorage, AK 99513-7564, 907-271-5568.

www.akd.uscourts.gov

Counties: Aleutian Islands-East, Aleutian Islands-West, Anchorage Borough, Bristol Bay Borough, Kenai Peninsula Borough, Kodiak Island Borough, Matanuska-Susitna Borough, Valdez-Cordova.

Indexing & Storage: Cases are indexed by defendant and plaintiff as well as by case number. New cases are available in the index immediately after filing date. Both computer and card indexes are maintained. An index card system was used to index files prior to May 1987. Records after May 1987 are on computer. Open records are located at this court. If a case was tried, the file will be sent to the Anchorage Federal Records Center. If the case did not go to trial, the file will be sent to the Seattle Federal Records Center. Case records are sent to a Center after the case is closed.

Fee & Payment: The fee is $15.00 per item (one party name or case number). Payment may be made by money order, cashier check, personal check. Prepayment is required. Payee: Clerk, US District Court. Certification fee: $5.00 per document. Copy fee: $.50 per page. You are allowed to make your own copies. These copies cost $.50 per page.

Phone Search: Only docket information is available by phone. An automated voice case information service (VCIS) is not available.

Mail Search: Always enclose a stamped self addressed envelope.

In Person Search: In person searching is available.

PACER: Sign-up number is 800-676-6856. Access fee is $.60 per minute. Toll-free access: 888-271-6212. Local access: 907-271-6212. Case records are available back to 1987. Records are purged every 6 months. New records are available online after 1 day.

Fairbanks Division Box 1, 101 12th Ave, Fairbanks, AK 99701, 907-451-5791.

www.akd.uscourts.gov

Counties: Bethel, Fairbanks North Star Borough, North Slope Borough, Northwest Arctic Borough, Southeast Fairbanks, Wade Hampton, Yukon-Koyukuk.

Indexing & Storage: Cases are indexed by defendant and plaintiff as well as by case number. New cases are available in the index 1-2 days after filing date. A computer index is maintained. Open records are located at this court.

Fee & Payment: The fee is $15.00 per item (one party name or case number). Payment may be made by money order, cashier check, personal check. Prepayment is required unless other arrangements have been made. Payee: US District Court. Certification fee: $5.00 per document. Copy fee: $.50 per page.

Phone Search: Only docket information is available by phone. An automated voice case information service (VCIS) is not available.

Mail Search: Always enclose a stamped self addressed envelope.

In Person Search: In person searching is available.

PACER: Sign-up number is 800-676-6856. Access fee is $.60 per minute. Toll-free access: 888-271-6212. Local access: 907-271-6212. Case records are available back to 1987. Records are purged every 6 months. New records are available online after 1 day.

Juneau Division PO Box 020349, Juneau, AK 99802-0349 (Courier Address: Room 979, Federal Bldg-US Courthouse, 709 W 9th, Juneau, AK 99802), 907-586-7458.

www.akd.uscourts.gov

Counties: Haines Borough, Juneau Borough, Prince of Wales-Outer Ketchikan, Sitka Borough, Skagway-Hoonah-Angoon, Wrangell-Petersburg.

Indexing & Storage: Cases are indexed by defendant and plaintiff as well as by case number. New cases are available in the index immediately after filing date. A computer index is maintained. Case files are indexed on computer and then stored in file cabinets. Open records are located at this court. If the case was tried, the file will be sent to the divison where it was filed. If the case did not go to trial, it will be sent to the Seattle Federal Records Center some time after the case is closed.

Fee & Payment: The fee is $15.00 per item (one party name or case number). Payment may be made by money order, cashier check, personal

check. Payee: Clerk, US District Court. Certification fee: $5.00 per document. Copy fee: $.50 per page.

Phone Search: Only docket information is available by phone. An automated voice case information service (VCIS) is not available.

Mail Search: Always enclose a stamped self addressed envelope.

In Person Search: In person searching is available.

PACER: Sign-up number is 800-676-6856. Access fee is $.60 per minute. Toll-free access: 888-271-6212. Local access: 907-271-6212. Case records are available back to 1987. Records are purged every 6 months. New records are available online after 1 day.

Ketchikan Division 648 Mission St, Room 507, Ketchikan, AK 99901, 907-247-7576.

www.akd.uscourts.gov

Counties: Ketchikan Gateway Borough.

Indexing & Storage: Cases are indexed by defendant and plaintiff as well as by case number. New cases are available in the index immediately after filing date. A computer index is maintained. Case files are indexed on computer and then stored in file cabinets. Open records are located at this court. If the case was tried, the file will be sent to the Anchorage Division. If the case did not go to trial, it will be sent to the Seattle Federal Records Center. Case records are sent to a Center after the case is closed.

Fee & Payment: The fee is $15.00 per item (one party name or case number). Payment may be made by money order, cashier check, business check. Personal checks are not accepted. Prepayment is required. Payee: Clerk, US District Court. Certification fee: $5.00 per document. Copy fee: $.50 per page.

Phone Search: Only docket information is available by phone. An automated voice case information service (VCIS) is not available.

Mail Search: Always enclose a stamped self addressed envelope.

In Person Search: In person searching is available.

PACER: Sign-up number is 800-676-6856. Access fee is $.60 per minute. Toll-free access: 888-271-6212. Local access: 907-271-6212. Case records are available back to 1987. Records are purged every 6 months. New records are available online after 1 day.

Nome Division PO Box 1110, Nome, AK 99762 (Courier Address: 2nd Floor, Federal Bldg, Front St, Nome, AK 99762), 907-443-5216, Fax: 907-443-2192.

www.akd.uscourts.gov

Counties: Nome.

Indexing & Storage: Cases are indexed by defendant and plaintiff as well as by case number. New cases are available in the index immediately after filing date. A card index is maintained. Open records are located at this court. Records have been retained at this court since 1960. No records have been sent to the repository.

Fee & Payment: The fee is $15.00 per item (one party name or case number). Payment may be made by money order, cashier check, personal check. Prepayment is not required, but is preferred. For copies, make checks payable to Alaska Court System. For searches and certified copies, make checks payable to US District Court. Certification fee: $5.00 per document. Copy fee: $.25 per page. The fee for copies made by court personnel is $.50 per page.

Phone Search: Only docket information is available by phone. The court prefers that requests be submitted in writing. An automated voice case information service (VCIS) is not available.

Fax Search: Will bill for fax search like a mail search. Fax requests should be sent AFTER hours. Prefer not to fax results, but will in expedited cases at cost of fax, search and copies. Fax copies cannot be certified.

Mail Search: A stamped self addressed envelope is not required.

In Person Search: In person searching is available.

PACER: Sign-up number is 800-676-6856. Access fee is $.60 per minute. Toll-free access: 888-271-6212. Local access: 907-271-6212. Case records are available back to 1987. Records are purged every 6 months. New records are available online after 1 day.

US Bankruptcy Court

District of Alaska

Anchorage Division Historic Courthouse, Suite 138, 605 W 4th Ave, Anchorage, AK 99501-2296, 907-271-2655.

www.akb.uscourts.gov

Counties: All boroughs and districts in Alaska.

Indexing & Storage: Cases are indexed by debtor as well as by case number. New cases are available in the index 1-2 days after filing date. To insure accuracy, the court advises including a social security number or tax ID number. A computer index is maintained. Open records are located at this court. If the case was tried, it will be sent to Anchorage Federal Records Center. If the case did not go to trial, it will be sent to Seattle Federal Records Center. Case records are sent to a Center 60 days after the case is closed.

Fee & Payment: The fee is $15.00 per item (one party name or case number). Payment may be made by money order, cashier check, personal check. Prepayment is required. Payee: Clerk, US Bankruptcy Court. Certification fee: $5.00 per

document. Copy fee: $.50 per page. You are allowed to make your own copies. These copies cost $.15 per page. The copy machine works on a debit card system. The cards may be purchased through the State Law Library. The card costs $.50 and can be credited with $1.00, $5.00, $10.00 or $20.00 amounts. Since files cannot be taken apart, it may be advisable to have

Phone Search: Accession numbers will be released over the phone if a case number is provided. If the case number is unknown, the information must be requested in writing with the $15.00 search fee. An automated voice case information service (VCIS) is available. Call VCIS at 888-878-3110 or 907-271-2658.

Mail Search: Always enclose a stamped self addressed envelope.

In Person Search: In person searching is available.

PACER: Sign-up number is 800-676-6856. Access fee is $.60 per minute. Toll-free access: 888-878-3110. Local access: 907-271-2695, 907-271-2696, 907-271-2697, 907-271-2698, 907-271-2699. Case records are available back to July 1991. Records are purged 6 months. New civil records are available online after 2 days. PACER is available on the Internet at http://pacer.akb.uscourts.gov.

Court	Jurisdiction	No. of Courts	How Organized
Superior Courts*	General		4 Districts
District Courts*	Limited	3	4 Districts
Combined Courts*		15	
Magistrate Courts*	Limited	32	4 Districts

* Profiled in this Sourcebook

Court	CIVIL								
	Tort	Contract	Real Estate	Min. Claim	Max. Claim	Small Claims	Estate	Eviction	Domestic Relations
Superior Courts*	X	X	X	$0	No Max		X	X	X
District Courts*	X	X		$0	$50,000	$5000		X	X
Magistrate Courts*	X	X	X	$0	$5000	$5000			

Court	CRIMINAL				
	Felony	Misdemeanor	DWI/DUI	Preliminary Hearing	Juvenile
Superior Courts*	X				X
District Courts*		X	X	X	X
Magistrate Courts*		X	X	X	

ADMINISTRATION   Office of the Administrative Director, 303 K St, Anchorage, AK, 99501; 907-264-0547, Fax: 907-264-0881. www.alaska.net/~akctlib/homepage.htm

COURT STRUCTURE   Alaska is not organized into counties, but rather into 15 boroughs (3 unified home rule municipalities that are combination borough and city, and 12 boroughs) and 12 home rule cities, which do not directly coincide with the 4 Judicial Districts into which the judicial system is divided, that is, judicial boundaries cross borough boundaries. We have listed the courts by their borough or home rule city in keeping with the format of this book. You should search through the city court location names to determine the correct court for your search. Probate is handled by the Superior Courts.

ONLINE ACCESS   There is no internal or external online statewide judicial computer system available.

ADDITIONAL INFORMATION   Documents may not be filed by fax in any Alaska court location without prior authorization of a judge.

The fees established by court rules for Alaska courts are: Search Fee - $15.00 per hour or fraction thereof; certification Fee - $5.00 per document and $2.00 per additional copy of the document; copy Fee - $.25 per page.

Magistrate Courts vary widely in how records are maintained and in the hours of operation (some are open only a few hours per week)

📖 📖 📖 📖 📖 📖 📖

Aleutian Islands

Sand Point Magistrate Court (3rd District) c/o Joanne Gilson, PO Box 127, Valdez, AK 99696-0127; 907-835-2266. *Misdemeanor, Civil Actions Under $5,000, Small Claims.*

Note: Court closed; records at Valdez Superior and District Court, address and phone here.

St Paul Island Magistrate Court (3rd District) c/o Joanne Gilson, PO Box 127, Valdez, AK 99696-0127; 907-835-2266. *Misdemeanor, Civil Actions Under $5,000, Small Claims.*

Note: Court closed. See Valdez Superior and District Court, address and phone here.

Unalaska Magistrate Court (3rd District) PO Box 245, Unalaska, AK 99685-

0245; 907-581-1266; Fax: 907-581-2809. Hours: 8:30AM-4:30PM (HT). *Misdemeanor, Civil Actions Under $5,000, Small Claims.*

Civil Records: Only the court conducts in person searches; visitors may not. **Criminal Records:** Only the court conducts in person searches; visitors may not. Search fee: $15.00 per hour. Required to search: name, years to search, DOB. **General Information:** Turnaround time 1-2 weeks. Fee payee: Unalaska Trial Courts. Prepayment is required.

Anchorage Borough

Superior & District Court (3rd District) 825 West 4th, Anchorage, AK 99501-2004; 907-264-0444; Probate phone:907-264-0435; Fax: 907-264-0873. Hours: 8AM-4:30PM (AK). *Felony, Misdemeanor, Civil, Eviction, Small Claims, Probate.*

Civil Records: Access: Phone, fax, mail, in person. Both court and visitors may perform in person searches. Search fee: $15.00 per hour. Required to search: name, years to search; also helpful-address. Civil cases indexed by defendant, plaintiff. Civil records on computer from 1990, on microfiche and archived from 1977 to 1989, on roll index from 1940s. **Criminal Records:** Access: Phone, fax, mail, in person. Both court and visitors may perform in person searches. Search fee: $15.00 per hour. Required to search: name, years to search; also helpful-address, DOB, SSN. Criminal records on computer from 1990, on microfiche and archived from 1977 to 1989, on roll index from 1940s. **General Information:** No adoption, juvenile, sealed or mental records released. SASE required. Turnaround time 1-3 days. Copy fee: $.25 per page. Certification fee: $5.00. Fee payee: Alaska Court System. Personal checks accepted. Prepayment is required. Public access terminal is available. Fax notes: No fee to fax results. Local fax only.

Bethel

Superior & District Court (4th District)

PO Box 130, Bethel, AK 99559-0130; 907-543-1117; Fax: 907-543-4419. Hours: 8AM-4:30PM (AK). *Felony, Misdemeanor, Civil, Eviction, Small Claims, Probate.*

Civil Records: Access: Phone, mail, in person. Both court and visitors may perform in person searches. Search fee: $15.00 per name. Required to search: name, years to search. Civil cases indexed by defendant, plaintiff. Civil records on computer from 1983, on microfiche, archived and on index from 1960s. **Criminal Records:** Access: Phone, mail, in person. Both court and visitors may perform in person searches. Search fee: $15.00 per name. Required to search: name, years to search; also helpful-DOB. Criminal records on computer from 1983, on microfiche, archived and on index from 1960s. **General Information:** No adoption, juvenile, guardianship or mental records released. SASE required. Turnaround time 2 weeks. Copy fee: $.25 per page. Certification fee: $5.00 plus $2.00 per page after first. Fee payee: Clerk of Court. Personal checks accepted. Prepayment is required.

Aniak District Court (4th District)

PO Box 147, Aniak, AK 99557-0147; 907-675-4325; Fax: 907-675-4278. Hours: 8AM-4:30PM (AK). *Misdemeanor, Civil Actions Under $7,500, Small Claims.*

Civil Records: Both court and visitors may perform in person searches. Search fee: $15.00 per search. **Criminal Records:** Both court and visitors may perform in person searches. Search fee: $15.00 per search. Required to search: name, years to search. **General Information:** Turnaround time 1-2 weeks. Fee payee: Aniak District Court. Prepayment is required.

Quinhagak Magistrate Court (Bethel Area)

c/o Bethel Clerk, PO Box 130, Bethel, AK 99559-0130; 907-543-1105. *Misdemeanor, Civil Actions Under $5,000, Small Claims.*

Note: Court closed; records at Bethel Clerk of Courts at address and phone here.

Bristol Bay Borough

Naknek Magistrate Court (3rd District)

PO Box 229, Naknek, AK 99633-0229; 907-246-6151; Fax: 907-246-7418. Hours: 8:30AM-4PM (AK). *Misdemeanor, Civil Actions Under $5,000, Small Claims.*

Civil Records: Only the court conducts in person searches; visitors may not. Search fee:. **Criminal Records:** Only the court conducts in person searches; visitors may not. Search fee: $15.00 per hour. Required to search: name, years to search. **General Information:** Turnaround time same day. Fee payee: Alaska Court System. Prepayment is required.

Denali

Healy Magistrate Court (4th District)

PO Box 298, Healy, AK 99743-0298; 907-683-2213; Fax: 907-683-1383. Hours: 8AM-4:30PM (AK). *Misdemeanor, Civil Actions Under $5,000, Small Claims.*

Civil Records: Only the court conducts in person searches; visitors may not. Search fee:. **Criminal Records:** Only the court conducts in person searches; visitors may not. Search fee: $15.00 per

hour. Required to search: name, years to search, DOB. **General Information:** Turnaround time 1-2 weeks. Fee payee: State of Alaska. Prepayment is required.

Dillingham

Dillingham Superior Court (3rd District)

PO Box 909, Dillingham, AK 99576-0909; 907-842-5215; Fax: 907-842-5746. Hours: 8AM-4:30PM (AK). *Felony, Misdemeanor, Civil, Small Claims.*

Civil Records: Only the court conducts in person searches; visitors may not. Search fee:. **Criminal Records:** Only the court conducts in person searches; visitors may not. Search fee: $15.00 per hour. Required to search: name, years to search, DOB. **General Information:** Turnaround time 1-2 weeks. Fee payee: Magistrate Court. Prepayment is required.

Fairbanks North Star Borough

Superior & District Court (4th District)

604 Barnette St, Fairbanks, AK 99701-4572; 907-452-9277; Fax: 907-452-9392. Hours: 8AM-4:30PM (AK). *Felony, Misdemeanor, Civil, Eviction, Small Claims, Probate.*

Civil Records: Access: Mail, in person. Both court and visitors may perform in person searches. Search fee: $15.00 per hour. Required to search: name, years to search. Civil cases indexed by defendant, plaintiff. Civil records on computer from 1988, on microfiche, archived and on index from 1900s. **Criminal Records:** Access: Mail, in person. Both court and visitors may perform in person searches. Search fee: $15.00 per hour. Required to search: name, years to search, DOB. Criminal records on computer from 1988, on microfiche, archived and on index from 1900s. **General Information:** No adoption, juvenile, guardianship or mental records released. SASE required. Turnaround time 2 weeks. Copy fee: $.25 per page. Certification fee: $5.00 plus $2.00 per copy after first. Fee payee: Clerk of Court. Personal checks accepted. Personals check must be preprinted. In person only. Prepayment is required. Public access terminal is available.

Haines Borough

District Court (1st District)

PO Box 169, Haines, AK 99827-0169; 907-766-2801; Fax: 907-766-3148. Hours: 8AM-4:30PM (AK). *Misdemeanor, Civil Actions Under $50,000, Small Claims.*

Civil Records: Access: Phone, fax, mail, in person. Only the court conducts in person searches; visitors may not. Search fee: $15.00 per hour. Required to search: name, years to search; also helpful-address. Civil cases indexed by defendant, plaintiff. Civil records on computer since 1993, index from 1960s. Limited information is available by phone. **Criminal Records:** Access: Phone, fax, mail, in person. Only the court conducts in person searches; visitors may not. Search fee: $15.00 per hour. Required to search: name, years to search; also helpful-address, DOB, SSN. Criminal records on computer since 1993, index from 1960s. **General Information:** No juvenile records released. SASE required. Turnaround time 1-2 days. Copy fee: $.25 per page. Certification fee: $5.00 plus $2.00 per each additional document requested at same time. Fee payee: Alaska Court System. Personal checks accepted. Prepayment is required.

Juneau Borough

Superior & District Court (1st District)

Dimond Courthouse, PO Box 114100, Juneau, AK 99811-4100; 907-463-4700; Fax: 907-463-3788. Hours: 8AM-4:30PM (AK). *Felony, Misdemeanor, Civil, Eviction, Small Claims, Probate.*

www.alaska.net/~akctlib/courtdir.htm#juneau

Civil Records: Access: Mail, in person. Both court and visitors may perform in person searches. Search fee: $15.00 per hour. Required to search: name, years to search. Civil cases indexed by defendant. Civil records on computer from 1988, on microfiche from 1960 to 1986, on index from 1959 to 1987. **Criminal Records:** Access: Mail, in person. Both court and visitors may perform in person searches. Search fee: $15.00 per hour. Required to search: name, years to search. Criminal records on computer from 1988, on microfiche from 1960 to 1986, on index from 1959 to 1987. **General Information:** No adoption, juvenile, guardianship or mental records released. SASE required. Turnaround time 10 days. Copy fee: $.25 per page. Certification fee: $5.00 plus $2.00 per page after first. Fee payee: Juneau Trial Court. Personal checks accepted. Prepayment is required. Public access terminal is available.

Kenai Peninsula Borough

Superior & District Court (3rd District)

125 Trading Bay Dr, Ste 100, Kenai, AK 99611; 907-283-3110; Fax: 907-283-8535. Hours: 8AM-4:30PM (AK). *Felony, Misdemeanor, Civil, Eviction, Small Claims, Probate.*

Civil Records: Access: Mail, in person. Both court and visitors may perform in person searches. Search fee: $15.00 per hour. Required to search: name, years to search. Civil cases indexed by defendant, plaintiff. Civil records on computer from 1983, on microfiche, archived and on index from 1959. **Criminal Records:** Access: Mail, in person. Both court and visitors may perform in person searches. Search fee: $15.00 per hour. Required to search: name, years to search, DOB. Criminal records on computer from 1983, on microfiche, archived and on index from 1959. **General Information:** No adoption, guardianship, children's, conservatorship or coroner records released. SASE required. Turnaround time 1 week. Copy fee: $.25 per page. Certification fee: $5.00 plus $2.00 per page after first. Fee payee: Clerk of Court. Personal checks accepted. Prepayment is required. Public access terminal is available.

District Court (3rd District)

3670 Lake St, Ste 400, Homer, AK 99603-9647; 907-235-8171; Fax: 907-235-4257. Hours: 8AM-4:30PM (AK). *Misdemeanor, Civil Actions Under $50,000, Small Claims.*

Civil Records: Access: Phone, mail, in person. Both court and visitors may perform in person searches. Search fee: $15.00 per hour. Required to search: name, years to search. Civil cases indexed by defendant, plaintiff. Civil records on computer from 1984. Phone access limited to name searches. **Criminal Records:** Access: Phone, mail, in person. Only the court conducts in person searches; visitors may not. Search fee: $15.00 per hour. Required to search: name, years to search. Criminal records on computer from 1984. **General Information:** No confidential or sealed records released. SASE required. Turnaround time 5 days. Copy fee: $.25 per page. Certification fee: $5.00. Fee payee: Alaska Court System. Personal checks accepted. Prepayment is required.

Seward Magistrate Court (3rd District)

PO Box 1929, Seward, AK 99664-1929; 907-224-3075; Fax: 907-227-7192. Hours: 8AM-4:30PM (AK). *Misdemeanor, Civil Actions Under $5,000, Small Claims.*

Civil Records: Both court and visitors may perform in person searches. Search fee:. **Criminal Records:** Both court and visitors may perform in person searches. Search fee: $15.00 per hour. Required to search: name, years to search, DOB. **General Information:** Turnaround time 1-2 weeks. Fee payee: State of Alaska. Prepayment is required.

Ketchikan Gateway Borough

Superior & District Court (1st District)

415 Main, Rm 400, Ketchikan, AK 99901-6399; 907-225-3195; Fax: 907-225-7849. Hours: 8AM-4:30PM (AK). *Felony, Misdemeanor, Civil, Eviction, Small Claims, Probate.*

Civil Records: Access: Fax, mail, in person. Both court and visitors may perform in person searches. Search fee: $15.00 per hour. Required to search: name, years to search. Civil cases indexed by defendant, plaintiff. Civil records on computer from 1983, on microfiche from 1972 to 1989, index from 1972. **Criminal Records:** Access: Fax, mail, in person. Both court and visitors may perform in person searches. Search fee: $15.00 per hour. Required to search: name, years to search, DOB. Criminal records on computer from 1983, on microfiche from 1972 to 1989, index from 1972. **General Information:** No confidential probate or childrens records released. SASE required. Turnaround time 2 weeks. Copy fee: $.25 per page. Certification fee: $5.00. Fee payee: Alaska Court System. Personal checks accepted. Prepayment is required. Public access terminal is available. Fax notes: No fee to fax results.

Kodiak Island Borough

Superior & District Court (3rd District)

204 Mission Road, Rm 10, Kodiak, AK 99615-7312; 907-486-1600; Fax: 907-486-1660. Hours: 8AM-4:30PM M,T,Th,F; 9AM-4:30PM W (AK). *Felony, Misdemeanor, Civil, Eviction, Small Claims, Probate.*

Civil Records: Access: Mail, in person. Both court and visitors may perform in person searches. Search fee: $15.00 per hour. Required to search: name, years to search; also helpful-address. Civil cases indexed by defendant, plaintiff. Civil records on computer from 1982, on microfiche, index and archived from 1959. **Criminal Records:** Access: Mail, in person. Both court and visitors may perform in person searches. Search fee: $15.00 per hour. Required to search: name, years to search; also helpful-address, DOB, SSN. Criminal records on computer from 1982, on microfiche, index and archived from 1959. **General Information:** No adoption, juvenile, guardianship or mental records released. SASE required. Turnaround time 1-3 weeks. Copy fee: $.25 per page. Certification fee: $5.00 plus $2.00 per add'l copy. Fee payee: Clerk of Court. Personal checks accepted. Prepayment is required. Public access terminal is available.

Matanuska-Susitna Borough

Superior & District Court (3rd District)

435 S Denali, Palmer, AK 99645-6437; 907-746-8109; Fax: 907-746-4151. Hours: 8AM-4:30PM (AK). *Felony, Misdemeanor, Civil, Eviction, Small Claims, Probate.*

Civil Records: Access: Mail, in person. Both court and visitors may perform in person searches. Search fee: $15.00 per hour. Required to search:

name, years to search; also helpful-address. Civil cases indexed by defendant, plaintiff. Civil records on computer from 1988, on microfiche, archived and index from 1974. **Criminal Records:** Access: Mail, in person. Both court and visitors may perform in person searches. Search fee: $15.00 per hour. Required to search: name, years to search; also helpful-address, DOB, SSN. Criminal records on computer from 1988, on microfiche, archived and index from 1974. **General Information:** No adoption, juvenile, guardianship or mental records released. SASE required. Turnaround time 1-3 weeks. Copy fee: $.25 per page. Certification fee: $5.00. Add $2.00 per document if from same case. Fee payee: State of Alaska. Personal checks accepted. Prepayment is required. Public access terminal is available.

Nome

Superior & District Court (2nd District)

PO Box 1110, Nome, AK 99762-1110; 907-443-5216; Fax: 907-443-2192. Hours: 8AM-4:30PM (AK). *Felony, Misdemeanor, Civil, Eviction, Small Claims, Probate.*

Civil Records: Access: Fax, mail, in person. Both court and visitors may perform in person searches. Search fee: $15.00 per hour. Required to search: name, years to search; also helpful-address. Civil cases indexed by defendant, plaintiff. Civil records on computer from 1983, on microfiche from 1960 to 1983, on index and archived from 1960. **Criminal Records:** Access: Fax, mail, in person. Both court and visitors may perform in person searches. Search fee: $15.00 per hour. Required to search: name, years to search; also helpful-address, DOB, SSN. Criminal records on computer from 1983, on microfiche from 1960 to 1983, on index and archived from 1960. **General Information:** No adoption, juvenile, guardianship or mental records released. SASE required. Turnaround time 5 days. Copy fee: $.25 per page. Certification fee: $5.00 plus $2.00 per copy after first. Fee payee: Nome Trial Courts. Personal checks accepted. Prepayment is required. Fax notes: Fax fee will be billed.

Gambell Magistrate Court (2nd District)

PO Box 1110, Nome, AK 99702-1110; 907-443-5216. *Misdemeanor, Civil Actions Under $5,000, Small Claims.*

Note: Court is vacant; records at Superior Court in Nome at address and phone here.

Unalakleet Magistrate Court (2nd District)

PO Box 250, Unalakleet, AK 99684-0250; 907-624-3015; Fax: 907-624-3118. Hours: 8AM-1:30PM (AK). *Misdemeanor, Civil Actions Under $5,000, Small Claims.*

Civil Records: Search fee:. **Criminal Records:** Only the court conducts in person searches; visitors may not. Search fee: $15.00 per hour. Required to search: name, years to search. **General Information:** Turnaround time 1-2 weeks. Fee payee: Magistrate Court. Prepayment is required.

North Slope Borough

Superior & District Court (2nd District)

PO Box 270, Barrow, AK 99723-0270; 907-852-4800 X80; Fax: 907-852-4804. Hours: 8AM-4:30PM (AK). *Felony, Misdemeanor, Civil, Eviction, Small Claims, Probate.*

Civil Records: Access: Fax, mail, in person. Only the court conducts in person searches; visitors may not. Search fee: $15.00 per hour. Required to search: name, years to search; also helpful-address. Civil cases indexed by defendant, plaintiff. Civil

records on computer from 1983, prior on microfiche. **Criminal Records:** Access: Fax, mail, in person. Only the court conducts in person searches; visitors may not. Search fee: $15.00 per hour. Required to search: name, years to search; also helpful-address, DOB, SSN. Criminal records on computer from 1983, prior on microfiche. **General Information:** No confidential records released. SASE required. Turnaround time 1-2 weeks. Copy fee: $.25 per page. Certification fee: $5.00 plus $2.00 per page after first. Fee payee: Alaska Court System. Personal checks accepted. Prepayment is required. Fax notes: No fee to fax results.

Northwest Arctic Borough

Superior & District Court (2nd District)

PO Box 317, Kotzebue, AK 99752-0317; 907-442-3208; Fax: 907-442-3974. Hours: 8AM-4:30PM (AK). *Felony, Misdemeanor, Civil, Eviction, Small Claims, Probate.*

Civil Records: Access: Fax, mail, in person. Both court and visitors may perform in person searches. Search fee: $15.00. Required to search: name, years to search. Civil cases indexed by defendant. Civil records on computer from 1983, prior records on microfilm, archived and index from 1966. Copy of check required for fax access. **Criminal Records:** Access: Mail, in person. Both court and visitors may perform in person searches. Search fee: $15.00. Required to search: name, years to search, DOB; also helpful-SSN. Criminal records on computer from 1983, prior records on microfilm, archived and index from 1966. **General Information:** No adoption, juvenile, guardianship or mental records released. Turnaround time 2-3 days. Copy fee: $1.00 for first page, $.25 each addl. Certification fee: $5.00 plus $2.00 per page after first. Certified Judgment $3.00 notary fee. Fee payee: Alaska Court System. Personal checks accepted. Prepayment is required.

Ambler Magistrate Court (2nd District)

PO Box 86028, Ambler, AK 99786; 907-445-2137; Fax: 907-445-2136. Hours: 9AM-2PM (AK). *Misdemeanor, Civil Actions Under $5,000, Small Claims.*

Civil Records: Only the court conducts in person searches; visitors may not. Search fee:. **Criminal Records:** Only the court conducts in person searches; visitors may not. Search fee: $15.00 per hour. Required to search: name, years to search. **General Information:** Turnaround time 1-2 weeks. Fee payee: Magistrate Court. Prepayment is required.

Kiana Magistrate Court (2nd District)

PO Box 317, Kotzebue, AK 99749-0170; 907-442-3208. Hours: 10AM-3PM M,W,F (AK). *Misdemeanor, Civil Actions Under $5,000, Small Claims.*

Note: Court is temporarily vacant; contact Kotzebue Court for records at address and phone here.

Prince of Wales-Outer Ketchikan

Craig Magistrate Court (1st District)

PO Box 646, Craig, AK 99921-0646; 907-826-3316/3306; Fax: 907-826-3904. Hours: 8AM-4:30PM (AK). *Misdemeanor, Civil Actions Under $5,000, Small Claims.*

Civil Records: Search fee:. **Criminal Records:** Only the court conducts in person searches; visitors may not. Search fee: $15.00 per hour. Required to search: name, years to search; also helpful-DOB. **General Information:** Turnaround time 2 weeks. Fee payee: Alaska Court System. Prepayment is required.

Sitka Borough

Superior & District Court (1st District)

304 Lake St, Rm 203, Sitka, AK 99835-7759; 907-747-3291; Fax: 907-747-6690. Hours: 8AM-4:30PM (AK). *Felony, Misdemeanor, Civil, Eviction, Small Claims, Probate.*

Civil Records: Access: Phone, fax, mail, in person. Both court and visitors may perform in person searches. Search fee: $15.00 per hour. Required to search: name. Civil cases indexed by defendant, plaintiff. Civil records on computer from 1983, on microfilm and archived from 1970 to 1987, on index from 1960. **Criminal Records:** Access: Phone, fax, mail, in person. Both court and visitors may perform in person searches. Search fee: $15.00 per hour. Required to search: name. Criminal records on computer from 1983, on microfilm and archived from 1970 to 1987, on index from 1960. **General Information:** No adoption, juvenile, guardianship or mental records released. SASE required. Turnaround time 1 week. Copy fee: $.25 per page. Certification fee: $5.00. Fee payee: Alaska Court System. Personal checks accepted. Prepayment is required. Public access terminal is available. Fax notes: No fee to fax results. Will fax collect.

Skagway-Yakutat-Angoon

District Court (1st District)

PO Box 430, Hoonah, AK 99829-0430; 907-945-3668; Fax: 907-945-3637. Hours: 8AM-Noon, 1-4:30PM (AK). *Misdemeanor, Civil Actions Under $50,000, Small Claims.*

www.alaska.net/~akctlib/homepage.htm

Note: This district encompases all of Southeast Alaska and includes 13 courts. Magistrates act as judicial officers. The 5 trial courts are in Ketchikan, Wrangell, Petersburg, Sitka and Juneau.

Civil Records: Access: Mail, in person. Only the court conducts in person searches; visitors may not. No search fee. Required to search: name, years to search. Civil cases indexed by defendant, plaintiff. Civil records on index from 1971 to present. **Criminal Records:** Access: Mail, in person. Only the court conducts in person searches; visitors may not. No search fee. Required to search: name, years to search; also helpful-DOB. Criminal records on index from 1971 to present. **General Information:** No confidential, juvenile or sex related records released. SASE not required. Turnaround time 2-3 days. Copy fee: $.25 per page. Certification fee: $5.00 plus $2.00 per page after first. Fee payee: Alaska Court System. Personal checks accepted. Prepayment is required.

Angoon Magistrate Court (1st District)

PO Box 250, Angoon, AK 99820-0123; 907-788-3229; Fax: 907-788-3108. Hours: 11AM-2PM (AK). *Misdemeanor, Civil Actions Under $5,000, Small Claims.*

Civil Records: Search fee:. **Criminal Records:** Only the court conducts in person searches; visitors may not. Search fee: $15.00 per hour. Required to search: name, years to search. **General Information:** Turnaround time 1-2 weeks. Fee payee: Alaska Court System. Prepayment is required.

Pelican Magistrate Court (1st District)

304 Lake St #203, Sitka, AK 99835; 907-747-

6271. *Misdemeanor, Civil Actions Under $5,000, Small Claims.*

Note: This court closed permanently on 12/31/99. All records are at the Sitka court, address & phone given here.

Civil Records: Only the court conducts in person searches; visitors may not. Search fee:. **Criminal Records:** Only the court conducts in person searches; visitors may not. Search fee: $15.00 per hour. Required to search: name, years to search, DOB. **General Information:** Turnaround time 3 days. Fee payee: Magistrate Court. Prepayment is required.

Skagway Magistrate Court (1st District)

PO Box 495, Skagway, AK 99840-0495; 907-983-2368; Fax: 907-983-3800. Hours: 9AM-Noon, 1-4:30PM M; 8AM-Noon, 1-4:30PM T-F (AK). *Misdemeanor, Civil Actions Under $7,500, Small Claims.*

Note: Hours will vary from summer to winter

Civil Records: Search fee:. **Criminal Records:** Only the court conducts in person searches; visitors may not. Search fee: $15.00 per hour. Required to search: name, years to search. **General Information:** Turnaround time 1-2 weeks. Fee payee: Magistrate Court. Prepayment is required.

Yakutat Magistrate Court (1st District)

PO Box 426, Yakutat, AK 99689-0426; 907-784-3274; Fax: 907-784-3257. Hours: 9AM-3:30PM (AK). *Misdemeanor, Civil Actions Under $7,500, Small Claims.*

Civil Records: Only the court conducts in person searches; visitors may not. Search fee:. **Criminal Records:** Only the court conducts in person searches; visitors may not. Search fee: $15.00 per hour. Required to search: name, years to search. **General Information:**. Fee payee: Magistrate Court. Prepayment is required.

Southeast Fairbanks

Delta Junction Magistrate Court (4th District)

PO Box 401, Delta Junction, AK 99737-0401; 907-895-4211; Fax: 907-895-4204. Hours: 8AM-Noon, 1-4:30PM (AK). *Misdemeanor, Civil Actions Under $7,500, Small Claims.*

Civil Records: Only the court conducts in person searches; visitors may not. Search fee:. **Criminal Records:** Only the court conducts in person searches; visitors may not. Search fee: $15.00 per hour. Required to search: name, years to search. **General Information:** Turnaround time 1 week. Fee payee: District Court. Prepayment is required.

Tok Magistrate Court (4th District)

PO Box 187, Tok, AK 99780-0187; 907-883-5171; Fax: 907-883-4367. Hours: 8AM-4:30PM (AK). *Misdemeanor, Civil Actions Under $7,500, Small Claims.*

Civil Records: Only the court conducts in person searches; visitors may not. Search fee:. **Criminal Records:** Only the court conducts in person searches; visitors may not. No search fee. Required to search: name, years to search, DOB. **General Information:** Turnaround time 5 days. Fee payee: State of Alaska. Prepayment is required.

Valdez-Cordova

Superior & District Court (3rd District)

PO Box 127, Valdez, AK 99686-0127; 907-835-2266; Fax: 907-835-3764. Hours: 8AM-4:30PM

(AK). *Felony, Misdemeanor, Civil, Eviction, Small Claims, Probate.*

Civil Records: Access: Fax, mail, in person. Both court and visitors may perform in person searches. Search fee: $15.00 per hour. Required to search: name, years to search; also helpful-address. Civil cases indexed by defendant, plaintiff. Civil records on computer from 1984, on microfiche, archived and index from 1960. **Criminal Records:** Access: Fax, mail, in person. Both court and visitors may perform in person searches. Search fee: $15.00 per hour. Required to search: name, years to search; also helpful-address, DOB, SSN. Criminal records on computer from 1984, on microfiche, archived and index from 1960. **General Information:** No adoption, juvenile, guardianship or mental records released. SASE required. Turnaround time 1-3 weeks. Copy fee: $.25 per page. Certification fee: $5.00. Fee payee: Valdez Trial Court of Alaska. Personal checks accepted. Prepayment is required.

Cordova Court (3rd District)

PO Box 898, Cordova, AK 99574-0898; 907-424-3378; Fax: 907-424-7581. Hours: 8AM-4:30PM (AK). *Felony, Misdemeanor, Civil, Small Claims, Probate.*

Civil Records: Both court and visitors may perform in person searches. Search fee:. Access by phone if time allows. **Criminal Records:** Both court and visitors may perform in person searches. Search fee: $15.00 per hour. Required to search: name, years to search, DOB; also helpful-SSN. Will take phone requests if time allows. **General Information:** Turnaround time 1 week. Fee payee: State of Alaska. Prepayment is required.

Glennallen District Court (3rd District)

PO Box 86, Glennallen, AK 99588-0086; 907-822-3405; Fax: 907-822-3601. Hours: 8AM-4:30PM (AK). *Misdemeanor, Civil Actions Under $10,000, Small Claims.*

Civil Records: Both court and visitors may perform in person searches. Search fee:. **Criminal Records:** Both court and visitors may perform in person searches. Search fee: $15.00 per hour. Required to search: name, years to search; also helpful-DOB. **General Information:** Turnaround time 1-2 weeks. Fee payee: Alaska Court System. Prepayment is required.

Whittier Magistrate Court (3rd District)

c/o Karla Utter, 825 W 4th Ave, Anchorage, AK 99500-2004; 907-264-0456. *Misdemeanor, Civil Actions Under $5,000, Small Claims.*

Note: Court closed; records available at the address and phone here.

Wade Hampton

Chevak Magistrate Court (Bethel Area)

PO Box 238, Chevak, AK 99563-0238; 907-858-7231; Fax: 907-858-7232. Hours: 9AM-3:30PM (AK). *Misdemeanor, Civil Actions Under $5,000, Small Claims.*

Civil Records: Only the court conducts in person searches; visitors may not. Search fee:. **Criminal Records:** Both court and visitors may perform in person searches. Search fee: $15.00 per hour. Required to search: name, years to search, address, DOB, SSN, signed release. **General Information:** Turnaround time 1-2 weeks. Fee payee: Magistrate Court. Prepayment is required.

Emmonak Magistrate Court (Bethel Area)

PO Box 176, Emmonak, AK 99581-0176; 907-949-1748; Fax: 907-949-1535. Hours: 8AM-4:30PM (AK). *Misdemeanor, Civil Actions Under $5,000, Small Claims.*

Civil Records: Only the court conducts in person searches; visitors may not. Search fee:. **Criminal Records:** Only the court conducts in person searches; visitors may not. Search fee: $15.00 per hour. Required to search: name, years to search, address, DOB, signed release; also helpful-SSN. **General Information:** Turnaround time 1-2 weeks. Fee payee: Magistrate Court. Prepayment is required.

St Mary's Magistrate Court (Bethel Area) PO Box 183, St Mary's, AK 99658-0183; 907-438-2912; Fax: 907-438-2819. Hours: 8AM-4:30PM (AK). *Misdemeanor, Civil Actions Under $7,500, Small Claims.*

Civil Records: Only the court conducts in person searches; visitors may not. Search fee:. **Criminal Records:** Only the court conducts in person searches; visitors may not. No search fee. Required to search: name, years to search; also helpful-DOB. **General Information:** Turnaround time 3 weeks. Fee payee: St Mary's District Court. Prepayment is required.

Wrangell-Petersburg

Petersburg Superior & District Court (1st District) PO Box 1009, Petersburg, AK 99833-1009; 907-772-3824; Fax: 907-772-3018. Hours: 8AM-4:30PM (AK). *Felony, Misdemeanor, Civil, Eviction, Small Claims, Probate.*

Civil Records: Access: Phone, fax, mail, in person. Both court and visitors may perform in person searches. No search fee. Required to search: name, years to search; also helpful-address. Civil cases indexed by defendant, plaintiff. Civil records on computer from 1988, on microfiche and index from 1960s, archived from 1920s. **Criminal Records:** Access: Phone, fax, mail, in person. Both court and visitors may perform in person searches. No search fee. Required to search: name, years to search; also helpful-address, DOB, SSN. Criminal records on computer from 1988, on microfiche and index from 1960s, archived from 1920s. **General Information:** No adoption, juvenile, guardianship or mental records released. SASE required. Turnaround time 1 week. Copy fee: $.25 per page. Certification fee: $5.00. Fee payee: Alaska Court System. Personal checks accepted. Prepayment is required. Fax notes: Outgoing fax limited to 10 pages; call for fee.

Wrangell Superior & District Court (1st District) PO Box 869, Wrangell, AK

99929-0869; 907-874-2311; Fax: 907-874-3509. Hours: 8AM-4:30PM (AK). *Felony, Misdemeanor, Civil, Eviction, Small Claims, Probate.*

Civil Records: Access: Phone, fax, mail, in person. Only the court conducts in person searches; visitors may not. Search fee: $15.00 per hour. Search fee is rarely charged. Required to search: name, years to search. Civil cases indexed by defendant, plaintiff. Civil records on computer from 1988, on microfiche and card files from 1959, archived from 1900s. **Criminal Records:** Access: Phone, fax, mail, in person. Only the court conducts in person searches; visitors may not. Search fee: $15.00 per hour. Required to search: name, years to search, DOB. Criminal records on computer from 1988, on microfiche and card files from 1959, archived from 1900s. **General Information:** No adoption, juvenile, guardianship or mental records released. SASE required. Turnaround time 3 days. Copy fee: $.25 per page. Certification fee: $5.00 plus $2.00 per copy after first. Fee payee: Alaska Court System or State of Alaska. Personal checks accepted. Prepayment is required. Fax notes: $.25 per page.

Kake Magistrate Court (1st District) PO Box 100, Kake, AK 99830-0100; 907-785-3651; Fax: 907-785-3152. Hours: 8AM-Noon (AK). *Misdemeanor, Civil Actions Under $7,500, Small Claims.*

Civil Records: Only the court conducts in person searches; visitors may not. Search fee:. **Criminal Records:** Only the court conducts in person searches; visitors may not. Search fee: $15.00 per hour. Required to search: name, years to search, DOB, SSN, signed release. **General Information:** Turnaround time 1-2 weeks. Fee payee: Alaska Court System. Prepayment is required.

Yukon-Koyukuk

Fort Yukon Magistrate Court (4th District) PO Box 211, Fort Yukon, AK 99740-0211; 907-662-2336; Fax: 907-662-2824. Hours: 9:30AM-3PM (AK). *Misdemeanor, Civil Actions Under $5,000, Small Claims.*

Civil Records: Only the court conducts in person searches; visitors may not. Search fee:. **Criminal Records:** Only the court conducts in person searches; visitors may not. Search fee: $15.00 per hour. Required to search: name, years to search. **General Information:** Turnaround time 1-2 weeks. Fee payee: District Court. Prepayment is required.

Galena Magistrate Court (4th District) PO Box 167, Galena, AK 99741-0167; 907-656-1322; Fax: 907-656-1546. Hours: 8AM-4:30PM (AK). *Misdemeanor, Civil Actions Under $5,000, Small Claims.*

Civil Records: Only the court conducts in person searches; visitors may not. Search fee:. **Criminal Records:** Only the court conducts in person searches; visitors may not. Search fee: $15.00 per hour. Required to search: name, years to search. **General Information:** Turnaround time 1-2 weeks. Fee payee: Magistrate Court. Prepayment is required.

McGrath Magistrate Court (4th District) PO Box 167, Galena, AK 99741-0167; 907-656-1322; Fax: 907-656-1546. Hours: 8:30AM-4:30PM (AK). *Misdemeanor, Civil Actions Under $5,000, Small Claims.*

Note: McGrath Court is vacant. Court records at Galena Magistrate Court, address and phone here.

Nenana Magistrate Court (4th District) PO Box 449, Nenana, AK 99760-0449; 907-832-5430; Fax: 907-832-5841. Hours: 8:30AM-4PM (AK). *Misdemeanor, Civil Actions Under $5,000, Small Claims.*

Civil Records: Only the court conducts in person searches; visitors may not. Search fee:. **Criminal Records:** Only the court conducts in person searches; visitors may not. No search fee. Required to search: name, years to search. **General Information:** Turnaround time 2 weeks. Fee payee: Alaska Court System. Prepayment is required.

Tanana Magistrate Court (4th District) PO Box 449, Nenana, AK 99777; 907-366-7243; Fax: 907-832-5841. Hours: Th-F 2nd full week each month (AK). *Misdemeanor, Civil Actions Under $5,000, Small Claims.*

Note: Magistrate may also be contacted by phone at 907-832-5430.

Civil Records: Only the court conducts in person searches; visitors may not. Search fee:. **Criminal Records:** Only the court conducts in person searches; visitors may not. Search fee: $15.00 per hour. Required to search: name, years to search, DOB, signed release. **General Information:** Turnaround time 1-2 weeks. Fee payee: Magistrate Court. Prepayment is required.

ORGANIZATION   23 boroughs, 34 recording offices. Recording is done by districts, which overlay the borough system. The recording officer is District Recorder. The entire state except the Aleutian Islands is in the Alaska Time Zone (AK).

REAL ESTATE RECORDS   Districts do **not** perform real estate searches. Certification fees are usually $5.00 per document. Copies usually cost $1.25 for the first page, $.25 per Add'l page.

UCC RECORDS   Financing statements are filed at the state level, except for consumer goods, farm collateral and real estate related collateral, which are filed with the District Recorder. All districts will perform UCC searches at $5.00 per debtor name for information and $15.00 with copies. Use search request form UCC-11. Copies ordered separately usually cost $2.00 per financing statement.

TAX LIEN RECORDS   All state and federal tax liens are filed with the District Recorder. Districts do **not** perform separate tax lien searches.

Aleutian Islands District
District Recorder, 3601 C Street, Suite 1140, Anchorage, AK 99503-5947. 907-269-8899.

Anchorage District
District Recorder, 3601 C Street, Suite 1140, Anchorage, AK 99503-5947. 907-269-8899.

Barrow District
District Recorder, 1648 S. Cushman St. #201, Fairbanks, AK 99701-6206. 907-452-3521.

Bethel District
District Recorder, P.O. Box 426, Bethel, AK 99559. 907-543-3391.

Bristol Bay District
District Recorder, 3601 C Street, Suite 1140, Anchorage, AK 99503-5947. 907-269-8899.

Cape Nome District
District Recorder, Box 431, Nome, AK 99762. 907-443-5178.

Chitina District
District Recorder, Box 86, Glennallen, AK 99588. 907-822-3726.

Cordova District
District Recorder, 3601 C Street, Suite 1140, Anchorage, AK 99503-5947. 907-269-8899.

Fairbanks District
District Recorder, 1648 S. Cushman St. #201, Fairbanks, AK 99701-6206. 907-452-3521.
www.co.fairbanks.ak.us
Online Access: Real Estate. Access to the City of Fairbanks Property database is available for free on the Internet at www.co.fairbanks.ak.us/database/aurora/default.asp.

Fairbanks North Star Borough
In Alaska, the proper place for real estate recording is based on Recording Districts, not Boroughs.

Fort Gibbon District
District Recorder, 1648 S. Cushman St. #201, Fairbanks, AK 99701-6206. 907-452-3521.

Haines District
District Recorder, 400 Willoughby, 3rd Floor, Juneau, AK 99801. 907-465-3449.

Homer District
District Recorder, 195 E. Bunnell Ave., Suite A, Homer, AK 99603. 907-235-8136.

Iliamna District
District Recorder, 3601 C Street, Suite 1140, Anchorage, AK 99503-5947. 907-269-8899.

Juneau District
District Recorder, 400 Willoughby, 3rd Floor, Juneau, AK 99801. 907-465-3449.
http://record.org/juneau_tax/search_tax_form.html

Online Access: Real Estate. Access to City of Juneau Property Records database is available free on the Internet. Also includes link access to Juneau rentals data and the Records home page.

Kenai District
District Recorder, 120 Trading Bay Road, Suite 230, Kenai, AK 99611. 907-283-3118.

Ketchikan District
District Recorder, 415 Main Street, Room 320, Ketchikan, AK 99901. 907-225-3142.

Kobuk Borough
In Alaska, the proper place for real estate recording is based on Recording Districts, not Boroughs.

Kodiak District
District Recorder, 204 Mission Road, Room 16, Kodiak, AK 99615. 907-486-9432.

Kotzebue District
District Recorder, 1648 S. Cushman St. #201, Fairbanks, AK 99701-6206. 907-452-3521.

Kuskokwim District
District Recorder, P.O. Box 426, Bethel, AK 99559. 907-543-3391.

Kvichak District
District Recorder, 3601 C Street, Suite 1140, Anchorage, AK 99503-5947. 907-269-8899.

Manley Hot Springs District
District Recorder, 1648 S. Cushman St. #201, Fairbanks, AK 99701-6206. 907-452-3521.

Matanuska-Susitna Borough
In Alaska, the proper place for real estate recording is based on Recording Districts, not Boroughs.

Mount McKinley District
District Recorder, 1648 S. Cushman St. #201, Fairbanks, AK 99701-6206. 907-452-3521.

Nenana District
District Recorder, 1648 S. Cushman St. #201, Fairbanks, AK 99701-6206. 907-452-3521.

Nome Borough
In Alaska, the proper place for real estate recording is based on Recording Districts, not Boroughs.

Northwest Arctic-North Slope Borough
In Alaska, the proper place for real estate recording is based on Recording Districts, not Boroughs.

Nulato District
District Recorder, 1648 S. Cushman St. #201, Fairbanks, AK 99701-6206. 907-452-3521.

Palmer District
District Recorder, 836 South Colony Way, Palmer, AK 99645. 907-745-3080.

Petersburg District
District Recorder, 415 Main Street, Room 320, Ketchikan, AK 99901. 907-225-3142.

Prince of Wales-Outer Ketchikan Borough
In Alaska, the proper place for real estate recording is based on Recording Districts, not Boroughs.

Rampart District
District Recorder, 1648 S. Cushman St. #201, Fairbanks, AK 99701-6206. 907-452-3521.

Seldovia District
District Recorder, 195 E. Bunnell Ave., Suite A, Homer, AK 99603. 907-235-8136.

Seward District
District Recorder, Box 1929, Seward, AK 99664. 907-224-3075.

Sitka District
District Recorder, 210C Lake Street, Sitka, AK 99835. 907-747-3275.

Skagway District
District Recorder, 400 Willoughby, 3rd Floor, Juneau, AK 99801. 907-269-8899.

Skagway-Yakutat-Angoon Borough
In Alaska, the proper place for real estate recording is based on Recording Districts, not Boroughs.

Southeast Fairbanks Borough
In Alaska, the proper place for real estate recording is based on Recording Districts, not Boroughs.

Talkeetna District
District Recorder, 836 South Colony Way, Palmer, AK 99645. 907-745-3080.

Valdez District
District Recorder, Box 127, Valdez, AK 99686. 907-835-2266.

Valdez-Cordova Borough
In Alaska, the proper place for real estate recording is based on Recording Districts, not Boroughs.

Wade Hampton Borough
In Alaska, the proper place for real estate recording is based on Recording Districts, not Boroughs.

Wrangell District
District Recorder, 415 Main Street, Room 320, Ketchikan, AK 99901. 907-225-3142.

You will usually be able to find the city name in the City/County Cross Reference below. In that case, it is a simple matter to determine the county from the cross reference. However, only the official US Postal Service city names are included in this index. There are an additional 40,000 place names that people use in their addresses. Therefore, we have also included a ZIP/City Cross Reference immediately following the City/County Cross Reference.

If you know the ZIP Code but the city name does not appear in the City/County Cross Reference index, look up the ZIP Code in the ZIP/City Cross Reference, find the city name, then look up the city name in the City/County Cross Reference. For example, you want to know the county for an address of Menands, NY 12204. There is no "Menands" in the City/County Cross Reference. The ZIP/City Cross Reference shows that ZIP Codes 12201-12288 are for the city of Albany. Looking back in the City/County Cross Reference, Albany is in Albany County.

City/County Cross Reference

AKIACHAK Bethel
AKIAK Bethel
AKUTAN Aleutian Islands, East
ALAKANUK Wade Hampton
ALEKNAGIK Dillingham
ALLAKAKET Yukon-Koyukuk
AMBLER Northwest Arctic
ANAKTUVUK PASS North Slope Borough
ANCHOR POINT Kenai Peninsula Borough
ANCHORAGE Anchorage Borough
ANDERSON Denali
ANGOON Skagway-Yakutat-Angoon
ANIAK Bethel
ANVIK Yukon-Koyukuk
ARCTIC VILLAGE Yukon-Koyukuk
ATKA Aleutian Islands, West
ATQASUK North Slope Borough
AUKE BAY Juneau Borough
BARROW North Slope Borough
BEAVER Yukon-Koyukuk
BETHEL Bethel
BETTLES FIELD Yukon-Koyukuk
BIG LAKE Matanuska-Susitna Borough
BREVIG MISSION Nome
BUCKLAND Northwest Arctic
CANTWELL Denali
CENTRAL Yukon-Koyukuk
CHALKYITSIK Yukon-Koyukuk
CHEFORNAK Bethel
CHEVAK Wade Hampton
CHICKEN Southeast Fairbanks
CHIGNIK Lake & Peninsula
CHIGNIK LAGOON Lake & Peninsula
CHIGNIK LAKE Lake & Peninsula
CHITINA Valdez-Cordova
CHUGIAK Anchorage Borough
CIRCLE Yukon-Koyukuk
CLAM GULCH Kenai Peninsula Borough
CLARKS POINT Dillingham
CLEAR Denali
COFFMAN COVE Prince of Wales-Outer
   Ketchikan
COLD BAY Aleutian Islands, East
COOPER LANDING Kenai Peninsula
   Borough
COPPER CENTER Valdez-Cordova
CORDOVA Valdez-Cordova
CRAIG Prince of Wales-Outer Ketchikan
CROOKED CREEK Bethel
DEERING Northwest Arctic
DELTA JUNCTION Southeast Fairbanks
DENALI NATIONAL PARK Denali
DILLINGHAM Dillingham
DOUGLAS Juneau Borough
DUTCH HARBOR Aleutian Islands, West
EAGLE Southeast Fairbanks
EAGLE RIVER Anchorage Borough
EEK Bethel
EGEGIK Lake & Peninsula
EIELSON AFB Fairbanks North Star
   Borough
EKWOK Dillingham

ELFIN COVE Skagway-Yakutat-Angoon
ELIM Nome
ELMENDORF AFB Anchorage Borough
EMMONAK Wade Hampton
ESTER Fairbanks North Star Borough
FAIRBANKS Fairbanks North Star Borough
FALSE PASS Aleutian Islands, East
FLAT Yukon-Koyukuk
FORT RICHARDSON Anchorage Borough
FORT WAINWRIGHT Fairbanks North Star
   Borough
FORT YUKON Yukon-Koyukuk
GAKONA Valdez-Cordova
GALENA Yukon-Koyukuk
GAMBELL Nome
GIRDWOOD Anchorage Borough
GLENNALLEN Valdez-Cordova
GOODNEWS BAY Bethel
GRAYLING Yukon-Koyukuk
GUSTAVUS Skagway-Yakutat-Angoon
HAINES (99827) Haines. Borough(98),
   Yakutat(2)
HEALY Denali
HOLY CROSS Yukon-Koyukuk
HOMER Kenai Peninsula Borough
HOONAH Skagway-Yakutat-Angoon
HOOPER BAY Wade Hampton
HOPE Kenai Peninsula Borough
HOUSTON Matanuska-Susitna Borough
HUGHES Yukon-Koyukuk
HUSLIA Yukon-Koyukuk
HYDABURG Prince of Wales-Outer
   Ketchikan
HYDER Prince of Wales-Outer Ketchikan
ILIAMNA Lake & Peninsula
INDIAN Anchorage Borough
JUNEAU Juneau Borough
KAKE Wrangell-Petersburg
KAKTOVIK North Slope Borough
KALSKAG Bethel
KALTAG Yukon-Koyukuk
KARLUK Kodiak Island Borough
KASIGLUK Bethel
KASILOF Kenai Peninsula Borough
KENAI Kenai Peninsula Borough
KETCHIKAN Ketchikan Gateway Borough
KIANA Northwest Arctic
KING COVE Aleutian Islands, East
KING SALMON Bristol Bay Borough
KIPNUK Bethel
KIVALINA Northwest Arctic
KLAWOCK Prince of Wales-Outer
   Ketchikan
KOBUK Northwest Arctic
KODIAK Kodiak Island Borough
KOTLIK Wade Hampton
KOTZEBUE Northwest Arctic
KOYUK Nome
KOYUKUK Yukon-Koyukuk
KWETHLUK Bethel
KWIGILLINGOK Bethel
LAKE MINCHUMINA Yukon-Koyukuk

LARSEN BAY Kodiak Island Borough
LEVELOCK Lake & Peninsula
LOWER KALSKAG Bethel
MANLEY HOT SPRINGS Yukon-Koyukuk
MANOKOTAK Dillingham
MARSHALL Wade Hampton
MC GRATH Yukon-Koyukuk
MEKORYUK Bethel
METLAKATLA Prince of Wales-Outer
   Ketchikan
MEYERS CHUCK Prince of Wales-Outer
   Ketchikan
MINTO Yukon-Koyukuk
MOOSE PASS Kenai Peninsula Borough
MOUNTAIN VILLAGE Wade Hampton
NAKNEK Bristol Bay Borough
NAPAKIAK Bethel
NENANA Yukon-Koyukuk
NEW STUYAHOK Dillingham
NIGHTMUTE Bethel
NIKISKI Kenai Peninsula Borough
NIKOLAI Yukon-Koyukuk
NIKOLSKI Aleutian Islands, West
NINILCHIK Kenai Peninsula Borough
NOATAK Northwest Arctic
NOME Nome
NONDALTON Lake & Peninsula
NOORVIK Northwest Arctic
NORTH POLE Fairbanks North Star
   Borough
NORTHWAY Southeast Fairbanks
NUIQSUT North Slope Borough
NULATO Yukon-Koyukuk
NUNAPITCHUK Bethel
OLD HARBOR Kodiak Island Borough
OUZINKIE Kodiak Island Borough
PALMER Matanuska-Susitna Borough
PEDRO BAY Lake & Peninsula
PELICAN Skagway-Yakutat-Angoon
PERRYVILLE Lake & Peninsula
PETERSBURG Wrangell-Petersburg
PILOT POINT Lake & Peninsula
PILOT STATION Wade Hampton
PLATINUM Bethel
POINT BAKER Prince of Wales-Outer
   Ketchikan
POINT HOPE North Slope Borough
POINT LAY North Slope Borough
PORT ALEXANDER Wrangell-Petersburg
PORT ALSWORTH Lake & Peninsula
PORT HEIDEN Lake & Peninsula
PORT LIONS Kodiak Island Borough
PRUDHOE BAY North Slope Borough
QUINHAGAK Bethel
RAMPART Yukon-Koyukuk
RED DEVIL Bethel
RUBY Yukon-Koyukuk
RUSSIAN MISSION Wade Hampton
SAINT GEORGE ISLAND Aleutian Islands,
   West
SAINT MARYS Wade Hampton
SAINT MICHAEL Nome

SAINT PAUL ISLAND Aleutian Islands,
   West
SALCHA Fairbanks North Star Borough
SAND POINT Aleutian Islands, East
SAVOONGA Nome
SCAMMON BAY Wade Hampton
SELAWIK Northwest Arctic
SELDOVIA Kenai Peninsula Borough
SEWARD Kenai Peninsula Borough
SHAGELUK Yukon-Koyukuk
SHAKTOOLIK Nome
SHELDON POINT Wade Hampton
SHISHMAREF Nome
SHUNGNAK Northwest Arctic
SITKA Sitka Borough
SKAGWAY Skagway-Yakutat-Angoon
SKWENTNA Matanuska-Susitna Borough
SLEETMUTE Bethel
SOLDOTNA Kenai Peninsula Borough
SOUTH NAKNEK Bristol Bay Borough
STEBBINS Nome
STERLING Kenai Peninsula Borough
STEVENS VILLAGE Yukon-Koyukuk
SUTTON Matanuska-Susitna Borough
TAKOTNA Yukon-Koyukuk
TALKEETNA Matanuska-Susitna Borough
TANACROSS Southeast Fairbanks
TANANA Yukon-Koyukuk
TATITLEK Valdez-Cordova
TELLER Nome
TENAKEE SPRINGS Skagway-Yakutat-
   Angoon
TETLIN Southeast Fairbanks
THORNE BAY Prince of Wales-Outer
   Ketchikan
TOGIAK Dillingham
TOK Southeast Fairbanks
TOKSOOK BAY Bethel
TRAPPER CREEK Matanuska-Susitna
   Borough
TULUKSAK Bethel
TUNTUTULIAK Bethel
TUNUNAK Bethel
TWO RIVERS Fairbanks North Star
   Borough
TYONEK Kenai Peninsula Borough
UNALAKLEET Nome
UNALASKA Aleutian Islands, West
VALDEZ Valdez-Cordova
VENETIE Yukon-Koyukuk
WAINWRIGHT North Slope Borough
WALES Nome
WARD COVE Ketchikan Gateway Borough
WASILLA Matanuska-Susitna Borough
WHITE MOUNTAIN Nome
WHITTIER Valdez-Cordova
WILLOW Matanuska-Susitna Borough
WRANGELL Wrangell-Petersburg
YAKUTAT Skagway-Yakutat-Angoon

ZIP/City Cross Reference

ZIP Range	City	ZIP Range	City	ZIP Range	City	ZIP Range	City
99501-99504	ANCHORAGE	99615-99619	KODIAK	99684-99684	UNALAKLEET	99762-99762	NOME
99505-99505	FORT RICHARDSON	99620-99620	KOTLIK	99685-99685	UNALASKA	99763-99763	NOORVIK
99506-99506	ELMENDORF AFB	99621-99621	KWETHLUK	99686-99686	VALDEZ	99764-99764	NORTHWAY
99507-99524	ANCHORAGE	99622-99622	KWIGILLINGOK	99687-99687	WASILLA	99765-99765	NULATO
99540-99540	INDIAN	99624-99624	LARSEN BAY	99688-99688	WILLOW	99766-99766	POINT HOPE
99547-99547	ATKA	99625-99625	LEVELOCK	99689-99689	YAKUTAT	99767-99767	RAMPART
99548-99548	CHIGNIK LAKE	99626-99626	LOWER KALSKAG	99690-99690	NIGHTMUTE	99768-99768	RUBY
99549-99549	PORT HEIDEN	99627-99627	MC GRATH	99691-99691	NIKOLAI	99769-99769	SAVOONGA
99550-99550	PORT LIONS	99628-99628	MANOKOTAK	99692-99692	DUTCH HARBOR	99770-99770	SELAWIK
99551-99551	AKIACHAK	99630-99630	MEKORYUK	99693-99693	WHITTIER	99771-99771	SHAKTOOLIK
99552-99552	AKIAK	99631-99631	MOOSE PASS	99694-99694	HOUSTON	99772-99772	SHISHMAREF
99553-99553	AKUTAN	99632-99632	MOUNTAIN VILLAGE	99695-99695	ANCHORAGE	99773-99773	SHUNGNAK
99554-99554	ALAKANUK	99633-99633	NAKNEK	99697-99697	KODIAK	99774-99774	STEVENS VILLAGE
99555-99555	ALEKNAGIK	99634-99634	NAPAKIAK	99701-99701	FAIRBANKS	99775-99775	FAIRBANKS
99556-99556	ANCHOR POINT	99635-99635	NIKISKI	99702-99702	EIELSON AFB	99776-99776	TANACROSS
99557-99557	ANIAK	99636-99636	NEW STUYAHOK	99703-99703	FORT WAINWRIGHT	99777-99777	TANANA
99558-99558	ANVIK	99637-99637	TOKSOOK BAY	99704-99704	CLEAR	99778-99778	TELLER
99559-99559	BETHEL	99638-99638	NIKOLSKI	99705-99705	NORTH POLE	99779-99779	TETLIN
99561-99561	CHEFORNAK	99639-99639	NINILCHIK	99706-99712	FAIRBANKS	99780-99780	TOK
99563-99563	CHEVAK	99640-99640	NONDALTON	99714-99714	SALCHA	99781-99781	VENETIE
99564-99564	CHIGNIK	99641-99641	NUNAPITCHUK	99716-99716	TWO RIVERS	99782-99782	WAINWRIGHT
99565-99565	CHIGNIK LAGOON	99643-99643	OLD HARBOR	99720-99720	ALLAKAKET	99783-99783	WALES
99566-99566	CHITINA	99644-99644	OUZINKIE	99721-99721	ANAKTUVUK PASS	99784-99784	WHITE MOUNTAIN
99567-99567	CHUGIAK	99645-99645	PALMER	99722-99722	ARCTIC VILLAGE	99785-99785	BREVIG MISSION
99568-99568	CLAM GULCH	99647-99647	PEDRO BAY	99723-99723	BARROW	99786-99786	AMBLER
99569-99569	CLARKS POINT	99648-99648	PERRYVILLE	99724-99724	BEAVER	99788-99788	CHALKYITSIK
99571-99571	COLD BAY	99649-99649	PILOT POINT	99725-99725	ESTER	99789-99789	NUIQSUT
99572-99572	COOPER LANDING	99650-99650	PILOT STATION	99726-99726	BETTLES FIELD	99790-99790	FAIRBANKS
99573-99573	COPPER CENTER	99651-99651	PLATINUM	99727-99727	BUCKLAND	99791-99791	ATQASUK
99574-99574	CORDOVA	99652-99652	BIG LAKE	99729-99729	CANTWELL	99801-99811	JUNEAU
99575-99575	CROOKED CREEK	99653-99653	PORT ALSWORTH	99730-99730	CENTRAL	99820-99820	ANGOON
99576-99576	DILLINGHAM	99654-99654	WASILLA	99732-99732	CHICKEN	99821-99821	AUKE BAY
99577-99577	EAGLE RIVER	99655-99655	QUINHAGAK	99733-99733	CIRCLE	99824-99824	DOUGLAS
99578-99578	EEK	99656-99656	RED DEVIL	99734-99734	PRUDHOE BAY	99825-99825	ELFIN COVE
99579-99579	EGEGIK	99657-99657	RUSSIAN MISSION	99736-99736	DEERING	99826-99826	GUSTAVUS
99580-99580	EKWOK	99658-99658	SAINT MARYS	99737-99737	DELTA JUNCTION	99827-99827	HAINES
99581-99581	EMMONAK	99659-99659	SAINT MICHAEL	99738-99738	EAGLE	99829-99829	HOONAH
99583-99583	FALSE PASS	99660-99660	SAINT PAUL ISLAND	99739-99739	ELIM	99830-99830	KAKE
99584-99584	FLAT	99661-99661	SAND POINT	99740-99740	FORT YUKON	99832-99832	PELICAN
99585-99585	MARSHALL	99662-99662	SCAMMON BAY	99741-99741	GALENA	99833-99833	PETERSBURG
99586-99586	GAKONA	99663-99663	SELDOVIA	99742-99742	GAMBELL	99835-99835	SITKA
99587-99587	GIRDWOOD	99664-99664	SEWARD	99743-99743	HEALY	99836-99836	PORT ALEXANDER
99588-99588	GLENNALLEN	99665-99665	SHAGELUK	99744-99744	ANDERSON	99840-99840	SKAGWAY
99589-99589	GOODNEWS BAY	99666-99666	SHELDON POINT	99745-99745	HUGHES	99841-99841	TENAKEE SPRINGS
99590-99590	GRAYLING	99667-99667	SKWENTNA	99746-99746	HUSLIA	99850-99850	JUNEAU
99591-99591	SAINT GEORGE ISLAND	99668-99668	SLEETMUTE	99747-99747	KAKTOVIK	99901-99901	KETCHIKAN
99599-99599	ANCHORAGE	99669-99669	SOLDOTNA	99748-99748	KALTAG	99903-99903	MEYERS CHUCK
99602-99602	HOLY CROSS	99670-99670	SOUTH NAKNEK	99749-99749	KIANA	99918-99918	COFFMAN COVE
99603-99603	HOMER	99671-99671	STEBBINS	99750-99750	KIVALINA	99919-99919	THORNE BAY
99604-99604	HOOPER BAY	99672-99672	STERLING	99751-99751	KOBUK	99921-99921	CRAIG
99605-99605	HOPE	99674-99674	SUTTON	99752-99752	KOTZEBUE	99922-99922	HYDABURG
99606-99606	ILIAMNA	99675-99675	TAKOTNA	99753-99753	KOYUK	99923-99923	HYDER
99607-99607	KALSKAG	99676-99676	TALKEETNA	99754-99754	KOYUKUK	99925-99925	KLAWOCK
99608-99608	KARLUK	99677-99677	TATITLEK	99755-99755	DENALI NATIONAL PARK	99926-99926	METLAKATLA
99609-99609	KASIGLUK	99678-99678	TOGIAK	99756-99756	MANLEY HOT SPRINGS	99927-99927	POINT BAKER
99610-99610	KASILOF	99679-99679	TULUKSAK	99757-99757	LAKE MINCHUMINA	99928-99928	WARD COVE
99611-99611	KENAI	99680-99680	TUNTUTULIAK	99758-99758	MINTO	99929-99929	WRANGELL
99612-99612	KING COVE	99681-99681	TUNUNAK	99759-99759	POINT LAY	99950-99950	KETCHIKAN
99613-99613	KING SALMON	99682-99682	TYONEK	99760-99760	NENANA		
99614-99614	KIPNUK	99683-99683	TRAPPER CREEK	99761-99761	NOATAK		

Arizona

General Help Numbers:

Governor's Office
State Capitol, 1700 W Washington   602-542-4331
Phoenix, AZ 85007   Fax 602-542-1381
www.governor.state.az.us   8AM-5PM

Attorney General's Office
1275 W Washington   602-542-5025
Phoenix, AZ 85007   Fax 602-542-4085
www.attorney_general.state.az.us   8AM-5PM

State Court Administrator
Arizona Supreme Court Bldg   602-542-9301
1501 W Washington   Fax 602-542-9484
Phoenix, AZ 85007-3231   8AM-5PM
www.supreme.state.az.us/aoc

State Archives
1700 W Washington, Room 342   602-542-4159
Phoenix, AZ 85007   Fax 602-542-4402
www.dlapr.lib.az.us/archives   8AM-5PM

State Specifics:

Capital:	Phoenix Maricopa County
Time Zone:	MST
Number of Counties:	15
Population:	4,554,966
Web Site:	www.state.az.us

State Agencies

Criminal Records

Department of Public Safety, Criminal History Records Unit, PO Box 18430, Phoenix, AZ 85005-6638 (Courier: 2320 N 20th Ave, Phoenix, AZ 85005); 602-223-2223, 8AM-5PM.

Note: Address requests to Applicant Team One.

Indexing & Storage: Records are available from 1988.

Searching: Record access is limited to agencies that have specific authorization by law including employers or pre-employment search firms located in AZ. Fingerprints are needed for a search.

Access by: mail.

Fee & Payment: Pay only by money order or cashier's check. Fee payee: Department of Public Safety. No credit cards accepted.

Mail search: Turnaround time: 2-3 days. Arizona employers may call 602-223-2223-request fingerprint cards and forms. No self addressed stamped envelope is required. Search costs $6.00 per name.

Corporation Records
Limited Liability Company Records

Corporation Commission, 1300 W Washington, Phoenix, AZ 85007; 602-542-3026 (Status), 602-542-3285 (Annual Reports), 602-542-3414 (Fax), 8AM-5PM.

www.cc.state.az.us

Note: Fictitious Name & Assumed Name records are found at the county level.

Indexing & Storage: Records are available from 1809 on. You must go through this office for records. If copies are needed for historical records, it can take as long as 4-6 weeks due to the filming process. It takes after 2-3 months before new records are available for inquiry. Records are indexed on microfiche, inhouse computer, microfilm.

Searching: Include the following in your request-full name of business, specific records that you need copies of. In addition to the articles of incorporation, corporation records include the following information: Annual Reports, Officers, Directors, Prior (Merged) Names, Inactive and Reserved Names.

Access by: mail, phone, fax, in person, online.

Fee & Payment: There is no charge for a search. Copies cost $.50 per page. Fee payee: Arizona Corporation Commission. Prepayment required. Phone and fax orders require deposit accounts. Personal checks accepted. No credit cards accepted.

Mail search: Turnaround time: 3-5 days. Enclose a check marked "Not to exceed $20."A self addressed stamped envelope is requested.

Phone search: Phone requests are limited to 3 inquiries per call.

Fax search: Established accounts may fax multiple requests per day.

In person search: Turnaround time is while you wait for up to 5 corporate names.

Online search: The commercial online system is called STARPAS. It functions 24 hours a day, 7 days a week. The initial set-up fee is $36 and access costs $.30 per minute. Call 602-542-0685 for a sign-up package. The agency also provides free access at the web site to basic information. The data is updated weekly.

Expedited service: Expedited service is available for mail, phone and in person searches. Turnaround time: 24 hours. Add $35.00 per request. The fee applies to large orders that must be completed within 24 hours. Generally, smaller orders or single document orders do not require this fee.

Fictitious Name
Assumed Name

Records not maintained by a state level agency.

Note: Records are found at the county level.

Trademarks/Servicemarks
Trade Names
Limited Partnership Records

Secretary of State, Trademarks/Tradenames/ Limited Partnership Division, 1700 W Washington, 7th Floor, Phoenix, AZ 85007; 602-542-6187, 602-542-7386 (Fax), 8AM-5PM.

www.sosaz.com

Indexing & Storage: Records are available from 1984-present on computer. It takes 1-3 days before new records are available for inquiry.

Searching: Provide the entity name, owner name or file number to search.

Access by: mail, phone, in person.

Fee & Payment: There is no search fee, but certification is $3.00 plus the copy fee of $.10 per page. Fee payee: Secretary of State. Prepayment

required. Personal checks accepted. No credit cards accepted.

Mail search: Turnaround time: 1-3 days. Trademarks may take longer.A self addressed stamped envelope is requested.

Phone search: They will give general information at no charge over the phone for up to 3 searches, such as owner's name, date of application, mailing address & expiration date.

In person search: If there are more than 5 pages of copy, service is overnight. You may view microfiche at no charge.

Other access: Bulk purchase is available on microfiche.

Expedited service: Expedited service is available for mail, phone and in person searches. Add $25.00 per filing.

Uniform Commercial Code
Federal Tax Liens
State Tax Liens

UCC Division, Secretary of State, State Capitol, West Wing, 7th Floor, Phoenix, AZ 85007; 602-542-6178, 602-542-7386 (Fax), 8AM - 5PM.

www.sosaz.com

Indexing & Storage: Records are available from 3/80-present on microfiche and from 06/95-present on the Internet.

Searching: Use search request form UCC-3. The search includes tax liens recorded here. Please note that tax liens recorded on individuals may be filed at the county level and not here. Include the following in your request-debtor name.

Access by: mail, phone, fax, in person, online.

Fee & Payment: The search fee is $6.00 per debtor name, except via the web which is no charge. Copies are $.10 each. Fee payee: Secretary of State. Prepayment required. Personal checks accepted. No credit cards accepted.

Mail search: Turnaround time: 5 days.

Phone search: Searching is available by phone.

Fax search: Searching is available by fax.

In person search: Searching is available in person.

Online search: UCC records can be searched for free over the web site. Searching can be done by debtor, secured party name, or file number. From this site you can also pull down a weekly microfiche file of filings (about 10 megabytes).

Other access: E-mail requests are accepted. Microfilm of filings is available for purchase.

Expedited service: Expedited service is available for mail and phone searches. Turnaround time: same day if possible. Add $25.00 per package.

Sales Tax Registrations

Revenue Department, Taxpayer Assistance, 1600 W Monroe, Phoenix, AZ 85007; 602-542-4656, 602-542-4772 (Fax), 8AM-5PM.

www.state.az.us/dor

Indexing & Storage: Records are available from 1980.

Searching: This agency will only confirm that a business is registered and whether it is active. It will provide no other information without a power of attorney. Include the following in your request-

business name. The tax permit number is very helpful.

Access by: mail, phone, in person.

Mail search: A self addressed stamped envelope is requested. No fee for mail request.

Phone search: No fee for telephone request.

In person search: No fee for request.

Birth Certificates

Department of Health Services, Vital Records Section, PO Box 3887, Phoenix, AZ 85030 (Courier: 2727 W Glendale Ave, Phoenix, AZ 85051); 602-255-3260, 602-249-3040 (Fax), 8AM-5PM.

Indexing & Storage: Records are available from late 1800's to present. Records are computerized from 1950-present. Records are indexed on file folders.

Searching: Must by 18 years of age or older to request a record and be the person named or that person's parent or legal guardian. Records 75 years or older available to the publice for a $2.00 fee. Include the following in your request-full name, names of parents, mother's maiden name, date of birth, place of birth, relationship to person of record, reason for information request.

Access by: mail, fax, in person.

Fee & Payment: Bring a government issued picture ID (or send a copy) with signature. For birth records prior to 1950, the fee for a certified photo copy is $9.00. For birth records after 1950, the fee for a certified computerized copy is $6.00. Fee payee: Vital Records Section. Prepayment required. Credit cards accepted: Mastercard, Visa, AmEx, Discover.

Mail search: Turnaround time: 2 weeks. No self addressed stamped envelope is required.

Fax search: Include the following additional information on the request: copy of government ID with your signature, return address, phone #, credit card #, and expiration date. Fee is $5.00 plus cost of copy. Turnaround time is 2 days.

In person search: Turnaround time is usually less than 1 hour.

Expedited service: Expedited service is available for mail and phone searches. Turnaround time: 1 day. The agency will not accept expedited requests over the phone. They must be sent by fax. There is $17.50 fee to have the results returned by Federal Express. Use of credit card required.

Death Records

Department of Health Services, Vital Records Section, PO Box 3887, Phoenix, AZ 85030 (Courier: 2727 W Glendale Ave, Phoenix, AZ 85051); 602-255-3260, 602-249-3040 (Fax), 8AM-5PM.

Indexing & Storage: Records are available from late 1800's to present. New records are available for inquiry immediately. Records are indexed on file folders.

Searching: Must have notarized release from immediate family. Only immediate family, attorney or funeral director acting for immediate family can get records. Records 50 years or older are available to the public for a $2.00 fee. Include the following in your request-full name, date of death, place of death, relationship to person of record, reason for information request. Send a copy of your ID or your signature must be notarized.

Access by: mail, fax, in person.

Fee & Payment: There is no search fee, but there is a certification fee of $6.00. Fee payee: Vital Records Section. Prepayment required. Personal checks accepted. Credit cards accepted: Mastercard, Visa, AmEx, Discover.

Mail search: Turnaround time: 2 weeks. A self addressed stamped envelope is requested.

Fax search: Include the following additional information on the request: copy of government ID with signature, return address, phone #, credit card #, and expiration date. Fee is $5.00 for processing/handling. Certification fee is $6.00.

In person search: Turnaround time is usually 30-50 minutes.

Expedited service: Expedited service is available for fax searches. Include your Fed Ex number. Expedited service is by fax only (must use credit card), the agency will not accept phone requests. Use of credit card required.

Marriage Certificates
Divorce Records

Records not maintained by a state level agency.

Note: These records are not available from the state, they must be requested from the county or court of issue.

Workers' Compensation Records

State Compensation Fund, 3031 N Second St, Phoenix, AZ 85012; 602-631-2000, 602-631-2213 (Fax), 8AM-5PM.

www.statefund.com

Indexing & Storage: Records are available from 1926 on. New records are available for inquiry immediately. Records are indexed on microfilm, inhouse computer.

Searching: Records that are closed or inactive are stored on microfilm. All active records are on the in-house computer. Claim and policy records are confidential, but you can get claim records with release form from claimant. Most other records are public. Include the following in your request-claimant name, Social Security Number, claim number. Requester must have signed release from claimant or policyholder prior to obtaining confidential records. Copies of legal, claims, and policy working files are not released otherwise.

Access by: mail, in person.

Fee & Payment: Copies are $.25 per page. There is no search fee. Fee payee: State Compensation Fund. Requesters will be billed. Personal checks accepted. No credit cards accepted.

Mail search: Turnaround time: 1-2 weeks. No self addressed stamped envelope is required.

In person search: Searching is available in person.

Driver Records

Motor Vehicle Division, Record Services Section, PO Box 2100, Mail Drop 539M, Phoenix, AZ 85001-2100 (Courier: Customer Records Services,

1801 W Jefferson, Rm 111, Phoenix, AZ 85007); 602-255-0072, 8AM-5PM.

www.dot.state.az.us/MVD/mvd.htm

Note: Arizona will suspend the license for unpaid out-of-state tickets.

Indexing & Storage: Records are available for either a thirty-nine month record or for a five-year record. CDL records may be available for ten years. It takes 2 weeks before new records are available for inquiry.

Searching: Any person requesting a motor vehicle record shall identify himself and state the reason for the request. ID may be required. Certain requesters, identified by law, are labeled as "exempt" (generally, in line with DPPA requirements). Include the following in your request-full name, date of birth, driver's license number. Exempt requesters need only supply 2 out of the 3 items required to search. The driver's mailing address is provided as part of the record to exempt requesters.

Access by: mail, in person, online.

Fee & Payment: The current fees are $3 for 39 month records and $5 for certified 5 year records. Insurers may only receive the 39 month record. All non-exempt requests must be signed and notarized. Fee payee: Motor Vehicle Division, Record Services. Prepayment required. Personal checks accepted. No credit cards accepted.

Mail search: Turnaround time: 1 week to 10 days. If express mail is requested, a pre-paid envelope is required. No self addressed stamped envelope is required.

In person search: There is a limit of 2 requests per trip to the window.

Online search: Arizona's online system is interactive. This system is primarily for those requesters who are exempt. For more information call "Third Party Programs" at 602-712-7235.

Other access: Overnight magnetic tape-to-tape ordering is available.

Vehicle Ownership
Vehicle Identification

Motor Vehicle Division, Record Services Section, PO Box 2100, Mail Drop 504M, Phoenix, AZ 85001-2100 (Courier: Customer Records Services, 1801 W Jefferson, Rm 111, Phoenix, AZ 85007); 602-255-0072, 8AM-5PM.

www.dot.state.az.us/MVD/mvd.htm

Indexing & Storage: Records are available for 5 years to present. It takes 2 weeks before new records are available for inquiry.

Searching: The record searcher must state the reason for the request and have his/her signature notarized. Records are not given by merely giving a plate license number or a name for ownership searches. The vehicle's owner, VIN, and plate number must be submitted to receive a vehicle history.

Access by: mail, in person, online.

Fee & Payment: The fee is $3.00, $2.00 if walk-in is willing to pick up the next day, and $5.00 if the record is certified. Fee payee: Motor Vehicle Division. Prepayment required. Money orders and checks are accepted through the mail. Walk-ins may pay with cash. Personal checks accepted. No credit cards accepted.

Mail search: Turnaround time: 1 week to 10 days. A self addressed stamped envelope is requested.

In person search: You may request information in person.

Online search: Online access is offered to permissible users. The system is open 24 hours a day, seven days a week. For more information, call 602-255-7235.

Other access: Commercial purpose mailing lists of license names and addresses or vehicle owners and addresses are available upon approval by the Division.

Accident Reports

Department of Public Safety, Accident Reports, PO Box 6638, Phoenix, AZ 85005 (Courier: 2102 W Encanto, 1st Floor, Phoenix, AZ 85005-6638); 602-223-2236, 602-223-2230, 8AM-5PM.

Indexing & Storage: It takes 2 weeks before new records are available for inquiry. Records are indexed on inhouse computer.

Searching: A written request is required and the requester must state his/her connection to the incident. Include the following in your request-relationship to person of record, date of accident, location of accident, full name, report number.

Access by: mail, in person.

Fee & Payment: The fee is $9.00 per record. Fee payee: Department of Public Safety Prepayment required; business check or money order. No credit cards accepted.

Mail search: Turnaround time: 1 week to 14 days. A self addressed stamped envelope is requested. No fee for mail request.

In person search: Turnaround time is while you wait.

Boat & Vessel Ownership
Boat & Vessel Registration

Game & Fish Dept, 2222 W Greenway Rd, Phoenix, AZ 85023-4399; 602-942-3000, 602-789-3729 (Fax), 8AM-5PM M-F.

www.azgf.com

Note: Lien information is recorded at the county level. Maricopa County has some liens from other counties.

Indexing & Storage: Records are available from 1977-present. Records are indexed on computer for the last 5 years. No titles are issued. All watercraft must be registered unless they are non-motorized.

Searching: To search, the following information is required: Arizona #, hull ID, owner's name, and a picture ID.

Access by: mail, phone, fax, in person.

Fee & Payment: There is no search fee.

Mail search: Turnaround time: Within 30 days. No self addressed stamped envelope is required.

Phone search: Only lawyers, private investigators, boat owners, and government representatives can search by phone or fax.

Fax search: Same criteria as phone searching.

In person search: Turnaround time is normally immediate.

Legislation-Current/Pending
Legislation-Passed

Arizona Legislature, State Senate - Room 203, 1700 W Washington, Phoenix, AZ 85007 (Courier: Senate Wing or, House Wing, Phoenix, AZ 85007); 602-542-3559 (Senate Information), 602-542-4221 (House Information), 602-542-3429 (Senate Fax), 602-542-3550 (Senate Resource Ctr), 602-542-4099 (Fax), 8AM-5PM.

www.azleg.state.az.us

Note: The phone number provides information on current session bills and on some previous bills.

Indexing & Storage: Records are available from 1969-1989 on microfilm for bill files. Committee minutes are available from 1967-present on hard copy.

Searching: Include the following in your request- bill number, year.

Access by: mail, fax, in person, online.

Fee & Payment: Copies are $.10 per page. Fee payee: State Senate or House of Representatives. Prepayment is requested for large photocopying projects. Personal checks accepted. No credit cards accepted.

Mail search: Turnaround time: 1 day. All research requests are processed ASAP, determined by the demands of the legislative sessions on the staff. No self addressed stamped envelope is required. No fee for mail request.

Fax search: Fee is $.10 per page, with a turnaround time of 1 day or sooner.

In person search: No fee for request. A desk is provided for reviewing files, reading minutes, etc. Staff will assist if time and workload permits.

Online search: Most information, beginning with 1997, is available through the Internet (i.e. bill text, committee minutes, committee assignments, member bios, etc.). There is no fee.

Other access: Name, address, and office # lists are available at no charge. Roll call vote histories of individuals per year are available at $.10 per page.

Voter Registration
Access to Records is Restricted

Secretary of State, Election Division, 1700 W Washington, 7th Floor, Phoenix, AZ 85007.

Note: Records are maintained at the county recorder offices. Records are permitted to be sold in bulk only for political related purposes; however, counties can confirm and release names and addresses on a single inquiry basis.

GED Certificates

Department of Education, GED Testing, 1535 W Jefferson, Phoenix, AZ 85007; 602-542-5802, 602-542-1161 (Fax), 8AM-5PM.

www.ade.state.az.us/programs

Searching: Include the following in your request- date of birth, Social Security Number, signed release. The year of the test is helpful. All requests must be in writing.

Access by: mail, fax, in person.

Fee & Payment: There is no fee for either a verification or a copy of transcript.

Mail search: Turnaround time: 5-7 days. No self addressed stamped envelope is required. No fee for mail request.

Fax search: Same criteria as mail searching.

In person search: No fee for request.

Hunting License Information
Fishing License Information

Game & Fish Department, Information & Licensing Division, 2221 W Greenway Rd, Phoenix, AZ 85023-4399; 602-942-3000, 602-789-3924 (Fax), 8AM-5PM.

www.azgfd.com

Note: This agency will also release watercraft registration information within specific legal constraints.

Indexing & Storage: Records are available for past 3 years.

Searching: Records are not available to the public except as a mailing list. They will release certain data to attorneys for pending litigation.

Access by: mail.

Fee & Payment: Prepayment required. Fee payee: AZ Game & Fish. Personal checks accepted. Credit cards accepted: Mastercard, Visa.

Mail search: Turnaround time: variable. Must complete a request form. No self addressed stamped envelope is required.

Other access: There is a program to purchase the database or portions of. You can get 3 years of approximately 160,000-190,000 names for $.05 per name, which includes addresses. This is available for commercial purposes only. Lists are completed within 30 days.

Licenses Searchable Online

Advance Fee Loan Broker #05 .... www.azbanking.com/Lists/Advance%20Fee%20Loan%20Broker%20List.HTML
Architect #29 .... www.btr.state.az.us
Assayer #29 .... www.btr.state.az.us
Attorney #30 .... www.azbar.org/MemberFinder
Bank #05 .... www.azbanking.com/Lists/State%20Bank%20List.HTML
Behavioral Health Emergency Service #47 .... www.hs.state.az.us/als/databases/index.html
Behavioral Health Residential #47 .... www.hs.state.az.us/als/databases/index.html
Behavioral Outpatient Clinic #47 .... www.hs.state.az.us/als/databases/index.html
Charity #71 .... www.sosaz.com/scripts/Charity_Search_engine.cgi
Collection Agency #05 .... www.azbanking.com/Lists/Collection%20Agency%20List.HTML
Commercial Mortgage Banker #05 .... www.azbanking.com/Lists/Commercial%20Mortgage%20Banker%20List.HTML
Consumer Lender #05 .... www.azbanking.com/Lists/Consumer%20Lender%20List.HTML
Contractor #70 .... www.rc.state.az.us/inquiry.htm
Credit Union #05 .... www.azbanking.com/Lists/Credit%20Union%20List.HTML
Day Care Establishment #45 .... www.hs.state.az.us/als/databases/index.html
Debt Management #05 .... www.azbanking.com/Lists/Debt%20Management%20Company%20List.HTML
Engineer #29 .... www.btr.state.az.us
Escrow Agent #05 .... www.azbanking.com/Lists/Escrow%20Agent%20List.HTML
Geologist #29 .... www.btr.state.az.us
Hearing Aid Dispenser #49 .... www.hs.state.az.us/als/databases/index.html
Home Inspector #29 .... www.btr.state.az.us
Landscape Architect #29 .... www.btr.state.az.us
Liquor Producer #52 .... www.azll.com/query.html
Liquor Retail #52 .... www.azll.com/query.html
Liquor Wholesaler #52 .... www.azll.com/query.html
Lobbyist #71 .... www.sosaz.com/scripts/lobbyist_engine.cgi
Marriage & Family Therapist #10 .... http://aspin.asu.edu/~azbbhe/directory/listing.html
Medical Doctor #17 .... www.docboard.org/az/df/azsearch.htm
Money Transmitter #05 .... www.azbanking.com/Lists/Money%20Transmitter%20List.HTML
Mortgage Banker #05 .... www.azbanking.com/Lists/Mortgage%20Banker%20List.HTML
Mortgage Broker #05 .... www.azbanking.com/Lists/Mortgage%20Broker%20List.HTML
Motor Vehicle Dealer & Sales Finance #05 .... www.azbanking.com/Lists/Motor%20Vehicle%20Dealer%20List.HTML
Notary Public #71 .... www.sosaz.com/scripts/Notary_Search_engine.cgi
Physician Assistant #18 .... www.docboard.org/az/df/azsearch.htm
Premium Finance Company #05 .... www.azbanking.com/Lists/Premium%20Finance%20Company%20List.HTML
Professional Counselor #10 .... http://aspin.asu.edu/~azbbhe/directory/listing.html
Property Tax Agent #08 .... www.appraisal.state.az.us/Directory/taxagent.html
Psychologist #27 .... www.goodnet.com/~azbpe/dir.html
Public Accountant-CPA #07 .... www.accountancy.state.az.us
Public Accountant-PA #07 .... www.accountancy.state.az.us
Public Accounting Firm-CPA & PA #07 .... www.accountancy.state.az.us
Real Estate Appraiser #08 .... www.appraisal.state.az.us/Directory/appr1.html
Social Worker #10 .... http://aspin.asu.edu/~azbbhe/directory/listing.html
Substance Abuse Counselor #10 .... http://aspin.asu.edu/~azbbhe/directory/listing.html
Surveyor #29 .... www.btr.state.az.us
Telemarketing Firm #71 .... www.sosaz.com/scripts/TS_Search_engine.cgi
Trust Company #05 .... www.azbanking.com/Lists/Trust%20Company%20List.HTML
Trust Divisions #05 .... www.azbanking.com/Lists/Trust%20Division%20List.HTML

Licensing Quick Finder

Acupuncturist #11 602-255-1444
Adult Care Home Manager #68 602-542-3095
Advance Fee Loan Broker #05 602-255-4421
Aesthetician #12 480-784-4539
Aesthetics Instructor #12 480-784-4539
Agricultural Aircraft Pilot #33 602-542-0904
Agricultural Grower Permit #33 602-542-0904
Agricultural Grower/Seller #33 602-542-0904
Agricultural Pest Control Advisor #33 .. 602-542-0904
Agricultural Seller Permit #33 602-542-0904
Air Pollution Source #39 602-207-2338
Air Quality #65 602-506-6970
Aircraft Dealer #57 602-255-7691

Aircraft Dealer for Wreckers or Salvage #57
.... 602-255-7691
Aircraft Distributor #57 602-255-7691
Aircraft Importer #57 602-255-7691
Aircraft Manufacturer #57 602-255-7691
Aircraft Owner #57 602-255-7691
Aircraft Pilot Trainer School or Instructor #57
.... 602-255-7691
Aircraft Retail #57 602-255-7691
Aircraft Transporter #57 602-255-7691
Aircraft Use Fuel Dealer/Manufacturer #56
.... 602-542-4565
Ambulance Service #48 602-861-0809

Ambulatory Surgical Center #43 602-674-9750
Amusement Park #56 602-542-4565
Amusement Printing & Advertising #56
.... 602-542-4565
Aquifer Protection Permit #41 602-207-4743
Architect #29 602-255-4053
Assayer #29 602-255-4053
Attorney #30 602-252-4804
Audiologist #49 602-674-4340
Bank #05 602-255-4421
Barber #09 602-542-4498
Barber Establishment #09 602-542-4498
Barber Instructor #09 602-542-4498

Barber School #09 ... 602-542-4498
Bedding/Furniture Manufacturer #65 ... 602-506-6970
Behavior Outpatient Rehab Center #47 ... 602-674-4300
Behavioral Health Emergency Service #47 ... 602-674-4300
Behavioral Health Residential #47 ... 602-674-4300
Behavioral Outpatient Clinic #47 ... 602-674-4300
Big & Small Game Resident Guide #59 ... 602-942-3000
Bingo Operation #56 ... 602-542-4565
Bondsman #51 ... 602-912-8470
Bottled Water Processor #65 ... 602-506-6970
Boxing #03 ... 602-542-1417
Boxing Announcer #03 ... 602-542-1417
Boxing Boxer #03 ... 602-542-1417
Boxing Judge #03 ... 602-542-1417
Boxing Manager #03 ... 602-542-1417
Boxing Matchmaker #03 ... 602-542-1417
Boxing Physician #03 ... 602-542-1417
Boxing Promoter #03 ... 602-542-1417
Boxing Referee #03 ... 602-542-1417
Boxing Second #03 ... 602-542-1417
Boxing Timekeeper #03 ... 602-542-1417
Boxing Trainer #03 ... 602-542-1417
Campground Membership Broker & Salesman #55 ... 602-468-1414
Cannabis & Controlled Substance Dealer #56 ... 602-542-4565
Cemetery Broker & Salesman #55 ... 602-468-1414
Charity #71 ... 602-542-6670
Child Adoption Agency #37 ... 602-542-2287
Child Foster Home #37 ... 602-542-2287
Child Placing Agency #37 ... 602-542-2375
Child Residential & Shelter Care #37 ... 602-542-2287
Chiropractor #11 ... 602-255-1444
Citrus Fruit Broker, Dealer, Packer, Shipper #35 ... 602-542-0943
Clinical Laboratory #44 ... 602-255-3454
Collection Agency #05 ... 602-255-4421
Commercial Leasing #56 ... 602-542-4565
Commercial Mortgage Banker #05 ... 602-255-4421
Community College Teacher #31 ... 602-255-5582
Concession on State Park Land #69 ... 602-542-2155
Consumer Lender #05 ... 602-255-4421
Contractor #70 ... 602-542-1525
Cosmetologist #12 ... 480-784-4539
Cosmetology Instructor #12 ... 480-784-4539
Cosmetology or Nail Technology Salon or School #12 ... 480-784-4539
Credit Union #05 ... 602-255-4421
Day Care Establishment #45 ... 602-674-4220
Debt Management #05 ... 602-255-4421
Degree Program #06 ... 602-542-5709
Dental Assistant #13 ... 602-242-1492
Dental Hygienist #13 ... 602-242-1492
Dentist #13 ... 602-242-1492
Denturist #13 ... 602-242-1492
Detoxification Service #47 ... 602-674-4300
Developmentally Disabled Group Home #49 ... 602-674-4340
Drug Manufacturer #24 ... 602-255-5125
Drug Wholesaler #24 ... 602-255-5125
Dry Well Registration #41 ... 602-207-4696
DUI Education Agency #47 ... 602-674-4300
DUI Screening Agency #47 ... 602-674-4300
DUI Treatment Agency #47 ... 602-674-4300
Elementary & Special Education Teacher #38 ... 602-542-4368
Embalmer #15 ... 602-542-3095
Emergency Medical Technician #48 ... 602-861-1188
Emergency Medical Technician Instructor #48 ... 602-861-1188
Engineer #29 ... 602-255-4053
Environmental Laboratory #44 ... 602-255-3454
Escrow Agent #05 ... 602-255-4421
Falconer #59 ... 602-942-3000
Family Day Care Home #37 ... 602-542-2287
Feed & Fertilizer #33 ... 602-542-0904
Feeds Distribution-Commercial #34 ... 602-242-0814
Fertilizer Distribution-Commercial #34 ... 602-253-0949
Field Trial License #59 ... 602-942-3000
Food Establishment #65 ... 602-506-6970
Food Packer or Grower/Shipper-Contract #35 ... 602-542-0943
Foster Care Home #49 ... 602-674-4340
Fruit & Vegetable Broker/Dealer #35 ... 602-542-0943
Funeral Director #15 ... 602-542-3095
Fur Dealer #59 ... 602-942-3000
Geologist #29 ... 602-255-4053
Groom #54 ... 602-277-1704
Guidance Counselor #38 ... 602-542-4368
Hazardous Waste Facility #40 ... 602-207-4197
Headstart Facility #45 ... 602-674-4220
Hearing Aid Dispenser #49 ... 602-674-4340
Home Health Agency #43 ... 602-674-9750
Home Inspector #29 ... 602-255-4053
Homeopathic Physician #16 ... 602-542-3095
Horse or Greyhound Racing #54 ... 602-277-1704
Horse Owner #54 ... 602-277-1704
Horse Trainer #54 ... 602-277-1704
Hospice #43 ... 602-674-9750
Hospital #43 ... 602-674-9750
Hotel, Motel & Tourist Court #65 ... 602-506-6970
Hunting & Fishing License Dealer #59 ... 602-942-3000
Industrial Laser #66 ... 602-255-4845
Infirmary #43 ... 602-674-9750
Insurance Agent #51 ... 602-912-8470
Insurance Broker P&C only #51 ... 602-912-8470
Intern & Resident #17 ... 602-255-3751 x7103
Investment Advisor Representatives #32 ... 602-542-0678
Investment Advisors #32 ... 602-542-0678
Jockey #54 ... 602-277-1704
Landscape Architect #29 ... 602-255-4053
Laser Light Show #56 ... 602-255-4845
Lay Midwife #50 ... 602-220-6550
Limited Travel Agent #51 ... 602-912-8470
Liquor Producer #52 ... 602-542-5141
Liquor Retail #52 ... 602-542-5141
Liquor Wholesaler #52 ... 602-542-5141
Lobbyist #71 ... 602-542-0229
Lottery Retailer #04 ... 480-921-4400
Marriage & Family Therapist #10 ... 602-542-1889
Medical Doctor #17 ... 602-255-3751 x7103
Medical Laser #66 ... 602-255-4845
Mental Health Screening, Evaluation & Treatment #47 ... 602-674-4300
Mining #56 ... 602-542-4565
Mining Elevator & Diesel #67 ... 602-542-5971
Mining Operator-Start-up #67 ... 602-542-5971
Minnow Dealer #59 ... 602-942-3000
Mobile Home Dealer/Broker #36 ... 602-255-4072 x251
Mobile Home Installer #36 ... 602-255-4072 x251
Mobile Home Manufacturer #36 ... 602-255-4072 x251
Mobile Home Salesperson #36 ... 602-255-4072 x251
Money Transmitter #05 ... 602-255-4421
Mortgage Banker #05 ... 602-255-4421
Mortgage Broker #05 ... 602-255-4421
Motor Vehicle Dealer & Sales Finance #05 .. 602-255-4421
MRI License #66 ... 602-255-4845
Nail Technician #12 ... 480-784-4539
Nail Technology Instructor #12 ... 480-784-4539
Naturopathic Physician #19 ... 602-542-8242
Notary Public #71 ... 602-542-4086
Nurse #20 ... 602-331-8111
Nurse #20 ... 602-331-8111
Nurses' Aide #20 ... 602-331-8111
Nursing Care Institution Administrator #68 ... 602-255-3095
Occupational Therapist/Assistant #21 ... 602-589-8352
Oil & Gas Production #56 ... 602-542-4565
Optical Establishment #14 ... 602-542-3095
Optician #14 ... 602-542-3095
Optometrist #22 ... 602-542-3095
Osteopathic Physician #23 ... 480-657-7703 x21
Outpatient Surgical Center #43 ... 602-674-9750
P & C Broker #51 ... 602-912-8470
P & C Managing Agent, also Life/Dis #51 ... 602-912-8470
Pesticide Applicator #33 ... 602-542-0904
Pesticide Applicator #72 ... 602-255-3664
Pesticide Applicator, Supervisor or Advisor #72 ... 602-255-3664
Pesticide Distribution #34 ... 602-253-0949
Pesticide Qualifying Party #72 ... 602-255-3664
Pharmacist #24 ... 602-255-5125
Pharmacy Intern #24 ... 602-255-5125
Physical Therapist #25 ... 602-542-3095
Physical Therapist Assistant #25 ... 602-542-3095
Physician Assistant #18 ... 602-255-3751 x7103
Physiotherapist #11 ... 602-255-1444
Pipeline #56 ... 602-542-4565
Plant Operator #41 ... 602-207-4643
Podiatrist #26 ... 602-542-3095
Pollutant Discharge Permit #41 ... 602-207-4665
Postsecondary Vocational Programs-Private #06 ... 602-542-5709
Premium Finance Company #05 ... 602-255-4421
Preschool #45 ... 602-674-4220
Private Car, Rail & Aircraft #56 ... 602-542-4565
Private Game Farm #59 ... 602-942-3000
Private Investigator #53 ... 602-223-2361
Professional Counselor #10 ... 602-542-1889
Property Broker #51 ... 602-912-8470
Property Tax Agent #08 ... 602-542-1539
Psychologist #27 ... 602-542-8162
Public & Semi-Public Bathing Place #65 ... 602-506-6970
Public Accountant-CPA #07 ... 602-255-3648
Public Accountant-PA #07 ... 602-255-3648
Public Accounting Firm-CPA & PA #07 ... 602-255-3648
Public Weighmaster #02 ... 602-255-5211
Publishing #56 ... 602-542-4565
Racing Kennel #54 ... 602-277-1704
Radiation Machine Possession Facility #66 ... 602-255-4845
Radiation Therapy Technologist #66 ... 602-255-4845
Radioactive Material Possessor #66 ... 602-255-4845
Radiologic Technologist #66 ... 602-255-4845
Radiology-Practical Technologist #66 ... 602-255-4845
Real & Personal Property Appraisal #56 ... 602-542-4565
Real Estate Appraiser #08 ... 602-542-1539
Real Estate Broker & Salesman #55 ... 602-468-1414
Real Estate Division #62 ... 602-542-1704
Real Estate School #55 ... 602-468-1414
Real Estate School Instructor & Course #55 ... 602-468-1414
Rehabilitation & Psychiatric Unit #47 ... 602-674-4300
Rehabilitation Agency #43 ... 602-674-9750
Renal Disease Facility #43 ... 602-674-9750
Renovator/Sterilizer/Spray Process Applicator #65 ... 602-506-6970
Rental of Personal Property #56 ... 602-542-4565
Respiratory Therapist #28 ... 602-542-5995
Restaurant & Bar #56 ... 602-542-4565
Retail Sales Outlet #56 ... 602-542-4565
Risk Management #51 ... 602-912-8470
Sanitarian #46 ... 602-230-5912
School Bus Driver (Certification) #01 ... 602-223-2646
School Bus Driver Instructor (Certification) #01 ... 602-223-2646
School Librarian #38 ... 602-542-4368
School Psychologist & Psychometrist #38 ... 602-542-4368
School Superintendent #38 ... 602-542-4368
School Supervisor #38 ... 602-542-4368
Scientific Collector #59 ... 602-942-3000

Securities Dealer #32	602-542-0678	
Securities Salesperson #32	602-542-0678	
Security Guard #53	602-223-2361	
Self Insured Employer #60	602-542-1836	
Sewage, Sludge & Septic Pumping Vehicle #40	602-207-4123	
Shooting Preserve License #59	602-942-3000	
Social Worker #10	602-542-1889	
Solid Waste Management Facility #40	602-207-4123	
Speech-Language Pathologist #49	602-674-4340	
Subdivision Public Report #55	602-468-1414	
Substance Abuse Counselor #10	602-542-1895	
Substance Abuse Treatment Service #47	602-674-4300	
Surety #51	602-912-8470	
Surplus Line Broker #51	602-912-8470	
Surveyor #29	602-255-4053	
Tanning Facility #66	602-255-4845	
Taxidermist #59	602-942-3000	
Telemarketing Firm #71	602-542-6670	
Timbering #56	602-542-4565	
Time Share Public Report #55	602-468-1414	
Tobacco Products Distributor #56	602-542-4565	
Trailer Coach Park #65	602-506-6970	
Transporting & Towing #56	602-542-4565	
Trust Company #05	602-255-4421	
Trust Divisions (of Chartered Financial Institutions) #05	602-255-4421	
Vehicle Emission-Fleet Inspection Station #42	602-207-7011	
Vehicle Emissions-Fleet Inspector #42	602-207-7011	
Veterinary Medicine & Surgery #73	602-542-3095	
Veterinary Premise (Hospital) #73	602-542-3095	
Veterinary Technician #73	602-542-3095	
Vocational Rehabilitation #61	602-542-3294	
Waste Water Collection, Treatment, Construction #41	602-207-4692	
Waste Water Facility Operator #41	602-207-4625	
Waste Water Reuse #41	602-207-4464	
Water Distribution System Operator #41	602-207-4643	
Water Quality Certification #41	602-207-4625	
Water Rights Assignment #58	602-417-2405	
Water Transporter (out of state) #58	602-417-2405	
Watercraft Registration Agent #59	602-942-3000	
Weights & Measures-Registered Representative #02	602-255-5211	
Weights & Measures-Registered Service Agency #02	602-255-5211	
Well Driller (Drilling Firm) #58	602-417-2470 x 7141	
Well Registration & Construction #58	602-417-2405	
White Amor Stocking License #59	602-942-3000	
Wholesale Feed #56	602-542-4565	
Wildlife Hobby License #59	602-942-3000	
Wildlife Holding Permit #59	602-942-3000	
Wildlife Rehab License #59	602-942-3000	
Wildlife Service License #59	602-942-3000	
X-ray Supplier #66	602-255-4845	
Zoo #59	602-942-3000	

Licensing Agency Information

01 Department of Public Safety, Student Transportation, PO Box 6638 (PO Box 6638 - Mail Drop 1250), Phoenix, AZ 85005-6638; 602-223-2646, Fax: 602-223-2923.

www.dps.state.az.us

02 Department of Weights & Measures, 4425 W Olive Av #134, Glendale, AZ 85302-3844; 602-255-5211, Fax: 602-255-1950.

03 Boxing Commission, 1400 W Washington, #210, Phoenix, AZ 85007; 602-542-1417, Fax: 602-542-1458.

04 Arizona State Lottery, 4740 E University Dr, Phoenix, AZ 85034; 800-921-4400, Fax: 480-921-4512.

www.arizonalottery.com

05 Banking Department, 2910 N 44th St, #310, Phoenix, AZ 85018; 602-255-4421, Fax: 602-381-1225.
www.azbanking.com
Direct URL to search licenses: www.azbanking.com/ListsofLicensees.htm You can search online using name.

06 Board for Private Postsecondary Education, 1400 W Washington, Rm 260, Phoenix, AZ 85007; 602-542-5709, Fax: 602-542-1253.

07 Board of Accountancy, 3877 N Seventh St, #106, Phoenix, AZ 85014; 602-255-3648, Fax: 602-255-1283.
www.accountancy.state.az.us
Direct URL to search licenses: www.accountancy.state.az.us You can search online using roster button, then search by name.

08 Board of Appraisal, 1400 W Washington, #360, Phoenix, AZ 85007; 602-542-1539, Fax: 602-542-1598.
www.appraisal.state.az.us
Direct URL to search licenses: www.appraisal.state.az.us/Directory/directory.html

09 Board of Barbers, 1400 W Washington, Rm 220, Phoenix, AZ 85007; 602-542-4498.

10 Board of Behavioral Health Examiners, 1400 E Washington St #320, Phoenix, AZ 85007; 602-542-1882, Fax: 602-542-1830.
www.aspin.asu/~azbbhe
Direct URL to search licenses: http://aspin.asu.edu/~azbbhe/directory/listing.html You can search online using name.

11 Board of Chiropractic Examiners, 5060 N 19th Ave #416, Phoenix, AZ 85015; 602-255-1444, Fax: 602-255-4289.

www.goodnet.com/~board/ Accupuncture and physciotherapy are certifications under a Chiropractic license.

12 Information Services, Board of Cosmetology, 1721 E Broadway Rd, Tempe, AZ 85282; 480-784-4539, Fax: 480-255-3680.

13 Board of Dental Examiners, 5060 N 19th Ave, #406, Phoenix, AZ 85015; 602-242-1492, Fax: 602-242-1445.

14 Board of Dispensing Opticians, 1400 W Washington, Rm 230, Phoenix, AZ 85007; 602-542-3095, Fax: 602-542-3093.

15 Board of Funeral Directors & Embalmers, 1400 W Washington, Room 230, Phoenix, AZ 85007; 602-542-3095, Fax: 602-542-3093.

16 Board of Homeopathic Medical Examiners, 1400 W Washington, Rm 230, Phoenix, AZ 85007; 602-542-3095, Fax: 602-542-3093.
www.goodnet.com/~bhme

17 Board of Medical Examiners, 9545 E Doubletree Ranch Dr, Scottsdale, AZ 85258-5514; 602-255-3751, Fax: 602-255-1848.

www.docboard.org/bomex/index.htm

18 Board of Medical Examiners, 9545 E Doubletree Ranch Rd, Scottsdale, AZ 85258-5514; 602-255-3751, Fax: 602-255-1848.
www.docboard.org/bomex/index.htm
Direct URL to search licenses: www.docboard.org/az/df/azsearch.htm You can search online using name and license number.

19 Board of Naturopathic Physicians Examiners, 1400 W Washington, Rm 230, Phoenix, AZ 85007; 602-542-8242, Fax: 602-542-3093.

20 Board of Nursing, 1651 E Morton, #150, Phoenix, AZ 85020; 602-331-8111, Fax: 602-906-9365.

www.nursing.state.az.us

21 Board of Occupational Therapy Examiners, 5060 N 19th Av #209, Phoenix, AZ 85015-3212; 602-589-8352, Fax: 602-589-8354.

www.primenet.com/~abote/index.html

22 Board of Optometry, 1400 W Washington, Rm 230, Phoenix, AZ 85007; 602-542-3095, Fax: 602-542-3093.

23 Board of Osteopathic Medicine & Surgery Examiners, 9535 E Doubletree Ranch Rd, Scottsdale, AZ 85258-5539; 480-657-7703 X21, Fax: 480-657-7715.

www.azosteoboard.org

24 Board of Pharmacy, 5060 N 19th Ave, #101, Phoenix, AZ 85015; 602-255-5125, Fax: 602-255-5740.

www.pharmacy.state.az.us

25 Board of Physical Therapy, 1400 W Washington, Rm 230, Phoenix, AZ 85007; 602-542-3095, Fax: 602-542-3093.

26 Board of Podiatry Examiners, 1400 W Washington, Rm 230, Phoenix, AZ 85007; 602-542-3095, Fax: 602-542-3093.

27 Board of Psychologist Examiners, 1400 W Washington St, Rm 235, Phoenix, AZ 85007; 602-542-8162, Fax: 602-542-8279.
www.goodnet.com/~azbpe
Direct URL to search licenses: www.goodnet.com/~azbpe/dir.html You can search online using name.

28 Board of Respiratory Care Examiners, 1400 W Washington, #200, Phoenix, AZ 85007; 602-542-5995, Fax: 602-542-5900.

29 Board of Technical Registration, 1990 W Camelback, #400, Phoenix, AZ 85015-7465; 602-255-4053, Fax: 602-255-4051.
www.btr.state.az.us
Direct URL to search licenses: www.btr.state.az.us

30 Committee on Examinations of Character & Fitness, 111 W Monroe, #1800, Phoenix, AZ 85003-1742; 602-252-4804, Fax: 602-271-4930.
www.azbar.org
Direct URL to search licenses: www.azbar.org/MemberFinder You can search online using name, firm, practice area, area of specialization, city, and county.

31 Community College Board of Directors, 3225 N Central, Century Plaza, #1220, Phoenix, AZ 85012; 602-255-5582, Fax: 602-279-3464.

www.stbd.cc.az.us

32 Registration Department, Securities Division, Corporation Commission, 1300 W Washington, 3rd Fl, Phoenix, AZ 85007; 602-542-4242, Fax: 602-594-7470.

www.ccsd.cc.state.az.us/licensing_and_ registration/index.asp

33 Department of Agriculture, Environmental Services Division, 1688 W Adams St, Phoenix, AZ 85007; 602-542-0904, Fax: 602-542-5420; 602-542-0466.

www.agriculture.state.az.us

34 Department of Agriculture, Environmental Services Division, 1688 W Adams St, 1st Fl, Phoenix, AZ 85007; 602-542-3579, Fax: 602-542-0466.

www.agriculture.state.az.us

35 Department of Agriculture, Plant Services, Citrus Fruits & Vegetables, 1688 W Adams, Phoenix, AZ 85007; 602-542-0943, Fax: 602-542-0281.

www.agriculture.state.az.us

36 Department of Building & Fire Safety, 99 E Virginia, Wildlife & Parks Bldg, #100, Phoenix, AZ 85004; 602-255-4072, Fax: 602-255-4962.

37 Department of Economic Security, Child Care Administration, Division of Children, Youth & Families Licensing, 1789 W Jefferson, Site Code 940A, 3rd Fl, Phoenix, AZ 85007; 602-542-2287, Fax: 602-542-3330.

38 Department of Education, Teacher Certification Unit, 1535 W Jefferson St, Bin 34, Phoenix, AZ 85007; 602-542-5529, Fax: 602-542-5388.

www.ade.state.az.us

39 Department of Environmental Quality, Office of Air Quality, 3033 N Central T5109B, Phoenix, AZ 85012; 602-207-2338, Fax: 602-207-2366.

www.adeq.state.az.us

40 Department of Environmental Quality, Office of Waste Programs, 3033 N Central Ave, 6th Fl, Phoenix, AZ 85012; 602-207-2300, Fax: 602-207-4138.

41 Department of Environmental Quality, Office of Water Quality, 3033 N Central, 2nd Fl, Phoenix, AZ 85012; 602-207-2300, Fax: 602-207-4674.

www.adeq.state.az.us

42 Department of Environmental Quality, Vehicle Emissions Section, 600 N 40th St, Phoenix, AZ 85008; 602-207-7000, Fax: 602-207-7020.

www.adeq.state.us

43 Department of Health Services, 1647 E Morten, #160, Phoenix, AZ 85020; 602-674-9750, Fax: 602-395-8913.

www.hs.state.az.us

44 Department of Health Services, Division of State Laboratory Services/Licensure/Cert, 3443 N Central Ave, #810, Phoenix, AZ 85012; 602-255-3454, Fax: 602-255-3462.

www.hs.state.az.us

45 Department of Health Services, Division of Child Care, 1647 E Morten, #230, Phoenix, AZ 85020; 602-674-4220, Fax: 602-861-0674.

www.hs.state.az.us

46 Department of Health Services, Food Protection & Institutional Sanitation Section, 3815 N Black Canyon Hwy, Phoenix, AZ 85015; 602-230-5912, Fax: 602-230-5817.

www.hs.state.az.us

47 Department of Health Services, Office of Behavioral Health Licensure, 1647 E Morten, #240, Phoenix, AZ 85020; 602-674-4300, Fax: 602-861-0643.

www.hs.state.az.us

Direct URL to search licenses: www.hs.state.az.us/als/databases/index.html You can search online using self extracting files, then by name.

48 Department of Health Services, Bureau of EMS, 1651 E Morten, #120, Phoenix, AZ 85020; 602-861-0708, Fax: 602-861-9812.

www.hs.state.az.us

49 Department of Health Services, Office of Health Care Licensure, 1647 E Morten Ave, Phoenix, AZ 85020; 602-674-4340, Fax: 602-861-0463.

www.hs.state.az.us

50 Department of Health Services, Office of Women & Children, 411 N 24th St, Phoenix, AZ 85008; 602-220-6550, Fax: 602-220-6551.

www.hs.state.az.us

51 Department of Insurance, Licensing Section, 2910 N 44th St, #210, Phoenix, AZ 85018-7256; 602-912-8470, Fax: 602-912-8453.

www.state.az.us/id

52 Department of Liquor License & Control, 800 W Washington, 5th Fl, Phoenix, AZ 85007; 602-542-5141, Fax: 602-542-5707.

www.az11.com

Direct URL to search licenses: www.azll.com/query.html You can search online using license number, business name, and location address. By visiting the web site, you can also search recently issued, expired, closed, suspended and inactive licenses.

53 Department of Public Safety, Security Guard & Private Investigator Licensing, PO Box 6328 (2102 W Encanto Blvd (85009)), Phoenix, AZ 85005-6328; 602-223-2361, Fax: 602-223-2938.

www.dps.state.az.us/mq/dpsmqpi.htm

54 Department of Racing, Licensing Division, 3877 N 7th St, #201, Phoenix, AZ 85014; 602-277-1704, Fax: 602-277-1165.

www.raccom.state.az.us

55 Department of Real Estate, 2910 N 44th St, Phoenix, AZ 85018; 602-468-1414, Fax: 602-468-0562.

www.adre.org

56 Department of Revenue, License & Registration, PO Box 29002 (PO Box 29002), Phoenix, AZ 85038-9069; 602-542-4565.

www.revenue.state.az.us

57 Department of Transportation, Aeronautics Division, 208 N Capitol Ave, Mutual Bldg, Phoenix, AZ 85002-3588; 602-254-6234, Fax: 602-254-6361.

www.dot.state.az.us

58 Department of Water Resources, 500 N 3rd St, Phoenix, AZ 85004-3903; 602-417-2400, Fax: 602-417-2421.

www.adwr.state.az.us

59 Game & Fish Department, 2222 W Greenway Rd, Phoenix, AZ 85023; 602-942-3000, Fax: 602-789-3921.

www.gf.state.az.us

60 Division of Administration, Industrial Commission of Arizona, 800 W Washington, 3rd Fl, Phoenix, AZ 85007; 602-542-4653, Fax: 602-542-3070.

61 Special Fund Division, Industrial Commission of Arizona, 800 W Washington, 4th Fl, Rm 401, Phoenix, AZ 85007; 602-542-3294, Fax: 602-542-3696.

65 Maricopa Environmental Services, 1001 N Central, #550, Phoenix, AZ 85004; 602-506-6970, Fax: 602-506-5141.

66 Medical Radiologic Technology Board of Examiners, 4814 S 40th St, Phoenix, AZ 85040; 602-255-4845, Fax: 602-437-0705.

67 Mine Inspector, 1700 W Washington, #400, Phoenix, AZ 85007-2805; 602-542-5971, Fax: 602-542-5335.

68 Nursing Care Board, 1400 W Washington, #230, Phoenix, AZ 85007; 602-542-3095, Fax: 602-542-3093.

69 Parks Board, 1300 W Washington, #221, Phoenix, AZ 85007; 602-542-2155, Fax: 602-542-4180.

70 Registrar of Contractors, 800 W Washington, 6th Fl, Phoenix, AZ 85007; 602-542-1525, Fax: 602-542-1599.

www.rc.state.az.us

Direct URL to search licenses: www.rc.state.az.us/Inquiry.htm You can search online using license number and name. The results of online searches are sent via fax.

71 Secretary of State, 1700 W Washington St, Exec Towers, 7th Fl, Phoenix, AZ 85007; 602-542-4285, Fax: 602-542-6172.

www.sosaz.com

Direct URL to search licenses: www.sosaz.com/ Online searching is only available for lobbyists and notaries. You can search lobbyists using the public body's name, the lobbyist's name or the lobbyist's employee's name. You can search notaries using name, ZIP Code and/or a range of dates.

72 Structural Pest Control Commission, 9535 E Doubletree Ranch Rd, Scottsdale, AZ 85258-5514; 602-255-3664.

www.sb.state.az.us/main.html

73 Veterinary Medical Examining Board, 1400 W Washington, #230, Phoenix, AZ 85007; 602-542-3095, Fax: 602-542-3093.

The following list indicates the district and division name for each county in the state. If the district or division name of the bankruptcy court is different from the civil/criminal court, it appears in parentheses.

County/Court Cross Reference

Apache	Prescott (Phoenix)	Mohave	Prescott (Yuma)
Cochise	Tucson	Navajo	Prescott (Phoenix)
Coconino	Prescott (Phoenix)	Pima	Tucson
Gila	Phoenix (Tucson)	Pinal	Phoenix (Tucson)
Graham	Tucson	Santa Cruz	Tucson
Greenlee	Tucson	Yavapai	Prescott (Phoenix)
La Paz	Phoenix (Yuma)	Yuma	Phoenix (Yuma)
Maricopa	Phoenix		

US District Court

District of Arizona

Phoenix Division Room 1400, 230 N 1st Ave, Phoenix, AZ 85025-0093, 602-514-7101.

www.azd.uscourts.gov

Counties: Gila, La Paz, Maricopa, Pinal, Yuma. Some Yuma cases handled by San Diego Division of the Southern District of California.

Indexing & Storage: Cases are indexed by defendant and plaintiff as well as by case number. New cases are available in the index 2-3 weeks after filing date. A computer index is maintained. Records are also indexed on microfiche. Open records are located at this court.

Fee & Payment: The fee is $15.00 per item (one party name or case number). Payment may be made by money order, cashier check, business check, Mastercard. In state personal checks are also accepted. Prepayment is required. Payee: Clerk, US District Court. Certification fee: $5.00 per document. Copy fee: $.50 per page.

Phone Search: If case number is known by the caller, basic information will be released over the phone.

Mail Search: All information is public unless the file is sealed. Always enclose a stamped self addressed envelope.

In Person Search: In person searching is available.

PACER: Sign-up number is 800-676-6856. Access fee is $.60 per minute. Toll-free access: 888-372-5707. Local access: 602-514-7113. Case records are available back to 1992. Records are purged every 12 months. New records are available online after 1-3 days. PACER is available on the Internet at http://pacer.azd.uscourts.gov.

Prescott Division c/o Phoenix Division, Room 1400, 230 N 1st Ave, Phoenix, AZ 85025-0093, 602-514-7101.

www.azd.uscourts.gov

Counties: Apache, Coconino, Mohave, Navajo, Yavapai.

Indexing & Storage: Cases are indexed by as well as by case number. New cases are available in the index after filing date. Open records are located at the Division.

Fee & Payment: The fee is $15.00 per item (one party name or case number). Payment may be made by money order, cashier check. Business

checks are not accepted. Personal checks are not accepted.

Phone Search: An automated voice case information service (VCIS) is not available.

In Person Search: In person searching is available.

PACER: Sign-up number is 800-676-6856. Access fee is $.60 per minute. Toll-free access: 888-372-5707. Local access: 602-514-7113. Case records are available back to 1992. Records are purged every 12 months. New records are available online after 1-3 days. PACER is available on the Internet at http://pacer.azd.uscourts.gov.

Tucson Division Room 202, 44 E Broadway Blvd, Tucson, AZ 85701-1711, 520-620-7200, Fax: 520-620-7199.

www.azd.uscourts.gov

Counties: Cochise, Graham, Greelee, Pima, Santa Cruz. The Globe Division was closed effective January 1994, and all case records for that division are now found here.

Indexing & Storage: Cases are indexed by defendant and plaintiff as well as by case number. New cases are available in the index immediately after filing date. A computer index is maintained. Open records are located at this court.

Fee & Payment: The fee is $15.00 per item (one party name or case number). Payment may be made by money order, cashier check, business check. In state personal checks are also accepted. A copy service at a much lower rate (currently $.07 per page) may be used in lieu of court staff. The copy service has a one day turnaround time. Prepayment is required. Payee: Clerk, US District Court. Certification fee: $5.00 per document. Copy fee: $.50 per page.

Phone Search: Only docket information is available by phone. An automated voice case information service (VCIS) is not available.

Mail Search: A stamped self addressed envelope is not required.

In Person Search: In person searching is available.

PACER: Sign-up number is 800-676-6856. Access fee is $.60 per minute. Toll-free access: 888-372-5707. Local access: 602-514-7113. Case records are available back to 1992. Records are purged every 12 months. New records are available online after 1-3 days. PACER is available on the Internet at http://pacer.azd.uscourts.gov.

US Bankruptcy Court

District of Arizona

Phoenix Division PO Box 34151, Phoenix, AZ 85067-4151, 602-640-5800.

www.azb.uscourts.gov

Counties: Apache, Coconino, Maricopa, Navajo, Yavapai.

Indexing & Storage: Cases are indexed by debtor as well as by case number. New cases are available in the index immediately after filing date. Creditors are also indexed from case # 95-1668 forward. A computer index is maintained. Case files are stored alphabetically. Open records are located at this court. Individuals cannot request files from the Federal Records Center themselves.

Fee & Payment: The fee is $15.00 per item (one party name or case number). Payment may be made by money order, cashier check, business check. Personal checks are not accepted. Prepayment is required. Payee: Clerk, US Bankruptcy Court. Certification fee: $5.00 per document. Copy fee: $.50 per page.

Phone Search: Only docket information is available by phone. An automated voice case information service (VCIS) is available.

Mail Search: Always enclose a stamped self addressed envelope.

In Person Search: In person searching is available.

PACER: Sign-up number is 800-676-6856. Access fee is $.60 per minute. Toll-free access: 800-556-9230. Local access: 602-640-5832. Use of PC Anywhere v4.0 suggested. Case records are available back to 1986. Records are purged every six months. New civil records are available online after 1 week.

Electronic Filing: Searching of electronically filed cases is NOT currently available online. Electronic filing information is available online at http://ecf.azb.uscourts.gov

Tucson Division Suite 8112, 110 S Church Ave, Tucson, AZ 85701-1608, 520-620-7500.

www.azb.uscourts.gov

Counties: Cochise, Gila, Graham, Greenlee, Pima, Pinal, Santa Cruz.

Indexing & Storage: Cases are indexed by debtor as well as by case number. New cases are available in the index immediately after filing date. Records are also indexed by adversary case number if applicable. A master list of creditors is available for each case from 1995 on. A computer index is maintained. Open records are located at this court.

Fee & Payment: The fee is $15.00 per item (one party name or case number). Payment may be made by money order, cashier check, business check. Personal checks are not accepted. Prepayment is required. Payee: Clerk, US Bankruptcy Court. Certification fee: $5.00 per document. Copy fee: $.50 per page.

Phone Search: Only docket and cover sheet information will be released over the phone. An automated voice case information service (VCIS) is available.

Mail Search: Always enclose a stamped self addressed envelope.

In Person Search: In person searching is available.

PACER: Sign-up number is 800-676-6856. Access fee is $.60 per minute. Toll-free access: 800-556-9224. Local access: 520-620-7470. Use of PC Anywhere v4.0 suggested. Case records are available back to 1914. Records are purged every

six months. New civil records are available online after 1 week.

Electronic Filing: Searching of electronically filed cases is NOT currently available online. Electronic filing information is available online at http://ecf.azb.uscourts.gov

Yuma Division Suite D, 325 W 19th St, Yuma, AZ 85364, 520-783-2288.

www.azb.uscourts.gov

Counties: La Paz, Mohave, Yuma.

Indexing & Storage: Cases are indexed by debtor as well as by case number. New cases are available in the index immediately after filing date. A computer index is maintained. Open records are located at this court.

Fee & Payment: The fee is $15.00 per item (one party name or case number). Payment may be made by money order, cashier check, business check. Personal checks are not accepted. Prepayment is required. Payee: Clerk, US

Bankruptcy Court. Certification fee: $5.00 per document. Copy fee: $.50 per page.

Phone Search: Only docket information is available by phone. An automated voice case information service (VCIS) is not available.

Mail Search: Always enclose a stamped self addressed envelope.

In Person Search: In person searching is available.

PACER: Sign-up number is 800-676-6856. Access fee is $.60 per minute. Toll-free access: 800-556-9227. Local access: 520-783-9535. Use of PC Anywhere v4.0 suggested. Case records are available back to the mid 1980's. Records are purged every six months. New civil records are available online after 1 day.

Electronic Filing: Searching of electronically filed cases is NOT currently available online. Electronic filing information is available online at http://ecf.azb.uscourts.gov

Court	Jurisdiction	No. of Courts	How Organized
Superior Courts*	General	15	15 Counties
Justice of the Peace Courts*	Limited	79	83 Precincts
Municipal Courts	Municipal	85	

* Profiled in this Sourcebook.

CIVIL									
Court	Tort	Contract	Real Estate	Min. Claim	Max. Claim	Small Claims	Estate	Eviction	Domestic Relations
Superior Courts*	X	X	X	$5000	No Max			X	
Justice of the Peace Courts*	X	X	X	$0	$10,000	$2500		X	X
Municipal Courts									X

CRIMINAL					
Court	Felony	Misdemeanor	DWI/DUI	Preliminary Hearing	Juvenile
Superior Courts*	X	X			X
Justice of the Peace Courts*		X	X	X	
Municipal Courts		X	X		

ADMINISTRATION

Administrative Office of the Courts, Arizona Supreme Court Bldg, 1501 W Washington, Phoenix, AZ, 85007; 602-542-9301, Fax: 602-542-9484. www.supreme.state.az.us

COURT STRUCTURE

The Superior is the court of general jurisdiction. Justice, and Municipal courts generally have separate jurisdiction over case types as indicated in the text. Most courts will search their records by plaintiff or defendant. Estate cases are handled by Superior Court. Fees are the same as for civil and criminal case searching.

ONLINE ACCESS

A system called ACAP (Arizona Court Automation Project) is implemented in over 100 courts. Mohave County is not a part of ACAP. ACAP is, fundamentally, a case and cash management information processing system. When fully implemented ACAP will provide all participating courts access to all records on the system. Current plans call for public availability later in late 2000. Access will be over the Internet. For more information, call Tim lawler at 602-542-9614.

The Maricopa and Pima county courts maintain their own systems, but will also, under current planning, be part of ACAP. These two counties provide ever-increasing online access to the public.

ADDITIONAL INFORMATION

Public access to all Maricopa County court case indexes is available at a central location - 1 W Madison Ave in Phoenix. Copies, however, must be obtained from the court where the case is heard.

Many offices do not perform searches due to personnel and/or budget constraints. As computerization of record offices increases across the state, more record offices are providing public access computer terminals.

Fees across all jurisdictions, as established by the Arizona Supreme Court and State Legislature, are as follows as of January 1, 1999: Search - Superior Court: $18.00 per name; lower courts: $17.00 per name; Certification - Superior Court: $18.00 per document; lower courts: $11.50 per document; Copies - $.50 per page. Courts may choose to charge no fees.

Apache County

Superior Court PO Box 365, St John's, AZ 85936; 520-337-4364 X262; Fax: 520-337-2771. Hours: 8AM-5PM (MST). *Felony, Civil Actions Over $5,000, Probate.*

Civil Records: Access: Mail, in person. Both court and visitors may perform in person searches. Search fee: $18.00 per name. Required to search:

name, years to search; also helpful-address. Civil cases indexed by defendant, plaintiff. Civil records on computer and docket books. **Criminal Records:** Access: Mail, in person. Both court and visitors may perform in person searches. Search fee: $18.00 per name. Required to search: name, years to search, DOB; also helpful-address, SSN. Criminal records on computer and docket books. **General Information:** No juvenile dependencies, mental health, victims, sealed or adoption records

released. SASE required. Copy fee: $.50 per page. Certification fee: $18.00. Fee payee: Clerk of the Courts. Business checks accepted. Prepayment is required. Public access terminal is available.

Chinle Justice Court PO Box 888, Chinle, AZ 86503; 520-674-5922; Fax: 520-674-5926. Hours: 8AM-5PM (MST). *Misdemeanor, Civil Actions Under $10,000, Eviction, Small Claims.*

86507-86507	LUKACHUKAI	86512-86512	SANDERS
86508-86508	LUPTON	86514-86514	TEEC NOS POS
86510-86510	PINON	86515-86515	WINDOW ROCK
86511-86511	SAINT MICHAELS	86520-86520	BLUE GAP

86535-86535	DENNEHOTSO	86545-86545	ROCK POINT
86538-86538	MANY FARMS	86547-86547	ROUND ROCK
86540-86540	NAZLINI	86549-86549	SAWMILL
86544-86544	RED VALLEY	86556-86556	TSAILE

Arkansas

General Help Numbers:

Governor's Office
State Capitol   501-682-2345
Little Rock, AR 72201   Fax 501-682-3597
www.state.ar.us/governor   8AM-5PM

Attorney General's Office
323 Center St #200   501-682-2007
Little Rock, AR 72201   Fax 501-682-8084
www.ag.state.ar.us   8AM-5PM

State Court Administrator
625 Marshall Street, 1100 Justice Bldg   501-682-9400
Little Rock, AR 72201-1078   Fax 501-682-9410
http://courts.state.ar.us/admin.htm   8AM-5PM

State Archives
State Archives   501-682-6900
One Capitol Mall
Little Rock, AR 72201   8AM-4:30PM M-SA
www.state.ar.us/ahc/ahc.html

State Specifics:

Capital:	Little Rock
	Pulaski County
Time Zone:	CST
Number of Counties:	75
Population:	2,522,819
Web Site:	www.state.ar.us

State Agencies

Criminal Records

Arkansas State Police, Identification Bureau, #1 State Police Plaza Dr, Little Rock, AR 72209; 501-618-8500, 501-618-8404 (Fax), 8AM-5PM.

www.asp.state.ar.us

Indexing & Storage: Records are available for the past 25 years. Older records are located in the off-site State Archives. It takes 2-3 weeks before new records are available for inquiry. Records are indexed on fingerprint cards.

Searching: Must have signed and notarized release from person of record. You must use the Bureau's form. Include the following in your request-name, date of birth, sex, Social Security Number, driver's license number.

Access by: mail, in person.

Fee & Payment: The fee is $15.00 per record. Fee payee: Arkansas State Police. Prepayment required. Personal checks accepted. No credit cards accepted.

Mail search: Turnaround time: 3-4 weeks. A self addressed stamped envelope is requested.

In person search: Bring in signed release. If applicant is subject, record is released immediately, otherwise it is mailed back.

Corporation Records
Fictitious Name
Limited Liability Company Records
Limited Partnerships

Secretary of State, Corporation Department-Aegon Bldg, 501 Woodlane, Rm 310, Little Rock, AR 72201-1094; 501-682-3409, 501-682-3437 (Fax), 8AM-4:30PM.

www.sosweb.state.ar.us/corps

Indexing & Storage: Records are available from late 1800's on. Corporation records are on computer from 1987 on. Prior records, such as dissolved corporations, may be in paper files. New records are available for inquiry immediately. Records are indexed on inhouse computer, file folders.

Searching: Franchise tax information is not released excpet for names and addresseses of parties involved and certain information about the shares of stock. Include the following in your request-full name of business. In addition to the articles of incorporation, corporation records include the following information: Prior (Merged) names, Reserved names, Good standing. Franchise tax information is not released.

Access by: mail, phone, in person, online.

Fee & Payment: There are no search fees. Certification of records costs $5.00. Fee payee: Secretary of State. Prepayment required. Personal checks accepted. No credit cards accepted.

Mail search: Turnaround time: same day if possible. Call first for copy fees. Records prior to 1988 will take longer to search. No self addressed stamped envelope is required. Copies cost $.50 per page.

Phone search: Copies cost $.50 per page. They will give incorporation dates, history, agent name, and status over the phone.

In person search: Copies cost $.50 per page.

Online search: The Internet site permits free searching of corporation records. You can search by name, registered agent, or filing number.

Other access: Bulk release of records is available for $.50 per page. Contact David Morrow at 501-682-3409 for details.

Trademarks/Servicemarks

Secretary of State, Trademarks Section-Aegon Bldg, 501 Woodlane, #310, Little Rock, AR 72201; 501-682-3409, 501-682-3437 (Fax), 8AM-5PM.

www.sosweb.state.ar.us/corps/trademk

Indexing & Storage: Records are available from the 1800s. It takes 2-3 weeks before new records are available for inquiry. Records are indexed on inhouse computer.

Searching: Include the following in your request-name.

Access by: mail, phone, in person, online.

Fee & Payment: There is no search fee, copy fees are $.50 per copy. Fee payee: Secretary of State. Prepayment required. Personal checks accepted. No credit cards accepted.

Mail search: Turnaround time: 3-4 working days. No self addressed stamped envelope is required.

Phone search: They will give information over the phone.

In person search: Turnaround time is within a few minutes.

Online search: Searching is available at no fee over the Internet site.

Other access: Records can be provided in bulk for $.50 per page. Contact David Morrow at 501-682-3409 for details.

Uniform Commercial Code Federal Tax Liens

UCC Division, Secretary of State-Aegon Bldg, 501 Woodlane, Rm 310, Little Rock, AR 72201-1094; 501-682-5078, 501-682-3500 (Fax), 8AM-5PM.

www.sosweb.state.ar.us/ucc.htm

Indexing & Storage: Records are available from 1962. Records are indexed on cards. You can make requests by fax, but they will be returned by mail. Records are not searched by phone, but they will inform if there is anything on file.

Searching: Use search request form UCC-11. A search includes tax liens on businesses, via a lien search certificate. Federal tax liens on individuals and all state tax liens (AKA municipal judgments before 1978) are filed at the county. Include the following in your request-debtor name.

Access by: mail, fax, in person.

Fee & Payment: A lien search certificate is $10.00. Photostat copies of financing statements are $10.00 for the first page, $.50 each additional, maximum $100.00. The fee for certification of a copy of a filed financing statement is $1.00. Fee payee: Secretary of State. Prepayment required. Personal checks accepted. No credit cards accepted.

Mail search: Turnaround time: 1-2 days. No self addressed stamped envelope is required.

Fax search: There is an additional fee of $5.00 plus $.50 per page.

In person search: Walk-in customers may view the index cards for no charge.

State Tax Liens

Records not maintained by a state level agency.

Note: Records are at the county level.

Sales Tax Registrations

Finance & Administration Department, Sales & Use Tax Office, PO Box 1272, Little Rock, AR 72203; 501-682-7104, 501-682-7900 (Fax), 8AM-4:30PM.

www.state.ar.us/salestax

Indexing & Storage: Records are available from the 1940s.

Searching: This agency will only confirm that a business is registered. They will provide no other information. All searches are based upon tax permit number

Access by: mail, phone, fax, in person.

Mail search: Turnaround time: 3-5 days. A self addressed stamped envelope is requested. No fee for mail request.

Phone search: No fee for telephone request. This is the recommended search request method.

Fax search: Fax searching available.

In person search: No fee for request.

Birth Certificates

Arkansas Department of Health, Division of Vital Records, 4815 W Markham St, Slot 44, Little Rock, AR 72205; 501-661-2134, 501-661-2336

(Message Number), 506-661-2726 (Credit Card Line), 501-663-2832 (Fax), 8AM-4:30PM.

Indexing & Storage: Records are available from 1914 on. New records are available for inquiry immediately. Records are indexed on microfiche, inhouse computer.

Searching: Must have a signed release from person of record if requester is not a member of parents, grandparents or spouse. Include your name, address and signature on the request. Include the following in your request-full name, names of parents, mother's maiden name, date of birth, place of birth, relationship to person of record, reason for information request. Also include your phone number.

Access by: mail, phone, fax, in person.

Fee & Payment: The fee is $5.00. Add $5.00 if you use a credit card. Fee payee: Division of Vital Records. Prepayment required. Personal checks accepted. Credit cards accepted: Mastercard, Visa, AmEx, Discover.

Mail search: Turnaround time: 3 weeks. No self addressed stamped envelope is required.

Phone search: You must use a credit card. Turnaround time is 1 week.

Fax search: Fax requests require the use of a credit card or prepayment. No certificates may be faxed back. Turnaround time is 1 week.

In person search: Search costs $5.00 for each name in request. Turnaround time: While you wait.

Other access: Research projects require the approval of the director.

Expedited service: Expedited service is available for mail, phone and fax searches. Turnaround time: next day. Add $21.25 for use of credit card and for express delivery. Overnight express is available.

Death Records

Arkansas Department of Health, Division of Vital Records, 4815 W Markham St, Slot 44, Little Rock, AR 72205; 501-661-2134, 501-661-2336 (Message number), 501-661-2726 (Credit Card Line), 501-663-2832 (Fax), 8AM-4:30PM.

Indexing & Storage: Records are available from 1914 on. New records are available for inquiry immediately. Records are indexed on microfiche, inhouse computer.

Searching: Must have a signed release from immediate family member if requester is not a member of family. Include the following in your request-full name, date of death, place of death, relationship to person of record, reason for information request, wife's maiden name. Include requester's signature and phone number.

Access by: mail, phone, fax, in person.

Fee & Payment: The fee is $4.00. Add $5.00 if ordered with a credit card. Fee payee: Division of Vital Records. Prepayment required. Personal checks accepted. Credit cards accepted: Mastercard, Visa, AmEx, Discover.

Mail search: Turnaround time: 3 weeks. Turnaround time with a credit card is 1 week. No self addressed stamped envelope is required.

Phone search: You must use a credit card.

Fax search: You must use a credit card or prepay before record is sent.

In person search: Search costs $4.00 for each name in request. Turnaround time is usually 1-2 hours.

Expedited service: Expedited service is available for mail, phone and fax searches. Turnaround time: overnight delivery. Add $21.25 for delivery and use of credit card.

Marriage Certificates

Arkansas Department of Health, Division of Vital Records, 4815 W Markham St, Slot 44, Little Rock, AR 72205; 501-661-2134, 501-661-2336 (Message Number), 501-661-2726 (Credit Card Line), 501-663-2832 (Fax), 8AM-4:30PM.

Indexing & Storage: Records are available from 1917 on. New records are available for inquiry immediately. Records are indexed on microfiche, inhouse computer.

Searching: Must have a signed release from person of record if requester is not a member of immediate family. Include the following in your request-names of husband and wife, registration number, date of marriage, place or county of marriage, wife's maiden name. Requester must sign request and provide phone number.

Access by: mail, phone, fax, in person.

Fee & Payment: The fee is $5.00. Add $5.00 if you use a credit card. Fee payee: Division of Vital Records. Prepayment required. Personal checks accepted. Credit cards accepted: Mastercard, Visa, AmEx, Discover.

Mail search: Turnaround time: 3 weeks. Turnaround time with a credit card is 1 week. No self addressed stamped envelope is required.

Phone search: You may call in your request, but you must use a credit card. Turnaround time is 1 week.

Fax search: A credit card is required or must prepay before records sent.

In person search: Search costs $5.00 per request. Turnaround time is 30 minutes to an hour.

Expedited service: Expedited service is available for mail, phone and fax searches. Turnaround time: overnight delivery. Add $21.25 for use of credit card and express delivery.

Divorce Records

Arkansas Department of Health, Department of Vital Records, 4815 W Markham St, Slot 44, Little Rock, AR 72205; 501-661-2134, 501-661-2336 (Message Number), 501-661-2726 (Credit Card Line), 501-663-2832 (Fax), 8AM-4:30PM.

Indexing & Storage: Records are available from 1914-present. New records are available for inquiry immediately.

Searching: Must have a signed release from person of record if requester is not a member of the immediate family. Include the following in your request-names of husband and wife, date of divorce, place of divorce. Signature of requester required.

Access by: mail, phone, fax, in person.

Fee & Payment: The fee is $5.00 per record. Add $5.00 if you use a credit card. Fee payee: Division of Public Records. Prepayment required. Personal checks accepted. Credit cards accepted: Mastercard, Visa, AmEx, Discover.

Mail search: Turnaround time: 3 weeks. Turnaround time with a credit card is 1 week. No self addressed stamped envelope is required.

Phone search: You must use a credit card. Turnaround time is 1 week.

Fax search: A credit card or prepayment is required.

In person search: Search costs $5.00 per request. Turnaround time is within 1 hour.

Expedited service: Expedited service is available for mail, phone and fax searches. Turnaround time: overnight delivery. The fee of $21.25 includes the $5.00 credit card fee and express delivery.

Workers' Compensation Records

Workers Compensation Department, 324 Spring Street, PO Box 950, Little Rock, AR 72203-0950; 501-682-3930, 800-622-4472, 501-682-6761 (Fax), 8AM-4:30PM M-F.

www.awcc.state.ar.us

Indexing & Storage: Records are available from 1940's on. New records are available for inquiry immediately. Records are indexed on microfilm, index cards, inhouse computer.

Searching: Only written requests are accepted. You may fax a request, but it is returned by mail. Include the following in your request-claimant name, Social Security Number, place of employment at time of accident, file number (if known). The following data is not released: Social Security Numbers or medical information.

Access by: mail, phone, fax, in person, online.

Fee & Payment: The fee is $5.00 per name searched and $.50 per page for copies. Fee payee: Workers' Compensation Commission. An invoice is mailed with the results of the request. Personal checks accepted. No credit cards accepted.

Mail search: Turnaround time: 10 days. No self addressed stamped envelope is required.

Phone search: Searching is available by phone.

Fax search: Same criteria as mail searching.

In person search: You may make copies at $.25 per page. You are allowed to look through the files without charge.

Online search: To perform an online claim search, one must be a subscriber to the Information Network of Arkansas (INA). Fee is $3.50 per claim per search. If 20 searches are reached in a month then fee goes to $2.50 per search. Records are from May 1, 1997 forward. There is an annual $50 subscriber fee to INA. For more information, visit the web site at www.state.ar.us/ina.html.

Driver Records

Department of Driver Services, Driving Records Division, PO Box 1272, Room 1130, Little Rock, AR 72203 (Courier: 1900 W 7th, #1130, Little Rock, AR 72201); 501-682-7207, 501-682-2075 (Fax), 8AM-4:30PM.

www.ahtd.state.ar.us

Note: Copies of tickets must be requested from the local jurisdiction where the ticket was issued.

Indexing & Storage: Records are available for 3 years for moving violations, 3 years for employment or insurance purposes and are retained indefinitely for departmental purposes.

DWI and suspensions show until all requirements are met. Records are indexed on inhouse computer.

Searching: Arkansas requires signed authorization by the driver to obtain a driving record. Volume requesters must have these authorizations on file. Violations on an interstate highway not exceeding 75 mph won't show on records requested for insurance purposes. Include the following in your request-full name, driver's license number, date of birth. Driver's address is included as part of the search report.

Access by: mail, in person, online.

Fee & Payment: Fees are $7.00 for insurance record and $10.00 for CDLs. There is a full charge for a "no record found." Fee payee: State of Arkansas, Driver Services. Prepayment required. Personal checks accepted. No credit cards accepted.

Mail search: Turnaround time: 24 hours. Requester must enclose written release, full name, DOB, driver's license number, and proper fees. No self addressed stamped envelope is required.

In person search: The state will process up to 5 requests while you wait.

Online search: Access is available through the Information Network of Arkansas (INA). The system offers both batch and interactive service. The system is only available to INA subscribers who have statutory rights to the data. The record fee is $8.00, or $11.00 for commercial drivers. Visit www.state.ar.us/ina.html.

Other access: High volume requesters use magnetic tape-to-tape for overnight access.

Vehicle Ownership Vehicle Identification

Office of Motor Vehicles, MV Title Records, PO Box 1272, Room 1100, Little Rock, AR 72203 (Courier: 7th & Battery Sts, Ragland Bldg, Room 1100, Little Rock, AR 72201); 501-682-4692, 8AM-4:30PM.

www.state.ar.us/dfa

Note: The state has plans to offer online access to permissible users soon. This will be through the Information Network of Arkansas.

Indexing & Storage: Records are available from 1950 for titles; license plate records from 1968 on microfilm; plate number and name from 1981 on microfiche. It takes 4-6 weeks before new records are available for inquiry.

Searching: Vehicle registration information cannot be sold or used for solicitation purposes. The following data is not released: Social Security Numbers or date of birth.

Access by: mail, phone, in person.

Fee & Payment: The fee for vehicle and/or ownership searches is $1.00 per copy and $1.00 per search. Fee payee: Department of Finance and Administration. Prepayment required. If mailing a check to open a new account, place "Attn: Search Account" on the request. If mailing an information request, place "Attn: Correspondence Desk" on the request. Personal checks accepted. No credit cards accepted.

Mail search: Turnaround time: 24 hours. No self addressed stamped envelope is required.

Phone search: Searching by phone is available for established accounts. A $25.00 deposit is required.

In person search: Turnaround time: while you wait.

Other access: The bulk purchase of records, except for recall or statistical purposes, is prohibited.

Accident Reports

Arkansas State Police, Accident Records Section, 1 State Police Plaza Drive, Little Rock, AR 72209; 501-618-8130, 501-618-8131 (Fax), 8AM-5PM.

www.asp.state.ar.us/ar/ar.html

Indexing & Storage: Records are available from 1958-present. Records are on microfilm from 1958-1982, off-line storage 1982-1994, and on computer 1994-present. It takes 2 weeks before new records are available for inquiry.

Searching: Include the following in your request-date of accident, location, name of at least on driver.

Access by: mail, phone, fax, in person.

Fee & Payment: The fee is $10.00 per record. There is no charge for a "no record found." Payment will be refunded. Fee payee: Arkansas State Police, Accident Records. Prepayment required. Personal checks accepted. No credit cards accepted.

Mail search: Turnaround time: 1-2 weeks. A self addressed stamped envelope is requested.

Phone search: Limited information is available.

Fax search: Searching is available by fax.

In person search: Turnaround time is while you wait if 1994 or newer, otherwise 1-2 weeks.

Boat & Vessel Ownership
Boat & Vessel Registration

Office of Motor Vehicles, Boat Registration, PO Box 1272, Little Rock, AR 72203; 501-682-4692, 8AM-4:30PM.

Note: Lien information is recorded at the Secretary of State.

Indexing & Storage: Records are available from 1980. All sail boats and all motorized boats must be registered. Vessels are not titled in this state.

Searching: Search by name or registration number or hull number. Anyone may request records, but personal information is not released.

Access by: mail, in person.

Fee & Payment: The search fee is $1.00. Fee payee: Office of Motor Vehicles. Prepayment required. No credit cards accepted.

Mail search: Turnaround time: 2 weeks. No self addressed stamped envelope is required.

In person search: Records are usually obtained at once, unless they require extensive research.

Legislation-Current/Pending
Legislation-Passed

Elections Department, State Capitol, Room 026, Little Rock, AR 72201; 501-682-5070, 501-682-3408 (Fax), 8AM-5PM.

www.arkleg.state.ar.us

Note: This agency will not do any research; they will only respond to requests by act number.

Indexing & Storage: Records are available from 1909-present.

Access by: mail, fax, in person, online.

Fee & Payment: You can purchase copies of bills for $.25 per page. They will return copies by Federal Express if you give your billing number. Fee payee: Secretary of State. Prepayment required. Personal checks accepted. No credit cards accepted.

Mail search: No self addressed stamped envelope is required.

Fax search: Fax searching available.

In person search: Searching is available in person.

Online search: Probably the best way to search is through the Interent site listed above. You may also search by subject matter.

Voter Registration
Access to Records is Restricted

Secretary of State, Voter Services, State Capitol, Room 026, Little Rock, AR 72201; 501-682-3526, 501-682-3548 (Fax), 8AM-5PM.

www.sosweb.state.ar.us/elect.html

Note: The state will sell the voter database for voting or election purposes. All individual search requests must be at the local County Clerk's office. The SSN will not be released.

GED Certificates

GED Testing, Dept of Workforce Education, Three Capitol Mall, Ste 200D, Little Rock, AR 72202; 501-682-1978 (Main Number), 501-682-1982 (Fax).

www.work-ed.state.ar.us

Searching: For verification or for a copy of a transcript, all of the following is required: a signed release, name, year of test, date of birth, and Social Security Number.

Access by: mail, fax.

Fee & Payment: There is no fee.

Mail search: Turnaround time is next day. No self addressed stamped envelope is required.

Fax search: Turnaround time is next day, but results returned by mail.

Hunting License Information
Fishing License Information

Game & Fish Commission, Two Natural Resource Dr, Little Rock, AR 72205; 501-223-6300, 501-223-6425 (Fax), 8AM-4:30PM.

www.agfc.state.ar.us

Note: Lists maintained here include fish farmers, put & take pay lakes, shell buyers, commercial game breeders, commercial shooting resorts, fur dealers, and bull frog permits.

Indexing & Storage: Records are available for 2-3 years then purged. It takes 4 days before new records are available for inquiry. Records are indexed on inhouse computer.

Searching: Must mention request is under the Freedom of Information Act. Include the following in your request-full name. Addresses are given and telephone numbers, if available.

Access by: mail, in person.

Fee & Payment: The search and copy fee is $2.00. Fee payee: Game & Fish Commission. Personal checks accepted. No credit cards accepted.

Mail search: Turnaround time: 1-2 days. No self addressed stamped envelope is required.

In person search: Some searches require 1-2 days to process.

Licenses Searchable Online

Anesthetician #15	www.state.ar.us/nurse/database/search.html
Architect #06	www.state.ar.us/arch/search.html
Attorney #43	http://courts.state.ar.us/attylist/index.html
Banks #38	www.sosweb.state.ar.us/corps/bkin
Cemeteries, Perpetual Care #39	www.state.ar.us/arsec
Child Care Provider #26	www.state.ar.us/childcare/search.html
Chiropractor #09	www.state.ar.us/asbce
Contractor #23	www.state.ar.us/clb/search.html
Dental Hygienist #11	www.asbde.org/hygenist.htm
Dentist #11	www.asbde.org/dentists.htm
Engineer #19	www.state.ar.us/pels/search.html
Engineer-in-Training #19	www.state.ar.us/pels/search.html
Home Inspector #38	www.sosweb.state.ar.us/corps/homeinsp
Homebuilder #38	www.sosweb.state.ar.us/corps/homebldr
Insurance Agency #38	www.sosweb.state.ar.us/corps/bkin
Insurance Sales Agent #02	www.state.ar.us/insurance/license/search.html
Investment Advisor #39	www.state.ar.us/arsec
Landscape Architect #06	www.state.ar.us/arch/search.html
Lobbyist #38	www.sosweb.state.ar.us/elect.html
Mortgage Loan Brokers/Companies #39	www.state.ar.us/arsec
Notary Public #38	www.sosweb.state.ar.us/corps/notary
Nurse #15	www.state.ar.us/nurse/database/search.html
Nurse Midwife #15	www.state.ar.us/nurse/database/search.html
Nurse-LPN #15	www.state.ar.us/nurse/database/search.html
Optometrist #16	www.arbo.org/nodb2000/licsearch.asp
Real Estate Broker #37	www.state.ar.us/arec/db
Real Estate Sales Agent #37	www.state.ar.us/arec/db
Securities Agent #39	www.state.ar.us/arsec
Securities Broker/Dealer #39	www.state.ar.us/arsec
Social Worker #40	www.state.ar.us/swlb/search/index.html
Surveyor #19	www.state.ar.us/pels/search.html
Surveyor-in-Training #19	www.state.ar.us/pels/search.html
Teacher #32	www.as-is.org/directory/search_lic.html

Licensing Quick Finder

Abstractor #48 ... 870-942-8064
Acupuncturist #46 ... 501-688-8851
Administrator #32 ... 501-682-4695
Agricultural Consultant #33 ... 501-225-1598
Agricultural Seed Dealer #33 ... 501-225-1598
Agriculture Education #32 ... 501-682-4695
Anesthetician #15 ... 501-686-2200
Architect #06 ... 501-682-3171
Armored Car Guard #42 ... 501-618-8600
Asbestos Abatement Inspector #28 ... 501-682-0718
Asbestos Abatement Management Planner #28 ... 501-682-0718
Asbestos Abatement Training Provider #28 ... 501-682-0718
Asbestos Removal Worker #28 ... 501-682-0718
Athletic Manager #04 ... 501-666-5544
Athletic Promoter/Matchmaker #04 ... 501-666-5544
Attorney #43 ... 501-682-6849
Auctioneer #05 ... 501-682-1156
Audiologist #41 ... 501-320-4319
Bail Bondsman #02 ... 501-686-9050
Banks #38 ... 501-682-3409
Barber #07 ... 501-682-4035
Barber Instructor #07 ... 501-682-4035
Barber Technician #07 ... 501-682-4035
Boiler Inspector #27 ... 501-682-4513
Boiler Installer #27 ... 501-682-4513
Boiler Operator #27 ... 501-682-4513
Boiler Repairer #27 ... 501-682-4513
Boxer #04 ... 501-666-5544
Boxing/Wrestling Referee #04 ... 501-666-5544
Burglar Alarm Systems Agent #42 ... 501-618-8600

Burglar Alarm Systems Manager #42 ... 501-618-8600
Business Education Teacher #32 ... 501-682-4695
Career Orientation Teacher #32 ... 501-682-4695
Cemeteries, Perpetual Care #39 ... 501-324-9260
Chauffeur #24 ... 501-371-1741
Check Cashers #10 ... 501-244-9194
Child Care Provider #26 ... 501-682-9699
Chiropractor #09 ... 501-682-9015
Claims Adjuster #02 ... 501-371-2750
Collection Agency #10 ... 501-376-9814
Collection Agency Collector #10 ... 501-376-9814
Collection Agency Manager #10 ... 501-376-9814
Combination Welder #35 ... 501-812-2254
Commercial Applicator #33 ... 501-225-1598
Contractor #23 ... 501-372-4661
Coordinated Career Education #32 ... 501-682-4695
Cosmetologist #49 ... 501-682-2168
Cosmetology Instructor #49 ... 501-682-2168
Counselor #51 ... 870-235-4131
Court Reporter #08 ... 501-682-6850
Custom Applicator #33 ... 501-225-1598
Dental Assistant #11 ... 501-682-2085
Dental Hygienist #11 ... 501-682-2085
Dentist #11 ... 501-682-2085
Dietitian #29 ... 501-374-8212
Egg Grader #53 ... 501-225-5138
Electrical Contractor #27 ... 501-682-4549
Electrologist #49 ... 501-682-2168
Electrolysis Instructor #49 ... 501-682-2168
Elevator/Lifting Device Inspector #27 ... 501-682-4531
Embalmer #12 ... 501-682-0574
Embalmer Apprentice #12 ... 501-682-0574

Emergency Medical Technician #25 ... 501-661-2262
Emergency Medical Technician-Paramedic #25 ... 501-661-2262
Employment Agency Manager #27 ... 501-682-4505
Employment Agent & Counselor #27 ... 501-682-4505
Engineer #19 ... 501-682-2824
Engineer-in-Training #19 ... 501-682-2824
Equine Dentist #36 ... 501-682-1467
Exterminator #33 ... 501-225-1598
Fire Equipment Inspector #56 ... 501-661-7903
Fire Extinguisher Repairer #56 ... 501-661-7903
Fire Extinguisher Sprinkler Inspector #56 ... 501-661-7903
Forester #20 ... 501-296-1998
Funeral Director #12 ... 501-682-0574
Funeral Director Apprentice #12 ... 501-682-0574
Gas Fitter #25 ... 501-661-2000
Gas Fitter Trainee #25 ... 501-661-2262
Geologist #21 ... 501-296-1877
Grain Warehouseman #33 ... 501-225-1598
Greyhound Racing #36 ... 501-682-1467
Hearing Instrument Dispenser #14 ... 501-663-5869
Home Inspector #38 ... 501-682-3409
Homebuilder #38 ... 501-682-3409
Horse Racing #36 ... 501-682-1467
Hospital Maintenance Plumber #25 ... 501-661-2262
Industrial Maintenance Electrician #27 ... 501-682-4549
Insurance Agency #38 ... 501-682-3409
Insurance Sales Agent #02 ... 501-371-2750
Investment Advisor #39 ... 501-324-9260
Landscape Architect #06 ... 501-682-3393

Liquor Distributor #01 501-682-1105	Occupational Therapist #31 501-296-1802	School Principal #32.........................501-682-4344
Lobbyist #38 501-682-1010	Occupational Therapy Assistant #31 501-296-1802	School Superintendant #32 501-682-4344
Manicurist #49 501-682-2168	Optician #50.....................................870-572-2847	Securities Agent #39 501-324-9260
Manufactured Home Dealer #54 501-324-9032	Optometrist #16 501-268-4351	Securities Broker/Dealer #39 501-324-9260
Manufactured Home Installer #54 501-324-9032	Osteopathic Physician #31 501-296-1802	Security Guard #42 501-618-8600
Manufactured Home Manufacturer #54	Permanent Cosmetic/Tattoo Artist #25	Septic Tank Cleaner #25 501-661-2000
....501-324-9032	501-661-2000	Social Worker #40 501-372-5071
Manufactured Home Salesperson #54	Petroleum Dealer #30 501-324-9228	Solid Waste Facility Operator #28.........501-682-0585
....501-324-9032	Pharmacist #17 501-682-0190	Speech Pathologist #41.....................501-320-4319
Marriage & Family Therapist #51 870-235-4131	Pharmacist Intern #17 501-682-0190	State Trooper #42 501-618-8600
Martial Arts #04................................501-666-5544	Physical Therapist #03 501-228-7100	Surveyor #19 501-682-2824
Medical Doctor/Surgeon #31 501-296-1802	Podiatrist #34 501-664-3668	Surveyor-in-Training #19 501-682-2824
Mortgage Loan Brokers/Companies #39	Polygraph Examiner #42 501-618-8600	Teacher #32......................................501-682-4695
....501-324-9260	Private Investigator #42 501-618-8600	Therapy Technician (Masseur/Masseuse) #22
Motor Vehicle Dealer/Salesperson-New #55	Psychological Examiner #13 501-682-6167	501-534-4734
....501-682-1428	Psychologist #13...............................501-682-6167	Veterinarian #44 501-224-2836
Motor Vehicle Dealer/Salesperson-Used #42	Public Accountant-CPA #18................501-682-1520	Veterinary Technician #44 501-224-2836
....501-618-8600	Pump Installer #45 501-682-1025	Waste Water Treatment Plant Operator #28
Notary Public #38.............................501-682-3409	Real Estate Appraiser #37 501-683-8010	501-682-2700
Nurse #15..501-686-2200	Real Estate Broker #37 501-683-8010	Water Supply Operator #25 501-661-2000
Nurse Midwife #15 501-686-2200	Real Estate Sales Agent #37 501-683-8010	Water Well Driller #45 501-682-1025
Nurse-Anesthetist #15.......................501-686-2200	Respiratory Care Practitioner #31 501-296-1802	Wrestler #04 501-666-5544
Nurse-LPN #15 501-686-2200	Ring Announcer #04...........................501-666-5544	
Nurseryman #33 501-225-1598	Safety Supervisor #30 501-324-9228	
Nursing Home Administrator #52 501-682-1001	School Counselor #32 501-682-4344	

Licensing Agency Information

01 Alcoholic Beverage Control Division, 100 Main St, #503, Little Rock, AR 72201; 501-682-1105, Fax: 501-682-2221.

02 Department of Insurance, Licensing Division, 1200 W 3rd St, Little Rock, AR 72201; 800-282-9134, Fax: 501-371-2618.

www.state.ar.us/insurance

03 Board of Physical Therapy, 9 Shackelford Plaza, #1, Little Rock, AR 72211; 501-228-7100, Fax: 501-228-5535.

04 Athletic Commission, 809 N Palm St, Little Rock, AR 72205-1946; 501-666-5544, Fax: 501-666-5546.

05 Auctioneers Licensing Board, 101 E Capital, #112B, Little Rock, AR 72201; 501-682-1156, Fax: 501-682-1158.

aalb.org

06 Board of Architecture, 101 E Capitol, #208, Little Rock, AR 72201; 501-682-3171, Fax: 501-682-3172.

www.state.ar.us/arch

Direct URL to search licenses: www.state.ar.us/arch/search.html You can search online using name, city, and organization name.

07 Board of Barber Examiners, 103 E 7th St Rm 212, Little Rock, AR 72201-4512; 501-682-4035, Fax: 501-682-2806.

08 Board of Certified Court Reporter Examiners, 625 Marshall St, Justice Bldg, Little Rock, AR 72201; 501-682-6850, Fax: 501-682-6877 c/o Renee.

09 Board of Chiropractic Examiners, 101 E Capital, #209, Little Rock, AR 72201; 501-682-9015, Fax: 501-682-9016.

www.state.ar.us/asbce

Direct URL to search licenses: www.state.ar.us/asbce/search.html You can search online using last name or city.

10 Board of Collection Agencies, 523 S Louisiana St, #460, Little Rock, AR 72201; 501-376-9814, Fax: 501-372-5383.

11 Board of Dental Examiners, 101 E Capitol Ave, #111, Little Rock, AR 72201; 501-682-2085, Fax: 501-682-3543.

www.asbde.org

Direct URL to search licenses: www.asbde.org/current.htm

12 Board of Embalmers & Funeral Directors, 101 E Capitol Ave, #113, Little Rock, AR 72201; 501-682-0574, Fax: 501-682-0575.

13 Board of Examiners in Psychology, 101 E Capitol Ave, #415, Little Rock, AR 72201; 501-682-6167, Fax: 501-682-6165.

www.state.ar.us/abep

14 Board of Hearing Instrument Dispensers, 305 N Monroe, Little Rock, AR 72205; 501-663-5869, Fax: 501-663-6359.

15 Board of Nursing, 1123 S University, University Tower Bldg, #800, Little Rock, AR 72204-1619; 501-686-2700, Fax: 501-686-2714.

www.state.ar.us/nurse

Direct URL to search licenses: www.state.ar.us/nurse/database/search.html You can search online using name and license number.

16 Board of Optometry, PO Box 512 (410 W Race St), Searcy, AR 72143; 501-268-4351, Fax: 501-268-5631.

www.state.ar.us/opt/arkopt.html

Direct URL to search licenses: www.arbo.org/nodb2000/licsearch.asp You can search online using national database by name, city, or state.

17 Board of Pharmacy, 101 E Capitol, #218, Little Rock, AR 72201; 501-682-0190, Fax: 501-682-0195.

www.state.ar.us/asbp

18 Board of Public Accountancy, 101 E Capitol, #430, Little Rock, AR 72201; 501-682-1520, Fax: 501-682-5538.

19 Board of Registration for Engineers/Land Surveyors, PO Box 3750 (PO Box 3750), Little Rock, AR 72203; 501-682-2824, Fax: 501-682-2827.

www.state.ar.us/pels

Direct URL to search licenses: www.state.ar.us/pels/search.html You can search online using name, company, city, company or license #

20 Board of Registration for Foresters, PO Box 7424 (PO Box 7424), Little Rock, AR 72217; 501-296-1998, Fax: 501-296-1949.

21 Board of Registration for Professional Geologists, 3815 W Roosevelt Rd, Little Rock, AR 72204; 501-296-1877, Fax: 501-663-7360.

www.state.ar.us/agc/BOR.htm

22 Board of Massage Therapy, 103 Airways (PO Box 20739), Hot Springs, AR 71903-0739; 501-623-0444, Fax: 501-623-4130.

23 Contractors Licensing Board, 621 E Capitol, Little Rock, AR 72202; 501-372-4661, Fax: 501-372-2247.

www.state.ar.us/clb

Direct URL to search licenses: www.state.ar.us/clb/search.html You can search online using name, city, class/description, and specialty.

24 Department of Finance & Administration, Division of Revenues, Ledbetter Bldg, 7th & Wolfe Streets #215, Little Rock, AR 72203; 501-324-9057, Fax: 501-682-7075.

25 Department of Health, 4815 W Markham, Slot 38, Little Rock, AR 72205-3867; 501-661-2262, Fax: 501-280-4901.

26 Department of Human Services, Division of Child Care & Early Childhood Education, 101 E Capitol, #106, Little Rock, AR 72201; 501-682-4891, Fax: 501-682-4897.

www.state.ar.us/childcare

Direct URL to search licenses: www.state.ar.us/childcare You can search online using name or company name, city, and ZIP Code.

27 Department of Labor, 10421 W Markham, Little Rock, AR 72205; 501-682-4500, Fax: 501-682-4535. www.state.ar.us/labor

28 Department of Pollution Control & Ecology, PO Box 8913 (PO Box 8913), Little Rock, AR 72219-8913; 501-682-0744, Fax: 501-682-0798.

www.adeq.state.ar.us

29 Dietetics Licensing Board, PO Box 1016 (PO Box 1016), Little Rock, AR 72115; 501-221-0566, Fax: 501-843-0878.

30 Liquefied Petroleum Gas Board, 1421 W 6th St, Little Rock, AR 72201; 501-324-9228, Fax: 501-324-9230.

31 Medical Board, 2100 Riverside, #200, Little Rock, AR 72202; 501-296-1802, Fax: 501-296-1805. They offer online verification using a modem system. To obtain more information on the program, fax a request including a contact name to the fax number listed above.

32 Department of Education, Office of Teacher Education & Licensure, State Education Bldg, Rm 106, Capitol Mall #4, Little Rock, AR 72201; 501-682-4695, Fax: 501-682-4898.

http://arkedu.state.ar.us/teacher.htm

33 Plant Board, PO Box 1069 (PO Box 1069), Little Rock, AR 72203; 501-225-1598, Fax: 501-225-3590.

34 Board of Podiatrical Medicine, 2001 Georgia Ave, Little Rock, AR 72207-5014; 501-664-3668, Fax: 501-666-3338.

35 Pulaski Technical College, 3000 W Scenic Dr, North Little Rock, AR 72118; 501-812-2254, Fax: 501-812-2316.

www.ptc.tec.ar.us

36 Racing Commission, PO Box 3076 (PO Box 3076), Little Rock, AR 72203; 501-682-1467, Fax: 501-682-5273.

37 Real Estate Commission, 612 Summit St, Little Rock, AR 72201; 501-683-8010, Fax: 501-682-2729.

www.state.ar.us/arec/frmain.htm

Direct URL to search licenses: www.state.ar.us/arec/db You can search online using name, city, and firm name.

38 Secretary of State, 256 State Capitol, Little Rock, AR 72201; 501-682-3409, Fax: 501-682-3437.

Direct URL to search licenses: www.sosweb.state.ar.us You can search online using name

39 Securities Department, 201 W Markham, Heritage West Bldg, 3rd Fl, Little Rock, AR 72201; 501-324-9260, Fax: 501-324-9268.
www.state.ar.us/arsec

Direct URL to search licenses: www.state.ar.us/arsec You can search online using alphabetical lists

40 Social Work Licensing Board, PO Box 250381 (2020 W 3rd St #503, POB 2560381), Little Rock, AR 72225; 501-372-5071, Fax: 501-372-6301.
www.state.ar.us/swlb

Direct URL to search licenses: www.state.ar.us/swlb/search/index.html You can search online using last name and city

41 Speech Pathology & Audiology, Arkansas Children's Hospital, 800 Marshall St., Little Rock, AR 72202; 501-320-4319, Fax: 501-320-6881.

42 Wes Adams, State Police, #1 State Police Plaza Drive, Little Rock, AR 72209; 501-618-8608.

43 Supreme Court, 625 Marshall, Justice Bldg, Little Rock, AR 72201; 501-682-6849, Fax: 501-682-6877.

44 Veterinary Medical Examining Board, PO Box 5497 (PO Box 8505), Little Rock, AR 72215; 501-224-2836, Fax: 501-224-1100.

45 Waterwell Construction Commission, 101 E Capitol #350, Little Rock, AR 72201; 501-682-1025, Fax: 501-682-3991.

46 Acupuncture Board, 5110 Kavanaugh Blvd, Little Ranch, AR 72207; 501-663-5006, Fax: 501-280-9203.

48 Abstractor's Board of Examiners, 71 Pinecrest Cir, Sheridan, AR 72150; 870-942-8064.

49 Board of Cosmetology, 101 E Capitol #108, Little Rock, AR 72201; 501-682-2168.

50 Board of Dispensing Opticians, Box 627, Helena, AR 72342; 870-572-2847.

51 Southern Arkansas University, Board of Examiners in Counseling, PO Box 1396, Magnolia, AR 71753-5000; 870-235-4131.

52 Department of Human Services, 7th & Main Streets, Little Rock, AR 72203; 501-682-1001.

53 Livestock & Poultry Commission, 1 Natural Resources Dr, PO Box 8505, Little Rock, AR 72215; 501-225-5138.

54 Manufactured Home Commission, 523 S Louisiana #500, Little Rock, AR 72201; 501-324-9032.

55 Motor Vehicle Commission, 101 E Capitol #210, Little Rock, AR 72201; 501-682-1428.

56 Fire Protection Licensing Board, 7509 Cantrell Rd #103-A, Little Rock, AR 72207; 501-661-7903.

The following list indicates the district and division name for each county in the state. If the district or division name of the bankruptcy court is different from the civil/criminal court, it appears in parentheses.

County/Court Cross Reference

County	District	Division
Arkansas	Eastern	Pine Bluff (Little Rock)
Ashley	Western (Eastern)	El Dorado (Little Rock)
Baxter	Western	Harrison (Fayetteville)
Benton	Western	Fayetteville
Boone	Western	Harrison (Fayetteville)
Bradley	Western (Eastern)	El Dorado (Little Rock)
Calhoun	Western (Eastern)	El Dorado (Little Rock)
Carroll	Western	Harrison (Fayetteville)
Chicot	Eastern	Pine Bluff (Little Rock)
Clark	Western (Eastern)	Hot Springs (Little Rock)
Clay	Eastern	Jonesboro (Little Rock)
Cleburne	Eastern	Batesville (Little Rock)
Cleveland	Eastern	Pine Bluff (Little Rock)
Columbia	Western (Eastern)	El Dorado (Little Rock)
Conway	Eastern	Little Rock
Craighead	Eastern	Jonesboro (Little Rock)
Crawford	Western	Fort Smith (Fayetteville)
Crittenden	Eastern	Jonesboro (Little Rock)
Cross	Eastern	Helena (Little Rock)
Dallas	Eastern	Pine Bluff (Little Rock)
Desha	Eastern	Pine Bluff (Little Rock)
Drew	Eastern	Pine Bluff (Little Rock)
Faulkner	Eastern	Little Rock
Franklin	Western	Fort Smith (Fayetteville)
Fulton	Eastern	Batesville (Little Rock)
Garland	Western (Eastern)	Hot Springs (Little Rock)
Grant	Eastern	Pine Bluff (Little Rock)
Greene	Eastern	Jonesboro (Little Rock)
Hempstead	Western (Eastern)	Texarkana (Little Rock)
Hot Spring	Western (Eastern)	Hot Springs (Little Rock)
Howard	Western (Eastern)	Texarkana (Little Rock)
Independence	Eastern	Batesville (Little Rock)
Izard	Eastern	Batesville (Little Rock)
Jackson	Eastern	Batesville (Little Rock)
Jefferson	Eastern	Pine Bluff (Little Rock)
Johnson	Western	Fort Smith (Fayetteville)
Lafayette	Western (Eastern)	Texarkana (Little Rock)
Lawrence	Eastern	Jonesboro (Little Rock)
Lee	Eastern	Helena (Little Rock)
Lincoln	Eastern	Pine Bluff (Little Rock)
Little River	Western (Eastern)	Texarkana (Little Rock)
Logan	Western	Fort Smith (Fayetteville)
Lonoke	Eastern	Little Rock
Madison	Western	Fayetteville
Marion	Western	Harrison (Fayetteville)
Miller	Western (Eastern)	Texarkana (Little Rock)
Mississippi	Eastern	Jonesboro (Little Rock)
Monroe	Eastern	Helena (Little Rock)
Montgomery	Western (Eastern)	Hot Springs (Little Rock)
Nevada	Western (Eastern)	Texarkana (Little Rock)
Newton	Western	Harrison (Fayetteville)
Ouachita	Western (Eastern)	El Dorado (Little Rock)
Perry	Eastern	Little Rock
Phillips	Eastern	Helena (Little Rock)
Pike	Western (Eastern)	Hot Springs (Little Rock)
Poinsett	Eastern	Jonesboro (Little Rock)
Polk	Western	Fort Smith (Fayetteville)
Pope	Eastern	Little Rock
Prairie	Eastern	Little Rock
Pulaski	Eastern	Little Rock
Randolph	Eastern	Jonesboro (Little Rock)
Saline	Eastern	Little Rock
Scott	Western	Fort Smith (Fayetteville)
Searcy	Western	Harrison (Fayetteville)
Sebastian	Western	Fort Smith (Fayetteville)
Sevier	Western (Eastern)	Texarkana (Little Rock)
Sharp	Eastern	Batesville (Little Rock)
St. Francis	Eastern	Helena (Little Rock)
Stone	Eastern	Batesville (Little Rock)
Union	Western (Eastern)	El Dorado (Little Rock)
Van Buren	Eastern	Little Rock
Washington	Western	Fayetteville
White	Eastern	Little Rock
Woodruff	Eastern	Helena (Little Rock)
Yell	Eastern	Little Rock

US District Court

Eastern District of Arkansas

Batesville Division c/o Little Rock Division, PO Box 869, Little Rock, AR 72201-3325 (Courier Address: 600 W Capital, Room 402, Little Rock, AR 72201), 501-324-5351.

www.are.uscourts.gov

Counties: Cleburne, Fulton, Independence, Izard, Jackson, Sharp, Stone.

Indexing & Storage: Cases are indexed by as well as by case number. New cases are available in the index after filing date. Open records are located at the Division.

Fee & Payment: The fee is no charge per item (one party name or case number). Payment may be made by money order, cashier check. Business checks are not accepted. Personal checks are not accepted.

Phone Search: Searching is not available by phone.

In Person Search: In person searching is available.

PACER: Sign-up number is 800-676-6856. Access fee is $.60 per minute. Toll-free access: 800-371-8842. Local access: 501-324-6190. Case records are available back to 1987-89. Records are purged every five years. New records are available online after 1 day.

Other Online Access: You can search records on the Internet using RACER. Currently the system is free and requires free registration. Simply visit www.are.uscourts.gov and click on "Case Information."

Helena Division 600 W Capital Rm 402, Little Rock, AR 72201-3325 (Courier Address: 600 W Capital, Room 402, Little Rock, AR 72201), 501-324-5351.

www.are.uscourts.gov

Counties: Cross, Lee, Monroe, Phillips, St. Francis, Woodruff.

Indexing & Storage: Cases are indexed by as well as by case number. New cases are available in the index after filing date. Open records are located at the Division.

Fee & Payment: The fee is no charge per item (one party name or case number). Payment may be made by money order, cashier check. Business checks are not accepted. Personal checks are not accepted.

Phone Search: Searching is not available by phone.

In Person Search: In person searching is available.

PACER: Sign-up number is 800-676-6856. Access fee is $.60 per minute. Toll-free access: 800-371-8842. Local access: 501-324-6190. Case records are available back to 1987-89. Records are purged every five years. New records are available online after 1 day.

Other Online Access: You can search records on the Internet using RACER. Currently the system is free and requires free registration. Simply visit www.are.uscourts.gov and click on "Case Information."

Jonesboro Division PO Box 7080, Jonesboro, AR 72403 (Courier Address: Federal Office Bldg, Room 312, 615 S Main St, Jonesboro, AR 72401), 870-972-4610, Fax: 870-972-4612.

www.are.uscourts.gov

Counties: Clay, Craighead, Crittenden, Greene, Lawrence, Mississippi, Poinsett, Randolph.

Indexing & Storage: Cases are indexed by defendant and plaintiff as well as by case number. New cases are available in the index immediately after filing date. A computer index is maintained. Open records are located at this court.

Fee & Payment: The fee is $15.00 per item (one party name or case number). Payment may be made by money order, cashier check, personal check. Prepayment is required. Payee: Clerk, US District Court. Certification fee: $5.00 per document. Copy fee: $.50 per page.

Phone Search: Docket information available by phone. An automated voice case information service (VCIS) is not available.

Fax Search: Fax requests accepted on same basis as mail requests.

Mail Search: A stamped self addressed envelope is not required.

In Person Search: In person searching is available.

PACER: Sign-up number is 800-676-6856. Access fee is $.60 per minute. Toll-free access: 800-371-8842. Local access: 501-324-6190. Case records are available back to 1987-89. Records are purged every five years. New records are available online after 1 day.

Other Online Access: You can search records on the Internet using RACER. Currently the system is free and requires free registration. Simply visit www.are.uscourts.gov and click on "Case Information."

Little Rock Division Room 402, 600 W Capitol, Little Rock, AR 72201, 501-324-5351.

www.are.uscourts.gov

Counties: Conway, Faulkner, Lonoke, Perry, Pope, Prairie, Pulaski, Saline, Van Buren, White, Yell.

Indexing & Storage: Cases are indexed by defendant and plaintiff as well as by case number. New cases are available in the index immediately after filing date. Both computer and card indexes are maintained. Records are also indexed on microfiche. Open records are located at this court.

Fee & Payment: The fee is $15.00 per item (one party name or case number). Payment may be made by money order, cashier check, personal check, Visa, Mastercard. Prepayment is required. Payee: Clerk, US District Court. Certification fee: $5.00 per document. Copy fee: $.50 per page.

Phone Search: Docket information available by phone. An automated voice case information service (VCIS) is not available.

Mail Search: Always enclose a stamped self addressed envelope.

In Person Search: In person searching is available.

PACER: Sign-up number is 800-676-6856. Access fee is $.60 per minute. Toll-free access: 800-371-8842. Local access: 501-324-6190. Case records are available back to 1987-89. Records are purged every five years. New records are available online after 1 day.

Other Online Access: You can search records on the Internet using RACER. Currently the system is free and requires free registration. Simply visit www.are.uscourts.gov and click on "Case Information."

Pine Bluff Division PO Box 8307, Pine Bluff, AR 71611-8307 (Courier Address: US Post Office & Courthouse, 100 E 8th St, Room 3103, Pine Bluff, AR 71601), 870-536-1190, Fax: 870-536-6330.

www.are.uscourts.gov

Counties: Arkansas, Chicot, Cleveland, Dallas, Desha, Drew, Grant, Jefferson, Lincoln.

Indexing & Storage: Cases are indexed by defendant and plaintiff as well as by case number. New cases are available in the index immediately after filing date. A computer index is maintained. Records are on the computer from 1989. Records are also indexed on microfiche. Open records are located at this court.

Fee & Payment: The fee is $15.00 per item (one party name or case number). Payment may be made by money order, cashier check, personal check. Prepayment is required for copies and certification. Payee: US District Clerk. Certification fee: $5.00 per document. Copy fee: $.50 per page.

Phone Search: Searching is not available by phone.

Mail Search: Always enclose a stamped self addressed envelope.

In Person Search: In person searching is available.

PACER: Sign-up number is 800-676-6856. Access fee is $.60 per minute. Toll-free access: 800-371-8842. Local access: 501-324-6190. Case records are available back to 1987-89. Records are purged every five years. New records are available online after 1 day.

Other Online Access: You can search records on the Internet using RACER. Currently the system is free and requires free registration. Simply visit www.are.uscourts.gov and click on "Case Information."

US Bankruptcy Court
Eastern District of Arkansas

Little Rock Division PO Drawer 3777, Little Rock, AR 72203 (Courier Address: Room 101, 600 W Capitol, Little Rock, AR 72201), 501-918-5500, Fax: 501-918-5520.

www.areb.uscourts.gov

Counties: Same counties as included in Eastern District of Arkansas, plus the counties included in the Western District divisions of El Dorado, Hot Springs and Texarkana. All bankruptcy cases in Arkansas prior to mid-1993 were heard here.

Indexing & Storage: Cases are indexed by debtor and creditors as well as by case number. New cases are available in the index immediately after filing date. Both computer and card indexes are maintained. Records are also indexed on microfiche. Open records are located at this court.

Fee & Payment: The fee is $15.00 per item (one party name or case number). Payment may be made by money order, cashier check, personal check, Visa or Mastercard. Prepayment is required. Debtor's checks are not accepted. Payee: Clerk, US Bankruptcy Court. Certification fee: $5.00 per document. Copy fee: $.50 per page.

Phone Search: Only the basic information not provided on the VCIS will be released over the phone. This includes the case number, chapter, judge, attorney, trustee, date if case closed, etc. An automated voice case information service (VCIS) is available. Call VCIS at 800-891-6741 or 501-918-5555.

Mail Search: Always enclose a stamped self addressed envelope.

In Person Search: In person searching is available.

PACER: Sign-up number is 800-676-6856. Access fee is $.60 per minute. Toll-free access: 800-891-6572. Local access: 501-918-6199. Case records are available back to May 1989. Records are purged every six months. New civil records are available online after 1 day. PACER is available on the Internet at http://pacer.areb.uscourts.gov.

US District Court
Western District of Arkansas

El Dorado Division PO Box 1566, El Dorado, AR 71731 (Courier Address: Room 205, 101 S Jackson, El Dorado, AR 71731), 870-862-1202.

www.arwd.uscourts.gov

Counties: Ashley, Bradley, Calhoun, Columbia, Ouachita, Union.

Indexing & Storage: Cases are indexed by defendant and plaintiff as well as by case number. New cases are available in the index immediately after filing date. A computer index is maintained. Files are maintained numerically by year. Open records are located at this court.

Fee & Payment: The fee is $15.00 per item (one party name or case number). Payment may be made by money order, cashier check, personal check, Visa, Mastercard. Prepayment is required for out of state searchers. Payee: Clerk, US District Court. Certification fee: $5.00 per document. Copy fee: $.50 per page.

Phone Search: Only docket information is available by phone. An automated voice case information service (VCIS) is not available.

Fax Search: Will accept fax request usually at no cost as long as results do not have to be in writing. Call for more information.

Mail Search: Always enclose a stamped self addressed envelope.

In Person Search: In person searching is available.

PACER: Sign-up number is 501-783-6833. Access fee is $.60 per minute. Case records are available back to September 1990. Records are purged every five years. New records are available online after 1 day.

Other Online Access: PACER via E-mail offers case information directly to your e-mailbox. Simply   visit www.arwd.uscourts.gov/mailform.html and input the information you are looking for, and the system will automatically send the results to you by e-mail.

Fayetteville Division PO Box 6420, Fayetteville, AR 72702 (Courier Address: Room 510, 35 E Mountain, Fayetteville, AR 72701), 501-521-6980, Fax: 501-575-0774.

www.arwd.uscourts.gov

Counties: Benton, Madison, Washington.

Indexing & Storage: Cases are indexed by defendant and plaintiff as well as by case number. New cases are available in the index immediately after filing date. A computer index is maintained. Files are maintained numerically by year. Open records are located at this court.

Fee & Payment: The fee is $15.00 per item (one party name or case number). Payment may be made by money order, cashier check, personal check, Visa, Mastercard. Prepayment is required for out of state searchers. Payee: Clerk, Western District of Arkansas. Certification fee: $5.00 per document. Copy fee: $.50 per page. You are allowed to make your own copies. These copies cost $.50 per page. Searches can be done in person at no charge to the searcher if no written record is furnished.

Phone Search: Only docket information is available by phone. An automated voice case information service (VCIS) is not available.

Fax Search: Will accept fax request on same basis as mail request. Call for information regarding fax results.

Mail Search: A stamped self addressed envelope is not required.

In Person Search: In person searching is available.

PACER: Sign-up number is 501-783-6833. Access fee is $.60 per minute. Case records are available back to September 1990. Records are purged every five years. New records are available online after 1 day.

Other Online Access: PACER via E-mail offers case information directly to your e-mailbox. Simply   visit www.arwd.uscourts.gov/mailform.html and input the information you are looking for, and the system will automatically send the results to you by e-mail.

Fort Smith Division PO Box 1547, Fort Smith, AR 72902 (Courier Address: Judge Isaac C. Parker Federal Bldg #1038, 6th & Rogers Ave, Fort Smith, AR 72901), 501-783-6833, Fax: 501-783-6308.

www.arwd.uscourts.gov

Counties: Crawford, Franklin, Johnson, Logan, Polk, Scott, Sebastian.

Indexing & Storage: Cases are indexed by defendant and plaintiff as well as by case number. New cases are available in the index immediately after filing date. A computer index is maintained. Files are maintained numerically by year. Open records are located at this court.

Fee & Payment: The fee is $15.00 per item (one party name or case number). Payment may be made by money order, cashier check, personal

check, Visa, Mastercard. Prepayment is required for out of state searchers. Payee: Clerk of Court. Certification fee: $5.00 per document. Copy fee: $.50 per page. You are allowed to make your own copies. These copies cost $.50 per page.

Phone Search: Only docket information is available by phone. An automated voice case information service (VCIS) is not available.

Mail Search: A stamped self addressed envelope is not required.

In Person Search: In person searching is available.

PACER: Sign-up number is 501-783-6833. Access fee is $.60 per minute. Case records are available back to September 1990. Records are purged every five years. New records are available online after 1 day.

Other Online Access: PACER via E-mail offers case information directly to your e-mailbox. Simply   visit www.arwd.uscourts.gov/mailform.html and input the information you are looking for, and the system will automatically send the results to you by e-mail.

Hot Springs Division PO Drawer I, Hot Springs, AR 71902 (Courier Address: Federal Bldg Room 347, 100 Reserve, Hot Springs, AR 71901), 501-623-6411.

www.arwd.uscourts.gov

Counties: Clark, Garland, Hot Springs, Montgomery, Pike.

Indexing & Storage: Cases are indexed by defendant and plaintiff as well as by case number. New cases are available in the index immediately after filing date. A computer index is maintained. Files are maintained numerically by year. Open records are located at this court.

Fee & Payment: The fee is $15.00 per item (one party name or case number). Payment may be made by money order, cashier check, personal check, Visa, Mastercard. Prepayment is required for out of state searchers. Payee: Clerk, Western District of Arkansas. Certification fee: $5.00 per document. Copy fee: $.50 per page.

Phone Search: Searching is not available by phone.

Mail Search: Always enclose a stamped self addressed envelope.

In Person Search: In person searching is available.

PACER: Sign-up number is 501-783-6833. Access fee is $.60 per minute. Case records are available back to September 1990. Records are purged every five years. New records are available online after 1 day.

Other Online Access: PACER via E-mail offers case information directly to your e-mailbox. Simply   visit www.arwd.uscourts.gov/mailform.html and input the information you are looking for, and the system will automatically send the results to you by e-mail.

Texarkana Division PO Box 2746, Texarkana, AR 75504-2746 (Courier Address: 500 State Line Ave, Texarkana, AR 71854), 870-773-3381.

www.arwd.uscourts.gov

Counties: Hempstead, Howard, Lafayette, Little River, Miller, Nevada, Sevier.

Indexing & Storage: Cases are indexed by defendant and plaintiff as well as by case number. New cases are available in the index immediately after filing date. A computer index is maintained. Files are maintained numerically by year. Records are also indexed by microfiche. Open records are located at this court.

Fee & Payment: The fee is $15.00 per item (one party name or case number). Payment may be made by money order, cashier check, personal check, Visa, Mastercard. Prepayment is required for out of state searchers. Payee: Clerk of the Court. Certification fee: $5.00 per document. Copy fee: $.50 per page. You are allowed to make your own copies. These copies cost $.50 per page.

Phone Search: Case numbers are released by phone. Anything else will depend on workload of deputy clerk. An automated voice case information service (VCIS) is not available.

Mail Search: A stamped self addressed envelope is not required.

In Person Search: In person searching is available.

PACER: Sign-up number is 501-783-6833. Access fee is $.60 per minute. Case records are available back to September 1990. Records are purged every five years. New records are available online after 1 day.

Other Online Access: PACER via E-mail offers case information directly to your e-mailbox. Simply   visit www.arwd.uscourts.gov/mailform.html and input the information you are looking for, and the system will automatically send the results to you by e-mail.

US Bankruptcy Court
Western District of Arkansas

Fayetteville Division PO Box 3097, Fayetteville, AR 72702-3097 (Courier Address: 35 E Mountain, Room 316, Fayetteville, AR 72701), 501-582-9800, Fax: 501-582-9825.

www.arb.uscourts.gov

Counties: Same counties as included in the Western District of Arkansas except that counties included in the divisions of El Dorado and Texarkana are heard in Little Rock.

Indexing & Storage: Cases are indexed by debtor and creditors as well as by case number. New cases are available in the index immediately after filing date. A computer index is maintained. Open records are located at this court.

Fee & Payment: The fee is $15.00 per item (one party name or case number). Payment may be made by money order, cashier check, personal check, Visa. Prepayment is required. Personal checks are not accepted from debtors. Licensed attorneys may be invoiced for copywork. Payee: Clerk, US Bankruptcy Court. Certification fee: $5.00 per document. Copy fee: $.50 per page.

Phone Search: Only the basic information not provided by the VCIS will be released over the phone. This includes the case number, chapter, judge, attorney, and trustee. An automated voice case information service (VCIS) is available. Call VCIS at 800-891-6741 or 501-918-5555.

Mail Search: Always enclose a stamped self addressed envelope.

In Person Search: In person searching is available.

PACER: Sign-up number is 800-676-6856. Access fee is $.60 per minute. Toll-free access: 800-891-6572. Local access: 501-918-6199. Case records are available back to May 1989. Records are purged every six months. New civil records are available online after 1 day.

Court	Jurisdiction	No. of Courts	How Organized
Circuit Courts*	General	1	24 Circuits
County Courts*	Limited		
Combined Courts*		47	
Chancery and Probate Courts*	Limited		24 Circuits
Combined Circuit/Chancery*		36	
Municipal Courts*	Municipal	77	
City Courts	Limited	94	
Court of Common Pleas	Limited	4	
Justice of the Peace Courts	Limited	55	
Police Courts	Limited	5	

* Profiled in this Sourcebook.

Court	CIVIL								
	Tort	Contract	Real Estate	Min. Claim	Max. Claim	Small Claims	Estate	Eviction	Domestic Relations
Circuit Courts*	X	X	X	$5000	No Max				
County Courts*			X						
Chancery and Probate Courts*	X	X	X				X		X
Municipal Courts*		X	X	$0	$3000	$5000		X	
City Courts		X	X	$0	$300				
Court of Common Pleas		X		$500	$1000				
Justice of the Peace Courts						$300			
Police Courts		X	X	$0	$300				

Court	CRIMINAL				
	Felony	Misdemeanor	DWI/DUI	Preliminary Hearing	Juvenile
Circuit Courts*	X				
County Courts*					
Chancery and Probate Courts*					X
Municipal Courts*		X	X	X	
City Courts		X	X	X	
Court of Common Pleas					
Justice of the Peace Courts		X			
Police Courts		X	X		

ADMINISTRATION
Administrative Office of Courts, 625 Marshall St, Justice Bldg, Little Rock, AR, 72201; 501-682-9400, Fax: 501-682-9410. http://courts.state.ar.us/

COURT STRUCTURE
28 Circuit Courts are the courts of general jurisdiction and can be combined with the County Courts. County Courts are, fundamentally, administrative courts dealing with county fiscal issues. Probate is handled by the Chancery and Probate Courts, or by the County Clerk in some counties. Civil limit raised to $5000 as of 8/2/97.

ONLINE ACCESS
There is a very limited internal online computer system at the Administrative Office of Courts.

ADD'L INFORMATION
Most courts that allow written search requests require an SASE. Fees vary widely across jurisdictions as do prepayment requirements.

Arkansas County

Circuit & Chancery Courts-Northern District PO Box 719, Stuttgart, AR 72160; 870-673-2056; Fax: 870-673-3869. Hours: 8AM-5PM (CST). *Felony, Civil Actions Over $5,000, Probate.*

Note: The court reports it is not bonded to search Civil or Chancery records

Civil Records: Access: In person only. Court does not conduct in person searches; visitors must perform searches for themselves. Search fee: No civil searches performed by court. Required to search: name, years to search. Civil cases indexed by defendant, plaintiff. Civil records in files from 1923, prior to 1930 records located in DeWitt (946-4219). **Criminal Records:** Access: Fax, mail, in person. Both court and visitors may perform in person searches. Search fee: $6.00 per name. Required to search: name, years to search, DOB. Criminal records in files from 1923, prior to 1930 records located in DeWitt (946-4219). Search request must be in writing. **General Information:** No juvenile records released. SASE required. Turnaround time 1-2 days. Copy fee: $.50 per page. Certification fee: $4.00. Fee payee: Tommy Suekeffer, Circuit Clerk. Personal checks accepted. Prepayment is required. Fax notes: $1.00 per page.

Circuit & Chancery Courts-Southern District 101 Courthouse Sq, De Witt, AR 72042; 870-946-4219; Fax: 870-946-1394. Hours: 8AM-5PM (CST). *Felony, Civil Actions Over $5,000.*

Civil Records: Access: Fax, mail, in person. Both court and visitors may perform in person searches. Search fee: $6.00 per name. Required to search: name, years to search. Civil cases indexed by defendant, plaintiff. Civil records in files from 1923, prior records (the two other courts in this county also) located at this court. **Criminal Records:** Access: Fax, mail, in person. Both court and visitors may perform in person searches. Search fee: $6.00 per name. Required to search: name, years to search, DOB; also helpful-SSN. Criminal records in files from 1923, prior records (the two other courts in this county also) located at this court. Search request must be in writing. **General Information:** No juvenile, expunged records released. SASE requested. Turnaround time 1-2 days. Copy fee: $.50 per page. Certification fee: $4.00. Fee payee: Arkansas County Circuit Clerk. Personal checks accepted. Prepayment is required. Fax notes: Fax fee $1.00 per copy; $6.00 per search.

Stuttgart Municipal Court PO Box 819, Stuttgart, AR 72160; 870-673-7951; Fax: 870-673-6522. Hours: 8AM-5PM (CST). *Misdemeanor, Civil Actions Under $5,000, Eviction, Small Claims.*

Civil Records: Both court and visitors may perform in person searches. Search fee:. **Criminal Records:** Both court and visitors may perform in person searches. No search fee. Required to search: name, years to search; also helpful-DOB, SSN. **General Information:** Turnaround time 3 days. Fee payee: Stuttgart Municipal Court. Prepayment is required.

Ashley County

Circuit & Chancery Courts Ashley County Courthouse, 205 E Jefferson, Hamburg, AR 71646; 870-853-2030; Fax: 870-853-2005. Hours: 8AM-4:30PM (CST). *Felony, Civil Actions Over $5,000, Probate.*

Civil Records: Access: Mail, in person. Both court and visitors may perform in person searches. Search fee: No civil searches performed by court. Required to search: name, years to search. Civil cases indexed by defendant, plaintiff. Civil records on files and index cards from 1950s. Mail requests must have case numbers. **Criminal Records:** Access: Mail, in person. Both court and visitors may perform in person searches. Search fee: No criminal searches performed by court. Required to search: name, years to search; also helpful-DOB, SSN. Criminal records on files and index cards from 1950s. No name searches by mail, must have case numbers. **General Information:** No juvenile records released. SASE required. Copy fee: $.50 per page. Certification fee: $2.50. Fee payee: Circuit Clerk's Office. Personal checks accepted. Prepayment is required.

Hamburg Municipal Court PO Box 558, City Hall, Hamburg, AR 71646; 870-853-8326; Fax: 870-853-8600. Hours: 7AM-4PM (CST). *Misdemeanor, Civil Actions Under $5,000, Eviction, Small Claims.*

Civil Records: Both court and visitors may perform in person searches. Search fee:. **Criminal Records:** Both court and visitors may perform in person searches. Search fee: $5.00. Required to search: name, years to search. **General Information:** Turnaround time 1-2 days. Fee payee: Municipal Court.

Baxter County

Circuit & Chancery Courts 1 E 7th St Courthouse Square, Mountain Home, AR 72653; 870-425-3475; Fax: 870-424-5105. Hours: 8AM-4:30PM (CST). *Felony, Civil Actions Over $5,000, Probate.*

Civil Records: Access: Fax, mail, in person. Both court and visitors may perform in person searches. Search fee: $6.00 per name. Required to search: name, years to search. Civil cases indexed by defendant, plaintiff. Civil records on computer from 1982, on criminal fee book from early 1900s. **Criminal Records:** Access: Mail, in person. Both court and visitors may perform in person searches. Search fee: $6.00 per name. Required to search: name, years to search, SSN. Criminal records on computer from 1982, on criminal fee book from early 1900s. **General Information:** No adoption or juvenile records released. SASE required. Turnaround time 1-2 days. Copy fee: $.25 per page. Certification fee: $3.00. Fee payee: Baxter County Clerk. Personal checks accepted. Prepayment is required.

Municipal Court 720 S Hickory, Mountain Home, AR 72653; 870-425-3140; Fax: 870-425-9290. Hours: 8AM-4:30PM (CST). *Misdemeanor, Civil Actions Under $5,000, Eviction, Small Claims.*

Civil Records: Only the court conducts in person searches; visitors may not. Search fee:. **Criminal Records:** Only the court conducts in person searches; visitors may not. No search fee. Required to search: name, years to search, DOB, SSN. **General Information:** Turnaround time 1-2 days. Fee payee: Municipal Court.

Benton County

Circuit & Chancery Courts 102 NE "A" St, Bentonville, AR 72712; 501-271-1015; Fax: 501-271-5719. Hours: 8AM-4:30PM (CST). *Felony, Civil Actions Over $5,000, Probate.*

Civil Records: Access: In person only. Court does not conduct in person searches; visitors must perform searches for themselves. Search fee: No civil searches performed by court. Required to search: name, years to search. Civil cases indexed by defendant, plaintiff. Civil records on computer from 1991, on dockets from 1880s. **Criminal Records:** Access: In person only. Court does not conduct in person searches; visitors must perform searches for themselves. Search fee: No criminal searches performed by court. Required to search: name, years to search. Criminal records on computer from 1991, on dockets from 1880s. **General Information:** No juvenile records released. Copy fee: $.50 per page. Certification fee: $2.00. Fee payee: Benton County Circuit Clerk. Personal checks accepted. Prepayment is required. Public access terminal is available.

Municipal Court 117 W Central, Bentonville, AR 72712; 501-271-3120; Fax: 501-271-3134. Hours: 8AM-4:30PM (CST). *Misdemeanor, Civil Actions Under $5,000, Small Claims.*

Civil Records: Both court and visitors may perform in person searches. Search fee:. **Criminal Records:** Both court and visitors may perform in person searches. No search fee. Required to search: name, years to search; also helpful-DOB. **General Information:** Turnaround time 5 days. Fee payee: Bentonville Municipal Court. Prepayment is required. Public access terminal is available.

Boone County

Circuit & Chancery Courts 100 N Main St #200, Harrison, AR 72601; 870-741-5560; Fax: 870-741-4335. Hours: 8AM-4:30PM (CST). *Felony, Civil Actions Over $5,000, Probate.*

Civil Records: Access: Mail, in person. Court does not conduct in person searches; visitors must perform searches for themselves. Search fee: $5.00 per name. Required to search: name, years to search. Civil cases indexed by defendant, plaintiff. Civil records archived from 1940, index from 1977. **Criminal Records:** Access: Mail, in person. Court does not conduct in person searches; visitors must perform searches for themselves. Search fee: $5.00 per name. Required to search: name, years to search. Criminal records archived from 1940, index from 1977. **General Information:** No indictments or juvenile records released. SASE required. Turnaround time 1 day. Copy fee: $.25 per page. Certification fee: $5.00. Fee payee: Circuit Clerk. Personal checks accepted. Prepayment is required.

Municipal Court PO Box 968, Harrison, AR 72602; 870-741-2788; Fax: 870-741-4329. Hours: 8:30AM-4PM (CST). *Misdemeanor, Civil Actions Under $5,000, Eviction, Small Claims.*

Civil Records: Both court and visitors may perform in person searches. Search fee:. **Criminal Records:** Both court and visitors may perform in person searches. No search fee. Required to search: name, years to search; also helpful-DOB. **General Information:** Turnaround time 2 weeks. Fee payee: Harrison Municipal Court.

Bradley County

Circuit & Chancery Courts Bradley County Courthouse - Records, 101 E Cedar, Warren, AR 71671; 870-226-2272; Fax: 870-226-8401. Hours: 8AM-4:30PM (CST). *Felony, Civil Actions Over $5,000, Probate.*

Civil Records: Access: In person only. Court does not conduct in person searches; visitors must perform searches for themselves. Search fee: No civil searches performed by court. Required to search: name, years to search. Civil cases indexed by defendant, plaintiff. Civil records (active cases) on dockets, retired cases on indexes from 1800s, no computerization. **Criminal Records:** Access: Mail, in person. Both court and visitors may perform in person searches. Search fee: $6.00. Required to search: name, years to search; also helpful-DOB, SSN. Criminal records (active cases) on dockets, retired cases on indexes from 1800s, no computerization. **General Information:** No juvenile released. SASE required. Turnaround time 1 week. Copy fee: $.25 per page. Certification fee: $3.00. Fee payee: Circuit Court. Personal checks accepted. Prepayment is required.

Municipal Court PO Box 352, Warren, AR 71671; 870-226-2567; Fax: 870-226-2567. Hours: 8AM-5PM (CST). *Misdemeanor, Civil Actions Under $5,000, Eviction, Small Claims.*

Civil Records: Only the court conducts in person searches; visitors may not. Search fee:. **Criminal Records:** Only the court conducts in person searches; visitors may not. Search fee: $5.00 per name. Required to search: name, years to search, SSN. **General Information:** Turnaround time 1 week. Fee payee: Municipal Court.

Calhoun County

Circuit & County Courts PO Box 1175, Hampton, AR 71744; 870-798-2517. Hours: 8:30AM-4:30PM (CST). *Felony, Civil Actions Over $5,000, Probate.*

Civil Records: Access: Mail, in person. Both court and visitors may perform in person searches. Search fee: $6.00 per name. Required to search: name, years to search. Civil cases indexed by defendant, plaintiff. Civil records on dockets from 1851. **Criminal Records:** Access: Mail, in person. Both court and visitors may perform in person searches. Search fee: $6.00 per name. Required to search: name, years to search, DOB, signed release; also helpful-SSN. Criminal records on dockets from 1851. **General Information:** No juvenile or adoption released. SASE required. Turnaround time 1-3 days. Copy fee: $.25 per page. Certification fee: $3.50. Fee payee: Calhoun County Clerk. Personal checks accepted. Prepayment is required.

Municipal Court PO Box 783, Hampton, AR 71744; 870-798-2753; Fax: 870-798-3665. Hours: 8AM-4:30PM (CST). *Misdemeanor, Civil Actions Under $5,000, Eviction, Small Claims.*

Civil Records: Both court and visitors may perform in person searches. Search fee:. **Criminal Records:** Both court and visitors may perform in person searches. No search fee. Required to search: name, years to search, SSN. **General Information:** Turnaround time 2 days. Fee payee: Municipal Court. Prepayment is required.

Carroll County

Berryville Circuit & Chancery Courts Berryville Circuit Court, PO Box 71, Berryville, AR 72616; 870-423-2422; Fax: 870-423-3866. Hours: 8:30AM-4:30PM (CST). *Felony, Civil Actions Over $5,000, Eviction, Probate.*

Civil Records: Access: Fax, mail, in person. Both court and visitors may perform in person searches. Search fee: $6.00 per name. Required to search: name, years to search. Civil cases indexed by defendant, plaintiff. Civil records on index books. **Criminal Records:** Access: Fax, mail, in person.

Both court and visitors may perform in person searches. Search fee: $6.00 per name. Required to search: name, years to search; also helpful-DOB, SSN. Criminal records on index books. **General Information:** No juvenile records released. SASE required. Turnaround time 1-2 days. Copy fee: $.25 per page. Certification fee: $2.00. Fee payee: Circuit Clerk of Carroll County. Personal checks accepted. Prepayment is required. Public access terminal is available. Fax notes: $1.00 per page.

Eureka Springs Circuit, County & Chancery Courts 44 S Main, PO Box 109, Eureka Springs, AR 72632; 501-253-8646. Hours: 8:30AM-4:30PM (CST). *Felony, Civil Actions Over $5,000, Eviction, Probate.*

Civil Records: Access: Phone, mail, in person. Both court and visitors may perform in person searches. Search fee: $6.00 per name. Required to search: name, years to search. Civil cases indexed by defendant, plaintiff. Civil records on indexes from 1883. **Criminal Records:** Access: Phone, mail, in person. Both court and visitors may perform in person searches. Search fee: $6.00 per name. Required to search: name, years to search; also helpful-DOB. Criminal records on indexes from 1883. **General Information:** No expunged criminal records released. SASE required. Turnaround time varies. Copy fee: $.50 by mail or $.25 in person. Certification fee: $2.00. $3.00 for Probate records. Fee payee: Circuit Clerk of Carroll County or County Clerk. Personal checks accepted. Prepayment is required.

Berryville Municipal Court 103 S Springs, Berryville, AR 72616; 870-423-6247; Fax: 870-423-7069. Hours: 8AM-4:30PM (CST). *Misdemeanor, Civil Actions Under $5,000, Small Claims.* **Criminal Records:** Both court and visitors may perform in person searches. No search fee. Required to search: name, years to search; also helpful-DOB. **General Information:** Turnaround time 1-2 days. Fee payee: Municipal Court. Prepayment is required.

Eureka Springs Municipal Court Courthouse, 44 S Main, Eureka Springs, AR 72632; 501-253-8574; Fax: 501-253-6887. Hours: 8AM-5PM (CST). *Misdemeanor, Civil Actions Under $5,000, Small Claims.*

www.cityofeureka.springs.org

Civil Records: Both court and visitors may perform in person searches. Search fee:. **Criminal Records:** Both court and visitors may perform in person searches. No search fee. Required to search: name, years to search. **General Information:** Turnaround time 1 week. Fee payee: Eureka Springs Municipal. Prepayment is required.

Chicot County

Circuit & Chancery Courts County Courthouse, Lake Village, AR 71653; 870-265-8010; Fax: 870-265-5102. Hours: 8AM-4:30PM (CST). *Felony, Civil Actions Over $5,000, Probate.*

Civil Records: Access: Mail, in person. Both court and visitors may perform in person searches. Search fee: $6.00 per name. Required to search: name, years to search. Civil cases indexed by defendant, plaintiff. Civil records on dockets and files from 1900s. **Criminal Records:** Access: Mail, in person. Both court and visitors may perform in person searches. Search fee: $6.00 per name. Required to search: name, years to search. Criminal records on dockets and files from 1900s. **General Information:** No juvenile records

released. SASE required. Turnaround time 1-2 days. Copy fee: $.50 per page. Certification fee: $2.00. Fee payee: Circuit Clerk. Personal checks accepted. Prepayment is required.

Lake Village Municipal Court PO Box 832, Lake Village, AR 71653; 870-265-3283. Hours: 9AM-5PM (CST). *Misdemeanor, Civil Actions Under $5,000, Eviction, Small Claims.*

Civil Records: Both court and visitors may perform in person searches. Search fee:. **Criminal Records:** Both court and visitors may perform in person searches. Search fee: $5.00 per name. Required to search: name, years to search; also helpful-DOB, SSN. **General Information:** Turnaround time ASAP. Fee payee: Lake Village Municipal Court.

Clark County

Circuit & Chancery Courts PO Box 576, Arkadelphia, AR 71923; 870-246-4281. Hours: 8:30AM-4:30PM (CST). *Felony, Civil Actions Over $5,000, Probate.*

Civil Records: Access: Mail, in person. Both court and visitors may perform in person searches. Search fee: $5.00 per name. Required to search: name, years to search. Civil cases indexed by defendant, plaintiff. Civil records on computer since 1985. **Criminal Records:** Access: Mail, in person. Both court and visitors may perform in person searches. Search fee: $5.00 per name. Required to search: name, years to search. Criminal records on computer since 1980. **General Information:** No juvenile records released. SASE requried. Turnaround time 1-2 days. Copy fee: $.50 per page. Certification fee: $5.00. Fee payee: Pamela King Circuit Clerk. Personal checks accepted. Prepayment is required.

Municipal Court PO Box 449, Arkadelphia, AR 71923; 870-246-9552. Hours: 8:30AM-4:30PM (CST). *Misdemeanor, Civil Actions Under $5,000, Eviction, Small Claims.*

Civil Records: Both court and visitors may perform in person searches. Search fee:. **Criminal Records:** Both court and visitors may perform in person searches. No search fee. Required to search: name, years to search; also helpful-DOB. **General Information:** Turnaround time same day. Prepayment is required.

Clay County

Corning Circuit & County Courts Courthouse, Corning, AR 72422; 870-857-3271; Fax: 870-857-9201. Hours: 8AM-4:30PM (CST). *Felony, Civil Actions Over $5,000, Probate.*

Civil Records: Access: Mail, in person. Both court and visitors may perform in person searches. Search fee: $6.00 per name. Required to search: name, years to search. Civil cases indexed by defendant, plaintiff. Civil records on books from 1893. **Criminal Records:** Access: Mail, in person. Both court and visitors may perform in person searches. Search fee: $6.00 per name. Required to search: name, years to search; also helpful-DOB, SSN. Criminal records on books from 1893. **General Information:** No juvenile records released. Turnaround time 1-2 days. Copy fee: $1.00 per page. Certification fee: $5.00. Fee payee: Circuit Clerk. Personal checks accepted. Prepayment is required.

Piggott Circuit & County Courts PO Box 29, Piggott, AR 72454; 870-598-2524; Fax: 870-598-2524. Hours: 8AM-4:30PM (CST). *Felony, Civil Actions Over $5,000.*

Civil Records: Access: Mail, in person. Search fee: $6.00 per name. Required to search: name, years to search. Civil cases indexed by defendant, plaintiff. Civil records on books from 1893. **Criminal Records:** Access: Mail, in person. Both court and visitors may perform in person searches. Search fee: $6.00 per name. Required to search: name, years to search. Criminal records on books from 1893. **General Information:** No expunged criminal records released. SASE required. Turnaround time 1-2 days. Copy fee: $1.00 per page. Certification fee: $5.00 per page. Fee payee: Circuit Clerk. Personal checks accepted. Prepayment is required. Fax notes: $5.00 per document.

Clay County Municipal Court 194 W Court St, Piggott, AR 72454; 870-598-2265. Hours: 8AM-4:30PM (CST). *Misdemeanor, Civil Actions Under $5,000, Eviction, Small Claims.*

Civil Records: Both court and visitors may perform in person searches. Search fee:. **Criminal Records:** Both court and visitors may perform in person searches. No search fee. Required to search: name, years to search, SSN; also helpful-DOB. **General Information:** Turnaround time 1-2 days. Fee payee: Municipal Court. Prepayment is required.

Cleburne County

Circuit & County Courts PO Box 543, Heber Springs, AR 72543; 501-362-8149; Fax: 501-362-4650. Hours: 8:30AM-4:30PM (CST). *Felony, Civil Actions Over $5,000, Probate, Eviction.*

Civil Records: Access: Phone, mail, in person. Both court and visitors may perform in person searches. Search fee: $6.00 per name. Required to search: name, years to search. Civil cases indexed by defendant, plaintiff. Civil records on dockets from 1883. **Criminal Records:** Access: Phone, mail, in person. Both court and visitors may perform in person searches. Search fee: $6.00 per name. Required to search: name, years to search. Criminal records on dockets from 1883. **General Information:** No juvenile records released. SASE required. Turnaround time 1-2 days. Copy fee: $.25 per page. Certification fee: $1.00. Fee payee: Circuit Clerk. Personal checks accepted. Prepayment is required.

Municipal Court 102 E Main, Heber Springs, AR 72543; 501-362-6585; Fax: 501-362-4661. Hours: 8:30AM-4:30PM (CST). *Misdemeanor, Civil Actions Under $5,000, Small Claims.*

Civil Records: Both court and visitors may perform in person searches. Search fee:. **Criminal Records:** Both court and visitors may perform in person searches. No search fee. Required to search: name, years to search, offense. **General Information:** Turnaround time 10 working days. Fee payee: Heber Springs Municipal Court. Prepayment is required.

Cleveland County

Circuit & County Courts PO Box 368, Rison, AR 71665; 870-325-6921; Fax: 870-325-6144. Hours: 8AM-4:30PM (CST). *Felony, Civil Actions Over $5,000, Probate.*

Civil Records: Access: In person only. Court does not conduct in person searches; visitors must perform searches for themselves. Search fee: No civil searches performed by court. Required to search: name, years to search. Civil cases indexed by defendant, plaintiff. Civil records from 1980. **Criminal Records:** Access: In person only. Both court and visitors may perform in person searches.

No search fee. Required to search: name, years to search, DOB. Criminal records from 1980. **General Information:** No juvenile or adoption records released. Copy fee: $.25 per page. Certification fee: $3.00. Fee payee: Clerk of Circuit Court. Personal checks accepted. Prepayment is required.

Municipal Court PO Box 405, City Hall, Rison, AR 71665; 870-325-7382; Fax: 870-325-6152. Hours: 8AM-4PM (CST). *Misdemeanor, Civil Actions Under $5,000, Eviction, Small Claims.*

Civil Records: Both court and visitors may perform in person searches. Search fee:. **Criminal Records:** Both court and visitors may perform in person searches. No search fee. Required to search: name, years to search, SSN. **General Information:**. Fee payee: Rison City Hall. Prepayment is required.

Columbia County

Circuit & County Courts 1 Court Square Ste 6, Magnolia, AR 71753-3595; 870-235-3700; Fax: 870-235-3786. Hours: 8AM-4:30PM (CST). *Felony, Civil Actions Over $5,000, Probate.*

Civil Records: Access: Mail, in person. Both court and visitors may perform in person searches. Search fee: $10.00 per name. Required to search: name, years to search. Civil cases indexed by defendant, plaintiff. Civil records on dockets and index cards. **Criminal Records:** Access: Mail, in person. Both court and visitors may perform in person searches. Search fee: $10.00 per name. Required to search: name, years to search, DOB, SSN. Criminal records on dockets and index cards. **General Information:** No juvenile or adoption. SASE required. Turnaround time 2-4 days. Copy fee: $1.00 per page. Certification fee: $3.00. Fee payee: Circuit Clerk. Personal checks accepted. Prepayment is required.

Magnolia Municipal Court PO Box 1126, Magnolia, AR 71753; 870-234-7312. Hours: 8AM-5PM (CST). *Misdemeanor, Civil Actions Under $5,000, Eviction, Small Claims.*

Civil Records: Both court and visitors may perform in person searches. Search fee:. **Criminal Records:** Only the court conducts in person searches; visitors may not. Search fee: $1.00 per name. Required to search: name, years to search; also helpful-address. **General Information:** Turnaround time 3 days. Fee payee: Municipal Court Clerk. Prepayment is required.

Conway County

Circuit & Chancery Courts Conway County Courthouse, Rm 206, Morrilton, AR 72110; 501-354-9617; Fax: 501-354-9612. Hours: 8AM-5PM (CST). *Felony, Civil Actions Over $5,000, Probate.*

Civil Records: Access: Phone, mail, in person. Both court and visitors may perform in person searches. Search fee: $8.00 per name. Required to search: name, years to search. Civil cases indexed by defendant, plaintiff. Civil records (child support) on computer. All others on dockets from 1930s. **Criminal Records:** Access: Phone, mail, in person. Both court and visitors may perform in person searches. Search fee: $8.00 per name. Required to search: name, years to search, DOB; also helpful-sex. indexed only in books, not computerized. **General Information:** No juvenile records released. SASE reqiured. Turnaround time 1-2 days. Copy fee: $1.00 per page. Certification fee: $2.00. Fee payee: Circuit Clerk. Personal

checks accepted. Prepayment is required. Public access terminal is available.

Municipal Court Conway County Courthouse, PO Box 127, Morrilton, AR 72110; 501-354-9615; Fax: 501-354-9633. Hours: 8AM-4:30PM (CST). *Misdemeanor, Civil Actions Under $5,000, Eviction, Small Claims.*

Civil Records: Both court and visitors may perform in person searches. Search fee:. **Criminal Records:** Only the court conducts in person searches; visitors may not. Search fee: $5.00 per name. Required to search: name, years to search; also helpful-DOB. **General Information:** Turnaround time 1-2 days. Fee payee: Municipal Court Clerk. Prepayment is required.

Craighead County

Jonesboro Circuit & Chancery Courts PO Box 120, Jonesboro, AR 72403; 870-933-4530; Fax: 870-933-4534. Hours: 8AM-5PM (CST). *Felony, Civil Actions Over $5,000, Probate.*

Civil Records: Access: Fax, mail, in person. Both court and visitors may perform in person searches. Search fee: $6.00 per name. Required to search: name, years to search. Civil cases indexed by defendant, plaintiff. Civil records on computer from 1972, on microfiche from 1800s. **Criminal Records:** Access: Fax, mail, in person. Both court and visitors may perform in person searches. Search fee: $6.00 per name. Required to search: name, years to search, DOB; also helpful-address, SSN. Criminal records on computer from 1972, on microfiche from 1800s. **General Information:** No juvenile records released. SASE required. Turnaround time 1-2 days. Copy fee: $.50 per page. Certification fee: $3.00. Fee payee: Circuit Clerk. Personal checks accepted. Prepayment is required. Public access terminal is available. Fax notes: $1.00 per page.

Lake City Circuit & County Courts PO Box 537, Lake City, AR 72437; 870-237-4342; Fax: 870-237-8174. Hours: 8AM-5PM (CST). *Felony, Civil Actions Over $5,000, Probate.*

Civil Records: Access: Phone, mail, in person. Both court and visitors may perform in person searches. Search fee: $6.00 per name. Required to search: name, years to search, address. Civil cases indexed by defendant, plaintiff. Civil records on computer from 1972, on microfiche from 1800s. **Criminal Records:** Access: Phone, mail, in person. Both court and visitors may perform in person searches. Search fee: $6.00 per name. Required to search: name, years to search, address, DOB; also helpful-SSN. Criminal records on computer from 1972, on microfiche from 1800s. **General Information:** No adoption records released. SASE required. Turnaround time 1-2 days. Copy fee: $.50 per page. Certification fee: $3.00 per page. Fee payee: Circuit Clerk. Business checks accepted. Prepayment is required.

Craighead County Municipal Court 410 W Washington, Jonesboro, AR 72401; 870-933-4508; Fax: 870-933-4582. Hours: 8AM-5PM (CST). *Misdemeanor, Civil Actions Under $5,000, Eviction, Small Claims.*

Civil Records: Both court and visitors may perform in person searches. Search fee:. **Criminal Records:** Both court and visitors may perform in person searches. No search fee. Required to search: name, years to search, SSN. **General Information:** Turnaround time 1-2 days. Fee payee: Municipal Court. Prepayment is required.

Crawford County

Circuit & Chancery Courts County Courthouse, 300 Main St, Rm 22, Van Buren, AR 72956; 501-474-1821; Fax: 501-471-0622. Hours: 8AM-5PM (CST). *Felony, Civil Actions Over $5,000, Probate.*

Civil Records: Access: Mail, in person. Both court and visitors may perform in person searches. Search fee: $6.00 per name. Required to search: name, years to search. Civil cases indexed by defendant, plaintiff. Civil records on computer from 1988, on dockets from 1877. **Criminal Records:** Access: Mail, in person. Both court and visitors may perform in person searches. Search fee: $6.00 per name. Required to search: name, years to search. Criminal records on computer from 1988, on dockets from 1877. **General Information:** No juvenile records released. SASE required. Turnaround time 1-2 days. Copy fee: $1.00 per page. Certification fee: $2.00. Fee payee: Circuit Clerk. Personal checks accepted. Prepayment is required. Public access terminal is available.

Municipal Court 1003 Broadway, Van Buren, AR 72956; 501-474-1671; Fax: 501-471-5010. Hours: 8AM-5PM (CST). *Misdemeanor, Civil Actions Under $5,000, Eviction, Small Claims.*

Civil Records: Both court and visitors may perform in person searches. Search fee:. **Criminal Records:** Both court and visitors may perform in person searches. Search fee: $10.00 per name. Required to search: name, years to search; also helpful-DOB, SSN. **General Information:** Turnaround time 2-3 days. Fee payee: Van Buren Municipal Court. Prepayment is required. Public access terminal is available.

Crittenden County

Circuit & County Courts 100 Court St, Marion, AR 72364; 870-739-3248. Hours: 8AM-4:30PM (CST). *Felony, Civil Actions Over $5,000, Probate.*

Civil Records: Access: Mail, in person. Both court and visitors may perform in person searches. Search fee: $6.00 per name. Required to search: name, years to search. Civil cases indexed by defendant, plaintiff. Civil records on dockets from 1930s. **Criminal Records:** Access: Mail, in person. Both court and visitors may perform in person searches. Search fee: $6.00 per name. Required to search: name, years to search, DOB. Criminal records on dockets from 1930s. **General Information:** No juvenile records released. SASE not required. Turnaround time 1-2 days. Copy fee: $1.00 per page. Certification fee: $3.00. Fee payee: Circuit Court. Personal checks accepted. Prepayment is required.

Municipal Court PO Box 766, West Memphis, AR 72301; 870-732-7560; Fax: 870-732-7538. Hours: 8AM-5PM (CST). *Misdemeanor, Civil Actions Under $5,000, Eviction, Small Claims.*

Civil Records: Both court and visitors may perform in person searches. Search fee:. **Criminal Records:** Both court and visitors may perform in person searches. No search fee. Required to search: name, years to search; also helpful-SSN, race, sex. **General Information:** Turnaround time 2-3 days. Fee payee: Municipal Court.

Cross County

Circuit & County Courts County Courthouse, 705 E Union, Rm 9, Wynne, AR 72396; 870-238-5720. Hours: 8AM-4PM (CST). *Felony, Civil Actions Over $5,000, Probate.*

Civil Records: Access: Mail, in person. Search fee: $6.00 per name. Required to search: name, years to search. Civil cases indexed by defendant. Civil records (child support) on computer. All on dockets from 1800s. **Criminal Records:** Access: Mail, in person. Both court and visitors may perform in person searches. Search fee: $6.00 per name. Required to search: name, years to search; also helpful-SSN. Criminal records (child support) on computer. All on dockets from 1800s. **General Information:** No juvenile records released. SASE required. Turnaround time same day. Copy fee: $.25 per page. Certification fee: $3.00. Fee payee: Cross County Circuit Court. Personal checks accepted. Prepayment is required.

Municipal Court 205 Mississippi St, Wynne, AR 72396; 870-238-9171; Fax: 870-238-3930. Hours: 8AM-4PM (CST). *Misdemeanor, Civil Actions Under $5,000, Eviction, Small Claims.*

Civil Records: Both court and visitors may perform in person searches. Search fee:. **Criminal Records:** Both court and visitors may perform in person searches. No search fee. Required to search: name, years to search; also helpful-SSN. **General Information:** Turnaround time 1-2 days. Fee payee: Wynne Municipal Court. Prepayment is required. Public access terminal is available.

Dallas County

Circuit & County Courts Dallas County Courthouse, Fordyce, AR 71742; 870-352-2307; Fax: 870-352-7179. Hours: 8:30AM-4:30PM (CST). *Felony, Civil Actions Over $5,000, Probate.*

Civil Records: Access: Fax, mail, in person. Both court and visitors may perform in person searches. Search fee: $6.00 per name. Required to search: name, years to search. Civil cases indexed by defendant, plaintiff. Civil records on dockets. **Criminal Records:** Access: Fax, mail, in person. Both court and visitors may perform in person searches. Search fee: $6.00 per name. Required to search: name, years to search, DOB; also helpful-SSN. Criminal records on dockets. **General Information:** No juvenile records released. SASE required. Turnaround time 1-2 days. Copy fee: $.50 per page. Certification fee: $3.00. Fee payee: Circuit Clerk. Business checks accepted. Law firm accounts, money orders and cashier checks allowed. Prepayment is required. Fax notes: $2.00 fax fee plus $.25 per page.

Municipal Court 202 W 3rd St, Fordyce, AR 71742; 870-352-2332; Fax: 870-352-3414. Hours: 8AM-4PM (CST). *Misdemeanor, Civil Actions Under $5,000, Eviction, Small Claims.*

Civil Records: Only the court conducts in person searches; visitors may not. Search fee:. **Criminal Records:** Only the court conducts in person searches; visitors may not. No search fee. Required to search: name, years to search, SSN; also helpful-DOB. **General Information:** Turnaround time 1-2 days. Fee payee: Dallas County Municipal Court.

Desha County

Circuit & Chancery Courts PO Box 309, Arkansas City, AR 71630; 870-877-2411; Fax: 870-877-3407. Hours: 8AM-4PM (CST). *Felony, Civil Actions Over $5,000, Probate.*

Civil Records: Access: Fax, mail, in person. Both court and visitors may perform in person searches. Search fee: $5.00 per name. Required to search:

name, years to search. Civil cases indexed by defendant, plaintiff. Civil records on dockets from 1920s. **Criminal Records:** Access: Fax, mail, in person. Both court and visitors may perform in person searches. Search fee: $5.00 per name. Required to search: name, years to search, SSN. Criminal records on dockets from 1920s. **General Information:** No juvenile records released. SASE required. Turnaround time 1-2 days. Copy fee: $.50 per page. Certification fee: $3.00. Fee payee: Skippy Leek, Circuit Court Clerk. Personal checks accepted. Prepayment is required. Fax notes: No fee to fax results.

Municipal Court 149 E Waterman, Dumas, AR 71639-2226; 870-382-6972; Fax: 870-382-1106. Hours: 8AM-4:30PM (CST). *Misdemeanor, Civil Actions Under $5,000, Eviction, Small Claims.*

Civil Records: Search fee:. **Criminal Records:** Only the court conducts in person searches; visitors may not. Search fee: $5.00 per name. Required to search: name, years to search, signed release; also helpful-address. **General Information:** Turnaround time 1-2 days. Fee payee: Dumas Municipal Court. Prepayment is required.

Drew County

Circuit & County Courts 210 S Main, Monticello, AR 71655; 870-460-6250; Fax: 870-460-6246. Hours: 8AM-4:30PM (CST). *Felony, Civil Actions Over $5,000, Probate.*

Civil Records: Access: Phone, fax, mail, in person. Both court and visitors may perform in person searches. No search fee. Required to search: name, years to search. Civil cases indexed by defendant, plaintiff. Civil records on dockets from 1846. **Criminal Records:** Access: Phone, fax, mail, in person. Both court and visitors may perform in person searches. Search fee: $6.00 per name. Required to search: name, years to search. Criminal records on dockets from 1846. **General Information:** No juvenile or expunged records released. SASE required. Turnaround time 1-2 days. Copy fee: $.50 per page. Certification fee: $2.00. Fee payee: Drew County Circuit Clerk. Personal checks accepted. Prepayment is required. Fax notes: $1.25 for first page, $1.00 each addl.

Municipal Court PO Box 505, Monticello, AR 71655; 870-367-4420; Fax: 870-367-8761. Hours: 8:30AM-5PM (CST). *Misdemeanor, Civil Actions Under $5,000, Eviction, Small Claims.*

Civil Records: Only the court conducts in person searches; visitors may not. Search fee:. **Criminal Records:** Only the court conducts in person searches; visitors may not. No search fee. Required to search: name, years to search, DOB; also helpful-sex. **General Information:** Turnaround time 1-2 days. Fee payee: Municipal Court.

Faulkner County

Circuit & Chancery Courts PO Box 9, Conway, AR 72033; 501-450-4911; Fax: 501-450-4948. Hours: 8AM-4:30PM (CST). *Felony, Civil Actions Over $5,000, Probate.*

Civil Records: Access: Fax, mail, in person. Both court and visitors may perform in person searches. Search fee: $6.00 per name. Required to search: name, years to search. Civil cases indexed by defendant, plaintiff. Civil records on computer since June 1989, on docket from 1800s. **Criminal Records:** Access: Fax, mail, in person. Both court and visitors may perform in person searches. Search fee: $6.00 per name. Required to search:

name, years to search. Criminal records on computer since June 1989, on docket from 1800s. **General Information:** No juvenile records released. SASE required. Turnaround time 1-2 days. Copy fee: $.25 per page. Certification fee: $3.00. Fee payee: Faulkner County Circuit Clerk. Personal checks accepted. Prepayment is required. Public access terminal is available. Fax notes: $1.00 if local, $3.50 plus $.25 per page if long distance.

Municipal Court 810 Parkway, Conway, AR 72032; 501-450-6112; Fax: 501-450-6184. Hours: 8AM-4:30PM (CST). *Misdemeanor, Civil Actions Under $5,000, Eviction, Small Claims.*

Civil Records: Both court and visitors may perform in person searches. Search fee:. **Criminal Records:** Both court and visitors may perform in person searches. Search fee: No search fee. Fee $15.00 3 years; $20.00 more than 3 years. Required to search: name, years to search, DOB, signed release; also helpful-address, SSN. **General Information:** Turnaround time 2 days. Fee payee: Conway Municipal Court.

Franklin County

Charleston Circuit & Chancery Courts PO Box 387, Charleston, AR 72933; 501-965-7332. Hours: 8AM-4:30PM (CST). *Felony, Civil Actions Over $5,000, Probate.*

Civil Records: Access: Mail, in person. Both court and visitors may perform in person searches. Search fee: $6.00 per name. Required to search: name, years to search. Civil cases indexed by defendant, plaintiff. Civil records on dockets from 1900s. **Criminal Records:** Access: Mail, in person. Both court and visitors may perform in person searches. Search fee: $6.00 per name. Required to search: name, years to search. Criminal records on dockets from 1900s. **General Information:** No juvenile records released. SASE required. Turnaround time 1-2 days. Copy fee: $.25 per page. Certification fee: $2.00. Fee payee: Franklin County. Personal checks accepted. Prepayment is required.

Ozark Circuit & Chancery Courts PO Box 1112, 211 W Commercial, Ozark, AR 72949; 501-667-3818; Probate phone:501-667-3607; Fax: 501-667-5174. Hours: 8AM-4:30PM (CST). *Felony, Civil Actions Over $5,000, Probate.*

Note: Probate is maintained at the County Clerk's Office

Civil Records: Access: Fax, mail, in person. Both court and visitors may perform in person searches. Search fee: $6.00 per name. Required to search: name, years to search. Civil cases indexed by plaintiff. Civil records on dockets from 1900s. **Criminal Records:** Access: Fax, mail, in person. Both court and visitors may perform in person searches. Search fee: $6.00 per name. Required to search: name, years to search. Criminal records on dockets from 1900s. **General Information:** No juvenile records released. SASE required. Turnaround time 1-2 days. Copy fee: $.25 per page. Certification fee: $2.00. Fee payee: Circuit Clerk. Personal checks accepted. Prepayment is required. Fax notes: $1.00 per page.

Municipal Court PO Box 426, Charleston, AR 72933; 501-965-7455; Fax: 501-965-2231. Hours: 8AM-5PM (CST). *Misdemeanor, Civil Actions Under $5,000, Eviction, Small Claims.*

Civil Records: Both court and visitors may perform in person searches. Search fee:. **Criminal Records:** Both court and visitors may perform in person searches. No search fee. Required to

search: name, years to search. **General Information:** Turnaround time 1-2 days. Fee payee: Charleston Municipal Court. Prepayment is required.

Fulton County

Circuit & Chancery Courts PO Box 485, Salem, AR 72576; 870-895-3310; Fax: 870-865-3362. Hours: 8AM-4:30PM (CST). *Felony, Civil Actions Over $5,000, Probate.*

Civil Records: Access: Phone, mail, in person. Both court and visitors may perform in person searches. Search fee: $6.00 per name. Required to search: name, years to search. Civil cases indexed by defendant, plaintiff. Civil records on dockets from 1900s. **Criminal Records:** Access: Phone, mail, in person. Both court and visitors may perform in person searches. Search fee: $6.00 per name. Required to search: name, years to search. Criminal records on dockets from 1900s. **General Information:** No juvenile records released. SASE required. Turnaround time 1-2 days. Copy fee: $.20 per page. Certification fee: No certification fee. Fee payee: Fulton County Clerks. Personal checks accepted. Prepayment is required.

Municipal Court PO Box 928, Salem, AR 72576; 870-895-4136; Fax: 870-895-4114. Hours: 8AM-4:30PM (CST). *Misdemeanor, Civil Actions Under $5,000, Eviction, Small Claims.*

Civil Records: Both court and visitors may perform in person searches. Search fee:. **Criminal Records:** Both court and visitors may perform in person searches. No search fee. Required to search: name, years to search, DOB. **General Information:** Turnaround time 1 week. Fee payee: Fulton Municipal Court.

Garland County

Circuit & Chancery Courts Garland County Courthouse, 501 Ouachita Ave, Room 207, Hot Springs, AR 71901;; Civil phone:501-622-3630; Criminal phone:501-622-3630; Probate phone:501-622-3610; Fax: 501-609-9043. Hours: 8AM-5PM (CST). *Felony, Civil Actions Over $5,000, Probate.*

Civil Records: Access: In person only. Court does not conduct in person searches; visitors must perform searches for themselves. No search fee. Required to search: name; also helpful-years to search. Civil cases indexed by defendant, plaintiff. Civil records on microfiche and docket from 1900s. **Criminal Records:** Access: Fax, mail, in person. Both court and visitors may perform in person searches. No search fee. Required to search: name, years to search; also helpful-DOB, maiden name, race, aliases, sex. Criminal records on microfiche and docket from 1900s. **General Information:** No expunged, sealed records released. SASE required. Turnaround time 1-2 days. Copy fee: $.25 per page. Certification fee: $.50. Fee payee: Garland County Circuit Clerk. Personal checks accepted. Prepayment is required. Fax notes: No fee to fax results.

Municipal Court PO Box 700, Hot Springs, AR 71902; 501-321-6761; Fax: 501-321-6809. Hours: 8AM-5PM (CST). *Misdemeanor, Civil Actions Under $5,000, Eviction, Small Claims.*

Civil Records: Both court and visitors may perform in person searches. Search fee:. **Criminal Records:** Both court and visitors may perform in person searches. No search fee. Required to search: name, years to search, offense. **General Information:** Turnaround time 1-2 days. Fee payee: Municipal Court. Prepayment is required.

Grant County

Circuit & County Courts Grant County Courthouse, 101 W Center, Rm 106, Sheridan, AR 72150; 870-942-2631; Fax: 870-942-3564. Hours: 8AM-4:30PM (CST). *Felony, Civil Actions Over $5,000, Probate.*

Civil Records: Access: In person only. Court does not conduct in person searches; visitors must perform searches for themselves. Search fee: No civil searches performed by court. Required to search: name, years to search. Civil cases indexed by defendant, plaintiff. Civil records on dockets and index from 1982. **Criminal Records:** Access: In person only. Court does not conduct in person searches; visitors must perform searches for themselves. Search fee: No criminal searches performed by court. Required to search: name, years to search. Criminal records on dockets and index from 1982. **General Information:** No juvenile, probate or adoption records released. Copy fee: $.25 per page. Certification fee: $3.00. Fee payee: Circuit Clerk. Personal checks accepted. Prepayment is required.

Municipal Court PO Box 603, Sheridan, AR 72150; 870-942-3464; Fax: 870-942-8885. Hours: 8AM-4:30PM (CST). *Misdemeanor, Civil Actions Under $5,000, Eviction, Small Claims.*

Civil Records: Both court and visitors may perform in person searches. Search fee:. **Criminal Records:** Both court and visitors may perform in person searches. No search fee. Required to search: name, years to search. **General Information:** Turnaround time 1-2 days.

Greene County

Circuit & County Courts 320 W Court #124, Paragould, AR 72450; 870-239-6330; Fax: 870-239-3550. Hours: 8AM-4:30PM (CST). *Felony, Civil Actions Over $5,000, Probate.*

Civil Records: Access: Fax, mail, in person. Both court and visitors may perform in person searches. Search fee: $6.00 per name. Required to search: name, years to search. Civil cases indexed by plaintiff. Civil records on computer from 1986, on index from 1930s. **Criminal Records:** Access: Fax, mail, in person. Both court and visitors may perform in person searches. Search fee: $6.00 per name. Required to search: name, years to search; also helpful-DOB, SSN. Criminal records computerized since 1990. **General Information:** No juvenile records released. SASE required. Turnaround time 1-2 days. Copy fee: $.50 per page. Certification fee: $3.00. Fee payee: Green County Circuit Clerk. Personal checks accepted. Prepayment is required. Fax notes: For fax back, $1.00 for first 3 pages then $.25 per page.

Municipal Court 320 W Court, Rm 227, Paragould, AR 72450; 870-239-7507; Fax: 870-239-7506. Hours: 8AM-4:30PM (CST). *Misdemeanor, Civil Actions Under $5,000, Eviction, Small Claims.*

Civil Records: Only the court conducts in person searches; visitors may not. Search fee:. **Criminal Records:** Only the court conducts in person searches; visitors may not. Search fee: $10.00 per name. Required to search: name, years to search. **General Information:** Turnaround time 2 days. Fee payee: Municipal Clerk. Prepayment is required.

Hempstead County

Circuit & Chancery Courts PO Box 1420, Hope, AR 71802; 870-777-2384; Probate phone:870-777-2241; Fax: 870-777-7827. Hours:

8AM-4PM (CST). *Felony, Civil Actions Over $5,000, Probate.*

Note: Probate is handled by the County Clerk at same address

Civil Records: Access: Phone, fax, mail, in person. Both court and visitors may perform in person searches. Search fee: $6.00 per name. Required to search: name, years to search. Civil cases indexed by defendant, plaintiff. Civil records on dockets from 1910. **Criminal Records:** Access: Phone, fax, mail, in person. Both court and visitors may perform in person searches. Search fee: $6.00 per name. Required to search: name, years to search, DOB, SSN. Criminal records on dockets from 1910. **General Information:** No juvenile records released. SASE required. Turnaround time 1-2 days. Copy fee: $.50 per page. Certification fee: $5.00. Fee payee: Circuit Clerk. Personal checks accepted. Prepayment is required. Public access terminal is available.

Municipal Court PO Box 1420, Hope, AR 71802-1420; 870-777-2525; Fax: 870-777-7830. Hours: 8AM-4:30PM (CST). *Misdemeanor, Civil Actions Under $5,000, Eviction, Small Claims.*

Civil Records: Both court and visitors may perform in person searches. Search fee:. **Criminal Records:** Both court and visitors may perform in person searches. Search fee: $5.00 per name. Required to search: name, years to search, SSN. **General Information:** Turnaround time less than 1 week. Fee payee: Municipal Court. Prepayment is required.

Hot Spring County

Circuit & Chancery Court 200 Locust St, PO Box 1200, Malvern, AR 72104; 501-332-2281. Hours: 8:00AM-4:30PM (CST). *Felony, Civil Actions Over $5,000, Probate.*

Civil Records: Access: Mail, in person. Both court and visitors may perform in person searches. Search fee: $5.00 per name. Required to search: name, years to search. Civil cases indexed by plaintiff. Civil records on dockets from 1800s. **Criminal Records:** Access: Mail, in person. Both court and visitors may perform in person searches. Search fee: $5.00 per name. Required to search: name, years to search. Criminal records on dockets from 1800s. **General Information:** No juvenile records released. SASE required. Turnaround time 1-2 days. Copy fee: $.50 per page. Certification fee: $5.00. Fee payee: Circuit Clerk. Personal checks accepted. Prepayment is required.

Malvern Municipal Court 305 Locust St, Rm 201, Malvern, AR 72104; 501-332-7604; Fax: 501-332-3144. Hours: 8AM-4:30PM (CST). *Misdemeanor, Civil Actions Under $5,000, Eviction, Small Claims.*

Civil Records: Court does not conduct in person searches; visitors must perform searches for themselves. Search fee:. **Criminal Records:** Court does not conduct in person searches; visitors must perform searches for themselves. Search fee: No criminal searches performed by court. Required to search: name, years to search; also helpful-address, SSN. **General Information:** Turnaround time 3 days.

Howard County

Circuit & County Courts 421 N Main, Rm 7, Nashville, AR 71852; 870-845-7506; Probate phone:870-845-7503. Hours: 8AM-4:30PM (CST). *Felony, Civil Actions Over $5,000, Probate.*

Note: Probate is handled by the County Clerk at this address

Civil Records: Access: Phone, mail, in person. Both court and visitors may perform in person searches. Search fee: $6.00 per name. Required to search: name, years to search. Civil cases indexed by defendant, plaintiff. Civil records on index cards and dockets from 1873. **Criminal Records:** Access: Phone, mail, in person. Only the court conducts in person searches; visitors may not. Search fee: $6.00 per name. Required to search: name, years to search, DOB. Criminal records on index cards and dockets from 1873. **General Information:** No juvenile or sealed records released. SASE required. Turnaround time 1 week. Copy fee: $.25 per page. Certification fee: $1.00. Fee payee: Circuit Clerk. Personal checks accepted. Prepayment is required.

Municipal Court 426 N Main, Suite #7, Nashville, AR 71852-2009; 870-845-7522; Fax: 870-845-3705. Hours: 8AM-4:30PM (CST). *Misdemeanor, Civil Actions Under $5,000, Eviction, Small Claims.*

Civil Records: Court does not conduct in person searches; visitors must perform searches for themselves. Search fee:. **Criminal Records:** Both court and visitors may perform in person searches. No search fee. Required to search: name, years to search, DOB; also helpful-address, SSN. **General Information:** Turnaround time 1-3 days. Fee payee: Howard County Municipal Court. Prepayment is required.

Independence County

Circuit & County Courts Main and Broad St, Batesville, AR 72501; 870-793-8833; Fax: 870-793-8888. Hours: 8AM-4:30PM (CST). *Felony, Civil Actions Over $5,000.*

Civil Records: Access: Phone, mail, in person. Both court and visitors may perform in person searches. Search fee: $6.00 per name. Required to search: name, years to search; also helpful-address. Civil cases indexed by defendant, plaintiff. Civil records on computer from 1980, all others on index books from 1970s. **Criminal Records:** Access: Mail, in person. Both court and visitors may perform in person searches. Search fee: $6.00 per name. Required to search: name, years to search, DOB; also helpful-address. Criminal records on index books from 1970s. **General Information:** No juvenile records released. SASE required. Turnaround time varies, but usually same day. Copy fee: $.50 per page. Certification fee: $.50. Fee payee: Circuit Clerk. Personal checks accepted. Prepayment is required.

Municipal Court 368 E Main, Rm 205, Batesville, AR 72501; 870-793-8817; Fax: 870-793-8875. Hours: 8AM-4:30PM (CST). *Misdemeanor, Civil Actions Under $5,000, Eviction, Small Claims.*

Civil Records: Both court and visitors may perform in person searches. Search fee:. **Criminal Records:** Both court and visitors may perform in person searches. No search fee. Required to search: name, years to search. **General Information:** Turnaround time 1-2 days. Fee payee: Municipal Court. Prepayment is required.

Izard County

Circuit & County Courts PO Box 95, Melbourne, AR 72556; 870-368-4316; Fax: 870-368-4748. Hours: 8:30AM-4:30PM (CST). *Felony, Civil Actions Over $5,000, Probate.*

Civil Records: Access: Fax, mail, in person. Both court and visitors may perform in person searches. Search fee: $6.00 per name. Required to search: name, years to search, address. Civil cases indexed by plaintiff. Civil records on judgment books from 1889. **Criminal Records:** Access: Fax, mail, in person. Both court and visitors may perform in person searches. Search fee: $6.00 per name. Required to search: name, years to search, DOB; also helpful-address. Criminal records on judgment books from 1889. **General Information:** No juvenile records released. SASE required. Turnaround time 2 weeks. Copy fee: $.20 per page. Certification fee: $3.00. Fee payee: Izard County and Circuit Clerk. Personal checks accepted. Prepayment is required. Fax notes: No fee to fax results.

Municipal Court PO Box 337, Melbourne, AR 72556; 870-368-4390; Fax: 870-368-5042. Hours: 8:30AM-4:30PM (CST). *Misdemeanor, Civil Actions Under $5,000, Eviction, Small Claims.*

Civil Records: Both court and visitors may perform in person searches. Search fee:. **Criminal Records:** Both court and visitors may perform in person searches. No search fee. Required to search: name, years to search. **General Information:** Turnaround time varies. Fee payee: Municipal Court. Prepayment is required.

Jackson County

Circuit & Chancery Courts Jackson County Courthouse, 208 Main St, Newport, AR 72112; 870-523-7423; Fax: 870-523-7404. Hours: 8AM-4:30PM (CST). *Felony, Civil Actions Over $5,000, Probate.*

Civil Records: Access: In person only. Court does not conduct in person searches; visitors must perform searches for themselves. Search fee: No civil searches performed by court. Required to search: name, years to search. Civil cases indexed by defendant, plaintiff. Civil records on dockets from 1800s. **Criminal Records:** Access: In person only. Court does not conduct in person searches; visitors must perform searches for themselves. Search fee: No criminal searches performed by court. Required to search: name, years to search. Criminal records on dockets from 1800s. **General Information:** No juvenile records released. Copy fee: $.25 per page. Certification fee: $3.00. Fee payee: Circuit Clerk. Personal checks accepted. Prepayment is required.

Municipal Court 615 3rd St, Newport, AR 72112; 870-523-9555; Fax: 870-523-4365. Hours: 8AM-4:30PM (CST). *Misdemeanor, Civil Actions Under $5,000, Eviction, Small Claims.*

Civil Records: Both court and visitors may perform in person searches. Search fee:. **Criminal Records:** Both court and visitors may perform in person searches. No search fee. Required to search: name, years to search, DOB, SSN. **General Information:** Turnaround time 5-7 days. Fee payee: Newport Municipal Court. Prepayment is required.

Jefferson County

Circuit & Chancery Courts PO Box 7433, Pine Bluff, AR 71611;; Civil phone:870-541-5307; Criminal phone:870-541-5307. Hours: 8:30PM-5PM (CST). *Felony, Civil Actions Over $5,000, Probate.*

Civil Records: Access: In person only. Court does not conduct in person searches; visitors must perform searches for themselves. Search fee: No civil searches performed by court. Required to search: name, years to search. Civil cases indexed by defendant, plaintiff. Civil records on dockets from 1950. **Criminal Records:** Access: In person only. Court does not conduct in person searches; visitors must perform searches for themselves. Search fee: No criminal searches performed by court. Required to search: name, years to search, DOB. Criminal records on dockets from 1950. **General Information:** No juvenile records released. Copy fee: $.50 per page. Certification fee: $2.00. Fee payee: Circuit Clerk. Personal checks accepted. Prepayment is required. Public access terminal is available.

Municipal Court 200 E 8th Ave, Pine Bluff, AR 71601; 870-543-1860; Fax: 870-543-1889. Hours: 8AM-5PM (CST). *Misdemeanor, Civil Actions Under $5,000, Eviction, Small Claims.*

Civil Records: Both court and visitors may perform in person searches. Search fee:. **Criminal Records:** Both court and visitors may perform in person searches. No search fee. Required to search: name, years to search; also helpful-DOB, SSN. **General Information:** Turnaround time 1-2 days. Fee payee: Pine Bluff Municipal Court. Prepayment is required.

Johnson County

Circuit Court PO Box 217, Clarksville, AR 72830; 501-754-2977; Probate phone:501-754-3967. Hours: 8AM-4:30PM (CST). *Felony, Civil Actions Over $5,000, Probate.*

Note: Probate is handled by County Clerk, PO Box 57

Civil Records: Access: Fax, mail, in person. Both court and visitors may perform in person searches. Search fee: $6.00 per name. Required to search: name, years to search. Civil cases indexed by defendant, plaintiff. Civil records on index from 1900s. Fax access limited to 800#'s. **Criminal Records:** Access: Fax, mail, in person. Both court and visitors may perform in person searches. Search fee: $6.00. Required to search: name, years to search, DOB; also helpful-SSN. Criminal records on index from 1900s. Fax access limited to 800#'s. **General Information:** No juvenile records released. SASE required. Turnaround time 1-2 days. Copy fee: $.50 per page. Certification fee: $1.00. Fee payee: Circuit. Personal checks accepted. Draft or two party checks not allowed. Fax notes: No fee to fax results. Will fax to 800 numbers only.

Municipal Court PO Box 581, Clarksville, AR 72830; 501-754-8533; Fax: 501-754-6014. Hours: 8AM-4PM (CST). *Misdemeanor, Civil Actions Under $5,000, Eviction, Small Claims.*

Civil Records: Both court and visitors may perform in person searches. Search fee:. **Criminal Records:** Both court and visitors may perform in person searches. No search fee. Required to search: name, years to search; also helpful-DOB, SSN. **General Information:** Turnaround time 1-2 days. Fee payee: Municipal Court. Prepayment is required.

Lafayette County

Circuit & Chancery Courts #3 Courthouse Square, Lewisville, AR 71845; 870-921-4878; Probate phone:870-921-4633; Fax: 870-921-4505. Hours: 8AM-4:30PM (CST). *Felony, Civil Actions Over $5,000, Probate.*

Civil Records: Access: Mail, in person. Both court and visitors may perform in person searches. Search fee: $6.00 per name. Required to search: name, years to search. Civil cases indexed by defendant, plaintiff. Civil records on dockets from

1950s. **Criminal Records:** Access: Mail, in person. Both court and visitors may perform in person searches. Search fee: $6.00 per name. Required to search: name, years to search. Criminal records on dockets from 1950s. **General Information:** No juvenile records released without written order form the judge. SASE required. Turnaround time 2 days. Copy fee: $.50 per page. Certification fee: $3.00. Fee payee: Circuit Clerk. Personal checks accepted. Prepayment is required.

Municipal Court 23 Courthouse Square, Lewisville, AR 71845; 870-921-5555; Fax: 870-921-4256. Hours: 8AM-4:30PM (CST). *Misdemeanor, Civil Actions Under $5,000, Eviction, Small Claims.*

Civil Records: Both court and visitors may perform in person searches. Search fee:. **Criminal Records:** Both court and visitors may perform in person searches. No search fee. Required to search: name, years to search, DOB, SSN. **General Information:**. Fee payee: Municipal Court. Prepayment is required.

Lawrence County

Circuit & Chancery Courts 126 W Green St #200, Walnut Ridge, AR 72476; 870-886-1112; Fax: 870-886-1128. Hours: 8AM-4:30PM (CST). *Felony, Civil Actions Over $5,000, Probate.*

Civil Records: Access: Phone, fax, mail, in person. Court does not conduct in person searches; visitors must perform searches for themselves. Search fee: $6.00 per name. Required to search: name, years to search. Civil cases indexed by defendant, plaintiff. Civil records on index from 1981, on docket sheets from 1960s. **Criminal Records:** Access: Phone, fax, mail, in person. Court does not conduct in person searches; visitors must perform searches for themselves. Search fee: $6.00 per name. Required to search: name, years to search. Criminal records on index from 1981, on docket sheets from 1960s. **General Information:** No juvenile records released. SASE required. Turnaround time 1 day. Copy fee: $.25 per page. Certification fee: $3.00. Fee payee: Circuit Clerk. Personal checks accepted. Prepayment is required. Fax notes: $1.00 per page.

Walnut Ridge Municipal Court 201 SW 2nd St, Walnut Ridge, AR 72476; 870-886-3905. Hours: 8AM-4:30PM (CST). *Misdemeanor, Civil Actions Under $5,000, Eviction, Small Claims.*

Civil Records: Both court and visitors may perform in person searches. Search fee:. **Criminal Records:** Both court and visitors may perform in person searches. No search fee. Required to search: name, years to search, offense. **General Information:** Turnaround time 2-3 days. Fee payee: Walnut Ridge Municipal Court.

Lee County

Circuit & Chancery Courts 15 E Chestnut, Marianna, AR 72360; 870-295-7710; Fax: 870-295-7766. Hours: 8:30AM-4:30PM (CST). *Felony, Civil Actions Over $5,000, Probate.*

Civil Records: Access: In person only. Only the court conducts in person searches; visitors may not. Search fee: No civil searches performed by court. Required to search: name, years to search. Civil cases indexed by defendant, plaintiff. Civil records on index books from 1873. **Criminal Records:** Access: In person only. Only the court conducts in person searches; visitors may not. Search fee: No criminal searches performed by court. Required to search: name, years to search, DOB. Criminal records on index books from 1873.

General Information: No juvenile records released. Copy fee: $.25 per page. Certification fee: $2.50. Fee payee: Circuit Court. Personal checks accepted. Prepayment is required.

Municipal Court 45 W Mississippi, Marianna, AR 72360; 870-295-3813; Fax: 870-295-5726. Hours: 8AM-Noon; 1-5PM (CST). *Misdemeanor, Civil Actions Under $5,000, Eviction, Small Claims.*

Civil Records: Only the court conducts in person searches; visitors may not. Search fee:. **Criminal Records:** Only the court conducts in person searches; visitors may not. No search fee. Required to search: name, years to search. **General Information:** Turnaround time 5 days. Fee payee: County of Marianna.

Lincoln County

Circuit & County Courts Courthouse, 300 S Drew, Star City, AR 71667; 870-628-3154; Probate phone:870-628-5114; Fax: 870-628-5546. Hours: 8AM-5PM (CST). *Felony, Civil Actions Over $5,000, Probate.*

Civil Records: Access: Mail, in person. Both court and visitors may perform in person searches. Search fee: $6.00 per name. Required to search: name, years to search. Civil cases indexed by defendant, plaintiff. Civil records on index from 1920, archived from 1920. **Criminal Records:** Access: In person only. Court does not conduct in person searches; visitors must perform searches for themselves. Search fee: $6.00 per name. Required to search: name, years to search. Criminal records on index from 1920, archived from 1920. **General Information:** No sealed records released. SASE required. Turnaround time 8 hours. Copy fee: $.50 per page. Certification fee: $3.00. Fee payee: Lincoln County Circuit Court. Personal checks accepted. Prepayment is required.

Lincoln County Municipal Court 300 S Drew St, Star City, AR 71667; 870-628-4904. Hours: 8AM-4:30PM (CST). *Misdemeanor, Civil Actions Under $5,000, Eviction, Small Claims.*

Civil Records: Both court and visitors may perform in person searches. Search fee:. **Criminal Records:** Both court and visitors may perform in person searches. Search fee: $6.00 per name. Required to search: name, years to search, DOB, signed release; also helpful-address, SSN. **General Information:** Turnaround time 3-5 days. Fee payee: Lincoln County Municipal Court. Prepayment is required.

Little River County

Circuit & County Courts PO Box 575, Ashdown, AR 71822; 870-898-7211; Fax: 870-898-7207. Hours: 8:30AM-4:30PM (CST). *Felony, Civil Actions Over $5,000, Probate.*

Civil Records: Access: Phone, mail, in person. Both court and visitors may perform in person searches. Search fee: $6.00 per name. Required to search: name, years to search. Civil cases indexed by plaintiff. Civil records docket books from early 1900s. **Criminal Records:** Access: Phone, mail, in person. Both court and visitors may perform in person searches. Search fee: $6.00 per name. Required to search: name, years to search, address, DOB, signed release. Criminal records on docket books back to 1868. **General Information:** No juvenile records released. SASE required. Turnaround time 1 day. Copy fee: $.50 per page. Certification fee: $5.00. Fee payee: Circuit Clerk. Personal checks accepted. Prepayment is required.

Municipal Court 351 N 2nd St, #8, Ashdown, AR 71822; 870-898-7230; Fax: 870-898-7262. Hours: 8:30AM-4:30PM (CST). *Misdemeanor, Civil Actions Under $5,000, Eviction, Small Claims.*

Civil Records: Both court and visitors may perform in person searches. Search fee:. **Criminal Records:** Both court and visitors may perform in person searches. No search fee. Required to search: name, years to search; also helpful-DOB, SSN. **General Information:** Turnaround time 1 week. Fee payee: Ashdown Municipal Court.

Logan County

Circuit & Chancery Courts Courthouse, 25 W Walnut, Paris, AR 72855; 501-963-2164; Fax: 501-963-3304. Hours: 8AM-4:30PM (CST). *Felony, Civil Actions Over $5,000, Probate.*

Civil Records: Access: Fax, mail, in person. Both court and visitors may perform in person searches. Search fee: $6.00 per name. Required to search: name, years to search. Civil cases indexed by defendant, plaintiff. Civil records on criminal index from 1901. **Criminal Records:** Access: Fax, mail, in person. Both court and visitors may perform in person searches. Search fee: $6.00 per name. Required to search: name, years to search. Criminal records on criminal index from 1901. **General Information:** No adoption or probate records released. SASE required. Turnaround time 1 days. Copy fee: $.50 per page. Certification fee: $5.00. Fee payee: Circuit Clerk. Personal checks accepted. Prepayment is required. Fax notes: $1.00 per page.

Paris Municipal Court Paris Courthouse, Paris, AR 72855; 501-963-3792; Fax: 501-963-2590. Hours: 8:30AM-4:30PM (CST). *Misdemeanor, Civil Actions Under $5,000, Eviction, Small Claims.*

Civil Records: Both court and visitors may perform in person searches. Search fee:. **Criminal Records:** Both court and visitors may perform in person searches. No search fee. Required to search: name, years to search; also helpful-DOB. **General Information:** Turnaround time 1-2 days. Fee payee: Paris Municipal Court. Public access terminal is available.

Lonoke County

Circuit & Chancery Courts PO Box 218 Attn: Circuit Clerk, Lonoke, AR 72086; 501-676-2316. Hours: 8AM-4:30PM (CST). *Felony, Civil Actions Over $5,000, Probate.*

Civil Records: Access: Mail, in person. Both court and visitors may perform in person searches. Search fee: $6.00 per name. Required to search: name, years to search. Civil cases indexed by defendant. Civil records on computer from 1989, on dockets from 1918's (not for public use). **Criminal Records:** Access: Mail, in person. Both court and visitors may perform in person searches. Search fee: $6.00 per name. Required to search: name, years to search, SSN. Criminal records on computer from 1989, on dockets from 1918's (not for public use). **General Information:** No juvenile records released. SASE required. Turnaround time 1-2 days. Copy fee: $.25 per page. Certification fee: $6.00. Fee payee: Circuit Clerk. Personal checks accepted. Prepayment is required.

Lonoke Municipal Court 107 W 2nd St, Lonoke, AR 72086-2701; 501-676-3585; Fax: 501-676-2500. Hours: 8AM-4:30PM (CST). *Misdemeanor, Civil Actions Under $5,000, Eviction, Small Claims.*

Civil Records: Both court and visitors may perform in person searches. Search fee:. **Criminal Records:** Both court and visitors may perform in person searches. Search fee: $6.00 per name. Required to search: name, years to search. **General Information:**. Fee payee: Municipal Court. Prepayment is required.

Madison County

Circuit & Chancery Courts PO Box 416, Huntsville, AR 72740; 501-738-2215; Fax: 501-738-1544. Hours: 8AM-4:30PM (CST). *Felony, Civil Actions Over $5,000, Probate.*

Note: Probate is in the County Clerk's office

Civil Records: Access: In person only. Court does not conduct in person searches; visitors must perform searches for themselves. Search fee: No civil searches performed by court. Required to search: name, years to search; also helpful-address. Civil cases indexed by defendant, plaintiff. Civil records on dockets back to 1906. **Criminal Records:** Access: In person only. Court does not conduct in person searches; visitors must perform searches for themselves. Search fee: No criminal searches performed by court. Required to search: name, years to search; also helpful-address, DOB, SSN. Criminal records on dockets back to 1906. **General Information:** No juvenile records released. Copy fee: $.25 per page. Certification fee: $5.00. Fee payee: Circuit Clerk. Personal checks accepted. Prepayment is required.

Municipal Court PO Box 549, Huntsville, AR 72740; 501-738-2911; Fax: 501-738-6846. Hours: 8AM-4:30PM (CST). *Misdemeanor, Civil Actions Under $5,000, Eviction, Small Claims.*

Civil Records: Both court and visitors may perform in person searches. Search fee:. **Criminal Records:** Both court and visitors may perform in person searches. No search fee. Required to search: name, years to search, DOB, SSN. **General Information:** Turnaround time 1 week. Fee payee: Municipal Court. Prepayment is required.

Marion County

Circuit & County Courts PO Box 385, Yellville, AR 72687; 870-449-6226; Fax: 870-449-4979. Hours: 8AM-4:30PM (CST). *Felony, Civil Actions Over $5,000, Eviction, Probate.*

Civil Records: Access: In person only. Court does not conduct in person searches; visitors must perform searches for themselves. Search fee: No civil searches performed by court. Required to search: name, years to search. Civil cases indexed by plaintiff. Civil records on dockets from 1956, records are not computerized. **Criminal Records:** Access: Mail, in person. Both court and visitors may perform in person searches. Search fee: $6.00 per name. Required to search: name, years to search. Criminal records on dockets from 1956, records are not computerized. **General Information:** No juvenile or adoption records released. SASE required. Turnaround time 1 day. Copy fee: $.50 per page. Certification fee: $3.00. Fee payee: Marion County Circuit Clerk. Personal checks accepted. Prepayment is required.

Municipal Court PO Box 301, Yellville, AR 72687; 870-449-6030. Hours: 8AM-4:30PM (CST). *Misdemeanor, Civil Actions Under $5,000, Small Claims.*

Civil Records: Both court and visitors may perform in person searches. Search fee:. **Criminal Records:** Both court and visitors may perform in person searches. No search fee. Required to search: name, years to search. **General Information:**.

Miller County

Circuit & County Courts 412 Laurel St Rm 109, Texarkana, AR 71854; 870-774-4501; Fax: 870-772-5293. Hours: 8AM-4:30PM (CST). *Felony, Civil Actions Over $5,000, Probate.*

Note: Probate is at the County Clerk's office

Civil Records: Access: Phone, mail, in person. Both court and visitors may perform in person searches. Search fee: $6.00 per name. Required to search: name, years to search. Civil cases indexed by defendant, plaintiff. Civil records on index from 1850s. **Criminal Records:** Access: Phone, mail, in person. Both court and visitors may perform in person searches. Search fee: $6.00 per name. Required to search: name, years to search. Criminal records on index from 1850s. **General Information:** No expunged records released. SASE required. Turnaround time 1-2 days. Copy fee: $1.00 per page. Certification fee: $3.50. Fee payee: Miller County Circuit Clerk. Personal checks accepted. Prepayment is required.

Municipal Court 400 Laurel Suite 101, Texarkana, AR 71854; 870-772-2780; Fax: 870-773-3595. Hours: 8AM-4:30PM (CST). *Misdemeanor, Civil Actions Under $5,000, Eviction, Small Claims.*

Civil Records: Both court and visitors may perform in person searches. Search fee:. **Criminal Records:** Both court and visitors may perform in person searches. No search fee. Required to search: name, years to search, DOB, SSN. **General Information:** Turnaround time 2 days. Fee payee: Miller County Court. Prepayment is required.

Mississippi County

Blytheville Circuit & Chancery Courts PO Box 1498, Blytheville, AR 72316; 870-762-2332; Fax: 870-763-0150. Hours: 9AM-4:30PM (CST). *Felony, Civil Actions Over $5,000, Probate.*

Civil Records: Access: In person only. Court does not conduct in person searches; visitors must perform searches for themselves. Search fee: No civil searches performed by court. Required to search: name, years to search. Civil cases indexed by plaintiff. Civil records on computer since 1990, prior on index from 1940. **Criminal Records:** Access: Phone, fax, mail, in person. Both court and visitors may perform in person searches. Search fee: $6.00 per name. Required to search: name, years to search, DOB, SSN. Criminal records on computer since 1990, prior on index from 1940. Will search 7 years. **General Information:** No juvenile records released. SASE required. Turnaround time 1-2 days. Copy fee: $.25 per page. Certification fee: $3.00. Fee payee: Circuit Clerk. Personal checks accepted. Prepayment is required. Fax notes: $5.00 per document.

Osceola Circuit & Chancery Courts County Courthouse, PO Box 471, Osceola, AR 72370; 870-563-6471. Hours: 9AM-4:30PM (CST). *Felony, Civil Actions Over $5,000, Probate.*

Civil Records: Access: Mail, in person. Court does not conduct in person searches; visitors must perform searches for themselves. Search fee: No civil searches performed by court. Required to search: name, years to search. Civil cases indexed by defendant, plaintiff. Civil records computerized since 1992, on index from 1940. **Criminal Records:** Access: Mail, in person. Court does not conduct in person searches; visitors must perform searches for themselves. Search fee: $6.00 per name. Required to search: name, years to search, DOB, SSN. Criminal records on computer (not for public use) since 1992. **General Information:** No juvenile records released. SASE required. Turnaround time 1-2 days. Copy fee: $.50 per page. Certification fee: $3.00. Fee payee: Circuit Clerk. Personal checks accepted. Prepayment is required.

Blytheville Municipal Court 121 N 2nd St, #104, Blytheville, AR 72315; 870-763-7513; Fax: 870-762-0443. Hours: 8AM-5PM (CST). *Misdemeanor, Civil Actions Under $5,000, Eviction, Small Claims.*

Civil Records: Both court and visitors may perform in person searches. Search fee:. **Criminal Records:** Both court and visitors may perform in person searches. Search fee: $5.00 per name. Required to search: name, years to search; also helpful-DOB, SSN. **General Information:** Turnaround time 1-2 days. Fee payee: City of Blythville.

Osceola Municipal Court 397 W Keiser, Osceola, AR 72370; 870-563-1303; Fax: 870-563-2543. Hours: 9AM-4:30PM (CST). *Misdemeanor, Civil Actions Under $5,000, Eviction, Small Claims.*

Civil Records: Court does not conduct in person searches; visitors must perform searches for themselves. Search fee:. **Criminal Records:** Court does not conduct in person searches; visitors must perform searches for themselves. Search fee: No criminal searches performed by court. Required to search: name, years to search; also helpful-address, DOB, SSN. **General Information:** Turnaround time 1-2 days. Fee payee: City of Osceola. Prepayment is required.

Monroe County

Circuit & Chancery Courts 123 Madison St, Courthouse, Clarendon, AR 72029; 870-747-3615; Fax: 870-747-3710. Hours: 8AM-4:30PM (CST). *Felony, Civil Actions Over $5,000, Probate.*

Civil Records: Access: Fax, mail, in person. Both court and visitors may perform in person searches. Search fee: $6.00 per name. Required to search: name, years to search. Civil cases indexed by defendant, plaintiff. Civil records on index books from 1900. **Criminal Records:** Access: Mail, in person. Both court and visitors may perform in person searches. Search fee: $6.00 per name. Required to search: name, years to search, DOB, SSN. Criminal records on index books from 1900. **General Information:** No juvenile records released. SASE required. Turnaround time 1-2 days. Copy fee: $.50 per page. Certification fee: $2.50. Fee payee: Monroe County Circuit Clerk. Personal checks accepted. Prepayment is required. Fax notes: $2.50 per document. Additional fee of $.50 if more than 10 pages.

Municipal Court Courthouse, 270 Madison St, Clarendon, AR 72029; 870-747-5200; Fax: 870-747-3903. Hours: 8AM-5PM (CST). *Misdemeanor, Civil Actions Under $5,000, Eviction, Small Claims.*

Civil Records: Both court and visitors may perform in person searches. Search fee:. **Criminal Records:** Both court and visitors may perform in person searches. No search fee. Required to search: name, years to search, DOB, SSN.

General Information: Turnaround time 2-3 days. Fee payee: Clarendon Municipal Court. Prepayment is required.

Montgomery County

Circuit & County Courts PO Box 369, Courthouse, Mount Ida, AR 71957; 870-867-3521; Fax: 870-867-2177. Hours: 8AM-4:30PM (CST). *Felony, Civil Actions Over $5,000, Probate.*

Civil Records: Access: Phone, fax, mail, in person. Both court and visitors may perform in person searches. Search fee: $3.00 per name. Required to search: name, years to search; also helpful-address. Civil cases indexed by defendant, plaintiff. Civil records on card files from 1960s. **Criminal Records:** Access: Phone, fax, mail, in person. Both court and visitors may perform in person searches. Search fee: $3.00 per name. Required to search: name, years to search; also helpful-address, DOB, SSN. Criminal records on card files from 1960s. **General Information:** No juvenile or adoption records released. SASE required. Turnaround time 1 day. Copy fee: $.50 per page. Certification fee: $3.00. Fee payee: Circuit Clerk. Personal checks accepted. Prepayment is required.

Municipal Court PO Box 548, Mount Ida, AR 71957; 870-867-2221. Hours: 8AM-4:30PM M-Th, other days hours may vary (CST). *Misdemeanor, Civil Actions Under $5,000, Eviction, Small Claims.*

Civil Records: Both court and visitors may perform in person searches. Search fee:. **Criminal Records:** Both court and visitors may perform in person searches. No search fee. Required to search: name, years to search. **General Information:** Turnaround time 1-2 days. Fee payee: Mount Ida Municipal Court. Prepayment is required.

Nevada County

Circuit & Chancery Courts PO Box 204, Prescott, AR 71857; 870-887-2511; Fax: 870-887-5795. Hours: 8AM-5PM (CST). *Felony, Civil Actions Over $5,000, Probate.*

Civil Records: Access: Phone, fax, mail, in person. Both court and visitors may perform in person searches. Search fee: $6.00 per name. Required to search: name, years to search. Civil cases indexed by defendant, plaintiff. Civil records on index since 1850. **Criminal Records:** Access: Phone, fax, mail, in person. Both court and visitors may perform in person searches. Search fee: $6.00 per name. Required to search: name, years to search, DOB. Criminal records on index since 1850. **General Information:** No juvenile records released. SASE required. Turnaround time 1-2 days. Copy fee: $.25 per page. Certification fee: $2.00. Fee payee: Nevada County Circuit Clerk. Personal checks accepted. Prepayment is required. Fax notes: $.25 per page.

Municipal Court PO Box 22, Prescott, AR 71857; 870-887-6016; Fax: 870-887-5795. Hours: 8AM-5PM (CST). *Misdemeanor, Civil Actions Under $5,000, Eviction, Small Claims.*

Civil Records: Both court and visitors may perform in person searches. Search fee:. **Criminal Records:** Both court and visitors may perform in person searches. No search fee. Required to search: name, years to search, DOB, SSN. **General Information:** Turnaround time 2-5 days. Fee payee: Municipal Court. Prepayment is required.

Newton County

Circuit & Chancery Courts PO Box 410, Jasper, AR 72641; 870-446-5125; Fax: 870-446-2106. Hours: 8AM-4:30PM (CST). *Felony, Civil Actions Over $5,000, Probate.*

Civil Records: Access: Fax, mail, in person. Both court and visitors may perform in person searches. Search fee: $5.00 per name. Required to search: name, years to search. Civil cases indexed by defendant, plaintiff. Civil records on dockets. **Criminal Records:** Access: Fax, mail, in person. Both court and visitors may perform in person searches. Search fee: $5.00 per name. Required to search: name, years to search, DOB. Criminal records on dockets. **General Information:** No juvenile records released. SASE required. Turnaround time varies. Copy fee: $.25 per page. Certification fee: $5.00. Fee payee: Circuit Clerk. Personal checks accepted. Prepayment is required. Fax notes: $2.50 for first page, $.50 each addl.

Municipal Court PO Box 550, Jasper, AR 72641; 870-446-5335; Fax: 870-446-2234. Hours: 8AM-4:30PM (CST). *Misdemeanor, Civil Actions Under $5,000, Eviction, Small Claims.*

Civil Records: Both court and visitors may perform in person searches. Search fee:. **Criminal Records:** Both court and visitors may perform in person searches. No search fee. Required to search: name, years to search. **General Information:**. Fee payee: Municipal Court.

Ouachita County

Circuit & Chancery Courts PO Box 667, Camden, AR 71701; 870-837-2230 (Circuit); Probate phone:870-837-2220; Fax: 870-837-2252. Hours: 8AM-4:30PM (CST). *Felony, Civil Actions Over $5,000, Probate.*

Civil Records: Access: Mail, in person. Both court and visitors may perform in person searches. Search fee: $6.00 per name. Add $1.00 per year searched. Required to search: name, years to search. Civil cases indexed by defendant, plaintiff. Civil records archived from 1950s. **Criminal Records:** Access: In person only. Both court and visitors may perform in person searches. Search fee: $6.00 per name. Add $1.00 per year searched. Required to search: name, years to search; also helpful-DOB, SSN. Criminal records archived from 1950s. **General Information:** No juvenile records released. SASE requested. Turnaround time 3-7 days. Copy fee: $1.00 per page. Certification fee: $2.50. Fee payee: Circuit Clerk of Ouachita County. Personal checks accepted. Prepayment is required.

Ouachita County Municipal Court 213 Madison St, Camden, AR 71701; 870-836-0331; Fax: 870-836-3369. Hours: 8AM-4:30PM (CST). *Misdemeanor, Civil Actions Under $5,000, Eviction, Small Claims.*

Civil Records: Both court and visitors may perform in person searches. Search fee:. **Criminal Records:** Both court and visitors may perform in person searches. Search fee: $5.00 per name. Required to search: name, years to search; also helpful-SSN. **General Information:** Turnaround time 1-2 days. Fee payee: Municipal Court. Prepayment is required.

Perry County

Circuit & Chancery Courts PO Box 358, Perryville, AR 72126; 501-889-5126; Fax: 501-889-5759. Hours: 8AM-4:30PM (CST). *Felony, Civil Actions Over $5,000, Probate.*

Civil Records: Access: In person only. Court does not conduct in person searches; visitors must perform searches for themselves. Search fee: No civil searches performed by court. Required to search: name, years to search. Civil cases indexed by defendant, plaintiff. Civil records on computer from 1991, on dockets from 1974. **Criminal Records:** Access: In person only. Court does not conduct in person searches; visitors must perform searches for themselves. Search fee: No criminal searches performed by court. Required to search: name, years to search, DOB. Criminal records on computer from 1991, on dockets from 1974. **General Information:** No juvenile or adoption records released. Copy fee: $.50 for first page, $.25 each addl. Certification fee: $5.00. Fee payee: Circuit Clerk. Personal checks accepted. Prepayment is required. Public access terminal is available.

Municipal Court PO Box 186, Perryville, AR 72126; 501-889-5296; Fax: 501-889-5835. Hours: 8AM-4:30PM (CST). *Misdemeanor, Civil Actions Under $5,000, Eviction, Small Claims.*

Civil Records: Both court and visitors may perform in person searches. Search fee:. **Criminal Records:** Both court and visitors may perform in person searches. No search fee. Required to search: name, years to search, DOB, SSN. **General Information:** Turnaround time 3-5 days. Fee payee: Municipal Court. Prepayment is required.

Phillips County

Circuit & Chancery Courts Courthouse, 620 Cherry St Suite 206, Helena, AR 72342; 870-338-5515; Probate phone:870-338-5505; Fax: 870-338-5513. Hours: 8AM-4:30PM (CST). *Felony, Civil Actions Over $5,000, Probate.*

Civil Records: Access: In person only. Court does not conduct in person searches; visitors must perform searches for themselves. Search fee: No civil searches performed by court. Required to search: name, years to search. Civil cases indexed by plaintiff. Civil records on fee books from 1970. **Criminal Records:** Access: Mail, in person. Both court and visitors may perform in person searches. Search fee: $6.00 per name. Required to search: name, years to search. Criminal records on fee books from 1970. **General Information:** No juvenile records released. SASE required. Turnaround time 1 day. Copy fee: $.25 per page. Certification fee: $3.00. Fee payee: Circuit Clerk. Personal checks accepted. Prepayment is required.

Municipal Court 226 Perry ST, City Hall, Helena, AR 72342; 870-338-9831; Fax: 870-338-9832. Hours: 8AM-4:30PM (CST). *Misdemeanor, Civil Actions Under $5,000, Eviction, Small Claims.*

Civil Records: Both court and visitors may perform in person searches. Search fee:. **Criminal Records:** Both court and visitors may perform in person searches. Search fee: $5.00 per name. Required to search: name, years to search, address, DOB, SSN. **General Information:** Turnaround time 3 days. Fee payee: City of Helena Municipal Court. Prepayment is required.

Pike County

Circuit & Chancery Courts PO Box 219, Murfreesboro, AR 71958; 870-285-2231; Fax: 870-285-3281. Hours: 8AM-4:30PM (CST). *Felony, Civil Actions Over $5,000, Probate.*

Civil Records: Access: Fax, mail, in person. Both court and visitors may perform in person searches. Search fee: $6.00 per name. Required to search:

name, years to search. Civil cases indexed by defendant. Civil records archived from 1895. Some records on dockets and fee books. **Criminal Records:** Access: Fax, mail, in person. Both court and visitors may perform in person searches. Search fee: $6.00 per name. Required to search: name, years to search, DOB. Criminal records archived from 1895. Some records on dockets and fee books. **General Information:** No juvenile or adoption records released. Turnaround time 1 week. Copy fee: $.50 per page. Certification fee: $3.00. Fee payee: Pike County Clerk. Prepayment is required. Fax notes: Fax fee $1.50 1st 3 pages, $.50 each additional page.

Municipal Court PO Box 197, Murfreesboro, AR 71958; 870-285-3865; Fax: 870-285-2660. Hours: 8AM-4:30PM (CST). *Misdemeanor, Civil Actions Under $5,000, Eviction, Small Claims.*

Civil Records: Both court and visitors may perform in person searches. Search fee:. **Criminal Records:** Both court and visitors may perform in person searches. Search fee: $6.00 per name. Required to search: name, years to search, offense. **General Information:** Turnaround time 2-3 days. Fee payee: Pike County Municipal Court. Prepayment is required.

Poinsett County

Circuit & Chancery Courts PO Box 46, Harrisburg, AR 72432; 870-578-4420; Fax: 870-578-2441. Hours: 8:30AM-4:30PM (CST). *Felony, Civil Actions Over $5,000, Probate.*

Civil Records: Access: Mail, in person. Both court and visitors may perform in person searches. Search fee: $6.00 per name. Required to search: name, years to search. Civil cases indexed by defendant, plaintiff. Civil records on computer from 1985. Some records on dockets. **Criminal Records:** Access: Mail, in person. Both court and visitors may perform in person searches. Search fee: $6.00 per name. Required to search: name, years to search, DOB. Criminal records on computer from 1985. Some records on dockets. **General Information:** No juvenile records released. SASE required. Turnaround time 1-2 days. Copy fee: $.25 per page. Certification fee: $2.00. Fee payee: Circuit Clerk. Personal checks accepted. Prepayment is required. Public access terminal is available.

Harrisburg Municipal Court 202 N East St, Harrisburg, AR 72432; 870-578-4110; Fax: 870-578-4113. Hours: 8AM-4:30PM (CST). *Misdemeanor, Civil Actions Under $5,000, Eviction, Small Claims.*

Civil Records: Both court and visitors may perform in person searches. Search fee:. **Criminal Records:** Both court and visitors may perform in person searches. No search fee. Required to search: name, years to search; also helpful-DOB, SSN. Court does not allow public access to computer index. **General Information:** Turnaround time 1-2 weeks. Fee payee: Harrisburg Municipal Court. Prepayment is required.

Polk County

Circuit & Chancery Courts 507 Church St, Mena, AR 71953; 501-394-8100; Probate phone:501-394-8123. Hours: 8AM-4:30PM (CST). *Felony, Civil Actions Over $5,000, Probate.*

Note: Probate is handled separately from the court

Civil Records: Access: Mail, in person. Both court and visitors may perform in person searches. Search fee: $6.00 per name. Required to search:

name, years to search. Civil cases indexed by defendant, plaintiff. Civil records on dockets and index from late 1800s. **Criminal Records:** Access: Mail, in person. Both court and visitors may perform in person searches. Search fee: $6.00 per name. Required to search: name, years to search, DOB. Criminal records on dockets and index from late 1800s. **General Information:** No juvenile records released. SASE required. Turnaround time 1-2 days. Copy fee: $.25 per page. $.50 for legal size copies. Certification fee: $2.00. Fee payee: Circuit Clerk. Personal checks accepted. Prepayment is required.

Municipal Court Courthouse, 507 Church St, Mena, AR 71953; 501-394-8140; Fax: 501-394-6199. Hours: 8AM-4:30PM (CST). *Misdemeanor, Civil Actions Under $5,000, Eviction, Small Claims.*

Civil Records: Court does not conduct in person searches; visitors must perform searches for themselves. Search fee:. **Criminal Records:** Court does not conduct in person searches; visitors must perform searches for themselves. Search fee: No criminal searches performed by court. Required to search: name, years to search, DOB; also helpful-SSN. **General Information:** Turnaround time 1-2 days. Fee payee: Polk Municipal Court.

Pope County

Circuit & Chancery Courts 100 W Main, Russellville, AR 72801; 501-968-7499. Hours: 8AM-5PM (CST). *Felony, Civil Actions Over $5,000, Probate.*

Note: This court will not do record searches; a local retriever must be hired

Civil Records: Access: In person only. Court does not conduct in person searches; visitors must perform searches for themselves. Search fee: No civil searches performed by court. Required to search: name, years to search. Civil cases indexed by defendant, plaintiff. Civil records on dockets from early 1900s. **Criminal Records:** Access: In person only. Court does not conduct in person searches; visitors must perform searches for themselves. Search fee: No criminal searches performed by court. Required to search: name, years to search, DOB; also helpful-SSN. Criminal records on dockets from early 1900s. **General Information:** No juvenile records released. Copy fee: If the court makes the copy, the fee is $1.00 per page, otherwise $.15. Certification fee: $3.00. Fee payee: Pope County. Personal checks accepted.

Municipal Court 205 S Commerce, Russellville, AR 72801; 501-968-1393; Fax: 501-968-8050. Hours: 8:30AM-5PM (CST). *Misdemeanor, Civil Actions Under $5,000, Eviction, Small Claims.*

Civil Records: Both court and visitors may perform in person searches. Search fee:. **Criminal Records:** Both court and visitors may perform in person searches. No search fee. Required to search: name, years to search; also helpful-DOB. **General Information:** Turnaround time 2-3 days. Fee payee: Municipal Court. Prepayment is required.

Prairie County

Circuit & Chancery Courts-Southern District PO Box 283, De Valls Bluff, AR 72041; 870-998-2314; Fax: 870-998-2314. Hours: 8AM-4:30PM (CST). *Felony, Civil Actions Over $5,000, Probate.*

Civil Records: Access: Phone, fax, mail, in person. Both court and visitors may perform in person searches. No search fee. Required to search: name, years to search. Civil cases indexed by defendant, plaintiff. Civil records on dockets from 1800s. **Criminal Records:** Access: Phone, fax, mail, in person. Both court and visitors may perform in person searches. No search fee. Required to search: name, years to search, DOB, SSN. Criminal records on dockets from 1800s. **General Information:** No juvenile or adoption records released. SASE required. Turnaround time 1 day. Copy fee: $.25 per page. Certification fee: $6.00. Fee payee: Circuit Clerk. Personal checks accepted. Prepayment is required. Fax notes: $1.00 per page.

Circuit & County Courts-Northern District PO Box 1011, Des Arc, AR 72040; 870-256-4434; Fax: 870-256-4434. Hours: 8AM-4:30PM (CST). *Felony, Civil Actions Over $5,000, Probate.*

Civil Records: Access: Phone, mail, in person. Both court and visitors may perform in person searches. Search fee: $6.00 per name. Required to search: name, years to search. Civil cases indexed by defendant, plaintiff. Civil records on dockets from 1800s. **Criminal Records:** Access: Phone, mail, in person. Both court and visitors may perform in person searches. Search fee: $6.00 per name. Required to search: name, years to search. Criminal records on dockets from 1800s. **General Information:** No juvenile, adoption records released. SASE required. Turnaround time 1 day. Copy fee: $.25 per page. Certification fee: $6.00. Fee payee: Circuit Clerk. Personal checks accepted. Prepayment is required.

Des Arc Municipal Court PO Box 389, Des Arc, AR 72040; 870-256-3011; Fax: 870-256-4612. Hours: 8AM-5PM (CST). *Misdemeanor, Civil Actions Under $5,000, Eviction, Small Claims.*

Civil Records: Both court and visitors may perform in person searches. Search fee:. **Criminal Records:** Both court and visitors may perform in person searches. No search fee. Required to search: name, years to search. **General Information:** Turnaround time 1-2 days. Fee payee: Municipal Court. Prepayment is required.

Pulaski County

Circuit & Chancery Courts Courthouse, Rm 102, 401 W Markham St, Ste 102, Little Rock, AR 72201; 501-340-8431; Probate phone:501-340-8411; Fax: 501-340-8420. Hours: 8:30AM-4:30PM (CST). *Felony, Civil Actions Over $5,000, Probate.*

Note: Probate is handled by the Chancery Court, Suite 120

Civil Records: Access: In person only. Court does not conduct in person searches; visitors must perform searches for themselves. Search fee: No civil searches performed by court. Required to search: name, years to search. Civil cases indexed by defendant, plaintiff. Civil records on computer from 1982, on microfiche from 1974 to 1982, archived from 1900. **Criminal Records:** Access: In person only. Court does not conduct in person searches; visitors must perform searches for themselves. Search fee: No criminal searches performed by court. Required to search: name, years to search, DOB, SSN. Criminal records on computer from 1982, on microfiche from 1974 to 1982, archived from 1900. **General Information:** No expunged records released. Copy fee: $.25 per page. Certification fee: $2.50. Fee payee: Circuit

Clerk. Personal checks accepted. Prepayment is required.

Pulaski County Municipal Court 3001 W Roosevelt, Little Rock, AR 72204; 501-340-6824; Fax: 501-340-6899. Hours: 8AM-4:30PM (CST). *Misdemeanor, Civil Actions Under $5,000, Eviction, Small Claims.*

Civil Records: Both court and visitors may perform in person searches. Search fee:. **Criminal Records:** Both court and visitors may perform in person searches. No search fee. Required to search: name, years to search; also helpful-SSN. **General Information:** Turnaround time 2-3 days. Fee payee: Municipal Court. Prepayment is required.

Randolph County

Circuit & Chancery Courts 107 West Broadway, Pocahontas, AR 72455; 870-892-5522; Fax: 870-892-8794. Hours: 8AM-4:30PM (CST). *Felony, Civil Actions Over $5,000, Probate.*

Civil Records: Access: Mail, in person. Both court and visitors may perform in person searches. Search fee: $6.00 per name. Required to search: name, years to search. Civil cases indexed by defendant, plaintiff. Civil records on criminal index from 1836. **Criminal Records:** Access: Mail, in person. Both court and visitors may perform in person searches. Search fee: $6.00 per name. Required to search: name, years to search, DOB. Criminal records on criminal index from 1836. **General Information:** No juvenile records released. SASE required. Turnaround time same day. Copy fee: $.25 per page. Certification fee: $2.00. Fee payee: Circuit Clerk. Personal checks accepted.

Municipal Court 1510 Pace Rd, Pocahontas, AR 72455; 870-892-4033; Fax: 870-892-4392. Hours: 7:30AM-4:30PM (CST). *Misdemeanor, Civil Actions Under $5,000, Eviction, Small Claims.*

Civil Records: Both court and visitors may perform in person searches. Search fee:. **Criminal Records:** Both court and visitors may perform in person searches. Search fee: No search fee. The court is considering a fee charge in the near future. Required to search: name, years to search, DOB, SSN. **General Information:** Turnaround time 1 day. Fee payee: Municipal Court. Prepayment is required.

Saline County

Circuit & Chancery Courts 200 Main St, Benton, AR 72018; 501-303-5615; Fax: 501-303-5675. Hours: 8AM-4:30PM (CST). *Felony, Civil Actions Over $5,000, Probate.*

www.salinecounty.org

Civil Records: Access: In person only. Court does not conduct in person searches; visitors must perform searches for themselves. Search fee: No civil searches performed by court. Required to search: name, years to search. Civil cases indexed by defendant, plaintiff. Civil records on computer since 9/94, prior on docket books. **Criminal Records:** Access: In person only. Court does not conduct in person searches; visitors must perform searches for themselves. Search fee: No criminal searches performed by court. Required to search: name, years to search, DOB, SSN. Criminal records on computer since 9/94, prior on docket books. **General Information:** No juvenile records released. Copy fee: $.25 per page. Certification fee: $3.00. Fee payee: Circuit Court. Personal checks accepted. Prepayment is required.

Benton Municipal Court 1605 Edison Ave, Benton, AR 72015; 501-303-5670/1 & 5975; Fax: 501-776-5696. Hours: 8AM-4:30PM (CST). *Misdemeanor, Civil Actions Under $5,000, Eviction, Small Claims.*

Civil Records: Both court and visitors may perform in person searches. Search fee:. **Criminal Records:** Both court and visitors may perform in person searches. No search fee. Required to search: name, years to search; also helpful-DOB, SSN. **General Information:** Turnaround time 1 day. Fee payee: Municipal Court. Prepayment is required.

Scott County

Circuit & Chancery Courts PO Box 2165, Waldron, AR 72958; 870-637-2642. Hours: 8AM-4:30PM (CST). *Felony, Civil Actions Over $5,000, Probate.*

Civil Records: Access: Mail, in person. Both court and visitors may perform in person searches. No search fee. Required to search: name, years to search. Civil cases indexed by defendant, plaintiff. Civil records on index books from 1882. **Criminal Records:** Access: Mail, in person. Both court and visitors may perform in person searches. No search fee. Required to search: name, years to search, DOB, SSN. Criminal records on index books from 1882. **General Information:** No juvenile or adoption records released. SASE required. Turnaround time 1 week. Copy fee: $.25 per page. Certification fee: $3.00. Fee payee: Scott County. Personal checks accepted. Prepayment is required.

Municipal Court 100 W 1st St, Box 15, Waldron, AR 72958; 501-637-4694; Fax: 501-437-4199. Hours: 8AM-4:30PM (CST). *Misdemeanor, Civil Actions Under $5,000, Eviction, Small Claims.*

Civil Records: Both court and visitors may perform in person searches. Search fee:. **Criminal Records:** Both court and visitors may perform in person searches. No search fee. Required to search: name, years to search. **General Information:** Turnaround time 1-2 days. Fee payee: Municipal Court.

Searcy County

Circuit & Chancery Courts PO Box 998, Marshall, AR 72650; 870-448-3807. Hours: 8AM-4:30PM (CST). *Felony, Civil Actions Over $5,000, Probate.*

Civil Records: Access: Mail, in person. Both court and visitors may perform in person searches. Search fee: $6.00 per name. Required to search: name, years to search. Civil cases indexed by defendant, plaintiff. Civil records archived from 1881. Some records on dockets. **Criminal Records:** Access: In person only. Court does not conduct in person searches; visitors must perform searches for themselves. Search fee: No criminal searches performed by court. Required to search: name, years to search, offense; also helpful-DOB, SSN. Criminal records archived from 1881. Some records on dockets. **General Information:** No juvenile or adoption records released. SASE required. Turnaround time 1-2 days. Copy fee: $.25 per page. Fee is for civil division only. Certification fee: $3.00. Fee payee: Searcy County Clerk. Personal checks accepted. Prepayment is required.

Municipal Court PO Box 837, Marshall, AR 72650; 870-448-5411; Fax: 870-448-5692. Hours: 9AM-5PM (CST). *Misdemeanor, Civil Actions Under $5,000, Eviction, Small Claims.*

Civil Records: Both court and visitors may perform in person searches. Search fee:. Criminal Records: Both court and visitors may perform in person searches. No search fee. Required to search: name, years to search, DOB, SSN. General Information: Turnaround time 1 week. Fee payee: Marshall Municipal Court. Prepayment is required.

Sebastian County

Circuit Court-Greenwood Division PO
Box 310, County Courthouse, Greenwood, AR 72936; 501-996-4175; Fax: 501-996-6885. Hours: 8AM-5PM (CST). *Felony, Civil Actions Over $5,000, Probate.*

Civil Records: Access: Mail, in person. Both court and visitors may perform in person searches. Search fee: $6.00 per name. Required to search: name, years to search. Civil cases indexed by defendant, plaintiff. Civil records on computer from 10/87, on dockets from 1900. Criminal Records: Access: Mail, in person. Both court and visitors may perform in person searches. Search fee: $6.00 per name. Required to search: name, years to search; also helpful-SSN. Criminal records on computer from 10/87, on dockets from 1900. General Information: No juvenile records released. SASE required. Turnaround time 1-2 weeks. Copy fee: $1.00 per page. Certification fee: $2.50. Fee payee: Circuit Clerk. Personal checks accepted. Prepayment is required. Public access terminal is available. Fax notes: $1.00 per page.

Circuit Court-Fort Smith 35 S 6th St, PO
Box 1179, Fort Smith, AR 72902; 501-782-1046. Hours: 8AM-5PM (CST). *Felony, Civil Actions Over $5,000, Probate.*

Civil Records: Access: Fax, mail, in person. Both court and visitors may perform in person searches. Search fee: $6.00 per name. Required to search: name, years to search; also helpful-address. Civil cases indexed by defendant, plaintiff. Civil records on computer from 1988, on dockets from 1900. Criminal Records: Access: Fax, mail, in person. Both court and visitors may perform in person searches. Search fee: $6.00 per name. Required to search: name, years to search; also helpful-address, DOB, SSN. Criminal records on computer from 1988, on dockets from 1900. General Information: No juvenile records released. SASE required. Turnaround time 1-2 weeks. Copy fee: $1.00 per page. The fee is $.50 if in person, $1.00 for mail requesters. Certification fee: $2.50. Fee payee: Circuit Clerk. Personal checks accepted. Prepayment is required. Public access terminal is available. Fax notes: $1.00 per page.

Fort Smith Municipal Court Courthouse,
35 S 6th St, Fort Smith, AR 72901; 501-784-2420; Fax: 501-784-2438. Hours: 8:30AM-5PM (CST). *Misdemeanor, Civil Actions Under $5,000, Eviction, Small Claims.*

Civil Records: Both court and visitors may perform in person searches. Search fee:. Criminal Records: Both court and visitors may perform in person searches. No search fee. Required to search: name, years to search, DOB; also helpful-SSN. General Information: Turnaround time 1-2 days. Fee payee: Fort Smith Municipal Court. Prepayment is required. Public access terminal is available.

Sevier County

Circuit Court 115 N 3rd, Courthouse, De
Queen, AR 71832; 870-584-3055; Fax: 870-642-9638. Hours: 8AM-4:30PM (CST). *Felony, Civil Actions Over $5,000, Probate.*

Civil Records: Access: In person only. Court does not conduct in person searches; visitors must perform searches for themselves. Search fee: No civil searches performed by court. Required to search: name, years to search. Civil cases indexed by defendant, plaintiff. Civil records archived from 1900. Criminal Records: Access: Mail, fax, in person. Both court and visitors may perform in person searches. Search fee: $6.00 per name. Required to search: name, years to search, DOB. Criminal records on record and index books. General Information: No juvenile records released. SASE required. Turnaround time 3 days. Copy fee: $.50 per page. Certification fee: $3.00. Fee payee: Circuit Clerk. Personal checks accepted. Prepayment is required. Fax notes: Fee to fax is $5.00 per document; free if to a toll-free number.

Municipal Court 115 N 3rd St, Rm 215, De
Queen, AR 71832; 870-584-7311; Fax: 870-642-9638. Hours: 8AM-4:30PM (CST). *Misdemeanor, Civil Actions Under $5,000, Eviction, Small Claims.*

Civil Records: Both court and visitors may perform in person searches. Search fee:. Criminal Records: Both court and visitors may perform in person searches. No search fee. Required to search: name, years to search, DOB. General Information: Turnaround time 1-2 weeks. Fee payee: Municipal Court.

Sharp County

Circuit & County Courts PO Box 307, Ash
Flat, AR 72513; 870-994-7361; Fax: 870-994-7712. Hours: 8AM-4PM (CST). *Felony, Civil Actions Over $5,000, Probate.*

Civil Records: Access: Fax, mail, in person. Both court and visitors may perform in person searches. Search fee: $6.00 per name. Required to search: name, years to search. Civil cases indexed by defendant, plaintiff. Civil records on card files from 1970s. Some records on dockets. Criminal Records: Access: Fax, mail, in person. Both court and visitors may perform in person searches. Search fee: $6.00 per name. Required to search: name, years to search; also helpful-DOB, SSN. Criminal records on card files from 1970s. Some records on dockets. General Information: No juvenile or expunged records released. SASE required. Turnaround time 1 day. Copy fee: $.15 per page. Certification fee: $3.00. Fee payee: Sharp County Clerk. Personal checks accepted. Prepayment is required. Fax notes: No fee to fax results. Will only fax to 800 numbers.

Municipal Court PO Box 2, Ash Flat, AR
72513; 870-994-2745; Fax: 870-994-7901. Hours: 8AM-4PM (CST). *Misdemeanor, Civil Actions Under $5,000, Eviction, Small Claims.*

Civil Records: Both court and visitors may perform in person searches. Search fee:. Criminal Records: Both court and visitors may perform in person searches. No search fee. Required to search: name, years to search; also helpful-DOB, SSN. General Information: Turnaround time 1 day. Fee payee: Sharp County Municipal Court. Prepayment is required.

St. Francis County

Circuit & County Courts PO Box 1775,
Forrest City, AR 72335; 870-261-1715; Fax: 870-261-1723. Hours: 8AM-4:30PM (CST). *Felony, Civil Actions Over $5,000, Probate.*

Civil Records: Access: Fax, mail, in person. Both court and visitors may perform in person searches. Search fee: $5.00 per name. Required to search:

name, years to search. Civil cases indexed by defendant, plaintiff. Civil records on index from 1982, archived from 1920s. Criminal Records: Access: Fax, mail, in person. Both court and visitors may perform in person searches. Search fee: $5.00 per name. Required to search: name, years to search, DOB, SSN. Criminal records on index from 1982, archived from 1920s. General Information: No juvenile records released. SASE required. Turnaround time 2-3 days. Copy fee: $.50 per page. Certification fee: $3.00. Fee payee: Circuit Clerk. Personal checks accepted. Fax notes: No fee to fax results. Local or toll free calls only.

Municipal Court 615 East Cross, Forrest City,
AR 72335; 870-261-1410; Fax: 870-261-1411. Hours: 8AM-4:30PM (CST). *Misdemeanor, Civil Actions Under $5,000, Eviction, Small Claims.*

Civil Records: Only the court conducts in person searches; visitors may not. Search fee:. Criminal Records: Only the court conducts in person searches; visitors may not. Search fee: $5.00 per name. Required to search: name, years to search. General Information: Turnaround time 5 days. Fee payee: Municipal Court. Prepayment is required.

Stone County

Circuit & Chancery Courts HC71 Box 1,
Mountain View, AR 72560; 870-269-3271; Fax: 870-269-2303. Hours: 8AM-4:30PM (CST). *Felony, Civil Actions Over $5,000, Probate.*

Civil Records: Access: In person only. Court does not conduct in person searches; visitors must perform searches for themselves. Search fee: No civil searches performed by court. Required to search: name, years to search. Civil cases indexed by defendant, plaintiff. Civil records on dockets from 1960s. Mountain View Abstract Corp does searches by mail. Call 870-269-8410. Criminal Records: Access: In person only. Court does not conduct in person searches; visitors must perform searches for themselves. Search fee: No criminal searches performed by court. Required to search: name, years to search, DOB; also helpful-SSN. Criminal records on dockets from 1960s. General Information: No juvenile or adoption records released. Copy fee: $.25 per page. Certification fee: $3.00. Fee payee: Stone County Clerk. Personal checks accepted. Prepayment is required.

Municipal Court HC 71 Box 4, Mountain
View, AR 72560; 870-269-3465. Hours: 8AM-4:30PM (CST). *Misdemeanor, Civil Actions Under $5,000, Eviction, Small Claims.*

Civil Records: Both court and visitors may perform in person searches. Search fee:. Criminal Records: Both court and visitors may perform in person searches. No search fee. Required to search: name, years to search. General Information: Turnaround time varies. Fee payee: Municipal Court.

Union County

Circuit & Chancery Courts PO Box 1626,
El Dorado, AR 71730; 870-864-1940. Hours: 8:30AM-5PM (CST). *Felony, Civil Actions Over $5,000, Probate.*

Civil Records: Access: Mail, in person. Both court and visitors may perform in person searches. Search fee: $6.00 per name. Required to search: name, years to search. Civil cases indexed by defendant, plaintiff. Civil records on computer from 1989, on dockets from 1800s. Criminal Records: Access: Mail, in person. Both court and visitors may perform in person searches. Search fee: $6.00 per name. Required to search: name, years to search, DOB. Criminal records on computer from 1989, on dockets from 1800s. **General Information:** No juvenile records released. SASE required. Turnaround time 2 days. Copy fee: $.50 per page. Certification fee: $1.00. Fee payee: Circuit Clerk. Personal checks accepted. Prepayment is required.

Municipal Court 101 N Washington, Suite 203, El Dorado, AR 71730; 870-864-1950; Fax: 870-864-1955. Hours: 8:30AM-5PM (CST). *Misdemeanor, Civil Actions Under $5,000, Eviction, Small Claims.*

Civil Records: Both court and visitors may perform in person searches. Search fee:. **Criminal Records:** Both court and visitors may perform in person searches. No search fee. Required to search: name, years to search, DOB; also helpful-SSN. **General Information:** Turnaround time 1-2 days. Fee payee: Union County Municipal Court. Prepayment is required.

Van Buren County

Circuit & County Courts Route 6 Box 254-9, Clinton, AR 72031; 501-745-4140. Hours: 8AM-5PM (CST). *Felony, Civil Actions Over $5,000, Probate.*

Civil Records: Access: Mail, in person. Both court and visitors may perform in person searches. Search fee: No civil searches performed by court. Required to search: name, years to search; also helpful-address. Civil cases indexed by defendant, plaintiff. Civil records on computer from 1987, archived from 1900s. **Criminal Records:** Access: Mail, in person. Both court and visitors may perform in person searches. Search fee: $6.00 per name. Required to search: name, years to search; also helpful-address, DOB, SSN. Criminal records on computer from 1987, archived from 1900s. **General Information:** No juvenile or adoption records released. SASE required. Turnaround time 7-10 days. Copy fee: $.25 per page. $.50 for microfilm copies. Certification fee: $3.00. Fee payee: Van Buren County Clerk's Office. Personal checks accepted. Prepayment is required.

Municipal Court PO Box 181, Clinton, AR 72031; 501-745-8894; Fax: 501-745-5810. Hours: 8:30AM-4:30PM (CST). *Misdemeanor, Civil Actions Under $5,000, Eviction, Small Claims.*

Civil Records: Court does not conduct in person searches; visitors must perform searches for themselves. Search fee:. **Criminal Records:** Both court and visitors may perform in person searches. Search fee: $5.00 per name. Required to search: name, years to search, DOB, SSN. **General Information:**. Fee payee: Clinton Municipal Court. Prepayment is required.

Washington County

Circuit & Chancery Courts 280 N College, Fayetteville, AR 72701; 501-444-1542; Fax: 501-444-1537. Hours: 8AM-4:30PM (CST). *Felony, Civil Actions Over $5,000, Probate.*

Civil Records: Access: Fax, mail, in person. Both court and visitors may perform in person searches. No search fee. Required to search: name, years to search. Civil cases indexed by defendant, plaintiff. Civil records on computer from 1992, on index from 1950. **Criminal Records:** Access: Fax, mail, in person. Both court and visitors may perform in person searches. No search fee. Required to search: name, years to search; also helpful-address, DOB, SSN. Criminal records on computer from 1992, on index from 1950. **General Information:**

No juvenile records released. Turnaround time 1-2 days. Copy fee: $.25 per page. Certification fee: $2.00. Fee payee: Circuit Clerk. Personal checks accepted. Prepayment is required. Public access terminal is available. Fax notes: $5.00 per document.

Fayetteville Municipal Court 100 B West Rock, Fayetteville, AR 72701; 501-587-3596; Fax: 501-444-3480. Hours: 8AM-5PM (CST). *Misdemeanor, Civil Actions Under $5,000, Small Claims.*

Civil Records: Both court and visitors may perform in person searches. Search fee:. **Criminal Records:** Both court and visitors may perform in person searches. Search fee: $5.00 per name. Required to search: name, years to search, address, DOB, SSN. **General Information:** Turnaround time 1 week. Fee payee: City of Fayetteville. Prepayment is required.

White County

Circuit & Chancery Courts 301 W Arch, Searcy, AR 72143; 501-279-6223; Probate phone:501-279-6204; Fax: 501-279-6218. Hours: 8AM-4:30PM (CST). *Felony, Civil Actions Over $5,000, Probate.*

Civil Records: Access: Phone, mail, in person. Both court and visitors may perform in person searches. Search fee: $6.00 per name. Required to search: name, years to search; also helpful-address. Civil cases indexed by plaintiff. Civil records on dockets from 1982. **Criminal Records:** Access: Phone, mail, in person. Both court and visitors may perform in person searches. Search fee: $6.00 per name. Required to search: name, years to search, DOB, SSN; also helpful-address. Criminal records on dockets from 1982. **General Information:** No juvenile records released. SASE required. Turnaround time 1 day. Copy fee: $.50 per page. Certification fee: $2.50. Fee payee: Chancery Clerk. Personal checks accepted. Prepayment is required. Public access terminal is available.

Searcy Municipal Court 311 N Gum, Searcy, AR 72143; 501-268-7622. Hours: 8:30AM-4:30PM (CST). *Misdemeanor, Civil Actions Under $5,000, Small Claims.*

Civil Records: Both court and visitors may perform in person searches. Search fee:. **Criminal Records:** Both court and visitors may perform in person searches. No search fee. Required to search: name, years to search, DOB, SSN. **General Information:** Turnaround time 5 days. Fee payee: Searcy Municipal Court.

Woodruff County

Circuit & County Courts PO Box 492, Augusta, AR 72006; 870-347-2391; Probate phone:870-347-2871; Fax: 870-347-2915. Hours: 8AM-4PM (CST). *Felony, Civil Actions Over $5,000, Probate.*

Note: Probate is handled by the County Clerk

Civil Records: Access: Phone, mail, in person. Both court and visitors may perform in person searches. No search fee. Required to search: name, years to search. Civil cases indexed by defendant, plaintiff. Civil records on dockets from 1982. **Criminal Records:** Access: Phone, mail, in person. Both court and visitors may perform in person searches. No search fee. Required to search: name, years to search. Criminal records on dockets from 1982. **General Information:** No juvenile records released. SASE required.

Turnaround time 1-2 days. Copy fee: $.50 per page. Certification fee: $3.00. Fee payee: Circuit Clerk. Personal checks accepted. Prepayment is required.

Municipal Court PO Box 381, Augusta, AR 72006; 870-347-2790; Fax: 870-347-2436. Hours: 8:30AM-5PM (CST). *Misdemeanor, Civil Actions Under $5,000, Eviction, Small Claims.*

Civil Records: Both court and visitors may perform in person searches. Search fee:. **Criminal Records:** Both court and visitors may perform in person searches. Search fee: $5.00 per name. Required to search: name, years to search. **General Information:** Turnaround time 10 days. Fee payee: Augusta Municipal Court. Prepayment is required.

Yell County

Danville Circuit & County Courts PO Box 219, Danville, AR 72833; 501-495-2414; Fax: 501-495-3495. Hours: 8AM-4PM (CST). *Felony, Civil Actions Over $5,000, Probate.*

Civil Records: Access: Mail, in person. Both court and visitors may perform in person searches. Search fee: $6.00 per name. Required to search: name, years to search; also helpful-address. Civil cases indexed by defendant. Civil records on computer from 1989, on dockets from 1800s. **Criminal Records:** Access: Mail, in person. Both court and visitors may perform in person searches. Search fee: $6.00 per name. Required to search: name, years to search, DOB; also helpful-address. Criminal records on computer from 1989, on dockets from 1800s. **General Information:** No juvenile or adoption records released. SASE required. Turnaround time 1 day. Copy fee: $.25 per page. Certification fee: $5.00. Fee payee: Circuit Clerk of Yell County. Personal checks accepted. Prepayment is required.

Dardanelle Circuit & County Courts County Courthouse, PO Box 457, Dardanelle, AR 72834; 501-229-4404. Hours: 8AM-4PM (CST). *Felony, Civil Actions Over $5,000, Probate.*

Civil Records: Access: Mail, in person. Both court and visitors may perform in person searches. Search fee: $6.00 per name. Required to search: name, years to search. Civil cases indexed by defendant. Civil records on computer from 1989, on dockets from 1800s. **Criminal Records:** Access: Mail, in person. Both court and visitors may perform in person searches. Search fee: $6.00 per name. Required to search: name, years to search; also helpful-DOB. Criminal records on computer from 1989, on dockets from 1800s. **General Information:** No adoption or juvenile records released. SASE required. Turnaround time 1 day. Copy fee: $.25 per page. Certification fee: $3.00. Fee payee: Circuit Clerk of Yell County. Personal checks accepted. Prepayment is required.

Municipal Court County Courthouse, Dardanelle, AR 72834; 501-229-1389. Hours: 8AM-4PM (CST). *Misdemeanor, Civil Actions Under $5,000, Eviction, Small Claims.*

Civil Records: Both court and visitors may perform in person searches. Search fee:. **Criminal Records:** Both court and visitors may perform in person searches. Search fee: $3.00 per name. Required to search: name, years to search; also helpful-address, DOB, SSN. **General Information:** Turnaround time 2-4 days. Fee payee: Municipal County. Prepayment is required.

ORGANIZATION

75 counties, 85 recording offices. The recording officer is the Clerk of Circuit Court, who is Ex Officio Recorder. **Ten counties have two recording offices**—Arkansas, Carroll, Clay, Craighead, Franklin, Logan, Mississippi, Prairie, Sebastian, and Yell. See the notes under each county for how to determine which office is appropriate to search. The entire state is in the Central Time Zone (CST).

REAL ESTATE RECORDS

Most counties do **not** perform real estate searches. Copy fees and certification fees vary.

UCC RECORDS

This is a **dual filing state**. Financing statements are filed at the state level and with the Circuit Clerk, except for consumer goods, farm and real estate related collateral, which are filed only with the Circuit Clerk. Most counties will perform UCC searches. Use search request form UCC-11. Search fees are usually $10.00 per debtor name. Copy fees vary.

TAX LIEN RECORDS

Federal tax liens on personal property of businesses are filed with the Secretary of State. Other federal and all state tax liens are filed with the Circuit Clerk. Many counties will perform separate tax lien searches. Search fees are usually $6.00 per name.

OTHER LIENS

Mechanics, lis pendens, judgments, hospital, child support, materialman.

Arkansas County (Northern District)
County Circuit Clerk, P.O. Box 719, Stuttgart, AR 72160. 870-673-2056. Fax: 870-673-3869.

Arkansas County (Southern District)
County Circuit Clerk, 101 Court Square, De Witt, AR 72042. 870-946-4219. Fax: 870-946-1394.

Ashley County
County Circuit Clerk, Jefferson Street, Courthouse, Hamburg, AR 71646. 870-853-2030. Fax: 870-853-2005.

Baxter County
County Circuit Clerk, Courthouse Square, 1 East 7th Street, Mountain Home, AR 72653. 870-425-3475. Fax: 870-425-5105.

Benton County
County Circuit Clerk, 215 East Central Street, Suite 6, Bentonville, AR 72712. 501-271-1017. Fax: 501-271-5719.
www.co.benton.ar.us
Online Access: Real Estate, Property Tax. Benton County Assessor, tax collector, & circuit court information is available for free on the Internet at http://208.154.254.51:5061 or, at the main site, click on the courthouse picture to access main menu.

Boone County
County Circuit Clerk, Courthouse, Suite 200, 100 N. Main, Harrison, AR 72601. 870-741-5560. Fax: 870-741-4335.

Bradley County
County Circuit Clerk, 101 E. Cedar Street, Courthouse, Warren, AR 71671. 870-226-2272. Fax: 870-226-8401.

Calhoun County
County Circuit Clerk, P.O. Box 626, Hampton, AR 71744. 870-798-2517. Fax: 870-798-2428.

Carroll County (Eastern District)
County Circuit Clerk, P.O. Box 71, Berryville, AR 72616. 870-423-2422. Fax: 870-423-4796.

Carroll County (Western District)
County Circuit Clerk, P.O. Box 109, Eureka Springs, AR 72632. 870-253-8646.

Chicot County
County Circuit Clerk, Courthouse, 108 Main St., Lake Village, AR 71653. 870-265-8010. Fax: 870-265-8012.

Clark County
County Circuit Clerk, P.O. Box 576, Arkadelphia, AR 71923. 870-246-4281.

Clay County (Eastern District)
County Circuit Clerk, P.O. Box 29, Piggott, AR 72454. 870-598-2524. Fax: 870-598-2524.

Clay County (Western District)
County Circuit Clerk, P.O. Box 176, Corning, AR 72422. 870-857-3271. Fax: 870-857-3271.

Cleburne County
County Circuit Clerk, P.O. Box 543, Heber Springs, AR 72543. 501-362-8149. Fax: 501-362-4650.

Cleveland County
County Circuit Clerk, P.O. Box 368, Rison, AR 71665. 870-325-6521. Fax: 870-325-6144.

Columbia County
County Circuit Clerk, P.O. Box 327, Magnolia, AR 71753. 870-235-3700. Fax: 870-235-3778.

Conway County
County Circuit Clerk, 115 S. Moose Street, County Courthouse - Room 206, Morrilton, AR 72110. 501-354-9617. Fax: 501-354-9612.

Craighead County (Eastern District)
County Circuit Clerk, P.O. Box 537, Lake City, AR 72437. 870-237-4342. Fax: 870-237-8174.

Craighead County (Western District)
County Circuit Clerk, P.O. Box 120, Jonesboro, AR 72401. 870-933-4530. Fax: 870-933-4534.

Crawford County
County Circuit Clerk, 300 Main, Courthouse Room 22, Van Buren, AR 72956-5799. 501-474-1821.

Crittenden County
County Circuit Clerk, 100 Court St., Marion, AR 72364. 870-739-3248. Fax: 870-739-3072.

Cross County
County Circuit Clerk, 705 East Union, Room 9, Wynne, AR 72396. 870-238-5720. Fax: 870-238-5739.

Dallas County
County Circuit Clerk, Courthouse, 206 West 3rd St, Fordyce, AR 71742-3299. 870-352-2307. Fax: 870-352-7179.

Desha County
County Circuit Clerk, P.O. Box 309, Arkansas City, AR 71630. 870-877-2411. Fax: 870-877-3407.

Drew County
County Circuit Clerk, 210 South Main, Monticello, AR 71655. 870-460-6250. Fax: 870-460-6246.

Faulkner County
County Circuit Clerk, P.O. Box 9, Conway, AR 72033. 501-450-4911. Fax: 501-450-4948.

Franklin County (Charleston District)
County Circuit Clerk, P.O. Box 387, Charleston, AR 72933. 501-965-7332.

Franklin County (Ozark District)
County Circuit Clerk, P.O. Box 1112, Ozark, AR 72949. 501-667-3818. Fax: 501-667-5174.

Fulton County
County Circuit Clerk, P.O. Box 485, Salem, AR 72576-0485. 870-895-3310. Fax: 870-895-3362.

Garland County
County Circuit Clerk, Courthouse - Room 207, Quachita and Hawthorn Streets, Hot Springs, AR 71901. 501-622-3630.

Grant County
County Circuit Clerk, Courthouse, 101 W. Center, Room 106, Sheridan, AR 72150. 870-942-2631. Fax: 870-942-3564.

Greene County
County Circuit Clerk, 320 W. Court St., Room 124, Paragould, AR 72450. 870-239-6330. Fax: 870-239-3550.

Hempstead County
County Circuit Clerk, P.O. Box 1420, Hope, AR 71802. 870-777-2384. Fax: 870-777-7827.

Hot Spring County
County Circuit Clerk, P.O. Box 1200, Malvern, AR 72104. 501-332-2281.

Howard County
County Circuit Clerk, 421 North Main Street, Room 7, Nashville, AR 71852. 870-845-7506.

Independence County
County Circuit Clerk, P.O. Box 2155, Batesville, AR 72503. 870-793-8865. Fax: 870-793-8888.

Izard County
County Circuit Clerk, P.O. Box 95, Melbourne, AR 72556. 870-368-4316. Fax: 870-368-4748.

Jackson County
County Circuit Clerk, Courthouse, Main Street, Newport, AR 72112. 870-523-7423.

Jefferson County
County Circuit Clerk, P.O. Box 7433, Pine Bluff, AR 71611. 870-541-5309.

Johnson County
County Circuit Clerk, P.O. Box 217, Clarksville, AR 72830. 501-754-2977. Fax: 501-754-4235.

Lafayette County
County Circuit Clerk, 3 Courthouse Square, Third & Spruce, Lewisville, AR 71845. 870-921-4878.

Lawrence County
County Circuit Clerk, P.O. Box 581, Walnut Ridge, AR 72476. 870-886-1112.

Lee County
County Circuit Clerk, 15 East Chestnut Street, Courthouse, Marianna, AR 72360. 870-295-7710. Fax: 870-295-7766.

Lincoln County
County Circuit Clerk, 300 South Drew St, Star City, AR 71667. 870-628-3154. Fax: 870-628-5546.

Little River County
County Circuit Clerk, P.O. Box 575, Ashdown, AR 71822-0575. 870-898-7211. Fax: 870-898-7207.

Logan County (Northern District)
County Circuit Clerk, Courthouse, Paris, AR 72855. 501-963-2164. Fax: 501-963-3304.

Logan County (Southern District)
County Circuit Clerk, Courthouse, 366 N Broadway #2, Booneville, AR 72927. 501-675-2894. Fax: 501-675-0577.

Lonoke County
County Circuit Clerk, P.O. Box 219, Lonoke, AR 72086-0219. 501-676-2316.

Madison County
County Circuit Clerk, P.O. Box 416, Huntsville, AR 72740. 501-738-2215. Fax: 501-738-1544.

Marion County
County Circuit Clerk, P.O. Box 385, Yellville, AR 72687. 870-449-6226. Fax: 870-449-4979.

Miller County
County Circuit Clerk, County Courthouse-Suite 109, 412 Laurel St., Texarkana, AR 71854. 870-774-4501. Fax: 870-772-5293.

Mississippi County (Chickasawba District)
County Circuit Clerk, P.O. Box 1498, Blytheville, AR 72316-1498. 870-762-2332. Fax: 870-762-8148.

Mississippi County (Osceola District)
County Circuit Clerk, P.O. Box 471, Osceola, AR 72370. 870-563-6471. Fax: 870-563-2543.

Monroe County
County Circuit Clerk, 123 Madison Street, Clarendon, AR 72029. 870-747-3615. Fax: 870-747-3710.

Montgomery County
County Circuit Clerk, P.O. Box 369, Mount Ida, AR 71957-0369. 870-867-3521. Fax: 870-867-4354.

Nevada County
County Circuit Clerk, PO Box 204, Prescott, AR 71857. 870-887-2511. Fax: 870-887-5795.

Newton County
County Circuit Clerk, P.O. Box 410, Jasper, AR 72641. 870-446-5125.

Ouachita County
County Circuit Clerk, P.O. Box 667, Camden, AR 71701. 870-837-2230. Fax: 870-837-2252.

Perry County
County Circuit Clerk, P.O. Box 358, Perryville, AR 72126. 501-889-5126. Fax: 501-889-5759.

Phillips County
County Circuit Clerk, Courthouse, Suite 206, 620 Cherry St., Helena, AR 72342. 870-338-5515. Fax: 870-338-5513.

Pike County
County Circuit Clerk, P.O. Box 219, Murfreesboro, AR 71958. 870-285-2231. Fax: 870-285-3281.

Poinsett County
County Circuit Clerk, P.O. Box 46, Harrisburg, AR 72432-0046. 870-578-4420. Fax: 870-578-2441.

Polk County
County Circuit Clerk, 507 Church, Courthouse, Mena, AR 71953. 501-394-8100.

Pope County
County Circuit Clerk, 100 West Main, 3rd Floor, County Courthouse, Russellville, AR 72801. 501-968-7499.

Prairie County (Northern District)
County Circuit Clerk, P.O. Box 1011, Des Arc, AR 72040. 870-256-4434. Fax: 870-256-4434.

Prairie County (Southern District)
County Circuit Clerk, P.O. Box 283, De Valls Bluff, AR 72041-0283. 870-998-2314. Fax: 870-998-2314.

Pulaski County
County Circuit Clerk, Room S216, 401 W. Markham St., Little Rock, AR 72201. 501-340-8433. Fax: 501-340-8420.

Randolph County
County Circuit Clerk, 107 W. Broadway, Pocahontas, AR 72455. 870-892-5522. Fax: 870-892-8794.

Saline County
County Circuit Clerk, P.O. Box 1560, Benton, AR 72018. 501-303-5615. Fax: 501-303-5675.

Scott County
County Circuit Clerk, P.O. Box 2165, Waldron, AR 72958-0464. 501-637-2642. Fax: 501-637-4199.

Searcy County
County Circuit Clerk, P.O. Box 935, Marshall, AR 72650. 870-448-3807.

Sebastian County (Fort Smith District)
County Circuit Clerk, P.O. Box 1179, Fort Smith, AR 72902-1179. 501-784-1581. Fax: 501-784-1580.

Sebastian County (Southern District)
County Circuit Clerk, P.O. Box 310, Greenwood, AR 72936. 501-996-4175. Fax: 501-996-6885.

Sevier County
County Circuit Clerk, 115 North 3rd Street, De Queen, AR 71832. 870-584-3055. Fax: 870-642-9638.

Sharp County
County Circuit Clerk, P.O. Box 307, Ash Flat, AR 72513. 870-994-7361. Fax: 870-994-7712.

St. Francis County
County Circuit Clerk, P.O. Box 1775, Forrest City, AR 72336-1775. 870-261-1715. Fax: 870-261-1725.

Stone County
County Circuit Clerk, Courthouse, HC 71 Box 1, Mountain View, AR 72560. 870-269-3271. Fax: 870-269-2303.

Union County
County Circuit Clerk, P.O. Box 1626, El Dorado, AR 71731-1626. 870-864-1940.

Van Buren County
County Circuit Clerk, RR6 Box 254-9, Clinton, AR 72031-9806. 501-745-4140. Fax: 501-745-7400.

Washington County
County Circuit Clerk, Courthouse, 280 N. College, Suite 302, Fayetteville, AR 72701. 501-444-1538. Fax: 501-444-1537.

White County
County Circuit Clerk, White County Courthouse, Spring St./East Entrance/Courthouse Sq., Searcy, AR 72143. 501-279-6203.

Woodruff County
County Circuit Clerk, P.O. Box 492, Augusta, AR 72006. 870-347-2391.

Yell County (Danville District)
County Circuit Clerk, P.O. Box 219, Danville, AR 72833. 501-495-2414. Fax: 501-495-3495.

Yell County (Dardanelle District)
County Circuit Clerk, P.O. Box 457, Dardanelle, AR 72834. 501-229-4404. Fax: 501-229-1130.

You will usually be able to find the city name in the City/County Cross Reference below. In that case, it is a simple matter to determine the county from the cross reference. However, only the official US Postal Service city names are included in this index. There are an additional 40,000 place names that people use in their addresses. Therefore, we have also included a ZIP/City Cross Reference immediately following the City/County Cross Reference.

If you know the ZIP Code but the city name does not appear in the City/County Cross Reference index, look up the ZIP Code in the ZIP/City Cross Reference, find the city name, then look up the city name in the City/County Cross Reference. For example, you want to know the county for an address of Menands, NY 12204. There is no "Menands" in the City/County Cross Reference. The ZIP/City Cross Reference shows that ZIP Codes 12201-12288 are for the city of Albany. Looking back in the City/County Cross Reference, Albany is in Albany County.

City/County Cross Reference

ADONA (72001) Perry(77), Conway(23)
ALCO (72610) Stone(88), Searcy(13)
ALEXANDER (72002) Saline(88), Pulaski(12)
ALICIA Lawrence
ALIX Franklin
ALLEENE Little River
ALMA Crawford
ALMYRA Arkansas
ALPENA (72611) Boone(76), Carroll(24)
ALPINE Clark
ALTHEIMER (72004) Jackson(88), Jefferson(12)
ALTUS (72821) Franklin(80), Johnson(19)
AMAGON Jackson
AMITY Clark
ANTOINE Pike
ARKADELPHIA (71923) Clark(97), Hot Spring(3)
ARKADELPHIA Clark
ARKANSAS CITY Desha
ARMOREL Mississippi
ASH FLAT (72513) Sharp(59), Fulton(30), Izard(12)
ASHDOWN Little River
ATKINS (72823) Pope(95), Conway(5)
ATKINS Pope
AUBREY Lee
AUGUSTA Woodruff
AUSTIN Lonoke
AVOCA Benton
BALCH Jackson
BALD KNOB White
BANKS Bradley
BARLING Sebastian
BARTON Phillips
BASS Newton
BASSETT Mississippi
BATES Scott
BATESVILLE Independence
BAUXITE Saline
BAY Craighead
BEARDEN (71720) Ouachita(85), Dallas(11), Calhoun(4)
BEAVER Carroll
BEE BRANCH Van Buren
BEEBE White
BEECH GROVE Greene
BEEDEVILLE Jackson
BEIRNE Clark
BELLA VISTA Benton
BELLEVILLE Yell
BEN LOMOND Sevier
BENTON Saline
BENTONVILLE Benton
BERGMAN Boone
BERRYVILLE Carroll
BEXAR Fulton
BIG FLAT (72617) Stone(75), Baxter(25)
BIGELOW (72016) Pulaski(56), Perry(44)
BIGGERS Randolph
BIRDEYE Cross

BISCOE Prairie
BISMARCK Hot Spring
BLACK OAK Craighead
BLACK ROCK Lawrence
BLAKELY Garland
BLEVINS Hempstead
BLUE MOUNTAIN Logan
BLUFF CITY Nevada
BLUFFTON (72827) Yell(96), Scott(4)
BLYTHEVILLE Mississippi
BOARD CAMP Polk
BOLES Scott
BONNERDALE (71933) Garland(69), Hot Spring(25), Montgomery(7)
BONO (72416) Craighead(77), Greene(23)
BOONEVILLE (72927) Logan(90), Sebastian(8), Scott(2)
BOSWELL Izard
BRADFORD (72020) Jackson(50), White(37), Independence(13)
BRADLEY Lafayette
BRANCH (72928) Franklin(96), Logan(4)
BRICKEYS Lee
BRIGGSVILLE Yell
BRINKLEY Monroe
BROCKWELL Izard
BROOKLAND Craighead
BRUNO Marion
BRYANT Saline
BUCKNER Lafayette
BULL SHOALS Marion
BURDETTE Mississippi
CABOT (72023) Lonoke(74), Pulaski(26)
CADDO GAP Montgomery
CALDWELL St. Francis
CALE Nevada
CALICO ROCK (72519) Baxter(79), Izard(19), Stone(2)
CALION Union
CAMDEN (71701) Ouachita(98), Calhoun(2)
CAMDEN Ouachita
CAMP Fulton
CANEHILL Washington
CARAWAY Craighead
CARLISLE (72024) Lonoke(97), Prairie(3)
CARTHAGE Dallas
CASA (72025) Perry(95), Conway(5)
CASH Craighead
CASSCOE Arkansas
CAVE CITY (72521) Sharp(64), Independence(36)
CAVE SPRINGS Benton
CECIL (72930) Sebastian(56), Franklin(44)
CEDARVILLE Crawford
CENTER RIDGE Conway
CENTERTON Benton
CENTERVILLE Yell
CHARLESTON (72933) Franklin(54), Sebastian(45)
CHARLOTTE Independence
CHATFIELD Crittenden

CHEROKEE VILLAGE Sharp
CHERRY VALLEY Cross
CHESTER Crawford
CHIDESTER Ouachita
CHOCTAW Van Buren
CLARENDON Monroe
CLARKEDALE Crittenden
CLARKRIDGE Baxter
CLARKSVILLE Johnson
CLEVELAND (72030) Conway(84), Van Buren(16)
CLINTON (72031) Van Buren(94), Conway(3), Stone(3)
COAL HILL Johnson
COLLEGE STATION Pulaski
COLLINS Drew
COLT St. Francis
COLUMBUS Hempstead
COMBS (72721) Madison(90), Franklin(10)
COMPTON (72624) Newton(84), Carroll(16)
CONCORD (72523) Cleburne(86), Independence(14)
CONWAY Faulkner
CORD Independence
CORNING Clay
COTTER Baxter
COTTON PLANT Woodruff
COVE Polk
COY Lonoke
CRAWFORDSVILLE Crittenden
CROCKETTS BLUFF Arkansas
CROSSETT Ashley
CRUMROD Phillips
CURTIS Clark
CUSHMAN Independence
DAMASCUS (72039) Faulkner(54), Van Buren(46)
DANVILLE Yell
DARDANELLE Yell
DATTO Clay
DE QUEEN Sevier
DE VALLS BLUFF Prairie
DE WITT Arkansas
DECATUR Benton
DEER Newton
DELAPLAINE Greene
DELAWARE Logan
DELIGHT Pike
DELL Mississippi
DENNARD (72629) Van Buren(96), Searcy(4)
DERMOTT (71638) Chicot(91), Drew(7), Desha(2)
DES ARC Prairie
DESHA Independence
DIAMOND CITY Boone
DIAZ Jackson
DIERKS Howard
DODDRIDGE Miller
DOLPH Izard
DONALDSON Hot Spring

DOVER Pope
DRASCO (72530) Cleburne(89), Stone(11)
DRIVER Mississippi
DUMAS (71639) Desha(97), Lincoln(3)
DYER Crawford
DYESS Mississippi
EARLE (72331) Crittenden(71), Cross(28)
EDGEMONT (72044) Cleburne(60), Stone(40)
EDMONDSON Crittenden
EGYPT Craighead
EL DORADO Union
EL PASO White
ELAINE Phillips
ELIZABETH (72531) Baxter(78), Fulton(22)
ELKINS (72727) Washington(90), Madison(10)
ELM SPRINGS Washington
EMERSON (71740) Columbia(69), Scott(31)
EMMET (71835) Nevada(62), Hempstead(38)
ENGLAND (72046) Lonoke(70), Jefferson(17), Pulaski(12)
ENOLA Faulkner
ETHEL Arkansas
ETOWAH Mississippi
EUDORA Chicot
EUREKA SPRINGS (72631) Carroll(77), Benton(23)
EUREKA SPRINGS Carroll
EVANSVILLE Washington
EVENING SHADE Sharp
EVERTON (72633) Marion(71), Boone(23), Searcy(6)
FAIRFIELD BAY (72088) Van Buren(92), Cleburne(8)
FARMINGTON Washington
FAYETTEVILLE Washington
FERNDALE Pulaski
FIFTY SIX Stone
FISHER Poinsett
FLIPPIN Marion
FLORAL (72534) Independence(87), Cleburne(13)
FORDYCE Dallas
FOREMAN Little River
FORREST CITY St. Francis
FORT SMITH Sebastian
FOUKE Miller
FOUNTAIN HILL (71642) Ashley(71), Drew(29)
FOX Stone
FRANKLIN Izard
FRENCHMANS BAYOU Mississippi
FRIENDSHIP Hot Spring
FULTON Hempstead
GAMALIEL Baxter
GARFIELD Benton
GARLAND CITY (71839) Miller(79), Lafayette(21)
GARNER White

Indexing & Storage: Cases are indexed by defendant and plaintiff as well as by case number. New cases are available in the index 3 days after filing date. Both computer and card indexes are maintained. Open records are located at this court.

Fee & Payment: The fee is $15.00 per item (one party name or case number). Payment may be made by money order, cashier check, business check. Personal checks are not accepted. Prepayment is required unless a deposit account is set up with the court. Payee: Clerk, US District Court. Certification fee: $5.00 per document. Copy fee: $.50 per page.

Phone Search: Only docket information is available by phone. An automated voice case information service (VCIS) is not available.

Mail Search: Always enclose a stamped self addressed envelope.

In Person Search: In person searching is available.

PACER: Sign-up number is 800-676-6856. Access fee is $.60 per minute. Toll-free access: 800-263-9358. Local access: 213-894-3625. Case records are available back to 1993. New records are available online after 2 days. PACER is available on the Internet at http://pacer.cacd.uscourts.gov.

Opinions Online: Court opinions are available online at www.cacd.uscourts.gov

US Bankruptcy Court

Central District of California

Los Angeles Division 255 E Temple St, Los Angeles, CA 90012, 213-894-3118, Fax: 213-894-1261.

www.cacb.uscourts.gov

Counties: Los Angeles. Certain Los Angeles ZIP Codes are assigned to a new location, San Fernando Valley Division, as of early 1995.

Indexing & Storage: Cases are indexed by debtor as well as by case number. New cases are available in the index immediately after filing date. A card index is maintained. Records are indexed on microfiche. Open records are located at this court.

Fee & Payment: The fee is $15.00 per item (one party name or case number). Payment may be made by money order, cashier check. Business checks are not accepted. Personal checks are not accepted. Prepayment is required. Payee: Clerk, US Bankruptcy Court. Certification fee: $5.00 per document. Copy fee: $.50 per page.

Phone Search: An automated voice case information service (VCIS) is available.

Fax Search: Handled like mail searches.

Mail Search: Always enclose a stamped self addressed envelope.

In Person Search: In person searching is available.

PACER: Sign-up number is 800-676-6856. Access fee is $.60 per minute. Toll-free access: 800-257-3887. Local access: 213-894-6199. Use of PC Anywhere v4.0 suggested. Case records are available back to 1992. Records are purged once a year. New civil records are available online after 1 day. You can access PACER via the Internet, using webPACER. For info and software visit www.cacb.uscourts.gov.

Riverside Division 3420 12th St #125, Riverside, CA 92501-3819, 909-774-1000.

www.cacb.uscourts.gov

Counties: Riverside, San Bernardino.

Indexing & Storage: Cases are indexed by debtor as well as by case number. New cases are available in the index immediately after filing date. A computer index is maintained. Files are stored in numerical sequence. Open records are located at this court. The time that records are kept at the Riverside court is varied. There is no set time limit before they are sent to the Los Angeles Federal Records Center.

Fee & Payment: The fee is $15.00 per item (one party name or case number). Payment may be made by money order, cashier check. Business checks are not accepted, Visa or Mastercard. Personal checks are not accepted. Prepayment is required. Payee: US Bankruptcy Court. Certification fee: $5.00 per document. Copy fee: $.50 per page.

Phone Search: Only docket information is available by phone. An automated voice case information service (VCIS) is available. Call VCIS at 888-457-0604 or 909-774-1150.

Mail Search: Include the case number, document title, document number (if available), your phone number, and any applicable fees. Always enclose a stamped self addressed envelope.

In Person Search: In person searching is available.

PACER: Sign-up number is 800-676-6856. Access fee is $.60 per minute. Toll-free access: 888-819-0233. Local access: 909-276-2914. Case records are available back to 1992. Records are purged once a year. New civil records are available online after 1 day. You can access PACER via the Internet, using webPACER. For info and software visit www.cacb.uscourts.gov.

Santa Ana Division Ronald Reagan Federal Bldg & US Courthouse, 411 W 4th St #2030, Santa Ana, CA 92701-4593, 714-836-2993.

www.cacb.uscourts.gov

Counties: Orange.

Indexing & Storage: Cases are indexed by debtor and creditors as well as by case number. New cases are available in the index 24-48 hours after filing date. A computer index is maintained. Open records are located at this court.

Fee & Payment: The fee is $15.00 per item (one party name or case number). Payment may be made by money order, cashier check, business check. Personal checks are not accepted. Prepayment is required unless prior arrangements have been made. Payee: US Bankruptcy Court. Certification fee: $5.00 per document. Copy fee: $.50 per page.

Phone Search: Docket information available by phone. An automated voice case information service (VCIS) is available.

Mail Search: Always enclose a stamped self addressed envelope.

In Person Search: In person searching is available.

PACER: Sign-up number is 800-676-6856. Access fee is $.60 per minute. Toll-free access: 888-819-0232. Local access: 714-836-2281, 714-836-2768. Case records are available back to June 3, 1991. New civil records are available online after 1 day. You can access PACER via the

Internet, using webPACER. For info and software visit www.cacb.uscourts.gov.

Santa Barbara (Northern) Division 1415 State St, Santa Barbara, CA 93101, 805-884-4800.

www.cacb.uscourts.gov

Counties: San Luis Obispo, Santa Barbara, Ventura. Certain Ventura ZIP Codes are assigned to the new office in San Fernando Valley.

Indexing & Storage: Cases are indexed by debtor as well as by case number. New cases are available in the index immediately after filing date. A computer index is maintained. Open records are located at this court. There is no set time for sending records to the repository.

Fee & Payment: The fee is $15.00 per item (one party name or case number). Payment may be made by money order, cashier check. Business checks are not accepted. Personal checks are not accepted. Prepayment is required. Payee: US Bankruptcy Court. Certification fee: $5.00 per document. Copy fee: $.50 per page.

Phone Search: An automated voice case information service (VCIS) is available.

Mail Search: Include case number, document title, document number (if available), your phone number and applicable fees. Always enclose a stamped self addressed envelope.

In Person Search: In person searching is available.

PACER: Sign-up number is 800-676-6856. Access fee is $.60 per minute. Toll-free access: 888-819-0231. Local access: 805-844-4806. Case records are available back to June 1992. New civil records are available online after 1 day. You can access PACER via the Internet, using webPACER. For info and software visit www.cacb.uscourts.gov.

US District Court

Eastern District of California

Fresno Division US Courthouse, Room 5000, 1130 "O" St, Fresno, CA 93721-2201, 559-498-7483.

www.caed.uscourts.gov

Counties: Fresno, Inyo, Kern, Kings, Madera, Mariposa, Merced, Stanislaus, Tulare, Tuolumne.

Indexing & Storage: Cases are indexed by defendant and plaintiff as well as by case number. New cases are available in the index 24 hours after filing date. A computer index is maintained. Records are stored by case type and case number. Open records are located at this court.

Fee & Payment: The fee is $15.00 per item (one party name or case number). Payment may be made by money order, cashier check, personal check. Prepayment is required. Payee: Clerk, US District Court. Certification fee: $5.00 per document. Copy fee: $.50 per page.

Phone Search: Only docket information is available by phone. An automated voice case information service (VCIS) is not available.

Mail Search: A stamped self addressed envelope is not required.

In Person Search: In person searching is available.

PACER: Sign-up number is 800-676-6856. Access fee is $.60 per minute. Toll-free access:

800-530-7682. Local access: 916-498-6567. Case records are available back to 1990 (some earlier). Records are purged at varying intervals. New records are available online after 1 day. PACER is available on the Internet at http://pacer.caed.uscourts.gov.

Opinions Online: Court opinions are available online at www.caed.uscourts.gov

Sacramento Division 501 I St, Sacramento, CA 95814, 916-930-4000, Fax: 916-930-4015.

www.caed.uscourts.gov

Counties: Alpine, Amador, Butte, Calaveras, Colusa, El Dorado, Glenn, Lassen, Modoc, Mono, Nevada, Placer, Plumas, Sacramento, San Joaquin, Shasta, Sierra, Siskiyou, Solano, Sutter, Tehama, Trinity, Yolo, Yuba.

Indexing & Storage: Cases are indexed by defendant and plaintiff as well as by case number. New cases are available in the index immediately after filing date. Archived records are stored by case number. A case number can be researched by the plaintiff's or defendant's name. A computer index is maintained. Archived case records are indexed on microfiche. Open records are located at this court.

Fee & Payment: The fee is $15.00 per item (one party name or case number). Payment may be made by money order, cashier check, business check. Personal checks are not accepted. Prepayment is required. Payee: Clerk, US District Court. Certification fee: $5.00 per document. Copy fee: $.50 per page. You are allowed to make your own copies. These copies cost $.15 per page. For copy service, call 916-448-8875. A 24-hour drop box is located on the premises.

Phone Search: Only docket information is available by phone. An automated voice case information service (VCIS) is not available.

Mail Search: Always enclose a stamped self addressed envelope.

In Person Search: In person searching is available.

PACER: Sign-up number is 800-676-6856. Access fee is $.60 per minute. Toll-free access: 800-530-7682. Local access: 916-498-6567. Case records are available back to 1990 (some earlier). Records are purged at varying intervals. New records are available online after 1 day. PACER is available on the Internet at http://pacer.caed.uscourts.gov.

Opinions Online: Court opinions are available online at www.caed.uscourts.gov

Court	Jurisdiction	No. of Courts	How Organized
Superior Courts*	General	51	
Limited Superior Courts*	General	67	
Municipal Courts*	Municipal	12	

* Profiled in this Sourcebook.

Court	CIVIL								
	Tort	Contract	Real Estate	Min. Claim	Max. Claim	Small Claims	Estate	Eviction	Domestic Relations
General Jurisdiction	X	X	X	$25,000	No Max		X		X
Municipal Jurisdiction	X	X	X	$0	$25,000	$5000		X	

Court	CRIMINAL				
	Felony	Misdemeanor	DWI/DUI	Preliminary Hearing	Juvenile
Sup/ComCourts*	X		X		X
Municipal and Limited Courts*		X	X	X	

ADMINISTRATION   Administrative Office of Courts, 455 Golden Gate Ave, San Francisco, CA, 94102; 415-865-4200, Fax: 415-865-4205. www.courtinfo.ca.gov

COURT STRUCTURE   In July 1998, the judges in individual counties were given the opportunity to vote on unification of superior and municipal courts within their respective counties. As of early 2000, 56 of 58 counties had voted to unify these courts. Court that were formally Municipal Courts are now known as Limited Jurisdiction Superior Courts. In some counties, superior and municipal courts were combined into one superior court. Civil under $25,000 is a Limited Civil Court, over $25,000 is an Unlimited Civil Court, and if both over and under then the court is a Combined Civil Court. Many counties are facing difficult challenges as they merge which, in turn, create hardships for record searchers.

It is important to note that Limited or Municipal Courts may try minor felonies not included under our felony definition.

ONLINE ACCESS   There is no statewide online computer access available, internal or external. However, a number of counties have developed their own online access sytems and provide Internet access at no fee. Also, the web site contains a lot of useful information about the state court system.

ADDITIONAL INFORMATION   If there is more than one court of a type within a county, where the case is tried and where the record is held depends on how a citation is written, where the infraction occurred, or where the filer chose to file the case.

Some courts now require signed releases from the subject in order to perform criminal searches, and will no longer allow the public to conduct such searches.

Personal checks are acceptable by state law.

Although fees are set by statute, courts interpret them differently. For example, the search fee is supposed to be $5.00 per name per year searched, but many courts charge only $5.00 per name. Generally, certification is $6.00 per document and copies are $.75 per page.

Alameda County

Southern Superior Court-Hayward Branch 24405 Amador St Rm 108, Hayward, CA 94544; 510-670-5060; Fax: 510-783-9456. Hours: 8:30AM-4:30PM (PST). *Civil Actions Over $25,000, Probate.*

www.co.alameda.ca.us/courts

Civil Records: Access: Mail, in person. Both court and visitors may perform in person searches. Search fee: $5.00 per name. Required to search: name, years to search. Civil cases indexed by defendant, plaintiff. Civil records on computer from 1976, on microfiche and archived from 1900s. **General Information:** No sealed files, paternity or adoption records released. SASE required. Turnaround time 4-6 weeks. Copy fee: $.75 per page. Certification fee: $6.00. Fee payee: Clerk of Superior Court. Personal checks accepted. Prepayment is required.

Alameda County Superior Court Northern Branch-Civil 1225 Fallon St Rm 109, Oakland, CA 94612; 510-272-6799. Hours: 8:30AM-4:30PM (PST). *Civil Actions Over $25,000, Probate.*

www.co.alameda.ca.us/courts/superior

Civil Records: Access: Mail, in person. Both court and visitors may perform in person searches.

Search fee: $5.00 per name per year. Additional $5.00 fee for years prior to 1974. Required to search: name, years to search. Civil cases indexed by defendant, plaintiff. Civil records on computer from 1974, on microfiche and archived from 1900s. **General Information:** No sealed records nor adoption records released unless court ordered. SASE required. Turnaround time 2 weeks. Copy fee: $.75 per page. Certification fee: $6.00. Fee payee: Superior Court. Personal checks accepted. Prepayment is required. Public access terminal is available.

Pleasanton Branch Superior Court 5672 Stoneridge Dr 1st Fl, Pleasanton, CA 94588;

925-551-6883. Hours: 8:30AM-4:30PM (PST). *Civil Actions Over $25,000, Probate.*

www.co.alameda.ca.us/courts

Civil Records: Access: Mail, in person. Both court and visitors may perform in person searches. Search fee: $5.00 per name per year. Required to search: name, years to search. Civil cases indexed by defendant, plaintiff. Civil records on computer from 1976, on microfiche and archived from 1900s. **General Information:** No sealed or confidential records released. SASE required. Turnaround time 2 weeks. Copy fee: $.75 per page. Certification fee: $6.00. Fee payee: Alameda County Superior Court. Personal checks accepted. Prepayment is required. Public access terminal is available.

Superior Court-Criminal 1225 Fallon St Rm 107, Oakland, CA 94612; 510-272-6777; Fax: 510-272-0796. Hours: 8:30AM-5PM (PST). *Felony.*

www.co.alameda.ca.us/courts **Criminal Records:** Access: Mail, in person. Both court and visitors may perform in person searches. Search fee: $5.00 per name per year. There is no fee if you do the search. Required to search: name, years to search; also helpful-DOB, SSN. Criminal records on computer from 1975, on microfiche from 1940, archived and indexed from 1880. **General Information:** No probation, medical, adoption, juvenile or sealed records released. SASE required. Turnaround time 1 week. Copy fee: $.75 per page. Certification fee: $6.00. Fee payee: Clerk of Superior Court. Personal checks accepted. Prepayment is required.

Alameda Branch - Superior Court 2233 Shoreline Dr (PO Box 1470), Alameda, CA 94501; 510-268-4208; Civil phone:510-268-4219; Criminal phone:510-268-4219; Fax: 510-523-7964. Hours: 8:30AM-4:30PM (PST). *Misdemeanor, Civil Actions Under $25,000, Eviction, Small Claims.*

www.co.alameda.ca.us/courts

Note: Co-extensive with the city limits of Alameda only

Civil Records: Access: Mail, in person. Both court and visitors may perform in person searches. Search fee: $5.00 per name. Required to search: name, years to search. Civil cases indexed by defendant, plaintiff. Civil records on computer since 1987. **Criminal Records:** Access: Mail, in person. Both court and visitors may perform in person searches. Search fee: $5.00 per name. Required to search: name, years to search, DOB, signed release; also helpful-SSN. Criminal records on computer 7 years back. Only seven year search available. **General Information:** No confidential records released. SASE required. Turnaround time 1 week. Copy fee: $.75 per page. Certification fee: $6.00. Fee payee: Alameda Superior Court. Personal checks accepted. Credit cards accepted. Accepted in person only. Prepayment is required.

Berkeley-Albany Branch -Criminal Division 2120 Martin Luther King Jr Way, Berkeley, CA 94704; 510-644-6917; Fax: 510-848-6916. Hours: 8:30AM-4:30PM (PST). *Misdemeanor.*

www.co.alameda.ca.us/courts

Note: Co-extensive with the city limits of Berkeley and Albany **Criminal Records:** Access: Mail, in person. Only the court conducts in person searches; visitors may not. Search fee: $5.00 per name. Required to search: name, years to search, DOB; also helpful-SSN. Criminal records on

computer from 1984. **General Information:** No sealed or confidential records released. SASE required. Turnaround time 1 week. Copy fee: $.75 per page. Certification fee: $6.00. Fee payee: Superior Court. Personal checks accepted. Prepayment is required.

Berkeley-Albany Superior Court-Civil Division 2000 Center St, Room 202, Berkeley, CA 94704; 510-644-6423. Hours: 8:30AM-4:30PM (PST). *Civil Actions Under $25,000, Eviction, Small Claims.*

www.co.alameda.ca.us/courts

Note: Co-extensive with the city limits of Berkeley and Albany

Civil Records: Access: Mail, in person. Both court and visitors may perform in person searches. Search fee: $5.00 per name. Required to search: name, years to search. Civil cases indexed by defendant, plaintiff. Civil records on computer from 1986. **General Information:** No sealed, judge's notes or confidential records released. SASE required. Turnaround time 1 week. Copy fee: $.75 per page. Certification fee: $6.00. Fee payee: Berkeley Superior Court. Personal checks accepted. Prepayment is required.

Fremont — Newark -- Union City Superior Court 39439 Paseo Padre Pky, Fremont, CA 94538;; Civil phone:510-795-2345; Criminal phone:510-795-2345; Fax: 510-795-2349. Hours: 8:30AM-5PM (PST). *Misdemeanor, Civil Actions Under $25,000, Eviction, Small Claims.*

www.co.alameda.ca.us/courts

Note: Jurisdiction includes Fremont, Newark and Union City

Civil Records: Access: Fax, mail, in person. Both court and visitors may perform in person searches. Search fee: $5.00 per name. Required to search: name, years to search. Civil cases indexed by defendant, plaintiff. Civil records on computer from 1990. **Criminal Records:** Access: Fax, mail, in person. Both court and visitors may perform in person searches. Search fee: $5.00 per name. Required to search: name, years to search, DOB, signed release. Criminal records on computer from 1990. **General Information:** No sealed or confidential records released. SASE required. Turnaround time 1 week. Copy fee: $.75 per page. Certification fee: $6.00. Fee payee: Fremont Superior Court. Personal checks accepted. Prepayment is required. Fax notes: $1.00 per page.

Livermore – Pleasanton - Dublin Superior Court 5672 Stoneridge Dr, Pleasanton, CA 94566-8678;; Civil phone:925-463-7948; Criminal phone:925-463-7948; Fax: 925-847-0863. Hours: 8:30AM-4:30PM (PST). *Misdemeanor, Civil Actions Under $25,000, Eviction, Small Claims.*

www.co.alameda.ca.us/courts

Note: Includes the cities of Livermore, Dublin, Sunol and Pleasanton and all areas east to San Joaquin County line, north of Highway 580 to Contra Costa line

Civil Records: Access: Mail, in person. Both court and visitors may perform in person searches. Search fee: $5.00 per name. Required to search: name, years to search. Civil cases indexed by defendant, plaintiff. Civil records on computer from 1990. **Criminal Records:** Access: Mail, in person. Both court and visitors may perform in person searches. Search fee: $5.00 per name. Required to search: name, years to search; also

helpful-address, DOB. Criminal records on computer from 1990. **General Information:** No records older than 10 years are released. SASE required. Turnaround time 1 week. Copy fee: $.75 per page. Certification fee: $6.00. Fee payee: Livermore Superior Court. Personal checks accepted. Credit cards accepted: Visa, Mastercard. Prepayment is required.

Oakland Piedmont Superior Court 600 Washington St, 4th Floor, Oakland, CA 94607;; Civil phone:510-268-7724; Criminal phone:510-268-7724; Fax: 510-268-7807. Hours: 8:30AM-4:30PM (PST). *Misdemeanor, Civil Actions Under $25,000, Eviction, Small Claims.*

www.co.alameda.ca.us/courts

Note: Comprises the cities of Oakland, Piedmont and Emeryville

Civil Records: Access: Mail, in person. Both court and visitors may perform in person searches. Search fee: $5.00 per name. Required to search: name, years to search. Civil cases indexed by defendant, plaintiff. Civil records on computer from 1990. **Criminal Records:** Access: Mail, in person. Both court and visitors may perform in person searches. Search fee: $5.00 per name. Required to search: name, years to search. Criminal records on computer from 1990. **General Information:** No sealed or confidential records released. SASE required. Turnaround time 1 week. Copy fee: $.75 per page. Certification fee: $6.00. Fee payee: Oakland Superior Court. Personal checks accepted. Prepayment is required.

San Leandro - Hayward Superior Court 24405 Amador St, Hayward, CA 94544;; Civil phone:510-670-6432; Criminal phone:510-670-6432; Fax: 510-670-5522. Hours: 8:30AM-4:30PM (PST). *Misdemeanor, Civil Actions Under $25,000, Eviction, Small Claims.*

www.co.alameda.ca.us/courts/hayward/index.htm

Note: Includes the cities of San Leandro, Hayward and adjoining unincorporated areas of Castro Valley and San Lorenzo

Civil Records: Access: Fax, mail, in person. Both court and visitors may perform in person searches. Search fee: $5.00 per name. Required to search: name, years to search. Civil cases indexed by defendant, plaintiff. Civil records on computer from 1987, on index files back 10 years. **Criminal Records:** Access: Fax, mail, in person. Both court and visitors may perform in person searches. Search fee: $5.00 per name. Fee is per case. Required to search: name, years to search, DOB, signed release; also helpful-SSN. Criminal records on paper index. **General Information:** No sealed or confidential records released. SASE required. Turnaround time 2 weeks. Copy fee: $.75 per page. Certification fee: $6.00. Fee payee: Clerk of the Court. Personal checks accepted. Credit cards accepted: Visa, Mastercard. ATM card accepted. Prepayment is required. Public access terminal is available. Fax notes: No fee to fax results.

Alpine County

Superior Court PO Box 518, Markleeville, CA 96120; 530-694-2113; Fax: 530-694-2119. Hours: 8AM-Noon, 1-5PM (PST). *Felony, Misdemeanor, Civil, Eviction, Small Claims, Probate.*

Civil Records: Access: Mail, in person. Both court and visitors may perform in person searches. Search fee: $5.00 per name per year. Required to search: name, years to search. Civil cases indexed by defendant, plaintiff. Civil records on index file from 1981, archived from 1800s. **Criminal**

Records: Access: Mail, in person. Both court and visitors may perform in person searches. Search fee: $5.00 per name per year. Required to search: name, years to search. Criminal records on index file from 1981, archived from 1800s. **General Information:** No juvenile, paternity, adoption or sealed released. SASE required. Turnaround time 2 days. Copy fee: $.50 per page. Certification fee: $6.00 per page. Fee payee: Alpine County Court Services. Personal checks accepted. Prepayment is required.

Amador County

Superior Court 108 Court St, Jackson, CA 95642; 209-223-6463. Hours: 8AM-5PM (PST). *Felony, Misdemeanor, Civil, Eviction, Small Claims, Probate.*

Civil Records: Access: Mail, in person. Both court and visitors may perform in person searches. Search fee: $5.00 per name. Required to search: name, years to search. Civil cases indexed by defendant, plaintiff. Civil records on computer from 1989, archived and indexed from 1800s. **Criminal Records:** Access: Phone, fax, mail, in person. Both court and visitors may perform in person searches. Search fee: $5.00 per name. $5.00 for search by case number. Required to search: name, years to search. Criminal records on computer from 1989, archived and indexed from 1800s. Phone & fax access limited to short searches. **General Information:** No adoption, juvenile or paternity records released. SASE required. Turnaround time 7-14 days. Copy fee: $1.00 for first page, $.20 each addl. Certification fee: $6.00. Fee payee: Superior Court Clerk. Personal checks accepted. Prepayment is required. Fax notes: Will fax results to 800 numbers only.

Butte County

Superior Court One Court St, Oroville, CA 95965; 530-538-7551; Fax: 530-538-2112. Hours: 8:30AM-4PM (PST). *Felony, Misdemeanor, Civil, Probate.*

www.courtinfo.ca.gov/trialcourts/butte

Note: This court physically holds all the files for all courts in the county; however, one can search the countywide computer index at any court. This court includes family law cases

Civil Records: Access: Fax, mail, in person. Both court and visitors may perform in person searches. Search fee: $5.00 per name. Required to search: name, years to search; also helpful-address. Civil cases indexed by defendant, plaintiff. Civil records on computer from 1988, on microfiche from 1983 thru 1988, archives at University, in index file from 1925. **Criminal Records:** Access: Mail, in person. Both court and visitors may perform in person searches. Search fee: $5.00 per name. Required to search: name, years to search; also helpful-DOB. Criminal records on computer from 1988, on microfiche from 1983 thru 1988, archives at University, in index file from 1925. **General Information:** No juvenile, paternity or adoption records released. SASE required. Turnaround time 1 week. Copy fee: $.50 per page. $1.00 minimum. Certification fee: $6.00. Fee payee: Butte County Superior Court. Personal checks accepted. Credit cards accepted: Visa, Mastercard. Prepayment is required. Public access terminal is available. Fax notes: $5.00 for first page, $1.00 each addl.

Chico Branch-Superior Court 655 Oleander Ave, Chico, CA 95926; 530-891-2716 (Traffic); Civil phone:530-891-2702; Criminal phone:530-891-2702. Hours: 8:30AM-4PM (PST).

Misdemeanor, Civil Actions Under $25,000, Eviction, Small Claims.

Civil Records: Access: Mail, in person. Only the court conducts in person searches; visitors may not. Search fee: $5.00 per name. Required to search: name, years to search. Civil cases indexed by defendant, plaintiff. Civil records in index files. Records destroyed after 10 years. **Criminal Records:** Access: Mail, in person. Only the court conducts in person searches; visitors may not. Search fee: $5.00 per name. Required to search: name, years to search; also helpful-DOB. Criminal records in index files. Records destroyed after 10 years. **General Information:** No sealed records released. SASE required. Turnaround time 2-3 days. Copy fee: $1.00 for first page, $.50 each addl. Certification fee: $6.00. Fee payee: Superior Court. Personal checks accepted. Prepayment is required.

Gridley Branch - Superior Court Gridley Courthouse, 239 Sycamore, Gridley, CA 95948; 530-846-5701. Hours: 8AM-1PM 2 days a month (PST). *Misdemeanor, Eviction, Small Claims.*

Note: Open the first "full week" Thursday and 3rd Thursday

Civil Records: Only the court conducts in person searches; visitors may not. Search fee:. **Criminal Records:** Only the court conducts in person searches; visitors may not. Search fee: $5.00 per name. Required to search: name, years to search. **General Information:** Turnaround time 2 days. Fee payee: Gridley Superior Court. Prepayment is required.

Paradise Branch - Superior Court 747 Elliott Rd, Paradise, CA 95969; 530-872-6347. Hours: 8AM-1PM M-W & F; 8AM-Noon, 1-5PM Th; Phone Hours: 9AM-Noon M-F (PST). *Misdemeanor, Eviction, Small Claims.*

Civil Records: Access: Mail, in person. Only the court conducts in person searches; visitors may not. Search fee: $5.00 per name. Required to search: name; also helpful-years to search. Civil cases indexed by defendant, plaintiff. Civil records are located in North Butte County Municipal Court. **Criminal Records:** Access: Mail, in person. Only the court conducts in person searches; visitors may not. Search fee: $5.00 per name. Required to search: name; also helpful-years to search. Civil records are located in North Butte County Municipal Court. **General Information:** No sealed records released. SASE required. Turnaround time 2-3 days. Copy fee: $1.00 for first page, $.50 each addl. Certification fee: $6.00. Fee payee: Superior Court. Personal checks accepted. Prepayment is required.

Calaveras County

Superior Court Dept One 891 Mt Ranch Rd, San Andreas, CA 95249; 209-754-6310/6311. Hours: 8AM-4PM (PST). *Civil Actions Over $25,000, Probate.*

www.co.calaveras.ca.us

Civil Records: Access: Phone, mail, in person. Both court and visitors may perform in person searches. Search fee: $5.00 per name. Fee is for each 15 year period. Required to search: name, years to search. Civil cases indexed by defendant, plaintiff. Civil records on computer since 6/96; in index books and microfiche from 1975. **General Information:** No juvenile or confidential records released. SASE required. Turnaround time 2-3 weeks. Copy fee: $.50 per page. Certification fee: $6.00. Fee payee: Calaveras Superior Court. Personal checks accepted. Prepayment is required.

Superior Court Dept Two 891 Mt Ranch Rd, San Andreas, CA 95249; 209-754-6338; Fax: 209-754-6689. Hours: 8AM-4PM (PST). *Misdemeanor, Civil Actions Under $25,000, Eviction, Small Claims.*

Civil Records: Access: Mail, in person. Both court and visitors may perform in person searches. Search fee: $5.00 per name. the fee covers 15 years. Required to search: name, years to search. Civil cases indexed by defendant, plaintiff. Civil records on computer from 1991, index files 10 years or less. **Criminal Records:** Access: Mail, in person. Both court and visitors may perform in person searches. Search fee: $5.00 per name. the fee covers 15 years. Required to search: name, years to search, DOB; also helpful-aliases. Criminal records on computer from 1991, index files 10 years or less. Driver license number is helpful in searching. **General Information:** No sealed records or probation reports released. SASE required. Turnaround time 2-4 weeks. Copy fee: $.50 per page. Certification fee: $6.00. Fee payee: Calaveras Superior Court. Personal checks accepted. Prepayment is required.

Colusa County

Colusa County Superior Court 547 Market St, Colusa, CA 95932; 530-458-0507; Fax: 530-458-2230. Hours: 8:30AM-5PM (PST). *Felony, Civil Actions Over $25,000, Probate.*

Note: Since 1995, the records have been combined for both courts in this county; prior records must be searched at the individual courts

Civil Records: Access: Mail, in person. Both court and visitors may perform in person searches. Search fee: $5.00 per name. Required to search: name, years to search. Civil cases indexed by defendant, plaintiff. Civil records on computer from 1986, in index files from 1800s. **Criminal Records:** Access: Mail, in person. Both court and visitors may perform in person searches. Search fee: $5.00 per name. Required to search: name, years to search. Criminal records on computer from 1986, in index files from 1800s. **General Information:** No juvenile, paternity (except Judgment) or adoption records released. SASE required. Turnaround time 2 days. Copy fee: $.50 per page. Certification fee: $6.00. Fee payee: Colusa County Superior Court. Personal checks accepted. Prepayment is required.

Colusa Superior Court 532 Oak St, Dept 2, Colusa, CA 95932; 530-458-5149; Fax: 530-458-2904. Hours: 8:30AM-Noon, 1-5PM (PST). *Misdemeanor, Civil Actions Under $25,000, Eviction, Small Claims.*

Note: Since 1995, records from both courts in this county have been combined; prior records must be searched at the individual courts

Civil Records: Access: Mail, in person. Both court and visitors may perform in person searches. Search fee: $5.00 per name per year. Required to search: name, years to search. Civil cases indexed by defendant, plaintiff. Civil records on computer from 1994, index books prior. **Criminal Records:** Access: Mail, in person. Both court and visitors may perform in person searches. Search fee: $5.00 per name per year. Required to search: name, years to search, DOB. Criminal records on computer from 1994, index books prior. **General Information:** No sealed records released. SASE required. Turnaround time 1-2 days. Copy fee: $.50 per page. Certification fee: $6.00. Fee payee: Colusa Superior Court. Personal checks accepted. Prepayment is required. Public access terminal is available.

Contra Costa County

Superior Court 725 Court St Rm 103, Martinez, CA 94553; 925-646-2950; Civil phone:925-646-2951; Criminal phone:925-646-2951. Hours: 8AM-4PM (PST). *Felony, Civil Actions Over $25,000, Probate.*

www.co.contra-costa.ca.us

Civil Records: Access: Mail, online, in person. Both court and visitors may perform in person searches. Search fee: $5.00 per name. Required to search: name, years to search. Civil cases indexed by defendant, plaintiff. Civil records on computer from 1987, on microfiche from 1900s. There is a free remote dial-up system for civil, probate and county law records. Call 925-646-2479 for details. **Criminal Records:** Access: Mail, in person. Both court and visitors may perform in person searches. Search fee: $5.00 per name. Required to search: name, years to search; also helpful-DOB. Criminal records on computer from 1987, on microfiche from 1900s. **General Information:** No adoption, juvenile or sealed records released. SASE required. Turnaround time 1 week. Copy fee: $1.00 per page. Certification fee: $6.00. Fee payee: Clerk of the Superior Court. Business checks accepted. Prepayment is required.

Walnut Creek Branch - Superior Court
640 Ygnacio Valley Rd (PO Box 5128), Walnut Creek, CA 94596-1128; 925-646-6578; Civil phone:925-646-6579; Criminal phone:925-646-6579. Hours: 8:30AM-4:30PM (PST). *Felony, Misdemeanor, Civil Actions Under $25,000, Eviction, Small Claims.*

Note: Includes Alamo, Canyon, Danville, Lafayette, Moraga, Orinda, Rheem, San Ramon, St Mary's College, Walnut Creek and Ygnacio Valley. Effective 01/01/99, this court has all civil records formally at the municipal court in Concord

Civil Records: Access: Phone, mail, online, in person. Both court and visitors may perform in person searches. Search fee: $5.00 per name. Add $5.00 archive retrieval fee for older cases. In person searching of microfiche is free. Required to search: name; also helpful-years to search. Civil cases indexed by defendant, plaintiff. Civil records on computer from 1991. Records are destroyed after 10 years. There is a free remote dial-up system for civil, probate and family law records. Call 925-646-2479 for sign-up. **Criminal Records:** Access: Mail, in person. Both court and visitors may perform in person searches. Search fee: $5.00 per name. Add $5.00 archive retrieval fee for older cases. Required to search: name, years to search, DOB. **General Information:** No probation reports or sealed case records released. SASE required. Turnaround time 2 days. Copy fee: $1.00 per page. Certification fee: $6.00. Fee payee: Walnut Creek Superior Court. Personal checks accepted. Credit cards accepted. Prepayment is required.

Pittsburg Branch - Superior Court
45 Civic Ave, Pittsburg, CA 94565-0431;; Civil phone:925-427-8159; Criminal phone:925-427-8159. Hours: 8AM-4:30PM (PST). *Misdemeanor, Civil Actions Under $25,000, Eviction, Small Claims.*

Note: Includes Antioch, Bethel Island, Bradford Island, Brentwood, Byron, Coney Island, Discovery Bay, Holland Tract, Jersey Island, Knightsen, Oakley, Pittsburg, Quimby Island, Shore Acres, Webb Tract, West Pittsburg, and parts of Clayton

Civil Records: Access: Mail, online, in person. Both court and visitors may perform in person

searches. Search fee: $5.00 per name. Required to search: name, years to search. Civil cases indexed by defendant, plaintiff. Civil records on computer from 1991. Records are destroyed after 10 years. There is a free remote dial-up system for civil, probate and family law records. Call 925-646-2479 for sign-up. **Criminal Records:** Access: Mail, in person. Both court and visitors may perform in person searches. Search fee: $5.00 per name. Required to search: name, years to search; also helpful-DOB. Criminal records on computer from 1991, index files for 10 years. Records are destroyed after 10 years. Visitor may search microfiche only. **General Information:** No probation reports released. SASE required. Turnaround time 2 days. Copy fee: $1.00 per page. Certification fee: $6.00. Fee payee: Superior Court. Personal checks accepted. Prepayment is required.

Richmond Superior Court
100 37th St Rm 185, Richmond, CA 94805;; Civil phone:510-374-3138; Criminal phone:510-374-3138. Hours: 8AM-4PM (PST). *Misdemeanor, Civil Actions Under $25,000, Eviction, Small Claims.*

Note: Includes Crockett, El Cerrito, El Sobrante, Hercules, Kensington, North Richmond, Pinole, Point Richmond, Port Costa, Richmond, Rodeo, Rollingwood and San Pablo

Civil Records: Access: Mail, online, in person. Both court and visitors may perform in person searches. Search fee: $5.00 per name. Fee is for retrieval of archive files only. Required to search: name. Civil cases indexed by defendant, plaintiff. Civil records on computer from 1991. Records are destroyed after 10 years. There is a free remote dial-up service for civil, probate and family law records. Call 925-646-2479 for sign-up. **Criminal Records:** Access: Mail, in person. Only the court conducts in person searches; visitors may not. Search fee: $5.00 per name. There is an additional fee for retrieval of archive files. Required to search: name, years to search; also helpful-address, DOB, SSN. Criminal records on computer from 1991, index files from 1983. Records are destroyed after 10 years. **General Information:** No probation reports released. SASE required. Turnaround time 5 days. Copy fee: $1.00 per page. Certification fee: $6.00. Fee payee: Richmond Superior Court. Personal checks accepted. Prepayment is required.

Del Norte County

Superior Court 450 "H" St Rm 182, Crescent City, CA 95531; 707-464-7205; Fax: 707-465-4005. Hours: 8AM-Noon,1-5PM (PST). *Felony, Misdemeanor, Civil, Eviction, Small Claims, Probate.*

Civil Records: Access: Phone, mail, in person. Both court and visitors may perform in person searches. Search fee: $1.75 per name per year. no fee if record is less than 5 years old. Required to search: name, years to search. Civil cases indexed by defendant, plaintiff. Civil records archived and in index file from 1970s. **Criminal Records:** Access: Mail, in person. Both court and visitors may perform in person searches. Search fee: $1.75 per name per year. no fee if record is less than 5 years old. Required to search: name, years to search. Criminal records archived and in index file from 1970s, index books prior in handwritten records. **General Information:** No adoption, juvenile, probate, LPS conservatorship released. SASE required. Turnaround time 1-2 days. Copy fee: $.50 per page. Certification fee: $6.00. Plus $.50 per page. Fee payee: Superior Court. Personal checks accepted. Prepayment is required.

El Dorado County

Placerville Branch-Superior Court 495 Main St, Placerville, CA 95667; 530-621-6460; Civil phone:530-621-6460; Criminal phone:530-621-6460; Fax: 530-622-9774. Hours: 8AM-4PM (PST). *Felony, Civil, Probate.*

http://co.el-dorado.ca.us/superiorcourts

Civil Records: Access: Mail, in person. Both court and visitors may perform in person searches. Search fee: $5.00 per name. Required to search: name, years to search. Civil cases indexed by defendant, plaintiff. Civil records on computer from 1989, in hardbound books from 1979 to 1989, prior archived in Placerville. **Criminal Records:** Access: Mail, in person. Both court and visitors may perform in person searches. Search fee: $5.00 per name. Required to search: name, years to search. Criminal records on computer from 1989, in hardbound books from 1979 to 1989, prior archived in Placerville. **General Information:** No adoption, juvenile, mental or confidential released. SASE required. Turnaround time 2 weeks. Copy fee: $.50 per page. Certification fee: $6.00. Fee payee: Clerk of Court. Personal checks accepted. Prepayment is required.

South Lake Tahoe Branch -Superior Court-Civil
1354 Johnson Blvd #2, South Lake Tahoe, CA 96150; 530-573-3075/3069; Fax: 916-544-6532. Hours: 8AM-4PM (PST). *Civil, Eviction, Probate.*

Civil Records: Access: Phone, mail, in person. Both court and visitors may perform in person searches. Search fee: $5.00 per name. Required to search: name, years to search. Civil cases indexed by defendant, plaintiff. Civil records on computer from 1989, in hardbound books from 1979 to 1989, prior archived in Placerville. **General Information:** No adoption, juvenile, mental or confidential released. SASE required. Turnaround time 2 weeks. Copy fee: $.50 per page. Certification fee: $6.00. Fee payee: Superior Court. Personal checks accepted. Prepayment is required.

South Lake Tahoe Branch -Superior Court-Criminal
1354 Johnson Blvd #1, South Lake Tahoe, CA 96150; 530-573-3047; Fax: 530-542-9102. Hours: 8AM-4PM (PST). *Felony, Misdemeanor.* **Criminal Records:** Access: Mail, in person. Both court and visitors may perform in person searches. Search fee: $5.00 per name. Required to search: name, years to search; also helpful-DOB, SSN. Criminal records on computer from 1991, index files from 1983. Records are destroyed after 10 years. **General Information:** No probation reports released. SASE required. Turnaround time 2 days. Copy fee: $.50 per page. Certification fee: $6.00. Fee payee: El Dorado Superior Court. Personal checks accepted. Prepayment is required.

Cameron Park Branch - Superior Court
3321 Cameron Park Dr, Cameron Park, CA 95682; 530-621-5867; Fax: 530-672-2413. Hours: 8AM-4PM (PST). *Misdemeanor.*

www.co.el-dorado.ca.us/superiorcourts/index.html

Note: Civil cases handled in Placerville **Criminal Records:** Access: Mail, in person. Both court and visitors may perform in person searches. Search fee: $5.00 per name. Required to search: name, years to search; also helpful-address, DOB. Criminal records on computer from 1991, index files from 1983. Records are destroyed after 10 years. **General Information:** No probation reports released. SASE required. Turnaround time 1 week.

Copy fee: $.50 per page. Certification fee: $6.00. Fee payee: Superior Court. Personal checks accepted. Prepayment is required.

Fairlane Branch - Superior Court 2850

Fairlane Ct, Placerville, CA 95667;; Civil phone:530-621-6460; Criminal phone:530-621-6460. Hours: 8AM-4PM (PST). *Misdemeanor, Small Claims, Traffic.*

Civil Records: Access: Mail, in person. Both court and visitors may perform in person searches. Search fee: $1.75 per name per year. Required to search: name, years to search. Civil cases indexed by defendant, plaintiff. Civil records on computer from 1991. Actual records after 1996 are kept at the main Superior Court in Placerville. Address to Dept. 8. **Criminal Records:** Access: Mail, in person. Both court and visitors may perform in person searches. Search fee: $5.00 per name. Required to search: name, years to search; also helpful-DOB. Criminal records on computer from 1994, prior on index books, index files from 1983. Records are destroyed after 10 years. Address to Dept 7. **General Information:** No probation reports released. SASE required. Turnaround time 2 weeks. Copy fee: $.50 per page. Certification fee: $6.00. Fee payee: El Dorado County Superior Courts. Personal checks accepted. Prepayment is required.

Fresno County

Superior Court 1100 Van Ness Ave, #401, Fresno, CA 93721; 559-488-3352; Fax: 559-488-1976. Hours: 8AM-4PM (PST). *Felony, Misdemeanor, Civil, Small Claims, Probate.*

www.fresno.ca.gov/2810/index.htm

Civil Records: Access: Phone, fax, mail, in person. Both court and visitors may perform in person searches. Search fee: $5.00 per name. Required to search: name, years to search. Civil cases indexed by defendant, plaintiff. Civil records on computer from 1976, on microfiche, index files and archived from 1800s. **Criminal Records:** Access: Phone, fax, mail, in person. Both court and visitors may perform in person searches. Search fee: $5.00 per name. Required to search: name, years to search. Criminal records on computer from 1976, microfiche, index files and archived from 1800s. **General Information:** No confidential, adoption or juvenile records released. SASE required. Turnaround time 3-5 days. Copy fee: $.50 per page. Certification fee: $6.00. Fee payee: Superior Court Clerk's Office. Personal checks accepted. Prepayment is required. Public access terminal is available.

Kingsburg Division -- Superior Court

1600 California St, Kingsburg, CA 93631; 559-897-2241; Fax: 559-897-1419. Hours: 8AM-Noon, 1-4PM (PST). *Felony, Misdemeanor, Civil Actions Under $25,000, Eviction, Small Claims.*

www.fresno.ca.gov/2810/kingsburg.htm

Note: This court includes records from the branch court closed in Riverdale

Civil Records: Access: Mail, in person. Only the court conducts in person searches; visitors may not. Search fee: $5.00 per name. Required to search: name, years to search. **Criminal Records:** Access: Mail, in person. Only the court conducts in person searches; visitors may not. Search fee: $5.00 per name. Required to search: name, years to search, DOB. Criminal records on computer from April, 1994, index cards prior. **General Information:** No confidential records released. SASE required. Turnaround time 1 week. Copy fee: $.50 per page. Certification fee: $6.00. Fee

payee: Superior Court. Personal checks accepted. Prepayment is required.

Clovis Division - Superior Court 1011

5th St, Clovis, CA 93612; 559-299-4964; Fax: 559-299-2595. Hours: 8AM-4PM (PST). *Misdemeanor, Civil Actions Under $25,000, Eviction, Small Claims.*

www.fresno.ca.gov/2810/clovis.htm

Note: Includes the city of Clovis and surrounding area

Civil Records: Access: Mail, in person. Only the court conducts in person searches; visitors may not. No search fee. Required to search: name, years to search. Civil cases indexed by defendant, plaintiff. Civil records on computer and index files from 1983. Records destroyed after 10 years. **Criminal Records:** Access: Mail, in person. Only the court conducts in person searches; visitors may not. No search fee. Required to search: name, years to search, DOB. Criminal records on computer and index files from 1983. Records destroyed after 10 years. **General Information:** No probation reports released. SASE required. Turnaround time 1 week. Copy fee: $.50 per page. Certification fee: $6.00. Fee payee: Clovis Superior Court. Personal checks accepted. Prepayment is required.

Coalinga Division-Superior Court 160

West Elm St, Coalinga, CA 93210; 559-935-2017/2018; Fax: 559-935-5324. Hours: 8AM-Noon, 1-4PM (PST). *Misdemeanor, Civil Actions Under $25,000, Eviction, Small Claims.*

www.fresno.ca.gov/2810/coalinga

Civil Records: Access: Mail, in person. Only the court conducts in person searches; visitors may not. Search fee: There is a $5.00 search fee if no case number is presented. Required to search: name, years to search; also helpful-address. Civil cases indexed by defendant, plaintiff. Civil records on index cards and are computerized since 1990. Will only search back 10 years. **Criminal Records:** Access: Mail, in person. Only the court conducts in person searches; visitors may not. Search fee: There is a $5.00 if no case number is presented. Required to search: name, years to search, DOB; also helpful-address, SSN. Criminal records on computer from 1990, on index cards prior. Will only search back 10 years, Traffic 7 years. **General Information:** No confidential records or cases not finished released. SASE required. Turnaround time 1 week. Copy fee: $.50 per page. Certification fee: $6.00. Fee payee: Superior Court. Personal checks accepted. Prepayment is required.

Firebaugh Division-Superior Court

1325 "O" St, Firebaugh, CA 93622; 559-659-2011/2012; Fax: 559-659-6228. Hours: 8AM-4:30 M; 8AM-4PM T-F (PST). *Misdemeanor, Civil Actions Under $25,000, Eviction, Small Claims.*

www.fresno.ca.gov/2810/firebaugh

Civil Records: Access: Phone, fax, mail, in person. Only the court conducts in person searches; visitors may not. Search fee: $5.00 per name. Required to search: name, years to search. Civil cases indexed by defendant, plaintiff. Civil records on computer from 1990, index cards prior. Will only search back 7 years. **Criminal Records:** Access: Phone, fax, mail, in person. Only the court conducts in person searches; visitors may not. Search fee: $5.00 per name. Required to search: name, years to search, DOB. Criminal records on computer from 1990, index cards prior. Will only search back 7 years. **General Information:** No

confidential records released. SASE required. Turnaround time 1 week. Copy fee: $.50 per page. Certification fee: $6.00. Fee payee: Firebaugh Superior Court. Personal checks accepted. Prepayment is required.

Fowler Division - Superior Court PO

Box 400, Fowler, CA 93625; 559-834-3215; Fax: 559-834-1645. Hours: 8AM-4PM (PST). *Misdemeanor, Civil Actions Under $25,000, Eviction, Small Claims.*

www.fresno.ca.gov/2810/fowler.htm

Note: This court holds the records for the closed courts in Caruthers and Parlier

Civil Records: Access: Mail, in person. Only the court conducts in person searches; visitors may not. Search fee: $5.00 per name. Required to search: name, years to search. Civil cases indexed by defendant, plaintiff. Civil records on index cards. Will only search back 7 years. **Criminal Records:** Access: Mail, in person. Only the court conducts in person searches; visitors may not. Search fee: $5.00 per name. Required to search: name, years to search; also helpful-DOB, SSN. Criminal records on computer from 1990, index cards prior. Will only search back 7 years. **General Information:** No confidential records released. SASE required. Turnaround time 1 week. Copy fee: $.50 per page. Certification fee: $6.00. Fee payee: Fowler Superior Court. Personal checks accepted. Prepayment is required.

Kerman Division-Superior Court 719 S

Madera Ave, Kerman, CA 93630; 559-846-7371/7372; Fax: 559-846-5751. Hours: 8AM-4PM M-F (2-4 for phone calls) (PST). *Misdemeanor, Civil Actions Under $25,000, Eviction, Small Claims.*

www.fresno.ca.gov/2810/default.htm

Note: The court holds preliminary hearings for felonies

Civil Records: Access: Phone, mail, in person. Both court and visitors may perform in person searches. No search fee. Required to search: name, years to search. Civil cases indexed by defendant, plaintiff. Civil records on index cards. Will only search back 7 years. **Criminal Records:** Access: Phone, mail, in person. Both court and visitors may perform in person searches. No search fee. Required to search: name, years to search. Criminal records on computer from 1990, index cards prior. Will only search back 7 years. **General Information:** No confidential records released. SASE required. Turnaround time 1 week. Copy fee: $.50 per page. Certification fee: $6.00. Fee payee: Superior Court. Personal checks accepted. Prepayment is required.

Reedley Division - Superior Court 815

"G" St, Reedley, CA 93654; 559-638-3114; Fax: 559-637-1534. Hours: 8AM-Noon, 1-4PM (2-4 for phone calls) (PST). *Misdemeanor, Civil Actions Under $25,000, Eviction, Small Claims.*

www.fresno.ca.gov/2810/reedley.htm

Civil Records: Access: Mail, in person. Both court and visitors may perform in person searches. Search fee: $5.00 per name. Required to search: name, years to search. Civil cases indexed by defendant, plaintiff. Civil records on computer since 1985, index cards prior. Will only search back 7 years. **Criminal Records:** Access: Mail, in person. Both court and visitors may perform in person searches. Search fee: $5.00 per name. Required to search: name, years to search, DOB. Criminal records on computer since 1985, index cards prior. Will only search back 7 years.

General Information: No confidential records released. SASE required. Turnaround time 1 week. Copy fee: $.50 per page. Certification fee: $6.00. Fee payee: Reedley Superior Court. Personal checks accepted. Prepayment is required.

Sanger Division - Superior Court 619
"N" St, Sanger, CA 93657; 559-875-7158/7159; Fax: 559-875-0002. Hours: 8AM-Noon, 1-4PM (PST). *Misdemeanor, Civil Actions Under $25,000, Eviction, Small Claims.*

www.fresno.ca.gov/2810/sanger.htm

Note: The clerk's office will only talk on the phone from 1-4pm

Civil Records: Access: Mail, in person. Only the court conducts in person searches; visitors may not. Search fee: $5.00 per name. Required to search: name, years to search. Civil cases indexed by defendant, plaintiff. Civil records on index cards. Will only search back 7 years. **Criminal Records:** Access: Mail, in person. Only the court conducts in person searches; visitors may not. Search fee: $5.00 per name. Required to search: name, years to search, DOB. Criminal records on computer from 1990, index cards prior. Will only search back 7 years. **General Information:** No confidential records released. SASE required. Turnaround time 1 week. Copy fee: $.50 per page. Certification fee: $6.00. Fee payee: Superior Court. Personal checks accepted.

Selma Division - Superior Court 2117
Selma St, Selma, CA 93662; 559-896-2123; Fax: 559-896-4465. Hours: 8AM-Noon, 1-4PM (PST). *Misdemeanor, Civil Actions Under $25,000, Eviction, Small Claims.*

www.fresno.ca.gov/2810/selma.htm

Civil Records: Access: Mail, in person. Only the court conducts in person searches; visitors may not. No search fee. Required to search: name, years to search. Civil cases indexed by defendant, plaintiff. Civil records on index cards. Will only search back 7 years. **Criminal Records:** Access: Mail, in person. Only the court conducts in person searches; visitors may not. No search fee. Required to search: name, years to search, DOB. Criminal records on computer from 1985, index cards prior. Will only search back 7 years. **General Information:** No confidential records released. SASE required. Turnaround time 1 week. Copy fee: $.50 per page. Certification fee: $6.00. Fee payee: Selma Superior Court. Personal checks accepted. Prepayment is required.

Glenn County

Superior Court 526 W Sycamore, Willows,
CA 95988; 530-934-6446; Fax: 530-934-6406. Hours: 8AM-5PM (PST). *Felony, Misdemeanor, Civil, Eviction, Small Claims, Probate.*

Note: Records from the municipal court were combined with this court when the courts were consolidated

Civil Records: Access: Mail, in person. Both court and visitors may perform in person searches. No search fee. Required to search: name, years to search. Civil cases indexed by defendant, plaintiff. Civil records on computer from 1987, on microfiche, archived and in index file from 1894. **Criminal Records:** Access: Mail, in person. Both court and visitors may perform in person searches. Search fee: No criminal searches performed by court. Required to search: name, years to search; also helpful-DOB. Criminal records on computer from 1987, on microfiche, archived and in index file from 1894. **General Information:** No adoption, juvenile or paternity released. SASE

required. Turnaround time 1 day. Copy fee: $.50 per page. Certification fee: $6.00. Fee payee: Superior Court. Personal checks accepted. Prepayment is required. Public access terminal is available.

Humboldt County

Superior Court 825 5th Street, Eureka, CA
95501; 707-445-7256. Hours: 8:30AM-Noon, 1-4PM (PST). *Felony, Civil, Probate.*

Note: County wide searching can be done from this court, records computerized for 10 years. The former Eureka, Eel River, and North Humboldt Municipal Court Divisions have been combined with this court. Physical address is at 421 I Street

Civil Records: Access: Mail, in person. Both court and visitors may perform in person searches. Search fee: $5.00 per name. Required to search: name, years to search. Civil cases indexed by defendant, plaintiff. Civil records computerized since 1992, on microfiche and archived from 1964. **Criminal Records:** Access: Mail, in person. Both court and visitors may perform in person searches. Search fee: $5.00 per name. Required to search: name, years to search; also helpful-DOB. Criminal records on computer from 1992, on microfiche and archived from 1964. **General Information:** No probation, medical, adoption, juvenile or sealed records released. SASE required. Turnaround time 3 weeks. Copy fee: $1.00 per page. Certification fee: $6.00. Fee payee: Humboldt Superior Court. Personal checks accepted. Prepayment is required.

Garberville Branch-Superior Court 483
Conger St, Garberville, CA 95542; 707-923-2141; Fax: 707-923-3133. Hours: 8:30AM-Noon, 1-5PM (PST). *Misdemeanor, Civil Actions Under $25,000, Eviction, Small Claims.*

Civil Records: Access: Mail, in person. Both court and visitors may perform in person searches. Search fee: $5.00 per name. Required to search: name, years to search. Civil cases indexed by defendant, plaintiff. Civil records on index cards. Will only search back 10 years. **Criminal Records:** Access: Mail, in person. Both court and visitors may perform in person searches. Search fee: $5.00 per name. Required to search: name, years to search, DOB. Criminal records on computer from 1990, index cards prior. Will only search back 10 years. **General Information:** No juvenile or adoption records released. SASE not required. Turnaround time 1 day to 1 week. Copy fee: $1.00 per page. Certification fee: $6.00. Fee payee: Humboldt Courts. Personal checks accepted. Prepayment is required.

Klamath/Trinity Branch-Superior Court PO Box 698, Hoopa, CA 95546; 530-625-4204. Hours: 8:30AM-Noon, 1-5PM M-TH (PST). *Misdemeanor, Civil Actions Under $25,000, Eviction, Small Claims.*

Civil Records: Access: Mail, in person. Both court and visitors may perform in person searches. Search fee: $5.00 per name. Required to search: name, years to search. Civil cases indexed by defendant, plaintiff. Civil records in index files from 1983. Records destroyed after 10 yrs. **Criminal Records:** Access: Mail, in person. Both court and visitors may perform in person searches. Search fee: $5.00 per name. Required to search: name, years to search. Criminal records on computer from 1987, index and dockets kept for 10 years, files kept for 5 years. **General Information:** No probation reports released. SASE required. Turnaround time 2 days. Copy fee: $1.00 per page. Certification fee: $6.00. Fee

payee: Humboldt Superior Court. Personal checks accepted. Prepayment is required.

Imperial County

Imperial Branch - Superior Court 939 W
Main St, El Centro, CA 92243;; Civil phone:760-339-4217; Criminal phone:760-339-4217; Fax: 760-352-3184. Hours: 8AM-4PM (PST). *Felony, Misdemeanor, Civil, Eviction, Small Claims, Probate.*

Note: All record searching for Imperial County must be done at each location

Civil Records: Access: Mail, in person. Both court and visitors may perform in person searches. Search fee: $5.00 per name. Required to search: name, years to search. Civil cases indexed by defendant, plaintiff. Civil records on microfiche from 1972, in index file from 1917. **Criminal Records:** Access: Mail, in person. Both court and visitors may perform in person searches. Search fee: $5.00 per name. Required to search: name, years to search. Criminal records on microfiche from 1972, index file from 1917. **General Information:** No adoptions, juvenile, medical, probation or sealed records released. SASE required. Turnaround time 2 weeks. Copy fee: $1.00 for first page, $.50 each addl. Certification fee: $6.00. Fee payee: Imperial County Superior Court. Personal checks accepted. Prepayment is required.

Brawley Branch - Superior Court 383
Main St, Brawley, CA 92227; 760-344-0710; Fax: 760-344-9231. Hours: 8AM-4PM (PST). *Misdemeanor, Civil Actions Under $25,000, Eviction, Small Claims.*

Note: There is no countywide database in this county

Civil Records: Access: Phone, fax, mail, in person. Both court and visitors may perform in person searches. Search fee: $5.00 per name. Required to search: name, years to search. Civil cases indexed by defendant, plaintiff. Civil records on computer (traffic only) from 1991, in index files from 1983. Records destroyed after 10 years. **Criminal Records:** Access: Phone, fax, mail, in person. Only the court conducts in person searches; visitors may not. Search fee: $5.00 per name. Required to search: name, years to search, DOB. Criminal records on computer (traffic only) from 1991, in index files from 1983. Records destroyed after 10 years. **General Information:** No probation reports released. SASE required. Turnaround time 1 week. Copy fee: $1.00 for first page, $.50 each addl. Certification fee: $6.00. Fee payee: Brawley Superior Court. Personal checks accepted. Prepayment is required.

Calexico Branch - Superior Court 415
4th St, Calexico, CA 92231; 760-357-3726; Fax: 760-357-6571. Hours: 8AM-4PM (PST). *Misdemeanor, Civil Actions Under $25,000, Eviction, Small Claims.*

Note: There is no countywide database in this county

Civil Records: Access: Fax, mail, in person. Both court and visitors may perform in person searches. Search fee: $5.00 per name. Required to search: name, years to search. Civil cases indexed by defendant, plaintiff. Civil records on computer from 1991, index files from 1983. Records destroyed after 10 years. **Criminal Records:** Access: Fax, mail, in person. Only the court conducts in person searches; visitors may not. Search fee: $5.00 per name. Required to search: name, years to search. Criminal records on computer from 1991, index files from 1983. Records destroyed after 10 years. **General Information:** No probation reports released. SASE required. Turnaround time within 2 weeks. Copy fee: $.50 per page. Certification fee: $6.00. Fee payee: Superior Court. Personal checks accepted. Write case # on check. Prepayment is required.

Winterhaven Branch -- Superior Court

PO Box 1087, Winterhaven, CA 92283; 760-572-0354; Fax: 760-572-2683. Hours: 8AM-Noon, 1-4PM (PST). *Eviction, Small Claims.*

Note: Misdemeanor and civil records have been moved to the Calexico Municipal Court. Only small claims and traffic records remain here

Civil Records: Access: Phone, fax, mail, in person. Both court and visitors may perform in person searches. Search fee: $5.00 per name. Required to search: name, years to search. Civil cases indexed by defendant, plaintiff. Civil records on computer from 1991, index files from 1983. Records destroyed after 10 years. **General Information:** SASE required. Turnaround time 2-3 days. Copy fee: $1.00 for first page, $.50 each addl. Certification fee: $6.00. Fee payee: Superior-Winterhaven. Personal checks accepted. Prepayment is required.

Inyo County

Superior Court 168 N Edwards St (PO Drawer 4), Independence, CA 93526; 760-878-0218. Hours: 9AM-5PM (PST). *Felony, Civil Actions Over $25,000, Probate.*

Note: There is no central record database, each court in the county has its own records

Civil Records: Access: Mail, in person. Both court and visitors may perform in person searches. Search fee: $5.00 per name. Required to search: name, years to search. Civil cases indexed by defendant, plaintiff. Civil records on computer from 1992, on microfiche and in index files from 1800s. **Criminal Records:** Access: Mail, in person. Both court and visitors may perform in person searches. Search fee: $5.00 per name. Required to search: name, years to search. Criminal records on computer from 1992, on microfiche and in index files from 1800s. **General Information:** No adoptions, juvenile, medical, probation or sealed records released. SASE required. Turnaround time 2-3 business days. Copy fee: $1.00 per page. Certification fee: $6.00. Fee payee: Inyo Superior Court. Personal checks accepted. Prepayment is required.

Bishop Branch - Superior Court 301 W

Line St, Bishop, CA 93514; 760-872-4971. Hours: 9AM-Noon, 1-5PM; Phone: 2-5PM (PST). *Misdemeanor, Civil Actions Under $25,000, Eviction, Small Claims.*

Note: There is no countywide database, each court must be searched

Civil Records: Access: Mail, in person. Only the court conducts in person searches; visitors may not. Search fee: $5.00 per name. Required to search: name, years to search. Civil cases indexed by defendant, plaintiff. Civil records on index cards. Will only search back 7 years. **Criminal Records:** Access: Mail, in person. Only the court conducts in person searches; visitors may not. Search fee: $5.00 per name. Required to search: name, years to search. Criminal records on computer from 1993, index cards prior. Will only search back 7 years. **General Information:** No confidential records released. SASE required. Turnaround time 1 week. Copy fee: $1.00 per

page. Certification fee: $6.00. Fee payee: Superior Court. Personal checks accepted. Prepayment is required.

Independence Limited Branch-Superior Court 168 N Edwards St (PO Box

518), Independence, CA 93526; 760-878-0319; Fax: 760-872-1060. Hours: 9AM-Noon, 1-5PM (PST). *Misdemeanor, Civil Actions Under $25,000, Eviction, Small Claims.*

Note: There is no countywide database, each court must be searched

Civil Records: Access: Mail, in person. Both court and visitors may perform in person searches. Search fee: $5.00 per name. Required to search: name, years to search. Civil cases indexed by defendant, plaintiff. Civil records computerized since 1999, in index books and index cards. Will only search back 7 years. **Criminal Records:** Access: Mail, in person. Both court and visitors may perform in person searches. Search fee: $5.00 per name. Required to search: name, years to search, DOB, SSN. Criminal records on computer from February, 1993, index books and index cards prior. Will only search back 7 years. **General Information:** No confidential records released. SASE required. Turnaround time 1 week. Copy fee: $.50 per page. Certification fee: $6.00. Fee payee: Inyo County Court. Personal checks accepted. Prepayment is required.

Kern County

Superior Court 1415 Truxtun Ave, Bakersfield, CA 93301; 661-861-2621; Fax: 661-634-4999. Hours: 8AM-5PM (PST). *Felony, Civil Actions Over $25,000, Probate.*

Civil Records: Access: Mail, in person. Court does not conduct in person searches; visitors must perform searches for themselves. Search fee: $10.00 per name. Required to search: name, years to search. Civil cases indexed by defendant, plaintiff. Civil records on microfiche from 1964, archived and in index file from 1800s. **Criminal Records:** Access: Mail, in person. Court does not conduct in person searches; visitors must perform searches for themselves. Search fee: $10.00 per name. Required to search: name, years to search, DOB. Criminal records on computer from 1989, on microfiche, archived, and in index files. **General Information:** No adoptions, juvenile, medical, probation or sealed records released. SASE required. Turnaround time 1 day to 1 week. Copy fee: $.75 per page. Certification fee: $6.00. Fee payee: Kern County Superior Court. Personal checks accepted. Prepayment is required.

Arvin/Lamont Branch-South Kern Municipal Court 12022 Main St, Lamont, CA

93241; 661-845-3460/3741; Fax: 661-845-9142. Hours: 8AM-4PM (PST). *Misdemeanor, Civil Actions Under $25,000, Eviction, Small Claims.*

Civil Records: Access: Fax, mail, in person. Only the court conducts in person searches; visitors may not. Search fee: $5.00 per name. Required to search: name, years to search. Civil cases indexed by defendant, plaintiff. Civil records on computer from 1991, in index files from 1983. Records destroyed after 10 years. **Criminal Records:** Access: Fax, mail, in person. Only the court conducts in person searches; visitors may not. Search fee: $5.00 per name. Required to search: name, years to search. Criminal records on computer from 1991, in index files from 1983. Records destroyed after 10 years. **General Information:** No probation reports released. SASE required. Turnaround time 2 days. Copy fee: $.75 per page. Certification fee: $6.00. Fee

payee: South Kern Municipal Court. Personal checks accepted. Credit cards accepted: Visa, AmEx. Prepayment is required. Fax notes: No fee to fax results.

Bakersfield Municipal Court 1215

Truxtun Ave, Bakersfield, CA 93301;; Civil phone:661-868-2456; Criminal phone:661-868-2456; Fax: 661-861-2005 (civ); 661-868-2695 (crim). Hours: 8AM-5PM (PST). *Misdemeanor, Civil Actions Under $25,000, Eviction, Small Claims.*

Note: Includes Bakersfield, Oildale, Edison, Glenville, Woody

Civil Records: Access: Fax, mail, in person. Both court and visitors may perform in person searches. Search fee: $10.00 per name per year. Required to search: name, years to search. Civil cases indexed by defendant, plaintiff. Civil records on index files from 1977 on microfilm. Records destroyed after 10 years. **Criminal Records:** Access: Fax, mail, in person. Both court and visitors may perform in person searches. Search fee: $10.00 per name per year. Required to search: name, years to search. Criminal records on computer since 1988, microfilm since 1952. **General Information:** No probation reports, rap sheets, medical or financial released. Mail requests not accepted. Turnaround time 2-5 days. Copy fee: $.75 per page. Certification fee: $6.00. Fee payee: Bakersfield Municipal Court. Personal checks accepted. Credit cards accepted: Visa, Discover. Prepayment is required. Public access terminal is available. Fax notes: No fee to fax results. Fax fee varies by quantity.

Delano/McFarland Branch - North Kern Municipal Court 1122 Jefferson St,

Delano, CA 93215; 661-720-5800; Fax: 661-721-1237. Hours: 8AM-Noon, 1-4:30PM (PST). *Misdemeanor, Civil Actions Under $25,000, Eviction, Small Claims.*

www.co.kern.ca.us

Civil Records: Access: Phone, fax, mail, in person. Both court and visitors may perform in person searches. Search fee: $5.00 per name per year. Required to search: name, years to search. Civil cases indexed by defendant, plaintiff. Civil records on computer from 1988, in index files from 1983. Records destroyed after 10 years. **Criminal Records:** Access: Phone, fax, mail, in person. Both court and visitors may perform in person searches. Search fee: $5.00 per name per year. Required to search: name, years to search; also helpful-DOB. Criminal records on computer from 1988, in index files from 1983. Records destroyed after 10 years. **General Information:** No probation reports released. SASE required. Turnaround time 2 days. Copy fee: $.75 per page. Certification fee: $6.00. Fee payee: North Kern Municipal Court-Delano/McFarland Branch. Personal checks accepted. Prepayment is required. Public access terminal is available.

East Kern Municipal Court 132 E Coso St,

Ridgecrest, CA 93555; 760-375-1397; Fax: 760-375-2112. Hours: 8AM-4PM M-T, 8AM-5PM F (PST). *Misdemeanor, Civil Actions Under $25,000, Eviction, Small Claims.*

Note: Includes Eastern Kern County, including Edwards Air Force Base, Lake Isabella, Kernville, China Lake NWC, California City, Ridgecrest, Mojave and Tehachapi

Civil Records: Access: Mail, in person. Both court and visitors may perform in person searches. Search fee: $5.00 per name. Required to search: name, years to search. Civil cases indexed by

Superior Court. Personal checks accepted. Prepayment is required.

San Benito County

Superior Court Courthouse, 440 5th St-Rm 205, Hollister, CA 95023; 831-636-4057; Fax: 831-636-2046. Hours: 8AM-4PM (PST). *Felony, Misdemeanor, Civil, Small Claims, Eviction, Probate.*

www.superior-court.co.san-benito.ca.us

Civil Records: Access: Mail, in person. Both court and visitors may perform in person searches. Search fee: $5.00 per name. If visitor does search, no fee. Required to search: name, years to search. Civil cases indexed by defendant, plaintiff. Civil records on computer for last 9 years, index books and archived from 1900. **Criminal Records:** Access: Mail, in person. Both court and visitors may perform in person searches. Search fee: $5.00 per name. If visitor does search, no fee. Required to search: name, years to search. Criminal records on computer for last 9 years, index books and archived from 1900. **General Information:** No adoptions, juvenile, medical, probation or sealed records released. SASE required. Turnaround time 1-2 weeks. Copy fee: $.50 per page. Certification fee: $7.00. Fee payee: Superior Court. Personal checks accepted. Prepayment is required.

San Bernardino County

Barstow Division - Superior Court 235 E Mountain View, Barstow, CA 92311;; Civil phone:760-256-4755; Criminal phone:760-256-4755. Hours: 8AM-4PM (PST). *Felony, Misdemeanor, Civil, Eviction, Small Claims.*

Note: Includes the City of Barstow and the unincorporated areas of Yermo, Lenwood, Daggett, Hinkley and Baker

Civil Records: Access: Mail, in person. Both court and visitors may perform in person searches. Search fee: $5.00 per name. Required to search: name, years to search. Civil cases indexed by defendant, plaintiff. Civil records on computer from 1991, index books and microfilm. Microfile is 3 to 4 weeks current. Records destroyed after 10 years. **Criminal Records:** Access: Mail, in person. Both court and visitors may perform in person searches. Search fee: $5.00 per name. Required to search: name, years to search. Criminal records on computer from 1991, index books and microfilm. Microfile is 3 to 4 weeks current. Records destroyed after 10 years. **General Information:** No probation or confidential reports released. SASE required. Turnaround time 2-5 days. Copy fee: $.50 per page. Certification fee: $6.00. Fee payee: Clerk of the Court. Only cashiers checks and money orders accepted. Credit cards accepted: Visa, Mastercard. Accepted for filings only. Prepayment is required.

Central District - Superior Court 351 N Arrowhead Ave, San Bernardino, CA 92415;; Civil phone:909-387-3922; Criminal phone:909-387-3922; Fax: 909-387-4428. Hours: 8AM-4PM (PST). *Felony, Misdemeanor, Civil, Eviction, Small Claims, Probate.*

www.co.san-bernardino.ca.us/ACR

Civil Records: Access: Mail, in person. Both court and visitors may perform in person searches. Search fee: $5.00 per name. Required to search: name, years to search. Civil cases indexed by defendant, plaintiff. Civil records on computer from 04/99, microfiche from 1972, archived and index file from 1856. Address mail search access requests to Research Dept. **Criminal Records:** Access: Mail, in person. Both court and visitors

may perform in person searches. Search fee: $5.00 per name. Required to search: name, years to search; also helpful-DOB. Criminal records on computer from 04/99, microfiche from 1972, archived and index file from 1856. **General Information:** No adoptions, juvenile, medical, probation or sealed records released. SASE required. Turnaround time 1-2 weeks. Copy fee: $.50 per page. Certification fee: $6.00. Fee payee: Clerk of the Court. Business checks accepted. Credit cards accepted: Visa, Discover. Prepayment is required. Public access terminal is available.

Joshua Tree Division - Superior Court 6527 White Feather Rd PO Box 6602, Joshua Tree, CA 92252; 760-366-4100; Fax: 760-366-4156. Hours: 8AM-4PM (PST). *Felony, Misdemeanor, Civil, Eviction, Small Claims.*

www.co.san-bernardino.ca.us/courts

Note: Includes the incorporated area of Twenty-Nine Palms, Yucca Valley and Morongo Valley

Civil Records: Access: Mail, in person. Only the court conducts in person searches; visitors may not. Search fee: $5.00 per name per year. Required to search: name, years to search. Civil cases indexed by defendant, plaintiff. Civil records on computer from 1991, index books from 1983. Records destroyed after 10 years. **Criminal Records:** Access: Mail, in person. Only the court conducts in person searches; visitors may not. Search fee: $5.00 per name per year. Required to search: name, years to search, DOB. Criminal records on computer from 1991, index books from 1983. Records destroyed after 10 years. **General Information:** No probation reports, confidential records released. SASE required. Turnaround time 1 week. Copy fee: $.50 per page. Certification fee: $6.00. Fee payee: Joshua Tree Superior Court. Personal checks accepted. Prepayment is required.

Twin Peaks Branch - Superior Court 26010 State Hwy 189, PO Box 394, Twin Peaks, CA 92391; 909-336-0620; Fax: 909-337-2101. Hours: 8AM-4PM (PST). *Felony, Misdemeanor, Civil to $25,000, Eviction, Small Claims.*

www.co.san-bernardino.ca.us/courts

Civil Records: Access: Mail, in person. Only the court conducts in person searches; visitors may not. Search fee: $5.00 per name per year. Required to search: name, years to search. Civil cases indexed by defendant, plaintiff. Civil records on index cards. Will only search back 7 years. **Criminal Records:** Access: Mail, in person. Only the court conducts in person searches; visitors may not. Search fee: $5.00 per name per year. Required to search: name, years to search, DOB. Criminal records on computer from 1990, index cards prior. Will only search back 7 years. **General Information:** No probation or arrest reports released. SASE required. Turnaround time 1 week. Copy fee: $.50 per page. Certification fee: $6.00. Fee payee: Superior Court. No checks accepted.

Victorville Division-Superior Court 14455 Civic Dr, Victorville, CA 92392;; Civil phone:760-243-8672; Criminal phone:760-243-8672; Fax: 760-243-8790 (civil); 8794 (criminal). Hours: 8AM-4PM (PST). *Felony, Misdemeanor, Civil, Eviction, Small Claims.*

Note: Includes the Cities of Victorville, Adelanto Hesperia and the unincorporated area of Apple Valley, El Mirage, Helendale, Lucerne Valley, Oro Grande, Phelan, Pinon Hill and Wrightwood

Civil Records: Access: Mail, in person. Both court and visitors may perform in person searches. Search fee: $5.00 per name. Required to search:

name, years to search. Civil cases indexed by defendant, plaintiff. Civil records on microfiche from 1982 to July 1999, on computer from 1989 to present, index books prior. Records destroyed after 10 years. **Criminal Records:** Access: Mail, in person. Only the court conducts in person searches; visitors may not. Search fee: $5.00 per name. Required to search: name, years to search; also helpful-DOB, date of offense. Criminal index books by defendant 1986 - present. Only court allowed to search computer index. **General Information:** No probation reports released. SASE required. Turnaround time within 1 week. Copy fee: $.50 per page. Certification fee: $6.00. Fee payee: Superior Court. Personal checks accepted. $5.00 minimum. Prepayment is required.

West District - Superior Court 8303 Haven Ave, Rancho Cucamonga, CA 91730;; Civil phone:909-945-4131; Criminal phone:909-945-4131; Fax: 909-945-4154. Hours: 8AM-4PM (PST). *Felony, Misdemeanor, Civil, Eviction, Small Claims, Probate.*

www.co.san-bernardino.ca.us/courts

Note: Includes the cities of Montclair, Ontario, Upland, Rancho Cucamonga and surrounding unincorporated area of Mt Baldy

Civil Records: Access: Phone, fax, mail, in person. Both court and visitors may perform in person searches. Search fee: $5.00 per name. Required to search: name, years to search. Civil cases indexed by defendant, plaintiff. Civil records on computer since April 1994, index cards prior. Records destroyed after 10 years. No charge for up to 3 inquires by phone. **Criminal Records:** Access: Phone, fax, mail, in person. Only the court conducts in person searches; visitors may not. Search fee: $5.00 per name. Required to search: name, years to search; also helpful-DOB. Criminal records computerized since 1994, also on index cards and microfiche. **General Information:** No probation reports released. SASE required. Turnaround time 2-4 days. Copy fee: $.50 per page. Certification fee: $6.00. Fee payee: West Valley Superior Court. Personal checks accepted. Checks over $10.00 accepted. Credit cards accepted: Visa, Discover. Prepayment is required.

Big Bear Lake Branch - Superior Court PO Box 2806, Big Bear Lake, CA 92315; 909-866-0150; Fax: 909-866-0160. Hours: 8AM-4PM (PST). *Misdemeanor, Civil Actions Under $25,000, Eviction, Small Claims.*

Civil Records: Access: Mail, in person. Both court and visitors may perform in person searches. Search fee: $5.00 per name. Required to search: name, years to search. Civil cases indexed by defendant, plaintiff. Civil records on computer since 9/1/96; prior on index books. Will only search back 7 years. **Criminal Records:** Access: Mail, in person. Both court and visitors may perform in person searches. Search fee: $5.00 per name. Required to search: name, years to search, DOB; also helpful-SSN. Criminal records on index books. Will only search back 7 years. **General Information:** No probation reports released. SASE required. Turnaround time 1 week. Copy fee: $.50 per page. Certification fee: $6.00. Fee payee: Superior Court. Personal checks accepted. Prepayment is required.

Central Division Branch - Superior Court 351 N Arrowhead, San Bernardino, CA 92415; 909-885-0139 (Small Claims); Civil phone:909-387-3922; Probate phone:909-387-3952; Fax: 909-387-4428. Hours: 8AM-4PM

(PST). *Misdemeanor, Civil Actions Under $25,000, Eviction, Small Claims.*

www.co.san-bernardino.ca.us/courts

Note: Includes the City of Bernardino, cities of Grand Terrace, Loma Linda, Colton and Highland and the unincorporated area of Del Rosa, Devore, Miscoy, Patton, Verdemont

Civil Records: Access: Mail, in person. Both court and visitors may perform in person searches. Search fee: $5.00 per name. Required to search: name, years to search. Civil cases indexed by defendant, plaintiff. Civil records on computer from 1991, index files from 1983, microfiche from 1972. Specify which city you are searching in. **Criminal Records:** Access: Mail, in person. Both court and visitors may perform in person searches. Search fee: $5.00 per name. Required to search: name, years to search; also helpful-DOB. Criminal records on computer from 1991, index files from 1983, microfiche from 1972. Specify which city you are searching in. **General Information:** No probation reports released. SASE required. Turnaround time 2 days. Copy fee: $.50 per page. Certification fee: $6.00. Fee payee: San Bernardino Superior Court. Personal checks accepted. Prepayment is required. Public access terminal is available.

Chino Division-Superior Court 13260 Central Ave, Chino, CA 91710; 909-465-5266 (Small Claims); Civil phone:909-465-5266; Criminal phone:909-465-5266; Fax: 909-465-5221. Hours: 8AM-4PM (PST). *Misdemeanor, Eviction, Small Claims.*

www.co.san-bernardino.ca.us/courts

Note: Includes City of Chino and surrounding unincorporated area. Rancho Cucamonga Courts handles all civil cases since 01/01/99

Civil Records: Access: Fax, mail, in person. Only the court conducts in person searches; visitors may not. Search fee: $5.00 per name. Required to search: name, years to search; also helpful-address. Civil cases indexed by defendant, plaintiff. Civil records on computer from 1991, index books from 1983. Records destroyed after 10 years. **Criminal Records:** Access: Mail, in person. Only the court conducts in person searches; visitors may not. Search fee: $5.00 per name. Required to search: name, years to search, DOB; also helpful-address. Criminal records on computer from 1991, index books from 1983. Records destroyed after 10 years. **General Information:** No probation reports released. SASE required. Turnaround time 2 days. Copy fee: $.50 per page. Certification fee: $6.00. Fee payee: Chino Superior Court. Personal checks accepted. Prepayment is required.

Fontana Division - Superior Court 17780 Arrow Blvd, Fontana, CA 92335; 909-356-3487; Civil phone:909-350-1590; Criminal phone:909-350-1590; Fax: 909-829-4149. Hours: 8AM-4PM (PST). *Misdemeanor, Civil Actions Under $25,000, Eviction, Small Claims.*

www.co.san-bernadino.ca.us/courts

Note: Includes the Cities of Fontana, Rialto, Crestmore and the unincorporated areas of Lytle Creek Canyon and Bloomington

Civil Records: Access: Mail, in person. Only the court conducts in person searches; visitors may not. Search fee: $5.00 per name. Required to search: name, years to search; also helpful-address. Civil cases indexed by defendant, plaintiff. Civil records on computer from 1987, microfilm prior. Records destroyed after 10 years. **Criminal Records:** Access: Mail, in person. Both court and

visitors may perform in person searches. Search fee: $5.00 per name. Required to search: name, years to search; also helpful-DOB. Criminal records on computer from 1987, microfilm prior. Records destroyed after 10 years. **General Information:** No probation reports or police records released. SASE required. Turnaround time 2-5 days. Copy fee: $.50 per page. Certification fee: $6.00. Fee payee: Fontana Courts. Personal checks accepted. Prepayment is required.

Needles Division - Superior Court 1111 Bailey Ave, Needles, CA 92363; 760-326-9245; Fax: 760-326-9254. Hours: 8AM-4PM (PST). *Misdemeanor, Civil Actions Under $25,000, Eviction, Small Claims.*

Civil Records: Access: Mail, in person. Only the court conducts in person searches; visitors may not. Search fee: $5.00 per name. Required to search: name, years to search. Civil cases indexed by plaintiff. Civil records in index books. Will only search back 7 years. **Criminal Records:** Access: Mail, in person. Only the court conducts in person searches; visitors may not. Search fee: $5.00 per name. Required to search: name, years to search. Criminal records on computer from 1990, index books prior. Will only search back 7 years. **General Information:** No probation reports released. SASE required. Turnaround time 1-2 weeks. Copy fee: $.50 per page. Certification fee: $6.00. Fee payee: Superior Court. Personal checks accepted. Prepayment is required.

Redlands District - Superior Court 216 Brookside Ave, Redlands, CA 92373;; Civil phone:909-888-4260; Criminal phone:909-888-4260; Fax: 909-798-8588. Hours: 8AM-4PM (PST). *Misdemeanor, Civil Actions Under $25,000, Eviction, Small Claims.*

Note: Includes Cities of Redlands, Yucaipa and the unincorporated areas of Angeles Oaks, Barton Flats, Forest Home and Mentone

Civil Records: Access: Mail, in person. Only the court conducts in person searches; visitors may not. Search fee: $5.00 per name. Required to search: name, years to search. Civil cases indexed by defendant, plaintiff. Civil records on computer from 1991, index books prior. Records destroyed after 10 years. **Criminal Records:** Access: Mail, in person. Both court and visitors may perform in person searches. Search fee: $5.00 per name. Required to search: name, years to search, DOB. Criminal records on computer from 1991, index books prior. Records destroyed after 10 years. **General Information:** No probation reports released. SASE required. Turnaround time 2 days. Copy fee: $.50 per page. Certification fee: $6.00. Fee payee: Superior Court. Business checks accepted. Prepayment is required.

San Diego County

East County Division - Superior Court 250 E Main St, El Cajon, CA 92020; 619-441-4622. Hours: 8AM-4:30PM (PST). *Felony, Misdemeanor, Civil, Small Claims, Eviction.*

www.sandiego.courts.ca.gov

Note: This court now houses the former municipal court records

Civil Records: Access: Mail, in person. Both court and visitors may perform in person searches. Search fee: $5.00 per name. Required to search: name, years to search. Civil cases indexed by defendant, plaintiff. Civil records on cmputer since 1974; microfilm prior. **Criminal Records:** Access: Mail, in person. Both court and visitors may perform in person searches. Search fee: $5.00

per name. Required to search: name, years to search; also helpful-DOB. Criminal records on cmputer since 1974; microfilm prior. **General Information:** No confidential or sealed records released. SASE required. Turnaround time 3-5 days. Copy fee: $.50 per page. Certification fee: $6.00. Fee payee: Clerk of Superior Court. Personal checks accepted. California checks with preprinted name and address only. Law firm business checks accepted. Prepayment is required. Public access terminal is available.

Superior Court PO Box 120128, San Diego, CA 92112-0128; 619-531-3151. Hours: 8:30AM-4:30PM (PST). *Felony, Civil Actions Over $25,000, Probate.*

www.sandiego.courts.ca.gov

Civil Records: Access: Mail, in person. Both court and visitors may perform in person searches. Search fee: $5.00 per name. Fee is per index. Required to search: name, years to search. Civil cases indexed by defendant, plaintiff. Civil records on computer from 1974 to present, paper ledgers from 1860s. **Criminal Records:** Access: Mail, in person. Both court and visitors may perform in person searches. Search fee: $5.00 per name. Fee is per index. Required to search: name, years to search. Criminal records on computer from 1974 to present, paper ledgers from 1860s. **General Information:** No adoptions, juvenile, medical, probation or sealed records released. SASE required. Turnaround time 1 week. Copy fee: $.50 per page. Certification fee: $6.00. Fee payee: San Diego Superior Court. Personal checks accepted. No out of state personal checks. Prepayment is required. Public access terminal is available.

Superior Court Hall of Justice, PO Box 10128, San Diego, CA 92112;; Civil phone:619-531-3151; Criminal phone:619-531-3151; Probate phone:619-685-6677. Hours: 8:30AM-4:30PM (PST). *Felony, Civil Actions Over $25,000, Probate.*

www.sandiego.courts.ca.gov/superior

Note: Specify which division when sending in written record request

Civil Records: Access: Mail, in person. Both court and visitors may perform in person searches. Search fee: $5.00 per name. Required to search: name, years to search. Civil cases indexed by defendant, plaintiff. Civil records index on computer from 06/74. The court offers for sale a CD-ROM of civil, domestic, mental health, and probate indices. **Criminal Records:** Access: Mail, in person. Both court and visitors may perform in person searches. Search fee: $5.00 per name. Required to search: name, years to search. Criminal records index on computer from 06/74. The court offers for sale a CD-ROM of a criminal record index. **General Information:** No probation reports released. SASE required. Turnaround time 1 day. Copy fee: $.50 per page. Certification fee: $6.00. Fee payee: Clerk of Superior Court. Personal checks accepted. Prepayment is required. Public access terminal is available.

North County Branch - Superior Court 325 S Melrose Dr, Suite 100, Vista, CA 92083-6627; 760-940-9595. Hours: 8:30AM-4:30PM (PST). *Felony, Misdemeanor, Civil, Eviction, Small Claims, Probate.*

www.sandiego.courts.ca.gov

Civil Records: Access: Mail, in person. Both court and visitors may perform in person searches. Search fee: $5.00 per name. Required to search: name, years to search. Civil cases indexed by

defendant, plaintiff. Civil records on computer, microfiche and index books. **Criminal Records:** Access: Mail, in person. Both court and visitors may perform in person searches. Search fee: $5.00 per name. Required to search: name, years to search. Criminal records on computer, microfiche and index books. **General Information:** No sealed or confidential documents released. SASE required. Turnaround time 2-3 days. Copy fee: $.50 per page. Certification fee: $6.00. Fee payee: Clerk of the Superior Court. Personal checks accepted. Out of state checks not accepted. Prepayment is required. Public access terminal is available.

South Bay Branch-Superior Court 500-

C 3rd Ave, Chula Vista, CA 91910;; Civil phone:619-691-4780; Criminal phone:619-691-4780; Fax: 619-691-4969 (Civil). Hours: 8:30AM-4:30PM (PST). *Felony, Civil Actions Over $25,000, Probate.*

www.sandiego.courts.ca.gov

Civil Records: Access: Fax, mail, in person. Both court and visitors may perform in person searches. Search fee: $5.00 per name per year. Required to search: name, years to search. Civil cases indexed by defendant, plaintiff. Civil records on computer; for case files prior to 1991, contact Superior Court's Main Records Division, Downtown. **Criminal Records:** Access: Phone, fax, mail, in person. Both court and visitors may perform in person searches. Search fee: $5.00 per name. Required to search: name, years to search, DOB. Criminal records on computer, cases files in or before 1986 on microfiche. **General Information:** No juvenile, medical, probation reports or pronouncement of judgment records released. SASE required. Turnaround time up to 1 week (civil)-Turnaround time depends on availability of clerk (criminal). Copy fee: $.60 per page. Certification fee: $6.00. Fee payee: Superior Court (Civil)-Clerk of the Court (Criminal). Personal checks accepted. Prepayment is required. Public access terminal is available.

North County Division - Superior

Court 325 S Melrose Dr Ste 120, Vista, CA 92083; 760-726-9595; Fax: 760-806-6121. Hours: 8AM-4:30PM (PST). *Misdemeanor, Civil Actions Under $25,000, Eviction, Small Claims.*

www.sandiego.courts.ca.gov

Note: Includes Cities of Oceanside, Del Mar, Carlsbad, Solana Beach, Encinitas, Escondido, San Marcos, Vista and unincorporated towns of Del Dios, Olivehain, San Luis Rey, San Pasqual, Rancho Santa Fe, Valley Center, Bonsall, Palomar Mountain, etc

Civil Records: Access: In person only. Only the court conducts in person searches; visitors may not. Search fee: $5.00 per name per year. Required to search: name, years to search. Civil records on computer from 1991, index files from 1983. Records destroyed after 10 years. **Criminal Records:** Access: Mail, in person. Only the court conducts in person searches; visitors may not. Search fee: $5.00 per name per year. Required to search: name, years to search, DOB, SSN. Criminal records on computer from 1991, index files from 1983. Records destroyed after 10 years. **General Information:** No probation reports released. SASE required. Turnaround time 2 days. Copy fee: $.50 per page. Certification fee: $6.00. Fee payee: Clerk of the Court. Personal checks accepted. Prepayment is required.

Ramona (East) Branch - Superior

Court 1428 Montecito Rd, Ramona, CA 92065; 760-738-2435. Hours: 8AM-4:30PM (PST). *Misdemeanor, Civil Actions Under $25,000, Eviction, Small Claims.*

www.sandiego.courts.ca.gov

Civil Records: Access: Fax, mail, in person. Both court and visitors may perform in person searches. Search fee: $5.00 per name. Required to search: name, years to search. Civil cases indexed by defendant, plaintiff. Civil records on computer from 1991, index files since 1983. Files destroyed after 10 years. **Criminal Records:** Access: Fax, mail, in person. Both court and visitors may perform in person searches. Search fee: $5.00 per name. Required to search: name, years to search, SSN; also helpful-DOB. Criminal records on computer from 1991, index files since 1983. Files destroyed after 10 years. **General Information:** No probation reports or DMV records released. SASE required. Turnaround time 2-3 days. Copy fee: $.50 per page. Certification fee: $6.00. Fee payee: Clerk of the Court. Personal checks accepted. Credit cards accepted: Visa, Mastercard. Prepayment is required. Fax notes: No fee to fax results.

San Diego Central Limited-Superior

Court 330 W Broadway 2nd Fl (Civil), 220 W Broadway Rm 2005 (Criminal), San Diego, CA 92101;; Civil phone:619-531-3141; Criminal phone:619-531-3141. Hours: 8:30AM-4:30PM (PST). *Misdemeanor, Civil Actions Under $25,000, Eviction, Small Claims.*

www.sandiego.courts.ca.gov

Note: Co-extensive with the boundaries of the City of San Diego including the precincts of Mission, Miramar and Poway and excluding that portion of the City of San Diego that lies within the boundaries of the South Bay Judicial District

Civil Records: Access: Mail, in person. Both court and visitors may perform in person searches. Search fee: $5.00 per name. Required to search: name, years to search. Civil cases indexed by defendant, plaintiff. Civil records on computer from 1991, index files from 1983. Records destroyed after 10 years. Visitors to the court require approval and a $25.00 fee before access is granted to the computerized index. **Criminal Records:** Access: Mail, in person. Both court and visitors may perform in person searches. Search fee: $5.00 per name. Required to search: name, years to search. Criminal records on microfiche. **General Information:** No probation reports released. SASE required. Turnaround time 2 days. Copy fee: $.50 per page. Certification fee: $6.00. Fee payee: Clerk of the Court. Personal checks accepted. Prepayment is required.

San Marcos Branch - Superior Court

338 Via Vera Cruz, San Marcos, CA 92069-2693; 760-940-2888; Fax: 760-940-2802. Hours: 8:30AM-4PM (PST). *Misdemeanor, Traffic.*

www.sandiego.courts.ca.gov

Civil Records: Access: Mail, in person. Both court and visitors may perform in person searches. Search fee: $5.00 per name. Required to search: name, years to search; also helpful-address. Civil records on computer since 1994. **Criminal Records:** Access: Mail, in person. Both court and visitors may perform in person searches. Search fee: $5.00 per name. Required to search: name, years to search; also helpful-address. Criminal records on computer since 1994. **General Information:** Juvenile and adoption records are not released. Turnaround time 3 days. Copy fee:

$.50 per page. Certification fee: $6.00. Fee payee: Clerk of the Court. Personal checks accepted. Prepayment is required.

South Bay Branch - Limited Superior

Court 500C 3rd Ave, Chula Vista, CA 91910;; Civil phone:619-691-4780; Criminal phone:619-691-4780; Fax: 619-691-4438. Hours: 8AM-4:30PM (PST). *Misdemeanor, Civil Actions Under $25,000, Eviction, Small Claims.*

www.sandiego.courts.ca.gov

Note: Includes National City, Chula Vista, Coronado, Imperial Beach and that portion of the City of San Diego lying south of the City of Chula Vista and contiguous unincorporated areas

Civil Records: Access: Mail, in person. Both court and visitors may perform in person searches. Search fee: $5.00 per name per year. Required to search: name, years to search. Civil cases indexed by defendant, plaintiff. Civil records on computer from 1991, index files from 1983. Records destroyed after 10 years. **Criminal Records:** Access: Mail, in person. Only the court conducts in person searches; visitors may not. Search fee: $5.00 per name per year. Required to search: name, years to search. Criminal records on computer from 1991, index files from 1983. Records destroyed after 10 years. In person search requires picture ID. **General Information:** No probation reports or unlawful detainer cases within 60 days of filing date records released. SASE required. Turnaround time 2 days. Copy fee: $.50 per page. Certification fee: $6.00. Fee payee: Clerk of Court. Personal checks accepted. Prepayment is required. Public access terminal is available. Public Access Terminal Note: Civil only.

San Francisco County

Superior Court - Criminal Division 850

Bryant St #306, San Francisco, CA 94107/94103; 415-553-1159. Hours: 8AM-4:30PM (PST). *Felony.*

www.ci.sf.ca.us/courts **Criminal Records:** Access: Fax, mail, in person. Both court and visitors may perform in person searches. Search fee: $4.00 per name per year. Add warehouse retrieval fee of $5.00. Required to search: name, years to search, DOB. **General Information:** No medical, probation or sealed records released. SASE required. Turnaround time 1 week. Copy fee: $.75 per page. Certification fee: $6.00. Fee payee: Clerk of the Superior Court. Personal checks accepted. Cashier checks and personal checks with ID only. Prepayment is required. Fax notes: No fee to fax results.

Superior Court - Civil Division 400

McAllister St, Rm 103, San Francisco, CA 94102; 415-551-3802; Probate phone:415-551-4040. Hours: 8AM-4PM (PST). *Civil, Probate.*

www.ci.sf.ca.us/courts

Civil Records: Access: Mail, in person. Both court and visitors may perform in person searches. Search fee: $4.00 per name per year. Required to search: name, years to search. Civil cases indexed by defendant, plaintiff. Civil records on computer since 1987; prior records on microfilm and microfiche. **General Information:** No medical, probation or sealed records released. SASE required. Turnaround time 2 weeks. Copy fee: $.75 per page. Certification fee: $6.00 plus $1.00 per page. Fee payee: Clerk of the Superior Court. Personal checks accepted. Credit cards accepted: Visa, Mastercard. Prepayment is required. Public access terminal is available.

Limited Superior - Civil Division 400 McAllister St, Rm 103, San Francisco, CA 94107; 415-551-4032 (Records Section); Civil phone:415-551-4047; Fax: 415-551-4041. Hours: 8AM-4:30PM (PST). *Civil Actions Under $25,000, Eviction, Small Claims.*

www.ci.sf.ca.us/courts

Note: Includes all of San Francisco County, including former municipal court on Folsom St

Civil Records: Access: Mail, in person. Both court and visitors may perform in person searches. Search fee: $5.00 per name per year. No charge if easily pulled from computer. Required to search: name, years to search. Civil cases indexed by defendant, plaintiff. Civil records on computer from 1991, index files from 1983. Records destroyed after 10 years. **General Information:** No sealed records released. SASE required. Turnaround time 2 days. Copy fee: $.75 per page. Certification fee: $6.00 plus $1.00 per page & copy fee. Fee payee: Superior Court. Personal checks accepted. Prepayment is required. Public access terminal is available.

Superior Court - Misdemeanor Division 850 Bryant St Rm 201, San Francisco, CA 94103; 415-553-1665 (Records Dept); Criminal phone:. Hours: 8AM-4:30PM (PST). *Misdemeanor.*

www.ci.sf.ca.us/courts

Note: Includes all of San Francisco County
Criminal Records: Access: Mail, in person. Both court and visitors may perform in person searches. Search fee: $5.00 per name per year. Required to search: name, years to search; also helpful-DOB. Criminal records (pending) on computer from 1991, index files from 1983. Records are destroyed after 10 years. **General Information:** No probation reports released. SASE required. Turnaround time 3-4 weeks. Copy fee: $.50 per page. Microfilm copies $1.50 per pg. Certification fee: $1.75. Fee payee: Superior Court. Personal checks accepted. Prepayment is required.

San Joaquin County

Superior Court-Civil 222 E Weber Ave, Rm 303, Stockton, CA 95202-2709; 209-468-2355; Fax: 209-468-0539. Hours: 7:30AM-5 M-F (office); 8AM-5PM M-F (phones) (PST). *Civil Actions, Eviction, Small Claims, Probate.*

www.stocktonet.com/courts

Note: Includes City of Stockton and suburban area, Farmington and Linden, Delta area and surrounding unincorporated areas

Civil Records: Access: Phone, mail, in person. Both court and visitors may perform in person searches. Search fee: $5.00 per name. No fee if search is done by customer. Required to search: name, years to search. Civil cases indexed by defendant, plaintiff. Civil records on computer from 1991, index files from 1983. Records destroyed after 10 years. **General Information:** No probation, confidential records released. SASE required. Turnaround time 5-7 days. Copy fee: $.50 per page. Certification fee: $6.00. Fee payee: Superior Court. Personal checks accepted. Prepayment is required. Public access terminal is available.

Superior Court - Criminal Division 222 E Weber St Rm 101, Stockton, CA 95202; 209-468-2935. Hours: 7:30AM-5PM (PST). *Felony, Misdemeanor.*

www.stocktonet.com/courts **Criminal Records:** Access: Mail, in person. Both court and visitors

may perform in person searches. Search fee: $5.00 per name. Required to search: name, years to search, signed release; also helpful-DOB, SSN. Criminal Records on computer since 1992, on microfiche since 1972, older records archived to 1800s. Mail access only available to authorized agencies. **General Information:** No juvenile, medical, probation, sealed records released. SASE required. Turnaround time 1 week. Copy fee: $.50 per page. Certification fee: $6.00. Fee payee: San Joaquin Superior Court. Personal checks accepted. Cash only for forms and kits. Prepayment is required. Public access terminal is available.

Lodi Division-Superior Court 315 W Elm St (Civil), 230 W Elm St (Criminal), Lodi, CA 95240; 209-333-6753; Civil phone:209-333-6755; Criminal phone:209-333-6755; Fax: 209-368-3157. Hours: 8AM-4PM (PST). *Misdemeanor, Civil Actions Under $25,000, Eviction, Small Claims.*

Note: Includes eight mile road to Sacramento County line, towns of Acampo, Clements, Lockeford, Terminous, Thornton, Woodbridge

Civil Records: Access: Mail, in person. Only the court conducts in person searches; visitors may not. Search fee: $6.00 per name. Required to search: name, years to search. Civil cases indexed by defendant, plaintiff. Civil records on computer from 1991, index files from 1983. Records destroyed after 10 years. **Criminal Records:** Access: Mail, in person. Only the court conducts in person searches; visitors may not. Search fee: $6.00 per name. Required to search: name, years to search, DOB; also helpful-address. Criminal records on computer from 1991, index files from 1983. Records destroyed after 10 years. **General Information:** No probation reports released. SASE required. Turnaround time 5 days. Copy fee: $.50 per page. Certification fee: $6.00. Fee payee: Superior Court. Personal checks accepted. Prepayment is required.

Manteca Branch - Superior Court 315 E Center St, Manteca, CA 95336; 209-239-9188 (Small Claims); Civil phone:209-239-9188; Criminal phone:209-239-9188. Hours: 8AM-4PM (PST). *Felony, Misdemeanor, Civil Actions Under $25,000, Eviction, Small Claims.*

Note: Includes Cities of Manteca, Ripon, Escalon, French Camp, Lathrop and surrounding unincorporated areas

Civil Records: Access: Mail, in person. Only the court conducts in person searches; visitors may not. Search fee: $5.00 per name. Fee is for cases more than 3 years old. Required to search: name, years to search. Civil cases indexed by defendant, plaintiff. Civil records on computer from 1991, microfiche since 1986, index files from 1983. Records destroyed after 10 years. **Criminal Records:** Access: Mail, in person. Only the court conducts in person searches; visitors may not. Search fee: $5.00 per name. Fee is for cases prior to 1990. Required to search: name, years to search; also helpful-DOB. Criminal records on computer since 1990, microfiche since 1986, index files from 1983. Records destroyed after 10 years. Special request form required to view files. **General Information:** No judge's notes, probation or police reports released. SASE required. Turnaround time 1-2 days. Copy fee: $.50 per page. Certification fee: $6.00. Fee payee: Superior Court. Personal checks accepted. Prepayment is required.

Tracy Branch-Superior Court 475 E 10th St, Tracy, CA 95376;; Civil phone:209-831-5902;

Criminal phone:209-831-5902; Fax: 209-831-5919. Hours: 8AM-4PM (PST). *Felony, Misdemeanor, Civil Actions Under $25,000, Eviction, Small Claims.*

Note: Includes Cities of Tracy, Banta, portion of Vernalis and surrounding unincorporated area

Civil Records: Access: Phone, mail, in person. Only the court conducts in person searches; visitors may not. Search fee: $5.00 per name. If on computer, no charge. Required to search: name, years to search. Civil cases indexed by defendant, plaintiff. Civil records on computer since 03/95; on index files from 1983. Records destroyed after 10 years. **Criminal Records:** Access: Mail, in person. Only the court conducts in person searches; visitors may not. Search fee: $5.00 per name. Required to search: name, years to search, DOB. Criminal records on computer from 1991; on index files from 1983. Records destroyed after 10 years. **General Information:** No probation reports, DMV history and criminal history records released. SASE required. Turnaround time 5-10 days. Copy fee: $.50 per page. Certification fee: $6.00. Fee payee: Tracy Superior Court. Personal checks accepted. Prepayment is required.

San Luis Obispo County

Superior Court Government Center, Rm 385, San Luis Obispo, CA 93408; 805-781-5241/5243. Hours: 8AM-5PM (PST). *Felony, Civil, Eviction, Probate.*

www.callamer.com/~slosc/court1.htm

Civil Records: Access: Mail, in person. Both court and visitors may perform in person searches. Search fee: $5.00 per name. Required to search: name, years to search. Civil cases indexed by defendant, plaintiff. Civil records on computer and microfiche from 1975, archived and index file from late 1800s. **Criminal Records:** Access: Mail, in person. Both court and visitors may perform in person searches. Search fee: $5.00 per name. Required to search: name, years to search. Criminal records on computer and microfiche from 1975, archived and index file from late 1800s. **General Information:** No adoptions, juvenile, medical, probation or sealed records released. SASE required. Turnaround time 1 week. Copy fee: $.50 per page. Certification fee: $6.00. Fee payee: Superior Court Civil or Criminal Court Operations. Personal checks accepted. Prepayment is required. Public access terminal is available.

Grover Beach Branch - Superior Court 214 S 16th St, Grover Beach, CA 93433-2299;; Civil phone:805-473-7077; Criminal phone:805-473-7077. Hours: 9AM-4PM (PST). *Misdemeanor, Civil Actions Under $25,000, Eviction, Small Claims.*

Note: Includes Nipomo, Grover Beach, Arroyo Grande, Pismo Beach, Ociano, South Coast unincorporated areas

Civil Records: Access: Phone, mail, in person. Only the court conducts in person searches; visitors may not. Search fee: First name is free, then $5.00 per name. Required to search: name, years to search. Civil cases indexed by defendant, plaintiff. Civil records on index cards. Records destroyed after 10 years. **Criminal Records:** Access: Phone, mail, in person. Only the court conducts in person searches; visitors may not. Search fee: First name is free, then $5.00 per name. Required to search: name, years to search. Criminal records on computer from 1990, index cards prior. Records destroyed after 10 years. **General Information:** No probation reports released. SASE required. Turnaround 2-3 weeks civil; 1 week criminal. Copy fee: $.50 per page. Certification fee: $6.00. Fee payee: Superior Court. Personal checks accepted. Prepayment is required.

Limited Jursidiction - Superior Court

1035 Palm St Rm 385, County Government Center, San Luis Obispo, CA 93408-2510; 805-781-5677; Criminal phone:. Hours: 9AM-4PM (PST). *Misdemeanor, Civil Actions Under $25,000, smal Claims, Evictions.*

Note: The San Luis Obispo County Superior Court has jurisdiction over all of San Luis Obispo County, San Luis Obispo, Morro Bay, Avila Beach areas

Civil Records: Access: Phone, mail, in person. Both court and visitors may perform in person searches. No search fee. Required to search: name, years to search. Civil cases indexed by defendant, plaintiff. Civil records on computer from 1991, index files from 1983. Records destroyed after 10 years. Criminal Records: Access: Phone, mail, in person. Both court and visitors may perform in person searches. No search fee. Required to search: name, years to search. Criminal records on computer since 1991. Phone access limited to short searches. General Information: No probation reports released. SASE required. Turnaround time 2-5 days. Copy fee: $.50 per page. Certification fee: $6.00. Fee payee: Superior Court. Personal checks accepted. Prepayment is required. Public access terminal is available.

Paso Robles Branch - Superior Court

549 10th St, Paso Robles, CA 93446-2593; 805-237-3080; Civil phone:805-237-3079; Criminal phone:805-237-3079. Hours: 8:30AM-4PM (PST). *Misdemeanor, Civil Actions Under $25,000, Eviction, Small Claims.*

Note: Includes Atascadero, Templeton, Paso Robles, San Miguel, Shandon, Cholame, areas north and east of the Cuesta Grade

Civil Records: Access: Phone, mail, in person. Only the court conducts in person searches; visitors may not. Search fee: $5.00 per name. Search is free if only one name. Required to search: name, years to search. Civil cases indexed by defendant, plaintiff. Civil records on computer from 1975, index files from 1983. Records destroyed after 10 years. Mail requests limited to 5 at a time. Criminal Records: Access: Phone, mail, in person. Only the court conducts in person searches; visitors may not. Search fee: $5.00. Search is free for only one name. Required to search: name, years to search; also helpful-DOB. Criminal records on computer from 1975, index files from 1983. Records destroyed after 10 years. Mail requests limited to 5 at a time. General Information: No driving histories, rap sheets, sealed or probation reports released. SASE required. Turnaround time 1-2 days. Copy fee: $.50 per page. Certification fee: $6.00. Fee payee: Superior Court. Personal checks accepted. Prepayment is required. Public access terminal is available.

San Mateo County

Superior Court 400 County Center, Redwood City, CA 94063; 650-363-4711; Civil phone:650-363-4711; Criminal phone:650-363-4711; Fax: 650-363-4914. Hours: 8AM-4PM (PST). *Felony, Civil Actions Over $25,000, Probate.*

www.co.sanmateo.ca.us/sanmateocourts/index.html

Civil Records: Access: Mail, in person. Both court and visitors may perform in person searches. Search fee: $5.00 per name. Required to search:

name, years to search. Civil cases indexed by defendant, plaintiff. Civil records on computer from 1978; index books prior. Criminal Records: Access: Mail, in person. Both court and visitors may perform in person searches. Search fee: $5.00 per name. Required to search: name, years to search; also helpful-address, DOB, SSN. Criminal records on computer since 1964; prior on books. General Information: No confidential jackets on conservatorships & guardianships, adoptions, juvenile, medical, probation or sealed records released. SASE required. Turnaround time 1 week. Copy fee: $.75 per page. Certification fee: $6.00. Fee payee: Superior Court. Personal checks accepted. Prepayment is required. Public access terminal is available.

Northern Branch - Superior Court 1050

Mission Rd, South San Francisco, CA 94080; 650-877-5773; Civil phone:650-877-5778. Hours: 8AM-4PM (PST). *Misdemeanor, Small Claims, Traffic.*

www.co.sanmateo.ca.us/sanmateocourts/index.html

Note: Includes Brisbane, Daly City (including Westlake), Pacifica, San Bruno, South San Francisco, the northern coastal towns and all unincorporated areas in the north end of the county including Colma and Broadmoor Criminal Records: Access: Mail, in person. Both court and visitors may perform in person searches. Search fee: $5.00 per name. Required to search: name, years to search; also helpful-DOB. Criminal records on computer from 1991, index files from 1983. Records destroyed after 10 years. General Information: No probation reports or confidential information records released. SASE required. Turnaround time 2 days-2 weeks. Copy fee: $.75 per page. Certification fee: $5.00. Fee payee: Superior Court. Personal checks accepted. Prepayment is required. Public access terminal is available.

San Mateo Combined Superior Court

400 County Center, Redwood City, CA 94063; 650-363-4302. Hours: 8AM-4PM (PST). *Misdemeanor, Civil, Eviction, Small Claims.*

www.co.sanmateo.ca.us/sanmateocourts/dome.htm

Note: Includes Atherton, Menlo Park, Portola Valley, Redwood City, San Carlos, Woodside, East Palo Alto and all unincorporated areas including La Honda and the southern coastal area south of Tunitas Creek Road which includes Pescadara and San Gregorio

Civil Records: Access: Mail, in person. Both court and visitors may perform in person searches. Search fee: $5.00 per name. Required to search: name, years to search. Civil cases indexed by defendant, plaintiff. Civil Records on cumputer since 1991. Criminal Records: Access: Mail, in person. Both court and visitors may perform in person searches. Search fee: $5.00 per name. Required to search: name, years to search. Criminal records on computer from 1991, index files from 1983. Records destroyed after 10 years. General Information: No probation reports or confidential information records released. SASE required. Turnaround time 2 weeks. Copy fee: $.75 per page. Certification fee: $6.00. Fee payee: Superior Court. Personal checks accepted. Write "not to exceed $x.xx" on check. Credit cards accepted: Visa, Mastercard. Credit card accepted in person only. Prepayment is required. Public access terminal is available.

Santa Barbara County

Superior Court Box 21107, Santa Barbara, CA 93121; 805-568-2237; Fax: 805-568-2219.

Hours: 8AM-4:45PM (PST). *Felony, Civil Actions Over $25,000, Probate.*

Civil Records: Access: Phone, fax, mail, in person. Both court and visitors may perform in person searches. No search fee. Required to search: name, years to search. Civil cases indexed by defendant, plaintiff. Civil records on computer and microfiche from 1975, archived and index file from 1920. Criminal Records: Access: Phone, fax, mail, in person. Both court and visitors may perform in person searches. Search fee: $5.00 per name. Required to search: name, years to search, DOB. Criminal records on computer and microfiche from 1975, archived and index file from 1920. General Information: No adoptions, juvenile, medical, probation or sealed records released. SASE required. Turnaround time 1 week. Copy fee: $.50 per page. Certification fee: $6.00. Fee payee: Superior Court. Personal checks accepted. Credit cards accepted: Visa, Mastercard. Prepayment is required.

Figueroa Division - SB Superior Court

118 E Figueroa St, Santa Barbara, CA 93101; 805-568-2735; Civil phone:805-568-2741; Criminal phone:805-568-2741; Fax: 805-568-2847. Hours: 7:45AM-4PM (PST). *Misdemeanor, Civil Actions Under $25,000, Eviction, Small Claims.*

Note: Includes the City of Santa Barbara, Goleta and adjacent unincorporated areas, Carpenteria, Montecito. For civil cases prior to 09/01/98, call 805-568-2750

Civil Records: Access: Mail, in person. Both court and visitors may perform in person searches. Search fee: $5.00 per name. Required to search: name, years to search. Civil cases indexed by defendant, plaintiff. Civil records on computer from 1991, index files from 1983, microfiche from 1975. Records destroyed after 10 years. Criminal Records: Access: Mail, in person. Both court and visitors may perform in person searches. Search fee: $5.00 per name. Required to search: name, years to search; also helpful-DOB. Criminal records on computer from 1991, index files from 1983, microfiche from 1975. Records destroyed after 10 years. General Information: No probation reports released. SASE required. Turnaround time 2 days. Copy fee: $.75 per page. Certification fee: $6.00. Fee payee: Clerk of the Court. Personal checks accepted. Prepayment is required.

Lompoc Division - Superior Court 115

Civic Center Plz, Lompoc, CA 93436; 805-737-7790; Civil phone:805-737-7796; Criminal phone:805-737-7796; Fax: 805-737-7786. Hours: 8:30AM-4:55PM (PST). *Misdemeanor, Civil Actions Under $25,000, Eviction, Small Claims.*

Note: Includes Lompoc and adjacent unincorporated areas, including sections of Vandenburg Air Force Base. The Santa Maria and Solvang courts (civil) were consolidated into this court in late 1995

Civil Records: Access: Phone, mail, in person. Both court and visitors may perform in person searches. No search fee. Required to search: name, years to search. Civil cases indexed by defendant, plaintiff. Civil records on computer from 1991, index files from 1983. Records destroyed after 10 years. Phone searches only for computerized records. Criminal Records: Access: Phone, mail, in person. Both court and visitors may perform in person searches. No search fee. Required to search: name, years to search, DOB; also helpful-address. Criminal records on computer from 1991, index files from 1983. Records destroyed after 10 years. Phone searches only for computerized records. **General Information:** No probation reports released. SASE required. Turnaround time 2 days. Copy fee: $.75 per page. Certification fee: $6.00. Fee payee: Clerk of the Superior Court. Personal checks accepted. Prepayment is required. Public access terminal is available.

Miller Division -- Superior Court 312-M
East Cook St, Santa Maria, CA 93454-5165; 805-346-7590; Civil phone:805-346-7565; Criminal phone:805-346-7565; Fax: 805-346-7591. Hours: 7:30AM-4:30PM (PST). *Misdemeanor, Civil Actions Under $25,000, Eviction, Small Claims.*

Note: Includes Betteravia, Casmalia, Cuyama, Guadalupe, Gary, Los Alamos, New Cuyama, Orcutt, Santa Maria, Sisquoc, Tepusquet and sections of the Vandenburg Air Force Base

Civil Records: Access: Mail, in person. Both court and visitors may perform in person searches. Search fee: $5.00 per name. Required to search: name, years to search. Civil cases indexed by defendant, plaintiff. Civil records in index files from 1983. Records destroyed after 10 years. **Criminal Records:** Access: Mail, in person. Both court and visitors may perform in person searches. Search fee: $5.00 per name. Required to search: name, years to search, DOB. Criminal records in index files from 1983. Records destroyed after 10 years. **General Information:** No probation reports, financial, judges notes, confidential or sealed records released. SASE required. Turnaround time 2 days. Copy fee: $.75 per page. Certification fee: $6.00. Fee payee: Clerk of Court. Personal checks accepted. Credit cards accepted: Visa, Mastercard. Prepayment is required.

Solvang Division - Superior Court 1745
Mission Dr, #C, Solvang, CA 93463; 805-686-5040; Fax: 805-686-5079. Hours: 8AM-4PM (PST). *Misdemeanor, Small Claims, Traffic.*

www.co.santa-barbara.ca.us

Civil Records: Access: Phone, mail, in person. Both court and visitors may perform in person searches. No search fee. Required to search: name, years to search. Civil cases indexed by defendant, plaintiff. Civil records on computer from 1990, index cards prior. Will only search back 7 years. **Criminal Records:** Access: Mail, in person. Only the court conducts in person searches; visitors may not. No search fee. Required to search: name, years to search, DOB. Criminal records on computer from 1988, index cards prior. **General Information:** No sealed or confidential records released. SASE required. Turnaround time 1 week. Copy fee: $.75 per page. Certification fee: $6.00. Fee payee: Superior Court. Personal checks accepted. Credit cards accepted: Visa, Mastercard. Credit cards are only accepted at the counter, not by mail. Prepayment is required.

Santa Clara County

Superior Court 190-200 W Hedding St, San
Jose, CA 95110-1774; 408-299-2974; Criminal phone:. Hours: 8:30AM-4PM (PST). *Felony, Civil, Small Claims, Eviction, Probate.*

www.sccsuperiorcourt.org

Note: On January 18, 2000, all civil matters except those filed in the South County Courthouse where transferred to this facility to be heard or filed

Civil Records: Access: Mail, in person. Both court and visitors may perform in person searches. Search fee: $5.00 per name per year. Required to search: name, years to search. Civil cases indexed by defendant, plaintiff. Civil records on microfiche from 1975-2000. Old files are kept in archives or on microfilm. **Criminal Records:** Access: Mail, in

person. Both court and visitors may perform in person searches. Search fee: $5.00 per name per year. Required to search: name, years to search, DOB. Criminal records on microfiche from 1975-2000. Old files are kept in archives or on microfilm. **General Information:** No probation, confidential or sealed records released. SASE required. Turnaround time 3-7 days. Copy fee: $1.00 per page. Postage also charged based on number of pages copied. Certification fee: $6.00. Fee payee: Santa Clara Superior Court. Personal checks accepted. Prepayment is required.

San Jose Facility - Superior Court 191
N 1st Street, San Jose, CA 95113-1-11; 408-299-2281; Civil phone:408-299-2964. Hours: 8:30AM-4PM (PST). *Felony, Misdemeanor.*

www.sccsuperiorcourt.org

Note: Handles cases for San Jose, Milpitas, Santa Clara, Los Gatos and Campbell areas

Civil Records: Access: Mail, in person. Both court and visitors may perform in person searches. Search fee: $5.00 per name per year. Required to search: name, years to search. **Criminal Records:** Access: Mail, in person. Both court and visitors may perform in person searches. Search fee: $5.00 per name per year. Required to search: name, years to search; also helpful-DOB. Criminal records on computer from 1986, microfiche prior. Records destroyed after 10 years. **General Information:** No probation reports or confidential records released. SASE required. Turnaround time 2 weeks. Copy fee: $1.00 per page. Certification fee: $6.00. Fee payee: Superior Court. Personal checks accepted. Prepayment is required.

South County Facility - Superior Court
12425 Monterey Rd, San Martin, CA 95046-9590;; Civil phone:408-686-3520; Criminal phone:408-686-3520. Hours: 8:30AM-4PM (PST). *Felony, Misdemeanor, Civil Actions Under $25,000, Eviction, Small Claims.*

http://sccsuperiorcourt.org

Note: Small Claims phone is 408-686-3520. Jurisdiction includes the Cities of Gilroy, Morgan Hill, San Martin and surrounding unincorporated areas.

Civil Records: Access: Mail, in person. Both court and visitors may perform in person searches. Search fee: $5.00 per name per year. Required to search: name, years to search. on microfiche. **Criminal Records:** Access: Mail, in person. Only the court conducts in person searches; visitors may not. Search fee: $5.00 per name per year. Required to search: name, years to search; also helpful-DOB. Same record keeping as civil. **General Information:** No adoptions, juvenile, medical, probation or sealed records released. SASE required. Turnaround time 1 week. Copy fee: $1.00 per page. Certification fee: $6.00. Fee payee: Superior Court. Personal checks accepted. Prepayment is required.

Palo Alto Facility - Superior Court 270
Grant Ave, Palo Alto, CA 94306; 650-324-0373. Hours: 8:30AM-4PM (PST). *Felony, Misdemeanor, Small Claims.*

www.scccsuperiorcourt.org

Note: Includes Palo Alto, Mountain View, Los Altos, Los Altos Hills, Stanford University and the surrounding unincorporated areas.

Civil Records: Access: Mail, in person. Both court and visitors may perform in person searches. Search fee: $5.00 per name per year. Required to search: name. **Criminal Records:** Access: Mail, in person. Both court and visitors may perform in

person searches. Search fee: $5.00 per name per year. Required to search: name, years to search; also helpful-DOB. Criminal Records on microfiche. **General Information:** No probation, doctor report, pretrial report records released. SASE required. Turnaround time 1 week. Copy fee: $1.00 per page. Certification fee: $6.00. Fee payee: Superior Court. Personal checks accepted. Prepayment is required.

Sunnyvale Facility-Superior Court 605
W El Camino Real, Sunnyvale, CA 94087; 408-739-1503. Hours: 8:30AM-4PM (PST). *Felony, Misdemeanor.*

www.sccsuperiorcourt.org

Note: Includes the cities of Sunnyvale and Cupertino. All traffic and small claims are filed at the San Jose Facility **Criminal Records:** Access: Mail, in person. Both court and visitors may perform in person searches. No search fee. Required to search: name, years to search, DOB. **General Information:** No probation reports, confidential or sealed records released. SASE required. Turnaround time 2-4 days. Copy fee: $1.00 per page. Certification fee: $6.00. Fee payee: Clerk of Court. Personal checks accepted. Prepayment is required.

Los Gatos Facility-Superior Court
14205 Capri Dr, Los Gatos, CA 95032; 408-866-8331. Hours: 8:30AM-4PM (PST). *Small Claims.*

http://sccsuperiorcourt.org

Note: Includes the towns of Los Gatos and Monte Sereno and the cities of Campbell, Saratoga, and surrounding unincorporated areas as well as San Jose, Milpitas and Santa Clara

Civil Records: Access: Phone, mail, in person. Both court and visitors may perform in person searches. Search fee: $5.00 per name per year. Required to search: name, years to search. Civil cases indexed by defendant, plaintiff. Civil Record index on microfiche. **General Information:** Copy fee: $1.00 per page. Certification fee: $6.00. Fee payee: Superior Court. Personal checks accepted. Prepayment is required.

Santa Cruz County

Superior Court - Civil 701 Ocean St Rm
110, Santa Cruz, CA 95060; 831-454-2020; Fax: 831-454-2215. Hours: 8AM-4PM (PST). *Civil, Probate.*

www.co.santa-cruz.ca.us/crt/courts.htm

Civil Records: Access: Mail, in person. Both court and visitors may perform in person searches. Search fee: $5.00 per name. Fee is per file. Required to search: name, years to search. Civil cases indexed by defendant, plaintiff. Civil records on computer since 1985, microfiche, archived and index books from 1820. **General Information:** No adoptions, juvenile, medical, probation or sealed records released. SASE required. Turnaround time 5-10 days. Copy fee: $.50 per page. Certification fee: $6.00 plus $1.00 per page. Fee payee: Clerk of Court. Personal checks accepted. Prepayment is required. Public access terminal is available.

Superior Court - Criminal 701 Ocean St
Rm 120, Santa Cruz, CA 95060; 831-454-2155; Fax: 831-454-2215. Hours: 8AM-4PM (PST). *Felony, Misdemeanor.*

www.co.santa-cruz.ca.us/crt/courts.htm   **Criminal Records:** Access: Phone, mail, in person. Both court and visitors may perform in person searches. Search fee: $5.00 per name. Required to search: name; also helpful-years to search, DOB. Criminal records on computer since 1985; also on microfiche index by party name. **General Information:** No juvenile, probation or sealed records released. SASE required. Turnaround time 1-2 weeks. Copy fee: $.50 per page. Certification fee: $6.00 plus $1.00 per page. Fee payee: Clerk of Court. Personal checks accepted. Prepayment is required. Public access terminal is available.

Watsonville Division - Superior Court

1430 Freedom Blvd, Watsonville, CA 95076;; Civil phone:831-763-8060; Criminal phone:831-763-8060. Hours: 8AM-4PM (PST). *Misdemeanor, Civil Actions Under $25,000, Eviction, Small Claims.*

www.co.santa-cruz.ca.us/crt/courts.htm

Note: Includes all of Santa Cruz County

Civil Records: Access: Mail, in person. Search fee: $5.00 per name. Required to search: name, years to search. Civil cases indexed by defendant, plaintiff. Civil records on computer from 1992, index books prior. Records destroyed after 10 years. **Criminal Records:** Access: Mail, in person. Both court and visitors may perform in person searches. Search fee: $5.00 per name. Required to search: name, years to search; also helpful-DOB. Criminal records on computer from 1992, index books prior. Records destroyed after 10 years. **General Information:** No probation or juvenile records released. SASE required. Turnaround time 2-5 days. Copy fee: $.50 per page. Certification fee: $6.00. Fee payee: Superior Court. Personal checks accepted. Prepayment is required.

Shasta County

Shasta County Superior Court 1500 Court St, Redding, CA 96001; 530-245-6789; Fax: 530-225-5564 Civil; 245-6483 Criminal. Hours: 8:30AM-Noon,1-4PM (PST). *Felony, Misdemeanor, Civil, Probate.*

Note: Address Room 319 for civil division and Room 219 for criminal division

Civil Records: Access: Mail, in person. Both court and visitors may perform in person searches. Search fee: $5.00 per name per year. Required to search: name, years to search. Civil cases indexed by defendant, plaintiff. Civil records on computer from 1993, index books prior. **Criminal Records:** Access: Mail, in person. Both court and visitors may perform in person searches. Search fee: $5.00 per name. Required to search: name, years to search. Criminal records on computer from 1993, index books prior. **General Information:** No probation or confidential records released. SASE required. Turnaround time 2-7 days. Copy fee: $.50 per page. Certification fee: $6.00. Fee payee: Superior Courts. Personal checks accepted. Prepayment is required.

Burney Branch - Superior Court

20509 Shasta St, Burney, CA 96013; 530-335-3571; Fax: 530-225-5684. Hours: 8:30AM-Noon, 1-4PM (PST). *Misdemeanor, Eviction, Small Claims.*

Note: Civil actions handled by Redding Branch since 1992. Prior civil records are maintained here

Civil Records: Access: Mail, in person. Only the court conducts in person searches; visitors may not. Search fee: $5.00 per name per year. Required to search: name, years to search. Civil cases indexed by defendant, plaintiff. Civil records on computer from 1993, index books prior. Records destroyed after 10 years. **Criminal Records:** Access: Mail, in person. Only the court conducts in person searches; visitors may not. Search fee: $5.00 per name. Required to search: name, years

to search, DOB. Criminal records on computer from 1993, index books prior. Records destroyed after 10 years. **General Information:** No probation, juvenile, or DMV reports released. SASE required. Turnaround time 2-14 days. Copy fee: $.50 per page. Certification fee: $6.00. Fee payee: Superior Court. Personal checks accepted. Prepayment is required.

Sierra County

Superior Court PO Box 476 Courthouse Square, Downieville, CA 95936; 530-289-3698; Fax: 530-289-0205. Hours: 8AM-Noon, 1-5PM (PST). *Felony, Misdemeanor, Civil, Eviction, Small Claims, Probate.*

Civil Records: Access: Phone, fax, mail, in person. Both court and visitors may perform in person searches. Search fee: $1.75 per name per year. Required to search: name, years to search. Civil cases indexed by defendant, plaintiff. Civil records on computer from 1985, index books from 1852. **Criminal Records:** Access: Phone, fax, mail, in person. Both court and visitors may perform in person searches. Search fee: $1.75 per name per year. Required to search: name, years to search. Criminal records on computer from 1985, index books from 1852. **General Information:** No adoptions, juvenile, medical, probation or sealed records released. SASE required. Turnaround time 2-4 days. Copy fee: $1.00 per page. Certification fee: $6.00. Fee payee: Superior Court. Personal checks accepted. Prepayment is required. Fax notes: $1.00 per page.

Siskiyou County

Superior Court 311 4th St PO Box 1026, Yreka, CA 96097;; Civil phone:530-842-8180; Criminal phone:530-842-8180; Fax: 530-842-0164(Civ); 530-842-8178(Crim). Hours: 8AM-5PM (PST). *Felony, Misdemeanor, Civil, Probate.*

Civil Records: Access: Phone, mail, in person. Both court and visitors may perform in person searches. Search fee: $5.00 per name. Fee is per 10 years searched. Required to search: name, years to search. Civil cases indexed by defendant, plaintiff. Civil records on computer since 1991, archived and index book from 1900. **Criminal Records:** Access: Phone, mail, in person. Both court and visitors may perform in person searches. Search fee: $5.00 per name. Fee is per 10 years searched. Required to search: name, years to search. Criminal records on computer since 1991, archived and index book from 1900. **General Information:** No adoptions, juvenile, medical, probation or sealed records released. SASE required. Turnaround time 1 week. Copy fee: $.50 per page. Certification fee: $6.00. Fee payee: Siskiyou Superior Court. Personal checks accepted. Prepayment is required.

Superior Court 550 Main St, Weed, CA 96094; 530-938-2483; Civil phone:530-938-3897; Fax: 530-842-0109. Hours: 8AM-5PM (PST). *Misdemeanor, Civil Actions Under $25,000, Eviction, Small Claims.*

Note: This court holds misdemeanor records for Dorris/Tulelake branch

Civil Records: Access: Mail, in person. Only the court conducts in person searches; visitors may not. Search fee: $5.00 per name per year. Required to search: name, years to search. Civil cases indexed by defendant, plaintiff. Civil records on computer since 1995. Will only search back 7 years. **Criminal Records:** Access: Mail, in person. Only the court conducts in person

searches; visitors may not. Search fee: $5.00 per name per year. Required to search: name, years to search, DOB, SSN. Criminal records on computer since 1995, index books prior. Will only search back 7 years. **General Information:** No probation reports released. SASE required. Turnaround time 10 days. Copy fee: $.50 per page. Certification fee: $1.75. Fee payee: Siskiyou Superior Court. Personal checks accepted. Prepayment is required.

Dorris Branch - Superior Court

PO Box 828, Dorris, CA 96023; 530-397-3161; Fax: 530-397-3169. Hours: 8AM-Noon, 1-4PM (PST). *Civil Actions Under $25,000, Eviction, Small Claims.*

Note: All new misdemeanor cases are referred to Southeastern branch in Weed, CA. Only maintains a few criminal records for a year

Civil Records: Access: Phone, mail, in person. Only the court conducts in person searches; visitors may not. Search fee: $5.00 per name. Required to search: name, years to search. **General Information:** No probation reports released. SASE required. Turnaround time 1 week. Copy fee: $.50 per page. Certification fee: $6.00. Fee payee: Siskiyou Superior Court. Personal checks accepted. Prepayment is required.

Solano County

Solano Superior Court - Civil 600 Union Ave, Fairfield, CA 94533; 707-421-6479; Probate phone:707-421-6486; Fax: 707-421-7817. Hours: 8AM-4PM (PST). *Civil, Eviction, Probate.*

Note: The Northern Solano Municipal Court has been combined with the Superior Court

Civil Records: Access: Phone, mail, in person. Both court and visitors may perform in person searches. Search fee: $5.00 per name. Required to search: name, years to search. Civil cases indexed by defendant, plaintiff. Civil records on computer since 1992, microfiche since 1971, archived and index files since 1800s. Phone access limited to short searches. **General Information:** No sealed records released. SASE required. Turnaround time 2-3 days. Copy fee: $1.00 per page. Certification fee: $6.00. Fee payee: Solano County Courts. Personal checks accepted. Prepayment is required. Public access terminal is available.

Solano Superior Court - Criminal

530 Union Ave #200, Fairfield, CA 94533; 707-421-7440; 421-7834 Sup Court Records; Fax: 707-421-7439. Hours: 8AM-4PM (PST). *Felony, Misdemeanor.*

www.co.solano.ca.us/courts

Note: The Northern Solano Municipal Court has been combined with the Superior Court **Criminal Records:** Access: Mail, in person. Both court and visitors may perform in person searches. Search fee: $5.00 per name. Required to search: name, years to search; also helpful-DOB, SSN. Superior Court records on computer since 1992, microfiche since 1971; Municipal Court records on computer for past 10 years. **General Information:** No probation reports released. SASE required. Turnaround time 1-3 weeks. Copy fee: $5.00 for first page. Certification fee: $6.00. Fee payee: Solano Superior Court. Personal checks accepted. Prepayment is required.

Vallejo Branch - Superior Court

321 Tuolumne St, Vallejo, CA 94590;; Civil phone:707-553-5346; Criminal phone:707-553-5346; Fax: 707-553-5661. Hours: 8AM-4PM (PST). *Misdemeanor, Civil, Eviction, Small Claims.*

www.co.solano.ca.us/courts

Note: Includes Cities of Vallejo and Benicia and the unincorporated area adjacent thereto

Civil Records: Access: Mail, in person. Both court and visitors may perform in person searches. Search fee: $5.00 per name. Required to search: name, years to search. Civil cases indexed by defendant, plaintiff. Civil records on computer from 1991, index files from 1983. Records destroyed after 10 years. **Criminal Records:** Access: Mail, in person. Only the court conducts in person searches; visitors may not. Search fee: $5.00 per name. Required to search: name, years to search. Criminal records on computer from 1991, index files from 1983. Records destroyed after 10 years. **General Information:** No probation reports released. SASE required. Turnaround time 2 days. Copy fee: $1.00 per page. Certification fee: $6.00. Fee payee: Superior Court. Personal checks accepted. Credit cards accepted: Visa, AmEx. Prepayment is required.

Sonoma County

Superior Court - Criminal 600 Administration Dr, Room 105J, Santa Rosa, CA 95403-0281; 707-565-1100. Hours: 8AM-4PM (PST). *Felony, Misdemeanor, Probate.*

www.sonomasuperiorcourt.com

Civil Records: Access: Phone, mail, in person. Both court and visitors may perform in person searches. Search fee: $15.00 per hour. Required to search: name, years to search. Civil cases indexed by defendant, plaintiff. Civil records on computer from 1984, microfiche and index books from 1850 to 1984. Phone access limited to 2 names or cases per call. **Criminal Records:** Access: Phone, mail, in person. Both court and visitors may perform in person searches. Search fee: $15.00 per hour. Required to search: name, years to search; also helpful-DOB. Criminal Records on computer since 1984, microfich and index books 1850 to 1984. Misdemeanor records destroyed after 10 years. **General Information:** No adoptions, juvenile, medical, probation or sealed records released. SASE required. Turnaround time 2-3 weeks. Copy fee: $1.00 per page. 10 page limit. If more than 10 pages must wait 3-5 days. Certification fee: $6.00. Fee payee: Superior Court. Personal checks accepted. No out of state personal checks accepted. Prepayment is required. Public access terminal is available.

Superior Court - Civil Division 600 Administration Dr, Rm 107J, Santa Rosa, CA 95403; 707-565-1100. Hours: 8AM-4PM (PST). *Civil, Eviction, Small Claims.*

www.sonomasuperiorcourt.com

Note: Area Code to change to 627 after May, 2001.

Civil Records: Access: Mail, in person. Both court and visitors may perform in person searches. Search fee: $15.00 per hour. Minimum fee is $5.00. Required to search: name, years to search. Civil cases indexed by defendant, plaintiff. Civil records on computer back 15 years, index files prior. Records destroyed after 10 years. **General Information:** No probation reports or sealed records released. SASE required. Turnaround time 2 days - 2 weeks. Copy fee: $1.00 per page. Certification fee: $6.00. Fee payee: Superior Court. Personal checks accepted. Prepayment is required. Public access terminal is available.

Stanislaus County

Superior Court-Criminal 800 11 Street, Rm 140, PO Box 1098, Modesto, CA 95353; 209-558-

6000. Hours: 8AM-Noon, 1-4PM (PST). *Felony, Misdemeanor.*

www.co.stanislaus.ca.us/courts

Note: Physical address Zip Code is 95354 **Criminal Records:** Access: Mail, in person. Both court and visitors may perform in person searches. Search fee: $5.00 per name per year. Required to search: name, years to search. Criminal Records on microfiche since 1974, archived back to 1800s. **General Information:** No adoptions, juvenile, medical, probation or sealed records released. SASE required. Turnaround time 1-2 weeks. Copy fee: $.50 per page. Certification fee: $6.00. Fee payee: Superior Court Clerk. Personal checks accepted. Prepayment is required.

Modesto Division - Superior Court 1100 "I" St PO Box 828, Modesto, CA 95353; 209-558-6000; Fax: 209-525-4348. Hours: 8AM-Noon, 1-4PM. *Civil, Eviction, Small Claims.*

www.co.stanislaus.ca.us/courts

Note: Ceres Branch has been closed and records transferred here

Civil Records: Access: Mail, in person. Both court and visitors may perform in person searches. Search fee: $5.00 per name. Required to search: name, years to search. Civil cases indexed by defendant, plaintiff. Civil records on computer from 1991, in index files from 1983. Records destroyed after 10 years. **General Information:** No probation or juvenile records released. SASE required. Turnaround time 2-5 days. Copy fee: $.50 per page. Certification fee: $6.00. Fee payee: Superior Court. Personal checks accepted. Prepayment is required.

Sutter County

Superior Court - Civil Division 463 2nd St, Rm 211, Yuba City, CA 95991; 530-822-7352; Fax: 530-822-7192. Hours: 8AM-5PM (PST). *Civil, Eviction, Small Claims, Probate.*

Civil Records: Access: Mail, in person. Both court and visitors may perform in person searches. Search fee: $5.00 per name. Required to search: name, years to search. Civil cases indexed by defendant, plaintiff. Civil records in index books and archived from 1800s, computerized since 01/94. **General Information:** No adoptions, juvenile, medical, probation or sealed records released. SASE required. Turnaround time 1 week. Copy fee: $.50 per page. Certification fee: $6.00. Fee payee: Superior Court. Personal checks accepted. Prepayment is required. Public access terminal is available.

Superior Court - Criminal Division 446 2nd St, Yuba City, CA 95991; 530-822-7360; Fax: 530-822-7159. Hours: 8AM-5PM (PST). *Felony, Misdemeanor.* **Criminal Records:** Access: Fax, mail, in person. Both court and visitors may perform in person searches. Search fee: $5.00 per name. Required to search: name, years to search. Criminal records in index books and archived from 1800s, computerized since 1995. **General Information:** No police reports or probation records released. SASE required. Turnaround time 1 week. Copy fee: $.50 per page. Certification fee: $6.00. Fee payee: Sutter Superior Court. Personal checks accepted. Prepayment is required. Public access terminal is available.

Tehama County

Superior Court PO Box 310, Red Bluff, CA 96080; 530-527-6441. Hours: 9AM-4PM (PST). *Civil, Small Claims, Eviction, Probate.*

Civil Records: Access: Mail, in person. Both court and visitors may perform in person searches. Search fee: $2.50 per name. Fee is $5.00 if years before 1991 are requested. Required to search: name, years to search. Civil cases indexed by defendant, plaintiff. Civil records on computer from January, 1991, archived and index books from 1900s. **General Information:** No adoptions, juvenile, mental, probation or sealed records released. SASE required. Turnaround time same day. Copy fee: $.50 per page. Certification fee: $6.00. Fee payee: Tehama County Superior Court Clerk. Personal checks accepted. Prepayment is required.

Superior Court - Criminal Division 445 Pine St PO Box 1170, Red Bluff, CA 96080; 530-527-3563; Criminal phone:; Fax: 530-527-0956. Hours: 8AM-5PM (PST). *Felony, Misdemeanor.* **Criminal Records:** Access: Mail, in person. Both court and visitors may perform in person searches. Search fee: $5.00 per name. Required to search: name, years to search; also helpful-DOB. Criminal records on computer from 1991, index cards prior. Will only search back 7 years. **General Information:** No probation reports released. SASE required. Turnaround time within 1 week. Copy fee: $.50 per page. Certification fee: $6.00. Fee payee: Superior Court. Personal checks accepted. Prepayment is required.

Corning Branch - Superior Court 720 Hoag St, Corning, CA 96021; 530-824-4601; Fax: 530-824-6457. Hours: 8AM-4PM (PST). *Misdemeanor, Civil Actions Under $25,000, Eviction, Small Claims.*

Civil Records: Access: Mail, in person. Search fee: $5.00 per name. Required to search: name, years to search. Civil cases indexed by defendant, plaintiff. Civil records on index cards. Will only search back 7 years. **Criminal Records:** Access: Mail, in person. Both court and visitors may perform in person searches. Search fee: $5.00 per name. Required to search: name, years to search; also helpful-DOB. Criminal records on computer from 1990, index cards prior. Will only search back 7 years. **General Information:** No probation reports released. SASE required. Turnaround time 1 week. Copy fee: $.50 per page. Certification fee: $6.00. Fee payee: Tehama Superior Court. Personal checks accepted. Prepayment is required.

Trinity County

Superior Court 101 Court St PO Box 1258, Weaverville, CA 96093; 530-623-1208; Fax: 530-623-3762. Hours: 9AM-4PM (PST). *Felony, Misdemeanor, Civil, Eviction, Small Claims, Probate.*

Civil Records: Access: Mail, in person. Both court and visitors may perform in person searches. Search fee: $5.00 per name per year. Required to search: name, years to search. Civil cases indexed by defendant, plaintiff. Civil records on microfiche, archived and index files from 1900s. **Criminal Records:** Access: Mail, in person. Both court and visitors may perform in person searches. Search fee: $5.00 per name per year. Required to search: name, years to search. Criminal records on microfiche, archived and index files from 1900s. **General Information:** No adoptions, juvenile, medical, probation or sealed records released. SASE required. Turnaround time 1 week. Copy fee: $.50 per page. Certification fee: $6.00. Fee payee: Superior Court. Personal checks accepted. Prepayment is required.

Tulare County

Superior Court Courthouse, 221 S Mooney, Visalia, CA 93291;; Civil phone:559-737-4488; Criminal phone:559-737-4488; Fax: 559-737-4547. Hours: 8AM-5PM (PST). *Felony, Civil, Eviction, Small Claims, Probate.*

Note: This court has records from Exeter, Woodlake, Farmersville, Goshen and Three Rivers. Address criminal record requests to Room 124 and civil to Room 201

Civil Records: Access: Mail, in person. Both court and visitors may perform in person searches. Search fee: $5.00 per name. Required to search: name, years to search. Civil cases indexed by defendant, plaintiff. Civil records on computer from 02/86, microfiche and index books from 1800s. **Criminal Records:** Access: Mail, in person. Both court and visitors may perform in person searches. Search fee: $5.00 per name. Required to search: name, years to search. Criminal records on computer from 02/86, microfiche and index books from 1800s. **General Information:** No adoptions, juvenile, mental, probation reports or sealed records released. SASE required. Turnaround time 1 week. Copy fee: $1.00 per page. Certification fee: $6.00. Fee payee: Tulare County Superior Court. Personal checks accepted. Prepayment is required. Public access terminal is available.

Dinuba Division - Superior Court 920 S College, Dinuba, CA 93618; 559-591-5815. Hours: 8AM-4PM (PST). *Misdemeanor, Civil Actions Under $25,000, Eviction, Small Claims.*

Note: Includes Dinuba, Cutler, Orosi, Seville, Traver, London, Delf, Orange Cove

Civil Records: Access: Mail, in person. Only the court conducts in person searches; visitors may not. Search fee: $5.00 per name. Required to search: name, years to search. Civil cases indexed by defendant, plaintiff. Civil records on computer from 1993, index files from 1983. Records destroyed after 10 years. **Criminal Records:** Access: Mail, in person. Only the court conducts in person searches; visitors may not. Search fee: $5.00 per name. Required to search: name, years to search, DOB. Criminal records on computer from 1993, index files from 1983. Records destroyed after 10 years. **General Information:** No probation reports released. SASE required. Turnaround time 2-3 days. Copy fee: $.50 per page. Certification fee: $6.00. Fee payee: Dinuba Superior Court. In-state checks accepted. Prepayment is required.

Porterville Division - Superior Court 87 E Morton Ave, Porterville, CA 93257; 559-782-4710; Fax: 559-782-4805. Hours: 8AM-4PM (PST). *Misdemeanor, Civil Actions Under $25,000, Eviction, Small Claims.*

Note: Includes Porterville, Springville, Camp Nelson, Johnsondale, Terra Bella, Ducor, Richgrove, Poplar, Lindsey, Strathmore and surrounding areas

Civil Records: Access: Mail, in person. Both court and visitors may perform in person searches. Search fee: $5.00 per name. also is per case. Required to search: name, years to search. Civil cases indexed by defendant, plaintiff. Civil records on computer from February, 1994, index book prior. Records destroyed after 10 years. **Criminal Records:** Access: Mail, in person. Both court and visitors may perform in person searches. Search fee: $5.00 per name. also is per case. Required to search: name, years to search; also helpful-DOB, SSN. Criminal records on computer from

February, 1994, index book prior. Records destroyed after 10 years. **General Information:** No probation reports released. SASE required. Turnaround time 2 days. Copy fee: $.50 per page. Certification fee: $6.00. Fee payee: Porterville Superior Court. Personal checks accepted. Prepayment is required. Public access terminal available.

Tulare/Pixley Division - Superior Court 425 E Kern St PO Box 1136, Tulare, CA 93275; 559-685-2556; Fax: 559-685-2663. Hours: 8AM-4PM (PST). *Misdemeanor, Civil Actions Under $25,000, Eviction, Small Claims.*

Note: Includes Tulare, Pixley, Tipton, Earlimart, Alpaugh, Allensworth, Woodville, Waukena and surrounding areas

Civil Records: Access: Mail, in person. Both court and visitors may perform in person searches. Search fee: $5.00 per name. Required to search: name, years to search. Civil cases indexed by defendant, plaintiff. Civil records in index books. Records destroyed after 10 years. **Criminal Records:** Access: Mail, in person. Both court and visitors may perform in person searches. Search fee: $5.00 per name. Required to search: name, years to search, DOB; also helpful-address, SSN. Criminal records in index books. Records destroyed after 10 years. **General Information:** No probation reports released. SASE required. Turnaround time 2 days. Copy fee: $.50 per page. Certification fee: $6.00. Fee payee: Superior Court. Personal checks accepted. Prepayment is required.

Tuolumne County

Superior Court 41 W Yaney, Sonora, CA 95370; 209-533-5555; Criminal phone:; Fax: 209-533-5618. Hours: 8AM-4:30PM (PST). *Felony, Misdemeanor, Civil, Probate.*

Civil Records: Access: Mail, in person. Both court and visitors may perform in person searches. Search fee: $5.00 per name. Fee is per record. Required to search: name, years to search. Civil cases indexed by defendant, plaintiff. Civil records on computer from January, 1994, microfiche and archived from 1900s, index files from 1800s. **Criminal Records:** Access: Mail, in person. Both court and visitors may perform in person searches. Search fee: $5.00 per name. Fee is per record. Required to search: name, years to search. Criminal records on computer from January, 1994, microfiche and archived from 1900s, index files from 1800s. **General Information:** No adoptions, juvenile, medical, probation or sealed records released. SASE required. Turnaround time 1 week. Copy fee: $.50 per page. Certification fee: $6.00. Fee payee: Superior Court Clerk. Personal checks accepted. Out of state checks not accepted. Prepayment is required.

Sonora Branch - Superior Court 60 N Washington St, Sonora, CA 95370; 209-533-5671; Fax: 209-533-5581. Hours: 8AM-3PM (PST). *Felony, Misdemeanor, Civil, Eviction, Small Claims.*

Civil Records: Access: Fax, mail, in person. Both court and visitors may perform in person searches. Search fee: $5.00 per name. Required to search: name, years to search. **Criminal Records:** Access: Mail, in person. Both court and visitors may perform in person searches. Search fee: $5.00 per name. Required to search: name, years to search, DOB. Criminal records on computer from 1990, index files prior. Will only search back 7 years. Records destroyed after 10 years. **General Information:** No sealed records released. Most records are public. SASE required. Turnaround

time 1 week. Copy fee: $.50 per page. Certification fee: $6.00. Fee payee: Tuolomne County Superior Court. Personal checks accepted. Prepayment is required. Public access terminal is available. Note: Will only fax to public agencies.

Ventura County

Ventura Superior Court 800 S Victoria Ave PO Box 6489, Ventura, CA 93006-6489; 805-662-6620; Fax: 805-650-4032. Hours: 8AM-5PM (PST). *Felony, Misdemeanor, Civil, Eviction, Small Claims, Probate.*

www.ventura.org/courts

Civil Records: Access: Phone, mail, online, in person. Both court and visitors may perform in person searches. Search fee: $5.00 per name. Required to search: name, years to search. Civil cases indexed by defendant, plaintiff. Civil records on computer 5 years back, microfiche prior. Free Internet access to records at www.efile-it.com/ventura. **Criminal Records:** Access: Phone, mail, in person. Both court and visitors may perform in person searches. Search fee: $5.00 per name. Required to search: name, years to search, DOB. Criminal records on computer back to 1989. **General Information:** No adoptions, mental health, paternity actions, juvenile, medical, probation or sealed records released. SASE required. Turnaround time 5-10 days. Copy fee: $.50 per page. Certification fee: $6.00. Fee payee: Superior Court. Personal checks accepted. Credit cards accepted: Visa, AmEx. Additional fee charged. Prepayment is required. Public access terminal is available.

East County Superior Court PO Box 1200, Simi Valley, CA 93062-1200; 805-582-8080. Hours: 8AM-5PM (PST). *Felony, Misdemeanor, Civil, Eviction, Small Claims, Probate.*

www.ventura.org/courts

Civil Records: Access: Phone, mail, online, in person. Both court and visitors may perform in person searches. Search fee: $5.00 per name. Fee is per court. Required to search: name, years to search. Free Internet access to records at www.efile-it.com/ventura. **Criminal Records:** Access: Phone, mail, in person. Both court and visitors may perform in person searches. Search fee: $5.00 per name. Fee is per court. Required to search: name, years to search, DOB. Same record keeping as civil. **General Information:** No adoptions, mental health, paternity actions, juvenile, medical, probation or sealed records released. SASE required. Turnaround time 5 days. Copy fee: $.50 per page. Certification fee: $6.00. Fee payee: Ventura County Superior Courts. Personal checks accepted. Credit cards accepted: Visa, Mastercard, Discover, AmEx. Additional fee charged. Prepayment is required. Public access terminal is available.

Yolo County

Superior Court 725 Court St, Rm 308, Woodland, CA 95695; 530-666-8598; Civil phone:530-666-8170; Criminal phone:530-666-8170; Fax: 530-666-8576. Hours: 8AM-Noon, 1-4PM (PST). *Felony, Misdemeanor, Civil, Eviction, Small Claims, Probate.*

www.yolocourts.com

Note: Address civil requests to Room 103 and criminal to Room 111

Civil Records: Access: Phone, mail, in person. Both court and visitors may perform in person searches. Search fee: $5.00 per name. Required to search: name, years to search. Civil cases indexed by defendant, plaintiff. Civil records on computer from 1995, microfiche, archived and index files from 1800s. **Criminal Records:** Access: Phone, mail, in person. Both court and visitors may perform in person searches. Search fee: $5.00 per name. Required to search: name, years to search; also helpful-DOB. Criminal records on computer from 1995, microfiche, archived and index files from 1800s. **General Information:** No adoptions, juvenile, medical, probation or sealed records released. SASE required. Turnaround time 2 weeks. Copy fee: $1.00 per page. Certification fee: $6.00. Fee payee: Yolo Superior Court. Personal checks accepted. Credit cards accepted: Visa, Mastercard. Prepayment is required.

Yuba County

Yuba County Superior Court 215 5th St, Marysville, CA 95901; 530-749-7600; Fax: 530-634-7681. Hours: 8:30AM-4:30PM. *Felony, Misdemeanor, Civil, Small Claims, Probate.*

Civil Records: Access: Mail, in person. Both court and visitors may perform in person searches. Search fee: $5.00 per name. Required to search: name, years to search. Civil cases indexed by defendant, plaintiff. Civil records on computer from 1992, index books through 1962, archives and index files from 1854. **Criminal Records:** Access: Mail, in person. Both court and visitors may perform in person searches. Search fee: $5.00 per name. Required to search: name, years to search. Criminal records on computer from 1992, index books through 1962, archives and index files from 1854. **General Information:** No adoptions, paternity, juvenile, medical, probation or sealed records released. SASE required. Turnaround time 1-4 weeks. Copy fee: $1.00 per page. Certification fee: $6.00. Fee payee: Yuba County Superior Court. Personal checks accepted. Prepayment is required. Public access terminal is available.

Marysville Civil Limited Superior Court 215 5th St, Marysville, CA 95901; 530-749-7600; Fax: 530-634-7687. Hours: 8:30AM-4:30PM (PST). *Civil Actions Under $25,000, Eviction, Small Claims.*

Civil Records: Access: Fax, mail, in person. Only the court conducts in person searches; visitors may not. Search fee: $5.00 per name. Required to search: name, years to search. Civil cases indexed by defendant, plaintiff. Civil records on computer through 1992, index books prior. Records destroyed after 10 years. **General Information:** No labor commissioner judgment, juvenile, or judge's records released. SASE required. Turnaround time 2 days. Copy fee: $1.00 per page. Certification fee: $6.00. Fee payee: Yuba County Superior Court. Personal checks accepted. Prepayment is required. Fax notes: $21.00 for first page, $1.00 each addl.

ORGANIZATION	58 counties, 58 recording offices. The recording officer is County Recorder. Recordings are usually located in a Grantor/Grantee or General index. The entire state is in the Pacific Time Zone (PST).
REAL ESTATE RECORDS	Most counties do **not** perform real estate searches. Copy fees and certification fees vary.
UCC RECORDS	Financing statements are filed at the state level, except for consumer goods, crops, and real estate related collateral, which are filed only with the County Recorder. All counties will perform UCC searches. Use search request form UCC-11. Search fees are usually $15.00 per debtor name. Copy costs vary.
TAX LIEN RECORDS	Federal and state tax liens on personal property of businesses are filed with the Secretary of State. Other federal and state tax liens are filed with the County Recorder. Some counties will perform separate tax lien searches. Fees vary for this type of search.
OTHER LIENS	Judgment (Note—Many judgments are also filed with the Secretary of State), child support, mechanics.

Alameda County

County Recorder, 1225 Fallon Street, Courthouse, Room 100, Oakland, CA 94612. 510-272-6363. Fax: 510-272-6382.

Alpine County

County Recorder, P.O. Box 217, Markleeville, CA 96120. 530-694-2286. Fax: 530-694-2491.

Amador County

County Recorder, 500 Argonaut Lane, Jackson, CA 95642. 209-223-6468.

Butte County

County Recorder, 25 County Center Drive, Oroville, CA 95965-3375. 530-538-7691. Fax: 530-538-7975.

Calaveras County

County Recorder, Government Center, 891 Mountain Ranch Rd, San Andreas, CA 95249. 209-754-6372.

Colusa County

County Recorder, 546 Jay Street, Colusa, CA 95932. www.colusanet.com/colusaclerk. 530-458-0500. Fax: 530-458-0512.

Contra Costa County

County Recorder, P.O. Box 350, Martinez, CA 94553. 925-646-2360.

Del Norte County

County Recorder, 457 F Street, Crescent City, CA 95531. 707-464-7216.

El Dorado County

County Recorder, 360 Fair Lane, Placerville, CA 95667-4197. 530-621-5490. Fax: 530-621-2147.

Fresno County

County Recorder, P.O. Box 766, Fresno, CA 93712. 559-488-3471. Fax: 559-488-6774.

Glenn County

County Recorder, 526 West Sycamore Street, Willows, CA 95988. 530-934-6412. Fax: 530-934-6305.

Humboldt County

County Recorder, 825 Fifth Street, Room 108, Eureka, CA 95501. 707-445-7593. Fax: 707-445-7324.

Imperial County

County Recorder, 940 Main Street, Room 202, El Centro, CA 92243-2865. 760-339-4272.

Inyo County

County Recorder, P.O. Box F, Independence, CA 93526. 760-878-0222. Fax: 760-872-2712.

Kern County

County Recorder, 1655 Chester Avenue, Hall of Records, Bakersfield, CA 93301. 661-868-6400. Fax: 661-868-6401.
www.co.kern.ca.us/assessor/search.htm
Online Access: Assessor. Records on the County of Kern Online Assessor database are available free on the Internet.

Kings County

County Recorder, 1400 West Lacey Blvd., Hanford, CA 93230. 559-582-3211x2475. Fax: 559-582-6639.

Lake County

County Recorder, 255 North Forbes, Room 223, Lakeport, CA 95453. 707-263-2293. Fax: 707-263-3703.

Lassen County

County Recorder, 220 S. Lassen Street, Suite 5, Susanville, CA 96130. 530-251-8234. Fax: 530-257-3480.

Los Angeles County

County Recorder, P.O. Box 53115, Los Angeles, CA 90053-0115. 562-462-2125.
Online Access: Assessor. The PDB Inquiry System is a dial-up service with a $100.00 monthly fee plus $1.00 per inquiry, also a $75 sign-up fee for 3-year dial-up. Usage fee is $6.50 per hour or 11 cents per minute. Contract must be approved. Send registration request letter, stating reason for request, to Data Systems Suerpvisor II Tech Admin, LA County Assessor's office, 500 W Temple St Rm 293, Los Angeles, CA 90012-2770. Further information: 213-974-3237 More information online at http://assessor.co.la.ca.us/html/online.htm

Madera County

County Recorder, 209 West Yosemite, Madera, CA 93637. 559-675-7724. Fax: 559-675-7870.

Marin County

County Recorder, 3501 Civic Center Dr., Room 234, San Rafael, CA 94903. 415-499-6092. Fax: 415-499-7893.

Mariposa County

County Recorder, P.O. Box 35, Mariposa, CA 95338. 209-966-5719.

Mendocino County

County Recorder, 501 Low Gap Rd. Room 1020, Ukiah, CA 95482. 707-463-4376. Fax: 707-463-4257. www.pacificsites.com/~mendocty/depts/clrkrec/recindex.htm

Merced County

County Recorder, 2222 M Street, Merced, CA 95340. 209-385-7627.

Modoc County

County Recorder, 204 Court Street, Alturas, CA 96101. 530-233-6205. Fax: 530-233-6666.

Mono County

County Recorder, P.O. Box 237, Bridgeport, CA 93517. 760-932-5240. Fax: 760-932-7035.

Monterey County

County Recorder, P.O. Box 29, Salinas, CA 93902. 831-755-5041. Fax: 831-755-5064.

Napa County

County Recorder, P.O. Box 298, Napa, CA 94559-0298. 707-253-4246. Fax: 707-259-8149.

Nevada County

County Recorder, 950 Maidu Avenue, Nevada City, CA 95959. 530-265-1221. Fax: 530-265-1497.

Orange County

County Recorder, P.O. Box 238, Santa Ana, CA 92702-0238. 714-834-2500. Fax: 714-834-2675.

Placer County

County Recorder, 2954 Richardson Dr., Auburn, CA 95603. 530-886-5600. Fax: 530-886-5687.

Plumas County

County Recorder, 520 Main Street, Room 102, Quincy, CA 95971. 530-283-6218. Fax: 530-283-6415.

Riverside County

County Recorder, P.O. Box 751, Riverside, CA 92502-0751. 909-486-7000. Fax: 909-486-7007.

Sacramento County

County Clerk and Recorder, P.O. Box 839, Sacramento, CA 95812-0839. 916-874-6334.

San Benito County

County Recorder, 440 Fifth Street, Room 206, Hollister, CA 95023. 831-636-4046. Fax: 831-636-2939.

San Bernardino County

County Recorder, 222 W. Hospitality Ln., 1st Floor, San Bernardino, CA 92415-0022. 909-387-8306. Fax: 909-386-8940.
www.co.san-bernardino.ca.us
Online Access: Recorder, Assessor, Fictitious Names. Records on the San Bernardino County Assessor database are available free on the Internet at www.co.san-bernardino.ca.us/tax/trsearch.asp. For automated call distribution, call 909-387-8306; for fictitious names information, call 909-386-8970.

San Diego County

County Recorder, P.O. Box 121750, San Diego, CA 92112. 619-237-0502. Fax: 619-557-4155.
www.co.san-diego.ca.us
Online Access: Assessor, Fictitious Names. Records on the San Diego County Assessor/Recorder/County Clerk Online Services site are available free on the Internet at www.co.san-diego.ca.us/cnty/cntydepts/general/assessor/online.html including fictitious business names, indexes, maps, property info Grantee/grantor index search by name for individual record data is free at http://arcc.co.san-diego.ca.us/services/grantorgrantee. Bulk data downloads are also available and require pre-payment or credit card payment.

San Francisco County

County Recorder, City Hall, Room 190, 1 Dr. Carlton E. Goodlet Pl., San Francisco, CA 94102. 415-554-4176. Fax: 415-554-4179.

San Joaquin County

County Recorder, P.O. Box 1968, Stockton, CA 95201. 209-468-3939. Fax: 209-468-8040.

San Luis Obispo County

County Recorder, 1144 Monterey St., Suite C, San Luis Obispo, CA 93408. 805-781-5080.

San Mateo County

County Recorder, 400 County Center, 6th Floor, Redwood City, CA 94063. 650-363-4213. Fax: 650-363-4843.
www.co.sanmateo.ca.us
Online Access: Property Tax, Fictious Name. Records on the San Mateo County Property Taxes database are available free on the Internet at www.co.sanmateo.ca.us/taxcollector/online/index.htm. Search by street name, number, city or parcel ID number Records on the Fictitious Business Name Center are available free on the Internet at www.care.co.sanmateo.ca.us/fbnc. Search by name.

Santa Barbara County

County Recorder, P.O. Box 159, Santa Barbara, CA 93102-0159. 805-568-2250. Fax: 805-568-2266. www.sb-democracy.com/ Online access to assessor parcel maps to be available 2001. Database will be free to view, but only subscribers will be able to download.

Santa Clara County

County Recorder, County Government Center, East Wing, 70 West Hedding St., San Jose, CA 95110. 408-299-2481. Fax: 408-280-1768.

Santa Cruz County

County Recorder, 701 Ocean Street, Room 230, Santa Cruz, CA 95060. 831-454-2800. Fax: 831-454-2445.

Shasta County

County Recorder, 1500 Court St., Room 102, Redding, CA 96001. 530-225-5671. Fax: 530-225-5673.
www.ci.redding.ca.us
Online Access: Assessor. Records on the City of Redding Parcel Search By Parcel Number Server are available free on the Internet. At the main site, look under "Online Services" to find "Property Lookup".

Sierra County

County Recorder, Drawer D, Downieville, CA 95936. 530-289-3295. Fax: 530-289-3300.

Siskiyou County

County Recorder, P.O. Box 8, Yreka, CA 96097. 530-842-8065. Fax: 530-842-8077.

Solano County

County Recorder, Old Courthouse, 580 Texas St., 1st Floor, Fairfield, CA 94533. 707-421-6290.

Sonoma County

County Recorder, P.O. Box 6124, Santa Rosa, CA 95406-0124. 707-527-2651. Fax: 707-527-3905.

Stanislaus County

County Recorder, P.O. Box 1008, Modesto, CA 95353. 209-525-5260. Fax: 209-525-5207.

Sutter County

County Recorder, P.O. Box 1555, Yuba City, CA 95992-1555. 530-822-7134. Fax: 530-822-7214.

Tehama County

County Recorder, P.O. Box 250, Red Bluff, CA 96080. 530-527-3350. Fax: 530-527-1140.

Trinity County

County Recorder, P.O. Box 1258, Weaverville, CA 96093-1258. 530-623-1215. Fax: 530-623-3762.

Tulare County

County Recorder, County Civic Center, Room 103, 221 S. Mooney Blvd., Visalia, CA 93291-4593. 559-733-6377.

Tuolumne County

County Recorder, 2 South Green Street, County Administration Center, Sonora, CA 95370. 209-533-5531. Fax: 209-533-5613.

Ventura County

County Recorder, 800 South Victoria Avenue, Ventura, CA 93009. 805-654-2292. Fax: 805-654-2392. www.ventura.org/assessor/index.html

Yolo County

County Recorder, P.O. Box 1130, Woodland, CA 95776-1130. 530-666-8130. Fax: 530-666-8109.

Yuba County

County Recorder, 935 14th Street, Marysville, CA 95901. 530-741-6547. Fax: 530-741-6285.

Searching: Handicap and disabled vet plate data are not released. To obtain vehicle or ownership information, the requester's driver license number, and Form DR 2489 are required. For title and lien records, use Form DR 2539.

Access by: mail, in person.

Fee & Payment: The fee for searches is $2.20 per record. Fee payee: Department of Revenue. Prepayment required. Personal checks accepted. No credit cards accepted.

Mail search: Turnaround time: 24 hours. A self addressed stamped envelope is requested.

In person search: Turnaround time is while you wait.

Other access: Bulk requests of vehicle information on magnetic tape, computer paper, and on microfiche are available. Direct inquires to the Data Services Section, Motor Vehicle Extractions, at the address listed above.

Boat & Vessel Ownership
Boat & Vessel Registration

Colorado State Parks, Registration, 13787 S Highway 85, Littleton, CO 80125; 303-791-1920, 303-470-0782 (Fax), 8AM-5PM.

www.dnr.state.co.us/parks

Note: Liens must be searched at the Secretary of State.

Indexing & Storage: Records are available for the past 5 years. Older records are available on microfiche. All sail and motorized vessels must be registered.

Searching: To search, submit the registration # or serial #, DOB and a Release of Registration Records Form must be completed and signed. The following data is not released: residence addresses.

Access by: mail, fax, in person.

Fee & Payment: There is a $2.00 charge per page. Fee payee: Colorado State Parks. Prepayment required. Personal checks accepted. No credit cards accepted.

Mail search: Turnaround time: 1 week. No self addressed stamped envelope is required.

Fax search: Turnaround time varies. Results are faxed or mailed back.

In person search: Searching is available in person.

Other access: Lists are available without addresses. The fee is $10.00 plus $.05 per record. It can take as long as 2 months to process.

Legislation-Current/Pending
Legislation-Passed

Colorado General Assembly, State Capitol, 200 E Colfax Ave, Denver, CO 80203-1784; 303-866-2316 (Senate), 303-866-3055 (Bill Data (if in session)), 303-866-2055 (Archives), 303-866-2904 (House), 8AM-4:30PM.

www.state.co.us/gov_dir/stateleg.html

Note: The House is room 271, the Senate room 248. The legislative Council Library can be reached at 303-866-4011.

Indexing & Storage: Records are available from 1993-present on computer and from 1967-1992 on microfiche. Records are indexed on inhouse computer, microfiche.

Searching: Include the following in your request-bill number, year.

Access by: mail, phone, in person, online.

Fee & Payment: There is no fee for searching the current year. Prior years or voluminous requests will require a fee determined on extent of request. Fee payee: State of Colorado. Personal checks accepted. No credit cards accepted.

Mail search: Turnaround time: same day if possible. Mail searches are done only if in-depth research is not required. No self addressed stamped envelope is required. No fee for mail request.

Phone search: No fee for telephone request. Only general information is provided over the phone. There is no fee.

In person search: No fee for request.

Online search: The web site gives access to bills, status, journals from the last two sessions, and much more.

Voter Registration

Department of State, Elections Department, 1560 Broadway #200, Denver, CO 80202; 303-894-2680, 303-894-7732 (Fax), 8:30AM-5PM.

www.state.co.us/gov_dir/sos

Indexing & Storage: Records are available for the current year only.

Searching: Voters may request not to have their information released. Provide name and address or DOB to search. The following data is not released: Social Security Numbers.

Access by: mail, fax, in person.

Fee & Payment: The fee is $.50 per name. Fee payee: Department of State. Prepayment required. No credit cards accepted.

Mail search: Turnaround time: 2-3 days. A self addressed stamped envelope is requested.

Fax search: Same criteria as mail searching.

In person search: Searching is available in person.

Other access: The entire database is available on tape or CD-ROM. The cost is $900. No customization is available.

GED Certificates

Colorado Dept of Education, GED Testing, 201 E Colfax Ave Rm 100, Denver, CO 80203; 303-866-6613.

www.colosys.net/click/ONLINE.html

Searching: All written requests must have a yes or no answer to the following question in the upper right hand corner of the request: Did the person who received the GED ever attend a Colorado public school (as in elementary or high school)? All of the following are required to search: a signed release, name, date/year of test, date of birth, Social Security Number, and location of testing.

Access by: mail, in person.

Fee & Payment: The search fee $2.00 per transcript. Fee payee: GED Testing. Prepayment required. Personal checks accepted. No credit cards accepted.

Mail search: Turnaround time: 7 days. No self addressed stamped envelope is required.

In person search: Turnaround time is 24 hours.

Hunting License Information
Fishing License Information
Access to Records is Restricted

Department of Natural Resources, Wildlife Division, 6060 Broadway, Denver, CO 80216; 303-291-7380 (Hunting Information), 303-291-7440 (Fishing Information), 303-294-0874 (Fax), 8AM-5PM.

Note: The state attorney general has decided that no information can be given to the public. It is only available to law enforcement officials or to the licensed individual.

Licenses Searchable Online

Acupuncturist #14	www.dora.state.co.us/real/plsql/ARMS_Search.Disclaimer_Page
Architect #15	www.dora.state.co.us/real/plsql/ARMS_Search.Disclaimer_Page
Architect Firms #15	www.dora.state.co.us/real/plsql/ARMS_Search.Disclaimer_Page
Audiologist #14	www.dora.state.co.us/audiologists
Barber #16	www.dora.state.co.us/real/plsql/ARMS_Search.Set_Up
Chiropractor #17	www.dora.state.co.us/real/plsql/ARMS_Search.Disclaimer_Page
Cosmetician #16	www.dora.state.co.us/real/plsql/ARMS_Search.Set_Up
Cosmetologist #16	www.dora.state.co.us/real/plsql/ARMS_Search.Set_Up
Credit Union #09	www.dora.state.co.us/financial-services/homeregu.html
Dental Hygienist #18	www.dora.state.co.us:81/real/owa/ARMS_Search.Disclaimer_Page
Dentist #18	www.dora.state.co.us:81/real/owa/ARMS_Search.Disclaimer_Page
Electrical Contractor #41	www.dora.state.co.us:81/real/owa/ARMS_Search.Disclaimer_Page
Electrician-Journeyman #41	www.dora.state.co.us:81/real/owa/ARMS_Search.Disclaimer_Page
Electrician-Master #41	www.dora.state.co.us:81/real/owa/ARMS_Search.Disclaimer_Page
Engineer #19	www.dora.state.co.us/real/plsql/ARMS_Search.Disclaimer_Page
Engineer-in-Training (Engineer Intern) #19	www.dora.state.co.us/real/plsql/ARMS_Search.Disclaimer_Page
Family Therapist #20	www.dora.state.co.us/real/plsql/ARMS_Search.Disclaimer_Page
Land Surveyor #19	www.dora.state.co.us/real/plsql/ARMS_Search.Disclaimer_Page
Land Surveyor Intern #19	www.dora.state.co.us/real/plsql/ARMS_Search.Disclaimer_Page
Lobbyist #37	www.sos.state.co.us/pubs/divinfo.html#Professional
Manicurist #16	www.dora.state.co.us/real/plsql/ARMS_Search.Set_Up
Manufactured Housing Dealer #22	www.state.co.us/gov_dir/loc_affairs_dir/dealers.htm
Marriage Therapist #20	www.dora.state.co.us/real/plsql/ARMS_Search.Disclaimer_Page
Medical Doctor #21	www.dora.state.co.us:81/real/owa/ARMS_Search.Disclaimer_Page
Midwife #28	www.dora.state.co.us/real/plsql/ARMS_Search.Disclaimer_Page
Nurse #01	www.dora.state.co.us:81/real/owa/ARMS_Search.Disclaimer_Page
Nurses' Aide #01	www.dora.state.co.us:81/real/owa/ARMS_Search.Disclaimer_Page
Nursing Care Facility #23	www.hfd.cdphe.state.co.us/criter.asp
Nursing Home Administrator #23	www.dora.state.co.us:81/real/owa/ARMS_Search.Disclaimer_Page
Optometrist #33	www.dora.state.co.us/real/plsql/arms_search.disclaimer_page
Outfitter #24	www.dora.state.co.us/real/plsql/ARMS_Search.Set_Up
Pharmacist #26	www.dora.state.co.us/real/plsql/ARMS_Search.Disclaimer_Page
Pharmacy #26	www.dora.state.co.us:81/real/owa/ARMS_Search.Set_Up
Pharmacy Intern #26	www.dora.state.co.us:81/real/owa/ARMS_Search.Set_Up
Physical Therapist #32	www.dora.state.co.us/real/plsql/ARMS_Search.Disclaimer_Page
Plumber Journeyman #35	www.dora.state.co.us:81/real/owa/ARMS_Search.Disclaimer_Page
Plumber, Master #35	www.dora.state.co.us:81/real/owa/ARMS_Search.Disclaimer_Page
Plumber-Residential #35	www.dora.state.co.us:81/real/owa/ARMS_Search.Disclaimer_Page
Podiatrist #27	www.dora.state.co.us/real/plsql/ARMS_Search.Disclaimer_Page
Professional Counselor #20	www.dora.state.co.us/real/plsql/ARMS_Search.Disclaimer_Page
Psychologist #20	www.dora.state.co.us/real/plsql/ARMS_Search.Disclaimer_Page
Public Accountant-CPA #13	www.dora.state.co.us/real/plsql/ARMS_Search.Disclaimer_Page
Real Estate Broker #12	www.dora.state.co.us/real/plsql/indiv_home?type=IND
Real Estate Salesperson #12	www.dora.state.co.us/real/plsql/indiv_home?type=IND
River Outfitter #38	www.dora.state.co.us/real/plsql/ARMS_Search.Disclaimer_Page
Savings & Loan Association #09	www.dora.state.co.us/financial-services/homeregu.html
Securities Broker #34	http://pdpi.nasdr.com/pdpi/disclaimer_frame.htm
Securities Dealer #34	http://pdpi.nasdr.com/pdpi/disclaimer_frame.htm
Social Worker #20	www.dora.state.co.us/real/plsql/ARMS_Search.Disclaimer_Page
Stock Broker #34	http://pdpi.nasdr.com/pdpi/disclaimer_frame.htm
Veterinarian #31	www.dora.state.co.us/real/plsql/ARMS_Search.Disclaimer_Page
Veterinary Student #31	www.dora.state.co.us/real/plsql/ARMS_Search.Disclaimer_Page

Licensing Quick Finder

Acupuncturist #14 303-894-2464	Asbestos Supervisor #05 303-692-3158	Bulk Milk Hauler #06 303-692-3643
Architect #15 303-894-7441	Asbestos Worker #05 303-692-3158	Child Care Facility #29 800-799-5876
Architect Firms #15 303-894-7441	Attorney #04 303-893-8096	Child Health Associate #21 303-894-7690
Artificial Inseminator #31 303-894-7755	Audiologist #14 303-894-2464	Chiropractor #17 303-894-7762
Asbestos Building Inspector #05 303-692-3158	Bail Bond Agent #10 303-894-7583	Collection Agency #03 303-866-5706
Asbestos Inspector Management Planner #05	Bank, Commercial #08 303-894-7575	Commercial Driving School #07 303-205-5841
.... 303-692-3158	Bank, Industrial #08 303-894-7575	Cosmetician #16 303-894-7772
Asbestos Project Designer #05 303-692-3158	Barber #16 303-894-7772	Cosmetologist #16 303-894-7772

Court Reporter #36	303-837-3695	
Credit Union #09	303-894-2336	
Dairy Farm #06	303-692-3643	
Dairy Plant #06	303-692-3643	
Debt Management Company #08	303-894-7575	
Dental Hygienist #18	303-894-7758	
Dentist #18	303-894-7758	
Egg Seller #02	303-239-4140	
Electrical Contractor #41	303-894-2300	
Electrician-Journeyman #41	303-894-2300	
Electrician-Master #41	303-894-2300	
Engineer #19	303-894-7788	
Engineer-in-Training (Engineer Intern) #19	303-894-7788	
Family Care Home #29	303-866-5958	
Family Therapist #20	303-894-7766	
Food Plant Operator #02	303-239-4140	
Greyhound Racing #11	303-205-2990	
Hearing Aid Dealer #14	303-894-2464	
Horse Racing #11	303-205-2990	
Insurance Agency #10	303-894-2419	
Insurance Producer #10	303-894-2419	
Investment Advisors #34	303-894-2320	
Kennel #02	303-239-4166	
Land Surveyor #19	303-894-7788	
Land Surveyor Intern #19	303-894-7788	
Liquor Control #39	303-205-2300	
Lobbyist #37	303-894-2200	
Manicurist #16	303-894-7772	
Manufactured Housing Dealer #22	303-442-4402	
Manufactured Housing Salesperson #22	303-442-4402	

Marriage Therapist #20	303-894-7766	
Medical Doctor #21	303-894-7690	
Midwife #28	303-894-2464	
Milk & Cream Sampler #06	303-692-3643	
Milk & Cream Tester #06	303-692-3643	
Money Order Company #08	303-894-7575	
Motor Vehicle Buyer #42	303-205-5604	
Motor Vehicle Franchised Dealer #42	303-205-5604	
Motor Vehicle Manufacturer Representative #42	303-205-5604	
Motor Vehicle Salesperson #42	303-205-5604	
Motor Vehicle Used Dealer #42	303-205-5604	
Motor Vehicle Wholesaler #42	303-205-5604	
Notary Public #37	303-894-2680	
Nurse #01	303-894-2430	
Nursery #02	303-239-4140	
Nurses' Aide #01	303-894-2816	
Nursing Home Administrator #23	303-894-7760	
Optometrist #33	303-894-7750	
Outfitter #24	303-894-7778	
Pesticide Applicator #02	303-239-4140	
Pet Animal/Bird Dealer #02	303-239-4166	
Pharmacist #26	303-894-7750	
Pharmacy #26	303-894-7750	
Pharmacy Intern #26	303-894-7750	
Physical Therapist #32	303-894-2440	
Physician Assistant #21	303-894-7690	
Physiotherapist #32	303-894-2440	
Plumber Journeyman #35	303-894-2300 x110	
Plumber, Master #35	303-894-2300 x110	
Plumber-Residential #35	303-894-2300 x110	

Podiatrist #27	303-894-2464	
Professional Counselor #20	303-894-7766	
Psychiatric Technician #01	303-894-2430	
Psychologist #20	303-894-7766	
Public Accountant-CPA #13	303-894-7441	
Public Adjuster #10	303-894-7499	
Real Estate Appraiser #12	303-894-2166	
Real Estate Broker #12	303-894-2166	
Real Estate Salesperson #12	303-894-2166	
Residential Wireman #41	303-894-2300	
River Outfitter #38	303-894-7772	
Savings & Loan Association #09	303-894-2336	
School Administrator/Principal #40	303-866-6628	
School Special Service Associate #40	303-866-6628	
Securities Broker #34	303-894-2320	
Securities Dealer #34	303-894-2320	
Securities Sales Promoter #34	303-894-2320	
Ski Lifts #25	303-894-7785	
Small Business Development Credit Corporation #09	303-894-2336	
Social Worker #20	303-894-7766	
Solicitor/Telemarketer #03	303-866-5079	
Stock Broker #34	303-894-2320	
Substitute Teacher #40	303-866-6968	
Teacher #40	303-866-6628	
Tramway #25	303-894-7785	
Trust Company #08	303-894-7575	
Veterinarian #31	303-894-7755	
Veterinary Student #31	303-894-7755	
Vocational Education Teacher #40	303-866-6628	

Licensing Agency Information

01 Board of Nursing, 1560 Broadway, #670, Denver, CO 80202; 303-894-2430, Fax: 303-894-2821.

Direct URL to search licenses: www.dora.state.co.us:81/real/owa/ARMS_Search. Disclaimer_Page You can search online using license number, name, and city.

02 Agriculture Department, 700 Kipling St, #4000, Lakewood, CO 80215-5894; 303-239-4100, Fax: 303-239-4125.

www.ag.state.co.us

03 Attorney General's Office, 1525 Sherman St, 5th Fl, Denver, CO 80203; 303-866-4500, Fax: 303-866-5691.

www.ago.state.co.us

04 Board of Law Examiners, 600 17th St, Dominion Plaza Bldg, #910S, Denver, CO 80202; 303-534-7841, Fax: 303-534-3643.

www.courts.state.co.us/ble/ble.htm

05 Department of Public Health & Environment, Air Pollution Control Division, 4300 Cherry Creek Dr S, Denver, CO 80246; 303-692-3150, Fax: 303-782-0278.

www.cdphe.state.co.us/ap/asbeshom.asp

06 Consumer Protection Division, Department of Public Health and Environment, 4300 Cherry Creek Dr S, Denver, CO 80222-1530; 303-692-3622, Fax: 303-753-6809.

www.cdphe2.state.co.us/cp/dairy.asp

07 Department of Revenue, 1375 Sherman St, Denver, CO 80261; 303-866-3091, Fax: 303-205-5634.

08 Division of Banking, 1560 Broadway, #1175, Denver, CO 80202; 303-894-7575, Fax: 303-894-7570.

www.dora.state.co.us/banking

09 Division of Financial Services, 1560 Broadway, #1520, Denver, CO 80202; 303-894-2336, Fax: 303-894-7886.

www.dora.state.co.us/financial-services

10 Division of Insurance, 1560 Broadway, #850, Denver, CO 80202; 303-894-7499, Fax: 303-894-7455.

www.dora.state.co.us/insurance

11 Division of Racing Events, 1881 Pierce St, #108, Lakewood, CO 80214; 303-205-2990, Fax: 303-205-2950.

www.state.co.us/gov_dir/revenue_dir/racing_dir/coracing.html

12 Division of Real Estate, 1900 Grant St, #600, Denver, CO 80203; 303-894-2166, Fax: 303-894-2683.

www.dora.state.co.us/Real-Estate

Direct URL to search licenses: www.dora.state.co.us/real/owa/re_estate_home You can search online using company or individual name.

13 Division of Registrations, 1560 Broadway, #1340, Denver, CO 80202; 303-894-7800, Fax: 303-894-7802.

www.dora.state.co.us/accountants

Direct URL to search licenses: www.dora.state.co.us/accountants You can search online using license number, name, and city. Click on "Locate Colo. CPAs & Firms Online."

14 Division of Registrations, 1560 Broadway, #680, Denver, CO 80202; 303-894-2464, Fax: 303-894-7885.

www.dora.state.co.us

Direct URL to search licenses: www.dora.state.co.us/real/plsql/ARMS_Search.Disclaimer_Page You can search online using license number, name, and city.

15 Division of Registrations, 1560 Broadway, #1340, Denver, CO 80202; 303-894-7801, Fax: 303-894-7802.

www.dora.state.co.us/Architects

Direct URL to search licenses: www.dora.state.co.us/architects You can search online using license number, name, and city. Click on "Locate Colorado Architects."

16 Division of Registrations, 1560 Broadway, #1340, Denver, CO 80202; 303-894-7772.

www.dora.state.co.us/Barbers_Cosmetologists

Direct URL to search licenses: www.dora.state.co.us/real/plsql/ARMS_Search.Set_Up You can search online using license number, name, and city.

17 Division of Registrations, 1560 Broadway, #1310, Denver, CO 80202; 303-894-7800.

www.state.co.us/gov_dir/regulatory_dir/chi.htm

Direct URL to search licenses: www.dora.state.co.us:81/real/owa/ARMS_Search. Disclaimer_Page You can search online using license number, name, and city.

18 Division of Registrations, 1560 Broadway, #1310, Denver, CO 80202; 303-894-7758, Fax: 303-894-7764.

www.dora.state.co.us/Dental

Direct URL to search licenses: www.dora.state.co.us:81/real/owa/ARMS_Search. Disclaimer_Page You can search online using license number, name, and city.

19 Division of Registrations, 1560 Broadway, #1370, Denver, CO 80202; 303-894-7788, Fax: 303-894-7790.

www.dora.state.co.us/Engineers_Surveyors

Direct URL to search licenses: www.dora.state.co.us/real/plsql/ARMS_Search.Disclaimer_Page You can search online using license number, name, and city.

20 Division of Registrations, 1560 Broadway, #1340, Denver, CO 80202; 303-894-7766. www.dora.state.co.us/Mental-Health

Direct URL to search licenses: www.dora.state.co.us/real/plsql/ARMS_Search.Disclaimer_Page You can search online using license number, name, and city.

21 Division of Registrations, 1560 Broadway, #1300, Denver, CO 80202; 303-894-7800, Fax: 303-894-7692.

www.dora.state.co.us/Medical

22 Division of Registrations, 525 Canyon Blvd, #A, Denver, CO 80302; 303-442-4402, Fax: 303-442-4430.

www.state.co.us/gov_dir/loc_affairs_dir/doh.htm

23 Division of Registrations, 1560 Broadway, #1310, Denver, CO 80202; 303-894-7800, Fax: 303-894-7764.
www.state.co.us/gov_dir/regulatory_dir/nha.htm

Direct URL to search licenses: www.dora.state.co.us:81/real/owa/ARMS_Search.Disclaimer_Page You can search online using license number, name, and city.

24 Division of Registrations, 1560 Broadway, #1340, Denver, CO 80202; 303-894-7778.
www.dora.state.co.us/Outfitters

Direct URL to search licenses: www.dora.state.co.us/real/plsql/ARMS_Search.Set_Up You can search online using license number, name, and city.

25 Division of Registrations, 1560 Broadway, #1370, Denver, CO 80202; 303-894-7785, Fax: 303-894-7790.

www.dora.state.co.us/tramway

26 Division of Registrations, 1560 Broadway, #1310, Denver, CO 80202-5146; 303-894-7750, Fax: 303-894-7764.
www.dora.state.co.us/pharmacy

Direct URL to search licenses: www.dora.state.co.us:81/real/plsql/ARMS_Search.Set_Up You can search online using license number, name, and city.

27 Division of Registrations, 1560 Broadway, #680, Denver, CO 80202; 303-894-2464, Fax: 303-894-2821.
www.dora.state.co.us/Podiatrists

Direct URL to search licenses: www.dora.state.co.us:81/real/owa/ARMS_Search.Disclaimer_Page You can search online using license number, name, or city.

28 Division of Registrations, Midwives Registration, 1560 Broadway, #1545, Denver, CO 80202; 303-894-2464, Fax: 303-894-7885.
www.dora.state.co.us/Midwives

Direct URL to search licenses: www.dora.state.co.us/real/plsql/arms-search.disclaimer.page You can search online using license number, name, and city.

29 Department of Human Services, Division of Child Care, 1575 Sherman St, Denver, CO 80202; 800-799-5876, Fax: 303-866-4453.

www.cdhs.state.co.us/cyf/ccare/index.html

31 Division of Registrations, 1560 Broadway, #1310, Denver, CO 80202-5146; 303-894-7755, Fax: 303-894-7764.
www.dora.state.co.us/veterinarians

Direct URL to search licenses: www.dora.state.co.us/real/plsql/ARMS_Search.Disclaimer_Page You can search online using license number, name, and city.

32 Division of Registrations, Physical Therapy Registration, 1560 Broadway, #680, Denver, CO 80202; 303-894-7800, Fax: 303-894-2821.
www.dora.state.co.us/Physical-Therapy

Direct URL to search licenses: www.dora.state.co.us/real/plsql/ARMS_Search.Disclaimer_Page You can search online using license number, name, and city.

33 Division of Registrations, Board of Optometry Examiners, 1560 Broadway, #1310, Denver, CO 80202-5146; 303-894-7800, Fax: 303-894-7764.
www.dora.state.co.us/optometry

Direct URL to search licenses: www.dora.state.co.us/real/plsql/arms_search.disclaimer_page You can search online using license number or last name, first name and city.

34 Department of Regulatory Agencies, Division of Securities, 1580 Lincoln, #420, Denver, CO 80203-1506; 303-894-2320, Fax: 303-861-2126.
www.dora.state.co.us/Securities/brokers.htm

Direct URL to search licenses: http://pdpi.nasdr.com/pdpi/disclaimer_frame.htm You can search online using NASD database and procedures

35 Examining Board of Plumbers, 1580 Logan St, #550, Denver, CO 80203-1941; 303-894-2300, Fax: 303-894-2310.
www.dora.state.co.us/plumbing

Direct URL to search licenses: www.dora.state.co.us:81/real/owa/ARMS_Search.Disclaimer_Page You can search online using license number, name, and city.

36 Judicial Department, Human Resources Office, 1301 Pennsylvania St, #300, Denver, CO 80203; 303-837-3695, Fax: 303-837-2340.

37 Office of Secretary of State, 1560 Broadway, #200, Denver, CO 80202; 303-894-2200, Fax: 303-894-2242.
www.sos.state.co.us

Direct URL to search licenses: www.sos.state.co.us/pubslbingo.html

38 Division of Registrations, Outfitters Registration, 1560 Broadway, #1340, Denver, CO 80202; 303-894-7778, Fax: 303-470-0782.
www.dora.state.co.us/Outfitters

Direct URL to search licenses: www.dora.state.co.us/real/plsql/ARMS_Search.Disclaimer_Page

39 Revenue Department, Alcohol Control Division, 1881 Pierce, #108A, Lakewood, CO 80214; 303-205-2300, Fax: 303-205-2341.

www.state.co.us/gov_dir/revenue_dir/liquor_dir/lic&permit.htm

40 Department of Education, 201 E Colifax, Denver, CO 80203; 303-866-6628, Fax: 303-866-6968.

www.cde.state.co.us/index_license.htm

41 Electrical Board, 1580 Logan St, #550, Denver, CO 80203-1939; 303-894-2300, Fax: 303-894-2310.
www.dora.state.co.us/electrical

Direct URL to search licenses: www.dora.state.co.us:81/real/owa/ARMS_Search.Disclaimer_Page You can search online using license number, name, and city.

42 Motor Vehicle Dealer Board, 1881 Pierce St Rm 142, Lakewood, CO 80215; 303-205-5604.

The following list indicates the district and division name for each county in the state. If the district or division name of the bankruptcy court is different from the civil/criminal court, it appears in parentheses.

County/Court Cross Reference

Adams	Denver	La Plata	Denver
Alamosa	Denver	Lake	Denver
Arapahoe	Denver	Larimer	Denver
Archuleta	Denver	Las Animas	Denver
Baca	Denver	Lincoln	Denver
Bent	Denver	Logan	Denver
Boulder	Denver	Mesa	Denver
Chaffee	Denver	Mineral	Denver
Cheyenne	Denver	Moffat	Denver
Clear Creek	Denver	Montezuma	Denver
Conejos	Denver	Montrose	Denver
Costilla	Denver	Morgan	Denver
Crowley	Denver	Otero	Denver
Custer	Denver	Ouray	Denver
Delta	Denver	Park	Denver
Denver	Denver	Phillips	Denver
Dolores	Denver	Pitkin	Denver
Douglas	Denver	Prowers	Denver
Eagle	Denver	Pueblo	Denver
El Paso	Denver	Rio Blanco	Denver
Elbert	Denver	Rio Grande	Denver
Fremont	Denver	Routt	Denver
Garfield	Denver	Saguache	Denver
Gilpin	Denver	San Juan	Denver
Grand	Denver	San Miguel	Denver
Gunnison	Denver	Sedgwick	Denver
Hinsdale	Denver	Summit	Denver
Huerfano	Denver	Teller	Denver
Jackson	Denver	Washington	Denver
Jefferson	Denver	Weld	Denver
Kiowa	Denver	Yuma	Denver
Kit Carson	Denver		

US District Court

District of Colorado

Denver Division US Courthouse, Room C-145, 1929 Stout St, Denver, CO 80294-3589, 303-844-3433.

www.co.uscourts.gov

Counties: All counties in Colorado.

Indexing & Storage: Cases are indexed by defendant and plaintiff as well as by case number. New cases are available in the index immediately after filing date. A computer index is maintained. Open records are located at this court.

Fee & Payment: The fee is $15.00 per item (one party name or case number). Payment may be made by money order, cashier check, personal check, Visa, Mastercard. There is no prepayment required for any copies unless the bill is over $100.00. Payee: Clerk, US District Court. Certification fee: $5.00 per document. Copy fee: $.50 per page.

Phone Search: Over the phone, the court will release anything of public record, although they will not read long excerpts over the phone. An automated voice case information service (VCIS) is not available.

Mail Search: Always enclose a stamped self addressed envelope.

In Person Search: In person searching is available.

PACER: Sign-up number is 800-676-6856. Access fee is $.60 per minute. Toll-free access: 888-481-7027. Local access: 303-844-3454. Case records are available back to 1990. Records are purged on a varying schedule. New records are available online after 1 day. PACER is available on the Internet at http://pacer.cod.uscourts.gov.

US Bankruptcy Court

District of Colorado

Denver Division US Custom House, Room 114, 721 19th St, Denver, CO 80202-2508, 303-844-4045.

www.co.uscourts.gov

Counties: All counties in Colorado.

Indexing & Storage: Cases are indexed by debtor as well as by case number. New cases are available in the index 24-48 hours after filing date. A computer index is maintained. Records are also on microfilm of all cases prior to June 1990. Open records are located at this court.

Fee & Payment: The fee is $15.00 per item (one party name or case number). Payment may be made by money order, cashier check, personal check. Prepayment is required. Personal checks are not accepted from debtors. Payee: Clerk, US Bankruptcy Court. Certification fee: $5.00 per document. Copy fee: $.50 per page. You are allowed to make your own copies. These copies cost $.10 per page. Records are available for viewing from 8:00 a.m. to 4:45 p.m., Monday through Friday in Room 114.

Phone Search: An automated voice case information service (VCIS) is available.

Mail Search: A stamped self addressed envelope is not required.

In Person Search: In person searching is available.

PACER: Sign-up number is 800-676-6856. Access fee is $.60 per minute. Toll-free access: 888-213-4715. Local access: 303-844-0263. Case records are available back to July 1981. New civil records are available online after 1 day. PACER is available on the Internet at http://pacer.cob.uscourts.gov.

Court	Jurisdiction	No. of Courts	How Organized
District Courts*	General	14	22 Districts
County Courts*	Limited	17	63 Counties
Combined Courts*		49	
Denver Probate Courts*	Probate	1	
Municipal Courts	Municipal	206	
Denver Juvenile Courts	Special	1	
Water Courts	Special	7	7 Districts

* Profiled in this Sourcebook.

Court	CIVIL								
	Tort	Contract	Real Estate	Min. Claim	Max. Claim	Small Claims	Estate	Eviction	Domestic Relations
District Courts*	X	X	X	$0	No Max		X		X
County Courts*	X	X	X	$0	$10,000	$3500		X	
Denver Probate Courts*							X		
Denver Juvenile Courts									
Water Courts			X	$0	No Max				

Court	CRIMINAL				
	Felony	Misdemeanor	DWI/DUI	Preliminary Hearing	Juvenile
District Courts*	X				X
County Courts*		X	X	X	
Denver Probate Courts*					
Denver Juvenile Courts					X
Water Courts					

ADMINISTRATION State Court Administrator, 1301 Pennsylvania St, Suite 300, Denver, CO, 80203; 303-861-1111, Fax: 303-837-2340. www.courts.state.co.us

COURT STRUCTURE The District and County Courts have overlapping jurisdiction over civil cases involving less than $10,000. The District and County Courts are combined in most counties. Combined courts usually search both civil or criminal indexes for a single fee, except as indicated in the profiles. Denver is the only county with a separate Probate Court.

Municipal courts only have jurisdiction over traffic, parking, and ordinance violations.

ONLINE ACCESS A statewide online computer system is under development in Colorado.

ADDITIONAL INFORMATION All state agencies require a self-addressed, stamped envelope (SASE) for return of information.

Co-located with seven district courts are divisions known as Water Courts. The Water Courts are located in Weld, Pueblo, Alamosa, Montrose, Garfield, Routt, and La Platta counties; see the District Court discussion for those counties to determine the jurisdictional area for the Water Court. Water Court records are maintained by the Water Clerk and fees are similar to those for other court records. To retrieve a Water Court record, one must furnish the Case Number or the Legal Description (section, township, and range) or the Full Name of the respondent (note that the case number or legal description are preferred).

Adams County

17th District Court 1100 Judicial Center Drive, Brighton, CO 80601; 303-659-1161; Fax: 303-654-3216. Hours: 8AM-5PM (MST). *Felony, Civil Actions Over $10,000, Probate.*

Note: District and County courts have combined, but records are searched separately unless requester asks to search both courts (no extra fee).

Civil Records: Access: Mail, in person. Both court and visitors may perform in person searches. Search fee: $5.00 per name. Fee is $10.00 for cases before 1976. There is no fee if search done by visitor. Required to search: name, years to search. Civil cases indexed by defendant, plaintiff. Civil records on computer from Jan 1976, index books back to early 1900s. **Criminal Records:** Access: Mail, in person. Both court and visitors may perform in person searches. Search fee: $5.00 per name. Fee is $8.00 for cases before 1976. Required to search: name, years to search, DOB. Criminal records on computer from Jan 1976, index books back to early 1900s. **General Information:** No adoptions, sealed, juvenile, mental health or expunged cases released. SASE required. Turnaround time 2 days. Copy fee: $.75 per page. Certification fee: $5.00. Fee payee: Clerk of the District Court. Personal checks accepted. Credit cards accepted. Accepted in person only. Prepayment is required.

County Court 1100 Judicial Center Drive, Brighton, CO 80601; 303-659-1161. Hours: 8AM-5PM (MST). *Misdemeanor, Civil Actions Under $10,000, Eviction, Small Claims.*

Note: District and County courts have combined, but records are searched separately unless requester asks to search both courts (no extra fee).

Civil Records: Access: Mail, in person. Both court and visitors may perform in person searches. Search fee: $5.00 per name. $8.00 per name for pre-computer records. Required to search: name, years to search. Civil cases indexed by defendant, plaintiff. Civil records on computer from Jan 1990, index books back to 1965. **Criminal Records:** Access: Mail, in person. Both court and visitors may perform in person searches. Search fee: $5.00 per name. $8.00 per name for pre-computer records. Required to search: name, years to search, DOB. Criminal records on computer from Jan 1990, index books back to 1965. **General Information:** No adoptions, sealed, juvenile, mental health or expunged cases released. SASE required. Turnaround time 2 working days. Copy fee: $.75 per page. Certification fee: $5.00. Fee payee: Adams County Combined Court. Personal checks accepted. Credit cards accepted: Visa, Mastercard. In person only. Prepayment is required.

Alamosa County

Alamosa Combined Court 702 4th St, Alamosa, CO 81101; 719-589-4996; Fax: 719-589-4998. Hours: 8AM-4:30PM (MST). *Felony, Civil, Eviction, Small Claims, Probate.*

Civil Records: Access: Mail, in person. Only the court conducts in person searches; visitors may not. Search fee: $5.00 per name. Required to search: name, years to search. Civil cases indexed by defendant. Civil records on computer from May 1978, index books back to 1913. **Criminal Records:** Access: Mail, in person. Only the court conducts in person searches; visitors may not. Search fee: $5.00 per name. Required to search: name, years to search, DOB. Criminal records on computer from May 1978, index books back to

1913. **General Information:** No adoptions, sealed, juvenile, mental health or expunged cases released. SASE required. Turnaround time 10 days. Copy fee: $.75 per page. Certification fee: $5.00. Fee payee: Clerk, Combined Court. Personal checks accepted. Prepayment is required. Public access terminal is available.

Arapahoe County

18th District Court 7325 S Potomac, Englewood, CO 80112; 303-649-6355. Hours: 8AM-5PM (MST). *Felony, Civil Actions Over $10,000, Probate.*

Civil Records: Access: Phone, mail, in person. Both court and visitors may perform in person searches. Search fee: $5.00 per name. Required to search: name, years to search. Civil cases indexed by defendant, plaintiff. Civil records on computer from 1990, microfiche back to 1903. **Criminal Records:** Access: Phone, mail, in person. Both court and visitors may perform in person searches. Search fee: $5.00 per name. Required to search: name, years to search, DOB. Criminal records on computer from 1990, microfiche back to 1903. **General Information:** No adoptions, sealed, juvenile, mental health or expunged cases released. SASE required. Turnaround time 1-2 days. Copy fee: $.75 per page. Certification fee: $5.00. Fee payee: Clerk of District Court. Personal checks accepted. Prepayment is required.

Arapahoe County Court Division B 15400 E 14th Pl, Aurora, CO 80011; 303-214-4000. Hours: 8AM-5PM (MST). *Misdemeanor, Civil Actions Under $10,000, Eviction, Small Claims.*

Civil Records: Access: Phone, mail, in person. Both court and visitors may perform in person searches. Search fee: $5.00 per name. Required to search: name, years to search. Civil cases indexed by defendant, plaintiff. Civil records on computer from April 1986, microfiche from 1980-1983, index cards from 1980. **Criminal Records:** Access: Phone, mail, in person. Both court and visitors may perform in person searches. Search fee: $5.00 per name. Required to search: name, years to search, DOB. Criminal records on computer from April 1986, microfiche from 1980-1983, index cards from 1980. **General Information:** No adoptions, sealed, juvenile, mental health or expunged cases released. SASE required. Turnaround time 2 days. Copy fee: $.75 per page. Certification fee: $5.00. Fee payee: Clerk of County Court. Personal checks accepted. Credit cards accepted: Visa, Mastercard. Prepayment is required.

Littleton County Court Division A 1790 W Littleton Blvd, Littleton, CO 80120-2060; 303-798-4591. Hours: 8AM-5PM (MST). *Misdemeanor, Civil Actions Under $10,000, Eviction, Small Claims.*

Civil Records: Access: Phone, mail, in person. Both court and visitors may perform in person searches. Search fee: $5.00 per name. Required to search: name, years to search. Civil cases indexed by defendant, plaintiff. Civil records on computer from 1986, index cards from 1965, microfiche from 1861 in District Court. Only court performs searches prior to March 1986. **Criminal Records:** Access: Mail, in person. Both court and visitors may perform in person searches. Search fee: $5.00 per name. Required to search: name, years to search, DOB. Criminal records on computer from 1986, index cards from 1965, microfiche from 1861 in District Court. Only court performs searches prior to March 1986. **General**

Information: No adoptions, sealed, juvenile, mental health or expunged cases released. SASE required. Turnaround time 2 weeks. Copy fee: $.75 per page. Certification fee: $5.00. Fee payee: Clerk of County Court. Personal checks accepted. Credit cards accepted: Visa, Mastercard. Prepayment is required. Public access terminal is available.

Archuleta County

6th District & County Courts PO Box 148, Pagosa Springs, CO 81147; 970-264-2400; Fax: 970-264-2407. Hours: 8AM-5PM (MST). *Felony, Misdemeanor, Civil, Eviction, Small Claims, Probate.*

Civil Records: Access: Mail, in person. Only the court conducts in person searches; visitors may not. Search fee: $5.00 per name. Specific case information is $2.00 per file. Required to search: name, years to search. Civil cases indexed by defendant, plaintiff. Civil records on index cards from 1976, index books back to 1885. **Criminal Records:** Access: Mail, in person. Only the court conducts in person searches; visitors may not. Search fee: $5.00 per name. Specific case information $2.00 per file. Required to search: name, years to search, DOB. Criminal records on index cards from 1976, index books back to 1885. **General Information:** No adoptions, sealed, juvenile, mental health or expunged cases released. SASE required. Turnaround time 5 days. Copy fee: $.75 per page. Certification fee: $5.00. Fee payee: Archuleta Combined Court. Personal checks accepted. Prepayment is required.

Baca County

Baca County District & County Courts 741 Main St, Springfield, CO 81073; 719-523-4555. Hours: 8AM-5PM (MST). *Felony, Misdemeanor, Civil, Eviction, Small Claims, Probate.*

Civil Records: Access: Mail, in person. Only the court conducts in person searches; visitors may not. Search fee: There is no search fee for a single record; however, multiple names or archived records are $20 per record. Required to search: name, years to search. Civil cases indexed by defendant, plaintiff. Civil records on index cards from 1945, index books back to 1910. **Criminal Records:** Access: Mail, in person. Only the court conducts in person searches; visitors may not. Search fee: Same fee structure as civil records. Required to search: name, years to search, DOB. Criminal records on index cards from 1945, index books back to 1910. **General Information:** No adoptions, sealed, juvenile, mental health or expunged cases released. SASE required. Turnaround time 1-2 days. Copy fee: $.75 per page. Certification fee: $5.00. Fee payee: Baca County Courts. Personal checks accepted. Prepayment is required.

Bent County

16th District Court Bent County Courthouse, 725 Bent, Las Animas, CO 81054; 719-456-1353; Fax: 719-456-0040. Hours: 8AM-12, 1-5PM (MST). *Felony, Misdemeanor, Civil, Eviction, Small Claims, Probate.*

www.courts.state.co.us/district/16th/dist-16.htm

Civil Records: Access: Mail, in person. Both court and visitors may perform in person searches. Search fee: $5.00 per name. Required to search: name, years to search. Civil cases indexed by defendant, plaintiff. Civil records on index cards from 1975, prior to 1975 some on microfilm, on computer from 11/95 forward- all indexes available at this office. **Criminal Records:**

Access: Mail, in person. Both court and visitors may perform in person searches. Search fee: $5.00 per name. Required to search: name, years to search, DOB, signed release. Criminal records on index cards from 1975, prior to 1975 some on microfilm, on computer from 11/95 forward- all indexes available at this office. **General Information:** No adoptions, sealed, juvenile, mental health or expunged cases released. SASE required. Turnaround time 4-5 days. Copy fee: $.75 per page. Certification fee: $5.00. Fee payee: Clerk of Combined Court. Personal checks accepted. Prepayment is required. Public access terminal is available.

Boulder County

20th District & County Courts 6th & Canyon, PO Box 4249, Boulder, CO 80306; 303-441-3750; Fax: 303-441-4862. Hours: 8AM-5PM (MST). *Felony, Misdemeanor, Civil, Eviction, Small Claims, Probate.*

Civil Records: Access: Mail, in person. Both court and visitors may perform in person searches. Search fee: $5.00 per name. Required to search: name, years to search. Civil cases indexed by defendant, plaintiff. Civil records on computer from 1989, microfiche prior from 1977, all prior records in books. **Criminal Records:** Access: Mail, in person. Both court and visitors may perform in person searches. Search fee: $5.00 per name. Required to search: name, years to search, SSN; also helpful-DOB. Criminal records on computer from 1989, microfiche prior from 1977, all prior records in books. **General Information:** No adoptions, sealed, juvenile, mental health or expunged cases released. SASE required. Turnaround time 5 days. Copy fee: $.75 per page. Certification fee: $5.00. Fee payee: 20th Judicial District. Business checks accepted. Attorney checks accepted. Credit cards accepted: Visa, Mastercard.

Chaffee County

11th District Court PO Box 279, Salida, CO 81201; 719-539-2561; Fax: 719-539-6281. Hours: 8AM-5PM (MST). *Felony, Civil Actions Over $10,000, Probate.*

Civil Records: Access: Fax, mail, in person. Only the court conducts in person searches; visitors may not. Search fee: $10.00 per name. Fee applies if 3 or more files involved. Required to search: name, years to search. Civil cases indexed by defendant, plaintiff. Civil records on index cards from April 1976, index books back to late 1800s. **Criminal Records:** Access: Fax, mail, in person. Only the court conducts in person searches; visitors may not. Search fee: $10.00 per name. Fee applies if 3 or more files involved. Required to search: name, years to search, DOB. Criminal records on index cards from April 1976, index books back to late 1800s. **General Information:** No adoptions, sealed, juvenile, mental health or expunged cases released. SASE required. Turnaround time 2-3 days. Copy fee: $.75 per page. Certification fee: $5.00. Fee payee: Clerk of District Court. Personal checks accepted. Prepayment is required. Fax notes: $1.00 per page.

County Court PO Box 279, Salida, CO 81201; 719-539-6031; Fax: 719-539-6281. Hours: 8AM-5PM (MST). *Misdemeanor, Civil Actions Under $10,000, Eviction, Small Claims.*

Civil Records: Access: Phone, fax, mail, in person. Both court and visitors may perform in person searches. No search fee. Required to search: name. Civil cases indexed by defendant, plaintiff. Civil records on computer since 1995;

prior on index cards from 1970s. **Criminal Records:** Access: Phone, fax, mail, in person. Both court and visitors may perform in person searches. No search fee. Required to search: name, years to search, DOB, aliases. Criminal records on computer since 1995; prior on index cards from 1970s. **General Information:** No adoptions, sealed, juvenile, mental health or expunged cases released. SASE required. Turnaround time 3-4 days. Copy fee: $.75 per page. Certification fee: $5.00. Fee payee: Clerk of County Court. Personal checks accepted. Prepayment is required. Fax notes: $1.00 per page.

Cheyenne County

15th District & County Courts PO Box 696, Cheyenne Wells, CO 80810; 719-767-5649. Hours: 8AM-4:30PM. *Felony, Misde-meanor, Civil, Eviction, Small Claims, Probate.*

Civil Records: Access: Mail, in person. Only the court conducts in person searches; visitors may not. Search fee: $5.00 per name. Required to search: name, years to search. Civil cases indexed by defendant, plaintiff. Civil records on computer since 11/1/95, index cards from 1960, index books back to early 1900s. **Criminal Records:** Access: Mail, in person. Only the court conducts in person searches; visitors may not. Search fee: $5.00 per name. Required to search: name, years to search, DOB. Criminal records on computer since 11/1/95, index cards from 1960, index books back to early 1900s. **General Information:** No adoptions, sealed, juvenile, mental health or expunged cases released. SASE required. Turnaround time 5-7 days. Copy fee: $.75 per page. Certification fee: $5.00. Fee payee: Cheyenne County Combined Court. Business checks accepted. Will bill attorneys only.

Clear Creek County

5th District & County Courts PO Box 367, Georgetown, CO 80444; 303-569-3273; Fax: 303-569-3274. Hours: 8AM-5PM (MST). *Felony, Misdemeanor, Civil, Eviction, Small Claims, Probate.*

Civil Records: Access: Mail, in person. Both court and visitors may perform in person searches. Search fee: $5.00 per name. Required to search: name, years to search. Civil cases indexed by defendant, plaintiff. Civil records on index cards from 1976, ledger books back to late 1800. No searches done on records prior to 1976. **Criminal Records:** Access: Mail, in person. Both court and visitors may perform in person searches. Search fee: $5.00 per name. Required to search: name, years to search, DOB. Criminal records on index cards from 1976, ledger books back to late 1800. **General Information:** No adoptions, sealed, juvenile, mental health or expunged cases released. SASE required. Turnaround time 1 week. Copy fee: $.75 per page. Certification fee: $5.00 per page. Fee payee: Clerk of Combined Court. Personal checks accepted. Prepayment is required.

Conejos County

12th District & County Courts PO Box 128, Conejos, CO 81129; 719-376-5466; Fax: 719-376-5465. Hours: 8AM-4PM (MST). *Felony, Misdemeanor, Civil, Eviction, Small Claims, Probate.*

Civil Records: Access: Mail, in person. Only the court conducts in person searches; visitors may not. Search fee: $10.00 per name. Required to search: name, years to search. Civil cases indexed by defendant, plaintiff. Civil records on computer since 6/94, on index cards from 1980. **Criminal**

Records: Access: Mail, in person. Only the court conducts in person searches; visitors may not. Search fee: $10.00 per name. Required to search: name, years to search, DOB. Criminal records on computer since 6/94, on index cards from 1980. **General Information:** No adoptions, sealed, juvenile, mental health or expunged cases released. SASE required. Turnaround time 1 week. Copy fee: $.75 per page. Certification fee: $5.00. Fee payee: Conejos Combined Court. Personal checks accepted. Prepayment is required.

Costilla County

12th District & County Courts PO Box 301, San Luis, CO 81152; 719-672-3681; Fax: 719-672-3681. Hours: 8AM-Noon, 1-4PM (MST). *Felony, Misdemeanor, Civil, Eviction, Small Claims, Probate.*

Civil Records: Access: Fax, mail, in person. Both court and visitors may perform in person searches. Search fee: $5.00 per name. There is no fee if the visitor performs the search. Required to search: name, years to search; also helpful-address. Civil cases indexed by defendant, plaintiff. Civil records on index cards from 1970, index books back to 1900s, indexed on computer since 1994. Archived prior to 1970. **Criminal Records:** Access: Fax, mail, in person. Only the court conducts in person searches; visitors may not. Search fee: $6.50 per name. Required to search: name, years to search; also helpful-address, DOB, SSN. Criminal records on index cards from 1970, index books back to 1900s, indexed on computer since 1994. Archived prior to 1970. **General Information:** No adoptions, sealed, juvenile, mental health, certain criminal cases or expunged cases released. SASE required. Turnaround time 1-2 weeks. Copy fee: $.75 per page. Certification fee: $5.00. Fee payee: Costilla Combined Courts. Personal checks accepted. Prepayment is required. Fax notes: $10.00 per document.

Crowley County

16th District & County Courts 110 E 6th St, #303, Ordway, CO 81063; 719-267-4468; Fax: 719-267-3753. Hours: 8AM-4:30PM (MST). *Felony, Misdemeanor, Civil, Eviction, Small Claims, Probate.*

www.courts.state.co.us/district/16th/dist-16.htm

Civil Records: Access: Mail, in person. Only the court conducts in person searches; visitors may not. Search fee: $5.00 per name. Required to search: name, years to search. Civil cases indexed by defendant, plaintiff. Civil records computerized from 1992, fiche since 1980'2, index books back to 1911. **Criminal Records:** Access: Mail, in person. Only the court conducts in person searches; visitors may not. Search fee: $5.00 per name. Required to search: name, years to search, DOB. Criminal records computerized from 1992, fiche since 1980'2, index books back to 1911. **General Information:** No adoptions, sealed, juvenile, mental health or expunged cases released. SASE required. Turnaround time 3-5 days. Copy fee: $.75 per page. Certification fee: $5.00. Fee payee: Crowley Combined Court. Personal checks accepted. Prepayment is required.

Custer County

11th District & County Courts PO Box 60, Westcliffe, CO 81252; 719-783-2274; Fax: 719-783-9782. Hours: 9AM-2PM (MST). *Felony, Misdemeanor, Civil, Eviction, Small Claims, Probate.*

Civil Records: Access: Mail, in person. Both court and visitors may perform in person searches.

Search fee: $5.00 per name. Required to search: name, years to search. Civil cases indexed by defendant, plaintiff. Civil records on index cards from 1973, ledger books back to 1965, archived from 1879-1965. **Criminal Records:** Access: Mail, in person. Both court and visitors may perform in person searches. Search fee: $5.00 per name. Required to search: name, years to search, DOB. Criminal records on index cards from 1973, ledger books back to 1965, archived from 1879-1965. **General Information:** No adoptions, sealed, juvenile, mental health or expunged cases released. SASE required. Turnaround time 1-2 weeks. Copy fee: $.75 per page. Certification fee: $5.00. Fee payee: Custer Combined Court. Personal checks accepted. Prepayment is required.

Delta County

District & County Courts, Delta County 501 Palmer St Rm 338, Delta, CO 81416; 970-874-4416. Hours: 8:30AM-4:30PM (MST). *Felony, Misdemeanor, Civil, Eviction, Small Claims, Probate.*

http://www.7thjudicialdistrictco.org/delta.html

Civil Records: Access: Mail, in person. Only the court conducts in person searches; visitors may not. Search fee: $5.00 per name. Required to search: name, years to search. Civil cases indexed by defendant, plaintiff. Civil records on computer from 1990, index cards from 1972, index books back to 1900. **Criminal Records:** Access: Mail, in person. Only the court conducts in person searches; visitors may not. Search fee: $5.00 per name. Required to search: name, years to search, DOB, signed release. Criminal records on computer from 1990, index cards from 1972, index books back to 1900. **General Information:** No adoptions, sealed, juvenile, mental health or expunged cases released. SASE required. Turnaround time 3 days. Copy fee: $.75 per page. Certification fee: $5.00. Fee payee: Clerk of Court. Only cashiers checks and money orders accepted. Prepayment is required.

Denver County

2nd District Court 1437 Bannock, Denver, CO 80202;; Civil phone:303-575-2491; Criminal phone:303-575-2491. Hours: 8AM-5PM (MST). *Felony, Civil Actions Over $10,000.*

www.courts.state.co.us/district/02nd/dcadmn02.htm

Civil Records: Access: Mail, in person. Both court and visitors may perform in person searches. No search fee. Required to search: name, years to search. Civil cases indexed by defendant, plaintiff. Civil records on computer from 1974, index books back to the late 1800s if convicted of criminal charges. **Criminal Records:** Access: Mail, in person. Both court and visitors may perform in person searches. No search fee. Required to search: name, years to search, DOB. Criminal records on computer from 1974, index books back to the late 1800s if convicted of criminal charges. **General Information:** No adoptions, sealed, juvenile, mental health or expunged cases released. SASE required. Turnaround time 1 week. Copy fee: $.75 per page. Certification fee: $5.00. Fee payee: Denver District Court. Personal checks accepted. Prepayment is required.

County Court-Civil Division 1515 Cleveland Pl 4th Floor, Denver, CO 80202; 303-640-5161; Fax: 303-640-4730. Hours: 8AM-5PM (MST). *Civil Actions Under $10,000, Eviction, Small Claims.*

www.courts.state.co.us/district/02nd/dcadmn02.htm

Civil Records: Access: Mail, in person, online. Both court and visitors may perform in person searches. No search fee. Required to search: name, years to search. Civil cases indexed by defendant, plaintiff. Civil records on computer from 1987, microfiche since 1965. Online searching of the Denver County Civil Division court cases is available at www.denvergov.org/civilcourts.asp. Search by name, business name, or case number. **General Information:** No adoptions, sealed, juvenile, mental health or expunged cases released. SASE required. Turnaround time 1 week. Copy fee: $1.00 per page. Certification fee: $5.00. Fee payee: Denver County Court. Personal checks accepted. Prepayment is required.

County Court - Criminal Division 1437 Bannock St Room 111A, Denver, CO 80202; 303-640-5911. Hours: 8AM-5PM (MST). *Misdemeanor.*

www.courts.state.co.us/district/02nd/dcadmn02.htm **Criminal Records:** Access: Mail, in person. Both court and visitors may perform in person searches. No search fee. Required to search: name, years to search, DOB; also helpful-address. Criminal records computerized since 1985. **General Information:** No adoptions, sealed, juvenile, mental health or expunged cases released. SASE required. Turnaround time 1 week. Copy fee: $.75 per page. Certification fee: $5.00. Fee payee: Denver County Court. Personal checks accepted. Prepayment is required.

Probate Court 1437 Bannock, Rm 230, Denver, CO 80202; 303-640-2327; Fax: 303-640-1002. Hours: 8AM-5PM (MST). *Probate.*

www.cpbar.org/probate.ct/index.htm

Dolores County

22nd District & County Courts PO Box 511, Dove Creek, CO 81324; 970-677-2258. Hours: 8AM-5PM M & T; 8AM-Noon W (MST). *Felony, Misdemeanor, Civil, Eviction, Small Claims, Probate.*

Civil Records: Access: Phone, mail, in person. Only the court conducts in person searches; visitors may not. No search fee. Required to search: name, years to search. Civil cases indexed by defendant, plaintiff. Civil records on index cards from 1972, index books back to 1895, on computer from 06/95 to present. **Criminal Records:** Access: Phone, mail, in person. Only the court conducts in person searches; visitors may not. No search fee. Required to search: name, years to search, DOB. Criminal records on index cards from 1972, index books back to 1895, on computer from 06/95 to present. **General Information:** No adoptions, sealed, juvenile, mental health or expunged cases released. SASE required. Turnaround time 1 week. Copy fee: $.75 per page. Certification fee: $5.00. Fee payee: Dolores County Combined. Only cashiers checks and money orders accepted. Prepayment is required.

Douglas County

Douglas County Combined Court 4000 Justice Way #2009, Castle Rock, CO 80104; 303-663-7200. Hours: 8AM-5PM (MST). *Felony, Misdemeanor, Civil, Eviction, Small Claims, Probate.*

Civil Records: Access: Mail, in person. Both court and visitors may perform in person searches. Search fee: $5.00 per name. $20.00 per hour for extensive search. Required to search: name, years to search. Civil cases indexed by defendant, plaintiff. Civil records on computer since Jan 1988, index cards from 1975, index books to 1880s. **Criminal Records:** Access: Mail, in person. Both court and visitors may perform in person searches. Search fee: $5.00 per name. Required to search: name, years to search, DOB. Criminal records on computer since Jan 1988, index cards from 1975, index books to 1880s. **General Information:** No adoptions, sealed, juvenile, mental health or expunged cases released. SASE required. Turnaround time 2 weeks. Copy fee: $.75 per page. Certification fee: $5.00. Fee payee: Clerk of Combined Courts. Only cashiers checks and money orders accepted. Prepayment is required.

Eagle County

Eagle Combined Court PO Box 597, Eagle, CO 81631; 970-328-6373; Fax: 970-328-6328. Hours: 8AM-5PM (MST). *Felony, Misdemeanor, Civil, Eviction, Small Claims, Probate.*

Civil Records: Access: Fax, mail, in person. Court does not conduct in person searches; visitors must perform searches for themselves. Search fee: $5.00 per name. Required to search: name, years to search. Civil cases indexed by defendant, plaintiff. Civil records on computer since 09/95; prior on fiche to 1970, books to 1930. **Criminal Records:** Access: Fax, mail, in person. Court does not conduct in person searches; visitors must perform searches for themselves. Search fee: $5.00 per name. Required to search: name, years to search, DOB. Criminal records on computer since 09/95; prior on fiche to 1970, books to 1930. **General Information:** No adoptions, sealed, juvenile, mental health or expunged cases released. SASE required. Turnaround time 5-7 days. Copy fee: $.75 per page. Certification fee: $5.00. Fee payee: Eagle Combined Courts. Personal checks accepted. Credit cards accepted: Visa, Mastercard. Prepayment is required. Public access terminal is available. Fax notes: $1.00 per page. Fax fee must be paid with credit card.

El Paso County

El Paso Combined Court 20 E Vermijo Rm 105, Colorado Springs, CO 80903; 719-448-7700; Fax: 719-448-7685. Hours: 8AM-5PM (MST). *Felony, Civil Actions Over $10,000, Probate.*

www.gofourth.org

Note: Records for the County and District Courts are combined

Civil Records: Access: Fax, mail, in person. Both court and visitors may perform in person searches. Search fee: $5.00 per name. Required to search: name, years to search. Civil cases indexed by defendant, plaintiff. Civil records on computer from Jan, 1975, index cards to 1975, index books to 1861. **Criminal Records:** Access: Fax, mail, in person. Both court and visitors may perform in person searches. Search fee: $5.00 per name. Required to search: name, years to search, DOB; also helpful-SSN. Criminal records on computer from Jan, 1975, index cards to 1975, index books to 1861. **General Information:** No adoptions, sealed, juvenile, mental health, expunged cases or other access restricted cases released. SASE required. Turnaround time 5-7 days. Copy fee: $.75 per page. Certification fee: $5.00. Fee payee: Clerk of District Court. Personal checks accepted. Credit cards accepted: Visa, Mastercard, Discover. Prepayment is required. Fax notes: Fee is $.75 per page plus $1.50 if long distance.

Elbert County

Elbert District & County Courts PO Box 232, Kiowa, CO 80117; 303-621-2131. Hours: 8AM-5PM (MST). *Felony, Misdemeanor, Civil, Eviction, Small Claims, Probate.*

Civil Records: Access: Phone, mail, in person. Only the court conducts in person searches; visitors may not. Search fee: $5.00 per name. Required to search: name, years to search. Civil cases indexed by defendant, plaintiff. Civil records on index cards from 1978, index books from 1920s, archived prior to 1920. **Criminal Records:** Access: Phone, mail, in person. Only the court conducts in person searches; visitors may not. Search fee: $5.00 per name. Required to search: name, years to search, DOB. Criminal records on index cards from 1978, index books from 1920s, archived prior to 1920. **General Information:** No adoptions, sealed, juvenile, mental health or expunged cases released. SASE required. Turnaround time 1-2 weeks. Copy fee: $.75 per page. Certification fee: $5.00. Fee payee: Elbert Combined Courts. Business checks accepted. Prepayment is required.

Fremont County

District & County Courts 136 Justice Center Rd, Rm 103, Canon City, CO 81212; 719-269-0100; Fax: 719-269-0134. Hours: 8AM-4PM (MST). *Felony, Misdemeanor, Civil, Eviction, Small Claims, Probate.*

Civil Records: Access: Mail, in person. Only the court conducts in person searches; visitors may not. Search fee: $5.00 per name. Required to search: name, years to search; also helpful-address. Civil cases indexed by defendant, plaintiff. Civil records on index cards from 1978, index books in Denver (except criminal) back to 1861. **Criminal Records:** Access: Mail, in person. Only the court conducts in person searches; visitors may not. Search fee: $5.00 per name. Required to search: name, years to search, DOB; also helpful-address. Criminal records on index cards from 1978, index books in Denver (except criminal) back to 1861. **General Information:** No adoptions, sealed, juvenile, mental health or expunged cases released. SASE required. Turnaround time 10 working days. Copy fee: $.75 per page. Certification fee: $5.00. Fee payee: Clerk of the Combined Courts. Personal checks accepted. Prepayment is required.

Garfield County

9th District & County Courts 109 8th St #104, Glenwood Springs, CO 81601; 970-945-5075; Fax: 970-945-8756. Hours: 8AM-5PM (MST). *Felony, Misdemeanor, Civil, Eviction, Small Claims, Probate.*

Note: This court handles cases in the county east of New Castle

Civil Records: Access: Mail, in person. Only the court conducts in person searches; visitors may not. Search fee: $5.00 per name. Required to search: name, years to search. Civil cases indexed by defendant, plaintiff. Civil records on computer from 1992, on fiche from 1970, index books back to late 1800s. **Criminal Records:** Access: Mail, in person. Only the court conducts in person searches; visitors may not. Search fee: $5.00 per name. Required to search: name, years to search. Criminal records on computer from 1992, on fiche from 1970, index books back to late 1800s. **General Information:** No adoptions, sealed, juvenile, mental health or expunged cases released. SASE required. Turnaround time 1-2 weeks. Copy fee: $.75 per page. Certification fee: $5.00. Fee

payee: Garfield Combined Courts. Personal checks accepted. Credit cards accepted: Visa, Mastercard. Prepayment is required. Public access terminal is available. Public Access Terminal Note: Records available since 09/98.

County Court-Rifle 110 E 18th St, Rifle, CO 81650; 970-625-5100; Fax: 970-625-1125. Hours: 8AM-5PM (MST). *Misdemeanor, Civil Actions Under $10,000, Eviction, Small Claims.*

Note: This court handles cases in the county from New Castle to the west

Civil Records: Access: Phone, fax, mail, in person. Only the court conducts in person searches; visitors may not. No search fee. Required to search: name, years to search. Civil cases indexed by defendant, plaintiff. Civil records on index cards from 1965, computerized since 1994. **Criminal Records:** Access: Phone, fax, mail, in person. Only the court conducts in person searches; visitors may not. No search fee. Required to search: name, years to search, DOB. Criminal records on index cards from 1965, computerized since 1994. **General Information:** No adoptions, sealed, juvenile, mental health or expunged cases released. SASE required. Turnaround time 1 week. Copy fee: $.75 per page. Certification fee: $5.00 per page. Fee payee: Associate County Court. Personal checks accepted. Credit cards accepted: Mastercard. Prepayment is required. Fax notes: $1.00 per page.

Gilpin County

1st District & County Courts 2960 Dory Hill Rd #200, Golden, CO 80403-8768; 303-582-5323; Fax: 303-582-3112. Hours: 8AM-5PM (MST). *Felony, Misdemeanor, Civil, Eviction, Small Claims, Probate.*

Civil Records: Access: Mail, in person. Only the court conducts in person searches; visitors may not. Search fee: $5.00 per name. Fee is for past 7 years. Required to search: name, years to search. Civil cases indexed by defendant, plaintiff. Civil records on computer (County-1993, District-1994), on index cards from 1970s, index books from 1950s. **Criminal Records:** Access: Mail, in person. Only the court conducts in person searches; visitors may not. Search fee: $10.00 per name. Fee is for past 7 years. Required to search: name, years to search, DOB. Criminal records on computer (County-1993, District-1994), on index cards from 1970s, index books from 1950s. **General Information:** No adoptions, sealed, juvenile, mental health or expunged cases released. SASE required. Turnaround time 5 days. Copy fee: $.75 per page. Certification fee: $5.00. Fee payee: Clerk of the Combined Courts. Personal checks accepted. Prepayment is required.

Grand County

14th District & County Courts PO Box 192, Hot Sulphur Springs, CO 80451; 970-725-3357. Hours: 8AM-5PM (MST). *Felony, Misdemeanor, Civil, Eviction, Small Claims, Probate.*

Civil Records: Access: Mail, in person. Only the court conducts in person searches; visitors may not. Search fee: $5.00 per name. Required to search: name, years to search. Civil cases indexed by defendant, plaintiff. Civil records on computer from July, 1991, fiche from 1970, index books from 1900. **Criminal Records:** Access: Mail, in person. Only the court conducts in person searches; visitors may not. Search fee: $5.00 per name. Required to search: name, years to search, DOB. Criminal records on computer from July,

1991, fiche from 1970, index books from 1900. **General Information:** No adoptions, sealed, juvenile, mental health or expunged cases released. SASE required. Turnaround time 1 week. Copy fee: $.75 per page. Certification fee: $5.00. Fee payee: Grand County Combined Court. Personal checks accepted. Prepayment is required.

Gunnison County

7th District & County Courts 200 E Virginia Ave, Gunnison, CO 81230; 970-641-3500; Fax: 970-641-6876. Hours: 8:30AM-4:30PM (MST). *Felony, Misdemeanor, Civil, Eviction, Small Claims, Probate.*

Civil Records: Access: Mail, in person. Only the court conducts in person searches; visitors may not. Search fee: $5.00 per name. Required to search: name, years to search. Civil cases indexed by defendant. Civil records on computer from 1994, index cards from 1977, index books back to 1877. **Criminal Records:** Access: Mail, in person. Only the court conducts in person searches; visitors may not. Search fee: $5.00 per name. Required to search: name, years to search, DOB. Criminal records on computer from 1994, index cards from 1977, index books back to 1877. **General Information:** No adoptions, sealed, juvenile, mental health or expunged cases released. SASE required. Turnaround time 1-2 days. Copy fee: $.75 per page. Certification fee: $5.00. Fee payee: Gunnison Combined Courts. Personal checks accepted. Prepayment is required.

Hinsdale County

7th District & County Courts PO Box 245, Lake City, CO 81235; 970-944-2227; Fax: 970-944-2289. Hours: 8:30-Noon MWF (Jun-Aug) 8:30-12:00 TF (Sept-May) (MST). *Felony, Misdemeanor, Civil, Eviction, Small Claims, Probate.*

Civil Records: Access: Phone, fax, mail, in person. Only the court conducts in person searches; visitors may not. No search fee. Required to search: name, years to search. Civil cases indexed by defendant, plaintiff. Civil records on index cards from 1975, index books back to 1900. **Criminal Records:** Access: Phone, fax, mail, in person. Only the court conducts in person searches; visitors may not. Search fee: No search fee. Fee depends on time required for search. Required to search: name, years to search, DOB. Criminal records on index cards from 1975, index books back to 1900. **General Information:** No adoptions, sealed, juvenile, mental health or expunged cases released. SASE required. Turnaround time 2-4 weeks. Copy fee: $.75 per page. Certification fee: $5.00. Fee payee: Clerk of the Combined Courts. Personal checks accepted. Prepayment is required. Fax notes: $.75 per page. 1-10 pgs $2.00, 11-20 pgs $5.00, 21-30 pgs $10.00.

Huerfano County

3rd District & County Courts 401 Main St, Suite 304, Walsenburg, CO 81089; 719-738-1040; Fax: 719-738-1267. Hours: 8AM-4PM (MST). *Felony, Misdemeanor, Civil, Eviction, Small Claims, Probate.*

Civil Records: Access: Mail, in person. Only the court conducts in person searches; visitors may not. Search fee: $5.00 per name. Required to search: name, years to search. Civil cases indexed by defendant, plaintiff. Civil records on computer from 1995 (county court only), index cards from 1978, index books from 1861. **Criminal Records:** Access: Mail, in person. Only the court conducts in person searches; visitors may not. Search fee: $5.00 per name. Required to search: name, years to search, DOB. Criminal records on computer from 1995 (county court only), index cards from 1978, index books from 1861. **General Information:** No adoptions, sealed, juvenile, mental health or expunged cases released. SASE required. Turnaround time 2 weeks. Copy fee: $.75 per page. Certification fee: $5.00. Fee payee: Huerfano County Combined Courts. Personal checks accepted. Prepayment is required.

Jackson County

8th District & County Courts PO Box 308, Walden, CO 80480; 970-723-4363. Hours: 9AM-1PM (MST). *Felony, Misdemeanor, Civil, Eviction, Small Claims, Probate.*

Civil Records: Access: Mail, in person. Only the court conducts in person searches; visitors may not. No search fee. Required to search: name, years to search. Civil cases indexed by defendant, plaintiff. Civil records on computer since 1994;prior on index cards from 1974, index books from the 1900s. **Criminal Records:** Access: Mail, in person. Only the court conducts in person searches; visitors may not. No search fee. Required to search: name, years to search, DOB. Criminal records on computer since 1994;prior on index cards from 1974, index books from the 1900s. **General Information:** No adoptions, sealed, juvenile, mental health or expunged cases released. SASE required. Turnaround time 1 week. Copy fee: $.75 per page. Will bill in excess of 10 pages. Certification fee: $5.00. Fee payee: Clerk of the Combined Courts. Personal checks accepted. If a file has been pulled, information found and it is in excess of 10 pages, will bill the requesting party providing the request is honorable.

Jefferson County

1st District & County Courts 100 Jefferson County Parkway, Golden, CO 80401-6002; 303-271-6267; Fax: 303-271-6188. Hours: 8AM-5PM (MST). *Felony, Misdemeanor, Civil, Eviction, Small Claims, Probate.*

Civil Records: Access: Mail, in person. Both court and visitors may perform in person searches. Search fee: $5.00 per name. Fee is per case. Required to search: name, years to search; also helpful-address. Civil cases indexed by defendant, plaintiff. Civil records on computer from 1985, microfiche from 1975, index books from 1963-1974, archived prior to 1963. **Criminal Records:** Access: Mail, in person. Both court and visitors may perform in person searches. Search fee: $5.00 per name. Fee varies depending on # of years searched. Required to search: name, years to search, DOB; also helpful-address. Criminal records on computer from 1985, microfiche from 1975, index books from 1963-1974, archived prior to 1963. **General Information:** No adoptions, sealed, juvenile, mental health or expunged cases released. SASE required. Turnaround time 1 week. Copy fee: $.75 per page. Certification fee: $5.00. Fee payee: Clerk of Combined Courts. Personal checks accepted. Prepayment is required.

Kiowa County

15th District & County Courts PO Box 353, Eads, CO 81036; 719-438-5558; Fax: 719-438-5300. Hours: 8AM-5PM (MST). *Felony, Misdemeanor, Civil, Eviction, Small Claims, Probate.*

Civil Records: Access: Phone, fax, mail, in person. Only the court conducts in person searches; visitors may not. Search fee: $5.00 per name. Required to search: name, years to search. Civil cases indexed by defendant, plaintiff. Civil records on index cards from the 1960s, index books from 1889. Recent records are computerized. **Criminal Records:** Access: Phone, fax, mail, in person. Only the court conducts in person searches; visitors may not. Search fee: $5.00 per name. Required to search: name, years to search, DOB. Criminal records on index cards from the 1960s, index books from 1889. Recent records are computerized. **General Information:** No adoptions, sealed, juvenile, mental health or expunged cases released. SASE required. Turnaround time 1 week. Copy fee: $.75 per page. Certification fee: $5.00. Fee payee: Kiowa County Court. Business checks accepted. Fax notes: $1.00 per page.

Kit Carson County

13th District & County Courts PO Box 547, Burlington, CO 80807; 719-346-5524. Hours: 8AM-4PM (MST). *Felony, Misdemeanor, Civil, Eviction, Small Claims, Probate.*

Civil Records: Access: Mail, in person. Only the court conducts in person searches; visitors may not. Search fee: $5.00 per name. Required to search: name, years to search. Civil cases indexed by defendant, plaintiff. Civil records on index cards from 1910, index books from 1889. **Criminal Records:** Access: Mail, in person. Only the court conducts in person searches; visitors may not. No search fee. Required to search: name, years to search, DOB. Criminal records on index cards from 1910, index books from 1889. Prefer mail search requests. **General Information:** No adoptions, sealed, juvenile, mental health or expunged cases released. SASE required. Turnaround time 1 week. Copy fee: $.75 per page. Certification fee: $5.00. Fee payee: Combined Courts. No personal checks accepted. Credit cards accepted. Prepayment is required.

La Plata County

6th District Court PO Box 3340, Durango, CO 81302-3340; 970-247-2304; Fax: 970-247-4348. Hours: 8AM-5PM (MST). *Felony, Civil Actions Over $10,000, Probate.*

Civil Records: Access: Mail, in person. Only the court conducts in person searches; visitors may not. Search fee: $5.00 per name. Fee is per case. Required to search: name, years to search. Civil cases indexed by defendant, plaintiff. Civil records on computer from 1990, index cards from 1976, index books from 1874. **Criminal Records:** Access: Mail, in person. Only the court conducts in person searches; visitors may not. Search fee: $5.00 per name. Required to search: name, years to search, DOB. Criminal records on computer from 1990, index cards from 1976, index books from 1874. **General Information:** No adoptions, sealed, juvenile, mental health or expunged cases released. SASE required. Turnaround time 3-7 days. Copy fee: $.75 per page. Certification fee: $5.00. Fee payee: Clerk of the Combined Courts. Personal checks accepted. Prepayment is required.

County Court PO Box 759, Durango, CO 81302; 970-247-2004; Fax: 970-247-4348. Hours: 8AM-5PM (MST). *Misdemeanor, Civil Actions Under $10,000, Eviction, Small Claims.*

Civil Records: Access: Mail, in person. Only the court conducts in person searches; visitors may not. Search fee: $5.00 per name. Fee is per case. Required to search: name, years to search. Civil cases indexed by defendant, plaintiff. Civil records on computer from February, 1990, index cards from 1965, index books in Denver prior to 1965.

$5.00 per name; $5.00 per case. **Criminal Records:** Access: Mail, in person. Only the court conducts in person searches; visitors may not. Search fee: $5.00 per name. Required to search: name, years to search, DOB. Criminal records on computer from February, 1990, index cards from 1965, index books in Denver prior to 1965. **General Information:** No adoptions, sealed, juvenile, mental health or expunged cases released. SASE required. Turnaround time 7-10 days. Copy fee: $.75 per page. Certification fee: $5.00. Fee payee: Clerk of the Combined Courts. Personal checks accepted. Prepayment is required.

Lake County

Lake County Combined Courts PO Box 55, Leadville, CO 80461; 719-486-0535. Hours: 8AM-Noon, 1-5PM (MST). *Felony, Misdemeanor, Civil, Eviction, Small Claims, Probate.*

Civil Records: Access: Mail, in person. Only the court conducts in person searches; visitors may not. Search fee: $10.00 per name. Required to search: name, years to search. Civil cases indexed by defendant, plaintiff. Civil records on index cards from 1988 (District), 1970 (County), index books from 1865. **Criminal Records:** Access: Mail, in person. Only the court conducts in person searches; visitors may not. Search fee: $10.00 per name. Required to search: name, years to search, DOB. Criminal records on index cards from 1988 (District), 1970 (County), index books from 1865. **General Information:** No adoptions, sealed, juvenile, mental health or expunged cases released. SASE required. Turnaround time 30 days. Copy fee: $.75 per page. Certification fee: $5.00. Fee payee: Lake County Court. Business checks accepted. Prepayment is required.

Larimer County

8th District Court PO Box 2066, Ft Collins, CO 80522; 970-498-7918; Fax: 970-498-7940. Hours: 8AM-5PM (MST). *Felony, Civil Actions Over $10,000, Probate.*

Civil Records: Access: Phone, mail, in person. Both court and visitors may perform in person searches. Search fee: $5.00 per name. Required to search: name; also helpful-years to search. Civil cases indexed by defendant, plaintiff. Civil records on computer from 1976, index books back to 1861. **Criminal Records:** Access: Mail, in person. Only the court conducts in person searches; visitors may not. Search fee: $5.00 per name. Required to search: name; also helpful-years to search, DOB, SSN. Criminal records on computer from 1976, index books back to 1861. Signed release required for certain cases. **General Information:** No adoptions, sealed, juvenile, mental health or expunged cases released. SASE required. Turnaround time 7-10 days. Copy fee: $.75 per page. Certification fee: $5.00. Fee payee: Clerk of District Court. Personal checks accepted. Prepayment is required.

County Court PO Box 800, Ft Collins, CO 80522; 970-498-7550; Fax: 970-498-7569. Hours: 8AM-5PM (MST). *Misdemeanor, Civil Actions Under $10,000, Eviction, Small Claims.*

Civil Records: Access: Fax, mail, in person. Only the court conducts in person searches; visitors may not. Search fee: $5.00 per name. Required to search: name, years to search; also helpful-address. Civil cases indexed by defendant, plaintiff. some records on computer from 1986, index cards from 1965. **Criminal Records:** Access: Fax, mail, in person. Only the court conducts in person searches; visitors may not. Search fee: $5.00 per name. Required to search: name, years to search, DOB, signed release, offense; also helpful-address. some records on computer from 1986, index cards from 1965. **General Information:** No sealed cases released. SASE required. Turnaround time 7-10 days. Copy fee: $.75 per page. Certification fee: $5.00. Fee payee: Larimer County Court Clerk. Personal checks accepted. Prepayment is required.

Las Animas County

3rd District Court 200 E 1st St Rm 304, Trinidad, CO 81082; 719-846-3316/2221; Fax: 719-846-9367. Hours: 8AM-5PM (MST). *Felony, Misdemeanor, Civil, Eviction, Small Claims, Probate.*

Civil Records: Access: Mail, in person. Only the court conducts in person searches; visitors may not. Search fee: $5.00 per name. Required to search: name, years to search. Civil cases indexed by defendant, plaintiff. Civil records on index cards from 1976, index books to 1950. **Criminal Records:** Access: Mail, in person. Only the court conducts in person searches; visitors may not. Search fee: $5.00 per name. Required to search: name, years to search, DOB; also helpful-SSN. Criminal records on index cards from 1976, index books to 1950. **General Information:** No adoptions, sealed, juvenile, mental health or expunged cases released. SASE required. Turnaround time 1 week. Copy fee: $.75 per page. Certification fee: $5.00. Fee payee: Combined courts. Only cashiers checks and money orders accepted. Prepayment is required.

Lincoln County

18th District & County Courts PO Box 128, Hugo, CO 80821; 719-743-2455. Hours: 8AM-4:30PM (MST). *Felony, Misdemeanor, Civil, Eviction, Small Claims, Probate.*

Civil Records: Access: Phone, mail, in person. Only the court conducts in person searches; visitors may not. Search fee: $5.00. Required to search: name, years to search. Civil cases indexed by defendant, plaintiff. Civil records on computer since 12/94, index cards from 1977, index books back to 1889, archived 10 years back. **Criminal Records:** Access: Phone, mail, in person. Only the court conducts in person searches; visitors may not. Search fee: $5.00. Required to search: name, years to search, DOB. Criminal records on computer since 12/94, index cards from 1977, index books back to 1889, archived 10 years back. **General Information:** No adoptions, sealed, juvenile, mental health or expunged cases released. SASE required. Turnaround time within 10 days. Copy fee: $.75 per page. Certification fee: $5.00. Fee payee: Lincoln County Combined Courts. Personal checks accepted. Prepayment is required.

Logan County

13th District Court PO Box 71, Sterling, CO 80751; 970-522-6565; Fax: 970-522-6566. Hours: 8AM-4PM (MST). *Felony, Civil Actions Over $10,000, Probate.*

Civil Records: Access: Mail, in person. Only the court conducts in person searches; visitors may not. Search fee: $5.00 per name. Required to search: name, years to search. Civil cases indexed by defendant, plaintiff. Civil records computerized since 08/95, on index cards from 1973, index books back to 1887. **Criminal Records:** Access: Mail, in person. Only the court conducts in person searches; visitors may not. Search fee: $5.00 per name. Required to search: name, years to search, DOB. Criminal records computerized since 08/95, on index cards from 1973, index books back to

1887. **General Information:** No adoptions, sealed, juvenile, mental health or expunged cases released. SASE required. Turnaround time 1-2 weeks. Copy fee: $.75 per page. Certification fee: $5.00. Fee payee: Logan District Court. Personal checks accepted. Prepayment is required.

County Court PO Box 1907, Sterling, CO 80751; 970-522-1572; Fax: 970-522-2875. Hours: 8AM-4PM (MST). *Misdemeanor, Civil Actions Under $10,000, Eviction, Small Claims.*

Civil Records: Access: Phone, mail, in person. Both court and visitors may perform in person searches. Search fee: $5.00 per name. Required to search: name, years to search. Civil cases indexed by defendant, plaintiff. Civil records on computer since 08/95; prior on index cards from 1972 and index books from 1965. **Criminal Records:** Access: Phone, mail, in person. Both court and visitors may perform in person searches. Search fee: $5.00 per name. Required to search: name, years to search, DOB. Criminal records on computer since 08/95; prior on index cards from 1972 and index books from 1965. **General Information:** No adoptions, sealed, juvenile, mental health or expunged cases released. SASE required. Turnaround time 1-2 weeks. Copy fee: $.75 per page. Certification fee: $5.00. Fee payee: Logan County Court. Business checks accepted. Credit cards accepted.

Mesa County

21st District Court Mesa County District Court, PO Box 20000, Grand Junction, CO 81502-5032; 970-257-3625; Fax: 970-257-3690. Hours: 8AM-5PM (MST). *Felony, Civil Actions Over $10,000, Probate.*

Civil Records: Access: Phone, mail, in person. Both court and visitors may perform in person searches. Search fee: $5.00 per name. Required to search: name, years to search. Civil cases indexed by defendant, plaintiff. Civil records on computer since 1989, on microfiche to 1976, books from late 1800s. **Criminal Records:** Access: Mail, in person. Only the court conducts in person searches; visitors may not. Search fee: $5.00 per name. Required to search: name, years to search, DOB. Criminal records on computer since 1989, on microfiche to 1976, books from late 1800s. **General Information:** No adoptions, sealed, juvenile, mental health or expunged cases released. SASE required. Turnaround time 5-7 days. Copy fee: $.75 per page. Certification fee: $5.00. Fee payee: Mesa County District Court. Business checks accepted. Credit cards accepted: Visa, Mastercard. Prepayment is required.

County Court PO Box 20000, Grand Junction, CO 81502-5032; 970-257-3640. Hours: 8AM-5PM (MST). *Misdemeanor, Civil Actions Under $10,000, Eviction, Small Claims.*

Civil Records: Access: Mail, in person. Only the court conducts in person searches; visitors may not. Search fee: $5.00 per name. Required to search: name, years to search. Civil cases indexed by defendant, plaintiff. Civil records on computer from 10/89. **Criminal Records:** Access: Mail, in person. Only the court conducts in person searches; visitors may not. Search fee: $5.00 per name. Required to search: name, years to search, DOB. Criminal records on computer from 10/89. **General Information:** No adoptions, sealed, juvenile, mental health or expunged cases released. SASE required. Turnaround time immediate if case is on computer. Copy fee: $.75 per page. Certification fee: $5.00. Fee payee: Mesa County Court. Personal checks accepted. Credit cards

accepted: Visa, Mastercard. Accepted in person only. Prepayment is required.

Mineral County

12th District & County Courts PO Box 337, Creede, CO 81130; 719-658-2575; Fax: 719-658-2575. Hours: 10AM-3PM (MST). *Felony, Misdemeanor, Civil, Eviction, Small Claims, Probate.*

Civil Records: Access: Mail, in person. Only the court conducts in person searches; visitors may not. Search fee: $5.00 per name. Required to search: name, years to search. Civil cases indexed by defendant, plaintiff. Civil records on computer since July 1993, on index cards from 1977, index books back to 1893. **Criminal Records:** Access: Mail, in person. Only the court conducts in person searches; visitors may not. Search fee: $5.00 per name. Required to search: name, years to search, DOB. Criminal records on computer since July 1993, on index cards from 1977, index books back to 1893. **General Information:** No adoptions, sealed, juvenile, mental health or expunged cases released. SASE required. Turnaround time 2-3 days. Copy fee: $.75 per page. Certification fee: $5.00. Fee payee: Mineral Combined Courts. Personal checks accepted. Prepayment is required.

Moffat County

Moffat County Combined Court 221 W Victory Wy, Craig, CO 81625; 970-824-8254. Hours: 8AM-5PM (MST). *Felony, Misdemeanor, Civil, Eviction, Small Claims, Probate.*

Civil Records: Access: Phone, mail, in person. Only the court conducts in person searches; visitors may not. Search fee: Search Fee: $5.00 1976-91; $20.00 prior to 1976. Required to search: name, years to search. Civil cases indexed by defendant, plaintiff. Civil records on computer from 1992, index cards from 1976, either microfilmed or archived back to 1911. **Criminal Records:** Access: Mail, in person. Only the court conducts in person searches; visitors may not. Search fee: $5.00 1976-1991; $20.00 prior to 1976. Required to search: name, years to search, DOB. Criminal records on computer from 1992, index cards from 1976, either microfilmed or archived back to 1911. **General Information:** No adoptions, sealed, juvenile, mental health or expunged cases released. SASE required. Turnaround time 1-2 weeks. Copy fee: $.75 per page. Certification fee: $5.00. Fee payee: Moffat County Combined Courts. Personal checks accepted. Prepayment is required.

Montezuma County

Montezuma (22nd) District Court 109 W Main St, #210, Cortez, CO 81321; 970-565-1111. Hours: 8AM-4:30PM (MST). *Felony, Civil Actions Over $10,000, Probate.*

Civil Records: Access: Mail, in person. Only the court conducts in person searches; visitors may not. Search fee: $5.00 per name or case number, or $20.00 per hour to search. Required to search: name, years to search. Civil cases indexed by defendant, plaintiff. Civil records on computer since 6/95, microfiche up to 1988, index cards from 1975, index books back to late 1890s. **Criminal Records:** Access: Mail, in person. Only the court conducts in person searches; visitors may not. Search fee: $5.00 per name or case number, or $20.00 per hour to search. Required to search: name, years to search, DOB. Criminal records on computer since 6/95, microfiche up to 1988, index cards from 1975, index books back to late 1890s. **General Information:** No adoptions, sealed, juvenile, mental health or expunged cases released. SASE required. Turnaround time 1-2 weeks. Copy fee: $.75 per page. Certification fee: $5.00. Fee payee: Montezuma District Court. Personal checks accepted. Will bill mailing and copy costs.

County Court 601 N Mildred Rd, Cortez, CO 81321; 970-565-7580; Fax: 970-565-8798. Hours: 8AM-4:30PM (MST). *Misdemeanor, Civil Actions Under $10,000, Eviction, Small Claims.*

Civil Records: Access: Mail, in person. Only the court conducts in person searches; visitors may not. No search fee. Required to search: name, years to search. Civil cases indexed by defendant, plaintiff. Civil records on computer since 1993. **Criminal Records:** Access: Mail, in person. Only the court conducts in person searches; visitors may not. No search fee. Required to search: name, years to search, DOB. Criminal records on index cards from 1975, index books prior. **General Information:** No adoptions, sealed, juvenile, mental health or expunged cases released. SASE required. Turnaround time 5-7 days. Copy fee: $.75 per page. Certification fee: $5.00. Fee payee: Montezuma County Court. Personal checks accepted. Prepayment is required.

Montrose County

7th District & County Courts 1200 N Grand Ave #A, Montrose, CO 81401-3164; 970-252-4300; 242-4309; Fax: 970-252-4345. Hours: 8:30AM-4:30PM (MST). *Felony, Misdemeanor, Civil, Eviction, Small Claims, Probate.*

www.courts.state.co.us

Civil Records: Access: Mail, in person. Search fee: $5.00 per name. Required to search: name, years to search. Civil cases indexed by defendant, plaintiff. Civil records on index cards from 1975, index books back to 1890. **Criminal Records:** Access: Mail, in person. Only the court conducts in person searches; visitors may not. Search fee: $5.00 per name. Required to search: name, years to search, DOB. Criminal records on index cards from 1975, index books back to 1890. **General Information:** No adoptions, sealed, juvenile, mental health or expunged cases released. SASE required. Turnaround time 1 week. Copy fee: $.75 per page. Certification fee: $5.00. Fee payee: Montrose Combined Courts. Personal checks accepted. Prepayment is required.

Morgan County

13th District Court PO Box 130, Ft Morgan, CO 80701; 970-542-3435; Fax: 970-542-3436. Hours: 8AM-4PM (MST). *Felony, Civil Actions Over $10,000, Probate.*

Civil Records: Access: Fax, mail, in person. Only the court conducts in person searches; visitors may not. No search fee. Required to search: name, years to search. Civil cases indexed by defendant, plaintiff. Civil records on index cards from 1967, index books back to 1906. **Criminal Records:** Access: Fax, mail, in person. Only the court conducts in person searches; visitors may not. No search fee. Required to search: name, years to search, DOB, SSN. Criminal records on index cards from 1967, index books back to 1906. **General Information:** No adoptions, sealed, juvenile, mental health or expunged cases released. SASE required. Turnaround time 2-3 days. Copy fee: $.75 per page. Certification fee: $5.00. Fee payee: Morgan District Court. Personal checks accepted. Will bill copy fees to attorneys.

County Court PO Box 695, Ft Morgan, CO 80701; 970-542-3414; Fax: 970-542-3416. Hours: 8AM-4PM (MST). *Misdemeanor, Civil Actions Under $10,000, Eviction, Small Claims.*

Civil Records: Access: Mail, in person. Only the court conducts in person searches; visitors may not. Search fee: $5.00 per name. Required to search: name, years to search. Civil cases indexed by defendant, plaintiff. Civil records on computer since 08/95; prior on index cards from 1980. **Criminal Records:** Access: Mail, in person. Only the court conducts in person searches; visitors may not. Search fee: $5.00 per name. Required to search: name, years to search, DOB. Criminal records on computer since 08/95; prior on index cards from 1980. **General Information:** No adoptions, sealed, juvenile, mental health or expunged cases released. SASE required. Turnaround time 2-3 days. Copy fee: $.75 per page. Certification fee: $5.00. Fee payee: Morgan County Court. Personal checks accepted. Prepayment is required.

Otero County

16th District Court Courthouse Rm 207, La Junta, CO 81050; 719-384-4951 (Dist) 384-4721 (County); Fax: 719-384-4991. Hours: 8AM-5PM (MST). *Felony, Civil, Probate.*

www.courts.state.co.us/district/16th/dist-16.htm

Civil Records: Access: Mail, in person. Only the court conducts in person searches; visitors may not. Search fee: $5.00 per name. Required to search: name, years to search. Civil cases indexed by defendant, plaintiff. Civil records on index cards from 1978, index books back to 1889, microfiche from 1889-1991. **Criminal Records:** Access: Mail, in person. Only the court conducts in person searches; visitors may not. Search fee: $5.00 per name. Required to search: name, years to search, DOB. Criminal records on index cards from 1978, index books back to 1889, microfiche from 1889-19791. **General Information:** No adoptions, sealed, juvenile, mental health or expunged cases released. SASE required. Turnaround time 1 week. Copy fee: $.75 per page. Certification fee: $5.00. Fee payee: Otero County Combined Courts. Personal checks accepted. Prepayment is required.

County Court Courthouse Rm 105, 13 West 3rd St, La Junta, CO 81050; 719-384-4721; Fax: 719-384-4991; 384-4772 (County Court). Hours: 8AM-Noon, 1-5PM (MST). *Misdemeanor, Civil Actions Under $10,000, Eviction, Small Claims.*

Civil Records: Access: Mail, in person. Only the court conducts in person searches; visitors may not. Search fee: $5.00 per name. Required to search: name, years to search. Civil cases indexed by defendant, plaintiff. Civil records on microfilm prior to 1991, index cards back to 1950s. **Criminal Records:** Access: Mail, in person. Only the court conducts in person searches; visitors may not. Search fee: $5.00 per name. Required to search: name; also helpful-years to search. Criminal records on microfilm prior to 1991, index cards back to 1950s. **General Information:** No adoptions, sealed, juvenile, sexual abuse, assault, mental health or expunged cases released. SASE required. Turnaround time 5 days. Copy fee: $.75 per page. Certification fee: $5.00. Fee payee: Otero County Courts. Personal checks accepted. Prepayment is required.

Ouray County

7th District & County Courts PO Box 643, Ouray, CO 81427; 970-325-4405; Fax: 970-

325-7364. Hours: 8:30AM-Noon, 1-4PM (MST). *Felony, Misdemeanor, Civil, Eviction, Small Claims, Probate.*

Civil Records: Access: Mail, in person. Only the court conducts in person searches; visitors may not. Search fee: $5.00 per name. Required to search: name, years to search. Civil cases indexed by defendant, plaintiff. Civil records on computer since 1994, index cards from 1976, index books back to 1886, archived prior to 1925. **Criminal Records:** Access: Mail, in person. Only the court conducts in person searches; visitors may not. Search fee: $5.00 per name. Required to search: name, years to search, DOB. Criminal records on computer since 1994, index cards from 1976, index books back to 1886, archived prior to 1925. **General Information:** No adoptions, sealed, juvenile, financial, drug/alcohol evaluations, mental health or expunged cases released. SASE not required. Turnaround time 1 week. Copy fee: $.75 per page. Certification fee: $5.00. Fee payee: Ouray Combined Courts. Personal checks accepted. Prepayment is required.

Park County

Park County Combined Courts PO Box 190, Fairplay, CO 80440; 719-836-2940; Fax: 719-836-2892. Hours: 8:30AM-4PM (MST). *Felony, Misdemeanor, Civil, Eviction, Small Claims, Probate.*

Civil Records: Access: Mail, in person. Only the court conducts in person searches; visitors may not. Search fee: $5.00 per name. Required to search: name, years to search. Civil cases indexed by defendant, plaintiff. Civil records computerized since 1995, on index cards from 1978, index books back to 1950, archived prior to 1950. **Criminal Records:** Access: Mail, in person. Only the court conducts in person searches; visitors may not. Search fee: $5.00 per name. Required to search: name, years to search, DOB, signed release. Criminal records computerized since 1995, on index cards from 1978, index books back to 1950, archived prior to 1950. Release needed for juvenile cases. **General Information:** No adoptions, sealed, juvenile, mental health or expunged cases released. SASE required. Turnaround time within 1 week. Copy fee: $.50 per page. Certification fee: $5.00. Fee payee: Park County Combined Court. Personal checks accepted. Prepayment is required.

Phillips County

13th District & County Courts 221 S Interocean, Holyoke, CO 80734; 970-854-3279; Fax: 970-854-3179. Hours: 8AM-Noon, 1-4PM (MST). *Felony, Misdemeanor, Civil, Eviction, Small Claims, Probate.*

Civil Records: Access: Phone, fax, mail, in person. Only the court conducts in person searches; visitors may not. No search fee. Required to search: name, years to search. Civil cases indexed by defendant, plaintiff. Civil records on computer since 08/85; prior on index cards from 1970, index books back to 1889. **Criminal Records:** Access: Phone, fax, mail, in person. Only the court conducts in person searches; visitors may not. No search fee. Required to search: name, years to search, DOB. Criminal records on computer since 08/85; prior on index cards from 1970, index books back to 1889. **General Information:** No adoptions, sealed, juvenile, mental health or expunged cases released. SASE required. Turnaround time 1-3 days. Copy fee: $.75 per page. Certification fee: $5.00. Fee payee: Phillips County Combined Court. Personal checks accepted. Prepayment is required.

Pitkin County

9th District & County Courts 506 E Main St, Ste 300, Aspen, CO 81611; 970-925-7635; Fax: 970-925-6349. Hours: 8AM-Noon, 1-5PM (MST). *Felony, Misdemeanor, Civil, Eviction, Small Claims, Probate.*

Civil Records: Access: Mail, in person. Both court and visitors may perform in person searches. Search fee: There is no fee for computer search. Required to search: name, years to search. Civil cases indexed by defendant. Civil records on computer from 1989, microfiche from 1940-1970, index cards from 1972. **Criminal Records:** Access: Mail, in person. Both court and visitors may perform in person searches. Search fee: There is no fee for searching computer, otherwise rate determined by time and volume. Required to search: name, years to search, DOB. Criminal records on computer from 1989, microfiche from 1940-1970, index cards from 1972. **General Information:** No adoptions, sealed, juvenile, mental health or expunged cases released. Turnaround time 1 week. Copy fee: $.75 per page. Certification fee: $5.00. Fee payee: Pitkin County Combined Court. Only cashiers checks and money orders accepted. Credit cards accepted: Visa, Mastercard. Prepayment is required.

Prowers County

15th District Court PO Box 1178, Lamar, CO 81052; 719-336-7424; Fax: 719-336-9757. Hours: 8AM-5PM (MST). *Felony, Civil Actions Over $10,000, Probate.*

Civil Records: Access: Fax, mail, in person. Only the court conducts in person searches; visitors may not. No search fee. Required to search: name, years to search. Civil cases indexed by defendant, plaintiff. Civil records computerized since 1995, on microfiche from 1920, index books from the late 1800s. **Criminal Records:** Access: Fax, mail, in person. Only the court conducts in person searches; visitors may not. No search fee. Required to search: name, years to search, DOB. Criminal records computerized since 1995, on microfiche from 1920, index books from the late 1800s. **General Information:** No adoptions, sealed, juvenile, mental health or expunged cases released. SASE required. Turnaround time 1 week. Copy fee: $.75 per page. Certification fee: $5.00. Fee payee: Clerk of District Court. Only cashiers checks and money orders accepted. Prepayment is required. Fax notes: $1.00 per page.

County Court PO Box 525, Lamar, CO 81052; 719-336-7416; Fax: 719-336-9757. Hours: 8AM-5PM (MST). *Misdemeanor, Civil Actions Under $10,000, Eviction, Small Claims.*

Civil Records: Access: Mail, in person. Both court and visitors may perform in person searches. No search fee. Required to search: name, years to search. Civil cases indexed by defendant, plaintiff. Civil records on computer since 10/95, prior on books. **Criminal Records:** Access: Mail, in person. Both court and visitors may perform in person searches. No search fee. Required to search: name, years to search; also helpful-DOB. Criminal records on computer since 10/95, prior on books. **General Information:** No adoptions, sealed, juvenile, mental health or expunged cases released. SASE required. Turnaround time 2-3 days. Copy fee: $.75 per page. Certification fee: $5.00. Fee payee: Prowers County Court. Personal checks accepted. Prepayment is required.

Pueblo County

Combined Courts 320 West 10th St, Pueblo, CO 81003; 719-583-7055; Fax: 719-583-7126. Hours: 8AM-5PM (MST). *Felony, Misdemeanor, Civil, Eviction, Small Claims, Probate.*

Civil Records: Access: Mail, in person. Only the court conducts in person searches; visitors may not. Search fee: $5.00 per name. Required to search: name, years to search; also helpful-address. Civil cases indexed by defendant, plaintiff. Civil records on computer from 1976, index books back to the 1890s. **Criminal Records:** Access: Mail, in person. Only the court conducts in person searches; visitors may not. Search fee: $5.00 per name. Required to search: name, years to search, DOB; also helpful-address, SSN. Criminal records on computer from 1976, index books back to the 1890s. **General Information:** No adoptions, sealed, juvenile, mental health or expunged cases released. SASE required. Turnaround time 3-5 days. Copy fee: $.75 per page. Certification fee: $5.00. Fee payee: Clerk of Court. Personal checks accepted. Prepayment is required.

Rio Blanco County

9th District & County Courts 555 Main St Rm 303, PO Box 1150, Meeker, CO 81641; 970-878-5622. Hours: 8AM-Noon, 1-5PM (MST). *Felony, Misdemeanor, Civil, Eviction, Small Claims, Probate.*

Civil Records: Access: Phone, mail, in person. Only the court conducts in person searches; visitors may not. Search fee: $5.00 per name. May charge for lengthy in-person search request. Required to search: name; also helpful-years to search. Civil cases indexed by defendant, plaintiff. Civil records on computer since August, 1994, on index cards from April 1976, index books back to 1889. **Criminal Records:** Access: Phone, mail, in person. Only the court conducts in person searches; visitors may not. Search fee: $5.00 per name. May charge for lengthy in-person search request. Required to search: name, years to search; also helpful-DOB. Criminal records on computer since August, 1994, on index cards from April 1976, index books back to 1889. **General Information:** No adoptions, sealed, juvenile, mental health or expunged cases released. SASE required. Turnaround time 2 days. Copy fee: $.75 per page. Certification fee: $5.00. Fee payee: Clerk of the Combined Courts. Business checks accepted. Prepayment is required.

Rio Grande County

12th District & County Courts 6th & Cherry, PO Box 427, Del Norte, CO 81132; 719-657-3394. Hours: 8AM-Noon, 1-4PM (MST). *Felony, Misdemeanor, Civil, Eviction, Small Claims, Probate.*

Civil Records: Access: Mail, in person. Only the court conducts in person searches; visitors may not. Search fee: $5.00 per name. Required to search: name, years to search. Civil cases indexed by defendant, plaintiff. Civil records on computer from June, 1994, County on index cards from 1950s, District from 1977. All on index books from the 1800s. **Criminal Records:** Access: Mail, in person. Only the court conducts in person searches; visitors may not. Search fee: $5.00 per name. Required to search: name, DOB; also helpful-years to search. Criminal records on computer from June, 1994, County on index cards from 1950s, District from 1977. All on index books from the 1800s. **General Information:** No adoptions, sealed, juvenile, mental health or

expunged cases released. SASE required. Turnaround time 2-4 days. Copy fee: $.75 per page. Certification fee: $5.00. Fee payee: Rio Grande Combined Court. Personal checks accepted. In-state personal & business checks accepted. Prepayment is required.

Routt County

Routt Combined Courts PO Box 773117, Steamboat Springs, CO 80477; 970-879-5020; Fax: 970-879-3531. Hours: 8AM-5PM (MST). *Felony, Misdemeanor, Civil, Eviction, Small Claims, Probate.*

Civil Records: Access: Mail, in person. Both court and visitors may perform in person searches. Search fee: Fee for 1976-1991 $5.00, prior to 1976 $20.00. There is no fee to search computer records. Required to search: name, years to search. Civil cases indexed by defendant. Civil records on computer since 1992, on index cards from 1977, microfiche from January 1977 to December 1990, archived from 1877. **Criminal Records:** Access: Mail, in person. Both court and visitors may perform in person searches. Search fee: Same fees as civil. Required to search: name, years to search, DOB, maiden name, aliases. Criminal records on computer since 1992, on index cards from 1977, microfiche from January 1977 to December 1990, archived from 1877. **General Information:** No adoptions, sealed, juvenile, mental health or expunged cases released. SASE required. Turnaround time is as time permits. Copy fee: $.75 per page. Certification fee: $5.00. Fee payee: Routt Combined Court. Personal checks accepted. Prepayment is required.

Saguache County

12th District & County Courts PO Box 164, Saguache, CO 81149; 719-655-2522; Fax: 719-655-2522. Hours: 8AM-Noon, 1-5PM (MST). *Felony, Misdemeanor, Civil, Eviction, Small Claims, Probate.*

Civil Records: Access: Mail, in person. Only the court conducts in person searches; visitors may not. Search fee: $5.00 per name. Required to search: name, years to search. Civil cases indexed by defendant, plaintiff. Civil records on computer since 06/94, on index cards from 1980s, index books back to 1866. **Criminal Records:** Access: Mail, in person. Only the court conducts in person searches; visitors may not. Search fee: $5.00 per name. Required to search: name, years to search, DOB. Criminal records on computer since 06/94, on index cards from 1980s, index books back to 1866. **General Information:** No adoptions, sealed, juvenile, mental health or expunged cases released. SASE required. Turnaround time within 10-12 days. Copy fee: $.75 per page. Certification fee: $5.00. Fee payee: Saguache Combined Courts. Personal checks accepted. Prepayment is required.

San Juan County

6th District & County Courts PO Box 900, Silverton, CO 81433; 970-387-5790. Hours: 8AM-4PM T & TH, 8AM-Noon W (MST). *Felony, Misdemeanor, Civil, Eviction, Small Claims, Probate.*

Civil Records: Access: Mail, in person. Both court and visitors may perform in person searches. Search fee: $20.00 per hour. Fee is for lengthy search. Required to search: name, years to search. Civil cases indexed by defendant, plaintiff. Civil records on computer since 1995; prior on index cards from 1975, index books back to 1876. **Criminal Records:** Access: Mail, in person. Both court and visitors may perform in person searches.

Search fee: $8.00 per name. Required to search: name, years to search; also helpful-DOB. Criminal records on computer since 1995; prior on index cards from 1975, index books back to 1876. **General Information:** No adoptions, sealed, juvenile, mental health, open domestic, probate or expunged cases released. SASE required. Turnaround time 1 week. Copy fee: $.75 per page. Certification fee: $5.00. Fee payee: San Juan County Court. Business checks accepted. Prepayment is required.

San Miguel County

7th District & County Courts PO Box 919, Telluride, CO 81435; 970-728-3891; Fax: 970-728-6216. Hours: 9AM-Noon, 1PM-4:30PM (MST). *Felony, Misdemeanor, Civil, Eviction, Small Claims, Probate.*

Civil Records: Access: Mail, in person. Only the court conducts in person searches; visitors may not. Search fee: $5.00 per name. Required to search: name, years to search. Civil cases indexed by defendant, plaintiff. Civil records on index cards from 1970, index books back to 1861, archived back to 1880. **Criminal Records:** Access: Mail, in person. Only the court conducts in person searches; visitors may not. Search fee: $5.00 per name. Required to search: name, years to search, DOB. Criminal records on index cards from 1970, index books back to 1861, archived back to 1880. **General Information:** No adoptions, sealed, juvenile, mental health or expunged cases released. SASE required. Turnaround time 30 days. Copy fee: $.75 per page. Certification fee: $5.00. Fee payee: Combined Courts. Personal checks accepted. Prepayment is required.

Sedgwick County

13th District & County Courts Third & Pine, Julesburg, CO 80737; 970-474-3627; Fax: 970-474-2026. Hours: 8AM-1PM (MST). *Felony, Misdemeanor, Civil, Eviction, Small Claims, Probate.*

Civil Records: Access: Fax, mail, in person. Both court and visitors may perform in person searches. No search fee. Required to search: name; also helpful-years to search. Civil cases indexed by defendant, plaintiff. Civil records on index cards from early 1970s, index books back to 1889. **Criminal Records:** Access: Fax, mail, in person. Both court and visitors may perform in person searches. Search fee: No search fee. The court reserves the right to charge if an extensive search is required. Required to search: name, DOB; also helpful-years to search. Criminal records on index cards from early 1970s, index books back to 1889. **General Information:** No adoptions, sealed, juvenile, mental health or expunged cases released. SASE required. Turnaround time 1-2 days. Copy fee: $.75 per page. Certification fee: $5.00. Fee payee: Sedgwick County Combined Court. Personal checks accepted. Prepayment is required. Fax notes: $5.00 per document.

Summit County

5th District & County Courts PO Box 185, Breckenridge, CO 80424; 970-453-2241. Hours: 8AM-5PM (MST). *Felony, Misdemeanor, Civil, Eviction, Small Claims, Probate.*

Note: District Court uses PO Box 269

Civil Records: Access: In person only. Court does not conduct in person searches; visitors must perform searches for themselves. Search fee: No civil searches performed by court. Required to search: name. Civil cases indexed by defendant, plaintiff. Civil records on index cards from the early 1970s, index books back to 1861, archived from 1980 and prior. **Criminal Records:** Access: In person only. Court does not conduct in person searches; visitors must perform searches for themselves. Search fee: No criminal searches performed by court. Required to search: name, DOB, signed release. name index on computer as of 09/95. **General Information:** No adoptions, sealed, juvenile, mental health or expunged cases released. Copy fee: $.75 per page. Certification fee: $5.00. Only cashiers checks and money orders accepted. Cash accepted in person. Prepayment is required.

Teller County

4th District & County Courts PO Box 997, Cripple Creek, CO 80813; 719-689-2543. Hours: 8:30AM-4PM (MST). *Felony, Misdemeanor, Civil, Eviction, Small Claims, Probate.*

Civil Records: Access: Mail, in person. Only the court conducts in person searches; visitors may not. Search fee: $5.00 per name. If not on computer, fee is $20.00 per hour. Required to search: name, years to search. Civil cases indexed by defendant, plaintiff. Civil records computerized since 1988, on index cards from 1960, index books back to 1899. **Criminal Records:** Access: Mail, in person. Only the court conducts in person searches; visitors may not. Search fee: $5.00 per name. If records not on computer, fee is $20.00 per hour. Required to search: name, years to search, DOB; also helpful-address, SSN. Criminal records computerized since 1988, on index cards from 1960, index books back to 1899. **General Information:** No adoptions, sealed, juvenile, mental health or expunged cases released. SASE required. Turnaround time 3-5 days, 4-6 weeks if not computerized. Copy fee: $.75 per page. Certification fee: $5.00. Fee payee: Teller County Combined Courts. Only cashiers checks and money orders accepted. Prepayment is required.

Washington County

Washington County Combined Court PO Box 455, Akron, CO 80720; 970-345-2756; Fax: 970-345-2829. Hours: 8AM-Noon, 1-5PM (MST). *Felony, Misdemeanor, Civil, Eviction, Small Claims, Probate.*

Civil Records: Access: Phone, mail, in person. Both court and visitors may perform in person searches. No search fee. Required to search: name,

years to search. Civil cases indexed by defendant. Civil records on index cards from 1970, index books back to 1887. **Criminal Records:** Access: Phone, mail, in person. Only the court conducts in person searches; visitors may not. No search fee. Required to search: name, years to search, DOB. Criminal records on index cards from 1970, index books back to 1887. **General Information:** No adoptions, sealed, juvenile, mental health or expunged cases released. SASE required. Turnaround time 2-3 days. Copy fee: $.75 per page. Certification fee: $5.00. Fee payee: Washington County Combined Court. Personal checks accepted. Prepayment is required.

Weld County

19th District & County Courts PO Box C, Greeley, CO 80632; 970-351-7300; Fax: 970-356-4356. Hours: 8AM-5PM (MST). *Felony, Misdemeanor, Civil, Eviction, Small Claims, Probate.*

Civil Records: Access: Mail, in person. Both court and visitors may perform in person searches. Search fee: $5.00 per name. Required to search: name, years to search. Civil cases indexed by defendant, plaintiff. Civil records on computer from 1975 (District), 1990 (County), index cards from 1958, index books back to 1876. **Criminal Records:** Access: Mail, in person. Both court and visitors may perform in person searches. Search fee: $5.00 per name. Required to search: name, years to search; also helpful-DOB. Criminal records on computer from 1975 (District), 1990 (County), index cards from 1958, index books back to 1876. **General Information:** No adoptions, sealed, juvenile, mental health or expunged cases released. SASE required. Turnaround time 3 days. Copy fee: $.75 per page. Certification fee: $5.00. Fee payee: Clerk of Court. Personal checks accepted. Prepayment is required.

Yuma County

13th District & County Courts PO Box 347, Wray, CO 80758; 970-332-4118; Fax: 970-332-4119. Hours: 8AM-4PM (MST). *Felony, Misdemeanor, Civil, Eviction, Small Claims, Probate.*

Civil Records: Access: Mail, in person. Only the court conducts in person searches; visitors may not. Search fee: $5.00 per name. Required to search: name, years to search. Civil cases indexed by defendant. Civil records on index cards from 1982, index books back to 1889. **Criminal Records:** Access: Mail, in person. Only the court conducts in person searches; visitors may not. Search fee: $5.00 per name. Required to search: name. Criminal records on index cards from 1982, index books back to 1889. **General Information:** No adoptions, sealed, juvenile, mental health or expunged cases released. SASE required. Turnaround time 2-5 days. Copy fee: $.75 per page. Certification fee: $5.00. Fee payee: Yuma County Combined Court. Personal checks accepted. Prepayment is required.

ORGANIZATION   63 counties, 63 recording offices. The recording officer is County Clerk and Recorder. The entire state is in the Mountain Time Zone (MST).

REAL ESTATE RECORDS   Counties do **not** perform real estate searches. Copy fees are usually $1.25 per page and certification fees are usually $1.00 per document. Tax records are located in the Assessor's Office.

UCC RECORDS   Financing statements are filed at the state level, except for consumer goods, farm and real estate related collateral, which are filed with the County Clerk and Recorder. All counties will perform UCC searches. Use search request form UCC-11. Search fees are usually $5.00 per debtor name for the first year and $2.00 for each additional year searched (or $13.00 for a five year search). Copies usually cost $1.25 per page.

TAX LIEN RECORDS   Federal and some state tax liens on personal property are filed with the Secretary of State. Other federal and state tax liens are filed with the County Clerk and Recorder. Many counties will perform tax lien searches, usually at the same fees as UCC searches. Copies usually cost $1.25 per page

OTHER LIENS   Judgments, motor vehicle, mechanics.

Adams County
County Clerk and Recorder, 450 South 4th Avenue, Administrative Building, Brighton, CO 80601-3197. 303-654-6020. Fax: 303-654-6009.

Alamosa County
County Clerk and Recorder, P.O. Box 630, Alamosa, CO 81101. 719-589-6681. Fax: 719-589-6118.

Arapahoe County
County Clerk and Recorder, 5334 South Prince Street, Littleton, CO 80166-0060. 303-795-4520. Fax: 303-794-4625.
www.co.arapahoe.co.us
Online Access: Assessor. Records on the Arapahoe County Assessor database are available free on the Internet at www.co.arapahoe.co.us/as/ResForm.htm.

Archuleta County
County Clerk and Recorder, P.O. Box 2589, Pagosa Springs, CO 81147-2589. 970-264-5633. Fax: 970-264-6423.

Baca County
County Clerk and Recorder, 741 Main Street, Courthouse, Springfield, CO 81073. 719-523-4372. Fax: 719-523-4881.

Bent County
County Clerk and Recorder, P.O. Box 350, Las Animas, CO 81054. 719-456-2009. Fax: 719-456-0375.

Boulder County
County Clerk and Recorder, 1750 33rd St #201, Boulder, CO 80301. 3034137770.

Chaffee County
County Clerk and Recorder, P.O. Box 699, Salida, CO 81201. 719-539-6913. Fax: 719-539-8588.

Cheyenne County
County Clerk and Recorder, P.O. Box 567, Cheyenne Wells, CO 80810. 719-767-5685. Fax: 719-767-5540.

Clear Creek County
County Clerk and Recorder, P.O. Box 2000, Georgetown, CO 80444-2000. 303-679-2339. Fax: 303-679-2441.

Conejos County
County Clerk and Recorder, P.O. Box 127, Conejos, CO 81129-0127. 719-376-5422. Fax: 719-376-5661.

Costilla County
County Clerk and Recorder, P.O. Box 308, San Luis, CO 81152. 719-672-3301. Fax: 719-672-3962.

Crowley County
County Clerk and Recorder, 110 W. 6th St., Ordway, CO 81063-1092. 719-267-4643. Fax: 719-267-4608.

Custer County
County Clerk and Recorder, P.O. Box 150, Westcliffe, CO 81252. 719-783-2441. Fax: 719-783-2885.

Delta County
County Clerk and Recorder, 501 Palmer Street, Suite 211, Delta, CO 81416. 970-874-2150. Fax: 970-874-2161.

Denver County
County Clerk and Recorder, 1437 Bannock Street #200, Denver, CO 80202. 303-640-7290. Fax: 303-640-3628.
www.denvergov.org
Online Access: Assessor. Records on the Denver City and Denver County Assessor database are available free on the Internet at www.denvergov.org/realproperty.asp.

Dolores County
County Clerk and Recorder, P.O. Box 58, Dove Creek, CO 81324-0058. 970-677-2381. Fax: 970-677-2815.

Douglas County
County Clerk and Recorder, P.O. Box 1360, Castle Rock, CO 80104. 303-660-7446. Fax: 303-688-3060.

Eagle County
County Clerk and Recorder, P.O. Box 537, Eagle, CO 81631. 970-328-8710. Fax: 970-328-8716.
http://208.14.222.204/HTDOCS/eaglecounty/assessor/input.cfm
Online Access: Assessor. Records on the Eagle County Assessor Database are available free on the Internet.

El Paso County
County Clerk and Recorder, P.O. Box 2007, Colorado Springs, CO 80901-2007. 719-520-6200. Fax: 719-520-6230.
www.co.el-paso.co.us
Online Access: Assessor. Records on the El Paso County Assessor database are available free on the Internet at www.co.el-paso.co.us/assessor/asr_location/srch.htm.

Elbert County
County Clerk and Recorder, P.O. Box 37, Kiowa, CO 80117. 303-621-3116. Fax: 303-621-3168.

Fremont County
County Clerk and Recorder, 615 Macon Avenue, Room 100, Canon City, CO 81212-3311. 719-275-1522. Fax: 719-275-1594.

Garfield County
County Clerk and Recorder, 109 8th Street, Suite 200, Glenwood Springs, CO 81601. 970-945-2377. Fax: 970-945-7785.

Gilpin County
County Clerk and Recorder, P.O. Box 429, Central City, CO 80427. 303-582-5321. Fax: 303-582-5440.

Grand County
County Clerk and Recorder, P.O. Box 120, Hot Sulphur Springs, CO 80451. 970-725-3347x273. Fax: 970-725-0100.

Gunnison County
County Clerk and Recorder, 200 East Virginia Avenue, Courthouse, Gunnison, CO 81230. 970-641-1516. Fax: 970-641-7690.

Hinsdale County
County Clerk and Recorder, P.O. Box 9, Lake City, CO 81235. 970-944-2228. Fax: 970-944-2202.

Huerfano County
County Clerk and Recorder, Courthouse, Suite 204, 410 Main St., Walsenburg, CO 81089. 719-738-2380. Fax: 719-738-2364.

Jackson County
County Clerk and Recorder, P.O. Box 337, Walden, CO 80480-0337. 970-723-4334.

Jefferson County
County Clerk and Recorder, 100 Jefferson County Parkway, #2530, Golden, CO 80419-2530. 303-271-8188. Fax: 303-271-8180.
http://buffy.co.jefferson.co.us
Online Access: Assessor. Records on the Jefferson County Assessor database are available free on the Internet at http://buffy.co.jefferson.co.us/cgi-bin/mis/ats/assr.

Kiowa County
County Clerk and Recorder, P.O. Box 37, Eads, CO 81036-0037. 719-438-5421. Fax: 719-438-5327.

Kit Carson County
County Clerk and Recorder, P.O. Box 249, Burlington, CO 80807-0249. 719-346-8638. Fax: 719-346-7242.

La Plata County
County Clerk and Recorder, P.O. Box 519, Durango, CO 81302-0519. 970-382-6281. Fax: 970-382-6299.
www.laplatainfo.com
Online Access: Assessor. Records on the La Plata County Assessor database are available free on the Internet at www.laplatainfo.com/search2.html.

Lake County
County Clerk and Recorder, P.O. Box 917, Leadville, CO 80461. 719-486-4131. Fax: 719-486-3972.

Larimer County
County Clerk and Recorder, P.O. Box 1280, Fort Collins, CO 80522-1280. 970-498-7860.
www.larimer.co.us/assessor/query/search.cfm
Online Access: Assessor. Records on the Larimer County Property Records database are available free on the Internet.

Las Animas County
County Clerk and Recorder, P.O. Box 115, Trinidad, CO 81082. 719-846-3314. Fax: 719-846-0333.

Lincoln County
County Clerk and Recorder, P.O. Box 67, Hugo, CO 80821-0067. 719-743-2444. Fax: 719-743-2838.

Logan County

County Clerk and Recorder, 315 Main Street, Logan County Courthouse, Sterling, CO 80751. 970-522-1544. Fax: 970-522-4357.

Mesa County

County Clerk and Recorder, P.O. Box 20000-5007, Grand Junction, CO 81502-5007. 970-244-1679. Fax: 970-256-1588.
www.co.mesa.co.us
Online Access: Assessor. Records on the Mesa County Assessor database are available free on the Internet at http://205.169.141.11/Assessor/Database/netsearch.html. An interactive Voice Response System lets callers access real property information at 970-256-1563. Information can be faxed directly to you if requested.

Mineral County

County Clerk and Recorder, P.O. Box 70, Creede, CO 81130. 719-658-2440. Fax: 719-658-2931.

Moffat County

County Clerk and Recorder, 221 West Victory Way, Craig, CO 81625-2716. 970-824-9104. Fax: 970-824-9191.

Montezuma County

County Clerk and Recorder, 109 West Main Street, Room 108, Cortez, CO 81321. 970-565-3728. Fax: 970-564-0215.

Montrose County

County Clerk and Recorder, P.O. Box 1289, Montrose, CO 81402. 970-249-3362. Fax: 970-249-0757.

Morgan County

County Clerk and Recorder, P.O. Box 1399, Fort Morgan, CO 80701. 970-867-5616. Fax: 970-867-6485.

Otero County

County Clerk and Recorder, P.O. Box 511, La Junta, CO 81050-0511. 719-383-3020. Fax: 719-383-3090.

Ouray County

County Clerk and Recorder, P.O. Bin C, Ouray, CO 81427. 970-325-4961. Fax: 970-325-0452.

Park County

County Clerk and Recorder, P.O. Box 220, Fairplay, CO 80440. 719-836-2771. Fax: 719-836-4348.
www.parkco.org
Online Access: Assessor. Records on the Park County Assessor database are available free on the Internet at www.parkco.org/Search2.asp? including tax information, owner, address, building characteristics, legal and deed information.

Phillips County

County Clerk and Recorder, 221 South Interocean, Holyoke, CO 80734. 970-854-3131. Fax: 970-664-3811.

Pitkin County

County Clerk and Recorder, 530 East Main St., #101, Aspen, CO 81611. 970-920-5180. Fax: 970-920-5196.
http://aimwebdomain.aspen.com
Online Access: Assessor. Records on the Pitkin County Assessor database are available free on the Internet at http://aimwebdomain.aspen.com/db/pca/pcareg1.asp.

Prowers County

County Clerk and Recorder, P.O. Box 889, Lamar, CO 81052. 719-336-8011. Fax: 719-336-5306.

Pueblo County

County Clerk and Recorder, P.O. Box 878, Pueblo, CO 81002-0878. 719-583-6625. Fax: 719-583-6549.

Rio Blanco County

County Clerk and Recorder, P.O. Box 1067, Meeker, CO 81641. 970-878-5068.

Rio Grande County

County Clerk and Recorder, P.O. Box 160, Del Norte, CO 81132. 719-657-3334. Fax: 719-657-2621.

Routt County

County Clerk and Recorder, P.O. Box 773598, Steamboat Springs, CO 80477. 970-870-5556. Fax: 970-870-1329.
www.co.routt.co.us/clerk/
Online Access: Real Estate, Assessor, Treasurer. Records on the Routt County Assessor/Treasurer Property Search database are available free on the

Internet at http://pioneer.yampa.com/asp/assessor/search.asp?. Records on the Routt County Clerk and Recorder Reception Search database are available free on the Internet at http://pioneer.yampa.com/asp/clerk/search.asp?.

Saguache County

County Clerk and Recorder, P.O. Box 176, Saguache, CO 81149-0176. 719-655-2512. Fax: 719-655-2635.

San Juan County

County Clerk and Recorder, P.O. Box 466, Silverton, CO 81433-0466. 970-387-5671. Fax: 970-387-5671.

San Miguel County

County Clerk and Recorder, P.O. Box 548, Telluride, CO 81435-0548. 970-728-3954. Fax: 970-728-4808.

Sedgwick County

County Clerk and Recorder, P.O. Box 50, Julesburg, CO 80737. 970-474-3346. Fax: 970-474-0954.

Summit County

County Clerk and Recorder, P.O. Box 1538, Breckenridge, CO 80424. 970-453-3475. Fax: 970-453-3540.

Teller County

County Clerk and Recorder, P.O. Box 1010, Cripple Creek, CO 80813-1010. 719-689-2951. Fax: 719-689-3524.

Washington County

County Clerk and Recorder, P.O. Box L, Akron, CO 80720-0380. 970-345-6565. Fax: 970-345-6607.

Weld County

County Clerk and Recorder, P.O. Box 459, Greeley, CO 80632-0459. 970-353-3065x3050. Fax: 970-353-1964.

Yuma County

County Clerk and Recorder, P.O. Box 426, Wray, CO 80758-0426. 970-332-5809.

You will usually be able to find the city name in the City/County Cross Reference below. In that case, it is a simple matter to determine the county from the cross reference. However, only the official US Postal Service city names are included in this index. There are an additional 40,000 place names that people use in their addresses. Therefore, we have also included a ZIP/City Cross Reference immediately following the City/County Cross Reference.

If you know the ZIP Code but the city name does not appear in the City/County Cross Reference index, look up the ZIP Code in the ZIP/City Cross Reference, find the city name, then look up the city name in the City/County Cross Reference. For example, you want to know the county for an address of Menands, NY 12204. There is no "Menands" in the City/County Cross Reference. The ZIP/City Cross Reference shows that ZIP Codes 12201-12288 are for the city of Albany. Looking back in the City/County Cross Reference, Albany is in Albany County.

City/County Cross Reference

AGATE Elbert
AGUILAR Las Animas
AKRON Washington
ALAMOSA (81101) Alamosa(99), Conejos(2)
ALAMOSA Alamosa
ALLENSPARK Boulder
ALMA Park
ALMONT Gunnison
AMHERST Phillips
ANTON Washington
ANTONITO Conejos
ARAPAHOE Cheyenne
ARBOLES Archuleta
ARLINGTON (81021) Kiowa(81), Lincoln(19)
ARRIBA Lincoln
ARVADA (80002) Jefferson(97), Adams(3)
ARVADA (80003) Jefferson(86), Adams(14)
ARVADA Jefferson
ASPEN Pitkin
ATWOOD Logan
AULT Weld
AURORA (80010) Adams(50), Arapahoe(50)
AURORA (80011) Arapahoe(58), Adams(42)
AURORA (80014) Arapahoe(96), Denver(4)
AURORA Adams
AURORA Arapahoe
AUSTIN Delta
AVON Eagle
AVONDALE Pueblo
BAILEY Park
BASALT (81621) Eagle(67), Pitkin(33)
BATTLEMENT MESA Garfield
BAYFIELD La Plata
BEDROCK Montrose
BELLVUE Larimer
BENNETT (80102) Adams(58), Arapahoe(37), Elbert(5)
BERTHOUD (80513) Larimer(90), Weld(10)
BETHUNE Kit Carson
BEULAH (81023) Pueblo(99), Custer(1)
BLACK HAWK Gilpin
BLANCA Costilla
BONCARBO Las Animas
BOND Eagle
BOONE Pueblo
BOULDER Boulder
BOYERO Lincoln
BRANSON Las Animas
BRECKENRIDGE Summit
BRIGGSDALE Weld
BRIGHTON (80601) Adams(88), Weld(12)
BRISTOL Prowers
BROOMFIELD (80020) Boulder(47), Adams(33), Jefferson(19)
BROOMFIELD (80021) Jefferson(96), Boulder(4)
BROOMFIELD Boulder

BRUSH (80723) Morgan(99), Washington(1)
BUENA VISTA Chaffee
BUFFALO CREEK Jefferson
BURLINGTON (80807) Kit Carson(98), Yuma(2)
BURNS Eagle
BYERS (80103) Arapahoe(83), Adams(17)
CAHONE Dolores
CALHAN (80808) El Paso(95), Elbert(5)
CAMPO Baca
CANON CITY Fremont
CAPULIN Conejos
CARBONDALE (81623) Garfield(62), Eagle(15), Gunnison(13), Pitkin(10)
CARR Weld
CASCADE El Paso
CASTLE ROCK Douglas
CEDAREDGE Delta
CENTER (81125) Saguache(66), Rio Grande(31), Alamosa(3)
CENTRAL CITY Gilpin
CHAMA Costilla
CHERAW Otero
CHEYENNE WELLS Cheyenne
CHIMNEY ROCK Archuleta
CHROMO Archuleta
CIMARRON (81220) Gunnison(91), Montrose(9)
CLARK Routt
CLIFTON Mesa
CLIMAX Lake
COAL CREEK Fremont
COALDALE Fremont
COALMONT Jackson
COKEDALE Las Animas
COLLBRAN Mesa
COLORADO CITY Pueblo
COLORADO SPRINGS (80926) El Paso(97), Fremont(3)
COLORADO SPRINGS El Paso
COMMERCE CITY Adams
COMO Park
CONEJOS Conejos
CONIFER Jefferson
COPE (80812) Washington(98), Yuma(3)
CORTEZ Montezuma
CORY Delta
COTOPAXI Fremont
COWDREY Jackson
CRAIG Moffat
CRAWFORD (81415) Delta(78), Montrose(22)
CREEDE Mineral
CRESTED BUTTE Gunnison
CRESTONE Saguache
CRIPPLE CREEK Teller
CROOK Logan
CROWLEY Crowley
DACONO Weld
DE BEQUE (81630) Garfield(61), Mesa(39)
DEER TRAIL (80105) Arapahoe(59), Elbert(30), Adams(11)

DEL NORTE (81132) Rio Grande(93), Saguache(7)
DELTA (81416) Delta(96), Montrose(4)
DENVER (80212) Denver(78), Jefferson(19), Adams(3)
DENVER (80214) Jefferson(99), Denver(1)
DENVER (80216) Denver(83), Adams(17)
DENVER (80221) Adams(92), Denver(8)
DENVER (80222) Denver(94), Arapahoe(6)
DENVER (80227) Jefferson(74), Denver(26)
DENVER (80231) Denver(75), Arapahoe(25)
DENVER (80235) Jefferson(58), Denver(42)
DENVER (80236) Denver(88), Arapahoe(12)
DENVER (80246) Denver(67), Arapahoe(34)
DENVER (80249) Denver(88), Adams(12)
DENVER Adams
DENVER Denver
DENVER Jefferson
DILLON Summit
DINOSAUR Moffat
DIVIDE Teller
DOLORES Montezuma
DOVE CREEK (81324) Dolores(97), San Miguel(3)
DRAKE Larimer
DUMONT Clear Creek
DUPONT Adams
DURANGO La Plata
EADS Kiowa
EAGLE Eagle
EASTLAKE Adams
EATON Weld
ECKERT Delta
ECKLEY Yuma
EDWARDS Eagle
EGNAR (81325) Dolores(63), San Miguel(38)
EL JEBEL Eagle
ELBERT (80106) El Paso(58), Elbert(40), Douglas(2)
ELDORADO SPRINGS Boulder
ELIZABETH Elbert
EMPIRE Clear Creek
ENGLEWOOD (80112) Arapahoe(97), Douglas(2)
ENGLEWOOD Arapahoe
ERIE (80516) Weld(79), Boulder(21)
ESTES PARK Larimer
EVANS Weld
EVERGREEN (80439) Jefferson(85), Clear Creek(15)
EVERGREEN Jefferson
FAIRPLAY (80440) Park(96), Adams(4)
FIRESTONE Weld
FLAGLER (80815) Kit Carson(87), Washington(13)
FLEMING Logan
FLORENCE Fremont

FLORISSANT (80816) Teller(79), Park(21)
FORT COLLINS (80525) Larimer(99), Boulder(1)
FORT COLLINS Larimer
FORT GARLAND Costilla
FORT LUPTON Weld
FORT LYON Bent
FORT MORGAN (80701) Morgan(93), Adams(7)
FOUNTAIN El Paso
FOWLER (81039) Otero(93), Pueblo(5), Crowley(1)
FOXTON Jefferson
FRANKTOWN Douglas
FRASER Grand
FREDERICK Weld
FRISCO Summit
FRUITA Mesa
GALETON Weld
GARCIA Costilla
GARDNER Huerfano
GATEWAY Mesa
GENOA (80818) Lincoln(79), Washington(21)
GEORGETOWN Clear Creek
GILCREST Weld
GILL Weld
GLADE PARK Mesa
GLEN HAVEN Larimer
GLENWOOD SPRINGS Garfield
GOLDEN (80403) Jefferson(67), Gilpin(28), Boulder(5)
GOLDEN Jefferson
GRANADA (81041) Prowers(92), Baca(8)
GRANBY Grand
GRAND JUNCTION Mesa
GRAND LAKE Grand
GRANITE (81228) Chaffee(75), Lake(25)
GRANT Park
GREELEY Weld
GREEN MOUNTAIN FALLS El Paso
GROVER Weld
GUFFEY Park
GULNARE Las Animas
GUNNISON Chaffee
GUNNISON Gunnison
GYPSUM (81637) Eagle(91), Garfield(9)
HAMILTON (81638) Moffat(59), Routt(32), Rio Blanco(9)
HARTMAN Prowers
HARTSEL Park
HASTY Bent
HASWELL (81045) Kiowa(71), Lincoln(17), Cheyenne(13)
HAXTUN (80731) Yuma(63), Logan(27), Phillips(10)
HAYDEN Routt
HENDERSON Adams
HEREFORD Weld
HESPERUS La Plata
HILLROSE Morgan
HILLSIDE Fremont
HOEHNE Las Animas

HOLLY (81047) Prowers(95), Kiowa(3), Baca(2)
HOLYOKE (80734) Phillips(95), Yuma(5)
HOMELAKE Rio Grande
HOOPER (81136) Alamosa(96), Saguache(4)
HOT SULPHUR SPRINGS Grand
HOTCHKISS Delta
HOWARD Fremont
HUDSON Weld
HUGO Lincoln
HYGIENE Boulder
IDAHO SPRINGS Clear Creek
IDALIA (80735) Yuma(80), Weld(21)
IDLEDALE Jefferson
IGNACIO La Plata
ILIFF Logan
INDIAN HILLS Jefferson
JAMESTOWN Boulder
JAROSO Costilla
JEFFERSON Park
JOES Yuma
JOHNSTOWN Weld
JULESBURG Sedgwick
KARVAL Lincoln
KEENESBURG Weld
KERSEY Weld
KIM Las Animas
KIOWA Elbert
KIRK (80824) Yuma(99), Kit Carson(1)
KIT CARSON Cheyenne
KITTREDGE Jefferson
KREMMLING (80459) Grand(99), Summit(1)
LA JARA Conejos
LA JUNTA Otero
LA SALLE Weld
LA VETA Huerfano
LAFAYETTE Boulder
LAKE CITY Hinsdale
LAKE GEORGE (80827) Teller(70), Park(30)
LAKEWOOD (80226) Jefferson(99), Denver(1)
LAKEWOOD Jefferson
LAMAR (81052) Prowers(99), Bent(1)
LAPORTE Larimer
LARKSPUR Douglas
LAS ANIMAS Bent
LAZEAR Delta
LEADVILLE Lake
LEWIS Montezuma
LIMON (80828) Lincoln(71), Elbert(29)
LIMON Lincoln
LINDON Washington
LITTLETON (80120) Arapahoe(98), Douglas(2)
LITTLETON (80123) Jefferson(53), Arapahoe(31), Denver(15)
LITTLETON (80124) Douglas(98), Arapahoe(2)
LITTLETON (80128) Jefferson(97), Arapahoe(3)
LITTLETON Arapahoe
LITTLETON Douglas
LITTLETON Jefferson
LIVERMORE Larimer
LOG LANE VILLAGE Morgan
LOMA Mesa
LONGMONT (80504) Weld(96), Boulder(4)

LONGMONT Boulder
LOUISVILLE Boulder
LOUVIERS Douglas
LOVELAND (80537) Larimer(99), Weld(2)
LOVELAND Larimer
LUCERNE Weld
LYONS (80540) Larimer(55), Boulder(45)
MACK Mesa
MAHER Delta
MANASSA Conejos
MANCOS (81328) Montezuma(96), La Plata(4)
MANITOU SPRINGS El Paso
MANZANOLA (81058) Otero(80), Crowley(20)
MARVEL La Plata
MASONVILLE Larimer
MATHESON Elbert
MAYBELL Moffat
MC CLAVE Bent
MC COY (80463) Eagle(75), Routt(25)
MEAD Weld
MEEKER (81641) Rio Blanco(94), Moffat(5), Garfield(2)
MEREDITH Pitkin
MERINO (80741) Logan(92), Washington(6), Morgan(2)
MESA Mesa
MESA VERDE NATIONAL PARK Montezuma
MILLIKEN Weld
MINTURN Eagle
MODEL (81059) Las Animas(76), Otero(24)
MOFFAT Saguache
MOLINA Mesa
MONARCH Chaffee
MONTE VISTA (81144) Rio Grande(97), Alamosa(4)
MONTROSE (81401) Montrose(97), Ouray(3)
MONTROSE Montrose
MONUMENT El Paso
MORRISON Jefferson
MOSCA Alamosa
NATHROP Chaffee
NATURITA Montrose
NEDERLAND Boulder
NEW CASTLE Garfield
NEW RAYMER (80742) Weld(89), Morgan(12)
NIWOT Boulder
NORWOOD San Miguel
NUCLA Montrose
NUNN Weld
OAK CREEK Routt
OHIO CITY (81237) Gunnison(75), Washington(25)
OLATHE Montrose
OLNEY SPRINGS (81062) Crowley(96), Pueblo(4)
OPHIR San Miguel
ORCHARD (80649) Morgan(57), Weld(43)
ORDWAY (81063) Crowley(96), Lincoln(4)
OTIS (80743) Washington(97), Logan(3)
OURAY Ouray
OVID Sedgwick
PADRONI Logan
PAGOSA SPRINGS Archuleta
PALISADE Mesa

PALMER LAKE (80133) El Paso(84), Douglas(16)
PAOLI Phillips
PAONIA Delta
PARACHUTE Garfield
PARADOX Montrose
PARKER (80134) Douglas(98), Elbert(2)
PARKER (80138) Douglas(74), Elbert(26)
PARLIN Gunnison
PARSHALL Grand
PEETZ Logan
PENROSE Fremont
PEYTON El Paso
PHIPPSBURG Routt
PIERCE Weld
PINE (80470) Jefferson(66), Park(34)
PINECLIFFE Boulder
PITKIN Gunnison
PLACERVILLE San Miguel
PLATTEVILLE Weld
PLEASANT VIEW Montezuma
PONCHA SPRINGS Chaffee
POWDERHORN Gunnison
PRITCHETT (81064) Baca(75), Las Animas(25)
PRYOR Huerfano
PUEBLO (81008) Pueblo(98), El Paso(2)
PUEBLO Pueblo
RAMAH (80832) Elbert(57), El Paso(39), Lincoln(5)
RAND Jackson
RANGELY Rio Blanco
RED CLIFF Eagle
RED FEATHER LAKES Larimer
RED WING Huerfano
REDVALE Montrose
RICO Dolores
RIDGWAY Ouray
RIFLE (81650) Garfield(95), Rio Blanco(5)
ROCKVALE Fremont
ROCKY FORD Otero
ROGGEN Weld
ROLLINSVILLE Gilpin
ROMEO Conejos
RUSH (80833) Lincoln(48), El Paso(43), Elbert(10)
RYE Pueblo
SAGUACHE Saguache
SALIDA Chaffee
SAN ACACIO Costilla
SAN LUIS Costilla
SAN PABLO Costilla
SANFORD (81151) Conejos(89), Costilla(9), Rio Grande(2)
SARGENTS Saguache
SEDALIA Douglas
SEDGWICK Sedgwick
SEGUNDO Las Animas
SEIBERT (80834) Kit Carson(89), Washington(11)
SEVERANCE Weld
SHAWNEE Park
SHERIDAN LAKE Kiowa
SILT Garfield
SILVER CLIFF Custer
SILVER PLUME Clear Creek
SILVERTHORNE Summit
SILVERTON San Juan
SIMLA (80835) Elbert(89), El Paso(11)
SLATER Moffat

SLICK ROCK San Miguel
SNOWMASS Pitkin
SNOWMASS VILLAGE Pitkin
SNYDER Morgan
SOMERSET (81434) Gunnison(93), Delta(8)
SOUTH FORK Rio Grande
SPRINGFIELD Baca
STARKVILLE Las Animas
STEAMBOAT SPRINGS Routt
STERLING Logan
STONEHAM Weld
STONINGTON Baca
STRASBURG (80136) Adams(70), Arapahoe(30)
STRATTON (80836) Kit Carson(99), Yuma(1)
SUGAR CITY (81076) Crowley(96), Kiowa(2), Lincoln(2)
SWINK Otero
TABERNASH Grand
TELLURIDE San Miguel
TIMNATH Larimer
TOPONAS Routt
TOWAOC Montezuma
TRINCHERA Las Animas
TRINIDAD Las Animas
TWIN LAKES Lake
TWO BUTTES (81084) Baca(90), Prowers(10)
U S A F ACADEMY El Paso
VAIL Eagle
VERNON Yuma
VICTOR Teller
VILAS Baca
VILLA GROVE Saguache
VONA Kit Carson
WALDEN Jackson
WALSENBURG Huerfano
WALSH Baca
WARD Boulder
WATKINS (80137) Arapahoe(60), Adams(40)
WELDONA Morgan
WELLINGTON (80549) Larimer(97), Weld(3)
WESTCLIFFE Custer
WESTMINSTER (80030) Adams(93), Jefferson(7)
WESTMINSTER Jefferson
WESTON Las Animas
WETMORE (81253) Custer(63), Fremont(30), Pueblo(7)
WHEAT RIDGE Jefferson
WHITEWATER Mesa
WIGGINS (80654) Morgan(98), Adams(3)
WILD HORSE Cheyenne
WILEY (81092) Prowers(60), Bent(38), Kiowa(2)
WINDSOR Weld
WINTER PARK Grand
WOLCOTT Eagle
WOODLAND PARK Teller
WOODROW Washington
WOODY CREEK Pitkin
WRAY Yuma
YAMPA Routt
YELLOW JACKET Montezuma
YODER El Paso
YUMA Yuma

ZIP/City Cross Reference

80001-80007	ARVADA	80033-80034	WHEAT RIDGE	80105-80105	DEER TRAIL
80010-80019	AURORA	80035-80036	WESTMINSTER	80106-80106	ELBERT
80020-80021	BROOMFIELD	80037-80037	COMMERCE CITY	80107-80107	ELIZABETH
80022-80022	COMMERCE CITY	80038-80038	BROOMFIELD	80110-80112	ENGLEWOOD
80024-80024	DUPONT	80040-80047	AURORA	80116-80116	FRANKTOWN
80025-80025	ELDORADO SPRINGS	80101-80101	AGATE	80117-80117	KIOWA
80026-80026	LAFAYETTE	80102-80102	BENNETT	80118-80118	LARKSPUR
80027-80028	LOUISVILLE	80103-80103	BYERS	80120-80128	LITTLETON
80030-80031	WESTMINSTER	80104-80104	CASTLE ROCK	80131-80131	LOUVIERS

80132-80132	MONUMENT
80133-80133	PALMER LAKE
80134-80134	PARKER
80135-80135	SEDALIA
80136-80136	STRASBURG
80137-80137	WATKINS
80138-80138	PARKER
80150-80155	ENGLEWOOD
80160-80166	LITTLETON

Zip Range	Place	Zip Range	Place	Zip Range	Place	Zip Range	Place
80201-80214	DENVER	80534-80534	JOHNSTOWN	80813-80813	CRIPPLE CREEK	81092-81092	WILEY
80215-80215	LAKEWOOD	80535-80535	LAPORTE	80814-80814	DIVIDE	81101-81102	ALAMOSA
80216-80225	DENVER	80536-80536	LIVERMORE	80815-80815	FLAGLER	81120-81120	ANTONITO
80226-80226	LAKEWOOD	80537-80539	LOVELAND	80816-80816	FLORISSANT	81121-81121	ARBOLES
80227-80227	DENVER	80540-80540	LYONS	80817-80817	FOUNTAIN	81122-81122	BAYFIELD
80228-80228	LAKEWOOD	80541-80541	MASONVILLE	80818-80818	GENOA	81123-81123	BLANCA
80229-80231	DENVER	80542-80542	MEAD	80819-80819	GREEN MOUNTAIN FALLS	81124-81124	CAPULIN
80232-80232	LAKEWOOD	80543-80543	MILLIKEN			81125-81125	CENTER
80233-80299	DENVER	80544-80544	NIWOT	80820-80820	GUFFEY	81126-81126	CHAMA
80301-80329	BOULDER	80545-80545	RED FEATHER LAKES	80821-80821	HUGO	81127-81127	CHIMNEY ROCK
80401-80419	GOLDEN	80546-80546	SEVERANCE	80822-80822	JOES	81128-81128	CHROMO
80420-80420	ALMA	80547-80547	TIMNATH	80823-80823	KARVAL	81129-81129	CONEJOS
80421-80421	BAILEY	80549-80549	WELLINGTON	80824-80824	KIRK	81130-81130	CREEDE
80422-80422	BLACK HAWK	80550-80551	WINDSOR	80825-80825	KIT CARSON	81131-81131	CRESTONE
80423-80423	BOND	80553-80553	FORT COLLINS	80826-80826	LIMON	81132-81132	DEL NORTE
80424-80424	BRECKENRIDGE	80601-80601	BRIGHTON	80827-80827	LAKE GEORGE	81133-81133	FORT GARLAND
80425-80425	BUFFALO CREEK	80610-80610	AULT	80828-80828	LIMON	81134-81134	GARCIA
80426-80426	BURNS	80611-80611	BRIGGSDALE	80829-80829	MANITOU SPRINGS	81135-81135	HOMELAKE
80427-80427	CENTRAL CITY	80612-80612	CARR	80830-80830	MATHESON	81136-81136	HOOPER
80428-80428	CLARK	80614-80614	EASTLAKE	80831-80831	PEYTON	81137-81137	IGNACIO
80429-80429	CLIMAX	80615-80615	EATON	80832-80832	RAMAH	81138-81138	JAROSO
80430-80430	COALMONT	80620-80620	EVANS	80833-80833	RUSH	81140-81140	LA JARA
80432-80432	COMO	80621-80621	FORT LUPTON	80834-80834	SEIBERT	81141-81141	MANASSA
80433-80433	CONIFER	80622-80622	GALETON	80835-80835	SIMLA	81143-81143	MOFFAT
80434-80434	COWDREY	80623-80623	GILCREST	80836-80836	STRATTON	81144-81144	MONTE VISTA
80435-80435	DILLON	80624-80624	GILL	80840-80841	U S A F ACADEMY	81146-81146	MOSCA
80436-80436	DUMONT	80631-80639	GREELEY	80860-80860	VICTOR	81147-81147	PAGOSA SPRINGS
80437-80437	EVERGREEN	80640-80640	HENDERSON	80861-80861	VONA	81148-81148	ROMEO
80438-80438	EMPIRE	80642-80642	HUDSON	80862-80862	WILD HORSE	81149-81149	SAGUACHE
80439-80439	EVERGREEN	80643-80643	KEENESBURG	80863-80863	WOODLAND PARK	81151-81151	SANFORD
80440-80440	FAIRPLAY	80644-80644	KERSEY	80864-80864	YODER	81152-81152	SAN LUIS
80442-80442	FRASER	80645-80645	LA SALLE	80866-80866	WOODLAND PARK	81153-81153	SAN PABLO
80443-80443	FRISCO	80646-80646	LUCERNE	80901-80997	COLORADO SPRINGS	81154-81154	SOUTH FORK
80444-80444	GEORGETOWN	80648-80648	NUNN	81001-81015	PUEBLO	81155-81155	VILLA GROVE
80446-80446	GRANBY	80649-80649	ORCHARD	81019-81019	COLORADO CITY	81157-81157	PAGOSA SPRINGS
80447-80447	GRAND LAKE	80650-80650	PIERCE	81020-81020	AGUILAR	81201-81201	SALIDA
80448-80448	GRANT	80651-80651	PLATTEVILLE	81021-81021	ARLINGTON	81210-81210	ALMONT
80449-80449	HARTSEL	80652-80652	ROGGEN	81022-81022	AVONDALE	81211-81211	BUENA VISTA
80451-80451	HOT SULPHUR SPRINGS	80653-80653	WELDONA	81023-81023	BEULAH	81212-81215	CANON CITY
80452-80452	IDAHO SPRINGS	80654-80654	WIGGINS	81024-81024	BONCARBO	81220-81220	CIMARRON
80453-80453	IDLEDALE	80701-80701	FORT MORGAN	81025-81025	BOONE	81221-81221	COAL CREEK
80454-80454	INDIAN HILLS	80705-80705	LOG LANE VILLAGE	81027-81027	BRANSON	81222-81222	COALDALE
80455-80455	JAMESTOWN	80720-80720	AKRON	81029-81029	CAMPO	81223-81223	COTOPAXI
80456-80456	JEFFERSON	80721-80721	AMHERST	81030-81030	CHERAW	81224-81225	CRESTED BUTTE
80457-80457	KITTREDGE	80722-80722	ATWOOD	81033-81034	CROWLEY	81226-81226	FLORENCE
80459-80459	KREMMLING	80723-80723	BRUSH	81036-81036	EADS	81227-81227	MONARCH
80461-80461	LEADVILLE	80726-80726	CROOK	81038-81038	FORT LYON	81228-81228	GRANITE
80463-80463	MC COY	80727-80727	ECKLEY	81039-81039	FOWLER	81230-81231	GUNNISON
80465-80465	MORRISON	80728-80728	FLEMING	81040-81040	GARDNER	81232-81232	HILLSIDE
80466-80466	NEDERLAND	80729-80729	GROVER	81041-81041	GRANADA	81233-81233	HOWARD
80467-80467	OAK CREEK	80731-80731	HAXTUN	81042-81042	GULNARE	81235-81235	LAKE CITY
80468-80468	PARSHALL	80732-80732	HEREFORD	81043-81043	HARTMAN	81236-81236	NATHROP
80469-80469	PHIPPSBURG	80733-80733	HILLROSE	81044-81044	HASTY	81237-81237	OHIO CITY
80470-80470	PINE	80734-80734	HOLYOKE	81045-81045	HASWELL	81239-81239	PARLIN
80471-80471	PINECLIFFE	80735-80735	IDALIA	81046-81046	HOEHNE	81240-81240	PENROSE
80473-80473	RAND	80736-80736	ILIFF	81047-81047	HOLLY	81241-81241	PITKIN
80474-80474	ROLLINSVILLE	80737-80737	JULESBURG	81049-81049	KIM	81242-81242	PONCHA SPRINGS
80475-80475	SHAWNEE	80740-80740	LINDON	81050-81050	LA JUNTA	81243-81243	POWDERHORN
80476-80476	SILVER PLUME	80741-80741	MERINO	81052-81052	LAMAR	81244-81244	ROCKVALE
80477-80477	STEAMBOAT SPRINGS	80742-80742	NEW RAYMER	81054-81054	LAS ANIMAS	81246-81246	CANON CITY
80478-80478	TABERNASH	80743-80743	OTIS	81055-81055	LA VETA	81247-81247	GUNNISON
80479-80479	TOPONAS	80744-80744	OVID	81057-81057	MC CLAVE	81248-81248	SARGENTS
80480-80480	WALDEN	80745-80745	PADRONI	81058-81058	MANZANOLA	81251-81251	TWIN LAKES
80481-80481	WARD	80746-80746	PAOLI	81059-81059	MODEL	81252-81252	WESTCLIFFE
80482-80482	WINTER PARK	80747-80747	PEETZ	81062-81062	OLNEY SPRINGS	81253-81253	WETMORE
80483-80483	YAMPA	80749-80749	SEDGWICK	81063-81063	ORDWAY	81290-81290	FLORENCE
80487-80488	STEAMBOAT SPRINGS	80750-80750	SNYDER	81064-81064	PRITCHETT	81301-81302	DURANGO
80498-80498	SILVERTHORNE	80751-80751	STERLING	81066-81066	RED WING	81320-81320	CAHONE
80501-80504	LONGMONT	80754-80754	STONEHAM	81067-81067	ROCKY FORD	81321-81321	CORTEZ
80510-80510	ALLENSPARK	80755-80755	VERNON	81069-81069	RYE	81323-81323	DOLORES
80511-80511	ESTES PARK	80757-80757	WOODROW	81071-81071	SHERIDAN LAKE	81324-81324	DOVE CREEK
80512-80512	BELLVUE	80758-80758	WRAY	81073-81073	SPRINGFIELD	81325-81325	EGNAR
80513-80513	BERTHOUD	80759-80759	YUMA	81074-81074	STARKVILLE	81326-81326	HESPERUS
80514-80514	DACONO	80801-80801	ANTON	81076-81076	SUGAR CITY	81327-81327	LEWIS
80515-80515	DRAKE	80802-80802	ARAPAHOE	81077-81077	SWINK	81328-81328	MANCOS
80516-80516	ERIE	80804-80804	ARRIBA	81081-81081	TRINCHERA	81329-81329	MARVEL
80517-80517	ESTES PARK	80805-80805	BETHUNE	81082-81082	TRINIDAD	81330-81330	MESA VERDE NATIONAL PARK
80520-80520	FIRESTONE	80807-80807	BURLINGTON	81084-81084	TWO BUTTES		
80521-80528	FORT COLLINS	80808-80808	CALHAN	81087-81087	VILAS	81331-81331	PLEASANT VIEW
80530-80530	FREDERICK	80809-80809	CASCADE	81089-81089	WALSENBURG	81332-81332	RICO
80532-80532	GLEN HAVEN	80810-80810	CHEYENNE WELLS	81090-81090	WALSH	81333-81333	SLICK ROCK
80533-80533	HYGIENE	80812-80812	COPE	81091-81091	WESTON	81334-81334	TOWAOC

81335-81335	YELLOW JACKET	81428-81428	PAONIA	81610-81610	DINOSAUR	81640-81640	MAYBELL
81401-81402	MONTROSE	81429-81429	PARADOX	81611-81612	ASPEN	81641-81641	MEEKER
81410-81410	AUSTIN	81430-81430	PLACERVILLE	81615-81615	SNOWMASS VILLAGE	81642-81642	MEREDITH
81411-81411	BEDROCK	81431-81431	REDVALE	81620-81620	AVON	81643-81643	MESA
81413-81413	CEDAREDGE	81432-81432	RIDGWAY	81621-81621	BASALT	81645-81645	MINTURN
81414-81414	CORY	81433-81433	SILVERTON	81623-81623	CARBONDALE	81646-81646	MOLINA
81415-81415	CRAWFORD	81434-81434	SOMERSET	81624-81624	COLLBRAN	81647-81647	NEW CASTLE
81416-81416	DELTA	81435-81435	TELLURIDE	81625-81626	CRAIG	81648-81648	RANGELY
81418-81418	ECKERT	81501-81506	GRAND JUNCTION	81628-81628	EL JEBEL	81649-81649	RED CLIFF
81419-81419	HOTCHKISS	81520-81520	CLIFTON	81630-81630	DE BEQUE	81650-81650	RIFLE
81420-81420	LAZEAR	81521-81521	FRUITA	81631-81631	EAGLE	81652-81652	SILT
81421-81421	MAHER	81522-81522	GATEWAY	81632-81632	EDWARDS	81653-81653	SLATER
81422-81422	NATURITA	81523-81523	GLADE PARK	81633-81633	DINOSAUR	81654-81654	SNOWMASS
81423-81423	NORWOOD	81524-81524	LOMA	81635-81635	PARACHUTE	81655-81655	WOLCOTT
81424-81424	NUCLA	81525-81525	MACK	81636-81636	BATTLEMENT MESA	81656-81656	WOODY CREEK
81425-81425	OLATHE	81526-81526	PALISADE	81637-81637	GYPSUM	81657-81658	VAIL
81426-81426	OPHIR	81527-81527	WHITEWATER	81638-81638	HAMILTON		
81427-81427	OURAY	81601-81602	GLENWOOD SPRINGS	81639-81639	HAYDEN		

Connecticut

General Help Numbers:

Governor's Office
State Capitol, 210 Capitol Ave   860-566-4840
Hartford, CT 06106   Fax 860-566-4677
www.state.ct.us/governor   8AM-5PM

Attorney General's Office
55 Elm St   860-808-5318
Hartford, CT 06106   Fax 860-808-5387
www.cslib.org/attygenl   8:30AM-4:30PM

State Court Administrator
231 Capitol Ave   860-566-4461
Hartford, CT 06106   Fax 860-566-3308
www.jud.state.ct.us   9AM-5PM

State Archives
History & Genealogy Unit   860-757-6580
231 Capitol Ave   Fax 860-757-6503
Hartford, CT 06106   9AM-5PM M-F
www.cslib.org

State Specifics:

Capital:	Hartford
	Hartford County
Time Zone:	EST
Number of Counties:	8
Population:	3,269,858
Web Site:	www.state.ct.us

State Agencies

Criminal Records

Department of Public Safety, Bureau of Identification, PO Box 2794, Middleton, CT 06759-9294 (Courier: 1111 Country Club Rd, Middleton, CT 06457); 860-685-8480, 860-685-8361 (Fax), 8:30AM-4:30PM.

www.state.ct.us/dps

Indexing & Storage: Records are available from the 1950's on. Records were first computerized in 1983. Also, the courts send their criminal records 3 months to 5 years after the eposition to the State Record Center (860-741-3714).

Searching: Records are open to the public. Forms can be mailed or downloaded from the web site.

The only information released to the public is conviction only criminal records. Include the following in your request-date of birth. The following data is not released: pending cases, dismissals or juvenile records.

Access by: mail.

Fee & Payment: The fee is $25.00 per request. The copy fee is $.25 per page. Fee payee: Commissioner of Public Safety. Prepayment required. Personal checks accepted. No credit cards accepted.

Mail search: Turnaround time: 2 weeks. Records can only be requested by mail. If you come in-person, the results are still mailed.

Corporation Records
Limited Partnership Records
Trademarks/Servicemarks
Limited Liability Company Records

Secretary of State, Commercial Recording Division, 30 Trinity St, Hartford, CT 06106; 860-509-6001, 860-509-6068 (Fax), 8:30AM-4:30PM.

www.sots.state.ct.us

Note: Assumed names are found at the town level.

Indexing & Storage: New records are available for inquiry immediately. Records are indexed on microfilm, inhouse computer.

Searching: Include the following in your request-full name of business, specific records that you need copies of. In addition to the articles of incorporation, corporation records include the following information: Annual Reports, Officers, Directors, Prior (merged) names, Inactive and Reserved names.

Access by: mail, phone, in person, online.

Fee & Payment: The search fee is $25.00 per business name for UCC searches performed by the office personnel. Fee payee: Secretary of State. Prepayment required. Personal checks accepted. Credit cards accepted: Mastercard, Visa.

Mail search: Turnaround time: 2-3 days. No self addressed stamped envelope is required.

Phone search: Only limited, basic information is available by phone.

In person search: Certain, limited information is available at no charge.

Online search: Click on the CONCORD option at the web site for free access to corporation and UCC records. The system is open from 7AM to 11PM.

Expedited service: Expedited service is available on limited filings for an add'l $25.00. Turnaround time: 24 hours. Add $25.00 per business name. The fee is per transaction requested; review is one transaction, copy is another, etc.

Uniform Commercial Code
Federal Tax Liens
State Tax Liens

UCC Division, Secretary of State, PO Box 150470, Hartford, CT 06115-0470 (Courier: 30 Trinity St, Hartford, CT 06106); 860-509-6004, 860-509-6068 (Fax), 8:30AM-4PM.

www.sots.state.ct.us

Indexing & Storage: Records are available from 8/94 on computer, earlier records are on microfilm from 10/80.

Searching: Use search request form UCC-11. The search includes tax liens. Include the following in your request-debtor name.

Access by: mail, in person, online.

Fee & Payment: UCC searches include tax liens and are free if requested in person, $25.00 per name by mail. Financing statements copies are $5.00 including 2 pages of attachments. Additional pages of attachments cost $5.00 each. Fee payee: Secretary of State. Prepayment required. Credit cards are accepted for in-person searching only. Personal checks accepted. Credit cards accepted: Mastercard, Visa.

Mail search: Turnaround time: 3-5 days. A self addressed stamped envelope is requested.

In person search: Searching is available in person.

Online search: Records may be accessed at no charge on the Internet. Click on the CONCORD option. The system is open 7AM to 11PM.

Sales Tax Registrations

Department of Revenue Services, Taxpayer Services Division, 25 Sigourney St, Hartford, CT

06106; 860-297-4885, 860-297-5714 (Fax), 8AM-5PM.

www.drs.state.ct.us

Searching: This agency will only confirm that the business is registered and active. They will provide no other information. Include the following in your request-business name. They will also search by tax permit number.

Access by: mail, phone, fax, in person.

Fee & Payment: There is no search fee

Mail search: Turnaround time: 1 day.

Phone search: Searching is available by phone.

Fax search: Same criteria as mail searches.

In person search: Searching is available in person.

Birth Certificates
Death Records
Marriage Certificates
Divorce Records
Access to Records is Restricted

Department of Public Health, Vital Records Section MS# 11VRS, PO Box 340308, Hartford, CT 06134-0308 (Courier: 410 Capitol Ave, Hartford, CT 06134); 860-509-7897, 860-509-7964 (Fax), 8:30AM-4:30PM M-F.

www.state.ct.us/dph

Note: The state is in the process of microfilming all records. You must contact the town/city clerk of occurance to obtain copies of records. The web site has a great list of towns and phone numbers. Records are $5.00 each.

Workers' Compensation Records

Workers Compensation Commission, 21 Oak Street, Hartford, CT 06106; 860-493-1500, 860-247-1361 (Fax), 7:45AM-4:30PM.

http://wcc.state.ct.us

Note: All files are kept at one of the eight district offices. This agency will forward the request to the proper district office.

Indexing & Storage: Records are available on microfilm from 1914 thru 1985 and computerized from 1985 forward, for insurance coverage files. The case files since 1995 are indexed on computer. It takes 1 month before new records are available for inquiry.

Searching: Claims information is not released without a signed release from the employee. Include the following in your request-claimant name, Social Security Number(if available), date of injury, name and address of employer. Include as much information as possible. The following data is not released: medical records.

Access by: mail, phone, fax, in person.

Fee & Payment: Fees vary depending upon the nature of the request and are determined at that time. Fee payee: Workers Compensation Commission. Personal checks accepted. No credit cards accepted.

Mail search: Turnaround time: variable. A self addressed stamped envelope is requested.

Phone search: You may call for information.

Fax search: A mail request must follow.

In person search: You may request information in person.

Other access: The agency will sell self-insured lists for $5.00.

Driver Records

Department of Motor Vehicles, Copy Records Unit, 60 State St., Wethersfield, CT 06109-1896; 860-263-5154, 8:30AM-4:30PM T,W,F; 8:30AM-7:30PM TH; 8:30AM-12:30 S.

http://dmvct.org

Note: Copies of tickets may be obtained from the Superior Court Records Center, 111 Phoenix Ave, Enfield, 06082, 860-741-3714 for a fee of $1.00, or $3.00 for certified. Written requests must include name, DOB, date of disposition, document # and court.

Indexing & Storage: Records are available for 3/5/10 years to present, dependent upon the type of violation. It takes 5-7 days before new records are available for inquiry. Records are normally destroyed after 5 years at the discretion of the commissioner. The state does not report accidents on the driving record.

Searching: Mail and in person requesters must complete From J-23. Casual requests must include evidence of the individual's consent. The form can be ordered from the web site at http://dmvct.org/formsrec.htm or by calling 860-263-5700. The driver's license number, name and address are needed when searching, the DOB is optional. A DWI first offense violation will not appear if the offender attends an "Accelerated Alcohol Class."

Access by: mail, in person, online.

Fee & Payment: The fee for walk-in or mail-in driving records is $10.00 per record. The fee for ordering online or on a tape-to-tape system is $5.00. The fee for a license status check is $5.50. Fee payee: Department of Motor Vehicles. Prepayment required. Personal checks accepted. No credit cards accepted.

Mail search: Turnaround time: 2 weeks. A self addressed stamped envelope is requested.

In person search: The state will process up to three requests for walk-in requesters who have a permissible use as stipulated in C.G.S.#14-10. Please note the office is closed on Mondays.

Online search: Online access is provided to approved businesses that enter into written contract. The contract requires a prepayment with minimum hits annually. Fee is $5.00 per record. The address is part of the record. For more information, call 203-805-6016

Other access: Magnetic tape ordering is available for approved users. The state will process tapes on Mondays. Input time is 11:00 AM, so service is essentially 2 days. Also, the state will sell its driver license file on a contract basis to permitted users only.

Vehicle Ownership
Vehicle Identification

Department of Motor Vehicles, Copy Record Unit, 60 State St, Wethersfield, CT 06109-1896; 860-263-5154, 8:AM-4:30PM T,W,TH,F; 8:30AM-12:30 S.

http://dmvct.org

Note: With the passage of Public Act 97-266, the release of records adheres to the DPPA guidelines.

Indexing & Storage: Records are available for 3 years to present. Any records prior to this period may be destroyed at the discretion of the commissioner. It takes six weeks before new records are available for inquiry. Records are normally destroyed after http://dmvct.org/formsrec.htm.

Searching: Only acceptable requesters are listed on back of Form J-23. This form can be ordered from the web site at http://dmvct.org/formsrec.htm or by calling 860-263-5700. Casual requests must include evidence of the individual's consent.; businesses may only use to confirm the accuracy of personal information submitted by an individual to them.

Access by: mail, in person, online.

Fee & Payment: Title searches-$17.50 per search; current owner searches-$7.00 per search; registration information-$4.50 per search; license file information-$5.50 per search; registration copies-$7.00. There is a full charge for a "no record found." Fee payee: Department of Motor Vehicles. Prepayment required. Personal checks accepted. No credit cards accepted.

Mail search: Turnaround time: 3-4 working days. The agency requests that you use their Form J-23.A self addressed stamped envelope is requested.

In person search: The office is closed on Mondays.

Online search: The Department has started a pilot program for online access that is not yet open to the general business public. This program, when available to all, will have the same restrictions and criteria as described in the Driving Records Section.

Other access: The state will sell the entire vehicle record database, upon approval of purpose, but the records cannot be resold.

Accident Reports

Department of Public Safety, Reports and Records Section, PO Box 2794, Middletown, CT 06457; 860-685-8250, 8:30AM-4:30PM.

Indexing & Storage: Records are available from 10 years to present. Searching by name only goes back 5 years.

Searching: The request should include data and location of incident, names of operators, and the 9 digit case number (if known). The following data is not released: pending cases or sealed records.

Access by: mail.

Fee & Payment: Prepayment required. Fee payee: Commissioner of Public Safety. Personal checks accepted. No credit cards accepted.

Mail search: Turnaround time: 2-4 weeks. A self addressed stamped envelope is requested. Search costs $8.00 per report.

Boat & Vessel Ownership
Boat & Vessel Registration

Department of Motor Vehicles, Boat Registration, 60 State Street, Wethersfield, CT 06161-3032; 860-263-5151, 860-263-5555 (Fax), 8-4:30 T,W,F; 8-7:30 Th, 8-12:30 Sat.

http://dmvct.org/BOATING.HTM

Note: Lien information is found at the Secretary of State.

Indexing & Storage: Records are available from 1981, records are maintained on computer for 4 years then placed on microfiche. All motorized boats and all vessels over 19.5 ft must be registered.

Searching: All requests must be in writing. Either the name, CT registration number or hull number is needed to do a search.

Access by: mail, in person.

Fee & Payment: The fee is $4.50 for a current owner search, $7.00 for a copy of the registration and $17.50 for a complete boat history. Fee payee: Department of Motor Vehicles. Prepayment required. No credit cards accepted.

Mail search: Turnaround time: 1-2 weeks. No self addressed stamped envelope is required.

In person search: Results are returned by mail. The agency is closed to the public on Mondays.

Other access: Bulk list information is available by contract. The fee depends on data requested. Call 860-263-5241 for ordering procedures.

Legislation-Current/Pending
Legislation-Passed

Connecticut General Assembly, State Library, 231 Capitol Ave, Bill Room, Hartford, CT 06106; 860-757-6550, 860-757-6594 (Fax), 9AM-5PM.

www.cga.state.ct.us/default.asp

Indexing & Storage: Records are available for the current session only. Records are indexed on inhouse computer.

Searching: Include the following in your request-bill number. You may also ask for bills by subject or statute number. Past bills are located in another office (call 860-566-4601 or 4544).

Access by: mail, phone, fax, in person, online.

Fee & Payment: Fees: No charge for current bills; $.25 per page if you request a large document or a bill that has not been printed. They will compute the charge. Fee payee: Connecticut State Library. Personal checks accepted. No credit cards accepted.

Mail search: Turnaround time: 4-7 days. No self addressed stamped envelope is required.

Phone search: You may call for information.

Fax search: Copies of bills totaling 30 pages or less can be returned by fax if local or toll free.

In person search: You may request information in person.

Online search: From the web site you can track bills, find update or status, and print copies of bills. Also, you can request via e-mail at billroom@cslib.org.

Voter Registration
Records not maintained by a state level agency.

Note: Records are open at the town level. There are 169 towns.

GED Certificates

Department of Education, GED Records, 25 Industrial Park Rd, Middletown, CT 06457; 860-807-2110, 860-807-2112 (Fax), 8AM-5PM.

Searching: Include the following in your request-signed release, Social Security Number, date of birth. The year of the test is helpful. For records prior to 1982, the location of the test is needed.

Access by: mail, fax, in person.

Fee & Payment: There is no search fee.

Mail search: Turnaround time: 2-3 days. No self addressed stamped envelope is required.

Fax search: There is no fee to fax back to a local phone number.

In person search: Photo ID is required.

Hunting License Information
Fishing License Information

Department of Environmental Protection, License Division, 79 Elm St, Hartford, CT 06106; 860-424-3105, 860-424-4072 (Fax), 9AM-3:30PM.

www.dep.state.ct.us

Indexing & Storage: Records are available for 1 year back. Records are indexed on inhouse computer.

Searching: Only deer tag information is released. Include the following in your request-full name, Social Security Number. Records are indexed by Social Security Number. All requests must be in writing.

Access by: mail, in person.

Fee & Payment: There is no search fee. Copies are $.50 per page. Fee payee: Department of Environmental Protection. Prepayment required. Personal checks accepted. No credit cards accepted.

Mail search: Turnaround time: 1-3 days. No self addressed stamped envelope is required.

In person search: Must have the request in writing.

Licenses Searchable Online

Acupuncturist #11	www.state.ct.us/dph/scripts/hlthprof.asp
Alcohol/Drug Counselor #11	www.state.ct.us/dph/scripts/hlthprof.asp
Asbestos Professional #11	www.state.ct.us/dph/scripts/hlthprof.asp
Audiologist #11	www.state.ct.us/dph/scripts/hlthprof.asp
Auto Adjuster #02	www.ct-clic.com/RsltKey.asp
Auto Appraiser #02	www.ct-clic.com/RsltKey.asp
Bail Bond Agent #02	www.ct-clic.com/RsltKey.asp
Bank #06	www.state.ct.us/dob/pages/banklist.htm
Bank & Trust Company #06	www.state.ct.us/dob/pages/bcharter.htm
Barber #11	www.state.ct.us/dph/scripts/hlthprof.asp
Branch Office-Bank #06	www.state.ct.us/dob/pages/branch1.htm
Casualty Adjuster #02	www.ct-clic.com/RsltKey.asp
Check Cashing Service #06	www.state.ct.us/dob/pages/chckcash.htm
Chiropractor #11	www.state.ct.us/dph/scripts/hlthprof.asp
Collection Agency #06	www.state.ct.us/dob/pages/collect.htm
Consumer Collection Agency #06	www.state.ct.us/dob/pages/collect.htm
Cosmetologist #11	www.state.ct.us/dph/scripts/hlthprof.asp
Credit Union #06	www.state.ct.us/dob/pages/culist.htm
Debt Adjuster #06	www.state.ct.us/dob/pages/debtadj.htm
Dental Anes/Consciou Sedation Permittee #11	www.state.ct.us/dph/scripts/hlthprof.asp
Dentist/Dental Hygienist #11	www.state.ct.us/dph/scripts/hlthprof.asp
Dietician/Nutritionist #11	www.state.ct.us/dph/scripts/hlthprof.asp
Embalmer #11	www.state.ct.us/dph/scripts/hlthprof.asp
Emergency Medical Technician #11	www.state.ct.us/dph/scripts/hlthprof.asp
EMS Professional #11	www.state.ct.us/dph/scripts/hlthprof.asp
Fraternal Agent #02	www.ct-clic.com/RsltKey.asp
Funeral Director #11	www.state.ct.us/dph/scripts/hlthprof.asp
Funeral Home #11	www.state.ct.us/dph/scripts/hlthprof.asp
Hairdresser #11	www.state.ct.us/dph/scripts/hlthprof.asp
Hearing Instrument Specialist #11	www.state.ct.us/dph/scripts/hlthprof.asp
Homeopathic Physician #11	www.state.ct.us/dph/scripts/hlthprof.asp
Hypertrichologist #11	www.state.ct.us/dph/scripts/hlthprof.asp
Insurance Agent/Broker #02	www.ct-clic.com/RsltKey.asp
Insurance Appraiser #02	www.ct-clic.com/RsltKey.asp
Insurance Adjuster #02	www.ct-clic.com/RsltKey.asp
Insurance Company #02	www.ct-clic.com/RsltKey.asp
Insurance Consultant #02	www.ct-clic.com/RsltKey.asp
Insurance Producer #02	www.ct-clic.com/RsltKey.asp
Lead Planner/Project Designer #11	www.state.ct.us/dph/scripts/hlthprof.asp
Lead Professional #11	www.state.ct.us/dph/scripts/hlthprof.asp
LPN #11	www.state.ct.us/dph/scripts/hlthprof.asp
Marriage & Family Therapist #11	www.state.ct.us/dph/scripts/hlthprof.asp
Massage Therapist #11	www.state.ct.us/dph/scripts/hlthprof.asp
Medical Doctor #11	www.state.ct.us/dph/scripts/hlthprof.asp
Medical Response Technician #11	www.state.ct.us/dph/scripts/hlthprof.asp
Midwife #11	www.state.ct.us/dph/scripts/hlthprof.asp
Money Forwarder #06	www.state.ct.us/dob/pages/$forward.htm
Mortgage Lender/Broker; First #06	www.state.ct.us/dob/pages/1stmtg.htm
Mortgage Lender/Broker; Secondary #06	www.state.ct.us/dob/pages/2ndmtg.htm
MVPD Appraiser #02	www.ct-clic.com/RsltKey.asp
Naturopathic Physician #11	www.state.ct.us/dph/scripts/hlthprof.asp
Nurse #11	www.state.ct.us/dph/scripts/hlthprof.asp
Nurse, Advance Registered Practice #11	www.state.ct.us/dph/scripts/hlthprof.asp
Nurse-LPN #11	www.state.ct.us/dph/scripts/hlthprof.asp
Nursing Home Administrator #11	www.state.ct.us/dph/scripts/hlthprof.asp
Occupational Therapist/Assistant #11	www.state.ct.us/dph/scripts/hlthprof.asp
Optical Shop #11	www.state.ct.us/dph/scripts/hlthprof.asp
Optician #11	www.state.ct.us/dph/scripts/hlthprof.asp
Optometrist #11	www.state.ct.us/dph/scripts/hlthprof.asp
Osteopathic Physician #11	www.state.ct.us/dph/scripts/hlthprof.asp
Paramedic #11	www.state.ct.us/dph/scripts/hlthprof.asp

Physical Therapist/Assistant #11 .... www.state.ct.us/dph/scripts/hlthprof.asp
Physician Assistant #11 .... www.state.ct.us/dph/scripts/hlthprof.asp
Podiatrist #11 .... www.state.ct.us/dph/scripts/hlthprof.asp
Professional Counselor #11 .... www.state.ct.us/dph/scripts/hlthprof.asp
Psychologist #11 .... www.state.ct.us/dph/scripts/hlthprof.asp
Public Adjuster #02 .... www.ct-clic.com/RsltKey.asp
Radiographer #11 .... www.state.ct.us/dph/scripts/hlthprof.asp
Reinsurance Intermediary #02 .... www.ct-clic.com/RsltKey.asp
Respiratory Care Practitioner #11 .... www.state.ct.us/dph/scripts/hlthprof.asp
Sales Finance Company #06 .... www.state.ct.us/dob/pages/salefinc.htm
Sanitarian #11 .... www.state.ct.us/dph/scripts/hlthprof.asp
Savings & Loan Association Bank #06 .... www.state.ct.us/dob/pages/bcharter.htm
Savings Bank #06 .... www.state.ct.us/dob/pages/bcharter.htm
Small Loan Company #06 .... www.state.ct.us/dob/pages/smalloan.htm
Social Worker #11 .... www.state.ct.us/dph/scripts/hlthprof.asp
Speech Pathologist #11 .... www.state.ct.us/dph/scripts/hlthprof.asp
Subsurface Sewage Cleaner/Installer #11 .... www.state.ct.us/dph/scripts/hlthprof.asp
Surplus Line Broker #02 .... www.ct-clic.com/RsltKey.asp
Veterinarian #11 .... www.state.ct.us/dph/scripts/hlthprof.asp
Viatical Settlement Broker #02 .... www.ct-clic.com/RsltKey.asp

Licensing Quick Finder

Acupuncturist #11 860-509-7603
Agent of Issuer #06 860-240-8299
Alcohol/Drug Counselor #11 860-509-7603
Antenna Service Dealer #05 860-566-3275
Antenna Technician #05 860-566-3275
Arborist #07 860-566-3290
Architect #03 860-566-2093
Asbestos Professional #11 860-509-7603
Athletic Promoter #07 860-566-6980
Attorney #01 860-756-7900
Audiologist #11 860-509-7603
Auto Adjuster #02 860-297-3845
Auto Appraiser #02 860-297-3845
Automobile Dealer #23 860-566-2796
Bail Bond Agent #02 860-297-3845
Bank #06 860-240-8299
Bank & Trust Company #06 860-240-8299
Barber #11 860-509-7603
Boxer #07 860-566-6980
Branch Office-Bank #06 860-240-8299
Broker-Dealer Agent #06 860-240-8299
Building Contractor #07 860-566-2825
Bus Driver #23 860-566-2796
Business Opportunity Offerings for Sale #06
.... 860-240-8299
Casino #12 860-594-0567
Casualty Adjuster #02 860-297-3845
Cattle Dealer #22 860-566-4845
Chauffeur/Driver #24 860-594-2865
Check Cashing Service #06 860-240-8299
Chiropractor #11 860-509-7603
Collection Agency #06 860-240-8299
Consumer Collection Agency #06 860-240-8299
Cosmetologist #11 860-509-7603
Credit Union #06 860-240-8299
Dairy Laboratory Analyst #22 860-566-4845
Dairy Sample Collector #22 860-566-4845
Dairy Transporter #22 860-566-4845
Day Care Provider #11 860-509-8000
Debt Adjuster #06 860-240-8299
Dental Anes/Consciou Sedation Permittee #11
.... 860-509-7603
Dentist/Dental Hygienist #11 860-509-7603
Dietician/Nutritionist #11 860-509-7603
Digger of Shellfish #20 203-874-0696
Dog Racing #12 860-594-0567
Driving Instructor #23 860-566-2796
Electrical Contractor #07 860-566-2825
Electrical Inspector #07 860-566-2825

Electrical Journeyman/Apprentice #04
.... 860-566-3290
Electrical Sign Installer #07 860-566-2825
Electrician #07 860-566-2825
Electrologist/Hypertricologist #11 860-509-7603
Electronics Service Dealer #05 860-566-3275
Electronics Service Technician #05 860-566-3275
Elevator Inpsector/Mechanic #04 860-566-3290
Embalmer #11 860-509-7603
Emergency Medical Technician #11 860-509-7603
EMS Professional #11 860-509-7603
Engineer #04 860-566-3290
Fire Protection Inspector #04 860-566-3290
Fish Dealer #10 860-424-3000
Fisher #10 860-424-3000
Fraternal Agent #02 860-297-3845
Funeral Director #11 860-509-7603
Funeral Home #11 860-509-7603
Fur Breeder #22 860-566-4845
Game Breeder #10 860-424-3000
Guard #19 860-685-8290
Guide, Hunting & Fishing #10 860-424-3000
Hairdresser #11 860-509-7603
Hearing Instrument Specialist #11 860-509-7603
Heating & Cooling Contractor #04 860-566-3290
Hoisting Equipment Operator #19 860-685-8290
Homeopathic Physician #11 860-509-7603
Hypertrichologist #11 860-509-7603
Insurance Agent/Broker #02 860-297-3845
Insurance Appraiser #02 860-297-3845
Insurance Asjuster #02 860-297-3845
Insurance Company #02 860-297-3845
Insurance Consultant #02 860-297-3845
Insurance Producer #02 860-297-3845
Interior Designer #07 860-566-2825
Investment Advisor/Agent #06 860-240-8299
Jai Alai #12 860-594-0567
Landscape Architect #07 860-566-2825
Lead Planner/Project Designer #11 860-509-7603
Lead Professional #11 860-509-7603
Liquor License #15 860-713-6200
Live Bait Seller #10 860-424-3000
Livestock Dealer #22 860-566-4845
Lobbyist #18 860-566-4472
Lobster Seller #10 860-424-3000
Lottery #12 860-594-0567
LPN #11 860-509-7603
Marriage & Family Therapist #11 860-609-7603
Massage Therapist #11 860-509-7603
Medical Doctor #11 860-509-7603

Medical Response Technician #11 860-509-7603
Midwife #11 860-509-7603
Milk Dealer #22 860-566-4845
Money Forwarder #06 860-240-8299
Mortgage Lender/Broker; First #06 860-240-8299
Mortgage Lender/Broker; Secondary #06
.... 860-240-8299
Motion Picture Operator #25 860-685-8470
MVPD Appraiser #02 860-297-3845
Naturopathic Physician #11 860-509-7603
Non-depository Banking Office #06 860-240-8299
Notary Public #16 860-509-6200
Nuisance Wildlife Control Operator #10
.... 860-424-3000
Nurse #11 860-509-7603
Nurse, Advance Registered Practice #11
.... 860-509-7603
Nurse-LPN #11 860-509-7603
Nurses' Aide #11 860-509-7603
Nursing Home Administrator #11 860-509-7603
Occupational Therapist/Assistant #11
.... 860-509-7603
Off Track Betting #12 860-594-0567
Optical Shop #11 860-509-7603
Optician #11 860-509-7603
Optometrist #11 860-509-7603
Osteopathic Physician #11 860-509-7603
Paramedic #11 860-509-7603
Pawnbroker #21 860-297-5962
Pesticide Dealer/Applicator #14 860-424-3369
Pet Store Operator #22 860-566-4845
Pharmacist #04 860-566-3290
Physical Therapist/Assistant #11 860-509-7603
Physician Assistant #11 860-509-7603
Pipefitter #07 860-566-2825
Plumber #04 860-566-3290
Podiatrist #11 860-509-7603
Private Investigator #13 860-685-8000
Professional Counselor #11 860-509-7603
Psychologist #11 860-509-7603
Public Accountant-CPA #16 860-509-6179
Public Adjuster #02 860-297-3845
Radio & TV Technician #07 860-566-2825
Radiographer #11 860-509-7603
Real Estate Appraiser #17 860-566-5130
Real Estate Broker #17 860-566-5130
Real Estate Salesperson #17 860-566-5130
Reinsurance Intermediary #02 860-297-3845
Respiratory Care Practitioner #11 860-509-7603
Sales Finance Company #06 860-240-8299

Sanitarian #11 860-509-7603
Savings & Loan Association Bank #06
....860-240-8299
Savings Bank #06 860-240-8299
School Administrator/Supervisor #09 860-566-5201
School Bus Driver #23 860-566-2796
School Guidance Counselor #09 860-566-5201
School Library Media Associate #09 860-566-5201
School Principal #09 860-566-5201
School Superintendent #09 860-566-5201
Securities Agent #06 860-240-8299
Securities Broker/Dealer #06 860-240-8299
Septic-Tank Cleaner #11 860-509-8000
Sewage Disposal System Installer #11
....860-509-8000
Small Loan Company #06 860-240-8299

Social Worker #11 860-509-7603
Solar Energy Contractor/Journeyman #04
....860-566-3290
Solid Waste Facility Operator #10 860-424-4051
Speech Pathologist #11 860-509-7603
Subsurface Sewage Cleaner/Installer #11
....860-509-7603
Surplus Line Broker #02 860-297-3845
Surveyor #04 860-566-3290
Tattoo Artist #11 860-509-8000
Taxi Driver #24 860-594-2865
Taxidermist #10 860-424-3000
Teacher #09 860-566-5201
Ticket Broker #12 860-667-5073
Trapper #10 860-424-3000
Tree Surgeon #07 860-566-2825

Truck Driver #23 860-566-2796
Veterinarian #11 860-509-7603
Viatical Settlement Broker #02 860-297-3845
Water Distribution System Operator #11
....860-509-8000
Water Treatment Plant Operator #11 860-509-8000
Weigher #08 860-713-6160
Weights & Measures Dealer/Repairer #08
....860-713-6160
Weights & Measures Device Regulator #08
....860-713-6160
Well Driller #07 860-566-2825
Wildlife Rehabilitator #10 860-424-3000
Wrestler #07 860-566-2825
Wrestling Manager #07 860-566-2825

Licensing Agency Information

01 Bar Examining Committee, 80 Washington St, Hartford, CT 06106-4424; 860-568-7900.

www.jud.state.ct.us/colp/Barexam.html

02 Department of Insurance, Licensing Division, PO Box 816 (153 Market St), Hartford, CT 06142-0816; 860-297-3845, Fax: 860-297-3872.

www.state.ct.us/cid

Direct URL to search licenses: www.ct-clic.com/RsltKey.asp

03 Consumer Protection Department, Board of Architects, 165 Capitol Ave, Hartford, CT 06106; 860-713-6135, Fax: 860-713-7239.

04 Consumer Protection Department, Board of Trades Division, 165 Capitol Ave, Hartford, CT 06106; 860-713-7239.

05 Consumer Protection Dept/Occupational Licensing, Board of Television & Radio Service Examiners, 165 Capitol Ave, Hartford, CT 06106; 860-713-6135, Fax: 860-713-7239.

06 Department of Banking, 260 Constitution Plaza, Hartford, CT 06106-1800; 860-240-8299, Fax: 860-240-8178.

www.state.ct.us/dob

07 Department of Consumer Protection, Occupational Licensing Division, 165 Capitol Ave, Hartford, CT 06106; 860-713-6300, Fax: 860-713-7239.

www.state.ct.us/dcp

08 Department of Consumer Protection, Food Standards Division, 165 Capitol Ave, State Office Bldg, Hartford, CT 06106-1630; 860-713-6160, Fax: 860-713-7244.

www.state.ct.us/dcp

09 Department of Education, Bureau of Certification & Professional Development, PO Box 150471 (PO Box 150471, Rm 243), Hartford, CT 06115-0471; 860-566-5201, Fax: 860-566-8929.

www.state.ct.us/sde

10 Department of Environmental Protection, 79 Elm St, Hartford, CT 06106; 860-424-3372, Fax: 860-424-4051.

www.state.ct/dep

11 Department of Public Health & Addiction Services, PO Box 340308 (410 Capital Ave, Mail Stop 12MQA), Hartford, CT 06134-0308; 860-509-7603, Fax: 860-509-7607.

www.state.ct.us/dph

Direct URL to search licenses: www.state.ct.us/dph/scripts/hlthprof.asp You can search online using license number, first and last name.

12 Division of Special Revenue, PO Box 11424 (PO Box 11424 (555 Russell Rd)), Newington, CT 06111; 860-594-0656, Fax: 860-594-0649.

www.state.ct.us/dosr

13 Division of State Police, 111 Country Club Rd, Middletown, CT 06457; 860-685-8046, Fax: 860-685-8496.

www.state.ct.us/dps

14 Environmental Protection Department, 79 Elm St, Hartford, CT 06134; 860-609-8000, Fax: 860-509-8457.

15 Liquor Control Department, 165 Capitol Ave, Hartford, CT 06106; 860-713-6200, Fax: 860-713-7235.

www.state.ct.us/dosr

16 Office of the Secretary of the State, PO Box 150470 (PO Box 150470), Hartford, CT 06115-0470; 860-509-6200, Fax: 860-509-6230.

www.state.ct.us/sots

17 Consumer Protection Department, Real Estate Division, 165 Capitol Ave, Rm 110, Hartford, CT 06106; 860-713-6150, Fax: 860-713-7239.

www.state.ct.us.dcp

18 Ethics Commission, 20 Trinity St, Hartford, CT 06106; 860-566-4472, Fax: 860-566-3806.

19 Department of Public Safety, Division of State Police, 1111 Country Club Rd, Middletown, CT 06457-9294; 860-685-8290.

20 Department of Agriculture, Bureau of Aquaculture, 190 Rogers Ave, Milford, CT 06460; 203-874-0696.

21 Department of Revenue Svcs, Audit Unit, 25 Sigourney St, Hartford, CT 06106; 860-297-5962.

22 Department of Agriculture, Bureau of Regulation & Inspection, 165 Capitol Ave, Hartford, CT 06106; 860-566-4845.

23 Department of Motor Vehicles, Dealers & Repairers Unit, 60 State St, Wethersfield, CT 06109; 860-566-2796.

24 Department of Transportation, Motor Transport Svcs, 2800 Berlin Turnpike, PO Box 317546, Newington, CT 06131-7546; 860-594-2865.

25 Department of Public Safety, Division of Fire, Emergency & Building Svcs, 1111 Country Club Rd, Middletown, CT 06457-9294; 860-685-8470.

The following list indicates the district and division name for each county in the state. If the district or division name of the bankruptcy court is different from the civil/criminal court, it appears in parentheses.

County/Court Cross Reference

Fairfield	Bridgeport	New Haven	New Haven
Hartford	Hartford	New London	New Haven
Litchfield	New Haven (Hartford)	Tolland	Hartford
Middlesex	New Haven (Hartford)	Windham	Hartford

US District Court

District of Connecticut

Bridgeport Division Office of the clerk, Room 400, 915 Lafayette Blvd, Bridgeport, CT 06604, 203-579-5861.

www.ctd.uscourts.gov

Counties: Fairfield (prior to 1993). Since January 1993, cases from any county may be assigned to any of the divisions in the district.

Indexing & Storage: Cases are indexed by defendant and plaintiff as well as by case number. New cases are available in the index immediately after filing date. A computer index is maintained. Records are stored by docket number, accession number and box number. Open records are located at this court.

Fee & Payment: The fee is $15.00 per item (one party name or case number). Payment may be made by money order, cashier check. Business checks are not accepted. Personal checks are not accepted. Prepayment is required. Payee: Clerk, US District Court. Certification fee: $5.00 per document. Copy fee: $.50 per page. You are allowed to make your own copies. These copies cost $.25 per page.

Phone Search: Only docket information is available by phone. An automated voice case information service (VCIS) is not available.

Mail Search: A stamped self addressed envelope is not required.

In Person Search: In person searching is available.

PACER: Sign-up number is 800-676-6856. Access fee is $.60 per minute. Toll-free access: 800-292-0658. Local access: 203-773-2451. Case records are available back to November 1, 1991. New records are available online after 1 day.

Hartford Division 450 Main St, Hartford, CT 06103, 860-240-3200.

www.ctd.uscourts.gov

Counties: Hartford, Tolland, Windham (prior to 1993). Since 1993, cases from any county may be assigned to any of the divisions in the district.

Indexing & Storage: Cases are indexed by defendant and plaintiff as well as by case number. New cases are available in the index immediately after filing date. A computer index is maintained. Records are kept where the assigned judge sits, and are stored by a federal record number system. Open records are located at this court.

Fee & Payment: The fee is $15.00 per item (one party name or case number). Payment may be made by money order, cashier check, personal check. Prepayment is required. Payee: Clerk, US District Court. Certification fee: $5.00 per document. Copy fee: $.50 per page. You are allowed to make your own copies. These copies cost $.25 per page.

Phone Search: Only docket information is available by phone. An automated voice case information service (VCIS) is not available.

Mail Search: Always enclose a stamped self addressed envelope.

In Person Search: In person searching is available.

PACER: Sign-up number is 800-676-6856. Access fee is $.60 per minute. Toll-free access: 800-292-0658. Local access: 203-773-2451. Case records are available back to November 1, 1991. New records are available online after 1 day.

New Haven Division 141 Church St, New Haven, CT 06510, 203-773-2140.

www.ctd.uscourts.gov

Counties: Litchfield, Middlesex, New Haven, New London (prior to 1993). Since 1993, cases from any county may be assigned to any of the divisions in the district.

Indexing & Storage: Cases are indexed by defendant and plaintiff as well as by case number. New cases are available in the index immediately after filing date. A computer index is maintained. Older records are indexed on microfiche. Open records are located at this court. District wide searches are available for information from 1982 to the present from this court.

Fee & Payment: The fee is no charge per item (one party name or case number). Payment may be made by money order, cashier check, business check. Personal checks are not accepted. There is a $15.00 search fee charged for each additional name after the first. Payee: District Court Clerk. Certification fee: $5.00 per document. Copy fee: $.50 per page. You are allowed to make your own copies. These copies cost $.25 per page.

Phone Search: Only docket information is available by phone. An automated voice case information service (VCIS) is not available.

Mail Search: Always enclose a stamped self addressed envelope.

In Person Search: In person searching is available.

PACER: Sign-up number is 800-676-6856. Access fee is $.60 per minute. Toll-free access: 800-292-0658. Local access: 203-773-2451. Case records are available back to November 1, 1991. New records are available online after 1 day.

US Bankruptcy Court

District of Connecticut

Bridgeport Division 915 Lafayette Blvd, Bridgeport, CT 06604, 203-579-5808.

www.ctb.uscourts.gov

Counties: Fairfield.

Indexing & Storage: Cases are indexed by debtor as well as by case number. New cases are available in the index immediately after filing date. A computer index is maintained. Open records are located at this court. District wide searches are available from this division.

Fee & Payment: The fee is $15.00 per item (one party name or case number). Payment may be made by money order, cashier check, business check. Personal checks are not accepted. Prepayment is required. Payee: Clerk, US Bankruptcy Court. Certification fee: $5.00 per document. Copy fee: $.50 per page. You are allowed to make your own copies. These copies cost $.25 per page.

Phone Search: An automated voice case information service (VCIS) is available. Call VCIS at 800-800-5113 or 860-240-3345.

Mail Search: Always enclose a stamped self addressed envelope.

In Person Search: In person searching is available.

PACER: Sign-up number is 800-676-6856. Access fee is $.60 per minute. Case records are available back to 1979. Records are purged every 6 months. New civil records are available online after 1 day. PACER is available on the Internet at http://pacer.ctb.uscourts.gov.

Hartford Division 450 Main St, Hartford, CT 06103, 860-240-3675.

www.ctb.uscourts.gov

Counties: Hartford, Litchfield, Middlesex, Tolland, Windham.

Indexing & Storage: Cases are indexed by debtor as well as by case number. New cases are available in the index within 1 week after filing date. A computer index is maintained. Open records are located at this court.

Fee & Payment: The fee is $15.00 per item (one party name or case number). Payment may be made by money order, cashier check, personal check. Prepayment is required. Payee: Clerk, US Bankruptcy Court. Certification fee: $5.00 per document. Copy fee: $.50 per page. You are

allowed to make your own copies. These copies cost $.25 per page.

Phone Search: Only docket information is available by phone. An automated voice case information service (VCIS) is available. Call VCIS at 800-800-5113 or 860-240-3345.

Mail Search: Always enclose a stamped self addressed envelope.

In Person Search: In person searching is available.

PACER: Sign-up number is 800-676-6856. Access fee is $.60 per minute. Case records are available back to 1979. Records are purged every 6 months. New civil records are available online after 1 day. PACER is available on the Internet at http://pacer.ctb.uscourts.gov.

New Haven Division The Connecticut Financial Center, 157 Church St, 18th Floor, New Haven, CT 06510, 203-773-2009.

www.ctb.uscourts.gov

Counties: New Haven, New London.

Indexing & Storage: Cases are indexed by debtor as well as by case number. New cases are available in the index within 1 week after filing date. A computer index is maintained. Open records are located at this court.

Fee & Payment: The fee is $15.00 per item (one party name or case number). Payment may be made by money order, cashier check, personal check. Prepayment is required. Payee: Clerk, US Bankruptcy Court. Certification fee: $5.00 per document. Copy fee: $.50 per page. You are

allowed to make your own copies. These copies cost $.25 per page.

Phone Search: Only docket information is available by phone. An automated voice case information service (VCIS) is available. Call VCIS at 800-800-5113 or 860-240-3345.

Mail Search: Always enclose a stamped self addressed envelope.

In Person Search: In person searching is available.

PACER: Sign-up number is 800-676-6856. Access fee is $.60 per minute. Case records are available back to 1979. Records are purged every 6 months. New civil records are available online after 1 day. PACER is available on the Internet at http://pacer.ctb.uscourts.gov.

Court	Jurisdiction	No. of Courts	How Organized
Superior Courts*	General	18	21 Geographic Areas
Geographic Area Courts*	Limited	19	21 Geographic Areas
Probate Courts*	Probate	129	

* Profiled in this Sourcebook.

Court	CIVIL								
	Tort	Contract	Real Estate	Min. Claim	Max. Claim	Small Claims	Estate	Eviction	Domestic Relations
Superior Courts*	X	X	X	$2500	No Max				X
Geographic Area Courts*						$2500		X	
Probate Courts*							X		X

Court	CRIMINAL				
	Felony	Misdemeanor	DWI/DUI	Preliminary Hearing	Juvenile
Superior Courts*	X				X
Geographic Area Courts*		X	X	X	
Probate Courts*					

ADMINISTRATION

Chief Court Administrator, 231 Capitol Av, Hartford, CT, 06106; 860-566-4461, Fax: 860-566-3308. www.jud.state.ct.us

COURT STRUCTURE

The Superior Court is the sole court of original jurisdiction for all causes of action, except for matters over which the probate courts have jurisdiction as provided by statute. The Geographic Area Courts are actually divisions of the Superior Court given jurisdiction over lesser offenses and actions. The Superior Court has five divisions: Criminal, Civil, Family, Juvenile, and Administrative Appeals

PROBATE COURTS

Probate is handled by city Probate Courts, which we have listed, and are not part of the state court system. Information request requirements are consistent across the state; requesters must provide full name of decedent, year and place of death, and. SASE. Written or in person searches are allowed, prepayment is required; there is no search fee; the certification fee is $5.00 for 1st 2 pages and $2.00 for each additional page; and, the copy fee is $1.00 per page.

ONLINE ACCESS

There are two online systems available for civil and family records only, statewide. www.jud2.state.ct.us/Civil_Inquiry/GetParty.asp is free internet access. However, it contains primarily active cases only but includes Supreme and Geographic Area courts.

The commercial system, which provides direct access to Superior Court records, is available through the Judicial Information Systems. User can access all civil and family records. The system is available from 8AM to 5PM Eastern Time Monday through Friday except on holidays. The fee is $30 per month network charge, $10.00 per use per month user authorization fee, plus a per minute usage fee. For information brochure or subscription information call the CT JIS Office at 860-566-8580. There is currently no online access to criminal records; however, criminal and motor vehicle data is available for purchase in database format. Also, there is a central criminal records repository (see below).

ADDITIONAL INFORMATION

Some courts do not perform criminal searches, but rather forward search requests to the Department of Public Safety, 1111 Country Club Rd, PO Box 2794, Middletown, CT 06457, 860-685-8480. The search fee is $25.00.

There is a State Record Center, which serves as the repository for criminal and some civil records, in Enfield CT open 9AM-5PM M-F. Case records are sent to the Record Center from 3 months to 5 years after disposition by the courts. These records are then maintained 10 years for misdemeanors and 20+ years for felonies. If a requester is certain that the record is at the Record Center, it is quicker to direct the request there rather than to the original court of record. Only written requests are accepted. Search requirements: full defendant name, docket number, disposition date, and court action. Fee is $5.00 for each docket. Fee payee is Treasurer-State of Connecticut. Direct Requests to: Connecticut Record Center, 111 Phoenix Avenue, Enfield CT 06082, 860-741-3714.

Personal checks must have name and address printed on the check; if requesting in person, check must have same address as drivers' license.

Many clerks state that they will send an extract of a record without copying originals or certification at no charge.

📖 📖 📖 📖 📖

Fairfield County

Danbury Superior Court 146 White St, Danbury, CT 06810; 203-207-8600. Hours: 9AM-1PM, 2:30-4PM (EST). *Felony, Civil Actions Over $2,500.*

Civil Records: Access: Mail, online, in person. Only the court conducts in person searches; visitors may not. No search fee. Required to search: name, years to search. Civil cases indexed by defendant. Civil records on microfilm from 11-87, prior on index cards, but only list docket number and disposal date, then referred to Records Center at Enfield, CT. See state introduction for online access info. Free access to civil case records is available on the Internet at www.jud2.state.ct.us/. **Criminal Records:** Access: Mail, in person. Only the court conducts in person searches; visitors may not. No search fee. Required to search: name, years to search, DOB. Criminal records on microfilm from 11-87, prior on index cards, but only list docket number and disposal date, then referred to Records Center at Enfield, CT. **General Information:** No sealed records released. Turnaround time 2-4 days for civil and family, 3-4 days for motor vehicle and criminal. Copy fee: $1.00 per page. Certification fee: $2.00. Fee payee: Clerk of Superior Court. Personal checks accepted. Require ID with personal check. Prepayment is required.

Fairfield Superior Court 1061 Main St Attn: criminal or civil, Bridgeport, CT 06604; 203-579-6527. Hours: 9AM-5PM (EST). *Felony, Civil Actions Over $2,500.*

Civil Records: Access: Mail, online, in person. Only the court conducts in person searches; visitors may not. No search fee. Required to search: name, years to search; also helpful-address. Civil cases indexed by defendant, plaintiff. Civil records on computer for 2 years, on microfiche from 1975 to 1990, prior on index cards. After 5 years sent to Records Center at Enfield, CT. Access to civil case records is available free on the Internet at www.jud2.state.ct.us/. **Criminal Records:** Access: Mail, in person. Only the court conducts in person searches; visitors may not. No search fee. Required to search: name, years to search, DOB. Criminal records on computer since 1991, on microfiche from 1975 to 1990. **General Information:** No sealed, adoption records released. SASE required. Turnaround time 2-3 weeks for civil, 4 weeks for criminal. Copy fee: $1.00 per page. Certification fee: $2.00. Fee payee: Chief Clerk Superior Court. Personal checks accepted. Prepayment is required.

Stamford-Norwalk Superior Court 123 Hoyt St, Stamford, CT 06905;; Civil phone:203-965-5307; Criminal phone:203-965-5307. Hours: 9AM-Noon, 1:30PM-4PM (EST). *Felony, Civil Actions Over $2,500.*

Civil Records: Access: Mail, online, in person. Both court and visitors may perform in person searches. No search fee. Required to search: name, years to search. Civil cases indexed by defendant, plaintiff. Only pending cases on computer, on microfiche from 1970s, on index cards from 1958. Access to civil case records is available free on the Internet at www.jud2.state.ct.us/. **Criminal Records:** Access: Phone, mail, in person. Only the

court conducts in person searches; visitors may not. No search fee. Required to search: name, years to search. Only pending cases on computer, on microfiche from 1970s, on index cards from 1958. **General Information:** No sealed records released. Copy fee: $1.00 per page. Certification fee: $2.00. Fee payee: Clerk of Superior Court. Personal checks accepted.

Geographical Area Court #2 172 Golden Hill St, Bridgeport, CT 06604; 203-579-6560. Hours: 9AM-4PM (EST). *Misdemeanor, Eviction, Small Claims.*

Civil Records: Access: Phone, mail, online, in person. Both court and visitors may perform in person searches. No search fee. Required to search: name, years to search. Civil cases indexed by defendant. Civil records pending and from 1990 on computer, on microfiche from 1982 to 1990, prior on index cards. After microfilmed and entered on index cards, sent to Records Center at Enfield, CT. Access to civil case records is available free on the Internet at www.jud2.state.ct.us/. **Criminal Records:** Access: In person only. Court does not conduct in person searches; visitors must perform searches for themselves. Search fee: No criminal searches performed by court. Required to search: name, years to search. Criminal records pending and from 1990 on computer, on microfiche from 1982. Mail requests are referred the state criminal records agency. **General Information:** No sealed records released. Turnaround time up to 4 weeks. Copy fee: $1.00 per page. Certification fee: $3.00. Fee payee: Clerk of Superior Court. Personal checks accepted. Prepayment is required.

Geographical Area Court #20 17 Belden Ave, Norwalk, CT 06850; 203-846-3237. Hours: 9AM-5PM (EST). *Misdemeanor, Eviction, Small Claims.*

Civil Records: Access: online, in person. Court does not conduct in person searches; visitors must perform searches for themselves. Search fee: No civil searches performed by court. Required to search: name, years to search. Civil cases indexed by defendant, plaintiff. Civil records on computer from 1986. Access to civil case records is available free on the Internet at www.jud2.state.ct.us/. **Criminal Records:** Access: In person only. Court does not conduct in person searches; visitors must perform searches for themselves. Search fee: No criminal searches performed by court. Required to search: name, years to search; also helpful-DOB. Criminal records on computer from 1986, prior records on index cards. **General Information:** Copy fee: $1.00 per page. Certification fee: $2.00. Fee payee: Superior Court GA #20. Only cashiers checks and money orders accepted. Prepayment is required.

Geographical Area Court #3 146 White St, Danbury, CT 06810; 203-207-8600. Hours: 9AM-5PM (EST). *Misdemeanor, Eviction, Small Claims.*

Civil Records: Access: Mail, online, in person. Only the court conducts in person searches; visitors may not. No search fee. Required to search: name, years to search. Civil cases indexed by defendant. Civil records on microfilm from 11-87, prior on index cards, but only list docket

number and disposal date, then referred to Records Center at Enfield, CT. In person searches returned by mail. Access to civil case records is available free on the Internet at www.jud2.state.ct.us/. **Criminal Records:** Access: Phone, mail, in person. Court does not conduct in person searches; visitors must perform searches for themselves. No search fee. Required to search: name, years to search; also helpful-DOB. Criminal records on computer from 11/9/87. The court refers all requests to one of the 2 statewide agencies. **General Information:** No youthful offender or dispositions by dismissal after 20 days from date of judgment records released. SASE required. Turnaround time up to 1 week. Copy fee: $1.00 per page. Certification fee: $2.00. Fee payee: Clerk of Superior Court. Personal checks accepted. Prepayment is required.

Bethel Probate Court 1 School St, PO Box 144, Bethel, CT 06801; 203-794-8508; Fax: 203-794-8564. Hours: 9AM-1:00PM *Probate.*

Bridgeport Probate District 202 State St, McLevy Hall, 3rd Floor, Bridgeport, CT 06604; 203-576-3945; Fax: 203-576-7898. Hours: 9AM-5PM M-Th; 9AM-4PM F (EST). *Probate.*

Brookfield Probate Court 100 Pocono Rd, PO Box 5192, Brookfield, CT 06804; 203-775-3700; Fax: 203-740-9008. Hours: 9AM-2PM (and by app't) (EST). *Probate.*

Danbury Probate Court 155 Deer Hill Ave, Danbury, CT 06810; 203-797-4521; Fax: 203-796-1526. Hours: 8:30AM-4:30PM (EST). *Probate.*

Darien Probate Court Town Hall, 2 Renshaw Rd, Darien, CT 06820; 203-656-7342; Fax: 203-656-0774. Hours: 9AM-12:30PM, 1:30-4:30PM; 9AM-12:30PM Fri July-Labor Day (EST). *Probate.*

Fairfield Probate Court Independence Hall, 725 Old Post Rd, Fairfield, CT 06430; 203-256-3041; Fax: 203-256-3044. Hours: 9AM-5PM, 9AM-4:30PM (July-Aug) (EST). *Probate.*

Greenwich Probate Court 101 Field Point Rd, PO Box 2540, Greenwich, CT 06836; 203-622-3766; Fax: 203-622-6451. Hours: 8AM-4PM, 8AM-Noon Fri July-Aug (EST). *Probate.*

New Canaan Probate Court PO Box 326, 77 Main St, New Canaan, CT 06840; 203-972-7500; Fax: 203-966-5555. Hours: 8:30AM-1PM 2-4:30PM; (8:30AM-1PM Fri July-Aug) (EST). *Probate.*

New Fairfield Probate Court 4 Brush Hill Rd, New Fairfield, CT 06812; 203-312-5627; Fax: 203-312-5612. Hours: 9AM-Noon W-Th (and by app't) (EST). *Probate.*

Newtown Probate Court Edmond Town Hall, 45 Main St, Newtown, CT 06470; 203-270-4280; Fax: 203-270-4205. Hours: 8:30AM-Noon,1-4:30PM (EST). *Probate.*

Norwalk Probate Court 125 East Ave, PO Box 2009, Norwalk, CT 06852-2009; 203-854-7737; Fax: 203-854-7825. Hours: 9AM-4:30PM (EST). *Probate.*

Note: District includes Town of Wilton

Redding Probate Court Town Hall, Lonetown Rd, PO Box 1125, Redding, CT 06875-

1125; 203-938-2326; Fax: 203-938-8816. Hours: 9AM-1PM (EST). *Probate.*

Ridgefield Probate Court Town Hall, 400 Main St, Ridgefield, CT 06877; 203-431-2776; Fax: 203-431-2772. Hours: 8:30AM-4:30PM (EST). *Probate.*

Shelton Probate Court 40 White St, PO Box 127, Shelton, CT 06484; 203-924-8462; Fax: 203-924-8943. Hours: 9AM-Noon, 1-4:30PM (EST). *Probate.*

Sherman Probate Court Mallory Town Hall, Rt. 39 Center, PO Box 39, Sherman, CT 06784; 860-355-1821; Fax: 860-350-5041. Hours: 9AM-Noon Tu (and by app't) (EST). *Probate.*

Stamford Probate Court 888 Washington Blvd, 8th Floor, PO Box 10152, Stamford, CT 06904-2152; 203-323-2149; Fax: 203-964-1830. Hours: 9AM-4PM (EST). *Probate.*

Stratford Probate Court 2725 Main St, Town Hall, Stratford, CT 06615; 203-385-4023; Fax: 203-375-6253. Hours: 9:30AM-4:30PM (EST). *Probate.*

Trumbull Probate Court Town Hall, 5866 Main St, Trumbull, CT 06611-5416; 203-452-5068; Fax: 203-452-5092. Hours: 9AM-4:30PM (EST). *Probate.*

Note: District includes Town of Easton

Westport Probate Court Town Hall, 110 Myrtle Ave, Westport, CT 06880; 203-341-1100; Fax: 203-341-1153. Hours: 9AM-4:30PM (EST). *Probate.*

Note: District includes Town of Weston

Hartford County

New Britain Superior Court 20 Franklin Square, New Britain, CT 06051;; Civil phone:860-515-5180; Criminal phone:860-515-5180. Hours: 9AM-5PM (EST). *Felony, Civil Actions Over $2,500.*

Civil Records: Access: online, in person. Court does not conduct in person searches; visitors must perform searches for themselves. Search fee: No civil searches performed by court. Required to search: name, years to search. Civil cases indexed by plaintiff. Civil records on computer up to one year after closing, index cards back to 1989, prior in Hartford. Access to civil case records is available free on the Internet at www.jud2.state.ct.us/. **Criminal Records:** Access: Mail, in person. Only the court conducts in person searches; visitors may not. Search fee: for judgments $10.00; if certified: $15.00. Required to search: name, years to search. Criminal records on computer for 2 years, then purged when cases sent to State Record Center. **General Information:** No paternity, family case studies or sealed records released. SASE required. Turnaround time 3 days. Copy fee: $1.00 per page. Certification fee: $2.00. Fee payee: Clerk of Superior Court. Personal checks accepted. Prepayment is required.

Geographical Area Court #12 410 Center St, Manchester, CT 06040; 860-647-1091. Hours: 9AM-5PM; Phone Hours: 9AM-4PM (EST). *Misdemeanor, Eviction, Small Claims.*

Note: Evictions are handled by a special Housing Court, 18 Trinity, Hartford, CT, 860-566-8550

Civil Records: Access: Mail, online, in person. Both court and visitors may perform in person searches. No search fee. Required to search: name, years to search. Civil cases indexed by defendant. Civil records on computer for 3 years. Access to civil case records is available free on the Internet

at www.jud2.state.ct.us/. **Criminal Records:** Access: Mail, in person. Only the court conducts in person searches; visitors may not. No search fee. Required to search: name, years to search, DOB. Criminal records on computer for 3 years. In person search results returned by mail only. **General Information:** No non disclosable records released. SASE required. Turnaround time 1-2 weeks. Copy fee: $1.00 per page. Certification fee: $2.00. Fee payee: Clerk of Superior Court.

Geographical Area Court #13 111 Phoenix, Enfield, CT 06082; 860-741-3727. Hours: 9AM-1PM, 2:30-4PM (EST). *Misdemeanor, Eviction.*

Civil Records: Access: online, in person. Court does not conduct in person searches; visitors must perform searches for themselves. Search fee: No civil searches performed by court. Required to search: name, years to search. Civil cases indexed by defendant. Civil records on computer for 1 year, microfiche by year, archived at Record Center at Enfield, CT. Access to civil case records is available free on the Internet at www.jud2.state.ct.us/. **Criminal Records:** Access: In person only. Court does not conduct in person searches; visitors must perform searches for themselves. Search fee: No criminal searches performed by court. Required to search: name, years to search, DOB. Criminal records on computer for 1 year, microfiche by year, archived at Record Center at Enfield, CT. **General Information:** No copy fee. Certification fee: No certification fee. Certification available from State Record Center. Fee payee: Clerk of Superior Court. Personal checks accepted. Prepayment is required.

Geographical Area Court #15 20 Franklin Square, New Britain, CT 06051;; Civil phone:860-515-5180; Criminal phone:860-515-5180. Hours: 8:15AM-5PM (EST). *Misdemeanor, Eviction, Small Claims.*

Civil Records: Access: Mail, online, in person. Only the court conducts in person searches; visitors may not. No search fee. Required to search: name, years to search. Civil cases indexed by defendant, plaintiff. Civil records on computer for 3 years, then on microfiche. All info in archives at Record Center at Enfield, CT. Access to civil case records is available free on the Internet at www.jud2.state.ct.us/. **Criminal Records:** Access: Mail, in person. Only the court conducts in person searches; visitors may not. No search fee. Required to search: name, years to search, DOB. Criminal records on computer from 1985, then on microfiche. All info in archives at Record Center @ Enfield, CT. Data is purged every two years. **General Information:** No sealed records released. SASE required. Turnaround time 1 month. Copy fee: $1.00 per page. Certification fee: $2.00. Certification fee is for criminal division. Civil fee varies. Fee payee: Clerk of Superior Court. Business checks accepted. Prepayment is required.

Geographical Area Court #17 131 N Main St, Bristol, CT 06010; 860-582-8111. Hours: 9AM-5PM (EST). *Misdemeanor, Eviction, Small Claims.*

www.jud2.state.ct.us **Criminal Records:** Access: Phone, mail, in person. Only the court conducts in person searches; visitors may not. No search fee. Required to search: name, years to search, DOB. Criminal records on computer from 1986, on microfiche from 1982, prior on index cards from 1979-1992, microfiche 1988-1992 and docket books. **General Information:** No dismissals, not

guilty, youthful offender or NOLLE records released. SASE required. Turnaround time 1-2 days. Copy fee: $1.00 per page. Certification fee: No certification fee. Fee payee: Clerk of Superior Court. Personal checks accepted. Prepayment is required.

Geographical Area Court #14 101 LaFayette St, Hartford, CT 06106; 860-566-1630. Hours: 1PM-2:30PM (EST). *Misdemeanor.* **Criminal Records:** Access: Phone, mail, in person. Only the court conducts in person searches; visitors may not. No search fee. Required to search: name, years to search. **General Information:** SASE required. Turnaround time 1 week. Copy fee: $1.00 per page. Certification fee: $2.00. Fee payee: Clerk of Superior Court. Personal checks accepted. Prepayment is required.

Geographical Area Court #16 105 Raymond Rd, West Hartford, CT 06107; 860-236-4551; Fax: 860-236-9311. Hours: 9AM-5PM (EST). *Misdemeanor.* **Criminal Records:** Access: Mail, in person. Only the court conducts in person searches; visitors may not. No search fee. Required to search: name, years to search, DOB, signed release. **General Information:** No dismissal, Nolles, YO records released. SASE required. Turnaround time 3-5 days. Copy fee: $1.00 per page. Certification fee: $3.00. Fee payee: Clerk of Superior Court. Personal checks accepted. Credit cards accepted: Visa, Mastercard. Accepted in person only. Prepayment is required.

Hartford Superior Court-Civil 95 Washington St, Hartford, CT 06106; 860-548-2700; Fax: 860-548-2711. Hours: 9AM-5PM (EST). *Civil.*

Civil Records: Access: Mail, online, in person. Both court and visitors may perform in person searches. No search fee. Required to search: name, years to search. Civil cases indexed by defendant, plaintiff. Civil records on computer if active, otherwise on microfiche, older records at Enfield Records Center. Access to active civil case records is available free on the Internet at www.jud2.state.ct.us/. **General Information:** No paternity, support agreement, sealed files, acknowledgments (filed before 10/01/95) records released. SASE required. Turnaround time 7-10 days. Copy fee: $1.00 per page. Certification fee: $2.00. Fee payee: Clerk of Superior Court. Personal checks accepted. Credit cards accepted: Visa, Mastercard. Accepted in person only. $10.00 minimum. Prepayment is required.

Hartford Superior Court-Criminal 101 LaFayette St, Hartford, CT 06106; 860-566-1634. Hours: 9AM-5PM (EST). *Felony.* **Criminal Records:** Access: Mail, in person. Only the court conducts in person searches; visitors may not. No search fee. Required to search: name, years to search; also helpful-DOB. Criminal records on computer from 1989. **General Information:** No youthful offender records or dismissals released. SASE required. Turnaround time 7-10 days. Copy fee: $1.00 per page. Certification fee: $2.50. Fee payee: Clerk of Superior Court. Personal checks accepted. Prepayment is required.

Avon Probate Court 60 W Main St, Avon, CT 06001-0578; 860-409-4348; Fax: 860-409-4368. Hours: 9AM-Noon (EST). *Probate.*

Berlin Probate Court 177 Columbus Blvd, PO Box 400, New Britain, CT 06050-0400; 860-826-2696; Fax: 860-826-2695. Hours: 9AM-4PM (EST). *Probate.*

Note: District includes Town of New Britain

Bloomfield Probate Court Town Hall, 800 Bloomfield Ave, Bloomfield, CT 06002; 860-769-3548; Fax: 860-769-3598. Hours: 9AM-1PM, 2AM-4:30PM (EST). *Probate.*

Bristol Probate Court 111 N Main St, City Hall, Bristol, CT 06010; 860-584-7650; Fax: 860-584-3818. Hours: 9AM-5PM (EST). *Probate.*

Burlington Probate Court 200 Spielman Highway, Burlington, CT 06013; 860-673-2108; Fax: 860-675-9312. Hours: 9AM-1PM Fri (and by app't) (EST). *Probate.*

Canton Probate Court Town Hall, 4 Market St, PO Box 175, Collinsville, CT 06022; 860-693-7851; Fax: 860-693-7889. Hours: 8:30AM-1PM Tu-Th (and by app't) (EST). *Probate.*

East Granby Probate Court PO Box 542, 9 Center St, East Granby, CT 06026-0542; 860-653-3434; Fax: 860-653-7085. Hours: 10AM-1PM Tu; 9AM-Noon W-Th (and by app't) (EST). *Probate.*

East Hartford Probate Court Town Hall, 740 Main St, East Hartford, CT 06108; 860-291-7278; Fax: 860-289-0831. Hours: 9AM-4PM (EST). *Probate.*

East Windsor Probate Court Town Hall, 1540 Sullivan Ave, South Windsor, CT 06074; 860-644-2511 X271; Fax: 860-648-5047. Hours: 8AM-2PM (EST). *Probate.*

Note: District includes Town of South Windsor

Enfield Probate Court 820 Enfield St, Enfield, CT 06082; 860-253-6305; Fax: 860-253-6388. Hours: 9AM-4:30PM (till 6:30PM 1st Monday) (EST). *Probate.*

Farmington Probate Court One Monteith Dr, Farmington, CT 06032; 860-673-2360; Fax: 860-673-8262. Hours: 9AM-4PM (EST). *Probate.*

Glastonbury Probate Court PO Box 6523, 2155 Main St, Glastonbury, CT 06033-6523; 860-652-7629; Fax: 860-652-7590. Hours: 9:30AM-4:30PM (EST). *Probate.*

Granby Probate Court 15 N Granby Rd, Town Hall, PO Box 240, Granby, CT 06035-0240; 860-653-8944; Fax: 860-653-4769. Hours: 9AM-Noon T,W,F (EST). *Probate.*

Hartford Probate Court 10 Prospect St, 4th Fl, Hartford, CT 06103; 860-522-1813; Fax: 860-724-1503. Hours: 9AM-4PM (4-6:30PM Mon. by app't) (EST). *Probate.*

Hartland Probate Court PO Box 158, West Hartland, CT 06027; 860-653-9710, 203-379-8625 (After hours); Fax: 860-738-1003. Hours: 10AM-1PM (and by app't) (EST). *Probate.*

Manchester Probate Court 66 Center St, Manchester, CT 06040; 860-647-3227; Fax: 860-647-3236. Hours: 8:30AM-Noon, 1-4:30PM (EST). *Probate.*

Marlborough Probate Court 26 N Main St, PO Box 29, Marlborough, CT 06447; 860-295-6239; Fax: 860-295-0317. Hours: 9AM-4:30PM M; 2:30-7PM T; 2PM-4:30 Th (and by app't) (EST). *Probate.*

Note: Hours are 9AM-4:30PM on Mon, 2:30PM-7PM on Tues, and 2PM-4:30PM on Thurs

Newington Probate Court 66 Cedar Street, Rear, Newington, CT 06111; 860-665-1285; Fax: 860-665-1331. Hours: 9AM-4PM M-W, F; 9AM-7PM Th (EST). *Probate.*

Note: District includes towns of Rocky Hill, Wethersfield

Plainville Probate Court 1 Central Square, Plainville, ct 06062; 860-793-0221 x250; Fax: 860-793-2424. Hours: 9AM-3PM M-Th; 9AM-1PM F (EST). *Probate.*

Simsbury Probate Court 933 Hopmeadow St, PO Box 495, Simsbury, CT 06070; 860-658-3277; Fax: 860-658-3206. Hours: 9AM-1PM, 2-4:30PM (and by app't) (EST). *Probate.*

Southington Probate Court Town Hall, 75 Main St, PO Box 165, Southington, CT 06489; 860-276-6253; Fax: 860-276-6255. Hours: 8:30AM-4:30PM M-W, F; 8:30AM-7PM Th (EST). *Probate.*

Suffield Probate Court 83 Mountain Rd, Town Hall, PO Box 234, Suffield, CT 06078; 860-668-3835; Fax: 860-668-3029. Hours: 9AM-1PM (and by app't) (EST). *Probate.*

West Hartford Probate Court 50 S Main St, West Hartford, CT 06107; 860-523-3174; Fax: 860-236-8352. Hours: 8:30AM-4:30PM (EST). *Probate.*

Windsor Locks Probate Court Town Office Bldg, 50 Church St, Windsor Locks, CT 06096; 860-627-1450; Fax: 860-627-1451. Hours: 9AM-2PM M-Th (EST). *Probate.*

Windsor Probate Court 275 Broad St, PO Box 342, Windsor, CT 06095; 860-285-1976; Fax: 860-285-1909. Hours: 8:30AM-4:30PM M-Th; 8:30AM-Noon Fri (EST). *Probate.*

Litchfield County

Litchfield Superior Court PO Box 247, Litchfield, CT 06759; 860-567-0885; Fax: 860-567-4779. Hours: 9AM-5PM (EST). *Felony, Civil Actions Over $2,500.*

Civil Records: Access: Fax, mail, online, in person. Only the court conducts in person searches; visitors may not. No search fee. Required to search: name, years to search. Civil cases indexed by defendant, plaintiff. Pending cases only on computer, on index cards from 1972. Access to civil case records is available free on the Internet at www.jud2.state.ct.us/. **Criminal Records:** Access: Fax, mail, in person. Only the court conducts in person searches; visitors may not. No search fee. Required to search: name, years to search; also helpful-DOB. Pending cases only on computer, on index cards from 1972. **General Information:** No sealed files released. SASE required. Turnaround time 3-4 weeks. Copy fee: $1.00 per page. Certification fee: $2.00. Fee payee: Clerk of Superior Court. Personal checks accepted. Prepayment is required. Fax notes: No fee to fax results.

Geographical Area Court #18 80 Doyle Rd (PO Box 667), Bantam, CT 06750; 860-567-3942. Hours: 9AM-5PM (EST). *Misdemeanor, Eviction, Small Claims.*

Civil Records: Access: Mail, online, in person. Both court and visitors may perform in person searches. No search fee. Required to search: name, years to search. Civil cases indexed by defendant. Civil records on computer for 1 yr, on microfiche from 1986. Access to civil case records is available free on the Internet at www.jud2.state.ct.us/. **Criminal Records:** Access: Mail, in person. Only the court conducts in person searches; visitors may not. No search fee. Required to search: name, years to search, DOB; also helpful-address. Criminal records on computer for 1 year, microfiche from 1986, on index cards for 40 years. Archived at Records Center at Enfield, CT. **General Information:** No

youthful offender or non-discloseable records released. SASE required. Turnaround time 1 week. Copy fee: $1.00 per page. Certification fee: $2.00. Fee payee: Clerk of Superior Court. Personal checks accepted.

Barkhamsted Probate Court 67 Ripley Rd, PO Box 185, Pleasant Valley, CT 06063-0185; 860-379-8665; Fax: 860-379-9284. Hours: 10AM-1PM M-W (and by app't) (EST). *Probate.*

Canaan Probate Court Town Hall, 100 Pease St, PO Box 905, Canaan, CT 06018-0905; 860-824-7114; Fax: 860-824-3139. Hours: 9AM-1PM (and by app't) (EST). *Probate.*

Cornwall Probate Court PO Box 157, Town Office Bldg, Cornwall, CT 06753-0157; 860-672-2677; Fax: 860-672-2677. Hours: 9AM-4PM M-Th (EST). *Probate.*

Harwinton Probate Court Town Hall, 100 Bentley Dr, Harwinton, CT 06791; 860-485-1403; Fax: 860-485-0051. Hours: 9AM-1PM Tu-W (and by app't) (EST). *Probate.*

Kent Probate Court Town Hall, 41 Kent Green Blvd, PO Box 185, Kent, CT 06757-0185; 860-927-3729; Fax: 860-927-1313. Hours: 9AM-Noon Tu & Th (and by app't) (EST). *Probate.*

Litchfield Probate Court 74 West St, PO Box 505, Litchfield, CT 06759; 860-567-8065; Fax: 860-567-2538. Hours: 9AM-1PM (and by app't) (EST). *Probate.*

Note: District includes towns of Morris, Warren, and Litchfield

New Hartford Probate Court Town Hall, 530 Main St, PO Box 308, New Hartford, CT 06057; 860-379-3254; Fax: 860-379-8560. Hours: 9AM-Noon M,W (and by app't) (EST). *Probate.*

New Milford Probate Court 10 Main St, New Milford, CT 06776; 860-355-6029; Fax: 860-355-6002. Hours: 9AM-Noon, 1-5PM M-Th, 9AM-Noon Fri (EST). *Probate.*

Note: District includes Town of Bridgewater

Norfolk Probate Court 19 Maple Ave, PO Box 648, Norfolk, CT 06058; 860-542-5134; Fax: 860-542-5876. Hours: 9AM-Noon Tu & Th (and by app't) (EST). *Probate.*

Plymouth Probate Court 80 Main St, Terryville, CT 06786; 860-585-4014. Hours: 9AM-2PM Tu & Th (and by app't) (EST). *Probate.*

Roxbury Probate Court Town Hall, 29 North St, PO Box 203, Roxbury, CT 06783; 860-354-1184; Fax: 860-354-0560. Hours: 9AM-3PM Tu-Th (and by app't) (EST). *Probate.*

Salisbury Probate Court Town Hall, 27 Main St, PO Box 525, Salisbury, CT 06068; 860-435-5183; Fax: 860-435-5172. Hours: 9AM-Noon (and by app't) (EST). *Probate.*

Sharon Probate Court 63 Main St, PO Box 1177, Sharon, CT 06069; 860-364-5514; Fax: 860-364-5789. Hours: 2-4PM M-W & F (and by app't) (EST). *Probate.*

Thomaston Probate Court 158 Main St, Town Hall Bldg, PO Box 136, Thomaston, CT 06787; 860-283-4874; Fax: 860-283-1013 (police dept). Hours: 3-6PM M-W (and by app't) (EST). *Probate.*

Torrington Probate Court Municipal Bldg, 140 Main St, Torrington, CT 06790; 860-489-2215; Fax: 860-496-5910. Hours: 9AM-4:30PM (EST). *Probate.*

Note: District includes Town of Goshen

Washington Probate Court Town Hall, 3 Bryan Mem. Plaza, PO Box 295, Washington Depot, CT 06794; 860-868-7974; Fax: 860-868-0512. Hours: 9AM-Noon, 1-3PM M,W,F (and by app't) (EST). *Probate.*

Watertown Probate Court 37 DeForest St, Town Hall, Watertown, CT 06795; 860-945-5237; Fax: 860-945-4741. Hours: 9AM-Noon, 1-3PM (EST). *Probate.*

Winchester Probate Court 338 Main St, PO Box 625, Winsted, CT 06098; 860-379-5576; Fax: 860-738-7053. Hours: 9AM-12,1-4PM M-W, 9Am-2PM, 3-7PM Th, til noon Fri (EST). *Probate.*

Note: District includes towns of Colebrook, Winsted

Woodbury Probate Court 281 Main St, South, PO Box 84, Woodbury, CT 06798; 203-263-2417; Fax: 203-263-2748. Hours: 9AM-4PM Tu,Th (and by app't) (EST). *Probate.*

Note: District includes Town of Bethlehem

Middlesex County

Middlesex Superior Court-Civil 1 Court St, 2nd Floor, Middletown, CT 06457-3374; 860-343-6400; Fax: 860-343-6423. Hours: 9AM-5PM (EST). *Civil.*

Civil Records: Access: Mail, online, in person. Only the court conducts in person searches; visitors may not. No search fee. Required to search: name, years to search. Civil cases indexed by defendant, plaintiff. Civil records on computer 1 year, on index card back 15 years, prior on docket books. Access to civil case records is available free on the Internet at www.jud2.state.ct.us/. **General Information:** No sealed records released. SASE required. Turnaround time 1 week. Copy fee: $1.00 per page. Certification fee: $2.00. Fee payee: Clerk, Superior Court. Personal checks accepted. Name & address must be pre-printed on check. Prepayment is required.

Middlesex Superior Court-Criminal 1 Court St, 1st Flr, Middletown, CT 06457-3348; 860-343-6445. Hours: 9AM-5PM (EST). *Felony.* **Criminal Records:** Access: Mail, in person. Only the court conducts in person searches; visitors may not. No search fee. Required to search: name, years to search, DOB, signed release; also helpful-address, SSN. Criminal records on computer for 1 year from disposition or sentence, on microfiche 1985 to present, prior on index cards. **General Information:** No youthful offender records or dismissals released. Turnaround time 3-4 days. Copy fee: $1.00 per page. Certification fee: $2.50. Fee payee: Clerk, Superior Court. Personal checks accepted. Prepayment is required.

Clinton Probate Court 50 E Main St, PO Box 130, Clinton, CT 06413-0130; 860-669-6447; Fax: 860-669-6447 (call first). Hours: 10AM-3PM M-Th (Fri. by app't) (EST). *Probate.*

Deep River Probate Court Town Hall, 174 Main St, PO Box 391, Deep River, CT 06417; 860-526-6026; Fax: 860-526-6094 (call first). Hours: 9AM-Noon, 1PM-4PM Tu,Th (and by app't) (EST). *Probate.*

East Haddam Probate Court PO Box 217, 7 Main St, East Haddam, CT 06423; 860-873-5028; Fax: 860-873-5025. Hours: 10AM-2PM (and by app't) (EST). *Probate.*

East Hampton Probate Court 20 East High St, Annex, East Hampton, CT 06424; 860-267-9262; Fax: 860-267-6453. Hours: 9AM-2PM T-Th (EST). *Probate.*

Essex Probate Court Town Hall, 29 West Ave, Essex, CT 06426; 860-767-4347; Fax: 860-767-8509. Hours: 9AM-1PM (and by app't) (EST). *Probate.*

Haddam Probate Court 30 Field Park Dr, Haddam, CT 06438; 860-345-8531; Fax: 860-345-3730. Hours: 10AM-2PM T-Th (and by app't) (EST). *Probate.*

Killingworth Probate Court 323 Route 81, Killingworth, CT 06419; 860-663-2304; Fax: 860-663-3305. Hours: 9AM-Noon M,W,F (and by app't) (EST). *Probate.*

Middletown Probate Court 94 Court St, Middletown, CT 06457; 860-347-7424; Fax: 860-346-1520. Hours: 8:30AM-4:30PM (EST). *Probate.*

Note: District includes towns of Cornwall, Durham, Middlefield

Old Saybrook Probate Court 263 Main St, #105, Old Saybrook, CT 06475; 860-395-3128; Fax: 860-395-3125. Hours: 9AM-1PM M,T,TH,F (Wed. eves by app't) (EST). *Probate.*

Note: Court is open on Wed. evenings, also

Portland Probate Court 33 E Main St, PO Box 71, Portland, CT 06480; 860-342-6739; Fax: 860-342-0001. Hours: 9AM-Noon (and by app't) (EST). *Probate.*

Saybrook Probate Court 65 Main St, PO Box 628, Chester, CT 06412; 860-526-0007; Fax: 860-526-0004. Hours: 9:30AM-12:30PM T,Th (and by app't) (EST). *Probate.*

Note: District includes Town of Chester

Westbrook Probate Court 1163 Boston Post Rd, PO Box 676, Westbrook, CT 06498; 860-399-5661; Fax: 860-399-9568. Hours: 1-4:30PM (EST). *Probate.*

New Haven County

Ansonia-Milford Superior Court 14 W River St (PO Box 210), Milford, CT 06460; 203-877-4293. Hours: 9AM-4PM (EST). *Felony, Civil Actions Over $2,500.*

Civil Records: Access: Mail, online, in person. Only the court conducts in person searches; visitors may not. No search fee. Required to search: name, years to search. Civil cases indexed by defendant, plaintiff. Civil records on computer only while case is active, on index cards from 1978. Purged computer records are on microfilm. Maintain 75 yrs at Records Center at Enfield, CT. Access to civil case records is available free on the Internet at www.jud2.state.ct.us/. **Criminal Records:** Access: Mail, in person. Only the court conducts in person searches; visitors may not. No search fee. Required to search: name, years to search, DOB. Criminal records on computer only while case is active, on index cards from 1978. Purged computer records are on microfilm. Maintain 75 yrs at Records Center at Enfield, CT. **General Information:** SASE required. Turnaround time 1-2 weeks. Copy fee: $1.00 per page. Certification fee: $2.00. Fee payee: Clerk of Superior Court. Personal checks accepted. Prepayment is required.

Superior Court 235 Church St, New Haven, CT 06510; 203-789-7908; Fax: 203-789-6424. Hours: 9AM-4PM (EST). *Felony, Civil Actions Over $2,500.*

www.jud2.state.ct.us

Civil Records: Access: Phone, mail, online, in person. Only the court conducts in person searches; visitors may not. No search fee. Required to search: name, years to search. Civil cases indexed by defendant, plaintiff. Pending cases on computer, disposed cases deleted after 1 year, on microfiche from 1972, prior on index cards. Access to civil case records is available free on the Internet at www.jud2.state.ct.us/. **Criminal Records:** Access: Mail, in person. Only the court conducts in person searches; visitors may not. No search fee. Required to search: name, years to search, DOB. Pending criminal cases on computer, disposed deleted after 1 year, prior on index cards. **General Information:** No sealed records released. SASE required. Turnaround time 2-5 weeks. Copy fee: $1.00 per page. Certification fee: $2.00. Fee payee: Clerk of Superior Court. Personal checks accepted. CT personal checks accepted if address on check matches address on drivers license. Prepayment is required. Public access terminal is available. Public Access Terminal Note: Live civil cases only.

Waterbury Superior Court 300 Grand St, Waterbury, CT 06702; 203-596-4023; Fax: 203-596-4032. Hours: 9AM-5PM (EST). *Felony, Civil Actions Over $2,500.*

Note: Address mail requests for criminal searches to 400 Grand St

Civil Records: Access: Phone, fax, mail, online, in person. Only the court conducts in person searches; visitors may not. No search fee. Required to search: name, years to search. Civil cases indexed by defendant. Civil records on computer since 1969. Phone access limited to one search. Access to civil case records is available free on the Internet at www.jud2.state.ct.us/. **Criminal Records:** Access: Fax, mail, in person. Only the court conducts in person searches; visitors may not. No search fee. Required to search: name, years to search, DOB. Criminal records on computer since 05/91; prior records in index books. **General Information:** SASE required. Turnaround time 1-2 weeks. Copy fee: $1.00 per page. Certification fee: $2.00. Fee payee: Clerk of Superior Court. Personal checks accepted. Prepayment is required.

Geographical Area Court #22 14 W River St, Milford, CT 06460; 203-874-0674 (Small Claims); Civil phone:203-877-4293; Criminal phone:203-877-4293. Hours: 1-2:30PM, 4-5PM. *Misdemeanor, Eviction, Small Claims.*

Civil Records: Access: Mail, online, in person. Only the court conducts in person searches; visitors may not. No search fee. Required to search: name, years to search. Civil cases indexed by defendant, plaintiff. Civil records on computer for 6 months, after disposal, on microfiche from 1986, prior on index cards and docket books. Access to civil case records is available free on the Internet at www.jud2.state.ct.us/. **Criminal Records:** Access: Mail, in person. Only the court conducts in person searches; visitors may not. No search fee. Required to search: name, years to search; also helpful-DOB. Criminal records on computer for 6 months, after disposal, on microfiche from 1986, prior on index cards and docket books. **General Information:** SASE required. Turnaround time 1 week. Copy fee: $1.00 per page. Certification fee: $2.00. Fee payee: Clerk of Superior Court. Personal checks accepted. Prepayment is required.

Geographical Area Court #4 400 Grand St, Waterbury, CT 06702; 203-236-8100; Fax: 203-236-8099. Hours: 9AM-5PM (EST). *Misdemeanor, Small Claims, Traffic.*

www.jud.state.ct.us **Criminal Records:** Access: Phone, mail, in person. Only the court conducts in person searches; visitors may not. No search fee. Required to search: name, years to search; also helpful-DOB. Criminal records on computer since 1985. **General Information:** No youthful offenders records or dismissals released. SASE required. Turnaround time 1-2 weeks. Copy fee: $1.00 per page. Certification fee: $2.00. Fee payee: Clerk of Superior Court. Personal checks accepted. Prepayment is required.

Geographical Area Court #5 106 Elizabeth St, Derby, CT 06418; 203-735-7438. Hours: 9AM-4PM (EST). *Misdemeanor, Eviction, Small Claims.*

Civil Records: Access: Mail, online, in person. Only the court conducts in person searches; visitors may not. No search fee. Required to search: name, years to search. Civil cases indexed by defendant, plaintiff. Pending and records for 1 yr after disposal on computer, on microfiche from 1986, prior on index cards. In person search results are mailed back. Access to civil case records is available free on the Internet at www.jud2.state.ct.us/. **Criminal Records:** Access: Mail, in person. Only the court conducts in person searches; visitors may not. No search fee. Required to search: name, years to search, DOB. Pending and records for 1 yr after disposal on computer, on microfiche from 1986, prior on index cards. In person search results returned by mail only. **General Information:** No sealed records released. SASE required. Turnaround time 1-2 weeks. Copy fee: $1.00 per page. Certification fee: $2.00. Fee payee: Clerk of Superior Court. Personal checks accepted. Prepayment is required.

Geographical Area Court #6 121 Elm St, New Haven, CT 06510; 203-789-7461; Fax: 203-789-6455. Hours: 9AM-5PM (EST). *Misdemeanor, Eviction, Small Claims.*

Civil Records: Access: Mail, online, in person. Only the court conducts in person searches; visitors may not. No search fee. Required to search: name, years to search. Civil records on log book for small claims. Access to civil case records is available free on the Internet at www.jud2.state.ct.us/. **Criminal Records:** Access: Mail, in person. Only the court conducts in person searches; visitors may not. No search fee. Required to search: name, years to search, DOB. Criminal records on computer back 13 months, microfiche from 1986, prior archived for criminal and motor vehicle. In person search results mailed back. **General Information:** No dismissals, juvenile records released. SASE required. Turnaround time 2-3 weeks. Copy fee: $1.00 per page. Certification fee: $2.00. Fee payee: Superior Court. Personal checks accepted. Prepayment is required.

Geographical Area Court #7 54 W Main St, Meriden, CT 06450;; Civil phone:203-238-6666; Criminal phone:203-238-6666; Fax: 203-238-6322. Hours: 9AM-5PM (EST). *Misdemeanor, Eviction, Small Claims.*

Civil Records: Access: Mail, online, in person. Only the court conducts in person searches; visitors may not. No search fee. Required to search: name, years to search. Civil cases indexed by defendant, plaintiff. Pending and 1 yr after disposed cases on computer, on microfiche from

1985, prior on index cards. All manual records by docket number. Access to civil case records is available free on the Internet at www.jud2.state.ct.us/. **Criminal Records:** Access: Phone, mail, in person. Only the court conducts in person searches; visitors may not. No search fee. Required to search: name, years to search, DOB. Criminal records on computer since 1986, purged every 6 months & maintained in Enfield, CT. **General Information:** No sealed records released. SASE required. Turnaround time 1-2 days. Copy fee: $1.00 per page. Certification fee: $10.00. Fee payee: Clerk of Superior Court. Personal checks accepted. Prepayment is required.

New Haven Superior Court-Meriden 54 W Main St, Meriden, CT 06451; 203-238-6666. Hours: 9AM-4PM (EST). *Civil Actions Over $2,500.*

Civil Records: Access: Mail, online, in person. Only the court conducts in person searches; visitors may not. No search fee. Required to search: name, years to search. Civil cases indexed by defendant, plaintiff. Pending and 1 yr after disposed cases on computer, on microfiche from 1984, prior on index cards. Access to civil case records is available free on the Internet at www.jud2.state.ct.us/. **General Information:** No acknowledgments of paternity, agreements to support prior to 10/01/95 records released. SASE required. Turnaround time 1-2 days. Copy fee: $1.00 per page. Certification fee: $2.00. Fee payee: Clerk of Superior Court. Personal checks accepted. In state personal checks accepted. Prepayment is required.

Bethany Probate Court Town Hall, 40 Peck Rd, Bethany, CT 06524; 203-393-3744; Fax: 203-393-0821. Hours: 9AM-Noon T,TH (EST). *Probate.*

Branford Probate Court PO Box 638, 1019 Main St, Branford, CT 06405-0638; 203-488-0318; Fax: 203-315-4715. Hours: 9AM-Noon, 1-4:30PM (till Noon, Fridays in Summer) (EST). *Probate.*

Cheshire Probate Court 84 S Main St, Cheshire, CT 06410; 203-271-6608; Fax: 203-271-6628. Hours: 8:30AM-12:30PM, 1:30PM-4PM M-Th; 8:30AM-12:30PM Fri (EST). *Probate.*

Note: District includes town of Prospect. On Fridays, they close at 12:30

Derby Probate Court 253 Main St, 2nd Fl, Ansonia, CT 06401; 203-734-1277; Fax: 203-734-0922. Hours: 9AM-5:30PM M-W; 8:30-6:30 PM Th (EST). *Probate.*

Note: District includes towns of Ansonia, Seymour

East Haven Probate Court 250 Main St, Town Hall, East Haven, CT 06512; 203-468-3895. Hours: 9AM-3:30PM, except 1PM on Fri (EST). *Probate.*

Guilford Probate Court Town Hall, 31 Park St, Guilford, CT 06437; 203-453-8006; Fax: 203-453-8017. Hours: 9AM-Noon,1-4PM M,T,Th,F; 9AM-Noon W (EST). *Probate.*

Hamden Probate Court 2372 Whitney Ave, Memorial Town Hall, Hamden, CT 06518; 203-287-2570; Fax: 203-287-2571. Hours: 8:30AM-4:30PM (EST). *Probate.*

Madison Probate Court 8 Campus Dr, PO Box 205, Madison, CT 06443; 203-245-5661; Fax: 203-245-5653. Hours: 9AM-3PM (and by app't) (EST). *Probate.*

Meriden Probate Court City Hall, E Main St, Rm 113, Meriden, CT 06450; 203-630-4150;

Fax: 203-630-4043. Hours: 8:30AM-7PM M; 8:30-4:30 T-F (EST). *Probate.*

Milford Probate Court Parsons Office Complex, 70 W River St, PO Box 414, Milford, CT 06460; 203-783-3205; Fax: 203-783-3364. Hours: 9AM-5PM (EST). *Probate.*

Naugatuck Probate Court Town Hall, 229 Church St, Naugatuck, CT 06770; 203-720-7046; Fax: 203-729-9452. Hours: 9AM-4PM M-Th; 9AM-3PM F (EST). *Probate.*

Note: District includes Town of Beacon Falls

New Haven Probate Court 200 Orange St, 1st Floor, PO Box 905, New Haven, CT 06504; 203-946-4880; Fax: 203-946-5962. Hours: 9AM-4PM (EST). *Probate.*

North Branford Probate Court 1599 Foxon Rd, PO Box 214, North Branford, CT 06471; 203-315-6007; Fax: 203-315-6025. Hours: 8:45AM-12:45PM (EST). *Probate.*

North Haven Probate Court 18 Church St, PO Box 175, North Haven, CT 06473-0175; 203-239-5321 X775; Fax: 203-239-1874. Hours: 8:30AM-4:30PM M-Th (and by app't) (EST). *Probate.*

Orange Probate Court 525 Orange Center Rd, Orange, CT 06477; 203-891-2160; Fax: 203-891-2161. Hours: 9AM-Noon (EST). *Probate.*

Oxford Probate Court Town Hall, Rt. 67, Oxford, CT 06478; 203-888-2543 x3014; Fax: 203-888-2136. Hours: 7-9PM Mon, 1-5PM Tu-W, 9AM-5PM, 7-9PM Th (EST). *Probate.*

Southbury Probate Court Townhall Annex, 421 Main St South, PO Box 674, Southbury, CT 06488; 203-262-0641; Fax: 203-264-9310. Hours: 9AM-4:30PM (and by app't) (EST). *Probate.*

Wallingford Probate Court Town Hall, 45 S Main St, Rm 114, Wallingford, CT 06492; 203-294-2100; Fax: 203-294-2109. Hours: 9AM-5PM (EST). *Probate.*

Waterbury Probate Court 236 Grand St, Waterbury, CT 06702; 203-755-1127; Fax: 203-597-0824. Hours: 9AM-4:45PM MTWF; 9AM-6PM Th; 9AM-Noon Sat (EST). *Probate.*

Note: District includes towns of Middlebury, Wolcott

West Haven Probate Court 355 Main St, PO Box 127, West Haven, CT 06516; 203-937-3552; Fax: 203-937-3556. Hours: 9AM-4PM (EST). *Probate.*

Woodbridge Probate Court Town Hall, 11 Meetinghouse Ln, Woodbridge, CT 06525; 203-389-3410; Fax: 203-389-3480. Hours: 3-7PM M, 9AM-1PM W (EST). *Probate.*

New London County

New London Superior Court 70 Huntington St, New London, CT 06320; 860-443-5363. Hours: 9AM-5PM (EST). *Felony, Civil Actions Over $2,500.*

Civil Records: Access: Mail, online, in person. No search fee. Required to search: name, years to search. Civil cases indexed by defendant, plaintiff. Civil records pending and 1 yr after disposed on computer, on microfiche from mid-70s. In person access limited to five names. Access to civil case records is available free on the Internet at www.jud2.state.ct.us/. **Criminal Records:** Access: Mail, in person. Only the court conducts in person searches; visitors may not. No search fee. Required to search: name, years to search; also helpful-DOB. Criminal records on computer from 1991, prior on index cards. **General Information:** No sealed or youthful offender records released. SASE required. Turnaround time 2 weeks. Copy fee: $1.00 per page. Certification fee: $2.00. Fee payee: Clerk of Superior Court. Personal checks accepted. Prepayment is required.

Geographical Area Court #10 112 Broad St, New London, CT 06320; 860-443-8343. Hours: 9AM-5PM (EST). *Misdemeanor, Eviction, Small Claims.*

www.jud.state.ct.us

Civil Records: Access: Mail, online, in person. Both court and visitors may perform in person searches. No search fee. Required to search: name, years to search. Civil cases indexed by defendant. Civil records on microfiche from early '85, prior on index cards and docket books. Access to civil case records is available free on the Internet at www.jud2.state.ct.us/. **Criminal Records:** Access: Mail, in person. Only the court conducts in person searches; visitors may not. No search fee. Required to search: name, years to search; also helpful-DOB, SSN. Criminal records on computer for 2 years; prior records on microfiche. **General Information:** No sealed, dismissed, youth or program records released. SASE required. Turnaround time up to 1 month. Copy fee: $1.00 per page. Certification fee: No certification. Certification available from State Record Center. Fee payee: Clerk, Superior Court. Personal checks accepted.

Geographical Area Court #21 1 Courthouse Sq, Norwich, CT 06360;; Civil phone:860-887-3515; Criminal phone:860-887-3515. Hours: 1-2:30PM, 4-5PM (EST). *Misdemeanor, Eviction, Small Claims.*

www.jud.state.ct.us

Civil Records: Access: Mail, online, in person. No search fee. Required to search: name, years to search. Civil cases indexed by defendant. Pending and 2-4 years history of disposed on computer, on microfiche from 1986, prior on index cards and docket books. Small claims, evictions not on computer. Access to civil case records is available free on the Internet at www.jud2.state.ct.us/. **Criminal Records:** Access: In person only. Court does not conduct in person searches; visitors must perform searches for themselves. Search fee: No criminal searches performed by court. Required to search: name, years to search, DOB. Pending and 2-4 years history of disposed on computer, on microfiche from 1986, prior on index cards and docket books. Small claims, evictions not on computer. Mail requests are referred to the Judicial Records Center in Enfield. **General Information:** No youthful offender or dismissed/erased records released. SASE required. Turnaround time 1-2 weeks. Copy fee: $1.00 per page. Certification fee: $2.00. Certified copy of Judgment $15.00. Fee payee: Superior Court GA #21. Personal checks accepted. Prepayment is required.

Norwich Superior Court 1 Courthouse Square, Norwich, CT 06360; 860-887-3515; Fax: 860-885-0509. Hours: 9AM-5PM (EST). *Civil Actions Over $2,500.*

Civil Records: Access: Phone, mail, online, in person. Only the court conducts in person searches; visitors may not. Search fee:. Required to search: name, years to search. Civil cases indexed by defendant, plaintiff. Pending and disposed cases on computer from 1992, on microfiche from 1975, prior on index cards. Access to civil case records is available free on the

Internet at www.jud2.state.ct.us/. **General Information:** No criminal search warrant, acknowledgment of paternity prior to 1995, sealed records released. SASE required. Turnaround time up to a month. Copy fee: $1.00 per page. Judgment copies $10.00. Certification fee: $2.00. Certified copy of Judgment $15.00. Fee payee: Clerk of Superior Court. Personal checks accepted. Checks must have imprinted name and address and match valid CT driver license. Prepayment is required. Public access terminal is available.

Bozrah Probate Court Town Hall, 2nd FL, One River Rd, Bozrah, CT 06334; 860-889-2958; Fax: 860-887-7571. Hours: 10AM-1PM M,W (and by app't) (EST). *Probate.*

Colchester Probate Court Town Hall, 127 Norwich Ave, Colchester, CT 06415; 860-537-7290; Fax: 860-537-0547. Hours: 12:30PM-4:30PM M,T,Th,F; 9AM-1PM Wed (EST). *Probate.*

East Lyme Probate Court PO Box 519, 108 Pennsylvania Ave, Niantic, CT 06357; 860-739-6931; Fax: 860-739-6930. Hours: 8:30AM-12:30PM (EST). *Probate.*

Griswold Probate Court Town Hall, 32 School St, PO Box 369, Jewett City, CT 06351; 860-376-0216; Fax: 860-376-0216. Hours: 5PM-8PM M; 1PM-5PM T-F (EST). *Probate.*

Lebanon Probate Court Town Hall, 579 Exeter Rd, Lebanon, CT 06249; 860-642-7429; Fax: 860-642-7716. Hours: 10AM-Noon, 1:30-4PM T; 4-6PM Th; 10AM-Noon F (and by appt.) (EST). *Probate.*

Ledyard Probate Court 741 Colonel Ledyard Hwy, Route 17, Ledyard, CT 06339; 860-464-3219; Fax: 860-464-8531. Hours: 9:30AM-1PM M,T; 9AM-4PM W; 9-11AM Th-F (and by app't) (EST). *Probate.*

Lyme Probate Court Town Hall, 480 Hamburg Rd, Lyme, CT 06371; 860-434-7733; Fax: 860-434-2989. Hours: 9AM-Noon (and by app't) (EST). *Probate.*

Montville Probate Court 310 Norwich-New London Turnpike, Uncasville, CT 06382; 860-848-9847; Fax: 860-848-4534. Hours: 9AM-1PM M,T,Th,F; 9AM-4:30PM W (EST). *Probate.*

New London Probate Court 181 Captain's Walk, Municipal Bldg, PO Box 148, New London, CT 06320; 860-443-7121; Fax: 860-437-8155. Hours: 9AM-4PM (EST). *Probate.*

Note: District includes Town of Waterford

North Stonington Probate Court 391 Norwich Westerly Rd #2, PO Box 204, North Stonington, CT 06359; 860-535-8441; Fax: 860-535-8441 (call first). Hours: 9AM-Noon M & W; 1-4PM T, F; 4-7PM Th (EST). *Probate.*

Norwich Probate Court 100 Broadway, Rm 101, PO Box 38, Norwich, CT 06360; 860-887-2160; Fax: 860-887-2401. Hours: 9AM-4:30PM (EST). *Probate.*

Note: District includes Towns of Franklin, Lisbon, Preston, Sprague, Voluntown

Old Lyme Probate Court 52 Lyme St, Memorial Town Hall, Old Lyme, CT 06371; 860-434-1406 X222; Fax: 860-434-9283. Hours: 9AM-Noon, 1-4PM (EST). *Probate.*

Salem Probate Court 270 Hartford Rd, Salem, CT 06420; 860-859-3873, 203-859-3036 (After hours); Fax: 860-537-0547. Hours: By app't (EST). *Probate.*

Stonington Probate Court 152 Elm St, PO Box 312, Stonington, CT 06378; 860-535-5090; Fax: 860-535-0520. Hours: 9AM-Noon, 1-4PM (EST). *Probate.*

Note: District includes Town of Mystic

Tolland County

Tolland Superior Court - Criminal Branch 20 Park St, Vernon, CT 06066; 860-870-3200. Hours: 9AM-5PM (EST). *Felony.*

Note: The address can use either Rockville or Vernon, but the US Posatl Service will sometimes return mail addressed to Rockville **Criminal Records:** Access: Mail, in person. Only the court conducts in person searches; visitors may not. No search fee. Required to search: name, years to search; also helpful-DOB. Criminal records are for active cases only. Completed cases must be searched in Enfield through DPS. **General Information:** No youthful offender, dismissed or not guilty verdict records released. SASE required. Turnaround time 1 week. Copy fee: $1.00 per page. Certification fee: $2.00. Fee payee: Clerk of Superior Court. Personal checks accepted. Prepayment is required.

Tolland Superior Court - Civil Branch 69 Brooklyn St, Rockville, CT 06066; 860-875-6294. Hours: 9AM-5PM (EST). *Civil Actions Over $2,500.*

Civil Records: Access: Mail, online, in person. Only the court conducts in person searches; visitors may not. No search fee. Required to search: name, years to search. Civil cases indexed by defendant, plaintiff. Civil records on computer from 1990, on microfiche from 1980, all prior on index cards. Access to civil case records is available free on the Internet at www.jud2.state.ct.us/. **General Information:** No youthful offender, dismissed or not guilty verdict records released. SASE required. Turnaround time 1-2 weeks. Copy fee: $1.00 per page. Certification fee: $2.00. Fee payee: Clerk of Superior Court. Personal checks accepted. Prepayment is required.

Geographical Area Court #19 20 Park St, PO Box 980, Rockville, CT 06066-0980; 860-870-3200. Hours: 9AM-4PM (EST). *Misdemeanor.*

www.jud2.state.ct.us **Criminal Records:** Access: Mail, in person. Only the court conducts in person searches; visitors may not. No search fee. Required to search: name, years to search, DOB. Criminal records on computer apprx. 2 yrs from disposition, on microfiche from 1985, prior on index cards. **General Information:** No youthful offender records released. SASE required. Turnaround time 1-7 days. Copy fee: $1.00 per page. Certification fee: $2.00. Fee payee: Clerk of Superior Court. Personal checks accepted. Prepayment is required.

Andover Probate Court 222 Bolton Center Rd, Bolton, CT 06043; 860-647-7979; Fax: 860-649-3187. Hours: 9AM-4PM M & W; 9AM-3PM F (EST). *Probate.*

Note: District includes towns of Andover, Bolton and Columbia

Ashford Probate Court 20 Pompey Hollow Rd, PO Box 61, Ashford, CT 06278; 860-429-4986. Hours: 1AM-3:30PM Th (and by app't) (EST). *Probate.*

Ellington Probate Court PO Box 268, 14 Park Place, Rockville, CT 06066; 860-872-0519; Fax: 860-870-5140. Hours: 8:30-4:30 M-W; 8:30-7PM TH; 8:30-1PM F (EST). *Probate.*

Note: District includes Town of Vernon

Hebron Probate Court 15 Gilead Rd, Hebron, CT 06248; 860-228-5971; Fax: 860-228-4859. Hours: 8AM-4PM Tu; 4-6PM Th (and by app't) (EST). *Probate.*

Mansfield Probate Court 4 South Eagleville Rd, Storrs, CT 06268; 860-429-3313; Fax: 860-429-6863. Hours: 9AM-5PM T; 2-5PM W; 2-6:30PM Th; 9AM-Noon F (EST). *Probate.*

Somers Probate Court , *Probate.*

Note: The Sommers Probate Court merged with the Stafford Probate Court on 1-6-99

Stafford Probate Court Town Hall, 1 Main St, PO Box 63, Stafford Springs, CT 06076; 860-684-3423; Fax: 860-684-7173. Hours: 9AM-Noon, 1-4:30PM M; 9AM-Noon Tu-F (and by app't) (EST). *Probate.*

Note: District includes towns of Union and Somers

Tolland Probate Court 21 Tolland Green, Tolland, CT 06084; 860-871-3640; Fax: 860-871-3641. Hours: 9AM-12:30 M-W; 5:30-8:30PM Th (and by app't) (EST). *Probate.*

Note: District includes Town of Willington

Windham County

Windham Superior Court 155 Church St, Putnam, CT 06260; 860-928-7749; Fax: 860-928-7076. Hours: 9AM-5PM (EST). *Felony, Civil Actions Over $2,500.*

Civil Records: Access: Phone, mail, online, in person. Only the court conducts in person searches; visitors may not. No search fee. Required to search: name, years to search. Civil cases indexed by defendant, plaintiff. Civil records on computer for 1 year, prior on index cards, prior to 70s archived. Access to civil case records is available free on the Internet at www.jud2.state.ct.us/. **Criminal Records:** Access: Phone, mail, in person. Only the court conducts in person searches; visitors may not. No search fee. Required to search: name, years to search. Criminal records on computer for 1 year, prior on index cards, prior to 70s archived. **General Information:** No sealed, dismissed criminal, not

guilty verdict records released. SASE required. Turnaround time 1-2 days. Copy fee: $1.00 per page. Certification fee: $2.00. Fee payee: Clerk of Superior Court. Personal checks accepted. Prepayment is required.

Geographical Area Court #11 120 School St #110, Danielson, CT 06239-3024; 860-779-8480; Fax: 860-779-8488. Hours: 9AM-5PM (EST). *Misdemeanor, Eviction, Small Claims.*

Civil Records: Access: Phone, mail, online, in person. Only the court conducts in person searches; visitors may not. No search fee. Required to search: name, years to search. Civil cases indexed by defendant. small claims records on computer since 08/96; all other records on index cards. Access to civil case records is available free on the Internet at www.jud2.state.ct.us/. **Criminal Records:** Access: Phone, mail, in person. Only the court conducts in person searches; visitors may not. No search fee. Required to search: name, years to search, DOB. Pending criminal and 1 year after disposed on computer, on microfiche from 1986, prior on index cards. **General Information:** No sealed records released. SASE required. Turnaround time 1-2 weeks. Copy fee: $1.00 per page. Certification fee: $2.00. Fee payee: Clerk of Superior Court. Personal checks accepted.

Brooklyn Probate Court Town Hall, 4 Wolf Den Rd, PO Box 356, Brooklyn, CT 06234-0356; 860-774-5973; Fax: 860-779-3744. Hours: 10AM-4:30PM T (and by app't) (EST). *Probate.*

Canterbury Probate Court 43 Maple Lane, Canterbury, CT 06331; 860-546-9605; Fax: 860-546-7805. Hours: 9AM-4:00PM Wed (and by app't) (EST). *Probate.*

Chaplin Probate Court c/o Eastford Probate District, PO Box 61, Ashford, CT 06278-0061; 860-974-1885; Fax: 860-974-0624. *Probate.*

Eastford Probate Court PO Box 207, 16 Westford Rd, Eastford, CT 06242-0207; 860-974-3024; Fax: 860-974-0624. Hours: 2-4PM Tu (and by app't) (EST). *Probate.*

Hampton Probate Court Town Hall, 164 Main St, PO Box 84, Hampton, CT 06247; 860-455-9132/0201; Fax: 860-455-0517. Hours: 10AM-Noon Th (and by app't) (EST). *Probate.*

Killingly Probate Court 172 Main St, Danielson, CT 06239; 860-779-5319; Fax: 860-779-5394. Hours: 8:30AM-Noon, 1-4PM (EST). *Probate.*

Plainfield Probate Court Town Hall, 8 Community Ave, Plainfield, CT 06374; 860-230-3031; Fax: 860-230-3033. Hours: 8:30-3:30PM M-Th; 8:30AM-Noon Fri (EST). *Probate.*

Pomfret Probate Court 5 Haven Rd, Rt. 44, Pomfret Center, CT 06259; 860-974-0186; Fax: 860-974-3950. Hours: 10AM-4PM Tu-Th (and by app't) (EST). *Probate.*

Putnam Probate Court Town Hall, 126 Church St, Putnam, CT 06260; 860-963-6868; Fax: 860-963-6814. Hours: 9AM-Noon M-Th (and by app't) (EST). *Probate.*

Sterling Probate Court 1114 Plainfield Pike, PO Box 157, Oneco, CT 06373; 860-564-8488; Fax: 860-564-1660. Hours: 8:30AM-Noon M,W (and by app't) (EST). *Probate.*

Thompson Probate Court 815 Riverside Dr, Town Hall, PO Box 74, North Grosvenordale, CT 06255; 860-923-2203; Fax: 860-923-3836. Hours: 9AM-Noon (and by app't) (EST). *Probate.*

Windham Probate Court 979 Main St, PO Box 34, Willimantic, CT 06226; 860-465-3049; Fax: 860-465-3012. Hours: 9AM-1PM M,Tu,Th; 9AM-1PM Fri (EST). *Probate.*

Note: District includes Town of Scotland

Woodstock Probate Court 415 Route 169, Woodstock, CT 06281; 860-928-2223; Fax: 860-963-7557. Hours: 3PM-6PM W, 1:30PM-4:30PM Th (and by app't) (EST). *Probate.*

ORGANIZATION   8 counties and 170 towns/cities. The recording officer is Town/City Clerk. **Counties have no administrative offices.** Be careful not to confuse searching in the following towns/cities as equivalent to a county-wide search : Fairfield, Hartford, Litchfield, New Haven, New London, Tolland, and Windham. The entire state is in the Eastern Time Zone (EST).

REAL ESTATE RECORDS   Towns do **not** perform real estate searches. Copy fees are usually $1.00 per page. Certification fees are usually $1.00 per document or per page.

UCC RECORDS   Financing statements are filed at the state level, except for real estate related collateral, which are filed only with the Town/City Clerk. Towns will **not** perform UCC searches. Copies usually cost $1.00 per page.

TAX LIEN RECORDS   All federal and state tax liens on personal property are filed with the Secretary of State. Federal and state tax liens on real property are filed with the Town/City Clerk. Towns will **not** perform tax lien searches.

OTHER LIENS   Mechanics, judgments, lis pendens, municipal, welfare, carpenter, sewer & water, city/town.

Andover Town
Town Clerk, PO Box 328, Andover, CT 06232-0328. 860-742-0188. Fax: 860-742-7535.

Ansonia City
City Clerk, 253 Main Street, City Hall, Ansonia, CT 06401. 203-736-5980.

Ashford Town
Town Clerk, 25 Pompey Hollow Road, Ashford, CT 06278. 860-429-7044. Fax: 860-487-2025.

Avon Town
Town Clerk, 60 West Main Street, Avon, CT 06001. 860-409-4310. Fax: 860-677-8428.

Barkhamsted Town
Town Clerk, P.O. Box 185, Pleasant Valley, CT 06063-0185. 860-379-8665. Fax: 860-379-9284.

Beacon Falls Town
Town Clerk, 10 Maple Avenue, Beacon Falls, CT 06403. 203-729-8254. Fax: 203-720-1078.

Berlin Town
Town Clerk, P.O. Box 1, Kensington, CT 06037. 860-828-7075. Fax: 860-828-7180.

Bethany Town
Town Clerk, 40 Peck Road, Bethany, CT 06524-3338. 203-393-0820. Fax: 203-393-0821.

Bethel Town
Town Clerk, 1 School St., Bethel, CT 06801. 203-794-8505. Fax: 203-794-8588.

Bethlehem Town
Town Clerk, P.O. Box 160, Bethlehem, CT 06751. 203-266-7510. Fax: 203-266-7670.

Bloomfield Town
Town Clerk, P.O. Box 337, Bloomfield, CT 06002. 860-769-3506. Fax: 860-769-3597.

Bolton Town
Town Clerk, 222 Bolton Center Road, Bolton, CT 06043-7698. 860-649-8066. Fax: 860-643-0021.

Bozrah Town
Town Clerk, P.O. Box 158, Bozrah, CT 06334. 860-889-2689. Fax: 860-887-5449.

Branford Town
Town Clerk, P.O. Box 150, Branford, CT 06405. 203-488-6305. Fax: 203-481-5561.

Bridgeport Town
City Clerk, 45 Lyon Terrace, City Hall, Room 124, Bridgeport, CT 06604. 203-576-7207.

Bridgewater Town
Town Clerk, P.O. Box 216, Bridgewater, CT 06752-0216. 860-354-5102. Fax: 860-350-5944.

Bristol City
City Clerk, P.O. Box 114, Bristol, CT 06010-0114. 860-584-7656. Fax: 860-584-3827.

Brookfield Town
Town Clerk, P.O. Box 5106, Brookfield, CT 06804-5106. 203-775-7313.

Brooklyn Town
Town Clerk, P.O. Box 356, Brooklyn, CT 06234. 860-774-9543. Fax: 860-779-3744.

Burlington Town
Town Clerk, 200 Spielman Highway, Burlington, CT 06013. 860-673-2108. Fax: 860-675-9312.

Canaan Town
Town Clerk, P.O. Box 47, Falls Village, CT 06031. 860-824-0707. Fax: 860-824-4506.

Canterbury Town
Town Clerk, P.O. Box 27, Canterbury, CT 06331-0027. 860-546-9377. Fax: 860-546-7805.

Canton Town
Town Clerk, P.O. Box 168, Collinsville, CT 06022. 860-693-7870. Fax: 860-693-7840.

Chaplin Town
Town Clerk, P.O. Box 286, Chaplin, CT 06235. 860-455-9455. Fax: 860-455-0027.

Cheshire Town
Town Clerk, 84 South Main Street, Town Hall, Cheshire, CT 06410. 203-271-6601.

Chester Town
Town Clerk, P.O. Box 328, Chester, CT 06412-0328. 860-526-0006. Fax: 860-526-0004.
Online Access: Assessor. Property records on the Assessor's Taxpayer Information System database are available free on the Internet at http://140.239.211.227/chesterct. User ID is required; registration is free. Search by street address, map, block, lot, unit, or account number.

Clinton Town
Town Clerk, 54 East Main Street, Clinton, CT 06413. 860-669-9101.

Colchester Town
Town Clerk, 127 Norwich Avenue, Colchester, CT 06415. 860-537-7215. Fax: 860-537-0547.

Colebrook Town
Town Clerk, P.O. Box 5, Colebrook, CT 06021. 860-379-3359. Fax: 860-379-7215.

Columbia Town
Town Clerk, 323 Jonathan Trumbull Hwy, Columbia, CT 06237. 860-228-3284. Fax: 860-228-1952.

Cornwall Town
Town Clerk, P.O. Box 97, Cornwall, CT 06753-0097. 860-672-2709.

Coventry Town
Town Clerk, 1712 Main Street, Coventry, CT 06238. 860-742-7966. Fax: 860-742-8911.

Cromwell Town
Town Clerk, 41 West Street, Cromwell, CT 06416-2100. 860-632-3440. Fax: 860-632-7048.

Danbury City
Town Clerk, 155 Deer Hill Avenue, City Hall, Danbury, CT 06810. 203-797-4531.

Darien Town
Town Clerk, 2 Renshaw Road, Darien, CT 06820-5397. 203-656-7307.

Deep River Town
Town Clerk, 174 Main Street, Town Hall, Deep River, CT 06417. 860-526-6024. Fax: 860-526-6023.

Derby City
City Clerk, 35 Fifth Street, Derby, CT 06418-1897. 203-736-1462. Fax: 203-736-1458.

Durham Town
Town Clerk, P.O. Box 428, Durham, CT 06422. 860-349-3452. Fax: 860-349-0547.

East Granby Town
Town Clerk, P.O. Box TC, East Granby, CT 06026-0459. 860-653-6528. Fax: 860-653-4017.

East Haddam Town
Town Clerk, Goodspeed Plaza, Town Office Building. PO Box K, East Haddam, CT 06423. 860-873-5027.

East Hampton Town
Town Clerk, 20 East High Street, Town Hall, East Hampton, CT 06424. 860-267-2519. Fax: 860-267-1027.

East Hartford Town
Town Clerk, 740 Main Street, East Hartford, CT 06108-3126. 860-291-7230. Fax: 860-289-0831.

East Haven Town
Town Clerk, 250 Main Street, East Haven, CT 06512-3034. 203-468-3201. Fax: 203-468-3372.

East Lyme Town
Town Clerk, P.O. Box 519, Niantic, CT 06357. 860-739-6931. Fax: 860-739-6930.

East Windsor Town
Town Clerk, P.O. Box 213, Broad Brook, CT 06016-0213. 860-623-9467.

Eastford Town
Town Clerk, P.O. Box 273, Eastford, CT 06242. 860-974-1885. Fax: 860-974-0624.

Easton Town
Town Clerk, 225 Center Road, Easton, CT 06612. 203-268-6291. Fax: 203-261-6080.

Ellington Town
Town Clerk, P.O. Box 187, Ellington, CT 06029-0187. 860-875-3190. Fax: 860-875-0788.

Enfield Town
Town Clerk, 820 Enfield Street, Enfield, CT 06082-2997. 860-253-6440. Fax: 860-253-6310.

Essex Town
Town Clerk, P.O. Box 98, Essex, CT 06426. 860-767-4344.

Fairfield County
There is no real estate recording at the county level. For real estate recording, you must determine the town or city where the property is located.

Fairfield Town
Town Clerk, 611 Old Post Road, Fairfield, CT 06430-6690. 203-256-3090.

Farmington Town
Town Clerk, 1 Monteith Drive, Farmington, CT 06032-1053. 860-673-8247. Fax: 860-675-7140.

Franklin Town
Town Clerk, 7 Meeting House Hill Road, Town Hall, North Franklin, CT 06254. 860-642-7352. Fax: 860-642-6606.

Glastonbury Town
Town Clerk, 2155 Main Street, Glastonbury, CT 06033. 860-652-7616. Fax: 860-652-7610.

Goshen Town
Town Clerk, P.O. Box 54, Goshen, CT 06756-0054. 860-491-3647.

Granby Town
Town Clerk, 15 North Granby Road, Granby, CT 06035. 860-653-8949.
Online Access: Assessor. Property tax records on the Assessor's database are available on the Internet at http://140.239.211.227/granbyct. User ID number is required is required to access the full database. Non-registered users can access a limited set of data.

Greenwich Town
Town Clerk, P.O. Box 2540, Greenwich, CT 06836. 203-622-7897.

Griswold Town
Town Clerk, P.O. Box 369, Jewett City, CT 06351. 860-376-7064. Fax: 860-376-7070.

Groton Town
Town Clerk, 45 Fort Hill Road, Groton, CT 06340. 860-441-6642.

Guilford Town
Town Clerk, 31 Park Street, Town Hall, Guilford, CT 06437. 203-453-8001.

Haddam Town
Town Clerk, P.O. Box 87, Haddam, CT 06438. 860-345-8531. Fax: 860-345-3730.

Hamden Town
Town Clerk, 2372 Whitney Avenue, Memorial Town Hall, Hamden, CT 06518. 203-287-2510. Fax: 203-287-2518.

Hampton Town
Town Clerk, P.O. Box 143, Hampton, CT 06247-0143. 860-455-9132. Fax: 860-455-0517.

Hartford City
City Clerk, 550 Main Street, Hartford, CT 06103-2992. 860-543-8580. Fax: 860-722-8041.

Hartford County
There is no real estate recording at the county level. For real estate recording, you must determine the town or city where the property is located.

Hartland Town
Town Clerk, Town Office Building, 22 South Road, East Hartland, CT 06027. 860-653-3542. Fax: 860-653-7919.

Harwinton Town
Town Clerk, 100 Bentley Drive, Town Hall, Harwinton, CT 06791. 860-485-9613. Fax: 860-485-0051.

Hebron Town
Town Clerk, P.O. Box 156, Hebron, CT 06248. 860-228-5971x124. Fax: 860-228-4859.

Kent Town
Town Clerk, P.O. Box 678, Kent, CT 06757-0678. 860-927-3433.

Killingly Town
Town Clerk, P.O. Box 6000, Danielson, CT 06239. 860-779-5307. Fax: 860-779-5394.

Killingworth Town
Town Clerk, 323 Route 81, Killingworth, CT 06419-1298. 860-663-1616. Fax: 860-663-3305.

Lebanon Town
Town Clerk, 579 Exeter Road, Town Hall, Lebanon, CT 06249. 860-642-7319.
Online Access: Assessor. Property Tax records on the Assessor's Database are available free on the Internet at http://140.239.211.227/lebanonct. User ID is required; registration is free.

Ledyard Town
Town Clerk, 741 Col. Ledyard Highway, Ledyard, CT 06339. 860-464-8740x230. Fax: 860-464-1126.

Lisbon Town
Town Clerk, 1 Newent Road, RD 2 Town Hall, Lisbon, CT 06351-9802. 860-376-2708. Fax: 860-376-6545.

Litchfield County
There is no real estate recording at the county level. For real estate recording, you must determine the town or city where the property is located.

Litchfield Town
Town Clerk, P.O. Box 488, Litchfield, CT 06759-0488. 860-567-7561.

Lyme Town
Town Clerk, 480 Hamburg Rd., Town Hall, Lyme, CT 06371. 860-434-7733. Fax: 860-434-2989.

Madison Town
Town Clerk, 8 Campus Dr., Madison, CT 06443-2538. 203-245-5672. Fax: 203-245-5613.

Manchester Town
Town Clerk, P.O. Box 191, Manchester, CT 06045-0191. 860-647-3037. Fax: 860-647-3029.

Mansfield Town
Town Clerk, 4 South Eagleville Road, Mansfield, CT 06268. 860-429-3302.

Marlborough Town
Town Clerk, P.O. Box 29, Marlborough, CT 06447. 860-295-6206. Fax: 860-295-0317.

Meriden City
City Clerk, 142 East Main Street, Meriden, CT 06450-8022. 203-630-4030. Fax: 203-630-4059.

Middlebury Town
Town Clerk, P.O. Box 392, Middlebury, CT 06762-0392. 203-758-2557.

Middlefield Town
Town Clerk, P.O. Box 179, Middlefield, CT 06455. 860-349-7116. Fax: 860-349-7115.

Middlesex County
There is no real estate recording at the county level. For real estate recording, you must determine the town or city where the property is located.

Middletown City
City Clerk, P.O. Box 1300, Middletown, CT 06457. 860-344-3459. Fax: 860-344-3591.

Milford City
City Clerk, 70 West River Street, Milford, CT 06460-3364. 203-783-3210.

Monroe Town
Town Clerk, 7 Fan Hill Road, Monroe, CT 06468-1800. 203-452-5417. Fax: 203-261-6197.

Montville Town
Town Clerk, 310 Norwich-New London Tpke., Town Hall, Uncasville, CT 06382. 860-848-1349. Fax: 860-848-1521.

Morris Town
Town Clerk, P.O. Box 66, Morris, CT 06763-0066. 860-567-7433. Fax: 860-567-7432.

Naugatuck Town
Town Clerk, Town Hall, 229 Church Street, Naugatuck, CT 06770. 203-720-7055. Fax: 203-720-7099.

New Britain Town
Town Clerk, 27 W. Main Street, New Britain, CT 06051. 860-826-3344.

New Canaan Town
Town Clerk, 77 Main Street, Town Hall, New Canaan, CT 06840. 203-972-2323. Fax: 203-966-0309.

New Fairfield Town
Town Clerk, P.O. Box 8896, New Fairfield, CT 06812. 203-312-5616.

New Hartford Town
Town Clerk, P.O. Box 426, New Hartford, CT 06057. 860-379-5037. Fax: 860-379-0940.

New Haven City
City Clerk, 200 Orange Street, Room 202, New Haven, CT 06510. 203-946-8339. Fax: 203-946-6974.

New Haven County
There is no real estate recording at the county level. For real estate recording, you must determine the town or city where the property is located.

New London City
City Clerk, 181 State Street, New London, CT 06320. 860-447-5205. Fax: 860-447-1644.
Online Access: Assessor. Property Tax records on the Assessor's database are available free on the Internet at http://140.239.211.227/newlondonct. User ID is required; registration is free.

New Milford Town
Town Clerk, P.O. Box 360, New Milford, CT 06776. 860-355-6020. Fax: 860-355-6002.
www.newmilford.org/agencies/home.htm

Newington Town
Town Clerk, 131 Cedar Street, Newington, CT 06111-2696. 860-665-8545.

Newtown Town
Town Clerk, 45 Main Street, Newtown, CT 06470. 203-270-4210.

Norfolk Town
Town Clerk, P.O. Box 552, Norfolk, CT 06058-0552. 860-542-5679.

North Branford Town
Town Clerk, P.O. Box 287, North Branford, CT 06471-0287. 203-315-6015.

North Canaan Town
Town Clerk, P.O. Box 338, North Canaan, CT 06018. 860-824-3138. Fax: 860-824-3139.

North Haven Town
Town Clerk, 18 Church Street, Town Hall, North Haven, CT 06473. 203-239-5321x541.

North Stonington Town
Town Clerk, 40 Main Street, North Stonington, CT 06359. 860-535-2877x21. Fax: 860-535-4554.

Norwalk City
Town Clerk, P.O. Box 5125, Norwalk, CT 06856-5125. 203-854-7746.

Norwich City
City Clerk, 100 Broadway, City Hall, Room 214, Norwich, CT 06360. 860-823-3732. Fax: 860-823-3790.
Online Access: Assessor. Property Tax records on the Assessor's database are available on the Internet at http://140.239.211.227/norwichct. User ID number is required is required to access the full database. Non-registered users can access a limited set of data.

Old Lyme Town
Town Clerk, P.O. Box 338, Old Lyme, CT 06371. 860-434-1655. Fax: 860-434-9283.

Old Saybrook Town
Town Clerk, 302 Main Street, Old Saybrook, CT 06475. 860-395-3135. Fax: 860-395-5014.
Online Access: Assessor. Property Tax records on the Assessor's database are available free on the Internet at http://140.239.211.227/oldsaybrookct. User ID is required; registration is free.

Orange Town
Town Clerk, Town Hall, 617 Orange Center Rd., Orange, CT 06477. 203-891-2122. Fax: 203-891-2185.

Oxford Town
Town Clerk, 486 Oxford Road, Oxford, CT 06478. 203-888-2543.

Plainfield Town
Town Clerk, 8 Community Avenue, Town Hall, Plainfield, CT 06374. 860-564-4075.

Plainville Town
Town Clerk, 1 Central Square, Municipal Center, Plainville, CT 06062. 860-793-0221.

Plymouth Town
Town Clerk, 80 Main Street, Town Hall, Terryville, CT 06786. 860-585-4039. Fax: 860-585-4015.

Pomfret Town
Town Clerk, 5 Haven Road, Pomfret Center, CT 06259. 860-974-0343. Fax: 860-974-3950.

Portland Town
Town Clerk, P.O. Box 71, Portland, CT 06480. 860-342-6743. Fax: 860-342-0001.

Preston Town
Town Clerk, 389 Route 2, Town Hall, Preston, CT 06365-8830. 860-887-9821. Fax: 860-885-1905.

Prospect Town
Town Clerk, 36 Center Street, Prospect, CT 06712-1699. 203-758-4461. Fax: 203-758-4466.

Putnam Town
Town Clerk, 126 Church Street, Putnam, CT 06260. 860-963-6807. Fax: 860-963-2001.

Redding Town
Town Clerk, P.O. Box 1028, Redding, CT 06875-1028. 203-938-2377. Fax: 203-938-8816.

Ridgefield Town
Town Clerk, 400 Main Street, Ridgefield, CT 06877 203-431-2783. Fax: 203-431-2722.
www.ridgefieldct.org/townhall/assessor.htm

Rocky Hill Town
Town Clerk, P.O. Box 657, Rocky Hill, CT 06067. 860-258-2705.

Roxbury Town
Town Clerk, 29 North St., Roxbury, CT 06783-1405. 860-354-3328. Fax: 860-354-0560.

Salem Town
Town Clerk, Town Office Building, 270 Hartford Road, Salem, CT 06420. 860-859-3873x170. Fax: 860-859-1184.

Salisbury Town
Town Clerk, P.O. Box 548, Salisbury, CT 06068. 860-435-5182. Fax: 860-435-5172.

Scotland Town
Town Clerk, P.O. Box 122, Scotland, CT 06264. 860-423-9634. Fax: 860-423-3666.

Seymour Town
Town Clerk, 1 First Street, Town Hall, Seymour, CT 06483-2817. 203-888-0519.

Sharon Town
Town Clerk, P.O. Box 224, Sharon, CT 06069-0224. 860-364-5224. Fax: 860-364-5789.

Shelton City
City Clerk, P.O. Box 364, Shelton, CT 06484-0364. 203-924-1555. Fax: 203-924-1721.

Sherman Town
Town Clerk, P.O. Box 39, Sherman, CT 06784-0039. 860-354-5281. Fax: 860-350-5041.

Simsbury Town
Town Clerk, P.O. Box 495, Simsbury, CT 06070. 860-658-3243. Fax: 860-658-3206.

Somers Town
Town Clerk, P.O. Box 308, Somers, CT 06071. 860-763-8206. Fax: 860-763-8228.

South Windsor Town
Town Clerk, 1540 Sullivan Avenue, South Windsor, CT 06074. 860-644-2511x225. Fax: 860-644-3781.

Southbury Town
Town Clerk, 501 Main Street South, Southbury, CT 06488-2295. 203-262-0657. Fax: 203-264-9762.

Southington Town
Town Clerk, P.O. Box 152, Southington, CT 06489. 860-276-6211. Fax: 860-628-8669.

Sprague Town
Town Clerk, P.O. Box 162, Baltic, CT 06330. 860-822-3001. Fax: 860-822-3013.

Stafford Town
Town Clerk, P.O. Box 11, Stafford Springs, CT 06076. 860-684-2532.

Stamford City
City Clerk, P.O. Box 891, Stamford, CT 06904-0891. 203-977-4054. Fax: 203-977-4943.

Sterling Town
Town Clerk, P.O. Box 157, Oneco, CT 06373-0157. 860-564-2657. Fax: 860-564-1660.

Stonington Town
Town Clerk, P.O. Box 352, Stonington, CT 06378. 860-535-5060. Fax: 860-535-1046.

Stratford Town
Town Clerk, 2725 Main Street, Room 101, Stratford, CT 06497-5892. 203-385-4020. Fax: 203-385-4108.

Suffield Town
Town Clerk, 83 Mountain Road, Town Hall, Suffield, CT 06078. 860-668-3880. Fax: 860-668-3898.
Online Access: Assessor. Property Tax records on the Assessor's database are available free on the Internet at http://140.239.211.227/suffieldct. User ID is required; registration is free.

Thomaston Town
Town Clerk, 158 Main Street, Thomaston, CT 06787. 860-283-4141. Fax: 860-283-1013.

Thompson Town
Town Clerk, P.O. Box 899, No. Grosvenor Dale, CT 06255. 860-923-9900. Fax: 860-923-3836.

Tolland County
There is no real estate recording at the county level. For real estate recording, you must determine the town or city where the property is located.

Tolland Town
Town Clerk, Hicks Memorial Municipal Center, 21 Tolland Green, Tolland, CT 06084. 860-871-3630.

Torrington City
Town Clerk, 140 Main Street, City Hall, Torrington, CT 06790. 860-489-2236. Fax: 860-489-2548.

Trumbull Town
Town Clerk, 5866 Main Street, Trumbull, CT 06611. 203-452-5035. Fax: 203-452-5038.

Union Town
Town Clerk, 1043 Buckley Highway, Route 171, Union, CT 06076-9520. 860-684-3770. Fax: 860-684-8830.

Vernon Town
Town Clerk, 14 Park Place, Rockville, CT 06066. 860-872-8591.

Voluntown Town
Town Clerk, P.O. Box 96, Voluntown, CT 06384-0096. 860-376-4089. Fax: 860-376-3295.

Wallingford Town
Town Clerk, P.O. Box 427, Wallingford, CT 06492. 203-294-2145. Fax: 203-294-2073.

Warren Town
Town Clerk, 7 Sackett Hill Road, Town Hall, Warren, CT 06754. 860-868-0090. Fax: 860-868-0090.

Washington Town
Town Clerk, P.O. Box 383, Washington Depot, CT 06794. 860-868-2786. Fax: 860-868-3103.

Waterbury City
City Clerk, 235 Grand Street, City Hall, Waterbury, CT 06702. 203-574-6806. Fax: 203-574-6887.

Waterford Town
Town Clerk, 15 Rope Ferry Road, Waterford, CT 06385. 860-444-5831. Fax: 860-437-0352.

Watertown Town
Town Clerk, 37 DeForest Street, Watertown, CT 06795. 860-945-5230.

West Hartford Town
Town Clerk, 50 South Main Street, Room 313 Town Hall Common, West Hartford, CT 06107-2431. 860-523-3148. Fax: 860-523-3522.

West Haven City
City Clerk, P.O. Box 526, West Haven, CT 06516. 203-937-3534. Fax: 203-937-3706.

Westbrook Town
Town Clerk, P.O. Box G, Westbrook, CT 06498-0676. 860-399-3044. Fax: 860-399-9568.

Weston Town
Town Clerk, P.O. Box 1007, Weston, CT 06883. 203-222-2616. Fax: 203-222-8871.

Westport Town
Town Clerk, P.O. Box 549, Westport, CT 06881. 203-341-1110. Fax: 203-341-1112.

Wethersfield Town
Town Clerk, 505 Silas Deane Highway, Wethersfield, CT 06109. 860-721-2880. Fax: 860-721-2994.

Willington Town
Town Clerk, 40 Old Farms Road, Willington, CT 06279. 860-429-9965. Fax: 860-429-8415.

Wilton Town
Town Clerk, 238 Danbury Road, Wilton, CT 06897. 203-563-0106. Fax: 203-563-0299.

Winchester Town
Town Clerk, 338 Main Street, Town Hall, Winsted, CT 06098-1697. 860-738-6963. Fax: 860-738-7053.

Windham County
There is no real estate recording at the county level. For real estate recording, you must determine the town or city where the property is located.

Windham Town
Town Clerk, P.O. Box 94, Willimantic, CT 06226. 860-465-3013. Fax: 860-465-3012.

Windsor Locks Town
Town Clerk, 50 Church Street, Town Office Building, Windsor Locks, CT 06096. 860-627-1441.

Windsor Town
Town Clerk, P.O. Box 472, Windsor, CT 06095-0472. 860-285-1902. Fax: 860-285-1909.
Online Access: Assessor. Records on the Assessor's Taxpayer Information System database are available free on the Internet at http://140.239.211.227/windsorct. Search by street address, map, block, lot, unit, or account number.

Wolcott Town
Town Clerk, 10 Kenea Avenue, Town Hall, Wolcott, CT 06716. 203-879-8100.

Woodbridge Town
Town Clerk, 11 Meetinghouse Lane, Woodbridge, CT 06525. 203-389-3422. Fax: 203-389-3480.

Woodbury Town
Town Clerk, P.O. Box 369, Woodbury, CT 06798-3407. 203-263-2144. Fax: 203-263-4755.

Woodstock Town
Town Clerk, Town Office Building, 415 Route 169, Woodstock, CT 06281. 860-928-6595. Fax: 860-963-7557.

You will usually be able to find the city name in the City/County Cross Reference below. In that case, it is a simple matter to determine the county from the cross reference. However, only the official US Postal Service city names are included in this index. There are an additional 40,000 place names that people use in their addresses. Therefore, we have also included a ZIP/City Cross Reference immediately following the City/County Cross Reference.

If you know the ZIP Code but the city name does not appear in the City/County Cross Reference index, look up the ZIP Code in the ZIP/City Cross Reference, find the city name, then look up the city name in the City/County Cross Reference. For example, you want to know the county for an address of Menands, NY 12204. There is no "Menands" in the City/County Cross Reference. The ZIP/City Cross Reference shows that ZIP Codes 12201-12288 are for the city of Albany. Looking back in the City/County Cross Reference, Albany is in Albany County.

City/County Cross Reference

ABINGTON Windham
AMSTON Tolland
ANDOVER Tolland
ANSONIA New Haven
ASHFORD Windham
AVON Hartford
BALLOUVILLE Windham
BALTIC (06330) New London(94),
   Windham(6)
BANTAM Litchfield
BEACON FALLS New Haven
BETHANY New Haven
BETHEL Fairfield
BETHLEHEM Litchfield
BLOOMFIELD Hartford
BOLTON Tolland
BOTSFORD Fairfield
BOZRAH New London
BRANFORD New Haven
BRIDGEPORT Fairfield
BRIDGEWATER Litchfield
BRISTOL Hartford
BROAD BROOK Hartford
BROOKFIELD Fairfield
BROOKLYN Windham
BURLINGTON Hartford
CANAAN Litchfield
CANTERBURY (06331) Windham(99),
   New London(1)
CANTON Hartford
CANTON CENTER Hartford
CENTERBROOK Middlesex
CENTRAL VILLAGE Windham
CHAPLIN Windham
CHESHIRE New Haven
CHESTER Middlesex
CLINTON Middlesex
COBALT Middlesex
COLCHESTER (06415) New London(90),
   Middlesex(10)
COLEBROOK Litchfield
COLLINSVILLE (06022) Hartford(92),
   Litchfield(8)
COLUMBIA Tolland
CORNWALL Litchfield
CORNWALL BRIDGE Litchfield
COS COB Fairfield
COVENTRY Tolland
CROMWELL Middlesex
DANBURY Fairfield
DANIELSON Windham
DARIEN Fairfield
DAYVILLE Windham
DEEP RIVER Middlesex
DERBY New Haven
DURHAM Middlesex
EAST BERLIN Hartford
EAST CANAAN Litchfield
EAST GLASTONBURY Hartford
EAST GRANBY Hartford
EAST HADDAM Middlesex
EAST HAMPTON Middlesex
EAST HARTFORD Hartford

EAST HARTLAND Hartford
EAST HAVEN New Haven
EAST KILLINGLY Windham
EAST LYME New London
EAST WINDSOR Hartford
EAST WINDSOR HILL Hartford
EAST WOODSTOCK Windham
EASTFORD (06242) Windham(97),
   Tolland(3)
EASTON Fairfield
ELLINGTON Tolland
ENFIELD Hartford
ESSEX Middlesex
FABYAN Windham
FAIRFIELD Fairfield
FALLS VILLAGE Litchfield
FARMINGTON Hartford
GALES FERRY New London
GAYLORDSVILLE Litchfield
GEORGETOWN Fairfield
GILMAN New London
GLASGO New London
GLASTONBURY Hartford
GOSHEN Litchfield
GRANBY Hartford
GREENS FARMS Fairfield
GREENWICH Fairfield
GROSVENOR DALE Windham
GROTON New London
GUILFORD New Haven
HADDAM Middlesex
HADLYME New London
HAMDEN New Haven
HAMPTON Windham
HANOVER New London
HARTFORD Hartford
HARWINTON Litchfield
HAWLEYVILLE Fairfield
HEBRON Tolland
HIGGANUM Middlesex
IVORYTON Middlesex
JEWETT CITY New London
KENSINGTON Hartford
KENT Litchfield
KILLINGWORTH Middlesex
LAKESIDE Litchfield
LAKEVILLE Litchfield
LEBANON New London
LEDYARD New London
LITCHFIELD Litchfield
MADISON New Haven
MANCHESTER (06040) Hartford(98),
   Tolland(2)
MANCHESTER Hartford
MANSFIELD CENTER (06250)
   Tolland(95), Windham(5)
MANSFIELD DEPOT Tolland
MARION Hartford
MARLBOROUGH Hartford
MELROSE Hartford
MERIDEN New Haven
MIDDLE HADDAM Middlesex
MIDDLEBURY New Haven

MIDDLEFIELD Middlesex
MIDDLETOWN Middlesex
MILFORD New Haven
MILLDALE Hartford
MONROE Fairfield
MONTVILLE New London
MOODUS Middlesex
MOOSUP Windham
MORRIS Litchfield
MYSTIC New London
NAUGATUCK New Haven
NEW BRITAIN Hartford
NEW CANAAN Fairfield
NEW FAIRFIELD Fairfield
NEW HARTFORD Litchfield
NEW HAVEN New Haven
NEW LONDON New London
NEW MILFORD Litchfield
NEW PRESTON MARBLE DALE Litchfield
NEWINGTON Hartford
NEWTOWN Fairfield
NIANTIC New London
NORFOLK Litchfield
NORTH BRANFORD New Haven
NORTH CANTON (06059) Litchfield(64),
   Hartford(36)
NORTH FRANKLIN New London
NORTH GRANBY Hartford
NORTH GROSVENORDALE Windham
NORTH HAVEN New Haven
NORTH STONINGTON New London
NORTH WESTCHESTER New London
NORTH WINDHAM Windham
NORTHFIELD Litchfield
NORTHFORD New Haven
NORWALK Fairfield
NORWICH New London
OAKDALE New London
OAKVILLE Litchfield
OLD GREENWICH Fairfield
OLD LYME New London
OLD MYSTIC New London
OLD SAYBROOK Middlesex
ONECO Windham
ORANGE New Haven
OXFORD New Haven
PAWCATUCK New London
PEQUABUCK Litchfield
PINE MEADOW Litchfield
PLAINFIELD Windham
PLAINVILLE Hartford
PLANTSVILLE Hartford
PLEASANT VALLEY Litchfield
PLYMOUTH Litchfield
POMFRET Windham
POMFRET CENTER Windham
POQUONOCK Hartford
PORTLAND Middlesex
PRESTON New London
PROSPECT New Haven
PUTNAM Windham
QUAKER HILL New London
QUINEBAUG Windham

REDDING Fairfield
REDDING CENTER Fairfield
REDDING RIDGE Fairfield
RIDGEFIELD Fairfield
RIVERSIDE Fairfield
RIVERTON Litchfield
ROCKFALL Middlesex
ROCKY HILL Hartford
ROGERS Windham
ROXBURY Litchfield
SALEM New London
SALISBURY Litchfield
SANDY HOOK Fairfield
SCOTLAND Windham
SEYMOUR New Haven
SHARON Litchfield
SHELTON Fairfield
SHERMAN (06784) Fairfield(99),
   Litchfield(1)
SIMSBURY Hartford
SOMERS Tolland
SOMERSVILLE Tolland
SOUTH BRITAIN New Haven
SOUTH GLASTONBURY Hartford
SOUTH KENT Litchfield
SOUTH LYME New London
SOUTH WILLINGTON Tolland
SOUTH WINDHAM Windham
SOUTH WINDSOR Hartford
SOUTH WOODSTOCK Windham
SOUTHBURY New Haven
SOUTHINGTON Hartford
SOUTHPORT Fairfield
STAFFORD Tolland
STAFFORD SPRINGS (06076)
   Tolland(92), Windham(8)
STAFFORDVILLE Tolland
STAMFORD Fairfield
STERLING Windham
STEVENSON Fairfield
STONINGTON New London
STORRS MANSFIELD Tolland
STRATFORD Fairfield
SUFFIELD Hartford
TACONIC Litchfield
TAFTVILLE New London
TARIFFVILLE Hartford
TERRYVILLE Litchfield
THOMASTON Litchfield
THOMPSON Windham
TOLLAND Tolland
TORRINGTON Litchfield
TRUMBULL Fairfield
UNCASVILLE New London
UNIONVILLE Hartford
VERNON ROCKVILLE Tolland
VERSAILLES New London
VOLUNTOWN (06384) New London(99),
   Windham(1)
W HARTFORD Hartford
WALLINGFORD New Haven
WASHINGTON DEPOT Litchfield
WATERBURY New Haven

WATERFORD New London
WATERTOWN Litchfield
WAUREGAN Windham
WEATOGUE Hartford
WEST CORNWALL Litchfield
WEST GRANBY Hartford
WEST HARTLAND Hartford
WEST HAVEN New Haven

WEST MYSTIC New London
WEST SIMSBURY Hartford
WEST SUFFIELD Hartford
WESTBROOK Middlesex
WESTON Fairfield
WESTPORT Fairfield
WETHERSFIELD Hartford

WILLIMANTIC (06226) Windham(99), Tolland(1)
WILLINGTON Tolland
WILTON Fairfield
WINCHESTER CENTER Litchfield
WINDHAM Windham
WINDSOR Hartford
WINDSOR LOCKS Hartford

WINSTED Litchfield
WOLCOTT New Haven
WOODBRIDGE New Haven
WOODBURY Litchfield
WOODSTOCK Windham
WOODSTOCK VALLEY Windham
YANTIC New London

ZIP/City Cross Reference

ZIP	City	ZIP	City	ZIP	City	ZIP	City
06001-06001	AVON	06107-06107	W HARTFORD	06339-06339	LEDYARD	06471-06471	NORTH BRANFORD
06002-06002	BLOOMFIELD	06108-06108	EAST HARTFORD	06340-06349	GROTON	06472-06472	NORTHFORD
06006-06006	WINDSOR	06109-06109	WETHERSFIELD	06350-06350	HANOVER	06473-06473	NORTH HAVEN
06010-06011	BRISTOL	06110-06110	W HARTFORD	06351-06351	JEWETT CITY	06474-06474	NORTH WESTCHESTER
06013-06013	BURLINGTON	06111-06111	NEWINGTON	06353-06353	MONTVILLE	06475-06475	OLD SAYBROOK
06016-06016	BROAD BROOK	06112-06115	HARTFORD	06354-06354	MOOSUP	06477-06477	ORANGE
06018-06018	CANAAN	06117-06117	W HARTFORD	06355-06355	MYSTIC	06478-06478	OXFORD
06019-06019	CANTON	06118-06118	EAST HARTFORD	06357-06357	NIANTIC	06479-06479	PLANTSVILLE
06020-06020	CANTON CENTER	06119-06119	W HARTFORD	06359-06359	NORTH STONINGTON	06480-06480	PORTLAND
06021-06021	COLEBROOK	06120-06126	HARTFORD	06360-06360	NORWICH	06481-06481	ROCKFALL
06022-06022	COLLINSVILLE	06127-06127	W HARTFORD	06365-06365	PRESTON	06482-06482	SANDY HOOK
06023-06023	EAST BERLIN	06128-06128	EAST HARTFORD	06370-06370	OAKDALE	06483-06483	SEYMOUR
06024-06024	EAST CANAAN	06129-06129	WETHERSFIELD	06371-06371	OLD LYME	06484-06484	SHELTON
06025-06025	EAST GLASTONBURY	06131-06131	NEWINGTON	06372-06372	OLD MYSTIC	06487-06487	SOUTH BRITAIN
06026-06026	EAST GRANBY	06132-06132	HARTFORD	06373-06373	ONECO	06488-06488	SOUTHBURY
06027-06027	EAST HARTLAND	06133-06133	W HARTFORD	06374-06374	PLAINFIELD	06489-06489	SOUTHINGTON
06028-06028	EAST WINDSOR HILL	06134-06134	HARTFORD	06375-06375	QUAKER HILL	06490-06490	SOUTHPORT
06029-06029	ELLINGTON	06137-06137	W HARTFORD	06376-06376	SOUTH LYME	06491-06491	STEVENSON
06030-06030	FARMINGTON	06138-06138	EAST HARTFORD	06377-06377	STERLING	06492-06494	WALLINGFORD
06031-06031	FALLS VILLAGE	06140-06199	HARTFORD	06378-06378	STONINGTON	06497-06497	STRATFORD
06032-06032	FARMINGTON	06226-06226	WILLIMANTIC	06379-06379	PAWCATUCK	06498-06498	WESTBROOK
06033-06033	GLASTONBURY	06230-06230	ABINGTON	06380-06380	TAFTVILLE	06501-06511	NEW HAVEN
06034-06034	FARMINGTON	06231-06231	AMSTON	06382-06382	UNCASVILLE	06512-06512	EAST HAVEN
06035-06035	GRANBY	06232-06232	ANDOVER	06383-06383	VERSAILLES	06513-06513	NEW HAVEN
06037-06037	KENSINGTON	06233-06233	BALLOUVILLE	06384-06384	VOLUNTOWN	06514-06514	HAMDEN
06039-06039	LAKEVILLE	06234-06234	BROOKLYN	06385-06386	WATERFORD	06515-06515	NEW HAVEN
06040-06041	MANCHESTER	06235-06235	CHAPLIN	06387-06387	WAUREGAN	06516-06516	WEST HAVEN
06043-06043	BOLTON	06237-06237	COLUMBIA	06388-06388	WEST MYSTIC	06517-06518	HAMDEN
06045-06045	MANCHESTER	06238-06238	COVENTRY	06389-06389	YANTIC	06519-06521	NEW HAVEN
06049-06049	MELROSE	06239-06239	DANIELSON	06401-06401	ANSONIA	06524-06524	BETHANY
06050-06053	NEW BRITAIN	06241-06241	DAYVILLE	06403-06403	BEACON FALLS	06525-06525	WOODBRIDGE
06057-06057	NEW HARTFORD	06242-06242	EASTFORD	06404-06404	BOTSFORD	06530-06540	NEW HAVEN
06058-06058	NORFOLK	06243-06243	EAST KILLINGLY	06405-06405	BRANFORD	06601-06610	BRIDGEPORT
06059-06059	NORTH CANTON	06244-06244	EAST WOODSTOCK	06409-06409	CENTERBROOK	06611-06611	TRUMBULL
06060-06060	NORTH GRANBY	06245-06245	FABYAN	06410-06411	CHESHIRE	06612-06612	EASTON
06061-06061	PINE MEADOW	06246-06246	GROSVENOR DALE	06412-06412	CHESTER	06650-06699	BRIDGEPORT
06062-06062	PLAINVILLE	06247-06247	HAMPTON	06413-06413	CLINTON	06701-06710	WATERBURY
06063-06063	PLEASANT VALLEY	06248-06248	HEBRON	06414-06414	COBALT	06712-06712	PROSPECT
06064-06064	POQUONOCK	06249-06249	LEBANON	06415-06415	COLCHESTER	06716-06716	WOLCOTT
06065-06065	RIVERTON	06250-06250	MANSFIELD CENTER	06416-06416	CROMWELL	06720-06749	WATERBURY
06066-06066	VERNON ROCKVILLE	06251-06251	MANSFIELD DEPOT	06417-06417	DEEP RIVER	06750-06750	BANTAM
06067-06067	ROCKY HILL	06254-06254	NORTH FRANKLIN	06418-06418	DERBY	06751-06751	BETHLEHEM
06068-06068	SALISBURY	06255-06255	NORTH GROSVENORDALE	06419-06419	KILLINGWORTH	06752-06752	BRIDGEWATER
06069-06069	SHARON	06256-06256	NORTH WINDHAM	06420-06420	SALEM	06753-06753	CORNWALL
06070-06070	SIMSBURY	06258-06258	POMFRET	06422-06422	DURHAM	06754-06754	CORNWALL BRIDGE
06071-06071	SOMERS	06259-06259	POMFRET CENTER	06423-06423	EAST HADDAM	06755-06755	GAYLORDSVILLE
06072-06072	SOMERSVILLE	06260-06260	PUTNAM	06424-06424	EAST HAMPTON	06756-06756	GOSHEN
06073-06073	SOUTH GLASTONBURY	06262-06262	QUINEBAUG	06426-06426	ESSEX	06757-06757	KENT
06074-06074	SOUTH WINDSOR	06263-06263	ROGERS	06430-06432	FAIRFIELD	06758-06758	LAKESIDE
06075-06075	STAFFORD	06264-06264	SCOTLAND	06436-06436	GREENS FARMS	06759-06759	LITCHFIELD
06076-06076	STAFFORD SPRINGS	06265-06265	SOUTH WILLINGTON	06437-06437	GUILFORD	06762-06762	MIDDLEBURY
06077-06077	STAFFORDVILLE	06266-06266	SOUTH WINDHAM	06438-06438	HADDAM	06763-06763	MORRIS
06078-06078	SUFFIELD	06267-06267	SOUTH WOODSTOCK	06439-06439	HADLYME	06770-06770	NAUGATUCK
06079-06079	TACONIC	06268-06269	STORRS MANSFIELD	06440-06440	HAWLEYVILLE	06776-06776	NEW MILFORD
06080-06080	SUFFIELD	06277-06277	THOMPSON	06441-06441	HIGGANUM	06777-06777	NEW PRESTON MARBLE DALE
06081-06081	TARIFFVILLE	06278-06278	ASHFORD	06442-06442	IVORYTON		
06082-06083	ENFIELD	06279-06279	WILLINGTON	06443-06443	MADISON	06778-06778	NORTHFIELD
06084-06084	TOLLAND	06280-06280	WINDHAM	06444-06444	MARION	06779-06779	OAKVILLE
06085-06087	UNIONVILLE	06281-06281	WOODSTOCK	06447-06447	MARLBOROUGH	06781-06781	PEQUABUCK
06088-06088	EAST WINDSOR	06282-06282	WOODSTOCK VALLEY	06450-06454	MERIDEN	06782-06782	PLYMOUTH
06089-06089	WEATOGUE	06320-06320	NEW LONDON	06455-06455	MIDDLEFIELD	06783-06783	ROXBURY
06090-06090	WEST GRANBY	06330-06330	BALTIC	06456-06456	MIDDLE HADDAM	06784-06784	SHERMAN
06091-06091	WEST HARTLAND	06331-06331	CANTERBURY	06457-06459	MIDDLETOWN	06785-06785	SOUTH KENT
06092-06093	WEST SIMSBURY	06332-06332	CENTRAL VILLAGE	06460-06460	MILFORD	06786-06786	TERRYVILLE
06093-06093	WEST SUFFIELD	06333-06333	EAST LYME	06461-06461	BRIDGEPORT	06787-06787	THOMASTON
06094-06094	WINCHESTER CENTER	06334-06334	BOZRAH	06466-06466	MILFORD	06790-06790	TORRINGTON
06095-06095	WINDSOR	06335-06335	GALES FERRY	06467-06467	MILLDALE	06791-06791	HARWINTON
06096-06096	WINDSOR LOCKS	06336-06336	GILMAN	06468-06468	MONROE	06793-06794	WASHINGTON DEPOT
06098-06098	WINSTED	06337-06337	GLASGO	06469-06469	MOODUS	06795-06795	WATERTOWN
06101-06106	HARTFORD			06470-06470	NEWTOWN	06796-06796	WEST CORNWALL

06798-06798 WOODBURY	06813-06817 DANBURY	06870-06870 OLD GREENWICH	06880-06881 WESTPORT
06801-06801 BETHEL	06820-06820 DARIEN	06875-06875 REDDING CENTER	06883-06883 WESTON
06804-06804 BROOKFIELD	06829-06829 GEORGETOWN	06876-06876 REDDING RIDGE	06888-06889 WESTPORT
06807-06807 COS COB	06830-06836 GREENWICH	06877-06877 RIDGEFIELD	06896-06896 REDDING
06810-06811 DANBURY	06840-06842 NEW CANAAN	06878-06878 RIVERSIDE	06897-06897 WILTON
06812-06812 NEW FAIRFIELD	06850-06860 NORWALK	06879-06879 RIDGEFIELD	06901-06928 STAMFORD

Delaware

General Help Numbers:

Governor's Office
820 N. French St, Carvel State Bldg   302-577-3210
Wilmington, DE 19801   Fax 302-577-3118
www.state.de.us/governor/index.htm   8AM-5:30PM

Attorney General's Office
Carvel State Office Bldg   302-577-8400
820 N French St   Fax 302-577-6630
Wilmington, DE 19801   8:30AM-4:30PM
www.state.de.us/attgen/index.htm

State Court Administrator
PO Box 8911   302-577-2480
Wilmington, DE 19899   Fax 302-577-3139
http://courts.state.de.us/supreme/index.htm 8:30AM-5PM

State Archives
121 Duke of York St   302-739-5318
Dover, DE 19901   Fax 302-739-2578
www.archives.lib.de.us   8:30AM-4:15PM M-F

State Specifics:

Capital:	Dover
	Kent County
Time Zone:	EST
Number of Counties:	3
Population:	731,581
Web Site:	www.state.de.us

State Agencies

Criminal Records

Delaware State Police Headquarters, Criminal Records Section, PO Box 430, Dover, DE 19903-0430 (Courier: 1407 N Dupont Highway, Dover, DE 19930); 302-739-5880, 302-739-5888 (Fax), 8AM-4PM.

Note: This agency will only release records with dispositions for pre-employment requesters.

Indexing & Storage: Records are available from 1935. New records are available for inquiry immediately.

Searching: You do not need to use the state's forms. Must have a signed release form for the fingerprint search and release of information. Include name and fingerprints in your request. The following data is not released: traffic ticket information.

Access by: mail, in person.

Fee & Payment: Prepayment required. Fee payee: Delaware State Police. Funds must be certified or money order. No credit cards accepted.

Mail search: Turnaround time: 14 days. Must have a signed release and full set of fingerprints. A self addressed stamped envelope is requested. Search costs $25.00 per request.

In person search: Search costs $25.00 per request. It can take up to 14 days before records are ready for pickup.

Corporation Records
Limited Partnership Records
Trademarks/Servicemarks
Limited Liability Company Records
Limited Liability Partnerships

Secretary of State, Division of Corporations, PO Box 898, Dover, DE 19903 (Courier: John G Townsend Bldg, 401 Federal Street #4, Dover, DE 19901); 302-739-3073, 302-739-3812 (Fax), 8AM-4:30PM.

www.state.de.us/corp

Note: There is no online access to the public; however, there is a system available to only registered agents.

Indexing & Storage: Records are available from the formation of the Division. Indexes are maintained on imaging system and in-house computer. Delaware Registered Agents have online access. New records are available for inquiry immediately.

Searching: Include the following in your request-full name of business. In addition to the articles of incorporation, corporation records include the following information: Annual Reports, Officers, Directors, Prior (merged) names, Inactive and Reserved names.

Access by: mail, phone, fax, in person.

Fee & Payment: Fees are $20.00 for a status of an entity; $20.00 for certified plus $1.00 per page; plain copies are $5.00 for the first page and $1.00 each additional. Fee payee: Delaware Secretary of State. Prepayment required. Personal checks accepted. Credit cards accepted: Mastercard, Visa, Discover.

Mail search: Turnaround time: 3 days. No self addressed stamped envelope is required.

Phone search: There is no fee for general information given over the phone.

Fax search: Fax requests can be received by fax, but are not returned by fax.

In person search: Requests are returned by regular mail unless expedite fee is paid.

Expedited service: Expedited service available for mail, fax, phone, and in person. Fees are up to $100.00 for 24 hour; up to $200.00 for same day; $500.00 for 2 hour.

Uniform Commercial Code
Federal Tax Liens

UCC Division, Secretary of State, PO Box 793, Dover, DE 19903 (Courier: Townsend Bldg, 401 Federal Street, Dover, DE 19901); 302-739-3077, 302-739-3813 (Fax), 8:30AM-4:30PM.

www.state.de.us/corp/ucc.htm

Indexing & Storage: Records are available from 1967. Records are computerized since 1992. Records are indexed on inhouse computer.

Searching: Use search request form UCC-11. The search includes federal tax liens on businesses since 1976. Federal tax liens on individuals may show here, also. All state tax liens are filed at the county level. Include the following in your request-debtor name.

Access by: mail, fax, in person.

Fee & Payment: Approved UCC-11 - $25.00 per debtor name; non-standard form - $35.00. Copies cost $2.00 per page with a minimum charge of $5.00. Certified copies are an additional $25.00. Fee payee: Secretary of State. Prepayment required. Volume users may establish an account. Personal checks accepted. Credit cards accepted: Mastercard, Visa, Discover.

Mail search: Turnaround time: 5-7 days. You may request information by mail. No self addressed stamped envelope is required.

Fax search: Same criteria as searching by mail.

In person search: Unless expedited fees are paid, results are mailed or you must come back in 5 days.

Other access: Bulk purchase of paper copies is $2.00 per page.

Expedited service: Expedited service is available for mail and phone searches. Three levels of expedited service are available at extra fees as follows: 24 hrs-$25.00; same day-$50.00; 2 hrs-$75.00.

State Tax Liens
Records not maintained by a state level agency.
Note: Records are at the county level.

Sales Tax Registrations

Finance Department, Revenue Division, PO Box 8911, Wilmington, DE 19899-8911 (Courier: Carvel State Office Bldg, 820 N French St, 8th Fl, Wilmington, DE 19801); 302-577-8450, 302-577-8662 (Fax), 8AM-4:30PM.

www.state.de.us/revenue/index.htm

Note: This state has a gross receipts tax, not a sales tax per se. They will release the information found on the face of the certificate issued to the business.

Indexing & Storage: Records are available from 1989 on computer and from 1973-1990 on microfiche.

Searching: This state will do an alpha search for a business name and will provide the business name, address and business license number, type of business, amount of license fee paid, and the federal ID#. They will not release business owner or officer names. Include the following in your request-business name. The federal tax ID can also be used.

Access by: mail, phone, fax, in person.

Mail search: Turnaround time: 1 week. A self addressed stamped envelope is requested. No fee for mail request.

Phone search: No fee for telephone request. There is a limit of 3 searches per phone call.

Fax search: There is no fee for fax searches. Turnaround time is 2 days.

In person search: No fee for request.

Birth Certificates

Department of Health, Office of Vital Statistics, PO Box 637, Dover, DE 19903 (Courier: William Penn & Federal Sts, Jesse Cooper Bldg, Dover, DE 19901); 302-739-4721, 8AM-4:30PM (Counter closes at 4:20 PM).

Indexing & Storage: Records are available from 1928-present. Records before 1928 are at the State Archives. Records are indexed on microfilm, microfiche.

Searching: Must have a signed release from person of record or immediate family member. Others may only obtain records if they demonstrate the record is needed for the determination or protection of their personal property rights or for genealogical uses. Include the following in your request-full name, names of parents, mother's maiden name, date of birth, place of birth, reason for information request, relationship to person of record.

Access by: mail, phone, in person.

Fee & Payment: Search fee is $6.00 per name for every 5 years searched. Add $5.00 if you use a credit card. Add $4.00 for each additional copy of the same record. Fee payee: Office of Vital Statistics. Prepayment required. Personal checks accepted. Credit cards accepted: Mastercard, Visa, AmEx, Discover.

Mail search: Turnaround time: 1 day to 1 week. No self addressed stamped envelope is required.

Phone search: You must use a credit card for a phone request for an additional fee.

In person search: Turnaround time is generally 10 minutes or less.

Expedited service: Expedited service is available for mail, phone and in person searches. Turnaround time: overnight delivery. Add $14.50 per package.

Death Records

Department of Health, Office of Vital Statistics, PO Box 637, Dover, DE 19903 (Courier: William Penn & Federal Sts, Jesse Cooper Bldg, Dover, DE 19901); 302-739-4721, 8AM-4:30PM.

Indexing & Storage: Records are available for the past 40 years. Prior records are at the State Archives. It takes 3 days before new records are available for inquiry. Records are indexed on microfilm, microfiche.

Searching: Must have a signed release from immediate family member. Include the following in your request-full name, date of death, place of death, names of parents, reason for information request, relationship to person of record.

Access by: mail, phone, in person.

Fee & Payment: The search fee is $6.00 per name for every 5 years searched. Add $5.00 if you use a credit card. Add $4.00 for each additional copy. Fee payee: Office of Vital Statistics. Prepayment required. Personal checks accepted. Credit cards accepted: Mastercard, Visa, AmEx, Discover.

Mail search: Turnaround time: 1 day. No self addressed stamped envelope is required.

Phone search: You must use a credit card for a phone request for an additional fee.

In person search: Turnaround time is 10-15 minutes.

Expedited service: Expedited service is available for mail, phone and in person searches. Turnaround time: overnight delivery. Add $14.50 per package.

Marriage Certificates

Department of Health, Office of Vital Statistics, PO Box 637, Dover, DE 19903 (Courier: William

Penn & Federal Sts, Jesse Cooper Bldg, Dover, DE 19901); 302-739-4721, 8AM-4:30PM.

Indexing & Storage: Records are available for 40 years. Prior records are in the State Archives. It takes 5 days before new records are available for inquiry. Records are indexed on microfilm, microfiche.

Searching: Must have a signed release from person or persons of record or immediate family member. Include the following in your request- names of husband and wife, wife's maiden name, date of marriage, place or county of marriage, relationship to person of record, reason for information request.

Access by: mail, phone, in person.

Fee & Payment: The search fee is $6.00 per name for every 5 years searched. Add $5.00 if you use a credit card. Add $4.00 for each additional copy. Fee payee: Office of Vital Statistics. Prepayment required. Personal checks accepted. Credit cards accepted: Mastercard, Visa, AmEx, Discover.

Mail search: Turnaround time: 1 day. No self addressed stamped envelope is required.

Phone search: You must use a credit card for a phone request for an additional fee.

In person search: Turnaround time is 10-15 minutes.

Expedited service: Expedited service is available for mail, phone and in person searches. Turnaround time: overnight delivery. Add $14.50 per package.

Divorce Records

Records not maintained by a state level agency.

Note: This agency will verify whether a divorce occurred after 1935, but will issue no copies of the record. For records 1976 to present, go to the Family Court at the county; prior to 1976, go to the Prothonotary at the county level.

Workers' Compensation Records

Labor Department, Industrial Accident Board, 4425 N Market Street, Wilmington, DE 19802; 302-761-8200, 302-761-6601 (Fax), 8AM-4:30PM.

Indexing & Storage: Records are available from 1985. New records are available for inquiry immediately.

Searching: Must have signed authorization from injured party in letter form or a court subpeona. They will not honor out-of-state requests. Information required includes claimant name, SSN, and date of accident.

Access by: mail.

Fee & Payment: There is no fee. Copies are $.25 each. Fee payee: DOL/IA. Prepayment required. Payment is for copies only. Personal checks accepted. No credit cards accepted.

Mail search: Turnaround time: 2-5 days. A self addressed stamped envelope is requested.

Driver Records

Division of Motor Vehicles, Driver Services, PO Box 698, Dover, DE 19903 (Courier: 303 Transportation Circle, Dover, DE 19901); 302-

744-2500, 302-739-2602 (Fax), 8AM-4:30PM M-T-TH-F; 12:00PM-8PM W.

Note: Delaware does not keep copies of tickets in a central repository for request purposes and suggests you go to the appropriate local jurisdiction.

Indexing & Storage: Records are available for 3 years to present for public record purposes. It takes 2-3 weeks before new records are available for inquiry.

Searching: Casual requesters can obtain records only with MV703 Form with notarized signature of subject. Include the following in your request- full name, driver's license number, date of birth. Authorized account holders must have an application and contract on file. The following data is not released: Social Security Numbers or medical information.

Access by: mail, in person, online.

Fee & Payment: The fee for all search modes is $4.00 per request. Fee payee: Division of Motor Vehicles. Prepayment required. Personal checks accepted. No credit cards accepted.

Mail search: Turnaround time: 3-5 days. A self addressed stamped envelope is requested.

In person search: Walk-in requesters may obtain records from centers in Wilmington, New Castle, Dover, and Georgetown.

Online search: Online searching is single inquiry only, no batch request mode is offered. Searching is done by driver's license number or name and DOB. A signed contract application and valid "business license" is required. Hours of operation are 8 AM to 4:30 PM. Access is provided through a 900 number at a fee of $1.00 per minute, plus the $4.00 per record fee. For more information, call 302-744-2606.

Other access: Tape-to-tape is offered for high volume, batch requesters. Also, the state will release data from the driver license file on tapes or cartridges, but this cannot be resold.

Vehicle Ownership
Vehicle Identification

Division of Motor Vehicles, Correspondence Section, PO Box 698, Dover, DE 19903 (Courier: 303 Transportation Circle, Dover, DE 19901); 302-744-2500, 302-739-2042 (Fax), 8:30AM-4:30PM M-T-TH-F; 12-8PM W.

Indexing & Storage: Records are available for 3 years to present. It takes 2-3 weeks before new records are available for inquiry.

Searching: Casual requesters can only obtain records with notarized consent. Causual requesters must use Form MV703. Those routinely seeking information must complete an Application and Contract for Direct Access to become an account holder.

Access by: mail, in person, online.

Fee & Payment: The fee for ownership, plate, and registration searches is $4.00 per record. Fee payee: Division of Motor Vehicles. Prepayment required. Personal checks accepted. No credit cards accepted.

Mail search: Turnaround time: 3-5 days. A self addressed stamped envelope is requested.

In person search: Turnaround time is while you wait.

Online search: There is an additional $1.00 per minute fee for using the on-line "900 number"

system. Records are $4.00 each. The system is single inquiry mode and open from 8 AM to 4:30 PM, except on Wed. from noon to 8PM. For more information, call 302-744-2606.

Other access: Bulk information can be obtained on a customized basis in tape, cartridge or paper format. However, the purpose of the request is carefully screened and information cannot be resold.

Accident Reports

Delaware State Police, Traffic Records, PO Box 430, Dover, DE 19903 (Courier: 1441 N Dupont Hwy, Dover, DE 19903); 302-739-5931, 302-739-5982 (Fax), 8AM-4PM.

Indexing & Storage: Records are available for 3 years as public record. It takes 2-3 weeks before new records are available for inquiry.

Searching: Include the following in your request- full name, date of accident, location of accident.

Access by: mail, in person.

Fee & Payment: The fee is $18.50 per report. You cannot search by phone, but you can verify by phone if a report exists. Fee payee: Delaware State Police. Prepayment required. Personal checks accepted. No credit cards accepted.

Mail search: Turnaround time: 3-5 days. A self addressed stamped envelope is requested.

In person search: Searching in person is discouraged. Personnel may not have time to perform an immediate search.

Boat & Vessel Ownership
Boat & Vessel Registration

Dept of Natural Resources & Environmental Control, Delaware Boat Registration Office, 89 Kings Highway, Dover, DE 19901; 302-739-3498, 302-739-6157 (Fax), 8AM-4:30PM.

www.dnrec.state.de.us

Note: Liens are filed with UCC filings, not at this location.

Indexing & Storage: Records are available from 1978-present. Records are registration only, no titles, and are indexed on microfiche from 1978-1989. Records are computer indexed from 1990-the present. All motorized craft are registered. There are no titles.

Searching: No searching of records is allowed. However, they will verify information over the phone using "yes" and "no" only. Either the owner's name, hull ID# or registration number must be submitted for a verification.

Access by: phone, in person.

Fee & Payment: There is no fee. No searching by mail.

Phone search: They will verify information over the phone using "yes" and "no" only.

In person search: Verification only.

Legislation-Current/Pending
Legislation-Passed

Legislative Hall, Division of Research, PO Box 1401, Dover, DE 19903; 302-739-4114, 302-739-5318 (Archives for old bills), 800-282-8545 (In-state), 8AM-4:30PM.

www.state.de.us/research/assembly.htm

Indexing & Storage: Records are available for current and 1 prior session only. Records are indexed on microfiche.

Searching: Include the following in your request- bill number.

Access by: mail, phone, in person, online.

Fee & Payment: There is no charge unless you want many copies or a copy of a large document. They will compute the charges. Fee payee: State of Delaware. Personal checks accepted. No credit cards accepted.

Mail search: Turnaround time: variable. No self addressed stamped envelope is required.

Phone search: You may call for copies.

In person search: You may request copies in person.

Online search: Access information at the Internet site, no fee.

Voter Registration

Commissioner of Elections, 32 W Lockerman, M-101, Dover, DE 19904; 302-739-4277, 8AM-4:30PM.

www.state.de.us/election

Indexing & Storage: Records are available for both active and inactive records.

Searching: There is no individual record searching permitted, except in person. The following data is not released: Social Security Numbers or telephone numbers.

Access by: in person.

Fee & Payment: There is no search fee, the copy fee is $.25 per copy. Fee payee: State of Delaware. Prepayment required. No credit cards accepted.

In person search: Searching is available in person.

Other access: The entire state database is available on tape for $250. Individual districts (378) are available on disk for $2.00 per district or $.025 per name on labels. Also, there are several different types of printed lists available.

GED Certificates

Department of Education, GED Testing, PO Box 1402, Dover, DE 19903; 302-739-3743, 302-739-2770 (Fax).

Searching: Include the following in your request- signed release, date of birth, Social Security Number. The year of the test is very helpful.

Access by: mail, fax, in person.

Fee & Payment: There is no fee.

Mail search: Turnaround time: 1-2 days. No self addressed stamped envelope is required.

Fax search: Same criteria as mail searching.

In person search: Requester must presenta photo ID.

Hunting License Information
Fishing License Information
Access to Records is Restricted

Natural Resources & Environmental Control Dept, Divsion of Fish & Wildlife, 89 Kings Hwy, Dover, DE 19901; 302-739-5296, 302-739-6157 (Fax), 8AM-4:30PM.

www.dnrec.state.de.us/fw/fwwel.htm

Note: Records are not on a computerized database, but kept on paper in boxes. Records may be rviewed, but research would be very tedious. They will release name, address, driver license number, and physical characteristics.

Licenses Searchable Online

Optometrist #11 .... www.arbo.org/nodb2000/licsearch.asp

Licensing Quick Finder

Administrative Supervisor/Assistant #04
....302-739-4601
Adult Entertainment #11 .... 302-739-4522 x207
Aesthetician #11 302-739-4522
Alarm Company/Employee #03 302-739-5991
Alcoholic Beverage Establishment #01 .302-577-5222
Ambulance Attendant #18 302-739-4773
Architect #11............................ 302-739-4522 x218
Armored Car Agencies/Employees #03
....302-739-5991
Asbestos Abatement Worker #15..........302-739-3930
Athletic Trainer #11 .... 302-739-4522 x205
Attorney #02..302-651-3113
Audiologist #11 302-739-4522
Barber #11................................. 302-739-4522 x204
Boiler Inspector #14 302-739-5889
Chiropractor #11 .... 302-739-4522 x204
Constables #03....................................302-739-5991
Cosmetologist #11 .... 302-739-4522 x204
Deadly Weapons Dealer #11 .... 302-739-4522 x209
Dental Hygienist #11 302-739-4522
Dental Radiographer #16......................302-739-3787
Dentist #11 .... 302-739-4522 x220
Dietician/Nutritionist #11 302-739-4522
Electrician #11 .... 302-739-4522 x203
Electrologist #11 302-739-4522
Emergency Medical Technician-Paramedic #07
....302-739-6637
Engineer #12 302-577-6500
Funeral Director #11................... 302-739-4522 x206
Gaming Control #11 .... 302-739-4522 x202

General Contractor #05 302-577-8778
Geologist #11............................ 302-739-4522 x207
Harness Racing #06.............................302-739-4811
Hearing Aid Dealer/Fitter #11 ...... 302-739-4522 x204
Human Relations Specialist #13 888-759-9133
Insurance Adjuster #08........................302-739-4254
Insurance Advisor #08..........................302-739-4254
Insurance Agent/Consultant #08...........302-739-4254
Insurance Broker #08 302-739-4254
Land Surveyor #11 .... 302-739-4522 x218
Landscape Architect #11 .... 302-739-4522 x218
Library Media Specialist #13.................888-759-9133
Lobbyist #09 302-739-2397
Massage #11 .... 302-739-4522 x203
Medical Doctor/Surgeon #11 .... 302-739-4522 x211
Mental Health Counselor #11 302-739-4522
Nail Technician #11..............................302-739-4522
Notary Public #09.................................302-739-4111
Nuclear Medicine Technologist #16 302-739-3787
Nurse #11 .... 302-739-4522 x216
Nurse-Midwife #11 302-739-4522
Nursing Home Administrator #11
.... 302-739-4522 x207
Occupational Therapist/Assistant #11
.... 302-739-4522 x207
Optometrist #11 .... 302-739-4522 x206
Osteopathic Physician #11 .... 302-739-4522 x211
Pesticide Applicator #10 302-739-4811
Pharmacist #07 302-739-4798
Pharmacist #11 .... 302-739-4522 x215
Physical Therapist/Assistant #11 . 302-739-4522 x206

Plumber #11 302-739-4522
Podiatrist #11 .... 302-739-4522 x207
Principal #13...888-759-9133
Private Investigative Agencies/Employees #03
....302-739-5991
Private Security Agencies/Employees #03
....302-739-5991
Professional Counselor #11 .... 302-739-4522 x220
Psychological Assistant #11 302-739-4522
Psychologist #11 .... 302-739-4522 x218
Public Accountant-CPA #11 .... 302-739-4522 x218
Radiation Therapist #16 302-739-3787
Real Estate Appraiser #11 .... 302-739-4522 x211
Real Estate Broker/Agent #11 ..... 302-739-4522 x219
River Pilot #11 .... 302-739-4522 x204
School Counselor #04 302-739-4601
School Principal #04.............................302-739-4601
School Superintendent #04 302-739-4601
Securities Agent #08............................302-739-4254
Securities Broker/Dealer #08 302-739-4254
Social Worker #11 .... 302-739-4522 x220
Speech Pathologist/Audiologist #11
.... 302-739-4522 x204
Superintendent #13..............................888-759-9133
Teacher #04...302-739-4601
Thorobred Racing #06..........................302-739-4811
Veterinarian #11......................... 302-739-4522 x206
Waste Water Operator #17 302-739-4860
Water Supply Operator #07 302-739-5410
X-ray Technician #07 302-739-3787

Licensing Agency Information

01 Alcoholic Beverage Control Division, 820 N French St, Carvel State Office Bldg, Wilmington, DE 19801; 302-577-5222, Fax: 302-577-3204.

02 Board of Bar Examiners, 200 W 9th St, #300B, Wilmington, DE 19801; 302-577-7038, Fax: 302-658-4605.

03 State Police, Detective Licensing, PO Box 430 (PO Box 430), Dover, DE 19903; 302-739-5991, Fax: 302-739-5888.

www.state.de.us/DSP

04 Department of Education, PO Box 1402 (PO Box 1402), Dover, DE 19903; 302-739-4601, Fax: 302-739-3092.

05 Division of Revenue, 820 N French St, Carvel State Office Bldg, Wilmington, DE 19801; 302-577-3363, Fax: 302-577-8203.

www.state.de.us/revenue/index.htm

06 Harness Racing Commission, 2320 S DuPont Hwy, Dover, DE 19901; 302-739-4811, Fax: 302-697-4748.

www.state.de.us/deptagri

07 Health & Social Services Department, Division of Public Health, PO Box 637 (PO Box 637), Dover, DE 19903-.

08 Insurance Department, 841 Silver Lake Blvd, Dover, DE 19904; 302-739-4254, Fax: 302-739-5280.

www.state.de.us/inscom

09 Notary Division, Office of Secretary of State, PO Box 898 (PO Box 898), Dover, DE 19903; 302-739-6479, Fax: 302-739-3812.

10 Department of Agriculture, Pesticide Section, 2320 S DuPont Hwy, Dover, DE 19901; 302-739-4811, Fax: 302-697-6287.

www.state.de.us/deptagri/index.htm

11 Division of Professional Regulations, 861 Silver Lake Blvd, Cannon Bldg #203, Dover, DE 19903; 302-739-4522, Fax: 302-739-2711.

12 Assoc. of Professional Engineers, Engineering Licensing Board, 56 W Main St #208, Wilmington, DE 19702-1500; 302-577-6500, Fax: 302-577-6502.

www.dape.org

13 Department of Public Instruction, Office of Certification, Townsend Bldg, PO Box 1402, Dover, DE 19903; 888-759-9133.

14 Division of Boiler Safety, PO Box 674, Dover, DE 19903-0674; 302-739-5889.

15 Division of Facilities Mgmt, O'Neill Bldg, PO Box 1401, Dover, DE 19903; 302-739-3930.

16 Division of Public Health, Office of Radiation Control, PO Box 637, Dover, DE 19903; 302-739-3787.

17 Department of Natural Resources & Environmental Control, Division of Water Resources, 89 Kings Hwy, Dover, DE 19901; 302-739-4860.

18 Fire Prevention Commission, 1461 Chestnut Grove Rd, Dover, DE 19904; 302-739-4773.

The following list indicates the district and division name for each county in the state. If the district or division name of the bankruptcy court is different from the civil/criminal court, it appears in parentheses.

County/Court Cross Reference

Kent... Wilmington
New Castle... Wilmington
Sussex.. Wilmington

US District Court

District of Delaware

Wilmington Division US Courthouse, Lock Box 18, 844 N King St, Wilmington, DE 19801 (Courier Address: US Courthouse, 844 N King St, Clerk's Office, 4th Floor, Room 4209, Wilmington, DE 19801), 302-573-6170.

Counties: All counties in Delaware.

Indexing & Storage: Cases are indexed by defendant and plaintiff as well as by case number. New cases are available in the index within 1 day after filing date. A computer index is maintained. Open records are located at this court.

Fee & Payment: The fee is $15.00 per item (one party name or case number). Payment may be made by money order, cashier check, personal check. Prepayment is required. A copy vendor is used for civil court documents. Parcels Incorporated, 1-800-343-1742 -- orders may be placed with them directly. Payee: Clerk, US District Court. Certification fee: $5.00 per document. Copy fee: $.50 per page.

Phone Search: They will search civil and criminal cases from 1982 to the present over the phone. The only information released over the phone is whether a case was found and, if so, its case number. An automated voice case information service (VCIS) is not available.

Mail Search: Search can include all computer, microfiche and judgment indexes. A stamped self addressed envelope is not required.

In Person Search: In person searching is available.

PACER: Sign-up number is 800-676-6856. Access fee is $.60 per minute. Toll-free access: 888-793-9488. Local access: 302-573-6651. Case records are available back to January 1991. Records are purged every few years (not since 1/91). New records are available online after 2 days. PACER is available on the Internet at http://pacer.ded.uscourts.gov.

Opinions Online: Court opinions are available online at www.lawlib.widener.edu/pages/deopind.htm

US Bankruptcy Court

District of Delaware

Wilmington Division 824 Market St, 5th Floor, Marine Midland Plaza, Wilmington, DE 19801, 302-573-6174.

www.deb.uscourts.gov

Counties: All counties in Delaware.

Indexing & Storage: Cases are indexed by debtor as well as by case number. New cases are available in the index 1 day after filing date. A computer index is maintained. Open records are located at this court.

Fee & Payment: The fee is $15.00 per item (one party name or case number). Payment may be made by money order, cashier check, personal check. Prepayment is required. Payee: Clerk, US Bankruptcy Court. Certification fee: $5.00 per document. Copy fee: $.50 per page. You are allowed to make your own copies. These copies cost $.50 per page. There is an in-house private copy service that you must use.

Phone Search: The only information that is released over the telephone is whether the search is positive or negative. If positive they will release the case number. An automated voice case information service (VCIS) is available. Call VCIS at 888-667-5530 or 302-573-6233.

Mail Search: Always enclose a stamped self addressed envelope.

In Person Search: In person searching is available.

PACER: Sign-up number is 800-676-6856. Access fee is $.60 per minute. Toll-free access: 800-249-9857. Local access: 302-573-6243. Use of PC Anywhere v4.0 suggested. Case records are available back to 1991. Records are purged every four years. New civil records are available online after 1 day.

Other Online Access: You can search case records using RACER at http://206.96.0.130/wconnect/WCI.DLL?usbcn_racer~main. Searching is currently free, but a fee may be charged in the future. You may need to sign up at the main web site prior to using RACER for the first time.

Court	Jurisdiction	No. of Courts	How Organized
Superior Courts*	General	3	
Chancery Courts*	General	3	
Court of Common Pleas*	Limited	3	
Justice of the Peace Courts*	Municipal	19	
Alderman's Courts	Municipal	9	
Family Courts	Special	3	

* Profiled in this Sourcebook.

Court	CIVIL								
	Tort	Contract	Real Estate	Min. Claim	Max. Claim	Small Claims	Estate	Eviction	Domestic Relations
Superior Courts*	X	X	X	$50000	No Max				
Chancery Courts*	X	X	X	$0	No Max		X		
Court of Common Pleas*	X	X	X	$0	$50000				
Justice of the Peace Courts*			X	$0	$15000	$5000		X	
Alderman's Courts						$2500			
Family Courts*									X

Court	CRIMINAL				
	Felony	Misdemeanor	DWI/DUI	Preliminary Hearing	Juvenile
Superior Courts*	X	X			
Chancery Courts*					
Court of Common Pleas*		X		X	
Justice of the Peace Courts*		X	X		
Alderman's Courts		X	X		
Family Courts*		X			X

ADMINISTRATION Administrative Office of the Courts, PO Box 8911, Wilmington, DE, 19899; 302-577-2480, Fax: 302-577-3139. www.state.de.us/dejudic.htm

COURT STRUCTURE Superior Courts have jurisdiction over felonies and all drug offenses, the Court of Common Pleas has jurisdiction over all misdemeanors except those involving drug offenses. The Common Pleas courts handle some minor felonies as defined in state statutes. Court of Chancery handles corporation and equity matters, as well as probate and estates. Guardianships are handled by the Register of Wills, corporate matters such as equity disputes and injunctions are handled by the Clerk of Chancery.

The Municipal Court of Wilmington merged with the Court of Common Pleas in New Castle in May 1998.

ONLINE ACCESS An online system called CLAD, developed by Mead Data Central and the New Castle Superior Court, is currently available in Delaware. CLAD contains only toxic waste, asbestos, and class action cases; however, based on CLAD's success, Delaware may pursue development of online availability of other public records by working in conjunction with private information resource enterprises.

ADDITIONAL INFORMATION Effective 1/15/95, the civil case limit of the Justice of the Peace Courts increased from $5,000 to $15,000; the Courts of Common Pleas' limit went from $15,000 to $50,000.

Criminal histories are available with a signed release from the offender at the State Police Headquaerts, Criminal Records Section in Dover DE. For information on criminal history retrieval requirements, call 302-739-5880.

Kent County

Chancery Court 38 The Green, Dover, DE 19901; 302-736-2242; Probate phone:302-744-2330; Fax: 302-736-2244. Hours: 8:30AM-4:30PM (EST). *Civil, Probate.*

Civil Records: Access: In person only. Court does not conduct in person searches; visitors must perform searches for themselves. Search fee: No civil searches performed by court. Required to search: name, years to search. Civil cases indexed by defendant, plaintiff. Civil records on index books. The Court of Chancery oversees corporate and equity matters and guardianship. The Register of Wills oversees estate, and probate matters. **General Information:** No juvenile, sealed or mental health records released. Turnaround time 24 hrs. Copy fee: $1.00 per page. Certification fee: $5.00 plus $1.00 per page. Fee payee: Register in Chancery (Register of Wills for Probate). Personal checks accepted. May bill law firms and businesses. Public access terminal is available.

Superior Court Office of Prothonotary, 38 The Green, Dover, DE 19901; 302-739-3184; Fax: 302-739-6717. Hours: 8AM-5PM (EST). *Felony, Misdemeanor, Civil Actions Over $50,000.*

Civil Records: Access: Mail, in person. Only the court conducts in person searches; visitors may not. Search fee: $10.00 per name. $25.00 for immediate service on non-microfiche files. Required to search: name, years to search. Civil cases indexed by defendant, plaintiff. judgment on computer from 1996, on microfiche from 1918. **Criminal Records:** Access: In person only. Court does not conduct in person searches; visitors must perform searches for themselves. Search fee: No criminal searches performed by court. $25.00 for immediate service on non-microfiche files. Required to search: name, years to search, DOB; also helpful-race. judgment on computer from 1996, on microfiche from 1918. Contact Dept of Records for search assistance. **General Information:** No sealed or psychological evaluation records released. SASE required. Copy fee: $1.00 per page. Certification fee: $6.00 fee for 3 pages and $1.00 each add'l page. Fee payee: Prothonotary. Personal checks accepted. Prepayment is required.

Court of Common Pleas 38 The Green, Dover, DE 19901; 302-739-4618; Fax: 302-739-4501. Hours: 8:30AM-4:30PM (EST). *Misdemeanor, Civil Actions Under $50,000.*

Civil Records: Access: Mail, in person. Both court and visitors may perform in person searches. No search fee. Required to search: name, years to search. Civil cases indexed by defendant, plaintiff. Civil records on computer from 1992, on microfiche from 10/85, archived prior. **Criminal Records:** Access: Mail, in person. Court does not conduct in person searches; visitors must perform searches for themselves. No search fee. Required to search: name, years to search, DOB, offense, date of offense. Criminal records on computer from 1/94, on microfiche from 10/85, archived prior. **General Information:** No sealed records released. SASE required. Turnaround time 1-3 days. Copy fee: $1.00 per page. Certification fee: $5.00. Fee payee: Court of Common Pleas. Personal checks accepted. Prepayment is required.

Dover Justice of the Peace 480 Bank Lane, Dover, DE 19904; 302-739-4316; Fax: 302-739-6797. Hours: 8AM-4PM (EST). *Civil Actions Under $15,000, Eviction, Small Claims.*

Civil Records: Access: Mail, in person. Both court and visitors may perform in person searches. Search fee:. Required to search: name, years to search. Civil cases indexed by defendant, plaintiff. Civil records computerized since 10/98. **General Information:** Copy fee: $.25 per page. Certification fee: $10.00. Fee payee: JCP Court 16. Personal checks accepted. Prepayment is required.

Dover Justice of the Peace 480 Bank Lane, Dover, DE 19903; 302-739-4554; Fax: 302-739-6797. Hours: Open 24 hours (EST). *Misdemeanor.* **Criminal Records:** Only the court conducts in person searches; visitors may not. Search fee: $7.00 per name. Fee is per charge. Required to search: name, years to search, DOB, signed release; also helpful-address, offense, date of offense. **General Information:.** Fee payee: State of Delaware. Prepayment is required.

Harrington Justice of the Peace #6 17111 South DuPont Hwy, Harrington, DE 19952; 302-398-8247. Hours: 8AM-4PM (EST). *Misdemeanor.* **Criminal Records:** Only the court conducts in person searches; visitors may not. No search fee. Required to search: name, years to search, DOB. Court form required for all searches. **General Information:** Turnaround time 2-3 days. Fee payee: State of Delaware. Prepayment is required.

Smyrna Justice of the Peace 100 Monrovia Ave, Smyrna, DE 19977; 302-653-7083; Fax: 302-653-2888. Hours: 8AM-4PM (EST). *Misdemeanor.* **Criminal Records:** Only the court conducts in person searches; visitors may not. No search fee. Required to search: name, years to search; also helpful-DOB. **General Information:.** Fee payee: State of Delaware. Prepayment is required.

New Castle County

Chancery Court 1020 N King St, Wilmington, DE 19801; 302-571-7540; Probate phone:302-571-7545; Fax: 302-571-7751. Hours: 8:30AM-5PM (EST). *Civil, Probate.*

Civil Records: Access: Phone, fax, mail, in person. Both court and visitors may perform in person searches. Search fee: No civil searches performed by court. Required to search: name; also helpful-years to search. Civil cases indexed by defendant, plaintiff. Civil records indexed on computer since 1963, in books prior to 1963. The civil records for the Court of Chancery deal with corporate and equity matters, there is no money jurisdiction. The Register of Wills oversees estates, guardianships and probate. **General Information:** No guardianship records released. SASE requested. Turnaround time 2 days. Copy fee: $1.00 per page. $2.00 if from microfilm. Certification fee: $5.00. Fee payee: Register in Chancery (Register of Wills for Probate). Personal checks accepted. Will bill fax requests. Public access terminal is available. Fax notes: $5.00 for first page, $2.00 each addl.

Superior Court Office of the Prothonotary, 1020 N King Street, Wilmington, DE 19801; 302-577-2400; Fax: 302-577-6487/577-6212. Hours: 8:30AM-5PM (EST). *Felony, Misdemeanor, Civil Actions Over $50,000.*

Civil Records: Access: In person only. Court does not conduct in person searches; visitors must perform searches for themselves. Search fee: No civil searches performed by court. Required to search: name, years to search. Civil cases indexed by defendant, plaintiff. Civil records on computer from 4/80, prior on microfiche. **Criminal Records:** Access: In person only. Court does not

conduct in person searches; visitors must perform searches for themselves. Search fee: No criminal searches performed by court. Required to search: name, DOB; also helpful-years to search. Criminal records on computer from 4/80, prior on microfiche. **General Information:** No psychological evaluation, sealed records released. Copy fee: $1.00 per page. Certification fee: $6.00. Fee payee: Prothonotary's Office. Personal checks accepted. Prepayment is required. Public access terminal is available. Public Access Terminal Note: Civil only.

Court of Common Pleas 1000 N King St, Wilmington, DE 19801-3348; 302-577-2430; Fax: 302-577-2193. Hours: 8:30AM-4:30PM (EST). *Misdemeanor, Civil Actions Under $50,000.*

Note: Fax for civil is 302-577-2431

Civil Records: Access: Phone, fax, mail, in person. Both court and visitors may perform in person searches. No search fee. Required to search: name, years to search. Civil cases indexed by defendant, plaintiff. Civil records on computer from 1993; prior records on docket books. **Criminal Records:** Access: Phone, fax, mail, in person. Both court and visitors may perform in person searches. No search fee. Required to search: name, years to search; also helpful-DOB. Criminal records on computer from 1993; prior records on docket books. **General Information:** No closed records released. SASE required. Turnaround time up tp a week. Copy fee: $1.00 per page. Certification fee: $5.00. Fee payee: Court of Common Pleas. Personal checks accepted. Prepayment is required. Fax notes: $1.00 per page.

Middletown Justice of the Peace Court #9 5355 Summitt Bridge Rd, Middletown, DE 19709; 302-378-5221. Hours: 8AM-4PM (EST). *Civil Under$15,000, Misdemeanor, Eviction, Small Claims.*

Civil Records: Access: In person only. Both court and visitors may perform in person searches. No search fee. Required to search: name, years to search. Civil cases indexed by defendant. The court will not do name searches, but will seach if a civil action # is presented. **Criminal Records:** Access: In person only. Court does not conduct in person searches; visitors must perform searches for themselves. Search fee: No criminal searches performed by court. Required to search: name, years to search, DOB. **General Information:** Copy fee: $.25 per page. Certification fee: Civil record certification is $7.00, criminal is $10.00.

Wilmington Justice of the Peace 212 Greenbank Rd, Wilmington, DE 19808; 302-995-8646; Fax: 302-995-8642. Hours: 8:30AM-4:30PM (EST). *Civil Actions Under $15,000, Eviction, Small Claims.*

Civil Records: Access: In person only. Court does not conduct in person searches; visitors must perform searches for themselves. Search fee: No civil searches performed by court. Required to search: name, years to search. **General Information:** No sealed, juvenile, adoption or mental health records released. Certification fee: $10.00. Fee payee: Justice of the Peace Court 12. Personal checks accepted. Prepayment is required.

Wilmington Justice of the Peace Court #13 1010 Concord Ave, Concord Professional Center, Wilmington, DE 19802; 302-577-2550; Fax: 302-577-2526. Hours: 8AM-4PM (EST). *Civil Actions Under $15,000, Eviction, Small Claims.*

Civil Records: Access: In person only. Court does not conduct in person searches; visitors must perform searches for themselves. Search fee: No civil searches performed by court. Required to search: name, years to search. Civil cases indexed by defendant, plaintiff. Civil Records are computerized since 09/01/99. The court will pull specific case data if CA# given, if and when time permitting. **General Information:** No sealed, juvenile, adoption or mental health records released. Copy fee: $.25 per page. Certification fee: $10.00. Fee payee: Justice of the Peace Court #13. Personal checks accepted. Prepayment is required.

New Castle Justice of the Peace Court #11 61 Christiana Rd, New Castle, DE 19720; 302-323-4450; Fax: 302-323-4452. Hours: Open 24 hours (EST). *Misdemeanor.* **Criminal Records:** Court does not conduct in person searches; visitors must perform searches for themselves. Search fee: $7.00 per name. Fee is per case. Required to search: name, years to search. **General Information:** Turnaround time 2-3 days. Fee payee: State of Delaware. Prepayment is required.

Wilmington Justice of the Peace 130 Hickman Rd #13, Wilmington, DE 19703; 302-798-5327. Hours: 8AM-4PM M; 8AM-Midnight T-F; 8AM-4PM Sat. *Misdemeanor.*

Note: Effective 06/01/99, the court assumed DUi and truancy cases. This court was formally located at 716 Phildelphia Pike in Wilmington **Criminal Records:** Only the court conducts in person searches; visitors may not. Search fee: $7.00 per name. Fee is per case & includes certification & copy fees. Required to search: name, years to search, DOB; also helpful-offense. **General Information:** Turnaround time 2-4 weeks. Fee payee: State of Delaware. Prepayment is required.

Wilmington Justice of the Peace 1301 E 12th St, Wilmington, DE 19809; 302-429-7740. Hours: 8:30AM-Midnight (EST). *Misdemeanor.* **Criminal Records:** Only the court conducts in person searches; visitors may not. Search fee: $7.50 per name. Required to search: name, years to search, DOB. **General Information:** Turnaround time varies.

Wilmington Justice of the Peace 210 Greenbank Rd, Wilmington, DE 19808; 302-995-8640; Fax: 302-995-8642. Hours: 8AM-11PM (EST). *Misdemeanor.* **Criminal Records:** Only the court conducts in person searches; visitors may not. Search fee: $7.00 per name. Required to search: name, years to search, DOB. **General Information:** Turnaround time 2 weeks. Fee payee: Justice of the Peace Court 10. Prepayment is required.

Wilmington Justice of the Peace #20 Public Safety Building, 300 N Walnut Street, Wilmington, DE 19801; 302-577-7234. Hours: 8AM-midnight (EST). *Misdemeanor.* **Criminal Records:** Court does not conduct in person searches; visitors must perform searches for themselves. Search fee: No criminal searches performed by court. Required to search: name, years to search. **General Information:.** Fee payee: Justice of the Peace Court #13.

Sussex County

Chancery Court PO Box 424, Georgetown, DE 19947; 302-855-7842; Probate phone:302-855-

7875. Hours: 8:30AM-4:30PM (EST). *Civil, Probate.*

Civil Records: Access: Phone, mail, in person. Both court and visitors may perform in person searches. No search fee. Required to search: name, years to search. Civil cases indexed by defendant, plaintiff. Civil records on index books. **General Information:** All records public. Turnaround time 1-3 days. Copy fee: $1.00 per page. Certification fee: $5.00 plus $1.00 per page. Fee payee: Register in Chancery (Register of Wills for Probate). Personal checks accepted. Prepayment is required.

Superior Court PO Box 756, Georgetown, DE 19947; 302-856-5740; Fax: 302-856-5739. Hours: 8AM-4:30PM (EST). *Felony, Misdemeanor, Civil Actions.*

Civil Records: Access: In person only. Court does not conduct in person searches; visitors must perform searches for themselves. Search fee: No civil searches performed by court. Required to search: name, years to search. Civil cases indexed by defendant, plaintiff. Civil records on computer from 6/91 or form 1980 if case was pending in 1991, microfiche prior. **Criminal Records:** Access: In person only. Court does not conduct in person searches; visitors must perform searches for themselves. Search fee: No criminal searches performed by court. Required to search: name, years to search. Criminal records on manual index. **General Information:** No divorce, victim info, sealed records, expungments, or CCDW permit records released. Copy fee: $.30 per page. Certification fee: $6.00 plus $1.00 per page after the first three. Fee payee: Prothonotary. Personal checks accepted. Prepayment is required. Public access terminal is available.

Court of Common Pleas PO Box 426, Georgetown, DE 19947; 302-856-5333; Fax: 302-856-5056. Hours: 8:30AM-4:30PM (EST). *Misdemeanor, Civil Actions Under $50,000.*

Civil Records: Access: Phone, fax, mail, in person. Only the court conducts in person searches; visitors may not. Search fee: $10.00 per name. Required to search: name, years to search. Civil cases indexed by defendant. Civil records on computer from 1993, on microfiche from 10/85, archives prior. **Criminal Records:** Access: Phone, fax, mail, in person. Only the court conducts in person searches; visitors may not. Search fee: $10.00 per name. Required to search: name, years to search, DOB, offense, date of offense. Criminal records on computer from 1994, on microfiche from 10/85, archives prior. **General Information:** No closed case records released. SASE required. Turnaround time 1-2 weeks. Copy fee: $1.00 per page. Certification fee: $1.00. Fee payee: Court of Common Pleas. Personal checks accepted. Prepayment is required. Fax notes: No fee to fax results.

Georgetown Justice of the Peace #17 17 Shortly Rd, Georgetown, DE 19947; 302-856-1447; Fax: 302-856-5923. Hours: 8AM-4PM (EST). *Civil Actions Under $15,000, Eviction, Small Claims.*

Civil Records: Access: Mail, in person. Both court and visitors may perform in person searches. No search fee. Required to search: name, years to search. Civil cases indexed by defendant, plaintiff. Civil records on index books from 1966 to present. **General Information:** SASE requested. Turnaround time 1-2 days. Copy fee: $10.00 per

page. Certification fee: $10.00. Fee payee: State of Delaware. Personal checks accepted. Prepayment is required.

Seaford Justice of the Peace Court #19 408 Stein Highway, Seaford, DE 19973; 302-629-5433; Fax: 302-628-2049. Hours: 8AM-4PM (EST). *Civil Actions Under $15,000, Eviction, Small Claims.*

Civil Records: Access: In person only. Court does not conduct in person searches; visitors must perform searches for themselves. Search fee: No civil searches performed by court. Required to search: name, years to search. Civil cases indexed by defendant, plaintiff. In person access requires identification. **General Information:** Copy fee: $1.00 per page. Certification fee: $10.00. Fee payee: State of Delaware. Personal checks accepted. Prepayment is required.

Milford Justice of the Peace #5 715 S DuPont Highway, Milford, DE 19963; 302-422-5922. Hours: 8AM-4PM (EST). *Misdemeanor.*

Note: Some old civil cases also located here **Criminal Records:** Access: In person only. Court does not conduct in person searches; visitors must perform searches for themselves. No search fee. Required to search: name, years to search, DOB. Court refers written requests to State Bureau of Investigation in Dover at 302-739-5882. **General Information:** No juvenile records released. Copy fee: $1.00 per page. Certification fee: $7.00. Fee payee: State of Delaware. Personal checks accepted. Credit cards accepted: Visa, Mastercard, Discover. Prepayment is required.

Georgetown Justice of the Peace #3 17 Shortly Rd, Georgetown, DE 19947; 302-856-1445. Hours: 24 hours daily (EST). *Misdemeanor.* **Criminal Records:** Only the court conducts in person searches; visitors may not. Search fee: $7.00 per name. Search fee includes certification. Also must be recent case. Required to search: name, years to search, DOB; also helpful-SSN. **General Information:.** Fee payee: State of Delaware. Prepayment is required.

Justice of the Peace Court 2 31 Route 24, Rehoboth Beach, DE 19971-9738; 302-645-6163; Fax: 302-645-8842. Hours: 8AM-4PM M & Sat; 8AM-Noon T-F (EST). *Misdemeanor.* **Criminal Records:** Both court and visitors may perform in person searches. No search fee. Required to search: name, years to search, DOB. **General Information:.** Fee payee: State of Delaware. Prepayment is required.

Millsboro Justice of the Peace Rt 113, 553 E DuPont Hwy, Millsboro, DE 19966; 302-934-7268; Fax: 302-934-1414. Hours: 8AM-4PM (EST). *Misdemeanor.* **Criminal Records:** Only the court conducts in person searches; visitors may not. No search fee. Required to search: name, years to search, DOB. **General Information:** Turnaround time same day. Prepayment is required.

Seaford Justice of the Peace #4 408 Stein Highway, Seaford, DE 19973; 302-628-2036; Fax: 302-528-2049. Hours: 8AM-4PM M & Sat; 8AM-Noon T-F (EST). *Misdemeanor.* **Criminal Records:** Court does not conduct in person searches; visitors must perform searches for themselves. Search fee: No criminal searches performed by court. Required to search: name, years to search.

ORGANIZATION   Delaware has 3 counties and 3 recording offices. The recording officer is County Recorder in both jurisdictions. Delaware is in the Eastern Time Zone (EST).

REAL ESTATE RECORDS   Counties do **not** perform real estate searches.

UCC RECORDS   Financing statements are filed at the state level, except for real estate related collateral, which are filed only with the County Recorder. All counties perform UCC searches. Copy and certification fees vary.

TAX LIEN RECORDS   Federal tax liens on personal property of businesses are filed with the Secretary of State. Other federal and all state tax liens on personal property are filed with the County Recorder. Copy and certification fees vary.

Kent County

County Recorder of Deeds, County Administration Bldg., Room 218, 414 Federal St., Dover, DE 19901. 302-736-2060. Fax: 302-736-2035.

New Castle County

County Recorder of Deeds, 800 French Street, 4th Floor, Wilmington, DE 19801. 302-571-7550. Fax: 302-571-7708.

www.2isystems.com/newcastle/frmain.htm

Online Access: Real Estate. Records on the City of New Castle Geographic Information System database are available free on the Internet at www.2isystems.com/newcastle/Search2.CFM.

Sussex County

County Recorder of Deeds, P.O. Box 827, Georgetown, DE 19947-0827. 302-855-7785. Fax: 302-855-7787.

You will usually be able to find the city name in the City/County Cross Reference below. In that case, it is a simple matter to determine the county from the cross reference. However, only the official US Postal Service city names are included in this index. There are an additional 40,000 place names that people use in their addresses. Therefore, we have also included a ZIP/City Cross Reference immediately following the City/County Cross Reference.

If you know the ZIP Code but the city name does not appear in the City/County Cross Reference index, look up the ZIP Code in the ZIP/City Cross Reference, find the city name, then look up the city name in the City/County Cross Reference. For example, you want to know the county for an address of Menands, NY 12204. There is no "Menands" in the City/County Cross Reference. The ZIP/City Cross Reference shows that ZIP Codes 12201-12288 are for the city of Albany. Looking back in the City/County Cross Reference, Albany is in Albany County.

City/County Cross Reference

BEAR New Castle
BETHANY BEACH Sussex
BETHEL Sussex
BRIDGEVILLE Sussex
CAMDEN WYOMING Kent
CHESWOLD Kent
CLAYMONT New Castle
CLAYTON (19938) Kent(86), New Castle(14)
DAGSBORO Sussex
DELAWARE CITY New Castle
DELMAR Sussex
DOVER Kent
DOVER AFB Kent
ELLENDALE Sussex
FARMINGTON Kent

FELTON Kent
FENWICK ISLAND Sussex
FRANKFORD Sussex
FREDERICA Kent
GEORGETOWN Sussex
GREENWOOD (19950) Kent(61), Sussex(39)
HARBESON (19951) Sussex(99), Kent(1)
HARRINGTON Kent
HARTLY Kent
HOCKESSIN New Castle
HOUSTON Kent
KENTON Kent
KIRKWOOD New Castle
LAUREL Sussex
LEWES Sussex

LINCOLN Sussex
LITTLE CREEK Kent
MAGNOLIA Kent
MARYDEL Kent
MIDDLETOWN New Castle
MILFORD (19963) Sussex(52), Kent(48)
MILLSBORO Sussex
MILLVILLE Sussex
MILTON Sussex
MONTCHANIN New Castle
NASSAU Sussex
NEW CASTLE New Castle
NEWARK New Castle
OCEAN VIEW Sussex
ODESSA New Castle
PORT PENN New Castle

REHOBOTH BEACH Sussex
ROCKLAND New Castle
SAINT GEORGES New Castle
SEAFORD Sussex
SELBYVILLE Sussex
SMYRNA (19977) Kent(88), New Castle(12)
TOWNSEND New Castle
VIOLA Kent
WILMINGTON New Castle
WINTERTHUR New Castle
WOODSIDE Kent
YORKLYN New Castle

ZIP/City Cross Reference

ZIP Range	City	ZIP Range	City	ZIP Range	City	ZIP Range	City
19701-19701	BEAR	19735-19735	WINTERTHUR	19943-19943	FELTON	19963-19963	MILFORD
19702-19702	NEWARK	19736-19736	YORKLYN	19944-19944	FENWICK ISLAND	19964-19964	MARYDEL
19703-19703	CLAYMONT	19801-19899	WILMINGTON	19945-19945	FRANKFORD	19966-19966	MILLSBORO
19706-19706	DELAWARE CITY	19901-19901	DOVER	19946-19946	FREDERICA	19967-19967	MILLVILLE
19707-19707	HOCKESSIN	19902-19902	DOVER AFB	19947-19947	GEORGETOWN	19968-19968	MILTON
19708-19708	KIRKWOOD	19903-19905	DOVER	19950-19950	GREENWOOD	19969-19969	NASSAU
19709-19709	MIDDLETOWN	19930-19930	BETHANY BEACH	19951-19951	HARBESON	19970-19970	OCEAN VIEW
19710-19710	MONTCHANIN	19931-19931	BETHEL	19952-19952	HARRINGTON	19971-19971	REHOBOTH BEACH
19711-19718	NEWARK	19933-19933	BRIDGEVILLE	19953-19953	HARTLY	19973-19973	SEAFORD
19720-19721	NEW CASTLE	19934-19934	CAMDEN WYOMING	19954-19954	HOUSTON	19975-19975	SELBYVILLE
19725-19726	NEWARK	19936-19936	CHESWOLD	19955-19955	KENTON	19977-19977	SMYRNA
19730-19730	ODESSA	19938-19938	CLAYTON	19956-19956	LAUREL	19979-19979	VIOLA
19731-19731	PORT PENN	19939-19939	DAGSBORO	19958-19958	LEWES	19980-19980	WOODSIDE
19732-19732	ROCKLAND	19940-19940	DELMAR	19960-19960	LINCOLN		
19733-19733	SAINT GEORGES	19941-19941	ELLENDALE	19961-19961	LITTLE CREEK		
19734-19734	TOWNSEND	19942-19942	FARMINGTON	19962-19962	MAGNOLIA		

District of Columbia

General Help Numbers:

Mayor's Office
1 Judiciary Square, 441 4th St NW #1100   202-727-2980
Washington, DC 20001   Fax 202-727-0505
www.washingtondc.gov/mayor/index.htm 8:30AM-5:30PM

District Court Administrator
500 Indiana Ave NW, Room 1500   202-879-1700
Washington, DC 20001   Fax 202-879-4829
www.dcsc.gov   8:30AM-5PM

District Archives
Office of Archives/Public Records   202-727-2052
1300 Naylor Ct NW   Fax 202-727-6076
Washington, DC 20001-4225

District Specifics:

Time Zone: EST

Population: 528,964

Web Site: www.washingtondc.gov

District Agencies

Criminal Records

Metropolitan Police Department, Identification and Records Section, 300 Indiana Ave NW, Rm 3055, Washington, DC 20001; 202-727-4302 (Police), 202-879-1373 (Superior Court), 8AM-5PM.

Note: The Superior Court, Criminal Division, is located at 500 Indiana NW, same zip. They do not charge a fee for a search and they will indicate over the phone if there is an existing record.

Indexing & Storage: Records are available for 10 years. Records at the Superior Court are indexed in microfilm from 1974 on, index cards from 1970 on, in house computer from 1978 on and District Archives from 1962 on. New records are available for inquiry immediately.

Searching: Must have release form from person of record. Neither location will supply records without dispositions. Include the following in your request-full name, date of birth, year. The SSN and case number, if known, are helpful. The following data is not released: pending cases.

Access by: mail, in person.

Fee & Payment: Prepayment required. Fee payee: Metropolitan Police. Personal checks accepted. No credit cards accepted.

Mail search: Turnaround time: 2-4 weeks. Search costs $5.00 per page.

In person search: Search costs $5.00 per page. Records are returned by mail.

Corporation Records
Limited Partnership Records
Limited Liability Company Records

Department of Consumer & Regulatory Affairs, 941 N Capitol St NE, Washington, DC 20002-4259; 202-442-4434, 9AM-3PM.

www.dcra.org

Indexing & Storage: Records are available from the 1850s. There is no trademark or servicemark statute. Records are indexed on inhouse computer.

Searching: Include the following in your request-full name of business. The web site provides download capability of forms.

Access by: mail, phone, in person.

Fee & Payment: Fees: $25.00 per legal document in folder. A document can be 1-100 pages. A Good Standing is $10.00, $20.00 if a not-for-profit. Fee payee: DC Treasury. Prepayment required. Personal checks accepted. Credit cards accepted: Mastercard, Visa, Discover.

Mail search: Turnaround time: 5-10 days.

Phone search: They will release agent's name and address, date of incorporation, and status over the phone at no fee. Names and addresses of Officers and Directors will not be released over the phone.

In person search: You may request information in person. There is no fee unless copies of documents are needed.

Other access: For information concerning lists and bulk file purchases, contact the office of Information Services.

Uniform Commercial Code
Federal Tax Liens
State Tax Liens

UCC Recorder, District of Columbia Recorder of Deeds, 515 D Street NW, Washington, DC 20001; 202-727-7116, 8:15AM-4:45PM.

www.dccfo.com

Note: Records from 1983 forward are located in Room 101, prior records are in Room 304. This agency will not perform name searches (you must do yourself or hire someone), but will provide certificates for a fee.

Indexing & Storage: Records are available from the 1900's. Records are indexed on microfiche.

Searching: Use search request form UCC-11. Local tax liens are called district tax liens. Include the following in your request-debtor name. Searches prior to 1973 need a book and page number. To search records after 1973, you must have an instrument number.

Access by: mail, in person.

Fee & Payment: There is no search fee; however, a certificate of search can be provided for $30.00. Copies cost $2.25 per page. Fee payee: DC Treasurer. Prepayment required. Personal checks accepted. No credit cards accepted.

Mail search: Turnaround time: 2 weeks. No name searches.

In person search: There is a public access terminal available to look up names to find instrument numbers.

Sales Tax Registrations

Office of Tax and Revenue, Audit Division, 941 N. Capitol Street NE, Washington, DC 20002; 202-727-4829, 202-442-6550 (Fax), 8:15AM-4:30PM.

www.dccfo.com/main.shtm

Indexing & Storage: Records are available from the 1980's. Records are computerized since 1990, otherwise are hard copies.

Searching: This agency will only confirm that the business is registered. They will provide no other information. Include the following in your request-business name, federal employer identification number, address. They will also search by tax permit number.

Access by: mail, phone, fax.

Mail search: Turnaround time: 3-5 days. A self addressed stamped envelope is requested. No fee for mail request.

Phone search: No fee for telephone request.

Fax search: Same criteria as mail searches.

Birth Certificates

Department of Health, Vital Records Division, 825 North Capitol St NE, 2st Fl, Washington, DC 20002; 202-442-9009, 202-783-1809 (Vital Chek), 8:30AM-3:30PM.

Indexing & Storage: Records are available from 1874-present. New records are available for

inquiry immediately. Records are indexed on microfiche, inhouse computer.

Searching: Records less than 100 years old are only released to person of record or immediate family members or to legal representative of family. Requester should include a copy of photo ID and daytime phone number. Include the following in your request-full name, date of birth, place of birth, names of parents, name of the hospital.

Access by: mail, phone, fax, in person.

Fee & Payment: The $12.00 fee is for the short form of birth certificate for every consecutive 3 years searched. The archival long form costs $18.00. All copies are certified. Fee payee: DC Treasurer. Prepayment required. Credit cards are only accepted for expedited services. Personal checks accepted. Credit cards accepted: Mastercard, Visa, AmEx, Discover.

Mail search: Turnaround time: 2 weeks. All genealogical searches must be done by mail and cannot be expedited. No self addressed stamped envelope is required.

Phone search: Phone requests are considered expedited and extra fees are involved.

Fax search: See expedited services.

In person search: Searching is available in person.

Expedited service: Expedited service is available for fax searches. Expedited service is available from VitalChek and requires a credit card and additional $8.95 fee for regular mail or $23.95 for overnight delivery after processing.

Death Records

Department of Health, Vital Records Division, 825 North Capitol St NE, 1st Fl, Washington, DC 20002; 202-442-9009, 202-783-1809 (Vital Chek), 8:30AM-3:30PM.

Indexing & Storage: Records are available from 1874 on. New records are available for inquiry immediately. Records are indexed on microfiche, inhouse computer.

Searching: Records up to 50 years old are only released to immediate family members of person of record or to legal representative of family. Requester should include copy of a photo ID and daytime phone number. Include the following in your request-full name, date of death, Social Security Number.

Access by: mail, phone, fax, in person.

Fee & Payment: All copies are certified. Fee payee: DC Treasurer. Prepayment required. Credit cards are only accepted for expedited services. Personal checks accepted. Credit cards accepted: Mastercard, Visa, AmEx, Discover.

Mail search: Turnaround time: 2 weeks. Genealogical searches must be in writing and cannot be expedited. No self addressed stamped envelope is required. Search costs $12.00 for each name in request.

Phone search: See expedited services.

Fax search: See expedited services.

In person search: Search costs $12.00 for each name in request. Turnaround time is 1/2 hour unless extensive search required.

Expedited service: Expedited service is available for fax searches. Expedited service is available from VitalChek, credit card required. Fee is an

additional $8.95 or $23.95 if overnight delivery is required.

Marriage Certificates

Superior Court House, Marriage Bureau, 500 Indiana Ave, NW, Room 4485, Washington, DC 20001; 202-879-4840, 202-879-1280 (Fax), 9AM-4PM.

www.dcbar.org/dcsc/fam.html

Indexing & Storage: Records are available from 1811 on. New records are available for inquiry immediately. Records are indexed on microfilm, books (volumes).

Searching: Include the following in your request-both names, wife's maiden name, date of marriage.

Access by: mail, in person.

Fee & Payment: Search fee is $10.00. Extra copies are $.50 per page. Fee payee: Clerk of the Superior Court. Prepayment required. Only money orders are accepted unless requester is an attorney or a minister/priest/rabbi. No credit cards accepted.

Mail search: Turnaround time: 1-2 weeks. A self addressed stamped envelope is requested.

In person search: Search costs $10.00 per request. Turnaround time is within the same day.

Divorce Records

Superior Court House, Divorce Records, 500 Indiana Ave, NW, Room 4230, Washington, DC 20001; 202-879-1261, 202-879-1572 (Fax), 9AM-4PM.

Indexing & Storage: Records are available from 1956 on. Records prior to 1956 are located at the US District Court at 202-273-0520. New records are available for inquiry immediately. Records are indexed on microfilm, books (volumes).

Searching: Include the following in your request-names of husband and wife, date of divorce, year divorce case began, case number (if known). The following data is not released: sealed records.

Access by: mail, fax, in person.

Fee & Payment: Search fee is $10.00. Certification is $5.00. Copy fee is $.50 per page. Fee payee: Clerk of the Superior Court. Prepayment required. Use either a money order or a cashier's check if ordering by mail. No credit cards accepted.

Mail search: Turnaround time: 3 weeks. Written requests must include requester's phone number so the court can call back with the charge.A self addressed stamped envelope is requested.

Fax search: Requesters must prepay before records are returned.

In person search: Turnaround time is same day for record after 1988. Prior records are kept off site and will take longer to retrieve.

Workers' Compensation Records

Office of Workers' Compensation, PO Box 56098 3rd Floor, Washington, DC 20011 (Courier: 1200 Upshur St NW, Washington, DC 20011); 202-576-6265, 202-541-3595 (Fax), 8:30AM-5PM.

http://does.ci.washington.dc.us

Indexing & Storage: Records are available from June 1982 on. Records are archived after a year

Licenses Searchable Online

Air Conditioning Contractor #16 .... www.state.fl.us/oraweb/owa/www_dbpr2.qry_lic_menu
Alcohol #06 .... www.state.fl.us/oraweb/owa/www_dbpr2.qry_lic_menu
Animal Registration (Livestock Marks & Brands) #03 http://doacs.state.fl.us/~ai/adcpmark.htm
Architect #06 .... www.state.fl.us/oraweb/owa/www_dbpr2.qry_lic_menu
Asbestos Remover/Contractor #16 .... www.state.fl.us/oraweb/owa/www_dbpr2.qry_lic_menu
Asbestos Surveyor Consultant #16 .... www.state.fl.us/oraweb/owa/www_dbpr2.qry_lic_menu
Assisted Living Facilities #26 .... www.floridahealthstat.com/qs/owa/facilitylocator.facllocator
Athletic Agent #06 .... www.state.fl.us/oraweb/owa/www_dbpr2.qry_lic_menu
Attorney #23 .... http://199.44.15.3/Members.nsf/ME+Search?OpenForm
Auction Company #22 .... www.state.fl.us/oraweb/owa/www_dbpr2.qry_lic_menu
Auctioneer #22 .... www.state.fl.us/oraweb/owa/www_dbpr2.qry_lic_menu
Barber/Barber Assistant/Barber Shop #06 .... www.state.fl.us/oraweb/owa/www_dbpr2.qry_lic_menu
Building Code Administrator #06 .... www.state.fl.us/oraweb/owa/www_dbpr2.qry_lic_menu
Building Contractor #16 .... www.state.fl.us/oraweb/owa/www_dbpr2.qry_lic_menu
Building Inspector #06 .... www.state.fl.us/oraweb/owa/www_dbpr2.qry_lic_menu
Care Facilities, Various #26 .... www.floridahealthstat.com/qs/owa/facilitylocator.facllocator
Community Association Manager #06 .... www.state.fl.us/oraweb/owa/www_dbpr2.qry_lic_menu
Construction Businees #16 .... www.state.fl.us/oraweb/owa/www_dbpr2.qry_lic_menu
Cosmetologist, Hair Braider, Nail Tech, Salon #06 .... www.state.fl.us/oraweb/owa/www_dbpr2.qry_lic_menu
Crematory #06 .... www.state.fl.us/oraweb/owa/www_dbpr2.qry_lic_menu
Electrical Contractor #16 .... www.state.fl.us/oraweb/owa/www_dbpr2.qry_lic_menu
Embalmer #06 .... www.state.fl.us/oraweb/owa/www_dbpr2.qry_lic_menu
Firearms Instructor #18 .... http://licgweb.dos.state.fl.us/access/individual.html
Funeral Director, Funeral Home #06 .... www.state.fl.us/oraweb/owa/www_dbpr2.qry_lic_menu
General Contractor #16 .... www.state.fl.us/oraweb/owa/www_dbpr2.qry_lic_menu
Geologist, Geology Business #06 .... www.state.fl.us/oraweb/owa/www_dbpr2.qry_lic_menu
Health Facility #26 .... www.floridahealthstat.com/qs/owa/facilitylocator.facllocator
Home Health Care Agency #26 .... www.floridahealthstat.com/qs/owa/facilitylocator.facllocator
Hospitals #26 .... www.floridahealthstat.com/qs/owa/facilitylocator.facllocator
Insurance Adjuster/Agent/Title Agent #14 .... www.doi.state.fl.us/Consumers/Agents_companies/Agents/index.htm
Interior Designer, Interior Design Business #06 .... www.state.fl.us/oraweb/owa/www_dbpr2.qry_lic_menu
Lab Licenses #26 .... www.floridahealthstat.com/qs/owa/facilitylocator.facllocator
Landscape Architect #06 .... www.state.fl.us/oraweb/owa/www_dbpr2.qry_lic_menu
Livestock Hauler #03 .... http://doacs.state.fl.us/~ai/adcplhp.htm
Lobbyist/Principal #28 .... www.leg.state.fl.us/session/lobbyist.html
Lodging Establishment #06 .... www.state.fl.us/oraweb/owa/www_dbpr2.qry_lic_menu
Mechanical Contractor #16 .... www.state.fl.us/oraweb/owa/www_dbpr2.qry_lic_menu
Nursing Home Administrator #26 .... www.floridahealthstat.com/qs/owa/facilitylocator.facllocator
Optometrist #06 .... www.arbo.org/nodb2000/licsearch.asp
Pesticide Applicator #32 .... http://doacs.state.fl.us/~aes/pstcert.html
Pesticide Dealer #32 .... http://doacs.state.fl.us/~aes/pstcert.html
Plumbing Contractor #16 .... www.state.fl.us/oraweb/owa/www_dbpr2.qry_lic_menu
Pool/Spa Contractor #16 .... www.state.fl.us/oraweb/owa/www_dbpr2.qry_lic_menu
Private Investigator #18 .... http://licgweb.dos.state.fl.us/access/individual.html
Private Investigator Agency #18 .... http://licgweb.dos.state.fl.us/access/agency.html
Public Accountant-CPA #21 .... www.state.fl.us/oraweb/owa/www_dbpr2.qry_lic_menu
Real Estate Appraiser #24 .... www.state.fl.us/oraweb/owa/www_dbpr2.qry_lic_menu
Real Estate Broker #24 .... www.state.fl.us/oraweb/owa/www_dbpr2.qry_lic_menu
Real Estate Salesperson #24 .... www.state.fl.us/oraweb/owa/www_dbpr2.qry_lic_menu
Recovery Agency #18 .... http://licgweb.dos.state.fl.us/access/agency.html
Recovery Agency Manager #18 .... http://licgweb.dos.state.fl.us/access/individual.html
Recovery Agent #18 .... http://licgweb.dos.state.fl.us/access/individual.html
Recovery Agent Intern #18 .... http://licgweb.dos.state.fl.us/access/individual.html
Recovery Agent School #18 .... http://licgweb.dos.state.fl.us/access/agency.html
Recovery School Instructor #18 .... http://licgweb.dos.state.fl.us/access/individual.html
Roofing Contractor #16 .... www.state.fl.us/oraweb/owa/www_dbpr2.qry_lic_menu
Security Officer #18 .... http://licgweb.dos.state.fl.us/access/individual.html
Security Officer School #18 .... http://licgweb.dos.state.fl.us/access/agency.html
Security Officer School Instructor #18 .... http://licgweb.dos.state.fl.us/access/individual.html
Solar Energy Contractor #16 .... www.state.fl.us/oraweb/owa/www_dbpr2.qry_lic_menu
Statewide Firearms License #18 .... http://licgweb.dos.state.fl.us/access/individual.html

Surveyor, Mapping #06 ... www.state.fl.us/oraweb/owa/www_dbpr2.qry_lic_menu
Talent Agency #06 ... www.state.fl.us/oraweb/owa/www_dbpr2.qry_lic_menu
Tobacco Wholesale #06 ... www.state.fl.us/oraweb/owa/www_dbpr2.qry_lic_menu
Underground Utility Contractor #16 ... www.state.fl.us/oraweb/owa/www_dbpr2.qry_lic_menu
Veterinarian, Veterinary Establishment #06 ... www.state.fl.us/oraweb/owa/www_dbpr2.qry_lic_menu

Licensing Quick Finder

Acupuncturist #06 ... 850-487-2253
Adoption Service #11 ... 850-488-8000
Adult & Foster Care #11 ... 850-488-1294
Air Conditioning Contractor #16 ... 904-727-6530
Alarm System Contractor #06 ... 850-455-6685
Alcohol #06 ... 850-487-6793
Ambulance Service #20 ... 850-487-1911
Animal Registration (Livestock Marks & Brands) #03 ... 850-922-0187
Architect #06 ... 850-488-6685
Architect Firm #30 ... 850-488-6685
Asbestos Remover/Contractor #16 ... 850-921-6347
Asbestos Surveyor Consultant #16 ... 850-921-6347
Assisted Living Facilities #26 ... 850-487-2515
Athletic Agent #06 ... 850-488-8500
Athletic Trainer #34 ... 850-487-1111
Attorney #23 ... 850-487-1292
Auction Company #22 ... 850-488-5189
Auctioneer #22 ... 850-488-5189
Auctioneer #06 ... 850-922-5335
Audiologist #09 ... 850-487-2253
Audiologist Assistant #09 ... 850-487-2253
Audiologist Provisional #09 ... 850-487-2253
Automobile Dealer-New Car #13 ... 850-488-4958
Automobile Repossession #18 ... 850-488-5381
Automobile Sales/Dealer #13 ... 850-488-4958
Bail Bondsman #14 ... 850-922-3137
Bank & Trust Company #05 ... 850-410-9805
Barber/Assistant/Shop #06 ... 850-488-6888
Boxer #06 ... 850-488-8500
Broker Dealer Associated Person #05 ... 850-410-9805
Broker Dealer/Branch Office #05 ... 850-410-9805
Building Code Administrator #06 ... 850-922-5335
Building Contractor #16 ... 904-727-6530
Building Inspector #06 ... 850-922-5335
Cemetery Lot Salesperson #17 ... 407-245-0800
Cemetery Lot Salesperson #05 ... 850-410-9898
Charter (Savings & Loan Association) #05 ... 850-410-9805
Child Care Center #10 ... 850-487-3166
Chiropractor #09 ... 850-487-2253
Clinical Laboratory #26 ... 850-487-3063
Clinical Laboratory Director #06 ... 850-488-2224
Clinical Laboratory Supervisor #06 ... 850-488-2224
Clinical Laboratory Technician #06 ... 850-657-1425
Clinical Laboratory Technologist #06 ... 850-488-2224
Commercial Feed Distributor #32 ... 850-488-7626
Commercial Fresh Water Fishing #125 ... 904-488-4066
Commercial Landscape Maint. Pest Management #04 ... 850-921-4177
Community Association Manager #06 ... 850-922-5335
Concealed Weapon License #18 ... 850-488-5381
Construction Businees #16 ... 904-727-6530
Consultant Pharmacist #06 ... 850-488-7176
Cosmetologist, Hair Braider, Nail Specialist, Salon #06 ... 850-488-5702
Credit Union #05 ... 850-410-9805
Crematory #06 ... 850-488-8690
Day Care/Child Care Center/Nursery School #10 ... 850-487-3166
Dentist/Dental Hygienist/Dental Laboratory #06 ... 850-488-6015
Dietitian/Nutrition Counselor #26 ... 850-487-3372
Electrical Contractor #16 ... 850-488-3109
Electrologist #34 ... 850-487-1111
Elevator Certificates of Operation #06 ... 904-488-9097
Embalmer #06 ... 850-488-8690
Emergency Medical Technician #20 ... 850-487-1911
Engineer #33 ... 850-521-0500
Engineering Business #33 ... 850-521-0500
Fertilizer Distributor #32 ... 850-487-2085
Financial Institution #05 ... 850-410-9805
Fire Equipment Dealer/Installer #14 ... 850-922-3172
Firearms Instructor #18 ... 850-488-5381
Food Services Establishment #06 ... 850-922-5335
Foster Family Home #11 ... 850-488-1294
Funeral Director, Funeral Home #06 ... 850-488-8690
General Contractor #16 ... 904-727-6530
Geologist, Geology Business #06 ... 850-488-1105
Guidance Counselor #02 ... 850-488-2317
Health Facility #26 ... 850-487-2527
Hearing Aid Specialist #06 ... 850-487-1813
Home Health Care Agency #26 ... 850-414-6010
Hospitals #26 ... 850-487-2717
Hotel/Restaurant #06 ... 850-488-7891
In Home Family Day Care Center #10 ... 850-487-3166
Insurance Adjuster/Agent #14 ... 904-922-3137
Interior Design Business #30 ... 850-488-6685
Interior Design Individual #30 ... 850-488-6685
Interior Designer, Interior Design Business #06 ... 850-488-6685
International Bank Office #05 ... 850-410-9805
Investment Advisor (Credit Unions) #05 ... 850-410-9805
Investment-Securities Dealer #05 ... 850-410-9805
Kickboxer #06 ... 850-488-8500
Lab Licenses #26 ... 850-487-3109
Laboratory Technician #11 ... 850-488-0595
Landscape Architect #06 ... 850-488-6685
Landscape Architecture, Business & Individual #30 ... 850-488-6685
Liquor Store #06 ... 850-488-8288
Livestock Hauler #03 ... 850-922-0187
Lobbyist/Principal #28 ... 850-922-4990
Lodging Establishment #06 ... 850-922-5335
LP Gas Licensing #32 ... 850-488-3022
Marriage Counselor/Mental Health Counselor #06 ... 850-487-2520
Massage Therapist #06 ... 850-488-6021
Mechanical Contractor #16 ... 904-727-6530
Medical Doctor/Surgeon #06 ... 850-488-0595
Midwife #06 ... 850-488-0595
Milk Hauler/Tester #31 ... 850-487-1450
Mobile Home Dealer/Broker #13 ... 850-488-4958
Mobile Home Manufacturer #13 ... 850-488-4958
Money Transmitter #05 ... 850-410-9805
Mortgage Broker #05 ... 850-410-9805
Motel/Restaurant #07 ... 904-488-1133
Nail Specialist #06 ... 850-922-5335
Naturopath #34 ... 850-487-1111
Notary Public #19 ... 850-488-7521
Nuclear Pharmacist #06 ... 850-488-7176
Nurse #06 ... 850-858-6940
Nursing Home Adminstrator #26 ... 850-488-6061
Occupational Therapist/Assistant #26 ... 850-487-3372
Optician #06 ... 850-487-2397
Optometrist #06 ... 850-488-7484
Organic Certifying Agent #32 ... 850-488-3863
Orphanage #11 ... 850-488-1294
Osteopathic Physician #26 ... 850-414-7209
Paramedic #20 ... 850-487-1911
Pari-Mutuel Wagering #07 ... 850-488-9161
Pest Control Operator #04 ... 850-921-4177
Pesticide Applicator (Commericial, Private, Public) #32 ... 850-488-6838
Pesticide Dealer #32 ... 850-488-6838
Pet Shop #25 ... 904-488-6253
Pharmacist/Pharmacy #06 ... 850-488-7176
Pharmacy #06 ... 850-488-7176
PHPC Public Health Pest Control #04 ... 850-921-4177
Physical Therapist/Assistant #26 ... 850-487-3372
Physician Asssitant #34 ... 850-487-1111
Pilot #06 ... 850-488-0698
Plumbing Contractor #16 ... 904-727-6530
Podiatrist #06 ... 850-487-1814
Pool/Spa Contractor #16 ... 904-727-6530
Private Investigator #18 ... 850-488-5381
Private Investigator Agency #18 ... 850-488-5381
Psychologist/School #06 ... 850-922-6728
Public Accountant-CPA #21 ... 352-955-2165
Racing-Dog/Horse #06 ... 850-488-9130
Radiology Technician/X-Ray Technologist #11 ... 850-487-3451
Real Estate Appraiser #24 ... 407-245-0800
Real Estate Broker #24 ... 407-245-0800
Real Estate Salesperson #24 ... 407-245-0800
Recovery Agency #18 ... 850-488-5381
Recovery Agency Manager #18 ... 850-488-5381
Recovery Agent #18 ... 850-488-5381
Recovery Agent Intern #18 ... 850-488-5381
Recovery Agent School #18 ... 850-488-5381
Recovery School Instructor #18 ... 850-488-5381
Recreational Vehicle Dealer #13 ... 850-488-4958
Respiratory Technician/Therapist #26 ... 850-487-3372
Roofing Contractor #16 ... 904-727-6530
School Administrator/Supervisor #02 ... 850-488-2317
School Educational Media Specialist #02 850-487-4822
School Principal #02 ... 850-488-2317
Securities Registration #05 ... 850-410-9805
Security Officer #18 ... 850-488-5381
Security Officer School #18 ... 850-488-5381
Security Officer School Instructor #18 ... 850-488-5381
Seed Dealer #32 ... 850-488-3863
Shorthand Reporter #29 ... 904-488-8628
Social Worker #06 ... 850-487-2520
Solar Energy Contractor #16 ... 904-727-6530
Solid Waste Facility Operator #08 ... 850-922-6104
Special ID For Fumigation Performance #04 ... 850-921-4177
Speech/Language Pathologist Assistant #06 ... 850-487-3041
Speech/Language Provisional Pathologist #06 ... 850-487-3041
Speech-Language Pathologist #06 ... 850-487-3041
Statewide Firearms License #18 ... 850-488-5381
Structural Pest Control #04 ... 850-921-4177
Surveyor, Mapping #06 ... 850-413-7480
Sweepstakes Operator (Registration) #18 ... 850-488-5381
Talent Agency #06 ... 850-922-5335
Teacher #02 ... 850-487-4822
Timeshare Agent #17 ... 407-245-0800
Timeshare Agent #05 ... 850-410-9805
Tobacco Wholesale #06 ... 850-487-6793
Underground Utility Contractor #16 ... 904-727-6530
Veterinarian, Veterinary Establishment #06 ... 850-487-1820
Yacht & Ship Broker/Salesman #06 ... 850-488-1636
Zoo #25 ... 904-488-6253

Licensing Agency Information

02 Education Center, Bureau of Teacher Certification, 325 W Gaines, #701, Tallahassee, FL 32399; 850-488-3352.

03 Department of Agriculture & Consumer Services, 407 S Calhoun, Mayo Bldg, Rm 332, Tallahassee, FL 32399-0800; 850-922-0187, Fax: 850-487-3641.

http://doacs.state.fl.us/~ai/aiindex.htm

04 Department of Agriculture & Consumer Services, Bureau of Entomology & Pest Control, 1203 Government Square Blvd #300, Tallahassee, FL 32301; 850-921-4177, Fax: 850-413-7044.

www.floridatermitehelp.org

05 Department of Banking & Finance, 101 E Gaines St, Fletcher Bldg #636, Tallahassee, FL 32399-0350; 850-410-9805, Fax: 850-410-9914.

06 Department of Business & Professional Regulation, 1940 N Monroe St #300, Tallahassee, FL 32399; 850-922-5335, Fax: 850-488-1514.

www.state.fl.us/dbpr

07 Department of Business Regulation, 1940 N Monroe, Tallahassee, FL 32399; 850-488-9161, Fax: 850-488-0550.

08 Department of Environmental Regulation, Division of Waste Management, 2600 Blair Stone Rd, Tallahassee, FL 32399-2400; 850-922-6104.

09 Department of Health, 2020 Capitol Circle SE Bin C01, Tallahassee, FL 32399-3257; 850-488-0595, Fax: 850-921-5389.

www.doh.state.fl.us

10 Department of Health, 3401 W Tharp, Tallahassee, FL 32303; 850-487-1111, Fax: 850-487-7956.

11 Department of Health & Rehabilitative Services, 1317 Winewood Blvd, Tallahassee, FL 32399-0700; 850-487-1111, Fax: 850-487-0688.

13 Department of Highway Safety & Motor Vehicles, Bureau of Motor Homes & Recreational Vehicles, 2900 Apalachee Pkwy MS66, Tallahassee, FL 32399-0600; 850-488-4958, Fax: 850-922-9840.

www.hsmv.state.fl.us

14 Department of Insurance & Treasurer, Bureau of Agents & Agency Licensing, 200 E Gaines St, Larsen Bldg, Tallahassee, FL 32399; 850-922-3137.

www.doi.state.fl.us

16 Department of Professional Regulation, Construction Industry Licensing Board, 7960 Arlington Expwy #300, Jacksonville, FL 32211-7467; 904-727-3689, Fax: 904-727-3677.
www.state.fl.us/dbpr
Direct URL to search licenses: www.state.fl.us/oraweb/owa/www_dbpr2.qry_lic_menu You can search online using personal name, business name, and license number.

18 Department of State, Division of Licensing, 2520 N Monroe St, Tallahassee, FL 32303; 850-488-5381, Fax: 850-487-7950.

http://licgweb.dos.state.fl.us

19 Department of State, Bureau of Notaries Public, The Capitol Bldg, Rm 1801, Tallahassee, FL 32399-0250; 850-488-7521, Fax: 850-488-1768.

20 Emergency Medical Services, 2002D Old St Augustine Rd, Tallahassee, FL 32301-4881; 850-487-1911, Fax: 850-488-2512.
www.doh.state.fl.us/ems
Direct URL to search licenses: www.doh.state.fl.us/ems You can search online using certification number, name

21 Department of Business & Professional Regulation, Board of Accounting, 2610 NW 43rd St, #1A, Gainesville, FL 32606; 352-955-2165, Fax: 352-955-2164.
Direct URL to search licenses: www.state.fl.us/oraweb/owa/www_dbpr2.qry_lic_menu

22 Department of Business & Professional Regulation, Board of Auctioneers, 1940 N Monroe St, Tallahassee, FL 32399; 850-488-5189.
www.state.fl.us/dbpr/prof/auc_index.shtml
Direct URL to search licenses: www.state.fl.us/oraweb/owa/www_dbpr2.qry_lic_menu You can search online using occupation, then name

23 Board of Bar Examiners, 1891 Elder Ct, Tallahassee, FL 32399-1750; 850-487-1292.

www.flabar.org

24 Department of Business & Professional Regulation, Real Estate Commission, 400 W Robinson, #N308, Orlando, FL 32801; 407-245-0800.
www.state.fl.us/dbpr
Direct URL to search licenses: www.state.fl.us/oraweb/owa/www_dbpr2.qry_lic_menu You can search online using personal name, business name, and license number.

25 Game & Fresh Water Fish Commission, 620 S Meridian St, Tallahassee, FL 32399-1600; 850-488-3641, Fax: 850-414-2628.

www.state.fl.us/ugsd_html/access.html

26 Facilities Licensing, Agency for Health Care Administration (AHCA), 2727 Mahan Dr, Tallahassee, FL 32308-5401; 850-487-2528, Fax: 850-410-1512.
www.floridahealthstat.com
Direct URL to search licenses: www.floridahealthstat.com/qs/owa/facilitylocator.facllocator You can search online using type and facility name, city, or county

28 Lobbyist Registration, 111 W Madison St Rm G-68, Tallahassee, FL 32399-1425; 850-922-4990.

Direct URL to search licenses: www.leg.state.fl.us

29 Supreme Court of Florida, 500 N Duvall, Tallahassee, FL 32399-1900; 850-488-8628.

30 Department of Professional Regulation, Bureau of Architects, Interior Designers & Landscape Architects, 1940 N Monroe St, Tallahassee, FL 32399-0751; 850-488-6685, Fax: 850-992-2918.
Direct URL to search licenses: www.state.fl.us/dbpr

31 Department of Agriculture & Consumer Services, Division of Dairy Industry, 3125 Conner Blvd, Mail Stop C-27, Tallahassee, FL 32399-1650; 850-487-1450, Fax: 850-922-9444.

http://doacs.state.fl.us/~dairy/index.html

32 Bureau of Compliance Monitoring, 3125 Conner Blvd, Tallahassee, FL 32399-1650; 850-488-3022, Fax: 850-488-8498.

http://doacs.state.fl.us/license.html

33 Board of Professional Engineers, 1208 Hays Street, Tallahassee, FL 32301; 850-521-0500, Fax: 850-521-0521.
www.fbpe.org
Direct URL to search licenses: www.fbpe.org/pesearch/Pesearch.htm You can search online using name or PE number.

34 Department of Health, Division of Medical Quality Assurance, 1940 N Monroe St, Tallahassee, FL 32399; 850-487-1111.

The following list indicates the district and division name for each county in the state. If the district or division name of the bankruptcy court is different from the civil/criminal court, it appears in parentheses.

County/Court Cross Reference

County	District	Division
Alachua	Northern	Gainesville (Tallahassee)
Baker	Middle	Jacksonville
Bay	Northern	Panama City (Tallahassee)
Bradford	Middle	Jacksonville
Brevard	Middle	Orlando
Broward	Southern	Fort Lauderdale (Miami)
Calhoun	Northern	Panama City (Tallahassee)
Charlotte	Middle	Fort Myers (Tampa)
Citrus	Middle	Ocala (Jacksonville)
Clay	Middle	Jacksonville
Collier	Middle	Fort Myers (Tampa)
Columbia	Middle	Jacksonville
Dade	Southern	Miami
De Soto	Middle	Fort Myers (Tampa)
Dixie	Northern	Gainesville (Tallahassee)
Duval	Middle	Jacksonville
Escambia	Northern	Pensacola
Flagler	Middle	Jacksonville
Franklin	Northern	Tallahassee
Gadsden	Northern	Tallahassee
Gilchrist	Northern	Gainesville (Tallahassee)
Glades	Middle	Fort Myers (Tampa)
Gulf	Northern	Panama City (Tallahassee)
Hamilton	Middle	Jacksonville
Hardee	Middle	Tampa
Hendry	Middle	Fort Myers (Tampa)
Hernando	Middle	Tampa
Highlands	Southern	Fort Pierce (Miami)
Hillsborough	Middle	Tampa
Holmes	Northern	Panama City (Tallahassee)
Indian River	Southern	Fort Pierce (Miami)
Jackson	Northern	Panama City (Tallahassee)
Jefferson	Northern	Tallahassee
Lafayette	Northern	Gainesville (Tallahassee)
Lake	Middle	Ocala (Orlando)
Lee	Middle	Fort Myers (Tampa)
Leon	Northern	Tallahassee
Levy	Northern	Gainesville (Tallahassee)
Liberty	Northern	Tallahassee
Madison	Northern	Tallahassee
Manatee	Middle	Tampa
Marion	Middle	Ocala (Jacksonville)
Martin	Southern	Fort Pierce (Miami)
Monroe	Southern	Key West (Miami)
Nassau	Middle	Jacksonville
Okaloosa	Northern	Pensacola
Okeechobee	Southern	Fort Pierce (Miami)
Orange	Middle	Orlando
Osceola	Middle	Orlando
Palm Beach	Southern	W. Palm Beach (Miami)
Pasco	Middle	Tampa
Pinellas	Middle	Tampa
Polk	Middle	Tampa
Putnam	Middle	Jacksonville
Santa Rosa	Northern	Pensacola
Sarasota	Middle	Tampa
Seminole	Middle	Orlando
St. Johns	Middle	Jacksonville
St. Lucie	Southern	Fort Pierce (Miami)
Sumter	Middle	Ocala (Jacksonville)
Suwannee	Middle	Jacksonville
Taylor	Northern	Tallahassee
Union	Middle	Jacksonville
Volusia	Middle	Orlando (Jacksonville)
Wakulla	Northern	Tallahassee
Walton	Northern	Pensacola
Washington	Northern	Panama City (Tallahassee)

US District Court

Middle District of Florida

Fort Myers Division 2110 First St, Room 2-194, Fort Myers, FL 33901, 941-461-2000.

www.flmd.uscourts.gov

Counties: Charlotte, Collier, De Soto, Glades, Hendry, Lee.

Indexing & Storage: Cases are indexed by defendant and plaintiff as well as by case number. New cases are available in the index immediately after filing date. The civil case index is computerized, but the criminal index is not. A card index is maintained. Records are also indexed on microfiche. Open records are located at this court.

Fee & Payment: The fee is $15.00 per item (one party name or case number). Payment may be made by money order, cashier check, personal check. Prepayment is required. Payee: Clerk, US District Court. Certification fee: $5.00 per document. Copy fee: $.50 per page. You are allowed to make your own copies. These copies cost Not Applicable per page.

Phone Search: Docket information is available by phone. An automated voice case information service (VCIS) is not available.

Mail Search: Always enclose a stamped self addressed envelope.

In Person Search: In person searching is available.

PACER: Sign-up number is 800-676-6856. Access fee is $.60 per minute. Toll-free access: 888-815-8701. Local access: 813-301-5820. Case records are available back to 1989-90. Records are purged three years after case closed. New records are available online after 1 day.

Jacksonville Division PO Box 53558, Jacksonville, FL 32201 (Courier Address: Suite 110, 311 W Monroe St, Jacksonville, FL 32202), 904-549-1900.

www.flmd.uscourts.gov

Counties: Baker, Bradford, Clay, Columbia, Duval, Flagler, Hamilton, Nassau, Putnam, St. Johns, Suwannee, Union.

Indexing & Storage: Cases are indexed by defendant and plaintiff as well as by case number. New cases are available in the index 1 day after filing date. A computer index is maintained. Open records are located at this court.

Fee & Payment: The fee is $15.00 per item (one party name or case number). Payment may be made by money order, cashier check, personal check. Prepayment is required. Payee: Clerk, US District Court. Certification fee: $5.00 per document. Copy fee: $.50 per page. You are allowed to make your own copies. These copies cost $.50 per page.

Phone Search: Searching is not available by phone.

Mail Search: Always enclose a stamped self addressed envelope.

In Person Search: In person searching is available.

PACER: Sign-up number is 800-676-6856. Access fee is $.60 per minute. Toll-free access: 888-815-8701. Local access: 813-301-5820. Case records are available back to 1989-90. Records are purged three years after case closed. New records are available online after 1 day.

Ocala Division c/o Jacksonville Division, PO Box 53558, Jacksonville, FL 32201 (Courier Address: 311 W Monroe St, Suite 110, Jacksonville, FL 32202), 904-232-2854.

www.flmd.uscourts.gov

Counties: Citrus, Lake, Marion, Sumter.

Indexing & Storage: Cases are indexed by as well as by case number. New cases are available in the index after filing date. Open records are located at the Division.

Fee & Payment: The fee is $15.00 per item (one party name or case number). Payment may be made by money order, cashier check. Business checks are not accepted. Personal checks are not accepted.

Phone Search: An automated voice case information service (VCIS) is not available.

In Person Search: In person searching is available.

PACER: Sign-up number is 800-676-6856. Access fee is $.60 per minute. Toll-free access: 888-815-8701. Local access: 813-301-5820. Case records are available back to 1989-90. Records are purged three years after case closed. New records are available online after 1 day.

Orlando Division Room 218, 80 North Hughey Ave, Orlando, FL 32801, 407-835-4200.

www.flmd.uscourts.gov

Counties: Brevard, Orange, Osceola, Seminole, Volusia.

Indexing & Storage: Cases are indexed by defendant and plaintiff as well as by case number. New cases are available in the index immediately after filing date. A computer index is maintained. Records are stored by case number according to year closed. Open records are located at this court.

Fee & Payment: The fee is $15.00 per item (one party name or case number). Payment may be made by money order, cashier check, personal check. The court will not bill. All checks, except foreign, are accepted. Payee: Clerk, US District Court. Certification fee: $5.00 per document. Copy fee: $.50 per page. You are allowed to make your own copies. These copies cost $.50 per page.

Phone Search: Docket information is available by phone. An automated voice case information service (VCIS) is not available.

Mail Search: Always enclose a stamped self addressed envelope.

In Person Search: In person searching is available.

PACER: Sign-up number is 800-676-6856. Access fee is $.60 per minute. Toll-free access: 888-815-8701. Local access: 813-301-5820. Case records are available back to 1989-90. Records are purged three years after case closed. New records are available online after 1 day.

Tampa Division Office of the clerk, 801 N Florida Ave #223, Tampa, FL 33602-4500, 813-301-5400.

www.flmd.uscourts.gov

Counties: Hardee, Hernando, Hillsborough, Manatee, Pasco, Pinellas, Polk, Sarasota.

Indexing & Storage: Cases are indexed by defendant and plaintiff as well as by case number. New cases are available in the index 1 day after

filing date. A computer index is maintained. Open records are located at this court.

Fee & Payment: The fee is $15.00 per item (one party name or case number). Payment may be made by money order, cashier check, personal check. Prepayment is required. Payee: Clerk, US District Court. Certification fee: $5.00 per document. Copy fee: $.50 per page. You are allowed to make your own copies. These copies cost $.25 per page.

Phone Search: Only docket information is available by phone. An automated voice case information service (VCIS) is not available.

Mail Search: Always enclose a stamped self addressed envelope.

In Person Search: In person searching is available.

PACER: Sign-up number is 800-676-6856. Access fee is $.60 per minute. Toll-free access: 888-815-8701. Local access: 813-301-5820. Case records are available back to 1989-90. Records are purged three years after case closed. New records are available online after 1 day.

US Bankruptcy Court
Middle District of Florida

Jacksonville Division PO Box 559, Jacksonville, FL 32201 (Courier Address: Room 206, 311 W Monroe, Jacksonville, FL 32202), 904-232-2852.

www.flmb.uscourts.gov

Counties: Baker, Bradford, Citrus, Clay, Columbia, Duval, Flagler, Hamilton, Marion, Nassau, Putnam, St. Johns, Sumter, Suwannee, Union, Volusia.

Indexing & Storage: Cases are indexed by debtor as well as by case number. New cases are available in the index immediately after filing date. A computer index is maintained. Open records are located at this court. This court has no specific time that they send closed records to the Atlanta Federal Records Center.

Fee & Payment: The fee is $15.00 per item (one party name or case number). Payment may be made by money order, cashier check, business check. Personal checks are not accepted. Prepayment is required. Pacific Photo is the contracted search and copy center for this district. They say it is fine to fax orders to them at 904-355-1062. Payee: Clerk, US Bankruptcy Court. Certification fee: $5.00 per document. Copy fee: $.50 per page.

Phone Search: An automated voice case information service (VCIS) is available.

Mail Search: A stamped self addressed envelope is not required.

In Person Search: In person searching is available.

PACER: Sign-up number is 800-676-6856. Access fee is $.60 per minute. You can search PACER via the Internet. Visit www.flmb.uscourts.gov/cgi/foxweb.dll/usbc/webpacer. Use of PC Anywhere V4.0 recommended. Case records are available back to 1981. Records are purged every year. New civil records are available online after 1 week. PACER is available on the Internet at www.flmb.uscourts.gov/cgi/foxweb.dll/usbc/webpacer.

Orlando Division Suite 950, 135 W Central Blvd, Orlando, FL 32801, 407-648-6365.

www.flmb.uscourts.gov

Counties: Brevard, Lake, Orange, Osceola, Seminole.

Indexing & Storage: Cases are indexed by debtor and creditors as well as by case number. New cases are available in the index 1-2 days after filing date. A computer index is maintained. Open records are located at this court. This court has no specific time that they send closed records to the Atlanta Federal Records Center.

Fee & Payment: The fee is $15.00 per item (one party name or case number). Payment may be made by money order, cashier check, business check. Personal checks are not accepted. Prepayment is required. Pacific Photo is the contracted search and copy center for this district. Orders may be faxed to them. Payee: Clerk, US Bankruptcy Court. Certification fee: $5.00 per document. Copy fee: $.50 per page.

Phone Search: An automated voice case information service (VCIS) is available.

Mail Search: Always enclose a stamped self addressed envelope.

In Person Search: In person searching is available.

PACER: Sign-up number is 800-676-6856. Access fee is $.60 per minute. Use of PC Anywhere V4.0 recommended. Case records are available back to 1986. Records are never purged. New civil records are available online after 1 day. PACER is available on the Internet at www.flmb.uscourts.gov/cgi/foxweb.dll/usbc/webpacer.

Tampa Division 801 N Florida Ave #727, Tampa, FL 33602, 813-301-5065.

www.flmb.uscourts.gov

Counties: Charlotte, Collier, De Soto, Glades, Hardee, Hendry, Hernando, Hillsborough, Lee, Manatee, Pasco, Pinellas, Polk, Sarasota.

Indexing & Storage: Cases are indexed by debtor as well as by case number. New cases are available in the index immediately after filing date. A computer index is maintained. Open records are located at this court. This court has no specific time that they send closed records to the Atlanta Federal Records Center.

Fee & Payment: The fee is $15.00 per item (one party name or case number). Payment may be made by money order, cashier check, business check. Personal checks are not accepted. Prepayment is required. Pacific Photo is the contracted search and copy center for this district. Payee: Clerk, US Bankruptcy Court. Certification fee: $5.00 per document. Copy fee: $.50 per page.

Phone Search: Searching is not available by phone.

Mail Search: Always enclose a stamped self addressed envelope.

In Person Search: In person searching is available.

PACER: Sign-up number is 800-676-6856. Access fee is $.60 per minute. Use of PC Anywhere V4.0 recommended. Case records are available back to 1992. Records are purged every six months. New civil records are available online after 1 day. PACER is available on the Internet at www.flmb.uscourts.gov/cgi/foxweb.dll/usbc/webpacer.

US District Court

Northern District of Florida

Gainesville Division 401 SE First Ave, Room 243, Gainesville, FL 32601, 352-380-2400, Fax: 352-380-2424.

www.flnd.uscourts.gov

Counties: Alachua, Dixie, Gilchrist, Lafayette, Levy. Records for cases prior to July 1996 are maintained at the Tallahassee Division.

Indexing & Storage: Cases are indexed by defendant and plaintiff as well as by case number. New cases are available in the index within 3 days after filing date. Both computer and card indexes are maintained. Open records are located at this court.

Fee & Payment: The fee is $15.00 per item (one party name or case number). Payment may be made by money order, cashier check, personal check. Prepayment is required. Payee: Clerk, US District Court. Certification fee: $5.00 per document. Copy fee: $.50 per page.

Phone Search: Only 1-3 names may be searched over the phone, and only docket information will be released. An automated voice case information service (VCIS) is not available.

Mail Search: Always enclose a stamped self addressed envelope.

In Person Search: In person searching is available.

PACER: Sign-up number is 800-676-6856. Access fee is $.60 per minute. Toll-free access: 800-844-0479. Local access: 850-942-8898. Case records are available back to 1992. Records are purged three years after case closed. New records are available online after 2 days.

Panama City Division c/o Pensacola Division, 1 N Palafox St, #226, Pensacola, FL 32501, 850-435-8440, Fax: 850-433-5972.

www.flnd.uscourts.gov

Counties: Bay, Calhoun, Gulf, Holmes, Jackson, Washington.

Indexing & Storage: Cases are indexed by as well as by case number. New cases are available in the index after filing date. Open records are located at the Division.

Fee & Payment: The fee is no charge per item (one party name or case number). Payment may be made by money order, cashier check. Business checks are not accepted. Personal checks are not accepted.

Phone Search: An automated voice case information service (VCIS) is not available.

Mail Search: Always enclose a stamped self addressed envelope.

In Person Search: In person searching is available.

PACER: Sign-up number is 800-676-6856. Access fee is $.60 per minute. Toll-free access: 800-844-0479. Local access: 850-942-8898. Case records are available back to 1992. Records are purged three years after case closed. New records are available online after 2 days.

Pensacola Division US Courthouse, 1 N Palafox St, #226, Pensacola, FL 32501, 850-435-8440, Fax: 850-433-5972.

www.flnd.uscourts.gov

Counties: Escambia, Okaloosa, Santa Rosa, Walton.

Indexing & Storage: Cases are indexed by defendant and plaintiff as well as by case number. New cases are available in the index 2-3 days after filing date. Both computer and card indexes are maintained. Records are indexed on computer as of August 1992. Open records are located at this court. District wide searches are available for information from August 1992 from this division. This division maintains records for the Panama City office.

Fee & Payment: The fee is $15.00 per item (one party name or case number). Payment may be made by money order, cashier check, personal check. Prepayment is required. Payee: Clerk, US District Court. Certification fee: $5.00 per document. Copy fee: $.50 per page.

Phone Search: Only basic information is released over the phone. They will not release all docket information over the phone. An automated voice case information service (VCIS) is not available.

Mail Search: Always enclose a stamped self addressed envelope.

In Person Search: In person searching is available.

PACER: Sign-up number is 800-676-6856. Access fee is $.60 per minute. Toll-free access: 800-844-0479. Local access: 850-942-8898. Case records are available back to 1992. Records are purged three years after case closed. New records are available online after 2 days.

Tallahassee Division Suite 122, 110 E Park Ave, Tallahassee, FL 32301, 850-942-8826, Fax: 850-942-8830.

www.flnd.uscourts.gov

Counties: Franklin, Gadsden, Jefferson, Leon, Liberty, Madison, Taylor, Wakulla.

Indexing & Storage: Cases are indexed by defendant and plaintiff as well as by case number. New cases are available in the index immediately after filing date. A computer index is maintained. Records are also indexed by year closed. Open records are located at this court.

Fee & Payment: The fee is $15.00 per item (one party name or case number). Payment may be made by money order, cashier check, personal check. Prepayment required. Payee: Clerk, US District Court. Certification fee: $5.00 per document. Copy fee: $.50 per page.

Phone Search: Basic information about a case requested by name (case number) or by case number (names of parties or their attorneys, date of complaint, or general status) is available by telephone at no charge. An automated voice case information service (VCIS) is not available.

Mail Search: A stamped self addressed envelope is not required.

In Person Search: In person searching is available.

PACER: Sign-up number is 800-676-6856. Access fee is $.60 per minute. Toll-free access: 800-844-0479. Local access: 850-942-8898. Case records are available back to 1992. Records are purged three years after case closed. New records are available online after 2 days.

US Bankruptcy Court

Northern District of Florida

Pensacola Division Suite 700, 220 W Garden St, Pensacola, FL 32501, 850-435-8475.

Counties: Escambia, Okaloosa, Santa Rosa, Walton.

Indexing & Storage: Cases are indexed by debtor as well as by case number. New cases are available in the index 5-7 days after filing date. Both computer and card indexes are maintained. Open records are located at this court.

Fee & Payment: The fee is $15.00 per item (one party name or case number). Payment may be made by money order, cashier check, business check. Personal checks are not accepted. Prepayment is required. Payee: Clerk, US Bankruptcy Court. Certification fee: $5.00 per document. Copy fee: $.50 per page.

Phone Search: Searching is not available by phone.

Mail Search: A stamped self addressed envelope is not required.

In Person Search: In person searching is available.

PACER: Sign-up number is 904-435-8475. Access fee is $.60 per minute. Toll-free access: 888-765-1751. Local access: 904-444-0189. Case records are available back to September 1985. Records are purged when cases are closed. New civil records are available online after 2 days.

Tallahassee Division Room 3120, 227 N Bronough St, Tallahassee, FL 32301-1378, 850-942-8933.

Counties: Alachua, Bay, Calhoun, Dixie, Franklin, Gadsden, Gilchrist, Gulf, Holmes, Jackson, Jefferson, Lafayette, Leon, Levy, Liberty, Madison, Taylor, Wakulla, Washington.

Indexing & Storage: Cases are indexed by debtor as well as by case number. New cases are available in the index 2-3 days after filing date. A computer index is maintained. Open records are located at this court.

Fee & Payment: The fee is $15.00 per item (one party name or case number). Payment may be made by money order, cashier check, business check. Personal checks are not accepted. Prepayment is required. Payee: Clerk, US Bankruptcy Court. Certification fee: $5.00 per document. Copy fee: $.50 per page.

Phone Search: Only docket information is available by phone.

Mail Search: Always enclose a stamped self addressed envelope.

In Person Search: In person searching is available.

PACER: Sign-up number is 800-676-6856. Access fee is $.60 per minute. Toll-free access: 888-765-1752. Local access: 904-942-8815. Use of PC Anywhere V4.0 recommended. Case records are available back to September 23, 1985. Records are purged every six months. New civil records are available online after 1 day.

US District Court

Southern District of Florida

Fort Lauderdale Division 299 E Broward Blvd, Fort Lauderdale, FL 33301, 954-769-5400.

www.netside.net/usdcfls

Counties: Broward.

Indexing & Storage: Cases are indexed by defendant and plaintiff as well as by case number. New cases are available in the index immediately after filing date. The full name of any party of the case, case number or case type is required to search for records. Both computer and card indexes are maintained. Civil cases are in the computer from August 1990 to present. Criminal cases are in the computer from January 1992. Cases from 1983 are on microfiche. Cases prior to 1983 are on microfilm. Open records are located at this court. Records that are more than 5 years old are, at the discretion of the clerk, sent to the Atlanta Federal Records Center. Call records department to get location of records.

Fee & Payment: The fee is $15.00 per item (one party name or case number). Payment may be made by money order, cashier check, business check, Visa, Mastercard. Personal checks are not accepted. Prepayment is required. Payee: U.S. Courts. Certification fee: $5.00 per document. Copy fee: $.50 per page. You are allowed to make your own copies. These copies cost $.25 per page. The copy service (954-832-0111) will pull records and make copies for $.25 per copy. Copy machines are also available in the lobby.

Phone Search: Only docket information is available by phone.

Mail Search: Always enclose a stamped self addressed envelope.

In Person Search: In person searching is available.

PACER: Sign-up number is 800-676-6856. Access fee is $.60 per minute. Toll-free access: 800-372-8846. Local access: 305-536-7265. Case records are available back to August 1990. Records are purged three years after case closed. New records are available online after 1 day. PACER is available on the Internet at http://pacer.flsd.uscourts.gov.

Fort Pierce Division c/o Miami Division, Room 150, 301 N Miami Ave, Miami, FL 33128, 305-523-5210.

www.netside.net/usdcfls

Counties: Highlands, Indian River, Martin, Okeechobee, St. Lucie.

Indexing & Storage: Cases are indexed by defendant and plaintiff as well as by case number. New cases are available in the index immediately after filing date. A computer index is maintained. Open records are located at the Division. Records are transferred to the Federal Records Center any time after 5 years at the discretion of the clerk.

Fee & Payment: The fee is $15.00 per item (one party name or case number). Payment may be made by money order, cashier check, personal check. Prepayment is required. Payee: US Court. Certification fee: $5.00 per document. Copy fee: $.50 per page.

Phone Search: Docket information is available by phone. An automated voice case information service (VCIS) is not available.

Mail Search: Always enclose a stamped self addressed envelope.

In Person Search: In person searching is available.

PACER: Sign-up number is 800-676-6856. Access fee is $.60 per minute. Toll-free access: 800-372-8846. Local access: 305-536-7265. Case records are available back to August 1990. Records are purged three years after case closed. New records are available online after 1 day. PACER is available on the Internet at http://pacer.flsd.uscourts.gov.

Key West Division c/o Miami Division, Room 150, 301 N Miami Ave, Miami, FL 33128-7788, 305-523-5100.

www.netside.net/usdcfls

Counties: Monroe.

Indexing & Storage: Cases are indexed by defendant and plaintiff as well as by case number. New cases are available in the index immediately after filing date. The full name of either party in the case, case number or case type is required to search for records. A computer index is maintained. Open records are located at the Division. Records that are more than 5 years old are, at the discretion of the clerk, are sent to the Atlanta Federal Records Center. Call records department to get location of records.

Fee & Payment: The fee is $15.00 per item (one party name or case number). Payment may be made by money order, cashier check, personal check. Prepayment is required. Payee: U.S. Courts. Certification fee: $5.00 per document. Copy fee: $.50 per page. You are allowed to make your own copies. These copies cost $.50 per page. The copy service will pull records and make copies for $.04 per copy. Copy machines are also available in the lobby.

Phone Search: Searching is not available by phone.

Mail Search: Always enclose a stamped self addressed envelope.

In Person Search: In person searching is available.

PACER: Sign-up number is 800-676-6856. Access fee is $.60 per minute. Toll-free access: 800-372-8846. Local access: 305-536-7265. Case records are available back to August 1990. Records are purged three years after case closed. New records are available online after 1 day. PACER is available on the Internet at http://pacer.flsd.uscourts.gov.

Miami Division Room 150, 301 N Miami Ave, Miami, FL 33128-7788, 305-523-5700.

www.netside.net/usdcfls

Counties: Dade.

Indexing & Storage: Cases are indexed by defendant and plaintiff as well as by case number. New cases are available in the index 1 day after filing date. The full name of either party in the case, case number or case type is required to search for records. A computer index is maintained. Open records are located at this court. Records that are more than 5 years old are, at the discretion of the clerk, sent to the Atlanta Federal Records Center. Call records department to get location of records.

Fee & Payment: The fee is $15.00 per item (one party name or case number). Payment may be made by money order, cashier check, personal check, Visa, Mastercard. Prepayment is required.

Payee: U.S. Courts. Certification fee: $5.00 per document. Copy fee: $.50 per page. You are allowed to make your own copies. These copies cost $.25 per page. Copy machines are also available in the lobby area of the Records and Docketing Section. There is also an on-site copy service that can pull records and make copies. Call for more information.

Phone Search: Only docket information is available by phone. An automated voice case information service (VCIS) is not available.

Mail Search: Always enclose a stamped self addressed envelope.

In Person Search: In person searching is available.

PACER: Sign-up number is 800-676-6856. Access fee is $.60 per minute. Toll-free access: 800-372-8846. Local access: 305-536-7265. Case records are available back to August 1990. Records are purged three years after case closed. New records are available online after 1 day. PACER is available on the Internet at http://pacer.flsd.uscourts.gov.

West Palm Beach Division Room 402, 701 Clematis St, West Palm Beach, FL 33401, 561-803-3400.

www.netside.net/usdcfls

Counties: Palm Beach.

Indexing & Storage: Cases are indexed by defendant and plaintiff as well as by case number. New cases are available in the index immediately after filing date. The full name of either party in the case, case number or case type is required to search for records. A computer index is maintained. Open records are located at this court.

Fee & Payment: The fee is $15.00 per item (one party name or case number). Payment may be made by money order, cashier check, business check, Visa, Mastercard. Personal checks are not accepted. Prepayment is required. Payee: U.S. Courts. Certification fee: $5.00 per document. Copy fee: $.50 per page. You are allowed to make your own copies. These copies cost $.50 per page. A copy service is available to pull records and make copies. Copy machines are also available in the lobby.

Phone Search: Docket information is available by phone. An automated voice case information service (VCIS) is not available.

Mail Search: Always enclose a stamped self addressed envelope.

In Person Search: In person searching is available.

PACER: Sign-up number is 800-676-6856. Access fee is $.60 per minute. Toll-free access: 800-372-8846. Local access: 305-536-7265. Case records are available back to August 1990. Records are purged three years after case closed. New records are available online after 1 day. PACER is available on the Internet at http://pacer.flsd.uscourts.gov.

US Bankruptcy Court

Southern District of Florida

Miami Division Room 1517, 51 SW 1st Ave, Miami, FL 33130, 305-536-5216.

www.flsb.uscourts.gov

Counties: Broward, Dade, Highlands, Indian River, Martin, Monroe, Okeechobee, Palm Beach, St. Lucie. Cases may also be assigned to Fort Lauderdale or to West Palm Beach.

Indexing & Storage: Cases are indexed by debtor and creditors as well as by case number. New cases are available in the index 48 hours after filing date. A computer index is maintained. Open records are located at this court. Open case records may be held in the Fort Lauderdale or West Palm Beach office, depending on the judge assigned.

Fee & Payment: The fee is $15.00 per item (one party name or case number). Payment may be made by money order, cashier check. Business checks are not accepted. Personal checks are not accepted. Prepayment is required. Checks from law firms are accepted. Payee: US Courts. Certification fee: $5.00 per document. Copy fee: $.50 per page.

Phone Search: An automated voice case information service (VCIS) is available. Call VCIS at 800-473-0226 or 305-536-5979.

Mail Search: Always enclose a stamped self addressed envelope.

In Person Search: In person searching is available.

PACER: Sign-up number is 800-676-6856. Access fee is $.60 per minute. Toll-free access: 888-443-0081. Local access: 305-536-7492, 305-536-7493, 305-536-7494, 305-536-7495, 305-536-7496. Case records are available back to 1986. Records are purged every six months. New civil records are available online after 1 day. PACER is available on the Internet at http://pacer.flsb.uscourts.gov.

Court	Jurisdiction	No. of Courts	How Organized
Circuit Courts*	General	10	20 Circuits
County Courts*	Limited	13	
Combined Courts*		81	

* Profiled in this Sourcebook.

	CIVIL								
Court	Tort	Contract	Real Estate	Min. Claim	Max. Claim	Small Claims	Estate	Eviction	Domestic Relations
Circuit Courts*	X	X	X	$15,000	No Max		X		X
County Courts*	X	X	X	$0	$15,000	$2500		X	

	CRIMINAL				
Court	Felony	Misdemeanor	DWI/DUI	Preliminary Hearing	Juvenile
Circuit Courts*	X				X
County Courts*		X	X	X	

ADMINISTRATION Office of State Courts Administrator, Supreme Court Bldg, 500 S Duval, Tallahassee, FL, 32399-1900; 850-922-5082, Fax: 850-488-0156. www.flcourts.org/

COURT STRUCTURE All counties have combined Circuit and County Courts. The Circuit Court is the court of general jurisdiction.

ONLINE ACCESS There is a statewide, online computer system for internal use only; there is no external access available nor planned currently. However, a number of courts do offer online access to the public.

ADDITIONAL INFORMATION All courts have one address and switchboard; however, the divisions within the court(s) are completely separate. Requesters should specify which court and which division, e.g., Circuit Civil, County Civil, etc., the request is directed to, even though some counties will automatically check both with one request.

Fees are set by statute and are as follows: Search Fee - $1.00 per name per year; Certification Fee - $1.00 per document plus copy fee; Copy Fee - $1.00 per certified page; $.15 per non-certified page.

Most courts have very lengthy phone recording systems.

📖 📖 📖 📖 📖 📖 📖

Alachua County

Circuit & County Courts PO Box 600, Gainesville, FL 32602; 352-374-3609; Civil phone:352-338-3207; Criminal phone:352-338-3207; Fax: 352-338-3201. Hours: 8:30AM-5PM (EST). *Felony, Misdemeanor, Civil, Eviction, Small Claims, Probate.*

http://circuit8.org

Civil Records: Access: Phone, fax, mail, online, in person. Both court and visitors may perform in person searches. Search fee: $1.00 per name per year. Required to search: name, years to search; also helpful-address. Civil cases indexed by defendant, plaintiff. Civil records on computer from 1979, some records on docket books. For information about the remote access system and requesting searches by e-mail, call Jack Crosetti at 352-338-7323. The annual fee is $360 plus a one time setup fee of $50. The system is open 24 hours daily. Records can be searched by name or case number. The Circuit's Civil open cases can be searched free on the web at http://circuit8.org/case/index.html by division. **Criminal Records:** Access: Phone, fax, mail, remote online, in person. Both court and visitors may perform in person searches. Search fee: $1.00 per name per year. Required to search: name, years to search, DOB; also helpful-address, SSN, race, sex. Criminal records on computer since 1974. The

same criteria for searching civil records online applies. The Circuit's criminal open cases can be searched free on the web at http://circuit8.org/case/index.html by division. **General Information:** No juvenile, child abuse or sexual battery records released. SASE required. Turnaround time 5 working days. Copy fee: $1.00 per page. Records can be searched by name or case number Certification fee: $1.00. Fee payee: Clerk of Circuit Court. Personal checks accepted. Credit cards accepted: Visa, Mastercard. Visa, MC. Prepayment is required. Public access terminal is available.

Baker County

Circuit & County Courts-Civil 339 E Macclenny Ave, Macclenny, FL 32063; 904-259-8449. Hours: 8:30AM-5PM (EST). *Civil, Eviction, Small Claims, Probate.*

http://circuit8.org

Civil Records: Access: Mail, in person. Search fee: $1.00 per name per year. Required to search: name, years to search; also helpful-address. Civil cases indexed by defendant, plaintiff. Civil records are computerized since 03/96, prior on index cards and docket books. **General Information:** No juvenile, child abuse or sexual battery records released. SASE preferred. Turnaround time 2 days. Copy fee: $1.00 per page. Certification fee: $1.00. Fee payee: Clerk of Circuit Court. Business checks

accepted. Prepayment is required. Public access terminal is available.

Circuit & County Courts-Criminal 339 E Macclenny Ave, Macclenny, FL 32063; 904-259-8449; Fax: 904-259-4176. Hours: 8:30AM-5PM (EST). *Felony, Misdemeanor.*

http://circuit8.org **Criminal Records:** Access: Mail, in person. Only the court conducts in person searches; visitors may not. Search fee: $1.00 per name per year. Required to search: name, years to search, DOB. Criminal records on computer since 1989. Some records on docket books. **General Information:** No juvenile or guardianship records released. SASE required. Turnaround time 1-2 days. Copy fee: $1.00 per page. Certification fee: $1.00. Fee payee: Clerk of Circuit Court. Business checks accepted. Prepayment is required.

Bay County

Circuit Court-Civil PO Box 2269, Panama City, FL 32402; 850-767-5715; Fax: 850-747-5188. Hours: 8AM-5PM (CST). *Civil Actions Over $15,000, Probate.*

www.baycoclerk.com

Civil Records: Access: Phone, fax, mail, in person. Both court and visitors may perform in person searches. Search fee: $1.00 per name per year. Required to search: name, years to search. Civil cases indexed by defendant, plaintiff. Civil records on computer from 1984, on microfiche from 1950 to 1980, archived from 1913 to 1979. Some records on dockets. **General Information:** No juvenile, adoption, child abuse or sexual battery records released. Turnaround time 2 days. Copy fee: $1.00 per page. Certification fee: $1.00. Fee payee: Clerk of Circuit Court. Personal checks accepted. Prepayment is required. Public access terminal is available. Fax notes: $2.00 per page.

Circuit Court-Criminal PO Box 2269, Panama City, FL 32402; 850-747-5123; Fax: 850-747-5188. Hours: 8AM-4:30PM (CST). *Felony.*

www.baycoclerk.com **Criminal Records:** Access: Fax, mail, in person. Both court and visitors may perform in person searches. Search fee: $1.00 per name per year. Required to search: name, years to search, DOB; also helpful-SSN. Criminal records on computer from 1982, on microfilm from 1938 to 1982, archived from 1938. **General Information:** No sealed, juvenile or expunged records released. SASE requested. Turnaround time 3-5 days. Copy fee: $1.00 per page. Certification fee: $1.00. Fee payee: Clerk of Circuit Court. Personal checks accepted. Prepayment is required. Public access terminal is available. Fax notes: $2.00 per document.

County Court-Civil PO Box 2269, Panama City, FL 32402; 850-747-5141; Fax: 850-747-5188. Hours: 8AM-4:30PM (CST). *Civil Actions Under $15,000, Eviction, Small Claims.*

www.baycoclerk.com

Civil Records: Access: Phone, fax, mail, in person. Both court and visitors may perform in person searches. Search fee: $1.00 per name per year. Required to search: name, years to search. Civil cases indexed by defendant, plaintiff. Civil records on computer from 1986, on microfiche from 1950 to 1980, archived from 1913 to 1979. Some records on docket books. **General Information:** No juvenile, child abuse or sexual battery records released. SASE requested. Turnaround time 2 days. Copy fee: $1.00 per page. Certification fee: $1.00. Fee payee: Clerk of Circuit Court. Personal checks accepted. Prepayment is required. Public access terminal is available. Fax notes: $2.00 per page.

County Court-Misdemeanor PO Box 2269, Panama City, FL 32402; 850-747-5144; Fax: 850-747-5188. Hours: 8AM-4:30PM (CST). *Misdemeanor.*

www.baycoclerk.com **Criminal Records:** Access: Phone, fax, mail, in person. Both court and visitors may perform in person searches. Search fee: $1.00 per name per year. Required to search: name, years to search; also helpful-DOB, SSN. Criminal records on computer from 1984, on microfiche from 1938 to 1991, archived from 1938. **General Information:** No sealed or expunged records released. SASE requested. Turnaround time 7-10 days. Copy fee: $1.00 per page. Certification fee: $1.00. Fee payee: Clerk of Circuit Court. Personal checks accepted. Prepayment is required. Public access terminal is available. Fax notes: $2.00 per document.

Bradford County

Circuit Court PO Drawer B, Starke, FL 32091; 904-964-6280; Fax: 904-964-4454. Hours: 8AM-5PM (EST). *Felony, Civil Actions Over $15,000, Probate.*

http://circuit8.org

Civil Records: Access: Phone, mail, in person. Both court and visitors may perform in person searches. Search fee: $1.00 per name per year. Required to search: name, years to search. Civil

cases indexed by defendant, plaintiff. Civil records on computer since late 1987, others on index books. **Criminal Records:** Access: Phone, mail, in person. Both court and visitors may perform in person searches. Search fee: $1.00 per name per year. Required to search: name, years to search, DOB, SSN. Criminal records on computer since 1989, others on index books. **General Information:** No juvenile, child abuse or sexual battery records released. SASE required. Turnaround time 1 week. Copy fee: $1.00 per page. Certification fee: $1.00. Fee payee: Clerk at Circuit Court. Business checks accepted. Prepayment is required.

County Court PO Drawer B, Starke, FL 32091; 904-964-6280; Fax: 904-964-4454. Hours: 8AM-5PM (EST). *Misdemeanor, Civil Actions Under $15,000, Eviction, Small Claims.*

www.co.alachua.fl.us/clerk

Civil Records: Access: Mail, in person. Both court and visitors may perform in person searches. Search fee: $1.00 per name per year. Required to search: name, years to search. Civil cases indexed by defendant, plaintiff. Civil records on computer from 1985. Some records on docket books. **Criminal Records:** Access: Mail, in person. Both court and visitors may perform in person searches. Search fee: $1.00 per name per year. Required to search: name, years to search, DOB. Criminal records on computer from 1985. Some records on docket books. **General Information:** No juvenile records released. SASE required. Turnaround time 2 days. Copy fee: $1.00 per page. Certification fee: $1.00. Fee payee: Clerk of Court. Business checks accepted. Prepayment is required.

Brevard County

Offical Records Copy Desk PO Box 2767, Titusville, FL 32781-2767; 321-633-1924; Fax: 321-617-7311. Hours: 8AM-5PM (EST). *Civil, Eviction, Small Claims, Probate.*

www.clerk.co.brevard.fl.us

Civil Records: Access: Phone, fax, mail, online, in person. Both court and visitors may perform in person searches. Search fee: $1.00 per name per year. Required to search: name, years to search. Civil cases indexed by defendant, plaintiff. Civil records on computer since 1987, on microfiche since early 1900s. Some records on docket books. Access to County Court records are available free from FACTSweb at www.clerk.co.brevard.fl.us/pages/facts1.htm. Online records back to 1988 can be searched by name, case number or citation number. **General Information:** No juvenile, child abuse or sexual battery victim records released. SASE not required. Turnaround time 1 week. Copy fee: $1.00 per page. Certification fee: $1.00. Fee payee: Circuit Clerk. Personal checks accepted. Check by fax or phone accepted. Credit cards accepted: Visa, Mastercard, Discover. Prepayment is required. Public access terminal is available. Fax notes: $2.00 for first page, $1.00 each addl. Fax fee for long distance $3.00 1st page, $1.00 each additional page.

Circuit Court-Felony PO Box 999, 700 S Park Ave, Titusville, FL 32781; 321-264-5350; Fax: 407-264-5395. Hours: 8AM-5PM (EST). *Felony.*

www.clerk.co.brevard.fl.us **Criminal Records:** Access: Phone, fax, mail, remote online, in person. Both court and visitors may perform in person searches. Search fee: $1.00 per name per year. Required to search: name, DOB, SSN. Criminal records on computer since 1988, on microfiche from early 1900s. Some records on docket books.

Online access to county criminal court records is available free through FACTSweb at www.clerk.co.brevard.fl.us/pages/facts1.htm. Search by name, case number or citation number. **General Information:** No juvenile, child abuse, sexual battery or adoption records released. SASE not required. Turnaround time 1 week, phone turnaround time same day. Copy fee: $1.00 per page. Certification fee: $1.00. Fee payee: Circuit Clerk. Personal checks accepted. Credit cards accepted: Visa, Mastercard. Prepayment is required. Public access terminal is available. Fax notes: $1.00 per page. Fax fee long distance $2.00.

County Court-Misdemeanor PO Box 999, 700 S Park Ave, Titusville, FL 32781; 321-264-5350; Fax: 321-264-5395. Hours: 8AM-4:30PM (EST). *Misdemeanor.*

www.clerk.co.brevard.fl.us **Criminal Records:** Access: Phone, fax, mail, remote online, in person. Both court and visitors may perform in person searches. Search fee: $1.00 per name per year. Required to search: name, years to search, DOB; also helpful-SSN, race, sex. Criminal records on computer since 1990, on microfiche from early 1900s. Some records on docket books and index cards. Access to County Court records are available free from FACTSweb at www.clerk.co.brevard.fl.us/pages/facts1.htm. Online records back to 1988 can be searched by name, case number or citation number. **General Information:** No juvenile, child abuse, sexual battery or adoption records released. SASE not required. Turnaround time 1 week, phone turnaround time 2 days. Copy fee: $1.00 per page. Certification fee: $1.00. Fee payee: Circuit Clerk. Personal checks accepted. Credit cards accepted: Visa, Mastercard. Prepayment is required. Public access terminal is available. Fax notes: $1.00 per page. Fax fee for long distance $2.00 for 1st page.

Broward County

Circuit & County Courts 201 SE 6th St, Ft Lauderdale, FL 33301; 954-765-4578; Civil phone:954-831-6610; Criminal phone:954-831-6610; Probate phone:954-831-7154; Fax: 954-831-7166. Hours: 9AM-4PM (EST). *Felony, Misdemeanor, Civil, Eviction, Small Claims, Probate.*

www.17th.flcourts.org

Civil Records: Access: Phone, mail, online, in person. Both court and visitors may perform in person searches. Search fee: $1.00 per name per year. Add $4.00 for written response (affidavit). Required to search: name, years to search. Civil cases indexed by defendant, plaintiff. Civil records on computer from 1986. Some records on dockets. Will search back 10 years. The online system has a $40.00 setup fee plus security deposit. The monthly access fee is $49.00 which includes 2 free hours, afterward there is a $.34 per minute charge. Search by name or case number or case type. Call 954-357-7022 for information. A telephone record search system is available for civil court records by calling 900-680-1510. Fee is $1.50 for 1st minute; each add'l minute is $.99. **Criminal Records:** Access: Phone, mail, remote online, in person. Both court and visitors may perform in person searches. Search fee: $1.00 per name per year. Add $4.00 for written response (affidavit). Required to search: name, years to search, DOB; also helpful-SSN. Criminal records on computer since 1980. Online access is same criteria as described for civil records. A telephone record search system is available for criminal court records by calling 900-680-1500. Fee is $1.50 fir 1st minute; each add'l minute is $.99. **General**

Information: Turnaround time 1-14 days. Copy fee: $1.00 per page. Certification fee: $1.00. Fee payee: Clerk of the Court. Only cashiers checks and money orders accepted. Public access terminal is available.

Calhoun County

Circuit & County Court 425 E Central Ave, Blountstown, FL 32424; 850-674-4545; Fax: 850-674-5553. Hours: 8AM-4PM (CST). *Felony, Misdemeanor, Civil, Eviction, Small Claims, Probate.*

Civil Records: Access: Phone, fax, mail, in person. Both court and visitors may perform in person searches. No search fee. Required to search: name, years to search. Civil cases indexed by defendant, plaintiff. Civil records on computer from 1985, on docket books from 1970s. **Criminal Records:** Access: Phone, fax, mail, in person. Both court and visitors may perform in person searches. No search fee. Required to search: name, years to search. Criminal records on computer from 1985, on docket books from 1970s. **General Information:** No juvenile, child abuse or sexual battery record released. SASE required. Turnaround time 2 days. Copy fee: $1.00 per page. Certification fee: $1.00. Fee payee: Clerk of Court. Personal checks accepted. Prepayment is required. Public access terminal is available. Fax notes: No fee to fax results.

Charlotte County

Circuit & County Courts - Civil Division PO Box 511687, Punta Gorda, FL 33951-1687; 941-637-2230; Probate phone:941-637-2210; Fax: 941-637-2116. Hours: 8AM-5PM (EST). *Civil, Eviction, Small Claims, Probate (Separate).*

http://co.charlotte.fl.us/clrkinfo/lcerk_default.htm

Note: Probate is handled by a separate court at the telephone given above.

Civil Records: Access: Mail, in person. Both court and visitors may perform in person searches. Search fee: $1.00 per name per year. Required to search: name, years to search. Civil cases indexed by defendant, plaintiff. Civil records on computer since 1984, on microfiche since 1987. **General Information:** No juvenile, child abuse, sexual battery, adoption records released. SASE requested. Turnaround time 1-2 days. Copy fee: $1.00 per page. Certification fee: $1.00. Fee payee: Clerk of Circuit Court. Personal checks accepted. Prepayment is required. Public access terminal is available.

Circuit & County Courts-Criminal Division PO Box 511687, Punta Gorda, FL 33951-1687; 941-637-2199; Fax: 941-637-2159. Hours: 8AM-5PM (EST). *Felony, Misdemeanor.*

http://co.charlotte.fl.us/clrkinfo/clerk_default.htm

Criminal Records: Access: Phone, mail, in person. Both court and visitors may perform in person searches. Search fee: $1.00 per name per year. Required to search: name, years to search, DOB; also helpful-address, SSN, race, sex. Criminal records on computer since 1985, misdemeanors on index cards, felonies on judgement books, imaging on disc. **General Information:** No juvenile, child abuse or sexual battery records released. SASE requested. Turnaround time 1 week. Copy fee: $1.00 per page. Certification fee: $1.00. Fee payee: Clerk of Circuit Court. Personal checks accepted. Prepayment is required. Public access terminal is available.

Citrus County

Circuit Court 110 N Apopka Rm 101, Inverness, FL 34450; 352-637-9400; Fax: 352-637-9413. Hours: 8AM-5PM (EST). *Felony, Civil Actions Over $15,000, Probate.*

www.clerk.citrus.fl.us

Civil Records: Access: Phone, fax, mail, in person. Both court and visitors may perform in person searches. Search fee: $1.00 per name per year. Required to search: name, years to search; also helpful-address. Civil cases indexed by defendant, plaintiff. Civil records on computer from 1989, archived from 1940 to 1988. Some records on docket books. By phone only back to 1989. Indicate on search request the type(s) of cases. **Criminal Records:** Access: Phone, fax, mail, in person. Both court and visitors may perform in person searches. Search fee: $1.00 per name per year. Required to search: name, years to search, DOB; also helpful-address, SSN, race, sex. Criminal records on computer from 1989, on microfiche from 1948 to 1987, archived from 1940-1988. By phone only back to 1989. **General Information:** No juvenile, adoption, child abuse or sexual battery records released. SASE required. Turnaround time 1-2 days. Copy fee: $1.00 per page. Certification fee: $1.00. Fee payee: Clerk of Circuit Court. Personal checks accepted. Prepayment is required. Public access terminal is available. Fax notes: $1.00 per page.

County Court 110 N Apopka, Rm 101, Inverness, FL 34450; 352-637-9400; Fax: 352-637-9413. Hours: 8AM-5PM (EST). *Misdemeanor, Civil Actions Under $15,000, Eviction, Small Claims.*

www.clerk.citrus.fl.us

Civil Records: Access: Phone, fax, mail, in person. Both court and visitors may perform in person searches. Search fee: $1.00 per name per year. Required to search: name, years to search; also helpful-address. Civil cases indexed by defendant, plaintiff. Civil records on computer from 1990, prior records on docket books. Indicate type of case(s) you are looking for on your search request. **Criminal Records:** Access: Mail, in person. Both court and visitors may perform in person searches. Search fee: $1.00 per name per year. Required to search: name, years to search, DOB; also helpful-address, SSN, race, sex. Criminal records on computer from 1990, prior records on docket books. **General Information:** No juvenile, child abuse or sexual battery records released. SASE required. Turnaround time 1-3 days. Copy fee: $1.00 per page. Certification fee: $1.00. Fee payee: Clerk of Circuit Court. Personal checks accepted. Prepayment is required. Public access terminal is available. Public Access Terminal Note: Criminal only. Fax notes: $1.00 per page. Fax fee for long distance $2.00 per page.

Clay County

Circuit Court PO Box 698, Green Cove Springs, FL 32043; 904-284-6302; Fax: 904-284-6390. Hours: 8:30AM-4:30PM (EST). *Felony, Civil Actions Over $15,000, Probate.*

http://clerk.co.clay.fl.us

Civil Records: Access: Mail, online, in person. Both court and visitors may perform in person searches. Search fee: $1.00 per name per year. Required to search: name, years to search; also helpful-address. Civil cases indexed by defendant, plaintiff. Civil records on computer from 1985, prior records on docket books. The court has free access to records from the web site. This has taken

the place of the commercial system. **Criminal Records:** Access: Mail, in person. Both court and visitors may perform in person searches. Search fee: $1.00 per name per year. Required to search: name, years to search, DOB; also helpful-address, SSN, race, sex. Criminal records (Felony) on computer from 1967, prior records on docket books. The agency hopes to have criminal records online at the web site before the close of 2000. Call 904-284-6371 for details. **General Information:** No juvenile, child abuse or sexual battery records released. Turnaround time 1-3 days. Copy fee: $1.00 per page. Certification fee: $1.00. Fee payee: Clerk of Circuit Court. Only cashiers checks and money orders accepted. Prepayment is required. Public access terminal is available.

County Court PO Box 698, Green Cove Springs, FL 32043; 904-284-6316; Fax: 904-284-6390. Hours: 8:30AM-4:30PM (EST). *Misdemeanor, Civil Actions Under $15,000, Eviction, Small Claims.*

http://clerk.co.clay.fl.us

Civil Records: Access: Mail, online, in person. Both court and visitors may perform in person searches. Search fee: $1.00 per name per year. Required to search: name, years to search; also helpful-address. Civil cases indexed by defendant, plaintiff. Civil records on computer from 1985, prior records on docket books. Online access to records is available at no fee from the web site. **Criminal Records:** Access: Mail, in person. Both court and visitors may perform in person searches. Search fee: $1.00 per name per year. Required to search: name, years to search, DOB; also helpful-address, SSN, race, sex. Criminal records on computer from 1985, prior records on docket books. **General Information:** No juvenile, child abuse or sexual battery records released. Turnaround time 1-2 days. Copy fee: $1.00 per page. Certification fee: $1.00. Fee payee: Clerk of Circuit Court. Personal checks accepted. Prepayment is required. Public access terminal is available.

Collier County

Circuit Court PO Box 413044, Naples, FL 34101-3044; 941-732-2646. Hours: 8AM-5PM (EST). *Felony, Civil Actions Over $15,000, Probate.*

www.clerk.collier.fl.us

Civil Records: Access: Mail, online, in person. Both court and visitors may perform in person searches. Search fee: $1.00 per name per year. Required to search: name, years to search. Civil cases indexed by defendant, plaintiff. Civil records on computer from 1990, on microfiche from 1922 to 1994, archived from 1922. The online access system has a $100.00 setup fee, a monthly $10.00 fee and a $.05 per minute access charge. The system is open 24 hours daily. Records include probate, traffic and domestic. Call Judy at 941-774-8339 for more information. **Criminal Records:** Access: Mail, remote online, in person. Both court and visitors may perform in person searches. Search fee: $1.00 per name per year. Required to search: name, years to search, DOB; also helpful-SSN. Criminal records on computer from 1990, on microfiche from 1922 to 1994, archived from 1922. The sames fees for online access apply as described for civil records. Searching is by name for both felony and misdemeanor records. Call 941-774-8339 for more information. **General Information:** No sealed by court or statute records released. Turnaround time within 1 week. Copy fee: $1.00 per page. Certification fee: $1.00. Fee payee: Clerk of Circuit Court. Personal checks accepted. Prepayment is required. Public access terminal is available.

County Court PO Box 413044, Naples, FL 34101-3044; 941-732-2646; Fax: 941-774-8020. Hours: 8AM-5PM (EST). *Misdemeanor, Civil Actions Under $15,000, Eviction, Small Claims.*

www.clerk.collier.fl.us

Civil Records: Access: Mail, online, in person. Both court and visitors may perform in person searches. Search fee: $1.00 per name per year. Required to search: name, years to search; also helpful-address. Civil cases indexed by defendant, plaintiff. Civil records on computer from 1990, on microfiche from 1922 to 1995. Fees for online access include $100.00 setup, $10.00 per month and $.05 per minute. This system also includes the Circuit Court records. Call 941-774-8339 for more information. **Criminal Records:** Access: Mail, remote online, in person. Both court and visitors may perform in person searches. Search fee: $1.00 per name per year. Required to search: name, years to search, DOB; also helpful-address, SSN, race, sex. Criminal records on computer from 1990, on microfiche from 1922 to 1995. Online access criteria is the same as described for civil records. **General Information:** No juvenile, child abuse or sexual battery records released. SASE required. Turnaround time 1 week. Copy fee: $1.00 per page. Certification fee: $1.00. Fee payee: Clerk of County Court. Personal checks accepted. Prepayment is required.

Columbia County

Circuit & County Courts PO Drawer 2069, Lake City, FL 32056; 904-758-1353. Hours: 8AM-5PM (EST). *Felony, Misdemeanor, Civil, Eviction, Small Claims, Probate.*

Civil Records: Access: Mail, in person. Both court and visitors may perform in person searches. Search fee: $1.00 per name per year. Fee is per department. Required to search: name, years to search. Civil cases indexed by defendant, plaintiff. Civil records on computer from 1990, archived from 1800s. DOB and SSN also helpful for searching. **Criminal Records:** Access: Mail, in person. Both court and visitors may perform in person searches. Search fee: $1.00 per name per year. Fee is per department. Required to search: name, years to search, DOB; also helpful-SSN. Criminal records on computer from mid-1988, archived from 1800s. **General Information:** No names of victims of sex related offenses, incompetency or mental health records released. SASE required. Turnaround time 1 day. Copy fee: $1.00 per page. Certification fee: $1.00. Fee payee: Clerk of Circuit Court. Personal checks accepted. No 2 party checks accepted. Prepayment is required.

Dade County

Circuit & County Courts - Civil 73 W Flagler St, Miami, FL 33130; 305-275-1155; Fax: 305-375-5819. Hours: 9AM-4PM (EST). *Civil, Eviction, Small Claims, Probate.*

http://jud11.flcourts.org

Civil Records: Access: Phone, fax, mail, online, in person. Both court and visitors may perform in person searches. Search fee: $1.00 per name per year. Required to search: name, years to search. Civil cases indexed by defendant, plaintiff. Civil records on computer from 1984, archived from 1836. Microfilm in county recorder's office.

Online access includes a $125.00 setup fee, $52.00 monthly and $.25 per minute after the first 208 minutes each month. Open 24 hours daily, docket information can be searched by case number or name. Call 305-596-8148 for more information. **General Information:** No juvenile, child abuse or sexual battery records released. SASE requested. Turnaround time 1 week. Copy fee: $1.00 per page. Certification fee: $1.00. Fee payee: Clerk of Circuit & County Courts. Personal checks accepted. Credit cards accepted: Visa, Mastercard. Visa, MC +$15.00 add'l charge. Prepayment is required. Public access terminal is available.

Circuit & County Courts-Criminal 1351 NW 12th St, Suite 9000, Miami, FL 33125; 305-275-1155; Fax: 305-548-5526. Hours: 9AM-4PM (EST). *Felony, Misdemeanor.*

http://jud11.flcourts.org

Criminal Records: Access: Phone, fax, mail, remote online, in person. Both court and visitors may perform in person searches. Search fee: $1.00 per name per year. Required to search: name, years to search, DOB; also helpful-address, SSN, race, sex. Criminal records on computer from 1971, on microfiche from 1975, archived from 1836. Fees for online access include a $125.00 setup, $52.00 per month for the first 208 minutes and a $.25 per minute charge thereafter. The system is open 24 hours daily. Searching is by name or case number. Call 305-596-8148 for more information. **General Information:** No juvenile, child abuse or sexual battery records released. SASE required. Turnaround time 10-15 days. Copy fee: $1.00 per page. Certification fee: $1.00. Fee payee: Clerk of Circuit and County Court. Personal checks accepted. Credit cards accepted: Visa, Mastercard. Credit cards accepted in person only. Prepayment is required. Public access terminal is available.

De Soto County

Circuit & County Courts 115 E Oak Street, Arcadia, FL 34266; 863-993-4876; Civil phone:863-993-4880; Probate phone:863-993-4880; Fax: 863-993-4669. Hours: 8AM-5PM (EST). *Felony, Misdemeanor, Civil, Eviction, Small Claims, Probate.*

http://12circuit.state.fl.us

Note: County Court & Evictions 863-993-4880

Civil Records: Access: Phone, fax, mail, in person. Both court and visitors may perform in person searches. Search fee: $1.00 per name per year. Required to search: name, years to search. Civil cases indexed by defendant, plaintiff. Civil records on computer from 1986, on microfiche from 1974, archived from 1887. **Criminal Records:** Access: Phone, fax, mail, in person. Both court and visitors may perform in person searches. Search fee: $1.00 per name per year. Required to search: name, years to search, DOB; also helpful-SSN, aliases. Criminal records on computer since 1986, archived since 1887. **General Information:** No juvenile or sex related records released. SASE requested. Turnaround time 2 days. Copy fee: $1.00 per page. Certification fee: $1.00. Fee payee: Clerk of the Court. Personal checks accepted. Prepayment is required. Public access terminal is available. Fax notes: $1.00 per page.

Dixie County

Circuit & County Courts PO Drawer 1206, Cross City, FL 32628-1206; 352-498-1200; Fax: 352-498-1201. Hours: 9AM-5PM (EST). *Felony, Misdemeanor, Civil, Eviction, Small Claims, Probate.*

Civil Records: Access: Mail, in person. Only the court conducts in person searches; visitors may not. Search fee: $1.00 per name per year. Required to search: name, years to search; also helpful-address. Civil cases indexed by defendant, plaintiff. Civil records on computer since 1987. **Criminal Records:** Access: Mail, in person. Only the court conducts in person searches; visitors may not. Search fee: $1.00 per name per year. Required to search: name, years to search, DOB; also helpful-address, SSN, race, sex. Criminal records on computer since 1989. **General Information:** No juvenile, child abuse or sexual battery records released. SASE required. Turnaround time 1 week. Copy fee: $1.00 per page. Certification fee: $1.00. Fee payee: Clerk of Circuit Court. Personal checks accepted. Prepayment is required.

Duval County

Circuit & County Courts - Civil Division 330 E Bay St, Jacksonville, FL 32202; 904-630-2039; Fax: 904-630-7506. Hours: 8AM-5PM (EST). *Civil, Eviction, Small Claims, Probate.*

www.coj.net/pub/clerk/default.htm

Civil Records: Access: Fax, mail, online, in person. Both court and visitors may perform in person searches. Search fee: $1.00 per name per year. Required to search: name, years to search; also helpful-address. Civil cases indexed by defendant, plaintiff. Civil records (Circuit) on computer from 1968, county from 1984. County civil on index books from 1975 to 1986, prior on docket books. Circuit civil on index books from 1900s to 1968. Online access is available 24 hours daily. There is a $100.00 setup fee, but no access charges. For more info, call Leslie Peterson at 904-630-1212 x5115. **General Information:** No juvenile, child abuse or sexual battery records released. Turnaround time for county records 5-7 days, circuit 2-4 days. Copy fee: $1.00 per page. Certification fee: $1.00. Fee payee: Clerk of Circuit Court. Business checks accepted. Prepayment is required. Fax notes: $1.00 per page.

Circuit & County Courts-Criminal Division 330 E Bay St, Rm M106, Jacksonville, FL 32202; 904-630-2070; Fax: 904-630-7505. Hours: 8AM-5PM (EST). *Felony, Misdemeanor.*

www.coj.net/pub/clerk/default.htm   **Criminal Records:** Access: Mail, remote online, in person. Court does not conduct in person searches; visitors must perform searches for themselves. Search fee: $1.00 per name per year. Required to search: name, years to search, DOB; also helpful-address, SSN, race, sex. Criminal records (Circuit) on computer from 1968, county from 1986. County civil on index books from 1975 to 1986, prior on docket books. Circuit civil on index books from 1900s to 1968. Contact Leslie Peterson at 904-630-1212 x5115 for information about remote access. Costs include $100 setup, $30 per month and $.25 per minute. System available 24 hours per day at minimum 9600 baud. Records go back to 1992. **General Information:** No juvenile, child abuse or sexual battery records released. SASE helpful. Turnaround time 2-3 days. Copy fee: $1.00 per page. Certification fee: $1.00. Fee payee: Clerk of the Court. Business checks accepted. Prepayment is required. Public access terminal is available.

Escambia County

Circuit & County Courts - Civil Division
190 Governmental Center, Pensacola, FL 32501; 850-595-4170; Probate phone:850-595-4300. Hours: 8AM-5PM (CST). *Civil, Eviction, Small Claims, Probate.*

www.clerk.co.escambia.fl.us

Civil Records: Access: Phone, fax, mail, in person. Both court and visitors may perform in person searches. Search fee: $1.00 per name per year. Add $4.00 for written response. Required to search: name, years to search; also helpful-address. Civil cases indexed by defendant, plaintiff. Civil records on computer from mid 1986, prior on index books. Judgements and small claims on microfiche from 1952, evictions from 1973. **General Information:** No juvenile, child abuse, adoption, mental health or sexual battery records released. SASE requested. Turnaround time 1-5 days. Copy fee: $1.00 per page. Certification fee: $1.00. Fee payee: Clerk of Circuit Court. Personal checks accepted. Prepayment is required. Public access terminal is available.

Circuit & County Courts-Criminal Division
190 Governmental Center, Pensacola, FL 32501; 850-595-4150; Fax: 850-595-4198. Hours: 8AM-5PM (CST). *Felony, Misdemeanor.*

www.clerk.co.escambia.fl.us

Note: Misdemeanor records phone is 850-595-4185 **Criminal Records:** Access: Fax, mail, in person. Only the court conducts in person searches; visitors may not. Search fee: $1.00 per name per year. Required to search: name, years to search, DOB; also helpful-address, SSN, race, sex. Criminal records on computer and microfiche from 1973, archived from 1940 to 1972. **General Information:** No juvenile, child abuse, mental health, adoption or sexual battery records released. SASE requested. Turnaround time within 1 week. Copy fee: $1.00 per page. Certification fee: $1.00. Fee payee: Clerk of Circuit Court. Personal checks accepted. Prepayment is required. Public access terminal is available. Fax notes: $1.00 per page. If more than 5 pages $2.00, each additional group of 5 pages charge increases by $1.00, plus phone charge.

Flagler County

Circuit & County Courts
PO Box 787, Bunnell, FL 32110; 904-437-7430; Fax: 904-437-7454. Hours: 8AM-5PM (EST). *Felony, Misdemeanor, Civil, Eviction, Small Claims, Probate.*

www.co.st-johns.fl.us/Const-Officers/Judicial

Civil Records: Access: Phone, fax, mail, in person. Both court and visitors may perform in person searches. Search fee: $1.00 per name per year. Required to search: name, years to search; also helpful-address. Civil cases indexed by defendant, plaintiff. Civil records on computer from 1990. All archived from 1917, some on index books. **Criminal Records:** Access: Phone, fax, mail, in person. Both court and visitors may perform in person searches. Search fee: $1.00 per name per year. Required to search: name, years to search, DOB; also helpful-address, SSN, race, sex. Criminal records on computer from 1990. All archived from 1917, some on index books. **General Information:** No juvenile, child abuse or sexual battery records released. Turnaround time 3-5 days. Copy fee: $1.00 per page. Certification fee: $1.00. Fee payee: Clerk of Circuit Court. Business checks accepted. Prepayment is required. Fax notes: $1.00 per page.

Franklin County

Circuit & County Courts
33 Market St, Suite 203, Apalachicola, FL 32321; 850-653-8862; Fax: 850-653-2261. Hours: 8:30AM-4:30PM (EST). *Felony, Misdemeanor, Civil, Eviction, Small Claims, Probate.*

www.co.leon.fl.us/court/court.htm

Civil Records: Access: Mail, in person. Both court and visitors may perform in person searches. Search fee: $1.00 per name per year. Required to search: name, years to search; also helpful-address. Civil cases indexed by defendant, plaintiff. Civil records on computer from 3/92. **Criminal Records:** Access: Mail, in person. Both court and visitors may perform in person searches. Search fee: $1.00 per name per year. Required to search: name, years to search, DOB; also helpful-address, SSN, race, sex. Criminal records on computer since 1989. **General Information:** No juvenile, child abuse or sexual battery records released. SASE requested. Turnaround time 2-5 days. Copy fee: $1.00 per page. Certification fee: $1.00. Fee payee: Clerk of Circuit Court. Personal checks accepted. Prepayment is required. Public access terminal is available.

Gadsden County

Circuit & County Courts - Civil Division
PO Box 1649, Quincy, FL 32353; 850-875-8621; Fax: 850-875-8612. Hours: 8:30AM-5PM (EST). *Civil, Eviction, Small Claims, Probate.*

Civil Records: Access: Phone, fax, mail, in person. Both court and visitors may perform in person searches. Search fee: $1.00 per name. Required to search: name, years to search. Civil cases indexed by defendant, plaintiff. Civil records on computer since 1984. **General Information:** No juvenile, child abuse or sexual battery records released. Turnaround time 1 week. Copy fee: $.15 per page. Certification fee: $2.00. Fee payee: Clerk of Circuit Court. Only cashiers checks and money orders accepted. Prepayment is required. Public access terminal is available. Fax notes: $1.00 per page.

Circuit & County Courts-Criminal Division
112 South Adams St, Quincy, FL 32351; 850-875-8609; Fax: 850-875-7625. Hours: 8:30AM-5PM (EST). *Felony, Misdemeanor.*

www.co.leon.fl.us/court/court.htm

Note: Requests may be sent to PO Box 1649, ZIP is 32353 **Criminal Records:** Access: Fax, mail, in person. Both court and visitors may perform in person searches. Search fee: $1.00 per name per year. Required to search: name, years to search, DOB; also helpful-SSN. Criminal records on computer from 1984, some on index books and cards. **General Information:** No juvenile or sex offender records released. Turnaround time 3-5 days. Copy fee: $.15 per page. Certification fee: $2.00. Fee payee: Clerk of Circuit Court. Personal checks accepted. Prepayment is required. Public access terminal available. Fax note: $1. per page.

Gilchrist County

Circuit & County Courts
Po Box 37, Trenton, FL 32693; 352-463-3170; Fax: 352-463-3166. Hours: 8AM-5PM (EST). *Felony, Misdemeanor, Civil, Eviction, Small Claims, Probate.*

http://circuit8.org

Civil Records: Access: Phone, fax, mail, in person. Both court and visitors may perform in

person searches. Search fee: $1.00 per name per year. Add $4.00 for written response (affidavit). Required to search: name, years to search; also helpful-address. Civil cases indexed by defendant, plaintiff. Civil records on computer from 1987, prior on index books. **Criminal Records:** Access: Phone, fax, mail, in person. Only the court conducts in person searches; visitors may not. Search fee: $1.00 per name per year. Add $4.00 for written response (affidavit). Required to search: name, years to search, DOB; also helpful-address, SSN, race, sex. Criminal records on computer since 1989, prior on index books. **General Information:** No juvenile, child abuse or sexual battery records released. Turnaround time 2-3 days. Copy fee: $1.00 per page. Certification fee: $1.00. Fee payee: Clerk of Circuit Court. Personal checks accepted. Prepayment is required. Fax notes: $1.00 per page. Available for civil only.

Glades County

Circuit & County Courts
PO Box 10, Moore Haven, FL 33471; 863-946-0113; Fax: 863-946-0560. Hours: 8AM-5PM (EST). *Felony, Misdemeanor, Civil, Eviction, Small Claims, Probate.*

Civil Records: Access: Phone, mail, in person. Only the court conducts in person searches; visitors may not. Search fee: $1.00 per name per year. Add $4.00 for written response (affidavit). Required to search: name, years to search; also helpful-address. Civil cases indexed by defendant, plaintiff. Civil records on computer from 1991. **Criminal Records:** Access: Mail, in person. Only the court conducts in person searches; visitors may not. Search fee: $1.00 per name per year. Add $4.00 for written response (affidavit). Required to search: name, years to search, DOB; also helpful-address, SSN, race, sex. Criminal records on computer from 1991. **General Information:** No juvenile, child abuse or sexual battery records released. SASE not required. Turnaround time 2-3 days. Copy fee: $1.00 per page. Certification fee: $1.00. Fee payee: Clerk of Circuit Court. Personal checks accepted. Prepayment is required.

Gulf County

Circuit & County Courts
1000 Cecil Costin Blvd, Port St Joe, FL 32456; 850-229-6112; Fax: 850-229-6174. Hours: 9AM-5PM (CST). *Felony, Misdemeanor, Civil, Eviction, Small Claims, Probate.*

Civil Records: Access: Fax, mail, in person. Both court and visitors may perform in person searches. Search fee: $1.00 per name per year. Required to search: name, years to search. Civil cases indexed by defendant, plaintiff. Civil records on computer from 1990. **Criminal Records:** Access: Fax, mail, in person. Both court and visitors may perform in person searches. Search fee: $1.00 per name per year. Required to search: name, years to search, DOB; also helpful-SSN. Criminal records on computer from 1990. **General Information:** No juvenile, adoption, child abuse or sexual battery records released. SASE required. Turnaround time 1-3 days. Copy fee: $.15 per page. Certification fee: $1.00. Fee payee: Clerk of Circuit Court. Personal checks accepted. Prepayment is required. Fax notes: $1.50 per page.

Hamilton County

Circuit & County Courts
207 NE 1st St #106, Jasper, FL 32052; 904-792-1288; Fax: 904-792-3524. Hours: 8:30AM-4:30PM (EST). *Felony, Misdemeanor, Civil, Eviction, Small Claims, Probate.*

Civil Records: Access: Mail, in person. Both court and visitors may perform in person searches. Search fee: $1.00 per name per year. Required to search: name, years to search; also helpful-address. Civil records on computer from 1/91, county civil from 3/91. **Criminal Records:** Access: Mail, in person. Both court and visitors may perform in person searches. Search fee: $1.00 per name per year. Required to search: name, years to search, DOB; also helpful-address, SSN, race, sex. Criminal records on computer-Felony since 3/90, Misdemeanor since 1/89. **General Information:** No juvenile, child abuse or sexual battery records released. SASE requested. Turnaround time 2-3 days. Copy fee: $1.00 per page. Certification fee: $1.00. Fee payee: Clerk of Circuit Court. Personal checks accepted. Prepayment is required.

Hardee County

Circuit & County Courts PO Drawer 1749, Wauchula, FL 33873-1749; 863-773-4174; Fax: 863-773-4422. Hours: 8:30AM-5PM (EST). *Felony, Misdemeanor, Civil, Eviction, Small Claims, Probate.*

http://jud10.flcourts.org

Civil Records: Access: Mail, in person. Both court and visitors may perform in person searches. Search fee: $1.00 per name per year. Required to search: name, years to search; also helpful-address. Civil records on computer from 1984. **Criminal Records:** Access: Mail, in person. Both court and visitors may perform in person searches. Search fee: $1.00 per name per year. Required to search: name, years to search, DOB; also helpful-address, SSN, race, sex. Criminal records on computer from 1984. **General Information:** No juvenile, child abuse or sexual battery records released. SASE requested. Turnaround time 3 days. Copy fee: $1.00 per page. Certification fee: $1.00. Fee payee: Clerk of Circuit Court. Business checks accepted. Prepayment is required. Public access terminal is available.

Hendry County

Circuit & County Courts PO Box 1760, LaBelle, FL 33975-1760; 863-675-5217; Fax: 863-675-5238. Hours: 8:30AM-5PM (EST). *Felony, Misdemeanor, Civil, Eviction, Small Claims, Probate.*

Civil Records: Access: Mail, in person. Both court and visitors may perform in person searches. Search fee: $1.00 per name per year. Required to search: name, years to search; also helpful-address. Civil cases indexed by defendant, plaintiff. Civil records on computer since 5/92, archived from 1923, on microfiche prior to 1989 if filed. **Criminal Records:** Access: Mail, in person. Both court and visitors may perform in person searches. Search fee: $1.00 per name per year. Required to search: name, years to search, DOB; also helpful-address, SSN, race, sex. Criminal records on computer since 1989, prior on microfiche, archived since 1923. **General Information:** No juvenile, child abuse or sexual battery records released. SASE helpful. Turnaround time varies. Copy fee: $1.00 per page. Certification fee: $1.00. Fee payee: Clerk of Circuit Court. Personal checks accepted. Prepayment is required.

Hernando County

Circuit & County Courts 20 N Main St, Brooksville, FL 34601; 352-754-4201; Fax: 352-754-4247. Hours: 8AM-5PM (EST). *Felony, Misdemeanor, Civil, Eviction, Small Claims, Probate.*

www.co.hernando.fl.us/ccc

Civil Records: Access: Mail, online, in person. Both court and visitors may perform in person searches. Search fee: $1.00 per name per year. Required to search: name, years to search. Civil cases indexed by defendant, plaintiff. Civil records on computer from 1982, archived from late 1800s. Contact Bob Piercy for more information about remote access. Costs include $100 setup, $25 per month and $.10 per minute. Modem speeds up to 28.8 accepted. A fax back service for specific pages is available for $1-$1.25 per page. **Criminal Records:** Access: Mail, remote online, in person. Both court and visitors may perform in person searches. Search fee: $1.00 per name per year. Required to search: name, years to search, DOB; also helpful-SSN. Criminal records on computer from 1982, archived from late 1800s. Online access for criminal records has the same criteria as described for civil records. Index and docket information is available for felony and misdemeanor records. **General Information:** No juvenile, child abuse or sexual battery records released. Turnaround time approx 5 days. Copy fee: $1.00 per page. Certification fee: $1.00. Fee payee: Clerk of Circuit Court. Personal checks accepted. Prepayment is required. Public access terminal is available.

Highlands County

Circuit & County Courts 590 S Commerce Ave, Sebring, FL 33870-3867;; Civil phone:863-386-6591; Criminal phone:863-386-6591; Fax: 863-386-6575. Hours: 8AM-4:30PM (EST). *Felony, Misdemeanor, Civil, Eviction, Small Claims, Probate.*

http://jud10.flcourts.org

Civil Records: Access: Mail, in person. Both court and visitors may perform in person searches. Search fee: $1.00 per name per year. Required to search: name, years to search. Civil cases indexed by defendant, plaintiff. Civil records on computer since 1992, prior on microfiche and film. **Criminal Records:** Access: Mail, in person. Both court and visitors may perform in person searches. Search fee: $1.00 per name per year. Required to search: name, years to search; also helpful-SSN. Criminal records on computer since 1991, prior on microfiche and film. **General Information:** No juvenile, child abuse or sexual battery records released. Turnaround time 1 week. Copy fee: $1.00 per page. Certification fee: $2.00. Fee payee: Clerk of Courts. Personal checks accepted. Prepayment is required. Public access terminal is available.

HillsBorough

Circuit & County Courts 419 Pierce St, Tampa, FL 33602; 813-276-8100; Fax: 813-272-7707. Hours: 8AM-5PM (EST). *Felony, Misdemeanor, Civil, Eviction, Small Claims, Probate.*

www.hillsclerk.com

Note: Extension for civil is 7252, for criminal is 7802.

Civil Records: Access: Fax, mail, online, in person. Both court and visitors may perform in person searches. Search fee: $1.00 per name per year. Required to search: name, years to search; also helpful-address. Civil cases indexed by defendant, plaintiff. Civil records on computer since 5/85, prior on microfiche since early 1900s. Online access has a $50.00 set-up/software fee plus initial $50.00 towards access charges ($.25 per minute). Probate, traffic and domestic records included. Call the help desk at 813-276-8100, Ext.

7000 for more info. **Criminal Records:** Access: Fax, mail, remote online, in person. Both court and visitors may perform in person searches. Search fee: $1.00 per name per year. Required to search: name, years to search, DOB; also helpful-address, SSN, race, sex. Criminal records on computer since 1989, prior on microfiche since 1975, archived from 1953 to 1974. Some felonies on docket books. The online system is the same as described for civil records. Contact the help desk at 813-276-8100, Ext. 7000 for more information. **General Information:** No juvenile, child abuse or sexual battery records released. Turnaround time 1-2 days. Copy fee: $1.00 per page. Certification fee: $1.00. Fee payee: Clerk of Circuit Court. Personal checks accepted. Local personal checks accepted. Prepayment is required. Public access terminal is available. Fax notes: No fee to fax results. Fax account required.

Holmes County

Circuit & County Courts PO Box 397, Bonifay, FL 32425; 850-547-1100; Fax: 850-547-6630. Hours: 8AM-4PM (CST). *Felony, Misdemeanor, Civil, Eviction, Small Claims, Probate.*

Civil Records: Access: Mail, in person. Both court and visitors may perform in person searches. Search fee: $1.00 per name per year. Required to search: name, years to search; also helpful-address. Civil cases indexed by defendant, plaintiff. Civil records on computer from 10/91, archived from early 1900s. **Criminal Records:** Access: Mail, in person. Both court and visitors may perform in person searches. Search fee: $1.00 per name per year. Required to search: name, years to search, DOB; also helpful-address, SSN, race, sex. Criminal records on computer since 1989, prior archived since early 1900s. **General Information:** No juvenile, child abuse or sexual battery records released. SASE required. Turnaround time 1 week. Copy fee: $1.00 per page. Certification fee: $1.00. Fee payee: Holmes County Clerk of Court. Personal checks accepted. Prepayment is required. Public access terminal is available.

Indian River County

Circuit & County Courts PO Box 1028, Vero Beach, FL 32961; 561-770-5185; Fax: 561-770-5008. Hours: 8:30AM-5PM (EST). *Felony, Misdemeanor, Civil, Eviction, Small Claims, Probate.*

Civil Records: Access: Mail, in person. Both court and visitors may perform in person searches. Search fee: $1.00 per name per year. Required to search: name, years to search; also helpful-address. Civil cases indexed by defendant, plaintiff. Civil records on computer since 1984, prior on microfiche. **Criminal Records:** Access: Mail, in person. Both court and visitors may perform in person searches. Search fee: $1.00 per name per year. Required to search: name, years to search, DOB; also helpful-address, SSN, race, sex. Criminal records on computer (Felony since 1986, Misdemeanor since 1983), both archived since 1925. **General Information:** No juvenile, child abuse or sexual battery records released. SASE helpful. Turnaround time 2 days. Copy fee: $1.00 per page. Certification fee: $1.00. Fee payee: Clerk of Circuit Court. Personal checks accepted. Prepayment is required. Public access terminal is available.

Jackson County

Circuit & County Courts PO Box 510, Marianna, FL 32447; 850-482-9552; Fax: 850-482-7849. Hours: 8AM-4:30PM (CST). *Felony, Misdemeanor, Civil, Eviction, Small Claims, Probate.*

Civil Records: Access: Fax, mail, in person. Both court and visitors may perform in person searches. Search fee: $1.00 per name per year. Required to search: name, years to search; also helpful-address. Civil cases indexed by defendant, plaintiff. Civil records on computer from 1991. **Criminal Records:** Access: Fax, mail, in person. Both court and visitors may perform in person searches. Search fee: $1.00 per name per year. Required to search: name, years to search, DOB; also helpful-address, SSN, race, sex. Criminal records on computer since 1989. **General Information:** No juvenile, child abuse or sexual battery records released. SASE helpful. Turnaround time 1-5 days. Copy fee: $1.00 per page. Certification fee: $1.00. Fee payee: Clerk of Circuit Court. Personal checks accepted. Credit cards accepted: Visa, Mastercard, AmEx. Prepayment is required. Public access terminal is available. Fax notes: $3.00 for first page, $1.00 each addl.

Jefferson County

Circuit & County Courts Jefferson County Courthouse, Rm 10, Monticello, FL 32344; 850-342-0218; Fax: 850-342-0222. Hours: 8AM-5PM (EST). *Felony, Misdemeanor, Civil, Eviction, Small Claims, Probate.*

www.co.leon.fl.us/court/court.htm

Civil Records: Access: Mail, in person. Both court and visitors may perform in person searches. Search fee: $1.00 per name per year. Required to search: name, years to search; also helpful-address. Civil cases indexed by defendant, plaintiff. Civil records on computer since 7/90, prior on dockets. **Criminal Records:** Access: Fax, mail, in person. Both court and visitors may perform in person searches. Search fee: $1.00 per name per year. Required to search: name, years to search, DOB; also helpful-address, SSN, race, sex. Criminal records on computer since 1989, prior on microfiche from 1969 to 1980, archived since 1950s, prior to 1950 on dockets. **General Information:** No juvenile, child abuse or sexual battery records released. Turnaround time 1 week. Copy fee: $1.00 per page. Certification fee: $1.00. Fee payee: Clerk of Circuit Court. Personal checks accepted. Prepayment is required. Public access terminal is available. Fax notes: $2.00 per page.

Lafayette County

Circuit & County Courts PO Box 88, Mayo, FL 32066; 904-294-1600; Fax: 904-294-4231. Hours: 8AM-5PM (EST). *Felony, Misdemeanor, Civil, Eviction, Small Claims, Probate.*

Civil Records: Access: Phone, mail, in person. Both court and visitors may perform in person searches. No search fee. Required to search: name, years to search; also helpful-address. Civil cases indexed by defendant, plaintiff. Civil records on computer since 1997, on books back to early 1900s. **Criminal Records:** Access: Phone, mail, in person. Both court and visitors may perform in person searches. No search fee. Required to search: name, years to search, DOB; also helpful-address, SSN, race, sex. recocrds computerized since 1989. **General Information:** No juvenile, child abuse or sexual battery records released. SASE required. Turnaround time 5-7 days. Copy

fee: $1.00 per page. Certification fee: $1.00. Fee payee: Clerk of Circuit Court. Personal checks accepted. Prepayment is required. Public access terminal is available.

Lake County

Circuit & County Courts 550 W Main St or PO Box 7800, Tavares, FL 32778; 352-742-4100; Fax: 352-742-4166. Hours: 8:30AM-5PM (EST). *Felony, Misdemeanor, Civil, Eviction, Small Claims, Probate.*

Civil Records: Access: Fax, mail, in person. Both court and visitors may perform in person searches. Search fee: $1.00 per name per year. Required to search: name, years to search; also helpful-address. Civil cases indexed by defendant, plaintiff. Civil records on computer since 1984, county civil on index books since 11/51, circuit civil since 1888. Dial in access available via modem. **Criminal Records:** Access: Fax, mail, in person. Both court and visitors may perform in person searches. Search fee: $1.00 per name per year. Required to search: name, years to search, DOB; also helpful-address, SSN, race, sex. Criminal records on computer since 1983, on microfiche since 1970s, archived since 1920s. Some on index books. **General Information:** No juvenile, child abuse or sexual battery records released. SASE helpful. Turnaround time 7-10 days. Copy fee: $1.00 per page. Certification fee: $1.00. Fee payee: Clerk of Circuit Court. Personal checks accepted. Prepayment is required. Public access terminal is available. Fax notes: $1.00 per page.

Lee County

Circuit & County Courts PO Box 2469, Ft Myers, FL 33902; 941-335-2283. Hours: 7:45AM-5PM (EST). *Felony, Misdemeanor, Civil, Eviction, Small Claims, Probate.*

Civil Records: Access: Mail, online, in person. Both court and visitors may perform in person searches. Search fee: $1.00 per name per year. Required to search: name; also helpful-years to search. Civil cases indexed by defendant, plaintiff. Civil records on computer since 1984, prior on microfilm and dockets. Online entails a $150.00 set up fee, $15.00 per month fee and a per minute access charge. The system is open 24 hours daily and includes probate records. Call Natalie at 941-335-2975 for more information. **Criminal Records:** Access: Mail, remote online, in person. Both court and visitors may perform in person searches. Search fee: $1.00 per name per year. Required to search: name; also helpful-years to search, address, DOB, SSN, race, sex. Criminal records on computer-(Felony since 1978, Misdemeanor since 1986), prior on microfilm. See Civil Records for description of online system. **General Information:** No juvenile, child abuse or sexual battery records released. SASE required. Turnaround time 2 days. Copy fee: $1.00 per page. Certification fee: $1.00. Fee payee: Clerk of Circuit Court. Personal checks accepted. Prepayment is required. Public access terminal is available.

Leon County

Circuit & County Courts PO Box 726, Tallahassee, FL 32302; 850-577-4000; Civil phone:850-577-4170; Criminal phone:850-577-4170; Probate phone:850-577-4180; Fax: 850-488-8863. Hours: 8:30AM-5PM (EST). *Felony, Misdemeanor, Civil, Eviction, Small Claims, Probate.*

www.co.leon.fl.us/court/court.htm

Civil Records: Access: Mail, online, in person. Both court and visitors may perform in person searches. Search fee: $1.00 per name per year. Required to search: name, years to search; also helpful-address. Civil cases indexed by defendant, plaintiff. Civil records on computer since 8/86, prior on docket books. Remote online access system, CHIPS, costs $50 for setup with an annual fee of $120. System includes civil and traffic indexes (as of 12/99) as well as property appraiser, tax assessor, probate and domestic data. Call Terry Turner at 941-741-4003 for more information. **Criminal Records:** Access: Mail, remote online, in person. Both court and visitors may perform in person searches. Search fee: $1.00 per name per year. Required to search: name, years to search, DOB; also helpful-address, SSN, race, sex. Criminal records on computer since 1976, on microfiche since 1937, archived since late 1800s/early 1900s. **General Information:** No juvenile, child abuse or sexual battery records released. SASE helpful. Turnaround time 1-5 days. Copy fee: $1.00 per page. Certification fee: $1.00. Fee payee: Clerk of Circuit Court. Personal checks accepted. Credit cards accepted: Visa, Mastercard. Prepayment is required. Public access terminal is available.

Levy County

Circuit & County Courts PO Box 610, Bronson, FL 32621; 352-486-5100; Fax: 352-486-5166. Hours: 8AM-5PM (EST). *Felony, Misdemeanor, Civil, Eviction, Small Claims, Probate.*

http://circuit8.org

Civil Records: Access: Mail, in person. Both court and visitors may perform in person searches. Search fee: $1.00 per name per year. Required to search: name, years to search; also helpful-address. Civil cases indexed by defendant, plaintiff. Civil records on computer from 1986, microfiche to 1981 (in process), prior on docket books. **Criminal Records:** Access: Mail, in person. Both court and visitors may perform in person searches. Search fee: $1.00 per name per year. Required to search: name, years to search, DOB, signed release; also helpful-address, SSN, race, sex. Criminal records on computer from 1986 to present, prior on docket books. **General Information:** No juvenile, child abuse or sexual battery records released. SASE required. Turnaround time 2-3 days. Copy fee: $1.00 per page. Certification fee: $1.00. Fee payee: Clerk of Circuit Court. Business checks accepted. Prepayment is required. Public access terminal is available.

Liberty County

Circuit & County Courts PO Box 399, Bristol, FL 32321; 850-643-2215; Fax: 850-643-2866. Hours: 8AM-5PM (EST). *Felony, Misdemeanor, Civil, Eviction, Small Claims, Probate.*

www.co.leon.fl.us/court/court.htm

Civil Records: Access: Mail, in person. Both court and visitors may perform in person searches. Search fee: $1.00 per name per year. Required to search: name, years to search; also helpful-address. Civil cases indexed by defendant, plaintiff. Civil records on docket books. **Criminal Records:** Access: Mail, in person. Both court and visitors may perform in person searches. Search fee: $1.00 per name per year. Required to search: name, years to search, DOB; also helpful-address, SSN, race, sex. Criminal records on docket books. **General Information:** No juvenile, child abuse or sexual battery records released. SASE required. Turnaround time 1 week. Copy fee: $1.00 per page. Certification fee: $1.00. Fee payee: Clerk of Circuit Court. Business checks accepted. Prepayment is required.

Madison County

Circuit & County Courts PO Box 237, Madison, FL 32341; 850-973-1500; Fax: 850-973-2059. Hours: 8AM-5PM (EST). *Felony, Misdemeanor, Civil, Eviction, Small Claims, Probate.*

Civil Records: Access: Phone, mail, in person. Both court and visitors may perform in person searches. Search fee: $1.00 per name per year. Required to search: name, years to search; also helpful-address. Civil cases indexed by defendant, plaintiff. Civil records on computer since 1990, prior on docket books. **Criminal Records:** Access: Phone, mail, in person. Both court and visitors may perform in person searches. Search fee: $1.00 per name per year. Required to search: name, years to search, DOB; also helpful-address, SSN, race, sex. Criminal records on computer since 1988, prior on docket books. **General Information:** No juvenile, child abuse or sexual battery records released. SASE requested. Turnaround time 1-3 days. Copy fee: $1.00 per page. Certification fee: $1.00. Fee payee: Clerk of Circuit Court. Personal checks accepted. Prepayment is required.

Manatee County

Circuit & County Courts PO Box 25400, Bradenton, FL 34206; 941-749-1800; Fax: 941-741-4082. Hours: 8:30AM-5PM (EST). *Felony, Misdemeanor, Civil, Eviction, Small Claims, Probate.*

www.clerkofcourts.com

Civil Records: Access: Phone, mail, online, in person. Both court and visitors may perform in person searches. Search fee: $1.00 per name per year. Required to search: name, years to search; also helpful-address. Civil cases indexed by defendant, plaintiff. Civil records on computer since 9/80, prior on microfilm. Two online options are available. Recorded documents from the clerk's office are available free on the internet at the web site. The second online access entails a $100.00 setup fee. The system is open during working hours only. ProComm Plus is required. Records available include civil/criminal, probate, traffic, domestic courts and marriage records. For more information, call 561-288-5985. **Criminal Records:** Access: Phone, mail, remote online, in person. Both court and visitors may perform in person searches. Search fee: $1.00 per name per year. Required to search: name, years to search; also helpful-address, DOB, race, sex. Criminal records on computer since 1981, prior on docket books. **General Information:** No juvenile, adoption, child abuse or sexual battery victim records released. SASE helpful. Turnaround time 2 days. Copy fee: $1.00 per page. Certification fee: $1.00. Fee payee: Clerk of Circuit Court. Personal checks accepted. Credit cards accepted: Visa, Mastercard, Discover. Prepayment is required. Public access terminal is available.

Marion County

Circuit & County Courts PO Box 1030, Ocala, FL 34478; 352-620-3904; Civil phone:352-620-3891; Criminal phone:352-620-3891; Fax: 352-620-3300 (civ); 840-5668 (crim). Hours: 8AM-5PM (EST). *Felony, Misdemeanor, Civil, Eviction, Small Claims, Probate.*

www.clerk.marioncountyfl.org

Civil Records: Access: Fax, mail, in person. Both court and visitors may perform in person searches. Search fee: $1.00 per name per year. Required to search: name, years to search; also helpful-address. Civil cases indexed by defendant, plaintiff. Civil records on computer since 1983, on microfiche since 1958. **Criminal Records:** Access: Fax, mail, in person. Both court and visitors may perform in person searches. Search fee: $1.00 per name per year. Required to search: name, years to search, DOB; also helpful-address, SSN, race, sex. Criminal records on computer. Felonies since 1984, on microfiche from 1950 to 1979, prior on index cards. Misdemeanors since 1983, on microfiche from 1900 to 1982, archived since 1900s, prior on index cards. **General Information:** No juvenile records released. SASE requested. Turnaround time 1-2 weeks. Copy fee: $1.00 per page. Certification fee: $1.00. Fee payee: Clerk of Court. Personal checks accepted. Prepayment is required. Public access terminal is available.

Martin County

Circuit & County Courts PO Box 9016, Stuart, FL 34995; 561-288-5576; Fax: 561-288-5990; 288-5991 (civil). Hours: 8AM-5PM (EST). *Felony, Misdemeanor, Civil, Eviction, Small Claims, Probate.*

www.martin.fl.us/GOVT/co/schack

Civil Records: Access: Phone, fax, mail, online, in person. Both court and visitors may perform in person searches. Search fee: $1.00 per name per year. Required to search: name, years to search; also helpful-address. Civil cases indexed by defendant, plaintiff. Civil records on computer since 10/86, prior on microfiche and archived. There is a dial-up online system that provides civil records from 1987 as well as probate, criminal, domestic and traffic records. The docket is listed. There is a $50 setup fee and a minimum charge of $35 per month. Call Cindy Johnson at 318-965-2336 for further details. **Criminal Records:** Access: Phone, fax, mail, remote online, in person. Both court and visitors may perform in person searches. Search fee: $1.00 per name per year. Required to search: name, years to search, DOB; also helpful-address, SSN. Criminal records on computer. Felonies since 1986, on microfiche since 1956, prior on index cards and docket books. Misdemeanors since 1985, on microfiche since 1973, prior on index cards and docket books. **General Information:** No juvenile, child abuse or sexual battery records released. Turnaround time 1 week. Copy fee: $1.00 per page. Certification fee: $1.00. Fee payee: Bossier Parish Clerk of Court. Personal checks accepted. Prepayment is required. Public access terminal is available. Fax notes: $1.25 per page.

Monroe County

Circuit & County Courts 500 Whitehead St, Key West, FL 33040; 305-294-4641; Civil phone:305-292-3310; Criminal phone:305-292-3310; Fax: 305-295-3623. Hours: 8:30AM-5PM (EST). *Felony, Misdemeanor, Civil, Eviction, Small Claims, Probate.*

Civil Records: Access: Mail, in person. Both court and visitors may perform in person searches. Search fee: $1.00 per name per year. Required to search: name, years to search; also helpful-address. Civil cases indexed by defendant, plaintiff. Civil records on computer since 1983, on microfiche since 1972, prior on docket books. Some records purged after 2 years. Probate from 1972. **Criminal**

Records: Access: Mail, in person. Both court and visitors may perform in person searches. Search fee: $1.00 per name per year. Required to search: name, years to search, DOB; also helpful-address, SSN, race, sex. Criminal records (pending felony and misdemeanors) on computer, others since 1992, non-pending on microfiche since 1945. **General Information:** No juvenile, child abuse or sexual battery records released. SASE helpful. Turnaround time 1-2 weeks. Copy fee: $1.00 per page. Certification fee: $1.00. Fee payee: Clerk of Circuit Court. Personal checks accepted. Prepayment is required. Public access terminal is available.

Nassau County

Circuit & County Courts PO Box 456, Fernandina Beach, FL 32035; 904-321-5700; Fax: 904-321-5723. Hours: 9AM-5PM (EST). *Felony, Misdemeanor, Civil, Eviction, Small Claims, Probate.*

Civil Records: Access: Phone, fax, mail, in person. Only the court conducts in person searches; visitors may not. Search fee: $1.00 per name per year. Required to search: name, years to search; also helpful-address. Civil cases indexed by defendant, plaintiff. Civil records on computer since 1993, on microfiche since 1982, prior on docket books. **Criminal Records:** Access: Phone, fax, mail, in person. Only the court conducts in person searches; visitors may not. Search fee: $1.00 per name per year. Required to search: name, years to search, DOB; also helpful-address, SSN, race, sex. Criminal records on computer since 1985, on microfiche since 1982, prior on docket books. Past 5 years only can be done on the phone. **General Information:** No juvenile, child abuse or sexual battery records released. SASE required. Turnaround time 1 week. Copy fee: $1.00 per page. Certification fee: $1.00. Fee payee: Clerk of Circuit Court. Personal checks accepted. Prepayment is required. Fax notes: $1.00 per page.

Okaloosa County

Circuit & County Courts 1250 Eglin Pkwy, Shalimar, FL 32579; 850-651-7200; Fax: 850-651-7230. Hours: 8AM-5PM (CST). *Felony, Misdemeanor, Civil, Eviction, Small Claims, Probate.*

www.co.okaloosa.fl.us/clerk.html

Civil Records: Access: Mail, online, in person. Both court and visitors may perform in person searches. Search fee: $6.00 per name. Add $1.00 for each year searched prior to 6/86. Required to search: name, years to search; also helpful-address. Civil cases indexed by defendant, plaintiff. Civil records on computer from 6/86, archived from 1915, prior on index cards. Online access is available 24 hours daily with a monthly fee of $100.00. Searching is by name or case number. Records include probate, traffic and domestic records. For more information, call 850-689-5821. **Criminal Records:** Access: Mail, remote online, in person. Both court and visitors may perform in person searches. Search fee: $6.00 per name. Add $1.00 for each year searched prior to 6/89. Required to search: name, years to search, DOB; also helpful-address, SSN, race, sex. Criminal records on computer from 6/86, archived from 1915, prior on index cards. Online access is the same as civil records. Both felony and misdemeanor indexes can be searched. **General Information:** No juvenile, child abuse or sexual battery records released. SASE required. Turnaround time 1 week. Copy fee: $1.00 per page. Certification fee: $1.00. Fee payee: Clerk of Circuit Court. Personal checks accepted. Prepayment is required. Public access terminal is available.

Okeechobee County

Circuit & County Courts 304 NW 2nd St Rm 101, Okeechobee, FL 34972; 863-763-2131. Hours: 8:30AM-5PM (EST). *Felony, Misdemeanor, Civil, Eviction, Small Claims, Probate.*

Civil Records: Access: Mail, in person. Both court and visitors may perform in person searches. Search fee: $1.00 per name per year. Required to search: name, years to search; also helpful-address. Civil cases indexed by defendant, plaintiff. Civil records on computer since 1990, on index cards from 1983 to 1988. **Criminal Records:** Access: Mail, in person. Both court and visitors may perform in person searches. Search fee: $1.00 per name per year. Required to search: name, years to search, DOB; also helpful-address, SSN, race, sex. Criminal records on computer since 1989, on index cards from 1932 to 1988. **General Information:** No juvenile, child abuse or sexual battery records released. SASE required. Turnaround time for criminal 2 weeks, civil 1-2 weeks. Copy fee: $1.00 per page. Certification fee: $1.00. Fee payee: Clerk of Circuit Court. Personal checks accepted. Prepayment is required.

Orange County

Circuit & County Courts 425 N Orange Ave, Orlando, FL 32801-1544; 407-836-2060. Hours: 8AM-5PM (EST). *Felony, Misdemeanor, Civil, Eviction, Small Claims, Probate.*

http://orangeclerk.ocfl.net

Note: Mail requests should use room numbers: civil circuit-310; civil county-358; crim circuit-210; crim county-250

Civil Records: Access: Mail, online, in person. Both court and visitors may perform in person searches. Search fee: $1.00 per name per year. Required to search: name, years to search. Civil cases indexed by defendant, plaintiff. Civil records are on computer as follows: Circuit civil-1992; Domestic civil-1990; probate-1993; traffic-1990. The Teleclerk remote online system costs are a $100 one time fee and $30 per month, for unlimited online time. The system is open 24 hours daily and includes probate, traffic and domestic records. For more information call 407-836-2064. **Criminal Records:** Access: Mail, remote online, in person. Both court and visitors may perform in person searches. Search fee: $1.00 per name per year. Required to search: name, years to search, DOB. Criminal records on computer from 1988. Online access is the same as described for civil records. **General Information:** No sex related or adoption records released. SASE helpful. Turnaround time 2 days. Copy fee: $1.00 per page. For more information call 407-836-2064. Certification fee: $1.00. Fee payee: Orange County Clerk of Courts. Personal checks accepted. Prepayment is required. Public access terminal is available. Public Access Terminal Note: Available in Records Management Division.

County Court #3 475 W Story Rd, Ocoee, FL 34761; 407-656-3229. Hours: 8AM-5PM (EST). *Misdemeanor, Civil Actions Under $15,000, Eviction, Small Claims.*

http://orangeclerk.ocfl.net

Civil Records: Access: Mail, in person. Both court and visitors may perform in person searches. Search fee: $5.00 per name per year. Required to

search: name, years to search. Civil cases indexed by defendant, plaintiff. Civil records (Pending) on computer. All dockets are on microfilm or microfiche. **Criminal Records:** Access: Mail, in person. Both court and visitors may perform in person searches. Search fee: $5.00 per name per year. Required to search: name, years to search, DOB; also helpful-SSN. Criminal records (Pending) on computer. All dockets are on microfilm or microfiche. **General Information:** No sex related or adoption records released. SASE helpful. Turnaround time 2 days (depending on file). Copy fee: $1.00 per page. Certification fee: $2.00 per page. Fee payee: Clerk of County Court. Personal checks accepted. Credit cards accepted: Visa, Mastercard. Accepted for civil payments only. Prepayment is required.

County Court - Apopka Branch 1111 N Rock Springs Rd, Apopka, FL 32712; 407-654-1030. Hours: 8AM-5PM (EST). *Misdemeanor, Civil Actions Under $15,000, Eviction, Small Claims.*

http://orangeclerk.ocfl.net

Note: Records maintained at Orlando office

Civil Records: Access: Mail, in person. Both court and visitors may perform in person searches. Search fee: $1.00 per name per year. Required to search: name, years to search. Civil cases indexed by defendant, plaintiff. Civil records (Pending) on computer. All dockets on microfilm or microfiche. Some records on index cards. **Criminal Records:** Access: Mail, in person. Both court and visitors may perform in person searches. Search fee: $5.00 per name. Required to search: name, years to search, DOB; also helpful-SSN. Criminal records (Pending) on computer. All dockets on microfilm or microfiche. Some records on index cards. **General Information:** No sex related or adoption records released. SASE helpful. Turnaround time 2 days. Copy fee: $1.00 per page. Certification fee: $2.00. Fee payee: Clerk of County Court. Personal checks accepted. Prepayment is required. Public access terminal is available.

County Court-NE Orange Division 450 N Lakemont Ave, Winter Park, FL 32792; 407-671-1116. Hours: 8AM-5PM (EST). *Misdemeanor, Civil Actions Under $15,000, Eviction, Small Claims.*

http://orangeclerk.ocfl.net

Civil Records: Access: Phone, mail, in person. Only the court conducts in person searches; visitors may not. Search fee: $1.00 per name per year. Required to search: name, years to search. Civil cases indexed by defendant, plaintiff. Civil records (Pending) on computer. All dockets on microfilm or microfiche. **Criminal Records:** Access: Phone, mail, in person. Only the court conducts in person searches; visitors may not. Search fee: $1.00 per name per year. Required to search: name, years to search, DOB; also helpful-SSN. Criminal records (Pending) on computer. All dockets on microfilm or microfiche. **General Information:** No sex related or adoption records released. SASE helpful. Turnaround time 2 days. Copy fee: $1.00 per page. Certification fee: $1.00. Fee payee: Clerk of County Court. Only cashiers checks and money orders accepted. Prepayment is required.

Osceola County

Circuit Court - Civil 17 S Vernon Ave, Kissimmee, FL 34741; 407-847-1300 #3 X1448. Hours: 8:30AM-5PM (EST). *Civil Actions Over $5,000.*

www.ninja9.net

Civil Records: Access: Mail, in person. Both court and visitors may perform in person searches. Search fee: $1.00 per name per year. Required to search: name, years to search. Civil cases indexed by defendant, plaintiff. Civil records on computer from 1990, on docket books from 1800s to 1990. **General Information:** No appeal records released. SASE required. Turnaround time 1-2 days. Copy fee: $1.00 per page. Certification fee: $1.00. Fee payee: Clerk of Court. Business checks accepted. Prepayment is required.

Circuit & County Courts-Criminal Division 17 S Vernon Ave, Kissimmee, FL 34741; 407-343-3543/3556. Hours: 8:30AM-5PM (EST). *Felony, Misdemeanor.*

www.ninja9.net **Criminal Records:** Access: Mail, in person. Only the court conducts in person searches; visitors may not. Search fee: $1.00 per name per year. Required to search: name, years to search, DOB, SSN. Criminal records on computer since 1986, on index since 1978, prior on docket books from 1800s to 1978. **General Information:** No juvenile or sealed records released. SASE requested. Turnaround time 1 week. Copy fee: $1.00 per page. Certification fee: $1.00. Fee payee: Money orders payable to Clerk of the Court. Business checks accepted. Prepayment is required.

County Court-Civil 17 S Vernon Ave, Kissimmee, FL 34741; 407-847-1300. Hours: 8:30AM-5PM (EST). *Eviction, Small Claims.*

www.ninja9.net

Civil Records: Access: Mail, in person. Both court and visitors may perform in person searches. Search fee: $1.00 per name per year. Required to search: name, years to search. Civil cases indexed by defendant, plaintiff. Civil records on computer from 1991, on index cards from 1972 to 1991, on docket books from 1800s to 1972. **General Information:** No juvenile records released. SASE helpful. Turnaround time 1 week. Copy fee: $1.00 per page. Certification fee: $1.00. Fee payee: Clerk of Court. Business checks accepted. Prepayment is required.

Palm Beach County

Circuit Court-Civil Division PO Box 4667, West Palm Beach, FL 33402; 561-355-2986; Fax: 561-355-4643. Hours: 8AM-5PM (EST). *Civil.*

www.pbcountyclerk.com

Civil Records: Access: Phone, mail, online, in person. Both court and visitors may perform in person searches. Search fee: $1.00 per name per year. Required to search: name, years to search; also helpful-address. Civil cases indexed by defendant, plaintiff. Civil records (Circuit) on computer from 1982, prior records on microfiche and dockets. County on computer from 1987, prior on microfilm. Contact Betty Jones at 561-355-6783 for information about remote access. Fees are $145 setup and $65 per month. Civil index goes back to 1988. Records available include probate, traffic and domestic. **General Information:** No juvenile, child abuse or sexual battery records released. SASE required. Turnaround time 1 week. Copy fee: $1.00 per page. Certification fee: $1.00. Fee payee: Clerk of Circuit Court. Personal checks accepted. Prepayment is required. Public access terminal is available.

Circuit & County Courts - Criminal Division 205 North Dixie Hwy, West Palm Beach, FL 33401; 561-355-2519; Fax: 561-355-

3802. Hours: 8AM-5PM (EST). *Felony, Misdemeanor.*

www.pbcountyclerk.com **Criminal Records:** Access: Phone, fax, mail, remote online, in person. Both court and visitors may perform in person searches. Search fee: $1.00 per name per year. Required to search: name, years to search, DOB, aliases. Criminal records on computer & microfiche (some files) from 1970s, archived from 1920s. Contact Ms. Kokollari at 561-355-4277 for information about remote access. Fees include $145 setup and $65 per month. Criminal records available back to 1988. The system is open 18 hours daily. **General Information:** No juvenile, child abuse or sexual battery records released. SASE not required. Turnaround time 1 day. Copy fee: $1.00 per page. Certification fee: $1.00. Fee payee: Clerk of Circuit Court. Personal checks accepted. Prepayment is required. Public access terminal is available.

County Court-Civil Division PO Box 3406, West Palm Beach, FL 33402; 561-355-2986; Fax: 561-355-4643. Hours: 8AM-5PM (EST). *Eviction, Small Claims.*

www.pbcountyclerk.com

Civil Records: Access: Phone, mail, online, in person. Both court and visitors may perform in person searches. Search fee: $1.00 per name per year. Required to search: name, years to search; also helpful-address. Civil cases indexed by defendant, plaintiff. Civil records (Circuit) on computer from 1982, prior records on microfiche and dockets. County on computer from 1987, prior on microfilm. Contact Ms. Kokollari at 561-355-4277 for information about remote access. Fees are $145 setup and $65 per month. **General Information:** No juvenile, child abuse or sexual battery records released. SASE required. Turnaround time 1 week. Copy fee: $1.00 per page. Certification fee: $1.00. Fee payee: Clerk of Circuit Court. Personal checks accepted. Prepayment is required. Public access terminal is available.

County Court-Probate Division PO Box 4238, West Palm Beach, FL 33402; 561-355-2986; Fax: 561-355-4643. Hours: 8AM-5PM (EST). *Probate.*

Pasco County

Circuit & County Courts - Civil Division 38053 Live Oak Ave, Dade City, FL 33523; 352-521-4482. Hours: 8:30AM-5PM (EST). *Civil, Eviction, Small Claims, Probate.*

www.jud6.org

Civil Records: Access: Mail, online, in person. Both court and visitors may perform in person searches. Search fee: $1.00 per name per year. Required to search: name, years to search. Civil cases indexed by defendant, plaintiff. Civil records on computer from 1985, on docket cards and docket books from 1900s. Online access requires a $100 deposit, $50 annual fee and minimum of $10.00 per month. There is a $.10 per screen charge. Probate records also available. Call 352-521-4201 for more information. **General Information:** No adoption records released. Turnaround time 2-4 days. Copy fee: $1.00 per page. Certification fee: $1.00. Fee payee: Clerk of Court. Personal checks accepted. Prepayment is required. Public access terminal is available.

Circuit & County Courts-Criminal Division 38053 Live Oak Ave, Dade City, FL 33523-3894; 352-521-4491. Hours: 8:30AM-5PM (EST). *Felony, Misdemeanor.*

www.jud6.org **Criminal Records:** Access: Mail, remote online, in person. Both court and visitors may perform in person searches. Search fee: $1.00 per name per year. Required to search: name, years to search, address, DOB; also helpful-SSN. Criminal records on computer since 1978. Online access requires a $100 deposit, $50 annual fee and $10 minimum per month. There is a $.10 per screen charge. The system is open 24 hours daily. Search by name or case number. Call Barbara Alford at 352-521-4201 for more information. **General Information:** No confidential, sealed or juvenile records released. Turnaround time 2-4 days. Copy fee: $1.00 per page. Certification fee: $1.00. Fee payee: Clerk of Courts. Personal checks accepted. Out of state personal checks not accepted. Prepayment is required. Public access terminal is available.

Pinellas County

Circuit & County Courts - Civil Division 315 Court St, Clearwater, FL 33756; 727-464-3267; Fax: 727-464-4070. Hours: 8AM-5PM (EST). *Civil, Eviction, Small Claims, Probate.*

www.jud6.org

Civil Records: Access: Phone, fax, mail, online, in person. Both court and visitors may perform in person searches. Search fee: $1.00 per name per year. Required to search: name, years to search. Civil cases indexed by defendant, plaintiff. Civil records on computer from 1980, on microfiche from 1900s to 1982, older data in warehouse. Call Sue Maskeny at 727-464-3779 for information about remote access. Setup fee is $60 plus $.05 per screen. Civil index goes back to 1973. The system is open 24 hours daily and includes probate and traffic records. **General Information:** No adoption or juvenile records released. SASE helpful. Turnaround time 1 week. Copy fee: $1.00 per page. Certification fee: $1.00. Fee payee: Clerk of the Court. Personal checks accepted. Prepayment is required. Public access terminal is available. Fax notes: $1.00 per page.

Criminal Justice Center Circuit Criminal Court Records, 14250 49th St N, Clearwater, FL 34622; 727-464-6793; Fax: 727-464-6233. Hours: 8AM-5PM (EST). *Felony.*

www.jud6.org **Criminal Records:** Access: Phone, fax, mail, remote online, in person. Both court and visitors may perform in person searches. Search fee: $1.00 per name per year. Required to search: name, years to search, DOB. Criminal records on computer from 1977, on microfilm from 1912 to 1976, on docket books from 1912. Contact Sue Maskeny at 727-464-3779 for information about remote access. The setup fee is $60 plus $.05 per screen. Criminal index goes back to 1972. Available 24 hours per day at 28.9 baud. **General Information:** Turnaround time 1 week. Copy fee: $1.00 per page. Certification fee: $1.00. Fee payee: Clerk of Circuit Court. Personal checks accepted. Prepayment is required. Public access terminal is available. Fax notes: $1.00 per page.

County Court - Criminal Division 14250 49th St N, Clearwater, FL 34622-2831; 727-464-7000; Fax: 727-464-7040. Hours: 8AM-5PM (EST). *Misdemeanor.*

www.jud6.org **Criminal Records:** Access: Mail, remote online, in person. Both court and visitors may perform in person searches. Search fee: $1.00 per name per year. Required to search: name, years to search; also helpful-address, DOB, SSN. Criminal records on computer since 10/77, prior on index books. Prior to 1993 on microfiche.

Contact Sue Maskeny at 727-464-3779 for information about remote access. Fees are $60 setup and per minute charge. Criminal index goes back to 1972. **General Information:** No sealed or non-arrested case records released. Turnaround time 3-5 days. Copy fee: $1.00 per page. Certification fee: $1.00. Fee payee: Clerk of Courts. Personal checks accepted. Prepayment is required. Public access terminal is available.

Polk County

Circuit Court-Civil Division PO Box 9000, Drawer CC2, Bartow, FL 33831-9000; 863-534-4488; Probate phone:863-534-4478; Fax: 863-534-7707. Hours: 8AM-5PM (EST). *Civil Actions Over $15,000, Probate.*

www.polk-county.net/clerk/clerk.html

Civil Records: Access: Phone, mail, online, in person. Both court and visitors may perform in person searches. Search fee: $1.00 per name per year. Required to search: name. Civil cases indexed by defendant, plaintiff. Civil Records on computer since 1978, on microfiche from 1800s to 1978. Two options are available. Online access to the complete database requires a $150 setup fee and $.15 per minute charge with a $50 minimum per quarter. Call 863-534-7575 for more information. Second, case index information is available free from the County Clerk's web site at www.polk-county.net/clerk/clerk.html. Search by name, case number, file number, book & page, or document type. Includes land and lien searching. **General Information:** No sex related cases, adoption, confidential, victims or child abuse records released. SASE required. Turnaround time 2-3 days. Copy fee: $1.00 per page. Certification fee: $1.00. Fee payee: Clerk of Court. Personal checks accepted. Prepayment is required.

Circuit & County Courts - Felony Division PO Box 9000 Drawer CC9, Bartow, FL 33830; 863-534-4000; Fax: 863-534-4137. Hours: 8AM-5PM (EST). *Felony.*

http://jud10.flcourts.org **Criminal Records:** Access: Phone, mail, remote online, in person. Both court and visitors may perform in person searches. Search fee: $1.00 per name per year. Required to search: name, years to search, DOB; also helpful-SSN. Criminal records on computer-felonies since 1977, misdemeanors purged periodically. Both on microfiche and archived since 1800s. Two options are available. Online access to the complete database requires a $150 setup fee and $.15 per minute charge with a $50 minimum per quarter. Call 863-534-7575 for more information. Second, case index information is available free from the County Clerk's web site at www.polk-county.net/clerk/clerk.html. Search by name, case number, file number, book & page, or document type. Includes land and lien searching. **General Information:** No sex related cases, victims or child abuse released. Turnaround time varies. Indicate on request when record is needed. Copy fee: $1.00 per page. Certification fee: $1.00. Fee payee: Clerk of Circuit Court. Personal checks accepted. Prepayment is required. Public access terminal is available.

Circuit & County Courts-Misdemeanor Division PO Box 9000 Drawer CC10, Bartow, FL 33831-9000; 863-534-4446; Fax: 863-534-4137. Hours: 8AM-5PM (EST). *Misdemeanor.*

www.polk-county.net/clerk/clerk.html **Criminal Records:** Access: Phone, mail, remote online, in person. Both court and visitors may perform in person searches. Search fee: 3 year search: $4.10; lifetime: $5.10. Required to search: name, years to search, DOB; also helpful-SSN. Criminal records on computer; felonies since 1977, misdemeanors purged periodically. Both on microfiche and archived since 1800s. Two options are available. Online access to the complete database requires a $150 setup fee and $.15 per minute charge with a $50 minimum per quarter. Call 863-534-7575 for more information. Second, case index information is available free from the County Clerk's web site at www.polk-county.net/clerk/clerk.html. Search by name, case number, file number, book & page, or document type. Includes land and lien searching. **General Information:** No sex related cases, victims or child abuse released. Turnaround time varies. Indicate on request when record is needed. Copy fee: $1.00 per page. Certification fee: $1.00. Fee payee: Clerk of Circuit Court. Personal checks accepted. Prepayment is required. Public access terminal is available.

County Court-Civil Division PO Box 9000 Drawer CC12, Bartow, FL 33830-9000; 863-534-4556; Fax: 863-534-4089. Hours: 8AM-5PM (EST). *Civil Actions Under $15,000, Eviction, Small Claims.*

www.polk-county.net/clerk/clerk.html

Civil Records: Access: Phone, mail, online, in person. Both court and visitors may perform in person searches. No search fee. Required to search: name, years to search. Civil cases indexed by defendant, plaintiff. Civil records on computer from 1983, on microfiche from 1961 to 1995. Two options are available. Online access to the complete database requires a $150 setup fee and $.15 per minute charge with a $50 minimum per quarter. Call 863-534-7575 for more information. Second, case index information is available free from the County Clerk's web site at www.polk-county.net/clerk/clerk.html. Search by name, case number, file number, book & page, or document type. Includes land and lien searching. **General Information:** Turnaround time 1-5 days. Copy fee: $1.00 per page. Certification fee: $1.00. Fee payee: Clerk of Court. Only cashiers checks and money orders accepted. Prepayment is required. Public access terminal is available.

Putnam County

Circuit & County Courts - Civil Division PO Box 758, Palatka, FL 32178; 904-329-0361; Fax: 904-329-0888. Hours: 8:30AM-5PM (EST). *Civil, Eviction, Small Claims, Probate.*

www.co.putnam.fl.us/clerkofcourt

Civil Records: Access: Mail, online, in person. Both court and visitors may perform in person searches. Search fee: $1.00 per name per year. Required to search: name, years to search. Civil cases indexed by defendant, plaintiff. Civil records on computer from 1984, on microfiche from 1973 to 1984, on index cards and docket books from 1900s to 1973. See Criminal Division for information about remote access. Civil index goes back to 1984. **General Information:** No juvenile or incompetency records released. SASE requested. Turnaround time 2-3 days. Copy fee: $1.00 per page. Certification fee: $1.00. Fee payee: Clerk of Court. Personal checks accepted. Prepayment is required. Public access terminal is available.

Circuit & County Courts-Criminal Division PO Box 758, Palatka, FL 32178; 904-329-0249; Fax: 904-329-0888. Hours: 8:30AM-5PM (EST). *Felony, Misdemeanor.*

www.co.putnam.fl.us/clerkofcourt   **Criminal Records:** Access: Phone, fax, mail, remote online, in person. Both court and visitors may perform in person searches. Search fee: $1.00 per name per year. Required to search: name, years to search; also helpful-DOB. Criminal records on computer from 1988, in files from 1930s to 1988. Write Ryel Christiansen to register; include a check for $400 as a setup fee. The monthly charge is $40 plus $.05 per minute over 20 hours. Criminal records go back to 1972. System includes civil and real property records and operates 24 hours daily. **General Information:** No juvenile records released. Turnaround time 2-3 days. Copy fee: $1.00 per page. Certification fee: $1.00. Fee payee: Clerk of Circuit Court. Personal checks accepted. Prepayment is required. Public access terminal is available.

Santa Rosa County

Circuit & County Courts - Civil Division PO Box 472, Milton, FL 32572; 850-623-0135; Fax: 850-626-7248. Hours: 8AM-4:30PM (CST). *Civil, Eviction, Small Claims, Probate.*

Civil Records: Access: Fax, mail, in person. Both court and visitors may perform in person searches. Search fee: $1.00 per name per year. Required to search: name, years to search. Civil cases indexed by defendant, plaintiff. Civil records (Circuit) on computer from 1990, archived and on docket books from 1900s. County on computer from 11/92, on microfiche from 1900s, on docket books from early 1900s. **General Information:** No adoption records released. SASE required. Turnaround time ASAP. Copy fee: $1.00 per page. Certification fee: $1.00. Fee payee: Clerk of Courts. Personal checks accepted. Prepayment is required. Public access terminal is available. Fax notes: $2.00 per page.

Circuit & County Courts-Criminal Division PO Box 472, Milton, FL 32572; 850-623-0135; Fax: 850-626-7248. Hours: 8AM-4:30PM (CST). *Felony, Misdemeanor.* **Criminal Records:** Access: Mail, in person. Both court and visitors may perform in person searches. Search fee: $1.00 per name per year. Required to search: name, years to search, DOB; also helpful-SSN. Criminal records on computer from 1989, felony on index cards from 1925, misdemeanors on docket books from 1900s. **General Information:** No records released before sentencing. SASE required. Turnaround time 1-5 days. Copy fee: $1.00 per page. Certification fee: $1.00. Fee payee: Clerk's Office. Personal checks accepted. Prepayment is required. Fax notes: $2.00 per page.

Sarasota County

Circuit & County Courts - Civil Division PO Box 3079, Sarasota, FL 34230; 941-951-5206. Hours: 8:30AM-5PM (EST). *Civil, Eviction, Small Claims, Probate.*

www.clerk.co.sarasota.fl.us/civilapp/civilinq.asp

Civil Records: Access: Mail, online, in person. Both court and visitors may perform in person searches. Search fee: $1.00 per name per year. Required to search: name, years to search. Civil cases indexed by defendant, plaintiff. Civil records on computer from 1983, circuit on docket books from 1900s to 1983, county from 1960s to 1983. Contact Tom Kay for information about remote access. Cost is $15 per month minimum against $.15 per minute, with an initial deposit of $300. System operates 8-5 daily at 9600 baud. Index goes back to 1983. Probate and domestic records

included. Probate court records are available free on the Internet at www.clerk.co.sarasota.fl.us/probapp/probinq.asp. **General Information:** No adoption or juvenile, sealed records released. SASE helpful. Turnaround time 1 week. Copy fee: $1.00 per page. Certification fee: $1.00. Fee payee: Clerk of Circuit Court. Personal checks accepted. Credit cards will be accepted as of 07/97. Prepayment is required. Public access terminal is available.

Circuit & County Courts-Criminal PO Box 3079, Sarasota, FL 34230; 941-362-4066. Hours: 8:30AM-5PM (EST). *Felony, Misdemeanor.*

www.clerk.co.sarasota.fl.us/crimdisclaim.htm

Criminal Records: Access: Mail, in person. Both court and visitors may perform in person searches. Search fee: $1.00 per name per year. Required to search: name, years to search, DOB, SSN. Criminal records on computer since 1983, (circuit) on docket books from 1900s to 1983, (county) on docket books from 1960s to 1983. **General Information:** No juvenile records released. SASE helpful. Turnaround time 1 week. Copy fee: $1.00 per page. Certification fee: $1.00. Fee payee: Clerk of Circuit Court. Personal checks accepted. Prepayment is required. Public access terminal is available.

Seminole County

Circuit & County Courts - Civil Division PO Drawer C, Sanford, FL 32772-0659; 407-665-4330; Fax: 407-330-7193. Hours: 8AM-4:30PM (EST). *Civil, Eviction, Small Claims, Probate.*

www.18thcircuit.state.fl.us

Civil Records: Access: Mail, in person. Both court and visitors may perform in person searches. Search fee: $1.00 per name per year. Required to search: name, years to search. Civil cases indexed by defendant, plaintiff. Civil records on computer since 1986, on microfiche since 1913. **General Information:** No confidential files pursuant to law or sealed records released. SASE required. Turnaround time 1 week. Copy fee: $1.00 per page. Certification fee: $1.00. Fee payee: Clerk of the Circuit Court. Personal checks accepted. Prepayment is required. Public access terminal is available.

Circuit & County Courts-Criminal Division 301 N Park Ave, Sanford, FL 32771; 407-665-4356 (Felony) 4377 (Misd). Hours: 8AM-4:30PM (EST). *Felony, Misdemeanor.*

www.18thcircuit.state.fl.us   **Criminal Records:** Access: Mail, in person. Both court and visitors may perform in person searches. Search fee: $1.00 per name per year. Required to search: name, years to search, DOB; also helpful-race, sex. Criminal records on computer from 1986. **General Information:** No records of investigations which have not resulted in an arrest released. SASE not required. Turnaround time 2 days for felonies, no set time for misdemeanors. Copy fee: $1.00 per page. Certification fee: $1.00. Fee payee: Clerk of Courts. Business checks accepted. Local personal and company checks allowed. Prepayment is required. Public access terminal is available.

St. Johns County

Circuit & County Courts - Civil Division PO Drawer 300, St Augustine, FL 32085-0300; 904-823-2333; Fax: 904-823-2294. Hours: 8AM-5PM (EST). *Civil, Eviction, Small Claims, Probate.* www.co.st-johns.fl.us

Civil Records: Access: Fax, mail, online, in person. Both court and visitors may perform in person searches. Search fee: $1.00 per name per year. Required to search: name, years to search. Civil cases indexed by defendant, plaintiff. Civil records on computer from 1984, on micrfiche from 1976 to 1986, on docket books from 1820 to 1983. County on computer from 1991, microfiche from 1983 to 1991, docket books from 1820 to 1983. Online access requires dedicated phone line. Setup is $200 and there is a monthly fee of $50. The index and dockets are available from 1984. Call Mark Dearing at 904-823-2333 x361 for more information. **General Information:** No confidential or sealed records released. SASE required. Turnaround time 4-5 days. Copy fee: $1.00 per page. Certification fee: $1.00. Fee payee: Clerk of Circuit Court. Personal checks accepted. Credit cards accepted: Visa, Mastercard. Prepayment is required. Public access terminal is available. Fax notes: Long distance: $2.25 for first page, $1.00 each add'l; Local: $1.25 1st page, $1.00 each add'l.

Circuit & County Courts-Criminal Division
PO Drawer 300, St Augustine, FL 32085-0300; 904-823-2333; Fax: 904-823-2294. Hours: 8AM-5PM (EST). *Felony, Misdemeanor.*

www.co.st-johns.fl.us **Criminal Records:** Access: Fax, mail, remote online, in person. Both court and visitors may perform in person searches. Search fee: $1.00 per name per year. Required to search: name, years to search, DOB; also helpful-address, SSN. Criminal Records on computer. Felony since 1986, Misdemeanor since 1984. Felony on log books from 1950 to 1984. Online requires a dedicated phone line. Setup is $200 plus a monthly fee of $50. The system is open 8-5 during the week. Searching is by name or case number. Call Mark Dearing at 904-823-2333 for more information. **General Information:** No juvenile or sexual offense records released. SASE required. Turnaround time 4-5 days. Copy fee: $1.00 per page. Certification fee: $1.00. Fee payee: Clerk of Circuit Court. Personal checks accepted. Credit cards accepted: Visa, Mastercard. Escrow & billing accounts available to government agencies. Public access terminal is available. Fax notes: Fax fee $1.25 ($2.25 if long distance) plus $1.00 per page.

St. Lucie County

Circuit & County Courts - Civil Division
PO Drawer 700, Ft Pierce, FL 34954; 561-462-2758; Civil phone:561-462-6950 (SC,Ev); Fax: 561-462-1283. Hours: 8AM-5PM (EST). *Civil, Eviction, Small Claims, Probate.*

www.martin.fl.us/GOVT/co/schack

Civil Records: Access: Mail, in person. Both court and visitors may perform in person searches. Search fee: $1.00 per name per year. Required to search: name, years to search. Civil cases indexed by defendant, plaintiff. Circuit on computer from 1986, county from 1986. Circuit on microfiche from 1981 to 1986, county from 1981 to 1989. Circuit on docket books from 1900s to 1981, county from 1900s to 1986. **General Information:** No sealed cases or adoption records released. Turnaround time 1 day. Copy fee: $1.00 per page. Certification fee: $1.00. Fee payee: Clerk of Court. Personal checks accepted. Drivers license & photo ID required. Prepayment is required.

Circuit & County Courts-Criminal Division
PO Drawer 700, Ft Pierce, FL 34954;

561-462-6900; Fax: 561-462-1174. Hours: 8AM-5PM (EST). *Felony, Misdemeanor.*

www.martin.fl.us/GOVT/co/schack **Criminal Records:** Access: Fax, mail, in person. Both court and visitors may perform in person searches. Search fee: $1.00 per name per year. Required to search: name, years to search, DOB, signed release; also helpful-address, SSN, race, sex. Criminal records are computerized for 10 years, then placed on microfiche to 1960, on books prior to 1900s. **General Information:** No sealed or expunged records released. Turnaround time 1-2 weeks, FAX turnaround time 1-5 days. Copy fee: $1.00 per page. Certification fee: $2.00. Fee payee: Clerk of Court. Personal checks accepted. Prepayment is required. Fax notes: $2.00 per page.

Sumter County

Circuit & County Courts - Civil Division
209 N Florida St, Bushnell, FL 33513; 352-793-0215; Fax: 352-793-0218. Hours: 8:30AM-5PM (EST). *Civil, Eviction, Small Claims, Probate.*

Civil Records: Access: Phone, fax, mail, in person. Both court and visitors may perform in person searches. Search fee: $1.00 per name per year. Required to search: name, years to search. Civil cases indexed by defendant, plaintiff. Civil records on computer from 1986 (circuit only), on docket books from 1800s. **General Information:** No juvenile or adoption records released. SASE requested. Turnaround time 1 week, phone turnaround 30 min. to 1 hour. Copy fee: $1.00 per page. Certification fee: $1.00. Fee payee: Clerk of Circuit Court. Personal checks accepted. Prepayment is required. Fax notes: $1.00 per page.

Circuit & County Courts-Criminal Division
209 N Florida St, Bushnell, FL 33513; 352-793-0211; Fax: 352-568-6608. Hours: 8:30AM-5PM (EST). *Felony, Misdemeanor.* **Criminal Records:** Access: Mail, in person. Only the court conducts in person searches; visitors may not. Search fee: $1.00 per name per year. Required to search: name, years to search, DOB. Criminal records (circuit) on computer since 1988, on index books from 1965 to 1988, prior in vaults. County on computer since 1982, on microfiche from 1960 to 1982, on docket books since early 1900s. **General Information:** No juvenile records released. SASE requested. Turnaround time 1 week, phone turnaround 30 min. to 1 hour. Copy fee: $1.00 per page. Certification fee: No certification fee. Fee payee: Clerk of Court. Only cashiers checks and money orders accepted. Prepayment is required. Fax notes: No fee to fax results.

Suwannee County

Circuit & County Courts
200 S Ohio Ave, Live Oak, FL 32060; 904-362-0500; Fax: 904-362-0548. Hours: 8AM-5PM (EST). *Felony, Misdemeanor, Civil, Eviction, Small Claims, Probate.*

www.suwanneeclerkofcourt.com

Civil Records: Access: Mail, in person. Both court and visitors may perform in person searches. Search fee: $1.00 per name per year. Fee is per index. Required to search: name, years to search; also helpful-address. Civil cases indexed by defendant, plaintiff. Civil records on computer from 1983, archived from 1859 to 1983. Written request with payment required. **Criminal Records:** Access: Mail, in person. Both court and visitors may perform in person searches. Search fee: $1.00 per name per year. Fee is per index.

Required to search: name, years to search, DOB; also helpful-address, SSN. Criminal records on computer from 1983, archived from 1859 to 1983. Written request with payment required. **General Information:** No juvenile or adoption records released. SASE required. Turnaround time 1 week. Copy fee: $1.00 per page. Certification fee: $1.00. Fee payee: Suwannee Court Clerk. Personal checks accepted. Prepayment is required. Public access terminal is available.

Taylor County

Circuit & County Courts
PO Box 620, Perry, FL 32348; 850-838-3506; Fax: 850-838-3549. Hours: 8AM-5PM (EST). *Felony, Misdemeanor, Civil, Eviction, Small Claims, Probate.*

Civil Records: Access: Phone, fax, mail, in person. Only the court conducts in person searches; visitors may not. No search fee. Required to search: name, years to search. Civil cases indexed by defendant, plaintiff. Civil records on computer from 1982 to present, on index from 1973 to 1991, prior on index books. **Criminal Records:** Access: Phone, fax, mail, in person. Only the court conducts in person searches; visitors may not. No search fee. Required to search: name, years to search, DOB; also helpful-SSN, race, sex. Criminal records on computer from 1982 to present, on index from 1973 to 1991, prior on index books. **General Information:** No juvenile records released. SASE helpful. Turnaround time 1 week. Copy fee: $1.00 per page. Certification fee: $1.00. Fee payee: Taylor County Clerk of Court. Business checks accepted. Prepayment is required.

Union County

Circuit & County Courts
Courthouse Rm 103, Lake Butler, FL 32054; 904-496-3711; Fax: 904-496-1718. Hours: 8AM-5PM (EST). *Felony, Misdemeanor, Civil, Eviction, Small Claims, Probate.*

http://circuit8.org

Civil Records: Access: Fax, mail, in person. Both court and visitors may perform in person searches. Search fee: $1.00 per name per year. Required to search: name, years to search. Civil cases indexed by defendant, plaintiff. Civil records on docket books from 1921. **Criminal Records:** Access: Fax, mail, in person. Both court and visitors may perform in person searches. Search fee: $1.00 per name per year. Required to search: name, years to search, DOB; also helpful-SSN. Criminal records on docket books from 1921. **General Information:** No juvenile records released. SASE preferred. Turnaround time 2-3 days. Copy fee: $1.00 per page. Certification fee: $1.00. Fee payee: Clerk of Court. Personal checks accepted. Prepayment is required. Fax notes: $1.00 per page.

Volusia County

Circuit & County Courts - Civil Division
PO Box 6043, De Land, FL 32721; 904-736-5915; Fax: 904-822-5711. Hours: 8AM-4:30PM *Civil, Eviction, Small Claims, Probate.*

http://volusia.org/courts

Civil Records: Access: Fax, mail, online, in person. Both court and visitors may perform in person searches. Search fee: $1.00 per name per year. Required to search: name, years to search. Civil cases indexed by defendant, plaintiff. Civil records on computer from 1986, on docket books from 1863 to 1986. **General Information:** No sealed records released. SASE requested.

Turnaround time 1-2 weeks. Copy fee: $1.00 per page. Certification fee: $1.00. Fee payee: Clerk of Circuit Court. Personal checks accepted. Prepayment is required. Public access terminal is available. Fax notes: $1.50 per page.

Circuit & County Courts-Criminal Division PO Box 43, De Land, FL 32721-0043; 904-736-5915; Fax: 904-822-5711. Hours: 8AM-4:30PM (EST). *Felony, Misdemeanor.*

http://volusia.org/courts **Criminal Records:** Access: Mail, remote online, in person. Both court and visitors may perform in person searches. Search fee: $1.00 per name per year. Required to search: name, years to search, DOB; also helpful-SSN, race, sex. Criminal records 1982 to present on computer, on microfiche from 1856 to 1988, on docket books prior to 1983. Online access is available from 8am to 4:30pm. Setup is $125 and the monthly fee is $25. Windows 95 or 98 is required. Search by name or case number back to 1988. Call Tom White for more information. **General Information:** No confidential, sexual battery and juvenile records released. SASE required. Turnaround time up to 1 week. Copy fee: $1.00 per page. Certification fee: $1.00. Fee payee: Clerk of Court. Personal checks accepted. Personal and out of state checks accepted with proper ID. Prepayment is required. Fax notes: $1.50 per page.

Wakulla County

Circuit & County Courts 3056 Crawfordville Hwy, Crawfordville, FL 32327; 850-926-0905; Fax: 850-926-0938 (Civil); 926-0936 (Crim). Hours: 8AM-5PM (EST). *Felony, Misdemeanor, Civil, Eviction, Small Claims, Probate.*

www.co.leon.fl.us/court/court.htm

Civil Records: Access: Phone, fax, mail, in person. Both court and visitors may perform in person searches. Search fee: $1.00 per name per year. Required to search: name, years to search. Civil cases indexed by defendant, plaintiff. Civil records on computer since 1990, on docket books from 1800s. **Criminal Records:** Access: Fax, mail, in person. Both court and visitors may perform in person searches. Search fee: $1.00 per name per year. Required to search: name, years to search, DOB; also helpful-SSN. Criminal records on computer since 1990, on docket books from 1800s. Visitors may review docket books, only court performs name searches. **General Information:** No juvenile, adoption records released. SASE helpful. Turnaround time 3-4 days. Copy fee: $1.00 per page. Certification fee: $1.00. Fee payee: Clerk of Court. Personal checks accepted. Prepayment is required. Fax notes: $1.00 per page.

Walton County

Circuit & County Courts PO Box 1260, De Funiak Springs, FL 32435; 850-892-8115; Fax: 850-892-7551. Hours: 8AM-4:30PM (CST). *Felony, Misdemeanor, Civil, Eviction, Small Claims, Probate.*

Civil Records: Access: Fax, mail, online, in person. Both court and visitors may perform in person searches. Search fee: $1.00 per name per year. Required to search: name, years to search. Civil cases indexed by defendant, plaintiff. Civil records on computer from 1988, on dockets from 1900s. Online access requires a setup fee of at least $30 plus a monthly fee of $100. The system is open 24 hours daily and also includes probate, traffic, domestic and criminal data. Search by name or case number. Call David Langford for more information. **Criminal Records:** Access: Fax, mail, remote online, in person. Both court and

visitors may perform in person searches. Search fee: $1.00 per name per year. Required to search: name, years to search, DOB. Criminal records on computer from 1988, on dockets from 1900s. Online access criteria is same as described for civil records. **General Information:** No sealed, expunged, or pre-sentence investigation records released. SASE helpful. Turnaround time 24 hours. Copy fee: $1.00 per page. Certification fee: $1.00. Fee payee: Clerk of Courts. Personal checks accepted. Prepayment is required. Public access terminal is available. Fax notes: $1.00 per page.

Washington County

Circuit & County Courts PO Box 647, Chipley, FL 32428-0647; 850-638-6285; Fax: 850-638-6297. Hours: 8AM-4PM (CST). *Felony, Misdemeanor, Civil, Eviction, Small Claims, Probate.*

Civil Records: Access: Phone, fax, mail, in person. Both court and visitors may perform in person searches. Search fee: $1.00 per name per year. Required to search: name, years to search. Civil cases indexed by defendant, plaintiff. Civil records on computer from 1981, on docket books from 1800s to 1986. **Criminal Records:** Access: Phone, fax, mail, in person. Only the court conducts in person searches; visitors may not. Search fee: $1.00 per name per year. Required to search: name, years to search. Criminal records on computer from 1981, on docket books from 1800s to 1986. **General Information:** No adoption or juvenile records released. SASE requested. Turnaround time 1 day. Copy fee: $1.00 per page. Certification fee: $1.00. Fee payee: Clerk of Court. Business checks accepted. Local personal checks accepted. Prepayment is required. Public access terminal is available. Public Access Terminal Note: In the civil department.

Include the following in your request-full name, date of accident, location of accident.

Access by: mail, in person.

Fee & Payment: The fee for a report is $5.00. There is no charge for a "no record found." Fee payee: Department of Public Safety. Prepayment required. Cash, money orders, certified checks, and cashier's checks are all accepted. No credit cards accepted.

Mail search: Turnaround time: 1 week to 10 days. No self addressed stamped envelope is required.

In person search: Request must be in writing. Turnaround time is within the hour.

Boat & Vessel Ownership
Boat & Vessel Registration

Georgia Dept of Natural Resources, 2189 Northlake Parkway Bldg 10 #108, Tucker, GA 30084; 770-414-3338, 770-414-3344 (Fax), 8AM-4:30PM.

www.ganet.org.dnr

Note: Liens are at the county level and will not show on records at this location.

Indexing & Storage: Records are available from 1986-present. Records are indexed on microfiche from 1986-1993 and on computer from 1994-present. All motorized boats must be registered. All sailboats 12 ft or longer must be registered.

Searching: Either the name, registration # or hull # must be submitted.

Access by: mail, phone, fax, in person.

Fee & Payment: There is no search fee.

Mail search: Turnaround time: 1-2 weeks. No self addressed stamped envelope is required.

Phone search: Verification only.

Fax search: Same criteria as mail searching.

In person search: Searching is available in person.

Legislation-Current/Pending
Legislation-Passed

General Assembly of Georgia, State Capitol, Atlanta, GA 30334; 404-656-5040 (Senate), 404-656-5015 (House), 404-656-2370 (Archives), 404-656-5043 (Fax), 8:30AM-4:30PM.

www.ganet.org/services/leg

Indexing & Storage: Records are available from 1967-present. Records are computerized since 1995, on hard copy 95-2000, and on microfilm 67-94. The older the document, the longer the turnaround time.

Searching: Include the following in your request-bill number, year. Either Senate or House Clerk can look up bills, but to receive copies of documents before 1967, go to respective area. State Archives has copies of all bills and has the same fee arrangement.

Access by: mail, phone, fax, in person, online.

Fee & Payment: The copy fee is $.10 per copy, after the first 100 copies. Fee payee: General Assembly of Georgia. Personal checks accepted. No credit cards accepted.

Mail search: Turnaround time: variable. Address questions to Senate to Room 351, House questions to Room 307. No self addressed stamped envelope is required.

Phone search: You may request bills by phone.

Fax search: Fax searching available.

In person search: You may request bills in person.

Online search: The Internet site has bill information back to 1995. Statutes are not available online.

Voter Registration

Secretary of State, Elections Division, 2 Martin Luther King Dr SE, Suite 1104, West Tower, Atlanta, GA 30334; 404-656-2871, 404-651-9531 (Fax), 8AM-5PM.

www.sos.state.ga.us/elections

Indexing & Storage: Records are available from 1995, on computer. Data is keyed in by county personnel onto the state computer.

Searching: Include the following in your request-Social Security Number if available, date of birth. All requests must be in writing. Records may be requested at county level, also. The following data is not released: Social Security Numbers or bulk information or lists for commercial purposes.

Access by: mail, fax.

Fee & Payment: There is no fee for individual requests.

Mail search: Turnaround time: 2-3 days. No self addressed stamped envelope is required.

Fax search: Fax searching available.

Other access: Tapes, disks, and paper lists are available for purchase for non-commercial purposes.

GED Certificates

GED Testing Services, 1800 Century Pl #555, Atlanta, GA 30345; 404-679-1644, 8:30AM-4:30PM M-F.

www.dtae.org

Searching: To search, all are required: a signed release, name, year of test, date of birth, and Social Security Number.

Access by: mail.

Fee & Payment: The fee for a verification or for a copy of a transcript is $5.00 per record. Fee payee: GED Testing Services. Prepayment required. Money orders are accepted. No credit cards accepted.

Mail search: Turnaround time: 2 weeks. No self addressed stamped envelope is required.

Hunting License Information
Fishing License Information
Records not maintained by a state level agency.

Note: They do not have a central database. You must contact the vendor where the license was purchased.

Licenses Searchable Online

Architect #15	www.sos.state.ga.us/ebd-architects/search.htm
Athletic Agent #42	www.sos.state.ga.us/ebd-agent/search.htm
Athletic Trainer #16	www.sos.state.ga.us/ebd-trainer/search.htm
Auction Dealer #13	www.sos.state.ga.us/ebd-auctioneer/search.htm
Auctioneer #13	www.sos.state.ga.us/ebd-auctioneer/search.htm
Bank #17	www.ganet.org/dbf/other_institutions.html
Barber #19	www.sos.state.ga.us/ebd-barber_cosmet/search.htm
Cardiac Technician #41	www.sos.state.ga.us/ebd-medical/medsearch2.htm
Charity #45	www.sos.state.ga.us/securities/charitysearch.htm
Check Casher/Seller #17	www.ganet.org/dbf/other_institutions.html
Chiropractor #18	www.sos.state.ga.us/ebd-chiro/search.htm
Conditioned Air Contractor #09	www.sos.state.ga.us/ebd-construct/search.htm
Cosmetologist #19	www.sos.state.ga.us/ebd-barber_cosmet/search.htm
Counselor #10	www.sos.state.ga.us/ebd-counselors/search.htm
Credit Union #17	www.ganet.org/dbf/other_institutions.html
Dental Hygienist #20	www.sos.state.ga.us/ebd-dentistry/search.htm
Dentist #20	www.sos.state.ga.us/ebd-dentistry/search.htm
Dietitian #23	www.sos.state.ga.us/ebd-dietitians/search.htm
EDP - Electronic Data Processors #17	www.ganet.org/dbf/other_institutions.html
Electrical Contractor #09	www.sos.state.ga.us/ebd-construct/search.htm
Embalmer #25	www.sos.state.ga.us/ebd-funeral/search.htm
Engineer #11	www.sos.state.ga.us/ebd-pels/search.htm
Esthetician #19	www.sos.state.ga.us/ebd-barber_cosmet/search.htm
Family Therapist #10	www.sos.state.ga.us/ebd-counselors/search.htm
Forester #36	www.sos.state.ga.us/ebd-foresters/search.htm
Funeral Apprentice #25	www.sos.state.ga.us/ebd-funeral/search.htm
Funeral Director #25	www.sos.state.ga.us/ebd-funeral/search.htm
Funeral Establishment #25	www.sos.state.ga.us/ebd-funeral/search.htm
General Contractor #09	www.sos.state.ga.us/ebd-construct/search.htm
Geologist #44	www.sos.state.ga.us/ebd-geologists/search.htm
Hearing Aid Dealer/Dispenser #26	www.sos.state.ga.us/ebd-hearingaid/search.htm
Holding Company/Representative Offices #17	www.ganet.org/dbf/other_institutions.html
Insurance Agent #08	www.inscomm.state.ga.us/main.consumers.agentsearch.html
Interior Designer #15	www.sos.state.ga.us/ebd-architects/search.htm
Landscape Architect #27	www.sos.state.ga.us/ebd-landscape/search.htm
Low Voltage Contractor #09	www.sos.state.ga.us/ebd-construct/search.htm
Manicurist #19	www.sos.state.ga.us/ebd-barber_cosmet/search.htm
Marriage Counselor #10	www.sos.state.ga.us/ebd-counselors/search.htm
Medical Doctor #41	www.sos.state.ga.us/ebd-medical/medsearch.htm
Mortgage Institution #17	www.ganet.org/dbf/mortgage.html
Nail Care #19	www.sos.state.ga.us/ebd-barber_cosmet/search.htm
Nuclear Pharmacist #31	www.sos.state.ga.us/ebd-pharmacy/search.htm
Nurse (Registered) #28	www.sos.state.ga.us/ebd-rn/search.htm
Nurse-LPN #02	www.sos.state.ga.us/ebd-lpn/search.htm
Nursing Home Administrator #29	www.sos.state.ga.us/ebd-nursinghome/search.htm
Occupational Therapist #30	www.sos.state.ga.us/ebd-ot/search.htm
Occupational Therapist Assistant #30	www.sos.state.ga.us/ebd-ot/search.htm
Optician, Dispensing #21	www.sos.state.ga.us/ebd-opticians/search.htm
Optometrist #22	www.sos.state.ga.us/ebd-optometry/search.htm
Osteopathic Physician #41	www.sos.state.ga.us/ebd-medical/medsearch.htm
Paramedic #41	www.sos.state.ga.us/ebd-medical/medsearch2.htm
Pharmacist #31	www.sos.state.ga.us/ebd-pharmacy/search.htm
Pharmacy School, Clinic Researcher #31	www.sos.state.ga.us/ebd-pharmacy/search.htm
Physical Therapist #32	www.sos.state.ga.us/ebd-pt/search.htm
Physical Therapist Assistant #32	www.sos.state.ga.us/ebd-pt/search.htm
Physician Assistant #41	www.sos.state.ga.us/ebd-medical/medsearch2.htm
Plumber Journeyman #09	www.sos.state.ga.us/ebd-construct/search.htm
Plumbing Contractor #09	www.sos.state.ga.us/ebd-construct/search.htm
Podiatrist #33	www.sos.state.ga.us/ebd-podiatry/search.htm
Poison Pharmacist #31	www.sos.state.ga.us/ebd-pharmacy/search.htm
Private Detective #35	www.sos.state.ga.us/ebd-detective/search.htm

Psychologist #24	www.sos.state.ga.us/ebd-psych/search.htm
Public Accountant-CPA #14	www.sos.state.ga.us/ebd-accountancy/search.htm
Respiratory Care Practitioner #41	www.sos.state.ga.us/ebd-medical/medsearch2.htm
Retail, Hospital Wholesale Manufacturer #31	www.sos.state.ga.us/ebd-pharmacy/search.htm
School Librarian #40	www.sos.state.ga.us/ebd-librarians/search.htm
Security Guard #35	www.sos.state.ga.us/ebd-detective/search.htm
Shop License #19	www.sos.state.ga.us/ebd-barber_cosmet/search.htm
Social Worker #10	www.sos.state.ga.us/ebd-counselors/search.htm
Speech Pathologist/Audiologist #38	www.sos.state.ga.us/ebd-speech/search.htm
Surveyor #11	www.sos.state.ga.us/ebd-pels/search.htm
Used Car Dealer #37	www.sos.state.ga.us/ebd-usedcar/search.htm
Used Car Parts Distributor #37	www.sos.state.ga.us/ebd-usedcar/search.htm
Utility Contractor #09	www.sos.state.ga.us/ebd-construct/search.htm
Veterinarian #39	www.sos.state.ga.us/ebd-veterinary/search.htm
Veterinary Faculty #39	www.sos.state.ga.us/ebd-veterinary/search.htm
Veterinary Technician #39	www.sos.state.ga.us/ebd-veterinary/search.htm
Waste Water Collection System Operator #43	www.sos.state.ga.us/ebd-water/search.htm
Waste Water Industrial #43	www.sos.state.ga.us/ebd-water/search.htm
Waste Water Laboratory Analyst #43	www.sos.state.ga.us/ebd-water/search.htm
Waste Water Operator Class 1-3 #43	www.sos.state.ga.us/ebd-water/search.htm
Waste Water Treatment System Operator #43	www.sos.state.ga.us/ebd-water/search.htm
Water Distribution System Operator #43	www.sos.state.ga.us/ebd-water/search.htm
Water Operator Class 1-3 #43	www.sos.state.ga.us/ebd-water/search.htm

Licensing Quick Finder

Acupuncturist #41	404-656-3913
Amusement Ride Inspector #48	404-656-2966
Animal Technician #39	912-207-1686
Architect #15	912-207-1400
Athletic Agent #42	912-207-1460
Athletic Trainer #16	404-656-3933
Attorney #47	404-527-8700
Auction Dealer #13	404-656-2282
Auctioneer #13	404-656-2282
Bank #17	770-986-1633
Barber #19	912-207-1430
Boiler Inspector #48	404-656-2966
Cardiac Technician #41	404-656-3923
Cemetery #45	404-656-3920
Charity #45	404-656-3920
Check Casher/Seller #17	770-986-1633
Chiropractor #18	912-207-1686
Conditioned Air Contractor #09	404-656-3939
Cosmetologist #19	912-207-1430
Counselor #10	404-656-3933
Credit Union #17	770-986-1637
Dental Hygienist #20	912-207-1680
Dentist #20	912-207-1680
Dietitian #23	404-656-3921
EDP - Electronic Data Processors #17	770-986-1633
Electrical Contractor #09	404-656-3939
Elevator Inspector #48	404-656-2966
Embalmer #25	404-656-3933
Emergency Medical Technician #49	404-657-6700
Engineer #11	478-207-1453
Esthetician #19	912-207-1430
Family Therapist #10	404-656-3933
Forester #36	912-207-1400
Funeral Apprentice #25	404-656-3933
Funeral Director #25	404-656-3933
Funeral Establishment #25	404-656-3933
General Contractor #09	404-656-3939
Geologist #44	912-207-1400
Hearing Aid Dealer/Dispenser #26	912-207-1686
Holding Company/Representative Offices #17	770-986-1633
Insurance Adjuster #08	404-656-2100
Insurance Agent #08	404-656-2100
Insurance Counselor #08	404-656-2100
Interior Designer #15	912-207-1400
Investment Advisor (Firm) #45	404-656-3920
Landfill Inspector/Operator #05	404-362-2696
Landscape Architect #27	912-207-1400
Liquor Control #06	404-656-0606
Low Voltage Contractor #09	404-656-3939
Manicurist #19	912-207-1430
Marriage Counselor #10	404-656-3933
Media Specialist #07	404-657-9000
Medical Doctor #41	404-656-3913
Mortgage Institution #17	770-986-1269
Nail Care #19	912-207-1430
Notary Public #03	404-327-6023
Nuclear Pharmacist #31	912-207-1686
Nurse (Registered) #28	404-657-0775
Nurse-LPN #02	404-656-3921
Nursing Home Administrator #29	404-656-3933
Occupational Therapist #30	404-656-3921
Occupational Therapist Assistant #30	404-656-3921
Optician, Dispensing #21	912-207-1686
Optometrist #22	912-207-1686
Osteopathic Physician #41	404-656-3913
Paramedic #41	404-656-3923
Pesticide Applicator #04	404-656-4958
Pesticide Contractor/Employee #04	404-656-4958
Pharmacist #31	912-207-1686
Pharmacy School, Clinic Researcher #31	912-207-1686
Physical Therapist #32	404-656-3921
Physical Therapist Assistant #32	404-656-3921
Physician Assistant #41	404-656-3913
Plumber Journeyman #09	404-656-3939
Plumbing Contractor #09	404-656-3939
Podiatrist #33	912-207-1686
Poison Pharmacist #31	912-207-1686
Private Detective #35	404-656-3921
Private Pesticide Application #04	404-656-4958
Psychologist #24	404-656-3933
Public Accountant-CPA #14	912-207-1400
Public Adjuster #08	404-656-2100
Real Estate Appraiser #46	404-656-3916
Real Estate Broker #46	404-656-3916
Real Estate Sales Agent #46	404-656-3916
Rebuilder #12	404-656-2282
Reporter #01	404-656-6422
Respiratory Care Practitioner #41	404-656-3914
Restricted Pesticide Dealer #04	404-656-4958
Retail, Hospital Wholesale Manufacturer #31	912-207-1686
Salvage Pool Operator #12	404-656-2282
Salvage Yard Dealer #12	404-656-2282
School Administrator/Supervisor #07	404-657-9000
School Bus Driver #51	404-624-7467
School Counselor #07	404-657-9000
School Librarian #40	912-207-1400
School Social Worker #07	404-657-9000
Securities Dealer #45	404-656-3920
Securities Salesperson #45	404-656-3920
Security Guard #35	404-656-3929
Shop License #19	912-207-1430
Shorthand Court Reporter/Stenomask #01	404-656-6422
Social Worker #10	404-656-3933
Speech Pathologist/Audiologist #38	404-656-3933
Surplus Line Broker #08	404-656-2100
Surveyor #11	478-207-1453
Teacher #07	404-657-9000
Timber Dealer & Processor #04	404-656-4958
Truck Driver #51	404-624-7467
Used Car Dealer #37	404-656-2282
Used Car Parts Distributor #37	404-656-2282
Utility Contractor #09	404-656-3939
Veterinarian #39	912-207-1686
Veterinary Faculty #39	912-207-1686
Veterinary Technician #39	912-207-1686
Waste Water Collection System Operator #43	912-207-1400
Waste Water Industrial #43	912-207-1400
Waste Water Laboratory Analyst #43	912-207-1400
Waste Water Operator Class 1-3 #43	912-207-1400
Waste Water Treatment System Operator #43	912-207-1400
Water Distribution System Operator #43	912-207-1400
Water Operator Class 1-3 #43	912-207-1400

Licensing Agency Information

01 Clerk of the Board, Board of Court Reporting, 244 Washington St SW, #550, Atlanta, GA 30334; 404-656-6422, Fax: 404-651-6449.

02 Board of Examiners of Licensed Practical Nurses, 166 Pryor St SW, Atlanta, GA 30303; 404-656-3921, Fax: 404-657-2002.
www.sos.state.ga.us/ebd-lpn

Direct URL to search licenses: www.sos.state.ga.us/ebd-lpn/search.htm You can search online using name and license number.

03 Clerks Authority, Notary Public Division, 1875 Century Blvd #100, Atlanta, GA 30345; 404-327-6023, Fax: 404-327-7887.

www2.gsccca.org/Projects/aboutnp.html

04 Department of Agriculture, Pesticide Division, Capitol Sq, Rm 550, Atlanta, GA 30334; 404-656-4958, Fax: 404-657-8378.

05 Department of Natural Resources, Environmental Protection Division, 4244 International Pky, #104, Atlanta, GA 30354; 404-362-2696, Fax: 404-362-2693.

www.dnr.state.ga.us/EPD

06 Department of Revenue, Centralized Tax Payer Registration, 270 Washington Rm 203, Atlanta, GA 30334-0390; 404-656-4060, Fax: 404-651-6705.

07 Education Department, Teacher Certification, 1452 Twin Towers East, Atlanta, GA 30334; 404-657-9000, Fax: 404-651-9185.

www.gapsc.com

08 Licensing Division, Insurance Commissioner's Office, 2 Martin Luther King Jr Dr, West Tower, #802, Atlanta, GA 30334; 404-656-2100, Fax: 404-656-0874.

09 State Construction Industry Licensing Board, 237 Coliseum Dr, Macon, GA 31217; 912-207-1416, Fax: 912-207-1425.
www.sos.state.ga.us/ebd-construct

Direct URL to search licenses: www.sos.state.ga.us/ebd-construct/search.htm You can search online using last name or license #

10 Examining Boards Division, Board of Prof. Counselors, Social Workers, & Marriage/Family Therapists, 166 Pryor St SW Rm 405, Atlanta, GA 30303; 404-656-3933, Fax: 404-656-3989.
www.sos.state.ga.us/ebd-counselors

Direct URL to search licenses: www.sos.state.ga.us/ebd-counselors/search.htm You can search online using name and license number.

11 Examining Boards Division, Professional Engineers & Land Surveyors Board, 237 Coliseum Dr, Macon, GA 31217-3858; 404-656-3926, Fax: 404-657-2003.
www.sos.state.ga.us/ebd-pel

Direct URL to search licenses: www.sos.state.ga.us/ebd-pels/search.htm You can search online using name and license number.

12 Licensing Boards, 166 Pryor St SW, Atlanta, GA 30303; 404-656-4220.

13 Examining Boards Division, Auctioneers Commission, 166 Pryor St SW, Atlanta, GA 30303; 404-656-2282, Fax: 404-657-4220/651-9532.
www.sos.state.ga.us/ebd-auctioneer

Direct URL to search licenses: www.sos.state.ga.us/ebd-auctioneer/search.htm

You can search online using name and license number.

14 Examining Boards Division, Board of Accountancy, 166 Pryor St SW, Rm 211, Atlanta, GA 30303; 912-207-1400, Fax: 912-207-1410.
www.sos.state.ga.us

Direct URL to search licenses: www.sos.state.ga.us/ebd-accountancy/search.htm

15 Examining Boards Division, Board of Architects and Interior Designers, 237 Coliseum Dr, Macon, GA 31217-3858; 912-207-1400, Fax: 912-207-1410.
www.sos.state.ga.us/ebd-architects

Direct URL to search licenses: www.sos.state.ga.us/ebd-architects/search.htm You can search online using last name and license number.

16 Examining Boards Division, Board of Athletic Trainers, 166 Pryor St SW, Atlanta, GA 30303-3465; 405-656-3933, Fax: 405-656-3989.
www.sos.state.ga.us/ebd-trainer

Direct URL to search licenses: www.sos.state.ga.us/ebd-trainer/search.htm You can search online using name and license number.

17 Department of Banking and Finance, Regulated Institutions, 2990 Brandywine Rd #200, Atlanta, GA 30341; 770-986-1633, Fax: 770-986-1654.
www.ganet.org/dbf/index.html

Direct URL to search licenses: www.ganet.org/dbf/regulated_institutions.html You can search online using alphabetical lists

18 Examining Boards Division, Board of Chiropractic Examiners, 237 Coliseum Dr, Macon, GA 31217; 912-207-1686, Fax: 912-207-1699.
www.sos.state.ga.us/ebd-chiro

Direct URL to search licenses: www.sos.state.ga.us/ebd-chiro/search.htm You can search online using name and license number.

19 Examining Boards Division, Board of Cosmetology, 237 Coliseum Drive, Macon, GA 31217; 912-207-1430, Fax: 912-207-1442.
www.sos.state.ga.us/ebd-barber_cosmet

Direct URL to search licenses: www.sos.state.ga.us/ebd-barber_cosmet/search.htm

20 Examining Boards Division, Board of Dentistry, 237 Coliseum Drive, Macon, GA 31217-3858; 912-207-1680, Fax: 912-207-1685.
www.sos.state.ga.us/ebd-dentistry

Direct URL to search licenses: www.sos.state.ga.us/ebd-dentistry/search.htm You can search online using name and license number.

21 Examining Boards Division, Board of Dispensing Opticians, 237 Coliseum Dr, Macon, GA 31217; 912-207-1686, Fax: 912-207-1699.
www.sos.state.ga.us/ebd-opticians

Direct URL to search licenses: www.sos.state.ga.us/ebd-opticians/search.htm You can search online using name and license number.

22 Examining Boards Division, Board of Examiners in Optometry, 237 Coliseum Dr, Macon, GA 31217; 912-207-1686, Fax: 912-207-1699.
www.sos.state.ga.us/ebd-optometry

Direct URL to search licenses: www.sos.state.ga.us/ebd-optometry/search.htm You can search online using name and license number.

23 Examining Boards Division, Board of Examiners of Licensed Dietitians, 166 Pryor St SW, Atlanta, GA 30303; 404-656-3921, Fax: 404-656-2002.
www.sos.state.ga.us/ebd-dieticians

Direct URL to search licenses: www.sos.state.ga.us/ebd-dieticians/search.htm You can search online using name and license number.

24 Examining Boards Division, Board of Examiners of Psychologists, 166 Pryor St SW, Atlanta, GA 30303-3465; 404-656-3933, Fax: 404-656-3989.
www.sos.state.ga.us/ebd-psych

Direct URL to search licenses: www.sos.state.ga.us/ebd-psych/search.htm You can search online using name and license number.

25 Examining Boards Division, Board of Funeral Service, 166 Pryor St SW, Atlanta, GA 30303; 404-656-3933, Fax: 404-656-3989.
www.sos.state.ga.us/ebd-funeral

Direct URL to search licenses: www.sos.state.ga.us/ebd-funeral/search.htm You can search online using name and license number.

26 Examining Boards Division, Board of Hearing Aid Dealers & Dispensers, 237 Coliseum Dr, Macon, GA 31217; 912-207-1686, Fax: 912-207-1699.
www.sos.state.ga.us/ebd-hearingaid/search.htm

Direct URL to search licenses: www.sos.state.ga.us/ebd-hearingaid/search.htm You can search online using name and license number.

27 Examining Boards Division, Board of Landscape Architects, 237 Colissum Dr, Macon, GA 31217-3858; 912-207-1400, Fax: 912-207-1400.
www.sos.state.ga.us/ebd-landscape

Direct URL to search licenses: www.sos.state.ga.us/ebd-landscape/search.htm You can search online using name and license number.

28 Examining Boards Division, Board of Nursing, 237 Coliseum Dr, Macon, GA 30217-3858; 478-207-1640, Fax: 478-207-1660.
www.sos.state.ga.us/ebd-rn

Direct URL to search licenses: www.sos.state.ga.us/ebd-rn/search.htm You can search online using name and license number.

29 Examining Boards Division, Board of Nursing Home Administrators, 166 Pryor St SW, Atlanta, GA 30303; 404-656-3933, Fax: 404-656-3989.
www.sos.state.ga.us/ebd-nursinghome

Direct URL to search licenses: www.sos.state.ga.us/ebd-nursinghome/search.htm You can search online using name and license number.

30 Examining Boards Division, Board of Occupational Therapy, 166 Pryor St SW, Atlanta, GA 30303-3465; 404-656-3921, Fax: 404-657-2002.
www.sos.state.ga.us/ebd-ot

Direct URL to search licenses: www.sos.state.ga.us/ebd-ot/search.htm You can search online using name and license number.

31 Examining Boards Division, Board of Pharmacy, 237 Coliseum Dr, Macon, GA 31217; 912-207-1686, Fax: 912-207-1699.
www.sos.state.ga.us/ebd-pharmacy

Direct URL to search licenses: www.sos.state.ga.us/ebd-pharmacy/search.htm You can search online using name and license number.

32 Examining Boards Division, Board of Physical Therapy, 166 Pryor St SW, Atlanta, GA 30303-3465; 404-656-3921, Fax: 404-657-2002. www.sos.state.ga.us/ebd-pt

Direct URL to search licenses: www.sos.state.ga.us/ebd-pt/search.htm You can search online using name and license number.

33 Examining Boards Division, Board of Podiatry Examiners, 237 Coliseum Dr, Macon, GA 31217; 912-207-1686, Fax: 912-207-1699. www.sos.state.ga.us/ebd-podiatry/search.htm

Direct URL to search licenses: www.sos.state.ga.us/ebd-podiatry/search.htm You can search online using name and license number.

35 Examining Boards Division, Board of Private Detectives & Security Agencies, 166 Pryor St SW, Rm 501, Atlanta, GA 30303; 404-656-2282, Fax: 404-657-4220. www.sos.state.ga.us/ebd-detective

Direct URL to search licenses: www.sos.state.ga.us/ebd-detective/search.htm You can search online using name and license number.

36 Examining Boards Division, Board of Registration for Foresters, 237 Coliseum Dr, Macon, GA 31217-3858; 912-207-1400, Fax: 912-207-1410. www.sos.state.ga.us/ebd-foresters

Direct URL to search licenses: www.sos.state.ga.us/ebd-foresters/search.htm You can search online using last name and licence number.

37 Examining Boards Division, Board of Registration of Used Car Dealers, 166 Pryor St SW, Atlanta, GA 30303; 404-656-2282, Fax: 404-657-4220/651-9532. www.sos.state.ga.us/ebd-usedcar

Direct URL to search licenses: www.sos.state.ga.us/ebd-usedcar/search.htm You can search online using name and license number.

38 Examining Boards Division, Board of Speech Pathology & Audiology, 166 Pryor St SW, Atlanta, GA 30303; 404-656-3933, Fax: 404-656-3989. www.sos.state.ga.us/ebd-speech

Direct URL to search licenses: www.sos.state.ga.us/ebd-speech/search.htm You can search online using name and license number.

39 Examining Boards Division, Board of Veterinary Medicine, 237 Coliseum Dr, Macon, GA 31217; 912-207-1686, Fax: 912-207-1699. www.sos.state.ga.us/ebd-veterinary/search.htm

Direct URL to search licenses: www.sos.state.ga.us/ebd-veterinary/search.htm You can search online using name and license number.

40 Examining Boards Division, Board for the Certification of Librarians, 166 Pryor St SW Rm 211, Atlanta, GA 30303; 912-207-1400, Fax: 912-207-1410. www.sos.state.ga.us/ebd-librarians

Direct URL to search licenses: www.sos.state.ga.us/ebd-librarians/search.htm

41 Examining Boards Division, Composite Board of Medical Examiners, 166 Pryor St SW, Atlanta, GA 30303; 404-656-3913, Fax: 404-656-9723. www.sos.state.ga.us/ebd-medical

42 Examining Boards Division, Athlete Agent Regulatory Commission, 166 Pryor St SW, Atlanta, GA 30303-3465; 912-207-1460, Fax: 912-207-1468. www.sos.state.ga.us/ebd-agent

Direct URL to search licenses: www.sos.state.ga.us/ebd-agent/search.htm You can search online using name or license number.

43 Examining Boards Division, 237 Coliseum Dr, Macon, GA 31217; 404-656-3933, Fax: 404-656-3989. www.sos.state.ga.us/ebd-water

Direct URL to search licenses: www.sos.state.ga.us/ebd-water/search.htm You can search online using name or license number.

44 Examining Boards Division, Board of Registration for Professional Geologists, 166 Pryor St SW, Rm 211, Atlanta, GA 30303; 912-207-1400, Fax: 912-207-1410. www.sos.state.ga.us/ebd-geologists

Direct URL to search licenses: www.sos.state.ga.us/ebd-geologists/search.htm You can search online using name and license number.

45 Securities & Business Regulation, Office of Secretary of State, 2 Martin Luther King Jr Dr, West Tower, #802, Atlanta, GA 30334-1530; 404-656-3920, Fax: 404-657-8410.

www.sos.state.ga.us/securities

46 Real Estate Commission/Appraiser Board, 229 Peachtree St NE, International Tower, #100, Atlanta, GA 30303-1605; 404-656-3916, Fax: 404-656-6650.

47 State Bar of Georgia, 50 Hurt Plaza, 800 The Hurt Bldg, Atlanta, GA 30303; 404-527-8700, Fax: 404-527-8700/8717. www.gabar.org

Direct URL to search licenses: www.gabar.org/ga_bar/searchpage.html You can search online using name, city, and state.

48 Department of Labor, Safety Engineering Division, 223 Courtland St NE #301, Atlanta, GA 30303-1751; 404-656-2966.

49 Emergency Medical Svcs, 47 Trinity Ave SW #104-LOB, Atlanta, GA 30334; 404-657-6700.

50 Board of Medical Examiners, 166 Pryor St SW Rm 424, Atlanta, GA 30303; 404-656-3913.

51 Department of Public Safety, Commercial Driver's License Unit, PO Box 1456, Atlanta, GA 30371; 404-624-7467.

The following list indicates the district and division name for each county in the state. If the district or division name of the bankruptcy court is different from the civil/criminal court, it appears in parentheses.

County/Court Cross Reference

County	District	Division
Appling	Southern	Brunswick (Savannah)
Atkinson	Southern	Waycross (Savannah)
Bacon	Southern	Waycross (Savannah)
Baker	Middle	Albany/Americus (Macon)
Baldwin	Middle	Macon
Banks	Northern	Gainesville
Barrow	Northern	Gainesville
Bartow	Northern	Rome
Ben Hill	Middle	Albany/Americus (Macon)
Berrien	Middle	Valdosta (Columbus)
Bibb	Middle	Macon
Bleckley	Middle	Macon
Brantley	Southern	Waycross (Savannah)
Brooks	Middle	Thomasville (Columbus)
Bryan	Southern	Savannah
Bulloch	Southern	Statesboro (Augusta)
Burke	Southern	Augusta
Butts	Middle	Macon
Calhoun	Middle	Albany/Americus (Macon)
Camden	Southern	Brunswick (Savannah)
Candler	Southern	Statesboro (Augusta)
Carroll	Northern	Newnan
Catoosa	Northern	Rome
Charlton	Southern	Waycross (Savannah)
Chatham	Southern	Savannah
Chattahoochee	Middle	Columbus
Chattooga	Northern	Rome
Cherokee	Northern	Atlanta
Clarke	Middle	Athens (Macon)
Clay	Middle	Columbus
Clayton	Northern	Atlanta
Clinch	Middle	Valdosta (Columbus)
Cobb	Northern	Atlanta
Coffee	Southern	Waycross (Savannah)
Colquitt	Middle	Thomasville (Columbus)
Columbia	Southern	Augusta
Cook	Middle	Valdosta (Columbus)
Coweta	Northern	Newnan
Crawford	Middle	Macon
Crisp	Middle	Albany/Americus (Macon)
Dade	Northern	Rome
Dawson	Northern	Gainesville
De Kalb	Northern	Atlanta
Decatur	Middle	Thomasville (Columbus)
Dodge	Southern	Dublin (Augusta)
Dooly	Middle	Macon
Dougherty	Middle	Albany/Americus (Macon)
Douglas	Northern	Atlanta
Early	Middle	Albany/Americus (Macon)
Echols	Middle	Valdosta (Columbus)
Effingham	Southern	Savannah
Elbert	Middle	Athens (Macon)
Emanuel	Southern	Statesboro (Augusta)
Evans	Southern	Statesboro (Augusta)
Fannin	Northern	Gainesville
Fayette	Northern	Newnan
Floyd	Northern	Rome
Forsyth	Northern	Gainesville
Franklin	Middle	Athens (Macon)
Fulton	Northern	Atlanta
Gilmer	Northern	Gainesville
Glascock	Southern	Augusta
Glynn	Southern	Brunswick (Savannah)
Gordon	Northern	Rome
Grady	Middle	Thomasville (Columbus)
Greene	Middle	Athens (Macon)
Gwinnett	Northern	Atlanta
Habersham	Northern	Gainesville
Hall	Northern	Gainesville
Hancock	Middle	Macon
Haralson	Northern	Newnan
Harris	Middle	Columbus
Hart	Middle	Athens (Macon)
Heard	Northern	Newnan
Henry	Northern	Atlanta
Houston	Middle	Macon
Irwin	Middle	Valdosta (Columbus)
Jackson	Northern	Gainesville
Jasper	Middle	Macon
Jeff Davis	Southern	Brunswick (Savannah)
Jefferson	Southern	Augusta
Jenkins	Southern	Statesboro (Augusta)
Johnson	Southern	Dublin (Augusta)
Jones	Middle	Macon
Lamar	Middle	Macon
Lanier	Middle	Valdosta (Columbus)
Laurens	Southern	Dublin (Augusta)
Lee	Middle	Albany/Americus (Macon)
Liberty	Southern	Savannah
Lincoln	Southern	Augusta
Long	Southern	Brunswick (Savannah)
Lowndes	Middle	Valdosta (Columbus)
Lumpkin	Northern	Gainesville
Macon	Middle	Macon
Madison	Middle	Athens (Macon)
Marion	Middle	Columbus
McDuffie	Southern	Augusta
McIntosh	Southern	Brunswick (Savannah)
Meriwether	Northern	Newnan
Miller	Middle	Albany/Americus (Macon)
Mitchell	Middle	Albany/Americus (Macon)
Monroe	Middle	Macon
Montgomery	Southern	Dublin (Augusta)
Morgan	Middle	Athens (Macon)
Murray	Northern	Rome
Muscogee	Middle	Columbus
Newton	Northern	Atlanta
Oconee	Middle	Athens (Macon)
Oglethorpe	Middle	Athens (Macon)
Paulding	Northern	Rome
Peach	Middle	Macon
Pickens	Northern	Gainesville

County	Division	County	Division
Pierce	Southern — Waycross (Savannah)	Tift	Middle — Valdosta (Columbus)
Pike	Northern — Newnan	Toombs	Southern — Statesboro (Augusta)
Polk	Northern — Rome	Towns	Northern — Gainesville
Pulaski	Middle — Macon	Treutlen	Southern — Dublin (Augusta)
Putnam	Middle — Macon	Troup	Northern — Newnan
Quitman	Middle — Columbus	Turner	Middle — Albany/Americus (Macon)
Rabun	Northern — Gainesville	Twiggs	Middle — Macon
Randolph	Middle — Columbus	Union	Northern — Gainesville
Richmond	Southern — Augusta	Upson	Middle — Macon
Rockdale	Northern — Atlanta	Walker	Northern — Rome
Schley	Middle — Albany/Americus (Macon)	Walton	Middle — Athens (Macon)
Screven	Southern — Statesboro (Augusta)	Ware	Southern — Waycross (Savannah)
Seminole	Middle — Thomasville (Columbus)	Warren	Southern — Augusta
Spalding	Northern — Newnan	Washington	Middle — Macon
Stephens	Northern — Gainesville	Wayne	Southern — Brunswick (Savannah)
Stewart	Middle — Columbus	Webster	Middle — Albany/Americus (Macon)
Sumter	Middle — Albany/Americus (Macon)	Wheeler	Southern — Dublin (Augusta)
Talbot	Middle — Columbus	White	Northern — Gainesville
Taliaferro	Southern — Augusta	Whitfield	Northern — Rome
Tattnall	Southern — Statesboro (Augusta)	Wilcox	Middle — Macon
Taylor	Middle — Columbus	Wilkes	Southern — Augusta
Telfair	Southern — Dublin (Augusta)	Wilkinson	Middle — Macon
Terrell	Middle — Albany/Americus (Macon)	Worth	Middle — Albany/Americus (Macon)
Thomas	Middle — Thomasville (Columbus)		

US District Court

Middle District of Georgia

Albany/Americus Division PO Box 1906, Albany, GA 31702 (Courier Address: Room 106, 345 Broad Ave, Albany, GA 31701), 912-430-8432, Fax: 912-430-8538.

www.gamd.uscourts.gov

Counties: Baker, Ben Hill, Calhoun, Crisp, Dougherty, Early, Lee, Miller, Mitchell, Schley, Sumter, Terrell, Turner, Webster, Worth. Ben Hill and Crisp were transferred from the Macon Division as of October 1, 1997.

Indexing & Storage: Cases are indexed by defendant and plaintiff as well as by case number. New cases are available in the index immediately after filing date. Both computer and card indexes are maintained. Records are on the computer from 1991. Prior records are indexed on index cards. District wide searches are available from any division in this district for files after 1/91. Open records are located at this court.

Fee & Payment: The fee is $15.00 per item (one party name or case number). Payment may be made by money order, cashier check, in-state business check. Personal checks are not accepted. Prepayment is required. Payee: Clerk, USDC. Certification fee: $5.00 per document. Copy fee: $.50 per page.

Phone Search: Only docket information is available by phone. An automated voice case information service (VCIS) is not available.

Mail Search: Always enclose a stamped self addressed envelope.

In Person Search: In person searching is available.

PACER: Sign-up number is 800-676-6856. Access fee is $.60 per minute. Toll-free access: 888-234-3839. Local access: 912-752-8170. Case records are available back to January 1991. Records are never purged. New records are available online after 1-2 days. Pacer is available online at http://pacer.gamd.uscourts.gov.

Athens Division PO Box 1106, Athens, GA 30603 (Courier Address: 115 E Hancock Ave, Athens, GA 30601), 706-227-1094, Fax: 706-546-2190.

www.gamd.uscourts.gov

Counties: Clarke, Elbert, Franklin, Greene, Hart, Madison, Morgan, Oconee, Oglethorpe, Walton. Closed cases before April 1997 are located in the Macon Division.

Indexing & Storage: Cases are indexed by defendant and plaintiff as well as by case number. New cases are available in the index 2 days after filing date. Both computer and card indexes are maintained. Open records are located at this court.

Fee & Payment: The fee is $15.00 per item (one party name or case number). Payment may be made by money order, cashier check, business check. Personal checks are not accepted. Payee: US District Court. Certification fee: $5.00 per document. Copy fee: $.50 per page.

Phone Search: Searching is not available by phone.

Mail Search: Always enclose a stamped self addressed envelope.

In Person Search: In person searching is available.

PACER: Sign-up number is 800-676-6856. Access fee is $.60 per minute. Toll-free access: 888-234-3839. Local access: 912-752-8170. Case records are available back to January 1991. Records are never purged. New records are available online after 1-2 days. Pacer is available online at http://pacer.gamd.uscourts.gov.

Columbus Division PO Box 124, Columbus, GA 31902 (Courier Address: Room 216, 120 12th St, Columbus, GA 31901), 706-649-7816.

www.gamd.uscourts.gov

Counties: Chattahoochee, Clay, Harris, Marion, Muscogee, Quitman, Randolph, Stewart, Talbot, Taylor.

Indexing & Storage: Cases are indexed by defendant and plaintiff as well as by case number. New cases are available in the index immediately after filing date. Both computer and card indexes are maintained. Open records are located at this court.

Fee & Payment: The fee is $15.00 per item (one party name or case number). Payment may be made by money order, cashier check, business check. Personal checks are not accepted. Prepayment is required. Payee: Clerk, US Courts. Certification fee: $5.00 per document. Copy fee: $.50 per page.

Phone Search: Only docket information is available by phone.

Mail Search: Always enclose a stamped self addressed envelope.

In Person Search: In person searching is available.

PACER: Sign-up number is 800-676-6856. Access fee is $.60 per minute. Toll-free access: 888-234-3839. Local access: 912-752-8170. Case records are available back to January 1991. Records are never purged. New records are available online after 1-2 days. Pacer is available online at http://pacer.gamd.uscourts.gov.

Macon Division PO Box 128, Macon, GA 31202-0128 (Courier Address: 475 Mulberry, Suite 216, Macon, GA 31201), 912-752-3497, Fax: 912-752-3496.

www.gamd.uscourts.gov

Counties: Baldwin, Ben Hill, Bibb, Bleckley, Butts, Crawford, Crisp, Dooly, Hancock, Houston, Jasper, Jones, Lamar, Macon, Monroe, Peach, Pulaski, Putnam, Twiggs, Upson, Washington, Wilcox, Wilkinson. Athens Division cases closed before April 1997 are also located here.

Indexing & Storage: Cases are indexed by defendant and plaintiff as well as by case number. New cases are available in the index immediately after filing date. Both computer and card indexes are maintained. Records after 1/91 can be searched from any court in this district. Open records are located at this court.

Fee & Payment: The fee is $15.00 per item (one party name or case number). Payment may be made by money order, cashier check, business check. Personal checks are not accepted. Payee: US Courts. Certification fee: $5.00 per document. Copy fee: $.50 per page.

Phone Search: Only docket information is available by phone. An automated voice case information service (VCIS) is not available.

Fax Search: Handled same as mail search. Will fax results at $3.00 per page.

Mail Search: Always enclose a stamped self addressed envelope.

In Person Search: In person searching is available.

PACER: Sign-up number is 800-676-6856. Access fee is $.60 per minute. Toll-free access: 888-234-3839. Local access: 912-752-8170. Case records are available back to January 1991. Records are never purged. New records are available online after 1-2 days.

Thomasville Division c/o Valdosta Division, PO Box 68, Valdosta, GA 31601 (Courier Address: Room 212, 401 N Patterson, Valdosta, GA 31603), 912-242-3616.

www.gamd.uscourts.gov

Counties: Brooks, Colquitt, Decatur, Grady, Seminole, Thomas.

Indexing & Storage: Cases are indexed by as well as by case number. New cases are available in the index after filing date. Open records are located at the Division.

Fee & Payment: The fee is $15.00 per item (one party name or case number). Payment may be made by money order, cashier check. Business checks are not accepted. Personal checks are not accepted.

Phone Search: An automated voice case information service (VCIS) is not available.

Mail Search: Always enclose a stamped self addressed envelope.

In Person Search: In person searching is available.

PACER: Sign-up number is 800-676-6856. Access fee is $.60 per minute. Toll-free access: 888-234-3839. Local access: 912-752-8170. Case records are available back to January 1991. Records are never purged. New records are available online after 1-2 days.

Valdosta Division PO Box 68, Valdosta, GA 31603 (Courier Address: Room 212, 401 N Patterson, Valdosta, GA 31601), 912-242-3616, Fax: 912-244-9547.

www.gamd.uscourts.gov

Counties: Berrien, Clinch, Cook, Echols, Irwin, Lanier, Lowndes, Tift.

Indexing & Storage: Cases are indexed by defendant and plaintiff as well as by case number. New cases are available in the index immediately after filing date. A computer index is maintained. Open records are located at this court.

Fee & Payment: The fee is $15.00 per item (one party name or case number). Payment may be

made by money order, cashier check, business check. Personal checks are not accepted. Prepayment is required. Payee: US Courts. Certification fee: $5.00 per document. Copy fee: $.50 per page. You are allowed to make your own copies. These copies cost Not Applicable per page.

Phone Search: Docket information is available by phone. An automated voice case information service (VCIS) is not available.

Mail Search: A stamped self addressed envelope is not required.

In Person Search: In person searching is available.

PACER: Sign-up number is 800-676-6856. Access fee is $.60 per minute. Toll-free access: 888-234-3839. Local access: 912-752-8170. Case records are available back to January 1991. Records are never purged. New records are available online after 1-2 days.

US Bankruptcy Court

Middle District of Georgia

Columbus Division PO Box 2147, Columbus, GA 31902 (Courier Address: 901 Front Ave, 1 Arsenal Pl, Columbus, GA 31902), 706-649-7837.

www.gamb.uscourts.gov

Counties: Berrien, Brooks, Chattahoochee, Clay, Clinch, Colquitt, Cook, Decatur, Echols, Grady, Harris, Irwin, Lanier, Lowndes, Marion, Muscogee, Quitman, Randolph, Seminole, Stewart, Talbot, Taylor, Thomas, Tift.

Indexing & Storage: Cases are indexed by debtor as well as by case number. New cases are available in the index immediately after filing date. A computer index is maintained. An alias name of the debtor may be required to search for records. Open records are located at this court.

Fee & Payment: The fee is $15.00 per item (one party name or case number). Payment may be made by money order, cashier check, business check. Personal checks are not accepted. Prepayment is required. Payee: Clerk, US Bankruptcy Court. Certification fee: $5.00 per document. Copy fee: $.50 per page.

Phone Search: Docket information is available by phone. An automated voice case information service (VCIS) is available. Call VCIS at 800-211-3015 or 912-752-8183.

Mail Search: Always enclose a stamped self addressed envelope.

In Person Search: In person searching is available.

PACER: Sign-up number is 800-676-6856. Access fee is $.60 per minute. Toll-free access: 800-546-7343. Local access: 912-752-3551. Case records are available back to March 1990 (some back to 1985). Records are purged except last 12 months. New civil records are available online after 1 day. PACER is available online at http://pacer.gamb.uscourts.gov.

Macon Division PO Box 1957, Macon, GA 31201 (Courier Address: 433 Cherry St, Macon, GA 31202), 912-752-3506, Fax: 912-752-8157.

www.gamb.uscourts.gov

Counties: Baldwin, Baker, Ben Hill, Bibb, Bleckley, Butts, Calhoun, Clarke, Crawford, Crisp, Dooly, Dougherty, Early, Elbert, Franklin, Greene,

Hancock, Hart, Houston, Jasper, Jones, Lamar, Lee, Macon, Madison, Miller, Mitchell, Monroe, Morgan, Oconee, Oglethorpe, Peach, Pulaski, Putnam, Schley, Sumter, Terrell, Turner, Twiggs, Upson, Walton, Washington, Webster, Wilcox, Wilkinson, Worth.

Indexing & Storage: Cases are indexed by debtor and creditors as well as by case number. New cases are available in the index 1-2 days after filing date. Any alias name of the debtor may be required to search for records. A computer index is maintained. Open records are located at this court.

Fee & Payment: The fee is $15.00 per item (one party name or case number). Payment may be made by money order, cashier check, business check. Personal checks are not accepted. Prepayment is required. Payee: Clerk, US Bankruptcy Court. Certification fee: $5.00 per document. Copy fee: $.50 per page.

Phone Search: This court will only search for basic information by phone and limits the number of searches to 3 per phone call. An automated voice case information service (VCIS) is available. Call VCIS at 800-211-3015 or 912-752-8183.

Mail Search: Always enclose a stamped self addressed envelope.

In Person Search: In person searching is available.

PACER: Sign-up number is 800-676-6856. Access fee is $.60 per minute. Toll-free access: 800-546-7343. Local access: 912-752-3551. Case records are available back to March 1990 (some back to 1985). Records are purged except last 12 months. New civil records are available online after 1 day. PACER is available online at http://pacer.gamb.uscourts.gov.

US District Court

Northern District of Georgia

Atlanta Division 2211 US Courthouse, 75 Spring St SW, Atlanta, GA 30303-3361, 404-331-6496.

www.gand.uscourts.gov

Counties: Cherokee, Clayton, Cobb, De Kalb, Douglas, Fulton, Gwinnett, Henry, Newton, Rockdale.

Indexing & Storage: Cases are indexed by defendant and plaintiff as well as by case number. New cases are available in the index 1 day after filing date. A computer index is maintained. Open records are located at this court.

Fee & Payment: The fee is $15.00 per item (one party name or case number). Payment may be made by money order, cashier check. Business checks are not accepted. Personal checks are not accepted. Prepayment is required. Payee: Clerk, US District Court. Certification fee: $5.00 per document. Copy fee: $.50 per page.

Phone Search: Only docket information is available by phone. An automated voice case information service (VCIS) is not available.

Mail Search: A stamped self addressed envelope is not required.

In Person Search: In person searching is available.

PACER: Sign-up number is 800-676-6856. Access fee is $.60 per minute. Toll-free access: 800-801-6932. Local access: 404-730-9668. Case records are available back to August 1992.

Records are purged on a varied schedule. New records are available online after 1 day. PACER is available online at http://pacer.gand.uscourts.gov.

Gainesville Division
Federal Bldg, Room 201, 121 Spring St SE, Gainesville, GA 30501, 770-534-5954.

www.gand.uscourts.gov

Counties: Banks, Barrow, Dawson, Fannin, Forsyth, Gilmer, Habersham, Hall, Jackson, Lumpkin, Pickens, Rabun, Stephens, Towns, Union, White.

Indexing & Storage: Cases are indexed by defendant and plaintiff as well as by case number. New cases are available in the index 24 hours after filing date. A computer index is maintained. Open records are located at this court.

Fee & Payment: The fee is $15.00 per item (one party name or case number). Payment may be made by money order. Business checks are not accepted. Personal checks are not accepted. Prepayment is required. The court will only accept US Postal money orders, law firm checks and cashier's checks. Payee: Clerk, US District Court. Certification fee: $5.00 per document. Copy fee: $.50 per page.

Phone Search: Searching is not available by phone.

Mail Search: Always enclose a stamped self addressed envelope.

In Person Search: In person searching is available.

PACER: Sign-up number is 800-676-6856. Access fee is $.60 per minute. Toll-free access: 800-801-6932. Local access: 404-730-9668. Case records are available back to August 1992. Records are purged on a varied schedule. New records are available online after 1 day. PACER is available online at http://pacer.gand.uscourts.gov.

Newnan Division
PO Box 939, Newnan, GA 30264 (Courier Address: 18 Greenville St, #352, Newnan, GA 30263), 770-253-8847.

www.gand.uscourts.gov

Counties: Carroll, Coweta, Fayette, Haralson, Heard, Meriwether, Pike, Spalding, Troup.

Indexing & Storage: Cases are indexed by defendant and plaintiff as well as by case number. New cases are available in the index immediately after filing date. A computer index is maintained. Open records are located at this court.

Fee & Payment: The fee is $15.00 per item (one party name or case number). Payment may be made by money order, cashier check. Business checks are not accepted. Personal checks are not accepted. Prepayment is required. Only attorney firm checks will be accepted. Payee: Clerk, US District Court. Certification fee: $5.00 per document. Copy fee: $.50 per page.

Phone Search: Only docket information is available by phone. An automated voice case information service (VCIS) is not available.

Mail Search: A stamped self addressed envelope is not required.

In Person Search: In person searching is available.

PACER: Sign-up number is 800-676-6856. Access fee is $.60 per minute. Toll-free access: 800-801-6932. Local access: 404-730-9668. Case records are available back to August 1992. Records are purged on a varied schedule. New

records are available online after 1 day. PACER is available online at http://pacer.gand.uscourts.gov.

Rome Division
PO Box 1186, Rome, GA 30162-1186 (Courier Address: 600 E 1st St, Room 304, Rome, GA 30161), 706-291-5629.

www.gand.uscourts.gov

Counties: Bartow, Catoosa, Chattooga, Dade, Floyd, Gordon, Murray, Paulding, Polk, Walker, Whitfield.

Indexing & Storage: Cases are indexed by defendant and plaintiff as well as by case number. New cases are available in the index immediately after filing date. A computer index is maintained. Records are also indexed on microfiche. Only records prior to 1978 are on index cards. Open records are located at this court.

Fee & Payment: The fee is $15.00 per item (one party name or case number). Payment may be made by money order, cashier check. Business checks are not accepted. Personal checks are not accepted. Prepayment is required. Attorney checks also accepted. Payee: Clerk, US District Court. Certification fee: $5.00 per document. Copy fee: $.50 per page.

Phone Search: Only docket information showing if a suit has been filed, date of filing, and if case is pending or closed will be released over the phone. An automated voice case information service (VCIS) is not available.

Mail Search: Always enclose a stamped self addressed envelope.

In Person Search: In person searching is available.

PACER: Sign-up number is 800-676-6856. Access fee is $.60 per minute. Toll-free access: 800-801-6932. Local access: 404-730-9668. Case records are available back to August 1992. Records are purged on a varied schedule. New records are available online after 1 day. PACER is available online at http://pacer.gand.uscourts.gov.

US Bankruptcy Court
Northern District of Georgia

Atlanta Division
1340 US Courthouse, 75 Spring St SW, Atlanta, GA 30303-3361, 404-215-1000.

www.ganb.uscourts.gov

Counties: Cherokee, Clayton, Cobb, DeKalb, Douglas, Fulton, Gwinnett, Henry, Newton, Rockdale.

Indexing & Storage: Cases are indexed by debtor as well as by case number. New cases are available in the index 1-2 days after filing date. Both computer and card indexes are maintained. Records are also indexed on microfiche. Open records are located at this court.

Fee & Payment: The fee is $15.00 per item (one party name or case number). Payment may be made by money order, cashier check, business check. Personal checks are not accepted. Prepayment is required. Debtor's checks are not accepted. Payee: Clerk, US Bankruptcy Court. Certification fee: $5.00 per document. Copy fee: $.50 per page.

Phone Search: Docket information is available by phone. An automated voice case information service (VCIS) is available. Call VCIS at 888-510-8284 or 404-730-2866.

Fax Search: Fax requests are handled by a copy service. To set-up a fax request, call the service at 404-681-9125.

Mail Search: Always enclose a stamped self addressed envelope.

In Person Search: In person searching is available.

PACER: Sign-up number is 800-676-6856. Access fee is $.60 per minute. Toll-free access: 800-436-8395. Local access: 404-730-3264. Case records are available back to August 1986. Records are never purged. New civil records are available online after 2 days.

Electronic Filing: Only law firms and practicioners may file documents electronically. Anyone can search online; however, searches only include those cases which have been filed electronically. Use http://ecf.ganb.uscourts.gov/cgi-bin/PublicCaseFiled-Rpt.pl to search. Electronic filing information is available online at http://ecf.ganb.uscourts.gov

Gainesville Division
121 Spring St SE, Room 120, Gainesville, GA 30501, 770-536-0556.

www.ganb.uscourts.gov

Counties: Banks, Barrow, Dawson, Fannin, Forsyth, Gilmer, Habersham, Hall, Jackson, Lumpkin, Pickens, Rabun, Stephens, Towns, Union, White.

Indexing & Storage: Cases are indexed by debtor as well as by case number. New cases are available in the index 1-2 days after filing date. This court maintains index cards on older cases. Both computer and card indexes are maintained. Open records are located at this court.

Fee & Payment: The fee is $15.00 per item (one party name or case number). Payment may be made by money order, cashier check, personal check. Prepayment is required. Debtors checks not accepted. Payee: Clerk, US Bankruptcy Court. Certification fee: $5.00 per document. Copy fee: $.50 per page.

Phone Search: Docket information available by phone. An automated voice case information service (VCIS) is available. Call VCIS at 888-510-8284 or 404-730-2866.

Mail Search: Always enclose a stamped self addressed envelope.

In Person Search: In person searching is available.

PACER: Sign-up number is 800-676-6856. Access fee is $.60 per minute. Toll-free access: 800-436-8395. Local access: 404-730-3264. Case records are available back to August 1986. Records are never purged. New civil records are available online after 2 days.

Electronic Filing: Only law firms and practicioners may file documents electronically. Anyone can search online; however, searches only include those cases which have been filed electronically. Use http://ecf.ganb.uscourts.gov/cgi-bin/PublicCaseFiled-Rpt.pl to search. Electronic filing information is available online at http://ecf.ganb.uscourts.gov

Newnan Division
Clerk, PO Box 2328, Newnan, GA 30264 (Courier Address: Room 220, 18 Greenville St, Newnan, GA 30263), 770-251-5583.

www.ganb.uscourts.gov

Counties: Carroll, Coweta, Fayette, Haralson, Heard, Meriwether, Pike, Spalding, Troup.

Indexing & Storage: Cases are indexed by debtor as well as by case number. New cases are available in the index 1 day after filing date. A card index is maintained. Records are also indexed on microfiche. Open records are located at this court.

Fee & Payment: The fee is $15.00 per item (one party name or case number). Payment may be made by money order, cashier check, personal check. Prepayment is required. Debtor's checks are not accepted. Payee: Clerk, US Bankruptcy Court. Certification fee: $5.00 per document. Copy fee: $.50 per page.

Phone Search: Only docket information is available by phone. The debtor's address and social security number will not be released. There is no charge if a case number is provided. An automated voice case information service (VCIS) is available. Call VCIS at 888-510-8284 or 404-730-2866.

Mail Search: A stamped self addressed envelope is not required.

In Person Search: In person searching is available.

PACER: Sign-up number is 800-676-6856. Access fee is $.60 per minute. Toll-free access: 800-436-8395. Local access: 404-730-3264. Case records are available back to August 1986. Records are never purged. New civil records are available online after 2 days.

Electronic Filing: Only law firms and practicioners may file documents electronically. Anyone can search online; however, searches only include those cases which have been filed electronically. Use http://ecf.ganb.uscourts.gov/cgi-bin/PublicCaseFiled-Rpt.pl to search. Electronic filing information is available online at http://ecf.ganb.uscourts.gov

Rome Division
Clerk, 600 E 1st St, Room 339, Rome, GA 30161-3187, 706-291-5639.

www.ganb.uscourts.gov

Counties: Bartow, Catoosa, Chattooga, Dade, Floyd, Gordon, Murray, Paulding, Polk, Walker, Whitfield.

Indexing & Storage: Cases are indexed by debtor as well as by case number. New cases are available in the index 24 hours after filing date. A card index is maintained. Open records are located at this court.

Fee & Payment: The fee is $15.00 per item (one party name or case number). Payment may be made by money order, cashier check, personal check. Prepayment is required. Payee: Clerk, US Bankruptcy Court. Certification fee: $5.00 per document. Copy fee: $.50 per page.

Phone Search: Docket information is available by phone. An automated voice case information service (VCIS) is available. Call VCIS at 888-510-8284 or 404-730-2866.

Mail Search: Always enclose a stamped self addressed envelope.

In Person Search: In person searching is available.

PACER: Sign-up number is 800-676-6856. Access fee is $.60 per minute. Toll-free access: 800-436-8395. Local access: 404-730-3264. Case records are available back to August 1986. Records are never purged. New civil records are available online after 2 days.

Electronic Filing: Only law firms and practicioners may file documents electronically. Anyone can search online; however, searches only include those cases which have been filed

electronically. Use http://ecf.ganb.uscourts.gov/cgi-bin/PublicCaseFiled-Rpt.pl to search. Electronic filing information is available online at http://ecf.ganb.uscourts.gov

US District Court
Southern District of Georgia

Augusta Division
PO Box 1130, Augusta, GA 30903 (Courier Address: Use mail address for courier delivery., 500 E Ford St, First Floor,), 706-849-4400.

www.gasd.uscourts.gov

Counties: Burke, Columbia, Glascock, Jefferson, Lincoln, McDuffie, Richmond, Taliaferro, Warren, Wilkes.

Indexing & Storage: Cases are indexed by defendant and plaintiff as well as by case number. New cases are available in the index immediately after filing date. Records are alphabetically indexed and stored by chronological case number order. A computer index is maintained. Open records are located at this court.

Fee & Payment: The fee is $15.00 per item (one party name or case number). Payment may be made by money order, cashier check, personal check. Prepayment is required. Payee: US Courts. Certification fee: $5.00 per document. Copy fee: $.50 per page.

Phone Search: Docket information available by phone. An automated voice case information service (VCIS) is not available.

Mail Search: Always enclose a stamped self addressed envelope.

In Person Search: In person searching is available.

PACER: Sign-up number is 800-676-6856. Access fee is $.60 per minute. Toll-free access: 800-801-6934. Local access: 912-650-4046. Case records are available back to June 1995. New records are available online after 1 day. PACER is available online at http://pacer.gasd.uscourts.gov.

Brunswick Division
PO Box 1636, Brunswick, GA 31521 (Courier Address: Room 222, 801 Glouchester, Brunswick, GA 31520), 912-265-1758.

www.gasd.uscourts.gov

Counties: Appling, Camden, Glynn, Jeff Davis, Long, McIntosh, Wayne.

Indexing & Storage: Cases are indexed by defendant and plaintiff as well as by case number. New cases are available in the index immediately after filing date. A computer index is maintained. The records from the last 1 1/2 years are indexed on computer. Prior records are indexed on microfiche. Open records are located at this court.

Fee & Payment: The fee is $15.00 per item (one party name or case number). Payment may be made by money order, cashier check, personal check. Prepayment is required. Payee: Clerk, US District Court. Certification fee: $5.00 per document. Copy fee: $.50 per page.

Phone Search: Only docket information is available by phone. An automated voice case information service (VCIS) is not available.

Mail Search: Always enclose a stamped self addressed envelope.

In Person Search: In person searching is available.

PACER: Sign-up number is 800-676-6856. Access fee is $.60 per minute. Toll-free access: 800-801-6934. Local access: 912-650-4046. Case records are available back to June 1995. New records are available online after 1 day. PACER is available online at http://pacer.gasd.uscourts.gov.

Dublin Division
c/o Augusta Division, PO Box 1130, Augusta, GA 30903 (Courier Address: 500 E Ford St, Augusta, GA 30901), 706-849-4400.

www.gasd.uscourts.gov

Counties: Dodge, Johnson, Laurens, Montgomery, Telfair, Treutlen, Wheeler.

Indexing & Storage: Cases are indexed by as well as by case number. New cases are available in the index after filing date. Open records are located at the Division.

Fee & Payment: The fee is no charge per item (one party name or case number). Payment may be made by money order, cashier check. Business checks are not accepted. Personal checks are not accepted.

Phone Search: An automated voice case information service (VCIS) is not available.

In Person Search: In person searching is available.

PACER: Sign-up number is 800-676-6856. Access fee is $.60 per minute. Toll-free access: 800-801-6934. Local access: 912-650-4046. Case records are available back to June 1995. New records are available online after 1 day. PACER is available online at http://pacer.gasd.uscourts.gov.

Savannah Division
PO Box 8286, Savannah, GA 31412 (Courier Address: Room 306, 125 Bull St, Savannah, GA 31401), 912-650-4020, Fax: 912-650-4030.

www.gasd.uscourts.gov

Counties: Bryan, Chatham, Effingham, Liberty.

Indexing & Storage: Cases are indexed by defendant and plaintiff as well as by case number. New cases are available in the index immediately after filing date. A computer index is maintained. Records have been indexed on computer from 1992. Prior records are indexed on microfiche. Open records are located at this court.

Fee & Payment: The fee is $15.00 per item (one party name or case number). Payment may be made by money order, cashier check, personal check. Prepayment is required. Payee: Clerk, US District Court. Certification fee: $5.00 per document. Copy fee: $.50 per page.

Phone Search: Only docket information is available by phone.

Mail Search: A stamped self addressed envelope is not required.

In Person Search: In person searching is available.

PACER: Sign-up number is 800-676-6856. Access fee is $.60 per minute. Toll-free access: 800-801-6934. Local access: 912-650-4046. Case records are available back to June 1995. New records are available online after 1 day. PACER is available online at http://pacer.gasd.uscourts.gov.

Statesboro Division
c/o Savannah Division, PO Box 8286, Savannah, GA 31412, 912-650-4020.

www.gasd.uscourts.gov

Counties: Bulloch, Candler, Emanuel, Evans, Jenkins, Screven, Tattnall, Toombs.

Indexing & Storage: Cases are indexed by as well as by case number. New cases are available in the index after filing date. Open records are located at the Division.

Fee & Payment: The fee is no charge per item (one party name or case number). Payment may be made by money order, cashier check. Business checks are not accepted. Personal checks are not accepted.

Phone Search: An automated voice case information service (VCIS) is not available.

In Person Search: In person searching is available.

PACER: Sign-up number is 800-676-6856. Access fee is $.60 per minute. Toll-free access: 800-801-6934. Local access: 912-650-4046. Case records are available back to June 1995. New records are available online after 1 day. PACER is available online at http://pacer.gasd.uscourts.gov.

Waycross Division c/o Savannah Division, PO Box 8286, Savannah, GA 31412 (Courier Address: Room 306, 125 Bull St, Savannah, GA 31401), 912-650-4020.

www.gasd.uscourts.gov

Counties: Atkinson, Bacon, Brantley, Charlton, Coffee, Pierce, Ware.

Indexing & Storage: Cases are indexed by as well as by case number. New cases are available in the index after filing date. Open records are located at the Division.

Fee & Payment: The fee is no charge per item (one party name or case number). Payment may be made by money order, cashier check. Business checks are not accepted. Personal checks are not accepted.

Phone Search: An automated voice case information service (VCIS) is not available.

In Person Search: In person searching is available.

PACER: Sign-up number is 800-676-6856. Access fee is $.60 per minute. Toll-free access: 800-801-6934. Local access: 912-650-4046. Case records are available back to June 1995. New records are available online after 1 day. PACER is available online at http://pacer.gasd.uscourts.gov.

US Bankruptcy Court

Southern District of Georgia

Augusta Division PO Box 1487, Augusta, GA 30903 (Courier Address: Room 150, 827 Telfair St, Augusta, GA 30901), 706-724-2421.

www.gasb.uscourts.gov

Counties: Bulloch, Burke, Candler, Columbia, Dodge, Emanuel, Evans, Glascock, Jefferson, Jenkins, Johnson, Laurens, Lincoln, McDuffie, Montgomery, Richmond, Screven, Taliaferro, Tattnall, Telfair, Toombs, Treutlen, Warren, Wheeler, Wilkes.

Indexing & Storage: Cases are indexed by debtor as well as by case number. New cases are available in the index 24 hours after filing date. A computer index is maintained. Open records are located at this court. District wide searches are available for information from August 1986 from this court. This court handles files for the Statesboro and Dublin divisions as well as the Augusta files.

Fee & Payment: The fee is $15.00 per item (one party name or case number). Payment may be

made by money order, cashier check, business check. Personal checks are not accepted. Prepayment is required. Payee: Clerk, US Bankruptcy Court. Certification fee: $5.00 per document. Copy fee: $.50 per page.

Phone Search: If case number is provided over the phone, all docket information will be released. An automated voice case information service (VCIS) is not available.

Mail Search: Always enclose a stamped self addressed envelope.

In Person Search: In person searching is available.

PACER: Sign-up number is 800-676-6856. Access fee is $.60 per minute. Toll-free access: 800-259-8679. Local access: 706-722-9776. Use of PC Anywhere v4.0 suggested. Case records are available back to August 1986. Records are purged annually. PACER is available online at http://pacer.gasb.uscourts.gov.

Savannah Division PO Box 8347, Savannah, GA 31412 (Courier Address: Room 213, 125 Bull St, Savannah, GA 31412), 912-650-4100.

www.gasb.uscourts.gov

Counties: Appling, Atkinson, Bacon, Brantley, Bryan, Camden, Charlton, Chatham, Coffee, Effingham, Glynn, Jeff Davis, Liberty, Long, McIntosh, Pierce, Ware, Wayne.

Indexing & Storage: Cases are indexed by debtor as well as by case number. New cases are available in the index immediately after filing date. Cases are also indexed by Social Security number. A computer index is maintained. Open records are located at this court. District wide searches are available for information from August 1, 1985 at this court. This court handles files for the Waycross and Brunswick divisions as well as the Savannah files.

Fee & Payment: The fee is $15.00 per item (one party name or case number). Payment may be made by money order, cashier check, business check. Personal checks are not accepted. Prepayment is required. Payee: Clerk, US Bankruptcy Court. Certification fee: $5.00 per document. Copy fee: $.50 per page.

Phone Search: Phone search is limited to information on computer. An automated voice case information service (VCIS) is not available.

Mail Search: A stamped self addressed envelope is not required.

In Person Search: In person searching is available.

PACER: Sign-up number is 800-676-6856. Access fee is $.60 per minute. Toll-free access: 800-891-9583. Local access: 912-650-4190. Use of PC Anywhere v4.0 suggested. Case records are available back to 1988. Records are purged every six months. New civil records are available online after 1 day. PACER is available online at http://pacer.gasb.uscourts.gov.

Court	Jurisdiction	No. of Courts	How Organized
Superior Courts*	General	100	46 Circuits
State Courts*	Limited	16	
Combined Courts*		43	
Magistrate Courts*	Limited	142	
Combined Superior/ Magistrate Court*		17	
Civil Courts*	Limited	2	Bibb, Richmond
County Recorder's Courts	Limited	3	DeKalb, Gwinnett, Muskogee
Municipal Court	Municipal	1	Columbus
Municipal Courts	Municipal	474	Includes City Court of Atlanta
Probate Courts*	Probate	153	
Juvenile Courts	Special	159	

* Profiled in this Sourcebook.

CIVIL									
Court	Tort	Contract	Real Estate	Min. Claim	Max. Claim	Small Claims	Estate	Eviction	Domestic Relations
Superior Courts*	X	X	X	$5000	No Max				X
State Courts*	X	X		$5000	No Max				
Combined Courts*	X	X		$0	$5000	$5000		X	
Magistrate Courts*	X	X		$0	$15,000	$5000			
Combined Superior/ Magistrate Court*									
Civil Courts*	X	X		$0	$7500	$7500			
County Recorder's Courts									
Municipal Court	X	X			$0	$7500	$7500		
Probate Courts*									
Juvenile Courts									

CRIMINAL					
Court	Felony	Misdemeanor	DWI/DUI	Preliminary Hearing	Juvenile
Superior Courts*	X	X	X		
State Courts*		X	X	X	
Combined Courts*				X	
Magistrate Courts*				X	
Combined Superior/ Magistrate Court*			X	X	
Civil Courts*				X	
County Recorder's Courts			X	X	
Municipal Court		X		X	
Probate Courts*					
Juvenile Courts					X

ADMINISTRATION   Court Administrator, 244 Washington St SW, Suite 550, Atlanta, GA, 30334; 404-656-5171, Fax: 404-651-6449. www2.state.ga.us/Courts/Supreme

COURT STRUCTURE   There is a Superior Court in each county, which assumes the role of State Court if the county does not have one.

The Magistrate Court has jurisdiction over one type of misdemeanor related to passing bad checks. This court also issues arrest warrants and sets bond on all felonies.

ONLINE ACCESS   Cobb has has Internet access to records, but there is no online access available statewide.

📖 📖 📖 📖 📖 📖 📖

Appling County

Superior & State Court PO Box 269, Baxley, GA 31513; 912-367-8126. Hours: 8AM-5PM (EST). *Felony, Misdemeanor, Civil.*

Civil Records: Access: In person only. Court does not conduct in person searches; visitors must perform searches for themselves. Search fee: No civil searches performed by court. Required to search: name, years to search. Civil cases indexed by defendant, plaintiff. Civil records on docket books back to 1800s. **Criminal Records:** Access: In person only. Court does not conduct in person searches; visitors must perform searches for themselves. Search fee: No criminal searches performed by court. Required to search: name, years to search, DOB; also helpful-SSN, race, sex. Criminal records on docket books back to 1800s. **General Information:** No juvenile, adoption, sealed, sexual, mental health or expunged records released. Copy fee: $.25 for first page, $.10 each addl. Certification fee: $2.50 plus $.50 per page after first. Fee payee: Court Clerk. Personal checks accepted.

Magistrate Court Box 366, Baxley, GA 31515; 912-367-8116; Fax: 912-367-8182. Hours: 8:30AM-5PM (EST). *Civil Actions Under $15,000, Eviction, Small Claims.*

Probate Court 36 S Main St #B, Baxley, GA 31513; 912-367-8114; Fax: 912-367-8166. Hours: 8:30AM-5PM (EST). *Probate.*

Atkinson County

Superior Court PO Box 6, South Main, Courthouse Square, Pearson, GA 31642; 912-422-3343; Fax: 912-422-3429. Hours: 8AM-Noon, 1-5PM (EST). *Felony, Misdemeanor, Civil.*

Civil Records: Access: In person only. Court does not conduct in person searches; visitors must perform searches for themselves. Search fee: No civil searches performed by court. Required to search: name, years to search. Civil cases indexed by defendant. Civil records in docket books back to 1919. **Criminal Records:** Access: In person only. Court does not conduct in person searches; visitors must perform searches for themselves. Search fee: No criminal searches performed by court. Required to search: name, years to search. Criminal records in docket books back to 1919. **General Information:** No juvenile, adoption, sealed, sexual, mental health or expunged records released. Copy fee: $.25 per page. Certification fee: $2.50 plus $.50 per page after first. Fee payee: Clerk of Superior Court. Personal checks accepted. Prepayment is required.

Magistrate Court PO Box 674, Pearson, GA 31642; 912-422-7158; Fax: 912-422-3429. Hours: 9AM-4:30PM (EST). *Civil Actions Under $15,000, Eviction, Small Claims.*

Probate Court PO Box 855, Pearson, GA 31642; 912-422-3552; Fax: 912-422-7842. Hours: 8AM-5PM (EST). *Probate.*

Bacon County

Superior Court PO Box 376, Alma, GA 31510; 912-632-4915. Hours: 9AM-5PM (EST). *Felony, Misdemeanor, Civil.*

Civil Records: Access: Mail, in person. Both court and visitors may perform in person searches. No search fee. Required to search: name, years to search. Civil cases indexed by defendant, plaintiff. Civil records on index from 1915. **Criminal Records:** Access: Mail, in person. Both court and visitors may perform in person searches. No search fee. Required to search: name, years to search, DOB; also helpful-SSN, race, sex. Criminal records on index from 1915. **General Information:** No juvenile, adoption, sealed, sexual, mental health, expunged or first offender records released. SASE required. Turnaround time 1 week. Copy fee: $.25 per page. Certification fee: $2.50 plus $.50 per page after first. Fee payee: Clerk of Superior Court. Personal checks accepted. Prepayment is required.

Magistrate Court Box 389, Alma, GA 31510; 912-632-5961. Hours: 9AM-5PM (EST). *Civil Actions Under $15,000, Eviction, Small Claims.*

Probate Court PO Box 146, Alma, GA 31510; 912-632-7661; Fax: 912-632-7662. Hours: 9AM-5PM (EST). *Probate.*

Baker County

Superior Court PO Box 10, Governmental Bldg, Newton, GA 31770; 229-734-3004; Fax: 229-734-8822. Hours: 9AM-5PM (EST). *Felony, Misdemeanor, Civil.*

Civil Records: Access: In person only. Court does not conduct in person searches; visitors must perform searches for themselves. Search fee: No civil searches performed by court. Required to search: name, years to search. Civil cases indexed by defendant. Civil records on index from 1850. **Criminal Records:** Access: In person only. Court does not conduct in person searches; visitors must perform searches for themselves. Search fee: No criminal searches performed by court. Required to search: name, years to search, DOB; also helpful-SSN, race, sex. Criminal records on index from 1850. **General Information:** No juvenile, adoption, sealed, sexual or expunged records released. Copy fee: $.25 per page. Certification fee: $2.50 plus $.50 per page after first. Fee payee: Court Clerk. Personal checks accepted. Prepayment is required.

Magistrate Court Box 535, Newton, GA 31770; 229-734-3009; Fax: 229-734-8822. Hours: 9AM-5PM (EST). *Civil Actions Under $15,000, Eviction, Small Claims.*

Probate Court PO Box 548, Newton, GA 31770; 229-734-3007; Fax: 229-734-8822. Hours: 9AM-5PM M-W & F; 9AM-Noon Th (EST). *Probate.*

Baldwin County

Superior & State Court PO Drawer 987, Milledgeville, GA 31061; 912-445-4007; Fax: 912-445-1404. Hours: 8:30AM-5PM (EST). *Felony, Misdemeanor, Civil.*

Civil Records: Access: In person only. Court does not conduct in person searches; visitors must perform searches for themselves. Search fee: No civil searches performed by court. Required to search: name, years to search. Civil cases indexed by defendant, plaintiff. Civil records on docket from 1861. **Criminal Records:** Access: In person only. Court does not conduct in person searches; visitors must perform searches for themselves. Search fee: No criminal searches performed by court. Required to search: name, years to search. Criminal records on docket from 1861. **General Information:** No juvenile, adoption, sealed, sexual, mental health or expunged records released. Copy fee: $.25 per page. Certification fee: $2.50 plus $.50 per page after first. Personal checks accepted. Prepayment is required.

Magistrate Court PO Box 1565, Milledgeville, GA 31061; 912-445-4446; Fax: 912-445-5918. Hours: 8:30AM-5PM (EST). *Civil Actions Under $15,000, Eviction, Small Claims.*

Probate Court PO Box 964, Milledgeville, GA 31061; 912-445-4807; Fax: 912-445-5178. Hours: 8:30AM-5PM (EST). *Probate.*

Banks County

Superior Court PO Box 337, 144 Yorah Homer Road, Homer, GA 30547; 706-677-6240; Fax: 706-677-2337. Hours: 8:30AM-5PM (EST). *Felony, Misdemeanor, Civil.*

Civil Records: Access: In person only. Court does not conduct in person searches; visitors must perform searches for themselves. Search fee: No civil searches performed by court. Required to search: name, years to search. Civil cases indexed by defendant, plaintiff. Civil records on docket from 1960. **Criminal Records:** Access: In person only. Court does not conduct in person searches; visitors must perform searches for themselves. Search fee: No criminal searches performed by court. Required to search: name, years to search, DOB, signed release; also helpful-SSN, race, sex. Criminal records on docket from 1960. **General Information:** No juvenile, adoption, sealed, sexual, mental health or expunged records released. Copy fee: $.25 per page. Certification fee: $3.75. Fee payee: Clerk of Superior Court. Personal checks accepted.

Magistrate Court Box 364, Homer, GA 30547; 706-677-6270; Fax: 706-677-6215. Hours: 8:30AM-5PM (EST). *Civil Actions Under $15,000, Eviction, Small Claims.*

Probate Court PO Box 7, Homer, GA 30547; 706-677-6250; Fax: 706-677-2339. Hours: 80AM-5PM (EST). *Probate.*

Barrow County

Superior Court PO Box 1280, Winder, GA 30680; 770-307-3035; Fax: 770-867-4800. Hours: 8AM-5PM (EST). *Felony, Misdemeanor, Civil.*

Civil Records: Access: In person only. Court does not conduct in person searches; visitors must perform searches for themselves. Search fee: No civil searches performed by court. Required to search: name, years to search. Civil cases indexed by defendant, plaintiff. Civil records on computer from 1990, docket from 1914. **Criminal Records:** Access: In person only. Court does not conduct in person searches; visitors must perform searches for themselves. Search fee: No criminal searches performed by court. Required to search: name, years to search, DOB; also helpful-SSN, race, sex. Criminal records on computer from 1992, docket from 1914. **General Information:** No juvenile, adoption, sealed, sexual, mental health or expunged records released. Copy fee: $.25 per page. Certification fee: $2.50 plus $.50 per page after first. Fee payee: Clerk of Superior Court. Business checks accepted. Prepayment is required.

Magistrate Court 30 N Broad St, Ste 331, Winder, GA 30680; 770-307-3050; Fax: 770-868-1440. Hours: 8AM-5PM (EST). *Civil Actions Under $15,000, Eviction, Small Claims.*

Probate Court Barrow County Courthouse, 30 N Broad St, Winder, GA 30680; 770-867-8981; Fax: 770-867-4800. Hours: 8AM-5PM (EST). *Probate.*

Bartow County

Superior Court 135 W Cherokee #233, Cartersville, GA 30120; 770-387-5025; Fax: 770-386-0846. Hours: 8AM-5PM (EST). *Felony, Misdemeanor, Civil.*

Civil Records: Access: In person only. Court does not conduct in person searches; visitors must perform searches for themselves. Search fee: No civil searches performed by court. Required to search: name, years to search. Civil cases indexed by defendant, plaintiff. Civil records on computer from 9/92, on books from 1900s. **Criminal Records:** Access: In person only. Court does not conduct in person searches; visitors must perform searches for themselves. Search fee: No criminal searches performed by court. Required to search: name, years to search, address, DOB, SSN, signed release. Criminal records on computer for 10 years, prior on books. **General Information:** No juvenile, adoptions or sealed records released. Copy fee: $.25 per page. Certification fee: $2.50 plus $.25 each add'l page. Fee payee: Clerk of Superior Court. Personal checks accepted. Prepayment is required.

Magistrate Court 135 W Cherokee Ave #225, Cartersville, GA 30120; 770-387-5070. Hours: 7AM-5:30PM (EST). *Civil Actions Under $15,000, Eviction, Small Claims.*

Probate Court 135 W Cherokee #243A, Cartersville, GA 30120; 770-387-5075; Fax: 770-387-5074. Hours: 8AM-5PM (EST). *Probate.*

Ben Hill County

Superior Court PO Box 1104, 401 Central, Fitzgerald, GA 31750; 912-426-5135; Fax: 912-426-5487. Hours: 8:30AM-4:30PM (EST). *Felony, Misdemeanor, Civil.*

Civil Records: Access: In person only. Court does not conduct in person searches; visitors must perform searches for themselves. Search fee: No civil searches performed by court. Required to search: name, years to search. Civil cases indexed by defendant. Civil records on computer from 1994, archived from 1907, docket 1907. **Criminal Records:** Access: In person only. Court does not conduct in person searches; visitors must perform searches for themselves. Search fee: No criminal searches performed by court. Required to search: name, years to search, signed release; also helpful-DOB, SSN. Criminal records on computer from 1994, archived from 1907, docket 1907. **General Information:** No juvenile, adoption, sealed, sexual, mental health or expunged records released. Copy fee: $.25 per page; $1.00 per page if mailed. Certification fee: $2.00 plus $.50 per page. Fee payee: Clerk. Personal checks accepted. Prepayment is required.

Magistrate Court Box 1163, Fitzgerald, GA 31750; 912-426-5140. Hours: 8:30AM-5:30PM (EST). *Civil Actions Under $15,000, Eviction, Small Claims.*

Probate Court 401 E Central Ave, Fitzgerald, GA 31750; 229-426-5137; Fax: 228-426-5486. Hours: 9AM-5PM (EST). *Probate.*

Berrien County

Superior Court 101 E Marion Ave, Ste 3, Nashville, GA 31639; 229-686-5506. Hours: 8AM-5PM (EST). *Felony, Misdemeanor, Civil.*

Civil Records: Access: Mail, in person. Both court and visitors may perform in person searches. No search fee. Required to search: name, years to search. Civil cases indexed by defendant, plaintiff. Civil records on docket back to 1800. **Criminal Records:** Access: Mail, in person. Both court and visitors may perform in person searches. No search fee. Required to search: name, years to search, DOB; also helpful-SSN, race, sex. Criminal records on docket back to 1800. **General Information:** No juvenile, adoption, sealed, sexual, mental health or expunged records released. Turnaround time same day. Copy fee: $.25 per page. Certification fee: $2.50 plus $.50 per page after first. Fee payee: Court Clerk. Personal checks accepted. Prepayment is required.

Magistrate Court PO Box 103, Nashville, GA 31639; 229-686-7019; Fax: 229-686-6328. Hours: 8:30AM-4:30PM (EST). *Civil Actions Under $15,000, Eviction, Small Claims.*

Probate Court 101 E Marion Ave, Ste 2, Nashville, GA 31639; 229-686-5213; Fax: 229-686-9495. Hours: 7AM-5PM Sun-Sat (EST). *Probate.*

Bibb County

Superior Court PO Box 1015, 601 Mulberry St Rm 216, Macon, GA 31202; 478-749-6527. Hours: 8:30AM-5PM (EST). *Felony, Civil.*

Civil Records: Access: Mail, in person. Both court and visitors may perform in person searches. Search fee: $10.00 per name. Required to search: name, years to search. Civil cases indexed by defendant, plaintiff. Civil records on computer from 1993, on books from 1823. **Criminal Records:** Access: Mail, in person. Both court and visitors may perform in person searches. Search fee: $10.00 per name. Required to search: name, years to search, DOB, signed release; also helpful-SSN. Criminal records on computer since 1989. **General Information:** No adoption or sealed records released. Turnaround time same day. Copy fee: $.25 per page. Fee is $1.00 if court makes copy. Certification fee: $2.50 plus $.50 per page after first. Fee payee: Superior Court Clerk. Only cashiers checks and money orders accepted. Prepayment is required.

State Court PO Box 5086, Macon, GA 31213-7199; 478-749-6676; Fax: 478-748-6326. Hours: 8AM-5PM (EST). *Misdemeanor, Civil.*

Civil Records: Access: Mail, in person. Both court and visitors may perform in person searches. Search fee: $10.00 per name. Required to search: name, years to search. Civil cases indexed by defendant, plaintiff. Civil records on computer from 1989, docket from 1945. **Criminal Records:** Access: Mail, in person. Both court and visitors may perform in person searches. Search fee: $10.00 per name. Required to search: name, years to search, DOB; also helpful-SSN, race, sex. Criminal records on computer from 1989, docket from 1945. **General Information:** No juvenile, adoption, sealed, sexual, mental health or expunged records released. SASE required. Turnaround time 1 day. Copy fee: $.30 per page. Certification fee: $2.50 plus $.30 per page. Fee payee: Court Clerk. Business checks accepted. Prepayment is required.

Civil & Magistrate Court PO Box 121, Bibb County Courthouse, Macon, GA 31202-0121; 478-749-6495; Fax: 478-722-5861. Hours: 8AM-5PM (EST). *Civil Actions Under $25,000, Eviction, Small Claims.*

Probate Court 207 Bibb County Courthouse, PO Box 6518, Macon, GA 31208-6518; 478-749-6494; Fax: 478-749-6686. Hours: 8AM-5PM (EST). *Probate.*

Bleckley County

Superior Court 306 SE 2nd St, Cochran, GA 31014; 478-934-3210; Fax: 478-934-3205. Hours: 8:30AM-5PM (EST). *Felony, Misdemeanor, Civil.*

Civil Records: Access: In person only. Court does not conduct in person searches; visitors must perform searches for themselves. Search fee: No civil searches performed by court. Required to search: name, years to search. Civil cases indexed by defendant, plaintiff. Civil records archived from 1913, docket from 1913. **Criminal Records:** Access: In person only. Court does not conduct in person searches; visitors must perform searches for themselves. Search fee: No criminal searches performed by court. Required to search: name, years to search, DOB; also helpful-SSN, race, sex. Criminal records archived from 1913, docket from 1913. **General Information:** No juvenile, adoption, sealed, sexual, mental health or expunged records released. Copy fee: $.25 per page. Certification fee: $2.50 plus $.50 per page after first. Fee payee: Clerk of the Superior Court. Personal checks accepted. Prepayment is required.

Magistrate Court 101 Eighth St, Cochran, GA 31014; 478-934-3202; Fax: 478-934-3226. Hours: 8:30AM-5PM (EST). *Civil Actions Under $15,000, Eviction, Small Claims.*

Probate Court 306 SE Second St, Cochran, GA 31014; 478-934-3204; Fax: 478-934-3205. Hours: 8:30AM-5PM (EST). *Probate.*

Brantley County

Superior Court PO Box 1067, 117 Brantley St, Nahunta, GA 31553; 912-462-5635; Fax: 912-462-6247. Hours: 8AM-5PM (EST). *Felony, Misdemeanor, Civil.*

Civil Records: Access: In person only. Court does not conduct in person searches; visitors must perform searches for themselves. Search fee: No civil searches performed by court. Required to search: name, years to search. Civil cases indexed by defendant, plaintiff. Civil records on dockets from 1922. **Criminal Records:** Access: In person only. Court does not conduct in person searches; visitors must perform searches for themselves. Search fee: No criminal searches performed by court. Required to search: name, years to search, DOB, SSN, signed release; also helpful-race, sex. Criminal records on dockets from 1922. **General Information:** No juvenile, adoption, sealed, 1st offenders, expunged or confidential records released. Copy fee: $.25 per page. Certification fee: $2.50 plus $.50 per page after first. Fee payee: Superior Court Clerk. Personal checks accepted. Prepayment is required.

Magistrate Court PO Box 998, Nahunta, GA 31553; 912-462-6780; Fax: 912-462-5538. Hours: 8AM-4:30PM (EST). *Civil Actions Under $15,000, Eviction, Small Claims.*

Probate Court PO Box 207, Nahunta, GA 31553; 912-462-5192; Fax: 912-462-5538. Hours: 9AM-5PM (EST). *Probate.*

Brooks County

Superior Court PO Box 630, Quitman, GA 31643; 229-263-4747/5150; Fax: 229-263-5050. Hours: 8AM-5PM (EST). *Felony, Misdemeanor, Civil.*

www2.state.ga.us/courts/superior/dca/ dca2sohp.htm

Civil Records: Access: In person only. Court does not conduct in person searches; visitors must perform searches for themselves. Search fee: No civil searches performed by court. Required to search: name, years to search. Civil cases indexed by defendant, plaintiff. Civil records in books back to 1857. **Criminal Records:** Access: In person only. Court does not conduct in person searches; visitors must perform searches for themselves. Search fee: No criminal searches performed by court. Required to search: name, years to search, DOB; also helpful-SSN, race, sex. Criminal records in books back to 1857. **General Information:** No juvenile, adoption, sealed, sexual, mental health or expunged records released. Copy fee: $.25 per page. Certification fee: $2.50 plus $.50 per page after first. Fee payee: Clerk Superior Court. Business checks accepted.

Magistrate Court PO Box 387, Quitman, GA 31643; 229-263-9989; Fax: 229-263-7847. Hours: 8AM-5PM (EST). *Civil Actions Under $15,000, Eviction, Small Claims.*

Probate Court PO Box 665, Quitman, GA 31643; 229-263-5567; Fax: 229-263-7559. Hours: 8:30AM-5PM (EST). *Probate.*

Bryan County

Superior & State Court PO Drawer H, Pembroke, GA 31321; 912-653-3872; Fax: 912-653-3695. Hours: 8AM-5PM (EST). *Felony, Misdemeanor, Civil.*

Civil Records: Access: Mail, in person. Both court and visitors may perform in person searches. Search fee: No civil searches performed by court. Required to search: name, years to search. Civil cases indexed by defendant, plaintiff. Civil records on dockets from 1960, recent records are computerized. **Criminal Records:** Access: Mail, in person. Both court and visitors may perform in person searches. Search fee: No criminal searches performed by court. Required to search: name, years to search, DOB; also helpful-SSN, race, sex. Criminal records on dockets from 1960, recent records are computerized. **General Information:** No juvenile, adoption, sealed, sexual, mental health or expunged records released. SASE

requested. Turnaround time 1-2 days. Copy fee: $.25 per page. Certification fee: $2.50 plus $.25 per page after first. Fee payee: Clerk of Superior & State Court. Personal checks accepted. Prepayment is required. Public access terminal is available.

Magistrate Court Box 927, Pembroke, GA 31321; 912-653-3861; Fax: 912-653-4603. Hours: 8AM-5PM (EST). *Civil Actions Under $15,000, Eviction, Small Claims.*

Probate Court PO Box 418, Pembroke, GA 31321; 912-653-3856; Fax: 912-653-4691. Hours: 8AM-12, 1-5PM (EST). *Probate.*

Bulloch County

Superior & State Court Judicial Annex Bldg, 20 Siebald St, Statesboro, GA 30458; 912-764-9009. Hours: 8:30AM-5PM (EST). *Felony, Misdemeanor, Civil.*

Civil Records: Access: In person only. Court does not conduct in person searches; visitors must perform searches for themselves. Search fee: No civil searches performed by court. Required to search: name, years to search. Civil cases indexed by defendant. Civil records on computer from 1991, dockets back to 1796. **Criminal Records:** Access: In person only. Court does not conduct in person searches; visitors must perform searches for themselves. Search fee: No criminal searches performed by court. Required to search: name, years to search. Criminal records on computer from 1991, dockets back to 1796. **General Information:** No juvenile, adoption, sexual, mental health or expunged records released. Copy fee: $.25 per page. Certification fee: $2.50 plus $.50 per page after first. Fee payee: Court Clerk. Personal checks accepted. Prepayment is required. Public access terminal is available.

Magistrate Court Box 1004, Statesboro, GA 30459-1004; 912-764-6458; Fax: 912-489-6731. Hours: 8:30AM-5PM (EST). *Civil Actions Under $15,000, Eviction, Small Claims.*

Probate Court PO Box 1005, Statesboro, GA 30459; 912-489-8749; Fax: 912-764-8740. Hours: 8:30AM-5PM (EST). *Probate.*

Burke County

Superior & State Court PO Box 803, Waynesboro, GA 30830; 706-554-2279; Fax: 706-554-7887. Hours: 9AM-5PM (EST). *Felony, Misdemeanor, Civil.*

Civil Records: Access: In person only. Court does not conduct in person searches; visitors must perform searches for themselves. Search fee: No civil searches performed by court. Required to search: name, years to search. Civil cases indexed by defendant. Civil records on minute books back to 1856, indexed on computer since 1996. **Criminal Records:** Access: In person only. Court does not conduct in person searches; visitors must perform searches for themselves. Search fee: No criminal searches performed by court. Required to search: name, years to search, DOB; also helpful-SSN, race, sex. Criminal records on minute books back to 1856, indexed on computer since 1996. **General Information:** No juvenile, adoption, sexual, mental health or expunged records released. Copy fee: $.25 per page. Certification fee: $2.50 plus $.50 per page after first. Fee payee: Clerk of Superior Court. Personal checks accepted. Prepayment is required.

Magistrate Court Box 401, Waynesboro, GA 30830; 706-554-4281; Fax: 706-554-0530. Hours: 9AM-5PM (EST). *Civil Actions Under $15,000, Eviction, Small Claims.*

Probate Court PO Box 322, Waynesboro, GA 30830; 706-554-3000; Fax: 706-554-6693. Hours: 9AM-5PM (EST). *Probate.*

Butts County

Superior Court PO Box 320, 26 3rd St, Jackson, GA 30233; 770-775-8215. Hours: 8AM-5PM (EST). *Felony, Misdemeanor, Civil.*

Civil Records: Access: In person only. Court does not conduct in person searches; visitors must perform searches for themselves. Search fee: No civil searches performed by court. Required to search: name, years to search. Civil cases indexed by defendant, plaintiff. Civil records on dockets from 1966. **Criminal Records:** Access: In person only. Court does not conduct in person searches; visitors must perform searches for themselves. Search fee: No criminal searches performed by court. Required to search: name, years to search, signed release; also helpful-DOB, SSN, race, sex. Criminal records on dockets from 1966. **General Information:** No juvenile, adoption, sexual, mental health or expunged records released. Copy fee: $.25 per page. Certification fee: $2.50 plus $.50 per page. Fee payee: Clerk of Superior Court. Personal checks accepted. Prepayment is required.

Magistrate Court Box 457, Jackson, GA 30233; 770-775-8220; Fax: 770-775-8236. Hours: 8AM-5PM (EST). *Civil Actions Under $15,000, Eviction, Small Claims.*

Probate Court 25 Third Street, #7, Jackson, GA 30233; 770-775-8204; Fax: 770-775-8211. Hours: 8AM-5PM (EST). *Probate.*

Calhoun County

Superior Court PO Box 69, Morgan, GA 31766; 229-849-2715; Fax: 229-849-2971. Hours: 8AM-5PM (EST). *Felony, Misdemeanor, Civil.*

Civil Records: Access: Mail, in person. Both court and visitors may perform in person searches. No search fee. Required to search: name, years to search. Civil cases indexed by defendant, plaintiff. Civil records on dockets back to 1854. **Criminal Records:** Access: Mail, in person. Both court and visitors may perform in person searches. No search fee. Required to search: name, years to search, DOB, SSN. Criminal records on dockets back to 1854. **General Information:** No juvenile, adoption, sexual, mental health or expunged records released. SASE required. Turnaround time 1-2 days. Copy fee: $.25 per page. Certification fee: $3.00. Fee payee: Superior Court Clerk. Personal checks accepted. Prepayment is required. Public access terminal is available.

Magistrate & Probate Court PO Box 87, Morgan, GA 31766; 229-849-2115; Fax: 229-849-0072. Hours: 8AM-5PM (EST). *Civil Actions Under $15,000, Eviction, Small Claims, Probate.*

Camden County

Superior Court PO Box 578, 202 E 4th Street, Woodbine, GA 31569; 912-576-5624. Hours: 9AM-5PM (EST). *Felony, Misdemeanor, Civil.*

Civil Records: Access: In person only. Both court and visitors may perform in person searches. Search fee: No civil searches performed by court. Required to search: name, years to search. Civil cases indexed by defendant, plaintiff. Civil records on computer from 1989, on dockets from 1776. **Criminal Records:** Access: In person only. Court does not conduct in person searches; visitors must perform searches for themselves. Search fee: No criminal searches performed by court. Required to search: name, years to search, signed release; also helpful-DOB, SSN. Criminal records on computer from 1989, on dockets from 1776. **General Information:** No juvenile, adoption, sexual or expunged records released. Copy fee: $.25 per page. Certification fee: $2.00 plus $.50 per page after first. Fee payee: Clerk of Superior Court. Personal checks accepted. Prepayment is required. Public access terminal is available.

Magistrate Court Box 386, Woodbine, GA 31569; 912-576-5658. Hours: 9AM-5PM (EST). *Civil Actions Under $15,000, Eviction, Small Claims.*

Probate Court PO Box 818, Woodbine, GA 31569; 912-576-3785; Fax: 912-576-5484. Hours: 9AM-Noon, 1-5PM (EST). *Probate.*

Candler County

Superior & State Court PO Draawer 830, Metter, GA 30439; 912-685-5257; Fax: 912-685-2946. Hours: 8:30AM-5PM (EST). *Felony, Misdemeanor, Civil.*

Civil Records: Access: In person only. Court does not conduct in person searches; visitors must perform searches for themselves. Search fee: No civil searches performed by court. Required to search: name, years to search. Civil cases indexed by defendant, plaintiff. Civil records on dockets from 1914. **Criminal Records:** Access: In person only. Court does not conduct in person searches; visitors must perform searches for themselves. Search fee: No criminal searches performed by court. Required to search: name, years to search. Criminal records on dockets from 1914. **General Information:** No juvenile, adoption, mental health, expunged or sealed records released. Copy fee: $.25 per page. Certification fee: $2.00 plus $.50 per page. Fee payee: Clerk of Superior & State Court. Personal checks accepted. Prepayment is required.

Magistrate Court Box 682, 349 N Roundtree St, Metter, GA 30439; 912-685-2888; Fax: 912-685-6426. Hours: 9AM-5PM (EST). *Civil Actions Under $15,000, Eviction, Small Claims.*

Probate Court Courthouse Square, Metter, GA 30439; 912-685-2357; Fax: 912-685-5130. Hours: 8AM-5PM (EST). *Probate.*

Carroll County

Superior & State Court PO Box 1620, Carrollton, GA 30117; 770-830-5830; Fax: 770-830-5988. Hours: 8AM-5PM (EST). *Felony, Misdemeanor, Civil.*

Civil Records: Access: Mail, in person. Both court and visitors may perform in person searches. Search fee: $5.00 per name. Required to search: name, years to search. Civil cases indexed by defendant, plaintiff. Civil records on computer from 1986, docket. **Criminal Records:** Access: Mail, in person. Both court and visitors may perform in person searches. Search fee: $5.00 per name. Required to search: name, years to search, DOB; also helpful-SSN, race, sex. Criminal records on computer from 1986, docket. **General Information:** No juvenile, adoption, sexual, mental health or expunged records released. SASE required. Turnaround time 1 week. Copy fee: $1.00 per page. Certification fee: $2.50 plus $.50 per page after first. Fee payee: Clerk of Superior & State Court. Personal checks accepted. Prepayment is required.

Magistrate Court PO Box 338, Carrollton, GA 30117; 770-830-0116. Hours: 9AM-5PM (EST). *Civil Actions Under $15,000, Eviction, Small Claims.*

Probate Court Carroll County Courthouse, Rm 204, Carrollton, GA 30117; 770-830-5840; Fax: 770-830-5995. Hours: 8AM-5PM (EST). *Probate.*

Catoosa County

Superior & Magistrate Court 875 Lafayette St, Ringgold, GA 30736; 706-935-4231. Hours: 8:30AM-5PM (EST). *Felony, Misdemeanor, Civil, Eviction, Small Claims.*

Civil Records: Access: In person only. Court does not conduct in person searches; visitors must perform searches for themselves. Search fee: No civil searches performed by court. Required to search: name, years to search. Civil cases indexed by defendant, plaintiff. Civil records on dockets from 1800. **Criminal Records:** Access: In person only. Court does not conduct in person searches; visitors must perform searches for themselves. Search fee: No criminal searches performed by court. Required to search: name, years to search, DOB; also helpful-SSN, race, sex. Criminal records on dockets from 1800. **General Information:** No juvenile, adoption, sexual, mental health or expunged records released. Copy fee: $1.00 per page. Certification fee: $2.50 plus $.50 per page after first. Fee payee: Superior Court - Court Clerk. Personal checks accepted. Prepayment is required.

Probate Court 875 LaFayette St, Justice Bldg, Ringgold, GA 30736; 706-935-3511. Hours: 9AM-5PM (EST). *Probate.*

Charlton County

Superior Court Courthouse, Folkston, GA 31537; 912-496-2354. Hours: 8:30AM-5PM (EST). *Felony, Misdemeanor, Civil.*

Civil Records: Access: Mail, in person. Both court and visitors may perform in person searches. Search fee: No search fee. Required to search: name, years to search. Civil cases indexed by defendant. Civil records on index from 1954. **Criminal Records:** Access: Mail, in person. Both court and visitors may perform in person searches. No search fee. Required to search: name, years to search, DOB, SSN. Criminal records on index from 1954. **General Information:** No juvenile, adoption, sexual, mental health or expunged records released. Turnaround time 1 day. Copy fee: $.25 per page. Certification fee: $2.50 plus $.50 per page after first. Fee payee: Court Clerk. Personal checks accepted.

Magistrate Court 608 Pennsylvania Ave, Homeland, GA 31537; 912-496-7332; Fax: 912-496-3747. Hours: 8AM-5PM (EST). *Civil Actions Under $15,000, Eviction, Small Claims.*

Probate Court 100 S 3rd St, Folkston, GA 31537; 912-496-2230; Fax: 912-496-1156. Hours: 8AM-5PM (EST). *Probate.*

Chatham County

Superior Court PO Box 10227, 133 Montgomery St, Savannah, GA 31412; 912-652-7197; Fax: 912-652-7380. Hours: 8AM-5PM (EST). *Felony, Misdemeanor, Civil.*

Civil Records: Access: Mail, in person. Both court and visitors may perform in person searches. No search fee. Required to search: name, years to search. Civil cases indexed by defendant, plaintiff. Civil records on computer from 1984, archived back to 1900, dockets back to 1900s. **Criminal Records:** Access: Mail, in person. Both court and visitors may perform in person searches. No search fee. Required to search: name, years to search, signed release; also helpful-DOB, SSN. Criminal

records on computer from 1984, archived back to 1900, dockets back to 1900s. **General Information:** No juvenile, adoption or 1st offender records released. SASE requested. Turnaround time 1 week. Copy fee: $.25 per page. Certification fee: $2.00 plus $.50 per page. Fee payee: Court Clerk. Personal checks accepted. Prepayment is required. Public access terminal is available.

State Court County Courthouse 133 Montgomery St, Savannah, GA 31401; 912-652-7224; Fax: 912-652-7229. Hours: 8AM-5PM (EST). *Misdemeanor, Civil.*

www.chathamcourts.org

Civil Records: Access: Mail, in person. Both court and visitors may perform in person searches. No search fee. Required to search: name, years to search, address. Civil cases indexed by defendant, plaintiff. Civil records on computer from 1983, prior on books. **Criminal Records:** Access: Mail, in person. Both court and visitors may perform in person searches. No search fee. Required to search: name, years to search. Criminal records on computer from 1983, prior on books. **General Information:** No first time criminal offender or sealed civil records released. SASE required. Turnaround time 2 days. Copy fee: $1.00 per page. Certification fee: $2.50 plus $.50 per page. Fee payee: Clerk of State Court. Only cashiers checks and money orders accepted. Prepayment is required. Public access terminal is available.

Magistrate Court 133 Montgomery St Room 300, Savannah, GA 31401; 912-652-7187; Fax: 912-652-7550. Hours: 8AM-5PM (EST). *Civil Actions Under $15,000, Eviction, Small Claims.*

www.chathamcourts.org

Probate Court 133 Montgomery St, Rm 509, PO Box 509, Savannah, GA 31401; 912-652-7264; Fax: 912-652-7262. Hours: 8AM-5PM (EST). *Probate.*

www.chathamcourts.org

Chattahoochee County

Superior & Magistrate Court PO Box 120, Cusseta, GA 31805; 706-989-3424; Fax: 706-989-0396. Hours: 8AM-5PM (EST). *Felony, Misdemeanor, Civil, Eviction, Small Claims.*

Note: Magistrate Court is 706-989-3643

Civil Records: Access: In person only. Court does not conduct in person searches; visitors must perform searches for themselves. Search fee: No civil searches performed by court. Required to search: name, years to search. Civil cases indexed by defendant, plaintiff. Civil records on dockets from 1854. **Criminal Records:** Access: In person only. Court does not conduct in person searches; visitors must perform searches for themselves. Search fee: No criminal searches performed by court. Required to search: name, years to search, DOB; also helpful-SSN, race, sex. Criminal records on dockets from 1854. **General Information:** No juvenile, adoption, sexual, mental health or expunged records released. Copy fee: $.25 per page. Certification fee: $2.50 plus $.50 per page after first. Fee payee: Court Clerk. Business checks accepted. Prepayment is required. Public access terminal is available.

Probate Court PO Box 119, Cusseta, GA 31805; 706-989-3603; Fax: 706-989-2005. Hours: 8AM-Noon, 1-5PM (EST). *Probate.*

Chattooga County

Superior & State Court PO Box 159, Summerville, GA 30747; 706-857-0706. Hours: 8:30AM-5PM (EST). *Felony, Misdemeanor, Civil, Eviction, Small Claims.*

Civil Records: Access: In person only. Court does not conduct in person searches; visitors must perform searches for themselves. Search fee: No civil searches performed by court. Required to search: name, years to search. Civil cases indexed by defendant, plaintiff. Civil records on dockets from 1960. **Criminal Records:** Access: In person only. Court does not conduct in person searches; visitors must perform searches for themselves. Search fee: No criminal searches performed by court. Required to search: name, years to search, DOB; also helpful-SSN, race, sex. Criminal records on dockets from 1960. **General Information:** No juvenile, adoption, sexual, mental health or expunged records released. Copy fee: $.25 per page. Certification fee: $2.50 plus $.50 per page after first. Fee payee: Clerk of Court. Personal checks accepted. Prepayment is required.

Magistrate Court 10017 Commerce St, Summerville, GA 30747; 706-857-0711; Fax: 706-857-0675. Hours: 8AM-5PM (EST). *Civil Actions Under $15,000, Eviction, Small Claims.*

Probate Court PO Box 467, Summerville, GA 30747; 706-857-0709; Fax: 706-857-0709. Hours: 8:30AM-Noon, 1-5PM (EST). *Probate.*

Cherokee County

Superior & State Court 990 North St, Ste G170, Canton, GA 30114; 770-479-0538. Hours: 8:30AM-5PM (EST). *Felony, Misdemeanor, Civil.*

http://209.86.240.205/blueridgehp.shtml

Note: This court location also handles juvenile records

Civil Records: Access: In person only. Both court and visitors may perform in person searches. Search fee: No civil searches performed by court. Required to search: name. Civil cases indexed by defendant, plaintiff. Civil records on computer from 1976, archived 1900-1976, on dockets back to 1900. **Criminal Records:** Access: In person only. Both court and visitors may perform in person searches. Search fee: No criminal searches performed by court. Required to search: name, years to search, DOB; also helpful-SSN, race, sex. Criminal records on computer from 1976, archived 1900-1976, on dockets back to 1900. **General Information:** No juvenile, adoption, sexual, mental health, expunged or confidential records released. Copy fee: $.25 per page. Certification fee: $2.00 plus $.50 per add'l page. Fee payee: Clerk of Court. Only cashiers checks and money orders accepted. Prepayment is required. Public access terminal is available.

Magistrate Court 90 North St #150, Canton, GA 30114; 770-479-8516. Hours: 8:30AM-5PM (EST). *Civil Actions Under $15,000, Eviction, Small Claims.*

Probate Court 90 North St, Rm 340, Canton, GA 30114; 770-479-0541; Fax: 770-479-0567. *Probate.*

Clarke County

Superior & State Court PO Box 1805, Athens, GA 30603; 706-613-3190. Hours: 8AM-5PM (EST). *Felony, Misdemeanor, Civil.*

Civil Records: Access: In person only. Court does not conduct in person searches; visitors must perform searches for themselves. Search fee: No civil searches performed by court. Required to search: name, years to search. Civil cases indexed by defendant, plaintiff. Civil records on computer from 1993, docket books from 1801. **Criminal Records:** Access: In person only. Court does not conduct in person searches; visitors must perform searches for themselves. Search fee: No criminal searches performed by court. Required to search: name, years to search, DOB; also helpful-SSN, race, sex. Criminal records on computer from 1993, docket books from 1801. **General Information:** No juvenile, adoptions, sealed, sexual, mental health or expunged records released. Copy fee: In-house copies are $.25 each; by mail is $1.00 per page. Certification fee: $2.50 plus $.50 per page after first. Fee payee: County Clerk. Personal checks accepted. Prepayment is required. Public access terminal is available.

Magistrate Court PO Box 1868, 325 E Washington St, Athens, GA 30601; 706-613-3310; Fax: 706-613-3314. Hours: 8AM-5PM (EST). *Civil Actions Under $15,000, Eviction, Small Claims.*

Probate Court 325 E Washington St, Rm 215, Athens, GA 30601; 706-613-3320; Fax: 706-613-3323. Hours: 8AM-5PM (EST). *Probate.*

Clay County

Superior Court PO Box 550, Ft Gaines, GA 31751; 229-768-2631; Fax: 229-768-3047. Hours: 8AM-4:30PM (EST). *Felony, Misdemeanor, Civil, Eviction.*

Civil Records: Access: In person only. Court does not conduct in person searches; visitors must perform searches for themselves. Search fee: No civil searches performed by court. Required to search: name, years to search. Civil cases indexed by defendant, plaintiff. Civil records on computer from 1990, on dockets from 1854. **Criminal Records:** Access: In person only. Court does not conduct in person searches; visitors must perform searches for themselves. Search fee: No criminal searches performed by court. Required to search: name, years to search. Criminal records on computer from 1990, on dockets from 1854. **General Information:** No juvenile, adoption, sexual, mental health or expunged records released. Copy fee: $1.00 per page. Certification fee: $3.00. Fee payee: Superior Court Clerk. Personal checks accepted. Prepayment is required. Public access terminal is available.

Magistrate Court PO Box 73, Ft Gaines, GA 31751; 229-768-2841; Fax: 229-768-3443. Hours: 8AM-4:30PM (EST). *Civil Actions Under $15,000, Eviction, Small Claims.*

Probate Court 210 S Washington, Ft. Gaines, GA 31751; 229-768-2445; Fax: 229-768-2710. Hours: 8AM-4:30PM (EST). *Probate.*

Clayton County

Superior Court 9151 Tara Blvd, Jonesboro, GA 30236-4912; 770-477-3405. Hours: 8AM-5PM (EST). *Felony, Civil.*

www.co.clayton.ga.us/clerkofcourts/superior.htm

Civil Records: Access: In person only. Court does not conduct in person searches; visitors must perform searches for themselves. Search fee: No civil searches performed by court. Required to search: name, years to search. Civil cases indexed by defendant. Civil records on docket books for all records, on computer from 1992, on microfilm from 1990, archived from 1800-1982, dockets to 1800. **Criminal Records:** Access: In person only.

Court does not conduct in person searches; visitors must perform searches for themselves. Search fee: No criminal searches performed by court. Required to search: name, years to search, DOB; also helpful-SSN, race, sex. Criminal record keeping as civil. **General Information:** No adoption, sexual, mental health or expunged records released. Copy fee: $.25 per page. Certification fee: $2.50 plus $.50 per page after first. Fee payee: Clerk of Superior Court. Only cashiers checks and money orders accepted. Attorney checks accepted. Prepayment is required. Public access terminal is available.

State Court 121 S McDonough St, Jonesboro, GA 30236; 770-477-4522. Hours: 8AM-5PM (EST). *Misdemeanor.*

www.co.clayton.ga.us/clerkofcourts

Criminal Records: Access: In person only. Court does not conduct in person searches; visitors must perform searches for themselves. Search fee: No criminal searches performed by court. Required to search: name, years to search. Criminal records on computer from 1985. **General Information:** No juvenile, adoption, sexual, mental health or expunged records released. Copy fee: $.25 per page. Certification fee: $2.50 plus $.50 per page after first. Fee payee: Court Clerk. Business checks accepted.

Magistrate Court 121 S McDonough St, Jonesboro, GA 30236; 770-477-3444; Fax: 770-473-5750. Hours: 8AM-5PM (EST). *Civil Actions Under $15,000, Eviction, Small Claims.*

Probate Court 121 S McDonough St, Annex 3, Jonesboro, GA 30236-3694; 770-477-3299; Fax: 770-477-3306. Hours: 8AM-5PM (EST). *Probate.*

Clinch County

Superior & State Court PO Box 433, Homerville, GA 31634; 912-487-5854; Fax: 912-489-3083. Hours: 8AM-5PM (EST). *Felony, Misdemeanor, Civil.*

Civil Records: Access: Mail, in person. Both court and visitors may perform in person searches. No search fee. Required to search: name, years to search. Civil cases indexed by defendant, plaintiff. Civil records on dockets from 1900. **Criminal Records:** Access: Mail, in person. Both court and visitors may perform in person searches. No search fee. Required to search: name, years to search, DOB; also helpful-SSN, race, sex. Criminal records on dockets from 1900. **General Information:** No juvenile, adoption, sexual, mental health or expunged records released. SASE requested. Turnaround time 1-2 days. Copy fee: $.25 per page. Certification fee: $3.00. Fee payee: Court Clerk. Personal checks accepted.

Magistrate Court 100 Court Square, Homerville, GA 31634; 912-487-2514; Fax: 912-487-3658. Hours: 9AM-5PM (EST). *Civil Actions Under $15,000, Eviction, Small Claims.*

Probate Court PO Box 364, Homerville, GA 31634; 912-487-5523; Fax: 912-487-3083. Hours: 9AM-5PM (EST). *Probate.*

Cobb County

Superior Court PO Box 3370, Marietta, GA 30061; 770-528-1300; Fax: 770-528-1382. Hours: 8AM-5PM (EST). *Felony, Misdemeanor, Civil.*

www.cobbgasupctclk.com/courts

Civil Records: Access: online, in person. Court does not conduct in person searches; visitors must perform searches for themselves. Search fee: No civil searches performed by court. Required to search: name, years to search. Civil cases indexed by defendant, plaintiff. Civil records on computer from 1982, Records on dockets from 1958. One may search the online index of civil cases at www.cobbgasupctclk.com/courts/Civil.htm. Search by name, type or case number. The data is updated every Friday. **Criminal Records:** Access: Remote online, in person. Court does not conduct in person searches; visitors must perform searches for themselves. Search fee: No criminal searches performed by court. Required to search: name, years to search, signed release. Criminal records on computer from 1982, Records on dockets from 1958. One may search the online index of criminal record   at www.cobbgasupctclk.com/courts/Criminal.htm. Search by name, type or case number. The data is updated every Friday. **General Information:** No juvenile, adoption, sexual, mental health or expunged records released. Copy fee: $.25 per page. Certification fee: $2.00 plus $.50 per page. Fee payee: Clerk of Superior Court. Personal checks accepted. Prepayment is required.

State Court-Civil & Criminal Divisions

12 East Park Square, Marietta, GA 30090-9630; ; Civil phone:770-528-1219; Criminal phone:770-528-1219. Hours: 8AM-5PM (EST). *Misdemeanor, Civil, Eviction.*

www.cobbstatecourtclerk.com

Civil Records: Access: Mail, in person. Both court and visitors may perform in person searches. Search fee: No fee except $7.00 retrieval fee for older cases in off-site storage. Required to search: name, years to search. Civil cases indexed by defendant, plaintiff. Civil records on computer since 03/10/97, docket books from 1965. **Criminal Records:** Access: Mail, in person. Both court and visitors may perform in person searches. Search fee: No search fee unless pre-1981, then $7.00. Required to search: name, years to search, offense; also helpful-DOB, SSN. Criminal records on computer since 05/99, on microfiche 01/81 -04/99, off site storage for pre-1981 records. **General Information:** No juvenile, adoption, sexual, mental health, expunged or sealed records released. SASE required. Turnaround time 1 day to 2 weeks. Copy fee: $.25 per page. Certification fee: $3.00. Fee payee: State Court Clerk. Business checks accepted. Prepayment is required.

Magistrate Court 32 Waddell St, 3rd Fl, Marietta, GA 30090-9656; 770-528-8931; Fax: 770-528-8947. Hours: 8AM-5PM (EST). *Civil Actions Under $15,000, Small Claims.*

www.cobbmagistratecourt.org

Probate Court 32 Waddell St, Marietta, GA 30060; 770-528-1990; Fax: 770-528-1996. Hours: 8AM-4:30PM (EST). *Probate.*

Coffee County

Superior & State Court 101 S Peterson Ave, Douglas, GA 31533; 912-384-2865. Hours: 8:30AM-5PM (EST). *Felony, Misdemeanor, Civil.*

Civil Records: Access: In person only. Court does not conduct in person searches; visitors must perform searches for themselves. Search fee: No civil searches performed by court. Required to search: name. Civil cases indexed by defendant, plaintiff. Civil records on dockets. **Criminal Records:** Access: In person only. Court does not conduct in person searches; visitors must perform searches for themselves. Search fee: No criminal searches performed by court. Required to search:

name, years to search. Criminal records on dockets. **General Information:** No juvenile, adoption, sexual, mental health or expunged records released. Copy fee: $.25 per page. Certification fee: $3.00. Fee payee: Clerk Superior Court. Business checks accepted.

Magistrate Court 101 S Peterson Ave, Douglas, GA 31533; 912-384-1381; Fax: 912-384-0291. Hours: 8AM-5PM (EST). *Civil Actions Under $15,000, Eviction, Small Claims.*

Probate Court 109 S Peterson Ave, Douglas, GA 31533; 912-384-5213; Fax: 912-384-0291. Hours: 9AM-5PM (EST). *Probate.*

Colquitt County

Superior & State Court PO Box 2827, Moultrie, GA 31776; 229-891-7420. Hours: 8AM-5PM (EST). *Felony, Misdemeanor, Civil.*

www2.state.ga.us/courts/superior/dca/dca2sohp.htm

Civil Records: Access: In person only. Court does not conduct in person searches; visitors must perform searches for themselves. Search fee: No civil searches performed by court. Required to search: name, years to search. Civil cases indexed by defendant, plaintiff. Civil records on dockets books. **Criminal Records:** Access: In person only. Court does not conduct in person searches; visitors must perform searches for themselves. Search fee: No criminal searches performed by court. Required to search: name, years to search. Criminal records on dockets books. **General Information:** No juvenile, adoption, sexual, mental health or expunged records released. Copy fee: $.50 per page. Certification fee: $2.00. Fee payee: Court Clerk. Personal checks accepted. Prepayment is required.

Magistrate Court PO Box 70, Moultrie, GA 31776; 229-891-7450; Fax: 229-891-7494. Hours: 8AM-5PM (EST). *Civil Actions Under $15,000, Eviction, Small Claims.*

Probate Court PO Box 264, Moultrie, GA 31776-0264; 229-891-7415; Fax: 229-891-7403. Hours: 8AM-5PM (EST). *Probate.*

Columbia County

Superior Court PO Box 100, Appling, GA 30802; 706-541-1139; Fax: 706-541-4013. Hours: 8AM-5PM (EST). *Felony, Misdemeanor, Civil.*

Civil Records: Access: In person only. Court does not conduct in person searches; visitors must perform searches for themselves. Search fee: No civil searches performed by court. Required to search: name, years to search. Civil cases indexed by plaintiff. Civil records on computer from 1987, prior on docket books. **Criminal Records:** Access: In person only. Court does not conduct in person searches; visitors must perform searches for themselves. Search fee: No criminal searches performed by court. Required to search: name, years to search, DOB; also helpful-SSN, race, sex. Criminal records on computer from 1987, prior on docket books. **General Information:** No juvenile, adoption, sexual, mental health or expunged records released. Copy fee: $.25 per page. Certification fee: $2.00. Fee payee: Clerk of Superior Court. Personal checks accepted. Credit cards accepted.

Magistrate Court PO Box 777, Evans, GA 30809; 706-868-3316. Hours: 8AM-5PM (EST). *Civil Actions Under $15,000, Eviction, Small Claims.*

Probate Court PO Box 525, Appling, GA 30802; 706-541-1254; Fax: 706-541-4001. Hours: 8AM-5PM (EST). *Probate.*

Cook County

Superior Court 212 N Hutchinson Ave, Adel, GA 31620; 229-896-7717. Hours: 8:30AM-4:30PM (EST). *Felony, Misdemeanor, Civil.*

Civil Records: Access: Phone, mail, in person. Both court and visitors may perform in person searches. Search fee: Fee is $10.00 per name, per five year period. Required to search: name, years to search. Civil cases indexed by defendant. Civil records on dockets books, microfilm. **Criminal Records:** Access: Mail, in person. Both court and visitors may perform in person searches. Search fee: Fee is $10.00 per name, per 5 year period. Required to search: name, years to search, DOB, signed release; also helpful-SSN, race, sex. Criminal records on dockets books, microfilm. **General Information:** No juvenile, adoption, sexual, 1st offenders, mental health or expunged records released. SASE not required. Turnaround time same day. Copy fee: $1.00 per page. Certification fee: $2.50 plus $.50 per page after first. Fee payee: Court Clerk. Business checks accepted. Prepayment is required.

Magistrate Court 212 N Hutchinson Ave, Adel, GA 31620; 229-896-3151; Fax: 229-896-7629. Hours: 8AM-4:30PM (EST). *Civil Actions Under $15,000, Eviction, Small Claims.*

Probate Court 212 N Hutchinson Ave, Adel, GA 31620; 229-896-3941; Fax: 229-896-7629. Hours: 8:30AM-5PM (EST). *Probate.*

Coweta County

Superior & State Court 200 Court Square, Newnan, GA 30263; 770-254-2690; Fax: 770-254-3700. Hours: 8:30AM-5PM (EST). *Felony, Misdemeanor, Civil.*

Civil Records: Access: Phone, mail, in person. Both court and visitors may perform in person searches. No search fee. Required to search: name, years to search. Civil cases indexed by defendant, plaintiff. Civil records on computer from 1990, dockets books to 1970. **Criminal Records:** Access: Phone, mail, in person. Both court and visitors may perform in person searches. No search fee. Required to search: name, years to search, DOB; also helpful-SSN, race, sex. Criminal records on docket books back to 1919. Can only conduct felony searches from 1990 to present. **General Information:** No juvenile, adoption, sexual, mental health or expunged records released. Turnaround time 2 days. Copy fee: $.25 per page. Certification fee: $2.50 plus $.50 per page after first. Fee payee: Clerk of Superior & State Court. Business checks accepted. Prepayment is required. Public access terminal is available.

Magistrate Court 34 E Broad St, Newnan, GA 30263; 770-254-2610; Fax: 770-254-2606. Hours: 8AM-5PM (EST). *Civil Actions Under $15,000, Eviction, Small Claims.*

Probate Court 22 E Broad St, Newnan, GA 30263; 770-254-2640; Fax: 770-254-2648. Hours: 8AM-5PM (EST). *Probate.*

Crawford County

Superior Court PO Box 1037, Roberta, GA 31058; 478-836-3328. Hours: 9AM-5PM (EST). *Felony, Misdemeanor, Civil.*

Note: Magistrate Court is at PO Box 568, call at 912-836-5804

Civil Records: Access: In person only. Court does not conduct in person searches; visitors must perform searches for themselves. No search fee. Required to search: name, years to search. Civil cases indexed by defendant, plaintiff. Civil records on dockets books, recent records computerized. **Criminal Records:** Access: In person only. Court does not conduct in person searches; visitors must perform searches for themselves. No search fee. Required to search: name, years to search, DOB; also helpful-SSN, race, sex. Criminal records on dockets books, recent records computerized. **General Information:** No juvenile, adoption, sexual, mental health or expunged records released. Copy fee: $.25 per page. Certification fee: $2.50 plus $.50 per page after first. Fee payee: Clerk of Superior Court. Personal checks accepted. Prepayment is required. Public access terminal is available. Public Access Terminal Note: However records are for deeds from 01/99 to present.

Magistrate Court PO Box 568, Roberta, GA 31078; 478-836-5804; Fax: 478-836-4340. Hours: 8AM-5PM (EST). *Civil Actions Under $15,000, Eviction, Small Claims.*

Probate Court PO Box 1028, Roberta, GA 31078; 478-836-3313. Hours: 8:30AM-4:30PM (EST). *Probate.*

Note: The record search fee is $4.00.

Crisp County

Superior & Juvenile Court PO Box 747, Cordele, GA 31010-0747; 229-276-2616. Hours: 8:30AM-5PM (EST). *Felony, Misdemeanor, Civil Actions Over $15,000.*

Civil Records: Access: Mail, in person. Court does not conduct in person searches; visitors must perform searches for themselves. No search fee. Required to search: name, years to search. Civil cases indexed by defendant. Civil records on docket books. **Criminal Records:** Access: Mail, in person. Court does not conduct in person searches; visitors must perform searches for themselves. No search fee. Required to search: name, years to search; also helpful-SSN. Criminal records on docket books. **General Information:** No juvenile, adoption, sexual, mental health or expunged records released. SASE required. Turnaround time 1-2 days. Copy fee: $.25 per page. Certification fee: $2.00 plus $.50 per page. Fee payee: Clerk of Superior Court. Personal checks accepted. Prepayment is required.

Magistrate Court 210 S 7th St Room 102, Cordele, GA 31015; 229-276-2618. Hours: 8:30AM-5PM (EST). *Civil Actions Under $15,000, Eviction, Small Claims.*

Probate Court PO Box 26, Cordele, GA 31010-0026; 229-276-2621; Fax: 229-273-9184. Hours: 9AM-5PM (EST). *Probate.*

Dade County

Superior Court PO Box 417, Trenton, GA 30752; 706-657-4778. Hours: 8:30AM-5PM (EST). *Felony, Misdemeanor, Civil, Eviction, Small Claims.*

Civil Records: Access: Phone, mail, in person. Both court and visitors may perform in person searches. No search fee. Required to search: name, years to search. Civil cases indexed by defendant, plaintiff. Civil records on docket books. **Criminal Records:** Access: Mail, in person. Both court and visitors may perform in person searches. Search fee: $5.00 per name. Required to search: name, years to search, DOB; also helpful-SSN, race, sex. Criminal records on docket books. **General**

Information: No juvenile, adoption, sexual, mental health or expunged records released. SASE requested. Turnaround time 1 day. Copy fee: $1.32 per page. Certification fee: $2.50 plus $.50 per page after first. Fee payee: Superior Court. Personal checks accepted. Prepayment is required.

Magistrate Court PO Box 518, Trenton, GA 31083; 706-657-4113; Fax: 706-657-9618. Hours: 8AM-5PM (EST). *Civil Actions Under $15,000, Eviction, Small Claims.*

Probate Court PO Box 605, Trenton, GA 30752; 706-657-4414; Fax: 706-657-5116. Hours: 8:30AM-5PM (EST). *Probate.*

Dawson County

Superior Court 25 Tucker Ave, #106, Dawsonville, GA 30534; 706-344-3510 X227; Fax: 706-344-3511. Hours: 8AM-5PM (EST). *Felony, Misdemeanor, Civil.*

http://209.86.240.205/dca9nehp.shtml

Civil Records: Access: In person only. Court does not conduct in person searches; visitors must perform searches for themselves. Search fee: No civil searches performed by court. Required to search: name, years to search. Civil cases indexed by plaintiff. Civil records on computer from 1994, on dockets books. **Criminal Records:** Access: In person only. Court does not conduct in person searches; visitors must perform searches for themselves. Search fee: No criminal searches performed by court. Required to search: name, years to search, DOB; also helpful-SSN, race, sex. Criminal records on computer from 1994, on dockets books. **General Information:** No juvenile, adoption, sexual, mental health or expunged records released. Copy fee: $.25 per page. Certification fee: $2.50. Fee payee: Superior Court. Prepayment is required.

Magistrate Court PO Box 254, Dawsonville, GA 30534; 706-334-3730-8000; Fax: 706-344-3537. Hours: 10AM-8PM M,T; 10AM-2PM W; 8:30AM-5PM F (EST). *Civil Actions Under $15,000, Eviction, Small Claims.*

Probate Court 25 Tucker Ave #211, Dawsonville, GA 30534; 706-344-3580; Fax: 706-265-6155. Hours: 8AM-5PM (EST). *Probate.*

De Kalb County

Superior Court 556 N McDonough St, Decatur, GA 30030; 404-371-2836; Fax: 404-371-2635. Hours: 8:30AM-5PM (EST). *Felony, Misdemeanor, Civil.*

Civil Records: Access: In person only. Court does not conduct in person searches; visitors must perform searches for themselves. Search fee: No civil searches performed by court. Required to search: name, years to search. Civil cases indexed by defendant, plaintiff. Civil records on computer from 1988, prior archived. **Criminal Records:** Access: In person only. Court does not conduct in person searches; visitors must perform searches for themselves. Search fee: No criminal searches performed by court. Required to search: name, years to search, DOB; also helpful-SSN, race, sex. Criminal records on computer from 1980, on microfilm from 1947. **General Information:** No juvenile, adoption, sexual, mental health or expunged records released. Copy fee: Copies made by the court are $1.00 per page, do it yourself is $.25 per page. Certification fee: $2.50 plus $.50 per page after first. Fee payee: Clerk of Superior Court. Personal checks accepted. Prepayment is required. Public access terminal is available.

State Court 556 N McDonough St, Decatur, GA 30030; 404-371-2261; Fax: 404-371-3064. Hours: 8:30AM-5PM (EST). *Misdemeanor, Civil.*

www.co.dekalb.ga.us/statect

Civil Records: Access: Mail, in person. Both court and visitors may perform in person searches. Search fee: No civil searches performed by court. Required to search: name, years to search. Civil cases indexed by defendant, plaintiff. Civil records on docket books. The court will perform limited searches. **Criminal Records:** Access: In person only. Court does not conduct in person searches; visitors must perform searches for themselves. Search fee: No criminal searches performed by court. Required to search: name. Criminal records on docket books. **General Information:** Turnaround time 7 days. Copy fee: $.25 per page. Certification fee: $5.00. Fee payee: Court Clerk. Personal checks accepted. Prepayment is required. Public access terminal is available.

Magistrate Court 807 DeKalb County Courthouse, Decatur, GA 30030; 404-371-4766; Fax: 404-371-2986. Hours: 8:30AM-5PM (EST). *Civil Actions Under $15,000, Eviction, Small Claims.*

Probate Court 103 County Courthouse, 556 N McDonough St, Rm 103, Decatur, GA 30030; 404-371-2718; Fax: 404-371-7055. Hours: 8:30AM-4PM (EST). *Probate.*

http://co.dekalb.ga.us/probate

Decatur County

Superior & State Court PO Box 336, Bainbridge, GA 31718; 229-248-3025. Hours: 9AM-5PM (EST). *Felony, Misdemeanor, Civil.*

Civil Records: Access: In person only. Court does not conduct in person searches; visitors must perform searches for themselves. Search fee: No civil searches performed by court. Required to search: name, years to search. Civil cases indexed by defendant, plaintiff. Civil records on docket books. **Criminal Records:** Access: In person only. Court does not conduct in person searches; visitors must perform searches for themselves. Search fee: No criminal searches performed by court. Required to search: name, years to search, DOB; also helpful-SSN, race, sex. Criminal records on docket books. **General Information:** No juvenile, adoption, sexual, mental health or expunged records released. Copy fee: $.25 per page. Certification fee: $2.00 plus $.50 per page. Fee payee: Court Clerk. No personal checks accepted.

Magistrate Court 912 Spring Creek Rd Box #3, Bainbridge, GA 31717; 229-248-3014; Fax: 229-248-3862. Hours: 9AM-5PM (EST). *Civil Actions Under $15,000, Eviction, Small Claims.*

Probate Court PO Box 234, Bainbridge, GA 31718; 229-248-3016; Fax: 229-248-3858. Hours: 9AM-5PM (EST). *Probate.*

Dodge County

Superior Court PO Drawer 4276, 407 Anson Ave, Eastman, GA 31023; 478-374-2871. Hours: 9AM-5PM (EST). *Felony, Misdemeanor, Civil.*

Civil Records: Access: In person only. Court does not conduct in person searches; visitors must perform searches for themselves. Search fee: No civil searches performed by court. Required to search: name, years to search. Civil cases indexed by defendant. Civil records on docket books. **Criminal Records:** Access: In person only. Court does not conduct in person searches; visitors must perform searches for themselves. Search fee: No criminal searches performed by court. Required to search: name, years to search, DOB, signed release; also helpful-SSN, race, sex. Criminal records on docket books. **General Information:** No juvenile, adoption, sexual, mental health or expunged records released. Copy fee: $.25 per page. Certification fee: $2.00 plus $.50 per page after first. Fee payee: Court Clerk. Personal checks accepted. Prepayment is required.

Magistrate Court 5018 Courthouse Circle #202, Eastman, GA 31023; 478-374-5145; Fax: 478-374-5716. Hours: 8:30AM-4:30PM (EST). *Civil Actions Under $15,000, Eviction, Small Claims.*

Probate Court PO Box 514, Eastman, GA 31023; 478-374-3775; Fax: 478-374-9197. Hours: 9AM-Noon, 1-5PM (EST). *Probate.*

Dooly County

Superior Court PO Box 326, Vienna, GA 31092-0326; 229-268-4234; Fax: 229-268-1427, Hours: 8:30AM-5PM (EST). *Felony, Misdemeanor, Civil.*

Civil Records: Access: Fax, mail, in person. Both court and visitors may perform in person searches. No search fee. Required to search: name, years to search. Civil cases indexed by defendant, plaintiff. Civil records on computer since 1995. Prefer to have public do searches. **Criminal Records:** Access: Fax, mail, in person. Both court and visitors may perform in person searches. No search fee. Required to search: name, years to search, DOB, signed release; also helpful-SSN, race, sex. Criminal records on computer since 1994, docket books. Prefer to have public to perform searches. **General Information:** No juvenile, adoption, sexual, mental health or expunged records released. SASE required. Turnaround time varies. Copy fee: $.25 per page. Certification fee: $2.50. Fee payee: Dooly County Superior Court Clerk. Personal checks accepted. Prepayment is required. Public access terminal is available.

Magistrate Court PO Box 336, Vienna, GA 31092; 229-268-4324. Hours: 8AM-Noon, 1-5PM M,W,F (EST). *Civil Actions Under $15,000, Eviction, Small Claims.*

Probate Court PO Box 304, Vienna, GA 31092; 229-268-4217; Fax: 229-268-6142. Hours: 8AM-5PM M,T,Th,F; 8:30AM-Noon W & Sat or by appointment (EST). *Probate.*

Dougherty County

Superior & State Court PO Box 1827, Albany, GA 31703; 229-431-2198. Hours: 8:30AM-5PM (EST). *Felony, Misdemeanor, Civil.*

www.dougherty.ga.us/dococlk.htm

Civil Records: Access: online, in person. Court does not conduct in person searches; visitors must perform searches for themselves. Search fee: No civil searches performed by court. Required to search: name, years to search. Civil cases indexed by defendant, plaintiff. Civil records on computer from 1992. The Internet site provides free access to civil and criminal court docket data. The same system permits access to probate, ucc, tax, deeds, and death certificates. **Criminal Records:** Access: Remote online, in person. Court does not conduct in person searches; visitors must perform searches for themselves. Search fee: No criminal searches performed by court. Required to search: name, years to search; also helpful-SSN. Criminal records on computer from 1992. see civil. **General Information:** No juvenile, adoption, sexual,

mental health or expunged records released. Copy fee: If court makes copy then $1.00, if yourself then $.25. Certification fee: $3.00 first page then $1.00 each additional. Fee payee: Court Clerk. Personal checks accepted. Prepayment is required. Public access terminal is available.

Magistrate Court PO Box 1827, Albany, GA 31702; 229-431-3216; Fax: 229-434-2692. Hours: 8:30AM-5PM (EST). *Civil Actions Under $15,000, Eviction, Small Claims.*

Probate Court PO Box 1827, Albany, GA 31702; 229-431-2102; Fax: 229-434-2694. Hours: 8:30AM-5PM (EST). *Probate.*

www.dougherty.ga.us/dwinet/dwmain.htm

Douglas County

Superior Court Douglas County Courthouse, 8700 Hospital Dr, Douglasville, GA 30134; 770-920-7252. Hours: 8AM-5PM (EST). *Felony, Misdemeanor, Civil.*

Civil Records: Access: In person only. Court does not conduct in person searches; visitors must perform searches for themselves. Search fee: No civil searches performed by court. Required to search: name, years to search. Civil cases indexed by defendant, plaintiff. Civil records on computer from 1994, prior on docket books. **Criminal Records:** Access: In person only. Court does not conduct in person searches; visitors must perform searches for themselves. Search fee: No criminal searches performed by court. Required to search: name, years to search, DOB, signed release; also helpful-address, SSN. Criminal records on computer from 1994, prior on docket books. **General Information:** No juvenile, adoption, sexual, mental health or expunged records released. Copy fee: $.25 per page. Certification fee: $2.50 plus $.50 per page. Fee payee: Clerk of Superior Court. Personal checks accepted. Prepayment is required. Public access terminal is available.

Magistrate Court PO Box 99, Douglasville, GA 30133; 770-949-1115. Hours: 8AM-5PM (EST). *Civil Actions Under $15,000, Eviction, Small Claims.*

Probate Court 8700 Hospital Dr, Douglasville, GA 30134; 770-920-7249; Fax: 770-920-7381. Hours: 8AM-5PM (EST). *Probate.*

Early County

Superior & State Court PO Box 849, Blakely, GA 31723; 229-723-3033; Fax: 229-723-5246. Hours: 8AM-5PM (EST). *Felony, Misdemeanor, Civil.*

Civil Records: Access: In person only. Court does not conduct in person searches; visitors must perform searches for themselves. Search fee: No civil searches performed by court. Required to search: name, years to search. Civil cases indexed by defendant, plaintiff. Civil records on dockets. **Criminal Records:** Access: In person only. Court does not conduct in person searches; visitors must perform searches for themselves. Search fee: No criminal searches performed by court. Required to search: name, years to search, DOB; also helpful-SSN, race, sex. Criminal records on dockets. **General Information:** No juvenile, adoption, sexual, mental health or expunged records released. Copy fee: $.50 per page. Certification fee: $2.50 plus $.50 per page after first. Fee payee: Court Clerk. Personal checks accepted. Prepayment is required.

Magistrate Court Early County Courthouse, Rm 8, Blakely, GA 31723; 229-723-3454; Fax:

229-723-5246. Hours: 8AM-5PM (EST). *Civil Actions Under $15,000, Eviction, Small Claims.*

Echols County

Superior Court PO Box 213, Statenville, GA 31648; 229-559-5642; Fax: 229-559-5792. Hours: 8AM-Noon, 1-4:30PM (EST). *Felony, Misdemeanor, Civil.*

www2.state.ga.us/courts/superior/dca/dca2sohp.htm

Civil Records: Access: In person only. Court does not conduct in person searches; visitors must perform searches for themselves. Search fee: No civil searches performed by court. Required to search: name, years to search. Civil cases indexed by defendant, plaintiff. Civil records on dockets books. **Criminal Records:** Access: In person only. Court does not conduct in person searches; visitors must perform searches for themselves. Search fee: No criminal searches performed by court. Required to search: name, years to search. Criminal records on dockets books. **General Information:** No juvenile, adoption, sexual, mental health or expunged records released. Copy fee: $1.00 per page. Certification fee: Certification $2.00 1st page, $.50 each additional page. Fee payee: Court Clerk. Personal checks accepted. Prepayment is required.

Magistrate & Probate Court PO Box 397, Statenville, GA 31648; 229-559-7526; Fax: 229-559-5792. Hours: 8:30AM-4:30PM (EST). *Civil Actions Under $15,000, Eviction, Small Claims, Probate.*

Effingham County

Superior & State Court PO Box 387, Springfield, GA 31329; 912-754-2118. Hours: 8:30AM-5PM (EST). *Felony, Misdemeanor, Civil.*

Civil Records: Access: Mail, in person. Both court and visitors may perform in person searches. Search fee: $15.00 per name. Required to search: name, years to search. Civil cases indexed by defendant, plaintiff. Civil records on computer from 1991, dockets books. **Criminal Records:** Access: Mail, in person. Both court and visitors may perform in person searches. Search fee: $15.00 per name. Required to search: name, years to search, DOB; also helpful-SSN, race, sex. Criminal records on computer from 1991, dockets books. **General Information:** No juvenile, adoption, sexual, mental health or expunged records released. SASE required. Turnaround time 3-5 days. Copy fee: $.25 per page. Certification fee: $2.50 plus $.50 per page after first. Fee payee: Court Clerk. Business checks accepted. Prepayment is required.

Magistrate Court PO Box 819, Springfield, GA 31329; 912-754-2124; Fax: 912-754-4893. Hours: 8:15AM-4:15PM (EST). *Civil Actions Under $15,000, Eviction, Small Claims.*

Probate Court 901 Pine St, PO Box 387, Springfield, GA 31329; 912-754-2112; Fax: 912-754-3894. Hours: 8:30AM-5PM (EST). *Probate.*

Elbert County

Superior & State Court PO Box 619, Elberton, GA 30635; 706-283-2005; Fax: 706-213-7286. Hours: 8AM-5PM (EST). *Felony, Misdemeanor, Civil.*

Civil Records: Access: In person only. Court does not conduct in person searches; visitors must perform searches for themselves. Search fee: No civil searches performed by court. Required to search: name, years to search. Civil cases indexed by defendant, plaintiff. Civil records on computer from 1986 (excluding felonies), dockets books prior. **Criminal Records:** Access: In person only. Court does not conduct in person searches; visitors must perform searches for themselves. Search fee: No criminal searches performed by court. Required to search: name, years to search. Criminal records on computer from 1986 (excluding felonies), dockets books prior. **General Information:** No juvenile, adoption, sexual, mental health or expunged records released. Copy fee: $.25 per page. Certification fee: $2.00 plus $.50 per page. Fee payee: Clerk of Court. Personal checks accepted. Prepayment is required. Public access terminal is available.

Magistrate Court PO Box 763, Elberton, GA 30635; 706-283-2027; Fax: 706-283-2004. Hours: 8AM-5PM (EST). *Civil Actions Under $15,000, Eviction, Small Claims.*

Probate Court Elbert County Courthouse, Elberton, GA 30635; 706-283-2016; Fax: 706-283-8144. Hours: 8AM-5PM (EST). *Probate.*

Emanuel County

Superior & State Court PO Box 627, Swainsboro, GA 30401; 478-237-8911; Fax: 478-237-2173. Hours: 8AM-5PM (EST). *Felony, Misdemeanor, Civil.*

Civil Records: Access: In person only. Court does not conduct in person searches; visitors must perform searches for themselves. Search fee: No civil searches performed by court. Required to search: name, years to search. Civil cases indexed by defendant, plaintiff. Civil records computerized since 1999, earlier on dockets books. **Criminal Records:** Access: In person only. Court does not conduct in person searches; visitors must perform searches for themselves. Search fee: No criminal searches performed by court. Required to search: name, years to search, DOB; also helpful-SSN, race, sex. Criminal records computerized since 1999, earlier on dockets books. **General Information:** No juvenile, adoption, sexual, mental health or expunged records released. Copy fee: $.25 per page. Certification fee: $2.50 plus $.50 per page. Fee payee: Court Clerk. Personal checks accepted. Prepayment is required.

Magistrate Court 107 N Main St, Swainsboro, GA 30401; 478-237-7278; Fax: 478-237-2593. Hours: 8AM-5PM (EST). *Civil Actions Under $15,000, Eviction, Small Claims.*

Probate Court PO Drawer 70, Swainsboro, GA 30401; 478-237-7091; Fax: 478-237-2633. Hours: 8AM-5PM (EST). *Probate.*

Evans County

Superior & State Court PO Box 845, Claxton, GA 30417; 912-739-3868; Fax: 912-739-2504. Hours: 8AM-5PM (EST). *Felony, Misdemeanor, Civil.*

Civil Records: Access: In person only. Court does not conduct in person searches; visitors must perform searches for themselves. Search fee: No civil searches performed by court. Required to search: name, years to search. Civil cases indexed by defendant, plaintiff. Civil records on computer from 1989, dockets books. **Criminal Records:** Access: In person only. Court does not conduct in person searches; visitors must perform searches for themselves. Search fee: No criminal searches performed by court. Required to search: name, years to search, DOB; also helpful-SSN, race, sex. Criminal records on computer from 1989, dockets books. **General Information:** No juvenile, adoption, sexual, mental health or expunged

records released. Copy fee: $1.00 per page. Certification fee: $2.50 plus $.50 per page after first. Fee payee: Court Clerk. Personal checks accepted. Prepayment is required. Public access terminal is available.

Magistrate Court Courthouse Annex, Rm 7, Freeman St, Claxton, GA 30417; 912-739-3948; Fax: 912-739-8865. Hours: 8AM-5PM (EST). *Civil Actions Under $15,000, Eviction, Small Claims.*

Probate Court 123 W Main St, PO Box 852, Claxton, GA 30417; 912-739-4080; Fax: 912-739-4077. Hours: 8AM-5PM (EST). *Probate.*

Fannin County

Superior Court PO Box 1300, 420 W Main St, Blue Ridge, GA 30513; 706-632-2039. Hours: 9AM-5PM (EST). *Felony, Misdemeanor, Civil.*

http://209.86.240.205/dca9apphp.shtml

Civil Records: Access: In person only. Court does not conduct in person searches; visitors must perform searches for themselves. Search fee: No civil searches performed by court. Required to search: name, years to search. Civil cases indexed by defendant, plaintiff. Civil records on docket books. **Criminal Records:** Access: In person only. Court does not conduct in person searches; visitors must perform searches for themselves. Search fee: No criminal searches performed by court. Required to search: name, years to search, DOB, signed release; also helpful-SSN, race, sex. Criminal records on docket books. **General Information:** No juvenile, adoption, sexual, mental health or expunged records released. Copy fee: $.25 per page. $1.00 per page if the court make copies. Certification fee: $2.50 plus $.50 per page after first. Fee payee: Court Clerk. Personal checks accepted. Prepayment is required.

Magistrate Court 420 W Main St, #7, Blue Ridge, GA 30513; 706-632-5558; Fax: 706-632-8236. Hours: 9AM-5PM (EST). *Civil Actions Under $15,000, Eviction, Small Claims.*

Probate Court 420 W Main St #2, Blue Ridge, GA 30513; 706-632-3011; Fax: 706-632-7167. Hours: 8AM-5PM (EST). *Probate.*

Fayette County

Superior Court PO Box 130, Fayetteville, GA 30214; 770-461-4703. Hours: 8AM-5PM (EST). *Felony, Misdemeanor, Civil.*

Civil Records: Access: In person only. Court does not conduct in person searches; visitors must perform searches for themselves. Search fee: No civil searches performed by court. Required to search: name, years to search. Civil cases indexed by defendant, plaintiff. Civil records on computer since 1989; prior records on dockets books. **Criminal Records:** Access: In person only. Court does not conduct in person searches; visitors must perform searches for themselves. Search fee: No criminal searches performed by court. Required to search: name, years to search, DOB; also helpful-SSN, race, sex. Criminal records on computer since 1989; prior records on dockets books. **General Information:** No juvenile, adoption, sexual, mental health or expunged records released. Copy fee: $.25 per page. Certification fee: $2.00 plus $.50 per page after first. Fee payee: Court Clerk. Only cashiers checks and money orders accepted.

Magistrate Court PO Box 1076, Fayetteville, GA 30214; 770-461-4703. Hours: 8AM-5PM (EST). *Civil Actions Under $15,000, Eviction, Small Claims.*

Probate Court 145 Johnson Ave, Fayetteville, GA 30214; 770-461-9555; Fax: 770-460-8685. Hours: 8AM-5PM (EST). *Probate.*

Floyd County

Superior Court PO Box 1110, #3 Government Plaza #101, Rome, GA 30163; 706-291-5190; Fax: 706-233-0035. Hours: 8AM-5PM (EST). *Felony, Misdemeanor, Civil.*

www.floydsuperiorcourt.org

Civil Records: Access: Fax, mail, in person. Both court and visitors may perform in person searches. No search fee. Required to search: name, years to search. Civil cases indexed by defendant, plaintiff. Civil records on computer since 11/95; prior records on docket books. The court will not do name searches. **Criminal Records:** Access: Fax, mail, in person. Both court and visitors may perform in person searches. No search fee. Required to search: name, years to search, signed release. Criminal records on computer since 02/96. The court will not do name searches. **General Information:** No juvenile, adoption, sexual, mental health or expunged records released. Copy fee: $.50 per page. Certification fee: $2.00 plus $.50 per page after first. Fee payee: Court Clerk. Personal checks accepted. Prepayment is required. Public access terminal is available. Fax notes: $1.00 per page.

Magistrate Court 3 Government Plaza, Rm 227, 410 Tribute St, Rm 227, Rome, GA 30161; 706-291-5250; Fax: 706-291-5269. Hours: 9AM-5PM (EST). *Civil Actions Under $15,000, Eviction, Small Claims.*

Probate Court 3 Government Plaza #201, County Administrative Offices, Rome, GA 30162; 706-291-5138; Fax: 706-291-5189. Hours: 8AM-4:30PM (EST). *Probate.*

Forsyth County

Superior & State Court 100 Courthouse Square, Rm 010, Cumming, GA 30040; 770-781-2120. Hours: 8:30AM-5PM (EST). *Felony, Misdemeanor, Civil, Eviction, Small Claims.*

http://209.86.240.205/bellforsythhp.shtml

Civil Records: Access: In person only. Court does not conduct in person searches; visitors must perform searches for themselves. Search fee: No civil searches performed by court. Required to search: name, years to search. Civil cases indexed by defendant. Civil records on computer since 03/97; prior records on docket books. **Criminal Records:** Access: In person only. Court does not conduct in person searches; visitors must perform searches for themselves. Search fee: No criminal searches performed by court. Required to search: name, years to search; also helpful-SSN. Criminal records on computer since late 1989. **General Information:** No juvenile, adoption, sexual, mental health or expunged records released. Copy fee: $.25 per page. Certification fee: $2.50 plus $.50 per page after first. Fee payee: Court Clerk. Personal checks accepted. Prepayment is required.

Magistrate Court 121 Dahlonega St, Cumming, GA 30040; 770-781-2211; Fax: 770-844-7581. Hours: 8AM-5PM (EST). *Civil Actions Under $15,000, Eviction, Small Claims, Probate.*

Probate Court County Courthouse Annex, Rm 101, 112 W Maple St, Cumming, GA 30130; 770-781-2140; Fax: 770-886-2839. Hours: 8:30AM-5PM (EST). *Probate.*

Franklin County

Superior Court PO Box 70, Carnesville, GA 30521; 706-384-2514. Hours: 8AM-5PM (EST). *Felony, Misdemeanor, Civil.*

Civil Records: Access: In person only. Court does not conduct in person searches; visitors must perform searches for themselves. Search fee: No civil searches performed by court. Required to search: name, years to search. Civil cases indexed by defendant, plaintiff. Civil records on computer since 1995; prior records on docket books. **Criminal Records:** Access: In person only. Court does not conduct in person searches; visitors must perform searches for themselves. Search fee: No criminal searches performed by court. Required to search: name, years to search, DOB; also helpful-SSN, race, sex. Criminal records on computer since 1995; prior records on docket books. **General Information:** No juvenile, adoption, sexual, mental health or expunged records released. Copy fee: $.25 per page. Certification fee: $2.50. Fee payee: Court Clerk. Personal checks accepted. Prepayment is required. Public access terminal is available.

Magistrate Court PO Box 467, Carnesville, GA 30521; 706-384-7473; Fax: 706-384-4346. Hours: 8AM-5PM (EST). *Civil Actions Under $15,000, Eviction, Small Claims.*

Probate Court PO Box 207, Carnesville, GA 30521; 706-384-2403; Fax: 706-384-4346. Hours: 8AM-4:30PM (EST). *Probate.*

Fulton County

Superior Court 136 Pryor St SW, Rm 106, Atlanta, GA 30303; ; Civil phone:404-730-5344; Criminal phone:404-730-5344; Fax: 404-730-7993. Hours: 8:30AM-5PM (EST). *Felony, Misdemeanor, Civil, Eviction.*

Civil Records: Access: In person only. Court does not conduct in person searches; visitors must perform searches for themselves. Search fee: No civil searches performed by court. Required to search: name, years to search. Civil cases indexed by defendant, plaintiff. Civil records on computer since 1972. **Criminal Records:** Access: In person only. Court does not conduct in person searches; visitors must perform searches for themselves. Search fee: $15.00 per name. Search limited to 1972-present. Required to search: name, years to search, DOB, signed release; also helpful-SSN, race, sex. Criminal records on computer from 1973. **General Information:** No juvenile, adoption, sexual, mental health, sealed or expunged records released. Copy fee: $.25 per page. Certification fee: $2.00 plus $.50 per page. Fee payee: Court Clerk. Personal checks accepted. Prepayment is required. Public access terminal is available.

State Court TG100 Justice Center Tower, 185 Central Ave SW, Atlanta, GA 30303; 404-730-5000; Fax: 404-730-8141 Civil; 335-3521 Criminal. Hours: 8:30AM-5PM (EST). *Misdemeanor, Civil.*

http://fultonstatecourt.com

Civil Records: Access: In person only. Court does not conduct in person searches; visitors must perform searches for themselves. Search fee: No civil searches performed by court. Required to search: name, years to search. Civil cases indexed by defendant, plaintiff. Civil records on computer from 1984, dockets books back 20 years. **Criminal Records:** Access: In person only. Court does not conduct in person searches; visitors must perform searches for themselves. Search fee: No

criminal searches performed by court. Required to search: name, years to search, DOB; also helpful-SSN, race, aliases, date of offense, sex. Criminal records on computer from 1984, docket books back 30 years. Approximate arrest date helpful. **General Information:** No juvenile, adoption, sexual, mental health or expunged records released. Copy fee: $.25 per page. Certification fee: $2.50 plus $.50 each add'l pg. Fee payee: Court Clerk. Business checks accepted. Prepayment is required. Public access terminal is available.

Magistrate Court 136 Pryor St SW, #C-669, Fulton County Courthouse, Atlanta, GA 30303; 404-730-4552; Civil phone:404-730-5045; Criminal phone:404-730-5045; Fax: 404-893-2683. Hours: 8:30AM-5PM (EST). *Civil Actions Under $15,000, Eviction, Small Claims.*

Probate Court 185 Central Ave. SW, T2705 Justice Ctr Tower, Atlanta, GA 30303; 404-730-4690; Fax: 404-730-7998. Hours: 8:30AM-5PM (EST). *Probate.*

Gilmer County

Superior Court #1 Westside Square, Ellijay, GA 30540; 706-635-4462; Fax: 706-635-1462. Hours: 8:30AM-5PM (EST). *Felony, Misdemeanor, Civil.*

http://209.86.240.205/dca9apphp.shtml

Civil Records: Access: In person only. Court does not conduct in person searches; visitors must perform searches for themselves. Search fee: $1.00 per name per year. Required to search: name, years to search. Civil cases indexed by defendant, plaintiff. Civil records on docket books and computer. **Criminal Records:** Access: In person only. Court does not conduct in person searches; visitors must perform searches for themselves. Search fee: $1.00 per name per year. Required to search: name, years to search, signed release; also helpful-DOB, SSN. Criminal records on docket books and computer. **General Information:** No juvenile, adoption, sealed, sexual, mental health, expunged or sealed records released. Copy fee: $.25 per page. Certification fee: $2.50 plus $.50 per page after first. Fee payee: Superior Court Clerk. Personal checks accepted. Prepayment is required. Public access terminal is available.

Magistrate Court #1 Westside Square, Box 5, Ellijay, GA 30540; 706-635-2515; Fax: 706-635-7756. Hours: 8:30AM-5PM (EST). *Civil Actions Under $15,000, Eviction, Small Claims.*

Probate Court One Westside Square, Ellijay, GA 30540; 706-635-4763; Fax: 706-635-1461. Hours: 8:30AM-5PM (EST). *Probate.*

Glascock County

Superior Court PO Box 231, 62 E Main St, Gibson, GA 30810; 706-598-2084; Fax: 706-598-2577. Hours: 8AM-Noon, 1-5PM (EST). *Felony, Misdemeanor, Civil.*

Civil Records: Access: In person only. Court does not conduct in person searches; visitors must perform searches for themselves. Search fee: No civil searches performed by court. Required to search: name, years to search. Civil cases indexed by defendant, plaintiff. Civil records on computer from 1990, dockets books. **Criminal Records:** Access: In person only. Court does not conduct in person searches; visitors must perform searches for themselves. Search fee: No criminal searches performed by court. Required to search: name, years to search, DOB; also helpful-SSN, race, sex. Criminal records on computer from 1990, dockets

books. **General Information:** No juvenile, adoption, sexual, mental health or expunged records released. Copy fee: $.25 per page. Legal size copies $1.00 per page. Certification fee: $2.00 plus $.50 per page after first. Fee payee: Court Clerk. Personal checks accepted. Prepayment is required. Public access terminal is available.

Magistrate Court PO Box 201, Gibson, GA 30810; 706-598-2013. Hours: 4-8PM T; 9AM-1PM W & Sat (EST). *Civil Actions Under $15,000, Eviction, Small Claims.*

Probate Court PO Box 64, Gibson, GA 30810; 706-598-3241. Hours: 8AM-Noon, 1-5PM (EST). *Probate.*

Glynn County

Superior Court PO Box 1355, Brunswick, GA 31521; 912-554-7272; Fax: 912-267-5625. Hours: 8:30AM-5PM (EST). *Felony, Misdemeanor, Civil.*

Civil Records: Access: Phone, mail, in person. Both court and visitors may perform in person searches. No search fee. Required to search: name, years to search. Civil cases indexed by defendant, plaintiff. Civil records on computer from 1989, archived from 1917, dockets books. **Criminal Records:** Access: Phone, mail, in person. Both court and visitors may perform in person searches. No search fee. Required to search: name, years to search, DOB, signed release; also helpful-SSN, race, sex. Criminal records on computer from 1987. **General Information:** No juvenile, adoption, sexual, mental health or expunged records released. SASE requested. Turnaround time 1-3 days. Copy fee: $.25 per page. If court does copy, fee is $1.00 per page. Certification fee: $2.50 plus $.50 per page after first. Fee payee: Court Clerk. Personal checks accepted. Will bill copy & certification fees.

State Court PO Box 879, Brunswick, GA 31521; 912-267-5674; Fax: 912-261-3849. Hours: 9AM-5PM (EST). *Misdemeanor, Civil.*

Civil Records: Access: In person only. Court does not conduct in person searches; visitors must perform searches for themselves. Search fee: No civil searches performed by court. Required to search: name, years to search. Civil cases indexed by defendant. Civil records on dockets books. **Criminal Records:** Access: In person only. Court does not conduct in person searches; visitors must perform searches for themselves. Search fee: No criminal searches performed by court. Required to search: name, years to search. Criminal records on dockets books. **General Information:** No juvenile, adoption, sexual, mental health or expunged records released. Copy fee: $.25 per page. Certification fee: $2.00 plus $.50 per page. Fee payee: Clerk of State Court. Only cashiers checks and money orders accepted. Prepayment is required. Public access terminal is available.

Magistrate Court PO Box 879, Brunswick, GA 31521; 912-267-5650. Hours: 8:30AM-5PM (EST). *Civil Actions Under $15,000, Eviction, Small Claims.*

Probate Court PO Box 938, Brunswick, GA 31521; 912-554-7231; Fax: 912-466-8001. Hours: 8:30AM-5PM (EST). *Probate.*

Gordon County

Superior Court 100 Wall St #102, Calhoun, GA 30701; 706-629-9533; Fax: 706-629-2139. Hours: 8:30AM-5PM (EST). *Felony, Misdemeanor, Civil.*

Civil Records: Access: Fax, mail, in person. Both court and visitors may perform in person searches. No search fee. Required to search: name, years to search. Civil cases indexed by defendant, plaintiff. Civil records on computer since 03/97; prior records on docket books. **Criminal Records:** Access: Fax, mail, in person. Both court and visitors may perform in person searches. No search fee. Required to search: name, years to search. Criminal records on computer since 03/97; prior records on docket books. **General Information:** No sealed records released. SASE required. Turnaround time 1-2 days. Copy fee: $1.00 per page. Certification fee: $2.50 plus $.50 per page after first. Fee payee: Superior Court Clerk. Personal checks accepted. Prepayment is required.

Magistrate Court PO Box 1025, 100 Wall St, Calhoun, GA 30703; 706-629-6818 X121/122/143/144. Hours: 8:30AM-5PM (EST). *Civil Actions Under $15,000, Eviction, Small Claims.*

Probate Court PO Box 669, Calhoun, GA 30703; 706-629-7314; Fax: 706-629-4698. Hours: 8:30AM-5PM (EST). *Probate.*

Grady County

Superior Court 250 N Broad St, Box 8, Cairo, GA 31728; 229-377-2912. Hours: 8AM-5PM (EST). *Felony, Misdemeanor, Civil.*

Civil Records: Access: In person only. Court does not conduct in person searches; visitors must perform searches for themselves. Search fee: No civil searches performed by court. Required to search: name, years to search. Civil cases indexed by defendant, plaintiff. Civil records on computer since 1993; prior records on docket books. **Criminal Records:** Access: In person only. Court does not conduct in person searches; visitors must perform searches for themselves. Search fee: No criminal searches performed by court. Required to search: name, years to search. Criminal records on computer since 1993; prior records on docket books. **General Information:** No juvenile or adoption records released. Copy fee: $.25 per page. Certification fee: $2.00 plus $.50 per page. Fee payee: Superior Court Clerk. Personal checks accepted. Prepayment is required. Public access terminal is available.

Magistrate Court 250 N Broad St, Cairo, GA 31728; 229-377-4132; Fax: 229-377-4127. Hours: 8AM-5PM (EST). *Civil Actions Under $15,000, Eviction, Small Claims.*

Probate Court Courthouse, 250 N Broad St, Box 1, Cairo, GA 31728; 229-377-4621; Fax: 229-377-4127. Hours: 8AM-5PM (EST). *Probate.*

Greene County

Superior & Juvenile Court 113 North Main St, #109, Greensboro, GA 30642; 706-453-3340; Fax: 706-453-3341. Hours: 8AM-5PM (EST). *Felony, Misdemeanor, Civil, Eviction, Small Claims.*

Civil Records: Access: In person only. Court does not conduct in person searches; visitors must perform searches for themselves. Search fee: No civil searches performed by court. Required to search: name, years to search. Civil cases indexed by defendant, plaintiff. Civil records in books. **Criminal Records:** Access: In person only. Court does not conduct in person searches; visitors must perform searches for themselves. Search fee: No criminal searches performed by court. Required to search: name, years to search; also helpful-SSN. Criminal records in books. **General Information:** No juvenile or adoption records released. Copy

fee: $.25 per page. Certification fee: Fee is $2.50 plus $.25 per page. Fee payee: Superior Court Clerk. Personal checks accepted. Prepayment is required.

Magistrate & Probate Court 113 N Main St #113, Greensboro, GA 30642; 706-453-3346; Fax: 706-453-7649. Hours: 8AM-5PM (EST). *Civil Actions Under $15,000, Eviction, Small Claims, Probate.*

Gwinnett County

Superior & State Court PO Box 880, Lawrenceville, GA 30046; 770-822-8100. Hours: 8AM-5PM (EST). *Felony, Misdemeanor, Civil, Eviction, Small Claims.*

www.courts.co.gwinnett.ga.us

Civil Records: Access: In person only. Court does not conduct in person searches; visitors must perform searches for themselves. Search fee: No civil searches performed by court. Required to search: name, years to search. Civil cases indexed by defendant, plaintiff. Civil records on computer from 1980, prior records on card index. **Criminal Records:** Access: In person only. Court does not conduct in person searches; visitors must perform searches for themselves. Search fee: No criminal searches performed by court. Required to search: name, years to search. Criminal records on computer from 1980, prior records on card index. **General Information:** No sealed records released. Copy fee: $.25 per page. Certification fee: $2.50 plus $.50 per page. Fee payee: Superior Court Clerk. Personal checks accepted. Prepayment is required. Public access terminal is available.

Magistrate Court 75 Langley Dr, Justice & Admin. Ctr., Lawrenceville, GA 30045-6900; 770-822-8080; Fax: 770-822-8075. Hours: 8AM-5PM (EST). *Civil Actions Under $15,000, Eviction, Small Claims.*

Probate Court 75 Langley Dr, Justice & Admin. Ctr, Lawrenceville, GA 30045; 770-822-8250; Fax: 770-822-8267. Hours: 8:30AM-4:30PM (EST). *Probate.*

www.courts.co.gwinnett.ga.us/procourt/proindex.htm

Habersham County

Superior & State Court 555 Monroe St, Unit 35, Clarkesville, GA 30523; 706-754-2923. Hours: 8:30AM-5PM (EST). *Felony, Misdemeanor, Civil.*

http:209.86.240.205/mountainhp.shtml

Civil Records: Access: In person only. Court does not conduct in person searches; visitors must perform searches for themselves. Search fee: No civil searches performed by court. Required to search: name, years to search. Civil cases indexed by defendant, plaintiff. Civil records on index books from 1819. **Criminal Records:** Access: In person only. Court does not conduct in person searches; visitors must perform searches for themselves. Search fee: No criminal searches performed by court. Required to search: name, years to search. Criminal records on index books from 1819. **General Information:** No juvenile, adoption, sexual, mental health or expunged records released. Copy fee: $.25 per page. Certification fee: No certification fee. Fee payee: Court Clerk. Personal checks accepted. Prepayment is required. Public access terminal is available.

Magistrate Court PO Box 738, Cornelia, GA 30531; 706-754-4871. Hours: 8AM-5PM (EST). *Civil Actions Under $15,000, Eviction, Small Claims.*

Probate Court Habersham County Courthouse, PO Box 625, Clarkesville, GA 30523; 706-754-2013; Fax: 706-754-5093. Hours: 8AM-5PM (EST). *Probate.*

Hall County

Superior & State Court PO Box 1336, Gainesville, GA 30503; 770-531-7025; Fax: 770-531-7070; 536-0702 real estate. Hours: 8AM-5PM (EST). *Felony, Misdemeanor, Civil.*

http://209.86.240.205/dca9nehp.shtml

Civil Records: Access: In person only. Court does not conduct in person searches; visitors must perform searches for themselves. Search fee: No civil searches performed by court. Required to search: name, years to search. Civil cases indexed by defendant, plaintiff. Civil records on computer from 1989, dockets books from the late 1920s. **Criminal Records:** Access: In person only. Court does not conduct in person searches; visitors must perform searches for themselves. Search fee: No criminal searches performed by court. Required to search: name, years to search. Criminal records on computer from 1989, dockets books from the late 1920s. **General Information:** No juvenile, adoption, sexual, mental health or expunged records released. Copy fee: $1.00 per page. Certification fee: $2.00 plus $.50 per page. Fee payee: Court Clerk. Personal checks accepted. Prepayment is required.

Magistrate Court PO Box 1435, Gainesville, GA 30503; 770-531-6912; Fax: 770-531-6917. Hours: 8AM-5PM (EST). *Civil Actions Under $15,000, Eviction, Small Claims.*

www.hallcounty.org/clerkct.htm

Probate Court Hall County Courthouse, Rm 123, 116 Spring St, Gainesville, GA 30501; 770-531-6923; Fax: 770-531-4946. Hours: 8AM-5PM (EST). *Probate.*

http://hallcountyprobatect.com/clerkct.htm

Note: The search fee is $4.00 per record

Hancock County

Superior Court PO Box 451, Courthouse Square, Sparta, GA 31087; 706-444-6644; Fax: 706-444-6221. Hours: 8AM-5PM, 8AM-Noon Th (EST). *Felony, Misdemeanor, Civil.*

Civil Records: Access: Mail, in person. Both court and visitors may perform in person searches. Search fee: $5.00 per name. Required to search: name, years to search. Civil cases indexed by defendant, plaintiff. Civil records on docket books from 1991. **Criminal Records:** Access: Mail, in person. Both court and visitors may perform in person searches. Search fee: $5.00 per name. Required to search: name, years to search, DOB, signed release; also helpful-SSN, race, sex. Criminal records on books since 1991. **General Information:** No juvenile, adoptions, sealed, sexual, mental health or expunged records released. SASE required. Turnaround time 1 week. Copy fee: $.25 per page. Certification fee: 2 page doc is $2.50 plus $.25 per page; 3 pages and more are $4.50 plus $.25 per page after 3. Fee payee: Clerk of Superior Court. Personal checks accepted. Prepayment is required. Public access terminal is available. Public Access Terminal Note: But only includes deeds, UCCs and notary publics.

Magistrate Court 601 Courthouse Square, Sparta, GA 31087; 706-444-6234; Fax: 706-444-6221. Hours: 9AM-5PM (EST). *Civil Actions Under $15,000, Eviction, Small Claims.*

Records: Access: In person only. Court does not conduct in person searches; visitors must perform searches for themselves. Search fee: No criminal searches performed by court. Required to search: name, years to search, DOB. Criminal records on computer from 6/91, on docket books from 1900s. The court will not do searches. **General Information:** No juvenile, adoption, sexual, mental health or expunged records released. Copy fee: $.25 per page. Certification fee: $2.50 per page. Fee payee: Superior Court Clerk. Personal checks accepted. Prepayment is required.

Magistrate & Probate Court PO Box 201, Irwinton, GA 31042; 478-946-2222; Fax: 478-946-3767. Hours: 8AM-5PM (EST). *Civil Actions Under $15,000, Eviction, Small Claims, Probate.*

Worth County

Superior & State Court 201 N Main St, Rm 13, Sylvester, GA 31791; 229-776-8205; Fax: 229-776-8232. Hours: 8AM-5PM (EST). *Felony, Misdemeanor, Civil, Eviction, Small Claims.*

Civil Records: Access: In person only. Court does not conduct in person searches; visitors must perform searches for themselves. Search fee: No civil searches performed by court. Required to search: name, years to search. Civil cases indexed by defendant, plaintiff. civil records computerized since 1995, on books since 1880, real estate records from 9/93. **Criminal Records:** Access: In person only. Court does not conduct in person searches; visitors must perform searches for themselves. Search fee: No criminal searches performed by court. Required to search: name,

years to search; also helpful-SSN. Criminal records computerized since 1995. **General Information:** No juvenile, adoption, sexual, mental health or expunged records released. Copy fee: $.25 per page. Certification fee: $2.50 plus $.50 per page after first. Fee payee: Superior Court Clerk. Personal checks accepted. Prepayment is required. Public access terminal is available.

Magistrate Court PO Box 64, 201 N Main St, Sylvester, GA 31791; 229-776-8210. Hours: 8:30AM-5PM (EST). *Civil Actions Under $15,000, Eviction, Small Claims.*

Note: All records are maintained at the Superior Court, not here

Probate Court 201 N Main St, Rm 12, Sylvester, GA 31791; 229-776-8207; Fax: 229-776-1540. Hours: 8AM-5PM (EST). *Probate.*

ORGANIZATION   159 counties, 159 recording offices. The recording officer is Clerk of Superior Court. All transactions are recorded in a "General Execution Docket." The entire state is in the Eastern Time Zone (EST).

REAL ESTATE RECORDS   Most counties will **not** perform real estate searches. Copy fees are the same as for UCC. Certification fees are usually $2.00 per document—$1.00 for seal and $1.00 for stamp—plus $.50 per page.

UCC RECORDS   Financing statements are filed only with the Clerk of Superior Court in each county. **A new system is in effect as of January 1, 1995**, which merges all new UCC filings into a central statewide database, and which allows statewide searching for **new filings only** from any county office. However, filings prior to that date will remain at the county offices. Only a few counties will perform local UCC searches. Use search request form UCC-11 for local searches. Search fees vary from $2.50 to $25.00 per debtor name. Copies usually cost $.25 per page if you make it and $1.00 per page if the county makes it.

TAX LIEN RECORDS   All tax liens on personal property are filed with the county Clerk of Superior Court in a "General Execution Docket" (grantor/grantee) or "Lien Index." Most counties will **not** perform tax lien searches. Copy fees are the same as for UCC.

OTHER LIENS   Judgments, hospital, materialman, county tax, lis pendens, child support, labor, mechanics.

Appling County
County Superior Court Clerk, P.O. Box 269, Baxley, GA 31513. 912-367-8126.

Atkinson County
County Superior Court Clerk, P.O. Box 6, Pearson, GA 31642. 912-422-3343. Fax: 912-422-3429.

Bacon County
County Superior Court Clerk, P.O. Box 376, Alma, GA 31510. 912-632-4915. Fax: 912-632-2757.

Baker County
County Superior Court Clerk, P.O. Box 10, Newton, GA 31770. 2297343004.

Baldwin County
County Superior Court Clerk, P.O. Drawer 987, Milledgeville, GA 31061. 912-445-6327. Fax: 912-445-6320.

Banks County
County Superior Court Clerk, P.O. Box 337, Homer, GA 30547. 706-677-6243. Fax: 706-677-2337.

Barrow County
County Superior Court Clerk, P.O. Box 1280, Winder, GA 30680. 770-307-3035.

Bartow County
County Superior Court Clerk, 135 W. Cherokee Ave., Suite 233, Cartersville, GA 30120. 770-387-5025. Fax: 770-386-0846.

Ben Hill County
County Superior Court Clerk, P.O. Box 1104, Fitzgerald, GA 31750-1104. 912-426-5135. Fax: 912-426-5487.

Berrien County
County Superior Court Clerk, 101 E. Marion Ave. #3, Nashville, GA 31639. 229-686-5506.

Bibb County
County Superior Court Clerk, P.O. Box 1015, Macon, GA 31202-1015. 478-749-6527. Fax: 478-749-6539.

Bleckley County
County Superior Court Clerk, Courthouse, Cochran, GA 31014. 4789343210. Fax: 478-934-3205.

Brantley County
County Superior Court Clerk, P.O. Box 1067, Nahunta, GA 31553. 912-462-5635. Fax: 912-462-5538.

Brooks County
County Superior Court Clerk, P.O. Box 630, Quitman, GA 31643. 2292634747. Fax: 229-263-5050.

Bryan County
County Superior Court Clerk, P.O. Drawer H, Pembroke, GA 31321. 912-653-3872. Fax: 912-653-3695.

Bulloch County
County Superior Court Clerk, Judicial Annex, 20 Siebald St., Statesboro, GA 30458. 912-764-9009.

Burke County
County Superior Court Clerk, P.O. Box 803, Waynesboro, GA 30830-0803. 706-554-2279. Fax: 706-554-7887.

Butts County
County Superior Court Clerk, P.O. Box 320, Jackson, GA 30233. 770-775-8215. Fax: 770-775-8211.

Calhoun County
County Superior Court Clerk, P.O. Box 69, Morgan, GA 31766. 2298492715. Fax: 2298490072.

Camden County
County Superior Court Clerk, P.O. Box 578, Woodbine, GA 31569-0578. 912-576-5622.

Candler County
County Superior Court Clerk, P.O. Drawer 830, Metter, GA 30439. 912-685-5257. Fax: 912-685-2160.

Carroll County
County Superior Court Clerk, P.O. Box 1620, Carrollton, GA 30117. 770-830-5830. Fax: 770-214-3125.

Catoosa County
County Superior Court Clerk, 875 Lafayette Street, Courthouse, Ringgold, GA 30736. 706-935-4231.

Charlton County
County Superior Court Clerk, Courthouse, 100 S. Third St., Folkston, GA 31537. 912-496-2354. Fax: 912-496-3882.

Chatham County
County Superior Court Clerk, P.O. Box 10227, Savannah, GA 31412. 912-652-7219. Fax: 912-652-7380.

Chattahoochee County
County Superior Court Clerk, P.O. Box 120, Cusseta, GA 31805-0120. 706-989-3424. Fax: 706-989-0396.

Chattooga County
County Superior Court Clerk, P.O. Box 159, Summerville, GA 30747. 706-857-0706.

Cherokee County
County Superior Court Clerk, 90 North Street, Suite G-170, Canton, GA 30114. 770-479-0558.

Clarke County
County Superior Court Clerk, P.O. Box 1805, Athens, GA 30603. 706-613-3196. Fax: 706-613-3189.

Clay County
County Superior Court Clerk, P.O. Box 550, Fort Gaines, GA 31751-0550. 2297682631. Fax: 229-768-3047.

Clayton County
County Superior Court Clerk, 121 South McDonough Street, Room 202, Jonesboro, GA 30236. 770-477-3395.

Clinch County
County Superior Court Clerk, P.O. Box 433, Homerville, GA 31634. 912-487-5854. Fax: 912-487-3083.

Cobb County
County Superior Court Clerk, PO Box 3490, Marietta, GA 30061. 770-528-1363.
www.cobbgasupctclk.com/index.htm
Online Access: Real Estate. Real property records on the Cobb County Superior Court Clerk web site are available free on the internet at www.cobbgasupctclk.com/home.asp. You may also search court records.

Coffee County
County Superior Court Clerk, Courthouse, 101 S. Peterson Ave., Douglas, GA 31533. 912-384-2865.

Colquitt County
County Superior Court Clerk, P.O. Box 2827, Moultrie, GA 31776-2827. 229-891-7420.

Columbia County
County Superior Court Clerk, P.O. Box 100, Appling, GA 30802. 706-541-1139. Fax: 706-541-4013.

Cook County
County Superior Court Clerk, 212 North Hutchinson Avenue, Adel, GA 31620-2497. 2298967717.

Coweta County
County Superior Court Clerk, Courthouse, First FLoor, 200 Court Square, Newnan, GA 30263. 770-254-2690. Fax: 770-254-3700.

Crawford County
County Superior Court Clerk, P.O. Box 1037, Roberta, GA 31078-1037. 478-836-3328.

Crisp County
County Superior Court Clerk, P.O. Box 747, Cordele, GA 31010-0747. 229-276-2616.

Dade County
County Superior Court Clerk, P.O. Box 417, Trenton, GA 30752. 706-657-4778. Fax: 706-657-8284.

Dawson County
County Superior Court Clerk, P.O. Box 249, Dawsonville, GA 30534-0222. 706-344-3510. Fax: 706-344-3511.

De Kalb County

County Superior Court Clerk, 556 North McDonough Street, Courthouse, Room 208, Decatur, GA 30030. 404-371-2836.

Decatur County

County Superior Court Clerk, P.O. Box 336, Bainbridge, GA 31718. 229-248-3025. Fax: 229-248-3029.

Dodge County

County Superior Court Clerk, P.O. Box 4276, Eastman, GA 31023-4276. 478-374-2871.

Dooly County

County Superior Court Clerk, P.O. Box 326, Vienna, GA 31092-0326. 229-268-4234. Fax: 2292686142.

Dougherty County

County Superior Court Clerk, P.O. Box 1827, Albany, GA 31701. 2294312198. Fax: 2294312850. www.albany.ga.us
Online Access: Real Estate, Personal Property, Tax Records. Records on the Dougherty County and City of Albany Tax Department database are available free on the Internet at www.albany.ga.us/docotax.htm.

Douglas County

County Superior Court Clerk, Douglas County Courthouse, 8700 Hospital Dr., Douglasville, GA 30134. 770-920-7449.

Early County

County Superior Court Clerk, P.O. Box 849, Blakely, GA 31723. 229-723-3033. Fax: 2297235246.

Echols County

County Superior Court Clerk, P.O. Box 213, Statenville, GA 31648. 229-559-5642. Fax: 229-559-5792.

Effingham County

County Superior Court Clerk, P.O. Box 387, Springfield, GA 31329-0387. 912-754-2118.

Elbert County

County Superior Court Clerk, P.O. Box 619, Elberton, GA 30635. 706-283-2005. Fax: 706-213-7286.

Emanuel County

County Superior Court Clerk, P.O. Box 627, Swainsboro, GA 30401. 4782378911. Fax: 478-237-2173.

Evans County

County Superior Court Clerk, P.O. Box 845, Claxton, GA 30417. 912-739-3868. Fax: 912-739-2327.

Fannin County

County Superior Court Clerk, P.O. Box 1300, Blue Ridge, GA 30513. 706-632-2039.

Fayette County

County Superior Court Clerk, P.O. Box 130, Fayetteville, GA 30214. 770-461-4703. www.admin.co.fayette.ga.us
Online Access: Tax Records. Records on the Fayette County County Tax Digest database are available free on the Internet at www.admin.co.fayette.ga.us/intro.htm.

Floyd County

County Superior Court Clerk, P.O. Box 1110, Rome, GA 30162-1110. 706-291-5190. Fax: 706-233-0035.

Forsyth County

County Superior Court Clerk, 100 Courthouse Square, Room 010, Cumming, GA 30040. 770-781-2120. Fax: 770-886-2858.

Franklin County

County Superior Court Clerk, P.O. Box 70, Carnesville, GA 30521. 706-384-2514. Fax: 706-384-2185.

Fulton County

County Superior Court Clerk, 136 Pryor Street, Atlanta, GA 30303. 404-730-5553. Fax: 404-730-7993.

Gilmer County

County Superior Court Clerk, 1 West Side Square, Courthouse, Box #30, Ellijay, GA 30540. 706-635-4462. Fax: 706-635-1462.

Glascock County

County Superior Court Clerk, P.O. Box 231, Gibson, GA 30810. 706-598-2084.

Glynn County

County Superior Court Clerk, P.O. Box 1355, Brunswick, GA 31521-1355. 912-267-5769. Fax: 912-267-5625.

Gordon County

County Superior Court Clerk, Courthouse, Suite 102, 100 Wall St., Calhoun, GA 30701. 706-629-9533. Fax: 706-629-2139.

Grady County

County Superior Court Clerk, 250 North Broad Street, Box 8, Cairo, GA 31728. 2293772912.

Greene County

County Superior Court Clerk, Courthouse, Suite 109, 113 North Main St., Greensboro, GA 30642-1107. 706-453-3340. Fax: 706-453-9179.

Gwinnett County

County Superior Court Clerk, P.O. Box 2050, Lawrenceville, GA 30046. 770-822-8100.

Habersham County

County Superior Court Clerk, Highway 115, 555 Monroe St., Unit 35, Clarkesville, GA 30523. 706-754-2923. Fax: 706-754-8779.

Hall County

County Superior Court Clerk, P.O. Box 1336, Gainesville, GA 30503-1336. 770-531-7064. Fax: 770-536-0702.

Hancock County

County Superior Court Clerk, P.O. Box 451, Sparta, GA 31087. 706-444-6644. Fax: 706-444-6221.

Haralson County

County Superior Court Clerk, P.O. Drawer 849, Buchanan, GA 30113. 770-646-2005. Fax: 770-646-2035.

Harris County

County Superior Court Clerk, P.O. Box 528, Hamilton, GA 31811. 706-628-5570. Fax: 706-628-7039.

Hart County

County Superior Court Clerk, P.O.Box 386, Hartwell, GA 30643. 706-376-7189. Fax: 706-376-1277.

Heard County

County Superior Court Clerk, P.O. Box 249, Franklin, GA 30217. 706-675-3301. Fax: 706-675-0819.

Henry County

County Superior Court Clerk, Courthouse, #1 Courthouse Square, McDonough, GA 30253. 770-954-2121.

Houston County

County Superior Court Clerk, 800 Carroll Street, Perry, GA 31069. 478-987-2170. Fax: 478-987-3252.

Irwin County

County Superior Court Clerk, Courthouse, Suite 105, 301 S. Irwin Avenue, Ocilla, GA 31774. 229-468-5356.

Jackson County

County Superior Court Clerk, P.O. Box 7, Jefferson, GA 30549. 706-367-6360. Fax: 706-367-2468.

Jasper County

County Superior Court Clerk, Courthouse, Monticello, GA 31064. 706-468-4901. Fax: 706-468-4946.

Jeff Davis County

County Superior Court Clerk, P.O. Box 248, Hazlehurst, GA 31539. 912-375-6615. Fax: 912-375-0378.

Jefferson County

County Superior Court Clerk, P.O. Box 151, Louisville, GA 30434. 478-625-7922. Fax: 478-625-9589.

Jenkins County

County Superior Court Clerk, P.O. Box 659, Millen, GA 30442. 4789824683. Fax: 4789821274.

Johnson County

County Superior Court Clerk, P.O. Box 321, Wrightsville, GA 31096. 478-864-3484. Fax: 478-864-1343.

Jones County

County Superior Court Clerk, P.O. Box 39, Gray, GA 31032. 478-986-6671.

Lamar County

County Superior Court Clerk, 326 Thomaston Street, Courthouse, Barnesville, GA 30204-1669. 770-358-5145. Fax: 770-358-5149.

Lanier County

County Superior Court Clerk, County Courthouse, 100 Main Street, Lakeland, GA 31635. 229-482-3594. Fax: 229-482-8333.

Laurens County

County Superior Court Clerk, P.O. Box 2028, Dublin, GA 31040. 4782723210. Fax: 478-275-2595.

Lee County

County Superior Court Clerk, P.O. Box 597, Leesburg, GA 31763. 229-759-6018.

Liberty County

County Superior Court Clerk, P.O. Box 50, Hinesville, GA 31310. 912-876-3625. Fax: 912-369-5463.

Lincoln County

County Superior Court Clerk, P.O. Box 340, Lincolnton, GA 30817. 706-359-4444.

Long County

County Superior Court Clerk, P.O. Box 458, Ludowici, GA 31316. 912-545-2123.

Lowndes County

County Superior Court Clerk, P.O. Box 1349, Valdosta, GA 31601-1349. 229-333-5125. Fax: 229-333-7637.

Lumpkin County

County Superior Court Clerk, 99 Courthouse Hill, Suite D, Dahlonega, GA 30533-0541. 706-864-3736. Fax: 706-864-5298.

Macon County

County Superior Court Clerk, P.O. Box 337, Oglethorpe, GA 31068. 478-472-7661.

Madison County

County Superior Court Clerk, P.O. Box 247, Danielsville, GA 30633. 706-795-3351. Fax: 706-795-5668.

Marion County

County Superior Court Clerk, P.O. Box 41, Buena Vista, GA 31803. 229-649-7321. Fax: 229-649-2059.

McDuffie County

County Superior Court Clerk, P.O. Box 158, Thomson, GA 30824-0150. 706-595-2134. Fax: 706-595-9150.

McIntosh County

County Superior Court Clerk, P.O. Box 1661, Darien, GA 31305. 912-437-6641. Fax: 912-437-6673.

Meriwether County

County Superior Court Clerk, P.O. Box 160, Greenville, GA 30222-0160. 706-672-4416. Fax: 706-672-1886.

Miller County

County Superior Court Clerk, P.O. Box 66, Colquitt, GA 31737. 229-758-4102. Fax: 229-758-2229.

Mitchell County

County Superior Court Clerk, P.O. Box 427, Camilla, GA 31730. 229-336-2022. Fax: 229-336-2003.

Monroe County

County Superior Court Clerk, P.O. Box 450, Forsyth, GA 31029-0450. 478-994-7022. Fax: 478-994-7053.

Montgomery County

County Superior Court Clerk, P.O. Box 311, Mount Vernon, GA 30445. 912-583-4401.

Morgan County

County Superior Court Clerk, P.O. Box 130, Madison, GA 30650. 706-342-3605.

Murray County

County Superior Court Clerk, P.O. Box 1000, Chatsworth, GA 30705. 706-695-2932.

Muscogee County

County Superior Court Clerk, P.O. Box 2145, Columbus, GA 31902-2145. 706-653-4358. Fax: 706-653-4359.

Newton County

County Superior Court Clerk, Newton County Judicial Center, 1132 Usher St., 3rd Floor, Covington, GA 30014. 770-784-2035.

Oconee County

County Superior Court Clerk, P.O. Box 1099, Watkinsville, GA 30677. 706-769-3940. Fax: 706-769-3948.

Oglethorpe County

County Superior Court Clerk, P.O. Box 68, Lexington, GA 30648-0068. 706-743-5731. Fax: 706-743-5335.
www.gsccca.org
Online Access: UCC, Real Estate. UCC and real estate records are available online from the Oglethorpe County Clerk for a monthly subscription fee of $9.95 plus $.25 per printed page. Guest accounts are available. For information and to open an account, call 404-327-9058.

Paulding County

County Superior Court Clerk, 11 Courthouse Sq., Room G-2, Dallas, GA 30132. 770-443-7527.

Peach County

County Superior Court Clerk, P.O. Box 389, Fort Valley, GA 31030. 478-825-5331.

Pickens County

County Superior Court Clerk, P.O. Box 130, Jasper, GA 30143. 706-692-2014.

Pierce County

County Superior Court Clerk, P.O. Box 588, Blackshear, GA 31516. 912-449-2020.

Pike County

County Superior Court Clerk, P.O. Box 10, Zebulon, GA 30295. 770-567-2000.

Polk County

County Superior Court Clerk, P.O. Box 948, Cedartown, GA 30125. 770-749-2114. Fax: 770-749-2148.

Pulaski County

County Superior Court Clerk, P.O. Box 60, Hawkinsville, GA 31036. 478-783-1911. Fax: 478-892-3308.

Putnam County

County Superior Court Clerk, Courthouse, 100 S. Jefferson St., Eatonton, GA 31024-1087. 706-485-4501. Fax: 706-485-2515.

Quitman County

County Superior Court Clerk, P.O. Box 307, Georgetown, GA 31754. 229-334-2578. Fax: 229-334-2151.

Rabun County

County Superior Court Clerk, 25 Courthouse Square # 7, Clayton, GA 30525. 706-782-3615. Fax: 706-782-7588.

Randolph County

County Superior Court Clerk, P.O. Box 98, Cuthbert, GA 31740. 229-732-2216. Fax: 229-732-5881.

Richmond County

County Superior Court Clerk, P.O. Box 2046, Augusta, GA 30903. 706-821-2460. Fax: 706-821-2448.

Rockdale County

County Superior Court Clerk, P.O. Box 937, Conyers, GA 30207. 770-929-4069. Fax: 770-860-0381.

Schley County

County Superior Court Clerk, P.O. Box 7, Ellaville, GA 31806-0007. 229-937-5581. Fax: 229-937-5047.

Screven County

County Superior Court Clerk, P.O. Box 156, Sylvania, GA 30467. 912-564-2614. Fax: 912-564-2622.

Seminole County

County Superior Court Clerk, P.O. Box 672, Donalsonville, GA 31745. 229-524-2525. Fax: 229-524-8528.

Spalding County

County Superior Court Clerk, P.O. Box 1046, Griffin, GA 30224. 770-467-4356.

Stephens County

County Superior Court Clerk, Stephens County Courthouse, 150 West Doyle St., Toccoa, GA 30577-2310. 706-886-9496.

Stewart County

County Superior Court Clerk, P.O. Box 910, Lumpkin, GA 31815-0910. 229-838-6220.

Sumter County

County Superior Court Clerk, P.O. Box 333, Americus, GA 31709. 229-924-5626.

Talbot County

County Superior Court Clerk, P.O. Box 325, Talbotton, GA 31827-0325. 706-665-3239. Fax: 706-665-8637.

Taliaferro County

County Superior Court Clerk, P.O. Box 182, Crawfordville, GA 30631. 706-456-2123.

Tattnall County

County Superior Court Clerk, P.O. Box 39, Reidsville, GA 30453. 912-557-6716. Fax: 912-557-4552.

Taylor County

County Superior Court Clerk, P.O. Box 248, Butler, GA 31006. 478-862-5594. Fax: 478-862-5334.

Telfair County

County Superior Court Clerk, Courthouse, Oak Street, McRae, GA 31055-1604. 229-868-6525. Fax: 229-868-7956.

Terrell County

County Superior Court Clerk, P.O. Box 189, Dawson, GA 31742. 229-995-2631.

Thomas County

County Superior Court Clerk, P.O. Box 1995, Thomasville, GA 31799. 2292254108. Fax: 229-225-4110.

Tift County

County Superior Court Clerk, P.O. Box 354, Tifton, GA 31793. 229-386-7810. Fax: 229-386-7807.

Toombs County

County Superior Court Clerk, P.O. Drawer 530, Lyons, GA 30436. 912-526-3501. Fax: 912-526-1004.

Towns County

County Superior Court Clerk, 48 River St., Courthouse, Suite E, Hiawassee, GA 30546. 706-896-2130.

Treutlen County

County Superior Court Clerk, P.O. Box 356, Soperton, GA 30457. 912-529-4215. Fax: 912-529-6364.

Troup County

County Superior Court Clerk, P.O. Box 866, LaGrange, GA 30241-0866. 706-883-1740.

Turner County

County Superior Court Clerk, P.O. Box 106, Ashburn, GA 31714. 229-567-2011. Fax: 229-567-0450.

Twiggs County

County Superior Court Clerk, P.O. Box 228, Jeffersonville, GA 31044-0228. 478-945-3350.

Union County

County Superior Court Clerk, 114 Courthouse Street, Box 5, Blairsville, GA 30512. 706-745-2611. Fax: 706-745-3822.

Upson County

County Superior Court Clerk, P.O. Box 469, Thomaston, GA 30286. 706-647-7835. Fax: 706-647-8999.

Walker County

County Superior Court Clerk, P.O. Box 448, La Fayette, GA 30728. 706-638-1742.

Walton County

County Superior Court Clerk, P.O. Box 745, Monroe, GA 30655. 770-267-1304. Fax: 770-267-1441.

Ware County

County Superior Court Clerk, P.O. Box 776, Waycross, GA 31502-0776. 912-287-4340.

Warren County

County Superior Court Clerk, P.O. Box 227, Warrenton, GA 30828. 706-465-2262. Fax: 706-465-0232.

Washington County

County Superior Court Clerk, P.O. Box 231, Sandersville, GA 31082-0231. 478-552-3186.

Wayne County

County Superior Court Clerk, P.O. Box 918, Jesup, GA 31598-0918. 912-427-5930. Fax: 912-427-5939.

Webster County

County Superior Court Clerk, P.O. Box 117, Preston, GA 31824. 229-828-3525.

Wheeler County

County Superior Court Clerk, P.O. Box 38, Alamo, GA 30411-0038. 912-568-7137. Fax: 912-568-7453.

White County

County Superior Court Clerk, 59 South Main Street, Courthouse, Suite B, Cleveland, GA 30528. 706-865-2613. Fax: 706-865-7749.

Whitfield County

County Superior Court Clerk, P.O. Box 868, Dalton, GA 30722. 706-275-7450. Fax: 706-275-7456.

Wilcox County

County Superior Court Clerk, Courthouse, 103 North Broad St., Abbeville, GA 31001-1000. 229-467-2442. Fax: 229-467-2000.

Wilkes County

County Superior Court Clerk, 23 East Court Street, Room 205, Washington, GA 30673. 706-678-2423. Fax: 706-678-2115.

Wilkinson County

County Superior Court Clerk, P.O. Box 250, Irwinton, GA 31042-0250. 478-946-2221. Fax: 478-946-7274.

Worth County

County Superior Court Clerk, 201 North Main Street, Courthouse, Room 13, Sylvester, GA 31791. 229-776-8205.

You will usually be able to find the city name in the City/County Cross Reference below. In that case, it is a simple matter to determine the county from the cross reference. However, only the official US Postal Service city names are included in this index. There are an additional 40,000 place names that people use in their addresses. Therefore, we have also included a ZIP/City Cross Reference immediately following the City/County Cross Reference.

If you know the ZIP Code but the city name does not appear in the City/County Cross Reference index, look up the ZIP Code in the ZIP/City Cross Reference, find the city name, then look up the city name in the City/County Cross Reference. For example, you want to know the county for an address of Menands, NY 12204. There is no "Menands" in the City/County Cross Reference. The ZIP/City Cross Reference shows that ZIP Codes 12201-12288 are for the city of Albany. Looking back in the City/County Cross Reference, Albany is in Albany County.

City/County Cross Reference

ABBEVILLE Wilcox
ACWORTH (30101) Cobb(84), Bartow(8), Paulding(7)
ACWORTH (30102) Cherokee(52), Bartow(26), Cobb(22)
ADAIRSVILLE (30103) Bartow(61), Gordon(30), Floyd(9)
ADEL Cook
ADRIAN (31002) Emanuel(43), Johnson(31), Laurens(18), Treutlen(9)
AILEY Montgomery
ALAMO (30411) Wheeler(61), Laurens(39)
ALAPAHA Berrien
ALBANY (31701) Dougherty(98), Lee(2)
ALBANY (31705) Dougherty(88), Worth(10), Mitchell(2)
ALBANY (31707) Dougherty(93), Lee(5), Baker(1)
ALBANY Dougherty
ALLENHURST (31301) Liberty(79), Long(21)
ALLENTOWN Wilkinson
ALMA (31510) Bacon(97), Pierce(3)
ALPHARETTA (30004) Fulton(76), Forsyth(17), Cherokee(7)
ALPHARETTA (30005) Fulton(87), Forsyth(13)
ALPHARETTA Fulton
ALSTON Montgomery
ALTO (30510) Habersham(65), Banks(28), Hall(8)
ALTO Habersham
AMBROSE Coffee
AMERICUS Sumter
ANDERSONVILLE (31711) Sumter(84), Macon(15)
APPLING Columbia
ARABI (31712) Crisp(94), Worth(6)
ARAGON (30104) Polk(70), Floyd(26), Bartow(4)
ARGYLE Clinch
ARLINGTON (31713) Calhoun(60), Early(30), Baker(10)
ARMUCHEE (30105) Floyd(94), Chattooga(6)
ARNOLDSVILLE (30619) Oglethorpe(88), Oconee(12)
ASHBURN (31714) Turner(94), Worth(6)
ATHENS (30601) Clarke(98), Jackson(1), Madison(1)
ATHENS (30605) Clarke(99), Oconee(1)
ATHENS (30606) Clarke(92), Oconee(8)
ATHENS (30607) Jackson(64), Clarke(36)
ATHENS Clarke
ATLANTA (30306) Fulton(60), De Kalb(40)
ATLANTA (30307) De Kalb(74), Fulton(27)
ATLANTA (30316) De Kalb(72), Fulton(28)
ATLANTA (30317) De Kalb(99), Fulton(1)
ATLANTA (30319) De Kalb(92), Fulton(8)
ATLANTA (30324) Fulton(82), De Kalb(18)
ATLANTA (30337) Fulton(88), Clayton(13)
ATLANTA (30338) De Kalb(97), Fulton(3)

ATLANTA (30339) Cobb(97), Fulton(3)
ATLANTA (30340) De Kalb(88), Gwinnett(12)
ATLANTA (30349) Fulton(65), Clayton(35)
ATLANTA (30350) Fulton(99), De Kalb(1)
ATLANTA (30354) Fulton(91), Clayton(9)
ATLANTA (30360) De Kalb(79), Gwinnett(21)
ATLANTA De Kalb
ATLANTA Fulton
ATTAPULGUS Decatur
AUBURN (30011) Barrow(81), Gwinnett(19)
AUBURN Barrow
AUGUSTA (30907) Columbia(76), Richmond(24)
AUGUSTA Columbia
AUGUSTA Richmond
AUSTELL (30001) Cobb(93), Douglas(7)
AUSTELL (30106) Cobb(97), Douglas(3)
AUSTELL (30168) Cobb(90), Douglas(10)
AVERA Jefferson
AVONDALE ESTATES De Kalb
AXSON (31624) Atkinson(63), Ware(27), Coffee(11)
BACONTON Mitchell
BAINBRIDGE Decatur
BALDWIN (30511) Banks(97), Habersham(3)
BALL GROUND (30107) Cherokee(86), Pickens(11), Forsyth(3)
BARNESVILLE (30204) Lamar(95), Monroe(3), Upson(2)
BARNEY Brooks
BARTOW (30413) Jefferson(88), Washington(12)
BARWICK Brooks
BAXLEY Appling
BELLVILLE Evans
BERLIN Colquitt
BETHLEHEM (30620) Gwinnett(91), Barrow(8), Walton(2)
BISHOP (30621) Oconee(68), Morgan(32)
BLACKSHEAR Pierce
BLAIRSVILLE Union
BLAKELY (31723) Early(96), Miller(4)
BLOOMINGDALE (31302) Chatham(52), Effingham(48)
BLUE RIDGE Fannin
BLUFFTON (31724) Clay(88), Early(12)
BLYTHE (30805) Burke(54), Richmond(46)
BOGART (30622) Oconee(61), Clarke(30), Jackson(9)
BOLINGBROKE Monroe
BONAIRE Houston
BONEVILLE McDuffie
BOSTON (31626) Thomas(98), Brooks(2)
BOSTWICK Morgan
BOWDON (30108) Carroll(95), Heard(5)
BOWDON JUNCTION Carroll
BOWERSVILLE Hart

BOWMAN (30624) Elbert(79), Hart(13), Madison(9)
BOX SPRINGS (31801) Talbot(57), Muscogee(24), Marion(19)
BRASELTON (30517) Jackson(76), Hall(14), Barrow(5), Gwinnett(5)
BREMEN (30110) Haralson(93), Carroll(7)
BRINSON (31725) Decatur(99), Seminole(1)
BRISTOL (31518) Appling(58), Pierce(38), Wayne(4)
BRONWOOD Terrell
BROOKFIELD Tift
BROOKLET Bulloch
BROOKS (30205) Fayette(52), Spalding(48)
BROXTON (31519) Coffee(99), Jeff Davis(1)
BRUNSWICK Glynn
BUCHANAN (30113) Haralson(88), Polk(12)
BUCKHEAD (30625) Morgan(95), Putnam(5)
BUENA VISTA (31803) Marion(95), Schley(4)
BUFORD (30518) Gwinnett(85), Hall(15)
BUFORD Gwinnett
BUTLER Taylor
BYROMVILLE Dooly
BYRON (31008) Peach(83), Houston(10), Crawford(7)
CADWELL Laurens
CAIRO Grady
CALHOUN (30701) Gordon(99), Floyd(1)
CALHOUN Gordon
CALVARY Grady
CAMAK Warren
CAMILLA Mitchell
CANON (30520) Hart(58), Franklin(43)
CANTON Cherokee
CARLTON (30627) Oglethorpe(86), Madison(14)
CARNESVILLE (30521) Franklin(96), Banks(5)
CARROLLTON Carroll
CARTERSVILLE Bartow
CASSVILLE Bartow
CATAULA Harris
CAVE SPRING (30124) Floyd(95), Polk(5)
CECIL Cook
CEDAR SPRINGS Early
CEDARTOWN (30125) Polk(98), Floyd(2)
CENTERVILLE Houston
CHATSWORTH Murray
CHAUNCEY (31011) Dodge(96), Laurens(4)
CHERRYLOG Gilmer
CHESTER (31012) Dodge(65), Bleckley(32), Laurens(3)
CHESTNUT MOUNTAIN Hall
CHICKAMAUGA (30707) Walker(97), Catoosa(3)

CHULA (31733) Irwin(71), Tift(29)
CISCO Murray
CLARKDALE Cobb
CLARKESVILLE Habersham
CLARKSTON De Kalb
CLAXTON Evans
CLAYTON Rabun
CLERMONT (30527) Hall(94), White(6)
CLEVELAND (30528) White(96), Lumpkin(4)
CLIMAX Decatur
CLINCHFIELD Houston
CLYO Effingham
COBB Sumter
COBBTOWN (30420) Tattnall(50), Candler(48), Evans(2)
COCHRAN (31014) Bleckley(91), Dodge(7), Twiggs(2)
COCHRAN Dodge
COHUTTA (99999) Whitfield(99), Catoosa(1)
COLBERT (30628) Madison(90), Oglethorpe(10)
COLEMAN (31736) Randolph(81), Clay(19)
COLLINS Tattnall
COLQUITT (31737) Miller(95), Decatur(2), Baker(2), Early(1)
COLUMBUS Muscogee
COMER (30629) Madison(90), Oglethorpe(10)
COMMERCE (30529) Jackson(90), Banks(10)
COMMERCE (30530) Jackson(49), Madison(22), Banks(20), Franklin(9)
COMMERCE Jackson
CONCORD Pike
CONLEY (30288) Clayton(50), De Kalb(50)
CONLEY Clayton
CONYERS (30012) Rockdale(97), De Kalb(2)
CONYERS (30013) Rockdale(93), Newton(7)
CONYERS Rockdale
COOLIDGE (31738) Colquitt(69), Thomas(28), Telfair(3)
COOSA Floyd
CORDELE Crisp
CORNELIA Habersham
COTTON Mitchell
COVINGTON (30014) Newton(90), Walton(9), Jasper(1)
COVINGTON Newton
CRANDALL Murray
CRAWFORD Oglethorpe
CRAWFORDVILLE (30631) Taliaferro(91), Wilkes(7), Greene(2)
CRESCENT McIntosh
CULLODEN (31016) Monroe(56), Upson(30), Lamar(11), Crawford(3)
CUMMING (30040) Forsyth(93), Cherokee(7)
CUMMING Forsyth

CUSSETA (31805) Chattahoochee(96), Stewart(4)
CUTHBERT Randolph
DACULA (30019) Gwinnett(97), Walton(2)
DACULA Gwinnett
DAHLONEGA Lumpkin
DAISY Evans
DALLAS (30132) Paulding(98), Cobb(2)
DALTON Whitfield
DAMASCUS (31741) Early(74), Baker(20), Miller(7)
DANIELSVILLE Madison
DANVILLE (31017) Twiggs(76), Wilkinson(17), Bleckley(8)
DARIEN McIntosh
DAVISBORO Washington
DAWSON Terrell
DAWSONVILLE (30534) Dawson(86), Lumpkin(10), Forsyth(3)
DE SOTO (31743) Sumter(88), Lee(12)
DEARING McDuffie
DECATUR De Kalb
DEMOREST Habersham
DENTON Jeff Davis
DEWY ROSE (30634) Elbert(57), Hart(43)
DEXTER Laurens
DILLARD Rabun
DIXIE Brooks
DOERUN (31744) Colquitt(70), Worth(29), Mitchell(1)
DONALSONVILLE (31745) Seminole(96), Miller(3)
DOUGLAS Coffee
DOUGLASVILLE (30134) Douglas(68), Paulding(33)
DOUGLASVILLE Douglas
DOVER Screven
DRY BRANCH (31020) Twiggs(69), Bibb(31)
DU PONT (31630) Clinch(81), Echols(19)
DUBLIN Laurens
DUDLEY (31022) Laurens(96), Bleckley(3)
DULUTH (30097) Fulton(51), Gwinnett(45), Forsyth(4)
DULUTH Gwinnett
EAST ELLIJAY Gilmer
EASTANOLLEE (30538) Stephens(72), Franklin(28)
EASTMAN (31023) Dodge(99), Pulaski(1)
EATONTON Putnam
EDEN Effingham
EDISON (31746) Calhoun(91), Clay(7), Randolph(2)
ELBERTON (30635) Elbert(99), Hart(1)
ELKO Houston
ELLABELL (31308) Bryan(79), Bulloch(21)
ELLAVILLE Schley
ELLENTON Colquitt
ELLENWOOD (30294) De Kalb(39), Clayton(34), Henry(27)
ELLENWOOD Clayton
ELLERSLIE Harris
ELLIJAY Gilmer
EMERSON Bartow
ENIGMA (31749) Berrien(64), Tift(34), Irwin(2)
EPWORTH Fannin
ESOM HILL Polk
ETON Murray
EVANS Columbia
EXPERIMENT Spalding
FAIRBURN (30213) Fulton(87), Fayette(13)
FAIRMOUNT (30139) Gordon(71), Pickens(24), Bartow(5)
FARGO (31631) Clinch(64), Echols(29), Charlton(7)
FARMINGTON Oconee
FAYETTEVILLE (30215) Fayette(93), Clayton(7)
FAYETTEVILLE Fayette
FELTON Haralson

FITZGERALD (31750) Ben Hill(86), Irwin(14)
FLEMING Liberty
FLINTSTONE Walker
FLOVILLA Butts
FLOWERY BRANCH Hall
FOLKSTON (31537) Charlton(94), Camden(6)
FOREST PARK Clayton
FORSYTH Monroe
FORT BENNING Muscogee
FORT GAINES Clay
FORT OGLETHORPE Catoosa
FORT STEWART (31314) Liberty(98), Bryan(2)
FORT STEWART Liberty
FORT VALLEY (31030) Peach(93), Crawford(5), Macon(2)
FORTSON (31808) Harris(67), Muscogee(33)
FOWLSTOWN Decatur
FRANKLIN (30217) Heard(99), Troup(1)
FRANKLIN SPRINGS Franklin
FUNSTON Colquitt
GAINESVILLE (30506) Hall(96), Forsyth(4)
GAINESVILLE Hall
GARFIELD (30425) Emanuel(39), Bulloch(38), Jenkins(23)
GAY Meriwether
GENEVA Talbot
GEORGETOWN (31754) Quitman(90), Clay(10)
GIBSON (30810) Glascock(97), Jefferson(3), Warren(1)
GILLSVILLE (30543) Hall(57), Banks(30), Jackson(13)
GIRARD (30426) Burke(96), Screven(4)
GLENN Heard
GLENNVILLE (30427) Tattnall(95), Long(5)
GLENWOOD (30428) Wheeler(73), Laurens(27)
GOOD HOPE (30641) Walton(82), Morgan(18)
GORDON (31031) Wilkinson(88), Baldwin(10), Twiggs(1), Jones(1)
GOUGH Burke
GRACEWOOD Richmond
GRANTVILLE (30220) Meriwether(75), Coweta(26)
GRAY Jones
GRAYSON Gwinnett
GRAYSVILLE Catoosa
GREENSBORO Greene
GREENVILLE Meriwether
GRIFFIN (30224) Spalding(95), Pike(3), Lamar(2)
GRIFFIN Spalding
GROVETOWN (30813) Columbia(99), Richmond(1)
GUYTON Effingham
HADDOCK (31033) Jones(81), Baldwin(20)
HAGAN Evans
HAHIRA (31632) Lowndes(95), Cook(5)
HAMILTON Harris
HAMPTON (30228) Henry(69), Clayton(25), Spalding(6)
HARALSON Coweta
HARDWICK Baldwin
HARLEM (30814) Columbia(94), McDuffie(6)
HARRISON Washington
HARTSFIELD Colquitt
HARTWELL Hart
HAWKINSVILLE (31036) Pulaski(86), Houston(13)
HAZLEHURST Jeff Davis
HELEN White
HELENA (31037) Telfair(35), Wheeler(35), Dodge(26), Laurens(4)
HEPHZIBAH (30815) Richmond(77), Burke(23)
HIAWASSEE Towns

HIGH SHOALS (30645) Morgan(80), Oconee(20)
HILLSBORO (31038) Jasper(93), Jones(6)
HINESVILLE Liberty
HIRAM (30141) Paulding(88), Cobb(13)
HOBOKEN Brantley
HOGANSVILLE (30230) Troup(76), Heard(12), Meriwether(12)
HOLLY SPRINGS Cherokee
HOMER Banks
HOMERVILLE Clinch
HORTENSE (31543) Wayne(64), Brantley(32), Glynn(4)
HOSCHTON (30548) Jackson(83), Gwinnett(16)
HOWARD Taylor
HULL (30646) Madison(98), Jackson(2)
IDEAL Macon
ILA Madison
INMAN Fayette
IRON CITY (31759) Seminole(96), Miller(3)
IRWINTON (31042) Wilkinson(97), Laurens(3)
IRWINVILLE Irwin
JACKSON (30233) Butts(79), Monroe(15), Henry(3), Lamar(2)
JACKSONVILLE Telfair
JAKIN (31761) Early(97), Seminole(3)
JASPER (30143) Pickens(99), Cherokee(1)
JEFFERSON Jackson
JEFFERSONVILLE (31044) Twiggs(97), Wilkinson(3)
JEKYLL ISLAND Glynn
JENKINSBURG (30234) Butts(81), Henry(19)
JERSEY Walton
JESUP Wayne
JEWELL (31045) Hancock(64), Warren(36)
JONESBORO (30236) Clayton(94), Henry(6)
JONESBORO (30238) Clayton(95), Fayette(5)
JONESBORO Clayton
JULIETTE (31046) Monroe(98), Jones(2)
JUNCTION CITY (31812) Talbot(86), Taylor(14)
KATHLEEN Houston
KENNESAW Cobb
KEYSVILLE (30816) Burke(72), Jefferson(28)
KINGS BAY Camden
KINGSLAND Camden
KINGSTON (30145) Bartow(61), Floyd(39)
KITE (31049) Johnson(54), Emanuel(46)
KNOXVILLE Crawford
LA FAYETTE Walker
LAGRANGE Troup
LAKE PARK (31636) Lowndes(91), Echols(6), Catoosa(3)
LAKELAND (99999) Lanier(98), Clinch(1)
LAKEMONT Rabun
LAVONIA (30553) Franklin(72), Hart(28)
LAWRENCEVILLE Gwinnett
LEARY (31762) Calhoun(51), Baker(49)
LEBANON Cherokee
LEESBURG Lee
LENOX (31637) Cook(53), Berrien(20), Colquitt(18), Tift(9)
LESLIE Sumter
LEXINGTON Oglethorpe
LILBURN Gwinnett
LILLY Dooly
LINCOLNTON (30817) Lincoln(97), McDuffie(2), Wilkes(1)
LINDALE (30147) Floyd(96), Polk(4)
LITHIA SPRINGS Douglas
LITHONIA (30058) De Kalb(67), Gwinnett(30), Rockdale(3)
LITHONIA De Kalb
LIZELLA (31052) Bibb(91), Crawford(10)
LOCUST GROVE (30248) Henry(93), Spalding(5), Butts(2)

LOGANVILLE (30052) Walton(64), Gwinnett(34), Rockdale(1)
LOGANVILLE Gwinnett
LOOKOUT MOUNTAIN (30750) Walker(60), Dade(40)
LOUISVILLE (30434) Jefferson(96), Burke(4)
LOUVALE Stewart
LOVEJOY Clayton
LUDOWICI Long
LULA (30554) Hall(68), Banks(32)
LUMBER CITY (31549) Telfair(75), Wheeler(25)
LUMPKIN Stewart
LUTHERSVILLE Meriwether
LYERLY Chattooga
LYONS (30436) Toombs(94), Emanuel(5)
MABLETON Cobb
MACON (31210) Bibb(89), Monroe(11)
MACON (31211) Bibb(60), Jones(40)
MACON (31217) Bibb(84), Jones(9), Twiggs(8)
MACON (31220) Bibb(76), Monroe(24)
MACON Bibb
MADISON (30650) Morgan(93), Greene(5), Walton(2)
MANASSAS Tattnall
MANCHESTER Meriwether
MANOR Ware
MANSFIELD (30055) Jasper(55), Newton(41), Morgan(4)
MANSFIELD Jasper
MARBLE HILL (30148) Pickens(74), Dawson(26)
MARIETTA Cobb
MARSHALLVILLE Macon
MARTIN (30557) Franklin(70), Stephens(30)
MATTHEWS Jefferson
MAUK (31058) Marion(64), Taylor(36)
MAXEYS Oglethorpe
MAYSVILLE (30558) Jackson(56), Banks(44)
MC CAYSVILLE Fannin
MC INTYRE Wilkinson
MC RAE Telfair
MCDONOUGH (30252) Henry(98), Rockdale(2)
MCDONOUGH Henry
MEANSVILLE (30256) Pike(64), Upson(32), Lamar(4)
MEIGS (31765) Mitchell(48), Thomas(34), Colquitt(18)
MELDRIM Effingham
MENLO (30731) Chattooga(43), Walker(37), Dade(20)
MERIDIAN McIntosh
MERSHON (31551) Pierce(81), Bacon(19)
MESENA Warren
METTER Candler
MIDLAND (31820) Muscogee(88), Harris(12)
MIDVILLE (30441) Emanuel(70), Burke(30)
MIDWAY Liberty
MILAN (31060) Telfair(59), Dodge(42)
MILLEDGEVILLE (31061) Baldwin(94), Putnam(4), Wilkinson(2)
MILLEDGEVILLE Baldwin
MILLEN (30442) Jenkins(94), Burke(4), Screven(2)
MILLWOOD (31552) Ware(91), Coffee(6), Atkinson(3)
MILNER (30257) Lamar(87), Pike(13)
MINERAL BLUFF Fannin
MITCHELL (30820) Glascock(64), Warren(37)
MOLENA (30258) Pike(65), Upson(35)
MONROE Walton
MONTEZUMA (31063) Macon(98), Dooly(2)
MONTICELLO Jasper

MONTROSE (31065) Laurens(90), Bleckley(10)
MORELAND Coweta
MORGAN (31766) Calhoun(94), Randolph(6)
MORGANTON (30560) Fannin(82), Union(18)
MORRIS (31767) Quitman(63), Clay(29), Randolph(5), Stewart(4)
MORROW Clayton
MORVEN Brooks
MOULTRIE Colquitt
MOUNT AIRY Habersham
MOUNT BERRY Floyd
MOUNT VERNON Montgomery
MOUNT ZION Carroll
MOUNTAIN CITY Rabun
MURRAYVILLE (30564) Lumpkin(62), Hall(33), White(6)
MUSELLA (31066) Crawford(57), Bibb(43)
MYSTIC Irwin
NAHUNTA (31553) Brantley(98), Charlton(2)
NASHVILLE Berrien
NAYLOR (31641) Lowndes(85), Lanier(15)
NELSON Cherokee
NEWBORN (30056) Jasper(51), Newton(39), Morgan(10)
NEWBORN Newton
NEWINGTON (30446) Screven(66), Effingham(34)
NEWNAN Coweta
NEWTON Baker
NICHOLLS (31554) Coffee(62), Ware(21), Bacon(17)
NICHOLSON Jackson
NORCROSS (30092) Gwinnett(98), Fulton(2)
NORCROSS Gwinnett
NORMAN PARK (31771) Colquitt(98), Worth(3)
NORRISTOWN Emanuel
NORTH METRO Gwinnett
NORWOOD Warren
NUNEZ Emanuel
OAKFIELD Worth
OAKMAN Gordon
OAKWOOD Hall
OCHLOCKNEE (31773) Thomas(79), Grady(19), Colquitt(2)
OCILLA Irwin
OCONEE (31067) Washington(83), Laurens(17)
ODUM (31555) Wayne(85), Appling(15)
OFFERMAN Pierce
OGLETHORPE Macon
OLIVER Screven
OMAHA Stewart
OMEGA (31775) Colquitt(56), Tift(27), Worth(17)
ORCHARD HILL Spalding
OXFORD (30054) Newton(82), Walton(18)
OXFORD Newton
PALMETTO (30268) Fulton(81), Coweta(19)
PARROTT (31777) Terrell(82), Webster(18)
PATTERSON Pierce
PAVO (31778) Thomas(78), Brooks(18), Colquitt(4)
PEACHTREE CITY Fayette
PEARSON (31642) Atkinson(95), Clinch(3), Coffee(2)
PELHAM Mitchell
PEMBROKE (31321) Bryan(50), Bulloch(50)
PENDERGRASS (30567) Hall(98), Jackson(3)
PERKINS Jenkins
PERRY Houston
PINE LAKE De Kalb

PINE MOUNTAIN (31822) Harris(83), Troup(15), Meriwether(2)
PINE MOUNTAIN VALLEY Harris
PINEHURST Dooly
PINEVIEW (31071) Pulaski(56), Wilcox(43), Dooly(1)
PITTS (31072) Wilcox(87), Crisp(12), Dooly(1)
PLAINFIELD Dodge
PLAINS Sumter
PLAINVILLE (30733) Gordon(92), Floyd(9)
POOLER Chatham
PORTAL Bulloch
PORTERDALE Newton
POULAN Worth
POWDER SPRINGS (30127) Cobb(92), Paulding(8)
POWDER SPRINGS Cobb
PRESTON Webster
PULASKI Candler
PUTNEY Dougherty
QUITMAN Brooks
RABUN GAP Rabun
RANGER (30734) Gordon(73), Pickens(27)
RAY CITY (31645) Lanier(61), Berrien(36), Lowndes(4)
RAYLE (30660) Wilkes(78), Oglethorpe(19), Taliaferro(4)
REBECCA (31783) Turner(50), Irwin(40), Ben Hill(11)
RED OAK Fulton
REDAN De Kalb
REGISTER Bulloch
REIDSVILLE Tattnall
RENTZ Laurens
RESACA (30735) Gordon(71), Murray(21), Whitfield(8)
REX (30273) Clayton(92), Henry(8)
REYNOLDS (31076) Taylor(82), Macon(18)
RHINE (31077) Dodge(52), Telfair(48)
RICEBORO (31323) Liberty(93), Long(7)
RICHLAND (31825) Stewart(88), Webster(12)
RICHMOND HILL Bryan
RINCON Effingham
RINGGOLD (30736) Catoosa(97), Walker(2)
RISING FAWN (30738) Dade(72), Walker(28)
RIVERDALE (30296) Clayton(83), Fulton(10), Fayette(7)
RIVERDALE Clayton
ROBERTA Crawford
ROCHELLE (31079) Wilcox(89), Ben Hill(11)
ROCK SPRING (30739) Walker(88), Catoosa(12)
ROCKLEDGE Laurens
ROCKMART (30153) Polk(86), Paulding(8), Haralson(6)
ROCKY FACE (30740) Whitfield(85), Walker(15)
ROCKY FORD Screven
ROME Floyd
ROOPVILLE (30170) Heard(63), Carroll(38)
ROSSVILLE (30741) Walker(60), Catoosa(40)
ROSWELL (30075) Fulton(81), Cobb(17), Cherokee(1)
ROSWELL Fulton
ROYSTON (30662) Franklin(55), Hart(28), Madison(17), Elbert(1)
RUPERT (31081) Taylor(80), Macon(18), Schley(3)
RUTLEDGE (30663) Morgan(99), Walton(1)
RYDAL (30171) Bartow(77), Gordon(23)
SAINT GEORGE Charlton
SAINT MARYS Camden
SAINT SIMONS ISLAND Glynn

SALE CITY (31784) Mitchell(73), Colquitt(27)
SANDERSVILLE Washington
SAPELO ISLAND McIntosh
SARDIS Burke
SARGENT Coweta
SASSER Terrell
SAUTEE NACOOCHEE (30571) White(97), Habersham(3)
SAVANNAH Chatham
SCOTLAND Telfair
SCOTTDALE De Kalb
SCREVEN Wayne
SEA ISLAND Glynn
SENOIA (30276) Coweta(89), Fayette(6), Meriwether(6)
SEVILLE Wilcox
SHADY DALE Jasper
SHANNON Floyd
SHARON Taliaferro
SHARPSBURG Coweta
SHELLMAN (31786) Randolph(96), Terrell(3), Calhoun(2)
SHILOH (31826) Harris(74), Talbot(26)
SILOAM Greene
SILVER CREEK (30173) Floyd(94), Polk(6)
SMARR Monroe
SMITHVILLE (31787) Lee(90), Sumter(10)
SMYRNA Cobb
SNELLVILLE Gwinnett
SOCIAL CIRCLE (30025) Walton(67), Newton(32), Morgan(2)
SOCIAL CIRCLE Walton
SOPERTON (30457) Treutlen(94), Montgomery(4), Emanuel(2)
SPARKS Cook
SPARTA (31087) Hancock(96), Baldwin(4)
SPRINGFIELD Effingham
STAPLETON (30823) Jefferson(84), Warren(13), Glascock(3), McDuffie(1)
STATENVILLE Echols
STATESBORO Bulloch
STATHAM (30666) Barrow(67), Oconee(25), Jackson(8)
STEPHENS Oglethorpe
STILLMORE Emanuel
STOCKBRIDGE (30281) Henry(90), Rockdale(7), Clayton(3)
STOCKTON (31649) Lanier(95), Echols(5)
STONE MOUNTAIN (30087) De Kalb(56), Gwinnett(44)
STONE MOUNTAIN De Kalb
SUCHES (30572) Union(77), Fannin(22)
SUGAR VALLEY (30746) Gordon(97), Walker(4)
SUMMERTOWN Emanuel
SUMMERVILLE (30747) Chattooga(94), Walker(6)
SUMNER Worth
SUNNY SIDE Spalding
SURRENCY Appling
SUWANEE (30024) Gwinnett(75), Forsyth(24), Fulton(1)
SUWANEE Gwinnett
SWAINSBORO Emanuel
SYCAMORE Turner
SYLVANIA Screven
SYLVESTER (31791) Worth(99), Dougherty(1)
TALBOTTON Talbot
TALKING ROCK (30175) Pickens(58), Gilmer(42)
TALLAPOOSA Haralson
TALLULAH FALLS (30573) Rabun(83), Habersham(17)
TALMO (30575) Jackson(79), Hall(21)
TARRYTOWN (30470) Montgomery(88), Treutlen(12)
TATE Pickens
TAYLORSVILLE (30178) Bartow(82), Polk(18)

TEMPLE (30179) Carroll(45), Haralson(31), Paulding(25)
TENNGA Murray
TENNILLE (31089) Washington(98), Johnson(2)
THE ROCK (30285) Upson(59), Pike(23), Lamar(18)
THOMASTON Upson
THOMASVILLE (31792) Thomas(97), Grady(3)
THOMASVILLE Thomas
THOMSON (30824) McDuffie(98), Columbia(2)
TIFTON Tift
TIGER Rabun
TIGNALL (30668) Wilkes(84), Lincoln(17)
TOCCOA (30577) Stephens(81), Franklin(14), Habersham(5), Banks(1)
TOCCOA Stephens
TOOMSBORO Wilkinson
TOWNSEND McIntosh
TRENTON Dade
TRION (30753) Chattooga(68), Walker(32)
TUCKER (30084) De Kalb(79), Gwinnett(21)
TUCKER De Kalb
TUNNEL HILL (30755) Catoosa(54), Whitfield(46)
TURIN Coweta
TURNERVILLE Habersham
TWIN CITY (30471) Emanuel(80), Bulloch(13), Jenkins(7)
TY TY (31795) Tift(76), Worth(24)
TYBEE ISLAND Chatham
TYRONE Fayette
UNADILLA (31091) Dooly(99), Houston(1)
UNION CITY Fulton
UNION POINT (30669) Greene(79), Oglethorpe(11), Taliaferro(10)
UPATOI (31829) Muscogee(92), Harris(8)
UVALDA (30473) Toombs(62), Montgomery(38)
VALDOSTA (31602) Lowndes(95), Brooks(5)
VALDOSTA (31605) Lowndes(97), Brooks(3)
VALDOSTA Lowndes
VALONA McIntosh
VARNELL Whitfield
VIDALIA (30474) Toombs(88), Montgomery(10), Emanuel(1)
VIDALIA Toombs
VIENNA (31092) Dooly(98), Crisp(2)
VILLA RICA (30180) Carroll(76), Douglas(17), Paulding(7)
WACO (30182) Carroll(66), Haralson(35)
WADLEY Jefferson
WALESKA Cherokee
WALTHOURVILLE Liberty
WARESBORO Ware
WARM SPRINGS Meriwether
WARNER ROBINS Houston
WARRENTON Warren
WARTHEN Washington
WARWICK Worth
WASHINGTON Wilkes
WATKINSVILLE (30677) Oconee(97), Greene(3)
WAVERLY Camden
WAVERLY HALL (31831) Harris(96), Talbot(4)
WAYCROSS (31503) Ware(94), Brantley(5), Pierce(1)
WAYCROSS Ware
WAYNESBORO Burke
WAYNESVILLE (31566) Brantley(52), Camden(48)
WEST GREEN (31567) Jeff Davis(58), Coffee(42)
WEST POINT (31833) Troup(71), Harris(29)

WESTON (31832) Webster(81), Randolph(19)
WHIGHAM Grady
WHITE (30184) Bartow(68), Cherokee(32)
WHITE OAK Camden
WHITE PLAINS (30678) Greene(98), Hancock(2)
WHITESBURG (30185) Carroll(97), Douglas(4)
WILDWOOD Dade

WILEY Rabun
WILLACOOCHEE (31650) Coffee(93), Atkinson(7)
WILLIAMSON (30292) Pike(68), Spalding(32)
WINDER (30680) Barrow(99), Oconee(1)
WINSTON (30187) Douglas(99), Carroll(1)
WINTERVILLE (30683) Clarke(62), Oglethorpe(37), Madison(2)
WOODBINE Camden

WOODBURY Meriwether
WOODLAND Talbot
WOODSTOCK (30188) Cherokee(97), Cobb(3)
WOODSTOCK Cherokee
WRAY (31798) Irwin(87), Ben Hill(7), Coffee(7)
WRENS Jefferson
WRIGHTSVILLE (31096) Johnson(84), Washington(10), Laurens(6)

YATESVILLE (31097) Upson(90), Lamar(7), Monroe(3)
YOUNG HARRIS (30582) Towns(80), Union(20)
ZEBULON Pike

ZIP/City Cross Reference

ZIP	City	ZIP	City	ZIP	City	ZIP	City
30002-30002	AVONDALE ESTATES	30122-30122	LITHIA SPRINGS	30221-30221	GRAYSON	30417-30417	CLAXTON
30003-30003	NORCROSS	30123-30123	CASSVILLE	30222-30222	GREENVILLE	30420-30420	COBBTOWN
30004-30005	ALPHARETTA	30124-30124	CAVE SPRING	30223-30224	GRIFFIN	30421-30421	COLLINS
30006-30008	MARIETTA	30125-30125	CEDARTOWN	30226-30226	LILBURN	30423-30423	DAISY
30009-30009	ALPHARETTA	30126-30126	MABLETON	30227-30227	LAWRENCEVILLE	30424-30424	DOVER
30010-30010	NORCROSS	30127-30127	POWDER SPRINGS	30228-30228	HAMPTON	30425-30425	GARFIELD
30011-30011	AUBURN	30128-30128	CUMMING	30229-30229	HARALSON	30426-30426	GIRARD
30012-30013	CONYERS	30129-30129	COOSA	30230-30230	HOGANSVILLE	30427-30427	GLENNVILLE
30014-30016	COVINGTON	30130-30131	CUMMING	30232-30232	INMAN	30428-30428	GLENWOOD
30017-30017	GRAYSON	30132-30132	DALLAS	30233-30233	JACKSON	30429-30429	HAGAN
30018-30018	JERSEY	30133-30135	DOUGLASVILLE	30234-30234	JENKINSBURG	30434-30434	LOUISVILLE
30019-30019	DACULA	30136-30136	DULUTH	30235-30235	JERSEY	30436-30436	LYONS
30020-30020	CLARKDALE	30137-30137	EMERSON	30236-30238	JONESBORO	30438-30438	MANASSAS
30021-30021	CLARKSTON	30138-30138	ESOM HILL	30239-30239	ALPHARETTA	30439-30439	METTER
30022-30023	ALPHARETTA	30139-30139	FAIRMOUNT	30240-30241	LAGRANGE	30441-30441	MIDVILLE
30024-30024	SUWANEE	30140-30140	FELTON	30243-30246	LAWRENCEVILLE	30442-30442	MILLEN
30025-30025	SOCIAL CIRCLE	30141-30141	HIRAM	30247-30247	LILBURN	30445-30445	MOUNT VERNON
30026-30026	DULUTH	30142-30142	HOLLY SPRINGS	30248-30248	LOCUST GROVE	30446-30446	NEWINGTON
30027-30027	CONLEY	30143-30143	JASPER	30249-30249	LOGANVILLE	30447-30447	NORRISTOWN
30028-30028	CUMMING	30144-30144	KENNESAW	30250-30250	LOVEJOY	30448-30448	NUNEZ
30029-30029	DULUTH	30145-30145	KINGSTON	30251-30251	LUTHERSVILLE	30449-30449	OLIVER
30030-30037	DECATUR	30146-30146	LEBANON	30252-30253	MCDONOUGH	30450-30450	PORTAL
30038-30038	LITHONIA	30147-30147	LINDALE	30255-30255	MANSFIELD	30451-30451	PULASKI
30039-30039	SNELLVILLE	30148-30148	MARBLE HILL	30256-30256	MEANSVILLE	30452-30452	REGISTER
30040-30041	CUMMING	30149-30149	MOUNT BERRY	30257-30257	MILNER	30453-30453	REIDSVILLE
30042-30046	LAWRENCEVILLE	30150-30150	MOUNT ZION	30258-30258	MOLENA	30454-30454	ROCKLEDGE
30047-30048	LILBURN	30151-30151	NELSON	30259-30259	MORELAND	30455-30455	ROCKY FORD
30049-30049	ELLENWOOD	30152-30152	KENNESAW	30260-30260	MORROW	30456-30456	SARDIS
30050-30051	FOREST PARK	30153-30153	ROCKMART	30261-30261	LAGRANGE	30457-30457	SOPERTON
30052-30052	LOGANVILLE	30154-30154	DOUGLASVILLE	30262-30262	NEWBORN	30458-30461	STATESBORO
30054-30054	OXFORD	30155-30155	DULUTH	30263-30265	NEWNAN	30464-30464	STILLMORE
30055-30055	MANSFIELD	30158-30159	NORTH METRO	30266-30266	ORCHARD HILL	30466-30466	SUMMERTOWN
30056-30056	NEWBORN	30161-30165	ROME	30267-30267	OXFORD	30467-30467	SYLVANIA
30057-30057	LITHIA SPRINGS	30168-30168	AUSTELL	30268-30268	PALMETTO	30470-30470	TARRYTOWN
30058-30058	LITHONIA	30170-30170	ROOPVILLE	30269-30269	PEACHTREE CITY	30471-30471	TWIN CITY
30059-30059	MABLETON	30171-30171	RYDAL	30270-30270	PORTERDALE	30473-30473	UVALDA
30060-30069	MARIETTA	30172-30172	SHANNON	30271-30271	NEWNAN	30474-30475	VIDALIA
30070-30070	PORTERDALE	30173-30173	SILVER CREEK	30272-30272	RED OAK	30477-30477	WADLEY
30071-30071	NORCROSS	30174-30174	SUWANEE	30273-30273	REX	30499-30499	REIDSVILLE
30072-30072	PINE LAKE	30175-30175	TALKING ROCK	30274-30274	RIVERDALE	30501-30501	GAINESVILLE
30073-30073	POWDER SPRINGS	30176-30176	TALLAPOOSA	30275-30275	SARGENT	30502-30502	CHESTNUT MOUNTAIN
30074-30074	REDAN	30177-30177	TATE	30276-30276	SENOIA	30503-30507	GAINESVILLE
30075-30077	ROSWELL	30178-30178	TAYLORSVILLE	30277-30277	SHARPSBURG	30510-30510	ALTO
30078-30078	SNELLVILLE	30179-30179	TEMPLE	30278-30278	SNELLVILLE	30511-30511	BALDWIN
30079-30079	SCOTTDALE	30180-30180	VILLA RICA	30279-30279	SOCIAL CIRCLE	30512-30512	BLAIRSVILLE
30080-30082	SMYRNA	30182-30182	WACO	30281-30281	STOCKBRIDGE	30513-30513	BLUE RIDGE
30083-30083	STONE MOUNTAIN	30183-30183	WALESKA	30284-30284	SUNNY SIDE	30514-30514	BLAIRSVILLE
30084-30085	TUCKER	30184-30184	WHITE	30285-30285	THE ROCK	30515-30515	BUFORD
30086-30088	STONE MOUNTAIN	30185-30185	WHITESBURG	30286-30286	THOMASTON	30516-30516	BOWERSVILLE
30089-30089	DECATUR	30187-30187	WINSTON	30287-30287	MORROW	30517-30517	BRASELTON
30090-30090	MARIETTA	30188-30189	WOODSTOCK	30288-30288	CONLEY	30518-30519	BUFORD
30091-30093	NORCROSS	30195-30199	DULUTH	30289-30289	TURIN	30520-30520	CANON
30094-30094	CONYERS	30201-30202	ALPHARETTA	30290-30290	TYRONE	30521-30521	CARNESVILLE
30095-30099	DULUTH	30203-30203	AUBURN	30291-30291	UNION CITY	30522-30522	CHERRYLOG
30101-30102	ACWORTH	30204-30204	BARNESVILLE	30292-30292	WILLIAMSON	30523-30523	CLARKESVILLE
30103-30103	ADAIRSVILLE	30205-30205	BROOKS	30293-30293	WOODBURY	30525-30525	CLAYTON
30104-30104	ARAGON	30206-30206	CONCORD	30294-30294	ELLENWOOD	30527-30527	CLERMONT
30105-30105	ARMUCHEE	30207-30208	CONYERS	30295-30295	ZEBULON	30528-30528	CLEVELAND
30106-30106	AUSTELL	30209-30210	COVINGTON	30296-30296	RIVERDALE	30529-30530	COMMERCE
30107-30107	BALL GROUND	30211-30211	DACULA	30297-30298	FOREST PARK	30531-30531	CORNELIA
30108-30108	BOWDON	30212-30212	EXPERIMENT	30301-30399	ATLANTA	30533-30533	DAHLONEGA
30109-30109	BOWDON JUNCTION	30213-30213	FAIRBURN	30401-30401	SWAINSBORO	30534-30534	DAWSONVILLE
30110-30110	BREMEN	30214-30215	FAYETTEVILLE	30410-30410	AILEY	30535-30535	DEMOREST
30111-30111	CLARKDALE	30216-30216	FLOVILLA	30411-30411	ALAMO	30537-30537	DILLARD
30113-30113	BUCHANAN	30217-30217	FRANKLIN	30412-30412	ALSTON	30538-30538	EASTANOLLEE
30114-30115	CANTON	30218-30218	GAY	30413-30413	BARTOW	30539-30539	EAST ELLIJAY
30116-30119	CARROLLTON	30219-30219	GLENN	30414-30414	BELLVILLE	30540-30540	ELLIJAY
30120-30121	CARTERSVILLE	30220-30220	GRANTVILLE	30415-30415	BROOKLET	30541-30541	EPWORTH

Code	Name	Code	Name	Code	Name	Code	Name
30542-30542	FLOWERY BRANCH	30710-30710	COHUTTA	31030-31030	FORT VALLEY	31324-31324	RICHMOND HILL
30543-30543	GILLSVILLE	30711-30711	CRANDALL	31031-31031	GORDON	31326-31326	RINCON
30544-30544	DEMOREST	30719-30722	DALTON	31032-31032	GRAY	31327-31327	SAPELO ISLAND
30545-30545	HELEN	30724-30724	ETON	31033-31033	HADDOCK	31328-31328	TYBEE ISLAND
30546-30546	HIAWASSEE	30725-30725	FLINTSTONE	31034-31034	HARDWICK	31329-31329	SPRINGFIELD
30547-30547	HOMER	30726-30726	GRAYSVILLE	31035-31035	HARRISON	31331-31331	TOWNSEND
30548-30548	HOSCHTON	30728-30728	LA FAYETTE	31036-31036	HAWKINSVILLE	31332-31332	VALONA
30549-30549	JEFFERSON	30730-30730	LYERLY	31037-31037	HELENA	31333-31333	WALTHOURVILLE
30552-30552	LAKEMONT	30731-30731	MENLO	31038-31038	HILLSBORO	31401-31499	SAVANNAH
30553-30553	LAVONIA	30732-30732	OAKMAN	31039-31039	HOWARD	31501-31503	WAYCROSS
30554-30554	LULA	30733-30733	PLAINVILLE	31040-31040	DUBLIN	31510-31510	ALMA
30555-30555	MC CAYSVILLE	30734-30734	RANGER	31041-31041	IDEAL	31512-31512	AMBROSE
30557-30557	MARTIN	30735-30735	RESACA	31042-31042	IRWINTON	31513-31515	BAXLEY
30558-30558	MAYSVILLE	30736-30736	RINGGOLD	31044-31044	JEFFERSONVILLE	31516-31516	BLACKSHEAR
30559-30559	MINERAL BLUFF	30738-30738	RISING FAWN	31045-31045	JEWELL	31518-31518	BRISTOL
30560-30560	MORGANTON	30739-30739	ROCK SPRING	31046-31046	JULIETTE	31519-31519	BROXTON
30562-30562	MOUNTAIN CITY	30740-30740	ROCKY FACE	31047-31047	KATHLEEN	31520-31521	BRUNSWICK
30563-30563	MOUNT AIRY	30741-30741	ROSSVILLE	31049-31049	KITE	31522-31522	SAINT SIMONS ISLAND
30564-30564	MURRAYVILLE	30742-30742	FORT OGLETHORPE	31050-31050	KNOXVILLE	31523-31525	BRUNSWICK
30565-30565	NICHOLSON	30746-30746	SUGAR VALLEY	31051-31051	LILLY	31527-31527	JEKYLL ISLAND
30566-30566	OAKWOOD	30747-30747	SUMMERVILLE	31052-31052	LIZELLA	31532-31532	DENTON
30567-30567	PENDERGRASS	30750-30750	LOOKOUT MOUNTAIN	31054-31054	MC INTYRE	31533-31535	DOUGLAS
30568-30568	RABUN GAP	30751-30751	TENNGA	31055-31055	MC RAE	31537-31537	FOLKSTON
30571-30571	SAUTEE NACOOCHEE	30752-30752	TRENTON	31057-31057	MARSHALLVILLE	31539-31539	HAZLEHURST
30572-30572	SUCHES	30753-30753	TRION	31058-31058	MAUK	31542-31542	HOBOKEN
30573-30573	TALLULAH FALLS	30755-30755	TUNNEL HILL	31060-31060	MILAN	31543-31543	HORTENSE
30575-30575	TALMO	30756-30756	VARNELL	31061-31062	MILLEDGEVILLE	31544-31544	JACKSONVILLE
30576-30576	TIGER	30757-30757	WILDWOOD	31063-31063	MONTEZUMA	31545-31546	JESUP
30577-30577	TOCCOA	30802-30802	APPLING	31064-31064	MONTICELLO	31547-31547	KINGS BAY
30580-30580	TURNERVILLE	30803-30803	AVERA	31065-31065	MONTROSE	31548-31548	KINGSLAND
30581-30581	WILEY	30805-30805	BLYTHE	31066-31066	MUSELLA	31549-31549	LUMBER CITY
30582-30582	YOUNG HARRIS	30806-30806	BONEVILLE	31067-31067	OCONEE	31550-31550	MANOR
30596-30596	ALTO	30807-30807	CAMAK	31068-31068	OGLETHORPE	31551-31551	MERSHON
30597-30597	DAHLONEGA	30808-30808	DEARING	31069-31069	PERRY	31552-31552	MILLWOOD
30598-30598	TOCCOA	30809-30809	EVANS	31070-31070	PINEHURST	31553-31553	NAHUNTA
30599-30599	COMMERCE	30810-30810	GIBSON	31071-31071	PINEVIEW	31554-31554	NICHOLLS
30601-30613	ATHENS	30811-30811	GOUGH	31072-31072	PITTS	31555-31555	ODUM
30619-30619	ARNOLDSVILLE	30812-30812	GRACEWOOD	31073-31073	PLAINFIELD	31556-31556	OFFERMAN
30620-30620	BETHLEHEM	30813-30813	GROVETOWN	31075-31075	RENTZ	31557-31557	PATTERSON
30621-30621	BISHOP	30814-30814	HARLEM	31076-31076	REYNOLDS	31558-31558	SAINT MARYS
30622-30622	BOGART	30815-30815	HEPHZIBAH	31077-31077	RHINE	31560-31560	SCREVEN
30623-30623	BOSTWICK	30816-30816	KEYSVILLE	31078-31078	ROBERTA	31561-31561	SEA ISLAND
30624-30624	BOWMAN	30817-30817	LINCOLNTON	31079-31079	ROCHELLE	31563-31563	SURRENCY
30625-30625	BUCKHEAD	30818-30818	MATTHEWS	31081-31081	RUPERT	31564-31564	WARESBORO
30627-30627	CARLTON	30819-30819	MESENA	31082-31082	SANDERSVILLE	31565-31565	WAVERLY
30628-30628	COLBERT	30820-30820	MITCHELL	31083-31083	SCOTLAND	31566-31566	WAYNESVILLE
30629-30629	COMER	30821-30821	NORWOOD	31084-31084	SEVILLE	31567-31567	WEST GREEN
30630-30630	CRAWFORD	30822-30822	PERKINS	31085-31085	SHADY DALE	31568-31568	WHITE OAK
30631-30631	CRAWFORDVILLE	30823-30823	STAPLETON	31086-31086	SMARR	31569-31569	WOODBINE
30633-30633	DANIELSVILLE	30824-30824	THOMSON	31087-31087	SPARTA	31598-31599	JESUP
30634-30634	DEWY ROSE	30828-30828	WARRENTON	31088-31088	WARNER ROBINS	31601-31606	VALDOSTA
30635-30635	ELBERTON	30830-30830	WAYNESBORO	31089-31089	TENNILLE	31620-31620	ADEL
30638-30638	FARMINGTON	30833-30833	WRENS	31090-31090	TOOMSBORO	31622-31622	ALAPAHA
30639-30639	FRANKLIN SPRINGS	30901-30999	AUGUSTA	31091-31091	UNADILLA	31623-31623	ARGYLE
30641-30641	GOOD HOPE	31001-31001	ABBEVILLE	31092-31092	VIENNA	31624-31624	AXSON
30642-30642	GREENSBORO	31002-31002	ADRIAN	31093-31093	WARNER ROBINS	31625-31625	BARNEY
30643-30643	HARTWELL	31003-31003	ALLENTOWN	31094-31094	WARTHEN	31626-31626	BOSTON
30645-30645	HIGH SHOALS	31004-31004	BOLINGBROKE	31095-31095	WARNER ROBINS	31627-31627	CECIL
30646-30646	HULL	31005-31005	BONAIRE	31096-31096	WRIGHTSVILLE	31629-31629	DIXIE
30647-30647	ILA	31006-31006	BUTLER	31097-31097	YATESVILLE	31630-31630	DU PONT
30648-30648	LEXINGTON	31007-31007	BYROMVILLE	31098-31099	WARNER ROBINS	31631-31631	FARGO
30650-30650	MADISON	31008-31008	BYRON	31106-31199	ATLANTA	31632-31632	HAHIRA
30655-30656	MONROE	31009-31009	CADWELL	31201-31299	MACON	31634-31634	HOMERVILLE
30660-30660	RAYLE	31010-31010	CORDELE	31301-31301	ALLENHURST	31635-31635	LAKELAND
30662-30662	ROYSTON	31011-31011	CHAUNCEY	31302-31302	BLOOMINGDALE	31636-31636	LAKE PARK
30663-30663	RUTLEDGE	31012-31012	CHESTER	31303-31303	CLYO	31637-31637	LENOX
30664-30664	SHARON	31013-31013	CLINCHFIELD	31304-31304	CRESCENT	31638-31638	MORVEN
30665-30665	SILOAM	31014-31014	COCHRAN	31305-31305	DARIEN	31639-31639	NASHVILLE
30666-30666	STATHAM	31015-31015	CORDELE	31307-31307	EDEN	31641-31641	NAYLOR
30667-30667	STEPHENS	31016-31016	CULLODEN	31308-31308	ELLABELL	31642-31642	PEARSON
30668-30668	TIGNALL	31017-31017	DANVILLE	31309-31309	FLEMING	31643-31643	QUITMAN
30669-30669	UNION POINT	31018-31018	DAVISBORO	31310-31310	HINESVILLE	31645-31645	RAY CITY
30671-30671	MAXEYS	31019-31019	DEXTER	31312-31312	GUYTON	31646-31646	SAINT GEORGE
30673-30673	WASHINGTON	31020-31020	DRY BRANCH	31313-31313	HINESVILLE	31647-31647	SPARKS
30677-30677	WATKINSVILLE	31021-31021	DUBLIN	31314-31315	FORT STEWART	31648-31648	STATENVILLE
30678-30678	WHITE PLAINS	31022-31022	DUDLEY	31316-31316	LUDOWICI	31649-31649	STOCKTON
30680-30680	WINDER	31023-31023	EASTMAN	31318-31318	MELDRIM	31650-31650	WILLACOOCHEE
30683-30683	WINTERVILLE	31024-31024	EATONTON	31319-31319	MERIDIAN	31698-31699	VALDOSTA
30701-30703	CALHOUN	31025-31025	ELKO	31320-31320	MIDWAY	31701-31708	ALBANY
30705-30705	CHATSWORTH	31027-31027	DUBLIN	31321-31321	PEMBROKE	31709-31710	AMERICUS
30707-30707	CHICKAMAUGA	31028-31028	CENTERVILLE	31322-31322	POOLER	31711-31711	ANDERSONVILLE
30708-30708	CISCO	31029-31029	FORSYTH	31323-31323	RICEBORO	31712-31712	ARABI

31713-31713	ARLINGTON	31745-31745	DONALSONVILLE	31776-31776	MOULTRIE	31808-31808	FORTSON
31714-31714	ASHBURN	31746-31746	EDISON	31777-31777	PARROTT	31810-31810	GENEVA
31715-31715	ATTAPULGUS	31747-31747	ELLENTON	31778-31778	PAVO	31811-31811	HAMILTON
31716-31716	BACONTON	31749-31749	ENIGMA	31779-31779	PELHAM	31812-31812	JUNCTION CITY
31717-31718	BAINBRIDGE	31750-31750	FITZGERALD	31780-31780	PLAINS	31814-31814	LOUVALE
31720-31720	BARWICK	31751-31751	FORT GAINES	31781-31781	POULAN	31815-31815	LUMPKIN
31722-31722	BERLIN	31752-31752	FOWLSTOWN	31782-31782	PUTNEY	31816-31816	MANCHESTER
31723-31723	BLAKELY	31753-31753	FUNSTON	31783-31783	REBECCA	31820-31820	MIDLAND
31724-31724	BLUFFTON	31754-31754	GEORGETOWN	31784-31784	SALE CITY	31821-31821	OMAHA
31725-31725	BRINSON	31756-31756	HARTSFIELD	31785-31785	SASSER	31822-31822	PINE MOUNTAIN
31726-31726	BRONWOOD	31757-31758	THOMASVILLE	31786-31786	SHELLMAN	31823-31823	PINE MOUNTAIN VALLEY
31727-31727	BROOKFIELD	31759-31759	IRON CITY	31787-31787	SMITHVILLE	31824-31824	PRESTON
31728-31728	CAIRO	31760-31760	IRWINVILLE	31789-31789	SUMNER	31825-31825	RICHLAND
31729-31729	CALVARY	31761-31761	JAKIN	31790-31790	SYCAMORE	31826-31826	SHILOH
31730-31730	CAMILLA	31762-31762	LEARY	31791-31791	SYLVESTER	31827-31827	TALBOTTON
31732-31732	CEDAR SPRINGS	31763-31763	LEESBURG	31792-31792	THOMASVILLE	31829-31829	UPATOI
31733-31733	CHULA	31764-31764	LESLIE	31793-31793	TIFTON	31830-31830	WARM SPRINGS
31734-31734	CLIMAX	31765-31765	MEIGS	31795-31795	TY TY	31831-31831	WAVERLY HALL
31735-31735	COBB	31766-31766	MORGAN	31796-31796	WARWICK	31832-31832	WESTON
31736-31736	COLEMAN	31767-31767	MORRIS	31797-31797	WHIGHAM	31833-31833	WEST POINT
31737-31737	COLQUITT	31768-31768	MOULTRIE	31798-31798	WRAY	31836-31836	WOODLAND
31738-31738	COOLIDGE	31769-31769	MYSTIC	31799-31799	THOMASVILLE	31901-31904	COLUMBUS
31739-31739	COTTON	31770-31770	NEWTON	31801-31801	BOX SPRINGS	31905-31905	FORT BENNING
31740-31740	CUTHBERT	31771-31771	NORMAN PARK	31803-31803	BUENA VISTA	31906-31994	COLUMBUS
31741-31741	DAMASCUS	31772-31772	OAKFIELD	31804-31804	CATAULA	31995-31995	FORT BENNING
31742-31742	DAWSON	31773-31773	OCHLOCKNEE	31805-31805	CUSSETA	31997-31999	COLUMBUS
31743-31743	DE SOTO	31774-31774	OCILLA	31806-31806	ELLAVILLE	39901-39901	ATLANTA
31744-31744	DOERUN	31775-31775	OMEGA	31807-31807	ELLERSLIE		

Hawaii

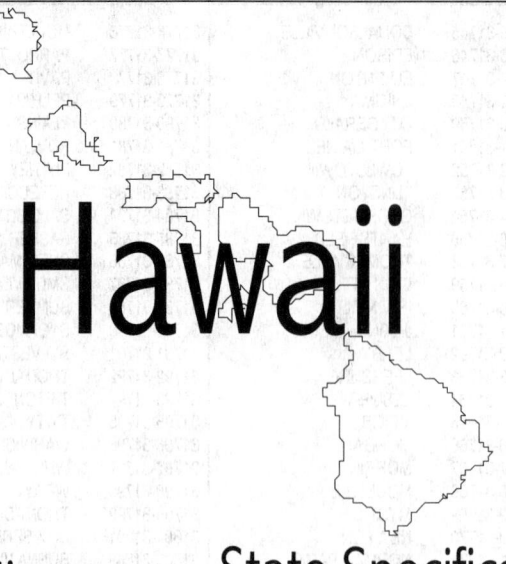

General Help Numbers:

Governor's Office
State Capitol   808-586-0034
415 S Beretania St   Fax 808-586-0006
Honolulu, HI 96813   7:45AM-5PM
http://gov.state.hi.us

Attorney General's Office
425 Queen St   808-586-1500
Honolulu, HI 96813   Fax 808-586-1239
www.state.hi.us/ag   7:45AM-4:30PM

State Court Administrator
417 S. King St   808-539-4900
Honolulu, HI 96813   Fax 808-539-4855
www.state.hi.us/jud   7:45AM-4:30PM

State Archives
Iolani Palace Grounds   808-586-0329
Honolulu, HI 96813   Fax 808-586-0330
www.state.hi.us/dags/archives   9AM-4PM

State Specifics:

Capital: Honolulu
Honolulu County

Time Zone: HT (Hawaii Standard Time)

Number of Counties: 4

Population: 1,186,602

Web Site: www.state.hi.us

State Agencies

Criminal Records

Hawaii Criminal Justice Data Center, Liane Moriyama, Administrator, 465 S King St, Room 101, Honolulu, HI 96813; 808-587-3106, 8AM-4PM.

www.state.hi.us/ag/hcjdc

Indexing & Storage: Records are available from the 1930's. Records are indexed on inhouse computer.

Searching: They will release only convictions and public sex offender information--arrests without dispositions are not released. Include the following in your request-any aliases, date of birth, Social Security Number.

Access by: mail, in person.

Fee & Payment: The search fee for a name-based criminal record search is $15.00. A fingerprint-based search is $25.00. A public access (convictions only) printout, available only in-person at this office or at main police stations, is $10.00. Fee payee: Hawaii Criminal Justice Data Center. Prepayment required. Money orders and cashiers' checks are the only acceptable methods of payment. No credit cards accepted.

Mail search: Turnaround time: 7-10 days. A self addressed stamped envelope is requested.

In person search: The public may access conviction information by computer on-site. Name, SSN, and gender are required. Date of birth

is optional. If SSN is unavailable, the staff will do the search.

Corporation Records
Fictitious Name
Limited Partnership Records
Assumed Name
Trademarks/Servicemarks
Limited Liability Company
   Records
Limited Liability
   Partnerships

Business Registration Division, PO Box 40, Honolulu, HI 96810 (Courier: 1010 Richard St, 1st Floor, Honolulu, HI 96813); 808-586-2727, 808-586-2733 (Fax), 7:45AM-4:30PM.

www.businessregistrations.com

Indexing & Storage: Records are available for active companies only. Inactive companies are archived. New records are available for inquiry immediately. Records are indexed on microfiche, hard copy.

Searching: There are no access restrictions. Records are open to the public. Include the following in your request-full name of business. In addition to the articles of incorporation, corporation records include the following information: Annual Reports, Officers, Directors, DBAs, Prior (merged) names, Inactive and Reserved names.

Access by: mail, phone, fax, in person, online.

Fee & Payment: The copy fee is $.25 per page. There is no search fee. Fee payee: Business Registration Division. Prepayment required. Personal checks accepted. No credit cards accepted.

Mail search: Turnaround time: 2 weeks. A self addressed stamped envelope is requested. No fee for mail request.

Phone search: No fee for telephone request. They will confirm data over the phone or let you know how many copies to prepay.

Fax search: Same criteria as mail searches.

In person search: No fee for request. Turnaround time is while you wait.

Online search: Online access is available through the Internet or via modem dial-up at 808-587-4800. There are no fees, the system is open 24 hours. For assistance during business hours, call 808-586-1919.

Uniform Commercial Code
Federal Tax Liens
State Tax Liens

UCC Division, Bureau of Conveyances, PO Box 2867, Honolulu, HI 96803 (Courier: Dept. of Land & Natural Resources, 1151 Punchbowl St, Honolulu, HI 96813); 808-587-0154, 808-587-0136 (Fax), 7:45AM-4:30PM.

www.hawaii.gov/dlnr/bc/bc.html

Indexing & Storage: Records are available from 1845. Records are on microfiche from 1976-present.

Searching: Use search request form UCC-3. Include the following in your request-debtor name. A UCC record does not include tax liens; a separate search is required.

Access by: mail, in person.

Fee & Payment: Fees are $25.00 per debtor name plus $5.00 for each financing statement and statement of assignment reported. Copies cost $1.00 per page. Fee payee: Bureau of Conveyances. Prepayment required. An initial fee of $25.00 must be paid in advance, additional fees will be invoiced. Personal checks accepted. No credit cards accepted.

Mail search: Turnaround time: 1 week. A self addressed stamped envelope is requested.

In person search: There is self-service in the public reference room.

Sales Tax Registrations
State does not impose sales tax.

Birth Certificates

State Department of Health, Vital Records Section, PO Box 3378, Honolulu, HI 96801 (Courier: 1250 Punchbowl St, Room 103, Honolulu, HI 96813); 808-586-4533, 808-586-4606 (Fax), 7:45AM-2:30PM.

www.hawaii.gov/doh

Indexing & Storage: Records are available from mid 1800's to present. New records are available for inquiry immediately. Records are indexed on microfilm, inhouse computer.

Searching: Must have a signed release form from person of record or immediate family member. Include the following in your request-full name, names of parents, mother's maiden name, date of birth, place of birth, relationship to person of record, reason for information request. Include a daytime phone number in your request. The Vital Records office will call you collect to verify information, if required. If your record is prior to July, 1909, you must know the island of event.

Access by: mail, in person.

Fee & Payment: Fees are $10.00 for first copy and $4.00 for each subsequent copy of same record. Fee payee: State Department of Health. Prepayment required. Money orders, certified checks, and cashier's checks are accepted. No credit cards accepted.

Mail search: Turnaround time: 4-6 weeks. No self addressed stamped envelope is required.

In person search: Turnaround time is 10 days or more.

Expedited service: Expedited service is available for mail and phone searches. You must send a pre-paid envelope going to requester.

Death Records

State Department of Health, Vital Records Section, PO Box 3378, Honolulu, HI 96801 (Courier: 1250 Punchbowl St, Room 103, Honolulu, HI 96813); 808-586-4533, 808-586-4606 (Fax), 7:45AM-2:30PM.

www.hawaii.gov/doh

Indexing & Storage: Records are available from mid 1800's on, but early records are not complete. New records are available for inquiry immediately. Records are indexed on microfilm, inhouse computer.

Searching: Must have a signed release form from immediate family member. Include the following in your request-full name, date of death, place of death, names of parents, relationship to person of record, reason for information request. Include a daytime phone number in your request. The agency may call you collect to verify information, if required. For records prior to July 1909, you must include the island of the event.

Access by: mail, in person.

Fee & Payment: The fee is $10.00 per record and $4.00 for each subsequent copy of same record. Fee payee: State Department of Health. Prepayment required. Cashier's checks and money orders accepted. No credit cards accepted.

Mail search: Turnaround time: 4-6 weeks.

In person search: Turnaround time is 10 days or more.

Marriage Certificates

State Department of Health, Vital Records Section, PO Box 3378, Honolulu, HI 96801 (Courier: 1250 Punchbowl St, Room 103, Honolulu, HI 96813); 808-586-4533, 808-586-4606 (Fax), 7:45AM-2:30PM.

www.hawaii.gov/doh

Indexing & Storage: Records are available from mid 1800's to present. New records are available for inquiry immediately. Records are indexed on microfilm, inhouse computer.

Searching: Must have a signed release form from person of record or immediate family member. Include the following in your request-names of husband and wife, wife's maiden name, date of marriage, place or county of marriage, names of parents, relationship to person of record, reason for information request. Include a daytime phone number. The office will call you collect to verify information, if required. For records prior to July 1909, include the island of the event.

Access by: mail, in person.

Fee & Payment: Fee is $10.00 per record and $4.00 for subsequent copy of same record. Fee payee: State Department of Health. Prepayment required. Cashier's check and money orders accepted. No credit cards accepted.

Mail search: Turnaround time: 4-6 weeks. No self addressed stamped envelope is required.

In person search: Turnaround time is 10 days or less.

Divorce Records

State Department of Health, Vital Records Section, PO Box 3378, Honolulu, HI 96801 (Courier: 1250 Punchbowl St, Room 103, Honolulu, HI 96813); 808-586-4533, 808-586-4606 (Fax), 7:45AM-2:30PM.

www.hawaii.gov/health

Indexing & Storage: Records are available from July 1951-present. Prior records are held by the clerk of the court granting the decree. New records are available for inquiry immediately. Records are indexed on microfilm, inhouse computer.

Searching: Must have a signed release form from person of record or immediate family member. Include the following in your request-names of husband and wife, date of divorce, place of divorce, relationship to person of record, reason for information request. Include a daytime phone number in your request. This office will call you collect to verify information, if required.

Access by: mail, in person.

Fee & Payment: The fee is $10.00 per rocrd and $4.00 each addional copy of same record. Fee payee: State Department of Health. Prepayment required. Cashier's check and money orders accepted. No credit cards accepted.

Mail search: Turnaround time: 4-6 weeks.

In person search: Results are mailed. Turnaround time is same day only if documented emergency.

Workers' Compensation Records

Labor & Industrial Relations, Disability Compensation Division, 830 Punchbowl St, Room 209, Honolulu, HI 96813; 808-586-9174, 808-586-9219 (Fax), 7:45AM-4:30PM.

Indexing & Storage: Records are available for the past 8 years. Prior records are in the State Archives but still must be requested through the Disability Compensation Division. It takes 2-4 days from receipt before new records are available for inquiry. Records are indexed on inhouse computer.

Searching: Must have a signed release from injured party or HI circuit court order signed by a judge. Include the following in your request-claimant name, Social Security Number, claim number.

Access by: mail, fax, in person.

Fee & Payment: There is no search fee, copy fee is $.05 per page. Fee payee: Director of Finance. Prepayment required. Personal checks accepted. No credit cards accepted.

Mail search: Turnaround time: 6-12 weeks. A self addressed stamped envelope is requested.

Fax search: Same criteria as mail searches.

In person search: In-person requests only saves mail time; results are mailed.

Driver Records

Traffic Violations Bureau, Abstract Section, 1111 Alakea St, Honolulu, HI 96813; 808-538-5510, 7:45AM-9:PM.

www.state.hi.us/jud

Note: Copies of tickets are available from the court where ticket was issued. The fees are $1.00 for first copy, $.50 each additional copy.

Indexing & Storage: Records are available for three years for moving violations, five years for no-faults, and ten years for DUIs. Accidents are only listed if a citation is issued for the accident. The driver's address is screened from the record.

Searching: Casual requsters can obtain records; however, personal information is not released. The driver's full name, DOB and either license number or SSN are needed when ordering.

Access by: mail, in person.

Fee & Payment: The fee is $7.00 per request. There is a full charge even if no record is found. Fee payee: TVB. Prepayment required. The state requires a money order or cashier's check for mail-in requests; in-person requesters may use cash, credit cards, personal or business checks.

Mail search: Turnaround time: 2-3 weeks. A self addressed stamped envelope is requested.

In person search: Walk-in requests can be processed in five to twenty minutes at any District Traffic Court or Traffic Violations Bureau Office.

Other access: Magnetic tape ordering is available in Hawaii for frequent or large orders. The fee is $7.00 per request. Turnaround time is 48 hours.

Accident Reports

Records not maintained by a state level agency.

Note: Accident reports are not available from the state. Records are maintained at the county level at the police departments.

Vehicle Ownership
Vehicle Identification
Access to Records is Restricted

Boat & Vessel Ownership
Boat & Vessel Registration

Land & Natural Resources, Division of Boating & Recreation, 333 Queen St Rm 300, Honolulu, HI 96813; 808-587-1963, 808-587-1977 (Fax), 7:45AM-4:30PM.

Indexing & Storage: Records are available 1950s, computerized since 1994, and on microfiche from 1987-1994.

Searching: Requests must be made in writing and must include a statement revealing the purpose for which the information will be used. Name or hull id number or registration number is required for search. The following data is not released: addresses or phone numbers.

Access by: mail, fax, in person.

Fee & Payment: There is no search fee.

Mail search: Turnaround time: 1-2 days. No self addressed stamped envelope is required.

Fax search: Same criteria as mail searching.

In person search: Turnaround time is usually the same day.

Legislation-Current/Pending
Legislation-Passed

Hawaii Legislature, 415 S Beretania St, Honolulu, HI 96813; 808-587-0700 (Bill # and Location), 808-586-6720 (Clerk's Office-Senate), 808-586-6400 (Clerk's Office-House), 808-586-0690 (State Library), 808-587-0720 (Fax), 7AM-6PM.

www.capitol.hawaii.gov

Indexing & Storage: Records are available from 1983-present. Records are indexed on inhouse computer.

Searching: Include the following in your request-bill number, year. Call the first phone number to get bill number and location of bill. Older bills are stored at the State Archives, 808-586-0329. Any bills that have become Acts can also be found at the library.

Access by: phone, in person, online.

Fee & Payment: There is no search fee nor a copy fee, unless extensive request is made.

Phone search: General information is available over the phone, copies can be requested.

In person search: Searching is available in person.

Online search: To dial online for current year bill information line, call 808-296-4636. Or, access the information through the Internet site. There is no fee, the system is up 24 hours.

Voter Registration

Records not maintained by a state level agency.

Note: Voter information is maintained by the County Clerks.

GED Certificates

Department of Education, GED Records, 634 Pensacola, #222, Honolulu, HI 96814; 808-594-0170, 808-594-0181 (Fax), 8AM-5PM.

Note: GED certificates are not issued by this agency. Instead, high school diplomas are issued to qualified individuals.

Searching: Include the following in your request-signed release, date of birth, Social Security Number. Knowing the approximate date and location of the test is helpful. The requirements are for both verifications and copies of transcripts.

Access by: mail, fax, in person.

Fee & Payment: Fees are not normally charged unless extensive search time involved.

Mail search: Turnaround time: 5-10 days. No self addressed stamped envelope is required.

Fax search: Same criteria as mail searching.

In person search: Same criteria as mail searching.

Hunting License Information
Fishing License Information
Access to Records is Restricted

Land & Natural Resources Department, 1151 Punchbowl St, Kalanimokui Bldg, Honolulu, HI 96813; 808-587-0100 (Fishing), 808-587-3257 (Hunting), 808-587-0115 (Fax), 7:45AM-4:30PM.

Note: Fishing information is kept by the Aquatic Resources Division; Hunting information by the Division of Forestry & Wildlife. Records are not released to the public, they are released only to law enforcement agencies.

Licenses Searchable Online

Lobbyist #41 .... www.state.hi.us/ethics/noindex/pubrec.htm
Optometrist #11 .... www.arbo.org/nodb2000/licsearch.asp

Licensing Quick Finder

Acupuncturist #04 808-586-3000
Airport Related #37 808-836-6533
Architect #19 808-587-3222
Attorney #38 808-537-1868
Banks #28 808-586-2820
Barber #05 808-587-3222
Barber Shop #05 808-587-3222
Beauty Operator #05 808-586-2699
Boxer #24 808-586-2701
Boxing Judge #24 808-586-2701
Boxing Manager #24 808-586-2701
Boxing Matchmaker #24 808-586-2701
Boxing Promoter #24 808-586-2701
Boxing Referee #24 808-586-2701
Boxing Second #24 808-586-2701
Boxing Timekeeper #24 808-586-2701
Bus Driver #39 808-487-5534
Cable Franchise #26 808-586-2620
Chiropractor #06 808-586-3000
Clinical Lab Director #40 808-453-6653
Clinical Laboratory Cytotechnologist #40
....808-453-6653
Clinical Laboratory Technician #40 808-453-6653
Clinical Laboratory Technologist/Specialist #40
....808-453-6653
Commercial Marine License #36........808-587-0100
Commercial Pesticide Applicator #02
.... 808-973-9414 or 9412
Condominium Hotel Operator #34........808-587-3222
Condominium Managing Agent #34 808-587-3222
Contractor #27 808-587-3222
Cosmetologist #05 808-587-3222
Credit Union #28 808-586-2820
Dental Hygienist #07 808-587-3222
Dentist #07 808-587-3222
Detective Agency #18 808-586-3000
Educational Administrator #35 808-586-3420
Electrician #29 808-587-3295

Electrologist #42 808-586-2699
Elevator Mechanic #29 808-587-3295
Embalmer #43 808-586-8000
Emergency Medical Personnel #13.......808-586-3000
Engineer #19 808-587-3222
Escrow depository Company #28..........808-586-2820
Financial Services Loan Company) #28
....808-586-2820
General Contractor #33 808-586-3000
Guard Agency #18 808-586-3000
Hearing Aid Dealer/Fitter #30 808-586-3000
Insurance Adjuster #31 808-586-2788
Insurance Agent #31 808-586-2788
Insurance Solicitor #31 808-586-2788
Investment Advisor/Representative #25
....808-586-2730
Landscape Architect #19 808-587-3222
Lobbyist #41 808-587-0460
Marriage & Family Therapist #42 808-586-2693
Massage Therapist #42 808-586-2699
Mechanic #42 808-586-2701
Medical Doctor #13 808-586-3000
Mortgage Broker #42 808-586-2709
Mortgage Solicitor #42 808-586-2709
Motor Vehicle Salesperson #42 808-586-2701
Naturopathic Physician #10 808-586-3000
Notary Public #03 808-586-1216
Nuclear Medicine Technologist #44 808-586-4700
Nurse #14 808-586-3000
Nurse Aide #14 808-586-3000
Nursing Home Administrator #12 808-586-3000
Optician, Dispensing #08....................808-586-3000
Optometrist #11 808-586-3000
Osteopathic Physician #13 808-586-3000
Out-of-state Pharmacy #16 808-586-3000
Pest Control Field Representative #32
....808-587-3295
Pest Control Operator #32 808-587-3295

Pesticide Dealer #02 .... 808-973-9414 or 9412
Pesticide Product #02 .... 808-973-9412 or 9414
Pharmacist #16 808-586-3000
Pharmacy #16 808-586-3000
Physical Therapist #17 808-586-3000
Physician Assistant #13 808-586-3000
Physician, Boxing #24 808-586-2701
Plumber #29 808-587-3295
Podiatrist #13 808-586-2708
Private Applicator (Pesticides) #02
.... 808-973-9412 or 9414
Private Detective #18 808-586-3000
Psychologist #20 808-586-3000
Public Accountant-CPA #21.................808-586-3222
Radiation Therapist #44 808-586-4700
Radiographer #44 808-586-4700
Real Estate Appraiser #34 808-587-3222
Real Estate Broker #34 808-587-3222
Real Estate Salesperson #34 808-587-3222
Sanitarian #43 808-586-8000
Savings & Loan Associations #28 808-586-2820
Savings Banks #28 808-586-2820
School Bus Driver #39.........................808-487-5534
Securities Salesperson #25 808-586-2730
Security Guard #18 808-586-3000
Shorthand Reporter #01 808-539-4226
Social Worker #42 808-586-2696
Speech Pathologist/Audiologist #22......808-586-3000
Surveyor #19 808-587-3222
Tattoo Artist #43.................................808-586-8000
Taxi Driver #39...................................808-532-2503
Teacher #35.......................................808-586-3392
Trust Company #28.............................808-586-2820
Veterinarian #23.................................808-587-3222
Wholesale Prescription, Drug Distributor #16
....808-586-3000

Licensing Agency Information

01 Board of Certified Shorthand Reporters, 777 Punchbowl St, Honolulu, HI 96813; 808-539-4226, Fax: 808-539-4149.

02 Department of Agriculture, PO Box 22159 (PO Box 22159), Honolulu, HI 96823-2159; 808-973-9401, Fax: 808-973-9410.

www.hawaiiag.org/212e3b.htm

03 Department of Attorney General, 425 Queen St, Honolulu, HI 96813; 808-586-1500, Fax: 808-586-1205.

www.state.hi.us/ag/notary/content.htm

04 Department of Commerce & Consumer Affairs, Board of Acupuncture, PO Box 3469 (PO Box 3469 (1010 Richards St, 96813)), Honolulu, HI 96801; 808-586-2698.

www.state.hi.us/dcca/dcca.html

05 Department of Commerce & Consumer Affairs, Board of Barbering & Cosmetology, PO Box 3469 (PO Box 3469 (1010 Richards St, 96813)), Honolulu, HI 96801; 808-586-3000.

06 Department of Commerce & Consumer Affairs, Board of Chiropractic Examiners, PO Box 3469 (PO Box 3469 (1010 Richards St, 96813)), Honolulu, HI 96801; 808-586-3000.

07 Department of Commerce & Consumer Affairs, Board of Dental Examiners, PO Box 3469 (PO Box 3469 (1010 Richards St 96813)), Honolulu, HI 96801; 808-586-3000.

08 Department of Commerce & Consumer Affairs, Dispensing Optician Program, PO Box 3469 (PO Box 3469 (1010 Richards St, 96813)), Honolulu, HI 96801; 808-586-2704, Fax: 808-586-3031.

www.state.hi.us/lrb/gd/gddoc.html

10 Department of Commerce & Consumer Affairs, Board of Examiners in Naturopathy, PO Box 3469 (PO Box 3469 (1010 Richards St, 96813)), Honolulu, HI 96801; 808-586-3000, Fax: 808-586-3031.

www.state.hi.us/dcca/dcca.html

11 Department of Commerce & Consumer Affairs, Board of Examiners in Optometry, PO Box 3469 (PO Box 3469 (1010 Richards St, 96813)), Honolulu, HI 96801; 808-586-2694.

Direct URL to search licenses: www.arbo.org/nodb2000/licsearch.asp You can search online using national database by name, city, or state

12 Department of Commerce & Consumer Affairs, Board of Examiners of Nursing Home Administrators, PO Box 3469 (PO Box 3469

(1010 Richards St, 96813)), Honolulu, HI 96801; 808-586-2695.

13 Department of Commerce & Consumer Affairs, Board of Medical Examiners, PO Box 3469 (PO Box 3469 (1010 Richards St, 96813)), Honolulu, HI 96801; 808-586-2708.

14 Department of Commerce & Consumer Affairs, Board of Nursing, PO Box 3469 (PO Box 3469 (1010 Richards St, 96813)), Honolulu, HI 96801; 808-586-2695.

16 Department of Commerce & Consumer Affairs, Board of Pharmacy, PO Box 3469 (PO Box 3469 (1010 Richards St, 96813)), Honolulu, HI 96801; 808-586-2694.

www.state.hi.us/dcca/dcca.html

17 Department of Commerce & Consumer Affairs, Board of Physical Therapy, PO Box 3469 (PO Box 3469 (1010 Richards St, 96813)), Honolulu, HI 96801; 808-586-2694.

www.state.hi.us/dcca/dcca.html

18 Department of Commerce & Consumer Affairs, Board of Private Detectives & Guards, PO Box 3469 (PO Box 3469 (1010 Richards St, 96813)), Honolulu, HI 96801; 808-586-2701, Fax: 808-586-2589.

19 Department of Commerce & Consumer Affairs, Architects & Surveyors, Board of Prof. Engineers, PO Box 3469 (PO Box 3469 (1010 Richards St, 96813)), Honolulu, HI 96801; 808-586-3000.

20 Department of Commerce & Consumer Affairs, Board of Psychology, PO Box 3469 (PO Box 3469 (1010 Richards St, 96813)), Honolulu, HI 96801; 808-586-2693.

21 Department of Commerce & Consumer Affairs, Board of Public Accountancy, PO Box 3469 (PO Box 3469 (1010 Richards St, 96813)), Honolulu, HI 96801; 808-586-2696, Fax: 808-586-2689.

www.state.hi.us/dcca/divisions.html

22 Department of Commerce & Consumer Affairs, Board of Speech Pathology & Audiology, PO Box 3469 (PO Box 3469 (1010 Richards St, 96813)), Honolulu, HI 96801; 808-586-3000.

23 Department of Commerce & Consumer Affairs, Board of Veterinary Examiners, PO Box 3469 (PO Box 3469 (1010 Richards St, 96813)), Honolulu, HI 96801; 808-586-3000.

24 Department of Commerce & Consumer Affairs, Boxing Commission, PO Box 3469 (PO Box 3469 (1010 Richards St, 96813)), Honolulu, HI 96801; 808-586-2701, Fax: 808-586-2689.

25 Department of Commerce & Consumer Affairs, Business Registration Division, Securities Compliance Branch, PO Box 40 (PO Box 3469 (1010 Richards St, 96813)), Honolulu, HI 96801; 808-586-2820, Fax: 808-586-2733.

26 Department of Commerce & Consumer Affairs, Cable TV Division, PO Box 541 (PO Box 541), Honolulu, HI 96809; 808-586-2620, Fax: 808-586-2625.

27 Department of Commerce & Consumer Affairs, Contractors License Board, PO Box 3469 (PO Box 3469 (1010 Richards St, 96813)), Honolulu, HI 96801; 808-586-2700, Fax: 808-586-3031.

www.state.hi.us/dcca

28 Department of Commerce & Consumer Affairs, Division of Financial Institutions, PO Box 2054 (PO Box 2054), Honolulu, HI 96805; 808-586-2820, Fax: 808-586-2818.

www.state.hi.us/dcca/dfi

29 Department of Commerce & Consumer Affairs, Board of Electricians, Plumbers & Elevator Mechanics Licensing, PO Box 3469 (PO Box 3469 (1010 Richards St, 96813)), Honolulu, HI 96801; 808-586-2705.

www.state.hi.us/dcca/ Online searching scheduled for late 2000.

30 Department of Commerce & Consumer Affairs, Hearing Aid Dealers & Fitters, PO Box 3469 (PO Box 3469 (1010 Richards St, 96813)), Honolulu, HI 96801; 808-586-2696.

31 Department of Commerce & Consumer Affairs, Insurance Division, Licensing Branch, 250 S King St, 5th Fl, Honolulu, HI 96813; 808-586-2790, Fax: 808-586-2806.

32 Department of Commerce & Consumer Affairs, Pest Control Board, PO Box 3469 (PO Box 3469), Honolulu, HI 96801; 808-586-2705.

www.state.hi.us/dcca

33 Department of Commerce & Consumer Affairs, Professional & Vocational Licensing Division, PO Box 3469 (PO Box 3469 (1010 Richards St, 96813)), Honolulu, HI 96801; 808-586-3000.

34 Department of Commerce & Consumer Affairs, Real Estate Commission, 250 S King St #702, Honolulu, HI 96813; 808-586-2643.

www.state.hi.us/hirec

35 Department of Education, Board of Education, PO Box 2360 (PO Box 2360), Honolulu, HI 96804; 808-586-3420, Fax: 808-586-3433.

36 Department of Land & Natural Resources, Division of Aquatic Resources, 1151 Punch Bowl St Rm 330, Honolulu, HI 96813; 808-587-0100, Fax: 808-587-0115.

www.state.hi.us/dlnr/dar

37 Department of Transportation, Airports Division, Airport District Manager, Honolulu Intl Airport, Honolulu, HI 96819; 808-836-6533.

www.state.hi.us/icsd/dot/guide.html

38 Bar Association, 1132 Bishop St #906, Honolulu, HI 96813-2814; 808-586-2660, Fax: 808-521-7936.

39 Motor Vehicle Licensing Division, 1199 Dillingham St, Honolulu, HI 96819; 808-536-2694.

40 Department of Health, Laboratory Licensing, 2725 Waimano Home Rd, Pearl City, HI 96782; 808-453-6653, Fax: 808-453-6662.

41 Ethics Commission, 1001 Bishop St, Pacific Tower #970, Honolulu, HI 96813; 808-587-0460, Fax: 808-587-0470.
www.state.hi.us/ethics

Direct URL to search licenses: www.state.hi.us/ethics/noindex/pubrec.htm

42 Department of Commerce & Consumer Affairs, Professional & Vocational Licensing Division, 1010 Richards St, Honolulu, HI 96813; 808-586-2699.

43 Department of Health, Sanitation Branch, 591 Ala Moana Blvd 1st Fl, Honolulu, HI 96813; 808-586-8000.

44 Department of Health, Radiologic Technology Board, 591 Ala Moana Blvd, Honolulu, HI 96813-4921; 808-586-4700.

The following list indicates the district and division name for each county in the state. If the district or division name of the bankruptcy court is different from the civil/criminal court, it appears in parentheses.

County/Court Cross Reference

Hawaii .... Honolulu
Honolulu .... Honolulu
Kalawao .... Honolulu
Kauai .... Honolulu
Maui .... Honolulu

US District Court

District of Hawaii

Honolulu Division 300 Ala Moana Blvd, Rm C-338, Honolulu, HI 96850, 808-541-1300, Fax: 808-541-1303.

www.hid.uscourts.gov

Counties: All counties.

Indexing & Storage: Cases are indexed by defendant and plaintiff as well as by case number. New cases are available in the index immediately after filing date. Both computer and card indexes are maintained. A microfiche index is also maintained. Open records are located at this court.

Fee & Payment: The fee is $15.00 per item (one party name or case number). Payment may be made by money order, cashier check, personal check. Prepayment is required. Payee: Clerk, US District Court. Certification fee: $5.00 per document. Copy fee: $.50 per page.

Phone Search: Searching is not available by phone.

Mail Search: Always enclose a stamped self addressed envelope.

In Person Search: In person searching is available.

PACER: Sign-up number is 800-676-6856. Access fee is $.60 per minute. Case records are available back to October 1991. Records are never purged. New civil records are available online after 1 day. New criminal records are available online after 3 days.

US Bankruptcy Court

District of Hawaii

Honolulu Division 1132 Bishop St, Suite 250-L, Honolulu, HI 96813, 808-522-8100.

www.hib.uscourts.gov

Counties: All counties.

Indexing & Storage: Cases are indexed by debtor as well as by case number. New cases are available in the index 24 hours after filing date. Both computer and card indexes are maintained. Open records are located at this court.

Fee & Payment: The fee is $15.00 per item (one party name or case number). Payment may be made by money order, cashier check, personal check. Prepayment is required. Debtor's checks are not accepted. Payee: US Bankruptcy Court. Certification fee: $5.00 per document. Copy fee: $.50 per page. You are allowed to make your own copies. These copies cost $.15 per page.

Phone Search: Only docket information is available by phone. An automated voice case information service (VCIS) is not available.

Mail Search: Always enclose a stamped self addressed envelope.

In Person Search: In person searching is available.

PACER: Sign-up number is 800-676-6856. Access fee is $.60 per minute. Use of PC Anywhere v4.0 suggested. Case records are available back to 1987. Records are purged varies. New civil records are available online after 1 day.

Court	Jurisdiction	No. of Courts	How Organized
Circuit Courts*	General	4	4 Circuits
District Courts*	Limited	7	4 Circuits

* Profiled in this Sourcebook.

CIVIL									
Court	Tort	Contract	Real Estate	Min. Claim	Max. Claim	Small Claims	Estate	Eviction	Domestic Relations
Circuit Courts*	X	X	X	$5000/ $10,000	No Max		X		X
District Courts*	X	X	X	$0	$20,000	$2500		X	

CRIMINAL					
Court	Felony	Misdemeanor	DWI/DUI	Preliminary Hearing	Juvenile
Circuit Courts*	X	X	X		X
District Courts*		X	X	X	

ADMINISTRATION   Administrative Director of Courts, Judicial Branch, 417 S King St, PO Box 2560, Honolulu, HI, 96813; 808-539-4900, Fax: 808-539-4855. www.state.hi.us/jud

COURT STRUCTURE   The Circuit Court is the court of general jurisdiction. There are 4 circuits in Hawaii: #1, #2, #3, and #5. The 4th Circuit merged with the 3rd Circuit in 1943. There are no records available for minor traffic offenses after 7/1/94.

The District Court handles some minor "felonies" and some civil cases up to $20,000.

ONLINE ACCESS   There is no online access to court records, but most courts offer a public access terminal to search records at the courthouse.

Hawaii County

3rd Circuit Court Legal Documents Section PO Box 1007, Hilo, HI 96721-1007; 808-961-7404; Fax: 808-961-7416. Hours: 7:45AM-4:30PM (HT). *Felony, Misdemeanor, Civil Actions Over $5,000, Probate.*

Civil Records: Access: Mail, in person. Both court and visitors may perform in person searches. Search fee: $5.00 per name. Required to search: name, years to search. Civil cases indexed by defendant, plaintiff. Civil records on computer from 1988, index card system prior to 1988. **Criminal Records:** Access: Mail, in person. Both court and visitors may perform in person searches. Search fee: $5.00 per name. Required to search: name, years to search. Criminal records on computer from 1988, index card system prior to 1988. **General Information:** No adoption, juvenile, dependencies, confidential records released. SASE required. Turnaround time 2 days depending upon staff coverage. Copy fee: $1.00 for first page, $.50 each addl. Certification fee: $2.00. Fee payee: Clerk, 3rd Circuit Court. Personal checks accepted. Prepayment is required. Public access terminal is available.

District Court PO Box 4879, Hilo, HI 96720; 808-961-7470; Fax: 808-961-7447. Hours: 7:45AM-4:30PM (HT). *Misdemeanor, Civil Actions Under $20,000, Eviction, Small Claims.*

www.state.hi.us/jud

Civil Records: Access: Phone, fax, mail, in person. Only the court conducts in person searches; visitors may not. Search fee: $5.00 per name. Required to search: name, years to search; also helpful-address. Civil cases indexed by defendant. Civil records on ledgers from statehood. **Criminal Records:** Access: Phone, fax, mail, in person. Only the court conducts in person searches; visitors may not. Search fee:. Required to search: name, years to search; also helpful-address, DOB, SSN. Criminal records on computer since March 1996. Public access terminal available for criminal abstracts. **General Information:** No family court records released. SASE requested. Turnaround time 1 week. Copy fee: $1.00 for first page, $.50 each addl. Off site storage- usual copy fees plus $5.00. Certification fee: $2.00. Fee payee: Clerk of the District Court. Personal checks accepted. Credit cards accepted: Visa, Mastercard. Public access terminal is available. Public Access Terminal Note: Available for criminal abstract record only. Fax notes: $2.00 for first page, $1.00 each addl. Extra fee for out of state faxing. Call for fee information.

Honolulu County

1st Circuit Court Legal Documents Branch, 777 Punchbowl St, Honolulu, HI 96813; 808-539-4300; Fax: 808-539-4314. Hours: 7:45AM-4:30PM (HT). *Felony, Civil Actions Over $5,000, Probate, Family.*

www.state.hi.us/jud/

Civil Records: Access: Mail, in person. Both court and visitors may perform in person searches. Search fee: $5.00 per name. Required to search: name, years to search. Civil cases indexed by defendant, plaintiff. Civil records on computer from 1983, on microfiche and archived from 1900. **Criminal Records:** Access: Mail, in person, online. Both court and visitors may perform in person searches. Search fee: $5.00 per name. Required to search: name, years to search, DOB; also helpful-SSN. Criminal records on computer from 1983, on microfiche and archived from 1900. **General Information:** No adoptions, paternity or sealed records released. SASE required. Turnaround time same day. Copy fee: $1.00 for first page, $.50 each addl. Microfilm service fee $5.00; cost of copies $1.00 per page. Certification fee: $2.00. Fee payee: 1st Circuit Court. Business checks accepted. Prepayment is required. Public access terminal is available.

District Court - Civil Division 1111 Alakea St, 3th Floor, Honolulu, HI 96813; 808-538-5151; Fax: 808-538-5444. Hours: 7:45AM-4:30PM (HT). *Civil Actions Under $20,000, Eviction, Small Claims.*

www.state.hi.us/jud/trials3.htm

Civil Records: Access: Phone, mail, in person. Both court and visitors may perform in person searches. Search fee: $5.00 per name. Required to search: name, years to search. Civil cases indexed by defendant. Civil records on computer from 1990; plaintiff index only on computer records. **General Information:** No sealed records released. SASE required. Turnaround time 1 week. Certification fee: No certification fee. Fee payee: District Court of the 1st Circuit. Personal checks accepted. Credit cards accepted: Visa, Mastercard,

Discover. Prepayment is required. Public access terminal is available. Fax notes: Call for fax fee.

District Court - Criminal Division

1111 Alakea St, 9th Floor Records, Honolulu, HI 96813; 808-538-5300 X1686; Fax: 808-538-5309. Hours: 7:45AM-4:30PM (HT). *Misdemeanor.* **Criminal Records:** Access: Fax, mail, in person. Only the court conducts in person searches; visitors may not. Search fee: $5.00 per name. Required to search: name, years to search, SSN, signed release, aliases; also helpful-address, DOB. **General Information:** No sealed records released. SASE required. Turnaround time 1 week. Copy fee: No copy fee. Certification fee: No certification. Fee payee: District Court of the 1st Circuit. Business checks accepted. Prepayment is required.

Kauai County

5th Circuit Court

3059 Umi St Rm #101, Lihue, HI 96766; 808-246-3300; Fax: 808-246-3310. Hours: 7:45AM-4:30PM (HT). *Felony, Misdemeanor, Civil Actions Over $10,000, Probate.*

Civil Records: Access: Mail, in person. Both court and visitors may perform in person searches. Search fee: $5.00 per name. Required to search: name, years to search. Civil cases indexed by defendant. Civil records on computer from 1987, microfiche from 1960. **Criminal Records:** Access: Mail, in person. Both court and visitors may perform in person searches. Search fee: $5.00 per name. Required to search: name, years to search, DOB; also helpful-SSN. Criminal records on computer from 1987, microfiche from 1960. **General Information:** No juvenile, dependencies records released. SASE required. Turnaround time 1 week. Copy fee: $1.00 for first page, $.50 each addl. Certification fee: $2.00. Fee payee: 5th Circuit Court. Only cashiers checks and money orders accepted. Prepayment is required. Public access terminal is available.

District Court of the 5th Circuit

3059 Umi St, Room 111, Lihue, HI 96766; 808-246-3330; Fax: 808-246-3309. Hours: 7:45AM-4:30PM (HT). *Misdemeanor.* **Criminal Records:** Access: Phone, fax, mail, in person. Only the court conducts in person searches; visitors may not. Search fee: $15.00. Required to search: name, years to search, DOB; also helpful-SSN. **General Information:** Copy fee: $1.00 for first page, $.50 each addl. Certification fee: $2.00. Fax notes: $2.00 for first page, $1.00 each addl.

District Court of the 5th Circuit

4357 Rice St, #101, Lihue, HI 96766; 808-246-3301; Fax: 808-241-7103. Hours: 7:45AM-4:30PM (HT). *Civil Actions Under $20,000, Eviction, Small Claims.*

www.state.hi.us/jud

Civil Records: Access: Phone, fax, mail, in person. Both court and visitors may perform in person searches. Search fee: $5.00 per case. Required to search: name, years to search. Civil cases indexed by defendant. Civil records on index books. **General Information:** No juvenile records released. SASE requested. Turnaround time 1-7 days. Copy fee: $1.00 for first page, $.50 each addl. Certification fee: No certification fee. Fee payee: District Court of the Fifth Circuit. Personal checks accepted. In-state personal check accepted. No third party checks. Credit cards accepted: Visa, Mastercard. Credit cards accepted. Fax notes: $2.00 for first page, $1.00 each addl.

Maui County

2nd Circuit Court

2145 Main St, #106, Wailuku, HI 96793; 808-244-2929; Fax: 808-244-2932. Hours: 7:45AM-4:30PM (HT). *Felony, Misdemeanor, Civil Actions Over $5,000, Probate.*

www.state.hi.us/jud

Note: This court also covers the counties of Lanai and Molokai

Civil Records: Access: Mail, in person. Both court and visitors may perform in person searches. Search fee: $5.00 per name. Required to search: name, years to search. Civil cases indexed by defendant, plaintiff. Civil records on computer from 10/88, some prior on microfiche. **Criminal Records:** Access: Mail, in person. Both court and visitors may perform in person searches. Search fee: $5.00 per name. Required to search: name, years to search; also helpful-DOB, SSN. Criminal records on computer from 10/88, some prior on microfiche. **General Information:** No juvenile or paternity records released. SASE required. Turnaround time 1 week. Copy fee: File marked pages are $1.00 per page; non-file marked are $.50. Certification fee: $2.00. Fee payee: Clerk, 2nd Circuit Court. Personal checks accepted. Prepayment is required. Public access terminal is available.

Lanai District Court

PO Box 630070, Lanai City, HI 96763; 808-565-6447. Hours: 7:45AM-4:30PM (HT). *Misdemeanor, Civil Actions Under $20,000, Eviction, Small Claims.*

Civil Records: Access: Mail, in person. Only the court conducts in person searches; visitors may not. Search fee: $5.00 per search. Required to search: name, years to search. Civil cases indexed by defendant, plaintiff. Civil records on index and docket books back to statehood. **Criminal Records:** Access: Mail, in person. Only the court conducts in person searches; visitors may not. Search fee: $5.00 per search. Required to search:

name, years to search; also helpful-DOB, SSN. Criminal records on computer since 1980. **General Information:** Turnaround time 2-3 weeks. Copy fee: $1.00 for first page, $.50 each addl. Certification fee: $1.00. Fee payee: Lanai District Court. Personal checks accepted. Credit cards accepted: Visa, Mastercard. Prepayment is required.

Molokai District Court

PO Box 284, Kaunakakai, HI 96748; 808-533-5451; Fax: 808-553-3374. Hours: 7:45AM-4PM (HT). *Misdemeanor, Civil Actions Under $20,000, Eviction, Small Claims.*

Civil Records: Access: Mail, in person. Only the court conducts in person searches; visitors may not. Search fee: $2.00 per name. Required to search: name, years to search. Civil cases indexed by defendant, plaintiff. Civil records on index and docket books back to statehood. **Criminal Records:** Access: Mail, in person. Only the court conducts in person searches; visitors may not. Search fee: $2.00 per name. Required to search: name, years to search; also helpful-address, DOB, SSN. Criminal records on computer since 1980. **General Information:** No juvenile or paternity records released. SASE requested. Turnaround time 2-3 weeks. Copy fee: $1.00 for first page, $.50 each addl. Certification fee: $5.00. Fee payee: Molokai District Court. Business checks accepted. Prepayment is required.

Wailuku District Court

2145 Main St, Ste 137, Wailuku, HI 96793; 808-244-2800; Fax: 808-244-2849. Hours: 7:45AM-4:30PM (HT). *Misdemeanor, Civil Actions Under $20,000, Eviction, Small Claims.*

http://1.49.41.1/mauidc/web/indexnew.html

Civil Records: Access: Fax, mail, in person. Only the court conducts in person searches; visitors may not. Search fee: $5.00 per name. Required to search: name, years to search; also helpful-address. Civil cases indexed by defendant, plaintiff. Civil records on index and docket books. **Criminal Records:** Access: Fax, mail, in person. Only the court conducts in person searches; visitors may not. Search fee: $5.00 per name. Required to search: name, years to search, DOB; also helpful-address, SSN. Criminal records on computer since 1980. **General Information:** SASE required. Turnaround time 2-3 weeks. Copy fee: $1.00 for first page, $.50 each addl. Certification fee: No certification. Fee payee: District Court 2nd Circuit. Personal checks accepted. Credit cards accepted: Visa, Mastercard. Prepayment is required. Fax notes: $5.00 for first page, $2.00 each addl. Within HI; $2.00 first page, $1.00 each add'l.

ORGANIZATION   All UCC financing statements, tax liens, and real estate documents are filed centrally with the Bureau of Conveyances. The entire state is in the Hawaii Time Zone (HT).

Bureau of Conveyances

Bureau of Conveyances, P.O. Box 2867, Honolulu, HI 96803. 808-587-0154. Fax: 808-587-0136.

Online Access: Property. Property records on the Honolulu Property Information database are available at http://caro.esri.com/honolulu/prperty.htm.

You will usually be able to find the city name in the City/County Cross Reference below. In that case, it is a simple matter to determine the county from the cross reference. However, only the official US Postal Service city names are included in this index. There are an additional 40,000 place names that people use in their addresses. Therefore, we have also included a ZIP/City Cross Reference immediately following the City/County Cross Reference.

If you know the ZIP Code but the city name does not appear in the City/County Cross Reference index, look up the ZIP Code in the ZIP/City Cross Reference, find the city name, then look up the city name in the City/County Cross Reference. For example, you want to know the county for an address of Menands, NY 12204. There is no "Menands" in the City/County Cross Reference. The ZIP/City Cross Reference shows that ZIP Codes 12201-12288 are for the city of Albany. Looking back in the City/County Cross Reference, Albany is in Albany County.

City/County Cross Reference

AIEA Honolulu
ANAHOLA Kauai
BARBERS POINT N A S Honolulu
CAMP H M SMITH Honolulu
CAPTAIN COOK Hawaii
ELEELE Kauai
EWA BEACH Honolulu
FORT SHAFTER Honolulu
HAIKU Maui
HAKALAU Hawaii
HALEIWA Honolulu
HANA Maui
HANALEI Kauai
HANAMAULU Kauai
HANAPEPE Kauai
HAUULA Honolulu
HAWAII NATIONAL PARK Hawaii
HAWI Hawaii
HICKAM AFB Honolulu
HILO Hawaii
HOLUALOA Hawaii
HONAUNAU Hawaii
HONOKAA Hawaii
HONOLULU Honolulu

HONOMU Hawaii
HOOLEHUA Maui
KAAAWA Honolulu
KAHUKU Honolulu
KAHULUI Maui
KAILUA Honolulu
KAILUA KONA Hawaii
KALAHEO Kauai
KALAUPAPA Maui
KAMUELA Hawaii
KANEOHE Honolulu
KAPAA Kauai
KAPAAU Hawaii
KAPOLEI Honolulu
KAUMAKANI Kauai
KAUNAKAKAI Maui
KEAAU Hawaii
KEALAKEKUA Hawaii
KEALIA Kauai
KEAUHOU Hawaii
KEKAHA Kauai
KIHEI Maui
KILAUEA Kauai
KOLOA Kauai

KUALAPUU Maui
KULA Maui
KUNIA Honolulu
KURTISTOWN Hawaii
LAHAINA Maui
LAIE Honolulu
LANAI CITY Maui
LAUPAHOEHOE Hawaii
LAWAI Kauai
LIHUE Kauai
M C B H KANEOHE BAY Honolulu
MAKAWAO Maui
MAKAWELI Kauai
MAUNALOA Maui
MILILANI Honolulu
MOUNTAIN VIEW Hawaii
NAALEHU Hawaii
NINOLE Hawaii
OCEAN VIEW Hawaii
OOKALA Hawaii
PAAUHAU Hawaii
PAAUILO Hawaii
PAHALA Hawaii
PAHOA Hawaii

PAIA Maui
PAPAALOA Hawaii
PAPAIKOU Hawaii
PEARL CITY Honolulu
PEARL HARBOR Honolulu
PEPEEKEO Hawaii
PRINCEVILLE Kauai
PUKALANI Maui
PUUNENE Maui
SCHOFIELD BARRACKS Honolulu
TRIPLER ARMY MEDICAL CTR Honolulu
VOLCANO Hawaii
WAHIAWA Honolulu
WAIALUA Honolulu
WAIANAE Honolulu
WAIKOLOA Hawaii
WAILUKU Maui
WAIMANALO Honolulu
WAIMEA Kauai
WAIPAHU Honolulu
WAKE ISLAND Honolulu
WHEELER ARMY AIRFIELD Honolulu

ZIP/City Cross Reference

ZIP	City	ZIP	City	ZIP	City	ZIP	City
96701-96701	AIEA	96731-96731	KAHUKU	96760-96760	KURTISTOWN	96785-96785	VOLCANO
96703-96703	ANAHOLA	96732-96733	KAHULUI	96761-96761	LAHAINA	96786-96786	WAHIAWA
96704-96704	CAPTAIN COOK	96734-96734	KAILUA	96762-96762	LAIE	96788-96788	PUKALANI
96705-96705	ELEELE	96737-96737	OCEAN VIEW	96763-96763	LANAI CITY	96789-96789	MILILANI
96706-96706	EWA BEACH	96738-96738	WAIKOLOA	96764-96764	LAUPAHOEHOE	96790-96790	KULA
96707-96707	KAPOLEI	96739-96739	KEAUHOU	96765-96765	LAWAI	96791-96791	WAIALUA
96708-96708	HAIKU	96740-96740	KAILUA KONA	96766-96766	LIHUE	96792-96792	WAIANAE
96709-96709	KAPOLEI	96741-96741	KALAHEO	96767-96767	LAHAINA	96793-96793	WAILUKU
96710-96710	HAKALAU	96742-96742	KALAUPAPA	96768-96768	MAKAWAO	96795-96795	WAIMANALO
96712-96712	HALEIWA	96743-96743	KAMUELA	96769-96769	MAKAWELI	96796-96796	WAIMEA
96713-96713	HANA	96744-96744	KANEOHE	96770-96770	MAUNALOA	96797-96797	WAIPAHU
96714-96714	HANALEI	96745-96745	KAILUA KONA	96771-96771	MOUNTAIN VIEW	96801-96850	HONOLULU
96715-96715	HANAMAULU	96746-96746	KAPAA	96772-96772	NAALEHU	96853-96853	HICKAM AFB
96716-96716	HANAPEPE	96747-96747	KAUMAKANI	96773-96773	NINOLE	96854-96854	WHEELER ARMY AIRFIELD
96717-96717	HAUULA	96748-96748	KAUNAKAKAI	96774-96774	OOKALA		
96718-96718	HAWAII NATIONAL PARK	96749-96749	KEAAU	96775-96775	PAAUHAU	96857-96857	SCHOFIELD BARRACKS
96719-96719	HAWI	96750-96750	KEALAKEKUA	96776-96776	PAAUILO	96858-96858	FORT SHAFTER
96720-96721	HILO	96751-96751	KEALIA	96777-96777	PAHALA	96859-96859	TRIPLER ARMY MEDICAL CTR
96722-96722	PRINCEVILLE	96752-96752	KEKAHA	96778-96778	PAHOA		
96725-96725	HOLUALOA	96753-96753	KIHEI	96779-96779	PAIA	96860-96860	PEARL HARBOR
96726-96726	HONAUNAU	96754-96754	KILAUEA	96780-96780	PAPAALOA	96861-96861	CAMP H M SMITH
96727-96727	HONOKAA	96755-96755	KAPAAU	96781-96781	PAPAIKOU	96862-96862	BARBERS POINT N A S
96728-96728	HONOMU	96756-96756	KOLOA	96782-96782	PEARL CITY	96863-96863	M C B H KANEOHE BAY
96729-96729	HOOLEHUA	96757-96757	KUALAPUU	96783-96783	PEPEEKEO	96898-96898	WAKE ISLAND
96730-96730	KAAAWA	96759-96759	KUNIA	96784-96784	PUUNENE		

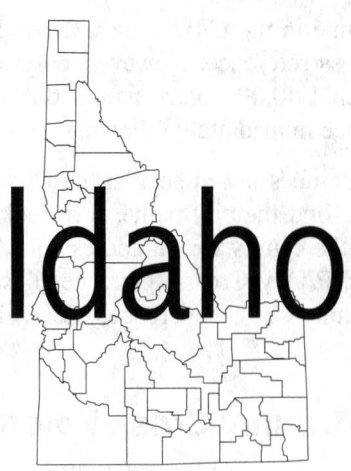

Idaho

General Help Numbers:

Governor's Office
PO Box 83720   208-334-2100
Boise, ID 83720-0034   Fax 208-334-3454
www2.state.id.us/gov/govhmpg.htm   8AM-6PM

Attorney General's Office
PO Box 83720   208-334-2400
Boise, ID 83720-0010   Fax 208-334-2530
www2.state.id.us/ag   8AM-5PM

State Court Administrator
451 W State St, Supreme Court Bldg   208-334-2246
Boise, ID 83720   Fax 208-334-2146
www2.state.id.us/judicial   9AM-5PM

State Archives
Historical Library & Archives   208-334-3356
450 N 4th Street   Fax 208-334-3198
Boise, ID 83702-6027   9AM-5PM
www2.state.id.us/ishs/index.html

State Specifics:

Capital: Boise
Ada County

Time Zone: MST*

* Idaho's ten northwestern-most counties are PST: They are: Benewah, Bonner, Boundary, Clearwater, Idaho, Kootenai, Latah, Lewis, Nez Perce, Shoshone.

Number of Counties: 44

Population: 1,210,232

Web Site: www.state.id.us

State Agencies

Criminal Records

State Repository, Bureau of Criminal Identification, PO Box 700, Meridian, ID 83680-0700 (Courier: 700 S Stratford Dr, Meridian, ID 83642); 208-884-7130, 208-884-7193 (Fax), 8AM-5PM.

Indexing & Storage: Records are available from 1960 on. New records are available for inquiry immediately.

Searching: A signed release is not required; however, a record of an arrest without disposition after 12 months from date of arrest will only be given if signed release presented. Requests without the release will recieve all records with dispositions. Name and DOB are required to search, SSN and alias will aid in identification. Fingerprints may be required to establish positive identification. Fingerprint searches take 5-7 days.

Access by: mail, in person.

Fee & Payment: Fees: $5.00 per person for name search only; $10.00 for a fingerprint search. Fee payee: BCI. Prepayment required. Cashier check or money order is preferred form of payment. No credit cards accepted.

Mail search: Turnaround time: 3-5 days.

In person search: You may request information in person, but results are still mailed.

Corporation Records
Limited Partnerships
Trademarks/Servicemarks
Limited Liability Company Records
Assumed Name

Secretary of State, Corporation Division, PO Box 83720, Boise, ID 83720-0080 (Courier: 700 W Jefferson, Boise, ID 83720); 208-334-2301, 208-334-2847 (Fax), 8AM-5PM.

www.idsos.state.id.us

Note: Effective 1/1/97, fictitious or assumed names are found at this office. (Previously they had recorded at the county level.)

Indexing & Storage: Records are available for all entities. New records are available for inquiry immediately. Records are indexed on inhouse computer.

Searching: Include the following in your request- full name of business, specific records that you need copies of. In addition to the articles of incorporation, corporation records include the following information: Annual Reports, Officers, Directors, Prior names, Inactive and Reserved names, and Filing History. Cross reference of owners/officers is not avail.

Access by: mail, phone, fax, in person, online.

Fee & Payment: There is no search fee. The fee for copies is $.25 per page. Certification is $10.00 as is a Certification of Existence. Fee payee: Secretary of State. Prepayment required. Agency will invoice for payment. Personal checks accepted. No credit cards accepted.

Mail search: Turnaround time: 1-2 days. No self addressed stamped envelope is required.

Phone search: There is a limit of 3 entities per call.

Fax search: Copies cost an additional $.50 each if returned by fax.

In person search: Call first to make an appointment so that they can pull file.

Online search: There are 2 systems. To subscribe to PAIS, you must pre-pay. An initial deposit of $25 is requested. There is a monthly subscription of $10.00 and an online usage charge of $.10 per minute. The system is available from 8AM-5PM M-F. Business Entity Searches is a free Internet service open 24 hours daily. This system offers an excellent array of reports and information.

Other access: There are a variety of formats and media avaible for bulk purchase requesters.

Expedited service: Expedited service is available for mail, phone and in person searches. Turnaround time: 1 day. Add $20.00 per document.

Uniform Commercial Code
Federal Tax Liens
State Tax Liens

UCC Division, Secretary of State, PO Box 83720, Boise, ID 83720-0080 (Courier: 700 W Jefferson, Boise, ID 83720); 208-334-3191, 208-334-2847 (Fax), 8AM-5PM.

www.idsos.state.id.us

Indexing & Storage: Records are available from 1967. It takes 1-2 days before new records are available for inquiry. Records are indexed on inhouse computer.

Searching: Use search request form UCC-4. The search includes federal tax liens, farm filings, and seed and labor filings. There is alaso an agricultural commodity lien search. Federal tax liens on individuals are filed at the county level. Include the following in your request-debtor name. For state tax liens that closed prior to 01/07/98, one must search at the county. On that date, the state took over the filing and database of state tax liens.

Access by: mail, phone, fax, in person, online.

Fee & Payment: Information request only by type of search is $6.00 per name, two or more file types is $10.00. Copies are $6.00. Individual copies are available at $1.00 per page. The Commodity lien search is a $5.00 flat fee. Fee payee: Secretary of State. Prepayment is not required, but preferred. Personal checks accepted. No credit cards accepted.

Mail search: Turnaround time: 3-5 days. No self addressed stamped envelope is required.

Phone search: They will tell whether a filing exists.

Fax search: You must call first to establish an account.

In person search: You may request information in person.

Online search: The deposit is $25-200 is required with a monthly subscription fee of $10.00 and a usage fee of $.10 per minute. This is the same system described under Corporation Records.

Other access: A summary data file on current filing is available on 4mm data tape.

Expedited service: Expedited service is available for mail and phone searches. The 24 hour service is available for an extra $10.00.

Sales Tax Registrations

Revenue Operations Division, Records Management, PO Box 36, Boise, ID 83722 (Courier: 800 Park, Boise, ID 83722); 208-334-7660, 208-334-7792 (Records Management), 208-334-7650 (Fax), 8AM-5:00PM.

http://www2.state.id.us/tax/site.htm

Indexing & Storage: Records are available from 1983. The agency maintains records on computer since 1995 and on microfiche from 1983-present.

Searching: This agency will only confirm that a business is registered if a tax permit number is provided. They will provide no other information. The only information released is that within public domain. They will also search if provided with a tax permit number, a DBA or an EIN.

Access by: mail, phone, fax, in person, online.

Fee & Payment: There is no search fee, but there is a fee for postage for mail requests or for faxing. Fee payee: ISTC, PO Box 36, Boise, ID 83732. Prepayment required. Personal checks accepted. No credit cards accepted.

Mail search: Turnaround time: 1-3 days. The copy fee is $.10 per page, after 20 pages. No self addressed stamped envelope is required.

Phone search: No fee for telephone request. Only general information is released.

Fax search: The fee is $1.00 per page. Turnaround time 24 hours.

In person search: No fee for request.

Online search: E-mail requests are accepted at rmcmichael@tax.state.id.us.

Birth Certificates

State Department of Health & Welfare, Center for Vital Statistics & Health Policy, PO Box 83720, Boise, ID 83720-0036 (Courier: 450 W State St, 1st Floor, Boise, ID 83702); 208-334-5988, 208-389-9096 (Fax), 8AM-5PM.

www2.state.id.us/dhw/hwgd_www/home.html

Indexing & Storage: Records are available on computer from July 1911-present.

Searching: Records are confidential for 100 years. Only immediate family or legal representative may receive records as well as those who have a notarized release from persons of record or an immediate family member. Include the following in your request-full name, names of parents, mother's maiden name, date of birth, place of birth, relationship to person of record, reason for information request. Also include a copy of a photo ID and sign the request. The following data is not released: adoption records or sealed records.

Access by: mail, fax, in person.

Fee & Payment: Requesters must include their signature and a copy of a driver's license or photo ID. Fee is $10.00 per name, add $10.00 per name requested for additional copies. Fee payee: Vital Statistics. Prepayment required. Credit cards accepted for fax requests only. Personal checks accepted. Credit cards accepted: Mastercard, Visa, AmEx, Discover.

Mail search: Turnaround time: 2-3 weeks. No self addressed stamped envelope is required.

Fax search: Fax requests require use of a credit card which is an additional $10.00 fee. They are processed within one week, unless express mail pre-paid, then process within 24 hours. Include a daytime phone number.

In person search: Turnaround time is 5-10 minutes.

Expedited service: Expedited service is available for fax searches. The fee is $20.00 plus cost of return express mail. Requests received by noon will be processed same day if pre-paid express delivery included or added to credit card charge; otherwise 1 week turnaround.

Death Records

State Department of Health, Center for Vital Statistics & Health Policy, PO Box 83720, Boise, ID 83720-0036 (Courier: 450 W State St, 1st Floor, Boise, ID 83702); 208-334-5988, 208-389-9096 (Fax), 8AM-5PM.

www2.state.id.us/dhw/hwgd_www/home.html

Indexing & Storage: Records are available from July 1911-present. Records are indexed on microfilm, inhouse computer.

Searching: Records are confidential for 50 years and are available only to family members or legal representatives or a person who has a notarized release form from persons of record or an immediate family member. Include the following in your request-full name, date of death, place of death, relationship to person of record, reason for information request.

Access by: mail, fax, in person.

Fee & Payment: Include a copy of your driver's license or photo ID and signature with request. The fee is $10.00 per name or additional copy. Fee payee: Vital Statistics. Prepayment required. Credit cards are accepted with fax requests only. Personal checks accepted. Credit cards accepted: Mastercard, Visa, AmEx, Discover.

Mail search: Turnaround time: 2-3 weeks. No self addressed stamped envelope is required.

Fax search: See expedited service.

In person search: Turnaround time is 5-10 minutes.

Expedited service: Expedited service is available for fax searches. Fee is an extra $10.00, processed by credit card and if received by noon will be sent the same day if arrangement made for overnight delivery, otherwise 1 week.

Marriage Certificates

State Department of Health, Center for Vital Statistics & Health Policy, PO Box 83720, Boise, ID 83720-0036 (Courier: 450 W State St, 1st Floor, Boise, ID 83702); 208-334-5988, 208-389-9096 (Fax), 8AM-5PM.

www2.state.id.us/dhw/hwgd_www/home.html

Indexing & Storage: Records are available from May 1947-present. Records are indexed on microfilm, inhouse computer.

Searching: Indexes are not available to the public for 50 years. Only immediate family members and legal representatives may obtain recent records, others may obtain records with a notarized release from a family member or person of record. Include the following in your request-names of husband and wife, date of marriage, place or county of marriage.

Access by: mail, fax, in person.

Fee & Payment: Include a copy of a photo ID or driver's license and a signature with request. The fee is $10.00 per name and per each additional copy. Fee payee: Vital Statistics. Prepayment required. Credit cards accepted with fax requests only. Personal checks accepted. Credit cards accepted: Mastercard, Visa, AmEx, Discover.

Mail search: Turnaround time: 2-3 weeks. No self addressed stamped envelope is required.

Fax search: See expedited service.

In person search: Turnaround time is 5-10 minutes.

Expedited service: Expedited service is available for fax searches. Expedited service is by fax service for an additional $10.00. If express delivery is desired, charges are added.

Divorce Records

State Department of Health, Center for Vital Statistics & Health Policy, PO Box 83720, Boise, ID 83720-0036 (Courier: 450 W State St, 1st Floor, Boise, ID 83702); 208-334-5988, 208-389-9096 (Fax), 8AM-5PM.

www2.state.id.us/dhw/hwgd_www/home.html

Note: This agency only maintains certificates of divorce; copies of decrees are available through the court system.

Indexing & Storage: Records are available from May 1947-present. New records are available for inquiry immediately. Records are indexed on microfilm, inhouse computer.

Searching: Indexes are not available to the public for 50 years and are available only to immediate family members, legal representatives, and a person with a notarzied signed release form from persons of record or immediate family. Include the following in your request-names of husband and wife, date of divorce, year divorce case began, case number (if known).

Access by: mail, fax, in person.

Fee & Payment: Include a copy of a driver's license or photo ID and include a signature with request. The fee is $10.00 per name. Fee payee: Vital Statistics. Prepayment required. Credit cards are accepted with fax requests only. Personal checks accepted. Credit cards accepted: Mastercard, Visa, AmEx, Discover.

Mail search: Turnaround time: 2-3 weeks. No self addressed stamped envelope is required.

Fax search: See expedited service.

In person search: Searching is available in person.

Expedited service: Expedited service is available for fax searches. Expedited service can be ordered by fax with a credit card for an additional $10.00 and costs of express delivery.

Workers' Compensation Records

Industrial Commission of Idaho, Attn: Records Management, PO Box 83720, Boise, ID 83720-0041; 208-334-6000, 208-334-2321 (Fax), 8AM-5PM.

www2.state.id.us/iic

Indexing & Storage: Records are available from 1917 on. New records are available for inquiry immediately. Records are indexed on microfilm, index cards, inhouse computer.

Searching: Must have a certified release form if you are not a party to the claim. Pre-employment screening companies must also provide an ADA certification and contingent job offer, and cannot get copies of files, only a work history report. Include the following in your request-claimant name, Social Security Number, date of accident and claim number. It is suggested to use their request form, found on the web site under Benefits Administration`. The following data is not released: psychiatric information.

Access by: mail, fax, in person.

Fee & Payment: Copy costs depend upon file size which are those that exceed 100 copied pages or 50 microfilmed pages. Larger files cost $.05 per page on paper and $.10 per page on microfilm. If file is off site, shipping fees of $2.00 per file apply. Fee payee: Industrial Commission. Charges that total under $5.00 are waived. Personal checks accepted. No credit cards accepted.

Mail search: Turnaround time: 3 days. There is a charge for postage. No self addressed stamped envelope is required.

Fax search: Fax searching available.

In person search: One may request information in person. However, not all files are available the same day because some files are not on site and must be ordered from storage.

Other access: There is no bulk data access as per Idaho law.

Driver Records

Idaho Transportation Department, Driver's Services, PO Box 34, Boise, ID 83731-0034 (Courier: 3311 W State, Boise, ID 83703); 208-334-8736, 208-334-8739 (Fax), 8:30AM-5PM.

www2.state.id.us/itd/dmv/ds.htm

Note: Copies of tickets may be available from the address listed above for a $4.00 fee per record.

Indexing & Storage: Records are available for at least 3 years for moving violations, DUIs and suspensions. Accidents are not shown on the record. It takes 1 day from receipt before new records are available for inquiry. Records are normally destroyed after 10 years and archived to tape.

Searching: Personal information is not released to casual requesters unless the requestor claims a valid authorization. The driver's license number and DOB are used for the primary search. If no record is found, a secondary search is performed using the name and DOB, or name and license number. The following data is not released: Social Security Numbers or medical information.

Access by: mail, fax, in person, online.

Fee & Payment: The fee is $4.00 per record. Convenience fees are added for online and batch searches. Fee payee: Idaho Transportation Department. Prepayment required. Ongoing requesters can set up an account. Personal checks accepted. Credit cards accepted: Mastercard, Visa.

Mail search: Turnaround time: 3-5 days. Mail-in requesters are asked to use the state form. No self addressed stamped envelope is required.

Fax search: Fax requests for records are accepted, if paid by a credit card or by account. Call 208-334-8761-set up an account.

In person search: Walk-in requesters may receive up to ten records while they wait, the rest are processed overnight.

Online search: Idaho offers on-line access (CICS) to the driver license files through its portal provider, Access Idaho. Fee is $4.00 per record. For more information, call 208-332-0102.

Other access: Idaho offers bulk retrieval of basic drivers license information with a signed contract. For information, call 208-334-8601

Vehicle Ownership
Vehicle Identification

Idaho Transportation Department, Vehicle Services, PO Box 34, Boise, ID 83731-0034 (Courier: 3311 W State St, Boise, ID 83707); 208-334-8773, 208-334-8542 (Fax), 8:30AM-5PM.

www2.state.id.us/itd/dmv/vs.htm

Indexing & Storage: Records are available from 1981. It takes 1 day before new records are available for inquiry.

Searching: Personal information is not released to casual requesters unless the requestor claims a valid authorization. Submit the name, VIN, license plate number for search, current address is also helpful. The following data is not released: Social Security Numbers or medical records.

Access by: mail, fax, in person, online.

Fee & Payment: The fee is $4.00 for current title with lien information or for a registration search. A complete title history (using the microfilm) is $8.00. Convenience fees are added for online and batch searches. Fee payee: Idaho Transportation Department. Prepayment required. Motor vehicle record accounts may be established by calling 208-334-8761. Personal checks accepted. Credit cards accepted: Mastercard, Visa.

Mail search: Turnaround time: 5-10 days. Information request forms are available. No self addressed stamped envelope is required.

Fax search: You may fax a request with a major credit card. Results, except for history records, can returned by fax for no additional fee. Turnaround time is three days.

In person search: You may request information in person.

Online search: Idaho offers online and batch access to registration and title files through its portal provider, Access Idaho. Records are $4.00

each plus a additional access fees. For more information, call 208-332-0102.

Other access: Idaho offers bulk retrieval of registration, ownership, and vehicle information with a signed contract. For more information, call 208-334-8601.

Accident Reports

Idaho Transportation Department, Office of Highway Safety-Accident Records, PO Box 7129, Boise, ID 83707-1129 (Courier: 3311 W State St, Boise, ID 83707); 208-334-8100, 208-334-4430 (Fax), 8AM-12:00PM; 1PM-5PM.

Indexing & Storage: Records are available from 1970's (on microfilm) to present. Starting in 2000, records are stored on an imaging system. It takes 4-5 weeks before new records are available for inquiry.

Searching: Include the following in your request-full name, date of accident, location of accident, driver's license number.

Access by: mail, phone, fax, in person.

Fee & Payment: The fee is $4.00 per report plus handling and tax. Fee payee: Idaho Transportation Department, Financial Control. Do not send a check with a request, you will be billed. Personal checks accepted. No credit cards accepted.

Mail search: Turnaround time: 2 weeks. A self addressed stamped envelope is requested.

Phone search: No fee for telephone request. Turnaround time: 2 weeks.

Fax search: Turnaround time 2 weeks.

In person search: It is suggested that walk-in requesters call first before going to department should the state have to locate the records on microfilm.

Other access: Computer files may be purchased with prepaid deposit plus computer charges. However, the file will not contain addresses, citation information, or drivers' license numbers.

Boat & Vessel Ownership
Boat & Vessel Registration

Idaho Parks & Recreation, PO Box 83720, Boise, ID 83720-0065 (Courier: 5657 Warm Springs, Boise, ID 83712); 208-334-4199, 208-334-3741 (Fax), 8AM-5PM.

www.idahoparks.org

Note: Liens must be searched at the UCC Division at the Secretary of State office.

Indexing & Storage: Records are available from 1987-present. Older records are available, but to search them, you must know the registration #.

Records are indexed on computer. All boats with motors and/or sails must be registered.

Searching: To search, a signed release is required along with one of the following: owner's name, hull #, or registration #.

Access by: mail, in person.

Fee & Payment: There is no search fee.

Mail search: Turnaround time: 2-3 weeks. No self addressed stamped envelope is required.

In person search: This is the preferred method.

Legislation-Current/Pending
Legislation-Passed

Legislative Services Office, Research and Legislation, PO Box 83720, Boise, ID 83720-0054 (Courier: 700 W Jefferson, Lower Level, East, Boise, ID 83720); 208-334-2475, 208-334-2125 (Fax), 8AM-5PM.

www.state.id.us/legislat/legislat.html

Note: Sessions are from January to the end of March.

Indexing & Storage: Records are available from 1971-present. The current and previous year are available on the Internet.

Searching: Include the following in your request-bill number. During session, current bills are in the mailroom on the lower level, State Capitol Bldg.

Access by: mail, phone, fax, in person, online.

Fee & Payment: There is no charge unless the bill is very long. The first 10 pages are free and the fee for pages in excess of 10 is $.20 per page. They will compute the charge. Fee payee: Legislative Services. Will bill for copy charges. Personal checks accepted. No credit cards accepted.

Mail search: Turnaround time: 3 days. Turnaround time may be longer from December through April. No self addressed stamped envelope is required.

Phone search: You may call for information. Information can be returned using your Fedex account number.

Fax search: Same criteria as phone searches. Up to 15 pages can be returned by fax.

In person search: You may request information in person.

Online search: Statutes, bill information, and subject are available from the web site. They also will answer questions via e-mail. (kford@lso.state.id.us)

Voter Registration
Records not maintained by a state level agency.

Note: Records are maintained by the County Clerks. The counties will generally release name, address, and voting precinct on individual request.

GED Certificates

Department of Education, GED Testing, PO Box 83720, Boise, ID 83720-0027; 208-332-6980, 208-334-4664 (Fax), 8AM-5PM.

www.sde.state.id.us

Searching: Include the following in your request-Social Security Number, date of birth. A signed release is necessary for copies of transcripts or for scores.

Access by: mail, phone, fax, in person.

Mail search: Turnaround time: 2-3 days. No self addressed stamped envelope is required. No fee for mail request.

Phone search: No fee for telephone request. Verification only over the phone.

Fax search: Turnaround time is 1 day.

In person search: No fee for request. Information is released immediately.

Hunting License Information
Fishing License Information

Fish & Game Department, Fish & Game Licenses Division, PO Box 25, Boise, ID 83707-0025 (Courier: 1075 Park Blvd, Boise, ID 83707); 208-334-3717 (License Department), 208-334-3736 (Enforcement Office), 208-334-2114 (Fax), 8AM-5PM.

www.state.id.us/fishgame/fishgame.html

Note: The license division says that if you want an individual name, you must call the Enforcement Office. This office will not release individual records with addresses, they will only confirm is there is a license issued.

Indexing & Storage: Records are available from January 1993-present.

Searching: Use of their request form is required.

Access by: mail, phone, in person.

Fee & Payment: There is no fee unless the search is extensive.

Mail search: Turnaround time: variable. No self addressed stamped envelope is required.

Phone search: They will only confirm.

In person search: Searching is available in person.

Licenses Searchable Online

Attorney #29	www2.state.id.us/isb/roster_search.htm
Bank #21	www2.state.id.us/finance/idbklst.htm
Collection Agency/Collector #21	www2.state.id.us/finance/icc/icclist.htm
Consumer Loans & Credit Sale #21	www2.state.id.us/finance/icc/icclist.htm
Credit Union #21	www2.state.id.us/finance/culist.htm
Dental Hygienist #13	www2.state.id.us/isbd/isbdqry.htm
Dentist #13	www2.state.id.us/isbd/isbdqry.htm
Electrical Inspector/Contractor #10	www2.state.id.us/dbs
Engineer #17	www.state.id.us/ipels/pelsnumb.htm
Finance Company #21	www2.state.id.us/finance/icc/icclist.htm
Guide #15	www.state.id.us/oglb/oglbhome.htm
Investment Advisor #21	www2.state.id.us/finance/culist.htm
Lobbyist #28	www.idsos.state.id.us/elect/lobbyist/lobinfo.htm
Mortgage Broker/Banker #21	www2.state.id.us/finance/mort/mortlist.htm
Mortgage Company #21	www2.state.id.us/finance/mort/mortlist.htm
Optometrist #19	www.arbo.org/nodb2000/licsearch.asp
Oral Surgeon #13	www2.state.id.us/isbd/isbdqry.htm
Orthodontist #13	www2.state.id.us/isbd/isbdqry.htm
Outfitter #15	www.state.id.us/oglb/oglbhome.htm
Public Accountant-CPA #12	www2.state.id.us/boa/HTM/cpalist.htm
Public Accountant-LPA #12	www2.state.id.us/boa/HTM/lpalist.htm
Savings & Loan Association #21	www2.state.id.us/finance/s&l-lst.htm
Securities Broker/Dealers Seller & Issuer #21	www2.state.id.us/finance/sec/seclist.htm
Surveyor #17	www.state.id.us/ipels/pelsnumb.htm
Trust Company #21	www2.state.id.us/finance/idbklst.htm#trust

Licensing Quick Finder

Aquaculture (Commercial) #20	208-332-8500
Architect #19	208-334-3233
Artificial Inseminator #20	208-332-8500
Asbestos Worker #10	208-334-2129
Athletic Trainer #30	208-334-2822
Attorney #29	208-344-4500
Bakery #11	208-327-7499
Bank #21	208-332-8005
Barber School Instructor #19	208-334-3233
Barber/Shop/School #19	208-334-3233
Bed & Breakfast #11	208-327-7450
Beekeeper #20	208-332-8500
Boiler Inspector #10	208-334-2129
Boiler Safety Code #10	208-334-2129
Bottling Plant #11	208-327-7450
Boxer #32	208-334-3888
Brewery License #25	208-334-7060
Brokerage Dealer #12	208-334-2490
Building Inspector #10	208-334-3950
Chemigator #20	208-332-8500
Child Care Institution/Agency #07	208-334-5700
Child Care Licensure #07	208-334-5700
Chiropractor #19	208-334-3233
Clinical Laboratory Registration #02	208-334-2235
Clinical Nurse Specialist #14	208-334-3110 X34
Collection Agency/Collector #21	208-332-8002
Collector/Solicitor #21	208-332-8002
Commercial Applicator #20	208-332-8500
Commercial Feed Manufacturer #20	208-332-8500
Commercial Fertilizer Manufacturer #20	208-332-8500
Commercial Fishing #22	208-334-3717
Commission Merchant #20	208-332-8500
Commodity Dealer #20	208-332-8500
Consumer Loans & Credit Sale #21	208-332-8002
Contractor #31	208-327-7326
Controlled Substance #16	208-334-2356
Cosmetologist, Salon, School #19	208-334-3233
Cosmetology Instructor #19	208-334-3233
Counselor #19	208-334-3233
Credit Union #21	208-332-8003
Crematory #03	208-334-3233
Dairy Product Processor/Milk Hauler/Dairy Farm #20	208-332-8500
Day Care Center Inspector #11	208-327-7499
Day Care Center/Home #07	208-334-5700
Dental Assistant #13	208-334-2369
Dental Hygienist #13	208-334-2369
Dentist #13	208-334-2369
Denturist #19	208-334-3233
Dietitian #30	208-334-2822
Director of Special Education #05	208-332-6800
Domestic & Mutual Insurer #24	208-334-4250
Drug Manufacturer #16	208-334-2356
Drug Outlet (i.e. Nursing Home) #16	208-334-2356
Drug Repackaging #16	208-334-2356
Drug Store/Pharmacy #16	208-334-2356
Drug Wholesaler #16	208-334-2356
Egg Distributor/Grader #20	208-332-8500
Electrical Inspector/Contracto#10	208-334-3950
Electrolysis #19	208-334-3233
Elevator Installation & Repairmen #10	208-334-2129
Emergency Medical Technician #09	208-334-5500
Engineer #17	208-334-3860
Environmental Health Specialist #19	208-334-3233
Esthetician #19	208-334-3233
Euthanasia Agency #01	208-332-8588
Euthanasia Technician #01	208-332-8588
Exceptional Child School Program Advisor #05	208-332-6800
Farm Produce Dealer/Broker #20	208-332-8500
Finance Company #21	208-332-8002
Fire Sprinkler System Contractor #23	208-334-4370
Florist/Nurseryman #20	208-332-8500
Food Processing/Manufacturing Plant #11	208-327-7499
Food Warehouse, Cold Storage #11	208-327-7499
Foreign & Alien Insurer #24	208-334-4250
Foster Home #07	208-334-5700
Funeral Establishment #03	208-334-3233
Fur Buyer #22	208-334-3717
Game Farm #22	208-334-3717
Geologist #18	208-334-2268
Grocery Store #11	208-327-7499
Guide #15	208-327-7380
Handling of Critical Material #11	208-327-7499
Hearing Aid Dealer/Fitter #19	208-334-3233
Horse Racing #33	208-884-7080
Hospital #08	208-334-5500
Insurance Agent #24	208-334-4250
Insurance Agent Corporation or Partnership #24	208-334-4250
Insurance Broker License #24	208-334-4250
Intermediate Care Facility for Mentally Retarded #08	208-334-5500
Investment Advisor #21	208-332-8004
Jr. Trapper #22	208-334-3717
Labor Relations #10	208-332-7452
Landscape Architect #19	208-334-3233
Livestock Auction Market #20	208-332-8500
Livestock Brand #25	208-884-7070
Loan Agent #12	208-334-2490
Loan Collection Officer #12	208-334-2490
Lobbyist #28	208-334-2852
Logging #10	208-334-6000
Mail Service Pharmacy #16	208-334-2356
Mammography #02	208-334-2235
Manufactured Commercial Building #10	208-334-3950
Manufactured Homes & Housing #10	208-334-3950
Manufactured Housing Dealer/Broker/Manufacturer #10	208-334-3950
Manufactured Recreational Vehicle #10	208-334-3950
Medical Doctor #30	208-334-2822
Medical Resident #30	208-334-2822
Milk Storage & Handling of Milk & Dairy Product #20	208-332-8500
Mine Safety Training #10	208-334-3950
Mixer-Loader #20	208-332-8500
Mortgage Broker/Banker #21	208-332-8004
Mortgage Company #21	208-332-8004
Mortician #19	208-334-3233
Mortician License #03	208-334-3233
Mortician Resident Trainee #03	208-334-3233
Non-Pharmacy Drug Sales (i.e. Grocery Store) #16	208-334-2356
Non-resident Insurance Agent #24	208-334-4320

Notary Public #28.............................208-334-2810
Nurse #14......................................208-334-3110 X34
Nurse Anesthetist #14 ....208-334-3110 X25
Nurse Midwife #14 ....208-334-3110 X34
Nurse-LPN #14................................208-334-3110
Nursing Assistant #14 208-334-3110
Nursing Home Administrator #19 208-334-3233
Occupational Therapist/Assistant #30 ...208-334-2822
Optometrist #19 208-334-3233
Oral Surgeon #13............................208-334-2369
Organic Certification #20 208-332-8500
Orthodontist #13 208-334-2369
Osteopathic Physician #30 208-334-2822
Outfitter #15...................................208-327-7380
Paramedic (EMT) #09 208-334-5500
Peace Officer #25 208-884-7000
Pest Control Consultant #20 208-332-8500
Pesticide Applicator/Operator/Dealer/Manufacturer #20
....208-332-8500
Pharmacist, Intern, Preceptor #16........208-334-2356
Physical Therapist/Assistant #30 208-334-2822
Physician Assistant #30...................208-334-2822
Plumbing Inspector/Contractor #10....208-334-3950
Podiatrist #19.................................208-334-3233
Private Applicator #20 208-332-8500
Professional Counselor #19................208-334-3233

Psychologist #19.............................208-334-3233
Public Accountant-CPA #12...................208-334-2490
Public Accountant-LPA #12 208-334-2490
Public Commodity Warehouse #20 208-332-8500
Radiation Equipment #03 208-334-3945
Real Estate Appraiser #19.................208-334-3233
Rehabilitation Facility #08..................208-334-5500
Residential Care Administrator #19....208-334-3233
Residential Care Facility #08 208-334-5500
Residential School #07.....................208-334-5700
Respiratory Therapist #30 208-334-2822
Restaurant Sanitation Standard #11 208-327-7499
Retail Beer & Wine License #25 208-884-7060
Retail Liquor License #25 208-884-7060
Rotary Driller #26............................208-327-7900
Savings & Loan Association #21.........208-332-8005
School Counselor #05.......................208-332-6800
School Nurse #05.............................208-332-6800
School Principal #05.........................208-332-6800
School Superintendent #05 208-332-6800
Securities Broker/Dealer #21.............208-332-8004
Seed Company #20 208-332-8500
Septic Tank Pumper #11 208-327-7499
Shooting Preserve #22.....................208-334-3717
Shorthand Reporter #04 208-334-2517
Skilled Nursing Care Facility #08 208-334-5500

Social Worker #19............................208-334-3233
Soil & Plant Amendment Manufacturer #20
....208-332-8500
Substance Abuse Treatment Center #07
....208-334-5700
Subsurface Sewage Installer #11.........208-327-7499
Surveyor #17..................................208-334-3860
Swimming Pool Installer #11.............208-327-7499
Taxidermist #22 208-334-3717
Teacher #05....................................208-332-6800
Trapper #22 208-334-3736
Trust Company #21.........................208-332-8005
Utility Regulation #27 208-334-0300
Veterinarian #01.............................208-332-8588
Veterinary Drug Outlet & Technician #16
....208-334-2356
Veterinary Technician #01 208-332-8588
Water Laboratory #02.......................208-334-2235
Water Rights Examiner #26 208-327-7900
Water Well Driller #26 208-327-7900
Weighmaster #20............................208-332-8500
Wholesale Beer & Wine License #25 208-884-7060
Winery #25 208-884-7060
Wrestler #32 208-334-3888
X-ray Equipment #02.........................208-334-2235

Licensing Agency Information

01 Board of Veterinary Medicine, PO Box 7249 (PO Box 7249), Boise, ID 83707; 208-332-8588, Fax: 208-334-4062.

02 Bureau of Laboratories, 2220 Old Penitentiary Rd, Boise, ID 83712; 208-334-2235.

03 Bureau of Occupational Licenses, Mortician Board of Examiners, 1109 Main St, #220, Boise, ID 83702-5642; 208-334-3233, Fax: 208-334-3945.

http://www2.state.id.us/ibol The ability to search is planned. Once available, you should be able to access it from the following web address: http://www2.state.id.us/ibol/mor.htm.

04 Certified Shorthand Reporters Board, 550 W State St, Boise, ID 83720-0017; 208-334-2517.

05 Department of Education, PO Box 83720 (PO Box 83720), Boise, ID 83720-0027; 208-332-6800, Fax: 208-334-4664.

07 Department of Health & Welfare, 450 W State St, 10th Fl, Boise, ID 83720; 208-334-5700, Fax: 208-334-6558.

08 Department of Health & Welfare, Division of Environmental Quality, 1410 N Hilton, Boise, ID 83706-1255; 208-373-0502, Fax: 208-373-0342.

www.state.id.us/DEQ

09 Department of Health & Welfare, 450 W State St, Boise, ID 83720; 208-334-5500, Fax: 208-334-4015.

10 Division of Building Safety, PO Box 83720 (PO Box 83720), Boise, ID 83720-0048; 208-334-3950, Fax: 208-334-2683.

http://www2.state.id.us/dbs/dbs.html

11 Environmental Health Department, Bakery & Related Licensing, 707 N Armstrong Place, Boise, ID 83704; 208-327-7450, Fax: 208-327-8553.

12 Board of Accountancy, PO Box 83720 (1109 Main #470), Boise, ID 83702-0002; 208-334-2490, Fax: 208-334-2615.

www2.state.id.us/boa

13 Board of Dentistry, PO Box 83720, Boise, ID 83720-0021; 208-334-2369, Fax: 208-334-3247.

www2.state.id.us/isbd

Direct URL to search licenses: www2.state.id.us/isbd/isbdqry.htm You can search online using status, name, city and license number.

14 Board of Nursing, 280 N 8th St #210, Boise, ID 83720; 208-334-3110, Fax: 208-334-3262.

www.state.id.us/ibn/ibnhome.htm

15 Board of Outfitters & Guides, 1365 N Orchard St, Rm 172, Boise, ID 83706; 208-327-7380, Fax: 208-327-7382.

www.state.id.us/oglb/oglbhome.htm

Direct URL to search licenses: www.state.id.us/oglb/oglbhome.htm You can search online using type and unit. Scroll to the bottom of the page to find the appropriate links for searching.

16 Board of Pharmacy, PO Box 83720 (280 N 8th St, #204), Boise, ID 83720-0067; 208-334-2356, Fax: 208-334-3536.

www.state.id.us/bop

17 Board of Professional Engineers & Surveyors, 600 S Orchard, #A, Boise, ID 83705; 208-334-3860, Fax: 208-334-2008.

www.state.id.us/ipels/index.htm

Direct URL to search licenses: www.state.id.us/ipels/pelsnumb.htm You can search online using name and license number.

18 Board of Professional Geologists, 550 W State St, Boise, ID 83720-0033; 208-334-2268.

19 Bureau of Occupational Licenses, 1109 Main St, Owyhee Plaza, #220, Boise, ID 83702; 208-334-3233, Fax: 208-334-3945.

www.state.id.us/ibol/boards.htm

20 Department of Agriculture, 2270 Old Penitentiary Rd, Boise, ID 83712; 208-332-8500.

www.agri.state.id.us/agresource/licensing.htm

21 Department of Finance, PO Box 83720 (700 W State St), Boise, ID 83720-0031; 208-332-8000, Fax: 208-332-8098.

www.state.id.us/finance/dof.htm

22 Department of Fish & Game, PO Box 25 (PO Box 25), Boise, ID 83707; 208-334-3700, Fax: 208-334-2114.

www.state.id.us/fishgame

23 Department of Insurance, PO Box 83720 (700 W State St, 3rd Fl), Boise, ID 83720-0043; 208-334-4370, Fax: 208-334-4375.

24 Department of Insurance, PO Box 30254 (7150 Harris Dr), Boise, ID 83720-0043; 208-334-4250, Fax: 208-334-4398.

25 State Police, PO Box 700 (PO Box 700), Meridian, ID 83680; 208-884-7000, Fax: 208-884-7098.

26 Department of Water Resources, 1301 N Orchard St, Boise, ID 83706; 208-327-7900, Fax: 208-327-7866.

www.idwr.state.id.us

27 Public Utilities Commission, 472 W Washington St, Boise, ID 83702; 208-334-0300, Fax: 208-334-3762.

28 Secretary of State, Rm 203, Statehouse, PO Box 83720, Boise, ID 83720; 208-334-2300, Fax: 208-334-2282.

www.idsos.state.id.us

Direct URL to search licenses: www.idsos.state.id.us You can search online using surname, company name

29 State Bar, PO Box 895 (PO Box 895), Boise, ID 83701; 208-334-4500, Fax: 208-334-4515.
www.state.id.us/isb

30 Board of Medicine, PO Box 83720 (280 N 8th St #202), Boise, ID 83720-0058; 208-334-2822, Fax: 208-334-2801.

31 Public Works Contractors Board, PO Box 83720 (PO Box 83720), Boise, ID 83720-0073; 208-327-7326, Fax: 208-327-7377.

32 State Athletic Department, 10 S Lath, #208, Boise, ID 83705; 208-334-3888, Fax: 208-345-1145.

33 Horse Racing Commission, PO Box 700 (700 Stratford Dr), Meridian, ID 83642; 208-884-7080, Fax: 208-884-7098.

www.state.id.us/race

The following list indicates the district and division name for each county in the state. If the district or division name of the bankruptcy court is different from the civil/criminal court, it appears in parentheses.

County/Court Cross Reference

County	District/Division	County	District/Division
Ada	Boise	Gem	Boise
Adams	Boise	Gooding	Boise
Bannock	Pocatello	Idaho	Pocatello (Moscow)
Bear Lake	Pocatello	Jefferson	Pocatello
Benewah	Coeur d' Alene	Jerome	Boise
Bingham	Pocatello	Kootenai	Coeur d' Alene
Blaine	Boise	Latah	Moscow
Boise	Boise	Lemhi	Pocatello
Bonner	Coeur d' Alene	Lewis	Moscow
Bonneville	Pocatello	Lincoln	Boise
Boundary	Coeur d' Alene	Madison	Pocatello
Butte	Pocatello	Minidoka	Boise
Camas	Boise	Nez Perce	Moscow
Canyon	Boise	Oneida	Pocatello
Caribou	Pocatello	Owyhee	Boise
Cassia	Boise	Payette	Boise
Clark	Pocatello	Power	Pocatello
Clearwater	Moscow	Shoshone	Coeur d' Alene
Custer	Pocatello	Teton	Pocatello
Elmore	Boise	Twin Falls	Boise
Franklin	Pocatello	Valley	Boise
Fremont	Pocatello	Washington	Boise

US District Court

District of Idaho

Boise Division MSC 039, Federal Bldg, 550 W Fort St, Room 400, Boise, ID 83724, 208-334-1361, Fax: 208-334-9362.

www.id.uscourts.gov

Counties: Ada, Adams, Blaine, Boise, Camas, Canyon, Cassia, Elmore, Gem, Gooding, Jerome, Lincoln, Minidoka, Owyhee, Payette, Twin Falls, Valley, Washington.

Indexing & Storage: Cases are indexed by defendant and plaintiff as well as by case number. New cases are available in the index immediately after filing date. Both computer and card indexes are maintained. Open records are located at this court.

Fee & Payment: The fee is $15.00 per item (one party name or case number). Payment may be made by money order, cashier check, personal check. Prepayment is only required for large requests. Payee: US District Court Clerk. Certification fee: $5.00 per document. Copy fee: $.50 per page.

Phone Search: All public information will be released over the phone. An automated voice case information service (VCIS) is not available.

Fax Search: Handled same as mail request. Check will Court Copy Service.

Mail Search: A stamped self addressed envelope is not required.

In Person Search: In person searching is available.

PACER: Sign-up number is 208-334-9342. Access fee is No charge. Case records are available back to January 1990. Records are purged varies. New civil records are available online after 2 days. New criminal records are available online after 1 day.

Opinions Online: Court opinions are available online at www.id.uscourts.gov

Other Online Access: You can search records on the Internet using RACER. Currently the system is free and requires free registration. Simply visit www.id.uscourts.gov/wconnect/wc.dll?usdc_racer~main.

Coeur d' Alene Division c/o Boise Division, MSD 039, Federal Bldg, 550 W Fort St, Room 400, Boise, ID 83724, 208-334-1361.

www.id.uscourts.gov

Counties: Benewah, Bonner, Boundary, Kootenai, Shoshone.

Indexing & Storage: Cases are indexed by as well as by case number. New cases are available in the index after filing date. Open records are located at the Division.

Fee & Payment: The fee is $15.00 per item (one party name or case number). Payment may be made by money order, cashier check. Business checks are not accepted. Personal checks are not accepted.

Phone Search: An automated voice case information service (VCIS) is not available.

Mail Search: Always enclose a stamped self addressed envelope.

In Person Search: In person searching is available.

PACER: Sign-up number is 208-334-9342. Access fee is No charge. Case records are available back to January 1990. Records are purged varies. New civil records are available online after 2 days. New criminal records are available online after 1 day.

Opinions Online: Court opinions are available online at www.id.uscourts.gov

Other Online Access: You can search records on the Internet using RACER. Currently the system is free and requires free registration. Simply visit www.id.uscourts.gov/wconnect/wc.dll?usdc_racer~main.

Moscow Division c/o Boise Division, PO Box 039, Federal Bldg, 550 W Fort St, Boise, ID 83724, 208-334-1361.

www.id.uscourts.gov

Counties: Clearwater, Latah, Lewis, Nez Perce.

Indexing & Storage: Cases are indexed by as well as by case number. New cases are available in the index after filing date. Open records are located at the Division.

Fee & Payment: The fee is $15.00 per item (one party name or case number). Payment may be made by money order, cashier check. Business checks are not accepted. Personal checks are not accepted.

Phone Search: Searching is not available by phone.

Mail Search: Always enclose a stamped self addressed envelope.

In Person Search: In person searching is available.

PACER: Sign-up number is 208-334-9342. Access fee is No charge. Case records are available back to January 1990. Records are purged varies. New civil records are available online after 2 days. New criminal records are available online after 1 day.

Opinions Online: Court opinions are available online at www.id.uscourts.gov

Other Online Access: You can search records on the Internet using RACER. Currently the system is free and requires free registration. Simply visit www.id.uscourts.gov/wconnect/wc.dll?usdc_racer ~main.

Pocatello Division c/o Boise Division, 801 E Sherman, 550 W Fort St, Pocatello, ID 83201, 208-478-4123.

www.id.uscourts.gov

Counties: Bannock, Bear Lake, Bingham, Bonneville, Butte, Caribou, Clark, Custer, Franklin, Fremont, Idaho, Jefferson, Lemhi, Madison, Oneida, Power, Teton.

Indexing & Storage: Cases are indexed by as well as by case number. New cases are available in the index after filing date. Open records are located at the Division.

Fee & Payment: The fee is $15.00 per item (one party name or case number). Payment may be made by money order, cashier check. Business checks are not accepted. Personal checks are not accepted.

Phone Search: Searching is not available by phone.

Mail Search: Always enclose a stamped self addressed envelope.

In Person Search: In person searching is available.

PACER: Sign-up number is 208-334-9342. Access fee is No charge. Case records are available back to January 1990. Records are purged varies. New civil records are available online after 2 days. New criminal records are available online after 1 day.

Opinions Online: Court opinions are available online at www.id.uscourts.gov

Other Online Access: You can search records on the Internet using RACER. Currently the system is free and requires free registration. Simply visit www.id.uscourts.gov/wconnect/wc.dll?usdc_racer ~main.

US Bankruptcy Court

District of Idaho

Boise Division MSC 042, US Courthouse, 550 W Fort St, Room 400, Boise, ID 83724, 208-334-1074, Fax: 208-334-9362.

www.id.uscourts.gov

Counties: Ada, Adams, Blaine, Boise, Camas, Canyon, Cassia, Elmore, Gem, Gooding, Jerome, Lincoln, Minidoka, Owyhee, Payette, Twin Falls, Valley, Washington.

Indexing & Storage: Cases are indexed by debtor as well as by case number. New cases are available in the index immediately after filing date. A computer index is maintained. Open records are located at this court.

Fee & Payment: The fee is $15.00 per item (one party name or case number). Payment may be made by money order, cashier check. Business checks are not accepted. Personal checks are not accepted. Prepayment is required. Make all search and copy arrangements with private vendor Court Copy Services, 208-334-9463. Payee: Coourt Copy Services. Certification fee: $5.00 per document. Copy fee: $.25 per page. The fee for copies made by court personnel is $.50 per page.

Phone Search: Only docket information is available by phone. An automated voice case information service (VCIS) is available.

Fax Search: Fax requests are handled by a copy service. Call 208-334-9463 to arrange a fax request.

Mail Search: A stamped self addressed envelope is not required.

In Person Search: In person searching is available.

PACER: Sign-up number is 208-334-9342. Access fee is No charge. Case records are available back to September 1990. Records are purged immediately when case closed. New civil records are available online after 1 day.

Opinions Online: Court opinions are available online at www.id.uscourts.gov

Other Online Access: You can search records on the Internet using RACER. Currently the system is free and requires free registration. Simply visit www.id.uscourts.gov/wconnect/wc.dll?usbc_racer ~main. Fednet also available; to access, dial 208-334-9476.

Coeur d' Alene Division 205 N 4th St, 2nd Floor, Coeur d'Alene, ID 83814, 208-664-4925, Fax: 208-765-0270.

www.id.uscourts.gov

Counties: Benewah, Bonner, Boundary, Kootenai, Shoshone.

Indexing & Storage: Cases are indexed by debtor as well as by case number. New cases are available in the index immediately after filing date. A computer index is maintained. Open records are located at this court.

Fee & Payment: The fee is $15.00 per item (one party name or case number). Payment may be made by money order, cashier check, business check. Personal checks are not accepted. Prepayment is required. Payee: US Bankruptcy Court. Certification fee: $5.00 per document. Copy fee: $.50 per page.

Phone Search: Only docket information is available by phone. An automated voice case information service (VCIS) is available.

Fax Search: Fax search handled same as mail.

Mail Search: Always enclose a stamped self addressed envelope.

In Person Search: In person searching is available.

PACER: Sign-up number is 208-334-9342. Access fee is No charge. Case records are available back to September 1990. Records are purged immediately when case closed. New civil records are available online after 1 day.

Opinions Online: Court opinions are available online at www.id.uscourts.gov

Other Online Access: You can search records on the Internet using RACER. Currently the system is free and requires free registration. Simply visit www.id.uscourts.gov/wconnect/wc.dll?usbc_racer ~main.

Moscow Division 220 E 5th St, Moscow, ID 83843, 208-882-7612, Fax: 208-883-1576.

www.id.uscourts.gov

Counties: Clearwater, Idaho, Latah, Lewis, Nez Perce.

Indexing & Storage: Cases are indexed by debtor as well as by case number. New cases are available in the index immediately after filing date. A computer index is maintained. Open records are located at this court.

Fee & Payment: The fee is $15.00 per item (one party name or case number). Payment may be made by money order, cashier check, business check. Personal checks are not accepted. Prepayment is required. Payee: US Bankruptcy Court. Certification fee: $5.00 per document. Copy fee: $.50 per page.

Phone Search: Only docket information is available by phone. An automated voice case information service (VCIS) is available.

Mail Search: Always enclose a stamped self addressed envelope.

In Person Search: In person searching is available.

PACER: Sign-up number is 208-334-9342. Access fee is No charge. Case records are available back to September 1990. Records are purged immediately when case closed. New civil records are available online after 1 day.

Opinions Online: Court opinions are available online at www.id.uscourts.gov

Other Online Access: You can search records on the Internet using RACER. Currently the system is free and requires free registration. Simply visit www.id.uscourts.gov/wconnect/wc.dll?usbc_racer ~main. Fednet also available; to access, dial 208-334-9476.

Pocatello Division 801 E Sherman, Pocatello, ID 83201, 208-478-4123, Fax: 208-478-4106.

www.id.uscourts.gov

Counties: Bannock, Bear Lake, Bingham, Bonneville, Butte, Caribou, Clark, Custer, Franklin, Fremont, Jefferson, Lemhi, Madison, Oneida, Power, Teton.

Indexing & Storage: Cases are indexed by debtor as well as by case number. New cases are available in the index immediately after filing date. A computer index is maintained. Open records are located at this court. No cases have been sent to the Federal Records Center yet.

Fee & Payment: The fee is $15.00 per item (one party name or case number). Payment may be made by money order, cashier check, business check. Personal checks are not accepted. Copy service will bill after first order. Payee: US Bankruptcy Court. Certification fee: $5.00 per document. Copy fee: $.50 per page.

Phone Search: Only docket information is available by phone. A VCIS is available.

Fax Search: Fax searching available with a deposit account. Call for special procedures. Copy service will fax documents at $.50 per page.

Mail Search: Always enclose an SASE.

In Person Search: In person searching is available.

PACER: Sign-up number is 208-334-9342. Access fee is No charge. Case records are available back to September 1990. Records are purged immediately when case closed. New civil records are available online after 1 day.

Opinions Online: Court opinions are available online at www.id.uscourts.gov

Other Online Access: You can search records on the Internet using RACER. Currently the system is free and requires free registration. Simply visit www.id.uscourts.gov/wconnect/wc.dll?usbc_racer ~main.

Court	Jurisdiction	No. of Courts	How Organized
District Courts*	General		7 Districts
Magistrates Division*	Limited	3	7 Districts
Combined Courts*		44	

* Profiled in this Sourcebook.

Court	CIVIL								
	Tort	Contract	Real Estate	Min. Claim	Max. Claim	Small Claims	Estate	Eviction	Domestic Relations
District Courts*	X	X	X	$0	No Max				
Magistrates Division*	X	X	X	$0	$10,000	$3000	X	X	X

Court	CRIMINAL				
	Felony	Misdemeanor	DWI/DUI	Preliminary Hearing	Juvenile
District Courts*	X	X	X	X	
Magistrates. Division*		.	X	X	X

ADMINISTRATION   Administrative Director of Courts, Supreme Court Building, 451 W State St, Boise, ID, 83720; 208-334-2246, Fax: 208-334-2146
www.idwr.state.id.us/judicial/judicial.html

COURT STRUCTURE   The District Court oversees felony and most civil cases. Small claims are handled by the Magistrate Division of the District Court. Probate is handled by the Magistrate Division of the District Court.

ONLINE ACCESS   There is no statewide computer system offering external access. ISTARS is a statewide intra-court/intra-agency system run and managed by the State Supreme Court. All counties are on ISTARS, and all courts provide public access terminals on-site.

ADDITIONAL INFORMATION   A statewide court administrative rule states that record custodians do not have a duty to "compile or summarize information contained in a record, nor ... to create new records for the requesting party." Under this rule, some courts will not perform searches.

Many courts require a signed release for employment record searches.

The following fees are mandated statewide: Search Fee - none; Certification Fee - $1.00 per document plus copy fee; Copy Fee - $1.00 per page. Not all jurisdictions currently follow these guidelines.

Ada County

District & Magistrate Courts-I 514 W. Jefferson St, Boise, ID 83702-5931; 208-364-2000. Hours: 8:30AM-5PM (MST). *Felony, Misdemeanor, Civil, Eviction, Small Claims, Probate.*

www2.state.is.us/fourthjudicial

Civil Records: Access: Mail, in person. Both court and visitors may perform in person searches. No search fee. Required to search: name, years to search; also helpful-address. Civil cases indexed by defendant, plaintiff. Civil records on computer since 1985, microfiche and docket books from 1860s. **Criminal Records:** Access: Mail, in person. Both court and visitors may perform in person searches. No search fee. Required to search: name, years to search; also helpful-address, DOB, SSN. Criminal records on computer since 1985, microfiche and docket books from 1860s. **General Information:** No juvenile, adoption, child protection records released. SASE required. Turnaround time 1-7 days. Copy fee: $1.00 per page. Certification fee: $1.00 per page. Fee payee:

Ada County. Personal checks accepted. Public access terminal is available.

Ada County Traffic Court 7180 Barrister, Boise, ID 83704; 208-327-5352. Hours: 8AM-5PM (MST). *Misdemeanor.* **Criminal Records:** Access: Mail, in person. Both court and visitors may perform in person searches. No search fee. Required to search: name, years to search; also helpful-address, DOB, SSN. Criminal records on computer from 1985, microfiche from 1983, docket books back to statehood. **General Information:** No alcohol level or confidential evaluation records released. SASE required. Turnaround time up to 1-2 weeks. Copy fee: $1.00 per page. Certification fee: $1.50. Fee payee: Ada County. Personal checks accepted. Prepayment is required. Public access terminal is available.

Adams County

District & Magistrate Courts PO Box 48, Council, ID 83612; 208-253-4561/4233; Fax: 208-253-4880. Hours: 8AM-Noon, 1-5PM (MST). *Felony, Misdemeanor, Civil, Eviction, Small Claims, Probate.*

Civil Records: Access: Fax, mail, in person. Both court and visitors may perform in person searches. No search fee. Required to search: name, years to search. Civil cases indexed by defendant, plaintiff. Civil records on computer from 1993, microfiche from 1972, docket books from 1911. **Criminal Records:** Access: Fax, mail, in person. Both court and visitors may perform in person searches. No search fee. Required to search: name, years to search, signed release. Criminal records on computer from 1993, microfiche from 1972, docket books from 1911. Submit DOB and/or SSN. **General Information:** No juvenile, sealed cases records released. SASE requested. Turnaround time 2 days. Copy fee: $1.00 per page. Certification fee: $1.00. Fee payee: Adams County. Personal checks accepted. Prepayment is required. Public access terminal is available. Fax notes: $4.00 per page.

Bannock County

District & Magistrate Courts PO Box 4847, Pocatello, ID 83205; 208-236-7350, 7351, 7352; Fax: 208-236-7013. Hours: 8AM-5PM

(MST). *Felony, Misdemeanor, Civil, Eviction, Small Claims, Probate.*

www.co.bannock.id.us/clkcrt1.htm

Civil Records: Access: Fax, mail, in person. Both court and visitors may perform in person searches. No search fee. Required to search: name, years to search. Civil cases indexed by defendant, plaintiff. Civil records on computer from 1986, on docket books from 1970s. **Criminal Records:** Access: Fax, mail, in person. Both court and visitors may perform in person searches. No search fee. Required to search: name, years to search; also helpful-DOB, SSN. Criminal records on computer from 1986, on docket books from 1970s. **General Information:** No adoption, mental, juvenile, termination, domestic violence or "open" domestic relations records released. SASE required. Turnaround time 1 day to 2 weeks. Copy fee: $1.00 per page. Certification fee: $1.00. Fee payee: Bannock County District Court. Personal checks accepted. Public access terminal is available. Fax notes: $1.00 per page.

Bear Lake County

District & Magistrate Courts PO Box 190, Paris, ID 83261; 208-945-2208; Fax: 208-945-2780. Hours: 8:30AM-5PM (MST). *Felony, Misdemeanor, Civil, Eviction, Small Claims, Probate.*

Civil Records: Access: Fax, mail, in person. Only the court conducts in person searches; visitors may not. No search fee. Required to search: name, years to search. Civil cases indexed by defendant, plaintiff. Civil records on computer from 1991, docket books from early 1900s. **Criminal Records:** Access: Fax, mail, in person. Only the court conducts in person searches; visitors may not. No search fee. Required to search: name, years to search, DOB, signed release; also helpful-SSN. Criminal records on computer from 1991, docket books from early 1900s. **General Information:** No juvenile, CPA, divorce records released. SASE required. Turnaround time 2-3 days. Copy fee: $1.00 per page. Certification fee: $1.50. Fee payee: Clerk of the Court. Business checks accepted. Prepayment is required. Fax notes: $1.00 per page.

Benewah County

District & Magistrate Courts Courthouse, 701 College Ave, St Maries, ID 83861; 208-245-3241; Fax: 208-245-3046. Hours: 9AM-5PM (PST). *Felony, Misdemeanor, Civil, Eviction, Small Claims, Probate.*

Civil Records: Access: Fax, mail, in person. Only the court conducts in person searches; visitors may not. No search fee. Required to search: name, years to search. Civil cases indexed by defendant, plaintiff. Civil records on computer from 1991, index cards and docket books from early 1900s. **Criminal Records:** Access: In person only. Court does not conduct in person searches; visitors must perform searches for themselves. Search fee: No search fee. If printout required $1.00 per page. Required to search: name, years to search. Criminal records on computer from 1991, index cards and docket books from early 1900s. The cousrt sends all written requests to BCI-Idaho 208-884-7140. **General Information:** No juvenile, adoptions, mental commitments or sealed records released. SASE required. Turnaround time 10-14 days. Copy fee: $1.00 per page. Certification fee: $1.00. Fee payee: District Court. Personal checks accepted. Prepayment is required. Fax notes: $3.00 for first page, $1.00 each addl. No fax fee if 800 number provided.

Bingham County

District & Magistrate Courts 501 N Maple St, #402, Blackfoot, ID 83221-1700; 208-785-5005 X342(Dist) X389(Magis); Fax: 208-785-8057. Hours: 8AM-Noon, 1-5PM (MST). *Felony, Misdemeanor, Civil, Eviction, Small Claims, Probate.*

Civil Records: Access: Phone, fax, mail, in person. Both court and visitors may perform in person searches. No search fee. Required to search: name, years to search; also helpful-address. Civil cases indexed by defendant, plaintiff. Civil records on computer from 1989, from microfiche from 1865. **Criminal Records:** Access: Phone, fax, mail, in person. Both court and visitors may perform in person searches. No search fee. Required to search: name, years to search, signed release; also helpful-address, DOB, SSN. Criminal records on computer from 1989, from microfiche from 1865. **General Information:** No juvenile, adoption, mental records released. SASE required. Turnaround time 1-2 weeks. Copy fee: $1.00 per page. Certification fee: $1.00. Fee payee: Clerk of the District Court. Personal checks accepted. Prepayment is required. Public access terminal is available. Fax notes: $1.25 per page.

Blaine County

District & Magistrate Courts 201 2nd Ave S #110, Hailey, ID 83333; 208-788-5548; Fax: 208-788-5512. Hours: 9AM-5PM (MST). *Felony, Misdemeanor, Civil, Eviction, Small Claims, Probate.*

Note: The Magistrate Court (Misdemeanor, Small Claims, Eviction, Probate) is in suite #106; Magistrate Court phone is 208-788-5525; fax 208-788-5527.

Civil Records: Access: Phone, fax, mail, in person. Both court and visitors may perform in person searches. No search fee. Required to search: name, years to search. Civil cases indexed by defendant, plaintiff. Civil records on computer from 1992. **Criminal Records:** Access: Phone, fax, mail, in person. Both court and visitors may perform in person searches. No search fee. Required to search: name, years to search, DOB, SSN. Criminal records on computer since 1988. **General Information:** No juvenile records released. SASE required. Turnaround time 3-10 days. Copy fee: $1.00 per page. Certification fee: $1.00 per document. Fee payee: Clerk of District Court. Personal checks accepted. Prepayment is required. Fax notes: $1.00 per page.

Boise County

District & Magistrate Courts PO Box 126, Idaho City, ID 83631; 208-392-4452; Fax: 208-392-6712. Hours: 8AM-5PM (MST). *Felony, Misdemeanor, Civil, Eviction, Small Claims, Probate.*

Civil Records: Access: Fax, mail, in person. Both court and visitors may perform in person searches. Search fee: $5.00 per hour. Required to search: name, years to search. Civil cases indexed by defendant, plaintiff. Civil records on computer from 6/90, on docket books from 1863. **Criminal Records:** Access: Fax, mail, in person. Both court and visitors may perform in person searches. Search fee: $5.00 per hour. Required to search: name, years to search, SSN; also helpful-DOB. Criminal records on computer from 6/90, on docket books from 1863. **General Information:** No juvenile, adoption records released. SASE required. Turnaround time 5 days. Copy fee: $1.00 per page. Certification fee: $1.50 per page. Fee

payee: Boise County. Personal checks accepted. Prepayment is required. Public access terminal is available. Fax notes: $5.00 for first page, $1.00 each addl.

Bonner County

District & Magistrate Courts 215 S. First Ave, Bonner Courthouse, Sandpoint, ID 83864; 208-265-1432; Fax: 208-265-1447. Hours: 9AM-5PM (PST). *Felony, Misdemeanor, Civil, Eviction, Small Claims, Probate.*

Civil Records: Access: Mail, in person. Both court and visitors may perform in person searches. No search fee. Required to search: name, years to search; also helpful-address. Civil cases indexed by defendant, plaintiff. Civil records on computer from 1990, index and docket books from 1907. **Criminal Records:** Access: Mail, in person. Both court and visitors may perform in person searches. No search fee. Required to search: name, years to search; also helpful-address, DOB, SSN. Criminal records on computer from 1990, index and docket books from 1907. **General Information:** No juvenile records released. SASE required. Turnaround time 1 week. Copy fee: $1.00 per page. Certification fee: $1.00. Fee payee: Bonner County Recorder or Clerk. Personal checks accepted. Prepayment is required. Public access terminal is available.

Bonneville County

District & Magistrate Courts 605 N. Capital, Idaho Falls, ID 83402; 208-529-1350; Fax: 208-529-1300. Hours: 8AM-5PM (MST). *Felony, Misdemeanor, Civil, Eviction, Small Claims, Probate.*

www.co.bonneville.id.us

Civil Records: Access: In person only. Court does not conduct in person searches; visitors must perform searches for themselves. No search fee. Required to search: name, years to search. Civil cases indexed by defendant, plaintiff. Criminal misdemeanor records on computer from 1983, felony on computer from 1991, civil from 1991. Criminal on microfiche from 1977, civil from 1923. Docket books by case number ongoing. Actual case records are archived before 10/91. **Criminal Records:** Access: In person only. Court does not conduct in person searches; visitors must perform searches for themselves. Search fee: No criminal searches performed by court. Required to search: name, years to search, DOB, signed release; also helpful-SSN. Criminal misdemeanor records on computer from 1983, felony on computer from 1991, civil from 1991. Criminal on microfiche from 1977, civil from 1923. Docket books by case number ongoing. Actual case records are archived before 10/91. **General Information:** No child protective, protection orders, juvenile, sanity, adoption or termination records released. Copy fee: $1.00 per page. Certification fee: $1.00. Fee payee: Bonneville County. Personal checks accepted. Credit cards accepted: Visa, Mastercard, Discover, AmEx. For criminal and traffic records only. Prepayment is required. Public access terminal is available.

Boundary County

District & Magistrate Courts Boundary County Courthouse, PO Box 419, Bonners Ferry, ID 83805; 208-267-5504; Fax: 208-267-7814. Hours: 9AM-5PM (PST). *Felony, Misdemeanor, Civil, Eviction, Small Claims, Probate.*

www.boundary-idaho.com

Civil Records: Access: Mail, in person. Both court and visitors may perform in person searches. No search fee. Required to search: name, years to search; also helpful-address. Civil cases indexed by defendant, plaintiff. Civil records on computer from 1989, on docket books by case number, index books and cards by name from early 1900s. Mail access only available if specifics are given; otherwise court will not do a search. **Criminal Records:** Access: Mail, in person. Both court and visitors may perform in person searches. No search fee. Required to search: name, years to search, SSN; also helpful-DOB. Criminal records on computer from 1989, on docket books by case number, index books and cards by name from early 1900s. Mail access only if specific case information given; the court will not do name searches. **General Information:** No sealed records released. SASE required. Turnaround time 5 days. Copy fee: $1.00 per page. Certification fee: $1.00. Fee payee: Clerk of the Court. Personal checks accepted. Prepayment is required. Public access terminal is available.

Butte County

District & Magistrate Courts PO Box 737, Arco, ID 83213; 208-527-3021; Fax: 208-527-3448. Hours: 9AM-5PM (MST). *Felony, Misdemeanor, Civil, Eviction, Small Claims, Probate.*

Civil Records: Access: Phone, fax, mail, in person. Both court and visitors may perform in person searches. No search fee. Required to search: name, years to search; also helpful-address. Civil cases indexed by defendant, plaintiff. Civil records on computer from 1989, archives prior. Docket books by case number from early 1910s. **Criminal Records:** Access: Phone, fax, mail, in person. Both court and visitors may perform in person searches. No search fee. Required to search: name, years to search; also helpful-address, DOB, SSN. Criminal records on computer from 1989, archives prior. Docket books by case number from early 1910s. **General Information:** No juvenile records released. SASE required. Turnaround time 1 week. Copy fee: $1.00 per page. Certification fee: $1.50. Fee payee: Butte County Magistrate Court. Personal checks accepted. Prepayment is required. Public access terminal is available. Fax notes: $2.00 per page.

Camas County

District & Magistrate Courts PO Box 430, Fairfield, ID 83327; 208-764-2238; Fax: 208-764-2349. Hours: 8:30AM-Noon, 1-5PM (MST). *Felony, Misdemeanor, Civil, Eviction, Small Claims, Probate.*

Civil Records: Access: Mail, in person. Both court and visitors may perform in person searches. No search fee. Required to search: name, years to search; also helpful-address. Civil cases indexed by defendant, plaintiff. Civil records from archives from 1917. Register of actions by case number. **Criminal Records:** Access: Mail, in person. Both court and visitors may perform in person searches. No search fee. Required to search: name, years to search; also helpful-address, DOB, SSN. Criminal records from archives from 1917. Register of actions by case number. **General Information:** No juvenile or domestic violence records released. SASE required. Turnaround time 1 day. Copy fee: $1.00 per page. Certification fee: $1.00. Fee payee: Camas County Courthouse. Personal checks accepted. Prepayment is required. Public access terminal is available.

Canyon County

District & Magistrate Courts 1115 Albany, Caldwell, ID 83605; ; Civil phone:208-454-7570; Criminal phone:208-454-7570. Hours: 8:30AM-5PM (MST). *Felony, Misdemeanor, Civil, Eviction, Small Claims, Probate.*

www.webpak.net/~tca3sec

Civil Records: Access: In person only. Court does not conduct in person searches; visitors must perform searches for themselves. Search fee: No civil searches performed by court. Required to search: name, years to search. Civil cases indexed by defendant, plaintiff. Civil records on computer from 1989, microfiche from 1800s, and docket books. **Criminal Records:** Access: In person only. Court does not conduct in person searches; visitors must perform searches for themselves. Search fee: No criminal searches performed by court. Required to search: name, years to search; also helpful-DOB, SSN. Criminal records on computer from 1989, microfiche from 1800s, and docket books. **General Information:** No adoption, mental, domestic violence records not released. Copy fee: $1.00 per page. Certification fee: $1.00. Fee payee: Clerk of Court. Only cashiers checks and money orders accepted. Public access terminal is available.

Caribou County

District & Magistrate Courts 159 S. Main, Soda Springs, ID 83276; 208-547-4342; Fax: 208-547-4759. Hours: 9AM-5PM (MST). *Felony, Misdemeanor, Civil, Eviction, Small Claims, Probate.*

Civil Records: Access: Phone, fax, mail, in person. Only the court conducts in person searches; visitors may not. No search fee. Required to search: name, years to search. Civil cases indexed by defendant, plaintiff. Civil records on computer from 1989, from archives from 1919 by case number. **Criminal Records:** Access: Phone, fax, mail, in person. Only the court conducts in person searches; visitors may not. No search fee. Required to search: name, years to search, DOB, SSN; also helpful-address. Criminal records on computer from 1989, from archives from 1919 by case number. **General Information:** No adoption, guardianship records released. SASE required. Turnaround time to 1 week. Copy fee: $1.00 per page. Certification fee: $1.00. Fee payee: Magistrate Court. Business checks accepted. Out of state checks not accepted. Prepayment is required. Fax notes: $2.00 for first page, $1.00 each addl.

Cassia County

District & Magistrate Courts 1459 Overland, Burley, ID 83318; 208-878-7351 Magistrate; 878-4367 Dist; Fax: 208-878-1003. Hours: 8:30AM-5PM (MST). *Felony, Misdemeanor, Civil, Eviction, Small Claims, Probate.*

www.safelink.net/ccounty/clerkof.htm

Civil Records: Access: Phone, fax, mail, in person. Both court and visitors may perform in person searches. No search fee. Required to search: name, years to search; also helpful-address. Civil cases indexed by defendant, plaintiff. Civil records on computer from 1990, archives from 1900s. **Criminal Records:** Access: Fax, mail, in person. Both court and visitors may perform in person searches. No search fee. Required to search: name, years to search; also helpful-address, DOB, SSN. Criminal records on computer from 1990, archives from 1900s. **General Information:**

No juvenile, adoption, mental commitment, child protection records released. SASE required. Turnaround time to 1-2 days. Copy fee: $1.00 per page. Certification fee: $1.50. Fee payee: Magistrate Court. Personal checks accepted. Prepayment is required. Public access terminal is available. Fax notes: $2.50 per page.

Clark County

District & Magistrate Courts PO Box 205, DuBois, ID 83423; 208-374-5402; Fax: 208-374-5609. Hours: 9AM-5PM (MST). *Felony, Misdemeanor, Civil, Eviction, Small Claims, Probate.*

Civil Records: Access: Fax, mail, in person. Both court and visitors may perform in person searches. No search fee. Required to search: name, years to search; also helpful-address. Civil cases indexed by defendant, plaintiff. Civil records on computer from 1985, on microfiche for civil judgements and from archives from 1919. **Criminal Records:** Access: Fax, mail, in person. Both court and visitors may perform in person searches. No search fee. Required to search: name, years to search; also helpful-address, DOB, SSN. Criminal records on computer from 1985, on microfiche for civil judgements and from archives from 1919. **General Information:** No juvenile, adoption records released. SASE required. Turnaround time 3 days. Copy fee: $1.00 per page. Certification fee: $1.00. Fee payee: Clerk of the District Court. Personal checks accepted. Prepayment is required. Public access terminal is available. Fax notes: $.50 per page.

Clearwater County

District & Magistrate Courts PO Box 586, Orofino, ID 83544; 208-476-5596; Fax: 208-476-5159. Hours: 8AM-5PM (PST). *Felony, Misdemeanor, Civil, Eviction, Small Claims, Probate.*

Civil Records: Access: Phone, fax, mail, in person. Only the court conducts in person searches; visitors may not. No search fee. Required to search: name, years to search. Civil cases indexed by defendant, plaintiff. Civil records on computer from 8/91, in docket books prior. **Criminal Records:** Access: Phone, fax, mail, in person. Only the court conducts in person searches; visitors may not. No search fee. Required to search: name, years to search. Criminal records on computer from 8/91, in docket books prior. **General Information:** No juvenile, domestic violence, adoption, social records released. SASE requested. Turnaround time 7 days. Copy fee: $1.00 per page. Certification fee: $1.00. Fee payee: Clerk of Court. Business checks accepted. Prepayment is required. Fax notes: $1.00 per page.

Custer County

District & Magistrate Courts PO Box 385, Challis, ID 83226; 208-879-2359; Fax: 208-879-5246. Hours: 8AM-5PM (MST). *Felony, Misdemeanor, Civil, Eviction, Small Claims, Probate.*

Civil Records: Access: Phone, mail, in person. Only the court conducts in person searches; visitors may not. Search fee: $5.00 per name. Required to search: name, years to search. Civil cases indexed by defendant. Civil records on computer from 1989, archived from early 1900s. **Criminal Records:** Access: Phone, mail, in person. Only the court conducts in person searches; visitors may not. Search fee: $5.00 per name. Required to search: name, years to search,

DOB, signed release; also helpful-SSN. Criminal records on computer from 1989, archived from early 1900s. **General Information:** No juvenile, adoption records released. Turnaround time 1 week. Copy fee: $1.00 per page. Certification fee: $1.00 per page. Fee payee: Custer County. Personal checks accepted. Prepayment is required.

Elmore County

District & Magistrate Courts 150 S 4th East, Ste 5, Mountain Home, ID 83647; 208-587-2133; Fax: 208-587-1320. Hours: 9AM-5PM (MST). *Felony, Misdemeanor, Civil, Eviction, Small Claims, Probate.*

Civil Records: Access: In person only. Court does not conduct in person searches; visitors must perform searches for themselves. No search fee. Required to search: name; also helpful-years to search. Civil cases indexed by defendant, plaintiff. Civil records on computer from 1992, on microfiche from 1972, archived from early 1900s. **Criminal Records:** Access: In person only. Court does not conduct in person searches; visitors must perform searches for themselves. No search fee. Required to search: name, DOB, signed release; also helpful-years to search, SSN. Criminal records on computer from 1992, on microfiche from 1972, archived from early 1900s. **General Information:** No juvenile, adoption, domestic violence, mental commitment records released. Copy fee: $1.00 per page. Certification fee: $1.00 per page. Fee payee: Elmore County. Personal checks accepted. Prepayment is required. Public access terminal is available. Fax notes: $1.00 per page.

Franklin County

District & Magistrate Courts 39 West Oneida, Preston, ID 83263; 208-852-0877; Fax: 208-852-2926. Hours: 9AM-5PM (MST). *Felony, Misdemeanor, Civil, Eviction, Small Claims, Probate.*

Civil Records: Access: Phone, fax, mail, in person. Both court and visitors may perform in person searches. Search fee: $2.00 per name. Fee is for years prior to 1990. No fee for 1990 to present. Required to search: name, years to search. Civil cases indexed by defendant, plaintiff. Civil records on computer from 1990, on microfiche from 1920, archived from 1920. **Criminal Records:** Access: Phone, fax, mail, in person. Both court and visitors may perform in person searches. Search fee: $2.00 per name. Fee is for years prior to 1990. No fee for 1990 to present. Required to search: name, years to search; also helpful-DOB, SSN. Criminal records on computer from 1990, on microfiche from 1920, archived from 1920. **General Information:** No adoption records released. SASE required. Turnaround time 2-3 days. Copy fee: $1.00 per page. Certification fee: $1.00. Fee payee: Magistrate Court. Personal checks accepted. Prepayment is required. Public access terminal is available. Fax notes: No fee to fax results. Local calls only.

Fremont County

District & Magistrate Courts 151 W 1st North, St Anthony, ID 83445; 208-624-7401; Fax: 208-624-4607. Hours: 9AM-5PM (MST). *Felony, Misdemeanor, Civil, Eviction, Small Claims, Probate.*

Civil Records: Access: Fax, mail, in person. Both court and visitors may perform in person searches. No search fee. Required to search: name, years to search; also helpful-address. Civil cases indexed by defendant, plaintiff. Civil records on computer from 1990, microfiche for last 20 years, prior archives. Thursday is the best day for in person searches. **Criminal Records:** Access: Fax, mail, in person. Both court and visitors may perform in person searches. No search fee. Required to search: name, years to search, DOB; also helpful-SSN. Criminal records on computer from 1990, microfiche for last 20 years, prior archives. Same as civil. **General Information:** No adoption or juvenile records released. SASE required. Turnaround time 1 week. Copy fee: $1.00 per page. Certification fee: $1.50. Fee payee: Clerk of the Court. Personal checks accepted. Prepayment is required. Public access terminal is available. Fax notes: $2.00 per page.

Gem County

District & Magistrate Courts 415 East Main St, Emmett, ID 83617; 208-365-4561; Fax: 208-365-6172. Hours: 8AM-5PM (MST). *Felony, Misdemeanor, Civil, Eviction, Small Claims, Probate.*

Note: Felony and misdemeanor records in different offices; therefore, a search fee is charged for each

Civil Records: Access: Mail, in person. Both court and visitors may perform in person searches. Search fee: $5.00 per name. Required to search: name, years to search; also helpful-address. Civil cases indexed by defendant, plaintiff. Civil records on computer from 1990, on microfiche, and archived from 1916. **Criminal Records:** Access: Mail, in person. Both court and visitors may perform in person searches. Search fee: $5.00 per name. Required to search: name, years to search; also helpful-address, DOB, SSN. Criminal records on computer from 1990, on microfiche, and archived from 1916. **General Information:** No juvenile, adoption records or domestic violence released. SASE required. Turnaround time 10 days. Copy fee: $1.00 per page. Certification fee: $1.00 plus $.50 per page. Fee payee: Gem County. Personal checks accepted. Prepayment is required. Public access terminal is available.

Gooding County

District & Magistrate Courts PO Box 477, Gooding, ID 83330; 208-934-4261; Fax: 208-934-4408. Hours: 8AM-5PM (MST). *Felony, Misdemeanor, Civil, Eviction, Small Claims, Probate.*

Civil Records: Access: Phone, fax, mail, in person. Court does not conduct in person searches; visitors must perform searches for themselves. Search fee: $1.00 per name. Required to search: name, years to search. Civil cases indexed by defendant, plaintiff. Civil records on computer from 1994, on microfiche, docket books from 1860s. **Criminal Records:** Access: In person only. Court does not conduct in person searches; visitors must perform searches for themselves. Search fee: No criminal searches performed by court. Required to search: name, years to search, DOB, SSN. Criminal records on computer from 1994, on microfiche, docket books from 1860s. **General Information:** No juvenile, adoption, domestic violence records released. SASE required. Turnaround time 5-10 days. Copy fee: $1.00 per page. Certification fee: $1.00. Fee payee: Gooding County Clerk. Personal checks accepted. Prepayment is required. Public access terminal is available. Fax notes: No fee to fax results.

Idaho County

District & Magistrate Courts 320 West Main, Grangeville, ID 83530; 208-983-2776; Fax: 208-983-2376. Hours: 8:30AM-5PM (PST). *Felony, Misdemeanor, Civil, Eviction, Small Claims, Probate.*

Civil Records: Access: Phone, fax, mail, in person. Only the court conducts in person searches; visitors may not. No search fee. Required to search: name, years to search. Civil cases indexed by defendant, plaintiff. Civil records on computer from 1989, on microfiche and archived from late 1800s. **Criminal Records:** Access: Phone, fax, mail, in person. Only the court conducts in person searches; visitors may not. No search fee. Required to search: name, years to search. Criminal records on computer from 1989, on microfiche and archived from late 1800s. **General Information:** No domestic violence, juvenile, hospitalization, adoption, termination records released. SASE not required but appreciated. Turnaround time same week. Copy fee: $1.00 per page. Certification fee: $1.00. Fee payee: Idaho County. Personal checks accepted. Prepayment is required. Fax notes: $2.00 per page.

Jefferson County

District & Magistrate Courts PO Box 71, Rigby, ID 83442; 208-745-7736; Fax: 208-745-6636. Hours: 9AM-5PM (MST). *Felony, Misdemeanor, Civil, Eviction, Small Claims, Probate.*

Civil Records: Access: In person. Both court and visitors may perform in person searches. No search fee. Required to search: name, years to search. Civil cases indexed by defendant, plaintiff. Civil records archived from early 1900s. Type of case also helpful with request. **Criminal Records:** Access: In person. Both court and visitors may perform in person searches. No search fee. Required to search: name, years to search, DOB. Criminal records archived from early 1900s. Type of case also helpful with request. **General Information:** No juvenile, adoption, some domestic records released. Copy fee: $1.00 per page. Certification fee: $1.00 per page. Fee payee: Magistrate Court. Personal checks accepted. Prepayment is required. Public access terminal is available. Fax notes: $1.00 per page.

Jerome County

District & Magistrate Courts 300 N Lincoln St, Jerome, ID 83338; 208-324-8811; Fax: 208-324-2719. Hours: 8:30AM-5PM (MST). *Felony, Misdemeanor, Civil, Eviction, Small Claims, Probate.*

Civil Records: Access: Fax, mail, in person. Both court and visitors may perform in person searches. No search fee. Required to search: name, years to search. Civil cases indexed by defendant, plaintiff. Criminal records on computer from 1985, civil from 1988, prior on microfiche. **Criminal Records:** Access: Fax, mail, in person. Both court and visitors may perform in person searches. No search fee. Required to search: name, years to search, address, DOB, SSN. Criminal records on computer from 1985, civil from 1988, prior on microfiche. Will not do background searches. **General Information:** No juvenile records released. SASE required. Turnaround time 2 days. Copy fee: $1.00 per page. Certification fee: $1.50 per page. Fee payee: Clerk of District Court. Personal checks accepted. Prepayment is required. Fax notes: $3.00 for first page, $2.50 each addl.

Kootenai County

District Court 324 West Garden Ave PO Box 9000, Coeur d'Alene, ID 83816-9000; 208-769-4440; Civil phone:208-769-4430; Criminal phone:208-769-4430; Fax: 208-664-0639. Hours:

9AM-5PM (PST). *Felony, Misdemeanor, Civil, Eviction, Small Claims, Probate.*

www.co.kootenai.id.us/court

Civil Records: Access: Fax, mail, in person. Both court and visitors may perform in person searches. No search fee. Required to search: name, years to search. Civil cases indexed by defendant, plaintiff. Civil records on computer from 1989, on microfiche from 1881, archived from 1819. **Criminal Records:** Access: Fax, mail, in person. Both court and visitors may perform in person searches. No search fee. Required to search: name, years to search; also helpful-DOB, SSN. Criminal records on computer from 1989, on microfiche from 1881, archived from 1819. **General Information:** No sealed, juvenile, adoption, parental termination, mentally incapacitated, domestic violence records released. SASE required. Turnaround time 1 week. Copy fee: $1.00 per page. Certification fee: $1.00. Fee payee: Clerk of Court. Personal checks accepted. Credit cards accepted. Prepayment is required. Public access terminal is available. Fax notes: $3.00 for first page, $1.00 each addl.

Latah County

District & Magistrate Courts PO Box 8068, Moscow, ID 83843; 208-883-2255; Fax: 208-883-2259. Hours: 8:30AM-5PM M-W, 8AM-5PM TH,F (PST). *Felony, Misdemeanor, Civil, Eviction, Small Claims, Probate.*

Civil Records: Access: Phone, fax, mail, in person. Only the court conducts in person searches; visitors may not. Search fee: $4.00 per name. Required to search: name, years to search; also helpful-address. Civil cases indexed by defendant, plaintiff. Civil records on computer from 1986, archived from May 1888. **Criminal Records:** Access: Phone, fax, mail, in person. Only the court conducts in person searches; visitors may not. Search fee: $4.00 per name. Required to search: name, years to search; also helpful-address, DOB, SSN. Criminal records on computer from 1986, archived from May 1888. **General Information:** No adoption, juvenile, hospitalization records released. Turnaround time 1-2 days. Copy fee: $1.00 per page. Certification fee: $1.00. Fee payee: Clerk of District Court. Personal checks accepted. Prepayment is required.

Lemhi County

District & Magistrate Courts 206 Courthouse Dr, Salmon, ID 83467; 208-756-2815; Fax: 208-756-8424. Hours: 9AM-5PM (MST). *Felony, Misdemeanor, Civil, Eviction, Small Claims, Probate.*

Civil Records: Access: Phone, fax, mail, in person. Both court and visitors may perform in person searches. Search fee: $5.00 per name. Required to search: name, years to search; also helpful-address. Civil cases indexed by defendant, plaintiff. Civil records on computer from 1991, on microfiche from 1964, archives from 1869. **Criminal Records:** Access: Phone, fax, mail, in person. Both court and visitors may perform in person searches. Search fee: $5.00 per name. Required to search: name, years to search; also helpful-address, DOB, SSN. Criminal records on computer from 1991, on microfiche from 1964, archives from 1869. **General Information:** No PSI, sealed records released. SASE requested. Turnaround time 1 day. Copy fee: $1.00 per page. Certification fee: $1.00. Fee payee: Lemhi County Clerk. Personal checks accepted. Credit cards accepted: Visa, Mastercard, Discover, AmEx. This is through a service. Prepayment is required.

Public access terminal is available. Fax notes: $1.00 per page.

Lewis County

District & Magistrate Courts 510 Oak St (PO Box 39), Nezperce, ID 83543; 208-937-2251; Fax: 208-937-9223. Hours: 9AM-5PM (PST). *Felony, Misdemeanor, Civil, Eviction, Small Claims, Probate.*

Civil Records: Access: Phone, fax, mail, in person. Both court and visitors may perform in person searches. No search fee. Required to search: name, years to search. Civil cases indexed by defendant, plaintiff. Civil records on computer from 1991, archived from late 1911. **Criminal Records:** Access: Phone, fax, mail, in person. Both court and visitors may perform in person searches. No search fee. Required to search: name, years to search; also helpful-DOB, SSN. Criminal records on computer from 1991, archived from late 1911. **General Information:** No juvenile, adoption records released. SASE required. Turnaround time 1 week. Copy fee: $1.00 per page. Certification fee: $1.00. Fee payee: Clerk of Court. Only cashiers checks and money orders accepted. Two-party checks not accepted. Prepayment is required. Fax notes: $1.00 per page.

Lincoln County

District & Magistrate Courts Drawer A, Shoshone, ID 83352; 208-886-2173; Fax: 208-886-2458. Hours: 8:30AM-5PM (MST). *Felony, Misdemeanor, Civil, Eviction, Small Claims, Probate.*

Civil Records: Access: In person only. Court does not conduct in person searches; visitors must perform searches for themselves. Search fee: No civil searches performed by court. Required to search: name, years to search. Civil cases indexed by defendant, plaintiff. Civil records on computer from 1991, archives from 1800s. **Criminal Records:** Access: In person only. Court does not conduct in person searches; visitors must perform searches for themselves. Search fee: No criminal searches performed by court. Required to search: name, years to search; also helpful-DOB, SSN. Criminal records on computer from 1991, archives from 1800s. **General Information:** No juvenile, domestic violence, sealed records released. Copy fee: $1.00 per page. Certification fee: $1.00. Fee payee: Lincoln County Courts. Personal checks accepted.

Madison County

District & Magistrate Courts PO Box 389, Rexburg, ID 83440; 208-356-9383; Fax: 208-356-5425. Hours: 9AM-5PM (MST). *Felony, Misdemeanor, Civil, Eviction, Small Claims, Probate.*

Civil Records: Access: Mail, in person. Both court and visitors may perform in person searches. No search fee. Required to search: name, years to search; also helpful-address. Civil cases indexed by defendant, plaintiff. Civil records on computer from 1991, microfiche and archives from early 1900s. **Criminal Records:** Access: In person only. Court does not conduct in person searches; visitors must perform searches for themselves. Search fee: No criminal searches performed by court. Required to search: name, years to search; also helpful-address, DOB, SSN. Criminal records on computer from 1991, microfiche and archives from early 1900s. **General Information:** No juvenile records released. SASE required. Turnaround time 1-2 days. Copy fee: $1.00 per page. Certification fee: $1.00. Fee payee:

Magistrate Court. Personal checks accepted. Prepayment is required. Public access terminal is available.

Minidoka County

District & Magistrate Courts PO Box 368, Rupert, ID 83350; 208-436-9041 (Dist) 436-7186 (Magis); Fax: 208-436-5857. Hours: 8:30AM-5PM (MST). *Felony, Misdemeanor, Civil, Eviction, Small Claims, Probate.*

Civil Records: Access: Phone, fax, mail, in person. Only the court conducts in person searches; visitors may not. No search fee. Required to search: name, years to search. Civil cases indexed by defendant, plaintiff. Criminal records on computer from 1989, archives from early 1900s. **Criminal Records:** Access: Phone, fax, mail, in person. Only the court conducts in person searches; visitors may not. No search fee. Required to search: name, years to search, DOB, SSN, signed release. Criminal records on computer from 1989, archives from early 1900s. **General Information:** No juvenile records released. Turnaround time 1-3 days. Copy fee: $1.00 per page. Certification fee: $.50 per page. Fee payee: Clerk of Court. Personal checks accepted. Fax notes: $.50 per page.

Nez Perce County

District Court PO Box 896, Lewiston, ID 83501; 208-799-3040; Fax: 208-799-3058. Hours: 8AM-5PM (PST). *Felony, Misdemeanor, Civil, Eviction, Small Claims, Probate.*

www.co.nezperce.id.us/clerk/clerk.htm

Civil Records: Access: Phone, fax, mail, in person. Both court and visitors may perform in person searches. No search fee. Required to search: name; also helpful-years to search. Civil cases indexed by defendant, plaintiff. Civil records on computer from 1990, microfiche from 1970 and archives from late 1800s. **Criminal Records:** Access: Phone, fax, mail, in person. Both court and visitors may perform in person searches. No search fee. Required to search: name; also helpful-years to search, DOB, SSN. Criminal records on computer from 1990, microfiche from 1970 and archives from late 1800s. **General Information:** SASE not required. Turnaround time 10 day waiting period. Copy fee: $1.00 per page. Certification fee: $1.00 per page. Fee payee: District Court. Personal checks accepted. Prepayment is required. Public access terminal is available. Fax notes: $1.00 for first page, $1.00 each addl.

Oneida County

District & Magistrate Courts 10 Court St, Malad City, ID 83252; 208-766-4285 X111,112,114,105; Fax: 208-766-2990. Hours: 9AM-5PM (MST). *Felony, Misdemeanor, Civil, Eviction, Small Claims, Probate.*

Civil Records: Access: Phone, fax, mail, in person. Both court and visitors may perform in person searches. No search fee. Required to search: name, years to search; also helpful-address. Civil cases indexed by case number, defendant, plaintiff. Civil records on computer from 1990, archives from 1887. **Criminal Records:** Access: Phone, fax, mail, in person. Both court and visitors may perform in person searches. No search fee. Required to search: name, years to search; also helpful-address, DOB, SSN. Criminal records on computer from 1990, archives from 1887. **General Information:** No juvenile, adoption records released. SASE requested. Turnaround time 1-2 days. Copy fee: $1.00 per page. Certification fee:

$1.00. Fee payee: Clerk of Court. Personal checks accepted. Prepayment is required. Fax notes: $1.00 per page.

Owyhee County

District & Magistrate Courts-I Courthouse, Murphy, ID 83650; 208-495-2806; Fax: 208-495-1226. Hours: 8:30AM-5PM (MST). *Felony, Misdemeanor, Civil, Eviction, Small Claims, Probate.*

Civil Records: Access: Fax, mail, in person. Both court and visitors may perform in person searches. No search fee. Required to search: name, years to search. Civil cases indexed by defendant, plaintiff. Civil records on computer from 1992, archives from 1800s. **Criminal Records:** Access: Fax, mail, in person. Both court and visitors may perform in person searches. No search fee. Required to search: name, years to search; also helpful-DOB. Criminal records on computer from 1992, archives from 1800s. Signed release required for search of juvenile records. **General Information:** No adoption, juvenile (except for some that are open), domestic violence records released. Turnaround time 5-7 days. Copy fee: $1.00 per page. Certification fee: $1.00 per page. Fee payee: Owyhee County. Only cashiers checks and money orders accepted. Prepayment is required.

Homedale Magistrate Court 31 W Wyoming Ave, Homedale, ID 83628-3402; 208-337-4540; Fax: 208-337-3035. Hours: 8:30AM-5PM (MST). *Misdemeanor, Civil Actions Under $10,000, Eviction, Small Claims.*

Civil Records: Access: In person only. Only the court conducts in person searches; visitors may not. No search fee. Required to search: name, years to search; also helpful-address. Civil cases indexed by defendant. Civil records on computer from 1992, archives from 1975. **Criminal Records:** Access: In person only. Only the court conducts in person searches; visitors may not. No search fee. Required to search: name, years to search; also helpful-address, DOB, SSN. Criminal records on computer from 1992, archives from 1975. **General Information:** No juvenile or mental records released. Copy fee: $1.00 per page. Certification fee: $1.00 plus $.50 per page. Fee payee: Magistrate Court. Personal checks accepted. Prepayment is required.

Payette County

District & Magistrate Courts 1130 3rd Ave N, Payette, ID 83661; 208-642-6000 (Dist) 642-6010(Magis); Fax: 208-642-6011. Hours: 9AM-5PM (MST). *Felony, Misdemeanor, Civil, Eviction, Small Claims, Probate.*

Civil Records: Access: Fax, mail, in person. Both court and visitors may perform in person searches. Search fee: $5.00 per name. Required to search: name, years to search; also helpful-address. Civil cases indexed by defendant, plaintiff. Civil records on computer from 1992, prior microfiched or archived from 1913. **Criminal Records:** Access: Fax, mail, in person. Both court and visitors may perform in person searches. Search fee: $5.00 per name. Required to search: name, years to search, signed release; also helpful-address, DOB, SSN. Criminal records on computer from 1992, prior microfiched or archived from 1913. **General Information:** No juvenile, adoption records released. SASE required. Turnaround time 1 day. Copy fee: $1.00 per page. Certification fee: $1.00. Fee payee: Clerk of District Court. Personal checks accepted. Prepayment is required. Public

access terminal is available. Fax notes: $3.00 for first page, $.50 each addl.

Power County

District & Magistrate Courts 543 Bannock Ave, American Falls, ID 83211; 208-226-7611 (Dist) 226-7618(Magistrate); Fax: 208-226-7612. Hours: 9AM-5PM (MST). *Felony, Misdemeanor, Civil, Eviction, Small Claims, Probate.*

Civil Records: Access: Phone, fax, mail, in person. Only the court conducts in person searches; visitors may not. No search fee. Required to search: name, years to search. Civil cases indexed by defendant. Civil records on computer from 1986, prior archived from early 1900s. **Criminal Records:** Access: Phone, fax, mail, in person. Only the court conducts in person searches; visitors may not. No search fee. Required to search: name, years to search, DOB, SSN. Criminal records on computer from 1986, prior archived from early 1900s. **General Information:** No juvenile, mental committment records released. SASE required. Turnaround time 10 days. Copy fee: $1.00 per page. Certification fee: $1.50. Fee payee: Power County Magistrate Court. Personal checks accepted. Prepayment is required. Fax notes: $1.00 per page.

Shoshone County

District & Magistrate Courts 700 Bank St, Wallace, ID 83873; 208-752-1266; Fax: 208-753-0921. Hours: 9AM-5PM (PST). *Felony, Misdemeanor, Civil, Eviction, Small Claims, Probate.*

Civil Records: Access: Phone, fax, mail, in person. Both court and visitors may perform in person searches. No search fee. Required to search: name, years to search; also helpful-address. Civil cases indexed by defendant, plaintiff. Civil records on computer from 1988, archives from 1971. Juvenile case information not available by fax. **Criminal Records:** Access: Phone, mail, in person. Both court and visitors may perform in person searches. No search fee. Required to search: name, years to search; also helpful-address, DOB, SSN. Criminal records on computer from 1988, archives from 1971. **General Information:** No special proceeding, juvenile records released. SASE required. Turnaround time 1-2 days. Copy fee: $1.00 per page. Certification fee: $1.00. Fee payee: Clerk of Court. Personal checks accepted. Prepayment is required. Public access terminal is available. Public Access Terminal Note: For records from 1995. Fax notes: $2.00 for first page, $1.00 each addl. Add $1.00 1st page if long distance.

Teton County

District & Magistrate Courts 89 N Main #5, Driggs, ID 83422; 208-354-2239; Fax: 208-354-8496. Hours: 9AM-5PM (MST). *Felony, Misdemeanor, Civil, Eviction, Small Claims, Probate.*

Note: Address and telephone given above are for District Court. If you wish to access only the Magistrate Court and call 208-354-2239

Civil Records: Access: Phone, fax, mail, in person. Both court and visitors may perform in person searches. Search fee: $6.00 per name. Required to search: name, years to search; also helpful-address. Civil cases indexed by defendant, plaintiff. Civil records on computer from 1988, archives from 1974, I-Star since 1993. **Criminal Records:** Access: Phone, fax, mail, in person. Both court and visitors may perform in person searches. Search fee: $6.00 per name. Required to

search: name, years to search; also helpful-address, DOB, SSN. Criminal records on computer from 1988, archives from 1974, I-Star since 1993. **General Information:** No juvenile, DV records released. SASE required. Turnaround time 3 days. Copy fee: $1.00 per page. Certification fee: $1.00. Fee payee: Clerk of the Court. Personal checks accepted. Prepayment is required. Public access terminal is available. Fax notes: $2.00 per page.

Twin Falls County

District & Magistrate Courts PO Box 126, Twin Falls, ID 83303-0126; 208-736-4013; Fax: 208-736-4155. Hours: 8AM-5PM (MST). *Felony, Misdemeanor, Civil, Eviction, Small Claims, Probate.*

www.co.twin-falls.id.us/5thdistrict

Civil Records: Access: Phone, fax, mail, in person. Both court and visitors may perform in person searches. No search fee. Required to search: name, years to search; also helpful-address. Civil cases indexed by defendant, plaintiff. Civil records on computer from 1989, archives from early 1900s. **Criminal Records:** Access: Phone, fax, mail, in person. Both court and visitors may perform in person searches. No search fee. Required to search: name, years to search; also helpful-address, DOB, SSN. Criminal records on computer from 1989, archives from early 1900s. **General Information:** No adoption, termination, juvenile records released. Turnaround time 1-10 days. Copy fee: $1.00 per page. Certification fee: $1.00 per page. Fee payee: Court Services. Personal checks accepted. Prepayment is required. Public access terminal is available. Fax notes: $2.50 per page.

Valley County

District & Magistrate Courts-I PO Box 1350, Cascade, ID 83611; 208-382-7178; Fax: 208-382-7184. Hours: 9AM-5PM (MST). *Felony, Misdemeanor, Civil, Eviction, Small Claims, Probate.*

Civil Records: Access: Phone, fax, mail, in person. Both court and visitors may perform in person searches. No search fee. Required to search: name, years to search; also helpful-address. Civil cases indexed by defendant, plaintiff. Civil records on computer from 1990, microfiche and archives from early 1900s. **Criminal Records:** Access: Phone, fax, mail, in person. Both court and visitors may perform in person searches. No search fee. Required to search: name, years to search; also helpful-address, DOB, SSN. Criminal records on computer from 1990, microfiche and archives from early 1900s. **General Information:** No juvenile records released. SASE required. Turnaround time 1-3 days. Copy fee: $1.00 per page. Certification fee: $1.50 per page. Fee payee: Valley County. Personal checks accepted. Two-party or out of country (w/o printed-stamped US Funds) not accepted. Prepayment is required. Public access terminal is available. Fax notes: No fee to fax results.

Magistrate Court II Valley County Courthouse Annex, 550 Deinhard Lane, McCall, ID 83638; 208-634-8102; Fax: 208-634-4040. Hours: 9AM-5PM (MST). *Misdemeanor, Civil Actions Under $10,000, Eviction, Small Claims.*

Civil Records: Access: Phone, fax, mail, in person. Only the court conducts in person searches; visitors may not. No search fee. Required to search: name, years to search; also helpful-address. Civil cases indexed by defendant. Civil records on computer from 1990, archives from 1984. **Criminal Records:** Access: Phone, fax, mail, in person. Only the court conducts in person searches; visitors may not. No search fee. Required to search: name, years to search; also helpful-address, DOB, SSN. Criminal records on computer from 1990, archives from 1984. **General Information:** No juvenile records released. SASE required. Turnaround time 1-5 days. Copy fee: $1.00 per page. Certification fee: $1.00 per page. Fee payee: McCall Court. Personal checks accepted. Fax notes: $5.00 for first page, $2.00 each addl.

Washington County

District & Magistrate Courts PO Box 670, Weiser, ID 83672; 208-549-2092; Fax: 208-549-3925. Hours: 8:30AM-5PM (MST). *Felony, Misdemeanor, Civil, Eviction, Small Claims, Probate.*

Civil Records: Access: In person only. Court does not conduct in person searches; visitors must perform searches for themselves. Search fee:. Required to search: name. Civil cases indexed by defendant, plaintiff. Civil records on computer from 02/90, archives from late 1800s. **Criminal**

Records: Access: In person only. Court does not conduct in person searches; visitors must perform searches for themselves. Search fee:. Required to search: name; also helpful-DOB, SSN. Criminal records on computer from 02/90, archives from late 1800s. **General Information:** No juvenile, adoption, hospitalization, child protection-termination of parental rights records released. Copy fee: $1.00 per page. Certification fee: $1.00. Fee payee: Washington County. Local business checks only. Prepayment is required. Public access terminal is available.

ORGANIZATION	44 counties, 44 recording offices. The recording officer is County Recorder. Many counties utilize a grantor/grantee index containing all transactions recorded with them. 34 counties are in the Mountain Time Zone (MST), and 10 are in the Pacific Time Zone (PST).	
REAL ESTATE RECORDS	Most counties will **not** perform real estate searches. Certification of copies usually costs $1.00 per document.	
UCC RECORDS	Financing statements are filed at the state level except for real estate related filings. All counties will perform UCC searches. Use search request form UCC-4. Search fees are usually $6.00 per debtor name for a listing of filings and $12.00 per debtor name for a listing plus copies at no additional charge. Separately ordered copies usually cost $1.00 per page.	
TAX LIEN RECORDS	Federal tax liens on personal property of businesses are filed with the Secretary of State. Other federal tax liens are filed with the County Recorder. Some counties will perform a combined tax lien search for $5.00 while others will **not** perform tax lien searches.	
OTHER LIENS	Judgments, hospital, labor, mechanics.	

Ada County
County Clerk and Recorder, 650 Main Street, Boise, ID 83702-5960. 208-364-2223.

Adams County
County Clerk and Recorder, P.O. Box 48, Council, ID 83612. 208-253-4561. Fax: 208-253-4880.

Bannock County
County Clerk and Recorder, 624 East Center, Courthouse, Room 211, Pocatello, ID 83201. 208-236-7340. Fax: 208-236-7345.

Bear Lake County
County Clerk and Recorder, P.O. Box 190, Paris, ID 83261. 208-945-2212. Fax: 208-945-2780.

Benewah County
County Clerk and Recorder, 701 College, St. Maries, ID 83861. 208-245-3212. Fax: 208-245-3046.

Bingham County
County Clerk and Recorder, 501 North Maple #205, Blackfoot, ID 83221. 208-785-5005. Fax: 208-785-4131.

Blaine County
County Clerk and Recorder, Courthouse, Suite 200, 206 1st Ave. South, Hailey, ID 83333. 208-788-5505. Fax: 208-788-5501.

Boise County
County Clerk and Recorder, P.O. Box B.C., Idaho City, ID 83631. 208-392-4431. Fax: 208-392-4473.

Bonner County
County Clerk and Recorder, 215 South First, Sandpoint, ID 83864. 208-265-1432. Fax: 208-265-1447.

Bonneville County
County Clerk and Recorder, 605 North Capital, Idaho Falls, ID 83402-3582. 208-529-1350x1350. Fax: 208-529-1353.

Boundary County
County Clerk and Recorder, P.O. Box 419, Bonners Ferry, ID 83805. 208-267-2242. Fax: 208-267-7814.

Butte County
County Clerk and Recorder, P.O. Box 737, Arco, ID 83213. 208-527-3021. Fax: 208-527-3295.

Camas County
County Clerk and Recorder, P.O. Box 430, Fairfield, ID 83327-0430. 208-764-2242. Fax: 208-764-2349.

Canyon County
County Recorder, 1115 Albany Street, Caldwell, ID 83605. 208-454-7556.

Caribou County
County Clerk and Recorder, P.O. Box 775, Soda Springs, ID 83276-0775. 208-547-4324. Fax: 208-547-4759.

Cassia County
County Clerk and Recorder, 1459 Overland Ave., Room 105, Burley, ID 83318. 208-878-5240. Fax: 208-878-1003.

Clark County
County Clerk and Recorder, P.O. Box 205, Dubois, ID 83423. 208-374-5304. Fax: 208-374-5609.

Clearwater County
County Clerk and Recorder, P.O. Box 586, Orofino, ID 83544-0586. 208-476-5615. Fax: 208-476-9315.

Custer County
County Clerk and Recorder, P.O. Box 385, Challis, ID 83226. 208-879-2360. Fax: 208-879-5246.

Elmore County
County Clerk and Recorder, 150 South 4th East, Suite #3, Mountain Home, ID 83647-3097. 208-587-2130. Fax: 208-587-2159.

Franklin County
County Clerk and Recorder, 39 West Oneida, Preston, ID 83263. 208-852-1090. Fax: 208-852-1094.

Fremont County
County Clerk and Recorder, 151 West 1st N. Room 12, St. Anthony, ID 83445. 208-624-7332. Fax: 208-624-4607.

Gem County
County Clerk and Recorder, 415 East Main, Emmett, ID 83617. 208-365-4561. Fax: 208-365-6172.

Gooding County
County Clerk and Recorder, P.O. Box 417, Gooding, ID 83330. 208-934-4841.

Idaho County
County Clerk and Recorder, 320 W. Main, Room 5, Grangeville, ID 83530. 208-983-2751. Fax: 208-983-1428.

Jefferson County
County Clerk and Recorder, P.O. Box 275, Rigby, ID 83442. 208-745-7756. Fax: 208-745-6636.

Jerome County
County Clerk and Recorder, 300 North Lincoln, Courthouse, Room 301, Jerome, ID 83338. 208-324-8811. Fax: 208-324-2719.

Kootenai County
County Clerk and Recorder, P.O. Box 9000, Coeur d'Alene, ID 83816-9000. 208-666-8162.

Latah County
County Clerk and Recorder, P.O. Box 8068, Moscow, ID 83843-0568. 208-882-8580x379. Fax: 208-883-7203.

Lemhi County
County Clerk and Recorder, 206 Courthouse Drive, Salmon, ID 83467. 208-756-2815. Fax: 208-756-8424.

Lewis County
County Clerk and Recorder, P.O. Box 39, Nezperce, ID 83543. 208-937-2661.

Lincoln County
County Clerk and Recorder, P.O. Drawer A, Shoshone, ID 83352-2774. 208-886-7641. Fax: 208-886-2707.

Madison County
County Clerk and Recorder, P.O. Box 389, Rexburg, ID 83440. 208-356-3662. Fax: 208-356-8396.

Minidoka County
County Clerk and Recorder, P.O. Box 474, Rupert, ID 83350-0474. 208-436-9511. Fax: 208-436-0737.

Nez Perce County
County Clerk and Recorder, P.O. Box 896, Lewiston, ID 83501-0896. 208-799-3020. Fax: 208-799-3070.

Oneida County
County Clerk and Recorder, 10 Court Street, Malad, ID 83252. 208-766-4116x10. Fax: 208-766-2448.

Owyhee County
County Clerk and Recorder, P.O. Box 128, Murphy, ID 83650. 208-495-2421. Fax: 208-495-1173.

Payette County
County Clerk and Recorder, P.O. Drawer D, Payette, ID 83661. 208-642-6000. Fax: 208-642-6011.

Power County
County Clerk and Recorder, 543 Bannock, American Falls, ID 83211. 208-226-7611. Fax: 208-226-7612.

Shoshone County
County Clerk and Recorder, Courthouse, Suite 120, 700 Bank St., Wallace, ID 83873-2348. 208-752-1264. Fax: 208-753-2711.

Teton County
County Clerk and Recorder, 89 North Main #1, Driggs, ID 83422. 208-354-2905. Fax: 208-354-8410.

Twin Falls County
County Clerk and Recorder, P.O. Box 126, Twin Falls, ID 83303-0126. 208-736-4004. Fax: 208-736-4182.

Valley County
County Clerk and Recorder, P.O. Box 737, Cascade, ID 83611-0737. 208-382-4297. Fax: 208-382-4955.

Washington County
County Clerk and Recorder, P.O. Box 670, Weiser, ID 83672-0670. 208-549-2092. Fax: 208-549-3925.

You will usually be able to find the city name in the City/County Cross Reference below. In that case, it is a simple matter to determine the county from the cross reference. However, only the official US Postal Service city names are included in this index. There are an additional 40,000 place names that people use in their addresses. Therefore, we have also included a ZIP/City Cross Reference immediately following the City/County Cross Reference.

If you know the ZIP Code but the city name does not appear in the City/County Cross Reference index, look up the ZIP Code in the ZIP/City Cross Reference, find the city name, then look up the city name in the City/County Cross Reference. For example, you want to know the county for an address of Menands, NY 12204. There is no "Menands" in the City/County Cross Reference. The ZIP/City Cross Reference shows that ZIP Codes 12201-12288 are for the city of Albany. Looking back in the City/County Cross Reference, Albany is in Albany County.

City/County Cross Reference

ABERDEEN Bingham
AHSAHKA Clearwater
ALBION Cassia
ALMO Cassia
AMERICAN FALLS Power
ARBON Power
ARCO Butte
ARIMO Bannock
ASHTON Fremont
ATHOL (83801) Kootenai(85), Bonner(15)
ATLANTA Elmore
ATOMIC CITY Bingham
AVERY Shoshone
BANCROFT Caribou
BANKS Boise
BASALT Bingham
BAYVIEW (83803) Kootenai(59), Bonner(41)
BELLEVUE Blaine
BERN Bear Lake
BLACKFOOT Bingham
BLANCHARD Bonner
BLISS Gooding
BLOOMINGTON Bear Lake
BOISE (83706) Ada(98), Boise(2)
BOISE Ada
BONNERS FERRY Boundary
BOVILL Latah
BRUNEAU Owyhee
BUHL Twin Falls
BURLEY Cassia
CALDER Shoshone
CALDWELL (83605) Canyon(98), Payette(2)
CALDWELL Canyon
CAMBRIDGE Washington
CAREY Blaine
CAREYWOOD Bonner
CARMEN Lemhi
CASCADE Valley
CASTLEFORD Twin Falls
CATALDO (83810) Kootenai(98), Shoshone(2)
CHALLIS (83226) Custer(98), Lemhi(2)
CHESTER Fremont
CLARK FORK Bonner
CLARKIA Shoshone
CLAYTON Custer
CLIFTON Franklin
COBALT Lemhi
COCOLALLA Bonner
COEUR D ALENE Kootenai
COLBURN Bonner
CONDA Caribou
COOLIN Bonner
CORRAL Camas
COTTONWOOD Idaho
COUNCIL Adams
CRAIGMONT Lewis
CULDESAC (83524) Nez Perce(86), Lewis(14)
DAYTON Franklin

DEARY Latah
DECLO Cassia
DESMET Benewah
DIETRICH Lincoln
DINGLE Bear Lake
DONNELLY Valley
DOVER Bonner
DOWNEY Bannock
DRIGGS Teton
DUBOIS Clark
EAGLE Ada
EASTPORT Boundary
EDEN Jerome
ELBA Cassia
ELK CITY Idaho
ELK RIVER Clearwater
ELLIS (83235) Custer(73), Lemhi(27)
EMMETT Gem
FAIRFIELD Camas
FELT Teton
FENN Idaho
FERDINAND Idaho
FERNWOOD Benewah
FILER Twin Falls
FIRTH Bingham
FISH HAVEN Bear Lake
FORT HALL Bingham
FRANKLIN Franklin
FRUITLAND Payette
FRUITVALE Adams
GARDEN VALLEY Boise
GENESEE (83832) Latah(85), Nez Perce(15)
GENEVA Bear Lake
GEORGETOWN Bear Lake
GIBBONSVILLE Lemhi
GLENNS FERRY Elmore
GOODING Gooding
GRACE (99999) Caribou(99), Franklin(1)
GRAND VIEW Owyhee
GRANGEVILLE Idaho
GREENCREEK Idaho
GREENLEAF Canyon
HAGERMAN (83332) Gooding(81), Twin Falls(19)
HAILEY Blaine
HAMER Jefferson
HAMMETT Elmore
HANSEN Twin Falls
HARRISON Kootenai
HARVARD Latah
HAYDEN Kootenai
HAZELTON Jerome
HEADQUARTERS Clearwater
HEYBURN (83336) Minidoka(81), Cassia(19)
HILL CITY Camas
HOLBROOK Oneida
HOMEDALE Owyhee
HOPE Bonner
HORSESHOE BEND (83629) Gem(69), Boise(31)

HOWE Butte
HUSTON Canyon
IDAHO CITY Boise
IDAHO FALLS Bonneville
INDIAN VALLEY (83632) Adams(87), Washington(13)
INKOM Bannock
IONA Bonneville
IRWIN Bonneville
ISLAND PARK Fremont
JEROME (83338) Jerome(99), Gooding(1)
JULIAETTA (83535) Latah(65), Nez Perce(35)
KAMIAH (83536) Idaho(73), Lewis(27)
KELLOGG Shoshone
KENDRICK (83537) Latah(52), Nez Perce(36), Clearwater(12)
KETCHUM (83340) Blaine(98), Custer(2)
KIMBERLY Twin Falls
KING HILL Elmore
KINGSTON Shoshone
KOOSKIA Idaho
KOOTENAI Bonner
KUNA (83634) Ada(95), Canyon(5)
LACLEDE Bonner
LAKE FORK Valley
LAPWAI (83540) Nez Perce(99), Benewah(1)
LAVA HOT SPRINGS Bannock
LEADORE (83464) Lemhi(83), Clark(17)
LEMHI Lemhi
LENORE (83541) Nez Perce(51), Clearwater(49)
LETHA Gem
LEWISTON Nez Perce
LEWISVILLE Jefferson
LOWMAN Boise
LUCILE Idaho
MACKAY Custer
MACKS INN Fremont
MALAD CITY Oneida
MALTA Cassia
MARSING Owyhee
MAY (83253) Lemhi(71), Custer(29)
MC CALL Valley
MC CAMMON Bannock
MEDIMONT Kootenai
MELBA (83641) Canyon(70), Owyhee(17), Ada(14)
MENAN (83434) Jefferson(91), Madison(9)
MERIDIAN Ada
MESA Adams
MIDDLETON Canyon
MIDVALE Washington
MINIDOKA Minidoka
MONTEVIEW Jefferson
MONTPELIER Bear Lake
MOORE (83255) Butte(72), Custer(28)
MOORE Butte
MORELAND Bingham
MOSCOW Latah
MOUNTAIN HOME Elmore

MOUNTAIN HOME A F B Elmore
MOYIE SPRINGS Boundary
MULLAN Shoshone
MURPHY Owyhee
MURRAY Shoshone
MURTAUGH (83344) Twin Falls(80), Cassia(21)
NAMPA (83687) Canyon(98), Ada(2)
NAMPA Canyon
NAPLES Boundary
NEW MEADOWS (83654) Adams(98), Idaho(2)
NEW PLYMOUTH Payette
NEWDALE (83436) Madison(56), Teton(28), Fremont(17)
NEZPERCE Lewis
NORDMAN Bonner
NORTH FORK Lemhi
NOTUS Canyon
OAKLEY Cassia
OLA Gem
OLDTOWN Bonner
OROFINO Clearwater
OSBURN Shoshone
OVID Bear Lake
PALISADES Bonneville
PARIS Bear Lake
PARKER Fremont
PARMA (83660) Canyon(90), Payette(10)
PAUL (83347) Lincoln(57), Minidoka(28), Jerome(15)
PAYETTE Payette
PECK Nez Perce
PICABO Blaine
PIERCE Clearwater
PINEHURST Shoshone
PINGREE Bingham
PLACERVILLE Boise
PLUMMER Benewah
POCATELLO (83202) Bannock(96), Bingham(4)
POCATELLO (83204) Bannock(95), Power(5)
POCATELLO Bannock
POLLOCK (83547) Idaho(83), Adams(17)
PONDERAY Bonner
PORTHILL Boundary
POST FALLS Kootenai
POTLATCH Latah
PRESTON Franklin
PRIEST RIVER Bonner
PRINCETON Latah
RATHDRUM Kootenai
REUBENS (83548) Lewis(53), Nez Perce(47)
REXBURG Madison
RICHFIELD Lincoln
RIGBY Jefferson
RIGGINS Idaho
RIRIE (83443) Jefferson(51), Bonneville(49)
ROBERTS Jefferson

ROCKLAND Power
ROGERSON Twin Falls
RUPERT Minidoka
SAGLE Bonner
SAINT ANTHONY Fremont
SAINT CHARLES Bear Lake
SAINT MARIES Benewah
SALMON Lemhi
SAMUELS Bonner
SANDPOINT Bonner
SANTA Benewah
SHELLEY Bingham
SHOSHONE Lincoln
SHOUP Lemhi
SILVERTON Shoshone

SMELTERVILLE Shoshone
SODA SPRINGS (83276) Caribou(91),
   Bear Lake(9)
SPALDING Nez Perce
SPENCER Clark
SPIRIT LAKE (83869) Kootenai(70),
   Bonner(30)
SPRINGFIELD Bingham
SQUIRREL Fremont
STANLEY Custer
STAR (83669) Ada(90), Canyon(11)
STITES Idaho
STONE Oneida
SUGAR CITY (83448) Madison(88),
   Fremont(12)

SUN VALLEY Blaine
SWAN VALLEY Bonneville
SWANLAKE Bannock
SWEET Gem
TENDOY Lemhi
TENSED Benewah
TERRETON Jefferson
TETON (83451) Fremont(64), Madison(36)
TETONIA Teton
THATCHER (83283) Franklin(98),
   Oneida(2)
TROY Latah
TWIN FALLS Twin Falls
UCON Bonneville
VICTOR Teton

VIOLA Latah
WALLACE Shoshone
WARREN Idaho
WAYAN (83285) Bonneville(52),
   Caribou(48)
WEIPPE Clearwater
WEISER Washington
WENDELL Gooding
WESTON Franklin
WHITE BIRD Idaho
WILDER Canyon
WINCHESTER Lewis
WORLEY Kootenai
YELLOW PINE Valley

ZIP/City Cross Reference

ZIP	City	ZIP	City	ZIP	City	ZIP	City
83201-83202	POCATELLO	83320-83320	CAREY	83464-83464	LEADORE	83638-83638	MC CALL
83203-83203	FORT HALL	83321-83321	CASTLEFORD	83465-83465	LEMHI	83639-83639	MARSING
83204-83209	POCATELLO	83322-83322	CORRAL	83466-83466	NORTH FORK	83641-83641	MELBA
83210-83210	ABERDEEN	83323-83323	DECLO	83467-83467	SALMON	83642-83642	MERIDIAN
83211-83211	AMERICAN FALLS	83324-83324	DIETRICH	83468-83468	TENDOY	83643-83643	MESA
83212-83212	ARBON	83325-83325	EDEN	83469-83469	SHOUP	83644-83644	MIDDLETON
83213-83213	ARCO	83326-83326	ELBA	83501-83501	LEWISTON	83645-83645	MIDVALE
83214-83214	ARIMO	83327-83327	FAIRFIELD	83520-83520	AHSAHKA	83647-83647	MOUNTAIN HOME
83215-83215	ATOMIC CITY	83328-83328	FILER	83522-83522	COTTONWOOD	83648-83648	MOUNTAIN HOME A F B
83217-83217	BANCROFT	83330-83330	GOODING	83523-83523	CRAIGMONT	83650-83650	MURPHY
83218-83218	BASALT	83332-83332	HAGERMAN	83524-83524	CULDESAC	83651-83653	NAMPA
83220-83220	BERN	83333-83333	HAILEY	83525-83525	ELK CITY	83654-83654	NEW MEADOWS
83221-83221	BLACKFOOT	83334-83334	HANSEN	83526-83526	FERDINAND	83655-83655	NEW PLYMOUTH
83223-83223	BLOOMINGTON	83335-83335	HAZELTON	83530-83530	GRANGEVILLE	83656-83656	NOTUS
83226-83226	CHALLIS	83336-83336	HEYBURN	83531-83531	FENN	83657-83657	OLA
83227-83227	CLAYTON	83337-83337	HILL CITY	83533-83533	GREENCREEK	83660-83660	PARMA
83228-83228	CLIFTON	83338-83338	JEROME	83535-83535	JULIAETTA	83661-83661	PAYETTE
83229-83229	COBALT	83340-83340	KETCHUM	83536-83536	KAMIAH	83666-83666	PLACERVILLE
83230-83230	CONDA	83341-83341	KIMBERLY	83537-83537	KENDRICK	83669-83669	STAR
83232-83232	DAYTON	83342-83342	MALTA	83538-83538	COTTONWOOD	83670-83670	SWEET
83233-83233	DINGLE	83343-83343	MINIDOKA	83539-83539	KOOSKIA	83671-83671	WARREN
83234-83234	DOWNEY	83344-83344	MURTAUGH	83540-83540	LAPWAI	83672-83672	WEISER
83235-83235	ELLIS	83346-83346	OAKLEY	83541-83541	LENORE	83676-83676	WILDER
83236-83236	FIRTH	83347-83347	PAUL	83542-83542	LUCILE	83677-83677	YELLOW PINE
83237-83237	FRANKLIN	83348-83348	PICABO	83543-83543	NEZPERCE	83680-83680	MERIDIAN
83238-83238	GENEVA	83349-83349	RICHFIELD	83544-83544	OROFINO	83686-83687	NAMPA
83239-83239	GEORGETOWN	83350-83350	RUPERT	83545-83545	PECK	83701-83788	BOISE
83241-83241	GRACE	83352-83352	SHOSHONE	83546-83546	PIERCE	83801-83801	ATHOL
83243-83243	HOLBROOK	83353-83354	SUN VALLEY	83547-83547	POLLOCK	83802-83802	AVERY
83244-83244	HOWE	83355-83355	WENDELL	83548-83548	REUBENS	83803-83803	BAYVIEW
83245-83245	INKOM	83401-83415	IDAHO FALLS	83549-83549	RIGGINS	83804-83804	BLANCHARD
83246-83246	LAVA HOT SPRINGS	83420-83420	ASHTON	83551-83551	SPALDING	83805-83805	BONNERS FERRY
83250-83250	MC CAMMON	83421-83421	CHESTER	83552-83552	STITES	83806-83806	BOVILL
83251-83251	MACKAY	83422-83422	DRIGGS	83553-83553	WEIPPE	83808-83808	CALDER
83252-83252	MALAD CITY	83423-83423	DUBOIS	83554-83554	WHITE BIRD	83809-83809	CAREYWOOD
83253-83253	MAY	83424-83424	FELT	83555-83555	WINCHESTER	83810-83810	CATALDO
83254-83254	MONTPELIER	83425-83425	HAMER	83601-83601	ATLANTA	83811-83811	CLARK FORK
83255-83255	MOORE	83427-83427	IONA	83602-83602	BANKS	83812-83812	CLARKIA
83256-83256	MORELAND	83428-83428	IRWIN	83604-83604	BRUNEAU	83813-83813	COCOLALLA
83261-83261	PARIS	83429-83429	ISLAND PARK	83605-83606	CALDWELL	83814-83816	COEUR D ALENE
83262-83262	PINGREE	83431-83431	LEWISVILLE	83610-83610	CAMBRIDGE	83821-83821	COOLIN
83263-83263	PRESTON	83433-83433	MACKS INN	83611-83611	CASCADE	83822-83822	OLDTOWN
83271-83271	ROCKLAND	83434-83434	MENAN	83612-83612	COUNCIL	83823-83823	DEARY
83272-83272	SAINT CHARLES	83435-83435	MONTEVIEW	83615-83615	DONNELLY	83824-83824	DESMET
83274-83274	SHELLEY	83436-83436	NEWDALE	83616-83616	EAGLE	83825-83825	DOVER
83276-83276	SODA SPRINGS	83438-83438	PARKER	83617-83617	EMMETT	83826-83826	EASTPORT
83277-83277	SPRINGFIELD	83440-83441	REXBURG	83619-83619	FRUITLAND	83827-83827	ELK RIVER
83278-83278	STANLEY	83442-83442	RIGBY	83620-83620	FRUITVALE	83830-83830	FERNWOOD
83280-83280	STONE	83443-83443	RIRIE	83622-83622	GARDEN VALLEY	83832-83832	GENESEE
83281-83281	SWANLAKE	83444-83444	ROBERTS	83623-83623	GLENNS FERRY	83833-83833	HARRISON
83283-83283	THATCHER	83445-83445	SAINT ANTHONY	83624-83624	GRAND VIEW	83834-83834	HARVARD
83285-83285	WAYAN	83446-83446	SPENCER	83626-83626	GREENLEAF	83835-83835	HAYDEN
83286-83286	WESTON	83447-83447	SQUIRREL	83627-83627	HAMMETT	83836-83836	HOPE
83287-83287	FISH HAVEN	83448-83448	SUGAR CITY	83628-83628	HOMEDALE	83837-83837	KELLOGG
83301-83301	TWIN FALLS	83449-83449	SWAN VALLEY	83629-83629	HORSESHOE BEND	83839-83839	KINGSTON
83302-83302	ROGERSON	83450-83450	TERRETON	83630-83630	HUSTON	83840-83840	KOOTENAI
83303-83303	TWIN FALLS	83451-83451	TETON	83631-83631	IDAHO CITY	83841-83841	LACLEDE
83311-83311	ALBION	83452-83452	TETONIA	83632-83632	INDIAN VALLEY	83842-83842	MEDIMONT
83312-83312	ALMO	83454-83454	UCON	83633-83633	KING HILL	83843-83844	MOSCOW
83313-83313	BELLEVUE	83455-83455	VICTOR	83634-83634	KUNA	83845-83845	MOYIE SPRINGS
83314-83314	BLISS	83460-83460	REXBURG	83635-83635	LAKE FORK	83846-83846	MULLAN
83316-83316	BUHL	83462-83462	CARMEN	83636-83636	LETHA	83847-83847	NAPLES
83318-83318	BURLEY	83463-83463	GIBBONSVILLE	83637-83637	LOWMAN	83848-83848	NORDMAN

Zip Range	City	Zip Range	City	Zip Range	City	Zip Range	City
83849-83849	OSBURN	83857-83857	PRINCETON	83867-83867	SILVERTON	83876-83876	WORLEY
83850-83850	PINEHURST	83858-83858	RATHDRUM	83868-83868	SMELTERVILLE	83877-83877	POST FALLS
83851-83851	PLUMMER	83860-83860	SAGLE	83869-83869	SPIRIT LAKE		
83852-83852	PONDERAY	83861-83861	SAINT MARIES	83870-83870	TENSED		
83853-83853	PORTHILL	83862-83862	SAMUELS	83871-83871	TROY		
83854-83854	POST FALLS	83864-83864	SANDPOINT	83872-83872	VIOLA		
83855-83855	POTLATCH	83865-83865	COLBURN	83873-83873	WALLACE		
83856-83856	PRIEST RIVER	83866-83866	SANTA	83874-83874	MURRAY		

Illinois

General Help Numbers:

Governor's Office
207 Statehouse   217-782-0244
Springfield, IL 62706   Fax 217-524-4049
www.state.il.us/gov   8:30AM-5PM

Attorney General's Office
500 S 2nd St   217-782-1090
Springfield, IL 62706   Fax 217-524-4701
www.ag.state.il.us/toc.htm   8:45AM-4:45PM

State Court Administrator
222 N. Lasalle - 13th Floor   312-793-3250
Chicago, IL 60601   Fax 312-793-1335
    8AM-5PM

State Archives
Archives Division   217-782-4682
Norton Bldg, Capitol Complex   Fax 217-524-3930
Springfield, IL 62756   8AM-4:30PM M-F
www.sos.state.il.us/depts/archives/arc_home.html

State Specifics:

Capital: Springfield
Sangamon County

Time Zone: CST

Number of Counties: 102

Population: 11,895,849

Web Site: www.state.il.us

State Agencies

Criminal Records

Illinois State Police, Bureau of Identification, 260 N Chicago St, Joliet, IL 60432-4075; 815-740-5164, 815-740-5193 (Fax), 8AM-4PM M-F.

www.state.il.us/isp/isphpage.htm

Indexing & Storage: Records are available from 1930's on. New records are available for inquiry immediately. Records are indexed on microfilm, index cards, inhouse computer.

Searching: No records are released without a disposition of conviction. Requester must use the state's Uniform Conviction Information Form signed by person of record. A request for a non-business purpose will be honored. Include the following in your request-name, date of birth, sex, race. Fingerprint cards are an option.

Access by: mail, in person, online.

Fee & Payment: The search fee is $12.00 per form. A fingerprint search is $14.00. Fee payee: Illinois State Police. Prepayment required. Modem users and ongoing UCIA requesters must prepay for records in groups of 35 at a time. Personal checks accepted. No credit cards accepted.

Mail search: Turnaround time: 15-20 days. No self addressed stamped envelope is required.

In person search: Going in person saves mailing time only.

Online search: Online access costs $7.00 per name. Upon signing an interagency agreement with ISP and establishing a $200 escrow account, users can submit inquiries over modem. Replies are still sent via U.S. mail. Turnaround time is approximately 4 business days for a "no record" response. Modem access is available from 7AM-4PM M-F, excluding holidays. Users must utilize LAPLINK version 6.0 or later. The system is called UCIA; call 815-740-5185 for more information, ask for Lynn Johnson.

Corporation Records
Limited Partnership Records
Trade Names
Assumed Name
Limited Liability Company
    Records

Department of Business Services, Corporate Department, Howlett Bldg, 3rd Floor, Copy Section, Springfield, IL 62756 (Courier: 501 S 2nd St, Springfield, IL 62756); 217-782-7880, 217-782-4528 (Fax), 8AM-4:30PM.

www.sos.state.il.us

Indexing & Storage: Records are available from mid-1800's on. Closed records are stored at the State Archives. Only limited information is available for corporations dissolved before 1986. New records are available for inquiry immediately. Records are indexed on inhouse computer.

Searching: Records are on micro-film from 1984. In-house computer has name of agent, state and date of incorporation, etc. Include the following in your request-full name of business, corporation file number. In addition to the articles of incorporation, corporation records include the following information: Annual Reports, Officers, Directors, Prior (merged) names, Assumed names, and Inactive names.

Access by: mail, phone, in person, online.

Fee & Payment: The search fee is $5.00 per name. Certification is $10.00 which includes search fee. Copies are $.50 per page after the initial $5.00. Fee payee: Secretary of State. Prepayment required. There is an additional $.50 charge to use a credit card. Personal checks accepted. Credit cards accepted: Mastercard, Visa, Discover.

Mail search: Turnaround time: 5-7 days. A self addressed stamped envelope is requested.

Phone search: Expedited copy service is available using a credit card.

In person search: Searching is available in person.

Online search: The web site gives free access to records, except the web does not offer not-for-profit records. A commercial access program is available. Potential users must submit in writing the purpose of the request. Submit to: Sharon Thomas, Dept. of Business Srvs, 330 Howlett Bldg, Springfield, IL 62756. Also, call 217-782-4104 for more information. Fees vary.

Other access: List or bulk file purchases are available. Call 217-782-4101 for more information.

Expedited service: Expedited service is available for mail, phone and fax searches. Turnaround time: 24 hours. Add $25.00 per business name.

Uniform Commercial Code
Federal Tax Liens

Secretary of State, UCC Division, 2nd & Edwards St, Howlett Bldg, Room 030, Springfield, IL 62756; 217-782-7518, 8AM-4:30PM.

www.sos.state.il.us

Indexing & Storage: Records are available from 1962. Records are computerized since 1972.

Searching: Use search request form UCC-11. Request searches for federal tax liens on businesses since 1988 separately with a fee of $5.00. Federal tax liens on individuals and all state tax liens are filed at the county level. Include the following in your request-debtor name and address.

Access by: mail, in person.

Fee & Payment: A UCC search is $10.00 per debtor name. A federal tax lien search only is available for $5.00 plus $.50 per page of copies. Copies are $1.00 per page. Fee payee: Secretary of State. Prepayment required. Personal checks accepted. Credit cards accepted: Mastercard, Visa, Discover.

Mail search: Turnaround time: 5-6 weeks. A self addressed stamped envelope is requested.

In person search: Documents can be viewed at no charge.

Other access: The entire database can be purchased and the state offers a microfilm update service for $250 per month.

State Tax Liens
Records not maintained by a state level agency.

Note: All state tax liens are filed at the county.

Sales Tax Registrations

Revenue Department, Taxpayer Services, PO Box 19044, Springfield, IL 62794-9044 (Courier: 101 W Jefferson, Springfield, IL 62702); 800-732-8866, 217-782-3336, 217-782-4217 (Fax), 8AM-5PM.

www.revenue.state.il.us

Indexing & Storage: Records are available for all active businesses with the state, records can go back to the 1930s.

Searching: This agency will only confirm that a business is registered if an Illinois business tax number is provided, often, the business name is not enough. They provide no other information. The state tax permit or federal tax ID is also helpful.

Access by: mail, phone, in person.

Fee & Payment: There is no fee. No credit cards accepted.

Mail search: Turnaround time: 7-10 days. A self addressed stamped envelope is requested.

Phone search: Will do up to 5 confirmations at a time.

In person search: Searching is available in person.

Birth Certificates

State Department of Health, Division of Vital Records, 605 W Jefferson St, Springfield, IL 62702-5097; 217-782-6553, 217-523-2648 (Fax), 8AM-5PM M-F.

www.idph.state.il.us/vital/home.htm

Indexing & Storage: Records are available from 1916-present. New records are available for inquiry immediately. Records are indexed on microfiche, inhouse computer.

Searching: Birth records are not considered public records. Copies are available to subject if 18 years old, parents, or legal guardian. Include the

following in your request-full name, date of birth, place of birth, relationship to person of record, names of parents, mother's maiden name. Place of birth can be city or county. Include name of hospital, if known. The following data is not released: sealed records.

Access by: mail, phone, fax, in person.

Fee & Payment: Fees are $10.00 per name for a computer abstract and $15.00 per name for a certified copy of original. Add $2.00 for each additional copy. Add $6.00 service fee to use a credit card. Fee payee: Illinois Department of Public Health. Prepayment required. Personal checks accepted. Credit cards accepted: Mastercard, Visa, AmEx, Discover.

Mail search: Turnaround time: 15 days. No self addressed stamped envelope is required.

Phone search: Use a credit card is required for extra fee of $6.00. Normal turnaround time is 2 days.

Fax search: Same criteria as phone searching.

In person search: Turnaround time 1-2 hours.

Expedited service: Expedited service is available for mail, phone and fax searches. Add $6.00 for using a credit card, $13.00 for express delivery.

Death Records

State Department of Health, Division of Vital Records, 605 W Jefferson St, Springfield, IL 62702-5097; 217-782-6553, 217-523-2648 (Fax), 8AM-5PM.

www.idph.state.il.us/vital/home.htm

Indexing & Storage: Records are available from 1916-present. New records are available for inquiry immediately. Records are indexed on microfiche.

Searching: Include the following in your request-full name, date of death, place of death, relationship to person of record, parents' names.

Access by: mail, phone, fax, in person.

Fee & Payment: Fees are $15.00 for a certified Death Certificate. Fee payee: Illinois Department of Public Health. Prepayment required. Personal checks accepted. Credit cards accepted: Mastercard, Visa, AmEx, Discover.

Mail search: Turnaround time: 1 month. No self addressed stamped envelope is required.

Phone search: Requires use of a credit card for an additional fee of $6.00. Turnaround time is 2 days.

Fax search: Same criteria as phone searching.

In person search: Turnaround time 1-2 hours.

Expedited service: Expedited service is available for mail, phone and fax searches. The fee is $6.00 for the credit card use and $13.00 for express delivery. If you send your request in by express delivery, they will turnaround in one day.

Marriage Certificates
Divorce Records
Records not maintained by a state level agency.

Note: State will verify marriage or divorce from 1962-present, but will not issue certificate. Verification requests must be in writing and there is a fee of $5.00 per event requested. Records of marriage and divorce are found at the county of issue.

Workers' Compensation Records

Industrial Commission, 100 W Randolph, 8th Floor, Chicago, IL 60601; 312-814-6611, 8:30AM-5PM.

www.state.il.us/agency/iic

Note: The web site lists cases that are up for a hearing status.

Indexing & Storage: Records are available on computer from 1982-present, on microfiche from 1927-1981. Settled file copies are kept in Springfield, but must be requested from Chicago. Data is indexed by name and file number. Records are indexed on file folders. Records are normally destroyed after five years.

Searching: Include the following in your request-claimant name, Social Security Number, date of accident. Include case number and company name.

Access by: mail, phone, in person.

Fee & Payment: There is no charge for a small file. For "large files," the office will contact you and suggest you use a record retrieval service. If your request is large enough to warrant the use of a copy service, the service will have its own fees that must be paid by you.

Mail search: Turnaround time: 2 weeks. Send a name as well as any other information you may have, such as company name and date of accident, to determine if any files existA self addressed stamped envelope is requested.

Phone search: Information about a case is accessed by the file number. The staff will do a name search if you have enough information for them to do so.

In person search: There are several public access terminals available in the office.

Driver Records

Abstract Information Unit, Drivers Services Department, 2701 S Dirksen Prky, Springfield, IL 62723; 217-782-2720, 8AM-4:30PM.

www.sos.state.il.us

Note: Copies of tickets can be obtained from the county of the incident for $1.00 or copies may be requested at the above address for a fee of $.50 per copy.

Indexing & Storage: Records are available for 4 years for moving violations; 7 years for suspension; lifetime for DWI. Commercial Driver records can go back 10 years for serious violations. It takes 2 weeks before new records are available for inquiry.

Searching: No personal identifiable information is provided on record unless requester is exempt. Exempt requesters include business representatives with a legitimate business need (e.g. insurance, financial institutions, employers, etc.). Include the following in your request-full name, date of birth, sex. There is a 10 day waiting period when requesting an abstract of another individual's driving record unless the requester is "exempt." This is so the person of record can be informed of the name of the requesting individual.

Access by: mail, in person.

Fee & Payment: The fee is $6.00 per record, which includes certification. There is a full charge for a "no record found." Fee payee: Secretary of State. Prepayment required. Personal checks accepted. No credit cards accepted.

Mail search: Turnaround time: 10 days. No self addressed stamped envelope is required.

In person search: Up to five requests will be processed immediately if requester meets the access requirement (see above). Requests are available from any Driver Services Facility statewide.

Other access: Overnight magnetic tape processing is available to high volume users (there is a 200 request minimum per day). Call (217) 785-2384 for more information.

Vehicle Ownership
Vehicle Identification

Vehicle Services Department, Vehicle Record Inquiry, 501 S 2nd Street #408, Springfield, IL 62756; 217-782-6992, 217-524-0122 (Fax), 8AM-4:30PM.

www.sos.state.il.us

Indexing & Storage: Records are available generally for 8 years to present.

Searching: Personal information is not released for non-business purposes. Bulk sales are not permitted for solicitation purposes.

Access by: mail, in person.

Fee & Payment: The fee is $5.00 per record search. Fee payee: Secretary of State. Prepayment required. Personal checks accepted. MasterCard, Visa, Discover accepted.

Mail search: Turnaround time: 4-7 days. You may search by mail, but there is a 10 day delay if the requester is not "exempt."A self addressed stamped envelope is requested.

In person search: Walk-in requesters may retrieve data immediately; however, if requester is not exempt there is a 10 day delay.

Other access: The state will sell customized, bulk requests upon approval of purpose and with a signed contract.

Accident Reports

Illinois State Police, Traffic Records Team, 500 Iles Park Place, Ste 200, Springfield, IL 62718; 217-785-0612, 8AM-5PM.

Note: If crash occurred on IL Tollway System, send check or money order payable to: IL Toll Highway Authority, Attn: State Police District 15, One Authority Drive, Downers Grove, IL 60515.

Indexing & Storage: Records are available from 1976-present.

Searching: Crash reports are considered public record and are available without restriction. Items needed by the requester include date, names of drivers involved, report number, and an exact location.

Access by: mail, phone, in person.

Fee & Payment: The fee is $5.00 per report or $20.00 for a reconstruction report. Fee payee: Illinois State Police. Prepayment required. Personal checks accepted. No credit cards accepted.

Mail search: Turnaround time: 7-10 days. If requester provides express envelope & label, the request will be returned quicker.A self addressed stamped envelope is requested.

Phone search: You may call to get information, but copies of records are only released with written requests.

In person search: Turnaround time is immediate.

Boat & Vessel Ownership
Boat & Vessel Registration

Department of Natural Resources, 524 S 2nd St, Springfield, IL 62701; 800-382-1696, 217-782-5016 (Fax), 8AM-5PM.

http://dnr.state.il.us

Note: Lien information will show on the history report.

Indexing & Storage: Records are available from 1982-the present. Snow mobile records are also available. Records are indexed on computer. All boats must be titled and registered unless if only used on a private lake.

Searching: To search, one of the following is required: name, hull id #, or registration #.

Access by: mail, phone.

Fee & Payment: There is a $5.00 fee for any search, including a title history search. Fee payee: IL Dept of Natural Resources. Prepayment required. Personal checks accepted. No credit cards accepted.

Mail search: Turnaround time: 4-6 weeks. No self addressed stamped envelope is required.

Phone search: They will give limited name search and verification information, time permitting.

Legislation-Current/Pending
Legislation-Passed

Illinois General Assembly, State House, House (or Senate) Bills Division, Springfield, IL 62706; 217-782-3944 (Bill Status Only), 217-782-7017 (Index Div-Older Bills), 217-782-5799 (House Bills), 217-782-9778 (Senate Bills), 217-524-6059 (Fax), 8AM-4:30PM.

www.legis.state.il.us

Note: Previous session bills must be obtained from: Senate 217-792-6970; House 217-782-7192. Cost is $.10 per page.

Indexing & Storage: Records are available from 1997-present on computer. Records are indexed on microfiche.

Searching: Include the following in your request-bill number. For statutes, it is suggested to go to a local law library or visit the Internet site. Complete statutes are not available here.

Access by: mail, phone, in person, online.

Fee & Payment: All copies of documents are considered as certified. There is no search fee, copies are free if from the last two sessions, otherwise $0.10 each. Fee payee: Illinois General Assembly. Personal checks accepted. No credit cards accepted.

Mail search: No self addressed stamped envelope is required.

Phone search: Searching is available by phone.

In person search: Searching is available in person.

Online search: The Legislative Information System is available for subscription through a standard modem. The sign-up fee is $500.00 which includes 100 free minutes of access.

Thereafter, access time is billed at $1.00 per minute. The hours of availability are 8 AM - 10 PM when in session and 8 AM - 5 PM when not in session, M-F. Contact Craig Garret at 217- 782-4083-set-up an account. The Internet site offers free access, but the state has a disclaimer which says the site should not be relied upon as an offical record of action.

Other access: A prepayment of $500.00 is required to obtain a printed copy of all bills.

Voter Registration

Access to Records is Restricted

Board of Elections, 1020 S Spring, Springfield, IL 62704; 217-782-4141, 217-782-5959 (Fax), 8AM-4:30PM.

www.elections.state.il.us

Note: The data is not considered public record at the state level and is only available in bulk format to political committees and government agencies. County Clerks control the information at the local level.

GED Certificates

Access to Records is Restricted

State Board of Education, 100 N 1st St, Springfield, IL 62777; 217-782-3370 (Main Number).

Note: All GED information is kept at the county level. You must contact the county where the test was taken. If you need assistance determining which county, contact the State Board of Education at the number listed here.

Hunting License Information
Fishing License Information

Records not maintained by a state level agency.

Note: They do not have a central database. The vendors hold license records.

Licenses Searchable Online

Architect #11	www.dpr.state.il.us/licenselookup/defaultn.htm
Athletic Trainer #11	www.dpr.state.il.us/licenselookup/defaultn.htm
Auctioneer #29	www.obre.state.il.us/lookup/
Bank #29	www.obre.state.il.us/CBT/REGENTY/BTREG.HTM
Barber #11	www.dpr.state.il.us/licenselookup/defaultn.htm
Check Printer #29	www.obre.state.il.us/CBT/REGENTY/BTREG.HTM
Chiropractor #11	www.dpr.state.il.us/licenselookup/defaultn.htm
Collection Agency #11	www.dpr.state.il.us/licenselookup/defaultn.htm
Controlled Substance #11	www.dpr.state.il.us/licenselookup/defaultn.htm
Corporate Fiduciary #29	www.obre.state.il.us/CBT/REGENTY/BTREG.HTM
Cosmetologist #11	www.dpr.state.il.us/licenselookup/defaultn.htm
Dentist/Dental Hygienist #11	www.dpr.state.il.us/licenselookup/defaultn.htm
Detection of Deception Examiner #11	www.dpr.state.il.us/licenselookup/defaultn.htm
Dietitian/Nutrition Counselor #11	www.dpr.state.il.us/licenselookup/defaultn.htm
Employee Leasing Company #04	www.state.il.us/INS/elc.htm
Engineer #11	www.dpr.state.il.us/licenselookup/defaultn.htm
Engineer, Structural #11	www.dpr.state.il.us/licenselookup/defaultn.htm
Environmental Health Practitioner #11	www.dpr.state.il.us/licenselookup/defaultn.htm
Esthetician #11	www.dpr.state.il.us/licenselookup/defaultn.htm
Firearms Regulation #27	www.dpr.state.il.us/licenselookup/defaultn.htm
Funeral Director/Embalmer #11	www.dpr.state.il.us/licenselookup/defaultn.htm
HMO #04	www.state.il.us/INS/bycty.htm
Interior Designer #11	www.dpr.state.il.us/licenselookup/defaultn.htm
Landscape Architect #11	www.dpr.state.il.us/licenselookup/defaultn.htm
Lead Contractors #17	http://163.191.194.35/envhealth/lead/leadcnt.asp
Lead Risk Assessor/Inspector/Supervisor #17	http://163.191.194.35/envhealth/lead/leadinsp.asp
Liquor License (Retail, Distributor, Manufacturer) #25	www.state.il.us/distributors/search.htm
Long Term Care Insurance Company #04	www.state.il.us/INS/longtermcareframe.htm
Marriage & Family Therapist #11	www.dpr.state.il.us/licenselookup/defaultn.htm
Medical Corporation #11	www.dpr.state.il.us/licenselookup/defaultn.htm
Medical Doctor/Physician's Assistant #11	www.dpr.state.il.us/licenselookup/defaultn.htm
Mortgage Banker/Broker #29	www.obre.state.il.us/RESFIN/liclistc.pdf
Nail Technician #11	www.dpr.state.il.us/licenselookup/defaultn.htm
Naprapath #11	www.dpr.state.il.us/licenselookup/defaultn.htm
Nurse #11	www.dpr.state.il.us/licenselookup/defaultn.htm
Nursing Home Administrator #17	www.medicare.gov/Nursing/Overview.asp
Occupational Therapist #11	www.dpr.state.il.us/licenselookup/defaultn.htm
Optometrist #11	www.dpr.state.il.us/licenselookup/defaultn.htm
Osteopathic Physician #11	www.dpr.state.il.us/licenselookup/defaultn.htm
Pawnbroker #29	www.obre.state.il.us/CBT/REGENTY/BTREG.HTM
Pharmacist/Pharmacy #11	www.dpr.state.il.us/licenselookup/defaultn.htm
Physical Therapist #11	www.dpr.state.il.us/licenselookup/defaultn.htm
Podiatrist #11	www.dpr.state.il.us/licenselookup/defaultn.htm
Private Detective #11	www.dpr.state.il.us/licenselookup/defaultn.htm
Private Security Contractor #11	www.dpr.state.il.us/licenselookup/defaultn.htm
Professional Counselor/Clinical Professional Counselor #11	www.dpr.state.il.us/licenselookup/defaultn.htm
Psychologist #11	www.dpr.state.il.us/licenselookup/defaultn.htm
Public Accountant-CPA #11	www.dpr.state.il.us/licenselookup/defaultn.htm
Real Estate Appraiser #29	www.obre.state.il.us/lookup/
Real Estate Broker #29	www.obre.state.il.us/lookup/
Real Estate Salesperson #29	www.obre.state.il.us/lookup/
Roofer #11	www.dpr.state.il.us/licenselookup/defaultn.htm
Shorthand Reporter #11	www.dpr.state.il.us/licenselookup/defaultn.htm
Social Worker #11	www.dpr.state.il.us/licenselookup/defaultn.htm
Speech-Language Pathologist/Audiologist #11	www.dpr.state.il.us/licenselookup/defaultn.htm
Surveyor #11	www.dpr.state.il.us/licenselookup/defaultn.htm
Timeshare/Land Sales #29	www.obre.state.il.us/lookup/
Trust Company #29	www.obre.state.il.us/CBT/REGENTY/BTREG.HTM
Veterinarian #11	www.dpr.state.il.us/licenselookup/defaultn.htm
Wholesale Drug Distributor #11	www.dpr.state.il.us/licenselookup/defaultn.htm

Licensing Quick Finder

Accident Reconstruction Specialist #19	217-782-4540
Alcohol Abuse Counselor #21	217-698-8110
Ambulance Provider #13	217-785-2080
Animal Breeder #06	217-785-3423
Aquaculturist #06	217-785-3423
Architect #11	217-785-0800
Asbestos Contractor #17	217-782-3517
Athletic Trainer #11	217-785-0800
Attorney #01	217-522-6838
Auctioneer #29	312-793-8704
Automotive Parts Recycler #30	217-782-7817
Bank #29	312-793-3000
Barber #11	217-785-0800
Bingo #18	217-785-5864
Blacksmith (Farrier) #26	312-814-2600
Blaster #07	217-782-4970
Boat Operator #05	217-782-2138
Boiler Inspector #36	217-782-2696
Boxing/Wrestling #11	217-785-0800
Breath Analyzer Operator #13	217-782-1571
Check Printer #29	312-793-3000
Chief School Business Official #35	217-782-2805
Child Care Facility #02	217-785-2688
Chiropractor #11	217-785-0800
Coal Mine Worker #08	217-782-6791
Collection Agency #11	217-785-0800
Commercial Fisherman #06	217-785-3423
Controlled Substance #11	217-785-0800
Corporate Fiduciary #29	312-793-3000
Cosmetologist #11	217-785-0800
County Coroner #19	217-782-4540
County Correction Officer #19	217-782-4540
County Sheriff Law Enforcement Officer #19	217-782-4540
Cross-Connection Control Device Inspector #24	217-782-1020
Day Care #02	217-785-2688
Dentist/Dental Hygienist #11	217-785-0800
Detection of Deception Examiner #11	217-785-0800
Dietitian/Nutrition Counselor #11	217-785-0800
Distribution System Operator #24	217-782-1869
Driving Instructor #31	847-437-3953
Early Childhood Teacher #35	217-782-2805
Electronic Criminal Surveillance Officer #19	217-782-4540
Emergency Medical Technician #13	217-785-2080
Employee Leasing Company #04	217-782-6366
Employment Agency #23	312-793-2810
Engineer #11	217-785-0800
Engineer, Structural #11	217-785-0800
Environmental Health Practitioner #11	217-785-0800
Esthetician #11	217-785-0800
Explosive - General Use #08	217-782-9976
Explosive Magazine Storage #08	217-782-9976
Firearms Regulation (Firearm Owner's Regulation) #27	217-782-7980
Fish Dealer #06	217-785-3423
Food Processing Plants & Warehouse #13	217-785-2439
Food Service Sanitation Manager #13	217-785-2439
Funeral Director/Embalmer #11	217-785-0800
Fur Buyer, Tanner or Dyer #05	217-782-7305
Gambling Employee #20	312-814-4702
Hearing Instrument Dispenser #13	217-782-1232
Hearing Instrument Dispenser #15	217-782-4733
High School Teacher #35	217-782-2805
Home Health Aide #13	217-782-7412
Home Health Care Agency #13	217-782-7412
Horseshoeing #26	312-814-2600
Hospital #13	217-782-7412
Hunting Area Operator #05	217-782-7305
Industrial Radiographer #09	217-785-9913
Insurance Adjuster/Agent #04	217-782-6366
Interior Designer #11	217-785-0800
Investment Adviser #33	217-785-4929
Laboratory Analysis Technician #13	217-785-8820
Land Sale #11	217-785-0800
Landfill Chief Operator #24	217-785-8604
Landscape Architect #11	217-785-0800
Lead Contractors #17	217-782-3517
Lead Risk Assessor/Inspector/Supervisor #17	217-782-3517
Liquor License (Retail, Distributor, Manufacturer) #25	312-814-3930
Lobbyist #32	217-782-0705
Marriage & Family Therapist #11	217-785-0800
Medical Corporation #11	217-785-0800
Medical Doctor/Physician's Assistant #11	217-785-0800
Mine Engineer #08	217-782-6791
Mine Foreman #08	217-782-6791
Mine Rescue Supervisor/Assistant #08	217-782-6791
Mine Supervisor #08	217-782-6791
Mortgage Banker/Broker #29	217-793-1409
Nail Technician #11	217-785-0800
Naprapath #11	217-785-0800
New Vehicle Dealer #30	217-782-7817
Notary Public #32	217-782-0641
Nuclear Medicine Technologist #09	217-785-9913
Nurse #11	217-785-0800
Nurses' Aide #13	217-785-5133
Nursing Home Administrator #17	217-782-0514
Occupational Aide #12	217-782-0545
Occupational Therapist #11	217-785-0800
Optometrist #11	217-785-0800
Osteopathic Physician #11	217-785-0800
Pawnbroker #29	312-793-3000
Pest Control Technician/Business/Non-commercial #17	217-782-4674
Pesticide Applicator #17	217-782-5830
Pharmacist/Pharmacy #11	217-785-0800
Physical Aide #12	217-782-0545
Physical Therapist #11	217-785-0800
Plumber #17	217-524-0791
Plumber Apprentice #13	217-785-1153
Podiatrist #11	217-785-0800
Private Detective #11	217-785-0800
Private Security Contractor #11	217-785-0800
Professional Counselor #11	217-785-0800
Psychologist #11	217-785-0800
Public Accountant-CPA #11	217-785-0800
Radiation Therapist #10	217-785-9913
Radiographer #10	217-785-9913
Radon Measurement Specialist #10	217-785-9935
Real Estate Appraiser #29	312-793-8704
Real Estate Broker #29	312-793-8704
Real Estate Salesperson #29	312-793-8704
Rehabilitation Aide #12	217-782-0545
Restaurant & Retail Food Store #17	217-785-2439
Riverboat Employee #20	312-814-4702
Roofer #11	217-785-0800
Salvage Firm #13	217-785-2439
Saving Bank #29	217-782-9043
Savings & Loan Association #29	217-782-9043
School Administrator #35	217-782-2805
School Guidance Counselor #35	217-782-2805
School Media Specialist/Librarian #35	217-782-2805
School Nurse #35	217-782-2805
School Principal #35	217-782-2805
School Psychologist #35	217-782-2805
School Superintendent #35	217-782-2805
School Supervisor #35	217-782-2805
Scrap Processor #30	217-782-7817
Securities Dealer/Salesperson #33	217-782-2256
Serviceman, Weighing & Measuring Devices #22	217-782-3817
Sewage System Contractor #17	217-782-5830
Shorthand Reporter #11	217-785-0800
Social Worker #11	217-785-0800
Special Teacher #35	217-782-2805
Speech-Language Pathologist/Audiologist #11	217-785-0800
Stock Broker #33	217-782-2256
Substitute Teacher #35	217-782-2805
Surveyor #11	217-785-0800
Tanning Facility #17	217-785-2439
Taxidermist #06	217-785-3423
Teacher #35	217-782-2805
Timber Buyer #03	217-782-2361
Time Share #11	217-785-0800
Timeshare/Land Sales #29	312-793-8704
Track #26	312-814-2600
Transitional Bilingual Teacher #35	217-782-2805
Trust Company #29	312-793-3000
Underground Shot Firer #08	217-782-6791
Used Vehicle Dealer #30	217-782-7817
Vehicle Auctioneer #30	217-782-7817
Vehicle Rebuilder #30	217-782-7817
Vehicle Repair #30	217-782-7817
Veterinarian #11	217-785-0800
Vision & Hearing Screening Technician #15	217-782-4733
Waste Water Treatment Plant Operator #24	217-782-1654
Water Supply Operator #24	217-782-1654
Water Well & Pump Installation Contractor #17	217-782-5830
Water Well Contractor/IDPH #17	217-782-5830
Wholesale Drug Distributor #11	217-785-0800

Licensing Agency Information

01 Attorney Registration & Disciplinary Commission of Supreme Court of IL, 700 E Adams St, Hilton Offices, #201, Springfield, IL 62701; 217-522-6838, Fax: 217-522-2417.

02 Department of Children & Family Services, 406 E Monroe St, Springfield, IL 62701; 217-785-2509, Fax: 217-785-1052.

03 Department of Commerce, Division of Forest Services, PO Box 19225 (600 N Grande Ave W), Springfield, IL 62794-9225; 217-782-2361, Fax: 217-785-5517.

04 Department of Insurance, 320 W Washington, Springfield, IL 62767-0001; 217-782-4515, Fax: 217-782-5020.

www.state.il.us/INS

05 Department of Natural Resources, 524 S 2nd St, Springfield, IL 62701; 217-782-2138, Fax: 217-782-5016.

http://dnr.state.il.us

06 Department of Natural Resources, 524 S 2nd St, Springfield, IL 62701; 217-785-3423, Fax: 217-782-5016.

http://dnr.state.il.us

08 Department of Natural Resources, Office of Mine & Minerals, 300 W Jefferson St, #300, Springfield, IL 62791; 217-782-9976, Fax: 217-524-4819.

http://dnr.state.il.us/mines/index.html

09 Department of Nuclear Safety, 1035 Outer Park Dr, Springfield, IL 62704; 217-785-9900, Fax: 217-785-9962.

www.state.il.us/idns

11 Department of Professional Regulation, Professions/Occupations/Entities, 320 W Washington, 3rd Fl, Springfield, IL 62786; 217-785-0800, Fax: 217-782-7645.
www.state.il.us/dpr

Direct URL to search licenses: www.dpr.state.il.us/licenselookup/defaultn.htm You can search online using name or license number.

12 Department of Public Aid, Bureau of Long-Term Care, 201 Grand Ave, Springfield, IL 62763-0001; 217-782-0545, Fax: 217-524-7114.

13 Department of Public Health, Education & Training Section, 525 W Jefferson St 4th Fl, Springfield, IL 62761; 217-782-4977, Fax: 217-782-3987.

www.idph.state.il.us

15 Department of Public Health, Division of Health Assessment & Screening, 535 W Jefferson St, Springfield, IL 62761; 217-782-4733, Fax: 217-524-2831.

www.idph.state.il.us

17 Department of Public Health, Environmental Health, 525 W Jefferson St, 3rd Fl, Springfield, IL 62761; 217-782-5830, Fax: 217-785-0253.

www.idph.state.il.us

18 Department of Revenue, Bingo Division, 101 W Jefferson RM3011, Springfield, IL 62794; 217-785-5864.

19 Law Enforcement & Standards Training Board, 600 S 2nd St, #300, Springfield, IL 62704; 217-782-4540, Fax: 217-524-5350.

http://cait.wiu.edu/iletsb

20 Gaming Board, 160 N Lasalle #300, Chicago, IL 60601; 312-814-4700, Fax: 312-814-1581.

21 Alcoholism Counselor-Executive Director Certification Board, 1305 Wabash Ave #L, Springfield, IL 62704-4938; 217-698-8110, Fax: 217-698-8234.

www.iaodapca.org

22 Department of Agriculture, State Fairgrounds, PO Box 19281 (PO Box 19281), Springfield, IL 62794-9281; 217-782-2172, Fax: 217-524-7801.

23 Department of Labor, 160 N LaSalle, 13th Fl, #C1300, Chicago, IL 60601; 312-793-2800, Fax: 312-793-5257.

www.state.il.us/agency/idol

24 Environmental Protection Agency, PO Box 19276 (1021 N Grand Ave), Springfield, IL 62794-9276; 217-782-1869, Fax: 217-557-1407.

www.epa.state.il.us

25 Freedom of Information Compliance Officer, Liquor Control Commission, 100 W Randolph, #5-300, Chicago, IL 60601; 312-814-2206, Fax: 312-814-2241.
www.state.il.us/lcc/default.htm

Direct URL to search licenses: www.state.il.us/distributors/search.htm You can search online using license year, license class, and license number.

26 Racing Board, 100 W Randolph, #11-100, Chicago, IL 60601; 312-814-2600, Fax: 312-814-5062.

www.state.il.us/agency/irb

27 State Police, 103 Armory Bldg, Springfield, IL 62708; 217-782-7980, Fax: 217-785-2821.

www.state.il.us/isp

29 Office of Banks & Real Estate, Bureaus of Res. Finance; Banks & Trusts; Real Estate Professions, 500 E Monroe, Springfield, IL 62701-1509; 217-782-3000, Fax: 217-524-5941.
www.obre.state.il.us

Direct URL to search licenses: www.obre.state.il.us/lookup/ You can search online using name, business name, license #. Lists Real Estate Professions.

30 Secretary of State, Howlett Bldg, Rm 8, Springfield, IL 62756; 217-782-2201, Fax: 217-524-0120.

www.sos.state.il.us

31 Secretary of State, Commercial Driver Training, 650 Roppolo Dr, Elk Grove, IL 60007; 847-437-3953, Fax: 847-437-3911.

32 Secretary of State, Index Department, 111 E Monroe St, Springfield, IL 62756; 217-782-7017, Fax: 217-524-0930.

33 Secretary of State, Securities Department, 520 S 2nd St, Lincoln Tower, #200, Springfield, IL 62701; 217-782-2256, Fax: 217-524-2172.

35 Board of Education, 100 N 1st St, Springfield, IL 62777; 217-782-2805, Fax: 217-524-1289.

www.isbe.state.il.us/teachers

36 State Fire Marshall, 1035 Stevenson Dr, Springfield, IL 62703; 217-785-0969, Fax: 217-782-1062.

The following list indicates the district and division name for each county in the state. If the district or division name of the bankruptcy court is different from the civil/criminal court, it appears in parentheses.

County/Court Cross Reference

County	District	Division
Adams	Central	Springfield
Alexander	Southern	Benton
Bond	Southern	East St Louis
Boone	Northern	Rockford
Brown	Central	Springfield
Bureau	Central	Peoria
Calhoun	Southern	East St Louis
Carroll	Northern	Rockford
Cass	Central	Springfield
Champaign	Central	Danville/Urbana (Danville)
Christian	Central	Springfield
Clark	Southern	Benton (East St Louis)
Clay	Southern	Benton (East St Louis)
Clinton	Southern	East St Louis
Coles	Central	Danville/Urbana (Danville)
Cook	Northern	Chicago (Eastern)
Crawford	Southern	Benton (East St Louis)
Cumberland	Southern	Benton
De Kalb	Northern	Rockford
De Witt	Central	Springfield
Douglas	Central	Danville/Urbana (Danville)
Du Page	Northern	Chicago (Eastern)
Edgar	Central	Danville/Urbana (Danville)
Edwards	Southern	Benton
Effingham	Southern	Benton (East St Louis)
Fayette	Southern	East St Louis
Ford	Central	Danville/Urbana (Danville)
Franklin	Southern	Benton
Fulton	Central	Peoria
Gallatin	Southern	Benton
Greene	Central	Springfield
Grundy	Northern	Chicago (Eastern)
Hamilton	Southern	Benton
Hancock	Central	Peoria
Hardin	Southern	Benton
Henderson	Central	Rock Island (Peoria)
Henry	Central	Rock Island (Peoria)
Iroquois	Central	Danville/Urbana (Danville)
Jackson	Southern	Benton
Jasper	Southern	Benton (East St Louis)
Jefferson	Southern	Benton
Jersey	Southern	East St Louis
Jo Daviess	Northern	Rockford
Johnson	Southern	Benton
Kane	Northern	Chicago (Eastern)
Kankakee	Central	Danville/Urbana (Danville)
Kendall	Northern	Chicago (Eastern)
Knox	Central	Peoria
La Salle	Northern	Chicago (Eastern)
Lake	Northern	Chicago (Eastern)
Lawrence	Southern	Benton (East St Louis)
Lee	Northern	Rockford
Livingston	Central	Peoria (Danville)
Logan	Central	Springfield
Macon	Central	Danville/Urbana (Spngfld)
Macoupin	Central	Springfield
Madison	Southern	East St Louis
Marion	Southern	East St Louis
Marshall	Central	Peoria
Mason	Central	Springfield
Massac	Southern	Benton
McDonough	Central	Peoria
McHenry	Northern	Rockford
McLean	Central	Peoria (Springfield)
Menard	Central	Springfield
Mercer	Central	Rock Island (Peoria)
Monroe	Southern	East St Louis
Montgomery	Central	Springfield
Morgan	Central	Springfield
Moultrie	Central	Danville/Urbana (Danville)
Ogle	Northern	Rockford
Peoria	Central	Peoria
Perry	Southern	Benton
Piatt	Central	Danville/Urbana (Danville)
Pike	Central	Springfield
Pope	Southern	Benton
Pulaski	Southern	Benton
Putnam	Central	Peoria
Randolph	Southern	East St Louis
Richland	Southern	Benton (East St Louis)
Rock Island	Central	Rock Island (Peoria)
Saline	Southern	Benton
Sangamon	Central	Springfield
Schuyler	Central	Springfield
Scott	Central	Springfield
Shelby	Central	Springfield
St. Clair	Southern	East St Louis
Stark	Central	Peoria
Stephenson	Northern	Rockford
Tazewell	Central	Peoria
Union	Southern	Benton
Vermilion	Central	Danville/Urbana (Danville)
Wabash	Southern	Benton
Warren	Central	Rock Island (Peoria)
Washington	Southern	East St Louis (Benton)
Wayne	Southern	Benton
White	Southern	Benton
Whiteside	Northern	Rockford
Will	Northern	Chicago (Eastern)
Williamson	Southern	Benton
Winnebago	Northern	Rockford
Woodford	Central	Peoria

US District Court

Central District of Illinois

Danville/Urbana Division 201 S Vine, Room 218, Urbana, IL 61801, 217-373-5830.

www.ilcd.uscourts.gov

Counties: Champaign, Coles, Douglas, Edgar, Ford, Iroquois, Kankakee, Macon, Moultrie, Piatt, Vermilion.

Indexing & Storage: Cases are indexed by defendant and plaintiff as well as by case number. New cases are available in the index immediately after filing date. Both computer and card indexes are maintained. Open records are located at this court. District wide searches are availiable for civil records from October 1989 and criminal records from April 1992 from this court.

Fee & Payment: The fee is $15.00 per item (one party name or case number). Payment may be made by money order, cashier check, business check. Personal checks are not accepted. Prepayment is required. Payee: Clerk, US District Court. Certification fee: $5.00 per document. Copy fee: $.50 per page.

Phone Search: Only docket information is available by phone. An automated voice case information service (VCIS) is not available.

Mail Search: A stamped self addressed envelope is not required.

In Person Search: In person searching is available.

PACER: Sign-up number is 800-676-6856. Access fee is $.60 per minute. Toll-free access: 800-258-3678. Local access: 217-492-4997. Case records are available back to 1995. Records are purged after 5-7 years. New records are available online after 1 day. PACER is available on the Internet at http://pacer.ilcd.uscourts.gov.

Peoria Division US District Clerk's Office, 309 Federal Bldg, 100 NE Monroe St, Peoria, IL 61602, 309-671-7117.

www.ilcd.uscourts.gov

Counties: Bureau, Fulton, Hancock, Knox, Livingston, McDonough, McLean, Marshall, Peoria, Putnam, Stark, Tazewell, Woodford.

Indexing & Storage: Cases are indexed by defendant and plaintiff as well as by case number. New cases are available in the index immediately after filing date. District-wide searches are available for civil cases from November 1989 and for criminal records from April 1992. Both computer and card indexes are maintained. Open records are located at this court.

Fee & Payment: The fee is $15.00 per item (one party name or case number). Payment may be made by money order, cashier check. Business checks are not accepted. Personal checks are not accepted. Prepayment is required. Law firm checks are accepted. Payee: Clerk,US District Court. Certification fee: $5.00 per document. Copy fee: $.50 per page.

Phone Search: Searching is not available by phone.

Mail Search: Always enclose a stamped self addressed envelope.

In Person Search: In person searching is available.

PACER: Sign-up number is 800-676-6856. Access fee is $.60 per minute. Toll-free access:

800-258-3678. Local access: 217-492-4997. Case records are available back to 1995. Records are purged after 5-7 years. New records are available online after 1 day. PACER is available on the Internet at http://pacer.ilcd.uscourts.gov.

Rock Island Division US District Clerk's Office, Room 40, Post Office Bldg, 211 19th St, Rock Island, IL 61201, 309-793-5778.

www.ilcd.uscourts.gov

Counties: Henderson, Henry, Mercer, Rock Island, Warren.

Indexing & Storage: Cases are indexed by defendant and plaintiff as well as by case number. New cases are available in the index immediately after filing date. A computer index is maintained. Open records are located at this court.

Fee & Payment: The fee is $15.00 per item (one party name or case number). Payment may be made by money order, cashier check, business check. Personal checks are not accepted. Prepayment is required. Payee: Clerk of US District Court. Certification fee: $5.00 per document. Copy fee: $.50 per page.

Phone Search: All information that is not sealed is available for release over the phone. An automated voice case information service (VCIS) is not available.

Mail Search: Always enclose a stamped self addressed envelope.

In Person Search: In person searching is available.

PACER: Sign-up number is 800-676-6856. Access fee is $.60 per minute. Toll-free access: 800-258-3678. Local access: 217-492-4997. Case records are available back to 1995. Records are purged after 5-7 years. New records are available online after 1 day. PACER is available on the Internet at http://pacer.ilcd.uscourts.gov.

Springfield Division Clerk, 151 US Courthouse, 600 E Monroe, Springfield, IL 62701, 217-492-4020.

www.ilcd.uscourts.gov

Counties: Adams, Brown, Cass, Christian, De Witt, Greene, Logan, Macoupin, Mason, Menard, Montgomery, Morgan, Pike, Sangamon, Schuyler, Scott, Shelby.

Indexing & Storage: Cases are indexed by defendant and plaintiff as well as by case number. New cases are available in the index immediately after filing date. Both computer and card indexes are maintained. Open records are located at this court. District wide searches are available for civil records from November 1989 and criminal records from 1992 from this court.

Fee & Payment: The fee is $15.00 per item (one party name or case number). Payment may be made by money order, cashier check, business check. Personal checks are not accepted. Prepayment is required. Payee: US District Court Clerk. Certification fee: $5.00 per document. Copy fee: $.50 per page. You are allowed to make your own copies. These copies cost $.50 per page.

Phone Search: Searching is not available by phone.

Mail Search: A stamped self addressed envelope is not required.

In Person Search: In person searching is available.

PACER: Sign-up number is 800-676-6856. Access fee is $.60 per minute. Toll-free access:

800-258-3678. Local access: 217-492-4997. Case records are available back to 1995. Records are purged after 5-7 years. New records are available online after 1 day. PACER is available on the Internet at http://pacer.ilcd.uscourts.gov.

US Bankruptcy Court

Central District of Illinois

Danville Division 201 N Vermilion #130, Danville, IL 61832-4733, 217-431-4820, Fax: 217-431-2694.

www.ilcb.uscourts.gov

Counties: Champaign, Coles, Douglas, Edgar, Ford, Iroquois, Kankakee, Livingston, Moultrie, Piatt, Vermilion.

Indexing & Storage: Cases are indexed by debtor as well as by case number. New cases are available in the index 24 hours after filing date. A computer index is maintained. Open records are located at this court.

Fee & Payment: The fee is $15.00 per item (one party name or case number). Payment may be made by money order, cashier check, business check. Personal checks are not accepted. Prepayment is required. Payee: US Bankruptcy Court. Certification fee: $5.00 per document. Copy fee: $.50 per page.

Phone Search: Docket information available by phone. An automated voice case information service (VCIS) is available. Call VCIS at 800-827-9005 or 217-492-4550.

Fax Search: You may request a fee quotation by fax. Court will add $25.00 if records are in Chicago. Will fax results for $15.00 plus other fees.

Mail Search: Always enclose a stamped self addressed envelope.

In Person Search: In person searching is available.

PACER: Sign-up number is 800-676-6856. Access fee is $.60 per minute. Toll-free access: 800-454-9893. Local access: 217-492-4260. Case records are available back to 1989-90. Records are purged immediately when case is closed. New civil records are available online after 2 days.

Peoria Division 131 Federal Bldg, 100 NE Monroe, Peoria, IL 61602, 309-671-7035, Fax: 309-671-7076.

www.ilcb.uscourts.gov

Counties: Bureau, Fulton, Hancock, Henderson, Henry, Knox, Marshall, McDonough, Mercer, Peoria, Putnam, Rock Island, Stark, Tazewell, Warren, Woodford.

Indexing & Storage: Cases are indexed by debtor as well as by case number. New cases are available in the index 24 hours after filing date. A computer index is maintained. Open records are located at this court.

Fee & Payment: The fee is $15.00 per item (one party name or case number). Payment may be made by money order, cashier check, business check. Personal checks are not accepted. Prepayment is required. A bill can be sent for copies. Payee: US Bankruptcy Court. Certification fee: $5.00 per document. Copy fee: $.50 per page.

Phone Search: An automated voice case information service (VCIS) is available. Call VCIS at 800-827-9005 or 217-492-4550.

Fax Search: You may request a quotation of fees by fax.

Mail Search: Always enclose a stamped self addressed envelope.

In Person Search: In person searching is available.

PACER: Sign-up number is 800-676-6856. Access fee is $.60 per minute. Toll-free access: 800-454-9893. Local access: 217-492-4260. Case records are available back to 1989-90. Records are purged immediately when case is closed. New civil records are available online after 2 days.

Springfield Division 226 US Courthouse, Springfield, IL 62701 (Courier Address: 600 E Monroe St, Springfield, IL 62701), 217-492-4551, Fax: 217-492-4556.

www.ilcb.uscourts.gov

Counties: Adams, Brown, Cass, Christian, De Witt, Greene, Logan, Macon, Macoupin, Mason, McLean, Menard, Montgomery, Morgan, Pike, Sangamon, Schuyler, Scott, Shelby.

Indexing & Storage: Cases are indexed by debtor as well as by case number. New cases are available in the index 24 hours after filing date. A computer index is maintained. Open records are located at this court.

Fee & Payment: The fee is $15.00 per item (one party name or case number). Payment may be made by money order, cashier check, business check. Personal checks are not accepted. Prepayment is required. A bill will be sent for copies. Payee: US Bankruptcy Court. Certification fee: $5.00 per document. Copy fee: $.50 per page.

Phone Search: An automated voice case information service (VCIS) is available. Call VCIS at 800-827-9005 or 217-492-4550.

Fax Search: Fax requests are handled the same as mail requests.

Mail Search: Always enclose a stamped self addressed envelope.

In Person Search: In person searching is available.

PACER: Sign-up number is 800-676-6856. Access fee is $.60 per minute. Toll-free access: 800-454-9893. Local access: 217-492-4260. Case records are available back to 1989-90. Records are purged immediately when case is closed. New civil records are available online after 2 days.

US District Court

Northern District of Illinois

Chicago (Eastern) Division 20th Floor, 219 S Dearborn St, Chicago, IL 60604, 312-435-5698.

www.ilnd.uscourts.gov

Counties: Cook, Du Page, Grundy, Kane, Kendall, Lake, La Salle, Will.

Indexing & Storage: Cases are indexed by defendant and plaintiff as well as by case number. New cases are available in the index 2 days after filing date. A computer index is maintained. Records are also indexed on microfiche. Open records are located at this court.

Fee & Payment: The fee is $15.00 per item (one party name or case number). Payment may be made by money order, cashier check, personal check, Visa, Mastercard. Except for criminal bail

bonds, all types of checks or money orders are accepted. Prepayment is required. Credit cards are only accepted in person. Payee: Clerk, US District Court. Certification fee: $5.00 per document. Copy fee: $.50 per page. You are allowed to make your own copies. These copies cost $.25 per page.

Phone Search: Only docket information is available by phone. Phone inquiries may be made from 8:15AM-5PM.

Mail Search: Always enclose a stamped self addressed envelope.

In Person Search: In person searching is available.

PACER: Sign-up number is 800-676-6856. Access fee is $.60 per minute. Toll-free access: 800-621-7029. Local access: 312-408-7777. Case records are available back to 1988. Records are purged varies. New records are available online after 1-2 days. If you are a registered PACER subscriber, you can access this court through the Internet at http://pacer.ilnd.uscourts.gov.

Rockford Division Room 211, 211 S Court St, Rockford, IL 61101, 815-987-4355.

www.ilnd.uscourts.gov

Counties: Boone, Carroll, De Kalb, Jo Daviess, Lee, McHenry, Ogle, Stephenson, Whiteside, Winnebago.

Indexing & Storage: Cases are indexed by defendant and plaintiff as well as by case number. New cases are available in the index 1-3 days after filing date. A computer index is maintained. Open records are located at this court.

Fee & Payment: The fee is $15.00 per item (one party name or case number). Payment may be made by money order, cashier check, personal check. Prepayment is required. Payee: Clerk, US District Court. Certification fee: $5.00 per document. Copy fee: $.50 per page.

Phone Search: Searching is not available by phone.

Mail Search: Any indictments, pending information, case numbers and docket sheets (if specifically requested) will be released. A stamped self addressed envelope is not required.

In Person Search: In person searching is available.

PACER: Sign-up number is 800-676-6856. Access fee is $.60 per minute. Toll-free access: 800-621-7029. Local access: 312-408-7777. Case records are available back to 1988. Records are purged varies. New records are available online after 1-2 days. If you are a registered PACER subscriber, you can access this court through the Internet at http://pacer.ilnd.uscourts.gov.

US Bankruptcy Court

Northern District of Illinois

Chicago (Eastern) Division 219 S Dearborn St, Chicago, IL 60604-1802, 312-435-5694.

www.ilnb.uscourts.gov

Counties: Cook, Du Page, Grundy, Kane, Kendall, La Salle, Lake, Will.

Indexing & Storage: Cases are indexed by debtor as well as by case number. New cases are available in the index 1 day after filing date. A computer index is maintained. Open records are located at this court.

Fee & Payment: The fee is $15.00 per item (one party name or case number). Payment may be made by money order, cashier check, business check. Personal checks are not accepted. Prepayment is required. Payee: Clerk, US Bankruptcy Court. Certification fee: $5.00 per document. Copy fee: $.50 per page. You are allowed to make your own copies. These copies cost $.28 per page. Copies are available through Ikon Copy Service, 312-913-9508.

Phone Search: If the searcher has a case number, any information contained on the docket will be released. An automated voice case information service (VCIS) is available.

Mail Search: Always enclose a stamped self addressed envelope.

In Person Search: In person searching is available.

PACER: Sign-up number is 800-676-6856. Access fee is $.60 per minute. Toll-free access: 888-541-1078. Local access: 312-408-5101. Use of PC Anywhere v4.0 suggested. Case records are available back to July 1, 1993. Records are never purged. New civil records are available online after 1 day.

Other Online Access: You can search using RACER on the Internet. Currently the system is free but a fee has been approved and may be applied in the future. Visit http://207.41.17.23/wconnect/wc.dll?usbcn_racer~main to log on.

Rockford Division Room 110, 211 S Court St, Rockford, IL 61101, 815-987-4350, Fax: 815-987-4205.

www.ilnb.uscourts.gov

Counties: Boone, Carroll, De Kalb, Jo Daviess, Lee, McHenry, Ogle, Stephenson, Whiteside, Winnebago.

Indexing & Storage: Cases are indexed by debtor and creditors as well as by case number. New cases are available in the index immediately after filing date. A computer index is maintained. Open records are located at this court.

Fee & Payment: The fee is $15.00 per item (one party name or case number). Payment may be made by money order, cashier check, personal check. Debtor's checks are not accepted. Payee: Clerk, US Bankruptcy Court. Certification fee: $5.00 per document. Copy fee: $.50 per page.

Phone Search: Only docket information is available by phone. An automated voice case information service (VCIS) is available. Call VCIS at 888-293-3698 or.

Mail Search: Always enclose a stamped self addressed envelope.

In Person Search: In person searching is available.

PACER: Sign-up number is 800-676-6856. Access fee is $.60 per minute. Use of PC Anywhere v4.0 suggested. Case records are available back to 1992. New civil records are available online after 1 day.

Other Online Access: You can search using RACER on the Internet. Currently the system is free but a fee has been approved and may be applied in the future. Visit http://207.41.17.23/wconnect/wc.dll?usbcn_racer~main to log on.

US District Court

Southern District of Illinois

Benton Division 301 W Main St, Benton, IL 62812, 618-438-0671.

www.ilsd.uscourts.gov

Counties: Alexander, Clark, Clay, Crawford, Cumberland, Edwards, Effingham, Franklin, Gallatin, Hamilton, Hardin, Jackson, Jasper, Jefferson, Johnson, Lawrence, Massac, Perry, Pope, Pulaski, Richland, Saline, Union, Wabash, Wayne, White, Williamson. Cases mayalso be allocated to the Benton Division.

Indexing & Storage: Cases are indexed by defendant and plaintiff as well as by case number. New cases are available in the index immediately after filing date. The name and date are required to search for records. Both computer and card indexes are maintained. Records are also indexed on microfiche. Open records are located at this court.

Fee & Payment: The fee is $15.00 per item (one party name or case number). Payment may be made by money order, cashier check, personal check. Except in an emergency, prepayment is required. Payee: Clerk, US District Court. Certification fee: $5.00 per document. Copy fee: $.50 per page. You are allowed to make your own copies. These copies cost $.50 per page.

Phone Search: Docket information available by phone. An automated voice case information service (VCIS) is not available.

Mail Search: Always enclose a stamped self addressed envelope.

In Person Search: In person searching is available.

PACER: Sign-up number is 800-676-6856. Access fee is $.60 per minute. Toll-free access: 800-426-7523. Local access: 618-482-9430. Case records are available back to 1985. Records are purged when deemed necessary. New civil records are available online after 1 day. New criminal records are available online after 1-2 days. PACER is available on the Internet at http://pacer.ilsd.uscourts.gov.

East St Louis Division PO Box 249, East St Louis, IL 62202 (Courier Address: 750 Missouri Ave, East St Louis, IL 62201), 618-482-9371.

www.ilsd.uscourts.gov

Counties: Bond, Calhoun, Clinton, Fayette, Jersey, Madison, Marion, Monroe, Randolph, St. Clair, Washington. Cases for these counties may also be allocated to the Benton Division.

Indexing & Storage: Cases are indexed by defendant and plaintiff as well as by case number. New cases are available in the index immediately after filing date. Name and date are required to search for records. Both computer and card indexes are maintained. Records are also indexed on microfiche. Open records are located at this court.

Fee & Payment: The fee is $15.00 per item (one party name or case number). Payment may be made by money order, cashier check, personal check. Except in an emergency, prepayment is required. Cash is also accepted. Payee: Clerk, US District Court. Certification fee: $5.00 per document. Copy fee: $.50 per page.

Phone Search: Docket information available by phone. An automated voice case information service (VCIS) is not available.

Mail Search: Always enclose a stamped self addressed envelope.

In Person Search: In person searching is available.

PACER: Sign-up number is 800-676-6856. Access fee is $.60 per minute. Toll-free access: 800-426-7523. Local access: 618-482-9430. Case records are available back to 1985. Records are purged when deemed necessary. New civil records are available online after 1 day. New criminal records are available online after 1-2 days. PACER is available on the Internet at http://pacer.ilsd.uscourts.gov.

US Bankruptcy Court

Southern District of Illinois

Benton Division 301 W Main, Benton, IL 62812, 618-435-2200.

www.ilsb.uscourts.gov

Counties: Alexander, Edwards, Franklin, Gallatin, Hamilton, Hardin, Jackson, Jefferson, Johnson, Massac, Perry, Pope, Pulaski, Randolph, Saline, Union, Wabash, Washington, Wayne, White, Williamson.

Indexing & Storage: Cases are indexed by debtor as well as by case number. New cases are available in the index immediately after filing date. Both computer and card indexes are maintained. Open records are located at this court.

Fee & Payment: The fee is $15.00 per item (one party name or case number). Payment may be made by money order, cashier check, business check. Personal checks are not accepted. Prepayment is required. Payee: Clerk, US Bankruptcy Court. Certification fee: $5.00 per document. Copy fee: $.50 per page.

Phone Search: An automated voice case information service (VCIS) is available. Call VCIS at 800-726-5622 or 618-482-9365.

Mail Search: Always enclose a stamped self addressed envelope.

In Person Search: In person searching is available.

PACER: Sign-up number is 800-676-6856. Access fee is $.60 per minute. Toll-free access: 800-933-9148. Local access: 618-482-9114, 618-482-9115, 618-482-9116. Case records are available back to January 1989. Records are purged as deemed necessary. New civil records are available online after 1 day. PACER is available on the Internet at http://pacer.ilsb.uscourts.gov.

East St Louis Division PO Box 309, East St Louis, IL 62202-0309 (Courier Address: 750 Missouri Ave, East St Louis, IL 62201), 618-482-9400.

www.ilsb.uscourts.gov

Counties: Bond, Calhoun, Clark, Clay, Clinton, Crawford, Cumberland, Effingham, Fayette, Jasper, Jersey, Lawrence, Madison, Marion, Monroe, Richland, St. Clair.

Indexing & Storage: Cases are indexed by debtor as well as by case number. New cases are available in the index 1 working day after filing date. Both computer and card indexes are maintained. Records are also indexed on microfiche. Open records are located at this court. District wide searches are available from this court.

Fee & Payment: The fee is $15.00 per item (one party name or case number). Payment may be made by money order, cashier check, personal check. Prepayment is required. Debtor's checks are not accepted. Payee: Clerk, US Bankruptcy Court. Certification fee: $5.00 per document. Copy fee: $.50 per page.

Phone Search: An automated voice case information service (VCIS) is available. Call VCIS at 800-726-5622 or 618-482-9365.

Mail Search: A stamped self addressed envelope is not required.

In Person Search: In person searching is available.

PACER: Sign-up number is 800-676-6856. Access fee is $.60 per minute. Toll-free access: 800-933-9148. Local access: 618-482-9114, 618-482-9115, 618-482-9116. Case records are available back to January 1989. Records are purged as deemed necessary. New civil records are available online after 1 day. PACER is available on the Internet at http://pacer.ilsb.uscourts.gov.

Court	Jurisdiction	No. of Courts	How Organized
Circuit Courts*	General	106	22 Circuits

* Profiled in this Sourcebook.

	CIVIL								
Court	Tort	Contract	Real Estate	Min. Claim	Max. Claim	Small Claims	Estate	Eviction	Domestic Relations
Circuit Courts*	X	X	X	$0	No Max	$5000	X	X	X

	CRIMINAL				
Court	Felony	Misdemeanor	DWI/DUI	Preliminary Hearing	Juvenile
Circuit Courts*	X	X	X	X	X

ADMINISTRATION Administative Office of Courts, 222 N LaSalle 13th Floor, Chicago, IL, 60601; 312-793-3250, Fax: 312-793-1335.

COURT STRUCTURE Illinois is divided into 22 judicial circuits; 3 are single county Cook, Du Page (18th Circuit) and Will (12th Circuit). The other 19 consist of 2 or more contiguous counties. The circuit court of Cook County is the largest unified court system in the world. Its 2300-person staff handles approximately 2.4 million cases each year. The civil part of the various Circuit Courts in Cook County is divided as follows: under $30,000 are "civil cases" and over $30,000 are "civil law division cases."

Probate is handled by the Circuit Court in all counties.

ONLINE ACCESS While there is no statewide public online system available, a number of Illinois Circuit Courts offer online access.

ADDITIONAL INFORMATION The search fee is set by statute and has three levels based on the county population. The higher the population, the larger the fee. In most courts, both civil and criminal data is on computer from the same starting date. In most Illinois courts the search fee is charged on a per name per year basis.

📖 📖 📖 📖 📖 📖

Adams County

Circuit Court 521 Vermont St, Quincy, IL 62301; 217-277-2100; Fax: 217-277-2116. Hours: 8:30AM-4:30PM (CST). *Felony, Misdemeanor, Civil, Eviction, Small Claims, Probate.*

Civil Records: Access: Mail, in person. Both court and visitors may perform in person searches. Search fee: $2.00 per name. Fee is $4.00 for years prior to 1987. Required to search: name, years to search. Civil cases indexed by defendant, plaintiff. Civil records on computer from 1987, books and index cards from 1920. **Criminal Records:** Access: Mail, in person. Both court and visitors may perform in person searches. Search fee: $2.00 per name. Fee is $4.00 for years prior to 1987. Required to search: name, years to search, DOB. Criminal records on computer from 1987, books and index cards from 1920. **General Information:** No juvenile or adoption records released. SASE required. Turnaround time 2-3 days. Copy fee: $1.00 for first page, $.50 each addl. Certification fee: $4.00. Fee payee: Clerk of Circuit Court. Personal checks accepted. Prepayment is required. Public access terminal is available.

Alexander County

Circuit Court 2000 Washington Ave, Cairo, IL 62914; 618-734-0107; Fax: 618-734-7003. Hours: 8AM-4PM (CST). *Felony, Misdemeanor, Civil, Eviction, Small Claims, Probate.*

Civil Records: Access: Fax, mail, in person. Both court and visitors may perform in person searches. Search fee: $4.00 per name per year. Required to search: name. Civil cases indexed by defendant, plaintiff. Civil records on computer from 1987, books and index cards from 1800s. **Criminal Records:** Access: Fax, mail, in person. Both court and visitors may perform in person searches. Search fee: $4.00 per name per year. Required to search: name. Criminal records on computer from 1987, books and index cards from 1800s. **General Information:** No juvenile or adoption records released. SASE required. Turnaround time 1 day. Copy fee: $1.00 for first page, $.50 each addl. Certification fee: $2.50. Fee payee: Clerk of Circuit Court. Personal checks accepted. Prepayment required. Public terminal is available.

Bond County

Circuit Court 200 W College Ave, Greenville, IL 62246; 618-664-3208; Fax: 618-664-4676. Hours: 8AM-4PM (CST). *Felony, Misdemeanor, Civil, Eviction, Small Claims, Probate.*

Civil Records: Access: Mail, in person. Both court and visitors may perform in person searches. Search fee: $4.00 per name per year. Required to search: name, years to search. Civil cases indexed by defendant, plaintiff. Civil records on computer are from 04/87 and are limited, index books from 1900s. **Criminal Records:** Access: Mail, in person. Both court and visitors may perform in person searches. Search fee: $4.00 per name per year. Required to search: name, years to search; also helpful-DOB. Criminal records on computer are from 04/87 and are limited, index books from 1900s. **General Information:** No juvenile or adoption records released. SASE required. Turnaround time 1-2 weeks. Copy fee: $.50 per page. Certification fee: $2.00 plus $.50 per page. Fee payee: Clerk of Circuit Court. Personal checks accepted. Prepayment is required. Public access terminal is available.

Boone County

Circuit Court 601 N Main, Belvidere, IL 61008; 815-544-0371. Hours: 8:30AM-5PM (CST). *Felony, Misdemeanor, Civil, Eviction, Small Claims, Probate.*

Civil Records: Access: Mail, in person. Both court and visitors may perform in person searches. Search fee: $4.00 per name per year. Required to search: name, years to search. Civil cases indexed by defendant, plaintiff. Civil records on computer since August, 1993, on index books from 1800s. **Criminal Records:** Access: Mail, in person. Both court and visitors may perform in person searches. Search fee: $4.00 per name per year. Required to search: name, years to search, DOB; also helpful-SSN. Criminal records on computer since August, 1993, on index books from 1800s. **General Information:** No juvenile or adoption records released. SASE required. Turnaround time 1-2 days. Copy fee: $1.00 for first page, $.50 each addl. Certification fee: $2.00. Fee payee: Clerk of Circuit Court. Only cashiers checks and money orders accepted. Prepayment is required. Public access terminal is available.

Brown County

Circuit Court County Courthouse, Mt Sterling, IL 62353; 217-773-2713. Hours: 8:30AM-4:30PM (CST). *Felony, Misdemeanor, Civil, Eviction, Small Claims, Probate.*

Civil Records: Access: Phone, fax, mail, in person. Both court and visitors may perform in person searches. Search fee: $4.00 per name per year. Required to search: name, years to search. Civil cases indexed by defendant, plaintiff. Civil records on computer since 1994, on index books from 1830s. **Criminal Records:** Access: Phone, fax, mail, in person. Both court and visitors may perform in person searches. Search fee: $4.00 per name per year. Required to search: name, years to search, DOB, signed release. Criminal records on computer since 1994, on index books from 1830s. **General Information:** No juvenile or adoption records released. SASE required. Turnaround time 1 week. Copy fee: $.35 per page. Certification fee: $2.00. Fee payee: Clerk of Circuit Court. Only cashiers checks and money orders accepted. Prepayment is required. Public access terminal is available.

Bureau County

Circuit Court 700 S Main, Princeton, IL 61356; 815-872-2001; Fax: 815-872-0027. Hours: 8AM-4PM (CST). *Felony, Misdemeanor, Civil, Eviction, Small Claims, Probate.*

Civil Records: Access: online, in person. Court does not conduct in person searches; visitors must perform searches for themselves. Search fee: No civil searches performed by court. Required to search: name, years to search. Civil cases indexed by defendant, plaintiff. Civil records on computer from 1989, prior on index books. Online access is primarily for local attorney firms and retrievers. The service is free. Call the Clerk's office for details. **Criminal Records:** Access: Mail, remote online, in person. Both court and visitors may perform in person searches. Search fee: $4.00 per name per year. Required to search: name, years to search, DOB. Criminal records on computer from 1989, prior on index books. Online access to available for primarily local attorney firms and retrievers. There is no access fee. Call the Clerk's office for further details. **General Information:** No juvenile or adoption records released. SASE required. Turnaround time 1 week. Copy fee: $.25 per page. Certification fee: $2.00. Fee payee: Bureau County Circuit Clerk. Personal checks accepted. Prepayment is required. Public access terminal is available.

Calhoun County

Circuit Court PO Box 486, Hardin, IL 62047; 618-576-2451; Fax: 618-576-9541. Hours: 8:30AM-4:30PM (CST). *Felony, Misdemeanor, Civil, Eviction, Small Claims, Probate.*

Civil Records: Access: Phone, fax, mail, in person. Both court and visitors may perform in person searches. Search fee: $4.00 per name per year. Required to search: name, years to search. Civil cases indexed by defendant, plaintiff. Civil records on index books from 1800s, computerized since 07/98. **Criminal Records:** Access: Phone, fax, mail, in person. Both court and visitors may perform in person searches. Search fee: $4.00 per name per year. Required to search: name, years to search, DOB. Criminal records on index books from 1800s, computerized since 07/98. **General Information:** No juvenile or adoption records released. SASE required. Turnaround time 1-2 days. Copy fee: $1.00 for first page. $.50 per page,

pages 2-19; $.25 each additional page. Certification fee: $2.00. Fee payee: Clerk of Circuit Court. Only cashiers checks and money orders accepted. Prepayment is required. Fax notes: No fee to fax results.

Carroll County

Circuit Court 301 N Main St, PO Box 32, Mt Carroll, IL 61053; 815-244-0230 X27; Fax: 815-244-3869. Hours: 8:30AM-4:30PM (CST). *Felony, Misdemeanor, Civil, Eviction, Small Claims, Probate.*

Civil Records: Access: Mail, in person. Both court and visitors may perform in person searches. Search fee: $4.00 per name per year. Required to search: name, years to search. Civil cases indexed by defendant. Civil records on computer from 1988, prior on index books. Will respond by fax if possible. **Criminal Records:** Access: Mail, in person. Both court and visitors may perform in person searches. Search fee: $4.00 per name per year. Required to search: name, years to search, DOB. Criminal records on computer from 1988, prior on index books. Will respond by fax if possible. **General Information:** No juvenile, mental health or adoption records released. SASE required. Turnaround time 2-3 days. Copy fee: $1.00 for first page, $.50 each addl. Certification fee: $2.00. Fee payee: Clerk of Circuit Court. Personal checks accepted. Prepayment is required. Public access terminal is available.

Cass County

Circuit Court PO Box 203, Virginia, IL 62691; 217-452-7225. Hours: 8:30AM-4:30PM (CST). *Felony, Misdemeanor, Civil, Eviction, Small Claims, Probate.*

Civil Records: Access: Mail, in person. Both court and visitors may perform in person searches. Search fee: $4.00 per name per year. Required to search: name, years to search. Civil cases indexed by defendant, plaintiff. Civil records on index books from 1800s. **Criminal Records:** Access: Mail, in person. Both court and visitors may perform in person searches. Search fee: $4.00 per name per year. Required to search: name, years to search, DOB; also helpful-SSN. Criminal records on index books from 1800s. **General Information:** No juvenile or adoption records released. SASE required. Turnaround time 1-2 weeks. Copy fee: $1.00 for first page, $.50 each addl. Certification fee: $2.00. Fee payee: Cass County Circuit Clerk. Personal checks accepted. Prepayment is required.

Champaign County

Circuit Court 101 E Main, Urbana, IL 61801; Civil phone:217-384-3725; Criminal phone:217-384-3725; Fax: 217-384-3879. Hours: 8:30AM-4:30PM (CST). *Felony, Misdemeanor, Civil, Eviction, Small Claims, Probate.*

Civil Records: Access: Mail, online, in person. Both court and visitors may perform in person searches. Search fee: $4.00 per name per year. Required to search: name, years to search. Civil cases indexed by defendant, plaintiff. Civil records on computer from 1986, index books from 1800s. Online available for cases back to 1992. The system is called PASS. There is a setup fee and an annual user fee. Contact Jo Kelly at 217-384-3767 for subscription information. **Criminal Records:** Access: Mail, remote online, in person. Both court and visitors may perform in person searches. Search fee: $4.00 per name per year. Required to search: name, years to search; also helpful-DOB, SSN. Criminal records on computer from 1988,

index books from 1800s. The online access is the same as civil. **General Information:** No juvenile or adoption records released. SASE required. Turnaround time 1-2 weeks. Copy fee: $.25 per page. Certification fee: $2.00. Fee payee: Clerk of Cicuit Court. Personal checks accepted. Prepayment is required. Public access terminal is available.

Christian County

Circuit Court PO Box 617, Taylorville, IL 62568; 217-824-4966; Fax: 217-824-5105. Hours: 8AM-4PM (CST). *Felony, Misdemeanor, Civil, Eviction, Small Claims, Probate.*

Civil Records: Access: Phone, mail, in person. Both court and visitors may perform in person searches. Search fee: $5.00 per name per year. Required to search: name; also helpful-years to search. Civil cases indexed by defendant, plaintiff. Civil records on computer from 1988, index books from 1840. **Criminal Records:** Access: Phone, mail, in person. Both court and visitors may perform in person searches. Search fee: $5.00 per name per year. Required to search: name; also helpful-years to search, DOB. Criminal records on computer from 1988, index books from 1840. **General Information:** No juvenile or adoption records released. SASE required. Turnaround time 1-2 days. Copy fee: $1.00 for first page, $.50 each addl. Certification fee: $2.00. Fee payee: Clerk of Circuit Court. Business checks accepted. Prepayment is required.

Clark County

Circuit Court PO Box 187, Marshall, IL 62441; 217-826-2811. Hours: 8AM-4PM (CST). *Felony, Misdemeanor, Civil, Eviction, Small Claims, Probate.*

Civil Records: Access: Mail, in person. Both court and visitors may perform in person searches. Search fee: $4.00 per name per year. Required to search: name, years to search; also helpful-address. Civil cases indexed by defendant, plaintiff. Civil records on computer from 1989, index books from 1800s. **Criminal Records:** Access: Mail, in person. Both court and visitors may perform in person searches. Search fee: $4.00 per name per year. Required to search: name, years to search, DOB, signed release; also helpful-address, SSN. Criminal records on computer from 1989, index books from 1800s. **General Information:** No juvenile or adoption records released. Turnaround time 1 week. Copy fee: $1.00 for first page, $.50 each addl. After 20 pages, fee is $.25 per page. Certification fee: $2.00. Fee payee: Clerk of Circuit Court. Only cashiers checks and money orders accepted. Public access terminal is available.

Clay County

Circuit Court PO Box 100, Louisville, IL 62858; 618-665-3523; Fax: 618-665-3543. Hours: 8AM-4PM (CST). *Felony, Misdemeanor, Civil, Eviction, Small Claims, Probate.*

Civil Records: Access: Fax, mail, in person. Both court and visitors may perform in person searches. Search fee: $4.00 per name. Fee is $4.00 per year prior to 1988. Required to search: name, years to search. Civil cases indexed by defendant. Civil records on computer from 1988, index books from 1850s. **Criminal Records:** Access: Fax, mail, in person. Both court and visitors may perform in person searches. Search fee: $4.00 per name. Fee is $4.00 per year prior to 1988. Required to search: name, years to search; also helpful-DOB. Criminal records on computer from 1988, index books from

1850s. **General Information:** No juvenile or adoption records released. SASE required. Turnaround time 2-3 days. Copy fee: $1.00 for first page, $.50 each addl 19; $.25 each thereafter. Certification fee: $2.00. Fee payee: Clerk of Circuit Court. Personal checks accepted. Prepayment is required. Public access terminal is available. Fax notes: $1.00 for first page, $.50 each addl.

Clinton County

Circuit Court County Courthouse, PO Box 407, Carlyle, IL 62231; 618-594-2464. Hours: 8AM-4PM (CST). *Felony, Misdemeanor, Civil, Eviction, Small Claims, Probate.*

Civil Records: Access: Mail, in person. Both court and visitors may perform in person searches. Search fee: $10.00 per name. Fee is for 10 year search. Required to search: name, years to search. Civil cases indexed by defendant, plaintiff. Civil records on computer from 1988, index books from 1800s. **Criminal Records:** Access: Mail, in person. Both court and visitors may perform in person searches. Search fee: $10.00 per name. Flat fee for 10 year search. Required to search: name, years to search, DOB; also helpful-SSN. Criminal records on computer from 1988, index books from 1800s. **General Information:** No juvenile or adoption records released. SASE required. Turnaround time 2-4 days. Copy fee: $.50 per page. Certification fee: $2.00. Fee payee: Clerk of Circuit Court. Personal checks accepted. Prepayment is required. Public access terminal is available.

Coles County

Circuit Court PO Box 48, Charleston, IL 61920; 217-348-0516. Hours: 8:30AM-4:30PM (CST). *Felony, Misdemeanor, Civil, Eviction, Small Claims, Probate.*

Civil Records: Access: Fax, mail, in person. Both court and visitors may perform in person searches. Search fee: $5.00 per name. Required to search: name, years to search. Civil cases indexed by defendant, plaintiff. Civil records on computer from 1989, index books from 1800s. **Criminal Records:** Access: Fax, mail, in person. Both court and visitors may perform in person searches. Search fee: $5.00 per name. Required to search: name, years to search, DOB; also helpful-SSN. Criminal records on computer from 1989, index books from 1800s. **General Information:** No juvenile or adoption records released. SASE required. Turnaround time 1-2 days. Copy fee: $.50 per page. Certification fee: $2.00. Fee payee: Clerk of Circuit Court. Personal checks accepted. Prepayment is required. Public access terminal is available.

Cook County

Circuit Court-Criminal Division 2650 S California Ave, Chicago, IL 60608; Criminal phone:773-869-3140; Fax: 773-869-4444. Hours: 9AM-5PM (CST). *Felony.*

www.cookcountyclerkofcourt.org

Note: Cases are heard in six district courts within the county and each court has a central index, eventually all case files are maintained here. **Criminal Records:** Access: Mail, remote online, in person. Both court and visitors may perform in person searches. Search fee: $6.00 per name per year. Required to search: name, years to search; also helpful-DOB, SSN. Criminal records on computer since 1964; prior records on microfiche from 1800s. Online case searching for limited case information, called case snapshots, is available

free online at www.cookcountyclerkofcourt.org/Terms/terms.html. Search by name, case number or court date. Information included is parties (up to 3), attorneys, case type, the filing date, the ad damnum (amount of damages sought), division and district, and the most current court date. **General Information:** No juvenile or adoption records released. SASE required. Turnaround time 2 weeks. Copy fee: $2.00 for first page, $.50 each addl. $.25 per page after 20. Certification fee: $6.00. Fee payee: Clerk of Circuit Court. Personal checks accepted. Personal checks accepted with drivers license# or attorney code. Prepayment is required. Public access terminal is available.

Circuit Court-Civil; Chicago District 50 W Washington Rm 601, Chicago, IL 60602; Civil phone:312-603-5145; criminal:312-603-5145; Civil phone:312-603-5116 (admin). Fax: 312-443-4557. Hours: 8:30AM-4:30PM (CST). *Misdemeanor, Civil Action Under $100,000, Eviction, Small Claims, Probate.*

www.cookcountyclerkofcourt.org

Note: Cases are heard in six district courts within the county and each court has a central index, eventually all case files are maintained here. Probate is a separate division at the same address, phone: 312-603-6441.

Civil Records: Access: Phone, mail, online, in person. Both court and visitors may perform in person searches. Search fee: $6.00 per name per year. Required to search: name, years to search. Civil cases indexed by defendant, plaintiff. Civil records on computer from 1983, index books from 1800s. Online case searching for limited case information, called case snapshots, is available free online at www.cookcountyclerkofcourt.org/Terms/terms.html. Search by name, case number or court date. Information included is parties (up to 3), attorneys, case type, the filing date, the ad damnum (amount of damages sought), division and district, and the most current court date. Phone inquires to check status only. **Criminal Records:** Access: Mail, in person. Court does not conduct in person searches; visitors must perform searches for themselves. No search fee. Required to search: name, years to search, DOB. **General Information:** No juvenile or adoption records released. SASE required. Turnaround time 1 week. Copy fee: $2.00 for first page, $.50 each addl. Certification fee: $6.00. Fee payee: Clerk of Circuit Court. Personal checks accepted. Prepayment is required. Public access terminal is available.

Bridgeview District 10220 S 76th Ave Rm 121, Bridgeview Court Bldg, Bridgeview, IL 60455; Civil phone:708-974-6500; Criminal phone:708-974-6500. *Felony, Civil Action Under $100,000, Eviction, Small Claims.*

www.cookcountyclerkofcourt.org

Jurisdictions: Alsip, Bedford Park, Bridgeview, Burbank, Burr Ridge, Chicago Ridge, Countryside, Evergreen Park, Forest View, Hickory Hills, Hinsdale, Hodgkins, Hometown, Indian Head Park, Justice, Lagrange, Lemont, Lyons, Merrionette Park, McCook, Oak Lawn, Orland Hills, Orland Park, Palos Heights, Palos Hills, Palos Park, Stickney, Summit, Western Springs, West Haven, Willow Springs, Worth.

Civil Records: Access: In person only. Court does not conduct in person searches; visitors must perform searches for themselves. Search fee: No civil searches performed by court. Required to search: name, years to search. Civil cases indexed by defendant, plaintiff. Computerized since 1985,

microfiched to early 1970s. **Criminal Records:** Access: In person only. Court does not conduct in person searches; visitors must perform searches for themselves. Search fee: No criminal searches performed by court. Required to search: name. **General Information:** Copy fee: $2.00 for first page, $.50 each addl. Certification fee: $6.00. Fee payee: Clerk of Circuit Court. Personal checks accepted. Public access terminal is available.

Markham District 16501 S Kedzie Pkwy Rm119, Markham, IL 60426-5509; Civil phone:708-210-4581; Criminal phone:708-210-4581. *Felony, Civil Action Under $30,000, Eviction, Small Claims.*

www.cookcountyclerkofcourt.org

Jurisdictions: Blue Island, Burnham, Calumet City, Calumet Park, Chicago Heights, Country Club Hills, Crestwood, Crete, Dixmoor, Dolton, East Hazelcrest, Flossmoor, Ford Heights, Glenwood, Harvey, Hazelcrest, Homewood, Lansing, Lynwood, Markham, Matteson, Midlothian, Oak Forest, Olympia Fields, Park Forest, Phoenix, Posen, Richton Park, Riverdale, Robbins, Sauk Village, South Chicago Heights, South Holland, Steger, Thornton, Tinley Park.

Civil Records: Access: In person only. Court does not conduct in person searches; visitors must perform searches for themselves. Search fee: No civil searches performed by court. Required to search: name. Civil cases indexed by defendant, plaintiff. Computerized since 1989. **Criminal Records:** Access: Mail, in person. Court does not conduct in person searches; visitors must perform searches for themselves. No search fee. Required to search: name, years to search. **General Information:** Turnaround time 2 weeks. Copy fee: $2.00 for first page, $.50 each addl. Certification fee: $6.00. Fee payee: Clerk of Circuit Court. Personal checks accepted. Public access terminal is available.

Maywood Division 1500 S Maybrook Dr, Rm 236, Maywood, IL 60153-2410; Civil phone:708-865-4973; Criminal phone:708-865-4973. Hours: 9AM-5PM (CST). *Felony, Civil Action Under $100,000, Eviction, Small Claims.*

www.cookcountyclerkofcourt.org

Jurisdictions: Bellwood, Berkeley, Berwyn, Broadview, Brookfield, Cicero, Elmwood Park, Forest Park, Franklin Park, Hillside, La Grange Park, Maywood, Melrose Park, Northlake, North Riverside, Oak Park, River Forest, River Grove, Riverside, Stone Park, Westchester.

Civil Records: Access: Mail, in person. Court does not conduct in person searches; visitors must perform searches for themselves. Search fee: $6.00. Required to search: name; also helpful-years to search. Civil cases indexed by defendant, plaintiff. computerized since 1982, docket books to 1970s, prior archived. **Criminal Records:** Access: In person only. Court does not conduct in person searches; visitors must perform searches for themselves. Search fee: No criminal searches performed by court. Required to search: name, years to search, DOB. **General Information:** Turnaround time 1 week. Copy fee: $2.00 for first page, $.50 each addl. Certification fee: $6.00. Fee payee: Clerk of Circuit Court. Personal checks accepted. Prepayment is required. Public access terminal is available.

Rolling Meadows Division 2121 Euclid Ave, Rolling Meadows, IL 60008-1566; Civil phone:847-818-2300; Criminal phone:847-818-2300. Hours: 8:30AM-4:30PM *Felony, Civil Action Under $100,000, Eviction, Small Claims.*

www.cookcountyclerkofcourt.org

Jurisdictions: Arlington Heights, Barrington, Barrington Hills, Bartlett, Bensonville, Buffalo Grove, Elgin, Elk Grove Village, Hanover Park, Harwood Heights, Hoffman Estates, Inverness, Mount Prospect, Norridge, Palatine, Prospect Heights, Rolling Meadows, Roselle, Rosemont, Schaumburg, Schiller Park, South Barrington, Streamwood, Wheeling, Cook County Sheriff and Forest Preserve, State Police 2, 3, and 15.

Civil Records: Access: Mail, in person. Court does not conduct in person searches; visitors must perform searches for themselves. Search fee: $6.00 per name. Required to search: name; also helpful-years to search. Civil cases indexed by defendant, plaintiff. Civil Records are computerized since 1986. **Criminal Records:** Access: In person only. Court does not conduct in person searches; visitors must perform searches for themselves. Search fee: No criminal searches performed by court. Required to search: name, years to search; also helpful-DOB, SSN. **General Information:** Turnaround time 2 weeks. Copy fee: $2.00 for first page, $.50 each addl. Certification fee: $6.00. Fee payee: Clerk of Circuit Court. Personal checks accepted. Public access terminal is available.

Skokie Division Skokie Court Bldg Rm 136, 5600 Old Orchard Rd, Skokie, IL 60076-1023; 847-470-7250. Hours: 8:30AM-4:30PM (CST). *Misdemeanor, Civil Action Under $100,000, Eviction, Small Claims.*

www.cookcountyclerkofcourt.org

Jurisdictions: Deerfield, Des Palines, Evanston, Glencoe, Glenview, Golf, Kenilworth, Lincolnwood, Morton Grove, Niles, Northbrook, Northfield, Park Ridge, Prospect Heights, Skokie, Wilmette, Winnetka, Cook County Sheriff, Cook County Forest Preserve, State 15 and 03..

Civil Records: Access: Phone, mail, in person. Court does not conduct in person searches; visitors must perform searches for themselves. Search fee: $6.00 per name per year. Required to search: name, years to search. Civil cases indexed by defendant, plaintiff. Civil records computerized since 1983. **Criminal Records:** Access: Phone, mail, in person. Both court and visitors may perform in person searches. Search fee: $6.00 per name per year. Required to search: name, years to search; also helpful-DOB, SSN. **General Information:** All records are public. SASE not required. Turnaround time 1 week to 1 month. Copy fee: $2.00 for first page, $.50 each addl. Certification fee: $6.00. Fee payee: Clerk of Circuit Court. Personal checks accepted. Prepayment required. Public terminal is available.

Crawford County

Circuit Court PO Box 655, Robinson, IL 62454-0655; 618-544-3512; Fax: 618-546-5628. Hours: 8AM-4PM (CST). *Felony, Misdemeanor, Civil, Eviction, Small Claims, Probate.*

Civil Records: Access: Fax, mail, in person. Both court and visitors may perform in person searches. Search fee: $4.00 per name per year. Required to search: name, years to search. Civil cases indexed by defendant, plaintiff. Civil records on computer from 1989, index books from 1800s. **Criminal Records:** Access: Fax, mail, in person. Both court and visitors may perform in person searches. Search fee: $4.00 per name per year. Required to search: name, years to search, DOB. Criminal records on computer from 1989, index books from 1800s. **General Information:** No juvenile or adoption records released. SASE required. Turnaround time up to 1 week. Copy fee: $1.00 for

first page, $.50 each addl. Certification fee: $2.00. Fee payee: Circuit Clerk. Personal checks accepted. Prepayment is required. Fax notes: $2.00 per page.

Cumberland County

Circuit Court PO Box 145, Toledo, IL 62468; 217-849-3601; Fax: 217-849-3183. Hours: 8AM-4PM (CST). *Felony, Misdemeanor, Civil, Eviction, Small Claims, Probate.*

Civil Records: Access: Phone, mail, in person. Both court and visitors may perform in person searches. Search fee: $4.00 per name per year. Required to search: name, years to search. Civil cases indexed by defendant, plaintiff. Civil records on computer from 1990, index books from 1885. **Criminal Records:** Access: Phone, mail, in person. Both court and visitors may perform in person searches. Search fee: $4.00 per name per year. Required to search: name, years to search; also helpful-DOB, SSN. Criminal records on computer from 1990, index books from 1885. **General Information:** No juvenile or adoption records released. SASE required. Turnaround time up to 1 week. Copy fee: $1.00 for 1st page, $.50 per page next 19, then $.25 per page. Certification fee: $2.00. Fee payee: Clerk of Circuit Court. Only cashiers checks and money orders accepted. Prepayment is required.

De Kalb County

Circuit Court 133 W State St, Sycamore, IL 60178; Civil phone:815-895-7131; Criminal phone:815-895-7131; Fax: 815-895-7140. Hours: 8:30AM-4:30PM (CST). *Felony, Misdemeanor, Civil, Eviction, Small Claims, Probate.*

Civil Records: Access: Mail, in person. Both court and visitors may perform in person searches. Search fee: $4.00 per name per year. Required to search: name, years to search; also helpful-address. Civil cases indexed by defendant, plaintiff. Civil records on computer since 9/91, on index books back 60 years. Court planning to offer online access. Call 1-800-307-1100 for more information. **Criminal Records:** Access: Mail, in person. Both court and visitors may perform in person searches. Search fee: $4.00 per name per year. Required to search: name, years to search, signed release; also helpful-address, DOB. Criminal records on computer since 9/91, on index books back 60 years. Court planning to offer online access. Call 1-800-307-1100 for more information. **General Information:** No juvenile or adoption records released. SASE required. Turnaround time 2 weeks. Copy fee: $1.00 for first page, $.50 each addl. After 20 pages, copies are $.25 each. Certification fee: $3.50. Fee payee: DeKalb County Circuit Clerk. Personal checks accepted. Credit cards accepted: Visa, Mastercard. Accepted in person only. Prepayment is required. Public access terminal is available.

De Witt County

Circuit Court 201 Washington St, Clinton, IL 61727; 217-935-2195; Fax: 217-935-3310. Hours: 8:30AM-4:30PM (CST). *Felony, Misdemeanor, Civil, Eviction, Small Claims, Probate.*

Civil Records: Access: Mail, in person. Both court and visitors may perform in person searches. Search fee: $4.00 per name per year. Required to search: name, years to search. Civil cases indexed by defendant. Civil records on computer from 1989, index books from 1839. **Criminal Records:** Access: Mail, in person. Both court and visitors may perform in person searches. Search fee: $4.00 per name per year. Required to search: name, years

to search, DOB. Criminal records on computer from 1989, index books from 1839. **General Information:** No juvenile or adoption records released. SASE required. Turnaround time 1-2 weeks. Copy fee: $.50 for first page, $.25 each addl. Certification fee: $2.00. Fee payee: Clerk of Circuit Court. Only cashiers checks and money orders accepted. Prepayment is required.

Douglas County

Circuit Court PO Box 50, Tuscola, IL 61953; 217-253-2352. Hours: 8:30AM-4:30PM (CST). *Felony, Misdemeanor, Civil, Eviction, Small Claims, Probate.*

Civil Records: Access: Mail, in person. Both court and visitors may perform in person searches. Search fee: $4.00 per name per year. Required to search: name, years to search. Civil cases indexed by defendant, plaintiff. Civil records on computer from 1989, index books from 1964. **Criminal Records:** Access: Mail, in person. Both court and visitors may perform in person searches. Search fee: $4.00 per name per year. Required to search: name, years to search, DOB; also helpful-SSN. Criminal records on computer from 1989, index books from 1964. **General Information:** No juvenile or adoption records released. SASE required. Turnaround time 1 week. Copy fee: $1.00 for first page, $.50 each addl. $.25 per pg after 20 pages. Certification fee: $2.00. Fee payee: Douglas County Circuit Clerk. Personal checks accepted. Prepayment is required. Public access terminal is available.

Du Page County

Circuit Court PO Box 707, Wheaton, IL 60189-0707; Civil phone:630-682-7100; Criminal phone:630-682-7100; Fax: 630-682-7082. Hours: 8:30AM-4:30PM (CST). *Felony, Misdemeanor, Civil, Eviction, Small Claims, Probate.*

www.co.dupage.il.us

Civil Records: Access: Phone, mail, in person. Both court and visitors may perform in person searches. Search fee: $4.00 per name per year. Required to search: name, years to search. Civil cases indexed by defendant, plaintiff. Civil and criminal record on-line from 1976, microfilm records back to 1939, index records back to 1839. All document files after 01/01/92 are on optical disk. **Criminal Records:** Access: Phone, mail, in person. Both court and visitors may perform in person searches. Search fee: $4.00 per name per year. Required to search: name, years to search, DOB. Civil and criminal record on-line from 1976, microfilm records back to 1939, index records back to 1839. All document files after 01/01/92 are on optical disk. **General Information:** No juvenile or adoption records released. SASE required. Turnaround time 1 week. Copy fee: $2.00 for first page, $.50 each addl. Certification fee: $4.00. Fee payee: Clerk of Circuit Court. Personal checks accepted. Credit cards accepted: Visa, Mastercard. Prepayment is required. Public access terminal is available.

Edgar County

Circuit Court County Courthouse, 115 W Court, Paris, IL 61944; 217-466-7447. Hours: 8AM-4PM (CST). *Felony, Misdemeanor, Civil, Eviction, Small Claims, Probate.*

Civil Records: Access: Mail, in person. Both court and visitors may perform in person searches. Search fee: $4.00 per name per year. Required to search: name, years to search. Civil cases indexed by defendant, plaintiff. Civil records on computer from 1992, index books from 1823. **Criminal**

Records: Access: Mail, in person. Both court and visitors may perform in person searches. Search fee: $4.00 per name per year. Required to search: name, years to search, DOB. Criminal records on computer from 1992, index books from 1823. **General Information:** No juvenile or adoption records released. SASE required. Turnaround time 1 week. Copy fee: $.50 for first page, $.25 each addl. Certification fee: $1.00. Fee payee: Janis K Nebergall, Circuit Clerk. Personal checks accepted. Prepayment is required.

Edwards County

Circuit Court County Courthouse, Albion, IL 62806; 618-445-2016; Fax: 618-445-4943. Hours: 8AM-4PM (CST). *Felony, Misdemeanor, Civil, Eviction, Small Claims, Probate.*

Civil Records: Access: Mail, in person. Both court and visitors may perform in person searches. Search fee: $4.00 per name per year. Required to search: name, years to search. Civil cases indexed by defendant. Civil records on computer from 1988, books and index cards from 1815. **Criminal Records:** Access: Mail, in person. Both court and visitors may perform in person searches. Search fee: $4.00 per name per year. Required to search: name, years to search, DOB. Criminal records on computer from 1988, index books from 1815. **General Information:** No juvenile or adoption records released. SASE required. Turnaround time 1 week. Copy fee: $.30 per page. Certification fee: $2.00. Fee payee: Clerk of Circuit Court. Only cashiers checks and money orders accepted. Prepayment is required. Public access terminal is available.

Effingham County

Circuit Court 100 E Jefferson, PO Box 586, Effingham, IL 62401; 217-342-4065; Fax: 217-342-6183. Hours: 8AM-4PM (CST). *Felony, Misdemeanor, Civil, Small Claims, Probate.*

Civil Records: Access: Mail, in person. Both court and visitors may perform in person searches. Search fee: $4.00 per name per year. Required to search: name, years to search; also helpful-address. Civil cases indexed by defendant, plaintiff. Civil records on computer from 1988, index books from 1800s. **Criminal Records:** Access: Mail, in person. Both court and visitors may perform in person searches. Search fee: $4.00 per name per year. Required to search: name, years to search, DOB; also helpful-address. Criminal records on computer from 1988, index books from 1800s. **General Information:** No juvenile or adoption records released. SASE required. Turnaround time 1 week. Copy fee: $1.00 for first page, $.50 each addl. $.25 per page after 20. Certification fee: $2.00. Fee payee: Effingham County Circuit Clerk. Business checks accepted. Prepayment is required. Public access terminal is available.

Fayette County

Circuit Court 221 S 7th St, Vandalia, IL 62471; 618-283-5009. Hours: 8AM-4PM (CST). *Felony, Misdemeanor, Civil, Eviction, Small Claims, Probate.*

Civil Records: Access: Mail, in person. Both court and visitors may perform in person searches. Search fee: $4.00 per name per year. Required to search: name, years to search. Civil cases indexed by defendant. Civil records on computer from 1988, index books from 1800s. **Criminal Records:** Access: Mail, in person. Both court and visitors may perform in person searches. Search fee: $4.00 per name per year. Required to search: name, years to search, DOB. Criminal records on

computer from 1988, index books from 1800s. **General Information:** No juvenile, impounded or adoption records released. SASE required. Turnaround time 1 week. Copy fee: $1.00 for first page, $.50 each addl. Certification fee: $1.00. Fee payee: Clerk of Circuit Court. Business checks accepted. Prepayment is required. Public access terminal is available.

Ford County

Circuit Court 200 W State St, Paxton, IL 60957; 217-379-2641; Fax: 217-379-3445. Hours: 8:30AM-4:30PM (CST). *Felony, Misdemeanor, Civil, Eviction, Small Claims, Probate.*

Civil Records: Access: Mail, in person. Both court and visitors may perform in person searches. Search fee: $4.00 per name per year. Required to search: name, years to search. Civil cases indexed by defendant. Civil records on index books from 1800s. **Criminal Records:** Access: Mail, in person. Both court and visitors may perform in person searches. Search fee: $4.00 per name per year. Required to search: name, years to search, DOB. Criminal records on index books from 1800s. **General Information:** No juvenile or adoption records released. SASE required. Turnaround time 2 days. Copy fee: $1.00 for first page, $.50 each addl. after 20 pages then $.25 per page. Certification fee: $2.00. Fee payee: Clerk of Circuit Court. Personal checks accepted. Prepayment is required.

Franklin County

Circuit Court County Courthouse, Benton, IL 62812; 618-439-2011. Hours: 8AM-4PM (CST). *Felony, Misdemeanor, Civil, Eviction, Small Claims, Probate.*

Civil Records: Access: Mail, in person. Both court and visitors may perform in person searches. Search fee: $4.00 per name per year. Required to search: name, years to search. Civil cases indexed by defendant, plaintiff. Civil records on computer from 1987, index books from 1800s. **Criminal Records:** Access: Mail, in person. Both court and visitors may perform in person searches. Search fee: $4.00 per name per year. Required to search: name, years to search, DOB. Criminal records on computer from 1987, index books from 1800s. **General Information:** No juvenile or adoption records released. SASE required. Turnaround time 1 week. Copy fee: $1.00 for first page, $.50 each addl. Certification fee: $2.00. Fee payee: Franklin County Circuit Clerk. Only cashiers checks and money orders accepted. Prepayment is required.

Fulton County

Circuit Court PO Box 152, Lewistown, IL 61542; 309-547-3041; Fax: 309-547-3674. Hours: 8AM-4PM (CST). *Felony, Misdemeanor, Civil, Eviction, Small Claims, Probate.*

Civil Records: Access: Mail, in person. Both court and visitors may perform in person searches. Search fee: $4.00 per name per year. Required to search: name, years to search. Civil cases indexed by defendant, plaintiff. Civil records on computer from 1989, index books from 1800s. **Criminal Records:** Access: Mail, in person. Both court and visitors may perform in person searches. Search fee: $4.00 per name per year. Required to search: name, years to search; also helpful-DOB. Criminal records on computer from 1989, index books from 1800s. **General Information:** No juvenile, impounded or adoption records released. SASE required. Turnaround time 1-2 days. Copy fee: $1.00 for first page, $.50 each addl. Certification fee: $2.00. Fee payee: Fulton County Circuit

Clerk. Business checks accepted. Prepayment is required. Public access terminal is available.

Gallatin County

Circuit Court County Courthouse, PO Box 249, Shawneetown, IL 62984; 618-269-3140; Fax: 618-269-4324. Hours: 8AM-4PM (CST). *Felony, Misdemeanor, Civil, Eviction, Small Claims, Probate.*

Civil Records: Access: Fax, mail, in person. Court does not conduct in person searches; visitors must perform searches for themselves. Search fee: $4.00 per name per year. Required to search: name, years to search. Civil cases indexed by defendant. Civil records on index books from 1800s. **Criminal Records:** Access: Fax, mail, in person. Court does not conduct in person searches; visitors must perform searches for themselves. Search fee: $4.00 per name per year. Required to search: name, years to search, DOB, signed release. Criminal records on index books from 1800s. **General Information:** No juvenile or adoption records released. SASE required. Turnaround time 1 week. Copy fee: $.25 per page. Certification fee: $1.00. Fee payee: Clerk of Circuit Court. Business checks accepted. Prepayment is required. Fax notes: $1.00 per page.

Greene County

Circuit Court 519 N Main, County Courthouse, Carrollton, IL 62016; 217-942-3421; Fax: 217-942-6211. Hours: 8AM-4PM (CST). *Felony, Misdemeanor, Civil, Eviction, Small Claims, Probate.*

Civil Records: Access: Phone, mail, in person. Both court and visitors may perform in person searches. Search fee: $5.00 per name. Required to search: name, years to search. Civil cases indexed by defendant, plaintiff. Civil records on index books from 1800s. **Criminal Records:** Access: Phone, fax, mail, in person. Both court and visitors may perform in person searches. Search fee: $5.00 per name. Required to search: name, years to search, DOB. Criminal records on index books from 1800s. No felonies by phone. Include signed release with felony search requests. **General Information:** No juvenile or adoption records released. SASE required. Turnaround time 1-2 days. Copy fee: $.25 per page. Certification fee: $2.00. Fee payee: Clerk of Circuit Court. Personal checks accepted. Prepayment is required. Fax notes: $.25 per page.

Grundy County

Circuit Court PO Box 707, Morris, IL 60450; 815-941-3256; Fax: 815-942-2222. Hours: 8AM-4:30PM (CST). *Felony, Misdemeanor, Civil, Eviction, Small Claims, Probate.*

Civil Records: Access: Mail, in person. Both court and visitors may perform in person searches. Search fee: $4.00 per name per year. Required to search: name, years to search. Civil cases indexed by defendant, plaintiff. Civil records on computer from 1988. **Criminal Records:** Access: Mail, in person. Both court and visitors may perform in person searches. Search fee: $4.00 per name per year. Required to search: name, years to search, DOB, signed release. Criminal records on computer from 1988. **General Information:** No juvenile or adoption records released. SASE required. Turnaround time 1-2 days. Copy fee: $.50 per page. Certification fee: $2.00. Fee payee: Clerk of Circuit Court. Personal checks accepted. Prepayment is required. Public access terminal is available.

Hamilton County

Circuit Court County Courthouse, McLeansboro, IL 62859; 618-643-3224; Fax: 618-643-3455. Hours: 8AM-4:30PM (CST). *Felony, Misdemeanor, Civil, Eviction, Small Claims, Probate.*

Civil Records: Access: Mail, in person. Both court and visitors may perform in person searches. Search fee: $4.00 per name per year. Required to search: name, years to search. Civil cases indexed by defendant, plaintiff. Civil records on index books from 1800s. **Criminal Records:** Access: Mail, in person. Both court and visitors may perform in person searches. Search fee: $4.00 per name per year. Required to search: name, years to search, DOB. Criminal records on index books from 1800s. **General Information:** No juvenile or adoption records released. SASE required. Turnaround time 1-2 days. Copy fee: $.30 per page. Certification fee: $2.00. Fee payee: Clerk of Circuit Court. No personal checks accepted. Prepayment is required.

Hancock County

Circuit Court PO Box 189, Carthage, IL 62321; 217-357-2616; Fax: 217-357-2231. Hours: 8AM-4PM (CST). *Felony, Misdemeanor, Civil, Eviction, Small Claims, Probate.*

Civil Records: Access: Mail, in person. Both court and visitors may perform in person searches. Search fee: $5.00 per name per year. Required to search: name, years to search. Civil cases indexed by defendant, plaintiff. Civil records on computer from 1992, index books from 1800s. **Criminal Records:** Access: Mail, in person. Both court and visitors may perform in person searches. Search fee: $5.00 per name per year. Required to search: name, years to search, DOB; also helpful-SSN. Criminal records on computer from 1992, index books from 1800s. **General Information:** No juvenile or adoption records released. SASE required. Turnaround time 1 week. Copy fee: $.50 per page. Certification fee: $5.00. Fee payee: Clerk of Circuit Court. Personal checks accepted. Prepayment is required. Public access terminal is available.

Hardin County

Circuit Court County Courthouse, Elizabethtown, IL 62931; 618-287-2735; Fax: 618-287-7833. Hours: 8AM-4PM (CST). *Felony, Misdemeanor, Civil, Eviction, Small Claims, Probate.*

Civil Records: Access: Mail, in person. Both court and visitors may perform in person searches. Search fee: $4.00 per name per year. Required to search: name, years to search. Civil cases indexed by defendant, plaintiff. Civil records on computer since 09/62, on index books from 1800s. **Criminal Records:** Access: Mail, in person. Both court and visitors may perform in person searches. Search fee: $4.00 per name per year. Required to search: name, years to search, DOB. Criminal records on computer since 09/62, on index books from 1800s. **General Information:** No juvenile or adoption records released. SASE required. Turnaround time 1 week. Copy fee: $.25 per page. Certification fee: $1.00 plus $.50 each add'l page. Fee payee: Circuit Clerk. Only cashiers checks and money orders accepted. Prepayment is required.

Henderson County

Circuit Court County Courthouse, PO Box 546, Oquawka, IL 61469; 309-867-3121; Fax: 309-867-3207. Hours: 8AM-4PM (CST). *Felony,*

Misdemeanor, Civil, Eviction, Small Claims, Probate.

Civil Records: Access: Phone, mail, in person. Both court and visitors may perform in person searches. No search fee. Required to search: name, years to search. Civil cases indexed by defendant, plaintiff. Civil records on computer from 1991, index books from 1800s. **Criminal Records:** Access: Phone, mail, in person. Both court and visitors may perform in person searches. No search fee. Required to search: name, years to search, DOB; also helpful-SSN. Criminal records on computer from 1991, index books from 1800s. **General Information:** No juvenile or adoption records released. SASE required. Turnaround time 1 day to 1 week. Copy fee: $.25 per page. Certification fee: $1.00 plus $.50 each add'l page. Fee payee: Clerk of Circuit Court. Personal checks accepted. Prepayment is required. Public access terminal is available.

Henry County

Circuit Court Henry County Courthouse, PO Box 9, Cambridge, IL 61238; 309-937-3572. Hours: 8AM-4:30PM (CST). *Felony, Misdemeanor, Civil, Eviction, Small Claims, Probate.*

Civil Records: Access: Mail, in person. Both court and visitors may perform in person searches. Search fee: $4.00 per name per year. Required to search: name, years to search. Civil cases indexed by defendant. Civil records on computer from 1989, index books from 1800s. **Criminal Records:** Access: Mail, in person. Both court and visitors may perform in person searches. Search fee: $4.00 per name per year. Required to search: name, years to search, DOB. Criminal records on computer from 1989, index books from 1800s. **General Information:** No juvenile or adoption records released. SASE not required. Turnaround time 2 weeks. Copy fee: $.50 per page. Certification fee: $2.00. Fee payee: Clerk of Circuit Court. Only cashiers checks and money orders accepted. Prepayment is required. Public access terminal is available.

Iroquois County

Circuit Court 550 S 10th St, Watseka, IL 60970; 815-432-6950 (6952 Traff) (6991 Ch Supp); Fax: 815-432-6953. Hours: 8:30AM-4:30PM (CST). *Felony, Misdemeanor, Civil, Eviction, Small Claims, Probate.*

Civil Records: Access: Fax, mail, in person. Both court and visitors may perform in person searches. Search fee: $4.00 per name per year. Required to search: name, years to search. Civil cases indexed by defendant. Civil records on index books from 1865. **Criminal Records:** Access: Fax, mail, in person. Both court and visitors may perform in person searches. Search fee: $4.00 per name per year. Required to search: name, years to search, DOB. Criminal records on index books from 1865. **General Information:** No juvenile or adoption records released. SASE required. Turnaround time 1-2 days. Copy fee: $.50 per page. Certification fee: $1.00. Fee payee: Clerk of Circuit Court. Personal checks accepted. Prepayment is required. Fax notes: $1.00 for first page, $.50 each addl.

Jackson County

Circuit Court County Courthouse, 1001 Walnut, PO Box 730, Murphysboro, IL 62966; 618-687-7300. Hours: 8AM-4PM (CST). *Felony, Misdemeanor, Civil, Eviction, Small Claims, Probate.*

www.circuitclerk.co.jackson.il.us

Civil Records: Access: Mail, in person. Both court and visitors may perform in person searches. Search fee: $4.00 per name. Fee is for 1986 to present. $4.00 per year prior to 1986. Required to search: name, years to search. Civil cases indexed by defendant, plaintiff. Civil records on computer from 1986, index books from 1860. **Criminal Records:** Access: Mail, in person. Both court and visitors may perform in person searches. Search fee: $4.00 per name. Required to search: name, years to search. Criminal records on computer from 1986, index books from 1860. **General Information:** No juvenile or adoption records released. SASE required. Turnaround time 1-2 weeks. Copy fee: $.50 per page. Certification fee: $2.50. Fee payee: Circuit Clerk. Personal checks accepted. Prepayment is required. Public access terminal is available.

Jasper County

Circuit Court 100 W Jourdan St, Newton, IL 62448; 618-783-2524. Hours: 8AM-4:30PM (CST). *Felony, Misdemeanor, Civil, Eviction, Small Claims, Probate.*

Civil Records: Access: Mail, in person. Both court and visitors may perform in person searches. Search fee: $4.00 per name per year. Required to search: name, years to search; also helpful-address. Civil cases indexed by defendant, plaintiff. Civil records on computer from 1988, index books from 1835. **Criminal Records:** Access: Mail, in person. Both court and visitors may perform in person searches. Search fee: $4.00 per name per year. Required to search: name, years to search, DOB, signed release. Criminal records on computer from 1988, index books from 1835. **General Information:** No juvenile or adoption records released. SASE required. Turnaround time 1 week. Copy fee: $.50 per page. Certification fee: $2.00. Fee payee: Clerk of Circuit Court. Personal checks accepted. Prepayment is required.

Jefferson County

Circuit Court PO Box 1266, Mt Vernon, IL 62864; 618-244-8008; Fax: 618-244-8029. Hours: 8AM-5PM (CST). *Felony, Misdemeanor, Civil, Eviction, Small Claims, Probate.*

Civil Records: Access: Phone, fax, mail, in person. Both court and visitors may perform in person searches. No search fee. Required to search: name, years to search. Civil cases indexed by defendant. Civil records on computer from 1988, index books from 1800s. Fax requests must be followed by original, before being processed. **Criminal Records:** Access: Phone, fax, mail, in person. Both court and visitors may perform in person searches. Search fee: $8.00. Required to search: name, years to search, DOB. Criminal records on computer from 1988, index books from 1800s. **General Information:** No juvenile or adoption records released. SASE required. Turnaround time 1 week. Copy fee: $.25 per page. Certification fee: No certification fee. Fee payee: Clerk of Circuit Court. Only cashiers checks and money orders accepted. Prepayment is required. Fax notes: $.25 per page. Add phone charge.

Jersey County

Circuit Court 201 W Pearl St, Jerseyville, IL 62052; 618-498-5571; Fax: 618-498-6128. Hours: 8:30AM-4:30PM (CST). *Felony, Misdemeanor, Civil, Eviction, Small Claims, Probate.*

Civil Records: Access: Mail, in person. Both court and visitors may perform in person searches. Search fee: $5.00 per name. Required to search: name, years to search. Civil cases indexed by

defendant. Civil records on computer from 1991, index books from 1800s. **Criminal Records:** Access: Mail, in person. Both court and visitors may perform in person searches. Search fee: $5.00 per name. Required to search: name, years to search; also helpful-DOB. Criminal records on computer from 1991, index books from 1800s. **General Information:** No juvenile or adoption records released. SASE required. Turnaround time 1 week. Copy fee: $.50 per page. Certification fee: $2.00 for first 2 pages then $.50 each additional. Fee payee: Clerk of Circuit Court. Personal checks accepted. Prepayment is required.

Jo Daviess County

Circuit Court 330 N Bench St, Galena, IL 61036; 815-777-2295/0037. Hours: 8AM-4PM (CST). *Felony, Misdemeanor, Civil, Eviction, Small Claims, Probate.*

Civil Records: Access: In person only. Court does not conduct in person searches; visitors must perform searches for themselves. Search fee: No civil searches performed by court. Required to search: name. Civil cases indexed by defendant, plaintiff. Civil records on computer since 1992, on index books from 1930s. **Criminal Records:** Access: Fax, mail, in person. Both court and visitors may perform in person searches. Search fee: $4.00 per name. Fee is for 1992 to present. Prior to 1992 $4.00 per name per year. Required to search: name, years to search, DOB. Criminal records on computer since 1992, on index books from 1930s. Will only fax back to a local number. **General Information:** No juvenile or adoption records released. SASE required. Turnaround time 1 week. Copy fee: $.25 per page. Certification fee: $2.00. Fee payee: Circuit Clerk. Business checks accepted. Prepayment is required. Public access terminal is available.

Johnson County

Circuit Court PO Box 517, Vienna, IL 62995; 618-658-4751; Fax: 618-658-2908. Hours: 8AM-4PM (CST). *Felony, Misdemeanor, Civil, Eviction, Small Claims, Probate.*

Civil Records: Access: Mail, in person. Both court and visitors may perform in person searches. Search fee: $4.00 per name per year. Required to search: name, years to search. Civil cases indexed by defendant, plaintiff. Civil records on computer from 1987, index books from 1930s. **Criminal Records:** Access: Mail, in person. Both court and visitors may perform in person searches. Search fee: $4.00 per name per year. Required to search: name, years to search, DOB. Criminal records on computer from 1987, index books from 1930s. **General Information:** No juvenile or adoption records released. SASE required. Turnaround time 1 week. Copy fee: $.25. Certification fee: $3.00. Fee payee: Circuit Clerk. Business checks accepted. Prepayment is required. Public access terminal is available.

Kane County

Circuit Court PO Box 112, Geneva, IL 60134; 630-232-3413; Civil phone:630-208-3323; Criminal phone:630-208-3323; Fax: 630-208-2172. Hours: 8:30AM-4:30PM (CST). *Felony, Misdemeanor, Civil, Eviction, Small Claims, Probate.*

www.co.kane.il.us/circuitclerk

Civil Records: Access: Phone, fax, mail, in person. Both court and visitors may perform in person searches. Search fee: $4.00 per name per year. Fee is for past 5 years. $8.00 for past 6 years or more. Required to search: name, years to

search. Civil cases indexed by defendant, plaintiff. Civil records on computer from 1986, index books from 1800s. **Criminal Records:** Access: Phone, fax, mail, in person. Both court and visitors may perform in person searches. Search fee: $4.00 per name per year. Required to search: name, years to search, DOB. Criminal records on computer past 5-7 years, index books from 1800s. Same as civil. **General Information:** No juvenile, mental health or adoption records released. SASE required. Turnaround time 1 week. Copy fee: $2.00 for first page, $.50 each addl. Certification fee: $4.00. Judgment orders certification fee $10.00. Fee payee: Clerk of Circuit Court. Personal checks accepted. Credit cards accepted: Visa, Mastercard. Prepayment is required. Public access terminal is available. Fax notes: $2.00 for first page, $.50 each addl.

Kankakee County

Circuit Court 450 E Court St, County Courthouse, Kankakee, IL 60901; 815-937-2905; Fax: 815-939-8830. Hours: 8:30AM-4:30PM (CST). *Felony, Misdemeanor, Civil, Eviction, Small Claims, Probate.*

Civil Records: Access: Mail, in person. Both court and visitors may perform in person searches. Search fee: $4.00 per name per year. Required to search: name, years to search. Civil cases indexed by defendant, plaintiff. Civil records on computer from 1990, index books from 1800s. **Criminal Records:** Access: Mail, in person. Both court and visitors may perform in person searches. Search fee: $4.00 per name per year. Required to search: name, years to search, DOB. Criminal records on computer from 1990, index books from 1800s. **General Information:** No juvenile, impounded, expunged or adoption records released. SASE required. Turnaround time 1-2 weeks. Copy fee: $1.00 for first page, $.50 each addl. Certification fee: $2.00. Fee payee: Clerk of Circuit Court. Personal checks accepted. Prepayment is required. Public access terminal is available.

Kendall County

Circuit Court PO Drawer M, 807 W John St, Yorkville, IL 60560; 630-553-4183. Hours: 8AM-4:30PM (CST). *Felony, Misdemeanor, Civil, Eviction, Small Claims, Probate.*

Civil Records: Access: Mail, in person. Both court and visitors may perform in person searches. Search fee: $4.00 per name per year. Required to search: name, years to search. Civil cases indexed by defendant, plaintiff. Civil records on computer since 1992, on index books from 1800s. **Criminal Records:** Access: Mail, in person. Both court and visitors may perform in person searches. Search fee: $4.00 per name per year. Required to search: name, years to search, DOB. Criminal records on computer since 1992, on index books from 1800s. **General Information:** No juvenile or adoption records released. SASE required. Turnaround time 2-3 days. Copy fee: $1.00 for first page, $.50 each addl. $2.00 per page when hard copy printouts when cases are maintained on an automated medium. Certification fee: $2.00. Fee payee: Clerk of Circuit Court. Only cashiers checks and money orders accepted. Prepayment is required. Public access terminal is available.

Knox County

Circuit Court County Courthouse, Galesburg, IL 61401; 309-345-3817. Hours: 8:30AM-4:30PM (CST). *Felony, Misdemeanor, Civil, Eviction, Small Claims, Probate.*

Civil Records: Access: Phone, mail, in person. Both court and visitors may perform in person searches. No search fee. Required to search: name, years to search. Civil cases indexed by defendant, plaintiff. Civil records on index books from 1800s. **Criminal Records:** Access: Phone, mail, in person. Both court and visitors may perform in person searches. No search fee. Required to search: name, years to search, DOB. Criminal records on index books from 1800s. **General Information:** No juvenile or adoption records released. SASE not required. Turnaround time 1 week. Copy fee: $1.00 for first page, $.50 each addl. Certification fee: $2.00. Fee payee: Clerk of Circuit Court. Personal checks accepted. Prepayment is required.

La Salle County

Circuit Court-Civil Division PO Box 617, Ottawa, IL 61350-0617; 815-434-8671; Fax: 815-433-9198. Hours: 8AM-4:30PM (CST). *Civil, Eviction, Small Claims, Probate.*

Civil Records: Access: Mail, in person. Both court and visitors may perform in person searches. Search fee: $4.00 per name per year. Required to search: name, years to search. Civil cases indexed by defendant, plaintiff. some records on computer since late 1980s; prior records on index books from 1800s. **General Information:** No juvenile or adoption records released. SASE required. Turnaround time 1-2 weeks. Copy fee: $1.00 for first page, $.50 each addl. Certification fee: $2.00. Fee payee: Clerk of Circuit Court. Personal checks accepted. Credit cards accepted: Visa, Mastercard. Prepayment is required. Public access terminal is available. Fax notes: No fee to fax results.

Circuit Court-Criminal Division 707 Etna Rd, Ottawa, IL 61360; 815-434-8271; Fax: 815-434-8299. Hours: 8AM-4:30PM (CST). *Felony, Misdemeanor.*

www.lasallecounty.com **Criminal Records:** Access: Fax, mail, in person. Court does not conduct in person searches; visitors must perform searches for themselves. No search fee. Required to search: name, years to search; also helpful-DOB. **General Information:** No juvenile or adoption records released. SASE required. Turnaround time 1-2 weeks. Copy fee: $1.00 for first page, $.50 each addl. Certification fee: $2.00. Fee payee: Clerk of Circuit Court. Personal checks accepted. Credit cards accepted: Visa, Mastercard. Prepayment is required. Public access terminal is available. Fax notes: No fee to fax results.

Lake County

Circuit Court 18 N County St, Waukegan, IL 60085; 847-360-6794. Hours: 8:30AM-5PM (CST). *Felony, Misdemeanor, Civil, Eviction, Small Claims, Probate.*

Civil Records: Access: Phone, mail, in person. Both court and visitors may perform in person searches. Search fee: $4.00 per name per year. Required to search: name, years to search. Civil cases indexed by defendant, plaintiff. Civil records on computer or microfiche from 1968, index books from 1800s. **Criminal Records:** Access: Phone, mail, in person. Both court and visitors may perform in person searches. Search fee: $4.00 per name per year. Required to search: name, years to search, DOB. Criminal records on computer or microfiche from 1968, index books from 1800s. **General Information:** No juvenile or adoption records released. SASE required. Turnaround time 1-2 days. Copy fee: $2.00 for first page, $.50 each addl. Certification fee: $4.00. Fee payee: Circuit Clerk. No personal checks accepted. Credit cards accepted: Discover. Discover. Prepayment is required.

Lawrence County

Circuit Court County Courthouse, Lawrenceville, IL 62439; 618-943-2815; Fax: 618-943-5205. Hours: 9AM-5PM *Felony, Misdemeanor, Civil, Eviction, Small Claims, Probate.*

Civil Records: Access: Mail, in person. Both court and visitors may perform in person searches. Search fee: $4.00 per name per year. Required to search: name, years to search, address. Civil cases indexed by defendant, plaintiff. Civil records on computer from 1988, index books from 1800s. **Criminal Records:** Access: Mail, in person. Both court and visitors may perform in person searches. Search fee: $4.00 per name per year. Required to search: name, years to search, address, DOB, SSN, signed release. Criminal records on computer from 1988, index books from 1800s. **General Information:** No juvenile or adoption records released. SASE required. Turnaround time 2-3 days. Copy fee: $1.00 for first page, $.50 each addl. Certification fee: $2.00. Fee payee: Clerk of Circuit Court. Only cashiers checks and money orders accepted. Prepayment is required.

Lee County

Circuit Court PO Box 325, Dixon, IL 61021; 815-284-5234. Hours: 8:30AM-4:30PM (CST). *Felony, Misdemeanor, Civil, Eviction, Small Claims, Probate.*

Civil Records: Access: Mail, in person. Both court and visitors may perform in person searches. Search fee: $4.00 per name per year. Required to search: name, years to search. Civil cases indexed by defendant, plaintiff. Civil records on computer from 1989, index books from 1800s. **Criminal Records:** Access: Mail, in person. Both court and visitors may perform in person searches. Search fee: $4.00 per name per year. Required to search: name, years to search, DOB; also helpful-SSN. Criminal records on computer from 1989, index books from 1800s. **General Information:** No juvenile, impounded or adoption records released. SASE required. Turnaround time 1 week. Copy fee: $.50 per page. Certification fee: $2.00. Fee payee: Clerk of Circuit Court. Personal checks accepted. Prepayment is required. Public access terminal is available.

Livingston County

Circuit Court 112 W Madison St, Box 320, Pontiac, IL 61764; 815-844-2602. Hours: 8AM-4:30PM (CST). *Felony, Misdemeanor, Civil, Eviction, Small Claims, Probate.*

Civil Records: Access: Mail, in person. Both court and visitors may perform in person searches. Search fee: $4.00 per name per year. Required to search: name, years to search; also helpful-address. Civil cases indexed by defendant, plaintiff. Civil records on computer from 1989 (child support since 1988), index books from 1800s. **Criminal Records:** Access: Mail, in person. Both court and visitors may perform in person searches. Search fee: $4.00 per name per year. Required to search: name, years to search, DOB, SSN; also helpful-address. Criminal records on computer from 1989 (child support since 1988), index books from 1800s. Signed release required for juvenile cases. **General Information:** No juvenile, impound or adoption records released. SASE required. Turnaround time 3-5 days. Copy fee: $1.00 for 1st pg; $.50 per pg, pages 2-19; $.25 each additional page. Certification fee: $2.00. Fee payee: Livingston County Circuit Clerk. Personal checks

accepted. Prepayment is required. Public access terminal is available. Public Access Terminal Note: Terminal will be available in the future.

Logan County

Circuit Court County Courthouse, Lincoln, IL 62656; 217-735-2376; Fax: 217-732-1231. Hours: 8:30AM-4:30PM (CST). *Felony, Misdemeanor, Civil, Eviction, Small Claims, Probate.*

Civil Records: Access: Mail, in person. Both court and visitors may perform in person searches. Search fee: $4.00 per name per year. Required to search: name, years to search. Civil cases indexed by defendant, plaintiff. Civil records on computer from 1990, index books from 1800s. **Criminal Records:** Access: Mail, in person. Both court and visitors may perform in person searches. Search fee: $4.00 per name per year. Required to search: name, years to search, DOB. Criminal records on computer from 1990, index books from 1800s. **General Information:** No juvenile or adoption records released. SASE not required. Turnaround time 1 week. Copy fee: $1.00 for first page, $.50 each addl. After 20 pages, the fee is $.25 per page. Certification fee: $2.00. Fee payee: Carla Bender, Circuit Clerk. Business checks accepted. Prepayment is required.

Macon County

Circuit Court 253 E Wood St, Decatur, IL 62523; 217-424-1454; Fax: 217-424-1350. Hours: 8AM-4:30PM (CST). *Felony, Misdemeanor, Civil, Eviction, Small Claims, Probate.*

www.court.co.macon.il.us

Civil Records: Access: Phone, mail, online, in person. Both court and visitors may perform in person searches. Search fee: $4.00 per name per year. Required to search: name, years to search; also helpful-address. Civil cases indexed by defendant, plaintiff. Civil records on computer from 1989, index books from 1800s. The online system is open 24 hours daily on the Internet. Docket information is viewable since 04/96. Search by name or case number. There is no fee. **Criminal Records:** Access: Phone, mail, remote online, in person. Both court and visitors may perform in person searches. Search fee: $4.00 per name per year. Required to search: name, years to search; also helpful-address, DOB, SSN. Criminal records on computer from 1989, index books from 1800s. Online access is open 24 hours daily via the Internet. Docket information from 04/96 forward is searchable by name or case number. There is no fee. **General Information:** No juvenile or adoption records released. SASE required. Turnaround time 1 week. Copy fee: $1.00 for first page, $.50 each addl. Certification fee: $2.00. Fee payee: Macon County Circuit Clerk. Business checks accepted. Prepayment is required. Public access terminal is available.

Macoupin County

Circuit Court PO Box 197, Carlinville, IL 62626; 217-854-3211; Fax: 217-854-8461. Hours: 8:30AM-4:30PM (CST). *Felony, Misdemeanor, Civil, Eviction, Small Claims, Probate.*

Civil Records: Access: Mail, in person. Both court and visitors may perform in person searches. Search fee: $4.00 per name per year. Required to search: name, years to search. Civil cases indexed by defendant, plaintiff. Civil records on computer from 1994, index books from 1837. **Criminal Records:** Access: Mail, in person. Both court and visitors may perform in person searches. Search fee: $4.00 per name per year. Required to search: name, years to search; also helpful-DOB, SSN.

Criminal records on computer from 1994, index books from 1837. **General Information:** No juvenile or adoption records released. SASE required. Turnaround time 1 month to 6 weeks. Copy fee: $1.00 for first page, $.50 each addl. Certification fee: $2.00. Fee payee: Mike Mathis Circuit Clerk. Personal checks accepted. Prepayment required. Public terminal is available.

Madison County

Circuit Court 155 N Main St, Edwardsville, IL 62025; 618-692-6240; Fax: 618-692-0676. Hours: 8AM-5PM (CST). *Felony, Misdemeanor, Civil, Eviction, Small Claims, Probate.*

Civil Records: Access: Mail, in person. Both court and visitors may perform in person searches. Search fee: $4.00 per name per year. Required to search: name, years to search. Civil cases indexed by defendant, plaintiff. Civil records on computer from 1990, index books from 1800s. **Criminal Records:** Access: Mail, in person. Both court and visitors may perform in person searches. Search fee: $4.00 per name per year. Required to search: name, years to search, DOB. Criminal records on computer from 1990, index books from 1800s. **General Information:** No juvenile, mental health, adoption records released. SASE required. Turnaround time 2-3 days. Copy fee: $2.00 for 1st pg; $.50 per pg for pgs 2-19; $.25 ea add'l pg. Certification fee: $4.00. Fee payee: Clerk of Circuit Court. Personal checks accepted. Prepayment is required. Public terminal available.

Marion County

Circuit Court 100 E Main, PO Box 130, Salem, IL 62881; 618-548-3856; Fax: 618-548-2358. Hours: 8AM-4PM (CST). *Felony, Misdemeanor, Civil, Eviction, Small Claims, Probate.*

Civil Records: Access: In person only. Court does not conduct in person searches; visitors must perform searches for themselves. Search fee: No civil searches performed by court. Required to search: name, years to search. Civil cases indexed by defendant, plaintiff. Civil records on computer from 1988, index books from 1800s. **Criminal Records:** Access: In person only. Court does not conduct in person searches; visitors must perform searches for themselves. Search fee: No criminal searches performed by court. Required to search: name, years to search; also helpful-DOB. Criminal records on computer from 1988, index books from 1800s. **General Information:** No juvenile or adoption records released. Copy fee: $1.00 for first page, $.50 each addl. Certification fee: $2.00. Fee payee: Clerk of Circuit Court. Only cashiers checks and money orders accepted. Will bill to attorneys.

Marshall County

Circuit Court PO Box 328, Lacon, IL 61540-0328; 309-246-6435; Fax: 309-246-2173. Hours: 8:30AM-Noon, 1-4:30PM (CST). *Felony, Misdemeanor, Civil, Eviction, Small Claims, Probate.*

Civil Records: Access: Mail, in person. Both court and visitors may perform in person searches. Search fee: $4.00 per name per year. Required to search: name, years to search. Civil cases indexed by defendant, plaintiff. Civil records on computer from 1988, microfiche since 1964, index books from 1800s. **Criminal Records:** Access: Mail, in person. Both court and visitors may perform in person searches. Search fee: $4.00 per name per year. Required to search: name, years to search, DOB. Criminal records on computer from 1988, microfiche since 1964, index books from 1800s.

General Information: No juvenile or adoption records released. SASE required. Turnaround time 1 week. Copy fee: $.50 per page. Certification fee: $2.00. Fee payee: Clerk of Circuit Court. Personal checks accepted. Prepayment is required. Public access terminal is available.

Mason County

Circuit Court 125 N Plum, Havana, IL 62644; 309-543-6619; Fax: 309-543-4214. Hours: 8AM-4PM (CST). *Felony, Misdemeanor, Civil, Eviction, Small Claims, Probate.*

Civil Records: Access: Mail, in person. Both court and visitors may perform in person searches. Search fee: $4.00 per name per year. Required to search: name, years to search. Civil cases indexed by defendant, plaintiff. Civil records on computer from 1989, index books from 1800s. **Criminal Records:** Access: Mail, in person. Both court and visitors may perform in person searches. Search fee: $4.00 per name per year. Required to search: name, years to search, DOB. Criminal records on computer from 1989, index books from 1800s. **General Information:** No juvenile or adoption records released. SASE required. Turnaround time 1 week. Copy fee: $1.00 for first page, $.50 each addl. Certification fee: $2.00. Fee payee: Clerk of Circuit Court. Only cashiers checks and money orders accepted. Prepayment is required. Public access terminal is available.

Massac County

Circuit Court PO Box 152, Metropolis, IL 62960; 618-524-9359; Fax: 618-524-4850. Hours: 8AM-Noon, 1-4PM (CST). *Felony, Misdemeanor, Civil, Eviction, Small Claims, Probate.*

Civil Records: Access: Mail, in person. Both court and visitors may perform in person searches. Search fee: $4.00 per name per year. Required to search: name, years to search. Civil cases indexed by defendant. Civil records on computer from 1986, index books from 1800s. **Criminal Records:** Access: Mail, in person. Both court and visitors may perform in person searches. Search fee: $4.00 per name per year. Required to search: name, years to search, DOB. Criminal records on computer from 1986, index books from 1800s. **General Information:** No juvenile or adoption records released. SASE required. Turnaround time 5 business days. Copy fee: $.25 per page. Certification fee: $3.00. Fee payee: Clerk of Circuit Court. Only cashiers checks and money orders accepted. Prepayment is required. Public access terminal is available.

McDonough County

Circuit Court County Courthouse, PO Box 348, Macomb, IL 61455; 309-837-4889; Fax: 309-836-3013. Hours: 8AM-4PM *Felony, Misdemeanor, Civil, Eviction, Small Claims, Probate.*

Civil Records: Access: Phone, fax, mail, in person. Both court and visitors may perform in person searches. Search fee: $5.00 per name per year. Required to search: name, years to search. Civil cases indexed by defendant, plaintiff. Civil records on computer from 1991, index books from 1800s. **Criminal Records:** Access: Phone, fax, mail, in person. Both court and visitors may perform in person searches. Search fee: $5.00 per name per year. Required to search: name, years to search; also helpful-SSN. Criminal records on computer from 1991, index books from 1800s. **General Information:** No juvenile or adoption records released. SASE required. Turnaround time 1 week. Copy fee: $1.00 for first page, $.50 each addl. Certification fee: $2.00. Fee payee: Clerk of

Circuit Court. Personal checks accepted. Prepayment is required. Public access terminal is available. Fax notes: $2.00 per page.

McHenry County

Circuit Court 2200 N Seminary Ave, Woodstock, IL 60098; 815-334-4307; Fax: 815-338-8583. Hours: 8AM-4:30PM *Felony, Misdemeanor, Civil, Eviction, Small Claims, Probate.*

www.co.mchenry.il.us

Civil Records: Access: Phone, mail, online, in person. Both court and visitors may perform in person searches. Search fee: $4.00 per name per year. Required to search: name, years to search. Civil cases indexed by defendant, plaintiff. Civil records on computer from 1991, index books from 1800s. Online is available 24 hours daily, $750 license fee plus $50 per month. Records date back to 1990. Civil, criminal, probate, traffic, and domestic records are available. For more information, call Kathy Keefe at 815-334-4193. **Criminal Records:** Access: Phone, mail, remote online, in person. Both court and visitors may perform in person searches. Search fee: $4.00 per name per year. Required to search: name, years to search, DOB; also helpful-SSN. Criminal records on computer from 1994, index books from 1800s. For online access, see civil records. **General Information:** No juvenile or adoption records released. SASE required. Turnaround time 1 week; criminal same day. Copy fee: $2.00 for first page, $.50 each addl. Over 20 copies then fee is $.25 per page. Certification fee: $4.00. Fee payee: Clerk of Circuit Court. Personal checks accepted. Credit cards accepted: Visa, Mastercard, Discover. Visa, MC, Discover. Prepayment is required. Public access terminal is available.

McLean County

Circuit Court PO Box 2420, Bloomington, IL 61702-2420; Civil phone:309-888-5341; Criminal phone:309-888-5341. Hours: 8:30AM-4:30PM (CST). *Felony, Misdemeanor, Civil, Eviction, Small Claims, Probate.*

www.mclean.gov

Civil Records: Access: Mail, in person. Both court and visitors may perform in person searches. Search fee: $4.00 per name per year. Required to search: name, years to search. Civil cases indexed by defendant, plaintiff. Civil records on computer from 1991, index books from 1800s. **Criminal Records:** Access: Mail, in person. Both court and visitors may perform in person searches. Search fee: $4.00 per name per year. Required to search: name, years to search, DOB; also helpful-address, SSN. Criminal records on computer from 1991, index books from 1800s. **General Information:** No juvenile or adoption records released. SASE required. Turnaround time 10 days. Copy fee: $1.00 for first page, $.50 each addl. Certification fee: $2.00. Fee payee: McLean County Circuit Clerk. Personal checks accepted. Prepayment is required. Public access terminal is available. Public Access Terminal Note: Criminal only.

Menard County

Circuit Court PO Box 466, Petersburg, IL 62675; 217-632-2615. Hours: 8:30AM-4:30PM (CST). *Felony, Misdemeanor, Civil, Eviction, Small Claims, Probate.*

Civil Records: Access: Mail, in person. Both court and visitors may perform in person searches. Search fee: $4.00 per name per year. Required to search: name, years to search. Civil cases indexed by defendant. Civil records on computer from

March, 1994, on index books from 1839. **Criminal Records:** Access: Mail, in person. Both court and visitors may perform in person searches. Search fee: $4.00 per name per year. Required to search: name, years to search, DOB. Criminal records on computer from March, 1994, on index books from 1839. **General Information:** No juvenile or adoption records released. SASE required. Turnaround time 2 days. Copy fee: $1.00 for first page, $.50 each addl. Certification fee: $1.00. Fee payee: Clerk of Circuit Court. Only cashiers checks and money orders accepted. Prepayment is required.

Mercer County

Circuit Court PO Box 175, Aledo, IL 61231; 309-582-7122; Fax: 309-582-7121. Hours: 8AM-4PM (CST). *Felony, Misdemeanor, Civil, Eviction, Small Claims, Probate.*

Note: 1988 forward records are available for search on the public access terminal

Civil Records: Access: Phone, fax, mail, in person. Only the court conducts in person searches; visitors may not. Search fee: $5.00 per name per year. Required to search: name, years to search. Civil cases indexed by defendant, plaintiff. Civil records on computer from 1989, index books from 1800s. **Criminal Records:** Access: Phone, fax, mail, in person. Only the court conducts in person searches; visitors may not. Search fee: $5.00 per name per year. Required to search: name, years to search, DOB. Criminal records on computer from 1989, index books from 1800s. **General Information:** No juvenile or adoption records released. SASE required. Turnaround time 2-3 days. Copy fee: $.25 per page. Certification fee: $3.50. Fee payee: Clerk of Circuit Court. Business checks accepted. Prepayment is required. Public terminal available. Fax note: $.25 per page.

Monroe County

Circuit Court 100 S Main St, Waterloo, IL 62298; 618-939-8681; Fax: 618-939-5132. Hours: 8AM-4:30PM (CST). *Felony, Misdemeanor, Civil, Eviction, Small Claims, Probate.*

http://ns.htc.net/~jacobdj/mcc

Civil Records: Access: Phone, fax, mail, in person. Both court and visitors may perform in person searches. Search fee: $4.00 per name per year. Required to search: name, years to search. Civil cases indexed by defendant, plaintiff. Civil records on computer from 1992, index books from 1800s. **Criminal Records:** Access: Phone, fax, mail, in person. Both court and visitors may perform in person searches. Search fee: $4.00 per name per year. Required to search: name, years to search, DOB. Criminal records on computer from 1992, index books from 1800s. **General Information:** No juvenile or adoption records released. SASE required. Turnaround time 1 week. Copy fee: $1.00 for first page, $.50 each addl. If over 20 pages, fee is $.25 per page (from 20 on). Certification fee: $2.00. Fee payee: Circuit Clerk. Business checks accepted. Public access terminal is available. Fax notes: No fee to fax results.

Montgomery County

Circuit Court County Courthouse, PO Box C, Hillsboro, IL 62049; 217-532-9546. Hours: 8AM-4PM (CST). *Felony, Misdemeanor, Civil, Eviction, Small Claims, Probate.*

Civil Records: Access: Mail, in person. Both court and visitors may perform in person searches. Search fee: $4.00 per name per year. Required to search: name, years to search. Civil cases indexed by defendant, plaintiff. Civil records on computer from 1988, index books from 1821, microfiche (probate only) since 1939. **Criminal Records:** Access: Mail, in person. Both court and visitors may perform in person searches. Search fee: $4.00 per name per year. Required to search: name, years to search, DOB. Criminal records on computer from 1988, index books from 1821, microfiche (probate only) since 1939. **General Information:** No juvenile or adoption records released. SASE required. Turnaround time 1 week. Copy fee: $1.00 for first page, $.50 each addl. Certification fee: $2.00. Fee payee: Clerk of Circuit Court. Only cashiers checks and money orders accepted. Prepayment is required. Public access terminal is available.

Morgan County

Circuit Court 300 W State St, Jacksonville, IL 62650; 217-243-5419; Fax: 217-243-2009. Hours: 8:30AM-4:30PM (CST). *Felony, Misdemeanor, Civil, Eviction, Small Claims, Probate.*

Civil Records: Access: Mail, in person. Both court and visitors may perform in person searches. Search fee: $4.00 per name per year. Required to search: name, years to search. Civil cases indexed by defendant. Civil records on computer from 1990, index books from 1890s. **Criminal Records:** Access: Mail, in person. Both court and visitors may perform in person searches. Search fee: $4.00 per name per year. Required to search: name, years to search, DOB. Criminal records on computer from 1990, index books from 1890s. **General Information:** No juvenile or adoption records released. SASE required. Turnaround time 1 week. Copy fee: $1.00 for first page, $.50 each addl. Certification fee: $2.00. Fee payee: Clerk of Circuit Court. Only cashiers checks and money orders accepted. Prepayment is required. Public access terminal is available.

Moultrie County

Moultrie County Courthouse 10 S Main, #7, Sullivan, IL 61951; 217-728-4622. Hours: 8:30AM-4:30PM (CST). *Felony, Misdemeanor, Civil, Eviction, Small Claims, Probate.*

www.circuit-clerk.moultrie.il.us

Civil Records: Access: Mail, in person. Both court and visitors may perform in person searches. Search fee: $4.00 per name per year. Required to search: name, years to search. Civil cases indexed by defendant. Civil records on computer from 1990, index books from 1850. **Criminal Records:** Access: Mail, in person. Both court and visitors may perform in person searches. Search fee: $4.00 per name per year. Required to search: name, years to search, DOB. Criminal records on computer from 1990, index books from 1850. **General Information:** No juvenile or adoption records released. SASE required. Turnaround time 1 week. Copy fee: $.25 per page. Certification fee: $2.00. Fee payee: Clerk of Circuit Court. Business checks accepted. Prepayment is required.

Ogle County

Circuit Court PO Box 337, Oregon, IL 61061; 815-732-1130. Hours: 8:30AM-4:30PM (CST). *Felony, Misdemeanor, Civil, Eviction, Small Claims, Probate.*

Civil Records: Access: Mail, in person. Both court and visitors may perform in person searches. Search fee: $4.00 per name per year. Required to search: name, years to search. Civil cases indexed by defendant, plaintiff. Civil records on computer since 1994; prior records on microfiche last 10 years, index books from 1800s. **Criminal**

Records: Access: Mail, in person. Both court and visitors may perform in person searches. Search fee: $4.00 per name per year. Required to search: name, years to search, DOB. Criminal records on computer since 1994; prior records on microfiche last 10 years, index books from 1800s. **General Information:** No juvenile or adoption records released. SASE required. Turnaround time 2-3 weeks. Copy fee: $1.00 for first page, $.50 each addl. $.25 per page after 20. Certification fee: $2.00. Fee payee: Clerk of Circuit Court. Only cashiers checks and money orders accepted. Local checks accepted. Prepayment is required. Public access terminal is available.

Peoria County

Circuit Court 324 Main St, Peoria, IL 61602; 309-672-6953; Fax: 309-677-6228. Hours: 8:30AM-5PM (CST). *Felony, Misdemeanor, Civil, Eviction, Small Claims, Probate.*

Civil Records: Access: Phone, mail, in person. Both court and visitors may perform in person searches. Search fee: $4.00 per name per year. Required to search: name, years to search. Civil cases indexed by defendant, plaintiff. Civil records on computer from 1986 (traffic), from 1987 (civil), archived from 1800s. **Criminal Records:** Access: Phone, mail, in person. Both court and visitors may perform in person searches. Search fee: $4.00 per name per year. Required to search: name, years to search, DOB; also helpful-SSN. Criminal records on computer from 1978, archived from 1800s. **General Information:** No juvenile or adoption records released. SASE required. Turnaround time 1 week. Copy fee: $2.00 for first page, $.50 each addl. Certification fee: $4.00. Fee payee: Clerk of Circuit Court. Personal checks accepted. Credit cards accepted: Visa, Mastercard. Prepayment is required. Public access terminal is available.

Perry County

Circuit Court PO Box 219, Pinckneyville, IL 62274; 618-357-6726. Hours: 8AM-4PM (CST). *Felony, Misdemeanor, Civil, Eviction, Small Claims, Probate.*

Civil Records: Access: Mail, in person. Both court and visitors may perform in person searches. Search fee: $4.00 per name per year. Required to search: name, years to search. Civil cases indexed by defendant, plaintiff. Civil records on computer from 1990, index books from 1800s. **Criminal Records:** Access: Mail, in person. Both court and visitors may perform in person searches. Search fee: $4.00 per name per year. Required to search: name, years to search; also helpful-DOB. Criminal records on computer from 1990, index books from 1800s. **General Information:** No juvenile or adoption records released. SASE required. Turnaround time 1 week. Copy fee: $.25 per page. Certification fee: $2.00. Fee payee: Clerk of Circuit Court. Only cashiers checks and money orders accepted. Prepayment is required. Public access terminal is available.

Piatt County

Circuit Court PO Box 288, Monticello, IL 61856; 217-762-4966; Fax: 217-762-8394. Hours: 8:30AM-4:30PM (CST). *Felony, Misdemeanor, Civil, Eviction, Small Claims, Probate.*

www.co.piatt.il.us

Civil Records: Access: Phone, fax, mail, in person. Both court and visitors may perform in person searches. No search fee. Required to search: name, years to search. Civil cases indexed by defendant, plaintiff. Civil records on computer

since 1988, index books from 1800s. **Criminal Records:** Access: Phone, fax, mail, in person. Both court and visitors may perform in person searches. No search fee. Required to search: name, years to search, DOB; also helpful-SSN. Criminal records on computer since 1988, index books from 1800s. **General Information:** No juvenile or adoption records released. SASE not required. Turnaround time 2-3 days. Copy fee: $1.00 for first page, $.50 each addl. Certification fee: $1.00 plus $.50 each add'l page. Fee payee: Clerk of Circuit Court. Business checks accepted. Prepayment is required. Fax notes: $1.00 for first page, $.50 each addl.

Pike County

Circuit Court Pike County Courthouse, Pittsfield, IL 62363; 217-285-6612; Fax: 217-285-4726. Hours: 8:30AM-4:30PM (CST). *Felony, Misdemeanor, Civil, Eviction, Small Claims, Probate.*

Civil Records: Access: Mail, in person. Both court and visitors may perform in person searches. Search fee: $4.00 per name per year. Required to search: name, years to search. Civil cases indexed by defendant, plaintiff. Civil records on computer since 1992, index books from 1800s. **Criminal Records:** Access: Mail, in person. Both court and visitors may perform in person searches. Search fee: $4.00 per name per year. Required to search: name, years to search; also helpful-SSN. Criminal records on computer since 1992, index books from 1800s. **General Information:** No juvenile or adoption records released. SASE required. Turnaround time as soon as possible. Copy fee: $1.00 for first page, $.50 each addl. $.25 per page after 19 pages. Certification fee: $3.00. Fee payee: Circuit Clerk. Personal checks accepted. Prepayment is required. Public access terminal is available.

Pope County

Circuit Court County Courthouse, Golconda, IL 62938; 618-683-3941; Fax: 618-683-3018. Hours: 8AM-4PM (CST). *Felony, Misdemeanor, Civil, Eviction, Small Claims, Probate.*

Civil Records: Access: Phone, fax, mail, in person. Both court and visitors may perform in person searches. No search fee. Required to search: name, years to search. Civil cases indexed by defendant. Civil records on computer from 1989, index books from 1800s. **Criminal Records:** Access: Phone, fax, mail, in person. Both court and visitors may perform in person searches. No search fee. Required to search: name, years to search, DOB. Criminal records on computer from 1989, index books from 1800s. **General Information:** No juvenile or adoption records released. SASE required. Turnaround time 2-3 days. Copy fee: $.25 per page. Certification fee: $2.00. Fee payee: Circuit Clerk. Business checks accepted. Prepayment is required. Public access terminal is available. Fax notes: $.50 per page.

Pulaski County

Circuit Court PO Box 88, Mound City, IL 62963; 618-748-9300; Fax: 618-748-9338. Hours: 8AM-4PM (CST). *Felony, Misdemeanor, Civil, Eviction, Small Claims, Probate.*

Civil Records: Access: Mail, in person. Both court and visitors may perform in person searches. Search fee: $4.00 per name. Required to search: name, years to search. Civil cases indexed by defendant, plaintiff. Civil records on computer since 1987, on books prior. **Criminal Records:**

Access: Mail, in person. Both court and visitors may perform in person searches. Search fee: $4.00 per name per year. Required to search: name, years to search, signed release; also helpful-DOB, SSN. Criminal records on computer since 1987, on books prior. **General Information:** No juvenile, adoption records released. SASE required. Turnaround time 1 week. Copy fee: $1.00 for first page, $.50 each addl. If over 20 pages, fee becomes $.25 per copy. Certification fee: $2.00. Fee payee: Clerk of Circuit Court. Only cashiers checks and money orders accepted. Prepayment is required.

Putnam County

Circuit Court 120 N 4th St, Hennepin, IL 61327; 815-925-7016; Fax: 815-925-7549. Hours: 9AM-4PM (CST). *Felony, Misdemeanor, Civil, Eviction, Small Claims, Probate.*

Civil Records: Access: Mail, in person. Both court and visitors may perform in person searches. Search fee: $5.00 per name. Fee is per 5 years searched. Required to search: name, years to search. Civil cases indexed by defendant. Civil records on computer from 1991, index books from 1836. **Criminal Records:** Access: Mail, in person. Both court and visitors may perform in person searches. Search fee: $5.00 per name. Fee is per 5 years searched. Required to search: name, years to search, DOB. Criminal records on computer from 1991, index books from 1836. **General Information:** No juvenile or adoption records released. SASE required. Turnaround time 3 days. Copy fee: $.50 per page. $.25 per page after 20. Certification fee: $2.00. Fee payee: Clerk of Circuit Court. Only cashiers checks and money orders accepted. Prepayment is required. Public access terminal is available.

Randolph County

Circuit Court County Courthouse, Chester, IL 62233; 618-826-5000 X150. Hours: 8AM-4PM (CST). *Felony, Misdemeanor, Civil, Eviction, Small Claims, Probate.*

Civil Records: Access: Mail, in person. Both court and visitors may perform in person searches. Search fee: $4.00 per name per year. Required to search: name, years to search. Civil cases indexed by defendant, plaintiff. Civil records on computer from 1992, index books from 1800s. Visitors can search computer index only. **Criminal Records:** Access: Mail, in person. Both court and visitors may perform in person searches. Search fee: $4.00 per name per year. Required to search: name, years to search, DOB. Criminal records on computer from 1992, index books from 1800s. Visitors can search computer index only. **General Information:** No juvenile or adoption records released. SASE required. Turnaround time 1-2 days. Copy fee: $.25 per page. Certification fee: $2.50. Fee payee: Clerk of Circuit Court. Business checks accepted. Prepayment is required.

Richland County

Circuit Court 103 W Main #21, Olney, IL 62450; 618-392-2151; Fax: 618-392-5041. Hours: 8AM-4PM (CST). *Felony, Misdemeanor, Civil, Eviction, Small Claims, Probate.*

Civil Records: Access: Mail, in person. Both court and visitors may perform in person searches. Search fee: $4.00 per name per year. Required to search: name, years to search. Civil cases indexed by defendant. Civil records on index books from 1800s. **Criminal Records:** Access: Mail, in person. Both court and visitors may perform in person searches. Search fee: $4.00 per name per

year. Required to search: name, years to search, DOB. Criminal records on index books from 1800s. **General Information:** No juvenile or adoption records released. SASE required. Turnaround time 1-2 weeks. Copy fee: $1.00 for first page, $.50 each addl. Certification fee: $.50. Fee payee: Clerk of Circuit Court. Only cashiers checks and money orders accepted. Prepayment is required. Public access terminal is available.

Rock Island County

Circuit Court 210 15th St, PO Box 5230, Rock Island, IL 61204-5230; 309-786-4451; Fax: 309-786-3029. Hours: 8AM-4:30PM (CST). *Felony, Misdemeanor, Civil, Eviction, Small Claims, Probate.*

www.co.rock-island.il.us

Civil Records: Access: Mail, online, in person. Both court and visitors may perform in person searches. Search fee: $4.00 per name per year. Required to search: name, years to search. Civil cases indexed by defendant, plaintiff. Civil records on computer from 1989, index books from 1950s. Online access is open 24 hours daily. There is a $200 setup fee and additional deposit required. The access fee is $1.00 per minute. Civil, criminal, probate, traffic, and domestic records can be accessed by name or case number. **Criminal Records:** Access: Fax, mail, remote online, in person. Both court and visitors may perform in person searches. Search fee: $4.00 per name per year. Required to search: name, years to search, DOB; also helpful-SSN. Criminal records on computer from 1989, index books from 1950s. Same online criteria as civil records. **General Information:** No juvenile or adoption records released. SASE required. Turnaround time 1 week. Copy fee: $1.00 for first page, $.50 each addl. Certification fee: $2.00. Fee payee: Circuit Clerks Office. Personal checks accepted. Prepayment is required. Public access terminal is available. Fax notes: $1.00 for first page, $.50 each addl.

Saline County

Circuit Court County Courthouse, Harrisburg, IL 62946; 618-253-5096 & 253-3904; Fax: 618-252-8438. Hours: 8AM-4PM (CST). *Felony, Misdemeanor, Civil, Eviction, Small Claims, Probate.*

Civil Records: Access: Fax, mail, in person. Both court and visitors may perform in person searches. Search fee: $5.00 per name per year. Required to search: name, years to search. Civil cases indexed by defendant, plaintiff. Civil records on computer from 1986, index books from 1800s. **Criminal Records:** Access: Fax, mail, in person. Both court and visitors may perform in person searches. Search fee: $5.00 per name per year. Required to search: name, years to search, DOB. Criminal records on computer from 1986, index books from 1800s. **General Information:** No juvenile or adoption records released. SASE required. Turnaround time 1-2 weeks. Copy fee: $1.00 for first page, $.50 each addl. Certification fee: $2.00. Fee payee: Clerk of Circuit Court. Business checks accepted. Prepayment is required. Public access terminal is available. Fax notes: $2.00 for first page, $1.00 each addl.

Sangamon County

Circuit Court 200 S Ninth St Rm 405, Springfield, IL 62701; 217-753-6674; Fax: 217-753-6665. Hours: 8:30AM-4:30PM (CST). *Felony, Misdemeanor, Civil, Eviction, Small Claims, Probate.*

Civil Records: Access: Fax, mail, in person. Both court and visitors may perform in person searches. Search fee: $4.00 per name per year. Required to search: name, years to search. Civil cases indexed by defendant, plaintiff. Civil records on computer from 1982, index books from 1800s. **Criminal Records:** Access: Fax, mail, in person. Both court and visitors may perform in person searches. Search fee: $4.00 per name per year. Required to search: name, years to search, DOB. Criminal records on computer from 1982, index books from 1800s. **General Information:** No juvenile, mental health, adoption records released. SASE required. Turnaround time 1-2 weeks. Copy fee: $1.00 for first page, $.50 each addl. $.25 per page after 19. Certification fee: $2.00. Fee payee: Circuit Clerk. Personal checks accepted. Public access terminal is available. Fax notes: No fee to fax results.

Schuyler County

Circuit Court PO Box 80, Rushville, IL 62681; 217-322-4633; Fax: 217-322-6164. Hours: 8AM-4PM (CST). *Felony, Misdemeanor, Civil, Eviction, Small Claims, Probate.*

Civil Records: Access: Mail, in person. Both court and visitors may perform in person searches. Search fee: $4.00 per name per year. Required to search: name, years to search. Civil cases indexed by defendant. Civil records on computer from 1988, index books from 1800s. **Criminal Records:** Access: Mail, in person. Both court and visitors may perform in person searches. Search fee: $4.00 per name per year. Required to search: name, years to search, DOB. Criminal records on computer from 1988, index books from 1800s. **General Information:** No juvenile or adoption records released. SASE required. Turnaround time 1 week. Copy fee: $1.00 for first page, $.50 each addl. $.25 after 20. Certification fee: $2.00. Fee payee: Clerk of Circuit Court. Only cashiers checks and money orders accepted. Prepayment is required.

Scott County

Circuit Court 35 E Market St, Winchester, IL 62694; 217-742-5217; Fax: 217-742-5853. Hours: 8AM-Noon, 1-4PM (CST). *Felony, Misdemeanor, Civil, Eviction, Small Claims, Probate.*

Civil Records: Access: Mail, in person. Both court and visitors may perform in person searches. Search fee: $4.00 per name per year. Required to search: name, years to search. Civil cases indexed by defendant, plaintiff. Civil records on index books from 1800s. **Criminal Records:** Access: Mail, in person. Both court and visitors may perform in person searches. Search fee: $4.00 per name per year. Required to search: name, years to search, DOB. Criminal records on index books from 1800s. **General Information:** No juvenile or adoption records released. SASE required. Turnaround time 1 week. Copy fee: $1.00 for first page, $.50 each addl. After 20 pages, copies are $.25 each. Certification fee: $2.00. Fee payee: Clerk of Circuit Court. Only cashiers checks and money orders accepted. Prepayment is required.

Shelby County

Circuit Court County Courthouse, PO Box 469, Shelbyville, IL 62565; 217-774-4212; Fax: 217-774-4109. Hours: 8AM-4PM (CST). *Felony, Misdemeanor, Civil, Eviction, Small Claims, Probate.*

Civil Records: Access: Phone, mail, in person. Search fee: $4.00 per name. Required to search: name, years to search. Civil cases indexed by defendant, plaintiff. Civil records on computer from 1988, index books from 1848. **Criminal Records:** Access: Phone, mail, in person. Both court and visitors may perform in person searches. Search fee: $4.00 per name. Required to search: name, years to search, DOB. Criminal records on computer from 1988, index books from 1848. **General Information:** No juvenile or adoption records released. SASE required. Turnaround time 1-2 weeks. Copy fee: $1.00 for first page, $.50 each addl. Certification fee: $2.00. Fee payee: Circuit Clerk.

St. Clair County

Circuit Court 10 Public Square, Belleville, IL 62220-1623; 618-277-6832; Fax: 618-277-1562. Hours: 9AM-4PM (CST). *Felony, Misdemeanor, Civil, Eviction, Small Claims, Probate.*

Civil Records: Access: Mail, in person. Both court and visitors may perform in person searches. Search fee: $4.00 per name per year. Required to search: name, years to search; also helpful-address. Civil cases indexed by defendant, plaintiff. Civil records on computer from 1990, microfiche from 1800s. **Criminal Records:** Access: Mail, in person. Both court and visitors may perform in person searches. Search fee: $4.00 per name per year. Required to search: name, years to search, DOB. Criminal records on computer from 1990, microfiche from 1800s. **General Information:** No juvenile or adoption records released. SASE required. Turnaround time 1-2 days. Copy fee: $2.00 for first page, $.50 each addl. $.25 per pg after 20. Certification fee: $4.00. Fee payee: Clerk of Circuit Court. Only cashiers checks and money orders accepted. Prepayment is required.

Stark County

Circuit Court 130 W Main St, Toulon, IL 61483; 309-286-5941. Hours: 8AM-4:30PM (CST). *Felony, Misdemeanor, Civil, Eviction, Small Claims, Probate.*

Civil Records: Access: Mail, in person. Both court and visitors may perform in person searches. Search fee: $4.00 per name per year. Required to search: name, years to search. Civil cases indexed by defendant. Civil records on index books from 1800s. **Criminal Records:** Access: Mail, in person. Both court and visitors may perform in person searches. Search fee: $4.00 per name per year. Required to search: name, years to search, DOB. Criminal records on index books from 1800s. **General Information:** No juvenile or adoption records released. SASE required. Turnaround time 2-3 days. Copy fee: $1.00 for first page, $.50 each addl. Certification fee: $2.00. Fee payee: Clerk of Circuit Court. Personal checks accepted. Prepayment is required.

Stephenson County

Circuit Court 15 N Galena Ave, Freeport, IL 61032; 815-235-8266. Hours: 8:30AM-4:30PM (CST). *Felony, Misdemeanor, Civil, Eviction, Small Claims, Probate.*

Civil Records: Access: Mail, in person. Both court and visitors may perform in person searches. Search fee: $4.00 per name per year. Required to search: name, years to search. Civil cases indexed by defendant, plaintiff. Civil records on computer from 1989, index books from 1900. **Criminal Records:** Access: Mail, in person. Both court and visitors may perform in person searches. Search fee: $4.00 per name per year. Required to search: name, years to search, DOB. Criminal records on computer from 1989, index books from 1900. **General Information:** No juvenile or adoption records released. SASE required. Turnaround time

5-15 days. Copy fee: $1.00 for first page, $.50 each addl. Certification fee: $2.00. Fee payee: Clerk of Circuit Court. Business checks accepted. Prepayment is required. Public access terminal is available.

Tazewell County

Circuit Court Courthouse, 4th & Court Sts, Pekin, IL 61554; 309-477-2214. Hours: 8:30AM-5PM (CST). *Felony, Misdemeanor, Civil, Small Claims, Probate.*

Civil Records: Access: Mail, in person. Both court and visitors may perform in person searches. Search fee: $4.00 per name per year. Required to search: name, years to search. Civil cases indexed by defendant, plaintiff. Civil records on computer from 02/89 index books from 1800s. **Criminal Records:** Access: Mail, in person. Both court and visitors may perform in person searches. Search fee: $4.00 per name per year. Required to search: name, years to search, DOB. Criminal records on computer from 02/89 index books from 1800s. **General Information:** No juvenile or adoption records released. SASE required. Turnaround time 3-4 days. Copy fee: $1.00 for first page, $.50 each addl. After 20 pages, $.10 per page. Certification fee: $2.00. Fee payee: Clerk of Circuit Court. Only cashiers checks and money orders accepted. Prepayment is required. Public access terminal is available.

Union County

Circuit Court Union County Courthouse, 309 W Market, Rm 101, Jonesboro, IL 62952; 618-833-5913; Fax: 618-833-5223. Hours: 8AM-Noon,1-4PM (CST). *Felony, Misdemeanor, Civil, Eviction, Small Claims, Probate.*

Civil Records: Access: Fax, mail, in person. Both court and visitors may perform in person searches. Search fee: $4.00 per name per year. Required to search: name, years to search. Civil cases indexed by defendant, plaintiff. Civil records on computer from 1986, index books from 1800s. Public can only search paper records up to 1986. Only court personnel have access to computer records. **Criminal Records:** Access: Fax, mail, in person. Both court and visitors may perform in person searches. Search fee: $4.00 per name per year. Required to search: name, years to search; also helpful-DOB. Criminal records on computer from 1986, index books from 1800s. Same search procedures as civil. **General Information:** No juvenile or adoption records released. SASE required. Turnaround time 1 week. Copy fee: $.25 per page. Certification fee: $1.00. $.50 each page after first. Fee payee: Lorraine Moreland, Circuit Clerk. Business checks accepted. Prepayment is required. Fax notes: $5.00 per page.

Vermilion County

Circuit Court 7 N Vermilion, Danville, IL 61832; 217-431-2534; Fax: 217-431-2538. Hours: 8:30AM-4:30PM (CST). *Felony, Misdemeanor, Civil, Eviction, Small Claims, Probate.*

Civil Records: Access: Phone, mail, in person. Both court and visitors may perform in person searches. Search fee: $4.00 per name per year. Required to search: name, years to search. Civil cases indexed by defendant, plaintiff. Civil records on computer from 1989; microfilm from March 1949 to May 1989; index books from 1800s. **Criminal Records:** Access: Phone, mail, in person. Both court and visitors may perform in person searches. Search fee: $4.00 per name per year. Required to search: name, years to search, DOB; also helpful-SSN. Criminal records on

computer from 1989; microfilm from March 1949 to May 1989; index books from 1800s. **General Information:** No juvenile, impounded, mental health or adoption records released. SASE required. Turnaround time 1 week. Copy fee: $1.00 for first page, $.50 each addl. Certification fee: $4.00. Fee payee: Clerk of Circuit Court. Business checks accepted. Prepayment is required. Public access terminal is available.

Wabash County

Circuit Court PO Box 997, 401 Market St, Mt Carmel, IL 62863; 618-262-5362; Fax: 618-263-4441. Hours: 8AM-5PM (CST). *Felony, Misdemeanor, Civil, Eviction, Small Claims, Probate.*

Civil Records: Access: Mail, in person. Both court and visitors may perform in person searches. Search fee: $4.00 per name per year. Required to search: name, years to search. Civil cases indexed by defendant, plaintiff. Civil records on computer from 1988, index books from 1800s. **Criminal Records:** Access: Mail, in person. Both court and visitors may perform in person searches. Search fee: $4.00 per name per year. Required to search: name, years to search, DOB. Criminal records on computer from 1988, index books from 1800s. **General Information:** No juvenile or adoption records released. SASE required. Turnaround time 10 days. Copy fee: $.50 for 1st 20 pages; $.25 each add'l. Certification fee: $2.00. Fee payee: Clerk of Circuit Court. Only cashiers checks and money orders accepted. Prepayment is required. Public access terminal is available. Fax notes: Will fax back if all fees prepaid.

Warren County

Circuit Court 100 W Broadway, Monmouth, IL 61462; 309-734-5179. Hours: 8AM-4:30PM (CST). *Felony, Misdemeanor, Civil, Eviction, Small Claims, Probate.*

Civil Records: Access: Mail, in person. Both court and visitors may perform in person searches. Search fee: $5.00 per name per year. Required to search: name, years to search. Civil cases indexed by defendant. Civil records on computer from 1990, index books from 1800s. **Criminal Records:** Access: Mail, in person. Both court and visitors may perform in person searches. Search fee: $5.00 per name per year. Required to search: name, years to search, DOB. Criminal records on computer from 1990, index books from 1800s. **General Information:** No juvenile or adoption records released. SASE required. Turnaround time 1-2 weeks. Copy fee: $.50 per page. Certification fee: $2.00. Fee payee: Clerk of Circuit Court. Only cashiers checks and money orders accepted. Prepayment is required.

Washington County

Circuit Court 101 E St Louis St, Nashville, IL 62263; 618-327-4800 X305; Fax: 618-327-3583. Hours: 8AM-4PM (CST). *Felony, Misdemeanor, Civil, Eviction, Small Claims, Probate.*

Civil Records: Access: Mail, in person. Both court and visitors may perform in person searches. Search fee: $5.00 per name per year. Required to search: name, years to search. Civil cases indexed by defendant, plaintiff. Civil records on computer since 1998; 1988 for child support; prior records on index books from 1800s. **Criminal Records:** Access: Mail, in person. Both court and visitors may perform in person searches. Search fee: $5.00 per name per year. Required to search: name, years to search; also helpful-DOB. Criminal records on computer since 1998; 1988 for child support; prior records on index books from 1800s. **General Information:** No juvenile or adoption records released. SASE required. Turnaround time 3-5 days. Copy fee: $1.00 per page. Certification fee: $2.00. Fee payee: Washington County Circuit Clerk. Personal checks accepted. Will bill to attorneys.

Wayne County

Circuit Court County Courthouse, PO Box 96, Fairfield, IL 62837; 618-842-7684; Fax: 618-842-2556. Hours: 8AM-4:30PM (CST). *Felony, Misdemeanor, Civil, Eviction, Small Claims, Probate.*

Civil Records: Access: Mail, in person. Both court and visitors may perform in person searches. Search fee: $4.00 per name per year. Required to search: name, years to search. Civil cases indexed by defendant, plaintiff. Civil records on computer from 11/88, index books from 1800s. **Criminal Records:** Access: Mail, in person. Both court and visitors may perform in person searches. Search fee: $4.00 per name per year. Required to search: name, years to search, DOB. Criminal records computerized since 1990. **General Information:** No juvenile or adoption records released. SASE required. Turnaround time 1 week. Copy fee: $.50 per page. Certification fee: $2.00. Fee payee: Clerk of Circuit Court. Only cashiers checks and money orders accepted. Prepayment is required. Public access terminal is available.

White County

Circuit Court PO Box 310, County Courthouse, Carmi, IL 62821; 618-382-2321; Fax: 618-382-2322. Hours: 8AM-4PM (CST). *Felony, Misdemeanor, Civil, Small Claims, Probate.*

Civil Records: Access: Fax, mail, in person. Both court and visitors may perform in person searches. Search fee: $4.00 per name per year. Required to search: name, years to search. Civil cases indexed by defendant, plaintiff. Civil records on computer from 1991, index books from 1800s. **Criminal Records:** Access: Fax, mail, in person. Both court and visitors may perform in person searches. Search fee: $4.00 per name per year. Required to search: name, years to search; also helpful-DOB. Criminal records on computer from 1991, index books from 1800s. **General Information:** No juvenile or adoption records released. SASE required. Turnaround time 1-2 weeks. Copy fee: $.25 per page. Certification fee: $1.00 plus $.50 per add'l page. Fee payee: Clerk of Circuit Court. Personal checks accepted. Prepayment is required. Public access terminal is available. Fax notes: $2.00 per page.

Whiteside County

Circuit Court 200 E Knox St, Morrison, IL 61270-2698; 815-772-5188; Fax: 815-772-5187. Hours: 8:30AM-4:30PM (CST). *Felony, Misdemeanor, Civil, Eviction, Small Claims, Probate.*

Civil Records: Access: Phone, fax, mail, in person. Both court and visitors may perform in person searches. Search fee: $4.00 per name. Required to search: name, years to search. Civil cases indexed by defendant. Civil records on computer from 1989, index books from 1800s. **Criminal Records:** Access: Phone, fax, mail, in person. Both court and visitors may perform in person searches. Search fee: $4.00 per name. Required to search: name, years to search, DOB. Criminal records on computer from 1989, index books from 1800s. **General Information:** No juvenile or adoption records released. SASE

required. Turnaround time 1 week. Copy fee: $.25 per page. Certification fee: $2.00. Fee payee: Clerk of Circuit Court. Personal checks accepted. Prepayment is required. Fax notes: No fee to fax results. Local call only.

Will County

Circuit Court 14 W Jefferson St, Joliet, IL 60432; 815-727-8592; Fax: 815-727-8896. Hours: 8:30AM-4:30PM (CST). *Felony, Misdemeanor, Civil, Eviction, Small Claims, Probate.*

www.willcountycircuitcourt.com

Civil Records: Access: Fax, mail, in person. Both court and visitors may perform in person searches. Search fee: $4.00 per name per year. Required to search: name, years to search. Civil cases indexed by defendant, plaintiff. Civil records on computer from 1980, index books from 1800s. **Criminal Records:** Access: Fax, mail, in person. Both court and visitors may perform in person searches. Search fee: $4.00 per name per year. Required to search: name, years to search, DOB. Criminal records on computer from 1980, index books from 1800s. **General Information:** No juvenile, adoption, mental health records released. SASE required. Turnaround time 2 weeks. Copy fee: $2.00 for first page, $.50 each addl. Certification fee: $4.00. Fee payee: Pamela J McGuire, Clerk of Circuit Court. Only cashiers checks and money orders accepted. Prepayment is required. Public access terminal is available.

Williamson County

Circuit Court 200 W Jefferson St, Marion, IL 62959; 618-997-1301 X114. Hours: 8AM-4:30PM (CST). *Felony, Misdemeanor, Civil, Eviction, Small Claims, Probate.*

Civil Records: Access: Mail, in person. Both court and visitors may perform in person searches. Search fee: $4.00 per name per year. Required to search: name, years to search. Civil cases indexed by defendant, plaintiff. Civil records on computer from 07/86, index books from 1800s. **Criminal Records:** Access: Mail, in person. Both court and visitors may perform in person searches. Search fee: $4.00 per name per year. Required to search: name, years to search, DOB. Criminal records on computer from 07/86, index books from 1800s. **General Information:** No juvenile or adoption records released. SASE required. Turnaround time 1 week. Copy fee: $1.00 for first page, $.50 each addl. Certification fee: $2.00. Fee payee: Clerk of Circuit Court. Business checks accepted. Prepayment is required.

Winnebago County

Circuit Court 400 W State St, Rockford, IL 61101; Civil phone:815-987-2510; Criminal phone:815-987-2510; Fax: 815-987-3012. Hours: 8AM-5PM (CST). *Felony, Misdemeanor, Civil, Eviction, Small Claims, Probate.*

Civil Records: Access: Phone, mail, online, in person. Both court and visitors may perform in person searches. Search fee: $4.00 per name per year. Required to search: name, years to search. Civil cases indexed by defendant, plaintiff. Civil records on computer past 3 years; prior records on index books from 1800s. **Criminal Records:** Access: Phone, mail, remote online, in person. Both court and visitors may perform in person searches. Search fee: $4.00 per name per year. Required to search: name, years to search, DOB. Criminal records on computer past 3 years; prior records on index books from 1800s. **General Information:** No juvenile, mental or adoption records released. SASE required. Turnaround time

1 week. Copy fee: $2.00 for first page, $.50 each addl. After 20 pgs, fee is $.25 per pg. Certification fee: $4.00 plus $.50 per add'l page. Fee payee: Clerk of Circuit Court. Only cashiers checks and money orders accepted.

Woodford County

Circuit Court County Courthouse, PO Box 284, 115 N Main, Suite 201, Eureka, IL 61530; 309-467-3312. Hours: 8AM-5PM (CST). *Felony, Misdemeanor, Civil, Eviction, Small Claims, Probate.*

Civil Records: Access: Mail, in person. Both court and visitors may perform in person searches. Search fee: $4.00 per name per year. Required to search: name, years to search. Civil cases indexed by defendant, plaintiff. Civil records on computer from 1990, index books from 1800s. **Criminal Records:** Access: Mail, in person. Both court and visitors may perform in person searches. Search fee: $4.00 per name per year. Required to search: name, years to search, DOB. Criminal records on computer from 1990, index books from 1800s. **General Information:** No juvenile or adoption records released. SASE required. Turnaround time 2-3 days. Copy fee: $.50 per page. Certification fee: $2.00. Fee payee: Woodford County Circuit Clerk. Personal checks accepted.

ORGANIZATION   102 counties, 103 recording offices. **Cook County** has separate offices for UCC and real estate recording. The recording officer is Recorder of Deeds. Many counties utilize a grantor/grantee index containing all transactions. The entire state is in the Central Time Zone (CST).

REAL ESTATE RECORDS   Most counties will **not** perform real estate searches. Cost of certified copies varies widely, but many counties charge the same as the cost of recording the document. Tax records are usually located at the Treasurer's Office.

UCC RECORDS   Financing statements are filed at the state level except for real estate related filings. Most counties will perform UCC searches. Use search request form UCC-11. Search fees are usually $10.00 per debtor name/address combination. Copies usually cost $1.00 per page.

TAX LIEN RECORDS   Federal tax liens on personal property of businesses are filed with the Secretary of State. Other federal and all state tax liens on personal property are filed with the County Recorder of Deeds. Some counties will perform tax lien searches for $5.00-$10.00 per name (state and federal are separate searches in many of these counties) and $1.00 per page of copy.

OTHER LIENS   Judgments, mechanics, contractor, medical, lis pendens, oil & gas, mobile home.

Adams County
County Recorder, P.O. Box 1067, Quincy, IL 62306. 217-277-2125.

Alexander County
County Recorder, 2000 Washington Avenue, Cairo, IL 62914. 618-734-7000. Fax: 618-734-7002.

Bond County
County Recorder, 203 West College Avenue, Greenville, IL 62246. 618-664-0449. Fax: 618-664-9414.

Boone County
County Recorder, 601 North Main Street, Suite 202, Belvidere, IL 61008. 815-544-3103. Fax: 815-547-8701.

Brown County
County Recorder, Courthouse - Room 4, #1 Court Street, Mount Sterling, IL 62353-1285. 217-773-3421. Fax: 217-773-2233.

Bureau County
County Recorder, 700 South Main St., Courthouse, Princeton, IL 61356. 815-875-3239. Fax: 815-879-4803.

Calhoun County
County Clerk and Recorder, P.O. Box 187, Hardin, IL 62047. 618-576-2351. Fax: 618-576-2895.

Carroll County
County Recorder, P.O. Box 152, Mount Carroll, IL 61053. 815-244-0223. Fax: 815-244-3709.

Cass County
County Recorder, Courthouse, Virginia, IL 62691. 217-452-7217. Fax: 217-452-7219.

Champaign County
County Recorder, 1776 E. Washington, Urbana, IL 61802. 217-384-3774. Fax: 217-344-1663.

Christian County
County Recorder, P.O. Box 647, Taylorville, IL 62568. 217-824-4960. Fax: 217-824-5105.

Clark County
County Recorder, Courthouse, Marshall, IL 62441. 217-826-8311.

Clay County
County Recorder, P.O. Box 160, Louisville, IL 62858-0160. 618-665-3626. Fax: 618-665-3607.

Clinton County
County Recorder, P.O. Box 308, Carlyle, IL 62231. 618-594-2464. Fax: 618-594-8715.

Coles County
County Recorder, 651 Jackson Ave., Room 122, Charleston, IL 61920. 217-348-7325. Fax: 217-348-7337.

Cook County
County Clerk, 118 North Clark Street, Room 120, Chicago, IL 60602-1387. 312-603-7524. Fax: 312-603-5063.
www.assessor.co.cook.il.us
Online Access: Property Tax Records. Records on the Cook County Assessor Residential Assessment Search database are available free on the Internet at www.assessor.co.cook.il.us/starsearch.html. Database is offered as a tax assessment comparison service.

Cook County Recorder
County Recorder, 118 North Clark St., Room 230, Chicago, IL 60602. 312-603-5134. Fax: 312-603-5063.

Crawford County
County Recorder, P.O. Box 602, Robinson, IL 62454-0602. 618-546-1212. Fax: 618-546-0140.

Cumberland County
County Recorder, P.O. Box 146, Toledo, IL 62468. 217-849-2631. Fax: 217-849-2968.

De Kalb County
County Recorder, 110 East Sycamore Street, Sycamore, IL 60178. 815-895-7156.
Online Access: Real Estate, Liens. The DeKalb County online system requires a $350 subscription fee, with a per minute charge of $.25, $.50 if printing. Records date back to 1980. The system operates 8:30AM-4:30PM and supports baud rate of 28.8. Lending agency information is available For further information, contact Sheila Larson at 815-895-7152.

De Witt County
County Recorder, P.O. Box 439, Clinton, IL 61727-0439. 217-935-2119. Fax: 217-935-4596.

Douglas County
County Recorder, P.O. Box 467, Tuscola, IL 61953-0467. 217-253-4410. Fax: 217-253-2233.

Du Page County
County Recorder, P.O. Box 936, Wheaton, IL 60189. 630-682-7200. Fax: 630-682-7204.
www.co.dupage.il.us
Online Access: Real Estate, Liens, Tax Assessor Records. For access to the Du Page County database, one must lease a live interface telephone line from a carrier to establish a connection. Additionally, there is a fee of $.05 per transaction. An IBM 3270 emulator is required; supports a baud rate of 56k For information, contact Fred Kieltcka at 630-682-7030. System hours are 12AM-6:30PM. Records date back to 1977.

Edgar County
County Recorder, Courthouse - Room "J", 115 W. Court St., Paris, IL 61944-1785. 217-466-7433. Fax: 217-466-7430.

Edwards County
County Recorder, 50 East Main Street, Courthouse, Albion, IL 62806-1294. 618-445-2115. Fax: 618-445-3505.

Effingham County
County Clerk and Recorder, P.O. Box 628, Effingham, IL 62401-0628. 217-342-6535. Fax: 217-342-3577.

Fayette County
County Recorder, P.O. Box 401, Vandalia, IL 62471-0401. 618-283-5000. Fax: 618-283-5004.

Ford County
County Recorder, 200 West State Street, Room 101, Paxton, IL 60957. 217-379-2721. Fax: 217-379-3258.

Franklin County
County Clerk & Recorder, P.O. Box 607, Benton, IL 62812. 618-438-3221. Fax: 618-439-4119.

Fulton County
County Recorder, P.O. Box 226, Lewistown, IL 61542. 309-547-3041.

Gallatin County
County Recorder, P.O. Box 550, Shawneetown, IL 62984. 618-269-3025. Fax: 618-269-3343.

Greene County
County Recorder, 519 North Main Street, Courthouse, Carrollton, IL 62016-1033. 217-942-5443.

Grundy County
County Recorder, P.O. Box 675, Morris, IL 60450-0675. 815-941-3224. Fax: 815-942-2220.

Hamilton County
County Recorder, Courthouse, Room 2, Mcleansboro, IL 62859-1489. 618-643-2721.

Hancock County
County Recorder, P.O. Box 39, Carthage, IL 62321-0039. 217-357-3911.

Hardin County
County Recorder, P.O. Box 187, Elizabethtown, IL 62931. 618-287-2251. Fax: 618-287-7833.

Henderson County
County Recorder, P.O. Box 308, Oquawka, IL 61469-0308. 309-867-2911. Fax: 309-867-2033.

Henry County
County Recorder, 100 South Main, Cambridge, IL 61238. 309-937-2426. Fax: 309-937-2796.
www.henrycty.com/recorder.htm

Iroquois County
County Recorder, 1001 East Grant Street, Watseka, IL 60970. 815-432-6962. Fax: 815-432-6984.

Jackson County
County Recorder, The Courthouse, 1001 & Walnut, Murphysboro, IL 62966. 618-687-7360.

Jasper County
County Recorder, 100 West Jourdan, Newton, IL 62448. 618-783-3124. Fax: 618-783-4137.

Jefferson County
County Recorder, Courthouse, 100 S. 10th St., Room 105, Mount Vernon, IL 62864. 618-244-8020.

Jersey County
County Recorder, P.O. Box 216, Jerseyville, IL 62052. 618-498-5571x117/8. Fax: 618-498-6128.

Jo Daviess County
County Recorder, 330 North Bench Street, Galena, IL 61036. 815-777-9694. Fax: 815-777-3688.

Johnson County
County Recorder, P.O. Box 96, Vienna, IL 62995. 618-658-3611. Fax: 618-658-2908.

Kane County
County Recorder, P.O. Box 71, Geneva, IL 60134. 630-232-5935. Fax: 630-232-5945.

Kankakee County
County Recorder, 189 East Court Street, Kankakee, IL 60901. 815-937-2980. Fax: 815-937-3657.

Kendall County
County Recorder, 111 West Fox Street, Yorkville, IL 60560. 630-553-4112. Fax: 630-553-4119.

Knox County
County Recorder, County Court House, Galesburg, IL 61401. 309-345-3818. Fax: 309-343-7002.

La Salle County
County Recorder, P.O. Box 189, Ottawa, IL 61350. 815-434-8226. Fax: 815-434-8260.

Lake County
County Recorder, 18 North County Street, Courthouse - 2nd Floor, Waukegan, IL 60085-4358. 847-360-6673. Fax: 847-625-7200. www.co.lake.il.us/recorder/

Lawrence County
County Recorder, Courthouse, Lawrenceville, IL 62439. 618-943-5126. Fax: 618-943-5205.

Lee County
County Recorder, P.O. Box 329, Dixon, IL 61021-0329. 815-288-3309. Fax: 815-288-6492.

Livingston County
County Recorder, 112 West Madison, Courthouse, Pontiac, IL 61764-1871. 815-844-2006. Fax: 815-842-1844.

Logan County
County Recorder, P.O. Box 278, Lincoln, IL 62656. 217-732-4148. Fax: 217-732-6064.

Macon County
County Recorder, 141 S. Main St., Room 201, Decatur, IL 62523-1293. 217-424-1359. Fax: 217-428-2908.

Macoupin County
County Recorder, P.O. Box 107, Carlinville, IL 62626. 217-854-3214. Fax: 217-854-8461.

Madison County
County Recorder, P.O. Box 308, Edwardsville, IL 62025-0308. 618-692-7040x4772. Fax: 618-692-9843.

Marion County
County Recorder, P.O. Box 637, Salem, IL 62881. 618-548-3400. Fax: 618-548-2226.

Marshall County
County Recorder, P.O. Box 328, Lacon, IL 61540. 309-246-6325. Fax: 309-246-3667.

Mason County
County Recorder, P.O. Box 77, Havana, IL 62644. 309-543-6661. Fax: 309-543-2085.

Massac County
County Recorder, P.O. Box 429, Metropolis, IL 62960. 618-524-5213. Fax: 618-524-4230.

McDonough County
County Recorder, 1 Courthouse Square, Macomb, IL 61455. 309-833-2474. Fax: 309-836-3368.

McHenry County
County Recorder, 2200 North Seminary Avenue, Room A280, Woodstock, IL 60098. 815-334-4110. Fax: 815-338-9612.
Online Access: Assessor/Treasurer. Records on the McMenry County Treasuer Inquiry site are available at http://209.172.155.14/cidnet.publictre1.htm free on the internet.

McLean County
County Recorder, P.O. Box 2400, Bloomington, IL 61702-2400. 309-888-5170. Fax: 309-888-5927. www.mclean.gov/Departments/recorder/recordr.html

Menard County
County Recorder, P.O. Box 465, Petersburg, IL 62675. 217-632-2415. Fax: 217-632-4124.

Mercer County
County Recorder, P.O. Box 66, Aledo, IL 61231. 309-582-7021. Fax: 309-582-7022.

Monroe County
County Recorder, 100 South Main, Courthouse, Waterloo, IL 62298-1399. 618-939-8681. Fax: 618-939-8639.

Montgomery County
County Recorder, Historic Courthouse, 1 Courthouse Square, Hillsboro, IL 62049-1196. 217-532-9532. Fax: 217-532-9581.

Morgan County
County Recorder, P.O. Box 1387, Jacksonville, IL 62651. 217-243-8581.

Moultrie County
County Recorder, Courthouse, Suite 6, 10 S. Main, Sullivan, IL 61951. 217-728-4389. Fax: 217-728-8178.

Ogle County
County Recorder, P.O. Box 357, Oregon, IL 61061. 815-732-1115x270/1.

Peoria County
County Recorder, County Courthouse - Room G04, 324 Main Street, Peoria, IL 61602. 309-672-6090.

Perry County
County Recorder, P.O. Box 438, Pinckneyville, IL 62274. 618-357-5116. Fax: 618-357-3194.

Piatt County
County Recorder, P.O. Box 558, Monticello, IL 61856-0558. 217-762-9487. Fax: 217-762-7563.

Pike County
County Recorder, Courthouse, 100 E. Washington St., Pittsfield, IL 62363. 217-285-6812. Fax: 217-285-5820.

Pope County
County Recorder, P.O. Box 216, Golconda, IL 62938. 618-683-4466. Fax: 618-683-6231.

Pulaski County
County Recorder, P.O. Box 109, Mound City, IL 62963. 618-748-9360.

Putnam County
County Recorder, P.O. Box 236, Hennepin, IL 61327. 815-925-7129. Fax: 815-925-7549.

Randolph County
County Recorder, P.O. Box 309, Chester, IL 62233-0309. 618-826-5000x191. Fax: 618-826-3750.

Richland County
County Recorder, 103 West Main, Courthouse, Olney, IL 62450. 618-392-3111. Fax: 618-393-4005.

Rock Island County
County Recorder, P.O. Box 3067, Rock Island, IL 61204. 309-786-4451x357.

Saline County
County Recorder, 10 E. Poplar, Harrisburg, IL 62946. 618-253-8197.

Sangamon County
County Recorder, P.O.Box 669, Springfield, IL 62705-0669. 217-535-3150. Fax: 217-535-3159.

Schuyler County
County Recorder, P.O. Box 200, Rushville, IL 62681. 217-322-4734. Fax: 217-322-6164.

Scott County
County Recorder, Courthouse, Winchester, IL 62694. 217-742-3178. Fax: 217-742-5853.

Shelby County
County Recorder, P.O. Box 230, Shelbyville, IL 62565. 217-774-4421. Fax: 217-774-5291.

St. Clair County
County Recorder, P.O. Box 543, Belleville, IL 62220. 618-277-6600.

Stark County
County Recorder, P.O. Box 97, Toulon, IL 61483. 309-286-5911. Fax: 309-286-4039.

Stephenson County
County Recorder, 15 North Galena Ave., Suite 1, Freeport, IL 61032. 815-235-8385.

Tazewell County
County Recorder, P.O. Box 36, Pekin, IL 61555-0036. 309-477-2210. Fax: 309-477-2321.

Union County
County Recorder, P.O. Box H, Jonesboro, IL 62952. 618-833-5711. Fax: 618-833-8712.

Vermilion County
County Recorder, 6 North Vermilion Street, Danville, IL 61832-5877. 217-431-2604. Fax: 217-431-7460.

Wabash County
County Recorder, P.O. Box 277, Mount Carmel, IL 62863. 618-262-4561.

Warren County
County Recorder, Courthouse, 100 W. Broadway, Monmouth, IL 61462-1797. 309-734-8592. Fax: 309-734-7406.

Washington County
County Recorder, County Courthouse, 101 E. St. Louis Street, Nashville, IL 62263-1105. 618-327-4800x300. Fax: 618-327-3582.

Wayne County
County Recorder, P.O. Box 187, Fairfield, IL 62837. 618-842-5182. Fax: 618-842-2556.
http://assessor.wayne.il.us/OPID.asp
Online Access: Assessor. Records on the Wayne Township Assessor Office database are available free on the Internet.

White County
County Recorder, P.O. Box 339, Carmi, IL 62821. 618-382-7211.

Whiteside County

County Recorder, 200 East Knox, Morrison, IL 61270. 815-772-5192.

Will County

County Recorder, 302 N. Chicago Street, Joliet, IL 60432. 815-740-4637. Fax: 815-740-4697.

Williamson County

County Recorder, P.O. Box 1108, Marion, IL 62959-1108. 618-997-1301. Fax: 618-993-2071.

Winnebago County

County Recorder, 404 Elm St., Room 405, Rockford, IL 61101. 815-987-3100. Fax: 815-961-3261.

Woodford County

County Recorder, 115 North Main, Courthouse, Room 202, Eureka, IL 61530-1273. 309-467-2822.

You will usually be able to find the city name in the City/County Cross Reference below. In that case, it is a simple matter to determine the county from the cross reference. However, only the official US Postal Service city names are included in this index. There are an additional 40,000 place names that people use in their addresses. Therefore, we have also included a ZIP/City Cross Reference immediately following the City/County Cross Reference.

If you know the ZIP Code but the city name does not appear in the City/County Cross Reference index, look up the ZIP Code in the ZIP/City Cross Reference, find the city name, then look up the city name in the City/County Cross Reference. For example, you want to know the county for an address of Menands, NY 12204. There is no "Menands" in the City/County Cross Reference. The ZIP/City Cross Reference shows that ZIP Codes 12201-12288 are for the city of Albany. Looking back in the City/County Cross Reference, Albany is in Albany County.

City/County Cross Reference

ABINGDON (61410) Knox(98), Warren(2)
ADAIR McDonough
ADDIEVILLE Washington
ADDISON Du Page
ADRIAN Hancock
AKIN Franklin
ALBANY Whiteside
ALBERS Clinton
ALBION Edwards
ALDEN McHenry
ALEDO Mercer
ALEXANDER Morgan
ALEXIS (61412) Mercer(80), Warren(20)
ALGONQUIN (60102) McHenry(92), Kane(8)
ALHAMBRA Madison
ALLENDALE (62410) Wabash(98), Lawrence(2)
ALLERTON (61810) Vermilion(68), Douglas(15), Edgar(14), Champaign(3)
ALMA Marion
ALPHA Henry
ALSEY Scott
ALSIP Cook
ALTAMONT (62411) Effingham(98), Fayette(2)
ALTO PASS (62905) Union(78), Jackson(22)
ALTON Madison
ALTONA (61414) Knox(69), Henry(31)
ALVIN Vermilion
AMBOY Lee
AMF OHARE Cook
ANCHOR (61720) McLean(76), Ford(24)
ANCONA Livingston
ANDALUSIA Rock Island
ANDOVER Henry
ANNA Union
ANNAPOLIS (62413) Crawford(94), Clark(6)
ANNAWAN Henry
ANTIOCH Lake
APPLE RIVER Jo Daviess
ARCOLA (61910) Douglas(89), Coles(11)
ARENZVILLE (62611) Cass(79), Morgan(21)
ARGENTA Macon
ARLINGTON Bureau
ARLINGTON HEIGHTS Cook
ARMINGTON (61721) Tazewell(92), Logan(7)
ARMSTRONG Vermilion
AROMA PARK Kankakee
ARROWSMITH McLean
ARTHUR (61911) Douglas(62), Moultrie(34), Coles(3)
ASHKUM Iroquois
ASHLAND (62612) Cass(58), Morgan(41)
ASHLEY (62808) Washington(82), Jefferson(18)
ASHMORE Coles
ASHTON (61006) Lee(69), Ogle(31)

ASSUMPTION (62510) Christian(87), Shelby(13)
ASTORIA Fulton
ATHENS (62613) Menard(93), Logan(5), Sangamon(2)
ATKINSON Henry
ATLANTA (61723) Logan(98), McLean(2)
ATWATER (62511) Macoupin(97), Montgomery(3)
ATWOOD (61913) Douglas(80), Piatt(19)
AUBURN Sangamon
AUGUSTA (62311) Hancock(93), Schuyler(6), Adams(1)
AURORA (60504) Du Page(82), Kane(14), Will(3)
AURORA (60506) Kane(97), Du Page(3)
AURORA Du Page
AURORA Kane
AVA Jackson
AVISTON Clinton
AVON (61415) Fulton(79), Warren(21)
BAILEYVILLE (61007) Ogle(69), Stephenson(31)
BALDWIN Randolph
BARDOLPH McDonough
BARNHILL Wayne
BARRINGTON (60010) Lake(58), Cook(36), McHenry(5)
BARRINGTON Lake
BARRY (62312) Pike(93), Adams(8)
BARSTOW Rock Island
BARTELSO Clinton
BARTLETT (60103) Cook(51), Du Page(49)
BASCO Hancock
BATAVIA Kane
BATCHTOWN Calhoun
BATH Mason
BAYLIS (62314) Pike(90), Adams(9), Brown(2)
BEARDSTOWN Cass
BEASON (62512) Logan(94), De Witt(6)
BEAVERVILLE (60912) Kankakee(53), Iroquois(47)
BECKEMEYER Clinton
BEDFORD PARK Cook
BEECHER (60401) Will(98), Kankakee(2)
BEECHER CITY (62414) Effingham(62), Fayette(28), Shelby(10)
BELKNAP (62908) Massac(55), Johnson(45)
BELLE RIVE (62810) Jefferson(94), Hamilton(4), Wayne(3)
BELLEVILLE St. Clair
BELLFLOWER McLean
BELLMONT Wabash
BELLWOOD Cook
BELVIDERE Boone
BEMENT Piatt
BENLD Macoupin
BENSENVILLE Du Page
BENSON Woodford

BENTON Franklin
BERKELEY Cook
BERWICK Warren
BERWYN Cook
BETHALTO Madison
BETHANY Moultrie
BIG ROCK (60511) Kane(94), De Kalb(5)
BIGGSVILLE Henderson
BINGHAM Fayette
BIRDS Lawrence
BISHOP HILL Henry
BISMARCK Vermilion
BLACKSTONE Livingston
BLANDINSVILLE (61420) McDonough(91), Hancock(9)
BLOOMINGDALE Du Page
BLOOMINGTON McLean
BLUE ISLAND Cook
BLUE MOUND (62513) Macon(76), Christian(24)
BLUFF SPRINGS Cass
BLUFFS (62621) Scott(89), Morgan(11)
BLUFORD (62814) Jefferson(99), Wayne(1)
BOLES Johnson
BOLINGBROOK (60440) Du Page(68), Will(32)
BOLINGBROOK (60490) Du Page(59), Will(41)
BONDVILLE Champaign
BONE GAP Edwards
BONFIELD Kankakee
BONNIE Jefferson
BOODY Macon
BOURBONNAIS Kankakee
BOWEN (62316) Hancock(99), Adams(1)
BRACEVILLE (60407) Will(54), Grundy(45), Kankakee(1)
BRADFORD (61421) Stark(72), Bureau(23), Marshall(5)
BRADLEY Kankakee
BRADLEY Livingston
BRAIDWOOD Will
BREESE Clinton
BRIDGEPORT Lawrence
BRIDGEVIEW Cook
BRIGHTON (62012) Macoupin(44), Jersey(40), Madison(16)
BRIMFIELD Peoria
BRISTOL Kendall
BROADLANDS (61816) Champaign(97), Douglas(4)
BROCTON (61917) Edgar(97), Douglas(3)
BROOKFIELD Cook
BROOKPORT (62910) Massac(96), Pope(4)
BROUGHTON Hamilton
BROWNING (62624) Schuyler(96), Fulton(5)
BROWNS (62818) Edwards(77), Wabash(23)
BROWNSTOWN Fayette
BRUSSELS Calhoun

BRYANT Fulton
BUCKINGHAM (60917) Kankakee(88), Livingston(12)
BUCKLEY Iroquois
BUCKNER Franklin
BUDA Bureau
BUFFALO Sangamon
BUFFALO GROVE (60089) Lake(50), Cook(50)
BUFFALO PRAIRIE Rock Island
BULPITT Christian
BUNCOMBE (62912) Johnson(55), Union(45)
BUNKER HILL Macoupin
BURBANK Cook
BUREAU Bureau
BURLINGTON Kane
BURNSIDE Hancock
BURNT PRAIRIE (62820) White(83), Wayne(17)
BUSHNELL McDonough
BUTLER Montgomery
BYRON Ogle
CABERY (60919) Ford(43), Livingston(37), Kankakee(21)
CACHE Alexander
CAIRO Alexander
CALEDONIA (61011) Boone(72), Winnebago(29)
CALHOUN Richland
CALUMET CITY Cook
CAMARGO Douglas
CAMBRIA Williamson
CAMBRIDGE Henry
CAMDEN Schuyler
CAMERON Warren
CAMP GROVE Marshall
CAMP POINT Adams
CAMPBELL HILL (62916) Jackson(77), Randolph(14), Perry(9)
CAMPUS Livingston
CANTON Fulton
CANTRALL Sangamon
CAPRON Boone
CARBON CLIFF Rock Island
CARBONDALE (62901) Jackson(89), Williamson(11)
CARBONDALE Jackson
CARLINVILLE Macoupin
CARLOCK (61725) McLean(76), Woodford(24)
CARLYLE Clinton
CARMAN Henderson
CARMI White
CAROL STREAM Du Page
CARPENTERSVILLE Kane
CARRIER MILLS (62917) Saline(89), Williamson(11)
CARROLLTON Greene
CARTERVILLE Williamson
CARTHAGE Hancock
CARY (60013) McHenry(95), Lake(5)

CASEY (62420) Clark(83), Cumberland(15), Coles(1)
CASEYVILLE St. Clair
CASTLETON Stark
CATLIN Vermilion
CAVE IN ROCK Hardin
CEDAR POINT La Salle
CEDARVILLE Stephenson
CENTRALIA (62801) Marion(68), Clinton(21), Washington(7), Jefferson(4)
CERRO GORDO Piatt
CHADWICK (61014) Carroll(82), Whiteside(18)
CHAMBERSBURG (62323) Pike(92), Brown(8)
CHAMPAIGN Champaign
CHANA Ogle
CHANDLERVILLE (62627) Cass(52), Mason(48)
CHANNAHON Will
CHAPIN (62628) Morgan(93), Scott(7)
CHARLESTON Coles
CHATHAM Sangamon
CHATSWORTH (60921) Livingston(99), Ford(1)
CHEBANSE (60922) Kankakee(64), Iroquois(36)
CHENOA (61726) McLean(94), Livingston(6)
CHERRY Bureau
CHERRY VALLEY (61016) Winnebago(89), Boone(11)
CHESTER Randolph
CHESTERFIELD (62630) Macoupin(96), Greene(3), Jersey(1)
CHESTNUT Logan
CHICAGO Cook
CHICAGO HEIGHTS Cook
CHICAGO RIDGE Cook
CHILLICOTHE Peoria
CHRISMAN Edgar
CHRISTOPHER Franklin
CICERO Cook
CISCO (61830) Piatt(87), Macon(13)
CISNE Wayne
CISSNA PARK Iroquois
CLARE De Kalb
CLAREMONT (62421) Richland(95), Crawford(4), Lawrence(1)
CLARENDON HILLS Du Page
CLAY CITY (62824) Clay(93), Wayne(7)
CLAYTON (62324) Adams(92), Brown(8)
CLAYTONVILLE Iroquois
CLIFTON Iroquois
CLINTON De Witt
COAL CITY Grundy
COAL VALLEY (61240) Rock Island(78), Henry(22)
COATSBURG Adams
COBDEN Union
COELLO Franklin
COFFEEN Montgomery
COLCHESTER (62326) McDonough(98), Hancock(2)
COLETA Whiteside
COLFAX McLean
COLLINSVILLE (62234) Madison(91), St. Clair(9)
COLLISON Vermilion
COLMAR McDonough
COLONA Henry
COLP Williamson
COLUMBIA (62236) Monroe(94), St. Clair(6)
COLUSA Hancock
COMPTON Lee
CONCORD Morgan
CONGERVILLE Woodford
COOKSVILLE McLean
CORDOVA Rock Island
CORNELL Livingston
CORNLAND Logan

CORTLAND De Kalb
COTTAGE HILLS Madison
COULTERVILLE (62237) Randolph(44), Washington(30), Perry(26)
COUNTRY CLUB HILLS Cook
COWDEN (62422) Shelby(76), Fayette(23), Fulton(1)
CREAL SPRINGS (62922) Williamson(72), Johnson(28)
CRESCENT CITY Iroquois
CRESTON Ogle
CRETE Will
CREVE COEUR Tazewell
CROPSEY (61731) McLean(63), Ford(36), Livingston(2)
CROSSVILLE White
CRYSTAL LAKE McHenry
CUBA Fulton
CULLOM (60929) Livingston(88), Ford(12)
CUTLER (62238) Perry(97), Randolph(3)
CYPRESS (62923) Johnson(89), Pulaski(9), Union(2)
DAHINDA Knox
DAHLGREN (62828) Hamilton(97), Wayne(3)
DAKOTA Stephenson
DALE Hamilton
DALLAS CITY (62330) Hancock(92), Henderson(8)
DALTON CITY (61925) Moultrie(62), Macon(38)
DALZELL Bureau
DANA (61321) La Salle(87), Livingston(6), Woodford(5), Marshall(3)
DANFORTH Iroquois
DANVERS (61732) McLean(62), Tazewell(38)
DANVILLE Vermilion
DARIEN Du Page
DAVIS (61019) Stephenson(60), Winnebago(40)
DAVIS JUNCTION (61020) Ogle(91), Winnebago(9)
DAWSON Sangamon
DE KALB De Kalb
DE LAND (61839) Vermilion(54), Piatt(47)
DE SOTO (62924) Jackson(80), Williamson(20)
DECATUR Macon
DEER CREEK Tazewell
DEER GROVE Whiteside
DEERE CO GROUP CLAIMS Rock Island
DEERFIELD (60015) Lake(95), Cook(6)
DEERFIELD Cook
DELAVAN Tazewell
DENNISON (62423) Clark(87), Edgar(13)
DEPUE Bureau
DES PLAINES Cook
DEWEY (61840) Champaign(97), Ford(3)
DEWITT De Witt
DIETERICH (62424) Effingham(90), Jasper(11)
DIVERNON Sangamon
DIX (62830) Jefferson(94), Marion(6)
DIXON (61021) Lee(90), Ogle(10)
DOLTON Cook
DONGOLA (62926) Union(91), Pulaski(8)
DONNELLSON (62019) Montgomery(75), Bond(25)
DONOVAN Iroquois
DORSEY (62021) Madison(99), Macoupin(1)
DOVER Bureau
DOW Jersey
DOWELL Jackson
DOWNERS GROVE Du Page
DOWNS McLean
DU BOIS (62831) Washington(91), Perry(8)
DU QUOIN (62832) Perry(97), Jackson(3)
DUNDAS (62425) Richland(87), Jasper(13)
DUNDEE (60118) Kane(98), Cook(2)
DUNFERMLINE Fulton

DUNLAP Peoria
DUPO St. Clair
DURAND Winnebago
DWIGHT (60420) Livingston(93), Grundy(7)
EAGARVILLE Macoupin
EARLVILLE (60518) La Salle(82), De Kalb(15), Lee(3)
EAST ALTON Madison
EAST CARONDELET (62240) St. Clair(98), Monroe(2)
EAST DUBUQUE Jo Daviess
EAST GALESBURG Knox
EAST LYNN Vermilion
EAST MOLINE Rock Island
EAST PEORIA (61611) Tazewell(87), Woodford(14)
EAST SAINT LOUIS St. Clair
EASTON Mason
EDDYVILLE Pope
EDELSTEIN (61526) Peoria(92), Marshall(6), Stark(2)
EDGEWOOD (62426) Effingham(68), Clay(23), Fayette(10)
EDINBURG Christian
EDWARDS Peoria
EDWARDSVILLE Madison
EFFINGHAM Effingham
EL PASO (61738) Woodford(96), McLean(3)
ELBURN Kane
ELCO Alexander
ELDENA Lee
ELDORADO (62930) Saline(98), Gallatin(2)
ELDRED Greene
ELEROY Stephenson
ELGIN (60120) Kane(55), Cook(45)
ELGIN Kane
ELIZABETH (61028) Jo Daviess(98), Carroll(2)
ELIZABETHTOWN (62931) Hardin(80), Gallatin(20)
ELK GROVE VILLAGE (60007) Cook(96), Du Page(4)
ELK GROVE VILLAGE Cook
ELKHART Logan
ELKVILLE Jackson
ELLERY (62833) Edwards(57), Wayne(43)
ELLIOTT Ford
ELLIS GROVE Randolph
ELLISVILLE Fulton
ELLSWORTH McLean
ELMHURST Du Page
ELMWOOD (61529) Peoria(97), Knox(3)
ELMWOOD PARK Cook
ELSAH Jersey
ELVASTON Hancock
ELWIN Macon
ELWOOD Will
EMDEN (62635) Tazewell(58), Logan(42)
EMINGTON Livingston
EMMA White
ENERGY Williamson
ENFIELD (62835) White(94), Hamilton(6)
EOLA Du Page
EQUALITY (62934) Gallatin(69), Saline(31)
ERIE (61250) Whiteside(94), Henry(6)
ESMOND (60129) Ogle(73), De Kalb(27)
ESSEX (60935) Kankakee(98), Will(2)
EUREKA Woodford
EVANSTON Cook
EVANSVILLE Randolph
EVERGREEN PARK Cook
EWING (62836) Franklin(98), Jefferson(2)
FAIRBURY (61739) Livingston(90), McLean(10)
FAIRFIELD Wayne
FAIRMOUNT Vermilion
FAIRVIEW Fulton
FAIRVIEW HEIGHTS St. Clair
FARINA (62838) Fayette(53), Clay(24), Marion(22), Effingham(1)

FARMER CITY (61842) De Witt(91), McLean(9)
FARMERSVILLE Montgomery
FARMINGTON (61531) Fulton(92), Peoria(5), Knox(2)
FENTON (61251) Whiteside(99), Rock Island(2)
FERRIS Hancock
FIATT Fulton
FIDELITY Jersey
FIELDON (62031) Jersey(94), Greene(6)
FILLMORE Montgomery
FINDLAY Shelby
FISHER (61843) Champaign(93), McLean(7)
FITHIAN Vermilion
FLANAGAN Livingston
FLAT ROCK (62427) Crawford(95), Lawrence(5)
FLORA Clay
FLOSSMOOR Cook
FOOSLAND (61845) Champaign(77), Ford(15), McLean(8)
FOREST CITY Mason
FOREST PARK Cook
FORREST Livingston
FORRESTON Ogle
FORSYTH Macon
FORT SHERIDAN Lake
FOWLER Adams
FOX LAKE Lake
FOX RIVER GROVE McHenry
FOX VALLEY Du Page
FRANKFORT Will
FRANKFORT HEIGHTS Franklin
FRANKLIN (62638) Morgan(99), Macoupin(1)
FRANKLIN GROVE (61031) Lee(95), Ogle(5)
FRANKLIN PARK Cook
FREDERICK Schuyler
FREEBURG St. Clair
FREEMAN SPUR Williamson
FREEPORT Stephenson
FULTON Whiteside
FULTS Monroe
GALATIA (62935) Saline(98), Hamilton(2)
GALATIA Saline
GALENA Jo Daviess
GALESBURG (61401) Knox(99), Warren(1)
GALESBURG Knox
GALT Whiteside
GALVA (61434) Henry(98), Knox(2)
GARDEN PRAIRIE (61038) Boone(85), McHenry(15)
GARDNER Grundy
GAYS (61928) Moultrie(61), Coles(26), Shelby(13)
GEFF Wayne
GENESEO Henry
GENEVA Kane
GENOA De Kalb
GEORGETOWN Vermilion
GERLAW Warren
GERMAN VALLEY (61039) Stephenson(61), Ogle(39)
GERMANTOWN Clinton
GIBSON CITY (60936) Ford(99), Champaign(1)
GIFFORD Champaign
GILBERTS Kane
GILLESPIE Macoupin
GILMAN Iroquois
GILSON Knox
GIRARD (62640) Macoupin(99), Montgomery(1)
GLADSTONE Henderson
GLASFORD (61533) Peoria(73), Fulton(27)
GLEN CARBON Madison
GLEN ELLYN Du Page
GLENARM Sangamon
GLENCOE Cook

GLENDALE HEIGHTS Du Page
GLENVIEW Cook
GLENVIEW NAS Cook
GLENWOOD Cook
GODFREY (62035) Madison(95), Jersey(5)
GOLCONDA (62938) Pope(86), Hardin(7), Massac(7)
GOLDEN Adams
GOLDEN EAGLE Calhoun
GOLDEN GATE Wayne
GOLF Cook
GOOD HOPE McDonough
GOODFIELD Woodford
GOODWINE Iroquois
GOREVILLE (62939) Johnson(92), Williamson(5), Union(3)
GORHAM Jackson
GRAFTON Jersey
GRAND CHAIN (62941) Pulaski(56), Massac(44)
GRAND RIDGE La Salle
GRAND TOWER Jackson
GRANITE CITY Madison
GRANT PARK (60940) Kankakee(97), Will(3)
GRANTSBURG (62943) Johnson(78), Massac(18), Pope(4)
GRANVILLE (61326) Putnam(88), La Salle(12)
GRAYMONT Livingston
GRAYSLAKE Lake
GRAYVILLE (62844) White(59), Edwards(41)
GREAT LAKES Lake
GREEN VALLEY (99999) Tazewell(99), Mason(1)
GREENFIELD Greene
GREENUP Cumberland
GREENVIEW Menard
GREENVILLE Bond
GRIDLEY (61744) McLean(90), Livingston(9)
GRIGGSVILLE Pike
GROVELAND Tazewell
GURNEE Lake
HAGARSTOWN Fayette
HAMBURG Calhoun
HAMEL Madison
HAMILTON Hancock
HAMLETSBURG Pope
HAMMOND (61929) Piatt(98), Moultrie(2)
HAMPSHIRE (99999) Kane(99), De Kalb(1)
HAMPTON Rock Island
HANNA CITY Peoria
HANOVER Jo Daviess
HARDIN Calhoun
HARMON (61042) Lee(99), Whiteside(1)
HARRISBURG Saline
HARRISTOWN Macon
HARTFORD Madison
HARTSBURG (62643) Montgomery(62), Logan(38)
HARVARD McHenry
HARVEL (62538) Montgomery(82), Christian(19)
HARVEY Cook
HAVANA (62644) Mason(95), Fulton(5)
HAZEL CREST Cook
HEBRON McHenry
HECKER Monroe
HENDERSON Knox
HENNEPIN Putnam
HENNING Vermilion
HENRY Marshall
HERALD White
HEROD (62947) Saline(44), Hardin(32), Pope(24)
HERRICK (62431) Shelby(69), Fayette(31)
HERRIN Williamson
HERSCHER (60941) Kankakee(96), Iroquois(3), Ford(2)

HETTICK (62649) Macoupin(99), Greene(1)
HEYWORTH (61745) McLean(97), De Witt(3)
HICKORY HILLS Cook
HIDALGO Jasper
HIGHLAND (62249) Madison(95), Clinton(4)
HIGHLAND PARK Lake
HIGHWOOD Lake
HILLSBORO Montgomery
HILLSDALE Rock Island
HILLSIDE Cook
HILLVIEW Greene
HINCKLEY De Kalb
HINDSBORO (61930) Douglas(84), Coles(16)
HINES Cook
HINSDALE (60521) Du Page(89), Cook(11)
HINSDALE (60523) Du Page(98), Cook(2)
HINSDALE Du Page
HOFFMAN Clinton
HOFFMAN ESTATES Cook
HOLCOMB Ogle
HOMER (61849) Champaign(79), Vermilion(21)
HOMETOWN Cook
HOMEWOOD Cook
HOOPESTON (60942) Vermilion(92), Iroquois(9)
HOOPPOLE Henry
HOPEDALE Tazewell
HOPKINS PARK Kankakee
HOYLETON Washington
HUDSON (61748) McLean(98), Woodford(2)
HUEY Clinton
HULL (62343) Pike(94), Adams(6)
HUMBOLDT Coles
HUME Edgar
HUNTLEY (60142) McHenry(80), Kane(20)
HUNTSVILLE Schuyler
HURST Williamson
HUTSONVILLE Crawford
ILLINOIS CITY (61259) Rock Island(98), Mercer(2)
ILLIOPOLIS (62539) Sangamon(93), Macon(6)
INA (62846) Jefferson(96), Franklin(4)
INDIANOLA (61850) Vermilion(98), Edgar(2)
INDUSTRY (61440) McDonough(98), Schuyler(2)
INGLESIDE Lake
INGRAHAM (62434) Jasper(79), Clay(21)
IOLA Clay
IPAVA Fulton
IROQUOIS Iroquois
IRVING Montgomery
IRVINGTON Washington
ISLAND LAKE (60042) Lake(56), McHenry(44)
ITASCA Du Page
IUKA Marion
IVESDALE (61851) Champaign(82), Piatt(14), Douglas(5)
JACKSONVILLE Morgan
JACOB Jackson
JANESVILLE Cumberland
JEFFERSON BANK Peoria
JERSEYVILLE Jersey
JEWETT (62436) Jasper(60), Cumberland(40)
JOHNSONVILLE Wayne
JOHNSTON CITY Williamson
JOLIET Will
JONESBORO Union
JOPPA Massac
JOY (61260) Mercer(93), Rock Island(7)
JUNCTION Gallatin
JUSTICE Cook

KAMPSVILLE (62053) Calhoun(97), Pike(3)
KANE (62054) Greene(86), Jersey(14)
KANEVILLE Kane
KANKAKEE Kankakee
KANSAS (61933) Edgar(84), Clark(13), Coles(2)
KARBERS RIDGE Hardin
KARNAK (62956) Massac(57), Pulaski(43)
KASBEER Bureau
KEENES (62851) Wayne(65), Jefferson(27), Marion(8)
KEENSBURG Wabash
KEITHSBURG (61442) Mercer(94), Henderson(6)
KELL (62853) Marion(98), Jefferson(2)
KEMPTON (60946) Ford(77), Livingston(23)
KENILWORTH Cook
KENNEY (61749) De Witt(79), Logan(22)
KENT (61044) Stephenson(72), Jo Daviess(28)
KEWANEE Henry
KEYESPORT (62253) Bond(54), Clinton(42), Fayette(4)
KILBOURNE Mason
KINCAID Christian
KINDERHOOK Pike
KINGS Ogle
KINGSTON (60145) De Kalb(93), Boone(7)
KINGSTON MINES Peoria
KINMUNDY (62854) Marion(98), Clay(1), Fayette(1)
KINSMAN (60437) Grundy(98), La Salle(3)
KIRKLAND (60146) De Kalb(90), Boone(8), Ogle(1), Winnebago(1)
KIRKWOOD (61447) Warren(91), Henderson(9)
KNOXVILLE Knox
LA FAYETTE (61449) Stark(79), Knox(21)
LA GRANGE Cook
LA GRANGE PARK Cook
LA HARPE (61450) Hancock(61), McDonough(37), Henderson(2)
LA MOILLE (61330) Bureau(70), Lee(30)
LA PLACE Piatt
LA PRAIRIE (62346) Adams(73), Schuyler(24), Hancock(3)
LA ROSE Marshall
LA SALLE La Salle
LACON Marshall
LADD Bureau
LAFOX Kane
LAKE BLUFF Lake
LAKE FOREST Lake
LAKE FORK Logan
LAKE VILLA Lake
LAKE ZURICH Lake
LAKEWOOD Shelby
LANARK Carroll
LANCASTER Wabash
LANE De Witt
LANSING Cook
LATHAM (62543) Logan(72), Macon(28)
LAURA (61451) Peoria(90), Stark(10)
LAWNDALE Logan
LAWRENCEVILLE Lawrence
LE ROY McLean
LEAF RIVER (61047) Ogle(97), Stephenson(2), Winnebago(2)
LEBANON St. Clair
LEE (60530) De Kalb(55), Lee(45)
LEE CENTER Lee
LELAND (60531) La Salle(67), De Kalb(33)
LEMONT (60439) Du Page(73), Cook(24), Will(3)
LENA (61048) Stephenson(97), Jo Daviess(3)
LENZBURG (62255) St. Clair(92), Washington(8)
LEONORE La Salle

LERNA (62440) Coles(71), Cumberland(29)
LEWISTOWN Fulton
LEXINGTON McLean
LIBERTY Adams
LIBERTYVILLE Lake
LIMA Adams
LINCOLN Logan
LINCOLN'S NEW SALEM Menard
LINCOLNSHIRE Lake
LINDENWOOD Ogle
LISLE Du Page
LITCHFIELD (62056) Montgomery(98), Macoupin(2)
LITERBERRY Morgan
LITTLE YORK (61453) Warren(87), Henderson(13)
LITTLETON (61452) Schuyler(83), McDonough(17)
LIVERPOOL Fulton
LIVINGSTON Madison
LOAMI Sangamon
LOCKPORT Will
LODA (60948) Iroquois(89), Ford(11)
LOGAN Franklin
LOMAX Henderson
LOMBARD Du Page
LONDON MILLS Fulton
LONG GROVE Lake
LONG POINT Livingston
LONGVIEW (61852) Champaign(87), Douglas(13)
LOOGOOTEE Fayette
LORAINE (62349) Adams(88), Hancock(12)
LOSTANT (61334) La Salle(96), Putnam(4)
LOUISVILLE (62858) Clay(98), Effingham(2)
LOVEJOY St. Clair
LOVES PARK Winnebago
LOVINGTON (61937) Moultrie(97), Piatt(3)
LOWDER Sangamon
LOWPOINT Woodford
LUDLOW (60949) Champaign(90), Ford(10)
LYNDON Whiteside
LYNN CENTER (61262) Henry(92), Mercer(8)
LYONS Cook
MACEDONIA (62860) Franklin(89), Hamilton(11)
MACHESNEY PARK Winnebago
MACKINAW Tazewell
MACOMB McDonough
MACON Macon
MADISON Madison
MAEYSTOWN Monroe
MAGNOLIA (61336) Putnam(59), Marshall(33), La Salle(9)
MAHOMET (61853) Champaign(98), Piatt(2)
MAKANDA (62958) Jackson(72), Williamson(15), Union(13)
MALDEN Bureau
MALTA De Kalb
MANCHESTER Scott
MANHATTAN Will
MANITO (61546) Mason(90), Tazewell(10)
MANLIUS Bureau
MANSFIELD Piatt
MANTENO (60950) Kankakee(98), Will(2)
MAPLE PARK (60151) Kane(88), De Kalb(12)
MAPLETON Peoria
MAQUON Knox
MARENGO McHenry
MARIETTA (61459) Fulton(60), McDonough(40)
MARINE Madison
MARION Williamson
MARISSA (62257) St. Clair(70), Washington(28), Randolph(2)

12 Grain Buyers & Warehouse Licensing Agency, 150 W Market St, Rm 416, Indianapolis, IN 46204-2810; 317-232-1356, Fax: 317-232-1362.

www.state.in.us/igbwla

13 Horse Racing Licensing, PO Box 942877 (150 W Market St), Indianapolis, IN 46204; 317-233-3119, Fax: 317-233-4470.

www.state.in.us/ihrc

14 Professional Standards Board, 251 E Ohio, #201, Indianapolis, IN 46204-2133; 317-232-9010, Fax: 317-232-9023.

15 Clerk of the Indiana Supreme Court, 217 State House, 20th Fl, Indianapolis, IN 46204; 317-232-1930, Fax: 317-232-8365.

www.state.in.us/judiciary

16 Lottery Commission of Indiana, 201 S Capitol Av #1100, Indianapolis, IN 46225; 317-264-4800, Fax: 317-264-4908.

17 Office of Secretary of State, Statehouse, #201, Indianapolis, IN 46204; 317-232-6542, Fax: 317-233-3283.

www.state.in.us/sos/bus_service/notary

18 Professional Licensing Agency, Boards & Commissions, 302 W Washington St, Rm E034, Indianapolis, IN 46204; 317-232-2980, Fax: 31733-5559.

www.state.in.us/pla

19 Secretary of State, Securities Division, 302 W Washington RME 111, Indianapolis, IN 46204; 317-232-6681, Fax: 317-233-3675.

www.state.in.us/sos/security

Direct URL to search licenses: www.state.in.us/serv/sos_securities You can search online using name, registration #

20 Division of End. & Radiologic Health, Board of Health, 2 N Meridian St, Indianapolis, IN 46204-3003; 317-233-7150.

21 State Police, 100 N Senate Ave, Government Center N, #302, Indianapolis, IN 46204-2259; 317-232-8263, Fax: 317-232-0652.

The following list indicates the district and division name for each county in the state. If the district or division name of the bankruptcy court is different from the civil/criminal court, it appears in parentheses.

County/Court Cross Reference

County	District	Division
Adams	Northern	Fort Wayne
Allen	Northern	Fort Wayne
Bartholomew	Southern	Indianapolis
Benton	Northern	Lafayette (Hammond at Lafayette)
Blackford	Northern	Fort Wayne
Boone	Southern	Indianapolis
Brown	Southern	Indianapolis
Carroll	Northern	Lafayette (Hammond at Lafayette)
Cass	Northern	South Bend
Clark	Southern	New Albany
Clay	Southern	Terre Haute
Clinton	Southern	Indianapolis
Crawford	Southern	New Albany
Daviess	Southern	Evansville
DeKalb	Northern	Fort Wayne
Dearborn	Southern	New Albany
Decatur	Southern	Indianapolis
Delaware	Southern	Indianapolis
Dubois	Southern	Evansville
Elkhart	Northern	South Bend
Fayette	Southern	Indianapolis
Floyd	Southern	New Albany
Fountain	Southern	Indianapolis
Franklin	Southern	Indianapolis
Fulton	Northern	South Bend
Gibson	Southern	Evansville
Grant	Northern	Fort Wayne
Greene	Southern	Terre Haute
Hamilton	Southern	Indianapolis
Hancock	Southern	Indianapolis
Harrison	Southern	New Albany
Hendricks	Southern	Indianapolis
Henry	Southern	Indianapolis
Howard	Southern	Indianapolis
Huntington	Northern	Fort Wayne
Jackson	Southern	New Albany
Jasper	Northern	Lafayette (Hammond at Lafayette)
Jay	Northern	Fort Wayne
Jefferson	Southern	New Albany
Jennings	Southern	New Albany
Johnson	Southern	Indianapolis
Knox	Southern	Terre Haute
Kosciusko	Northern	South Bend
La Porte	Northern	South Bend
LaGrange	Northern	Fort Wayne
Lake	Northern	Hammond (Hammond. at Gary)
Lawrence	Southern	New Albany
Madison	Southern	Indianapolis
Marion	Southern	Indianapolis
Marshall	Northern	South Bend
Martin	Southern	Evansville
Miami	Northern	South Bend
Monroe	Southern	Indianapolis
Montgomery	Southern	Indianapolis
Morgan	Southern	Indianapolis
Newton	Northern	Lafayette (Hammond at Lafayette)
Noble	Northern	Fort Wayne
Ohio	Southern	New Albany
Orange	Southern	New Albany
Owen	Southern	Terre Haute
Parke	Southern	Terre Haute
Perry	Southern	Evansville
Pike	Southern	Evansville
Porter	Northern	Hammond (Hammond. at Gary)
Posey	Southern	Evansville
Pulaski	Northern	South Bend
Putnam	Southern	Terre Haute
Randolph	Southern	Indianapolis
Ripley	Southern	New Albany
Rush	Southern	Indianapolis
Scott	Southern	New Albany
Shelby	Southern	Indianapolis
Spencer	Southern	Evansville
St. Joseph	Northern	South Bend
Starke	Northern	South Bend
Steuben	Northern	Fort Wayne
Sullivan	Southern	Terre Haute
Switzerland	Southern	New Albany
Tippecanoe	Northern	Lafayette (Hammond at Lafayette)
Tipton	Southern	Indianapolis
Union	Southern	Indianapolis
Vanderburgh	Southern	Evansville
Vermillion	Southern	Terre Haute
Vigo	Southern	Terre Haute
Wabash	Northern	South Bend
Warren	Northern	Lafayette (Hammond at Lafayette)
Warrick	Southern	Evansville
Washington	Southern	New Albany
Wayne	Southern	Indianapolis
Wells	Northern	Fort Wayne
White	Northern	Lafayette (Hammond at Lafayette)
Whitley	Northern	Fort Wayne

US District Court

Northern District of Indiana

Fort Wayne Division Room 1108, Federal Bldg, 1300 S Harrison St, Fort Wayne, IN 46802, 219-424-7360.

www.innd.uscourts.gov

Counties: Adams, Allen, Blackford, DeKalb, Grant, Huntington, Jay, Lagrange, Noble, Steuben, Wells, Whitley.

Indexing & Storage: Cases are indexed by defendant and plaintiff as well as by case number. New cases are available in the index 1-2 days after filing date. Both computer and card indexes are maintained. Open records are located at this court.

Fee & Payment: The fee is $15.00 per item (one party name or case number). Payment may be made by money order, cashier check, personal check. Prepayment is required. Payee: Clerk, US District Court. Certification fee: $5.00 per document. Copy fee: $.50 per page.

Phone Search: Only case names and numbers will be released over the phone. An automated voice case information service (VCIS) is not available.

Mail Search: Always enclose a stamped self addressed envelope.

In Person Search: In person searching is available.

PACER: Sign-up number is 800-676-6856. Access fee is $.60 per minute. Toll-free access: 800-371-8843. Local access: 219-246-8200. Case records are available back to 1994. Records are purged as deemed necessary. New records are available online after 2 days.

Hammond Division Room 101, 507 State St, Hammond, IN 46320, 219-937-5235.

www.innd.uscourts.gov

Counties: Lake, Porter.

Indexing & Storage: Cases are indexed by defendant and plaintiff as well as by case number. New cases are available in the index 1-3 days after filing date. A computer index is maintained. Open records are located at this court.

Fee & Payment: The fee is $15.00 per item (one party name or case number). Payment may be made by money order, cashier check, personal check. Prepayment is required. Payee: Clerk, US District Court. Certification fee: $5.00 per document. Copy fee: $.50 per page.

Phone Search: Only docket information is available by phone. An automated voice case information service (VCIS) is not available.

Mail Search: Always enclose a stamped self addressed envelope.

In Person Search: In person searching is available.

PACER: Sign-up number is 800-676-6856. Access fee is $.60 per minute. Toll-free access: 800-371-8843. Local access: 219-246-8200. Case records are available back to 1994. Records are purged as deemed necessary. New records are available online after 2 days.

Lafayette Division PO Box 1498, Lafayette, IN 47902 (Courier Address: 230 N 4th St, Lafayette, IN 47901), 765-420-6250.

www.innd.uscourts.gov

Counties: Benton, Carroll, Jasper, Newton, Tippecanoe, Warren, White.

Indexing & Storage: Cases are indexed by defendant and plaintiff as well as by case number. New cases are available in the index 24 hours after filing date. A computer index is maintained. Microfiche is also available. Open records are located at this court.

Fee & Payment: The fee is $15.00 per item (one party name or case number). Payment may be made by money order, cashier check, personal check. Prepayment is required. Payee: Clerk, US District Court. Certification fee: $5.00 per document. Copy fee: $.50 per page.

Phone Search: Only docket information is available by phone. An automated voice case information service (VCIS) is not available.

Fax Search: Will accept fax only to ask if a person is a defendant or plaintiff in any cases.

Mail Search: Always enclose a stamped self addressed envelope.

In Person Search: In person searching is available.

PACER: Sign-up number is 800-676-6856. Access fee is $.60 per minute. Toll-free access: 800-371-8843. Local access: 219-246-8200. Case records are available back to 1994. Records are purged as deemed necessary. New records are available online after 2 days.

South Bend Division Room 102, 204 S Main, South Bend, IN 46601, 219-246-8000, Fax: 219-246-8002.

www.innd.uscourts.gov

Counties: Cass, Elkhart, Fulton, Kosciusko, La Porte, Marshall, Miami, Pulaski, St. Joseph, Starke, Wabash.

Indexing & Storage: Cases are indexed by defendant and plaintiff as well as by case number. New cases are available in the index 2 days after filing date. A computer index is maintained. Open records are located at this court.

Fee & Payment: The fee is $15.00 per item (one party name or case number). Payment may be made by money order, cashier check, personal check. Prepayment is required. Payee: Clerk, US District Court. Certification fee: $5.00 per document. Copy fee: $.50 per page.

Phone Search: Only docket information is available by phone. An automated voice case information service (VCIS) is not available.

Mail Search: Always enclose a stamped self addressed envelope.

In Person Search: In person searching is available.

PACER: Sign-up number is 800-676-6856. Access fee is $.60 per minute. Toll-free access: 800-371-8843. Local access: 219-246-8200. Case records are available back to 1994. Records are purged as deemed necessary. New records are available online after 2 days.

US Bankruptcy Court
Northern District of Indiana

Fort Wayne Division PO Box 2547, Fort Wayne, IN 46801-2547 (Courier Address: 1188 Federal Bldg, 1300 S Harrison St, Fort Wayne, IN 46802), 219-420-5100.

www.innb.uscourts.gov

Counties: Adams, Allen, Blackford, DeKalb, Grant, Huntington, Jay, Lagrange, Noble, Steuben, Wells, Whitley.

Indexing & Storage: Cases are indexed by debtor and creditors as well as by case number. New cases are available in the index 24 hours after filing date. A computer index is maintained. A card index of debtor names is also maintained. Open records are located at this court. Records in closed cases are only kept locally for a brief period. Records are shipped to the Chicago FRC annually. At the time a case is closed, both the date of filing and the date of closing are factors in determining when the case is shipped.

Fee & Payment: The fee is $15.00 per item (one party name or case number). Payment may be made by money order, cashier check, personal check. Prepayment is required. Debtor's checks are not accepted. Payee: Clerk, US Bankruptcy Court. Certification fee: $5.00 per document. Copy fee: $.50 per page.

Phone Search: Only docket information is available by phone. An automated voice case information service (VCIS) is available. Call VCIS at 800-755-8393 or 219-968-2275.

Mail Search: Always enclose a stamped self addressed envelope.

In Person Search: In person searching is available.

PACER: Sign-up number is 800-676-6856. Access fee is $.60 per minute. Toll-free access: 888-917-2237. Local access: 219-968-2270. Case records are available back to 1992. Records are purged every 6 months. New civil records are available online after 2 days. PACER is available on the Internet at http://pacer.innb.uscourts.gov.

Hammond at Gary Division 221 Federal Bldg, 610 Connecticut St, Gary, IN 46402-2595, 219-881-3335, Fax: 219-881-3307.

www.innb.uscourts.gov

Counties: Lake, Porter.

Indexing & Storage: Cases are indexed by debtor and creditors as well as by case number. New cases are available in the index 24 hours after filing date. A computer index is maintained. Open records are located at this court. Records in closed cases are only kept locally for a brief period. Records are shipped to the FRC twice a year. At the time a case is closed, both the date of filing and the date of closing are factors in determining when the case is shipped.

Fee & Payment: The fee is $15.00 per item (one party name or case number). Payment may be made by money order, cashier check, personal check, Visa or Mastercard. Prepayment is required. Debtor's checks and credit cards are not accepted. Payee: Clerk, US Bankruptcy Court. Certification fee: $5.00 per document. Copy fee: $.50 per page. You are allowed to make your own copies. These copies cost $.15 per page.

Phone Search: Only docket information is available by phone. An automated voice case information service (VCIS) is available. Call VCIS at 800-755-8393 or 219-968-2275.

Mail Search: Always enclose a stamped self addressed envelope.

In Person Search: In person searching is available.

PACER: Sign-up number is 800-676-6856. Access fee is $.60 per minute. Toll-free access: 888-917-2237. Local access: 219-968-2270. Case records are available back to 1992. Records are purged every 6 months. New civil records are available online after 2 days. PACER is available on the Internet at http://pacer.innb.uscourts.gov.

Hammond at Lafayette Division c/o Fort Wayne Division, PO Box 2547, Fort Wayne, IN 46801-2547, 219-420-5100.

www.innb.uscourts.gov

Counties: Benton, Carroll, Jasper, Newton, Tippecanoe, Warren, White.

Indexing & Storage: Cases are indexed by as well as by case number. New cases are available in the index after filing date. All the files for the Hammond Division at Lafayette are physically kept in the Fort Wayne office. All papers pertaining to Hammond Division at Lafayette cases after the initial filing, including claims, should be sent to the Fort Wayne office. Open records are located at the Division.

Fee & Payment: The fee is $15.00 per item (one party name or case number). Payment may be made by money order, cashier check. Business checks are not accepted. Personal checks are not accepted.

Phone Search: An automated voice case information service (VCIS) is available. Call VCIS at 800-755-8393 or 219-968-2275.

Mail Search: Always enclose a stamped self addressed envelope.

In Person Search: In person searching is available.

PACER: Sign-up number is 800-676-6856. Access fee is $.60 per minute. Toll-free access: 888-917-2237. Local access: 219-968-2270. Case records are available back to 1992. Records are purged every 6 months. New civil records are available online after 2 days. PACER is available on the Internet at http://pacer.innb.uscourts.gov.

South Bend Division PO Box 7003, South Bend, IN 46634-7003 (Courier Address: 401 S Michigan St, South Bend, IN 46601), 219-968-2100, Fax: 219-968-2205.

www.innb.uscourts.gov

Counties: Cass, Elkhart, Fulton, Kosciusko, La Porte, Marshall, Miami, Pulaski, St. Joseph, Starke, Wabash.

Indexing & Storage: Cases are indexed by debtor and creditors as well as by case number. New cases are available in the index 24 hours after filing date. A computer index is maintained. Open records are located at this court. Records in closed cases are only kept locally for a brief period. Records are shipped to the Chicago FRC semi-annually. At the time a case is closed, both the date of filing and the date of closing are factors in determining when the case is shipped.

Fee & Payment: The fee is $15.00 per item (one party name or case number). Payment may be made by money order, cashier check, personal check, Visa or Mastercard. Prepayment is required. Debtor's checks are not accepted. Payee: Clerk, US Bankruptcy Court. Certification fee: $5.00 per document. Copy fee: $.50 per page. You are allowed to make your own copies. These copies cost $.15 per page. A self service copy machine is available.

Phone Search: Only docket information is available by phone. An automated voice case information service (VCIS) is available. Call VCIS at 800-755-8393 or 219-968-2275.

Mail Search: Always enclose a stamped self addressed envelope.

In Person Search: In person searching is available.

PACER: Sign-up number is 800-676-6856. Access fee is $.60 per minute. Toll-free access: 888-917-2237. Local access: 219-968-2270. Case records are available back to 1992. Records are purged every 6 months. New civil records are available online after 2 days. PACER is available on the Internet at http://pacer.innb.uscourts.gov.

US District Court

Southern District of Indiana

Evansville Division 304 Federal Bldg, 101 NW Martin Luther King Blvd, Evansville, IN 47708, 812-465-6426, Fax: 812-465-6428.

www.insd.uscourts.gov

Counties: Daviess, Dubois, Gibson, Martin, Perry, Pike, Posey, Spencer, Vanderburgh, Warrick.

Indexing & Storage: Cases are indexed by defendant and plaintiff as well as by case number. New cases are available in the index immediately after filing date. Cases prior to 1992 are indexed by name only on index cards. Open records are located at this court.

Fee & Payment: The fee is $15.00 per item (one party name or case number). Payment may be made by money order, cashier check, personal check. Prepayment is required. Payee: Clerk, US District Court. Certification fee: $5.00 per document. Copy fee: $.50 per page.

Phone Search: Searching is not available by phone.

Mail Search: A stamped self addressed envelope is not required.

In Person Search: In person searching is available.

PACER: There is no PACER access to this court.

Other Online Access: You can search records using the Internet. Searching is currently free. Visit www.insd.uscourts.gov/casesearch.htm to search.

Indianapolis Division Clerk, Room 105, 46 E Ohio St, Indianapolis, IN 46204, 317-229-3700, Fax: 317-229-3959.

www.insd.uscourts.gov

Counties: Bartholomew, Boone, Brown, Clinton, Decatur, Delaware, Fayette, Fountain, Franklin, Hamilton, Hancock, Hendricks, Henry, Howard, Johnson, Madison, Marion, Monroe, Montgomery, Morgan, Randolph, Rush, Shelby, Tipton, Union, Wayne.

Indexing & Storage: Cases are indexed by defendant and plaintiff as well as by case number. New cases are available in the index 24 hours after filing date. A computer index is maintained. Open records are located at this court. District wide searches are available from this court for cases from 1996 to the present.

Fee & Payment: The fee is $15.00 per item (one party name or case number). Payment may be made by money order. Business checks are not accepted, Visa, Mastercard. Personal checks are not accepted. Prepayment is required. Payee: Clerk, US District Court. Certification fee: $5.00 per document. Copy fee: $.50 per page.

Phone Search: Only information contained on the face of the docket sheet will be released over the phone. Anything from the remaining pages requires that the search fee be paid. An automated voice case information service (VCIS) is not available.

Mail Search: A stamped self addressed envelope is not required.

In Person Search: In person searching is available.

PACER: There is no PACER access to this court.

Other Online Access: You can search records using the Internet. Searching is currently free. Visit www.insd.uscourts.gov/casesearch.htm to search.

New Albany Division Room 210, 121 W Spring St, New Albany, IN 47150, 812-948-5238.

www.insd.uscourts.gov

Counties: Clark, Crawford, Dearborn, Floyd, Harrison, Jackson, Jefferson, Jennings, Lawrence, Ohio, Orange, Ripley, Scott, Switzerland, Washington.

Indexing & Storage: Cases are indexed by defendant and plaintiff as well as by case number. New cases are available in the index immediately after filing date. A card index is maintained. Open records are located at this court. Files may also be in Indianapolis or Evansville.

Fee & Payment: The fee is $15.00 per item (one party name or case number). Payment may be made by money order, cashier check, personal check. Prepayment is required. Payee: Clerk, US District Court. Certification fee: $5.00 per document. Copy fee: $.50 per page.

Phone Search: Searching is not available by phone.

Mail Search: Always enclose a stamped self addressed envelope.

In Person Search: In person searching is available.

PACER: There is no PACER access to this court.

Other Online Access: You can search records using the Internet. Searching is currently free. Visit www.insd.uscourts.gov/casesearch.htm to search.

Terre Haute Division 207 Federal Bldg, 30 N 7th St, Terre Haute, IN 47808, 812-234-9484.

www.insd.uscourts.gov

Counties: Clay, Greene, Knox, Owen, Parke, Putnam, Sullivan, Vermillion, Vigo.

Indexing & Storage: Cases are indexed by defendant and plaintiff as well as by case number. New cases are available in the index immediately after filing date. A computer index is maintained. Open records are located at this court.

Fee & Payment: The fee is $15.00 per item (one party name or case number). Payment may be made by money order, cashier check, personal check. Prepayment is required. Payee: Clerk, US District Court. Certification fee: $5.00 per document. Copy fee: $.50 per page.

Phone Search: All information that is not sealed is available for release over the phone. An automated voice case information service (VCIS) is not available.

Mail Search: Always enclose a stamped self addressed envelope.

In Person Search: In person searching is available.

PACER: There is no PACER access to this court.

Other Online Access: You can search records using the Internet. Searching is currently free. Visit www.insd.uscourts.gov/casesearch.htm to search.

US Bankruptcy Court

Southern District of Indiana

Evansville Division 352 Federal Building, 101 NW Martin Luther King Blvd, Evansville, IN 47708, 812-465-6440, Fax: 812-465-6453.

www.insb.uscourts.gov

Counties: Daviess, Dubois, Gibson, Martin, Perry, Pike, Posey, Spencer, Vanderburgh, Warrick.

Indexing & Storage: Cases are indexed by debtor as well as by case number. New cases are available in the index 1-2 days after filing date. Both computer and card indexes are maintained. Open records are located at this court.

Fee & Payment: The fee is $15.00 per item (one party name or case number). Payment may be made by money order, cashier check, personal check. Prepayment is required. Debtor's checks are not accepted. Payee: Clerk, US Bankruptcy Court. Certification fee: $5.00 per document. Copy fee:

$.50 per page. You are allowed to make your own copies. These copies cost $.50 per page.

Phone Search: Only docket information is available by phone. An automated voice case information service (VCIS) is available. Call VCIS at 800-335-8003 or.

Mail Search: Always enclose a stamped self addressed envelope.

In Person Search: In person searching is available.

PACER: Sign-up number is 317-229-3845. Access fee is $.60 per minute. NIBS system: First number is for Carbon Copy users and second is for Procomm users. Use of Carbon Copy Plus required. Case records are available back to 1988. Records are purged every 3 months. New civil records are available online after 2-3 days.

Other Online Access: You can search records online at www.insb.uscourts.gov/public/casesearch.asp. You may search using case number, party name, social security number and/or tax ID number. The system is currently free.

Indianapolis Division US Courthouse, Rm 116, 46 E Ohio St, Indianapolis, IN 46204, 317-229-3800, Fax: 317-229-3801.

www.insb.uscourts.gov

Counties: Bartholomew, Boone, Brown, Clinton, Decatur, Delaware, Fayette, Fountain, Franklin, Hamilton, Hancock, Hendricks, Henry, Howard, Johnson, Madison, Marion, Monroe, Montgomery, Morgan, Randolph, Rush, Shelby, Tipton, Union, Wayne.

Indexing & Storage: Cases are indexed by debtor as well as by case number. New cases are available in the index 48 hours after filing date. A computer index is maintained. Records are stored electronically since 1986. Open records are located at this court.

Fee & Payment: The fee is $15.00 per item (one party name or case number). Payment may be made by money order, cashier check, personal check. Checks are accepted from debtors. Payee: Clerk, US Bankruptcy Court (SDIN). Certification fee: $5.00 per document. Copy fee: $.50 per page.

Phone Search: Only docket information is available by phone. An automated voice case information service (VCIS) is available. Call VCIS at 800-335-8003 or.

Mail Search: Always enclose a stamped self addressed envelope.

In Person Search: In person searching is available.

PACER: Sign-up number is 317-229-3845. Access fee is $.60 per minute. NIBS system: First number is for Carbon Copy users and second is for Procomm users. Use of Carbon Copy Plus required. Case records are available back to 1988. Records are purged every 3 months. New civil records are available online after 2-3 days.

Other Online Access: You can search records online at www.insb.uscourts.gov/public/casesearch.asp. You may search using case number, party name, social security number and/or tax ID number. The system is currently free.

New Albany Division US Courthouse, Rm 110, 121 W Spring St, New Albany, IN 47150, 812-948-5254, Fax: 812-948-5262.

www.insb.uscourts.gov

Counties: Clark, Crawford, Dearborn, Floyd, Harrison, Jackson, Jefferson, Jennings, Lawrence, Ohio, Orange, Ripley, Scott, Switzerland, Washington.

Indexing & Storage: Cases are indexed by debtor as well as by case number. New cases are available in the index 48 hours after filing date. A computer index is maintained. Open records are located at this court.

Fee & Payment: The fee is $15.00 per item (one party name or case number). Payment may be made by money order, cashier check, personal check. Checks are not accepted from debtors. Payee: Clerk, US Bankruptcy Court (SDIN). Certification fee: $5.00 per document. Copy fee: $.50 per page.

Phone Search: Only docket information is available by phone. An automated voice case information service (VCIS) is available. Call VCIS at 800-335-8003 or.

Mail Search: Always enclose a stamped self addressed envelope.

In Person Search: In person searching is available.

PACER: Sign-up number is 317-229-3845. Access fee is $.60 per minute. NIBS system: First number is for Carbon Copy users and second is for Procomm users. Use of Carbon Copy Plus required. Case records are available back to 1988.

Records are purged every 3 months. New civil records are available online after 2-3 days.

Other Online Access: You can search records online at www.insb.uscourts.gov/public/casesearch.asp. You may search using case number, party name, social security number and/or tax ID number. The system is currently free.

Terre Haute Division Federal Bldg Rm 207, 30 N 7th St, Terre Haute, IN 47808, 812-238-1550, Fax: 812-238-1831.

www.insb.uscourts.gov

Counties: Clay, Greene, Knox, Owen, Parke, Putnam, Sullivan, Vermillion, Vigo.

Indexing & Storage: Cases are indexed by debtor as well as by case number. New cases are available in the index 48 hours after filing date. A computer index is maintained. Records are stored electronically since 1986. Open records are located at this court.

Fee & Payment: The fee is $15.00 per item (one party name or case number). Payment may be made by money order, cashier check, personal check. Prepayment is required. A search fee will only be charged if a detailed search is required. Personal checks are not accepted from debtors. Payee: Clerk, US Bankruptcy Court. Certification fee: $5.00 per document. Copy fee: $.50 per page.

Phone Search: Only docket information is available by phone. An automated voice case information service (VCIS) is available. Call VCIS at 800-335-8003 or.

Mail Search: Always enclose a stamped self addressed envelope.

In Person Search: In person searching is available.

PACER: Sign-up number is 317-229-3845. Access fee is $.60 per minute. NIBS system: First number is for Carbon Copy users and second is for Procomm users. Use of Carbon Copy Plus required. Case records are available back to 1988. Records are purged every 3 months. New civil records are available online after 2-3 days.

Other Online Access: You can search records online at www.insb.uscourts.gov/public/casesearch.asp. You may search using case number, party name, social security number and/or tax ID number. The system is currently free.

Court	Jurisdiction	No. of Courts	How Organized
Circuit Courts*	General	24	
Superior Courts*	General	4	
Combined Courts*		68	
County Courts*	Limited		
Combined Circuit/County*		4	
City Courts	Limited	47	
Small Claims -Marion County	Special	9	
Town Courts	Municipal	25	
Probate Court	Special	1	St. Joseph County

* Profiled in this Sourcebook.

Court					CIVIL				
	Tort	Contract	Real Estate	Min. Claim	Max. Claim	Small Claims	Estate	Eviction	Domestic Relations
Circuit Courts*	X	X	X	$0	No Max	$3000	X		X
Superior Courts*	X	X	X	$0	No Max	$3000	X		X
County Courts*	X	X	X	$0	$10,000	$3000		X	X
City Courts	X	X		$0	$2500			X	X
Small Claims - Marion County						$3000			
Town Courts									X
Probate Court							X		

Court		CRIMINAL			
	Felony	Misdemeanor	DWI/DUI	Preliminary Hearing	Juvenile
Circuit Courts*	X	X	X	X	X
Superior Courts*	X	X	X	X	X
County Courts*	X	X	X	X	
City Courts		X	X	X	
Small Claims - Marion County					
Town Courts		X	X	X	
Probate Court					X

ADMINISTRATION   State Court Administrator, 115 W Washington St Suite 1080, Indianapolis, IN, 46204; 317-232-2542, Fax: 317-233-6586. www.state.in.us/judiciary/

COURT STRUCTURE   There are 92 judical circuits with Circuit Courts or Combined Circuit and Superior Courts. In addition, there are 47 City Courts and 25 Town Courts. County courts are gradually being restructered into divisions of the Superior Courts. Note that Small Claims in Marion County are heard at the township and records are maintained at that level. The phone number for the township offices are indicated in Marion County.

ONLINE ACCESS   No online access computer system, internal or external, is available, except for Marion County through CivicNet/Access Indiana Information Network, which is available on the Internet at www.civicnet.net. Account and password are required. No charge for civil court name searches. Fees range from $2.00 to $5.00 for civil case summaries, civil justice name searches, criminal case summaries, and party booking details.

ADDITIONAL INFORMATION   The Circuit Court Clerk/County Clerk in every county is the same individual and is responsible for keeping all county judicial records. However, it is recommended that, when requesting a record, the request indicate which court heard the case (Circuit, Superior, or County).

Many courts are no longer performing searches, especially criminal searches, based on a 7/8/96 statement by the State Board of Accounts.

Certification and copy fees are set by statute as $1.00 per document plus copy fee for certification and $1.00 per page for copies.

Adams County

Circuit & Superior Court 2nd St Courthouse, Decatur, IN 46733; 219-724-2600 X206; Fax: 219-724-3848. Hours: 8AM-4:30PM (EST). *Felony, Misdemeanor, Civil, Eviction, Small Claims, Probate.*

Civil Records: Access: In person only. Court does not conduct in person searches; visitors must perform searches for themselves. Search fee: No civil searches performed by court. Required to search: name, years to search. Civil cases indexed by defendant, plaintiff. Civil records on computer from 1992, archived from 1876. Some records on index cards. **Criminal Records:** Access: In person only. Court does not conduct in person searches; visitors must perform searches for themselves. Search fee: No criminal searches performed by court. Required to search: name, years to search, DOB; also helpful-SSN. Criminal records on computer from 1992, archived from 1876. Some records on index cards. **General Information:** No juvenile, adoption, mental health or sealed records released. Copy fee: $1.00 per page. Certification fee: $2.00 per page. Fee payee: Adams County Clerk. Only cashiers checks and money orders accepted. Prepayment is required. Public access terminal is available. Public Access Terminal Note: Limited.

Allen County

Circuit & Superior Court 715 S. Calhoun St. Rm 200 Courthouse, Ft Wayne, IN 46802; 219-449-7245. Hours: 8AM-4:30PM (EST). *Felony, Misdemeanor, Civil, Eviction, Small Claims, Probate.*

http://www.co.allen.in.us/clerk/Default.htm

Civil Records: Access: In person only. Court does not conduct in person searches; visitors must perform searches for themselves. Search fee: No civil searches performed by court. Required to search: name, years to search. Civil cases indexed by defendant, plaintiff. recent cases on computer; prior records on microfiche, archived and index from 1824. **Criminal Records:** Access: In person only. Court does not conduct in person searches; visitors must perform searches for themselves. Search fee: No criminal searches performed by court. Required to search: name, years to search; also helpful-DOB, SSN. recent cases on computer; prior records on microfiche, archived and index from 1824. **General Information:** No juvenile, adoption or sealed records released. Copy fee: $1.00 per page. Certification fee: $1.00 per page. Fee payee: Clerk of Allen Circuit Court. Business checks accepted. Prepayment is required. Public access terminal is available.

Bartholomew County

Circuit & Superior Court PO Box 924, Columbus, IN 47202-0924; 812-379-1600; Fax: 812-379-1675. Hours: 8AM-5PM (EST). *Felony, Misdemeanor, Civil, Eviction, Small Claims, Probate.*

Civil Records: Access: In person only. Court does not conduct in person searches; visitors must perform searches for themselves. Search fee: No civil searches performed by court. Required to

search: name. Civil cases indexed by plaintiff. Civil records on computer from 1985, on microfilm from 1940, on index from 1821. **Criminal Records:** Access: Fax, mail, in person. Both court and visitors may perform in person searches. No search fee. Required to search: name, years to search, DOB; also helpful-SSN, race, sex. Criminal records on computer from 1985, on microfilm from 1940, on index from 1821. **General Information:** No juvenile, mental health, adoption or sealed released. All searches 1985 to present. SASE required. Turnaround time 1 day. Copy fee: $1.00 per page. Certification fee: $1.00. Fee payee: Bartholomew County Clerk. Personal checks accepted. Prepayment is required. Public access terminal is available. Fax notes: $5.00 per page. No fee to fax to 800 number.

Benton County

Circuit Court 706 E 5th St, Suite 37, Fowler, IN 47944-1556; 765-884-0930; Fax: 765-884-0322. Hours: 8:30AM-4PM (EST). *Felony, Misdemeanor, Civil, Eviction, Small Claims, Probate.*

www.bentoncounty.org

Civil Records: Access: In person only. Court does not conduct in person searches; visitors must perform searches for themselves. Search fee: No civil searches performed by court. Required to search: name, years to search. Civil cases indexed by defendant, plaintiff. Civil records on computer from 1992, on index books from 1860. **Criminal Records:** Access: Mail, in person. Court does not conduct in person searches; visitors must perform searches for themselves. No search fee. Required to search: name, years to search, DOB. Criminal records on computer from 1992, on index books from 1860. **General Information:** No juvenile, mental, adoption or sealed released. SASE required. Turnaround time 2-3 days. Copy fee: $1.00 per page. Certification fee: $1.00. Fee payee: Benton County Clerk. Only cashiers checks and money orders accepted. Prepayment is required.

Blackford County

Circuit & County Court 110 W Washington St, Hartford City, IN 47348; 765-348-1130. Hours: 8AM-4PM (EST). *Felony, Misdemeanor, Civil, Eviction, Small Claims, Probate.*

Civil Records: Access: Mail, in person. Both court and visitors may perform in person searches. No search fee. Required to search: name, years to search. Civil cases indexed by defendant, plaintiff. court records on computer from 1991, on index from 1800. **Criminal Records:** Access: Mail, in person. Both court and visitors may perform in person searches. No search fee. Required to search: name, years to search, DOB; also helpful-SSN. court records on computer from 1991, on index from 1800. **General Information:** No juvenile, mental, adoption or sealed released. Turnaround time 1 week. Copy fee: $1.00 per page. Certification fee: $2.00. Fee payee: Clerk of Blackford County. Business checks accepted. Prepayment is required. Public access terminal is available.

Boone County

Circuit & Superior Court I & II Rm 212, Courthouse Sq, Lebanon, IN 46052; 765-482-3510. Hours: 7AM-4PM (EST). *Felony, Misdemeanor, Civil, Eviction, Small Claims, Probate.*

Civil Records: Access: Mail, in person. Both court and visitors may perform in person searches. Search fee: $10.00 per name. Required to search: name, years to search. Civil cases indexed by defendant, plaintiff. Civil records on index from 1900. **Criminal Records:** Access: Mail, in person. Both court and visitors may perform in person searches. Search fee: $10.00 per name. Required to search: name, years to search; also helpful-SSN. Criminal records on index from 1900. **General Information:** No juvenile, mental, adoption or sealed released. SASE required. Turnaround time 1 week. Copy fee: $1.00 per page. Certification fee: $1.00. Fee payee: Boone County Clerk. Business checks accepted. Prepayment is required.

Brown County

Circuit Court Box 85, Nashville, IN 47448; 812-988-5510; Fax: 812-988-5562. Hours: 8AM-4PM (EST). *Felony, Misdemeanor, Civil, Eviction, Small Claims, Probate.*

Civil Records: Access: In person only. Court does not conduct in person searches; visitors must perform searches for themselves. Search fee: No civil searches performed by court. Required to search: name, years to search. Civil cases indexed by defendant, plaintiff. Civil records on open cases on computer from 1993, in entry books from early 1800s. Records are not indexed by SSN, but SSNs can be viewed. **Criminal Records:** Access: In person only. Court does not conduct in person searches; visitors must perform searches for themselves. Search fee: No criminal searches performed by court. Required to search: name, years to search, DOB; also helpful-SSN. Criminal records on open cases on computer from 1993, in entry books from early 1800s. Records are not indexed by SSN, but SSNs can be viewed. **General Information:** No juvenile, mental, adoption or sealed records released. Copy fee: $1.00 per page. Certification fee: $2.00. Fee payee: County Clerk. Personal checks accepted. Prepayment is required. Public access terminal is available.

Carroll County

Circuit & Superior Court Courthouse, 101 W Main, Delphi, IN 46923; 765-564-4485; Fax: 765-564-6907. Hours: 8AM-5PM M,T,Th,F; 8AM-Noon W (EST). *Felony, Misdemeanor, Civil, Eviction, Small Claims, Probate.*

Civil Records: Access: Mail, in person. Both court and visitors may perform in person searches. Search fee: $4.00 per name. Required to search: name, years to search. Civil cases indexed by defendant, plaintiff. Civil records archived from 1981, on index from 1828. **Criminal Records:** Access: Mail, in person. Both court and visitors may perform in person searches. Search fee: $4.00 per name. Required to search: name, years to search. Criminal records archived from 1981, on index from 1828. **General Information:** No juvenile, mental, adoption or sealed released. SASE required. Turnaround time 2-3 days. Copy fee: $1.00 per page. Certification fee: $1.00. Fee payee: Carroll County Clerk. Personal checks accepted. Prepayment is required.

Cass County

Circuit & Superior Court 200 Court Park, Logansport, IN 46947; 219-753-7870. Hours: 8AM-4PM (EST). *Felony, Misdemeanor, Civil, Eviction, Small Claims, Probate.*

Civil Records: Access: Mail, in person. Both court and visitors may perform in person searches. No search fee. Required to search: name, years to search. Civil cases indexed by defendant, plaintiff. Civil records on computer from 1989, on index from 1900s. **Criminal Records:** Access: Mail, in person. Both court and visitors may perform in person searches. No search fee. Required to search: name, years to search, DOB; also helpful-SSN. Criminal records on computer from 1989, on index from 1900s. **General Information:** No juvenile, mental, adoption or sealed released. SASE requested. Turnaround time 2 weeks. Copy fee: $1.00 per page. Fee is for criminal division only. Certification fee: $1.00. Fee payee: Cass County Clerk. Personal checks accepted. Checks accepted up to $10.00 only. Prepayment is required. Public access terminal is available.

Clark County

Circuit, Superior, & County Court 501 E Court, Rm 137, Jeffersonville, IN 47130; 812-285-6244. Hours: 8:30AM-4:30PM M-F, 8:30-Noon S (EST). *Felony, Misdemeanor, Civil, Eviction, Small Claims, Probate.*

Civil Records: Access: In person only. Court does not conduct in person searches; visitors must perform searches for themselves. Search fee: No civil searches performed by court. Required to search: name, years to search; also helpful-address. Civil cases indexed by defendant, plaintiff. Civil records on computer since 8/92, on index cards from 1900. **Criminal Records:** Access: In person only. Court does not conduct in person searches; visitors must perform searches for themselves. Search fee: No criminal searches performed by court. Required to search: name, years to search; also helpful-DOB, SSN. Criminal records on computer since 8/92, on index cards from 1900. **General Information:** No juvenile, mental, adoption or sealed released. Copy fee: $1.00 per page. Certification fee: $1.00. Fee payee: County Clerk. Business checks accepted. Prepayment is required. Public access terminal is available.

Clay County

Circuit & Superior Court Box 33, Brazil, IN 47834; 812-448-8727. Hours: 8AM-4PM (EST). *Felony, Misdemeanor, Civil, Eviction, Small Claims, Probate.*

Civil Records: Access: Mail, in person. Search fee: $6.00 per name. Required to search: name, years to search; also helpful-address. Civil cases indexed by defendant, plaintiff. Civil records on index from 1850. **Criminal Records:** Access: Mail, in person. Court does not conduct in person searches; visitors must perform searches for themselves. Search fee: $6.00 per name. Required to search: name, years to search, address, DOB, SSN, signed release. Criminal records on index from 1850. **General Information:** No juvenile, mental, adoption or sealed released. SASE required. Turnaround time 1 week. Copy fee: $1.00 per page. Certification fee: $1.00. Fee

payee: County Clerk. Business checks accepted. Prepayment is required.

Clinton County

Circuit & Superior Court 265 Courthouse Square, Frankfort, IN 46041; 765-659-6335. Hours: 8AM-4PM M-TH,8AM-5PM F (EST). *Felony, Misdemeanor, Civil, Eviction, Small Claims, Probate.*

Civil Records: Access: Mail, in person. Both court and visitors may perform in person searches. Search fee: $4.00 per name. Required to search: name, years to search. Civil cases indexed by defendant, plaintiff. Civil records on computer from 1991, on microfiche and index from 1900s. **Criminal Records:** Access: Mail, in person. Both court and visitors may perform in person searches. Search fee: $4.00 per name. Required to search: name, years to search, signed release; also helpful-DOB. Criminal records on computer from 1991, on microfiche and index from 1900s. **General Information:** No juvenile, mental, adoption or sealed released. SASE required. Turnaround time 1 week. Copy fee: $1.00 per page. Certification fee: $1.00. Fee payee: County Clerk. Business checks accepted. Prepayment is required. Public access terminal is available.

Crawford County

Circuit Court Box 375, English, IN 47118; 812-338-2565; Fax: 812-338-2507. Hours: 8AM-4PM M,F; 8AM-6PM T-Th (EST). *Felony, Misdemeanor, Civil, Eviction, Small Claims, Probate.*

Civil Records: Access: In person only. Court does not conduct in person searches; visitors must perform searches for themselves. Search fee: No civil searches performed by court. Required to search: name, years to search. Civil cases indexed by defendant, plaintiff. Civil records on index from 1900s. **Criminal Records:** Access: Fax, mail, in person. Only the court conducts in person searches; visitors may not. Search fee: $5.00 per name. Required to search: name, years to search, DOB, SSN, signed release. Criminal records on index from 1900s. **General Information:** No juvenile, mental, adoption or sealed released. SASE required. Turnaround time 1 week. Copy fee: $1.00 per page. Fee is for criminal division only. Certification fee: $2.00. Fee payee: County Clerk. Business checks accepted. Prepayment is required. Fax notes: No fee to fax results.

Daviess County

Circuit & Superior Court PO Box 739, Washington, IN 47501; 812-254-8664; Fax: 812-254-8698. Hours: 8AM-4PM (EST). *Felony, Misdemeanor, Civil, Eviction, Small Claims, Probate.*

Civil Records: Access: Mail, in person. Both court and visitors may perform in person searches. No search fee. Required to search: name, years to search. Civil cases indexed by defendant, plaintiff. Civil records on index from 1900s. **Criminal Records:** Access: Mail, in person. Both court and visitors may perform in person searches. No search fee. Required to search: name, years to search. Criminal records on index from 1900s. **General Information:** No juvenile, mental, adoption or sealed records released. SASE required. Turnaround time varies. Copy fee: $1.00 per page. Certification fee: $1.00. Fee payee: Daviess County Clerk. Business checks accepted. Prepayment is required.

Dearborn County

Circuit & County Court Courthouse, 215 W High St, Lawrenceburg, IN 47025; 812-537-8867; Fax: 812-537-4295. Hours: 8:30AM-4:30PM (EST). *Felony, Misdemeanor, Civil, Eviction, Small Claims, Probate.*

Civil Records: Access: In person only. Court does not conduct in person searches; visitors must perform searches for themselves. Search fee: No civil searches performed by court. Required to search: name, years to search. Civil cases indexed by defendant, plaintiff. Civil records on computer from 1992, on index from 1970s. **Criminal Records:** Access: In person only. Court does not conduct in person searches; visitors must perform searches for themselves. Search fee: No criminal searches performed by court. Required to search: name, years to search, DOB; also helpful-SSN. Criminal records on computer from 1992, on index from 1970s. **General Information:** No juvenile, mental, adoption or sealed records released. Copy fee: $1.00 per page. Fee is for civil division only. Certification fee: $1.00. Fee payee: Circuit Court Clerk. Only cashiers checks and money orders accepted. Prepayment is required.

Decatur County

Circuit & Superior Court 150 Courthouse Square, Suite 244, Greensburg, IN 47240; 812-663-8223/8642; Fax: 812-663-7957. Hours: 8AM-4PM, 8AM-5PM F (EST). *Felony, Misdemeanor, Civil, Eviction, Small Claims, Probate.*

Civil Records: Access: Mail, in person. Court does not conduct in person searches; visitors must perform searches for themselves. Search fee: No civil searches performed by court. Required to search: name, years to search. Civil cases indexed by defendant, plaintiff. Civil records on index from 1823. **Criminal Records:** Access: Mail, in person. Court does not conduct in person searches; visitors must perform searches for themselves. Search fee: No criminal searches performed by court. Required to search: name, years to search, DOB; also helpful-SSN. Criminal records on index from 1823. **General Information:** No juvenile, mental, adoption or sealed released. Turnaround time 2-7 days. Copy fee: $1.00 per page. Certification fee: $1.00. Fee payee: Court Clerk. Personal checks accepted. Prepayment is required.

DeKalb County

Circuit & Superior Court PO Box 230, Auburn, IN 46706; 219-925-0912; Fax: 219-925-5126. Hours: 8:30AM-4:30PM (EST). *Felony, Misdemeanor, Civil, Eviction, Small Claims, Probate.*

Civil Records: Access: In person only. Court does not conduct in person searches; visitors must perform searches for themselves. Search fee: No civil searches performed by court. Required to search: name, years to search. Civil cases indexed by defendant, plaintiff. Civil records on computer from 1987, on index from 1800s. **Criminal Records:** Access: In person only. Court does not conduct in person searches; visitors must perform searches for themselves. Search fee: No criminal searches performed by court. Required to search: name, years to search. Criminal records on computer from 1987, on index from 1800s. **General Information:** No juvenile, mental, adoption or sealed released. Copy fee: $1.00 per page. Certification fee: $1.00. Fee payee: Court Clerk. Only cashiers checks and money orders accepted. Prepayment is required. Public access terminal is available.

Delaware County

Circuit & Superior Court Box 1089, Muncie, IN 47308; 765-747-7726; Fax: 765-747-7768. Hours: 8:30AM-4:30PM (EST). *Felony, Misdemeanor, Civil, Eviction, Small Claims, Probate.*

www.dcclerk.org

Civil Records: Access: Phone, fax, mail, in person. Both court and visitors may perform in person searches. No search fee. Required to search: name, years to search. Civil cases indexed by defendant, plaintiff. Civil records on computer from 1989, on microfiche, archived and on index from 1800. **Criminal Records:** Access: Mail, in person. Both court and visitors may perform in person searches. No search fee. Required to search: name, years to search, DOB, SSN. Criminal records on computer from 1989, on microfiche, archived and on index from 1800. Indicate suffixes such as "Jr" and "Sr" in your search request. **General Information:** No juvenile, mental, adoption or sealed released. Turnaround time 1-2 days. Copy fee: $.25 per page. Certification fee: $1.00. Fee payee: Court Clerk. Business checks accepted. Prepayment is required. Public access terminal is available. Fax notes: $1.00 per page.

Dubois County

Circuit & Superior Court 1 Courthouse Square, Jasper, IN 47546; 812-481-7070/7035/7020; Fax: 812-481-7030. Hours: 8AM-4PM (EST). *Felony, Misdemeanor, Civil, Eviction, Small Claims, Probate.*

Civil Records: Access: In person only. Court does not conduct in person searches; visitors must perform searches for themselves. Search fee: No civil searches performed by court. Required to search: name; also helpful-years to search. Civil cases indexed by defendant, plaintiff. Civil records on computer from 8\93, on index books from 1930. **Criminal Records:** Access: In person only. Court does not conduct in person searches; visitors must perform searches for themselves. Search fee: No criminal searches performed by court. Required to search: name; also helpful-years to search. Criminal records on computer from 8\93, on index books from 1930. **General Information:** No juvenile, mental, adoption or sealed records released. Copy fee: $.25 per page. Certification fee: $1.00. Fee payee: Court Clerk. Personal checks accepted. Prepayment is required. Public access terminal is available.

Elkhart County

Circuit, Superior, & County Court Courthouse, 101 N. Main St, Goshen, IN 46526; 219-535-6431; Fax: 219-535-6471. Hours: 8AM-4PM M-Th, 8AM-5PM F (EST). *Felony, Misdemeanor, Civil, Eviction, Small Claims, Probate.*

Civil Records: Access: In person only. Court does not conduct in person searches; visitors must perform searches for themselves. Search fee: No civil searches performed by court. Required to search: name, years to search. Civil cases indexed by defendant, plaintiff. Civil records archived from 1800. Some records on index books. **Criminal Records:** Access: In person only. Court does not conduct in person searches; visitors must perform searches for themselves. Search fee: No criminal searches performed by court. Required to search: name, years to search, DOB; also helpful-SSN. Criminal records archived from 1800. Some records on index books. **General Information:**

No juvenile, mental, adoption or sealed released. Certification fee: $1.00. Fee payee: Court Clerk. Personal checks accepted. Prepayment is required.

Fayette County

Circuit & Superior Court PO Box 607, Connersville, IN 47331-0607; 765-825-1813. Hours: 8:30AM-4PM (5PM on Wed) (EST). *Felony, Misdemeanor, Civil, Eviction, Small Claims, Probate.*

http://courthouse.co.fayette.in.us

Civil Records: Access: In person only. Court does not conduct in person searches; visitors must perform searches for themselves. Search fee: No civil searches performed by court. Required to search: name, years to search. Civil cases indexed by defendant, plaintiff. Civil records on computer from 1988 (Circuit), 1992 (Superior). **Criminal Records:** Access: In person only. Court does not conduct in person searches; visitors must perform searches for themselves. Search fee: No criminal searches performed by court. Required to search: name, years to search. Criminal records on computer from 1988 (Circuit), 1992 (Superior). **General Information:** No juvenile, mental, adoption or sealed released. Copy fee: $1.00 per page. Certification fee: $1.00. Fee payee: Fayette County Clerk. Only cashiers checks and money orders accepted. Prepayment is required. Public access terminal is available.

Floyd County

Circuit, Superior, & County Court Box 1056, City County Bldg, New Albany, IN 47150; 812-948-5414; Fax: 812-948-4711. Hours: 8AM-4PM (EST). *Felony, Misdemeanor, Civil, Eviction, Small Claims, Probate.*

Civil Records: Access: Mail, in person. Search fee: $5.00 per name. Required to search: name, years to search. Civil cases indexed by defendant, plaintiff. Civil records on computer from 1988, archived from 1978, on index from 1819. **Criminal Records:** Access: Mail, in person. Court does not conduct in person searches; visitors must perform searches for themselves. Search fee: $5.00 per name. Required to search: name, years to search; also helpful-SSN. Criminal records on computer from 1988, archived from 1978, on index from 1819. **General Information:** No juvenile, mental, adoption or sealed released. SASE required. Turnaround time 1-2 days. Copy fee: $1.00 per page. Certification fee: $1.00. Fee payee: Court Clerk. Personal checks accepted. Prepayment is required. Public access terminal is available.

Fountain County

Circuit Court Box 183, Covington, IN 47932; 765-793-2192; Fax: 765-793-5002. Hours: 8AM-4PM (EST). *Felony, Misdemeanor, Civil, Eviction, Small Claims, Probate.*

Civil Records: Access: Mail, in person. Both court and visitors may perform in person searches. No search fee. Required to search: name, years to search. Civil cases indexed by defendant, plaintiff. Civil records on computer from 1989. **Criminal Records:** Access: Mail, in person. Both court and visitors may perform in person searches. No search fee. Required to search: name, years to search; also helpful-SSN. Criminal records on computer from 1989. **General Information:** No juvenile, mental, adoption or sealed released. SASE required. Turnaround time 1-2 days if records after 1989, 4-5 days if prior. Copy fee: $1.00 per page. Certification fee: $2.00. Fee payee: Court Clerk.

Personal checks accepted. Prepayment is required. Public access terminal is available.

Franklin County

Circuit Court 459 Main, Brookville, IN 47012; 765-647-5111; Fax: 765-647-3224. Hours: 8:30AM-4PM (EST). *Felony, Misdemeanor, Civil, Eviction, Small Claims, Probate.*

Civil Records: Access: In person only. Court does not conduct in person searches; visitors must perform searches for themselves. Search fee: No civil searches performed by court. Required to search: name, years to search. Civil cases indexed by defendant, plaintiff. Civil on index from 1978. **Criminal Records:** Access: In person only. Court does not conduct in person searches; visitors must perform searches for themselves. Search fee: No criminal searches performed by court. Required to search: name, years to search. Criminal records on index from 1950. **General Information:** No juvenile, mental, adoption or sealed released. Copy fee: $.50 per page. Certification fee: $1.00. Fee payee: Court Clerk. Personal checks accepted. Prepayment is required.

Fulton County

Circuit Court 815 Main St, PO Box 524, Rochester, IN 46975; 219-223-2911; Fax: 219-223-8304. Hours: 8AM-4PM M-TH, 8AM-5PM F (EST). *Felony, Misdemeanor, Civil, Eviction, Small Claims, Probate.*

Civil Records: Access: Mail, in person. Both court and visitors may perform in person searches. No search fee. Required to search: name, years to search. Civil cases indexed by defendant, plaintiff. Civil records on computer from 1989, on microfiche, archived and on index from 1845. **Criminal Records:** Access: Mail, in person. Both court and visitors may perform in person searches. No search fee. Required to search: name, years to search. Criminal records on computer from 1989, on microfiche, archived and on index from 1845. **General Information:** No juvenile, mental, adoption or sealed released. SASE Required. Turnaround time 3-4 days. Copy fee: $1.00 per page. Certification fee: $1.00. Fee payee: Court Clerk. Business checks accepted. Prepayment is required. Public access terminal is available.

Gibson County

Circuit & Superior Court Courthouse, Princeton, IN 47670; 812-386-8401; Fax: 812-386-5025. Hours: 8AM-4PM (CST). *Felony, Misdemeanor, Civil, Eviction, Small Claims, Probate.*

Civil Records: Access: In person only. Court does not conduct in person searches; visitors must perform searches for themselves. Search fee: No civil searches performed by court. Required to search: name, years to search. Civil cases indexed by defendant, plaintiff. Civil records on computer from 1990, on microfiche from 1940, on index from 1813. **Criminal Records:** Access: In person only. Court does not conduct in person searches; visitors must perform searches for themselves. Search fee: No criminal searches performed by court. Required to search: name, years to search. Criminal records on computer from 1990, on microfiche from 1940, on index from 1813. **General Information:** No juvenile, mental, adoption or sealed records released. Copy fee: $1.00 per page. Certification fee: $2.00. Fee payee: Court Clerk. No personal checks accepted. Prepayment is required.

Grant County

Circuit & Superior Court Courthouse 101 E 4th St, Marion, IN 46952; 765-668-8121; Fax: 765-668-6541. Hours: 8AM-4PM (EST). *Felony, Misdemeanor, Civil, Eviction, Small Claims, Probate.*

Civil Records: Access: In person only. Court does not conduct in person searches; visitors must perform searches for themselves. Search fee: No civil searches performed by court. Required to search: name, years to search; also helpful-address. Civil cases indexed by defendant, plaintiff. Civil records on computer from 1989, on index from 1881. **Criminal Records:** Access: In person only. Court does not conduct in person searches; visitors must perform searches for themselves. Search fee: No criminal searches performed by court. Required to search: name, years to search; also helpful-DOB, SSN. Criminal records on computer from 1989, on index from 1881. **General Information:** No juvenile, adoption, mental health or sealed records released. Copy fee: $.10 per page. Certification fee: $1.00. Fee payee: Court Clerk. Personal checks accepted. Prepayment is required.

Greene County

Circuit & Superior Court PO Box 229, Bloomfield, IN 47424; 812-384-8532; Fax: 812-384-8458. Hours: 8AM-4PM (EST). *Felony, Misdemeanor, Civil, Eviction, Small Claims, Probate.*

Civil Records: Access: In person only. Court does not conduct in person searches; visitors must perform searches for themselves. Search fee: No civil searches performed by court. Required to search: name, years to search. Civil cases indexed by defendant, plaintiff. Civil records on computer from 1989, all other records in books. **Criminal Records:** Access: In person only. Court does not conduct in person searches; visitors must perform searches for themselves. Search fee: No criminal searches performed by court. Required to search: name, years to search. Criminal records in books. **General Information:** No juvenile, mental, adoption or sealed released. Copy fee: $1.00 per page. Certification fee: $1.00. Fee payee: Court Clerk. Only cashiers checks and money orders accepted. Prepayment is required.

Hamilton County

Circuit & Superior Court One Hamilton County Square, Suite 106, Noblesville, IN 46060-2233; 317-776-9629; Fax: 317-776-9727. Hours: 8AM-4:30PM (EST). *Felony, Misdemeanor, Civil, Eviction, Small Claims, Probate.*

Civil Records: Access: In person only. Court does not conduct in person searches; visitors must perform searches for themselves. Search fee: No civil searches performed by court. Required to search: name, years to search. Civil cases indexed by defendant, plaintiff. Civil records on computer from 1986, on index from 1840s. **Criminal Records:** Access: In person only. Court does not conduct in person searches; visitors must perform searches for themselves. Search fee: No criminal searches performed by court. Required to search: name, years to search. Criminal records on computer from 1986, on index from 1840s. **General Information:** No juvenile, mental, adoption or sealed released. Copy fee: $.50 per page. Certification fee: $1.00 plus $.50 per page. Fee payee: Court Clerk. Business checks accepted. Prepayment is required. Public access terminal is available.

Hancock County

Circuit & Superior Court 9 E Main St, Rm 201, Greenfield, IN 46140; 317-462-1109; Fax: 317-462-1163. Hours: 8AM-4PM (EST). *Felony, Misdemeanor, Civil, Eviction, Small Claims, Probate.*

Civil Records: Access: Phone, mail, in person. Both court and visitors may perform in person searches. No search fee. Required to search: name, years to search. Civil cases indexed by defendant, plaintiff. Civil records on computer from 07/88, on index and archived from 1883. **Criminal Records:** Access: Phone, mail, in person. Both court and visitors may perform in person searches. No search fee. Required to search: name, years to search, DOB; also helpful-SSN. Criminal records on computer from 07/88, on index and archived from 1883. **General Information:** No juvenile, mental, adoption or sealed released. SASE required. Turnaround time 3-7 days, same day or next for phone requests. Copy fee: $1.00 per page for case history, otherwise $.25 per page. Certification fee: $1.00. Fee payee: Court Clerk. Personal checks accepted. Prepayment is required.

Harrison County

Circuit & Superior Court 300 N Capitol, Corydon, IN 47112; 812-738-4289. Hours: 8AM-4PM M,T,Th,F; 8AM-Noon W,S (EST). *Felony, Misdemeanor, Civil, Eviction, Small Claims, Probate.*

Civil Records: Access: Mail, in person. Both court and visitors may perform in person searches. Search fee: No civil searches performed by court. Required to search: name, years to search. Civil cases indexed by defendant, plaintiff. Civil records on index from 1900. Court personnel will only do record searching when they have time, strongly urge using a retriever. **Criminal Records:** Access: Mail, in person. Court does not conduct in person searches; visitors must perform searches for themselves. Search fee: No criminal searches performed by court. Required to search: name, years to search. Criminal records on index from 1900. Court personnel only do record searching when they have time, suggest to use a retriever. **General Information:** No juvenile, mental, adoption or sealed released. Searches will only be done as time permits. Copy fee: $.50 per page. Certification fee: $2.00. Fee payee: Court Clerk. Only cashiers checks and money orders accepted. Prepayment is required.

Hendricks County

Circuit & Superior Court PO Box 599, Danville, IN 46122; 317-745-9231; Fax: 317-745-9306. Hours: 8AM-4PM (EST). *Felony, Misdemeanor, Civil, Eviction, Small Claims, Probate.*

Civil Records: Access: In person only. Court does not conduct in person searches; visitors must perform searches for themselves. Search fee: No civil searches performed by court. Required to search: name, years to search. Civil cases indexed by defendant, plaintiff. Civil records on computer since late 1992, on index from 1800s. **Criminal Records:** Access: In person only. Court does not conduct in person searches; visitors must perform searches for themselves. Search fee: No criminal searches performed by court. Required to search: name, years to search; also helpful-DOB, SSN. Criminal records on computer since late 1992, on index from 1800s. **General Information:** No juvenile, mental, adoption or sealed released. Copy fee: $1.00 per page. Certification fee: $1.00. Fee

payee: Court Clerk. Business checks accepted. Prepayment is required.

Henry County

Circuit & Superior Court PO Box B, New Castle, IN 47362; 765-529-6401. Hours: 8AM-4PM (EST). *Felony, Misdemeanor, Civil, Eviction, Small Claims, Probate.*

Civil Records: Access: Mail, in person. Both court and visitors may perform in person searches. No search fee. Required to search: name, years to search. Civil cases indexed by plaintiff. Civil records on computer from 1991, archived from 1979, on index from 1976. **Criminal Records:** Access: Mail, in person. Both court and visitors may perform in person searches. No search fee. Required to search: name, years to search. Criminal records on computer from 1991, archived from 1979, on index from 1976. **General Information:** No juvenile, mental, adoption or sealed released. SASE Required. Turnaround time 1-2 days. Copy fee: $1.00 per page. Certification fee: $1.00. Fee payee: County Clerk. Only cashiers checks and money orders accepted. Prepayment is required. Public access terminal is available.

Howard County

Circuit & Superior Court PO Box 9004, Kokomo, IN 46904; 765-456-2201; Fax: 765-456-2267. Hours: 8AM-4PM (EST). *Felony, Misdemeanor, Civil, Eviction, Small Claims, Probate.*

Civil Records: Access: In person only. Court does not conduct in person searches; visitors must perform searches for themselves. Search fee: No civil searches performed by court. Required to search: name, years to search. Civil cases indexed by defendant, plaintiff. Civil records on computer since 1994, on microfiche from early 1800s. **Criminal Records:** Access: In person only. Court does not conduct in person searches; visitors must perform searches for themselves. Search fee: No criminal searches performed by court. Required to search: name, years to search; also helpful-DOB, SSN. Criminal records on computer since 1994, on microfiche from early 1800s. **General Information:** No juvenile, mental, adoption or sealed records released. Copy fee: $.20 per page. Certification fee: $1.00. Fee payee: County Clerk. Only cashiers checks and money orders accepted.

Huntington County

Circuit & Superior Court PO Box 228, Huntington, IN 46750; 219-358-4817. Hours: 8AM-4:40PM (EST). *Felony, Misdemeanor, Civil, Eviction, Small Claims, Probate.*

Civil Records: Access: Phone, mail, in person. Both court and visitors may perform in person searches. No search fee. Required to search: name, years to search. Civil cases indexed by defendant, plaintiff. Civil records on computer from 1990, on microfiche from 1970, on index and archived from 1800s. **Criminal Records:** Access: In person only. Court does not conduct in person searches; visitors must perform searches for themselves. Search fee: No criminal searches performed by court. Required to search: name, years to search. Criminal records on computer from 1990, on microfiche from 1970, on index and archived from 1800s. **General Information:** No juvenile, mental, adoption or sealed released. SASE not required. Turnaround time 1-2 days. Copy fee: $1.00 per page. Certification fee: $1.00. Fee payee: County Clerk. Personal checks accepted. Prepayment is required. Public access terminal is available.

Jackson County

Circuit Court PO Box 318, Brownstown, IN 47220; 812-358-6117; Fax: 812-358-6197. Hours: 8AM-4:30PM (EST). *Felony, Misdemeanor, Civil, Eviction, Small Claims, Probate.*

Civil Records: Access: Fax, mail, in person. Both court and visitors may perform in person searches. Search fee: $5.00 per name. Required to search: name, years to search. Civil cases indexed by defendant, plaintiff. Civil records on computer from 1989, on index from 1800s. **Criminal Records:** Access: Fax, mail, in person. Both court and visitors may perform in person searches. Search fee: $5.00 per name. Required to search: name, years to search; also helpful-DOB, SSN. Criminal records on computer from 1989, on index from 1800s. **General Information:** No juvenile, mental, adoption or sealed released. SASE required. Turnaround time 2-3 days. Copy fee: $1.00 per page. Certification fee: $2.00. Fee payee: Jackson County Clerk. Personal checks accepted. Public access terminal is available. Fax notes: $5.00 per document; no fee to toll-free number.

Superior Court PO Box 788, Seymour, IN 47274; 812-522-9676; Fax: 812-523-6065. Hours: 8AM-4:30PM (EST). *Felony, Misdemeanor, Civil, Eviction, Small Claims.*

Civil Records: Access: Fax, mail, in person. Both court and visitors may perform in person searches. Search fee: $5.00 per name. Required to search: name, years to search. Civil cases indexed by defendant, plaintiff. Civil records on computer from 1989, on index from 1800s. **Criminal Records:** Access: Fax, mail, in person. Both court and visitors may perform in person searches. Search fee: $5.00 per name. Required to search: name, years to search; also helpful-DOB, SSN. Criminal records on computer from 1989, on index from 1800s. **General Information:** No juvenile, mental, adoption or sealed released. SASE required. Turnaround time 2-3 days. Copy fee: $1.00 per page. Certification fee: $2.00. Fee payee: Jackson County Clerk. Personal checks accepted. Public access terminal is available. Fax notes: $5.00 per document; no fee to toll-free number.

Jasper County

Circuit Court 115 W Washington, Rensselaer, IN 47978; 219-866-4941. Hours: 8AM-4PM (CST). *Felony, Misdemeanor, Civil, Eviction, Small Claims, Probate.*

Note: This court also handles juvenile, paternity and adoption

Civil Records: Access: Mail, in person. Both court and visitors may perform in person searches. No search fee. Required to search: name, years to search. Civil cases indexed by defendant, plaintiff. County records on computer from 1976, circuit from 1989. Some records on index from 1900s. **Criminal Records:** Access: Mail, in person. Both court and visitors may perform in person searches. No search fee. Required to search: name, years to search; also helpful-DOB, SSN. County records on computer from 1976, circuit from 1989. Some records on index from 1900s. **General Information:** No juvenile, mental, adoption or sealed released. SASE required. Turnaround time 1 day. Copy fee: $1.00 per page. Certification fee: $2.00. Fee payee: Jasper County Clerk. Business checks accepted. Prepayment is required. Public access terminal is available.

Superior Court I 115 W Washington St, Rensselaer, IN 47978; 219-866-4922. Hours: 8AM-4PM (CST). *Felony, Misdemeanor, Civil, Probate.*

Civil Records: Access: Mail, in person. Both court and visitors may perform in person searches. No search fee. Required to search: name, years to search. Civil cases indexed by defendant, plaintiff. County records on computer from 1976, circuit from 1989. Some records on index from 1900s. **Criminal Records:** Access: Mail, in person. Both court and visitors may perform in person searches. No search fee. Required to search: name, years to search. County records on computer from 1976, circuit from 1989. Some records on index from 1900s. **General Information:** No juvenile, mental, adoption or sealed released. SASE required. Turnaround time 1 day to 1 week. Copy fee: $.50 per page. Non-case related copies are $.10 per page. Certification fee: $1.00. Per page. Fee payee: County Clerk. Only cashiers checks and money orders accepted. Prepayment is required. Public access terminal is available.

Jay County

Circuit & Superior Court Courthouse, Portland, IN 47371; 219-726-4951. Hours: 8:30AM-4:30PM (EST). *Felony, Misdemeanor, Civil, Eviction, Small Claims, Probate.*

Civil Records: Access: Mail, in person. Both court and visitors may perform in person searches. No search fee. Required to search: name, years to search; also helpful-address. Civil cases indexed by defendant, plaintiff. Civil records on computer from 8\94, prior on microfiche from 1979, on index books from 1900. **Criminal Records:** Access: Mail, in person. Both court and visitors may perform in person searches. No search fee. Required to search: name, years to search, DOB, SSN; also helpful-address. Criminal records on computer from 8\94, prior on microfiche from 1979, on index books from 1900. **General Information:** No juvenile, mental, adoption or sealed records released. SASE required. Turnaround time 1-2 days. Copy fee: $1.00 per page. Certification fee: $1.00. Fee payee: Court Clerk. Only cashiers checks and money orders accepted. Prepayment is required. Public access terminal is available.

Jefferson County

Circuit & Superior Court Courthouse 300E Main St, Madison, IN 47250; 812-265-8923; Fax: 812-265-8950. Hours: 8AM-4PM (EST). *Felony, Misdemeanor, Civil, Eviction, Small Claims, Probate.*

Civil Records: Access: In person only. Court does not conduct in person searches; visitors must perform searches for themselves. Search fee: No civil searches performed by court. Required to search: name, years to search. Civil cases indexed by defendant, plaintiff. Civil records on index from 1975, computerized since 1995. **Criminal Records:** Access: In person only. Court does not conduct in person searches; visitors must perform searches for themselves. Search fee: No criminal searches performed by court. Required to search: name, years to search, address, DOB, SSN, signed release. Criminal records on index from 1975, computerized since 1995. **General Information:** No juvenile, mental, adoption or sealed released. Copy fee: $1.00 per page. Certification fee: $1.00. Fee payee: County Clerk. Only cashiers checks and money orders accepted. Prepayment is required. Public access terminal is available.

Jennings County

Circuit Court Courthouse, PO Box 385, Vernon, IN 47282; 812-346-5977. Hours: 8AM-4PM (EST). *Felony, Misdemeanor, Civil, Eviction, Small Claims, Probate.*

Civil Records: Access: Mail, in person. Both court and visitors may perform in person searches. No search fee. Required to search: name, years to search. Civil cases indexed by defendant, plaintiff. Civil records on index from 1930. **Criminal Records:** Access: Mail, in person. Both court and visitors may perform in person searches. No search fee. Required to search: name, years to search, DOB; also helpful-SSN. Criminal records on index from 1930. **General Information:** No juvenile, mental, adoption or sealed released. SASE required. Turnaround time 2 weeks. Copy fee: $.25 per page. Certification fee: $1.00. Fee payee: County Clerk. Personal checks accepted. Prepayment is required.

Johnson County

Circuit & Superior Court Courthouse, PO Box 368, Franklin, IN 46131; 317-736-3708; Fax: 317-736-3749. Hours: 8AM-4:30PM (EST). *Felony, Misdemeanor, Civil, Eviction, Small Claims, Probate.*

Civil Records: Access: Phone, fax, mail, in person. Both court and visitors may perform in person searches. No search fee. Required to search: name, years to search. Civil cases indexed by defendant, plaintiff. Civil records on computer from 1989, on index from 1968, on microfiche from 1800s. **Criminal Records:** Access: Phone, fax, mail, in person. Both court and visitors may perform in person searches. No search fee. Required to search: name, years to search; also helpful-DOB, SSN. Criminal records on computer from 1989, on index from 1968, on microfiche from 1800s. **General Information:** No juvenile, mental, adoption or sealed released. Turnaround time 1-2 days. Copy fee: $1.00 per page. Certification fee: $1.00. Fee payee: County Clerk. Business checks accepted. Prepayment is required. Public access terminal is available. Fax notes: $1.00 for first page, $.50 each addl.

Knox County

Circuit & Superior Court 101 N 7th St, Vincennes, IN 47591; 812-885-2521. Hours: 8AM-4PM (EST). *Felony, Misdemeanor, Civil, Eviction, Small Claims, Probate.*

Civil Records: Access: Mail, in person. Court does not conduct in person searches; visitors must perform searches for themselves. No search fee. Required to search: name, years to search. Civil cases indexed by defendant, plaintiff. Civil records on index books from 1800s. **Criminal Records:** Access: Mail, in person. Court does not conduct in person searches; visitors must perform searches for themselves. No search fee. Required to search: name, years to search. Criminal records on index books from 1800s. **General Information:** No juvenile, mental, adoption or sealed released. Turnaround time 1 week. Copy fee: $1.00 per page. Certification fee: $1.00. Fee payee: Knox County Clerk. Personal checks accepted.

Kosciusko County

Circuit & Superior Court 121 N Lake, Warsaw, IN 46580; 219-372-2331. Hours: 8AM-4PM (EST). *Felony, Misdemeanor, Civil, Eviction, Small Claims, Probate.*

Civil Records: Access: Mail, in person. Both court and visitors may perform in person searches.

No search fee. Required to search: name, years to search. Civil cases indexed by defendant, plaintiff. Civil records on computer from 10/1/93, general index from 1908. **Criminal Records:** Access: Mail, in person. Both court and visitors may perform in person searches. No search fee. Required to search: name, years to search. Criminal records on computer from 10/1/93, general index from 1908. **General Information:** No juvenile, mental, adoption or sealed released. SASE required. Turnaround time 1-3 weeks. Copy fee: $1.00 per page. Certification fee: $1.00. Fee payee: County Clerk. Personal checks accepted. Prepayment is required. Public access terminal is available.

La Porte County

Circuit & Superior Court 813 Lincolnway, La Porte, IN 46350; 219-326-6808. Hours: 8:30AM-5PM (CST). *Felony, Misdemeanor, Civil, Eviction, Probate.*

Civil Records: Access: In person only. Court does not conduct in person searches; visitors must perform searches for themselves. Search fee: No civil searches performed by court. Required to search: name, years to search. Civil cases indexed by defendant, plaintiff. Civil records on microfiche and index from 1900. **Criminal Records:** Access: In person only. Court does not conduct in person searches; visitors must perform searches for themselves. Search fee: No criminal searches performed by court. Required to search: name, years to search. Criminal records on microfiche and index from 1900. **General Information:** No juvenile, mental, adoption or sealed released. Copy fee: $1.00 per page. Certification fee: $1.00 per page. Fee payee: Court Clerk. Business checks accepted. Will bill dissolutions. Public access terminal is available.

LaGrange County

Circuit & Superior Court 105 N Detroit St, Courthouse, LaGrange, IN 46761; 219-463-3442. Hours: 8AM-4PM M-TH, 8AM-5PM F (EST). *Felony, Misdemeanor, Civil, Eviction, Small Claims, Probate.*

Civil Records: Access: Phone, mail, in person. Both court and visitors may perform in person searches. No search fee. Required to search: name, years to search. Civil cases indexed by defendant, plaintiff. Civil records on computer from 1990, on books from 1900. **Criminal Records:** Access: Phone, mail, in person. Both court and visitors may perform in person searches. No search fee. Required to search: name, years to search; also helpful-DOB, SSN. Criminal records on computer from 1990, on books from 1900. **General Information:** No juvenile, mental, adoption or sealed released. SASE requested. Turnaround time 1-2 days from 1/1/90. 30 days if prior to 1/1/90. Copy fee: $1.00 per page. Certification fee: $1.00. Fee payee: LaGrange County Clerk. Personal checks accepted. Prepayment is required.

Lake County

Circuit & Superior Court 2293 N Main St, Courthouse, Crown Point, IN 46307; 219-755-3000. Hours: 8:30AM-4:20PM (CST). *Felony, Misdemeanor, Civil, Eviction, Small Claims, Probate.*

Civil Records: Access: Mail, in person. Both court and visitors may perform in person searches. Search fee: $1.00 per name. Required to search: name, years to search; also helpful-address. Civil cases indexed by defendant, plaintiff. Civil records on computer and microfiche from 1983, archived

and on index from 1900. **Criminal Records:** Access: Mail, in person. Both court and visitors may perform in person searches. Search fee: $7.00 per name. Required to search: name, years to search, DOB, SSN; also helpful-address. Criminal records on computer & microfiche from 1987. **General Information:** No juvenile, mental, adoption or sealed released. Turnaround time 1 week. Copy fee: $1.00 per page. Fee is for 1991 to present. $2.00 per page for 1990 and before. Certification fee: $2.00. Fee payee: Lake County Clerk. Business checks accepted. Prepayment is required.

Lawrence County

Circuit, Superior, & County Court 31 Courthouse, PO Box 99, Bedford, IN 47421; 812-275-7543; Fax: 812-277-2024. Hours: 8:30AM-4:30PM (EST). *Felony, Misdemeanor, Civil, Eviction, Small Claims, Probate.*

Note: Superior Court I is located at 1410 I Street, 812-275-3124. Superior Court II is located at 1420 I Street, 812-275-4161. All small claims are filed in Superior II

Civil Records: Access: In person only. Court does not conduct in person searches; visitors must perform searches for themselves. Search fee: No civil searches performed by court. Required to search: name, years to search. Civil cases indexed by plaintiff. Civil records on computer from 1987, on index from 1817. **Criminal Records:** Access: In person only. Court does not conduct in person searches; visitors must perform searches for themselves. Search fee: No criminal searches performed by court. Required to search: name, years to search, DOB; also helpful-SSN. Criminal records on computer from 1987, on index from 1817. **General Information:** No juvenile, mental, adoption or sealed released. Copy fee: $1.00 per page. Certification fee: $1.00. Fee payee: Lawrence County Clerk. Only cashiers checks and money orders accepted. Prepayment is required.

Madison County

Circuit, Superior, & County Court PO Box 1277, Anderson, IN 46015-1277; 765-641-9443; Fax: 765-640-4203. Hours: 8AM-4PM (EST). *Felony, Misdemeanor, Civil, Eviction, Small Claims, Probate.*

Civil Records: Access: In person only. Court does not conduct in person searches; visitors must perform searches for themselves. Search fee: No civil searches performed by court. Required to search: name, years to search. Civil cases indexed by defendant. Civil records on microfiche and archived from 1950, on index from 1900. **Criminal Records:** Access: In person only. Court does not conduct in person searches; visitors must perform searches for themselves. Search fee: No criminal searches performed by court. Required to search: name, years to search, signed release. Criminal records on microfiche and archived from 1950, on index from 1900. **General Information:** No juvenile, mental, adoption or sealed released. Copy fee: $1.00 per page. Certification fee: $1.00. Fee payee: County Clerk. Business checks accepted. Prepayment is required. Public access terminal is available.

Marion County

Circuit & Superior Court 200 E Washington St, Indianapolis, IN 46204; 317-327-4740; Civil phone:317-327-4724; Criminal phone:317-327-4724. Hours: 8AM-4:30PM (EST). *Felony, Misdemeanor, Civil, Eviction, Small Claims, Probate.*

Note: The Municipal Court of Marion County, once separate, is now part of the Superior Court. All records are merged with the Superiors Court

Civil Records: Access: Mail, online, in person. Both court and visitors may perform in person searches. No search fee. Required to search: name, years to search. Civil cases indexed by defendant, plaintiff. Civil records on computer from 1991, on microfiche, archived and on index from 1912. Small claims records are held by the township in which they were filed; the phone numbers are listed below. Remote access available through www.civicnet.net (Internet). The setup fee is $50, other fees vary by type of record or search. **Criminal Records:** Access: Mail, remote online, in person. Both court and visitors may perform in person searches. Search fee: $7.00 per name. Fee is $3.00 for in person request. Required to search: name, years to search, DOB; also helpful-SSN. Criminal records on computer from 1991, on microfiche, archived and on index from 1912. Small claims records are held by the township in which they were filed; the phone numbers are listed below. Remote access available through www.civicnet.net. Fees vary by search, there is a $50 setup fee. Criminal records go back to 1988. **General Information:** No juvenile, mental, adoption or sealed released. SASE not required. Turnaround time 1-2 days. Copy fee: $1.00 per page. Certification fee: $1.00. Fee payee: County Clerk. Personal checks accepted. Public access terminal is available.

Marshall County

Circuit & Superior Court 211 W Madison St, Plymouth, IN 46563; 219-936-8922; Fax: 219-936-8893. Hours: 8AM-4PM (EST). *Felony, Misdemeanor, Civil, Eviction, Small Claims, Probate.*

Civil Records: Access: Mail, in person. Both court and visitors may perform in person searches. Search fee: $1.00 per name. Required to search: name, years to search; also helpful-address. Civil cases indexed by defendant, plaintiff. Civil records on computer from 1989, on microfiche, archived and on index from 1835. **Criminal Records:** Access: Mail, in person. Both court and visitors may perform in person searches. Search fee: $10.00 per name. Required to search: name, years to search, signed release; also helpful-address, DOB, SSN. Criminal records on computer from 1989, on microfiche, archived and on index from 1835. **General Information:** No juvenile, mental, adoption or sealed released. SASE required. Turnaround time within 1 week. Copy fee: $1.00 per page. Certification fee: $1.00. Fee payee: County Clerk. Business checks accepted. Prepayment is required. Public access terminal is available.

Martin County

Circuit Court PO Box 120, Shoals, IN 47581; 812-247-3651; Fax: 812-247-3901. Hours: 8AM-4PM (EST). *Felony, Misdemeanor, Civil, Eviction, Small Claims, Probate.*

Civil Records: Access: Mail, in person. Both court and visitors may perform in person searches. No search fee. Required to search: name, years to search. Civil cases indexed by defendant, plaintiff. Civil records on index books. **Criminal Records:** Access: Mail, in person. Both court and visitors may perform in person searches. No search fee. Required to search: name, years to search. Criminal records on index books. **General Information:** No juvenile, mental, adoption, or sealed records released. Turnaround time 4 days.

Copy fee: $1.00 per page. Certification fee: $2.00. Fee payee: County Clerk. Business checks accepted. Prepayment is required.

Miami County

Circuit & Superior Court PO Box 184, Peru, IN 46970; 765-472-3901; Fax: 765-472-1778. Hours: 8AM-4PM (EST). *Felony, Misdemeanor, Civil, Eviction, Small Claims, Probate.*

Civil Records: Access: Fax, mail, in person. Both court and visitors may perform in person searches. Search fee: $10.00 per name. Required to search: name, years to search. Civil cases indexed by defendant, plaintiff. Civil records archived from 1900s. Some records on docket books by case number and alpha. **Criminal Records:** Access: Fax, mail, in person. Both court and visitors may perform in person searches. Search fee: $10.00 per name. Required to search: name, years to search, DOB, signed release; also helpful-SSN. Criminal records archived from 1900s. Some records on docket books by case number and alpha. **General Information:** No juvenile, mental, adoption, or sealed released. Turnaround time 1-2 days. Copy fee: $1.00 per page. Certification fee: $1.00. Fee payee: Miami County Clerk. Personal checks accepted. Prepayment is required. Fax notes: $1.00 per page. No fee for toll free or local calls.

Monroe County

Circuit Court PO Box 547, Bloomington, IN 47402; 812-349-2614; Fax: 812-349-2610. Hours: 8AM-4PM (EST). *Felony, Misdemeanor, Civil, Eviction, Small Claims, Probate.*

Civil Records: Access: Mail, in person. Both court and visitors may perform in person searches. No search fee. Required to search: name, years to search. Civil cases indexed by defendant, plaintiff. Civil records on computer from 1986, archived from 1919. Some records on docket books by case number and alpha. In the process of putting records on microfiche. **Criminal Records:** Access: Mail, in person. Both court and visitors may perform in person searches. No search fee. Required to search: name, years to search, DOB; also helpful-SSN. Criminal records on computer from 1986, archived from 1919. Some records on docket books by case number and alpha. In the process of putting records on microfiche. **General Information:** No juvenile, mental, adoption or sealed released. Turnaround time 48 hours. Copy fee: $1.00 per page. Certification fee: $1.00. Fee payee: Monroe County Clerk. Personal checks accepted. Prepayment is required. Public access terminal is available.

Montgomery County

Circuit, Superior, & County Court PO Box 768, Crawfordsville, IN 47933; 765-364-6430; Fax: 765-364-6355. Hours: 8:30AM-4:30PM (EST). *Felony, Misdemeanor, Civil, Eviction, Small Claims, Probate.*

Civil Records: Access: Phone, fax, mail, in person. Both court and visitors may perform in person searches. Search fee: $1.00 per page document fee. Required to search: name, years to search. Civil cases indexed by defendant, plaintiff. Civil records on computer from 1990, some on microfiche and docket books, and archived from 1800s. Indicate type(s) of cases sought in search request. **Criminal Records:** Access: Mail, in person. Both court and visitors may perform in person searches. Search fee:. Required to search: name, years to search, DOB; also helpful-SSN. Criminal records on computer from 1990, some on

microfiche and docket books, and archived from 1800s. **General Information:** No juvenile, mental, adoption or sealed released. SASE not required. Turnaround time 1 week. Copy fee: $1.00 per page. Certification fee: $2.00. Fee payee: Montgomery County Clerk. Personal checks accepted. Prepayment is required. Public access terminal is available. Fax notes: $1.00 per page. Additional fax fee $3.25.

Morgan County

Circuit, Superior, & County Court PO Box 1556, Martinsville, IN 46151; 765-342-1025; Fax: 765-342-1111. Hours: 8AM-4PM (EST). *Felony, Misdemeanor, Civil, Eviction, Small Claims, Probate.*

Civil Records: Access: In person only. Court does not conduct in person searches; visitors must perform searches for themselves. Search fee: No civil searches performed by court. Required to search: name, years to search. Civil cases indexed by defendant, plaintiff. Civil records archived from 1970. Some records on index cards. **Criminal Records:** Access: In person only. Court does not conduct in person searches; visitors must perform searches for themselves. Search fee: No criminal searches performed by court. Required to search: name, years to search, DOB; also helpful-SSN. Criminal records archived from 1970. Some records on index cards. **General Information:** No juvenile, mental, adoption or sealed released. Certification fee: $1.00 per page. Fee payee: Morgan County Clerk. Personal checks accepted. Prepayment is required.

Newton County

Circuit & Superior Court PO Box 49, Kentland, IN 47951; 219-474-6081. Hours: 8AM-4PM (CST). *Felony, Misdemeanor, Civil, Eviction, Small Claims, Probate.*

Civil Records: Access: Mail, in person. Both court and visitors may perform in person searches. Search fee: $3.00 per name. Required to search: name, years to search. Civil cases indexed by defendant, plaintiff. Civil records on index from 1950, partial on microfiche. **Criminal Records:** Access: Mail, in person. Both court and visitors may perform in person searches. Search fee: $3.00 per name. Required to search: name, years to search, DOB; also helpful-SSN. Criminal records on index from 1950, partial on microfiche. **General Information:** No juvenile, mental, adoption or sealed records released. SASE required. Turnaround time 1-2 weeks. Copy fee: $1.00 per page. Certification fee: $2.00. Fee payee: Clerk of Newton Circuit Court. Business checks accepted. Prepayment is required.

Noble County

Circuit, Superior, & County Court 101 N Orange St, Albion, IN 46701; 219-636-2736; Fax: 219-636-3053. Hours: 8AM-4PM (EST). *Felony, Misdemeanor, Civil, Eviction, Small Claims, Probate.*

Civil Records: Access: Fax, mail, in person. Both court and visitors may perform in person searches. No search fee. Required to search: name, years to search. Civil cases indexed by defendant, plaintiff. Civil records on index cards and docket books. Preparing computer and microfiche records. **Criminal Records:** Access: Fax, mail, in person. Both court and visitors may perform in person searches. Search fee: No criminal searches performed by court. Required to search: name, years to search; also helpful-DOB, SSN. Criminal records on index cards and docket books.

Preparing computer and microfiche records. **General Information:** No juvenile, mental, adoption or sealed released. SASE required. Turnaround time 1 week. Copy fee: $1.00 per page. Certification fee: $2.00. Fee payee: Noble County Clerk. No personal checks accepted. Prepayment is required. Public access terminal is available. Fax notes: No fee to fax results.

Ohio County

Circuit & Superior Court PO Box 185, Rising Sun, IN 47040; 812-438-2610; Fax: 812-438-4590. Hours: 9AM-4PM M,T,Th,F 9AM-Noon S (EST). *Felony, Misdemeanor, Civil, Eviction, Small Claims, Probate.*

Civil Records: Access: Phone, fax, mail, in person. Both court and visitors may perform in person searches. No search fee. Required to search: name, years to search. Civil cases indexed by defendant, plaintiff. Civil records archived from 1844. Recent records on computerized. **Criminal Records:** Access: Phone, fax, mail, in person. Both court and visitors may perform in person searches. No search fee. Required to search: name, years to search. Criminal records not computerized. **General Information:** No juvenile, mental, adoption or sealed released. Copy fee: $1.00 per page. Certification fee: $2.00. Fee payee: Ohio County Clerk. Personal checks accepted. Prepayment is required. Fax notes: $3.00 for first page, $1.00 each addl.

Orange County

Circuit & County Court Courthouse, Court St, Paoli, IN 47454; 812-723-2649. Hours: 8AM-4PM (EST). *Felony, Misdemeanor, Civil, Eviction, Small Claims, Probate.*

Note: The physical location of the County Court is 205 E Main Street. The County Court handles msdemenaor, evicition and small claims

Civil Records: Access: Mail, in person. Both court and visitors may perform in person searches. No search fee. Required to search: name, years to search. Civil cases indexed by defendant, plaintiff. Civil records archived from 1874. Some records on docket books. **Criminal Records:** Access: Mail, in person. Both court and visitors may perform in person searches. No search fee. Required to search: name, years to search. Criminal records archived from 1874. Some records on docket books. **General Information:** No juvenile, mental, adoption or sealed released. SASE required. Turnaround time 2 weeks. Copy fee: $1.00 per page. Certification fee: $2.00. Fee payee: Orange Circuit Clerk. Only cashiers checks and money orders accepted.

Owen County

Circuit Court PO Box 146, Courthouse, Spencer, IN 47460; 812-829-5015; Fax: 812-829-5028. Hours: 8AM-4PM (EST). *Felony, Misdemeanor, Civil, Eviction, Small Claims, Probate.*

Civil Records: Access: Fax, in person. Court does not conduct in person searches; visitors must perform searches for themselves. Search fee: No civil searches performed by court. Required to search: name, years to search. Civil cases indexed by defendant, plaintiff. Civil records archived from 1800s. Some records on docket books. **Criminal Records:** Access: Fax, in person. Court does not conduct in person searches; visitors must perform searches for themselves. Search fee: No criminal searches performed by court. Required to search: name, years to search. Criminal records archived from 1800s. Some records on docket books.

General Information: No juvenile, mental, adoption or sealed records released. Copy fee: $1.00 per page. Certification fee: $2.00. Fee payee: Owen County Clerk. Business checks accepted. Prepayment is required. Fax notes: No fee to fax results.

Parke County

Circuit Court 116 W High St, Rm 204, Rockville, IN 47872; 765-569-5132. Hours: 8AM-4PM (EST). *Felony, Misdemeanor, Civil, Eviction, Small Claims, Probate.*

Civil Records: Access: In person only. Court does not conduct in person searches; visitors must perform searches for themselves. Search fee: No civil searches performed by court. Required to search: name, years to search. Civil cases indexed by defendant, plaintiff. Civil records archived from 1880s. Some records on docket books. **Criminal Records:** Access: In person only. Court does not conduct in person searches; visitors must perform searches for themselves. Search fee: No criminal searches performed by court. Required to search: name, years to search. Criminal records archived from 1880s. Some records on docket books. **General Information:** No juvenile, mental, adoption or sealed released. Copy fee: $1.00 per page. Certification fee: $2.00. Fee payee: Parke County Clerk. Personal checks not accepted.

Perry County

Circuit Court 2219 Payne St, Courthouse, Tell City, IN 47586; 812-547-3741. Hours: 8AM-4PM (EST). *Felony, Misdemeanor, Civil, Eviction, Small Claims, Probate.*

Civil Records: Access: In person only. Both court and visitors may perform in person searches. No search fee. Required to search: name, years to search. Civil cases indexed by defendant, plaintiff. Civil records archived from 1900s. Some records on dockets. **Criminal Records:** Access: In person only. Both court and visitors may perform in person searches. No search fee. Required to search: name, years to search. Criminal records archived from 1900s. Some records on dockets. **General Information:** No juvenile, mental, adoption or sealed released. Copy fee: $.50 per page. Certification fee: $1.00. Fee payee: Perry County Clerk. Business checks accepted. Prepayment is required.

Pike County

Circuit Court 801 Main St. Courthouse, Petersburg, IN 47567-1298; 812-354-6025; Fax: 812-354-3552. Hours: 8AM-4PM (EST). *Felony, Misdemeanor, Civil, Eviction, Small Claims, Probate.*

Civil Records: Access: Mail, in person. Both court and visitors may perform in person searches. No search fee. Required to search: name, years to search. Civil cases indexed by defendant, plaintiff. Civil records archived from 1817. Some records on docket books and index file. **Criminal Records:** Access: Mail, in person. Both court and visitors may perform in person searches. No search fee. Required to search: name, years to search. Criminal records archived from 1817. Some records on docket books and index file. **General Information:** No juvenile, mental, adoption or sealed released. SASE required. Turnaround time 1-2 days. Copy fee: $1.00 per page. Certification fee: $2.00. Fee payee: Pike County Clerk. Only cashiers checks and money orders accepted. Prepayment is required.

Porter County

Circuit Court Records Division, Courthouse Suite 217, 16 E Lincolnway, Valparaiso, IN 46383-5659; 219-465-3453; Fax: 219-465-3592. Hours: 8:30AM-4:30PM (CST). *Felony, Misdemeanor, Civil, Eviction, Small Claims, Probate.*

Civil Records: Access: Mail, in person. Both court and visitors may perform in person searches. No search fee. Required to search: name, years to search. Civil cases indexed by defendant, plaintiff. Civil records on computer index from 1990. Circuit Court records kept from 1844, Superior Court records from 1895. Probate records from Circuit Court kept from 1853, Superior Court from 1900. **Criminal Records:** Access: Mail, in person. Both court and visitors may perform in person searches. No search fee. Required to search: name, years to search. Criminal records on computer index since 1990. Cicuit Court criminal records kept from 1877, Superior Court from 1895. **General Information:** No juvenile, mental, adoption or sealed released. SASE required. Turnaround time 1-2 weeks. Copy fee: $1.00 per page. Certification fee: $1.00. Fee payee: Porter County Clerk. Only cashiers checks and money orders accepted. Prepayment is required.

Superior Court 3560 Willow Creek Dr, Portage, IN 46368; 219-759-2501. Hours: 8:30AM-4:30PM (CST). *Misdemeanor, Civil, Small Claims, Probate.*

Civil Records: Access: Mail, in person. Both court and visitors may perform in person searches. No search fee. Required to search: name, years to search. Civil cases indexed by defendant, plaintiff. Civil records on computer since 1991; prior records on manual index. **Criminal Records:** Access: Mail, in person. Both court and visitors may perform in person searches. No search fee. Required to search: name, years to search; also helpful-DOB, SSN. Civil records on computer since 1991; prior records on manual index. **General Information:** No juvenile, mental, adoption or sealed records released. Copy fee: $1.00 per page. Certification fee: $1.00. Fee payee: Porter County Clerk. Only cashiers checks and money orders accepted. Prepayment is required.

Posey County

Circuit & Superior Court PO Box 606, 300 Main St, Mount Vernon, IN 47620-0606; 812-838-1306; Fax: 812-838-1307. Hours: 8AM-4PM (CST). *Felony, Misdemeanor, Civil, Eviction, Small Claims, Probate.*

Civil Records: Access: In person only. Court does not conduct in person searches; visitors must perform searches for themselves. Search fee: No civil searches performed by court. Required to search: name, years to search; also helpful-address. Civil cases indexed by defendant, plaintiff. Civil records on computer since 8/88, prior on docket books. **Criminal Records:** Access: In person only. Court does not conduct in person searches; visitors must perform searches for themselves. Search fee: No criminal searches performed by court. Required to search: name, years to search; also helpful-DOB, SSN. Criminal records on computer since 8/88, prior on docket books. **General Information:** No juvenile, mental, adoption or sealed released. Copy fee: $1.00 per page. Certification fee: $1.00. Fee payee: Posey County Clerk. Only cashiers checks and money orders accepted. Prepayment is required. Public access

terminal is available. Public Access Terminal Note: Available in Superior Court.

Pulaski County

Circuit & Superior Court 112 E Main, Room 230, Winamac, IN 46996; 219-946-3313; Fax: 219-946-4953. Hours: 8AM-4PM (EST). *Felony, Misdemeanor, Civil, Eviction, Small Claims, Probate.*

Civil Records: Access: In person only. Court does not conduct in person searches; visitors must perform searches for themselves. Search fee: No civil searches performed by court. Required to search: name, years to search. Civil cases indexed by defendant. Civil records archived from 1850s. Some records on docket books. **Criminal Records:** Access: In person only. Court does not conduct in person searches; visitors must perform searches for themselves. Search fee: No criminal searches performed by court. Required to search: name, years to search; also helpful-SSN. Criminal records archived from 1850s. Some records on docket books. **General Information:** No juvenile, mental, adoption or sealed records released. Copy fee: $.50 per page. Certification fee: $2.00. Fee payee: Pulaski County Clerk. Only cashiers checks and money orders accepted. Prepayment is required.

Putnam County

Circuit & Superior Court PO Box 546, Greencastle, IN 46135; 765-653-2648. Hours: 8AM-4PM (EST). *Felony, Misdemeanor, Civil, Eviction, Small Claims, Probate.*

Civil Records: Access: Mail, in person. Both court and visitors may perform in person searches. No search fee. Required to search: name, years to search. Civil cases indexed by defendant, plaintiff. Civil records on index books from 1991, archived from 1800s. Some records on docket books. **Criminal Records:** Access: In person only. Court does not conduct in person searches; visitors must perform searches for themselves. Search fee: No criminal searches performed by court. Required to search: name, years to search; also helpful-DOB, SSN. Criminal records on index books from 1991, archived from 1800s. Some records on docket books. **General Information:** No juvenile, mental, adoption or sealed released. Turnaround time 1 week. Copy fee: $1.00 per page. Certification fee: $1.00. Fee payee: Putnam County Clerk. Business checks accepted. Prepayment is required.

Randolph County

Circuit & Superior Court PO Box 230 Courthouse, Winchester, IN 47394-0230; 765-584-7070 X231; Fax: 765-584-2958. Hours: 8AM-4PM (EST). *Felony, Misdemeanor, Civil, Eviction, Small Claims, Probate.*

Civil Records: Access: Fax, mail, in person. Both court and visitors may perform in person searches. No search fee. Required to search: name, years to search. Civil cases indexed by defendant, plaintiff. Civil records archived from early 1800s. Records on docket books and microfiche. **Criminal Records:** Access: Fax, mail, in person. Both court and visitors may perform in person searches. No search fee. Required to search: name, years to search. Criminal records archived from early 1800s. Records on docket books and microfiche. **General Information:** No juvenile, mental, adoption or sealed released. SASE required. Turnaround time 3 days. Copy fee: $1.00 per page. Certification fee: $1.00. Fee payee: Randolph County Clerk. Only cashiers checks and money orders accepted. Prepayment is required. Public access terminal is available. Fax notes: $4.00 for first page, $.75 each addl.

Ripley County

Circuit Court PO BOX 177, Versailles, IN 47042; 812-689-6115. Hours: 8AM-4PM (EST). *Felony, Misdemeanor, Civil, Eviction, Small Claims, Probate.*

Civil Records: Access: Mail, in person. Both court and visitors may perform in person searches. No search fee. Required to search: name, years to search. Civil cases indexed by defendant, plaintiff. Civil records on computer since 1994, archived from 1900s. Some records on docket books. **Criminal Records:** Access: Mail, in person. Both court and visitors may perform in person searches. No search fee. Required to search: name, years to search, DOB; also helpful-SSN. Criminal records on computer since 1994, archived from 1900s. Some records on docket books. **General Information:** No juvenile, mental, adoption or sealed records released. Turnaround time 1 week. Copy fee: $1.00 per page. Certification fee: $1.00. Fee payee: Clerk of Ripley Circuit Court. Personal checks accepted. Prepayment is required. Public access terminal is available.

Rush County

Circuit & County Court PO Box 429, Rushville, IN 46173; 765-932-2086; Fax: 765-932-2357. Hours: 8AM-4PM (EST). *Felony, Misdemeanor, Civil, Eviction, Small Claims, Probate.*

Civil Records: Access: In person only. Court does not conduct in person searches; visitors must perform searches for themselves. Search fee: No civil searches performed by court. Required to search: name, years to search. Civil cases indexed by defendant, plaintiff. Civil records archived from 1822. Some records on docket books. **Criminal Records:** Access: In person only. Court does not conduct in person searches; visitors must perform searches for themselves. Search fee: No criminal searches performed by court. Required to search: name, years to search, DOB, SSN. Criminal records archived from 1822. Some records on docket books. **General Information:** No juvenile, mental, adoption or sealed records released. Copy fee: $1.00 per page. Certification fee: $2.00. Fee payee: Rush County Clerk. Business checks accepted. Prepayment is required.

Scott County

Circuit & Superior Court 1 E McClain Ave, #120, Scottsburg, IN 47170; 812-752-8420; Fax: 812-752-5459. Hours: 8:30AM-4:30PM (EST). *Felony, Misdemeanor, Civil, Eviction, Small Claims, Probate.*

Civil Records: Access: In person only. Court does not conduct in person searches; visitors must perform searches for themselves. Search fee: No civil searches performed by court. Required to search: name, years to search; also helpful-address. Civil cases indexed by defendant, plaintiff. Civil records on computer from 2/90, on docket books from 1970. **Criminal Records:** Access: In person only. Court does not perform searches for themselves. Search fee: No criminal searches performed by court. Required to search: name, years to search; also helpful-DOB, SSN. Criminal records on computer from 2/90, on docket books from 1970. **General Information:** No juvenile, mental, adoption or sealed released. Copy fee: $1.00 per page. Certification fee: $2.00. Fee payee: Scott

County Clerk. Business checks accepted. Prepayment is required.

Shelby County

Circuit & Superior Court PO Box 198, Shelbyville, IN 46176; 317-392-6320. Hours: 8AM-4PM (EST). *Felony, Misdemeanor, Civil, Eviction, Small Claims, Probate.*

Civil Records: Access: In person only. Court does not conduct in person searches; visitors must perform searches for themselves. Search fee: No civil searches performed by court. Required to search: name, years to search. Civil cases indexed by defendant, plaintiff. Civil records on computer since 07/95. **Criminal Records:** Access: In person only. Court does not conduct in person searches; visitors must perform searches for themselves. Search fee: No criminal searches performed by court. Required to search: name, years to search. Criminal records on computer since 07/95. **General Information:** No juvenile, mental, adoption or sealed released. Copy fee: $1.00 per page. Certification fee: $1.00. Fee payee: Clerk of Court. Personal checks accepted. Prepayment is required. Public access terminal is available.

Spencer County

Circuit Court PO Box 12, Rockport, IN 47635; 812-649-6027; Fax: 812-649-6030. Hours: 8AM-4PM (CST). *Felony, Misdemeanor, Civil, Eviction, Small Claims, Probate.*

Civil Records: Access: In person only. Court does not conduct in person searches; visitors must perform searches for themselves. Search fee: No civil searches performed by court. Required to search: name, years to search. Civil cases indexed by defendant, plaintiff. Civil records archived from early 1900s. Some records on docket books. Child support cases on computer. **Criminal Records:** Access: In person only. Court does not conduct in person searches; visitors must perform searches for themselves. Search fee: No criminal searches performed by court. Required to search: name, years to search. Criminal records archived from early 1900s. Some records on docket books. Child support cases on computer. **General Information:** No juvenile, mental, adoption or sealed released. Copy fee: $1.00 per page. Certification fee: $1.00. Fee payee: Spencer Circuit Court. Only cashiers checks and money orders accepted. Prepayment is required.

St. Joseph County

Circuit & Superior Court 101 South Main St, South Bend, IN 46601; 219-235-9635; Fax: 219-235-9838. Hours: 8AM-4:30PM (EST). *Felony, Misdemeanor, Civil, Eviction, Small Claims, Probate.*

Civil Records: Access: Mail, in person. Both court and visitors may perform in person searches. No search fee. Required to search: name, years to search. Civil cases indexed by defendant, plaintiff. Civil records on general index from 1962. **Criminal Records:** Access: In person only. Court does not conduct in person searches; visitors must perform searches for themselves. Search fee: No criminal searches performed by court. Required to search: name, years to search; also helpful-address, DOB, SSN. Criminal records on general index from 1962. **General Information:** No juvenile, mental, adoption or sealed released. SASE required. Turnaround time 1-2 days. Copy fee: $1.00 per page. Certification fee: $1.00. Fee payee: St Joseph County Clerk. Business checks accepted. Public access terminal is available.

Starke County

Circuit Court Courthouse, 53 E Washington St, Knox, IN 46534; 219-772-9128. Hours: 8:30AM-4PM (CST). *Felony, Misdemeanor, Civil, Eviction, Small Claims, Probate.*

Civil Records: Access: In person only. Court does not conduct in person searches; visitors must perform searches for themselves. Search fee: No civil searches performed by court. Required to search: name, years to search. Civil cases indexed by defendant, plaintiff. Civil records archived from 1900s. Some records on docket books. **Criminal Records:** Access: In person only. Court does not conduct in person searches; visitors must perform searches for themselves. Search fee: No criminal searches performed by court. Required to search: name, years to search, DOB; also helpful-SSN. Criminal records archived from 1900s. Some records on docket books. Same as civil. **General Information:** No juvenile, mental, adoption or sealed released. Copy fee: $1.00 per page. Certification fee: $2.00. Fee payee: Clerk of Stark Circuit Court. Business checks accepted. Prepayment is required.

Steuben County

Circuit & Superior Court Courthouse, 55 S. Public Square, Angola, IN 46703; 219-668-1000 X2240. Hours: 8AM-4:30PM (EST). *Felony, Misdemeanor, Civil, Eviction, Small Claims, Probate.*

Civil Records: Access: In person only. Court does not conduct in person searches; visitors must perform searches for themselves. Search fee: No civil searches performed by court. Required to search: name, years to search. Civil cases indexed by defendant, plaintiff. Civil records archived from 1800s. Some records on docket books. **Criminal Records:** Access: In person only. Court does not conduct in person searches; visitors must perform searches for themselves. Search fee: No criminal searches performed by court. Required to search: name, years to search. Criminal records archived from 1800s. Some records on docket books. **General Information:** No juvenile, mental, adoption, some probate, or sealed released. Copy fee: $1.00 per page. Certification fee: $2.00. Fee payee: Steuben County Clerk. Only cashiers checks and money orders accepted. Prepayment is required. Public access terminal is available.

Sullivan County

Circuit & Superior Court Courthouse, 3rd Fl, PO Box 370, Sullivan, IN 47882-0370; 812-268-4657. Hours: 8AM-4PM (EST). *Felony, Misdemeanor, Civil, Eviction, Small Claims, Probate.*

Civil Records: Access: Mail, in person. Both court and visitors may perform in person searches. No search fee. Required to search: name, years to search; also helpful-address. Civil cases indexed by defendant, plaintiff. Civil records on docket books or general index. **Criminal Records:** Access: In person only. Court does not conduct in person searches; visitors must perform searches for themselves. Search fee: No criminal searches performed by court. Required to search: name, years to search, DOB, signed release; also helpful-address, SSN. Criminal records on docket books or general index. **General Information:** No juvenile, mental, adoption or sealed released. SASE required. Turnaround time 1-2 days. Copy fee: $1.00 per page. Certification fee: $2.00. Fee payee: Sullivan County. Personal checks accepted. Prepayment is required.

Expedited service: Expedited service is available for fax searches. Account is required. Turnaround time: same day if possible.

Corporation Records
Limited Liability Company Records
Fictitious Name
Limited Partnership Records
Trademarks/Servicemarks

Secretary of State, Corporation Division, 2nd Floor, Hoover Bldg, Des Moines, IA 50319; 515-281-5204, 515-242-5953 (Fax), 8AM-4:30PM.

www.sos.state.ia.us

Indexing & Storage: Records are available from the late 1800s. New records are available for inquiry immediately. Records are indexed on microfilm, inhouse computer, on-line.

Searching: Include the following in your request-full name of business, specific records that you need copies of. In addition to the articles of incorporation, the following information is released: Annual/Biennial Reports, Officers, Directors, DBAs, Prior (merged) names, Inactive and Reserved names.

Access by: mail, phone, fax, in person, online.

Fee & Payment: Copies are $1.00 each. Fee payee: Secretary of State. Prepayment required. A charge account may be established for ongoing requesters. Call 515-281-5204 for more details. Personal checks accepted. Credit cards accepted: Mastercard, Visa.

Mail search: Turnaround time: 2-3 days. A self addressed stamped envelope is requested. No fee for mail request.

Phone search: No fee for telephone request. You are restricted to 3 requests per call.

Fax search: Copies cost $1.00 per page, plus $1.00 for each page that is faxed. Turnaround time: 2 days.

In person search: No fee for request.

Online search: The state offers the DataShare On-line System. Fees are $175.00 per year plus $.30 per minute. The system is open 5 AM to 8 PM daily. All records are available, including UCCs. Call 515-281-5204 and ask for Cheryl Allen for more information. Another online option is via the Internet. Access to information is free; however, the data is not as current as the DataShare System.

Other access: The state will sell the records in database format. Call the number listed above and ask for Karen Ubaldo for more information.

Uniform Commercial Code
Federal Tax Liens

UCC Division, Secretary of State, Hoover Bldg, 2nd Floor, Des Moines, IA 50319; 515-281-5204, 515-242-5953 (Other Fax Line), 515-242-6556 (Fax), 8AM-4:30PM.

www.sos.state.ia.us/business/services.html

Indexing & Storage: Records are available from 1966 and are computerized. All current records are on optical disk. It takes 1-3 before new records are available for inquiry.

Searching: Use search request form UCC-11. Specify if you also want federal tax liens and include another search fee. Federal tax liens on individuals and all state tax liens are filed at the county level. Include the following in your request-debtor name. Copies of filings may be requested at time of search, but do not ask for copies with your initial request unless you have a charge account.

Access by: mail, phone, fax, in person, online.

Fee & Payment: The fee is $5.00 per debtor name, $6.00 for federal liens. Copies are $1.00 per page. Fee payee: Secretary of State. Prepayment required. Personal checks accepted. Credit cards accepted: Mastercard, Visa.

Mail search: Turnaround time: 1-2 days. A self addressed stamped envelope is requested.

Phone search: A telephone search is available with a prepaid or charge account, or with credit card.

Fax search: urnaround time usually same day, fee is $1.00 per page.

In person search: Searching is available in person.

Online search: All information is available online for no fee at www.sos.state.ia.us/uccweb.

State Tax Liens

Records not maintained by a state level agency.

Note: Records are found at the county recorder's offices.

Sales Tax Registrations

Department of Revenue, Taxpayer Services Division, Hoover State Office Bldg, Des Moines, IA 50306-0465; 515-281-3114, 515-242-6487 (Fax), 8AM-4PM.

www.state.ia.us/tax

Indexing & Storage: Records are available for 5 years. Records are indexed on computer, microfiche.

Searching: This agency will provide any information found on the face of the Tax Permit-business name, business address, and tax permit number. Information not released includes telephone numbers, tax liabilities, taxes collected, officers, federal ID#s, etc. Include the following in your request-business name. They will also search by tax permit number.

Access by: mail, phone, fax, in person.

Fee & Payment: There is no search fee; however, there is a $5.00 copy fee per document. Fee payee: Treasurer of State of Iowa. Prepayment required. Personal checks accepted. No credit cards accepted.

Mail search: Turnaround time: 7-10 days. No self addressed stamped envelope is required.

Phone search: Limited information is available by phone.

Fax search: There is no fee for fax searches. Turnaround time: 24 hours.

In person search: Searching is available in person.

Other access: The agency will provide the database on lists, fees vary from $20-$45.

Birth Certificates

Iowa Department of Public Health, Bureau of Vital Records, 321 E 12th St, Lucas Bldg, Des Moines, IA 50319-0075; 515-281-4944, 515-281-5871 (Message Recording), 7AM-4:45PM.

www.idph.state.ia.us

Note: All vital records are open for inspection at the county level, usually for a $10.00 fee.

Indexing & Storage: Records are available from 1880-present. It takes 30 days to 6 weeks before new records are available for inquiry. Records are indexed on microfiche, inhouse computer.

Searching: Adoption records are not released. Include the following in your request-full name, names of parents, mother's maiden name, date of birth, place of birth, relationship to person of record, reason for information request. Must have copy of a photo ID (mail) or a photo ID (in person) to search.

Access by: mail, phone, in person.

Fee & Payment: The search fee is $10.00, There is an additional $5.00 fee to use a credit card. For records 1880-1915, a $10.00 per year fee is charged. Fee payee: Iowa Department of Public Health. Prepayment required. Personal checks accepted. Credit cards accepted: Mastercard, Visa, AmEx, Discover.

Mail search: Turnaround time: within 1 month.

Phone search: Searching is available by phone.

In person search: Same day service is not available. Turnaround time is 48 hours.

Expedited service: Expedited mail service is available for phone searches. Add $11.00 per package. Must use a credit card which is an extra $5.00. Normal turnaround time is 10-14 days.

Death Records

Iowa Department of Public Health, Vital Records, 321 E 12th St, Lucas Bldg, Des Moines, IA 50319-0075; 515-281-4944, 515-281-5871 (Message Recording), 7AM-4:45PM.

www.idph.state.ia.us

Indexing & Storage: Records are available from 1880-present. From 1880-1895 there is no index. It takes up to 60 days before new records are available for inquiry. Records are indexed on microfiche, inhouse computer.

Searching: Include the following in your request-full name, date of death, place of death, relationship to person of record, reason for information request. Must have a copy of a photo ID (mail) or a photo ID (in person) to search.

Access by: mail, phone, in person.

Fee & Payment: The search fee is $10.00 for each index searched. There is an additional $5.00 fee when using a credit card. Fee payee: Iowa Department of Public Health. Prepayment required. Personal checks accepted. Credit cards accepted: Mastercard, Visa, AmEx, Discover.

Mail search: Turnaround time: within 1 month. A self addressed stamped envelope is requested.

Phone search: Searching is available by phone.

In person search: Same day service in not available. Turnaround time is 48 hours.

Expedited service: Expedited mail service is available phone searches. Add fee for express delivery. Also, be sure to include the extra credit card fee. Turnaround time is 7-10 days.

Marriage Certificates

Iowa Department of Public Health, Vital Records, 321 E 12th St, Lucas Bldg, Des Moines, IA 50319-0075; 515-281-4944, 515-281-5871 (Message Recording), 7AM-4:45PM.

www.idph.state.ia.us

Indexing & Storage: Records are available from 1880. Records from 1880-1915 have to be searched by year. 1916 forward are indexed. New records are available for inquiry immediately. Records are indexed on microfiche, inhouse computer.

Searching: Include the following in your request-names of husband and wife, date of marriage, place or county of marriage.

Access by: mail, phone, in person.

Fee & Payment: The search fee is $10.00 per index searched. There is an additional $5.00 fee when using a credit card. Fee payee: Iowa Department of Public Health. Prepayment required. Personal checks accepted. Credit cards accepted: Mastercard, Visa, AmEx, Discover.

Mail search: Turnaround time: within 1 month. A self addressed stamped envelope is requested.

Phone search: Searching is available by phone.

In person search: Same day service is not available. Turnaround time is 48 hours.

Expedited service: Expedited mail service is available for phone searches. Add fee for express delivery. Also, there is an additional $5.00 for use of credit card. Turnaround time is 7-10 days.

Divorce Records

Records not maintained by a state level agency.

Note: Divorce records are found at the county court issuing the decree. In general, records are available from 1880.

Workers' Compensation Records

Iowa Workforce Development, Division of Workers' Compensation, 1000 E Grand Ave, Des Moines, IA 50319; 515-281-5387, 515-281-6501 (Fax), 8AM-4:30PM.

www.state.ia.us/iwd/wc

Note: Regular, ongoing requesters may apply for charge accounts.

Indexing & Storage: Records are available for the past 20 years. New records are available for inquiry immediately.

Searching: Include the following in your request-claimant name, Social Security Number, place of employment at time of accident. Older records may take as long as 6 weeks to research.

Access by: mail, phone, fax, in person.

Fee & Payment: There is no search fee, copies are $.50 per page. Fee payee: Workers' Compensation. Prepayment required. Personal checks accepted. No credit cards accepted.

Mail search: Turnaround time: 3-5 days. A self addressed stamped envelope is requested.

Phone search: No fee for telephone request. They will let you know if a record exists. Limit is 4 requests per day. Callers are required to provide

their name, company, and SSN or FEIN (whichever applicable). These are permanently recorded.

Fax search: Response to fax requests is made by mail.

In person search: Files are available for personal viewing only if requested in advance.

Other access: This agency sells its entire database.

Driver Records

Department of Transportation, Driver Service Records Section, PO Box 9204, Des Moines, IA 50306-9204 (Courier: Park Fair Mall, 100 Euclid, Des Moines, IA 50306); 515-244-9124, 515-237-3152 (Fax), 8AM-4:30PM.

www.dot.state.ia.us/mvd/ovs/index.htm

Note: Copies of tickets can be requested from this address for $.50 per copy.

Indexing & Storage: Records are available for 5-7 years for moving violations; 12 years for DWIs; 5-7 years after closed for suspensions. The driver's address is shown on the record. Accidents are listed, but fault is not shown. It takes 2-3 days before new records are available for inquiry.

Searching: Casual requesters may not obtain personal information on the record without consent of the subject. Include the following in your request-full name, driver's license number, date of birth. County sheriffs in Iowa are authorized to furnish copies of driving records, but not all do. There are DOT "Super Stations" in Cedar Rapids, Council Bluff, Davenport, and Sioux City that offer a public access terminal.

Access by: mail, in person.

Fee & Payment: The fee for certified mail-in or walk-in requests and tape-to-tape records is $5.50 per record. There is no charge for a no record found. Fee payee: Treasurer, State of Iowa. Prepayment required. Personal checks accepted. No credit cards accepted.

Mail search: Turnaround time: 4-7 days. An account can be established for on-going requesters. No self addressed stamped envelope is required.

In person search: Iowa permits walk-in requesters to view driving records at a terminal. The fee for an on-screen look-up is $1.00 per record for the first 5 records viewed and $2.00 for each additional record viewed. These prints are not considered certified.

Other access: Iowa offers magnetic tape processing for high volume users. Iowa will sell the master data file, without driver history information, as well as a suspension/revocation file. Call Carol Padgett at 515-237-3146 for more information.

Vehicle Ownership
Vehicle Identification

Department of Transportation, Office of Vehicle Services, PO Box 9278, Des Moines, IA 50306-9278 (Courier: Park Fair Mall, 100 Euclid, Des Moines, IA 50306); 515-237-3148, 515-237-3049, 515-237-3118 (Fax), 8AM-4:30PM.

www.dot.state.ia.us/mvd/ovs/index.htm

Note: Vehicle lien information is not maintained by this department.

Indexing & Storage: Records are available from 1968-present for registration and title. Title records are indexed on computer from 1986-present.

Searching: Vehicle registration information is released to casual requesters, but personal information not given without consent. Plate searches will release only the vehicle information.

Access by: mail, phone, fax, in person.

Fee & Payment: Fees: $.50 per certified record; photocopy of record is $.10 per copy; record search-$2.70 per quarter hour or fraction thereof. Fee payee: Iowa Department of Transportation. Prepayment required. Personal checks accepted. No credit cards accepted.

Mail search: Turnaround time: 3-5 days. No self addressed stamped envelope is required.

Phone search: Searching is available by phone.

Fax search: Fax searching available.

In person search: You may request information in person.

Other access: Iowa makes the entire vehicle file or selected data available for purchase. Weekly updates are also available for those purchasers. For more information, call 515-237-3110.

Accident Reports

Department of Transportation, Office of Driver Services, PO Box 9204, (Park Fair Mall, 100 Euclid), Des Moines, IA 50306-9204; 515-244-9124, 800-532-1121, 515-239-1837 (Fax), 8AM-4:30PM.

Indexing & Storage: Records are available for five years.

Searching: Accident reports are available only to the person involved in accident or the person's insurance company or attorney. Include the following in your request-full name, date of accident, location of accident.

Access by: mail, fax, in person.

Fee & Payment: The fee is $4.00 per officer report. Fee payee: Treasurer, State of Iowa. Prepayment required. The state allows regular, ongoing requesters to open a deposit account. Personal checks accepted. No credit cards accepted.

Mail search: Turnaround time: 2-3 weeks. No self addressed stamped envelope is required.

Fax search: Same criteria as mail searches.

In person search: Turnaround time for walk-in requesters is generally immediate.

Boat & Vessel Ownership
Boat & Vessel Registration

Records not maintained by a state level agency.

Note: Vessels are registered at the county level.

Legislation-Current/Pending
Legislation-Passed

Iowa General Assembly, Legislative Information Office, State Capitol, Des Moines, IA 50319; 515-281-5129, 8AM-4:30PM.

www.legis.state.ia.us

Note: For copies of older bills, it is suggested to go to a local law library.

Indexing & Storage: Records are available for the current year. Records are indexed on inhouse computer.

Searching: Include the following in your request- bill number.

Access by: mail, phone, in person, online.

Fee & Payment: There is no fee for copies of current and pending legislation. Fee payee: Treasurer, State of Iowa. Prepayment required. Personal checks accepted. No credit cards accepted.

Mail search: Turnaround time: variable. A maximum of 20 bills will be sent by mail. No self addressed stamped envelope is required.

Phone search: You may request bills by phone or receive status information.

In person search: You may request bills in person.

Online search: Access is available through the Legislative Computer Support Bureau or through their web site.

Other access: The state sells a weekly summary called the Session Brief. The fee is $10.60.

Voter Registration

Secretary of State, Elections Division, Hoover State Office Building, Des Moines, IA 50319; 515-281-5760, 515-242-5953 (Fax), 8AM-4:30PM.

www.sos.state.ia.us

Indexing & Storage: Records are available for active records and two elections back for inactive.

Searching: The following data is not released: Social Security Numbers or bulk information or lists for commercial purposes.

Access by: phone, in person.

Fee & Payment: There is no fee for confirmation. No searching by mail.

Phone search: Will only confirm.

In person search: Records may be viewed.

Other access: Information is available, on tape or disk, for political purposes only. Data can be sorted by any field on the registration file.

GED Certificates

Department of Education, GED Records, Grimes State Office Building, Des Moines, IA 50319-0146; 515-281-7308, 515-281-3636, 515-281-6544 (Fax), 8AM-5PM.

Searching: Include the following in your request- signed release, Social Security Number, date of birth. The year and city of test are also helpful.

Access by: mail, phone, fax, in person.

Fee & Payment: There is a $5.00 fee for a copy (and $3.00 for 2nd copy) of a transcript or a diploma. There is no fee for a verification. Fee payee: IA Department of Education. Prepayment required. Money orders are accepted. No personal checks accepted. No credit cards accepted.

Mail search: Turnaround time: 1-3 days. A self addressed stamped envelope is requested.

Phone search: Limited information is available.

Fax search: They will return verification data by fax to local or toll-free numbers.

In person search: Searching is available in person.

Hunting License Information
Fishing License Information

Department of Natural Resources, Wallace Building, E 9th & Grand Ave, 4th Floor, Des Moines, IA 50319-0034; 515-281-8688, 515-281-6794 (Fax), 8:15AM-4:15PM.

www.state.ia.us

Indexing & Storage: Records are available for current year on computer, past years on microfiche. Records are indexed on inhouse computer.

Searching: Include the following in your request- full name, date of birth, Social Security Number. This agency only maintains records for deer (except bow & free landowners) and turkey.

Access by: mail, phone, in person.

Fee & Payment: There is no charge for a search of one record for personal use. Lists will incur a fee based on length and how search must be done. Fee payee: Iowa Department of Natural Resources. Personal checks accepted. No credit cards accepted.

Mail search: Turnaround time: 1-3 days. No self addressed stamped envelope is required.

Phone search: You may call for information.

In person search: You may request information in person.

Licenses Searchable Online

Architect #08	www.state.ia.us/government/com/prof/arch/archrost.htm
Bank #04	www.idob.state.ia.us
Credit Union #06	www.iacudiv.state.ia.us/Public/fieldofmembership/membersearch.htm
Debt Management Company #04	www.idob.state.ia.us/license/lic_default.htm
Delayed Deposit Service Business #04	www.idob.state.ia.us/license/lic_default.htm
Engineer #08	www.state.ia.us/government/com/prof/engx/rosters.htm
Finance Company #04	www.idob.state.ia.us/license/lic_default.htm
Landscape Architect #10	www.state.ia.us/government/com/prof/lands/lanscros.htm
Medical Doctor #14	www.docboard.org/ia/find_ia.htm
Money Transmitter #04	www.idob.state.ia.us/license/lic_default.htm
Mortgage Banker #04	www.idob.state.ia.us/license/lic_default.htm
Mortgage Broker #04	www.idob.state.ia.us/license/lic_default.htm
Mortgage Loan Service #04	www.idob.state.ia.us/license/lic_default.htm
Notary Public #31	www.sos.state.ia.us/NotaryWeb
Optometrist #22	www.arbo.org/nodb2000/licsearch.asp
Public Accountant-CPA #08	www.state.ia.us/government/com/prof/acct/acctrost.htm
Real Estate Appraiser #32	www.state.ia.us/government/com/prof/realappr/approst.htm
Surveyor #08	www.state.ia.us/government/com/prof/engx/rosters.htm
Trust Company #04	www.idob.state.ia.us/license/lic_default.htm

Licensing Quick Finder

Acupuncturist #14 515-281-5171
Adoption Investigator #18 515-281-8746
Alcoholic Beverage Licensing Retail/Wholesale #05
.... 515-281-7430
Alcoholic Beverage Manufacturer #05
.... 515-281-7430
Amusement Ride Inspection #27 515-281-5415
Architect #08 515-281-4126
Asbestos Abatement Contractor/Worker #27
.... 515-281-6175
Asbestos Inspector #27 515-281-6175
Asbestos Project Designer/Management Planner #27
.... 515-281-6175
Athletic Agents #31 515-281-5204
Athletic Trainer #22 515-281-4401
Attorney #30 515-281-5911
Audiologist #22 515-281-4408
Bank #04 515-281-4014
Barber #22 515-281-4416
Boiler Inspector #27 515-281-6533
Bus Driver #34 515-237-3079
Chiropractor #22 515-281-4287
Coach #12 800-788-7856
Community & Institutional Pharmacy #16
.... 515-281-5944
Contractor #27 515-281-6175
Controlled Substances Registrant #16
.... 515-281-5944
Cosmetologist #22 515-281-4416
Cosmetology Instructor #22 515-281-4416
Credit Union #06 515-281-6514
Day Care #17 515-242-5994
Debt Management Company #04 515-281-4014
Delayed Deposit Service Business #04
.... 515-281-4014
Dental Hygienist #13 515-281-5157
Dentist #13 515-281-5157
Dietitian #22 515-281-6959
Drug Distributor/Drug Wholesaler #16 .. 515-281-5944
Drug Manufacturer #16 515-281-5944
Drug Wholesaler #16 515-281-5944
Electrologist #33 515-242-6385
Elevator Inspection #27 515-281-5415
Emergency Medical Technician-Basic #27
.... 515-281-3239
Emergency Medical Technician-Intermediate #27
.... 515-281-3239

Emergency Medical Technician-Paramedic #27
.... 515-281-3239
Engineer #08 515-281-5602
Esthetician #33 515-242-6385
Excursion Boat Gambling #19 515-281-7352
Excursion Gambling #19 515-281-7352
Finance Company #04 515-281-4014
First Response Paramedic #27 515-281-4958
Funeral Director #22 515-281-4287
Group Foster Care #17 515-281-4625
Hearing Aid Dealer #22 515-281-6959
Instructional Schools #31 515-281-5204
Instructor-Community College #12 800-788-7856
Insurance Agency/Corporation/Broker #07
.... 515-281-4037
Insurance Agent #07 515-281-4037
Landfill Operator #20 515-281-8688
Landscape Architect #10 515-281-4126
Lottery Retailer #26 515-281-7900
Manicurist #33 515-242-6385
Marriage & Family Therapist #22 515-281-4422
Massage Therapist #22 515-281-6959
Medical Doctor #14 515-281-5171
Mental Health Counselor #22 515-281-4422
Money Transmitter #04 515-281-4014
Mortgage Banker #04 515-281-4014
Mortgage Broker #04 515-281-4014
Mortgage Loan Service #04 515-281-4014
Mortuary Science #22 515-281-4287
Nail Technologist #33 515-242-6385
Notary Public #31 515-281-5204
Nuclear Medicine Technologist #29 515-281-4942
Nurse #15 .... 515-281-3264 or 4826
Nurse, Advance Registered Practice #15
.... 515-281-3264 or 4826
Nurse-LPN #15 .... 515-281-3264 or 4826
Nursing Home Administrator #22 515-281-4401
Occupational Therapist/Assistant #22 ... 515-281-4401
Optometrist #22 515-281-4287
Osteopathic Physician #14 515-281-5171
Pari-Mutuel Wagering Facility #19 515-281-7352
Pesticide Commercial Applicator #03 515-281-5601
Pesticide Dealer/Applicator #03 515-281-5601
Pesticide Private Applicator #03 515-281-4339
Pharmacist #16 515-281-5944
Pharmacist Tech/Intern #16 515-281-5944
Pharmacy #16 515-281-5944

Physical & Occupational Therapist #22 . 515-281-4401
Physical Therapist/Assistant #22 515-281-4401
Physician Assistant #22 515-242-4408
Podiatrist #22 515-242-4422
Polygraph Examiner #25 515-281-7610
Post-Secondary Schools #31 515-281-5204
Private Investigator #25 515-281-7610
Private Security Guard #25 515-281-7610
Psychologist #22 515-281-4401
Public Accountant-CPA #08 515-281-4126
Racing Worker/Riverboat Gambling Worker #19
.... 515-281-7352
Radiation Therapist #29 515-281-4942
Radioactive Material #29 515-281-3478
Radiographer (Medical) #29 515-281-4942
Radon Measurement Specialist #29 515-281-6549
Radon Mitigation Specialist #29 515-281-6549
Real Estate Appraiser #32 515-281-7393
Real Estate Broker/Salesman #11 515-281-5910
Respiratory Therapist #22 515-281-4408
School Counselor #12 800-788-7856
School Principal #12 800-788-7856
Securities Agent/Registered Rep./Broker #07
.... 515-281-4441
Sheep Dealer #02 515-281-8601
Shorthand Reporter #30 515-246-8076
Social Worker #22 515-281-4422
Solid Waste Incinerator Operator #20 ... 515-281-8688
Speech Pathologist/Audiologist #22 515-281-4408
Superintendent of Schools #12 800-788-7856
Surveyor #08 515-281-5602
Tattoo Artist #22 515-242-5149
Taxi Driver #34 515-237-3079
Teacher #12 800-788-7856
Transient Merchant #31 515-281-5204
Travel Agencies #31 515-281-5204
Trust Company #04 515-281-4014
Veterinarian #02 515-281-5304
Veterinary Technician #02 515-281-5304
Voting Booth #01 515-281-0145
Voting Equipment #01 515-281-0145
Waste Water Lagoon/Treatment Operator #20
.... 515-281-8688
Water Distribution Operator #20 515-281-8688
Water Treatment Operator #20 515-281-8688
Well Driller #20 515-281-8688

Licensing Agency Information

01 Attn: Sandy Steinbach, Secretary of State's Office, Board of Voting Systems Examiners, Hoover Bldg, 2nd Fl, Des Moines, IA 50319; 515-281-0145, Fax: 515-242-5953.

www.sos.state.ia.us

02 Department of Agriculture, Animal Industrial Bureau, Regulatory Division, PO Box 4009 (E 9th & Grand Ave, Wallace Bldg, 2nd Fl), Des Moines, IA 50319; 515-281-7074, Fax: 515-281-3121.

03 Department of Agriculture, Laboratory Division, Wallace State Office Bldg, Des Moines, IA 50319; 515-281-5001, Fax: 515-242-6497.

04 Department of Commerce, 200 E Grand Ave, Des Moines, IA 50309; 515-281-4014, Fax: 515-281-4862.

www.idob.state.ia.us

Direct URL to search licenses: www.idob.state.ia.us/license/lic_default.htm You can search online using corporate name, license name, license number or address.

05 Department of Commerce, Alcoholic Beverage Division, 1918 SE Hulsizer Ave, Ankeny, IA 50021; 515-281-7430, Fax: 515-281-7375.

www.iowaabd.com

06 Department of Commerce, Credit Union Division, 200 E Grand Ave #370, Des Moines, IA 50309; 515-281-6514, Fax: 515-281-7595.

www.iacudiv.state.ia.us

Direct URL to search licenses: www.iacudiv.state.ia.us/Public/fieldofmembership/membersearch.htm You can search online using name, credit union #, charter #, city, zip code

07 Department of Commerce, Insurance Division, 35 Anthony Ave, State House Station 158, Des Moines, IA 50319; 515-281-7758, Fax: 515-281-3059.

www.state.ia.us/government/com/ins/agent/agent.htm

08 Department of Commerce, Professional Licensing & Regulation Division, 1918 SE Hulsizer Ave, Ankeny, IA 50021; 515-281-5602, Fax: 515-281-7411.

www.state.ia.us/government/com/prof/search.htm

Direct URL to search licenses: www.state.ia.us/government/com/prof/search.htm You can search online using name and county.

10 Department of Commerce, Professional Licensing & Regulation Division, 1918 SE Hulsizer Ave, Ankeny, IA 50021; 515-281-3183, Fax: 515-281-7411.

www.state.ia.us/government/com/prof/lands/lands.htm

Direct URL to search licenses: www.state.ia.us/government/com/prof/lands/lanscros.htm You can search online using name.

11 Department of Commerce, Professional Licensing & Regulation Division, 1918 SE Hulsizer, Ankeny, IA 50021; 515-281-3183, Fax: 515-281-7411.

www.state.ia.us/government/com/prof/realesta/realesta.htm

12 Department of Education, Board of Educational Examiners, Grimes State Office Bldg, Des Moines, IA 50319-0147; 515-281-5849, Fax: 515-281-7669.

www.state.ia.us/educate/programs/boee

13 Board of Dental Examiners, PO Box 64975 (400 SW 8th St, #D), Des Moines, IA 50309-4687; 515-281-5157, Fax: 515-281-7969.

www.state.ia.us/dentalboard

14 Department of Health, Board of Medical Examiners, 1209 E Court Ave, Executive Hills West, Des Moines, IA 50319-0810; 515-281-5171, Fax: 515-242-5908.

www.docboard.org/ia/ia_home.htm

15 Department of Health, Board of Nursing, 1223 E Court Ave, Des Moines, IA 50319; 515-281-3255, Fax: 515-281-4825.

www.state.ia.us/government/nursing

Direct URL to search licenses: www.state.ia.us/government/nursing You can search online using name. IVR telephone verifications available at 515-281-3255

16 Department of Health, Board of Pharmacy, 1209 E Court Ave, Executive Hills West, Des Moines, IA 50319-0187; 515-281-5944, Fax: 515-281-4609.

17 Department of Human Services, Adult & Family Services, Hoover State Office Bldg, 5th Fl, Des Moines, IA 50319-0114; 515-281-5521, Fax: 515-281-4597.

18 Department of Human Services, Children & Family Services, Adoption Certifier, Hoover State Office Bldg, 5th Fl, Des Moines, IA 50319-0114; 515-281-8746, Fax: 515-281-4597.

19 Department of Inspections & Appeals, Racing & Gaming Commission, 717 E Court Av #B, Des Moines, IA 50309; 515-281-7352, Fax: 515-242-6560.

www3.state.ia.us/irgc/

20 Department of Natural Resources, 502 E 9th St, Wallace State Office Bldg, Des Moines, IA 50319-0035; 515-281-8688, Fax: 515-281-6794.

www.state.ia.us/dnr

22 Department of Public Health, Division of Professional Licensing, Lucas State Office Bldg, Des Moines, IA 50319; 515-281-7074, Fax: 515-281-3121.

25 Department of Public Safety, Wallace State Office Bldg, Des Moines, IA 50319; 515-281-7610, Fax: 515-281-8921.

26 Department of Revenue & Finance, Lottery Board, PO Box 10474 (2015 Grand Av), Des Moines, IA 50312; 515-281-7900, Fax: 515-281-7882.

www.ialottery.com

27 Division of Labor, Workforce Development, 1000 E Grand Ave, Des Moines, IA 50319-0209; 515-281-6175, Fax: 515-281-7995.

www.state.ia.us/iwd/labor/index.html

29 Department of Public Health, Bureau of Radiological Health, 321 E 12th St, Lucas State Office Bldg, Des Moines, IA 50319-0075; 515-281-3478, Fax: 515-242-6284.

30 Supreme Court Clerk's Office, Legal Boards, Statehouse, Des Moines, IA 50319; 515-281-5911, Fax: 515-242-6164.

www.judicial.state.ia.us/regs

31 Office of Secretary of State, Hoover Office Bldg, 2nd Fl, Des Moines, IA 50319; 515-281-5204, Fax: 515-242-5953 or 6556.

www.sos.state.ia.us/new/sos/notaries.html

Direct URL to search licenses: www.sos.state.ia.us/NotaryWeb You can search online using name, business, city, and language.

32 Real Estate Commission, 1918 SE Hulsizer, Ankeny, IA 50021-3941; 515-281-7393.

www.state.ia.us/government/com/prof/realappr/realappr.htm

Direct URL to search licenses: www.state.ia.us/government/com/prof/realappr/approst.htm You can search online using name and county.

33 Department of Professional Licensure, Board of Cosmetology Arts & Sciences Examiners, 321 E 12th St, Lucas State Office Bldg 4th Fl, Des Moines, IA 50319-0075; 515-242-6385.

34 Department of Transportation, Motor Vehicle Division, Office of Driver Svcs, 100 Euclid, Park Fair Mall, Des Moines, IA 50306-9204; 515-237-3079.

The following list indicates the district and division name for each county in the state. If the district or division name of the bankruptcy court is different from the civil/criminal court, it appears in parentheses.

County/Court Cross Reference

County	District	Division
Adair	Southern	Council Bluffs (Des Moines)
Adams	Southern	Council Bluffs (Des Moines)
Allamakee	Northern	Dubuque (Cedar Rapids)
Appanoose	Southern	Des Moines (Central)
Audubon	Southern	Council Bluffs (Des Moines)
Benton	Northern	Cedar Rapids
Black Hawk	Northern	Dubuque (Cedar Rapids)
Boone	Southern	Des Moines (Central)
Bremer	Northern	Dubuque (Cedar Rapids)
Buchanan	Northern	Dubuque (Cedar Rapids)
Buena Vista	Northern	Sioux Cty (Cedar Rapids)
Butler	Northern	Sioux Cty (Cedar Rapids)
Calhoun	Northern	Sioux Cty (Cedar Rapids)
Carroll	Northern	Sioux Cty (Cedar Rapids)
Cass	Southern	Council Bluffs (Des Moines)
Cedar	Northern	Cedar Rapids
Cerro Gordo	Northern	Cedar Rapids
Cherokee	Northern	Sioux Cty (Cedar Rapids)
Chickasaw	Northern	Dubuque (Cedar Rapids)
Clarke	Southern	Council Bluffs (Des Moines)
Clay	Northern	Sioux Cty (Cedar Rapids)
Clayton	Northern	Dubuque (Cedar Rapids)
Clinton	Southern	Council Bluffs (Des Moines)
Crawford	Northern	Sioux Cty (Cedar Rapids)
Dallas	Southern	Des Moines (Central)
Davis	Southern	Des Moines (Central)
Decatur	Southern	Council Bluffs (Des Moines)
Delaware	Northern	Dubuque (Cedar Rapids)
Des Moines	Southern	Des Moines (Central)
Dickinson	Northern	Sioux Cty (Cedar Rapids)
Dubuque	Northern	Dubuque (Cedar Rapids)
Emmet	Northern	Sioux Cty (Cedar Rapids)
Fayette	Northern	Dubuque (Cedar Rapids)
Floyd	Northern	Dubuque (Cedar Rapids)
Franklin	Northern	Sioux Cty (Cedar Rapids)
Fremont	Southern	Council Bluffs (Des Moin
Greene	Southern	Des Moines (Central)
Grundy	Northern	Cedar Rapids
Guthrie	Southern	Des Moines (Central)
Hamilton	Northern	Sioux Cty (Cedar Rapids)
Hancock	Northern	Sioux Cty (Cedar Rapids)
Hardin	Northern	Cedar Rapids
Harrison	Southern	Council Bluffs (Des Moines)
Henry	Southern	Davenport (Des Moines)
Howard	Northern	Dubuque (Cedar Rapids)
Humboldt	Northern	Sioux Cty (Cedar Rapids)
Ida	Northern	Sioux Cty (Cedar Rapids)
Iowa	Northern	Cedar Rapids
Jackson	Northern	Dubuque (Cedar Rapids)
Jasper	Southern	Des Moines (Central)
Jefferson	Southern	Des Moines (Central)
Johnson	Southern	Davenport (Des Moines)
Jones	Northern	Cedar Rapids
Keokuk	Southern	Des Moines (Central)
Kossuth	Northern	Sioux Cty (Cedar Rapids)
Lee	Southern	Davenport (Des Moines)
Linn	Northern	Cedar Rapids
Louisa	Southern	Davenport (Des Moines)
Lucas	Southern	Council Bluffs (Des Moines)
Lyon	Northern	Sioux Cty (Cedar Rapids)
Madison	Southern	Des Moines (Central)
Mahaska	Southern	Des Moines (Central)
Marion	Southern	Des Moines (Central)
Marshall	Southern	Des Moines (Central)
Mills	Southern	Council Bluffs (Des Moines)
Mitchell	Northern	Dubuque (Cedar Rapids)
Monona	Northern	Sioux Cty (Cedar Rapids)
Monroe	Southern	Des Moines (Central)
Montgomery	Southern	Council Bluffs (Des Moines)
Muscatine	Southern	Davenport (Des Moines)
O'Brien	Northern	Sioux Cty (Cedar Rapids)
Osceola	Northern	Sioux Cty (Cedar Rapids)
Page	Southern	Council Bluffs (Des Moines)
Palo Alto	Northern	Sioux Cty (Cedar Rapids)
Plymouth	Northern	Sioux Cty (Cedar Rapids)
Pocahontas	Northern	Sioux Cty (Cedar Rapids)
Polk	Southern	Des Moines (Central)
Pottawattamie	Southern	Council Bluffs (Des Moines)
Poweshiek	Southern	Des Moines (Central)
Ringgold	Southern	Council Bluffs (Des Moines)
Sac	Northern	Sioux Cty (Cedar Rapids)
Scott	Southern	Davenport (Des Moines)
Shelby	Southern	Council Bluffs (Des Moines)
Sioux	Northern	Sioux Cty (Cedar Rapids)
Story	Southern	Des Moines (Central)
Tama	Northern	Cedar Rapids
Taylor	Southern	Council Bluffs (Des Moines)
Union	Southern	Council Bluffs (Des Moines)
Van Buren	Southern	Davenport (Des Moines)
Wapello	Southern	Des Moines (Central)
Warren	Southern	Des Moines (Central)
Washington	Southern	Davenport (Des Moines)
Wayne	Southern	Council Bluffs (Des Moines)
Webster	Northern	Sioux Cty (Cedar Rapids)
Winnebago	Northern	Sioux Cty (Cedar Rapids)
Winneshiek	Northern	Dubuque (Cedar Rapids)
Woodbury	Northern	Sioux Cty (Cedar Rapids)
Worth	Northern	Sioux Cty (Cedar Rapids)
Wright	Northern	Sioux Cty (Cedar Rapids)

US District Court

Northern District of Iowa

Cedar Rapids Division Court Clerk, PO Box 74710, Cedar Rapids, IA 52407-4710 (Courier Address: Federal Bldg, US Courthouse, 101 1st St SE, Room 313, Cedar Rapids, IA 52401), 319-286-2300.

www.iand.uscourts.gov

Counties: Benton, Cedar, Cerro Gordo, Grundy, Hardin, Iowa, Jones, Linn, Tama.

Indexing & Storage: Cases are indexed by defendant and plaintiff as well as by case number. New cases are available in the index immediately after filing date. A computer index is maintained. Open records are located at this court.

Fee & Payment: The fee is $15.00 per item (one party name or case number). Payment may be made by money order, cashier check, personal check. Prepayment is required. Payee: Clerk, US District Court. Certification fee: $5.00 per document. Copy fee: $.50 per page.

Phone Search: Anything that is public record will be released over the phone, but only for one name per call. An automated voice case information service (VCIS) is not available.

Mail Search: A stamped self addressed envelope is not required.

In Person Search: In person searching is available.

PACER: Sign-up number is 800-676-5856. Access fee is $.60 per minute. Toll-free access: 888-845-4528. Local access: 319-362-3256. Case records are available back to November 1992. New records are available online after 1 day.

Dubuque Division c/o Cedar Rapids Division, PO Box 74710, Cedar Rapids, IA 52407-4710 (Courier Address: Federal Bldg, US Courthouse, 101 1st St SE, Room 313, Cedar Rapids, IA 52401), 319-286-2300.

www.iand.uscourts.gov

Counties: Allamakee, Black Hawk, Bremer, Buchanan, Chickasaw, Clayton, Delaware, Dubuque, Fayette, Floyd, Howard, Jackson, Mitchell, Winneshiek.

Indexing & Storage: Cases are indexed by as well as by case number. New cases are available in the index after filing date. Open records are located at the Division.

Fee & Payment: The fee is $15.00 per item (one party name or case number). Payment may be made by money order, cashier check. Business checks are not accepted. Personal checks are not accepted.

Phone Search: An automated voice case information service (VCIS) is not available.

Mail Search: A stamped self addressed envelope is not required.

In Person Search: In person searching is available.

PACER: Sign-up number is 800-676-5856. Access fee is $.60 per minute. Toll-free access: 888-845-4528. Local access: 319-362-3256. Case records are available back to November 1992. New records are available online after 1 day.

Sioux City Division Room 301, Federal Bldg, 320 6th St, Sioux City, IA 51101, 712-233-3900.

www.iand.uscourts.gov

Counties: Buena Vista, Cherokee, Clay, Crawford, Dickinson, Ida, Lyon, Monona, O'Brien, Osceola, Plymouth, Sac, Sioux, Woodbury.

Indexing & Storage: Cases are indexed by defendant and plaintiff as well as by case number. New cases are available in the index immediately after filing date. A computer index is maintained. Open records are located at this court.

Fee & Payment: The fee is $15.00 per item (one party name or case number). Payment may be made by money order, cashier check, personal check. Prepayment is required. Payee: Clerk, US District Court. Certification fee: $5.00 per document. Copy fee: $.50 per page.

Phone Search: Only docket information is available by phone. An automated voice case information service (VCIS) is not available.

Mail Search: Always enclose a stamped self addressed envelope.

In Person Search: In person searching is available.

PACER: Sign-up number is 800-676-5856. Access fee is $.60 per minute. Toll-free access: 888-845-4528. Local access: 319-362-3256. Case records are available back to November 1992. New records are available online after 1 day.

US Bankruptcy Court

Northern District of Iowa

Cedar Rapids Division PO Box 74890, Cedar Rapids, IA 52407-4890 (Courier Address: 8th Floor, 425 2nd St SE, Cedar Rapids, IA 52401), 319-286-2200, Fax: 319-286-2280.

Counties: Allamakee, Benton, Black Hawk, Bremer, Buchanan, Buena Vista, Butler, Calhoun, Carroll, Cedar, Cerro Gordo, Cherokee, Chickasaw, Clay, Clayton, Crawford, Delaware, Dickinson, Dubuque, Emmet, Fayette, Floyd, Franklin, Grundy, Hamilton, Hancock, Hardin, Howard, Humboldt, Ida, Iowa, Jackson, Jones, Kossuth, Linn, Lyon, Mitchell, Monona, O'Brien, Osceola, Palo Alto, Plymouth, Pocahontas, Sac, Sioux, Tama, Webster, Winnebago, Winneshiek, Woodbury, Worth, Wright.

Indexing & Storage: Cases are indexed by debtor and creditors as well as by case number. New cases are available in the index immediately after filing date. A computer index is maintained. Open records are located at this court. District wide searches are available for information from 1988 to the present from this court. This court handles records for the Sioux City division.

Fee & Payment: The fee is $15.00 per item (one party name or case number). Payment may be made by money order, cashier check, business check, Visa or Mastercard. Personal checks are not accepted. Prepayment is required. Checks are accepted from in-state law firms only. Payee: Clerk, US Bankruptcy Court. Certification fee: $5.00 per document. Copy fee: $.50 per page. You are allowed to make your own copies. These copies cost $.25 per page.

Phone Search: Only minimal information will be released over the phone. Not all docket information will be released. An automated voice case information service (VCIS) is available.

Mail Search: Always enclose a stamped self addressed envelope.

In Person Search: In person searching is available.

PACER: PACER is available on the Internet at http://pacer.ianb.uscourts.gov.

US District Court

Southern District of Iowa

Council Bluffs Division PO Box 307, Council Bluffs, IA 51502 (Courier Address: Room 313, 8 S 6th St, Council Bluffs, IA 51501), 712-328-0283, Fax: 712-328-1241.

www.iasd.uscourts.gov

Counties: Audubon, Cass, Fremont, Harrison, Mills, Montgomery, Page, Pottawattamie, Shelby.

Indexing & Storage: Cases are indexed by defendant and plaintiff as well as by case number. New cases are available in the index immediately after filing date. A computer index is maintained. Open records are located at this court.

Fee & Payment: The fee is $15.00 per item (one party name or case number). Payment may be made by money order, cashier check, personal check. The search fee will be charged only if the clerk's staff is required to spend more than 5 minutes searching. Payee: Clerk, US District Court. Certification fee: $5.00 per document. Copy fee: $.50 per page. You are allowed to make your own copies. These copies cost $.50 per page.

Phone Search: All information available will be released over the phone. An automated voice case information service (VCIS) is not available.

Mail Search: Always enclose a stamped self addressed envelope.

In Person Search: In person searching is available.

PACER: Sign-up number is 800-676-6856. Access fee is $.60 per minute. Case records are available back to mid 1989. Records are purged every six months. New records are available online after 3 days. PACER is available on the Internet at http://pacer.iasd.uscourts.gov.

Davenport Division PO Box 256, Davenport, IA 52805 (Courier Address: Room 215, 131 E 4th St, Davenport, IA 52801), Fax: 319-322-2962.

www.iasd.uscourts.gov

Counties: Henry, Johnson, Lee, Louisa, Muscatine, Scott, Van Buren, Washington.

Indexing & Storage: Cases are indexed by defendant and plaintiff as well as by case number. New cases are available in the index 1 week after filing date. All criminal cases are handled in Des Moines Division. Civil cases are handled here. Both computer and card indexes are maintained. Open records are located at this court.

Fee & Payment: The fee is $15.00 per item (one party name or case number). Payment may be made by money order, cashier check, personal check. Will bill fees. Payee: Clerk, US District Court. Certification fee: $5.00 per document. Copy fee: $.50 per page. You are allowed to make your own copies. These copies cost $.50 per page. You are only allowed to search the index cards.

Phone Search: Docket information available by phone. An automated voice case information service (VCIS) is not available.

Fax Search: Fax requests are processed the same as mail searches. Will fax documents for $3.00 up to 9 pages and $5.00 if more, plus copy fees.

Mail Search: A stamped self addressed envelope is not required.

In Person Search: In person searching is available.

PACER: Sign-up number is 800-676-6856. Access fee is $.60 per minute. Case records are available back to mid 1989. Records are purged every six months. New records are available online after 3 days. PACER is available on the Internet at http://pacer.iasd.uscourts.gov.

Des Moines (Central) Division PO Box 9344, Des Moines, IA 50306-9344, 515-284-6248, Fax: 515-284-6418.

www.iasd.uscourts.gov

Counties: Adair, Adams, Appanoose, Boone, Clarke, Clinton, Dallas, Davis, Decatur, Des Moines, Greene, Guthrie, Jasper, Jefferson, Keokuk, Lucas, Madison, Mahaska, Marion, Marshall, Monroe, Polk, Poweshiek, Ringgold, Story, Taylor, Union, Wapello, Warren, Wayne.

Indexing & Storage: Cases are indexed by defendant and plaintiff as well as by case number. New cases are available in the index immediately after filing date. A computer index is maintained. Records are stored by date filed and closed. Open records are located at this court.

Fee & Payment: The fee is $15.00 per item (one party name or case number). Payment may be made by money order, cashier check, personal check. A bill can be sent by mail. Payee: Clerk, US District Court. Certification fee: $5.00 per document. Copy fee: $.50 per page.

Phone Search: Requests for searches must be in writing.

Fax Search: Fax search handled same as mail. Will fax documents for $3.00 up to 9 pages and $5.00 if more, plus copy fee.

Mail Search: A stamped self addressed envelope is not required.

In Person Search: In person searching is available.

PACER: Sign-up number is 800-676-6856. Access fee is $.60 per minute. Case records are available back to mid 1989. Records are purged every six months. New records are available online after 3 days. PACER is available on the Internet at http://pacer.iasd.uscourts.gov.

US Bankruptcy Court

Southern District of Iowa

Des Moines Division PO Box 9264, Des Moines, IA 50306-9264 (Courier Address: 300 US Courthouse Annex, 110 East Court Ave, Des Moines, IA 50309), 515-284-6230, Fax: 515-284-6404.

Counties: Adair, Adams, Appanoose, Audubon, Boone, Cass, Clarke, Clinton, Dallas, Davis, Decatur, Des Moines, Fremont, Greene, Guthrie, Harrison, Henry, Jasper, Jefferson, Johnson, Keokuk, Lee, Louisa, Lucas, Madison, Mahaska, Marion, Marshall, Mills, Monroe,Montgomery, Muscatine, Page, Polk, Pottawattamie, Poweshiek, Ringgold, Scott, Shelby, Story, Taylor, Union, Van Buren, Wapello, Warren, Washington, Wayne.

Indexing & Storage: Cases are indexed by debtor as well as by case number. New cases are available in the index immediately after filing date. A computer index is maintained. Open records are located at this court.

Fee & Payment: The fee is $15.00 per item (one party name or case number). Payment may be made by money order, cashier check, business check. Personal checks are not accepted. Copy requests must be directed to CopyCat Photocopy Center at 515-288-6843. Payee: CopyCat Photocopy Center. Certification fee: $5.00 per document. Copy fee: $.50 per page.

Phone Search: The information released over the phone is: name, case number, chapter date file, assets, attorney, attorney's telephone number, trustee, judge, status and discharge. Information is available from June 1987. An automated voice case information service (VCIS) is available. Call VCIS at 800-597-5917 or 515-284-6427.

Mail Search: Always enclose a stamped self addressed envelope.

In Person Search: In person searching is available.

PACER: Sign-up number is 800-676-6856. Access fee is $.60 per minute. Toll-free access: 800-597-5917. Local access: 515-284-6466. Case records are available back to June 1987. Records are purged every six months. New civil records are available online after 1 day.

Court	Jurisdiction	No. of Courts	How Organized
District Courts*	General	100	8 Districts

* Profiled in this Sourcebook.

CIVIL									
Court	Tort	Contract	Real Estate	Min. Claim	Max. Claim	Small Claims	Estate	Eviction	Domestic Relations
District Courts*	X	X	X	$0	No Max	$4000	X	X	X

CRIMINAL					
Court	Felony	Misdemeanor	DWI/DUI	Preliminary Hearing	Juvenile
District Courts*	X	X	X	X	X

ADMINISTRATION

State Court Administrator, State Capitol, Des Moines, IA, 50319; 515-281-5241, Fax: 515-242-0014. www.judicial.state.ia.us

COURT STRUCTURE

The District Court is the court of general jurisdiction. Effective 7/1/95, the Small Claims limit increased to $4000 from $3000.

Vital records were moved from courts to the County Recorder's office in each county.

ONLINE ACCESS

There is a statewide online computer system called the Iowa Court Information System (ICIS), which is for internal use only. There is no public access system.

ADDITIONAL INFORMATION

In most courts, the Certification Fee is $10.00 plus copy fee. Copy Fee is $.50 per page. Most courts do not do searches and recommend either in person searches or use of a record retriever. Courts that accept written search requests usually require an SASE.

Most courts have a public access terminal for access to that court's records.

Adair County

5th District Court PO Box L, Greenfield, IA 50849; 641-743-2445; Fax: 641-743-2974. Hours: 8AM-4:30PM (CST). *Felony, Misdemeanor, Civil, Eviction, Small Claims, Probate.*

Civil Records: Access: In person only. Court does not conduct in person searches; visitors must perform searches for themselves. Search fee: No civil searches performed by court. Required to search: name, years to search. Civil cases indexed by defendant, plaintiff. Civil records on docket books from late 1800s. **Criminal Records:** Access: In person only. Court does not conduct in person searches; visitors must perform searches for themselves. Search fee: No criminal searches performed by court. Required to search: name, years to search, DOB, signed release; also helpful-SSN. Criminal records on docket books from late 1800s. **General Information:** No juvenile, sealed, dissolution of marriage, mental health domestic abuse or deferred records released. Copy fee: $.50 per page. Certification fee: $10.00. Fee payee: Clerk of Court. Personal checks accepted. Prepayment is required. Public access terminal is available.

Adams County

5th District Court Courthouse, PO Box 484, Corning, IA 50841; 641-322-4711; Fax: 515-322-4523. Hours: 8AM-4:30PM (CST). *Felony, Misdemeanor, Civil, Eviction, Small Claims, Probate.*

Civil Records: Access: In person only. Court does not conduct in person searches; visitors must perform searches for themselves. Search fee: No civil searches performed by court. Required to search: name, years to search. Civil cases indexed by defendant, plaintiff. Civil records on docket books from late 1800s. **Criminal Records:** Access: In person only. Court does not conduct in person searches; visitors must perform searches for themselves. Search fee: No criminal searches performed by court. Required to search: name, years to search, signed release. Criminal records on docket books from late 1800s. **General Information:** No juvenile, sealed, dissolution of marriage, mental health, domestic abuse or deferred records released. Copy fee: $.50 per page. Certification fee: $10.00. Fee payee: Clerk of Court. Personal checks accepted. Prepayment is required. Public access terminal is available.

Allamakee County

1st District Court PO Box 248, Waukon, IA 52172; 319-568-6351. Hours: 8AM-4:30PM (CST). *Felony, Misdemeanor, Civil, Eviction, Small Claims, Probate.*

Civil Records: Access: In person only. Court does not conduct in person searches; visitors must perform searches for themselves. Search fee: No civil searches performed by court. Required to search: name, years to search. Civil cases indexed by defendant, plaintiff. All judgments on computer, vital records (at county recorder's office) on index books back to 1880, probate back to 1852. **Criminal Records:** Access: In person only. Court does not conduct in person searches; visitors must perform searches for themselves. Search fee: No criminal searches performed by court. Required to search: name, years to search, signed release. Criminal records on docket books from 1800s. **General Information:** No juvenile, adoption, sealed, dissolution of marriage, mental health, domestic abuse or deferred records released. Copy fee: $.50 per page. Certification fee: $10.00. Fee payee: Clerk of Court. Personal checks accepted. Prepayment is required.

Appanoose County

8th District Court PO Box 400, Centerville, IA 52544; 641-856-6101; Fax: 641-856-2282. Hours: 8AM-4:30PM (CST). *Felony, Misdemeanor, Civil, Eviction, Small Claims, Probate.*

Civil Records: Access: In person only. Court does not conduct in person searches; visitors must perform searches for themselves. Search fee: No civil searches performed by court. Required to search: name, years to search. Civil cases indexed by defendant, plaintiff. Civil records on docket books from 1847. **Criminal Records:** Access: In person only. Court does not conduct in person searches; visitors must perform searches for themselves. Search fee: No criminal searches performed by court. Required to search: name, years to search, signed release. Criminal records on docket books from 1847. **General Information:** No juvenile, sealed, dissolution of marriage, mental health, domestic abuse or deferred records released. Copy fee: $.25 per page. Certification fee: $10.00. Fee payee: Clerk of Court. Personal checks accepted. Prepayment is required. Public access terminal is available.

Audubon County

4th District Court 318 Leroy St #6, Audubon, IA 50025; 712-563-4275; Fax: 712-563-4276. Hours: 8AM-4:30PM (CST). *Felony, Misdemeanor, Civil, Eviction, Small Claims, Probate.*

Civil Records: Access: Mail, in person. Both court and visitors may perform in person searches. Search fee: $10.00 per name. Required to search:

name, years to search; also helpful-address. Civil cases indexed by defendant, plaintiff. Civil records on docket books from 1930s, computerized since 1996. **Criminal Records:** Access: Mail, in person. Both court and visitors may perform in person searches. Search fee: $10.00 per name. Required to search: name, years to search, DOB, SSN, signed release; also helpful-address. Criminal records on docket books from late 1800s. SSNs are not released to the public. **General Information:** No juvenile, sealed, dissolution of marriage, mental health, domestic abuse or deferred records released. SASE required. Turnaround time 10 days. Copy fee: $.50 per page. Certification fee: $10.00. Fee payee: Clerk of Court. Personal checks accepted. Credit cards accepted. Prepayment is required.

Benton County

6th District Court PO Box 719, Vinton, IA 52349; 319-472-2766; Fax: 319-472-2747. Hours: 8AM-4:30PM (CST). *Felony, Misdemeanor, Civil, Eviction, Small Claims, Probate.*

Civil Records: Access: In person only. Court does not conduct in person searches; visitors must perform searches for themselves. Search fee: No civil searches performed by court. Required to search: name, years to search. Civil cases indexed by defendant, plaintiff. Civil records on original record books from 1800s, index is on computer since 06/95. **Criminal Records:** Access: In person only. Court does not conduct in person searches; visitors must perform searches for themselves. Search fee: No criminal searches performed by court. Required to search: name, years to search. Criminal records on original record books from 1800s, index is on computer since 06/95. **General Information:** No juvenile, sealed, dissolution of marriage, mental health, domestic abuse or deferred records released. Copy fee: $.25 per page. Certification fee: $10.00. Fee payee: Clerk of Court. Personal checks accepted. Prepayment is required. Public access terminal is available.

Black Hawk County

1st District Court 316 E 5th St, Waterloo, IA 50703; 319-291-2612. Hours: 8AM-4:30PM (CST). *Felony, Misdemeanor, Civil, Eviction, Small Claims, Probate.*

Civil Records: Access: In person only. Court does not conduct in person searches; visitors must perform searches for themselves. Search fee: No civil searches performed by court. Required to search: name, years to search. Civil cases indexed by defendant, plaintiff. Civil records on computer from 1992, docket books from early 1900s. **Criminal Records:** Access: In person only. Court does not conduct in person searches; visitors must perform searches for themselves. Search fee: No criminal searches performed by court. Required to search: name, years to search; also helpful-DOB, SSN. Criminal records on computer from 1992, docket books from early 1900s. **General Information:** No juvenile, sealed, dissolution of marriage, mental health, domestic abuse or deferred records released. Copy fee: $.50 per page. Certification fee: $10.00. Fee payee: District Court. Personal checks accepted. Prepayment is required. Public access terminal is available.

Boone County

2nd District Court 201 State St, Boone, IA 50036; 515-433-0561; Fax: 515-433-0563. Hours: 8AM-4:30PM (CST). *Felony, Misdemeanor, Civil, Eviction, Small Claims, Probate.*

Civil Records: Access: In person only. Court does not conduct in person searches; visitors must perform searches for themselves. Search fee: No civil searches performed by court. Required to search: name, years to search. Civil cases indexed by defendant, plaintiff. Civil records on docket books from 1890s. **Criminal Records:** Access: In person only. Court does not conduct in person searches; visitors must perform searches for themselves. Search fee: No criminal searches performed by court. Required to search: name, years to search, offense, date of offense. Criminal records on docket books from 1890s. **General Information:** No juvenile, sealed, dissolution of marriage, mental health, domestic abuse or deferred records released. Copy fee: $.50 per page. Certification fee: $10.00. Fee payee: Clerk of Court. Personal checks accepted. Prepayment is required.

Bremer County

2nd District Court PO Box 328, Waverly, IA 50677; 319-352-5661; Fax: 319-352-1054. Hours: 8AM-4:30PM (CST). *Felony, Misdemeanor, Civil, Eviction, Small Claims, Probate.*

Civil Records: Access: In person only. Court does not conduct in person searches; visitors must perform searches for themselves. Search fee: No civil searches performed by court. Required to search: name, years to search. Civil cases indexed by defendant, plaintiff. Civil records on computer since 07/96; prior records on docket books from 1880s. **Criminal Records:** Access: In person only. Court does not conduct in person searches; visitors must perform searches for themselves. Search fee: No criminal searches performed by court. Required to search: name, years to search. Criminal records on computer since 07/96; prior records on docket books from 1880s. **General Information:** No juvenile, sealed, dissolution of marriage, mental health, domestic abuse or deferred records released. Copy fee: $.50 per page. Certification fee: $10.00. Fee payee: Clerk of Court. Personal checks accepted. Credit cards accepted: Visa, Mastercard. Prepayment is required. Public access terminal is available. Terminal has records since 1996 only.

Buchanan County

1st District Court PO Box 259, Independence, IA 50644; 319-334-2196; Fax: 319-334-7455. Hours: 8AM-4:30PM (CST). *Felony, Misdemeanor, Civil, Eviction, Small Claims, Probate.*

Civil Records: Access: Mail, in person. Both court and visitors may perform in person searches. No search fee. Required to search: name, years to search. Civil cases indexed by defendant, plaintiff. Civil records on docket books from 1900s. **Criminal Records:** Access: Mail, in person. Both court and visitors may perform in person searches. No search fee. Required to search: name, years to search. Criminal records on docket books from 1900s. **General Information:** No juvenile, sealed, dissolution of marriage, mental health, domestic abuse or deferred records released. SASE required. Turnaround time 2 days. Copy fee: $.50 per page. Certification fee: $10.00. Fee payee: Clerk of Court. Personal checks accepted. Credit cards accepted: Visa, Mastercard. Prepayment is required.

Buena Vista County

3rd District Court PO Box 1186, Storm Lake, IA 50588; 712-749-2546; Fax: 712-749-2700. Hours: 8AM-4:30PM (CST). *Felony,*

Misdemeanor, Civil, Eviction, Small Claims, Probate.

Civil Records: Access: In person only. Court does not conduct in person searches; visitors must perform searches for themselves. Search fee: No civil searches performed by court. Required to search: name, years to search. Civil cases indexed by defendant, plaintiff. Civil records on index cards from early 1900s. **Criminal Records:** Access: In person only. Court does not conduct in person searches; visitors must perform searches for themselves. Search fee: No criminal searches performed by court. Required to search: name, years to search. Criminal records on index cards from early 1900s. **General Information:** No juvenile, sealed, dissolution of marriage, mental health, domestic abuse or deferred records released. Copy fee: $.50 per page. Certification fee: $10.00. Fee payee: Clerk of Court. Personal checks accepted. Prepayment is required. Public access terminal is available.

Butler County

2nd District Court PO Box 307, Allison, IA 50602; 319-267-2487; Fax: 319-267-2488. Hours: 8AM-4:30PM (CST). *Felony, Misdemeanor, Civil, Eviction, Small Claims, Probate.*

Civil Records: Access: In person only. Court does not conduct in person searches; visitors must perform searches for themselves. Search fee: No civil searches performed by court. Required to search: name, years to search. Civil cases indexed by defendant, plaintiff. Civil records on docket books from 1800s. **Criminal Records:** Access: In person only. Court does not conduct in person searches; visitors must perform searches for themselves. Search fee: No criminal searches performed by court. Required to search: name, years to search. Criminal records on docket books from 1800s. **General Information:** No juvenile, sealed, dissolution of marriage, mental health, domestic abuse or deferred records released. Copy fee: $1.00 for first page, $.50 each addl. Certification fee: $10.00. Fee payee: Clerk of Court. Personal checks accepted. Prepayment is required. Public access terminal is available.

Calhoun County

2nd District Court Box 273, Rockwell City, IA 50579; 712-297-8122; Fax: 712-297-5082. Hours: 8AM-4:30PM (CST). *Felony, Misdemeanor, Civil, Eviction, Small Claims, Probate.*

Civil Records: Access: In person only. Court does not conduct in person searches; visitors must perform searches for themselves. Search fee: No civil searches performed by court. Required to search: name, years to search. Civil cases indexed by defendant, plaintiff. Civil records on docket books, computerized since 07/97. **Criminal Records:** Access: In person only. Court does not conduct in person searches; visitors must perform searches for themselves. Search fee: No criminal searches performed by court. Required to search: name, years to search, DOB, signed release; also helpful-SSN. Criminal records on docket books, computerized since 07/97. **General Information:** No juvenile, sealed, dissolution of marriage, mental health, domestic abuse or deferred records released. Copy fee: $.50 per page. Certification fee: $10.00. Fee payee: Clerk of the Court. Personal checks accepted. Credit cards accepted: Visa, Mastercard. Prepayment is required.

Carroll County

2nd District Court PO Box 867, Carroll, IA 51401; 712-792-4327; Fax: 712-792-4328. Hours: 8AM-4:30PM *Felony, Misdemeanor, Civil, Eviction, Small Claims, Probate.*

Civil Records: Access: In person only. Court does not conduct in person searches; visitors must perform searches for themselves. Search fee: No civil searches performed by court. Required to search: name, years to search. Civil cases indexed by defendant, plaintiff. Civil records on index books from 1800s. **Criminal Records:** Access: In person only. Court does not conduct in person searches; visitors must perform searches for themselves. Search fee: No criminal searches performed by court. Required to search: name, years to search. Criminal records on computer from June, 1994, index books from 1800s. **General Information:** No juvenile, sealed, dissolution of marriage, mental health, domestic abuse or deferred records released. Copy fee: $.50 per page. Certification fee: $10.00. Fee payee: Clerk of Court. Personal checks accepted. Credit cards accepted. Prepayment is required. Public access terminal is available.

Cass County

4th District Court 5 W 7th St, Courthouse, Atlantic, IA 50022; 712-243-2105. Hours: 8AM-4:30PM (CST). *Felony, Misdemeanor, Civil, Eviction, Small Claims, Probate.*

Civil Records: Access: In person only. Court does not conduct in person searches; visitors must perform searches for themselves. Search fee: No civil searches performed by court. Required to search: name, years to search. Civil cases indexed by defendant, plaintiff. Civil records on docket books from early 1900s. **Criminal Records:** Access: In person only. Court does not conduct in · person searches; visitors must perform searches for themselves. Search fee: No criminal searches performed by court. Required to search: name, years to search, signed release; also helpful-DOB, SSN. Criminal records on docket books from early 1900s. **General Information:** No juvenile, sealed, dissolution of marriage, mental health, domestic abuse or deferred records released. Copy fee: $.50 per page. Certification fee: $10.00. Fee payee: Clerk of Court. Personal checks accepted. Prepayment is required. Public access terminal is available.

Cedar County

7th District Court PO Box 111, Tipton, IA 52772; 319-886-2101. Hours: 8AM-4:30PM (CST). *Felony, Misdemeanor, Civil, Eviction, Small Claims, Probate.*

Civil Records: Access: Mail, in person. Both court and visitors may perform in person searches. Search fee: $10.00 per name. Required to search: name, years to search. Civil cases indexed by defendant, plaintiff. Civil records on microfiche and docket books from 1839. **Criminal Records:** Access: Mail, in person. Both court and visitors may perform in person searches. Search fee: $10.00 per name. Required to search: name, years to search; also helpful-DOB, SSN. Criminal records on computer since 1993, microfiche and docket books from 1839. **General Information:** No juvenile, sealed, dissolution of marriage, mental health, domestic abuse or deferred records released. SASE required. Turnaround time 1 week. Copy fee: $.50 per page. Certification fee: $10.00. Fee payee: Clerk of Court. Only cashiers checks or money orders accepted. Prepayment is required.

Cerro Gordo County

2nd District Court 220 W Washington, Mason City, IA 50401; 641-424-6431. Hours: 8AM-4:30PM (CST). *Felony, Misdemeanor, Civil, Eviction, Small Claims, Probate.*

Civil Records: Access: In person only. Court does not conduct in person searches; visitors must perform searches for themselves. Search fee: No civil searches performed by court. Required to search: name, years to search. Civil cases indexed by defendant, plaintiff. Civil records on computer since 1996; prior records on docket books from early 1900s. **Criminal Records:** Access: In person only. Court does not conduct in person searches; visitors must perform searches for themselves. Search fee: No criminal searches performed by court. Required to search: name, years to search; also helpful-DOB, SSN. Criminal records on computer since 4/95; prior records on index cards from 1977. **General Information:** No juvenile, sealed, dissolution of marriage, mental health, domestic abuse or deferred records released. Copy fee: $.50 per page. Certification fee: $10.00. Fee payee: Clerk of Court. Personal checks accepted. Credit cards accepted. Prepayment is required. Public access terminal is available.

Cherokee County

3rd District Court Courthouse Drawer F, Cherokee, IA 51012; 712-225-6744; Fax: 712-225-6749. Hours: 8AM-4:30PM (CST). *Felony, Misdemeanor, Civil, Eviction, Small Claims, Probate.*

Civil Records: Access: In person only. Court does not conduct in person searches; visitors must perform searches for themselves. Search fee: No civil searches performed by court. Required to search: name, years to search. Civil cases indexed by defendant, plaintiff. Civil records on docket books from 1800s, indexed on computer since 1997. **Criminal Records:** Access: In person only. Court does not conduct in person searches; visitors must perform searches for themselves. Search fee: No criminal searches performed by court. Required to search: name, years to search. index is computerized since 06/90. **General Information:** No juvenile, sealed, dissolution of marriage, mental health, domestic abuse or deferred records released. Copy fee: $.50 per page. Certification fee: $10.00. Fee payee: Clerk of Court. Personal checks accepted. Prepayment is required. Public access terminal is available.

Chickasaw County

1st District Court County Courthouse, 8 E Prospect, New Hampton, IA 50659; 641-394-2106; Fax: 641-394-5106. Hours: 8AM-4:30PM (CST). *Felony, Misdemeanor, Civil, Eviction, Small Claims, Probate.*

Civil Records: Access: In person only. Court does not conduct in person searches; visitors must perform searches for themselves. Search fee: No civil searches performed by court. Required to search: name, years to search. Civil cases indexed by defendant, plaintiff. Civil records on docket books from late 1800s. **Criminal Records:** Access: In person only. Court does not conduct in person searches; visitors must perform searches for themselves. Search fee: No criminal searches performed by court. Required to search: name, years to search, signed release. Criminal records on docket books from late 1800s. **General Information:** No juvenile, sealed, dissolution of marriage, adoption, mental health, domestic abuse or deferred records released. Copy fee: $.50. $.25

per page after first 10. Certification fee: $10.00. Fee payee: Clerk of District Court. Personal checks accepted. Prepayment is required. Public access terminal is available.

Clarke County

5th District Court Clarke County Courthouse, Osceola, IA 50213; 641-342-6096; Fax: 641-342-2463. Hours: 8AM-4:30PM (CST). *Felony, Misdemeanor, Civil, Eviction, Small Claims, Probate.*

Civil Records: Access: In person only. Both court and visitors may perform in person searches. No search fee. Required to search: name, years to search. Civil cases indexed by defendant, plaintiff. Civil records on docket books from early 1900s. **Criminal Records:** Access: In person only. Both court and visitors may perform in person searches. No search fee. Required to search: name, years to search; also helpful-SSN. Criminal records on docket books from early 1900s. **General Information:** No juvenile, sealed, dissolution of marriage, mental health, domestic abuse or deferred records released. Copy fee: $.25 per page. Certification fee: $10.00. Fee payee: Clerk of Court. Personal checks accepted. Prepayment is required. Public access terminal is available.

Clay County

3rd District Court Courthouse 215 W 4th St, Spencer, IA 51301; 712-262-4335. Hours: 8AM-4:30PM (CST). *Felony, Misdemeanor, Civil, Eviction, Small Claims, Probate.*

Civil Records: Access: In person only. Court does not conduct in person searches; visitors must perform searches for themselves. Search fee: No civil searches performed by court. Required to search: name, years to search. Civil cases indexed by defendant, plaintiff. Civil records on microfilm from to 1972 to 1995, docket books from 1800s. **Criminal Records:** Access: In person only. Court does not conduct in person searches; visitors must perform searches for themselves. Search fee: No criminal searches performed by court. Required to search: name, years to search. Criminal records on microfilm from to 1972 to 1995, docket books from 1800s. **General Information:** No juvenile, sealed, pending dissolution of marriage, mental health, sealed domestic abuse or deferred records released. Copy fee: $.50 per page. Certification fee: $10.00. Fee payee: Clerk of Court. Personal checks accepted. Credit cards accepted: Visa, Mastercard. Public access terminal is available.

Clayton County

1st District Court PO Box 418, Clayton County Courthouse, Elkader, IA 52043; 319-245-2204; Fax: 319-245-2825. Hours: 8AM-4:30PM (CST). *Felony, Misdemeanor, Civil, Eviction, Small Claims, Probate.*

Civil Records: Access: In person only. Court does not conduct in person searches; visitors must perform searches for themselves. Search fee: No civil searches performed by court. Required to search: name, years to search. Civil cases indexed by defendant, plaintiff. Civil records on docket books from late 1880s. **Criminal Records:** Access: In person only. Court does not conduct in person searches; visitors must perform searches for themselves. Search fee: No criminal searches performed by court. Required to search: name, years to search. Criminal records on docket books from late 1880s. **General Information:** No juvenile, sealed, dissolution of marriage, mental health, domestic abuse or deferred records released. Copy fee: $.50 per page. Certification fee: $10.00. Fee payee: Clerk of Court. Personal checks accepted. Prepayment is required. Public access terminal is available.

Clinton County

7th District Court Courthouse (PO Box 2957), Clinton, IA 52733; 319-243-6210; Fax: 319-243-3655. Hours: 8AM-4:30PM (CST). *Felony, Misdemeanor, Civil, Eviction, Small Claims, Probate.*

Civil Records: Access: In person only. Court does not conduct in person searches; visitors must perform searches for themselves. Search fee: No civil searches performed by court. Required to search: name, years to search. Civil cases indexed by defendant. Civil records on computer since 1980, on docket books prior. **Criminal Records:** Access: In person only. Court does not conduct in person searches; visitors must perform searches for themselves. Search fee: No criminal searches performed by court. Required to search: name, years to search, DOB, signed release; also helpful-SSN. Criminal records on computer since 1980, on docket books prior. **General Information:** No juvenile, adoption, sealed, disssolution of marriage before decree, mental health, domestic abuse or deferred records released. Copy fee: $.50 per page. Certification fee: $10.00. Fee payee: Clerk of Court. Personal checks accepted. Credit cards accepted: Visa, Mastercard. Prepayment is required. Public access terminal is available.

Crawford County

3rd District Court 1202 Broadway, Denison, IA 51442; 712-263-2242; Fax: 712-263-5753. Hours: 8AM-4:30PM (CST). *Felony, Misdemeanor, Civil, Eviction, Small Claims, Probate.*

Civil Records: Access: In person only. Court does not conduct in person searches; visitors must perform searches for themselves. Search fee: No civil searches performed by court. Required to search: name, years to search. Civil cases indexed by defendant, plaintiff. Civil records available since 1937, on docket books from 1869. **Criminal Records:** Access: In person only. Court does not conduct in person searches; visitors must perform searches for themselves. Search fee: No criminal searches performed by court. Required to search: name, years to search. Criminal records available since 1937, on docket books from 1869. **General Information:** No juvenile, sealed, disssolution of marriage, mental health, domestic abuse or deferred records released. Copy fee: $.50 per page. Certification fee: $10.00. Fee payee: Clerk of Court. Personal checks accepted. Prepayment is required. Public access terminal is available.

Dallas County

5th District Court 801 Court St, Adel, IA 50003; 515-993-5816; Fax: 515-993-4752. Hours: 8AM-4:30PM (CST). *Felony, Misdemeanor, Civil, Eviction, Small Claims, Probate.*

Civil Records: Access: In person only. Court does not conduct in person searches; visitors must perform searches for themselves. Search fee: No civil searches performed by court. Required to search: name, years to search. Civil cases indexed by defendant, plaintiff. Civil records on docket books from 1800s. **Criminal Records:** Access: In person only. Court does not conduct in person searches; visitors must perform searches for themselves. Search fee: No criminal searches performed by court. Required to search: name, years to search. Criminal records on docket books from 1800s. **General Information:** No juvenile,

sealed, dissolution of marriage, mental health, domestic abuse or deferred records released. Copy fee: $.50 per page. Certification fee: $10.00. Fee payee: Clerk of Court. Personal checks accepted. Prepayment is required. Public access terminal is available.

Davis County

8th District Court Davis County Courthouse, Bloomfield, IA 52537; 641-664-2011; Fax: 641-664-2041. Hours: 8AM-4:30PM (CST). *Felony, Misdemeanor, Civil, Eviction, Small Claims, Probate.*

Civil Records: Access: In person only. Court does not conduct in person searches; visitors must perform searches for themselves. Search fee: No civil searches performed by court. Required to search: name, years to search. Civil cases indexed by defendant, plaintiff. Civil records on docket books from late 1800s. **Criminal Records:** Access: In person only. Court does not conduct in person searches; visitors must perform searches for themselves. Search fee: No criminal searches performed by court. Required to search: name, years to search, DOB. Criminal records on docket books from late 1800s. **General Information:** No juvenile, sealed, dissolution of marriage, mental health, domestic abuse or deferred records released. Copy fee: $.25 per page. Certification fee: $10.00. Fee payee: Clerk of Court. Personal checks accepted. Prepayment is required. Public access terminal is available. Public Access Terminal Note: Records available since 1997.

Decatur County

5th District Court 207 N Main St, Leon, IA 50144; 641-446-4331; Fax: 641-446-3759. Hours: 8AM-4:30PM (CST). *Felony, Misdemeanor, Civil, Eviction, Small Claims, Probate.*

Civil Records: Access: Fax, mail, in person. Both court and visitors may perform in person searches. No search fee. Required to search: name, years to search. Civil cases indexed by defendant, plaintiff. Civil records on docket books since 1880. **Criminal Records:** Access: Fax, mail, in person. Both court and visitors may perform in person searches. No search fee. Required to search: name, years to search, DOB. Criminal records on docket books since 1880. **General Information:** No juvenile, sealed, dissolution of marriage, mental health, domestic abuse or deferred records released. SASE required. Turnaround time same day. Copy fee: $.25 per page. Certification fee: $10.00. Fee payee: Clerk of Court. Personal checks accepted. Fax notes: No fee to fax results.

Delaware County

District Court Delaware County Courthouse, PO Box 527, Manchester, IA 52057; 319-927-4942; Fax: 319-927-3074. Hours: 8AM-4:30PM (CST). *Felony, Misdemeanor, Civil, Eviction, Small Claims, Probate.*

Civil Records: Access: In person only. Court does not conduct in person searches; visitors must perform searches for themselves. Search fee: No civil searches performed by court. Required to search: name, years to search. Civil cases indexed by defendant, plaintiff. Civil records on docket books from late 1800s. **Criminal Records:** Access: In person only. Court does not conduct in person searches; visitors must perform searches for themselves. Search fee: No criminal searches performed by court. Required to search: name, years to search. Criminal records on docket books from late 1800s. **General Information:** No juvenile, sealed, dissolution of marriage, mental

health, domestic abuse or deferred records released. Copy fee: $.50 per page. Certification fee: $10.00. Fee payee: Clerk of Court. Personal checks accepted. Prepayment is required.

Des Moines County

8th District Court 513 Main St, PO Box 158, Burlington, IA 52601; 319-753-8262/8242; Fax: 319-753-8253. Hours: 8AM-4:30PM (CST). *Felony, Misdemeanor, Civil, Eviction, Small Claims, Probate.*

Civil Records: Access: In person only. Court does not conduct in person searches; visitors must perform searches for themselves. Search fee: No civil searches performed by court. Required to search: name, years to search; also helpful-address. Civil cases indexed by defendant, plaintiff. Civil records on computer from July, 1992, docket books prior. **Criminal Records:** Access: In person only. Court does not conduct in person searches; visitors must perform searches for themselves. Search fee: No criminal searches performed by court. Required to search: name, years to search, aliases; also helpful-DOB, SSN. Criminal records on computer from July, 1992, docket books prior. **General Information:** No juvenile, sealed, dissolution of marriage, mental health, domestic abuse or deferred records released. Copy fee: $.25 per page. Certification fee: $10.00. Fee payee: Clerk of Court. Personal checks accepted. Credit cards accepted: Visa, Mastercard. Public access terminal is available.

Dickinson County

3rd District Court PO Drawer O N, Spirit Lake, IA 51360; 712-336-1138; Fax: 712-336-4005. Hours: 8AM-4:30PM (CST). *Felony, Misdemeanor, Civil, Eviction, Small Claims, Probate.*

Civil Records: Access: In person only. Court does not conduct in person searches; visitors must perform searches for themselves. Search fee: No civil searches performed by court. Required to search: name, years to search. Civil cases indexed by defendant, plaintiff. Early information on microfiche, docket books from 1800s. **Criminal Records:** Access: In person only. Court does not conduct in person searches; visitors must perform searches for themselves. Search fee: No criminal searches performed by court. Required to search: name, years to search. Early information on microfiche, docket books from 1800s. **General Information:** No juvenile, sealed, dissolution of marriage, mental health, domestic abuse or deferred records released. Copy fee: $.50 per page. Certification fee: $10.00. Fee payee: Clerk of Court. Personal checks accepted. Public access terminal is available.

Dubuque County

1st District Court 720 Central, Dubuque, IA 52001; 319-589-4418. Hours: 8AM-4:30PM (CST). *Felony, Misdemeanor, Civil, Eviction, Small Claims, Probate.*

Civil Records: Access: In person only. Court does not conduct in person searches; visitors must perform searches for themselves. Search fee: No civil searches performed by court. Required to search: name, years to search. Civil cases indexed by defendant, plaintiff. Civil records on computer since July, 1994, on docket books from 1900s. **Criminal Records:** Access: In person only. Court does not conduct in person searches; visitors must perform searches for themselves. Search fee: No criminal searches performed by court. Required to search: name, years to search; also helpful-DOB,

SSN. Criminal records on computer since July, 1994, on docket books from 1900s. **General Information:** No juvenile, sealed, dissolution of marriage, mental health, domestic abuse or expunged records released. Copy fee: $.50 per page. Certification fee: $10.00. Fee payee: Clerk of District Court. Local checks accepted. Credit cards accepted: Visa, Mastercard. Prepayment is required. Public access terminal is available.

Emmet County

3rd District Court Emmet County, 609 1st Ave N, Estherville, IA 51334; 712-362-3325. Hours: 8AM-4:30PM (CST). *Felony, Misdemeanor, Civil, Eviction, Small Claims, Probate.*

Civil Records: Access: In person only. Court does not conduct in person searches; visitors must perform searches for themselves. Search fee: No civil searches performed by court. Required to search: name, years to search. Civil cases indexed by defendant, plaintiff. Civil records on docket books from 1900s. **Criminal Records:** Access: In person only. Court does not conduct in person searches; visitors must perform searches for themselves. Search fee: No criminal searches performed by court. Required to search: name, years to search. Criminal records on docket books from 1900s. **General Information:** No juvenile, sealed, dissolution of marriage, mental health, domestic abuse or deferred records released. Copy fee: $.25 per page. Certification fee: $10.00. Fee payee: Clerk of Court. Personal checks accepted. Public access terminal is available. Public Access Terminal Note: Records available since 1996.

Fayette County

Fayette County District Court PO Box 458, West Union, IA 52175; 319-422-5694; Fax: 319-422-3137. Hours: 8AM-4:30PM (CST). *Felony, Misdemeanor, Civil, Eviction, Small Claims, Probate, Traffic.*

Civil Records: Access: In person only. Court does not conduct in person searches; visitors must perform searches for themselves. Search fee: No civil searches performed by court. Required to search: name, years to search. Civil cases indexed by defendant, plaintiff. Civil records on docket books from 1900s. **Criminal Records:** Access: In person only. Court does not conduct in person searches; visitors must perform searches for themselves. Search fee: No criminal searches performed by court. Required to search: name, years to search. Criminal records on docket books from 1900s. Contact Fayette Co Abstract Co, West Union, IA 52175. **General Information:** No juvenile, sealed, dissolution of marriage, mental health, domestic abuse or deferred records released. Copy fee: $.50 per page. Certification fee: $10.00. Fee payee: Clerk of Court. Personal checks accepted. Prepayment is required. Public access terminal is available.

Floyd County

2nd District Court 101 S Main St, Charles City, IA 50616; 641-257-6122; Fax: 641-257-6125. Hours: 8AM-4:30PM (CST). *Felony, Misdemeanor, Civil, Eviction, Small Claims, Probate.*

Civil Records: Access: In person only. Court does not conduct in person searches; visitors must perform searches for themselves. Search fee: No civil searches performed by court. Required to search: name, years to search. Civil cases indexed by defendant, plaintiff. Civil records in docket books, are computerized since 1996. **Criminal**

Records: Access: In person only. Court does not conduct in person searches; visitors must perform searches for themselves. Search fee: No criminal searches performed by court. Required to search: name, years to search, DOB, signed release; also helpful-SSN. Criminal records in docket books, are computerized since 1996. **General Information:** No juvenile, sealed, dissolution of marriage, mental health, domestic abuse or deferred records released. Copy fee: $.50 per page. Certification fee: $10.00. Fee payee: Clerk of Court. Personal checks accepted. Credit cards accepted. Public access terminal is available.

Franklin County

2nd Judicial District Court 12 1st Ave NW, PO Box 28, Hampton, IA 50441; 641-456-5626; Fax: 641-456-5628. Hours: 8AM-4:30PM (CST). *Felony, Misdemeanor, Civil, Eviction, Small Claims, Probate.*

Civil Records: Access: In person only. Court does not conduct in person searches; visitors must perform searches for themselves. Search fee: No civil searches performed by court. Required to search: name, years to search. Civil cases indexed by defendant, plaintiff. Civil records on microfiche and/or microfilm from 1860 to 1984, on docket books from 1984 to present. **Criminal Records:** Access: In person only. Court does not conduct in person searches; visitors must perform searches for themselves. Search fee: No criminal searches performed by court. Required to search: name, years to search. Criminal records on microfiche and/or microfilm from 1860 to 1984, on docket books from 1984 to present. **General Information:** No juvenile, sealed, dissolution of marriage, mental health, domestic abuse or deferred records released. Copy fee: $.50 per page. Certification fee: $10.00. Fee payee: Clerk of District Court. Personal checks accepted. Credit cards accepted: Visa, Mastercard. Credit cards accepted for traffic fees only. Prepayment is required.

Fremont County

4th District Court PO Box 549, Sidney, IA 51652; 712-374-2232; Fax: 712-374-3330. Hours: 8AM-4:30PM (CST). *Felony, Misdemeanor, Civil, Eviction, Small Claims, Probate.*

Civil Records: Access: In person only. Court does not conduct in person searches; visitors must perform searches for themselves. Search fee: No civil searches performed by court. Required to search: name, years to search. Civil cases indexed by defendant, plaintiff. Civil records in docket books and microfiche since 1927. **Criminal Records:** Access: In person only. Court does not conduct in person searches; visitors must perform searches for themselves. Search fee: No criminal searches performed by court. Required to search: name, years to search. Criminal records in docket books and microfiche since 1927. **General Information:** No juvenile, sealed, dissolution of marriage, mental health, domestic abuse or deferred records released. Copy fee: $.25 per page. Certification fee: $10.00. Fee payee: Clerk of Court. Personal checks accepted. Prepayment is required. Public access terminal is available.

Greene County

2nd District Court Greene County Courthouse, 114 N Chestnut, Jefferson, IA 50129; 515-386-2516. Hours: 8AM-4:30PM (CST). *Felony, Misdemeanor, Civil, Eviction, Small Claims, Probate.*

Civil Records: Access: In person only. Court does not conduct in person searches; visitors must perform searches for themselves. Search fee: No civil searches performed by court. Required to search: name, years to search. Civil cases indexed by defendant, plaintiff. Civil records on microfiche from 1981 back to establishment of court, docket books from 1800s. **Criminal Records:** Access: In person only. Court does not conduct in person searches; visitors must perform searches for themselves. Search fee: No criminal searches performed by court. Required to search: name, years to search. Criminal records on microfiche from 1981 back to establishment of court, docket books from 1800s. **General Information:** No juvenile, sealed, dissolution of marriage, mental health, domestic abuse or deferred records released. Copy fee: $.50 per page. Certification fee: $10.00. Fee payee: Clerk of Court. Personal checks accepted. Credit cards accepted: Visa, Mastercard. Credit cards accepted for traffic fees only. Prepayment is required. Public access terminal is available.

Grundy County

1st District Court Grundy County Courthouse, 706 G Ave, Grundy Center, IA 50638; 319-824-5229; Fax: 319-824-3447. Hours: 8AM-4:30PM (CST). *Felony, Misdemeanor, Civil, Eviction, Small Claims, Probate.*

Civil Records: Access: In person only. Court does not conduct in person searches; visitors must perform searches for themselves. Search fee: No civil searches performed by court. Required to search: name, years to search. Civil cases indexed by defendant, plaintiff. Civil records on docket books from 1881. **Criminal Records:** Access: In person only. Court does not conduct in person searches; visitors must perform searches for themselves. Search fee: No criminal searches performed by court. Required to search: name, years to search. Criminal records on docket books from 1881. **General Information:** No juvenile, sealed, dissolution of marriage, mental health, domestic abuse or deferred records released. Copy fee: $.50 per page. Certification fee: $10.00. Fee payee: Clerk of Court. Personal checks accepted. Credit cards accepted: Visa, Mastercard. Prepayment is required. Public access terminal is available.

Guthrie County

5th District Court Courthouse, 200 N 5th St, Guthrie Center, IA 50115; 641-747-3415. Hours: 8AM-4:30PM (CST). *Felony, Misdemeanor, Civil, Eviction, Small Claims, Probate.*

Civil Records: Access: In person only. Court does not conduct in person searches; visitors must perform searches for themselves. Search fee: No civil searches performed by court. Required to search: name, years to search. Civil cases indexed by defendant, plaintiff. Civil records on computer since 11/96; prior records on docket books from 1880s. **Criminal Records:** Access: In person only. Court does not conduct in person searches; visitors must perform searches for themselves. Search fee: No criminal searches performed by court. Required to search: name, years to search. Criminal records on computer since 11/96; prior records on docket books from 1880s. **General Information:** No juvenile, sealed, dissolution of marriage, mental health, domestic abuse or deferred records released. Copy fee: $.50 per page. Certification fee: $10.00. Fee payee: Clerk of Court. Personal checks accepted. Prepayment is required. Public access terminal is available.

Hamilton County

2nd District Court Courthouse PO Box 845, Webster City, IA 50595; 515-832-9600. Hours: 8AM-4:30PM (CST). *Felony, Misdemeanor, Civil, Eviction, Small Claims, Probate.*

Civil Records: Access: In person only. Court does not conduct in person searches; visitors must perform searches for themselves. Search fee: No civil searches performed by court. Required to search: name, years to search. Civil cases indexed by defendant, plaintiff. Civil records on microfiche from 1939, docket books from 1880s. **Criminal Records:** Access: In person only. Court does not conduct in person searches; visitors must perform searches for themselves. Search fee: No criminal searches performed by court. Required to search: name, years to search. Criminal records on microfiche from 1939, docket books from 1880s. **General Information:** No juvenile, sealed, dissolution of marriage, mental health, domestic abuse records released. Copy fee: $.50 per page. Certification fee: $10.00. Fee payee: Clerk of Court. Personal checks accepted. Credit cards accepted. Prepayment is required. Public access terminal is available.

Hancock County

2nd District Court 855 State St, Garner, IA 50438; 641-923-2532; Fax: 641-923-3521. Hours: 8AM-4:30PM (CST). *Felony, Misdemeanor, Civil, Eviction, Small Claims, Probate.*

Civil Records: Access: In person only. Court does not conduct in person searches; visitors must perform searches for themselves. Search fee: No civil searches performed by court. Required to search: name, years to search. Civil cases indexed by defendant, plaintiff. Civil records on docket books from 1880s. **Criminal Records:** Access: In person only. Court does not conduct in person searches; visitors must perform searches for themselves. Search fee: No criminal searches performed by court. Required to search: name, years to search. Criminal records on docket books from 1880s. **General Information:** No juvenile, sealed, dissolution of marriage, mental health, domestic abuse or deferred records released. Copy fee: $.50 per page. Certification fee: $10.00. Fee payee: Clerk of Court. Personal checks accepted. Prepayment is required. Public access terminal is available.

Hardin County

2nd District Court Courthouse, PO Box 495, Eldora, IA 50627; 641-858-2328; Fax: 641-858-2320. Hours: 8AM-4:30PM (CST). *Felony, Misdemeanor, Civil, Eviction, Small Claims, Probate.*

Civil Records: Access: In person only. Court does not conduct in person searches; visitors must perform searches for themselves. Search fee: No civil searches performed by court. Required to search: name, years to search. Civil cases indexed by defendant, plaintiff. Civil records on docket books from 1880s. **Criminal Records:** Access: In person only. Court does not conduct in person searches; visitors must perform searches for themselves. Search fee: No criminal searches performed by court. Required to search: name, years to search. Criminal records on docket books from 1880s. **General Information:** No juvenile, sealed, dissolution of marriage, mental health, domestic abuse or deferred records released. Copy fee: $.50 per page. Certification fee: $10.00. Fee payee: Clerk of Court. Personal checks accepted. Credit cards accepted: Visa, Mastercard.

Prepayment is required. Public access terminal is available.

Harrison County

District Court Court House, Logan, IA 51546; 712-644-2665. Hours: 8AM-4:30PM (CST). *Felony, Misdemeanor, Civil, Eviction, Small Claims, Probate.*

Civil Records: Access: In person only. Court does not conduct in person searches; visitors must perform searches for themselves. Search fee: No civil searches performed by court. Required to search: name, years to search. Civil cases indexed by defendant, plaintiff. Recent death and birth certificates on microfiche, docket books from 1840s. **Criminal Records:** Access: In person only. Court does not conduct in person searches; visitors must perform searches for themselves. Search fee: No criminal searches performed by court. Required to search: name, years to search. Recent death and birth certificates on microfiche, docket books from 1840s. **General Information:** No juvenile, sealed, dissolution of marriage, mental health, domestic abuse or deferred records released. Copy fee: $.50 per page. Certification fee: $10.00. Fee payee: Clerk of Court. Personal checks accepted. Prepayment is required.

Henry County

8th District Court PO Box 176, Mount Pleasant, IA 52641; Civil phone:319-385-2632; Criminal phone:319-385-2632; Fax: 319-385-4144. Hours: 8AM-4:30PM (CST). *Felony, Misdemeanor, Civil, Eviction, Small Claims, Probate.*

Civil Records: Access: In person only. Court does not conduct in person searches; visitors must perform searches for themselves. Search fee: No civil searches performed by court. Required to search: name, years to search. Civil cases indexed by defendant, plaintiff. Civil records on docket books from 1880s. **Criminal Records:** Access: In person only. Court does not conduct in person searches; visitors must perform searches for themselves. Search fee: No criminal searches performed by court. Required to search: name, years to search, DOB; also helpful-address, SSN. Criminal records on docket books from 1880s. **General Information:** No juvenile, sealed, dissolution of marriage, mental health, domestic abuse or deferred records released. Copy fee: $.25 per page. Certification fee: $10.00. Fee payee: Clerk of Court. Personal checks accepted. Prepayment is required. Public access terminal is available.

Howard County

1st District Court Courthouse, 137 N Elm St, Cresco, IA 52136; 319-547-2661. Hours: 8AM-4:30PM (CST). *Felony, Misdemeanor, Civil, Eviction, Small Claims, Probate.*

Civil Records: Access: In person only. Court does not conduct in person searches; visitors must perform searches for themselves. Search fee: No civil searches performed by court. Required to search: name, years to search. Civil cases indexed by defendant, plaintiff. Civil records on docket books from 1900s. **Criminal Records:** Access: In person only. Court does not conduct in person searches; visitors must perform searches for themselves. Search fee: No criminal searches performed by court. Required to search: name, years to search, DOB. Criminal records on docket books from 1900s. **General Information:** No juvenile, sealed, dissolution of marriage, mental health, domestic abuse or deferred records

released. Copy fee: $.50 per page. Certification fee: $10.00. Fee payee: Clerk of Court. Personal checks accepted. Prepayment is required.

Humboldt County

2nd District Court Courthouse, Dakota City, IA 50529; 515-332-1806; Fax: 515-332-7100. Hours: 8AM-4:30PM (CST). *Felony, Misdemeanor, Civil, Eviction, Small Claims, Probate.*

Civil Records: Access: In person only. Court does not conduct in person searches; visitors must perform searches for themselves. Search fee: No civil searches performed by court. Required to search: name, years to search. Civil cases indexed by defendant, plaintiff. Civil records on docket books from early 1900s. **Criminal Records:** Access: In person only. Court does not conduct in person searches; visitors must perform searches for themselves. Search fee: No criminal searches performed by court. Required to search: name, years to search. Criminal records on docket books from early 1900s. **General Information:** No juvenile, sealed, dissolution of marriage, mental health, domestic abuse or deferred records released. Copy fee: $.50 per page. Certification fee: $10.00. Fee payee: Clerk of Court. Personal checks accepted. Prepayment is required. Public access terminal is available.

Ida County

3rd District Court Courthouse, 401 Moorehead St, Ida Grove, IA 51445; 712-364-2628; Fax: 712-364-2699. Hours: 8AM-4:30PM (CST). *Felony, Misdemeanor, Civil, Eviction, Small Claims, Probate.*

Civil Records: Access: In person only. Court does not conduct in person searches; visitors must perform searches for themselves. Search fee: No civil searches performed by court. Required to search: name, years to search. Civil cases indexed by defendant, plaintiff. Civil records on docket books from early 1800s. **Criminal Records:** Access: In person only. Court does not conduct in person searches; visitors must perform searches for themselves. Search fee: No criminal searches performed by court. Required to search: name, years to search. Criminal records on docket books from early 1800s. **General Information:** No juvenile, sealed, dissolution of marriage, mental health, domestic abuse or deferred records released. Copy fee: $.50 per page. Certification fee: $10.00. Fee payee: Clerk of Court. Personal checks accepted. Prepayment is required. Public access terminal is available.

Iowa County

6th District Court PO Box 266, Marengo, IA 52301; 319-642-3914. Hours: 8AM-4:30PM (CST). *Felony, Misdemeanor, Civil, Eviction, Small Claims, Probate.*

Civil Records: Access: In person only. Court does not conduct in person searches; visitors must perform searches for themselves. Search fee: No civil searches performed by court. Required to search: name, years to search. Civil cases indexed by defendant, plaintiff. Civil records on docket books from early 1800s. **Criminal Records:** Access: In person only. Court does not conduct in person searches; visitors must perform searches for themselves. Search fee: No criminal searches performed by court. Required to search: name, years to search. Criminal records on docket books from early 1800s. **General Information:** No juvenile, sealed, dissolution of marriage, mental health, domestic abuse or deferred records released. Copy fee: $.50 per page. Certification fee: $10.00. Fee payee: Clerk of Court. Personal checks accepted. Prepayment is required. Public access terminal is available.

Jackson County

7th District Court 201 West Platt, Maquoketa, IA 52060; 319-652-4946; Fax: 319-652-2708. Hours: 8AM-4:30PM (CST). *Felony, Misdemeanor, Civil, Eviction, Small Claims, Probate.*

Civil Records: Access: In person only. Court does not conduct in person searches; visitors must perform searches for themselves. Search fee: No civil searches performed by court. Required to search: name, years to search. Civil cases indexed by defendant, plaintiff. Civil records on computer since 1994, on docket books from 1900s. **Criminal Records:** Access: In person only. Court does not conduct in person searches; visitors must perform searches for themselves. Search fee: No criminal searches performed by court. Required to search: name, years to search, DOB; also helpful-SSN. Criminal records on computer since 1994, on docket books from 1900s. **General Information:** No juvenile, sealed, dissolution of marriage, mental health, domestic abuse or deferred records released. Copy fee: $.50 per page. Certification fee: $10.00 per page. Fee payee: Clerk of Court. Personal checks accepted. Prepayment is required. Public access terminal is available.

Jasper County

5th District Court 101 1st Street North, Rm 104, Newton, IA 50208; 641-792-3255; Fax: 641-792-2818. Hours: 8AM-4:30PM (CST). *Felony, Misdemeanor, Civil, Eviction, Small Claims, Probate.*

http://www.judicial.state.ia.us/decisions/district/d5.asp

Civil Records: Access: In person only. Court does not conduct in person searches; visitors must perform searches for themselves. Search fee: No civil searches performed by court. Required to search: name, years to search. Civil cases indexed by defendant, plaintiff. Civil records on computer since 1994, docket books from 1900s. **Criminal Records:** Access: In person only. Court does not conduct in person searches; visitors must perform searches for themselves. Search fee: No criminal searches performed by court. Required to search: name, years to search. Criminal records on computer since 1994, docket books from 1900s. **General Information:** No juvenile, sealed, dissolution of marriage, mental health, domestic abuse or deferred records released. Copy fee: $.50 per page. Certification fee: $10.00. Fee payee: Clerk of Court. Personal checks accepted. Prepayment is required. Public access terminal is available.

Jefferson County

8th District Court PO Box 984, Fairfield, IA 52556; 641-472-3454; Fax: 641-472-9472. Hours: 8AM-4:30PM (CST). *Felony, Misdemeanor, Civil, Eviction, Small Claims, Probate.*

Civil Records: Access: In person only. Court does not conduct in person searches; visitors must perform searches for themselves. Search fee: No civil searches performed by court. Required to search: name, years to search. Civil cases indexed by defendant, plaintiff. Civil records on docket books from 1800s. **Criminal Records:** Access: In person only. Court does not conduct in person searches; visitors must perform searches for themselves. Search fee: No criminal searches

performed by court. Required to search: name, years to search, DOB. Criminal records on docket books from 1800s. **General Information:** No juvenile, sealed, dissolution of marriage, mental health, domestic abuse or deferred records released. Copy fee: $.25 per page. Certification fee: $10.00. Fee payee: Clerk of Court. Personal checks accepted. Public access terminal is available.

Johnson County

6th District Court PO Box 2510, Iowa City, IA 52244; 319-356-6060; Fax: 319-339-6153. Hours: 8AM-4:30PM (CST). *Felony, Misdemeanor, Civil, Eviction, Small Claims, Probate.*

Civil Records: Access: In person only. Court does not conduct in person searches; visitors must perform searches for themselves. Search fee: No civil searches performed by court. Required to search: name, years to search. Civil cases indexed by defendant, plaintiff. Civil records on docket books and microfilm from 1880s. **Criminal Records:** Access: In person only. Court does not conduct in person searches; visitors must perform searches for themselves. Search fee: No criminal searches performed by court. Required to search: name, years to search; also helpful-address, DOB, SSN. Criminal records on docket books and microfilm from 1880s. **General Information:** No juvenile, sealed, dissolution of marriage, mental health, domestic abuse or deferred records released. Copy fee: $.50 per page. Certification fee: $10.00. Fee payee: Clerk of Court. Personal checks accepted. Public access terminal is available.

Jones County

6th District Court PO Box 19, Anamosa, IA 52205; 319-462-4341. Hours: 8AM-4:30PM (CST). *Felony, Misdemeanor, Civil, Eviction, Small Claims, Probate.*

Civil Records: Access: In person only. Court does not conduct in person searches; visitors must perform searches for themselves. Search fee: No civil searches performed by court. Required to search: name, years to search. Civil cases indexed by defendant, plaintiff. Civil records on docket books from mid 1800s. **Criminal Records:** Access: In person only. Court does not conduct in person searches; visitors must perform searches for themselves. No search fee. Required to search: name, years to search. Criminal records on docket books from early 1900s. **General Information:** No juvenile, sealed, dissolution of marriage (prior to decree), mental health or deferred records released. Copy fee: $.50 per page. Certification fee: $10.00. Fee payee: Clerk of Court. Personal checks accepted. Prepayment is required. Public access terminal is available.

Keokuk County

8th District Court Courthouse, Sigourney, IA 52591; 641-622-2210; Fax: 641-622-2171. Hours: 8AM-4:30PM (CST). *Felony, Misdemeanor, Civil, Eviction, Small Claims, Probate.*

Civil Records: Access: In person only. Court does not conduct in person searches; visitors must perform searches for themselves. Search fee: No civil searches performed by court. Required to search: name, years to search. Civil cases indexed by defendant, plaintiff. Civil records on docket books from 1888. **Criminal Records:** Access: In person only. Court does not conduct in person searches; visitors must perform searches for themselves. Search fee: No criminal searches

performed by court. Required to search: name, years to search. Criminal records on docket books from 1888. **General Information:** No juvenile, sealed, dissolution of marriage, mental health, domestic abuse or deferred records released. Copy fee: $.25 per page. Certification fee: $10.00. Fee payee: Clerk of Court. Personal checks accepted. Prepayment is required. Public access terminal is available.

Kossuth County

3rd District Court Kossuth County Courthouse, 114 W State St, Algona, IA 50511; 515-295-3240. Hours: 8AM-4PM (CST). *Felony, Misdemeanor, Civil, Eviction, Small Claims, Probate.*

Civil Records: Access: In person only. Court does not conduct in person searches; visitors must perform searches for themselves. Search fee: No civil searches performed by court. Required to search: name, years to search. Civil cases indexed by defendant, plaintiff. Civil records on computer since 09/97; prior records on dockets. **Criminal Records:** Access: In person only. Court does not conduct in person searches; visitors must perform searches for themselves. Search fee: No criminal searches performed by court. Required to search: name, years to search. Criminal records on computer since 09/97; prior records on dockets. **General Information:** No juvenile, sealed, dissolution of marriage, mental health, domestic abuse or deferred records released. Copy fee: $.50 per page. Certification fee: $10.00. Fee payee: Clerk of Court. Personal checks accepted. Prepayment is required.

Lee County

8th District Court PO Box 1443, Ft Madison, IA 52627; 319-372-3523. Hours: 8AM-4:30PM (CST). *Felony, Misdemeanor, Civil, Eviction, Small Claims, Probate.*

Civil Records: Access: In person only. Court does not conduct in person searches; visitors must perform searches for themselves. Search fee: No civil searches performed by court. Required to search: name, years to search. Civil cases indexed by defendant, plaintiff. Civil records on docket books from early 1800s. **Criminal Records:** Access: In person only. Court does not conduct in person searches; visitors must perform searches for themselves. Search fee: No criminal searches performed by court. Required to search: name, years to search. Criminal records on docket books from early 1800s. **General Information:** No juvenile, sealed, dissolution of marriage, mental health, domestic abuse or deferred records released. Copy fee: $.25 per page. Certification fee: $10.00. Fee payee: Clerk of Court. Personal checks accepted. Prepayment is required. Public access terminal is available.

Linn County

District Court Linn County Courthouse, PO Box 1468, Cedar Rapids, IA 52406-1468; 319-398-3411; Fax: 319-398-3964. Hours: 8AM-4:30PM (CST). *Felony, Misdemeanor, Civil, Eviction, Small Claims, Probate.*

Civil Records: Access: In person only. Court does not conduct in person searches; visitors must perform searches for themselves. Search fee:. Required to search: name, years to search. Civil cases indexed by defendant, plaintiff. Civil records on computer since 1995, docket books from early 1900s. **Criminal Records:** Access: In person only. Court does not conduct in person searches; visitors must perform searches for themselves. Search fee:.

Required to search: name, years to search; also helpful-address, DOB. Criminal records on computer since 1993. **General Information:** No juvenile, sealed, pending dissolution of marriage, mental health, domestic abuse or deferred records released. Copy fee: $.50 per page. Certification fee: $10.00. Fee payee: Clerk of Court. Personal checks accepted. Prepayment is required. Public access terminal is available.

Louisa County

8th District Court PO Box 268, Wapello, IA 52653; 319-523-4541; Fax: 319-523-4542. Hours: 8AM-4:30PM (CST). *Felony, Misdemeanor, Civil, Eviction, Small Claims, Probate.*

Civil Records: Access: In person only. Both court and visitors may perform in person searches. No search fee. Required to search: name, years to search. Civil cases indexed by defendant, plaintiff. Civil records on docket books from 1920s, on computer since 02/97. **Criminal Records:** Access: In person only. Both court and visitors may perform in person searches. No search fee. Required to search: name, years to search, DOB, signed release; also helpful-SSN. Criminal records on docket books from 1920s, on computer since 02/97. **General Information:** No juvenile, sealed, dissolution of marriage, mental health, domestic abuse or deferred records released. Copy fee: $.25 per page. Certification fee: $10.00. Fee payee: Clerk of Court. Personal checks accepted. Prepayment is required. Public access terminal is available.

Lucas County

5th District Court Courthouse, Chariton, IA 50049; 641-774-4421; Fax: 641-774-8669. Hours: 8AM-4:30PM (CST). *Felony, Misdemeanor, Civil, Eviction, Small Claims, Probate.*

Civil Records: Access: In person only. Court does not conduct in person searches; visitors must perform searches for themselves. Search fee: No civil searches performed by court. Required to search: name, years to search. Civil cases indexed by defendant, plaintiff. Civil records on docket books from 1880s. **Criminal Records:** Access: In person only. Court does not conduct in person searches; visitors must perform searches for themselves. Search fee: No criminal searches performed by court. Required to search: name, years to search; also helpful-SSN. Criminal records on docket books from 1880s. **General Information:** No juvenile, adoption, sealed, dissolution of marriage, mental health, domestic abuse or deferred records released. Copy fee: $.50 per page. Certification fee: $10.00. Fee payee: Clerk of District Court. Personal checks accepted. Credit cards accepted: Visa, Mastercard. Prepayment is required.

Lyon County

3rd District Court Courthouse, Rock Rapids, IA 51246; 712-472-2623; Fax: 712-472-2422. Hours: 8AM-4:30PM (CST). *Felony, Misdemeanor, Civil, Eviction, Small Claims, Probate.*

Civil Records: Access: In person only. Court does not conduct in person searches; visitors must perform searches for themselves. Search fee: No civil searches performed by court. Required to search: name, years to search. Civil cases indexed by defendant, plaintiff. Civil records on docket books from 1880s. **Criminal Records:** Access: In person only. Court does not conduct in person searches; visitors must perform searches for themselves. Search fee: No criminal searches

performed by court. Required to search: name, years to search. Criminal records on docket books from 1880s. **General Information:** No juvenile, sealed, dissolution of marriage, mental health, domestic abuse or deferred records released. Copy fee: $.50 per page. Certification fee: $10.00. Fee payee: Clerk of Court. Personal checks accepted. Public access terminal is available.

Madison County

5th District Court PO Box 152, Winterset, IA 50273; 515-462-4451; Fax: 515-462-9825. Hours: 8AM-4:30PM (CST). *Felony, Misdemeanor, Civil, Eviction, Small Claims, Probate.*

Civil Records: Access: In person only. Court does not conduct in person searches; visitors must perform searches for themselves. Search fee: No civil searches performed by court. Required to search: name, years to search. Civil cases indexed by plaintiff. Civil records on docket books from 1880s. Misdemeanor records from 1974 to present. Other criminal same record keeping as civil. **Criminal Records:** Access: In person only. Court does not conduct in person searches; visitors must perform searches for themselves. Search fee: No criminal searches performed by court. Required to search: name, years to search; also helpful-DOB. Criminal records on docket books from 1880s. Misdemeanor records from 1974 to present. Other criminal same record keeping as civil. **General Information:** No juvenile, sealed, dissolution of marriage, mental health, domestic abuse of deferred records released. Copy fee: $.25 per page. Certification fee: $10.00. Fee payee: Clerk of Court. Personal checks accepted. Prepayment is required. Public access terminal is available.

Mahaska County

8th District Court Courthouse, PO Box 1168, Oskaloosa, IA 52577; 641-673-7786; Fax: 641-672-1256. Hours: 8AM-4:30PM (CST). *Felony, Misdemeanor, Civil, Eviction, Small Claims, Probate.*

Civil Records: Access: In person only. Court does not conduct in person searches; visitors must perform searches for themselves. Search fee: No civil searches performed by court. Required to search: name, years to search. Civil cases indexed by defendant, plaintiff. Civil records on docket books from 1880s. **Criminal Records:** Access: In person only. Court does not conduct in person searches; visitors must perform searches for themselves. Search fee: No criminal searches performed by court. Required to search: name, years to search. Criminal records on docket books from 1880s. **General Information:** No juvenile, sealed, dissolution of marriage, mental health, domestic abuse or deferred records released. Copy fee: $.25 per page. Docket Copy Fee: $1.00 per page. Certification fee: $10.00. Fee payee: Clerk of Court. Personal checks accepted. Prepayment is required. Public access terminal is available.

Marion County

5th District Court PO Box 497, Knoxville, IA 50138; 641-828-2207; Fax: 641-828-7580. Hours: 8AM-4:30PM (CST). *Felony, Misdemeanor, Civil, Eviction, Small Claims, Probate.*

Civil Records: Access: In person only. Court does not conduct in person searches; visitors must perform searches for themselves. Search fee: No civil searches performed by court. Required to search: name, years to search. Civil cases indexed by defendant, plaintiff. Civil records on computer since 1992, docket books from 1896. **Criminal Records:** Access: In person only. Court does not

conduct in person searches; visitors must perform searches for themselves. Search fee: No criminal searches performed by court. Required to search: name, years to search. Criminal records on computer since 1992, docket books from 1896. **General Information:** No juvenile, sealed, dissolution of marriage, mental health, domestic abuse or defered records released. Copy fee: $.50 per page. Certification fee: $10.00. Fee payee: Clerk of Court. Personal checks accepted. Prepayment is required.

Marshall County

2nd District Court Courthouse, Marshalltown, IA 50158; 641-754-6373; Fax: 641-754-6376. Hours: 8AM-4:30PM (CST). *Felony, Misdemeanor, Civil, Eviction, Small Claims, Probate.*

Civil Records: Access: In person only. Court does not conduct in person searches; visitors must perform searches for themselves. Search fee: No civil searches performed by court. Required to search: name, years to search. Civil cases indexed by defendant, plaintiff. Civil records on computer since June, 1994, docket books from late 1800s. **Criminal Records:** Access: In person only. Court does not conduct in person searches; visitors must perform searches for themselves. Search fee: No criminal searches performed by court. Required to search: name, years to search; also helpful-DOB, SSN. Criminal records on computer since August, 1992, docket books from late 1800s. **General Information:** No juvenile, sealed, pending dissolution of marriage, mental health, domestic abuse and deferred records released. Copy fee: $.25 per page. Probate copies $.50 per page. Certification fee: $10.00. Fee payee: Clerk of Court. Personal checks accepted. Credit cards accepted. Prepayment is required. Public access terminal is available.

Mills County

4th District Court 418 Sharp St, Courthouse, Glenwood, IA 51534; 712-527-4880; Fax: 712-527-4936. Hours: 8AM-4:30PM (CST). *Felony, Misdemeanor, Civil, Eviction, Small Claims, Probate.*

Civil Records: Access: In person only. Both court and visitors may perform in person searches. Search fee: $6.00 per name. Required to search: name, years to search. Civil cases indexed by defendant, plaintiff. Civil records on docket books since 1880s. **Criminal Records:** Access: In person only. Both court and visitors may perform in person searches. Search fee: $6.00 per name. Required to search: name, years to search, DOB; also helpful-SSN. Criminal records on docket books since 1880s. **General Information:** No juvenile, sealed, dissolution of marriage, mental health, domestic abuse or deferred records released. Copy fee: $.25 per page. Certification fee: $10.00. Fee payee: Clerk of Court. Personal checks accepted. Prepayment is required. Public access terminal is available.

Mitchell County

2nd District Court 508 State St, Osage, IA 50461; 641-732-3726; Fax: 641-732-3728. Hours: 8AM-4:30PM (CST). *Felony, Misdemeanor, Civil, Eviction, Small Claims, Probate.*

Civil Records: Access: In person only. Court does not conduct in person searches; visitors must perform searches for themselves. Search fee: No civil searches performed by court. Required to search: name, years to search. Civil cases indexed by defendant, plaintiff. Civil records on docket

ZIP Range	City	ZIP Range	City	ZIP Range	City	ZIP Range	City
50483-50483	WESLEY	50606-50606	ARLINGTON	50848-50848	GRAVITY	51240-51240	INWOOD
50484-50484	WODEN	50607-50607	AURORA	50849-50849	GREENFIELD	51241-51241	LARCHWOOD
50501-50501	FORT DODGE	50608-50608	AUSTINVILLE	50851-50851	LENOX	51242-51242	LESTER
50510-50510	ALBERT CITY	50609-50609	BEAMAN	50853-50853	MASSENA	51243-51243	LITTLE ROCK
50511-50511	ALGONA	50611-50611	BRISTOW	50854-50854	MOUNT AYR	51244-51244	MATLOCK
50514-50514	ARMSTRONG	50612-50612	BUCKINGHAM	50857-50857	NODAWAY	51245-51245	PRIMGHAR
50515-50515	AYRSHIRE	50613-50614	CEDAR FALLS	50858-50858	ORIENT	51246-51246	ROCK RAPIDS
50516-50516	BADGER	50616-50616	CHARLES CITY	50859-50859	PRESCOTT	51247-51247	ROCK VALLEY
50517-50517	BANCROFT	50619-50619	CLARKSVILLE	50860-50860	REDDING	51248-51248	SANBORN
50518-50518	BARNUM	50620-50620	COLWELL	50861-50861	SHANNON CITY	51249-51249	SIBLEY
50519-50519	BODE	50621-50621	CONRAD	50862-50862	SHARPSBURG	51250-51250	SIOUX CENTER
50520-50520	BRADGATE	50622-50622	DENVER	50863-50863	TINGLEY	51301-51301	SPENCER
50521-50521	BURNSIDE	50623-50623	DEWAR	50864-50864	VILLISCA	51330-51330	ALLENDORF
50522-50522	BURT	50624-50624	DIKE	50936-50981	DES MOINES	51331-51331	ARNOLDS PARK
50523-50523	CALLENDER	50625-50625	DUMONT	51001-51001	AKRON	51333-51333	DICKENS
50524-50524	CLARE	50626-50626	DUNKERTON	51002-51002	ALTA	51334-51334	ESTHERVILLE
50525-50525	CLARION	50627-50627	ELDORA	51003-51003	ALTON	51338-51338	EVERLY
50527-50527	CURLEW	50628-50628	ELMA	51004-51004	ANTHON	51340-51340	FOSTORIA
50528-50528	CYLINDER	50629-50629	FAIRBANK	51005-51005	AURELIA	51341-51341	GILLETT GROVE
50529-50529	DAKOTA CITY	50630-50630	FREDERICKSBURG	51006-51006	BATTLE CREEK	51342-51342	GRAETTINGER
50530-50530	DAYTON	50631-50631	FREDERIKA	51007-51007	BRONSON	51343-51343	GREENVILLE
50531-50531	DOLLIVER	50632-50632	GARWIN	51008-51008	BRUNSVILLE	51344-51344	GRUVER
50532-50532	DUNCOMBE	50633-50633	GENEVA	51009-51009	CALUMET	51345-51345	HARRIS
50533-50533	EAGLE GROVE	50634-50634	GILBERTVILLE	51010-51010	CASTANA	51346-51346	HARTLEY
50535-50535	EARLY	50635-50635	GLADBROOK	51011-51011	CHATSWORTH	51347-51347	LAKE PARK
50536-50536	EMMETSBURG	50636-50636	GREENE	51012-51012	CHEROKEE	51349-51349	MAY CITY
50538-50538	FARNHAMVILLE	50638-50638	GRUNDY CENTER	51014-51014	CLEGHORN	51350-51350	MELVIN
50539-50539	FENTON	50641-50641	HAZLETON	51015-51015	CLIMBING HILL	51351-51351	MILFORD
50540-50540	FONDA	50642-50642	HOLLAND	51016-51016	CORRECTIONVILLE	51354-51354	OCHEYEDAN
50541-50541	GILMORE CITY	50643-50643	HUDSON	51017-51017	CRAIG	51355-51355	OKOBOJI
50542-50542	GOLDFIELD	50644-50644	INDEPENDENCE	51018-51018	CUSHING	51357-51357	ROYAL
50543-50543	GOWRIE	50645-50645	IONIA	51019-51019	DANBURY	51358-51358	RUTHVEN
50544-50544	HARCOURT	50647-50647	JANESVILLE	51020-51020	GALVA	51360-51360	SPIRIT LAKE
50545-50545	HARDY	50648-50648	JESUP	51022-51022	GRANVILLE	51363-51363	SUPERIOR
50546-50546	HAVELOCK	50649-50649	KESLEY	51023-51023	HAWARDEN	51364-51364	TERRIL
50548-50548	HUMBOLDT	50650-50650	LAMONT	51024-51024	HINTON	51365-51365	WALLINGFORD
50551-50551	JOLLEY	50651-50651	LA PORTE CITY	51025-51025	HOLSTEIN	51366-51366	WEBB
50552-50552	KNIERIM	50652-50652	LINCOLN	51026-51026	HORNICK	51401-51401	CARROLL
50554-50554	LAURENS	50653-50653	MARBLE ROCK	51027-51027	IRETON	51430-51430	ARCADIA
50556-50556	LEDYARD	50654-50654	MASONVILLE	51028-51028	KINGSLEY	51431-51431	ARTHUR
50557-50557	LEHIGH	50655-50655	MAYNARD	51029-51029	LARRABEE	51432-51432	ASPINWALL
50558-50558	LIVERMORE	50657-50657	MORRISON	51030-51030	LAWTON	51433-51433	AUBURN
50559-50559	LONE ROCK	50658-50658	NASHUA	51031-51031	LE MARS	51436-51436	BREDA
50560-50560	LU VERNE	50659-50659	NEW HAMPTON	51033-51033	LINN GROVE	51439-51439	CHARTER OAK
50561-50561	LYTTON	50660-50660	NEW HARTFORD	51034-51034	MAPLETON	51440-51440	DEDHAM
50562-50562	MALLARD	50661-50661	NORTH WASHINGTON	51035-51035	MARCUS	51441-51441	DELOIT
50563-50563	MANSON	50662-50662	OELWEIN	51036-51036	MAURICE	51442-51442	DENISON
50565-50565	MARATHON	50664-50664	ORAN	51037-51037	MERIDEN	51443-51443	GLIDDEN
50566-50566	MOORLAND	50665-50665	PARKERSBURG	51038-51038	MERRILL	51444-51444	HALBUR
50567-50567	NEMAHA	50666-50666	PLAINFIELD	51039-51039	MOVILLE	51445-51445	IDA GROVE
50568-50568	NEWELL	50667-50667	RAYMOND	51040-51040	ONAWA	51446-51446	IRWIN
50569-50569	OTHO	50668-50668	READLYN	51041-51041	ORANGE CITY	51447-51447	KIRKMAN
50570-50570	OTTOSEN	50669-50669	REINBECK	51044-51044	OTO	51448-51448	KIRON
50571-50571	PALMER	50670-50670	SHELL ROCK	51045-51045	OYENS	51449-51449	LAKE CITY
50573-50573	PLOVER	50671-50671	STANLEY	51046-51046	PAULLINA	51450-51450	LAKE VIEW
50574-50574	POCAHONTAS	50672-50672	STEAMBOAT ROCK	51047-51047	PETERSON	51451-51451	LANESBORO
50575-50575	POMEROY	50673-50673	STOUT	51048-51048	PIERSON	51452-51452	LIDDERDALE
50576-50576	REMBRANDT	50674-50674	SUMNER	51049-51049	QUIMBY	51453-51453	LOHRVILLE
50577-50577	RENWICK	50675-50675	TRAER	51050-51050	REMSEN	51454-51454	MANILLA
50578-50578	RINGSTED	50676-50676	TRIPOLI	51051-51051	RODNEY	51455-51455	MANNING
50579-50579	ROCKWELL CITY	50677-50677	WAVERLY	51052-51052	SALIX	51458-51458	ODEBOLT
50581-50581	ROLFE	50680-50680	WELLSBURG	51053-51053	SCHALLER	51459-51459	RALSTON
50582-50582	RUTLAND	50681-50681	WESTGATE	51054-51054	SERGEANT BLUFF	51460-51460	RICKETTS
50583-50583	SAC CITY	50682-50682	WINTHROP	51055-51055	SLOAN	51461-51461	SCHLESWIG
50585-50585	SIOUX RAPIDS	50701-50706	WATERLOO	51056-51056	SMITHLAND	51462-51462	SCRANTON
50586-50586	SOMERS	50707-50707	EVANSDALE	51057-51057	STRUBLE	51463-51463	TEMPLETON
50587-50587	RINARD	50799-50799	WATERLOO	51058-51058	SUTHERLAND	51465-51465	VAIL
50588-50588	STORM LAKE	50801-50801	CRESTON	51059-51059	TURIN	51466-51466	WALL LAKE
50590-50590	SWEA CITY	50830-50830	AFTON	51060-51060	UTE	51467-51467	WESTSIDE
50591-50591	THOR	50831-50831	ARISPE	51061-51061	WASHTA	51501-51503	COUNCIL BLUFFS
50592-50592	TRUESDALE	50833-50833	BEDFORD	51062-51062	WESTFIELD	51510-51510	CARTER LAKE
50593-50593	VARINA	50835-50835	BENTON	51063-51063	WHITING	51520-51520	ARION
50594-50594	VINCENT	50836-50836	BLOCKTON	51101-51111	SIOUX CITY	51521-51521	AVOCA
50595-50595	WEBSTER CITY	50837-50837	BRIDGEWATER	51201-51201	SHELDON	51523-51523	BLENCOE
50597-50597	WEST BEND	50839-50839	CARBON	51230-51230	ALVORD	51525-51525	CARSON
50598-50598	WHITTEMORE	50840-50840	CLEARFIELD	51231-51231	ARCHER	51526-51526	CRESCENT
50599-50599	WOOLSTOCK	50841-50841	CORNING	51232-51232	ASHTON	51527-51527	DEFIANCE
50601-50601	ACKLEY	50842-50842	CROMWELL	51234-51234	BOYDEN	51528-51528	DOW CITY
50602-50602	ALLISON	50843-50843	CUMBERLAND	51235-51235	DOON	51529-51529	DUNLAP
50603-50603	ALTA VISTA	50845-50845	DIAGONAL	51237-51237	GEORGE	51530-51530	EARLING
50604-50604	APLINGTON	50846-50846	FONTANELLE	51238-51238	HOSPERS	51531-51531	ELK HORN
50605-50605	AREDALE	50847-50847	GRANT	51239-51239	HULL	51532-51532	ELLIOTT

Range	Name	Range	Name	Range	Name	Range	Name
51533-51533	EMERSON	52049-52049	GARNAVILLO	52225-52225	ELBERON	52501-52501	OTTUMWA
51534-51534	GLENWOOD	52050-52050	GREELEY	52226-52226	ELWOOD	52530-52530	AGENCY
51535-51535	GRISWOLD	52052-52052	GUTTENBERG	52227-52227	ELY	52531-52531	ALBIA
51536-51536	HANCOCK	52053-52053	HOLY CROSS	52228-52228	FAIRFAX	52533-52533	BATAVIA
51537-51537	HARLAN	52054-52054	LA MOTTE	52229-52229	GARRISON	52534-52534	BEACON
51540-51540	HASTINGS	52055-52055	LITTLEPORT	52230-52230	HALE	52535-52535	BIRMINGHAM
51541-51541	HENDERSON	52056-52056	LUXEMBURG	52231-52231	HARPER	52536-52536	BLAKESBURG
51542-51542	HONEY CREEK	52057-52057	MANCHESTER	52232-52232	HARTWICK	52537-52537	BLOOMFIELD
51543-51543	KIMBALLTON	52060-52060	MAQUOKETA	52233-52233	HIAWATHA	52538-52538	WEST GROVE
51544-51544	LEWIS	52064-52064	MILES	52235-52235	HILLS	52540-52540	BRIGHTON
51545-51545	LITTLE SIOUX	52065-52065	NEW VIENNA	52236-52236	HOMESTEAD	52542-52542	CANTRIL
51546-51546	LOGAN	52066-52066	NORTH BUENA VISTA	52237-52237	HOPKINTON	52543-52543	CEDAR
51548-51548	MC CLELLAND	52068-52068	PEOSTA	52240-52240	IOWA CITY	52544-52544	CENTERVILLE
51549-51549	MACEDONIA	52069-52069	PRESTON	52241-52241	CORALVILLE	52548-52548	CHILLICOTHE
51550-51550	MAGNOLIA	52070-52070	SABULA	52242-52246	IOWA CITY	52549-52549	CINCINNATI
51551-51551	MALVERN	52071-52071	SAINT DONATUS	52247-52247	KALONA	52550-52550	DELTA
51552-51552	MARNE	52072-52072	SAINT OLAF	52248-52248	KEOTA	52551-52551	DOUDS
51553-51553	MINDEN	52073-52073	SHERRILL	52249-52249	KEYSTONE	52552-52552	DRAKESVILLE
51554-51554	MINEOLA	52074-52074	SPRAGUEVILLE	52250-52250	KINROSS	52553-52553	EDDYVILLE
51555-51555	MISSOURI VALLEY	52075-52075	SPRINGBROOK	52251-52251	LADORA	52554-52554	ELDON
51556-51556	MODALE	52076-52076	STRAWBERRY POINT	52252-52252	LANGWORTHY	52555-52555	EXLINE
51557-51557	MONDAMIN	52077-52077	VOLGA	52253-52253	LISBON	52556-52556	FAIRFIELD
51558-51558	MOORHEAD	52078-52078	WORTHINGTON	52254-52254	LOST NATION	52560-52560	FLORIS
51559-51559	NEOLA	52079-52079	ZWINGLE	52255-52255	LOWDEN	52561-52561	FREMONT
51560-51560	OAKLAND	52101-52101	DECORAH	52257-52257	LUZERNE	52562-52562	HAYESVILLE
51561-51561	PACIFIC JUNCTION	52130-52130	ALPHA	52301-52301	MARENGO	52563-52563	HEDRICK
51562-51562	PANAMA	52131-52131	BURR OAK	52302-52302	MARION	52565-52565	KEOSAUQUA
51563-51563	PERSIA	52132-52132	CALMAR	52305-52305	MARTELLE	52566-52566	KIRKVILLE
51564-51564	PISGAH	52133-52133	CASTALIA	52306-52306	MECHANICSVILLE	52567-52567	LIBERTYVILLE
51565-51565	PORTSMOUTH	52134-52134	CHESTER	52307-52307	MIDDLE AMANA	52568-52568	MARTINSBURG
51566-51566	RED OAK	52135-52135	CLERMONT	52308-52308	MILLERSBURG	52569-52569	MELROSE
51570-51570	SHELBY	52136-52136	CRESCO	52309-52309	MONMOUTH	52570-52570	MILTON
51571-51571	SILVER CITY	52140-52140	DORCHESTER	52310-52310	MONTICELLO	52571-52571	MORAVIA
51572-51572	SOLDIER	52141-52141	ELGIN	52312-52312	MORLEY	52572-52572	MOULTON
51573-51573	STANTON	52142-52142	FAYETTE	52313-52313	MOUNT AUBURN	52573-52573	MOUNT STERLING
51574-51574	TENNANT	52144-52144	FORT ATKINSON	52314-52314	MOUNT VERNON	52574-52574	MYSTIC
51575-51575	TREYNOR	52146-52146	HARPERS FERRY	52315-52315	NEWHALL	52576-52576	OLLIE
51576-51576	UNDERWOOD	52147-52147	HAWKEYE	52316-52316	NORTH ENGLISH	52577-52577	OSKALOOSA
51577-51577	WALNUT	52149-52149	HIGHLANDVILLE	52317-52317	NORTH LIBERTY	52580-52580	PACKWOOD
51578-51578	WESTPHALIA	52151-52151	LANSING	52318-52318	NORWAY	52581-52581	PLANO
51579-51579	WOODBINE	52154-52154	LAWLER	52319-52319	OAKDALE	52583-52583	PROMISE CITY
51591-51591	RED OAK	52155-52155	LIME SPRINGS	52320-52320	OLIN	52584-52584	PULASKI
51593-51593	HARLAN	52156-52156	LUANA	52321-52321	ONSLOW	52585-52585	RICHLAND
51601-51603	SHENANDOAH	52157-52157	MC GREGOR	52322-52322	OXFORD	52586-52586	ROSE HILL
51630-51630	BLANCHARD	52158-52158	MARQUETTE	52323-52323	OXFORD JUNCTION	52588-52588	SELMA
51631-51631	BRADDYVILLE	52159-52159	MONONA	52324-52324	PALO	52590-52590	SEYMOUR
51632-51632	CLARINDA	52160-52160	NEW ALBIN	52325-52325	PARNELL	52591-52591	SIGOURNEY
51636-51636	COIN	52161-52161	OSSIAN	52326-52326	QUASQUETON	52593-52593	UDELL
51637-51637	COLLEGE SPRINGS	52162-52162	POSTVILLE	52327-52327	RIVERSIDE	52594-52594	UNIONVILLE
51638-51638	ESSEX	52163-52163	PROTIVIN	52328-52328	ROBINS	52595-52595	UNIVERSITY PARK
51639-51639	FARRAGUT	52164-52164	RANDALIA	52329-52329	ROWLEY	52601-52601	BURLINGTON
51640-51640	HAMBURG	52165-52165	RIDGEWAY	52330-52330	RYAN	52619-52619	ARGYLE
51645-51645	IMOGENE	52166-52166	SAINT LUCAS	52331-52331	SCOTCH GROVE	52620-52620	BONAPARTE
51646-51646	NEW MARKET	52168-52168	SPILLVILLE	52332-52332	SHELLSBURG	52621-52621	CRAWFORDSVILLE
51647-51647	NORTHBORO	52169-52169	WADENA	52333-52333	SOLON	52623-52623	DANVILLE
51648-51648	PERCIVAL	52170-52170	WATERVILLE	52334-52334	SOUTH AMANA	52624-52624	DENMARK
51649-51649	RANDOLPH	52171-52171	WAUCOMA	52335-52335	SOUTH ENGLISH	52625-52625	DONNELLSON
51650-51650	RIVERTON	52172-52172	WAUKON	52336-52336	SPRINGVILLE	52626-52626	FARMINGTON
51651-51651	SHAMBAUGH	52175-52175	WEST UNION	52337-52337	STANWOOD	52627-52627	FORT MADISON
51652-51652	SIDNEY	52201-52201	AINSWORTH	52338-52338	SWISHER	52630-52630	HILLSBORO
51653-51653	TABOR	52202-52202	ALBURNETT	52339-52339	TAMA	52631-52631	HOUGHTON
51654-51654	THURMAN	52203-52204	AMANA	52340-52340	TIFFIN	52632-52632	KEOKUK
51656-51656	YORKTOWN	52205-52205	ANAMOSA	52341-52341	TODDVILLE	52635-52635	LOCKRIDGE
52001-52004	DUBUQUE	52206-52206	ATKINS	52342-52342	TOLEDO	52637-52637	MEDIAPOLIS
52030-52030	ANDREW	52207-52207	BALDWIN	52344-52344	TROY MILLS	52638-52638	MIDDLETOWN
52031-52031	BELLEVUE	52208-52208	BELLE PLAINE	52345-52345	URBANA	52639-52639	MONTROSE
52032-52032	BERNARD	52209-52209	BLAIRSTOWN	52346-52346	VAN HORNE	52640-52640	MORNING SUN
52033-52033	CASCADE	52210-52210	BRANDON	52347-52347	VICTOR	52641-52641	MOUNT PLEASANT
52035-52035	COLESBURG	52211-52211	BROOKLYN	52348-52348	VINING	52642-52642	ROME
52036-52036	DELAWARE	52212-52212	CENTER JUNCTION	52349-52349	VINTON	52644-52644	MOUNT UNION
52037-52037	DELMAR	52213-52213	CENTER POINT	52350-52350	VIOLA	52645-52645	NEW LONDON
52038-52038	DUNDEE	52214-52214	CENTRAL CITY	52351-52351	WALFORD	52646-52646	OAKVILLE
52039-52039	DURANGO	52215-52215	CHELSEA	52352-52352	WALKER	52647-52647	OLDS
52040-52040	DYERSVILLE	52216-52216	CLARENCE	52353-52353	WASHINGTON	52648-52648	PILOT GROVE
52041-52041	EARLVILLE	52217-52217	CLUTIER	52354-52354	WATKINS	52649-52649	SALEM
52042-52042	EDGEWOOD	52218-52218	COGGON	52355-52355	WEBSTER	52650-52650	SPERRY
52043-52043	ELKADER	52219-52219	PRAIRIEBURG	52356-52356	WELLMAN	52651-52651	STOCKPORT
52044-52044	ELKPORT	52220-52220	CONROY	52358-52358	WEST BRANCH	52652-52652	SWEDESBURG
52045-52045	EPWORTH	52221-52221	GUERNSEY	52359-52359	WEST CHESTER	52653-52653	WAPELLO
52046-52046	FARLEY	52222-52222	DEEP RIVER	52361-52361	WILLIAMSBURG	52654-52654	WAYLAND
52047-52047	FARMERSBURG	52223-52223	DELHI	52362-52362	WYOMING	52655-52655	WEST BURLINGTON
52048-52048	GARBER	52224-52224	DYSART	52401-52499	CEDAR RAPIDS	52656-52656	WEST POINT

52657-52657 SAINT PAUL	52731-52731 CHARLOTTE	52752-52752 GRANDVIEW	52768-52768 PRINCETON	
52658-52658 WEVER	52732-52736 CLINTON	52753-52753 LE CLAIRE	52769-52769 STOCKTON	
52659-52659 WINFIELD	52737-52737 COLUMBUS CITY	52754-52754 LETTS	52771-52771 TEEDS GROVE	
52660-52660 YARMOUTH	52738-52738 COLUMBUS JUNCTION	52755-52755 LONE TREE	52772-52772 TIPTON	
52701-52701 ANDOVER	52739-52739 CONESVILLE	52756-52756 LONG GROVE	52773-52773 WALCOTT	
52720-52720 ATALISSA	52742-52742 DE WITT	52757-52757 LOW MOOR	52774-52774 WELTON	
52721-52721 BENNETT	52745-52745 DIXON	52758-52758 MC CAUSLAND	52776-52776 WEST LIBERTY	
52722-52722 BETTENDORF	52746-52746 DONAHUE	52759-52759 MONTPELIER	52777-52777 WHEATLAND	
52726-52726 BLUE GRASS	52747-52747 DURANT	52760-52760 MOSCOW	52778-52778 WILTON	
52727-52727 BRYANT	52748-52748 ELDRIDGE	52761-52761 MUSCATINE	52801-52809 DAVENPORT	
52728-52728 BUFFALO	52749-52749 FRUITLAND	52765-52765 NEW LIBERTY		
52729-52729 CALAMUS	52750-52750 GOOSE LAKE	52766-52766 NICHOLS		
52730-52730 CAMANCHE	52751-52751 GRAND MOUND	52767-52767 PLEASANT VALLEY		

Kansas

General Help Numbers:

Governor's Office
State Capitol Bldg, Room 212S   785-296-3232
Topeka, KS 66612-1590   Fax 785-296-7973
www.ink.org/public/governor   8AM-5PM

Attorney General's Office
Memorial Hall   785-296-2215
120 SW 10th Ave, 2nd Floor   Fax 785-296-6296
Topeka, KS 66612-1597   8AM-5PM
www.ink.org/public/ksag

State Court Administrator
Kansas Judicial Center, 301 SW 10th St   785-296-4873
Topeka, KS 66612-1507   Fax 785-296-7076
www.kscourts.org   8AM-5PM

State Archives
Library and Archives Division   785-272-8681
6425 SW 6th Ave   Fax 785-272-8682
Topeka, KS 66615-1099   9AM-4:30PM M-SA
http://hs4.kshs.org

State Specifics:

Capital: Topeka
          Shawnee County

Time Zone: CST*
*Kansas' five western-most counties are MST:
They are: Greeley, Hamilton, Kearny, Sherman, Wallace,

Number of Counties: 105

Population: 2,594,840

Web Site: www.state.ks.us

State Agencies

Criminal Records

Kansas Bureau of Investigation, Criminal Records Division, 1620 SW Tyler, Crim. History Record Sec., Topeka, KS 66612-1837; 785-296-8200, 785-296-6781 (Fax), 8AM-5PM.

www.kbi.state.ks.us

Note: Non-criminal justice agencies, organizations, individuals and commercial companies are entitled to receive recorded conviction information. Arrests with no convictions are not shown, unless arrest is less than 12 months old and there is no disposition.

Indexing & Storage: New records are available for inquiry immediately. Records are indexed on Kansas Central Repository database, which is syncronized with the automated fingerprint ID system db.

Searching: Each request must be on a separate "Records Check Request Form." First time requesters must complete a user's agreement. Include the following in your request-full name, sex, race, date of birth, Social Security Number. Turnaround time may be several weeks if the record is not currently automated. The following data is not released: expunged records, non-conviction information or juvenile records.

Access by: mail, fax.

Fee & Payment: Fees: $10.00 for a name check; $17.00 for fingerprint search. All requests are allowed one additional alias name per person. However, add $5.00 per third and each additional alias name. Fee payee: KBI Records Fees Fund. Prepayment required. Personal checks accepted. No credit cards accepted.

Mail search: Turnaround time: 2-4 weeks. A self addressed stamped envelope is requested.

Fax search: Prior arrangement is required, same criteria as mail.

Other access: Currently constructing web site that allows record checks with credit card payment system.

Corporation Records
Limited Partnerships
Limited Liability Company Records

Secretary of State, Memorial Hall, 120 SW 10th Ave, 1st Floor, Topeka, KS 66612-1594; 785-296-4564, 785-296-4570 (Fax), 8AM-5PM.

www.kssos.org

Indexing & Storage: Records are available since the applicable laws have been in effect. All Annual Reports before 1995 are at the Historical Society. New records are available for inquiry immediately. Records are indexed on inhouse computer.

Searching: Items not released include confidential annual report balance sheets and copies of extensions. Include the following in your request-full name of business, specific records that you need copies of. In addition to the articles of incorporation, corporation records include the following information: Annual Reports, Officers, Directors and Prior (merged) names. They do not keep Inactive or Reserved names.

Access by: mail, phone, fax, in person, online.

Fee & Payment: Fees: Certificate of good standing - $7.50; letter of status - $5.00; written record search $5.00. Copies are $1.00 per page. Fee payee: Secretary of State. Prepayment required. When requesting by mail, send check for $5.00 or $10.00. They will refund any excess. Prepaid accounts are available. Personal checks accepted. Credit cards accepted: Mastercard, Visa.

Mail search: Turnaround time: 1-2 days. No self addressed stamped envelope is required.

Phone search: General information is given without charge.

Fax search: Items can be returned by fax for an addtional $2.00 for the first page and $1.00 each additional page.

In person search: No fee for request. Turnaround time 10 minutes.

Online search: Corporate data can be ordered from the Information Network of Kansas (INK), a state sponsored interface at www.ink.org/public/corps. There is no fee to search or view records, but there is a fee to order copies of certificates or good standings. You must also subscribe to INK which entails an annual feeof $6.00 plus an initial subscription fee.

Expedited service: Expedited service is available for fax searches. Turnaround time: same day if possible. Add $20.00 per package.

Trademarks/Servicemarks

Secretary of State, Trademarks/Servicemarks Division, 120 SW 10th Ave, Rm 100, Topeka, KS 66612-1240; 785-296-4564, 785-296-4570 (Fax), 8AM-5PM.

www.kssos.org

Indexing & Storage: Records are available from the 1950s, all on computer. It takes 2-3 days before new records are available for inquiry.

Searching: All information recorded is available to the public. However, Kansas law prohibits the use of names and/or addresses derived from public record for solicitation purposes. Include the following in your request-trademark/servicemark name, name of owner. The search provides the names and addresses of owners, date of filing, and class code of filing.

Access by: mail, phone, fax, in person.

Fee & Payment: There is no search fee. Copies are $1.00 per page. Certification is $7.50 plus the copy fees. Fee payee: Secretary of State. Prepayment required. The Secretary of State's office offers prepaid accounts for all regular, ongoing requesters. Personal checks accepted. Credit cards accepted: Mastercard, Visa.

Mail search: Turnaround time: 1-2 days. A mail request must include the name of trademark/servicemark and/or the owner's name. No self addressed stamped envelope is required. No fee for mail request.

Phone search: No fee for telephone request. They will give you limited information from the computer index.

Fax search: Turnaround time 24 hours.

In person search: No fee for request. If you call ahead of time, they will have information ready when you come in.

Other access: For bulk file purchase, there is a $20-75 program set-up fee, plus $1.00 per page. Files are also available on CD for $40 and $20 program set-up fee.

Expedited service: Expedited service is available for mail, phone and in person searches. Expedited requesters are required to have a pre-paid account, $150-start.

Uniform Commercial Code
Federal Tax Liens
State Tax Liens

UCC Division, Secretary of State, Memorial Hall, 120 SW 10th Ave, Topeka, KS 66612; 785-296-1849, 785-296-3659 (Fax), 8AM-5PM.

www.ink.org/public/sos

Indexing & Storage: Records are available from 1978 on computer, from Sept. 1983-present on microfiche.

Searching: Use search request form UCC-3. The search includes federal tax liens on businesses. Federal tax liens on individuals can be filed here or at county, all state tax liens are filed at the county level. Include the following in your request-debtor name. You must order copies to receive collateral information. No collateral data is given over the phone.

Access by: mail, phone, fax, in person, online.

Fee & Payment: Copies are $1.00 per page, search varies with type of access. Fee payee: Secretary of State. Prepayment required. Personal checks accepted. Credit cards accepted: Mastercard, Visa.

Mail search: Turnaround time: 1 day. A self addressed stamped envelope is requested. Search costs $8.00 per debtor name.

Phone search: Search costs $15.00 per debtor name.

Fax search: Same criteria as mail searching. You can have information returned by fax for an additional $2.00 for the first page and $1.00 each additional page.

In person search: Search costs $8.00 per debtor name. Copies cost $1.00 per page.

Online search: Online service is provided the Information Network of Kansas (INK). The system is open 24 hours daily. There is an annual fee. Network charges are $.10 a minute unless access is through their Internet site (www.ink.org) which has no network fee. UCC records are $8.00 per record. This is the same online system used for corporation records. For more information, call INK at 800-4-KANSAS.

Other access: INK also provides records in a bulk or database format.

Sales Tax Registrations
Access to Records is Restricted

Kansas Department of Revenue, Customer Relations, Docking State Office Bldg, 915 SW Harrison, Topeka, KS 66612-1588; 785-296-0222, 785-291-3614 (Fax), 7AM-5PM.

www.ink.org/public/kdor

Note: Sales tax registration information is considered confidential and not public record.

Birth Certificates

Kansas Department of Health & Environment, Office of Vital Statistics, 900 SW Jackson, #151, Topeka, KS 66612-2221; 785-296-1400, 785-296-3253 (Credit Card Orders), 785-357-4332 (Fax), 8AM-5PM.

www.kdhe.state.ks.us/vital

Note: Vital records are not considered public records in Kansas.

Indexing & Storage: Records are available from 1911-present. Delayed birth registrations from the mid-1800s are available. Records are indexed on microfiche, index cards, inhouse computer.

Searching: Must have a signed release from person of record or have direct interest for personal or property right. Include the following in your request-full name, names of parents, mother's maiden name, date of birth, place of birth, relationship to person of record, reason for information request. Include a daytime phone number.

Access by: mail, phone, fax, in person.

Fee & Payment: The fee is $10.00 for first certified copy; add $5.00 for each additional copy of same record. Fee payee: Vital Statistics. Prepayment required. There is an additional $8.00 VitalChek fee with the use of a credit card. Personal checks accepted. Credit cards accepted: Mastercard, Visa, AmEx, Discover.

Mail search: Turnaround time: 2-3 weeks. Include copy of personal ID.A self addressed stamped envelope is requested.

Phone search: You must use a credit card for an additional $8.00 fee. Turnaround time is next business day. Phone service hours are from 8am to 4pm.

Fax search: The fee must include $8.00 for use of a credit card. Turnaround time: 2-3 business days.

In person search: You must complete an application and provide ID. Turnaround time: 20-30 minutes.

Expedited service: Expedited service is available for fax searches. Turnaround time: overnight delivery. Overnight mail services for return of documents is available for an additional fee. Requests may require up to 24 business hours to process. Use of credit card required.

Death Records

Kansas State Department of Health & Environment, Office of Vital Statistics, 900 SW Jackson, #151, Topeka, KS 66612-2221; 785-296-1400, 785-296-3253 (Credit Card Orders), 785-357-4332 (Fax), 8AM-5PM.

www.kdhe.state.ks.us/vital

Note: Vital records are not considered public records in Kansas.

Indexing & Storage: Records are available from July 1, 1911-present. New records are available for inquiry immediately. Records are indexed on microfiche, index cards, inhouse computer.

Searching: Must have a signed release from immediate family member or show direct interest for personal or property right. Include the following in your request-full name, date of death, place of death, relationship to person of record, reason for information request. Please include a daytime phone number.

Access by: mail, phone, fax, in person.

Fee & Payment: The search fee is $10.00 for 1 certified copy; add $5.00 per copy requested at the same time. The search fee covers five years, if year not known. Fee payee: Vital Statistics. Prepayment required. Money orders are accepted. There is a $7.00 VitalChek fee for the use of a credit card. Personal checks accepted. Credit cards accepted: Mastercard, Visa, AmEx, Discover.

Mail search: Turnaround time: 3-5 days. Must include a personal ID.A self addressed stamped envelope is requested.

Phone search: Use a credit card required for an additional $8.00 fee. Turnaround time is next business day.

Fax search: Same criteria as phone searches.

In person search: Must complete an application and provide personal ID. Turnaround time: 20-30 minutes.

Expedited service: Expedited service is available for fax searches. Overnight service is available for an additional fee. Use of credit card required.

Marriage Certificates

Kansas State Department of Health & Environment, Office of Vital Statistics, 900 SW Jackson, #151, Topeka, KS 66612-2221; 785-296-1400, 785-357-4332 (Fax), 8AM-5PM.

www.kdhe.state.ks.us/vital

Note: Vital records are not considered public records in Kansas.

Indexing & Storage: Records are available from May 1, 1913-present. Records prior to 1913 are found at county of issue. Records are computerized from 1993. Records are indexed on microfiche, index cards, inhouse computer.

Searching: Must have a signed release from person of record or have direct interest in personal or property right. Include the following in your request-names of husband and wife, date of marriage, place or county of marriage, relationship to person of record, reason for information request. Include a daytime phone number.

Access by: mail, phone, fax, in person.

Fee & Payment: The search fee is $10.00 for 1 certified copy; add $5.00 per name for addl copy. Fee payee: Vital Statistics. Prepayment required. Money orders are accepted. Personal checks accepted. Credit cards accepted: Mastercard, Visa, AmEx, Discover.

Mail search: Turnaround time: 3-5 days. Must include a personal ID number.A self addressed stamped envelope is requested.

Phone search: You must use a credit card for an additional $8.00 fee. Turnaround time is next business day.

Fax search: Same criteria as phone searches.

In person search: Turnaround time 20-30 minutes.

Expedited service: Expedited service is available for fax searches. Overnight mail service is available for an additional fee. Overnight requests may require up to 24 business hours to process. Use of credit card required.

Divorce Records

Kansas State Department of Health & Environment, Office of Vital Statistics, 900 SW Jackson, #151, Topeka, KS 66612-2221; 785-296-1400, 785-296-3253 (Credit Card Orders), 785-357-4332 (Fax), 8AM-5PM.

www.kdhe.state.ks.us/vital

Note: The agency will issue a divorce certificate, but a copy of the decree must be ordered from the county of issue.

Indexing & Storage: Records are available from July 1, 1951-present. Records prior to July 1, 1951 are found at county of issue. New records are available for inquiry immediately. Records are indexed on microfiche, index cards, inhouse computer.

Searching: Must have a signed release from person of record or show direct interest in personal or property right. Include the following in your request-names of husband and wife, date of divorce, relationship to person of record, reason for information request.

Access by: mail, phone, fax, in person.

Fee & Payment: The search fee is $10.00 for 1 certified copy; add $5.00 per additional copy. Fee payee: Vital Statistics. Prepayment required. Money orders are accepted. Personal checks accepted. Credit cards accepted: Mastercard, Visa, AmEx, Discover.

Mail search: Turnaround time: 3-5 days. A self addressed stamped envelope is requested.

Phone search: Must use a credit card for an additional $8.00 fee. Turnaround time is next business day.

Fax search: Same criteria as phone searches.

In person search: Turnaround time is 20-30 minutes.

Expedited service: Expedited service is available for fax searches. Overnight mail service is available for an additional fee and may require up to 24 business hours to process. Use of credit card required.

Workers' Compensation Records

Human Resources Department, Workers Compensation Division, 800 SW Jackson, Suite 600, Topeka, KS 66612-1227; 785-296-3441, 800-332-0353 (Claims Advisor), 785-296-0025 (Fax), 8AM-5PM.

www.hr.state.ks.us/wc/html/wc.htm

Indexing & Storage: Records are available from the mid-1970's on. New records are available for inquiry immediately. Records are indexed on inhouse computer, file folders.

Searching: Information not released includes financial information submitted by employer, peer review records, records related to safety inspections. Medical records are only released to those authorized by law, and are not open to the general public. Include the following in your request-claimant name, Social Security Number. Employers may receive medical records if a job has been conditionally offered and there is a signed release by the subject.

Access by: mail, phone, fax, in person.

Fee & Payment: There is no search fee.

Mail search: Turnaround time: 1 week to 10 days. No self addressed stamped envelope is required.

Phone search: Searching is available by phone.

Fax search: Fax searching available.

In person search: Requests maintained off premises will take 2 days to obtain.

Other access: Release of bulk lists or portions of the database is available per special written request. Call for more information.

Driver Records
Accident Reports

Department of Revenue, Driver Control Bureau, PO Box 12021, Topeka, KS 66612-2021 (Courier: Docking State Office Building, 915 Harrison, 1st Floor, Topeka, KS 66612); 785-296-3671, 785-296-6851 (Fax), 8AM-4:45PM.

Indexing & Storage: Records are available for 3 years for minor violations and 5 years for DWIs. The state does not record speeding violations of 10 mph or less over in a 70 speed zone or 5 mph or less in all other speed zones. It takes 2-21 days before new records are available for inquiry.

Searching: Casual requesters cannot obtain records. Statutes prohibit acquiring records for the purpose of obtaining addresses and lists for the sale of property or services. An explanation of intended use may be required. The driver license number and either full name or DOB are required when ordering a driving record. The driver's address will show on the record. For an accident report, include the full name, DOB and/or VIN number, and date of accident. The following data is not released: medical information.

Access by: mail, in person, online.

Fee & Payment: The fee is $5.00 for a walk-in or mail-in request for a driving record. An accident report is available for $3.50 per page. Fee payee: Department of Revenue. Prepayment required. Personal checks accepted. No credit cards accepted.

Mail search: Turnaround time: 2-5 days. A self addressed stamped envelope is requested.

In person search: Walk-in requests are usually processed within 30 minutes. Local law enforcement agencies may also honor driving record requests at a higher cost.

Online search: Kansas has contracted with the Information Network of Kansas (INK) (800-452-

6727) to service all electronic media requests of driver license histories. INK offers connection through an "800 number" or can be reached via the Internet (www.ink.org). The fee is $3.50 per record.There is an initial $75 subscription fee and an annual $60 fee to access records from INK. The system is open 24 hours a day, 7 days a week. Batch requests are available at 7:30 am (if ordered by 10 pm the previous day).

Other access: Tape-to-tape request records are available on an overnight basis through INK.

Vehicle Ownership
Vehicle Identification

Division of Vehicles, Title and Registration Bureau, 915 Harrison, Rm 155, Topeka, KS 66612; 785-296-3621, 785-296-3852 (Fax), 7:30AM-4:45PM.

www.ink.org/public/kdor/kdorvehicle

Indexing & Storage: Records are available from approximately 1940. Older records are on microfilm, on microfiche from 1970-1987, and computerized since 1988.

Searching: Casual requesters can obtain records, no personal information is released if subject opted out. Records are restricted from purchase for the purpose of obtaining address mail lists for selling property or services. Mail and walk-in search requesters are asked to use Form TR-18.

Access by: mail, in person, online.

Fee & Payment: The fee for a title/registration verification depends on the request mode, noted as below. Fee payee: Kansas Department of Revenue. Prepayment required. Personal checks accepted. No credit cards accepted.

Mail search: Turnaround time: 2 days. The fee for a title or registration verification is $5.00 ($3.50, if your own record). The fee for a title application copy of a vehicle title history is $10.00.A self addressed stamped envelope is requested.

In person search: Inquires are processed while you wait; however, requests must be in writing. Same fees as by mail.

Online search: Online batch inquires are $3.00 per record; online interactive requests are $4.00 per record. See the Driving Records Section for a complete description of the Information Network of Kansas (800-452-6727), the state authorized vendor. There is an initial $75 subscription fee and an annual $60 fee to access records from INK.

Other access: The state has several programs available to sell data in bulk format. Contact Cathy Reardon at the Dept of Revenue's Bureau of Research & Analysis.

Boat & Vessel Ownership
Boat & Vessel Registration

Kansas Wildlife & Parks Department, Boat Registration, 512 SE 25th Ave, Pratt, KS 67124-

8174; 316-672-5911, 316-672-6020 (Fax), 8AM-5PM M-F.

www.kdwp.state.ks.us

Note: Liens must be searched at the county level.

Indexing & Storage: Records are available from 1967-present. Records are indexed on computer. Titles are not required. All motorized or sailboats must be reqistered.

Searching: All requests must be submitted in writing with specific reason given for the request. No information is released for solicitation purposes. To search, either the hull ID or name is required.

Access by: mail, fax, in person.

Fee & Payment: There is no search fee, unless extensive searching is requested.

Mail search: Turnaround time: 3 weeks. No self addressed stamped envelope is required.

Fax search: Same criteria as mail searching.

In person search: Searching is available in person.

Legislation-Current/Pending
Legislation-Passed

Kansas State Library, Capitol Bldg, 300 SW 10th Ave, Topeka, KS 66612; 785-296-2149, 785-296-6650 (Fax), 8AM-5PM.

www.ink.org

Note: A second url is http://skways.lib.ks.us/ksl

Indexing & Storage: Records are available from 1908-present. Records are on computer since 1991.

Searching: Include either bill number or bill topic.

Access by: mail, phone, fax, in person, online.

Fee & Payment: First 20 pages are free for all searches. Copies are $.10 a page. Fee payee: Kansas State Library. Personal checks accepted. No credit cards accepted.

Mail search: Turnaround time: 1-2 days. No self addressed stamped envelope is required. No fee for mail request.

Phone search: No fee for telephone request.

Fax search: Fax searching available.

In person search: No fee for request.

Online search: The web site has bill information for the current session. The site also contains access to the state statutes.

Voter Registration
Access to Records is Restricted

Secretary of State, Department of Elections, 300 SW 10th Street, 2nd Fl, Topeka, KS 66612; 785-296-4564, 785-291-3051 (Fax), 8AM-5PM.

http://www.kssos.org

Note: Individual records must be searched at the county level. This agency will sell the database on disk, CD or tape format only for political purposes.

GED Certificates

Kansas Board of Regents, GED,,; 785-296-3191, 785-296-0983 (Fax).

www.kansasregents.com

Searching: Include the following in your request-Social Security Number, signed release. Also include the date of the test.

Access by: mail, fax, in person.

Fee & Payment: There is no fee for a verification, the fee for a transcript is $5.00. Fee payee: Kansas Board of Regents. Prepayment required. Cash and money orders are accepted. No credit cards accepted.

Mail search: Turnaround time: 1 week. No self addressed stamped envelope is required.

Fax search: Same criteria as mail searching.

In person search: Searching is available in person.

Hunting License Information

Dept of Wildlife & Parks, Operations Office, Fish & Wildlife, 512 SE 25th Ave, Pratt, KS 67124-8174; 316-672-5911, 316-672-6020 (Fax), 8AM-5PM.

www.kdwp.state.ks.us

Indexing & Storage: Records are available for 2 years. Boat statistics are available. Records are indexed on hard copy.

Searching: You can get big game information only. You must submit request in writing indicating what information you require and its intended use. Requests for information to be used for the sale of products or services will not be answered. Include the following in your request-full name, date of birth.

Access by: mail, in person.

Fee & Payment: You must have Department approval. The agency reserves the right to recover costs for voluminous requests.

Mail search: Turnaround time: 1-3 days. No self addressed stamped envelope is required.

In person search: You may request information in person.

Fishing License Information
Records not maintained by a state level agency.

Licenses Searchable Online

Athletic Trainer #10 .... www.docboard.org/ks/df/kssearch.htm
Chiropractor #10 .... www.docboard.org/ks/df/kssearch.htm
Insurance Company #22 .... www.ksinsurance.org/company/main.html
Medical Doctor #10 .... www.docboard.org/ks/df/kssearch.htm
Mortician #11 .... www.ink.org/public/ksbma/listings.html
Occupational Therapist/Assistant #10 .... www.docboard.org/ks/df/kssearch.htm
Optometrist #26 .... www.arbo.org/nodb2000/licsearch.asp
Physician Assistant #10 .... www.docboard.org/ks/df/kssearch.htm
Podiatrist #10 .... www.docboard.org/ks/df/kssearch.htm
Respiratory Therapist #10 .... www.docboard.org/ks/df/kssearch.htm

Licensing Quick Finder

Abstractor #01 316-544-2311
Adult Care Home Administrator #16 785-296-0061
Alcohol Vendor License #20 785-296-7015
Alcohol/Drug Counselor #03 785-296-3240
Ambulance Attendant #08 785-296-7299
Animal Keeper #02 785-296-2326
Architect #14 785-296-3053
Athletic Trainer #10 785-296-7413
Attorney #18 785-296-8409
Audiologist #16 785-296-0061
Barber #05 785-296-2211
Body Piercers #06 785-296-3155
Child Care Attendant #30 785-296-1240
Chiropractor #10 785-296-7413
Cosmetic Facilities #06 785-296-3155
Cosmetologist #06 785-296-3155
Cosmetology School Instructor #06 785-296-3155
Dental Hygienist #19 785-273-0780
Dentist/Dental Hygienist #19 785-273-0780
Dietitian #16 785-296-0061
Electrologist #06 785-296-3155
Embalmer #11 785-296-3980
Emergency Medical Technician #08 785-296-7299
Engineer #14 785-296-3053
Esthetics #06 785-296-3155
Funeral Branch Establishment #11 785-296-3980
Funeral Director #11 785-296-3980
Funeral Director Assistant #11 785-296-3980

Funeral Establishment #11 785-296-3980
General Contractor #21 785-296-4460
Geologist #14 785-296-3054
Hearing Aid Dispenser #09 316-263-0774
Home Health Aide #16 785-296-1250
Insurance Agent #22 785-296-7859
Investment Advisor #29 785-296-3307
Landscape Architect #14 785-296-3053
Livestock Brand #02 785-296-2326
Lobbyist #27 785-296-3488
Marriage & Family Therapist #03 785-296-3240
Medical Doctor #10 785-296-7413
Medication Aide #16 785-296-1250
Mortician #11 785-296-3980
Nail Technician #06 785-296-3155
Notary Public #27 785-296-2239
Nurse #12 785-296-4929
Nurse Aide #16 785-296-1250
Nursing Home Administrator #16 785-296-0061
Occupational Therapist/Assistant #10 .. 785-296-7413
Optometrist #26 785-832-9986
Osteopathic Physician #10 785-296-7413
Permanent Cosmetic Technician #06 785-296-3155
Pesticide Applicator #24 785-296-2263
Pesticide Dealer #24 785-296-2263
Pharmacist #13 785-296-8420
Physical Therapist/Assistant #10 785-296-7413
Physician Assistant #10 785-296-7413

Podiatrist #10 785-296-7413
Private Investigator #23 785-296-4436
Professional Counselor #03 785-296-3240
Psychologist #03 785-296-3240
Public Accountant-CPA #04 785-296-2162
Racing Concessionaire #25 785-296-5800
Racing Occupation License #25 785-296-5800
Real Estate Agent #28 785-296-0706
Real Estate Appraiser #28 785-296-0706
Real Estate Broker #28 785-296-0706
Respiratory Care Practitioner #10 785-296-7413
Respiratory Therapist #10 785-296-7413
School Administrator #07 785-296-2288
School Counselor #07 785-296-2288
School Library Media Specialist #07 785-296-2288
School Nurse #07 785-296-2288
Securities Agent #29 785-296-3307
Securities Broker/Dealer #29 785-296-3307
Shorthand Reporter #17 785-296-8410
Social Worker #03 785-296-3240
Speech/Language Pathologist #16 785-296-0061
Surveyor #14 785-296-3053
Tanning Facilities #06 785-296-3155
Tattoo Artist #06 785-296-3155
Teacher #07 785-296-2288
Track Occupation License #25 785-296-5800
Veterinarian #15 785-355-6358

Licensing Agency Information

01 Abstracters Board of Examiners, 525 W Jefferson St, Box 549, 4th Fl, Hugoton, KS 67951-0549; 316-544-2311, Fax: 316-544-8029.

02 Animal Health Department, 708 S Jackson, Topeka, KS 66603-3714; 785-296-2326, Fax: 785-296-1765.

03 Behavioral Sciences Regulatory Board, 712 S Kansas, Topeka, KS 66603; 785-296-3240, Fax: 785-296-3112.

04 Board of Accountancy, 900 SW Jackson, Topeka, KS 66612-1239; 785-296-2162.

05 Board of Barbering, 700 SW Jackson #1002, Topeka, KS 66603; 785-296-2211, Fax: 785-296-2211.

06 Board of Cosmetology, 2708 NW Topeka Blvd, Topeka, KS 66617-1139; 785-296-3155, Fax: 785-296-3002.

07 Board of Education, 120 SE 10th Ave, Topeka, KS 66612-1182; 785-296-2288, Fax: 785-296-7933.

08 Board of Emergency Medical Services, 109 SW 6th, Topeka, KS 66603-3826; 785-296-7299, Fax: 785-296-6212.

09 Board of Examiners for Hearing Aid Dispensers, PO Box 252 (600 N St Francis), Wichita, KS 67201-0252; 316-263-0774, Fax: 316-264-2681.

10 Board of Healing Arts, 235 S Topeka Blvd, Topeka, KS 66603-3059; 785-296-7413, Fax: 785-296-0852.

www.ink.org/public/boha

11 Board of Mortuary Arts, 700 SW Jackson, #904, Topeka, KS 66603-3733; 785-296-3980, Fax: 785-296-0891.

www.ink.org/public/ksbma

Direct URL to search licenses: www.ink.org/public/ksbma/listings.html

12 Board of Nursing, 900 SW Jackson, Rm 5515, Topeka, KS 66612-1230; 785-296-2967, Fax: 785-296-3929.

www.ink.org/public/ksbn There is a searchable database of licenses available online, but you must be a registered user of INK (Information Network of Kansas).

13 Board of Pharmacy, 900 Jackson, Landon State Office Bldg, Rm 513, Topeka, KS 66612; 785-296-4056, Fax: 785-296-8420.

14 Board of Technical Professions, 900 SW Jackson, Rm 507, Topeka, KS 66612-1257; 785-296-3053.

www.state.ks.us/public/ksbtp/roster.html

15 Board of Veterinary Examiners, PO Box 242 (PO Box 242), Wamego, KS 66547-0242; 785-456-8781, Fax: 785-456-8782.

16 Department of Health & Environment, Bureau of Health Facilities, 900 SW Jackson #1051-S, Topeka, KS 66612-1290; 785-296-0056, Fax: 785-296-3075.

www.kdhe.state.ks.us/hoc/index.html

17 Clerk of Appellate Court, 301 W 10th St, Topeka, KS 66612; 785-296-8410, Fax: 785-296-1028.

www.kscourts.org

18 Clerk of the Supreme Court, 301 SW 10th Ave, Topeka, KS 66612; 785-296-8409, Fax: 785-296-1028.

www.kscourts.org

19 Dental Board, 3601 SW 29th St #134, Topeka, KS 66614-2062; 785-273-0780, Fax: 785-273-7545.

20 Department of Revenue, Alcoholic Beverage Control, 200 SE 6th St, 4 Townsite Plaza, #210, Topeka, KS 66603-3512; 785-296-7015, Fax: 785-296-1279.

www.ink.org/public/kdor/abc/

21 Department of Revenue, PO Box 30008 (Robert B Docking, State Office Bldg), Topeka, KS 66625-0001; 785-296-3160.

www.state.ks.us/ink-index.cgi?type=byserv&

22 Insurance Department, 420 SW 9th, Topeka, KS 66612-1678; 785-296-7859, Fax: 785-368-7019.
www.ksinsurance.org

Direct URL to search licenses: www.ksinsurance.org/company/main.html You can search online using company name, type, class, or state Searching is fee but there are fees to download from their database.

23 Bureau of Investigation, 1620 SW Tyler, Topeka, KS 66612-1837; 785-296-8200, Fax: 785-296-6781.

www.ink.org/public/kbi

24 Department of Agriculture, Division of Taxation, 901 S Kansas Ave,, Topeka, KS 66612-1280; 785-296-2263, Fax: 785-296-0673.

www.state.ks.us/ink-index.cgi?type=byserv&which=agencies

25 Racing Commission, 3400 SW Van Buren, Topeka, KS 66611-2228; 785-296-5800, Fax: 785-296-0900.

www.state.ks.us/ink-index.cgi?type=byserv&which=agencies

26 Board of Examiners in Optometry, 3111 W 6th #A, Lawrence, KS 66049; 785-832-9986, Fax: 785-832-9986.
www.terraworld.net/kssbeo/

Direct URL to search licenses: www.arbo.org/nodb2000/licsearch.asp You can search online using national database by name, city, or state

27 Office of Secretary of State, State Capitol, 2nd Fl, Topeka, KS 66612; 785-296-1848, Fax: 785-296-4570.

www.state.ks.us/ink-index.cgi?type=byserv&which=agencies

28 Real Estate Commission, Real Estate Appraisal Board, PO Box 36104-94 (820 S Quincy Rm 314), Topeka, KS 66612; 785-296-0706, Fax: 785-296-1771.

www.state.ks.us/ink-index.cgi?type=byserv&which=agencies

29 Securities Commissioner of Kansas, PO Box 94064 (618 S Kansas 2nd Fl), Topeka, KS 66603-3804; 785-296-3307, Fax: 785-296-6872.

www.ink.org/public/ksecom

30 Child Care Licensing & Registration, 900 SW Jackson #260, Topeka, KS 66612; 785-296-1240.

The following list indicates the district and division name for each county in the state. If the district or division name of the bankruptcy court is different from the civil/criminal court, it appears in parentheses.

County/Court Cross Reference

County	Court	County	Court
Allen	Topeka	Linn	Kansas City
Anderson	Topeka	Logan	Wichita
Atchison	Kansas City	Lyon	Topeka
Barber	Wichita	Marion	Topeka
Barton	Wichita	Marshall	Kansas City
Bourbon	Kansas City	McPherson	Wichita
Brown	Kansas City	Meade	Wichita
Butler	Wichita	Miami	Kansas City
Chase	Topeka	Mitchell	Topeka
Chautauqua	Wichita	Montgomery	Wichita
Cherokee	Kansas City	Morris	Topeka
Cheyenne	Wichita	Morton	Wichita
Clark	Wichita	Nemaha	Kansas City
Clay	Topeka	Neosho	Topeka
Cloud	Topeka	Ness	Wichita
Coffey	Topeka	Norton	Wichita
Comanche	Kansas City (Wichita)	Osage	Topeka
Cowley	Wichita	Osborne	Wichita
Crawford	Kansas City	Ottawa	Topeka
Decatur	Wichita	Pawnee	Wichita
Dickinson	Topeka	Phillips	Wichita
Doniphan	Kansas City	Pottawatomie	Topeka
Douglas	Topeka	Pratt	Wichita
Edwards	Wichita	Rawlins	Wichita
Elk	Wichita	Reno	Wichita
Ellis	Wichita	Republic	Topeka
Ellsworth	Wichita	Rice	Wichita
Finney	Wichita	Riley	Topeka
Ford	Wichita	Rooks	Wichita
Franklin	Topeka	Rush	Wichita
Geary	Topeka	Russell	Wichita
Gove	Wichita	Saline	Topeka
Graham	Wichita	Scott	Wichita
Grant	Wichita	Sedgwick	Wichita
Gray	Wichita	Seward	Wichita
Greeley	Wichita	Shawnee	Topeka
Greenwood	Wichita	Sheridan	Wichita
Hamilton	Wichita	Sherman	Wichita
Harper	Wichita	Smith	Wichita
Harvey	Wichita	Stafford	Wichita
Haskell	Wichita	Stanton	Wichita
Hodgeman	Wichita	Stevens	Wichita
Jackson	Topeka	Sumner	Wichita
Jefferson	Wichita	Thomas	Wichita
Jewell	Topeka	Trego	Wichita
Johnson	Kansas City	Wabaunsee	Topeka
Kearny	Wichita	Wallace	Wichita
Kingman	Wichita	Washington	Topeka
Kiowa	Wichita	Wichita	Wichita
Labette	Kansas City	Wilson	Topeka
Lane	Wichita	Woodson	Topeka
Leavenworth	Kansas City	Wyandotte	Kansas City
Lincoln	Topeka		

US District Court

District of Kansas

Kansas City Division Clerk, 500 State Ave, Kansas City, KS 66101, 913-551-6719.

www.ksd.uscourts.gov

Counties: Atchison, Bourbon, Brown, Cherokee, Crawford, Doniphan, Johnson, Labette, Leavenworth, Linn, Marshall, Miami, Nemaha, Wyandotte.

Indexing & Storage: Cases are indexed by defendant and plaintiff as well as by case number. New cases are available in the index immediately after filing date. Both computer and card indexes are maintained. Records are also indexed on microfiche. Open records are located at this court.

Fee & Payment: The fee is no charge per item (one party name or case number). Payment may be made by money order, cashier check, personal check. No search fee is charged unless certification is required. All certification searches are conducted by the Wichita office. Payee: Clerk, US District Court. Certification fee: $5.00 per document. Copy fee: $.50 per page.

Phone Search: Only docket information will be released over the phone if you have a case number.

Mail Search: A stamped self addressed envelope is not required.

In Person Search: In person searching is available.

PACER: Sign-up number is 800-676-6856. Access fee is $.60 per minute. Toll-free access: 800-898-3078. Local access: 913-551-6556. Case records are available back to 1991. Records are never purged. New civil records are available online after 2 days. New criminal records are available online after 3 days. PACER is available on the Internet at http://pacer.ksd.uscourts.gov.

Topeka Division Clerk, US District Court, Room 490, 444 SE Quincy, Topeka, KS 66683, 785-295-2610.

www.ksd.uscourts.gov

Counties: Allen, Anderson, Chase, Clay, Cloud, Coffey, Dickinson, Douglas, Franklin, Geary, Jackson, Jewell, Lincoln, Lyon, Marion, Mitchell, Morris, Neosho, Osage, Ottawa, Pottawatomie, Republic, Riley, Saline, Shawnee, Wabaunsee, Washington, Wilson, Woodson.

Indexing & Storage: Cases are indexed by defendant and plaintiff as well as by case number. New cases are available in the index 24 hours after filing date. A full name, the case number and a date are very helpful to obtain records. Both computer and card indexes are maintained. Open records are located at this court.

Fee & Payment: The fee is $15.00 per item (one party name or case number). Payment may be made by money order, cashier check, personal check. Prepayment is required. Payee: Clerk of US District Court. Certification fee: $5.00 per document. Copy fee: $.50 per page.

Phone Search: Docket information available by phone. An automated voice case information service (VCIS) is not available.

Mail Search: Always enclose a stamped self addressed envelope.

In Person Search: In person searching is available.

PACER: Sign-up number is 800-676-6856. Access fee is $.60 per minute. Toll-free access: 800-898-3078. Local access: 913-551-6556. Case records are available back to 1991. Records are never purged. New civil records are available online after 2 days. New criminal records are available online after 3 days. PACER is available on the Internet at http://pacer.ksd.uscourts.gov.

Wichita Division 204 US Courthouse, 401 N Market, Wichita, KS 67202-2096, 316-269-6491.

www.ksd.uscourts.gov

Counties: All counties in Kansas. Cases may be heard from counties in the other division.

Indexing & Storage: Cases are indexed by defendant and plaintiff as well as by case number. New cases are available in the index immediately after filing date. Both computer and card indexes are maintained. Records are indexed on the computer since 1990. Prior records are indexed on microfiche or index cards. Open records are located at this court. District wide searches are available from this court.

Fee & Payment: The fee is $15.00 per item (one party name or case number). Payment may be made by money order, cashier check, personal check. Prepayment is required. Payee: Clerk, US District Court. Certification fee: $5.00 per document. Copy fee: $.50 per page.

Phone Search: Will do computer search on one name over the phone. An automated voice case information service (VCIS) is not available.

Mail Search: Always enclose a stamped self addressed envelope.

In Person Search: In person searching is available.

PACER: Sign-up number is 800-676-6856. Access fee is $.60 per minute. Toll-free access: 800-898-3078. Local access: 913-551-6556. Case records are available back to 1991. Records are never purged. New civil records are available online after 2 days. New criminal records are available online after 3 days. PACER is available on the Internet at http://pacer.ksd.uscourts.gov.

US Bankruptcy Court

District of Kansas

Kansas City Division 500 State Ave, Room 161, Kansas City, KS 66101, 913-551-6732.

www.ksb.uscourts.gov

Counties: Atchison, Bourbon, Brown, Cherokee, Comanche, Crawford, Doniphan, Johnson, Labette, Leavenworth, Linn, Marshall, Miami, Nemaha, Wyandotte.

Indexing & Storage: Cases are indexed by debtor as well as by case number. New cases are available in the index 1 day after filing date. Approximate year of filing will also help in the search for files. A computer index is maintained. Bankruptcy searches can be performed from any bankruptcy court in the district for case files from 1989 forward; master listing for pre-1989 cases are available from the Topeka Office. Open records are located at this court.

Fee & Payment: The fee is $15.00 per item (one party name or case number). Payment may be made by money order, cashier check, personal check. Prepayment is required. Debtor's checks are not accepted. Payee: Clerk of US Bankruptcy Court. Certification fee: $5.00 per document. Copy

fee: $.50 per page. You are allowed to make your own copies. These copies cost $.25 per page.

Phone Search: Only docket information is available by phone. An automated voice case information service (VCIS) is available. Call VCIS at 800-827-9028 or 316-269-6668.

Mail Search: Always enclose a stamped self addressed envelope.

In Person Search: In person searching is available.

PACER: Sign-up number is 800-676-6856. Access fee is $.60 per minute. Toll-free access: 800-613-7052. Local access: 316-269-6258. Case records are available back to 1988. Records are purged every 6 months. New civil records are available online after 1 day. PACER is available on the Internet at http://pacer.ksb.uscourts.gov.

Topeka Division 240 US Courthouse, 444 SE Quincy, Topeka, KS 66683, 785-295-2750.

www.ksb.uscourts.gov

Counties: Allen, Anderson, Chase, Clay, Cloud, Coffey, Dickinson, Douglas, Franklin, Geary, Jackson, Jewell, Lincoln, Lyon, Marion, Mitchell, Morris, Neosho, Osage, Ottawa, Pottawatomie, Republic, Riley, Saline, Shawnee, Wabaunsee, Washington, Wilson, Woodson.

Indexing & Storage: Cases are indexed by debtor as well as by case number. New cases are available in the index 1 day after filing date. A computer index is maintained. Approximate year of filing will also help in the search for files. Open records are located at this court.

Fee & Payment: The fee is $15.00 per item (one party name or case number). Payment may be made by money order, cashier check, personal check. Prepayment is required. Debtor's checks are not accepted. Payee: Clerk, US Bankruptcy Court. Certification fee: $5.00 per document. Copy fee: $.50 per page. You are allowed to make your own copies. These copies cost $.25 per page.

Phone Search: Only docket information is available by phone. An automated voice case information service (VCIS) is available. Call VCIS at 800-827-9028 or 316-269-6668.

Mail Search: A stamped self addressed envelope is not required.

In Person Search: In person searching is available.

PACER: Sign-up number is 800-676-6856. Access fee is $.60 per minute. Toll-free access: 800-613-7052. Local access: 316-269-6258. Case records are available back to 1988. Records are purged every 6 months. New civil records are available online after 1 day. PACER is available on the Internet at http://pacer.ksb.uscourts.gov.

Wichita Division 167 US Courthouse, 401 N Market, Wichita, KS 67202, 316-269-6486.

www.ksb.uscourts.gov

Counties: Barber, Barton, Butler, Chautauqua, Cheyenne, Clark, Comanche, Cowley, Decatur, Edwards, Elk, Ellis, Ellsworth, Finney, Ford, Gove, Graham, Grant, Gray, Greeley, Greenwood, Hamilton, Harper, Harvey, Haskell, Hodgeman, Jefferson, Kearny, Kingman, Kiowa, Lane, Logan, Mcpherson, Meade, Montgomery, Morton, Ness, Norton, Osborne, Pawnee, Phillips, Pratt, Rawlins, Reno, Rice, Rooks, Rush, Russell, Scott, Sedgwick, Seward, Sheridan, Smith, Stafford, Stanton, Stevens, Sumner, Thomas, Trego, Wallace, Wichita.

Indexing & Storage: Cases are indexed by debtor as well as by case number. New cases are available in the index 1 day after filing date. A computer index is maintained. Records are also indexed on microfiche. Open records are located at this court. District wide searches are available from this division.

Fee & Payment: The fee is $15.00 per item (one party name or case number). Payment may be made by money order, cashier check, personal check. Prepayment is required. Payee: Clerk, US Bankruptcy Court. Certification fee: $5.00 per document. Copy fee: $.50 per page. You are allowed to make your own copies. These copies cost $.25 per page.

Phone Search: Only the attorneys, trustees, hearing dates and file dates will be released over the phone. An automated voice case information service (VCIS) is available. Call VCIS at 800-827-9028 or 316-269-6668.

Mail Search: A stamped self addressed envelope is not required.

In Person Search: In person searching is available.

PACER: Sign-up number is 800-676-6856. Access fee is $.60 per minute. Toll-free access: 800-613-7052. Local access: 316-269-6258. Case records are available back to 1988. Records are purged every 6 months. New civil records are available online after 1 day. PACER is available on the Internet at http://pacer.ksb.uscourts.gov.

Court	Jurisdiction	No. of Courts	How Organized
District Courts*	General	109	31 Districts
Municipal Courts	Municipal	350	

* Profiled in this Sourcebook.

CIVIL									
Court	Tort	Contract	Real Estate	Min. Claim	Max. Claim	Small Claims	Estate	Eviction	Domestic Relations
District Courts*	X	X	X	$0	No Max	$1800	X	X	
Municipal Courts									

CRIMINAL					
Court	Felony	Misdemeanor	DWI/DUI	Preliminary Hearing	Juvenile
District Courts*	X	X	X	X	X
Municipal Courts			X		

ADMINISTRATION Judicial Administrator, Kansas Judicial Center, 301 SW 10th St, Topeka, KS, 66612; 785-296-4873, Fax: 785-296-7076. www.kscourts.html

COURT STRUCTURE The District Court is the court of general jurisdiction. There are 109 courts in 31 districts in 105 counties.

ONLINE ACCESS Commercial online access is available for District Court Records in 3 counties - Johnson, Sedgwick, and Wyandotte - through the Information Network of Kansas (INK) Services. Franklin and Finney counties may be available by late 2000. A user can access INK through their Internet site at www.ink.org or via a dial-up system. The INK subscription fee is $75.00, and the annual renewal fee is $60.00. There is no per minute connect charge, but there is a transaction fee. Othe information from INK includes Drivers License, Title, Registration, Lien, and UCC searches. For additional information or a registration packet, call 800-4-KANSAS (800-452-6727).

ADDITIONAL INFORMATION Five counties - Cowley, Crawford, Labette, Montgomery and Neosho - have two hearing locations, but only one record center, which is the location included in this Sourcebook.

Many Kansas courts do not do criminal record searches and will refer any criminal requests to the Kansas Bureau of Investigation.

Allen County

District Court PO Box 630, Iola, KS 66749; 316-365-1425; Fax: 316-365-1429. Hours: 8AM-5PM (CST). *Felony, Misdemeanor, Civil, Eviction, Small Claims, Probate.*

Civil Records: Access: Fax, mail, in person. Both court and visitors may perform in person searches. Search fee: $10.80 per hour. Required to search: name, years to search. Civil cases indexed by defendant, plaintiff. Civil records on computer from 1993, manual index from 1800s. **Criminal Records:** Access: In person only. Court does not conduct in person searches; visitors must perform searches for themselves. Search fee: No criminal searches performed by court. Required to search: name, years to search. Criminal records on computer from 1993, manual index from 1800s. **General Information:** No juvenile (under the age of 15), mental health, sealed or expunged records released. SASE required. Turnaround time 1 week. Copy fee: $.25 per page. Certification fee: $1.00. Fee payee: Clerk of Court. Personal checks accepted. Prepayment is required. Public access terminal is available. Fax notes: $3.00 for first page, $1.00 each addl.

Anderson County

District Court PO Box 305, Garnett, KS 66032; 785-448-6886; Fax: 785-448-3230. Hours: 8AM-5PM (CST). *Felony, Misdemeanor, Civil, Eviction, Small Claims, Probate.*

www.kscourts.org.dstcts/4dstct.htm

Civil Records: Access: Fax, mail, in person. Both court and visitors may perform in person searches. No search fee. Required to search: name, years to search. Civil cases indexed by defendant, plaintiff. Civil records on computer from 1977, index books from 1800s. **Criminal Records:** Access: In person only. Court does not conduct in person searches; visitors must perform searches for themselves. Search fee: No criminal searches performed by court. Required to search: name, years to search. Criminal records on computer from 1977, index books from 1800s. The court urges requesters to contact the KS Bureau of Investigations. **General Information:** No juvenile, mental health, sealed or expunged records released. SASE required. Turnaround time same day. Copy fee: $.25 per page. Certification fee: $1.00. Fee payee: District Court. Personal checks accepted. Public access terminal is available. Public Access Terminal Note: Not on statewide system. Fax notes: $2.00 for first page, $.50 each addl.

Atchison County

District Court PO Box 408, Atchison, KS 66002; 913-367-7400; Fax: 913-367-1171. Hours: 8AM-5PM (CST). *Felony, Misdemeanor, Civil, Eviction, Small Claims, Probate.*

Civil Records: Access: Fax, mail, in person. Both court and visitors may perform in person searches. Search fee: $10.80 per hour. Required to search: name, years to search. Civil cases indexed by defendant, plaintiff. Civil records on computer from 1991, microfiche from 1860s, index books from 1900s, archives from 1860s. **Criminal Records:** Access: In person only. Court does not conduct in person searches; visitors must perform searches for themselves. Search fee: No criminal searches performed by court. Required to search: name, years to search; also helpful-SSN. Criminal records on computer from 1991, microfiche from 1860s, index books from 1900s, archives from 1860s. **General Information:** No juvenile, mental health, sealed or expunged records released. SASE required. Turnaround time 1-5 days. Copy fee: $.25 per page. Certification fee: $1.00. Fee payee: District Court. Personal checks accepted. Prepayment is required. Public access terminal is available. Fax notes: $1.25 per page.

Barber County

District Court 118 E Washington, Medicine Lodge, KS 67104; 316-886-5639; Fax: 316-886-5854. Hours: 8AM-Noon,1-5PM (CST). *Felony, Misdemeanor, Civil, Eviction, Small Claims, Probate.*

Civil Records: Access: In person only. Court does not conduct in person searches; visitors must perform searches for themselves. Search fee: No civil searches performed by court. Required to search: name, years to search. Civil cases indexed by defendant, plaintiff. Civil records on computer from 1987, microfiche from 1900-1976, index cards from 1800s. **Criminal Records:** Access: In person only. Court does not conduct in person searches; visitors must perform searches for themselves. Search fee: No criminal searches performed by court. Required to search: name, years to search, SSN; also helpful-DOB. Criminal records on computer from 1987, microfiche from 1900-1976, index cards from 1800s. **General Information:** No juvenile, mental health, sealed or expunged records released. Copy fee: $.25 per page. Certification fee: $1.00. Fee payee: District Court. Personal checks accepted. Public access terminal is available.

Barton County

District Court 1400 Main, Rm 306, Great Bend, KS 67530; 316-793-1856; Fax: 316-793-1860. Hours: 8AM-5PM (CST). *Felony, Misdemeanor, Civil, Eviction, Small Claims, Probate.*

Civil Records: Access: Fax, mail, in person. Both court and visitors may perform in person searches. Search fee: $10.80 per hour. Required to search: name, years to search. Civil cases indexed by defendant, plaintiff. Civil records on computer 1990, microfiche and archives from 1800s, index from 1987. **Criminal Records:** Access: Fax, mail, in person. Both court and visitors may perform in person searches. Search fee: $10.80 per hour. Required to search: name, years to search. Criminal records on computer 1990, microfiche and archives from 1800s, index from 1987. **General Information:** No juvenile, mental health, sealed or expunged records released. Turnaround time 3 days. Copy fee: $.35 per page. Certification fee: No certification fee. Fee payee: Clerk of Court. Personal checks accepted. Prepayment is required. Public access terminal is available. Fax notes: No fee to fax results.

Bourbon County

District Court PO Box 868, Ft Scott, KS 66701; 316-223-0780; Fax: 316-223-5303. Hours: 8:30AM-4:30PM (CST). *Felony, Misdemeanor, Civil, Eviction, Small Claims, Probate.*

Civil Records: Access: Fax, mail, in person. Both court and visitors may perform in person searches. Search fee: $10.80 per hour. Required to search: name, years to search. Civil cases indexed by defendant, plaintiff. Civil records on computer since 1990, index on computer since 1985. **Criminal Records:** Access: Fax, mail, in person. Both court and visitors may perform in person searches. Search fee: $10.80 per hour. Required to search: name, years to search; also helpful-SSN. Criminal records on computer since 1990, index on computer since 1985. **General Information:** No juvenile, mental health, sealed or expunged records released. SASE required. Turnaround time 3 days. Copy fee: $.25 per page. Certification fee: $1.00. Fee payee: Clerk of Court. Personal checks

accepted. Prepayment is required. Fax notes: $1.00 per page.

Brown County

District Court PO Box 417, Hiawatha, KS 66434; 785-742-7481; Fax: 785-742-3506. Hours: 8AM-5PM (CST). *Felony, Misdemeanor, Civil, Eviction, Small Claims, Probate.*

Civil Records: Access: Phone, fax, mail, in person. Both court and visitors may perform in person searches. Search fee: $9.00 per hour. Required to search: name, years to search. Civil cases indexed by defendant, plaintiff. Civil records on computer from 1982, microfiche from 1900s, index books from 1900s. **Criminal Records:** Access: Phone, fax, mail, in person. Both court and visitors may perform in person searches. Search fee: $9.00 per hour. Required to search: name, years to search; also helpful-SSN. Criminal records on computer from 1982, microfiche from 1900s, index books from 1900s. **General Information:** No juvenile, mental health, sealed or expunged records released. SASE required. Turnaround time 1-2 days. Copy fee: $.50 for first page, $.25 each addl. Certification fee: $1.00. Fee payee: District Court. Personal checks accepted. Prepayment is required. Public access terminal is available. Fax notes: $2.00 for first page, $1.00 each addl.

Butler County

District Court PO Box 432, El Dorado, KS 67042; 316-322-4370; Fax: 316-321-9486. Hours: 8:30AM-5PM (CST). *Felony, Misdemeanor, Civil, Eviction, Small Claims, Probate.*

Civil Records: Access: In person only. Court does not conduct in person searches; visitors must perform searches for themselves. Search fee: No civil searches performed by court. Required to search: name, years to search. Civil cases indexed by defendant, plaintiff. Civil records on computer from 1992, index cards from 1800s. **Criminal Records:** Access: In person only. Court does not conduct in person searches; visitors must perform searches for themselves. Search fee: No criminal searches performed by court. Required to search: name, years to search, SSN. Criminal records on computer from 1992, index cards from 1800s. **General Information:** No juvenile, mental health, sealed or expunged records released. Copy fee: $.25 per page. Certification fee: $1.00. Fee payee: Clerk of District Court. Personal checks accepted. Fax fees billed. Public access terminal is available.

Chase County

District Court PO Box 207, Cottonwood Falls, KS 66845; 316-273-6319; Fax: 316-273-6890. Hours: 8AM-5PM (CST). *Felony, Misdemeanor, Civil, Eviction, Small Claims, Probate.*

Civil Records: Access: In person only. Court does not conduct in person searches; visitors must perform searches for themselves. Search fee: No civil searches performed by court. Required to search: name, years to search. Civil cases indexed by defendant, plaintiff. Civil records on computer from late 1990, microfiche from 1860, index books from 1860. **Criminal Records:** Access: In person only. Court does not conduct in person searches; visitors must perform searches for themselves. Search fee: No criminal searches performed by court. Required to search: name, years to search. Criminal records on computer from late 1990, microfiche from 1860, index books from 1860. **General Information:** No juvenile, mental health, sealed or expunged records released. Copy fee: $.25 per page.

Certification fee: $2.00. Fee payee: District Court. Personal checks accepted. Prepayment is required.

Chautauqua County

District Court 215 N Chautauqua, PO Box 306, Sedan, KS 67361; 316-725-5870; Fax: 316-725-3027. Hours: 8AM-5PM (CST). *Felony, Misdemeanor, Civil, Eviction, Small Claims, Probate.*

Civil Records: Access: Mail, in person. Both court and visitors may perform in person searches. Search fee: $10.80 per hour. Required to search: name, years to search. Civil cases indexed by defendant, plaintiff. Civil records on computer from 1994, microfiche and archives from 1950, index cards from 1870. **Criminal Records:** Access: Mail, in person. Both court and visitors may perform in person searches. Search fee: $10.80 per hour. Required to search: name, years to search; also helpful-DOB. Criminal records on computer from 1994, microfiche and archives from 1950, index cards from 1870. **General Information:** No juvenile, mental health, sealed or expunged records released. SASE required. Turnaround time 1-2 weeks. Copy fee: $.25 per page. Certification fee: $1.00. Fee payee: District Court. Personal checks accepted. Public access terminal is available.

Cherokee County

District Court PO Box 189, Columbus, KS 66725; 316-429-3880; Fax: 316-429-1130. Hours: 8AM-5PM (CST). *Felony, Misdemeanor, Civil, Eviction, Small Claims, Probate.*

Civil Records: Access: In person only. Court does not conduct in person searches; visitors must perform searches for themselves. Search fee: No civil searches performed by court. Required to search: name, years to search. Civil cases indexed by defendant, plaintiff. Civil records on computer from 1990, index books from 1867. **Criminal Records:** Access: In person only. Court does not conduct in person searches; visitors must perform searches for themselves. Search fee: No criminal searches performed by court. Required to search: name, years to search; also helpful-SSN. Criminal records on computer from 1990, index books from 1867. **General Information:** No juvenile, mental health, sealed or expunged records released. Certification fee: $1.00. Fee payee: District Court. Personal checks accepted. Prepayment is required. Public access terminal is available.

Cheyenne County

District Court PO Box 646, St Francis, KS 67756; 785-332-8850; Fax: 785-332-8851. Hours: 8AM-Noon,1-5PM (CST). *Felony, Misdemeanor, Civil, Eviction, Small Claims, Probate.*

Civil Records: Access: Fax, mail, in person. Both court and visitors may perform in person searches. No search fee. Required to search: name, years to search. Civil cases indexed by defendant, plaintiff. Civil records on strip index from 1989, index cards from 1870. **Criminal Records:** Access: Fax, mail, in person. Both court and visitors may perform in person searches. No search fee. Required to search: name, years to search. Criminal records on strip index from 1989, index cards from 1870. **General Information:** No juvenile, adoptions, mental health, sealed or expunged records released. SASE not required. Turnaround time 2 days. Copy fee: $.25 per page. Certification fee: $1.00. Fee payee: Clerk of Court. Personal checks accepted. Prepayment is required. Fax notes: $1.00 per page unless toll free line used.

511

The Sourcebook to Public Record Information

County Courts - Kansas

Clark County

District Court PO Box 790, Ashland, KS 67831; 316-635-2753; Fax: 316-635-2155. Hours: 8AM-5PM (CST). *Felony, Misdemeanor, Civil, Eviction, Small Claims, Probate.*

Civil Records: Access: Mail, in person. Both court and visitors may perform in person searches. Search fee: $9.00 per hour. Required to search: name, years to search. Civil cases indexed by defendant, plaintiff. Civil records on computer from 1992 (Child support only), microfiche and archives from 1800s, index cards from 1800s. **Criminal Records:** Access: Mail, in person. Both court and visitors may perform in person searches. Search fee: $9.00 per hour. Required to search: name, years to search; also helpful-SSN. Criminal records on index cards. **General Information:** No juvenile, mental health, sealed or expunged records released. SASE required. Turnaround time 1 day. Copy fee: $.25 per page. Certification fee: $1.25. Fee payee: District Court. Personal checks accepted. Prepayment is required.

Clay County

District Court PO Box 203, Clay Center, KS 67432; 785-632-3443; Fax: 785-632-2651. Hours: 8AM-5PM (CST). *Felony, Misdemeanor, Civil, Eviction, Small Claims, Probate.*

Civil Records: Access: Mail, in person. Both court and visitors may perform in person searches. Search fee: No civil searches performed by court. Required to search: name, years to search. Civil cases indexed by defendant, plaintiff. Civil records on computer from July, 1994, index books from late 1800s. **Criminal Records:** Access: In person only. Court does not conduct in person searches; visitors must perform searches for themselves. Search fee: No criminal searches performed by court. Required to search: name. Criminal records on computer from July, 1994, index books from late 1800s. **General Information:** No juvenile, adoption, mental health, sealed or expunged records released. SASE required. Turnaround time 2 days. Copy fee: $.25 per page. Certification fee: $1.00. Fee payee: Clerk of District Court. Personal checks accepted. Prepayment is required. Public access terminal is available.

Cloud County

District Court 811 Washington, Concordia, KS 66901; 785-243-8124; Fax: 785-243-8188. Hours: 8:00AM-5PM (CST). *Felony, Misdemeanor, Civil, Eviction, Small Claims, Probate.*

Civil Records: Access: Phone, fax, mail, in person. Court does not conduct in person searches; visitors must perform searches for themselves. Search fee: $10.80 per hour. Required to search: name, years to search. Civil cases indexed by defendant, plaintiff. Civil records in strip indexes from 1992, index books prior to 1992, index cards from 1800s. **Criminal Records:** Access: Fax, mail, in person. Both court and visitors may perform in person searches. Search fee: $10.80 per hour. Required to search: name, years to search; also helpful-SSN. Criminal records in strip indexes from 1992, index books prior to 1992, index cards from 1800s. **General Information:** No juvenile, mental health, sealed or expunged records released. SASE required. Turnaround time 3-4 days. Copy fee: $.25 per page. Certification fee: $1.00. Fee payee: Clerk of Court. Personal checks accepted. Prepayment is required. Fax notes: $3.00 per page.

Coffey County

District Court PO Box 330, Burlington, KS 66839; 316-364-8628; Fax: 316-364-8535. Hours: 8AM-5PM (CST). *Felony, Misdemeanor, Civil, Eviction, Small Claims, Probate.*

Civil Records: Access: Mail, in person. Both court and visitors may perform in person searches. Search fee: $10.60 per hour. Required to search: name, years to search. Civil cases indexed by defendant, plaintiff. Civil records on computer back to 1800s, index cards from 1800s. **Criminal Records:** Access: Mail, in person. Both court and visitors may perform in person searches. Search fee: $10.60 per hour. Required to search: name, years to search, SSN. Criminal records on computer back to 1800s, index cards from 1800s. The court will not do name searches nor search for employment purposes. **General Information:** No juvenile, mental health, sealed or expunged records released. SASE required. Turnaround time 1 day. Copy fee: $.25 per page. Certification fee: $1.00. Fee payee: Clerk of District Court. Personal checks accepted. Prepayment is required. Public access terminal is available.

Comanche County

District Court PO Box 722, Coldwater, KS 67029; 316-582-2182; Fax: 316-582-2603. Hours: 8AM-5PM (CST). *Felony, Misdemeanor, Civil, Eviction, Small Claims, Probate.*

Civil Records: Access: Fax, mail, in person. Both court and visitors may perform in person searches. Search fee: $10.80 per hour. Required to search: name, years to search. Civil cases indexed by defendant, plaintiff. Civil records on computer since 1992 (child support only), index cards from 1886. **Criminal Records:** Access: Fax, mail, in person. Both court and visitors may perform in person searches. Search fee: $10.80 per hour. Required to search: name, years to search; also helpful-SSN. Criminal records on index cards from 1886. **General Information:** No juvenile, mental health, sealed or expunged records released. SASE required. Turnaround time 3 days. Copy fee: $.25 per page. Certification fee: $1.00. Fee payee: District Court. Personal checks accepted. Prepayment is required. Public access terminal is available. Fax notes: $1.00 per page.

Cowley County

Arkansas City District Court PO Box 1152, Arkansas City, KS 67005; 316-441-4520; Fax: 316-442-7213. Hours: 8AM-Noon,1-4PM (CST). *Felony, Misdemeanor, Civil, Eviction, Small Claims, Probate.*

Note: This court covers the southern part of the county. All felony records are kept at Winfield.

Civil Records: Access: Mail, in person. Both court and visitors may perform in person searches. Search fee: $10.80 per hour. Required to search: name, years to search. Civil cases indexed by defendant, plaintiff. Civil records from 1977. This Court facility has only been in existence since 1977, so no records prior to that date, index cards only. Computer records commencing 1994. **Criminal Records:** Access: Mail, in person. Both court and visitors may perform in person searches. Search fee: $10.80 per hour. Required to search: name, years to search, SSN. Criminal records from 1977. This Court facility has only been in existence since 1977, so no records prior to that date, index cards only. Computer records commencing 1994. **General Information:** No juvenile, mental health, sealed or expunged

records released. SASE not required. Turnaround time 1 week. Copy fee: $.50 per page. Certification fee: $1.00. Fee payee: Clerk of Court. Personal checks accepted. Prepayment is required.

Winfield District Court PO Box 472, Winfield, KS 67156; 316-221-5470; Fax: 316-221-1097. Hours: 8AM-Noon,1-4PM (CST). *Felony, Misdemeanor, Civil, Eviction, Small Claims, Probate.*

Note: This court covers northern part of county

Civil Records: Access: Fax, mail, in person. Both court and visitors may perform in person searches. Search fee: $10.80 per hour. Required to search: name, years to search. Civil cases indexed by defendant, plaintiff. Civil records on computer since 1994, index cards from 1874. **Criminal Records:** Access: Fax, mail, in person. Both court and visitors may perform in person searches. Search fee: $10.80 per hour. Required to search: name, years to search. Criminal records on computer since 1994, index cards from 1874. **General Information:** No juvenile, mental health, sealed or expunged records released. SASE not required. Turnaround time 1 week. Copy fee: $.50 per page. Certification fee: $1.00. Fee payee: Clerk of Court. Personal checks accepted. Prepayment is required. Fax notes: $1.00 per page.

Crawford County

Girard District Court PO Box 69, Girard, KS 66743; 316-724-6211; Fax: 316-724-4987. Hours: 8:30AM-4:30PM (CST). *Felony, Misdemeanor, Civil, Eviction, Small Claims, Probate.*

Note: Records are maintained here for the Pittsburg District Court as well since 8/92. For prior cases, search both courts separately

Civil Records: Access: Fax, mail, in person. Both court and visitors may perform in person searches. Search fee: $10.80 per hour. Required to search: name, years to search. Civil cases indexed by defendant, plaintiff. Civil records on computer since August, 1992, microfiche from 1977, index cards from 1977. **Criminal Records:** Access: In person only. Both court and visitors may perform in person searches. No search fee. Required to search: name, years to search. Criminal records on computer since August, 1992, microfiche from 1977, index cards from 1977. All mail inquires are referred to the Kansas Bureau of Investigation. **General Information:** No juvenile, mental health, sealed or expunged records released. SASE required. Turnaround time 3-7 days. Copy fee: $.25 per page. Certification fee: $1.00. Fee payee: Clerk of Court. Personal checks accepted. Prepayment is required. Public access terminal is available. Fax notes: $2.50 per page.

Decatur County

District Court PO Box 89, Oberlin, KS 67749; 785-475-8107; Fax: 785-475-8170. Hours: 8AM-5PM (CST). *Felony, Misdemeanor, Civil, Eviction, Small Claims, Probate.*

Civil Records: Access: In person only. Court does not conduct in person searches; visitors must perform searches for themselves. Search fee: No civil searches performed by court. Required to search: name, years to search. Civil cases indexed by defendant, plaintiff. Civil records on index books from 1870. **Criminal Records:** Access: In person only. Court does not conduct in person searches; visitors must perform searches for themselves. Search fee: No criminal searches performed by court. Required to search: name, years to search. Criminal records on index books from 1870. **General Information:** No adoption, juvenile, mental health, sealed or expunged records released. Copy fee: $.25 per page. Certification fee: $1.00.

Dickinson County

District Court PO Box 127, Abilene, KS 67410; 785-263-3142; Fax: 785-263-4407. Hours: 8AM-5PM (CST). *Felony, Misdemeanor, Civil, Eviction, Small Claims, Probate.*

Civil Records: Access: Mail, in person. Both court and visitors may perform in person searches. Search fee: $10.80 per hour. Required to search: name, years to search. Civil cases indexed by defendant, plaintiff. Civil records on computer since 7/92, on index books prior. **Criminal Records:** Access: Mail, in person. Both court and visitors may perform in person searches. Search fee: $10.80 per hour. Required to search: name, years to search; also helpful-SSN. Criminal records on computer since 7/92, on index books prior. **General Information:** No juvenile, mental health, sealed or expunged records released. SASE required. Turnaround time 1 week. Copy fee: $1.00. Fee for first 4 pages. Add $.25 per page thereafter. Certification fee: $1.00. Fee payee: Clerk of District Court. Personal checks accepted. Prepayment is required. Public access terminal is available.

Doniphan County

District Court PO Box 295, Troy, KS 66087; 785-985-3582; Fax: 785-985-2402. Hours: 8AM-5PM (CST). *Felony, Misdemeanor, Civil, Eviction, Small Claims, Probate.*

Civil Records: Access: Phone, mail, in person. Both court and visitors may perform in person searches. Search fee: $10.80 per hour. Required to search: name, years to search. Civil cases indexed by defendant, plaintiff. Civil records on computer from 1989-1990, index cards from 1856. **Criminal Records:** Access: Phone, mail, in person. Only the court conducts in person searches; visitors may not. Search fee: $10.80 per hour. Required to search: name, years to search; also helpful-address, DOB. Criminal records on computer from 1989-1990, index cards from 1856. **General Information:** No juvenile, mental health, sealed or expunged records released. SASE required. Turnaround time 1-2 days. Copy fee: $.50 for first page, $.25 each addl. Certification fee: $1.00. Fee payee: Clerk of Court. Personal checks accepted.

Douglas County

District Court 111 E 11th St Rm 144, Lawrence, KS 66044-2966; 785-841-7700 X141; Fax: 785-832-5174. Hours: 8:30AM-4PM (CST). *Felony, Misdemeanor, Civil, Eviction, Small Claims, Probate.*

Civil Records: Access: Phone, mail, in person. Both court and visitors may perform in person searches. Search fee: $11.00 per hour. Required to search: name, years to search. Civil cases indexed by defendant, plaintiff. Civil records on index cards from 1863, archived from 1865 on film, indexed on computer since 1989. All written requests must include a phone number. In person requests take 48 hours to process, if court does search. **Criminal Records:** Access: Phone, mail, in person. Both court and visitors may perform in person searches. Search fee: $11.00 per hour. Required to search: name, years to search; also helpful-DOB. Criminal records on computer from 1991, index cards 1860, archived from 1865. All background checks must be in writing. **General Information:** No juvenile, mental health, sealed or expunged records released. SASE not required.

Turnaround time 3 days. Copy fee: $.50 per page. After first 100 pages, then $.25 per page. Certification fee: $1.00. Authenications are $2.00 each. Fee payee: Clerk of Court. Personal checks accepted. Prepayment is required. Public access terminal is available.

Edwards County

District Court PO Box 232, Kinsley, KS 67547; 316-659-2442; Fax: 316-659-2998. Hours: 8AM-5PM (CST). *Felony, Misdemeanor, Civil, Eviction, Small Claims, Probate.*

Civil Records: Access: Mail, in person. Both court and visitors may perform in person searches. Search fee: $10.80 per hour. Required to search: name, years to search. Civil cases indexed by defendant, plaintiff. Civil records on index books from 1800s. **Criminal Records:** Access: In person only. Court does not conduct in person searches; visitors must perform searches for themselves. Search fee: No criminal searches performed by court. Required to search: name, years to search. Criminal records on index books from 1800s. **General Information:** No juvenile, adoption, mental health, sealed or expunged records released. SASE required. Turnaround time 1-2 days. Copy fee: $.25 per page. Certification fee: $1.00. Fee payee: Clerk District Court. Personal checks accepted. Prepayment is required.

Elk County

District Court PO Box 306, Howard, KS 67349; 316-374-2370; Fax: 316-374-3531. Hours: 8AM-4:30PM (CST). *Felony, Misdemeanor, Civil, Eviction, Small Claims, Probate.*

Civil Records: Access: In person only. Court does not conduct in person searches; visitors must perform searches for themselves. Search fee: No civil searches performed by court. Required to search: name, years to search. Civil cases indexed by defendant, plaintiff. Civil records on index books from 1907. **Criminal Records:** Access: In person only. Court does not conduct in person searches; visitors must perform searches for themselves. Search fee: No criminal searches performed by court. Required to search: name, years to search. Criminal records on index books from 1907. **General Information:** No juvenile, mental health, sealed or expunged records released. Copy fee: $.25 per page. Certification fee: $1.00. Fee payee: Clerk of District Court. Personal checks accepted. Prepayment is required.

Ellis County

District Court PO Box 8, Hays, KS 67601; 785-628-9415; Fax: 785-628-8415. Hours: 8AM-5PM (CST). *Felony, Misdemeanor, Civil, Eviction, Small Claims, Probate.*

Civil Records: Access: Mail, in person. Both court and visitors may perform in person searches. Search fee: $10.80 per hour. Required to search: name, years to search. Civil cases indexed by defendant, plaintiff. Civil records on computer from 1991, microfiche from 1900s, index cards from 1800s, archives from 1800s. **Criminal Records:** Access: In person only. Court does not conduct in person searches; visitors must perform searches for themselves. Search fee: No criminal searches performed by court. Required to search: name, years to search. Criminal records on computer from 1991, microfiche from 1900s, index cards from 1800s, archives from 1800s. **General Information:** No juvenile, mental health, sealed or expunged records released. SASE required. Turnaround time 7 days. Copy fee: $.25 per page. Certification fee: $1.00. Fee payee: Clerk

of Court. Personal checks accepted. Prepayment is required. Public access terminal is available.

Ellsworth County

District Court 210 N Kansas, Ellsworth, KS 67439-3118; 785-472-3832; Fax: 785-472-5712. Hours: 8AM-5PM (CST). *Felony, Misdemeanor, Civil, Eviction, Small Claims, Probate.*

Civil Records: Access: Phone, fax, mail, in person. Both court and visitors may perform in person searches. No search fee. Required to search: name, years to search. Civil cases indexed by defendant, plaintiff. Civil records on computer from 1994, microfiche from 1900s, books from late 1800s. **Criminal Records:** Access: Phone, fax, mail, in person. Both court and visitors may perform in person searches. No search fee. Required to search: name, years to search; also helpful-SSN. Criminal records on computer from 1994, microfiche from 1900s, books from late 1800s. **General Information:** No juvenile, mental health, sealed or expunged records released. SASE required. Turnaround time 1-2 days. Copy fee: $.35 per page. Certification fee: No certification fee. Fee payee: District Court. Personal checks accepted. Prepayment is required. Fax notes: $.50 per page.

Finney County

District Court PO Box 798, Garden City, KS 67846; Civil phone:316-271-6121; Criminal phone:316-271-6121; Fax: 316-271-6140. Hours: 8AM-4:30PM (CST). *Felony, Misdemeanor, Civil, Eviction, Small Claims, Probate.*

Civil Records: Access: In person only. Court does not conduct in person searches; visitors must perform searches for themselves. Search fee: No civil searches performed by court. Required to search: name, years to search. Civil cases indexed by defendant, plaintiff. Civil records on computer from 1991, microfiche from 1900s, index books from 1900s. **Criminal Records:** Access: In person only. Court does not conduct in person searches; visitors must perform searches for themselves. Search fee: No criminal searches performed by court. Required to search: name, years to search. Criminal records on computer from 1991, microfiche from 1900s, index books from 1900s. **General Information:** No juvenile, Mental health, sealed or expunged records released. Copy fee: $.25 per page. Certification fee: $1.00. Fee payee: District Court. Personal checks accepted. Prepayment is required. Public access terminal is available.

Ford County

District Court 101 W Spruce, Dodge City, KS 67801; 316-227-4609; Civil phone:316-227-4610; Criminal phone:316-227-4610; Fax: 316-227-6799. Hours: 8AM-5PM (CST). *Felony, Misdemeanor, Civil, Eviction, Small Claims, Probate.*

Civil Records: Access: Fax, mail, in person. Both court and visitors may perform in person searches. Search fee: $10.80 per hour. Required to search: name, years to search. Civil cases indexed by defendant, plaintiff. Civil records on computer from end of 1991, microfiche from 1900s, index books from 1900s. **Criminal Records:** Access: Fax, mail, in person. Both court and visitors may perform in person searches. Search fee: $10.80 per hour. Required to search: name, years to search; also helpful-SSN. Criminal records on computer from end of 1991, microfiche from 1900s, index books from 1900s. **General Information:** No juvenile, mental health, sealed or expunged records released. SASE required. Turnaround time 3 days. Copy fee: $.25 per page. Certification fee: $1.00. Fee payee: Clerk of District Court. Personal checks accepted. Prepayment is required. Public access terminal is available. Fax notes: $1.00 per page.

Franklin County

District Court PO Box 637, Ottawa, KS 66067; 785-242-6000; Fax: 785-242-5970. Hours: 8AM-12, 1PM-5PM (CST). *Felony, Misdemeanor, Civil, Eviction, Small Claims, Probate.*

www.kscourts.org/dstcts/4dstct.htm

Civil Records: Access: Mail, in person. Both court and visitors may perform in person searches. Search fee: $10.60 per hour. Required to search: name, years to search. Civil cases indexed by defendant, plaintiff. Civil records on computer from 1982, index books from 1800s. **Criminal Records:** Access: In person only. Court does not conduct in person searches; visitors must perform searches for themselves. Search fee: No criminal searches performed by court. Required to search: name, years to search, SSN. Criminal records on computer from 1982, index books from 1800s. **General Information:** No juvenile, mental health, sealed or expunged records released. SASE required. Turnaround time 3-5 days. Copy fee: $.25 per page. Certification fee: $1.00. Fee payee: Clerk of District Court. Personal checks accepted. Prepayment is required. Public access terminal is available.

Geary County

District Court PO Box 1147, Junction City, KS 66441; 785-762-5221; Fax: 785-762-4420. Hours: 8AM-5PM (CST). *Felony, Misdemeanor, Civil, Eviction, Small Claims, Probate.*

Civil Records: Access: Mail, in person. Both court and visitors may perform in person searches. Search fee: $10.00 per hour. Required to search: name, years to search. Civil cases indexed by defendant, plaintiff. Civil records on computer from 1992, microfiche, index books and archives from 1894. **Criminal Records:** Access: Mail, in person. Both court and visitors may perform in person searches. Search fee: $10.00 per hour. Required to search: name, years to search; also helpful-SSN. Criminal records on computer from 1992, microfiche, index books and archives from 1894. **General Information:** No juvenile, adoption, mental health, sealed or expunged records released. SASE not required. Turnaround time 3 days. Copy fee: $.25 per page. Certification fee: $1.00. Fee payee: Clerk of Court. Personal checks accepted. Prepayment is required. Public access terminal is available.

Gove County

District Court PO Box 97, Gove, KS 67736; 785-938-2310; Fax: 785-938-2312. Hours: 8AM-Noon, 1-5PM (CST). *Felony, Misdemeanor, Civil, Eviction, Small Claims, Probate.*

Civil Records: Access: Fax, mail, in person. Both court and visitors may perform in person searches. Search fee: $9.00 per hour. Required to search: name, years to search. Civil cases indexed by defendant, plaintiff. Civil records on computer from 1993, index books from 1890 through present. **Criminal Records:** Access: Fax, mail, in person. Both court and visitors may perform in person searches. Search fee: $9.00 per hour. Required to search: name, years to search. Criminal records on computer from 1993, index books from 1890 through present. **General**

Information: No juvenile, mental health, sealed or expunged records released. SASE required. Turnaround time 1-2 days. Copy fee: $.25 per page. Certification fee: No certification fee. Fee payee: Clerk of District Court. Personal checks accepted. Prepayment is required. Fax notes: $1.00 for first page, $.50 each addl.

Graham County

District Court 410 N Pomeroy, Hill City, KS 67642; 785-421-3458; Fax: 785-421-5463. Hours: 8AM-5PM (CST). *Felony, Misdemeanor, Civil, Eviction, Small Claims, Probate.*

Civil Records: Access: In person only. Court does not conduct in person searches; visitors must perform searches for themselves. Search fee: No civil searches performed by court. Required to search: name, years to search. Civil cases indexed by defendant, plaintiff. Civil records on index books from 1880s. **Criminal Records:** Access: In person only. Court does not conduct in person searches; visitors must perform searches for themselves. Search fee: No criminal searches performed by court. Required to search: name, years to search; also helpful-SSN. Criminal records on index books from 1880s. **General Information:** No juvenile, mental health, sealed or expunged records released. Copy fee: $.25 per page. Certification fee: $1.00. Fee payee: Clerk of District Court. Personal checks accepted.

Grant County

District Court 108 S Glenn, Ulysses, KS 67880; 316-356-1526; Fax: 316-353-2131. Hours: 8:30AM-5PM (CST). *Felony, Misdemeanor, Civil, Eviction, Small Claims, Probate.*

Civil Records: Access: In person only. Court does not conduct in person searches; visitors must perform searches for themselves. Search fee: No civil searches performed by court. Required to search: name, years to search. Civil cases indexed by defendant, plaintiff. Civil records on computer from 1977, microfiche index from 1880s. **Criminal Records:** Court does not conduct in person searches; visitors must perform searches for themselves. Search fee: No criminal searches performed by court. Required to search: name, years to search. Civil records on computer from 1977, microfiche index from 1880s. The court refers all searchers to the state Bureau of investigations, including in-person searchers. **General Information:** No juvenile, mental health, sealed or expunged records released. SASE required. Turnaround time same day. Copy fee: $.50 per page. Certification fee: $1.00. Fee payee: District Court. Personal checks accepted. Prepayment is required. Public access terminal is available.

Gray County

District Court PO Box 487, Cimarron, KS 67835; 316-855-3812; Fax: 316-855-7037. Hours: 8AM-5PM (CST). *Felony, Misdemeanor, Civil, Eviction, Small Claims, Probate.*

Civil Records: Access: In person only. Court does not conduct in person searches; visitors must perform searches for themselves. Search fee: No civil searches performed by court. Required to search: name; also helpful-years to search. Civil cases indexed by defendant, plaintiff. Civil records on computer from 1990, index books from 1800s. **Criminal Records:** Access: In person only. Court does not conduct in person searches; visitors must perform searches for themselves. Search fee: No criminal searches performed by court. Required to search: name, years to search; also helpful-address,

DOB. Criminal records on computer from 1990, index books from 1800s. **General Information:** No juvenile, mental health, sealed or expunged records released. Copy fee: $.50 per page. Certification fee: $1.00. Fee payee: Clerk of District Court. Personal checks accepted. Public access terminal is available.

Greeley County

District Court PO Box 516, Tribune, KS 67879; 316-376-4292. Hours: 8AM-Noon, 1-5PM (MST). *Felony, Misdemeanor, Civil, Eviction, Small Claims, Probate.*

Civil Records: Access: In person only. Court does not conduct in person searches; visitors must perform searches for themselves. Search fee: No civil searches performed by court. Required to search: name, years to search. Civil cases indexed by defendant, plaintiff. Civil records on hardcopy index from beginning. **Criminal Records:** Access: In person only. Court does not conduct in person searches; visitors must perform searches for themselves. Search fee: No criminal searches performed by court. Required to search: name, years to search; also helpful-SSN. Criminal records on hardcopy index from beginning. **General Information:** No juvenile, mental health, sealed or expunged records released. Copy fee: $.50 per page. Certification fee: $1.00. Fee payee: Clerk of the District Court. Personal checks accepted. Prepayment is required. Public access terminal is available.

Greenwood County

District Court 311 N Main, Eureka, KS 67045; 316-583-8153; Fax: 316-583-6818. Hours: 8AM-5PM (CST). *Felony, Misdemeanor, Civil, Eviction, Small Claims, Probate.*

Civil Records: Access: Mail, in person. Both court and visitors may perform in person searches. Search fee: $10.80 per hour. Required to search: name, years to search. Civil cases indexed by defendant, plaintiff. Civil records on computer from 1983, index cards from 1800s. **Criminal Records:** Access: Mail, in person. Both court and visitors may perform in person searches. Search fee: $10.80 per hour. Required to search: name, years to search. Criminal records on computer from 1983, index cards from 1800s. **General Information:** No juvenile, mental health, sealed or expunged records released. SASE required. Turnaround time 1-2 days. Copy fee: $.25 per page. Certification fee: $1.00. Fee payee: Clerk of Court. Personal checks accepted. Prepayment is required. Public access terminal is available.

Hamilton County

District Court PO Box 745, Syracuse, KS 67878; 316-384-5159; Fax: 316-384-7806. Hours: 8AM-5PM (MST). *Felony, Misdemeanor, Civil, Eviction, Small Claims, Probate.*

Civil Records: Access: In person only. Court does not conduct in person searches; visitors must perform searches for themselves. Search fee: No civil searches performed by court. Required to search: name, years to search. Civil cases indexed by defendant, plaintiff. Civil records on computer from 1989, microfiche, archives and index cards from 1880s. **Criminal Records:** Access: In person only. Court does not conduct in person searches; visitors must perform searches for themselves. Search fee: No criminal searches performed by court. Required to search: name, years to search. Criminal records on computer from 1989, microfiche, archives and index cards from 1880s. **General Information:** No juvenile, mental health, sealed or expunged records released. Copy fee: $.25 per page. Certification fee: $1.00. Fee payee: Clerk of District Court. Personal checks accepted. Prepayment is required. Public access terminal is available.

Harper County

District Court PO Box 467, Anthony, KS 67003; 316-842-3721; Fax: 316-842-5937. Hours: 8AM-Noon, 1-5PM (CST). *Felony, Misdemeanor, Civil, Eviction, Small Claims, Probate.*

Civil Records: Access: Fax, mail, in person. Both court and visitors may perform in person searches. Search fee: $10.80 per hour. Required to search: name, years to search. Civil cases indexed by defendant, plaintiff. Civil records on computer from 1976, microfiche, index books and archives from 1887. **Criminal Records:** Access: Fax, mail, in person. Both court and visitors may perform in person searches. Search fee: $10.80 per hour. Required to search: name, years to search, SSN. Criminal records on computer from 1976, microfiche, index books and archives from 1887. **General Information:** No juvenile, mental health, sealed or expunged records released. SASE not required. Turnaround time same day. Copy fee: $.25 per page. Certification fee: $1.00. Fee payee: Clerk of District Court. Personal checks accepted. Public access terminal is available. Fax notes: $1.00 per page.

Harvey County

District Court PO Box 665, Newton, KS 67114-0665; 316-284-6890; Civil phone:316-284-6894; Criminal phone:316-284-6894; Fax: 316-283-4601. Hours: 8AM-5PM (CST). *Felony, Misdemeanor, Civil, Eviction, Small Claims, Probate.*

Civil Records: Access: Mail, in person. Both court and visitors may perform in person searches. Search fee: $10.80 per hour. Required to search: name, years to search. Civil cases indexed by defendant, plaintiff. Civil records on index books from 1800s. **Criminal Records:** Access: Mail, in person. Both court and visitors may perform in person searches. Search fee: $10.80 per hour. Required to search: name, years to search. Criminal records on index books from 1800s. Call KBI for thorough search. **General Information:** No juvenile, mental health, sealed or expunged records released. SASE not required. Turnaround time 3-5 days. Copy fee: $.50 per page. Certification fee: $1.00. Fee payee: Clerk of District Court. Personal checks accepted. Public access terminal is available.

Haskell County

District Court PO Box 146, Sublette, KS 67877; 316-675-2671; Fax: 316-675-8599. Hours: 8AM-5PM (CST). *Felony, Misdemeanor, Civil, Eviction, Small Claims, Probate.*

Civil Records: Access: Mail, in person. Both court and visitors may perform in person searches. Search fee: $10.80 per hour. Required to search: name, years to search. Civil cases indexed by defendant, plaintiff. Civil records on computer from 1989, index books from 1874. **Criminal Records:** Access: In person only. Court does not conduct in person searches; visitors must perform searches for themselves. Search fee: No criminal searches performed by court. Required to search: name, years to search. Criminal records on computer from 1989, index books from 1874. **General Information:** No juvenile, mental health, sealed or expunged records released. SASE not required. Turnaround time same day. Copy fee:

$.25 per page. Certification fee: $1.00. Fee payee: Clerk of District Court. Personal checks accepted. Prepayment is required. Public access terminal is available.

Hodgeman County

District Court PO Box 187, Jetmore, KS 67854; 316-357-6522; Fax: 316-357-6216. Hours: 8:30AM-5PM (CST). *Felony, Misdemeanor, Civil, Eviction, Small Claims, Probate.*

Civil Records: Access: Phone, fax, mail, in person. Both court and visitors may perform in person searches. Search fee: $9.00 per hour. Required to search: name, years to search. Civil cases indexed by defendant, plaintiff. Civil records on index cards and books from 1800s. **Criminal Records:** Access: In person only. Court does not conduct in person searches; visitors must perform searches for themselves. Search fee: No criminal searches performed by court. Required to search: name, years to search; also helpful-SSN. Criminal records on index cards and books from 1800s. **General Information:** No juvenile, mental health, sealed or expunged records released. SASE not required. Turnaround time 1-2 days. Copy fee: $.25 per page. Certification fee: $1.00. Fee payee: Clerk of Court. Personal checks accepted. Must prepay for mail and fax. Fax notes: $.50 per page.

Jackson County

District Court PO Box 1026, Holton, KS 66436; 785-364-2191; Fax: 785-364-3804. Hours: 8AM-4:30PM (CST). *Felony, Misdemeanor, Civil, Eviction, Small Claims, Probate.*

Civil Records: Access: In person only. Court does not conduct in person searches; visitors must perform searches for themselves. Search fee: No civil searches performed by court. Required to search: name, years to search. Civil cases indexed by defendant, plaintiff. Civil records on index cards from 1800s (working on installation of computer at this time). **Criminal Records:** Access: In person only. Court does not conduct in person searches; visitors must perform searches for themselves. Search fee: No criminal searches performed by court. Required to search: name, years to search. Criminal records on index cards from 1800s (working on installation of computer at this time). **General Information:** No juvenile, mental health, sealed or expunged records released. Copy fee: $.25 per page. Certification fee: $1.00. Fee payee: Clerk of District Court. Personal checks accepted.

Jefferson County

District Court PO Box 327, Oskaloosa, KS 66066; 785-863-2461; Fax: 785-863-2369. Hours: 8AM-4:30PM (CST). *Felony, Misdemeanor, Civil, Eviction, Small Claims, Probate.*

Civil Records: Access: In person only. Court does not conduct in person searches; visitors must perform searches for themselves. Search fee: No civil searches performed by court. Required to search: name, years to search. Civil cases indexed by defendant, plaintiff. Civil records on computer since 5/94, on index books from 1855. **Criminal Records:** Access: In person only. Court does not conduct in person searches; visitors must perform searches for themselves. Search fee: No criminal searches performed by court. Required to search: name, years to search; also helpful-SSN. Criminal records on index books from 1855. **General Information:** No juvenile, mental health, sealed or expunged records released. Copy fee: $.25 per page. Certification fee: $1.00. Fee payee: District

Court. Personal checks accepted. Prepayment is required. Public access terminal is available.

Jewell County

District Court 307 N Commercial, Mankato, KS 66956; 785-378-4030; Fax: 785-378-4035. Hours: 8AM-5PM (CST). *Felony, Misdemeanor, Civil, Eviction, Small Claims, Probate.*

Civil Records: Access: Phone, fax, mail, in person. Both court and visitors may perform in person searches. Search fee: $10.80 per hour. Required to search: name, years to search. Civil cases indexed by defendant, plaintiff. Civil records on index books from 1871. **Criminal Records:** Access: Phone, fax, mail, in person. Both court and visitors may perform in person searches. Search fee: $10.80 per hour. Required to search: name, years to search. Criminal records on index books from 1871. **General Information:** No juvenile, mental health, sealed or expunged records released. SASE required. Turnaround time 1-2 days. Copy fee: $.25 per page. Certification fee: $1.00. Fee payee: District Court. Personal checks accepted. Prepayment is required. Fax notes: $3.00 per page.

Johnson County

District Court 100 N Kansas, Olathe, KS 66061; 913-715-3500; Civil phone:913-715-3400; Criminal phone:913-715-3400; Fax: 913-715-3481. Hours: 8:30AM-5PM (CST). *Felony, Misdemeanor, Civil, Eviction, Small Claims, Probate.*

www.jocoks.com/jococourts

Note: Search requests should be made to the Records Center, phone 913-715-3480.

Civil Records: Access: Fax, mail, online, in person. Both court and visitors may perform in person searches. Search fee: $10.80 per hour. Required to search: name, years to search. Civil cases indexed by defendant, plaintiff. Civil records on computer from 1980, microfiche, archives and index prior. Index online through INK of Kansas. See www.ink.org for subscription information. **Criminal Records:** Access: Fax, mail, in person. Both court and visitors may perform in person searches. Search fee: $10.80 per hour. Required to search: name, years to search. Criminal records on computer from 1980, microfiche, archives and index prior. Criminal fax number is 913-715-3461. **General Information:** No juvenile, mental health, sealed or expunged records released. No employment searches. SASE required. Turnaround time 1-2 days if current records, 1-2 weeks for very old document. Copy fee: $.50 per page. Copy fee for records prior to 1993 $10.00 flat fee. Certification fee: $1.00. Fee payee: Clerk of the District Court. Only cashiers checks and money orders accepted. Prepayment is required. Public access terminal is available. Fax notes: $2.50 per page.

Kearny County

District Court PO Box 64, Lakin, KS 67860; 316-355-6481; Fax: 316-355-7462. Hours: 8AM-Noon,1-5PM (CST). *Felony, Misdemeanor, Civil, Eviction, Small Claims, Probate.*

Civil Records: Access: Mail, in person. Both court and visitors may perform in person searches. Search fee: $10.80 per hour. Required to search: name, years to search. Civil cases indexed by defendant, plaintiff. Civil records on computer from 1991, index books from 1900s. **Criminal Records:** Access: Mail, in person. Both court and visitors may perform in person searches. Search fee: $10.80 per hour. Required to search: name, years to search, SSN. Criminal records on computer from 1991, index books from 1900s. **General Information:** No juvenile, mental health, adoption, sealed or expunged records released. SASE required. Turnaround time 3 days. Copy fee: $.25 per page. Certification fee: $1.00. Fee payee: District Court. Personal checks accepted. Prepayment is required. Public access terminal is available.

Kingman County

District Court PO Box 495, Kingman, KS 67068; 316-532-5151; Fax: 316-532-2952. Hours: 8AM-Noon, 1-5PM (CST). *Felony, Misdemeanor, Civil, Eviction, Small Claims, Probate.*

Civil Records: Access: Mail, in person. Both court and visitors may perform in person searches. Search fee: $10.80 per hour. Required to search: name, years to search. Civil cases indexed by defendant, plaintiff. Civil records on computer from 1990, microfiche, archives and index cards from 1800s. **Criminal Records:** Access: Mail, in person. Both court and visitors may perform in person searches. Search fee: $10.80 per hour. Required to search: name, years to search, SSN. Criminal records on computer from 1990, microfiche, archives and index cards from 1800s. **General Information:** No juvenile, mental health, sealed or expunged records released. SASE required. Turnaround time 1-2 days. Copy fee: $.25 per page. Certification fee: $1.00. Fee payee: Clerk of Court. Personal checks accepted. Prepayment is required. Public access terminal is available.

Kiowa County

District Court 211 E Florida, Greensburg, KS 67054; 316-723-3317; Fax: 316-723-2970. Hours: 8AM-5PM (CST). *Felony, Misdemeanor, Civil, Eviction, Small Claims, Probate.*

Civil Records: Access: Fax, mail, in person. Both court and visitors may perform in person searches. Search fee: $10.80 per hour. Required to search: name, years to search. Civil cases indexed by defendant, plaintiff. Civil records archived and on index books from 1900s. **Criminal Records:** Access: Fax, mail, in person. Both court and visitors may perform in person searches. Search fee: $10.80 per hour. Required to search: name, years to search, signed release; also helpful-DOB. Criminal records archived and on index books from 1900s. **General Information:** No juvenile, mental health, sealed or expunged records released. SASE required. Turnaround time 7 days. Copy fee: $.25 per page. Certification fee: $1.00. Fee payee: Clerk of District Court. Personal checks accepted. Fax notes: Fee to fax results is $1.00 per page.

Labette County

District Court Courthouse, 517 Merchant, Oswego, KS 67356; 316-795-4533 (316-421-4120 Parsons); Fax: 316-795-3056 (316-421-3633 Parsons). Hours: 8AM-5PM (CST). *Felony, Misdemeanor, Civil, Eviction, Small Claims, Probate.*

Civil Records: Access: Mail, in person. Both court and visitors may perform in person searches. No search fee. Required to search: name, years to search. Civil cases indexed by defendant, plaintiff. Civil records on computer since 1992. **Criminal Records:** Access: Mail, in person. Both court and visitors may perform in person searches. No search fee. Required to search: name, years to search; also helpful-DOB, SSN. Criminal records on computer

since 1992. **General Information:** no juvenile, adoption, mental health, sealed or expunged records released. Copy fee: $.25 per page. Certification fee: $1.00. Fee payee: Clerk of District Court. Personal checks accepted. Prepayment is required. Public access terminal is available.

District Court 201 South Central, Parsons, KS 67357; 316-421-4120; Fax: 316-421-3633. Hours: 8AM-5PM (CST). *Felony, Misdemeanor, Civil, Eviction, Small Claims, Probate.*

Civil Records: Access: Mail, in person. Both court and visitors may perform in person searches. Search fee: $10.80 per hour. Required to search: name, years to search. Civil cases indexed by defendant, plaintiff. Civil records on computer from 1992, index books from 1874. **Criminal Records:** Access: Mail, in person. Both court and visitors may perform in person searches. Search fee: $9.00 per hour. Required to search: name, years to search. Criminal records on computer from 1992, index books from 1874. **General Information:** No juvenile, adoption, mental health, sealed or expunged records released. SASE required. Turnaround time 1-2 days. Copy fee: $.25 per page. Certification fee: $1.00. Fee payee: Clerk of District Court. Personal checks accepted. Prepayment is required. Public access terminal is available.

Lane County

District Court PO Box 188, Dighton, KS 67839; 316-397-2805; Fax: 316-397-5526. Hours: 8AM-5PM (CST). *Felony, Misdemeanor, Civil, Eviction, Small Claims, Probate.*

Civil Records: Access: Mail, in person. Both court and visitors may perform in person searches. Search fee: $9.00 per hour. Required to search: name, years to search. Civil cases indexed by defendant, plaintiff. Civil records on computer since 1993; prior records from 1800s. **Criminal Records:** Access: In person only. Court does not conduct in person searches; visitors must perform searches for themselves. Search fee: No criminal searches performed by court. Required to search: name, years to search; also helpful-SSN. Criminal records on computer since 1993; prior records from 1800s. **General Information:** No juvenile, mental health, sealed or expunged records released. SASE required. Turnaround time 1-2 weeks. Copy fee: $.25 per page. Certification fee: $1.00. Fee payee: Clerk of Court. Personal checks accepted. Prepayment is required.

Leavenworth County

District Court 601 S Third Street, Leavenworth, KS 66048; 913-684-0700; Civil phone:913-684-0701; Criminal phone:913-684-0701; Fax: 913-684-0492. Hours: 8AM-5PM (CST). *Felony, Misdemeanor, Civil, Eviction, Small Claims, Probate.*

Civil Records: Access: In person only. Both court and visitors may perform in person searches. No search fee. Required to search: name, years to search. Civil cases indexed by defendant, plaintiff. Civil records on computer from 1990, microfiche and index books from 1960. **Criminal Records:** Access: Mail, in person. Both court and visitors may perform in person searches. No search fee. Required to search: name, years to search; also helpful-SSN. Criminal records on computer from 1990, microfiche and index books from 1960. **General Information:** No juvenile, mental health, sealed or expunged records released. SASE required. Turnaround time 1-2 days. Copy fee: $.25 per page. Certification fee: $1.00. Fee payee:

Clerk of District Court. Personal checks accepted. Prepayment is required. Public access terminal is available.

Lincoln County

District Court 216 E Lincoln Ave, Lincoln, KS 67455; 785-524-4057; Fax: 785-524-3204. Hours: 8AM-12, 1_5PM (CST). *Felony, Misdemeanor, Civil, Eviction, Small Claims, Probate.*

Civil Records: Access: Fax, mail, in person. Both court and visitors may perform in person searches. Search fee: $9.00 per hour. Required to search: name; also helpful-years to search. Civil cases indexed by defendant, plaintiff. all records on computer. **Criminal Records:** Access: Fax, mail, in person. Both court and visitors may perform in person searches. Search fee: $9.00 per hour. Required to search: name; also helpful-years to search, DOB, SSN. Criminal records on computer since 1980, on index cards from 1880. **General Information:** No juvenile, mental health, sealed or expunged records released. SASE required. Turnaround time 3 days. Copy fee: $.25 per page. Certification fee: $1.00. Fee payee: Clerk of Court. Personal checks accepted. Prepayment is required. Fax notes: $3.00 per page.

Linn County

District Court PO Box 350, Mound City, KS 66056-0350; 913-795-2660; Fax: 913-795-2004. Hours: 8AM-5PM (CST). *Felony, Misdemeanor, Civil, Eviction, Small Claims, Probate.*

Civil Records: Access: In person only. Court does not conduct in person searches; visitors must perform searches for themselves. Search fee: No civil searches performed by court. Required to search: name, years to search. Civil cases indexed by defendant, plaintiff. Civil records on computer from 1990, archives and index books from 1886. **Criminal Records:** Access: In person only. Court does not conduct in person searches; visitors must perform searches for themselves. Search fee: No criminal searches performed by court. Required to search: name, years to search. Criminal records on computer from 1990, archives and index books from 1886. **General Information:** No juvenile, mental health, sealed or expunged records released. Copy fee: $.25 per page. Certification fee: $1.00. Fee payee: Clerk of District Court. Personal checks accepted. Prepayment is required.

Logan County

District Court 710 W 2nd St, Oakley, KS 67748-1233; 785-672-3654; Fax: 785-672-3517. Hours: 8:30AM-Noon, 1-5PM (CST). *Felony, Misdemeanor, Civil, Eviction, Small Claims, Probate.*

Civil Records: Access: In person only. Court does not conduct in person searches; visitors must perform searches for themselves. Search fee: No civil searches performed by court. Required to search: name, years to search. Civil cases indexed by defendant, plaintiff. Civil records on computer from 1948, index cards from 1889. **Criminal Records:** Access: In person only. Court does not conduct in person searches; visitors must perform searches for themselves. Search fee: No criminal searches performed by court. Required to search: name, years to search; also helpful-SSN. Criminal records on computer from 1948, index cards from 1889. **General Information:** No juvenile, mental health, sealed or expunged records released. Copy fee: $.25 per page. Certification fee: $1.00. Fee payee: Clerk of District Court. Personal checks accepted. Prepayment is required. Public access terminal is available.

Lyon County

District Court 402 Commercial St, Emporia, KS 66801; 316-342-4950; Fax: 316-342-8005. Hours: 8AM-4PM (CST). *Felony, Misdemeanor, Civil, Eviction, Small Claims, Probate.*

Civil Records: Access: Fax, mail, in person. Both court and visitors may perform in person searches. Search fee: $10.80 per hour. Required to search: name, years to search. Civil cases indexed by defendant, plaintiff. **Criminal Records:** Access: In person only. Court does not conduct in person searches; visitors must perform searches for themselves. Search fee: No criminal searches performed by court. Required to search: name, years to search, SSN. **General Information:** No mental health, sealed or expunged records released. SASE required. Turnaround time 3 days. Copy fee: $.50 per page. Certification fee: $2.00. Fee payee: Clerk of District Court. Personal checks accepted. Prepayment is required. Fax notes: $1.00 per page.

Marion County

District Court PO Box 298, Marion, KS 66861; 316-382-2104; Fax: 316-382-2259. Hours: 8AM-5PM (CST). *Felony, Misdemeanor, Civil, Eviction, Small Claims, Probate.*

Civil Records: Access: In person. Both court and visitors may perform in person searches. Search fee: $10.80 per hour. Required to search: name, years to search. Civil cases indexed by defendant, plaintiff. Civil records on computer from July, 1992, on index cards from 1800s. **Criminal Records:** Access: In person. Both court and visitors may perform in person searches. Search fee: $10.80 per hour. Required to search: name, years to search. Criminal records on computer from July, 1992, on index cards from 1800s. **General Information:** No juvenile, mental health, sealed or expunged records released. Copy fee: $1.00 per page. Certification fee: $1.00. Fee payee: District Court. Personal checks accepted. Prepayment is required. Public access terminal is available.

Marshall County

District Court PO Box 86, Marysville, KS 66508; 785-562-5301; Fax: 785-562-2458. Hours: 8AM-5PM; Search hours: 8:30AM-4:30PM (CST). *Felony, Misdemeanor, Civil, Eviction, Small Claims, Probate.*

Civil Records: Access: Fax, mail, in person. Both court and visitors may perform in person searches. Search fee: $9.00 per hour. Required to search: name, years to search. Civil cases indexed by defendant, plaintiff. Civil records on computer from 1990, microfiche from 1977 (earlier records on roll-marriage licenses on computer index 1860s, forward/naturalizations on computer index). **Criminal Records:** Access: Fax, mail, in person. Both court and visitors may perform in person searches. Search fee: $9.00 per hour. Required to search: name, years to search. Criminal records on computer from 1988, microfiche from 1977. **General Information:** No juvenile, mental health, sealed or expunged records released. SASE required. Turnaround time 1-2 days. Copy fee: $.50 for first page, $.25 each addl. Certification fee: $1.00. Fee payee: Clerk of Court. Personal checks accepted. Prepayment is required. Public access terminal is available. Fax notes: $2.00 for first page, $1.00 each addl. Prepayment required.

McPherson County

District Court PO Box 1106, McPherson, KS 67460; 316-241-3422; Fax: 316-241-1372. Hours: 8AM-5PM (CST). *Felony, Misdemeanor, Civil, Eviction, Small Claims, Probate.*

Civil Records: Access: Mail, in person. Both court and visitors may perform in person searches. Search fee: $10.80 per hour. Required to search: name, years to search. Civil cases indexed by defendant, plaintiff. Civil records on microfilm from 1953, index cards from 1900s. **Criminal Records:** Access: Mail, in person. Both court and visitors may perform in person searches. Search fee: $10.80 per hour. Required to search: name, years to search; also helpful-SSN. Criminal records on microfilm from 1953, index cards from 1900s. **General Information:** No juvenile, mental health, sealed or expunged records released. SASE required. Turnaround time 1-3 days. Copy fee: $.50 per page. Certification fee: $.50 per document. Fee payee: District Court. Personal checks accepted. Prepayment is required. Public access terminal is available.

Meade County

Meade County District Court PO Box 623, Meade, KS 67864; 316-873-8750; Fax: 316-873-8759. Hours: 8AM-5PM (CST). *Felony, Misdemeanor, Civil, Eviction, Small Claims, Probate.*

Note: All employment background checks requested by mail, phone, or fax are refered to the KBI (state agency for criminal records).

Civil Records: Access: Mail, in person. Both court and visitors may perform in person searches. Search fee: $10.00 per hour. Required to search: name, years to search. Civil cases indexed by defendant, plaintiff. Civil records on computer from 1990, index cards from 1896. **Criminal Records:** Access: Mail, in person. Both court and visitors may perform in person searches. Search fee: $10.00 per hour. Required to search: name, years to search. Criminal records on computer from 1990, index cards from 1896. **General Information:** No juvenile, mental health, sealed or expunged records released. SASE required. Turnaround time 1-2 days. Copy fee: $.25 per page. Certification fee: $1.00. Fee payee: Clerk of Court. Only cashiers checks and money orders accepted. Prepayment is required. Public access terminal is available.

Miami County

District Court PO Box 187, Paola, KS 66071; 913-294-3326; Fax: 913-294-2535. Hours: 8AM-4:30PM (CST). *Felony, Misdemeanor, Civil, Eviction, Small Claims, Probate.*

Civil Records: Access: In person only. Both court and visitors may perform in person searches. Search fee: $10.80 per hour. Required to search: name, years to search. Civil cases indexed by defendant, plaintiff. Civil records on computer from 1984, index cards from 1890s. **Criminal Records:** Access: In person only. Both court and visitors may perform in person searches. Search fee: $10.80 per hour. Required to search: name, years to search; also helpful-SSN. Criminal records on computer from 1984, index cards from 1890s. **General Information:** No juvenile, mental health, sealed or expunged records released. Copy fee: $.25 per page. Certification fee: $1.00. Fee payee: District Court. Personal checks accepted. Prepayment is required. Public access terminal is available.

Mitchell County

District Court 115 S Hersey, Beloit, KS 67420; 785-738-3753; Fax: 785-738-4101. Hours: 8AM-5PM (CST). *Felony, Misdemeanor, Civil, Eviction, Small Claims, Probate.*

Civil Records: Access: Mail, in person. Both court and visitors may perform in person searches. Search fee: $9.00 per hour. Required to search: name, years to search. Civil cases indexed by defendant, plaintiff. Civil records on index cards from 1870. **Criminal Records:** Access: Mail, in person. Both court and visitors may perform in person searches. Search fee: $9.00 per hour. Required to search: name, years to search. Criminal records on index cards from 1870. **General Information:** No juvenile, mental health, sealed or expunged records released. SASE required. Turnaround time 1-2 days. Copy fee: $.25 per page. Certification fee: $1.00. Fee payee: Clerk of Court. Personal checks accepted. Prepayment is required.

Montgomery County

Independence District Court PO Box 768, Independence, KS 67301; 316-330-1070; Fax: 316-331-6120. Hours: 8AM-5PM (CST). *Felony, Misdemeanor, Civil, Eviction, Small Claims, Probate.*

Note: This court covers civil cases for the northern part of the county. It is suggested to search both courts

Civil Records: Access: Fax, mail, in person. Both court and visitors may perform in person searches. Search fee: $10.80 per hour. $5.00 minimum. Required to search: name, years to search. Civil cases indexed by defendant, plaintiff. Civil records on computer since 1992, on microfiche from 1870-1930, archives 1930-1992, index cards from 1870. **Criminal Records:** Access: Fax, mail, in person. Both court and visitors may perform in person searches. Search fee: $10.80 per hour. $5.00 minimum. Required to search: name, years to search; also helpful-SSN. Criminal records on computer since 1992, on microfiche from 1870-1930, archives 1930-1992, index cards from 1870. **General Information:** No juvenile, adoptions, mental health, sealed or expunged records released. SASE not required. Turnaround time 72 hours. Copy fee: $.25 per page. Certification fee: $1.00. Fee payee: Clerk of Court. Personal checks accepted. Prepayment is required. Public access terminal is available. Fax notes: $5.00 for first page, $1.00 each addl.

Coffeyville District Court PO Box 409, Coffeyville, KS 67337; 316-251-1060; Fax: 316-251-2734. Hours: 8AM-5PM (CST). *Civil, Eviction, Small Claims, Probate.*

Note: This court covers civil cases for the southern part of the county, although cases can be filed in either court. It is recommended to search both courts

Civil Records: Access: Fax, mail, in person. Both court and visitors may perform in person searches. Search fee: $10.80 per hour. Required to search: name, years to search. Civil cases indexed by defendant, plaintiff. Civil records on computer since 1992, on paper, fiche, etc. since 1924. **General Information:** No juvenile, mental health, sealed, adoption, or expunged records released. Turnaround time 72 hours. Copy fee: $.25 per page. Certification fee: $1.00. Fee payee: Clerk of Court. Personal checks accepted. Public access terminal is available. Fax notes: Require $1.00 per page fax fee in advance plus search fee.

ZIP Range	City	ZIP Range	City	ZIP Range	City	ZIP Range	City
67053-67053	GOESSEL	67351-67351	LIBERTY	67522-67522	BUHLER	67672-67672	WA KEENEY
67054-67054	GREENSBURG	67352-67352	LONGTON	67523-67523	BURDETT	67673-67673	WALDO
67055-67055	GREENWICH	67353-67353	MOLINE	67524-67524	CHASE	67674-67674	WALKER
67056-67056	HALSTEAD	67354-67354	MOUND VALLEY	67525-67525	CLAFLIN	67675-67675	WOODSTON
67057-67057	HARDTNER	67355-67355	NIOTAZE	67526-67526	ELLINWOOD	67701-67701	COLBY
67058-67058	HARPER	67356-67356	OSWEGO	67529-67529	GARFIELD	67730-67730	ATWOOD
67059-67059	HAVILAND	67357-67357	PARSONS	67530-67530	GREAT BEND	67731-67731	BIRD CITY
67060-67060	HAYSVILLE	67360-67360	PERU	67543-67543	HAVEN	67732-67732	BREWSTER
67061-67061	HAZELTON	67361-67361	SEDAN	67544-67544	HOISINGTON	67733-67733	EDSON
67062-67062	HESSTON	67363-67363	SYCAMORE	67545-67545	HUDSON	67734-67734	GEM
67063-67063	HILLSBORO	67364-67364	TYRO	67546-67546	INMAN	67735-67735	GOODLAND
67065-67065	ISABEL	67401-67402	SALINA	67547-67547	KINSLEY	67736-67736	GOVE
67066-67066	IUKA	67410-67410	ABILENE	67548-67548	LA CROSSE	67737-67737	GRAINFIELD
67067-67067	KECHI	67414-67414	ADA	67550-67550	LARNED	67738-67738	GRINNELL
67068-67068	KINGMAN	67416-67416	ASSARIA	67552-67552	LEWIS	67739-67739	HERNDON
67070-67070	KIOWA	67417-67417	AURORA	67553-67553	LIEBENTHAL	67740-67740	HOXIE
67071-67071	LAKE CITY	67418-67418	BARNARD	67554-67554	LYONS	67741-67741	KANORADO
67072-67072	LATHAM	67420-67420	BELOIT	67556-67556	MC CRACKEN	67743-67743	LEVANT
67073-67073	LEHIGH	67422-67422	BENNINGTON	67557-67557	MACKSVILLE	67744-67744	LUDELL
67074-67074	LEON	67423-67423	BEVERLY	67559-67559	NEKOMA	67745-67745	MC DONALD
67101-67101	MAIZE	67425-67425	BROOKVILLE	67560-67560	NESS CITY	67747-67747	MONUMENT
67102-67102	MAPLE CITY	67427-67427	BUSHTON	67561-67561	NICKERSON	67748-67748	OAKLEY
67103-67103	MAYFIELD	67428-67428	CANTON	67563-67563	OFFERLE	67749-67749	OBERLIN
67104-67104	MEDICINE LODGE	67430-67430	CAWKER CITY	67564-67564	OLMITZ	67751-67751	PARK
67105-67105	MILAN	67431-67431	CHAPMAN	67565-67565	OTIS	67752-67752	QUINTER
67106-67106	MILTON	67432-67432	CLAY CENTER	67566-67566	PARTRIDGE	67753-67753	REXFORD
67107-67107	MOUNDRIDGE	67436-67436	DELPHOS	67567-67567	PAWNEE ROCK	67755-67755	RUSSELL SPRINGS
67108-67108	MOUNT HOPE	67437-67437	DOWNS	67568-67568	PLEVNA	67756-67756	SAINT FRANCIS
67109-67109	MULLINVILLE	67438-67438	DURHAM	67570-67570	PRETTY PRAIRIE	67757-67757	SELDEN
67110-67110	MULVANE	67439-67439	ELLSWORTH	67572-67572	RANSOM	67758-67758	SHARON SPRINGS
67111-67111	MURDOCK	67441-67441	ENTERPRISE	67573-67573	RAYMOND	67761-67761	WALLACE
67112-67112	NASHVILLE	67442-67442	FALUN	67574-67574	ROZEL	67762-67762	WESKAN
67114-67114	NEWTON	67443-67443	GALVA	67575-67575	RUSH CENTER	67764-67764	WINONA
67117-67117	NORTH NEWTON	67444-67444	GENESEO	67576-67576	SAINT JOHN	67801-67801	DODGE CITY
67118-67118	NORWICH	67445-67445	GLASCO	67578-67578	STAFFORD	67831-67831	ASHLAND
67119-67119	OXFORD	67446-67446	GLEN ELDER	67579-67579	STERLING	67834-67834	BUCKLIN
67120-67120	PECK	67447-67447	GREEN	67581-67581	SYLVIA	67835-67835	CIMARRON
67122-67122	PIEDMONT	67448-67448	GYPSUM	67583-67583	TURON	67836-67836	COOLIDGE
67123-67123	POTWIN	67449-67449	HERINGTON	67584-67584	UTICA	67837-67837	COPELAND
67124-67124	PRATT	67450-67450	HOLYROOD	67585-67585	YODER	67838-67838	DEERFIELD
67127-67127	PROTECTION	67451-67451	HOPE	67601-67601	HAYS	67839-67839	DIGHTON
67128-67128	RAGO	67452-67452	HUNTER	67621-67621	AGRA	67840-67840	ENGLEWOOD
67131-67131	ROCK	67454-67454	KANOPOLIS	67622-67622	ALMENA	67841-67841	ENSIGN
67132-67132	ROSALIA	67455-67455	LINCOLN	67623-67623	ALTON	67842-67842	FORD
67133-67133	ROSE HILL	67456-67456	LINDSBORG	67625-67625	BOGUE	67844-67844	FOWLER
67134-67134	SAWYER	67457-67457	LITTLE RIVER	67626-67626	BUNKER HILL	67846-67846	GARDEN CITY
67135-67135	SEDGWICK	67458-67458	LONGFORD	67627-67627	CATHARINE	67849-67849	HANSTON
67137-67137	SEVERY	67459-67459	LORRAINE	67628-67628	CEDAR	67850-67850	HEALY
67138-67138	SHARON	67460-67460	MCPHERSON	67629-67629	CLAYTON	67851-67851	HOLCOMB
67140-67140	SOUTH HAVEN	67464-67464	MARQUETTE	67631-67631	COLLYER	67853-67853	INGALLS
67142-67142	SPIVEY	67466-67466	MILTONVALE	67632-67632	DAMAR	67854-67854	JETMORE
67143-67143	SUN CITY	67467-67467	MINNEAPOLIS	67634-67634	DORRANCE	67855-67855	JOHNSON
67144-67144	TOWANDA	67468-67468	MORGANVILLE	67635-67635	DRESDEN	67856-67856	KALVESTA
67146-67146	UDALL	67470-67470	NEW CAMBRIA	67637-67637	ELLIS	67857-67857	KENDALL
67147-67147	VALLEY CENTER	67473-67473	OSBORNE	67638-67638	GAYLORD	67858-67858	KINGSDOWN
67149-67149	VIOLA	67474-67474	PORTIS	67639-67639	GLADE	67859-67859	KISMET
67150-67150	WALDRON	67475-67475	RAMONA	67640-67640	GORHAM	67860-67860	LAKIN
67151-67151	WALTON	67476-67476	ROXBURY	67642-67642	HILL CITY	67861-67861	LEOTI
67152-67152	WELLINGTON	67478-67478	SIMPSON	67643-67643	JENNINGS	67862-67862	MANTER
67154-67154	WHITEWATER	67480-67480	SOLOMON	67644-67644	KIRWIN	67863-67863	MARIENTHAL
67155-67155	WILMORE	67481-67481	SYLVAN GROVE	67645-67645	LENORA	67864-67864	MEADE
67156-67156	WINFIELD	67482-67482	TALMAGE	67646-67646	LOGAN	67865-67865	MINNEOLA
67159-67159	ZENDA	67483-67483	TAMPA	67647-67647	LONG ISLAND	67867-67867	MONTEZUMA
67201-67220	WICHITA	67484-67484	TESCOTT	67648-67648	LUCAS	67868-67868	PIERCEVILLE
67221-67221	MC CONNELL A F B	67485-67485	TIPTON	67649-67649	LURAY	67869-67869	PLAINS
67223-67278	WICHITA	67487-67487	WAKEFIELD	67650-67650	MORLAND	67870-67870	SATANTA
67301-67301	INDEPENDENCE	67490-67490	WILSON	67651-67651	NATOMA	67871-67871	SCOTT CITY
67330-67330	ALTAMONT	67491-67491	WINDOM	67653-67653	NORCATUR	67876-67876	SPEARVILLE
67332-67332	BARTLETT	67492-67492	WOODBINE	67654-67654	NORTON	67877-67877	SUBLETTE
67333-67333	CANEY	67501-67504	HUTCHINSON	67656-67656	OGALLAH	67878-67878	SYRACUSE
67334-67334	CHAUTAUQUA	67505-67505	SOUTH HUTCHINSON	67657-67657	PALCO	67879-67879	TRIBUNE
67335-67335	CHERRYVALE	67510-67510	ABBYVILLE	67658-67658	PARADISE	67880-67880	ULYSSES
67336-67336	CHETOPA	67511-67511	ALBERT	67659-67659	PENOKEE	67882-67882	WRIGHT
67337-67337	COFFEYVILLE	67512-67512	ALDEN	67660-67660	PFEIFER	67901-67905	LIBERAL
67340-67340	DEARING	67513-67513	ALEXANDER	67661-67661	PHILLIPSBURG	67950-67950	ELKHART
67341-67341	DENNIS	67514-67514	ARLINGTON	67663-67663	PLAINVILLE	67951-67951	HUGOTON
67342-67342	EDNA	67515-67515	ARNOLD	67664-67664	PRAIRIE VIEW	67952-67952	MOSCOW
67344-67344	ELK CITY	67516-67516	BAZINE	67665-67665	RUSSELL	67953-67953	RICHFIELD
67345-67345	ELK FALLS	67518-67518	BEELER	67667-67667	SCHOENCHEN	67954-67954	ROLLA
67346-67346	GRENOLA	67519-67519	BELPRE	67669-67669	STOCKTON		
67347-67347	HAVANA	67520-67520	BISON	67670-67670	STUTTGART		
67349-67349	HOWARD	67521-67521	BROWNELL	67671-67671	VICTORIA		

Kentucky

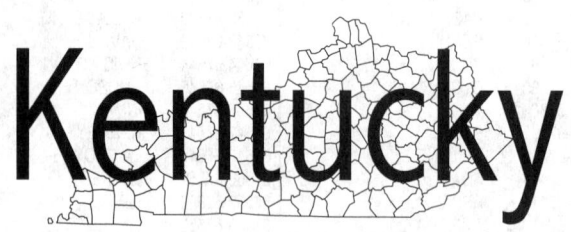

General Help Numbers:

Governor's Office
700 Capitol Ave, Room 100　　　502-564-2611
Frankfort, KY 40601　　　　　　Fax 502-564-2517
www.state.ky.us/agencies/gov/govmenu6.htm

Attorney General's Office
1024 Capital Center Drive　　　502-696-5300
Frankfort, KY 40601　　　　　　Fax 502-573-8317
www.law.state.ky.us　　　　　　8AM-5PM

State Court Administrator
100 Mill Creek Park　　　　　　502-573-2350
Frankfort, KY 40601　　　　　　Fax 502-695-1759
www.aoc.state.ky.us/aoc/default.htm　　8AM-4:30PM

State Archives
300 Coffee Tree Rd　　　　　　502-564-8300
Frankfort, KY 40601　　　　　　Fax 502-564-5773
www.kdla.state.ky.us　　　　　8AM-4PM T-SA

State Specifics:

Capital:　　　　　　　　　　　　　　Frankfort
　　　　　　　　　　　　　　Franklin County

Time Zone:　　　　　　　　　　　　　EST*
* Kentucky's forty western-most counties are CST: They are: Adair, Allen, Ballard, Barren, Breckinridge, Butler, Caldwell, Calloway, Carlisle, Christian, Clinton, Crittenden, Cumberland, Daviess, Edmonson, Fulton, Graves, Grayson, Hancock, Hart, Henderson, Hickman, Hopkins, Livingstone, Logan, Marshall, McCracken, McLean, Metcalfe, Monroe, Muhlenberg, Ohio,Russell, Simpson, Todd, Trigg, Union, Warren, Wayne, Webster.

Number of Counties:　　　　　　　　120

Population:　　　　　　　　　　　3,908.124

Web Site:　　　　　　　　　　www.state.ky.us

State Agencies

Criminal Records

Kentucky State Police, Records Section, 1250 Louisville Rd, Frankfort, KY 40601; 502-227-8713, 502-227-8734 (Fax), 8AM-4PM.

www.state.ky.us/agencies/ksp/ksphome.htm

Note: Kentucky courts at the local level will not do criminal searches and refer all requesters to the Administrative Office of Courts in Frankfurt, then to KY State Police who will do record checks for $10.00 per name. Records go back to 1988.

Indexing & Storage: Records are available from 1952 on for criminal records. It takes 30 days from arrest date before new records are available for inquiry. Records are indexed on inhouse computer, fingerprint cards.

Searching: Access only as mandated by Kentucky Revised Statutes. Requests accepted for employment purposes, nursing homes and adoptive/foster parent background searches. Include the following in your request-full name, date of birth, Social Security Number, reason for information request. A signed release is also required. Statistical information about criminal offenses and accidents is available from 1971 on. The following data is not released: juvenile records, dismissals or pending cases.

Access by: mail, in person.

Fee & Payment: The fee is $4.00 per individual. Fee payee: Kentucky State Treasury. Prepayment required. Personal checks accepted. No credit cards accepted.

Mail search: Turnaround time: 2-3 weeks. A self addressed stamped envelope is requested.

In person search: Turnaround time is while you wait. There is a limit of 5 searches.

Corporation Records
Limited Partnerships
Assumed Name
Limited Liability Company Records

Secretary of State, Corporate Records, PO Box 718, Frankfort, KY 40602-0718 (Courier: 700 Capitol Ave, Room 156, Frankfort, KY 40601); 502-564-7330, 502-564-4075 (Fax), 8AM-4PM.

www.sos.state.ky.us

Indexing & Storage: Records are available from the 1977 forward on computer index. Hard copies are on microfilm. Records inactive by 1976 are archived and it takes 3 weeks to research. New records are available for inquiry immediately.

Searching: Computer records are limited, they contain name, dates, current registered agent and initial incorporators and initial directors. They do contain current lists of officers and directors when available. Include the following in your request-full name of business.

Access by: mail, phone, in person, online.

Fee & Payment: There is no search fee, but there is a $5.00 certification fee. Copies are $1.00 (minimum) for up to first to 10 pages, and $.10 per each additional page. Pages can be certified for $.50 each. A Certificate of Good Standing is $10.00. Fee payee: Secretary of State. Prepayment required. Send at least $1.00 in the mail for copies. If certified copies are needed, call first. Personal checks accepted. No credit cards accepted.

Mail search: Turnaround time: 2-3 days. No self addressed stamped envelope is required.

Phone search: Only information on the computer system is released over the phone.

In person search: Turnaround time while you wait. If you order 5 or more, they will mail the records to you.

Online search: The Internet site, open 24 hours, has a searchable database with over 340,000 KY businesses. The site also offers downloading of filing forms.

Other access: Monthly lists of new corporations are available for $10.00 per month.

Trademarks/Servicemarks

Secretary of State, Legal Department, 700 Capitol Ave, Room 86, Frankfort, KY 40601; 502-564-7330, 502-564-4075 (Fax), 8AM-4:30PM.

www.sos.state.ky.us

Searching: Include the trademark/servicemark name or applicant name or certification number.

Access by: mail, in person.

Fee & Payment: There is no fee, unless extensive searching is required. Fee payee: KY State Treasurer. Prepayment required. Personal checks accepted. No credit cards accepted.

Mail search: Turnaround time: 1 week. A self addressed stamped envelope is requested.

In person search: Searching is available in person.

Uniform Commercial Code

UCC Division, Secretary of State, PO Box 1470, Frankfort, KY 40602-0718 (Courier: State Capitol Bldg, Rm 79, Frankfort, KY 40601); 502-564-2848, 502-564-5687 (Fax), 8AM-4:30PM.

www.sos.state.ky.us

Note: Important--UCC statements filed at the county clerks office on or before 01/04/99 plus all out-of-state debtor filings are available from this agency. All tax liens are filed at the county level.

Searching: Records are open; however, this agency does not conduct searches itself. You must contact a search company or do in-person. Mail requests are referred to the county level. Include the following in your request-debtor name.

Access by: in person, online.

Fee & Payment: There is no search fee. The copy fee is a minimum of $1.00 which includes the first 10 pages, then $.10 per page thereafter. Fee payee: KY State Treasurer. Personal checks accepted. No credit cards accepted. No searching by mail.

In person search: Searching is available in person.

Online search: The Kentucky Lien Information Search System is offered free of charge at the web site. Search by debor name, secured party name, location or date of filing, or county identification number.

Federal Tax Liens
State Tax Liens
Records not maintained by a state level agency.

Note: All tax liens are at the county level.

Sales Tax Registrations

Revenue Cabinet, Tax Compliance Department, Sales Tax Section, Station 53, PO Box 181, Frankfort, KY 40602-0181 (Courier: 200 Fair Oaks, Bldg 2, Frankfort, KY 40602); 502-564-5170, 502-564-2041 (Fax), 8AM-4:30PM.

www.state.ky.us/agencies/revenue/revhome.htm

Indexing & Storage: Records are available from the 1970's. Records are indexed on computer from 1996-present, and on microfilm from 1985-1995.

Searching: This agency will only confirm if a business is registered, and they will confirm if a tax permit exists. They will provide no other information. Include the following in your request-business name, owner name and address, federal employer identification number. They will also search by tax permit number.

Access by: mail, phone, in person.

Mail search: Turnaround time: 2-3 months. A self addressed stamped envelope is requested. No fee for mail request.

Phone search: No fee for telephone request.

In person search: No fee for request.

Birth Certificates

Department for Public Health, Vital Statistics, 275 E Main St - IE-A, Frankfort, KY 40621-0001; 502-564-4212, 502-227-0032 (Fax), 8AM-4PM.

http://publichealth.state.ky.us/vital.htm

Indexing & Storage: Records are available from 1911-present. It takes 1 month before new records are available for inquiry. Records are indexed on microfiche, inhouse computer, books (volumes).

Searching: Include the following in your request-full name, names of parents, mother's maiden name, date of birth, place of birth. Provide a daytime phone number.

Access by: mail, phone, fax, in person.

Fee & Payment: Searches are $9.00 per name. Add $5.00 if using a credit card. Fee payee: Kentucky State Treasurer. Prepayment required. Personal checks accepted. Credit cards accepted: Mastercard, Visa, AmEx, Discover.

Mail search: Turnaround time: 3-4 weeks. No self addressed stamped envelope is required.

Phone search: Must use a credit card (add $5.00 fee) for a phone request. Turnaround time is 3-5 days.

Fax search: Same fees as telephone search.

In person search: Turnaround time 1 1/2 hour.

Expedited service: Expedited service is available for mail, phone and fax searches. Turnaround time: overnight delivery. Add $10.70 per package. Also, be sure to include extra credit card use fee.

Death Records

Department for Public Health, Vital Statistics, 275 E Main St - IE-A, Frankfort, KY 40621-0001; 502-564-4212, 502-227-0032 (Fax), 8AM-3PM.

http://publichealth.state.ky.us/vital.htm

Indexing & Storage: Records are available from 1911 on. It takes 1 month before new records are available for inquiry. Records are indexed on microfiche, inhouse computer, books (volumes).

Searching: Include the following in your request-full name, date of death, place of death. Provide a daytime phone number.

Access by: mail, phone, fax, in person, online.

Fee & Payment: The fee is $6.00 per name. Fee payee: Kentucky State Treasurer. Prepayment required. Personal checks accepted. Credit cards accepted: Mastercard, Visa, AmEx, Discover.

Mail search: Turnaround time: 3-4 weeks. No self addressed stamped envelope is required.

Phone search: Must use a credit card (add $5.00 fee) to make phone request. Turnaround time is 2-3 days.

Fax search: Same fees and turnaround time as telephone requests.

In person search: Turnaround time 1 1/2 hour.

Online search: In cooperation with the University of Kentucky, there is a searchable death index at http://ukcc.uky.edu:80/~vitalrec/. This is for non-commercial use only. Records are from 1911 through 1992.

Expedited service: Expedited service is available for mail, phone and fax searches. Turnaround time: overnight delivery. Add $10.70 per package. Also, be sure to include extra credit card use fee.

Marriage Certificates

Department for Public Health, Vital Statistics, 275 E Main St - IE-A, Frankfort, KY 40621-0001; 502-564-4212, 502-227-0032 (Fax), 8AM-3PM.

http://publichealth.state.ky.us/vital.htm

Indexing & Storage: Records are available from June 1958-present. It takes 1-2 months before new records are available for inquiry. Records are indexed on microfiche, inhouse computer, books (volumes).

Searching: Include the following in your request- names of husband and wife, date of marriage, place or county of marriage. Must also include where marriage license was obtained and a daytime phone number.

Access by: mail, phone, fax, in person, online.

Fee & Payment: The fee is $6.00 per name. Fee payee: Kentucky State Treasurer. Prepayment required. Personal checks accepted. Credit cards accepted: Mastercard, Visa, AmEx, Discover.

Mail search: Turnaround time: 3-4 weeks. No self addressed stamped envelope is required.

Phone search: Must use a credit card (add $5.00 fee) for a phone request. Turnaround time is 3-5 days.

Fax search: Same criteria as phone orders.

In person search: Turnaround time 1 1/2 hour.

Online search: In cooperation with the University of Kentucky, a searchable index is available on the Internet at http://ukcc.uky.edu:80/~vitalrec/. The index runs from 1973 through 1993. This is for non-commercial use only.

Other access: Records are available on microfiche for $6.00 per set. Records are separated by either wife or husband and run 1973 through 1993.

Expedited service: Expedited service is available for mail, phone and fax searches. Turnaround time: overnight delivery. Add $10.70 per package. Also, be sure to include extra credit card use fee.

Divorce Records

Department for Public Health, Vital Statistics, 275 E Main St - IE-A, Frankfort, KY 40621-0001; 502-564-4212, 502-227-0032 (Fax), 8AM-3PM.

http://publichealth.state.ky.us/vital.htm

Indexing & Storage: Records are available from June, 1958-present. It takes 1-2 months before new records are available for inquiry. Records are indexed on microfiche, inhouse computer, books (volumes).

Searching: Include the following in your request- names of husband and wife, date of divorce, place of divorce. Provide a daytime phone number.

Access by: mail, phone, fax, in person, online.

Fee & Payment: The fee is $6.00 per name. Fee payee: Kentucky State Treasurer. Prepayment required. Personal checks accepted. Credit cards accepted: Mastercard, Visa, AmEx, Discover.

Mail search: Turnaround time: 3-4 weeks. No self addressed stamped envelope is required.

Phone search: Must use a credit card (add $5.00 fee) for a phone request. Turnaround time 3-5 days.

Fax search: Same criteria as phone requests.

In person search: Turnaround time 1 1/2 hour.

Online search: In cooperation with the University of Kentucky, there is a searchable index on the Internet at http://ukcc.uky.edu:80/~vitalrec/. This is for non-commercial use only. The index is for 1973-1993.

Other access: Records are available on microfiche for $6.00 per set. They are separated by either husband or wife and are available from 1974 through 1993.

Expedited service: Expedited service is available for mail, phone and fax searches. Turnaround time: overnight delivery. Add $10.70 per package.

Workers' Compensation Records

Kentucky Department of Workers' Claims, Perimeter Park West, 1270 Louisville Rd, Bldg C, Frankfort, KY 40601; 502-564-5550, 502-564-5732 (Fax), 8AM-4:30PM.

www.state.ky/us/agencies/labor/wkrclaims.htm

Indexing & Storage: Records are available from 1982-present on computer. New records are available for inquiry immediately.

Searching: Must have a signed release from claimant only for copies of first report. Otherwise, information is open to the public per KRS 61.870 through 61.884. Include the following in your request-claimant name, Social Security Number, date of accident, place of employment at time of accident. The following data is not released: Social Security Numbers, addresses or personal information (height, weight, sex, eye color, etc.).

Access by: mail, fax, in person.

Fee & Payment: Fees are $.50 per page from microfilm and photocopies are $.10 per page. Fee payee: Kentucky State Treasurer. Payment may be submitted at the time records are picked up. Otherwise, an invoice will be mailed at the end of the month. Personal checks accepted. No credit cards accepted.

Mail search: Turnaround time: 2-4 weeks. Requests are processed in order by the date received. A self addressed stamped envelope is requested.

Fax search: Fax requests are processed by date of receipt asame as requests that are mailed.

In person search: The office will have the records ready for you if you call ahead first and make an appointment.

Other access: A listing of file contents may be requested. Call for details.

Driver Records

Division of Driver Licensing, State Office Bldg, MVRS, 501 High Street, 2nd Floor, Frankfort, KY 40622; 502-564-6800 x2250, 502-564-5787 (Fax), 8AM-4:30PM.

www.kytc.state.ky.us

Note: Requests for copies of tickets must be submitted in writing to; Cabinets Record Custodian, Department of Administrative Services, State Office Building, Frankfort 40622. There is a $.10 fee per document.

Indexing & Storage: Records are available for 3 years for moving violations, DWIs and suspensions. Accidents are not reported. Any entry over 3 years old is "masked for insurance and employers." Records of surrendered licenses are available for 3 years. Records computer indexed for past 5 years.

Searching: There is no opt out. Casual requesters can obtain record information, but no personal information is provided. The SSN can be used as the DL#. That number, the full name and DOB are needed when ordering. The driver's address is not included as part of the search report without a release from the driver.

Access by: mail, in person, online.

Fee & Payment: The fee is $3.00 per record. Fee payee: Kentucky State Treasurer. Prepayment required. Personal checks accepted. No credit cards accepted.

Mail search: Turnaround time: 3 days.

In person search: Walk-in requesters may receive up to 5 records immediately at the address listed above or at any one of 11 field offices in the state.

Online search: This is a batch method for higher volume users. There is a minimum order of 150 requests per batch. Input received by 3 PM will be available the next morning. Either the DL# or SSN is needed for ordering. The state will bill monthly.

Other access: The state will sell its entire database of driver license names and addresses to certain vendors. Records are not available for commercial purposes.

Vehicle Ownership
Vehicle Identification

Department of Motor Vehicles, Division of Motor Vehicle Licensing, State Office Bldg, 3rd Floor, Frankfort, KY 40622; 502-564-4076 (Title History), 502-564-3298 (Other Requests), 502-564-1686 (Fax), 8AM-4:30PM.

www.kytc.state.ky.us

Indexing & Storage: Records are available for 10 years to present. Records are indexed on computer from 1983-present, and on microfiche from 1978-1982.

Searching: Vehicle and ownership records are made available to the public; however, personal information is not released to the general public or for marketing purposes without consent. This agency will not do a search by SSN.

Access by: mail, in person, online.

Fee & Payment: The fee is $2.00 per record request. The state reporst current lien information. There is a full charge for a "no record found." Fee payee: Division of Motor Vehicles. Prepayment required. Cash and money orders are accepted. Personal checks accepted. No credit cards accepted.

Mail search: Turnaround time: 5-7 days. A self addressed stamped envelope is requested.

In person search: Turnaround time is while you wait (typically, 15 minutes to 1 hour).

Online search: Online access costs $2.00 per record. The online mode is interactive. Title, lien and registration searches are available. Records include those for mobile homes. For more information, contact Gale Warfield at 502-564-4076.

Other access: Kentucky has the ability to supply customized bulk delivery of vehicle registration information. The request must be in writing with the intended use outlined. For more information, call 502- 564-3298.

Accident Reports

Department of State Police, Records Section, 1250 Louisville Rd, Frankfort, KY 40601; 502-227-8700, 502-227-8734 (Fax), 8AM-4:30PM.

Indexing & Storage: Records are available from 4 years back at this location. However, there is limited access to accident reports less than 2 years old. It is suggested to go to the agency that filed the report for the record.

Searching: Some requests must be made through "open records." Detailed listing of accidents at specific location without personal identifying information is available for a fee with a written request. For more information phone 502-227-

8700 ext. 8259 for details. Search requirements include the exact date, county, roadway and mile post, and the driver's name and DOB. All requests must be in writing.

Access by: mail.

Fee & Payment: The charge is $.10 per page with a $.20 minimum. Fee payee: KY State Treasurer. Prepayment required. Personal checks accepted. No credit cards accepted.

Mail search: Turnaround time: 2-3 weeks. A self addressed stamped envelope is requested.

Other access: Specific accident statistics may be obtained by phoning the statistics coordinator.

Boat & Vessel Ownership
Boat & Vessel Registration

Division of Motor Vehicle Licensing, Vessel Titles and Registration, State Office Building, 3rd Floor, Frankfort, KY 40622; 502-564-5301, 8AM-5PM.

www.kytc.state.ky.us

Indexing & Storage: Records are available for titles from 1990, for registration from 1985. Prior records are kept by Circuit Clerks. Only motorized vessels must be titled and registered. Personal information is not released to casual requesters.

Searching: The hull number, title number or KY number must be submitted.

Access by: mail, in person.

Fee & Payment: The fee is $2.00 per record. Fee payee: Kentucky State Treasurer. Prepayment required. No credit cards accepted.

Mail search: Turnaround time: 1 week.

In person search: Most of the time results will be mailed.

Legislation-Current/Pending
Legislation-Passed

Kentucky General Assembly, Legislative Research Commission, 700 Capitol Ave, Room 300, Frankfort, KY 40601; 502-372-7181 (Bill Status Only), 502-564-8100 x323 (Bill Room), 502-564-8100 x340 (LRC Library), 502-223-5094 (Fax), 8AM-4:30PM.

www.lrc.state.ky.us

Indexing & Storage: Records are available from 1986 on computer, and from 1950 in hard copy.

Kentucky Acts from 1820-present are available in hard copy. Records are indexed on inhouse computer.

Searching: Include the following in your request-bill number.

Access by: mail, phone, fax, in person, online.

Fee & Payment: Minimum fee $1.00. Fees over $1.00 are invoiced. You pay postage/UPS charges over 8 ounces. Copies are $.15 each. Fee payee: LRC. Personal checks accepted. No credit cards accepted.

Mail search: Turnaround time: variable.

Phone search: Searching is available by phone.

Fax search: The fee is $.65 per page.

In person search: Searching is available in person.

Online search: The web site has an extensive searching mechanism for bills, actions, summaries, and statutes.

Voter Registration

State Board of Elections, 140 Walnut, Frankfort, KY 40601; 502-573-7100, 502-573-4369 (Fax), 8AM-4:30PM.

www.sos.state.ky.us/elecdiv.htm

Note: For individual searches, it is best to go to the county level.

Searching: The state will allow viewing and verification of records and voting histories. The SSN or DOB is required when doing a verification. The following data is not released: Social Security Numbers or bulk information or lists for commercial purposes.

Access by: mail, fax, in person.

Fee & Payment: There is no search fee. There is a $.10 per page copy fee, if visiting in person.

Mail search: Turnaround time: 3 days. No self addressed stamped envelope is required.

Fax search: For confirmation purposes only.

In person search: Searching is available in person.

Other access: Data is available on disk, tape, labels or lists for political purposes only.

GED Certificates

Adult Education and Literacy, GED Program, Capitol Plaze Tower, 500 Mero St Rm 335,

Frankfort, KY 40601; 502-564-5117, 502-564-5436 (Fax).

www.state.ky.us/agencies/wforce/index.htm

Searching: To verify or to get copy of transcript or diploma, all of the following is required: a signed release, name, date/year of test, date of birth, Social Security Number, and city of test.

Access by: mail, fax, in person.

Fee & Payment: There is no fee for verification. Copies of transcript or duplicate diplomas are $5.00 each. Fee payee: KY State Treasurer. Prepayment required. Money orders are accepted. No credit cards accepted.

Mail search: Turnaround time is 1 week. No self addressed stamped envelope is required.

Fax search: Same criteria as mail searching.

In person search: In person searchers must bring a photo id. Turnaround time: Same day.

Hunting License Information
Fishing License Information

Fish & Wildlife Resources Department, Division of Administrative Services, 1 Game Farm Rd, Arnold Mitchell Bldg, Frankfort, KY 40601; 502-564-4224, 502-564-6508 (Fax), 8AM-4:30PM.

www.state.ky.us/agencies/fw/kdfwr.htm

Note: A database has been created, starting in 1996. Records are not released without written request and for good reason. Records are not available for commercial mail lists. Older records are archived in boxes. Record retrieval extremely difficult.

Indexing & Storage: Records are available for current year only. Records are indexed on hard copy.

Searching: Requests must be in writing and adddressed to the Commissioner's Office. Include the following in your request-full name, Social Security Number.

Access by: mail, in person.

Fee & Payment: Fees will vary by type of request.

Mail search: Searching is available by mail.

In person search: Searching is available in person.

Licenses Searchable Online

Architect #07	http://kybera.com/roster.shtml
Check Seller/ Casher #18	www.dfi.state.ky.us/ConsumerLoan/List%20of%20Check%20Cashers.xls
Engineer #39	http://kyboels.state.ky.us/roster.htm
Engineer & Land Surveyor Firm #39	http://kyboels.state.ky.us/roster.htm
Geologist #15	www.state.ky.us/agencies/finance/boards/geology/pages/geol.html
Loan Company #18	www.dfi.state.ky.us/ConsumerLoan/Small%20Loan%20Companies.xls
Mortgage Broker #18	www.dfi.state.ky.us/aspscripts/mort_brokers.asp
Mortgage Loan Company #18	www.dfi.state.ky.us/aspscripts/mort_company.asp
Optometrist #11	http://optometry.state.ky.us/Search/OptomLookUp.asp
Physical Therapist #38	http://web.state.ky.us/gbc/LicenseSearch.asp?AGY=4
Physical Therapist Assistant #38	http://web.state.ky.us/gbc/LicenseSearch.asp?AGY=4
Public Accountant-CPA #03	www.state.ky.us/agencies/boa/Locate.html
Real Estate Broker #33	http://web.state.ky.us/krecweb/Search/LicenseeLookUp.asp
Real Estate Broker Firm #33	http://web.state.ky.us/krecweb/Search/FirmLookUp.asp
Real Estate Sales Associate #33	http://web.state.ky.us/krecweb/Search/LicenseeLookUp.asp
Surveyor #39	http://kyboels.state.ky.us/roster.htm

Licensing Quick Finder

Animal Technician #15 502-564-3296
Architect #07 606-246-2069
Art Therapist #15 502-564-3296
Association Employee #31 606-246-2040
Athletic Manager #15 502-564-3296
Athletic Trainer #15 502-564-3296
Attorney #02 502-564-3795
Auction House Operator #04 502-339-9453
Auctioneer #04 502-339-9453
Auctioneer, Apprentice #04 502-339-9453
Bank #18 502-573-3390
Barber #05 502-429-8841
Blacksmith #31 606-246-2040
Boiler Contractor #26 502-564-3626
Boiler Installer/Inspector #26 502-564-3626
Boxer #15 502-564-3296
Broker/Dealer/Agent #18 502-573-3390
Building Inspector #26 502-564-8090
Check Seller/ Casher #18 502-573-3390
Child Care Facility #13 502-564-2800
Chiropractor #35 888-605-1368
Claiming License #31 606-246-2040
Commercial Fishing #20 800-858-1549
Compost Operator #24 502-565-6716
Coroner #17 606-622-6165
Cosmetologist #37 502-564-4262
Dental Hygienist #06 502-423-0573
Dental Laboratory #06 502-423-0573
Dental Laboratory Technician #06 502-423-0573
Dentist #06 502-423-0573
Dietitian/Nutritionist #15 502-564-3296
Drinking Water Treatment/Distribution System
     Operator #29 502-564-3410
Driver Training Instructor #42 502-226-7404
Electrical Contractor #26 502-564-3626
Electrical Inspector #26 502-564-3626
Elevator Inspector #26 502-564-3626
Embalmer #36 502-241-3918
Emergency Medical Technician-Basic #14
     502-564-8950
Emergency Medical Technician-First Response #14
     502-564-8950
Engineer #39 502-573-2680
Engineer & Land Surveyor Firm #39 502-573-2680
Farm Manager/Agent #31 606-246-2040
Fire Alarm Sys. Inspector #26 502-564-3626
Fire Protection Sprinkler Installer #26 502-564-3626
Funeral Director #36 502-241-3918
Fur Buyer #20 800-858-1549
Fur Processor #20 800-858-1549
Geologist #15 .... 502-564-3296 x227

Guide, Hunting & Fishing #20 800-858-1549
Health Care Facility #13 502-564-2800
Hearing Instrument Specialist #15 502-564-3296
Horse Owner/Trainer #31 606-246-2040
Horse Trainer/Assistant Trainer #31 606-246-2040
Insurance Adjuster #21 502-564-3630
Insurance Agent #21 502-564-3630
Insurance Consultant #21 502-564-3630
Insurance Solicitor #21 502-564-3630
Investment Advisor/Representative #18
     502-573-3390
Jockey Agent #31 606-246-2040
Jockey/Jockey Apprentice #31 606-246-2040
Landfarm Operator #24 502-564-6716
Landfill Manager #24 502-564-6716
Landfill Operator #24 502-564-6716
Law Enforcement Training Instructor #17
     606-622-6165
Limited Livestock Auctioneer #04 502-339-9453
Limited Tobacco Auctioneer #04 502-339-9453
Liquor License #01 502-573-4850
Loan Company #18 502-573-3390
Malt Beverage Distributor #01 502-573-4850
Manufacturer #12 502-573-1580
Marriage & Family Therapist #15 502-564-3296
Medical Doctor/Surgeon #41 502-429-8046
Milk Sampler-Weigher #43 606-257-2785
Milk Tester #43 606-257-2785
Miner #22 606-246-2026
Mining Blaster #22 606-246-2026
Mining Fire Boss #22 606-246-2026
Mining Foreman #22 606-246-2026
Mining Inspector #22 606-246-2026
Mining Safety Instructor #22 606-246-2026
Mortgage Broker #18 502-573-3390
Mortgage Loan Company #18 502-573-3390
Mutuel Employee #31 606-246-2040
Nail Technician #37 502-564-4262
Notary Public #30 502-564-3490
Nurse #09 502-329-7000
Nurse Anesthetist #09 502-329-7000
Nurse Clinical Specialist #09 502-329-7000
Nurse Midwife #09 502-329-7000
Nurse-RN & LPN #09 502-329-7000
Nurses Aide Instructor #09 502-329-7048
Nurses' Aide Instructor #40 502-564-2800
Nursing Home Administrator #15 502-564-3296
Occupational License #31 606-246-2040
Occupational Therapist/Assistant #15 502-564-3296
Onsite Septic System Installers #45 502-564-4856

Ophthalmic Dispenser/Optician/Apprentice #10
     502-564-3296
Optometrist #11 502-863-5816
Osteopathic Physician #41 502-429-8046
Paramedic #14 502-564-8950
Pay Lake Operator #20 800-858-1549
Pesticide Applicator #16 502-564-7274
Pesticide Dealer #16 502-564-7274
Pesticide Exterminator #16 502-564-7274
Pharmacist #12 502-573-1580
Pharmacy #12 502-573-1580
Physical Therapist #38 502-327-8497
Physical Therapist Assistant #38 502-327-8497
Physician Assistant #41 502-429-8046
Plans & Specifications Inspector #26 502-564-8090
Plumber #47 502-564-3580
Plumber #26 502-564-3580
Podiatrist #27 207-759-0007
Police Officer #17 606-622-6165
Polygraph Examiner #28 502-564-7110
Polygraph Examiner-Trainee #28 502-564-7110
Profesional Couneslor #15 502-564-3296
Property Valuation Administrator #34 502-564-5620
Proprietary Education School #15 502-564-3296
Psychologist #15 502-564-3296
Public Accountant-CPA #03 502-595-3037
Racing Official #31 606-246-2040
Racing-Authorized Agent #31 606-246-2040
Radiation Operator #44 502-564-3700
Real Estate Appraiser #32 502-573-0091
Real Estate Broker #33 502-425-4273
Real Estate Broker Firm #33 502-425-4273
Real Estate Sales Associate #33 502-425-4273
Rehabilitation Counselor #23 502-564-6745
Respiratory Care Practitioner #15 502-564-3296
Respiratory Therapist #15 502-564-3296
Sanitarian #45 502-564-7398
Savings & Loan #18 502-573-3390
School Administrator #25 502-573-4606
School Bus Driver #46 502-564-4718
School Guidance Counselor #25 502-573-4606
School Media Librarian #25 502-573-4606
School Nurse #25 502-573-4606
School Social Worker/Psychologist #25 502-573-4606
Securities Agent #18 502-573-3370
Securities Broker/Dealer #18 502-573-3370
Sexual Assault Nurse Examiner #09 502-329-7000
Social Worker #15 502-564-3296
Speech-Language Pathologist/Audiologist #15
     .... 502-564-3296 x227
Stable Employee #31 606-246-2040

Suppression System Inspector #26	502-564-8090
Surveyor #39	502-573-2680
Taxidermist #20	800-858-1549
Teacher #25	502-573-4606
Track Occupational Employee #31	606-246-2040

Vendor Employee #31	606-246-2040
Vendors #31	606-246-2040
Veterinarian #15	502-564-3296
Veterinarian/Veterinary Assistant #31	606-246-2040
Veterinary Dental Technician #31	606-246-2040

Waste Water System Operator #29	502-564-3410
Water Well Driller #29	502-564-3410
Wholesaler #12	502-573-1580
Wrestler #15	502-564-3296

Licensing Agency Information

01 Alcoholic Beverage Control Department, 1003 Twilight Trail, #A2, Frankfort, KY 40601; 502-564-4850, Fax: 502-564-1442.

02 Bar Association, 514 W Main St, Frankfort, KY 40601-1883; 502-564-3795, Fax: 502-564-3225. www.kybar.org

03 Board of Accountancy, 332 W Broadway, #310, Louisville, KY 40202; 502-595-3037, Fax: 502-595-4281. www.state.ky.us/agencies/boa

Direct URL to search licenses: www.state.ky.us/agencies/boa/Locate.html You can search online using name and address. The online search is actually e-mail based, meaning that you visit the URL listed, enter the search criteria, and an e-mail is sent to the board. The results of your inquiry are e-mailed to you.

04 Board of Auctioneers, 9112 Leesgate Rd, Louisville, KY 40222-5089; 502-339-9453, Fax: 502-423-1854.

05 Board of Barbering, 9114 Leesgate Rd, #6, Louisville, KY 40222-5055; 502-429-8841, Fax: 502-429-5223.

06 Board of Dentistry, 10101 Linn Station Rd, #540, Louisville, KY 40223; 502-423-0573, Fax: 502-423-1239.

07 Board of Examiners & Registration of Architects, 841 Corporate Dr, #200B, Lexington, KY 40503; 606-246-2069, Fax: 606-246-2431. http://kybera.com

Direct URL to search licenses: http://kybera.com/roster.shtml You can search online using name, city, other

09 Board of Nursing, 312 Whittington Pky, #300, Louisville, KY 40222-5172; 502-329-7000, Fax: 502-329-7011.

www.kbn.state.ky.us/index.htm

10 Board of Ophthalmic Dispensers, PO Box 456 (PO Box 456), Frankfort, KY 40602; 502-564-3296 X227, Fax: 502-564-4818.

11 Board of Optometric Examiners, 1000 W Main St, Georgetown, KY 40324; 502-863-5816, Fax: 502-868-0176.

Direct URL to search licenses: http://optometry.state.ky.us/Search/OptomLookUp.asp You can search online using name and license number.

12 Board of Pharmacy, 1024 Capital Center Dr, #210, Frankfort, KY 40601-8204; 502-573-1580, Fax: 502-573-1582.

13 Division of Licensing & Regulations, Cabinet for Health Services, CHR Bldg, 4th Fl East, Frankfort, KY 40621-0001; 502-564-2800, Fax: 502-564-6546. www.cfc-chs.chr.state.ky.us

14 Cabinet for Health Services, Emergency Medical Services Branch, 275 Main St, Frankfort, KY 40621; 502-564-8950, Fax: 502-564-6533.

http://publichealth.state.ky.us/ems.htm

15 Department of Administration, Division of Occupations & Professions, PO Box 456 (PO Box 456), Frankfort, KY 40602; 502-564-3296, Fax: 502-564-4818.

www.state.ky.us/agencies/finance/descript/deptaddm.htm

16 Department of Agriculture, Division of Pesticide, 100 Fair Oak Ln, Frankfort, KY 40601; 502-564-7274, Fax: 502-564-3773.

www.state.ky.us/agencies/agr/kyagr.htm

17 Department of Criminal Justice Training, 3137 Kit Carson Dr, Richmond, KY 40475-3137; 606-622-6165, Fax: 606-622-2740.

www.jus.state.ky.us

18 Department of Financial Institutions, Division of Law & Regulatory Compliance, 1025 Capitol Center Dr #200, Frankfort, KY 40601; 800-223-2579, Fax: 502-573-8787.

www.dfi.state.ky.us

20 Department of Fish & Wildlife, 1 Game Farm Rd, Frankfort, KY 40601; 800-858-1549, Fax: 502-564-9136. www.kdfwr.state.ky.us

21 Department of Insurance, Licensing Division, PO Box 517, 215 W Main St, Frankfort, KY 40602-0517; 502-564-3630. www.doi.state.ky.us

22 Department of Mines & Minerals, PO Box 14080 (PO Box 2244), Frankfort, KY 40602-2244; 502-573-0140, Fax: 502-573-0152.

www.caer.uky.edu/kdmm/homepage.htm

23 Department of Vocational Rehabilitation, 209 St Clair St, Frankfort, KY 40601; 502-564-4440, Fax: 502-564-6745. http://kydvr.state.ky.us

24 Division of Waste Management, 14 Reilly Rd, Frankfort, KY 40601; 502-564-6716, Fax: 502-564-4049.

25 Education Department, Teacher Education/Certification Office, 1025 Capitol Center Dr, Frankfort, KY 40601; 502-573-4606, Fax: 502-573-4606.

www.kde.state.ky.us

26 Buildings & Construction Department, Housing, 1047 US 127 S, #1, Frankfort, KY 40601; 502-564-8044.

www.state.ky.us/agencies/housing/hbchome.htm

27 Board of Podiatry, 906B South 12th St, Murray, KY 42071-2949; 270-759-0007, Fax: 270-753-0684.

28 State Police, Polygraph Unit, 1250 Louisville Rd, Frankfort, KY 40601; 502-564-7110, Fax: 502-564-5956.

www.state.ky.us/agencies/ksp/ksphome.htm

29 Division of Water, Natural Resources & Environmental Protection, 14 Reilly Rd, Frankfort Office Park, Frankfort, KY 40601; 502-564-3410, Fax: 502-564-9720.

http://water.nr.state.ky.us/dow/dwhome.htm

30 Office of Secretary of State, Notary Commissions, PO Box 821 (Capitol Bldg), Frankfort, KY 40602-0821; 502-564-3490 X413, Fax: 502-564-4075.

www.sos.state.ky.us/ADMIN/NOTARY/NOTARY.HTM

31 National Horse Center - Bldg B, Racing Commission, 4063 Iron Works Pike, Lexington, KY 40511; 606-246-2040, Fax: 606-246-2039.

32 Real Estate Appraisers Board, 1025 Capitol Center Dr #100, Frankfort, KY 40601-8205; 502-573-0091, Fax: 502-573-0093.

33 Real Estate Commission, 10200 Linn Station Rd, #201, Louisville, KY 40223; 502-425-4273, Fax: 502-426-2717. www.krec.net

34 Department of Property Taxation, Revenue Cabinet, 592 Main St, Frankfort, KY 40620; 502-564-5620, Fax: 502-564-5620.

www.state.ky.us/agencies/revenue/revhome.htm

35 Board of Chiropractic Examiners, PO Box 183 (209 S Green St (PO Box 183)), Glasgow, KY 42142-0183; 270-651-2522, Fax: 270-651-8784.

36 Board of Embalmers & Funeral Directors, PO Box 324 (PO Box 324), Crestwood, KY 40014; 502-241-3918, Fax: 502-241-4297.

37 Board of Hairdressers & Cosmetologists, 111 St James Court #A, Frankfort, KY 40601; 502-564-4262, Fax: 502-564-0481.

38 Board of Physical Therapy, 9110 Leesgate Rd, #6, Louisville, KY 40222-5159; 502-327-8497, Fax: 502-423-0934. http://kbpt.state.ky.us

Direct URL to search licenses: http://web.state.ky.us/gbc/LicenseSearch.asp?AGY=4 You can search online using last name or license number

39 Professional Engineers & Land Surveyors, Board of Licensure, 160 Democrat Dr, Frankfort, KY 40601; 502-573-2680, Fax: 502-573-6687. http://kyboels.state.ky.us

Direct URL to search licenses: http://kyboels.state.ky.us/roster.htm You can search online using name.

41 Board of Medical Licensure, 310 Whittington Pky, #1B, Louisville, KY 40222; 502-429-8046, Fax: 502-429-9923.

42 State Police Driver Testing Section, 919 Versailles Rd, Frankfort, KY 40601; 502-226-7404, Fax: 502-226-7412.

43 Division of Regulatory Services, 103 Regulatory Service Bldg, Lexington, KY 40546-0275; 606-257-2785, Fax: 606-323-9931.

www.rs.uky.edu

44 Radiation Health & Toxic Agents, 275 E Main St, Frankfort, KY 40621; 502-564-3700, Fax: 502-564-6533.

45 Department for Public Health, Sanitarian Examining Committee, 275 E Main, 2nd Fl E, HS 2EA, Frankfort, KY 40621; 502-564-7398, Fax: 502-564-6533.

46 Department of Education, Pupil Transportation, 500 Mero St 15th Fl, Frankfort, KY 40601; 502-564-4718.

47 Division of Plumbing, 1047 US 127 S #1, Frankfort, KY 40601-4337.

The following list indicates the district and division name for each county in the state. If the district or division name of the bankruptcy court is different from the civil/criminal court, it appears in parentheses.

County/Court Cross Reference

County	District	Division
Adair	Western	Bowling Green (Louisville)
Allen	Western	Bowling Green (Louisville)
Anderson	Eastern	Frankfort (Lexington)
Ballard	Western	Paducah (Louisville)
Barren	Western	Bowling Green (Louisville)
Bath	Eastern	Lexington
Bell	Eastern	London (Lexington)
Boone	Eastern	Covington (Lexington)
Bourbon	Eastern	Lexington
Boyd	Eastern	Ashland (Lexington)
Boyle	Eastern	Lexington
Bracken	Eastern	Covington (Lexington)
Breathitt	Eastern	Pikeville (Lexington)
Breckinridge	Western	Louisville
Bullitt	Western	Louisville
Butler	Western	Bowling Green (Louisville)
Caldwell	Western	Paducah (Louisville)
Calloway	Western	Paducah (Louisville)
Campbell	Eastern	Covington (Lexington)
Carlisle	Western	Paducah (Louisville)
Carroll	Eastern	Frankfort (Lexington)
Carter	Eastern	Ashland (Lexington)
Casey	Western	Bowling Green (Louisville)
Christian	Western	Paducah (Louisville)
Clark	Eastern	Lexington
Clay	Eastern	London (Lexington)
Clinton	Western	Bowling Green (Louisville)
Crittenden	Western	Paducah (Louisville)
Cumberland	Western	Bowling Green (Louisville)
Daviess	Western	Owensboro (Louisville)
Edmonson	Western	Bowling Green (Louisville)
Elliott	Eastern	Ashland (Lexington)
Estill	Eastern	Lexington
Fayette	Eastern	Lexington
Fleming	Eastern	Lexington
Floyd	Eastern	Pikeville (Lexington)
Franklin	Eastern	Frankfort (Lexington)
Fulton	Western	Paducah (Louisville)
Gallatin	Eastern	Covington (Lexington)
Garrard	Eastern	Lexington
Grant	Eastern	Covington (Lexington)
Graves	Western	Paducah (Louisville)
Grayson	Western	Owensboro (Louisville)
Green	Western	Bowling Green (Louisville)
Greenup	Eastern	Ashland (Lexington)
Hancock	Western	Owensboro (Louisville)
Hardin	Western	Louisville
Harlan	Eastern	London (Lexington)
Harrison	Eastern	Lexington
Hart	Western	Bowling Green (Louisville)
Henderson	Western	Owensboro (Louisville)
Henry	Eastern	Frankfort (Lexington)
Hickman	Western	Paducah (Louisville)
Hopkins	Western	Owensboro (Louisville)
Jackson	Eastern	London (Lexington)
Jefferson	Western	Louisville
Jessamine	Eastern	Lexington
Johnson	Eastern	Pikeville (Lexington)
Kenton	Eastern	Covington (Lexington)
Knott	Eastern	Pikeville (Lexington)
Knox	Eastern	London (Lexington)
Larue	Western	Louisville
Laurel	Eastern	London (Lexington)
Lawrence	Eastern	Ashland (Lexington)
Lee	Eastern	Lexington
Leslie	Eastern	London (Lexington)
Letcher	Eastern	Pikeville (Lexington)
Lewis	Eastern	Ashland (Lexington)
Lincoln	Eastern	Lexington
Livingston	Western	Paducah (Louisville)
Logan	Western	Bowling Green (Louisville)
Lyon	Western	Paducah (Louisville)
Madison	Eastern	Lexington
Magoffin	Eastern	Pikeville (Lexington)
Marion	Western	Louisville
Marshall	Western	Paducah (Louisville)
Martin	Eastern	Pikeville (Lexington)
Mason	Eastern	Covington (Lexington)
McCracken	Western	Paducah (Louisville)
McCreary	Eastern	London (Lexington)
McLean	Western	Owensboro (Louisville)
Meade	Western	Louisville
Menifee	Eastern	Lexington
Mercer	Eastern	Lexington
Metcalfe	Western	Bowling Green (Louisville)
Monroe	Western	Bowling Green (Louisville)
Montgomery	Eastern	Lexington
Morgan	Eastern	Ashland (Lexington)
Muhlenberg	Western	Owensboro (Louisville)
Nelson	Western	Louisville
Nicholas	Eastern	Lexington
Ohio	Western	Owensboro (Louisville)
Oldham	Western	Louisville
Owen	Eastern	Frankfort (Lexington)
Owsley	Eastern	London (Lexington)
Pendleton	Eastern	Covington (Lexington)
Perry	Eastern	Pikeville (Lexington)
Pike	Eastern	Pikeville (Lexington)
Powell	Eastern	Lexington
Pulaski	Eastern	London (Lexington)
Robertson	Eastern	Covington (Lexington)
Rockcastle	Eastern	London (Lexington)
Rowan	Eastern	Ashland (Lexington)
Russell	Western	Bowling Green (Louisville)
Scott	Eastern	Lexington
Shelby	Eastern	Frankfort (Lexington)
Simpson	Western	Bowling Green (Louisville)
Spencer	Western	Louisville
Taylor	Western	Bowling Green (Louisville)
Todd	Western	Bowling Green (Louisville)
Trigg	Western	Paducah (Louisville)
Trimble	Eastern	Frankfort (Lexington)
Union	Western	Owensboro (Louisville)
Warren	Western	Bowling Green (Louisville)
Washington	Western	Louisville
Wayne	Eastern	London (Lexington)
Webster	Western	Owensboro (Louisville)
Whitley	Eastern	London (Lexington)
Wolfe	Eastern	Lexington
Woodford	Eastern	Lexington

US District Court

Eastern District of Kentucky

Ashland Division Suite 336, 1405 Greenup Ave, Ashland, KY 41101, 606-329-2465.

www.kyed.uscourts.gov

Counties: Boyd, Carter, Elliott, Greenup, Lawrence, Lewis, Morgan, Rowan.

Indexing & Storage: Cases are indexed by defendant and plaintiff as well as by case number. New cases are available in the index 1-2 days after filing date. Lexington Division has a master index for the district. Both computer and card indexes are maintained. The index is computerized from 1992. Open records are located at this court.

Fee & Payment: The fee is $15.00 per item (one party name or case number). Payment may be made by money order, cashier check, personal check. Prepayment is required. Payee: Clerk, USDC. Certification fee: $5.00 per document. Copy fee: $.50 per page.

Phone Search: Only docket information from active cases will be released over the phone. An automated voice case information service (VCIS) is not available.

Mail Search: A stamped self addressed envelope is not required.

In Person Search: In person searching is available.

PACER: Sign-up number is 800-676-6856. Access fee is $.60 per minute. Toll-free access: 800-361-0442. Local access: 606-233-2787. Case records are available back to September 1991. Records are never purged. New records are available online after 1 day. PACER is available on the Internet at http://pacer.kyed.uscourts.gov.

Covington Division Clerk, PO Box 1073, Covington, KY 41012 (Courier Address: US Courthouse, Room 201, 35 W 5th St, Covington, KY 41011), 606-392-7925.

www.kyed.uscourts.gov

Counties: Boone, Bracken, Campbell, Gallatin, Grant, Kenton, Mason, Pendleton, Robertson.

Indexing & Storage: Cases are indexed by defendant and plaintiff as well as by case number. New cases are available in the index immediately after filing date. Both computer and card indexes are maintained. Open records are located at this court.

Fee & Payment: The fee is $15.00 per item (one party name or case number). Payment may be made by money order, cashier check, personal check. Prepayment is required. The turnaround time for written requests varies. Payee: Clerk, US District Court. Certification fee: $5.00 per document. Copy fee: $.50 per page.

Phone Search: Searching is not available by phone.

Mail Search: Always enclose a stamped self addressed envelope.

In Person Search: In person searching is available.

PACER: Sign-up number is 800-676-6856. Access fee is $.60 per minute. Toll-free access: 800-361-0442. Local access: 606-233-2787. Case records are available back to September 1991. Records are never purged. New records are

available online after 1 day. PACER is available on the Internet at http://pacer.kyed.uscourts.gov.

Frankfort Division Room 313, 330 W Broadway, Frankfort, KY 40601, 502-223-5225.

www.kyed.uscourts.gov

Counties: Anderson, Carroll, Franklin, Henry, Owen, Shelby, Trimble.

Indexing & Storage: Cases are indexed by defendant and plaintiff as well as by case number. New cases are available in the index immediately after filing date. Both computer and card indexes are maintained. Records have been indexed on computer since January, 1993. Open records are located at this court.

Fee & Payment: The fee is $15.00 per item (one party name or case number). Payment may be made by money order, cashier check, personal check. Prepayment is required. Payee: Clerk, US District Court. Certification fee: $5.00 per document. Copy fee: $.50 per page.

Phone Search: Only docket information is available by phone. An automated voice case information service (VCIS) is not available.

Mail Search: A stamped self addressed envelope is not required.

In Person Search: In person searching is available.

PACER: Sign-up number is 800-676-6856. Access fee is $.60 per minute. Toll-free access: 800-361-0442. Local access: 606-233-2787. Case records are available back to September 1991. Records are never purged. New records are available online after 1 day. PACER is available on the Internet at http://pacer.kyed.uscourts.gov.

Lexington Division PO Box 3074, Lexington, KY 40588 (Courier Address: Room 206, 101 Barr St, Lexington, KY 40507), 606-233-2503.

www.kyed.uscourts.gov

Counties: Bath, Bourbon, Boyle, Clark, Estill, Fayette, Fleming, Garrard, Harrison, Jessamine, Lee, Lincoln, Madison, Menifee, Mercer, Montgomery, Nicholas, Powell, Scott, Wolfe, Woodford. Lee and Wolfe counties were part of the Pikeville Division before 10/31/92. Perry became part of Pikeville after 1992.

Indexing & Storage: Cases are indexed by defendant and plaintiff as well as by case number. New cases are available in the index 24 hours after filing date. Both computer and card indexes are maintained. Civil cases filed after October 1, 1992 are on the computer. Cases prior to October 1992 are on index cards. Open records are located at this court.

Fee & Payment: The fee is $15.00 per item (one party name or case number). Payment may be made by money order, cashier check, personal check. Prepayment is required. Payee: Clerk, USDC. Certification fee: $5.00 per document. Copy fee: $.50 per page.

Phone Search: Only docket information from active cases will be released over the phone. An automated voice case information service (VCIS) is not available.

Mail Search: A stamped self addressed envelope is not required.

In Person Search: In person searching is available.

PACER: Sign-up number is 800-676-6856. Access fee is $.60 per minute. Toll-free access:

800-361-0442. Local access: 606-233-2787. Case records are available back to September 1991. Records are never purged. New records are available online after 1 day. PACER is available on the Internet at http://pacer.kyed.uscourts.gov.

London Division PO Box 5121, London, KY 40745-5121 (Courier Address: 124 US Courthouse, 300 S Main, London, KY 40741), 606-864-5137.

www.kyed.uscourts.gov

Counties: Bell, Clay, Harlan, Jackson, Knox, Laurel, Leslie, McCreary, Owsley, Pulaski, Rockcastle, Wayne, Whitley.

Indexing & Storage: Cases are indexed by defendant and plaintiff as well as by case number. New cases are available in the index 1 day after filing date. A computer index is maintained. Open records are located at this court.

Fee & Payment: The fee is $15.00 per item (one party name or case number). Payment may be made by money order, cashier check, personal check. Prepayment is required. Payee: Clerk, USDC. Certification fee: $5.00 per document. Copy fee: $.50 per page.

Phone Search: Only docket information is available by phone. An automated voice case information service (VCIS) is not available.

Mail Search: Always enclose a stamped self addressed envelope.

In Person Search: In person searching is available.

PACER: Sign-up number is 800-676-6856. Access fee is $.60 per minute. Toll-free access: 800-361-0442. Local access: 606-233-2787. Case records are available back to September 1991. Records are never purged. New records are available online after 1 day. PACER is available on the Internet at http://pacer.kyed.uscourts.gov.

Pikeville Division Office of the clerk, 203 Federal Bldg, 110 Main St, Pikeville, KY 41501, 606-437-6160.

www.kyed.uscourts.gov

Counties: Breathitt, Floyd, Johnson, Knott, Letcher, Magoffin, Martin, Perry, Pike. Lee and Wolfe Counties were part of this division until 10/31/92, when they were moved to the Lexington Division.

Indexing & Storage: Cases are indexed by defendant and plaintiff as well as by case number. New cases are available in the index immediately after filing date. A computer index is maintained. Open records are located at this court.

Fee & Payment: The fee is $15.00 per item (one party name or case number). Payment may be made by money order, cashier check, personal check. Prepayment required except for Kentucky attorneys. Payee: Clerk, US District Court. Certification fee: $5.00 per document. Copy fee: $.50 per page. You are allowed to make your own copies. These copies cost $.50 per page.

Phone Search: Only the date the case was filed and the status of the case will be released over the phone. An automated voice case information service (VCIS) is not available.

Mail Search: A stamped self addressed envelope is not required.

In Person Search: In person searching is available.

PACER: Sign-up number is 800-676-6856. Access fee is $.60 per minute. Toll-free access:

800-361-0442. Local access: 606-233-2787. Case records are available back to September 1991. Records are never purged. New records are available online after 1 day. PACER is available on the Internet at http://pacer.kyed.uscourts.gov.

US Bankruptcy Court
Eastern District of Kentucky

Lexington Division PO Box 1111, Lexington, KY 40589-1111 (Courier Address: Community Trust Bldg, Suite 202, 100 E Vine St, Lexington, KY 40507), 606-233-2608.

www.kyeb.uscourts.gov

Counties: Anderson, Bath, Bell, Boone, Bourbon, Boyd, Boyle, Bracken, Breathitt, Campbell, Carroll, Carter, Clark, Clay, Elliott, Estill, Fayette, Fleming, Floyd, Franklin, Gallatin, Garrard, Grant, Greenup, Harlan, Harrison, Henry, Jackson, Jessamine, Johnson,Kenton, Knott, Knox, Laurel, Lawrence, Lee, Leslie, Letcher, Lewis, Lincoln, Madison, Magoffin, Martin, Mason, McCreary, Menifee, Mercer, Montgomery, Morgan, Nicholas, Owen, Owsley, Pendleton, Perry, Pike, Powell, Pulaski, Robertson, Rockcastle, Rowan,Scott, Shelby, Trimble, Wayne, Whitley, Wolfe, Woodford.

Indexing & Storage: Cases are indexed by debtor as well as by case number. New cases are available in the index 3 days after filing date. Both computer and card indexes are maintained. Open records are located at this court.

Fee & Payment: The fee is $15.00 per item (one party name or case number). Payment may be made by money order, cashier check, business check. Personal checks are not accepted. Prepayment is required (excluding pauper filings). Payee: Clerk, US Bankruptcy Court. Certification fee: $5.00 per document. Copy fee: $.50 per page. You are allowed to make your own copies. These copies cost $.15 per page.

Phone Search: Only docket information is available by phone. An automated voice case information service (VCIS) is available. Call VCIS at 800-998-2650 or 606-233-2650.

Mail Search: Always enclose a stamped self addressed envelope.

In Person Search: In person searching is available.

PACER: Sign-up number is 800-676-6856. Access fee is $.60 per minute. Toll-free access: 800-497-2777. Local access: 606-233-2777. Case records are available back to July 1992. Records are purged every six months. New civil records are available online after 1 day. PACER is available on the Internet at http://pacer.kyeb.uscourts.gov.

US District Court
Western District of Kentucky

Bowling Green Division US District Court, 241 E Main St, Room 120, Bowling Green, KY 42101-2175, 270-781-1110.

www.kywd.uscourts.gov

Counties: Adair, Allen, Barren, Butler, Casey, Clinton, Cumberland, Edmonson, Green, Hart, Logan, Metcalfe, Monroe, Russell, Simpson, Taylor, Todd, Warren.

Indexing & Storage: Cases are indexed by defendant and plaintiff as well as by case number. New cases are available in the index 1-2 days after filing date. Both computer and card indexes are maintained. Open records are located at this court.

Fee & Payment: The fee is $15.00 per item (one party name or case number). Payment may be made by money order, cashier check, personal check. Prepayment is required. Payee: Clerk, US District Court. Certification fee: $5.00 per document. Copy fee: $.50 per page. You are allowed to make your own copies. These copies cost $.50 per page.

Phone Search: Only docket information is available by phone. An automated voice case information service (VCIS) is not available.

Mail Search: Always enclose a stamped self addressed envelope.

In Person Search: In person searching is available.

PACER: Sign-up number is 800-676-6856. Access fee is $.60 per minute. Case records are available back to 1992. New records are available online after 1 day. PACER is available on the Internet at http://38.244.24.105/webpacer.html.

Electronic Filing: Only law firms and practitioners may file cases electronically. Electronic filing information is available online at www.kywd.uscourts.gov/scripts/usdckyw/ecf/ecf.pl

Louisville Division Clerk, US District Court, 450 US Courthouse, 601 W Broadway, Louisville, KY 40202, 502-582-5156, Fax: 502-582-6302.

www.kywd.uscourts.gov

Counties: Breckinridge, Bullitt, Hardin, Jefferson, Larue, Marion, Meade, Nelson, Oldham, Spencer, Washington.

Indexing & Storage: Cases are indexed by defendant and plaintiff as well as by case number. New cases are available in the index immediately after filing date. Both computer and card indexes are maintained. Records are indexed on index cards from 1938 to 1979. Records are indexed on microfiche from 1979 to 4/92. Records after 4/92 are on the automated system. Open records are located at this court. District wide searches are available from this court for information from 1938.

Fee & Payment: The fee is $15.00 per item (one party name or case number). Payment may be made by money order, cashier check, personal check. Prepayment is required. Payee: Clerk, US District Court. Certification fee: $5.00 per document. Copy fee: $.50 per page.

Phone Search: Only docket information is available by phone.

Mail Search: Always enclose a stamped self addressed envelope.

In Person Search: In person searching is available.

PACER: Sign-up number is 800-676-6856. Access fee is $.60 per minute. Case records are available back to 1992. New records are available online after 1 day. PACER is available on the Internet at http://38.244.24.105/webpacer.html.

Electronic Filing: Only law firms and practitioners may file cases electronically. Electronic filing information is available online at www.kywd.uscourts.gov/scripts/usdckyw/ecf/ecf.pl

Opinions Online: Court opinions are available online at www.kywd.uscourts.gov

Owensboro Division Federal Bldg, Room 126, 423 Frederica St, Owensboro, KY 42301, 270-683-0221, Fax: 502-685-4601.

www.kywd.uscourts.gov

Counties: Daviess, Grayson, Hancock, Henderson, Hopkins, McLean, Muhlenberg, Ohio, Union, Webster.

Indexing & Storage: Cases are indexed by defendant and plaintiff as well as by case number. New cases are available in the index 1-2 days after filing date. The court needs the correct name, date and/or criminal or civil case number to search for a record. A computer index is maintained. Open records are located at this court.

Fee & Payment: The fee is $15.00 per item (one party name or case number). Payment may be made by money order, cashier check, personal check. The court will only bill to in state searchers. Payee: Clerk, US District Court. Certification fee: $5.00 per document. Copy fee: $.50 per page. You are allowed to make your own copies. These copies cost $.50 per page.

Phone Search: Only docket information is available by phone. An automated voice case information service (VCIS) is not available.

Mail Search: A stamped self addressed envelope is not required.

In Person Search: In person searching is available.

PACER: Sign-up number is 800-676-6856. Access fee is $.60 per minute. Case records are available back to 1992. New records are available online after 1 day. PACER is available on the Internet at http://38.244.24.105/webpacer.html.

Electronic Filing: Only law firms and practitioners may file cases electronically. Electronic filing information is available online at www.kywd.uscourts.gov/scripts/usdckyw/ecf/ecf.pl

Paducah Division 127 Federal Building, 501 Broadway, Paducah, KY 42001, 270-443-1337.

www.kywd.uscourts.gov

Counties: Ballard, Caldwell, Calloway, Carlisle, Christian, Crittenden, Fulton, Graves, Hickman, Livingston, Lyon, McCracken, Marshall, Trigg.

Indexing & Storage: Cases are indexed by defendant and plaintiff as well as by case number. New cases are available in the index 1-2 days after filing date. Both computer and card indexes are maintained. Open records are located at this court.

Fee & Payment: The fee is $15.00 per item (one party name or case number). Payment may be made by money order, cashier check, personal check. Prepayment is required. Payee: Clerk, US District Court. Certification fee: $5.00 per document. Copy fee: $.50 per page. You are allowed to make your own copies. These copies cost $.50 per page.

Phone Search: Only docket information is available by phone. An automated voice case information service (VCIS) is not available.

Fax Search: You may fax for a fee quote.

Mail Search: Always enclose a stamped self addressed envelope.

In Person Search: In person searching is available.

PACER: Sign-up number is 800-676-6856. Access fee is $.60 per minute. Case records are available back to 1992. New records are available online after 1 day. PACER is available on the Internet at http://38.244.24.105/webpacer.html.

Electronic Filing: Only law firms and practictioners may file cases electronically. Electronic filing information is available online at www.kywd.uscourts.gov/scripts/usdckyw/ecf/ecf.pl

US Bankruptcy Court

Western District of Kentucky

Louisville Division 546 US Courthouse, 601 W Broadway, Louisville, KY 40202, 502-582-5145.

www.kywb.uscourts.gov

Counties: Adair, Allen, Ballard, Barren, Breckinridge, Bullitt, Butler, Caldwell, Calloway, Carlisle, Casey, Christian, Clinton, Crittenden, Cumberland, Daviess, Edmonson, Fulton, Graves, Grayson, Green, Hancock, Hardin, Hart, Henderson, Hickman, Hopkins,Jefferson, Larue, Livingston, Logan, Lyon, Marion, Marshall, McCracken, McLean, Meade, Metcalfe, Monroe, Muhlenberg, Nelson, Ohio, Oldham, Russell, Simpson, Spencer, Taylor, Todd, Trigg, Union, Warren, Washington, Webster.

Indexing & Storage: Cases are indexed by debtor as well as by case number. New cases are available in the index 1-2 days after filing date. A card index is maintained. Open records are located at this court. District wide searches are available from this division. This division maintains records for all of the divisions in this district.

Fee & Payment: The fee is $15.00 per item (one party name or case number). Payment may be made by money order, cashier check. Business checks are not accepted. Personal checks are not accepted. Prepayment is required. Payee: Clerk, US Bankruptcy Court. Certification fee: $5.00 per document. Copy fee: $.50 per page.

Phone Search: Only docket information is available by phone. An automated voice case information service (VCIS) is available. Call VCIS at 800-263-9385 or 502-625-7391.

Mail Search: Always enclose a stamped self addressed envelope.

In Person Search: In person searching is available.

PACER: Sign-up number is 800-676-6856. Access fee is $.60 per minute. Toll-free access: 800-263-9389. Local access: 502-627-5664. Case records are available back to July 1992. Records are purged every six months. New civil records are available online after 1-2 days. PACER is available online at http://pacer.kywb.uscourts.gov.

Court	Jurisdiction	No. of Courts	How Organized
Circuit Courts*	General	19	56 Judicial Circuits
District Courts*	Limited	19	59 Judicial Districts
Combined*		102	

* Profiled in this Sourcebook.

Court	CIVIL								
	Tort	Contract	Real Estate	Min. Claim	Max. Claim	Small Claims	Estate	Eviction	Domestic Relations
Circuit Courts*	X	X	X	$4000	No Max				X
District Courts*	X	X	X	$0	$4000	$1500	X	X	X

Court	CRIMINAL				
	Felony	Misdemeanor	DWI/DUI	Preliminary Hearing	Juvenile
Circuit Courts*	X				
District Courts*		X	X	X	X

ADMINISTRATION Administrative Office of Courts, 100 Mill Creek Park, Frankfort, KY, 40601; 502-573-2350, Fax: 502-573-1448. www.aoc.state.ky.us

COURT STRUCTURE The Circuit Court is the court of general jurisdiction and the District Court is the limited jurisdiction court. Most of Kentucky's counties combined the courts into one location and records are co-mingled. Probate is handled by the Circuit Court if contested and by the District Court if uncontested.

ONLINE ACCESS There is a statewide, online computer system called SUSTAIN available for internal judicial/state agency use only. No courts offer online access.

ADDITIONAL INFORMATION Until 1978, county judges handled all cases; therefore, in many cases, District and Circuit Court records go back only to 1978. Records prior to that time are archived.

Adair County

Circuit & District Court 500 Public Square, Columbia, KY 42728; 270-384-2626; Fax: 270-384-4299. Hours: 8AM-4PM (CST). *Felony, Misdemeanor, Civil, Eviction, Small Claims, Probate.*

Civil Records: Access: Mail, in person. Both court and visitors may perform in person searches. No search fee. Required to search: name, years to search. Civil records on computer since June 1993, prior records on docket books since 1978. **Criminal Records:** Access: Mail, in person. Both court and visitors may perform in person searches. No search fee. Required to search: name, years to search, SSN. Criminal records on computer since June 1993, prior records on docket books since 1978. **General Information:** No adoption, mental, juvenile, or sealed records released. SASE required. Turnaround time same day. Copy fee: $.15 per page. Certification fee: No certification fee. Fee payee: Adair County Circuit Clerk. Personal checks accepted. Public access terminal is available.

Allen County

Circuit & District Court Box 477, Scottsville, KY 42164; 270-237-3561. Hours: 8AM-4:30PM (CST). *Felony, Misdemeanor, Civil, Eviction, Small Claims, Probate.*

Civil Records: Access: In person only. Court does not conduct in person searches; visitors must perform searches for themselves. Search fee: No civil searches performed by court. Required to search: name, years to search. Civil cases indexed by defendant, plaintiff. Civil records on computer since 1992, records on index cards from 1978 to 1992, prior records on books. **Criminal Records:** Access: In person only. Court does not conduct in person searches; visitors must perform searches for themselves. Search fee: No criminal searches performed by court. Required to search: name, years to search; also helpful-SSN. Criminal records on computer since 1992, records on index cards from 1978 to 1992, prior records on books. **General Information:** No adoption, mental, juvenile, or sealed records released. Copy fee: $.15 per page. Certification fee: $1.00. Fee payee: Circuit Clerk. Personal checks accepted. Prepayment is required.

Anderson County

Circuit Court Courthouse 151 S Main St, Lawrenceburg, KY 40342; 502-839-3508. Hours: 8:30AM-5PM (EST). *Felony, Civil Actions Over $4,000.*

Civil Records: Access: In person only. Only the court conducts in person searches; visitors may not. Search fee: No civil searches performed by court. Required to search: name, years to search. Civil cases indexed by defendant, plaintiff. Civil

records on computer since August 1994, prior records on docket books since 1978. **Criminal Records:** Access: In person only. Court does not conduct in person searches; visitors must perform searches for themselves. Search fee: No criminal searches performed by court. Required to search: name, years to search; also helpful-DOB, SSN. All record requests are referred to the state agency at 502-573-2350. **General Information:** No adoption, mental, juvenile, or sealed records released. Certification fee: $1.00. Fee payee: Clerk of Circuit Clerk. Personal checks accepted. Prepayment is required. Public access terminal is available.

District Court 151 S Main, Lawrenceburg, KY 40342; 502-839-5445. Hours: 8:30AM-5PM M-TH, 8:30AM-6PM F (EST). *Misdemeanor, Civil Actions Under $4,000, Eviction, Small Claims, Probate.*

Civil Records: Access: In person only. Only the court conducts in person searches; visitors may not. Search fee: $10.00 per name. Required to search: name, years to search. Civil cases indexed by defendant, plaintiff. Civil records on computer since August 1994, prior records on index cards. **Criminal Records:** Access: In person only. Court does not conduct in person searches; visitors must perform searches for themselves. Search fee: No criminal searches performed by court. Required to search: name, years to search; also helpful-DOB, SSN. All requests are referred to the state agency at 502-573-2350. **General Information:** No adoption, mental, juvenile, or sealed records released. Copy fee: $.15 per page. Certification fee: $1.00. Fee payee: Anderson County District Court. Business checks accepted. Prepayment is required.

Ballard County

Circuit & District Court Box 265, Wickliffe, KY 42087; 270-335-5123; Fax: 270-335-3849. Hours: 8AM-4PM (CST). *Felony, Misdemeanor, Civil, Eviction, Small Claims, Probate.*

Civil Records: Access: Mail, in person. Both court and visitors may perform in person searches. No search fee. Required to search: name, years to search. Civil cases indexed by defendant, plaintiff. Civil records on computer since 1992, prior records on books. **Criminal Records:** Access: In person only. Court does not conduct in person searches; visitors must perform searches for themselves. Search fee: No criminal searches performed by court. Required to search: name, years to search. Criminal records on computer since 1992, prior records on books. **General Information:** No adoption, mental, juvenile, or sealed records released. SASE required. Turnaround time 2 days. Copy fee: $.15 per page. Certification fee: $1.50. Fee payee: Circuit Clerk. Only cashiers checks and money orders accepted. Prepayment is required. Public access terminal is available.

Barren County

Circuit & District Court PO Box 1359, Glasgow, KY 42142-1359; 270-651-3763; Civil phone:270-651-9830; Criminal phone:270-651-9830; Fax: 270-651-6203. Hours: 8AM-4:30PM (CST). *Felony, Misdemeanor, Civil, Eviction, Small Claims, Probate.*

Civil Records: Access: In person only. Court does not conduct in person searches; visitors must perform searches for themselves. Search fee: No civil searches performed by court. Required to search: name, years to search. Civil cases indexed by defendant, plaintiff. Civil records on computer since October 1991, prior records on index books since 1800s. **Criminal Records:** Access: In person only. Court does not conduct in person searches; visitors must perform searches for themselves. Search fee: No criminal searches performed by court. Required to search: name, years to search, DOB; also helpful-SSN. Criminal records on computer since October 1991, prior records on index books since 1800s. **General Information:** No adoption, mental, juvenile, or sealed records released. Copy fee: $.15 per page. Certification fee: $1.00. Fee payee: Barren Circuit Clerk. Personal checks accepted. Prepayment is required. Public access terminal is available.

Bath County

Circuit & District Court Box 558, Owingsville, KY 40360; 606-674-2186 X6821; Fax: 606-674-3996. Hours: 8AM-4PM (EST). *Felony, Misdemeanor, Civil, Eviction, Small Claims, Probate.*

Civil Records: Access: Mail, in person. Both court and visitors may perform in person searches. Search fee: $6.00 per name. Required to search: name, years to search. Civil cases indexed by defendant, plaintiff. Civil records computerized since 1994, on docket books since 1978, prior records archived. **Criminal Records:** Access: Mail, in person. Both court and visitors may perform in person searches. Search fee: $6.00 per name. Required to search: name, years to search, DOB, SSN. Criminal records computerized since 1994, on docket books since 1978, prior records archived. **General Information:** No adoption, mental, juvenile, or sealed records released. SASE required. Turnaround time 2-3 days. Copy fee: $.15 per page. Certification fee: $1.00. Fee payee: Bath Circuit Clerk. Personal checks accepted. Prepayment is required. Public access terminal is available.

Bell County

Circuit & District Court Box 306, Pineville, KY 40977; 606-337-2942/9900; Fax: 606-337-8850. Hours: 8:30AM-4PM (EST). *Felony, Misdemeanor, Civil, Eviction, Small Claims, Probate.*

Civil Records: Access: Phone, mail, in person. Both court and visitors may perform in person searches. No search fee. Required to search: name, years to search. Civil cases indexed by defendant, plaintiff. Civil records on computer since 1991, prior records on docket books since 1978. **Criminal Records:** Access: Phone, mail, in person. Both court and visitors may perform in person searches. No search fee. Required to search: name, years to search. Criminal records on computer since 1991, prior records on docket books since 1978. **General Information:** No adoption, mental, juvenile, or sealed records released. SASE required. Turnaround time 1 day. Copy fee: $.15 per page. Certification fee: $3.00. Fee payee: Bell Circuit Clerk. Personal checks accepted. Prepayment is required. Public access terminal is available.

Boone County

Circuit & District Court Box 480, Burlington, KY 41005; 606-334-2237; Fax: 606-586-9413. Hours: 8:30AM-5:30PM (EST). *Felony, Misdemeanor, Civil, Eviction, Small Claims, Probate.*

Civil Records: Access: Mail, in person. Both court and visitors may perform in person searches. No search fee. Required to search: name, years to search. Civil cases indexed by defendant, plaintiff. Civil records on computer since July 1990, on index card file since 1978, prior records on books. **Criminal Records:** Access: In person only. Court does not conduct in person searches; visitors must perform searches for themselves. Search fee: No criminal searches performed by court. Required to search: name, years to search; also helpful-SSN. Criminal records on computer since July 1990, on index card file since 1978, prior records on books. **General Information:** No adoption, mental, juvenile, or sealed records released. SASE required. Copy fee: $.15 per page. Certification fee: $1.00. Fee payee: Clerk of Circuit Court. Only cashiers checks and money orders accepted.

Bourbon County

Circuit & District Court Box 740, Paris, KY 40361; 606-987-2624. Hours: 8:30AM-4PM M-TH, 8:30AM-6PM F (EST). *Felony, Misdemeanor, Civil, Eviction, Small Claims, Probate.*

Civil Records: Access: In person only. Court does not conduct in person searches; visitors must perform searches for themselves. Search fee: No civil searches performed by court. Required to search: name, years to search. Civil cases indexed by defendant, plaintiff. Civil records on computer since November 1991, prior records on books. **Criminal Records:** Access: In person only. Court does not conduct in person searches; visitors must perform searches for themselves. Search fee: No criminal searches performed by court. Required to search: name, years to search; also helpful-SSN. Criminal records on computer since November 1991, prior records on books. **General Information:** No adoption, mental, juvenile, or sealed records released. Copy fee: District Ct documents are $.15 per page, Circuit Ct $.25 per page. Certification fee: $1.00. Fee payee: Circuit Clerk. Personal checks accepted. Prepayment is required. Public access terminal is available.

Boyd County

Circuit & District Court Box 694, Catlettsburg, KY 41129-0694; 606-739-4131; Fax: 606-739-5793. Hours: 8:30AM-4PM (EST). *Felony, Misdemeanor, Civil, Eviction, Small Claims, Probate.*

Civil Records: Access: In person only. Court does not conduct in person searches; visitors must perform searches for themselves. Search fee: No civil searches performed by court. Required to search: name, years to search. Civil cases indexed by defendant, plaintiff. Civil records on computer since 1991, prior records on index cards since 1975. **Criminal Records:** Access: In person only. Court does not conduct in person searches; visitors must perform searches for themselves. Search fee: No criminal searches performed by court. Required to search: name, years to search, signed release; also helpful-DOB, SSN. Criminal records on computer since 1991, on index cards since 1978; misdemeanor & traffic from 1987. **General Information:** No adoption, mental, juvenile, or sealed records released. Copy fee: $.15 per page. Certification fee: $1.00. Fee payee: Boyd County Circuit Court. Personal checks accepted. Prepayment is required. Public access terminal is available.

Boyle County

Circuit Court Courthouse, Main St, Danville, KY 40422; 859-239-7442; Fax: 859-239-7807. Hours: 8AM-5PM (EST). *Felony, Civil Actions Over $4,000.*

Civil Records: Access: Phone, mail, in person. Both court and visitors may perform in person searches. No search fee. Required to search: name, years to search. Civil cases indexed by defendant, plaintiff. Civil records on computer since 08/91, prior records on index cards. **Criminal Records:** Access: Fax, mail, in person. Both court and visitors may perform in person searches. No search fee. Required to search: name, years to search, DOB, SSN. Criminal records on computer since 08/91, prior records on index cards. **General Information:** No adoption, mental, juvenile, or sealed records released. SASE required. Turnaround time 2-4 days. Copy fee: $.15 per page. Certification fee: $1.00. Fee payee: Circuit Clerk. Personal checks accepted. Prepayment is required. Public access terminal is available.

District Court Courthouse, 3rd Floor, Danville, KY 40422; 606-239-7362; Fax: 606-236-9807. Hours: 8AM-4:30PM (EST). *Misdemeanor, Civil Actions Under $4,000, Eviction, Small Claims, Probate.*

Civil Records: Access: Mail, in person. Both court and visitors may perform in person searches. No search fee. Required to search: name, years to search. Civil cases indexed by defendant, plaintiff. Civil records on computer since August 1991, prior records on index cards since 1978. **Criminal Records:** Access: Mail, in person. Both court and visitors may perform in person searches. No search fee. Required to search: name, DOB, SSN. Criminal records on computer since08/91; prior records on card index. **General Information:** No adoption, mental, juvenile, or sealed records released. SASE required. Turnaround time 3-4 days. Copy fee: $.15 per page. Certification fee: $1.00. Fee payee: Circuit Clerk. Personal checks accepted. Prepayment is required. Public access terminal is available.

Bracken County

Circuit & District Court Box 132 Courthouse, Brooksville, KY 41004; 606-735-3328; Fax: 606-735-3900. Hours: 9AM-4PM M,T,TH,F, 9AM-Noon W & Sat (EST). *Felony, Misdemeanor, Civil, Eviction, Small Claims, Probate.*

Civil Records: Access: Mail, in person. Both court and visitors may perform in person searches. No search fee. Required to search: name, years to search. Civil cases indexed by defendant, plaintiff. Civil records on computer since 1993, prior records on docket books since the 1800s. **Criminal Records:** Access: In person only. Court does not conduct in person searches; visitors must perform searches for themselves. Search fee: No criminal searches performed by court. Required to search: name, years to search; also helpful-SSN. Criminal records on computer since 1993, prior records on docket books since the 1800s. **General Information:** No adoption, mental, juvenile, or sealed records released. SASE required. Copy fee: $.15 per page. Certification fee: $1.00. Fee payee: Circuit Clerk. Prepayment is required. Public access terminal is available.

Breathitt County

Circuit & District Court 1137 Main St, Jackson, KY 41339; 606-666-5768; Fax: 606-666-4893. Hours: 8AM-4PM M,T,TH,F; 8AM-Noon W; 9AM-Noon Sat (EST). *Felony, Misdemeanor, Civil, Eviction, Small Claims, Probate.*

Civil Records: Access: Phone, mail, in person. Both court and visitors may perform in person searches. No search fee. Required to search: name, years to search. Civil cases indexed by defendant, plaintiff. Civil records in files since 1978. **Criminal Records:** Access: Phone, mail, in person. Both court and visitors may perform in person searches. No search fee. Required to search: name, years to search, DOB, SSN, signed release. Criminal records in files since 1978. **General Information:** No adoption, mental, juvenile, or sealed records released. SASE required. Turnaround time 2-3 days. Copy fee: $.25 per page. Certification fee: $1.00. Fee payee: Breathitt Circuit Clerk. Personal checks accepted. Prepayment is required. Public access terminal is available.

Breckinridge County

Circuit & District Court Box 111, Hardinsburg, KY 40143; 270-756-2239; Fax: 270-756-1129. Hours: 8AM-4PM (CST). *Felony, Misdemeanor, Civil, Eviction, Small Claims, Probate.*

Civil Records: Access: In person only. Court does not conduct in person searches; visitors must perform searches for themselves. Search fee: No civil searches performed by court. Required to search: name, years to search. Civil cases indexed by defendant, plaintiff. Civil records on computer since August 1994, on index cards since 1978, prior records on docket books since the 1800s. **Criminal Records:** Access: In person only. Court does not conduct in person searches; visitors must perform searches for themselves. Search fee: No criminal searches performed by court. Required to

search: name, years to search, DOB, SSN. Criminal records on computer since August 1994, on index cards since 1978, prior records on docket books since the 1800s. **General Information:** No adoption, mental, juvenile, or sealed records released. Copy fee: $.15 per page. Certification fee: $1.00. Fee payee: Clerk of Circuit Court. Personal checks accepted. Prepayment is required. Public access terminal is available.

Bullitt County

Circuit & District Court Box 746, Shephardsville, KY 40165; 502-543-7104; Fax: 502-543-7158. Hours: 8AM-4PM (EST). *Felony, Misdemeanor, Civil, Eviction, Small Claims, Probate.*

Civil Records: Access: Fax, mail, in person. Both court and visitors may perform in person searches. Search fee: $1.00 per name. Required to search: name. Civil cases indexed by defendant, plaintiff. Civil records on computer since 11/91, prior records on index cards since the 1800s. **Criminal Records:** Access: Fax, mail, in person. Both court and visitors may perform in person searches. Search fee: $1.00 per name. Required to search: name. Criminal records on computer since 11/91, prior records on index cards since the 1800s. Access by mail with authorization. **General Information:** No adoption, mental, juvenile, or sealed records released. SASE required. Turnaround time 1-2 days. Copy fee: $.15 per page. Certification fee: $1.00. Fee payee: Clerk of Circuit Court. Personal checks accepted. Prepayment is required. Public access terminal is available. Fax notes: $1.00 per page. Send copy of check with fax.

Butler County

Circuit & District Court Box 625, Morgantown, KY 42261; 270-526-5631. Hours: 8AM-4:30PM M-F; 9AM-Noon Sat (CST). *Felony, Misdemeanor, Civil, Eviction, Small Claims, Probate.*

Civil Records: Access: Mail, in person. No search fee. Required to search: name, years to search. Civil cases indexed by defendant, plaintiff. Civil records on computer since 1993, prior records on index cards since the 1800s. **Criminal Records:** Access: Mail, in person. Both court and visitors may perform in person searches. No search fee. Required to search: name, years to search, DOB; also helpful-SSN. Criminal records on computer since 1993, prior records on index cards since the 1800s. **General Information:** No adoption, mental, juvenile, or sealed records released. SASE required. Turnaround time 1 week. Copy fee: $.25 per page. Certification fee: No certification fee. Fee payee: Clerk of Circuit Court. Personal checks accepted. Prepayment is required. Public access terminal is available.

Caldwell County

Circuit & District Court 105 West Court Sq, Princeton, KY 42445; 270-365-6884; Fax: 270-365-9171. Hours: 8AM-4PM (CST). *Felony, Misdemeanor, Civil, Eviction, Small Claims, Probate.*

Civil Records: Access: Mail, fax, in person. Court does not conduct in person searches; visitors must perform searches for themselves. Search fee: No civil searches performed by court. Required to search: name, years to search. Civil cases indexed by defendant, plaintiff. Civil records on index cards; on computer since 09/94. **Criminal Records:** Access: Fax, in person. Court does not conduct in person searches; visitors must perform

searches for themselves. Search fee: No criminal searches performed by court. Required to search: name, years to search; also helpful-DOB, SSN. Criminal records on index cards; on computer since 09/94. **General Information:** No adoption, mental, juvenile, or sealed records released. SASE required. Turnaround time 2 days. Copy fee: $.15 per page. Copy request must include postage. Certification fee: $1.00. Fee payee: Circuit Clerk. Personal checks accepted. Prepayment is required. Public access terminal is available. Fax notes: $2.00 for first page, $1.00 each addl.

Calloway County

Circuit & District Court 312 N 4th St, Murray, KY 42071; 270-753-2714; Fax: 270-759-9822. Hours: 8AM-4:30PM (CST). *Felony, Misdemeanor, Civil, Eviction, Small Claims, Probate.*

Civil Records: Access: Mail, in person. Both court and visitors may perform in person searches. No search fee. Required to search: name, years to search. Civil cases indexed by defendant, plaintiff. Civil records on computer since 06/92, on index cards since 1978. Prior to 1978 records are archived in Frankfurt. **Criminal Records:** Access: Mail, in person. Both court and visitors may perform in person searches. No search fee. Required to search: name, years to search, DOB; also helpful-SSN. Criminal records on computer since 06/92, on index cards since 1978. Prior to 1978 records are archived in Frankfurt. **General Information:** No adoption, mental, juvenile, or sealed records released. SASE required. Turnaround time 2-4 days. Copy fee: $.20 per page. Certification fee: $1.50. Fee payee: Clerk of Circuit Court. Personal checks accepted. Prepayment is required. Public access terminal is available.

Campbell County

Circuit Court 330 York St Rm 8, Newport, KY 41071; 606-292-6314; Fax: 606-431-0816. Hours: 8:30AM-4PM (EST). *Felony, Civil Actions Over $4,000.*

Civil Records: Access: In person only. Court does not conduct in person searches; visitors must perform searches for themselves. Search fee: No civil searches performed by court. Required to search: name, years to search. Civil cases indexed by defendant, plaintiff. Civil records on computer since 1992, prior records on index cards since 1978. **Criminal Records:** Access: In person only. Court does not conduct in person searches; visitors must perform searches for themselves. Search fee: No criminal searches performed by court. Required to search: name, years to search; also helpful-SSN. Criminal records on computer since 1992, prior records on index cards since 1978. **General Information:** No adoption, mental, juvenile, or sealed records released. Copy fee: $.15 per page. Certification fee: $1.50. Fee payee: Campbell Circuit Court. Personal checks accepted. Prepayment is required. Public access terminal is available.

District Court 600 Columbia St, Newport, KY 41071-1816; 606-292-6305; Fax: 606-292-6593. Hours: 8:30AM-4PM (EST). *Misdemeanor, Civil Actions Under $4,000, Eviction, Small Claims, Probate.*

Civil Records: Access: Mail, in person. Both court and visitors may perform in person searches. Search fee: $10.00 per name. Required to search: name, years to search. Civil cases indexed by defendant, plaintiff. Civil records on computer since 1992, prior records on index cards. **Criminal**

Records: Access: In person only. Court does not conduct in person searches; visitors must perform searches for themselves. Search fee: No criminal searches performed by court. Required to search: name, years to search, SSN. Criminal records on computer since 1992, prior records on index cards. **General Information:** No adoption, mental, juvenile, or sealed records released. SASE required. Turnaround time 7 days. Copy fee: $.15 per page. Certification fee: $1.00. Fee payee: District Clerk. Business checks accepted. Prepayment is required. Public access terminal is available.

Carlisle County

Circuit & District Court Box 337, Bardwell, KY 42023; 270-628-5425; Fax: 270-628-5456. Hours: 8AM-4PM (CST). *Felony, Misdemeanor, Civil, Eviction, Small Claims, Probate.*

Civil Records: Access: Phone, mail, in person. Both court and visitors may perform in person searches. No search fee. Required to search: name, years to search. Civil cases indexed by defendant, plaintiff. Civil records on computer since May 1993, records on docket books since 1978, prior records archived. **Criminal Records:** Access: Phone, mail, in person. Both court and visitors may perform in person searches. No search fee. Required to search: name, years to search. Criminal records on computer since May 1993, records on docket books since 1978, prior records archived. **General Information:** No adoption, mental, juvenile, or sealed records released. SASE required. Turnaround time 1-5 days. Copy fee: $.15 per page. Certification fee: $1.00. Fee payee: Clerk of Circuit Court. Personal checks accepted. Prepayment is required. Public access terminal is available.

Carroll County

Circuit & District Court 802 Clay St, Carrollton, KY 41008; 502-732-4305. Hours: 8AM-5PM (EST). *Felony, Misdemeanor, Civil, Eviction, Small Claims, Probate.*

Civil Records: Access: Phone, mail, in person. Both court and visitors may perform in person searches. No search fee. Required to search: name, years to search. Civil cases indexed by defendant, plaintiff. Civil records on computer since 1994, on docket books since 1980. Records before 1980 are archived in Frankfurt. **Criminal Records:** Access: Phone, mail, in person. Both court and visitors may perform in person searches. No search fee. Required to search: name, years to search, DOB; also helpful-SSN. Criminal records on computer since 1994, on docket books since 1980. Records before 1980 are archived in Frankfurt. **General Information:** No adoption, mental, juvenile, or sealed records released. SASE required. Turnaround time 2-4 days. Copy fee: $.15 per page. Certification fee: $1.00. Fee payee: Carroll County Circuit Clerk. Personal checks accepted. Prepayment is required. Public access terminal is available.

Carter County

Circuit Court 300 W Main St, Rm 308, Grayson, KY 41143; 606-474-5191; Fax: 606-474-8826. Hours: 8:30AM-4PM M-F; 9AM-Noon Sat (EST). *Felony, Civil Actions Over $4,000.*

Civil Records: Access: Mail, in person. Both court and visitors may perform in person searches. No search fee. Required to search: name, years to search. Civil cases indexed by defendant, plaintiff. Civil records on computer since 1994, records archived since 1978, prior records are archived.

Criminal Records: Access: Mail, in person. Both court and visitors may perform in person searches. No search fee. Required to search: name, years to search, DOB, SSN. Criminal records on computer since 1994, records archived since 1978, prior records are archived. **General Information:** No adoption, mental, juvenile, or sealed records released. SASE required. Turnaround time 1-2 days. Copy fee: $.15 per page. Certification fee: $2.00. Fee payee: Carter County Circuit Clerk. Personal checks accepted. Prepayment is required. Public access terminal is available.

District Court Courthouse, Rm 203, 300 West Main, Grayson, KY 41143; 606-474-6572; Fax: 606-474-8826. Hours: 8:30AM-4PM (EST). *Misdemeanor, Civil Actions Under $4,000, Eviction, Small Claims, Probate.*

Civil Records: Access: Mail, in person. Both court and visitors may perform in person searches. Search fee: $2.00 per name. Required to search: name, years to search. Civil cases indexed by defendant, plaintiff. Civil records on computer since 1994, prior records on index cards. **Criminal Records:** Access: In person only. Court does not conduct in person searches; visitors must perform searches for themselves. Search fee: No criminal searches performed by court. Required to search: name, years to search, DOB; also helpful-SSN. Criminal records on computer since 1994, prior records on index cards. **General Information:** No adoption, mental, juvenile, or sealed records released. SASE required. Turnaround time 2-4 days. Copy fee: $.15 per page. Certification fee: $1.00. Fee payee: District Clerk. Personal checks accepted. Prepayment is required. Public access terminal is available.

Casey County

Circuit & District Court Box 147, Liberty, KY 42539; 606-787-6510. Hours: 8AM-4:30PM M-W, 8AM-4PM TH, 8AM-Noon Sat (EST). *Felony, Misdemeanor, Civil, Eviction, Small Claims, Probate.*

Note: This court asks all pre-trial record requests go to the Administrative office of the Courts in Frankfort

Civil Records: Access: Mail, in person. Both court and visitors may perform in person searches. No search fee. Required to search: name, years to search. Civil cases indexed by defendant, plaintiff. Civil records on index cards since 1978, prior records archived. **Criminal Records:** Access: In person only. Court does not conduct in person searches; visitors must perform searches for themselves. Search fee: No criminal searches performed by court. Required to search: name, years to search; also helpful-SSN. Criminal records on index cards since 1978, prior records archived. **General Information:** No adoption, mental, juvenile, or sealed records released. SASE required. Turnaround time 1-2 days. Copy fee: $.15 per page. Certification fee: $1.50. Fee payee: Circuit Clerk. Personal checks accepted. Prepayment is required. Public access terminal is available.

Christian County

Circuit & District Court 511 S Main St Rm 301, Hopkinsville, KY 42240-2368; 270-889-6539; Fax: 270-889-6564. Hours: 8AM-4:30PM (CST). *Felony, Misdemeanor, Civil, Eviction, Small Claims, Probate.*

Civil Records: Access: Mail, in person. Both court and visitors may perform in person searches. No search fee. Required to search: name, years to

search. Civil cases indexed by defendant, plaintiff. Civil records on computer since 1991, prior records on index cards since 1978. **Criminal Records:** Access: In person only. Court does not conduct in person searches; visitors must perform searches for themselves. Search fee: No criminal searches performed by court. Required to search: name, years to search; also helpful-DOB, SSN. Criminal records on computer since 1991, prior records on index cards since 1978. **General Information:** No adoption, mental, juvenile, or sealed records released. SASE required. Turnaround time 2-4 days. Copy fee: $.15 per page. Certification fee: $1.00. Fee payee: Circuit Clerk. Personal checks accepted. Prepayment is required. Public access terminal is available.

Clark County

Circuit Court Box 687, Winchester, KY 40391; 606-737-7264. Hours: 8AM-4PM (EST). *Felony, Civil Actions Over $4,000.*

Civil Records: Access: Mail, in person. Both court and visitors may perform in person searches. No search fee. Required to search: name, years to search; also helpful-address. Civil cases indexed by defendant, plaintiff. Civil records on computer since 1989, on index cards since 1950, prior records archived since the 1700s. **Criminal Records:** Access: In person only. Court does not conduct in person searches; visitors must perform searches for themselves. Search fee: No criminal searches performed by court. Required to search: name, years to search; also helpful-address, DOB, SSN. Criminal records on computer since 1989, on index cards since 1950, prior records archived since the 1700s. **General Information:** No adoption, mental, juvenile, or sealed records released. SASE required. Turnaround time 2-4 days. Copy fee: $.25 per page. Certification fee: $1.00. Fee payee: Circuit Clerk. Personal checks accepted. Prepayment is required. Public access terminal is available.

District Court PO Box 687, Winchester, KY 40392-0687; 859-737-7264; Fax: 859-737-7005. Hours: 8AM-4PM (EST). *Misdemeanor, Civil Actions Under $4,000, Eviction, Small Claims, Probate.*

Civil Records: Access: Mail, fax, in person. Both court and visitors may perform in person searches. No search fee. Required to search: name, years to search. Civil cases indexed by defendant, plaintiff. Civil records on computer since 1989, on docket books since 1978, prior records on archived. **Criminal Records:** Access: Mail, fax, in person. Both court and visitors may perform in person searches. No search fee. Required to search: name, years to search; also helpful-DOB, SSN. Criminal records on computer since 1989, on docket books since 1978, prior records on archived. **General Information:** No adoption, mental, juvenile, or sealed records released. SASE required. Turnaround time 1-3 days. Copy fee: $.25 per page. Certification fee: $1.00. Fee payee: District Clerk. Personal checks accepted. Prepayment is required. Public access terminal is available.

Clay County

Circuit & District Court 316 Main Street, #108, Manchester, KY 40962; 606-598-3663; Fax: 606-598-4047. Hours: 8AM-4PM (EST). *Felony, Misdemeanor, Civil, Eviction, Small Claims, Probate.*

Civil Records: Access: In person only. Court does not conduct in person searches; visitors must perform searches for themselves. Search fee: No civil searches performed by court. Required to

search: name, years to search. Civil cases indexed by defendant, plaintiff. Civil records on computer since 1992, on index cards since 1978, prior records archived. **Criminal Records:** Access: In person only. Court does not conduct in person searches; visitors must perform searches for themselves. Search fee: No criminal searches performed by court. Required to search: name, years to search, DOB; also helpful-SSN. Criminal records on computer since 1992, on index cards since 1978, prior records archived. **General Information:** No adoption, mental, juvenile, or sealed records released. Copy fee: $.15 per page. Certification fee: $1.00. Fee payee: Circuit Clerk. Personal checks accepted. Prepayment is required. Public access terminal is available.

Clinton County

Circuit & District Court Courthouse 2nd Fl, Albany, KY 42602; 606-387-6424; Fax: 606-387-8154. Hours: 8AM-4PM M-F; 8AM-Noon Sat (CST). *Felony, Misdemeanor, Civil, Eviction, Small Claims, Probate.*

Civil Records: Access: Phone, mail, in person. Both court and visitors may perform in person searches. No search fee. Required to search: name, years to search. Civil cases indexed by defendant, plaintiff. Civil records on computer since 08/92, on docket books since 1978, prior records archived. **Criminal Records:** Access: Phone, mail, in person. Both court and visitors may perform in person searches. No search fee. Required to search: name, years to search, SSN; also helpful-DOB. Criminal records on computer since 08/92, on docket books since 1978, prior records archived. **General Information:** No adoption, mental, juvenile, or sealed records released. SASE required. Turnaround time 5 days. Copy fee: $.15 per page. Certification fee: $1.00. Fee payee: Circuit Clerk. Personal checks accepted. Prepayment is required. Public access terminal is available.

Crittenden County

Circuit & District Court 107 S Main, Marion, KY 42064; 270-965-4200. Hours: 8AM-4:30PM (CST). *Felony, Misdemeanor, Civil, Eviction, Small Claims, Probate.*

Civil Records: Access: Mail, in person. Both court and visitors may perform in person searches. No search fee. Required to search: name, years to search. Civil cases indexed by defendant, plaintiff. Civil records on index cards since 1977. **Criminal Records:** Access: In person. Court does not conduct in person searches; visitors must perform searches for themselves. No search fee. Required to search: name, years to search. Criminal records on index cards since 1977. **General Information:** No adoption, mental, juvenile, or sealed records released. SASE required. Turnaround time 10 days. Copy fee: $.15 per page. Certification fee: $1.00. Fee payee: Circuit Clerk. Checks not accepted. Prepayment is required. Public access terminal is available.

Cumberland County

Circuit & District Court Box 395, Burkesville, KY 42717; 270-864-2611. Hours: 8AM-4PM (CST). *Felony, Misdemeanor, Civil, Eviction, Small Claims, Probate.*

Civil Records: Access: Mail, in person. Both court and visitors may perform in person searches. No search fee. Required to search: name, years to search. Civil cases indexed by defendant, plaintiff. Civil records on computer since 06/93, on docket cards from 1978, prior records archived. **Criminal**

Records: Access: Mail, in person. Both court and visitors may perform in person searches. No search fee. Required to search: name, years to search, DOB; also helpful-SSN. Criminal records on computer since 06/93, on docket cards from 1978, prior records archived. **General Information:** No adoption, mental, juvenile, or sealed records released. SASE required. Turnaround time 3-5 days. Copy fee: $.15 per page. Certification fee: $1.00. Fee payee: Circuit Clerk. Personal checks accepted. Prepayment is required. Public access terminal is available.

Daviess County

Circuit & District Court Box 277, Owensboro, KY 42302; 270-687-7333. Hours: 8AM-4PM (CST). *Felony, Misdemeanor, Civil, Eviction, Small Claims, Probate.*

Civil Records: Access: In person only. Court does not conduct in person searches; visitors must perform searches for themselves. Search fee: No civil searches performed by court. Required to search: name, years to search. Civil cases indexed by defendant, plaintiff. Civil records on computer since 04/91, on index cards since 1978, prior records on docket books since 1809. Search in person only on Tuesday or Thursday. **Criminal Records:** Access: In person only. Court does not conduct in person searches; visitors must perform searches for themselves. Search fee: No criminal searches performed by court. Required to search: name, years to search, DOB, SSN. Criminal records on computer since 04/91, on index cards since 1978, prior records on docket books since 1809. Search in person only on Tuesday or Thursday. **General Information:** No adoption, mental, juvenile, or sealed records released. Copy fee: $.15 per page. Certification fee: $1.00. Fee payee: Circuit Clerk. Business checks accepted. Prepayment is required. Public access terminal is available.

Edmonson County

Circuit & District Court Box 130, Brownsville, KY 42210; 270-597-2584; Fax: 270-597-2884. Hours: 8AM-5PM M-W,F; 8AM-Noon Sat (CST). *Felony, Misdemeanor, Civil, Eviction, Small Claims, Probate.*

Civil Records: Access: In person only. Court does not conduct in person searches; visitors must perform searches for themselves. Search fee: No civil searches performed by court. Required to search: name, years to search, address. Civil cases indexed by defendant, plaintiff. Civil records computerized since 1995, on index cards and docket books from 1800s. **Criminal Records:** Access: In person only. Court does not conduct in person searches; visitors must perform searches for themselves. Search fee: No criminal searches performed by court. Required to search: name, years to search, DOB, SSN. Criminal records computerized since 1995, on index cards and docket books from 1800s. **General Information:** No adoption, mental, juvenile, or sealed records released. Copy fee: $.15 per page. Certification fee: $1.00. Fee payee: Circuit Clerk. Personal checks accepted. Prepayment is required.

Elliott County

Circuit & District Court Box 788, Sandy Hook, KY 41171; 606-738-5238; Fax: 606-738-6962. Hours: 8AM-4PM M-F; 9AM-Noon Sat (EST). *Felony, Misdemeanor, Civil, Eviction, Small Claims, Probate.*

Civil Records: Access: Phone, mail, in person. Both court and visitors may perform in person

searches. No search fee. Required to search: name, years to search. Civil cases indexed by defendant, plaintiff. Civil records on computer since October 1992, prior records on index cards since 1978. **Criminal Records:** Access: Phone, mail, in person. Both court and visitors may perform in person searches. No search fee. Required to search: name, years to search; also helpful-SSN. Criminal records on computer since October 1992, prior records on index cards since 1978. **General Information:** No adoption, mental, juvenile, or sealed records released. SASE required. Turnaround time 1-2 days. Copy fee: $.15 per page. Certification fee: $1.00. Fee payee: Circuit Clerk. Personal checks accepted. Prepayment is required. Public access terminal is available.

Estill County

Circuit & District Court 130 Main St, Rm 207, Irvine, KY 40336; 606-723-3970; Fax: 606-723-1158. Hours: 8AM-4PM (EST). *Felony, Misdemeanor, Civil, Eviction, Small Claims, Probate.*

Civil Records: Access: Phone, fax, mail, in person. Both court and visitors may perform in person searches. No search fee. Required to search: name, years to search. Civil cases indexed by defendant, plaintiff. Civil records on index cards. **Criminal Records:** Access: Phone, fax, mail, in person. Both court and visitors may perform in person searches. No search fee. Required to search: name, years to search, DOB; also helpful-SSN. Criminal records on index cards. **General Information:** No adoption, mental, juvenile, or sealed records released. SASE required. Turnaround time 2-4 days. Copy fee: $.15 per page. Certification fee: $1.00. Fee payee: Circuit Clerk. Personal checks accepted. Prepayment is required. Public access terminal is available. Fax notes: $2.00 for first page, $1.00 each addl.

Fayette County

Circuit Court-Criminal & Civil Divisions 215 W Main (Civil-Rm 200), Lexington, KY 40507; Civil phone:606-246-2141; Criminal phone:606-246-2141. Hours: 8:30AM-4:30PM (EST). *Felony, Civil Actions Over $4,000.*

Civil Records: Access: Mail, in person. Both court and visitors may perform in person searches. Search fee: $5.00 per name. Required to search: name, years to search. Civil cases indexed by defendant, plaintiff. Civil records on computer since April 1993, on index cards since 1978, prior records on books and archived. **Criminal Records:** Access: Mail, in person. Both court and visitors may perform in person searches. Search fee: $5.00 per name. Required to search: name, years to search; also helpful-DOB, SSN. Criminal records on computer since April 1993, on index cards since 1978, prior records on books and archived. **General Information:** No adoption, juvenile, mental, or sealed records released. SASE required. Turnaround time 1-2 days. Copy fee: $.50 per page. Certification fee: $1.50. Fee payee: Fayette County Circuit Clerk. No personal checks accepted. Prepayment is required. Public access terminal is available.

District Court-Criminal & Civil 140 N ML King Blvd (Criminal), 136 N ML King Blvd (Civil), Lexington, KY 40507; Civil phone:606-246-2240; Criminal phone:606-246-2240. Hours: 8AM-4PM (EST). *Misdemeanor, Civil Actions Under $4,000, Eviction, Small Claims, Probate.*

Civil Records: Access: Mail, in person. Both court and visitors may perform in person searches. No search fee. Required to search: name, years to search. Civil cases indexed by defendant, plaintiff. Civil records on computer since 1992, prior records on index cards since 1977. **Criminal Records:** Access: Mail, in person. Both court and visitors may perform in person searches. No search fee. Required to search: name, years to search, DOB; also helpful-SSN. Criminal records on computer since 1977. **General Information:** No adoption, mental, juvenile, or sealed records released. SASE required. Turnaround time 3 days. Copy fee: $.25 per page. Certification fee: $1.00. Fee payee: District Clerk. Personal checks accepted. Prepayment is required. Public access terminal is available.

Fleming County

Circuit & District Court Courthouse 100 Court Square, Flemingsburg, KY 41041; 606-845-7011; Fax: 606-849-2400. Hours: 8AM-4:30PM (EST). *Felony, Misdemeanor, Civil, Eviction, Small Claims, Probate.*

Civil Records: Access: Phone, fax, mail, in person. Both court and visitors may perform in person searches. No search fee. Required to search: name, years to search. Civil cases indexed by defendant, plaintiff. Civil records on computer since May 1994, prior records on index cards since 1978. **Criminal Records:** Access: Phone, fax, mail, in person. Both court and visitors may perform in person searches. No search fee. Required to search: name, years to search, DOB; also helpful-SSN. Criminal records on computer since May 1994, prior records on index cards since 1978. **General Information:** No adoption, mental, juvenile, or sealed records released. SASE required. Turnaround time 1-2 days. Copy fee: $.15 per page. Certification fee: $1.00. Fee payee: Clerk of Circuit Court. Personal checks accepted. Prepayment is required. Public access terminal is available. Fax notes: $1.00 per page.

Floyd County

Circuit Court PO Bix 3368, (127 S Lake Dr), Prestonsburg, KY 41653-3368; 606-886-3090; Fax: 606-886-9075. Hours: 8AM-4PM (EST). *Felony, Civil Actions Over $4,000.*

Civil Records: Access: Mail, in person. Both court and visitors may perform in person searches. No search fee. Required to search: name, years to search. Civil cases indexed by defendant, plaintiff. Civil records on computer since September 1991, prior records on index cards since 1978. **Criminal Records:** Access: Mail, in person. Both court and visitors may perform in person searches. No search fee. Required to search: name, years to search, DOB, SSN. Criminal records on computer since September 1991, prior records on index cards since 1978. **General Information:** No adoption, mental, juvenile, or sealed records released. SASE required. Turnaround time 2-4 days. Copy fee: $.25 per page. Certification fee: $1.00. Fee payee: Clerk of Circuit Court. Personal checks accepted. Prepayment is required.

District Court PO Box 3368, (127 S Lake Dr), Prestonsburg, KY 41653-3368; 606-886-9114. Hours: 8AM-4PM (EST). *Misdemeanor, Small Claims.*

Note: Small cliams can be reached at 606-886-2124 **Criminal Records:** Access: Phone, mail, in person. Only the court conducts in person searches; visitors may not. No search fee. Required to search: name, years to search; also helpful-SSN. Criminal records on computer since

1991, prior records in index cards since 1989. Records are only kept for five years in this office. **General Information:** No adoption, mental, juvenile, or sealed records released. SASE required. Turnaround time 2-4 days. Copy fee: $.15 per page. Certification fee: $1.75. Fee payee: Floyd District Court. Personal checks accepted. Prepayment is required.

Franklin County

Circuit Court Box 678, Frankfort, KY 40602; 502-564-8380; Fax: 502-564-8188. Hours: 8AM-4:30PM (EST). *Felony, Civil Actions Over $4,000.*

Civil Records: Access: Fax, mail, in person. Both court and visitors may perform in person searches. No search fee. Required to search: name, years to search. Civil cases indexed by defendant, plaintiff. Civil records on computer since 1990, prior records on index cards since 1978. **Criminal Records:** Access: Fax, in person. Court does not conduct in person searches; visitors must perform searches for themselves. No search fee. Required to search: name, years to search, DOB, SSN. Criminal records on computer since 1990, prior records on index cards since 1978. All requests are referred to the state Administrator's Office of Courts. **General Information:** No adoption, mental, juvenile, or sealed records released. SASE required. Turnaround time 2 days. Copy fee: $.15 per page. Certification fee: $1.00. Fee payee: Circuit Clerk. Personal checks accepted. Prepayment is required. Public access terminal is available. Fax notes: $2.00 for first page, $1.00 each addl.

District Court Box 678, Frankfort, KY 40601; 502-564-7013; Fax: 502-564-8188. Hours: 8AM-4:30PM (EST). *Misdemeanor, Civil Actions Under $4,000, Eviction, Small Claims, Probate.*

Civil Records: Access: In person only. Court does not conduct in person searches; visitors must perform searches for themselves. Search fee: No civil searches performed by court. Required to search: name, years to search. Civil cases indexed by defendant, plaintiff. Civil records on computer since 1990, records on index cards since 1978, prior records archived. **Criminal Records:** Access: In person only. Court does not conduct in person searches; visitors must perform searches for themselves. No search fee. Required to search: name, years to search, DOB. Criminal records on computer since 1990, records on index cards since 1978, prior records archived. **General Information:** No adoption, mental, juvenile, or sealed records released. Copy fee: $.15 per page. Certification fee: $1.00. Fee payee: Franklin Circuit Clerk. Personal checks accepted. Prepayment is required. Public access terminal is available.

Fulton County

Circuit & District Court Box 198, Hickman, KY 42050; 270-236-3944; Fax: 270-236-3729. Hours: 8:30AM-4PM (CST). *Felony, Misdemeanor, Civil, Eviction, Small Claims, Probate.*

Civil Records: Access: Mail, in person. Both court and visitors may perform in person searches. No search fee. Required to search: name, years to search. Civil cases indexed by defendant, plaintiff. Civil records on index and archived since 1843. **Criminal Records:** Access: In person only. Court does not conduct in person searches; visitors must perform searches for themselves. Search fee: No criminal searches performed by court. Required to search: name, years to search. Criminal records on

index and archived since 1843. **General Information:** No adoption, mental, juvenile, or sealed records released. SASE required. Copy fee: $.15 per page. Certification fee: $1.00. Fee payee: Circuit Clerk. Personal checks accepted. Prepayment is required. Public access terminal is available.

Gallatin County

Circuit Court Box 256, Warsaw, KY 41095; 859-567-5241. Hours: 8AM-5PM M,T,Th,F; Closed W (EST). *Felony, Civil Actions Over $4,000.*

Civil Records: Access: Mail, in person. Both court and visitors may perform in person searches. No search fee. Required to search: name, years to search. Civil cases indexed by defendant, plaintiff. Civil records on index cards since 1978. **Criminal Records:** Access: Mail, in person. Both court and visitors may perform in person searches. No search fee. Required to search: name, years to search; also helpful-SSN. Criminal records on index cards since 1978. **General Information:** No adoption, mental, juvenile, or sealed records released. SASE required. Turnaround time 4 days. Copy fee: $.15 per page. Certification fee: $1.00. Fee payee: Circuit Clerk. Personal checks accepted. Prepayment is required. Public access terminal is available.

District Court Box 256, Warsaw, KY 41095; 606-567-2388. Hours: 8AM-5PM T,Th,F; 8AM-6PM M; 8AM-Noon Sat (EST). *Misdemeanor, Civil Actions Under $4,000, Eviction, Small Claims, Probate.*

Civil Records: Access: Mail, in person. Both court and visitors may perform in person searches. No search fee. Required to search: name, years to search. Civil cases indexed by defendant, plaintiff. Civil records on computer since November 1994, prior records on index cards since 1978. **Criminal Records:** Access: Mail, in person. Both court and visitors may perform in person searches. No search fee. Required to search: name, years to search, DOB; also helpful-SSN. Criminal records on computer since November 1994, prior records on index cards since 1978. **General Information:** No adoption, mental, juvenile, or sealed records released. Turnaround time 1-2 days. Copy fee: $.15 per page. Certification fee: $1.00. Fee payee: District Clerk. Personal checks accepted. Prepayment is required. Public access terminal is available.

Garrard County

Circuit & District Court 7 Public Square, Courthouse Annex, Lancaster, KY 40444; 606-792-6032; Fax: 606-792-6414. Hours: 8AM-4PM M,T,TH,F, 8AM-Noon Wed & Sat (EST). *Felony, Misdemeanor, Civil, Eviction, Small Claims, Probate.*

Civil Records: Access: In person only. Court does not conduct in person searches; visitors must perform searches for themselves. Search fee: No civil searches performed by court. Required to search: name, years to search. Civil cases indexed by defendant, plaintiff. Civil records in index since 1900s. **Criminal Records:** Access: In person only. Court does not conduct in person searches; visitors must perform searches for themselves. Search fee: No criminal searches performed by court. Required to search: name, years to search; also helpful-address, DOB, SSN. Criminal records in index since 1900s. **General Information:** No adoption, mental, juvenile, or sealed records released. Copy fee: $.15 per page. Certification fee: $1.00. Fee payee: Circuit Clerk. Personal checks accepted. Prepayment is required. Public access terminal is available.

Grant County

Circuit & District Court Courthouse 101 N Main, Williamstown, KY 41097; 606-824-4467. Hours: 8AM-4PM (EST). *Felony, Misdemeanor, Civil, Eviction, Small Claims, Probate.*

Civil Records: Access: In person only. Court does not conduct in person searches; visitors must perform searches for themselves. Search fee: No civil searches performed by court. Required to search: name, years to search. Civil cases indexed by defendant, plaintiff. Civil records on computer since 1992, prior records on index cards since 1978. **Criminal Records:** Access: In person only. Court does not conduct in person searches; visitors must perform searches for themselves. Search fee: No criminal searches performed by court. Required to search: name, years to search, DOB; also helpful-SSN. Criminal records on computer since 1992, prior records on index cards since 1978. **General Information:** No adoption, mental, juvenile, or sealed records released. Copy fee: $.15 per page. Certification fee: $1.00. Fee payee: Circuit Clerk. Personal checks accepted. Prepayment is required. Public access terminal is available.

Graves County

Circuit & District Court Courthouse 100 E Broadway, Mayfield, KY 42066; 270-247-1733; Fax: 270-247-7358. Hours: 8AM-4:30PM (CST). *Felony, Misdemeanor, Civil, Eviction, Small Claims, Probate.*

Civil Records: Access: In person only. Court does not conduct in person searches; visitors must perform searches for themselves. Search fee: No civil searches performed by court. Required to search: name, years to search. Civil cases indexed by defendant, plaintiff. Civil records on computer since June, 1994, prior records on index cards since 1978. **Criminal Records:** Access: In person only. Court does not conduct in person searches; visitors must perform searches for themselves. Search fee: No criminal searches performed by court. Required to search: name, years to search, DOB; also helpful-SSN. Criminal records on computer since June, 1994, prior records on index cards since 1978. **General Information:** No adoption, mental, juvenile, or sealed records released. Copy fee: $.25 per page. Certification fee: $1.00. Fee payee: Circuit Clerk. Personal checks accepted. Prepayment is required.

Grayson County

Circuit & District Court 125 E White Oak, Leitchfield, KY 42754; 270-259-3040; Fax: 270-259-9866. Hours: 8AM-4PM M-F; 8AM-Noon Sat (CST). *Felony, Misdemeanor, Civil, Eviction, Small Claims, Probate.*

Civil Records: Access: Mail, in person. Both court and visitors may perform in person searches. Search fee: $10.00 per name. Required to search: name, years to search. Civil cases indexed by defendant, plaintiff. Civil records on computer since 05/94, prior records on index cards since 1978. **Criminal Records:** Access: Mail, in person. Both court and visitors may perform in person searches. Search fee: $10.00. Required to search: name, years to search; also helpful-DOB, SSN. Criminal records on computer since 05/94, prior records on index cards since 1978. **General Information:** No adoption, mental, juvenile, or sealed records released. SASE requird. Turnaround time 2 days. Copy fee: $.15 per page.

Certification fee: $1.50. Fee payee: Clerk of Circuit Court. Personal checks accepted. Prepayment is required. Public access terminal is available.

Green County

Circuit & District Court 203 W Court St, Greensburg, KY 42743; 270-932-5631; Fax: 270-932-6468. Hours: 8AM-4PM M-W, F; 8AM-12:30PM Sat (EST). *Felony, Misdemeanor, Civil, Eviction, Small Claims, Probate.*

Civil Records: Access: Fax, mail, in person. Both court and visitors may perform in person searches. No search fee. Required to search: name, years to search; also helpful-address. Civil cases indexed by defendant, plaintiff. Civil records on index cards since 1978. **Criminal Records:** Access: Fax, mail, in person. Both court and visitors may perform in person searches. No search fee. Required to search: name, years to search; also helpful-address, DOB, SSN. Criminal records on index cards since 1978. **General Information:** No adoption, mental, juvenile, or sealed records released. SASE required. Turnaround time 1-2 days. Copy fee: $.15 per page. Certification fee: $1.00. Fee payee: Green County Circuit or District Clerk. Personal checks accepted. Prepayment is required. Public access terminal is available. Fax notes: No fee to fax results. Will only fax to 800 numbers.

Greenup County

Circuit & District Court Courthouse Annex, Greenup, KY 41144; 606-473-9869; Fax: 606-473-7388. Hours: 9AM-4:30PM M-F (EST). *Felony, Misdemeanor, Civil, Eviction, Small Claims, Probate.*

Civil Records: Access: In person only. Both court and visitors may perform in person searches. Search fee: No civil searches performed by court. Required to search: name, years to search. Civil cases indexed by defendant, plaintiff. Civil records on computer since 1990, prior records on index cards since 1978. **Criminal Records:** Access: In person only. Court does not conduct in person searches; visitors must perform searches for themselves. Search fee: No criminal searches performed by court. Required to search: name, years to search, DOB; also helpful-SSN. Criminal records on computer since 1990, prior records on index cards since 1978. **General Information:** No adoption, mental, juvenile, or sealed records released. Copy fee: $.15 per page. Certification fee: $1.00. Fee payee: Circuit Clerk. Personal checks accepted. Prepayment is required. Public access terminal is available.

Hancock County

Circuit & District Court Courthouse, PO Box 250, Hawesville, KY 42348; 270-927-8144; Fax: 270-927-8629. Hours: 8AM-4PM M,T,W,F; 8AM-5:30PM Th (CST). *Felony, Misdemeanor, Civil, Eviction, Small Claims, Probate.*

Civil Records: Access: Mail, in person. Both court and visitors may perform in person searches. No search fee. Required to search: name, years to search. Civil cases indexed by defendant, plaintiff. Civil records on computer since August, 1994, prior records on index cards. **Criminal Records:** Access: Mail, in person. Both court and visitors may perform in person searches. No search fee. Required to search: name, years to search; also helpful-DOB, SSN. Criminal records on computer since August, 1994, prior records on index cards. **General Information:** No adoption, mental, juvenile, or sealed records released. SASE

required. Turnaround time 1-2 days. Copy fee: $.15 per page. Certification fee: $1.00. Fee payee: Circuit Clerk. Personal checks accepted. Prepayment is required. Public access terminal is available.

Hardin County

Circuit & District Court Hardin County Justice Center, 120 E Dixie Ave, Elizabethtown, KY 42701; 270-766-5000; Fax: 270-766-5243. Hours: 8AM-4:30PM; (EST). *Felony, Misdemeanor, Civil, Eviction, Small Claims, Probate.*

Civil Records: Access: In person only. Court does not conduct in person searches; visitors must perform searches for themselves. Search fee: No civil searches performed by court. Required to search: name, years to search. Civil cases indexed by defendant, plaintiff. Civil records on computer since 03/28/94, prior records on index cards since 1978. **Criminal Records:** Access: In person only. Court does not conduct in person searches; visitors must perform searches for themselves. Search fee: No criminal searches performed by court. Required to search: name, years to search, DOB. Criminal records on computer since 03/28/94, prior records on index cards since 1978. **General Information:** No adoption, mental, juvenile, or sealed records released. Copy fee: $.15 per page. Certification fee: $1.00. Fee payee: Circuit Clerk. Personal checks accepted. Prepayment is required. Public access terminal is available.

Radcliff District Court 220 Freedom Way, Radcliff, KY 40160; 270-351-1299; Fax: 270-351-1301. Hours: 8:30AM-12, 12:20-4PM (EST). *Probate, Evictions.* **Criminal Records:** Both court and visitors may perform in person searches. Search fee:. Required to search: name. **General Information:**.

Harlan County

Circuit & District Court Box 190, Harlan, KY 40831; 606-573-2680. Hours: 8AM-4:30PM (EST). *Felony, Misdemeanor, Civil, Eviction, Small Claims, Probate.*

Civil Records: Access: In person only. Court does not conduct in person searches; visitors must perform searches for themselves. Search fee: No civil searches performed by court. Required to search: name, years to search. Civil cases indexed by defendant, plaintiff. Civil records on computer since August, 1991, on index cards since 1978, records prior to 1983 are archived in Frankfort. **Criminal Records:** Access: In person only. Court does not conduct in person searches; visitors must perform searches for themselves. Search fee: No criminal searches performed by court. Required to search: name, years to search, DOB; also helpful-SSN. Criminal records on computer since August, 1991, on index cards since 1978, records prior to 1983 are archived in Frankfort. **General Information:** No adoption, mental, juvenile, sealed or domestic violence records released. Copy fee: $.25 per page. Certification fee: $3.50. Fee payee: Circuit Clerk. Personal checks accepted. Prepayment is required. Public access terminal is available. Fax notes: $2.00 fee to fax 1st page; $1.00 each add'l.

Harrison County

Circuit & District Court Courthouse Box 10, Cynthiana, KY 41031; 606-234-1914. Hours: 8:30AM-4:30PM M-F, 9AM-12PM Sat (EST). *Felony, Misdemeanor, Civil, Eviction, Small Claims, Probate.*

CROMONA Letcher
CROMWELL (42333) Ohio(86), Butler(14)
CROWN Letcher
CRYSTAL (40420) Lee(83), Estill(17)
CUB RUN (42729) Hart(75), Edmonson(25)
CULVER Elliott
CUMBERLAND (40823) Harlan(99),
    Letcher(1)
CUNDIFF Adair
CUNNINGHAM (42035) Carlisle(58),
    Graves(42)
CURDSVILLE Daviess
CUSTER Breckinridge
CUTSHIN Leslie
CYNTHIANA Harrison
DABOLT Jackson
DAISY Perry
DANA Floyd
DANVILLE Boyle
DAVID Floyd
DAWSON SPRINGS (42408) Hopkins(88),
    Caldwell(9), Christian(3)
DAYHOIT Harlan
DAYTON Campbell
DE MOSSVILLE Pendleton
DEANE (41812) Knott(77), Letcher(23)
DEBORD Martin
DECOY (41321) Knott(80), Breathitt(20)
DEFOE Henry
DELPHIA Perry
DELTA Wayne
DEMA Knott
DENNISTON Menifee
DENTON (41132) Carter(96), Lawrence(3),
    Boyd(1)
DENVER Johnson
DEWITT Knox
DEXTER (42036) Calloway(99),
    Marshall(1)
DICE Perry
DINGUS Morgan
DIXON Webster
DIZNEY Harlan
DORTON Pike
DOVER (41034) Mason(97), Bracken(3)
DRAFFIN Pike
DRAKE Warren
DRAKESBORO Muhlenberg
DREYFUS Madison
DRIFT Floyd
DRY RIDGE Grant
DUBRE (42731) Cumberland(84),
    Metcalfe(16)
DUNBAR Butler
DUNDEE Ohio
DUNMOR (42339) Muhlenberg(93),
    Butler(7)
DUNNVILLE (42528) Casey(97), Russell(3)
DWALE Floyd
DWARF Perry
DYCUSBURG Crittenden
EARLINGTON Hopkins
EAST BERNSTADT Laurel
EAST POINT (41216) Floyd(66),
    Johnson(34)
EASTERN Floyd
EASTVIEW Hardin
EASTWOOD Jefferson
EDDYVILLE Lyon
EDMONTON (42129) Metcalfe(94),
    Adair(6)
EDNA Magoffin
EGYPT Jackson
EIGHTY EIGHT Barren
EKRON Meade
ELIZABETHTOWN Hardin
ELIZAVILLE Fleming
ELK HORN (42733) Taylor(76), Casey(23),
    Adair(1)
ELKFORK Morgan
ELKHORN CITY Pike
ELKTON (42220) Todd(98), Muhlenberg(2)

ELLIOTTVILLE Rowan
ELSIE Magoffin
EMERSON Lewis
EMINENCE (40019) Henry(98), Shelby(2)
EMLYN Whitley
EMMA Floyd
EMMALENA Knott
ENDICOTT Floyd
EOLIA Letcher
ERILINE Clay
ERLANGER Kenton
ERMINE Letcher
ESSIE (40827) Leslie(96), Adair(4)
ESTILL Floyd
ETOILE Barren
EUBANK (42567) Pulaski(86), Lincoln(14)
EVARTS Harlan
EWING Fleming
EZEL Morgan
FAIRDALE Jefferson
FAIRFIELD Nelson
FAIRPLAY Adair
FAIRVIEW Christian
FALCON Magoffin
FALL ROCK Clay
FALLS OF ROUGH (40119) Grayson(59),
    Breckinridge(39), Ohio(2)
FALMOUTH Pendleton
FANCY FARM (42039) Graves(54),
    Hickman(28), Carlisle(18)
FARMERS Rowan
FARMINGTON (42040) Graves(78),
    Calloway(22)
FAUBUSH (42532) Pulaski(59),
    Russell(35), Wayne(6)
FEDSCREEK Pike
FERGUSON Pulaski
FILLMORE Lee
FINCHVILLE Shelby
FINLEY (42736) Taylor(57), Marion(43)
FIREBRICK Lewis
FISHERVILLE (40023) Jefferson(59),
    Spencer(38), Shelby(3)
FISTY Knott
FLAT FORK Magoffin
FLAT LICK Knox
FLATGAP Johnson
FLATWOODS Greenup
FLEMINGSBURG Fleming
FLORENCE Boone
FOGERTOWN Clay
FORD Clark
FORDS BRANCH Pike
FORDSVILLE (42343) Ohio(68),
    Hancock(31)
FOREST HILLS Pike
FORT CAMPBELL Christian
FORT KNOX Hardin
FORT THOMAS Campbell
FOSTER Bracken
FOUNTAIN RUN (42133) Monroe(49),
    Barren(32), Allen(19)
FOURMILE Knox
FRAKES (40940) Bell(64), Whitley(36)
FRANKFORT (40601) Franklin(97),
    Woodford(2), Shelby(1)
FRANKFORT Franklin
FRANKLIN (42134) Simpson(94), Allen(5)
FRANKLIN Simpson
FRAZER Wayne
FREDONIA (42411) Caldwell(57),
    Crittenden(38), Lyon(5)
FREDVILLE Magoffin
FREEBURN Pike
FRENCHBURG Menifee
FRITZ Magoffin
FT MITCHELL Kenton
FUGET Johnson
FULTON (42041) Fulton(72), Graves(17),
    Hickman(11)
GALVESTON Floyd
GAMALIEL Monroe

GAPVILLE Magoffin
GARFIELD (40140) Breckinridge(85),
    Hardin(15)
GARNER Knott
GARRARD Clay
GARRETT (41630) Knott(55), Floyd(45)
GARRISON (41141) Lewis(61),
    Greenup(25), Carter(14)
GAYS CREEK Perry
GEORGETOWN Scott
GERMANTOWN (41044) Bracken(51),
    Mason(50)
GHENT Carroll
GILBERTSVILLE Marshall
GILLMORE Wolfe
GIRDLER Knox
GLASGOW Barren
GLENCOE (41046) Grant(74), Gallatin(26)
GLENDALE Hardin
GLENS FORK (42741) Adair(93),
    Russell(8)
GLENVIEW Jefferson
GOODY Pike
GOOSE ROCK Clay
GORDON Letcher
GOSHEN Oldham
GRACEY (42232) Christian(77), Trigg(23)
GRADYVILLE Adair
GRAHAM Muhlenberg
GRAHN Carter
GRAND RIVERS Livingston
GRATZ Owen
GRAVEL SWITCH (40328) Marion(46),
    Boyle(32), Casey(20), Washington(2)
GRAY (40734) Knox(87), Laurel(13)
GRAY HAWK Jackson
GRAYS KNOB Harlan
GRAYSON (41143) Carter(99), Greenup(1)
GREEN HALL Owsley
GREEN ROAD Knox
GREENSBURG (42743) Green(97),
    Adair(2), Taylor(2)
GREENUP Greenup
GREENVILLE Muhlenberg
GRETHEL Floyd
GULSTON Harlan
GUNLOCK Magoffin
GUSTON (40142) Meade(96),
    Breckinridge(4)
GUTHRIE Todd
GYPSY Magoffin
HADDIX Breathitt
HADLEY Warren
HAGERHILL Johnson
HALDEMAN Rowan
HALFWAY Allen
HALLIE Letcher
HALO Floyd
HAMLIN Calloway
HAMPTON Livingston
HANSON Hopkins
HAPPY Perry
HARDBURLY Perry
HARDIN (42048) Marshall(95), Calloway(5)
HARDINSBURG Breckinridge
HARDY Pike
HARDYVILLE (42746) Hart(80), Green(12),
    Metcalfe(8)
HARLAN Harlan
HARNED Breckinridge
HAROLD Floyd
HARRODS CREEK Jefferson
HARRODSBURG (40330) Mercer(96),
    Washington(4)
HARTFORD Ohio
HAWESVILLE (42348) Hancock(98),
    Daviess(2)
HAZARD (41701) Perry(91), Knott(9)
HAZARD Perry
HAZEL Calloway
HAZEL GREEN (41332) Wolfe(82),
    Morgan(18)

HEBRON Boone
HEIDELBERG Lee
HEIDRICK Knox
HELLIER Pike
HELTON (40840) Leslie(77), Harlan(23)
HENDERSON Henderson
HENDRICKS Magoffin
HERD Jackson
HERNDON (42236) Christian(86), Trigg(15)
HESTAND (42151) Monroe(97),
    Metcalfe(3)
HI HAT Floyd
HICKMAN Fulton
HICKORY Graves
HILLSBORO Fleming
HIMA Clay
HINDMAN Knott
HINKLE Knox
HIPPO Floyd
HISEVILLE Barren
HITCHINS Carter
HODGENVILLE Larue
HOLLAND Allen
HOLLYBUSH Knott
HOLMES MILL Harlan
HONAKER Floyd
HOPE (40334) Bath(87), Montgomery(13)
HOPKINSVILLE Christian
HORSE BRANCH (42349) Ohio(82),
    Grayson(18)
HORSE CAVE (42749) Hart(94),
    Metcalfe(4), Barren(2)
HOSKINSTON Leslie
HOWARDSTOWN (40028) Nelson(84),
    Larue(16)
HUDDY Pike
HUDSON Breckinridge
HUEYSVILLE (41640) Knott(80), Floyd(20)
HUFF Edmonson
HULEN Bell
HUNTER Floyd
HUNTSVILLE Butler
HUSTONVILLE (40437) Lincoln(69),
    Casey(31)
HYDEN Leslie
INDEPENDENCE Kenton
INEZ Martin
INGLE Pulaski
INGRAM Bell
INSKO Morgan
IRVINE (40336) Estill(98), Lee(1)
IRVINGTON (40146) Breckinridge(98),
    Meade(2)
ISLAND McLean
ISLAND CITY Owsley
ISOM Letcher
ISONVILLE Elliott
IVEL Floyd
IVYTON Magoffin
JACKHORN Letcher
JACKSON (41339) Breathitt(94), Knott(6)
JACOBS Carter
JAMBOREE Pike
JAMESTOWN Russell
JEFF Perry
JEFFERSONVILLE Montgomery
JENKINS (41537) Letcher(97), Pike(3)
JEREMIAH Letcher
JETSON Butler
JOB Martin
JOHNS RUN Carter
JONANCY Pike
JONESVILLE Grant
JUNCTION CITY Boyle
KEATON Johnson
KEAVY Laurel
KEENE Jessamine
KEITH Harlan
KENTON Kenton
KENVIR Harlan
KERBY KNOB Jackson
KETTLE Cumberland

KETTLE ISLAND Bell
KEVIL (42053) McCracken(53), Ballard(47)
KIMPER Pike
KINGS MOUNTAIN (40442) Lincoln(64), Casey(36)
KIRKSEY (42054) Calloway(80), Marshall(14), Graves(6)
KITE Knott
KNIFLEY Adair
KNOB LICK (42154) Metcalfe(86), Barren(14)
KONA Letcher
KRYPTON (41754) Perry(97), Leslie(3)
KUTTAWA Lyon
LA CENTER Ballard
LA FAYETTE Christian
LA GRANGE (40031) Oldham(95), Henry(5)
LA GRANGE Oldham
LACKEY (41643) Knott(84), Floyd(16)
LAMB (42155) Barren(61), Monroe(39)
LAMBRIC Breathitt
LAMERO Rockcastle
LANCASTER (40444) Garrard(97), Lincoln(3)
LANCASTER Garrard
LANGLEY Floyd
LATONIA Kenton
LAWRENCEBURG Anderson
LEANDER Johnson
LEATHERWOOD Perry
LEBANON Marion
LEBANON JUNCTION (40150) Bullitt(78), Hardin(22)
LEBURN Knott
LEDBETTER Livingston
LEE CITY Wolfe
LEECO Lee
LEITCHFIELD (42754) Grayson(94), Breckinridge(6)
LEITCHFIELD Grayson
LEJUNIOR Harlan
LENOX Morgan
LEROSE Owsley
LETCHER Letcher
LEWISBURG (42256) Logan(86), Todd(10), Butler(3), Muhlenberg(1)
LEWISPORT (42351) Hancock(92), Daviess(8)
LEXINGTON (40509) Fayette(98), Clark(2)
LEXINGTON (40511) Fayette(98), Scott(1)
LEXINGTON (40514) Fayette(94), Jessamine(7)
LEXINGTON (40516) Fayette(85), Bourbon(15)
LEXINGTON Fayette
LIBERTY Casey
LICK CREEK Pike
LILY Laurel
LINDSEYVILLE Edmonson
LINEFORK Letcher
LITTCARR Knott
LITTLE Breathitt
LIVERMORE (42352) McLean(95), Ohio(5)
LIVINGSTON (40445) Rockcastle(98), Laurel(2)
LLOYD Greenup
LOCKPORT Henry
LOLA Livingston
LONDON Laurel
LONE Lee
LOOKOUT Pike
LORETTO (40037) Marion(75), Washington(17), Nelson(8)
LOST CREEK (41348) Breathitt(77), Perry(23)
LOUISA (41230) Lawrence(98), Martin(2)
LOUISVILLE (40229) Jefferson(62), Bullitt(38)
LOUISVILLE (40241) Jefferson(98), Oldham(2)

LOUISVILLE (40245) Jefferson(88), Shelby(11), Oldham(1)
LOUISVILLE (40272) Jefferson(99), Bullitt(2)
LOUISVILLE (40299) Jefferson(98), Bullitt(2)
LOUISVILLE Jefferson
LOVELACEVILLE Ballard
LOVELY Martin
LOWES Graves
LOWMANSVILLE (41232) Lawrence(68), Johnson(32)
LOYALL Harlan
LUCAS Barren
LYNCH Harlan
LYNNVILLE Graves
MACEDONIA Breathitt
MACEO Daviess
MACKVILLE Washington
MADISONVILLE Hopkins
MAGNOLIA (42757) Hart(53), Larue(39), Green(8)
MAJESTIC Pike
MALLIE Knott
MALONE Morgan
MAMMOTH CAVE Edmonson
MANCHESTER Clay
MANITOU Hopkins
MANNSVILLE Taylor
MAPLE MOUNT Daviess
MARIBA Menifee
MARION Crittenden
MARROWBONE Cumberland
MARSHALLVILLE Magoffin
MARSHES SIDING McCreary
MARTHA (41159) Lawrence(93), Johnson(8)
MARTIN Floyd
MARY ALICE (40964) Harlan(93), Adair(7)
MARYDELL Laurel
MASON Grant
MASONIC HOME Jefferson
MAYFIELD Graves
MAYKING Letcher
MAYSLICK Mason
MAYSVILLE Mason
MAZIE Lawrence
MC ANDREWS Pike
MC CARR Pike
MC COMBS (41545) Pike(90), Floyd(10)
MC DANIELS Breckinridge
MC DOWELL Floyd
MC HENRY Ohio
MC KEE (40447) Jackson(97), Rockcastle(2), Estill(1)
MC KINNEY Lincoln
MC QUADY Breckinridge
MC ROBERTS Letcher
MC VEIGH Pike
MEALLY Johnson
MEANS (40346) Menifee(81), Bath(11), Montgomery(9)
MELBER (42069) Graves(90), McCracken(9), Carlisle(1)
MELBOURNE Campbell
MELVIN Floyd
MIDDLEBURG Casey
MIDDLESBORO Bell
MIDWAY (40347) Woodford(92), Franklin(4), Scott(3)
MILBURN Carlisle
MILFORD Bracken
MILL SPRINGS Wayne
MILLERSBURG Bourbon
MILLS Knox
MILLSTONE Letcher
MILLTOWN Adair
MILLWOOD Grayson
MILTON (40045) Trimble(86), Carroll(14)
MIMA Morgan
MINERVA Mason
MINNIE Floyd

MIRACLE Bell
MISTLETOE Owsley
MITCHELLSBURG Boyle
MIZE Morgan
MONTICELLO Wayne
MONTPELIER Adair
MOON Morgan
MOOREFIELD Nicholas
MOORMAN Muhlenberg
MOREHEAD Rowan
MORGANFIELD (42437) Union(98), Webster(2)
MORGANTOWN Butler
MORNING VIEW Kenton
MORRILL Jackson
MORTONS GAP Hopkins
MOUNT EDEN (40046) Spencer(59), Anderson(37), Shelby(4)
MOUNT HERMON Monroe
MOUNT OLIVET Robertson
MOUNT SHERMAN (42764) Green(52), Larue(48)
MOUNT STERLING (40353) Montgomery(98), Clark(1)
MOUNT VERNON Rockcastle
MOUNT WASHINGTON Bullitt
MOUSIE Knott
MOUTHCARD Pike
MOZELLE Leslie
MULDRAUGH Meade
MUNFORDVILLE Hart
MURRAY Calloway
MUSES MILLS Fleming
MYRA Pike
NANCY (42544) Pulaski(72), Wayne(18), Russell(9)
NARROWS Ohio
NAZARETH Nelson
NEAFUS Grayson
NEBO (42441) Hopkins(95), Webster(5)
NELSE Pike
NEON (41840) Letcher(98), Knott(2)
NERINX Marion
NEVISDALE Whitley
NEW CASTLE Henry
NEW CONCORD Calloway
NEW HAVEN (40051) Nelson(84), Larue(16)
NEW HOPE (40052) Nelson(86), Larue(12), Marion(2)
NEW LIBERTY Owen
NEWPORT Campbell
NICHOLASVILLE Jessamine
NOCTOR Breathitt
NORTH MIDDLETOWN Bourbon
NORTONVILLE (42442) Hopkins(95), Christian(5)
OAK GROVE Christian
OAKLAND Warren
OAKVILLE Logan
OFFUTT Johnson
OIL SPRINGS Johnson
OLATON (42361) Ohio(88), Grayson(12)
OLD LANDING Lee
OLDTOWN Greenup
OLIVE HILL (41164) Carter(97), Elliott(3)
OLLIE Edmonson
OLMSTEAD (42265) Logan(90), Todd(10)
OLYMPIA Bath
ONEIDA Clay
OPHIR Morgan
ORLANDO Rockcastle
OVEN FORK Letcher
OWENSBORO Daviess
OWENTON Owen
OWINGSVILLE (40360) Bath(94), Montgomery(6)
PADUCAH McCracken
PAINT LICK (40461) Garrard(61), Madison(39)
PAINTSVILLE Johnson
PARIS Bourbon

PARK CITY (42160) Barren(80), Edmonson(20)
PARKERS LAKE McCreary
PARKSVILLE (40464) Boyle(92), Casey(8)
PARROT Jackson
PARTRIDGE Letcher
PATHFORK Harlan
PAW PAW Pike
PAYNEVILLE (40157) Meade(99), Breckinridge(1)
PELLVILLE Hancock
PEMBROKE (42266) Christian(93), Todd(7)
PENDLETON (40055) Trimble(45), Henry(40), Oldham(16)
PENROD Muhlenberg
PEOPLES Jackson
PERRY PARK Owen
PERRYVILLE (40468) Boyle(93), Washington(4), Mercer(2)
PETERSBURG Boone
PEWEE VALLEY Oldham
PEYTONSBURG Cumberland
PHELPS Pike
PHILPOT (42366) Daviess(94), Hancock(4), Ohio(3)
PHYLLIS Pike
PIKEVILLE Pike
PILGRIM Martin
PINE KNOT McCreary
PINE RIDGE (41360) Wolfe(85), Powell(15)
PINE TOP Knott
PINEVILLE Bell
PINSONFORK Pike
PIPPA PASSES Knott
PITTSBURG Laurel
PLANK Clay
PLEASUREVILLE (40057) Henry(89), Shelby(11)
PLUMMERS LANDING Fleming
POMEROYTON Menifee
POOLE Webster
PORT ROYAL Henry
POWDERLY Muhlenberg
PREMIUM Letcher
PRESTON Bath
PRESTONSBURG Floyd
PRIMROSE Lee
PRINCETON (42445) Caldwell(93), Lyon(3), Hopkins(2), Trigg(2)
PRINTER Floyd
PROSPECT (40059) Jefferson(67), Oldham(33)
PROVIDENCE (42450) Webster(91), Hopkins(5), Crittenden(5)
PROVO Butler
PRYSE Estill
PUTNEY Harlan
QUALITY (42268) Butler(73), Logan(27)
QUICKSAND Breathitt
QUINCY Lewis
RACCOON Pike
RADCLIFF Hardin
RANSOM Pike
RAVEN Knott
RAVENNA Estill
RAYWICK Marion
REDFOX Knott
REED Henderson
REGINA Pike
RENFRO VALLEY Rockcastle
REVELO McCreary
REYNOLDS STATION (42368) Hancock(78), Ohio(22)
RHODELIA (40161) Meade(90), Breckinridge(11)
RICETOWN Owsley
RICHARDSON Lawrence
RICHARDSVILLE Warren
RICHMOND Madison
RINEYVILLE Hardin
RIVER (41254) Johnson(95), Lawrence(5)

ROARK Leslie
ROBARDS (42452) Henderson(85), Webster(16)
ROBINSON CREEK Pike
ROCHESTER Butler
ROCKFIELD (42274) Warren(92), Logan(8)
ROCKHOLDS (40759) Whitley(91), Knox(9)
ROCKHOUSE Pike
ROCKPORT Ohio
ROCKY HILL Edmonson
ROCKYBRANCH Wayne
ROGERS Wolfe
ROSINE Ohio
ROUNDHILL (42275) Butler(71), Edmonson(30)
ROUSSEAU Breathitt
ROWDY Perry
ROWLETTS Hart
ROXANA Letcher
ROYALTON Magoffin
RUMSEY McLean
RUSH (41168) Carter(72), Boyd(27)
RUSSELL Greenup
RUSSELL SPRINGS (42642) Russell(91), Adair(6), Casey(2)
RUSSELLVILLE Logan
SACRAMENTO (42372) Muhlenberg(51), McLean(50)
SADIEVILLE (40370) Scott(75), Harrison(26)
SAINT CATHARINE Washington
SAINT CHARLES Hopkins
SAINT FRANCIS Marion
SAINT HELENS Lee
SAINT JOSEPH Daviess
SAINT MARY Marion
SAINT PAUL Lewis
SALDEE Breathitt
SALEM (42078) Livingston(62), Crittenden(38)
SALT LICK (40371) Bath(92), Menifee(8)
SALVISA (40372) Mercer(94), Anderson(6)
SALYERSVILLE (41465) Magoffin(98), Floyd(2)
SANDERS Carroll
SANDGAP Jackson
SANDY HOOK Elliott
SASSAFRAS Knott
SAUL Perry
SAWYER McCreary
SCALF Knox
SCIENCE HILL Pulaski
SCOTTSVILLE Allen
SCUDDY Perry
SE REE Breckinridge
SEBREE Webster
SECO Letcher
SEDALIA Graves
SEITZ Magoffin
SEXTONS CREEK (40983) Clay(67), Owsley(33)
SHARON GROVE Todd
SHARPSBURG (40374) Bath(91), Bourbon(5), Nicholas(4)
SHELBIANA Pike
SHELBY GAP Pike
SHELBYVILLE Shelby
SHEPHERDSVILLE Bullitt
SHOPVILLE Pulaski
SIDNEY Pike

SILER (40763) Whitley(80), Bell(20)
SILVER GROVE Campbell
SILVERHILL Morgan
SIMPSONVILLE Shelby
SITKA Johnson
SIZEROCK Leslie
SLADE Powell
SLAUGHTERS (42456) Webster(72), Hopkins(28)
SLEMP Perry
SLOANS VALLEY Pulaski
SMILAX Leslie
SMITH Harlan
SMITH MILLS Henderson
SMITHFIELD (40068) Henry(87), Shelby(8), Oldham(5)
SMITHLAND Livingston
SMITHS GROVE (42171) Warren(49), Edmonson(29), Barren(23)
SOLDIER Carter
SOMERSET Pulaski
SONORA (42776) Hardin(67), Larue(34)
SOUTH CARROLLTON Muhlenberg
SOUTH PORTSMOUTH Greenup
SOUTH SHORE Greenup
SOUTH UNION Logan
SOUTH WILLIAMSON Pike
SPARTA (41086) Owen(52), Gallatin(48)
SPEIGHT Pike
SPOTTSVILLE Henderson
SPRING LICK Grayson
SPRINGFIELD Washington
STAB Pulaski
STAFFORDSVILLE Johnson
STAMBAUGH Johnson
STAMPING GROUND (40379) Scott(82), Owen(14), Franklin(5)
STANFORD Lincoln
STANLEY Daviess
STANTON (40380) Powell(97), Estill(3)
STANVILLE (41659) Floyd(97), Pike(3)
STEARNS McCreary
STEELE Pike
STEFF Grayson
STEPHENS Elliott
STEPHENSBURG Hardin
STEPHENSPORT Breckinridge
STEUBENVILLE Wayne
STINNETT Leslie
STONE Pike
STONEY FORK (40988) Bell(54), Harlan(46)
STOPOVER Pike
STRUNK McCreary
STURGIS (42459) Union(94), Crittenden(6)
SULLIVAN Union
SULPHUR Henry
SUMMER SHADE (42166) Metcalfe(72), Barren(16), Monroe(13)
SUMMERSVILLE (42782) Green(95), Hart(5)
SUMMIT Hardin
SUNFISH Edmonson
SWAMP BRANCH Johnson
SWEEDEN Edmonson
SYMSONIA (42082) Graves(74), Marshall(23), McCracken(3)
TALBERT Breathitt
TALCUM (41765) Knott(86), Perry(14)
TALLEGA Lee
TATEVILLE Pulaski

TAYLORSVILLE (40071) Spencer(80), Bullitt(18), Shelby(2)
TEABERRY Floyd
THELMA Johnson
THORNTON Letcher
THOUSANDSTICKS Leslie
THREEFORKS Martin
TILINE Livingston
TOLER Pike
TOLLESBORO Lewis
TOLU Crittenden
TOMAHAWK Martin
TOMPKINSVILLE Monroe
TOPMOST Knott
TOTZ Harlan
TRAM Floyd
TRENTON (42286) Todd(96), Christian(4)
TROSPER Knox
TURKEY CREEK (41570) Pike(96), Martin(4)
TURNERS STATION (40075) Henry(72), Carroll(28)
TUTOR KEY Johnson
TYNER (40486) Jackson(97), Clay(3)
TYPO Perry
ULYSSES Lawrence
UNION Boone
UNION STAR Breckinridge
UNIONTOWN (42461) Union(97), Henderson(3)
UPTON (42784) Hardin(53), Larue(28), Hart(19)
UTICA (42376) Daviess(74), Ohio(20), McLean(6)
VAN LEAR Johnson
VANCEBURG (41179) Lewis(94), Carter(6)
VANCLEVE Breathitt
VARNEY Pike
VENTRESS Hardin
VERONA Boone
VERSAILLES (40383) Woodford(99), Jessamine(2)
VERSAILLES Woodford
VEST Knott
VICCO (41773) Perry(63), Knott(37)
VINCENT Owsley
VINE GROVE (40175) Hardin(65), Meade(35)
VIPER Perry
VIRGIE Pike
VOLGA Johnson
WACO (40385) Madison(98), Estill(3)
WADDY (40076) Shelby(72), Franklin(16), Anderson(10), Spencer(2)
WALKER Knox
WALLINGFORD Fleming
WALLINS CREEK Harlan
WALNUT GROVE Pulaski
WALTON (41094) Boone(99), Kenton(1)
WANETA Jackson
WARBRANCH Leslie
WARFIELD Martin
WARSAW (41095) Gallatin(96), Boone(4)
WASHINGTON Mason
WATER VALLEY (42085) Graves(69), Hickman(31)
WATERVIEW Cumberland
WAVERLY (42462) Union(91), Henderson(10)
WAX Grayson
WAYLAND Floyd

WAYNESBURG (40489) Lincoln(80), Pulaski(12), Casey(8)
WEBBVILLE (41180) Lawrence(54), Carter(45), Elliott(1)
WEBSTER (40176) Breckinridge(66), Meade(34)
WEEKSBURY Floyd
WELCHS CREEK Butler
WELLINGTON Menifee
WENDOVER Leslie
WEST LIBERTY (41472) Morgan(98), Elliott(2)
WEST LOUISVILLE Daviess
WEST PADUCAH McCracken
WEST POINT (40177) Hardin(91), Bullitt(7), Jefferson(2)
WEST PRESTONSBURG Floyd
WEST SOMERSET Pulaski
WEST VAN LEAR Johnson
WESTPORT Oldham
WESTVIEW Breckinridge
WHEATCROFT Webster
WHEATLEY Owen
WHEELWRIGHT Floyd
WHICK Breathitt
WHITE MILLS Hardin
WHITE OAK Morgan
WHITE PLAINS (42464) Hopkins(74), Muhlenberg(17), Christian(10)
WHITEHOUSE Johnson
WHITESBURG Letcher
WHITESVILLE (42378) Daviess(53), Ohio(47)
WHITLEY CITY McCreary
WICKLIFFE Ballard
WIDECREEK Breathitt
WILDIE Rockcastle
WILLARD Carter
WILLIAMSBURG Whitley
WILLIAMSPORT Johnson
WILLIAMSTOWN Grant
WILLISBURG (40078) Washington(96), Mercer(2), Anderson(2)
WILLOW SHADE Metcalfe
WILMORE (40390) Jessamine(98), Woodford(2)
WINCHESTER Clark
WIND CAVE Jackson
WINDSOR (42565) Casey(99), Russell(1)
WINDY Wayne
WINGO (42088) Graves(85), Hickman(15)
WINSTON Estill
WITTENSVILLE Johnson
WOODBINE (40771) Knox(84), Whitley(16)
WOODBURN (42170) Warren(64), Simpson(36)
WOODBURY Butler
WOODMAN Pike
WOOLLUM Knox
WOOTON Leslie
WORTHINGTON Greenup
WORTHVILLE (41098) Owen(96), Carroll(4)
WRIGLEY Morgan
YEADDISS Leslie
YERKES Perry
YOSEMITE Casey
ZACHARIAH Lee
ZOE Lee

ZIP/City Cross Reference

40003-40003	BAGDAD	40011-40011	CAMPBELLSBURG	40022-40022	FINCHVILLE	40036-40036	LOCKPORT
40004-40004	BARDSTOWN	40012-40012	CHAPLIN	40023-40023	FISHERVILLE	40037-40037	LORETTO
40006-40006	BEDFORD	40013-40013	COXS CREEK	40025-40025	GLENVIEW	40040-40040	MACKVILLE
40007-40007	BETHLEHEM	40014-40014	CRESTWOOD	40026-40026	GOSHEN	40041-40041	MASONIC HOME
40008-40008	BLOOMFIELD	40018-40018	EASTWOOD	40027-40027	HARRODS CREEK	40045-40045	MILTON
40009-40009	BRADFORDSVILLE	40019-40019	EMINENCE	40031-40032	LA GRANGE	40046-40046	MOUNT EDEN
40010-40010	BUCKNER	40020-40020	FAIRFIELD	40033-40033	LEBANON	40047-40047	MOUNT WASHINGTON

Zip	City	Zip	City	Zip	City	Zip	City
40048-40048	NAZARETH	40350-40350	MOOREFIELD	40813-40813	CALVIN	41016-41016	COVINGTON
40049-40049	NERINX	40351-40351	MOREHEAD	40815-40815	CAWOOD	41017-41017	FT MITCHELL
40050-40050	NEW CASTLE	40353-40353	MOUNT STERLING	40816-40816	CHAPPELL	41018-41018	ERLANGER
40051-40051	NEW HAVEN	40355-40355	NEW LIBERTY	40818-40818	COALGOOD	41019-41019	COVINGTON
40052-40052	NEW HOPE	40356-40356	NICHOLASVILLE	40819-40819	COLDIRON	41022-41022	FLORENCE
40055-40055	PENDLETON	40357-40357	NORTH MIDDLETOWN	40820-40820	CRANKS	41030-41030	CRITTENDEN
40056-40056	PEWEE VALLEY	40358-40358	OLYMPIA	40823-40823	CUMBERLAND	41031-41031	CYNTHIANA
40057-40057	PLEASUREVILLE	40359-40359	OWENTON	40824-40824	DAYHOIT	41033-41033	DE MOSSVILLE
40058-40058	PORT ROYAL	40360-40360	OWINGSVILLE	40825-40825	DIZNEY	41034-41034	DOVER
40059-40059	PROSPECT	40361-40362	PARIS	40826-40826	EOLIA	41035-41035	DRY RIDGE
40060-40060	RAYWICK	40363-40363	PERRY PARK	40827-40827	ESSIE	41037-41037	ELIZAVILLE
40061-40061	SAINT CATHARINE	40366-40366	PRESTON	40828-40828	EVARTS	41039-41039	EWING
40062-40062	SAINT FRANCIS	40370-40370	SADIEVILLE	40829-40829	GRAYS KNOB	41040-41040	FALMOUTH
40063-40063	SAINT MARY	40371-40371	SALT LICK	40830-40830	GULSTON	41041-41041	FLEMINGSBURG
40065-40066	SHELBYVILLE	40372-40372	SALVISA	40831-40831	HARLAN	41042-41042	FLORENCE
40067-40067	SIMPSONVILLE	40374-40374	SHARPSBURG	40840-40840	HELTON	41043-41043	FOSTER
40068-40068	SMITHFIELD	40376-40376	SLADE	40843-40843	HOLMES MILL	41044-41044	GERMANTOWN
40069-40069	SPRINGFIELD	40379-40379	STAMPING GROUND	40844-40844	HOSKINSTON	41045-41045	GHENT
40070-40070	SULPHUR	40380-40380	STANTON	40845-40845	HULEN	41046-41046	GLENCOE
40071-40071	TAYLORSVILLE	40383-40384	VERSAILLES	40847-40847	KENVIR	41048-41048	HEBRON
40075-40075	TURNERS STATION	40385-40385	WACO	40849-40849	LEJUNIOR	41049-41049	HILLSBORO
40076-40076	WADDY	40386-40386	VERSAILLES	40854-40854	LOYALL	41051-41051	INDEPENDENCE
40077-40077	WESTPORT	40387-40387	WELLINGTON	40855-40855	LYNCH	41052-41052	JONESVILLE
40078-40078	WILLISBURG	40390-40390	WILMORE	40856-40856	MIRACLE	41053-41053	KENTON
40104-40104	BATTLETOWN	40391-40392	WINCHESTER	40858-40858	MOZELLE	41054-41054	MASON
40106-40106	BIG SPRING	40402-40402	ANNVILLE	40862-40862	PARTRIDGE	41055-41055	MAYSLICK
40107-40107	BOSTON	40403-40404	BEREA	40863-40863	PATHFORK	41056-41056	MAYSVILLE
40108-40108	BRANDENBURG	40405-40405	BIGHILL	40865-40865	PUTNEY	41059-41059	MELBOURNE
40109-40109	BROOKS	40409-40409	BRODHEAD	40867-40867	SMITH	41061-41061	MILFORD
40110-40110	CLERMONT	40410-40410	BRYANTSVILLE	40868-40868	STINNETT	41062-41062	MINERVA
40111-40111	CLOVERPORT	40419-40419	CRAB ORCHARD	40870-40870	TOTZ	41063-41063	MORNING VIEW
40115-40115	CUSTER	40421-40421	DABOLT	40873-40873	WALLINS CREEK	41064-41064	MOUNT OLIVET
40117-40117	EKRON	40422-40423	DANVILLE	40874-40874	WARBRANCH	41065-41065	MUSES MILLS
40118-40118	FAIRDALE	40434-40434	GRAY HAWK	40902-40902	ARJAY	41071-41072	NEWPORT
40119-40119	FALLS OF ROUGH	40437-40437	HUSTONVILLE	40903-40903	ARTEMUS	41073-41073	BELLEVUE
40121-40121	FORT KNOX	40440-40440	JUNCTION CITY	40906-40906	BARBOURVILLE	41074-41074	DAYTON
40140-40140	GARFIELD	40442-40442	KINGS MOUNTAIN	40913-40913	BEVERLY	41075-41075	FORT THOMAS
40142-40142	GUSTON	40444-40444	LANCASTER	40914-40914	BIG CREEK	41076-41076	NEWPORT
40143-40143	HARDINSBURG	40445-40445	LIVINGSTON	40915-40915	BIMBLE	41080-41080	PETERSBURG
40144-40144	HARNED	40446-40446	LANCASTER	40921-40921	BRYANTS STORE	41081-41081	PLUMMERS LANDING
40145-40145	HUDSON	40447-40447	MC KEE	40923-40923	CANNON	41083-41083	SANDERS
40146-40146	IRVINGTON	40448-40448	MC KINNEY	40927-40927	CLOSPLINT	41085-41085	SILVER GROVE
40150-40150	LEBANON JUNCTION	40452-40452	MITCHELLSBURG	40930-40930	DEWITT	41086-41086	SPARTA
40152-40152	MC DANIELS	40456-40456	MOUNT VERNON	40931-40931	ERILINE	41091-41091	UNION
40153-40153	MC QUADY	40460-40460	ORLANDO	40932-40932	FALL ROCK	41092-41092	VERONA
40155-40155	MULDRAUGH	40461-40461	PAINT LICK	40935-40935	FLAT LICK	41093-41093	WALLINGFORD
40157-40157	PAYNEVILLE	40464-40464	PARKSVILLE	40939-40939	FOURMILE	41094-41094	WALTON
40159-40160	RADCLIFF	40467-40467	PEOPLES	40940-40940	FRAKES	41095-41095	WARSAW
40161-40161	RHODELIA	40468-40468	PERRYVILLE	40941-40941	GARRARD	41096-41096	WASHINGTON
40162-40162	RINEYVILLE	40472-40472	RAVENNA	40943-40943	GIRDLER	41097-41097	WILLIAMSTOWN
40164-40164	SE REE	40473-40473	RENFRO VALLEY	40944-40944	GOOSE ROCK	41098-41098	WORTHVILLE
40165-40165	SHEPHERDSVILLE	40475-40476	RICHMOND	40946-40946	GREEN ROAD	41099-41099	NEWPORT
40170-40170	STEPHENSPORT	40481-40481	SANDGAP	40949-40949	HEIDRICK	41101-41114	ASHLAND
40171-40171	UNION STAR	40484-40484	STANFORD	40951-40951	HIMA	41121-41121	ARGILLITE
40175-40175	VINE GROVE	40486-40486	TYNER	40953-40953	HINKLE	41124-41124	BLAINE
40176-40176	WEBSTER	40488-40488	WANETA	40955-40955	INGRAM	41125-41125	BRUIN
40177-40177	WEST POINT	40489-40489	WAYNESBURG	40958-40958	KETTLE ISLAND	41127-41127	CAMP DIX
40178-40178	WESTVIEW	40492-40492	WILDIE	40962-40962	MANCHESTER	41128-41128	CARTER
40201-40299	LOUISVILLE	40495-40495	WINSTON	40964-40964	MARY ALICE	41129-41129	CATLETTSBURG
40309-40309	BOWEN	40501-40596	LEXINGTON	40965-40965	MIDDLESBORO	41131-41131	CONCORD
40310-40310	BURGIN	40601-40622	FRANKFORT	40972-40972	ONEIDA	41132-41132	DENTON
40311-40311	CARLISLE	40701-40702	CORBIN	40977-40977	PINEVILLE	41135-41135	EMERSON
40312-40312	CLAY CITY	40724-40724	BUSH	40979-40979	ROARK	41137-41137	FIREBRICK
40313-40313	CLEARFIELD	40729-40729	EAST BERNSTADT	40981-40981	SAUL	41139-41139	FLATWOODS
40316-40316	DENNISTON	40730-40730	EMLYN	40982-40982	SCALF	41141-41141	GARRISON
40317-40317	ELLIOTTVILLE	40734-40734	GRAY	40983-40983	SEXTONS CREEK	41142-41142	GRAHN
40319-40319	FARMERS	40737-40737	KEAVY	40988-40988	STONEY FORK	41143-41143	GRAYSON
40320-40320	FORD	40740-40740	LILY	40995-40995	TROSPER	41144-41144	GREENUP
40322-40322	FRENCHBURG	40741-40745	LONDON	40997-40997	WALKER	41146-41146	HITCHINS
40324-40324	GEORGETOWN	40751-40751	MARYDELL	40999-40999	WOOLLUM	41149-41149	ISONVILLE
40328-40328	GRAVEL SWITCH	40754-40754	NEVISDALE	41001-41001	ALEXANDRIA	41150-41150	JACOBS
40329-40329	HALDEMAN	40755-40755	PITTSBURG	41002-41002	AUGUSTA	41156-41156	LLOYD
40330-40330	HARRODSBURG	40759-40759	ROCKHOLDS	41003-41003	BERRY	41159-41159	MARTHA
40334-40334	HOPE	40763-40763	SILER	41004-41004	BROOKSVILLE	41160-41160	MAZIE
40336-40336	IRVINE	40769-40769	WILLIAMSBURG	41005-41005	BURLINGTON	41164-41164	OLIVE HILL
40337-40337	JEFFERSONVILLE	40771-40771	WOODBINE	41006-41006	BUTLER	41166-41166	QUINCY
40339-40339	KEENE	40801-40801	AGES BROOKSIDE	41007-41007	CALIFORNIA	41168-41168	RUSH
40340-40340	NICHOLASVILLE	40803-40803	ASHER	41008-41008	CARROLLTON	41169-41169	RUSSELL
40342-40342	LAWRENCEBURG	40806-40806	BAXTER	41009-41009	CONSTANCE	41170-41170	SAINT PAUL
40346-40346	MEANS	40807-40807	BENHAM	41010-41010	CORINTH	41171-41171	SANDY HOOK
40347-40347	MIDWAY	40808-40808	BIG LAUREL	41011-41014	COVINGTON	41173-41173	SOLDIER
40348-40348	MILLERSBURG	40810-40810	BLEDSOE	41015-41015	LATONIA	41174-41174	SOUTH PORTSMOUTH

41175-41175	SOUTH SHORE	41465-41465	SALYERSVILLE	41667-41667	WEEKSBURY	42029-42029	CALVERT CITY
41179-41179	VANCEBURG	41472-41472	WEST LIBERTY	41668-41668	WEST PRESTONSBURG	42031-42031	CLINTON
41180-41180	WEBBVILLE	41477-41477	WRIGLEY	41669-41669	WHEELWRIGHT	42032-42032	COLUMBUS
41181-41181	WILLARD	41501-41502	PIKEVILLE	41701-41702	HAZARD	42033-42033	CRAYNE
41183-41183	WORTHINGTON	41503-41503	SOUTH WILLIAMSON	41712-41712	ARY	42035-42035	CUNNINGHAM
41189-41189	TOLLESBORO	41512-41512	ASHCAMP	41713-41713	AVAWAM	42036-42036	DEXTER
41201-41201	ADAMS	41513-41513	BELCHER	41714-41714	BEAR BRANCH	42037-42037	DYCUSBURG
41203-41203	BEAUTY	41514-41514	BELFRY	41719-41719	BONNYMAN	42038-42038	EDDYVILLE
41204-41204	BOONS CAMP	41517-41517	BURDINE	41721-41721	BUCKHORN	42039-42039	FANCY FARM
41214-41214	DEBORD	41519-41519	CANADA	41722-41722	BULAN	42040-42040	FARMINGTON
41215-41215	DENVER	41520-41520	DORTON	41723-41723	BUSY	42041-42041	FULTON
41216-41216	EAST POINT	41522-41522	ELKHORN CITY	41725-41725	CARRIE	42044-42044	GILBERTSVILLE
41219-41219	FLATGAP	41524-41524	FEDSCREEK	41727-41727	CHAVIES	42045-42045	GRAND RIVERS
41222-41222	HAGERHILL	41526-41526	FORDS BRANCH	41729-41729	COMBS	42046-42046	HAMLIN
41224-41224	INEZ	41527-41527	FOREST HILLS	41730-41730	CONFLUENCE	42047-42047	HAMPTON
41226-41226	KEATON	41528-41528	FREEBURN	41731-41731	CORNETTSVILLE	42048-42048	HARDIN
41228-41228	LEANDER	41531-41531	HARDY	41735-41735	DELPHIA	42049-42049	HAZEL
41230-41230	LOUISA	41534-41534	HELLIER	41736-41736	DICE	42050-42050	HICKMAN
41231-41231	LOVELY	41535-41535	HUDDY	41739-41739	DWARF	42051-42051	HICKORY
41232-41232	LOWMANSVILLE	41536-41536	JAMBOREE	41740-41740	EMMALENA	42053-42053	KEVIL
41234-41234	MEALLY	41537-41537	JENKINS	41743-41743	FISTY	42054-42054	KIRKSEY
41238-41238	OIL SPRINGS	41538-41538	JONANCY	41745-41745	GAYS CREEK	42055-42055	KUTTAWA
41240-41240	PAINTSVILLE	41539-41539	KIMPER	41746-41746	HAPPY	42056-42056	LA CENTER
41250-41250	PILGRIM	41540-41540	LICK CREEK	41747-41747	HARDBURLY	42058-42058	LEDBETTER
41254-41254	RIVER	41542-41542	LOOKOUT	41749-41749	HYDEN	42060-42060	LOVELACEVILLE
41255-41255	SITKA	41543-41543	MC ANDREWS	41751-41751	JEFF	42061-42061	LOWES
41256-41256	STAFFORDSVILLE	41544-41544	MC CARR	41754-41754	KRYPTON	42063-42063	LYNNVILLE
41257-41257	STAMBAUGH	41546-41546	MC VEIGH	41759-41759	SASSAFRAS	42064-42064	MARION
41260-41260	THELMA	41547-41547	MAJESTIC	41760-41760	SCUDDY	42066-42066	MAYFIELD
41262-41262	TOMAHAWK	41548-41548	MOUTHCARD	41762-41762	SIZEROCK	42069-42069	MELBER
41263-41263	TUTOR KEY	41549-41549	MYRA	41763-41763	SLEMP	42070-42070	MILBURN
41264-41264	ULYSSES	41553-41553	PHELPS	41764-41764	SMILAX	42071-42071	MURRAY
41265-41265	VAN LEAR	41554-41554	PHYLLIS	41766-41766	THOUSANDSTICKS	42076-42076	NEW CONCORD
41267-41267	WARFIELD	41555-41555	PINSONFORK	41772-41772	VEST	42078-42078	SALEM
41268-41268	WEST VAN LEAR	41557-41557	RACCOON	41773-41773	VICCO	42079-42079	SEDALIA
41269-41269	WHITEHOUSE	41558-41558	RANSOM	41774-41774	VIPER	42081-42081	SMITHLAND
41271-41271	WILLIAMSPORT	41559-41559	REGINA	41775-41775	WENDOVER	42082-42082	SYMSONIA
41274-41274	WITTENSVILLE	41560-41560	ROBINSON CREEK	41776-41776	WOOTON	42083-42083	TILINE
41301-41301	CAMPTON	41561-41561	ROCKHOUSE	41777-41777	YEADDISS	42084-42084	TOLU
41307-41307	ATHOL	41562-41562	SHELBIANA	41778-41778	YERKES	42085-42085	WATER VALLEY
41310-41310	BAYS	41563-41563	SHELBY GAP	41804-41804	BLACKEY	42086-42086	WEST PADUCAH
41311-41311	BEATTYVILLE	41564-41564	SIDNEY	41810-41810	CROMONA	42087-42087	WICKLIFFE
41313-41313	BETHANY	41566-41566	STEELE	41812-41812	DEANE	42088-42088	WINGO
41314-41314	BOONEVILLE	41567-41567	STONE	41815-41815	ERMINE	42101-42104	BOWLING GREEN
41317-41317	CLAYHOLE	41568-41568	STOPOVER	41817-41817	GARNER	42120-42120	ADOLPHUS
41332-41332	HAZEL GREEN	41569-41569	TOLER	41819-41819	GORDON	42122-42122	ALVATON
41333-41333	HEIDELBERG	41571-41571	VARNEY	41821-41821	HALLIE	42123-42123	AUSTIN
41338-41338	ISLAND CITY	41572-41572	VIRGIE	41822-41822	HINDMAN	42124-42124	BEAUMONT
41339-41339	JACKSON	41601-41601	ALLEN	41824-41824	ISOM	42127-42127	CAVE CITY
41342-41342	LEE CITY	41602-41602	AUXIER	41825-41825	JACKHORN	42128-42128	DRAKE
41344-41344	LEROSE	41603-41603	BANNER	41826-41826	JEREMIAH	42129-42129	EDMONTON
41347-41347	LONE	41604-41604	BEAVER	41828-41828	KITE	42130-42130	EIGHTY EIGHT
41348-41348	LOST CREEK	41605-41605	BETSY LAYNE	41831-41831	LEBURN	42131-42131	ETOILE
41351-41351	MISTLETOE	41606-41606	BEVINSVILLE	41832-41832	LETCHER	42133-42133	FOUNTAIN RUN
41352-41352	MIZE	41607-41607	BLUE RIVER	41833-41833	LINEFORK	42134-42135	FRANKLIN
41360-41360	PINE RIDGE	41612-41612	BYPRO	41834-41834	LITTCARR	42140-42140	GAMALIEL
41362-41362	PRIMROSE	41615-41615	DANA	41835-41835	MC ROBERTS	42141-42142	GLASGOW
41364-41364	RICETOWN	41616-41616	DAVID	41836-41836	MALLIE	42150-42150	HALFWAY
41365-41365	ROGERS	41619-41619	DRIFT	41837-41837	MAYKING	42151-42151	HESTAND
41366-41366	ROUSSEAU	41621-41621	DWALE	41838-41838	MILLSTONE	42152-42152	HISEVILLE
41367-41367	ROWDY	41622-41622	EASTERN	41839-41839	MOUSIE	42153-42153	HOLLAND
41368-41368	SAINT HELENS	41626-41626	ENDICOTT	41840-41840	NEON	42154-42154	KNOB LICK
41377-41377	TALBERT	41630-41630	GARRETT	41843-41843	PINE TOP	42156-42156	LUCAS
41385-41385	VANCLEVE	41631-41631	GRETHEL	41844-41844	PIPPA PASSES	42157-42157	MOUNT HERMON
41386-41386	VINCENT	41632-41632	GUNLOCK	41845-41845	PREMIUM	42159-42159	OAKLAND
41390-41390	WHICK	41635-41635	HAROLD	41847-41847	REDFOX	42160-42160	PARK CITY
41397-41397	ZOE	41636-41636	HI HAT	41848-41848	ROXANA	42163-42163	ROCKY HILL
41408-41408	CANNEL CITY	41639-41639	HONAKER	41849-41849	SECO	42164-42164	SCOTTSVILLE
41410-41410	CISCO	41640-41640	HUEYSVILLE	41855-41855	THORNTON	42166-42166	SUMMER SHADE
41413-41413	CROCKETT	41642-41642	IVEL	41858-41858	WHITESBURG	42167-42167	TOMPKINSVILLE
41419-41419	EDNA	41643-41643	LACKEY	41859-41859	DEMA	42170-42170	WOODBURN
41421-41421	ELKFORK	41645-41645	LANGLEY	41861-41861	RAVEN	42171-42171	SMITHS GROVE
41422-41422	ELSIE	41647-41647	MC DOWELL	41862-41862	TOPMOST	42201-42201	ABERDEEN
41425-41425	EZEL	41649-41649	MARTIN	42001-42003	PADUCAH	42202-42202	ADAIRVILLE
41426-41426	FALCON	41650-41650	MELVIN	42020-42020	ALMO	42203-42203	ALLEGRE
41427-41427	FLAT FORK	41651-41651	MINNIE	42021-42021	ARLINGTON	42204-42204	ALLENSVILLE
41433-41433	GAPVILLE	41653-41653	PRESTONSBURG	42022-42022	BANDANA	42206-42206	AUBURN
41444-41444	IVYTON	41655-41655	PRINTER	42023-42023	BARDWELL	42207-42207	BEE SPRING
41451-41451	MALONE	41659-41659	STANVILLE	42024-42024	BARLOW	42209-42209	BROOKLYN
41452-41452	MARSHALLVILLE	41660-41660	TEABERRY	42025-42025	BENTON	42210-42210	BROWNSVILLE
41459-41459	OPHIR	41663-41663	TRAM	42027-42027	BOAZ	42211-42211	CADIZ
41464-41464	ROYALTON	41666-41666	WAYLAND	42028-42028	BURNA	42214-42214	CENTER

42215-42215	CERULEAN	42333-42333	CROMWELL	42441-42441	NEBO	42653-42653	WHITLEY CITY
42216-42216	CLIFTY	42334-42334	CURDSVILLE	42442-42442	NORTONVILLE	42701-42702	ELIZABETHTOWN
42217-42217	CROFTON	42337-42337	DRAKESBORO	42444-42444	POOLE	42711-42711	BAKERTON
42219-42219	DUNBAR	42338-42338	DUNDEE	42445-42445	PRINCETON	42712-42712	BIG CLIFTY
42220-42220	ELKTON	42339-42339	DUNMOR	42450-42450	PROVIDENCE	42713-42713	BONNIEVILLE
42221-42221	FAIRVIEW	42343-42343	FORDSVILLE	42451-42451	REED	42715-42715	BREEDING
42223-42223	FORT CAMPBELL	42344-42344	GRAHAM	42452-42452	ROBARDS	42716-42716	BUFFALO
42232-42232	GRACEY	42345-42345	GREENVILLE	42453-42453	SAINT CHARLES	42717-42717	BURKESVILLE
42234-42234	GUTHRIE	42347-42347	HARTFORD	42455-42455	SEBREE	42718-42719	CAMPBELLSVILLE
42235-42235	HADLEY	42348-42348	HAWESVILLE	42456-42456	SLAUGHTERS	42720-42720	CANE VALLEY
42236-42236	HERNDON	42349-42349	HORSE BRANCH	42457-42457	SMITH MILLS	42721-42721	CANEYVILLE
42240-42241	HOPKINSVILLE	42350-42350	ISLAND	42458-42458	SPOTTSVILLE	42722-42722	CANMER
42251-42251	HUNTSVILLE	42351-42351	LEWISPORT	42459-42459	STURGIS	42724-42724	CECILIA
42252-42252	JETSON	42352-42352	LIVERMORE	42460-42460	SULLIVAN	42726-42726	CLARKSON
42254-42254	LA FAYETTE	42354-42354	MC HENRY	42461-42461	UNIONTOWN	42728-42728	COLUMBIA
42256-42256	LEWISBURG	42355-42355	MACEO	42462-42462	WAVERLY	42729-42729	CUB RUN
42257-42257	LINDSEYVILLE	42356-42356	MAPLE MOUNT	42463-42463	WHEATCROFT	42731-42731	DUBRE
42259-42259	MAMMOTH CAVE	42361-42361	OLATON	42464-42464	WHITE PLAINS	42732-42732	EASTVIEW
42261-42261	MORGANTOWN	42364-42364	PELLVILLE	42501-42503	SOMERSET	42733-42733	ELK HORN
42262-42262	OAK GROVE	42365-42365	PENROD	42516-42516	BETHELRIDGE	42735-42735	FAIRPLAY
42265-42265	OLMSTEAD	42366-42366	PHILPOT	42518-42518	BRONSTON	42740-42740	GLENDALE
42266-42266	PEMBROKE	42367-42367	POWDERLY	42519-42519	BURNSIDE	42741-42741	GLENS FORK
42267-42267	PROVO	42368-42368	REYNOLDS STATION	42528-42528	DUNNVILLE	42742-42742	GRADYVILLE
42270-42270	RICHARDSVILLE	42369-42369	ROCKPORT	42533-42533	FERGUSON	42743-42743	GREENSBURG
42273-42273	ROCHESTER	42370-42370	ROSINE	42539-42539	LIBERTY	42746-42746	HARDYVILLE
42274-42274	ROCKFIELD	42371-42371	RUMSEY	42541-42541	MIDDLEBURG	42748-42748	HODGENVILLE
42275-42275	ROUNDHILL	42372-42372	SACRAMENTO	42544-42544	NANCY	42749-42749	HORSE CAVE
42276-42276	RUSSELLVILLE	42374-42374	SOUTH CARROLLTON	42553-42553	SCIENCE HILL	42753-42753	KNIFLEY
42280-42280	SHARON GROVE	42375-42375	STANLEY	42555-42555	SLOANS VALLEY	42754-42755	LEITCHFIELD
42283-42283	SOUTH UNION	42376-42376	UTICA	42558-42558	TATEVILLE	42757-42757	MAGNOLIA
42285-42285	SWEEDEN	42377-42377	WEST LOUISVILLE	42564-42564	WEST SOMERSET	42758-42758	MANNSVILLE
42286-42286	TRENTON	42378-42378	WHITESVILLE	42565-42565	WINDSOR	42759-42759	MARROWBONE
42287-42287	WELCHS CREEK	42402-42402	BASKETT	42566-42566	YOSEMITE	42761-42761	MILLTOWN
42288-42288	WOODBURY	42403-42403	BLACKFORD	42567-42567	EUBANK	42762-42762	MILLWOOD
42301-42304	OWENSBORO	42404-42404	CLAY	42602-42602	ALBANY	42764-42764	MOUNT SHERMAN
42320-42320	BEAVER DAM	42406-42406	CORYDON	42603-42603	ALPHA	42765-42765	MUNFORDVILLE
42321-42321	BEECH CREEK	42408-42408	DAWSON SPRINGS	42629-42629	JAMESTOWN	42776-42776	SONORA
42322-42322	BEECH GROVE	42409-42409	DIXON	42631-42631	MARSHES SIDING	42780-42780	STEFF
42323-42323	BEECHMONT	42410-42410	EARLINGTON	42632-42632	MILL SPRINGS	42782-42782	SUMMERSVILLE
42324-42324	BELTON	42411-42411	FREDONIA	42633-42633	MONTICELLO	42783-42783	SUMMIT
42325-42325	BREMEN	42413-42413	HANSON	42634-42634	PARKERS LAKE	42784-42784	UPTON
42326-42326	BROWDER	42419-42420	HENDERSON	42635-42635	PINE KNOT	42786-42786	WATERVIEW
42327-42327	CALHOUN	42431-42431	MADISONVILLE	42638-42638	REVELO	42788-42788	WHITE MILLS
42328-42328	CENTERTOWN	42436-42436	MANITOU	42642-42642	RUSSELL SPRINGS		
42330-42330	CENTRAL CITY	42437-42437	MORGANFIELD	42647-42647	STEARNS		
42332-42332	CLEATON	42440-42440	MORTONS GAP	42649-42649	STRUNK		

General Help Numbers:

Governor's Office
PO Box 94004   225-342-7015
Baton Rouge, LA 70804-9004   Fax 225-342-7099
www.gov.state.la.us   8AM-5PM

Attorney General's Office
LA Department of Justice   225-342-7013
PO Box 94005   Fax 225-342-7335
Baton Rouge, LA 70804-9005   8:30AM-5PM
www.ag.state.la.us

State Court Administrator
Judicial Council of the Supreme Court   504-568-5747
1555 Poydras Street, Suite 1540
New Orleans, LA 70112-1814   9AM-5PM
www.lajao.org

State Archives
Division of Archives   225-922-1000
3851 Essen Lane   Fax 225-922-0433
Baton Rouge, LA 70809-2137   8AM-4:30PM, 9-5 SA
www.sec.state.la.us/archives/archives/archives-index.htm

State Specifics:

Capital: Baton Rouge
                                          East Baton Rouge Parish

Time Zone: CST

Number of Parishes: 64

Population: 4,372,035

Web Site: www.state.la.us

State Agencies

Criminal Records

State Police, Bureau of Criminal Identification, 265 S Foster, Baton Rouge, LA 70806; 225-925-6095, 225-925-7005 (Fax), 8AM-4:30PM.

www.lsp.org

Note: Records are available for employment screening purposes only if the employment falls under a state statute requiring a criminal record check.

Indexing & Storage: Records are available from the early 1900's. Records are indexed by name on computer from 1974-present.

Searching: Records are not available to the public in general or to employers who do not qualify under a specific legislative act (such as childcare or schools). Include the following in your request-set of fingerprints, signed release. The following data is not released: pending records or juvenile records.

Access by: mail, in person.

Fee & Payment: Fees vary by type of requester. Dealing with children or health care is $10; dealing with state licensing boards is $10-no charge. We recommend calling first. Fee payee: State Police. Prepayment required. Business

checks, cashiers' checks, and money orders are accepted. No credit cards accepted.

Mail search: Turnaround time: 30 days. No self addressed stamped envelope is required.

In person search: Searching is available in person.

Corporation Records
Limited Partnership Records
Limited Liability Company Records
Trademarks/Servicemarks

Commercial Division, Corporation Department, PO Box 94125, Baton Rouge, LA 70804-9125 (Courier: 3851 Essen Lane, Baton Rouge, LA 70809); 225-925-4704, 225-925-4726 (Fax), 8AM-4:30PM.

www.sec.state.la.us

Note: Fictitious Names and Assumed Names are found at the parish level.

Indexing & Storage: Records are available from mid-1800s. New records are available for inquiry immediately. Records are indexed on microfilm, inhouse computer, index cards, on-line.

Searching: Include the following in your request-full name of business. In addition to the articles of incorporation, corporation records include the following information: Annual Reports, Officers, Directors, Prior (merged) names, Inactive names, Reserved names and (possibly) US Tax ID number.

Access by: mail, phone, fax, in person, online.

Fee & Payment: The search fee is $10.00. Copies cost $10.00 without amendments and $20.00 with amendments and a fee of $.25 per page after 40 pages for specific query searches on computer. Fee payee: Secretary of State. Prepayment required. Personal checks accepted. Credit cards accepted: Mastercard, Visa, AmEx.

Mail search: Turnaround time: 5-10 working days. No self addressed stamped envelope is required. No fee for mail request.

Phone search: You may call for information; however, only limited information is available.

Fax search: There is an additional $1.00 per page fee if returned by fax. Turnaround time is 5-10 working days.

In person search: There is a free public access terminal.

Online search: There are 2 ways to go: free on the Internet or pay. Free but limited information is available on the web site; go to "Commercial Division, Corporations Section," then "Search Corporations Database." The pay system is $360 per year for unlimited access. Almost any communications software will work with up to a 14,400 baud rate. The system is open from 6:30 am to 11pm. For more information, call Brenda Wright at (225) 922-1475.

Other access: The state offers corporation, LLC, partnership, and trademark information on tape cartridges. For more info, call 225-925-4792.

Expedited service: Expedited service is available for mail and phone searches. Turnaround time: 1 day. Add $20.00 per business name.

Uniform Commercial Code

Secretary of State, UCC Records, PO Box 94125, Baton Rouge, LA 70804-9125; 800-256-3758, 225-342-9011 (Fax), 8AM-4:30PM.

www.sec.state.la.us/comm/ucc-index.htm

Note: The statewide index of UCC filings is available in each parish office. All tax liens and financial statements are filed at the parish level. IRS liens show up on UCC records.

Indexing & Storage: Records are available for all active listings. Records are indexed on computer since 1990. It takes 2 days before new records are available for inquiry.

Searching: All filing information including debtor names, property descriptions, and subsequent filings and amendments are available.

Access by: mail, in person, online.

Fee & Payment: Copy fee is $1.00 per page at the Secretary of State Office. There may be variations at the parish level. Fee payee: Secretary of State. Prepayment required. The payment information outlined here applies only to online access. Personal checks accepted. Credit cards accepted: Mastercard, Visa.

Mail search: Mail-in requests are sent to the parish involved.

In person search: Walk-in searches are accepted.

Online search: An annual $400 fee gives unlimited access to UCC filing information. The dial-up service is open from 6:30 AM to 11 PM daily. Minimum baud rate is 9600. Most any software communications program can be configured to work. For further information, call Brenda Wright at 225-922-1475, or visit the web site.

Federal Tax Liens
State Tax Liens

Records not maintained by a state level agency.

Note: Records are filed with the Clerk of Court at the parish level.

Sales Tax Registrations

Access to Records is Restricted

Revenue and Tax Department, Sales Tax Division, PO Box 201, Baton Rouge, LA 70821-0201 (Courier: 330 N Ardenwwod Blvd, Baton Rouge, LA 70806); 225-925-7356, 225-925-3860 (Fax), 8AM-4:30PM.

www.rev.state.la.us

Note: This agency will only provide registration information to the registrant itself.

Birth Certificates

Vital Records Registry, PO Box 60630, New Orleans, LA 70160 (Courier: 325 Loyola Ave Room 102, New Orleans, LA 70112); 504-568-5152, 504-568-5167 (For adoptions), 504-568-5391 (Fax), 8AM-4PM.

www.dhh.state.la.us/OPH/vrinfo.htm

Note: Some certificates (all types of vital records) contain information at the bottom of the document that is confidential and not released to anyone. This information is used for statistical purposes and varies depending on legislative action.

Indexing & Storage: Records are available from 1914 on. Birth records for only the City of New Orleans are available from 1900 on. Records older than 100 years should be ordered from the State Archives. New records are available for inquiry immediately. Records are indexed on microfiche, index cards, inhouse computer.

Searching: Birth certificates are considered confidential for 100 years. Requesters must be related to the person of record or have a signed release. Include the following in your request-full name, names of parents, mother's maiden name, date of birth, place of birth, relationship to person of record, reason for information request. Older records must be searched at the State Archives 225-922-1184.

Access by: mail, fax, in person.

Fee & Payment: A "long form" birth certificate is $15.00, while a "birth card" is $9.00. Fee payee: Vital Records Registry. Prepayment required. Credit cards are not accepted for mail requests. Personal checks accepted. Credit cards accepted: Mastercard, Visa.

Mail search: Turnaround time: 3 weeks. No self addressed stamped envelope is required.

Fax search: Fax requests are with a credit card number only. See expedited service.

In person search: Photo ID required, turnaround time immediate.

Expedited service: Expedited service is available for mail and phone searches. Turnaround time: 24-48 hours. Add $15.50 per package. You must include written authorization to charge document fee and shipment fee to your credit card. The extra fee is over overnight delivery.

Death Records

Vital Records Registry, PO Box 60630, New Orleans, LA 70160 (Courier: 325 Loyola Ave Room 102, New Orleans, LA 70112); 504-568-5152, 504-568-5273 (Corrections), 504-568-5391 (Fax), 8AM-4PM.

www.dhh.state.la.us/OPH/vrinfo.htm

Indexing & Storage: Records are available from 1950 on. Older records must be obtained from the State Archives. New records are available for inquiry immediately. Records are indexed on microfiche, index cards, inhouse computer.

Searching: Death records are considered confidential for 50 years. Must show how related or have a signed release from immediate family member if for investigative purposes. Include the following in your request-full name, date of death, place of death, relationship to person of record, reason for information request. Records older than 50 years must be searched at the State Archives 225-922-1184.

Access by: mail, fax, in person.

Fee & Payment: The search fee is $5.00. Fee payee: Department of Vital Records. Prepayment required. Credit cards accepted for fax and in person requests only. Personal checks accepted. Credit cards accepted: Mastercard, Visa.

Mail search: Turnaround time: 3 weeks. No self addressed stamped envelope is required.

Fax search: Fax requests require use of credit card and are charged expedited fees.

In person search: In person search requires a photo ID. Turnaround time usually 45 minutes.

Expedited service: Expedited service is available for mail and phone searches. Turnaround time: 24-48 hours. Add $15.50 per package. You must include written authorization to charge document fee and shipping fee to credit card.

Licenses Searchable Online

Acupuncturist #20	www.lsbme.org/bmeSearch/licenseesearch.asp
Athletic Trainer #20	www.lsbme.org/bmeSearch/licenseesearch.asp
Bank #32	www.ofi.state.la.us/newbanks.htm
Bond For Deed #32	www.ofi.state.la.us/newbfd.htm
Check Casher #32	www.ofi.state.la.us/newcheckcash.htm
Clinical Exercise Physiologist #20	www.lsbme.org/bmeSearch/licenseesearch.asp
Clinical Lab Personnel #20	www.lsbme.org/bmeSearch/licenseesearch.asp
Collection Agency #32	www.ofi.state.la.us/newcolagn.htm
Consumer Credit #32	www.ofi.state.la.us/newliclen.htm
Credit Repair #32	www.ofi.state.la.us/newcredrep.htm
Dental Hygienist #09	www.lsbd.org/fpDentistSearch.asp
Dentist #09	www.lsbd.org/dentistsearch.asp
Engineer #40	www.lapels.com/indv_reg.html
Land Surveyor #40	www.lapels.com/indv_reg.html
Licensed Lenders #32	www.ofi.state.la.us/newliclen.htm
Licensed Professional Counselor (LPC) #46	www.lpcboard.org/lpc_alpha_list.htm
Lobbyist #66	www.ethics.state.la.us/lobs.htm
Medical Doctor #20	www.lsbme.org/bmeSearch/licenseesearch.asp
Midwife #20	www.lsbme.org/bmeSearch/licenseesearch.asp
Notary Public #54	www.sec.state.la.us/notary-pub/NTRINQ.htm
Notification Filers #32	www.ofi.state.la.us/newnotif.htm
Occupational Therapist #20	www.lsbme.org/bmeSearch/licenseesearch.asp
Occupational Therapist Technologist #20	www.lsbme.org/bmeSearch/licenseesearch.asp
Optometrist #22	www.arbo.org/nodb2000/licsearch.asp
Osteopathic Physician #20	www.lsbme.org/bmeSearch/licenseesearch.asp
Pawnbroker #32	www.ofi.state.la.us/newpawn.htm
Physician Assistant #20	www.lsbme.org/bmeSearch/licenseesearch.asp
Podiatrist #20	www.lsbme.org/bmeSearch/licenseesearch.asp
Private Radiologic Technologist #20	www.lsbme.org/bmeSearch/licenseesearch.asp
Residential Mortgage Lenders/Brokers #32	www.ofi.state.la.us/newrml.htm
Respiratory Therapist #20	www.lsbme.org/bmeSearch/licenseesearch.asp
Respiratory Therapy Technician #20	www.lsbme.org/bmeSearch/licenseesearch.asp
Savings & Loan & Credit Union #32	www.ofi.state.la.us/newcus.htm
Thrifts #32	www.ofi.state.la.us/newthrift.htm
Wholesale Drug Distributor #64	www.ntgasp.com/ldwdd/search.asp

Licensing Quick Finder

Acupuncturist #20	504-524-6820
Adult Day Care #35	225-022-0015
Adult Education Instructor #42	225-342-3490
Adult Residential Care #35	225-022-0015
Agricultural Consultant #31	225-925-3787
Agricultural Consultant #56	225-925-3787
Alcoholic Beverage Vendor #03	225-925-4041
Amusement Ride/Attraction Inspectors #55	225-925-7045
Amusement Ride/Attraction Owner/Operator #55	225-925-7045
Appraiser #29	225-925-4771
Arborist/Utility Arborist #39	225-925-7772
Architect #50	225-925-4802
Architect Firms #50	225-925-4802
Art Therapist #42	225-342-3490
Athletic Trainer #20	504-524-6820
Attorney #49	504-566-1600
Auction Business #44	225-992-2329
Auctioneer #44	225-922-2329
Bank #32	225-925-4660
Barber #04	225-925-1701
Barber Instructor #04	225-925-1701
Barber School #04	225-925-1701
Barber Shop #04	225-925-1701
Blood Alcohol Analyst #01	225-925-6216
Boiler Inspector #55	225-925-4344
Boiler Installer/Boiler Installer #55	225-925-4344
Bond For Deed #32	225-925-4660
Boxing & Wrestling Personnel #27	337-828-7154
Burglar Alarm Contractor #55	225-925-6766
Cemetery #02	504-838-5267
Check Casher #32	225-925-4660
Check Seller #32	225-925-4660
Chemical Engineer #40	225-925-6291
Child Nutrition Program Supervisor #42	225-342-3490
Child Residential Care #35	225-022-0015
Chiropractor #07	225-765-2322
Clinical Exercise Physiologist #20	504-524-6820
Clinical Lab Personnel #20	504-524-6820
Collection Agency #32	225-925-4660
Consumer Credit #32	225-925-4667
Contractor (Residential/Commercial) #41	225-765-2301
Cosmetologist #08	225-756-3404
Cosmetology Instructor #08	225-756-3404
Credit Repair #32	225-925-4660
Day Care Facilities #35	225-922-0015
Dental Hygienist #09	504-568-8574
Dentist #09	504-568-8574
Dietitian/Nutritionist #13	225-763-5490
Electrical Engineer #40	225-925-6291
Electrologist #10	318-463-6180
Embalmer #12	504-838-5109
Emergency Medical Technician #20	504-524-6820
Emergency Shelters #35	225-922-0015
Engineer #40	225-925-6291
Engineering Intern #40	225-925-6291
Environmental Engineer #40	225-925-6291
Equine Dentists #45	225-342-2176
Esthetician #08	225-756-3404
Euthanasia Technician #45	225-342-2176
Explosives Dealer #38	225-925-6178
Explosives Handler #38	225-925-6178
Family Support #35	225-022-0015
Fire Alarm Contractors #55	225-925-6766
Fire Extinguisher Contractors #55	225-925-6766
Fire Protection Sprinkler Contractor #55	225-925-6766
Fire Suppression Contractors #55	225-925-6766
Foster Care/Adoption Care #35	225-922-0015
Funeral Director #12	504-838-5109
Funeral Establishment #12	504-838-5109
Funeral Home Internship #12	504-838-5109
Funeral Home Work Permit #12	504-838-5109
General Contractor #30	504-736-7125
Groom #52	504-483-4000
Guidance Counselor #42	225-342-3490
Hearing Aid Dealer #19	318-362-3014
Horse Owner #52	504-483-4000
Horse Racing #52	504-483-4000
Horse Trainer #52	504-483-4000
Horticulturist #39	225-925-7772
Infant Intervention Services #35	225-022-0015
Insurance Agent #33	225-342-1216
Insurance Agent-LHA #33	225-342-0806

Insurance Broker #33 225-342-1216
Interior Designer #14 225-925-3921
Investment Advisor #53 225-568-5515
Jockey #52 504-483-4000
Jockey Agent #52 504-483-4000
Jockey Apprentice #52 504-483-4000
Juvenile Detention #35 225-022-0015
Land Surveying Intern #40 225-925-6291
Land Surveyor #40 225-925-6291
Landscape Architect #39 225-925-7772
Landscape Contractor #39 225-925-7772
Licensed Lenders #32 225-925-4660
Licensed Professional Counselor (LPC) #46
....225-765-2515
Livestock Branding #43 225-925-3980
Loan Brokers #32 225-925-4660
Lobbyist #66 225-992-1400
Lottery #47 225-297-2000
Lottery Claims Center #48 504-889-0031
Manicurist #08 225-756-3404
Manufactured Home Developers #55...225-925-4911
Manufactured Home Installers #55 225-925-4911
Manufactured Home Manufacturer #55.225-925-4911
Manufactured Housing Dealer/Salesman #55
....225-925-4911
Massage Therapist #62 225-922-1435
Maternity Homes #35 225-922-0015
Medical Doctor #20 504-524-6820
Medical Gas Piping Installer #51 504-826-2382
Midwife #20 504-524-6820
Montessori Teacher #42 225-342-3490
Motor Vehicle Agent/Salesman # 59 504-838-5207
Motor Vehicle Dealer; New or Used #59
....504-838-5207
Motor Vehicle Inspector #01 225-925-6984
Motor Vehicle Leasing/Rental Company # 59
....504-838-5207
Motor Vehicle Sales Finance Company #59
....504-838-5207
Music Therapist #42 225-342-3490
Mutuel Employee #52 504-483-4000
Notary Public #54 225-342-4981
Notification Filers #32 225-992-0634

Nuclear Medicine Technologist #16 504-838-5231
Nurse #21 504-838-5332
Nurse-LPN #25 504-568-6480
Nursing Home Administrator #36 225-925-4132
Nursing School #21 504-838-5332
Occupational Therapist #20 504-524-6820
Occupational Therapist Technologist #20
....504-524-6820
Optometrist #22 318-335-2989
Osteopathic Physician #20 504-524-6820
Outrider #52 504-483-4000
Parish or City School Superintendent #42
....225-342-3490
Pawnbroker #32 225-925-4660
Payday Lenders #32 225-925-4660
Personal Care Attendant #35 225-922-0015
Pesticide Applicator #31 225-925-3787
Pesticide Dealer #56 225-925-3796
Pesticide Operator #56 225-925-3796
Pharmacist #23 225-925-6496
Pharmacy #23 225-925-6496
Physical Therapist #24 318-262-1043
Physician Assistant #20 504-524-6820
Plater #52 504-483-4000
Plumber (Plumber, Master) #51 504-826-2382
Plumber Journeyman #51 504-826-2382
Podiatrist #20 504-524-6820
Polygraph Examiner #57 504-389-3836
Pony Person #52 504-483-4000
Practical Nurse School #25 504-568-6480
Private Investigation Company #58.......225-763-3556
Private Investigator #58 225-763-3556
Private Radiologic Technologist #20 504-524-6820
Private Security #26 225-295-8486
Psychologist #15 225-763-3935
Public Accountant-CPA #05 504-566-1244
Radiation Therapy Technologist #16 504-838-5231
Radio & TV Technician #40 225-925-6291
Radiographer #16 504-838-5231
Radiologic Technologist #16 504-838-5231
Reading Specialist #42 225-342-3490
Real Estate Appraiser #60 225-925-4771
Real Estate Broker #60 225-925-4771

Real Estate Salesperson #60 225-925-4771
Repairman; Radio/TV/Recording Device #34
....225-231-4710
Repite Care #35 225-022-0015
Residential Mortgage Lenders/Brokers #32
....225-925-4662
Respiratory Therapist #20 504-524-6820
Respiratory Therapy Technician #20.....504-524-6820
Retail and Wholesale Florist #39..........225-925-7772
Sanitarian #17 318-676-7489
Savings & Loan & Credit Union #32 225-925-4660
School Counselor #42 225-342-3490
School Librarian #42 225-342-3490
School Nurse #42 225-342-3490
School Principal #42 225-342-3490
School Psychologist #42 225-342-3490
School Therapist #42 225-342-3490
Securities Dealer #53 225-568-5515
Securities Salesperson #53 225-568-5515
Security Guard #26 225-295-8486
Shorthand Reporter #37 225-219-4732
Social Worker #06 225-763-5470
Solicitor #33 225-342-1216
Speech Pathologist/Audiologist #18 225-763-5480
Speech/Language/Hearing Teachers #42
....225-342-3490
Stable Foreman #52 504-483-4000
Substance Abuse Counselor #28..........225-927-7600
Supervised Independent Living #35 225-022-0015
Surveyor #40 225-925-6291
Teacher/Teacher Aide #11 225-342-3490
Temporary Teacher #42 225-342-3490
Thrifts #32...225-925-4660
Timeshare Interest Salesperson #60.....225-925-4771
Used Vehicle Salesperson #61 225-925-3870
Veterinarian #45 225-342-2176
Veterinary Technician #45 225-342-2176
Vocational Rehabilitative Counselor #63
....225-924-4935
Water Supply #51 504-826-2382
Wholesale Drug Distributor #64 225-295-8567

Licensing Agency Information

01 State Police Safety & Enforcement, PO Box 66614 (PO Box 66614), Baton Rouge, LA 70896; 225-925-6984, Fax: 225-925-3966.

02 Cemetery Board, 2901 Ridgelake Dr, #101, Metairie, LA 70002-4946; 504-838-5267, Fax: 504-838-5289.

03 Board of Alcohol & Tobacco, PO Box 66404 (PO Box 66404), Baton Rouge, LA 70896-6404; 225-925-4041, Fax: 225-925-3975.

www.atcla.com/home.cfm

04 Board of Barber Examiners, PO Box 14029 (PO Box 14029), Baton Rouge, LA 70898-4029; 225-925-1701, Fax: 225-925-1703.

05 Board of Certified Public Accountants, 601 Poydras St, #1770, New Orleans, LA 70130; 504-566-1244, Fax: 504-566-1252.

06 Board of Certified Social Work Examiners, 11930 Perkins Rd, #B, Baton Rouge, LA 70810; 225-763-5470, Fax: 225-763-5400.

www.eatel.net/~bcsw/main.html

07 Board of Chiropractic Examiners, 8621 Summa Ave, Baton Rouge, LA 70809; 225-765-2322, Fax: 225-765-2640.

www.dhh.state.la.us/boards.htm

08 Board of Cosmetology, 11622 Sunbelt Court, Baton Rouge, LA 70809; 225-756-3404, Fax: 225-756-3410/3109.

09 Board of Dentistry, 365 Canal Street, Suite 2680, New Orleans, LA 70112; 504-568-8574, Fax: 504-568-8598.

www.lsbd.org

Direct URL to search licenses: www.lsbd.org/DentistSearch.asp You can search online using name or license #

10 Board of Electrolysis Examiners, PO Box 67 (PO Box 67), DeRidder, LA 70634-0067; 318-463-6180, Fax: 318-463-3991.

11 Board of Elementary & Secondary Education, 626 N 4th St, Baton Rouge, LA 70804-9064; 225-342-3441, Fax: 225-342-3499.

12 Board of Embalmers & Funeral Directors, 3500 N Causeway Blvd, #1232, New Orleans, LA 70002; 504-838-5109, Fax: 504-838-5112.

http://www.lsbefd.state.la.us

13 Board of Examiners of Dietitics & Nutrition, 11930 Perkins Rd, #B, Baton Rouge, LA 70810; 225-763-5490, Fax: 225-763-5400.

14 Board of Examiners of Interior Designers, 2900 Westfork Dr #200, Baton Rouge, LA 70827-0004; 225-925-3921, Fax: 225-925-1892.

15 Board of Examiners of Psychologists, 8280 YMCA Plaza Dr, Bldg 8B, Baton Rouge, LA 70810; 225-763-3935, Fax: 225-763-3968. www.lsbep.org

Direct URL to search licenses: www.lsbep.org You can search online using A list of current members is available on the web site, updated infrequently.

16 Board of Examiners of Radiologic Technologists, 3108 Cleary Ave, #207, Metairie, LA 70002; 504-838-5231, Fax: 504-780-1740.

17 Board of Examiners of Sanitarians, 1525 Fairfield Ave, Rm 569, Shreveport, LA 71101-4388; 318-676-7489, Fax: 318-676-7560.

18 Board of Examiners of Speech/Language Pathology & Audiology, 11930 Perkins Rd, #B, Baton Rouge, LA 70810; 225-763-5480, Fax: 225-763-5400.

www.lbespa.org/

19 Board of Hearing Aid Dealers, PO Box 6016 (2205 Liberty St), Monroe, LA 71211-6016; 318-362-3014, Fax: 318-362-3019.

20 Executive Director, Board of Medical Examiners, 630 Camp St, New Orleans, LA 70130; 504-524-6820, auto response: dial 1, Fax: 504-568-8893.

www.lsbme.org

Direct URL to search licenses: www.lsbme.org/bmeSearch/licenseesearch.asp

21 Board of Nursing, 3510 N Causeway Blvd, #501, Metairie, LA 70002; 504-838-5332, Fax: 504-838-5349.

www.lsbn.state.la.us

22 Board of Optometry Examiners, PO Box 555 (115 B N 13th St), Oakdale, LA 71463; 318-335-2989, Fax: 318-335-2989.

Direct URL to search licenses: www.arbo.org/nodb2000/licsearch.asp You can search online using national database by name, city or state.

23 Board of Pharmacy, 5615 Corporate Blvd, #8E, Baton Rouge, LA 70808; 225-925-6496, Fax: 225-925-6499.

www.labp.com

24 Board of Physical Therapy Examiners, 2014 W Pinhook Rd, #701, Lafayette, LA 70508; 318-262-1043, Fax: 318-262-1054.

www.laptboard.org

25 Board of Practical Nurse Examiners, 3421 N Causeway Blvd, #203, Metairie, LA 70002; 504-838-5791, Fax: 504-838-5279.

26 Board of Private Security Examiners, PO Box 86510 (PO Box 86510), Baton Rouge, LA 70879-6510; 225-295-8486, Fax: 225-295-8498.

27 Boxing & Wrestling Commission, PO Box 251, Franklin, LA 70538; 337-828-7154.

28 Board of Certification for Substance Abuse Counselors, 4637 Jamestown #2A, Baton Rouge, LA 70808; 225-927-7600, Fax: 225-927-8150.

29 Real Estate Appraisers State Board of Certification, PO Box 14785 (9071 Interline Ave), Baton Rouge, LA 70809-4785; 225-925-4771, Fax: 225-925-4431.

30 Contractors Licensing Board, 1221 Elmwood Pk Blvd, New Orleans, LA 70141; 504-736-7125, Fax: 504-736-7125 *Key.

32 Department of Economic Development, Office of Financial Institutions, 8660 United Plaza Blvd, 2nd Floor, Baton Rouge, LA 70809; 225-925-4660, Fax: 225-925-4548.

www.ofi.state.la.us

33 Department of Insurance, Agent's License Division, 950 N 5th, Baton Rouge, LA 70802; 225-342-1216, Fax: 225-342-3078.

34 Radio And Television Technicians Board, 6554 Florida Boulevard #109, Baton Rouge, LA 70806; 225-231-4710.

35 Department of Social Services, Bureau of Licensing, PO Box 3078 (PO Box 3078), Baton Rouge, LA 70821; 225-922-0015, Fax: 225-922-0014.

www.dss.state.la.us/offos/html/licensing.html

36 Examiners of Nursing Facility Administrators, 5615 Corporate Blvd, #8D, Baton Rouge, LA 70808; 225-922-0009, Fax: 225-925-0006.

37 Examiners of Certified Shorthand Reporters, PO Box 3257 (PO Box 3257), Baton Rouge, LA 70821-3257; 225-219-4732, Fax: 225-219-4731.

www.lacourtreporterboard.com

38 Explosives Control Unit, PO Box 66614 (PO Box 66614), Baton Rouge, LA 70896; 225-925-6178 x208, Fax: 225-925-4048.

39 Department of Agriculture, Horticulture Commission, PO Box 3118 (PO Box 3596), Baton Rouge, LA 70821-3596; 225-925-7772, Fax: 225-925-3760.

40 Professional Engineers & Land Surveying Board, 9643 Brookline Ave #121, Baton Rouge, LA 70809-1433; 225-925-6291, Fax: 225-925-6292.

www.lapels.com

Direct URL to search licenses: www.lapels.com/indv_reg.html You can search online using alphabetical lists

41 Licensing Board for Contractors, PO Box 14419 (PO Box 14419), Baton Rouge, LA 70898-4419; 225-765-2301, Fax: 225-765-2431.

42 Department of Education, Licensing Bureau of Higher Education Certification, 626 N 4th St, Baton Rouge, LA 70804-9064; 225-342-3490, Fax: 225-342-3499.

www.doe.state.la.us

43 Livestock Brand Commission, 5825 Florida Blvd, Baton Rouge, LA 70806; 225-925-3980, Fax: 225-925-4103.

44 Auctioneers Licensing Board, 8017 Jefferson Hwy, #A-2, Baton Rouge, LA 70809; 225-922-2329, Fax: 225-925-1892.

45 Board of Veterinary Medicine, 263 3rd St, #104, Baton Rouge, LA 70801; 225-342-2176, Fax: 225-342-2142.

46 Licensed Professional Counselors, Board of Examiners, 8631 Summa Ave, #A, Baton Rouge, LA 70809; 225-765-2515, Fax: 225-765-2514.
www.lpcboard.org

Direct URL to search licenses: www.lpcboard.org/lpc_alpha_list.htm

47 Lottery Corporation, State Headquarters, 11200 Industriplex, #190, Baton Rouge, LA 70809; 225-297-2000, Fax: 225-297-2005.

48 Lottery Corporation, 2222 Clearview Parkway, Metairie, LA 70001; 504-889-0031, Fax: 504-889-0490.

www.louisianalottery.com

49 State Bar Association, PO Box 37200 (614 H St NW, 9th Fl), New Orleans, LA 70130; 504-566-1600, Fax: 504-566-0930.

www.lsba.org

50 Board of Architectural Examiners, 8017 Jefferson Hwy B-2, Baton Rouge, LA 70809; 225-925-4802, Fax: 225-925-4804.
www.lastbdarchs.com

Direct URL to search licenses: www.lastbdarchs.com/roster.htm You can search online using name.

51 Plumbing Board, 2714 Canal St, #512, New Orleans, LA 70119; 504-826-2382, Fax: 504-826-2175.

52 Racing Commission, 320 N Carrollton Ave, #2B, New Orleans, LA 70119-5100; 504-483-4000, Fax: 504-483-4898.

www.lded.state.la.us/new/lrc/lrcmain.htm

53 Securities, Office of Financial Institutions, 8660 United Plaza Blvd, 2nd Fl, Baton Rouge, LA 70809; 225-568-5515.

www.state.la.us/state/dept.htm

54 Office of Secretary of State, PO Box 94125 (PO Box 94125), Baton Rouge, LA 70804-9125; 225-342-4981, Fax: 225-342-2066.
www.sec.state.la.us/notary-pub/notary.htm

Direct URL to search licenses: www.sec.state.la.us/notary-pub/NTRINQ.htm You can search online using alpha or zip code

55 Office of the State Fire Marshall, 5150 Florida Blvd, Baton Rouge, LA 70806; 225-925-4911; 800-256-5452, Fax: 225-925-4241.

www.dps.state.la.us/sfm

56 Agricultural & Environmental Sciences, Pest Control Commission, 5825 Florida Blvd, Baton Rouge, LA 70806; 225-925-3796, Fax: 225-925-3760.

www.ldaf.state.la.us

57 Polygraph Board, 9746 W Wheaton Circle, New Orleans, LA 70127-2236; 504-389-3836.

58 Board of Private Investigators Examiners, 2051 Silverside Dr. #109, Baton Rouge, LA 70808; 225-763-3556, Fax: 225-763-3536.

www.lsbpie.com/

59 Motor Vehicle Commission, 3519 12th Street, Metairie, LA 70002-3427; 504-838-5207.

60 Real Estate Commission, 9071 Interline Ave, Baton Rouge, LA 70809; 225-925-4771, Fax: 225-925-4431.

www.lrec.state.la.us

61 Used Motor Vehicle & Parts Commission, 3132 Valley Creek Drive, Baton Rouge, LA 70808; 225-925-3870, Fax: 225-925-3869.

62 Professional Licensing Boards, Board of Massage Therapy, PO Box 1279 (4707 Main St), Zachary, LA 70791; 225-922-1435, Fax: 225-922-1352.

www.lrcboard.org

63 Board of Examiners, Board of Vocational Rehabilitative Counselors, PO Box 41594 (PO Box 41594), Baton Rouge, LA 70801; 225-924-4935, Fax: 225-924-5073.

64 Board of Wholesale Drug Distributors, 12046 Justice Ave, #C, Baton Rouge, LA 70816; 225-295-8567, Fax: 225-295-8568.
www.lsbwdd.org

Direct URL to search licenses: www.ntgasp.com/ldwdd/search.asp You can search online using name of licensee, dba, or license number.

66 Ethics Board, 8401 United Plaza Blvd #200, Baton Rouge, LA 70809; 225-992-1400 1-800-842-6630, Fax: 225-922-1414.
www.ethics.state.la.us

Direct URL to search licenses: www.ethics.state.la.us/lobs.htm You can search online using Lobbyist and company list; lists are updated irregularly.

The following list indicates the district and division name for each parish in the state. If the district or division name of the bankruptcy court is different from the civil/criminal court, it appears in parentheses.

Parish/Court Cross Reference

Parish	District	Division
Acadia Parish	Western	Lafayette (Lafayette-Opelousas)
Allen Parish	Western	Lake Charles
Ascension Parish	Middle	Baton Rouge
Assumption Parish	Eastern	New Orleans
Avoyelles Parish	Western	Alexandria
Beauregard Parish	Western	Lake Charles
Bienville Parish	Western	Shreveport
Bossier Parish	Western	Shreveport
Caddo Parish	Western	Shreveport
Calcasieu Parish	Western	Lake Charles
Caldwell Parish	Western	Monroe
Cameron Parish	Western	Lake Charles
Catahoula Parish	Western	Alexandria
Claiborne Parish	Western	Shreveport
Concordia Parish	Western	Alexandria
De Soto Parish	Western	Shreveport
East Baton Rouge Parish	Parish	Middle Baton Rouge
East Carroll Parish	Western	Monroe
East Feliciana Parish	Middle	Baton Rouge
Evangeline Parish	Western	Lafayette (Lafayette-Opelousas)
Franklin Parish	Western	Monroe
Grant Parish	Western	Alexandria
Iberia Parish	Western	Lafayette (Lafayette-Opelousas)
Iberville Parish	Middle	Baton Rouge
Jackson Parish	Western	Monroe
Jefferson Davis Parish	Western	Lake Charles
Jefferson Parish	Eastern	New Orleans
La Salle Parish	Western	Alexandria
Lafayette Parish	Western	Lafayette (Lafayette-Opelousas)
Lafourche Parish	Eastern	New Orleans
Lincoln Parish	Western	Monroe
Livingston Parish	Middle	Baton Rouge
Madison Parish	Western	Monroe
Morehouse Parish	Western	Monroe
Natchitoches Parish	Western	Alexandria
Orleans Parish	Eastern	New Orleans
Ouachita Parish	Western	Monroe
Plaquemines Parish	Eastern	New Orleans
Pointe Coupee Parish	Middle	Baton Rouge
Rapides Parish	Western	Alexandria
Red River Parish	Western	Shreveport
Richland Parish	Western	Monroe
Sabine Parish	Western	Shreveport
St. Bernard Parish	Eastern	New Orleans
St. Charles Parish	Eastern	New Orleans
St. Helena Parish	Middle	Baton Rouge
St. James Parish	Eastern	New Orleans
St. John the Baptist Parish	Parish	EasternNew Orleans
St. Landry Parish	Western	Lafayette (Lafayette-Opelousas)
St. Martin Parish	Western	Lafayette (Lafayette-Opelousas)
St. Mary Parish	Western	Lafayette (Lafayette-Opelousas)
St. Tammany Parish	Eastern	New Orleans
Tangipahoa Parish	Eastern	New Orleans
Tensas Parish	Western	Monroe
Terrebonne Parish	Eastern	New Orleans
Union Parish	Western	Monroe
Vermilion Parish	Western	Lafayette (Lafayette-Opelousas)
Vernon Parish	Western	Alexandria
Washington Parish	Eastern	New Orleans
Webster Parish	Western	Shreveport
West Baton Rouge Parish	Parish	Middle Baton Rouge
West Carroll Parish	Western	Monroe
West Feliciana Parish	Middle	Baton Rouge
Winn Parish	Western	Alexandria

US District Court

Eastern District of Louisiana

New Orleans Division Clerk, Room 151, 500 Camp St, New Orleans, LA 70130, 504-589-7650.

www.laed.uscourts.gov

Counties: Assumption Parish, Jefferson Parish, Lafourche Parish, Orleans Parish, Plaquemines Parish, St. Bernard Parish, St. Charles Parish, St. James Parish, St. John the Baptist Parish, St. Tammany Parish, Tangipahoa Parish, Terrebonne Parish, Washington Parish.

Indexing & Storage: Cases are indexed by defendant and plaintiff as well as by case number. New cases are available in the index 1-2 days after filing date. Both computer and card indexes are maintained. Open records are located at this court.

Fee & Payment: The fee is $15.00 per item (one party name or case number). Payment may be made by money order, cashier check, personal check. Prepayment is required. Payee: Clerk, US District Court. Certification fee: $5.00 per document. Copy fee: $.50 per page.

Phone Search: Only docket information is available by phone.

Mail Search: Always enclose a stamped self addressed envelope.

In Person Search: In person searching is available.

PACER: Sign-up number is 800-676-6856. Access fee is $.60 per minute. Toll-free access: 888-257-1175. Local access: 504-589-6714. Case records are available back to 1989. Records are purged every six months. New records are available online after 1-2 days. PACER is available online at http://pacer.laed.uscourts.gov.

US Bankruptcy Court

Eastern District of Louisiana

New Orleans Division Hale Boggs Federal Bldg, 501 Magazine St, #601, New Orleans, LA 70130, 504-589-7878.

www.laeb.uscourts.gov

Counties: Assumption Parish, Jefferson Parish, Lafourche Parish, Orleans Parish, Plaquemines Parish, St. Bernard Parish, St. Charles Parish, St. James Parish, St. John the Baptist Parish, St. Tammany Parish, Tangipahoa Parish, Terrebonne Parish, Washington Parish.

Indexing & Storage: Cases are indexed by debtor as well as by case number. New cases are available in the index 2 days after filing date. Both computer and card indexes are maintained. Records are also indexed on microfiche. Open records are located at this court. District wide searches are available from this court from November 1985 for information in the computer and from 1979 to 1985 on card index.

Fee & Payment: The fee is $15.00 per item (one party name or case number). Payment may be made by money order, cashier check, business check. Personal checks are not accepted. Prepayment is required. Payee: Clerk, US Bankruptcy Court. Certification fee: $5.00 per document. Copy fee: $.50 per page.

Phone Search: Information is available from 9:00 to 10:30 a.m. and 1:00 to 2:30 p.m. over the phone. There is no fee for case status information. Only docket information will be released. An automated voice case information service (VCIS) is available.

Mail Search: Always enclose a stamped self addressed envelope.

In Person Search: In person searching is available.

PACER: Sign-up number is 800-676-6856. Access fee is $.60 per minute. Toll-free access: 800-743-2464. Local access: 504-589-6761. Case records are available back to 1985. Records are purged every six months. New civil records are available online after 2 days. PACER is available on the Internet at http://pacer.laeb.uscourts.gov.

US District Court

Middle District of Louisiana

Baton Rouge Division PO Box 2630, Baton Rouge, LA 70821-2630 (Courier Address: 777 Florida St, Baton Rouge, LA 70801), 225-389-3500, Fax: 225-389-3501.

www.lamd.uscourts.gov

Counties: Ascension Parish, East Baton Rouge Parish, East Feliciana Parish, Iberville Parish, Livingston Parish, Pointe Coupee Parish, St. Helena Parish, West Baton Rouge Parish, West Feliciana Parish.

Indexing & Storage: Cases are indexed by defendant and plaintiff as well as by case number. New cases are available in the index immediately after filing date. A computer index is maintained. Index prior to 1992 is on microfiche and computer. Open records are located at this court.

Fee & Payment: The fee is $15.00 per item (one party name or case number). Payment may be made by money order, cashier check, business check, Visa, Mastercard. Personal checks are not accepted. Prepayment is required. The court has no billing procedures. Payee: Clerk, US District Court. Certification fee: $5.00 per document. Copy fee: $.50 per page. You are allowed to make your own copies. These copies cost $.25 per page. A coin operated copier is installed for the public.

Phone Search: Only docket information is available by phone. If the information is at the Federal Records Center, the court will provide the information needed to review a record. An automated voice case information service (VCIS) is not available.

Mail Search: A stamped self addressed envelope is not required.

In Person Search: In person searching is available.

PACER: Sign-up number is 800-676-6856. Access fee is $.60 per minute. Toll-free access: 800-616-8757. Local access: 225-389-3547. Case records are available back to October 1993. New records are available online after 1 day. PACER is available online at http://pacer.lamd.uscourts.gov.

US Bankruptcy Court

Middle District of Louisiana

Baton Rouge Division Room 119, 707 Florida St, Baton Rouge, LA 70801, 225-389-0211.

www.lamb.uscourts.gov

Counties: Ascension Parish, East Baton Rouge Parish, East Feliciana Parish, Iberville Parish, Livingston Parish, Pointe Coupee Parish, St. Helena Parish, West Baton Rouge Parish, West Feliciana Parish.

Indexing & Storage: Cases are indexed by debtor and creditors as well as by case number. New cases are available in the index immediately after filing date. A computer index is maintained. Open records are located at this court.

Fee & Payment: The fee is $15.00 per item (one party name or case number). Payment may be made by money order, cashier check, business check. Personal checks are not accepted. Prepayment is required. Payee: Clerk, US Bankruptcy Court. Certification fee: $5.00 per document. Copy fee: $.50 per page. You are allowed to make your own copies. These copies cost $.25 per page.

Phone Search: Only docket information is available by phone. An automated voice case information service (VCIS) is available.

Mail Search: Always enclose a stamped self addressed envelope.

In Person Search: In person searching is available.

PACER: Sign-up number is 800-676-6856. Access fee is $.60 per minute. Case records are available back to May 15, 1992. New civil records are available online after 1 day. PACER is available online at http://pacer.lamb.uscourts.gov.

US District Court

Western District of Louisiana

Alexandria Division PO Box 1269, Alexandria, LA 71309 (Courier Address: 515 Murray, Alexandria, LA 71301), 318-473-7415, Fax: 318-473-7345.

www.lawd.uscourts.gov

Counties: Avoyelles Parish, Catahoula Parish, Concordia Parish, Grant Parish, La Salle Parish, Natchitoches Parish, Rapides Parish, Winn Parish.

Indexing & Storage: Cases are indexed by defendant and plaintiff as well as by case number. New cases are available in the index 3 days after filing date. A computer index is maintained. Open records are located at this court.

Fee & Payment: The fee is $15.00 per item (one party name or case number). Payment may be made by money order, cashier check, personal check. Prepayment is required. Payee: Clerk, US District Court. Certification fee: $5.00 per document. Copy fee: $.50 per page.

Phone Search: Only docket information is available by phone. An automated voice case information service (VCIS) is not available.

Mail Search: Always enclose a stamped self addressed envelope.

In Person Search: In person searching is available.

PACER: Sign-up number is 800-676-6856. Access fee is $.60 per minute. Toll-free access: 888-263-2679. Local access: 318-676-3958. Case records are available back to October 1993. Records are purged as deemed necessary. New records are available online after 1 day. PACER is available online at https://pacer.lawd.uscourts.gov.

Lafayette Division Room 113, Federal Bldg, 705 Jefferson St, Lafayette, LA 70501, 337-593-5000.

www.lawd.uscourts.gov

Counties: Acadia Parish, Evangeline Parish, Iberia Parish, Lafayette Parish, St. Landry Parish, St. Martin Parish, St. Mary Parish, Vermilion Parish.

Indexing & Storage: Cases are indexed by defendant and plaintiff as well as by case number. New cases are available in the index 1 day after filing date. A computer index is maintained. Open records are located at this court.

Fee & Payment: The fee is no charge per item (one party name or case number). Payment may be made by money order, cashier check, business check. Personal checks are not accepted. Prepayment is required. Payee: Clerk, US District Court. Certification fee: $5.00 per document. Copy fee: $.50 per page.

Phone Search: Only docket information is available by phone. An automated voice case information service (VCIS) is not available.

Mail Search: Certified name searches can only be performed from the Shreveport office. A stamped self addressed envelope is not required.

In Person Search: In person searching is available.

PACER: Sign-up number is 800-676-6856. Access fee is $.60 per minute. Toll-free access: 888-263-2679. Local access: 318-676-3958. Case records are available back to October 1993. Records are purged as deemed necessary. New records are available online after 1 day. PACER is available online at https://pacer.lawd.uscourts.gov.

Lake Charles Division 611 Broad St, Suite 188, Lake Charles, LA 70601, 337-437-3870.

www.lawd.uscourts.gov

Counties: Allen Parish, Beauregard Parish, Calcasieu Parish, Cameron Parish, Jefferson Davis Parish, Vernon Parish.

Indexing & Storage: Cases are indexed by defendant and plaintiff as well as by case number. New cases are available in the index 3 days after filing date. A computer index is maintained. Open records are located at this court.

Fee & Payment: The fee is $15.00 per item (one party name or case number). Payment may be made by money order, cashier check, business check. Personal checks are not accepted. Prepayment is required. Payee: Clerk, US District Court. Certification fee: $5.00 per document. Copy fee: $.50 per page.

Phone Search: Only docket information is available by phone. An automated voice case information service (VCIS) is not available.

Mail Search: Always enclose a stamped self addressed envelope.

In Person Search: In person searching is available.

PACER: Sign-up number is 800-676-6856. Access fee is $.60 per minute. Toll-free access: 888-263-2679. Local access: 318-676-3958. Case records are available back to October 1993. Records are purged as deemed necessary. New records are available online after 1 day. PACER is available online at https://pacer.lawd.uscourts.gov.

Monroe Division PO Drawer 3087, Monroe, LA 71210 (Courier Address: Room 215, 201 Jackson St, Monroe, LA 71201), 318-322-6740.

www.lawd.uscourts.gov

Counties: Caldwell Parish, East Carroll Parish, Franklin Parish, Jackson Parish, Lincoln Parish, Madison Parish, Morehouse Parish, Ouachita

Parish, Richland Parish, Tensas Parish, Union Parish, West Carroll Parish.

Indexing & Storage: Cases are indexed by defendant and plaintiff as well as by case number. New cases are available in the index 3 days after filing date. The Shreveport computerized index is used for searching. A computer index is maintained. Open records are located at this court. This division has been without a judge since 1996, and may not be getting one. Therefore, there are very few case records held here any longer. It is recommended to search at the Shreveport division.

Fee & Payment: The fee is $15.00 per item (one party name or case number). Payment may be made by money order, cashier check, business check. Personal checks are not accepted. Prepayment is required. Payee: Clerk, US District Court. Certification fee: $5.00 per document. Copy fee: $.50 per page.

Phone Search: Only docket information is available by phone. An automated voice case information service (VCIS) is not available.

Mail Search: Always enclose a stamped self addressed envelope.

In Person Search: In person searching is available.

PACER: Sign-up number is 800-676-6856. Access fee is $.60 per minute. Toll-free access: 888-263-2679. Local access: 318-676-3958. Case records are available back to October 1993. Records are purged as deemed necessary. New records are available online after 1 day. PACER is available online at https://pacer.lawd.uscourts.gov.

Shreveport Division
US Courthouse, Suite 1167, 300 Fannin St, Shreveport, LA 71101-3083, 318-676-4273.

www.lawd.uscourts.gov

Counties: Bienville Parish, Bossier Parish, Caddo Parish, Claiborne Parish, De Soto Parish, Red River Parish, Sabine Parish, Webster Parish.

Indexing & Storage: Cases are indexed by defendant and plaintiff as well as by case number. New cases are available in the index immediately after filing date. A computer index is maintained. On computer are cases that were filed in 1977 or later. Copies from closed records in cases filed in 1977 or later are available from microfiche located at this court. Open records are located at this court.

Fee & Payment: The fee is $15.00 per item (one party name or case number). Payment may be made by money order, cashier check, business check. Personal checks are not accepted. Prepayment is required. Payee: Clerk, US District Court. Certification fee: $5.00 per document. Copy fee: $.50 per page.

Phone Search: Only docket information is available by phone. If the information is at the Federal Records Center, the court will provide the information needed to review a record. An automated voice case information service (VCIS) is not available.

Mail Search: A stamped self addressed envelope is not required.

In Person Search: In person searching is available.

PACER: Sign-up number is 800-676-6856. Access fee is $.60 per minute. Toll-free access: 888-263-2679. Local access: 318-676-3958. Case records are available back to October 1993. Records are purged as deemed necessary. New records are available online after 1 day. PACER is available online at https://pacer.lawd.uscourts.gov.

US Bankruptcy Court
Western District of Louisiana

Alexandria Division 300 Jackson St, Suite 116, Alexandria, LA 71301-8357 (Courier Address: Hemenway Bldg, 300 Jackson St, Alexandria, LA 71301), 318-445-1890.

www.lawb.uscourts.gov

Counties: Avoyelles Parish, Catahoula Parish, Concordia Parish, Grant Parish, La Salle Parish, Natchitoches Parish, Rapides Parish, Vernon Parish, Winn Parish.

Indexing & Storage: Cases are indexed by debtor as well as by case number. New cases are available in the index 1 day after filing date. Chapter 7 and 11 cases from the Monroe Division are now at this court. Chapter 12 and Chapter 13 continue to be handled by Shreveport. A computer index is maintained. Open records are located at this court.

Fee & Payment: The fee is $15.00 per item (one party name or case number). Payment may be made by money order, cashier check, personal check. A copy service will also do the search and copies at $5.00 for the search fee and $.25 per page plus cost of postage. The copy service will bill law firms. Payee: Clerk, US Bankruptcy Court or copy service. Certification fee: $5.00 per document. The fee for copies made by court personnel is $.50 per page.

Phone Search: Only docket information is available by phone. An automated voice case information service (VCIS) is available. Call VCIS at 800-326-4026 or 318-676-4234.

Mail Search: A stamped self addressed envelope is not required.

In Person Search: In person searching is available.

PACER: Sign-up number is 800-676-6856. Access fee is $.60 per minute. Toll-free access: 888-523-1976. Local access: 318-676-4235. Case records are available back to 1992. New civil records are available online after 1 day. PACER is available online at http://pacer.lawb.uscourts.gov.

Lafayette-Opelousas Division PO Box J, Opelousas, LA 70571-1909 (Courier Address: Room 205, 250 S Union, Opelousas, LA 70570), 318-948-3451, Fax: 318-948-4426.

www.lawb.uscourts.gov

Counties: Acadia Parish, Evangeline Parish, Iberia Parish, Lafayette Parish, St. Landry Parish, St. Martin Parish, St. Mary Parish, Vermilion Parish.

Indexing & Storage: Cases are indexed by debtor as well as by case number. New cases are available in the index 1 day after filing date. Both computer and card indexes are maintained. Records are indexed on index cards for pre-1987 files only. Records are also indexed on microfiche. Open records are located at this court. District wide searches are available for information from January 1, 1986 from this division. This office handles case records for the Lake Charles Division also.

Fee & Payment: The fee is $15.00 per item (one party name or case number). Payment may be made by money order, cashier check, business check. Personal checks are not accepted. Prepayment is required. Payee: Clerk, US Bankruptcy Court. Certification fee: $5.00 per document. Copy fee: $.50 per page.

Phone Search: Only docket information is available by phone. An automated voice case information service (VCIS) is available. Call VCIS at 800-326-4026 or 318-676-4234.

Mail Search: A stamped self addressed envelope is not required.

In Person Search: In person searching is available.

PACER: Sign-up number is 800-676-6856. Access fee is $.60 per minute. Toll-free access: 888-523-1976. Local access: 318-676-4235. Case records are available back to 1992. New civil records are available online after 1 day. PACER is available online at http://pacer.lawb.uscourts.gov.

Lake Charles Division c/o Lafayette-Opelousas Division, PO Box J, Opelousas, LA 70571-1909 (Courier Address: Room 205, 250 S Union, Opelousas, LA 70570), 318-948-3451.

www.lawb.uscourts.gov

Counties: Allen Parish, Beauregard Parish, Calcasieu Parish, Cameron Parish, Jefferson Davis Parish.

Indexing & Storage: Cases are indexed by as well as by case number. New cases are available in the index after filing date. Open records are located at the Division.

Fee & Payment: The fee is no charge per item (one party name or case number). Payment may be made by money order, cashier check. Business checks are not accepted. Personal checks are not accepted.

Phone Search: An automated voice case information service (VCIS) is available. Call VCIS at 800-326-4026 or 318-676-4234.

In Person Search: In person searching is available.

PACER: Sign-up number is 800-676-6856. Access fee is $.60 per minute. Toll-free access: 888-523-1976. Local access: 318-676-4235. Case records are available back to 1992. New civil records are available online after 1 day. PACER is available online at http://pacer.lawb.uscourts.gov.

Monroe Division c/o Shreveport Division, Suite 2201, 300 Fannin St, Shreveport, LA 71101, 318-676-4267.

www.lawb.uscourts.gov

Counties: Caldwell Parish, East Carroll Parish, Franklin Parish, Jackson Parish, Lincoln Parish, Madison Parish, Morehouse Parish, Ouachita Parish, Richland Parish, Tensas Parish, Union Parish, West Carroll Parish.

Indexing & Storage: Cases are indexed by as well as by case number. New cases are available in the index after filing date. This court is an unmanned office. Cases are housed as follows: Chapter 7 and Chapter 11 cases to Alexandria; Chapter 12 and Chapter 13 cases to Shreveport. Open records are located at the Division.

Fee & Payment: The fee is no charge per item (one party name or case number). Payment may be made by money order. Business checks are not accepted. Personal checks are not accepted.

Phone Search: An automated voice case information service (VCIS) is available. Call VCIS at 800-326-4026 or 318-676-4234.

In Person Search: In person searching is available.

PACER: Sign-up number is 800-676-6856. Access fee is $.60 per minute. Toll-free access: 888-523-1976. Local access: 318-676-4235. Case records are available back to 1992. New civil records are available online after 1 day. PACER is available online at http://pacer.lawb.uscourts.gov.

Shreveport Division Suite 2201, 300 Fannin St, Shreveport, LA 71101-3089, 318-676-4267.

www.lawb.uscourts.gov

Counties: Bienville Parish, Bossier Parish, Caddo Parish, Claiborne Parish, De Soto Parish, Red River Parish, Sabine Parish, Webster Parish.

Indexing & Storage: Cases are indexed by as well as by case number. New cases are available in the index immediately after filing date. A computer index is maintained. Open records are located at this court.

Fee & Payment: The fee is $15.00 per item (one party name or case number). Payment may be made by money order, business check. Personal checks are not accepted. Prepayment is required. Debtor's checks are not accepted. Payee: Clerk, US Bankruptcy Court. Certification fee: $5.00 per document. Copy fee: $.50 per page.

Phone Search: An automated voice case information service (VCIS) is available. Call VCIS at 800-326-4026 or 318-676-4234.

Mail Search: Always enclose a stamped self addressed envelope.

In Person Search: In person searching is available.

PACER: Sign-up number is 800-676-6856. Access fee is $.60 per minute. Toll-free access: 888-523-1976. Local access: 318-676-4235. Case records are available back to 1992. New civil records are available online after 1 day. PACER is available online at http://pacer.lawb.uscourts.gov.

Court	Jurisdiction	No. of Courts	How Organized
District Courts*	General	65	42 Districts
New Orleans City Court*	Limited	1	City of New Orleans
City and Parish Courts	Limited	52	
Justice of the Peace Courts	Municipal	390	
Mayor's Courts	Municipal	250	
Family Court	Special	1	Baton Rouge
Juvenile Courts	Special	4	

* Profiled in this Sourcebook.

Court	CIVIL								
	Tort	Contract	Real Estate	Min. Claim	Max. Claim	Small Claims	Estate	Eviction	Domestic Relations
District Courts*	X	X	X	$0	No Max		X		X
New Orleans City Court*	X	X	X	$0	$20,000	$2000			X
City and Parish Courts	X	X	X	$0	$15,000	$2000		X	X
Justice of the Peace Courts	X	X	X	$0	$2000	$2000		X	
Mayor's Courts									
Family Court									X
Juvenile Courts									X

Court	CRIMINAL				
	Felony	Misdemeanor	DWI/DUI	Preliminary Hearing	Juvenile
District Courts*	X	X	X		X
New Orleans City Court*		X	X	X	X
City and Parish Courts		X	X	X	X
Justice of the Peace Courts					
Mayor's Courts					
Family Court					X
Juvenile Courts					X

ADMINISTRATION   Judicial Administrator, Judicial Council of the Supreme Court, 301 Loyola Av Room 109, New Orleans, LA, 70012-1814; 504-568-5747 www.lasc.org

COURT STRUCTURE   A District Court Clerk in each Parish holds all the records for that Parish. Each Parish has its own clerk and courthouse.

ONLINE ACCESS   The online computer system, Case Management Information System (CMIS), is operating and development is continuing. It is for internal use only; there is no plan to permit online access to the public. There are a number of Parishes that do offer a means of remote online access to the public.

Acadia Parish

15th District Court PO Box 922, Crowley, LA 70527; 337-788-8881; Fax: 337-788-1048. Hours: 8:30AM-4:30PM (CST). *Felony, Misdemeanor, Civil, Probate.*

Civil Records: Access: Phone, fax, mail, in person. Both court and visitors may perform in person searches. Search fee: $11.00 per name per year. Required to search: name, years to search. Civil cases indexed by defendant, plaintiff. Civil records on computer from 1979, archived from 1800s. Copy of check must be faxed with request. **Criminal Records:** Access: Phone, fax, mail, in person. Both court and visitors may perform in person searches. Search fee: $11.00 per name per year. Required to search: name, years to search, DOB; also helpful-SSN. Criminal records on computer from 1979, archived from 1800s. Copy of check must be faxed with request. **General Information:** No adoption or juvenile records released. SASE required. Turnaround time 1-2 days. Copy fee: $2.00 per page. Certification fee: $6.00. Fee payee: Acadia Parish Clerk of Court. Personal checks accepted. Prepayment is required. Public access terminal is available.

Allen Parish

33rd District Court PO Box 248, Oberlin, LA 70655; 337-639-4351; Fax: 337-639-2030. Hours: 8AM-4:30PM (CST). *Felony, Misdemeanor, Civil, Probate.*

Civil Records: Access: Fax, mail, in person. Both court and visitors may perform in person searches. Search fee: $10.00 per name. Fee is for a 10 year search. Required to search: name, years to search. Civil cases indexed by defendant, plaintiff. Civil records archived back to 1913. **Criminal Records:** Access: Mail, in person. Both court and visitors may perform in person searches. Search fee: $10.00 per name. Fee is for a 10 year search. Required to search: name, years to search, DOB, SSN. Criminal records archived back to 1913. **General Information:** No adoption or juvenile records released. SASE requested. Turnaround time 2 days. Copy fee: $1.00 per page. Certification fee: $2.00. Fee payee: Allen Parish Clerk of Court. Personal checks accepted. Prepayment is required. Fax notes: $2.00 per page.

Ascension Parish

23rd District Court PO Box 192, Donaldsonville, LA 70346; 225-473-9866; Fax: 225-473-8641. Hours: 8:30AM-4:30PM (CST). *Felony, Misdemeanor, Civil, Probate.*

Civil Records: Access: Fax, mail, in person. Both court and visitors may perform in person searches. Search fee: $10.00 per name. Required to search: name, years to search. Civil cases indexed by defendant, plaintiff. Civil records on computer from 1987, index books back to 1800s, proprty tax since 1994, mortgage sice 11/77. **Criminal Records:** Access: Fax, mail, in person. Both court and visitors may perform in person searches. Search fee: $10.00 per name. Required to search: name, years to search, DOB; also helpful-SSN. Criminal Records computerized since 11/86. **General Information:** No adoption or juvenile records released. SASE requested. Turnaround time 2 days. Copy fee: $1.00 per page. Certification fee: $3.00. Fee payee: Ascension Parish Clerk of Court. Personal checks accepted. Prepayment is required. Public access terminal is available. Fax notes: $5.00 for first page, $1.00 each addl. Add $5.00 on search fee if request by fax.

Assumption Parish

23rd District Court PO Box 249, Napoleonville, LA 70390; 504-369-6653; Fax: 504-369-2032. Hours: 8:30AM-4:30PM (CST). *Felony, Misdemeanor, Civil, Probate.*

Civil Records: Access: Fax, mail, in person. Both court and visitors may perform in person searches. Search fee: $10.00 per name. Required to search: name, years to search. Civil cases indexed by defendant, plaintiff. Civil records archived back to 1800s. **Criminal Records:** Access: Fax, mail, in person. Both court and visitors may perform in person searches. Search fee: $10.00 per name. Required to search: name, years to search, DOB. Criminal records archived back to 1800s. **General Information:** No adoption or juvenile records released. SASE requested. Turnaround time 1 day. Copy fee: $1.00 per page. Certification fee: $4.00. Fee payee: Assumption Parish Clerk of Court. Personal checks accepted. Prepayment is required. Fax notes: $2.00 for first page, $1.00 each addl.

Avoyelles Parish

12th District Court PO Box 219, Marksville, LA 71351; 318-253-7523. Hours: 8:30AM-4:30PM (CST). *Felony, Misdemeanor, Civil, Probate.*

Civil Records: Access: Mail, in person. Both court and visitors may perform in person searches. Search fee: $10.00 per name. Required to search: name, years to search. Civil cases indexed by defendant, plaintiff. Civil records on computer from 1985, microfiche back to 1800s. **Criminal Records:** Access: Mail, in person. Both court and visitors may perform in person searches. Search fee: $10.00 per name. Required to search: name, years to search, DOB; also helpful-SSN. Criminal records on computer from 1985, microfiche back to 1800s. **General Information:** No adoption or juvenile records released. SASE not required. Turnaround time 1 day. Copy fee: $1.00 per page. Certification fee: $3.00 per page. Fee payee: Clerk of Court. Personal checks accepted. Prepayment is required.

Beauregard Parish

36th District Court PO Box 1148, DeRidder, LA 70634; 337-463-8595; Fax: 337-462-3916. Hours: 8AM-4:30PM (CST). *Felony, Misdemeanor, Civil, Probate.*

Civil Records: Access: Mail, in person. Both court and visitors may perform in person searches. Search fee: $15.00 per name. Fee is per 10 years searched. Required to search: name, years to search. Civil cases indexed by defendant, plaintiff. Civil records on computer since 1985, archived from 1913. **Criminal Records:** Access: Mail, in person. Both court and visitors may perform in person searches. Search fee: $15.00 per name. Fee is per 10 years searched. Required to search: name, years to search, DOB; also helpful-SSN. Criminal records on computer since 1985, archived from 1913. **General Information:** No adoption or juvenile records released. SASE required. Turnaround time 1 wk. Copy fee: $.50 per page. Certification fee: $2.25. Fee payee: Clerk of Court. Personal checks accepted. Prepayment is required.

Bienville Parish

2nd District Court 100 Courthouse Dr, #100, Arcadia, LA 71001; 318-263-2123; Fax: 318-263-7405. Hours: 8:30AM-4:30PM (CST). *Felony, Misdemeanor, Civil, Probate.*

Civil Records: Access: Fax, mail, in person. Both court and visitors may perform in person searches.

Search fee: $10.00 per name. Required to search: name, years to search. Civil cases indexed by defendant, plaintiff. Civil records on computer from 1991, index books prior. **Criminal Records:** Access: Fax, mail, in person. Both court and visitors may perform in person searches. Search fee: $10.00 per name. Required to search: name, years to search, DOB; also helpful-SSN. Criminal records on computer from 1991, index books prior. **General Information:** No adoption or juvenile records released. SASE not required. Turnaround time 2-3 days. Copy fee: $.50 per page. Certification fee: $2.50. Fee payee: Clerk of Court. Personal checks accepted. Prepayment is required. Fax notes: $3.00 per page.

Bossier Parish

26th District Court PO Box 430, Benton, LA 71006; 318-965-2336; Fax: 318-965-2713. Hours: 8:30AM-4:30PM (CST). *Felony, Misdemeanor, Civil, Probate.*

www.ebrclerkofcourt.org

Civil Records: Access: Mail, online, in person. Both court and visitors may perform in person searches. Search fee: $15.00 per name. Required to search: name, years to search. Civil cases indexed by defendant, plaintiff. Civil records on computer from 1987, index books back to 1843. The online system for Parish Clerk of Court records is open 24 hours daily. The setup fee is $100, the monthly minimum is $15 plus $.33 per minute if you view, $.50 if you print. Civil, criminal, probate (1988 forward), traffic and domestic index information is available by name or case number. Call Wendie Gibbs at 225-389-5295 for more information. **Criminal Records:** Access: Mail, remote online, in person. Both court and visitors may perform in person searches. Search fee: $15.00 per name. Required to search: name, years to search. Criminal records on computer since 1982. **General Information:** No adoption or juvenile records released. SASE requested. Turnaround time 4-5 days. Copy fee: $.50 per page. Certification fee: $2.00. Fee payee: Clerk of Court. Business checks accepted. Prepayment is required. Public access terminal is available.

Caddo Parish

1st District Court 501 Texas St, Rm 103, Shreveport, LA 71101-5408; 318-226-6780; Fax: 318-227-9080. Hours: 8:30AM-5PM (CST). *Felony, Misdemeanor, Civil, Probate.*

Civil Records: Access: Mail, in person. Both court and visitors may perform in person searches. Search fee: $10.00 per name. Fee is $5.00 for second name on same search request. Required to search: name, years to search. Civil cases indexed by defendant, plaintiff. Civil records on computer from 1984. **Criminal Records:** Access: Mail, in person. Both court and visitors may perform in person searches. Search fee: $10.00 per name. Fee is $5.00 for second name on same search request. Required to search: name, years to search, DOB; also helpful-SSN. Criminal records on computer from 1984. **General Information:** No adoption or juvenile records released. SASE required. Turnaround time 1-2 days. Copy fee: $.50 per page. Certification fee: $2.00. Fee payee: Clerk of Court. Personal checks accepted. Prepayment is required. Public access terminal is available.

Calcasieu Parish

14th District Court PO Box 1030, Lake Charles, LA 70602; 337-437-3550; Fax: 337-437-3350/3833. Hours: 8:30AM-4:30PM (CST). *Felony, Misdemeanor, Civil, Probate.*

Civil Records: Access: Fax, mail, in person. Both court and visitors may perform in person searches. Search fee: $10.00 per name. Additional fee of $2.00 per year after 1st 10 years. Required to search: name, years to search. Civil cases indexed by defendant, plaintiff. Civil records on computer since 1987. Criminal Records: Access: Mail, in person. Both court and visitors may perform in person searches. Search fee: $10.00 per name. Additional fee of $2.00 per year after 1st 10 years. Required to search: name, years to search, DOB; also helpful-SSN. Criminal records on computer since 1987. General Information: No adoption or juvenile records released. SASE required. Turnaround time 1 wk. Copy fee: $1.00 per page. Certification fee: $5.00. Fee payee: Clerk of Court. Personal checks accepted. Prepayment is required. Public access terminal is available. Fax notes: $7.00 for first page, $2.00 each addl. Fax available for civil division only.

Caldwell Parish

37th District Court PO Box 1327, Columbia, LA 71418; 318-649-2272; Fax: 318-649-2037. Hours: 8AM-4:30PM (CST). *Felony, Misdemeanor, Civil, Probate.*

Note: All record requests must be in writing

Civil Records: Access: Fax, mail, in person. Both court and visitors may perform in person searches. Search fee: $10.00 per name. Required to search: name, years to search. Civil cases indexed by defendant, plaintiff. Civil records on books from 1970, computerized since 11/84. Criminal Records: Access: Mail, in person. Only the court conducts in person searches; visitors may not. Search fee: $10.00 per name. Required to search: name, years to search, DOB; also helpful-SSN. Criminal Records kept on books since 1970. General Information: No adoption or juvenile records released. SASE not required. Turnaround time 1 week. Copy fee: $1.00 per page. Certification fee: $2.00 plus $1.00 per page. Fee payee: Clerk of Court. Personal checks accepted. Prepayment is required. Fax notes: $3.00 for first page, $1.00 each addl.

Cameron Parish

38th District Court PO Box 549, Cameron, LA 70631; 337-775-5316; Fax: 337-775-7172. Hours: 8:30AM-4:30PM (CST). *Felony, Misdemeanor, Civil, Probate.*

Civil Records: Access: Mail, in person. Both court and visitors may perform in person searches. No search fee. Required to search: name, years to search. Civil cases indexed by defendant, plaintiff. Civil records from 1874. Criminal Records: Access: Fax, mail, in person. Only the court conducts in person searches; visitors may not. No search fee. Required to search: name, years to search, DOB. Criminal records from 1874. General Information: No adoption, interdiction or juvenile records released. SASE required. Turnaround time 2 days. Copy fee: $1.00 per page. Certification fee: $5.00. Fee payee: Cameron Parish Clerk of Court. Personal checks accepted. Fax notes: $1.00 per page.

Catahoula Parish

7th District Court PO Box 198, Harrisonburg, LA 71340; 318-744-5222; Fax: 318-744-5488. Hours: 8AM-4:30PM (CST). *Felony, Misdemeanor, Civil, Probate.*

Civil Records: Access: Mail, in person. Both court and visitors may perform in person searches. Search fee: $25.00 per name. Fee is for 10 year search. Required to search: name, years to search.

Civil cases indexed by defendant, plaintiff. Minute entries back to 1800s. Criminal Records: Access: Mail, in person. Both court and visitors may perform in person searches. Search fee: $25.00 per name. Fee is for 10 year search. Required to search: name, years to search, DOB. Minute entries back to 1800s. General Information: No adoption or juvenile records released. SASE required. Turnaround time 1-2 weeks. Copy fee: $1.00 per page. Certification fee: $5.00. Fee payee: Clerk of Court. Personal checks accepted. Prepayment is required.

Claiborne Parish

2nd District Court PO Box 330, Homer, LA 71040; 318-927-9601; Fax: 318-927-2345. Hours: 8:30AM-4:30PM (CST). *Felony, Misdemeanor, Civil, Probate.*

Civil Records: Access: Mail, in person. Both court and visitors may perform in person searches. Search fee: $10.00 per name. Required to search: name, years to search. Civil cases indexed by defendant, plaintiff. Civil records on index books back to early 1900s. Criminal Records: Access: Mail, in person. Both court and visitors may perform in person searches. Search fee: $10.00 per name. Required to search: name, years to search, DOB; also helpful-SSN. Criminal records on computer since 1993, archived prior. General Information: No adoption or juvenile records released. SASE required. Turnaround time 1-2 days. Copy fee: $1.00 per page. Certification fee: $2.50. Fee payee: Clerk of Court. Personal checks accepted. Prepayment is required.

Concordia Parish

7th District Court PO Box 790, Vidalia, LA 71373; 318-336-4204; Fax: 318-336-8217. Hours: 8:30AM-4:30PM (CST). *Felony, Misdemeanor, Civil, Probate.*

Civil Records: Access: Fax, mail, in person. Both court and visitors may perform in person searches. Search fee: $25.00 per name. Required to search: name, years to search. Civil cases indexed by defendant, plaintiff. Civil records on computer from 1983, index books back to 1800s. Criminal Records: Access: Mail, in person. Both court and visitors may perform in person searches. Search fee: $25.00 per name. Required to search: name, years to search, DOB; also helpful-SSN. Criminal records on computer from 1983, index books back to 1800s. General Information: No adoption or juvenile records released. SASE not required. Turnaround time 3-4 days. Copy fee: $1.00 per page. Certification fee: $6.50. Fee payee: Clerk of Court. Personal checks accepted. Prepayment is required. Public access terminal is available. Fax notes: $5.00 per document. Fax available for civil division only.

De Soto Parish

11th District Court PO Box 1206, Mansfield, LA 71052; 318-872-3110; Fax: 318-872-4202. Hours: 8AM-4:30PM (CST). *Felony, Misdemeanor, Civil, Probate.*

Civil Records: Access: Mail, in person. Both court and visitors may perform in person searches. Search fee: $10.00 per name. Required to search: name, years to search. Civil cases indexed by defendant, plaintiff. Civil records on computer from 1985, index books back to 1800s. Criminal Records: Access: Mail, in person. Both court and visitors may perform in person searches. Search fee: $10.00 per name. Required to search: name, years to search, DOB. Criminal records on computer since 1991, archived or in books prior.

General Information: No adoption or juvenile records released. SASE Required. Turnaround time 1-2 days. Copy fee: $1.00 per page. Certification fee: $3.50. Fee payee: Clerk of Court. Personal checks accepted. Prepayment is required. Public access terminal is available.

East Baton Rouge Parish

19th District Court PO Box 1991, Baton Rouge, LA 70821; 225-389-3950; Fax: 225-389-3392. Hours: 7:30AM-5:30PM (CST). *Felony, Misdemeanor, Civil, Probate.*

www.16thcircuit.org

Civil Records: Access: Fax, mail, online, in person. Both court and visitors may perform in person searches. Search fee: $3.00 per name per year. Required to search: name, years to search. Civil cases indexed by defendant, plaintiff. Civil records in index books from 1942. Contact Becki Fortune at 816-881-3411 for information about remote access. No fee for service, but request to sign up must be on company letterhead and include indication of the business you are in. Fax requests to 816-851-3148. This court also participates in a free Internet access to name, case number or filing date queries at http://168.166.59.61/casenet/welcome.asp. Criminal Records: Access: Fax, mail, remote online, in person. Both court and visitors may perform in person searches. Search fee: $20.00 per name. Required to search: name, years to search, DOB; also helpful-SSN. Criminal records in index books from 1942. General Information: No adoption or juvenile records released. SASE required. Turnaround time 2-3 days. Copy fee: $.50 per page. Criminal record copy fee is $1.00 per page. Certification fee: $5.00. Fee payee: Civil Records. Personal checks accepted. Prepayment is required. Public access terminal is available. Fax notes: $2.00 per page.

East Carroll Parish

6th District Court 400 1st St, Lake Providence, LA 71254; 318-559-2388. Hours: 8:30AM-4:30PM (CST). *Felony, Misdemeanor, Civil, Probate.*

Civil Records: Access: Mail, in person. Both court and visitors may perform in person searches. Search fee: $10.00 per name. Required to search: name, years to search. Civil cases indexed by defendant, plaintiff. Civil records on index books back to 1832. Criminal Records: Access: Mail, in person. Both court and visitors may perform in person searches. Search fee: $10.00 per name. Required to search: name, years to search, DOB; also helpful-SSN. Criminal records on index books back to 1832. General Information: No adoption or juvenile records released. SASE required. Turnaround time same day. Copy fee: $1.00 per page. Certification fee: $2.00. Fee payee: Clerk of Court. Personal checks accepted. Prepayment is required.

East Feliciana Parish

20th District Court PO Box 599, Clinton, LA 70722; 225-683-5145; Fax: 225-683-3556. Hours: 8AM-4:30PM (CST). *Felony, Misdemeanor, Civil, Probate.*

Civil Records: Access: Fax, mail, in person. Both court and visitors may perform in person searches. Search fee: $10.00 per name per year. Required to search: name, years to search; also helpful-address. Civil cases indexed by defendant, plaintiff. Civil records on computer from 1988, index books back to 1800s. State which years to search. Criminal Records: Access: Fax, mail, in person. Both court and visitors may perform in person searches. Search fee: $10.00 per name per year. Required to search: name, years to search; also helpful-address, DOB. Criminal records on computer from 1988, index books back to 1800s. State which years to search. **General Information:** No adoption or juvenile records released. Turnaround time 1-2 days. Copy fee: $1.00 per page. Certification fee: $5.00. Fee payee: Clerk of Court. Personal checks accepted. Prepayment is required. Public access terminal is available. Fax notes: $5.00 for first page, $1.00 each addl.

Evangeline Parish

13th District Court PO Drawer 347, Ville Platte, LA 70586; 337-363-5671; Fax: 337-363-5780. Hours: 8AM-4:30PM (CST). *Felony, Misdemeanor, Civil, Probate.*

Civil Records: Access: Fax, mail, in person. Both court and visitors may perform in person searches. Search fee: $10.00 per name. Fee is for first 7 years searched. Add $2.00 per additional year. Required to search: name, years to search. Civil cases indexed by defendant, plaintiff. Civil records on computer since 1/1/89; prior records archived from 1911. **Criminal Records:** Access: Fax, mail, in person. Both court and visitors may perform in person searches. Search fee: $10.00 per name. Fee is for first 7 years searched. Add $2.00 per additional year. Required to search: name, years to search; also helpful-DOB, SSN. Criminal records on computer since 11/1/97, prior records archived from 1911. **General Information:** No adoption or juvenile records released. Turnaround time 1-2 days. Copy fee: $.75 per page. Certification fee: $2.00 per page. Fee payee: Clerk of Court. Personal checks accepted. Prepayment is required. Public access terminal is available. Fax notes: $6.00 for first page, $1.00 each addl.

Franklin Parish

5th District Court PO Box 431, Winnsboro, LA 71295; 318-435-5133; Fax: 318-435-5134. Hours: 8:30AM-4:30PM (CST). *Felony, Misdemeanor, Civil, Probate.*

Civil Records: Access: Fax, mail, in person. Both court and visitors may perform in person searches. Search fee: $10.00 per name. Required to search: name, years to search. Civil cases indexed by defendant, plaintiff. Civil records on computer from 1988, index books back to 1800s. **Criminal Records:** Access: Mail, in person. Both court and visitors may perform in person searches. Search fee: $10.00 per name. Fee includes 10 year search. Required to search: name, years to search, DOB; also helpful-SSN. Criminal records on computer since 1995. **General Information:** No adoption or juvenile records released. SASE required. Turnaround time 1-2 days. Copy fee: $1.00 per page. Certification fee: $2.00. Fee payee: Clerk of Court. Business checks accepted. Prepayment is required. Fax notes: $1.00 for first page, $.50 each addl.

Grant Parish

35th District Court PO Box 263, Colfax, LA 71417; 318-627-3246. Hours: 8:30AM-4:30PM (CST). *Felony, Misdemeanor, Civil, Probate.*

Civil Records: Access: Phone, mail, in person. Only the court conducts in person searches; visitors may not. Search fee: $5.00 per name. Required to search: name, years to search. Civil cases indexed by defendant, plaintiff. Civil records on computer from 1990, index books back to 1878. **Criminal Records:** Access: Phone, mail, in person. Only the court conducts in person

searches; visitors may not. Search fee: $5.00 per name. Required to search: name, years to search, DOB; also helpful-SSN. Criminal records on computer since 1996. **General Information:** No adoption or juvenile records released without approval of a judge. SASE required. Turnaround time 1-2 days. Copy fee: $.75 per page. Certification fee: $5.00. Fee payee: Grant Parish Clerk of Court. Personal checks accepted.

Iberia Parish

16th District Court PO Drawer 12010, New Iberia, LA 70562-2010; 337-365-7282; Fax: 337-365-0737. Hours: 8:30AM-4:30PM (CST). *Felony, Misdemeanor, Civil, Probate.*

Civil Records: Access: Phone, fax, mail, online, in person. Both court and visitors may perform in person searches. Search fee: $10.00 per name. Required to search: name, years to search; also helpful-address. Civil cases indexed by defendant, plaintiff. Civil records on computer from 1994, index books back to 1800s. Online access is open 24 hours daily. There is a monthly fee of $50. Can search civil or probate records by name or case number. Call Mike Thibodeaux for more information. **Criminal Records:** Access: Phone, fax, mail, in person. Both court and visitors may perform in person searches. Search fee: $10.00 per name. Required to search: name, years to search, DOB; also helpful-address, SSN. Criminal records on computer from 1994, index books back to 1800s. **General Information:** No adoption or juvenile records released. SASE required. Turnaround time 1-2 days. Copy fee: $.50 per page. Certification fee: $5.50. Fee payee: Clerk of Court. Personal checks accepted. Prepayment is required. Public access terminal is available.

Iberville Parish

18th District Court PO Box 423, Plaquemine, LA 70764; 225-687-5160; Fax: 225-687-5260. Hours: 8:30AM-4:30PM (CST). *Felony, Misdemeanor, Civil, Probate.*

Civil Records: Access: Fax, mail, in person. Both court and visitors may perform in person searches. Search fee: $10.00 per name. Required to search: name, years to search. Civil cases indexed by defendant, plaintiff. Civil records on books back to 1800s. **Criminal Records:** Access: Fax, mail, in person. Both court and visitors may perform in person searches. Search fee: $10.00 per name. Required to search: name, years to search, DOB; also helpful-SSN. Criminal records on books back to 1800s. **General Information:** No adoption or juvenile records released. SASE required. Turnaround time 1-2 days. Copy fee: $.75 per page. Certification fee: $5.00. Fee payee: Clerk of Court. Personal checks accepted. Prepayment is required. Fax notes: $5.00 for first page, $2.00 each addl.

Jackson Parish

2nd District Court PO Drawer 730, Jonesboro, LA 71251; 318-259-2424; Fax: 318-259-5681. Hours: 8:30AM-4:30PM (CST). *Felony, Misdemeanor, Civil, Probate.*

Civil Records: Access: Phone, mail, in person. Both court and visitors may perform in person searches. Search fee: $10.00 per name. Fee is per 10 years searched. Required to search: name, years to search. Civil cases indexed by defendant, plaintiff. Civil records on index books from 1880 and on computer since 1988. **Criminal Records:** Access: Phone, mail, in person. Both court and visitors may perform in person searches. Search fee: $10.00 per name. Fee is per 10 years searched.

Required to search: name, years to search, DOB; also helpful-SSN. Criminal records on computer since 1988. **General Information:** No adoption or juvenile records released. SASE required. Turnaround time 1-2 days. Copy fee: $1.00 for first page, $.50 each addl. Certification fee: $2.50. Fee payee: Clerk of Court. Personal checks accepted. Prepayment is required. Public access terminal is available.

Jefferson Davis Parish

31st District Court PO Box 799, Jennings, LA 70546; 337-824-1160; Fax: 337-824-1354. Hours: 8:30AM-4:30PM (CST). *Felony, Misdemeanor, Civil, Probate.*

Civil Records: Access: Mail, in person. Both court and visitors may perform in person searches. Search fee: $10.00 per name. Required to search: name, years to search; also helpful-address. Civil cases indexed by defendant, plaintiff. Civil records archived from 1913, on computer since 1991. **Criminal Records:** Access: Mail, in person. Both court and visitors may perform in person searches. Search fee: $10.00 per name. Required to search: name, years to search; also helpful-DOB, SSN. Criminal records archived from 1913, on computer since 1991. Include city of residence of subject in your search request. **General Information:** No adoption or juvenile records released. SASE not required. Turnaround time 2 days. Copy fee: $1.00 per page. Certification fee: $4.00. Fee payee: Clerk of Court. Personal checks accepted. Prepayment is required. Public access terminal is available.

Jefferson Parish

24th District Court PO Box 10, Gretna, LA 70053; 504-364-2992; Fax: 504-364-3797. Hours: 8:30AM-4:30PM (CST). *Felony, Misdemeanor, Civil, Probate.*

www.clerkofcourt.co.jefferson.la.us

Civil Records: Access: Fax, mail, in person. Both court and visitors may perform in person searches. Search fee: $20.00 per name per year. Required to search: name, years to search. Civil cases indexed by defendant, plaintiff. Civil records on computer from 1986, in index books back to 1972, prior records archived. **Criminal Records:** Access: Fax, mail, in person. Both court and visitors may perform in person searches. Search fee: $10.00 per name. Required to search: name, years to search, DOB; also helpful-SSN. Criminal records on computer from 1994 to present, active cases are in books from 1972. **General Information:** No adoption, juvenile or grand jury records released. Turnaround time 1-2 days. Copy fee: $.75 per page. Add postage. Certification fee: $1.25 per page. Fee payee: Clerk of Court. Personal checks accepted. Out of state personal checks not accepted. Prepayment is required. Public access terminal is available. Fax notes: $5.00 for first page, $1.00 each addl.

La Salle Parish

28th District Court PO Box 1316, Jena, LA 71342; 318-992-2158; Fax: 318-992-2157. Hours: 8:30AM-4:30PM (CST). *Felony, Misdemeanor, Civil, Probate.*

Civil Records: Access: Phone, mail, in person. Both court and visitors may perform in person searches. Search fee: $17.00 per name. Fee is for 10 year search per name with certificate. Required to search: name, years to search. Civil cases indexed by defendant, plaintiff. Civil records archived from 1916. **Criminal Records:** Access: Phone, mail, in person. Both court and visitors may perform in person searches. Search fee:

$17.00 per name per year. Fee is for 10 year search per name with certificate. Required to search: name, years to search, DOB; also helpful-SSN. Criminal records archived from 1916. **General Information:** No adoption or juvenile records released. SASE not required. Turnaround time 1-2 wks, will release info sooner by phone. Copy fee: $1.00 per page. Certification fee: $3.30 plus $1.10 per add'l page. Fee payee: Clerk of Court. Personal checks accepted. Prepayment is required.

Lafayette Parish

15th District Court PO Box 2009, Lafayette, LA 70502; 337-233-0150; Fax: 337-269-6392. Hours: 8:30AM-4:30PM (CST). *Felony, Misdemeanor, Civil, Probate.*

www.lafayetteparishclerk.com

Civil Records: Access: Phone, mail, online, in person. Both court and visitors may perform in person searches. Search fee: $11.00 per name. Required to search: name, years to search. Civil cases indexed by defendant, plaintiff. Civil records archived from 1966. Remote access available for $100 setup fee plus $15 per month and $.50 per minute. Civil index back to 1986. Modem speeds up to 9600 supported 24 hours per day. For more information, call Mike Prejean at 337-291-6232. **Criminal Records:** Access: Phone, mail, remote online, in person. Both court and visitors may perform in person searches. Search fee: $11.00 per name. Required to search: name, years to search, DOB. Criminal records archived from 1966. For online access, see civil records. **General Information:** No adoption or juvenile records released. SASE not required. Turnaround time 1-2 days. Copy fee: $.50 per page. Certification fee: The fee is $1.00 for criminal records and $5.00 for civil. Fee payee: Clerk of Court. Personal checks accepted. Prepayment is required. Public access terminal is available.

Lafourche Parish

17th District Court PO Box 818, Thibodaux, LA 70302; 504-447-4841; Fax: 504-447-5800. Hours: 8:30AM-4:30PM (CST). *Felony, Misdemeanor, Civil, Probate.*

Civil Records: Access: Fax, mail, in person. Both court and visitors may perform in person searches. Search fee: $15.00 per name. Fee is for 10 year search. Required to search: name, years to search. Civil cases indexed by defendant, plaintiff. Civil records on computer from 1982, microfiche from 1968, index books back to 1800s. **Criminal Records:** Access: Fax, mail, in person. Both court and visitors may perform in person searches. Search fee: $15.00 per name. Fee is for 10 year search. Required to search: name, years to search, DOB; also helpful-SSN, race, sex. Criminal records on computer from 1982, microfiche from 1968, index books back to 1800s. **General Information:** No adoption or juvenile records released. SASE requested. Turnaround time 1-2 days. Copy fee: $.55 per page. Certification fee: Minimum certification fee with copies is $3.30. Fee payee: Lafourche Parish Clerk of Court. Personal checks accepted. Prepayment is required. Public access terminal is available. Fax notes: $5.00 for first page, $1.00 each addl.

Lincoln Parish

3rd District Court PO Box 924, Ruston, LA 71273-0924; 318-251-5130; Fax: 318-255-6004. Hours: 8:30AM-4:30PM (CST). *Felony, Misdemeanor, Civil, Probate.*

Civil Records: Access: Mail, in person. Both court and visitors may perform in person searches.

Search fee: $10.00 per name. Fee is per 10 years searched. Required to search: name, years to search. Civil cases indexed by defendant, plaintiff. Civil records on computer since 1985, index books back to 1800s. **Criminal Records:** Access: Mail, in person. Both court and visitors may perform in person searches. Search fee: $10.00 per name. Fee is per 10 years searched. Required to search: name, years to search, DOB; also helpful-SSN. Criminal records on computer since 1992. **General Information:** No adoption or juvenile records released. SASE not required. Turnaround time 1-2 days. Copy fee: $1.00 per page. Certification fee: $2.00. Fee payee: Clerk of Court. Personal checks accepted. Prepayment is required. Public access terminal is available.

Livingston Parish

21st District Court PO Box 1150, Livingston, LA 70754; 225-686-2216. Hours: 8AM-4:30PM (CST). *Felony, Misdemeanor, Civil, Probate.*

Civil Records: Access: In person only. Court does not conduct in person searches; visitors must perform searches for themselves. Search fee: No civil searches performed by court. Required to search: name, years to search. Civil cases indexed by defendant, plaintiff. Civil records on index books since 1800s. **Criminal Records:** Access: In person only. Court does not conduct in person searches; visitors must perform searches for themselves. Search fee: No criminal searches performed by court. Required to search: name, years to search, DOB; also helpful-SSN, race, sex. Criminal records on index books since 1800s. **General Information:** No adoption or juvenile records released. Copy fee: $1.00 per page. Certification fee: $5.00. Fee payee: 21st District Court. Personal checks accepted. Prepayment is required. Public access terminal is available.

Madison Parish

6th District Court PO Box 1710, Tallulah, LA 71282; 318-574-0655; Fax: 318-574-0656. Hours: 8:30AM-4:30PM (CST). *Felony, Misdemeanor, Civil, Probate.*

Civil Records: Access: Phone, mail, in person. Both court and visitors may perform in person searches. Search fee: $10.00 per name. Required to search: name, years to search. Civil cases indexed by defendant, plaintiff. Civil records kept on computer since 7/93. **Criminal Records:** Access: Phone, mail, in person. Both court and visitors may perform in person searches. Search fee: $10.00 per name. Required to search: name, years to search, DOB; also helpful-SSN. Criminal records on index. **General Information:** No adoption or juvenile records released. SASE required. Turnaround time 1-2 days. Copy fee: No copy fee. Certification fee: $5.50. Fee does not include any copy fees. Fee payee: Clerk of Court. Personal checks accepted. Prepayment is required.

Morehouse Parish

4th District Court PO Box 1543, Bastrop, LA 71221; 318-281-3343/3346/3349; Fax: 318-281-3775. Hours: 8:30AM-4:30PM (CST). *Felony, Misdemeanor, Civil, Probate.*

Civil Records: Access: Phone, fax, mail, in person. Both court and visitors may perform in person searches. Search fee: $10.00 per name. Fee is per 10 years searched. Required to search: name, years to search; also helpful-address. Civil cases indexed by defendant, plaintiff. Civil records on computer since 1987, in books since 1898, some on microfilm. **Criminal Records:** Access: Phone,

fax, mail, in person. Both court and visitors may perform in person searches. Search fee: $10.00 per name. Fee is per 10 years searched. Required to search: name, years to search, DOB; also helpful-address, SSN. Criminal records in books since 1926 and on microfilm since 1974. **General Information:** No adoption, juvenile or judicial commitment records released. SASE required. Turnaround time 2-3 days. Copy fee: $1.00 per page. Certification fee: $2.50. Fee payee: Clerk of Court. Personal checks accepted. Prepayment is required. Public access terminal is available. Fax notes: $5.00 for first page, $1.00 each addl.

Natchitoches Parish

10th District Court PO Box 476, Natchitoches, LA 71458; 318-352-8152; Fax: 318-352-9321. Hours: 8:15AM-4:30PM (CST). *Felony, Misdemeanor, Civil, Probate.*

Civil Records: Access: Phone, fax, mail, in person. Both court and visitors may perform in person searches. Search fee: $10.00 per name. Required to search: name, years to search. Civil cases indexed by defendant, plaintiff. Civil records on computer from June 1991, archived from 1950, index books back to 1800s. **Criminal Records:** Access: Phone, fax, mail, in person. Both court and visitors may perform in person searches. Search fee: $10.00 per name. Required to search: name, years to search, DOB; also helpful-SSN. Criminal records on computer from June 1991, archived from 1950, index books back to 1800s. **General Information:** No adoption or juvenile records released. SASE required. Turnaround time 1 week. Copy fee: $.50 per page. Certification fee: $5.00. Fee payee: Clerk of Court. Personal checks accepted. Prepayment is required. Public access terminal is available. Fax notes: $5.00 for first page, $2.00 each addl. Fax available for civil division only.

Orleans Parish

Civil District Court 421 Loyola Ave, Rm 402, New Orleans, LA 70112; 504-592-9100 X122; Fax: 504-592-9128. Hours: 8AM-5PM (CST). *Civil, Probate.*

www.orleanscdc.gov

Civil Records: Access: Phone, mail, online, in person. Both court and visitors may perform in person searches. No search fee. Required to search: name, years to search. Civil cases indexed by defendant, plaintiff. Civil records on computer since 1985, in books back to early 1800s. CDC Remote provides access to civil cases from 1985 and First City Court cases from 1988, as well as mortgage and conveyance indexes for the parish. The fee is $250 per year. Call 504-592-9264 for more information. **General Information:** No adoptions or juvenile released. SASE required. Turnaround time 1-2 days. Copy fee: $.75 per page. Certification fee: $2.00 per document. Fee payee: Clerk of Court. Only cashiers checks and money orders accepted. Prepayment is required. Public access terminal is available.

New Orleans City Court 421 Loyola Ave, Rm 201, New Orleans, LA 70112; 504-592-9155; Fax: 504-592-9281. Hours: 8:30AM-4PM (CST). *Civil Actions Under $20,000, Small Claims.*

Civil Records: Access: Mail, in person. Both court and visitors may perform in person searches. No search fee. Required to search: name, years to search. Civil cases indexed by defendant, plaintiff. Civil records on computer since 1988. **General Information:** No sealed records released. SASE requested. Turnaround time 5-10 days. Copy fee:

$1.00 per page. Certification fee: $3.00. Fee payee: New Orleans City Court. Personal checks accepted. Credit cards accepted: Visa, Mastercard. Prepayment is required. Public access terminal is available.

4th District Court-Criminal Division

2700 Tulane Ave, Rm 115, New Orleans, LA 70119; 504-827-3520; Fax: 504-827-3385. Hours: 8:15AM-3:30PM (CST). *Felony, Misdemeanor.*

Criminal Records: Access: Mail, in person. Both court and visitors may perform in person searches. Search fee: $10.00 per name. Expedited search available for $20.00 per name. Required to search: name, years to search, DOB; also helpful-SSN. Criminal records on computer past 8 years, books and files go back to early 1900s. **General Information:** No adoption or juvenile records released. SASE required. Turnaround time 2 days. Copy fee: No copy fee. Certification fee: $1.50 per page. Fee payee: Clerk of Court. Business checks accepted. Prepayment is required. Public access terminal is available.

Ouachita Parish

4th District Court PO Box 1862, Monroe, LA 71210-1862; 318-327-1444; Fax: 318-327-1462. Hours: 8:30AM-5PM (CST). *Felony, Misdemeanor, Civil, Probate.*

Civil Records: Access: Fax, mail, in person. Both court and visitors may perform in person searches. Search fee: $10.00 per name. Required to search: name, years to search. Civil cases indexed by defendant, plaintiff. Civil records on computer from 1991, index books back to 1800s. **Criminal Records:** Access: Fax, mail, in person. Both court and visitors may perform in person searches. Search fee: $10.00 per name. Required to search: name, years to search, DOB; also helpful-SSN. Criminal records on computer from 1991, index books back to 1800s. **General Information:** No adoption or juvenile records released. SASE required. Turnaround time 1-2 days. Copy fee: $.50 per page. Certification fee: $2.00. Fee payee: Clerk of Court. Business checks accepted. Checks accepted up to $50.00. Prepayment is required. Fax notes: $2.00 for first page, $1.00 each addl.

Plaquemines Parish

25th District Court PO Box 129, Pointe A La Hache, LA 70082; 504-333-4377; Fax: 504-333-9202. Hours: 8:30AM-4:30PM (CST). *Felony, Misdemeanor, Civil, Probate.*

Civil Records: Access: In person only. Court does not conduct in person searches; visitors must perform searches for themselves. Search fee: No civil searches performed by court. Required to search: name, years to search. Civil cases indexed by defendant, plaintiff. Civil records on index books back to 1800s. **Criminal Records:** Access: In person only. Court does not conduct in person searches; visitors must perform searches for themselves. Search fee: No criminal searches performed by court. Required to search: name, years to search, DOB. Criminal records on index books back to 1966. **General Information:** No adoption or juvenile records released. Copy fee: $.50 per page. Certification fee: $3.00. Fee payee: Clerk of Court. Personal checks accepted. Prepayment is required.

Pointe Coupee Parish

18th District Court PO Box 38, New Roads, LA 70760; 225-638-9596. Hours: 8:30AM-4:30PM (CST). *Felony, Misdemeanor, Civil, Probate.*

Civil Records: Access: Mail, in person. Both court and visitors may perform in person searches. Search fee: $10.00 per name. Required to search: name, years to search. Civil cases indexed by defendant, plaintiff. Civil records on index books back to 1800s. **Criminal Records:** Access: In person only. Court does not conduct in person searches; visitors must perform searches for themselves. Search fee: No criminal searches performed by court. Required to search: name, years to search, DOB; also helpful-SSN. Criminal records on index books back to 1800s. **General Information:** No adoption or juvenile records released. SASE not required. Turnaround time 2 weeks. Copy fee: $1.25 per page. Certification fee: $3.00. Fee payee: Clerk of Court. Personal checks accepted. Prepayment is required. Public access terminal is available.

Rapides Parish

9th District Court PO Box 952, Alexandria, LA 71309; 318-473-8153; Fax: 318-473-4667. Hours: 8:30AM-4:30PM (CST). *Felony, Misdemeanor, Civil, Probate.*

Civil Records: Access: Mail, in person. Both court and visitors may perform in person searches. Search fee: $11.00 per name. Fee is per separate index. Required to search: name, years to search. Civil cases indexed by defendant, plaintiff. Civil records on index books since 1864, civil in computer since 1985. **Criminal Records:** Access: Mail, in person. Both court and visitors may perform in person searches. Search fee: $11.00 per name. Fee is per separate index. Required to search: name, years to search, DOB; also helpful-SSN. Criminal records on computer since 1984; prior records in index books back to 1864. **General Information:** No adoption, juvenile, or judicial commitment records released. SASE not required. Turnaround time 2-4 days. Copy fee: $.50 per page. Certification fee: $2.00. Fee payee: Rapides Parish Clerk of Court. Personal checks accepted. Prepayment is required. Public access terminal is available.

Red River Parish

39th District Court PO Box 485, Coushatta, LA 71019; 318-932-6741. Hours: 8:30AM-4:30PM (CST). *Felony, Misdemeanor, Civil, Probate.*

Civil Records: Access: Mail, in person. Both court and visitors may perform in person searches. Search fee: $10.00 per name. Required to search: name, years to search. Civil cases indexed by defendant, plaintiff. Civil records on index books. **Criminal Records:** Access: Mail, in person. Only the court conducts in person searches; visitors may not. Search fee: $10.00 per name. Required to search: name, years to search, DOB; also helpful-SSN. The index is kept in the DA's office. **General Information:** No adoption or juvenile records released. SASE required. Turnaround time 1-2 days. Copy fee: $1.00 per page. Certification fee: $5.00. Fee payee: Clerk of Court. Personal checks accepted. Prepayment is required.

Richland Parish

5th District Court PO Box 119, Rayville, LA 71269; 318-728-4171. Hours: 8:30AM-4:30PM (CST). *Felony, Misdemeanor, Civil, Probate.*

Civil Records: Access: Mail, in person. Both court and visitors may perform in person searches. Search fee: $10.00 per name. Required to search: name, years to search. Civil cases indexed by defendant, plaintiff. Civil records on since 1/94, prior on books to 1800s. **Criminal Records:**

Access: Mail, in person. Both court and visitors may perform in person searches. Search fee: $10.00 per name. Required to search: name, years to search, DOB, SSN. Criminal records on since 1/94, prior on books to 1800s. **General Information:** No adoption or juvenile records released. SASE required. Turnaround time 1-2 days. Copy fee: $1.00 per page. Certification fee: $3.00. Fee payee: Clerk of Court. Personal checks accepted. Prepayment is required.

Sabine Parish

11th District Court PO Box 419, Many, LA 71449; 318-256-6223; Fax: 318-256-9037. Hours: 8AM-4:30PM (CST). *Felony, Misdemeanor, Civil, Probate.*

Civil Records: Access: Fax, mail, in person. Both court and visitors may perform in person searches. Search fee: $10.00 per name. Required to search: name, years to search. Civil cases indexed by defendant, plaintiff. Civil records on index books back to 1843's. **Criminal Records:** Access: Fax, mail, in person. Both court and visitors may perform in person searches. Search fee: $10.00 per name. Required to search: name, years to search. Criminal Records available for 10 years. **General Information:** No adoption or juvenile records released. SASE required. Turnaround time 5-10 days. Copy fee: $1.25 per page. Certification fee: $4.00. Fee payee: Sabine Parish Clerk. Personal checks accepted. Prepayment is required. Public access terminal is available. Fax notes: $5.00 for first page, $2.00 each addl.

St. Bernard Parish

34th District Court PO Box 1746, Chalmette, LA 70044; 504-271-3434. Hours: 8:30AM-4:30PM (CST). *Felony, Misdemeanor, Civil, Probate.*

Civil Records: Access: Mail, in person. Both court and visitors may perform in person searches. Search fee: $5.00 per name. Fee is per 10 years searched. Required to search: name, years to search. Civil cases indexed by defendant, plaintiff. Civil records on index books back to 1800s, on computer since 1989. **Criminal Records:** Access: Mail, in person. Both court and visitors may perform in person searches. Search fee: $5.00 per name. Fee is per 10 years searched. Required to search: name, years to search, DOB; also helpful-SSN. Criminal records on index books back to 1800s, on computer since 1989. **General Information:** No adoption or juvenile. SASE required. Turnaround time 2-3 days. Copy fee: $1.00 per page. Certification fee: $3.00. Fee payee: Clerk of Court. Personal checks accepted. Prepayment is required. Public access terminal is available.

St. Charles Parish

29th District Court PO Box 424, Hahnville, LA 70057; 504-783-6632; Fax: 504-783-2005. Hours: 8:30AM-4:30PM (CST). *Felony, Misdemeanor, Civil, Probate.*

Civil Records: Access: Mail, in person. Both court and visitors may perform in person searches. Search fee: $5.00 per name. Required to search: name, years to search. Civil cases indexed by defendant, plaintiff. Civil records on computer since 1981, on index books back to 1800s. **Criminal Records:** Access: Mail, in person. Both court and visitors may perform in person searches. Search fee: $5.00 per name. Required to search: name, years to search, DOB; also helpful-SSN, race, sex. Criminal records on computer since 1981, on index books back to 1800s. **General**

Information: No adoption or juvenile records released. Turnaround time 1 day. Copy fee: $.50 per page. Certification fee: $2.00 per page. Fee payee: Clerk of Court. Personal checks accepted. Prepayment is required. Public access terminal is available.

St. Helena Parish

21st District Court PO Box 308, Greensburg, LA 70441; 225-222-4514. Hours: 8:30AM-4:30PM (CST). *Felony, Misdemeanor, Civil, Probate.*

Civil Records: Access: Phone, mail, fax, in person. Both court and visitors may perform in person searches. Search fee: $10.00 per name. Required to search: name, years to search. Civil cases indexed by defendant, plaintiff. Civil records on index books back to 1800s. **Criminal Records:** Access: Mail, in person. Both court and visitors may perform in person searches. Search fee: $10.00 per name. Required to search: name, years to search, DOB; also helpful-SSN. Criminal records on index books back to 1800s. **General Information:** No adoption or juvenile records released. SASE required. Turnaround time 1-2 days. Copy fee: No copy fee. Certification fee: $5.00. Fee payee: Clerk of Court. Personal checks accepted.

St. James Parish

23rd District Court PO Box 63, Convent, LA 70723; 225-562-7496; Fax: 504-562-2383. Hours: 8AM-4:30PM (CST). *Felony, Misdemeanor, Civil, Probate.*

Civil Records: Access: Mail, in person. Both court and visitors may perform in person searches. Search fee: $15.00 per name. Required to search: name, years to search. Civil cases indexed by defendant, plaintiff. Civil records on index books back to early 1900s. **Criminal Records:** Access: Mail, in person. Both court and visitors may perform in person searches. Search fee: $15.00 per name. Required to search: name, years to search, DOB. Criminal records on index books back to early 1900s. **General Information:** No adoption or juvenile records released. SASE required. Turnaround time 1-2 days. Copy fee: $.75 per page. Certification fee: $3.00. Fee payee: Clerk of Court. Only cashiers checks and money orders accepted. Prepayment is required.

St. John the Baptist Parish

40th District Court PO Box 280, Edgard, LA 70049; 504-497-3331. Hours: 8:30AM-4:30PM (CST). *Felony, Misdemeanor, Civil, Probate.*

Civil Records: Access: Mail, in person. Both court and visitors may perform in person searches. Search fee: $5.00 per name. Fee is for first 5 years. Add $1.00 per additional year. Required to search: name, years to search. Civil cases indexed by defendant, plaintiff. Civil records on computer since 1983. **Criminal Records:** Access: Mail, in person. Both court and visitors may perform in person searches. Search fee: $5.00 per name. Fee is for first 5 years. Add $1.00 per additional year. Required to search: name, years to search, DOB; also helpful-SSN. Felony records on computer since 1983, misdemeanors since 3/91. **General Information:** No adoption or juvenile records released. SASE required. Turnaround time 3-4 days. Copy fee: $1.00 per page. Certification fee: $5.00. Fee payee: Clerk of Court. Personal checks accepted. Prepayment is required.

St. Landry Parish

27th District Court PO Box 750, Opelousas, LA 70570; 337-942-5606; Fax: 337-948-1653. Hours: 8AM-4:30PM (CST). *Felony, Misdemeanor, Civil, Probate.*

Civil Records: Access: Mail, in person. Both court and visitors may perform in person searches. Search fee: $15.00 per name. Additional $1.00 fee per year after 1st 10 years. Required to search: name, years to search. Civil cases indexed by defendant, plaintiff. Civil records on index books back to 1800s, computerized since 1992. **Criminal Records:** Access: Mail, in person. Both court and visitors may perform in person searches. Search fee: $15.00 per name. Additional $1.00 fee per year after 1st 10 years. Required to search: name, years to search, DOB; also helpful-SSN. Criminal records on index books back to 1800s, computerized since 1992. **General Information:** No adoption or juvenile records released. SASE required. Turnaround time 1-2 days. Copy fee: $.75 per page. Certification fee: $5.50. Fee payee: Clerk of Court. Personal checks accepted. Prepayment is required.

St. Martin Parish

16th District Court PO Box 308, St. Martinville, LA 70582; 337-394-2210; Fax: 337-394-7772. Hours: 8:30AM-4:30PM (CST). *Felony, Misdemeanor, Civil, Probate.*

Civil Records: Access: Fax, mail, in person. Both court and visitors may perform in person searches. Search fee: $10.00 per name. Required to search: name, years to search; also helpful-address. Civil cases indexed by defendant, plaintiff. Civil records archived from 1760, on computer since 1990. **Criminal Records:** Access: Fax, mail, in person. Both court and visitors may perform in person searches. Search fee: $10.00 per name. Required to search: name, years to search, DOB; also helpful-address, SSN. Criminal records archived from 1760, on computer since 1990. **General Information:** No adoption, sealed records, expunged or juvenile records released. SASE required. Turnaround time 1-2 days. Copy fee: $.50 per page. Certification fee: $6.00. Fee payee: Clerk of Court. Personal checks accepted. Prepayment is required. Public access terminal is available. Fax notes: $.75 per page.

St. Mary Parish

16th District Court PO Box 1231, Franklin, LA 70538; 337-828-4100 X200; Fax: 337-828-2509. Hours: 8:30AM-4:30PM (CST). *Felony, Misdemeanor, Civil, Probate.*

Civil Records: Access: In person only. Court does not conduct in person searches; visitors must perform searches for themselves. Search fee: No civil searches performed by court. Required to search: name, years to search. Civil cases indexed by defendant, plaintiff. Civil records on index books back to 1800s. **Criminal Records:** Access: In person only. Court does not conduct in person searches; visitors must perform searches for themselves. Search fee: No criminal searches performed by court. Required to search: name, years to search, DOB; also helpful-SSN. Criminal records on index books back to 1800s. **General Information:** No adoption or juvenile records released. Copy fee: $1.00 per page. Certification fee: $5.00. Fee payee: St. Mary Parish Clerk of Court. Personal checks accepted. Prepayment is required.

St. Tammany Parish

22nd District Court PO Box 1090, Covington, LA 70434; 504-898-2430. Hours: 8:30AM-4:30PM (CST). *Felony, Misdemeanor, Civil, Probate.*

http://stp.pa.st.tammany.la.us/othergov/clerk

Civil Records: Access: Mail, in person. Both court and visitors may perform in person searches. Search fee: $10.00 per name. Add $5.00 for each add'l name. Required to search: name, years to search. Civil cases indexed by defendant, plaintiff. Civil records on index books back to 1800s, on computer since 1967. **Criminal Records:** Access: Mail, in person. Both court and visitors may perform in person searches. Search fee: $10.00 per name. Add $5.00 for each add'l name. Required to search: name, years to search, DOB; also helpful-SSN. Criminal records on computer since 10/87. **General Information:** No adoption or juvenile records released. SASE required. Turnaround time 2-3 days. Copy fee: $1.00 per page. Certification fee: $2.00 per page. Fee payee: Clerk of Court. Personal checks accepted. Prepayment is required. Public access terminal is available.

Tangipahoa Parish

21st District Court PO Box 667, Amite, LA 70422; 504-748-4146; Fax: 504-748-6503. Hours: 8:30AM-4:30PM (CST). *Felony, Misdemeanor, Civil, Probate.*

Civil Records: Access: Phone, fax, mail, in person. Both court and visitors may perform in person searches. Search fee: $10.00 per name. Required to search: name, years to search. Civil cases indexed by defendant, plaintiff. Civil records archived back to early 1900s. Online access is possible before the end of 2000. For more information, call 504-748-4146. **Criminal Records:** Access: Phone, fax, mail, in person. Both court and visitors may perform in person searches. Search fee: $10.00 per name. Required to search: name, years to search, DOB; also helpful-SSN. Criminal records archived back to early 1900s. **General Information:** No adoption or juvenile records released. SASE required. Turnaround time 3-4 days. Copy fee: $1.00 per page. Certification fee: $5.00. Fee payee: Clerk of Court. Personal checks accepted. Prepayment is required. Public access terminal is available. Fax notes: $5.00 for first page, $1.00 each addl.

Tensas Parish

6th District Court PO Box 78, St. Joseph, LA 71366; 318-766-3921. Hours: 8AM-4:30PM (CST). *Felony, Misdemeanor, Civil, Probate.*

Civil Records: Access: In person only. Court does not conduct in person searches; visitors must perform searches for themselves. Search fee: No civil searches performed by court. Required to search: name, years to search. Civil cases indexed by defendant, plaintiff. Civil records archived back to 1800s, on computer since 1989. **Criminal Records:** Access: In person only. Court does not conduct in person searches; visitors must perform searches for themselves. Search fee: No criminal searches performed by court. Required to search: name, years to search, DOB; also helpful-SSN. Criminal records not on computer, archived back to 1800s. **General Information:** No adoption or juvenile records released. Certification fee: $5.50. Fee payee: Clerk of Court. Personal checks accepted. Prepayment is required.

Terrebonne Parish

32nd District Court PO Box 1569, Houma, LA 70361; 504-868-5660. Hours: 8:30AM-4:30PM (CST). *Felony, Misdemeanor, Civil, Probate.*

Civil Records: Access: Mail, in person. Both court and visitors may perform in person searches. Search fee: $15.00 per name. Required to search: name, years to search. Civil cases indexed by defendant, plaintiff. Civil records on computer since 1986, in books to 1823. **Criminal Records:** Access: Mail, in person. Both court and visitors may perform in person searches. Search fee: $15.00 per name. Required to search: name, years to search, DOB; also helpful-SSN, race, sex. Criminal records archived to 1800s. **General Information:** No adoption or juvenile records released. SASE required. Turnaround time 2-3 days. Copy fee: $.75 per page. Certification fee: $5.00. Fee payee: Terrebonne Parish Clerk of Court. Personal checks accepted. Prepayment is required.

Union Parish

3rd District Court Courthouse Bldg, 100 E Bayou #105, Farmerville, LA 71241; 318-368-3055; Fax: 318-368-2487. Hours: 8:30AM-4:30PM (CST). *Felony, Misdemeanor, Civil, Probate.*

Civil Records: Access: Mail, in person. Search fee: $5.00 per name. Required to search: name, years to search. Civil cases indexed by defendant, plaintiff. Civil records on index books back to 1839. **Criminal Records:** Access: Mail, in person. Both court and visitors may perform in person searches. Search fee: $10.00 per name. Required to search: name, years to search. Criminal records on index books back to 1839. **General Information:** No adoption or juvenile records released. SASE required. Turnaround time 2-3 days. Copy fee: $.75 per page. Certification fee: $2.00. Fee payee: Clerk of Court. Personal checks accepted. Prepayment is required.

Vermilion Parish

15th District Court 100 N. State St, #101, Abbeville, LA 70511-0790; 337-898-1992; Fax: 337-898-0404. Hours: 8:30AM-4:30PM (CST). *Felony, Misdemeanor, Civil, Probate.*

Civil Records: Access: Phone, fax, mail, in person. Both court and visitors may perform in person searches. Search fee: $12.00 per name. Fee for second name on same search request is $6.50. Required to search: name, years to search. Civil cases indexed by defendant, plaintiff. Civil records on computer since 1982, in books since 1885, on microfilm since 1885. **Criminal Records:** Access: Phone, fax, mail, in person. Both court and visitors may perform in person searches. Search fee: $12.00 per name. Fee for second name on same search request is $6.50. Required to search: name, years to search, DOB; also helpful-SSN, race, sex. Criminal records on computer since 1982, in books since 1885, on microfilm since 1885. **General Information:** No adoption or juvenile records released. SASE required. Turnaround time 1-2 days after payment. Copy fee: $1.00 per page. Certification fee: $5.00. Fee payee: Vermilion Parish Clerk of Court. Personal checks accepted. Prepayment is required. Public access terminal is available. Fax notes: $2.00 for first page, $1.00 each addl.

Vernon Parish

30th District Court PO Box 40, Leesville, LA 71496; 337-238-1384; Fax: 337-238-9902. Hours: 8AM-4:30PM (CST). *Felony, Misdemeanor, Civil, Probate.*

Civil Records: Access: Mail, in person. Both court and visitors may perform in person searches. Search fee: $10.00 per name. Required to search: name, years to search. Civil cases indexed by defendant, plaintiff. Civil records on computer from November 1985, archived back to 1900. **Criminal Records:** Access: Mail, in person. Both court and visitors may perform in person searches. Search fee: $10.00 per name. Required to search: name, years to search, DOB. Criminal records on computer from November 1985, archived back to 1900. **General Information:** No adoption or juvenile records released. SASE required. Turnaround time same day. Copy fee: $1.25 per page. Certification fee: $3.00. Fee payee: Clerk of Court. Personal checks accepted. Prepayment is required. Public access terminal is available.

Washington Parish

22nd District Court PO Box 607, Franklinton, LA 70438; 504-839-4663/7821. Hours: 8AM-4:30PM (CST). *Felony, Misdemeanor, Civil, Probate.*

Civil Records: Access: Mail, in person. Both court and visitors may perform in person searches. Search fee: $10.00 per name. Required to search: name, years to search. Civil cases indexed by defendant, plaintiff. Civil records on computer from August 1989, archived April 1967, index books back to 1800s. **Criminal Records:** Access: Mail, in person. Both court and visitors may perform in person searches. Search fee: $10.00 per name. Required to search: name, years to search, DOB, SSN. Criminal records on computer from August 1989, archived April 1967, index books back to 1800s. **General Information:** No adoption or juvenile records released. SASE requested. Turnaround time 1-2 days. Copy fee: $1.00 per page. Certification fee: $5.00. Fee payee: Washington Parish Clerk of Court. Personal checks accepted. Prepayment is required.

Webster Parish

26th District Court PO Box 370, Minden, LA 71058; 318-371-0366; Fax: 318-371-0226. Hours: 8:30AM-4:30PM (CST). *Felony, Misdemeanor, Civil, Probate.*

Civil Records: Access: Fax, mail, in person. Both court and visitors may perform in person searches. Search fee: $10.00 per name. Required to search: name, years to search. Civil cases indexed by defendant, plaintiff. Civil records archived back to 1800s, on computer since 1986. **Criminal Records:** Access: Fax, mail, in person. Both court and visitors may perform in person searches. Search fee: $10.00 per name. Required to search: name; also helpful-years to search. Criminal records not on computer, in books to 1800s. **General Information:** No adoption or juvenile records released. SASE not required. Turnaround time 2-3 days. Copy fee: $1.00 per page. Certification fee: $5.00. Fee payee: Clerk of Court. Personal checks accepted. Prepayment is required. Fax notes: $5.00 per page.

West Baton Rouge Parish

18th District Court PO Box 107, Port Allen, LA 70767; 225-383-0378. Hours: 8:30AM-4:30PM (CST). *Felony, Misdemeanor, Civil, Probate.*

Civil Records: Access: Phone, mail, in person. Both court and visitors may perform in person searches. Search fee: $10.00 per name. Required to search: name, years to search. Civil cases indexed by defendant, plaintiff. Civil records on computer from 1983. **Criminal Records:** Access: Phone, mail, in person. Both court and visitors may perform in person searches. Search fee: $10.00 per name. Required to search: name, years to search, DOB; also helpful-SSN. Criminal records on computer from 1983. **General Information:** No adoption or juvenile records released. SASE required. Turnaround time 1-2 days. Copy fee: $.50 per page. Certification fee: $2.00. Fee payee: Clerk of Court. Personal checks accepted. Prepayment is required.

West Carroll Parish

5th District Court PO Box 1078, Oak Grove, LA 71263; 318-428-3281. Hours: 8:30AM-4:30PM (CST). *Felony, Misdemeanor, Civil, Probate.*

Civil Records: Access: Mail, in person. Both court and visitors may perform in person searches. Search fee: $1.00 per name per year. Required to search: name, years to search. Civil cases indexed by defendant, plaintiff. Civil records on index books back to 1800s. **Criminal Records:** Access: Mail, in person. Both court and visitors may perform in person searches. Search fee: $1.00 per name per year. Required to search: name, years to search, DOB. Criminal records on index books back to 1800s. **General Information:** No adoption or juvenile records released. SASE required. Turnaround time 1-2 days. Copy fee: $1.00 per page. Certification fee: $3.00. Fee payee: Clerk of Court. Only cashiers checks and money orders accepted. Prepayment is required.

West Feliciana Parish

20th District Court PO Box 1843, St Francisville, LA 70775; 225-635-3794; Fax: 225-635-3770. Hours: 8:30AM-4:30PM (CST). *Felony, Misdemeanor, Civil, Probate.*

Civil Records: Access: Mail, in person. Both court and visitors may perform in person searches. Search fee: $10.00 per name. Fee is per 5 years searched. Required to search: name, years to search; also helpful-address. Civil cases indexed by defendant, plaintiff. Civil records on computer from 1984, index books back to 1800s. **Criminal Records:** Access: Mail, in person. Both court and visitors may perform in person searches. Search fee: $10.00 per name. Fee is per 5 years searched. Required to search: name, years to search, DOB; also helpful-address. Criminal records on computer since 1992; prior on cards and dockets back to 1800s. **General Information:** No adoption, juvenile or juvenile records released. SASE required. Turnaround time 3-5 days. Copy fee: $1.00 per page. Certification fee: $5.00. Fee payee: Clerk of Court. Business checks accepted. Prepayment is required.

Winn Parish

8th District Court 100 Main St, #103, Winnfield, LA 71483; 318-628-3515. Hours: 8AM-4:30PM (CST). *Felony, Misdemeanor, Civil, Probate.*

Civil Records: Access: Mail, in person. Both court and visitors may perform in person searches. Search fee: $10.00 per name. Fee is for 10 year search. Required to search: name, years to search, address. Civil cases indexed by defendant, plaintiff. Civil records on books from 1886 to present, on computer from 1988, mortgages since

Licenses Searchable Online

Employee Leasing Company #15	www.state.me.us/pfr/ins/emplease.htm
Health Maintenance Organization #15	www.state.me.us/pfr/ins/inshmo.htm
Medical Doctor #23	www.docboard.org/me/df/mesearch.htm
Notary Public #24	www.state.me.us/sos/cec/rcn/notary/notlist.htm
Optometrist #18	www.arbo.org/nodb2000/licsearch.asp
Osteopathic Physician #26	www.docboard.org/me-osteo
Osteopathic Resident/Intern #26	www.docboard.org/me-osteo
Preferred Provider Organization #15	www.state.me.us/pfr/ins/insppo.htm
Registration-ATV, Watercraft, Snowmobile #11	www.mefishwildlife.com
Utilitization Review Entity #15	www.state.me.us/pfr/ins/insmedur.htm

Licensing Quick Finder

Acupuncturist #13	207-624-8632
Adult Care Home #09	207-624-5250
Adult Day Services #09	207-624-5250
Aesthetician #13	207-624-8603
Air Quality Control (Business) #05	207-287-2437
Alcohol & Drug Abuse Counselor #13	207-624-8603
Alcoholic Beverage Distributor #21	207-624-8745
Ambulance Attendant #20	207-287-3953
Ambulatory Surgical Center #09	207-624-5443
Animal Medical Technician #13	207-624-8603
Arborist #13	207-624-8629
Architect #13	207-624-8522
Assisted Living Facilities #09	207-624-5250
Athletic Trainer #13	207-624-8624
Attorney #22	207-623-1121
Auctioneer #13	207-624-8521
Bank Personnel #14	207-624-8648
Barber #13	207-624-8620
Bedding/Upholstering/Furniture & Stuffed Toy Manufacturer #12	207-624-6411
Beekeeper #03	207-287-3117
Boiler, Elevator, Tramway Contractor #13	207-624-8615
Boxer #13	207-624-8603
Charitable Solicitation #13	207-624-8624
Chiropractor #13	207-624-8634
Contract Security Company #25	207-624-8775
Cosmetologist #13	207-624-8620
Counselor #13	207-624-8626
Dental Hygienist #16	207-287-3333
Dental Radiographer #16	207-287-3333
Dentist #16	207-287-3333
Denturist #16	207-287-3333
Dietitian #13	207-624-8611
Drug Analyzer #07	207-287-3201
Electrician #13	207-624-8611
Electrologist #07	207-287-5338
Emergency Medical Technician #10	207-287-3953
Employee Leasing Company #15	207-624-8475
End State Renal Disease Facilities #09	207-624-5443
Engineer #17	207-287-3236
Firearm Permit (Resident-Concealed) #25	207-624-8775
First Responder #10	207-287-3953
Forester #13	207-624-8628
Funeral Home #13	207-624-8603

Funeral Service #13	207-624-8611
General Real Estate Appraiser #13	207-624-8616
Geologist & Soil Scientist #13	207-624-8616
Hazardous Material/Solid Waste Operator #06	207-287-7865
Health Maintenance Organization #15	207-624-8475
Hearing Aid Dealer/Fitter #13	207-624-8628
Home Health Agencies #09	207-624-5443
Home Health Care Service Agencies #09	207-624-5443
Hospice #09	207-624-5443
Hospital #09	207-624-5443
Insurance Advisor #13	207-624-8603
Insurance Agent #13	207-624-8603
Intermediate Care Facility for Mentally Retarded #09	207-624-5443
Investment Advisor #13	207-624-8603
Itinerant Vendor #13	207-624-8624
Kickboxer #13	207-624-8603
Landscape Architect #13	207-624-8616
Library Media Specialist #04	207-287-5944
Loan Broker #13	207-624-8603
Lobbyist #01	207-287-6221
Lottery Combined Instant & Online Vendor #21	207-287-6824
Lottery Instant Ticket Vendor #21	207-287-6824
Lottery Retailer #02	207-287-6824
Lottery Vending #21	207-287-6824
Manicurist #13	207-624-8603
Manufactured Housing #13	207-582-8612
Marriage & Family Therapist #13	207-624-8634
Massage Therapist #13	207-624-8624
Medical Doctor #23	207-287-3601
Non-Resident Concealed Firearm Permit #25	207-624-8775
Notary Public #24	207-287-4173
Nurse #08	207-287-1133
Nursing Home #09	207-624-5443
Nursing Home Administrator #13	207-624-8611
Occupational Therapist #13	207-624-8616
Oil & Solid Fuel #13	207-624-8631
Optometrist #18	207-624-8691
Osteopathic Physician #26	207-287-2480
Osteopathic Physician Assistant #26	207-287-2480
Osteopathic Physician Extender #26	207-287-2480

Osteopathic Resident/Intern #26	207-287-2480
Paramedic #10	207-287-3953
Pastoral Counselor #13	207-624-8634
Pesticide Applicator #03	207-287-2731
Pesticide Dealer #03	207-287-2731
Pharmacist #13	207-624-8616
Physical Therapist #13	207-624-8628
Physician Assistant #23	207-287-3601
Pilot #13	207-624-8620
Plumber #13	207-624-8628
Podiatrist #13	207-624-8626
Polygraph Examiner #20	207-624-7074
Preferred Provider Organization #15	207-624-8475
Private Investigator #25	207-624-8775
Psychologist #13	207-624-8628
Public Accountant-CPA #13	207-582-8627
Radiologic Technician #13	207-624-8628
Real Estate Appraiser #13	207-624-8616
Real Estate Appraiser (Trainee) #13	207-624-8616
Real Estate Broker #13	207-624-8603
Registration-ATV, Watercraft, Snowmobile #11	207-287-2043
Residential Child Care Provider #07	207-287-5060
Residential Real Estate Appraiser #13	207-624-8616
Respiratory Care Therapist #13	207-624-8616
School Guidance Counselor #04	207-287-5944
School Library Media Specialist #04	207-287-5944
School Principal #04	207-287-5944
School Superintendent #04	207-287-5944
Sea Urchin Harvester #27	207-624-6550
Seaweed Harvester #27	207-624-6550
Self Insurance Company #15	207-624-8475
Social Worker #13	207-624-8631
Soil Scientist #13	207-624-8603
Speech Pathologist/Audiologist #13	207-624-8634
Sprinkler Inspector #20	207-287-3473
Substance Abuse Counselor #13	207-624-8634
Surveyor #13	207-624-8611
Tattoo Artist #07	207-287-3201
Taxidermist #11	207-287-2751
Teacher #04	207-287-5944
Utilitization Review Entitity #15	207-624-8475
Veterinarian #13	207-624-8628
Veterinary Technician #13	207-624-8603

Licensing Agency Information

01 Registrar, Commission on Governmental Ethics & Elections, State House Station 135, Augusta, ME 04333; 207-287-6221, Fax: 207-287-6775.

www.state.me.us/ethics

02 Department of Administrative & Financial Services, Bureau of Alcoholic Beverages & Lottery Operations, 8 State House Station, Augusta, ME 04333-0008; 207-287-6824, Fax: 207-287-6769. www.mainelottery.com

03 Department of Agriculture, Food & Rural Resources, Board of Pesticides Control, PO Box 83720 (280 State House Station), Augusta, ME 04332-0028; 207-287-2731, Fax: 207-287-7548.

www.state.me.us/agriculture/pesticides

04 Department of Education, Certification Office, 23 State House Station, Augusta Complex, Augusta, ME 04333-0023; 207-287-5944, Fax: 207-287-3910.

www.state.me.us/agencies.htm

05 Department of Environmental Protection, Bureau of Air Quality Control, 17 State House Station, Augusta, ME 04333-0017; 207-287-2437, Fax: 207-287-7641.

www.state.me.us/agencies.htm

06 Department of Environmental Protection, Bureau/Hazardous Materials & Solid Waste

Control, State House Station 17, Augusta, ME 04333; 207-287-7865, Fax: 207-287-7826.

www.state.me.us/agencies.htm

07 Department of Human Services, 221 State St, 11 State House Station, Augusta, ME 04333-0011; 207-287-5060, Fax: 207-287-5282.

www.state.me.us/agencies.htm

08 Department of Professional & Financial Regulation, Board of Nursing, 24 Stone Street, # 158 State House Station, Augusta, ME 04333-0158; 207-287-1133, Fax: 207-287-1149.

www.state.me.us/nursingbd

09 Department of Human Services, Division of Licensure, 35 SHS, Augusta, ME 04333; 207-624-5443, Fax: 207-624-5378.

http://maineprofessionalreg.org

10 Department of Human Services, Medical Services Bureau Licensing & Certification, 16 Edison Dr, Augusta, ME 04333; 207-287-3953, Fax: 207-289-6251.

http://janus.state.me.us/dps/ems

11 Department of Inland Fisheries & Wildlife, Licensing & Registration Division, 284 State St, 41 Statehouse Station, Augusta, ME 04333-0041; 207-287-8000, Fax: 207-287-8094. www.mefishwildlife.com

Direct URL to search licenses: www.mefishwildlife.com You can search online using name.

12 Department of Labor, 45 State House Station, Augusta, ME 04333-0045; 207-624-6411, Fax: 207-624-6449.

http://janus.state.me.us/labor

13 Department of Professional & Financial Regulation, Bureau of Licensing, 35 State House Station, Augusta, ME 04333-0035; 207-624-8500, Fax: 207-624-8590.

www.state.me.us/pfr/led/list.htm

14 Department of Professional & Financial Regulation, Bureau of Banking, 36 State House Station, Augusta, ME 04333-0036; 207-624-8500, Fax: 207-624-8590.

15 Department of Professional & Financial Regulation, Bureau of Insurance, State House Station 34, Augusta, ME 04333-0034; 207-624-8475, Fax: 207-624-8599.

www.state.me.us/pfr/ins/inshome2.htm

16 Board of Dental Examiners, 143 Statehouse Station, 2 Bangor St, Augusta, ME 04333-0143; 207-287-3333, Fax: 207-287-8140.

17 Department of Professional & Financial Regulation, Professional Engineers Reg. Board, 92 State House Station, Augusta, ME 04333; 207-287-3236, Fax: 207-626-2309.

www.state.me.us/pfr/auxboards/enghome.htm

18 Department of Professional & Financial Regulation, Bureau of Optometry, 113 State House Station, Augusta, ME 04333; 207-624-8691, Fax: 207-624-8691.

Direct URL to search licenses: www.arbo.org/nodb2000/licsearch.asp You can search online using national database by name, city, or state.

20 Department of Public Safety, 42 State House Station, 36 Hospital St, Augusta, ME 04333-0042; 207-624-7094, Fax: 207-624-7088.

www.state.me.us/agencies.htm

21 Department of Public Safety, Licensing & Inspection-Liquor, 164 State House Station, Augusta, ME 04333; 207-624-8745, Fax: 207-624-8767.

22 Board of Bar Examiners, PO Box 30 (PO Box 30), Augusta, ME 04332-0030; 207-623-2464, Fax: 207-623-4175.

23 Medical Doctor & Physician Assistant Licensing & Investigation, Board of Licensure & Medicine, 137 State House Station, Augusta, ME 04333; 207-287-3601, Fax: 207-287-6590.

www.docboard.org/me/df/find_me.htm

24 Department of Secretary of State, Division of Rules, Commissions & Administration, Notary Office, PO Box 2054 (101 State House Station), Augusta, ME 04333-0101; 207-287-4181, Fax: 207-287-5874.

www.state.me.us/sos/rec.rcn/notary/not.htm

Direct URL to search licenses: www.state.me.us/sos/notary.htm You can search online using town and name.

25 State Police Licensing Division, 164 State House Station, Augusta, ME 04333; 207-624-8775, Fax: 207-624-8767.

26 State of Maine, Board of Osteopathic Licensure, 142 State House Station, Augusta, ME 04333-0142; 207-287-2480, Fax: 207-287-2480.

Direct URL to search licenses: www.docboard.org/me-osteo You can search online using name or license number.

27 Department of Marine Resources, Bureau of Marine Patrol, Licensing Division, 21 State House Station, Hallowell Annex-Baker Bldg, Augusta, ME 04333-0021; 207-624-6550.

The following list indicates the district and division name for each county in the state. If the district or division name of the bankruptcy court is different from the civil/criminal court, it appears in parentheses.

County/Court Cross Reference

Androscoggin	Portland	Oxford	Portland
Aroostook	Bangor	Penobscot	Bangor
Cumberland	Portland	Piscataquis	Bangor
Franklin	Bangor	Sagadahoc	Portland
Hancock	Bangor	Somerset	Bangor
Kennebec	Bangor	Waldo	Bangor
Knox	Portland (Bangor)	Washington	Bangor
Lincoln	Portland (Bangor)	York	Portland

US District Court

District of Maine

Bangor Division Court Clerk, PO Box 1007, Bangor, ME 04402-1007 (Courier Address: Room 357, 202 Harlow St, Bangor, ME 04401), 207-945-0575.

www.med.uscourts.gov

Counties: Aroostook, Franklin, Hancock, Kennebec, Penobscot, Piscataquis, Somerset, Waldo, Washington.

Indexing & Storage: Cases are indexed by defendant and plaintiff as well as by case number. New cases are available in the index immediately after filing date. A computer index is maintained. Records are indexed and stored by year, then docket number for case files and by name for electronic index system. Open records are located at this court.

Fee & Payment: The fee is $15.00 per item (one party name or case number). Payment may be made by money order, cashier check, personal check. Prepayment is required. Payee: Clerk, US District Court. Certification fee: $5.00 per document. Copy fee: $.50 per page.

Phone Search: Any public record information will be released over the phone including the accession number. An automated voice case information service (VCIS) is not available.

Mail Search: A stamped self addressed envelope is not required.

In Person Search: In person searching is available.

PACER: Sign-up number is 800-676-6856. Access fee is $.60 per minute. Toll-free access: 800-260-9774. Local access: 207-780-3392. Case records are available back to August 1991. Records are purged every 6 months. New records are available online after 1 day. PACER is available online at https://pacer.med.uscourts.gov.

Portland Division Court Clerk, 156 Federal St, Portland, ME 04101, 207-780-3356.

www.med.uscourts.gov

Counties: Androscoggin, Cumberland, Knox, Lincoln, Oxford, Sagadahoc, York.

Indexing & Storage: Cases are indexed by defendant and plaintiff as well as by case number. New cases are available in the index immediately after filing date. A computer index is maintained. Records are indexed and stored by year, then docket number for case files and by name for electronic index system. Open records are located at this court.

Fee & Payment: The fee is $15.00 per item (one party name or case number). Payment may be made by money order, cashier check, personal check. Prepayment is required. Payee: Clerk, US District Court. Certification fee: $5.00 per document. Copy fee: $.50 per page.

Phone Search: Any public record information will be released over the phone including accession numbers. An automated voice case information service (VCIS) is not available.

Mail Search: A stamped self addressed envelope is not required.

In Person Search: In person searching is available.

PACER: Sign-up number is 800-676-6856. Access fee is $.60 per minute. Toll-free access: 800-260-9774. Local access: 207-780-3392. Case records are available back to August 1991. Records are purged every 6 months. New records are available online after 1 day. PACER is available online at https://pacer.med.uscourts.gov.

US Bankruptcy Court

District of Maine

Bangor Division PO Box 1109, Bangor, ME 04402-1109 (Courier Address: 202 Harlow St, Bangor, ME 04401), 207-945-0348, Fax: 207-945-0304.

www.meb.uscourts.gov

Counties: Aroostook, Franklin, Hancock, Kennebec, Knox, Lincoln, Penobscot, Piscataquis, Somerset, Waldo, Washington.

Indexing & Storage: Cases are indexed by debtor as well as by case number. New cases are available in the index immediately after filing date. A computer index is maintained. Archived records are available within 2 weeks of shipment to the archives. Open records are located at this court. The length of time records are retained depends on space; files are usually retained 3 years before being sent to the Boston Federal Records Center.

Fee & Payment: The fee is $15.00 per item (one party name or case number). Payment may be made by money order, cashier check, business check. Personal checks are not accepted. Prepayment is required. Payee: United States Courts. Certification fee: $5.00 per document. Copy fee: $.50 per page.

Phone Search: An automated voice case information service (VCIS) is available. Call VCIS at 800-650-7253 or 207-780-3755.

Mail Search: A stamped self addressed envelope is not required.

In Person Search: In person searching is available.

PACER: Sign-up number is 800-676-6856. Access fee is $.60 per minute. Toll-free access: 800-733-8797. Local access: 207-780-3268, 207-780-3269. Case records are available back to December 1988. Records are purged every two years. New civil records are available online after 1 day. PACER is available online at http://pacer.meb.uscourts.gov.

Portland Division 537 Congress St, Portland, ME 04101, 207-780-3482, Fax: 207-780-3679.

www.meb.uscourts.gov

Counties: Androscoggin, Cumberland, Oxford, Sagadahoc, York.

Indexing & Storage: Cases are indexed by debtor as well as by case number. New cases are available in the index immediately after filing date. Searches for cases filed prior to 1988 require the debtor's name. Automated searches require either the case number or debtor's name. A computer index is maintained. Records from the court are available from the court immediately after docketing. Information through VCIS and Pacer is available 24 hours after docketing. Open records are located at this court.

Fee & Payment: The fee is $15.00 per item (one party name or case number). Payment may be made by money order, cashier check, business check. Personal checks are not accepted. Prepayment is required for individual requesters. Payee: US Bankruptcy Court. Certification fee: $5.00 per document. Copy fee: $.50 per page.

Phone Search: Only docket information is available by phone. An automated voice case information service (VCIS) is available. Call VCIS at 800-650-7253 or 207-780-3755.

Mail Search: Always enclose a stamped self addressed envelope.

In Person Search: In person searching is available.

PACER: Sign-up number is 800-676-6856. Access fee is $.60 per minute. Toll-free access: 800-733-8797. Local access: 207-780-3268, 207-780-3269. Case records are available back to December 1988. Records are purged every two years. New civil records are available online after 1 day. PACER is available online at http://pacer.meb.uscourts.gov.

Court	Jurisdiction	No. of Courts	How Organized
Superior Courts*	General	18	16 Counties
District Courts*	Limited	33	13 Districts
Probate Courts*	Special	16	

* Profiled in this Sourcebook.

CIVIL									
Court	Tort	Contract	Real Estate	Min. Claim	Max. Claim	Small Claims	Estate	Eviction	Domestic Relations
Superior Courts*	X	X	X	$30,000	No Max				X
District Courts*	X	X	X	$0	$30,000	$5000		X	X
Probate Courts*							X		X

CRIMINAL					
Court	Felony	Misdemeanor	DWI/DUI	Preliminary Hearing	Juvenile
Superior Courts*	X	X	X		
District Courts*		X	X	X	X
Probate Courts*					

ADMINISTRATION   State Court Administrator, PO Box 4820, Portland, ME, 04112; 207-822-0792, Fax: 207-822-0781. www.courts.state.me.us

COURT STRUCTURE   The Superior Court is the court of general jurisdiction. While District Courts accept civil cases involving claims less than $30,000, the plaintiff may file at the Superior, also, judge permitting. District Courts handle some minor "felonies." The small claims limit was raised from $3000 to $4500 as of 7/1/97.

Probate Courts are part of the county court system, not the state system. Even though the Probate Court may be housed with other state courts, it is on a different phone system and calls may not be transferred.

ONLINE ACCESS   Development of a statewide judicial computer system is in progress and will be available statewide sometime in the future. The system will be initially for judicial and law enforcement agencies and will not include public access in the near term. Some counties are online through a private vendor.

ADDITIONAL INFORMATION   Many courts will refer written requests for criminal searches to the Maine State Police.

📖 📖 📖 📖 📖 📖 📖

Androscoggin County

Androscoggin Superior Court PO Box 3660, Auburn, ME 04212-3660; 207-783-5450. Hours: 8AM-4:30PM (EST). *Felony, Misdemeanor, Civil Actions Over $30,000.*

Civil Records: Access: Phone, mail, in person. Only the court conducts in person searches; visitors may not. No search fee. Required to search: name, years to search; also helpful-address. Civil cases indexed by defendant, plaintiff. Civil records on index cards since 1977, docket books from 1961-1977. **Criminal Records:** Access: In person only. Court does not conduct in person searches; visitors must perform searches for themselves. Search fee: No criminal searches performed by court. Required to search: name, years to search; also helpful-DOB. Criminal records go back to 1920s. **General Information:** No adoption, juvenile, impounded by judge, certain domestic matters. SASE required.

Turnaround time 1 week. Copy fee: $1.00 per page. Certification fee: $1.00. Fee payee: Androscoggin Superior Court. Personal checks accepted. Prepayment is required.

District Court North Androscoggin District 11 2 Main St, Livermore Falls, ME 04254; 207-897-3800. Hours: 8AM-4PM T-Th (EST). *Misdemeanor, Civil Actions Under $30,000, Eviction, Small Claims.*

Civil Records: Access: Mail, in person. Only the court conducts in person searches; visitors may not. No search fee. Required to search: name, years to search. Civil cases indexed by defendant. Civil records on docket books. **Criminal Records:** Access: Mail, in person. Only the court conducts in person searches; visitors may not. No search fee. Sourcequired to search: name, years to search; also helpful-DOB. Criminal records on computer since 1988. **General Information:** No juvenile, protective custody records released. SASE

requested. Turnaround time up to 1 week. Copy fee: $1.00 per page. Certification fee: $1.00. Fee payee: Maine District Court. Personal checks accepted. Prepayment is required.

Lewiston District Court - South #8 PO Box 1345, 85 Park St, Lewiston, ME 04243; Civil phone:207-783-5403; Criminal phone:207-783-5403. Hours: 8AM-4PM (EST). *Misdemeanor, Civil Actions Under $30,000, Eviction, Small Claims.*

Civil Records: Access: Mail, in person. Both court and visitors may perform in person searches. No search fee. Required to search: name, years to search; also helpful-address. Civil cases indexed by defendant. Civil records on docket books from 1956-1987. **Criminal Records:** Access: Mail, in person. Both court and visitors may perform in person searches. No search fee. Required to search: name, years to search, DOB; also helpful-address, SSN. Criminal records on computer since

1987, docket books from 1956-1987. **General Information:** No juvenile, protective custody records released. SASE required. Turnaround time 1-2 days. Copy fee: $1.00 per page. Divorce Copy Fees: $2.00 first page, $1.00 each add'l page. Certification fee: $1.00. Fee payee: Maine District Court. Personal checks accepted. Prepayment is required. Public access terminal is available.

Waterville District Court -District 7 18
Colby St, PO Box 397, Waterville, ME 04903; 207-873-2103. Hours: 8AM-4PM (EST). *Misdemeanor, Civil Actions Under $30,000, Eviction, Small Claims.*

Civil Records: Access: Mail, in person. Both court and visitors may perform in person searches. No search fee. Required to search: name, years to search; also helpful-address. Civil cases indexed by defendant. Civil records on docket books from 1956-1998. **Criminal Records:** Access: Mail, in person. Both court and visitors may perform in person searches. No search fee. Required to search: name, years to search, DOB; also helpful-address, SSN. Criminal records on computer since 1986, docket books from 1956-1986. **General Information:** No juvenile, protective custody records released. SASE required. Turnaround time 1 week. Copy fee: $1.00 per page. Certification fee: $1.00. Fee payee: Maine. Personal checks accepted. Prepayment is required.

Probate Court 2 Turner St, Auburn, ME
04210; 207-782-0281; Fax: 207-782-5367. Hours: 8:30AM-5PM (EST). *Probate.*

Aroostook County

Caribou Superior Court 144 Sweden St,
Suite 101, Caribou, ME 04736; 207-498-8125. Hours: 8AM-4PM (EST). *Felony, Misdemeanor, Civil Actions Over $30,000.*

Civil Records: Access: Mail, in person. Only the court conducts in person searches; visitors may not. No search fee. Required to search: name, years to search. Civil cases indexed by defendant, plaintiff. Civil records on docket books since 1951. Pending cases 1990 forward stored in Caribou Court. **Criminal Records:** Access: Mail, in person. Only the court conducts in person searches; visitors may not. Search fee:. Required to search: name, years to search; also helpful-DOB. Criminal records on docket books since 1951. Pending cases 1990 forward stored in Caribou Court. **General Information:** No juvenile, protective custody records released. SASE required. Turnaround time 1 week. Copy fee: $1.00 per page. Certification fee: $2.00. Fee payee: Treasurer, State of Maine or Superior Court. Personal checks accepted. Prepayment is required.

Houlton Superior Court PO Box 457,
Houlton, ME 04730; 207-532-6563. Hours: 8AM-4PM (EST). *Felony, Misdemeanor, Civil Actions Over $30,000.*

Civil Records: Access: Mail, in person. Both court and visitors may perform in person searches. No search fee. Required to search: name, years to search. Civil cases indexed by defendant, plaintiff. Civil records on docket books since 1951. Non-pending closed case records are stored at the Houlton Court. **Criminal Records:** Access: Mail, in person. Both court and visitors may perform in person searches. No search fee. Required to search: name, years to search, DOB. Criminal records on docket books since 1951. Non-pending closed case records are stored at the Houlton Court. **General Information:** No juvenile or protective custody records released. SASE

required. Turnaround time 2-3 days. Copy fee: $2.00 for first page, $.50 each addl. Certification fee: $2.00. Fee payee: Maine Superior Court. No personal checks accepted. Prepayment is required.

Caribou District Court - East #1 144
Sweden St, Caribou, ME 04736; 207-493-3144. Hours: 8AM-4PM (EST). *Misdemeanor, Civil Actions Under $30,000, Eviction, Small Claims.*

Civil Records: Access: Mail, in person. Only the court conducts in person searches; visitors may not. No search fee. Required to search: name, years to search. Civil cases indexed by defendant. Civil records on docket books since 1963. **Criminal Records:** Access: In person only. Court does not conduct in person searches; visitors must perform searches for themselves. Search fee: No criminal searches performed by court. Required to search: name, years to search; also helpful-DOB. Criminal records on computer since 1987 (includes traffic), docket books since 1963. **General Information:** No juvenile or child protective records released. SASE required. Turnaround time 1 week. Copy fee: $1.00 per page. Certification fee: $2.00 plus $1.00 each additional page. Fee payee: Maine District Court. Personal checks accepted. Prepayment is required. Public access terminal is available.

District Court PO Box 794 (27 Riverside Dr),
Presque Isle, ME 04769; 207-764-2055. Hours: 8AM-4PM (EST). *Misdemeanor, Civil Actions Under $30,000, Eviction, Small Claims.*

Civil Records: Access: Mail, in person. Both court and visitors may perform in person searches. No search fee. Required to search: name, years to search. Civil cases indexed by defendant. Civil records on docket books since 1962. **Criminal Records:** Access: In person only. Court does not conduct in person searches; visitors must perform searches for themselves. Search fee: No criminal searches performed by court. Required to search: name, years to search; also helpful-DOB. Criminal records on computer since 1987, docket books since 1962. **General Information:** No juvenile or child protective records released. SASE required. Turnaround time 1 week. Copy fee: $1.00 per page. Include $1.00 for postage or SASE. Certification fee: $1.00. Fee payee: Maine District Court. Personal checks accepted. Prepayment is required. Public access terminal is available.

Fort Kent District Court - District 1
Division of Western Aroostook, PO Box 473, Fort Kent, ME 04743; 207-834-5003. Hours: 8AM-4PM (EST). *Misdemeanor, Civil Actions Under $30,000, Eviction, Small Claims.*

Civil Records: Access: Phone, mail, in person. Both court and visitors may perform in person searches. No search fee. Required to search: name, years to search. Civil cases indexed by defendant, plaintiff. few records are computerized. **Criminal Records:** Access: Phone, mail, in person. Both court and visitors may perform in person searches. No search fee. Required to search: name, years to search. Criminal records on computer from 1988, on docket books from 1960-1988. **General Information:** No juvenile, protective custody, impounded, mental health records released. SASE required. Turnaround time 2-3 days. Copy fee: $1.00 per page. Certification fee: $1.00. Fee payee: Maine District Court. Personal checks accepted. Prepayment is required.

Houlton District Court - South #2 PO
Box 457, Houlton, ME 04730; 207-532-2147. Hours: 8AM-4PM (EST). *Misdemeanor, Civil Actions Under $30,000, Eviction, Small Claims.*

Civil Records: Access: Mail, in person. Only the court conducts in person searches; visitors may not. No search fee. Required to search: name, years to search; also helpful-address. Civil cases indexed by defendant, plaintiff. Civil records on docket books since 1960. **Criminal Records:** Access: Mail, in person. Only the court conducts in person searches; visitors may not. No search fee. Required to search: name, years to search; also helpful-address, DOB. Criminal records on computer since June 1987, docket books since 1960. **General Information:** No Juvenile or protective custody records released. SASE required. Turnaround time 2-3 days. Copy fee: $1.00 per page. Certification fee: $1.00. Fee payee: Maine District Court. Personal checks accepted. Prepayment is required. Public access terminal is available. Public Access Terminal Note: Since June 1987.

Madawaska District Court - West PO
Box 127, 123 E Main St, Madawaska, ME 04756; 207-728-4700. Hours: 8AM-4PM M,T,F (EST). *Misdemeanor, Civil Actions Under $30,000, Eviction, Small Claims.*

Civil Records: Access: Phone, mail, in person. Only the court conducts in person searches; visitors may not. No search fee. Required to search: name, years to search. Civil cases indexed by defendant, plaintiff. Civil records on docket books from 1966-67. **Criminal Records:** Access: Phone, mail, in person. Only the court conducts in person searches; visitors may not. No search fee. Required to search: name, years to search; also helpful-DOB. Criminal records on computer since 1988, docket books from 1966-67. **General Information:** No juvenile, protected custody, impounded or mental health records released. SASE required. Turnaround time 2-3 days. Copy fee: $1.00 per page. Additional fee $1.00 if no SASE. Certification fee: $1.00. Fee payee: Maine District Court. Personal checks accepted. Prepayment is required.

Probate Court 26 Court St #103, Houlton, ME
04730; 207-532-1502. Hours: 8AM-4:30PM (EST). *Probate.*

Cumberland County

Superior Court - Civil PO Box 287-DTS,
Portland, ME 04112; 207-822-4105. Hours: 8AM-4:30PM (EST). *Civil Actions Over $30,000.*

Civil Records: Access: Phone, mail, in person. Both court and visitors may perform in person searches. No search fee. Required to search: name, years to search. Civil cases indexed by defendant, plaintiff. Civil records on index cards since 1900s. **General Information:** No juvenile, medical malpractice, impounded records released. SASE required. Turnaround time 1 day to 1 week. Copy fee: $1.00 per page. Include $1.00 for postage unless pre-paid envelope already enclosed. Certification fee: $1.00. Fee payee: Superior Court. Personal checks accepted. Prepayment is required.

Superior Court - Criminal PO Box 287,
Portland, ME 04112; 207-822-4113. Hours: 8AM-4:30PM (EST). *Felony, Misdemeanor.* **Criminal Records:** Access: In person only. Both court and visitors may perform in person searches. No search fee. Required to search: name, years to search, DOB. Criminal records on index cards since 1900s, some records form 08/98 to present are computerized. **General Information:** No juvenile records released. SASE required. Turnaround time 2-3 days. Copy fee: $1.00 per page. Certification

fee: $1.00. Fee payee: Clerk of Courts. Personal checks accepted. Prepayment is required.

Portland District Court - South #9-Civil
PO Box 412, 205 Newbury St, Portland, ME 04112; 207-822-4200. Hours: 8AM-4:30PM (EST). *Civil Actions Under $30,000, Eviction, Small Claims.*

Note: Also see Sagadahoc District Court, which handles cases from the eastern part of Cumberland County.

Civil Records: Access: Mail, in person. Both court and visitors may perform in person searches. No search fee. Required to search: name, years to search. Civil cases indexed by defendant. **General Information:** No child custody records released. SASE required. Turnaround time 1 week. Copy fee: $1.00 per page. Certification fee: $1.00. Fee payee: Maine District Court. Personal checks accepted. Prepayment is required.

Portland District Court-South #9-Criminal
PO Box 412, Portland, ME 04112; 207-822-4205. Hours: 8AM-4:30PM (EST). *Misdemeanor.* **Criminal Records:** Access: Mail, in person. Both court and visitors may perform in person searches. No search fee. Required to search: name, years to search, DOB, offense, date of offense. Criminal records on computer since 09/86, prior records archived. **General Information:** No impounded records released. SASE required. Turnaround time 3-4 days. Copy fee: $1.00 per page. Certification fee: $1.00. Fee payee: Maine District Court. Personal checks accepted. Prepayment is required. Public access terminal is available.

Bath District Court - East #6
RR 1, Box 310, Bath, ME 04530; 207-442-0200. Hours: 8AM-4PM (EST). *Misdemeanor, Civil Actions Under $30,000, Eviction, Small Claims.*

Civil Records: Access: Mail, in person. Only the court conducts in person searches; visitors may not. No search fee. Required to search: name, years to search. Civil cases indexed by defendant, plaintiff. Civil records on docket books since 1960s. **Criminal Records:** Access: Mail, in person. Court does not conduct in person searches; visitors must perform searches for themselves. No search fee. Required to search: name, years to search; also helpful-DOB. Criminal records on computer since 1987, docket books since 1960s. **General Information:** No juvenile, child protective or impounded records released. SASE not required. Turnaround time up to 1 week. Copy fee: $1.00 per page. Certification fee: $1.00. Fee payee: Maine District Court. Personal checks accepted. Prepayment is required.

Bridgton District Court - North #9
2 Chase Common, Bridgton, ME 04009; 207-647-3535. Hours: 8AM-4PM (EST). *Misdemeanor, Civil Actions Under $30,000, Eviction, Small Claims.*

Civil Records: Access: Phone, in person. Both court and visitors may perform in person searches. Search fee: No civil searches performed by court. Required to search: name, years to search. Civil cases indexed by defendant. Civil records on docket books since 1960. **Criminal Records:** Access: Phone, in person. Both court and visitors may perform in person searches. Search fee: No criminal searches performed by court. Required to search: name, years to search; also helpful-DOB. Criminal records on computer since 1988, docket books since 1960. **General Information:** No juvenile, protective custody, financial affidavits, impounded or domestic records released. Copy

fee: $1.00 per page. Certification fee: $1.00. Fee payee: Maine District Court. Personal checks accepted. Prepayment is required. Public access terminal is available. Public Access Terminal Note: Criminal only.

Probate Court
142 Federal St, Portland, ME 04101-4196; 207-871-8382. Hours: 8:30AM-4:30PM (EST). *Probate.*

Franklin County

Superior Court
38 Main St, Farmington, ME 04938; 207-778-3346; Fax: 207-778-8261. Hours: 8AM-4PM (EST). *Felony, Misdemeanor, Civil Actions Over $30,000.*

Civil Records: Access: Phone, in person. Court does not conduct in person searches; visitors must perform searches for themselves. Search fee: No civil searches performed by court. Required to search: name, years to search. Civil cases indexed by defendant, plaintiff. Civil records on docket books and index cards since 1900s. **Criminal Records:** Access: In person only. Court does not conduct in person searches; visitors must perform searches for themselves. Search fee: No criminal searches performed by court. Required to search: name, years to search; also helpful-DOB, SSN. Criminal records on docket books and index cards since 1900s. **General Information:** No juvenile, impounded or medical malpractice records released. Copy fee: $1.00 per page. Certification fee: $1.00. Fee payee: Superior Court. Personal checks accepted. Prepayment is required.

District Court #12
25 Main St, Farmington, ME 04938; 207-778-8200. Hours: 8AM-4PM (EST). *Misdemeanor, Civil Actions Under $30,000, Eviction, Small Claims.*

Civil Records: Access: In person only. Court does not conduct in person searches; visitors must perform searches for themselves. Search fee: No civil searches performed by court. Required to search: name, years to search. Civil cases indexed by defendant. Civil records on docket books since 1965 (index cards in front). **Criminal Records:** Access: In person only. Court does not conduct in person searches; visitors must perform searches for themselves. Search fee: No criminal searches performed by court. Required to search: name, years to search, DOB. Criminal records on computer since 1987, on docket books since 1965 (index cards in front). **General Information:** No impounded records released. Copy fee: $1.00 per page. Certification fee: $1.00. Fee payee: Maine District Court. Personal checks accepted. Prepayment is required.

Probate Court
County Courthouse, 38 Main St, Farmington, ME 04938; 207-778-5888; Fax: 207-778-5899. Hours: 8:30AM-4PM (EST). *Probate.*

Hancock County

Superior Court
50 State St, Ellsworth, ME 04605-1926; 207-667-7176. Hours: 8AM-4PM (EST). *Felony, Misdemeanor, Civil Actions Over $30,000.*

Civil Records: Access: Mail, in person. Only the court conducts in person searches; visitors may not. No search fee. Required to search: name, years to search. Civil cases indexed by defendant, plaintiff. Civil records on card files since 1960. **Criminal Records:** Access: Mail, in person. Only the court conducts in person searches; visitors may not. No search fee. Required to search: name, years to search, DOB. Criminal records on card files since 1960. **General Information:** No protective custody records released. Mail requests

not accepted. Turnaround time varies. Copy fee: $1.00 per page. Certification fee: $1.00. Fee payee: State of Maine. Personal checks accepted. Prepayment is required.

Bar Harbor District Court - South #5
93 Cottage St, Bar Harbor, ME 04609; 207-288-3082. Hours: 8AM-4PM (EST). *Misdemeanor, Civil Actions Under $30,000, Eviction, Small Claims.*

Civil Records: Access: Mail, in person. Both court and visitors may perform in person searches. Search fee: $1.00 per name. Required to search: name, years to search. Civil cases indexed by defendant, plaintiff. Civil records on docket books since 1970. **Criminal Records:** Access: Mail, in person. Both court and visitors may perform in person searches. Search fee: $1.00 per name. Required to search: name, years to search, DOB. Criminal records on computer since 1987, on docket books since 1970. **General Information:** No juvenile or impounded records released. SASE required. Turnaround time 2-3 days. Copy fee: $1.00 per page. Certification fee: $1.00. Fee payee: Maine District Court. Personal checks accepted. Prepayment is required. Public access terminal is available.

Ellsworth District Court-Central #5
50 State St, Ellsworth, ME 04605; 207-667-7141. Hours: 8AM-4PM (EST). *Misdemeanor, Civil Actions Under $30,000, Eviction, Small Claims.*

Civil Records: Access: Mail, in person. Both court and visitors may perform in person searches. No search fee. Required to search: name, years to search. Civil cases indexed by defendant, plaintiff. Civil records on docket books since 1965; need to know names of both parties to search. **Criminal Records:** Both court and visitors may perform in person searches. Search fee: No criminal searches performed by court. Required to search: name, years to search. Criminal records on computer since 1987, docket books since 1965. The court will aloow no access to criminal records. **General Information:** No juvenile, child protection, adoption or mental health records released. SASE required. Turnaround time 1 week. Copy fee: $1.00 per page. Certification fee: $1.00. Fee payee: Maine District Court. Personal checks accepted. Prepayment is required. Public access terminal is available. Public Access Terminal Note: Criminal only.

Probate Court
50 State St, Ellsworth, ME 04605; 207-667-8434. Hours: 8:30AM-4PM (EST). *Probate.*

Kennebec County

Superior Court
95 State St, Clerk of Court, Augusta, ME 04330; 207-622-9357. Hours: 8AM-4PM (EST). *Felony, Misdemeanor, Civil Actions Over $30,000.*

Civil Records: Access: Mail, in person. Only the court conducts in person searches; visitors may not. No search fee. Required to search: name, years to search. Civil cases indexed by defendant, plaintiff. Civil records on index cards since 1977, docket books since 1950. **Criminal Records:** Access: In person only. Court does not conduct in person searches; visitors must perform searches for themselves. Search fee: No criminal searches performed by court. Required to search: name, years to search; also helpful-DOB. Criminal records on index cards since 1977, docket books since 1950. **General Information:** No protective custody records released. SASE not required. Turnaround time 1 week. Copy fee: $1.00 per page. Certification fee: $1.00. Fee payee:

Treasurer State of Maine. Personal checks accepted. Prepayment is required.

Maine District Court District 7
Division of Southern Kennebec, 145 State St, Augusta, ME 04330-7495; 207-287-8075. Hours: 8AM-4PM (EST). *Misdemeanor, Civil Actions Under $30,000, Eviction, Small Claims.*

Civil Records: Access: Mail, in person. Both court and visitors may perform in person searches. No search fee. Required to search: name, years to search. Civil cases indexed by defendant. Civil records on docket books since 1963. **Criminal Records:** Access: Mail, in person. Both court and visitors may perform in person searches. No search fee. Required to search: name, years to search, DOB; also helpful-SSN. Criminal records on computer since 1987, docket books since 1963. **General Information:** No juvenile, mental health, protective custody and closed proceeding case records released. SASE required. Turnaround time 1 week. Copy fee: $1.00 per page. Certification fee: $1.00. Fee payee: Maine District Court. Personal checks accepted. Prepayment is required.

Probate Court 95 State St, Augusta, ME 04330; 207-622-7558; Fax: 207-621-1639. Hours: 8AM-4PM (EST). *Probate.*

Knox County

Superior Court 62 Union St, Rockland, ME 04841-2836; 207-594-2576. Hours: 8AM-4PM (EST). *Felony, Misdemeanor, Civil Actions Over $30,000.*

Civil Records: Access: Phone, mail, in person. Both court and visitors may perform in person searches. No search fee. Required to search: name, years to search. Civil cases indexed by defendant, plaintiff. Civil records on docket books since 1930s, index cards (in office) since mid-1970s. **Criminal Records:** Access: In person only. Court does not conduct in person searches; visitors must perform searches for themselves. Search fee: No criminal searches performed by court. Required to search: name, years to search; also helpful-DOB. Criminal records on docket books since 1930s, index cards (in office) since mid-1970s. **General Information:** No Impounded or pre-sentence records released. SASE not required. Turnaround time 1 week. Copy fee: $1.00 per page. Certification fee: $1.00. Fee payee: State Treasurer. In-state checks only. Out-of-state money orders only. Prepayment is required.

District Court #6 62 Union St, Rockland, ME 04841; 207-596-2240. Hours: 8AM-4PM (EST). *Misdemeanor, Civil Actions Under $30,000, Eviction, Small Claims.*

Civil Records: Access: Phone, mail, in person. Both court and visitors may perform in person searches. No search fee. Required to search: name, years to search. Civil cases indexed by defendant, plaintiff. Civil records on docket books. **Criminal Records:** Access: Phone, mail, in person. Both court and visitors may perform in person searches. No search fee. Required to search: name, years to search, DOB. Criminal records on docket books. **General Information:** No impounded records released. SASE required. Turnaround time 1 week. Copy fee: $1.00 per page. Certification fee: $1.00. Fee payee: Maine District Court. Personal checks accepted. Prepayment is required. Public access terminal is available.

Probate Court 62 Union St, Rockland, ME 04841; 207-594-0427; Fax: 207-594-0443. Hours: 8AM-4PM (EST). *Probate.*

http://knoxcounty.midcoast.com

Lincoln County

Lincoln County Superior Court High St, PO Box 249, Wiscasset, ME 04578; 207-882-7517; Fax: 207-882-7741. Hours: 8AM-4PM (EST). *Felony, Misdemeanor, Civil Actions Over $30,000.*

Civil Records: Access: Mail, in person. Only the court conducts in person searches; visitors may not. No search fee. Required to search: name, years to search. Civil cases indexed by defendant, plaintiff. Civil records on docket books and index cards since 1960s. **Criminal Records:** Access: Mail, in person. Only the court conducts in person searches; visitors may not. No search fee. Required to search: name, years to search, DOB. Criminal records on docket books and index cards since 1960s. **General Information:** No protective custody records released. SASE not required. Copy fee: $1.00 per page. Certification fee: $2.00. Personal checks accepted. Prepayment is required.

District Court #6 32 High St, PO Box 249, Wiscasset, ME 04578; 207-882-6363; Fax: 207-882-5980. Hours: 8AM-4PM (EST). *Misdemeanor, Civil Actions Under $30,000, Eviction, Small Claims.*

Civil Records: Access: Phone, mail, in person. Both court and visitors may perform in person searches. No search fee. Required to search: name, years to search. Civil cases indexed by defendant, plaintiff. Civil records on docket books since 1960. **Criminal Records:** Access: Mail, in person. Only the court conducts in person searches; visitors may not. No search fee. Required to search: name, years to search, DOB. Criminal records on computer since 1987, docket books since 1960. **General Information:** No juvenile, child protective or impounded records released. SASE required. Turnaround time 1 week. Copy fee: $1.00 per page. Certification fee: $1.00. Fee payee: Maine District Court. Personal checks accepted. Prepayment is required.

Probate Court High St, PO Box 249, Wiscasset, ME 04578; 207-882-7392; Fax: 207-882-4061. Hours: 8AM-4PM (EST). *Probate.*

Oxford County

Superior Court Courthouse, 26 Western Ave, PO Box 179, South Paris, ME 04281-0179; 207-743-8936; Fax: 207-743-7346. Hours: 8AM-4PM (EST). *Felony, Misdemeanor, Civil Actions Over $30,000.*

Civil Records: Access: Mail, in person. Both court and visitors may perform in person searches. No search fee. Required to search: name, years to search. Civil cases indexed by defendant, plaintiff. Civil records on docket books since 1951. **Criminal Records:** Access: Mail, in person. Both court and visitors may perform in person searches. No search fee. Required to search: name, years to search, DOB. Criminal records on docket books since 1951. **General Information:** No protective custody or protection from abuse records released. SASE required. Turnaround time 3-4 days. Copy fee: $1.00 per page. Certification fee: $1.00. Fee payee: Clerk of Superior Court. Personal checks accepted.

Rumford District Court - North #11
Municipal Bldg, 145 Congress St, Rumford, ME 04276; 207-364-7171. Hours: 8AM-4PM (EST). *Misdemeanor, Civil Actions Under $30,000, Eviction, Small Claims.*

Civil Records: Access: Phone, mail, in person. Both court and visitors may perform in person searches. No search fee. Required to search: name,

years to search. Civil cases indexed by defendant, plaintiff. Civil records on docket books since 1966. **Criminal Records:** Access: Mail, in person. Both court and visitors may perform in person searches. No search fee. Required to search: name, years to search, DOB. Criminal records on computer since March 1988, docket books since 1966. **General Information:** No impounded records released. SASE required. Turnaround time 1 week. Copy fee: $1.00 per page. Certification fee: $2.00. Fee payee: Maine District Court. Personal checks accepted.

South Paris District Court - South #11
26 Western Ave, South Paris, ME 04281; 207-743-8942. Hours: 8AM-4PM (EST). *Misdemeanor, Civil Actions Under $30,000, Eviction, Small Claims.*

Civil Records: Access: Mail, in person. Only the court conducts in person searches; visitors may not. No search fee. Required to search: name, years to search. Civil cases indexed by defendant. Civil records on docket books back 5 years. **Criminal Records:** Access: Mail, in person. Both court and visitors may perform in person searches. No search fee. Required to search: name, years to search; also helpful-DOB. Criminal records on computer since 1988, docket books back 5 years. **General Information:** No juvenile or child protective records released. SASE required. Turnaround time 1-2 days. Copy fee: $1.00 per page. Certification fee: $2.00. Fee payee: Maine District Court. Personal checks accepted. Prepayment is required. Public access terminal is available. Public Access Terminal Note: Criminal only.

Probate Court 26 Western Ave, PO Box 179, South Paris, ME 04281; 207-743-6671; Fax: 207-743-6671. Hours: 8AM-4PM (EST). *Probate.*

Penobscot County

Superior Court 97 Hammond St, Bangor, ME 04401; 207-947-0751. Hours: 8AM-4:30PM (EST). *Felony, Misdemeanor, Civil Actions Over $30,000.*

Civil Records: Access: Mail, in person. Only the court conducts in person searches; visitors may not. No search fee. Required to search: name, years to search. Civil cases indexed by defendant, plaintiff. Civil records on docket books since 1975. **Criminal Records:** Access: In person. Only the court conducts in person searches; visitors may not. Search fee: No criminal searches performed by court. Required to search: name, years to search, DOB. Criminal records on docket books since 1975. **General Information:** No impounded records released. SASE required. Copy fee: $1.00 per page. Certification fee: $1.00. Fee payee: Treasurer, State of Maine. Personal checks accepted. Prepayment is required.

Bangor District Court 73 Hammond St, Bangor, ME 04401; 207-941-3040. Hours: 8AM-4PM (EST). *Misdemeanor, Civil Actions Under $30,000, Eviction, Small Claims.*

Civil Records: Access: Mail, in person. Both court and visitors may perform in person searches. No search fee. Required to search: name, years to search. Civil cases indexed by defendant. Civil records on docket books since 1962. Court suggests using central state repository. **Criminal Records:** Access: Mail, in person. Both court and visitors may perform in person searches. No search fee. Required to search: name, years to search; also helpful-DOB. Criminal records on computer since late 1986, docket books since 1962. **General Information:** No protective custody records released. SASE required. Turnaround time 1 week. Copy fee: $1.00 per page. Certification fee: $1.00. Fee payee: Maine District Court. Personal checks accepted. Prepayment is required. Public access terminal is available. Public Access Terminal Note: Criminal only.

Central District Court - Central #13 66

Maine St, Lincoln, ME 04457; 207-794-8512. Hours: 8AM-4PM (EST). *Misdemeanor, Civil Actions Under $30,000, Eviction, Small Claims.*

Civil Records: Access: In person only. Only the court conducts in person searches; visitors may not. No search fee. Required to search: name, years to search. Civil cases indexed by defendant. Civil records on docket books since 1964. **Criminal Records:** Access: In person only. Only the court conducts in person searches; visitors may not. No search fee. Required to search: name, years to search, DOB. Criminal records on computer since 1987, docket books since 1964. **General Information:** No juvenile or protective custody records released. Copy fee: $1.00 per page. Certification fee: $1.00. Fee payee: Maine District Court. Personal checks accepted. Prepayment is required. Public access terminal is available.

Millinocket District Court - North #13

207 Penobscot Ave, Millinocket, ME 04462; 207-723-4786. Hours: 8AM-4PM (EST). *Misdemeanor, Civil Actions Under $30,000, Eviction, Small Claims.*

Civil Records: Access: Mail, in person. Court does not conduct in person searches; visitors must perform searches for themselves. No search fee. Required to search: name, years to search. Civil cases indexed by defendant, plaintiff. Civil records on docket books since 1970s. **Criminal Records:** Access: Mail, in person. Both court and visitors may perform in person searches. No search fee. Required to search: name, years to search, DOB. Criminal records on computer since 1987, docket books since 1964. **General Information:** No juvenile or protective custody records released. SASE required. Turnaround time 1 week. Copy fee: $1.00 per page. Certification fee: $1.00. Fee payee: Maine District Court. Personal checks accepted. Prepayment is required.

Newport District Court - West #3 16

Water St, Newport, ME 04953; 207-368-5778. Hours: 8AM-4PM (EST). *Misdemeanor, Civil Actions Under $30,000, Eviction, Small Claims.*

Civil Records: Access: Mail, in person. Both court and visitors may perform in person searches. No search fee. Required to search: name, years to search. Civil cases indexed by defendant, plaintiff. Civil records on docket books since 1965. **Criminal Records:** Access: Mail, in person. Both court and visitors may perform in person searches. No search fee. Required to search: name, years to search; also helpful-DOB. Criminal records on computer since 1987, docket books since 1965. **General Information:** No impounded records released. SASE required. Turnaround time 1 week. Copy fee: $1.00 per page. Certification fee: $1.00. Fee payee: Maine District Court. Personal checks accepted. Prepayment is required.

Probate Court 97 Hammond St, Bangor, ME

04401-4996; 207-942-8769; Fax: 207-941-8499. Hours: 8AM-4:30PM (EST). *Probate.*

Piscataquis County

Superior Court 51 E Main St, Dover-

Foxcroft, ME 04426; 207-564-8419; Fax: 207-564-3363. Hours: 8AM-4PM (EST). *Felony, Misdemeanor, Civil Actions Over $30,000.*

Civil Records: Access: Mail, in person. Only the court conducts in person searches; visitors may not. No search fee. Required to search: name, years to search. Civil cases indexed by defendant, plaintiff. Civil records on docket books since 1960. **Criminal Records:** Access: Mail, in person. Only the court conducts in person searches; visitors may not. No search fee. Required to search: name, years to search; also helpful-DOB. Criminal records on docket books since 1960. **General Information:** No pre-sentence report records released. SASE required. Turnaround time 1 week. Copy fee: $1.00 per page. Certification fee: $1.00. Fee payee: State of Maine Superior Court. Personal checks accepted. Prepayment is required.

District Court #13 59 E Main St, Dover-

Foxcroft, ME 04426; 207-564-2240. Hours: 8AM-4PM (EST). *Misdemeanor, Civil Actions Under $30,000, Eviction, Small Claims.*

Civil Records: Access: Mail, in person. Both court and visitors may perform in person searches. No search fee. Required to search: name, years to search. Civil cases indexed by defendant, plaintiff. Civil records on docket books since 1963. **Criminal Records:** Access: Mail, in person. Both court and visitors may perform in person searches. No search fee. Required to search: name, years to search; also helpful-DOB. Criminal records on computer since 1987, docket books since 1963. **General Information:** No protective custody or juvenile records released. SASE required. Turnaround time 1 week. Copy fee: $1.00 per page. Certification fee: $1.00. Fee payee: Maine District Court. Personal checks accepted. Prepayment is required.

Probate Court 51 E Main St, Dover-Foxcroft,

ME 04426; 207-564-2431; Fax: 207-564-3022. Hours: 8:30AM-4PM (EST). *Probate.*

Sagadahoc County

Superior Court 752 High St, PO Box 246,

Bath, ME 04530; 207-443-9733. Hours: 8AM-4:30PM (EST). *Felony, Misdemeanor, Civil Actions Over $30,000.*

Civil Records: Access: In person only. Court does not conduct in person searches; visitors must perform searches for themselves. Search fee: No civil searches performed by court. Required to search: name, years to search. Civil cases indexed by defendant, plaintiff. Civil records on docket books since 1900s. **Criminal Records:** Access: In person only. Court does not conduct in person searches; visitors must perform searches for themselves. Search fee: No criminal searches performed by court. Required to search: name, years to search. Criminal records on docket books since 1900s. **General Information:** No impounded records released. Copy fee: $1.00 per page. Certification fee: $1.00. Fee payee: Clerk of Superior Court. Only cashiers checks and money orders accepted. Prepayment is required.

District Court #6 RR 1, Box 310, New

Meadows Rd, Bath, ME 04530; 207-442-0200. Hours: 8AM-4PM (EST). *Misdemeanor, Civil Actions Under $30,000, Eviction, Small Claims.*

Note: This court handles the eastern part of Cumberland County & all of Sagadahoc County.

Civil Records: Access: Mail, in person. Only the court conducts in person searches; visitors may not. No search fee. Required to search: name, years to search. Civil cases indexed by defendant, plaintiff. Civil records on docket books since 1960s. **Criminal Records:** Access: Mail, in person. Only the court conducts in person searches; visitors may not. No search fee. Required to search: name, years to search; also helpful-DOB. Criminal records on computer since 1987, docket books from 1987 back to 1960s. Search requests are referred to central state repository. **General Information:** No protective custody or juvenile records released. SASE not required. Turnaround time 1 week. Copy fee: $1.00 per page. Certification fee: $1.00. Fee payee: Maine District Court. Personal checks accepted. Prepayment is required.

Probate Court 752 High St, PO Box 246,

Bath, ME 04530; 207-443-8218; Fax: 207-443-8217. Hours: 8:30AM-4:30PM (EST). *Probate.*

Somerset County

Superior Court PO Box 725, Skowhegan, ME

04976; 207-474-5161. Hours: 8AM-4PM (EST). *Felony, Misdemeanor, Civil Actions Over $30,000.*

Civil Records: Access: In person only. Court does not conduct in person searches; visitors must perform searches for themselves. Search fee: No civil searches performed by court. Required to search: name, years to search. Civil cases indexed by defendant, plaintiff. Civil records archived in Augusta back to 1800s, docket books and index cards back to 1900s. **Criminal Records:** Access: In person only. Court does not conduct in person searches; visitors must perform searches for themselves. Search fee: No criminal searches performed by court. Required to search: name, years to search; also helpful-DOB. Criminal records archived in Augusta back to 1800s, docket books and index cards back to 1900s. **General Information:** No impounded, present investigations, psychological evaluations or child support records released. Copy fee: $1.00 per page. Certification fee: $1.00. Fee payee: Clerk of Superior Court. Personal checks accepted. Prepayment is required.

District Court #12 PO Box 525, 88 Water St,

Skowhegan, ME 04976; 207-474-9518. Hours: 8AM-4PM (EST). *Misdemeanor, Civil Actions Under $30,000, Eviction, Small Claims.*

Civil Records: Access: Mail, in person. Both court and visitors may perform in person searches. No search fee. Required to search: name, years to search. Civil cases indexed by defendant. Civil records on docket books since 1960s, divorces since 1970s. **Criminal Records:** Access: Mail, in person. Both court and visitors may perform in person searches. No search fee. Required to search: name, years to search; also helpful-DOB. Criminal records on computer since 1987, docket books since 1960s. **General Information:** No juvenile records released. SASE required. Turnaround time 2-4 weeks. Copy fee: $1.00 per page. Certification fee: $1.00. Fee payee: Maine District Court. Personal checks accepted. Prepayment is required. Public access terminal is available. Public Access Terminal Note: Criminal only.

Probate Court Court St, Skowhegan, ME

04976; 207-474-3322. Hours: 8:30AM-4:30PM (EST). *Probate.*

Waldo County

Superior Court 137 Church St, PO Box 188, Belfast, ME 04915; 207-338-1940; Fax: 207-338-1086. Hours: 8AM-4PM (EST). *Felony, Misdemeanor, Civil Actions Over $30,000.*

Civil Records: Access: Mail, in person. Only the court conducts in person searches; visitors may not. No search fee. Required to search: name, years to search. Civil cases indexed by defendant, plaintiff. Civil records archived back to 1980 (not in office), on docket books since 1980. **Criminal Records:** Access: Mail, in person. Only the court conducts in person searches; visitors may not. No search fee. Required to search: name, years to search, DOB. Criminal records archived back to 1975 (not in office), on docket books since 1975. **General Information:** No protective custody records released. SASE required. Turnaround time 1 week. Copy fee: $1.00 per page. Certification fee: $1.00. Fee payee: State Treasurer. Personal checks accepted. Prepayment is required.

District Court #5 PO Box 382, 103 Church St, Belfast, ME 04915; 207-338-3107. Hours: 8AM-4PM (EST). *Misdemeanor, Civil Actions Under $30,000, Eviction, Small Claims.*

Civil Records: Access: Mail, in person. Both court and visitors may perform in person searches. No search fee. Required to search: name, years to search. Civil cases indexed by defendant, plaintiff. Civil records on docket books since 1966. **Criminal Records:** Access: Mail, in person. Both court and visitors may perform in person searches. No search fee. Required to search: name, years to search, DOB. Criminal records on computer since 1987, docket books since 1966. **General Information:** No juvenile or impounded records released. SASE required. Turnaround time 1 week. Copy fee: $1.00 per page. Certification fee: $1.00. Fee payee: Maine District Court. Personal checks accepted.

Probate Court 172 High St, PO Box 323, Belfast, ME 04915; 207-338-2780; Fax: 207-338-6360. Hours: 9AM-4PM (EST). *Probate.*

Washington County

Superior Court Clerk of Court, PO Box 526, Machias, ME 04654; 207-255-3326. Hours: 8AM-4PM (EST). *Felony, Misdemeanor, Civil.*

Civil Records: Access: Mail, in person. Both court and visitors may perform in person searches. No search fee. Required to search: name, years to search. Civil cases indexed by defendant, plaintiff. Civil records on docket books and index cards since 1940s. **Criminal Records:** Access: Mail, in person. Both court and visitors may perform in person searches. No search fee. Required to search: name, years to search, DOB. Criminal records on docket books and index cards since 1940s. **General Information:** No impounded records released. SASE required. Turnaround time 1 week. Copy fee: $1.00 per page. Certification fee: $1.00. Fee payee: Treasurer, State of Maine. Personal checks accepted. Prepayment is required.

Calais District Court - North #4 PO Box 929, Calais, ME 04619; 207-454-2055. Hours: 8AM-4PM (EST). *Misdemeanor, Civil Actions Under $30,000, Eviction, Small Claims.*

Civil Records: Access: In person only. Court does not conduct in person searches; visitors must perform searches for themselves. Search fee: No civil searches performed by court. Required to search: name, years to search. Civil cases indexed by defendant, plaintiff. Civil records on docket books since 1964. **Criminal Records:** Access: In person only. Court does not conduct in person searches; visitors must perform searches for themselves. Search fee: No criminal searches performed by court. Required to search: name, years to search, DOB. Criminal records on computer since 1987, docket books since 1964. **General Information:** No juvenile or protective custody records released. Copy fee: $1.00 per page. Certification fee: $1.00. Fee payee: Maine District Court. Personal checks accepted. Prepayment is required. Public access terminal is available.

Maine District Court - 4th District 47 Court St, PO Box 297, Machias, ME 04654; 207-255-3044. Hours: 8AM-4PM (EST). *Misdemeanor, Civil Actions Under $30,000, Eviction, Small Claims.*

Civil Records: Access: Mail, in person. Both court and visitors may perform in person searches. No search fee. Required to search: name, years to search. Civil cases indexed by defendant, plaintiff. Civil records on docket books since 1964. **Criminal Records:** Access: Mail, in person. Both court and visitors may perform in person searches. No search fee. Required to search: name, years to search, DOB. Criminal records on computer since 1987, docket books since 1964. **General Information:** No protective custody or juvenile records released. SASE required. Turnaround time 4 days. Copy fee: $1.00 per page. Add $1.00 processing fee. Certification fee: $1.00. Fee payee: Maine District Court. Personal checks accepted. Prepayment is required. Public access terminal is available.

Probate Court PO Box 297, Machias, ME 04654; 207-255-6591. Hours: 8AM-4PM (EST). *Probate.*

York County

Superior Court Clerk of Court, PO Box 160, Alfred, ME 04002; 207-324-5122. Hours: 8AM-4:30PM (EST). *Felony, Misdemeanor, Civil Actions Over $30,000.*

Civil Records: Access: In person only. Court does not conduct in person searches; visitors must perform searches for themselves. Search fee: No civil searches performed by court. Required to search: name, years to search. Civil cases indexed by defendant, plaintiff. Civil records on docket books since 1930. **Criminal Records:** Access: In person only. Court does not conduct in person searches; visitors must perform searches for themselves. Search fee: No criminal searches performed by court. Required to search: name, years to search, DOB. Criminal records on docket books since 1930. **General Information:** No juvenile, or protective custody records released. Copy fee: $1.00 per page. Add $1.00 handling fee. Certification fee: $2.00. Fee payee: Clerk of Courts. Only cashiers checks and money orders accepted. Prepayment is required.

Biddeford District Court - East #10 25 Adams St, Biddeford, ME 04005; 207-283-1147. Hours: 8AM-4PM (EST). *Misdemeanor, Civil Actions Under $30,000, Eviction, Small Claims.*

Civil Records: Access: In person only. Both court and visitors may perform in person searches. Search fee: No civil searches performed by court. Required to search: name, years to search. Civil cases indexed by defendant. Civil records on docket books since 1989. Court will do up to 3 searches. **Criminal Records:** Access: In person only. Both court and visitors may perform in person searches. Search fee: No criminal searches performed by court. Required to search: name, years to search; also helpful-DOB. Criminal records on computer since 1986. Court will do up to 3 searches. **General Information:** No child protection or juvenile records released. Copy fee: $1.00 per page. Certification fee: $1.00. Fee payee: Maine District Court. Personal checks accepted. Prepayment is required.

Springvale District Court - West #10 PO Box 95, Butler St, Springvale, ME 04083; 207-324-6737. Hours: 8AM-4PM (EST). *Misdemeanor, Civil Actions Under $30,000, Eviction, Small Claims.*

Civil Records: Access: In person only. Court does not conduct in person searches; visitors must perform searches for themselves. Search fee: No civil searches performed by court. Required to search: name, years to search. Civil cases indexed by defendant. Civil records on docket books since 1965. **Criminal Records:** Access: Mail, in person. Only the court conducts in person searches; visitors may not. No search fee. Required to search: name, years to search, DOB. Criminal records on computer since 1987, dockets books since 1965. **General Information:** No impounded, juvenile, mental health or protective custody records released. SASE required. Turnaround time 3-4 days. Copy fee: $1.00 per page. Certification fee: $1.00. Fee payee: Maine District Court. Personal checks accepted. Prepayment is required.

York District Court - South #10 PO Box 770, Chase's Pond Rd, York, ME 03909-0770; 207-363-1230. Hours: 8AM-4PM (EST). *Misdemeanor, Civil Actions Under $30,000, Eviction, Small Claims.*

Civil Records: Access: In person only. Court does not conduct in person searches; visitors must perform searches for themselves. Search fee: No civil searches performed by court. Required to search: name, years to search. Civil cases indexed by defendant, plaintiff. Civil records on docket books since 1965. **Criminal Records:** Access: In person only. Court does not conduct in person searches; visitors must perform searches for themselves. Search fee: No criminal searches performed by court. Required to search: name, years to search, DOB. Criminal records on computer since 1987, docket books since 1965. **General Information:** No impounded, juvenile and protective custody records released. Copy fee: $1.00 per page. Certification fee: $2.00. Fee payee: Maine District Court. Personal checks accepted. Prepayment is required.

Probate Court PO Box 399, 45 Kennebunk Rd, Alfred, ME 04002; 207-324-1577; Fax: 207-324-0163. Hours: 8:30AM-4:30PM (EST). *Probate.*

ORGANIZATION

16 counties, 17 recording offices. The recording officer is County Register of Deeds. Counties maintain a general index of all transactions recorded. **Aroostock and Oxford Counties each have two recording offices.** There are no county assessors; each town has its own. The entire state is in the Eastern Time Zone (EST).

REAL ESTATE RECORDS

Counties do **not** usually perform real estate searches, but some will look up a name informally. Copy and certification fees vary widely. Assessor and tax records are located at the town/city level.

UCC RECORDS

Financing statements are filed both at the state level, except for real estate related filings, which are filed only with the Register of Deeds. Counties do **not** perform UCC searches. Copy fees are usually $1.00 per page.

TAX LIEN RECORDS

All tax liens on personal property are filed with the Secretary of State. All tax liens on real property are filed with the Register of Deeds.

OTHER LIENS

Municipal, bail bond, mechanics.

Androscoggin County

County Register of Deeds, 2 Turner Street, Courthouse, Auburn, ME 04210-5978. 207-782-0191. Fax: 207-784-3163.

Aroostook County (Northern District)

County Register of Deeds, P.O. Box 47, Fort Kent, ME 04743. 207-834-3925. Fax: 207-834-3138.

Aroostook County (Southern District)

County Register of Deeds, 26 Court St., Suite 102, Houlton, ME 04730. 207-532-1500.

Cumberland County

County Register of Deeds, P.O. Box 7230, Portland, ME 04112. 207-871-8389. Fax: 207-772-4162.
Online Access: Assessor. Records on the Cape Elizabeth Town Assessor database are available free on the Internet at www.capeelizabeth.com/taxdata.html. Records on the Freeport Town Assessor property database are available free on the Internet at www.freeportmaine.com/assessordb/db.cgi.

Franklin County

County Register of Deeds, 38 Main Street, Courthouse, Farmington, ME 04938-1818. 207-778-5889. Fax: 207-778-5899.

Hancock County

County Register of Deeds, P.O. Box 784, Ellsworth, ME 04605. 207-667-8353. Fax: 207-667-1410.

Kennebec County

County Register of Deeds, P.O. Box 1053, Augusta, ME 04332-1053. 207-622-0431. Fax: 207-622-1598.
Online Access: Assessor. Records on the Winslow Town Property Records database are available free on the Internet at www.winslowmaine.org. Records on the Town of Waterville Assessor's Database are available free on the Internet at http://140.239.211.227/watervilleme. User ID is required; registration is free.

Knox County

County Register of Deeds, 62 Union Street, Rockland, ME 04841. 207-594-0422. Fax: 207-594-0446.

Lincoln County

County Register of Deeds, P.O. Box 249, 32 High St., Wiscasset, ME 04578-0249. 207-882-7515. Fax: 207-882-4061.

Oxford County

County Register of Deeds, P.O. Box 179, South Paris, ME 04281-0179. 207-743-6211. Fax: 207-743-2656.

Penobscot County

County Register of Deeds, P.O. Box 2070, Bangor, ME 04402-2070. 207-942-8797. Fax: 207-945-4920.

Piscataquis County

County Register of Deeds, 51 East Main Street, Dover-Foxcroft, ME 04426. 207-564-2411. Fax: 207-564-7708.

Sagadahoc County

County Register of Deeds, P.O. Box 246, Bath, ME 04530. 207-443-8214. Fax: 207-443-8216.
www.cityofbath.com
Online Access: Assessor. Records on the City of Bath Assessor database are available free on the Internet at www.cityofbath.com/assessing/INDEX.HTM.

Somerset County

County Register of Deeds, P.O. Box 248, Skowhegan, ME 04976-0248. 207-474-3421. Fax: 207-474-2793.

Waldo County

County Register of Deeds, P.O. Box D, Belfast, ME 04915. 207-338-1710. Fax: 207-338-6360.

Washington County

County Register of Deeds, P.O. Box 297, Machias, ME 04654-0297. 207-255-6512. Fax: 207-255-3838.

York County

County Register of Deeds, P.O. Box 339, Alfred, ME 04002-0339. 207-324-1576. Fax: 207-324-2886.
www.raynorshyn.com/yorknet
Online Access: Assessor. Records on the Town of York Assessor Database Lookup are availabel free on the Internet at www.raynorshyn.com/yorknet/accsel.cfm. Records on the Town of Eliot Assessor database are available free on the Internet at http://140.239.211.227/edliotme. Search by street name & number, map/block/lot/unit, or account number.

You will usually be able to find the city name in the City/County Cross. Reference below. In that case, it is a simple matter to determine the county from the cross reference. However, only the official US Postal Service city names are included in this index. There are an additional 40,000 place names that people use in their addresses. Therefore, we have also included a ZIP/City Cross. Reference immediately following the City/County Cross. Reference.

If you know the ZIP Code but the city name does not appear in the City/County Cross. Reference index, look up the ZIP Code in the ZIP/City Cross. Reference, find the city name, then look up the city name in the City/County Cross. Reference. For example, you want to know the county for an address of Menands, NY 12204. There is no "Menands" in the City/County Cross. Reference. The ZIP/City Cross. Reference shows that ZIP Codes 12201-12288 are for the city of Albany. Looking back in the City/County Cross. Reference, Albany is in Albany County.

City/County Cross Reference

ABBOT VILLAGE Piscataquis
ACTON York
ADDISON Washington
ALBION Kennebec
ALFRED York
ALNA Lincoln
ANDOVER Oxford
ANSON Somerset
ASHLAND Aroostook
ATHENS Somerset
ATLANTIC Hancock
AUBURN Androscoggin
AUGUSTA Kennebec
AURORA Hancock
BAILEY ISLAND Cumberland
BANGOR Penobscot
BAR HARBOR Hancock
BAR MILLS York
BASS HARBOR Hancock
BATH Sagadahoc
BAYVILLE Lincoln
BEALS Washington
BELFAST Waldo
BELGRADE Kennebec
BELGRADE LAKES Kennebec
BENEDICTA Aroostook
BERNARD Hancock
BERWICK York
BETHEL Oxford
BIDDEFORD York
BIDDEFORD POOL York
BINGHAM Somerset
BIRCH HARBOR Hancock
BLAINE Aroostook
BLUE HILL Hancock
BLUE HILL FALLS Hancock
BOOTHBAY Lincoln
BOOTHBAY HARBOR Lincoln
BOWDOINHAM Sagadahoc
BRADFORD (04410) Penobscot(97), Piscataquis(3)
BRADLEY Penobscot
BREMEN Lincoln
BREWER Penobscot
BRIDGEWATER Aroostook
BRIDGTON Cumberland
BRISTOL Lincoln
BROOKLIN Hancock
BROOKS Waldo
BROOKSVILLE Hancock
BROOKTON Washington
BROWNFIELD Oxford
BROWNVILLE Piscataquis
BROWNVILLE JUNCTION Piscataquis
BRUNSWICK Cumberland
BRYANT POND Oxford
BUCKFIELD Oxford
BUCKS HARBOR Washington
BUCKSPORT (04416) Hancock(89), Waldo(11)
BURLINGTON Penobscot
BURNHAM Waldo

BUSTINS ISLAND Cumberland
CALAIS Washington
CAMBRIDGE (04923) Somerset(97), Piscataquis(3)
CAMDEN Knox
CANAAN Somerset
CANTON Oxford
CAPE ELIZABETH Cumberland
CAPE NEDDICK York
CAPE PORPOISE York
CARATUNK Somerset
CARDVILLE Penobscot
CARIBOU Aroostook
CARMEL Penobscot
CASCO Cumberland
CASTINE Hancock
CENTER LOVELL Oxford
CHAMBERLAIN Lincoln
CHARLESTON Penobscot
CHEBEAGUE ISLAND Cumberland
CHERRYFIELD (04622) Washington(98), Hancock(2)
CHINA Kennebec
CLAYTON LAKE Aroostook
CLIFF ISLAND Cumberland
CLINTON Kennebec
COLUMBIA FALLS Washington
COOPERS MILLS Lincoln
COREA Hancock
CORINNA Penobscot
CORNISH York
COSTIGAN Penobscot
CRANBERRY ISLES Hancock
CROUSEVILLE Aroostook
CUMBERLAND CENTER Cumberland
CUMBERLAND FORESIDE Cumberland
CUSHING Knox
CUTLER Washington
DAMARISCOTTA Lincoln
DANFORTH Washington
DANVILLE Androscoggin
DEER ISLE Hancock
DENMARK Oxford
DENNYSVILLE Washington
DETROIT Somerset
DEXTER (04930) Penobscot(96), Somerset(4)
DIXFIELD Oxford
DIXMONT Penobscot
DOVER FOXCROFT Piscataquis
DRESDEN Lincoln
DRYDEN Franklin
DURHAM Androscoggin
EAGLE LAKE Aroostook
EAST ANDOVER Oxford
EAST BALDWIN Cumberland
EAST BLUE HILL Hancock
EAST BOOTHBAY Lincoln
EAST CORINTH Penobscot
EAST DIXFIELD Franklin
EAST LIVERMORE Androscoggin
EAST MACHIAS Washington

EAST MILLINOCKET Penobscot
EAST NEWPORT Penobscot
EAST ORLAND Hancock
EAST PARSONFIELD York
EAST POLAND Androscoggin
EAST STONEHAM Oxford
EAST VASSALBORO Kennebec
EAST WATERBORO York
EAST WATERFORD Oxford
EAST WILTON Franklin
EAST WINTHROP Kennebec
EASTON Aroostook
EASTPORT Washington
EDDINGTON Penobscot
EDGECOMB Lincoln
ELIOT York
ELLSWORTH Hancock
ENFIELD Penobscot
ESTCOURT STATION Aroostook
ETNA Penobscot
EUSTIS Franklin
EXETER Penobscot
FAIRFIELD (04937) Kennebec(99), Somerset(1)
FALMOUTH Cumberland
FARMINGDALE Kennebec
FARMINGTON Franklin
FARMINGTON FALLS Franklin
FORT FAIRFIELD Aroostook
FORT KENT Aroostook
FORT KENT MILLS Aroostook
FRANKFORT Waldo
FRANKLIN Hancock
FREEDOM Waldo
FREEPORT Cumberland
FRENCHBORO Hancock
FRENCHVILLE Aroostook
FRIENDSHIP Knox
FRYE Oxford
FRYEBURG Oxford
GARDINER Kennebec
GARLAND Penobscot
GEORGETOWN Sagadahoc
GLEN COVE Knox
GORHAM Cumberland
GOULDSBORO Hancock
GRAND ISLE Aroostook
GRAND LAKE STREAM Washington
GRAY Cumberland
GREENE Androscoggin
GREENVILLE Piscataquis
GREENVILLE JUNCTION (04442) Piscataquis(86), Somerset(14)
GROVE Washington
GUILFORD Piscataquis
HALLOWELL Kennebec
HAMPDEN Penobscot
HANCOCK Hancock
HANOVER Oxford
HARBORSIDE Hancock
HARMONY Somerset
HARPSWELL Cumberland

HARRINGTON Washington
HARRISON Cumberland
HARTLAND Somerset
HAYNESVILLE Aroostook
HEBRON Oxford
HINCKLEY Somerset
HIRAM Oxford
HOLDEN (04429) Penobscot(98), Hancock(2)
HOLLIS CENTER York
HOPE Knox
HOULTON Aroostook
HOWLAND Penobscot
HUDSON Penobscot
HULLS COVE Hancock
ISLAND FALLS Aroostook
ISLE AU HAUT Knox
ISLE OF SPRINGS Lincoln
ISLESBORO Waldo
ISLESFORD Hancock
JACKMAN Somerset
JAY Franklin
JEFFERSON Lincoln
JONESBORO Washington
JONESPORT Washington
KENDUSKEAG Penobscot
KENNEBUNK York
KENNEBUNKPORT York
KENTS HILL Kennebec
KINGFIELD Franklin
KINGMAN Penobscot
KITTERY York
KITTERY POINT York
LAGRANGE (04453) Penobscot(90), Piscataquis(10)
LAMBERT LAKE Washington
LEBANON York
LEE Penobscot
LEEDS Androscoggin
LEVANT Penobscot
LEWISTON Androscoggin
LIBERTY (04949) Waldo(80), Knox(20)
LILLE Aroostook
LIMERICK York
LIMESTONE Aroostook
LIMINGTON York
LINCOLN Penobscot
LINCOLN CENTER Penobscot
LINCOLNVILLE Waldo
LINCOLNVILLE CENTER Waldo
LISBON Androscoggin
LISBON CENTER Androscoggin
LISBON FALLS Androscoggin
LITCHFIELD Kennebec
LITTLE DEER ISLE Hancock
LIVERMORE Androscoggin
LIVERMORE FALLS Androscoggin
LOCKE MILLS Oxford
LONG ISLAND Cumberland
LOVELL Oxford
LUBEC Washington
MACHIAS Washington

MACHIASPORT Washington
MADAWASKA Aroostook
MADISON Somerset
MANCHESTER Kennebec
MANSET Hancock
MAPLETON Aroostook
MARS HILL Aroostook
MASARDIS Aroostook
MATINICUS Knox
MATTAWAMKEAG Penobscot
MECHANIC FALLS Androscoggin
MEDDYBEMPS Washington
MEDWAY Penobscot
MEREPOINT Cumberland
MEXICO Oxford
MILBRIDGE Washington
MILFORD Penobscot
MILLINOCKET Penobscot
MILO (04463) Piscataquis(98),
    Penobscot(2)
MINOT Androscoggin
MINTURN Hancock
MONHEGAN Lincoln
MONMOUTH Kennebec
MONROE Waldo
MONSON Piscataquis
MONTICELLO Aroostook
MOODY York
MORRILL Waldo
MOUNT DESERT Hancock
MOUNT VERNON Kennebec
NAPLES Cumberland
NEW GLOUCESTER Cumberland
NEW HARBOR Lincoln
NEW LIMERICK Aroostook
NEW PORTLAND Somerset
NEW SHARON (04955) Franklin(96),
    Kennebec(3), Somerset(1)
NEW SWEDEN Aroostook
NEW VINEYARD Franklin
NEWAGEN Lincoln
NEWCASTLE Lincoln
NEWFIELD York
NEWPORT (04953) Penobscot(99),
    Somerset(1)
NEWRY Oxford
NOBLEBORO Lincoln
NORRIDGEWOCK Somerset
NORTH AMITY Aroostook
NORTH ANSON Somerset
NORTH BERWICK York
NORTH BRIDGTON Cumberland
NORTH BROOKLIN Hancock
NORTH FRYEBURG Oxford
NORTH HAVEN Knox
NORTH JAY Franklin
NORTH MONMOUTH Kennebec
NORTH NEW PORTLAND Somerset
NORTH SHAPLEIGH York
NORTH TURNER Androscoggin
NORTH VASSALBORO Kennebec
NORTH WATERBORO York
NORTH WATERFORD Oxford
NORTH YARMOUTH Cumberland
NORTHEAST HARBOR Hancock
NORWAY Oxford
OAKFIELD Aroostook
OAKLAND Kennebec

OCEAN PARK York
OGUNQUIT York
OLAMON Penobscot
OLD ORCHARD BEACH York
OLD TOWN Penobscot
OQUOSSOC (04964) Franklin(94),
    Oxford(6)
ORIENT Aroostook
ORLAND Hancock
ORONO Penobscot
ORRINGTON Penobscot
ORRS ISLAND Cumberland
OTTER CREEK Hancock
OWLS HEAD Knox
OXBOW Aroostook
OXFORD Oxford
PALERMO Waldo
PALMYRA Somerset
PARIS Oxford
PARSONSFIELD York
PASSADUMKEAG Penobscot
PATTEN (04765) Penobscot(97),
    Aroostook(3)
PEAKS ISLAND Cumberland
PEJEPSCOT Sagadahoc
PEMAQUID Lincoln
PEMBROKE Washington
PENOBSCOT Hancock
PERHAM Aroostook
PERRY Washington
PERU Oxford
PHILLIPS Franklin
PHIPPSBURG Sagadahoc
PITTSFIELD Somerset
PLAISTED Aroostook
PLYMOUTH Penobscot
POLAND Androscoggin
PORT CLYDE Knox
PORTAGE Aroostook
PORTER Oxford
PORTLAND Cumberland
POWNAL Cumberland
PRESQUE ISLE Aroostook
PRINCETON Washington
PROSPECT HARBOR Hancock
QUIMBY Aroostook
RANDOLPH Kennebec
RANGELEY Franklin
RAYMOND Cumberland
READFIELD Kennebec
RICHMOND Sagadahoc
ROBBINSTON Washington
ROCKLAND Knox
ROCKPORT Knox
ROCKWOOD (04478) Somerset(86),
    Piscataquis(14)
ROUND POND Lincoln
ROXBURY Oxford
RUMFORD Oxford
RUMFORD CENTER Oxford
RUMFORD POINT Oxford
SABATTUS Androscoggin
SACO York
SAINT AGATHA Aroostook
SAINT ALBANS Somerset
SAINT DAVID Aroostook
SAINT FRANCIS Aroostook
SAINT GEORGE Knox

SALSBURY COVE Hancock
SANDY POINT Waldo
SANFORD York
SANGERVILLE Piscataquis
SARGENTVILLE Hancock
SCARBOROUGH Cumberland
SEAL COVE Hancock
SEAL HARBOR Hancock
SEARSMONT Waldo
SEARSPORT Waldo
SEBAGO Cumberland
SEBAGO LAKE Cumberland
SEBASCO ESTATES Sagadahoc
SEBEC Piscataquis
SEDGWICK Hancock
SHAPLEIGH York
SHAWMUT Somerset
SHERIDAN Aroostook
SHERMAN MILLS Aroostook
SHERMAN STATION (04777)
    Penobscot(73), Aroostook(27)
SHIRLEY MILLS Piscataquis
SINCLAIR Aroostook
SKOWHEGAN Somerset
SMALL POINT Sagadahoc
SMITHFIELD Somerset
SMYRNA MILLS Aroostook
SOLDIER POND Aroostook
SOLON Somerset
SORRENTO Hancock
SOUTH BERWICK York
SOUTH BRISTOL Lincoln
SOUTH CASCO Cumberland
SOUTH CHINA Kennebec
SOUTH FREEPORT Cumberland
SOUTH GARDINER Kennebec
SOUTH GOULDSBORO Hancock
SOUTH HIRAM Oxford
SOUTH PARIS Oxford
SOUTH PORTLAND Cumberland
SOUTH THOMASTON Knox
SOUTH WATERFORD Oxford
SOUTH WINDHAM Cumberland
SOUTHWEST HARBOR Hancock
SPRINGFIELD Penobscot
SPRINGVALE York
SPRUCE HEAD Knox
SQUIRREL ISLAND Lincoln
STACYVILLE Penobscot
STANDISH Cumberland
STEEP FALLS Cumberland
STETSON Penobscot
STEUBEN Washington
STILLWATER Penobscot
STOCKHOLM Aroostook
STOCKTON SPRINGS Waldo
STONINGTON Hancock
STRATTON Franklin
STRONG Franklin
SULLIVAN Hancock
SUMNER Oxford
SUNSET Hancock
SURRY Hancock
SWANS ISLAND Hancock
TEMPLE Franklin
TENANTS HARBOR Knox
THOMASTON Knox
THORNDIKE Waldo

TOPSFIELD Washington
TOPSHAM Sagadahoc
TREVETT Lincoln
TROY Waldo
TURNER Androscoggin
TURNER CENTER Androscoggin
UNION Knox
UNITY Waldo
UPPER FRENCHVILLE Aroostook
VAN BUREN Aroostook
VANCEBORO Washington
VASSALBORO Kennebec
VIENNA Kennebec
VINALHAVEN Knox
WAITE Washington
WALDOBORO Lincoln
WALPOLE Lincoln
WARREN Knox
WASHBURN Aroostook
WASHINGTON Knox
WATERBORO York
WATERFORD Oxford
WATERVILLE Kennebec
WAYNE Kennebec
WEEKS MILLS Kennebec
WELD Franklin
WELLS York
WESLEY Washington
WEST BALDWIN Cumberland
WEST BETHEL Oxford
WEST BOOTHBAY HARBOR Lincoln
WEST BOWDOIN Sagadahoc
WEST BUXTON York
WEST ENFIELD Penobscot
WEST FARMINGTON Franklin
WEST FORKS Somerset
WEST KENNEBUNK York
WEST MINOT Androscoggin
WEST NEWFIELD York
WEST PARIS Oxford
WEST POLAND Androscoggin
WEST ROCKPORT Knox
WEST SOUTHPORT Lincoln
WEST TREMONT Hancock
WESTBROOK Cumberland
WESTFIELD Aroostook
WHITEFIELD Lincoln
WHITING Washington
WHITNEYVILLE Washington
WILTON Franklin
WINDHAM Cumberland
WINDSOR Kennebec
WINN Penobscot
WINTER HARBOR Hancock
WINTERPORT Waldo
WINTERVILLE Aroostook
WINTHROP Kennebec
WISCASSET Lincoln
WOODLAND Washington
WOOLWICH Sagadahoc
WYTOPITLOCK Aroostook
YARMOUTH Cumberland
YORK York
YORK BEACH York
YORK HARBOR York

ZIP/City Cross Reference

03901-03901	BERWICK	03911-03911	YORK HARBOR	04010-04010	BROWNFIELD	04022-04022	DENMARK
03902-03902	CAPE NEDDICK	04001-04001	ACTON	04011-04011	BRUNSWICK	04024-04024	EAST BALDWIN
03903-03903	ELIOT	04002-04002	ALFRED	04013-04013	BUSTINS ISLAND	04027-04027	LEBANON
03904-03904	KITTERY	04003-04003	BAILEY ISLAND	04014-04014	CAPE PORPOISE	04028-04028	EAST PARSONFIELD
03905-03905	KITTERY POINT	04004-04004	BAR MILLS	04015-04015	CASCO	04029-04029	SEBAGO
03906-03906	NORTH BERWICK	04005-04005	BIDDEFORD	04016-04016	CENTER LOVELL	04030-04030	EAST WATERBORO
03907-03907	OGUNQUIT	04006-04006	BIDDEFORD POOL	04017-04017	CHEBEAGUE ISLAND	04032-04034	FREEPORT
03908-03908	SOUTH BERWICK	04007-04007	BIDDEFORD	04019-04019	CLIFF ISLAND	04037-04037	FRYEBURG
03909-03909	YORK	04008-04008	BOWDOINHAM	04020-04020	CORNISH	04038-04038	GORHAM
03910-03910	YORK BEACH	04009-04009	BRIDGTON	04021-04021	CUMBERLAND CENTER	04039-04039	GRAY

ZIP	Location
04040-04040	HARRISON
04041-04041	HIRAM
04042-04042	HOLLIS CENTER
04043-04043	KENNEBUNK
04046-04046	KENNEBUNKPORT
04047-04047	PARSONSFIELD
04048-04048	LIMERICK
04049-04049	LIMINGTON
04050-04050	LONG ISLAND
04051-04051	LOVELL
04053-04053	MEREPOINT
04054-04054	MOODY
04055-04055	NAPLES
04056-04056	NEWFIELD
04057-04057	NORTH BRIDGTON
04061-04061	NORTH WATERBORO
04062-04062	WINDHAM
04063-04063	OCEAN PARK
04064-04064	OLD ORCHARD BEACH
04066-04066	ORRS ISLAND
04068-04068	PORTER
04069-04069	POWNAL
04070-04070	SCARBOROUGH
04071-04071	RAYMOND
04072-04072	SACO
04073-04073	SANFORD
04074-04074	SCARBOROUGH
04075-04075	SEBAGO LAKE
04076-04076	SHAPLEIGH
04077-04077	SOUTH CASCO
04078-04078	SOUTH FREEPORT
04079-04079	HARPSWELL
04081-04081	SOUTH WATERFORD
04082-04082	SOUTH WINDHAM
04083-04083	SPRINGVALE
04084-04084	STANDISH
04085-04085	STEEP FALLS
04086-04086	TOPSHAM
04087-04087	WATERBORO
04088-04088	WATERFORD
04090-04090	WELLS
04091-04091	WEST BALDWIN
04092-04092	WESTBROOK
04093-04093	WEST BUXTON
04094-04094	WEST KENNEBUNK
04095-04095	WEST NEWFIELD
04096-04096	YARMOUTH
04097-04097	NORTH YARMOUTH
04098-04098	WESTBROOK
04101-04104	PORTLAND
04105-04105	FALMOUTH
04106-04106	SOUTH PORTLAND
04107-04107	CAPE ELIZABETH
04108-04108	PEAKS ISLAND
04109-04109	PORTLAND
04110-04110	CUMBERLAND FORESIDE
04112-04112	PORTLAND
04116-04116	SOUTH PORTLAND
04122-04124	PORTLAND
04210-04212	AUBURN
04216-04216	ANDOVER
04217-04217	BETHEL
04219-04219	BRYANT POND
04220-04220	BUCKFIELD
04221-04221	CANTON
04222-04222	DURHAM
04223-04223	DANVILLE
04224-04224	DIXFIELD
04225-04225	DRYDEN
04226-04226	EAST ANDOVER
04227-04227	EAST DIXFIELD
04228-04228	EAST LIVERMORE
04230-04230	EAST POLAND
04231-04231	EAST STONEHAM
04234-04234	EAST WILTON
04236-04236	GREENE
04237-04237	HANOVER
04238-04238	HEBRON
04239-04239	JAY
04240-04243	LEWISTON
04250-04250	LISBON
04252-04252	LISBON FALLS
04253-04253	LIVERMORE
04254-04254	LIVERMORE FALLS
04255-04255	LOCKE MILLS
04256-04256	MECHANIC FALLS
04257-04257	MEXICO
04258-04258	MINOT
04259-04259	MONMOUTH
04260-04260	NEW GLOUCESTER
04261-04261	NEWRY
04262-04262	NORTH JAY
04263-04263	LEEDS
04265-04265	NORTH MONMOUTH
04266-04266	NORTH TURNER
04267-04267	NORTH WATERFORD
04268-04268	NORWAY
04270-04270	OXFORD
04271-04271	PARIS
04274-04274	POLAND
04275-04275	ROXBURY
04276-04276	RUMFORD
04278-04278	RUMFORD CENTER
04279-04279	RUMFORD POINT
04280-04280	SABATTUS
04281-04281	SOUTH PARIS
04282-04282	TURNER
04283-04283	TURNER CENTER
04284-04284	WAYNE
04285-04285	WELD
04286-04286	WEST BETHEL
04287-04287	WEST BOWDOIN
04288-04288	WEST MINOT
04289-04289	WEST PARIS
04290-04290	PERU
04291-04291	WEST POLAND
04292-04292	SUMNER
04294-04294	WILTON
04330-04338	AUGUSTA
04341-04341	COOPERS MILLS
04342-04342	DRESDEN
04343-04343	EAST WINTHROP
04344-04344	FARMINGDALE
04345-04345	GARDINER
04346-04346	RANDOLPH
04347-04347	HALLOWELL
04348-04348	JEFFERSON
04349-04349	KENTS HILL
04350-04350	LITCHFIELD
04351-04351	MANCHESTER
04352-04352	MOUNT VERNON
04353-04353	WHITEFIELD
04354-04354	PALERMO
04355-04355	READFIELD
04357-04357	RICHMOND
04358-04358	SOUTH CHINA
04359-04359	SOUTH GARDINER
04360-04360	VIENNA
04361-04361	WEEKS MILLS
04363-04363	WINDSOR
04364-04364	WINTHROP
04401-04402	BANGOR
04406-04406	ABBOT VILLAGE
04408-04408	AURORA
04410-04410	BRADFORD
04411-04411	BRADLEY
04412-04412	BREWER
04413-04413	BROOKTON
04414-04414	BROWNVILLE
04415-04415	BROWNVILLE JUNCTION
04416-04416	BUCKSPORT
04417-04417	BURLINGTON
04418-04418	CARDVILLE
04419-04419	CARMEL
04420-04421	CASTINE
04422-04422	CHARLESTON
04423-04423	COSTIGAN
04424-04424	DANFORTH
04426-04426	DOVER FOXCROFT
04427-04427	EAST CORINTH
04428-04428	EDDINGTON
04429-04429	HOLDEN
04430-04430	EAST MILLINOCKET
04431-04431	EAST ORLAND
04434-04434	ETNA
04435-04435	EXETER
04438-04438	FRANKFORT
04441-04441	GREENVILLE
04442-04442	GREENVILLE JUNCTION
04443-04443	GUILFORD
04444-04444	HAMPDEN
04448-04448	HOWLAND
04449-04449	HUDSON
04450-04450	KENDUSKEAG
04451-04451	KINGMAN
04453-04453	LAGRANGE
04454-04454	LAMBERT LAKE
04455-04455	LEE
04456-04456	LEVANT
04457-04457	LINCOLN
04459-04459	MATTAWAMKEAG
04460-04460	MEDWAY
04461-04461	MILFORD
04462-04462	MILLINOCKET
04463-04463	MILO
04464-04464	MONSON
04467-04467	OLAMON
04468-04468	OLD TOWN
04469-04469	ORONO
04471-04471	ORIENT
04472-04472	ORLAND
04473-04473	ORONO
04474-04474	ORRINGTON
04475-04475	PASSADUMKEAG
04476-04476	PENOBSCOT
04478-04478	ROCKWOOD
04479-04479	SANGERVILLE
04481-04481	SEBEC
04485-04485	SHIRLEY MILLS
04487-04487	SPRINGFIELD
04488-04488	STETSON
04489-04489	STILLWATER
04490-04490	TOPSFIELD
04491-04491	VANCEBORO
04492-04492	WAITE
04493-04493	WEST ENFIELD
04495-04495	WINN
04496-04496	WINTERPORT
04497-04497	WYTOPITLOCK
04530-04530	BATH
04535-04535	ALNA
04536-04536	BAYVILLE
04537-04537	BOOTHBAY
04538-04538	BOOTHBAY HARBOR
04539-04539	BRISTOL
04541-04541	CHAMBERLAIN
04543-04543	DAMARISCOTTA
04544-04544	EAST BOOTHBAY
04547-04547	FRIENDSHIP
04548-04548	GEORGETOWN
04549-04549	ISLE OF SPRINGS
04551-04551	BREMEN
04552-04552	NEWAGEN
04553-04553	NEWCASTLE
04554-04554	NEW HARBOR
04555-04555	NOBLEBORO
04556-04556	EDGECOMB
04558-04558	PEMAQUID
04562-04562	PHIPPSBURG
04563-04563	CUSHING
04564-04564	ROUND POND
04565-04565	SEBASCO ESTATES
04567-04567	SMALL POINT
04568-04568	SOUTH BRISTOL
04570-04570	SQUIRREL ISLAND
04571-04571	TREVETT
04572-04572	WALDOBORO
04573-04573	WALPOLE
04574-04574	WASHINGTON
04575-04575	WEST BOOTHBAY HARBOR
04576-04576	WEST SOUTHPORT
04578-04578	WISCASSET
04579-04579	WOOLWICH
04605-04605	ELLSWORTH
04606-04606	ADDISON
04607-04607	GOULDSBORO
04609-04609	BAR HARBOR
04611-04611	BEALS
04612-04612	BERNARD
04613-04613	BIRCH HARBOR
04614-04614	BLUE HILL
04615-04615	BLUE HILL FALLS
04616-04616	BROOKLIN
04617-04617	BROOKSVILLE
04619-04619	CALAIS
04622-04622	CHERRYFIELD
04623-04623	COLUMBIA FALLS
04624-04624	COREA
04625-04625	CRANBERRY ISLES
04626-04626	CUTLER
04627-04627	DEER ISLE
04628-04628	DENNYSVILLE
04629-04629	EAST BLUE HILL
04630-04630	EAST MACHIAS
04631-04631	EASTPORT
04634-04634	FRANKLIN
04635-04635	FRENCHBORO
04637-04637	GRAND LAKE STREAM
04640-04640	HANCOCK
04642-04642	HARBORSIDE
04643-04643	HARRINGTON
04644-04644	HULLS COVE
04645-04645	ISLE AU HAUT
04646-04646	ISLESFORD
04648-04648	JONESBORO
04649-04649	JONESPORT
04650-04650	LITTLE DEER ISLE
04652-04652	LUBEC
04653-04653	BASS HARBOR
04654-04654	MACHIAS
04655-04655	MACHIASPORT
04656-04656	MANSET
04657-04657	MEDDYBEMPS
04658-04658	MILBRIDGE
04659-04659	MINTURN
04660-04660	MOUNT DESERT
04662-04662	NORTHEAST HARBOR
04664-04664	SULLIVAN
04665-04665	OTTER CREEK
04666-04666	PEMBROKE
04667-04667	PERRY
04668-04668	PRINCETON
04669-04669	PROSPECT HARBOR
04671-04671	ROBBINSTON
04672-04672	SALSBURY COVE
04673-04673	SARGENTVILLE
04674-04674	SEAL COVE
04675-04675	SEAL HARBOR
04676-04676	SEDGWICK
04677-04677	SORRENTO
04679-04679	SOUTHWEST HARBOR
04680-04680	STEUBEN
04681-04681	STONINGTON
04683-04683	SUNSET
04684-04684	SURRY
04685-04685	SWANS ISLAND
04686-04686	WESLEY
04690-04690	WEST TREMONT
04691-04691	WHITING
04693-04693	WINTER HARBOR
04694-04694	WOODLAND
04730-04730	HOULTON
04732-04732	ASHLAND
04733-04733	BENEDICTA
04734-04734	BLAINE
04735-04735	BRIDGEWATER
04736-04736	CARIBOU
04737-04737	CLAYTON LAKE
04738-04738	CROUSEVILLE
04739-04739	EAGLE LAKE
04740-04740	EASTON
04741-04741	ESTCOURT STATION
04742-04742	FORT FAIRFIELD
04743-04743	FORT KENT
04744-04744	FORT KENT MILLS
04745-04745	FRENCHVILLE

Civil Records: Access: Mail, online, in person. No search fee. Required to search: name, years to search. Civil cases indexed by defendant, plaintiff. Civil records on computer since 11/97. Case index available through SJIS. See state introduction. **Criminal Records:** Access: Mail, in person. Both court and visitors may perform in person searches. No search fee. Required to search: name, years to search, DOB. Civil records on computer since 11/97. **General Information:** No adoptions, juvenile, sealed, expunged or mental records released. SASE not required. Turnaround time 1 day. Copy fee: $.50 per page. Certification fee: $5.00 per page. Fee payee: David K Martin, Clerk. Personal checks accepted. Prepayment is required. Public access terminal is available.

District Court 205 S 3rd St, Oakland, MD 21550; 301-334-8164. Hours: 8:30AM-4:30PM (EST). *Misdemeanor, Civil Actions Under $25,000, Eviction, Small Claims.*

Civil Records: Access: Mail, online, in person. Both court and visitors may perform in person searches. No search fee. Required to search: name, years to search. Civil cases indexed by defendant. Civil records on computer from 1990, on card index from 1971. Online access available through SJIS. See state introduction. **Criminal Records:** Access: Remote online, in person. Court does not conduct in person searches; visitors must perform searches for themselves. Search fee: No criminal searches performed by court. Required to search: name, years to search, DOB. Criminal records on computer from 1981. Online access available through SJIS. See state introduction. **General Information:** No adoptions, juvenile, sealed, expunged or mental records released. SASE required. Turnaround time 1 week. Copy fee: $.25 per page. Certification fee: $5.00 per page. Fee payee: District Court. Personal checks accepted. Prepayment is required.

Register of Wills Courthouse, 313 E Alder St, Room 103, Oakland, MD 21550; 301-334-1999; Fax: 301-334-1984. Hours: 8AM-4:30PM (EST). *Probate.*

www.registers.state.md.us/county/garrett

Harford County

3rd Judicial Circuit 20 W Courtland St, Bel Air, MD 21014; 410-638-3426. Hours: 8:30AM-4:30PM (EST). *Felony, Misdemeanor, Civil Actions Over $25,000.*

www.courts.state.md.us

Civil Records: Access: online, in person. Court does not conduct in person searches; visitors must perform searches for themselves. Search fee: No civil searches performed by court. Required to search: name, years to search; also helpful-address. Civil cases indexed by defendant, plaintiff. Civil records on computer since 08/92 and on books prior. Case index available through SJIS. See state introduction. **Criminal Records:** Access: In person only. Court does not conduct in person searches; visitors must perform searches for themselves. Search fee: No criminal searches performed by court. Required to search: name, years to search; also helpful-DOB. Criminal records on computer since 08/92 and on books prior. **General Information:** No adoptions, presentence investigations, juvenile, sealed, expunged or mental records released. Copy fee: $.50 per page. Certification fee: $5.00. Fee payee: Clerk of the Circuit Court. Only cashiers checks and money orders accepted. Prepayment is required. Public access terminal is available.

District Court 2 S Bond St, Bel Air, MD 21014; 410-838-2300. Hours: 8:30AM-4:30PM (EST). *Misdemeanor, Civil Actions Under $25,000, Eviction, Small Claims.*

Civil Records: Access: Mail, online, in person. Both court and visitors may perform in person searches. No search fee. Required to search: name, years to search. Civil cases indexed by defendant. Civil records on computer from 1981, on microfiche from 1972, archived from 1900. Online access available through SJIS. See state introduction. **Criminal Records:** Access: Mail, remote online, in person. Both court and visitors may perform in person searches. No search fee. Required to search: name, years to search; also helpful-address, DOB. Criminal records on computer from 1981, on microfiche from 1972, archived from 1900. Online access available through SJIS. See state introduction. **General Information:** No adoptions, motor vehicle, juvenile, sealed, expunged or mental records released. SASE required. Turnaround time 3-4 days. Copy fee: $.25 per page. Certification fee: $5.00. Fee payee: District Court of MD. Personal checks accepted. Credit cards accepted: Visa. Prepayment is required. Public access terminal is available.

Register of Wills 20 W Courtland St, Room 304, Bel Air, MD 21014; 410-638-3275; Fax: 410-893-3177. Hours: 8:30AM-4:30PM (EST). *Probate.*

www.registers.state.md.us/county/harford.html

Howard County

5th Judicial Circuit Court 8360 Court Ave, Ellicott City, MD 21043; 410-313-2111. Hours: 8:30AM-4:30PM (EST). *Felony, Misdemeanor, Civil Actions Over $25,000.*

Civil Records: Access: online, in person. Court does not conduct in person searches; visitors must perform searches for themselves. Search fee: No civil searches performed by court. Required to search: name, years to search; also helpful-address. Civil cases indexed by defendant, plaintiff. Civil records on computer from 1984, archived from 1900, on card index from 1900. Case index available through SJIS. See state introduction. **Criminal Records:** Access: In person only. Court does not conduct in person searches; visitors must perform searches for themselves. Search fee: No criminal searches performed by court. Required to search: name, years to search; also helpful-address, DOB, SSN. Criminal records on card index. **General Information:** No adoptions, juvenile, sealed, expunged or mental records released. Certification fee: $5.00 per page. Fee payee: Office of Clerk. Personal checks accepted. Public access terminal is available.

District Court 3451 Courthouse Dr, Ellicott City, MD 21043; 410-461-0200. Hours: 8:30AM-4:30PM (EST). *Misdemeanor, Civil Actions Under $25,000, Eviction, Small Claims.*

Civil Records: Access: Mail, online, in person. Both court and visitors may perform in person searches. No search fee. Required to search: name, years to search. Civil cases indexed by defendant. Civil records on computer from 1989, on card index prior. Online access available through SJIS. See state introduction. **Criminal Records:** Access: Mail, remote online, in person. Both court and visitors may perform in person searches. No search fee. Required to search: name, years to search. Criminal records on computer from 1989, on card index prior. Online access available through SJIS. See state introduction. **General Information:** No adoptions, juvenile, sealed, expunged or mental records released. SASE required if return receipt requested. Turnaround time before 1989 4-6 weeks, 1989-present 7 days. Copy fee: $.25 per page. Certification fee: $5.00. Fee payee: District Court of MD. Personal checks accepted. Credit cards accepted: Visa. Public access terminal is available.

Register of Wills 8360 Court Ave, Ellicott City, MD 21043; 410-313-2133; Fax: 410-313-3409. Hours: 8:30AM-4:30PM (EST). *Probate.*

www.registers.state.md.us/pamphlets.html

Kent County

2nd Judicial Circuit Court 103 N Cross St Courthouse, Chestertown, MD 21620; 410-778-7460; Fax: 410-778-7412. Hours: 8:30AM-4:30PM (EST). *Felony, Misdemeanor, Civil Actions Over $25,000.*

Civil Records: Access: online, in person. Court does not conduct in person searches; visitors must perform searches for themselves. Search fee: No civil searches performed by court. Required to search: name, years to search. Civil cases indexed by defendant, plaintiff. Civil records on computer from 1991, on card index from 1656. Case index available through SJIS. See state introduction. **Criminal Records:** Access: Remote online, in person. Court does not conduct in person searches; visitors must perform searches for themselves. Search fee: No criminal searches performed by court. Required to search: name, years to search; also helpful-DOB, SSN. Civil records on computer from 1991, on card index from 1656. Online access available through SJIS. **General Information:** No adoptions, juvenile, sealed, expunged or mental records released. Copy fee: $.50 per page. Certification fee: $5.00. Fee payee: Mark L Mumford, Clerk. Personal checks accepted. Prepayment is required. Public access terminal is available.

District Court 103 N Cross St, Chestertown, MD 21620; 410-778-1830; Fax: 410-778-3474. Hours: 8:30AM-4:30PM (EST). *Misdemeanor, Civil Actions Under $25,000, Eviction, Small Claims.*

Civil Records: Access: online, in person. Court does not conduct in person searches; visitors must perform searches for themselves. Search fee: No civil searches performed by court. Required to search: name, years to search. Civil cases indexed by defendant. Civil records on computer from 1988; on card index from 1971. Online access available through SJIS. See state introduction. **Criminal Records:** Access: Remote online, in person. Court does not conduct in person searches; visitors must perform searches for themselves. Search fee: No criminal searches performed by court. Required to search: name, years to search. Criminal records on computer from 1981, on card index from 1971. Online access available through SJIS. See state introduction. **General Information:** No sealed, expunged, mental records or judge's notes released. Copy fee: $.25 per page. Certification fee: $5.00 per page. Fee payee: District Court of MD. Personal checks accepted. Credit cards accepted: Visa, Discover.

Register of Wills 103 N Cross St, Chestertown, MD 21620; 410-778-7466 & 1-888-778-0179(w/in MD); Fax: 410-778-2466. Hours: 8AM-4:30PM (EST). *Probate.*

www.registers.state.md.us/county/kent.html

Montgomery County

6th Judicial Circuit Court 50 Maryland Ave, Rockville, MD 20850; 240-777-9466. Hours: 8:30AM-4:30PM (EST). *Felony, Misdemeanor, Civil Actions Over $25,000.*

www.co.mo.md.us/judicial

Civil Records: Access: In person only. Court does not conduct in person searches; visitors must perform searches for themselves. Search fee: No civil searches performed by court. Required to search: name, years to search; also helpful-address. Civil cases indexed by defendant, plaintiff. Civil records on computer from 1977, archived from 1900, on card index from 1977. **Criminal Records:** Access: In person only. Court does not conduct in person searches; visitors must perform searches for themselves. Search fee: No criminal searches performed by court. Required to search: name, years to search, DOB; also helpful-address, SSN. Criminal records on computer from 1977, archived from 1900, on card index from 1977. **General Information:** No adoptions, juvenile, sealed, expunged or mental records released. Copy fee: $.50. Certification fee: $5.00. Plus $.50 per page. Fee payee: Clerk of Circuit Court. Personal checks accepted. Prepayment is required. Public access terminal is available.

District Court 8665 Georgia Ave, Silver Spring, MD 20910; 301-608-0660. Hours: 8:30AM-4:30PM (EST). *Misdemeanor, Civil Actions Under $25,000, Eviction, Small Claims.*

Civil Records: Access: Mail, online, in person. Both court and visitors may perform in person searches. No search fee. Required to search: name, years to search. Civil cases indexed by defendant, plaintiff. Civil records on computer from 1986, on card index and case folder. Online access available through SJIS. See state introduction. **Criminal Records:** Access: Mail, remote online, in person. Both court and visitors may perform in person searches. No search fee. Required to search: name, years to search. Criminal records on computer, index book and case folder. Online access available through SJIS. See state introduction. **General Information:** No juvenile, sealed, expunged or mental records or judge's notes released. SASE required. Turnaround time 2-4 weeks. Copy fee: $.25 per page. Certification fee: $5.00. Fee payee: District Court. Personal checks accepted. Prepayment is required. Public access terminal is available.

Rockville District Court 27 Courthouse Square, Rockville, MD 20850; Civil phone:301-279-1500; Criminal phone:301-279-1500. Hours: 8:30AM-4:30PM (EST). *Misdemeanor, Civil Actions Under $25,000, Eviction, Small Claims.*

Civil Records: Access: Mail, online, in person. Both court and visitors may perform in person searches. No search fee. Required to search: name, years to search. Civil cases indexed by defendant. Civil records on computer from 1986, prior in case folder. Online access available through SJIS. See state introduction. **Criminal Records:** Access: Mail, remote online, in person. Both court and visitors may perform in person searches. No search fee. Required to search: name, years to search; also helpful-DOB, SSN. Criminal records on computer, case folder, index book. Online access available through SJIS. See state introduction. **General Information:** No juvenile, sealed, expunged, mental records or judge's notes released. SASE required. Turnaround time 2-4 weeks. Copy fee: $.25 per page. Certification fee: $5.00 per page. Fee payee: District Court. Personal checks

accepted. Prepayment is required. Public access terminal is available.

Register of Wills Maryland Ave, Suite 322, Rockville, MD 20850; 301-217-7150; Fax: 301-217-7306. Hours: 8:30AM-4:30PM (EST). *Probate.*

www.co.mo.md.us/judicial

Prince George's County

7th Judicial Circuit Court 14735 Main St, Upper Marlboro, MD 20772; Civil phone:301-952-3240; Criminal phone:301-952-3240. Hours: 8:30AM-4:30PM (EST). *Felony, Misdemeanor, Civil Actions Over $25,000.*

Civil Records: Access: Mail, in person. Court does not conduct in person searches; visitors must perform searches for themselves. No search fee. Required to search: name, years to search. Civil cases indexed by defendant, plaintiff. Civil records on computer from 1981, on microfiche from 1979, on card index prior. **Criminal Records:** Access: Mail, in person. Court does not conduct in person searches; visitors must perform searches for themselves. No search fee. Required to search: name, years to search, DOB; also helpful-SSN. Criminal records on computer from 1981, on microfiche from 1979, on card index prior. **General Information:** No adoptions, juvenile, sealed, expunged or mental records released. SASE not required. Copy fee: $.50 per page. Certification fee: $5.00 per page. Fee payee: Clerk of Circuit Court. Personal checks accepted. Prepayment is required.

District Court 14735 Main St, Rm 173B, Upper Marlboro, MD 20772; 301-952-4080. Hours: 8:30AM-4:30PM (EST). *Misdemeanor, Civil Actions Under $25,000, Eviction, Small Claims.*

Civil Records: Access: Mail, online, in person. No search fee. Required to search: name, years to search. Civil cases indexed by defendant. Civil records on computer from 1988, on card index from 1970. Online access available through SJIS. See state introduction. **Criminal Records:** Access: Mail, remote online, in person. Court does not conduct in person searches; visitors must perform searches for themselves. No search fee. Required to search: name, years to search. Criminal records on computer from 1984, on cards from 1970. Online access available through SJIS. See state introduction. **General Information:** No adoptions, juvenile, sealed, expunged or mental records released. SASE required. Turnaround time 1-2 weeks. Copy fee: $.25 per page. Certification fee: $5.00 per page. Fee payee: District Court of Maryland. Personal checks accepted. Prepayment is required. Public access terminal is available.

Register of Wills PO Box 1729, Upper Marlboro, MD 20773; 301-952-3250; Fax: 301-952-4489. Hours: 8:30AM-4:30PM (EST). *Probate.*

www.registers.state.md.us/county/princegeorges.html

Queen Anne's County

2nd Judicial Circuit Court Courthouse, 100 Courthouse Sq, Centreville, MD 21617; 410-758-1773. Hours: 8:30AM-4:30PM (EST). *Felony, Misdemeanor, Civil Actions Over $25,000.*

Note: Misdemeanor case files at District Court until appealed by jury trial

Civil Records: Access: online, in person. Court does not conduct in person searches; visitors must perform searches for themselves. Search fee: No

civil searches performed by court. Required to search: name, years to search. Civil cases indexed by defendant, plaintiff. Civil records on computer from 11/92; on index books from 1978. Case index available through SJIS. See state introduction. **Criminal Records:** Access: Remote online, in person. Court does not conduct in person searches; visitors must perform searches for themselves. Search fee: No criminal searches performed by court. Required to search: name, years to search, SSN. Criminal records on computer from 11/92; on index books from 1978. **General Information:** No adoptions, juvenile, sealed, expunged or mental records released. Certification fee: $5.00. Fee payee: Clerk of Circuit Court. Personal checks accepted. Prepayment is required. Public access terminal is available.

District Court 120 Broadway, Centreville, MD 21617; 410-758-5200. Hours: 8:30AM-4:30PM (EST). *Misdemeanor, Civil Actions Under $25,000, Eviction, Small Claims.*

Civil Records: Access: online, in person. Court does not conduct in person searches; visitors must perform searches for themselves. Search fee: No civil searches performed by court. Required to search: name, years to search; also helpful-address. Civil cases indexed by defendant. Civil records on computer from 1988, archived from 1974, prior on index books. Online access available through SJIS. See state introduction. **Criminal Records:** Access: Remote online, in person. Court does not conduct in person searches; visitors must perform searches for themselves. Search fee: No criminal searches performed by court. Required to search: name, years to search; also helpful-address, DOB, SSN. Criminal records on computer from 1981, prior on index books. Online access available through SJIS. See state introduction. **General Information:** No adoptions, juvenile, sealed, expunged or mental records released. Certification fee: $5.00. Fee payee: District Court of Maryland. Personal checks accepted. Credit cards accepted: Visa, Discover. Prepayment is required. Public access terminal is available.

Register of Wills Liberty Bldg, 107 N Liberty St #220, PO Box 59, Centreville, MD 21617; 410-758-0585; Fax: 410-758-4408. Hours: 8AM-4:30PM (EST). *Probate.*

www.registers.state.md.us/county/queenannes.html

Somerset County

1st Judicial Circuit Court PO Box 99, Princess Anne, MD 21853; 410-651-1555; Fax: 410-651-1048. Hours: 8:30AM-4:30PM (EST). *Felony, Misdemeanor, Civil Actions Over $25,000.*

Civil Records: Access: online, in person. Court does not conduct in person searches; visitors must perform searches for themselves. Search fee: No civil searches performed by court. Required to search: name, years to search; also helpful-address. Civil cases indexed by defendant, plaintiff. Civil records on computer from 9/93, archived and on index books from 1665. Case index available through SJIS. See state introduction. **Criminal Records:** Access: In person only. Court does not conduct in person searches; visitors must perform searches for themselves. Search fee: No criminal searches performed by court. Required to search: name, years to search; also helpful-address, DOB, SSN. Criminal records on computer from 9/93, archived and on index books from 1665. **General Information:** No adoptions, juvenile, sealed, expunged or mental records released. Copy fee: $.50 per page. Certification fee: $5.00. Fee payee:

Clerk of Circuit Court. Personal checks accepted. Prepayment is required. Public access terminal is available.

District Court 11559 Somerset Ave, Princess Anne, MD 21853; 410-651-2713. Hours: 8:30AM-4:30PM (EST). *Misdemeanor, Civil Actions Under $25,000, Eviction, Small Claims.*

Note: Misdemeanor cases go to Circuit Court if preliminary hearing waived. Records held at court where trial heard

Civil Records: Access: online, in person. Court does not conduct in person searches; visitors must perform searches for themselves. Search fee: No civil searches performed by court. Required to search: name, years to search. Civil cases indexed by defendant, plaintiff. Civil records on computer from 1987, archived and on index books from 1971. Online access available through SJIS. See state introduction. **Criminal Records:** Access: Remote online, in person. Court does not conduct in person searches; visitors must perform searches for themselves. Search fee: No criminal searches performed by court. Required to search: name, years to search; also helpful-SSN. Criminal records on computer from 1987, archived and on index books from 1971. Online access available through SJIS. See state introduction. **General Information:** No adoptions, juvenile, sealed, expunged or mental records released. Copy fee: $.50 per page. Certification fee: $5.00. Fee payee: District Court. Personal checks accepted. Prepayment is required. Public access terminal is available.

Register of Wills 30512 Prince William St, Princess Anne, MD 21853; 410-651-1696; Fax: 410-651-3873. Hours: 8:30AM-4:30PM (EST). *Probate.*

www.registers.state.md.us/county/somerset.html

St. Mary's County

7th Judicial Circuit Court PO Box 676, Leonardtown, MD 20650; 301-475-5621. Hours: 8:30AM-4:30PM (EST). *Felony, Misdemeanor, Civil Actions Over $25,000.*

Civil Records: Access: online, in person. Court does not conduct in person searches; visitors must perform searches for themselves. Search fee: No civil searches performed by court. Required to search: name, years to search. Civil cases indexed by defendant, plaintiff. Civil records on computer from 1987, on card index from 1970. Case index available through SJIS. See state introduction. **Criminal Records:** Access: In person only. Court does not conduct in person searches; visitors must perform searches for themselves. Search fee: No criminal searches performed by court. Required to search: name, years to search; also helpful-SSN. Criminal records on computer from 1987, on card index from 1970. **General Information:** No adoptions, juvenile, sealed, expunged or mental records released. Copy fee: $.50 per page. Certification fee: $5.00. Fee payee: Clerk of the Circuit Court. Personal checks accepted. Prepayment is required. Public access terminal is available.

District Court Carter State Office Bldg, 23110 Leonard Hall Dr, PO Box 653, Leonardtown, MD 20650; 301-475-4530; Fax: 301-475-4535. Hours: 8:30AM-4:30PM (EST). *Misdemeanor, Civil Actions Under $25,000, Eviction, Small Claims.*

Civil Records: Access: online, in person. Court does not conduct in person searches; visitors must perform searches for themselves. Search fee: No civil searches performed by court. Required to

search: name, years to search. Civil cases indexed by defendant. Civil records on computer from 1985, archived from 1979. Online access available through SJIS. See state introduction. **Criminal Records:** Access: Remote online, in person. Court does not conduct in person searches; visitors must perform searches for themselves. Search fee: No criminal searches performed by court. Required to search: name, years to search; also helpful-DOB. Criminal records on computer from 1985, archived from 1979. Online access available through SJIS. See state introduction. **General Information:** No adoptions, juvenile, sealed, expunged or mental records released. Copy fee: $.25 per page. Certification fee: $10.00. Fee payee: District Court of Maryland. Personal checks accepted. Public access terminal is available.

Register of Wills PO Box 602, Leonardtown, MD 20650; 301-475-5566; Fax: 301-475-4968. Hours: 8:30AM-4:30PM (EST). *Probate.*

Talbot County

Circuit Court PO Box 723, Easton, MD 21601; 410-822-2611; Fax: 410-820-8168. Hours: 8:30AM-4:30PM (EST). *Felony, Misdemeanor, Civil Actions Over $25,000.*

Civil Records: Access: online, in person. Court does not conduct in person searches; visitors must perform searches for themselves. Search fee: No civil searches performed by court. Required to search: name, years to search; also helpful-address. Civil cases indexed by defendant, plaintiff. Civil records on card index from 1993. Case index available through SJIS. See state introduction. **Criminal Records:** Access: In person only. Court does not conduct in person searches; visitors must perform searches for themselves. Search fee: No criminal searches performed by court. Required to search: name, years to search; also helpful-address, DOB, SSN. Criminal records on card index from 1993. **General Information:** No adoptions, juvenile, sealed, expunged or mental records released. Copy fee: $.50 per page. Certification fee: $5.00. Fee payee: Maryann Shorall, Clerk of Court. Personal checks accepted. Prepayment is required. Public access terminal is available.

District Court 108 W Dover St, Easton, MD 21601; 410-822-2750; Fax: 410-822-1607. Hours: 8:30AM-4:30PM (EST). *Misdemeanor, Civil Actions Under $25,000, Eviction, Small Claims.*

Civil Records: Access: online, in person. Court does not conduct in person searches; visitors must perform searches for themselves. Search fee: No civil searches performed by court. Required to search: name, years to search. Civil cases indexed by defendant. Civil records on computer from 1988, archived and on card index from 1971. Online access available through SJIS. See state introduction. **Criminal Records:** Access: Remote online, in person. Court does not conduct in person searches; visitors must perform searches for themselves. Search fee: No criminal searches performed by court. Required to search: name, years to search. Criminal records on computer from 1984. Online access available through SJIS. See state introduction. **General Information:** No adoptions, juvenile, sealed, expunged or mental records released. Copy fee: $.25 per page. Certification fee: $5.00. Fee payee: District Court of MD. Personal checks accepted.

Register of Wills PO Box 816, Easton, MD 21601; 410-822-2470; Fax: 410-822-5452. Hours: 8AM-4:30PM (EST). *Probate.*

www.registers.state.md.us/county/talbot.html

Washington County

Washington County Circuit Court Box 229, Hagerstown, MD 21741; 301-733-8660; Fax: 301-791-1151. Hours: 8:30AM-4:30PM (EST). *Felony, Misdemeanor, Civil Actions Over $25,000.*

Civil Records: Access: online, in person. Court does not conduct in person searches; visitors must perform searches for themselves. Search fee: No civil searches performed by court. Required to search: name, years to search. Civil cases indexed by defendant. Civil records on case files, docket books. Case index available through SJIS. See state introduction. **Criminal Records:** Access: In person only. Court does not conduct in person searches; visitors must perform searches for themselves. Search fee: No criminal searches performed by court. Required to search: name, years to search; also helpful-DOB. Criminal records on case files, docket books. **General Information:** No adoptions, juvenile, sealed, expunged or mental records released. Copy fee: $.50 per page. Certification fee: $5.00. Fee payee: Clerk of Circuit Court. Personal checks accepted. Prepayment is required. Public access terminal is available.

District Court 35 W Washington St, Hagerstown, MD 21740; 301-791-4740. Hours: 8:30AM-4:30PM (EST). *Misdemeanor, Civil Actions Under $25,000, Eviction, Small Claims.*

Civil Records: Access: Mail, online, in person. Both court and visitors may perform in person searches. No search fee. Required to search: name, years to search; also helpful-address. Civil cases indexed by defendant. Civil records on computer from 1986, archived and on index books from 1971. Online access available through CJIS. See state introduction. **Criminal Records:** Access: Remote online, in person. Court does not conduct in person searches; visitors must perform searches for themselves. Search fee: No criminal searches performed by court. Required to search: name, years to search; also helpful-address, DOB, SSN. Criminal records on computer from 1982, on index books from 1971. Online access available through CJIS. See state introduction. **General Information:** No adoptions, juvenile, sealed, expunged or mental records released. SASE required. Turnaround time less than 30 days. Copy fee: $.25 per page. Fee applies to civil division only. Certification fee: $5.00. Fee payee: District Court. Personal checks accepted. Credit cards accepted: Visa, Discover. Prepayment is required. Public access terminal is available.

Register of Wills 95 W Washington, Hagerstown, MD 21740; 301-739-3612; Fax: 301-733-8636. Hours: 8:30AM-4:30PM (EST). *Probate.*

www.registers.state.md.us/county/washington.html

Wicomico County

1st Judicial Circuit Court PO Box 198, Salisbury, MD 21803-0198; 410-543-6551; Fax: 410-548-5150. Hours: 8:30AM-4:30PM (EST). *Felony, Misdemeanor, Civil Actions Over $25,000.*

Civil Records: Access: Phone, mail, online, in person. Both court and visitors may perform in person searches. Search fee: No civil searches performed by court. Required to search: name, years to search. Civil cases indexed by defendant, plaintiff. Civil records on books, cases filed after 05/93 on computer. All phone requests must include case number. Case index available through

SJIS. See state introduction. **Criminal Records:** Access: Phone, mail, in person. Both court and visitors may perform in person searches. No search fee. Required to search: name, years to search; also helpful-DOB, SSN. Criminal records on books, cases filed after 05/93 on computer. Phone requests must include case number. **General Information:** No adoptions, juvenile, sealed, expunged or mental records released. SASE not required. Turnaround time 1-2 days. Copy fee: $.50 per page. Certification fee: $5.00. Fee payee: Clerk of Circuit Court. Personal checks accepted. Out of state checks not accepted. Prepayment is required. Public access terminal is available.

District Court 201 Baptist St, Salisbury, MD 21801; 410-543-6600. Hours: 8:30AM-4:30PM (EST). *Misdemeanor, Civil Actions Under $25,000, Eviction, Small Claims.*

Civil Records: Access: online, in person. Court does not conduct in person searches; visitors must perform searches for themselves. Search fee: No civil searches performed by court. Required to search: name, years to search; also helpful-address. Civil cases indexed by defendant, plaintiff. Civil records on computer from 1985, archived from 1984, on card index from 1976. Online access available through SJIS. See state introduction. **Criminal Records:** Access: Remote online, in person. Court does not conduct in person searches; visitors must perform searches for themselves. Search fee: No criminal searches performed by court. Required to search: name, years to search; also helpful-address, DOB. Criminal records on computer since 1983. Online access available through SJIS. See state introduction. **General**

Information: No adoptions, juvenile, sealed, expunged or mental records released. Copy fee: $.50. Certification fee: $5.00. Fee payee: District Court. Personal checks accepted. Prepayment is required. Public access terminal is available.

Register of Wills PO Box 787, Salisbury, MD 21803-0787; 410-543-6635; Fax: 410-334-3440. Hours: 8:30AM-4:30PM (EST). *Probate.*

www.registers.state.md.us/county/wicomico.html

Worcester County

1st Judicial Circuit Court Box 40, Snow Hill, MD 21863; 410-632-1221; Civil phone:410-632-1222; Criminal phone:410-632-1222. Hours: 8:30AM-4:30PM (EST). *Felony, Misdemeanor, Civil Actions Over $25,000.*

Civil Records: Access: online, in person. Court does not conduct in person searches; visitors must perform searches for themselves. Search fee: No civil searches performed by court. Required to search: name, years to search. Civil cases indexed by defendant. Civil records on computer since 7/93, on docket books prior. Case index available through SJIS. See state introduction. **Criminal Records:** Access: In person only. Court does not conduct in person searches; visitors must perform searches for themselves. Search fee: No criminal searches performed by court. Required to search: name, years to search. Criminal records on computer since 7/93, on docket books prior. **General Information:** No adoptions, juvenile, sealed or expunged records released. Copy fee: $.50 per page. Certification fee: $5.00. Fee payee: Clerk of Circuit Court. Personal checks accepted.

Will bill copy fees to Maryland attorneys. Public access terminal is available.

District Court 301 Commerce St, Snow Hill, MD 21863-1007; 410-632-2525; Fax: 410-632-2718. Hours: 8:30AM-4:30PM (EST). *Misdemeanor, Civil Actions Under $25,000, Eviction, Small Claims.*

Civil Records: Access: online, in person. Court does not conduct in person searches; visitors must perform searches for themselves. Search fee: No civil searches performed by court. Required to search: name, years to search; also helpful-address. Civil cases indexed by defendant. Civil records on computer since 1988. Online access available through SJIS. See state introduction. **Criminal Records:** Access: Remote online, in person. Court does not conduct in person searches; visitors must perform searches for themselves. Search fee: No criminal searches performed by court. Required to search: name, years to search; also helpful-address, DOB, SSN. Criminal records on computer since 1982. Online access available through SJIS. See state introduction. **General Information:** No sealed or juvenile records released. Copy fee: $.50 per page. Certification fee: $5.00 per page. Fee payee: District Court. Personal checks accepted. Prepayment is required. Public access terminal is available.

Register of Wills Courthouse, Room 102, One W Market St, Snow Hill, MD 21863-1074; 410-632-1529; Fax: 410-632-5600. Hours: 8AM-4:30PM (EST). *Probate.*

www.registers.state.md.us/county/worcester.html

ORGANIZATION   23 counties and **one independent city**, 24 recording offices. The recording officer is Clerk of the Circuit Court. **Baltimore City has a recording office separate from the county of Baltimore.** See the City/County Locator section at the end of this chapter for ZIP Codes that include both the city and the county. The entire state is in the Eastern Time Zone (EST).

REAL ESTATE RECORDS   Counties will **not** perform real estate searches. Copies usually cost $.50 per page, and certification fees $5.00 per document.

UCC RECORDS   This was a **dual filing state** until July 1995. As of July 1995, **all new** UCC filings are submitted only to the central filing office. Financing statements are usually filed both at the state level and with the Clerk of Circuit Court, except for consumer goods, farm related and real estate related filings, which will still be filed with the Clerk after June 1995. Only one county performs UCC searches. Copy fees vary.

TAX LIEN RECORDS   All tax liens are filed with the county Clerk of Circuit Court. Counties will **not** perform searches.

OTHER LIENS   Judgment, mechanics, county, hospital, condominium.

Allegany County
County Clerk of the Circuit Court, P.O. Box 359, Cumberland, MD 21502. 301-777-5922. Fax: 301-777-2100.

Anne Arundel County
County Clerk of the Circuit Court, P.O. Box 71, Annapolis, MD 21404. 410-222-1425. Fax: 410-222-1087.

Baltimore City
City Clerk, 100 North Calvert Street, Room 610, Baltimore, MD 21202. 410-333-3760.

Baltimore County
County Clerk of the Circuit Court, P.O. Box 6754, Baltimore, MD 21285. 410-887-2652. Fax: 410-887-3062.

Calvert County
County Clerk of the Circuit Court, 175 Main Street, Courthouse, Prince Frederick, MD 20678. 410-535-1660.

Caroline County
County Clerk of the Circuit Court, P.O. Box 458, Denton, MD 21629. 410-479-1811. Fax: 410-479-1142.

Carroll County
County Clerk of the Circuit Court, 55 North Court Street, Room G8, Westminster, MD 21157. 410-386-2022. Fax: 410-876-0822.

Cecil County
County Clerk of the Circuit Court, 129 East Main St., Room 108, Elkton, MD 21921-5971. 410-996-5375.

Charles County
County Clerk of the Circuit Court, P.O. Box 970, La Plata, MD 20646. 301-932-3255.

Dorchester County
County Clerk of the Circuit Court, P.O. Box 150, Cambridge, MD 21613. 410-228-0481.

Frederick County
County Clerk of the Circuit Court, 100 West Patrick Street, Frederick, MD 21701. 301-694-1964. Fax: 301-846-2245.

Garrett County
County Clerk of the Circuit Court, P.O. Box 447, Oakland, MD 21550-0447. 301-334-1937. Fax: 301-334-5017.

Harford County
County Clerk of the Circuit Court, 20 West Courtland Street, Bel Air, MD 21014. 410-638-3244.

Howard County
County Clerk of the Circuit Court, 8360 Court Avenue, Ellicott City, MD 21043. 410-313-2111.

Kent County
County Clerk of the Circuit Court, Courthouse, 103 N. Cross St., Chestertown, MD 21620. 410-778-7431.

Montgomery County
County Clerk of the Circuit Court, 50 Maryland Ave., County Courthouse, Rockville, MD 20850. 301-217-7116. Fax: 301-217-1635.

Prince George's County
County Clerk of the Circuit Court, 14735 Main Street, Upper Marlboro, MD 20772. 301-952-3352.

Queen Anne's County
County Clerk of the Circuit Court, 100 Court House Square, Centreville, MD 21617. 410-758-1773.

Somerset County
County Clerk of the Circuit Court, P.O. Box 99, Princess Anne, MD 21853. 410-651-1555. Fax: 410-651-1048.

St. Mary's County
County Clerk of the Circuit Court, P.O. Box 676, Leonardtown, MD 20650. 301-475-4567.

Talbot County
County Clerk of the Circuit Court, P.O. Box 723, Easton, MD 21601. 410-822-2611. Fax: 410-820-8168.

Washington County
County Clerk of the Circuit Court, P.O. Box 229, Hagerstown, MD 21741-0229. 301-733-8660. Fax: 301-791-1151.

Wicomico County
County Clerk of the Circuit Court, P.O. Box 198, Salisbury, MD 21803-0198. 410-543-6551.

Worcester County
County Clerk of the Circuit Court, P.O. Box 40, Snow Hill, MD 21863-0040. 410-632-1221.

You will usually be able to find the city name in the City/County Cross Reference below. In that case, it is a simple matter to determine the county from the cross reference. However, only the official US Postal Service city names are included in this index. There are an additional 40,000 place names that people use in their addresses. Therefore, we have also included a ZIP/City Cross Reference immediately following the City/County Cross Reference.

If you know the ZIP Code but the city name does not appear in the City/County Cross Reference index, look up the ZIP Code in the ZIP/City Cross Reference, find the city name, then look up the city name in the City/County Cross. Reference. For example, you want to know the county for an address of Menands, NY 12204. There is no "Menands" in the City/County Cross Reference. The ZIP/City Cross Reference shows that ZIP Codes 12201-12288 are for the city of Albany. Looking back in the City/County Cross Reference, Albany is in Albany County.

City/County Cross Reference

ABELL St. Mary's
ABERDEEN Harford
ABERDEEN PROVING GROUND Harford
ABINGDON Harford
ACCIDENT Garrett
ACCOKEEK (20607) Prince George's(99), Charles(1)
ADAMSTOWN Frederick
ALESIA (21107) Carroll(59), Baltimore(41)
ALLEN Wicomico
ANDREWS AIR FORCE BASE Prince George's
ANNAPOLIS Anne Arundel
ANNAPOLIS JUNCTION (20701) Howard(85), Anne Arundel(15)
AQUASCO Prince George's
ARNOLD Anne Arundel
ASHTON Montgomery
AVENUE St. Mary's
BALDWIN (21013) Baltimore(68), Harford(32)
BALTIMORE (21206) Baltimore City(83), Baltimore(17)
BALTIMORE (21209) Baltimore(52), Baltimore City(49)
BALTIMORE (21210) Baltimore City(93), Baltimore(7)
BALTIMORE (21212) Baltimore City(63), Baltimore(37)
BALTIMORE (21215) Baltimore City(91), Baltimore(10)
BALTIMORE (21224) Baltimore City(85), Baltimore(15)
BALTIMORE (21229) Baltimore City(83), Baltimore(17)
BALTIMORE (21239) Baltimore City(80), Baltimore(20)
BALTIMORE Anne Arundel
BALTIMORE Baltimore
BALTIMORE Baltimore City
BARCLAY Queen Anne's
BARNESVILLE Montgomery
BARSTOW Calvert
BARTON (21521) Allegany(72), Garrett(28)
BEALLSVILLE Montgomery
BEL AIR Harford
BEL ALTON Charles
BELCAMP Harford
BELTSVILLE Prince George's
BENEDICT Charles
BENSON Harford
BERLIN Worcester
BETHESDA Montgomery
BETHLEHEM Caroline
BETTERTON Kent
BIG POOL Washington
BISHOPVILLE Worcester
BITTINGER Garrett
BIVALVE Wicomico
BLADENSBURG Prince George's
BLOOMINGTON Garrett
BOONSBORO Washington

BORING Baltimore
BOWIE Prince George's
BOYDS Montgomery
BOZMAN Talbot
BRADDOCK HEIGHTS Frederick
BRADSHAW Baltimore
BRANDYWINE (20613) Prince George's(92), Charles(8)
BRENTWOOD Prince George's
BRINKLOW Montgomery
BROOKEVILLE (20833) Montgomery(97), Howard(3)
BROOKLANDVILLE Baltimore
BROOKLYN (21225) Baltimore City(54), Anne Arundel(46)
BROOMES ISLAND Calvert
BROWNSVILLE Washington
BRUNSWICK Frederick
BRYANS ROAD Charles
BRYANTOWN Charles
BUCKEYSTOWN Frederick
BURKITTSVILLE Frederick
BURTONSVILLE Montgomery
BUSHWOOD St. Mary's
BUTLER Baltimore
CABIN JOHN Montgomery
CALIFORNIA St. Mary's
CALLAWAY St. Mary's
CAMBRIDGE Dorchester
CAPITOL HEIGHTS Montgomery
CAPITOL HEIGHTS Prince George's
CARDIFF Harford
CASCADE (21719) Washington(99), Frederick(1)
CATONSVILLE Baltimore
CAVETOWN Washington
CECILTON Cecil
CENTREVILLE Queen Anne's
CHANCE Somerset
CHAPTICO St. Mary's
CHARLESTOWN Cecil
CHARLOTTE HALL (20622) Charles(67), St. Mary's(33)
CHASE Baltimore
CHELTENHAM Prince George's
CHESAPEAKE BEACH Calvert
CHESAPEAKE CITY Cecil
CHESTER Queen Anne's
CHESTERTOWN Kent
CHESTERTOWN Queen Anne's
CHEVY CHASE Montgomery
CHEWSVILLE Washington
CHILDS Cecil
CHURCH CREEK Dorchester
CHURCH HILL Queen Anne's
CHURCHTON Anne Arundel
CHURCHVILLE Harford
CLAIBORNE Talbot
CLARKSBURG (20871) Montgomery(90), Frederick(10)
CLARKSVILLE Howard
CLEAR SPRING Washington

CLEMENTS St. Mary's
CLINTON Prince George's
COBB ISLAND Charles
COCKEYSVILLE Baltimore
COLLEGE PARK Prince George's
COLORA Cecil
COLTONS POINT St. Mary's
COLUMBIA Howard
COMPTON St. Mary's
CONOWINGO Cecil
COOKSVILLE Howard
CORDOVA Talbot
CORRIGANVILLE Allegany
CRAPO Dorchester
CRISFIELD Somerset
CROCHERON Dorchester
CROFTON Anne Arundel
CROWNSVILLE Anne Arundel
CRUMPTON Queen Anne's
CUMBERLAND Allegany
CURTIS BAY (21226) Baltimore City(59), Anne Arundel(41)
DAMASCUS Montgomery
DAMERON St. Mary's
DAMES QUARTER Somerset
DARLINGTON Harford
DAVIDSONVILLE Anne Arundel
DAYTON Howard
DEAL ISLAND Somerset
DEALE Anne Arundel
DELMAR Wicomico
DENTON Caroline
DERWOOD Montgomery
DETOUR Carroll
DICKERSON (20842) Montgomery(86), Frederick(14)
DISTRICT HEIGHTS Prince George's
DOWELL Calvert
DRAYDEN St. Mary's
DUNDALK (21222) Baltimore(97), Baltimore City(3)
DUNKIRK (20754) Calvert(85), Anne Arundel(15)
EARLEVILLE Cecil
EAST NEW MARKET Dorchester
EASTON Talbot
ECKHART MINES Allegany
EDEN (21822) Worcester(94), Somerset(6)
EDGEWATER Anne Arundel
EDGEWOOD Harford
ELK MILLS Cecil
ELKRIDGE (99999) Howard(99), Carroll(1)
ELKTON Cecil
ELLERSLIE Allegany
ELLICOTT CITY (21043) Howard(98), Baltimore(2)
ELLICOTT CITY Howard
EMMITSBURG Frederick
ESSEX Baltimore
EWELL Somerset
FAIRPLAY Washington
FALLSTON Harford

FAULKNER Charles
FEDERALSBURG Caroline
FINKSBURG Carroll
FISHING CREEK Dorchester
FLINTSTONE Allegany
FOREST HILL Harford
FORK Baltimore
FORT GEORGE G MEADE Anne Arundel
FORT HOWARD Baltimore
FORT WASHINGTON Prince George's
FREDERICK Frederick
FREELAND Baltimore
FRIENDSHIP Anne Arundel
FRIENDSVILLE Garrett
FROSTBURG (21532) Allegany(84), Garrett(16)
FRUITLAND Wicomico
FULTON Howard
FUNKSTOWN Washington
GAITHER Carroll
GAITHERSBURG Montgomery
GALENA Kent
GALESVILLE Anne Arundel
GAMBRILLS Anne Arundel
GAPLAND Washington
GARRETT PARK Montgomery
GARRISON Baltimore
GEORGETOWN Cecil
GERMANTOWN Montgomery
GIBSON ISLAND Anne Arundel
GIRDLETREE Worcester
GLEN ARM Baltimore
GLEN BURNIE Anne Arundel
GLEN ECHO Montgomery
GLENELG Howard
GLENN DALE Prince George's
GLENWOOD Howard
GLYNDON Baltimore
GOLDSBORO Caroline
GRANTSVILLE Garrett
GRASONVILLE Queen Anne's
GREAT MILLS St. Mary's
GREENBELT Prince George's
GREENSBORO Caroline
GUNPOWDER Harford
GWYNN OAK (21207) Baltimore(66), Baltimore City(34)
GWYNN OAK Baltimore
HAGERSTOWN Washington
HALETHORPE (21227) Baltimore(95), Baltimore City(5)
HAMPSTEAD Carroll
HANCOCK Washington
HANOVER (21076) Anne Arundel(91), Howard(9)
HANOVER Anne Arundel
HARMANS Anne Arundel
HARWOOD Anne Arundel
HAVRE DE GRACE Harford
HEBRON Wicomico
HELEN St. Mary's
HENDERSON Caroline

HENRYTON Carroll
HIGHLAND (20777) Howard(95), Montgomery(5)
HILLSBORO Caroline
HOLLYWOOD St. Mary's
HUGHESVILLE Charles
HUNT VALLEY Baltimore
HUNTINGTOWN Calvert
HURLOCK Dorchester
HYATTSVILLE (20783) Prince George's(98), Montgomery(2)
HYATTSVILLE Prince George's
HYDES (21082) Baltimore(96), Harford(4)
IJAMSVILLE Frederick
INDIAN HEAD Charles
INGLESIDE Queen Anne's
IRONSIDES Charles
ISSUE Charles
JARRETTSVILLE Harford
JEFFERSON Frederick
JESSUP (20794) Howard(84), Anne Arundel(16)
JOPPA Harford
KEEDYSVILLE Washington
KENNEDYVILLE Kent
KENSINGTON Montgomery
KEYMAR (21757) Frederick(51), Carroll(49)
KINGSVILLE (21087) Baltimore(86), Harford(14)
KITZMILLER Garrett
KNOXVILLE (21758) Frederick(56), Washington(45)
LA PLATA Charles
LADIESBURG Frederick
LANHAM Prince George's
LAUREL Anne Arundel
LAUREL Howard
LAUREL Prince George's
LEONARDTOWN St. Mary's
LEXINGTON PARK St. Mary's
LIBERTYTOWN Frederick
LINEBORO Carroll
LINKWOOD Dorchester
LINTHICUM HEIGHTS Anne Arundel
LINWOOD Carroll
LISBON Howard
LITTLE ORLEANS Allegany
LONACONING (21539) Allegany(69), Garrett(31)
LONG GREEN Baltimore
LOTHIAN Anne Arundel
LOVEVILLE St. Mary's
LUKE Allegany
LUSBY Calvert
LUTHERVILLE TIMONIUM Baltimore
LYNCH Kent
MADISON Dorchester
MAGNOLIA Harford
MANCHESTER (21102) Carroll(98), Baltimore(2)
MANOKIN Somerset
MARBURY Charles
MARDELA SPRINGS Wicomico
MARION STATION Somerset
MARRIOTTSVILLE (21104) Howard(48), Carroll(43), Baltimore(9)
MARYDEL Caroline
MARYLAND LINE Baltimore
MASSEY Kent

MAUGANSVILLE Washington
MAYO Anne Arundel
MC HENRY Garrett
MCDANIEL Talbot
MECHANICSVILLE (20659) St. Mary's(98), Charles(2)
MIDDLE RIVER Baltimore
MIDDLEBURG Carroll
MIDDLETOWN Frederick
MIDLAND Allegany
MIDLOTHIAN Allegany
MILLERSVILLE Anne Arundel
MILLINGTON Kent
MONKTON (21111) Baltimore(87), Harford(13)
MONROVIA Frederick
MONTGOMERY VILLAGE Montgomery
MORGANZA St. Mary's
MOUNT AIRY (21771) Frederick(46), Carroll(36), Howard(15), Montgomery(2)
MOUNT RAINIER Prince George's
MOUNT SAVAGE Allegany
MOUNT VICTORIA Charles
MYERSVILLE Frederick
NANJEMOY Charles
NANTICOKE Wicomico
NEAVITT Talbot
NEW MARKET Frederick
NEW MIDWAY Frederick
NEW WINDSOR (21776) Carroll(83), Frederick(17)
NEWARK Worcester
NEWBURG Charles
NEWCOMB Talbot
NIKEP Allegany
NORTH BEACH (20714) Calvert(89), Anne Arundel(11)
NORTH EAST Cecil
NOTTINGHAM Baltimore
OAKLAND Garrett
OCEAN CITY Worcester
ODENTON Anne Arundel
OLDTOWN Allegany
OLNEY Montgomery
OWINGS Calvert
OWINGS MILLS Baltimore
OXFORD Talbot
OXON HILL Prince George's
PARK HALL St. Mary's
PARKTON Baltimore
PARKVILLE (21234) Baltimore(89), Baltimore City(11)
PARSONSBURG Wicomico
PASADENA Anne Arundel
PATUXENT RIVER St. Mary's
PERRY HALL Baltimore
PERRY POINT Cecil
PERRYMAN Harford
PERRYVILLE Cecil
PHOENIX Baltimore
PIKESVILLE (21208) Baltimore(93), Baltimore City(7)
PINEY POINT St. Mary's
PINTO Allegany
PITTSVILLE Wicomico
POCOMOKE CITY (21851) Worcester(88), Somerset(12)
POINT OF ROCKS Frederick
POMFRET Charles
POOLESVILLE Montgomery

PORT DEPOSIT Cecil
PORT REPUBLIC Calvert
PORT TOBACCO Charles
POTOMAC Montgomery
POWELLVILLE Wicomico
PRESTON Caroline
PRINCE FREDERICK Calvert
PRINCESS ANNE Somerset
PYLESVILLE Harford
QUANTICO Wicomico
QUEEN ANNE Queen Anne's
QUEENSTOWN Queen Anne's
RANDALLSTOWN Baltimore
RAWLINGS Allegany
REHOBETH Somerset
REISTERSTOWN (21136) Baltimore(97), Carroll(3)
RHODES POINT Somerset
RHODESDALE Dorchester
RIDERWOOD Baltimore
RIDGE St. Mary's
RIDGELY Caroline
RISING SUN Cecil
RIVA Anne Arundel
RIVERDALE Prince George's
ROCK HALL Kent
ROCK POINT Charles
ROCKVILLE Montgomery
ROCKY RIDGE Frederick
ROHRERSVILLE Washington
ROSEDALE (21237) Baltimore(96), Baltimore City(4)
ROYAL OAK Talbot
SABILLASVILLE (21780) Frederick(94), Washington(6)
SAINT INIGOES St. Mary's
SAINT JAMES (21781) Frederick(50), Washington(50)
SAINT LEONARD Calvert
SAINT MARYS CITY St. Mary's
SAINT MICHAELS Talbot
SALISBURY Wicomico
SANDY SPRING Montgomery
SAVAGE Howard
SCOTLAND St. Mary's
SECRETARY Dorchester
SEVERN Anne Arundel
SEVERNA PARK Anne Arundel
SHADY SIDE Anne Arundel
SHARPSBURG Washington
SHARPTOWN Wicomico
SHERWOOD Talbot
SHOWELL Worcester
SILVER SPRING (20903) Montgomery(85), Prince George's(15)
SILVER SPRING Montgomery
SIMPSONVILLE Howard
SMITHSBURG (21783) Washington(76), Frederick(24)
SNOW HILL Worcester
SOLOMONS Calvert
SOUTHERN MD FACILITY Prince George's
SPARKS GLENCOE Baltimore
SPARROWS POINT Baltimore
SPENCERVILLE Montgomery
SPRING GAP Allegany
STEVENSON Baltimore
STEVENSVILLE Queen Anne's
STILL POND Kent

STOCKTON Worcester
STREET Harford
SUBURB MARYLAND FAC Montgomery
SUDLERSVILLE Queen Anne's
SUITLAND Prince George's
SUNDERLAND Calvert
SWANTON Garrett
SYKESVILLE (21784) Carroll(94), Howard(6)
TAKOMA PARK (20912) Montgomery(92), Prince George's(8)
TAKOMA PARK Prince George's
TALL TIMBERS St. Mary's
TANEYTOWN (21787) Carroll(90), Frederick(10)
TAYLORS ISLAND Dorchester
TEMPLE HILLS Prince George's
TEMPLEVILLE Caroline
THURMONT Frederick
TILGHMAN Talbot
TODDVILLE Dorchester
TOWSON Baltimore
TRACYS LANDING Anne Arundel
TRAPPE Talbot
TUSCARORA Frederick
TYASKIN Wicomico
TYLERTON Somerset
UNION BRIDGE (21791) Frederick(52), Carroll(48)
UNIONVILLE Frederick
UPPER FAIRMOUNT Somerset
UPPER FALLS Baltimore
UPPER HILL Somerset
UPPER MARLBORO Prince George's
UPPERCO (21155) Baltimore(92), Carroll(8)
VALLEY LEE St. Mary's
VIENNA Dorchester
WALDORF (20601) Charles(95), Prince George's(5)
WALDORF Charles
WALKERSVILLE Frederick
WARWICK Cecil
WASHINGTON Prince George's
WASHINGTON GROVE Montgomery
WELCOME Charles
WENONA Somerset
WEST FRIENDSHIP Howard
WEST RIVER Anne Arundel
WESTERNPORT Allegany
WESTMINSTER Carroll
WESTOVER Somerset
WHALEYVILLE Worcester
WHITE HALL (21161) Baltimore(60), Harford(40)
WHITE MARSH Baltimore
WHITE PLAINS Charles
WHITEFORD Harford
WILLARDS Wicomico
WILLIAMSPORT Washington
WINGATE Dorchester
WITTMAN Talbot
WOODBINE (21797) Howard(62), Carroll(38)
WOODSBORO Frederick
WOODSTOCK (21163) Baltimore(71), Howard(29)
WOOLFORD Dorchester
WORTON Kent
WYE MILLS Talbot

ZIP/City Cross Reference

ZIP	City	ZIP	City	ZIP	City	ZIP	City
20601-20604	WALDORF	20613-20613	BRANDYWINE	20622-20622	CHARLOTTE HALL	20630-20630	DRAYDEN
20606-20606	ABELL	20615-20615	BROOMES ISLAND	20623-20623	CHELTENHAM	20632-20632	FAULKNER
20607-20607	ACCOKEEK	20616-20616	BRYANS ROAD	20624-20624	CLEMENTS	20634-20634	GREAT MILLS
20608-20608	AQUASCO	20617-20617	BRYANTOWN	20625-20625	COBB ISLAND	20635-20635	HELEN
20609-20609	AVENUE	20618-20618	BUSHWOOD	20626-20626	COLTONS POINT	20636-20636	HOLLYWOOD
20610-20610	BARSTOW	20619-20619	CALIFORNIA	20627-20627	COMPTON	20637-20637	HUGHESVILLE
20611-20611	BEL ALTON	20620-20620	CALLAWAY	20628-20628	DAMERON	20639-20639	HUNTINGTOWN
20612-20612	BENEDICT	20621-20621	CHAPTICO	20629-20629	DOWELL	20640-20640	INDIAN HEAD

Zip	City	Zip	City	Zip	City	Zip	City
20643-20643	IRONSIDES	20781-20788	HYATTSVILLE	21050-21050	FOREST HILL	21287-21298	BALTIMORE
20645-20645	ISSUE	20790-20791	CAPITOL HEIGHTS	21051-21051	FORK	21401-21412	ANNAPOLIS
20646-20646	LA PLATA	20794-20794	JESSUP	21052-21052	FORT HOWARD	21501-21505	CUMBERLAND
20650-20650	LEONARDTOWN	20797-20797	SOUTHERN MD FACILITY	21053-21053	FREELAND	21520-21520	ACCIDENT
20653-20653	LEXINGTON PARK	20799-20799	CAPITOL HEIGHTS	21054-21054	GAMBRILLS	21521-21521	BARTON
20656-20656	LOVEVILLE	20800-20800	SUBURB MARYLAND FAC	21055-21055	GARRISON	21522-21522	BITTINGER
20657-20657	LUSBY			21056-21056	GIBSON ISLAND	21523-21523	BLOOMINGTON
20658-20658	MARBURY	20812-20812	GLEN ECHO	21057-21057	GLEN ARM	21524-21524	CORRIGANVILLE
20659-20659	MECHANICSVILLE	20813-20814	BETHESDA	21060-21062	GLEN BURNIE	21528-21528	ECKHART MINES
20660-20660	MORGANZA	20815-20815	CHEVY CHASE	21071-21071	GLYNDON	21529-21529	ELLERSLIE
20661-20661	MOUNT VICTORIA	20816-20817	BETHESDA	21074-21074	HAMPSTEAD	21530-21530	FLINTSTONE
20662-20662	NANJEMOY	20818-20818	CABIN JOHN	21075-21075	ELKRIDGE	21531-21531	FRIENDSVILLE
20664-20664	NEWBURG	20824-20824	BETHESDA	21076-21076	HANOVER	21532-21532	FROSTBURG
20667-20667	PARK HALL	20825-20825	CHEVY CHASE	21077-21077	HARMANS	21536-21536	GRANTSVILLE
20670-20670	PATUXENT RIVER	20827-20827	BETHESDA	21078-21078	HAVRE DE GRACE	21538-21538	KITZMILLER
20674-20674	PINEY POINT	20830-20832	OLNEY	21080-21080	HENRYTON	21539-21539	LONACONING
20675-20675	POMFRET	20833-20833	BROOKEVILLE	21082-21082	HYDES	21540-21540	LUKE
20676-20676	PORT REPUBLIC	20837-20837	POOLESVILLE	21084-21084	JARRETTSVILLE	21541-21541	MC HENRY
20677-20677	PORT TOBACCO	20838-20838	BARNESVILLE	21085-21085	JOPPA	21542-21542	MIDLAND
20678-20678	PRINCE FREDERICK	20839-20839	BEALLSVILLE	21087-21087	KINGSVILLE	21543-21543	MIDLOTHIAN
20680-20680	RIDGE	20841-20841	BOYDS	21088-21088	LINEBORO	21545-21545	MOUNT SAVAGE
20682-20682	ROCK POINT	20842-20842	DICKERSON	21090-21090	LINTHICUM HEIGHTS	21550-21550	OAKLAND
20684-20684	SAINT INIGOES	20847-20853	ROCKVILLE	21092-21092	LONG GREEN	21555-21555	OLDTOWN
20685-20685	SAINT LEONARD	20854-20854	POTOMAC	21093-21094	LUTHERVILLE TIMONIUM	21556-21556	PINTO
20686-20686	SAINT MARYS CITY	20855-20855	DERWOOD	21098-21098	HANOVER	21557-21557	RAWLINGS
20687-20687	SCOTLAND	20857-20857	ROCKVILLE	21101-21101	MAGNOLIA	21560-21560	SPRING GAP
20688-20688	SOLOMONS	20859-20859	POTOMAC	21102-21102	MANCHESTER	21561-21561	SWANTON
20689-20689	SUNDERLAND	20860-20860	SANDY SPRING	21104-21104	MARRIOTTSVILLE	21562-21562	WESTERNPORT
20690-20690	TALL TIMBERS	20861-20861	ASHTON	21105-21105	MARYLAND LINE	21601-21606	EASTON
20692-20692	VALLEY LEE	20862-20862	BRINKLOW	21106-21106	MAYO	21607-21607	BARCLAY
20693-20693	WELCOME	20866-20866	BURTONSVILLE	21108-21108	MILLERSVILLE	21609-21609	BETHLEHEM
20695-20695	WHITE PLAINS	20868-20868	SPENCERVILLE	21111-21111	MONKTON	21610-21610	BETTERTON
20697-20697	SOUTHERN MD FACILITY	20871-20871	CLARKSBURG	21113-21113	ODENTON	21612-21612	BOZMAN
20701-20701	ANNAPOLIS JUNCTION	20872-20872	DAMASCUS	21114-21114	CROFTON	21613-21613	CAMBRIDGE
20703-20703	LANHAM	20874-20876	GERMANTOWN	21117-21117	OWINGS MILLS	21617-21617	CENTREVILLE
20704-20705	BELTSVILLE	20877-20879	GAITHERSBURG	21120-21120	PARKTON	21619-21619	CHESTER
20706-20706	LANHAM	20880-20880	WASHINGTON GROVE	21122-21123	PASADENA	21620-21620	CHESTERTOWN
20707-20709	LAUREL	20882-20885	GAITHERSBURG	21128-21128	PERRY HALL	21622-21622	CHURCH CREEK
20710-20710	BLADENSBURG	20886-20886	MONTGOMERY VILLAGE	21130-21130	PERRYMAN	21623-21623	CHURCH HILL
20711-20711	LOTHIAN	20889-20889	BETHESDA	21131-21131	PHOENIX	21624-21624	CLAIBORNE
20712-20712	MOUNT RAINIER	20890-20890	SUBURB MARYLAND FAC	21132-21132	PYLESVILLE	21625-21625	CORDOVA
20714-20714	NORTH BEACH			21133-21133	RANDALLSTOWN	21626-21626	CRAPO
20715-20721	BOWIE	20891-20891	KENSINGTON	21136-21136	REISTERSTOWN	21627-21627	CROCHERON
20722-20722	BRENTWOOD	20892-20894	BETHESDA	21139-21139	RIDERWOOD	21628-21628	CRUMPTON
20723-20726	LAUREL	20895-20895	KENSINGTON	21140-21140	RIVA	21629-21629	DENTON
20731-20731	CAPITOL HEIGHTS	20896-20896	GARRETT PARK	21144-21144	SEVERN	21631-21631	EAST NEW MARKET
20732-20732	CHESAPEAKE BEACH	20897-20897	SUBURB MARYLAND FAC	21146-21146	SEVERNA PARK	21632-21632	FEDERALSBURG
20733-20733	CHURCHTON			21150-21150	SIMPSONVILLE	21634-21634	FISHING CREEK
20735-20735	CLINTON	20898-20899	GAITHERSBURG	21152-21152	SPARKS GLENCOE	21635-21635	GALENA
20736-20736	OWINGS	20901-20911	SILVER SPRING	21153-21153	STEVENSON	21636-21636	GOLDSBORO
20737-20738	RIVERDALE	20912-20913	TAKOMA PARK	21154-21154	STREET	21638-21638	GRASONVILLE
20740-20742	COLLEGE PARK	20914-20997	SILVER SPRING	21155-21155	UPPERCO	21639-21639	GREENSBORO
20743-20743	CAPITOL HEIGHTS	21001-21001	ABERDEEN	21156-21156	UPPER FALLS	21640-21640	HENDERSON
20744-20744	FORT WASHINGTON	21005-21005	ABERDEEN PROVING GROUND	21157-21158	WESTMINSTER	21641-21641	HILLSBORO
20745-20745	OXON HILL	21009-21009	ABINGDON	21160-21160	WHITEFORD	21643-21643	HURLOCK
20746-20746	SUITLAND	21010-21010	GUNPOWDER	21161-21161	WHITE HALL	21644-21644	INGLESIDE
20747-20747	DISTRICT HEIGHTS	21012-21012	ARNOLD	21162-21162	WHITE MARSH	21645-21645	KENNEDYVILLE
20748-20748	TEMPLE HILLS	21013-21013	BALDWIN	21163-21163	WOODSTOCK	21647-21647	MCDANIEL
20749-20749	FORT WASHINGTON	21014-21015	BEL AIR	21201-21203	BALTIMORE	21648-21648	MADISON
20750-20750	OXON HILL	21017-21017	BELCAMP	21204-21204	TOWSON	21649-21649	MARYDEL
20751-20751	DEALE	21018-21018	BENSON	21205-21206	BALTIMORE	21650-21650	MASSEY
20752-20752	SUITLAND	21020-21020	BORING	21207-21207	GWYNN OAK	21651-21651	MILLINGTON
20753-20753	DISTRICT HEIGHTS	21021-21021	BRADSHAW	21208-21208	PIKESVILLE	21652-21652	NEAVITT
20754-20754	DUNKIRK	21022-21022	BROOKLANDVILLE	21209-21218	BALTIMORE	21653-21653	NEWCOMB
20755-20755	FORT GEORGE G MEADE	21023-21023	BUTLER	21219-21219	SPARROWS POINT	21654-21654	OXFORD
20757-20757	TEMPLE HILLS	21024-21024	CARDIFF	21220-21220	MIDDLE RIVER	21655-21655	PRESTON
20758-20758	FRIENDSHIP	21027-21027	CHASE	21221-21221	ESSEX	21656-21656	CHURCH HILL
20759-20759	FULTON	21028-21028	CHURCHVILLE	21222-21222	DUNDALK	21657-21657	QUEEN ANNE
20762-20762	ANDREWS AIR FORCE BASE	21029-21029	CLARKSVILLE	21223-21224	BALTIMORE	21658-21658	QUEENSTOWN
20763-20763	SAVAGE	21030-21030	COCKEYSVILLE	21225-21225	BROOKLYN	21659-21659	RHODESDALE
20764-20764	SHADY SIDE	21031-21031	HUNT VALLEY	21226-21226	CURTIS BAY	21660-21660	RIDGELY
20765-20765	GALESVILLE	21032-21032	CROWNSVILLE	21227-21227	HALETHORPE	21661-21661	ROCK HALL
20768-20768	GREENBELT	21034-21034	DARLINGTON	21228-21228	CATONSVILLE	21662-21662	ROYAL OAK
20769-20769	GLENN DALE	21035-21035	DAVIDSONVILLE	21229-21233	BALTIMORE	21663-21663	SAINT MICHAELS
20770-20771	GREENBELT	21036-21036	DAYTON	21234-21234	PARKVILLE	21664-21664	SECRETARY
20772-20775	UPPER MARLBORO	21037-21037	EDGEWATER	21235-21235	BALTIMORE	21665-21665	SHERWOOD
20776-20776	HARWOOD	21040-21040	EDGEWOOD	21236-21236	NOTTINGHAM	21666-21666	STEVENSVILLE
20777-20777	HIGHLAND	21041-21043	ELLICOTT CITY	21237-21237	ROSEDALE	21667-21667	STILL POND
20778-20778	WEST RIVER	21044-21046	COLUMBIA	21239-21241	BALTIMORE	21668-21668	SUDLERSVILLE
20779-20779	TRACYS LANDING	21047-21047	FALLSTON	21244-21244	GWYNN OAK	21669-21669	TAYLORS ISLAND
		21048-21048	FINKSBURG	21250-21285	BALTIMORE	21670-21670	TEMPLEVILLE
				21286-21286	TOWSON	21671-21671	TILGHMAN

21672-21672	TODDVILLE	21755-21755	JEFFERSON	21795-21795	WILLIAMSPORT	21862-21862	SHOWELL
21673-21673	TRAPPE	21756-21756	KEEDYSVILLE	21797-21797	WOODBINE	21863-21863	SNOW HILL
21675-21675	WINGATE	21757-21757	KEYMAR	21798-21798	WOODSBORO	21864-21864	STOCKTON
21676-21676	WITTMAN	21758-21758	KNOXVILLE	21801-21804	SALISBURY	21865-21865	TYASKIN
21677-21677	WOOLFORD	21759-21759	LADIESBURG	21810-21810	ALLEN	21866-21866	TYLERTON
21678-21678	WORTON	21762-21762	LIBERTYTOWN	21811-21811	BERLIN	21867-21867	UPPER FAIRMOUNT
21679-21679	WYE MILLS	21764-21764	LINWOOD	21813-21813	BISHOPVILLE	21869-21869	VIENNA
21681-21688	RIDGELY	21765-21765	LISBON	21814-21814	BIVALVE	21870-21870	WENONA
21690-21690	CHESTERTOWN	21766-21766	LITTLE ORLEANS	21816-21816	CHANCE	21871-21871	WESTOVER
21701-21709	FREDERICK	21767-21767	MAUGANSVILLE	21817-21817	CRISFIELD	21872-21872	WHALEYVILLE
21710-21710	ADAMSTOWN	21769-21769	MIDDLETOWN	21820-21820	DAMES QUARTER	21874-21874	WILLARDS
21711-21711	BIG POOL	21770-21770	MONROVIA	21821-21821	DEAL ISLAND	21875-21875	DELMAR
21713-21713	BOONSBORO	21771-21771	MOUNT AIRY	21822-21822	EDEN	21890-21890	WESTOVER
21714-21714	BRADDOCK HEIGHTS	21773-21773	MYERSVILLE	21824-21824	EWELL	21901-21901	NORTH EAST
21715-21715	BROWNSVILLE	21774-21774	NEW MARKET	21826-21826	FRUITLAND	21902-21902	PERRY POINT
21716-21716	BRUNSWICK	21775-21775	NEW MIDWAY	21829-21829	GIRDLETREE	21903-21903	PERRYVILLE
21717-21717	BUCKEYSTOWN	21776-21776	NEW WINDSOR	21830-21830	HEBRON	21904-21904	PORT DEPOSIT
21718-21718	BURKITTSVILLE	21777-21777	POINT OF ROCKS	21835-21835	LINKWOOD	21911-21911	RISING SUN
21719-21719	CASCADE	21778-21778	ROCKY RIDGE	21836-21836	MANOKIN	21912-21912	WARWICK
21720-21720	CAVETOWN	21779-21779	ROHRERSVILLE	21837-21837	MARDELA SPRINGS	21913-21913	CECILTON
21721-21721	CHEWSVILLE	21780-21780	SABILLASVILLE	21838-21838	MARION STATION	21914-21914	CHARLESTOWN
21722-21722	CLEAR SPRING	21781-21781	SAINT JAMES	21840-21840	NANTICOKE	21915-21915	CHESAPEAKE CITY
21723-21723	COOKSVILLE	21782-21782	SHARPSBURG	21841-21841	NEWARK	21916-21916	CHILDS
21727-21727	EMMITSBURG	21783-21783	SMITHSBURG	21842-21843	OCEAN CITY	21917-21917	COLORA
21733-21733	FAIRPLAY	21784-21784	SYKESVILLE	21849-21849	PARSONSBURG	21918-21918	CONOWINGO
21734-21734	FUNKSTOWN	21787-21787	TANEYTOWN	21850-21850	PITTSVILLE	21919-21919	EARLEVILLE
21736-21736	GAPLAND	21788-21788	THURMONT	21851-21851	POCOMOKE CITY	21920-21920	ELK MILLS
21737-21737	GLENELG	21790-21790	TUSCARORA	21852-21852	POWELLVILLE	21921-21922	ELKTON
21738-21738	GLENWOOD	21791-21791	UNION BRIDGE	21853-21853	PRINCESS ANNE	21930-21930	GEORGETOWN
21740-21749	HAGERSTOWN	21792-21792	UNIONVILLE	21856-21856	QUANTICO		
21750-21750	HANCOCK	21793-21793	WALKERSVILLE	21857-21857	REHOBETH		
21754-21754	IJAMSVILLE	21794-21794	WEST FRIENDSHIP	21861-21861	SHARPTOWN		

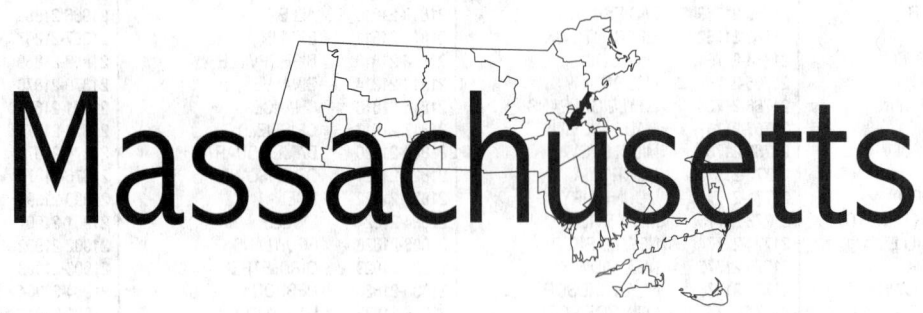

Massachusetts

General Help Numbers:

Governor's Office
State House, Room 360   617-727-6250
Boston, MA 02133   Fax 617-727-9725
www.state.ma.us/gov   8AM-6PM

Attorney General's Office
One Ashburton Place, Room 2010   617-727-2200
Boston, MA 02108-1698   Fax 617-727-5768
www.ago.state.ma.us   9AM-5PM

State Court Administrator
2 Center Plaza, Room 540   617-742-8575
Boston, MA 02108   Fax 617-742-0968
www.magnet.state.ma.us/courts/TrialC/trial.htm

State Archives
Archives Division   617-727-2816
220 Morrissey Blvd   Fax 617-288-8429
Boston, MA 02125   9AM-5PM M-F; 9-3 SA
www.state.ma.us/sec/arc/arcidx.htm

State Specifics:

Capital: Boston
                                     Suffolk County

Time Zone: EST

Number of Counties: 14

Population: 6,175,169

Web Site: www.state.ma.us

State Agencies

Criminal Records

Criminal History Systems Board, 200 Arlington Street, #2200, Chelsea, MA 02150; 617-660-4600, 617-660-4613 (Fax), 9AM-5PM.

www.state.ma.us/chsb/pubs.htm

Note: There are 3 searches offered: Personal; Certified Agency; and Publicly Accessible (PUBAC). Certified Agency requests are pre-approved via statute or by the Board. PUBAC is open to the public.

Indexing & Storage: Records are available for at least 50 years. New records are available for inquiry immediately. Records are indexed on inhouse computer, file folders.

Searching: PUBAC requesters are limited to adult records. The crime must include a sentance of 5 years or more OR sentenced and convicted for any term if, at the time of request, the subject is on probation or has been released within 2 years of felony conv. Include the following in your request-name, date of birth. The Certified Agency record includes all conviction and all open or pending actions. The Personal request (on one's self) requires a notarized signature.

Access by: mail.

Fee & Payment: The Personal request is free. The Certified Agency request is $10.00. The PUBAC request is $25.00. No fingerprints are used, thus no fingerprint fees. Fee payee: The Commonwealth of

Massachusetts. Prepayment required. Personal checks accepted. No credit cards accepted.

Mail search: Turnaround time: 2 weeks. A self addressed stamped envelope is requested.

Corporation Records
Trademarks/Servicemarks
Limited Liability
Partnerships
Limited Partnership Records

Secretary of the Commonwealth, Corporation Division, One Ashburton Pl, 17th Floor, Boston, MA 02108; 617-727-9640 (Corporations), 617-727-2850 (Records), 617-727-8329 (Trademarks), 617-727-9440 (Forms request line), 617-742-4538 (Fax), 8:45AM-5PM.

www.state.ma.us/sec/cor/coridx.htm

Indexing & Storage: Records are available for corporations and business entities organized since 1978 on computer. Corporations and business entities organized prior to 1978 may or may not be available. Annual reports are maintained for 10 years. New records are available for inquiry immediately. Records are indexed on microfilm, inhouse computer.

Searching: Include the following in your request-full name of business. In addition to the articles of incorporation, corporation records include the following information: Annual Reports, Officers and Directors names and addresses, Prior (merged) names, Inactive and Reserved names and US Tax ID numbers.

Access by: mail, phone, in person, online.

Fee & Payment: Uncertified copies cost $.20 per page. Certified copies cost $7.00 for the first page and $2.00 for each additional page. Certified copies of articles of incorporation are $12.00 per organization. Fee payee: Commonwealth of Massachusetts. Prepayment required. Personal checks accepted. No credit cards accepted.

Mail search: Turnaround time: 3-5 days. A self addressed stamped envelope is requested.

Phone search: No fee for telephone request. Telephone room hours are 8:45AM-5PM.

In person search: Turnaround time: while you wait.

Online search: The agency offers "Direct Access." The annual subscription fee is $149.00 and there is a $.40 a minute access fee. System is available from 8 AM to 10 PM. This system also provides UCC record data. Call (617) 727-7655 for a sign-up packet.

Uniform Commercial Code
State Tax Liens

UCC Division, Secretary of the Commonwealth, One Ashburton Pl, Room 1711, Boston, MA 02108; 617-727-2860, 900-555-4500 (Computer Prints), 900-555-4600 (Copies), 8:45AM-5PM.

www.state.ma.us/sec/cor/corucc/uccinf.htm

Indexing & Storage: Records are available from 09/01/81 on computer and 01/01/84 on microfiche. Records are indexed on inhouse computer.

Searching: Use search request form UCC-11. Federal tax liens are filed at the US District Courts, PO & Courthouse Bldg, Boston, MA 02109 (617-233-9152). A list of state tax liens is available here, but must be searched in person separately from UCC filings. Include the following in your request-debtor name. Only active filings are available.

Access by: mail, phone, fax, in person, online.

Fee & Payment: Information listing only is $5.00. Search with copies is $15.00 for first 15 pages, $1.00 per page of copies after 15. State tax liens cost $0.20 per copy made. The state does not certify any state tax lien. Fee payee: Commonwealth of Massachusetts. Prepayment required. Personal checks accepted. No credit cards accepted.

Mail search: Turnaround time: 2 days. Information requests are available.

Phone search: See expedited service.

Fax search: Results can be returned by fax, if arrangements are made, only by 900 calls. Call number above for more information.

In person search: You may request information in person, but turnaround time for certified documents is 24 hours.

Online search: "Direct Access" is available for $149 per year plus a $.40 per minute network fee. The system is open from 8 AM to 9:50 PM. Call 617-727-2853-obtain information packet.

Other access: Microfiche may be purchased.

Expedited service: Expedited service is available for fax searches. Turnaround time: 24 hours. A 24 hours express search of financial statements (900-555-4600) is $50.00. An express search of computer printouts is $25.00 per debter name (900-555-4500), from 10AM-4PM.

Sales Tax Registrations

Revenue Department, Taxpayer Assistance Office, PO Box 7010, Boston, MA 02204 (Courier: 200 Arlington Street, 4th Floor, Chelsea, MA 02150); 617-887-6100, 8AM-5PM.

www.state.ma.us/dor

Note: There are actually 6 offices in the state that will allow walk-in researchers. The office in Chelsea will not let you in the building.

Searching: This agency will only confirm that a business is registered. They will provide no other information. Include the following in your request-business name. They will also search by tax permit number.

Access by: mail, phone, fax, in person.

Mail search: Turnaround time: 5-10 days. A self addressed stamped envelope is requested. No fee for mail request.

Phone search: No fee for telephone request.

Fax search: They ask that you call first to get the number, they do not wish to publish their fax number.

In person search: No fee for request.

Birth Certificates

Registry of Vital Records and Statistics, 150 Mt. Vernon St, 1st FL, Dorchester, MA 02125; 617-740-2600, 617-740-2606, 8:45AM-4:45PM.

www.state.ma.us/dph/vitrecs.htm

Indexing & Storage: Records are available from 1906-present. Records from 1841-1905 are located at the Massachusetts Archives, 220 Morrissey Blvd., Boston, MA 02125. Records prior to 1841 are located at the town/city level. It takes 6 months before new records are available for inquiry.

Searching: Access to out-of-wedlock birth records and health information is strictly limited. A court order is required for adopted children's records. Otherwise, records are open. Include the following

in your request-full name, names of parents, mother's maiden name, date of birth, place of birth. Must present a photo ID or provide a copy of a photo ID to search. Phone and fax searchers must give exact place and date of event.

Access by: mail, phone, fax, in person.

Fee & Payment: Prepayment required. Fee payee: Commonwealth of Massachusetts. Personal checks accepted. Credit cards accepted: Mastercard, Visa, AmEx, Discover.

Mail search: Turnaround time: 3-4 weeks. A self addressed stamped envelope is requested. Search costs $11.00 for each 10 years searched.

Phone search: Search costs $19.00 for each 10 years searched. Must use a credit card.

Fax search: Search costs $19.00 for each 10 years searched. Must use a credit card.

In person search: Search costs $6.00 for each 10 years searched. Turnaround time is immediate. You can also do your own searching of records. First 20 minutes is free, then there is a $3.00 fee. The research center is open 9AM-12PM and 2PM-4:30PM, M-F.

Expedited service: Expedited service is available for mail, phone and fax searches. Turnaround time: 2 days. Use of credit card required, add $16.00 for express delivery.

Death Records

Registry of Vital Records and Statistics, 150 Mt Vernon St, 1st FL, Dorchester, MA 02125; 617-740-2600, 617-740-2606, 8:45AM-4:45PM.

www.state.ma.us/dph/vitrecs.htm

Indexing & Storage: Records are available from 1906-present. Prior records at State Archives to 1841. It takes 4 months before new records are available for inquiry.

Searching: Fetal death records are not available. A court order is required to access the originals of amended records. Include the following in your request-full name, date of death, place of death. Name of spouse and age at time of death will help facilitate the search. Phone and fax requesters must supply exact place and date of event.

Access by: mail, phone, fax, in person.

Fee & Payment: Prepayment required. Fee payee: Commonwealth of Massachusetts. Personal checks accepted. Credit cards accepted: Mastercard, Visa, AmEx, Discover.

Mail search: Turnaround time: 3-4 weeks. A self addressed stamped envelope is requested. Search costs $11.00 for each 10 years searched.

Phone search: Search costs $19.00 per record. You must use a credit card.

Fax search: Same criteria as phone searches.

In person search: Search costs $6.00 for each 10 years searched. There is a research center open 9AM-12PM and 2PM-4:30PM M-F. Searching is free the first 20 minutes, then it is $3.00 per hour.

Expedited service: Expedited service is available for mail, phone and fax searches. Turnaround time: 2 days. Add $16.00 for express delivery. Use of credit card required.

Marriage Certificates

Registry of Vital Records and Statistics, 150 Mt Vernon St, 1st FL, Dorchester, MA 02125; 617-740-2600, 617-740-2606, 8:45AM-4:45PM.

www.state.ma.us/dph/vitrecs.htm

Indexing & Storage: Records are available from 1906-present. Prior records to 1841 are at State Archives. It takes 5 months before new records are available for inquiry.

Searching: A court order is required for originals of amended records. Include the following in your request-names of husband and wife, date of marriage, place or county of marriage. Phone or fax searchers must submit exact place and date of event. Also helpful is parents' names.

Access by: mail, phone, fax, in person.

Fee & Payment: Prepayment required. Fee payee: Commonwealth of Massachusetts. Personal checks accepted. Credit cards accepted: Mastercard, Visa, AmEx, Discover.

Mail search: Turnaround time: 3-4 weeks. A self addressed stamped envelope is requested. Search costs $11.00 for each 10 years searched.

Phone search: Search costs $19.00 per record. You must use a credit card.

Fax search: Same search criteria as phone searching.

In person search: Search costs $6.00 for each 10 years searched. There is a research center open from 9AM-12PM and 2PM-4:30PM, M-F. The first 20 minutes are free, then a $3.00 per hour fee is charged.

Expedited service: Expedited service is available for mail, phone and fax searches. Turnaround time: 2 days. Add $16.00 for express delivery. Use of credit card required.

Divorce Records

Registry of Vital Records and Statistics, 150 Mt. Vernon St, 1st FL, Dorchester, MA 02125; 617-740-2600, 617-740-2606.

www.state.ma.us/dph/vitrecs.htm

Note: Divorce records are found at county of issue. However, this agency maintains an index from 1952-present. The state will do a search for free by mail only to determine the county.

Workers' Compensation Records

Keeper of Records, Department of Industrial Accidents, 600 Washington St, 7th Floor, Boston, MA 02111; 617-727-4900 x301, 617-727-1161 (Fax), 8AM-4PM.

Indexing & Storage: Records are available from 1993 on. The index is computerized since 1981. Older records are located at the State Archives. Records are indexed on inhouse computer.

Searching: You need a signed release from claimant to receive data regarding body parts, DOB and SSN. Include the following in your request-claimant name, Social Security Number, date of accident. The following data is not released: medical records, date of birth or Social Security Numbers.

Access by: mail, in person.

Fee & Payment: There is no fee to do a name search, copies are $.20 per page. If you require the

injury codes and body parts data (which requires a signed release), the fee is $3.00 per name. These requests are within 10 days. Fee payee: Comm of Mass. Prepayment required. Personal checks accepted. No credit cards accepted.

Mail search: Turnaround time: 2 weeks. No self addressed stamped envelope is required.

In person search: All requests must be in writing.

Driver Records-Registry

Registry of Motor Vehicles, Driver Control Unit, Box 199150, Roxbury, MA 02119-9100; 617-351-9213 (Registry), 617-351-9219 (Fax), 8AM-4:30PM M-T-W-F; 8AM-7PM TH.

www.state.ma.us/rmv

Note: The driving records provided by the Registry are for employment or general business use. Both the Registry and the Merit Rating Board use the same database of driving record histories.

Indexing & Storage: Records are available for 6 years plus current year for moving violations. It takes 1 week before new records are available for inquiry.

Searching: Casual requesters can only obtain records without personal information. Include the following in your request-full name, driver's license number, date of birth. The address of the requester should also be included. The following data is not released: bulk information or lists for commercial purposes.

Access by: mail, phone, in person.

Fee & Payment: The fee is $10.00 per record. Fee payee: Registry of Motor Vehicles. Prepayment required. Personal checks accepted. No credit cards accepted.

Mail search: Turnaround time: 10 working days. No self addressed stamped envelope is required.

Phone search: The Registry offers a phone-in request line at 617-351-4500. Orders can be paid with a credit card, results are mailed.

In person search: Up to 10 requests will be processed immediately; the rest are available the next day. You may request a record from any field office.

Driver Records-Insurance

Merit Rating Board, Attn: Driving Records, PO Box 199100, Boston, MA 02119-9100; 617-351-4400, 617-351-9660 (Fax), 8:45AM-5:00PM.

www.state.ma.us/rmv

Note: The Merit Rating Board processes driving records for the insurance industry in accordance with state statutes.

Indexing & Storage: Records are available for 6 years for moving violations and at fault accidents (process date). The license number and name are validated against the Registry license file.

Searching: These records do not show revocation or suspension action. Include the following in your request-driver's license number, full name, date of birth. All requests must be on the agency form.

Access by: mail, in person.

Fee & Payment: The fee is $10.00 per record. Fee payee: Commonwealth of Massachusetts. Prepayment required. Personal checks accepted. No credit cards accepted.

Mail search: Turnaround time: 2 days. No self addressed stamped envelope is required.

In person search: Turnaround time while you wait.

Other access: The Merit Rating Board provides both on-line and tape inquiry to the insurance industry for rating and issuance of new and renewal automobile insuarnce policies. Per statute, this method of retrieval is not open to the public.

Vehicle Ownership
Vehicle Identification

Registry of Motor Vehicles, Customer Assistance-Mail List Dept., PO Box 199100, Boston, MA 02119-9100; 617-351-9384, 617-351-9524 (Fax), 8AM-4:30PM.

www.state.ma.us/rmv

Indexing & Storage: Records are available from the 1940's for licenses, from 1963 for registrations and names. Records are computerized from 1986.

Searching: In general, license, ownership, and registration information is available to the public. Personal information is not available to casual requesters without consent. The state does not do VIN look-ups. Lien information is provided as part of the record.

Access by: mail, fax, in person, online.

Fee & Payment: The current fee is $5.00 for per record request if on computer, $10.00 if on microfiche. Fee payee: Commonwealth of Massachusetts. Prepayment required. Personal checks accepted. No credit cards accepted.

Mail search: Turnaround time: 7-10 days. A self addressed stamped envelope is requested.

Fax search: Searching is available by fax.

In person search: In person requesters may get computer records immediately, microfiche records take 3 days.

Online search: Searching is limited to Massachusetts based insurance companies and agents for the purpose of issuing or renewing insurance. This system is not open to the public. There is no fee, but line charges will be incurred.

Other access: The state offers an extensive array of customized bulk record requests. For further information, contact the Production Control Office.

Accident Reports

Accident Records Section, Registry of Motor Vehicles, PO Box 199100, Roxbury, MA 02119-9100; 617-351-9434, 617-351-9401 (Fax), 8:45AM-5PM.

www.state.ma.us/rmv

Note: Accident reports may also be obtained from the local police department in the investigating jurisdiction. Normal fee is $1.00 per page.

Indexing & Storage: Records are available for 2 years to present. Records are indexed on computer.

Searching: Criminal Offender Record Information (CORI) will not be released. Items required for search include; full name, date of accident, location of accident, and license or registration number.

Access by: mail, in person.

Fee & Payment: The charge is $10.00 per report. Fee payee: Registry of Motor Vehicles. Prepayment required. Personal checks accepted. No credit cards accepted.

Mail search: Turnaround time: 7-10 days.

In person search: Walk-in location is Copley Place, Tower One, 5th Floor, Boston, MA 02116. Turnaround time is immediate if on system.

Boat & Vessel Ownership
Boat & Vessel Registration

Massachusetts Environmental Police, 175 Portland St, Boston, MA 02114; 617-727-3900, 617-727-8897 (Fax), 8:45AM-5PM.

Indexing & Storage: Records are available from 1988-present. All motor powered boats and jet skis must be registered with this agency. All boats over 14ft must be titled. Records are indexed on computer.

Searching: To search, you need name and registration or hull number. The following data is not released: Social Security Numbers or phone numbers.

Access by: mail, fax.

Fee & Payment: There is no search fee.

Mail search: Turnaround time: 1 week. No self addressed stamped envelope is required.

Fax search: Turnaround time is usually 5 minutes.

Other access: To obtain printed lists or tapes, contact Robert Morley.

Legislation-Current/Pending
Legislation-Passed

Massachusetts General Court, State House, Beacon St, Room 428 (Document Room), Boston, MA 02133; 617-722-2860 (Document Room), 9AM-5PM.

www.state.ma.us/legis.legis.htm

Indexing & Storage: Records are available for usually two years on computer. Older years are available from the State House Library at 617-727-2590. Records are computer indexed from 1995-present.

Searching: The document room only has information on current bills. Include the following in your request-bill number, date of debate.

Access by: mail, phone, in person, online.

Fee & Payment: There is no fee.

Mail search: Turnaround time: same day if possible. A self addressed stamped envelope is requested.

Phone search: Searching is available by phone.

In person search: Turnaround time same day.

Online search: The web site has bill information for the current session and the previous session.

Other access: The state does make available a listing of all bills filed and several bulletins; call 617-722-2340 for more information.

Voter Registration
Records not maintained by a state level agency.

Note: Records are maintained at the local city and town level. In general, they are open to the public.

GED Certificates

Massachusetts Dept of Education, GED Processing, 350 Main St, Malden, MA 02148; 781-338-6636, 781-338-3391, 781-338-3391 (Fax).

www.doe.mass.edu/ged

Searching: They will not release copies of transcripts (you must go to the educational institution). This agency will verify or confirm receipt of GED diploma information. All of the following are required: a signed release, date of birth, and Social Security Number. The year and the name of institution are also helpful.

Access by: mail, fax, in person.

Fee & Payment: The fee is $2.00 per verification or letter of certification. Fee payee: Commonwealth of Massachusetts. Prepayment required. Only money orders or business checks are accepted. No credit cards accepted.

Mail search: Turnaround time 1-2 days. No self addressed stamped envelope is required.

Fax search: Fax is only available to companies and educational institutions.

In person search: Turnaround time can be immediate, depending on workload.

Hunting License Information
Fishing License Information

Division of Fisheries & Wildlife, 100 Cambridge St, Room 1902, Boston, MA 02202; 617-626-1590, 617-626-1517 (Fax), 8:45AM-5PM.

www.state.ma.us/dfwele

Indexing & Storage: Records are available for 1 year back only. Older records are maintained at one of several locations off premises and take longer to research.

Searching: All requests must be in writing and on their form. You may call to request the form. Need to know the store where license was purchased and month it was purchased. They are filed by license number only.

Access by: mail, in person.

Fee & Payment: There is no search fee.

Mail search: Turnaround time: same day if possible. No self addressed stamped envelope is required.

In person search: You must complete their form.

Licenses Searchable Online

Acupuncturist #05	www.docboard.org/ma/df/masearch.htm
Alarm (Burglar & Fire) Installer #07	http://license.reg.state.ma.us/pubLic/licque.asp?color=red&Board=EL
Allied Health Professions #07	http://license.reg.state.ma.us/pubLic/licque.asp?color=red&Board=AH
Allied Mental Health & Human Svcs Prof #07	http://license.reg.state.ma.us/pubLic/licque.asp?query=personal&color=red&board=MH
Amusement Device Inspector #27	www.state.ma.us/dps/Lic_srch.htm
Architect #42	http://license.reg.state.ma.us/pubLic/licque.asp?color=red&Board=AR
Athletic Trainer #07	http://license.reg.state.ma.us/pubLic/licque.asp?color=red&Board=AH
Auctioneer School #43	www.magnet.state.ma.us/standards/auc-sch.htm
Barber #07	http://license.reg.state.ma.us/pubLic/licque.asp?color=red&Board=BR
Barber Shop #07	http://license.reg.state.ma.us/pubLic/licque.asp?color=red&Board=BR
Boxer #50	www.state.ma.us/mbc/ranking.htm
Building Producer #03	www.state.ma.us/bbrs/mfg98.pdf
Chiropractor #07	http://license.reg.state.ma.us/pubLic/licque.asp?color=red&Board=CH
Concrete Technician #03	www.state.ma.us/bbrs/concretetestlabs.PDF
Concrete-Testing Laboratory #03	www.state.ma.us/bbrs/concretetestlabs.PDF
Construction Supervisor #18	www.state.ma.us/bbrs/cslsearch.htm
Cosmetologist (Hairdresser/Manicurist/etc.) #07	http://license.reg.state.ma.us/pubLic/licque.asp?color=red&Board=HD
Dental Hygienist #07	http://license.reg.state.ma.us/pubLic/licque.asp?color=red&Board=DN
Dentist #07	http://license.reg.state.ma.us/pubLic/licque.asp?color=red&Board=DN
Dispensing Optician #07	http://license.reg.state.ma.us/pubLic/licque.asp?color=red&Board=DO
Drinking Water Supply Facilities Operators #07	http://license.reg.state.ma.us/pubLic/licque.asp?color=red&Board=DW
Educational Psychologist #07	http://license.reg.state.ma.us/pubLic/licque.asp?query=personal&color=red&board=MH
Electrician #07	http://license.reg.state.ma.us/pubLic/licque.asp?color=red&Board=EL
Electrologist #07	http://license.reg.state.ma.us/pubLic/licque.asp?color=red&Board=ET
Embalmer & Funeral Director #40	http://license.reg.state.ma.us/pubLic/licque.asp?color=red&Board=EM
Engineer #07	http://license.reg.state.ma.us/pubLic/licque.asp?color=red&Board=EN
Fire Protection Sprinkler System Contractor/Fitter #27	www.state.ma.us/dps/Lic_srch.htm
Firemen / Engineer #27	www.state.ma.us/dps/Lic_srch.htm
Gas Fitter #07	http://license.reg.state.ma.us/pubLic/licque.asp?color=red&Board=PL
Health Officer (Certified) #12	http://license.reg.state.ma.us/pubLic/licque.asp?color=red&Board=HO
HMO #38	www.state.ma.us/doi/Consumer/css_health_HMO.html
Hoisting Machinery Operator #27	www.state.ma.us/dps/Lic_srch.htm
Home Improvement Contractor #18	www.state.ma.us/bbrs/Hicsearch.htm
Inspector of Bldgs/Local Inspector #03	www.state.ma.us/bbrs/bocert.PDF
Inspector of Boilers & Amusement Devices #27	www.state.ma.us/dps/Lic_srch.htm
Insurance, Domestic & Foreign Company #38	www.state.ma.us/doi/companies/companies_home.html
Land Surveyor #07	http://license.reg.state.ma.us/pubLic/licque.asp?color=red&Board=EN
Landscape Architect #07	http://license.reg.state.ma.us/pubLic/licque.asp?color=red&Board=LA
Lobbyist #21	www.state.ma.us/scripts/sec/pre/search.asp
Marriage & Family Therapist #07	http://license.reg.state.ma.us/pubLic/licque.asp?query=personal&color=red&board=MH
Medical Doctor #53	www.docboard.org/ma/df/masearch.htm
Mental Health Counselor #07	http://license.reg.state.ma.us/pubLic/licque.asp?query=personal&color=red&board=MH
Native Lumber Producer #03	www.state.ma.us/bbrs/lumber99.PDF
Nuclear Power Plant Engineer/Operator #27	www.state.ma.us/dps/Lic_srch.htm
Nurse (LPN, RN, Midwife) #07	http://license.reg.state.ma.us/pubLic/licque.asp?color=red&Board=RN
Nursing Home Administrator #12	http://license.reg.state.ma.us/pubLic/licque.asp?color=red&Board=NH
Occupational Therapist #07	http://license.reg.state.ma.us/pubLic/licque.asp?color=red&Board=AH
Occupational Therapist Assistant #07	http://license.reg.state.ma.us/pubLic/licque.asp?color=red&Board=AH
Oil Burner Technician/Contractor #27	www.state.ma.us/dps/Lic_srch.htm
Optometrist #07	http://license.reg.state.ma.us/pubLic/licque.asp?color=red&Board=OP
Pharmacist #07	http://license.reg.state.ma.us/pubLic/licque.asp?color=red&Board=PH
Physical Therapist #07	http://license.reg.state.ma.us/pubLic/licque.asp?color=red&Board=AH
Physical Therapist Assistant #07	http://license.reg.state.ma.us/pubLic/licque.asp?color=red&Board=AH
Physician Assistant #13	http://license.reg.state.ma.us/pubLic/licque.asp?color=red&Board=AP
Pipefitter #27	www.state.ma.us/dps/Lic_srch.htm
Plumber #07	http://license.reg.state.ma.us/pubLic/licque.asp?color=red&Board=PL
Podiatrist #07	http://license.reg.state.ma.us/pubLic/licque.asp?color=red&Board=PD
Psychologist/Provider #13	http://license.reg.state.ma.us/pubLic/licque.asp?color=red&Board=PY
Public Accountant-CPA #07	http://license.reg.state.ma.us/pubLic/licque.asp?color=red&Board=PA
Radio/TV Repair Technician #07	http://license.reg.state.ma.us/pubLic/licque.asp?color=red&Board=TV
Real Estate Appraiser #07	http://license.reg.state.ma.us/pubLic/licque.asp?color=red&Board=RA

Real Estate Broker & Salesperson #07 ....http://license.reg.state.ma.us/pubLic/licque.asp?color=red&Board=RE
Refrigeration Technician/Contractor #27 ....www.state.ma.us/dps/Lic_srch.htm
Rehabilitation Therapist #07 ....http://license.reg.state.ma.us/pubLic/licque.asp?query=personal&color=red&board=MH
Respiratory Care Therapist #07 ....http://license.reg.state.ma.us/pubLic/licque.asp?color=red&Board=RC
Sanitarian #07 ....http://license.reg.state.ma.us/pubLic/licque.asp?color=red&Board=SA
Social Worker #07 ....http://license.reg.state.ma.us/pubLic/licque.asp?color=red&Board=SW
Speech-Language Pathologist/Audiologist #07 ....http://license.reg.state.ma.us/pubLic/licque.asp?color=red&Board=SP
Veterinarian #07 ....http://license.reg.state.ma.us/pubLic/licque.asp?color=red&Board=VT

Licensing Quick Finder

Acupuncturist #05 617-727-3086
Administrator #17 ....781-388-3300 x665
Aesthetician #07 617-727-9940
Agent, Entertainment #27 617-727-3296
Aircraft #46 617-973-8881
Airport #46 617-973-8881
Airport Manager #46 617-973-8881
Alarm (Burglar & Fire) Installer #07 617-727-9931
Alcoholic Beverage Manufacturer #15
............617-727-3040
Alcoholic Beverage Solicitor #15 617-727-3040
Alcoholic Beverage Wholesaler #15 617-727-3040
Allied Health Professions #07 617-727-3071
Allied Mental Health & Human Services Profession #07
............617-727-3071
Ambulance Service #14 617-753-8300
Ambulatory Surgical Center #45 617-753-8000
Amusement Device Inspector #27
............617-727-3200 x607
Appraiser of Motor Vehicle Damage #47
............617-521-7453
Architect #42 617-727-3072
Architect #07 617-727-3072
Asbestos & Lead Abatement #24 617-727-7047
Athletic Trainer #07 617-727-3071
Attorney #02 617-728-8800
Auctioneer #43 617-727-3480
Auctioneer School #43 617-727-3480
Auto Sales Finance Company #48
............617-956-1500 X501
Bank/Savings #35 617-727-3141
Barber #07 617-727-7367
Barber Shop #07 617-727-7367
Birthing Center #45 617-753-8000
Blood Bank #45 617-753-8000
Boiler Engineer #27 617-727-3200
Boxer #50 ....617-727-3200 x657
Boxing Judge #50 ....617-727-3200 x657
Boxing Manager #50 ....617-727-3200 x657
Boxing Matchmaker #50 ....617-727-3200 x657
Boxing Physician #50 ....617-727-3200 x657
Boxing Promoter #50 ....617-727-3200 x657
Boxing Referee #50 ....617-727-3200 x657
Boxing Second #50 ....617-727-3200 x657
Boxing Timekeeper #50 ....617-727-3200 x657
Brokerage Firm #49 617-727-3548
Building Producer #03 617-727-3200
Bus Driver-Motor Coach #31 617-305-3559
Car Dealer #48 ....617-956-1500 X501
Cattle Dealer & Transporter #19
............617-727-3018 x158
Chair Lift #27 ....617-727-3200 x662
Chiropractor #07 617-727-3093
Clinic #45 617-753-8000
Collection Agency #35 617-727-3141
Commercial Finfishing #34 617-626-1520
Commercial Shellfishing #34 617-626-1520
Comprehensive Out-Patient Rehabilitation Facility #45
............617-753-8000
Concrete Technician #03 ....617-727-3200 x642
Concrete-Testing Laboratory #03
............617-727-3200 x614
Construction Supervisor #18 ....617-727-3200 x607

Construction/Maintenance of Elevator #27
............617-727-3200 x25238
Consumer Credit Grantor #35 617-727-3141
Cooperative Bank #35 617-727-3141
Cosmetologist (Hairdresser/Manicurist/Aesthetician) #07
............617-727-9940
Credit Union #35 617-727-3141
Day Care Center Director #52 617-626-2010
Day Care Teacher #52 617-626-2010
Dental Examiner #41 617-727-9928
Dental Hygienist #07 617-727-9928
Dentist #07 617-727-9928
Dispensing Optician #07 617-727-3093
Drinking Water Supply Facilities Operators #07
............617-727-3074
Drug/Alcoholism Facility #01 617-727-3040
Drug/Alcoholism Program #01 617-727-3040
Educational Psychologist #07 617-727-3071
Electrician #07 617-727-9931
Electrologist #07 617-727-9957
Elevator Operator #27 ....617-727-3200 x25238
Embalmer & Funeral Director #40 617-727-1718
Emergency Medical Technician #14 617-753-8300
Employment Agency #23 617-727-3696
End Stage Renal Dialysis #45 617-753-8000
Engineer #07 617-727-9957
Equine Dealer #19 ....617-727-3018 x168
Exterminator #19 ....617-727-3020 x104
Family Child Care Assistant #52 617-626-2010
Family Child Care Provider #52 617-626-2010
Fire Protection Sprinkler System Contractor/Fitter #27
............617-727-3200 x607
Firemen / Engineer #27 ....617-727-3200 x607
Funeral Director #07 617-727-1718
Fur Buyer #34 617-727-3151
Gas Fitter #07 617-727-9952
Gas Station Owner #43 617-727-3480
Guard or Hearing Dog Business #19
............617-727-3018 x157
Hairdresser #07 617-727-9940
Hawker/Peddler #43 617-727-3480
Health Officer (Certified) #12 617-727-9925
Heliport #46 617-973-8881
Hoisting Machinery Operator #27
............617-727-3200 x607
Home Improvement Contractor #18
............617-727-3200 x605
Horse/Greyhound #16 617-568-3336
Hospice & Hospital #45 617-753-8000
Inspector of Bldgs/Local Inspector #03..617-727-3200
Inspector of Boilers/Pressure Vessels &
 Amusement Devices #27 ....617-727-3200 x607
Insurance Advisor/Adjuster #38 617-727-7189
Insurance Agent #38 617-727-7189
Insurance Broker #38 617-727-7189
Insurance, Domestic & Foreign Company #38
............617-321-7391
Jockey #16 617-568-3336
Justice of the Peace #44 ....617-727-2795 X3
Laboratory #45 617-753-8000
Land Surveyor #07 617-727-9957
Landscape Architect #07 617-727-3072
Lead Inspector #25 617-753-8400

Library Media Specialist #17 781-388-3300
Lobbyist #21 617-878-3434
Lobstering #34 617-626-1520
Mammography Radiologic Technologist #26
............617-727-6214
Manicurist #07 617-727-9940
Marriage & Family Therapist #07 617-727-3071
Medical Doctor #53 617-727-3086
Mental Health Counselor #07 617-727-3071
Milk Plant #19 ....617-727-3018 x174
Modeling Agency #23 617-727-3696
Modeling Industry #22 617-727-3696
Mortgage Broker & Lender #48 ....617-956-1500 X501
Motion Picture Operator #27 ....617-727-3200 x25223
Motor Vehicle Repair Shop
 (Auto Body, Auto Glass, etc) #43..617-727-3480
Nanny Agency #22 617-727-3696
Native Lumber Producer #03 ....617-727-3636 x561
Notary Public #44 ....617-727-2795 X1
Nuclear Medicine Technologist (Radiologic
 Technologist-
 Nuclear Medicine) #26 617-727-6214
Nuclear Power Plant Engineer/Operator #27
............617-727-3200 x607
Nurse (LPN. RN & Midwife) #07 617-727-9961
Nursery #19 617-626-1801
Nursery Agent #19 617-626-1801
Nurses' Aide in Long-term Care Facility #37
............617-753-8140
Nursing Home & Rest Home #45 617-753-8000
Nursing Home Administrator #12 617-727-9925
Occupational Therapist #07 617-727-3071
Occupational Therapist Assistant #07
............617-727-3071
Oil Burner Technician/Contractor #27
............617-727-3200 x607
Optometrist #07 617-727-3093
Pasteurization Plant #19 ....617-727-3018 x174
Personal Agent #27 ....617-727-3200 x637
Pesticide Applicator or Dealer #19 617-626-1777
Pet Shop #19 ....617-727-3018 x158
Pharmacist #07 617-727-9953
Physical Therapist #07 617-727-3071
Physical Therapist Assistant #07 617-727-3071
Physician Assistant #13 617-727-3069
Pipefitter #27 ....617-727-3200 x607
Placement/Temporary Employment Agency #22
............617-727-3696
Plumber #07 617-727-9952
Podiatrist #07 617-727-1747
Private Detective #33 617-727-6128
Private Investigator #33 617-727-6128
Psychologist/Provider #13 617-727-9925
Public Accountant-CPA #07 617-727-1806
Radio/TV Repair Technician #07 617-727-3074
Radiographer #26 617-727-6214
Radiologic Technologist/Radiographer #26
............617-727-6214
Radiologic Technologist-Radiation Therapy #26
............617-727-6214
Railroad, Airlines & Steamship Transportation &
 Warehouse #01 617-727-3040
Real Estate Appraiser #07 617-727-3055

Real Estate Broker & Salesperson #07 617-727-2373
Refrigeration Technician/Contractor #27 .... 617-727-3200 x607
Rehabilitation Therapist #07 617-727-3071
Respiratory Care Therapist #07 617-727-1747
Riding Instructor #19 .... 617-727-3018 x161
Riding School #19 .... 617-727-3018 x161
Sales Finance Company #48 .... 617-956-1500 X501
Sanitarian #07 617-727-3072
School Bus #31 617-305-3559
School Guidance Counselor #17 . 781-388-3300 x665
Seafood Dealers #34 617-626-1520
Securities Agent #49 617-727-3548
Securities Broker/Dealer #49 617-727-3548

Security Guard Agency #33 617-727-6128
Simulcast & Inter-Track Wagering #16 .. 617-727-2581
Ski Tow #27 .... 617-727-3200 x662
Skimobile #27 .... 617-727-3200 x662
Small Loan Company #48 .... 617-956-1500 X501
Social Worker #07 617-727-3073
Speech-Language Pathologist/Audiologist #07 617-727-1747
Stable (Horse & Buggy Operator) #19 .... 617-727-3018 x161
Stock Broker #49 617-727-3548
Swine Dealer #19 .... 617-727-3018 x158
Taxidermist #34 617-727-3151
Teacher #17 .... 781-388-3300 x665
Theatrical Booking Agent #27 ...... 617-727-3200 x637

Ticket Broker #27 617-727-3296
Ticket Reseller #27 .... 617-727-3200 x637
Track #16 617-727-2581
Trainer #16 617-568-3336
Tramway Inspector #27 .... 617-727-3200 x662
Transient Vendor #43 617-727-3480
Trapping #34 617-626-1590
Trust Company #35 617-727-3141
Two & Multi-Car Aerial Passenger Cable Car #27 .... 617-727-3200 x662
Vending Machine #25 617-522-6712
Veterinarian #07 617-727-3080
Weights & Measures #43 617-727-3480
Wholesale or Retail Cigarette Seller #32 617-887-5090

Licensing Agency Information

01 Division of Substance Abuse Services, Alcoholic Beverages Control Commission, 239 Causeway St #200, Boston, MA 02114-2130; 617-727-3040, Fax: 617-727-1258.

02 Board of Overseers Registry Dept, Board of Bar Examiners, 75 Federal St, 5th Fl, Boston, MA 02110; 617-728-8800, Fax: 617-357-1872.

Direct URL to search licenses: www.state.ma.us/obcbbo/bboreg You can search online using name. Registry gives attorney name, office and residence address

03 Board of Building Regulations & Standards, Executive Office of Public Safety, 1 Ashburton Place, Rm 2133, Boston, MA 02108; 617-727-3200, Fax: 617-727-4764.
www.state.ma.us/eops/index.htm

Direct URL to search licenses: www.state.ma.us/bbrs/programs.htm You can search online using aslphabetical list

05 Board of Registration in Medicine, 100 Cambridge St, 3rd Fl, Boston, MA 02111; 617-727-3086, Fax: 617-426-9358.
www.docboard.org/ma/ma_home.htm

Direct URL to search licenses: www.docboard.org/ma/df/masearch.htm You can search online using name and town name.

07 Division of Registration, Boards of Registration & Examination, 239 Causeway St #400, Boston, MA 02114-2130; 617-727-3074, Fax: 617-727-2197.
www.state.ma.us/reg/home.htm

Direct URL to search licenses: http://license.reg.state.ma.us/pubLic/licque.asp You can search online using license number, name, city, state and ZIP Code.

12 Division of Registration, Boards of Registration of Nursing Home Admin., 239 Causeway St #400, Boston, MA 02114-2130; 617-727-9925, Fax: 617-727-2366.
www.state.ma.us/reg/home.htm

Direct URL to search licenses: http://license.reg.state.ma.us/pubLic/licque.asp You can search online using license number, name, city, state and ZIP Code.

13 Division of Registration, Boards of Registration of Physicians Assistants, 100 Cambridge St, 15th Fl, Boston, MA 02202; 617-727-3074, Fax: 617-727-2197.
www.state.ma.us/reg/boards.htm#P

Direct URL to search licenses: http://license.reg.state.ma.us/pubLic/licque.asp You can search online using name, city, ZIP Code, and license number.

14 Bureau of Health Care Systems - Public Health, Office of Emergency Medical Services, PO Box 83720 (150 Mount Vernon St #1), Dorchester, MA 02125-3135; 617-753-8300, Fax: 617-753-8350.

15 Consumer Department, Alcoholic Beverages Control Commission, 236 Causeway St #200, Boston, MA 02114-2130; 617-727-3040, Fax: 617-727-1258.

16 Consumer Department, Racing Commission, 1 Ashburton Place, 13th Fl, Rm 1313, Boston, MA 02108; 617-727-2581, Fax: 617-227-6062.

17 Division of Educational Personnel, Department of Education & Arts, 350 Main St, Malven, MA 02148; 781-388-3300 x665, Fax: 781-388-3475.
www.doe.mass.edu

18 Home Improvement Contractor/Construction Supervisor Licensing, Board of Build Regulations and Standards, 1 Ashburton Pl, Rm 1301, Boston, MA 02108; 617-727-7532.
www.state.ma.us/bbrs/programs.htm

Direct URL to search licenses: www.state.ma.us/bbrs/programs.htm You can search online using name, city/town, license #

19 Department of Food & Agriculture, Pesticide Bureau, 251 Causeway St, 5th Fl, Boston, MA 02114-2151; 617-626-1700, Fax: 617-626-1850.
www.massdfa.org/pesticide.htm

21 Secretary of the Commonwealth, Lobbyist & Lobbyist Employer Directory, One Ashburton Place, Room 1719, Boston, MA 02108; 617-878-3434, Fax: 617-727-5914.
www.state.ma.us/sec/pre/prelob/lobidx.htm

Direct URL to search licenses: www.state.ma.us/scripts/sec/pre/search.asp You can search online using agent last name, employer, and year.

22 Licensing Division, Department of Labor & Industries, 100 Cambridge St, 11th Fl, Boston, MA 02202; 617-727-3696, Fax: 617-727-7568.

24 Department of Occupational Safety, Licensing Division, Labor & Workforce Development, 399 Washington St, 5th Fl, Boston, MA 02100-5212; 617-727-7047, Fax: 617-727-7568.

25 Department of Public Health, 305 S St, Jamaica Plain, MA 02130; 617-522-3700, Fax: 617-753-8436.
www.state.ma.us/dph/dphhome.htm

26 Radiation Control Program, Department of Public Health, 305 South St, Jamaica Plain, MA 02130; 617-522-3700, Fax: 617-727-2098.
www.state.ma.us/dph/dphhome.htm

27 Department of Public Safety, 1 Ashburton Pl, 13th Fl, Rm 1301, Boston, MA 02108; 617-727-3200 x623, Fax: 617-248-0813.
www.state.ma.us/dps

31 Department of Telecommunications and Energy, Transportation Division, 1 South Sta #2, Boston, MA 02110-2208; 617-305-3559, Fax: 617-478-2598.

32 Department of Revenue, Excises Unit, PO Box 7012 (PO Box 7012), Boston, MA 02204; 617-887-5090, Fax: 617-887-5039.
www.state.ma.us/dor/dorpg.htm

33 Department of State Police, Certification Unit, 485 Maple St, Danvers, MA 01923; 617-538-6128.
www.state.ma.us/eops/index.htm

34 Department of Fisheries, Wildlife & Environment, 251 Causeway St #S-400, Boston, MA 02114-2104; 617-727-1614, Fax: 617-727-7988.
www.state.ma.us/dfwele/dpt_toc.htm

35 Division of Banks & Loan Agencies, 1 South Station, 3rd FL, Boston, MA 02110; 617-727-3141, Fax: 617-727-0607.
www.state.ma.us/dob

37 Division of Health Care Quality, Department of Public Health, 10 W St, #5th Fl., Boston, MA 02111; 617-753-8000, Fax: 617-753-8095.
www.state.ma.us/dph

38 Division of Insurance, 470 Atlantic Ave, Boston, MA 02110-2223; 617-521-7794, Fax: 617-521-7772.
www.state.ma.us/doi

Direct URL to search licenses: www.state.ma.us/doi/doi_site_alt.html You can search online using site map to locate directory lists

40 Division of Registration, Board of Funeral Directors & Embalmers, 239 Causeway St #400, Boston, MA 02114-2130; 617-727-3074, Fax: 617-727-2197.
www.state.ma.us/reg/home.htm

Direct URL to search licenses: http://license.reg.state.ma.us/pubLic/licque.asp?color=red&Board=EM You can search online using name, city, ZIP Code, and license number.

42 Division of Regulation of Architecture, 100 Cambridge St, #1406, Boston, MA 02202; 617-727-3072, Fax: 617-727-2197.
www.magnet.state.ma.us/reg/boards/ar/default.htm

Direct URL to search licenses: http://license.reg.state.ma.us/pubLic/licque.asp?color=red&Board=AR You can search online using name, state, ZIP Code, and license number.

43 Executive Office of Public Safety, Division of Standards, 1 Ashburton Pl, Boston, MA 02108; 617-727-3480, Fax: 617-727-5705. www.magnet.state.ma.us/standards

Direct URL to search licenses: www.magnet.state.ma.us/standards/license.htm You can search online using alphabetical lists

44 Governor's Council, State House, Rm 184, Boston, MA 02133; 617-727-2795.

www.state.ma.us/gov/govco.htm

45 Department of Public Health, Health Care Quality, 100 Cambridge St, Boston, MA 02111; 617-753-8000, Fax: 617-753-8095.

www.state.ma.us/dph/hcqskel.htm

46 Massachusetts Aeronautics Commission, 10 Park Plaza Rm 6620, Boston, MA 02116-3966; 617-973-8881, Fax: 617-973-8889.

47 Division of Insurance, Motor Vehicle Damage Appraisers Licensing Board, 1 South Station, 5th Fl, Boston, MA 02110; 617-521-7446, Fax: 617-521-7772.

www.state.ma.us/doi

48 Division of Banks, 1 South Station, 3rd Fl, Boston, MA 02110; 617-956-1500 X501, Fax: 617-956-1599.

www.state.ma.us/dob

49 Securities Division, Office of the Secretary of State, PO Box 30017 (McCormack Bldg, 17th Fl), Boston, MA 02108; 617-727-3548, Fax: 617-248-0177.

www.state.ma.us/sec/sct/sctidx.htm

50 Boxing Commission, 1 Ashburton Pl Rm 1301, Boston, MA 02108; 617-727-3200 x657, Fax: 617-727-5732.

www.state.ma.us/dps/Boxing.htm

Direct URL to search licenses: www.state.ma.us/mbc/ranking.htm You can search online using boxer ranking lists

52 Executive Office of Human Svcs, Office for Children, Staff Qualifications, 1 Ashburton Pl Rm 1105, Boston, MA 02108-1518; 617-626-2010.

53 Board of Registration in Medicine, 10 West St, Boston, MA 02111; 617-727-3086.

www.massmedboard.org.

The following list indicates the district and division name for each county in the state. If the district or division name of the bankruptcy court is different from the civil/criminal court, it appears in parentheses.

County/Court Cross. Reference

Barnstable .... Boston	Hampshire .... Springfield (Worcester)
Berkshire .... Springfield (Worcester)	Middlesex .... Boston
Bristol .... Boston	Nantucket .... Boston
Dukes... Boston	Norfolk.. Boston
Essex .... Boston	Plymouth.. Boston
Franklin .... Springfield (Worcester)	Suffolk... Boston
Hampden................................... Springfield (Worcester)	Worcester .... Worcester

US District Court

District of Massachusetts

Boston Division US Courthouse, 1 Courthouse Way, Boston, MA 02210, 617-748-9152, Fax: 617-748-9096.

www.mad.uscourts.gov

Counties: Barnstable, Bristol, Dukes, Essex, Middlesex, Nantucket, Norfolk, Plymouth, Suffolk.

Indexing & Storage: Cases are indexed by defendant and plaintiff as well as by case number. New cases are available in the index 1 day to 1 week after filing date. A computer index is maintained. The civil and criminal database dates from the early 1900's until the present. Records are available when they are not in the possession of the judge or his/her clerks. Open records are located at this court.

Fee & Payment: The fee is $15.00 per item (one party name or case number). Payment may be made by money order, cashier check, personal check. Prepayment is required. Payee: Clerk, US District Court. Certification fee: $5.00 per document. Copy fee: $.50 per page. You are allowed to make your own copies. These copies cost $.25 per page.

Phone Search: Searching is not available by phone.

Mail Search: A stamped self addressed envelope is not required.

In Person Search: In person searching is available.

PACER: Sign-up number is 800-676-6856. Access fee is $.60 per minute. Toll-free access: 888-399-4639. Local access: 617-223-4294. Case records are available back to January 1990. Records are purged every 12 months. New records are available online after 1 day. PACER is available online at http://pacer.mad.uscourts.gov.

Springfield Division 1550 Main St, Springfield, MA 01103, 413-785-0214, Fax: 413-785-0204.

www.mad.uscourts.gov

Counties: Berkshire, Franklin, Hampden, Hampshire.

Indexing & Storage: Cases are indexed by defendant and plaintiff as well as by case number. New cases are available in the index immediately after filing date. There is a microfiche index for pre-1989 cases. A computer index is maintained.

The civil and criminal database dates from July 1979. Open records are located at this court. Records are not available when they are in the possession of a judge or a judge's clerk.

Fee & Payment: The fee is $15.00 per item (one party name or case number). Payment may be made by money order, cashier check, personal check. Will bill if total fee is less than $25.00. Payee: Clerk, US District Court. Certification fee: $5.00 per document. Copy fee: $.50 per page.

Phone Search: Docket information available over the phone if Clerk has time. An automated voice case information service (VCIS) is not available.

Fax Search: Will charge for fax search request only if copies and certification requested. Will fax results at $.50 per page.

Mail Search: A stamped self addressed envelope is not required.

In Person Search: In person searching is available.

PACER: Sign-up number is 800-676-6856. Access fee is $.60 per minute. Toll-free access: 888-399-4639. Local access: 617-223-4294. Case records are available back to January 1990. Records are purged every 12 months. New records are available online after 1 day. PACER is available online at http://pacer.mad.uscourts.gov.

Worcester Division 595 Main St., Room 502, Worcester, MA 01608, 508-793-0552.

www.mad.uscourts.gov

Counties: Worcester.

Indexing & Storage: Cases are indexed by defendant and plaintiff as well as by case number. New cases are available in the index immediately after filing date. Indexes are on computer from 1988 and on microfiche from 1981. Earlier indexes are in storage from the early 1900's. Open records are located at this court. Records are not available when in the possession of a judge or the judge's clerks.

Fee & Payment: The fee is $15.00 per item (one party name or case number). Payment may be made by money order, cashier check, personal check. Payee: Clerk, US District Court. Certification fee: $5.00 per document. Copy fee: $.50 per page.

Phone Search: Only docket information available by telephone. An automated voice case information service (VCIS) is not available.

Fax Search: Invoice will be sent with copies of records for a fax request.

Mail Search: Always enclose a stamped self addressed envelope.

In Person Search: In person searching is available.

PACER: Sign-up number is 800-676-6856. Access fee is $.60 per minute. Toll-free access: 888-399-4639. Local access: 617-223-4294. Case records are available back to January 1990. Records are purged every 12 months. New records are available online after 1 day. PACER is available online at http://pacer.mad.uscourts.gov.

US Bankruptcy Court

District of Massachusetts

Boston Division Room 1101, 10 Causeway, Boston, MA 02222-1074, 617-565-6051, Fax: 617-565-6087.

www.mab.uscourts.gov

Counties: Barnstable, Bristol, Dukes, Essex (except towns assigned to Worcester Division), Nantucket, Norfolk (except towns assigned to Worcester Division), Plymouth, Suffolk, and the following towns in Middlesex: Arlington, Belmont, Burlington, Everett,Lexington, Malden, Medford, Melrose, Newton, North Reading, Reading, Stoneham, Wakefield, Waltham, Watertown, Wilmington, Winchester and Woburn.

Indexing & Storage: Cases are indexed by debtor as well as by case number. New cases are available in the index immediately after filing date. A computer index is maintained. Open records are located at this court.

Fee & Payment: The fee is $15.00 per item (one party name or case number). Payment may be made by money order, cashier check, personal check. Copy fees will be billed after the search is completed. Checks are not accepted from debtors. Payee: US Bankruptcy Court. Certification fee: $5.00 per document. Copy fee: $.50 per page. You are allowed to make your own copies. These copies cost $.50 per page.

Phone Search: Only general information will be released over the phone. An automated voice case information service (VCIS) is available. Call VCIS at 888-201-3572 or 617-565-6025.

Fax Search: Fax requests are processed the same as mail requests.

Mail Search: Always enclose a stamped self addressed envelope.

In Person Search: In person searching is available.

PACER: Sign-up number is 800-676-6856. Access fee is $.60 per minute. Toll-free access: 888-201-3571. Local access: 617-565-7593, 617-

565-7594, 617-565-6021, 617-565-6022, 617-565-6023. Case records are available back to April 1, 1987. Records are purged every 12 months. New civil records are available online after 1 day. PACER is available on the Internet at http://pacer.mab.uscourts.gov.

Worcester Division
595 Main St, Room 211, Worcester, MA 01608, 508-770-8900, Fax: 508-793-0541.

www.mab.uscourts.gov

Counties: Berkshire, Franklin, Hampden, Hampshire, Middlesex (except the towns assigned to the Boston Division), Worcester and the following towns: in Essex-Andover, Haverhill, Lawrence, Methuen and North Andover; in

Norfolk-Bellingham, Franklin, Medway,Millis and Norfolk.

Indexing & Storage: Cases are indexed by debtor as well as by case number. New cases are available in the index immediately after filing date. A computer index is maintained. Open records are located at this court.

Fee & Payment: The fee is $15.00 per item (one party name or case number). Payment may be made by money order, cashier check, personal check. Prepayment is required. Checks are not accepted from debtors. Payee: US Bankruptcy Court. Certification fee: $5.00 per document. Copy fee: $.50 per page. You are allowed to make your own copies. These copies cost $.25 per page.

Phone Search: Only docket information is available by phone. An automated voice case

information service (VCIS) is available. Call VCIS at 888-201-3572 or 617-565-6025.

Mail Search: A stamped self addressed envelope is not required.

In Person Search: In person searching is available.

PACER: Sign-up number is 800-676-6856. Access fee is $.60 per minute. Toll-free access: 888-201-3571. Local access: 617-565-7593, 617-565-7594, 617-565-6021, 617-565-6022, 617-565-6023. Case records are available back to April 1, 1987. Records are purged every 12 months. New civil records are available online after 1 day. PACER is available on the Internet at http://pacer.mab.uscourts.gov.

Court	Jurisdiction	No. of Courts	How Organized
Superior Courts*	General	19	14 Counties
District Courts*	General	68	68 Geographic Divisions
Boston Municipal Court*	General	1	
Housing Courts	General	7	
Probate and Family Courts*	Probate	15	14 Counties
Juvenile Courts	Special	7	
Land Court	Special	1	

* Profiled in this Sourcebook.

	CIVIL								
Court	Tort	Contract	Real Estate	Min. Claim	Max. Claim	Small Claims	Estate	Eviction	Domestic Relations
Superior Courts*	X	X	X	$25,000	No Max				
District Courts*	X	X	X	$0	No Max	$2000	X	X	X
Boston Municipal Court*	X	X	X	$0	No Max	$2000			X
Housing Courts			X	$0	No Max	$2000			
Probate and Family Courts*							X		X
Juvenile Courts									
Land Court			X						

	CRIMINAL				
Court	Felony	Misdemeanor	DWI/DUI	Preliminary Hearing	Juvenile
Superior Courts*	X				
District Courts*	X	X	X	X	X
Boston Municipal Court*		X	X		
Housing Courts		X		X	
Probate and Family Courts*					
Juvenile Courts					X
Land Court					

ADMINISTRATION   Chief Justice for Administration and Management, 2 Center Plaza, Room 540, Boston, MA, 02108; 617-742-8575, Fax: 617-742-0968. www.state.ma.us/courts/courts.htm

COURT STRUCTURE   The various court sections are called "Departments." The small claims limit changed in 1993 to $2000 from $1500.

While Superior and District Courts have concurrent jurisdiction in civil cases, the practice is to assign cases less than $25,000 to the District Court and those over $25,000 to Superior Court.

In addition to misdemeanors, the District Courts and Boston Municipal Courts have jurisdiction over certain minor felonies.

There are more than 20 Probate and Family Court locations in MA - one per county plus 2 in Bristol, a Middlesex satellite in Cambridge and Lawrence.

ONLINE ACCESS   There is no online access computer system, internal or external.

Barnstable County

Superior Court 3195 Main St, PO Box 425, Barnstable, MA 02630; 508-362-2511. Hours: 8AM-4:30PM (EST). *Felony, Civil Actions Over $25,000.*

Civil Records: Access: Mail, in person. Both court and visitors may perform in person searches. No search fee. Required to search: name, years to search; also helpful-address. Civil cases indexed by defendant, plaintiff. Civil records on index cards from 1985 and books from 1830s. **Criminal Records:** Access: Mail, in person. Both court and visitors may perform in person searches. No search fee. Required to search: name, years to search, DOB; also helpful-address, SSN. Criminal records on index cards from 1985 and books from 1830s. **General Information:** No victims names released. SASE not required. Copy fee: $.50 per page. Certification fee: $1.50. Fee payee: Barnstable Superior Court. Business checks accepted. Prepayment is required.

Barnstable Division District Court Route 6A, PO Box 427, Barnstable, MA 02630; 508-362-2511 X445. Hours: 8:30AM-4:30PM (EST). *Felony, Misdemeanor, Civil, Eviction, Small Claims.*

Civil Records: Access: Phone, mail, in person. Only the court conducts in person searches; visitors may not. No search fee. Required to search: name, years to search. Civil cases indexed by defendant, plaintiff. Civil records on index cards and docket books. **Criminal Records:** Access: Phone, mail, in person. Only the court conducts in person searches; visitors may not. No search fee. Required to search: name, years to search; also helpful-DOB. Criminal records on computer since 1996; prior records on index cards and docket books. **General Information:** No impounded records released. Turnaround time 1-2 weeks. Copy fee: $.50 per page. Certification fee: $1.50. Fee payee: District Court. Only cashiers checks and money orders accepted. Prepayment is required.

Orleans Division District Court 237 Rock Harbor Rd, Orleans, MA 02653; 508-255-4700. Hours: 8:30AM-4:30PM (EST). *Felony, Misdemeanor, Civil, Eviction, Small Claims.*

Note: Includes Brewster, Chatham, Dennis, Eastham, Orleans, Truro, Wellfleet, Harwich, and Provincetown

Civil Records: Access: In person only. Court does not conduct in person searches; visitors must perform searches for themselves. Search fee: No civil searches performed by court. Required to search: name, years to search. Civil cases indexed by defendant, plaintiff. Civil records kept in storage from 1978. Some prior records destroyed. **Criminal Records:** Access: In person only. Court does not conduct in person searches; visitors must perform searches for themselves. Search fee: No criminal searches performed by court. Required to search: name, years to search. Criminal records kept in storage from 1978. Some prior records destroyed. **General Information:** No impounded records released. Copy fee: $.50 per page. Certification fee: $1.50. Fee payee: Orleans District Court. Personal checks accepted. Prepayment is required.

Probate & Family Court PO Box 346, Barnstable, MA 02630; 508-362-2511 X265; Fax: 508-362-3662. Hours: 8:30AM-4:30PM (EST). *Probate.*

Berkshire County

Superior Court 76 East St, Pittsfield, MA 01201; 413-499-7487; Fax: 413-442-9190. Hours: 8:30AM-4:30PM (EST). *Felony, Civil Actions Over $25,000.*

Civil Records: Access: Mail, in person. Both court and visitors may perform in person searches. No search fee. Required to search: name, years to search. Civil cases indexed by defendant, plaintiff. Civil records on index cards from 1980s and books from 1700s. **Criminal Records:** Access: Mail, in person. Both court and visitors may perform in person searches. No search fee. Required to search: name, years to search, DOB, SSN. Criminal records on index cards from 1980s and books from 1700s. **General Information:** No impounded records released. Turnaround time 1 week. Copy fee: $.50 per page. Certification fee: $1.50. Fee payee: Clerk of Superior Court. Personal checks accepted. Prepayment is required.

North Berkshire Division District Court #28 City Hall, North Adams, MA 01247; 413-663-5339; Fax: 413-664-7209. Hours: 8:30AM-4:30PM (EST). *Felony, Misdemeanor, Civil, Eviction, Small Claims.*

Note: Handles cases for Clarksburg, Florida, Hancock, New Ashford, North Adams, and Williamstown

Civil Records: Access: Phone, mail, in person. Only the court conducts in person searches; visitors may not. No search fee. Required to search: name, years to search. Civil cases indexed by defendant, plaintiff. Civil records on index cards from 1983, docket books to 1900. **Criminal Records:** Access: Phone, mail, in person. Only the court conducts in person searches; visitors may not. No search fee. Required to search: name, years to search; also helpful-DOB. Criminal records on index cards from 1983, docket books to 1900. **General Information:** No impounded records released. Turnaround time 1-2 weeks. Copy fee: $.50 per page. Certification fee: $1.50. Fee payee: District Court. Business checks accepted. Prepayment is required.

North Berkshire Division District Court #30 65 Park St, Adams, MA 01220; 413-743-0021; Fax: 413-743-4848. Hours: 8AM-4:30PM (EST). *Felony, Misdemeanor, Civil, Eviction, Small Claims.*

Note: Handles cases for Adams, Cheshire, Savoy, and Windsor

Civil Records: Access: Mail, fax. Only the court conducts in person searches; visitors may not. No search fee. Required to search: name, years to search; also helpful-address. Civil cases indexed by defendant, plaintiff. Civil records on index cards from 1990, small claims from 1988. Prior stored. **Criminal Records:** Access: Mail, fax. Only the court conducts in person searches; visitors may not. No search fee. Required to search: name, years to search; also helpful-DOB, SSN. Criminal records on computer since 1976/77, listes on docket books until 1985. **General Information:** No juvenile, mental health, impounded case records released. SASE required. Turnaround time 7 days. Copy fee: $.50 per page. Certification fee: $1.50. Fee payee: District Court. No personal checks accepted. Prepayment is required.

Pittsfield Division District Court #27 24 Wendell Ave, Pittsfield, MA 01201; 413-442-5468; Fax: 413-499-7327. Hours: 8:30AM-4:30PM (EST). *Felony, Misdemeanor, Civil, Eviction, Small Claims.*

Civil Records: Access: Phone, mail, in person. Only the court conducts in person searches; visitors may not. No search fee. Required to search: name, years to search. Civil cases indexed by defendant, plaintiff. Civil records on docket books to 1900. Records purged every 6 years. **Criminal Records:** Access: Phone, mail, in person. Only the court conducts in person searches; visitors may not. No search fee. Required to search: name, years to search; also helpful-DOB. Criminal records on docket books to 1900. Records purged every 6 years. **General Information:** No juvenile or sealed records released. SASE required. Turnaround time 1-2 weeks. Copy fee: $.50 per page. Certification fee: $1.50. Fee payee: Pittsfield District Court. Personal checks accepted. Prepayment is required.

South Berkshire Division District Court 9 Gilmore Ave, Great Barrington, MA 01230; 413-528-3520; Fax: 413-528-0757. Hours: 8AM-4PM (EST). *Felony, Misdemeanor, Civil, Eviction, Small Claims.*

Civil Records: Access: Phone, mail, in person. Both court and visitors may perform in person searches. No search fee. Required to search: name, years to search. Civil cases indexed by defendant, plaintiff. Civil records on index cards from 1984, docket books to 1900. Court will only perform search if given the docket number. **Criminal Records:** Access: Phone, mail, in person. Only the court conducts in person searches; visitors may not. No search fee. Required to search: name, years to search. Criminal records on index cards from 1984, docket books to 1900. Court will only do search if given docket number. **General Information:** No juvenile, impounded records released. SASE required. Turnaround time 1-2 weeks. Copy fee: $.50 per page. Certification fee: $1.50. Fee payee: District Court. Personal checks accepted. Prepayment is required.

Probate & Family Court 44 Bank Row, Pittsfield, MA 01201; 413-442-6941; Fax: 413-443-3430. Hours: 8:30AM-4PM (EST). *Probate.*

Bristol County

Superior Court-Taunton 9 Court St, Taunton, MA 02780; 508-823-6588 X1. Hours: 8AM-4:30PM (EST). *Felony, Civil Actions Over $25,000.*

Civil Records: Access: Mail, in person. Both court and visitors may perform in person searches. No search fee. Required to search: name, years to search. Civil cases indexed by defendant, plaintiff. Civil records on computer link to Boston from 1985, index books from 1935. **Criminal Records:** Access: Mail, in person. Both court and visitors may perform in person searches. No search fee. Required to search: name, years to search; also helpful-DOB. Criminal records on computer link to Boston from 1985, index books from 1935. **General Information:** No impounded records released. Turnaround time 2 weeks. Copy fee: $.50 per page. Certification fee: $1.50. Fee payee: Clerk of Superior Court of Bristol County. Personal checks accepted. Prepayment is required. Public access terminal is available.

Attleboro Division District Court 34 Courthouse, 88 N Main St, Attleboro, MA 02703; 508-222-5900; Fax: 508-223-3916. Hours: 8AM-4:30PM (EST). *Felony, Misdemeanor, Civil, Eviction, Small Claims.*

Civil Records: Access: Phone, mail, in person. Only the court conducts in person searches; visitors may not. No search fee. Required to search: name, years to search. Civil cases indexed by defendant, plaintiff. Civil records on computer since 1995; prior records on index cards from 1983, docket books from 1900. **Criminal Records:** Access: Phone, mail, in person. Only the court conducts in person searches; visitors may not. No search fee. Required to search: name, years to search, DOB, SSN. Criminal records on computer since 1995; prior records on index cards from 1983, docket books from 1900. **General Information:** No impounded records released. Turnaround time 1-2 weeks. Copy fee: $.50 per page. Certification fee: $1.50. Fee payee: District Court, Attleboro District Court. Business checks accepted. Prepayment is required.

Fall River Division District Court 45 Rock St, Fall River, MA 02720; 508-679-8161; Fax: 508-675-5477. Hours: 8AM-4:30PM (EST). *Felony, Misdemeanor, Civil, Eviction, Small Claims.*

Civil Records: Access: In person only. Court does not conduct in person searches; visitors must perform searches for themselves. Search fee: No civil searches performed by court. Required to search: name, years to search. Civil cases indexed by defendant, plaintiff. Civil records on index on computer from 1989, on docket books in vault from 1985. **Criminal Records:** Access: Mail, in person. Only the court conducts in person searches; visitors may not. No search fee. Required to search: name, years to search. Criminal records on index on computer from 1989, on docket books in vault from 1985. **General Information:** No sealed, minor, confidential address records released. SASE requested. Turnaround time 1-2 weeks. Copy fee: $.50 per page. Certification fee: $1.50. Fee payee: District Court. Only cashiers checks and money orders accepted. Prepayment is required.

New Bedford Division District Court 33 75 N 6th St, New Bedford, MA 02740; 508-999-9700. Hours: 8:30AM-4PM (EST). *Felony, Misdemeanor, Civil, Eviction, Small Claims.*

Civil Records: Access: Mail, in person. Only the court conducts in person searches; visitors may not. No search fee. Required to search: name, years to search. Civil cases indexed by defendant, plaintiff. Civil records filed from 1989, prior on docket books. **Criminal Records:** Access: Mail, in person. Only the court conducts in person searches; visitors may not. No search fee. Required to search: name, years to search, DOB; also helpful-SSN. Criminal records filed from 1989, prior on docket books. Searches are limited to pending charges, this agency recommends searching elsewhere for closed case files. **General Information:** No impounded records released. Turnaround time 1-2 weeks. Copy fee: $.50 per page. Certification fee: $1.50. Fee payee: District Court. Business checks accepted. Prepayment is required.

Taunton Division District Court 15 Court St, Taunton, MA 02780; 508-824-4032; Fax: 508-824-2282. Hours: 8AM-4:30PM (EST). *Felony, Misdemeanor, Civil, Eviction, Small Claims.*

Civil Records: Access: Phone, mail, in person. Only the court conducts in person searches; visitors may not. No search fee. Required to search: name, years to search. Civil cases indexed by defendant, plaintiff. Civil records on index cards for 6 years. **Criminal Records:** Access: Phone, mail, in person. Only the court conducts in

person searches; visitors may not. No search fee. Required to search: name, years to search, DOB. Criminal records on index cards for 6 years. **General Information:** Turnaround time 1-2 days. Copy fee: $.50 per page. Certification fee: $1.50. Fee payee: District Court. Personal checks accepted. Prepayment is required.

New Bedford Probate & Family Court 505 Pleasant St, New Bedford, MA 02740; 508-999-5249; Fax: 508-991-7421. Hours: 8AM-4:30PM (EST). *Probate.*

Taunton Probate & Family Court 11 Court St, PO Box 567, Taunton, MA 02780; 508-824-4004; Fax: 508-822-9837. Hours: 8AM-4:30PM (EST). *Probate.*

Dukes County

Superior Court PO Box 1267, Edgartown, MA 02539; 508-627-4668; Fax: 508-627-7571. Hours: 8AM-4PM (EST). *Felony, Civil Actions Over $25,000.*

Civil Records: Access: Mail, in person. Both court and visitors may perform in person searches. No search fee. Required to search: name, years to search. Civil cases indexed by defendant, plaintiff. Civil records on index cards from 1976 and books from 1695. **Criminal Records:** Access: Mail, in person. Both court and visitors may perform in person searches. No search fee. Required to search: name, years to search. Criminal records on index cards from 1976 and books from 1695. **General Information:** No sealed records released. SASE required. Turnaround time 1-2 days. Copy fee: $.50 per page. Certification fee: $1.50. Fee payee: Clerk of Superior Court. Personal checks accepted. Prepayment is required.

Edgartown District Court Courthouse, 81 Main St, Edgartown, MA 02539-1284; 508-627-3751/4622. Hours: 8:30AM-4:30PM (EST). *Felony, Misdemeanor, Civil, Eviction, Small Claims.*

Civil Records: Access: In person only. Only the court conducts in person searches; visitors may not. No search fee. Required to search: name, years to search. Civil cases indexed by defendant, plaintiff. Civil records on index cards from 1983, docket books to 1900. **Criminal Records:** Access: In person only. Only the court conducts in person searches; visitors may not. No search fee. Required to search: name, years to search, DOB; also helpful-SSN. Criminal records on index cards from 1983, docket books to 1900. **General Information:** No sealed records released. Copy fee: $.50 per page. Certification fee: $1.50. Fee payee: District Court. Personal checks accepted. Prepayment is required.

Probate & Family Court PO Box 237, Edgartown, MA 02539; 508-627-4703; Fax: 508-627-7664. Hours: 8:30AM-4:30PM (EST). *Probate.*

Essex County

Superior Court-Lawrence 43 Appleton Way, Lawrence, MA 01840; 978-687-7463. Hours: 8AM-4:30PM (EST). *Civil Actions Over $25,000.*

Note: Index cards are found in the Salem office (records prior to 1985)

Civil Records: Access: Mail, in person. Both court and visitors may perform in person searches. No search fee. Required to search: name, years to search. Civil cases indexed by defendant, plaintiff. Civil Records on computer since 1985; prior records on index cards in Salem office. **General**

Information: No impounded records released. Turnaround time 1-2 days. Copy fee: $.50 per page. Certification fee: $1.50. Fee payee: Clerk of Superior Court. Personal checks accepted. Prepayment is required.

Superior Court - Newburyport 145 High St, Newburyport, MA 01950; 978-462-4474. Hours: 8AM-4:30PM (EST). *Felony, Civil Actions Over $25,000.*

Note: All finished criminal record files are in Salem and civil case records Session A in Salem, Session B in Newburyport and Session C & D inr Lawrence

Civil Records: Access: Mail, in person. Both court and visitors may perform in person searches. No search fee. Required to search: name, years to search. Civil cases indexed by defendant, plaintiff. **Criminal Records:** Access: Mail, in person. Both court and visitors may perform in person searches. No search fee. Required to search: name, years to search. **General Information:** No impounded records released. Turnaround time 1-2 days. Copy fee: $.50 per page. Certification fee: $1.50. Fee payee: Clerk of Superior Court. Personal checks accepted. Prepayment is required.

Superior Court-Salem 34 Federal St, Salem, MA 01970; Civil phone:978-744-5500 X223; Criminal phone:978-744-5500 X223; Fax: 978-741-0691 (civ); 978-825-9989 (crim). Hours: 8:00AM-4:30PM (EST). *Felony, Civil Actions Over $25,000.*

Civil Records: Access: Mail, in person. Only the court conducts in person searches; visitors may not. No search fee. Required to search: name, years to search. Civil cases indexed by defendant, plaintiff. Civil records are entered on computer for civil actions from all three Superior courts in this county. Records go back to 1985 on computer. **Criminal Records:** Access: In person only. Court does not conduct in person searches; visitors must perform searches for themselves. Search fee: No criminal searches performed by court. Required to search: name, years to search. Criminal records are entered on computer for civil actions from all three Superior courts in this county. Records go back to 1985 on computer. **General Information:** Impounded cases are not released. Turnaround time 1-2 days. Copy fee: $.50 per page. Certification fee: $1.50. Fee payee: Clerk of Superior Court. Only cashiers checks and money orders accepted. Prepayment is required.

Haverhill Division District Court PO Box 1389, Haverhill, MA 01831; 978-373-4151; Fax: 978-521-6886. Hours: 8:30AM-4:30PM (EST). *Felony, Misdemeanor, Civil, Eviction, Small Claims.*

Civil Records: Access: Phone, fax, mail, in person. Both court and visitors may perform in person searches. No search fee. Required to search: name, years to search. Civil cases indexed by defendant, plaintiff. Civil records on index cards from 1983. Non-active in storage. **Criminal Records:** Access: Phone, fax, mail, in person. Both court and visitors may perform in person searches. No search fee. Required to search: name, years to search; also helpful-DOB. Criminal records on index cards from 1983. Non-active in storage. **General Information:** No juvenile, sealed cases, confidential records released. SASE required. Turnaround time 1-2 weeks. Copy fee: $.50 per page. Certification fee: $1.50. Fee payee: District Court. Personal checks accepted. Prepayment is required.

Ipswich Division District Court 30 South Main St, PO Box 246, Ipswich, MA 01938; 978-356-2681; Fax: 978-356-4396. Hours: 8:30AM-4:30PM (EST). *Felony, Misdemeanor, Civil, Eviction, Small Claims.*

Civil Records: Access: In person only. Court does not conduct in person searches; visitors must perform searches for themselves. Search fee: No civil searches performed by court. Required to search: name, years to search. Civil cases indexed by defendant, plaintiff. Civil records on index cards, small claims from 1984, civil from 1964. Civil on docket books from 1970. **Criminal Records:** Access: In person only. Court does not conduct in person searches; visitors must perform searches for themselves. Search fee: No criminal searches performed by court. Required to search: name, years to search; also helpful-DOB. Criminal records on index cards from 1979. **General Information:** No juvenile records released. Copy fee: $.50 per page. Certification fee: Certification fee is $1.50 per page. Fee payee: District Court. Personal checks accepted. Prepayment is required.

Lawrence Division District Court 381 Common St, Lawrence, MA 01840; 978-687-7184; Civil phone:978-689-2810. Hours: 8AM-4:30PM (EST). *Felony, Misdemeanor, Civil, Eviction, Small Claims.*

Civil Records: Access: Mail, in person. Both court and visitors may perform in person searches. No search fee. Required to search: name, years to search. Civil cases indexed by defendant, plaintiff. Civil records on index cards from 1983, docket books from 1900, on computer since 1990. **Criminal Records:** Access: Mail, in person. Only the court conducts in person searches; visitors may not. No search fee. Required to search: name, years to search, DOB; also helpful-address, SSN. Criminal records on index cards from 1983, docket books from 1900, on computer since 1990. **General Information:** No medical, police reports, impounded, juvenile records released. SASE requested. Turnaround time 1-2 weeks. Copy fee: $.50 per page. Certification fee: $1.50. Fee payee: District Court. Personal checks accepted. Prepayment is required.

Lynn Division District Court 580 Essex St, Lynn, MA 01901; 781-598-5200. Hours: 8AM-4:30PM (EST). *Felony, Misdemeanor, Civil, Eviction, Small Claims.*

Civil Records: Access: Mail, in person. Both court and visitors may perform in person searches. No search fee. Required to search: name, years to search. Civil cases indexed by defendant, plaintiff. Civil records on index cards from 1983, docket books from approx 1900. Records older than 15 years are difficult to find and may take longer. **Criminal Records:** Access: Mail, in person. Only the court conducts in person searches; visitors may not. No search fee. Required to search: name, years to search; also helpful-DOB, SSN. Criminal records on index cards from 1983, docket books from approx 1900. Records older than 15 years are difficult to find and may take longer. **General Information:** No juvenile, impounded or sealed records released. Copy fee: $.50 per page. Certification fee: $1.50. Fee payee: District Court. Personal checks accepted. Prepayment is required.

Newburyport Division District Court 22 188 State St, Newburyport, MA 01950; 978-462-2652. Hours: 8:30AM-4:30PM (EST). *Felony, Misdemeanor, Civil, Eviction, Small Claims.*

Civil Records: Access: Phone, mail, in person. Both court and visitors may perform in person searches. No search fee. Required to search: name, years to search. Civil cases indexed by defendant, plaintiff. Civil records on index cards from 1983, prior archived in Worcester. **Criminal Records:** Access: Phone, mail, in person. Only the court conducts in person searches; visitors may not. No search fee. Required to search: name, years to search, DOB. Criminal records on index cards from 1983, prior archived in Worcester. **General Information:** No juvenile or impounded records released. Turnaround time 1-2 weeks. Copy fee: $.50 per page. Certification fee: $1.50. Fee payee: District Court. Personal checks accepted. Prepayment is required.

Peabody Division District Court 86 PO Box 666, Peabody, MA 01960; 978-532-3100. Hours: 8:30AM-4:30PM (EST). *Felony, Misdemeanor, Civil, Eviction, Small Claims.*

Civil Records: Access: Phone, mail, in person. Only the court conducts in person searches; visitors may not. No search fee. Required to search: name, years to search. Civil cases indexed by defendant, plaintiff. Civil records stored in office for 10 years, prior stored in basement and are difficult to find. **Criminal Records:** Access: Phone, mail, in person. Only the court conducts in person searches; visitors may not. No search fee. Required to search: name, years to search, DOB. Criminal records stored in office for 10 years, prior stored in basement and are difficult to find. **General Information:** No juvenile or impounded records released. Turnaround time 1-2 weeks. Copy fee: $.50 per page. Certification fee: $1.50. Fee payee: District Court. Personal checks accepted. Prepayment is required.

Salem Division District Court 36 65 Washington St, Salem, MA 01970; 978-744-1167. Hours: 8:30AM-4:30PM (EST). *Felony, Misdemeanor, Civil, Eviction, Small Claims.*

Civil Records: Access: Mail, in person. Only the court conducts in person searches; visitors may not. No search fee. Required to search: name, years to search. Civil cases indexed by defendant, plaintiff. Civil records on index cards and docket books. **Criminal Records:** Access: Mail, in person. Only the court conducts in person searches; visitors may not. No search fee. Required to search: name, years to search, DOB, SSN. Criminal records on index cards and docket books. **General Information:** No juvenile or impounded records released. Turnaround time 1-2 weeks. Copy fee: $.50 per page. Certification fee: $1.50. Fee payee: District Court. Personal checks accepted. Prepayment is required.

Probate & Family Court 36 Federal St, Salem, MA 01970; 978-744-1020; Fax: 978-741-2957. Hours: 8:00AM-4:30PM (EST). *Probate.*

Franklin County

Superior Court PO Box 1573, Greenfield, MA 01302; 413-774-5535; Fax: 413-774-4770. Hours: 8:30AM-4:30PM (EST). *Felony, Civil Actions Over $25,000.*

Civil Records: Access: Phone, mail, in person. Both court and visitors may perform in person searches. No search fee. Required to search: name, years to search. Civil cases indexed by defendant, plaintiff. Civil records in files. **Criminal Records:** Access: Phone, mail, in person. Only the court conducts in person searches; visitors may not. No search fee. Required to search: name, years to search. Criminal records in files. **General Information:** No impounded or juvenile records

released. SASE required. Turnaround time 1 week. Copy fee: $.50 per page. Certification fee: $1.50. Fee payee: Franklin County Superior Court. Personal checks accepted. Prepayment is required. Fax notes: Fee to fax results is $1.50 per page.

Greenfield District Court 425 Main St, Greenfield, MA 01301; 413-774-5533; Fax: 413-774-5328. Hours: 8:30AM-4:30PM (EST). *Felony, Misdemeanor, Civil, Eviction, Small Claims.*

Civil Records: Access: In person. Both court and visitors may perform in person searches. No search fee. Required to search: name, years to search. Civil cases indexed by defendant, plaintiff. Civil records on docket books or index cards. **Criminal Records:** Access: In person. Both court and visitors may perform in person searches. No search fee. Required to search: name, years to search, DOB. Criminal records on docket books or index cards. **General Information:** No juvenile records released. Copy fee: $.50 per page. Certification fee: $1.50. Fee payee: Greenfield District Court. Personal checks accepted. Prepayment is required.

Orange Division District Court #42 One Court Square, Orange, MA 01364; 978-544-8277; Fax: 978-544-5204. Hours: 8:30AM-4:30PM (EST). *Felony, Misdemeanor, Civil, Eviction, Small Claims.*

Civil Records: Access: Phone, mail, in person. Both court and visitors may perform in person searches. No search fee. Required to search: name, years to search. Civil cases indexed by defendant, plaintiff. Civil records on docket books from 1975. **Criminal Records:** Access: Phone, mail, in person. Only the court conducts in person searches; visitors may not. No search fee. Required to search: name, years to search. Criminal records on docket books from 1975. **General Information:** No juvenile records released. Turnaround time 1-2 weeks. Copy fee: $.50 per page. Certification fee: $1.50. Fee payee: District Court. Personal checks accepted. Prepayment is required.

Probate & Family Court PO Box 590, Greenfield, MA 01302; 413-774-7011; Fax: 413-774-3829. Hours: 8AM-4:30PM (EST). *Probate.*

http://aotweb.jud.state.ma.us

Hampden County

Superior Court 50 State St, PO Box 559, Springfield, MA 01102-0559; 413-748-8600; Fax: 413-737-1611. Hours: 8:30AM-4:30PM (EST). *Felony, Civil Actions Over $25,000.*

Civil Records: Access: Phone, mail, in person. Both court and visitors may perform in person searches. No search fee. Required to search: name, years to search. Civil cases indexed by defendant, plaintiff. Civil records on computer from 1989 to present; prior on index cards from 1930s, books from 1812. **Criminal Records:** Access: Mail, in person. Both court and visitors may perform in person searches. No search fee. Required to search: name, years to search. Criminal records on computer from 1989 to present; prior on index cards from 1930s, books from 1812. **General Information:** No impounded case records released. SASE requested. Turnaround time 1 week. Copy fee: $.50 per page. Certification fee: $1.50. Fee payee: Clerk of Superior Court. Personal checks accepted. Prepayment is required.

Chicopee Division District Court #20 30 Church St, Chicopee, MA 01020; 413-598-0099; Fax: 413-598-8176. Hours: 8AM-4PM

(EST). *Felony, Misdemeanor, Civil, Eviction, Small Claims.*

Civil Records: Access: Phone, mail, in person. Both court and visitors may perform in person searches. No search fee. Required to search: name, years to search. Civil cases indexed by defendant, plaintiff. Civil records on index cards from 1983, docket books to 1900. **Criminal Records:** Access: Phone, mail, in person. Both court and visitors may perform in person searches. No search fee. Required to search: name, years to search, DOB. Criminal records on index cards from 1983, docket books to 1900. **General Information:** No juvenile records released. Turnaround time 1-2 weeks. Copy fee: $.50 per page. Certification fee: $1.50. Fee payee: District Court. Personal checks accepted. Prepayment is required.

Holyoke Division District Court 20 Court Sq, Holyoke, MA 01041-5075; 413-538-9710; Fax: 413-533-7165. Hours: 8:30AM-4:30PM (EST). *Felony, Misdemeanor, Civil, Eviction, Small Claims.*

Civil Records: Access: Phone, mail, in person. Both court and visitors may perform in person searches. No search fee. Required to search: name, years to search. Civil cases indexed by defendant, plaintiff. Civil records on index cards and docket books. **Criminal Records:** Access: Phone, mail, in person. Both court and visitors may perform in person searches. No search fee. Required to search: name, years to search. Criminal records on index cards and docket books. **General Information:** No juvenile, sealed records released. SASE requested. Turnaround time 1-2 weeks. Copy fee: $.50 per page. Certification fee: $1.50. Fee payee: District Court. Only cashiers checks and money orders accepted. Prepayment is required.

Palmer Division District Court 235 Sykes St, Palmer, MA 01069; 413-283-8916; Fax: 413-283-6775. Hours: 8:30AM-4:30PM (EST). *Felony, Misdemeanor, Civil, Eviction, Small Claims.*

Civil Records: Access: Phone, mail, in person. Both court and visitors may perform in person searches. No search fee. Required to search: name, years to search. Civil cases indexed by defendant, plaintiff. Civil records on index cards for 10 years. **Criminal Records:** Access: Phone, mail, in person. Both court and visitors may perform in person searches. No search fee. Required to search: name, years to search. Criminal records on index cards for 10 years. **General Information:** No sealed or juvenile records released. Turnaround time 1-2 weeks. Copy fee: $.50 per page. Certification fee: $1.50. Fee payee: District Court. Personal checks accepted. Prepayment is required.

Springfield Division District Court 50 State St, Springfield, MA 01103; 413-748-7613; Civil phone:413-748-8659; Criminal phone:413-748-8659; Fax: 413-747-4841. Hours: 8:00AM-4:30PM (EST). *Felony, Misdemeanor, Civil, Eviction, Small Claims.*

Civil Records: Access: Phone, mail, in person. Both court and visitors may perform in person searches. No search fee. Required to search: name, years to search. Civil cases indexed by defendant, plaintiff. Civil records on index cards. **Criminal Records:** Access: Phone, mail, in person. Both court and visitors may perform in person searches. No search fee. Required to search: name, years to search. Criminal records on index cards. **General Information:** No sealed, expunged, or adoption records released. Turnaround time 1-2 weeks.

Copy fee: $.50 per page. Certification fee: $1.50. Fee payee: District Court. Business checks accepted. Prepayment is required.

Westfield Division District Court 27 Washington St, Westfield, MA 01085; 413-568-8946; Fax: 413-568-4863. Hours: 8AM-4PM (EST). *Felony, Misdemeanor, Civil, Eviction, Small Claims.*

Civil Records: Access: Mail, in person. Both court and visitors may perform in person searches. No search fee. Required to search: name, years to search. Civil cases indexed by defendant, plaintiff. Civil records on index cards and in files. **Criminal Records:** Access: Mail, in person. Both court and visitors may perform in person searches. No search fee. Required to search: name, years to search. Criminal records on index cards and in files. **General Information:** No sealed or juvenile records released. Turnaround time 1-2 weeks. Copy fee: $.50 per page. Certification fee: $1.50. Fee payee: District Court. Personal checks accepted. Prepayment is required.

Probate & Family Court 50 State St, Springfield, MA 01103-0559; 413-748-7759; Fax: 413-781-5605. Hours: 8AM-4:25PM (EST). *Probate.*

Hampshire County

Superior Court PO Box 1119, Northampton, MA 01061; 413-584-5810; Fax: 413-586-8217. Hours: 9AM-4PM (EST). *Felony, Civil Actions Over $25,000.*

Civil Records: Access: Mail, in person. Both court and visitors may perform in person searches. No search fee. Required to search: name, years to search. Civil cases indexed by defendant, plaintiff. Civil records in files, index cards from 1800s. **Criminal Records:** Access: Mail, in person. Both court and visitors may perform in person searches. No search fee. Required to search: name, years to search. Criminal records in files, index cards from 1800s. **General Information:** No impounded case records released. Turnaround time 1 week. Copy fee: $.50 per page. Certification fee: $1.50. Fee payee: Clerk of Superior Court. Personal checks accepted. Prepayment is required. Public access terminal is available. Public Access Terminal Note: Civil only.

Northampton District Court Courthouse, 15 Gothic St, Northampton, MA 01060; 413-584-7400/7405 413-584-7776; Criminal phone:; Fax: 413-586-1980. Hours: 8:30AM-4PM (EST). *Felony, Misdemeanor, Civil, Eviction, Small Claims.*

Civil Records: Access: Phone, fax, mail, in person. Only the court conducts in person searches; visitors may not. No search fee. Required to search: name, years to search, address. Civil cases indexed by defendant, plaintiff. Civil records on index cards and docket books. **Criminal Records:** Access: Fax, mail, in person. Only the court conducts in person searches; visitors may not. No search fee. Required to search: name, years to search, DOB. Criminal records on index cards and docket books. **General Information:** No CHINS-care & protection, show cause-mental health records released. SASE requested. Turnaround time 1-2 weeks. Copy fee: $.50 per page. Certification fee: $1.50 per page. Fee payee: District Court. Personal checks accepted. Prepayment is required. Fax notes: No fee to fax results.

Ware Division District Court PO Box 300, Ware, MA 01082; 413-967-3301; Fax: 413-

967-7986. Hours: 8AM-4:30PM (EST). *Felony, Misdemeanor, Civil, Eviction, Small Claims.*

Civil Records: Access: Phone, fax, mail, in person. Only the court conducts in person searches; visitors may not. No search fee. Required to search: name, years to search. Civil cases indexed by defendant, plaintiff. Civil records on index cards or docket books. Some records sent to archives in Worcester. **Criminal Records:** Access: Phone, fax, mail, in person. Only the court conducts in person searches; visitors may not. No search fee. Required to search: name, years to search; also helpful-DOB, SSN. Criminal records on index cards or docket books. Some records sent to archives in Worcester. **General Information:** No sealed, impounded, confidential or juvenile records released. Turnaround time 1-2 weeks. Copy fee: $.50 per page. Certification fee: $1.50. Fee payee: Ware District Court. Personal checks accepted. Prepayment is required.

Probate & Family Court 33 King St, Northampton, MA 01060; 413-586-8500; Fax: 413-584-1132. Hours: 9AM-4:30PM (EST). *Probate.*

Middlesex County

Superior Court-East Cambridge 40 Thorndike St, East Cambridge, MA 02141; 617-494-4010. Hours: 8:30AM-4:30PM (EST). *Felony, Civil Actions Over $25,000.*

Note: The court is planning to have Internet access to records by the end of 1999

Civil Records: Access: Mail, in person. Both court and visitors may perform in person searches. No search fee. Required to search: name, years to search; also helpful-address. Civil cases indexed by defendant, plaintiff. Civil records on computer from 1986, rest on card indexes. **Criminal Records:** Access: Mail, in person. Both court and visitors may perform in person searches. No search fee. Required to search: name, years to search; also helpful-address. Criminal records on computer back to 1991, rest on card indexes. **General Information:** No impounded or those restricted by statute records released. Turnaround time 3-5 days for criminal records. Copy fee: $.50 per page. Certification fee: $1.50. Fee payee: Clerk of Superior Court. Personal checks accepted. Prepayment is required. Public access terminal is available.

Superior Court-Lowell 360 Gorham St, Lowell, MA 01852; 978-453-0201. Hours: 8:30AM-4:30PM (EST). *Felony, Civil Actions Over $25,000.*

Civil Records: Access: Mail, in person. Both court and visitors may perform in person searches. No search fee. Required to search: name, years to search. Civil cases indexed by defendant, plaintiff. Civil records on computer since 1990; prior records kept at East Cambridge Middlesex Superior Court, 40 Thorndike, Cambridge, MA 02141. **Criminal Records:** Access: Mail, in person. Both court and visitors may perform in person searches. No search fee. Required to search: name, years to search. Criminal records on computer since 1990; prior records kept at East Cambridge Middlesex Superior Court, 40 Thorndike, Cambridge, MA 02141. **General Information:** Turnaround time 1-2 days. Copy fee: $.50 per page. Certification fee: $1.50. Fee payee: Clerk of Superior Court. Personal checks accepted. Prepayment is required.

Ayer Division District Court 25 E Main St, Ayer, MA 01432; 978-772-2100; Fax: 978-772-

5345. Hours: 8:30AM-4:30PM (EST). *Felony, Misdemeanor, Civil, Eviction, Small Claims.*

Civil Records: Access: Mail, in person. No search fee. Required to search: name, years to search. Civil cases indexed by defendant, plaintiff. Civil records on index cards from 1977 to present, computerization to begin in late 1999. DOB required on subject. **Criminal Records:** Access: Phone, mail, in person. Both court and visitors may perform in person searches. No search fee. Required to search: name, years to search, DOB. Index cards from 1977 to 1995, computerized 1996 forward. **General Information:** Juvenile records not released. Turnaround time 1-2 weeks. Copy fee: $.50 per page. Certification fee: $1.50. Fee payee: Ayer District Court. Personal checks accepted. Prepayment is required.

Cambridge Division District Court 52
PO Box 338, East Cambridge, MA 02141; 617-494-4310; Probate phone:617-494-5233. Hours: 8:30AM-4:30PM (EST). *Felony, Misdemeanor, Civil, Eviction, Small Claims.*

Civil Records: Access: Mail, in person. Both court and visitors may perform in person searches. No search fee. Required to search: name, years to search. Civil cases indexed by defendant, plaintiff. Civil records on index cards or docket books. State law requires records be retained for 10 years. **Criminal Records:** Access: In person only. Court does not conduct in person searches; visitors must perform searches for themselves. Search fee: No criminal searches performed by court. Required to search: name, years to search, DOB. Criminal records on index cards or docket books. State law requires records be retained for 10 years. **General Information:** No sealed or juvenile records released. Turnaround time 1-2 weeks. Copy fee: $.50 per page. Certification fee: $1.50. Fee payee: District Court. Personal checks accepted. Prepayment is required.

Concord Division District Court 47 305 Walden St, Concord, MA 01742; 978-369-0500. Hours: 8:30AM-4:30PM (EST). *Felony, Misdemeanor, Civil, Eviction, Small Claims.*

Civil Records: Access: Mail, in person. Both court and visitors may perform in person searches. No search fee. Required to search: name, years to search; also helpful-address. Civil cases indexed by defendant, plaintiff. Civil records on computer from 1991, index cards and books from 1950, archived from 1643. In person searches performed from 1-2PM only. **Criminal Records:** Access: Mail, in person. Both court and visitors may perform in person searches. No search fee. Required to search: name, years to search; also helpful-address, DOB, SSN. Criminal records on computer from 1991, index cards and books from 1950, archived from 1643. In person searches performed from 1-2PM only. **General Information:** No impounded files released. SASE requested. Turnaround time 1 week. Copy fee: $.50 per page. Certification fee: $1.50. Fee payee: Commonwealth of Massachusetts. Personal checks accepted. Prepayment is required.

Framingham Division District Court
600 Concord St, Framingham, MA 01701; 508-875-7461. Hours: 8:30AM-4:30PM (EST). *Felony, Misdemeanor, Civil, Eviction, Small Claims.*

Civil Records: Access: Mail, in person. Both court and visitors may perform in person searches. No search fee. Required to search: name, years to search. Civil cases indexed by defendant, plaintiff. Civil records on index cards or docket books. State

law requires records be retained for 10 years. Special form required for mail request. **Criminal Records:** Access: Mail, in person. Both court and visitors may perform in person searches. No search fee. Required to search: name, years to search. Criminal records on index cards or docket books. State law requires records be retained for 10 years. Special form required for mail request. **General Information:** No sealed, expunged or juvenile records released. Copy fee: $.50 per page. Certification fee: $1.50. Fee payee: District Court. Only cashiers checks and money orders accepted. Prepayment is required.

Lowell Division District Court 41 Hurd St, Lowell, MA 01852; 978-459-4101. Hours: 8:30AM-4:30PM (EST). *Felony, Misdemeanor, Civil, Eviction, Small Claims.*

Civil Records: Access: In person only. Court does not conduct in person searches; visitors must perform searches for themselves. Search fee: No civil searches performed by court. Required to search: name, years to search. Civil cases indexed by defendant, plaintiff. Civil records on index cards or docket books. State law requires records be retained for 10 years. **Criminal Records:** Access: In person only. Court does not conduct in person searches; visitors must perform searches for themselves. Search fee: No criminal searches performed by court. Required to search: name, years to search, DOB. Criminal records on index cards or docket books. State law requires records be retained for 10 years. **General Information:** No impounded records released. Copy fee: $.50 per page. Certification fee: $1.50. Fee payee: District Court, Lowell Division. Business checks accepted. Prepayment is required.

Malden Division District Court 89 Summer, Malden, MA 02148; 508-653-4332. Hours: 8:30AM-4:30PM (EST). *Felony, Misdemeanor, Civil, Eviction, Small Claims.*

Civil Records: Access: Phone, mail, in person. Both court and visitors may perform in person searches. No search fee. Required to search: name, years to search. Civil cases indexed by defendant, plaintiff. Civil records on index cards or docket books. State law requires records be retained for 10 years. **Criminal Records:** Access: Phone, mail, in person. Both court and visitors may perform in person searches. No search fee. Required to search: name, years to search; also helpful-DOB. Criminal records on index cards or docket books. State law requires records be retained for 10 years. **General Information:** No juvenile records released. Turnaround time 1-2 weeks. Copy fee: $.50 per page. Certification fee: $1.50. Fee payee: District Court. Personal checks accepted. Prepayment is required.

Marlborough Division District Court 21 45 Williams St, Marlborough, MA 01752; 508-485-3700. Hours: 8AM-4:30PM (EST). *Felony, Misdemeanor, Civil, Eviction, Small Claims.*

Civil Records: Access: Phone, mail, in person. Both court and visitors may perform in person searches. No search fee. Required to search: name, years to search. Civil cases indexed by defendant, plaintiff. Civil records on index cards or docket books. State law requires records be retained for 10 years. **Criminal Records:** Access: Phone, mail, in person. Both court and visitors may perform in person searches. No search fee. Required to search: name, years to search, DOB. Criminal records on index cards or docket books. State law requires records be retained for 10 years. **General Information:** No juvenile records released. Turnaround time 1-2 weeks. Copy fee: $.50 per

page. Certification fee: $1.50. Fee payee: District Court. Personal checks accepted. Prepayment is required.

Natick Division District Court 117 E Central, Natick, MA 01760; 508-653-4332. Hours: 8:30AM-4:30PM (EST). *Felony, Misdemeanor, Civil, Eviction, Small Claims.*

Civil Records: Access: Phone, mail, in person. Only the court conducts in person searches; visitors may not. No search fee. Required to search: name, years to search. Civil cases indexed by defendant, plaintiff. Civil records on index cards and docket books, back for 10 years. **Criminal Records:** Access: Phone, mail, in person. Only the court conducts in person searches; visitors may not. No search fee. Required to search: name, years to search, DOB. Criminal records on index cards and docket books, back for 10 years. **General Information:** No juvenile records released. Turnaround time 1-2 weeks. Copy fee: $.50 per page. Certification fee: $1.50. Fee payee: District Court. Personal checks accepted. Prepayment is required.

Newton Division District Court 1309 Washington, West Newton, MA 02165; 617-244-3600; Fax: 617-965-7584. Hours: 8:30AM-4:30PM (EST). *Felony, Misdemeanor, Civil, Eviction, Small Claims.*

Civil Records: Access: Phone, fax, mail, in person. Both court and visitors may perform in person searches. No search fee. Required to search: name, years to search. Civil cases indexed by defendant, plaintiff. Civil records on index cards going back 10 years or more. **Criminal Records:** Access: Phone, fax, mail, in person. Both court and visitors may perform in person searches. No search fee. Required to search: name, years to search. Criminal records on index cards going back 10 years or more. **General Information:** No juvenile, (some) 209-A cases or mental health records released. Turnaround time 1 week. Copy fee: $.50 per page. Certification fee: $1.50. Fee payee: District Court of Newton. Personal checks accepted.

Somerville Division District Court 175 Fellsway, Somerville, MA 02145; 617-666-8000. Hours: 8:30AM-4:30PM (EST). *Felony, Misdemeanor, Civil, Eviction, Small Claims.*

Civil Records: Access: Phone, mail, in person. Only the court conducts in person searches; visitors may not. No search fee. Required to search: name, years to search. Civil cases indexed by defendant, plaintiff. Civil records on index cards or docket books. State law requires records be retained for 10 years. **Criminal Records:** Access: Phone, mail, in person. Only the court conducts in person searches; visitors may not. No search fee. Required to search: name, years to search, DOB. Criminal records on computer since 1997; prior records on index cards or docket books. State law requires records be retained for 10 years. **General Information:** No juvenile or impounded records released. Turnaround time 1-2 weeks. Copy fee: $.50 per page. Certification fee: $1.50. Fee payee: District Court. Personal checks accepted. Prepayment is required.

Waltham Division District Court 51 38 Linden St, Waltham, MA 02154; 617-894-4500. Hours: 8:30AM-4:30PM (EST). *Felony, Misdemeanor, Civil, Eviction, Small Claims.*

Civil Records: Access: Mail, in person. Both court and visitors may perform in person searches. No search fee. Required to search: name, years to search. Civil cases indexed by defendant, plaintiff.

Civil records on index cards and docket books, back for 10 years. **Criminal Records:** Access: Mail, in person. Both court and visitors may perform in person searches. No search fee. Required to search: name, years to search; also helpful-DOB. Criminal records on index cards and docket books, back for 10 years. **General Information:** No juvenile records released. Turnaround time 1 week. Copy fee: $.50 per page. Certification fee: $1.50. Fee payee: District Court. Personal checks accepted. Prepayment is required.

Woburn Division District Court 53 30 Pleasant St, Woburn, MA 01801; 617-935-4000. Hours: 8:30AM-4:30PM (EST). *Felony, Misdemeanor, Civil, Eviction, Small Claims.*

Civil Records: Access: Mail, in person. Both court and visitors may perform in person searches. No search fee. Required to search: name, years to search. Civil cases indexed by defendant, plaintiff. Civil records on index cards, computer listing or docket books. State law requires records be retained for 30 years. **Criminal Records:** Access: Mail, in person. Only the court conducts in person searches; visitors may not. No search fee. Required to search: name, years to search; also helpful-DOB. Criminal records on index cards, computer listing or docket books. State law requires records be retained for 30 years. Court searches only for records prior to 1996. **General Information:** No statutorily non-public records released. SASE requested. Turnaround time 1-2 weeks. Copy fee: $.50 per page. Certification fee: $1.50. Fee payee: District Court. Personal checks accepted. Prepayment is required. Public access terminal is available. Public Access Terminal Note: For files after 1996.

Probate & Family Court 208 Cambridge St, PO Box 410480, East Cambridge, MA 02141-0005; 617-494-4530; Fax: 617-225-0781. Hours: 8AM-4PM (EST). *Probate.*

Nantucket County

Superior Court PO Box 967, Nantucket, MA 02554; 508-228-2559; Fax: 508-228-3725. Hours: 8:30AM-4PM (EST). *Felony, Civil Actions Over $25,000.*

Civil Records: Access: Phone, fax, mail, in person. Both court and visitors may perform in person searches. No search fee. Required to search: name, years to search. Civil cases indexed by defendant, plaintiff. Civil records on index books from 1762. **Criminal Records:** Access: Phone, fax, mail, in person. Both court and visitors may perform in person searches. No search fee. Required to search: name, years to search. Criminal records on index books from 1762. **General Information:** No impounded records released. SASE required. Turnaround time 1 week. Copy fee: $.50 per page. Certification fee: $1.50. Fee payee: Nantucket Superior Court. Personal checks accepted. Prepayment is required. Fax notes: No fee to fax results. In-state faxing only.

Nantucket Division District Court 16 Broad Street, PO Box 1800, Nantucket, MA 02554; 508-228-0460. Hours: 8AM-4PM (EST). *Felony, Misdemeanor, Civil, Eviction, Small Claims.*

Civil Records: Access: In person only. Court does not conduct in person searches; visitors must perform searches for themselves. Search fee: No civil searches performed by court. Required to search: name, years to search. Civil cases indexed by defendant, plaintiff. Civil records on index cards or docket books. State law requires records be retained for 10 years. **Criminal Records:**

Access: In person only. Court does not conduct in person searches; visitors must perform searches for themselves. Search fee: No criminal searches performed by court. Required to search: name, years to search. Criminal records on index cards or docket books. State law requires records be retained for 10 years. **General Information:** Copy fee: $.50 per page. Certification fee: $1.50. Fee payee: Nantucket District Court. Prepayment is required.

Probate & Family Court PO Box 1116, Nantucket, MA 02554; 508-228-2669; Fax: 508-228-3662. Hours: 8:30AM-4PM (EST). *Probate.*

Norfolk County

Superior Court 650 High St, Dedham, MA 02026; Civil phone:781-326-1600 X1; Criminal phone:781-326-1600 X1; Fax: 781-326-3871(Civ); 781-320-9726(Crim). Hours: 8:30AM-4:30PM (EST). *Felony, Civil Actions Over $25,000.*

Civil Records: Access: Phone, mail, in person. Both court and visitors may perform in person searches. No search fee. Required to search: name, years to search. Civil cases indexed by defendant, plaintiff. Civil records on index books from 1900, recent records on computer. **Criminal Records:** Access: Mail, in person. Only the court conducts in person searches; visitors may not. No search fee. Required to search: name, years to search; also helpful-address, DOB, SSN. Criminal records on index books from 1900, recent records on computer. After faxing call back later that day for information. **General Information:** No impounded records released. No one may view a file of a sex-related crime without authorization from a judge. SASE not requried. Turnaround time 1 week, 1-2 days for criminal phone in requests. Copy fee: $.50 per page. Certification fee: $1.50. Fee payee: Clerk of Superior Court. Personal checks accepted. Prepayment is required.

Brookline Division District Court 360 Washington St, Brookline, MA 02146; 617-232-4660; Fax: 617-739-0734. Hours: 8:30AM-4:30PM (EST). *Felony, Misdemeanor, Civil, Eviction, Small Claims.*

Civil Records: Access: Mail, in person. Only the court conducts in person searches; visitors may not. No search fee. Required to search: name, years to search. Civil cases indexed by defendant, plaintiff. Civil records on index cards and docket books, back for 10 years or more. **Criminal Records:** Access: Mail, in person. Only the court conducts in person searches; visitors may not. No search fee. Required to search: name, years to search; also helpful-DOB. Criminal records on index cards and docket books, back for 10 years or more. **General Information:** No sealed case records released. Turnaround time 1-2 weeks. Copy fee: $.50 per page. Certification fee: $1.50. Fee payee: District Court Clerk. Personal checks accepted. Prepayment is required.

Dedham Division District Court 631 High St, Dedham, MA 02026; 781-329-4777. Hours: 8:15AM-4:30PM (EST). *Felony, Misdemeanor, Civil, Eviction, Small Claims.*

Civil Records: Access: In person only. Court does not conduct in person searches; visitors must perform searches for themselves. Search fee: No civil searches performed by court. Required to search: name, years to search. Civil cases indexed by defendant, plaintiff. Civil records on computer since 1997, and on index cards or docket books prior to that. State law requres records be retained for 10 years. **Criminal Records:** Access: In person only. Court does not conduct in person

searches; visitors must perform searches for themselves. Search fee: No criminal searches performed by court. Required to search: name, years to search. Criminal records on computer since 1997, and on index cards or docket books prior to that. State law requres records be retained for 10 years. Access is available after 10AM. **General Information:** No juvenile records released. Copy fee: $.50 per page. Certification fee: $1.50. Fee payee: District Court. Personal checks accepted. Prepayment is required.

Quincy Division District Court One Dennis Ryan Parkway, Quincy, MA 02169; 617-471-1650. Hours: 8:30AM-4:30PM (EST). *Felony, Misdemeanor, Civil, Eviction, Small Claims.*

Civil Records: Access: In person only. Court does not conduct in person searches; visitors must perform searches for themselves. Search fee: No civil searches performed by court. Required to search: name, years to search. Civil cases indexed by defendant, plaintiff. Civil records on index cards or docket books. State law requires records be retained for 10 years. **Criminal Records:** Access: In person only. Court does not conduct in person searches; visitors must perform searches for themselves. Search fee: No criminal searches performed by court. Required to search: name, years to search; also helpful-DOB. Criminal records on computer since 1996; prior records on index cards or docket books. State law requires records be retained for 10 years. **General Information:** No juvenile records released. Copy fee: $.50 per page. Certification fee: $1.50. Fee payee: District Court. Only cashiers checks and money orders accepted. Prepayment is required.

Stoughton Division District Court 1288 Central St, Stoughton, MA 02072; 781-344-2131. Hours: 8:30AM-4:30PM (EST). *Felony, Misdemeanor, Civil, Eviction, Small Claims.*

Civil Records: Access: Mail, in person. Both court and visitors may perform in person searches. No search fee. Required to search: name, years to search. Civil cases indexed by defendant, plaintiff. Civil records on index cards or docket books for 10 years or more. **Criminal Records:** Access: Mail, in person. Only the court conducts in person searches; visitors may not. No search fee. Required to search: name, years to search; also helpful-DOB. Criminal records on computer since 1996; prior records on index cards or docket books for 10 years or more. **General Information:** No juvenile records released. Turnaround time 1 week. Copy fee: $.50 per page. Certification fee: $1.50. Fee payee: District Court. Personal checks accepted. Prepayment is required.

Wrentham Division District Court PO Box 248, Wrentham, MA 02093; 508-384-3106; Fax: 508-384-5052. Hours: 8:30AM-4:30PM (EST). *Felony, Misdemeanor, Civil, Eviction, Small Claims.*

Civil Records: Access: Mail, in person. Both court and visitors may perform in person searches. No search fee. Required to search: name, years to search. Civil cases indexed by defendant, plaintiff. Civil records on index cards or docket books. State law requires records be retained for 10 years. **Criminal Records:** Access: Mail, in person. Both court and visitors may perform in person searches. No search fee. Required to search: name, years to search; also helpful-DOB. Criminal records on index cards or docket books. State law requires records be retained for 10 years. **General Information:** No show cause hearing or juvenile records released. Mail requests not accepted.

Turnaround time up to 2 weeks. Copy fee: $.50 per page. Certification fee: $1.50. Fee payee: District Court. Personal checks accepted. Prepayment is required.

Probate & Family Court 649 High St, PO Box 269, Dedham, MA 02027; 781-326-7200; Fax: 781-326-5575. Hours: 8AM-4:30PM (EST). *Probate.*

Plymouth County

Superior Court-Brockton 72 Belmont St, Brockton, MA 02401; 508-583-8250. Hours: 8:30AM-4:30PM (EST). *Felony, Civil Actions Over $25,000.*

Civil Records: Access: Mail, in person. Both court and visitors may perform in person searches. No search fee. Required to search: name, years to search. Civil cases indexed by defendant, plaintiff. Civil records for current civil cases are here, closed case are in Plymouth, some pending. **Criminal Records:** Access: Mail, in person. Both court and visitors may perform in person searches. No search fee. Required to search: name, years to search. Civil records for current civil cases are here, closed case are in Plymouth, some pending. **General Information:** No impounded records released. Turnaround time 1-2 days. Copy fee: $.50 per page. Certification fee: $1.50. Fee payee: Clerk of Superior Court. Personal checks accepted. Prepayment is required.

Superior Court-Plymouth Court St, Plymouth, MA 02360; 508-747-6911. Hours: 8:30AM-4:30PM (EST). *Felony, Civil Actions Over $25,000.*

Civil Records: Access: Mail, in person. Only the court conducts in person searches; visitors may not. No search fee. Required to search: name, years to search. Civil cases indexed by defendant, plaintiff. Civil records for all closed cases are kept here. **Criminal Records:** Access: Mail, in person. Only the court conducts in person searches; visitors may not. No search fee. Required to search: name, years to search. Criminal records 10 years or older are here, for recent cases go to the Superior Court in Brockton. **General Information:** No impounded records released. Turnaround time 1 week, immediate four phone requests. Copy fee: $.50 per page. Certification fee: $1.50. Fee payee: Clerk of Superior Court. Personal checks accepted. Prepayment is required.

Brockton Division District Court 155 West Elm St, Brockton, MA 02401; 508-587-8000. Hours: 8:30AM-4:30PM (EST). *Felony, Misdemeanor, Civil, Eviction, Small Claims.*

Civil Records: Access: Mail, in person. Both court and visitors may perform in person searches. No search fee. Required to search: name, years to search. Civil cases indexed by defendant, plaintiff. Civil records on index cards or docket books, retained for 10 years. **Criminal Records:** Access: Mail, in person. Both court and visitors may perform in person searches. No search fee. Required to search: name, years to search; also helpful-DOB. Criminal records on index cards or docket books, retained for 10 years. **General Information:** No juvenile or impounded records released. Turnaround time 1-2 weeks. Copy fee: $.50 per page. Certification fee: $1.50. Fee payee: District Court. Personal checks accepted. Prepayment is required.

Hingham Division District Court 28 George Washington Blvd, Hingham, MA 02043; 781-749-7000; Fax: 617-740-8390. Hours:

8:30AM-4:30PM (EST). *Felony, Misdemeanor, Civil, Eviction, Small Claims.*

Civil Records: Access: Mail, in person. Only the court conducts in person searches; visitors may not. No search fee. Required to search: name, years to search. Civil cases indexed by defendant, plaintiff. Civil records on index cards or docket books, retained for 10 years or more. **Criminal Records:** Access: Mail, in person. Only the court conducts in person searches; visitors may not. No search fee. Required to search: name, years to search; also helpful-DOB. Criminal records on index cards or docket books, retained for 10 years or more. **General Information:** No juvenile records released. Turnaround time 1-2 weeks. Copy fee: $.50 per page. Certification fee: $1.50. Fee payee: District Court. Personal checks accepted. Prepayment is required.

Plymouth 3rd Division District Court Courthouse, South Russell St, Plymouth, MA 02360; 508-747-0500 X300. Hours: 8:30AM-4:30PM (EST). *Felony, Misdemeanor, Civil, Eviction, Small Claims.*

Civil Records: Access: Mail, in person. Both court and visitors may perform in person searches. No search fee. Required to search: name, years to search. Civil cases indexed by defendant, plaintiff. Civil records on index cards or docket books. State law requires records be retained for 10 years. Visitors can only access the index cards. **Criminal Records:** Access: Mail, in person. Both court and visitors may perform in person searches. No search fee. Required to search: name, years to search; also helpful-DOB. Criminal records on index cards or docket books. State law requires records be retained for 10 years. Visitors can only access the index cards. **General Information:** No juvenile or impounded records released. Turnaround time 3-4 days. Copy fee: $.50 per page. Certification fee: $1.50. Fee payee: Plymouth District Court. Personal checks accepted. Prepayment is required.

Wareham Division District Court 2200 Cranberry Hwy, Junction Routes 28 & 58, West Wareham, MA 02576; 508-295-8300; Fax: 508-291-6376. Hours: 8:30AM-4:30PM (EST). *Felony, Misdemeanor, Civil, Eviction, Small Claims.*

Civil Records: Access: Phone, mail, in person. Both court and visitors may perform in person searches. No search fee. Required to search: name, years to search. Civil cases indexed by defendant, plaintiff. Civil records on index cards or docket books. State law requires records be retained for 10 years. **Criminal Records:** Access: Phone, mail, in person. Only the court conducts in person searches; visitors may not. No search fee. Required to search: name, years to search; also helpful-DOB. Criminal records on index cards or docket books. State law requires records be retained for 10 years. **General Information:** No juvenile records released. SASE requested. Turnaround time 1-2 weeks. Copy fee: $.50 per page. Certification fee: $1.50. Fee payee: District Court. Personal checks accepted. Prepayment is required.

Probate & Family Court 11 Russell, PO Box 3640, Plymouth, MA 02361; 508-747-6204; Fax: 508-588-8483. Hours: 8:30AM-4PM (EST). *Probate.*

Suffolk County

Superior Court-Civil 90 Devonshire St, Rm 810, Boston, MA 02109; 617-788-7677. Hours: 8:30AM-5PM (EST). *Civil.*

Civil Records: Access: Mail, in person. Both court and visitors may perform in person searches. No search fee. Required to search: name, years to search. Civil cases indexed by defendant, plaintiff. Civil records on computer from 1991, index cards and books from 1860. **General Information:** No impounded records released. Turnaround time 1 week. Copy fee: $.50 per page. Certification fee: $1.50. Fee payee: Clerk of Superior Court. Business checks accepted. Prepayment is required. Public access terminal is available.

Superior Court - Criminal New Courthouse, 712 Pemberton, Boston, MA 02108; 617-725-8160; Fax: 617-227-8834. Hours: 9AM-5PM (EST). *Felony.* **Criminal Records:** Access: Mail, in person. Both court and visitors may perform in person searches. No search fee. Required to search: name, years to search. Criminal records on computer since 1991, index cards and books from 1950, archived from 1864. **General Information:** Turnaround time 1-2 weeks. Copy fee: $.50 per page. Certification fee: $1.50. Fee payee: Superior Court. Personal checks accepted. Prepayment is required. Public access terminal is available.

Brighton Division District Court Department 52 Academy Hill Rd, Brighton, MA 02135; 617-782-6521; Fax: 617-254-2127. Hours: 8:30AM-4:30PM (EST). *Felony, Misdemeanor, Civil, Eviction, Small Claims.*

Civil Records: Access: Phone, mail, in person. Both court and visitors may perform in person searches. No search fee. Required to search: name, years to search. Civil cases indexed by defendant, plaintiff. Civil records on index cards or docket books. State law requires records be retained for 10 years. **Criminal Records:** Access: Phone, mail, in person. Both court and visitors may perform in person searches. No search fee. Required to search: name, years to search. Criminal records on index cards or docket books. State law requires records be retained for 10 years. **General Information:** No sealed or impounded records released. Turnaround time 1-2 weeks. Copy fee: $.50 per page. Certification fee: $1.50 per page. Fee payee: District Court. Personal checks accepted. Prepayment is required.

Charleston Division District Court 3 City Square, Charleston, MA 02129; 617-242-5400; Fax: 617-242-1677. Hours: 8:30AM-4:30PM (EST). *Felony, Misdemeanor, Civil, Eviction, Small Claims.*

Civil Records: Access: Fax, mail, in person. Only the court conducts in person searches; visitors may not. No search fee. Required to search: name, years to search. Civil cases indexed by defendant, plaintiff. Civil records on index cards or docket books. State law requires records be retained for 10 years. **Criminal Records:** Access: Fax, mail, in person. Only the court conducts in person searches; visitors may not. No search fee. Required to search: name, years to search; also helpful-DOB. Criminal records on index cards or docket books. State law requires records be retained for 10 years. **General Information:** No juvenile records released. Turnaround time 1-2 weeks. Copy fee: $.50 per page. Certification fee: $1.50. Fee payee: District Court. Personal checks accepted. Prepayment is required.

Chelsea Division District Court 121 3rd St, Cambridge, MA 02141-1710; 617-252-0960; Fax: 617-621-9743. Hours: 8:30AM-4:30PM (EST). *Felony, Misdemeanor, Civil, Eviction, Small Claims.*

Civil Records: Access: Phone, mail, in person. Both court and visitors may perform in person searches. No search fee. Required to search: name, years to search. Civil cases indexed by defendant, plaintiff. Civil records on index cards or docket books. State law requires records be retained for 10 years. **Criminal Records:** Access: Phone, mail, in person. Both court and visitors may perform in person searches. No search fee. Required to search: name, years to search; also helpful-address, DOB. Criminal records on index cards or docket books. State law requires records be retained for 10 years. **General Information:** No closed cases, impounded, sealed, mental health commitment, dismissed cases, alcoholic or victim of sexual offense records released. SASE required. Turnaround time 1-2 weeks. Copy fee: $.50 per page. Certification fee: $1.50. Fee payee: District Court. Personal checks accepted. Prepayment is required.

Dorchester Division District Court
510 Washington St, Dorchester, MA 02124; 617-288-9500. Hours: 8:30AM-4:30PM (EST). *Felony, Misdemeanor, Civil, Eviction, Small Claims.*

Civil Records: Access: Mail, in person. Both court and visitors may perform in person searches. No search fee. Required to search: name, years to search. Civil cases indexed by defendant, plaintiff. Civil records on index cards or docket books. State law requires records be retained for 10 years. **Criminal Records:** Access: Mail, in person. Only the court conducts in person searches; visitors may not. No search fee. Required to search: name, years to search; also helpful-DOB. Criminal records on index cards or docket books. State law requires records be retained for 10 years. **General Information:** No juvenile records released. Turnaround time 1-2 weeks. Copy fee: $.50 per page. Certification fee: $1.50. Fee payee: District Court. Personal checks accepted. Prepayment is required.

East Boston Division District Court
37 Meridian St, East Boston, MA 02128; 617-569-7550; Fax: 617-561-4988. Hours: 8:30AM-4:30PM (EST). *Misdemeanor, Civil Actions Under $25,000, Eviction, Small Claims.*

Civil Records: Access: Mail, in person. Both court and visitors may perform in person searches. No search fee. Required to search: name, years to search. Civil cases indexed by defendant, plaintiff. Civil records on index cards or docket books. State law requires records be retained for 10 years. **Criminal Records:** Access: Mail, in person. Both court and visitors may perform in person searches. No search fee. Required to search: name, years to search. Criminal records on index cards or docket books. State law requires records be retained for 10 years. **General Information:** No juvenile records released. Turnaround time 1-2 weeks. Copy fee: $.50 per page. Certification fee: $1.50. Fee payee: District Court. Personal checks accepted. Prepayment is required.

Roxbury Division District Court
85 Warren St, Roxbury, MA 02119; 617-427-7000; Fax: 617-541-0286. Hours: 8:30AM-5:30PM (EST). *Felony, Misdemeanor, Civil, Eviction, Small Claims.*

Civil Records: Access: Phone, fax, mail, in person. Both court and visitors may perform in person searches. No search fee. Required to search: name, years to search. Civil cases indexed by defendant, plaintiff. Civil records on index cards or docket books. State law requires records be retained for 10 years. **Criminal Records:** Access: Phone, fax, mail, in person. Both court

and visitors may perform in person searches. No search fee. Required to search: name, years to search; also helpful-address, DOB. Criminal records on index cards or docket books. State law requires records be retained for 10 years. **General Information:** No juvenile records released. Turnaround time 1-2 weeks. Copy fee: $1.00 per page. Certification fee: $1.50. Fee payee: District Court. Personal checks accepted. Prepayment is required. Fax notes: $1.00 per page.

South Boston Division District Court
535 East Broadway, South Boston, MA 02127; 617-268-9292/9293; Fax: 617-268-7321. Hours: 8:30AM-4:30PM (EST). *Felony, Misdemeanor, Civil, Eviction, Small Claims.*

Civil Records: Access: In person only. Court does not conduct in person searches; visitors must perform searches for themselves. Search fee: No civil searches performed by court. Required to search: name, years to search, address. Civil cases indexed by defendant, plaintiff. Civil records on index cards or docket books. State law requires records be retained for 10 years. **Criminal Records:** Access: In person only. Court does not conduct in person searches; visitors must perform searches for themselves. Search fee: No criminal searches performed by court. Required to search: name, years to search, address, DOB. Indexed by defendent name. **General Information:** No juvenile or medical records released. Copy fee: $.50 per page. Certification fee: $1.50. Fee payee: District Court. Personal checks accepted. Prepayment is required.

Suffolk County Courthouse Boston Municipal Court
55 Pemberpon Square, Boston, MA 02108; 617-725-8000; Civil phone:617-725-8404; Criminal phone:617-725-8404. Hours: 8:30AM-4:30PM (EST). *Misdemeanor, Civil, Small Claims.*

Civil Records: Access: Mail, in person. Both court and visitors may perform in person searches. No search fee. Required to search: name, years to search. Civil cases indexed by defendant, plaintiff. Civil records on computer from 1995 to present, and only court searches those records. Public can search prior records on index cards and look-up. State law requires records be retained for 10 years. **Criminal Records:** Access: Mail, in person. Both court and visitors may perform in person searches. No search fee. Required to search: name, years to search; also helpful-DOB. Criminal records on computer from 1995 to present, and only court searches those records. Public can search prior records on index cards and look-up. State law requires records be retained for 10 years. **General Information:** No impounded records released. Turnaround time 1-2 weeks. Copy fee: $.50 per page. Certification fee: $1.50. Fee payee: District Court. Personal checks accepted. Prepayment is required.

West Roxbury Division District Court
Courthouse, 445 Arborway, Jamaica Plain, MA 02130; 617-971-1200. Hours: 8:30AM-4:30PM (EST). *Felony, Misdemeanor, Civil, Eviction, Small Claims.*

Civil Records: Access: Mail, in person. Only the court conducts in person searches; visitors may not. No search fee. Required to search: name, years to search; also helpful-address. Civil cases indexed by defendant, plaintiff. Civil records on index cards or docket books. State law requires records be retained for 10 years. Include type of civil action to be searched. **Criminal Records:** Access: Mail, in person. Only the court conducts in person searches; visitors may not. No search

fee. Required to search: name, years to search; also helpful-DOB. Criminal records on index cards or docket books. State law requires records be retained for 10 years. **General Information:** No juvenile records released. Turnaround time 1-2 weeks. Copy fee: $.50 per page. Certification fee: $1.50. Fee payee: District Court. Personal checks accepted. Prepayment is required.

Probate & Family Court
24 New Chardon St, Boston, MA 02114-4703; 617-788-8300; Fax: 617-788-8926. Hours: 8:30AM-4:30PM (EST). *Probate.*

Worcester County

Superior Court
2 Main St Rm 21, Worcester, MA 01608; 508-770-1899. Hours: 8AM-4:30PM (EST). *Felony, Civil Actions Over $25,000.*

Civil Records: Access: Mail, in person. Both court and visitors may perform in person searches. No search fee. Required to search: name, years to search. Civil cases indexed by defendant, plaintiff. Civil records on computer from 1990, index books from 1900. **Criminal Records:** Access: Mail, in person. Both court and visitors may perform in person searches. No search fee. Required to search: name, years to search. Criminal records on computer from 1990, index books from 1900. **General Information:** No impounded or juvenile records released. Turnaround time 1 week. Copy fee: $.50 per page. Certification fee: $1.50. Fee payee: Clerk of Superior Court. Personal checks accepted. Prepayment is required. Public access terminal is available.

Clinton Division District Court
300 Boylston St, Clinton, MA 01510; 978-368-7811; Fax: 978-368-7827. Hours: 8:30AM-4:30PM (EST). *Felony, Misdemeanor, Civil, Eviction, Small Claims.*

Civil Records: Access: Mail, in person. Only the court conducts in person searches; visitors may not. No search fee. Required to search: name, years to search; also helpful: DOB, SSN. Civil cases indexed by defendant, plaintiff. Civil records on index cards or docket books. State law requires records be retained for 10 years. **Criminal Records:** Access: Mail, in person. Only the court conducts in person searches; visitors may not. No search fee. Required to search: name, years to search, address, DOB, SSN, signed release. Criminal records on index cards or docket books. State law requires records be retained for 10 years. **General Information:** No juvenile records released. SASE required. Turnaround time 1-2 weeks. Copy fee: $1.00 per page. Certification fee: $1.50. Fee payee: District Court Clerk Magistrate. Prepayment is required.

Dudley Division District Court
64 PO Box 100, Dudley, MA 01571; 508-943-7123; Fax: 508-949-0015. Hours: 8AM-4:30PM (EST). *Felony, Misdemeanor, Civil, Eviction, Small Claims.*

Civil Records: Access: Phone, mail, in person. Both court and visitors may perform in person searches. No search fee. Required to search: name, years to search. Civil cases indexed by defendant, plaintiff. Civil records on index cards or docket books. State law requires records be retained for 10 years. **Criminal Records:** Access: Phone, mail, in person. Both court and visitors may perform in person searches. No search fee. Required to search: name, years to search, DOB. Criminal records on computer since 06/96; prior records on index cards or docket books. State law requires records be retained for 10 years. **General Information:** No juvenile records released. SASE not required. Turnaround time 1-2 weeks. Copy fee: $.50 per page. Certification fee: $1.50. Fee payee: District Court. Business checks accepted. Prepayment is required.

Fitchburg District Court 16 100 Elm St, Fitchburg, MA 01420; 978-345-2111; Fax: 978-342-2461. Hours: 8:30AM-4:30PM (EST). *Felony, Misdemeanor, Civil, Eviction, Small Claims.*

Civil Records: Access: In person only. Court does not conduct in person searches; visitors must perform searches for themselves. Search fee: No civil searches performed by court. Required to search: name, years to search. Civil cases indexed by defendant, plaintiff. Civil records on index cards or docket books. State law requires records be retained for 10 years. **Criminal Records:** Access: In person only. Court does not conduct in person searches; visitors must perform searches for themselves. Search fee: No criminal searches performed by court. Required to search: name, years to search. Criminal records on index cards or docket books. State law requires records be retained for 10 years. **General Information:** No juvenile or mental health records released. Copy fee: $.50 per page. Certification fee: $1.50. Fee payee: District Court. Personal checks accepted. Prepayment is required.

Leominster Division District Court 25 School St, Leominster, MA 01453; 978-537-3722; Fax: 978-537-3970. Hours: 8:30AM-4:30PM (EST). *Felony, Misdemeanor, Civil, Eviction, Small Claims.*

Civil Records: Access: Phone, mail, in person. Both court and visitors may perform in person searches. No search fee. Required to search: name, years to search. Civil cases indexed by defendant, plaintiff. Civil records on index cards or docket books. State law requires records be retained for 10 years. **Criminal Records:** Access: Phone, mail, in person. Both court and visitors may perform in person searches. No search fee. Required to search: name, years to search; also helpful-DOB. Criminal records on computer since 1987; Prior records on index cards or docket books. State law requires records be retained for 10 years. **General Information:** No juvenile or impounded records released. Turnaround time 1-2 weeks. Copy fee: $.50 per page. Certification fee: $1.50. Fee payee: District Court. Personal checks accepted. Prepayment is required.

Milford Division District Court PO Box 370, Milford, MA 01757; 508-473-1260. Hours: 8:30AM-4:30PM (EST). *Felony, Misdemeanor, Civil, Eviction, Small Claims.*

Civil Records: Access: Mail, in person. Both court and visitors may perform in person searches. No search fee. Required to search: name, years to search. Civil cases indexed by defendant, plaintiff. Civil records on index cards or docket books. State law requires records be retained for 10 years. Some indexes can only be searches by court. Mail requests require the docket number, suggest using a retriever. **Criminal Records:** Access: Mail, in person. Both court and visitors may perform in person searches. No search fee. Required to search: name, years to search, DOB; also helpful-SSN, aliases. Criminal records on computer since 1995; prior records on index cards & docket books; some indexes only searchable by court. Mail reqeusts require the docket number, local retriever is suggested. **General Information:** No mental health, impounded, alcohol, commitment, sexual abuse victim, waivers of fees or costs for indigents, delinquency, C & P, CHINS, 209A

minor or 209A address records released. Turnaround time 1-5 days. Copy fee: $.50 per page. Certification fee: $1.50. Fee payee: District Court. Business checks accepted. Prepayment is required.

Spencer Division District Court 544 E Main St, East Brookfield, MA 01515-1701; 508-885-6305/6306; Fax: 508-885-7623. Hours: 8:30AM-4:30PM (EST). *Felony, Misdemeanor, Civil, Eviction, Small Claims.*

Civil Records: Access: Phone, mail, in person. Both court and visitors may perform in person searches. No search fee. Required to search: name, years to search. Civil cases indexed by defendant, plaintiff. Civil records on index cards or docket books. State law requires records be retained for 10 years. **Criminal Records:** Access: Phone, mail, in person. Both court and visitors may perform in person searches. No search fee. Required to search: name, years to search; also helpful-DOB. Criminal records on index cards or docket books. State law requires records be retained for 10 years. **General Information:** No juvenile, mental health records released. SASE requested. Turnaround time 1-2 weeks, strongly suggest to use a retriever when possible. Copy fee: $.50 per page. Certification fee: $1.50. Fee payee: District Court. Personal checks accepted. Prepayment is required.

Trial Court of the Commonwealth-Gardner Division 108 Matthews St, PO Box 40, Gardner, MA 01440-0040; 978-632-2373; Fax: 978-630-3902. Hours: 8:30AM-4:30PM (EST). *Felony, Misdemeanor, Civil, Eviction, Small Claims.*

Civil Records: Access: Phone, fax, mail, in person. Both court and visitors may perform in person searches. No search fee. Required to search: name, years to search, address. Civil cases indexed by defendant, plaintiff. Civil records on index cards or docket books. State law requires records be retained for 10 years. **Criminal Records:** Access: Phone, fax, mail, in person. Both court and visitors may perform in person searches. No search fee. Required to search: name, years to search; also helpful-DOB. Criminal records on index cards or docket books. State law requires records be retained for 10 years. **General Information:** No juvenile records released. Turnaround time 1-2 weeks, quicker for phone and FAX verifications. Copy fee: $.50 per page. Certification fee: $1.50. Fee payee: District Court. Personal checks accepted. Prepayment is required. Fax notes: No fee to fax results.

Uxbridge Division District Court PO Box 580, Uxbridge, MA 01569; 508-278-2454; Fax: 508-278-2929. Hours: 8:30AM-4:30PM (EST). *Felony, Misdemeanor, Civil, Eviction, Small Claims.*

Civil Records: Access: Phone, mail, in person. Only the court conducts in person searches; visitors may not. No search fee. Required to search: name, years to search. Civil cases indexed by defendant, plaintiff. Civil records on index cards or docket books. State law requires records be retained for 10 years. **Criminal Records:** Access: Phone, mail, in person. Only the court conducts in person searches; visitors may not. No search fee. Required to search: name, years to search; also helpful-DOB. Criminal records on index cards or docket books. State law requires records be retained for 10 years. **General Information:** No juvenile records released. Turnaround time 1-2 weeks. Copy fee: $.50 per page. Certification fee: $1.50. Fee payee: District

Court. Personal checks accepted. Prepayment is required.

Westborough Division District Court 175 Milk St, Westborough, MA 01581; 508-366-8266; Fax: 508-366-8268. Hours: 8AM-4:30PM (EST). *Felony, Misdemeanor, Civil, Eviction, Small Claims.*

Civil Records: Access: Mail, in person. Both court and visitors may perform in person searches. No search fee. Required to search: name, years to search. Civil cases indexed by defendant, plaintiff. Civil records go back to 1986, on books and cards. **Criminal Records:** Access: Mail, in person. Both court and visitors may perform in person searches. No search fee. Required to search: name, years to search; also helpful-DOB. Criminal records go back to 1986, on books and cards. **General Information:** No impounded, juvenile records released. SASE required. Turnaround time 5 days. Copy fee: $.50 per page. Certification fee: $1.50. Fee payee: District Court Westborough Division. Personal checks accepted. Prepayment is required.

Winchendon Division District Court PO Box 309, Winchendon, MA 01475; 978-297-0156; Fax: 978-297-0161. Hours: 8:30AM-4:30PM (EST). *Felony, Misdemeanor, Civil, Eviction, Small Claims.*

Civil Records: Access: Phone, mail, in person. Both court and visitors may perform in person searches. No search fee. Required to search: name, years to search. Civil cases indexed by defendant, plaintiff. Civil records on index cards or docket books. State law requires records be retained for 10 years. **Criminal Records:** Access: Phone, mail, in person. Both court and visitors may perform in person searches. No search fee. Required to search: name, years to search; also helpful-DOB. Criminal records on index cards or docket books. State law requires records be retained for 10 years. **General Information:** Turnaround time 1-2 weeks. Copy fee: $.50 per page. Certification fee: $1.50. Fee payee: District Court. Personal checks accepted. Prepayment is required.

Worcester Division District Court 50 Harvard St, Worcester, MA 01608; 508-757-8350; Fax: 508-797-0716. Hours: 8AM-4:30PM (EST). *Felony, Misdemeanor, Civil, Eviction, Small Claims.*

Civil Records: Access: Mail, in person. Only the court conducts in person searches; visitors may not. No search fee. Required to search: name, years to search. Civil cases indexed by defendant, plaintiff. Civil records on index cards or docket books. State law requires records be retained for 10 years. **Criminal Records:** Access: Mail, in person. Only the court conducts in person searches; visitors may not. No search fee. Required to search: name, years to search. Criminal records on computer since 1996; prior records on docket books. State law requires records be retained for 10 years. **General Information:** No sealed, expunged, adoption or sex offense records released. Turnaround time 1-2 weeks. Copy fee: $.50 per page. Certification fee: $1.50. Fee payee: District Court. Personal checks accepted. Prepayment is required.

Probate & Family Court 2 Main St, Worcester, MA 01608; 508-770-0825 X217; Fax: 508-752-6138. Hours: 8AM-4:30PM (EST). *Probate.*

02167-02167 CHESTNUT HILL	02345-02345 MANOMET	02565-02565 SILVER BEACH	02668-02668 WEST BARNSTABLE
02168-02168 WABAN	02346-02346 MIDDLEBORO	02568-02568 VINEYARD HAVEN	02669-02669 WEST CHATHAM
02169-02171 QUINCY	02347-02347 LAKEVILLE	02571-02571 WAREHAM	02670-02670 WEST DENNIS
02172-02172 WATERTOWN	02348-02349 MIDDLEBORO	02573-02573 VINEYARD HAVEN	02671-02671 WEST HARWICH
02173-02173 LEXINGTON	02350-02350 MONPONSETT	02574-02574 WEST FALMOUTH	02672-02672 WEST HYANNISPORT
02174-02174 ARLINGTON	02351-02351 ABINGTON	02575-02575 WEST TISBURY	02673-02673 WEST YARMOUTH
02175-02175 ARLINGTON HEIGHTS	02355-02355 NORTH CARVER	02576-02576 WEST WAREHAM	02675-02675 YARMOUTH PORT
02176-02177 MELROSE	02356-02357 NORTH EASTON	02584-02584 NANTUCKET	02702-02702 ASSONET
02178-02178 BELMONT	02358-02358 NORTH PEMBROKE	02601-02601 HYANNIS	02703-02703 ATTLEBORO
02179-02179 WAVERLEY	02359-02359 PEMBROKE	02630-02630 BARNSTABLE	02712-02712 CHARTLEY
02180-02180 STONEHAM	02360-02363 PLYMOUTH	02631-02631 BREWSTER	02713-02713 CUTTYHUNK
02181-02181 WELLESLEY	02364-02364 KINGSTON	02632-02632 CENTERVILLE	02714-02714 DARTMOUTH
02184-02185 BRAINTREE	02366-02366 SOUTH CARVER	02633-02633 CHATHAM	02715-02715 DIGHTON
02186-02186 MILTON	02367-02367 PLYMPTON	02634-02634 CENTERVILLE	02717-02717 EAST FREETOWN
02187-02187 MILTON VILLAGE	02368-02368 RANDOLPH	02635-02635 COTUIT	02718-02718 EAST TAUNTON
02188-02191 WEYMOUTH	02370-02370 ROCKLAND	02636-02636 CENTERVILLE	02719-02719 FAIRHAVEN
02192-02192 NEEDHAM	02375-02375 SOUTH EASTON	02637-02637 CUMMAQUID	02720-02724 FALL RIVER
02193-02193 WESTON	02379-02379 WEST BRIDGEWATER	02638-02638 DENNIS	02725-02726 SOMERSET
02194-02194 NEEDHAM	02381-02381 WHITE HORSE BEACH	02639-02639 DENNIS PORT	02738-02738 MARION
02195-02195 NEWTON	02382-02382 WHITMAN	02641-02641 EAST DENNIS	02739-02739 MATTAPOISETT
02196-02222 BOSTON	02401-02499 BROCKTON	02642-02642 EASTHAM	02740-02742 NEW BEDFORD
02238-02239 CAMBRIDGE	02532-02532 BUZZARDS BAY	02643-02643 EAST ORLEANS	02743-02743 ACUSHNET
02241-02241 BOSTON	02534-02534 CATAUMET	02644-02644 FORESTDALE	02744-02746 NEW BEDFORD
02254-02254 WALTHAM	02535-02535 CHILMARK	02645-02645 HARWICH	02747-02747 NORTH DARTMOUTH
02258-02258 NEWTON	02536-02536 EAST FALMOUTH	02646-02646 HARWICH PORT	02748-02748 SOUTH DARTMOUTH
02266-02266 BOSTON	02537-02537 EAST SANDWICH	02647-02647 HYANNIS PORT	02754-02754 NORTH DIGHTON
02269-02269 QUINCY	02538-02538 EAST WAREHAM	02648-02648 MARSTONS MILLS	02760-02761 NORTH ATTLEBORO
02272-02277 WATERTOWN	02539-02539 EDGARTOWN	02649-02649 MASHPEE	02762-02762 PLAINVILLE
02293-02297 BOSTON	02540-02541 FALMOUTH	02650-02650 NORTH CHATHAM	02763-02763 ATTLEBORO FALLS
02322-02322 AVON	02542-02542 BUZZARDS BAY	02651-02651 NORTH EASTHAM	02764-02764 NORTH DIGHTON
02324-02325 BRIDGEWATER	02543-02543 WOODS HOLE	02652-02652 NORTH TRURO	02766-02766 NORTON
02327-02327 BRYANTVILLE	02552-02552 MENEMSHA	02653-02653 ORLEANS	02767-02767 RAYNHAM
02330-02330 CARVER	02553-02553 MONUMENT BEACH	02655-02655 OSTERVILLE	02768-02768 RAYNHAM CENTER
02331-02332 DUXBURY	02554-02554 NANTUCKET	02657-02657 PROVINCETOWN	02769-02769 REHOBOTH
02333-02333 EAST BRIDGEWATER	02556-02556 NORTH FALMOUTH	02659-02659 SOUTH CHATHAM	02770-02770 ROCHESTER
02334-02334 EASTON	02557-02557 OAK BLUFFS	02660-02660 SOUTH DENNIS	02771-02771 SEEKONK
02337-02337 ELMWOOD	02558-02558 ONSET	02661-02661 SOUTH HARWICH	02777-02777 SWANSEA
02338-02338 HALIFAX	02559-02559 POCASSET	02662-02662 SOUTH ORLEANS	02779-02779 BERKLEY
02339-02339 HANOVER	02561-02561 SAGAMORE	02663-02663 SOUTH WELLFLEET	02780-02780 TAUNTON
02341-02341 HANSON	02562-02562 SAGAMORE BEACH	02664-02664 SOUTH YARMOUTH	02790-02790 WESTPORT
02343-02343 HOLBROOK	02563-02563 SANDWICH	02666-02666 TRURO	02791-02791 WESTPORT POINT
02344-02344 MIDDLEBORO	02564-02564 SIASCONSET	02667-02667 WELLFLEET	05501-05544 ANDOVER

Michigan

General Help Numbers:

Governor's Office
PO Box 30013   517-373-3400
Lansing, MI 48909   Fax 517-335-6863
www.migov.state.mi.us   8AM-5PM

Attorney General's Office
PO Box 30212   517-373-1110
Lansing, MI 48909   Fax 517-373-3042
www.ag.state.mi.us   8AM-5PM

State Court Administrator
309 N Washington Sq   517-373-2222
Lansing, MI 48909   Fax 517-373-2112
www.supremecourt.state.mi.us   8:30AM-5PM

State Archives
Michigan Historical Center   517-373-1408
Michigan Library & Historical Ctr   Fax 517-241-1658
717 W Allegan   10AM-4PM
Lansing, MI 48918-1837
www.sos.state.mi.us/history/archive/index.html

State Specifics:

Capital: Lansing
Ingham County

Time Zone: EST*
* Four north-western Michigan counties are CST:
They are: Dickinson, Gogebic, Iron, Menominee.

Number of Counties: 83

Population: 9,863,775

Web Site: www.state.mi.us

State Agencies

Criminal Records

Michigan State Police, Ident. Section, Criminal Justice Information Center, 7150 Harris Dr, Lansing, MI 48913; 517-322-5531, 517-322-0635 (Fax), 8AM-5PM.

www.msp.state.mi.us

Note: Non-profit organizations may submit a copy of Federal Form 501C3 in lieu of payment for a name search.

Indexing & Storage: Records are available until the subject's DOB indicates 99 years or a death is reported. It takes 1-2 weeks before new records are available for inquiry. Records are indexed on inhouse computer.

Searching: Include the following in your request- full name, sex, race, date of birth. A SSN or maiden-previous name is very helpful. Records can be searched with or without a fingerprint card. The following data is not released: non-conviction information.

Access by: mail, fax.

Fee & Payment: The search fee is $5.00 per name without a fingerprint card, $15.00 with a fingerprint card, and $39.00 with state and FBI fingerprint cards. Fee payee: State of Michigan. Prepayment required. Payment required in advance unless a prepaid account has been arranged with Division cashier. Personal checks accepted. No credit cards accepted.

Mail search: Turnaround time: 2-4 weeks.

Fax search: The state will permit ongoing requesters to set up a pre-paid account and submit requests by fax.

Corporation Records
Limited Liability Company Records
Limited Partnership Records
Assumed Name

Department of Consumer & Industrial Svcs, Corporation & Land ve. Bureau, PO Box 30044, Lansing, MI 48909-7554 (Courier: 6546 Mercantile Way, Lansing, MI 48910); 517-241-6470, 517-334-8329 (Fax), 8AM-5PM.

www.cis.state.mi.us/corp

Note: Forms, policies, and procedures may be viewed at their web site. The fax listed above is for record requests. the fax for copies or certificates is 517-334-7145.

Indexing & Storage: Records are available from the first corporation in Michigan. Older records were indexed on cards. The index to records for actiive entities are maintained on computer. It takes 24 hours or less before new records are available for inquiry.

Searching: Include the following in your request-full name of business, corporation file number. The directors are only listed on the annual report.

Access by: mail, phone, fax, in person.

Fee & Payment: There is no search fee. The minimum charge for copies is $6.00 per record and $1.00 per page if over 6 pages. The minimum charge for a certificate is $10.00. Fee payee: State of Michigan. Credit cards are accepted for in person requests only. Personal checks accepted. Credit cards accepted: Mastercard, Visa.

Mail search: Turnaround time: 5-7 days. There is no fee unless copies or certificates are needed, then there is a minimum $6.00 fee.No self addressed stamped envelope is required. Copies cost $1.00 per page.

Phone search: You can order copies or certificates.

Fax search: Only current database records are available by fax.

In person search: The agency has a public access terminal for viewing records.

Other access: The database is for sale on tape or microfiche.

Trademarks/Servicemarks

Department of Consumer & Industry Srvs, Securities Examination Division, PO Box 30054, Lansing, MI 48909-7554 (Courier: 6546 Mercantile Way, Lansing, MI 48910); 517-241-6000, 8AM-5PM.

www.cis.state.mi.us/corp

Note: This agency will not do record checks (unless you are applying for a mark). They suggest several outside firms to come in person.

Indexing & Storage: Records are available for current records. The index is available since 1990.

Access by: phone, in person. No searching by mail.

Phone search: No fee for telephone request. Limited - words only, no designs.

In person search: No fee for request. There is a public access terminal. They strongly urge to call in first and schedule usage time.

Uniform Commercial Code
Federal Tax Liens
State Tax Liens

UCC Section, Department of State, PO Box 30197, Lansing, MI 48909-7697 (Courier: 7064 Crowner Dr, Dimondale, MI 48821); 517-322-1144, 517-322-5434 (Fax), 8AM-5PM.

Indexing & Storage: Records are available from 1964. Records are computerized since 1990.

Searching: Use search request form UCC-11. The search includes federal and state tax liens on businesses. Federal and state tax liens on individuals are filed at the county level. Include the following in your request-debtor name, Social Security or federal employer number.

Access by: mail, phone, fax, in person.

Fee & Payment: The search fee is $3.00; however there is an additional $1.00 fee if the Social Security Number or federal ID is not provided. Also, there is an additional $3.00 fee if a non-standard form is used for the request. The copy fee is $1.00. Fee payee: State of Michigan. Prepayment required. Personal checks accepted. No credit cards accepted.

Mail search: Turnaround time: 1 week. A self addressed stamped envelope is requested.

Phone search: Phone searching is available on a prepaid account basis, results are returned by mail.

Fax search: See expedited services.

In person search: Must be scheduled in advance and subject to availability of equipment.

Expedited service: Expedited service is available for fax searches. Expedited searches are provided on a prepaid account basis at $25.00 + $3.00 per debtor name. If request is received by 11 AM, search is mailed that same day.

Sales Tax Registrations

Records not maintained by a state level agency.

Note: The agency has recently determined it will not release information to the public nor verify or confirm data.

Birth Certificates

Department of Community Health, Vital Records Requests, PO Box 30721, Lansing, MI 48909 (Courier: 3423 Martin Luther King, Jr Blvd, Lansing, MI 48909); 517-335-8656 (Instructions), 517-335-8666 (Request Unit), 517-321-5884 (Fax), 8AM-5PM.

www.mdch.state.mi.us/Pha/Osr/vitframe.htm

Indexing & Storage: Records are available from 1867 on. It takes 90-120 days after birth. before new records are available for inquiry. Records are indexed on microfiche, inhouse computer.

Searching: Certified copies of birth records are only issued to the individual to whom the record pertains, the parent(s) named on the record, an heir, legal guardian or legal rep. of an eligible person, or through court order Records over 110 yrs old are open Include the following in your request-full name, names of parents, mother's maiden name, date of birth, place of birth, relationship to person of record. The signature and relationship to the subject are required items on the

request form. The following data is not released: sealed records.

Access by: mail, phone, in person, online.

Fee & Payment: The fee is $13.00 per name for every 3 years searched. The fee is $4.00 for each additional year. Additional copies of the same record are $4.00 each. Use of a credit card is additional $5.00. Fee payee: State of Michigan. Prepayment required. Personal checks accepted. Credit cards accepted: Mastercard, Visa, AmEx, Discover.

Mail search: Turnaround time: 2-3 weeks. No self addressed stamped envelope is required.

Phone search: You can use a credit card when ordering by phone.

In person search: Turnaround time up to 3 hours. Counter closes at 3:30 PM.

Online search: Records may be ordered from the web site. Step-by-step instructions given, use of credit card required.

Expedited service: Expedited service is available for mail, phone, and online searches. The total fee is $32.50 (includes express delivery) and payment must be on credit card. Turnaround is next day if ordered by noon.

Death Records

Department of Health, Vital Records Requests, PO Box 30721, Lansing, MI 48909 (Courier: 3423 Martin Luther King, Jr Blvd, Lansing, MI 48909); 517-335-8656 (Instructions), 517-335-8666 (Request Unit), 517-321-5884 (Fax), 8AM-5PM.

www.mdch.state.mi.us/Pha/Osr/vitrame.htm

Indexing & Storage: Records are available from 1867-present. New records are available for inquiry immediately. Records are indexed on microfiche, inhouse computer.

Searching: Records are open to the public. Include the following in your request-full name, date of death, place of death, relationship to person of record. The following data is not released: sealed records.

Access by: mail, phone, in person, online.

Fee & Payment: The fee for a certified copy is $13.00 for a 3 year search, add $4.00 for each additional year searched. Add $4.00 per name per copy for additional copies. Use of credit card is additional $5.00 fee. Fee payee: State of Michigan. Prepayment required. Personal checks, money orders accepted. Credit cards accepted: Mastercard, Visa, AmEx, Discover.

Mail search: Turnaround time: 2-3 weeks. No self addressed stamped envelope is required.

Phone search: Credit cards are accepted over the phone for an additional fee.

In person search: Turnaround time 2-3 hours. Counter closes at 3:30 PM.

Online search: Records may be ordered from the web. Use of a credit card is required. Records are returned by mail or express delivery.

Expedited service: Expedited service is available for mail, phone and online searches. The total fee is $32.50 (includes express delivery) and a credit card is required. Turnaround time is 24 hours if order in by noon.

Marriage Certificates

Department of Health, Vital Records Requests, PO Box 30721, Lansing, MI 48909 (Courier: 3423 Martin Luther King, Jr Blvd, Lansing, MI 48909); 517-335-8656 (Instructions), 517-335-8666 (Requests Unit), 517-321-5884 (Fax), 8AM-5PM.

www.mdch.state.mi.us/pha/osr/vitframe.htm

Indexing & Storage: Records are available from 1867-present. New records are available for inquiry immediately. Records are indexed on microfiche, inhouse computer.

Searching: Records are open to the public. Include the following in your request-names of husband and wife, date of marriage, place or county of marriage, relationship to person of record. The following data is not released: sealed records.

Access by: mail, phone, in person, online.

Fee & Payment: The fee for a certified copy is $13.00 which includes 3 years searched. Each additional year searched is another $4.00. Additional copies of the same records are $4.00 each. use of credit card is an additional $5.00 fee. Fee payee: State of Michigan. Prepayment required. Personal checks accepted. Credit cards accepted: Mastercard, Visa, AmEx, Discover.

Mail search: Turnaround time: 2-3 weeks. No self addressed stamped envelope is required.

Phone search: You can order by credit card over the phone.

In person search: Turnaround time up to 3 hours minutes. Counter closes at 3:30 PM.

Online search: Records can be ordered from the web site, credit card is required.

Expedited service: Expedited service is available for mail and phone searches. The total fee is $32.50 (includes express delivery) and use of a credit card is required. Turnaround time is 24 hours if ordered by noon.

Divorce Records

Department of Health, Vital Records Requests, PO Box 30721, Lansing, MI 48909 (Courier: 3423 Martin Luther King, Jr Blvd, Lansing, MI 48909); 517-335-8656 (Instructions), 517-335-8666 (Requests Unit), 517-321-5884 (Fax), 8AM-5PM.

www.mdch.state.mi.us/pha/osr/vitframe.htm

Indexing & Storage: Records are available from 1897-present. New records are available for inquiry immediately. Records are indexed on microfiche, inhouse computer.

Searching: Records are open to the public. Include the following in your request-names of husband and wife, date of divorce, year divorce case began, case number (if known), relationship to person of record.

Access by: mail, phone, in person.

Fee & Payment: The fee for a certified copy is $13.00, which includes 3 years searched. Each additional year is another $4.00. Extra copies of the same record are $4.00 each. Use of a credit card is an additional $5.00. Fee payee: State of Michigan. Prepayment required. Personal checks accepted. Credit cards accepted: Mastercard, Visa, AmEx, Discover.

Mail search: Turnaround time: 2-3 weeks. No self addressed stamped envelope is required.

Phone search: You can order over the phone by credit card.

In person search: Turnaround time 45 minutes. Counter closes at 3:30 PM.

Expedited service: Expedited service is available for mail, phone and fax searches. The total fee is $32.50 (includes express delivery), use of credit card is required. Turnaround time is overnight if ordered by noon.

Workers' Compensation Records

Department of Consumer & Industry Services, Bureau of Workers Disability Compensation, 7150 Harris Dr, Lansing, MI 48909; 517-322-1884, 888-396-5041, 517-322-1808 (Fax), 8AM-5PM.

www.cis.state.mi.us/wkrcomp/bwdc

Note: In person requests are discouraged due to confidentiality of records and records may not be on site. Injured employee may review their own records, but should call first and make arrangements.

Indexing & Storage: Records are available from 1981 on computer and from 1976-1981 records on microfilm. You can request by fax, but results are mailed.

Searching: Request must be in writing and cannot be for pre-employment screening. Only litigated cases are released. Include the following in your request-claimant name, Social Security Number.

Access by: mail.

Fee & Payment: Fee is $.25 per page plus postage and research labor cost if over 30 pages. Fee payee: Consumer & Industry Services, Bureau of Workers Dist. Comp. Personal checks accepted. No credit cards accepted.

Mail search: Turnaround time: 1-2 weeks. Turnaround time may be longer if records must be searched at archives.No self addressed stamped envelope is required.

Driver Records

Department of State Police, Record Look-up Unit, 7064 Crowner Dr, Lansing, MI 48918; 517-322-1624, 517-322-1181 (Fax), 8AM-4:45PM.

www.sos.state.mi.us/dv

Note: Copies of court abstracts of convictions may be purchased at the same address for a fee of $6.55 per copy. Copies of tickets must be obtained from the courts involved.

Indexing & Storage: Records are available for 7 years from conviction date; unless there is an alcohol or controlled substance conviction which will remain on record for 10 years. Accidents are reported on the record only if the driver is cited. It takes 14 days before new records are available for inquiry.

Searching: Casual requesters can only obtain records without personal information.

Access by: mail, phone, fax, in person, online.

Fee & Payment: The fee for obtaining a record is $6.55 per search. If certification is needed, there is an additional $1.00 fee. Fee payee: State of Michigan. The fee may accompany the request for mail-in, or a bill can be sent with the records. There is a full charge for a "no record found." Credit cards are accepted for fax and phone requests only. Personal checks accepted. Credit cards accepted: Mastercard, Visa.

Mail search: Turnaround time: 10 working days. No self addressed stamped envelope is required.

Phone search: Phone requesting is available for pre-approved accounts and government agencies or with a credit card.

Fax search: Established accounts can order by fax, results are returned by mail.

In person search: Search costs $6.55 per record. Turnaround time is up to 14 days (they mail the record back) unless you are the actual driver, then the record is immediately available.

Online search: Online ordering is available on an interactive basis. The system is open 7 days a week. Ordering is by DL or name and DOB. An account must be established and billing is monthly. Access is also available from the Internet. Fee is $6.55 per record.

Other access: Magnetic tape inquiry is available. Also, the state offers the license file for bulk purchase. Customized runs are $64 per thousand records; the complete database can be purchased for $16 per thousand. A $10,000 surety bond is required.

Vehicle Ownership
Vehicle Identification
Boat & Vessel Ownership
Boat & Vessel Registration

Department of State Police, Record Look-up Unit, 7064 Crowner Dr, Lansing, MI 48918; 517-322-1624, 517-322-1181 (Fax), 8AM-4:45PM.

www.sos.state.mi.us/dv

Indexing & Storage: Records are available for 10 years to present for vehicle information and 3 years to present for registration information. Vessel titles are on computer since 1974. All motorized boats must be registered, if 20 ft or over they must also be titled. It takes 14 days before new records are available for inquiry.

Searching: Requests for vehicle and ownership records must be submitted in writing with a statement of intended use. Large volume users or fax requesters must be pre-approved. There is no opt out provision.

Access by: mail, phone, fax, in person, online.

Fee & Payment: The fee is $6.55 per transaction. Normal searching requires the plate or VIN number. Records to be accessed include mobile homes and boats. Copy fee is $1.00 per record. Fee payee: State of Michigan. The fee may accompany the request for mail-in, or a bill can be sent with the records. Requests made by fax will be sent a bill with the records. There is a full charge for a "no record found." Personal checks accepted. Credit cards accepted: Mastercard, Visa.

Mail search: Turnaround time: 10 days. A self addressed stamped envelope is requested.

Phone search: Call-in requests are for established, approved accounts only. Records may be mailed or faxed back. They will usually also accept a credit card.

Fax search: Established accounts may order by fax and receive results by fax.

In person search: You can make your request in person, but they will mail back the records in 4 or 5 days. Requests must be in writing.

Online search: Online searching is single inquiry and requires a VIN or plate number. A $25,000 surety bond is required. Direct dialup or Internet access is offered. For more information, call Carol Lycos at 517-322-1591.

Other access: Michigan offers bulk retrieval from the VIN and plate database. A written request letter, stating purpose, must be approved. A surety bond is required upon approval. Please call 517-241-2781.

Accident Reports

Department of State Police, Central Justice Information Center, 7150 Harris Dr, Lansing, MI 48913; 517-322-5509, 517-323-5350 (Fax), 8AM-5PM.

www.msp.state.mi.us

Indexing & Storage: Records are available from 1983-present for state police records. UD10's for all law enforcement agencies in Michigan are available for the current year plus 2 years back, first page only. It takes 3-4 weeks before new records are available for inquiry.

Searching: Include the following in your request- full name, date of accident, location of accident.

Access by: mail, in person.

Fee & Payment: Fee is $5.00 per report. Fee payee: State of Michigan. Prepayment required. Personal checks accepted. No credit cards accepted.

Mail search: Turnaround time: 10 days. A self addressed stamped envelope is requested.

In person search: You may request information in person, but it is discouraged.

Legislation-Current/Pending
Legislation-Passed

Michigan Legislature Document Room, State Capitol, PO Box 30036, Lansing, MI 48909 (Courier: North Capitol Annex, Lansing, MI 48909); 517-373-0169, 8:30AM-5PM.

www.michiganlegislature.org

Note: Older passed bills found at the State Law Library, 517-373-0630.

Indexing & Storage: Records are available from 1997 on computer.

Searching: Search by bill numner, sponser or subject.

Access by: mail, phone, in person, online.

Fee & Payment: There are no fees involved. No credit cards accepted.

Mail search: Turnaround time: 1 day. No self addressed stamped envelope is required.

Phone search: Only current and past session information is available.

In person search: Searching is available in person.

Online search: Access is available from their Internet site. Adobe Acrobat Reader is required. Information available includes status of bills, bill text, joint resolution text, journals, calendars, session and committee schedules, and MI complied laws.

Voter Registration

Records not maintained by a state level agency.

Note: The city or township keeps all records. In general, the records are open to the public.

GED Certificates

MI Department of Career Development, Adult Education - GED Testing, PO Box 30008, Lansing, MI 48909 (Courier: 608 W Allegan, Lansing, MI 48933); 517-373-1692, 517-335-3630 (Fax), 8AM-5PM.

Searching: To search, include the SSN, DOB and date and location of test. For a copy of a transcript, also include a signed release.

Access by: mail, phone, fax, in person.

Fee & Payment: There are no fees.

Mail search: Turnaround time: 1 week. No self addressed stamped envelope is required.

Phone search: You request a verification by leaving a message and the agency will call back with the information.

Fax search: Same criteria as mail searching.

In person search: The building is also known as the John Hannah Building.

Hunting License Information
Fishing License Information
Access to Records is Restricted

Dept of Natural Resources, License Control, PO Box 30181, Lansing, MI 48909 (Courier: 530 W Allegan St, Lansing, MI 48933); 517-373-1204, 517-373-0784 (Fax), 8AM-5PM.

Note: Hunting and fishing license information is no longer released. All FOIA requests are now being denied because it is personal information. They will release name, DOB, type of license and date of purchase.

Licenses Searchable Online

Architect #08	www.cis.state.mi.us:8020/public/lic_reg$.startup
Athletic Control #08	www.cis.state.mi.us:8020/public/lic_reg$.startup
Aviation Medical Examiners #24	www.mdot.state.mi.us/aero/resources/ame.htm
Barber #08	www.cis.state.mi.us:8020/public/lic_reg$.startup
Carnival-Amusement #08	www.cis.state.mi.us:8020/public/lic_reg$.startup
Cemetery #08	www.cis.state.mi.us:8020/public/lic_reg$.startup
Child Caring Institution #26	www.cis.state.mi.us/brs/cwl/cwllist.htm
Child Welfare Agency (Child Placing Agency) #26	www.cis.state.mi.us/brs/cwl/cwllist.htm
Chiropractor #15	www.cis.state.mi.us./bhser
Collection Manager #08	www.cis.state.mi.us:8020/public/lic_reg$.startup
Community Planner-Professional #08	www.cis.state.mi.us:8020/public/lic_reg$.startup
Cosmetologist #08	www.cis.state.mi.us:8020/public/lic_reg$.startup
Counselor #15	www.cis.state.mi.us./bhser
Dentist #15	www.cis.state.mi.us./bhser
Employment Agency #08	www.cis.state.mi.us:8020/public/lic_reg$.startup
Forensic Polygraph Examiner #08	www.cis.state.mi.us:8020/public/lic_reg$.startup
Hearing Aid Dealer #08	www.cis.state.mi.us:8020/public/lic_reg$.startup
Marriage & Family Therapist #15	www.cis.state.mi.us./bhser
Medical Doctor #15	www.cis.state.mi.us./bhser
Mortuary Science #08	www.cis.state.mi.us:8020/public/lic_reg$.startup
Notary Public #22	www.sos.state.mi.us/greatse/notaries/notaries.html
Nurse #15	www.cis.state.mi.us./bhser
Nursing Home Administrator #08	www.cis.state.mi.us:8020/public/lic_reg$.startup
Occupational Therapist #15	www.cis.state.mi.us./bhser
Optometrist #15	www.cis.state.mi.us./bhser
Osteopathic Physician #15	www.cis.state.mi.us./bhser
Pharmacist #15	www.cis.state.mi.us./bhser
Physical Therapist #15	www.cis.state.mi.us./bhser
Physician Assistant #15	www.cis.state.mi.us./bhser
Pilot Examiner #24	www.mdot.state.mi.us/aero/resources/dpe.htm
Podiatric Medicine & Surgery #15	www.cis.state.mi.us./bhser
Psychologist #15	www.cis.state.mi.us./bhser
Public Accountant-CPA #08	www.cis.state.mi.us:8020/public/lic_reg$.startup
Real Estate #08	www.cis.state.mi.us:8020/public/lic_reg$.startup
Sanitarian #15	www.cis.state.mi.us./bhser
Social Worker #08	www.cis.state.mi.us:8020/public/lic_reg$.startup
Veterinarian #15	www.cis.state.mi.us./bhser

Licensing Quick Finder

Adoption Service #13	517-373-8383
Adult Foster Care #13	517-373-8580
Aeronautics #24	517-335-9719
Alarm System Service #23	517-336-3440
Ambulance Attendant #10	517-241-3018
Architect #08	517-241-9253
Asbestos Accreditation-Individual #11	517-322-1320
Asbestos Licensing #11	517-322-1320
Assessor #25	517-373-8320
Athletic Control #08	517-241-9246
Attorney #27	517-372-9030
Automobile dealers/mechanics/repair facilities #28	517-373-9082
Aviation Medical Examiners #24	517-335-9943
Bank & Trust #14	517-373-6950
Barber #08	517-241-9261
Boiler Repairer #07	517-241-9334
Boilermaker (Boiler Installer) #07	517-241-9334
Carnival-Amusement #08	517-241-9246
Cemetery #08	517-241-9244
Charitable Gaming (Supplier) #01	517-335-5781
Child Caring Institution #26	517-373-8383
Child Day Care #13	517-373-8300
Child Welfare Agency (Child Placing Agency) #26	517-373-8383
Children's Camp/Adult Camp #26	517-373-0697

Chiropractor #15	900-555-8374
Collection Manager #08	517-241-9258
Community Planner-Professional #08	517-241-9253
Corrections Officer #18	517-335-1426
Cosmetologist #08	517-373-9234
Counselor #15	900-555-8374
Credit Union #14	517-373-6930
Dentist #15	900-555-8374
Electrician (various types) #07	517-241-9320
Elevator Service (types) #07	517-241-9337
Employment Agency #08	517-241-9246
EMT Instructor #10	517-241-3018
EMT, EMT Advanced, EMT Specialist #10	517-241-3018
Engineer #09	517-241-9253
Food Licensing #02	517-373-1060
Forensic Polygraph Examiner #08	517-241-9234
Foster Care Program #21	517-335-6108
Foster Family Home #21	517-335-6108
Guidance Counselor #19	517-373-6505
Health Facilities/Laboratory #13	517-241-2648
Hearing Aid Dealer #08	517-241-9234
Insurance Adjuster #05	517-373-0234
Insurance Agent/Counselor/Solicitor/Administrator #05	517-373-0234
Investment Adviser #12	517-334-6215

Liquor Distributor/Wholesale/Manufacturer #06	517-322-1420
Liquor Licensing director #06	517-322-1408
Lottery Retailer #01	517-335-5619
Manufactured Home Communities #16	517-241-6300
Manufactured Home Installer/Services #16	517-241-6300
Manufactured Home Retailers #16	517-241-6300
Marriage & Family Therapist #15	900-555-8374
Mechanical Construction #07	517-241-9325
Medical Doctor #15	900-555-8374
Medical First Responder #10	517-241-3018
Millionaire Party-Vegas Night #01	517-335-5781
Mortuary Science #08	517-241-9252
Notary Public #22	517-373-2531
Nurse #15	900-555-8374
Nursing Home Administrator #08	517-335-4403
Occupational Therapist #15	900-555-8374
Optometrist #15	900-555-8374
Osteopathic Physician #15	900-555-8374
Paramedic #10	517-241-3018
Pesticide Licensing (types) #02	517-373-1087
Pharmacist #15	900-555-8374
Physical Therapist #15	900-555-8374
Physician Assistant #15	900-555-8374
Pilot Examiner #24	517-335-9943

Plumber #07 517-241-9304	Racing #04 734-462-2400	Social Worker #15 900-555-8374
Podiatric Medicine & Surgery #15 900-555-8374	Raffle #01 517-335-5781	Special Bingo #01 517-335-5781
Prepaid Funeral Contract Salesperson #09	Railroad Commissions #23 517-336-3440	Surveyor-Professional #09 517-241-9253
....517-241-9258	Real Estate #08 517-241-9288	Teacher #19 517-373-6505
Private Detective #23 517-336-3440	Real Estate Broker/Salesperson #09 517-241-9288	Veterinarian #15 900-555-8374
Private Security #23 517-336-3440	Sanitarian #15 900-555-8374	Weekly Bingo #01 517-335-5781
Private Security Arrest Authority #23 517-336-3440	School Librarian #19 517-373-6505	Well Contractor #20 517-335-8299
Psychologist #15 900-555-8374	Securities Agent #17 517-334-6211	
Public Accountant-CPA #08 517-373-0682	Securities Broker/Dealer #12 517-334-6215	
Pump Installer #20 517-335-8299	Social Worker #08 517-241-9245	

Licensing Agency Information

01 Bureau of State Lottery, PO Box 33023 (101 E Hillsdale), Lansing, MI 48909; 517-335-5781, Fax: 517-373-6863.

www.state.mi.us

02 Department of Agriculture, Food & Dairy Division, PO Box 30017 (Ottawa Bldg, 4th Fl), Lansing, MI 48909; 517-373-1060, Fax: 517-373-3333.

www.state.mi.us

04 Department of Agriculture, Office of Racing Commissioner, 37650 Professional Center Dr, Livonia, MI 48154-1100; 734-462-2400, Fax: 734-462-2429.

www.state.mi.us

05 Department of Commerce, Insurance Bureau, PO Box 23127 (PO Box 23127), Lansing, MI 48909-3127; 517-373-0234, Fax: 517-335-4978.

www.cis.state.mi.us/ins

06 Department of Consumer & Industry Services, Liquor Control Commission, PO Box 30005 (PO Box 30005, 7150 Harris Dr), Lansing, MI 48909-7505; 517-322-1345, Fax: 517-322-6137.

www.cis.state.mi.us/lcc

07 Department of Consumer & Industry Services, Bureau of Construction Codes, PO Box 30254 (7150 Harris Dr), Lansing, MI 48909; 517-241-9302, Fax: 517-241-9308.

www.state.mi.us

08 Department of Consumer & Industry Services, Commercial Services/Licensing Division, PO Box 30018 (PO Box 30018), Lansing, MI 48909; 517-241-9288, Fax: 517-241-9280.

www.cis.state.mi.us

09 Department of Consumer & Industry Services, Commercial Services/Licensing Division, PO Box 30018 (Ottawa Bldg, 1st Fl), Lansing, MI 48909; 517-373-0580, Fax: 517-373-2795.

10 Department of Consumer & Industry Services, Division of Emergency Medical Services, PO Box 30664 (525 W Ottawa), Lansing, MI 48909; 517-241-3018, Fax: 517-241-2895.

11 Department of Consumer & Industry Services, Occupational Health Division, PO Box 30671 (PO Box 30671), Lansing, MI 48909-8171; 517-322-1320, Fax: 517-322-1713.

www.cis.state.mi.us/bsr/divisions/occ/asbestos.htm

12 Department of Consumer & Industry Services, Securities Division, PO Box 30222 (PO Box 30222), Lansing, MI 48909; 517-334-6200, Fax: 517-334-7813.

www.cis.state.mi.us/corp/sec-info.htm

13 Department of Consumer & Industry Services, Family Independence Agency, PO Box 30037 (PO Box 30037), Lansing, MI 48909; 517-373-1820, Fax: 517-333-6121.

www.state.mi.us

14 Department of Consumer & Industry Services, Office of Financial & Insurance Services, PO Box 30224 (PO Box 30224), Lansing, MI 48909; 517-373-3460, Fax: 517-335-0908.

www.commerce.state.mi.us/ofis/home.htm

15 Department of Consumer & Industry Services, Health Services Licensing Division, PO Box 30670 (611 W Ottawa, 1st Fl), Lansing, MI 48909-8170; 517-335-0918, Fax: 517-373-2179.

www.cis.state.mi.us./bhser

Direct URL to search licenses: www.cis.state.mi.us./bhser You can search online using name or license number.

16 Department of Consumer & Industry Services, Manufactured Home & Land Development Division, PO Box 30222 (PO Box 30703), Lansing, MI 48909; 517-241-6300, Fax: 517-241-6301.

www.cis.state.mi.us/corp/

18 Department of Corrections, 206 E Michigan Ave, Lansing, MI 48933; 517-335-1426.

19 Department of Education, Office of Professional Preparation & Certification, PO Box 30008 (Hannah Bldg, 3rd Fl), Lansing, MI 48909; 517-373-3310, Fax: 517-373-0542.

20 Department of Environmental Quality, Ground Water Supply Section, 3423 N Martin Luther King Jr Blvd, Lansing, MI 48909-8130; 517-335-8299, Fax: 517-335-9434.

21 Department of Consumer & Industry Services, Bureau of Resulatory Services-Div of Child Welfare Licensing/Child Foster Home Licensing, PO Box 30650 (7109 W Saginaw, 2nd Floor), Lansing, MI 48909-8150; 517-335-6108.

www.cis.state.mi.us/brs

22 Department of State, Office of the Great Seal, 717 W Allegan St, Lansing, MI 48918; 517-373-2531, Fax: 517-373-3706.

www.sos.state.mi.us/greatse/index.html

Direct URL to search licenses: www.sos.state.mi.us/greatse/notaries/notaries.html You can search online using only lists counrty clerks

23 Department of State Police, Private Security & Investigator Unit, PO Box 30635 (4000 Collins Rd), Lansing, MI 48909; 517-336-3440, Fax: 517-336-3441.

www.state.mi.us

24 Department of Transportation, Bureau of Aeronautics, 2700 E Airport Service Dr, Lansing, MI 48906; 517-335-9943, Fax: 517-321-6522.

www.mdot.state.mi.us/aero

25 Department of Treasury, Treasury Bldg, Lansing, MI 48922; 517-373-3200, Fax: 517-373-3553.

www.state.mi.us

26 Michigan Department of Consumer & Industry Services, Bureau of Regulatory Services, PO Box 30650 (7109 W Saginaw, 2nd Fl), Lansing, MI 48909-8150; 517-373-8383, Fax: 517-335-6121.

www.cis.state.mi.us/brs

Direct URL to search licenses: www.cis.state.mi.us/brs/cwl/cwllist.htm You can search online using name of facility

27 State Bar, 306 Townsend, Lansing, MI 48933; 517-372-9030, Fax: 517-482-6248.

28 Business Licensing Section, Bureau of Automobile Regulation, 208 N Capitol Ave, Lansing, MI 48918; 517-373-9082, Fax: 517-373-0964.

www.sos.state.mi.us/bar

The following list indicates the district and division name for each county in the state. If the district or division name of the bankruptcy court is different from the civil/criminal court, it appears in parentheses.

County/Court Cross Reference

County	District	Division
Alcona	Eastern	Bay City
Alger	Western	Marquette-Northern (Marquette)
Allegan	Western	Kalamazoo (Grand Rapids)
Alpena	Eastern	Bay City
Antrim	Western	Grand Rapids
Arenac	Eastern	Bay City
Baraga	Western	Marquette-Northern (Marquette)
Barry	Western	Grand Rapids
Bay	Eastern	Bay City
Benzie	Western	Grand Rapids
Berrien	Western	Kalamazoo (Grand Rapids)
Branch	Western	Lansing (Grand Rapids)
Calhoun	Western	Kalamazoo (Grand Rapids)
Cass	Western	Kalamazoo (Grand Rapids)
Charlevoix	Western	Grand Rapids
Cheboygan	Eastern	Bay City
Chippewa	Western	Marquette-Northern (Marquette)
Clare	Eastern	Bay City
Clinton	Western	Lansing (Grand Rapids)
Crawford	Eastern	Bay City
Delta	Western	Marquette-Northern (Marquette)
Dickinson	Western	Marquette-Northern (Marquette)
Eaton	Western	Lansing (Grand Rapids)
Emmet	Western	Grand Rapids
Genesee	Eastern	Flint
Gladwin	Eastern	Bay City
Gogebic	Western	Marquette-Northern (Marquette)
Grand Traverse	Western	Grand Rapids
Gratiot	Eastern	Bay City
Hillsdale	Western	Lansing (Grand Rapids)
Houghton	Western	Marquette-Northern (Marquette)
Huron	Eastern	Bay City
Ingham	Western	Lansing (Grand Rapids)
Ionia	Western	Grand Rapids
Iosco	Eastern	Bay City
Iron	Western	Marquette-Northern (Marquette)
Isabella	Eastern	Bay City
Jackson	Eastern	Ann Arbor (Detroit)
Kalamazoo	Western	Kalamazoo (Grand Rapids)
Kalkaska	Western	Grand Rapids
Kent	Western	Grand Rapids
Keweenaw	Western	Marquette-Northern (Marquette)
Lake	Western	Grand Rapids
Lapeer	Eastern	Flint
Leelanau	Western	Grand Rapids
Lenawee	Eastern	Ann Arbor (Detroit)
Livingston	Eastern	Flint
Luce	Western	Marquette-Northern (Marquette)
Mackinac	Western	Marquette-Northern (Marquette)
Macomb	Eastern	Detroit
Manistee	Western	Grand Rapids
Marquette	Western	Marquette-Northern (Marquette)
Mason	Western	Grand Rapids
Mecosta	Western	Grand Rapids
Menominee	Western	Marquette-Northern (Marquette)
Midland	Eastern	Bay City
Missaukee	Western	Grand Rapids
Monroe	Eastern	Ann Arbor (Detroit)
Montcalm	Western	Grand Rapids
Montmorency	Eastern	Bay City
Muskegon	Western	Grand Rapids
Newaygo	Western	Grand Rapids
Oakland	Eastern	Ann Arbor (Detroit)
Oceana	Western	Grand Rapids
Ogemaw	Eastern	Bay City
Ontonagon	Western	Marquette-Northern (Marquette)
Osceola	Western	Grand Rapids
Oscoda	Eastern	Bay City
Otsego	Eastern	Bay City
Ottawa	Western	Grand Rapids
Presque Isle	Eastern	Bay City
Roscommon	Eastern	Bay City
Saginaw	Eastern	Bay City
Sanilac	Eastern	Detroit
Schoolcraft	Western	Marquette-Northern (Marquette)
Shiawassee	Eastern	Flint
St. Clair	Eastern	Detroit
St. Joseph	Western	Kalamazoo (Grand Rapids)
Tuscola	Eastern	Bay City
Van Buren	Western	Kalamazoo (Grand Rapids)
Washtenaw	Eastern	Ann Arbor (Detroit)
Wayne	Eastern	Detroit
Wexford	Western	Grand Rapids

US District Court

Eastern District of Michigan

Ann Arbor Division PO Box 8199, Ann Arbor, MI 48107 (Courier Address: 200 E Liberty, Room 120, Ann Arbor, MI 48104), 734-741-2380, Fax: 734-741-2065.

www.mied.uscourts.gov

Counties: Jackson, Lenawee, Monroe, Oakland, Washtenaw, Wayne. Civil cases in these counties are assigned randomly to the Detroit, Flint or Port Huron Divisions. Case files are maintained where the case is assigned.

Indexing & Storage: Cases are indexed by defendant and plaintiff as well as by case number. New cases are available in the index immediately after filing date. A computer index is maintained. Open records are located at this court.

Fee & Payment: The fee is $15.00 per item (one party name or case number). Payment may be made by money order, cashier check, personal check. Prepayment is required. Payee: Clerk, US District Court. Certification fee: $5.00 per document. Copy fee: $.50 per page.

Phone Search: Only docket information is available by phone. An automated voice case information service (VCIS) is not available.

Mail Search: Always enclose a stamped self addressed envelope.

In Person Search: In person searching is available.

PACER: Sign-up number is 800-676-6856. Access fee is $.60 per minute. Toll-free access: 800-229-8015. Local access: 313-234-5376. Case records are available back to 1988. New records are available online after 2 days. PACER is available online at http://pacer.mied.uscourts.gov.

Bay City Division 1000 Washington Ave Rm 304, PO Box 913, Bay City, MI 48707, 517-894-8800, Fax: 517-894-8804.

www.mied.uscourts.gov

Counties: Alcona, Alpena, Arenac, Bay, Cheboygan, Clare, Crawford, Gladwin, Gratiot, Huron, Iosco, Isabella, Midland, Montmorency, Ogemaw, Oscoda, Otsego, Presque Isle, Roscommon, Saginaw, Tuscola.

Indexing & Storage: Cases are indexed by defendant and plaintiff as well as by case number. New cases are available in the index 24 hours after filing date. Both computer and card indexes are maintained. Records are also indexed on microfiche. Open records are located at this court. District wide searches are available for information from 1985 from this division.

Fee & Payment: The fee is $15.00 per item (one party name or case number). Payment may be made by money order, cashier check, personal check. Prepayment is required. Payee: Clerk, US District Court. Certification fee: $5.00 per document. Copy fee: $.50 per page.

Phone Search: Only docket information is available by phone. An automated voice case information service (VCIS) is not available.

Mail Search: Always enclose a stamped self addressed envelope.

In Person Search: In person searching is available.

PACER: Sign-up number is 800-676-6856. Access fee is $.60 per minute. Toll-free access: 800-229-8015. Local access: 313-234-5376. Case records are available back to 1988. New records are available online after 2 days. PACER is available online at http://pacer.mied.uscourts.gov.

Detroit Division 231 W Lafayette Blvd, Detroit, MI 48226, 313-234-5050, Fax: 313-234-5393.

www.mied.uscourts.gov

Counties: Macomb, St. Clair, Sanilac. Civil cases for these counties are assigned randomly among the Flint, Ann Arbor and Detroit divisions. Port Huron cases may also be assigned here. Case files are kept where the case is assigned.

Indexing & Storage: Cases are indexed by defendant and plaintiff as well as by case number. New cases are available in the index 2 days after filing date. Both computer and card indexes are maintained. A card index is maintained for older cases. Open records are located at this court. Court is in process of adding older records to the PACER system.

Fee & Payment: The fee is $15.00 per item (one party name or case number). Payment may be made by money order, cashier check, personal check. Prepayment is required for all copying. All checks should be made out for the exact amount. Payee: Clerk, US District Court. Certification fee: $5.00 per document. Copy fee: $.50 per page.

Phone Search: Only docket information on active cases will be released over the phone. An automated voice case information service (VCIS) is not available.

Fax Search: Court will call with costs.

Mail Search: A stamped self addressed envelope is not required.

In Person Search: In person searching is available.

PACER: Sign-up number is 800-676-6856. Access fee is $.60 per minute. Toll-free access: 800-229-8015. Local access: 313-234-5376. Case records are available back to 1988. New records are available online after 2 days. PACER is available online at http://pacer.mied.uscourts.gov.

Flint Division Clerk, Federal Bldg, Room 140, 600 Church St, Flint, MI 48502, 810-341-7840.

Counties: Genesee, Lapeer, Livingston, Shiawassee. This office handles all criminal cases for these counties. Civil cases are assigned randomly among the Detroit, Ann Arbor and Flint divisions.

Indexing & Storage: Cases are indexed by defendant and plaintiff as well as by case number. New cases are available in the index 2-5 days after filing date. As of July 3, 1995, cases from these counties may also be assigned to Detroit, Ann Arbor or Port Huron. Case files are maintained where the case is handled. Both computer and card indexes are maintained. Records are also indexed on microfiche. The only records indexed on index cards are old Flint cases. Open records are located at this court. District wide searches are available from this division. The date the information is available varies.

Fee & Payment: The fee is $15.00 per item (one party name or case number). Payment may be made by money order, cashier check, personal check. Prepayment is required. Payee: Clerk, US District Court. Certification fee: $5.00 per document. Copy fee: $.50 per page.

Phone Search: Only general information and a reasonable number of requests will be released over the phone. All docket information will not be released. An automated voice case information service (VCIS) is not available.

Mail Search: A stamped self addressed envelope is not required.

In Person Search: In person searching is available.

PACER: Sign-up number is 800-676-6856. Access fee is $.60 per minute. Toll-free access: 800-229-8015. Local access: 313-234-5376. Case records are available back to 1988. New records are available online after 2 days. PACER is available online at http://pacer.mied.uscourts.gov.

US Bankruptcy Court
Eastern District of Michigan

Bay City Division PO Box 911, Bay City, MI 48707 (Courier Address: 111 1st St, Bay City, MI 48708), 517-894-8840.

www.mieb.uscourts.gov

Counties: Alcona, Alpena, Arenac, Bay, Cheboygan, Clare, Crawford, Gladwin, Gratiot, Huron, Iosco, Isabella, Midland, Montmorency, Ogemaw, Oscoda, Otsego, Presque Isle, Roscommon, Saginaw, Tuscola.

Indexing & Storage: Cases are indexed by debtor as well as by case number. New cases are available in the index immediately after filing date. Both computer and card indexes are maintained. Open records are located at this court. District wide searches are available from this division for records filed on or after 10/1/92.

Fee & Payment: The fee is $15.00 per item (one party name or case number). Payment may be made by money order, cashier check, personal check. Prepayment is required. Payee: US Bankruptcy Court. Certification fee: $5.00 per document. Copy fee: $.50 per page.

Phone Search: Use VCIS to obtain docket information. An automated voice case information

service (VCIS) is available. Call VCIS at 877-422-3066 or 313-961-4940.

Mail Search: Always enclose a stamped self addressed envelope.

In Person Search: In person searching is available.

PACER: Sign-up number is 800-676-6856. Access fee is $.60 per minute. Case records are available back to October 1, 1992. New civil records are available online after 1-2 days. PACER is available on the Internet at http://pacer.mieb.uscourts.gov.

Detroit Division Clerk, 21st Floor, 21 W Fort St, Detroit, MI 48226, 313-234-0065.

www.mieb.uscourts.gov

Counties: Jackson, Lenawee, Macomb, Monroe, Oakland, Sanilac, St. Clair, Washtenaw, Wayne.

Indexing & Storage: Cases are indexed by debtor as well as by case number. New cases are available in the index immediately after filing date. A computer index is maintained. Open records are located at this court. District wide searches are available from this division for records filed on or after 10/1/92.

Fee & Payment: The fee is $15.00 per item (one party name or case number). Payment may be made by money order, cashier check, business check. Personal checks are not accepted. Prepayment is required. Payee: US Bankruptcy Court. Certification fee: $5.00 per document. Copy fee: $.50 per page.

Phone Search: Only the case number, case name, filing date, chapter, 341 date, attorney and trustee names will be released. An automated voice case information service (VCIS) is available. Call VCIS at 877-422-3066 or 313-961-4940.

Mail Search: Always enclose a stamped self addressed envelope.

In Person Search: In person searching is available.

PACER: Sign-up number is 800-676-6856. Access fee is $.60 per minute. Case records are available back to October 1, 1992. New civil records are available online after 1-2 days. PACER is available on the Internet at http://pacer.mieb.uscourts.gov.

Flint Division 226 W 2nd St, Flint, MI 48502, 810-235-4126.

www.mieb.uscourts.gov

Counties: Genesee, Lapeer, Livingston, Shiawassee.

Indexing & Storage: Cases are indexed by debtor as well as by case number. New cases are available in the index immediately after filing date. Both computer and card indexes are maintained. Open records are located at this court. District wide searches are available from this division for records filed on or after 10/1/92.

Fee & Payment: The fee is $15.00 per item (one party name or case number). Payment may be made by money order, cashier check, business check. Personal checks are not accepted. Prepayment is required. Payee: Clerk, US Bankruptcy Court. Certification fee: $5.00 per document. Copy fee: $.50 per page.

Phone Search: Only the case number, case name, filing date, chapter, 341 date, attorney and trustee names will be released. An automated voice case information service (VCIS) is available. Call VCIS at 877-422-3066 or 313-961-4940.

Mail Search: Always enclose a stamped self addressed envelope.

In Person Search: In person searching is available.

PACER: Sign-up number is 800-676-6856. Access fee is $.60 per minute. Case records are available back to October 1, 1992. New civil records are available online after 1-2 days. PACER is available on the Internet at http://pacer.mieb.uscourts.gov.

US District Court

Western District of Michigan

Grand Rapids Division PO Box 3310, Grand Rapids, MI 49501 (Courier Address: Gerald Ford Federal Building, 1110 Michigan St NW, Rm 299, Grand Rapids, MI 49503), 616-456-2693.

www.miw.uscourts.gov

Counties: Antrim, Barry, Benzie, Charlevoix, Emmet, Grand Traverse, Ionia, Kalkaska, Kent, Lake, Leelanau, Manistee, Mason, Mecosta, Missaukee, Montcalm, Muskegon, Newaygo, Oceana, Osceola, Ottawa, Wexford. The Lansing and Kalamazoo Divisions also handle cases from these counties.

Indexing & Storage: Cases are indexed by defendant and plaintiff as well as by case number. New cases are available in the index 24-48 hours after filing date. Both computer and card indexes are maintained. Open records are located at this court. Cases in these counties may also be tried in the Kalamazoo or Lansing courts.

Fee & Payment: The fee is $15.00 per item (one party name or case number). Payment may be made by money order, cashier check, personal check. Will bill businesses and law firms for search and copy fees only; otherwise, prepayment is required. Payee: Clerk, US District Court. Certification fee: $5.00 per document. Copy fee: $.50 per page.

Phone Search: Only docket information is available by phone. An automated voice case information service (VCIS) is not available.

Mail Search: Always enclose a stamped self addressed envelope.

In Person Search: In person searching is available.

PACER: Sign-up number is 800-676-6856. Access fee is $.60 per minute. Toll-free access: 800-547-6398. Local access: 616-732-2765. Case records are available back to September 1989. Records are never purged. New records are available online after 1-2 days. PACER is available online at http://pacer.miwd.uscourts.gov.

Kalamazoo Division 410 W Michigan, Kalamazoo, MI 49007, 616-349-2922.

www.miw.uscourts.gov

Counties: Allegan, Berrien, Calhoun, Cass, Kalamazoo, St. Joseph, Van Buren. Also handle cases from the counties in the Grand Rapids Division.

Indexing & Storage: Cases are indexed by defendant and plaintiff as well as by case number. New cases are available in the index 24-48 hours after filing date. Both computer and card indexes are maintained. Open records are located at this court.

Fee & Payment: The fee is $15.00 per item (one party name or case number). Payment may be made by money order, cashier check, personal check, Visa, Mastercard. Prepayment is required, except for law firms. Payee: Clerk, US District Court. Certification fee: $5.00 per document. Copy fee: $.50 per page.

Phone Search: Only docket information is available by phone. An automated voice case information service (VCIS) is not available.

Mail Search: Always enclose a stamped self addressed envelope.

In Person Search: In person searching is available.

PACER: Sign-up number is 800-676-6856. Access fee is $.60 per minute. Toll-free access: 800-547-6398. Local access: 616-732-2765. Case records are available back to September 1989. Records are never purged. New records are available online after 1-2 days. PACER is available online at http://pacer.miwd.uscourts.gov.

Lansing Division US Post Office & Courthouse Bldg, 315 W Allegan, Rm 101, Lansing, MI 48933, 517-377-1559.

www.miw.uscourts.gov

Counties: Branch, Clinton, Eaton, Hillsdale, Ingham. Also handle cases from the counties in the Grand Rapids Division.

Indexing & Storage: Cases are indexed by defendant and plaintiff as well as by case number. New cases are available in the index 24-48 hours after filing date. Both computer and card indexes are maintained. Open records are located at this court.

Fee & Payment: The fee is $15.00 per item (one party name or case number). Payment may be made by money order, cashier check, personal check, Visa, Mastercard. Prepayment is required except from businesses and law firms. Payee: Clerk, US District Court. Certification fee: $5.00 per document. Copy fee: $.50 per page.

Phone Search: Only docket information is available by phone. An automated voice case information service (VCIS) is not available.

Mail Search: Always enclose a stamped self addressed envelope.

In Person Search: In person searching is available.

PACER: Sign-up number is 800-676-6856. Access fee is $.60 per minute. Toll-free access: 800-547-6398. Local access: 616-732-2765. Case records are available back to September 1989. Records are never purged. New records are available online after 1-2 days. PACER is available online at http://pacer.miwd.uscourts.gov.

Marquette-Northern Division PO Box 909, Marquette, MI 49855 (Courier Address: 202 W Washington, Room 229, Marquette, MI 49855), 906-226-2117, Fax: 906-226-6735.

www.miw.uscourts.gov

Counties: Alger, Baraga, Chippewa, Delta, Dickinson, Gogebic, Houghton, Iron, Keweenaw, Luce, Mackinac, Marquette, Menominee, Ontonagon, Schoolcraft.

Indexing & Storage: Cases are indexed by defendant and plaintiff as well as by case number. New cases are available in the index 24-48 hours after filing date. Both computer and card indexes are maintained. Open records are located at this court.

Fee & Payment: The fee is $15.00 per item (one party name or case number). Payment may be made by money order, cashier check, personal check, Visa, Mastercard. Prepayment is required, except from businesses and law firms. Payee: Clerk, US District Court. Certification fee: $5.00 per document. Copy fee: $.50 per page.

Phone Search: Use a credit card for telephone searching. Copies will be mailed. An automated voice case information service (VCIS) is not available.

Mail Search: A stamped self addressed envelope is not required.

In Person Search: In person searching is available.

PACER: Sign-up number is 800-676-6856. Access fee is $.60 per minute. Toll-free access: 800-547-6398. Local access: 616-732-2765. Case records are available back to September 1989. Records are never purged. New records are available online after 1-2 days. PACER is available online at http://pacer.miwd.uscourts.gov.

US Bankruptcy Court

Western District of Michigan

Grand Rapids Division PO Box 3310, Grand Rapids, MI 49501 (Courier Address: 110 Michigan NW, Grand Rapids, MI 49503), 616-456-2693, Fax: 616-456-2919.

www.miw.uscourts.gov

Counties: Allegan, Antrim, Barry, Benzie, Berrien, Branch, Calhoun, Cass, Charlevoix, Clinton, Eaton, Emmet, Grand Traverse, Hillsdale, Ingham, Ionia, Kalamazoo, Kalkaska, Kent, Lake, Leelanau, Manistee, Mason, Mecosta, Missaukee, Montcalm, Muskegon, Newaygo, Oceana, Osceola, Ottawa, St. Joseph, Van Buren, Wexford.

Indexing & Storage: Cases are indexed by debtor and creditors as well as by case number. New cases are available in the index immediately after filing date. A computer index is maintained. Records are on the computer from 1990. Open records are located at this court.

Fee & Payment: The fee is $15.00 per item (one party name or case number). Payment may be made by money order, cashier check, personal check, Visa or Mastercard. Will bill for charges less than $10.00. Checks will not be accepted from debtors. Payee: US Bankruptcy Court. Certification fee: $5.00 per document. Copy fee: $.50 per page.

Phone Search: The court will only verify by phone whether a case was filed. An automated voice case information service (VCIS) is available.

Fax Search: Will accept fax requests for $15.00 in advance. Will fax back results of a search.

Mail Search: Always enclose a stamped self addressed envelope.

In Person Search: In person searching is available.

PACER: Sign-up number is 800-676-6856. Access fee is $.60 per minute. Toll-free access: 800-526-0342. Local access: 616-732-2739. Case records are available back to September 1989. Records are purged six months after case closed. New civil records are available online after 1 day. PACER is available online at http://pacer.miwb.uscourts.gov.

Marquette Division PO Box 909, Marquette, MI 49855 (Courier Address: 202 W Washington, Room 314, Marquette, MI 49855), 906-226-2117, Fax: 906-226-7388.

www.miw.uscourts.gov

Counties: Alger, Baraga, Chippewa, Delta, Dickinson, Gogebic, Houghton, Iron, Keweenaw, Luce, Mackinac, Marquette, Menominee, Ontonagon, Schoolcraft.

Indexing & Storage: Cases are indexed by debtor as well as by case number. New cases are available in the index immediately after filing date. A computer index is maintained. Records are on computer from 1990. Open records are located at this court.

Fee & Payment: The fee is $15.00 per item (one party name or case number). Payment may be made by money order, cashier check, personal check, Visa or Mastercard. Court will bill for charges totaling less than $10.00. Checks from a debtor are not accepted. Payee: US Bankruptcy Court. Certification fee: $5.00 per document. Copy fee: $.50 per page.

Phone Search: The court will only verify by phone if a case is filed. An automated voice case information service (VCIS) is available.

Fax Search: Will accept searches by fax with a credit card. Will fax copies at $.50 per page plus search fee.

Mail Search: For the fee, the following items will be sent: Case number, list of creditors, and when the first meeting of creditors is scheduled. A stamped self addressed envelope is not required.

In Person Search: In person searching is available.

PACER: Sign-up number is 800-676-6856. Access fee is $.60 per minute. Toll-free access: 800-526-0342. Local access: 616-732-2739. Case records are available back to September 1989. Records are purged six months after case closed. New civil records are available online after 1 day. PACER is available on the Internet at http://pacer.miwb.uscourts.gov.

Court	Jurisdiction	No. of Courts	How Organized
Circuit Courts*	General	83	57 Circuits
District Courts*	Limited	150	101 Districts
Municipal Courts	Municipal	5	
Probate Courts*	Probate	82	

* Profiled in this Sourcebook.

CIVIL									
Court	Tort	Contract	Real Estate	Min. Claim	Max. Claim	Small Claims	Estate	Eviction	Domestic Relations
Circuit Courts*	X	X	X	$25,000	No Max				X
District Courts*	X	X	X	$0	$25,000	$1750		X	
Municipal Courts	X	X	X	$0	$1500	$1750			
Probate Courts*							X		

CRIMINAL					
Court	Felony	Misdemeanor	DWI/DUI	Preliminary Hearing	Juvenile
Circuit Courts*	X				X
District Courts*		X	X	X	
Municipal Courts		X	X	X	
Probate Courts*					

ADMINISTRATION

State Court Administrator, 309 N. Washington Sq, PO Box 30048, Lansing, MI, 48909; 517-373-2222, Fax: 517-373-2112. www.supremecourt.state.mi.us

COURT STRUCTURE

The Circuit Court is the court of general jurisdiction. District Courts and Municipal Courts have jurisdiction over certain minor felonies and handle all preliminary hearings.

There is a Court of Claims in Lansing which is a function of the 30th Circuit Court with jurisdiction over claims against the state of Michigan.

A Recorder's Court in Detroit was abolished as of October 1, 1997.

As of January 1, 1998, the Family Division of the Circuit Court was created. Domestic relations actions and juvenile cases, including criminal and abuse/neglect, formerly adjudicated in the Probate Court, were transferred to the Family Division of the Circuit Court. Mental health and estate cases continue to be handled by the Probate Courts.

As of January 1, 1998, the limit for civil actions brought in District Court was raised from $10,000 to $25,000. The minimum for civil actions brought in Circuit Court was also raised to $25,000 at that time.

ONLINE ACCESS

There is a wide range of online computerization of the judicial system from "none" to "fairly complete," but there is no statewide network. Some Michigan courts provide public access terminals in clerk's offices, and some courts are developing off-site electronic filing and searching capability, but none offer remote online to the public.

ADDITIONAL INFORMATION

Court records are considered public except for specific categories: controlled substances, spousal abuse, Holmes youthful trainee, parental kidnapping, set aside convictions and probation, and sealed records. Courts will, however, affirm that cases exist and provide case numbers.

Some courts will not conduct criminal searches. Rather, they refer requests to the State Police.

Note that costs, search requirements, and procedures vary widely because each jurisdiction may create its own administrative orders.

Alcona County

26th Circuit Court PO Box 308, Harrisville, MI 48740; 517-724-6807; Fax: 517-724-5684 (Treasurer's office). Hours: 8:30AM-Noon, 1-4:30PM *Felony, Civil Actions Over $25,000.*

Civil Records: Access: Phone, mail, in person. Only the court conducts in person searches; visitors may not. No search fee. Required to search: name, years to search. Civil cases indexed by defendant, plaintiff. Civil records on computer since 1990, pleading headings in books since 1869. **Criminal Records:** Access: Phone, mail, in person. Only the court conducts in person searches; visitors may not. No search fee. Required to search: name, years to search, DOB. Criminal records on computer since 1990, pleading headings in books since 1869. **General Information:** No suppressed, juvenile, sex offenders, mental health, or adoption records released. SASE required. Turnaround time 1-2 days. Copy fee: $1.00 per page. Certification fee: $10.00 plus $1.00 per page after first. Fee payee: Alcona County Clerk. Personal checks accepted. Prepayment is required.

82nd District Court PO Box 385, Harrisville, MI 48740; 517-724-5313; Fax: 517-724-5397. Hours: 8:30AM-4:30PM *Misdemeanor, Civil Actions Under $25,000, Eviction, Small Claims.*

Civil Records: Access: Phone, fax, mail, in person. Both court and visitors may perform in person searches. Search fee: $2.00. Required to search: name, years to search. Civil cases indexed by defendant, plaintiff. Civil records on books since 1980. **Criminal Records:** Access: Phone, fax, mail, in person. Both court and visitors may perform in person searches. Search fee: $2.00. Required to search: name, years to search, DOB; also helpful-SSN. Criminal records on books since 1980. **General Information:** No suppressed, juvenile, sex offenders, mental health, or adoption records released. SASE required. Turnaround time 1 week. Copy fee: $1.00 per page. Certification fee: $15.00. Fee payee: 82nd District Court. Personal checks accepted. Prepayment is required. Fax notes: $10.00 for first page, $1.00 each addl.

Probate Court PO Box 328, Harrisville, MI 48740; 517-724-6880; Fax: 517-724-6397. Hours: 8:30AM-4:30PM (EST). *Probate.*

Alger County

11th Circuit Court 101 Court St, PO Box \ 538, Munising, MI 49862; 906-387-2076; Fax: 906-387-2156. Hours: 8AM-4PM (EST). *Felony, Civil Actions Over $25,000.*

www.courts.net/mi/alger.htm

Civil Records: Access: Phone, mail, in person. Only the court conducts in person searches; visitors may not. No search fee. Required to search: name, years to search. Civil cases indexed by defendant, plaintiff. Civil records on index books. **Criminal Records:** Access: Phone, mail, in person. Only the court conducts in person searches; visitors may not. No search fee. Required to search: name, years to search, DOB; also helpful-SSN. Criminal records on index books. **General Information:** No juvenile, sex offenders, mental health, or adoption records released. Turnaround time 1 week. Copy fee: $.25 per page. Certification fee: $10.00 plus $1.00 per page after first. Fee payee: Alger County Clerk. Personal checks accepted.

93rd District Court PO Box 186, Munising, MI 49862; 906-387-3879; Fax: 906-387-3289.

Hours: 8AM-4PM (EST). *Misdemeanor, Civil Actions Under $25,000, Eviction, Small Claims.*

Civil Records: Access: Phone, mail, in person. Only the court conducts in person searches; visitors may not. No search fee. Required to search: name, years to search. Civil cases indexed by defendant, plaintiff. Civil records on index books from 1984. **Criminal Records:** Access: Phone, mail, in person. Only the court conducts in person searches; visitors may not. No search fee. Required to search: name, years to search, DOB; also helpful-SSN. Criminal records on index books from 1984. **General Information:** No suppressed records released. SASE required. Turnaround time 5-7 days. Copy fee: $.25 per page. Certification fee: $15.00. Fee payee: District Court. Business checks accepted.

Probate Court 101 Court St, Munising, MI 49862; 906-387-2080; Fax: 906-387-2200. Hours: 8AM-Noon, 1-4PM (EST). *Probate.*

Allegan County

48th Circuit Court 113 Chestnut St, Allegan, MI 49010; 616-673-0300; Fax: 616-673-0298. Hours: 8AM-5PM (EST). *Felony, Civil Actions Over $25,000.*

Civil Records: Access: Mail, in person. Both court and visitors may perform in person searches. No search fee. Required to search: name, years to search. Civil cases indexed by defendant, plaintiff. Civil records on computer since 1985, indexed in books to 1839. Public can only search docket books. **Criminal Records:** Access: Mail, in person. Both court and visitors may perform in person searches. No search fee. Required to search: name, years to search, DOB; also helpful-SSN. Criminal records on computer since 1985, indexed in books to 1839. Public can only search docket books. **General Information:** No suppressed, juvenile, sex offenders, mental health, or adoption records released. SASE not required. Turnaround time 1-2 days. Copy fee: $1.00 per page. Certification fee: $10.00. Fee payee: Allegan County Clerk. Personal checks accepted. Credit cards accepted: Visa, Mastercard. Accepted for fax filings only. Prepayment is required.

57th District Court 113 Chestnut St, Allegan, MI 49010; 616-673-0400. Hours: 8AM-5PM (EST). *Misdemeanor, Civil Actions Under $25,000, Eviction, Small Claims.*

Civil Records: Access: Mail, in person. Both court and visitors may perform in person searches. No search fee. Required to search: name, years to search. Civil cases indexed by defendant, plaintiff. Civil records on index books. **Criminal Records:** Access: Mail, in person. Both court and visitors may perform in person searches. No search fee. Required to search: name, years to search, DOB; also helpful-SSN. Criminal records on index books. **General Information:** No suppressed, juvenile, sex offenders, mental health, or adoption records released. SASE required. Turnaround time 1 week. Copy fee: $1.00 per page. Certification fee: $10.00. Fee payee: Allegan County Clerk. Personal checks accepted. Prepayment is required. Public access terminal is available.

Probate Court 2243 33rd St, Allegan, MI 49010; 616-673-0250; Fax: 616-673-2200. Hours: 8AM-5PM (EST). *Probate.*

Alpena County

26th Circuit Court 720 West Chisholm, Alpena, MI 49707; 517-356-0115; Fax: 517-356-6559. Hours: 8:30AM-4:30PM (EST). *Felony, Civil Actions Over $25,000.*

Civil Records: Access: Fax, mail, in person. Only the court conducts in person searches; visitors may not. Search fee: $5.00 per name. Required to search: name, years to search. Civil cases indexed by defendant, plaintiff. Civil records on computer since 1988. **Criminal Records:** Access: Fax, mail, in person. Only the court conducts in person searches; visitors may not. Search fee: $5.00 per name. Required to search: name, years to search. Criminal records on computer since 1988. **General Information:** No suppressed, juvenile, sex offenders, mental health, or adoption records released. SASE required. Turnaround time 3-4 days. Copy fee: $1.00 per page. Certification fee: $10.00 plus $1.00 per page after first. Fee payee: County Clerk. Personal checks accepted. Prepayment is required. Fax notes: Fax fee $5.00 per document plus $1.00 per page.

88th District Court 719 West Chisholm #3, Alpena, MI 49707; 517-354-3330; Fax: 517-358-9127. Hours: 8:30AM-4:30PM (EST). *Misdemeanor, Civil Actions Under $25,000, Eviction, Small Claims.*

Civil Records: Access: Fax, mail, in person. Only the court conducts in person searches; visitors may not. No search fee. Required to search: name, years to search. Civil cases indexed by defendant, plaintiff. Civil records on computer since June, 1989, in books prior. **Criminal Records:** Access: Fax, mail, in person. Only the court conducts in person searches; visitors may not. No search fee. Required to search: name, years to search, DOB; also helpful-SSN. Criminal records on computer and on cards. **General Information:** No suppressed, juvenile, sex offenders, mental health, or adoption records released. SASE required. Turnaround time 1-2 days. Copy fee: $1.00 per page. Certification fee: No certification fee. Fee payee: 88th District Court. Only cashiers checks and money orders accepted. Prepayment is required.

Probate Court 719 West Chisholm St, Alpena, MI 49707; 517-354-8785; Fax: 517-356-3665. Hours: 8:30AM-4:30PM (EST). *Probate.*

Antrim County

13th Circuit Court PO Box 520, Bellaire, MI 49615; 231-533-8607; Fax: 231-533-6935. Hours: 8:30AM-5PM (EST). *Felony, Civil Actions Over $25,000.*

Civil Records: Access: Fax, mail, in person. Both court and visitors may perform in person searches. Search fee: $5.00 per name. Required to search: name, years to search. Civil cases indexed by defendant, plaintiff. Civil records on computer since 1977, prior on books. Only court can search on computer, in person searchers may look at old records on docket books. **Criminal Records:** Access: Fax, mail, in person. Both court and visitors may perform in person searches. Search fee: $5.00 per name. Required to search: name, years to search, DOB; also helpful-SSN. Criminal records on books from 1800s, on computer since 1997. Only court can search on computer, in person searchers may review old docket books. **General Information:** No suppressed, juvenile, sex offenders, mental health, or adoption records released. SASE required. Turnaround time 1 week. Copy fee: $1.00 per page. Certification fee: $10.00 plus $1.00 per page after first. Fee payee: Antrim County Clerk. Personal checks accepted. Credit cards accepted: Visa, Mastercard. Prepayment is required. Fax notes: $5.00 per document.

86th District Court PO Box 597, Bellaire, MI 49615; 231-533-6441; Fax: 231-533-6322. Hours:

8AM-4:30PM (EST). *Misdemeanor, Civil Actions Under $25,000, Eviction, Small Claims.*

Civil Records: Access: Fax, mail, in person. Only the court conducts in person searches; visitors may not. No search fee. Required to search: name, years to search. Civil cases indexed by defendant, plaintiff. Civil records on computer since 1985, prior on cards. **Criminal Records:** Access: Fax, mail, in person. Only the court conducts in person searches; visitors may not. No search fee. Required to search: name, years to search, DOB; also helpful-SSN. Criminal records on computer since 1985, prior on cards. **General Information:** No suppressed, sex offenders records released. SASE not required. Turnaround time same day. Copy fee: $.30 per page. Certification fee: $10.00. Fee payee: District Court. Business checks accepted. Prepayment is required.

Probate Court 205 Cayuga St, PO Box 130, Bellaire, MI 49615; 231-533-6681; Fax: 231-533-6600. Hours: 8:30AM-4:30PM (EST). *Probate.*

Arenac County

34th Circuit Court 120 N Grove St, PO Box 747, Standish, MI 48658; 517-846-9186; Fax: 517-846-6757. Hours: 8:30AM-5PM (EST). *Felony, Civil Actions Over $25,000.*

Civil Records: Access: Mail, in person. Only the court conducts in person searches; visitors may not. Search fee: $5.00 per name. Required to search: name, years to search. Civil cases indexed by defendant, plaintiff. Civil records on computer since 1990, prior on index books. **Criminal Records:** Access: Mail, in person. Only the court conducts in person searches; visitors may not. Search fee: $5.00 per name. Required to search: name, years to search, DOB; also helpful-SSN. Criminal records on computer since 1990, prior on index books. **General Information:** No suppressed, juvenile, mental health, or adoption records released. SASE required. Turnaround time 1-5 days. Copy fee: $1.00 per page. Certification fee: $10.00 plus $1.00 per page after first. Fee payee: Arenac County Clerk. Personal checks accepted. Prepayment is required.

81st District Court PO Box 129, Standish, MI 48658; 517-846-9538; Fax: 517-846-2008. Hours: 8:30AM-5PM (EST). *Misdemeanor, Civil Actions Under $25,000, Eviction, Small Claims.*

Civil Records: Access: Phone, fax, mail, in person. Only the court conducts in person searches; visitors may not. No search fee. Required to search: name, years to search. Civil cases indexed by defendant, plaintiff. Civil records on computer since 1990, prior on docket books. **Criminal Records:** Access: Phone, fax, mail, in person. Only the court conducts in person searches; visitors may not. No search fee. Required to search: name, years to search, DOB; also helpful-SSN. Criminal records on computer since 1990, prior on cards by name. **General Information:** No suppressed, juvenile, sex offenders, mental health, or adoption records released. SASE required. Turnaround time 5 days. Copy fee: $.25 per page. Certification fee: No certification fee. Fee payee: 81st District Court. Personal checks accepted. Prepayment is required. Fax notes: $2.00 for first page, $.50 each addl. No charge for fax cover sheet.

Probate Court 120 N Grove, PO Box 666, Standish, MI 48658; 517-846-6941; Fax: 517-846-6757. Hours: 9AM-5PM (EST). *Probate.*

Baraga County

12th Circuit Court 16 North 3rd St, L'Anse, MI 49946; 906-524-6183; Fax: 906-524-6186. Hours: 8:30AM-4:30PM (EST). *Felony, Civil Actions Over $25,000.*

Civil Records: Access: Phone, mail, in person. Both court and visitors may perform in person searches. No search fee. Required to search: name, years to search. Civil cases indexed by defendant, plaintiff. Civil records on docket books and are not computerized. **Criminal Records:** Access: Phone, mail, in person. Both court and visitors may perform in person searches. No search fee. Required to search: name, years to search, DOB; also helpful-SSN. Criminal records on docket books and are not computerized. **General Information:** No suppressed records released. SASE required. Turnaround time same day. Copy fee: $2.00 per page. Certification fee: $10.00 plus $2.00 per page after first. Fee payee: County Clerk. Personal checks accepted. Prepayment is required.

97th District Court 16 North 3rd St, L'Anse, MI 49946; 906-524-6109; Fax: 906-524-6186. Hours: 8:30AM-Noon,1-4:30PM (EST). *Misdemeanor, Civil Actions Under $25,000, Eviction, Small Claims.*

Civil Records: Access: Mail, in person. Only the court conducts in person searches; visitors may not. No search fee. Required to search: name, years to search. Civil cases indexed by defendant, plaintiff. Civil records listed on docket books since 1968. **Criminal Records:** Access: Mail, in person. Only the court conducts in person searches; visitors may not. No search fee. Required to search: name, years to search, DOB; also helpful-SSN. Criminal records listed on docket books since 1968. **General Information:** No suppressed, juvenile, sex offenders, mental health, or adoption records released. SASE requested. Turnaround time 2-3 days. Copy fee: $5.00 per page. Certification fee: $10.00 plus $1.00 per page after first. Fee payee: 97th District Court. Personal checks accepted. Prepayment is required.

Probate Court County Courthouse, 16 N 3rd St, L'Anse, MI 49946; 906-524-6390; Fax: 906-524-6186. Hours: 8:30AM-Noon, 1-4:30PM (EST). *Probate.*

Barry County

5th Circuit Court 220 West State St, Hastings, MI 49058; 616-948-4810; Fax: 616-945-0209. Hours: 8AM-5PM (EST). *Felony, Civil Actions Over $25,000.*

Civil Records: Access: Fax, mail, in person. Only the court conducts in person searches; visitors may not. Search fee: $5.00 per name. Required to search: name, years to search. Civil cases indexed by defendant, plaintiff. Civil records on computer since 1992, card index back to 1977, prior on books. **Criminal Records:** Access: Fax, mail, in person. Only the court conducts in person searches; visitors may not. Search fee: $5.00 per name. Required to search: name, years to search, DOB; also helpful-SSN. Criminal records on computer since 1992, card index back to 1977, prior on books. **General Information:** No suppressed, juvenile, sex offenders, mental health, or adoption records released. SASE required. Turnaround time 2 days. Copy fee: $1.00 per page. Certification fee: $10.00. Fee payee: County Clerk. Personal checks accepted. Prepayment is required. Fax notes: $1.00 per page.

56B District Court 220 West Court St, Suite 202, Hastings, MI 49058; 616-948-4835; Fax: 616-948-3314. Hours: 8AM-5PM (EST). *Misdemeanor, Civil Actions Under $25,000, Eviction, Small Claims.*

Civil Records: Access: Phone, fax, mail, in person. Only the court conducts in person searches; visitors may not. Search fee: $5.00 per name. Required to search: name, years to search. Civil cases indexed by defendant, plaintiff. Civil records on computer since 1990, prior on index books. **Criminal Records:** Access: Phone, fax, mail, in person. Only the court conducts in person searches; visitors may not. Search fee: $5.00 per name. Required to search: name, years to search, DOB; also helpful-SSN. Criminal records on computer since 1990, prior on index books. **General Information:** No suppressed, sex offenders, or mental health records released. SASE required. Turnaround time 2 days. Copy fee: $.25 per page. Certification fee: $10.00 plus $1.00 per page after first. Fee payee: 56th District Court. Personal checks accepted. Prepayment is required. Fax notes: $1.00 per page.

Probate Court 220 West Court St, Suite 302, Hastings, MI 49058; 616-948-4842; Fax: 616-948-3322. Hours: 8AM-5PM (EST). *Probate.*

Bay County

18th Circuit Court 1200 Washington Ave, Bay City, MI 48708; 517-895-2066; Fax: 517-895-4099. Hours: 8AM-5PM Winter; 7:30AM-4PM Summer (EST). *Felony, Civil Actions Over $25,000.*

Civil Records: Access: Phone, fax, mail, in person. Only the court conducts in person searches; visitors may not. No search fee. Required to search: name, years to search. Civil cases indexed by defendant, plaintiff. Civil records on computer for the last since 1986. **Criminal Records:** Access: Phone, fax, mail, in person. Only the court conducts in person searches; visitors may not. No search fee. Required to search: name, years to search, DOB; also helpful-SSN. Criminal records on computer for the last since 1986. **General Information:** No suppressed records released. SASE requested. Turnaround time same day. Copy fee: $.25 per page. Certification fee: $10.00 plus $1.00 each add'l page. Fee payee: County Clerk. Personal checks accepted. Prepayment is required. Fax notes: $5.00 per document.

74th District Court 1230 Washington Ave, Bay City, MI 48708; 517-895-4232; Fax: 517-895-4233. Hours: 8AM-5PM (EST). *Misdemeanor, Civil Actions Under $25,000, Eviction, Small Claims.*

Civil Records: Access: In person only. Court does not conduct in person searches; visitors must perform searches for themselves. Search fee: No civil searches performed by court. Required to search: name, years to search. Civil cases indexed by defendant, plaintiff. Civil records on computer since 1992, listed on index cards prior. **Criminal Records:** Access: In person only. Court does not conduct in person searches; visitors must perform searches for themselves. Search fee: No criminal searches performed by court. Required to search: name, years to search, DOB; also helpful-SSN. Criminal records on computer since 1992, listed on index cards prior. **General Information:** No suppressed, juvenile, sex offenders, mental health, or adoption records released. Copy fee: $1.00 per page. Certification fee: $10.00. Fee payee: 74th

District Court. Personal checks accepted. Prepayment is required.

Probate Court 1230 Washington, Ste 715, Bay City, MI 48708; 517-895-4205; Fax: 517-895-4194. Hours: 8AM-5PM; Summer hours 7:30AM-4PM (EST). *Probate.*

Benzie County

19th Circuit Court PO Box 398, Beulah, MI 49617; 231-882-9671 & 800-315-3593; Fax: 231-882-5941. Hours: 8AM-5PM (EST). *Felony, Civil Actions Over $25,000.*

Civil Records: Access: Phone, fax, mail, in person. Both court and visitors may perform in person searches. No search fee. Required to search: name, years to search. Civil cases indexed by defendant, plaintiff. Civil records on computer since 1980, prior on docket books. **Criminal Records:** Access: Phone, fax, mail, in person. Both court and visitors may perform in person searches. No search fee. Required to search: name, years to search. Criminal records on computer since 1980, prior listed in docket books. **General Information:** No suppressed or home-youthful training case records released. SASE not required. Turnaround time 1-2 days. Copy fee: $.50 per page. Certification fee: $10.00 plus $1.00 per page after first. Fee payee: Benzie County Clerk. Personal checks accepted. Prepayment is required. Public access terminal is available. Fax notes: $3.00 for first page, $1.00 each addl.

85th District Court PO Box 398, Beulah, MI 49617; 800-759-5175 231-882-0019; Fax: 231-882-0022. Hours: 9AM-5PM (EST). *Misdemeanor, Civil Actions Under $25,000, Eviction, Small Claims.*

Civil Records: Access: Fax, mail, in person. Only the court conducts in person searches; visitors may not. Search fee: $3.00 per name. Required to search: name, years to search. Civil cases indexed by defendant, plaintiff. Civil records on computer since 1990, prior on cards to 1965. **Criminal Records:** Access: Fax, mail, in person. Only the court conducts in person searches; visitors may not. Search fee: $3.00 per name. Required to search: name, years to search, DOB; also helpful-SSN. Criminal records on computer since 1990, prior on cards to 1965. **General Information:** No suppressed, juvenile, sex offenders, mental health, or adoption records released. SASE required. Turnaround time 1 week. Copy fee: $1.00 per page. Certification fee: $10.00. Fee payee: 85th District Court. Personal checks accepted. Out of state checks not accepted. Prepayment is required. Fax notes: $3.00 for first page, $1.00 each addl.

Probate Court 448 Court Place, County Gov't Ctr., PO Box 377, Beulah, MI 49617; 231-882-9675; Fax: 231-882-5987. Hours: 8:30AM-Noon, 1-5PM (EST). *Probate.*

Berrien County

2nd Circuit Court 811 Port St, St Joseph, MI 49085; 616-983-7111 X8574; Fax: 616-982-8647. Hours: 8:30AM-4PM (EST). *Felony, Civil Actions Over $25,000.*

Civil Records: Access: Mail, in person. Only the court conducts in person searches; visitors may not. Search fee: $5.00 per name. Required to search: name, years to search. Civil cases indexed by defendant, plaintiff. Civil records on computer since 1981, prior on books (domestic) back to 1835, (civil & criminal) back to 1837. **Criminal Records:** Access: Mail, in person. Only the court conducts in person searches; visitors may not. Search fee: $5.00 per name. Required to search:

name, years to search, DOB; also helpful-SSN. Criminal records on computer since 1981, prior on books (domestic) back to 1835, (civil & criminal) back to 1837. **General Information:** No suppressed, juvenile, sex offenders, mental health, or adoption records released. SASE required. Turnaround time 2-3 days. Copy fee: $1.00 per page. Certification fee: $10.00 plus $1.00 per page after first. Fee payee: Berrien County Clerk. Personal checks accepted. Prepayment is required.

5th District Court Attn: Records, 811 Port St, St Joseph, MI 49085; 616-983-7111; Fax: 616-982-8643. Hours: 8:30AM-4PM (EST). *Misdemeanor, Civil Actions Under $25,000, Eviction, Small Claims.*

Civil Records: Access: Mail, in person. Only the court conducts in person searches; visitors may not. Search fee: $5.00 per name. Required to search: name, years to search; also helpful-address. Civil cases indexed by defendant, plaintiff. Civil records on computer since 1988, on logs from 1976-87, on index cards from 1969-75. Will do civil record check searches for only seven years. **Criminal Records:** Access: Mail, in person. Only the court conducts in person searches; visitors may not. Search fee: $5.00 per name. Required to search: name, years to search, DOB; also helpful-address, SSN. Criminal records on computer since 1979, on mircofiche prior to 1986. **General Information:** No suppressed or mental health records released. SASE not required. Turnaround time 5 days. Copy fee: $1.00 per page. Certification fee: $10.00 plus $1.00 per page after first. Fee payee: 5th District Court. Personal checks accepted. Prepayment is required.

Probate Court 811 Port St., St Joseph, MI 49085; 616-983-7111 X8365; Fax: 616-982-8644. Hours: 8:30AM-5PM (EST). *Probate.*

Branch County

15th Circuit Court 31 Division St, Coldwater, MI 49036; 517-279-4306; Fax: 517-278-5627. Hours: 9AM-5PM (EST). *Felony, Civil Actions Over $25,000.*

Civil Records: Access: Mail, in person. Both court and visitors may perform in person searches. Search fee: $1.00 per name per year. Required to search: name, years to search. Civil cases indexed by defendant, plaintiff. Civil records on computer since 1988, prior in books back to 1830s. **Criminal Records:** Access: Mail, in person. Both court and visitors may perform in person searches. Search fee: $1.00 per name per year. Required to search: name, years to search, DOB. Criminal records on computer since 1988, prior in books back to 1830s. **General Information:** No suppressed records released. SASE not required. Turnaround time 1-5 days. Copy fee: $1.00 per page. Certification fee: $10.00 plus $1.00 per page. Fee payee: Branch County Clerk. Business checks accepted. Prepayment is required.

3A District Court 31 Division St., Coldwater, MI 49036; 517-279-4308; Fax: 517-279-4333. Hours: 8AM-5PM (EST). *Misdemeanor, Civil Actions Under $25,000, Eviction, Small Claims.*

www.branchcountycourts.com

Civil Records: Access: Phone, mail, in person. Only the court conducts in person searches; visitors may not. Search fee: $10.00 per name. Required to search: name, years to search. Civil cases indexed by defendant, plaintiff. Civil records on computer since June 1991, prior on index books. **Criminal Records:** Access: Phone, mail, in person. Only the court conducts in person

searches; visitors may not. Search fee: $10.00 per name. Required to search: name, years to search, DOB; also helpful-SSN. Criminal records on computer since Oct. 1988. **General Information:** No suppressed, juvenile, sex offenders, mental health, or adoption records released. SASE requested. Turnaround time immediate if possible, otherwise 2-3 days. Copy fee: $1.00 per page. Certification fee: $10.00. Fee payee: 3A District Court. Personal checks accepted. Credit cards accepted. Prepayment is required.

Probate Court 31 Division St., Coldwater, MI 49036; 517-279-4318; Fax: 517-278-4130. Hours: 9AM-Noon, 1-5PM (EST). *Probate.*

Calhoun County

37th Circuit Court 161 East Michigan, Battle Creek, MI 49014-4066; 616-969-6518. Hours: 8AM-5PM (EST). *Felony, Civil Actions Over $25,000.*

http://courts.co.calhoun.mi.us

Civil Records: Access: Mail, in person. Court does not conduct in person searches; visitors must perform searches for themselves. Search fee: No civil searches performed by court. Required to search: name, years to search. Civil cases indexed by defendant, plaintiff. Civil records on computer since 1984, prior on microfilm. The court will provide case number, filed date, case title, case status, and date of final judgement for the search fee. **Criminal Records:** Access: In person only. Court does not conduct in person searches; visitors must perform searches for themselves. Search fee: No criminal searches performed by court. Required to search: name, years to search, DOB; also helpful-SSN. Criminal records on computer since 1984, prior on microfilm. The court refers requests to the State Police (517-322-5531). Searcher may view public court file if case number known. **General Information:** No suppressed, juvenile, sex offenders, mental health, or adoption records released. SASE required. Turnaround time 1 week. Copy fee: $1.00 per page. Certification fee: $10.00 plus $1.00 per page after first. Fee payee: 37th Circuit Court Clerk. Personal checks accepted. Prepayment is required.

10th District Court 161 E Michigan Ave, Battle Creek, MI 49014; 616-969-6666; Fax: 616-969-6663. Hours: 8:00AM-4PM (EST). *Misdemeanor, Civil Actions Under $25,000, Eviction, Small Claims.*

Civil Records: Access: Fax, mail, in person. Both court and visitors may perform in person searches. No search fee. Required to search: name, years to search. Civil cases indexed by defendant, plaintiff. Civil records on computer since 1986, prior on docket books. Public access terminal searches back to 10/1997. Fax requests must be signed. **Criminal Records:** Access: Fax, mail, in person. Both court and visitors may perform in person searches. No search fee. Required to search: name, years to search, DOB. Criminal records on computer since 1986, prior on docket books. Public access terminal searches back to 10/1997. Fax requests must be signed. **General Information:** No suppressed, juvenile, sex offenders, mental health, or adoption records released. SASE required. Turnaround time 48 hours. Copy fee: $.25 per page. Certification fee: $10.00 plus $1.00 per page after first. Fee payee: 10th District Court. Personal checks accepted. Credit cards accepted: Visa, Mastercard. Prepayment is required. Fax notes: No fee to fax results to toll-free number.

10th District Court - Marshall Branch

315 West Arlen, Marshall, MI 49068; 616-969-6678; Fax: 616-969-6663. Hours: 8:30AM-4PM (EST). *Misdemeanor, Civil Actions Under $25,000, Eviction, Small Claims.*

Civil Records: Access: Fax, mail, in person. Both court and visitors may perform in person searches. No search fee. Required to search: name, years to search. Civil cases indexed by defendant, plaintiff. Civil records on computer since 1989, prior on books. **Criminal Records:** Access: Fax, mail, in person. Both court and visitors may perform in person searches. Search fee: $4.00 per name per year. Required to search: name, years to search, DOB; also helpful-SSN. Criminal records on computer since 1989, prior on books. **General Information:** No suppressed, juvenile, sex offenders, mental health, or adoption records released. SASE not required. Turnaround time 1-2 days. Copy fee: $.25 per page. Certification fee: $10.00 plus $1.00 per page after first. Fee payee: County Clerk. Personal checks accepted. Prepayment is required. Fax notes: No fee to fax results.

Probate Court Justice Center, 161 E Michigan Ave, Battle Creek, MI 49014; 616-969-6794; Fax: 616-969-6797. Hours: 8AM-5PM (EST). *Probate.*

Cass County

43rd Circuit Court 120 North Broadway, File Room, Cassopolis, MI 49031-1398; 616-445-4416 X3201; Fax: 616-445-8978. Hours: 9AM-12; 1PM-4PM (EST). *Felony, Civil Actions Over $25,000.*

Civil Records: Access: Fax, mail, in person. Both court and visitors may perform in person searches. No search fee. Required to search: name, years to search. Civil cases indexed by defendant, plaintiff. Civil records on computer since 1989, in books since 1963. **Criminal Records:** Access: Fax, mail, in person. Both court and visitors may perform in person searches. No search fee. Required to search: name, years to search, DOB; also helpful-SSN. Criminal records on computer since 1989, in books since 1963. **General Information:** No suppressed, juvenile, sex offenders, mental health, or adoption records released. SASE helpful. Turnaround time 2 weeks. Copy fee: $1.00 per page. Certification fee: $10.00. Fee payee: Cass County Clerk. Business checks accepted. Prepayment is required. Public access terminal is available.

4th District Court 110 North Broadway, Cassopolis, MI 49031; 616-445-4424; Fax: 616-445-4486. Hours: 8AM-5PM (EST). *Misdemeanor, Civil Actions Under $25,000, Eviction, Small Claims.*

Civil Records: Access: Phone, mail, in person. Both court and visitors may perform in person searches. No search fee. Required to search: name, years to search; also helpful-address. Civil cases indexed by defendant, plaintiff. Civil records on computer since 1988, indexed on cards prior. You can fax requests, but results will not be returned by fax. **Criminal Records:** Access: Phone, mail, in person. Both court and visitors may perform in person searches. No search fee. Required to search: name, years to search, DOB; also helpful-address. Criminal records on computer since 1988, indexed on cards prior. You can fax requests, but results will not be returned by fax. **General Information:** No suppressed, juvenile, sex offenders, mental health, or adoption records released. SASE not required. Turnaround time 2 weeks. Copy fee: $1.00 for first page, $.10 each

addl. Certification fee: $10.00 plus $1.00 per page after first. Fee payee: 4th District Court. Personal checks accepted. Prepayment is required.

Probate Court 110 North Broadway, Rm 202, Cassopolis, MI 49031; 616-445-4454; Fax: 616-445-4453. Hours: 8AM-Noon, 1-5PM (EST). *Probate.*

Charlevoix County

33rd Circuit Court 203 Antrim St, Charlevoix, MI 49720; 231-547-7200; Fax: 231-547-7217. Hours: 9AM-5PM (EST). *Felony, Civil Actions Over $25,000.*

Civil Records: Access: Mail, in person. Only the court conducts in person searches; visitors may not. No search fee. Required to search: name, years to search. Civil cases indexed by defendant, plaintiff. Civil records on computer from 1991, microfiche and archives from 1868. **Criminal Records:** Access: Mail, in person. Only the court conducts in person searches; visitors may not. No search fee. Required to search: name, years to search, DOB; also helpful-SSN. Criminal records on computer from 1991, microfiche and archives from 1868. **General Information:** No suppressed, juvenile, adoption records released. SASE requested. Turnaround time 1 week. Copy fee: $1.00 per page. Certification fee: $10.00. Fee payee: Charlevoix County Clerk. Personal checks accepted. Prepayment is required.

90th District Court 301 State St, Court Bldg, Charlevoix, MI 49720; 231-547-7227; Fax: 231-547-7253. Hours: 9AM-5PM (EST). *Misdemeanor, Civil Actions Under $25,000, Eviction, Small Claims.*

Civil Records: Access: Mail, in person. Both court and visitors may perform in person searches. No search fee. Required to search: name, years to search. Civil cases indexed by defendant, plaintiff. Civil records on computer since 1987, listed on index cards to 1963. **Criminal Records:** Access: Mail, in person. Both court and visitors may perform in person searches. No search fee. Required to search: name, years to search, DOB, SSN. Criminal records on computer since 1987, listed on index cards to 1963. **General Information:** No suppressed records released. SASE helpful. Turnaround time 1-2 days. Copy fee: $1.00 per page. Fee payee: 90th District Court. Personal checks accepted. Prepayment is required.

Probate Court 301 State St, County Bldg, Charlevoix, MI 49720; 231-547-7214; Fax: 231-547-7256. Hours: 9AM-5PM (EST). *Probate.*

Note: Shares the same judge with Emmet County Probate Court.

Cheboygan County

53rd District Court PO Box 70, Cheboygan, MI 49721; 231-627-8808. Hours: 9AM-5PM (EST). *Felony, Civil Actions Over $25,000.*

Civil Records: Access: Phone, mail, in person. Only the court conducts in person searches; visitors may not. No search fee. Required to search: name, years to search. Civil cases indexed by defendant, plaintiff. Civil records on computer from 1985, index cards from 1884. **Criminal Records:** Access: Phone, mail, in person. Only the court conducts in person searches; visitors may not. No search fee. Required to search: name, years to search, DOB. Criminal records on computer from 1985, index cards from 1884. **General Information:** No suppressed records released. SASE requested. Turnaround time 3-4

days. Copy fee: $1.00 for first page, $.20 each addl. Certification fee: $10.00 plus $1.00 each additional page. Fee payee: County Clerk. Personal checks accepted. Prepayment is required.

89th District Court PO Box 70, Cheboygan, MI 49721; 231-627-8809; Fax: 231-627-8444. Hours: 8:30AM-4PM (EST). *Misdemeanor, Civil Actions Under $25,000, Eviction, Small Claims.*

Civil Records: Access: Phone, fax, mail, in person. Only the court conducts in person searches; visitors may not. No search fee. Required to search: name, years to search. Civil cases indexed by defendant, plaintiff. Civil records on computer since 1988, microfilmed prior. **Criminal Records:** Access: Phone, fax, mail, in person. Only the court conducts in person searches; visitors may not. No search fee. Required to search: name, years to search, DOB; also helpful-SSN. Criminal records on computer since 1986. **General Information:** No suppressed, juvenile, sex offenders, mental health, or adoption records released. SASE required. Turnaround time 3-4 days. Copy fee: $1.00 per page. Certification fee: $10.00 plus $1.00 per page after first. Fee payee: 89th District Court. Personal checks accepted. Prepayment is required. Fax notes: No fee to fax results.

Probate Court 870 S Main St, PO Box 70, Cheboygan, MI 49721; 231-627-8823; Fax: 231-627-8868. Hours: 9AM-5PM (EST). *Probate.*

Chippewa County

50th Circuit Court 319 Court St, Sault Ste Marie, MI 49783; 906-635-6300; Fax: 906-635-6851. Hours: 8:30AM-5PM (EST). *Felony, Civil Actions Over $25,000.*

Civil Records: Access: Mail, in person. Only the court conducts in person searches; visitors may not. Search fee: $5.00 per name. Fee is for 10 year search. Required to search: name, years to search. Civil cases indexed by defendant, plaintiff. Civil records on computer since 1990, prior on index books. **Criminal Records:** Access: Mail, in person. Only the court conducts in person searches; visitors may not. Search fee: $5.00 per name. Fee is for 10 year search. Required to search: name, years to search, DOB; also helpful-SSN. Criminal records on computer since 1990, prior on index books. **General Information:** No suppressed, juvenile, sex offenders, mental health, or adoption records released. SASA not required. Turnaround time 1-2 days. Copy fee: $1.00 per page. Certification fee: $10.00 plus $1.00 per page after first. Fee payee: County Clerk. Personal checks accepted. Prepayment is required.

91st District Court 325 Court St, Sault Ste Marie, MI 49783; 906-635-6320; Fax: 906-635-7605. Hours: 9AM-4:30PM (EST). *Misdemeanor, Civil Actions Under $25,000, Eviction, Small Claims.*

Civil Records: Access: Mail, in person. Both court and visitors may perform in person searches. Search fee: $5.00 per name. Required to search: name, years to search. Civil cases indexed by defendant, plaintiff. Civil records on computer since 1989, prior on index books to 1968. **Criminal Records:** Access: Mail, in person. Both court and visitors may perform in person searches. Search fee: $5.00 per name. Required to search: name, years to search, DOB; also helpful-SSN. Criminal records on computer since 1989, prior on index books to 1968. **General Information:** No suppressed, juvenile, sex offenders, mental health, or adoption records released. SASE required. Turnaround time 10 days. Copy fee: $1.00 per page. Certification fee: $10.00. Only cashiers checks and money orders accepted. Prepayment is required. Public access terminal is available.

Probate Court 319 Court St., Sault Ste Marie, MI 49783; 906-635-6314; Fax: 906-635-6852. Hours: 9AM-5PM (EST). *Probate.*

Clare County

55th Circuit Court 225 West Main St, PO Box 438, Harrison, MI 48625; 517-539-7131; Fax: 517-539-6616. Hours: 8AM-4:30PM (EST). *Felony, Civil Actions Over $25,000.*

Civil Records: Access: Mail, in person. Only the court conducts in person searches; visitors may not. Search fee: $5.00 per name. Add $1.00 per year if more than five. Required to search: name, years to search. Civil cases indexed by defendant, plaintiff. Civil records on computer since 1992, on books from 1925. **Criminal Records:** Access: Mail, in person. Only the court conducts in person searches; visitors may not. Search fee: $5.00 per name. Add $1.00 per year if more than five. Required to search: name, years to search, DOB; also helpful-SSN. Criminal records on computer since 1992, on books from 1925. **General Information:** No suppressed, juvenile, sex offenders, mental health, or adoption records released. SASE required. Turnaround time 1-5 days. Copy fee: $1.00 per page. Certification fee: $10.00 per document plus $1.00 per page. Fee payee: Clare County Clerk. Personal checks accepted. Prepayment is required.

80th District Court 225 W. Main St, Harrison, MI 48625; 517-539-7173; Fax: 517-539-4036. Hours: 8AM-4:30PM (EST). *Misdemeanor, Civil Actions Under $25,000, Eviction, Small Claims.*

Civil Records: Access: Mail, in person. Both court and visitors may perform in person searches. No search fee. Required to search: name, years to search. Civil cases indexed by defendant, plaintiff. Civil records on computer since 1988. **Criminal Records:** Access: Mail, in person. Only the court conducts in person searches; visitors may not. No search fee. Required to search: name, years to search, DOB. Criminal records on computer since 1988. **General Information:** No suppressed, juvenile, sex offenders, mental health, or adoption records released. SASE required. Turnaround time 1-2 days. Copy fee: $1.00 per page. Certification fee: No certification fee. Fee payee: 80th District Court. Personal checks accepted. Prepayment is required.

Probate Court 225 W. Main St., PO Box 96, Harrison, MI 48625; 517-539-7109. Hours: 8AM-4:30PM (EST). *Probate.*

Note: This is combined with Gladwin County Probate Court.

Clinton County

29th Circuit Court PO Box 69, St Johns, MI 48879-0069; 517-224-5140; Fax: 517-224-5254. Hours: 8AM-5PM (EST). *Felony, Civil Actions Over $25,000.*

www.clinton-county.org

Civil Records: Access: Mail, in person. Both court and visitors may perform in person searches. Search fee: $10.00 per name. Fee is for 10 year search. Required to search: name, years to search. Civil cases indexed by defendant, plaintiff. Civil records in calendar books since 1800s, some on microfiche. **Criminal Records:** Access: Mail, in person. Both court and visitors may perform in person searches. Search fee: $10.00 per name. Fee

is for 10 year search. Required to search: name, years to search; also helpful-DOB. Criminal records in calendar books since 1800s, some on microfiche. **General Information:** No suppressed or non public records released. SASE required. Turnaround time 24 hrs. Copy fee: $1.00 per page. Certification fee: $10.00 plus $1.00 per page. Fee payee: Clinton County Clerk. Personal checks accepted. Prepayment is required.

65th District Court 409 South Whittemore St., St Johns, MI 48879; 517-224-5150; Fax: 517-224-5154. Hours: 8AM-5PM (EST). *Misdemeanor, Civil Actions Under $25,000, Eviction, Small Claims.*

Civil Records: Access: Mail, in person. Both court and visitors may perform in person searches. No search fee. Required to search: name, years to search. Civil cases indexed by defendant, plaintiff. Civil records on computer since 1989-90. **Criminal Records:** Access: Mail, in person. Both court and visitors may perform in person searches. No search fee. Required to search: name, years to search, DOB, SSN. Criminal records on computer since 1986. **General Information:** No suppressed, juvenile, sex offenders, mental health, or adoption records released. SASE required. Turnaround time 1 week. Copy fee: $.25 per page. Certification fee: No certification fee. Fee payee: 65th District Court. Personal checks accepted. Prepayment is required.

Probate Court 101 E State St, St Johns, MI 48879; 517-224-5190; Fax: 517-224-5254. Hours: 8AM-Noon, 1-5PM (EST). *Probate.*

www.clinton-county.org

Crawford County

46th Circuit Court 200 West Michigan Ave, Grayling, MI 49738; 517-348-2841; Fax: 517-344-3443. Hours: 8:30AM-4:30PM (EST). *Felony, Civil Actions Over $25,000.*

www.Circuit46.org

Civil Records: Access: Mail, in person. No search fee. Required to search: name, years to search. Civil cases indexed by defendant, plaintiff. Civil records on computer since 1990, prior on books. **Criminal Records:** Access: Mail, in person. Both court and visitors may perform in person searches. No search fee. Required to search: name, years to search, DOB. Criminal records on computer since 1990, prior on books. **General Information:** No suppressed records released. SASE required. Turnaround time 2-3 days. Copy fee: $1.00 per page. Certification fee: $10.00 plus $1.00 per page after first. Fee payee: Crawford County. Personal checks accepted. Prepayment is required.

83rd District Court 200 West Michigan Ave., Grayling, MI 49738; 517-348-2841 X242; Fax: 517-344-3290. Hours: 8AM-4:30PM (EST). *Misdemeanor, Civil Actions Under $25,000, Eviction, Small Claims.*

www.Circuit46.org

Civil Records: Access: Mail, in person. Only the court conducts in person searches; visitors may not. No search fee. Required to search: name, years to search. Civil cases indexed by defendant, plaintiff. Civil records on computer since 1990, books from 1969. **Criminal Records:** Access: Mail, in person. Only the court conducts in person searches; visitors may not. No search fee. Required to search: name, years to search, DOB. Criminal records on computer since 1989. **General Information:** No suppressed, juvenile, sex offenders, mental health, or adoption records released. SASE not required. Turnaround time 1-4

days. Copy fee: $.25 per page. Certification fee: $10.00 plus $1.00 each additional page. Fee payee: Crawford County 83rd District Court. Personal checks accepted. Credit cards accepted: Visa, Mastercard. Prepayment is required.

Probate Court 200 N Michigan Ave., Grayling, MI 49738; 517-348-2841 X237; Fax: 517-348-7582. Hours: 8:30AM-4:30PM (EST). *Probate.*

www.Circuit46.org

Delta County

47th Circuit Court 310 Ludington St, Escanaba, MI 49829; 906-789-5105; Fax: 906-789-5196. Hours: 8AM-4PM (EST). *Felony, Civil Actions Over $25,000.*

Civil Records: Access: Mail, in person. Both court and visitors may perform in person searches. Search fee: $5.00 per name. Required to search: name; also helpful-years to search, address. Civil cases indexed by defendant, plaintiff. Civil records on computer from 1989, archived into 1800s. **Criminal Records:** Access: Mail, in person. Both court and visitors may perform in person searches. Search fee: $5.00 per name. Required to search: name; also helpful-years to search, DOB, SSN. Criminal records on computer from 1989, archived into 1800s. **General Information:** No suppressed, juvenile, sex offenders, mental health, or adoption records released. SASE required. Turnaround time same day. Copy fee: $10.00 for first page, $1.00 each addl. Certification fee: $10.00 plus $1.00 per page after first. Fee payee: Delta County. Personal checks accepted. Prepayment is required.

94th District Court 310 Ludington St., Escanaba, MI 49829; 906-789-5106; Fax: 906-789-5198. Hours: 8AM-4PM (EST). *Misdemeanor, Civil Actions Under $25,000, Eviction, Small Claims.*

Civil Records: Access: Mail, in person. Only the court conducts in person searches; visitors may not. No search fee. Required to search: name, years to search; also helpful-address. Civil cases indexed by defendant, plaintiff. Civil records on computer since 1988, prior on books to 1968. **Criminal Records:** Access: Mail, in person. Only the court conducts in person searches; visitors may not. No search fee. Required to search: name, years to search, DOB; also helpful-address, SSN. Criminal records on computer since 1988, prior on books to 1968. **General Information:** No suppressed, juvenile, sex offenders, mental health, or adoption records released. SASE required. Turnaround time 3 days. Copy fee: $.25 per page. Certification fee: $10.00. Fee payee: 94th District Court. Personal checks accepted. Prepayment is required.

Probate Court 310 Ludington St., Escanaba, MI 49829; 906-789-5112; Fax: 906-789-5140. Hours: 8AM-Noon, 1-4PM (EST). *Probate.*

Dickinson County

41st Circuit Court PO Box 609, Iron Mountain, MI 49801; 906-774-0988; Fax: 906-774-4660. Hours: 8AM-4:30PM (CST). *Felony, Civil Actions Over $25,000.*

Civil Records: Access: Mail, in person. Both court and visitors may perform in person searches. Search fee: $15.00 per name. Fee is for 10 year search. Required to search: name, years to search. Civil cases indexed by defendant, plaintiff. Civil records on docket books since 1891. **Criminal Records:** Access: Mail, in person. Both court and visitors may perform in person searches. Search fee: $5.00 per name. Fee is for 10 year search. Required to search: name, years to search, DOB; also helpful-SSN. Criminal records on docket books since 1891. **General Information:** No suppressed, juvenile, sex offenders, mental health, or adoption records released. SASE required. Turnaround time 1-2 days. Copy fee: $.15 per page. Certification fee: $10.00 plus $1.00 per page. Fee payee: County Clerk. Business checks accepted. Prepayment is required.

95 B District Court County Courthouse, Iron Mountain, MI 49801; 906-774-0506; Fax: 906-774-3686. Hours: 8AM-4:30PM (CST). *Misdemeanor, Civil Actions Under $25,000, Eviction, Small Claims.*

Note: May require a signed release for certain records

Civil Records: Access: Mail, in person. Both court and visitors may perform in person searches. Search fee: $25.00 per name. Required to search: name, years to search; also helpful-address. Civil cases indexed by defendant, plaintiff. Civil records on index cards from 1976. **Criminal Records:** Access: Mail, in person. Both court and visitors may perform in person searches. Search fee: $25.00 per name. Required to search: name, years to search, DOB; also helpful-address, SSN. Criminal records on index cards from 1976. **General Information:** No suppressed, juvenile, sex offenders, mental health, or adoption records released. Turnaround time 1 week. Copy fee: $1.00 per page. Certification fee: $10.00. Fee payee: 95-B District Court. Only cashiers checks and money orders accepted. Prepayment is required.

Probate Court PO Box 609, Iron Mountain, MI 49801; 906-774-1555; Fax: 906-774-1561. Hours: 8AM-4:30PM (CST). *Probate.*

Eaton County

56th Circuit Court 1045 Independence Blvd, Charlotte, MI 48813; 517-543-7500 X396; Fax: 517-543-4475. Hours: 8AM-5PM (EST). *Felony, Civil Actions Over $25,000.*

www.co.eaton.mi.us/COURTS/COURTS.HTM

Civil Records: Access: Phone, fax, mail, in person. Both court and visitors may perform in person searches. Search fee: $5.00 per name. Required to search: name, years to search. Civil cases indexed by defendant, plaintiff. Civil records on computer since 1987, microfilm since 1930s, books from 1848. **Criminal Records:** Access: Fax, mail, in person. Both court and visitors may perform in person searches. Search fee: $5.00 per name. Required to search: name, years to search, DOB; also helpful-SSN. Criminal records on computer since 1985, microfolm since 1930s, books from 1860s. **General Information:** No suppressed, juvenile, sex offenders, mental health, or adoption records released. SASE required. Turnaround time 1-3 days. Copy fee: $1.00 for first page, $.50 each addl. Certification fee: $10.00 plus $1.00 per page after first. Fee payee: Eaton County Circuit Court Clerk. Personal checks accepted. Prepayment is required.

56th District Court - Civil Division 1045 Independence Blvd, Charlotte, MI 48813; 517-543-7500 X294. Hours: 8AM-5PM (EST). *Civil Actions Under $25,000, Eviction, Small Claims.*

www.co.eaton.mi.us/COURTS/COURTS.HTM

Civil Records: Access: Mail, in person. Both court and visitors may perform in person searches. No search fee. Required to search: name, years to search. Civil cases indexed by defendant, plaintiff.

Civil records on computer since 1997; prior records on books. **General Information:** No suppressed, juvenile, sex offenders, mental health, or adoption records. Turnaround time 1 week. Copy fee: $.25 per page. Certification fee: $10.00. Fee payee: 56th District. Personal checks accepted. Prepayment is required. Public access terminal is available.

56th District Court - Criminal 1045 Independence Blvd, Charlotte, MI 48813; 517-543-7500 X282; Fax: 517-543-7377. Hours: 8AM-5PM (EST). *Misdemeanor.*

www.co.eaton.mi.us/COURTS/COURTS.HTM

Criminal Records: Access: Mail, in person. Only the court conducts in person searches; visitors may not. Search fee:. Required to search: name, years to search, DOB; also helpful-SSN. Criminal records on computer since 1989, prior on books. **General Information:** No suppressed, juvenile, sex offenders, mental health, or adoption records released. SASE required. Turnaround time 2-3 days. Copy fee: $.25 per page. Certification fee: $10.00. Fee payee: 56th-2 District Court. Personal checks accepted. Prepayment is required.

Emmet County

57th Circuit Court 200 Division St, Petoskey, MI 49770; 231-348-1744; Fax: 231-348-0633. Hours: 8AM-5PM (EST). *Felony, Civil Actions Over $25,000.*

Civil Records: Access: Mail, in person. Only the court conducts in person searches; visitors may not. Search fee: $5.00 per name. Required to search: name, years to search. Civil cases indexed by defendant, plaintiff. Civil records on computer from 1867 to present. **Criminal Records:** Access: Mail, in person. Only the court conducts in person searches; visitors may not. Search fee: $5.00 per name. Required to search: name, years to search, DOB. Criminal records on computer from 1867 to present. **General Information:** No suppressed records released. SASE required. Turnaround time 5 days. Copy fee: $1.00 per page. Certification fee: $10.00. Fee payee: Emmet County Clerk. Personal checks accepted. Credit cards accepted: Visa, Mastercard. Prepayment is required.

90th District Court 200 Division St., Petoskey, MI 49770; 231-348-1750; Fax: 231-348-0616. Hours: 8AM-5PM (EST). *Misdemeanor, Civil Actions Under $25,000, Eviction, Small Claims.*

Civil Records: Access: Fax, mail, in person. Only the court conducts in person searches; visitors may not. No search fee. Required to search: name, years to search. Civil cases indexed by defendant, plaintiff. Civil records on computer since 1981, prior listed in books. **Criminal Records:** Access: Fax, mail, in person. Only the court conducts in person searches; visitors may not. No search fee. Required to search: name, years to search, DOB; also helpful-SSN. Criminal records on computer since 1981, prior listed in books. **General Information:** No suppressed, juvenile, sex offenders, mental health, or adoption records released. Turnaround time 2-3 days. Copy fee: $2.00 per page. Fee is for non-parties. Certification fee: $10.00. Fee payee: 90th District Court. Business checks accepted. Prepayment is required. Fax notes: $6.00 for first page, $1.00 each addl.

Probate Court 200 Division St., Petoskey, MI 49770; 231-348-1707; Fax: 231-348-0672. Hours: 8AM-5PM (EST). *Probate.*

Note: Shares the same judge with Charlevoix County Probate Court.

Genesee County

7th Circuit Court 900 South Saginaw, Flint, MI 48502; 810-257-3220. Hours: 8AM-5PM (EST). *Felony, Civil Actions Over $25,000.*

Civil Records: Access: Mail, in person. Both court and visitors may perform in person searches. Search fee: $5.00 per name. Required to search: name, years to search. Civil cases indexed by defendant, plaintiff. Civil records on computer since 1978, prior on index cards. **Criminal Records:** Access: Mail, in person. Both court and visitors may perform in person searches. Search fee: $5.00 per name. Required to search: name, years to search, DOB; also helpful-SSN, sex. Criminal records on computer since 1978, prior on index cards. **General Information:** No suppressed, juvenile, adoption, or mental health records released. SASE required. Turnaround time 1-2 weeks. Copy fee: $1.00 per page. Certification fee: $10.00. Fee payee: Genesee County Clerk. Prepayment is required. Public access terminal is available.

67th District Court 630 South Saginaw, Flint, MI 48502; 810-257-3170 (67th), 810-766-8968 (68th). Hours: 8AM-4PM (EST). *Misdemeanor, Civil Actions Under $25,000, Eviction, Small Claims.*

Civil Records: Access: Mail, in person. Only the court conducts in person searches; visitors may not. No search fee. Required to search: name, years to search; also helpful-address. Civil cases indexed by defendant, plaintiff. Civil records on computer since 1983, on microfilm since 1969, prior archived. **Criminal Records:** Access: Mail, in person. Only the court conducts in person searches; visitors may not. No search fee. Required to search: name, years to search, DOB, offense; also helpful-address, SSN. Criminal records on computer since 1983, on microfilm since 1969, prior archived. **General Information:** No drug related case records released. SASE helpful. Turnaround time 1 week. Copy fee: $1.00 per page. Certification fee: $11.00. Fee payee: 67th District Court. Only cashiers checks and money orders accepted. Prepayment is required.

Probate Court 919 Beach St, Flint, MI 48502; 810-257-3528; Fax: 810-257-3299. Hours: 8AM-4PM (EST). *Probate.*

Gladwin County

55th Circuit Court 401 West Cedar, Gladwin, MI 48624; 517-426-7351; Fax: 517-426-6917. Hours: 8:30AM-4:30PM (EST). *Felony, Civil Actions Over $25,000.*

Civil Records: Access: Fax, mail, in person. Both court and visitors may perform in person searches. No search fee. Required to search: name, years to search. Civil cases indexed by defendant, plaintiff. Civil records on computer since 1994, prior on books. **Criminal Records:** Access: Fax, mail, in person. Both court and visitors may perform in person searches. No search fee. Required to search: name, years to search, DOB; also helpful-SSN. Criminal records on computer since 1994, prior on books. **General Information:** No suppressed, juvenile, sex offenders, mental health, or adoption records released. SASE required. Turnaround time 2-3 days. Copy fee: $1.00 per page. Certification fee: $10.00 plus $1.00 per page after first. Fee payee: Gladwin County Clerk. Personal checks accepted. Prepayment is required.

Gladwin County

80th District Court 401 West Cedar, Gladwin, MI 48624; 517-426-9207; Fax: 517-426-6949. Hours: 8:30AM-4:30PM (EST). *Misdemeanor, Civil Actions Under $25,000, Eviction, Small Claims.*

Civil Records: Access: Mail, in person. Only the court conducts in person searches; visitors may not. No search fee. Required to search: name, years to search. Civil cases indexed by defendant, plaintiff. Civil records on computer since 1988, prior on index cards and docket books, archived to late 1968. **Criminal Records:** Access: Mail, in person. Only the court conducts in person searches; visitors may not. No search fee. Required to search: name, years to search, DOB; also helpful-SSN. Criminal records on computer since 1988, prior on index cards and docket books, archived to late 1968. **General Information:** No suppressed, juvenile, sex offenders, mental health, or adoption records released. SASE required. Turnaround time same day when possible. Copy fee: $2.00 per page. Certification fee: $10.00 plus $1.00 per page after first. Fee payee: 80th District Court. Personal checks accepted. Prepayment is required.

Probate Court 401 West Cedar, Gladwin, MI 48624; 517-426-7451; Fax: 517-426-5478. Hours: 8:30AM-4:30PM (EST). *Probate.*

Note: This is combined with Clare County Probate Court.

Gogebic County

32nd Circuit Court 200 North Moore St, Bessemer, MI 49911; 906-663-4518; Fax: 906-663-4660. Hours: 8:30AM-4:30PM (CST). *Felony, Civil Actions Over $25,000.*

Civil Records: Access: Mail, in person. Both court and visitors may perform in person searches. Search fee: $5.00 per name. Required to search: name, years to search. Civil cases indexed by defendant, plaintiff. Civil records in books since 1887. **Criminal Records:** Access: Mail, in person. Both court and visitors may perform in person searches. Search fee: $5.00 per name. Required to search: name, years to search, DOB; also helpful-SSN. Criminal records in books since 1887. **General Information:** No suppressed, juvenile, sex offenders, mental health, or adoption records released. SASE requested. Turnaround time 1-2 days. Copy fee: $1.00 per page. Certification fee: $10.00. Fee payee: Gogebic County Clerk's Office. Personal checks accepted. Prepayment is required.

98th District Court 200 North Moore St, Bessemer, MI 49911; 906-663-4611; Fax: 906-663-4660. Hours: 8:30AM-4PM (CST). *Misdemeanor, Civil Actions Under $25,000, Eviction, Small Claims.*

Civil Records: Access: Mail, in person. Only the court conducts in person searches; visitors may not. Search fee: $5.00 per name. Required to search: name, years to search. Civil cases indexed by defendant, plaintiff. Civil records on computer since 6/88. **Criminal Records:** Access: Mail, in person. Only the court conducts in person searches; visitors may not. Search fee: $5.00 per name. Required to search: name, years to search, DOB, SSN. Criminal records on computer since 6/88. **General Information:** No suppressed, juvenile, sex offenders, mental health, or adoption records released. SASE not required. Turnaround time 10 days. Copy fee: $1.00 per page. Certification fee: $10.00 plus $1.00 per page after

first. Fee payee: District Court. Business checks accepted. Prepayment is required.

Probate Court 200 North Moore St., Bessemer, MI 49911; 906-667-0421; Fax: 906-663-4660. Hours: 8:30AM-Noon, 1-4:30PM (CST). *Probate.*

Grand Traverse County

13th Circuit Court 328 Washington St, Traverse City, MI 49684; 231-922-4710. Hours: 8AM-5PM (EST). *Felony, Civil Actions Over $25,000.*

Civil Records: Access: Phone, mail, in person. Both court and visitors may perform in person searches. No search fee. Required to search: name, years to search. Civil cases indexed by defendant, plaintiff. Civil records on computer since 1971, prior on books since 1859. **Criminal Records:** Access: Phone, mail, in person. Both court and visitors may perform in person searches. No search fee. Required to search: name, years to search; also helpful-DOB, SSN. Criminal records on computer since 1981. **General Information:** No suppressed records released. SASE required. Turnaround time 1 week. Copy fee: $1.00 for first page, $.25 each addl. Certification fee: $10.00 plus $1.00 per page after first. Fee payee: 13th Circuit Court. Personal checks accepted. Prepayment is required.

86th District Court 328 Washington St., Traverse City, MI 49684; 231-922-4580; Fax: 231-922-4454. Hours: 8AM-5PM (EST). *Misdemeanor, Civil Actions Under $25,000, Eviction, Small Claims.*

Civil Records: Access: Phone, mail, in person. Only the court conducts in person searches; visitors may not. No search fee. Required to search: name, years to search. Civil cases indexed by defendant, plaintiff. Civil records on computer since 1988, prior on books. **Criminal Records:** Access: Phone, mail, in person. Only the court conducts in person searches; visitors may not. No search fee. Required to search: name, years to search, DOB; also helpful-SSN. Most criminal records on computer. **General Information:** No suppressed, juvenile, sex offenders, mental health, or adoption records released. SASE required. Turnaround time 2-3 days. Copy fee: $.25 per page. Certification fee: $10.00. Fee payee: 86th District Court. Business checks accepted. Prepayment is required.

Probate Court 400 Boardman St, Traverse City, MI 49684; 231-922-4640; Fax: 231-922-6893. Hours: 8AM-5PM (EST). *Probate.*

Gratiot County

29th Circuit Court 214 East Center St, Ithaca, MI 48847; 517-875-5215. Hours: 8:30AM-5PM (EST). *Felony, Civil Actions Over $25,000.*

Civil Records: Access: Mail, in person. Only the court conducts in person searches; visitors may not. Search fee: $10.00 per name. Fee is for 5 years, $1.00 each additional year. Required to search: name, years to search. Civil cases indexed by defendant, plaintiff. **Criminal Records:** Access: Mail, in person. Only the court conducts in person searches; visitors may not. Search fee: $10.00 per name. Fee is for 5 years, $1.00 each additional year. Required to search: name, years to search. **General Information:** No suppressed, juvenile, sex offenders, mental health, or adoption records released. SASE required. Turnaround time 1-3 days. Copy fee: $1.00 per page. Certification fee: $10.00. Fee payee: Gratiot County Clerk. Personal checks accepted. Prepayment is required.

65-B District Court 245 East Newark St, Ithaca, MI 48847; 517-875-5240; Fax: 517-875-5290. Hours: 8AM-4:30PM (EST). *Misdemeanor, Civil Actions Under $25,000, Eviction, Small Claims.*

Civil Records: Access: In person only. Court does not conduct in person searches; visitors must perform searches for themselves. Search fee: No civil searches performed by court. Required to search: name, years to search. Civil cases indexed by defendant, plaintiff. Civil records on index books from 1969 to present. **Criminal Records:** Access: In person only. Court does not conduct in person searches; visitors must perform searches for themselves. Search fee: No criminal searches performed by court. Required to search: name, years to search, DOB; also helpful-SSN. Criminal records on computer since 02/20/96. **General Information:** No non-public records released. Copy fee: $1.00 per page. Certification fee: $10.00 plus $1.00 per page after first. Fee payee: 65B District Court. Personal checks accepted. Prepayment is required.

Probate Court 214 E Center St, PO Box 217, Ithaca, MI 48847; 517-875-5231; Fax: 517-875-5331. Hours: 8:30AM-5PM (EST). *Probate.*

Hillsdale County

1st Circuit Court 29 North Howell, Hillsdale, MI 49242; 517-437-3391; Fax: 517-437-3392. Hours: 8:30AM-5PM (EST). *Felony, Civil Actions Over $25,000.*

Civil Records: Access: Mail, in person. Only the court conducts in person searches; visitors may not. Search fee: $1.00 per name per year. Required to search: name, years to search. Civil cases indexed by defendant, plaintiff. Civil records on computer from 1985, prior on docket books, archived to 1844. **Criminal Records:** Access: Mail, in person. Only the court conducts in person searches; visitors may not. Search fee: $1.00 per name per year. Required to search: name, years to search, DOB; also helpful-SSN. Criminal records on computer from 1985, prior on docket books, archived to 1844. **General Information:** No suppressed, juvenile, sex offenders, mental health, or adoption records released. SASE required. Turnaround time 2-3 days. Copy fee: $1.00 per page. Certification fee: $10.00. Fee payee: Hillsdale County Clerk. Personal checks accepted. Out-of-state personal checks not accepted. Prepayment is required.

2nd District Court 49 North Howell, Hillsdale, MI 49242; 517-437-7329; Fax: 517-437-2908. Hours: 8AM-4:30PM; 8AM-5PM Traffic (EST). *Misdemeanor, Civil Actions Under $25,000, Eviction, Small Claims.*

Civil Records: Access: Phone, mail, in person. Both court and visitors may perform in person searches. No search fee. Required to search: name, years to search. Civil cases indexed by defendant, plaintiff. Civil records kept in docket books and files. A request in writing may be required. **Criminal Records:** Access: Phone, mail, in person. Only the court conducts in person searches; visitors may not. No search fee. Required to search: name, years to search, DOB; also helpful-SSN. Criminal records kept in docket books and files. **General Information:** No suppressed records released. Turnaround time 1 week. Copy fee: $.15 per page. Certification fee: $10.00 plus $1.00 each add'l page. Fee payee: Hillsdale District Court. Personal checks accepted. Prepayment is required.

Probate Court 29 North Howell, Hillsdale, MI 49242; 517-437-4643. Hours: 8:30AM-Noon, 1-5PM (EST). *Probate.*

Houghton County

12th Circuit Court 401 East Houghton Ave, Houghton, MI 49931; 906-482-5420. Hours: 8AM-4:30PM (EST). *Felony, Civil Actions Over $25,000.*

Civil Records: Access: Mail, in person. Only the court conducts in person searches; visitors may not. No search fee. Required to search: name, years to search. Civil cases indexed by defendant, plaintiff. Civil records kept on docket books, cards; are computerized as of 1997. **Criminal Records:** Access: Mail, in person. Only the court conducts in person searches; visitors may not. No search fee. Required to search: name, years to search, DOB; also helpful-SSN. Criminal records kept on docket books, cards; are computerized as of 1997. **General Information:** No suppressed, juvenile, sex offenders, mental health, or adoption records released. SASE required. Turnaround time 1-2 days. Copy fee: $1.00 per page. Certification fee: $10.00 plus $1.00 per page after first. Fee payee: Clerk of Circuit Court. Personal checks accepted. Prepayment is required.

97th District Court 401 East Houghton Ave., Houghton, MI 49931; 906-482-4980; Fax: 906-482-7238. Hours: 8AM-4:30PM (EST). *Misdemeanor, Civil Actions Under $25,000, Eviction, Small Claims.*

Civil Records: Access: Mail, in person. Both court and visitors may perform in person searches. No search fee. Required to search: name, years to search; also helpful-address. Civil cases indexed by defendant, plaintiff. Civil records listed in "Registers of Actions". **Criminal Records:** Access: Mail, in person. Both court and visitors may perform in person searches. No search fee. Required to search: name, years to search, DOB; also helpful-address. Criminal records listed in "Registers of Actions". **General Information:** No conviction records released. SASE required. Turnaround time 1 week. Copy fee: $1.00 for first page, $.25 each addl. Certification fee: $10.00 plus $1.00 per page after first. Fee payee: 97th District Court. Business checks accepted. Prepayment is required.

Probate Court 401 E. Houghton Ave., Houghton, MI 49931; 906-482-3120; Fax: 906-487-5964. Hours: 8AM-4:30PM (EST). *Probate.*

Huron County

52nd Circuit Court 250 East Huron Ave, Bad Axe, MI 48413; 517-269-9942; Fax: 517-269-6160. Hours: 8:30AM-5PM (EST). *Felony, Civil Actions Over $25,000.*

Civil Records: Access: Phone, mail, in person. Both court and visitors may perform in person searches. Search fee: $5.00 per name. Required to search: name, years to search. Civil cases indexed by defendant, plaintiff. Civil records on computer since 1992, prior on books to 1867. **Criminal Records:** Access: Phone, mail, in person. Both court and visitors may perform in person searches. Search fee: $5.00 per name. Required to search: name, years to search, DOB; also helpful-SSN. Criminal records on computer since 1992, prior on books to 1867. **General Information:** No suppressed, juvenile, sex offenders, mental health, or adoption records released. SASE required. Turnaround time 2-3 days. Copy fee: $1.00 per page. Certification fee: $10.00 plus $1.00 per page

after first. Fee payee: Huron County Clerk. No personal checks accepted. Prepayment is required.

73B District Court 250 East Huron Ave., Bad Axe, MI 48413; 517-269-9987; Fax: 517-269-6167. Hours: 8:30AM-5PM *Misdemeanor, Civil Actions Under $25,000, Eviction, Small Claims.*

Civil Records: Access: Phone, fax, mail, in person. Only the court conducts in person searches; visitors may not. Search fee: $5.00 per name. Required to search: name, years to search. Civil cases indexed by defendant, plaintiff. Civil records on computer since June 1992, prior on books since 1969. **Criminal Records:** Access: Phone, fax, mail, in person. Only the court conducts in person searches; visitors may not. Search fee: $5.00 per name. Required to search: name, years to search, DOB; also helpful-SSN. Criminal records on computer since June 1992, prior on books since 1969. **General Information:** No suppressed, juvenile, sex offenders, mental health, or adoption records released. SASE required. Turnaround time 1-5 days. Copy fee: $1.00 per page. Certification fee: No certification fee. Fee payee: 73B District Court. Business checks accepted. Prepayment is required. Fax notes: No fee to fax results.

Probate Court 250 E. Huron Ave., Bad Axe, MI 48413; 517-269-9944; Fax: 517-269-0004. Hours: 8:30AM-Noon, 1-5PM (EST). *Probate.*

Ingham County

30th Circuit Court 333 South Capital Ave, Ste C, Lansing, MI 48933; 517-483-6500; Fax: 517-483-6501. Hours: 9AM-Noon, 1-5PM M,T,Th,F; 8AM-Noon, 1-5PM W (EST). *Felony, Civil Actions Over $25,000.*

Civil Records: Access: Phone, mail, in person. Both court and visitors may perform in person searches. No search fee. Required to search: name, years to search. Civil cases indexed by defendant, plaintiff. Civil records on computer since 1986. **Criminal Records:** Access: Phone, mail, in person. Both court and visitors may perform in person searches. No search fee. Required to search: name, years to search; also helpful-DOB. Criminal records on computer since 1986. **General Information:** All circuit Court files are public record unless specifically suppressed by Judge. SASE not required. Turnaround time 1-2 days, unless file is in storage then 1 week. Copy fee: $.50 per page 1st 10 pages, each additional page $.20 per page. Certification fee: $10.00 plus $1.00 per page after first. Fee payee: Ingham County Circuit Court. Personal checks accepted. Prepayment is required.

54 A District Court 124 West Michigan Ave, Lansing, MI 48933; 517-483-4433; Civil phone:517-483-4426; Criminal phone:517-483-4426; Fax: 517-483-4108. Hours: 8AM-4:35PM (EST). *Misdemeanor, Civil Actions Under $25,000, Eviction, Small Claims.*

Note: This court covers the city of Lansing

Civil Records: Access: In person only. Court does not conduct in person searches; visitors must perform searches for themselves. Search fee: No civil searches performed by court. Required to search: name, years to search. Civil cases indexed by defendant, plaintiff. Civil records on computer since 1990, microfiche from 1985, prior archived. **Criminal Records:** Access: In person only. Court does not conduct in person searches; visitors must perform searches for themselves. Search fee: No criminal searches performed by court. Required to search: name, years to search, DOB, offense, date

of offense; also helpful-SSN. Criminal records on computer since 1990, microfiche from 1985, prior archived. **General Information:** No suppressed, juvenile, sex offenders, mental health, or adoption, non-public records released. Copy fee: $.50 per page. Certification fee: $10.00 plus $1.00 per page after first. Fee payee: 54A District Court. No personal checks accepted. Credit cards accepted: Visa, Mastercard. Prepayment is required. Public access terminal is available.

54 B District Court 101 Linden, East Lansing, MI 48823; 517-351-7000; Civil phone:517-351-1730; Criminal phone:517-351-1730; Fax: 517-351-3371. Hours: 8AM-4:30PM (EST). *Misdemeanor, Civil Actions Under $25,000, Eviction, Small Claims.*

Note: This court covers the city of East Lansing

Civil Records: Access: Mail, in person. Both court and visitors may perform in person searches. No search fee. Required to search: name, years to search. Civil cases indexed by defendant, plaintiff. Civil records on computer since 1991, ROA's are kept indefinitely. **Criminal Records:** Access: Mail, in person. Both court and visitors may perform in person searches. No search fee. Required to search: name, years to search, DOB; also helpful-SSN. Criminal records on computer since 1989, files stored prior. **General Information:** No suppressed, juvenile, sex offenders, mental health, or adoption records released. Turnaround time up 1 hour to 1 week, depends on availability. Copy fee: $.25 per page. Certification fee: $10.00 plus $1.00 per page after first. Fee payee: 54-B District Court. Personal checks accepted. Two party or payroll checks not allowed. Credit cards accepted: Visa, Mastercard. Debit card. Prepayment is required. Public access terminal is available.

55th District Court 700 Buhl, Mason, MI 48854; 517-676-8400. Hours: 8:30AM-4:30PM (EST). *Misdemeanor, Civil Actions Under $25,000, Eviction, Small Claims.*

Note: This court covers all of Ingham County except for Lansing and East Lansing

Civil Records: Access: Mail, in person. Both court and visitors may perform in person searches. No search fee. Required to search: name, years to search. Civil records on computer since 11/91, prior listed in index books. **Criminal Records:** Access: Mail, in person. Both court and visitors may perform in person searches. No search fee. Required to search: name, years to search, DOB; also helpful-SSN. Criminal records on computer since 1994, prior on books. **General Information:** No suppressed, juvenile, sex offenders, mental health, or adoption records released. SASE required. Turnaround time 5 days. Copy fee: $1.00 per page. Certification fee: $10.00 plus $1.00 each additional page. Fee payee: 55th District court. Personal checks accepted. Prepayment is required.

Ingham County Probate Court PO Box 176, Mason, MI 48854; 517-676-7276; Fax: 517-676-7344. Hours: 8AM-Noon, 1-5PM (EST). *Probate.*

Lansing Probate Court 303 West Kalamazoo, Lansing, MI 48933; 517-483-6300; Fax: 517-483-6150. Hours: 8AM-Noon, 1-5PM (EST). *Probate.*

Ionia County

8th Circuit Court 100 Main, Ionia, MI 48846; 616-527-5322; Fax: 616-527-5323. Hours: 8:30AM-5PM (EST). *Felony, Civil Actions Over $25,000.*

Civil Records: Access: Phone, fax, mail, in person. Only the court conducts in person searches; visitors may not. No search fee. Required to search: name, years to search. Civil cases indexed by defendant, plaintiff. Civil records on computer since 7/91; prior records kept in books and files, archived to 1800s. **Criminal Records:** Access: Phone, fax, mail, in person. Only the court conducts in person searches; visitors may not. No search fee. Required to search: name, years to search; also helpful-DOB, SSN. Criminal records on computer since 6/84; in books and files prior. **General Information:** No suppressed records released. SASE not required. Turnaround time 1 week. Copy fee: $1.00 per page. Certification fee: $10.00 plus $1.00 per page after first. Fee payee: Ionia County Clerk. Personal checks accepted. Prepayment is required. Fax notes: $1.00 per page.

64 A District Court 101 West Main, Ionia, MI 48846; 616-527-5346; Fax: 616-527-5343. Hours: 7:45AM-5:30PM (EST). *Misdemeanor, Civil Actions Under $25,000, Eviction, Small Claims.*

Civil Records: Access: Fax, mail, in person. Only the court conducts in person searches; visitors may not. Search fee: $3.00 per name. Required to search: name, years to search. Civil cases indexed by defendant, plaintiff. Files and books available since 1969. Fax request must be followed up by originals. **Criminal Records:** Access: Fax, mail, in person. Only the court conducts in person searches; visitors may not. Search fee: $3.00 per name. Required to search: name, years to search, DOB; also helpful-address. Files and books available since 1969. Fax must be followed up by originals. **General Information:** No suppressed, juvenile, sex offenders, mental health, or adoption records released. SASE requested. Turnaround time 10 days. Copy fee: $.50 per page. Certification fee: $10.00 plus $1.00 per page after first. Fee payee: 64-A District Court. Personal checks accepted. Prepayment is required.

Probate Court 100 Main, Ionia, MI 48846; 616-527-5326; Fax: 616-527-5321. Hours: 8:30AM-5PM (EST). *Probate.*

Iosco County

23rd Circuit Court PO Box 838, Tawas City, MI 48764; 517-362-3497; Fax: 517-362-1444. Hours: 9AM-5PM (EST). *Felony, Civil Actions Over $25,000.*

Civil Records: Access: Phone, mail, in person. Both court and visitors may perform in person searches. No search fee. Required to search: name, years to search. Civil records on computer since 1987, prior on books. **Criminal Records:** Access: Phone, mail, in person. Both court and visitors may perform in person searches. No search fee. Required to search: name, years to search, DOB; also helpful-SSN. Criminal records on computer since 1983. **General Information:** No suppressed, parental waivers, mental health, or adoption records released. SASE not required. Turnaround time 1 week. Copy fee: $.25 per page. Certification fee: $10.00 plus $1.00 per page after first. Fee payee: Iosco County Clerk. Only cashiers checks and money orders accepted. Prepayment is required.

81st District Court PO Box 388, Tawas City, MI 48764; 517-362-4441; Fax: 517-362-3494. Hours: 8AM-5PM (EST). *Misdemeanor, Civil Actions Under $25,000, Eviction, Small Claims.*

Civil Records: Access: Mail, in person. Only the court conducts in person searches; visitors may

not. No search fee. Required to search: name, years to search. Civil cases indexed by defendant, plaintiff. Civil records on computer since 1987, prior on books. **Criminal Records:** Access: Mail, in person. Only the court conducts in person searches; visitors may not. No search fee. Required to search: name, years to search, DOB; also helpful-SSN. Criminal records on computer since 1987, prior on books. **General Information:** No suppressed, juvenile, sex offenders, mental health, or adoption records released. SASE required. Turnaround time 2-3 days. Copy fee: $2.00 for first page, $.50 each addl. Certification fee: $10.00 plus $1.00 per page after first. Fee payee: 81st District Court. Personal checks accepted. Prepayment is required.

Probate Court PO Box 421, Tawas City, MI 48764; 517-362-3991; Fax: 517-362-1459. Hours: 8AM-5PM (EST). *Probate.*

Iron County

41st Circuit Court 2 South 6th St, Crystal Falls, MI 49920; 906-875-3221; Fax: 906-875-6675. Hours: 8AM-4PM (CST). *Felony, Civil Actions Over $25,000.*

Civil Records: Access: Fax, mail, in person. Only the court conducts in person searches; visitors may not. Search fee: $5.00 per name. Required to search: name, years to search. Civil cases indexed by defendant, plaintiff. Most records on books, on microfiche 1958-67. **Criminal Records:** Access: Fax, mail, in person. Only the court conducts in person searches; visitors may not. Search fee: $5.00 per name. Required to search: name, years to search, DOB; also helpful-SSN. Most records on books, on microfiche 1958-67. **General Information:** No suppressed, juvenile, sex offenders, mental health, or adoption records released. SASE required. Turnaround time 2-3 days. Copy fee: $.25 per page. Certification fee: $10.00 plus $1.00 per page after first. Fee payee: Iron County Clerk. Personal checks accepted. Prepayment is required. Fax notes: $1.50 per page.

95 B District Court 2 South 6th St., Crystal Falls, MI 49920; 906-875-6658; Fax: 906-875-6775. Hours: 8AM-4PM *Misdemeanor, Civil Actions Under $25,000, Eviction, Small Claims.*

Civil Records: Access: Mail, in person. Only the court conducts in person searches; visitors may not. Search fee: $5.00. Required to search: name, years to search. Civil cases indexed by defendant, plaintiff. Civil records computerized since 1999, earlier records index kept on cards, accessible from 1982. **Criminal Records:** Access: Mail, in person. Only the court conducts in person searches; visitors may not. No search fee. Required to search: name, years to search, DOB; also helpful-SSN. Criminal records computerized since 1999, earlier records index kept on cards, accessible from 1982. **General Information:** No suppressed, juvenile, sex offenders, mental health, or adoption records released. SASE required. Turnaround time 1 week. Copy fee: $.25 per page. Certification fee: $10.00 plus $1.00 per page after first. Fee payee: 95-B District Court. Personal checks accepted. Prepayment is required.

Probate Court 2 South 6th St, Suite 10, Crystal Falls, MI 49920; 906-875-3121; Fax: 906-875-6775. 8AM-Noon, 12:30-4PM *Probate.*

Isabella County

21st Circuit Court 200 North Main St, Mount Pleasant, MI 48858; 517-772-0911 X308. Hours: 8AM-4:30PM (EST). *Felony, Civil Actions Over $25,000.*

Civil Records: Access: Mail, in person. Both court and visitors may perform in person searches. Search fee: Search fee from 1980 to present $5.00. Prior years $1.00 per year. Required to search: name, years to search. Civil cases indexed by defendant, plaintiff. Civil records on computer since 1980, archived from 1900. **Criminal Records:** Access: Mail, in person. Both court and visitors may perform in person searches. Search fee: from 1980 to present $5.00. Prior years $1.00 per year. Required to search: name, years to search, DOB; also helpful-SSN. Criminal records on computer since 1980, archived from 1900. **General Information:** No suppressed, juvenile, sex offenders, mental health, or adoption records released. Turnaround time 1-2 weeks. Copy fee: $10.00 for first page, $1.00 each addl. Certification fee: $10.00 plus $1.00 per page after first. Fee payee: County Clerk. Personal checks accepted. Prepayment is required.

76th District Court 200 North Main St., Mount Pleasant, MI 48858; 517-772-0911 X320; Fax: 517-773-2419. Hours: 8AM-4:30PM (EST). *Misdemeanor, Civil Actions Under $25,000, Eviction, Small Claims.*

Civil Records: Access: Mail, in person. Both court and visitors may perform in person searches. Search fee: $5.00 per name. Required to search: name, years to search. Civil cases indexed by defendant, plaintiff. Civil records on computer since 1988, on books since 1960s. **Criminal Records:** Access: Mail, in person. Both court and visitors may perform in person searches. Search fee: $5.00 per name. Required to search: name, years to search, DOB; also helpful-SSN. Criminal records on computer since 1988, on books since 1960s. **General Information:** No suppressed, juvenile, sex offenders, mental health, or adoption records released. SASE required. Turnaround time 5-7 days. Copy fee: $1.00 per page. Certification fee: $10.00 plus $1.00 per page after first. Fee payee: 76th District Court. Business checks accepted. Prepayment is required.

Probate Court 200 N Main St, Mount Pleasant, MI 48858; 517-772-0911 X310; Fax: 517-773-2419. Hours: 8AM-4:30PM (EST). *Probate.*

Jackson County

4th Circuit Court 312 South Jackson St, Jackson, MI 49201; 517-788-4268. Hours: 8AM-5PM (EST). *Felony, Civil Actions Over $25,000.*

www.co.jackson.mi.us

Civil Records: Access: Phone, mail, in person. Only the court conducts in person searches; visitors may not. Search fee: $10.50 per hour. Required to search: name, years to search. Civil cases indexed by defendant, plaintiff. Civil records on computer since 1982, prior on index cards and docket books since 1800s. **Criminal Records:** Access: Phone, mail, in person. Only the court conducts in person searches; visitors may not. Search fee: $10.50 per hour. Required to search: name, years to search; also helpful-DOB, SSN. Criminal records on computer since 1982, prior on index cards and docket books since 1800s. **General Information:** No adoption or juvenile records released. Turnaround time 1 week. Copy fee: $.25 per page. Certification fee: $10.00 plus $1.00 per page after first. Fee payee: Jackson County Clerk. Only cashiers checks and money orders accepted. Credit cards accepted: Visa, Mastercard. Prepayment of fax and mail service required. Fees billed to Attorney's.

12th District Court 312 South Jackson St., Jackson, MI 49201; 517-788-4260; Fax: 517-788-

4262. Hours: 7AM-6PM (EST). *Misdemeanor, Civil Actions Under $25,000, Eviction, Small Claims.*

www.d12.com

Civil Records: Access: Fax, mail, in person. Only the court conducts in person searches; visitors may not. No search fee. Required to search: name, years to search. Civil cases indexed by defendant, plaintiff. Civil records on computer since 1986. **Criminal Records:** Access: Fax, mail, in person. Only the court conducts in person searches; visitors may not. No search fee. Required to search: name, years to search, DOB; also helpful-SSN. Criminal records on computer since 1986. **General Information:** No suppressed, juvenile, sex offenders, mental health, or probation records released. Turnaround time 5 days. Copy fee: $.25 per page. Certification fee: $10.00 plus $1.00 per page after first. Fee payee: 12th District Court. Personal checks accepted. Third party checks not allowed. Prepayment is required. Fax notes: $5.00 for first page, $1.00 each addl.

Probate Court 312 S Jackson St, 1st Fl, Jackson, MI 49201; 517-788-4290. Hours: 8AM-5PM (EST). *Probate.*

Kalamazoo County

9th Circuit Court 227 West Michigan St, Kalamazoo, MI 49007; 616-384-8250, 616-383-8837. Hours: 9AM-4PM (EST). *Felony, Civil Actions Over $25,000.*

Civil Records: Access: Mail, in person. Only the court conducts in person searches; visitors may not. Search fee: $1.00 per name. Required to search: name, years to search. Civil cases indexed by defendant, plaintiff. Civil records stored as hard copies, some records kept off-site. **Criminal Records:** Access: Mail, in person. Only the court conducts in person searches; visitors may not. Search fee: $1.00 per name. Required to search: name, years to search, DOB; also helpful-SSN. Criminal records stored as hard copies, some records kept off-site. **General Information:** No suppressed or non-public records released. Turnaround time 2 days. Copy fee: $1.00 per page. Certification fee: $13.00. Fee payee: Circuit Court Clerk. Personal checks accepted. Prepayment is required.

8th District Court 227 West Michigan St., Kalamazoo, MI 49007; 616-384-8171; Fax: 616-384-8047. Hours: 8:30AM-4PM (EST). *Misdemeanor, Civil Actions Under $25,000, Eviction, Small Claims.*

Note: This court covers the areas in Kalamazoo County not handled by the 9th District Courts

Civil Records: Access: Fax, mail, in person. Both court and visitors may perform in person searches. No search fee. Required to search: name, years to search, address. Civil cases indexed by defendant, plaintiff. Civil records on computer since 1991, prior on books. **Criminal Records:** Access: Fax, mail, in person. Both court and visitors may perform in person searches. No search fee. Required to search: name, years to search, DOB; also helpful-SSN. Criminal records on computer since 1991, prior on books. **General Information:** No suppressed or non-public records released. SASE requested. Turnaround time 2 days. Copy fee: $.50 per page. Certification fee: $10.00. Fee payee: 8th District Court. Personal checks accepted. Credit cards accepted: Visa, Mastercard. Prepayment is required. Public access terminal is available. Fax notes: No fee to fax results.

8th District Court Division 1 416 S. Rose, Kalamazoo, MI 49007; 616-384-8020; Fax: 616-383-8899. Hours: 8AM-4:15PM (EST). *Misdemeanor, Civil Actions Under $25,000, Eviction, Small Claims.*

Note: This court covers city of Kalamazoo

Civil Records: Access: Fax, mail, in person. Both court and visitors may perform in person searches. No search fee. Required to search: name, years to search. Civil cases indexed by defendant, plaintiff. Civil records on computer since 1988, prior on index books. **Criminal Records:** Access: Fax, mail, in person. Both court and visitors may perform in person searches. No search fee. Required to search: name, years to search, DOB; also helpful-SSN. Criminal records on computer since 1988, prior on index books. **General Information:** No suppressed records released. SASE not required. Turnaround time 1-3 days. Copy fee: $.50 per page. Certification fee: $10.00. Fee payee: 8th District Court. Personal checks accepted. Credit cards accepted: Visa, Mastercard.

9th District Court Division 2 7810 Shaver Rd., Portage, MI 49002; 616-329-4590; Fax: 616-329-4519. Hours: 8AM-4:30PM (EST). *Misdemeanor, Civil Actions Under $25,000, Eviction, Small Claims.*

Note: This court covers the city of Portage

Civil Records: Access: Mail, in person. Only the court conducts in person searches; visitors may not. Search fee: $20.00 per name. Required to search: name, years to search. Civil cases indexed by defendant, plaintiff. Civil records on computer since 1992, prior on index books. **Criminal Records:** Access: Mail, in person. Only the court conducts in person searches; visitors may not. Search fee: $20.00 per name. Required to search: name, years to search, DOB; also helpful-SSN. Criminal records on computer since 1992, prior on index books. **General Information:** No suppressed, juvenile, sex offenders, mental health, or adoption records released. SASE required. Turnaround time 5 days. Copy fee: $.50 per page. Certification fee: $10.00 plus $1.00 per page after first. Fee payee: 9th District Court Division 2. Personal checks accepted. Prepayment is required.

Probate Court 227 West Michigan Ave., Kalamazoo, MI 49007; 616-383-8666/8933; Fax: 616-383-8685. Hours: 9AM-Noon, 1-5PM M; 8AM-Noon, 1-5PM T-F (EST). *Probate.*

Kalkaska County

46th Circuit Court PO Box 10, Kalkaska, MI 49646; 231-258-3300. Hours: 9AM-5PM (EST). *Felony, Civil Actions Over $25,000.*

www.Circuit46.org

Civil Records: Access: Mail, in person. Only the court conducts in person searches; visitors may not. Search fee: $5.00 per name. Required to search: name, years to search. Civil cases indexed by defendant, plaintiff. Civil records on computer since 1989, prior on books, indexed to 1800s. **Criminal Records:** Access: Mail, in person. Only the court conducts in person searches; visitors may not. Search fee: $5.00 per name. Required to search: name, years to search, DOB; also helpful-SSN. Criminal records on computer since 1989, prior on books, indexed to 1800s. **General Information:** No suppressed records released. SASE required. Turnaround time 2-3 days. Copy fee: $.30 per page. Certification fee: $10.00 plus $1.00 per page after first. Fee payee: County Clerk. Personal checks accepted. Prepayment is required.

87th District Court PO Box 780, Kalkaska, MI 49646; 231-258-9031; Fax: 231-258-2424. Hours: 8AM-4:30PM (EST). *Misdemeanor, Civil Actions Under $25,000, Eviction, Small Claims.*

www.Circuit46.org

Civil Records: Access: Phone, mail, in person. Only the court conducts in person searches; visitors may not. No search fee. Required to search: name, years to search. Civil cases indexed by defendant, plaintiff. Civil records on computer since 1989, prior on books. **Criminal Records:** Access: Phone, mail, in person. Only the court conducts in person searches; visitors may not. No search fee. Required to search: name, years to search, DOB. Criminal records on computer since 1989, prior on books. **General Information:** No suppressed records released. SASE required. Turnaround time 4 days. Copy fee: $1.00 per page. Certification fee: $10.00 plus $1.00 per page after first. Fee payee: 87th District Court. Personal checks accepted. Prepayment is required.

Circuit Trial Court - Probate Division 605 North Birch, PO Box 780, Kalkaska, MI 49646; 231-258-3330; Fax: 231-258-3329. Hours: 9AM-Noon, 1-5PM (EST). *Probate.*

www.Circuit46.org

Kent County

17th Circuit Court 333 Monroe Ave NW, Grand Rapids, MI 49503; 616-336-3679; Fax: 616-336-3349. Hours: 8AM-5PM (EST). *Felony, Civil Actions Over $25,000.*

www.co.kent.mi.us/courts.htm

Civil Records: Access: Mail, in person. Only the court conducts in person searches; visitors may not. Search fee: $5.00 per name. Required to search: name, years to search. Civil cases indexed by defendant, plaintiff. Civil records on computer since 1986, prior on books. **Criminal Records:** Access: Mail, in person. Only the court conducts in person searches; visitors may not. Search fee: $5.00 per name. Required to search: name, years to search, DOB. Criminal records on computer since 1986, prior on books. **General Information:** No supressed records released. SASE not required. Turnaround time 2-3 days. Copy fee: $1.00 per page. Certification fee: $10.00 plus $1.00 per page after first. Fee payee: Kent County Clerk. Personal checks accepted. Prepayment is required.

59th District Court - Grandville & Walker 3181 Wilson Ave SW, Grandville, MI 49418; 616-538-9660; Fax: 616-538-5144. Hours: 8:30AM-Noon,1-5PM (EST). *Misdemeanor, Civil Actions Under $25,000, Eviction, Small Claims.*

Civil Records: Access: Mail, in person. Only the court conducts in person searches; visitors may not. Search fee: $1.00 per name. Add $.50 per year requested. Required to search: name, years to search; also helpful-address. Civil cases indexed by defendant, plaintiff. Civil records on computer from 1990, docket books and cards prior. **Criminal Records:** Access: Mail, in person. Only the court conducts in person searches; visitors may not. Search fee: $1.00 per name. Add $.50 per year requested. Required to search: name, years to search, DOB; also helpful-address, SSN. Criminal records on computer from 1990, docket books and cards prior. **General Information:** No suppressed, juvenile, sex offenders, mental health, or adoption records released. SASE required. Turnaround time varies. Copy fee: $1.00 per page. Certification fee: $10.00 plus $1.00 per page after first. Fee payee: 59th District Court. Personal checks accepted. Prepayment is required.

61st District Court - Grand Rapids 333

Monroe Ave NW, Grand Rapids, MI 49503;; Civil phone:616-456-3370; Criminal phone:616-456-3370; Fax: 616-456-3311. Hours: 7:45AM-4:45PM (EST). *Misdemeanor, Civil Actions Under $25,000, Eviction, Small Claims.*

Civil Records: Access: Mail, in person. Only the court conducts in person searches; visitors may not. No search fee. Required to search: name, years to search. Civil cases indexed by defendant, plaintiff. Civil records kept in files and books. **Criminal Records:** Access: Mail, in person. Only the court conducts in person searches; visitors may not. Search fee: $1.00 per name per year. Required to search: name, years to search, DOB; also helpful-SSN. Criminal records are automated from 1985, microfiche from 1980. **General Information:** No suppressed, juvenile, sex offenders, mental health, or adoption records released. SASE not required. Turnaround time 7-10 days. Copy fee: $1.00 for first page, $.50 each addl. Certification fee: $10.00 plus $1.00 per page after first. Fee payee: 61st District Court. Personal checks accepted. Prepayment of mail service required.

62 A District Court - Wyoming 2650 De

Hoop Ave SW, Wyoming, MI 49509; 616-530-7385; Fax: 616-249-3419. Hours: 8AM-5PM (EST). *Misdemeanor, Civil Actions Under $25,000, Eviction, Small Claims.*

Civil Records: Access: Mail, in person. Both court and visitors may perform in person searches. Search fee: Search fee $1.00 per name & $.50 per year. Required to search: name, years to search. Civil cases indexed by defendant, plaintiff. Civil records kept on docket books. The judge must approve all requests from collection agencies. **Criminal Records:** Access: In person only. Both court and visitors may perform in person searches. Search fee: $1.00 per name & $.50 per year. Required to search: name, years to search, DOB; also helpful-SSN. Criminal records kept on docket books. The court suggests mail requests be sent to the state police. **General Information:** No suppressed, juvenile, sex offenders, mental health, or adoption records released. SASE required. Turnaround time 2-3 days. Copy fee: $1.00 per page. Certification fee: $10.00 plus $1.00 per page after first. Fee payee: 62 A District Court. Personal checks accepted. Credit cards accepted: Visa. Accepted in person only. Prepayment is required. Public access terminal is available. Public Access Terminal Note: Available 01/97.

62 B District Court - Kentwood PO

Box 8848, Kentwood, MI 49518; 616-698-9310; Fax: 616-698-8199. Hours: 8AM-5PM (EST). *Misdemeanor, Civil Actions Under $25,000, Eviction, Small Claims.*

Civil Records: Access: Mail, in person. Only the court conducts in person searches; visitors may not. Search fee: $5.00 per name. Required to search: name, years to search. Civil cases indexed by defendant, plaintiff. Civil records on computer since 11/88, prior on books. **Criminal Records:** Access: Fax, mail, in person. Only the court conducts in person searches; visitors may not. Search fee: $5.00 per name. Required to search: name, years to search, DOB. Criminal records on computer since 11/88, prior on books. **General Information:** No suppressed, juvenile, sex offenders, mental health, or adoption records released. SASE required. Turnaround time 1-2 days. Copy fee: $2.00 for first page, $.25 each addl. Certification fee: $15.00. Fee payee: 62 B

District Court. Personal checks accepted. Prepayment is required.

63rd District Court - 1st Division 105

Maple St, Rockford, MI 49341; 616-866-1576; Fax: 616-866-3080. Hours: 8AM-5PM (EST). *Misdemeanor, Civil Actions Under $25,000, Eviction, Small Claims.*

Civil Records: Access: Mail, in person. Both court and visitors may perform in person searches. No search fee. Required to search: name, years to search. Civil cases indexed by defendant, plaintiff. Civil records on computer since 8/94, prior on books. **Criminal Records:** Access: Mail, in person. Both court and visitors may perform in person searches. No search fee. Required to search: name, years to search, DOB; also helpful-SSN. Criminal records on computer since 8/94, prior on books. **General Information:** No suppressed, juvenile, sex offenders, mental health, or adoption records released. SASE required. Turnaround time 1 week. Copy fee: $1.00 per page. Certification fee: $10.00. Fee payee: 63rd District Court. Personal checks accepted. Prepayment is required. Public access terminal is available.

Probate Court 320 Ottawa Ave. NW, Grand Rapids, MI 49503; 616-336-3630; Fax: 616-336-3574. Hours: 8:30AM-5PM (EST). *Probate.*

Keweenaw County

12th Circuit Court HCI Box 607, Eagle

River, MI 49924; 906-337-2229; Fax: 906-337-2795. Hours: 9AM-4PM (EST). *Felony, Civil Actions Over $25,000.*

Civil Records: Access: Mail, in person. Only the court conducts in person searches; visitors may not. No search fee. Required to search: name, years to search. Civil cases indexed by defendant, plaintiff. Civil records kept on index books. **Criminal Records:** Access: Mail, in person. Only the court conducts in person searches; visitors may not. No search fee. Required to search: name, years to search, DOB. Criminal records kept on index books. **General Information:** No suppressed, juvenile, sex offenders, mental health, or adoption records released. SASE required. Turnaround time 1-2 days. Copy fee: $.50 per page. Certification fee: $10.00. Fee payee: Keweenaw County. Personal checks accepted. Prepayment is required.

97th District Court HCI Box 607, Eagle

River, MI 49950; 906-337-2229; Fax: 906-337-2795. Hours: 9AM-4PM (EST). *Misdemeanor, Civil Actions Under $25,000, Eviction, Small Claims.*

Civil Records: Access: Fax, mail, in person. Only the court conducts in person searches; visitors may not. No search fee. Required to search: name, years to search. Civil cases indexed by defendant, plaintiff. Civil records kept on books. Results cannot be faxed. **Criminal Records:** Access: Fax, mail, in person. Only the court conducts in person searches; visitors may not. No search fee. Required to search: name, years to search, DOB; also helpful-SSN. Criminal records kept on books. Results cannot be faxed. **General Information:** No suppressed, juvenile, sex offenders, mental health, or adoption records released. SASE required. Turnaround time 1-2 days. Copy fee: $.50 per page. Certification fee: $10.00. Fee payee: Keweenaw County. Personal checks accepted. Prepayment is required.

Probate Court HC1 Box 607, Courthouse, Eagle River, MI 49924; 906-337-1927; Fax: 906-337-2795. Hours: 9AM-4PM (EST). *Probate.*

Lake County

51st Circuit Court PO Drawer B, Baldwin,

MI 49304; 231-745-4614. Hours: 8:30AM-5PM (EST). *Felony, Civil Actions Over $25,000.*

Civil Records: Access: Mail, in person. Only the court conducts in person searches; visitors may not. Search fee: $5.00 per name. Required to search: name, years to search. Civil cases indexed by defendant, plaintiff. Civil records on computer since 7/90, prior on index books since 1900s. **Criminal Records:** Access: Mail, in person. Only the court conducts in person searches; visitors may not. Search fee: $5.00 per name. Required to search: name, years to search. Criminal records on computer since 7/90, prior on index books since 1900s. **General Information:** No sealed records released. SASE required. Turnaround time 2 days. Copy fee: $1.00 per page. Certification fee: $10.00. Fee payee: Lake County Trial Court. Personal checks accepted. Prepayment is required.

Lake County Trial Court PO Box 1330,

Baldwin, MI 49304; 231-745-4614. Hours: 8:30AM-5PM (EST). *Misdemeanor, Civil Actions Under $25,000, Eviction, Small Claims.*

Civil Records: Access: Mail, in person. Only the court conducts in person searches; visitors may not. Search fee: $5.00 per name per year. Required to search: name, years to search. Civil cases indexed by defendant, plaintiff. Civil records on computer since 7/89, prior on books. **Criminal Records:** Access: Mail, in person. Only the court conducts in person searches; visitors may not. Search fee: $5.00 per name per year. Required to search: name, years to search, DOB; also helpful-SSN. Criminal records on computer since 7/89, prior on books. **General Information:** No suppressed, juvenile, sex offenders, mental health, or adoption records released. SASE not required. Turnaround time 3-7 days. No copy fee. Certification fee: No certification fee. Fee payee: Lake County Trial Court. Personal checks accepted. Prepayment is required.

Lake County Trial Court PO Box 1330,

Baldwin, MI 49304; 231-745-4614; Fax: 231-745-2241. Hours: 8:30AM-5PM (EST). *Probate.*

Lapeer County

40th Circuit Court 255 Clay St, Lapeer, MI

48446; 810-667-0358. Hours: 8AM-5PM (EST). *Felony, Civil Actions Over $25,000.*

Civil Records: Access: Phone, mail, in person. Both court and visitors may perform in person searches. Search fee: $5.00 search fee covers 10 year span. Required to search: name, years to search. Civil cases indexed by defendant, plaintiff. Civil records on computer since 1985, prior on index cards. **Criminal Records:** Access: Phone, mail, in person. Both court and visitors may perform in person searches. Search fee: $5.00 search fee covers 10 year span. Required to search: name, years to search. Criminal records on computer since 1985, prior on index cards. **General Information:** No suppressed, juvenile, sex offenders, mental health, or adoption records released. SASE required. Turnaround time 1-3 days. Copy fee: $1.00 per page. Certification fee: $10.00 plus $1.00 per page after first. Fee payee: 40th Circuit Court. Personal checks accepted. Prepayment is required.

71 A District Court 255 Clay St., Lapeer, MI 48446; 810-667-0300. Hours: 8AM-5PM (EST).

Misdemeanor, Civil Actions Under $25,000, Eviction, Small Claims.

Civil Records: Access: Mail, in person. Only the court conducts in person searches; visitors may not. Search fee: $5.00 per name. Required to search: name, years to search. Civil cases indexed by defendant, plaintiff. Civil records on computer since 1992, cards and dockets from 1969. **Criminal Records:** Access: Mail, in person. Only the court conducts in person searches; visitors may not. Search fee: $5.00 per name. Required to search: name, years to search, DOB; also helpful-SSN. Criminal records on computer since 1992, cards and dockets from 1969. **General Information:** No suppressed, juvenile, sex offenders, mental health, or adoption records released. SASE requires. Turnaround time 10 days. Copy fee: $1.00 per page. Certification fee: $10.00 plus $1.00 per page after first. Fee payee: 71 A District Court. Personal checks accepted. Third party checks not accepted. Prepayment is required.

Probate Court 255 Clay St., Lapeer, MI 48446; 810-667-0261; Fax: 810-667-0390. Hours: 8AM-5PM (EST). *Probate.*

Leelanau County

13th Circuit Court PO Box 467, Leland, MI 49654; 231-256-9824; Fax: 231-256-7850. Hours: 9AM-5PM (EST). *Felony, Civil Actions Over $25,000.*

Civil Records: Access: Mail, in person. Both court and visitors may perform in person searches. Search fee: $3.00 per name. Required to search: name, years to search. Civil cases indexed by defendant, plaintiff. Civil records on computer since 1/93, prior on docket books. **Criminal Records:** Access: Mail, in person. Both court and visitors may perform in person searches. Search fee: $3.00 per name. Required to search: name, years to search. Criminal records on computer since 1/97; prior records on books. **General Information:** No suppressed, juvenile, sex offenders, mental health, or adoption records released. SASE required. Turnaround time 2-3 days. Copy fee: $.50 per page. Certification fee: $10.00 plus $1.00 per page after first. Fee payee: County Clerk. Personal checks accepted. Prepayment is required.

86th District Court PO Box 486, Leland, MI 49654; 231-256-8250; Fax: 231-256-8275. Hours: 8AM-4PM (EST). *Misdemeanor, Civil Actions Under $25,000, Eviction, Small Claims.*

Civil Records: Access: Fax, mail, in person. Only the court conducts in person searches; visitors may not. No search fee. Required to search: name, years to search. Civil cases indexed by defendant, plaintiff. Civil records on computer since 1991, prior on books to 1969. **Criminal Records:** Access: Phone, fax, mail, in person. Only the court conducts in person searches; visitors may not. No search fee. Required to search: name, years to search, DOB; also helpful-SSN. Criminal records on computer since 1991, prior on books to 1969. **General Information:** No suppressed, sex offenders records released. SASE requested. Turnaround time 3 days. Copy fee: $.25 per page. Certification fee: $10.00. Business checks accepted. Prepayment is required. Fax notes: $.25 per page.

Probate Court/Juvenile Division PO Box 595, Leland, MI 49654; 231-256-9803; Fax: 231-256-9845. Hours: 9AM-5PM (EST). *Probate.*

Lenawee County

39th Circuit Court 425 North Main St, Adrian, MI 49221; 517-264-4597. Hours: 8AM-4:30PM (EST). *Felony, Civil Actions Over $25,000.*

Civil Records: Access: Mail, in person. Only the court conducts in person searches; visitors may not. Search fee: $10.00 per name. Fee is for ten years. Required to search: name, years to search. Civil records on computer since 01/89, prior on books. **Criminal Records:** Access: Mail, in person. Only the court conducts in person searches; visitors may not. Search fee: $10.00 per name. Fee is for 10 years. Required to search: name, years to search. Criminal records on computer since 01/89, prior on books. **General Information:** No suppressed, juvenile, sex offenders, mental health, or adoption records released. SASE helpful. Turnaround time 1-2 days. Copy fee: $.50 per page. Certification fee: $1.00 per page. Fee payee: Lenawee County Clerk or 39th Circuit Court. Personal checks accepted. Prepayment is required.

2A District Court 425 North Main St., Adrian, MI 49221; 517-264-4673 & 264-4668; Fax: 517-264-4665 Probation; 264-4681. Hours: 8AM-4:30PM (EST). *Misdemeanor, Civil Actions Under $25,000, Eviction, Small Claims.*

Civil Records: Access: Fax, mail, in person. Both court and visitors may perform in person searches. Search fee: $10.00 per name. Required to search: name, years to search. Civil cases indexed by defendant, plaintiff. Civil records on computer since 1988, prior on index books, cards and microfilm. **Criminal Records:** Access: In person. Both court and visitors may perform in person searches. Search fee: $10.00 per name. Required to search: name, years to search, DOB. Criminal records on computer since 1988, prior on index books, cards and microfilm. **General Information:** No suppressed, juvenile, sex offenders, mental health, or adoption records released. SASE required. Turnaround time 1 week. Copy fee: $.25 per page. Certification fee: $10.00. Fee payee: 2nd District Court. Personal checks accepted. Prepayment is required.

Probate Court 425 North Main St., Adrian, MI 49221; 517-264-4614; Fax: 517-264-4616. Hours: 8AM-4:30PM (EST). *Probate.*

Livingston County

44th Circuit Court 210 South Highlander Way, Howell, MI 48843; 517-546-9816. Hours: 8AM-5PM (EST). *Felony, Civil Actions Over $25,000.*

Note: Juvenile Unit records are at 517-546-1500

Civil Records: Access: Mail, in person. Both court and visitors may perform in person searches. No search fee. Required to search: name, years to search. Civil cases indexed by defendant, plaintiff. Civil records computerized from 1987, microfiched and archived from 1900s. **Criminal Records:** Access: Mail, in person. Both court and visitors may perform in person searches. No search fee. Required to search: name, years to search. Criminal records computerized from 1987, microfiched and archived from 1900s. **General Information:** All records released, none are restricted. SASE required. Turnaround time 5 days. Copy fee: $1.00 per page. Certification fee: $10.00 plus $1.00 ea add'l pg. Fee payee: Livingston County Clerk. Personal checks accepted. Out of state checks not accepted.

Prepayment is required. Public access terminal is available.

53 A District Court 300 South Highlander Way, Howell, MI 48843; 517-548-1000; Fax: 517-548-9445. Hours: 8AM-4:45PM (EST). *Misdemeanor, Civil Actions Under $25,000, Eviction, Small Claims.*

Civil Records: Access: Mail, in person. Only the court conducts in person searches; visitors may not. No search fee. Required to search: name, years to search; also helpful-address. Civil cases indexed by defendant, plaintiff. Civil records on computer since 1982. **Criminal Records:** Access: Mail, in person. Only the court conducts in person searches; visitors may not. No search fee. Required to search: name, years to search, DOB; also helpful-address, SSN. Criminal records on computer since 1982. **General Information:** No suppressed, juvenile, sex offenders, mental health, or adoption records released. SASE preferred. Turnaround time 1 week. Copy fee: $1.00 for first page, $.50 each addl. Certification fee: $10.00. Fee payee: 53 District Court. Personal checks accepted. Prepayment is required.

53 B District Court 224 N First, Brighton, MI 48116;; Civil phone:810-229-6615; Criminal phone:810-229-6615; Fax: 810-229-1770. Hours: 8AM-4:45PM (EST). *Misdemeanor, Civil Actions Under $25,000, Eviction, Small Claims.*

Civil Records: Access: Mail, in person. Only the court conducts in person searches; visitors may not. No search fee. Required to search: name, years to search. Civil cases indexed by defendant, plaintiff. Civil records on computer since 1985, prior on index books. **Criminal Records:** Access: Mail, in person. Only the court conducts in person searches; visitors may not. No search fee. Required to search: name, years to search, DOB; also helpful-SSN. Criminal records on computer since 1985, prior on index books. **General Information:** No suppressed, juvenile, sex offenders, mental health, or adoption records released. SASE required. Turnaround time 1 week. Copy fee: $1.00 for first page, $.50 each addl. Certification fee: $10.00. Fee payee: 53rd District Court. Personal checks accepted.

Probate Court 200 E. Grand River, Howell, MI 48843; 517-546-3750; Fax: 517-546-3731. Hours: 8AM-5PM (EST). *Probate.*

Luce County

11th Circuit Court 407 W Harrie, Newberry, MI 49868; 906-293-5521; Fax: 906-293-3581. Hours: 8AM-4PM (EST). *Felony, Civil Actions Over $25,000.*

Civil Records: Access: Mail, in person. Only the court conducts in person searches; visitors may not. No search fee. Required to search: name, years to search. Civil cases indexed by defendant, plaintiff. Civil records listed on cards since 1876. **Criminal Records:** Access: Mail, in person. Only the court conducts in person searches; visitors may not. No search fee. Required to search: name, years to search, DOB. Criminal records listed on cards since 1876. **General Information:** No suppressed, juvenile, sex offenders, mental health, or adoption records released. SASE required. Turnaround time 4-5 days. Copy fee: $1.00 per page. Certification fee: $10.00. Fee payee: 11th Circuit Court. Personal checks accepted. Prepayment is required.

92nd District Court 407 W Harrie, Newberry, MI 49868; 906-293-5531; Fax: 906-293-3581. Hours: 8AM-4PM (EST). *Misdemeanor,*

Civil Records: Access: Mail, in person. Only the court conducts in person searches; visitors may not. No search fee. Required to search: name, years to search. Civil cases indexed by defendant, plaintiff. Civil records on computer since 11/93; prior records on cards. **Criminal Records:** Access: Mail, in person. Only the court conducts in person searches; visitors may not. No search fee. Required to search: name, years to search, DOB. Criminal records on computer since 1993, prior on index cards. **General Information:** No suppressed records released. SASE required. Turnaround time 1 week. Copy fee: $1.00 per page. No certification fee. Fee payee: 26-1 District Court. No personal checks accepted. Prepayment is required.

26-2 District Court 3869 W Jefferson, Ecorse, MI 48229; 313-386-7900; Fax: 313-386-4316. Hours: 9AM-4PM (EST). *Misdemeanor, Civil Actions Under $25,000, Eviction, Small Claims.*

Civil Records: Access: Mail, in person. Only the court conducts in person searches; visitors may not. No search fee. Required to search: name, years to search. Civil cases indexed by defendant, plaintiff. Civil records on computer since 1992, prior on index cards. **Criminal Records:** Access: Mail, in person. Only the court conducts in person searches; visitors may not. No search fee. Required to search: name, years to search, DOB; also helpful-SSN. Criminal records on computer since 1992, prior on index cards. **General Information:** No suppressed records released. SASE not required. Turnaround time 1 week. Copy fee: $.50 per page. Certification fee: $10.00. Fee payee: 26-2 District Court. Business checks accepted.

27-1 District Court 2015 Biddle Ave, Wyandotte, MI 48192; 734-324-4475; Fax: 734-324-4472. Hours: 8:30AM-4:30PM (EST). *Misdemeanor, Civil Actions Under $25,000, Eviction, Small Claims.*

Civil Records: Access: Mail, in person. Only the court conducts in person searches; visitors may not. No search fee. Required to search: name, years to search. Civil cases indexed by defendant, plaintiff. Civil records on computer since 1988, prior on index cards. **Criminal Records:** Access: Mail, in person. Only the court conducts in person searches; visitors may not. No search fee. Required to search: name, years to search, DOB. Criminal records on computer since 1988, prior on index cards. **General Information:** No suppressed records released. SASE required. Turnaround time 1 week. Copy fee: $1.00 per page. Certification fee: $10.00 plus $1.00 per page after first. Fee payee: 27-1 District Court. Personal checks accepted. Prepayment is required.

27-2 District Court 14100 Civic Park Dr, Riverview, MI 48192; 734-281-4204. Hours: 8:30AM-4:30PM (EST). *Misdemeanor, Civil Actions Under $25,000, Eviction, Small Claims.*

Civil Records: Access: Mail, in person. Both court and visitors may perform in person searches. No search fee. Required to search: name, years to search. Civil cases indexed by defendant, plaintiff. Civil records on computer since 1988. **Criminal Records:** Access: Mail, in person. Both court and visitors may perform in person searches. No search fee. Required to search: name, years to search, DOB. Criminal records on computer since 1988. **General Information:** No suppressed records released. Turnaround time 1 week. Copy fee: $1.00 per page. Certification fee: $10.00 plus $1.00 per page after first. Fee payee: 27-2 District

Court. Personal checks accepted. Prepayment is required.

28th District Court 14720 Reaume Parkway, Southgate, MI 48195; 734-246-1360; Civil phone:734-246-1366; Criminal phone:734-246-1366; Fax: 734-246-1405. Hours: 8:30AM-4:30PM (EST). *Misdemeanor, Civil Actions Under $25,000, Eviction, Small Claims.*

Civil Records: Access: Fax, mail, in person. Both court and visitors may perform in person searches. No search fee. Required to search: name, years to search; also helpful-address. Civil cases indexed by defendant, plaintiff. Civil records on computer since 1987, prior on card files by party. **Criminal Records:** Access: Fax, mail, in person. Only the court conducts in person searches; visitors may not. No search fee. Required to search: name, years to search, DOB; also helpful-address, SSN. Criminal records on computer since 1987, prior on card files by party. **General Information:** No suppressed, probation, juvenile, sex offenders, mental health, or adoption records released. SASE required. Turnaround time 2 days. Copy fee: $1.00 per page. Certification fee: $10.00. Fee payee: 28th District Court. Only cashiers checks and money orders accepted. Credit cards accepted: Visa, Mastercard. In person only. Prepayment is required.

29th District Court 34808 Sims Ave, Wayne, MI 48184; 734-722-5220; Fax: 734-722-7003. Hours: 8AM-4:30PM (EST). *Misdemeanor, Civil Actions Under $25,000, Eviction, Small Claims.*

Civil Records: Access: Mail, in person. Only the court conducts in person searches; visitors may not. No search fee. Required to search: name, years to search. Civil cases indexed by defendant, plaintiff. Civil records on computer since 1990. **Criminal Records:** Access: Mail, in person. Only the court conducts in person searches; visitors may not. No search fee. Required to search: name, years to search, DOB; also helpful-address, SSN. Criminal records on computer since 1990. **General Information:** No suppressed, juvenile, sex offenders, mental health, or adoption records released. SASE required. Turnaround time 1 week, phone turnaround time 1 day. Copy fee: $.50 per page. Certification fee: $25.00. Fee payee: 29th District Court. Personal checks accepted. Credit cards accepted: Visa, Mastercard. Prepayment is required.

30th District Court 28 Gerard Ave, Highland Park, MI 48203; 313-252-0300; Fax: 313-865-1115. Hours: 8AM-4:30PM (EST). *Misdemeanor, Civil Actions Under $25,000, Eviction, Small Claims.*

Civil Records: Access: Mail, in person. Both court and visitors may perform in person searches. Search fee: $5.00 per name. Required to search: name, years to search. Civil cases indexed by defendant, plaintiff. Civil records on computer since 1989, prior on index cards. **Criminal Records:** Access: Mail, in person. Both court and visitors may perform in person searches. Search fee: $5.00 per name. Required to search: name, years to search, DOB. Criminal records on computer since 1989, prior on index cards. **General Information:** No suppressed records released. SASE required. Turnaround time 1 week. Copy fee: $1.00 per page. Certification fee: $5.00. Fee payee: 30th District Court. Personal checks accepted. Prepayment is required.

31st District Court 3401 Evaline Ave, Hamtramck, MI 48212; 313-876-7710; Fax: 313-876-7724. Hours: 8AM-4PM (EST).

Misdemeanor, Civil Actions Under $25,000, Eviction, Small Claims.

Civil Records: Access: Mail, in person. Only the court conducts in person searches; visitors may not. No search fee. Required to search: name, years to search. Civil cases indexed by defendant, plaintiff. Civil records on computer since 1989, prior on index cards. **Criminal Records:** Access: Mail, in person. Only the court conducts in person searches; visitors may not. No search fee. Required to search: name, years to search, DOB; also helpful-SSN. Criminal records on computer since 1989, prior on index cards. **General Information:** No suppressed records released. SASE required. Turnaround time 1-2 days. Copy fee: $1.00 per page. Certification fee: $10.00 plus $1.00 per page after first. Fee payee: 31st District Court. Personal checks accepted. Prepayment is required.

32 A District Court 19617 Harper Ave, Harper Woods, MI 48225; 313-343-2590; Fax: 313-343-2594. Hours: 8:30AM-4:30PM (EST). *Misdemeanor, Civil Actions Under $25,000, Small Claims.*

Civil Records: Access: Phone, fax, mail, in person. Only the court conducts in person searches; visitors may not. No search fee. Required to search: name, years to search. Civil cases indexed by defendant, plaintiff. Civil records indexed by name and case number on computer, microfiche, and paper. **Criminal Records:** Access: Phone, fax, mail, in person. Only the court conducts in person searches; visitors may not. No search fee. Required to search: name, years to search. Criminal records indexed by name and case number on computer, microfiche, and paper. **General Information:** No suppressed records released. SASE requested. Turnaround time same day. Copy fee: $.50 per page. Certification fee: No certification fee. Fee payee: 32A District Court. Personal checks accepted. Credit cards accepted: Visa, Mastercard. Prepayment is required. Fax notes: No fee to fax results.

33rd District Court 19000 Van Horn Rd, Woodhaven, MI 48183;; Civil phone:734-671-0225; Criminal phone:734-671-0225; Fax: 734-671-0307. Hours: 8:30AM-4:30PM (EST). *Misdemeanor, Civil Actions Under $25,000, Eviction, Small Claims.*

Civil Records: Access: Mail, in person. Only the court conducts in person searches; visitors may not. No search fee. Required to search: name, years to search; also helpful-address. Civil cases indexed by defendant, plaintiff. Civil records on computer since 1995, prior on microfilm and microfiche. **Criminal Records:** Access: Mail, in person. Only the court conducts in person searches; visitors may not. No search fee. Required to search: name, years to search, DOB; also helpful-address. Criminal records on computer since 1995, prior on microfilm and microfiche. **General Information:** No suppressed records released. SASE required. Turnaround time 1-5 days. Copy fee: $.25 per page. Certification fee: $10.00 plus $1.00 per page after first. Fee payee: 33rd District Court. Business checks accepted. Credit cards accepted: Visa, Mastercard. Prepayment is required.

34th District Court 11131 S Wayne Rd, Romulus, MI 48174; 734-941-4462; Fax: 734-941-7530. Hours: 8:30AM-4PM (EST). *Misdemeanor, Civil Actions Under $25,000, Eviction, Small Claims.*

Civil Records: Access: Mail, in person. Only the court conducts in person searches; visitors may not. No search fee. Required to search: name, years to search. Civil cases indexed by defendant, plaintiff. Civil records on computer since 1984, prior on index cards and docket books. **Criminal Records:** Access: Mail, in person. Only the court conducts in person searches; visitors may not. No search fee. Required to search: name, years to search, DOB; also helpful-SSN. Criminal records on computer since 1984, prior on index cards and docket books. **General Information:** No suppressed records released. SASE required. Turnaround time 1 week. Copy fee: $1.00 per page. Certification fee: $10.00 per page. Fee payee: 34th District Court. Personal checks accepted. Prepayment is required.

35th District Court 660 Plymouth Rd, Plymouth, MI 48170; 734-459-4740; Fax: 734-454-9303. Hours: 8:30AM-4:25PM (EST). *Misdemeanor, Civil Actions Under $25,000, Eviction, Small Claims.*

Civil Records: Access: Mail, in person. Both court and visitors may perform in person searches. No search fee. Required to search: name, years to search. Civil cases indexed by defendant, plaintiff. Civil records on computer since 1990; prior records archived. **Criminal Records:** Access: Mail, in person. Both court and visitors may perform in person searches. No search fee.

Required to search: name, years to search, DOB; also helpful-SSN. Criminal records on computer since 1990; prior records archived. **General Information:** No suppressed, juvenile, sex offenders, mental health, or adoption records released. Turnaround time 1 week. Copy fee: $1.00 per page. Certification fee: No certification fee. Fee payee: 35th District Court. Personal checks accepted. Third party checks not allowed. Debit cards accepted. Prepayment is required.

Wexford County

28th Circuit Court PO Box 490, Cadillac, MI 49601; 231-779-9450. Hours: 8:30AM-5PM (EST). *Felony, Civil Actions Over $25,000.*

Civil Records: Access: Mail, in person. Only the court conducts in person searches; visitors may not. Search fee: $1.00 per name. Required to search: name, years to search. Civil cases indexed by defendant, plaintiff. Civil records on computer since 1977. **Criminal Records:** Access: Mail, in person. Only the court conducts in person searches; visitors may not. Search fee: $5.00 per name. Fee is for first 3 years. Add $2.00 for each add'l year. Required to search: name, years to search. Criminal records on computer since 1977. **General Information:** No suppressed, YTA files, juvenile, sex offenders, mental health, or adoption records released. SASE required. Turnaround time same day. Copy fee: $1.00 per page. Certification

fee: $10.00. Fee payee: Wexford County Clerk. Only cashiers checks and money orders accepted. Prepayment is required.

84th District Court 501 S Garfield, Cadillac, MI 49601; 231-779-9515; Fax: 231-779-9485. Hours: 8:30AM-5PM (EST). *Misdemeanor, Civil Actions Under $25,000, Eviction, Small Claims.*

Civil Records: Access: Phone, mail, in person. Both court and visitors may perform in person searches. Search fee: $1.00 per name. Required to search: name, years to search. Civil cases indexed by defendant, plaintiff. Civil records on computer since 1984; on index from 1969 to 1984. **Criminal Records:** Access: Mail, in person. Both court and visitors may perform in person searches. Search fee: $1.00 per name. Required to search: name, years to search, DOB; also helpful-SSN. Criminal records on computer since 1984; prior records on blue cards. **General Information:** No suppressed, juvenile, sex offenders, mental health, or adoption records released. SASE required. Turnaround time 1 week. Copy fee: $1.00 per page. Certification fee: $10.00. Fee payee: 84th District Court. Personal checks accepted. Prepayment is required.

Probate Court 503 S Garfield, Cadillac, MI 49601; 231-779-9510; Fax: 231-779-9485. Hours: 8:30AM-5PM (EST). *Probate.*

ORGANIZATION   83 counties, 83 recording offices. The recording officer is County Register of Deeds. 79 counties are in the Eastern Time Zone (EST) and 4 are in the Central Time Zone (CST).

REAL ESTATE RECORDS   Some counties will perform real estate searches. Copies usually cost $1.00 per page. and certification fees vary. Ownership records are located at the Equalization Office, designated "Assessor" in this section. Tax records are located at the Treasurer's Office.

UCC RECORDS   Financing statements are filed at the state level except for consumer goods, farm related and real estate related filings. All counties will perform UCC searches. Use search request form UCC-11. Search fees are usually $3 per debtor name if federal tax identification number or Social Security number are given, or $6 without the number. Copies usually cost $1 per page.

TAX LIEN RECORDS   Federal and state tax liens on personal property of businesses are filed with the Secretary of State. Other federal and state tax liens are filed with the Register of Deeds. Most counties search each tax lien index separately. Some charge one fee to search both, while others charge a separate fee for each one. When combining a UCC and tax lien search, total fee is usually $9 for all three searches. Some counties require tax id number as well as name to do a search. Copy fees are usually $1 per page.

OTHER LIENS   Construction, lis pendens.

Alcona County
County Register of Deeds, P.O. Box 269, Harrisville, MI 48740-0269. 517-724-6802. Fax: 517-724-5684.

Alger County
County Register of Deeds, P.O. Box 538, Munising, MI 49862. 906-387-2076. Fax: 906-387-2156.

Allegan County
County Register of Deeds, 113 Chestnut Street, County Court House, Allegan, MI 49010-1360. 616-673-0390. Fax: 616-673-0289.

Alpena County
County Register of Deeds, 720 West Chisholm Street, Courthouse, Alpena, MI 49707-2487. 517-356-3887. Fax: 517-356-6559.

Antrim County
County Register of Deeds, P.O. Box 295, Bellaire, MI 49615. 231-533-6683. Fax: 231-533-8317.

Arenac County
County Register of Deeds, P.O. Box 296, Standish, MI 48658. 517-846-9201.

Baraga County
County Register of Deeds, Courthouse, 16 N. 3rd St., L'Anse, MI 49946-1085. 906-524-6183. Fax: 906-524-6186.

Barry County
County Register of Deeds, P.O. Box 7, Hastings, MI 49058-0007. 616-948-4824. Fax: 616-948-4820.

Bay County
County Register of Deeds, 515 Center Avenue, Bay City, MI 48708-5994. 517-895-4228. Fax: 517-895-4296.

Benzie County
County Register of Deeds, P.O. Box 398, Beulah, MI 49617. 231-882-0016. Fax: 231-882-0167.

Berrien County
County Register of Deeds, Berrien County Administration Center, 701 Main St., St. Joseph, MI 49085. 616-983-7111x8562. Fax: 616-982-8659.

Branch County
County Register of Deeds, 31 Division Street, Coldwater, MI 49036. 517-279-4320.

Calhoun County
County Register of Deeds, 315 West Green Street, Marshall, MI 49068. 616-781-0718. Fax: 616-781-0721. www.co.calhoun.mi.us/docs/documents.html

Cass County
County Register of Deeds, P.O. Box 355, Cassopolis, MI 49031-0355. 616-445-4464x3207. Fax: 616-445-8978.

Charlevoix County
County Register of Deeds, 301 State Street, County Building, Charlevoix, MI 49720. 231-547-7204. Fax: 231-547-7246.

Cheboygan County
County Register of Deeds, P.O. Box 70, Cheboygan, MI 49721. 231-627-8866.

Chippewa County
County Register of Deeds, Courthouse, 319 Court St., Sault Ste. Marie, MI 49783. 906-635-6312. Fax: 906-635-6855.

Clare County
County Register of Deeds, P.O. Box 438, Harrison, MI 48625. 517-539-7131. Fax: 517-539-6616.

Clinton County
County Register of Deeds, P.O. Box 435, St. Johns, MI 48879-0435. 517-224-5270. Fax: 517-224-5254.

Crawford County
County Register of Deeds, 200 West Michigan, Grayling, MI 49738. 517-348-2841. Fax: 517-344-3223.

Delta County
County Register of Deeds, 310 Ludington Street, Suite 104, Escanaba, MI 49829-4039. 906-789-5116. Fax: 906-789-5196.

Dickinson County
County Register of Deeds, P.O. Box 609, Iron Mountain, MI 49801. 906-774-0955. Fax: 906-774-4660.

Eaton County
County Register of Deeds, 1045 Independence Blvd., Room 104, Charlotte, MI 48813-1095. 517-543-7500x232. Fax: 517-543-7377.
www.co.eaton.mi.us/cntsrv/online.htm
Online Access: Assessor, Tax Records. Two levels of service are available on the Eaton County Online Data Service site. For free information, click on the Free Limited Public Information on the main page; then, on the Access System Page, at "User" enter PUBLIC. For "password," enter PUBLIC The more sophisticated Enhanced Records Access requires registration, a password, and an associated fee. Access to Enhanced information is restricted Access fees are billable monthly and can be prepaid to cover usage for any length of time. Fees are non-refundable

Emmet County
County Register of Deeds, 200 Division, Petoskey, MI 49770. 231-348-1761. Fax: 231-348-0633.

Genesee County
County Register of Deeds, 1101 Beach Street, Administration Building, Flint, MI 48502. 810-257-3060. Fax: 810-768-7965.

Gladwin County
County Register of Deeds, 401 West Cedar Ave., Ste 7, Gladwin, MI 48624-2093. 517-426-7551.

Gogebic County
County Register of Deeds, Courthouse, 200 N. Moore St., Bessemer, MI 49911. 906-667-0381. Fax: 906-663-4660.

Grand Traverse County
County Register of Deeds, 400 Boardman Avenue, Traverse City, MI 49684-2577. 231-922-4750. Fax: 231-922-4658.

Gratiot County
County Register of Deeds, P.O. Box 5, Ithaca, MI 48847. 517-875-5217.

Hillsdale County
County Register of Deeds, Courthouse, 29 N. Howell, Room 3, Hillsdale, MI 49242. 517-437-2231. Fax: 517-437-3139.

Houghton County
County Register of Deeds, 401 East Houghton Avenue, Houghton, MI 49931. 906-482-1311. Fax: 906-483-0364.

Huron County
County Register of Deeds, P.O. Box 126, Bad Axe, MI 48413. 517-269-9941.

Ingham County
County Register of Deeds, P.O. Box 195, Mason, MI 48854-0195. 517-676-7216. Fax: 517-676-7287.

Ionia County
County Register of Deeds, P.O. Box 35, Ionia, MI 48846. 616-527-5320. Fax: 616-527-5380.

Iosco County
County Register of Deeds, P.O. Box 367, Tawas City, MI 48764. 517-362-2021. Fax: 517-362-1443.

Iron County
County Register of Deeds, 2 South Sixth Street, Courthouse Annex, Suite 11, Crystal Falls, MI 49920-1413. 906-875-3321. Fax: 906-875-4626.

Isabella County
County Register of Deeds, 200 North Main Street, Mt. Pleasant, MI 48858. 517-772-0911x253. Fax: 517-773-7431.

Jackson County

County Register of Deeds, 120 West Michigan Avenue, 11th Floor, Jackson, MI 49201. 517-788-4350. Fax: 517-788-4686.

Online Access: Real Estate, Liens. Access to Jackson County online records requires pre-payment and $1 per minute of use (this may be revised). The system operates 24 hours daily and supports a baud rate of 28.8. Records date back to 1985. Indexes include grantor/grantee, deeds, mortgages For information, contact Mindy at 517-768-6682. Lending agency information is available. Vital records will be added to the system when it is upgraded.

Kalamazoo County

County Register of Deeds, 201 West Kalamazoo Avenue, Kalamazoo, MI 49007. 616-383-8970.

Kalkaska County

County Register of Deeds, P.O. Box 780, Kalkaska, MI 49646. 231-258-3315. Fax: 231-258-3318.

Kent County

County Register of Deeds, 300 Monroe Avenue NW, Grand Rapids, MI 49503-2286. 616-336-3558. www.ci.walker.mi.us/assess.htm

Online Access: Assessor. Records on the Walker City Assessing Dept. database are available free on the Internet at http://walker.data-web.net/query.php3. In most cases, sales and permit histories only go back to 1993. Database contains residential assessment and structural info Records on the Alpine Charter Township Assessment database are available free on the Internet at http://alpine.data-web.net. Search by parcel number or street name.

Keweenaw County

County Register of Deeds, HC 1 Box 607, Eagle River, MI 49924-9700. 906-337-2229. Fax: 906-337-2795.

Lake County

County Register of Deeds, Drawer B, Baldwin, MI 49304. 231-745-4641. Fax: 231-745-2241.

Lapeer County

County Register of Deeds, 279 North Court Street, Lapeer, MI 48446. 810-667-0211. Fax: 810-667-0293.

Leelanau County

County Register of Deeds, P.O. Box 595, Leland, MI 49654. 231-256-9682. Fax: 231-256-8149.

Lenawee County

County Register of Deeds, 301 N. Main St., Adrian, MI 49221. 517-264-4538. Fax: 517-264-4543.

Livingston County

County Register of Deeds, P.O. Box 197, Howell, MI 48844. 517-546-0270. Fax: 517-546-5966.

Online Access: Real Estate, Liens, Tas Assessor Records. Access to Livingston County online records is available for occasional users; a dedicated line is available for $1200 for professional users. Annual fee for occasional use is $400, plus $.000043 per second. The system supports a baud rate of 28.8 For information, contact Judy Eplee at 517-546-2530. Records date back to 1984. System operates 5:30AM-11PM daily. Lending agency information is available.

Luce County

County Register of Deeds, County Government Building, Newberry, MI 49868. 906-293-5521. Fax: 906-293-0050.

Mackinac County

County Register of Deeds, 100 Marley Street, Saint Ignace, MI 49781. 906-643-7306. Fax: 906-643-7302.

Macomb County

County Register of Deeds, 10 North Main, Mt. Clemens, MI 48043. 810-469-5342. Fax: 810-469-5130.

Manistee County

County Register of Deeds, 415 Third Street, Courthouse, Manistee, MI 49660-1606. 231-723-2146. Fax: 231-723-9069.

Marquette County

County Register of Deeds, 234 West Baraga Avenue, C-105, Marquette, MI 49855. 906-225-8415. Fax: 906-225-8203.

Mason County

County Register of Deeds, P.O. Box 57, Ludington, MI 49431-0057. 231-843-4466. Fax: 231-843-1972.

Mecosta County

County Register of Deeds, P.O. Box 718, Big Rapids, MI 49307. 231-592-0148.

Menominee County

County Register of Deeds, Courthouse, 839 10th Ave., Menominee, MI 49858-3000. 906-863-2822. Fax: 906-863-8839.

Midland County

County Register of Deeds, 220 West Ellsworth Street, County Services Building, Midland, MI 48640-5194. 517-832-6820. Fax: 517-832-6608.

Missaukee County

County Register of Deeds, P.O. Box 800, Lake City, MI 49651. 231-839-4967. Fax: 231-839-3684.

Monroe County

County Register of Deeds, 106 East First Street, Monroe, MI 48161. 313-243-7390.

Montcalm County

County Register of Deeds, P.O. Box 368, Stanton, MI 48888. 517-831-7337. Fax: 517-831-7320.

Online Access: Real Estate, Liens. Two online variations are available. To view the index, the monthly fee is $250. To view both the index and document image, the monthly fee is $650. Records date back to 1/1/1988. The system operates 24 hours daily and supports baud rates up to 28.8 For information, contact Laurie Wilson at 517-831-7321. Lending agency information is available.

Montmorency County

County Register of Deeds, P.O. Box 789, Atlanta, MI 49709. 517-785-3374. Fax: 517-785-2825.

Muskegon County

County Register of Deeds, 990 Terrace St., Muskegon, MI 49442. 231-724-6271. Fax: 231-724-6842.

Newaygo County

County Register of Deeds, P.O. Box 885, White Cloud, MI 49349. 231-689-7246. Fax: 231-689-7205.

Oakland County

County Register of Deeds, 1200 North Telegraph Road, Dept 480, Pontiac, MI 48341-0480. 248-858-0599.

Oceana County

County Register of Deeds, P.O. Box 111, Hart, MI 49420. 231-873-4158.

Ogemaw County

County Register of Deeds, 806 West Houghton Ave, Room 104, West Branch, MI 48661. 517-345-0728.

Ontonagon County

County Register of Deeds, 725 Greenland Road, Ontonagon, MI 49953-1492. 906-884-4255. Fax: 906-884-2916.

Osceola County

County Register of Deeds, P.O. Box 208, Reed City, MI 49677-0208. 231-832-6113.

Oscoda County

County Register of Deeds, P.O. Box 399, Mio, MI 48647. 517-826-1116. Fax: 517-826-3657.

Otsego County

County Register of Deeds, 225 West Main St., Room 108, Gaylord, MI 49735. 517-732-6484x301-2. Fax: 517-732-1562.

Ottawa County

County Register of Deeds, P.O. Box 265, Grand Haven, MI 49417-0265. 616-846-8240. Fax: 616-846-8131.

Presque Isle County

County Register of Deeds, P.O. Box 110, Rogers City, MI 49779-0110. 517-734-2676. Fax: 517-734-0506.

Roscommon County

County Register of Deeds, P.O. Box 98, Roscommon, MI 48653. 517-275-5931. Fax: 517-275-8640.

Saginaw County

County Register of Deeds, 111 South Michigan Avenue, Saginaw, MI 48602. 517-790-5270. Fax: 517-790-5278.

Online Access: Assessor. Records on the Saginaw Charter Township Assessor's Property Data page are available free on the Internet at www.sagtwp.org/pt_scripts/search.cfm. Search by address, taxroll #, or owner name.

Sanilac County

County Register of Deeds, Box 168, Sandusky, MI 48471-0168. 810-648-2313. Fax: 810-648-5461.

Schoolcraft County

County Register of Deeds, 300 Walnut Street, Room 164, Manistique, MI 49854. 906-341-3618. Fax: 906-341-5680.

Shiawassee County

County Register of Deeds, P.O. Box 103, Corunna, MI 48817. 517-743-2216. Fax: 517-743-2459.

St. Clair County

County Register of Deeds, 201 McMorran Blvd., Room 116, Port Huron, MI 48060. 810-985-2275. Fax: 810-985-4297.

St. Joseph County

County Register of Deeds, P.O. Box 388, Centreville, MI 49032-0388. 616-467-5553x553. Fax: 616-467-5628.

Tuscola County

County Register of Deeds, 440 North State Street, Caro, MI 48723. 517-672-3840. Fax: 517-672-4266.

Van Buren County

County Register of Deeds, 212 Paw Paw Street, Paw Paw, MI 49079. 616-657-8242. Fax: 616-657-7573.

Washtenaw County

County Register of Deeds, P.O. Box 8645, Ann Arbor, MI 48107. 734-994-2517.

Wayne County

County Register of Deeds, 400 Monroe, Room 620, Detroit, MI 48226. 313-224-5860. Fax: 313-224-5884.

Online Access: Assessor. Records on the City of Dearborn Residential property Assessment Database are available free on the Internet at www.dearbornol.net/city/dbnCitySearch.asp. Search by street name and number.

Wexford County

County Register of Deeds, 437 East Division Street, Cadillac, MI 49601. 231-779-9455. Fax: 231-779-0292.

You will usually be able to find the city name in the City/County Cross Reference below. In that case, it is a simple matter to determine the county from the cross reference. However, only the official US Postal Service city names are included in this index. There are an additional 40,000 place names that people use in their addresses. Therefore, we have also included a ZIP/City Cross Reference immediately following the City/County Cross Reference.

If you know the ZIP Code but the city name does not appear in the City/County Cross Reference index, look up the ZIP Code in the ZIP/City Cross Reference, find the city name, then look up the city name in the City/County Cross Reference. For example, you want to know the county for an address of Menands, NY 12204. There is no "Menands" in the City/County Cross Reference. The ZIP/City Cross Reference shows that ZIP Codes 12201-12288 are for the city of Albany. Looking back in the City/County Cross Reference, Albany is in Albany County.

City/County Cross Reference

ACME Grand Traverse
ADA Kent
ADDISON Lenawee
ADRIAN Lenawee
AFTON Cheboygan
AHMEEK Keweenaw
AKRON Tuscola
ALANSON (49706) Emmet(82), Cheboygan(18)
ALBA Antrim
ALBION Calhoun
ALDEN (49612) Antrim(73), Kalkaska(27)
ALGER (48610) Ogemaw(36), Arenac(33), Gladwin(32)
ALGONAC St. Clair
ALLEGAN Allegan
ALLEN Hillsdale
ALLEN PARK Wayne
ALLENDALE Ottawa
ALLENTON St. Clair
ALLOUEZ Keweenaw
ALMA Gratiot
ALMONT Lapeer
ALPENA (49707) Alpena(98), Presque Isle(3)
ALPHA Iron
ALTO Kent
AMASA Iron
ANCHORVILLE St. Clair
ANN ARBOR Washtenaw
APPLEGATE Sanilac
ARCADIA (49613) Manistee(76), Benzie(24)
ARGYLE Sanilac
ARMADA (48005) Macomb(96), St. Clair(4)
ARNOLD Marquette
ASHLEY Gratiot
ATHENS (49011) Calhoun(96), Branch(2), St. Joseph(2)
ATLANTA Montmorency
ATLANTIC MINE Houghton
ATLAS Genesee
ATTICA Lapeer
AU GRES Arenac
AU TRAIN Alger
AUBURN Bay
AUBURN HILLS Oakland
AUGUSTA Kalamazoo
AVOCA St. Clair
AZALIA Monroe
BAD AXE Huron
BAILEY (49303) Muskegon(89), Newaygo(10), Kent(1)
BALDWIN Lake
BANCROFT Shiawassee
BANGOR Van Buren
BANNISTER (48807) Gratiot(76), Saginaw(24)
BARAGA Baraga
BARBEAU Chippewa
BARK RIVER (49807) Delta(45), Dickinson(35), Menominee(20)

BARODA Berrien
BARRYTON (49305) Mecosta(92), Isabella(8)
BARTON CITY Alcona
BATH Clinton
BATTLE CREEK (49016) Calhoun(98), Kalamazoo(2)
BATTLE CREEK (49017) Calhoun(95), Barry(5)
BATTLE CREEK Calhoun
BAY CITY Bay
BAY PORT Huron
BAY SHORE Charlevoix
BEAR LAKE Manistee
BEAVER ISLAND Charlevoix
BEAVERTON (48612) Gladwin(96), Clare(2), Midland(2)
BEDFORD Calhoun
BELDING Ionia
BELLAIRE Antrim
BELLEVILLE Wayne
BELLEVUE (49021) Eaton(69), Barry(24), Calhoun(7)
BELMONT Kent
BENTLEY (48613) Bay(87), Gladwin(11), Arenac(2)
BENTON HARBOR (49022) Berrien(99), Van Buren(1)
BENTON HARBOR Berrien
BENZONIA (49616) Benzie(98), Manistee(2)
BERGLAND Ontonagon
BERKLEY Oakland
BERRIEN CENTER (49102) Berrien(96), Cass(5)
BERRIEN SPRINGS Berrien
BESSEMER Gogebic
BEULAH Benzie
BIG BAY Marquette
BIG RAPIDS (49307) Mecosta(97), Newaygo(3)
BIRCH RUN (48415) Saginaw(96), Tuscola(2), Genesee(1)
BIRMINGHAM Oakland
BITELY (49309) Newaygo(94), Lake(6)
BLACK RIVER Alcona
BLANCHARD (49310) Isabella(58), Mecosta(39), Montcalm(3)
BLISSFIELD Lenawee
BLOOMFIELD HILLS Oakland
BLOOMINGDALE (49026) Van Buren(88), Allegan(12)
BOON Wexford
BOYNE CITY (49712) Charlevoix(98), Antrim(2)
BOYNE FALLS (49713) Charlevoix(91), Emmet(9)
BRADLEY Allegan
BRANCH (49402) Lake(47), Mason(45), Oceana(8)
BRANT Saginaw

BRECKENRIDGE (48615) Gratiot(72), Midland(28)
BREEDSVILLE Van Buren
BRETHREN Manistee
BRIDGEPORT Saginaw
BRIDGEWATER Washtenaw
BRIDGMAN Berrien
BRIGHTON Livingston
BRIMLEY Chippewa
BRITTON (49229) Lenawee(89), Monroe(9), Washtenaw(3)
BROHMAN Newaygo
BRONSON Branch
BROOKLYN Jackson
BROWN CITY (48416) Sanilac(61), Lapeer(36), St. Clair(3)
BRUCE CROSSING Ontonagon
BRUNSWICK (49313) Muskegon(78), Newaygo(22)
BRUTUS (49716) Emmet(64), Cheboygan(36)
BUCHANAN Berrien
BUCKLEY (49620) Wexford(60), Grand Traverse(40)
BURLINGTON Calhoun
BURNIPS Allegan
BURR OAK (49030) St. Joseph(92), Branch(8)
BURT Saginaw
BURT LAKE Cheboygan
BURTON Genesee
BYRON (48418) Shiawassee(60), Genesee(30), Livingston(10)
BYRON CENTER (49315) Kent(93), Ottawa(4), Allegan(3)
CADILLAC Wexford
CADMUS Lenawee
CALEDONIA (49316) Kent(88), Allegan(9), Barry(3)
CALUMET Houghton
CAMDEN Hillsdale
CANNONSBURG Kent
CANTON Wayne
CAPAC (48014) St. Clair(98), Lapeer(2)
CARLETON Monroe
CARNEY Menominee
CARO Tuscola
CARP LAKE (49718) Emmet(67), Cheboygan(33)
CARROLLTON Saginaw
CARSON CITY (48811) Montcalm(68), Gratiot(32)
CARSONVILLE Sanilac
CASCO St. Clair
CASEVILLE Huron
CASNOVIA (49318) Muskegon(70), Newaygo(18), Kent(12)
CASPIAN Iron
CASS CITY (48726) Tuscola(85), Sanilac(12), Huron(3)
CASSOPOLIS Cass
CEDAR Leelanau

CEDAR LAKE Montcalm
CEDAR RIVER Menominee
CEDAR SPRINGS Kent
CEDARVILLE Mackinac
CEMENT CITY (49233) Lenawee(77), Jackson(23)
CENTER LINE Macomb
CENTRAL LAKE Antrim
CENTREVILLE St. Joseph
CERESCO Calhoun
CHAMPION Marquette
CHANNING Dickinson
CHARLEVOIX (49720) Charlevoix(98), Antrim(2)
CHARLOTTE Eaton
CHASE Lake
CHASSELL Houghton
CHATHAM Alger
CHEBOYGAN Cheboygan
CHELSEA Washtenaw
CHESANING (48616) Saginaw(99), Shiawassee(1)
CHIPPEWA LAKE Mecosta
CLARE (48617) Clare(79), Isabella(21)
CLARKLAKE Jackson
CLARKSTON Oakland
CLARKSVILLE (48815) Ionia(96), Kent(4)
CLAWSON Oakland
CLAYTON Lenawee
CLIFFORD (48727) Lapeer(60), Tuscola(40)
CLIMAX Kalamazoo
CLINTON (49236) Lenawee(83), Washtenaw(18)
CLINTON TOWNSHIP Macomb
CLIO (48420) Genesee(98), Tuscola(2)
CLOVERDALE Barry
COHOCTAH Livingston
COLDWATER Branch
COLEMAN (48618) Midland(84), Isabella(13), Gladwin(3)
COLOMA (49038) Berrien(93), Van Buren(7)
COLON (49040) St. Joseph(99), Branch(1)
COLUMBIAVILLE (48421) Lapeer(96), Genesee(4)
COLUMBUS St. Clair
COMINS (48619) Oscoda(77), Montmorency(23)
COMMERCE TOWNSHIP Oakland
COMSTOCK Kalamazoo
COMSTOCK PARK Kent
CONCORD Jackson
CONKLIN (49403) Ottawa(90), Muskegon(5), Kent(5)
CONSTANTINE St. Joseph
CONWAY Emmet
COOKS (49817) Schoolcraft(83), Delta(17)
COOPERSVILLE (49404) Ottawa(97), Muskegon(3)
COPEMISH (49625) Manistee(93), Wexford(7)

COPPER CITY Houghton
COPPER HARBOR Keweenaw
CORAL Montcalm
CORNELL (49818) Delta(93), Marquette(8)
CORUNNA Shiawassee
COVERT Van Buren
COVINGTON Baraga
CROSS VILLAGE Emmet
CROSWELL Sanilac
CRYSTAL (48818) Montcalm(99), Gratiot(1)
CRYSTAL FALLS Iron
CURRAN (48728) Alcona(86), Oscoda(14)
CURTIS Mackinac
CUSTER Mason
DAFTER Chippewa
DAGGETT Menominee
DANSVILLE Ingham
DAVISBURG Oakland
DAVISON (99999) Genesee(99), Lapeer(1)
DE TOUR VILLAGE Chippewa
DEARBORN Wayne
DEARBORN HEIGHTS Wayne
DECATUR (49045) Van Buren(92), Cass(8)
DECKER (48426) Sanilac(94), Tuscola(6)
DECKERVILLE Sanilac
DEERFIELD Lenawee
DEERTON (49822) Alger(98), Marquette(2)
DEFORD (48729) Tuscola(99), Sanilac(1)
DELTON Barry
DETROIT Wayne
DEWITT Clinton
DEXTER Washtenaw
DIMONDALE (48821) Eaton(95), Ingham(5)
DODGEVILLE Houghton
DOLLAR BAY Houghton
DORR (49323) Allegan(97), Kent(3)
DOUGLAS Allegan
DOWAGIAC (49047) Cass(94), Van Buren(6)
DOWLING Barry
DRAYTON PLAINS Oakland
DRUMMOND ISLAND Chippewa
DRYDEN Lapeer
DUNDEE Monroe
DURAND (48429) Shiawassee(99), Genesee(1)
EAGLE Clinton
EAGLE RIVER Keweenaw
EAST CHINA St. Clair
EAST JORDAN (49727) Charlevoix(70), Antrim(30)
EAST LANSING (48823) Ingham(98), Clinton(2)
EAST LANSING Ingham
EAST LEROY Calhoun
EAST TAWAS Iosco
EASTLAKE Manistee
EASTPOINTE Macomb
EASTPORT Antrim
EATON RAPIDS (48827) Eaton(94), Ingham(6)
EAU CLAIRE (49111) Berrien(85), Cass(15)
EBEN JUNCTION Alger
ECKERMAN Chippewa
ECORSE Wayne
EDENVILLE Midland
EDMORE (48829) Montcalm(99), Isabella(1)
EDWARDSBURG Cass
ELBERTA Benzie
ELK RAPIDS Antrim
ELKTON Huron
ELLSWORTH (49729) Antrim(86), Charlevoix(14)
ELM HALL Gratiot
ELMIRA (49730) Antrim(73), Otsego(21), Charlevoix(6)
ELSIE (48831) Clinton(52), Shiawassee(25), Saginaw(19), Gratiot(4)

ELWELL Gratiot
EMMETT St. Clair
EMPIRE (49630) Leelanau(98), Benzie(3)
ENGADINE Mackinac
ERIE Monroe
ESCANABA Delta
ESSEXVILLE Bay
EUREKA Clinton
EVART (49631) Osceola(92), Mecosta(8)
EWEN Ontonagon
FAIR HAVEN St. Clair
FAIRGROVE Tuscola
FAIRVIEW Oscoda
FALMOUTH Missaukee
FARMINGTON Oakland
FARWELL (48622) Clare(81), Isabella(19)
FELCH Dickinson
FENNVILLE Allegan
FENTON (48430) Genesee(78), Livingston(17), Oakland(5)
FENWICK (48834) Montcalm(60), Ionia(40)
FERNDALE Oakland
FERRYSBURG Ottawa
FIFE LAKE (49633) Kalkaska(60), Grand Traverse(32), Wexford(6), Missaukee(3)
FILER CITY Manistee
FILION Huron
FLAT ROCK Wayne
FLINT Genesee
FLUSHING Genesee
FORESTVILLE Sanilac
FORT GRATIOT St. Clair
FOSTER CITY Dickinson
FOSTORIA (48435) Tuscola(55), Lapeer(45)
FOUNTAIN Mason
FOWLER (48835) Clinton(99), Gratiot(1)
FOWLERVILLE Livingston
FRANKENMUTH (48734) Saginaw(98), Tuscola(2)
FRANKENMUTH Saginaw
FRANKFORT Benzie
FRANKLIN Oakland
FRASER Macomb
FREDERIC (49733) Crawford(74), Otsego(26)
FREE SOIL (49411) Mason(98), Manistee(2)
FREELAND (48623) Saginaw(79), Midland(11), Bay(10)
FREEPORT (49325) Barry(75), Ionia(14), Kent(10)
FREMONT (49412) Newaygo(98), Oceana(2)
FREMONT Newaygo
FRONTIER Hillsdale
FRUITPORT (49415) Muskegon(89), Ottawa(11)
FULTON (49052) Kalamazoo(79), Calhoun(17), St. Joseph(5)
GAASTRA Iron
GAGETOWN (48735) Tuscola(64), Huron(36)
GAINES (48436) Genesee(96), Shiawassee(4)
GALESBURG Kalamazoo
GALIEN Berrien
GARDEN (99999) Delta(99), Schoolcraft(1)
GARDEN CITY Wayne
GAYLORD Otsego
GENESEE Genesee
GERMFASK (49836) Schoolcraft(52), Mackinac(48)
GILFORD Tuscola
GLADSTONE Delta
GLADWIN (48624) Gladwin(92), Clare(6), Roscommon(2)
GLEN ARBOR Leelanau
GLENN Allegan
GLENNIE (48737) Alcona(91), Iosco(9)
GOBLES (49055) Van Buren(93), Allegan(7)

GOETZVILLE Chippewa
GOOD HART Emmet
GOODELLS St. Clair
GOODRICH (48438) Genesee(86), Lapeer(14)
GOULD CITY Mackinac
GOWEN (49326) Kent(74), Montcalm(26)
GRAND BLANC Genesee
GRAND HAVEN Ottawa
GRAND JUNCTION (49056) Van Buren(73), Allegan(27)
GRAND LEDGE (48837) Eaton(90), Clinton(9)
GRAND MARAIS Alger
GRAND RAPIDS (49544) Kent(79), Ottawa(21)
GRAND RAPIDS Kent
GRANDVILLE (49418) Kent(84), Ottawa(16)
GRANDVILLE Kent
GRANT Newaygo
GRASS LAKE (49240) Jackson(92), Washtenaw(8)
GRAWN Grand Traverse
GRAYLING (49738) Crawford(96), Kalkaska(4)
GRAYLING Crawford
GREENBUSH (48738) Alcona(89), Iosco(11)
GREENLAND Ontonagon
GREENVILLE (48838) Montcalm(91), Kent(9)
GREGORY (48137) Livingston(99), Washtenaw(1)
GROSSE ILE Wayne
GROSSE POINTE Wayne
GULLIVER Schoolcraft
GWINN Marquette
HADLEY Lapeer
HAGAR SHORES Berrien
HALE (48739) Iosco(76), Ogemaw(25)
HAMBURG Livingston
HAMILTON Allegan
HAMTRAMCK Wayne
HANCOCK Houghton
HANOVER Jackson
HARBERT Berrien
HARBOR BEACH Huron
HARBOR SPRINGS Emmet
HARPER WOODS Wayne
HARRIETTA (49638) Wexford(90), Manistee(10)
HARRIS Menominee
HARRISON Clare
HARRISON TOWNSHIP Macomb
HARRISVILLE Alcona
HARSENS ISLAND St. Clair
HART Oceana
HARTFORD Van Buren
HARTLAND Livingston
HASLETT (48840) Ingham(96), Clinton(4)
HASTINGS Barry
HAWKS Presque Isle
HAZEL PARK Oakland
HEMLOCK (48626) Saginaw(94), Midland(6)
HENDERSON (48841) Shiawassee(78), Saginaw(22)
HERMANSVILLE Menominee
HERRON Alpena
HERSEY (49639) Osceola(87), Mecosta(13)
HESPERIA (49421) Oceana(72), Newaygo(28)
HESSEL Mackinac
HICKORY CORNERS (49060) Barry(95), Kalamazoo(5)
HIGGINS LAKE Roscommon
HIGHLAND Oakland
HIGHLAND PARK Wayne
HILLMAN (49746) Montmorency(91), Alpena(9)

HILLSDALE Hillsdale
HOLLAND (49423) Ottawa(71), Allegan(29)
HOLLAND Ottawa
HOLLY (48442) Oakland(98), Genesee(2)
HOLT Ingham
HOLTON (49425) Muskegon(81), Oceana(13), Newaygo(7)
HOMER Calhoun
HONOR Benzie
HOPE (48628) Midland(81), Gladwin(19)
HOPKINS Allegan
HORTON (49246) Jackson(98), Hillsdale(2)
HOUGHTON Houghton
HOUGHTON LAKE Roscommon
HOUGHTON LAKE HEIGHTS Roscommon
HOWARD CITY (49329) Montcalm(87), Newaygo(13)
HOWELL Livingston
HUBBARD LAKE (49747) Alpena(56), Alcona(44)
HUBBARDSTON (48845) Ionia(53), Clinton(23), Montcalm(16), Gratiot(8)
HUBBELL Houghton
HUDSON (49247) Lenawee(72), Hillsdale(29)
HUDSONVILLE Ottawa
HULBERT Chippewa
HUNTINGTON WOODS Oakland
IDA Monroe
IDLEWILD Lake
IMLAY CITY (48444) Lapeer(99), St. Clair(1)
INDIAN RIVER Cheboygan
INGALLS Menominee
INKSTER Wayne
INTERLOCHEN (49643) Grand Traverse(75), Benzie(25)
IONIA Ionia
IRON MOUNTAIN Dickinson
IRON RIVER Iron
IRONS (49644) Lake(92), Manistee(7)
IRONWOOD Gogebic
ISHPEMING Marquette
ITHACA Gratiot
JACKSON Jackson
JAMESTOWN Ottawa
JASPER Lenawee
JEDDO (48032) St. Clair(81), Sanilac(19)
JENISON Ottawa
JEROME (49249) Hillsdale(93), Jackson(7)
JOHANNESBURG (49751) Otsego(86), Montmorency(14)
JONES Cass
JONESVILLE Hillsdale
KALAMAZOO Kalamazoo
KALEVA Manistee
KALKASKA Kalkaska
KARLIN Grand Traverse
KAWKAWLIN Bay
KEARSARGE Houghton
KEEGO HARBOR Oakland
KENDALL Van Buren
KENT CITY (49330) Kent(92), Newaygo(5), Muskegon(2), Ottawa(2)
KENTON Houghton
KEWADIN Antrim
KINCHELOE Chippewa
KINDE Huron
KINGSFORD Dickinson
KINGSLEY (49649) Grand Traverse(96), Wexford(4)
KINGSTON (48741) Tuscola(93), Sanilac(7)
KINROSS Chippewa
LA SALLE Monroe
LACHINE Alpena
LACOTA Van Buren
LAINGSBURG (48848) Shiawassee(69), Clinton(31)
LAKE (48632) Clare(74), Isabella(24), Osceola(2)
LAKE ANN Benzie

LAKE CITY Missaukee
LAKE GEORGE Clare
LAKE LEELANAU Leelanau
LAKE LINDEN (49945) Houghton(97),
   Keweenaw(3)
LAKE ODESSA (48849) Ionia(82),
   Barry(15), Eaton(3)
LAKE ORION Oakland
LAKELAND Livingston
LAKESIDE Berrien
LAKEVIEW (48850) Montcalm(81),
   Mecosta(19)
LAKEVILLE Oakland
LAMBERTVILLE Monroe
LAMONT Ottawa
LANSE Baraga
LANSING (48906) Ingham(63), Clinton(35),
   Eaton(2)
LANSING (48911) Ingham(86), Eaton(14)
LANSING (48917) Eaton(80), Ingham(21)
LANSING Eaton
LANSING Ingham
LAPEER Lapeer
LAWRENCE Van Buren
LAWTON Van Buren
LELAND Leelanau
LENNON (48449) Shiawassee(56),
   Genesee(44)
LEONARD Oakland
LEONIDAS St. Joseph
LEROY (49655) Osceola(98), Lake(2)
LESLIE Ingham
LEVERING (49755) Emmet(66),
   Cheboygan(34)
LEWISTON (49756) Montmorency(73),
   Oscoda(27)
LEXINGTON Sanilac
LINCOLN Alcona
LINCOLN PARK Wayne
LINDEN (48451) Genesee(92),
   Livingston(8)
LINWOOD Bay
LITCHFIELD Hillsdale
LITTLE LAKE Marquette
LIVONIA Wayne
LONG LAKE (48743) Iosco(93),
   Ogemaw(7)
LORETTO Dickinson
LOWELL (49331) Kent(92), Ionia(8)
LUDINGTON Mason
LUNA PIER Monroe
LUPTON Ogemaw
LUTHER Lake
LUZERNE Oscoda
LYONS Ionia
MACATAWA Ottawa
MACKINAC ISLAND Mackinac
MACKINAW CITY Cheboygan
MACOMB Macomb
MADISON HEIGHTS Oakland
MANCELONA (49659) Antrim(81),
   Kalkaska(19)
MANCHESTER Washtenaw
MANISTEE (49660) Manistee(97),
   Mason(3)
MANISTIQUE (49854) Schoolcraft(99),
   Delta(1)
MANITOU BEACH Lenawee
MANTON (49663) Wexford(79),
   Missaukee(21)
MAPLE CITY Leelanau
MAPLE RAPIDS Clinton
MARCELLUS (49067) Cass(66), St.
   Joseph(24), Van Buren(10)
MARENISCO (49947) Gogebic(85),
   Ontonagon(15)
MARINE CITY St. Clair
MARION (49665) Osceola(86), Clare(10),
   Missaukee(4)
MARLETTE (48453) Sanilac(98),
   Tuscola(2)
MARNE (49435) Ottawa(96), Kent(4)

MARQUETTE Marquette
MARSHALL Calhoun
MARTIN Allegan
MARYSVILLE St. Clair
MASON Ingham
MASS CITY Ontonagon
MATTAWAN (49071) Van Buren(81),
   Kalamazoo(19)
MAYBEE Monroe
MAYFIELD Grand Traverse
MAYVILLE (48744) Tuscola(88),
   Lapeer(12)
MC BAIN Missaukee
MC MILLAN (49853) Luce(96), Mackinac(4)
MCBRIDES Montcalm
MEARS Oceana
MECOSTA Mecosta
MELVIN (99999) Sanilac(99), Tuscola(1)
MELVINDALE Wayne
MEMPHIS (48041) St. Clair(79),
   Macomb(21)
MENDON St. Joseph
MENOMINEE Menominee
MERRILL (48637) Saginaw(70),
   Midland(15), Gratiot(15)
MERRITT Missaukee
MESICK (49668) Wexford(98), Manistee(2)
METAMORA Lapeer
MICHIGAMME (49861) Baraga(70),
   Marquette(30)
MICHIGAN CENTER Jackson
MIDDLETON Gratiot
MIDDLEVILLE (49333) Barry(96), Kent(3)
MIDLAND (48642) Midland(97), Bay(3)
MIDLAND Midland
MIKADO (48745) Alcona(93), Iosco(7)
MILAN (48160) Monroe(97), Washtenaw(3)
MILFORD (48380) Oakland(73),
   Livingston(27)
MILFORD Oakland
MILLBROOK Mecosta
MILLERSBURG Presque Isle
MILLINGTON (48746) Tuscola(93),
   Genesee(7)
MINDEN CITY (48456) Sanilac(79),
   Huron(21)
MIO Oscoda
MOHAWK Keweenaw
MOLINE Allegan
MONROE Monroe
MONTAGUE (49437) Muskegon(81),
   Oceana(19)
MONTGOMERY (49255) Branch(96),
   Hillsdale(4)
MONTROSE (48457) Genesee(74),
   Saginaw(26)
MORAN Mackinac
MORENCI Lenawee
MORLEY (49336) Mecosta(92),
   Montcalm(9)
MORRICE Shiawassee
MOSCOW Hillsdale
MOSHERVILLE Hillsdale
MOUNT CLEMENS Macomb
MOUNT MORRIS Genesee
MOUNT PLEASANT Isabella
MUIR Ionia
MULLETT LAKE Cheboygan
MULLIKEN (48861) Eaton(88), Ionia(12)
MUNGER (48747) Bay(94), Saginaw(6)
MUNISING Alger
MUNITH Jackson
MUSKEGON Muskegon
NADEAU Menominee
NAHMA Delta
NAPOLEON Jackson
NASHVILLE (49073) Barry(90), Eaton(10)
NATIONAL CITY Iosco
NATIONAL MINE Marquette
NAUBINWAY Mackinac
NAZARETH Kalamazoo
NEGAUNEE Marquette

NEW BALTIMORE Macomb
NEW BOSTON Wayne
NEW BUFFALO Berrien
NEW ERA Oceana
NEW HAVEN Macomb
NEW HUDSON Oakland
NEW LOTHROP (48460) Shiawassee(62),
   Saginaw(36), Genesee(2)
NEW RICHMOND Allegan
NEW TROY Berrien
NEWAYGO (49337) Newaygo(97),
   Mecosta(2), Montcalm(2)
NEWBERRY Luce
NEWPORT Monroe
NILES (49120) Berrien(84), Cass(16)
NILES Berrien
NISULA Houghton
NORTH ADAMS Hillsdale
NORTH BRANCH Lapeer
NORTH STAR Gratiot
NORTH STREET St. Clair
NORTHLAND Marquette
NORTHPORT Leelanau
NORTHVILLE (48167) Wayne(64),
   Oakland(31), Washtenaw(5)
NORVELL Jackson
NORWAY Dickinson
NOTTAWA St. Joseph
NOVI Oakland
NUNICA (49448) Ottawa(83),
   Muskegon(17)
OAK GROVE Livingston
OAK PARK Oakland
OAKLAND Oakland
OAKLEY (48649) Saginaw(94),
   Shiawassee(6)
ODEN Emmet
OKEMOS Ingham
OLD MISSION Grand Traverse
OLIVET (49076) Eaton(69), Calhoun(31)
OMENA Leelanau
OMER Arenac
ONAWAY (49765) Presque Isle(68),
   Cheboygan(32)
ONEKAMA Manistee
ONONDAGA (49264) Ingham(71),
   Jackson(22), Eaton(7)
ONSTED Lenawee
ONTONAGON Ontonagon
ORLEANS Ionia
ORTONVILLE (48462) Oakland(95),
   Lapeer(3), Genesee(1)
OSCODA Iosco
OSHTEMO Kalamazoo
OSSEO Hillsdale
OSSINEKE Alpena
OTISVILLE (99999) Genesee(99),
   Lapeer(1)
OTSEGO (49078) Allegan(97), Van
   Buren(2), Kalamazoo(2)
OTTAWA LAKE (49267) Monroe(87),
   Lenawee(13)
OTTER LAKE (48464) Lapeer(80),
   Tuscola(15), Genesee(5)
OVID (48866) Clinton(62), Shiawassee(38)
OWENDALE Huron
OWOSSO Shiawassee
OXFORD (48371) Oakland(94), Lapeer(6)
OXFORD Oakland
PAINESDALE Houghton
PALMER Marquette
PALMS Sanilac
PALMYRA Lenawee
PALO Ionia
PARADISE Chippewa
PARIS (49338) Mecosta(56), Newaygo(37),
   Osceola(7)
PARMA Jackson
PAW PAW Van Buren
PECK Sanilac
PELKIE (49958) Houghton(65), Baraga(35)

PELLSTON (49769) Emmet(82),
   Cheboygan(18)
PENTWATER (49449) Oceana(78),
   Mason(22)
PERKINS Delta
PERRINTON Gratiot
PERRONVILLE (49873) Menominee(86),
   Dickinson(14)
PERRY (48872) Shiawassee(91),
   Ingham(8), Livingston(1)
PETERSBURG Monroe
PETOSKEY Emmet
PEWAMO (48873) Ionia(62), Clinton(38)
PICKFORD (49774) Chippewa(88),
   Mackinac(12)
PIERSON Montcalm
PIGEON Huron
PINCKNEY Livingston
PINCONNING (48650) Bay(95), Arenac(5)
PITTSFORD Hillsdale
PLAINWELL (49080) Allegan(70),
   Barry(19), Kalamazoo(11)
PLEASANT LAKE Jackson
PLEASANT RIDGE Oakland
PLYMOUTH (48170) Wayne(96),
   Washtenaw(4)
POINTE AUX PINS Mackinac
POMPEII Gratiot
PONTIAC Oakland
PORT AUSTIN Huron
PORT HOPE Huron
PORT HURON St. Clair
PORT SANILAC Sanilac
PORTAGE Kalamazoo
PORTLAND (48875) Ionia(93), Clinton(7)
POSEN (49776) Presque Isle(75),
   Alpena(25)
POTTERVILLE Eaton
POWERS Menominee
PRATTVILLE Hillsdale
PRESCOTT Ogemaw
PRESQUE ISLE Presque Isle
PRUDENVILLE Roscommon
PULLMAN Allegan
QUINCY (49082) Branch(94), Hillsdale(6)
QUINNESEC Dickinson
RALPH Dickinson
RAMSAY Gogebic
RAPID CITY (49676) Kalkaska(59),
   Antrim(41)
RAPID RIVER (49878) Delta(96), Alger(4)
RAVENNA (49451) Muskegon(96),
   Ottawa(4)
RAY Macomb
READING Hillsdale
REDFORD Wayne
REED CITY (49677) Osceola(83),
   Lake(14), Newaygo(3)
REESE (48757) Tuscola(67), Saginaw(30),
   Bay(4)
REMUS (49340) Mecosta(69), Isabella(31)
REPUBLIC (49879) Marquette(99), Iron(1)
RHODES (48652) Gladwin(61), Bay(22),
   Midland(17)
RICHLAND Kalamazoo
RICHMOND Macomb
RICHVILLE Tuscola
RIDGEWAY Lenawee
RIGA (49276) Lenawee(71), Monroe(29)
RIVER ROUGE Wayne
RIVERDALE (48877) Gratiot(58),
   Montcalm(32), Isabella(10)
RIVERSIDE Berrien
RIVES JUNCTION Jackson
ROCHESTER (48306) Oakland(98),
   Macomb(2)
ROCHESTER Oakland
ROCK (49880) Delta(67), Marquette(33)
ROCKFORD Kent
ROCKLAND Ontonagon
ROCKWOOD Wayne
RODNEY Mecosta

ROGERS CITY Presque Isle
ROLLIN Lenawee
ROMEO Macomb
ROMULUS Wayne
ROSCOMMON (48653) Roscommon(80), Crawford(20)
ROSE CITY (48654) Ogemaw(77), Oscoda(23)
ROSEBUSH Isabella
ROSEVILLE Macomb
ROTHBURY Oceana
ROYAL OAK Oakland
RUDYARD (49780) Chippewa(94), Mackinac(6)
RUMELY Alger
RUTH (48470) Huron(99), Sanilac(1)
SAGINAW Saginaw
SAGOLA Dickinson
SAINT CHARLES Saginaw
SAINT CLAIR St. Clair
SAINT CLAIR SHORES Macomb
SAINT HELEN Roscommon
SAINT IGNACE Mackinac
SAINT JOHNS Clinton
SAINT JOSEPH Berrien
SAINT LOUIS (48880) Gratiot(93), Midland(7)
SALEM Washtenaw
SALINE Washtenaw
SAMARIA Monroe
SAND CREEK Lenawee
SAND LAKE (49343) Kent(58), Newaygo(26), Montcalm(16)
SANDUSKY Sanilac
SANFORD Midland
SARANAC Ionia
SAUGATUCK Allegan
SAULT SAINTE MARIE Chippewa
SAWYER Berrien
SCHOOLCRAFT (49087) Kalamazoo(95), Van Buren(4)
SCOTTS Kalamazoo
SCOTTVILLE Mason
SEARS Osceola
SEBEWAING (48759) Huron(99), Tuscola(1)
SENECA Lenawee
SENEY (49883) Schoolcraft(75), Alger(25)
SHAFTSBURG Shiawassee
SHELBY Oceana
SHELBYVILLE (49344) Allegan(57), Barry(43)
SHEPHERD (48883) Isabella(76), Midland(22), Gratiot(2)
SHERIDAN Montcalm
SHERWOOD Branch

SHINGLETON Alger
SIDNAW Houghton
SIDNEY Montcalm
SILVERWOOD (48760) Tuscola(62), Lapeer(38)
SIX LAKES (48886) Montcalm(97), Mecosta(3)
SKANDIA (49885) Marquette(80), Alger(20)
SKANEE Baraga
SMITHS CREEK St. Clair
SMYRNA Ionia
SNOVER Sanilac
SODUS Berrien
SOMERSET Hillsdale
SOMERSET CENTER Hillsdale
SOUTH BOARDMAN Kalkaska
SOUTH BRANCH (48761) Iosco(38), Ogemaw(30), Alcona(28), Oscoda(4)
SOUTH HAVEN (49090) Van Buren(96), Allegan(5)
SOUTH LYON (48178) Oakland(68), Livingston(21), Washtenaw(11)
SOUTH RANGE Houghton
SOUTH ROCKWOOD Monroe
SOUTHFIELD Oakland
SOUTHGATE Wayne
SPALDING Menominee
SPARTA Kent
SPRING ARBOR Jackson
SPRING LAKE (49456) Ottawa(96), Muskegon(4)
SPRINGPORT (49284) Jackson(57), Calhoun(32), Eaton(11)
SPRUCE (48762) Alcona(89), Alpena(11)
STALWART Chippewa
STAMBAUGH Iron
STANDISH (48658) Arenac(95), Bay(5)
STANTON Montcalm
STANWOOD Mecosta
STEPHENSON Menominee
STERLING (48659) Arenac(96), Bay(4)
STERLING HEIGHTS Macomb
STEVENSVILLE Berrien
STOCKBRIDGE (49285) Ingham(84), Jackson(7), Livingston(5), Washtenaw(4)
STRONGS Chippewa
STURGIS St. Joseph
SUMNER (48889) Gratiot(98), Montcalm(2)
SUNFIELD (48890) Eaton(57), Ionia(43)
SUTTONS BAY Leelanau
SWARTZ CREEK Genesee
TAWAS CITY (48763) Iosco(97), Arenac(3)
TAWAS CITY Iosco
TAYLOR Wayne
TECUMSEH Lenawee

TEKONSHA (49092) Calhoun(82), Branch(18)
TEMPERANCE Monroe
THOMPSONVILLE (49683) Benzie(62), Manistee(32), Grand Traverse(6)
THREE OAKS Berrien
THREE RIVERS St. Joseph
TIPTON Lenawee
TOIVOLA (49965) Houghton(87), Ontonagon(13)
TOPINABEE Cheboygan
TOWER Cheboygan
TRAUNIK Alger
TRAVERSE CITY (49684) Grand Traverse(77), Leelanau(23)
TRAVERSE CITY Grand Traverse
TRENARY Alger
TRENTON Wayne
TROUT CREEK (49967) Ontonagon(87), Houghton(13)
TROUT LAKE Chippewa
TROY Oakland
TRUFANT (49347) Montcalm(94), Kent(7)
TURNER (48765) Arenac(69), Iosco(31)
TUSCOLA Tuscola
TUSTIN (49688) Osceola(93), Lake(5), Wexford(3)
TWIN LAKE Muskegon
TWINING (48766) Arenac(97), Iosco(3)
UBLY (48475) Huron(58), Sanilac(42)
UNION Cass
UNION CITY (49094) Branch(99), Calhoun(1)
UNION LAKE Oakland
UNION PIER Berrien
UNIONVILLE (48767) Tuscola(97), Huron(3)
UNIVERSITY CENTER Bay
UTICA Macomb
VANDALIA Cass
VANDERBILT (49795) Otsego(81), Cheboygan(17), Charlevoix(2)
VASSAR Tuscola
VERMONTVILLE Eaton
VERNON Shiawassee
VESTABURG (48891) Montcalm(99), Isabella(1)
VICKSBURG (49097) Kalamazoo(99), St. Joseph(2)
VULCAN (49892) Dickinson(76), Menominee(24)
WABANINGO Muskegon
WAKEFIELD Gogebic
WALDRON Hillsdale
WALHALLA Mason

WALKERVILLE (49459) Oceana(92), Newaygo(9)
WALLACE Menominee
WALLED LAKE Oakland
WALLOON LAKE Charlevoix
WARREN Macomb
WASHINGTON Macomb
WATERFORD Oakland
WATERS Otsego
WATERSMEET Gogebic
WATERVLIET (49098) Berrien(89), Van Buren(11)
WATTON Baraga
WAYLAND (49348) Allegan(83), Barry(17)
WAYNE Wayne
WEBBERVILLE (48892) Ingham(77), Livingston(23)
WEIDMAN Isabella
WELLS Delta
WELLSTON (49689) Manistee(85), Wexford(15)
WEST BLOOMFIELD Oakland
WEST BRANCH Ogemaw
WEST OLIVE Ottawa
WESTLAND Wayne
WESTON Lenawee
WESTPHALIA Clinton
WETMORE (49895) Alger(70), Delta(24), Schoolcraft(7)
WHEELER (48662) Gratiot(85), Midland(15)
WHITE CLOUD Newaygo
WHITE LAKE Oakland
WHITE PIGEON (49099) St. Joseph(89), Cass(11)
WHITE PINE Ontonagon
WHITEHALL Muskegon
WHITMORE LAKE (48189) Washtenaw(57), Livingston(43)
WHITTAKER Washtenaw
WHITTEMORE (48770) Iosco(95), Arenac(3), Ogemaw(2)
WILLIAMSBURG (49690) Grand Traverse(88), Antrim(7), Kalkaska(6)
WILLIAMSTON Ingham
WILLIS Washtenaw
WILSON Menominee
WINN Isabella
WIXOM Oakland
WOLVERINE Cheboygan
WOODLAND Barry
WYANDOTTE Wayne
YALE (48097) St. Clair(83), Sanilac(17)
YPSILANTI Washtenaw
ZEELAND Ottawa

ZIP/City Cross Reference

ZIP	City	ZIP	City	ZIP	City	ZIP	City
48001-48001	ALGONAC	48037-48037	SOUTHFIELD	48066-48066	ROSEVILLE	48113-48113	ANN ARBOR
48002-48002	ALLENTON	48038-48038	CLINTON TOWNSHIP	48067-48068	ROYAL OAK	48114-48114	BRIGHTON
48003-48003	ALMONT	48039-48039	MARINE CITY	48069-48069	PLEASANT RIDGE	48115-48115	BRIDGEWATER
48004-48004	ANCHORVILLE	48040-48040	MARYSVILLE	48070-48070	HUNTINGTON WOODS	48116-48116	BRIGHTON
48005-48005	ARMADA	48041-48041	MEMPHIS	48071-48071	MADISON HEIGHTS	48117-48117	CARLETON
48006-48006	AVOCA	48042-48042	MACOMB	48072-48072	BERKLEY	48118-48118	CHELSEA
48007-48007	TROY	48043-48043	MOUNT CLEMENS	48073-48073	ROYAL OAK	48120-48121	DEARBORN
48009-48012	BIRMINGHAM	48044-48044	MACOMB	48074-48074	SMITHS CREEK	48122-48122	MELVINDALE
48014-48014	CAPAC	48045-48045	HARRISON TOWNSHIP	48075-48076	SOUTHFIELD	48123-48124	DEARBORN
48015-48015	CENTER LINE	48046-48046	MOUNT CLEMENS	48079-48079	SAINT CLAIR	48125-48125	DEARBORN HEIGHTS
48017-48017	CLAWSON	48047-48047	NEW BALTIMORE	48080-48082	SAINT CLAIR SHORES	48126-48126	DEARBORN
48021-48021	EASTPOINTE	48048-48048	NEW HAVEN	48083-48084	TROY	48127-48127	DEARBORN HEIGHTS
48022-48022	EMMETT	48049-48049	NORTH STREET	48086-48086	SOUTHFIELD	48128-48128	DEARBORN
48023-48023	FAIR HAVEN	48050-48050	NEW HAVEN	48089-48093	WARREN	48130-48130	DEXTER
48025-48025	FRANKLIN	48051-48051	NEW BALTIMORE	48094-48095	WASHINGTON	48131-48131	DUNDEE
48026-48026	FRASER	48054-48054	EAST CHINA	48096-48096	RAY	48133-48133	ERIE
48027-48027	GOODELLS	48059-48059	FORT GRATIOT	48097-48097	YALE	48134-48134	FLAT ROCK
48028-48028	HARSENS ISLAND	48060-48061	PORT HURON	48098-48099	TROY	48135-48136	GARDEN CITY
48030-48030	HAZEL PARK	48062-48062	RICHMOND	48101-48101	ALLEN PARK	48137-48137	GREGORY
48032-48032	JEDDO	48063-48063	COLUMBUS	48103-48109	ANN ARBOR	48138-48138	GROSSE ILE
48034-48034	SOUTHFIELD	48064-48064	CASCO	48110-48110	AZALIA	48139-48139	HAMBURG
48035-48036	CLINTON TOWNSHIP	48065-48065	ROMEO	48111-48112	BELLEVILLE	48140-48140	IDA

48141-48141	INKSTER	48393-48393	WIXOM	48626-48626	HEMLOCK	48787-48787	FRANKENMUTH
48143-48143	LAKELAND	48397-48397	WARREN	48627-48627	HIGGINS LAKE	48801-48802	ALMA
48144-48144	LAMBERTVILLE	48398-48398	CLAWSON	48628-48628	HOPE	48804-48804	MOUNT PLEASANT
48145-48145	LA SALLE	48401-48401	APPLEGATE	48629-48629	HOUGHTON LAKE	48805-48805	OKEMOS
48146-48146	LINCOLN PARK	48410-48410	ARGYLE	48630-48630	HOUGHTON LAKE	48806-48806	ASHLEY
48150-48154	LIVONIA	48411-48411	ATLAS		HEIGHTS	48807-48807	BANNISTER
48157-48157	LUNA PIER	48412-48412	ATTICA	48631-48631	KAWKAWLIN	48808-48808	BATH
48158-48158	MANCHESTER	48413-48413	BAD AXE	48632-48632	LAKE	48809-48809	BELDING
48159-48159	MAYBEE	48414-48414	BANCROFT	48633-48633	LAKE GEORGE	48811-48811	CARSON CITY
48160-48160	MILAN	48415-48415	BIRCH RUN	48634-48634	LINWOOD	48812-48812	CEDAR LAKE
48161-48162	MONROE	48416-48416	BROWN CITY	48635-48635	LUPTON	48813-48813	CHARLOTTE
48164-48164	NEW BOSTON	48417-48417	BURT	48636-48636	LUZERNE	48815-48815	CLARKSVILLE
48165-48165	NEW HUDSON	48418-48418	BYRON	48637-48637	MERRILL	48816-48816	COHOCTAH
48166-48166	NEWPORT	48419-48419	CARSONVILLE	48640-48642	MIDLAND	48817-48817	CORUNNA
48167-48167	NORTHVILLE	48420-48420	CLIO	48647-48647	MIO	48818-48818	CRYSTAL
48169-48169	PINCKNEY	48421-48421	COLUMBIAVILLE	48649-48649	OAKLEY	48819-48819	DANSVILLE
48170-48170	PLYMOUTH	48422-48422	CROSWELL	48650-48650	PINCONNING	48820-48820	DEWITT
48173-48173	ROCKWOOD	48423-48423	DAVISON	48651-48651	PRUDENVILLE	48821-48821	DIMONDALE
48174-48174	ROMULUS	48426-48426	DECKER	48652-48652	RHODES	48822-48822	EAGLE
48175-48175	SALEM	48427-48427	DECKERVILLE	48653-48653	ROSCOMMON	48823-48826	EAST LANSING
48176-48176	SALINE	48428-48428	DRYDEN	48654-48654	ROSE CITY	48827-48827	EATON RAPIDS
48177-48177	SAMARIA	48429-48429	DURAND	48655-48655	SAINT CHARLES	48829-48829	EDMORE
48178-48178	SOUTH LYON	48430-48430	FENTON	48656-48656	SAINT HELEN	48830-48830	ELM HALL
48179-48179	SOUTH ROCKWOOD	48432-48432	FILION	48657-48657	SANFORD	48831-48831	ELSIE
48180-48180	TAYLOR	48433-48433	FLUSHING	48658-48658	STANDISH	48832-48832	ELWELL
48182-48182	TEMPERANCE	48434-48434	FORESTVILLE	48659-48659	STERLING	48833-48833	EUREKA
48183-48183	TRENTON	48435-48435	FOSTORIA	48661-48661	WEST BRANCH	48834-48834	FENWICK
48184-48184	WAYNE	48436-48436	GAINES	48662-48662	WHEELER	48835-48835	FOWLER
48185-48186	WESTLAND	48437-48437	GENESEE	48663-48663	SAGINAW	48836-48836	FOWLERVILLE
48187-48188	CANTON	48438-48438	GOODRICH	48667-48686	MIDLAND	48837-48837	GRAND LEDGE
48189-48189	WHITMORE LAKE	48439-48439	GRAND BLANC	48701-48701	AKRON	48838-48838	GREENVILLE
48190-48190	WHITTAKER	48440-48440	HADLEY	48703-48703	AU GRES	48840-48840	HASLETT
48191-48191	WILLIS	48441-48441	HARBOR BEACH	48705-48705	BARTON CITY	48841-48841	HENDERSON
48192-48192	WYANDOTTE	48442-48442	HOLLY	48706-48708	BAY CITY	48842-48842	HOLT
48195-48195	SOUTHGATE	48444-48444	IMLAY CITY	48710-48710	UNIVERSITY CENTER	48843-48844	HOWELL
48197-48198	YPSILANTI	48445-48445	KINDE	48720-48720	BAY PORT	48845-48845	HUBBARDSTON
48201-48202	DETROIT	48446-48446	LAPEER	48721-48721	BLACK RIVER	48846-48846	IONIA
48203-48203	HIGHLAND PARK	48449-48449	LENNON	48722-48722	BRIDGEPORT	48847-48847	ITHACA
48204-48211	DETROIT	48450-48450	LEXINGTON	48723-48723	CARO	48848-48848	LAINGSBURG
48212-48212	HAMTRAMCK	48451-48451	LINDEN	48724-48724	CARROLLTON	48849-48849	LAKE ODESSA
48213-48217	DETROIT	48453-48453	MARLETTE	48725-48725	CASEVILLE	48850-48850	LAKEVIEW
48218-48218	RIVER ROUGE	48454-48454	MELVIN	48726-48726	CASS CITY	48851-48851	LYONS
48219-48219	DETROIT	48455-48455	METAMORA	48727-48727	CLIFFORD	48852-48852	MCBRIDES
48220-48220	FERNDALE	48456-48456	MINDEN CITY	48728-48728	CURRAN	48853-48853	MAPLE RAPIDS
48221-48224	DETROIT	48457-48457	MONTROSE	48729-48729	DEFORD	48854-48854	MASON
48225-48225	HARPER WOODS	48458-48458	MOUNT MORRIS	48730-48730	EAST TAWAS	48856-48856	MIDDLETON
48226-48228	DETROIT	48460-48460	NEW LOTHROP	48731-48731	ELKTON	48857-48857	MORRICE
48229-48229	ECORSE	48461-48461	NORTH BRANCH	48732-48732	ESSEXVILLE	48858-48859	MOUNT PLEASANT
48230-48230	GROSSE POINTE	48462-48462	ORTONVILLE	48733-48733	FAIRGROVE	48860-48860	MUIR
48231-48235	DETROIT	48463-48463	OTISVILLE	48734-48734	FRANKENMUTH	48861-48861	MULLIKEN
48236-48236	GROSSE POINTE	48464-48464	OTTER LAKE	48735-48735	GAGETOWN	48862-48862	NORTH STAR
48237-48237	OAK PARK	48465-48465	PALMS	48736-48736	GILFORD	48863-48863	OAK GROVE
48238-48238	DETROIT	48466-48466	PECK	48737-48737	GLENNIE	48864-48864	OKEMOS
48239-48240	REDFORD	48467-48467	PORT AUSTIN	48738-48738	GREENBUSH	48865-48865	ORLEANS
48242-48299	DETROIT	48468-48468	PORT HOPE	48739-48739	HALE	48866-48866	OVID
48301-48304	BLOOMFIELD HILLS	48469-48469	PORT SANILAC	48740-48740	HARRISVILLE	48867-48867	OWOSSO
48306-48309	ROCHESTER	48470-48470	RUTH	48741-48741	KINGSTON	48870-48870	PALO
48310-48314	STERLING HEIGHTS	48471-48471	SANDUSKY	48742-48742	LINCOLN	48871-48871	PERRINTON
48315-48318	UTICA	48472-48472	SNOVER	48743-48743	LONG LAKE	48872-48872	PERRY
48320-48320	KEEGO HARBOR	48473-48473	SWARTZ CREEK	48744-48744	MAYVILLE	48873-48873	PEWAMO
48321-48321	AUBURN HILLS	48475-48475	UBLY	48745-48745	MIKADO	48874-48874	POMPEII
48322-48325	WEST BLOOMFIELD	48476-48476	VERNON	48746-48746	MILLINGTON	48875-48875	PORTLAND
48326-48326	AUBURN HILLS	48501-48507	FLINT	48747-48747	MUNGER	48876-48876	POTTERVILLE
48327-48329	WATERFORD	48509-48529	BURTON	48748-48748	NATIONAL CITY	48877-48877	RIVERDALE
48330-48330	DRAYTON PLAINS	48531-48559	FLINT	48749-48749	OMER	48878-48878	ROSEBUSH
48331-48336	FARMINGTON	48601-48609	SAGINAW	48750-48753	OSCODA	48879-48879	SAINT JOHNS
48340-48343	PONTIAC	48610-48610	ALGER	48754-48754	OWENDALE	48880-48880	SAINT LOUIS
48346-48348	CLARKSTON	48611-48611	AUBURN	48755-48755	PIGEON	48881-48881	SARANAC
48350-48350	DAVISBURG	48612-48612	BEAVERTON	48756-48756	PRESCOTT	48882-48882	SHAFTSBURG
48353-48353	HARTLAND	48613-48613	BENTLEY	48757-48757	REESE	48883-48883	SHEPHERD
48356-48357	HIGHLAND	48614-48614	BRANT	48758-48758	RICHVILLE	48884-48884	SHERIDAN
48359-48362	LAKE ORION	48615-48615	BRECKENRIDGE	48759-48759	SEBEWAING	48885-48885	SIDNEY
48363-48363	OAKLAND	48616-48616	CHESANING	48760-48760	SILVERWOOD	48886-48886	SIX LAKES
48366-48366	LAKEVILLE	48617-48617	CLARE	48761-48761	SOUTH BRANCH	48887-48887	SMYRNA
48367-48367	LEONARD	48618-48618	COLEMAN	48762-48762	SPRUCE	48888-48888	STANTON
48370-48371	OXFORD	48619-48619	COMINS	48763-48764	TAWAS CITY	48889-48889	SUMNER
48374-48377	NOVI	48620-48620	EDENVILLE	48765-48765	TURNER	48890-48890	SUNFIELD
48380-48381	MILFORD	48621-48621	FAIRVIEW	48766-48766	TWINING	48891-48891	VESTABURG
48382-48382	COMMERCE TOWNSHIP	48622-48622	FARWELL	48767-48767	UNIONVILLE	48892-48892	WEBBERVILLE
48383-48386	WHITE LAKE	48623-48623	FREELAND	48768-48768	VASSAR	48893-48893	WEIDMAN
48387-48387	UNION LAKE	48624-48624	GLADWIN	48769-48769	TUSCOLA	48894-48894	WESTPHALIA
48390-48391	WALLED LAKE	48625-48625	HARRISON	48770-48770	WHITTEMORE	48895-48895	WILLIAMSTON

Zip Range	City	Zip Range	City	Zip Range	City	Zip Range	City
48896-48896	WINN	49101-49101	BARODA	49302-49302	ALTO	49453-49453	SAUGATUCK
48897-48897	WOODLAND	49102-49102	BERRIEN CENTER	49303-49303	BAILEY	49454-49454	SCOTTVILLE
48901-48980	LANSING	49103-49104	BERRIEN SPRINGS	49304-49304	BALDWIN	49455-49455	SHELBY
49001-49001	KALAMAZOO	49106-49106	BRIDGMAN	49305-49305	BARRYTON	49456-49456	SPRING LAKE
49002-49002	PORTAGE	49107-49107	BUCHANAN	49306-49306	BELMONT	49457-49457	TWIN LAKE
49003-49009	KALAMAZOO	49111-49111	EAU CLAIRE	49307-49307	BIG RAPIDS	49458-49458	WALHALLA
49010-49010	ALLEGAN	49112-49112	EDWARDSBURG	49309-49309	BITELY	49459-49459	WALKERVILLE
49011-49011	ATHENS	49113-49113	GALIEN	49310-49310	BLANCHARD	49460-49460	WEST OLIVE
49012-49012	AUGUSTA	49115-49115	HARBERT	49311-49311	BRADLEY	49461-49461	WHITEHALL
49013-49013	BANGOR	49116-49116	LAKESIDE	49312-49312	BROHMAN	49463-49463	WABANINGO
49014-49018	BATTLE CREEK	49117-49117	NEW BUFFALO	49314-49314	BURNIPS	49464-49464	ZEELAND
49019-49019	KALAMAZOO	49119-49119	NEW TROY	49315-49315	BYRON CENTER	49468-49468	GRANDVILLE
49020-49020	BEDFORD	49120-49121	NILES	49316-49316	CALEDONIA	49501-49599	GRAND RAPIDS
49021-49021	BELLEVUE	49125-49125	SAWYER	49317-49317	CANNONSBURG	49601-49601	CADILLAC
49022-49023	BENTON HARBOR	49126-49126	SODUS	49318-49318	CASNOVIA	49610-49610	ACME
49024-49024	PORTAGE	49127-49127	STEVENSVILLE	49319-49319	CEDAR SPRINGS	49611-49611	ALBA
49026-49026	BLOOMINGDALE	49128-49128	THREE OAKS	49320-49320	CHIPPEWA LAKE	49612-49612	ALDEN
49027-49027	BREEDSVILLE	49129-49129	UNION PIER	49321-49321	COMSTOCK PARK	49613-49613	ARCADIA
49028-49028	BRONSON	49130-49130	UNION	49322-49322	CORAL	49614-49614	BEAR LAKE
49029-49029	BURLINGTON	49201-49204	JACKSON	49323-49323	DORR	49615-49615	BELLAIRE
49030-49030	BURR OAK	49220-49220	ADDISON	49325-49325	FREEPORT	49616-49616	BENZONIA
49031-49031	CASSOPOLIS	49221-49221	ADRIAN	49326-49326	GOWEN	49617-49617	BEULAH
49032-49032	CENTREVILLE	49224-49224	ALBION	49327-49327	GRANT	49618-49618	BOON
49033-49033	CERESCO	49227-49227	ALLEN	49328-49328	HOPKINS	49619-49619	BRETHREN
49034-49034	CLIMAX	49228-49228	BLISSFIELD	49329-49329	HOWARD CITY	49620-49620	BUCKLEY
49035-49035	CLOVERDALE	49229-49229	BRITTON	49330-49330	KENT CITY	49621-49621	CEDAR
49036-49036	COLDWATER	49230-49230	BROOKLYN	49331-49331	LOWELL	49622-49622	CENTRAL LAKE
49038-49038	COLOMA	49232-49232	CAMDEN	49332-49332	MECOSTA	49623-49623	CHASE
49039-49039	HAGAR SHORES	49233-49233	CEMENT CITY	49333-49333	MIDDLEVILLE	49625-49625	COPEMISH
49040-49040	COLON	49234-49234	CLARKLAKE	49335-49335	MOLINE	49626-49626	EASTLAKE
49041-49041	COMSTOCK	49235-49235	CLAYTON	49336-49336	MORLEY	49627-49627	EASTPORT
49042-49042	CONSTANTINE	49236-49236	CLINTON	49337-49337	NEWAYGO	49628-49628	ELBERTA
49043-49043	COVERT	49237-49237	CONCORD	49338-49338	PARIS	49629-49629	ELK RAPIDS
49045-49045	DECATUR	49238-49238	DEERFIELD	49339-49339	PIERSON	49630-49630	EMPIRE
49046-49046	DELTON	49239-49239	FRONTIER	49340-49340	REMUS	49631-49631	EVART
49047-49047	DOWAGIAC	49240-49240	GRASS LAKE	49341-49341	ROCKFORD	49632-49632	FALMOUTH
49050-49050	DOWLING	49241-49241	HANOVER	49342-49342	RODNEY	49633-49633	FIFE LAKE
49051-49051	EAST LEROY	49242-49242	HILLSDALE	49343-49343	SAND LAKE	49634-49634	FILER CITY
49052-49052	FULTON	49245-49245	HOMER	49344-49344	SHELBYVILLE	49635-49635	FRANKFORT
49053-49053	GALESBURG	49246-49246	HORTON	49345-49345	SPARTA	49636-49636	GLEN ARBOR
49055-49055	GOBLES	49247-49247	HUDSON	49346-49346	STANWOOD	49637-49637	GRAWN
49056-49056	GRAND JUNCTION	49248-49248	JASPER	49347-49347	TRUFANT	49638-49638	HARRIETTA
49057-49057	HARTFORD	49249-49249	JEROME	49348-49348	WAYLAND	49639-49639	HERSEY
49058-49058	HASTINGS	49250-49250	JONESVILLE	49349-49349	WHITE CLOUD	49640-49640	HONOR
49060-49060	HICKORY CORNERS	49251-49251	LESLIE	49351-49351	ROCKFORD	49642-49642	IDLEWILD
49061-49061	JONES	49252-49252	LITCHFIELD	49355-49357	ADA	49643-49643	INTERLOCHEN
49062-49062	KENDALL	49253-49253	MANITOU BEACH	49401-49401	ALLENDALE	49644-49644	IRONS
49063-49063	LACOTA	49254-49254	MICHIGAN CENTER	49402-49402	BRANCH	49645-49645	KALEVA
49064-49064	LAWRENCE	49255-49255	MONTGOMERY	49403-49403	CONKLIN	49646-49646	KALKASKA
49065-49065	LAWTON	49256-49256	MORENCI	49404-49404	COOPERSVILLE	49648-49648	KEWADIN
49066-49066	LEONIDAS	49257-49257	MOSCOW	49405-49405	CUSTER	49649-49649	KINGSLEY
49067-49067	MARCELLUS	49258-49258	MOSHERVILLE	49406-49406	DOUGLAS	49650-49650	LAKE ANN
49068-49069	MARSHALL	49259-49259	MUNITH	49408-49408	FENNVILLE	49651-49651	LAKE CITY
49070-49070	MARTIN	49261-49261	NAPOLEON	49409-49409	FERRYSBURG	49653-49653	LAKE LEELANAU
49071-49071	MATTAWAN	49262-49262	NORTH ADAMS	49410-49410	FOUNTAIN	49654-49654	LELAND
49072-49072	MENDON	49263-49263	NORVELL	49411-49411	FREE SOIL	49655-49655	LEROY
49073-49073	NASHVILLE	49264-49264	ONONDAGA	49412-49413	FREMONT	49656-49656	LUTHER
49074-49074	NAZARETH	49265-49265	ONSTED	49415-49415	FRUITPORT	49657-49657	MC BAIN
49075-49075	NOTTAWA	49266-49266	OSSEO	49416-49416	GLENN	49659-49659	MANCELONA
49076-49076	OLIVET	49267-49267	OTTAWA LAKE	49417-49417	GRAND HAVEN	49660-49660	MANISTEE
49077-49077	OSHTEMO	49268-49268	PALMYRA	49418-49418	GRANDVILLE	49663-49663	MANTON
49078-49078	OTSEGO	49269-49269	PARMA	49419-49419	HAMILTON	49664-49664	MAPLE CITY
49079-49079	PAW PAW	49270-49270	PETERSBURG	49420-49420	HART	49665-49665	MARION
49080-49080	PLAINWELL	49271-49271	PITTSFORD	49421-49421	HESPERIA	49666-49666	MAYFIELD
49081-49081	PORTAGE	49272-49272	PLEASANT LAKE	49422-49424	HOLLAND	49667-49667	MERRITT
49082-49082	QUINCY	49274-49274	READING	49425-49425	HOLTON	49668-49668	MESICK
49083-49083	RICHLAND	49275-49275	RIDGEWAY	49426-49426	HUDSONVILLE	49670-49670	NORTHPORT
49084-49084	RIVERSIDE	49276-49276	RIGA	49427-49427	JAMESTOWN	49673-49673	OLD MISSION
49085-49085	SAINT JOSEPH	49277-49277	RIVES JUNCTION	49428-49429	JENISON	49674-49674	OMENA
49087-49087	SCHOOLCRAFT	49278-49278	ROLLIN	49430-49430	LAMONT	49675-49675	ONEKAMA
49088-49088	SCOTTS	49279-49279	SAND CREEK	49431-49431	LUDINGTON	49676-49676	RAPID CITY
49089-49089	SHERWOOD	49280-49280	SENECA	49434-49434	MACATAWA	49677-49677	REED CITY
49090-49090	SOUTH HAVEN	49281-49281	SOMERSET	49435-49435	MARNE	49679-49679	SEARS
49091-49091	STURGIS	49282-49282	SOMERSET CENTER	49436-49436	MEARS	49680-49680	SOUTH BOARDMAN
49092-49092	TEKONSHA	49283-49283	SPRING ARBOR	49437-49437	MONTAGUE	49682-49682	SUTTONS BAY
49093-49093	THREE RIVERS	49284-49284	SPRINGPORT	49440-49445	MUSKEGON	49683-49683	THOMPSONVILLE
49094-49094	UNION CITY	49285-49285	STOCKBRIDGE	49446-49446	NEW ERA	49684-49686	TRAVERSE CITY
49095-49095	VANDALIA	49286-49286	TECUMSEH	49448-49448	NUNICA	49688-49688	TUSTIN
49096-49096	VERMONTVILLE	49287-49287	TIPTON	49449-49449	PENTWATER	49689-49689	WELLSTON
49097-49097	VICKSBURG	49288-49288	WALDRON	49450-49450	PULLMAN	49690-49690	WILLIAMSBURG
49098-49098	WATERVLIET	49289-49289	WESTON	49451-49451	RAVENNA	49696-49696	TRAVERSE CITY
49099-49099	WHITE PIGEON	49301-49301	ADA	49452-49452	ROTHBURY	49701-49701	MACKINAW CITY

49705-49705 AFTON	49765-49765 ONAWAY	49835-49835 GARDEN	49903-49903 AMASA
49706-49706 ALANSON	49766-49766 OSSINEKE	49836-49836 GERMFASK	49905-49905 ATLANTIC MINE
49707-49707 ALPENA	49768-49768 PARADISE	49837-49837 GLADSTONE	49908-49908 BARAGA
49709-49709 ATLANTA	49769-49769 PELLSTON	49838-49838 GOULD CITY	49910-49910 BERGLAND
49710-49710 BARBEAU	49770-49770 PETOSKEY	49839-49839 GRAND MARAIS	49911-49911 BESSEMER
49711-49711 BAY SHORE	49774-49774 PICKFORD	49840-49840 GULLIVER	49912-49912 BRUCE CROSSING
49712-49712 BOYNE CITY	49775-49775 POINTE AUX PINS	49841-49841 GWINN	49913-49913 CALUMET
49713-49713 BOYNE FALLS	49776-49776 POSEN	49845-49845 HARRIS	49915-49915 CASPIAN
49715-49715 BRIMLEY	49777-49777 PRESQUE ISLE	49847-49847 HERMANSVILLE	49916-49916 CHASSELL
49716-49716 BRUTUS	49778-49778 BRIMLEY	49848-49848 INGALLS	49917-49917 COPPER CITY
49717-49717 BURT LAKE	49779-49779 ROGERS CITY	49849-49849 ISHPEMING	49918-49918 COPPER HARBOR
49718-49718 CARP LAKE	49780-49780 RUDYARD	49852-49852 LORETTO	49919-49919 COVINGTON
49719-49719 CEDARVILLE	49781-49781 SAINT IGNACE	49853-49853 MC MILLAN	49920-49920 CRYSTAL FALLS
49720-49720 CHARLEVOIX	49782-49782 BEAVER ISLAND	49854-49854 MANISTIQUE	49921-49921 DODGEVILLE
49721-49721 CHEBOYGAN	49783-49783 SAULT SAINTE MARIE	49855-49855 MARQUETTE	49922-49922 DOLLAR BAY
49722-49722 CONWAY	49784-49788 KINCHELOE	49858-49858 MENOMINEE	49924-49924 EAGLE RIVER
49723-49723 CROSS VILLAGE	49790-49790 STRONGS	49861-49861 MICHIGAMME	49925-49925 EWEN
49724-49724 DAFTER	49791-49791 TOPINABEE	49862-49862 MUNISING	49927-49927 GAASTRA
49725-49725 DE TOUR VILLAGE	49792-49792 TOWER	49863-49863 NADEAU	49929-49929 GREENLAND
49726-49726 DRUMMOND ISLAND	49793-49793 TROUT LAKE	49864-49864 NAHMA	49930-49930 HANCOCK
49727-49727 EAST JORDAN	49795-49795 VANDERBILT	49865-49865 NATIONAL MINE	49931-49931 HOUGHTON
49728-49728 ECKERMAN	49796-49796 WALLOON LAKE	49866-49866 NEGAUNEE	49934-49934 HUBBELL
49729-49729 ELLSWORTH	49797-49797 WATERS	49868-49868 NEWBERRY	49935-49935 IRON RIVER
49730-49730 ELMIRA	49799-49799 WOLVERINE	49869-49869 NORTHLAND	49938-49938 IRONWOOD
49733-49733 FREDERIC	49801-49801 IRON MOUNTAIN	49870-49870 NORWAY	49942-49942 KEARSARGE
49734-49735 GAYLORD	49802-49802 KINGSFORD	49871-49871 PALMER	49943-49943 KENTON
49736-49736 GOETZVILLE	49805-49805 ALLOUEZ	49872-49872 PERKINS	49945-49945 LAKE LINDEN
49737-49737 GOOD HART	49806-49806 AU TRAIN	49873-49873 PERRONVILLE	49946-49946 LANSE
49738-49739 GRAYLING	49807-49807 BARK RIVER	49874-49874 POWERS	49947-49947 MARENISCO
49740-49740 HARBOR SPRINGS	49808-49808 BIG BAY	49876-49876 QUINNESEC	49948-49948 MASS CITY
49743-49743 HAWKS	49812-49812 CARNEY	49877-49877 RALPH	49950-49950 MOHAWK
49744-49744 HERRON	49813-49813 CEDAR RIVER	49878-49878 RAPID RIVER	49952-49952 NISULA
49745-49745 HESSEL	49814-49814 CHAMPION	49879-49879 REPUBLIC	49953-49953 ONTONAGON
49746-49746 HILLMAN	49815-49815 CHANNING	49880-49880 ROCK	49955-49955 PAINESDALE
49747-49747 HUBBARD LAKE	49816-49816 CHATHAM	49881-49881 SAGOLA	49958-49958 PELKIE
49748-49748 HULBERT	49817-49817 COOKS	49883-49883 SENEY	49959-49959 RAMSAY
49749-49749 INDIAN RIVER	49818-49818 CORNELL	49884-49884 SHINGLETON	49960-49960 ROCKLAND
49751-49751 JOHANNESBURG	49819-49819 ARNOLD	49885-49885 SKANDIA	49961-49961 SIDNAW
49752-49752 KINROSS	49820-49820 CURTIS	49886-49886 SPALDING	49962-49962 SKANEE
49753-49753 LACHINE	49821-49821 DAGGETT	49887-49887 STEPHENSON	49963-49963 SOUTH RANGE
49755-49755 LEVERING	49822-49822 DEERTON	49891-49891 TRENARY	49964-49964 STAMBAUGH
49756-49756 LEWISTON	49825-49825 EBEN JUNCTION	49892-49892 VULCAN	49965-49965 TOIVOLA
49757-49757 MACKINAC ISLAND	49826-49826 RUMELY	49893-49893 WALLACE	49967-49967 TROUT CREEK
49759-49759 MILLERSBURG	49827-49827 ENGADINE	49894-49894 WELLS	49968-49968 WAKEFIELD
49760-49760 MORAN	49829-49829 ESCANABA	49895-49895 WETMORE	49969-49969 WATERSMEET
49761-49761 MULLETT LAKE	49831-49831 FELCH	49896-49896 WILSON	49970-49970 WATTON
49762-49762 NAUBINWAY	49833-49833 LITTLE LAKE	49901-49901 AHMEEK	49971-49971 WHITE PINE
49764-49764 ODEN	49834-49834 FOSTER CITY	49902-49902 ALPHA	

Minnesota

General Help Numbers:

Governor's Office
130 State Capitol Bldg   651-296-3391
75 Constitution Ave   Fax 651-296-2089
St Paul, MN 55155   7:30AM-5PM
www.mainserver.state.mn.us/governor

Attorney General's Office
102 State Capitol   651-296-6196
St Paul, MN 55155   Fax 651-297-4193
www.ag.state.mn.us/home/mainhi.shtml   8AM-5PM

State Court Administrator
135 Minnesota Judicial Center   651-296-2474
25 Constitution Ave   Fax 651-297-5636
St Paul, MN 55155   8AM-4:30PM
www.courts.state.mn.us

State Archives
Divison of Library & Archives   651-296-6126
345 Kellogg Blvd West   Fax 651-297-7436
St Paul, MN 55102-1906   9AM-5PM M-SA; till 9PM TU
www.mnhs.org

State Specifics:

Capital:	St. Paul Ramsey County
Time Zone:	CST
Number of Counties:	87
Population:	4,775,508
Web Site:	www.state.mn.us

State Agencies

Criminal Records

Bureau of Criminal Apprehension, Records & Identification, 1246 University Ave, St Paul, MN 55104; 651-642-0670, 8:15AM-4PM.

www.dps.state.mn.us/bca

Indexing & Storage: Records are available from 1924. New records are available for inquiry immediately. Records are indexed on microfilm, inhouse computer.

Searching: For most requesters, to obtain the entire adult history, including all arrests, you must have a notarized release form signed by person of

record. To get a 15 year record of convictions only, a consent form is not required. Include the following in your request-name, date of birth. The following data is not released: juvenile records.

Access by: mail, in person.

Fee & Payment: The fee for the full adult history is $15.00, for non-profits the fee is $8.00. The fee for the 15 year record is $4.00. Fee payee: BCA. Prepayment required. Business checks, persoanl checks, money orders and certified funds are accepted. No credit cards accepted.

Mail search: Turnaround time: 1-2 weeks. A self addressed stamped envelope is requested.

In person search: Turnaround time is 2 days, unless you are the person of record, then it is immediate. Public access (15 year search) is also immediate.

Other access: A public database is available on CD-ROM. Monthly updates can be purchased. Data is in ASCII format and is raw data. Fee is $250.00.

Corporation Records
Limited Liability Company Records
Assumed Name
Trademarks/Servicemarks
Limited Partnerships

Business Records Services, Secretary of State, 180 State Office Bldg, 100 Constitution Ave, St Paul, MN 55155-1299; 651-296-2803 (Information), 651-297-7067 (Fax), 8AM-4:30PM.

www.sos.state.mn.us

Indexing & Storage: Records are available from 1850's on. All records are indexed together. It takes one day before new records are available for inquiry.

Searching: Part II of foreign corporation annual reports are not released. Include the following in your request-full name of business, corporation file number. In addition to articles of incorporation, corporation records include the following information: Annual Reports, Prior (merged) names, Inactive and Reserved names.

Access by: mail, phone, in person, online.

Fee & Payment: There is no search fee. Certification is $5.00 per copy. Copies are $1.00 per page. Fee payee: Secretary of State. Prepayment required. Personal checks accepted. No credit cards accepted.

Mail search: Turnaround time: 1-2 days. No self addressed stamped envelope is required.

Phone search: Limited verification information, only on corporation data, is given over the phone.

In person search: You may make copies at $6.00 per business name. There is no fee to view the database or microfilm. However, if you walk-in and wish copies immediately, there is an additional $20.00 fee.

Online search: The program is called Direct Access and is available 24 hours. There is an annual subscription fee of $50.00. Records are $1-4, depending on item needed. Please call 651-297-9096 for more information.

Other access: Information can be purchased in bulk format. Call 651-297-9100 for more information.

Uniform Commercial Code
Federal Tax Liens
State Tax Liens

UCC Division, Secretary of State, 180 State Office Bldg, St Paul, MN 55155-1299; 651-296-2803, 651-297-5844 (Fax), 8AM-4:30PM.

www.sos.state.mn.us

Indexing & Storage: Records are available from 1987 on computer. Records on microfiche from 1966-present. Records are indexed on inhouse computer.

Searching: Use search request form UCC-11 for UCC filings. Use a separate UCC-12 request form to obtain federal and state tax liens on businesses. All tax liens on individuals are filed at the county level. Include the following in your request-debtor name.

Access by: mail, in person, online.

Fee & Payment: Search using approved form is $15.00; other forms $20.00. The search fee includes 10 copies, after which copies are $1.00 per page. Fee payee: Secretary of State. Prepayment required. Personal checks accepted. No credit cards accepted.

Mail search: Turnaround time: 2-3 days. A self addressed stamped envelope is requested.

In person search: A free public access terminal is available.

Online search: The program is called Direct Access and is available 24 hours. There is a subscription fee is $50.00 per year, plus $3.00 per UCC search or $4.00 per business search. Call 651-297-9097 for more information.

Other access: The state will provide information in bulk form on paper or disk. Call 651-297-9100 for more information.

Sales Tax Registrations

Minnesota Department of Revenue, Sales & Use Tax Division, 600 N Robert Street MS:6330, St Paul, MN 55146-6330; 651-296-6181, 651-282-5225 (To Register), 651-296-1938 (Fax), 7:30AM-5PM.

www.taxes.state.mn.us

Indexing & Storage: Records are available for current registration records only. Records have been computerized since 1992.

Searching: This agency will only confirm that a business is registered, business name and location, and date permit was isssued. They will provide no other information. Include the following in your request-business name. They also require the MN business identification number.

Access by: mail, phone, fax, in person.

Fee & Payment: There is no fee. No credit cards accepted.

Mail search: Turnaround time: 7 days. No self addressed stamped envelope is required.

Phone search: Turnaround time for a written reply is approximately 7 days from the request date.

Fax search: Fax searching available.

In person search: Searching is available in person.

Birth Certificates

Minnesota Department of Health, Vital Records, PO Box 9441, Minneapolis, MN 55440-9441 (Courier: 717 Delaware St SE, Minneapolis, MN 55414); 612-676-5120, 612-331-5776 (Fax), 8AM-4:30PM.

www.health.state.mn.us

Note: For information pertaining to adoption records, call 612-676-5129,

Indexing & Storage: Records are available from 1900 on. Prior records must be obtained from the county level. It takes 3 months before new records are available for inquiry. Records are indexed on microfiche, inhouse computer.

Searching: As of 08/01/2000, only those with a "tanglible interest" may request a record. Out of wedlock birth certificates require a notarized release from parent or child. Include the following in your request-full name, date of birth, place of birth, names of parents, mother's maiden name. Also, requester's signature must be notarized.

Access by: mail, fax, in person.

Fee & Payment: Fees are: $11.00 for a non-certified copy, $14.00 for a certified copy and $8.00 for an additional certified copy of the same name. Fee payee: Minnesota Department of Health. Prepayment required. Credit cards may be used for mail, phone and fax requesters. Personal checks accepted. Credit cards accepted: Mastercard, Visa, AmEx, Discover.

Mail search: Turnaround time: 6-8 weeks. No self addressed stamped envelope is required.

Fax search: See expeditied services.

In person search: Turnaround time is 10-20 minutes.

Expedited service: Expedited service is available for fax searches. Turnaround time: 4 weeks. Use of credit card required. Add $5.00 for use of credit card and $14.00 for overnight delivery.

Death Records

Minnesota Department of Health, Section of Vital Records, PO Box 9441, Minneapolis, MN 55440-9441 (Courier: 717 Delaware St SE, Minneapolis, MN 55414); 612-676-5120, 612-331-5776 (Fax), 8AM-4:30PM.

www.health.state.mn.us

Indexing & Storage: Records are available from 1908 on. Prior records must be obtained at the county level. It takes 3 months before new records are available for inquiry. Records are indexed on microfiche.

Searching: As of 08/01/2000, only those with a "tangible interest" may request a record. Include the following in your request-full name, date of death, place of death. Also, requester's signature must be notarized. If date or place not known, include last year known to be alive.

Access by: mail, fax, in person.

Fee & Payment: The search fees are $11.00 for a certified record and $5.00 for certified identical copy of same name. Fee payee: Minnesota Department of Health. Prepayment required. Credit cards may be used for ordering by fax, phone or mail. Personal checks accepted. Credit cards accepted: Mastercard, Visa, AmEx, Discover.

Mail search: Turnaround time: 6-8 weeks. No self addressed stamped envelope is required.

Fax search: See expeditied services.

In person search: Turnaround time is 10-20 minutes.

Expedited service: Expedited service is available for fax searches. Turnaround time: 4 weeks. Use of credit card is required. Add $5.00 for credit card and $14.00 for overnight express.

Marriage Certificates
Divorce Records

Records not maintained by a state level agency.

Note: Marriage and divorce records are found at the county level. The Section of Vital Records has an index and they will direct you to the proper county (Marriage since 1958, Divorce since 1970). Call the Section of Vital Records at 651-676-5120.

Workers' Compensation Records

Labor & Industry Department, Workers Compensation Division - Records Section, 443 Lafayette Rd, St Paul, MN 55155; 651-296-6845, 651-215-0170 (Fax), 8AM-4:30PM.

Indexing & Storage: Records are available on microfilm for 18 years after file closure. Imaged records are available for 50 years. New records are available for inquiry immediately. Records are indexed on microfilm, microfiche, inhouse computer. Records are normally destroyed after 19 years old or more.

Searching: Must have a signed release from claimant to obtain all files. Include the following in your request-claimant name, Social Security Number, date of injury, employer. Include any and all dates of injury in your request.

Access by: mail, phone, in person.

Fee & Payment: There is no search fee. Copies are $.65 each. Add 6.5% tax and postage. There is a $6.00 fee for records retrieved from archives. Fee payee: Department of Labor & Industry. Prepayment required. Personal checks accepted. No credit cards accepted.

Mail search: Turnaround time: 2-4 weeks. No self addressed stamped envelope is required.

Phone search: Phone searching is limited to employees involved within a case.

In person search: If you request in person, they will mail requested copies.

Driver Records

Driver & Vehicle Services, Records Section, 445 Minnesota St, #180, St Paul, MN 55101; 651-296-6911, 8AM-4:30PM.

www.dps.state.mn.us/dvs/index.html

Note: Copies of tickets can be requested from the same address. The fee is $4.00 per reocrd, $5.00 if certified.

Indexing & Storage: Records are available for 5 years minimum for moving violations and suspensions; 10 years for open revocation; retained indefinitely for DWIs for 2 or more convictions. Accidents and up to 10 mph over in a 55 zone on interstate roads are not shown. It takes no more than 15 days before new records are available for inquiry.

Searching: A casual requester can only receive the driver's address with consent of driver. The driver's license number or full name and DOB is required for a search. Surrendered licenses will be purged after one year if clear; after five years if the record has convictions. The following data is not released: medical information.

Access by: mail, in person, online.

Fee & Payment: Fees: $5.50 per certified record; $4.50 per non-certified record. Fee payee: Department of Public Safety. Prepayment required. Personal checks accepted. No credit cards accepted.

Mail search: Turnaround time: 1 week. No self addressed stamped envelope is required.

In person search: Up to 3 requests will be processed for walk-in requesters, the rest are available the next day.

Online search: Online access costs $2.50 per record. Online inquiries can be processed either as interactive or as batch files (overnight) 24 hours a day, 7 days a week. Requesters operate from a "bank." Records are accessed by either DL number or full name and DOB. Call 651-297-1714 for more information.

Other access: Minnesota will sell its entire database of driving record information with monthly updates. Customized request sorts are available. Fees vary by type with programming and computer time and are quite reasonable.

Vehicle Ownership
Vehicle Identification

Driver & Vehicle Services, Records Section, 445 Minnesota St, St Paul, MN 55101; 651-296-6911 (General Information), 8AM-4:30PM.

www.dps.state.mn.us/dvs/index.html

Indexing & Storage: Records are available for past 7 years. It takes 5 days before new records are available for inquiry.

Searching: The state places no restrictions on obtaining vehicle or ownership information; however, the licensee has the option to restrict access to his/her record from sale to mail list vendors or to individual requesters not on DPPA approval list.

Access by: mail, in person, online.

Fee & Payment: The fee is $4.50 per record for current information and $5.50 per certified copy for mail or walk-in requesters. Fee payee: Department of Public Safety. Prepayment required. Personal checks accepted. No credit cards accepted.

Mail search: Turnaround time: 1 week. A self addressed stamped envelope is requested.

In person search: Turnaround time is immediate for walk-in requesters.

Online search: Online access costs $2.50 per record. There is an additional monthly charge for dial-in access. The system is the same as described for driving record requests. It is open 24 hours a day, 7 days a week. Lien information is included. Call 651-297-1714 for more information.

Accident Reports

Driver & Vehicle Services, Accident Records, 445 Minnesota St, Suite 181, St Paul, MN 55101-5181; 651-296-2060, 651-282-2360 (Fax), 8AM-4:30PM.

Indexing & Storage: Records are available from 1987-1996 on microfilm, and from 1992-present can be located by computer. It takes 3 weeks from date of accident before new records are available for inquiry.

Searching: Police reports may be obtained with the written and signed authorization from the person involved in the accident. Include the following in your request-date of accident, full name, date of birth, driver's license number. Records are indexed by driver names.

Access by: mail, phone, fax, in person.

Fee & Payment: The fee is $4 per police report. Fee payee: DVS. Prepayment required. Personal checks accepted. No credit cards accepted.

Mail search: Turnaround time: 1 week. A self addressed stamped envelope is requested.

Phone search: No fee for telephone request. They will acknowledge by phone if a file exists if file number can be found on driver license database. Ongoing requesters may set-up an account and request records by fax.

Fax search: Fax requests require an account with the agency. Turnaround time 3 days if the request is received after the file has become available.

In person search: Walk-in requesters may obtain copies of accident reports with the authorization of the individual(s) involved in the accident. Turnaround time: while you wait (typically, 5-10 minutes).

Boat & Vessel Ownership
Boat & Vessel Registration

Department of Natural Resources, License Bureau, 500 Lafayette Rd, St Paul, MN 55155-4026; 651-296-2316, 800-285-2000, 651-297-8851 (Fax), 8AM-4:30PM.

www.dnr.state.mn.us

Note: Lien information shows on title records obtained at this agency.

Indexing & Storage: Records are available for the last 15 years. Records are maintained for watercraft, snow mobiles, and off-highway vehicles (all terrain) and off-highway motorcycles. A watercraft must be titled if over 16 ft and 1980 model or newer, registered if over 9 ft.

Searching: The name and hull number or registration number is required to complete a search.

Access by: mail, phone, fax, in person.

Fee & Payment: There is no search fee.

Mail search: Turnaround time: 1 week.

Phone search: Up to 2 names may be searched over the phone.

Fax search: Same criteria as mail searching.

In person search: Turnaround time is usually immediate.

Other access: Bulk requests are offered in several media types. Call 651-297-4928 for more information.

Legislation-Current/Pending
Legislation-Passed

Minnesota Legislature, State Capitol, House-Room 211, Senate-Room 231, St Paul, MN 55155; 651-296-2887 (Senate Bills), 651-296-6646 (House Bill Status), 651-296-2314 (House Bill Copies), 651-296-2146 (House Information), 651-296-1563 (Fax), 8AM-5PM.

www.leg.state.mn.us

Note: When sessions, the hours are extended to 5:30 PM. Sessions start in January in odd numbered years and in February in even numbered years.

Indexing & Storage: Records are available for current session only. For Senate bill status & general legis. questions, call 651-296-0504; Senate bill copies, 651-296-2343. For historical records, call the legislative reference library at 612-296-3398, and there will be a fee involved. Records are indexed on inhouse computer, hard copy.

Searching: Include the following in your request-bill number.

Access by: mail, phone, in person, online.

Fee & Payment: There is no search fee. There is no expedited service; however, they will help requesters who have their own Federal Express account.

Mail search: Turnaround time: variable. No self addressed stamped envelope is required.

Phone search: No fee for telephone request.

In person search: No fee for request.

Online search: Information available through the Internet site includes full text of bills, status, previous 4 years of bills, and bill tracking.

Voter Registration

Access to Records is Restricted

Secretary of State, Elections Division, 180 State Office Bldg, 100 Constitution Ave, St Paul, MN 55155; 651-215-1440, 651-296-9073 (Fax), 8AM-4:30PM.

www.sos.state.mn.us

Note: Records are sold by the state only for political, election, or government purposes and only to MN registered voters. Some counties will honor record requests.

GED Certificates

Department of Children, Families & Learning, GED Testing, 1500 Highway 36 West, Roseville, MN 55113; 651-582-8445, 651-582-8496 (Fax), 7AM-3:30PM.

http://cfl.state.mn.us

Searching: The SSN and year of the test are needed to search. A signed release is needed for a copy of a transcript, scores or graduation verification.

Access by: mail, phone, fax, in person.

Mail search: Turnaround time: 1-2 days. No self addressed stamped envelope is required. No fee for mail request.

Phone search: No fee for telephone request. For verification only.

Fax search: Same criteria as mail searching.

In person search: No fee for request. Records must be picked up the next day.

Hunting License Information
Fishing License Information

Fish & Wildlife Division, DNR Information Center, 500 Lafayette Rd, St Paul, MN 55155-4040; 651-296-6157, 651-297-3618 (Fax), 8AM-4:30PM.

www.dnr.state.mn.us

Indexing & Storage: Records are available on computer from 1979 for doe, turkey - Spring permits; 1985 for moose, 1982 for bear and 1990 for turkey-Fall permits.

Searching: Records are open to public; all information is released. Include the following in your request-full name, date of birth. The driver's license is also helpful.

Access by: mail, phone, fax, in person.

Fee & Payment: There is no search fee. Fee payee: DNR. Prepayment required. Personal checks accepted. No credit cards accepted.

Mail search: Turnaround time: 1-3 days. No self addressed stamped envelope is required.

Phone search: They will confirm information over the phone.

Fax search: They will confirm information, turnaround time is 1 week.

In person search: Searching is available in person.

Other access: They have mailing lists available for purchase. Call Sue Klecker at 651-297-4928 for details.

Licenses Searchable Online

Acupuncturist #09	www.docboard.org/mn/df/mndf.htm
Architect #37	www.aelslagid.state.mn.us/lic.html
Athletic Trainer #09	www.docboard.org/mn/df/mndf.htm
Bingo Hall #35	www.gcb.state.mn.us/
Chiropractor #04	www.mn-chiroboard.state.mn.us/main-licensing.htm
Crematory #27	www.health.state.mn.us/divs/hpsc/Mortsci/contact.htm
Engineer #37	www.aelslagid.state.mn.us/lic.html
Funeral Establishment #27	www.health.state.mn.us/divs/hpsc/Mortsci/contact.htm
Gambling Equipment Distributor #35	www.gcb.state.mn.us/
Geologist #37	www.aelslagid.state.mn.us/lic.html
Interior Designer #37	www.aelslagid.state.mn.us/lic.html
Landscape Architect #37	www.aelslagid.state.mn.us/lic.html
Lobbyist #19	www.cfboard.state.mn.us/lobby/index.html
Lottery (Retail) #42	www.lottery.state.mn.us/retailer/lookup.html
Manufacturer of Gambling Equipment #35	www.gcb.state.mn.us/
Medical Doctor #09	www.docboard.org/mn/df/mndf.htm
On-sale Retail #34	www.dps.state.mn.us/alcgamb/alcenf/liquorlic/liquorlic.html
On-sale Retail Municipal Liquor Store #34	www.dps.state.mn.us/alcgamb/alcenf/liquorlic/liquorlic.html
Optometrist #11	www.arbo.org/nodb2000/licsearch.asp
Organization, Lawful Gambling #35	www.gcb.state.mn.us/
Physical Therapist #09	www.docboard.org/mn/df/mndf.htm
Physician Assistant #09	www.docboard.org/mn/df/mndf.htm
Political Candidates #19	www.cfboard.state.mn.us/legcand.html
Respiratory Care Practitioner #09	www.docboard.org/mn/df/mndf.htm
Soil Scientist #37	www.aelslagid.state.mn.us/lic.html
Surgeon #09	www.docboard.org/mn/df/mndf.htm
Surveyor #37	www.aelslagid.state.mn.us/lic.html
Teacher #17	http://cfl.state.mn.us/licen/licinfo.html
Underground Storage Tank Contractor #43	www.pca.state.mn.us/cleanup/ust.html#certification

Licensing Quick Finder

Abstractor #25	800-657-3978
Abstractor Company #25	800-657-3978
Accredited Minnesota Assessor #01	651-296-0209
Acupuncturist #09	612-617-2130
Adoption & Guardianship #31	651-296-3971
Alarm & Communication System Contractor #06	651-642-0800
Alarm & Communication System Installer #06	651-642-0800
Alcohol/Drug Counselor #29	651-282-5619
All-Terrain Vehicle Registration #32	651-296-2316
Amateur Boxing Coach #03	651-296-2501
Amateur Boxing Referee #03	651-296-2501
Amateur Boxing Show #03	651-296-5310
Ambulance Service/Personnel #28	612-627-6000
Applicant Background Study & Investigation #30	651-296-3971
Architect #37	651-297-2208
Asbestos Abatement Worker/Contractor #26	651-215-0900
Assessor #01	651-296-0209
Athletic Trainer #09	612-617-2130
Attorney #40	651-296-2254
Audiologist #29	651-282-5629
Auditor #39	651-296-7937
Bank #24	651-297-3779
Barber #02	651-642-0489
Bingo Hall #35	651-639-4000
Boat & Canoe Registration #32	651-296-2316
Boat Title #32	651-297-2316
Boiler Inspector #36	651-296-4531
Bondsman #23	651-296-6319
Boxer #03	651-296-2501
Chemical Dependency #30	651-296-3991
Child Care Facility #31	651-296-3971
Children's Service #30	651-296-3800
Chiropractor #04	612-617-2223

Consumer Credit, Credit Union & Savings Association #24	651-296-2297
Consumption & Display Information #34	651-296-6439
Cosmetologist #23	651-296-6319
Cosmetology School/Shop #23	651-296-6319
County Fair #41	952-496-7950
Credit Union #24	651-296-2297
Crematory #27	651-282-3829
Dental Assistant #05	612-617-2250
Dental Hygienist #05	612-617-2250
Dentist #05	612-617-2250
Developmental Disabilities Licensing #30	651-297-4112
Dietitian #46	612-617-2175
Electrician #06	651-642-0800
Elevator Inspector #36	651-297-1644
Emergency Medical Technician #28	612-627-6000
Employment Agency Counselor #36	651-296-2282
Employment Agency Manager #36	651-296-2282
Engineer #37	651-296-2388
Equipment Manufacturing & Distribution #33	651-296-6159
Esthetician #23	651-296-6319
Foster Care Program #31	651-296-3971
Funeral Director #27	651-282-3829
Funeral Establishment #27	651-282-3829
Gambling Equipment Distributor #35	651-639-4000
Geologist #37	651-296-2388
Grain Licensing #21	651-296-2980
Hearing Aid Dispenser #29	651-282-5620
High Pressure Inspector #36	651-296-4531
Insurance Agent/Salesman #23	651-296-6319
Interior Designer #37	651-296-2388
Kick Karate Professional #03	651-296-2501
Landscape Architect #37	651-296-2388
Licensure Information #45	651-649-5736

Livestock Weighing #21	651-296-2980
Lobbyist #19	651-296-5148
Lottery (Retail) #42	651-635-8119
LPA #39	651-296-7937
Manicurist #23	800-657-3978
Manufactured Home Installer #38	651-296-8458
Manufactured Home Manufacturer & Dealer #38	651-296-4628
Manufactured Structures Section #38	651-296-4628
Manufacturer of Gambling Equipment #35	651-639-4000
Marriage & Family Therapist #08	612-617-2220
Medical Doctor #09	612-617-2130
Mental Health, Chemical Dependency #30	651-296-4497
Minnesota Assessor Specialist #01	651-296-0209
Mortician #27	651-282-3829
Notary Public #23	651-296-6319
Nurse-LPN #10	612-617-2270
Nurse-RN #10	612-617-2270
Nursing Home Administrator #07	612-617-2117
Nutritionist #46	612-617-2175
Occupational Therapist/Assistant #29	651-282-5624
Off Sale Retail & Wine Retail #34	651-296-9519
Off-Highway Motorcycle #32	651-296-2316
Off-Road Vehicle #32	651-296-2316
On-sale Retail #34	651-296-6939
On-sale Retail Municipal Liquor Store #34	651-215-6209
Optometrist #11	612-617-2173
Organization, Lawful Gambling #35	651-639-4000
Part-time Peace Officer #12	651-643-3060
Peace Officer #12	651-643-3060
Pesticide Applicator #22	651-296-6121
Pharmacist #13	612-617-2201
Physical Therapist #09	612-617-2130
Physician Assistant #09	612-617-2130

Plumber #26 651-215-0836
Podiatrist (Licensed & Temporary Permit) #14
....612-617-2200
Political Candidates #19 651-296-5148
Private Detective/Investigator #44.........651-215-1753
Professional Cornermen #03 651-296-2501
Professional Referee #03 651-296-2501
Protective Agent #44 651-215-1753
Psychological Practitioner #15 651-617-2230
Psychologist #15.................................651-617-2230
Public Accountant-CPA #39.................651-296-7937
Public Water Supply Operator #26........651-215-0770
Race Track/Card Club Operator #41 952-496-7950
Racing (Racing Class "A"- Owners of Track) #41
....952-496-7950
Racing/Card Club Occupational #41 952-496-7950
Real Estate Broker/Dealer #23 651-296-6319

Residential Mortgage Originators/Servicers #24
....651-282-9855
Residential Remodeler/Contractor #23
....651-296-6319
Respiratory Care Practitioner #09 612-617-2130
Sanitarian #26....................................651-215-0836
Securities/Investment Advisor #23 651-296-6319
Snowmobile Registration #32 651-296-2316
Social Worker #16................................612-617-2100
Soil Scientist #37.................................651-296-2388
Speech-Language Pathologist #29 651-282-5629
Surgeon #09 612-617-2130
Surveyor #37 651-296-2388
Teacher #17...651-582-8691
Underground Storage Tank Contractor/Supervisor #43
....651-297-8616

Unlicensed Mental Health Practitioneers #29
....651-282-5621
Veterinarian #18.................................612-617-2170
Waste Disposal Facility Inspector #43
....651-296-7162
Waste Water Disposal Facility Operator #43
....651-296-7162
Water Conditioning Installer/Contractor #26
....651-215-0836
Water Well Contractor #26 651-215-0870
Watercraft #32 651-296-2316
Weather Modifier #21 651-296-0591
Wholesaler, Manufacturer, Labels & Import #34
....651-296-6939
X-ray Operator #20 651-215-0941

Licensing Agency Information

01 Board of Assessors, Mail Station 3340, St Paul, MN 55146-3340; 651-296-0209, Fax: 651-297-2166.

02 Board of Barber Examiners, 1885 University Ave W, #335, St Paul, MN 55104-3403; 651-642-0489, Fax: 651-649-5997.

03 Board of Boxing, 133 E 7th St, St Paul, MN 55101; 651-296-2501, Fax: 651-297-5310.

04 Board of Chiropractic Examiners, 2829 University Ave SE, Minneapolis, MN 55414-3220; 612-617-2222, Fax: 612-617-2224.
www.mn-chiroboard.state.mn.us

Direct URL to search licenses: www.mn-chiroboard.state.mn.us/main-licensing.htm You can search online using alphabetical lists

05 Board of Dentistry, 2829 University Ave SE, #450, Minneapolis, MN 55414; 612-617-2250, Fax: 612-617-2260.
www.dentalboard.state.mn.us

06 Board of Electricity, 1821 University - RM S-128, St Paul, MN 55104; 651-642-0800, Fax: 651-642-0441.

07 Board of Examiners for Nursing Home Administrators, 2829 University Ave SE #440, Minneapolis, MN 55414; 612-617-2117, Fax: 612-617-2119.
www.benha.state.mn.us

08 Board of Marriage & Family Therapy, 2829 University Ave SE #330, Minneapolis, MN 55414-3222; 612-617-2220, Fax: 612-617-2221.
www.bmft.state.mn.us

09 Board of Medical Practice, 2829 University Ave SE, #400, Minneapolis, MN 55414-3246; 612-617-2130, Fax: 612-617-2166.
www.bmp.state.mn.us

Direct URL to search licenses: www.docboard.org/mn/df/mndf.htm You can search online using name, town name, and license number.

10 Board of Nursing, 2829 University Ave SE, #500, Minneapolis, MN 55414-3253; 612-617-2181, Fax: 612-617-2190.
www.nursingboard.state.mn.us

11 Board of Optometry, 2829 University Av SE #550, Minneapolis, MN 55414; 612-617-2173, Fax: 612-617-2174.

Direct URL to search licenses: www.arbo.org/nodb2000/licsearch.asp You can search online using national database by name, city or state.

12 Board of Peace Officers Standards & Training, 1600 University Av #200, St Paul, MN 55104-3825; 651-643-3060, Fax: 651-643-3072.
www.dps.state.mn.us/post

13 Board of Pharmacy, 2829 University Ave SE, #530, Minneapolis, MN 55414-3251; 612-617-2201, Fax: 612-617-2212.
www.phcybrd.state.mn.us

14 Board of Podiatric Medicine, 2829 University Av SE #430, Minneapolis, MN 55414; 612-617-2200, Fax: 612-617-2698.

15 Board of Psychology, 2829 University Ave. SE, #320, Minneapolis, MN 55414-3237; 612-612-2230, Fax: 612-617-2240.

16 Board of Social Work, 2829 University Ave SE, #340, Minneapolis, MN 55414-3239; 612-617-2100, Fax: 612-617-2103.
www.socialwork.state.mn.us

17 Licensing Unit, Board of Teaching, 1500 Highway 36 W, Roseville, MN 55113; 651-582-8691, Fax: 651-582-8809.
http://cfl.state.mn.us/teachbrd

Direct URL to search licenses: http://cfl.state.mn.us/licen/licinfo.html You can search online using file folder number or first & last name

18 Board of Veterinary Medicine, 2829 University Ave SE, Minneapolis, MN 55414; 612-617-2170, Fax: 612-617-2172.

19 Division of Plant Health, Campaign Finance Board, 638 Cedar St, Centennial Bld, 1st Fl, St Paul, MN 55155; 651-296-5148, Fax: 651-296-1722.
www.cfboard.state.mn.us

Direct URL to search licenses: www.cfboard.state.mn.us/

20 Department of Health, Radiation Division, 121 E 7th Pl #220, St Paul, MN 55101; 651-215-0930, Fax: 651-215-0976.

21 Department of Agriculture, Livestock Weighing & Licensing, 90 W Plato Blvd, St Paul, MN 55107; 651-296-2980, Fax: 651-297-2504.

22 Department of Agriculture, Pesticide Registration, 90 W Plato Blvd, St Paul, MN 55107; 651-296-6121, Fax: 651-297-2271.
www.state.mn.us/govtoffice/index.html

23 Department of Commerce, 133 E 7th St, St Paul, MN 55101; 800-657-3978, Fax: 651-296-8591.
www.state.mn.us/govtoffice/index.html

24 Department of Commerce, Division of Financial Examinations, 133 E 7th St, St Paul, MN 55101; 651-296-2135, Fax: 651-296-8591.
www.commerce.state.mn.us

25 Department of Commerce, Licensing Unit for Abstractors, 133 E 7th St, St Paul, MN 55101; 800-657-3978.
www.state.mn.us/govtoffice/index.html

26 Department of Health, Environmental Health Division, PO Box 64975 (121 E 7th Pl #220), St Paul, MN 55164-0975; 651-215-0900, Fax: 651-215-0975.
www.health.state.mn.us/divs/eh/eh.html

27 Department of Health, Mortuary Science Section, PO Box 64975 (PO Box 64975), St Paul, MN 55164-0975; 651-282-3829, Fax: 651-282-3839.
www.health.state.mn.us/divs/hpsc/Mortsci/contact.htm

Direct URL to search licenses: www.health.state.mn.us/divs/hpsc/Mortsci/contact.htm Online searching is under construction.

28 Emergency Medical Services, Regulatory Board, 2829 University Av SE #310, Minneapolis, MN 55414-3222; 612-627-6000, Fax: 612-627-5442.
www.emsrb@state.mn.us

29 Health Occupation Programs, Health Policy & Systems Compliance, PO Box 64975 (121 E 7th Pl #450, Metro Square Bldg), St Paul, MN 55164-0975; 651-282-6366, Fax: 651-282-5628.
www.health.state.mn.us/divs/hpsc/hop/home/homepg.html

Direct URL to search licenses: www.health.state.mn.us/divs/hpsc/hop/home/homepg.html Online searching is under construction at the web site.

30 Department of Human Services, 444 Lafayette Rd, St Paul, MN 55155; 651-296-6117, Fax: 651-297-1490.
www.state.mn.us/govtoffice/index.html

31 Department of Human Services, 444 Lafayette Rd, St Paul, MN 55155; 651-296-6117, Fax: 651-297-1490.

32 Department of Natural Resources, License Bureau, 500 Lafayette Rd, St Paul, MN 55155; 651-296-2316, Fax: 651-297-8851.
www.dnr.state.mn.us/license_bureau/licenses.html

33 Department of Public Safety, Division of Gambling Enforcement, 444 Cedar St, #133, St Paul, MN 55101-5133; 651-296-6159, Fax: 651-297-5259.

www.dps.state.ms.us

34 Department of Public Safety, Alcohol & Gambling Enforcement, 444 Cedar St #133, St Paul, MN 55101-5133; 651-296-6159, Fax: 651-297-5259.
http://www.dps.state.mn.us/alcgamb/alcenf/alcenf.html

Direct URL to search licenses: www.dps.state.mn.us/alcgamb/alcenf/liquorlic.html You can search online using licensee, business name, city - for liquor licenses

35 Gambling Control Board, 1711 W County B, #300 South, Roseville, MN 55113; 651-639-4000. www.gcb.state.mn.us

Direct URL to search licenses: www.gcb.state.mn.us You can search online using alphabetical lists

36 Labor & Industry, Code & Inspection Services, 443 Lafayette Rd, St Paul, MN 55155-4304; 651-296-4531, Fax: 651-296-1140.

37 Board of AELSLAGID, Licensing Boards, 85 E 7th Pl #160, St Paul, MN 55101; 651-296-2388, Fax: 651-297-5310.
www.aelslagid.state.mn.us

Direct URL to search licenses: http://www.aelslagid.state.mn.us/lic.html You can search online using extractable lists, searchable by various criteria

38 Building Codes & Standards Division, 408 Metro Square Bldg, St Paul, MN 55101-2181; 800-657-3944, Fax: 651-297-1973.

www.admin.state.mn.us/buildingcodes

39 Board of Accountancy, 8 SE 7th Pl #125, St Paul, MN 55101; 651-296-7937, Fax: 651-282-2644.

40 Judicial Center, Board of Law Examiners, 25 Constitution Ave #110, St Paul, MN 55155; 651-297-1800, Fax: 651-297-4149.

www.ble.state.mn.us

41 Racing Commission, PO Box 630 (PO Box 630), Shakopee, MN 55379; 952-496-7950, Fax: 952-496-7954.

www.mnrace.commission.state.mn.us/

42 State Lottery, 2645 Long Lake Rd, Roseville, MN 55113; 651-635-8100, Fax: 651-297-7498.
www.lottery.state.mn.us

Direct URL to search licenses: www.lottery.state.mn.us/retailer/lookup.html You can search online using city or zip code

43 Pollution Control Agency, 520 Lafayette Rd N, St Paul, MN 55155-4194; 651-297-8367, Fax: 651-282-6247.

www.pca.state.mn.us/netscape4.html

44 Private Detective & Protective Agent Services Board, 445 Minnesota St, St Paul, MN 55101-5530; 651-215-1753, Fax: 651-296-7096.

www.dps.state.mn.us/pdb/

45 State College & University Section, Licensing Unit, MNSCU - ETC Bldg #300, 1450 Energy Park Dr, St Paul, MN 55108; 651-649-5736, Fax: 651-649-5749.

www.mnscu.edu

46 Board of Dietetics & Nutrition Practice, 2829 University Ave SE #555, Minneapolis, MN 55414-3250; 612-617-2175.

The following list indicates the district and division name for each county in the state. If the district or division name of the bankruptcy court is different from the civil/criminal court, it appears in parentheses.

County/Court Cross Reference

County	Court	County	Court
Aitkin	Duluth	Martin	Minneapolis (St Paul)
Anoka	Minneapolis	McLeod	Minneapolis
Becker	Minneapolis (Fergus Falls)	Meeker	Minneapolis
Beltrami	Minneapolis (Fergus Falls)	Mille Lacs	Duluth
Benton	Duluth	Morrison	Duluth
Big Stone	Minneapolis (Fergus Falls)	Mower	Minneapolis (St Paul)
Blue Earth	Minneapolis (St Paul)	Murray	Minneapolis (St Paul)
Brown	Minneapolis (St Paul)	Nicollet	Minneapolis (St Paul)
Carlton	Duluth	Nobles	Minneapolis (St Paul)
Carver	Minneapolis	Norman	Minneapolis (Fergus Falls)
Cass	Duluth	Olmsted	Minneapolis (St Paul)
Chippewa	Minneapolis	Otter Tail	Minneapolis (Fergus Falls)
Chisago	Minneapolis (St Paul)	Pennington	Minneapolis (Fergus Falls)
Clay	Minneapolis (Fergus Falls)	Pine	Duluth
Clearwater	Minneapolis (Fergus Falls)	Pipestone	Minneapolis (St Paul)
Cook	Duluth	Polk	Minneapolis (Fergus Falls)
Cottonwood	Minneapolis (St Paul)	Pope	Minneapolis (Fergus Falls)
Crow Wing	Duluth	Ramsey	St Paul
Dakota	Minneapolis (St Paul)	Red Lake	Minneapolis (Fergus Falls)
Dodge	Minneapolis (St Paul)	Redwood	Minneapolis (St Paul)
Douglas	Minneapolis (Fergus Falls)	Renville	Minneapolis
Faribault	Minneapolis (St Paul)	Rice	Minneapolis (St Paul)
Fillmore	Minneapolis (St Paul)	Rock	Minneapolis (St Paul)
Freeborn	Minneapolis (St Paul)	Roseau	Minneapolis (Fergus Falls)
Goodhue	Minneapolis (St Paul)	Scott	Minneapolis (St Paul)
Grant	Minneapolis (Fergus Falls)	Sherburne	Minneapolis
Hennepin	Minneapolis	Sibley	Minneapolis (St Paul)
Houston	Minneapolis (St Paul)	St. Louis	Duluth
Hubbard	Minneapolis (Fergus Falls)	Stearns	Minneapolis (Fergus Falls)
Isanti	Minneapolis	Steele	Minneapolis (St Paul)
Itasca	Duluth	Stevens	Minneapolis (Fergus Falls)
Jackson	Minneapolis (St Paul)	Swift	Minneapolis
Kanabec	Duluth	Todd	Minneapolis (Fergus Falls)
Kandiyohi	Minneapolis	Traverse	Minneapolis (Fergus Falls)
Kittson	Minneapolis (Fergus Falls)	Wabasha	Minneapolis (St Paul)
Koochiching	Duluth	Wadena	Minneapolis (Fergus Falls)
Lac qui Parle	Minneapolis (St Paul)	Waseca	Minneapolis (St Paul)
Lake	Duluth	Washington	Minneapolis (St Paul)
Lake of the Woods	Minneapolis (Fergus Falls)	Watonwan	Minneapolis (St Paul)
Le Sueur	Minneapolis (St Paul)	Wilkin	Minneapolis (Fergus Falls)
Lincoln	Minneapolis (St Paul)	Winona	Minneapolis (St Paul)
Lyon	Minneapolis (St Paul)	Wright	Minneapolis
Mahnomen	Minneapolis (Fergus Falls)	Yellow Medicine	Minneapolis (St Paul)
Marshall	Minneapolis (Fergus Falls)		

US District Court

District of Minnesota

Duluth Division Clerk's Office, 417 Federal Bldg, Duluth, MN 55802, 218-529-3500, Fax: 218-720-5622.

www.mnd.uscourts.gov

Counties: Aitkin, Becker*, Beltrami*, Benton, Big Stone*, Carlton, Cass, Clay*, Clearwater*, Cook, Crow Wing, Douglas*, Grant*, Hubbard*, Itasca, Kanabec, Kittson*, Koochiching, Lake, Lake of the Woods*, Mahnomen*, Marshall*, Mille Lacs, Morrison, Norman*, Otter*,Tail, Pennington*, Pine, Polk*, Pope*, Red Lake*, Roseau*, Stearns*, Stevens*, St. Louis, Todd*, Traverse*, Wadena*, Wilkin*. From March 1, 1995, to 1998, cases from the counties marked with an asterisk (*) were heard here.Before and after that period, cases were and are allocated between St. Paul and Minneapolis.

Indexing & Storage: Cases are indexed by defendant and plaintiff as well as by case number. New cases are available in the index immediately after filing date. A computer index is maintained. Open records are located at this court.

Fee & Payment: The fee is $15.00 per item (one party name or case number). Payment may be made by money order, cashier check, personal check. Prepayment is required. Payee: Clerk, US District Court. Certification fee: $5.00 per document. Copy fee: $.50 per page.

Phone Search: Only docket information is available by phone. An automated voice case information service (VCIS) is not available.

Mail Search: A stamped self addressed envelope is not required.

In Person Search: In person searching is available.

PACER: Sign-up number is 800-676-6856. Access fee is $.60 per minute. Toll-free access: 800-818-8761. Local access: 612-664-5170. Case records are available back to February 1990. New records are available online after 1 day. PACER is available online at http://pacer.mnd.uscourts.gov.

Minneapolis Division Court Clerk, Room 202, 300 S 4th St, Minneapolis, MN 55415, 612-664-5000.

www.mnd.uscourts.gov

Counties: All counties not covered by the Duluth Division. Cases are allocated between Minneapolis and St Paul.

Indexing & Storage: Cases are indexed by defendant and plaintiff as well as by case number. New cases are available in the index immediately after filing date. Both computer and card indexes are maintained. Records are also indexed on microfiche. Open records are located at this court.

Fee & Payment: The fee is $15.00 per item (one party name or case number). Payment may be made by money order, cashier check, personal check. Prepayment is required. Payee: Clerk, US District Court. Certification fee: $5.00 per document. Copy fee: $.50 per page.

Phone Search: The case number and parties involved will be released over the phone. An automated voice case information service (VCIS) is not available.

Mail Search: A stamped self addressed envelope is not required.

In Person Search: In person searching is available.

PACER: Sign-up number is 800-676-6856. Access fee is $.60 per minute. Toll-free access: 800-818-8761. Local access: 612-664-5170. Case records are available back to February 1990. New records are available online after 1 day. PACER is available online at http://pacer.mnd.uscourts.gov.

St Paul Division 708 Federal Bldg, 316 N Robert, St Paul, MN 55101, 651-848-1100, Fax: 651-848-1108.

www.mnd.uscourts.gov

Counties: All counties not covered by the Duluth Division. Cases are allocated between Minneapolis and St Paul.

Indexing & Storage: Cases are indexed by defendant and plaintiff as well as by case number. New cases are available in the index immediately after filing date. Both computer and card indexes are maintained. Records are also indexed on microfiche. Open records are located at this court.

Fee & Payment: The fee is $15.00 per item (one party name or case number). Payment may be made by money order, cashier check, personal check. Prepayment is required. Payee: Clerk, US District Court. Certification fee: $5.00 per document. Copy fee: $.50 per page.

Phone Search: Only the case number and parties involved will be released over the phone. An automated voice case information service (VCIS) is not available.

Fax Search: Fax requests will be accepted, but results that involve copies will not be faxed or mailed back until after payment has been received.

Mail Search: A stamped self addressed envelope is not required.

In Person Search: In person searching is available.

PACER: Sign-up number is 800-676-6856. Access fee is $.60 per minute. Toll-free access: 800-818-8761. Local access: 612-664-5170. Case records are available back to February 1990. New records are available online after 1 day. PACER is available online at http://pacer.mnd.uscourts.gov.

US Bankruptcy Court

District of Minnesota

Duluth Division 416 US Courthouse, 515 W 1st St, Duluth, MN 55802, 218-720-5253.

www.mnb.uscourts.gov

Counties: Aitkin, Benton, Carlton, Cass, Cook, Crow Wing, Itasca, Kanabec, Koochiching, Lake, Mille Lacs, Morrison, Pine, St. Louis. A petition commencing Chapter 11 or 12 proceedings may initially be filed in any of the four divisons, but may be assigned toanother division.

Indexing & Storage: Cases are indexed by debtor as well as by case number. New cases are available in the index 1-2 days after filing date. Chapter 7 and 13 cases in Benton, Kanabec, Mille Lacs, Morrison and Pine may also be filed in St. Paul. A computer index is maintained. Open records are located at this court.

Fee & Payment: The fee is $15.00 per item (one party name or case number). Payment may be made by money order, personal check. Prepayment

is required. Payee: Clerk, US Bankruptcy Court. Certification fee: $5.00 per document. Copy fee: $.50 per page. You are allowed to make your own copies. These copies cost $.15 per page.

Phone Search: Only basic information is released over the phone. An automated voice case information service (VCIS) is available. Call VCIS at 800-959-9002 or 612-664-5302.

Mail Search: A stamped self addressed envelope is not required.

In Person Search: In person searching is available.

PACER: Sign-up number is 800-676-6856. Access fee is $.60 per minute. Case records are available back to January 1993. Records are purged up to April 1996. New civil records are available online after 1 day.

Electronic Filing: Electronic filing information is available online at www.mnb.uscourts.gov/cgi-bin/mnb-500-file.pl

Other Online Access: You can search records using the Internet. Searching is currently free. Visit www.mnb.uscourts.gov/cgi-bin/mnb-500-main.pl.

Fergus Falls Division 204 US Courthouse, 118 S Mill St, Fergus Falls, MN 56537, 218-739-4671.

www.mnb.uscourts.gov

Counties: Becker, Beltrami, Big Stone, Clay, Clearwater, Douglas, Grant, Hubbard, Kittson, Lake of the Woods, Mahnomen, Marshall, Norman, Otter Tail, Pennington, Polk, Pope, Red Lake, Roseau, Stearns, Stevens, Todd, Traverse, Wadena, Wilkin. A petition commencingChapter 11 or 12 proceedings may be filed initially in any of the four divisions, but may then be assigned to another division.

Indexing & Storage: Cases are indexed by debtor as well as by case number. New cases are available in the index immediately after filing date. A computer index is maintained. Open records are located at this court.

Fee & Payment: The fee is $15.00 per item (one party name or case number). Payment may be made by money order, cashier check, personal check. Prepayment is required. Payee: US Bankruptcy Court. Certification fee: $5.00 per document. Copy fee: $.50 per page.

Phone Search: Only docket information is available by phone. An automated voice case information service (VCIS) is available. Call VCIS at 800-959-9002 or 612-664-5302.

Mail Search: A stamped self addressed envelope is not required.

In Person Search: In person searching is available.

PACER: Sign-up number is 800-676-6856. Access fee is $.60 per minute. Case records are available back to January 1993. Records are purged up to April 1996. New civil records are available online after 1 day.

Electronic Filing: Electronic filing information is available online at www.mnb.uscourts.gov/cgi-bin/mnb-500-file.pl

Other Online Access: You can search records using the Internet. Searching is currently free. Visit www.mnb.uscourts.gov/cgi-bin/mnb-500-main.pl.

Minneapolis Division 301 US Courthouse, 300 S 4th St, Minneapolis, MN 55415, 612-664-5200.

www.mnb.uscourts.gov

Counties: Anoka, Carver, Chippewa, Hennepin, Isanti, Kandiyohi, McLeod, Meeker, Renville, Sherburne, Swift, Wright. Initial petitions for Chapter 11 or 12 may be filed initially at any of the four divisions, but may then be assigned to a judge in another division.

Indexing & Storage: Cases are indexed by as well as by case number. New cases are available in the index immediately after filing date. A computer index is maintained. Records are also indexed on microfiche. Open records are located at this court. District wide searches are available for information from January 2, 1992 from this court. This division holds closed cases from St. Paul for 4 years (no indexing available at this office).

Fee & Payment: The fee is $15.00 per item (one party name or case number). Payment may be made by money order, cashier check, personal check. Prepayment is required. Payee: Clerk, US Bankruptcy Court. Certification fee: $5.00 per document. Copy fee: $.50 per page. You are allowed to make your own copies. These copies cost $.15 per page.

Phone Search: Only basic information is released over the phone. An automated voice case information service (VCIS) is available. Call VCIS at 800-959-9002 or 612-664-5302.

Mail Search: A stamped self addressed envelope is not required.

In Person Search: In person searching is available.

PACER: Sign-up number is 800-676-6856. Access fee is $.60 per minute. Case records are available back to January 1993. Records are purged up to April 1996. New civil records are available online after 1 day.

Electronic Filing: Electronic filing information is available online at www.mnb.uscourts.gov/cgi-bin/mnb-500-file.pl

Other Online Access: You can search records using the Internet. Searching is currently free. Visit www.mnb.uscourts.gov/cgi-bin/mnb-500-main.pl.

St Paul Division 200 Federal Bldg, 316 N Robert St, St Paul, MN 55101, 651-848-1000.

www.mnb.uscourts.gov

Counties: Blue Earth, Brown, Chisago, Cottonwood, Dakota, Dodge, Faribault, Fillmore, Freeborn, Goodhue, Houston, Jackson, Lac qui Parle, Le Sueur, Lincoln, Lyon, Martin, Mower, Murray, Nicollet, Nobles, Olmsted, Pipestone, Ramsey, Redwood, Rice, Rock, Scott,Sibley, Steele, Wabasha, Waseca, Washington, Watonwan, Winona, Yellow Medicine. Cases from Benton, Kanabec, Mille Lacs, Morrison and Pine may also be heard here. A petition commencing Chapter 11 or 12 proceedings may be filed initially with any of thefour divisions, but may then be assigned to another division.

Indexing & Storage: Cases are indexed by debtor as well as by case number. New cases are available in the index 1 day after filing date. A computer index is maintained. Open records are located at this court.

Fee & Payment: The fee is $15.00 per item (one party name or case number). Payment may be made by money order, cashier check, personal check. Payee: Clerk, US Bankruptcy Court. Certification fee: $5.00 per document. Copy fee: $.50 per page. You are allowed to make your own copies. These copies cost $.15 per page.

Phone Search: Only docket information is available by phone. An automated voice case information service (VCIS) is available. Call VCIS at 800-959-9002 or 612-664-5302.

Mail Search: A stamped self addressed envelope is not required.

In Person Search: In person searching is available.

PACER: Sign-up number is 800-676-6856. Access fee is $.60 per minute. Case records are available back to January 1993. Records are purged up to April 1996. New civil records are available online after 1 day.

Electronic Filing: Electronic filing information is available online at www.mnb.uscourts.gov/cgi-bin/mnb-500-file.pl

Other Online Access: You can search records using the Internet. Searching is currently free. Visit www.mnb.uscourts.gov/cgi-bin/mnb-500-main.pl.

Court	Jurisdiction	No. of Courts	How Organized
District Courts*	General	97	10 Districts

* Profiled in this Sourcebook.

CIVIL									
Court	Tort	Contract	Real Estate	Min. Claim	Max. Claim	Small Claims	Estate	Eviction	Domestic Relations
Circuit Courts*	X	X	X	$0	No Max	$7500	X	X	X

CRIMINAL					
Court	Felony	Misdemeanor	DWI/DUI	Preliminary Hearing	Juvenile
Circuit Courts*	X	X	X		X

ADMINISTRATION State Court Adminstrator, 135 Minn. Judicial Center, 25 Constitution Ave, St Paul, MN, 55155; 651-296-2474, Fax: 651-297-5636. www.courts.state.mn.us

COURT STRUCTURE There are 97 District Courts comprising 10 judicial districts. Effective July 1, 1996, the limit for small claims was raised from $5000 to $7500.

ONLINE ACCESS There is an online system in place that allows internal and external access. Some criminal information is available online from St Paul through the Bureau of Criminal Apprehension (BCA), 1246 University Ave, St. Paul, MN 55104. Additional information is available from BCA by calling 651-642-0670.

ADDITIONAL INFORMATION Statewide certification and copy fees are as follows: Certification Fee: $10.00 per document, Copy Fee: $5.00 per document (not per page).

An exact name is required to search, e.g., a request for "Robert Smith" will not result in finding "Bob Smith." The requester must request both names and pay two search and copy fees.

When a search is permitted by "plaintiff or defendant," most jurisdictions stated that a case is indexed by only the 1st plaintiff or defendant, and a 2nd or 3rd party would not be sufficient to search.

The 3rd, 5th, 8th and 10th Judicial Districts no longer will perform criminal record searches for the public.

Most courts take personal checks. Exceptions are noted.

Aitkin County

9th Judicial District Court 209 Second St NW, Aitkin, MN 56431; 218-927-7350; Fax: 218-927-4535. Hours: 8AM-4:30PM (CST). *Felony, Misdemeanor, Civil, Eviction, Small Claims, Probate.*

Civil Records: Access: Mail, in person. Both court and visitors may perform in person searches. Search fee: $5.00 per name. Required to search: name, years to search. Civil cases indexed by defendant, plaintiff. Civil records on computer from 2/90, cards to 1982, index books prior. **Criminal Records:** Access: Mail, in person. Both court and visitors may perform in person searches. Search fee: $5.00 per name. Required to search: name, years to search, DOB. Criminal records on computer from 2/90, cards to 1982, index books prior. **General Information:** No adoption, juvenile, sex offender or sealed records released. SASE required. Turnaround time 1 week. Copy fee: $5.00 per document. Certification fee: $10.00. Fee payee: Aitkin District Court. Personal checks accepted. Prepayment is required. Public access terminal is available.

Anoka County

10th Judicial District Court 325 E Main St, Anoka, MN 55303; 612-422-7350; Criminal phone:; Fax: 612-422-6919. Hours: 8AM-4:30PM (CST). *Felony, Misdemeanor, Civil, Eviction, Small Claims, Probate.*

Civil Records: Access: In person only. Court does not conduct in person searches; visitors must perform searches for themselves. Search fee: No civil searches performed by court. Required to search: name, years to search. Civil cases indexed by defendant, plaintiff. Civil records on computer from 1985, prior on microfiche. **Criminal Records:** Access: In person only. Court does not conduct in person searches; visitors must perform searches for themselves. Search fee: No criminal searches performed by court. Required to search: name, years to search, DOB; also helpful-SSN. Criminal records on computer from 1985, prior on microfiche. **General Information:** No adoption, juvenile, sex offender or sealed records released. Copy fee: $5.00 per document. Certification fee: $10.00. Fee payee: Court Administrator. Personal checks accepted. Credit cards accepted: Visa, Mastercard. Prepayment is required. Public access terminal is available.

Becker County

7th Judicial District Court PO Box 787, Detroit Lakes, MN 56502; 218-846-7305; Fax: 218-847-7620. Hours: 8AM-4:30PM (CST). *Felony, Misdemeanor, Civil, Eviction, Small Claims, Probate.*

Civil Records: Access: Phone, fax, mail, in person. Both court and visitors may perform in person searches. No search fee. Required to search: name; also helpful-years to search. Civil cases indexed by defendant, plaintiff. Civil records on computer from 8/86, prior on books from 1891. **Criminal Records:** Access: In person only. Court does not conduct in person searches; visitors must perform searches for themselves. Search fee: No criminal searches performed by court. Required to search: name, years to search. Criminal records on computer from 8/86, prior on books from 1891. **General Information:** No adoption, juvenile, sex offender or sealed records released. SASE required. Turnaround time same day. Copy fee: $5.00 per document. Certification fee: $10.00. Fee payee: Becker County. Personal checks accepted. Credit cards accepted: Visa, Mastercard. Prepayment is required. Public access terminal is available. Fax notes: $5.00 per document.

Beltrami County

District Court 619 Beltrami Ave NW, Bemidji, MN 56601; 218-759-4531; Fax: 218-759-4209. Hours: 8AM-4:30PM (CST). *Felony, Misdemeanor, Civil, Eviction, Small Claims, Probate.*

Civil Records: Access: Mail, in person. Both court and visitors may perform in person searches. Search fee: $5.00 per name. Required to search: name, years to search. Civil cases indexed by defendant, plaintiff. Civil records on computer from 1983. **Criminal Records:** Access: Mail, in person. Both court and visitors may perform in person searches. Search fee: $5.00 per name. Required to search: name, years to search, DOB. Criminal records on computer from 1983. **General**

Information: No adoption, juvenile, sex offender or sealed records released. SASE not required. Turnaround time 1-2 days. Copy fee: $5.00 per document. Certification fee: $10.00. Fee payee: Court Administrator. Personal checks accepted. Prepayment is required. Public access terminal is available.

Benton County

7th Judicial District Court 615 High-way 23, PO Box 189, Foley, MN 563290189; 320-968-5205; Fax: 320-968-5353. Hours: 8AM-4:30PM (CST). *Felony, Misdemeanor, Civil, Eviction, Small Claims, Probate.*

Civil Records: Access: In person only. Court does not conduct in person searches; visitors must perform searches for themselves. Search fee: No civil searches performed by court. Required to search: name, years to search. Civil cases indexed by defendant, plaintiff. Civil records on computer from 1986. **Criminal Records:** Access: In person only. Court does not conduct in person searches; visitors must perform searches for themselves. Search fee: No criminal searches performed by court. Required to search: name, years to search, DOB. Criminal records on computer from 1986. **General Information:** No adoption, juvenile records released. Copy fee: $5.00 per document. Certification fee: $10.00. Fee payee: Court Administrator. Personal checks accepted. Prepayment is required. Public access terminal is available.

Big Stone County

8th Judicial District Court 20 SE 2nd St, Ortonville, MN 56278; 320-839-2536; Fax: 320-839-2537. Hours: 8AM-4:30PM (CST). *Felony, Misdemeanor, Civil, Eviction, Small Claims, Probate.*

Civil Records: Access: Mail, in person. Both court and visitors may perform in person searches. Search fee: $5.00 per name. Required to search: name, years to search. Civil cases indexed by defendant, plaintiff. Civil records on computer from 1989, prior on cards and in books. **Criminal Records:** Access: In person only. Court does not conduct in person searches; visitors must perform searches for themselves. Search fee: No criminal searches performed by court. Required to search: name, years to search, DOB; also helpful-SSN. Criminal records on computer from 1989, prior on cards and in books. **General Information:** No adoption, juvenile, sex offender or sealed records released. SASE required. Turnaround time 3 days. Copy fee: $5.00 per document. Certification fee: $10.00. Fee payee: Court Administrator. Personal checks accepted. Prepayment is required. Public access terminal is available.

Blue Earth County

5th Judicial District Court 204 S 5th St (PO Box 0347), Mankato, MN 56002-0347; 507-389-8310; Fax: 507-389-8437. Hours: 8AM-5PM (CST). *Felony, Misdemeanor, Civil, Eviction, Small Claims, Probate.*

Civil Records: Access: Mail, in person. Both court and visitors may perform in person searches. Search fee: $10.00 per name. Required to search: name, years to search. Civil cases indexed by defendant, plaintiff. Civil records on computer from 8/85, prior in books and cards. **Criminal Records:** Access: In person only. Court does not conduct in person searches; visitors must perform searches for themselves. Search fee: No criminal searches performed by court. Required to search: name, years to search; also helpful-DOB. Criminal records on computer from 8/85, prior in books and cards. The county forwards mail requests to the state Bureau of Criminal Apprehension. **General Information:** No juvenile, adoption, sealed records released. SASE not required. Turnaround time is same day. Copy fee: $5.00 per document. Certification fee: $10.00. Fee payee: Court Administrator. Personal checks accepted. Prepayment is required. Public access terminal is available.

Brown County

5th Judicial District Court PO Box 248, New Ulm, MN 56073-0248; 507-233-6670; Fax: 507-359-9562. Hours: 8AM-5PM (CST). *Felony, Misdemeanor, Civil, Eviction, Small Claims, Probate.*

Civil Records: Access: Mail, in person. Both court and visitors may perform in person searches. Search fee: $10.00 per name. Required to search: name, years to search. Civil cases indexed by defendant, plaintiff. Civil records on computer from 1988, microfiche 1981-1988, prior on books. **Criminal Records:** Access: In person only. Court does not conduct in person searches; visitors must perform searches for themselves. Search fee: No criminal searches performed by court. Required to search: name, years to search. Criminal records on computer from 1988, microfiche 1981-1988, prior on books. Requests must be made to the state Bureau of Criminal Apprehension. **General Information:** No adoption, juvenile, sex offender or sealed records released. SASE required. Turnaround time 3 days. Copy fee: $5.00 per document. Certification fee: $10.00. Fee payee: Court Administrator. Personal checks accepted. Credit cards accepted: Visa, Mastercard. Prepayment is required. Public access terminal is available.

Carlton County

6th Judicial District Court PO Box 190, Carlton, MN 55718; 218-384-4281; Fax: 218-384-9182. Hours: 8AM-4PM (CST). *Felony, Misdemeanor, Civil, Eviction, Small Claims, Probate.*

Civil Records: Access: Mail, in person. Both court and visitors may perform in person searches. Search fee: $5.00 per name. Required to search: name, years to search; also helpful-address. Civil cases indexed by defendant, plaintiff. Civil records on computer from 1985, in books from 1900. **Criminal Records:** Access: In person only. Court does not conduct in person searches; visitors must perform searches for themselves. Search fee: No criminal searches performed by court. Required to search: name, years to search; also helpful-address, DOB. Criminal records on computer from 1985, in books from 1900. **General Information:** No adoption, juvenile, sex offender or sealed records released. SASE required. Turnaround time 1 day. Copy fee: $5.00 per document. Certification fee: $10.00. Fee payee: Court Administrator. Personal checks accepted. Prepayment is required. Public access terminal is available.

Carver County

1st Judicial District Court 600 E 4th St, Box 4, Chaska, MN 55318-2183; 612-361-1420; Fax: 612-361-1491. Hours: 8AM-4:30PM (CST). *Felony, Misdemeanor, Civil, Eviction, Small Claims, Probate.*

Civil Records: Access: Mail, in person. Both court and visitors may perform in person searches. Search fee: $5.00 per name. Required to search: name, years to search. Civil cases indexed by

defendant, plaintiff. Civil records on computer from 2/92, prior on books. **Criminal Records:** Access: Mail, in person. Both court and visitors may perform in person searches. Search fee: $5.00 per name. Required to search: name, years to search, DOB. Criminal records on computer from 2/92, prior on books. **General Information:** No adoption, juvenile, sex offender or sealed records released. SASE not required. Turnaround time 3-4 days. Copy fee: $5.00 per document. Certification fee: $10.00. Fee payee: Court Administrator. Personal checks accepted. Prepayment is required. Public access terminal is available.

Cass County

9th Judicial District Court 300 Minnesota Ave, PO Box 3000, Walker, MN 56484; 218-547-7200; Fax: 218-547-1904. Hours: 8AM-4:30PM (CST). *Felony, Misdemeanor, Civil, Eviction, Small Claims, Probate.*

Civil Records: Access: Mail, in person. Both court and visitors may perform in person searches. Search fee: $5.00 per name. Required to search: name, years to search; also helpful-address. Civil cases indexed by defendant, plaintiff. Civil records on computer from mid-1990, on index cards from 1983-1990, on books to 1983. **Criminal Records:** Access: Mail, in person. Both court and visitors may perform in person searches. Search fee: $5.00 per name. Required to search: name, years to search, DOB; also helpful-address. Criminal records on computer from mid-1990, on index cards from 1983-1990, on books to 1983. **General Information:** No adoption, juvenile or sealed records released. SASE required. Turnaround time 1 week. Copy fee: $5.00 per document. Certification fee: $10.00. Fee payee: District Court. Personal checks accepted. Prepayment is required. Public access terminal is available.

Chippewa County

8th Judicial District Court PO Box 697, Montevideo, MN 56265; 320-269-7774; Fax: 320-269-7733. Hours: 8AM-4:30PM (CST). *Felony, Misdemeanor, Civil, Eviction, Small Claims, Probate.*

Civil Records: Access: Mail, in person. Only the court conducts in person searches; visitors may not. Search fee: $5.00 per name. Required to search: name, years to search. Civil cases indexed by defendant, plaintiff. Civil records on computer from 1988, in books from 1870. **Criminal Records:** Access: In person only. Court does not conduct in person searches; visitors must perform searches for themselves. Search fee: No criminal searches performed by court. Required to search: name, years to search, DOB. Criminal records on computer from 1988, in books from 1870. **General Information:** No adoption, juvenile, sex offender or sealed records released. SASE required. Turnaround time same day. Copy fee: $5.00 per page. Certification fee: $10.00. Fee payee: Court Administrator. Personal checks accepted. Prepayment is required.

Chisago County

10th Judicial District Court 313 N Main St, Rm 358, Center City, MN 55012; 651-257-1300; Fax: 651-257-0359. Hours: 8AM-4:30PM (CST). *Felony, Misdemeanor, Civil, Eviction, Small Claims, Probate.*

Civil Records: Access: Mail, in person. Both court and visitors may perform in person searches. Search fee: $5.00 per name. Required to search: name, years to search. Civil cases indexed by defendant, plaintiff. Civil records on computer from 1984, prior on index cards. **Criminal Records:** Access: In person only. Court does not conduct in person searches; visitors must perform searches for themselves. Search fee: No criminal searches performed by court. Required to search: name, years to search; also helpful-DOB. Criminal records on computer from 1984, prior on index cards. **General Information:** No adoption, juvenile, sex offender or sealed records released. SASE required. Turnaround time 1-2 days. Copy fee: $5.00 per document. Certification fee: $10.00. Fee payee: Court Administrator. Personal checks accepted. Prepayment is required. Public access terminal is available.

Clay County

7th Judicial District Court PO Box 280, Moorhead, MN 56561; 218-299-5065; Fax: 218-299-7307. Hours: 8AM-4:30PM (CST). *Felony, Misdemeanor, Civil, Eviction, Small Claims, Probate.*

Civil Records: Access: Mail, in person. Both court and visitors may perform in person searches. Search fee: $5.00 per name. Required to search: name; also helpful-years to search. Civil cases indexed by defendant, plaintiff. Civil records on computer from 1982; prior on microfiche and microfilm. **Criminal Records:** Access: In person only. Court does not conduct in person searches; visitors must perform searches for themselves. Search fee: No criminal searches performed by court. Required to search: name, DOB; also helpful-years to search, SSN. Criminal records on computer from 1982; prior on microfiche and microfilm. Court no longer performs searches as of July 1, 1997. **General Information:** No adoption, juvenile, sex offender or sealed records released. SASE required. Turnaround time 3 days. Copy fee: $5.00 per document. Certification fee: $10.00. Fee payee: Court Administrator. Personal checks accepted. Prepayment is required. Public access terminal is available.

Clearwater County

9th Judicial District Court 213 Main Ave North, Bagley, MN 56621; 218-694-6177; Fax: 218-694-6213. Hours: 8AM-4:30PM (CST). *Felony, Misdemeanor, Civil, Eviction, Small Claims, Probate.*

Civil Records: Access: Phone, mail, fax, in person. Both court and visitors may perform in person searches. Search fee: $5.00 per name, by court. Required to search: name, years to search. Civil cases indexed by defendant, plaintiff. Civil records on computer from 1990, on cards and books prior back to 1903. **Criminal Records:** Access: Phone, mail, fax, in person. Both court and visitors may perform in person searches. Search fee: $5.00 per name, by court. Required to search: name, years to search; also helpful-DOB. Criminal records on computer from 1990, on cards and books prior back to 1903. **General Information:** No adoption, juvenile or sealed records released. SASE not required. Turnaround time 3-5 days. Copy fee: $5.00 per document. Certification fee: $10.00. Fee payee: Court Administrator. Personal checks accepted. Prepayment is required. Public access terminal is available.

Cook County

6th Judicial District Court Po Box 1150, Grand Marais, MN 55604-1150; 218-387-3000; Fax: 218-387-3007. Hours: 8AM-4PM (CST). *Felony, Misdemeanor, Civil, Eviction, Small Claims, Probate.*

Civil Records: Access: In person only. Both court and visitors may perform in person searches. Search fee: $5.00 per name if court conducts search. Required to search: name, years to search. Civil cases indexed by defendant, plaintiff. Civil records on computer from 2/91, prior on card files. **Criminal Records:** Access: In person only. Court does not conduct in person searches; visitors must perform searches for themselves. Search fee: No criminal searches performed by court. Required to search: name, years to search, DOB. Criminal records on computer from 2/91, prior on card files. **General Information:** No adoption, juvenile, sex offender or sealed records released. Copy fee: $5.00 per document. Certification fee: $10.00. Fee payee: Court Administrator. Business checks accepted. Prepayment is required. Public access terminal is available.

Cottonwood County

5th Judicial District Court PO Box 97, Windom, MN 56101; 507-831-4551; Fax: 507-831-1425. Hours: 8AM-4:30PM (CST). *Felony, Misdemeanor, Civil, Eviction, Small Claims, Probate.*

Civil Records: Access: Mail, in person. Only the court conducts in person searches; visitors may not. Search fee: $10.00 per name. Required to search: name; also helpful-years to search. Civil cases indexed by defendant, plaintiff. Civil records on computer from 1989, judgments on card file, probate on microfilm. **Criminal Records:** Access: Mail, in person. Both court and visitors may perform in person searches. Search fee: No criminal searches performed by court. Required to search: name, years to search; also helpful-DOB, SSN. Criminal records on computer since 1989; prior records on card file. Court will only do searches if caseload permits. **General Information:** No adoption, juvenile, sex offender or sealed records released. SASE required. Turnaround time 2-3 days. Copy fee: $5.00 per document. Certification fee: $10.00. Fee payee: Court Administrator. Personal checks accepted. Prepayment is required. Public access terminal is available.

Crow Wing County

District Court 326 Laurel St, Brainerd, MN 56401; 218-828-3959; Fax: 218-828-2905. Hours: 8AM-5PM (CST). *Felony, Misdemeanor, Civil, Eviction, Small Claims, Probate.*

Civil Records: Access: Mail, in person. Both court and visitors may perform in person searches. Search fee: $5.00 per name. Required to search: name, years to search. Civil cases indexed by defendant, plaintiff. Civil records on computer from 1989, prior in books from 1873. **Criminal Records:** Access: Mail, in person. Both court and visitors may perform in person searches. Search fee: $5.00 per name. Required to search: name, years to search; also helpful-DOB. Criminal records on computer from 1989, prior in books from 1873. **General Information:** No adoption, juvenile, sex offender or sealed records released. SASE required. Turnaround time 7-14 days. Copy fee: $5.00 per document. Certification fee: $10.00. Fee payee: Court Administrator. Personal checks accepted. Prepayment is required. Public access terminal is available.

Dakota County

1st Judicial District Court - Apple Valley 14955 Galaxie Ave, Apple Valley, MN 55124; 952-891-7256; Fax: 952-891-7285. Hours: 8AM-4:30PM (CST). *Felony, Misdemeanor, Civil, Eviction, Small Claims.*

Civil Records: Access: In person only. Court does not conduct in person searches; visitors must perform searches for themselves. Search fee: No civil searches performed by court. Required to search: name, years to search. Civil cases indexed by defendant, plaintiff. Civil records on computer from 1988, prior in files. **Criminal Records:** Access: In person only. Court does not conduct in person searches; visitors must perform searches for themselves. Search fee: No criminal searches performed by court. Required to search: name, years to search, DOB; also helpful-SSN. Criminal records on computer from 1988, prior in files. **General Information:** No adoption, juvenile, sex offender or sealed records released. Copy fee: $5.00 per document. Certification fee: $10.00. Fee payee: District Court. Personal checks accepted. Prepayment is required. Public access terminal is available.

1st Judicial District Court - South St Paul 125 3rd Ave North, South St Paul, MN 55075; 651-451-1791; Fax: 651-451-3526. Hours: 8AM-4:30PM (CST). *Felony, Misdemeanor, Civil, Eviction, Small Claims, Probate.*

Civil Records: Access: In person only. Court does not conduct in person searches; visitors must perform searches for themselves. Search fee: No civil searches performed by court. Required to search: name, years to search. Civil records on computer from 12/87, prior on ledgers. **Criminal Records:** Access: In person only. Court does not conduct in person searches; visitors must perform searches for themselves. Search fee: No criminal searches performed by court. Required to search: name, years to search. Criminal records on computer from 12/87, prior on ledgers. **General Information:** No adoption, juvenile, sex offender or sealed records released. Copy fee: $5.00 per document. Certification fee: $10.00. Fee payee: Court Administrator. Personal checks accepted. Prepayment is required.

District Court Judicial Center, 1560 Hwy 55, Hastings, MN 55033; 651-438-8100; Fax: 651-438-8162. Hours: 8AM-4:30PM (CST). *Felony, Misdemeanor, Civil, Eviction, Small Claims, Probate.*

Civil Records: Access: In person only. Court does not conduct in person searches; visitors must perform searches for themselves. Search fee: No civil searches performed by court. Required to search: name, years to search. Civil cases indexed by defendant, plaintiff. Civil records on computer from 1/88, on ledgers prior. **Criminal Records:** Access: In person only. Court does not conduct in person searches; visitors must perform searches for themselves. Search fee: No criminal searches performed by court. Required to search: name, years to search. Criminal records on computer from 1/88, on ledgers prior. **General Information:** No adoption, juvenile, sealed records released. Copy fee: $5.00 per document. Certification fee: $10.00. Fee payee: District Court. Personal checks accepted. Prepayment is required. Public access terminal is available.

Dodge County

3rd Judicial District Court PO Box 96, Mantorville, MN 55955; 507-635-6260; Fax: 507-635-6271. Hours: 8AM-4:30PM (CST). *Felony, Misdemeanor, Civil, Eviction, Small Claims, Probate.*

Civil Records: Access: Fax, mail, in person. Both court and visitors may perform in person searches.

Search fee: $5.00 per name. Required to search: name, years to search. Civil cases indexed by defendant, plaintiff. Civil records on computer from 1989, on cards from 1984, on books from 1972. **Criminal Records:** Access: In person only. Court does not conduct in person searches; visitors must perform searches for themselves. Search fee: No criminal searches performed by court. Required to search: name, years to search, DOB. Criminal records on computer from 1989, on cards from 1984, on books from 1972. **General Information:** No adoption, juvenile, sex offender or sealed records released. SASE required. Turnaround time 1-2 days. Copy fee: $5.00 per document. Certification fee: $10.00. Fee payee: Court Administrator. Personal checks accepted. Prepayment is required. Public access terminal is available. Fax notes: $5.00 per document.

Douglas County

7th Judicial District Court 305 8th Ave West, Alexandria, MN 56308; 320-762-3882; Fax: 320-762-8863. Hours: 8AM-4:30PM (CST). *Felony, Misdemeanor, Civil, Eviction, Small Claims, Probate.*

Civil Records: Access: Mail, in person. Both court and visitors may perform in person searches. Search fee: $5.00 per name. Required to search: name, years to search. Civil cases indexed by defendant, plaintiff. Civil records on computer from 1987, on microfiche from 1951, books prior. The books are grouped by letter, but not alphabetized. **Criminal Records:** Access: In person only. Both court and visitors may perform in person searches. Search fee: $5.00 per name. Required to search: name. Criminal records on computer from 1987, on microfiche from 1951, books prior. The books are grouped by letter, but not alphabetized. **General Information:** No adoption, juvenile or sealed records released. SASE required. Turnaround time 1-7 days. Copy fee: $5.00 per document. Certification fee: $10.00. Fee payee: Court Administrator. Personal checks accepted. Prepayment is required. Public access terminal is available.

Faribault County

5th Judicial District Court PO Box 130, Blue Earth, MN 56013; 507-526-6273; Fax: 507-526-3054. Hours: 8AM-4:30PM (CST). *Felony, Misdemeanor, Civil, Eviction, Small Claims, Probate.*

Civil Records: Access: Mail, in person. Only the court conducts in person searches; visitors may not. Search fee: $10.00 per name. $5.00 per name for judgment search. Required to search: name, years to search. Civil cases indexed by defendant, plaintiff. Civil records on computer from 1989, in books from 1870. **Criminal Records:** Access: In person only. Court does not conduct in person searches; visitors must perform searches for themselves. Search fee: No criminal searches performed by court. Required to search: name, years to search; also helpful-DOB. Criminal records on computer from 1989, in books from 1870. The county suggests sending requests to the state Bureau of Criminal Apprehension. **General Information:** No adoption, juvenile, sex offender or sealed records released. SASE required. Turnaround time 7 days or less. Copy fee: $5.00 per document. Certification fee: $10.00. Fee payee: Court Administrator. Personal checks accepted. Prepayment is required.

Fillmore County

3rd Judicial District Court 101 Fillmore St, PO Box 436, Preston, MN 55965; 507-765-4483; Fax: 507-765-4571. Hours: 8AM-4:30PM (CST). *Felony, Misdemeanor, Civil, Eviction, Small Claims, Probate.*

www.courts.state.mn.us/districts/third/fillmore/index.html

Civil Records: Access: Mail, in person. Both court and visitors may perform in person searches. Search fee: $5.00 per name. Required to search: name, years to search. Civil cases indexed by defendant, plaintiff. Civil records on computer from 1990, books from 1860s. **Criminal Records:** Access: In person only. Court does not conduct in person searches; visitors must perform searches for themselves. Search fee: No criminal searches performed by court. Required to search: name, years to search, DOB. Criminal records on computer from 1990, books from 1860s. **General Information:** No adoption, juvenile or sealed records released. SASE not required. Turnaround time 1-2 days. Copy fee: $5.00 per document. Certification fee: $10.00. Fee payee: Court Administrator. Personal checks accepted. Prepayment is required. Public access terminal is available.

Freeborn County

3rd Judicial District Court 411 S Broadway, Albert Lea, MN 56007; 507-377-5153; Fax: 507-377-5260. Hours: 8AM-5PM (CST). *Felony, Misdemeanor, Civil, Eviction, Small Claims, Probate.*

Civil Records: Access: Mail, in person. Both court and visitors may perform in person searches. Search fee: $5.00 per name. Required to search: name, years to search. Civil cases indexed by defendant, plaintiff. Civil records on computer from 11/89. **Criminal Records:** Access: In person only. Court does not conduct in person searches; visitors must perform searches for themselves. Search fee: No criminal searches performed by court. Required to search: name, years to search, DOB. Criminal records on computer from 11/89. **General Information:** No adoption, juvenile, sex offender or sealed records released. SASE required. Turnaround time 3-5 days. Copy fee: $5.00 per document. Certification fee: $10.00. Fee payee: Court Administrator. Personal checks accepted. Prepayment is required. Public access terminal is available.

Goodhue County

1st Judicial District Court PO Box 408, Rm 310, Red Wing, MN 55066; 651-385-3051; Fax: 651-385-3065. Hours: 8AM-4:30PM (CST). *Felony, Misdemeanor, Civil, Eviction, Small Claims, Probate.*

Civil Records: Access: Mail, in person. Both court and visitors may perform in person searches. Search fee: $5.00 per name. Required to search: name, years to search. Civil cases indexed by defendant, plaintiff. Civil records on computer from 3/92, prior records on docket books. **Criminal Records:** Access: In person only. Court does not conduct in person searches; visitors must perform searches for themselves. Search fee: No criminal searches performed by court. Required to search: name. Criminal records on computer from 3/92, prior records on docket books. **General Information:** No adoption, juvenile, sex offender or sealed records released. SASE required. Turnaround time same day. Copy fee: $5.00 per document. Certification fee: $10.00. Fee payee:

Court Administrator. Personal checks accepted. Prepayment is required. Public access terminal is available.

Grant County

8th Judicial District Court 10 2nd St NE, Elbow Lake, MN 56531; 218-685-4825. Hours: 8AM-4PM (CST). *Felony, Misdemeanor, Civil, Eviction, Small Claims, Probate.*

Civil Records: Access: Mail, in person. Only the court conducts in person searches; visitors may not. Search fee: $5.00 per name. Required to search: name, years to search. Civil cases indexed by defendant, plaintiff. Civil records on computer from 6/89, on cards from 1930, prior at Historical Society. **Criminal Records:** Access: In person only. Court does not conduct in person searches; visitors must perform searches for themselves. Search fee: No criminal searches performed by court. Required to search: name, years to search; also helpful-DOB. Criminal records on computer from 6/89, on cards from 1930, prior at Historical Society. **General Information:** No adoption, juvenile, sex offender or sealed records released. SASE required. Turnaround time 1-2 days. Copy fee: $5.00 per document. Certification fee: $10.00. Fee payee: Court Administrator. Personal checks accepted. Prepayment is required. Public access terminal is available.

Hennepin County

4th Judicial District Court-Division 2 Brookdale Area 6125 Shingle Creek Pkwy, Brooklyn Center, MN 55430; 612-569-2799; Fax: 612-569-3697. Hours: 7:45AM-4:30PM (CST). *Misdemeanor, Eviction, Small Claims.*

www.co.hennepin.mn.us

Civil Records: Access: Mail, in person. Search fee: $5.00 per name. Required to search: name, years to search. Civil cases indexed by defendant. **Criminal Records:** Access: Mail, in person. Both court and visitors may perform in person searches. Search fee: $5.00 per name. Required to search: name, years to search, DOB. Criminal records on computer since 1987. **General Information:** No juvenile court, unlawful detainers or sealed records released. SASE required. Turnaround time 1-7 days. Copy fee: $5.00 per document. Certification fee: $10.00. Fee payee: Hennepin County District Court. Personal checks accepted. Prepayment is required. Public access terminal is available.

4th Judicial District Court-Division 3 Ridgedale Area 12601 Ridgedale Dr, Minnetonka, MN 55305; 612-541-8500 (Recording) 541-7000; Fax: 612-541-6297. Hours: 8AM-4:30PM (CST). *Misdemeanor, Eviction, Small Claims.*

www.co.hennepin.mn.us

Civil Records: Access: Mail, in person. Both court and visitors may perform in person searches. Search fee: $5.00 per name. Required to search: name, years to search. Civil cases indexed by defendant. Civil records on computer. **Criminal Records:** Access: Mail, in person. Both court and visitors may perform in person searches. Search fee: $5.00 per name. Required to search: name, years to search; also helpful-DOB. Criminal records on computer since 1989; prior records on microfiche. **General Information:** No police reports, juvenile or sealed records released. SASE required. Turnaround time 3-4 weeks. Copy fee: $5.00 per document. Certification fee: $10.00. Fee payee: Hennepin County District Court. Personal checks accepted. Prepayment is required. Public access terminal is available. Public Access Terminal Note: Limited.

4th Judicial District Court -Division 4 Southdale Area
7009 York Ave South, Edina, MN 55435; 612-830-4905 (Recording) 830-4877; Fax: 612-830-4993. Hours: 8AM-4:30PM (CST). *Misdemeanor.*

www.co.hennepin.mn.us **Criminal Records:** Access: In person only. Court does not conduct in person searches; visitors must perform searches for themselves. Search fee: No criminal searches performed by court. Required to search: name, years to search, DOB; also helpful-offense, date of offense. Criminal records on computer since late 1970s, felonies on computer earlier. In person search with court assistance $10.00. **General Information:** No juvenile or sealed records released. Copy fee: $5.00 per document. Certification fee: $10.00. Fee payee: Hennepin County District Court. Personal checks accepted. Prepayment is required. Public access terminal is available. Public Access Terminal Note: Available for Traffic & Criminal.

4th Judicial District Court -Division 1
1251 C Government Center, 300 S 6th St, Minneapolis, MN 55487; 612-348-2611; Civil phone:612-348-3170; Criminal phone:612-348-3170; Fax: 612-348-6099. Hours: 8AM-4:30PM (CST). *Civil.*

www.co.hennepin.mn.us/courts/court.htm

Civil Records: Access: Fax, mail, in person. Both court and visitors may perform in person searches. No search fee. Required to search: name, years to search. Civil cases indexed by defendant, plaintiff. Civil records on computer from 1978, prior on microfilm. **General Information:** No sex offender or sealed records released, domestic abuse and paternity cases are limited. SASE required. Turnaround time 7-10 days. Copy fee: $.50 per document. Certification fee: $10.00. Fee payee: Court Administrator. Personal checks accepted. Prepayment is required. Public access terminal is available.

4th Judicial District Court -Division 1
300 S 6th St, Minneapolis, MN 55487;; Civil phone:612-348-3170; Criminal phone:612-348-3170; Fax: 612-317-6134. Hours: 8AM-4:30PM (CST). *Felony, Misdemeanor.*

www.co.hennepin.mn.us **Criminal Records:** Access: Fax, mail, in person. Both court and visitors may perform in person searches. Search fee: $5.00 per name if no record found; otherwise $10.00 per name. Required to search: name, years to search, DOB. same as civil. **General Information:** No adoption, juvenile, sex offender or sealed records released. SASE required. Turnaround time 7-10 days. Copy fee: $5.00 per document. Certification fee: $10.00. Fee payee: Court Administrator. Personal checks accepted. Prepayment is required. Public access terminal is available.

4th Judicial District Court -Division 1
C400 Government Center, 300 S 6th St, Minneapolis, MN 55487; 612-348-3244; Fax: 612-348-5799. Hours: 7AM-5PM (CST). *Probate.*

Houston County

3rd Judicial District Court
304 S Marshall, Caledonia, MN 55921; 507-724-5806; Fax: 507-724-5550. Hours: 8:30AM-5PM (CST). *Felony, Misdemeanor, Civil, Eviction, Small Claims, Probate.*

Civil Records: Access: Fax, mail, in person. Court does not conduct in person searches; visitors must perform searches for themselves. Search fee: $5.00 per name. Required to search: name, years to search. Civil cases indexed by defendant, plaintiff. Civil records on computer from 8/89, prior on cards and books. Probate on microfilm to 1982. **Criminal Records:** Access: In person only. Court does not conduct in person searches; visitors must perform searches for themselves. Search fee: No criminal searches performed by court. Required to search: name, years to search, DOB; also helpful-SSN. Criminal records on computer from 8/89, prior on cards and books. Probate on microfilm to 1982. Effective July 1, 1997, this court will no longer conduct criminal record searches. **General Information:** No adoption, juvenile, sex offender or sealed records released. SASE required. Turnaround time 2 days. Copy fee: $5.00 per document. Certification fee: $10.00. Fee payee: Court Administrator. Personal checks accepted. Prepayment is required. Public access terminal is available. Fax notes: $5.00 per document.

Hubbard County

9th Judicial District Court
301 Court St, Park Rapids, MN 56470; 218-732-3573; Fax: 218-732-0137. Hours: 8AM-4:30PM (CST). *Felony, Misdemeanor, Civil, Eviction, Small Claims, Probate.*

Civil Records: Access: Mail, in person. Both court and visitors may perform in person searches. Search fee: $5.00 per name. Required to search: name, years to search. Civil cases indexed by defendant, plaintiff. Civil records on computer since 1990, prior on index cards. **Criminal Records:** Access: Mail, in person. Both court and visitors may perform in person searches. Search fee: $5.00 per name. Required to search: name, DOB. Criminal records on computer since 1990, prior on index cards. **General Information:** No adoption, juvenile, sex offender or sealed records released. SASE required. Turnaround time 1 week. Copy fee: $5.00 per document. Certification fee: $10.00. Fee payee: Court Administrator. Personal checks accepted. Prepayment is required. Public access terminal is available.

Isanti County

10th Judicial District Court
555 18th Ave SW, Cambridge, MN 55008-9386; 763-689-2292; Fax: 763-689-8340. Hours: 8AM-4:30PM (CST). *Felony, Misdemeanor, Civil, Eviction, Small Claims, Probate.*

Civil Records: Access: Mail, in person. Both court and visitors may perform in person searches. Search fee: $5.00 per name. Required to search: name, years to search. Civil cases indexed by defendant, plaintiff. Civil records on computer from 12/84, prior on microfiche. **Criminal Records:** Access: In person only. Court does not conduct in person searches; visitors must perform searches for themselves. Search fee: No criminal searches performed by court. Required to search: name, years to search. Criminal records on computer from 12/84, prior on microfiche. **General Information:** No adoption, juvenile, sex offender or sealed records released. SASE required. Turnaround time 2 days. Copy fee: $5.00 per document. Certification fee: $10.00. Fee payee: Court Administrator. Personal checks accepted. Prepayment is required. Public access terminal is available. Fax notes: Will fax free to local or toll-free numbers.

Itasca County

9th Judicial District Court
123 4th St NE, Grand Rapids, MN 55744-2600; 218-327-2870; Fax: 218-327-2897. Hours: 8:30AM-4PM (CST). *Felony, Misdemeanor, Civil, Eviction, Small Claims, Probate.*

Civil Records: Access: Mail, in person. Only the court conducts in person searches; visitors may not. Search fee: $5.00 per name. Required to search: name, years to search. Civil cases indexed by defendant, plaintiff. Civil records on computer from 4-87, on microfich to 1982, on books prior. **Criminal Records:** Access: Mail, in person. Only the court conducts in person searches; visitors may not. Search fee: $5.00 per name. Required to search: name, years to search, DOB. Criminal records on computer from 4-87, on microfich to 1982, on books prior. **General Information:** No adoption, juvenile, sex offender or sealed records released. SASE required. Turnaround time 7 days, 24 hours required to pull from off-site storage. Copy fee: $5.00 per document. Certification fee: $10.00. Fee payee: Court Administrator. Personal checks accepted. Prepayment is required. Public access terminal is available.

Jackson County

5th Judicial District Court
PO Box 177, Jackson, MN 56143; 507-847-4400; Fax: 507-847-5433. Hours: 8:30AM-4:30PM (CST). *Felony, Misdemeanor, Civil, Eviction, Small Claims, Probate.*

Civil Records: Access: Fax, mail, in person. Only the court conducts in person searches; visitors may not. Search fee: $5.00 per name. Required to search: name, years to search, address. Civil cases indexed by defendant, plaintiff. Civil records on computer from 5/89. Probate on microfiche from 1870. **Criminal Records:** Access: Fax, mail, in person. Only the court conducts in person searches; visitors may not. Search fee: $10.00 per name. Required to search: name, years to search, DOB. Criminal records on computer from 5/89. Probate on microfiche from 1870. **General Information:** No adoption, juvenile, sex offender or sealed records released. SASE required. Turnaround time 2-3 days (including phone requests). Copy fee: $5.00 per document. Certification fee: $10.00. Fee payee: Court Administrator. Personal checks accepted. Prepayment is required. Fax notes: Fax fee 1-5 pages $5.00, each additional page $1.00.

Kanabec County

10th Judicial District Court
18 North Vine, Mora, MN 55051; 320-679-6400; Fax: 320-679-6411. Hours: 8AM-4PM (CST). *Felony, Misdemeanor, Civil, Eviction, Small Claims, Probate.*

Civil Records: Access: In person only. Court does not conduct in person searches; visitors must perform searches for themselves. Search fee: No civil searches performed by court. Required to search: name, years to search. Civil cases indexed by defendant, plaintiff. Civil records on computer from 1986, prior on books and microfiche. **Criminal Records:** Access: In person only. Court does not conduct in person searches; visitors must perform searches for themselves. Search fee: No criminal searches performed by court. Required to search: name, years to search; also helpful-DOB. Criminal records on computer from 1986, prior on books and microfiche. **General Information:** No adoption, juvenile or sealed records released. Copy fee: $5.00 per document. Certification fee: $10.00.

Fee payee: Court Administrator. Personal checks accepted. Prepayment is required. Public access terminal is available.

Kandiyohi County

8th Judicial District Court 505 Becker Ave SW, Willmar, MN 56201; 320-231-6206; Fax: 320-231-6276. Hours: 8AM-4:30PM (CST). *Felony, Misdemeanor, Civil, Eviction, Small Claims, Probate.*

Civil Records: Access: Mail, in person. Both court and visitors may perform in person searches. Search fee: $5.00 per name. Required to search: name, years to search. Civil cases indexed by defendant, plaintiff. Civil records on computer from 1986, prior on microfilm. **Criminal Records:** Access: In person only. Court does not conduct in person searches; visitors must perform searches for themselves. Search fee: No criminal searches performed by court. Required to search: name, years to search, DOB; also helpful-SSN. Criminal records on computer from 1986, prior on microfilm. **General Information:** No adoption, juvenile, sex offender or sealed records released. SASE required. Turnaround time 5 days. Copy fee: $5.00 per document. Certification fee: $10.00. Fee payee: Court Administrator. Personal checks accepted. Prepayment is required.

Kittson County

9th Judicial District Court PO Box 39, Hallock, MN 56728; 218-843-3632; Fax: 218-843-3634. Hours: 8:30AM-4:30PM (CST). *Felony, Misdemeanor, Civil, Eviction, Small Claims, Probate.*

Civil Records: Access: Fax, mail, in person. Both court and visitors may perform in person searches. Search fee: $5.00 per name. Will charge $20.00 per hour for extensive searches. Required to search: name, years to search. Civil cases indexed by defendant, plaintiff. Civil records on computer from 9/90, prior on books and index cards. Visitors may look at judgment docket. **Criminal Records:** Access: Fax, mail, in person. Only the court conducts in person searches; visitors may not. Search fee: $5.00 per name. Will charge $20.00 per hour for extensive searches. Required to search: name, years to search, DOB, offense. Criminal records on computer from 9/90, prior on books and index cards. **General Information:** No adoption, juvenile, sex offender or sealed records released. SASE required. Turnaround time 1-2 days. Copy fee: $5.00 per document. Certification fee: $10.00. Fee payee: Court Administrator. Personal checks accepted. Prepayment is required. Fax notes: No fee to fax results.

Koochiching County

9th Judicial District Court Court House, 715 4th St, International Falls, MN 56649; 218-283-6260; Fax: 218-283-6262. Hours: 8AM-5PM (CST). *Felony, Misdemeanor, Civil, Eviction, Small Claims, Probate.*

Civil Records: Access: Mail, in person. Both court and visitors may perform in person searches. Search fee: $5.00 per name. Required to search: name, years to search. Civil cases indexed by defendant, plaintiff. Civil records on computer from 9/90, on TCIS cards from 1984, on books from 1906. They will fax back results for an extra $5.00. **Criminal Records:** Access: Mail, in person. Both court and visitors may perform in person searches. Search fee: $5.00 per name. Required to search: name, years to search, DOB. Criminal records on computer from 9/90, on TCIS cards from 1984, on books from 1906. **General**

Information: No adoption, juvenile, sex offender or sealed records released. SASE required. Turnaround time 1 week. Copy fee: $5.00 per document. Certification fee: $10.00. Fee payee: Court Administrator. Personal checks accepted. Prepayment is required. Public access terminal is available.

Lac qui Parle County

8th Judicial District Court PO Box 36, Madison, MN 56256; 320-598-3536; Fax: 320-598-3915. Hours: 8:30AM-4:30PM (CST). *Felony, Misdemeanor, Civil, Eviction, Small Claims, Probate.*

Civil Records: Access: Fax, mail, in person. Only the court conducts in person searches; visitors may not. Search fee: $5.00 per name. Required to search: name, years to search. Civil cases indexed by defendant, plaintiff. Civil records on computer from 1988, prior on index cards. **Criminal Records:** Access: Fax, mail, in person. Only the court conducts in person searches; visitors may not. Search fee: $5.00 per name. Required to search: name, years to search, DOB; also helpful-SSN. Criminal records on computer from 1988, prior on index cards. **General Information:** No adoption, juvenile, sex offender or sealed records released. SASE required. Turnaround time 1-3 days. Copy fee: $5.00 per document. Certification fee: $10.00. Fee payee: Court Administrator. Personal checks accepted. Prepayment is required. Fax notes: $5.00 per document.

Lake County

6th Judicial District Court 601 3rd Ave, Two Harbors, MN 55616; 218-834-8330; Fax: 218-834-8397. Hours: 8AM-4:30PM (CST). *Felony, Misdemeanor, Civil, Eviction, Small Claims, Probate.*

Civil Records: Access: Fax, mail, in person. Both court and visitors may perform in person searches. Search fee: $5.00 per name. Required to search: name, years to search. Civil cases indexed by defendant, plaintiff. Civil records on computer from 1991, prior on index cards. **Criminal Records:** Access: In person only. Court does not conduct in person searches; visitors must perform searches for themselves. Search fee: No criminal searches performed by court. Required to search: name, years to search, DOB. Criminal records on computer from 1991, prior on index cards. **General Information:** No adoption, juvenile, sex offender or sealed records released. SASE required. Turnaround time 1 day. Copy fee: $5.00 per document. Certification fee: $10.00. Fee payee: Court Administrator. Personal checks accepted. Credit cards accepted: Visa, Mastercard. Prepayment is required. Public access terminal is available. Fax notes: $5.00 per document.

Lake of the Woods County

9th Judicial District Court PO Box 808, Baudette, MN 56623; 218-634-1451; Fax: 218-634-9444. Hours: 7:30AM-4PM (CST). *Felony, Misdemeanor, Civil, Eviction, Small Claims, Probate.*

Civil Records: Access: Fax, mail, in person. Both court and visitors may perform in person searches. Search fee: $10.00 per name. Required to search: name, years to search. Civil records on computer from 1990, on books from 1923. **Criminal Records:** Access: Fax, mail, in person. Only the court conducts in person searches; visitors may not. Search fee: $10.00 per name. Required to search: name, years to search. Criminal records on computer from 1990, on books from 1923.

General Information: No adoption, juvenile, sex offender or sealed records released. SASE not required. Turnaround time 2 days, no phone searches. Copy fee: $5.00 per document. Certification fee: $10.00. Fee payee: Court Administrator. Personal checks accepted. Prepayment is required. Fax notes: No fee to fax results.

Le Sueur County

1st Judicial District Court 88 S Park Ave, Le Center, MN 56057; 507-357-2251; Fax: 507-357-6375. Hours: 8AM-4:30PM (CST). *Felony, Misdemeanor, Civil, Eviction, Small Claims, Probate.*

Civil Records: Access: Fax, mail, in person. Both court and visitors may perform in person searches. Search fee: $5.00 per name. Required to search: name, years to search. Civil cases indexed by defendant, plaintiff. Civil records on computer from 1992, prior on books. **Criminal Records:** Access: Fax, mail, in person. Both court and visitors may perform in person searches. Search fee: $5.00 per name. Required to search: name, years to search, DOB, signed release. Criminal records on computer from 1992, prior on books. **General Information:** No adoption, juvenile, sex offender or sealed records released. SASE required. Turnaround time 1-2 days. Copy fee: $5.00 per document. Certification fee: $10.00. Fee payee: Court Administrator. Personal checks accepted. Prepayment is required. Public access terminal is available. Fax notes: No fee to fax results.

Lincoln County

5th Judicial District Court PO Box 15, Ivanhoe, MN 56142-0015; 507-694-1355; Fax: 507-694-1717. Hours: 8:30AM-Noon,1-4:30PM (CST). *Felony, Misdemeanor, Civil, Eviction, Small Claims, Probate.*

Civil Records: Access: Mail, in person. Only the court conducts in person searches; visitors may not. Search fee: $10.00 per name. Required to search: name, years to search. Civil cases indexed by defendant, plaintiff. Civil records on computer from 1989, on TCIS from 12/82, on books from late 1800. **Criminal Records:** Access: In person only. Court does not conduct in person searches; visitors must perform searches for themselves. Search fee: No criminal searches performed by court. Required to search: name, years to search, DOB. Criminal records on computer from 1989, on TCIS from 12/82, on books from late 1800. All written requests for criminal record information is referred to the Bureau of Criminal Apprehension (state agency). Call first for form, 650-642-0670. **General Information:** No adoption, juvenile, sex offender or sealed records released. SASE required. Turnaround time 1 week. Copy fee: $5.00 per document. Certification fee: $10.00. Fee payee: Court Administrator. Personal checks accepted. Prepayment is required.

Lyon County

5th Judicial District Court 607 W Main, Marshall, MN 56258; 507-537-6734; Fax: 507-537-6150. Hours: 8:30AM-4:30PM (CST). *Felony, Misdemeanor, Civil, Eviction, Small Claims, Probate.*

Civil Records: Access: Mail, in person. Both court and visitors may perform in person searches. Search fee: $10.00 per name. Required to search: name, years to search. Civil cases indexed by defendant, plaintiff. Civil records on computer from 1987, prior on index cards. **Criminal**

Records: Access: In person only. Court does not conduct in person searches; visitors must perform searches for themselves. Search fee: No criminal searches performed by court. Required to search: name, years to search. Criminal records on computer from 1987, prior on index cards. The court requires sending requests to the state Bureau of Criminal Apprehension. **General Information:** No adoption, juvenile, sex offender or sealed records released. SASE required. Turnaround time 2 days. Copy fee: $5.00 per document. Certification fee: $10.00. Fee payee: Court Administrator. Personal checks accepted. Credit cards accepted: Visa, Mastercard. Prepayment is required. Public access terminal is available.

Mahnomen County

9th Judicial District Court PO Box 459, Mahnomen, MN 56557; 218-935-2251; Fax: 218-935-2851. Hours: 8AM-4:30PM (CST). *Felony, Misdemeanor, Civil, Eviction, Small Claims, Probate.*

Civil Records: Access: Mail, in person. Only the court conducts in person searches; visitors may not. Search fee: $5.00 per name. Required to search: name, years to search. Civil cases indexed by defendant, plaintiff. Civil records on computer from 8/90, prior on books from 1907. **Criminal Records:** Access: Mail, in person. Only the court conducts in person searches; visitors may not. Search fee: $5.00 per name. Required to search: name, years to search. Criminal records on computer from 8/90, prior on books from 1907. **General Information:** No adoption, juvenile, sex offender or sealed records released. SASE required. Turnaround time 1-5 days. Copy fee: $5.00 per document. Certification fee: $10.00. Fee payee: Court Administrator. Personal checks accepted. Prepayment is required.

Marshall County

9th Judicial District Court 208 E Colvin, Warren, MN 56762; 218-745-4921; Fax: 218-745-4343. Hours: 8AM-4:30PM (CST). *Felony, Misdemeanor, Civil, Eviction, Small Claims, Probate.*

Civil Records: Access: Mail, in person. Only the court conducts in person searches; visitors may not. Search fee: $5.00 per name. Required to search: name, years to search; also helpful-address. Civil cases indexed by defendant, plaintiff. Civil records on computer from 5/90, on cards from 1982, on books from 1885. **Criminal Records:** Access: Mail, in person. Only the court conducts in person searches; visitors may not. Search fee: $5.00 per name. Required to search: name, years to search; also helpful-address, DOB. Criminal records on computer from 5/90, on cards from 1982, on books from 1885. **General Information:** No adoption, juvenile, sex offender or sealed records released. SASE required. Turnaround time same day. Copy fee: $5.00 per document. Certification fee: $10.00. Fee payee: Court Administrator. Personal checks accepted. Prepayment is required. Public access terminal is available.

Martin County

5th Judicial District Court 201 Lake Ave, Rm 304, Fairmont, MN 56031; 507-238-3205; Fax: 507-238-1913. Hours: 8AM-5PM (CST). *Felony, Misdemeanor, Civil, Eviction, Small Claims, Probate.*

Civil Records: Access: Mail, in person. Both court and visitors may perform in person searches. Search fee: $10.00 per name background search;

$5.00 per name judgments. Required to search: name, years to search; also helpful-address. Civil cases indexed by defendant, plaintiff. Civil records on computer from 7/89, on cards from 1986, on books from 1800s. **Criminal Records:** Access: In person only. Court does not conduct in person searches; visitors must perform searches for themselves. Search fee: No criminal searches performed by court. Required to search: name, years to search, DOB; also helpful-address, SSN. Criminal records on computer from 7/89, on cards from 1986, on books from 1800s. The court suggests sending requests to the state Bureau of Criminal Apprehension. **General Information:** No adoption, juvenile, sex offender or sealed records released. SASE required. Turnaround time 1-2 weeks. Copy fee: $5.00 per document. Certification fee: $10.00. Fee payee: Court Administrator. Personal checks accepted. Credit cards accepted: Visa, Mastercard. Prepayment is required. Public access terminal is available.

McLeod County

1st Judicial District Court 830 E 11th, Glencoe, MN 55336; 320-864-5551. Hours: 8AM-4:30PM (CST). *Felony, Misdemeanor, Civil, Eviction, Small Claims, Probate.*

Civil Records: Access: Mail, in person. Search fee: $5.00 per name. Required to search: name, years to search. Civil records on computer from 4/92, prior on books. **Criminal Records:** Access: In person only. Court does not conduct in person searches; visitors must perform searches for themselves. Search fee: No criminal searches performed by court. Required to search: name, years to search. Criminal records on computer from 4/92, prior on books. **General Information:** No adoption, juvenile, sex offender or sealed records released. SASE required. Copy fee: $5.00 per document. Certification fee: $10.00. Fee payee: Court Administrator. Personal checks accepted. Prepayment is required. Public access terminal is available.

Meeker County

8th Judicial District Court 325 N Sibley, Litchfield, MN 55355; 320-693-5230; Fax: 320-693-5254. Hours: 8AM-4:30PM (CST). *Felony, Misdemeanor, Civil, Eviction, Small Claims, Probate.*

Civil Records: Access: Fax, mail, in person. Both court and visitors may perform in person searches. Search fee: $5.00 per name. Required to search: name; also helpful-years to search, address. Civil cases indexed by defendant, plaintiff. Civil records on computer from 11/88, prior on index cards. **Criminal Records:** Access: In person only. Court does not conduct in person searches; visitors must perform searches for themselves. Search fee: No criminal searches performed by court. Required to search: name; also helpful-years to search, DOB. Criminal records on computer from 11/88, prior on index cards. **General Information:** No adoption, juvenile, sex offender or sealed records released. SASE required. Turnaround time 3 days. Copy fee: $5.00 per document. Certification fee: $10.00. Fee payee: Court Administrator. Personal checks accepted. Prepayment is required. Public access terminal is available. Fax notes: $5.00 per document.

Mille Lacs County

7th Judicial District Court Courthouse, Milaca, MN 56353; 320-983-8313; Fax: 320-983-8384. Hours: 8AM-4:30PM (CST). *Felony,*

Misdemeanor, Civil, Eviction, Small Claims, Probate.

Civil Records: Access: Fax, mail, in person. Both court and visitors may perform in person searches. Search fee: $5.00 per name. Required to search: name, years to search. Civil records on computer from 4/86, cards from 1981, books prior. **Criminal Records:** Access: Fax, in person. Court does not conduct in person searches; visitors must perform searches for themselves. Search fee: No criminal searches performed by court. Required to search: name, years to search. Criminal records on computer from 4/86, cards from 1981, books prior. **General Information:** No adoption, juvenile, sex offender or sealed records released. SASE required. Turnaround time 1 week. Copy fee: $5.00 per document. Certification fee: $10.00. Fee payee: District Court. Personal checks accepted. Prepayment is required. Public access terminal is available. Fax notes: $5.00 per document.

Morrison County

7th Judicial District Court 213 SE 1st Ave, Little Falls, MN 56345; 320-632-0325; Fax: 320-632-0340. Hours: 8AM-4:30PM (CST). *Felony, Misdemeanor, Civil, Eviction, Small Claims, Probate.*

Civil Records: Access: Fax, mail, in person. Both court and visitors may perform in person searches. Search fee: $5.00 per name. Required to search: name, years to search. Civil cases indexed by defendant, plaintiff. Civil records on computer from 5/86, prior on cards and books. **Criminal Records:** Access: In person only. Court does not conduct in person searches; visitors must perform searches for themselves. Search fee: No criminal searches performed by court. Required to search: name, years to search, DOB. Criminal records on computer from 5/86, prior on cards and books. **General Information:** No adoption, juvenile, sex offender or sealed records released. SASE required. Turnaround time 2-3 days. Copy fee: $5.00 per document. Certification fee: $10.00. Fee payee: Court Administrator. Personal checks accepted. Prepayment is required. Public access terminal is available. Fax notes: $5.00 per document.

Mower County

Mower County District Court 201 1st St NE, Austin, MN 55912; 507-437-9465; Fax: 507-437-9471. Hours: 8AM-5PM (CST). *Felony, Misdemeanor, Civil, Eviction, Small Claims, Probate.*

Civil Records: Access: Mail, in person. Both court and visitors may perform in person searches. Search fee: $5.00 per name. Required to search: name, years to search. Civil cases indexed by defendant, plaintiff. Civil records on computer from 1989. **Criminal Records:** Access: In person only. Court does not conduct in person searches; visitors must perform searches for themselves. Search fee: No criminal searches performed by court. Required to search: name, years to search, DOB. Criminal records on computer from 1989. Effective July 1, 1997, this court will no longer conduct criminal record searches. **General Information:** No adoption, juvenile, paternity or sealed records released. SASE required. Turnaround time 2-3 weeks for civil, 3-4 days for criminal. Copy fee: $5.00 per document. Certification fee: $10.00. Fee payee: Court Administrator. Personal checks accepted. Prepayment is required.

Murray County

5th Judicial District Court PO Box 57, Slayton, MN 56172-0057; 507-836-6163, 825-4550 (Administrator); Fax: 507-836-6019. Hours: 8AM-5PM (CST). *Felony, Misdemeanor, Civil, Eviction, Small Claims, Probate.*

Civil Records: Access: Fax, mail, in person. Both court and visitors may perform in person searches. Search fee: $5.00 per name. Required to search: name, years to search. Civil cases indexed by defendant, plaintiff. Civil records on computer from 7/88. **Criminal Records:** Access: In person only. Court does not conduct in person searches; visitors must perform searches for themselves. Search fee: No criminal searches performed by court. Required to search: name, years to search; also helpful-SSN. Criminal records on computer from 7/88. The court suggests sending requests to the state Bureau of Criminal Apprehension. **General Information:** No adoption, juvenile, or sealed records released. SASE required. Turnaround time 5 days. Copy fee: $5.00 per document. Certification fee: $10.00. Fee payee: Court Administrator. Personal checks accepted. Prepayment is required. Fax notes: $5.00 per document.

Nicollet County

5th Judicial District Court PO Box 496, St Peter, MN 56082; 507-931-6800; Fax: 507-931-4278. Hours: 8AM-5PM (CST). *Felony, Misdemeanor, Civil, Eviction, Small Claims, Probate.*

Note: Records for this county can also be found at the District Court Branch in Mankato

Civil Records: Access: Mail, in person. Both court and visitors may perform in person searches. Search fee: $10.00 per name. Required to search: name, years to search. Civil cases indexed by defendant, plaintiff. Civil records on computer from 9/25/88, on books from 1890. The civil records prior to 9/25/88 for the entire county are located here. **Criminal Records:** Access: In person only. Both court and visitors may perform in person searches. Search fee: No criminal searches performed by court. Required to search: name, years to search, DOB. Criminal records on computer since 9/25/88. Prior records for this court only are located here on books and cards. **General Information:** No adoption, juvenile, sex offender or sealed records released. SASE required. Turnaround time 2 days. Copy fee: $5.00 per document. Certification fee: $10.00. Fee payee: Court Administrator. Personal checks accepted. Prepayment is required. Public access terminal is available.

District Court-Branch PO Box 2055, North Mankato, MN 56002-2055; 507-625-3149; Fax: 507-345-1273. Hours: 8AM-5PM (CST). *Felony, Misdemeanor, Civil, Eviction, Small Claims, Probate.*

Note: Phone number for traffic is 507-625-7795

Civil Records: Access: Mail, in person. Both court and visitors may perform in person searches. Search fee: $10.00 per name. Required to search: name, years to search. Civil cases indexed by defendant, plaintiff. Civil records on computer from 9/25/88, prior in St Peters office. **Criminal Records:** Access: In person only. Court does not conduct in person searches; visitors must perform searches for themselves. Search fee: No criminal searches performed by court. Required to search: name, years to search, DOB; also helpful-SSN. Criminal records for both courts are on computer

since 9/25/88. Prior records are here for only this branch. **General Information:** No adoption, juvenile, sex offender or sealed records released. SASE required. Turnaround time 2 days. Copy fee: $5.00 per document. Certification fee: $10.00. Fee payee: District Court. Personal checks accepted. Prepayment is required. Public access terminal is available.

Nobles County

5th Judicial District Court PO Box 547, Worthington, MN 56187; 507-372-8263; Fax: 507-372-4994. Hours: 8AM-4:30PM (CST). *Felony, Misdemeanor, Civil, Eviction, Small Claims, Probate.*

Civil Records: Access: Mail, in person. Both court and visitors may perform in person searches. Search fee: $10.00 per name. Required to search: name, years to search. Civil cases indexed by defendant, plaintiff. Civil records on computer from 7/88, on books and index cards prior. **Criminal Records:** Access: In person only. Court does not conduct in person searches; visitors must perform searches for themselves. Search fee: No criminal searches performed by court. Required to search: name, years to search; also helpful-SSN. Criminal records on computer from 7/88, on books and index cards prior. The court suggests sending requests to the state Bureau of Criminal Apprehension. **General Information:** No adoption, juvenile, sex offender or sealed records released. SASE required. Turnaround time 1 week. Copy fee: $5.00 per document. Certification fee: $10.00. Fee payee: Court Administrator. Personal checks accepted. Credit cards accepted: Visa, Mastercard. In person only. Prepayment is required. Public access terminal is available.

Norman County

9th Judicial District Court 16 3rd Ave E, Ada, MN 56510-0146; 218-784-7131; Fax: 218-784-3110. Hours: 8:30AM-4:30PM (CST). *Felony, Misdemeanor, Civil, Eviction, Small Claims, Probate.*

Civil Records: Access: Mail, in person. Both court and visitors may perform in person searches. Search fee: $5.00 per name. Required to search: name, years to search. Civil records on computer since 5/90, prior on index cards. **Criminal Records:** Access: Mail, in person. Both court and visitors may perform in person searches. Search fee: $5.00 per name. Required to search: name, years to search, DOB. Criminal records on computer since 5/90, prior on index cards. **General Information:** No adoption, juvenile, sex offender or sealed records released. SASE required. Turnaround time 1-5 days. Copy fee: $5.00 per document. Certification fee: $10.00. Fee payee: Court Administrator. Business checks accepted. Prepayment is required.

Olmsted County

Olmsted County District Court 151 4th St SE, Rochester, MN 55904; 507-285-8210; Fax: 507-285-8996. Hours: 8AM-5PM (CST). *Felony, Misdemeanor, Civil, Eviction, Small Claims, Probate.*

Civil Records: Access: Mail, in person. Both court and visitors may perform in person searches. Search fee: $5.00 per name. Required to search: name, years to search. Civil cases indexed by defendant, plaintiff. Civil records on computer from mid-1989, prior on index cards. **Criminal Records:** Access: In person only. Court does not conduct in person searches; visitors must perform searches for themselves. Search fee: No criminal

searches performed by court. Required to search: name, DOB. Criminal records on computer from mid-1989, prior on index cards. **General Information:** No adoption, juvenile, sex offender or sealed records released. SASE required. Turnaround time 2-7 days. Copy fee: $5.00 per document. Certification fee: $10.00. Fee payee: Court Administrator. Personal checks accepted. Credit cards accepted: Visa, Mastercard, Discover. Prepayment is required. Public access terminal is available.

Otter Tail County

Otter Tail County District Court PO Box 417, Fergus Falls, MN 56538-0417; 218-739-2271; Fax: 218-739-4983. Hours: 8AM-5PM (CST). *Felony, Misdemeanor, Civil, Eviction, Small Claims, Probate.*

Civil Records: Access: Mail, in person. Both court and visitors may perform in person searches. Search fee: $5.00 per name. Required to search: name; also helpful-years to search. Civil cases indexed by defendant, plaintiff. Civil records on computer from 1987, prior on index books. **Criminal Records:** Access: In person only. Court does not conduct in person searches; visitors must perform searches for themselves. Search fee: No criminal searches performed by court. Required to search: name, years to search, DOB; also helpful-address. Criminal records on computer from 1987, prior on index books. **General Information:** No adoption, juvenile, sex offender or sealed records released. SASE required. Turnaround time 2-3 days. Copy fee: $5.00 per document. Certification fee: $10.00. Fee payee: Court Administrator. Personal checks accepted. Prepayment is required. Public access terminal is available.

Pennington County

9th Judicial District Court PO Box 619, Thief River Falls, MN 56701; 218-681-7023; Fax: 218-681-0907. Hours: 8AM-4:30PM (CST). *Felony, Misdemeanor, Civil, Eviction, Small Claims, Probate.*

Civil Records: Access: Mail, in person. Both court and visitors may perform in person searches. Search fee: $5.00 per name. Required to search: name, years to search. Civil cases indexed by defendant, plaintiff. Civil records on computer from 1990, prior on TCIS cards and books. **Criminal Records:** Access: Mail, in person. Both court and visitors may perform in person searches. Search fee: $5.00 per name. Required to search: name, years to search, DOB, offense. Criminal records on computer from 1990, prior on TCIS cards and books. **General Information:** No adoption, juvenile, sex offender or sealed records released. SASE required. Turnaround time 1 day. Copy fee: $5.00 per document. Certification fee: $10.00. Fee payee: Court Administrator. Personal checks accepted. Prepayment is required. Public access terminal is available.

Pine County

10th Judicial District Court 315 6th St, Pine City, MN 55063; 320-629-5634. Hours: 8AM-4:30PM (CST). *Felony, Misdemeanor, Civil, Eviction, Small Claims, Probate.*

Civil Records: Access: Mail, in person. Court does not conduct in person searches; visitors must perform searches for themselves. Search fee: $5.00 per name. Required to search: name, years to search. Civil records on computer from 2/85. **Criminal Records:** Access: In person only. Court does not conduct in person searches; visitors must perform searches for themselves. Search fee: No criminal searches performed by court. Required to search: name, years to search. Criminal records on computer from 2/85. **General Information:** No adoption, juvenile, sex offender or sealed records released. SASE required. Turnaround time 7-9 days. Copy fee: $5.00 per document. Certification fee: $10.00. Fee payee: Court Administrator. Personal checks accepted. Prepayment is required. Public access terminal is available.

Pipestone County

5th Judicial District Court 416 S Hiawatha Ave (PO Box 337), Pipestone, MN 56164; 507-825-6730; Fax: 507-825-6733. Hours: 8:30AM-4:30PM (CST). *Felony, Misdemeanor, Civil, Eviction, Small Claims, Probate.*

Civil Records: Access: Mail, in person. Both court and visitors may perform in person searches. Search fee: $5.00 per name. Required to search: name, years to search. Civil cases indexed by defendant, plaintiff. Civil records on computer from 1989, prior on books. **Criminal Records:** Access: In person only. Court does not conduct in person searches; visitors must perform searches for themselves. Search fee: No criminal searches performed by court. Required to search: name, years to search. Criminal records on computer from 1989, prior on books. The court suggests sending requests to the state Bureau of Criminal Apprehension. **General Information:** No adoption, juvenile, sex offender victims or sealed records released. SASE required. Turnaround time 1 week. Copy fee: $5.00 per document. Certification fee: $10.00. Fee payee: Court Administrator. Personal checks accepted. Prepayment is required. Public access terminal is available.

Polk County

9th Judicial District Court Court Administrator, 612 N Broadway #301, Crookston, MN 56716; 218-281-2332; Fax: 218-281-2204. Hours: 8AM-4:30PM (CST). *Felony, Misdemeanor, Civil, Eviction, Small Claims, Probate.*

Civil Records: Access: Mail, in person. Both court and visitors may perform in person searches. Search fee: $5.00 per name. Required to search: name, years to search. Civil cases indexed by defendant, plaintiff. Civil records on computer from 1990, prior on index cards or books. **Criminal Records:** Access: Mail, in person. Both court and visitors may perform in person searches. Search fee: $5.00 per name. Required to search: name, years to search, DOB. Criminal records on computer from 1990, prior on index cards or books. **General Information:** No adoption, non-felony under age 16 juvenile or sealed records released. SASE required. Turnaround time 3-5 days. Copy fee: $5.00 per document. Certification fee: $10.00. Fee payee: Court Administrator. Personal checks accepted. Prepayment is required. Public access terminal is available.

Pope County

8th Judicial District Court 130 E Minnesota Ave (PO Box 195), Glenwood, MN 56334; 320-634-5222. Hours: 8AM-4:30PM (CST). *Felony, Misdemeanor, Civil, Eviction, Small Claims, Probate.*

Civil Records: Access: Mail, in person. Search fee: $5.00 per name. Required to search: name, years to search. Civil cases indexed by defendant, plaintiff. Civil records on computer from 2/89, prior on TCIS cards ad books. **Criminal Records:** Access: In person only. Court does not conduct in

person searches; visitors must perform searches for themselves. Search fee: No criminal searches performed by court. Required to search: name, years to search. Criminal records on computer from 2/89, prior on TCIS cards ad books. **General Information:** No adoption, juvenile, sex offender or sealed records released. SASE required. Turnaround time 1-2 days. Copy fee: $5.00 per document. Certification fee: $10.00. Fee payee: Court Administrator. Personal checks accepted. Prepayment is required.

Ramsey County

2nd Judicial District Court 15 W Kellogg, Rm 1700, St Paul, MN 55102;; Civil phone:651-266-8266; Criminal phone:651-266-8266; Fax: 651-266-8278. Hours: 8AM-4:30PM (CST). *Felony, Misdemeanor, Civil, Probate.*

Civil Records: Access: Mail, in person. Both court and visitors may perform in person searches. Search fee: Civil name search $5.00, civil judgment search $10.00. Required to search: name, years to search. Civil cases indexed by defendant. Civil records on computer from 5/88, prior on books. **Criminal Records:** Access: In person only. Court does not conduct in person searches; visitors must perform searches for themselves. No search fee. Required to search: name, years to search; also helpful-DOB. Criminal records on computer from 5/88, prior on books. **General Information:** No adoption, juvenile, sex offender or sealed records released. SASE required. Turnaround time 3-5 days. Copy fee: $5.00 per document. Certification fee: $10.00. Fee payee: Court Administrator. Personal checks accepted. Prepayment is required. Public access terminal is available.

2nd Judicial District Court - Maplewood Area 2785 White Bear Ave, Maplewood, MN 55109; 651-777-9111; Fax: 651-777-3970. Hours: 8AM-4:30PM (CST). *Misdemeanor.*

www.co.ramsey.mn.us/courts/index.htm **Criminal Records:** Access: In person only. Court does not conduct in person searches; visitors must perform searches for themselves. Search fee: No criminal searches performed by court. Required to search: name; also helpful-address, DOB, offense, date of offense. Criminal records on computer from 11/90, prior on books or index cards. **General Information:** No adoption, juvenile, sex offender victim, sealed or medical records released. Copy fee: $5.00 per document. Certification fee: $10.00. Fee payee: Ramsey County District Court. Personal checks accepted. Credit cards accepted: Visa, Mastercard, Discover. Not accepted over the phone. Prepayment is required. Public access terminal is available.

2nd Judicial District Court-New Brighton Area 803 5th Ave NW, New Brighton, MN 55112; 651-636-7101; Fax: 651-635-0722. Hours: 8AM-4:30PM (CST). *Misdemeanor.* **Criminal Records:** Access: In person only. Court does not conduct in person searches; visitors must perform searches for themselves. No search fee. Required to search: name, years to search, DOB. Gross misdemeanor files microfilmed, index cards. **General Information:** No juvenile criminal or victim records released. SASE required. Turnaround time 3 days. Copy fee: $5.00 per document. Certification fee: $10.00. Fee payee: District Court. Personal checks accepted. Credit cards accepted: Visa, Mastercard, Discover. Public

access terminal is available. Fax notes: $5.00 per document.

Red Lake County

9th Judicial District Court PO Box 339, Red Lake Falls, MN 56750; 218-253-4281; Fax: 218-253-4287. Hours: 9AM-5PM (CST). *Felony, Misdemeanor, Civil, Eviction, Small Claims, Probate.*

Civil Records: Access: Mail, in person. Only the court conducts in person searches; visitors may not. Search fee: $5.00 per name. Required to search: name, years to search. Civil cases indexed by defendant, plaintiff. Civil records on computer and microfiche from 1990, on books from 1897. **Criminal Records:** Access: Mail, in person. Only the court conducts in person searches; visitors may not. Search fee: $5.00 per name. Required to search: name, years to search, DOB. Criminal records on computer and microfiche from 1990, on books from 1897. **General Information:** No adoption, juvenile, sex offender or sealed records released. SASE required. Turnaround time 1 week. Copy fee: $5.00 per document. Certification fee: $10.00. Fee payee: Court Administrator. Personal checks accepted. Prepayment is required.

Redwood County

5th Judicial District Court PO Box 130, Redwood Falls, MN 56283; 507-637-4020; Fax: 507-637-4021. Hours: 8AM-4:30PM (CST). *Felony, Misdemeanor, Civil, Eviction, Small Claims, Probate.*

Civil Records: Access: Mail, in person. Both court and visitors may perform in person searches. Search fee: $10.00 per name. Required to search: name, years to search. Civil cases indexed by defendant, plaintiff. Civil records on computer from 11/88, prior on card and books. **Criminal Records:** Access: In person only. Court does not conduct in person searches; visitors must perform searches for themselves. Search fee: No criminal searches performed by court. Required to search: name, years to search. Criminal records on computer from 11/88, prior on card and books. No felony or gross misdemeanor searches will be performed. **General Information:** No adoption, juvenile, sex offender or sealed records released. SASE required. Turnaround time 2-3 days. Copy fee: $5.00 per document. Certification fee: $10.00. Fee payee: Court Administrator. Personal checks accepted. Prepayment is required. Public access terminal is available.

Renville County

8th Judicial District Court 500 E DePue Ave, Olivia, MN 56277; 320-523-3680; Fax: 320-523-3689. Hours: 8AM-4:30PM (CST). *Felony, Misdemeanor, Civil, Eviction, Small Claims, Probate.*

Civil Records: Access: Mail, in person. Only the court conducts in person searches; visitors may not. Search fee: $5.00 per name. Required to search: name, years to search. Civil cases indexed by defendant, plaintiff. Civil records on computer from 1988, prior on index cards. **Criminal Records:** Access: In person only. Court does not conduct in person searches; visitors must perform searches for themselves. Search fee: No criminal searches performed by court. Required to search: name. Criminal records on computer from 1988, prior on index cards. **General Information:** No adoption, juvenile, sex offender, criminal or sealed records released. SASE required. Turnaround time 1-5 days. Copy fee: $5.00 per document. Certification fee: $10.00. Fee payee: Court

Administrator. Personal checks accepted. Prepayment is required. Public access terminal is available.

Rice County

3rd Judicial District Court 218 NW 3rd St, Suite 300, Faribault, MN 55021; 507-332-6107; Fax: 507-332-6199. Hours: 8AM-4:30PM (CST). *Felony, Misdemeanor, Civil, Eviction, Small Claims, Probate.*

Civil Records: Access: Mail, in person. Both court and visitors may perform in person searches. Search fee: $5.00 per name. Required to search: name, years to search. Civil cases indexed by defendant, plaintiff. Civil records on computer from 1990, prior on index cards. **Criminal Records:** Access: In person only. Court does not conduct in person searches; visitors must perform searches for themselves. Search fee: No criminal searches performed by court. Required to search: name, years to search; also helpful-SSN. Criminal records on computer from 1990, prior on index cards. **General Information:** No adoption, juvenile, sex offender or sealed records released. SASE required. Turnaround time 1-2 days. Copy fee: $5.00 per document. Certification fee: $10.00. Fee payee: Court Administrator. Personal checks accepted. Prepayment is required. Public access terminal is available.

Rock County

5th Judicial District Court PO Box 745, Luverne, MN 56156; 507-283-5020; Fax: 507-283-5017. Hours: 8AM-5PM (CST). *Felony, Misdemeanor, Civil, Eviction, Small Claims, Probate.*

Civil Records: Access: Mail, in person. Only the court conducts in person searches; visitors may not. Search fee: $10.00 per name. Required to search: name, years to search. Civil cases indexed by defendant, plaintiff. Civil records on computer from 1989, prior on books. **Criminal Records:** Access: Mail, in person. Court does not conduct in person searches; visitors must perform searches for themselves. Search fee: $10.00. Required to search: name, years to search; also helpful-SSN. Criminal records on computer from 1989, prior on books. The court will send requests to the state Bureau of Criminal Apprehension if busy. **General Information:** No adoption, juvenile, sex offender or sealed records released. SASE required. Turnaround time same day if possible. Copy fee: $5.00 per document. Certification fee: $10.00. Fee payee: Court Administrator. Personal checks accepted. Prepayment is required.

Roseau County

9th Judicial District Court 606 5th Ave SW Rm 20, Roseau, MN 56751; 218-463-2541; Fax: 218-463-1889. Hours: 8AM-4:30PM (CST). *Felony, Misdemeanor, Civil, Eviction, Small Claims, Probate.*

Civil Records: Access: Mail, in person. Both court and visitors may perform in person searches. Search fee: $5.00 per name. Required to search: name, years to search. Civil cases indexed by defendant, plaintiff. Civil records on computer from 1990, prior on index cards. **Criminal Records:** Access: Mail, in person. Both court and visitors may perform in person searches. Search fee: $5.00 per name. Required to search: name, years to search; also helpful-DOB. Criminal records on computer from 1990, prior on index cards. **General Information:** No adoption, juvenile, paternity or sealed records released. SASE required. Turnaround time same day if

possible. Copy fee: $5.00 per document. Certification fee: $10.00. Fee payee: Court Administrator. Personal checks accepted. Prepayment is required. Public access terminal is available.

Scott County

1st Judicial District Court Scott County Justice Center, 200 Fourth Ave W, Shakopee, MN 55379; 612-496-8200; Fax: 612-496-8211. Hours: 8AM-4:30PM (CST). *Felony, Misdemeanor, Civil, Eviction, Small Claims, Probate.*

Civil Records: Access: Mail, in person. Both court and visitors may perform in person searches. Search fee: $5.00 per name. Required to search: name, years to search. Civil cases indexed by defendant, plaintiff. Civil records on computer from 1981, prior on books. **Criminal Records:** Access: In person only. Court does not conduct in person searches; visitors must perform searches for themselves. Search fee: No criminal searches performed by court. Required to search: name, years to search, DOB. Criminal records on computer from 1981, prior on books. **General Information:** No adoption, juvenile or sealed records released. SASE required. Turnaround time 1-2 days. Copy fee: $5.00 per document. Certification fee: $10.00. Fee payee: Scott County. Personal checks accepted. Prepayment is required. Public access terminal is available.

Sherburne County

10th Judicial District Court Sherburne County Government Center, 13880 Hwy #10, Elkriver, MN 55330-4608; 612-241-2800; Fax: 612-241-2816. Hours: 8AM-5PM (CST). *Felony, Misdemeanor, Civil, Eviction, Small Claims, Probate.*

Civil Records: Access: Mail, in person. Both court and visitors may perform in person searches. Search fee: $5.00 per name. Required to search: name, years to search. Civil cases indexed by defendant, plaintiff. Civil records on computer from 02/85, prior on books. **Criminal Records:** Access: In person only. Court does not conduct in person searches; visitors must perform searches for themselves. Search fee: No criminal searches performed by court. Required to search: name, years to search, DOB. Criminal records on computer from 02/85, prior on books. **General Information:** No adoption, juvenile, confidential or sealed records released. SASE required. Turnaround time 5 days. Copy fee: $5.00 per document. Certification fee: $10.00. Fee payee: Court Administrator. Personal checks accepted. Prepayment is required. Public access terminal is available.

Sibley County

1st Judicial District Court PO Box 867, Gaylord, MN 55334; 507-237-4051; Fax: 507-237-4062. Hours: 8AM-5PM (CST). *Felony, Misdemeanor, Civil, Eviction, Small Claims, Probate.*

Civil Records: Access: Mail, in person. Both court and visitors may perform in person searches. Search fee: $5.00 per name. Required to search: name, years to search. Civil cases indexed by defendant, plaintiff. Civil records on computer from 5/92, prior on books. **Criminal Records:** Access: Mail, in person. Both court and visitors may perform in person searches. Search fee: $5.00 per name. Required to search: name, years to search, DOB. Criminal records on computer from 5/92, prior on books. **General Information:** No adoption, juvenile or sealed records released.

SASE required. Turnaround time 1-2 week. Copy fee: $5.00 per document. Certification fee: $10.00. Fee payee: Court Administrator. Personal checks accepted. Prepayment is required. Public access terminal is available.

St. Louis County

6th Judicial District Court 100 N 5th Ave W, Rm 320, Duluth, MN 55802-1294;; Civil phone:218-726-2431; Criminal phone:218-726-2431; Probate phone:218-726-2500; Fax: 218-726-2473. Hours: 8AM-4:30PM (CST). *Felony, Misdemeanor, Civil, Eviction, Small Claims, Probate.*

Note: All three St Louis County courts can access computer records for the county and direct you to the appropriate court to get the physical file

Civil Records: Access: Mail, in person. Search fee: $5.00 per name. Required to search: name, years to search. Civil records on computer from 1976. **Criminal Records:** Access: In person only. Court does not conduct in person searches; visitors must perform searches for themselves. Search fee: No criminal searches performed by court. Required to search: name. Civil records on computer from 1976. **General Information:** No adoption, juvenile, juvenile victim of sex offense, sealed records released. SASE not required. Turnaround time 5 days. Copy fee: $5.00 per document. Certification fee: $10.00. Fee payee: Court Administrator. Personal checks accepted. Prepayment is required. Public access terminal is available.

6th Judicial District Court-Hibbing Branch 1810 12th Ave East, Hibbing, MN 55746; 218-262-0100; Fax: 218-262-0219. Hours: 8AM-4:30PM (CST). *Felony, Misdemeanor, Civil, Eviction, Small Claims, Probate.*

Note: All three St Louis County courts can access computer records for the county and direct you to the appropriate court for the physical file

Civil Records: Access: Mail, in person. Both court and visitors may perform in person searches. Search fee: $5.00 per name. Required to search: name, years to search. Civil cases indexed by defendant, plaintiff. Civil records on computer from 1985, prior on card or books. **Criminal Records:** Access: In person only. Court does not conduct in person searches; visitors must perform searches for themselves. Search fee: No criminal searches performed by court. Required to search: name, years to search. Criminal records on computer from 1985, prior on card or books. **General Information:** No adoption, juvenile, sex offender or sealed records released. SASE required. Turnaround time 2 days. Copy fee: $5.00 per document. Certification fee: $10.00. Fee payee: Court Administrator. Personal checks accepted. Prepayment is required. Public access terminal is available.

6th Judicial District Court-Virginia Branch 300 S 5th Ave, Virginia, MN 55792; 218-749-7106; Fax: 218-749-7109. Hours: 8AM-4:30PM (CST). *Felony, Misdemeanor, Civil, Eviction, Small Claims, Probate.*

Note: All three St Louis County courts can access computer records for the county and direct you to the appropriate court for the physical files

Civil Records: Access: Mail, in person. Both court and visitors may perform in person searches. Search fee: $5.00 per name. Required to search: name, years to search. Civil cases indexed by defendant, plaintiff. Civil records on computer from 1991, prior on books. **Criminal Records:**

Access: In person only. Court does not conduct in person searches; visitors must perform searches for themselves. Search fee: No criminal searches performed by court. Required to search: name, years to search, DOB. Criminal records on computer from 1991, prior on books. **General Information:** No adoption, juvenile, sex offender or sealed records released. SASE required. Turnaround time 2-3 days. Copy fee: $5.00 per document. Certification fee: $10.00. Fee payee: Court Administrator. Personal checks accepted. Prepayment is required. Public access terminal is available.

Stearns County

Stearns County District Court PO Box 1168, St Cloud, MN 56302; 320-656-3620; Fax: 320-656-3626. Hours: 8AM-4:30PM (CST). *Felony, Misdemeanor, Civil, Eviction, Probate.*

Civil Records: Access: Mail, in person. Both court and visitors may perform in person searches. Search fee: $5.00 per name. Required to search: name, years to search. Civil cases indexed by defendant, plaintiff. Civil records on computer from 1984, on books from the 1920s. **Criminal Records:** Access: In person only. Court does not conduct in person searches; visitors must perform searches for themselves. Search fee: No criminal searches performed by court. Required to search: name, years to search, DOB. Criminal records on computer from 1984, on books from the 1920s. **General Information:** No adoption, juvenile, sex offender or sealed records released. SASE not required. Turnaround time 1-2 days. Copy fee: $5.00 per document. Certification fee: $10.00. Fee payee: District Court. Personal checks accepted. Credit cards accepted: Visa, Mastercard, Discover. Prepayment is required. Public access terminal is available.

Steele County

3rd Judicial District Court PO Box 487, Owatonna, MN 55060; 507-444-7700; Fax: 507-444-7491. Hours: 8AM-5PM (CST). *Felony, Misdemeanor, Civil, Eviction, Small Claims, Probate.*

Civil Records: Access: Mail, in person. Both court and visitors may perform in person searches. Search fee: $5.00 per name. Required to search: name, years to search. Civil cases indexed by defendant, plaintiff. Civil records on computer from 1990, on books from 1870. **Criminal Records:** Access: In person only. Court does not conduct in person searches; visitors must perform searches for themselves. Search fee: No criminal searches performed by court. Required to search: name, years to search; also helpful-SSN. Criminal records on computer from 1990, on books from 1870. **General Information:** No adoption, juvenile, sex offender or sealed records released. SASE required. Turnaround time 1-3 days. Copy fee: $5.00 per document. Certification fee: $10.00. Fee payee: Court Administrator. Personal checks accepted. Prepayment is required. Public access terminal is available.

Stevens County

8th Judicial District Court PO Box 530, Morris, MN 56267; 320-589-7287; Fax: 320-589-7288. Hours: 8AM-4:30PM (8AM-4PM Summer hours) (CST). *Felony, Misdemeanor, Civil, Eviction, Small Claims, Probate.*

Civil Records: Access: Mail, in person. Only the court conducts in person searches; visitors may not. Search fee: $5.00 per name. Required to search: name, years to search. Civil cases indexed

by defendant, plaintiff. Civil records on computer from 2/89, on cards from 5/86, on books from 1900. **Criminal Records:** Access: In person only. Court does not conduct in person searches; visitors must perform searches for themselves. Search fee: No criminal searches performed by court. Required to search: name, years to search. Criminal records on computer from 2/89, on cards from 5/86, on books from 1900. **General Information:** No adoption, juvenile, sex offender or sealed records released. SASE required. Turnaround time 1-2 days. Copy fee: $5.00 per document. Certification fee: $10.00. Fee payee: Court Administrator. Personal checks accepted. Prepayment is required.

Swift County

8th Judicial District Court PO Box 110, Benson, MN 56215; 320-843-2744; Fax: 320-843-4124. Hours: 8AM-4:30PM (CST). *Felony, Misdemeanor, Civil, Eviction, Small Claims, Probate.*

Civil Records: Access: Phone, mail, in person. Both court and visitors may perform in person searches. Search fee: $5.00 per name. Required to search: name, years to search. Civil cases indexed by defendant, plaintiff. Civil records on computer from 8-88, prior in files and books from 1800s. **Criminal Records:** Access: Phone, mail, in person. Court does not conduct in person searches; visitors must perform searches for themselves. Search fee:. Required to search: name, years to search; also helpful-DOB. Criminal records on computer from 8-88, prior in files and books from 1800s. **General Information:** No adoption, juvenile, minor victim of sex offense, sealed records released. SASE required. Turnaround time 1 week. Copy fee: $5.00 per document. Certification fee: $10.00. Fee payee: Court Administrator. Personal checks accepted. Prepayment is required.

Todd County

7th Judicial District Court 221 1st Ave South, Long Prairie, MN 56347; 320-732-7800; Fax: 320-732-2506. Hours: 8AM-4:30PM (CST). *Felony, Misdemeanor, Civil, Eviction, Small Claims, Probate.*

Civil Records: Access: Mail, in person. Both court and visitors may perform in person searches. Search fee: $5.00 per name. Required to search: name, years to search, address. Civil cases indexed by defendant, plaintiff. Civil records on computer 7/86, prior on index cards and books. **Criminal Records:** Access: In person only. Court does not conduct in person searches; visitors must perform searches for themselves. Search fee: No criminal searches performed by court. Required to search: name, years to search, address, DOB; also helpful-SSN. Criminal records on computer 7/86, prior on index cards and books. **General Information:** No adoption, juvenile or sealed records released. SASE required. Turnaround time 3-4 days. Copy fee: $5.00 per document. Certification fee: $10.00. Fee payee: Court Administrator. Personal checks accepted. Prepayment is required. Public access terminal is available.

Traverse County

8th Judicial District Court PO Box 867, 702 2nd Ave N, Wheaton, MN 56296; 320-563-4343; Fax: 320-563-4311. Hours: 8AM-Noon, 12:30-4:30PM (CST). *Felony, Misdemeanor, Civil, Eviction, Small Claims, Probate.*

Civil Records: Access: Mail, in person. Both court and visitors may perform in person searches.

Search fee: $5.00 per name. Available for judgments only. Required to search: name, years to search. Civil cases indexed by defendant, plaintiff. Civil records on computer from 6/89, prior on index cards and books. Only judgment searches accepted by mail. **Criminal Records:** Access: In person only. Court does not conduct in person searches; visitors must perform searches for themselves. Search fee: No criminal searches performed by court. Required to search: name, years to search. Criminal records on computer from 6/89, prior on index cards and books. **General Information:** No adoption, juvenile, sex offender or sealed records released. SASE required. Turnaround time 1 day. Copy fee: $5.00 per document. Certification fee: $10.00. Fee payee: Court Administrator. Personal checks accepted. Prepayment is required.

Wabasha County

3rd Judicial District Court 625 Jefferson Ave, Wabasha, MN 55981; 651-565-3579; Fax: 651-565-3524. Hours: 8AM-4PM (CST). *Felony, Misdemeanor, Civil, Eviction, Small Claims, Probate.*

Civil Records: Access: Mail, in person. Both court and visitors may perform in person searches. Search fee: $5.00 per name. Required to search: name, years to search. Civil cases indexed by defendant, plaintiff. Civil records on computer from 6/89, prior on index cards and books. **Criminal Records:** Access: In person only. Court does not conduct in person searches; visitors must perform searches for themselves. Search fee: No criminal searches performed by court. Required to search: name, years to search; also helpful-DOB. Criminal records on computer from 6/89, prior on index cards and books. **General Information:** No adoption, juvenile, sex offender or sealed records released. SASE required. Turnaround time same day usually. Copy fee: $5.00 per document. Certification fee: $10.00. Fee payee: Wabasha District Court. Personal checks accepted. Prepayment is required.

Wadena County

7th Judicial District Court County Courthouse, 415 South Jefferson St, Wadena, MN 56482; 218-631-7634; Fax: 218-631-7635. Hours: 8AM-4:30PM (CST). *Felony, Misdemeanor, Civil, Eviction, Small Claims, Probate.*

Civil Records: Access: In person only. Both court and visitors may perform in person searches. Search fee: $5.00 per name. Required to search: name, years to search. Civil cases indexed by defendant, plaintiff. Civil records on computer from 7/86; prior on books, cards and microfiche. **Criminal Records:** Access: In person only. Court does not conduct in person searches; visitors must perform searches for themselves. Search fee: No criminal searches performed by court. Required to search: name, years to search, DOB; also helpful-address. Criminal records on computer from 7/86; prior on books, cards and microfiche. **General Information:** No adoption, juvenile, or sealed records released. Copy fee: $.25 per page. Certification fee: $10.00. Fee payee: Court Administrator. Personal checks accepted. Prepayment is required. Public access terminal is available.

Waseca County

3rd Judicial District Court 307 N State St, Waseca, MN 56093; 507-835-0540; Fax: 507-835-0633. Hours: 8AM-4:30PM (CST). *Felony,*

Misdemeanor, Civil, Eviction, Small Claims, Probate.

Civil Records: Access: Mail, in person. Both court and visitors may perform in person searches. Search fee: $5.00 per name. Required to search: name, years to search. Civil cases indexed by defendant, plaintiff. Civil records on computer from 1990, prior on TCIS cards and books. **Criminal Records:** Access: In person only. Court does not conduct in person searches; visitors must perform searches for themselves. Search fee: No criminal searches performed by court. Required to search: name, years to search, DOB. Criminal records on computer from 1990, prior on TCIS cards and books. **General Information:** No adoption, juvenile, sex offender victim or sealed records released. SASE required. Turnaround time 2 days. Copy fee: $5.00 per document. Certification fee: $10.00. Fee payee: Court Administrator. Personal checks accepted. Prepayment is required. Public access terminal is available.

Washington County

10th Judicial District Court 14949 62nd St North, PO Box 3802, Stillwater, MN 55082-3802; 651-430-6263; Fax: 651-430-6300. Hours: 7:30AM-5PM (CST). *Felony, Misdemeanor, Civil, Eviction, Small Claims, Probate.*

www.co.washington.mn.us/crtadmn.htm

Civil Records: Access: Mail, in person. Both court and visitors may perform in person searches. Search fee: $5.00 per name. Required to search: name, years to search. Civil cases indexed by defendant, plaintiff. Civil records on computer from 12/83, prior on books. **Criminal Records:** Access: In person only. Court does not conduct in person searches; visitors must perform searches for themselves. Search fee: No criminal searches performed by court. Required to search: name, years to search, DOB. Criminal records on computer from 12/83, prior on books. Fax & mail access limited to statute requirements. **General Information:** No adoption, juvenile, sex offender or sealed records released. SASE required. Turnaround time 1 week. Copy fee: $5.00 per document. Certification fee: $10.00. Fee payee: Court Administrator. Personal checks accepted. Credit cards accepted: Visa, Mastercard. Prepayment is required. Public access terminal is available.

Watonwan County

5th Judicial District Court PO Box 518, St James, MN 56081; 507-375-1236; Fax: 507-375-5010. Hours: 8AM-5PM (CST). *Felony, Misdemeanor, Civil, Eviction, Small Claims, Probate.*

Civil Records: Access: Mail, in person. Both court and visitors may perform in person searches. Search fee: $5.00 per name. Required to search: name, years to search. Civil cases indexed by defendant, plaintiff. Civil records on computer from 5/89, prior on index cards. **Criminal Records:** Access: In person only. Both court and visitors may perform in person searches. Search fee: No criminal searches performed by court. Required to search: name, years to search; also helpful-DOB. Criminal records on computer from 5/89, prior on index cards. A signed release is necessary if court does search. **General Information:** No adoption, juvenile, sex offender or sealed records released. SASE required. Copy fee: $5.00 per document. Certification fee: $10.00. Fee payee: Court Administrator. Personal checks accepted. Prepayment is required. Public access terminal is available.

Wilkin County

8th Judicial District Court PO Box 219, Breckenridge, MN 56520; 218-643-4972; Fax: 218-643-5733. Hours: 8AM-4:30PM (CST). *Felony, Misdemeanor, Civil, Eviction, Small Claims, Probate.*

http://courtnet.courts.state.mn.us/dist08

Civil Records: Access: Mail, in person. Both court and visitors may perform in person searches. Search fee: $5.00 per name. Required to search: name; also helpful-years to search. Civil cases indexed by defendant, plaintiff. Civil records on computer from 1989, prior on books. **Criminal Records:** Access: In person only. Court does not conduct in person searches; visitors must perform searches for themselves. Search fee: No criminal searches performed by court. Required to search: name; also helpful-years to search. Criminal records on computer from 1989, prior on books. **General Information:** No adoption, juvenile, sex offender or sealed records released. SASE required. Turnaround time 3-5 days. Copy fee: $5.00 per document. Certification fee: $10.00. Fee payee: Court Administrator. Personal checks accepted. Prepayment is required. Public access terminal is available. Public Access Terminal Note: Not in complete use at this time.

Winona County

3rd Judicial District Court 171 West 3rd St, Winona, MN 55987; 507-457-6385; Fax: 507-457-6392. Hours: 8AM-4:30PM (CST). *Felony, Misdemeanor, Civil, Eviction, Small Claims, Probate.*

www.courts.state.mn.us/districts/third/winona.htm

Civil Records: Access: Mail, in person. Both court and visitors may perform in person searches. Search fee: $10.00 per hour. Required to search: name, years to search. Civil cases indexed by defendant, plaintiff. Civil records on computer from 1986, on books from 1888. **Criminal Records:** Access: In person only. Court does not conduct in person searches; visitors must perform searches for themselves. Search fee: No criminal searches performed by court. Required to search: name, years to search, DOB. Criminal records on computer from 1986, on books from 1888. **General Information:** No adoption, juvenile, sex offender or sealed records released. SASE not required. Turnaround time 5-10 working days. Copy fee: $5.00 per document. Certification fee: $10.00. Fee payee: Court Administrator. Personal checks accepted. Prepayment is required. Public access terminal is available.

Wright County

10th Judicial District Court 10 NW 2nd St, Room 201, Buffalo, MN 55313-1192; 763-682-7549; Fax: 763-682-7300. Hours: 8AM-4:30PM (CST). *Felony, Misdemeanor, Civil, Eviction, Small Claims, Probate.*

Civil Records: Access: In person only. Court does not conduct in person searches; visitors must perform searches for themselves. Search fee: No civil searches performed by court. Required to search: name, years to search. Civil cases indexed by defendant, plaintiff. Civil records on computer from 8/84, prior on books, cards & microfiche. **Criminal Records:** Access: In person only. Court does not conduct in person searches; visitors must perform searches for themselves. Search fee: No criminal searches performed by court. Required to search: name, years to search; also helpful-DOB. Criminal records on computer from 8/84, prior on books, cards & microfiche. **General Information:** No adoption, juvenile, confidential or sealed records released. Copy fee: $5.00 per document. Certification fee: $10.00. Fee payee: Court Administrator. Personal checks accepted. Prepayment is required. Public access terminal is available.

Yellow Medicine County

8th Judicial District Court 415 9th Ave, Granite Falls, MN 56241; 320-564-3325; Fax: 320-564-4435. Hours: 8AM-4PM (CST). *Felony, Misdemeanor, Civil, Eviction, Small Claims, Probate.*

Civil Records: Access: Mail, in person. Both court and visitors may perform in person searches. Search fee: $5.00 per name. Required to search: name, years to search; also helpful-address. Civil cases indexed by defendant, plaintiff. Civil records on computer from 1988. **Criminal Records:** Access: In person only. Court does not conduct in person searches; visitors must perform searches for themselves. Search fee: No criminal searches performed by court. Required to search: name, years to search. Criminal records on computer from 1988. **General Information:** No adoption, juvenile or sealed records released. SASE required. Turnaround time 2-3 days. Copy fee: $5.00 per document. Certification fee: $10.00. Fee payee: Court Administrator. Personal checks accepted. Prepayment is required. Public access terminal is available.

ORGANIZATION   87 counties, 87 recording offices. The recording officer is County Recorder. The entire state is in the Central Time Zone (CST).

REAL ESTATE RECORDS   Many Minnesota counties will perform real estate searches, especially short questions over the telephone. Copy fees vary, but do not apply to certified copies. Certification fees are usually $1.00 per page with a minimum of $5.00.

UCC RECORDS   Financing statements are filed at the state level except for consumer goods, farm related and real estate related filings. Counties enter all non-real estate filings into a central statewide database which can be accessed from any county office. All counties will perform UCC searches. Use search request form UCC-11. Search fees are usually $15.00 per debtor name if the standard UCC-12 request form is used, or $20.00 if a nonstandard form is used. A UCC search can include tax liens. The search fee usually includes 10 listings or copies. Additional copies usually cost $1.00 per page.

TAX LIEN RECORDS   Federal and state tax liens on personal property of businesses are filed with the Secretary of State. Other federal and state tax liens are filed with the County Recorder. A special search form UCC-12 is used for separate tax lien searches. Some counties search each tax lien index separately. Some charge one $15.00 fee to search both indexes, but others charge a separate fee for each index searched. Search and copy fees vary widely.

OTHER LIENS   Mechanics, hospital, judgment, attorneys.

Aitkin County
County Recorder, 209 Second Street NW, Aitkin, MN 56431. 218-927-7336.

Anoka County
County Recorder, 2100 3rd Ave., Anoka, MN 55303-2265. 763-323-5416. Fax: 763-323-5421.
www2.co.hennepin.mn.us
Online Access: Real Estate, Tax Assessor Records. Access to the Anoka County online records requires an annual fee of $35 and a $25 monthly fee and $.25 per transaction. The system operates from 8AM-4:30PM M-F and supports baud rates up to 33.6. Records date back to 1995 For information, contact Pam LeBlanc at 763-323-5424. Lending agency information is available.

Becker County
County Recorder, P.O. Box 595, Detroit Lakes, MN 56502-0595. 218-846-7304. Fax: 218-846-7323.

Beltrami County
County Recorder, 619 Beltrami Ave. NW, Courthouse, Bemidji, MN 56601. 218-759-4170. Fax: 218-759-4527.

Benton County
County Recorder, P.O. Box 129, Foley, MN 56329. 320-968-6254.

Big Stone County
County Recorder, P.O. Box 218, Ortonville, MN 56278. 320-839-2308. Fax: 320-839-2308.

Blue Earth County
County Recorder, P.O. Box 3567, Mankato, MN 56002-3567. 507-389-8222. Fax: 507-389-8808.

Brown County
County Recorder, P.O. Box 248, New Ulm, MN 56073-0248. 507-233-6653. Fax: 507-359-1430.

Carlton County
County Recorder, Box 70, Carlton, MN 55718. 218-384-9122. Fax: 218-384-9157.

Carver County
County Recorder, Carver County Govt Center, Admin Bldg, 600 East Fourth St, Chaska, MN 55318-2158. 952-361-1930. Fax: 952-361-1931.
www.co.carver.mn.us
Online Access: Property Tax Records. Records on the Carver County Property Tax Information database ar available free on the Internet at www.co.carvr.mn.us/Prop_Tax/default.asp. Information is updated bi-monthly.

Cass County
County Recorder, P.O. Box 3000, Walker, MN 56484. 218-547-7381. Fax: 218-547-2440.

Chippewa County
County Recorder, 629 No. 11th St., Montevideo, MN 56265. 320-269-9431. Fax: 320-269-7168.

Chisago County
County Recorder, Government Center, Room/Box 277, 313 N. Main St., Center City, MN 55012-9663. 651-213-0438. Fax: 651-213-0454.

Clay County
County Recorder, P.O. Box 280, Moorhead, MN 56561-0280. 218-299-5031. Fax: 218-299-7500.

Clearwater County
County Recorder, 213 Main Avenue North, Dept. 207, Bagley, MN 56621. 218-694-6129. Fax: 218-694-6244.

Cook County
County Recorder, P.O. Box 1150, Grand Marais, MN 55604-1150. 218-387-3000. Fax: 218-387-2610.

Cottonwood County
County Recorder, P.O. Box 326, Windom, MN 56101. 507-831-1458. Fax: 507-831-3675.

Crow Wing County
County Recorder, P.O. Box 383, Brainerd, MN 56401. 218-828-3965. Fax: 218-825-1808.

Dakota County
County Recorder, 1590 Highway 55, Hastings, MN 55033. 651-438-4355. Fax: 651-438-8176.
www.co.dakota.mn.us
Online Access: Real Estate. Records on the Dakota County Real Estate Inquiry database are available free on the Internet at www.co.dakota.mn.us/depart/property/index.htm. Information includes items such as address, estimated value, taxes, last sale price, building details.

Dodge County
County Recorder, P.O. Box 128, Mantorville, MN 55955-0128. 507-635-6250. Fax: 507-635-6265.

Douglas County
County Recorder, 305 8th Avenue West, Courthouse, Alexandria, MN 56308. 320-762-3877.

Faribault County
County Recorder, P.O. Box 130, Blue Earth, MN 56013. 507-526-6252. Fax: 507-526-6227.

Fillmore County
County Recorder, Box 465, Preston, MN 55965-0465. 507-765-3852. Fax: 507-765-4571.

Freeborn County
County Recorder, 411 South Broadway, Court House, Albert Lea, MN 56007-4506. 507-377-5130. Fax: 507-377-5260.

Goodhue County
County Recorder, Box 408, Red Wing, MN 55066. 651-385-3149. Fax: 651-385-3039.

Grant County
County Recorder, 10th Second Street NE, Courthouse, Elbow Lake, MN 56531-4300. 218-685-4133. Fax: 218-685-4521.

Hennepin County
County Recorder, 300 South 6th Street, 8-A Government Center, Minneapolis, MN 55487. 612-348-3049.
www2.co.hennepin.mn.us
Online Access: Real Estate, Liens. Two methods are available. Access to Hennepin County online records requires a $35 annual fee with a charge of $5 per hour from 7AM-7PM, or $4.15 per hour at other times. The system supports baud rates up to 28.8. Records date back to 1988 For information, contact Jerry Erickson at 612-348-3856. Only UCC & lending agency information is available. Property tax info is at the Treasurer office Records on the Hennepin County Property Information Search database are available free on the Internet at www2.co.hennepin.mn.us/pins/main.htm. Search by Property ID #, address, or addition name. An Automated phone system is also available; 612-348-3011

Houston County
County Recorder, P.O. Box 29, Caledonia, MN 55921-0029. 507-724-5813. Fax: 507-724-2647.

Hubbard County
County Recorder, Courthouse, Park Rapids, MN 56470. 218-732-3552.

Isanti County
County Recorder, Courthouse, Cambridge, MN 55008. 763-689-1191.

Itasca County
County Recorder, 123 NE 4th Street, Grand Rapids, MN 55744-2600. 218-327-2856. Fax: 218-327-0689.

Jackson County
County Recorder, Jackson County Recorder P.O. Box 209, Jackson, MN 56143. 507-847-2580. Fax: 507-847-4718.

Kanabec County
County Recorder, 18 North Vine Street, Mora, MN 55051. 320-679-6466. Fax: 320-679-6431.

Kandiyohi County
County Recorder, P.O. Box 736, Willmar, MN 56201-0736. 320-231-6223. Fax: 320-231-6284.

Kittson County
County Recorder, P.O. Box 639, Hallock, MN 56728. 218-843-2842. Fax: 218-843-2020.

Koochiching County
County Recorder, Courthouse, 715 4th St., International Falls, MN 56649. 218-283-6290. Fax: 218-283-6434.

Lac qui Parle County
County Recorder, P.O. Box 132, Madison, MN 56256-0132. 320-598-3724.

Lake County
County Recorder, 601 Third Avenue, Two Harbors, MN 55616. 218-834-8347. Fax: 218-834-8365.

Lake of the Woods County
County Recorder, P.O. Box 808, Baudette, MN 56623. 218-634-1902. Fax: 218-634-2509.

Le Sueur County
County Recorder, 88 South Park Avenue, Courthouse, Le Center, MN 56057-1620. 507-357-2251. Fax: 507-357-6375.

Lincoln County
County Recorder, P.O. Box 119, Ivanhoe, MN 56142. 507-694-1360. Fax: 507-694-1198.

Lyon County
County Recorder, 607 West Main Street, Marshall, MN 56258. 507-537-6722. Fax: 507-537-6091.

Mahnomen County
County Recorder, P.O. Box 380, Mahnomen, MN 56557. 218-935-5528. Fax: 218-935-5946.

Marshall County
County Recorder, 208 East Colvin, Warren, MN 56762. 218-745-4801. Fax: 218-745-4343.

Martin County
County Recorder, P.O. Box 785, Fairmont, MN 56031-0785. 507-238-3213. Fax: 507-238-3259.

McLeod County
County Recorder, P.O. Box 127, Glencoe, MN 55336. 320-864-5551. Fax: 320-864-1295.

Meeker County
County Recorder, 325 North Sibley Avenue, Courthouse, Litchfield, MN 55355. 320-693-5440. Fax: 320-693-5444.

Mille Lacs County
County Recorder, 635 2nd Street S.E., Milaca, MN 56353. 320-983-8309. Fax: 320-983-8388.

Morrison County
County Recorder, Administration Building, 213 SE 1st Ave., Little Falls, MN 56345. 320-632-0145. Fax: 320-632-0141.

Mower County
County Recorder, 201 First Street NE, Austin, MN 55912-3475. 507-437-9446. Fax: 507-437-9471.

Murray County
County Recorder, P.O. Box 57, Slayton, MN 56172-0057. 507-836-6148x144. Fax: 507-836-8904.

Nicollet County
County Recorder, P.O. Box 493, St. Peter, MN 56082-0493. 507-931-6800. Fax: 507-931-9220.

Nobles County
County Recorder, P.O. Box 757, Worthington, MN 56187. 507-372-8236. Fax: 507-372-8223.

Norman County
County Recorder, P.O. Box 146, Ada, MN 56510. 218-784-5481. Fax: 218-784-2399.

Olmsted County
County Recorder, 151 4th St. SE, Rochester, MN 55904. 507-285-8194. Fax: 507-287-7186.

Otter Tail County
County Recorder, P.O. Box 867, Fergus Falls, MN 56538. 218-739-2271.

Pennington County
County Recorder, P.O. Box 616, Thief River Falls, MN 56701. 218-683-7027. Fax: 218-683-7026.

Pine County
County Recorder, Courthouse, 315 Sixth St., Suite 3, Pine City, MN 55063. 320-629-5665. Fax: 320-629-7319.

Pipestone County
County Recorder, 416 S. Hiawatha Ave., Pipestone, MN 56164. 507-825-6755. Fax: 507-825-6741.

Polk County
County Recorder, P.O. Box 397, Crookston, MN 56716. 218-281-3464. Fax: 218-281-2204.

Pope County
County Recorder, 130 East Minnesota, Glenwood, MN 56334. 320-634-5723. Fax: 320-634-3087.

Ramsey County
County Recorder, 50 West Kellogg Blvd., Suite 812 RCGC-W, St. Paul, MN 55102-1693. 651-266-2060.

Red Lake County
County Recorder, Box 3, Red Lake Falls, MN 56750-0003. 218-253-2997. Fax: 218-253-4894.

Redwood County
County Recorder, P.O. Box 130, Redwood Falls, MN 56283. 507-637-4032. Fax: 507-637-4064.

Renville County
County Recorder, 500 East DePue, Olivia, MN 56277-1396. 320-523-1000. Fax: 795-231-1172.

Rice County
County Recorder, 320 NW 3rd St., Suite 10, Faribault, MN 55021-6146. 507-332-6114. Fax: 507-332-5999.

Rock County
County Recorder, P.O. Box 509, Luverne, MN 56156. 507-283-5014. Fax: 507-283-1343.

Roseau County
County Recorder, 606 5th Ave. SW, Room 170, Roseau, MN 56751-1477. 218-463-2061.

Scott County
County Recorder, 428 South Holmes Street, Shakopee, MN 55379. 952-496-8143. Fax: 952-496-8138.

Sherburne County
County Recorder, 13880 Highway 10, Elk River, MN 55330. 763-241-2915. Fax: 763-241-2995.

Sibley County
County Recorder, P.O. Box 44, Gaylord, MN 55334-0044. 507-237-4080. Fax: 507-237-4062.

St. Louis County
County Recorder, P.O. Box 157, Duluth, MN 55801-0157. 218-726-2677. Fax: 218-725-5052.

Stearns County
County Recorder, 705 Courthouse Square, Administration Center, Room 131, St. Cloud, MN 56303. 320-656-3855. Fax: 320-656-3916.

Steele County
County Recorder, P.O. Box 890, Owatonna, MN 55060. 507-444-7450. Fax: 507-444-7470.

Stevens County
County Recorder, P.O. Box 530, Morris, MN 56267. 320-589-7414. Fax: 320-589-2036.

Swift County
County Recorder, P.O. Box 246, Benson, MN 56215. 320-843-3377. Fax: 320-843-2275.

Todd County
County Recorder, 215 First Avenue South, Suite 300, Long Prairie, MN 56347-1391. 320-732-4428. Fax: 320-732-4001.

Traverse County
County Recorder, P.O. Box 487, Wheaton, MN 56296-0487. 320-563-4622. Fax: 320-563-4424.

Wabasha County
County Recorder, 625 Jefferson Avenue, Wabasha, MN 55981. 651-565-3623. Fax: 651-565-2774.

Wadena County
County Recorder, P.O. Box 415, Wadena, MN 56482. 218-631-7622. Fax: 218-631-7652.

Waseca County
County Recorder, 307 North State Street, Waseca, MN 56093. 507-835-0670. Fax: 507-835-0633.

Washington County
County Recorder, 14900 North 61st Street, P.O. Box 6, Stillwater, MN 55082. 651-430-6755. Fax: 651-430-6753.

Online Access: Real Estate, Liens, Tax Assessor Records. Access to Washington County online records requires a $250 set up fee; no fees apply to Recorder office information. The system operates 24 hours daily and supports baud rates up to 28.8. Records date back 3 years For information, contact Larry Haseman at 651-430-6423. Lending agency information is available, but UCC information is on a separate system.

Watonwan County
County Recorder, P.O. Box 518, St. James, MN 56081. 507-375-1216.

Wilkin County
County Recorder, P.O. Box 29, Breckenridge, MN 56520. 218-643-4012. Fax: 218-643-1617.

Winona County
County Recorder, 171 West 3rd Street, Winona, MN 55987-3102. 507-457-6340. Fax: 507-457-6469.

Wright County
County Recorder, 10 2nd Street NW, Room 210, Buffalo, MN 55313-1196. 763-682-7357.

Yellow Medicine County
County Recorder, 415 9th Avenue, Courthouse, Granite Falls, MN 56241. 320-564-2529. Fax: 320-564-3670.

You will usually be able to find the city name in the City/County Cross Reference below. In that case, it is a simple matter to determine the county from the cross reference. However, only the official US Postal Service city names are included in this index. There are an additional 40,000 place names that people use in their addresses. Therefore, we have also included a ZIP/City Cross Reference immediately following the City/County Cross Reference.

If you know the ZIP Code but the city name does not appear in the City/County Cross Reference index, look up the ZIP Code in the ZIP/City Cross Reference, find the city name, then look up the city name in the City/County Cross Reference. For example, you want to know the county for an address of Menands, NY 12204. There is no "Menands" in the City/County Cross Reference. The ZIP/City Cross Reference shows that ZIP Codes 12201-12288 are for the city of Albany. Looking back in the City/County Cross Reference, Albany is in Albany County.

City/County Cross Reference

ADA Norman
ADAMS Mower
ADOLPH St. Louis
ADRIAN Nobles
AFTON Washington
AH GWAH CHING Cass
AITKIN (56431) Aitkin(96), Crow Wing(4)
AKELEY (56433) Hubbard(51), Cass(49)
ALBANY (56307) Stearns(99), Morrison(2)
ALBERT LEA Freeborn
ALBERTA (56207) Stevens(96), Swift(4)
ALBERTVILLE Wright
ALBORN St. Louis
ALDEN (56009) Freeborn(98), Faribault(2)
ALDRICH Wadena
ALEXANDRIA Douglas
ALMELUND Chisago
ALPHA Jackson
ALTURA (55910) Winona(82), Wabasha(18)
ALVARADO (56710) Marshall(86), Polk(14)
AMBOY (56010) Blue Earth(96), Faribault(3), Martin(1)
AMIRET Lyon
ANGLE INLET Lake of the Woods
ANGORA St. Louis
ANGUS Polk
ANNANDALE Wright
ANOKA Anoka
APPLETON (56208) Swift(95), Lac qui Parle(3), Big Stone(1)
ARCO Lincoln
ARGYLE Marshall
ARLINGTON Sibley
ASHBY (56309) Grant(61), Otter Tail(30), Douglas(9)
ASKOV Pine
ATWATER (56209) Kandiyohi(83), Meeker(17)
AUDUBON Becker
AURORA St. Louis
AUSTIN (55912) Mower(98), Freeborn(2)
AVOCA Murray
AVON Stearns
BABBITT St. Louis
BACKUS (56435) Cass(97), Crow Wing(2)
BADGER Roseau
BAGLEY (56621) Clearwater(98), Polk(2)
BAKER Clay
BALATON (56115) Murray(53), Lyon(47)
BANGOR Pope
BARNESVILLE (56514) Clay(89), Wilkin(10)
BARNUM Carlton
BARRETT Grant
BARRY Big Stone
BATTLE LAKE Otter Tail
BAUDETTE (56623) Lake of the Woods(61), Koochiching(39)
BAXTER Crow Wing
BAYPORT Washington

BEARDSLEY (56211) Big Stone(66), Traverse(35)
BEAVER BAY Lake
BEAVER CREEK Rock
BECIDA Hubbard
BECKER Sherburne
BEJOU (56516) Mahnomen(74), Norman(26)
BELGRADE (56312) Stearns(67), Kandiyohi(33)
BELLE PLAINE (56011) Scott(89), Sibley(5), Carver(3), Le Sueur(3)
BELLINGHAM Lac qui Parle
BELTRAMI (56517) Polk(97), Norman(3)
BELVIEW (56214) Redwood(93), Yellow Medicine(7)
BEMIDJI (56601) Beltrami(98), Hubbard(2)
BEMIDJI Beltrami
BENA Cass
BENEDICT Hubbard
BENSON (56215) Swift(97), Pope(3)
BEROUN Pine
BERTHA (56437) Todd(90), Otter Tail(10)
BETHEL (55005) Anoka(96), Isanti(4)
BIG FALLS Koochiching
BIG LAKE Sherburne
BIGELOW (56117) Nobles(55), Sibley(45)
BIGFORK Itasca
BINGHAM LAKE (56118) Cottonwood(93), Jackson(8)
BIRCHDALE Koochiching
BIRD ISLAND Renville
BIWABIK St. Louis
BLACKDUCK (56630) Beltrami(84), Itasca(16)
BLOMKEST Kandiyohi
BLOOMING PRAIRIE (55917) Steele(83), Dodge(12), Mower(4)
BLUE EARTH (56013) Faribault(99), Martin(1)
BLUFFTON Otter Tail
BOCK Mille Lacs
BORUP (56519) Norman(63), Clay(38)
BOVEY Itasca
BOWLUS (56314) Morrison(97), Stearns(4)
BOWSTRING Itasca
BOY RIVER Cass
BOYD (56218) Lac qui Parle(59), Yellow Medicine(41)
BRAHAM (55006) Isanti(43), Kanabec(39), Pine(13), Chisago(6)
BRAINERD (56401) Crow Wing(96), Cass(4)
BRANDON (56315) Douglas(92), Otter Tail(8)
BRECKENRIDGE Wilkin
BREWSTER (56119) Nobles(67), Jackson(33)
BRICELYN Faribault
BRIMSON (55602) St. Louis(88), Lake(12)
BRITT St. Louis

BROOK PARK (55007) Pine(69), Kanabec(31)
BROOKS (56715) Red Lake(96), Polk(4)
BROOKSTON St. Louis
BROOTEN (56316) Pope(48), Stearns(39), Kandiyohi(12)
BROWERVILLE Todd
BROWNS VALLEY (56219) Traverse(62), Olmsted(37), Big Stone(1)
BROWNSDALE Mower
BROWNSVILLE Houston
BROWNTON McLeod
BRUNO Pine
BUCKMAN Morrison
BUFFALO Wright
BUFFALO LAKE (55314) Renville(85), Sibley(15)
BUHL St. Louis
BURNSVILLE Dakota
BURTRUM (56318) Todd(51), Morrison(49)
BUTTERFIELD Watonwan
BYRON Olmsted
CALEDONIA Houston
CALLAWAY Becker
CALUMET Itasca
CAMBRIDGE Isanti
CAMPBELL (56522) Wilkin(85), Otter Tail(12), Grant(3)
CANBY (56220) Yellow Medicine(85), Lac qui Parle(9), Lincoln(6)
CANNON FALLS (55009) Goodhue(92), Dakota(8)
CANTON Fillmore
CANYON St. Louis
CARLOS (56319) Douglas(87), Todd(13)
CARLTON Carlton
CARVER Carver
CASS LAKE (56633) Cass(72), Hubbard(14), Beltrami(14)
CASTLE ROCK Dakota
CEDAR Anoka
CENTER CITY Chisago
CEYLON Martin
CHAMPLIN Hennepin
CHANDLER (56122) Murray(97), Nobles(3)
CHANHASSEN Carver
CHASKA Carver
CHATFIELD (55923) Fillmore(52), Olmsted(48)
CHISAGO CITY Chisago
CHISHOLM St. Louis
CHOKIO (56221) Stevens(90), Big Stone(8), Traverse(2)
CIRCLE PINES Anoka
CLARA CITY Chippewa
CLAREMONT (55924) Dodge(57), Steele(43)
CLARISSA Todd
CLARKFIELD Yellow Medicine
CLARKS GROVE Freeborn
CLEAR LAKE Sherburne

CLEARBROOK (56634) Clearwater(55), Polk(45)
CLEARWATER (55320) Wright(83), Stearns(17)
CLEMENTS Redwood
CLEVELAND Le Sueur
CLIMAX Polk
CLINTON Big Stone
CLITHERALL Otter Tail
CLONTARF (56226) Swift(65), Pope(36)
CLOQUET (55720) Carlton(92), St. Louis(8)
COHASSET Itasca
COKATO Wright
COLD SPRING Stearns
COLERAINE Itasca
COLLEGEVILLE Stearns
COLOGNE Carver
COMFREY (56019) Brown(73), Cottonwood(25), Watonwan(3)
COMSTOCK Clay
CONGER Freeborn
COOK (55723) St. Louis(95), Itasca(5)
COOK (55788) Itasca(78), St. Louis(22)
CORRELL Big Stone
COSMOS (56228) Meeker(98), Renville(3)
COTTAGE GROVE Washington
COTTON St. Louis
COTTONWOOD (56229) Lyon(87), Yellow Medicine(14)
COURTLAND Nicollet
CRANE LAKE St. Louis
CROMWELL Carlton
CROOKSTON Polk
CROSBY Crow Wing
CROSSLAKE Crow Wing
CRYSTAL BAY Hennepin
CULVER St. Louis
CURRIE Murray
CUSHING (56443) Morrison(93), Todd(7)
CYRUS (56323) Pope(91), Stevens(9)
DAKOTA Winona
DALBO Isanti
DALTON (56324) Otter Tail(97), Grant(3)
DANUBE Renville
DANVERS Swift
DARFUR Watonwan
DARWIN Meeker
DASSEL (55325) Meeker(96), Wright(4)
DAWSON Lac qui Parle
DAYTON Hennepin
DE GRAFF (56233) Swift(82), Chippewa(18)
DEBS Beltrami
DEER CREEK Otter Tail
DEER RIVER (56636) Itasca(94), Cass(6)
DEERWOOD Crow Wing
DELANO (55328) Wright(89), Hennepin(6), Carver(5)
DELAVAN Faribault
DELFT Cottonwood
DENHAM Pine

DENHAM St. Louis
DENNISON (55018) Goodhue(87), Rice(12), Dakota(1)
DENT Otter Tail
DETROIT LAKES (56501) Becker(97), Otter Tail(3)
DETROIT LAKES Becker
DEXTER Mower
DILWORTH Clay
DODGE CENTER Dodge
DONALDSON Kittson
DONNELLY Stevens
DOVER Olmsted
DOVRAY Murray
DULUTH (55810) St. Louis(98), Carlton(2)
DULUTH St. Louis
DUMONT (56236) Traverse(54), Big Stone(46)
DUNDAS Rice
DUNDEE (56126) Nobles(65), Cottonwood(19), Murray(12), Jackson(4)
DUNNELL (56127) Martin(83), Jackson(17)
DUQUETTE Pine
EAGLE BEND (56446) Todd(86), Douglas(8), Otter Tail(6)
EAGLE LAKE Blue Earth
EAST GRAND FORKS Polk
EASTON Faribault
ECHO Yellow Medicine
EDEN PRAIRIE Hennepin
EDEN VALLEY (55329) Stearns(64), Meeker(36)
EDGERTON (56128) Pipestone(78), Rock(9), Nobles(7), Murray(6)
EFFIE (56639) Itasca(83), Koochiching(17)
EITZEN Houston
ELBOW LAKE Grant
ELGIN (55932) Olmsted(50), Wabasha(50)
ELIZABETH Otter Tail
ELK RIVER (55330) Sherburne(75), Wright(19), Anoka(6)
ELKO (55020) Scott(99), Rice(1)
ELKTON Mower
ELLENDALE (56026) Steele(69), Freeborn(18), Olmsted(12), Waseca(1)
ELLSWORTH (56129) Nobles(75), Rock(14), Lyon(11)
ELMORE (56027) Faribault(67), Olmsted(31), Martin(2)
ELROSA Stearns
ELY (55731) St. Louis(95), Lake(5)
ELYSIAN (56028) Le Sueur(84), Waseca(16)
EMBARRASS St. Louis
EMILY Crow Wing
EMMONS Freeborn
ERHARD Otter Tail
ERSKINE (56535) Polk(96), Red Lake(4)
ESKO (55733) Carlton(97), St. Louis(3)
ESSIG Brown
EUCLID Polk
EVAN (56238) Redwood(75), Brown(25)
EVANSVILLE (56326) Douglas(90), Otter Tail(8), Grant(2)
EVELETH St. Louis
EXCELSIOR (55331) Hennepin(77), Carver(23)
EYOTA Olmsted
FAIRFAX (55332) Renville(87), Nicollet(13)
FAIRMONT Martin
FARIBAULT Rice
FARMINGTON Dakota
FARWELL (56327) Douglas(58), Pope(42)
FEDERAL DAM Cass
FELTON Clay
FERGUS FALLS Otter Tail
FERTILE (56540) Polk(91), Norman(9)
FIFTY LAKES Crow Wing
FINLAND Lake
FINLAYSON (55735) Pine(79), Aitkin(21)
FISHER Polk
FLENSBURG Morrison

FLOM Norman
FLOODWOOD St. Louis
FOLEY (56329) Benton(89), Morrison(11)
FORBES St. Louis
FOREST LAKE (55025) Washington(81), Anoka(13), Chisago(6)
FORESTON (56330) Mille Lacs(85), Benton(15)
FORT RIPLEY (56449) Crow Wing(82), Morrison(18)
FOSSTON (56542) Polk(94), Mahnomen(6)
FOUNTAIN Fillmore
FOXHOME Wilkin
FRANKLIN (55333) Renville(92), Redwood(7), Brown(1)
FRAZEE (56544) Becker(85), Otter Tail(15)
FREEBORN Freeborn
FREEPORT (56331) Stearns(95), Morrison(4), Todd(1)
FRONTENAC Goodhue
FROST Faribault
FULDA (56131) Murray(96), Nobles(4)
GARDEN CITY Blue Earth
GARFIELD Douglas
GARRISON (56450) Mille Lacs(67), Crow Wing(34)
GARVIN (56132) Lyon(73), Murray(27)
GARY Norman
GATZKE Marshall
GAYLORD (55334) Sibley(94), Nicollet(6)
GENEVA Freeborn
GEORGETOWN Clay
GHENT Lyon
GIBBON (55335) Sibley(85), Nicollet(15)
GILBERT St. Louis
GILMAN Benton
GLENCOE (55336) McLeod(96), Sibley(4)
GLENVILLE Freeborn
GLENWOOD (56334) Pope(98), Douglas(2)
GLYNDON Clay
GONVICK (56644) Clearwater(96), Polk(4)
GOOD THUNDER Blue Earth
GOODHUE (55027) Goodhue(98), Wabasha(2)
GOODLAND Itasca
GOODRIDGE (56725) Pennington(74), Marshall(26)
GRACEVILLE (56240) Big Stone(80), Traverse(20)
GRANADA (56039) Martin(95), Faribault(5)
GRAND MARAIS Cook
GRAND MEADOW Mower
GRAND PORTAGE (55605) Cook(71), Lyon(29)
GRAND RAPIDS Itasca
GRANDY Isanti
GRANGER Fillmore
GRANITE FALLS (56241) Yellow Medicine(80), Chippewa(17), Renville(3)
GRASSTON (55030) Pine(89), Kanabec(11)
GREEN ISLE (55338) Sibley(86), Carver(14)
GREENBUSH Roseau
GREENWALD Stearns
GREY EAGLE (56336) Todd(96), Stearns(3), Morrison(2)
GROVE CITY Meeker
GRYGLA (56727) Beltrami(58), Marshall(42)
GULLY (56646) Polk(89), Clearwater(11)
HACKENSACK Cass
HADLEY Murray
HALLOCK Kittson
HALMA Kittson
HALSTAD Norman
HAMBURG (55339) Carver(79), Sibley(21)
HAMEL Hennepin
HAMMOND Wabasha
HAMPTON Dakota

HANCOCK (56244) Stevens(67), Pope(28), Swift(5)
HANLEY FALLS Yellow Medicine
HANOVER (55341) Wright(98), Hennepin(2)
HANSKA (56041) Brown(94), Watonwan(3), Blue Earth(3)
HARDWICK Rock
HARMONY Fillmore
HARRIS (55032) Chisago(99), Isanti(1)
HARTLAND (56042) Freeborn(85), Waseca(12), Steele(3)
HASTINGS (55033) Dakota(93), Washington(7)
HAWICK Kandiyohi
HAWLEY Clay
HAYFIELD (55940) Dodge(80), Olmsted(18), Mower(1)
HAYWARD Freeborn
HAZEL RUN Yellow Medicine
HECTOR (55342) Renville(92), Sibley(5), Kandiyohi(2), Meeker(1)
HENDERSON (56044) Sibley(94), Scott(7)
HENDRICKS (56136) Lincoln(70), Dodge(30)
HENDRUM Norman
HENNING Otter Tail
HENRIETTE Pine
HERMAN (56248) Grant(81), Stevens(11), Traverse(7)
HERON LAKE (56137) Jackson(46), Nobles(33), Cottonwood(21)
HEWITT (56453) Todd(71), Otter Tail(29)
HIBBING (55746) St. Louis(96), Itasca(4)
HIBBING St. Louis
HILL CITY (55748) Aitkin(86), Itasca(14)
HILLMAN (56338) Morrison(95), Crow Wing(5)
HILLS (56138) Rock(95), Lyon(4), Mower(1)
HINCKLEY (55037) Pine(95), Kanabec(5)
HINES Beltrami
HITTERDAL (56552) Clay(81), Becker(19)
HOFFMAN (56339) Grant(80), Douglas(20)
HOKAH Houston
HOLDINGFORD (56340) Stearns(82), Morrison(18)
HOLLAND Pipestone
HOLLANDALE Freeborn
HOLLOWAY Swift
HOLMES CITY Douglas
HOLYOKE (55749) Carlton(98), Pine(2)
HOMER (55942) Winona(86), Olmsted(14)
HOPE Steele
HOPKINS Hennepin
HOUSTON (55943) Houston(84), Winona(15)
HOVLAND Cook
HOWARD LAKE Hennepin
HOWARD LAKE Wright
HOYT LAKES St. Louis
HUGO (55038) Washington(64), Anoka(36)
HUMBOLDT Kittson
HUNTLEY Faribault
HUTCHINSON (55350) McLeod(96), Meeker(4)
IHLEN Pipestone
INTERNATIONAL FALLS Koochiching
INVER GROVE HEIGHTS Dakota
IONA Murray
IRON St. Louis
IRONTON Crow Wing
ISABELLA Lake
ISANTI Isanti
ISLE (56342) Mille Lacs(59), Aitkin(21), Kanabec(20)
IVANHOE Lincoln
JACKSON Jackson
JACOBSON (55752) Aitkin(90), Itasca(10)
JANESVILLE Waseca
JASPER (56144) Rock(48), Pipestone(40), Murray(10), Mower(2)

JEFFERS Cottonwood
JENKINS Crow Wing
JOHNSON (56250) Big Stone(71), Traverse(29)
JORDAN Scott
KANARANZI (56146) Nobles(95), Rock(5)
KANDIYOHI Kandiyohi
KARLSTAD (56732) Kittson(91), Marshall(6), Roseau(3)
KASOTA Le Sueur
KASSON (55944) Dodge(96), Olmsted(4)
KEEWATIN Itasca
KELLIHER Beltrami
KELLOGG Wabasha
KELSEY St. Louis
KENNEDY Kittson
KENNETH (56147) Rock(93), Nobles(7)
KENSINGTON (56343) Douglas(80), Pope(16), Stevens(4)
KENT Wilkin
KENYON (55946) Goodhue(84), Rice(13), Steele(2), Dodge(1)
KERKHOVEN (56252) Kandiyohi(56), Swift(33), Chippewa(11)
KERRICK (55756) Pine(96), Carlton(4)
KETTLE RIVER Carlton
KIESTER (56051) Faribault(99), Freeborn(2)
KILKENNY (56052) Le Sueur(60), Rice(40)
KIMBALL (55353) Stearns(77), Meeker(23)
KINNEY St. Louis
KLOSSNER Nicollet
KNIFE RIVER Lake
LA CRESCENT (55947) Houston(90), Winona(10)
LA SALLE Watonwan
LAFAYETTE (56054) Nicollet(86), Sibley(14)
LAKE BENTON (56149) Lincoln(95), Pipestone(5)
LAKE BRONSON Kittson
LAKE CITY (55041) Wabasha(80), Goodhue(20)
LAKE CRYSTAL Blue Earth
LAKE ELMO Washington
LAKE GEORGE Hubbard
LAKE HUBERT Crow Wing
LAKE ITASCA Clearwater
LAKE LILLIAN Kandiyohi
LAKE PARK (56554) Becker(94), Clay(6)
LAKE WILSON Murray
LAKEFIELD Jackson
LAKELAND Washington
LAKEVILLE (55044) Dakota(86), Scott(14)
LAMBERTON (56152) Redwood(88), Cottonwood(12)
LANCASTER (56735) Kittson(98), Roseau(3)
LANESBORO Fillmore
LANSING Mower
LAPORTE Hubbard
LASTRUP Morrison
LE CENTER Le Sueur
LE ROY (55951) Mower(64), Marshall(15), (12), Fillmore(9)
LE SUEUR (56058) Le Sueur(91), Sibley(7), Nicollet(2)
LENGBY (56651) Mahnomen(60), Polk(40)
LEONARD (56652) Clearwater(97), Beltrami(3)
LEOTA Nobles
LESTER PRAIRIE McLeod
LEWISTON Winona
LEWISVILLE (56060) Watonwan(93), Blue Earth(8)
LINDSTROM Chisago
LISMORE Nobles
LITCHFIELD Meeker
LITTLE FALLS Morrison
LITTLEFORK Koochiching
LOMAN Koochiching
LONDON Freeborn

LONG LAKE Hennepin
LONG PRAIRIE (56347) Todd(98), Morrison(2)
LONG PRAIRIE Todd
LONGVILLE Cass
LONSDALE Rice
LORETTO Hennepin
LOUISBURG Lac qui Parle
LOWRY (56349) Pope(77), Douglas(23)
LUCAN Redwood
LUTSEN Cook
LUVERNE Rock
LYLE (55953) Mower(64), Rice(32), Freeborn(4)
LYND Lyon
MABEL (55954) Fillmore(96), Houston(4)
MADELIA (56062) Watonwan(91), Blue Earth(8), Brown(2)
MADISON Lac qui Parle
MADISON LAKE (56063) Blue Earth(57), Le Sueur(29), Waseca(14)
MAGNOLIA (56158) Rock(94), Nobles(6)
MAHNOMEN (56557) Mahnomen(96), Norman(3), Clearwater(2)
MAHTOWA Carlton
MAKINEN St. Louis
MANCHESTER Freeborn
MANHATTAN BEACH Crow Wing
MANKATO Blue Earth
MANKATO Nicollet
MANTORVILLE Dodge
MAPLE LAKE Wright
MAPLE PLAIN Hennepin
MAPLE PLAIN Wright
MAPLETON (56065) Blue Earth(93), Faribault(4), Waseca(3)
MARBLE Itasca
MARCELL Itasca
MARGIE Koochiching
MARIETTA (56257) Lac qui Parle(87), Dodge(10), Grant(3)
MARINE ON SAINT CROIX Washington
MARSHALL (56258) Lyon(99), Redwood(1)
MAX Itasca
MAYER Carver
MAYNARD (56260) Chippewa(90), Renville(10)
MAZEPPA (55956) Wabasha(73), Goodhue(25), Olmsted(1)
MC GRATH Aitkin
MC KINLEY St. Louis
MCGREGOR Aitkin
MCINTOSH Polk
MEADOWLANDS St. Louis
MEDFORD (55049) Steele(92), Rice(8)
MELROSE Stearns
MELRUDE St. Louis
MENAHGA (56464) Wadena(55), Becker(28), Hubbard(15), Otter Tail(3)
MENDOTA Dakota
MENTOR (56736) Polk(87), Red Lake(13)
MERIDEN (56067) Waseca(69), Steele(31)
MERRIFIELD Crow Wing
MIDDLE RIVER Marshall
MILACA (56353) Mille Lacs(97), Isanti(3)
MILAN (56262) Chippewa(90), Swift(10)
MILLVILLE Wabasha
MILROY (56263) Redwood(89), Lyon(11)
MILTONA (56354) Douglas(99), Todd(1)
MINNEAPOLIS (55421) Anoka(87), Ramsey(11), Hennepin(1)
MINNEAPOLIS (55449) Anoka(93), Ramsey(4), Hennepin(3)
MINNEAPOLIS Anoka
MINNEAPOLIS Carver
MINNEAPOLIS Hennepin
MINNEOTA (56264) Lyon(99), Yellow Medicine(1)
MINNESOTA CITY Winona
MINNESOTA LAKE (56068) Faribault(44), Waseca(41), Blue Earth(15)
MINNETONKA Hennepin

MINNETONKA BEACH Hennepin
MIZPAH Koochiching
MONTEVIDEO (56265) Chippewa(93), Lac qui Parle(5), Yellow Medicine(2)
MONTGOMERY (56069) Le Sueur(69), Rice(31)
MONTICELLO Carver
MONTICELLO Wright
MONTROSE (55363) Wright(97), Carver(3)
MOORHEAD Clay
MOOSE LAKE (55767) Carlton(94), Pine(6)
MORA Kanabec
MORGAN (56266) Redwood(88), Brown(12)
MORRIS Stevens
MORRISTOWN (55052) Rice(91), Waseca(8), Steele(2)
MORTON (56270) Renville(61), Redwood(39)
MOTLEY (56466) Morrison(76), Cass(19), Todd(5)
MOUND Hennepin
MOUNTAIN IRON St. Louis
MOUNTAIN LAKE (56159) Cottonwood(96), Jackson(3)
MURDOCK (56271) Swift(83), Chippewa(17)
MYRTLE Freeborn
NASHUA (56565) Wilkin(82), Grant(19)
NASHWAUK Itasca
NASSAU Lac qui Parle
NAVARRE Hennepin
NAYTAHWAUSH Mahnomen
NELSON Douglas
NERSTRAND (55053) Rice(80), Goodhue(20)
NETT LAKE St. Louis
NEVIS Hubbard
NEW AUBURN Sibley
NEW GERMANY (55367) Carver(98), McLeod(2)
NEW LONDON Kandiyohi
NEW MARKET Scott
NEW MUNICH Stearns
NEW PRAGUE (56071) Scott(59), Le Sueur(38), Rice(4)
NEW RICHLAND (56072) Waseca(94), Steele(4), Freeborn(2)
NEW ULM (56073) Brown(94), Nicollet(5), Blue Earth(1)
NEW YORK MILLS Otter Tail
NEWFOLDEN Marshall
NEWPORT Washington
NICOLLET Nicollet
NIELSVILLE (56568) Polk(85), Norman(15)
NIMROD Wadena
NISSWA (56468) Crow Wing(73), Cass(27)
NORCROSS (56274) Grant(69), Traverse(32)
NORTH BRANCH (55056) Chisago(74), Isanti(26)
NORTHFIELD (55057) Rice(83), Dakota(17)
NORTHHOME (56661) Koochiching(72), Itasca(22), Beltrami(6)
NORTHROP Martin
NORWOOD (55368) Carver(96), McLeod(2), Hennepin(2)
NORWOOD Carver
NOYES Kittson
OAK ISLAND Lake of the Woods
OAK PARK (56357) Benton(88), Mille Lacs(12)
OAKLAND Freeborn
ODESSA (56276) Big Stone(64), Lac qui Parle(36)
ODIN (56160) Watonwan(43), Martin(37), Jackson(20)
OGEMA Becker
OGILVIE (56358) Kanabec(81), Mille Lacs(19), Isanti(1)
OKABENA Jackson

OKLEE (56742) Red Lake(65), Pennington(33), Polk(2)
OLIVIA Renville
ONAMIA Mille Lacs
ORMSBY (56162) Martin(65), Watonwan(36)
ORONOCO Olmsted
ORR (55771) St. Louis(91), Koochiching(9)
ORTONVILLE Big Stone
OSAGE Becker
OSAKIS (56360) Douglas(54), Todd(46)
OSLO (56744) Marshall(84), Polk(16)
OSSEO Hennepin
OSTRANDER (55961) Mower(60), Fillmore(40)
OTISCO Waseca
OTTERTAIL Otter Tail
OUTING Cass
OWATONNA Steele
PALISADE Aitkin
PARK RAPIDS (56470) Hubbard(95), Becker(5)
PARKERS PRAIRIE (56361) Otter Tail(77), Douglas(23)
PARKVILLE St. Louis
PAYNESVILLE (56362) Stearns(88), Meeker(9), Kandiyohi(3)
PEASE Mille Lacs
PELICAN RAPIDS (56572) Otter Tail(97), Becker(3)
PEMBERTON (56078) Waseca(68), Blue Earth(33)
PENGILLY Itasca
PENNINGTON Beltrami
PENNOCK Kandiyohi
PEQUOT LAKES (56472) Crow Wing(85), Cass(15)
PERHAM Otter Tail
PERLEY (56574) Norman(98), Clay(2)
PETERSON (55962) Fillmore(95), Winona(6)
PIERZ (56364) Morrison(97), Crow Wing(3)
PILLAGER Cass
PINE CITY Pine
PINE ISLAND (55963) Goodhue(55), Olmsted(37), Dodge(9)
PINE RIVER (56474) Cass(81), Crow Wing(19)
PIPESTONE (56164) Pipestone(94), Murray(6)
PITT Lake of the Woods
PLAINVIEW (55964) Wabasha(96), Olmsted(2), Winona(2)
PLATO McLeod
PLUMMER (56748) Red Lake(83), Pennington(17)
PONEMAH Beltrami
PONSFORD Becker
PORTER (56280) Yellow Medicine(67), Lincoln(33)
PRESTON Fillmore
PRINCETON (55371) Mille Lacs(66), Sherburne(16), Isanti(13), Benton(5)
PRINSBURG Kandiyohi
PRIOR LAKE Scott
PUPOSKY Beltrami
RACINE (55967) Mower(98), Fillmore(2)
RANDALL Morrison
RANDOLPH (55065) Dakota(96), Goodhue(4)
RANIER Koochiching
RAY (56669) Koochiching(66), St. Louis(34)
RAYMOND (56282) Kandiyohi(80), Chippewa(20)
READING Nobles
READS LANDING Wabasha
RED LAKE FALLS (56750) Red Lake(93), Polk(4), Pennington(3)
RED WING Goodhue
REDBY Beltrami
REDLAKE Beltrami

REDWOOD FALLS (56283) Redwood(97), Renville(3)
REMER Cass
RENVILLE (56284) Renville(72), Kandiyohi(22), Redwood(6)
REVERE (56166) Redwood(74), Cottonwood(26)
RICE (56367) Benton(81), Stearns(19)
RICHMOND Stearns
RICHVILLE Otter Tail
RICHWOOD Becker
ROCHERT Becker
ROCHESTER Olmsted
ROCK CREEK Pine
ROCKFORD (55373) Wright(63), Hennepin(37)
ROCKVILLE Stearns
ROGERS (55374) Hennepin(70), Wright(30)
ROLLINGSTONE Winona
ROOSEVELT (56673) Lake of the Woods(60), Roseau(40)
ROSCOE Stearns
ROSE CREEK Mower
ROSEAU Roseau
ROSEMOUNT Dakota
ROTHSAY (56579) Wilkin(78), Otter Tail(22)
ROUND LAKE (56167) Nobles(63), Jackson(36), Sibley(1)
ROYALTON (56373) Morrison(91), Benton(10)
RUSH CITY (55069) Chisago(94), Pine(6)
RUSHFORD (55971) Fillmore(81), Winona(12), Houston(7)
RUSHMORE Nobles
RUSSELL (56169) Lyon(99), Wright(1)
RUTHTON (56170) Pipestone(65), Murray(28), Lyon(6), Lincoln(2)
RUTLEDGE Pine
SABIN Clay
SACRED HEART (56285) Renville(98), Chippewa(2)
SAGINAW St. Louis
SAINT BONIFACIUS Hennepin
SAINT CHARLES (55972) Winona(86), Olmsted(15)
SAINT CLAIR Blue Earth
SAINT CLOUD (56304) Sherburne(51), Benton(49)
SAINT CLOUD Stearns
SAINT FRANCIS (55070) Anoka(88), Isanti(12)
SAINT HILAIRE (56754) Pennington(92), Red Lake(8)
SAINT JAMES (99999) Watonwan(99), Brown(1)
SAINT JOSEPH Stearns
SAINT LEO Yellow Medicine
SAINT MARTIN Stearns
SAINT MICHAEL Wright
SAINT PAUL (55110) Ramsey(84), Washington(15), Anoka(1)
SAINT PAUL (55118) Dakota(99), Ramsey(1)
SAINT PAUL (55125) Washington(98), Dakota(2)
SAINT PAUL (55126) Ramsey(99), Anoka(1)
SAINT PAUL Dakota
SAINT PAUL Hennepin
SAINT PAUL Ramsey
SAINT PAUL Washington
SAINT PAUL PARK Washington
SAINT PETER (56082) Nicollet(96), Le Sueur(4)
SAINT STEPHEN Stearns
SAINT VINCENT Kittson
SALOL Roseau
SANBORN (56083) Redwood(78), Cottonwood(15), Brown(8)

SANDSTONE (55072) Pine(87), Kanabec(12), Aitkin(1)
SANTIAGO Sherburne
SARGEANT (55973) Mower(94), Dodge(6)
SARTELL (56377) Stearns(68), Benton(32)
SAUK CENTRE (56378) Stearns(86), Todd(14)
SAUK RAPIDS (56379) Benton(98), Stearns(2)
SAUM Beltrami
SAVAGE Scott
SAWYER Carlton
SCANDIA (55073) Washington(67), Chisago(33)
SCHROEDER Cook
SEAFORTH Redwood
SEARLES Brown
SEBEKA (56477) Wadena(73), Otter Tail(23), Cass(4)
SHAFER Chisago
SHAKOPEE Scott
SHELLY Norman
SHERBURN Martin
SHEVLIN (56676) Clearwater(52), Beltrami(48)
SIDE LAKE St. Louis
SILVER BAY Lake
SILVER CREEK Wright
SILVER LAKE (55381) McLeod(98), Martin(1)
SLAYTON Murray
SLEEPY EYE (56085) Brown(96), Redwood(4)
SOLWAY (56678) Beltrami(97), Clearwater(3)
SOUDAN St. Louis
SOUTH HAVEN (55382) Wright(53), Stearns(37), Meeker(9)
SOUTH INTERNATIONAL FALLS Koochiching
SOUTH SAINT PAUL Dakota
SPICER Kandiyohi
SPRING GROVE (55974) Houston(95), Fillmore(3), Becker(2)
SPRING LAKE Itasca
SPRING PARK Hennepin
SPRING VALLEY (55975) Fillmore(95), Mower(5)
SPRINGFIELD (56087) Brown(87), Redwood(13)
SQUAW LAKE Itasca
STACY (55079) Chisago(46), Anoka(32), Isanti(22)
STACY Washington
STANCHFIELD (55080) Isanti(64), Chisago(36)

STAPLES (56479) Todd(71), Wadena(23), Cass(6)
STARBUCK Pope
STEEN (56173) Rock(77), Lyon(23)
STEPHEN (56757) Marshall(98), Kittson(2)
STEWART (55385) McLeod(75), Renville(19), Sibley(6)
STEWARTVILLE (55976) Olmsted(98), Fillmore(1)
STILLWATER Washington
STOCKTON (55988) Winona(91), Olmsted(9)
STORDEN Cottonwood
STRANDQUIST Marshall
STRATHCONA (56759) Roseau(72), Marshall(28)
STURGEON LAKE (55783) Pine(90), Carlton(8), Aitkin(2)
SUNBURG (56289) Kandiyohi(74), Swift(24), Pope(2)
SWAN RIVER Itasca
SWANVILLE (56382) Morrison(82), Todd(18)
SWATARA Aitkin
SWIFT Roseau
TACONITE Itasca
TALMOON Itasca
TAMARACK (55787) Aitkin(53), Carlton(47)
TAOPI Mower
TAUNTON (56291) Lyon(62), Yellow Medicine(26), Lincoln(12)
TAYLORS FALLS Chisago
TENSTRIKE Beltrami
THEILMAN Wabasha
THIEF RIVER FALLS (56701) Pennington(96), Marshall(4)
TINTAH (56583) Traverse(72), Wilkin(28)
TOFTE Cook
TOWER St. Louis
TRACY (56175) Lyon(80), Redwood(12), Murray(8)
TRAIL (56684) Polk(48), Pennington(41), Red Lake(11)
TRIMONT Martin
TROSKY Pipestone
TRUMAN (56088) Martin(73), Watonwan(20), Blue Earth(8)
TWIG St. Louis
TWIN LAKES Freeborn
TWIN VALLEY (56584) Norman(99), Clay(1)
TWO HARBORS (55616) Lake(99), St. Louis(1)
TYLER (56178) Lincoln(91), Lyon(9)
ULEN (56585) Clay(75), Becker(23), Norman(2)

UNDERWOOD Otter Tail
UPSALA Morrison
UTICA (55979) Winona(96), Fillmore(4)
VERDI (56179) Lincoln(92), Pipestone(8)
VERGAS Otter Tail
VERMILLION Dakota
VERNDALE (56481) Wadena(79), Todd(18), Cass(3)
VERNON CENTER Blue Earth
VESTA (56292) Redwood(97), Yellow Medicine(3)
VICTORIA Carver
VIKING (56760) Marshall(98), Pennington(3)
VILLARD (56385) Pope(85), Stearns(8), Douglas(8)
VINING Otter Tail
VIRGINIA St. Louis
WABASHA Wabasha
WABASSO Redwood
WACONIA (55387) Carver(98), Hennepin(2)
WADENA (56482) Wadena(88), Otter Tail(12)
WAHKON Mille Lacs
WAITE PARK Stearns
WALDORF Waseca
WALKER (56484) Cass(97), Hubbard(3)
WALNUT GROVE (56180) Redwood(78), Murray(15), Cottonwood(7)
WALTERS (56092) Faribault(93), Freeborn(7)
WALTHAM (55982) Mower(98), Dodge(2)
WANAMINGO Goodhue
WANDA Redwood
WANNASKA Roseau
WARBA Itasca
WARREN (56762) Marshall(91), Polk(9)
WARROAD Roseau
WARSAW Rice
WASECA (56093) Waseca(94), Steele(5)
WASKISH Beltrami
WATERTOWN (55388) Carver(74), Wright(24), Hennepin(2)
WATERVILLE (56096) Le Sueur(88), Waseca(7), Rice(6)
WATKINS (55389) Meeker(78), Stearns(22)
WATSON Chippewa
WAUBUN (56589) Mahnomen(74), Becker(26)
WAVERLY Wright
WAWINA Itasca
WAYZATA Hennepin
WEBSTER (55088) Rice(67), Scott(32), Dakota(1)

WELCH (55089) Goodhue(92), Dakota(8)
WELCOME Martin
WELLS (56097) Faribault(94), Waseca(3), Freeborn(3)
WENDELL (56590) Grant(99), Otter Tail(2)
WEST CONCORD (55985) Dodge(88), Goodhue(8), Steele(4)
WEST UNION Todd
WESTBROOK (56183) Cottonwood(90), Murray(10)
WHALAN Fillmore
WHEATON Traverse
WHIPHOLT Cass
WHITE EARTH Becker
WILLERNIE Washington
WILLIAMS Lake of the Woods
WILLMAR Kandiyohi
WILLOW RIVER Pine
WILMONT Nobles
WILTON Beltrami
WINDOM (56101) Cottonwood(91), Jackson(9)
WINGER (56592) Polk(94), Mahnomen(6)
WINNEBAGO (56098) Faribault(94), Martin(6)
WINONA Winona
WINSTED (55395) McLeod(91), Carver(7), Wright(2)
WINTHROP (55396) Sibley(98), McLeod(1)
WINTON St. Louis
WIRT Itasca
WOLF LAKE Becker
WOLVERTON Wilkin
WOOD LAKE (56297) Yellow Medicine(92), Redwood(6), Lyon(2)
WOODSTOCK (56186) Murray(54), Pipestone(46)
WORTHINGTON (56187) Nobles(99), Jackson(1)
WRENSHALL (55797) Carlton(93), Pine(7)
WRIGHT Carlton
WYKOFF Fillmore
WYOMING (55092) Chisago(54), Anoka(46)
YOUNG AMERICA Carver
YOUNG AMERICA Hennepin
ZIM St. Louis
ZIMMERMAN (55398) Sherburne(90), Isanti(10)
ZUMBRO FALLS (55991) Wabasha(90), Olmsted(10)
ZUMBROTA Goodhue

ZIP/City Cross Reference

55001-55001	AFTON	55027-55027	GOODHUE	55054-55054	NEW MARKET	55085-55085	VERMILLION
55002-55002	ALMELUND	55029-55029	GRANDY	55055-55055	NEWPORT	55087-55087	WARSAW
55003-55003	BAYPORT	55030-55030	GRASSTON	55056-55056	NORTH BRANCH	55088-55088	WEBSTER
55005-55005	BETHEL	55031-55031	HAMPTON	55057-55057	NORTHFIELD	55089-55089	WELCH
55006-55006	BRAHAM	55032-55032	HARRIS	55060-55060	OWATONNA	55090-55090	WILLERNIE
55007-55007	BROOK PARK	55033-55033	HASTINGS	55063-55063	PINE CITY	55092-55092	WYOMING
55008-55008	CAMBRIDGE	55036-55036	HENRIETTE	55065-55065	RANDOLPH	55101-55146	SAINT PAUL
55009-55009	CANNON FALLS	55037-55037	HINCKLEY	55066-55066	RED WING	55150-55150	MENDOTA
55010-55010	CASTLE ROCK	55038-55038	HUGO	55067-55067	ROCK CREEK	55155-55191	SAINT PAUL
55011-55011	CEDAR	55040-55040	ISANTI	55068-55068	ROSEMOUNT	55301-55301	ALBERTVILLE
55012-55012	CENTER CITY	55041-55041	LAKE CITY	55069-55069	RUSH CITY	55302-55302	ANNANDALE
55013-55013	CHISAGO CITY	55042-55042	LAKE ELMO	55070-55070	SAINT FRANCIS	55303-55303	ANOKA
55014-55014	CIRCLE PINES	55043-55043	LAKELAND	55071-55071	SAINT PAUL PARK	55305-55305	HOPKINS
55016-55016	COTTAGE GROVE	55044-55044	LAKEVILLE	55072-55072	SANDSTONE	55306-55306	BURNSVILLE
55017-55017	DALBO	55045-55045	LINDSTROM	55073-55073	SCANDIA	55307-55307	ARLINGTON
55018-55018	DENNISON	55046-55046	LONSDALE	55074-55074	SHAFER	55308-55308	BECKER
55019-55019	DUNDAS	55047-55047	MARINE ON SAINT	55075-55075	SOUTH SAINT PAUL	55309-55309	BIG LAKE
55020-55020	ELKO		CROIX	55076-55077	INVER GROVE HEIGHTS	55310-55310	BIRD ISLAND
55021-55021	FARIBAULT	55049-55049	MEDFORD	55078-55079	STACY	55311-55311	OSSEO
55024-55024	FARMINGTON	55051-55051	MORA	55080-55080	STANCHFIELD	55312-55312	BROWNTON
55025-55025	FOREST LAKE	55052-55052	MORRISTOWN	55082-55083	STILLWATER	55313-55313	BUFFALO
55026-55026	FRONTENAC	55053-55053	NERSTRAND	55084-55084	TAYLORS FALLS	55314-55314	BUFFALO LAKE

Zip	City	Zip	City	Zip	City	Zip	City
55315-55315	CARVER	55401-55488	MINNEAPOLIS	55765-55765	MEADOWLANDS	55975-55975	SPRING VALLEY
55316-55316	CHAMPLIN	55550-55560	YOUNG AMERICA	55766-55766	MELRUDE	55976-55976	STEWARTVILLE
55317-55317	CHANHASSEN	55561-55561	MONTICELLO	55767-55767	MOOSE LAKE	55977-55977	TAOPI
55318-55318	CHASKA	55562-55562	YOUNG AMERICA	55768-55768	MOUNTAIN IRON	55979-55979	UTICA
55319-55319	CLEAR LAKE	55563-55563	MONTICELLO	55769-55769	NASHWAUK	55981-55981	WABASHA
55320-55320	CLEARWATER	55564-55564	YOUNG AMERICA	55771-55771	ORR	55982-55982	WALTHAM
55321-55321	COKATO	55565-55565	MONTICELLO	55772-55772	NETT LAKE	55983-55983	WANAMINGO
55322-55322	COLOGNE	55566-55568	YOUNG AMERICA	55775-55775	PENGILLY	55985-55985	WEST CONCORD
55323-55323	CRYSTAL BAY	55569-55569	OSSEO	55777-55777	VIRGINIA	55987-55987	WINONA
55324-55324	DARWIN	55570-55572	MAPLE PLAIN	55779-55779	SAGINAW	55988-55988	STOCKTON
55325-55325	DASSEL	55573-55573	YOUNG AMERICA	55780-55780	SAWYER	55990-55990	WYKOFF
55327-55327	DAYTON	55574-55574	MAPLE PLAIN	55781-55781	SIDE LAKE	55991-55991	ZUMBRO FALLS
55328-55328	DELANO	55575-55575	HOWARD LAKE	55782-55782	SOUDAN	55992-55992	ZUMBROTA
55329-55329	EDEN VALLEY	55576-55579	MAPLE PLAIN	55783-55783	STURGEON LAKE	56001-56006	MANKATO
55330-55330	ELK RIVER	55580-55582	MONTICELLO	55784-55784	SWAN RIVER	56007-56007	ALBERT LEA
55331-55331	EXCELSIOR	55583-55583	NORWOOD	55785-55785	SWATARA	56009-56009	ALDEN
55332-55332	FAIRFAX	55584-55591	MONTICELLO	55786-55786	TACONITE	56010-56010	AMBOY
55333-55333	FRANKLIN	55592-55593	MAPLE PLAIN	55787-55787	TAMARACK	56011-56011	BELLE PLAINE
55334-55334	GAYLORD	55594-55594	YOUNG AMERICA	55790-55790	TOWER	56013-56013	BLUE EARTH
55335-55335	GIBBON	55595-55599	LORETTO	55791-55791	TWIG	56014-56014	BRICELYN
55336-55336	GLENCOE	55601-55601	BEAVER BAY	55792-55792	VIRGINIA	56016-56016	CLARKS GROVE
55337-55337	BURNSVILLE	55602-55602	BRIMSON	55793-55793	WARBA	56017-56017	CLEVELAND
55338-55338	GREEN ISLE	55603-55603	FINLAND	55795-55795	WILLOW RIVER	56019-56019	COMFREY
55339-55339	HAMBURG	55604-55604	GRAND MARAIS	55796-55796	WINTON	56020-56020	CONGER
55340-55340	HAMEL	55605-55605	GRAND PORTAGE	55797-55797	WRENSHALL	56021-56021	COURTLAND
55341-55341	HANOVER	55606-55606	HOVLAND	55798-55798	WRIGHT	56022-56022	DARFUR
55342-55342	HECTOR	55607-55607	ISABELLA	55801-55816	DULUTH	56023-56023	DELAVAN
55343-55343	HOPKINS	55609-55609	KNIFE RIVER	55901-55906	ROCHESTER	56024-56024	EAGLE LAKE
55344-55344	EDEN PRAIRIE	55612-55612	LUTSEN	55909-55909	ADAMS	56025-56025	EASTON
55345-55345	MINNETONKA	55613-55613	SCHROEDER	55910-55910	ALTURA	56026-56026	ELLENDALE
55346-55347	EDEN PRAIRIE	55614-55614	SILVER BAY	55912-55912	AUSTIN	56027-56027	ELMORE
55348-55348	MAPLE PLAIN	55615-55615	TOFTE	55917-55917	BLOOMING PRAIRIE	56028-56028	ELYSIAN
55349-55349	HOWARD LAKE	55616-55616	TWO HARBORS	55918-55918	BROWNSDALE	56029-56029	EMMONS
55350-55350	HUTCHINSON	55701-55701	ADOLPH	55919-55919	BROWNSVILLE	56030-56030	ESSIG
55352-55352	JORDAN	55702-55702	ALBORN	55920-55920	BYRON	56031-56031	FAIRMONT
55353-55353	KIMBALL	55703-55703	ANGORA	55921-55921	CALEDONIA	56032-56032	FREEBORN
55354-55354	LESTER PRAIRIE	55704-55704	ASKOV	55922-55922	CANTON	56033-56033	FROST
55355-55355	LITCHFIELD	55705-55705	AURORA	55923-55923	CHATFIELD	56034-56034	GARDEN CITY
55356-55356	LONG LAKE	55706-55706	BABBITT	55924-55924	CLAREMONT	56035-56035	GENEVA
55357-55357	LORETTO	55707-55707	BARNUM	55925-55925	DAKOTA	56036-56036	GLENVILLE
55358-55358	MAPLE LAKE	55708-55708	BIWABIK	55926-55926	DEXTER	56037-56037	GOOD THUNDER
55359-55359	MAPLE PLAIN	55709-55709	BOVEY	55927-55927	DODGE CENTER	56039-56039	GRANADA
55360-55360	MAYER	55710-55710	BRITT	55929-55929	DOVER	56041-56041	HANSKA
55361-55361	MINNETONKA BEACH	55711-55711	BROOKSTON	55931-55931	EITZEN	56042-56042	HARTLAND
55362-55362	MONTICELLO	55712-55712	BRUNO	55932-55932	ELGIN	56043-56043	HAYWARD
55363-55363	MONTROSE	55713-55713	BUHL	55933-55933	ELKTON	56044-56044	HENDERSON
55364-55364	MOUND	55716-55716	CALUMET	55934-55934	EYOTA	56045-56045	HOLLANDALE
55365-55365	MONTICELLO	55717-55717	CANYON	55935-55935	FOUNTAIN	56046-56046	HOPE
55366-55366	NEW AUBURN	55718-55718	CARLTON	55936-55936	GRAND MEADOW	56047-56047	HUNTLEY
55367-55367	NEW GERMANY	55719-55719	CHISHOLM	55939-55939	HARMONY	56048-56048	JANESVILLE
55368-55368	NORWOOD	55720-55720	CLOQUET	55940-55940	HAYFIELD	56050-56050	KASOTA
55369-55369	OSSEO	55721-55721	COHASSET	55941-55941	HOKAH	56051-56051	KIESTER
55370-55370	PLATO	55722-55722	COLERAINE	55942-55942	HOMER	56052-56052	KILKENNY
55371-55371	PRINCETON	55723-55723	COOK	55943-55943	HOUSTON	56054-56054	LAFAYETTE
55372-55372	PRIOR LAKE	55724-55724	COTTON	55944-55944	KASSON	56055-56055	LAKE CRYSTAL
55373-55373	ROCKFORD	55725-55725	CRANE LAKE	55945-55945	KELLOGG	56056-56056	LA SALLE
55374-55374	ROGERS	55726-55726	CROMWELL	55946-55946	KENYON	56057-56057	LE CENTER
55375-55375	SAINT BONIFACIUS	55729-55729	DUQUETTE	55947-55947	LA CRESCENT	56058-56058	LE SUEUR
55376-55376	SAINT MICHAEL	55730-55730	GRAND RAPIDS	55949-55949	LANESBORO	56060-56060	LEWISVILLE
55377-55377	SANTIAGO	55731-55731	ELY	55950-55950	LANSING	56062-56062	MADELIA
55378-55378	SAVAGE	55732-55732	EMBARRASS	55951-55951	LE ROY	56063-56063	MADISON LAKE
55379-55379	SHAKOPEE	55733-55733	ESKO	55952-55952	LEWISTON	56064-56064	MANCHESTER
55380-55380	SILVER CREEK	55734-55734	EVELETH	55953-55953	LYLE	56065-56065	MAPLETON
55381-55381	SILVER LAKE	55735-55735	FINLAYSON	55954-55954	MABEL	56068-56068	MINNESOTA LAKE
55382-55382	SOUTH HAVEN	55736-55736	FLOODWOOD	55955-55955	MANTORVILLE	56069-56069	MONTGOMERY
55383-55383	NORWOOD	55738-55738	FORBES	55956-55956	MAZEPPA	56071-56071	NEW PRAGUE
55384-55384	SPRING PARK	55741-55741	GILBERT	55957-55957	MILLVILLE	56072-56072	NEW RICHLAND
55385-55385	STEWART	55742-55742	GOODLAND	55959-55959	MINNESOTA CITY	56073-56073	NEW ULM
55386-55386	VICTORIA	55744-55745	GRAND RAPIDS	55960-55960	ORONOCO	56074-56074	NICOLLET
55387-55387	WACONIA	55746-55747	HIBBING	55961-55961	OSTRANDER	56075-56075	NORTHROP
55388-55388	WATERTOWN	55748-55748	HILL CITY	55962-55962	PETERSON	56076-56076	OAKLAND
55389-55389	WATKINS	55749-55749	HOLYOKE	55963-55963	PINE ISLAND	56078-56078	PEMBERTON
55390-55390	WAVERLY	55750-55750	HOYT LAKES	55964-55964	PLAINVIEW	56080-56080	SAINT CLAIR
55391-55391	WAYZATA	55751-55751	IRON	55965-55965	PRESTON	56081-56081	SAINT JAMES
55392-55392	NAVARRE	55752-55752	JACOBSON	55967-55967	RACINE	56082-56082	SAINT PETER
55393-55393	MAPLE PLAIN	55753-55753	KEEWATIN	55968-55968	READS LANDING	56083-56083	SANBORN
55394-55394	YOUNG AMERICA	55756-55756	KERRICK	55969-55969	ROLLINGSTONE	56084-56084	SEARLES
55395-55395	WINSTED	55757-55757	KETTLE RIVER	55970-55970	ROSE CREEK	56085-56085	SLEEPY EYE
55396-55396	WINTHROP	55758-55758	KINNEY	55971-55971	RUSHFORD	56087-56087	SPRINGFIELD
55397-55397	YOUNG AMERICA	55760-55760	MCGREGOR	55972-55972	SAINT CHARLES	56088-56088	TRUMAN
55398-55398	ZIMMERMAN	55763-55763	MAKINEN	55973-55973	SARGEANT	56089-56089	TWIN LAKES
55399-55399	YOUNG AMERICA	55764-55764	MARBLE	55974-55974	SPRING GROVE	56090-56090	VERNON CENTER

56091-56091	WALDORF	56216-56216	BLOMKEST	56321-56321	COLLEGEVILLE	56456-56456	JENKINS
56093-56093	WASECA	56218-56218	BOYD	56323-56323	CYRUS	56458-56458	LAKE GEORGE
56096-56096	WATERVILLE	56219-56219	BROWNS VALLEY	56324-56324	DALTON	56459-56459	LAKE HUBERT
56097-56097	WELLS	56220-56220	CANBY	56325-56325	ELROSA	56460-56460	LAKE ITASCA
56098-56098	WINNEBAGO	56221-56221	CHOKIO	56326-56326	EVANSVILLE	56461-56461	LAPORTE
56101-56101	WINDOM	56222-56222	CLARA CITY	56327-56327	FARWELL	56464-56464	MENAHGA
56110-56110	ADRIAN	56223-56223	CLARKFIELD	56328-56328	FLENSBURG	56465-56465	MERRIFIELD
56111-56111	ALPHA	56224-56224	CLEMENTS	56329-56329	FOLEY	56466-56466	MOTLEY
56113-56113	ARCO	56225-56225	CLINTON	56330-56330	FORESTON	56467-56467	NEVIS
56114-56114	AVOCA	56226-56226	CLONTARF	56331-56331	FREEPORT	56468-56468	NISSWA
56115-56115	BALATON	56227-56227	CORRELL	56332-56332	GARFIELD	56469-56469	PALISADE
56116-56116	BEAVER CREEK	56228-56228	COSMOS	56333-56333	GILMAN	56470-56470	PARK RAPIDS
56117-56117	BIGELOW	56229-56229	COTTONWOOD	56334-56334	GLENWOOD	56472-56472	PEQUOT LAKES
56118-56118	BINGHAM LAKE	56230-56230	DANUBE	56335-56335	GREENWALD	56473-56473	PILLAGER
56119-56119	BREWSTER	56231-56231	DANVERS	56336-56336	GREY EAGLE	56474-56474	PINE RIVER
56120-56120	BUTTERFIELD	56232-56232	DAWSON	56338-56338	HILLMAN	56475-56475	RANDALL
56121-56121	CEYLON	56235-56235	DONNELLY	56339-56339	HOFFMAN	56477-56477	SEBEKA
56122-56122	CHANDLER	56236-56236	DUMONT	56340-56340	HOLDINGFORD	56478-56478	NIMROD
56123-56123	CURRIE	56237-56237	ECHO	56341-56341	HOLMES CITY	56479-56479	STAPLES
56125-56125	DOVRAY	56239-56239	GHENT	56342-56342	ISLE	56481-56481	VERNDALE
56127-56127	DUNNELL	56240-56240	GRACEVILLE	56343-56343	KENSINGTON	56482-56482	WADENA
56128-56128	EDGERTON	56241-56241	GRANITE FALLS	56344-56344	LASTRUP	56484-56484	WALKER
56129-56129	ELLSWORTH	56243-56243	GROVE CITY	56345-56345	LITTLE FALLS	56501-56502	DETROIT LAKES
56131-56131	FULDA	56244-56244	HANCOCK	56347-56347	LONG PRAIRIE	56510-56510	ADA
56132-56132	GARVIN	56245-56245	HANLEY FALLS	56349-56349	LOWRY	56511-56511	AUDUBON
56134-56134	HARDWICK	56246-56246	HAWICK	56350-56350	MC GRATH	56513-56513	BAKER
56136-56136	HENDRICKS	56248-56248	HERMAN	56352-56352	MELROSE	56514-56514	BARNESVILLE
56137-56137	HERON LAKE	56249-56249	HOLLOWAY	56353-56353	MILACA	56515-56515	BATTLE LAKE
56138-56138	HILLS	56251-56251	KANDIYOHI	56354-56354	MILTONA	56516-56516	BEJOU
56139-56139	HOLLAND	56252-56252	KERKHOVEN	56355-56355	NELSON	56517-56517	BELTRAMI
56140-56140	IHLEN	56253-56253	LAKE LILLIAN	56356-56356	NEW MUNICH	56518-56518	BLUFFTON
56141-56141	IONA	56255-56255	LUCAN	56357-56357	OAK PARK	56519-56519	BORUP
56142-56142	IVANHOE	56256-56256	MADISON	56358-56358	OGILVIE	56520-56520	BRECKENRIDGE
56143-56143	JACKSON	56257-56257	MARIETTA	56359-56359	ONAMIA	56521-56521	CALLAWAY
56144-56144	JASPER	56258-56258	MARSHALL	56360-56360	OSAKIS	56522-56522	CAMPBELL
56145-56145	JEFFERS	56260-56260	MAYNARD	56361-56361	PARKERS PRAIRIE	56523-56523	CLIMAX
56146-56146	KANARANZI	56262-56262	MILAN	56362-56362	PAYNESVILLE	56524-56524	CLITHERALL
56147-56147	KENNETH	56263-56263	MILROY	56363-56363	PEASE	56525-56525	COMSTOCK
56149-56149	LAKE BENTON	56264-56264	MINNEOTA	56364-56364	PIERZ	56527-56527	DEER CREEK
56150-56150	LAKEFIELD	56265-56265	MONTEVIDEO	56367-56367	RICE	56528-56528	DENT
56151-56151	LAKE WILSON	56266-56266	MORGAN	56368-56368	RICHMOND	56529-56529	DILWORTH
56152-56152	LAMBERTON	56267-56267	MORRIS	56369-56369	ROCKVILLE	56531-56531	ELBOW LAKE
56153-56153	LEOTA	56270-56270	MORTON	56371-56371	ROSCOE	56533-56533	ELIZABETH
56155-56155	LISMORE	56271-56271	MURDOCK	56372-56372	SAINT CLOUD	56534-56534	ERHARD
56156-56156	LUVERNE	56272-56272	NASSAU	56373-56373	ROYALTON	56535-56535	ERSKINE
56157-56157	LYND	56273-56273	NEW LONDON	56374-56374	SAINT JOSEPH	56536-56536	FELTON
56158-56158	MAGNOLIA	56274-56274	NORCROSS	56375-56375	SAINT STEPHEN	56537-56538	FERGUS FALLS
56159-56159	MOUNTAIN LAKE	56276-56276	ODESSA	56376-56376	SAINT MARTIN	56540-56540	FERTILE
56160-56160	ODIN	56277-56277	OLIVIA	56377-56377	SARTELL	56541-56541	FLOM
56161-56161	OKABENA	56278-56278	ORTONVILLE	56378-56378	SAUK CENTRE	56542-56542	FOSSTON
56162-56162	ORMSBY	56279-56279	PENNOCK	56379-56379	SAUK RAPIDS	56543-56543	FOXHOME
56164-56164	PIPESTONE	56280-56280	PORTER	56381-56381	STARBUCK	56544-56544	FRAZEE
56165-56165	READING	56281-56281	PRINSBURG	56382-56382	SWANVILLE	56545-56545	GARY
56166-56166	REVERE	56282-56282	RAYMOND	56384-56384	UPSALA	56546-56546	GEORGETOWN
56167-56167	ROUND LAKE	56283-56283	REDWOOD FALLS	56385-56385	VILLARD	56547-56547	GLYNDON
56168-56168	RUSHMORE	56284-56284	RENVILLE	56386-56386	WAHKON	56548-56548	HALSTAD
56169-56169	RUSSELL	56285-56285	SACRED HEART	56387-56387	WAITE PARK	56549-56549	HAWLEY
56170-56170	RUTHTON	56287-56287	SEAFORTH	56389-56389	WEST UNION	56550-56550	HENDRUM
56171-56171	SHERBURN	56288-56288	SPICER	56393-56398	SAINT CLOUD	56551-56551	HENNING
56172-56172	SLAYTON	56289-56289	SUNBURG	56401-56401	BRAINERD	56552-56552	HITTERDAL
56173-56173	STEEN	56291-56291	TAUNTON	56425-56425	BAXTER	56553-56553	KENT
56174-56174	STORDEN	56292-56292	VESTA	56430-56430	AH GWAH CHING	56554-56554	LAKE PARK
56175-56175	TRACY	56293-56293	WABASSO	56431-56431	AITKIN	56556-56556	MCINTOSH
56176-56176	TRIMONT	56294-56294	WANDA	56433-56433	AKELEY	56557-56557	MAHNOMEN
56177-56177	TROSKY	56295-56295	WATSON	56434-56434	ALDRICH	56560-56563	MOORHEAD
56178-56178	TYLER	56296-56296	WHEATON	56435-56435	BACKUS	56565-56565	NASHUA
56179-56179	VERDI	56297-56297	WOOD LAKE	56436-56436	BENEDICT	56566-56566	NAYTAHWAUSH
56180-56180	WALNUT GROVE	56301-56304	SAINT CLOUD	56437-56437	BERTHA	56567-56567	NEW YORK MILLS
56181-56181	WELCOME	56307-56307	ALBANY	56438-56438	BROWERVILLE	56568-56568	NIELSVILLE
56183-56183	WESTBROOK	56308-56308	ALEXANDRIA	56440-56440	CLARISSA	56569-56569	OGEMA
56185-56185	WILMONT	56309-56309	ASHBY	56441-56441	CROSBY	56570-56570	OSAGE
56186-56186	WOODSTOCK	56310-56310	AVON	56442-56442	CROSSLAKE	56571-56571	OTTERTAIL
56187-56187	WORTHINGTON	56311-56311	BARRETT	56443-56443	CUSHING	56572-56572	PELICAN RAPIDS
56201-56201	WILLMAR	56312-56312	BELGRADE	56444-56444	DEERWOOD	56573-56573	PERHAM
56207-56207	ALBERTA	56313-56313	BOCK	56446-56446	EAGLE BEND	56574-56574	PERLEY
56208-56208	APPLETON	56314-56314	BOWLUS	56447-56447	EMILY	56575-56575	PONSFORD
56209-56209	ATWATER	56315-56315	BRANDON	56448-56448	FIFTY LAKES	56576-56576	RICHVILLE
56210-56210	BARRY	56316-56316	BROOTEN	56449-56449	FORT RIPLEY	56577-56577	RICHWOOD
56211-56211	BEARDSLEY	56317-56317	BUCKMAN	56450-56450	GARRISON	56578-56578	ROCHERT
56212-56212	BELLINGHAM	56318-56318	BURTRUM	56452-56452	HACKENSACK	56579-56579	ROTHSAY
56214-56214	BELVIEW	56319-56319	CARLOS	56453-56453	HEWITT	56580-56580	SABIN
56215-56215	BENSON	56320-56320	COLD SPRING	56455-56455	IRONTON	56581-56581	SHELLY

56583-56583	TINTAH	56644-56644	GONVICK	56679-56679	SOUTH INTERNATIONAL	56728-56728	HALLOCK
56584-56584	TWIN VALLEY	56646-56646	GULLY		FALLS	56729-56729	HALMA
56585-56585	ULEN	56647-56647	HINES	56680-56680	SPRING LAKE	56731-56731	HUMBOLDT
56586-56586	UNDERWOOD	56649-56649	INTERNATIONAL FALLS	56681-56681	SQUAW LAKE	56732-56732	KARLSTAD
56587-56587	VERGAS	56650-56650	KELLIHER	56682-56682	SWIFT	56733-56733	KENNEDY
56588-56588	VINING	56651-56651	LENGBY	56683-56683	TENSTRIKE	56734-56734	LAKE BRONSON
56589-56589	WAUBUN	56652-56652	LEONARD	56684-56684	TRAIL	56735-56735	LANCASTER
56590-56590	WENDELL	56653-56653	LITTLEFORK	56685-56685	WASKISH	56736-56736	MENTOR
56591-56591	WHITE EARTH	56654-56654	LOMAN	56686-56686	WILLIAMS	56737-56737	MIDDLE RIVER
56592-56592	WINGER	56655-56655	LONGVILLE	56687-56687	WILTON	56738-56738	NEWFOLDEN
56593-56593	WOLF LAKE	56657-56657	MARCELL	56688-56688	WIRT	56740-56740	NOYES
56594-56594	WOLVERTON	56658-56658	MARGIE	56701-56701	THIEF RIVER FALLS	56741-56741	OAK ISLAND
56601-56619	BEMIDJI	56659-56659	MAX	56710-56710	ALVARADO	56742-56742	OKLEE
56621-56621	BAGLEY	56660-56660	MIZPAH	56711-56711	ANGLE INLET	56744-56744	OSLO
56623-56623	BAUDETTE	56661-56661	NORTHOME	56712-56712	ANGUS	56748-56748	PLUMMER
56626-56626	BENA	56662-56662	OUTING	56713-56713	ARGYLE	56750-56750	RED LAKE FALLS
56627-56627	BIG FALLS	56663-56663	PENNINGTON	56714-56714	BADGER	56751-56751	ROSEAU
56628-56628	BIGFORK	56666-56666	PONEMAH	56715-56715	BROOKS	56754-56754	SAINT HILAIRE
56629-56629	BIRCHDALE	56667-56667	PUPOSKY	56716-56716	CROOKSTON	56755-56755	SAINT VINCENT
56630-56630	BLACKDUCK	56668-56668	RANIER	56720-56720	DONALDSON	56756-56756	SALOL
56631-56631	BOWSTRING	56669-56669	RAY	56721-56721	EAST GRAND FORKS	56757-56757	STEPHEN
56633-56633	CASS LAKE	56670-56670	REDBY	56722-56722	EUCLID	56758-56758	STRANDQUIST
56634-56634	CLEARBROOK	56671-56671	REDLAKE	56723-56723	FISHER	56759-56759	STRATHCONA
56636-56636	DEER RIVER	56672-56672	REMER	56724-56724	GATZKE	56760-56760	VIKING
56637-56637	TALMOON	56673-56673	ROOSEVELT	56725-56725	GOODRIDGE	56761-56761	WANNASKA
56639-56639	EFFIE	56676-56676	SHEVLIN	56726-56726	GREENBUSH	56762-56762	WARREN
56641-56641	FEDERAL DAM	56678-56678	SOLWAY	56727-56727	GRYGLA	56763-56763	WARROAD

Mississippi

General Help Numbers:

Governor's Office
PO Box 139   601-359-3150
Jackson, MS 39205-0139   Fax 601-359-3741
www.governor.state.ms.us   8AM-5PM

Attorney General's Office
PO Box 220   601-359-3680
Jackson, MS 39201-0220   Fax 601-359-3796
www.ago.state.ms.us   8AM-5PM

State Court Administrator
Supreme Court, Box 117   601-359-3697
Jackson, MS 39205   Fax 601-359-2443
www.mssc.state.ms.us   8AM-5PM

State Archives
Archives & Library Division   601-359-6850
PO Box 571   Fax 601-359-6964
Jackson, MS 39205-0571 9AM-5PM M; 8AM-5PM TU-F
www.mdah.state.ms.us

State Specifics:

Capital:	Jackson
	Hinds County
Time Zone:	CST
Number of Counties:	82
Population:	2,768,619
Web Site:	www.state.ms.us

State Agencies

Criminal Records

Records not maintained by a state level agency.

Note: Mississippi does not have a central state repository of criminal records. They suggest that you obtain information at the county level.

Corporation Records
Limited Partnership Records
Limited Liability Company Records
Trademarks/Servicemarks

Corporation Commission, Secretary of State, PO Box 136, Jackson, MS 39205-0136 (Courier: 202 N Congress, Suite 601, Jackson, MS 39201); 601-359-1633, 800-256-3494, 601-359-1607 (Fax), 8AM-5PM.

www.sos.state.ms.us

Indexing & Storage: Records are available from the 1800's, computerized since 1995. New records are available for inquiry immediately. Records are indexed on microfilm, inhouse computer.

Searching: Include the following in your request-full name of business. In addition to the articles of incorporation, corporation records include the following information: Annual Reports, Officers, Directors, Prior (merged) names, Inactive and Reserved names. The following data is not released: federal id numbers or phone numbers.

Access by: mail, phone, fax, in person, online.

Fee & Payment: There is no search fee. The certification fee is $10.00 per package. Opies are $1.00 per page. Fee payee: Secretary of State.

Prepayment required. You must prepay if the invoice amount is over $50.00. If under $50.00 they will invoice. Personal checks accepted. Credit cards accepted: Mastercard, Visa.

Mail search: Turnaround time: 1-2 days.

Phone search: Will only verify if record exists.

Fax search: Requests only are accepted, will return to toll-free fax numbers.

In person search: Computer screen prints are free.

Online search: The system is called "CorpSnap" and is available from the Internet. There is no fee to view records, including officers and registered agents.

Other access: The Data Division offers bulk release of information on paper or disk.

Uniform Commercial Code
Federal Tax Liens

Business Services Division, Secretary of State, PO Box 136, Jackson, MS 39205-0136 (Courier: 202 N Congress St, Suite 601, Union Planters Bank Bldg, Jackson, MS 39201); 601-359-1633, 800-256-3494, 601-359-1607 (Fax), 8AM-5PM.

www.sos.state.ms.us

Indexing & Storage: Records are available from 1968. Records are computerized since 1987. Records are indexed on inhouse computer.

Searching: Use search request form UCC-11. The search includes federal tax liens on businesses. Federal tax liens on individuals and all state tax liens are filed at the county level. Include the following in your request-debtor name.

Access by: mail, phone, fax, in person, online.

Fee & Payment: The search fee is $5.00, copies are $2.00 each, financing statements are $2.00 each. Fee payee: Secretary of State. Prepayment required. The state offers ACH accounts for regular requesters. Personal checks accepted. Credit cards accepted: Mastercard, Visa.

Mail search: Turnaround time: 1 day. No self addressed stamped envelope is required.

Phone search: Limited information is released over the phone.

Fax search: Requester must first set-up a prepaid account.

In person search: Searching is available in person.

Online search: The PC system is called "Success" and is open 24 hours daily. There is a $250 set-up fee and usage fee of $.10 per screen. Users can access via the Internet to avoid any toll charges. Customers are billed quarterly. For more information, call Burrell Brown at 601-359-1633.

Other access: A monthly list of farm liens is available for purchase.

State Tax Liens

Records not maintained by a state level agency.

Note: All state tax liens are filed at the county level.

Sales Tax Registrations

Revenue Bureau, Sales Tax Division, PO Box 22828, Jackson, MS 39225-2828 (Courier: 1577 Springridge Rd, Raymond, MS 39154); 601-923-7000, 601-923-7300 (Fax), 8AM-5PM.

www.mstc.state.ms.us

Indexing & Storage: Records are available for the most current 3 years and are computerized.

Searching: The agency will only verify if a business is registered and will not release ownership data. Include the following in your request-business name. They will also search by tax permit number.

Access by: mail, phone, fax, in person.

Fee & Payment: Prepayment required. Fee payee: Revenue Bureau. Personal checks accepted. No credit cards accepted.

Mail search: Turnaround time: 5-10 working days. No self addressed stamped envelope is required. No fee for mail request. Copies cost $2.00 per page.

Phone search: No fee for telephone request.

Fax search: Same criteria as phone or mail searches.

In person search: No fee for request. Copies cost $2.00 per page.

Birth Certificates

State Department of Health, Vital Statistics & Records, PO Box 1700, Jackson, MS 39215-1700 (Courier: 2423 N State St, Jackson, MS 39216); 601-576-7960, 601-576-7988, 601-576-7505 (Fax), 7:30AM-5PM.

www.msdh.state.ms.us/phs/index.htm

Indexing & Storage: Records are available from November 1, 1912-present. New records are available for inquiry immediately. Records are indexed on microfiche, inhouse computer.

Searching: Employers need written release form from person of record. Records are not public access documents, they are only available to persons with legitimate and tangible interest. Include the following in your request-full name, names of parents, mother's maiden name, date of birth, place of birth, relationship to person of record, reason for information request. The following data is not released: original records of adoption.

Access by: mail, phone, fax, in person.

Fee & Payment: The $7.00 fee is for the short form. The fee for the long form certified is $12.00, plus is a $3.00 per for each additional copy. There is a $7.00 charge for no record found. Fee payee: Mississippi State Department of Health. Prepayment required. Use credit card for phone and/or expedited service only. Credit cards accepted: Mastercard, Visa, AmEx, Discover.

Mail search: Turnaround time: 7-10 days. No self addressed stamped envelope is required.

Phone search: Must use a credit card for an additional $5.00 fee. Turnaround time is same or next day.

Fax search: Same criteria as phone searches.

In person search: Turnaround time for Short Form-while you wait, Long Form-next day mail.

Expedited service: Expedited service is available for mail, phone and fax searches. Turnaround

time: overnight delivery. Add a $5.00 credit card fee and $12.75 for overnight shipping.

Death Records

State Department of Health, Vital Statistics & Records, PO Box 1700, Jackson, MS 39215-1700 (Courier: 2423 N State St, Jackson, MS 39216); 601-576-7960, 601-576-7988, 601-576-7505 (Fax), 7:30AM-5PM.

www.msdh.state.ms.us/phs/index.htm

Indexing & Storage: Records are available from November 1, 1912-present. New records are available for inquiry immediately. Records are indexed on microfiche, inhouse computer.

Searching: Employers need written release form from immediate family member. Records are not considered public access documents. They are only available to persons with legitimate and tangible interest. Include the following in your request-full name, date of death, place of death, Social Security Number, relationship to person of record, reason for information request.

Access by: mail, phone, fax, in person.

Fee & Payment: Fee is $10.00 if you want a certified copy, and an additional $2.00 for each additional copy ordered at same time. If no record is found, the fee is $6.00. Fee payee: Mississippi State Department of Health. Prepayment required. Use credit cards for phone, fax and/or expedited service only. Credit cards accepted: Mastercard, Visa, AmEx, Discover.

Mail search: Turnaround time: 7-10 days. No self addressed stamped envelope is required.

Phone search: Turnaround time 2-3 days. Must use a credit card for an additional fee of $5.00.

Fax search: Same criteria as phone searching.

In person search: Turnaround time next day mail.

Expedited service: Expedited service is available for mail, phone and fax searches. Turnaround time: 1 day. Add $5.00 for use of credit card and $12.75 for overnight shipping.

Marriage Certificates

State Department of Health, Vital Statistics & Records, PO Box 1700, Jackson, MS 39215-1700 (Courier: 2423 N State St, Jackson, MS 39216); 601-576-7960, 601-576-7988, 601-576-7505 (Fax), 7:30AM-5PM.

www.msdh.state.ms.us/phs/index.htm

Note: Records are also available at the county level, including those records from 1938-1942.

Indexing & Storage: Records are available from January 1926-June 1938 and January 1942-present. New records are available for inquiry immediately. Records are indexed on microfiche, inhouse computer.

Searching: Employers need written release from persons of record. Records are not considered public access documents. They are only available to persons with legitimate and tangible interest. Include the following in your request-names of husband and wife, date of marriage, place or county of marriage, relationship to person of record, reason for information request.

Access by: mail, phone, fax, in person.

Fee & Payment: The fee is $10.00 and $2.00 for each additional copy ordered at same time. If record not found fee is $6.00. Fee payee: Mississippi State Department of Health.

Prepayment required. Use credit cards for phone, fax and/or expedited service only. Credit cards accepted: Mastercard, Visa, AmEx, Discover.

Mail search: Turnaround time: 4-7 days. No self addressed stamped envelope is required.

Phone search: Turnaround time 2-3 days. Must use a credit card for an additional $5.00 fee.

Fax search: Same criteria as phone searching.

In person search: Search costs $10.00 per request. Turnaround time next day mail.

Expedited service: Expedited service is available for mail, phone and fax searches. Turnaround time: 1 day. Add $5.00 for use of credit card and $12.75 for overnight delivery.

Divorce Records

State Department of Health, Vital Statistics, PO Box 1700, Jackson, MS 39215-1700 (Courier: 2423 N State St, Jackson, MS 39216); 601-576-7960, 601-576-7988, 601-576-7505 (Fax), 7:30AM-5PM.

www.msdh.state.ms.us/phs/index.htm

Note: The state maintains a state-wide index and can refer to book and page number in county records. Requests for copies must be made to the county of record.

Indexing & Storage: Records are available from 1930-present in county of record. This office will only confirm that a record exists and where. New records are available for inquiry immediately. Records are indexed on microfiche, inhouse computer.

Searching: Employers need written release form from person of record. Records are not public access documents and are available only to persons with legitimate and tangible interest. Include the following in your request-names of husband and wife, date of divorce, year divorce case began, case number (if known), relationship to person of record, reason for information request.

Access by: mail, phone, fax, in person.

Fee & Payment: The fee to do an index search is $6.00. Copies are not released from this agency. Fee payee: Mississippi State Department of Health. Prepayment required. Personal checks accepted. Credit cards accepted: Mastercard, Visa, AmEx, Discover.

Mail search: Turnaround time: 1-3 days. No self addressed stamped envelope is required.

Phone search: Use of credit card, for an additional $5.00 fee, required.

Fax search: Same criteria as phone searching.

In person search: Turnaround time next day mail.

Expedited service: Expedited service is available for mail, phone and fax searches. Turnaround time: 1 day. Add $5.00 for use of credit card and $12.75 for overnight delivery.

Workers' Compensation Records

Workers Compensation Commission, PO Box 5300, Jackson, MS 39296-5300 (Courier: 1428 Lakeland Dr, Jackson, MS 39216); 601-987-4200, 8AM-5PM.

www.mwcc.state.ms.us

Note: The state does not provide electronic access, but has sold the database to a third party who does

provide online retrieval and the agency refers all calls to them. Call 601-664-1900 for details.

Indexing & Storage: Records are available for 10 years back to present. New records are available for inquiry immediately. Records are indexed on inhouse computer.

Searching: All requests must be in writing. Claimant's attorney must have contract or medical authorization. Employer/carrier must be party to action to obtain records. They do not conduct searches for pre-employment screening. Include the following in your request-claimant name, Social Security Number, docket number, place of employment at time of accident.

Access by: mail, in person.

Fee & Payment: Copy fee is $.50 with a $5.00 minimum, there is no search fee. Fee payee: Mississippi Workers' Compensation Commission. They will invoice. Personal checks accepted. No credit cards accepted.

Mail search: Turnaround time: 3-4 working days. No self addressed stamped envelope is required.

In person search: Anyone can come in to view. Medical information is not made available and copies cannot be made unless there is written authorization by party of record.

Other access: A first report of injury database is available on CD-ROM for $500.00.

Driver Records

Department of Public Safety, Driver Records, PO Box 958, Jackson, MS 39205 (Courier: 1900 E Woodrow Wilson, Jackson, MS 39216); 601-987-1274, 8AM-5PM.

Note: Copies of tickets may be obtained from the same address for a fee of $5.00 per record. A pre-addressed, stamped envelope is advised.

Indexing & Storage: Records are available for 3 years for moving violations, DUIs and suspensions. Accidents appear on driving records. The driver's address is provided on the record. It takes 45 days or more before new records are available for inquiry.

Searching: Casual requesters can obtain personal information only with consent of subject. The driver's full name, license number, and/or DOB are needed when ordering. The magnetic tape system requires only the driver's last name and number (first name and DOB are optional). Surrendered license records can only be obtained by a manual search.

Access by: mail, in person, online.

Fee & Payment: The fee is $7.00 per request. Fee payee: Department of Public Safety. Prepayment required. Personal checks accepted. No credit cards accepted.

Mail search: Turnaround time: 2 days. A self addressed stamped envelope is requested.

In person search: Walk-in requesters may submit up to 10 requests for immediate delivery; the rest are available the next day.

Online search: Both interactive and batch delivery is offer for high volume users only. Billing is monthly. Hook-up is through the Advantis System, fees apply. Lookup is by name only-not by driver license number. For more information, call 601-987-1337.

Other access: Overnight batch delivery by tape is available. The state will sell the driver record file

(without histories) to private or commercial parties.

Accident Reports

Safety Responsibility, Accident Records, PO Box 958, Jackson, MS 39205 (Courier: 1900 E Woodrow Wilson, Jackson, MS 39216); 601-987-1278, 601-987-1261 (Fax), 8AM-5PM.

Note: The above address is for Highway Patrol accident investigations only. Reports require authorization from person involved. You must go to the agency that did the investigation for reports not found with the Highway Patrol.

Indexing & Storage: Records are available for 3 years to present on computer. Records are on microfiche from 1990-present.

Searching: Must have authorization from individuals involved in the accident. Accident reports are only available to persons involved, their legal counsel and their insurance representative. Include the following in your request-date of accident, location of accident, full name. Requests must be in writing.

Access by: mail.

Fee & Payment: The fee is $10.00 per record. Fee payee: Department of Public Safety. Prepayment required. Personal checks accepted. No credit cards accepted.

Mail search: Turnaround time: 5 days. A self addressed stamped envelope is requested.

Vehicle Ownership
Vehicle Identification

Mississippi State Tax Commission, Registration Department, PO Box 1140, Jackson, MS 39215 (Courier: 1577 Springridge Rd, Raymond, MS 39154); 601-923-7143, 601-923-7134 (Fax), 8AM-5PM.

www.mstc.state.ms.us/mvl/main.htm

Note: Please note that title information (liens, histories) requests are processed by a different section than registration information. For mail requests, use PO Box 1033 for the Title Department.

Indexing & Storage: Records are available from July 1, 1969-present. Records are computer indexed from July 1, 1969-present, and on microfiche from July 1, 1969-present.

Searching: Personal information is not released to casual requesters without consent from the subject. The turnaround time will be one week longer if the request requires a search farther back than 5 years.

Access by: mail, in person.

Fee & Payment: Fees are $4.50 per search for title, $1.00 per search for VIN or registration, and $2.00 for lien history. Fee payee: Mississippi State Tax Commission. Prepayment required. No cash will be accepted for mail requests. Personal checks accepted. No credit cards accepted.

Mail search: Turnaround time: 2 days. A self addressed stamped envelope is requested.

In person search: Turnaround time is immediate.

Other access: Mississippi offers some standardized files as well as some customization for bulk requesters of VIN and registration information. For more information, contact Administrative Services, PO Box 22828 Jackson 39225.

Boat & Vessel Ownership
Boat & Vessel Registration

Dept of Wildlife, Fisheries, & Parks, PO Box 451, Jackson, MS 39205; 601-432-2070, 601-364-2048 (Fax), 8AM-5PM.

www.mdwfp.com

Note: Liens are recorded if the vessel has been titled. Starting July 1998, boats are titled at the option of the owner/lender.

Indexing & Storage: Records are available from 1981-present. Records are indexed on computer from 1985-present. All motorized boats and all sailboats must be registered. It takes 2 weeks or so before new records are available for inquiry.

Searching: The name or DL number or MS number or hull number is required to search.

Access by: mail, phone, fax, in person.

Fee & Payment: There is no search fee.

Mail search: Turnaround time is the same day, except during the summer, which can take 3-4 weeks. A self addressed stamped envelope is requested.

Phone search: Searching is available by phone.

Fax search: Results will be mailed back usually the same day.

In person search: Turnaround time is usually immediate.

Other access: The state makes records available on printed lists and magnetic tapes. Fees vary.

Legislation-Current/Pending
Legislation-Passed

Mississippi Legislature, PO Box 1018, Jackson, MS 39215 (Courier: New Capitol, 3rd Floor, Jackson, MS 39215-1018);, 601-359-3229 (Senate), 601-359-3358 (House), 8:30AM-5PM.

www.ls.state.ms.us

Note: The room number for Senate documents is 308, the room number for House documents is 305. The session begins the 1st Tuesday after the 1st Monday in January and usually lasts 3 months.

Indexing & Storage: Records are available from the beginning of the Legislature. Bills from 1991-present are on computer, prior bills are in file books. New records are available for inquiry immediately. Records are indexed on inhouse computer, books (volumes).

Searching: Include the following in your request-bill number.

Access by: mail, phone, fax, in person, online.

Fee & Payment: No charges for copies or searches.

Mail search: Turnaround time: same day. No self addressed stamped envelope is required.

Phone search: Searching is available by phone.

Fax search: Same day service is available.

In person search: Searching is available in person.

Online search: The Internet site has an excellent bill status and measure information program. Data includes current and the previous year.

Voter Registration
Records not maintained by a state level agency.

Note: Records are open to the public, but must be obtained at the county level. However, MS is going to a statewide system sometime in 2001.

GED Certificates

State Board for Community & Jr Colleges, GED Office, 3825 Ridgewood Rd, Jackson, MS 39211; 601-432-6338, 601-432-6363 (Fax), 8AM-5PM.

www.sbcjc.cc.ms.us

Searching: Transcripts are only available by written request. To search, all of the following is required: a signed release, name, date of birth, and Social Security Number. If known, the diploma number is helpful.

Access by: mail, fax, in person.

Fee & Payment: There is no fee for either a verification or a transcript.

Mail search: Turnaround time is 3 days. No self addressed stamped envelope is required.

Fax search: Same criteria as mail searching.

In person search: In person searchers must have a picture ID. Turnaround time: 2-3 minutes for a verification.

Hunting License Information
Fishing License Information

Department of Wildlife, Fisheries & Parks, PO Box 451, Jackson, MS 39205; 601-432-2055 (License Division), 601-432-2041 (Data Processing Div), 601-432-2071 (Fax), 8AM-5PM.

www.mdwfp.com

Indexing & Storage: Records are available for present data only.

Searching: Records are open to the public. They hold records on "sportsman" license holders which is a combination of hunting and fishing. Temporary license information is not maintained. You can search using the name or driver's license number.

Access by: mail, phone, fax, in person.

Fee & Payment: There is no search fee.

Mail search: Turnaround time: 10 days. No self addressed stamped envelope is required.

Phone search: Searching is available by phone.

Fax search: Same criteria as mail searches.

In person search: You can make the request in person but they will mail back your response.

Other access: They have available mailing lists. For a print-out the cost is $550.00 for all the names and addresses; for magnetic tape the cost is $300.00 plus $20.00 for the tape. You can provide your own tape; call first to find out type and how many tapes needed.

Licenses Searchable Online

Architect #03 .... www.archbd.state.ms.us/aroster.htm
Attorney #27 .... www.mslawyer.com/index.html
Attorney Firm #27 .... www.mslawyer.com/LawFirms
Engineer #09 .... http://dsitspe01.its.state.ms.us/pepls/EngSurveyors.nsf
General Contractor #06 .... www.msboc.state.ms.us/Search.cfm
HMO #25 .... www.doi.state.ms.us/hmolist.pdf
Insurance Company #25 .... www.doi.state.ms.us/compdir.html
Landscape Architect #03 .... www.archbd.state.ms.us/lroster.htm
Lobbyist #31 .... www.sos.state.ms.us/elections/Lobbyists/Lobbyist_Dir.html
Long Term Care Insurance Company #25 .... www.doi.state.ms.us/ltclist.html
Notary Public #31 .... www.sos.state.ms.us/busserv/notaries/NotarySearch.html
Optometrist #15 .... www.arbo.org/nodb2000/licsearch.asp
Surveyor #09 .... http://dsitspe01.its.state.ms.us/pepls/EngSurveyors.nsf

Licensing Quick Finder

Alcohol Beverage Employee #26 601-856-1330
Animal Technician #29 662-324-9380
Appraiser #30 601-987-4150
Architect #03 601-359-6020
Asbestos Contractor/Inspector #22 601-961-5100
Asbestos Management Planner/Project Designer #22
.... 601-961-5100
Asbestos Supervisor #22 601-961-5100
Asbestos Worker #22 601-961-5100
Athletic Trainer #37 601-987-4153
Attorney Firm #27 601-948-4471
Bank #04 601-359-1031
Barber #05 601-359-1015
Barber Instructor #05 601-359-1015
Barber School #05 601-359-1015
Barber Shop #05 601-359-1015
Boiler & Pressure Vessel Inspector #37
.... 601-960-7917
Child Care Facility #37 601-960-7613
Chiropractor #35 662-773-4478
Commercial Fishing #24 601-362-9212
Cosmetologist #07 601-354-6623
Cosmetology Instructor #07 601-354-6623
Counselor, Licensed Professional #10
.... 601-359-6630
Dental Hygienist #08 601-944-9622
Dental Radiologist #08 601-944-9622
Dentist #08 601-944-9622
Dietitian #37 601-987-4153
Emergency Medical Technician #37 601-987-3880
Emergency Medical Technician (Basic) #37
.... 601-987-3880

Emergency Medical Technician-Intermediate #37
.... 601-987-3880
Emergency Medical Technician-Paramedic #37
.... 601-987-3880
Engineer #09 601-359-6160
Esthetician #07 601-354-6623
Eye Enucleator #37 601-987-4153
Funeral Director #11 601-354-6903
Funeral Service Practitioner #11 601-354-6903
Gaming #26 601-351-2800
General Contractor #06 601-354-6161
General Real Estate Appraiser #30 601-987-4150
Health Facility #41 601-576-7300
Hearing Aid Dealer (Specialist) #38 601-987-4153
Insurance Sales Agent #25 601-359-3582
Insurance Solicitor/Advisor #25 601-359-3582
Landscape Architect #03 601-359-6020
Liquor Control #02 601-856-1310
Liquor Control, Alcoholic Beverage Retailer #02
.... 601-856-1330
Liquor Control, Alcoholic Beverage Retailer #01
.... 601-856-1330
Lobbyist #31 601-359-6353
Manicurist #07 601-354-6623
Marriage/Family Therapist #28 601-987-6806
Medical Doctor #12 601-987-3079
Notary Public #31 601-359-1615
Nurse #13 601-987-6858
Nurse-LPN #13 601-987-6858
Nursing Home Administrator #14 601-364-2310
Occupational Therapist/Assistant #33 ... 601-576-7260
Optometrist #15 601-684-6241

Osteopathic Physician #12 601-987-3079
Pharmacist #16 601-345-6750
Pharmacy Intern #16 601-345-6750
Physical Therapist/Assistant #33 601-576-7260
Podiatrist #12 601-987-3079
Polygraph Examiner #17 601-987-4202
Psychologist #18 601-321-4621
Public Accountant-CPA #19 601-354-7320
Radiation Technician #37 601-987-4153
Real Estate Broker #34 601-987-3969
Real Estate Salesperson #34 601-987-3969
Residential Real Estate Appraiser #30 .. 601-987-4150
Salon #07 601-354-6623
Savings Institution #23 601-354-6135
School Administrator #36 601-359-3483
Securities Agent #32 601-359-6363
Securities Broker/Dealer #32 601-359-6363
Shorthand Reporter #20 601-354-6580
Social Worker #28 601-987-6806
Speech Pathologist/Audiologist #39 601-987-4153
Speech-Language Pathologist/Audiologist #21
.... 601-576-7260
Surveyor #09 601-359-6160
Tattoo Artist #37 601-987-4153
Teacher #36 601-359-3483
Veterinarian #29 662-324-9380
Veterinary Facility #29 662-324-9380
Veterinary Technician #29 662-324-9380
Youth Camp #40 601-960-7740

Licensing Agency Information

02 Alcoholic Beverage Control Board, PO Box 540, Madison, MS 39110-0540; 601-856-1330, Fax: 601-856-1390.

03 Board of Architecture, 239 N Lamarr St, Rm 502, Jackson, MS 39201-1311; 601-359-6020, Fax: 601-359-6011.

www.archbd.state.ms.us

04 Board of Banking Review, 550 High St, 304 Sallers Bldg, Jackson, MS 39202; 601-359-1031, Fax: 601-359-3557.

www.dbcf.state.ms.us/review.htm

05 Board of Barber Examiners, 510 George St Rm 234, Jackson, MS 39205; 601-359-1015, Fax: 601-359-1050.

06 Board of Contractors, 2829 University Ave SE, #104, Jackson, MS 39208; 601-354-6161, Fax: 601-354-6915.
www.msboc.com

Direct URL to search licenses: www.bsoc.com

07 Board of Cosmetology, 2001 Airport Rd #101, Jackson, MS 39202; 601-354-6623, Fax: 601-354-7076.

08 Board of Dental Examiners, 600 E Amitest #100, Jackson, MS 39060; 601-944-9622, Fax: 601-924-9623 or 9624.

09 Board of Engineers & Land Surveyors, 239 N Lamar St, 1101 Robert E Lee Bldg, Jackson, MS 39201; 601-359-6160, Fax: 601-359-6159.

www.pepls.state.ms.us

10 Board of Examiners for Professional Counselors, 1101 Robert E Lee Bldg, 239 N Lamar St, Jackson, MS 39201; 601-359-6630, Fax: 601-359-6295.

11 Board of Funeral Service, 1307 E Fortification St, Jackson, MS 39202; 601-354-6903, Fax: 601-354-6934.

12 Board of Medical Licensure, 2600 Inusrance Center Dr #2008, Jackson, MS 39216; 601-987-3079, Fax: 601-987-4159.

www.msbml.state.ms.us

13 Board of Nursing, 2829 University Ave SE, #450, Jackson, MS 39201; 601-987-4188, Fax: 601-364-2352.

14 Board of Nursing Home Administrators, 1400 Lakeover Rd #120, Jackson, MS 39213; 601-364-2310, Fax: 601-364-2306.

15 Board of Optometry, PO Box 688, McComb, MS 39648; 601-684-6241.

16 Board of Pharmacy, PO Box 24507 (625 N State St, #202), Jackson, MS 39225-4507; 601-354-6750, Fax: 601-354-6071.

www.mbp.state.ms.us

17 Board of Polygraph Examiners, PO Box 958, Jackson, MS 39205; 601-987-4202.

18 Board of Psychological Examiners, 4273 I 55 N #104, Jackson, MS 39206-6157; 601-353-8871, Fax: 601-352-4384.

19 Board of Public Accountancy, 653 N State St, Jackson, MS 39202; 601-354-7320, Fax: 601-354-7290.

www.msbpa.state.ms.us

20 Board of Certified Court Reporters, PO Box 369, Jackson, MS 39205; 601-354-6580, Fax: 601-354-6058.

21 Department of Health, Council of Advisors in Speech Pathology/Audiology, PO Box 1700, Jackson, MS 39215-1700; 601-987-4153, Fax: 601-987-3784.

www.msdh.state.ms.us

22 Department of Environmental Quality, Pollution Control, PO Box 10385, Jackson, MS 39289-0385; 601-961-5171, Fax: 601-354-6612.

www.deq.state.ms.us/domino/pcweb.nsf

23 Department of Savings Institutions, 633 N State St #201, Jackson, MS 39202; 601-354-6135.

24 Department of Wildlife, Fisheries & Parks, 2906 N State St, Jackson, MS 39216; 601-362-9212, Fax: 601-364-2009;2008.

www.mdwfp.com/scrMDWFP/default.asp

25 Insurance Department, Licensing Division, PO Box 79 (1804 Sillers Bldg, 550 High St), Jackson, MS 39205; 601-359-3569, Fax: 601-359-2474.

www.doi.state.ms.us/agents.html

26 Misisippi Gaming Commission, 200 E Pearl St, Jackson, MS 39205; 601-351-2800, Fax: 601-351-2817.

www.msgaming.com

27 Mississippi Board of Bar Admissions, PO Box 1449 (156 N State St 1st Fl), Jackson, MS 39202; 601-948-4471, Fax: 601-355-8635.

www.ms.org

Direct URL to search licenses: www.mslawyer.com/LawFirms You can search online using name, city, address, phone, fax, practice area, and e-mail address.

28 Marriage & Family Therapists, Mississippi Board of Examiners for Social Workers, PO Box 480, Jackson, MS 39296-4508; 601-987-6806.

29 Mississippi Board of Veterinary Medicine, 209 S Lafayette, Starkville, MS 39759; 662-324-9380, Fax: 662-324-9380.

30 Mississippi Real Estate Appraiser, Licensing & Certification Board, PO Box 12865 (5176 Keele St), Jackson, MS 39236-2685; 601-987-4150, Fax: 601-987-4173.

31 Office of Secretary of State, PO Box 136, Jackson, MS 39205-0136; 601-359-1350, Fax: 601-359-1499.

www.sos.state.ms.us

32 Office of Secretary of State, Securities Department, PO Box 136 (3605 Missouri Blvd),

Jackson, MS 39205; 601-359-6364, Fax: 601-359-2894.

33 Professional Licensure Division, PO Box 1700 (2423 N State St), Jackson, MS 39215-1700; 601-987-4153, Fax: 601-960-7948.

34 Real Estate Commission, 1920 DunBarton Dr, Jackson, MS 39216; 601-987-3969, Fax: 601-987-4984.

35 Board of Chiropractic Examiners, PO Box 775, Louisville, MS 39339; 662-773-4478, Fax: 662-773-4433.

36 State Department of Education, Teacher Licensure/Certification, 359 N West Street, Jackson, MS 39201; 601-359-3483, Fax: 601-359-2778.

http://mde.k12.ms.us

37 State Department of Health, PO Box 1700 (2423 N State St), Jackson, MS 39216; 601-960-7917, Fax: 601-354-6189.

www.msdh.state.ms.us

38 State Department of Health, PO Box 1700 (2423 N State St), Jackson, MS 39216; 601-987-4153, Fax: 601-987-3784.

www.msdh.state.ms.us

39 State Department of Health, 500B E Woodrow Wilson Blvd, Jackson, MS 39216; 601-987-4153, Fax: 601-987-3784.

www.msdh.state.ms.us

41 State Department of Health, Health Facilities Licensure & Certification, PO Box 1700 (421 W Dascagoula), Jackson, MS 39215-1700; 601-354-7300, Fax: 601-354-7225.

www.msdh.state.ms.us

The following list indicates the district and division name for each county in the state. If the district or division name of the bankruptcy court is different from the civil/criminal court, it appears in parentheses.

County/Court Cross. Reference

County	District	Division
Adams	Southern	Vicksburg (Jackson)
Alcorn	Northern	Aberdeen-Eastern (Aberdeen)
Amite	Southern	Jackson
Attala	Northern	Aberdeen-Eastern (Aberdeen)
Benton	Northern	Oxford-Northern (Aberdeen)
Bolivar	Northern	Clarksdale/Delta (Aberdeen)
Calhoun	Northern	Oxford-Northern (Aberdeen)
Carroll	Northern	Greenville (Aberdeen)
Chickasaw	Northern	Aberdeen-Eastern (Aberdeen)
Choctaw	Northern	Aberdeen-Eastern (Aberdeen)
Claiborne	Southern	Vicksburg (Jackson)
Clarke	Southern	Meridian (Biloxi)
Clay	Northern	Aberdeen-Eastern (Aberdeen)
Coahoma	Northern	Clarksdale/Delta (Aberdeen)
Copiah	Southern	Jackson
Covington	Southern	Hattiesburg (Biloxi)
De Soto	Northern	Clarksdale/Delta (Aberdeen)
Forrest	Southern	Hattiesburg (Biloxi)
Franklin	Southern	Jackson
George	Southern	Biloxi-Southern (Biloxi)
Greene	Southern	Hattiesburg (Biloxi)
Grenada	Northern	Oxford-Northern (Aberdeen)
Hancock	Southern	Biloxi-Southern (Biloxi)
Harrison	Southern	Biloxi-Southern (Biloxi)
Hinds	Southern	Jackson
Holmes	Southern	Jackson
Humphreys	Northern	Greenville (Aberdeen)
Issaquena	Southern	Vicksburg (Jackson)
Itawamba	Northern	Aberdeen-Eastern (Aberdeen)
Jackson	Southern	Biloxi-Southern (Biloxi)
Jasper	Southern	Meridian (Biloxi)
Jefferson	Southern	Vicksburg (Jackson)
Jefferson Davis	Southern	Hattiesburg (Biloxi)
Jones	Southern	Hattiesburg (Biloxi)
Kemper	Southern	Meridian (Biloxi)
Lafayette	Northern	Oxford-Northern (Aberdeen)
Lamar	Southern	Hattiesburg (Biloxi)
Lauderdale	Southern	Meridian (Biloxi)
Lawrence	Southern	Hattiesburg (Biloxi)
Leake	Southern	Jackson
Lee	Northern	Aberdeen-Eastern (Aberdeen)
Leflore	Northern	Greenville (Aberdeen)
Lincoln	Southern	Jackson
Lowndes	Northern	Aberdeen-Eastern (Aberdeen)
Madison	Southern	Jackson
Marion	Southern	Hattiesburg (Jackson)
Marshall	Northern	Oxford-Northern (Aberdeen)
Monroe	Northern	Aberdeen-Eastern (Aberdeen)
Montgomery	Northern	Oxford-Northern (Aberdeen)
Neshoba	Southern	Meridian (Biloxi)
Newton	Southern	Meridian (Biloxi)
Noxubee	Southern	Meridian (Biloxi)
Oktibbeha	Northern	Aberdeen-Eastern (Aberdeen)
Panola	Northern	Clarksdale/Delta (Aberdeen)
Pearl River	Southern	Biloxi-Southern (Biloxi)
Perry	Southern	Hattiesburg (Biloxi)
Pike	Southern	Jackson
Pontotoc	Northern	Oxford-Northern (Aberdeen)
Prentiss	Northern	Aberdeen-Eastern (Aberdeen)
Quitman	Northern	Clarksdale/Delta (Aberdeen)
Rankin	Southern	Jackson
Scott	Southern	Jackson
Sharkey	Southern	Vicksburg (Jackson)
Simpson	Southern	Jackson
Smith	Southern	Jackson
Stone	Southern	Biloxi-Southern (Biloxi)
Sunflower	Northern	Greenville (Aberdeen)
Tallahatchie	Northern	Clarksdale/Delta (Aberdeen)
Tate	Northern	Clarksdale/Delta (Aberdeen)
Tippah	Northern	Oxford-Northern (Aberdeen)
Tishomingo	Northern	Aberdeen-Eastern (Aberdeen)
Tunica	Northern	Clarksdale/Delta (Aberdeen)
Union	Northern	Oxford-Northern (Aberdeen)
Walthall	Southern	Hattiesburg (Biloxi)
Warren	Southern	Vicksburg (Jackson)
Washington	Northern	Greenville (Aberdeen)
Wayne	Southern	Meridian (Biloxi)
Webster	Northern	Oxford-Northern (Aberdeen)
Wilkinson	Southern	Vicksburg (Jackson)
Winston	Northern	Aberdeen-Eastern (Aberdeen)
Yalobusha	Northern	Oxford-Northern (Aberdeen)
Yazoo	Southern	Vicksburg (Jackson)

US District Court

Northern District of Mississippi

Aberdeen-Eastern Division PO Box 704, Aberdeen, MS 39730 (Courier Address: 301 W Commerce, Room 310, Aberdeen, MS 39730), 662-369-4952.

www.msnd.uscourts.gov

Counties: Alcorn, Attala, Chickasaw, Choctaw, Clay, Itawamba, Lee, Lowndes, Monroe, Oktibbeha, Prentiss, Tishomingo, Winston.

Indexing & Storage: Cases are indexed by defendant and plaintiff as well as by case number.

New cases are available in the index 48 hours after filing date. Both computer and card indexes are maintained. Open records are located at this court.

Fee & Payment: The fee is $15.00 per item (one party name or case number). Payment may be made by money order, cashier check, personal check. Prepayment is required. Payee: Clerk, US District Court. Certification fee: $5.00 per document. Copy fee: $.50 per page. You are allowed to make your own copies. These copies cost $.25 per page.

Phone Search: If a case number is provided over the phone, the court will verify that the case number is correct.

Mail Search: Always enclose a stamped self addressed envelope.

In Person Search: In person searching is available.

PACER: Sign-up number is 800-676-6856. Access fee is $.60 per minute. Toll-free access: 888-227-0558. Local access: 662-236-4706. Case records are available back to 1990. Records are purged every six months. New records are available online after 1 day. PACER is available on the Internet at http://pacer.msnd.uscourts.gov.

Opinions Online: Court opinions are available online at http://sunset.backbone.olemiss.edu/~llibcoll/ndms

Clarksdale/Delta Division c/o Oxford-Northern Division, PO Box 727, Oxford, MS 38655 (Courier Address: Suite 369, 911 Jackson Ave, Oxford, MS 38655), 662-234-1971.

www.msnd.uscourts.gov

Counties: Bolivar, Coahoma, De Soto, Panola, Quitman, Tallahatchie, Tate, Tunica.

Indexing & Storage: Cases are indexed by as well as by case number. New cases are available in the index after filing date. Open records are located at the Division.

Fee & Payment: The fee is no charge per item (one party name or case number). Payment may be made by money order, cashier check. Business checks are not accepted. Personal checks are not accepted.

Phone Search: An automated voice case information service (VCIS) is not available.

In Person Search: In person searching is available.

PACER: Sign-up number is 800-676-6856. Access fee is $.60 per minute. Toll-free access: 888-227-0558. Local access: 662-236-4706. Case records are available back to 1990. Records are purged every six months. New records are available online after 1 day. PACER is available on the Internet at http://pacer.msnd.uscourts.gov.

Opinions Online: Court opinions are available online at http://sunset.backbone.olemiss.edu/~lilibcoll/ndms

Greenville Division
PO Box 190, Greenville, MS 38702-0190 (Courier Address: US Post Office & Federal Bldg, 305 Main, Greenville, MS 38701), 662-335-1651, Fax: 662-332-4292.

www.msnd.uscourts.gov

Counties: Carroll, Humphreys, Leflore, Sunflower, Washington.

Indexing & Storage: Cases are indexed by defendant and plaintiff as well as by case number. New cases are available in the index immediately after filing date. A computer index is maintained. Open records are located at this court.

Fee & Payment: The fee is $15.00 per item (one party name or case number). Payment may be made by money order, cashier check, personal check. Prepayment is required. Payee: Clerk, US District Court. Certification fee: $5.00 per document. Copy fee: $.50 per page. You are allowed to make your own copies. These copies cost $.25 per page.

Phone Search: Only docket information based on case number is available by phone. An automated voice case information service (VCIS) is not available.

Mail Search: Always enclose a stamped self addressed envelope.

In Person Search: In person searching is available.

PACER: Sign-up number is 800-676-6856. Access fee is $.60 per minute. Toll-free access: 888-227-0558. Local access: 662-236-4706. Case records are available back to 1990. Records are purged every six months. New records are available online after 1 day. PACER is available on the Internet at http://pacer.msnd.uscourts.gov.

Opinions Online: Court opinions are available online at http://sunset.backbone.olemiss.edu/~lilibcoll/ndms

Oxford-Northern Division
PO Box 727, Oxford, MS 38655 (Courier Address: Suite 369, 911 Jackson Ave, Oxford, MS 38655), 662-234-1971.

www.msnd.uscourts.gov

Counties: Benton, Calhoun, Grenada, Lafayette, Marshall, Montgomery, Pontotoc, Tippah, Union, Webster, Yalobusha.

Indexing & Storage: Cases are indexed by defendant and plaintiff as well as by case number. New cases are available in the index 48 hours after filing date. Both computer and card indexes are maintained. Records are also indexed on microfiche. Open records are located at this court. Civil records are sent to the Atlanta Federal Records Center 5 years after closing. Criminal records are sent to the Atlanta Federal Records Ce10 years after closing. All criminal records for the Delta Division (Clarksdale) are maintained in this office.

Fee & Payment: The fee is $15.00 per item (one party name or case number). Payment may be made by money order, cashier check, personal check. Prepayment is required. Payee: Clerk, US District Court. Certification fee: $5.00 per document. Copy fee: $.50 per page. You are allowed to make your own copies. These copies cost $.25 per page.

Phone Search: If a case number is provided over the phone, the court will verify that the case number is correct.

Mail Search: Always enclose a stamped self addressed envelope.

In Person Search: In person searching is available.

PACER: Sign-up number is 800-676-6856. Access fee is $.60 per minute. Toll-free access: 888-227-0558. Local access: 662-236-4706. Case records are available back to 1990. Records are purged every six months. New records are available online after 1 day. PACER is available on the Internet at http://pacer.msnd.uscourts.gov.

Opinions Online: Court opinions are available online at http://sunset.backbone.olemiss.edu/~lilibcoll/ndms

US Bankruptcy Court
Northern District of Mississippi

Aberdeen Division
PO Drawer 867, Aberdeen, MS 39730-0867 (Courier Address: 205 Federal Bldg, Aberdeen, MS 39730), 662-369-2596.

www.msnb.uscourts.gov

Counties: Alcorn, Attala, Benton, Bolivar, Calhoun, Carroll, Chickasaw, Choctaw, Clay, Coahoma, De Soto, Grenada, Humphreys, Itawamba, Lafayette, Lee, Leflore, Lowndes, Marshall, Monroe, Montgomery, Oktibbeha, Panola, Pontotoc, Prentiss, Quitman, Sunflower, Tallahatchie, Tate, Tippah, Tishomingo, Tunica, Union, Washington, Webster, Winston, Yalobusha.

Indexing & Storage: Cases are indexed by debtor as well as by case number. New cases are available in the index 1-2 days after filing date. A computer index is maintained. Open records are located at this court.

Fee & Payment: The fee is $15.00 per item (one party name or case number). Payment may be made by money order, cashier check, personal check. Prepayment is required. Payee: Clerk, US Bankruptcy Court, Northern District. Certification fee: $5.00 per document. Copy fee: $.50 per page. You are allowed to make your own copies. These copies cost $.50 per page. The $15.00 charge is per

name or item. You may not take case files from the court for copies.

Phone Search: Only docket information is available by phone. An automated voice case information service (VCIS) is available. Call VCIS at 800-392-8653 or.

Mail Search: Always enclose a stamped self addressed envelope.

In Person Search: In person searching is available.

PACER: Sign-up number is 800-676-6856. Access fee is $.60 per minute. Toll-free access: 888-372-5709. Local access: 662-369-9805, 622-369-9854. Case records are available back to April 1, 1987. Records are purged every 6 months. New civil records are available online after 2 days.

US District Court
Southern District of Mississippi

Biloxi-Southern Division
Room 243, 725 Dr. Martin Luther King Jr. Blvd, Biloxi, MS 39530, 228-432-8623, Fax: 601-436-9632.

www.mssd.uscourts.gov

Counties: George, Hancock, Harrison, Jackson, Pearl River, Stone.

Indexing & Storage: Cases are indexed by defendant and plaintiff as well as by case number. New cases are available in the index 48 hours after filing date. Both computer and card indexes are maintained. Open records are located at this court.

Fee & Payment: The fee is $15.00 per item (one party name or case number). Payment may be made by money order, cashier check, personal check. Prepayment is required. Payee: Clerk, US District Court. Certification fee: $5.00 per document. Copy fee: $.50 per page. You are allowed to make your own copies. These copies cost $.25 per page.

Phone Search: Only docket information is available by phone.

Mail Search: Always enclose a stamped self addressed envelope.

In Person Search: In person searching is available.

PACER: Sign-up number is 800-676-6856. Toll-free access: 800-839-6425. Local access: 601-965-5141. Case records are available back to 1992. New records are available online after 2 days.

Hattiesburg Division
Suite 200, 701 Main St, Hattiesburg, MS 39401, 601-583-2433.

www.mssd.uscourts.gov

Counties: Covington, Forrest, Greene, Jefferson Davis, Jones, Lamar, Lawrence, Marion, Perry, Walthall.

Indexing & Storage: Cases are indexed by defendant and plaintiff as well as by case number. New cases are available in the index 48 hours after filing date. Both computer and card indexes are maintained. Open records are located at this court.

Fee & Payment: The fee is $15.00 per item (one party name or case number). Payment may be made by money order, cashier check, personal check. Prepayment is required. Payee: Clerk, US District Court. Certification fee: $5.00 per document. Copy fee: $.50 per page. You are allowed to make your own copies. These copies cost $.25 per page.

Phone Search: Only docket information is available by case number over the phone. An automated voice case information service (VCIS) is not available.

Mail Search: Always enclose a stamped self addressed envelope.

In Person Search: In person searching is available.

PACER: Sign-up number is 800-676-6856. Toll-free access: 800-839-6425. Local access: 601-965-5141. Case records are available back to 1992. New records are available online after 2 days.

Jackson Division Suite 316, 245 E Capitol St, Jackson, MS 39201, 601-965-4439.

www.mssd.uscourts.gov

Counties: Amite, Copiah, Franklin, Hinds, Holmes, Leake, Lincoln, Madison, Pike, Rankin, Scott, Simpson, Smith.

Indexing & Storage: Cases are indexed by defendant and plaintiff as well as by case number. New cases are available in the index 48 hours after filing date. Both computer and card indexes are maintained. Microfiche index also maintained. Open records are located at this court.

Fee & Payment: The fee is $15.00 per item (one party name or case number). Payment may be made by money order, cashier check, personal check. Prepayment is required. Payee: Clerk, US District Court. Certification fee: $5.00 per document. Copy fee: $.50 per page. You are allowed to make your own copies. These copies cost $.25 per page.

Phone Search: Searching is not available by phone.

Mail Search: Always enclose a stamped self addressed envelope.

In Person Search: In person searching is available.

PACER: Sign-up number is 800-676-6856. Toll-free access: 800-839-6425. Local access: 601-965-5141. Case records are available back to 1992. New records are available online after 2 days.

Meridian Division c/o Jackson Division, Suite 316, 245 E Capitol St, Jackson, MS 39201, 601-965-4439.

www.mssd.uscourts.gov

Counties: Clarke, Jasper, Kemper, Lauderdale, Neshoba, Newton, Noxubee, Wayne.

Indexing & Storage: Cases are indexed by as well as by case number. New cases are available in the index after filing date. Open records are located at the Division.

Fee & Payment: The fee is no charge per item (one party name or case number). Payment may be made by money order, cashier check. Business checks are not accepted. Personal checks are not accepted.

Phone Search: An automated voice case information service (VCIS) is not available.

In Person Search: In person searching is available.

PACER: Sign-up number is 800-676-6856. Toll-free access: 800-839-6425. Local access: 601-965-5141. Case records are available back to 1992. New records are available online after 2 days.

Vicksburg Division c/o Jackson Division, Suite 316, 245 E Capitol St, Jackson, MS 39201, 601-965-4439.

www.mssd.uscourts.gov

Counties: Adams, Claiborne, Issaquena, Jefferson, Sharkey, Warren, Wilkinson, Yazoo.

Indexing & Storage: Cases are indexed by as well as by case number. New cases are available in the index after filing date. Open records are located at the Division.

Fee & Payment: The fee is no charge per item (one party name or case number). Payment may be made by money order, cashier check. Business checks are not accepted. Personal checks are not accepted.

Phone Search: An automated voice case information service (VCIS) is not available.

In Person Search: In person searching is available.

PACER: Sign-up number is 800-676-6856. Toll-free access: 800-839-6425. Local access: 601-965-5141. Case records are available back to 1992. New records are available online after 2 days.

US Bankruptcy Court

Southern District of Mississippi

Biloxi Division Room 117, 725 Dr. Martin Luther King Jr. Blvd, Biloxi, MS 39530, 228-432-5542.

Counties: Clarke, Covington, Forrest, George, Greene, Hancock, Harrison, Jackson, Jasper, Jefferson Davis, Jones, Kemper, Lamar, Lauderdale, Lawrence, Marion, Neshoba, Newton, Noxubee, Pearl River, Perry, Stone, Walthall, Wayne.

Indexing & Storage: Cases are indexed by debtor as well as by case number. New cases are available in the index a few hours after filing date. Both computer and card indexes are maintained. Open records are located at this court.

Fee & Payment: The fee is $15.00 per item (one party name or case number). Payment may be made by money order, cashier check, personal check. Prepayment is required. Payee: Clerk, US Bankruptcy Court. Certification fee: $5.00 per document. Copy fee: $.50 per page.

Phone Search: An automated voice case information service (VCIS) is available. Call VCIS at 800-293-2723 or 601-435-2905.

Mail Search: Always enclose a stamped self addressed envelope.

In Person Search: In person searching is available.

PACER: Sign-up number is 800-676-6856. Access fee is $.60 per minute. Toll-free access: 800-223-1078. Local access: 601-965-6103. Use of PC Anywhere V4.0 recommended. Case records are available back to 1986. New civil records are available online after 1 day.

Jackson Division PO Box 2448, Jackson, MS 39225-2448 (Courier Address: 100 E Capitol St, Jackson, MS 39201), 601-965-5301.

Counties: Adams, Amite, Claiborne, Copiah, Franklin, Hinds, Holmes, Issaquena, Jefferson, Leake, Lincoln, Madison, Pike, Rankin, Scott, Sharkey, Simpson, Smith, Warren, Wilkinson, Yazoo.

Indexing & Storage: Cases are indexed by debtor as well as by case number. New cases are available in the index a few hours after filing date. Both computer and card indexes are maintained. Open records are located at this court.

Fee & Payment: The fee is $15.00 per item (one party name or case number). Payment may be made by money order, cashier check, personal check. Prepayment is required. Payee: Clerk, US Bankruptcy Court. Certification fee: $5.00 per document. Copy fee: $.50 per page.

Phone Search: An automated voice case information service (VCIS) is available. Call VCIS at 800-601-8859 or 601-965-6106.

Mail Search: Always enclose a stamped self addressed envelope.

In Person Search: In person searching is available.

PACER: Sign-up number is 800-676-6856. Access fee is $.60 per minute. Toll-free access: 800-223-1078. Local access: 601-965-6103. Use of PC Anywhere V4.0 recommended.

Court	Jurisdiction	No. of Courts	How Organized
Circuit Courts*	General	70	22 Districts
County Courts*	Limited	3	19 Counties
Combined Courts*		20	
Chancery Courts*	General	91	20 Districts
Justice Courts	Limited	88	
Municipal Courts	Municipal	154	
Family Court	Special	1	

* Profiled in this Sourcebook.

Court	CIVIL								
	Tort	Contract	Real Estate	Min. Claim	Max. Claim	Small Claims	Estate	Eviction	Domestic Relations
Circuit Courts*	X	X	X	$2500	No Max			X	X
County Courts*	X	X	X	$0	$75,000			X	X
Combined Courts*									
Chancery Courts*	X	X	X	$0	No Max		X		X
Justice Courts*	X	X	X	$0	$2500	$2500		X	
Municipal Courts								X	
Family Court									X

Court	CRIMINAL				
	Felony	Misdemeanor	DWI/DUI	Preliminary Hearing	Juvenile
Circuit Courts*	X				
County Courts*		X	X	X	X
Combined Courts*					
Chancery Courts*					X
Justice Courts*		X	X	X	
Municipal Courts		X	X	X	
Family Court					X

ADMINISTRATION   Court Administrator, Supreme Court, Box 117, Jackson, MS, 39205; 601-359-3697, Fax: 601-359-2443. www.mssc.state.ms.us

COURT STRUCTURE   The court of general jurisdiction is the Circuit Court with 70 courts in 22 districts. Justice Courts were first created in 1984, replacing the Justice of the Peace. Prior to 1984, records were kept separately by each Justice of the Peace, so the location of such records today is often unknown. Probate is handled by the Chancery Courts as are property matters.

ONLINE ACCESS   A statewide online computer system is in use internally for court personnel. There are plans underway to make this system available to the public by early 2001. For further details, call Susan Anthony at 601-354-7449.

ADDITIONAL INFORMATION   A number of Mississippi counties have two Circuit Court Districts. A search of either court in such a county will include the index from the other court.

Full Name is a search requirement for all courts. DOB and SSN are very helpful for differentiating between like-named individuals.

Adams County

Circuit & County Court PO Box 1224, Natchez, MS 39121; 601-446-6326; Fax: 601-445-7955. Hours: 8AM-5PM (CST). *Felony, Misdemeanor, Civil Actions Over $2,500.*

Civil Records: Access: Phone, fax, mail, in person. Both court and visitors may perform in person searches. Search fee: $10.00 per name. Required to search: name, years to search. Civil cases indexed by defendant, plaintiff. Civil records on computer; docket books to 1950s; records stored in basement to 1799. **Criminal Records:** Access: Mail, in person. Both court and visitors may perform in person searches. Search fee: $10.00 per name. Required to search: name, years to search; also helpful-SSN. Criminal records on computer; docket books to 1950s; records stored in basement to 1799. **General Information:** No sealed, adoptions, mental health, juvenile, sex, or expunged records released. Turnaround time 1-2 days if on computer. Copy fee: $1.00 per page. No certification fee. Fee payee: Circuit Clerk. Personal checks accepted. Prepayment is required.

Justice Court 115 S Wall, Natchez, MS 39120; 601-446-6326; Fax: 601-445-7955. Hours: 8AM-5PM (CST). *Misdemeanor, Civil Actions Under $2,500, Eviction, Small Claims.*

Chancery Court PO Box 1006, Natchez, MS 39121; 601-446-6684; Fax: 601-445-7913. Hours: 8AM-5PM (CST). *Probate.*

Alcorn County

Circuit Court PO Box 430 Attn: Circuit Clerk, Corinth, MS 38835; 662-286-7740; Fax: 662-286-7767. Hours: 8AM-5PM (CST). *Felony, Civil Actions Over $2,500.*

Civil Records: Access: Mail, in person. Both court and visitors may perform in person searches. Search fee: $10.00 per name. Required to search: name, years to search. Civil cases indexed by defendant, plaintiff. Civil records on docket books from the 1930s. **Criminal Records:** Access: Mail, in person. Both court and visitors may perform in person searches. Search fee: $10.00 per name. Required to search: name, years to search; also helpful-SSN. Criminal records on docket books from the 1930s. **General Information:** No sealed, adoptions, mental health, juvenile, sex, or expunged records released. SASE required. Turnaround time varies. Copy fee: $.50 per page. Certification fee: No certification fee. Fee payee: Circuit Clerk. Personal checks accepted. Prepayment is required.

Justice Court PO Box 226, Corinth, MS 38834; 662-286-7776. Hours: 8AM-5PM (CST). *Misdemeanor, Civil Actions Under $2,500, Eviction, Small Claims.*

Chancery Court PO Box 69, Corinth, MS 38835-0069; 662-286-7702; Fax: 662-286-7706. *Probate.*

Amite County

Circuit Court PO Box 312, Liberty, MS 39645; 601-657-8932; Fax: 601-657-1082. Hours: 8AM-5PM (CST). *Felony, Civil Actions Over $2,500.*

Civil Records: Access: Fax, mail, in person. Both court and visitors may perform in person searches. Search fee: $10.00 per name. Required to search: name, years to search. Civil cases indexed by defendant, plaintiff. Civil records on books since 1976. **Criminal Records:** Access: Fax, mail, in person. Both court and visitors may perform in person searches. Search fee: $10.00 per name.

Required to search: name, years to search, DOB; also helpful-SSN. Criminal records on books since 1976. **General Information:** No sealed, adoptions, mental health, juvenile, sex, or expunged records released. SASE required. Turnaround time same day. Copy fee: $1.00 per page. Certification fee: $10.00. Fee payee: Circuit Clerk. Personal checks accepted. Fax notes: $3.00.

Justice Court PO Box 362, Liberty, MS 39645; 601-657-4527; Fax: 601-657-4527. Hours: 8AM-5PM (CST). *Misdemeanor, Civil Actions Under $2,500, Eviction, Small Claims.*

Chancery Court PO Box 680, Liberty, MS 39645; 601-657-8022; Fax: 601-657-8288. Hours: 8AM-5PM (CST). *Probate.*

Attala County

Circuit Court Courthouse, Kosciusko, MS 39090; 662-289-1471; Fax: 662-289-7666. Hours: 8AM-5PM (CST). *Felony, Civil Actions Over $2,500.*

Civil Records: Access: Phone, fax, mail, in person. Both court and visitors may perform in person searches. Search fee: $10.00 per name. Required to search: name, years to search. Civil cases indexed by defendant, plaintiff. Civil records kept on docket books since 1915. **Criminal Records:** Access: Phone, fax, mail, in person. Both court and visitors may perform in person searches. Search fee: $10.00 per name. Required to search: name, years to search, DOB; also helpful-SSN. Criminal records kept on docket books since 1915. **General Information:** No sealed, adoptions, mental health, juvenile, sex, or expunged records released. SASE required. Turnaround time same day. Copy fee: $.50 per page. Certification fee: $1.00. Fee payee: Circuit Clerk. Business checks accepted. Prepayment is required. Fax notes: $.50 per page.

Justice Court Attala County Courthouse, Kosciusko, MS 39090; 662-289-7272. Hours: 8AM-5PM (CST). *Misdemeanor, Civil Actions Under $2,500, Eviction, Small Claims.*

Chancery Court 230 W. Washington, Kosciusko, MS 39090; 662-289-2921; Fax: 662-289-7662. Hours: 8AM-5PM (CST). *Probate.*

Benton County

Circuit Court PO Box 262, Ashland, MS 38603; 662-224-6310; Fax: 662-224-6303. Hours: 8AM-5PM (CST). *Felony, Civil Actions Over $2,500.*

Civil Records: Access: Mail, in person. Both court and visitors may perform in person searches. Search fee: $10.00 per name. Required to search: name, years to search, address. Civil cases indexed by defendant, plaintiff. Civil records kept on index books since 1871. **Criminal Records:** Access: Mail, in person. Both court and visitors may perform in person searches. Search fee: $10.00 per name. Required to search: name, years to search, DOB; also helpful-SSN. Criminal records kept on index books since 1871. **General Information:** No sealed, adoptions, mental health, juvenile, sex, or expunged records released. Turnaround time same day. Copy fee: $.50 per page. Certification fee: $1.00. Fee payee: Circuit Court. Only cashiers checks and money orders accepted. Prepayment is required.

Justice Court PO Box 152, Ashland, MS 38603; 662-224-6320; Fax: 662-224-6313. Hours: 8AM-5PM (CST). *Misdemeanor, Civil Actions Under $2,500, Eviction, Small Claims.*

Chancery Court PO Box 218, Ashland, MS 38603; 662-224-6300; Fax: 662-224-6303. Hours: 8AM-5PM (CST). *Probate.*

Bolivar County

Circuit & County Court-1st District PO Box 205, Rosedale, MS 38769; 662-759-6521. Hours: 8AM-5PM (CST). *Felony, Misdemeanor, Civil.*

Civil Records: Access: Mail, in person. Both court and visitors may perform in person searches. Search fee: $10.00 per name. Fee is for 7 year search. Required to search: name, years to search. Civil cases indexed by defendant, plaintiff. Civil records on docket books since 1900s. **Criminal Records:** Access: Mail, in person. Both court and visitors may perform in person searches. Search fee: $10.00 per name. Fee is for 7 year search. Required to search: name, years to search. Criminal records on docket books since 1900s. **General Information:** No sealed, juvenile, sex, or expunged records released. Turnaround time 2-3 days. Copy fee: $.50 per page. Certification fee: $1.50. Fee payee: Circuit Clerk. Personal checks accepted. Prepayment is required.

Circuit & County Court - 2nd District PO Box 670, Cleveland, MS 38732; 662-843-2061; Fax: 662-846-2943. Hours: 8AM-5PM (CST). *Felony, Misdemeanor, Civil.*

Civil Records: Access: In person only. Court does not conduct in person searches; visitors must perform searches for themselves. Search fee: No civil searches performed by court. Required to search: name, years to search. Civil cases indexed by defendant, plaintiff. Civil records on docket books since 1940. **Criminal Records:** Access: Mail, in person. Both court and visitors may perform in person searches. Search fee: $10.00 per name. Fee is for 7 year search. Required to search: name, years to search. Criminal records on docket books since 1940. **General Information:** No sealed, juvenile or expunged records released. Turnaround time 2-3 days. Copy fee: $.50 per page. Certification fee: $1.50. Fee payee: Circuit Clerk. Personal checks accepted. Prepayment is required.

Justice Court PO Box 1507, Cleveland, MS 38732; 662-843-4008; Fax: 662-846-6783. Hours: 8:00AM-5:00PM (CST). *Misdemeanor, Civil Actions Under $2,500, Eviction, Small Claims.*

Cleveland Chancery Court PO Box 789, Cleveland, MS 38732; 662-843-2071; Fax: 662-846-5880. Hours: 8AM-5PM (CST). *Probate.*

Rosedale Chancery Court PO Box 238, Rosedale, MS 38769; 662-759-3762; Fax: 662-759-3467. Hours: 8AM-Noon, 1-5PM (CST). *Probate.*

Calhoun County

Circuit Court PO Box 25, Pittsboro, MS 38951; 662-412-3101; Fax: 662-412-3103. Hours: 8AM-5PM (CST). *Felony, Civil Actions Over $2,500.*

Civil Records: Access: Mail, in person. Both court and visitors may perform in person searches. Search fee: $10.00 per name. Required to search: name, years to search. Civil cases indexed by defendant, plaintiff. Civil records on docket books since 1923. **Criminal Records:** Access: Mail, in person. Both court and visitors may perform in person searches. Search fee: $10.00 per name. Required to search: name, years to search, DOB; also helpful-SSN. Criminal records on docket books since 1923. **General Information:** No sealed, adoptions, mental health, juvenile, sex, or expunged records released. SASE not required. Turnaround time same day, phone search info released when payment is received. Copy fee: $.50 per page. Certification fee: $1.50. Fee payee: Circuit Clerk. Personal checks accepted. Prepayment is required. Public access terminal is available. Public Access Terminal Note: Marriage Records & Judgment Roll.

Justice Court PO Box 7, Pittsboro, MS 38951; 662-412-3134; Fax: 662-412-3143. Hours: 8AM-5PM (CST). *Misdemeanor, Civil Actions Under $2,500, Eviction, Small Claims.*

Chancery Court PO Box 8, Pittsboro, MS 38951; 662-983-3117; Fax: 662-983-3128. Hours: 8AM-5PM (CST). *Probate.*

Carroll County

Circuit Court PO Box 6, Vaiden, MS 39176; 662-464-5476; Fax: 662-464-7745. Hours: 8AM-5PM (CST). *Felony, Civil Actions Over $2,500.*

Civil Records: Access: Mail, in person. Both court and visitors may perform in person searches. Search fee: $10.00 per name. Required to search: name, years to search. Civil cases indexed by defendant, plaintiff. Civil records on books since 1900s. **Criminal Records:** Access: Mail, in person. Both court and visitors may perform in person searches. Search fee: $10.00 per name. Required to search: name, years to search; also helpful-SSN. Criminal records on books since 1900s. **General Information:** No adoptions, mental health or juvenile records released. Turnaround time 2 days. Copy fee: $.50 per page. Certification fee: $2.00. Fee payee: Circuit Court. Personal checks accepted. Prepayment is required.

Justice Court PO Box 10, Carrollton, MS 38917; 662-237-9285. Hours: 8AM-4PM (CST). *Misdemeanor, Civil Actions Under $2,500, Eviction, Small Claims.*

Chancery Court PO Box 60, Carrollton, MS 38917; 662-237-9274; Fax: 662-237-9642. Hours: 8AM-12; 1-5PM (CST). *Probate.*

Chickasaw County

Circuit Court-1st District 1 Pinson Sq, Rm 2, Houston, MS 38851; 662-456-2331; Fax: 662-456-5295. Hours: 8AM-5PM (CST). *Felony, Civil Actions Over $2,500.*

Civil Records: Access: Fax, mail, in person. Both court and visitors may perform in person searches. Search fee: $10.00 per name. There is no fee if the visitor performs the search. Required to search: name, years to search; also helpful-address. Civil cases indexed by defendant, plaintiff. Civil records on docket books since mid-1800s. **Criminal Records:** Access: Fax, mail, in person. Both court and visitors may perform in person searches. Search fee: $10.00 per name. Required to search: name, years to search, DOB; also helpful-address, SSN. Criminal records on docket books since mid-1800s. **General Information:** No sealed, adoptions, mental health, juvenile, sex, or expunged records released. SASE required. Turnaround time 2-3 days. Copy fee: $.25 if visitor does; $.50 if court does. Certification fee: $1.00 plus $.50 per page after first. Fee payee: Circuit Clerk. Business checks accepted. Prepayment is required. Public access terminal is available. Fax notes: $1.00 per page.

Circuit Court-2nd District Courthouse, Okolona, MS 38860; 662-447-2838; Fax: 662-447-5024. Hours: 8AM-5PM (CST). *Felony, Civil Actions Over $2,500.*

Civil Records: Access: Fax, mail, in person. Both court and visitors may perform in person searches. Search fee: $10.00 per name. Required to search: name, years to search; also helpful-address. Civil cases indexed by defendant, plaintiff. Civil records on docket books. **Criminal Records:** Access: Fax, mail, in person. Both court and visitors may perform in person searches. Search fee: $10.00 per name. Required to search: name, years to search, DOB; also helpful-SSN. Criminal records on docket books. **General Information:** No sealed, adoptions, mental health, juvenile, sex, or expunged records released. SASE required. Turnaround time 2-3 days. Copy fee: $.50 per page. Certification fee: $1.00 plus $.50 per page after first. Fee payee: Circuit Clerk. Business checks accepted. Prepayment is required.

Justice Court Courthouse, Houston, MS 38851; 662-456-3941; Fax: 662-456-5295. Hours: 8AM-5PM (CST). *Misdemeanor, Civil Actions Under $2,500, Eviction, Small Claims.*

Justice Court District 2 234 W Main, Rm 207, Okolona, MS 38860; 662-447-3402. *Misdemeanor, Civil Actions Under $2,500, Eviction, Small Claims.*

Chancery Court Courthouse Bldg, 1 Pinson Square, Houston, MS 38851; 662-456-2513; Fax: 662-456-5295. *Probate.*

Chancery Court 234 W Main, Rm 201, Okolona, MS 38860-1438; 662-447-2092; Fax: 662-447-5024. *Probate.*

Choctaw County

Circuit Court PO Box 34, Ackerman, MS 39735; 662-285-6245; Fax: 662-285-3444. Hours: 8AM-5PM (CST). *Felony, Civil Actions Over $2,500.*

Civil Records: Access: Mail, in person. Both court and visitors may perform in person searches. Search fee: $10.00 per name. Required to search: name, years to search. Civil cases indexed by defendant, plaintiff. Civil records kept in books, unsure of starting date. **Criminal Records:** Access: Mail, in person. Both court and visitors may perform in person searches. Search fee: $10.00 per name. Same fee for in person search. Required to search: name, years to search; also helpful-DOB, SSN. Criminal records kept in books, unsure of starting date. **General Information:** No sealed, adoptions, mental health, juvenile, sex, or expunged records released. SASE required. Turnaround time 14 days legal maximum. Copy fee: $.50 per page. Certification fee: $1.00. Fee payee: Choctaw County Circuit Clerk. Personal checks accepted. Prepayment is required.

Justice Court PO Box 357, Ackerman, MS 39735; 662-285-3599; Fax: 662-285-3444. Hours: 8AM-5PM (CST). *Misdemeanor, Civil Actions Under $2,500, Eviction, Small Claims.*

Chancery Court PO Box 250, Ackerman, MS 39735; 662-285-6329; Fax: 662-285-3444. Hours: 8AM-5PM (CST). *Probate.*

Claiborne County

Circuit Court PO Box 549, Port Gibson, MS 39150; 601-437-5841. Hours: 8AM-5PM (CST). *Felony, Civil Actions Over $2,500.*

Civil Records: Access: Mail, in person. Both court and visitors may perform in person searches. Search fee: $10.00 per name. Required to search: name, years to search, address. Civil cases indexed by defendant, plaintiff. Civil records on docket books since 1820. **Criminal Records:** Access:

Mail, in person. Both court and visitors may perform in person searches. Search fee: $10.00 per name. Required to search: name, years to search, address, DOB, signed release. Criminal records on docket books since 1820. **General Information:** No sealed, adoptions, mental health, juvenile, sex, or expunged records released. Turnaround time varies. Copy fee: $1.00 per page. Certification fee: No certification fee. Fee payee: Sammie L Good, Circuit Clerk. Personal checks accepted. Prepayment is required.

Justice Court PO Box 497, Port Gibson, MS 39150; 601-437-4478. Hours: 8AM-5PM (CST). *Misdemeanor, Civil Actions Under $2,500, Eviction, Small Claims.*

Chancery Court PO Box 449, Port Gibson, MS 39150; 601-437-4992; Fax: 601-437-3137. Hours: 8AM-5PM (CST). *Probate.*

Clarke County

Circuit Court PO Box 216, Quitman, MS 39355; 601-776-3111; Fax: 601-776-1001. Hours: 8AM-5PM (CST). *Felony, Civil Actions Over $2,500.*

Civil Records: Access: Fax, mail, in person. Both court and visitors may perform in person searches. Search fee: $10.00 per name. Required to search: name, years to search; also helpful-address. Civil cases indexed by defendant, plaintiff. Civil records kept on docket books since 1950s. **Criminal Records:** Access: Fax, mail, in person. Both court and visitors may perform in person searches. Search fee: $10.00 per name. Required to search: name, years to search; also helpful-address, DOB, SSN. Criminal records kept on docket books since 1950s. **General Information:** No sealed, adoptions, mental health, juvenile, sex, or expunged records released. Turnaround time 1 day. No copy fee. Certification fee: No certification fee. Fee payee: Circuit Clerk. Personal checks accepted. Prepayment is required. Fax notes: No fee to fax results.

Justice Court PO Box 4, Quitman, MS 39355; 601-776-5371. Hours: 8AM-5PM (CST). *Misdemeanor, Civil Actions Under $2,500, Eviction, Small Claims.*

Chancery Court PO Box 689, Quitman, MS 39355; 601-776-2126. Hours: 8AM-5PM (CST). *Probate.*

Clay County

Circuit Court PO Box 364, West Point, MS 39773; 662-494-3384. Hours: 8AM-5PM (CST). *Felony, Civil Actions Over $2,500.*

Civil Records: Access: Mail, in person. Both court and visitors may perform in person searches. Search fee: $10.00 per name. Required to search: name, years to search. Civil cases indexed by defendant, plaintiff. Civil records on docket books since mid-1800s. **Criminal Records:** Access: Mail, in person. Both court and visitors may perform in person searches. Search fee: $10.00 per name. Required to search: name, years to search, address, DOB; also helpful-SSN. Criminal records on docket books since mid-1800s. **General Information:** No sealed, adoptions, mental health, juvenile, sex, or expunged records released. SASE required. Turnaround time same day. Copy fee: $.50 per page. Certification fee: $10.00. Fee payee: Clay County Circuit Clerk. Personal checks accepted. Prepayment is required.

Justice Court PO Box 674, West Point, MS 39773; 662-494-6141; Fax: 662-494-4034. Hours:

8AM-5PM (CST). *Misdemeanor, Civil Actions Under $2,500, Eviction, Small Claims.*

Chancery Court PO Box 815, West Point, MS 39773; 662-494-3124. Hours: 8AM-5PM (CST). *Probate.*

Coahoma County

Circuit & County Court PO Box 849, Clarksdale, MS 38614-0849; 662-624-3014; Fax: 662-624-3075. Hours: 8AM-5PM (CST). *Felony, Civil.*

Civil Records: Access: Fax, mail, in person. Both court and visitors may perform in person searches. Search fee: $10.00 per name. Required to search: name, years to search, address. Civil cases indexed by defendant, plaintiff. Civil records on docket since 1836. **Criminal Records:** Access: Mail, in person. Both court and visitors may perform in person searches. Search fee: $10.00 per name. Required to search: name, years to search, DOB, signed release; also helpful-address, SSN. Criminal records on docket since 1836. **General Information:** No sealed, adoptions, mental health, juvenile, sex, or expunged records released. SASE not required. Turnaround time 2 days. Copy fee: $.50 per page. Certification fee: $1.00. Fee payee: Circuit Clerk. Personal checks accepted. Prepayment is required. Fax notes: No fee to fax results.

Justice Court 144 Ritch, Clarksdale, MS 38614; 662-624-3060. Hours: 8AM-5PM (CST). *Misdemeanor, Civil Actions Under $2,500, Eviction, Small Claims.*

Chancery Court PO Box 98, Clarksdale, MS 38614; 662-624-3000; Fax: 662-624-3029. Hours: 8AM-5PM (CST). *Probate.*

Copiah County

Circuit Court PO Box 467, Hazlehurst, MS 39083; 601-894-1241; Fax: 601-894-3026. Hours: 8AM-5PM (CST). *Felony, Civil Actions Over $2,500.*

Civil Records: Access: Fax, mail, in person. Both court and visitors may perform in person searches. Search fee: $6.00 per name. Required to search: name, years to search. Civil cases indexed by defendant. Civil records on docket books since late 1800s. **Criminal Records:** Access: Fax, mail, in person. Both court and visitors may perform in person searches. Search fee: $6.00 per name. Required to search: name, years to search; also helpful-DOB, SSN. Criminal records on docket books since late 1800s. **General Information:** No sealed, adoptions, mental health, juvenile, sex, or expunged records released. Turnaround time 1-2 days. Copy fee: $.50 per page. Certification fee: $1.50. Fee payee: Circuit Clerk. Business checks accepted. Prepayment is required. Fax notes: No fee to fax results.

Justice Court PO Box 798, Hazlehurst, MS 39083; 601-894-3218; Fax: 601-894-1676. Hours: 8:00AM-5:00PM (CST). *Misdemeanor, Civil Actions Under $2,500, Eviction, Small Claims.*

Chancery Court PO Box 507, Hazlehurst, MS 39083; 601-894-3021; Fax: 601-894-3026. Hours: 8AM-5PM (CST). *Probate.*

Covington County

Circuit Court PO Box 667, Collins, MS 39428; 601-765-6506; Fax: 601-765-1052. Hours: 8AM-5PM (CST). *Felony, Civil Actions Over $2,500.*

Civil Records: Access: Fax, mail, in person. Both court and visitors may perform in person searches. Search fee: $10.00 per name. Required to search:

name, years to search. Civil cases indexed by defendant, plaintiff. Civil records on docket books since 1915. **Criminal Records:** Access: Fax, mail, in person. Both court and visitors may perform in person searches. Search fee: $10.00 per name. Required to search: name, years to search, DOB; also helpful-SSN. Criminal records on docket books since 1915. **General Information:** No sealed, adoptions, mental health, juvenile, sex, or expunged records released. Turnaround time 2-3 days. Copy fee: $.50 for first page, $.25 each addl. Certification fee: $3.00. Fee payee: Circuit Clerk. Personal checks accepted. Prepayment is required. Fax notes: No fee to fax results.

Justice Court PO Box 665, Collins, MS 39428; 601-765-6581. Hours: 8AM-5PM (CST). *Misdemeanor, Civil Actions Under $2,500, Eviction, Small Claims.*

Chancery Court PO Box 1679, Collins, MS 39428; 601-765-4242; Fax: 601-765-1052. Hours: 8AM-5PM (CST). *Probate.*

De Soto County

Circuit & County Court 2535 Hwy 51 South, Hernando, MS 38632; 662-429-1325. Hours: 8AM-5PM (CST). *Felony, Misdemeanor, Civil.*

Civil Records: Access: Fax, mail, in person. Both court and visitors may perform in person searches. Search fee: $10.00 per name. Required to search: name, years to search; also helpful-address. Civil cases indexed by defendant, plaintiff. Civil records on docket books since 1972. **Criminal Records:** Access: Fax, mail, in person. Both court and visitors may perform in person searches. Search fee: $10.00 per name. Required to search: name, years to search, DOB; also helpful-SSN. Criminal records on docket books since 1972. **General Information:** No sealed, adoptions, mental health, juvenile, sex, or expunged records released. Turnaround time 1-2 days. Copy fee: $.50 per page. Certification fee: $2.50. Fee payee: Circuit Clerk. Personal checks accepted. Prepayment is required.

Justice Court 8525 Highway 51 North, Southaven, MS 38671; 662-393-5810; Fax: 662-393-5859. Hours: 8AM-5PM (CST). *Misdemeanor, Civil Actions Under $2,500, Eviction, Small Claims.*

Chancery Court 2535 Hwy 51 South, Hernando, MS 38632; 662-429-1320; Fax: 662-429-1311. Hours: 8AM-5PM (CST). *Probate.*

Forrest County

Circuit & County Court PO Box 992, Hattiesburg, MS 39403; 601-582-3213; Fax: 601-545-6065. Hours: 8AM-5PM (CST). *Felony, Misdemeanor, Civil.*

Civil Records: Access: Phone, mail, in person. Both court and visitors may perform in person searches. Search fee: $10.00 per name. Required to search: name, years to search; also helpful-address. Civil cases indexed by defendant, plaintiff. Civil records on docket books since 1900s. Limited phone access. **Criminal Records:** Access: Mail, in person. Both court and visitors may perform in person searches. Search fee: $10.00 per name. Required to search: name, years to search, DOB, SSN; also helpful-address. Criminal records on docket books since 1900s; on computer since 1995. **General Information:** No juvenile or expunged records released. Turnaround time 10 days. Copy fee: $.50 per page. Certification fee: $1.50. Fee payee: Circuit Clerk. Business checks

accepted. Attorney's checks accepted. Prior approval required.

Justice Court 316 Forrest St, Hattiesburg, MS 39401; 601-544-3136. Hours: 8AM-5PM (CST). *Misdemeanor, Civil Actions Under $2,500, Eviction, Small Claims.*

Chancery Court PO Box 951, Hattiesburg, MS 39403; 601-545-6040. Hours: 8AM-5PM (CST). *Probate.*

Franklin County

Circuit Court PO Box 267, Meadville, MS 39653; 601-384-2320; Fax: 601-384-5864. Hours: 8AM-5PM (CST). *Felony, Civil Actions Over $2,500.*

Civil Records: Access: Mail, in person. Both court and visitors may perform in person searches. Search fee: $10.00 per name. Required to search: name, years to search. Civil cases indexed by defendant, plaintiff. Civil records on books since 1944. **Criminal Records:** Access: Mail, in person. Both court and visitors may perform in person searches. Search fee: $10.00 per name. Required to search: name, years to search, DOB; also helpful-address, SSN. Criminal records on books since 1944. **General Information:** No sealed, adoptions, mental health, juvenile, sex, or expunged records released. Turnaround time 2-3 days. Copy fee: $.50 per page. Certification fee: $1.50. Fee payee: Circuit Clerk. Personal checks accepted. Prepayment is required.

Justice Court PO Box 365, Meadville, MS 39653; 601-384-2002. Hours: 8AM-5PM (CST). *Misdemeanor, Civil Actions Under $2,500, Eviction, Small Claims.*

Chancery Court PO Box 297, Meadville, MS 39653; 601-384-2330; Fax: 601-384-5864. Hours: 8AM-5PM (CST). *Probate.*

George County

Circuit Court 355 Cox St, Suite C, Lucedale, MS 39452; 601-947-4881; Fax: 601-947-8804. Hours: 8AM-5PM M-F, 9AM-12PM Sat (CST). *Felony, Civil Actions Over $2,500.*

Civil Records: Access: Fax, mail, in person. Both court and visitors may perform in person searches. Search fee: $10.00 per name. Required to search: name, years to search. Civil cases indexed by defendant, plaintiff. Civil records on docket books since 1910. **Criminal Records:** Access: Fax, mail, in person. Both court and visitors may perform in person searches. Search fee: $10.00 per name. Required to search: name, years to search; also helpful-SSN. Criminal records on docket books since 1910. **General Information:** No sealed, adoptions, mental health, juvenile, sex, or expunged records released. SASE requested. Turnaround time 1-2 days. Copy fee: $.50 per page. Certification fee: $2.00 plus $1.00 each additional page. Fee payee: Circuit Clerk. Personal checks accepted. Fax notes: No fee to fax results.

Justice Court 356 A Cox St, Lucedale, MS 39452; 601-947-4834. Hours: 8AM-5PM (CST). *Misdemeanor, Civil Actions Under $2,500, Eviction, Small Claims.*

Chancery Court 355 Cox St, Suite Cre, Lucedale, MS 39452; 601-947-4881; Fax: 601-947-4812. Hours: 8AM-5PM (CST). *Probate.*

Greene County

Circuit Court PO Box 310, Leakesville, MS 39451; 601-394-2379; Fax: 601-394-2334. Hours: 8AM-5PM M-F (CST). *Felony, Civil Actions Over $2,500.*

Civil Records: Access: Phone, fax, mail, in person. Both court and visitors may perform in person searches. Search fee: $10.00 per name. Required to search: name, years to search; also helpful-address. Civil cases indexed by defendant, plaintiff. Civil records on docket books since early 1900s. **Criminal Records:** Access: Phone, fax, mail, in person. Both court and visitors may perform in person searches. Search fee: $10.00 per name. Required to search: name, years to search; also helpful-SSN. Criminal records on docket books since early 1900s. Misdemeanor records are kept in Greene County Justice Court, 601-394-2347. **General Information:** No sealed, adoptions, mental health, juvenile, sex, or expunged records released. SASE requested. Turnaround time 1-2 days. Copy fee: $.50 per page. Certification fee: $1.00. Fee payee: Circuit Clerk. Personal checks accepted. Prepayment is required. Fax notes: No fee to fax results.

Justice Court PO Box 547, Leakesville, MS 39451; 601-394-2347; Fax: 601-394-5939. Hours: 8AM-5PM (CST). *Misdemeanor, Civil Actions Under $2,500, Eviction, Small Claims.*

Chancery Court PO Box 610, Leakesville, MS 39451; 601-394-2377. Hours: 8AM-5PM (CST). *Probate.*

Grenada County

Circuit Court PO Box 1517, Grenada, MS 38902-1517; 662-226-1941; Fax: 662-227-2865. Hours: 8AM-5PM (CST). *Felony, Civil Actions Over $2,500.*

Civil Records: Access: In person only. Court does not conduct in person searches; visitors must perform searches for themselves. Search fee: No civil searches performed by court. Required to search: name, years to search. Civil cases indexed by defendant, plaintiff. Civil records on docket books since mid-1970s. **Criminal Records:** Access: In person only. Court does not conduct in person searches; visitors must perform searches for themselves. Search fee: No criminal searches performed by court. Required to search: name, years to search. Criminal records on docket books since mid-1970s. **General Information:** No sealed, juvenile, or expunged records released. Copy fee: $.50 per page. Certification fee: $1.50. Fee payee: Circuit Clerk. No personal checks accepted. Prepayment is required. Public access terminal is available. Public Access Terminal Note: Judgement roll on terminal from 1996.

Justice Court 16 First St, Grenada, MS 38901; 662-226-3331. Hours: 8AM-5PM (CST). *Misdemeanor, Civil Actions Under $2,500, Eviction, Small Claims.*

Chancery Court PO Box 1208, Grenada, MS 38902; 662-226-1821; Fax: 662-226-0427. Hours: 8AM-5PM (CST). *Probate.*

Hancock County

Circuit Court PO Box 249, 152 Main Street, Bay St. Louis, MS 39520; 228-467-5265; Fax: 228-467-2779. Hours: 8AM-5PM (CST). *Felony, Civil Actions Over $2,500.*

Civil Records: Access: Mail, in person. Both court and visitors may perform in person searches. Search fee: $10.00 per name. Required to search: name, years to search. Civil cases indexed by defendant, plaintiff. Civil records on docket books since 1975. **Criminal Records:** Access: Mail, in person. Both court and visitors may perform in person searches. Search fee: $10.00 per name. Required to search: name, years to search, DOB; also helpful-SSN. Criminal records on docket

books since 1918. **General Information:** No sealed, adoptions, mental health, juvenile, sex, or expunged records released. Turnaround time 1 week. Copy fee: $.50 per page. Certification fee: $1.50 per page. Fee payee: Circuit Clerk. Personal checks accepted. Prepayment is required.

Justice Court 306 Hwy 90, Bay St. Louis, MS 39520; 228-467-5573. Hours: 8AM-5PM (CST). *Misdemeanor, Civil Actions Under $2,500, Eviction, Small Claims.*

Chancery Court PO Box 429 Bay St., Bay St. Louis, MS 39520; 228-467-5404; Fax: 228-466-5994. Hours: 8AM-5PM (CST). *Probate.*

Harrison County

Circuit Court-1st District PO Box 998, Gulfport, MS 39502; 228-865-4147; Fax: 228-865-4099. Hours: 8AM-5PM (CST). *Felony, Civil Actions Over $75,000.*

Civil Records: Access: Mail, in person. Both court and visitors may perform in person searches. Search fee: $10.00 per name. Required to search: name, years to search. Civil cases indexed by defendant, plaintiff. Civil records on computer since 1991, prior on docket books, older records are archived. **Criminal Records:** Access: Mail, in person. Both court and visitors may perform in person searches. Search fee: $10.00 per name. Required to search: name, years to search, DOB; also helpful-SSN. Criminal records on computer since 1991, prior on docket books, older records are archived. **General Information:** No sealed, adoptions, mental health, juvenile, sex, or expunged records released. SASE requested. Turnaround time 1-2 days. Copy fee: $.50 per page. Certification fee: $1.50. Fee payee: Circuit Clerk. Business checks accepted. Prepayment is required. Public access terminal is available.

Circuit Court-2nd District PO Box 235, Biloxi, MS 39533; 228-435-8258; Fax: 228-435-8277. Hours: 8AM-5PM (CST). *Felony, Civil Actions Over $75,000.*

Civil Records: Access: Fax, mail, in person. Both court and visitors may perform in person searches. Search fee: $10.00 per name. Required to search: name, years to search. Civil cases indexed by defendant, plaintiff. Civil records on computer since July 1991. **Criminal Records:** Access: Fax, mail, in person. Both court and visitors may perform in person searches. Search fee: $10.00 per name. Required to search: name, years to search, DOB; also helpful-SSN. Criminal records on computer since July 1991. **General Information:** No sealed or expunged records released. SASE required. Turnaround time 3 days. Copy fee: $.50 per page. Certification fee: $1.00. Fee payee: Circuit Clerk. Business checks accepted. Attorney's checks accepted. Prepayment is required. Public access terminal is available. Fax notes: $.50 per page.

County Court-1st District PO Box 998, Gulfport, MS 39502; 228-865-4097; Fax: 228-865-4099. Hours: 8AM-5PM (CST). *Misdemeanor, Civil Actions Under $75,000.*

Civil Records: Access: Mail, in person. Both court and visitors may perform in person searches. No search fee. Required to search: name, years to search. Civil cases indexed by defendant, plaintiff. Civil records on computer since 1991, prior on docket books since early 1900s. **Criminal Records:** Access: Mail, in person. Both court and visitors may perform in person searches. Search fee: $10.00 per name. Required to search: name, years to search; also helpful-DOB. Criminal

records on computer since 1991, prior on docket books since early 1900s. **General Information:** No sealed, adoptions, mental health, juvenile, sex, or expunged records released. Turnaround time 1-2 days. Copy fee: $.50 per page. Certification fee: $1.00. Fee payee: County Clerk. Business checks accepted. Prepayment is required. Public access terminal is available.

County Court-2nd District PO Box 235, Biloxi, MS 39533; 228-435-8294/8232; Fax: 228-435-8277. Hours: 8AM-5PM (CST). *Misdemeanor, Civil Actions Under $75,000.*

Civil Records: Access: Fax, mail, in person. Both court and visitors may perform in person searches. Search fee: $10.00 per name. Required to search: name, years to search. Civil cases indexed by defendant, plaintiff. Civil records on computer since July 1991, prior on books. **Criminal Records:** Access: Fax, mail, in person. Both court and visitors may perform in person searches. Search fee: $10.00 per name. Required to search: name, years to search, DOB; also helpful-SSN, aliases. Criminal records on computer since July 1991, prior on books. **General Information:** No sealed or expunged records released. SASE required. Turnaround time 3 days. Copy fee: $.50 per page. Certification fee: $1.00. Fee payee: Circuit Clerk. Business checks accepted. Attorney's checks accepted. Prepayment is required. Public access terminal is available. Fax notes: No fee to fax results.

Justice Court PO Box 1754, Gulfport, MS 39502;; Civil phone:228-865-4193; Criminal phone:228-865-4193; Fax: 228-865-4216. Hours: 8AM-5PM (CST). *Misdemeanor, Civil Actions Under $2,500, Eviction, Small Claims.*

Biloxi Chancery Court PO Box 544, Biloxi, MS 39533; 228-435-8220; Fax: 228-435-8251. Hours: 8AM-Noon, 1-5PM (CST). *Probate.*

Gulfport Chancery Court PO Drawer CC, Gulfport, MS 39502; 228-865-4092; Fax: 228-865-1646. Hours: 8AM-Noon, 1-5PM (CST). *Probate.*

Hinds County

Circuit & County Court-1st District PO Box 327, Jackson, MS 39205; 601-968-6628. Hours: 8AM-5PM (CST). *Felony, Misdemeanor, Civil.*

Civil Records: Access: Mail, in person. Both court and visitors may perform in person searches. Search fee: $9.00 per name. Required to search: name, years to search. Civil cases indexed by defendant, plaintiff. Civil records on docket books back to 1900s. **Criminal Records:** Access: Mail, in person. Both court and visitors may perform in person searches. Search fee: $9.00 per name. Required to search: name, years to search, DOB; also helpful-SSN. Criminal records on docket books back to 1900s. **General Information:** No sealed, adoptions, mental health, juvenile, sex, or expunged records released. Turnaround time 14 days. Copy fee: $.50 per page. Certification fee: No certification fee. Fee payee: Circuit Clerk. Personal checks accepted. Prepayment is required. Public access terminal is available.

Circuit & County Court - 2nd District PO Box 999, Raymond, MS 39154; 601-968-6653. Hours: 8AM-Noon, 1-5PM (CST). *Felony, Misdemeanor, Civil.*

Civil Records: Access: Mail, in person. Both court and visitors may perform in person searches. Search fee: $9.00 per name. Required to search: name, years to search. Civil cases indexed by

defendant, plaintiff. Civil records on computer since 1994, prior on docket books since late 1800s. **Criminal Records:** Access: Mail, in person. Both court and visitors may perform in person searches. Search fee: $9.00 per name. Required to search: name, years to search; also helpful-DOB, SSN. Criminal records on computer since 1994, prior on docket books since late 1800s. **General Information:** No sealed, adoptions, mental health, juvenile, sex, expunged or some preliminary criminal records released. SASE not required. Turnaround time 1 week. Copy fee: $.50 per page. Certification fee: $1.50. Fee payee: Circuit Clerk. Personal checks accepted. Prepayment is required.

Justice Court 407 E Pascagoula, 3rd floor, PO Box 3490, Jackson, MS 39207; 601-968-6781; Fax: 601-973-5532. Hours: 8AM-Noon, 1-5PM (CST). *Misdemeanor, Civil Actions Under $2,500, Eviction, Small Claims.*

Jackson Chancery Court PO Box 686, Jackson, MS 39205; 601-968-6540. Hours: 8AM-5PM (CST). *Probate.*

Raymond Chancery Court PO Box 88, Raymond, MS 39154; 601-857-8055; Fax: 601-857-4953. Hours: 8AM-5PM (CST). *Probate.*

Holmes County

Circuit Court PO Box 718, Lexington, MS 39095; 662-834-2476; Fax: 662-834-3870. Hours: 8AM-5PM (CST). *Felony, Civil Actions Over $2,500.*

Civil Records: Access: Fax, mail, in person. Both court and visitors may perform in person searches. Search fee: $10.00 per name. Required to search: name, years to search. Civil cases indexed by defendant, plaintiff. Civil records on docket books since 1940s. **Criminal Records:** Access: Fax, mail, in person. Both court and visitors may perform in person searches. Search fee: $10.00 per name. Required to search: name, years to search; also helpful-DOB, SSN. Criminal records on docket books since 1940s. **General Information:** No sealed or expunged records released. Turnaround time 1-2 days. Copy fee: $1.00 per page. Certification fee: $1.50. Fee payee: Holmes County Circuit Clerk. Business checks accepted. Prepayment is required. Fax notes: $.25 per page.

Justice Court PO Box 99, Lexington, MS 39095; 662-834-4565. Hours: 8AM-Noon, 1-5PM (CST). *Misdemeanor, Civil Actions Under $2,500, Eviction, Small Claims.*

Chancery Court PO Box 239, Lexington, MS 39095; 662-834-2508; Fax: 662-834-3020. Hours: 8AM-5PM (CST). *Probate.*

Humphreys County

Circuit Court PO Box 696, Belzoni, MS 39038; 662-247-3065; Fax: 662-247-3906. Hours: 8AM-5PM (CST). *Felony, Civil Actions Over $2,500.*

Civil Records: Access: Fax, mail, in person. Both court and visitors may perform in person searches. Search fee: $10.00 per name. Required to search: name, years to search. Civil cases indexed by defendant, plaintiff. Civil records on books since 1918. **Criminal Records:** Access: Fax, mail, in person. Both court and visitors may perform in person searches. Search fee: $10.00 per name. Required to search: name, years to search; also helpful-DOB, SSN. Criminal records on books since 1918. **General Information:** No sealed, adoptions, mental health, juvenile, sex, or expunged records released. SASE not required. Turnaround time 1 day, phone turnaround 30

minutes. Copy fee: $1.00 per page. Certification fee: Certification is included in search fee, unless you do search yourself then $1.00. Fee payee: Circuit Clerk. Personal checks accepted. Prepayment is required. Fax notes: $.50 per page.

Justice Court 102 Castleman St, Belzoni, MS 39038; 662-247-4337; Fax: 662-247-1095. Hours: 8AM-Noon, 1-5PM (CST). *Misdemeanor, Civil Actions Under $2,500, Eviction, Small Claims.*

Chancery Court PO Box 547, Belzoni, MS 39038; 662-247-1740; Fax: 662-247-1010. Hours: 8AM-Noon, 1-5PM (CST). *Probate.*

Issaquena County

Circuit Court PO Box 27, Mayersville, MS 39113; 662-873-2761. Hours: 8AM-5PM (CST). *Felony, Civil Actions Over $2,500.*

Civil Records: Access: Mail, in person. Both court and visitors may perform in person searches. Search fee: $20.00 per name. Required to search: name, years to search. Civil cases indexed by defendant, plaintiff. Civil records on docket books since 1846. **Criminal Records:** Access: Mail, in person. Both court and visitors may perform in person searches. Search fee: $20.00 per name. Required to search: name, years to search; also helpful-DOB, SSN. Criminal records on docket books since 1846. **General Information:** No sealed, adoptions, mental health, juvenile, sex, or expunged records released. Turnaround time 1 week. Copy fee: $.50 per page. Certification fee: $1.00. Fee payee: Circuit Clerk. Personal checks accepted. Prepayment is required.

Justice Court PO Box 58, Mayersville, MS 39113; 662-873-6287. Hours: 8AM-Noon, 1-5PM (CST). *Misdemeanor, Civil Actions Under $2,500, Eviction, Small Claims.*

Chancery Court PO Box 27, Mayersville, MS 39113; 662-873-2761; Fax: 662-873-2061. Hours: 8AM-5PM (CST). *Probate.*

Itawamba County

Circuit Court 201 W Main, Fulton, MS 38843; 662-862-3511; Fax: 662-862-4006. Hours: 8AM-5PM (CST). *Felony, Civil Actions Over $2,500.*

Civil Records: Access: Phone, fax, mail, in person. Both court and visitors may perform in person searches. No search fee. Required to search: name, years to search. Civil cases indexed by defendant, plaintiff. Civil records on books since 1940s. **Criminal Records:** Access: Phone, fax, mail, in person. Both court and visitors may perform in person searches. No search fee. Required to search: name, years to search, DOB; also helpful-SSN. Criminal records on books since 1940s. **General Information:** sex or expunged records released. SASE required. Turnaround time 1 day. No copy fee. Certification fee: No certification fee. Fee payee: Itawamba County Circuit Clerk. Business checks accepted. Public access terminal is available. Fax notes: No fee to fax results.

Justice Court 201 W Main, Fulton, MS 38843; 662-862-4315; Fax: 662-862-5805. Hours: 8AM-Noon, 1-5PM (CST). *Misdemeanor, Civil Actions Under $2,500, Eviction, Small Claims.*

Chancery Court 201 W Main, Fulton, MS 38843; 662-862-3421; Fax: 662-862-4006. Hours: 8AM-5PM M-F; 8AM-Noon Sat (CST). *Probate.*

Jackson County

Circuit Court PO Box 998, Pascagoula, MS 39568-0998; 228-769-3025; Fax: 228-769-3180. Hours: 8AM-5PM (CST). *Felony, Civil.*

Civil Records: Access: Mail, in person. Both court and visitors may perform in person searches. Search fee: $10.00 per name per 10 years searched. Required to search: name, years to search. Civil cases indexed by defendant, plaintiff. Civil records on computer since 1993, prior on docket books since 1920s. **Criminal Records:** Access: Mail, in person. Both court and visitors may perform in person searches. Search fee: $10.00 per name, per 10 years searched. Required to search: name, years to search, DOB; also helpful-SSN. Criminal records on computer since 1992, prior on docket books since 1920s. **General Information:** No sealed or expunged records released. SASE required. Turnaround time varies. Copy fee: $1.0 per page. Certification fee: $2.50. Fee payee: Circuit Clerk. Business checks accepted. Prepayment is required. Public access terminal is available. Fax notes: $2.00 per page.

County Court PO Box 998, Pascagoula, MS 39568; 228-769-3181. Hours: 8AM-5PM (CST). *Misdemeanor, Civil Actions Under $75,000.*

Civil Records: Access: Mail, in person. Both court and visitors may perform in person searches. Search fee: $10.00 per name. Required to search: name, years to search. Civil cases indexed by defendant, plaintiff. Civil records on docket books since 1940s. **Criminal Records:** Access: Mail, in person. Both court and visitors may perform in person searches. Search fee: $10.00 per name. Required to search: name, years to search, DOB. Criminal records on docket books since 1940s. **General Information:** No sealed, adoptions, mental health, juvenile, sex, or expunged records released. Turnaround time 1 week. Copy fee: $1.00 per page. Certification fee: $2.50. Fee payee: Clerk of County Court. Only cashiers checks and money orders accepted. Prepayment is required.

Justice Court 5343 Jefferson St, Moss Point, MS 39563; 228-769-3080; Fax: 228-769-3364. Hours: 8AM-5PM (CST). *Misdemeanor, Civil Actions Under $2,500, Eviction, Small Claims.*

Chancery Court PO Box 998, Pascagoula, MS 39568; 228-769-3124; Fax: 228-769-3397. Hours: 8AM-5PM (CST). *Probate.*

Jasper County

Circuit Court-1st District PO Box 485, Paulding, MS 39348; 601-727-4941; Fax: 601-727-4475. Hours: 8AM-5PM (CST). *Felony, Civil Actions Over $2,500.*

Civil Records: Access: Fax, mail, in person. Both court and visitors may perform in person searches. Search fee: $10.00 per name. Fee includes a search of both districts in the county. Required to search: name, years to search. Civil cases indexed by defendant, plaintiff. Civil records on docket books since 1932. **Criminal Records:** Access: Fax, mail, in person. Both court and visitors may perform in person searches. Search fee: $10.00 per name. Fee includes a search of both districts in the county. Required to search: name, years to search; also helpful-DOB, SSN. Criminal records on docket books since 1932. **General Information:** No sealed or expunged records released. Turnaround time 1 week. Copy fee: $.50 per page. Certification fee: $1.50. Fee payee: Circuit Clerk. Personal checks accepted. Prepayment is required. Fax notes: $5.00 per document.

Circuit Court-2nd District PO Box 447, Bay Springs, MS 39422; 601-764-2245; Fax: 601-764-3078. Hours: 8AM-5PM (CST). *Felony, Civil Actions Over $2,500.*

Civil Records: Access: Mail, in person. Both court and visitors may perform in person searches. Search fee: $10.00 per name. Fee includes a search of both districts in the county. Required to search: name, years to search. Civil cases indexed by defendant, plaintiff. Civil records on docket books since 1932. **Criminal Records:** Access: Mail, in person. Both court and visitors may perform in person searches. Search fee: $10.00 per name. Fee includes a search of both districts in the county. Required to search: name, years to search; also helpful-SSN. Criminal records on docket books since 1932. **General Information:** No sealed, adoptions, mental health, juvenile, sex, or expunged records released. SASE requested. Turnaround time 1 day. Copy fee: $.50 per page. Certification fee: $1.50. Fee payee: Circuit Clerk. Personal checks accepted.

Justice Court PO Box 1054, Bay Springs, MS 39422; 601-764-2065; Fax: 601-764-3402. Hours: 8AM-Noon, 1-5PM (CST). *Misdemeanor, Civil Actions Under $2,500, Eviction, Small Claims.*

Bay Springs Chancery Court PO Box 1047, Bay Springs, MS 39422; 601-764-3368; Fax: 601-764-3026. Hours: 8AM-5PM (CST). *Probate.*

Paulding Chancery Court PO Box 38, Paulding, MS 39348; 601-727-4941; Fax: 601-727-4475. Hours: 8AM-5PM (CST). *Probate.*

Jefferson County

Circuit Court PO Box 305, Fayette, MS 39069; 601-786-3422; Fax: 601-786-9676. Hours: 8AM-5PM (CST). *Felony, Civil Actions Over $2,500.*

Civil Records: Access: Mail, in person. Both court and visitors may perform in person searches. Search fee: $10.00 per name. Required to search: name, years to search. Civil cases indexed by defendant, plaintiff. Civil records on docket books since 1966, prior archived. **Criminal Records:** Access: Mail, in person. Both court and visitors may perform in person searches. Search fee: $10.00 per name. Required to search: name, years to search, DOB; also helpful-SSN. Criminal records on docket books since 1971, prior archived. **General Information:** No sealed, adoptions, mental health, juvenile, sex, or expunged records released. SASE required. Turnaround time same day. Copy fee: $.50 per page. Certification fee: $1.50. Fee payee: Jefferson County Circuit Court. Business checks accepted. Prepayment is required.

Justice Court PO Box 1047, Fayette, MS 39069; 601-786-8594; Fax: 601-786-6017. Hours: 8AM-5PM (CST). *Misdemeanor, Civil Actions Under $2,500, Eviction, Small Claims.*

Chancery Court PO Box 145, Fayette, MS 39069; 601-786-3021; Fax: 601-786-6009. Hours: 8AM-5PM (CST). *Probate.*

Jefferson Davis County

Circuit Court PO Box 1082, Prentiss, MS 39474; 601-792-4231; Fax: 601-792-4957. Hours: 8AM-5PM (CST). *Felony, Civil Actions Over $2,500.*

Civil Records: Access: Fax, mail, in person. Both court and visitors may perform in person searches. Search fee: $10.00 per name. Required to search: name, years to search. Civil cases indexed by defendant, plaintiff. Civil records on docket books since 1907. **Criminal Records:** Access: Fax, mail, in person. Both court and visitors may perform in person searches. Search fee: $10.00 per name. Required to search: name, years to search; also

helpful-SSN. Criminal records on docket books since 1907. **General Information:** No sealed, adoptions, mental health, juvenile, sex, or expunged records released. Turnaround time 1-2 days. Copy fee: $1.00 per page. Certification fee: $2.50. Fee payee: Circuit Clerk. Personal checks accepted. Prepayment is required. Fax notes: No fee to fax results.

Justice Court PO Box 1407, Prentiss, MS 39474; 601-792-5129. Hours: 8AM-Noon, 1-5PM (CST). *Misdemeanor, Civil Actions Under $2,500, Eviction, Small Claims.*

Chancery Court PO Box 1137, Prentiss, MS 39474; 601-792-4204; Fax: 601-792-2894. Hours: 8AM-5PM (CST). *Probate.*

Jones County

Circuit & County Court-1st District 101 N. Court St, Ellisville, MS 39437; 601-477-8538. Hours: 8AM-5PM (CST). *Felony, Misdemeanor, Civil.*

Civil Records: Access: In person only. Court does not conduct in person searches; visitors must perform searches for themselves. Search fee: No civil searches performed by court. Required to search: name, years to search. Civil cases indexed by defendant, plaintiff. Civil records on docket books since 1960s. **Criminal Records:** Access: Mail, in person. Both court and visitors may perform in person searches. Search fee: $10.00 per name. Required to search: name, years to search. Criminal records on docket books since 1960s. **General Information:** No sealed, adoptions, mental health, juvenile, sex, or expunged records released. Turnaround time 1-2 days. Copy fee: $.50 per page. Certification fee: $1.00. Fee payee: Circuit Clerk. Personal checks accepted. Prepayment is required.

Circuit & County Court-2nd District PO Box 1336, Laurel, MS 39441; 601-425-2556. Hours: 8AM-5PM (CST). *Felony, Misdemeanor, Civil.*

Civil Records: Access: Mail, in person. Both court and visitors may perform in person searches. Search fee: $10.00 per name. Fee is per district. Required to search: name, years to search. Civil cases indexed by defendant, plaintiff. Civil records on docket books since 1960s. **Criminal Records:** Access: Mail, in person. Both court and visitors may perform in person searches. Search fee: $10.00 per name. Fee is per district. Required to search: name, years to search; also helpful-SSN. Criminal records on docket books since 1960s. **General Information:** No sealed or Juvenile Youth Court records released. Turnaround time 2 days. Copy fee: $.50 per page. Certification fee: $1.00. Fee payee: Jones County Circuit Clerk. Personal checks accepted. Prepayment is required.

Justice Court PO Box 1997, Laurel, MS 39441; 601-428-3137; Fax: 601-428-0526. Hours: 8AM-Noon, 1-5PM (CST). *Misdemeanor, Civil Actions Under $2,500, Eviction, Small Claims.*

Ellisville Chancery Court 101-D Court St., Ellisville, MS 39437; 601-477-3307. Hours: 8AM-Noon, 1-5PM (CST). *Probate.*

Laurel Chancery Court PO Box 1468, Laurel, MS 39441; 601-428-0527; Fax: 601-428-3602. Hours: 8AM-5PM (CST). *Probate.*

Kemper County

Circuit Court PO Box 130, De Kalb, MS 39328; 601-743-2224; Fax: 601-743-2789. Hours: 8AM-5PM (CST). *Felony, Civil Actions Over $2,500.*

Civil Records: Access: Phone, fax, mail, in person. Both court and visitors may perform in person searches. Search fee: $10.00 per name. Required to search: name, years to search, address. Civil cases indexed by defendant, plaintiff. Civil records on docket books since 1960s. **Criminal Records:** Access: Phone, fax, mail, in person. Both court and visitors may perform in person searches. Search fee: $10.00 per name. Required to search: name, years to search, address, DOB; also helpful-SSN. Criminal records on docket books since 1960s. **General Information:** No sealed, adoptions, mental health, juvenile, sex, or expunged records released. Turnaround time 1 week. Copy fee: $.25 per page. Certification fee: No certification fee. Fee payee: Circuit Clerk. Business checks accepted. Prepayment is required. Fax notes: $.25 per page.

Justice Court PO Box 661, De Kalb, MS 39328; 601-743-2793; Fax: 601-743-2789. Hours: 8AM-5PM (CST). *Misdemeanor, Civil Actions Under $2,500, Eviction, Small Claims.*

Chancery Court PO Box 188, De Kalb, MS 39328; 601-743-2460; Fax: 601-743-2789. Hours: 8AM-5PM (CST). *Probate.*

Lafayette County

Circuit Court LaFayette County Courthouse, Oxford, MS 38655; 662-234-4951; Fax: 662-236-0238. Hours: 8AM-5PM (CST). *Felony, Civil Actions Over $2,500.*

Civil Records: Access: Mail, in person. Both court and visitors may perform in person searches. Search fee: $10.00 per name. Fee is per 10 years searched. Required to search: name, years to search; also helpful-address. Civil cases indexed by defendant, plaintiff. Civil records on docket books from late 1800s. **Criminal Records:** Access: Mail, in person. Both court and visitors may perform in person searches. Search fee: $10.00 per name. Fee is per 10 years searched. Required to search: name, years to search, DOB; also helpful-address, SSN. Criminal records on docket books from late 1800s. **General Information:** No sealed, adoptions, mental health, juvenile, sex, or expunged records released. Turnaround time 1-2 days. Copy fee: $.50 per page. Certification fee: $1.50. Fee payee: Circuit Clerk. Business checks accepted. Prepayment is required. Public access terminal is available.

Justice Court 1219 Monroe, Oxford, MS 38655; 662-234-1545; Fax: 662-238-7990. Hours: 8AM-5PM (CST). *Misdemeanor, Civil Actions Under $2,500, Eviction, Small Claims.*

Chancery Court PO Box 1240, Oxford, MS 38655; 662-234-2131; Fax: 662-234-5402. Hours: 8AM-5PM (CST). *Probate.*

Lamar County

Circuit Court PO Box 369, Purvis, MS 39475; 601-794-8504; Fax: 601-794-3905. Hours: 8AM-5PM (CST). *Felony, Civil Actions Over $2,500.*

Civil Records: Access: Mail, in person. Both court and visitors may perform in person searches. Search fee: $10.00 per name. Required to search: name, years to search. Civil cases indexed by defendant, plaintiff. Civil records on docket books since 1904. **Criminal Records:** Access: Mail, in person. Both court and visitors may perform in person searches. Search fee: $10.00 per name. Required to search: name, years to search; also helpful-SSN. Criminal records on docket books since 1904. **General Information:** No sealed, adoptions, mental health, juvenile, sex, or expunged records released. SASE requested.

Turnaround time 1-2 days. Copy fee: $1.00 per page. Certification fee: No certification fee. Fee payee: Circuit Clerk. Business checks accepted. Prepayment is required.

Justice Court PO Box 1010, Purvis, MS 39475; 601-794-2950; Fax: 601-794-1076. Hours: 8AM-5PM (CST). *Misdemeanor, Civil Actions Under $2,500, Eviction, Small Claims.*

Chancery Court PO Box 247, Purvis, MS 39475; 601-794-8504; Fax: 601-794-3903. Hours: 8AM-5PM (CST). *Probate.*

Lauderdale County

Circuit & County Court PO Box 1005, Meridian, MS 39302-1005; 601-482-9738; Fax: 601-484-3970. Hours: 8AM-5PM (CST). *Felony, Civil Actions Over $2,500.*

Note: County Court can be reached at 601-482-9715

Civil Records: Access: Mail, in person. Both court and visitors may perform in person searches. Search fee: $10.00 per name. Required to search: name, years to search. Civil cases indexed by defendant, plaintiff. Civil records on docket books back to 1950s, computerized since 1992. **Criminal Records:** Access: Mail, in person. Both court and visitors may perform in person searches. Search fee: $10.00 per name. Required to search: name, years to search, DOB; also helpful-SSN. Criminal records on computer (Felony) since 1965. **General Information:** No sealed, adoptions, mental health, juvenile, sex, or expunged records released. SASE not required. Turnaround time 1 week, phone turnaround time 1 week. Copy fee: $.50 per page. Certification fee: No certification fee. Fee payee: Circuit Clerk. Business checks accepted. Will bill complete files to attorneys.

Justice Court PO Box 5126, Meridian, MS 39302; 601-482-9879; Fax: 601-482-9813. Hours: 8AM-5PM (CST). *Misdemeanor, Civil Actions Under $2,500, Eviction, Small Claims.*

Chancery Court PO Box 1587, Meridian, MS 39302; 601-482-9701; Fax: 601-486-4920. Hours: 8AM-Noon, 1-5PM (CST). *Probate.*

Lawrence County

Circuit Court PO Box 1249, Monticello, MS 39654; 601-587-4791; Fax: 601-587-0750. Hours: 8AM-5PM (CST). *Felony, Civil Actions Over $2,500.*

Civil Records: Access: Phone, fax, mail, in person. Both court and visitors may perform in person searches. Search fee: $10.00 per name. Required to search: name, years to search; also helpful-address. Civil cases indexed by defendant, plaintiff. Civil records on docket books since 1900s. For fax request send copy of check for fee. **Criminal Records:** Access: Phone, fax, mail, in person. Both court and visitors may perform in person searches. Search fee: $10.00 per name. Required to search: name, years to search, DOB; also helpful-address, SSN. Criminal records on docket books since 1900s. For fax request send copy of check for fee. **General Information:** No sealed, adoptions, mental health, juvenile, sex, or expunged records released. SASE requested. Turnaround time 1 week, phone turnaround time 1-2 days. No copy fee. Certification fee: No certification fee. Fee payee: Circuit Clerk. Personal checks accepted. Prepayment is required. Fax notes: $10.00 per document.

Justice Court PO Box 903, Monticello, MS 39654; 601-587-7183; Fax: 601-587-0755. Hours:

8AM-5PM (CST). *Misdemeanor, Civil Actions Under $2,500, Eviction, Small Claims.*

Chancery Court 517 Broad St, Courthouse Sq, PO Box 821, Monticello, MS 39654; 601-587-7162; Fax: 601-587-0750. Hours: 8AM-5PM (CST). *Probate.*

Leake County

Circuit Court PO Box 67, Carthage, MS 39051; 601-267-8357; Fax: 601-267-8889. Hours: 8AM-5PM (CST). *Felony, Civil Actions Over $2,500.*

Civil Records: Access: Mail, in person. Both court and visitors may perform in person searches. Search fee: $10.00 per name. Required to search: name, years to search. Civil cases indexed by defendant, plaintiff. Civil records on docket books since 1970s. **Criminal Records:** Access: Mail, in person. Both court and visitors may perform in person searches. Search fee: $10.00 per name. Required to search: name, years to search, DOB; also helpful-SSN. Criminal records on docket books since 1970s. **General Information:** No sealed, adoptions, mental health, juvenile, sex, or expunged records released. SASE required. Turnaround time 1-2 days. Copy fee: $.50 per page. Certification fee: $1.50. Fee payee: Circuit Clerk. Personal checks accepted. Prepayment is required. Public access terminal is available. Public Access Terminal Note: Voting & Judgments only.

Justice Court PO Box 69, Carthage, MS 39051; 601-267-5677; Fax: 601-267-6134. Hours: 8:00AM-5:00PM (CST). *Misdemeanor, Civil Actions Under $2,500, Eviction, Small Claims.*

Chancery Court PO Box 72, Carthage, MS 39051; 601-267-7371; Fax: 601-267-6137. Hours: 8AM-5PM (CST). *Probate.*

Lee County

Circuit & County Court Circuit Court-PO Box 762, County Court - PO Box 736, Tupelo, MS 38802; 662-841-9022/9023(Circuit) 9730 (County); Fax: 662-680-6079. Hours: 8AM-5PM (CST). *Felony, Civil Actions Over $2,500.*

Civil Records: Access: Mail, in person. Both court and visitors may perform in person searches. Search fee: $10.00 per name. Required to search: name, years to search. Civil cases indexed by defendant, plaintiff. Circuit records on computer since 1990, others on docket books since 1987. County records not on computer. **Criminal Records:** Access: Mail, in person. Both court and visitors may perform in person searches. Search fee: $10.00 per name. Required to search: name, years to search; also helpful-DOB, SSN. Circuit records on computer since 1990, others on docket books since 1987. County records not on computer. **General Information:** No sealed or expunged records released. SASE required. Turnaround time 1-2 days. Copy fee: $.25 per page. Certification fee: $1.50. Fee payee: Lee County & Circuit Court. Business checks accepted. Prepayment is required.

Justice Court PO Box 108, Tupelo, MS 38802; 662-841-9014; Fax: 662-680-6021. Hours: 8AM-5PM (CST). *Misdemeanor, Civil Actions Under $2,500, Eviction, Small Claims.*

Chancery Court PO Box 7127, Tupelo, MS 38802; 662-841-9100; Fax: 662-680-6091. Hours: 8AM-5PM (CST). *Probate.*

Leflore County

Circuit & County Court PO Box 1953, Greenwood, MS 38935-1953; 662-453-1041; Fax: 662-455-1278. Hours: 8AM-5PM (CST). *Felony, Civil Actions Over $2,500.*

Civil Records: Access: Fax, mail, in person. Both court and visitors may perform in person searches. Search fee: $10.00 per name. Required to search: name, years to search. Civil cases indexed by defendant, plaintiff. Civil records on computer since 1994; prior records on docket books since mid-1800s. **Criminal Records:** Access: Fax, mail, in person. Both court and visitors may perform in person searches. Search fee: $10.00 per name. Required to search: name, years to search; also helpful-DOB, SSN. Criminal records on computer since 1994; prior records on docket books since mid-1800s. **General Information:** No sealed or expunged records released. Turnaround time 1-2 days. Copy fee: $.50 per page. Certification fee: $1.50. Fee payee: Circuit Clerk. Personal checks accepted. Prepayment is required. Public access terminal is available. Fax notes: Call for fax fee.

Justice Court PO Box 8056, Greenwood, MS 38935; 662-453-1605. Hours: 8AM-5PM (CST). *Misdemeanor, Civil Actions Under $2,500, Eviction, Small Claims.*

Chancery Court PO Box 250, Greenwood, MS 38935-0250; 662-453-1041; 453-1432 (court admin); Fax: 662-455-7959. Hours: 8AM-5PM (CST). *Probate.*

Lincoln County

Circuit Court PO Box 357, Brookhaven, MS 39602; 601-835-3435; Fax: 601-835-3482. Hours: 8AM-5PM (CST). *Felony, Civil Actions Over $2,500.*

Civil Records: Access: Fax, mail, in person. Both court and visitors may perform in person searches. Search fee: $10.00 per name. Required to search: name, years to search. Civil cases indexed by defendant, plaintiff. Civil records on computer since 1986, prior on docket books. **Criminal Records:** Access: Fax, mail, in person. Both court and visitors may perform in person searches. Search fee: $10.00 per name. Required to search: name, years to search; also helpful-DOB, SSN. Criminal records on computer since 1986, prior on docket books. **General Information:** No sealed or expunged records released. Turnaround time 1-2 days. Copy fee: $.50 per page. Certification fee: $1.00. Fee payee: Circuit Clerk. Personal checks accepted. Out of state checks not accepted. Prepayment is required. Public access terminal is available. Fax notes: $10.00 per document.

Justice Court PO Box 767, Brookhaven, MS 39602; 601-835-3474. Hours: 8:00AM-5:00PM (CST). *Misdemeanor, Civil Actions Under $2,500, Eviction, Small Claims.*

Chancery Court PO Box 555, Brookhaven, MS 39602; 601-835-3412; Fax: 601-835-3423. Hours: 8AM-5PM (CST). *Probate.*

Lowndes County

Circuit & County Court PO Box 31, Columbus, MS 39703; 662-329-5900. Hours: 8AM-5PM (CST). *Felony, Civil.*

Civil Records: Access: Mail, in person. Both court and visitors may perform in person searches. Search fee: $10.00 per name. Required to search: name, years to search. Civil cases indexed by defendant, plaintiff. Civil records on computer from 2/94, on docket books from 1900s. **Criminal Records:** Access: Mail, in person. Both court and visitors may perform in person searches. Search fee: $10.00 per name per year. Required to search: name, years to search, DOB; also helpful-SSN. Criminal records on computer since 11/93; prior on docket books. **General Information:** No sealed, adoption, mental health, juvenile, sex or expunged cases released. Copy fee: $.50 per page. Certification fee: $1.50. Fee payee: Clerk of Court. Personal checks accepted. Prepayment is required. Public access terminal is available.

Justice Court 11 Airline Rd, Columbus, MS 39702; 662-329-5929; Fax: 662-245-4619. Hours: 8AM-5PM (CST). *Misdemeanor, Civil Actions Under $2,500, Eviction, Small Claims.*

Chancery Court PO Box 684, Columbus, MS 39703; 662-329-5800. Hours: 8AM-5PM (CST). *Probate.*

Madison County

Circuit & County Court PO Box 1626, Canton, MS 39046; 601-859-4365; Fax: 601-859-8555. Hours: 8AM-5PM (CST). *Felony, Civil.*

Civil Records: Access: Phone, fax, mail, in person. Both court and visitors may perform in person searches. No search fee. Required to search: name, years to search. Civil cases indexed by defendant, plaintiff. Civil records on computer since 1987, prior on docket books since 1950. **Criminal Records:** Access: Mail, in person. Both court and visitors may perform in person searches. Search fee: $10.00 per name. Required to search: name, years to search. Criminal records on computer since 1992, prior on docket books since 1945. **General Information:** No sealed, adoptions, mental health, juvenile, sex, or expunged records released. SASE requested. Turnaround time 1 week. Copy fee: $.25 per page. Certification fee: $1.00. Fee payee: Circuit Clerk. Personal checks accepted. Prepayment is required. Public access terminal is available.

Justice Court 175 N Union, Canton, MS 39046; 601-859-6337; Fax: 601-859-5878. Hours: 8AM-5PM (CST). *Misdemeanor, Civil Actions Under $2,500, Eviction, Small Claims.*

Chancery Court PO Box 404, Canton, MS 39046; 601-859-1177; Fax: 601-859-5875. Hours: 8AM-5PM (CST). *Probate.*

Marion County

Circuit Court 250 Broad St, Suite 1, Columbia, MS 39429; 601-736-8246. Hours: 8AM-5PM (CST). *Felony, Civil Actions Over $2,500.*

Civil Records: Access: Mail, in person. Both court and visitors may perform in person searches. Search fee: $10.00 per name. Required to search: name, years to search. Civil cases indexed by defendant, plaintiff. Civil records on docket books since 1800s. **Criminal Records:** Access: Mail, in person. Both court and visitors may perform in person searches. Search fee: $10.00 per name. Required to search: name, years to search; also helpful-SSN. Criminal records on docket books since 1800s. **General Information:** No sealed, adoptions, mental health, juvenile, sex, or expunged records released. SASE required. Turnaround time 1-2 days. Copy fee: $.50 per page. Certification fee: No certification fee. Fee payee: Circuit Clerk. Personal checks accepted. Prepayment is required.

Justice Court 500 Courthouse Square, Columbia, MS 39429; 601-736-2572; Fax: 601-736-2580. Hours: 8AM-5PM (CST). *Misdemeanor, Civil Actions Under $2,500, Eviction, Small Claims.*

Chancery Court 250 Broad St, Suite 2, Columbia, MS 39429; 601-736-2691; Fax: 601-736-1232. Hours: 8AM-5PM (CST). *Probate.*

Marshall County

Circuit Court PO Box 459, Holly Springs, MS 38635; 662-252-3434; Fax: 662-252-0004 & 252-5951. Hours: 8AM-5PM (CST). *Felony, Civil Actions Over $2,500.*

Civil Records: Access: Fax, mail, in person. Both court and visitors may perform in person searches. Search fee: $10.00 per name. Required to search: name, years to search. Civil cases indexed by defendant, plaintiff. Civil records on docket books since 1960s. **Criminal Records:** Access: Mail, in person. Both court and visitors may perform in person searches. Search fee: $10.00 per name. Required to search: name, years to search; also helpful-DOB, SSN. Criminal records on docket books since 1960s. **General Information:** No sealed or expunged records released. Turnaround time 1-2 days. Copy fee: $.50 per page. Certification fee: $2.50. Fee payee: Circuit Court Clerk. Personal checks accepted. Prepayment is required. Fax notes: No fee to fax results. Fax copy of search fee check.

Justice Court-North & South Districts PO Box 867, Holly Springs, MS 38635; 662-252-3585. Hours: 8AM-5PM (CST). *Misdemeanor, Civil Actions Under $2,500, Eviction, Small Claims.*

Chancery Court PO Box 219, Holly Springs, MS 38635; 662-252-4431; Fax: 662-252-0004. Hours: 8AM-5PM (CST). *Probate.*

Monroe County

Circuit Court PO Box 843, Aberdeen, MS 39730; 662-369-8695; Fax: 662-369-3684. Hours: 8AM-5PM (CST). *Felony, Civil Actions Over $2,500.*

Civil Records: Access: In person only. Court does not conduct in person searches; visitors must perform searches for themselves. Search fee: No civil searches performed by court. Required to search: name, years to search; also helpful-address. Civil cases indexed by defendant, plaintiff. Civil records on docket books since 1821. **Criminal Records:** Access: In person only. Court does not conduct in person searches; visitors must perform searches for themselves. Search fee: No criminal searches performed by court. Required to search: name, years to search, DOB; also helpful-address, SSN. Criminal records on docket books since 1821. **General Information:** No sealed, adoptions, mental health, juvenile, sex, or expunged records released. Copy fee: $.50 per page. Certification fee: $3.00. Fee payee: Monroe County Circuit Clerk. Only cashiers checks and money orders accepted. Prepayment is required.

Justice Court-District 1 & 3 101 9th St, Amory, MS 38821; 662-256-8493; Fax: 662-256-7876. *Misdemeanor, Civil Actions Under $2,500, Eviction, Small Claims.*

Justice Court-District 2 PO Box F, Aberdeen, MS 39730; 662-369-4971. Hours: 8AM-5PM (CST). *Misdemeanor, Civil Actions Under $2,500, Eviction, Small Claims.*

Chancery Court PO Box 578, Aberdeen, MS 39730; 662-369-8143; Fax: 662-369-7928. Hours: 8AM-5PM (CST). *Probate.*

Montgomery County

Circuit Court PO Box 765, Winona, MS 38967; 662-283-4161; Fax: 662-283-2233. Hours: 8AM-5PM (CST). *Felony, Civil Actions Over $2,500.*

Civil Records: Access: Mail, in person. Both court and visitors may perform in person searches. Search fee: $10.00 per name. Required to search: name, years to search. Civil cases indexed by defendant, plaintiff. Civil records on docket books since early 1900s. **Criminal Records:** Access: Mail, in person. Both court and visitors may perform in person searches. Search fee: $10.00 per name. Required to search: name, years to search. Criminal records on docket books since early 1900s. **General Information:** No sealed or expunged records released. SASE required. Turnaround time 1-2 days. Copy fee: $.25 per page. Certification fee: $2.00. Fee payee: Circuit Clerk. Personal checks accepted. Prepayment is required.

Justice Court PO Box 229, Winona, MS 38967; 662-283-2290; Fax: 662-283-2233. Hours: 8AM-5PM (CST). *Misdemeanor, Civil Actions Under $2,500, Eviction, Small Claims.*

Chancery Court PO Box 71, Winona, MS 38967; 662-283-2333; Fax: 662-283-2233. Hours: 8AM-5PM (CST). *Probate.*

Neshoba County

Circuit Court 401 E Beacon St Suite 110, Philadelphia, MS 39350; 601-656-4781; Fax: 601-650-3997. Hours: 8AM-5PM (CST). *Felony, Civil Actions Over $2,500.*

Civil Records: Access: Mail, in person. Both court and visitors may perform in person searches. Search fee: $10.00 per name. Required to search: name, years to search. Civil cases indexed by defendant. **Criminal Records:** Access: Mail, in person. Both court and visitors may perform in person searches. Search fee: $10.00 per name. Required to search: name, years to search, DOB; also helpful-SSN. Criminal records on docket books since 1877. **General Information:** No sealed, adoptions, mental health, juvenile, sex, or expunged records released. Turnaround time 1 day. Copy fee: $.50 per page. Certification fee: $2.00. Fee payee: Circuit Clerk. Business checks accepted.

Justice Court 401 E Beacon St, Philadelphia, MS 39350; 601-656-5361/1101. *Misdemeanor, Civil Actions Under $2,500, Eviction, Small Claims.*

Chancery Court 401 Beacon St Suite 107, Philadelphia, MS 39350; 601-656-3581. Hours: 8AM-5PM (CST). *Probate.*

Newton County

Circuit Court PO Box 447, Decatur, MS 39327; 601-635-2368; Fax: 601-635-3210. Hours: 8AM-5PM (CST). *Felony, Civil Actions Over $2,500.*

Civil Records: Access: Phone, mail, in person. Both court and visitors may perform in person searches. Search fee: $10.00 per name. Required to search: name, years to search. Civil cases indexed by defendant, plaintiff. Civil records on docket books. **Criminal Records:** Access: Phone, mail, in person. Both court and visitors may perform in person searches. Search fee: $10.00 per name. Required to search: name, years to search, DOB; also helpful-SSN. Criminal records on docket books. **General Information:** No sealed, adoptions, mental health, juvenile, sex, or expunged records released. SASE required. Turnaround time same day. Copy fee: $.50 per page. Certification fee: $1.50. Fee payee: Circuit

Court. Personal checks accepted. Prepayment is required.

Justice Court PO Box 69, Decatur, MS 39327; 601-635-2740. Hours: 8AM-5PM (CST). *Misdemeanor, Civil Actions Under $2,500, Eviction, Small Claims.*

Chancery Clerk's Office PO Box 68, Decatur, MS 39327; 601-635-2367. Hours: 8AM-5PM (CST). *Probate.*

Noxubee County

Circuit Court PO Box 431, Macon, MS 39341; 662-726-5737; Fax: 662-726-6041. Hours: 8AM-5PM (CST). *Felony, Civil Actions Over $2,500.*

Civil Records: Access: Mail, in person. Both court and visitors may perform in person searches. Search fee: $10.00 per name. Required to search: name, years to search. Civil cases indexed by defendant. Civil records on docket books since 1800s. Criminal Records: Access: Mail, in person. Both court and visitors may perform in person searches. Search fee: $10.00 per name. Required to search: name, years to search; also helpful-SSN. Criminal records on docket books since 1800s. General Information: No sealed, adoptions, mental health, juvenile, sex, or expunged records released. SASE required. Turnaround time 1 week. Copy fee: $.50 per page. Certification fee: $5.00. Fee payee: Circuit Clerk. Business checks accepted. Prepayment is required.

Justice Court - North & South Districts 507 S Jefferson, Macon, MS 39341; 662-726-5834; Fax: 662-726-2944. Hours: 8AM-5PM (CST). *Misdemeanor, Civil Actions Under $2,500, Eviction, Small Claims.*

Chancery Court PO Box 147, Macon, MS 39341; 662-726-4243; Fax: 662-726-2272. Hours: 8AM-5PM (CST). *Probate.*

Oktibbeha County

Circuit Court Courthouse, 101 E Main, Starkville, MS 39759; 662-323-1356. Hours: 8AM-5PM (CST). *Felony, Civil Actions Over $2,500.*

Civil Records: Access: Mail, in person. Both court and visitors may perform in person searches. Search fee: $10.00 per name. Required to search: name, years to search; also helpful-address. Civil cases indexed by defendant, plaintiff. Civil records on docket books since 1938. Criminal Records: Access: Mail, in person. Both court and visitors may perform in person searches. Search fee: $10.00 per name. Required to search: name, years to search; also helpful-DOB, SSN. Criminal records on docket since 1950. General Information: No sealed, adoptions, mental health, juvenile, sex, or expunged records released. Turnaround time 1 week. Copy fee: $.50 per page. Certification fee: $1.50. Fee payee: Circuit Clerk. Personal checks accepted. Prepayment is required.

Justice Court-Districts 1-3 104 Felix Long Dr, Starkville, MS 39759; 662-324-3032; Fax: 662-338-1060. Hours: 8AM-5PM (CST). *Misdemeanor, Civil Actions Under $2,500, Eviction, Small Claims.*

Chancery Court Courthouse, 101 E Main, Starkville, MS 39759; 662-323-5834. Hours: 8AM-5PM (CST). *Probate.*

Panola County

Circuit Court-1st District PO Box 130, Sardis, MS 38666; 662-487-2073; Fax: 662-487-3595. Hours: 8AM-5PM (CST). *Felony, Civil Actions Over $2,500.*

Civil Records: Access: Fax, mail, in person. Both court and visitors may perform in person searches. Search fee: $10.00 per name. Fee is for dual district search. Required to search: name, years to search. Civil cases indexed by defendant. Civil records on docket books since 1925. Criminal Records: Access: Fax, mail, in person. Both court and visitors may perform in person searches. Search fee: $10.00 per name. Fee is for dual district search. Required to search: name, years to search, DOB; also helpful-SSN. Criminal records on docket books since 1925. General Information: No sealed, adoptions, mental health, juvenile, sex, or expunged records released. SASE required. Turnaround time varies. Copy fee: $.50 per page. Certification fee: $1.50. Fee payee: Circuit Clerk. Business checks accepted. Prepayment is required. Fax notes: No fee to fax results. Fax copy of the search fee check.

Circuit Court-2nd District PO Box 346, Batesville, MS 38606; 662-563-6210; Fax: 662-563-8233. Hours: 8AM-5PM (CST). *Felony, Civil Actions Over $2,500.*

Civil Records: Access: Phone, fax, mail, in person. Both court and visitors may perform in person searches. Search fee: $10.00 per name. Fee is per district. Required to search: name, years to search. Civil cases indexed by defendant, plaintiff. Civil records on docket books since 1925. Criminal Records: Access: Phone, fax, mail, in person. Both court and visitors may perform in person searches. Search fee: $10.00 per name. Fee is per district. Required to search: name, years to search, address, DOB; also helpful-SSN. Criminal records on docket books since 1925. General Information: No sealed, adoptions, mental health, juvenile, sex, or expunged records released. Turnaround time same day. Copy fee: $.25 per page. Certification fee: $5.00. Fee payee: Circuit Clerk's Office. Personal checks accepted. Prepayment is required. Fax notes: $1.00 per page.

Justice Court PO Box 249, Sardis, MS 38666; 662-487-2080. Hours: 8AM-5PM (CST). *Misdemeanor, Civil Actions Under $2,500, Eviction, Small Claims.*

Panola County Chancery Clerk 151 Public Square, Batesville, MS 38606; 662-563-6205; Fax: 662-563-8233. Hours: 8AM-5PM (CST). *Probate.*

Sardis Chancery Court PO Box 130, Sardis, MS 38666; 662-487-2070; Fax: 662-487-3595. Hours: 8AM-Noon, 1-5PM (CST). *Probate.*

Pearl River County

Circuit Court Courthouse, Poplarville, MS 39470; 601-795-3059; Fax: 601-795-3084. Hours: 8AM-5PM (CST). *Felony, Civil Actions Over $2,500.*

Civil Records: Access: Mail, in person. Both court and visitors may perform in person searches. Search fee: $10.00 per name. Required to search: name, years to search. Civil cases indexed by defendant, plaintiff. Civil records on docket books since 1890. Criminal Records: Access: Mail, in person. Both court and visitors may perform in person searches. Search fee: $10.00 per name. Required to search: name, years to search. Criminal records on computer since late 1960s, prior on docket books since 1890. General Information: No sealed, adoptions, mental health, juvenile, sex, or expunged records released. Turnaround time 1-2 days. Copy fee: $.50 per page. Certification fee: $1.50. Fee payee: Circuit Clerk. Personal checks accepted. Prepayment is required.

Justice Court - Northern, South-eastern, & Southwestern Districts 204 Julia St, Poplarville, MS 39470; 601-795-8018; Fax: 601-795-3063. Hours: 8AM-5PM (CST). *Misdemeanor, Civil Actions Under $2,500, Eviction, Small Claims.*

Chancery Court PO Box 431, Poplarville, MS 39470; 601-795-2238; Fax: 601-795-3093. Hours: 8AM-5PM (CST). *Probate.*

Perry County

Circuit Court PO Box 198, New Augusta, MS 39462; 601-964-8663; Fax: 601-964-8265. Hours: 8AM-5PM (CST). *Felony, Civil Actions Over $2,500.*

Civil Records: Access: Mail, in person. Both court and visitors may perform in person searches. Search fee: $10.00 per name. Fee is per 10 years searched. Required to search: name, years to search. Civil cases indexed by defendant, plaintiff. Civil records on docket books since 1962. Criminal Records: Access: Mail, in person. Both court and visitors may perform in person searches. Search fee: $10.00 per name. Fee is per 10 years searched. Required to search: name, years to search. Criminal records on docket books since 1962. General Information: No sealed, adoptions, mental health, juvenile, sex, or expunged records released. Turnaround time 1-2 days. Copy fee: $.50 per page. Certification fee: $2.50. Fee payee: Circuit Clerk. Personal checks accepted. Prepayment is required.

Justice Court PO Box 455, New Augusta, MS 39462; 601-964-8366. Hours: 8AM-5PM (CST). *Misdemeanor, Civil Actions Under $2,500, Eviction, Small Claims.*

Justice Court-District 1 5091 Hwy 29, Petal, MS 39465; 601-544-3136. Hours: 8AM-5PM (CST). *Misdemeanor, Civil Actions Under $2,500, Eviction, Small Claims.*

Chancery Court PO Box 198, New Augusta, MS 39462; 601-964-8398; Fax: 601-964-8265. Hours: 8AM-5PM (CST). *Probate.*

Pike County

Circuit & County Court PO Drawer 31, Magnolia, MS 39652; 601-783-2581; Fax: 601-783-4101. Hours: 8AM-5PM (CST). *Felony, Misdemeanor, Civil.*

Civil Records: Access: Fax, mail, in person. Both court and visitors may perform in person searches. Search fee: $6.00 per name. Required to search: name, years to search. Civil cases indexed by defendant, plaintiff. Civil records on docket books since 1950s. Criminal Records: Access: Fax, mail, in person. Both court and visitors may perform in person searches. Search fee: $6.00 per name. Required to search: name, years to search; also helpful-SSN. Criminal records on docket books since 1950s. General Information: No sealed, adoptions, mental health, juvenile, sex, or expunged records released. SASE required. Turnaround time 1-2 days. Copy fee: $.50 per page. Certification fee: $1.50. Fee payee: Circuit Clerk. Personal checks accepted. Prepayment is required.

Justice Court - Divisions 1-3 PO Box 509, Magnolia, MS 39652; 601-783-5333; Fax: 601-783-4181. Hours: 8AM-5PM (CST). *Misdemeanor, Civil Actions Under $2,500, Eviction, Small Claims.*

Chancery Court PO Box 309, Magnolia, MS 39652; 601-783-3362; Fax: 601-783-4101. Hours: 8AM-5PM (CST). *Probate.*

Pontotoc County

Circuit Court PO Box 428, Pontotoc, MS 38863; 662-489-3908. Hours: 8AM-5PM (CST). *Felony, Civil Actions Over $2,500.*

Civil Records: Access: Mail, in person. Both court and visitors may perform in person searches. Search fee: $5.00 per name. Required to search: name, years to search. Civil cases indexed by defendant, plaintiff. Civil records on books from 1849. **Criminal Records:** Access: Mail, in person. Both court and visitors may perform in person searches. Search fee: $5.00 per name. Required to search: name, years to search, DOB; also helpful-SSN. Criminal records on books from 1849. **General Information:** No sealed, adoptions, mental health, juvenile, sex, or expunged records released. SASE required. Turnaround time 1 week. Copy fee: $.50 per page. Certification fee: No certification fee. Fee payee: Circuit Clerk. Prepayment is required.

Justice Court - East & West Districts 29 E Washington St, Pontotoc, MS 38863-2923; 662-489-3920; Fax: 662-489-3921. Hours: 8AM-5PM (CST). *Misdemeanor, Civil Actions Under $2,500, Eviction, Small Claims.*

Chancery Court 11 Washington, PO Box 209, Pontotoc, MS 38863; 662-489-3900; Fax: 662-489-3940. Hours: 8AM-5PM (CST). *Probate.*

Prentiss County

Circuit Court 101 N Main St, Booneville, MS 38829; 662-728-4611; Fax: 662-728-2006. Hours: 8AM-5PM (CST). *Felony, Civil Actions Over $2,500.*

Civil Records: Access: Mail, in person. Both court and visitors may perform in person searches. Search fee: $10.00 per name. Required to search: name, years to search. Civil cases indexed by defendant, plaintiff. Civil records on docket books from 1880, only judgements are on computer. **Criminal Records:** Access: Fax, mail, in person. Both court and visitors may perform in person searches. Search fee: $10.00 per name. Required to search: name, years to search; also helpful-DOB, SSN. Criminal records on docket books from 1880, only judgements are on computer. Prepaid account is required for fax access. **General Information:** No sealed, adoptions, mental health, juvenile, sex, or expunged records released. SASE required. Turnaround time varies. Copy fee: $.50 for first page, $.25 each addl. Certification fee: $2.00. Fee payee: Circuit Clerk. Personal checks accepted. Accounts available.

Prentiss County Justice Court 1901C East Chambers Dr, Booneville, MS 38829; 662-728-8696; Fax: 662-728-2009. Hours: 8AM-5PM (CST). *Misdemeanor, Civil Actions Under $2,500, Eviction, Small Claims.*

Chancery Court PO Box 477, Booneville, MS 38829; 662-728-8151; Fax: 662-728-2007. Hours: 8AM-5PM (CST). *Probate.*

Quitman County

Circuit Court Courthouse, Marks, MS 38646; 662-326-8003; Fax: 662-326-8004. Hours: 8AM-5PM (CST). *Felony, Civil Actions Over $2,500.*

Civil Records: Access: Fax, mail, in person. Both court and visitors may perform in person searches. Search fee: $10.00 per name. Required to search: name, years to search. Civil cases indexed by

defendant, plaintiff. Civil records on books and files since 1890. **Criminal Records:** Access: Fax, mail, in person. Both court and visitors may perform in person searches. Search fee: $10.00 per name. Required to search: name, years to search, DOB; also helpful-SSN. Criminal records on books and files since 1890. **General Information:** No sealed, adoptions, mental health, juvenile, sex, or expunged records released. SASE not required. Turnaround time 2 days, phone turnaround time 10 minutes. Copy fee: $.50 per page. Certification fee: $1.50. Fee payee: Circuit Clerk. Business checks accepted. Prepayment is required. Fax notes: No fax fee when $10.00 has been paid.

Justice Court-Districts 1 & 2 PO Box 100, Marks, MS 38646; 662-326-2104; Fax: 662-326-2330. Hours: 8AM-5PM (CST). *Misdemeanor, Civil Actions Under $2,500, Eviction, Small Claims.*

Chancery Court 230 Chestnut St, Marks, MS 38646; 662-326-2661; Fax: 662-326-8004. Hours: 8AM-Noon, 1-5PM (CST). *Probate.*

Rankin County

Circuit & County Court PO Drawer 1599, Brandon, MS 39043; 601-825-1466. Hours: 8AM-5PM (CST). *Felony, Misdemeanor, Civil.*

Civil Records: Access: Mail, in person. Both court and visitors may perform in person searches. Search fee: $5.00 per name. Required to search: name, years to search. Civil cases indexed by defendant, plaintiff. Civil records on computer since 1990, prior on docket books. **Criminal Records:** Access: Mail, in person. Both court and visitors may perform in person searches. Search fee: $5.00 per name. Required to search: name, years to search; also helpful-DOB, SSN. Criminal records on computer since 1990, prior on docket books. **General Information:** No sealed or expunged records released. Turnaround time 1-2 days. Copy fee: $.50 per page. Certification fee: $1.50. Fee payee: Circuit Clerk. Personal checks accepted. Prepayment is required. Public access terminal is available.

Justice Court-Districts 1-4 110 Paul Truitt Lane, Pearl, MS 39208; 601-939-1885; Fax: 601-939-2320. Hours: 8AM-5PM (CST). *Misdemeanor, Civil Actions Under $2,500, Eviction, Small Claims.*

Chancery Court 203 Town Sq, PO Box 700, Brandon, MS 39042; 601-825-1649; Fax: 601-824-2450. Hours: 8AM-5PM (CST). *Probate.*

Scott County

Circuit Court PO Box 371, Forest, MS 39074; 601-469-3601. Hours: 8AM-5PM (CST). *Felony, Civil Actions Over $2,500.*

Civil Records: Access: Mail, in person. Both court and visitors may perform in person searches. Search fee: $10.00 per name. Fee is for 7 year search. Required to search: name, years to search. Civil cases indexed by defendant, plaintiff. Civil records on docket books since 1865. **Criminal Records:** Access: Mail, in person. Both court and visitors may perform in person searches. Search fee: $10.00 per name. Fee is for 7 year search. Required to search: name, years to search, DOB; also helpful-SSN. Criminal records on docket books since 1865. **General Information:** No sealed, adoptions, mental health, juvenile, sex, or expunged records released. SASE required. Turnaround time 1 week. Copy fee: $.50 per page. Certification fee: $1.50. Fee payee: Circuit Clerk. Personal checks accepted. Prepayment is required.

Justice Court PO Box 371, Forest, MS 39074; 601-469-4555; Fax: 601-469-5193. Hours: 8AM-5PM (CST). *Misdemeanor, Civil Actions Under $2,500, Eviction, Small Claims.*

Chancery Court 100 Main St, PO Box 630, Forest, MS 39074; 601-469-1922; Fax: 601-469-5180. Hours: 8AM-5PM (CST). *Probate.*

Sharkey County

Circuit Court PO Box 218, Rolling Fork, MS 39159; 662-873-2766; Fax: 662-873-6045. Hours: 8AM-Noon, 1-5PM (CST). *Felony, Civil Actions Over $2,500.*

Civil Records: Access: Mail, in person. Both court and visitors may perform in person searches. Search fee: $10.00 per name. Required to search: name, years to search. Civil cases indexed by defendant, plaintiff. Civil records on docket books since 1893. **Criminal Records:** Access: Mail, in person. Both court and visitors may perform in person searches. Search fee: $10.00 per name. Required to search: name, years to search, DOB; also helpful-SSN. Criminal records on docket books since 1893. **General Information:** No sealed, adoptions, mental health, juvenile, sex, or expunged records released. Turnaround time 1 week. Copy fee: $.50 per page. Certification fee: $2.00. Fee payee: Circuit Clerk. Business checks accepted. Prepayment is required.

Justice Court PO Box 218, Rolling Fork, MS 39159; 662-873-6140. Hours: 8AM-5PM (CST). *Misdemeanor, Civil Actions Under $2,500, Eviction, Small Claims.*

Chancery Court 400 Locust St, PO Box 218, Rolling Fork, MS 39159; 662-873-2755; Fax: 662-873-6045. Hours: 8AM-Noon,1-5PM (CST). *Probate.*

Simpson County

Circuit Court PO Box 307, Mendenhall, MS 39114; 601-847-2474; Fax: 601-847-4011. Hours: 8AM-5PM (CST). *Felony, Civil Actions Over $2,500.*

Civil Records: Access: Fax, mail, in person. Both court and visitors may perform in person searches. Search fee: $9.00 per name. Required to search: name, years to search. Civil cases indexed by defendant, plaintiff. Civil records on docket books since 1978. **Criminal Records:** Access: Fax, mail, in person. Both court and visitors may perform in person searches. Search fee: $9.00 per name. Required to search: name, years to search; also helpful-DOB, SSN. Criminal records on docket books since 1978. **General Information:** No sealed or expunged records released. Turnaround time 1-2 days. Copy fee: $.50 per page. Certification fee: $1.50. Fee payee: Circuit Clerk. Business checks accepted. Prepayment is required. Fax notes: No fee to fax results.

Justice Court 159 Court Ave, Mendenhall, MS 39114; 601-847-5848; Fax: 601-847-5856. Hours: 8AM-5PM (CST). *Misdemeanor, Civil Actions Under $2,500, Eviction, Small Claims.*

Chancery Court Chancery Building, PO Box 367, Mendenhall, MS 39114; 601-847-2626. Hours: 8AM-5PM (CST). *Probate.*

Smith County

Circuit Court PO Box 517, Raleigh, MS 39153; 601-782-4751; Fax: 601-782-4007. Hours: 8AM-5PM (CST). *Felony, Civil Actions Over $2,500.*

Civil Records: Access: Mail, in person. Both court and visitors may perform in person searches.

Search fee: $10.00 per name. Required to search: name, years to search. Civil cases indexed by defendant, plaintiff. Civil records on docket books since 1912. **Criminal Records:** Access: Mail, in person. Both court and visitors may perform in person searches. Search fee: $10.00 per name. Required to search: name, years to search, DOB; also helpful-SSN. Criminal records on docket books since 1912. **General Information:** No sealed, adoptions, mental health, juvenile, sex, or expunged records released. SASE required. Turnaround time 2 days. Copy fee: $.50 per page. Certification fee: No certification fee. Fee payee: Circuit Clerk. Personal checks accepted.

Justice Court PO Box 171, Raleigh, MS 39153; 601-782-4334. Hours: 8AM-5PM (CST). *Misdemeanor, Civil Actions Under $2,500, Eviction, Small Claims.*

Chancery Court 123 Main St, PO Box 39, Raleigh, MS 39153; 601-782-9811. Hours: 8AM-Noon, 1-5PM (CST). *Probate.*

Stone County

Circuit Court Courthouse, 323 Cavers Ave, Wiggins, MS 39577; 601-928-5246; Fax: 601-928-5248. Hours: 8AM-5PM (CST). *Felony, Civil Actions Over $2,500.*

Civil Records: Access: Fax, mail, in person. Both court and visitors may perform in person searches. Search fee: $10.00 per name. Required to search: name, years to search. Civil cases indexed by defendant, plaintiff. Civil records on docket books since 1945. **Criminal Records:** Access: Fax, mail, in person. Both court and visitors may perform in person searches. Search fee: $10.00 per name. Required to search: name, years to search, DOB, notarized release; also helpful-SSN. Criminal records on docket books since 1945. **General Information:** No sealed, adoptions, mental health, juvenile, sex, or expunged records released. Turnaround time same day. Copy fee: $.50 per page. Certification fee: $1.50. Fee payee: Circuit Clerk. Business checks accepted. Prepayment is required. Fax notes: $3.00 for first page, $.50 each addl.

Justice Court 231 3rd Street, Wiggins, MS 39577; 601-928-4415; Fax: 601-928-2114. Hours: 8AM-5PM (CST). *Misdemeanor, Civil Actions Under $2,500, Eviction, Small Claims.*

Justice Court-West District 231 3rd St, Wiggins, MS 39577; 601-928-4415. Hours: 8AM-5PM (CST). *Misdemeanor, Civil Actions Under $2,500, Eviction, Small Claims.*

Chancery Court 323 E Cavers, PO Drawer 7, Wiggins, MS 39577; 601-928-5266; Fax: 601-928-5248. Hours: 8AM-5PM (CST). *Probate.*

Sunflower County

Circuit Court PO Box 576, Indianola, MS 38751; 662-887-1252; Fax: 662-887-7077. Hours: 8AM-5PM (CST). *Felony, Civil Actions Over $2,500.*

Civil Records: Access: Fax, mail, in person. Both court and visitors may perform in person searches. Search fee: $10.00 per name. Fee is for 7 year search. Required to search: name, years to search. Civil cases indexed by defendant, plaintiff. Civil records on docket books since 1881. **Criminal Records:** Access: Mail, in person. Both court and visitors may perform in person searches. Search fee: $10.00 per name. Fee is for 7 year search. Required to search: name, years to search, DOB; also helpful-SSN. Criminal records on docket books since 1881. **General Information:** No

sealed, adoptions, mental health, juvenile, sex, or expunged records released. Turnaround time 1-3 days. Copy fee: $.50 per page. Certification fee: $1.50. Fee payee: Circuit Clerk. Personal checks accepted. Prepayment is required. Fax notes: $1.00 per page.

Justice Court - Northern District PO Box 52, Ruleville, MS 38771; 662-756-2835. Hours: 8AM-Noon, 1-5PM (CST). *Misdemeanor, Civil Actions Under $2,500, Eviction, Small Claims.*

Justice Court - Southern District PO Box 487, Indianola, MS 38751; 662-887-6921. Hours: 8AM-5PM (CST). *Misdemeanor, Civil Actions Under $2,500, Eviction, Small Claims.*

Chancery Court 200 Main St, PO Box 988, Indianola, MS 38751; 662-887-4703; Fax: 662-887-7054. Hours: 8AM-5PM (CST). *Probate.*

Tallahatchie County

Charleston Circuit Court PO Box 86, Charleston, MS 38921; 662-647-8758; Fax: 662-647-8490. Hours: 8AM-5PM (CST). *Felony, Civil Actions Over $2,500.*

Civil Records: Access: Mail, in person. Both court and visitors may perform in person searches. Search fee: $10.00 per name. Required to search: name, years to search. Civil cases indexed by defendant, plaintiff. Civil records on books since 1920s. **Criminal Records:** Access: Mail, in person. Both court and visitors may perform in person searches. Search fee: $10.00 per name. Required to search: name, years to search, DOB; also helpful-SSN. Criminal records on books since 1920s. **General Information:** No sealed, adoptions, mental health, juvenile, sex, or expunged records released. SASE requested. Turnaround time 3 days. Copy fee: $2.00 per page. Certification fee: $3.00. Fee payee: Circuit Clerk. Personal checks accepted. Prepayment is required.

Justice Court PO Box 155, Sumner, MS 38957; 662-375-9452; Fax: 662-375-8200. Hours: 8AM-5PM (CST). *Misdemeanor, Civil Actions Under $2,500, Eviction, Small Claims.*

Chancery Court #1 Main St, PO Box 350, Charleston, MS 38921; 662-647-5551; Fax: 662-647-8490. Hours: 8AM-5PM (CST). *Probate.*

Chancery Court PO Box 180, Sumner, MS 38957; 662-375-8731; Fax: 662-375-7252. Hours: 8AM-Noon, 1-5PM (CST). *Probate.*

Tate County

Circuit Court 201 Ward St, Senatobia, MS 38668; 662-562-5211; Fax: 662-562-7486. Hours: 8AM-5PM (CST). *Felony, Civil Actions Over $2,500.*

Civil Records: Access: Mail, in person. Both court and visitors may perform in person searches. Search fee: $10.00 per name. Required to search: name, years to search. Civil cases indexed by defendant, plaintiff. Civil records on books since 1872. **Criminal Records:** Access: Mail, in person. Both court and visitors may perform in person searches. Search fee: $10.00 per name. Required to search: name, years to search; also helpful-SSN. Criminal records on books since 1872. **General Information:** No sealed, adoptions, mental health, juvenile, sex, or expunged records released. SASE requested. Turnaround time same day. Copy fee: $.50 for first page, $.25 each addl. Certification fee: $1.50. Fee payee: Circuit Clerk. Personal checks accepted. Prepayment is required.

Justice Court 111 Court St, Senatobia, MS 38668; 662-562-7626. Hours: 8AM-5PM (CST). *Misdemeanor, Civil Actions Under $2,500, Eviction, Small Claims.*

Chancery Court 201 Ward St, Senatobia, MS 38668; 662-562-5661; Fax: 662-562-7486. Hours: 8AM-5PM (CST). *Probate.*

Tippah County

Circuit Court Courthouse, Ripley, MS 38663; 662-837-7370; Fax: 662-837-1030. Hours: 8AM-5PM (CST). *Felony, Civil Actions Over $2,500.*

Civil Records: Access: Phone, fax, mail, in person. Both court and visitors may perform in person searches. Search fee: $5.00 per name. Required to search: name, years to search. Civil cases indexed by defendant. Civil records on docket books since 1800s. **Criminal Records:** Access: Phone, fax, mail, in person. Both court and visitors may perform in person searches. Search fee: $5.00 per name. Required to search: name, years to search, DOB; also helpful-SSN. Criminal records on docket books since 1800s. **General Information:** No sealed, adoptions, mental health, juvenile, sex or expunged records released. SASE not required. Turnaround time 1 week, phone turnaround time 30 minutes. Copy fee: $.50 per page. Certification fee: No certification fee. Fee payee: Circuit Clerk. Personal checks accepted. All fees may be billed. Fax notes: $1.00 per page.

Justice Court Justice Court, 205-B Spring Ave, Ripley, MS 38663; 662-837-8842. Hours: 8AM-5PM (CST). *Misdemeanor, Civil Actions Under $2,500, Eviction, Small Claims.*

Chancery Court PO Box 99, Ripley, MS 38663; 662-837-7374; Fax: 662-837-1030. Hours: 8AM-5PM (CST). *Probate.*

Tishomingo County

Circuit Court 1008 Battleground Dr, Iuka, MS 38852; 662-423-7026; Fax: 662-423-1667. Hours: 8AM-5PM (CST). *Felony, Civil Actions Over $2,500.*

Civil Records: Access: Mail, in person. Both court and visitors may perform in person searches. Search fee: $10.00 per name. Required to search: name, years to search. Civil cases indexed by defendant, plaintiff. Civil records on docket books since 1950s, others in storage. **Criminal Records:** Access: Mail, in person. Both court and visitors may perform in person searches. Search fee: $10.00 per name. Required to search: name, years to search, DOB; also helpful-SSN. Criminal records on docket books since 1950s, others in storage. **General Information:** No sealed, adoptions, mental health, juvenile, sex, or expunged records released. SASE requested. Turnaround time 1-2 days. Copy fee: $.25 per page. Certification fee: No certification fee. Fee payee: Circuit Clerk. Business checks accepted. Prepayment is required.

Justice Court - Northern & Southern Districts 1008 Battleground Drive, Iuka, MS 38852; 662-423-7033. Hours: 8AM-5PM (CST). *Misdemeanor, Civil Actions Under $2,500, Eviction, Small Claims.*

Chancery Court 1008 Battleground Dr, Iuka, MS 38852; 662-423-7010; Fax: 662-423-7005. Hours: 8AM-5PM (CST). *Probate.*

Tunica County

Circuit Court PO Box 184, Tunica, MS 38676; 662-363-2842. Hours: 8AM-5PM (CST). *Felony, Civil Actions Over $2,500.*

Civil Records: Access: Mail, in person. Both court and visitors may perform in person searches. Search fee: $10.00 per name. Required to search: name, years to search. Civil cases indexed by defendant, plaintiff. Civil records on docket books since 1959, archived prior. **Criminal Records:** Access: Mail, in person. Both court and visitors may perform in person searches. Search fee: $10.00 per name. Required to search: name, years to search, DOB; also helpful-SSN. Criminal records on docket books since 1954. **General Information:** No sealed, adoptions, mental health, juvenile, sex, or expunged records released. SASE requested. Turnaround time 1 week. Copy fee: $.50 per page. Add postage. Certification fee: $1.50. Fee payee: Circuit Clerk. Personal checks accepted. Prepayment is required.

Justice Court 1070 N Court St, Tunica, MS 38676; 662-363-2178; Fax: 662-363-4234. Hours: 8AM-5PM (CST). *Misdemeanor, Civil Actions Under $2,500, Eviction, Small Claims.*

Justice Court - Southern District 5130 Old Moon Landing, Tunica, MS 38676; 662-363-2178. Hours: 8AM-5PM (CST). *Misdemeanor, Civil Actions Under $2,500, Eviction, Small Claims.*

Chancery Court PO Box 217, Tunica, MS 38676; 662-363-2451; Fax: 662-357-5934. Hours: 8AM-Noon, 1-5PM (CST). *Probate.*

Union County

Circuit Court PO Box 298, New Albany, MS 38652; 662-534-1910; Fax: 662-534-2059. Hours: 8AM-5PM (CST). *Felony, Civil Actions Over $2,500.*

Civil Records: Access: Fax, mail, in person. Both court and visitors may perform in person searches. Search fee: $10.00 per name. Includes certification fee. Required to search: name, years to search, address. Civil cases indexed by defendant, plaintiff. Civil records on docket books since early 1900s. **Criminal Records:** Access: Fax, mail, in person. Both court and visitors may perform in person searches. Search fee: $10.00 per name. Fee includes certification. Required to search: name, years to search, DOB; also helpful-SSN. Criminal records on docket books since early 1900s. **General Information:** No adoptions, mental health or juvenile records released. SASE requested. Turnaround time 1 week. Copy fee: $.50 per page. Certification fee: $5.00. Fee payee: Helen Randle or Rhonda Dowdy. Personal checks accepted. Prepayment is required. Fax notes: No fee to fax results.

Justice Court-East & West Posts PO Box 27, New Albany, MS 38652; 662-534-1951; Fax: 662-534-1935. Hours: 8AM-5PM (CST). *Misdemeanor, Civil Actions Under $2,500, Eviction, Small Claims.*

Chancery Court PO Box 847, New Albany, MS 38652; 662-534-1900; Fax: 662-534-1907. Hours: 8AM-5PM (CST). *Probate.*

Walthall County

Circuit Court 200 Ball Ave, Tylertown, MS 39667; 601-876-5677; Fax: 601-876-6688. Hours: 8AM-Noon; 1-5PM (CST). *Felony, Civil Actions Over $2,500.*

Civil Records: Access: Mail, in person. Both court and visitors may perform in person searches. Search fee: $10.00 per name. Required to search: name, years to search. Civil cases indexed by defendant, plaintiff. Civil records on docket books since 1914. **Criminal Records:** Access: Mail, in person. Both court and visitors may perform in person searches. Search fee: $10.00 per name. Required to search: name, years to search; also helpful-SSN. Criminal records on docket books since 1914. **General Information:** No sealed, adoptions, mental health, juvenile, sex, or expunged records released. Turnaround time 1-2 days. Copy fee: $.25 per page. Certification fee: $1.50 plus $.50 per page. Fee payee: Circuit Clerk. Personal checks accepted. Prepayment is required.

Justice Court-Districts 1 & 2 PO Box 507, Tylertown, MS 39667; 601-876-2311. Hours: 8AM-5PM (CST). *Misdemeanor, Civil Actions Under $2,500, Eviction, Small Claims.*

Chancery Court 200 Ball Ave, PO Box 351, Tylertown, MS 39667; 601-876-3553; Fax: 601-876-7788. Hours: 8AM-5PM (CST). *Probate.*

Warren County

Circuit & County Court PO Box 351, Vicksburg, MS 39181; 601-636-3961; Fax: 601-630-4100. Hours: 8AM-5PM (CST). *Felony, Misdemeanor, Civil.*

Civil Records: Access: Mail, in person. Both court and visitors may perform in person searches. Search fee: $10.00 per name. Required to search: name, years to search. Civil cases indexed by defendant, plaintiff. Civil records on books since 1970s. **Criminal Records:** Access: Mail, in person. Both court and visitors may perform in person searches. Search fee: $10.00 per name. Required to search: name, years to search; also helpful-DOB, SSN. Criminal records on books since 1970s. **General Information:** No sealed or expunged records released. SASE required. Turnaround time 1 day. Copy fee: $1.00 per page. Certification fee: $1.50. Fee payee: Circuit Clerk. Personal checks accepted. Prepayment is required.

Justice Court - Northern, Central, & Southern Districts PO Box 1598, Vicksburg, MS 39181; 601-634-6402. Hours: 8AM-5PM (CST). *Misdemeanor, Civil Actions Under $2,500, Eviction, Small Claims.*

Chancery Court PO Box 351, Vicksburg, MS 39181; 601-636-4415; Fax: 601-630-8016. Hours: 8AM-5PM (CST). *Probate.*

Washington County

Circuit & County Court PO Box 1276, Greenville, MS 38702; 662-378-2747; Fax: 662-334-2698. Hours: 8AM-5PM (CST). *Felony, Misdemeanor, Civil.*

Civil Records: Access: Fax, mail, in person. Both court and visitors may perform in person searches. Search fee: $10.00 per name. Required to search: name, years to search. Civil cases indexed by defendant, plaintiff. Civil records on books since 1964. **Criminal Records:** Access: Fax, mail, in person. Both court and visitors may perform in person searches. Search fee: $10.00 per name. Required to search: name, years to search; also helpful-DOB, SSN. Criminal records on books since 1964. **General Information:** No sealed or expunged records released. SASE required. Turnaround time 5-10 days. Copy fee: $.50 per page. Certification fee: $3.00. Fee payee: Circuit Clerk. Business checks accepted. Prepayment is required. Fax notes: No fee to fax results.

Justice Court-Districts 1-3 905 W Alexander, Greenville, MS 38701; 662-332-0633. Hours: 8AM-5PM (CST). *Misdemeanor, Civil Actions Under $2,500, Eviction, Small Claims.*

Chancery Court PO Box 309, Greenville, MS 38702-0309; 662-332-1595; Fax: 662-334-2725. Hours: 8AM-5PM (CST). *Probate.*

Wayne County

Circuit Court PO Box 428, Waynesboro, MS 39367; 601-735-1171; Fax: 601-735-6261. Hours: 8AM-5PM (CST). *Felony, Civil Actions Over $2,500.*

Civil Records: Access: Fax, mail, in person. Both court and visitors may perform in person searches. Search fee: $10.00 per name. Required to search: name, years to search. Civil cases indexed by defendant, plaintiff. Civil records on docket books since 1971, others in storage. **Criminal Records:** Access: Fax, mail, in person. Both court and visitors may perform in person searches. Search fee: $10.00 per name. Required to search: name, years to search; also helpful-DOB, SSN. Criminal records on docket books since 1971, others in storage. **General Information:** No sealed or expunged records released. Turnaround time 1-2 days. Copy fee: $.50 per page. Certification fee: $1.50. Fee payee: Circuit Clerk. Business checks accepted. Fax notes: No fee to fax results.

Justice Court-Posts 1 & 2 810 Chickasawhay St, Waynesboro, MS 39367; 601-735-3118; Fax: 601-735-6266. *Misdemeanor, Civil Actions Under $2,500, Eviction, Small Claims.*

Chancery Court Courthouse, 609 Azalea Dr, Waynesboro, MS 39367; 601-735-2873; Fax: 601-735-6248. Hours: 8AM-5PM (CST). *Probate.*

Webster County

Circuit Court PO Box 308, Walthall, MS 39771; 662-258-6287; Fax: 662-258-6657. Hours: 8AM-5PM (CST). *Felony, Civil Actions Over $2,500.*

Civil Records: Access: Fax, mail, in person. Both court and visitors may perform in person searches. Search fee: $10.00 per name. Required to search: name, years to search. Civil cases indexed by defendant, plaintiff. Civil records on docket books since 1874. **Criminal Records:** Access: Fax, mail, in person. Both court and visitors may perform in person searches. Search fee: $10.00 per name. Required to search: name, years to search, DOB; also helpful-SSN. Criminal records on docket books since 1874. **General Information:** No sealed, adoptions, mental health, juvenile, sex, or expunged records released. Turnaround time 1-2 days. Copy fee: $.50 per page. Certification fee: $1.00. Fee payee: Circuit Clerk. Business checks accepted. Prepayment is required. Fax notes: No fee to fax results.

Justice Court-Districts 1 & 2 114 Hwy 9 N, Eupora, MS 39744; 662-258-2590. Hours: 8AM-5PM (CST). *Misdemeanor, Civil Actions Under $2,500, Eviction, Small Claims.*

Chancery Court PO Box 398, Walthall, MS 39771; 662-258-4131; Fax: 662-258-6657. Hours: 8AM-5PM (CST). *Probate.*

Wilkinson County

Circuit Court PO Box 327, Woodville, MS 39669; 601-888-6697; Fax: 601-888-6984. Hours: 8:00AM-5:00PM (CST). *Felony, Civil Actions Over $2,500.*

Civil Records: Access: Mail, in person. Both court and visitors may perform in person searches. Search fee: $10.00 per name. Required to search: name, years to search. Civil cases indexed by defendant, plaintiff. Civil records on docket books since 1940s. **Criminal Records:** Access: Mail, in person. Both court and visitors may perform in person searches. Search fee: $10.00 per name. Required to search: name, years to search; also helpful-DOB, SSN. Criminal records on docket books since 1940s. **General Information:** No sealed or expunged records released. Turnaround time 1-2 days. Copy fee: $.50 per page. Certification fee: $5.00. Fee payee: Circuit Clerk. Personal checks accepted. Prepayment is required.

Justice Court - East & West Districts
PO Box 40, Woodville, MS 39669; 601-888-3538; Fax: 601-888-6776. Hours: 8AM-5PM (CST). *Misdemeanor, Civil Actions Under $2,500, Eviction, Small Claims.*

Chancery Court
PO Box 516, Woodville, MS 39669; 601-888-4381; Fax: 601-888-6776. Hours: 8AM-5PM (CST). *Probate.*

Winston County

Circuit Court
PO Drawer 785, Louisville, MS 39339; 662-773-3581; Fax: 662-773-8825. Hours: 8AM-5PM (CST). *Felony, Civil Actions Over $2,500.*

Civil Records: Access: Phone, fax, mail, in person. Both court and visitors may perform in person searches. Search fee: $10.00 per name. Required to search: name, years to search. Civil cases indexed by defendant, plaintiff. Civil records on docket books since early 1950s. **Criminal Records:** Access: Phone, fax, mail, in person. Both court and visitors may perform in person searches. Search fee: $10.00 per name. Required to search: name, years to search, DOB; also helpful-SSN. Criminal records on docket books since early 1950s. **General Information:** No sealed, adoptions, mental health, juvenile or expunged records released. SASE requested. Turnaround time 14 days. Copy fee: $.50 per page. Certification fee: $1.50. Fee payee: Circuit Clerk. Personal checks accepted. Prepayment is required. Fax notes: $5.00 for first page, $1.00 each addl.

Justice Court
PO Box 327, Louisville, MS 39339; 662-773-6016. Hours: 8AM-5PM (CST). *Misdemeanor, Civil Actions Under $2,500, Eviction, Small Claims.*

Chancery Court
PO Drawer 69, Louisville, MS 39339; 662-773-3631; Fax: 662-773-8825. Hours: 8AM-5PM (CST). *Probate.*

Yalobusha County

Coffeeville Circuit Court
PO Box 260, Coffeeville, MS 38922; 662-675-8187; Fax: 662-675-8004. Hours: 8AM-5PM (CST). *Felony, Civil Actions Over $2,500.*

Civil Records: Access: Phone, fax, mail, in person. Both court and visitors may perform in person searches. Search fee: $10.00 per name. May mail request with check or fax request with copy of check to be mailed. Required to search: name, years to search. Civil cases indexed by defendant, plaintiff. Civil records on docket books since 1930s. **Criminal Records:** Access: Phone, fax, mail, in person. Both court and visitors may perform in person searches. Search fee: $10.00 per name. May mail request with check or fax request with copy of check to be mailed. Required to search: name, years to search; also helpful-DOB. Criminal records on docket books since 1930s. **General Information:** No sealed, adoptions, mental health, juvenile, sex, or expunged records released. SASE requested. Turnaround time 1-2 days. Copy fee: $.25 per page. Certification fee: $10.00. Fee payee: Circuit Clerk. Personal checks accepted. Prepayment is required.

Water Valley Circuit Court
PO Box 431, Water Valley, MS 38965; 662-473-1341; Fax: 662-473-5020. Hours: 8AM-5PM (CST). *Felony, Civil Actions Over $2,500.*

Civil Records: Access: Fax, mail, in person. Both court and visitors may perform in person searches. Search fee: $10.00 per name. Includes certification fee. Required to search: name, years to search. Civil cases indexed by defendant, plaintiff. Civil records on docket books since 1930s. **Criminal Records:** Access: Fax, mail, in person. Both court and visitors may perform in person searches. Search fee: $10.00 per name. Fee includes certification. Required to search: name, years to search, DOB; also helpful-SSN. Criminal records on docket books since 1930s. **General Information:** No sealed, adoptions, mental health, juvenile, sex, or expunged records released. Turnaround time 1 week. Copy fee: $.50 per page. Certification fee: $1.50. Fee payee: Circuit Clerk. Personal checks accepted. Fax notes: No fee to fax results.

Justice Court-District 1
Rt. 3, Box 237, Coffeeville, MS 38922; 662-675-8115. Hours: 8AM-5PM (CST). *Misdemeanor, Civil Actions Under $2,500, Eviction, Small Claims.*

Justice Court-Division 2
PO Box 272, Water Valley, MS 38965; 662-473-4502. Hours: 8AM-5PM (CST). *Misdemeanor, Civil Actions Under $2,500, Eviction, Small Claims.*

Chancery Court
PO Box 664, Water Valley, MS 38965; 662-473-2091; Fax: 662-473-5020. Hours: 8AM-5PM (CST). *Probate.*

Chancery Court
PO Box 260, Coffeeville, MS 38922; 662-675-2716; Fax: 662-675-8004. Hours: 8AM-Noon, 1-5PM (CST). *Probate.*

Yazoo County

Circuit & County Court
PO Box 108, Yazoo City, MS 39194; 662-746-1872. Hours: 8AM-5PM (CST). *Felony, Misdemeanor, Civil.*

Civil Records: Access: Mail, in person. Both court and visitors may perform in person searches. Search fee: $10.00 per name. Required to search: name, years to search. Civil cases indexed by defendant, plaintiff. Civil records for Civil Circuit on docket books since 1973; for Civil County on docket books since 1977. **Criminal Records:** Access: Mail, in person. Both court and visitors may perform in person searches. Search fee: $10.00 per name. Required to search: name, years to search, DOB; also helpful-SSN. Criminal records for Criminal Circuit from 1975; Criminal County on docket books since 1975. **General Information:** No sealed, adoptions, mental health, juvenile, sex, or expunged records released. SASE required. Turnaround time 1 day. Copy fee: $.50 per page. Certification fee: $1.00. Fee payee: Circuit Clerk. Business checks accepted. Prepayment is required.

Justice Court - Northern & Southern Districts
PO Box 798, Yazoo City, MS 39194; 662-746-8181. Hours: 8AM-5PM (CST). *Misdemeanor, Civil Actions Under $2,500, Eviction, Small Claims.*

Chancery Court
PO Box 68, Yazoo City, MS 39194; 662-746-2661. Hours: 8AM-5PM (CST). *Probate.*

ORGANIZATION   82 counties, 92 recording offices. The recording officers are Chancery Clerk and Clerk of Circuit Court (state tax liens). **Ten counties have two separate recording offices**—Bolivar, Carroll, Chickasaw, Craighead, Harrison, Hinds, Jasper, Jones, Panola, Tallahatchie, and Yalobusha. See the notes under each county for how to determine which office is appropriate to search. The entire state is in the Central Time Zone (CST).

REAL ESTATE RECORDS   A few counties will perform real estate searches. Copies usually cost $.50 per page and certification fees $1.00 per document. The Assessor maintains tax records.

UCC RECORDS   This is a **dual filing state**. Financing statements are filed both at the state level and with the Chancery Clerk, except for consumer goods, farm related and real estate related filings, which are filed only with the Chancery Clerk. All but one county will perform UCC searches. Use search request form UCC-11. Search fees are usually $5.00 per debtor name. Copy fees vary from $.25 to $2.00 per page.

TAX LIEN RECORDS   Federal tax liens on personal property of businesses are filed with the Secretary of State. Federal tax liens on personal property of individuals are filed with the county Chancery Clerk. State tax liens on personal property are filed with the county Clerk of Circuit Court. State tax liens on real property are filed with the Chancery Clerk. Most Chancery Clerk offices will perform a federal tax lien search for a fee of $5.00 per name. Copy fees vary.

OTHER LIENS   Mechanics, lis pendens, judgment (Circuit Court), construction.

Adams County
County Clerk of the Chancery Court, P.O. Box 1006, Natchez, MS 39121. 601-446-6684. Fax: 601-445-7913.

Alcorn County
County Clerk of the Chancery Court, P.O. Box 69, Corinth, MS 38835-0069. 662-286-7700. Fax: 662-286-7706.

Amite County
County Clerk of the Chancery Court, P.O. Box 680, Liberty, MS 39645-0680. 601-657-8022. Fax: 601-657-8288.

Attala County
County Clerk of the Chancery Court, Chancery Court Bldg., 230 W. Washington St., Kosciusko, MS 39090. 662-289-2921. Fax: 662-289-7662.

Benton County
County Clerk of the Chancery Court, P.O. Box 218, Ashland, MS 38603. 662-224-6300. Fax: 662-224-6303.

Bolivar County (1st District)
County Clerk of the Chancery Court, P.O. Box 238, Rosedale, MS 38769-0238. 662-759-3762. Fax: 662-759-3467.

Bolivar County (2nd District)
County Clerk of the Chancery Court, P.O. Box 789, Cleveland, MS 38732. 662-843-2071. Fax: 662-846-2940.

Calhoun County
County Clerk of the Chancery Court, P.O. Box 8, Pittsboro, MS 38951. 662-412-3117. Fax: 662-412-3128.

Carroll County (1st District)
County Clerk of the Chancery Court, P.O. Box 60, Carrollton, MS 38917. 662-237-9274. Fax: 662-237-9642.

Carroll County (2nd District)
County Clerk of the Chancery Court, P.O. Box 6, Vaiden, MS 39176. 662-464-5476. Fax: 662-464-7745.

Chickasaw County (1st District)
County Clerk of the Chancery Court, Courthouse, Houston, MS 38851. 662-456-2513. Fax: 662-456-5295.

Chickasaw County (2nd District)
County Clerk of the Chancery Court, 234 Main Street, Room 201, Okolona, MS 38860-1438. 662-447-2092. Fax: 662-447-5024.

Choctaw County
County Clerk of the Chancery Court, P.O. Box 250, Ackerman, MS 39735-0250. 662-285-6329. Fax: 662-285-3444.

Claiborne County
County Clerk of the Chancery Court, P.O. Box 449, Port Gibson, MS 39150. 662-437-4992. Fax: 662-437-3731.

Clarke County
County Clerk of the Chancery Court, P.O. Box 689, Quitman, MS 39355. 601-776-2126.

Clay County
County Clerk of the Chancery Court, P.O. Box 815, West Point, MS 39773. 662-494-3124.

Coahoma County
County Clerk of the Chancery Court, P.O. Box 98, Clarksdale, MS 38614. 662-624-3000. Fax: 662-624-3029.

Copiah County
County Clerk of the Chancery Court, P.O. Box 507, Hazlehurst, MS 39083-0507. 601-894-3021. Fax: 601-894-3026.

Covington County
County Clerk of the Chancery Court, P.O. Box 1679, Collins, MS 39428. 601-765-4242. Fax: 601-765-5016.

De Soto County
County Clerk of the Chancery Court, P.O. Box 949, Hernando, MS 38632. 662-429-1361.

Forrest County
County Clerk of the Chancery Court, P.O. Box 951, Hattiesburg, MS 39401. 601-545-6014. Fax: 601-545-6095.

Franklin County
County Clerk of the Chancery Court, P.O. Box 297, Meadville, MS 39653-0297. 601-384-2330. Fax: 601-384-5864.

George County
County Clerk of the Chancery Court, 355 Cox Street, Lucedale, MS 39452. 601-947-4801.

Greene County
County Clerk of the Chancery Court, P.O. Box 610, Leakesville, MS 39451. 601-394-2377.

Grenada County
County Clerk of the Chancery Court, P.O. Drawer 1208, Grenada, MS 38902-1208. 662-226-1821.

Hancock County
County Clerk of the Chancery Court, P.O. Box 429, Bay Saint Louis, MS 39520. 228-467-5404. Fax: 228-467-3159.

Harrison County (1st District)
County Clerk of the Chancery Court, P.O. Drawer CC, Gulfport, MS 39502. 228-865-4195. Fax: 228-868-1480.

Harrison County (2nd District)
County Clerk of the Chancery Court, P.O. Box 544, Biloxi, MS 39533. 228-435-8220. Fax: 228-435-8292.

Hinds County (1st District)
County Clerk of the Chancery Court, P.O. Box 686, Jackson, MS 39205-0686. 601-968-6516. Fax: 601-973-5535.

Hinds County (2nd District)
County Clerk of the Chancery Court, P.O. Box 88, Raymond, MS 39154. 601-857-8055.

Holmes County
County Clerk of the Chancery Court, P.O. Box 239, Lexington, MS 39095. 662-834-2508. Fax: 662-834-3020.

Humphreys County
County Clerk of the Chancery Court, P.O. Box 547, Belzoni, MS 39038. 662-247-1740. Fax: 662-247-0101.

Issaquena County
County Clerk of the Chancery Court, P.O. Box 27, Mayersville, MS 39113-0027. 662-873-2761. Fax: 662-873-2061.

Itawamba County
County Clerk of the Chancery Court, P.O. Box 776, Fulton, MS 38843. 662-862-3421. Fax: 662-862-3421.

Jackson County
County Clerk of the Chancery Court, P.O. Box 998, Pascagoula, MS 39568. 228-769-3131. Fax: 228-769-3135.

Jasper County (1st District)
County Clerk of the Chancery Court, P.O. Box 38, Paulding, MS 39348-0038. 601-727-4941. Fax: 601-727-4475.

Jasper County (2nd District)
County Clerk of the Chancery Court, P.O. Box 1047, Bay Springs, MS 39422. 601-764-3026. Fax: 601-764-3468.

Jefferson County
County Clerk of the Chancery Court, P.O. Box 145, Fayette, MS 39069. 601-786-3021. Fax: 601-786-6009.

Jefferson Davis County
County Clerk of the Chancery Court, P.O. Box 1137, Prentiss, MS 39474. 601-792-4204. Fax: 601-792-2894.

Jones County (1st District)
County Clerk of the Chancery Court, Court Street, Jones County Courthouse, Ellisville, MS 39437. 601-477-3307.

Jones County (2nd District)
County Clerk of the Chancery Court, P.O. Box 1468, Laurel, MS 39441. 601-428-0527. Fax: 601-428-3602.

Kemper County
County Clerk of the Chancery Court, P.O. Box 188, De Kalb, MS 39328. 601-743-2460. Fax: 601-743-2789.

Lafayette County
County Clerk of the Chancery Court, P.O. Box 1240, Oxford, MS 38655. 662-234-2131.

Lamar County
County Clerk of the Chancery Court, P.O. Box 247, Purvis, MS 39475. 601-794-8504. Fax: 601-794-1049.

Lauderdale County
County Clerk of the Chancery Court, P.O. Box 1587, Meridian, MS 39302-1587. 601-482-9701.

Lawrence County
County Clerk of the Chancery Court, P.O. Box 821, Monticello, MS 39654. 601-587-7162. Fax: 601-587-0750.

Leake County
County Clerk of the Chancery Court, P.O. Box 72, Carthage, MS 39051. 601-267-7371. Fax: 601-267-6137.

Lee County
County Clerk of the Chancery Court, P.O. Box 7127, Tupelo, MS 38802. 662-841-9100. Fax: 662-680-6091.

Leflore County
County Clerk of the Chancery Court, P.O. Box 250, Greenwood, MS 38935-0250. 662-455-7913. Fax: 662-455-7965.

Lincoln County
County Clerk of the Chancery Court, P.O. Box 555, Brookhaven, MS 39602. 601-835-3416.

Lowndes County
County Clerk of the Chancery Court, P.O. Box 684, Columbus, MS 39703. 662-329-5807.

Madison County
County Clerk of the Chancery Court, P.O. Box 404, Canton, MS 39046. 601-859-1177.
http://mcatax.com
Online Access: Ral Estate, Tas Assessor Records. Records from the Madison County Assessor office are available free on the Internet. At www.mcatax.mcasearch.asp, click on "Search The Database." Records include parcel number, address, legal description, value information, and tax district.

Marion County
County Clerk of the Chancery Court, 250 Broad Street, Suite 2, Columbia, MS 39429. 601-736-2691. Fax: 601-736-1232.

Marshall County
County Clerk of the Chancery Court, P.O. Box 219, Holly Springs, MS 38635. 662-252-4431. Fax: 662-252-0004.

Monroe County
County Clerk of the Chancery Court, P.O. Box 578, Aberdeen, MS 39730. 662-369-8143. Fax: 662-369-7928.

Montgomery County
County Clerk of the Chancery Court, P.O. Box 71, Winona, MS 38967. 662-283-2333. Fax: 662-283-2233.

Neshoba County
County Clerk of the Chancery Court, 401 Beacon Street, Suite 107, Philadelphia, MS 39350. 601-656-3581.

Newton County
County Clerk of the Chancery Court, P.O. Box 68, Decatur, MS 39327. 601-635-2367. Fax: 601-635-3210.

Noxubee County
County Clerk of the Chancery Court, P.O. Box 147, Macon, MS 39341. 601-726-4243. Fax: 601-726-2272.

Oktibbeha County
County Clerk of the Chancery Court, 101 East Main, Courthouse, Starkville, MS 39759. 662-323-5834.

Panola County (1st District)
County Clerk of the Chancery Court, P.O. Box 130, Sardis, MS 38666. 662-487-2070. Fax: 662-487-3595.

Panola County (2nd District)
County Clerk of the Chancery Court, 151 Public Square, Batesville, MS 38606. 662-563-6205. Fax: 662-563-8233.

Pearl River County
County Clerk of the Chancery Court, P.O. Box 431, Poplarville, MS 39470. 601-795-2237.

Perry County
County Clerk of the Chancery Court, P.O. Box 198, New Augusta, MS 39462. 601-964-8398. Fax: 601-964-8265.

Pike County
County Clerk of the Chancery Court, P.O. Box 309, Magnolia, MS 39652. 601-783-3362. Fax: 601-783-2001.

Pontotoc County
County Clerk of the Chancery Court, P.O. Box 209, Pontotoc, MS 38863. 662-489-3900.

Prentiss County
County Clerk of the Chancery Court, P.O. Box 477, Booneville, MS 38829. 662-728-8151. Fax: 662-728-2007.

Quitman County
County Clerk of the Chancery Court, Chestnut Street, Courthouse, Marks, MS 38646. 662-326-2661. Fax: 662-326-8004.

Rankin County
County Clerk of the Chancery Court, P.O. Box 700, Brandon, MS 39043. 601-825-1469. Fax: 601-824-7116.
www.rankincounty.org
Online Access: Real Estate, Tax Assessor Records. Records on the Rankin County land Roll Files database are available free on the Internet at www.rankincounty.org/tA/interact_LandRoll.asp. For other formats, contact MIS Division at 601-825-1642 or email webmaster@rankingcounty.org.

Scott County
County Clerk of the Chancery Court, P.O. Box 630, Forest, MS 39074. 601-469-1922. Fax: 601-469-5180.

Sharkey County
County Clerk of the Chancery Court, P.O. Box 218, Rolling Fork, MS 39159. 662-873-2755. Fax: 662-873-6045.

Simpson County
County Clerk of the Chancery Court, P.O. Box 367, Mendenhall, MS 39114. 601-847-2626. Fax: 601-847-7004.

Smith County
County Clerk of the Chancery Court, P.O. Box 39, Raleigh, MS 39153. 601-782-9811. Fax: 601-782-4690.

Stone County
County Clerk of the Chancery Court, P.O. Drawer 7, Wiggins, MS 39577. 601-928-5266. Fax: 601-928-5248.

Sunflower County
County Clerk of the Chancery Court, P.O. Box 988, Indianola, MS 38751-0988. 662-887-4703. Fax: 662-887-7054.

Tallahatchie County (1st District)
County Clerk of the Chancery Court, P.O. Box 350, Charleston, MS 38921. 662-647-5551.

Tallahatchie County (2nd District)
County Clerk of the Chancery Court, P.O. Box 180, Sumner, MS 38957. 662-375-8731. Fax: 662-375-7252.

Tate County
County Clerk of the Chancery Court, 201 Ward Street, Senatobia, MS 38668. 662-562-5661. Fax: 662-560-6205.

Tippah County
County Clerk of the Chancery Court, P.O. Box 99, Ripley, MS 38663. 662-837-7374. Fax: 662-837-1030.

Tishomingo County
County Clerk of the Chancery Court, 1008 Battleground Dr., Courthouse, Iuka, MS 38852. 662-423-7010. Fax: 662-423-7005.

Tunica County
County Clerk of the Chancery Court, P.O. Box 217, Tunica, MS 38676. 662-363-2451.

Union County
County Clerk of the Chancery Court, P.O. Box 847, New Albany, MS 38652. 662-534-1900. Fax: 662-534-1907.

Walthall County
County Clerk of the Chancery Court, P.O. Box 351, Tylertown, MS 39667. 601-876-3553. Fax: 601-876-6026.

Warren County
County Clerk of the Chancery Court, P.O. Box 351, Vicksburg, MS 39181. 601-636-4415. Fax: 601-634-4815.

Washington County
County Clerk of the Chancery Court, P.O. Box 309, Greenville, MS 38702-0309. 662-332-1595. Fax: 662-334-2725.

Wayne County
County Clerk of the Chancery Court, Wayne Co. Courthouse, 609 Azalea Dr., Waynesboro, MS 39367. 601-735-2873. Fax: 601-735-6224.

Webster County
County Clerk of the Chancery Court, P.O. Box 398, Walthall, MS 39771. 662-258-4131. Fax: 662-258-6657.

Wilkinson County
County Clerk of the Chancery Court, P.O. Box 516, Woodville, MS 39669. 601-888-4381. Fax: 601-888-6776.

Winston County

County Clerk of the Chancery Court, P.O. Drawer 69, Louisville, MS 39339. 662-773-3631. Fax: 662-773-8831.

Yalobusha County (1st District)

County Clerk of the Chancery Court, P.O. Box 260, Coffeeville, MS 38922. 662-675-2716. Fax: 662-675-8187.

Yalobusha County (2nd District)

County Clerk of the Chancery Court, P.O. Box 664, Water Valley, MS 38965. 662-473-2091. Fax: 662-473-5020.

Yazoo County

County Clerk of the Chancery Court, P.O. Box 68, Yazoo City, MS 39194. 662-746-2661.

You will usually be able to find the city name in the City/County Cross Reference below. In that case, it is a simple matter to determine the county from the cross reference. However, only the official US Postal Service city names are included in this index. There are an additional 40,000 place names that people use in their addresses. Therefore, we have also included a ZIP/City Cross Reference immediately following the City/County Cross Reference.

If you know the ZIP Code but the city name does not appear in the City/County Cross Reference index, look up the ZIP Code in the ZIP/City Cross Reference, find the city name, then look up the city name in the City/County Cross Reference. For example, you want to know the county for an address of Menands, NY 12204. There is no "Menands" in the City/County Cross Reference. The ZIP/City Cross Reference shows that ZIP Codes 12201-12288 are for the city of Albany. Looking back in the City/County Cross Reference, Albany is in Albany County.

City/County Cross Reference

ABBEVILLE Lafayette
ABERDEEN Monroe
ACKERMAN Choctaw
ALGOMA Pontotoc
ALLIGATOR (38720) Coahoma(71), Bolivar(29)
AMORY Monroe
ANGUILLA (38721) Sharkey(98), Humphreys(2)
ARCOLA Washington
ARKABUTLA Tate
ARTESIA Lowndes
ASHLAND Benton
AVALON (38912) Carroll(50), Grenada(50)
AVON Washington
BAILEY (39320) Lauderdale(79), Kemper(21)
BALDWYN (38824) Lee(76), Prentiss(17), Union(4), Itawamba(3)
BANNER (38913) Calhoun(93), Lafayette(7)
BASSFIELD (39421) Jefferson Davis(76), Marion(24)
BATESVILLE Panola
BAY SAINT LOUIS Hancock
BAY SPRINGS (39422) Jasper(82), Smith(19)
BEAUMONT Perry
BECKER Monroe
BELDEN Lee
BELEN Quitman
BELLEFONTAINE Webster
BELMONT Tishomingo
BELZONI Humphreys
BENOIT Bolivar
BENTON Yazoo
BENTONIA Yazoo
BEULAH Bolivar
BIG CREEK Calhoun
BIGBEE VALLEY Noxubee
BILOXI (39532) Harrison(80), Jackson(20)
BILOXI Harrison
BLUE MOUNTAIN (38610) Tippah(90), Union(8), Benton(2)
BLUE SPRINGS Union
BOGUE CHITTO Lincoln
BOLTON Hinds
BOONEVILLE Prentiss
BOYLE Bolivar
BRANDON Rankin
BRAXTON (39044) Simpson(61), Rankin(39)
BROOKHAVEN Lincoln
BROOKLYN (39425) Forrest(54), Perry(46)
BROOKSVILLE Noxubee
BRUCE (38915) Calhoun(98), Lafayette(2)
BUCKATUNNA Wayne
BUDE Franklin
BURNSVILLE Tishomingo
BYHALIA (38611) Marshall(98), De Soto(2)
CALEDONIA (39740) Monroe(89), Montgomery(11)

CALHOUN CITY (38916) Calhoun(97), Webster(3)
CAMDEN (39045) Madison(96), Attala(4)
CANTON Madison
CARLISLE Claiborne
CARRIERE Pearl River
CARROLLTON Carroll
CARSON Jefferson Davis
CARTHAGE (39051) Leake(97), Neshoba(2), Attala(1)
CARY Sharkey
CASCILLA Tallahatchie
CEDARBLUFF Clay
CENTREVILLE (39631) Wilkinson(75), Amite(26)
CHARLESTON Tallahatchie
CHATAWA Pike
CHATHAM Washington
CHUNKY (39323) Newton(77), Lauderdale(23)
CHURCH HILL Jefferson
CLARA Wayne
CLARKSDALE Coahoma
CLEVELAND (38732) Bolivar(98), Sunflower(2)
CLEVELAND Bolivar
CLINTON Hinds
COAHOMA Coahoma
COFFEEVILLE (38922) Yalobusha(83), Grenada(17)
COILA Carroll
COLDWATER Tate
COLLINS Covington
COLLINSVILLE (39325) Lauderdale(70), Kemper(14), Newton(11), Neshoba(5)
COLUMBIA Marion
COLUMBUS Lowndes
COMO (38619) Panola(63), Lafayette(34), Tate(3)
CONEHATTA (39057) Newton(90), Scott(10)
CORINTH Alcorn
COURTLAND Panola
CRAWFORD (39743) Lowndes(70), Oktibbeha(29), Noxubee(1)
CRENSHAW (38621) Panola(96), Quitman(3)
CROSBY Amite
CROWDER Quitman
CRUGER (38924) Holmes(92), Carroll(5), Leflore(3)
CRYSTAL SPRINGS (39059) Copiah(97), Hinds(3)
D LO Simpson
DALEVILLE (39326) Lauderdale(66), Kemper(34)
DARLING Quitman
DE KALB Kemper
DECATUR Newton
DELTA CITY Sharkey
DENNIS Tishomingo
DERMA Calhoun
DIAMONDHEAD Hancock

DODDSVILLE (38736) Sunflower(74), Leflore(26)
DREW (38737) Sunflower(96), Tallahatchie(4)
DUBLIN Coahoma
DUCK HILL (38925) Montgomery(72), Grenada(28)
DUMAS (38625) Tippah(82), Union(18)
DUNCAN Bolivar
DUNDEE (38626) Coahoma(96), Tunica(4)
DURANT Holmes
EASTABUCHIE Jones
EBENEZER Holmes
ECRU Pontotoc
EDWARDS Hinds
ELLIOTT Grenada
ELLISVILLE Jones
ENID (38927) Tallahatchie(82), Panola(17), Yalobusha(1)
ENTERPRISE (39330) Clarke(85), Lauderdale(12), Jasper(3)
ESCATAWPA Jackson
ETHEL Attala
ETTA Union
EUPORA Webster
FALCON Quitman
FALKNER (38629) Tippah(95), Benton(5)
FARRELL Coahoma
FAYETTE Jefferson
FERNWOOD Pike
FITLER Issaquena
FLORA (39071) Madison(98), Hinds(2)
FLORENCE (39073) Rankin(93), Simpson(7)
FOREST (39074) Scott(98), Smith(3)
FORKVILLE Scott
FOXWORTH Marion
FRENCH CAMP Choctaw
FRIARS POINT Coahoma
FULTON Itawamba
GALLMAN Copiah
GATTMAN (38844) Alcorn(82), Monroe(18)
GAUTIER Jackson
GEORGETOWN (39078) Copiah(95), Simpson(5)
GLEN (38846) Alcorn(79), Tishomingo(21)
GLEN ALLAN Washington
GLENDORA Tallahatchie
GLOSTER Amite
GOLDEN (38847) Itawamba(96), Tishomingo(4)
GOODMAN (39079) Madison(87), Holmes(7), Attala(6)
GORE SPRINGS (38929) Grenada(88), Webster(8), Calhoun(4)
GRACE Issaquena
GREENVILLE Bolivar
GREENVILLE Washington
GREENWOOD Leflore
GREENWOOD SPRINGS Monroe
GRENADA Grenada
GULFPORT Harrison
GUNNISON Bolivar

GUNTOWN Lee
HAMILTON Monroe
HARPERVILLE Scott
HARRISTON Jefferson
HARRISVILLE Simpson
HATTIESBURG (39402) Lamar(54), Forrest(46)
HATTIESBURG Forrest
HAZLEHURST Copiah
HEIDELBERG (39439) Jasper(51), Clarke(38), Jones(11)
HERMANVILLE (39086) Claiborne(70), Copiah(30)
HERNANDO De Soto
HICKORY (39332) Newton(97), Jasper(4)
HICKORY FLAT (38633) Benton(63), Union(37)
HILLSBORO Scott
HOLCOMB (38940) Grenada(93), Carroll(4), Tallahatchie(3)
HOLLANDALE (38748) Washington(96), Sharkey(4)
HOLLY BLUFF Yazoo
HOLLY RIDGE Sunflower
HOLLY SPRINGS (38635) Marshall(94), Tate(4), Benton(3)
HOLLY SPRINGS Marshall
HORN LAKE De Soto
HOULKA Chickasaw
HOUSTON Chickasaw
HURLEY Jackson
INDEPENDENCE Tate
INDIANOLA Sunflower
INVERNESS (38753) Sunflower(93), Humphreys(7)
ISOLA (38754) Humphreys(97), Sunflower(4)
ITTA BENA Leflore
IUKA Tishomingo
JACKSON (39213) Hinds(94), Madison(6)
JACKSON Hinds
JACKSON Rankin
JAYESS (39641) Lawrence(86), Walthall(14)
JONESTOWN Coahoma
KILMICHAEL Montgomery
KILN Hancock
KOKOMO (39643) Marion(84), Walthall(16)
KOSCIUSKO (39090) Attala(95), Leake(4), Winston(1)
LAKE (39092) Newton(93), Scott(7)
LAKE CORMORANT De Soto
LAKESHORE Hancock
LAMAR (38642) Marshall(80), Benton(21)
LAMBERT (38643) Quitman(97), Coahoma(3)
LAUDERDALE (39335) Lauderdale(94), Kemper(6)
LAUREL (39440) Jones(97), Wayne(2)
LAUREL Jones
LAWRENCE (99999) Newton(98), Jasper(1)
LEAKESVILLE Greene

LELAND Washington
LENA (39094) Leake(56), Scott(37), Rankin(8)
LEXINGTON (39095) Holmes(84), Yazoo(15)
LIBERTY Amite
LITTLE ROCK Newton
LONG BEACH Harrison
LORMAN (39096) Jefferson(64), Claiborne(36)
LOUIN (39338) Jasper(78), Smith(22)
LOUISE Humphreys
LOUISVILLE Winston
LUCEDALE (39452) George(77), Jackson(20), Greene(3)
LUDLOW Scott
LULA Coahoma
LUMBERTON (39455) Lamar(45), Pearl River(44), Stone(9), Marion(1)
LYON (38645) Coahoma(96), Quitman(4)
MABEN Webster
MACON (39341) Noxubee(98), Winston(2)
MADDEN Leake
MADISON Madison
MAGEE (39111) Simpson(96), Smith(4)
MAGNOLIA Pike
MANTACHIE Itawamba
MANTEE Calhoun
MARIETTA (38856) Prentiss(93), Itawamba(7)
MARION Lauderdale
MARKS Quitman
MATHISTON Webster
MATTSON Coahoma
MAYERSVILLE Issaquena
MAYHEW Lowndes
MC ADAMS Attala
MC CALL CREEK (39647) Franklin(95), Lincoln(5)
MC CARLEY Carroll
MC COMB Pike
MC CONDY Chickasaw
MC COOL (39108) Attala(39), Winston(38), Choctaw(23)
MC HENRY Stone
MC LAIN (39456) Perry(53), Greene(45), George(2)
MC NEILL Pearl River
MEADVILLE (39653) Franklin(98), Amite(1), Jefferson(1)
MENDENHALL (39114) Simpson(97), Rankin(2)
MERIDIAN (39301) Lauderdale(92), Clarke(8)
MERIDIAN Lauderdale
MERIGOLD (38759) Sunflower(89), Bolivar(11)
METCALFE Washington
MICHIGAN CITY Benton
MIDNIGHT Humphreys
MINERAL WELLS De Soto
MINTER CITY Leflore
MISSISSIPPI STATE Oktibbeha
MIZE Smith
MONEY Leflore
MONTICELLO Lawrence
MONTPELIER Clay
MOOREVILLE Lee
MOORHEAD Sunflower
MORGAN CITY Leflore
MORGANTOWN Marion
MORTON (39117) Scott(93), Smith(5), Rankin(2)
MOSELLE Jones
MOSS Jasper
MOSS POINT Jackson
MOUND BAYOU Bolivar
MOUNT OLIVE (39119) Covington(63), Smith(15), Simpson(14), Jefferson Davis(8)
MOUNT PLEASANT Marshall

MYRTLE (38650) Union(96), Benton(2), Tippah(2)
NATCHEZ Adams
NEELY Greene
NESBIT De Soto
NETTLETON (38858) Monroe(83), Itawamba(14), Lee(3)
NEW ALBANY Union
NEW AUGUSTA Perry
NEW SITE Prentiss
NEWHEBRON (39140) Lawrence(70), Jefferson Davis(19), Simpson(11)
NEWTON Newton
NICHOLSON Pearl River
NITTA YUMA Sharkey
NORTH CARROLLTON Carroll
NOXAPATER (39346) Winston(92), Neshoba(8)
OAK VALE (39656) Jefferson Davis(81), Lawrence(19)
OAKLAND (38948) Yalobusha(69), Tallahatchie(31)
OCEAN SPRINGS Jackson
OKOLONA (38860) Chickasaw(94), Lee(5)
OLIVE BRANCH De Soto
OSYKA (39657) Pike(99), Amite(1)
OVETT (39464) Perry(97), Jones(3)
OXFORD Lafayette
PACE Bolivar
PACHUTA (39347) Jasper(59), Clarke(41)
PANTHER BURN Sharkey
PARCHMAN Sunflower
PARIS Lafayette
PASCAGOULA Jackson
PASS CHRISTIAN (39571) Harrison(76), Hancock(24)
PATTISON (39144) Claiborne(79), Jefferson(14), Copiah(8)
PAULDING Jasper
PEARLINGTON Hancock
PELAHATCHIE (39145) Rankin(97), Scott(3)
PERKINSTON (39573) Stone(63), Hancock(25), Pearl River(4), George(4), Jackson(2)
PETAL (39465) Forrest(92), Perry(8)
PHEBA (39755) Clay(77), Oktibbeha(23)
PHILADELPHIA (39350) Neshoba(95), Winston(3), Kemper(1)
PHILIPP Tallahatchie
PICAYUNE Pearl River
PICKENS (39146) Yazoo(66), Madison(31), Holmes(3)
PINEY WOODS Rankin
PINOLA Simpson
PITTSBORO Calhoun
PLANTERSVILLE Lee
PLEASANT GROVE Panola
POCAHONTAS Hinds
PONTOTOC Pontotoc
POPE Panola
POPLARVILLE (39470) Pearl River(98), Hancock(2)
PORT GIBSON Claiborne
PORTERVILLE (39352) Kemper(99), Quitman(1)
POTTS CAMP (38659) Marshall(93), Benton(7)
PRAIRIE (39756) Clay(94), Monroe(5)
PRAIRIE POINT Noxubee
PRENTISS (99999) Jefferson Davis(99), Covington(1)
PRESTON (39354) Kemper(72), Winston(24), Neshoba(4)
PUCKETT Rankin
PULASKI (39152) Scott(52), Smith(48)
PURVIS Lamar
QUITMAN Clarke
RALEIGH Smith
RANDOLPH (38864) Pontotoc(90), Calhoun(10)
RAYMOND Hinds

RED BANKS Marshall
REDWOOD (39156) Warren(96), Yazoo(5)
REFORM Choctaw
RENA LARA Coahoma
RICH Coahoma
RICHTON (39476) Perry(64), Greene(25), Wayne(12)
RIDGELAND Madison
RIENZI Alcorn
RIPLEY Tippah
ROBINSONVILLE (39664) De Soto(87), Tunica(13)
ROLLING FORK (39159) Sharkey(93), Issaquena(7)
ROME Sunflower
ROSE HILL Jasper
ROSEDALE Bolivar
ROXIE (39661) Franklin(75), Adams(20), Jefferson(5)
RULEVILLE Sunflower
RUTH (39662) Lincoln(68), Lawrence(32)
SALLIS (39160) Attala(97), Leake(3)
SALTILLO Lee
SANATORIUM Simpson
SANDERSVILLE Jones
SANDHILL Rankin
SANDY HOOK (39478) Marion(88), Walthall(13)
SARAH Panola
SARDIS Panola
SATARTIA (39162) Warren(89), Yazoo(11)
SAUCIER Harrison
SCHLATER Leflore
SCOBEY (38953) Grenada(40), Yalobusha(33), Tallahatchie(27)
SCOOBA Kemper
SCOTT Bolivar
SEBASTOPOL Scott
SEMINARY (39479) Covington(91), Jones(9)
SENATOBIA Tate
SHANNON (38868) Lee(89), Pontotoc(7), Chickasaw(3)
SHARON Madison
SHAW (38773) Bolivar(76), Sunflower(24)
SHELBY Bolivar
SHERARD Coahoma
SHERMAN Pontotoc
SHUBUTA (39360) Clarke(77), Wayne(23)
SHUQUALAK (39361) Noxubee(98), Kemper(2)
SIBLEY Adams
SIDON (38954) Leflore(83), Carroll(18)
SILVER CITY Humphreys
SILVER CREEK (39663) Lawrence(86), Jefferson Davis(14)
SKENE Bolivar
SLATE SPRING Calhoun
SLEDGE (38670) Quitman(50), Tunica(50)
SMITHDALE (39664) Amite(55), Franklin(32), Lincoln(12)
SMITHVILLE (38870) Monroe(96), Itawamba(4)
SONTAG (39665) Lawrence(83), Lincoln(17)
SOSO (39480) Jones(97), Smith(3)
SOUTHAVEN De Soto
STAR Rankin
STARKVILLE Oktibbeha
STATE LINE (39362) Wayne(64), Greene(36)
STEENS Lowndes
STEWART Montgomery
STONEVILLE Washington
STONEWALL Clarke
STRINGER Jasper
STURGIS (39769) Oktibbeha(91), Winston(9)
SUMMIT (39666) Pike(68), Lincoln(26), Amite(6)
SUMNER Tallahatchie
SUMRALL (39482) Lamar(93), Jefferson

Davis(4), Marion(3)
SUNFLOWER Sunflower
SWAN LAKE Tallahatchie
SWIFTOWN Leflore
TAYLOR Lafayette
TAYLORSVILLE (39168) Smith(71), Jones(21), Covington(8)
TCHULA Holmes
TERRY Hinds
THAXTON (38871) Pontotoc(85), Lafayette(11), Union(4)
THOMASTOWN Leake
THORNTON Holmes
TIE PLANT Grenada
TILLATOBA (38961) Yalobusha(63), Tallahatchie(37)
TINSLEY Yazoo
TIPLERSVILLE Tippah
TIPPO Tallahatchie
TISHOMINGO Tishomingo
TOCCOPOLA Lafayette
TOOMSUBA Lauderdale
TOUGALOO Hinds
TREBLOC Chickasaw
TREMONT Itawamba
TRIBBETT Washington
TULA Lafayette
TUNICA Tunica
TUPELO Lee
TUTWILER (38963) Coahoma(76), Tallahatchie(22), Sunflower(1)
TYLERTOWN Walthall
UNION (39365) Newton(64), Neshoba(36)
UNION CHURCH (99999) Jefferson(98), Franklin(1), Lincoln(1)
UNIVERSITY Lafayette
UTICA (39175) Hinds(85), Copiah(13), Claiborne(2)
VAIDEN (39176) Carroll(65), Attala(25), Montgomery(10)
VALLEY PARK Issaquena
VAN VLEET Chickasaw
VANCE Quitman
VARDAMAN (38878) Calhoun(98), Chickasaw(2)
VAUGHAN Yazoo
VERONA Lee
VICKSBURG Warren
VICTORIA Marshall
VOSSBURG (39366) Clarke(51), Jasper(49)
WALLS De Soto
WALNUT (38683) Tippah(89), Alcorn(9), Benton(2)
WALNUT GROVE (39189) Leake(80), Scott(20)
WALTHALL Webster
WASHINGTON Adams
WATER VALLEY (38965) Yalobusha(82), Lafayette(12), Calhoun(5), Panola(1)
WATERFORD Lafayette
WAVELAND Hancock
WAYNESBORO (39367) Wayne(98), Clarke(2)
WAYSIDE Washington
WEBB Tallahatchie
WEIR Choctaw
WESSON (39191) Copiah(57), Lincoln(41), Lawrence(2)
WEST (39192) Attala(53), Holmes(42), Carroll(5)
WEST POINT (39773) Clay(99), Monroe(1)
WHEELER Prentiss
WHITFIELD Rankin
WIGGINS (39577) Stone(88), Forrest(12)
WINONA (38967) Montgomery(95), Carroll(5)
WINSTONVILLE Bolivar
WINTERVILLE Washington
WOODLAND Chickasaw
WOODVILLE Wilkinson
YAZOO CITY Yazoo

ZIP/City Cross Reference

ZIP	City	ZIP	City	ZIP	City	ZIP	City
38601-38601	ABBEVILLE	38745-38745	GRACE	38914-38914	BIG CREEK	39092-39092	LAKE
38602-38602	ARKABUTLA	38746-38746	GUNNISON	38915-38915	BRUCE	39094-39094	LENA
38603-38603	ASHLAND	38748-38748	HOLLANDALE	38916-38916	CALHOUN CITY	39095-39095	LEXINGTON
38606-38606	BATESVILLE	38749-38749	HOLLY RIDGE	38917-38917	CARROLLTON	39096-39096	LORMAN
38609-38609	BELEN	38751-38751	INDIANOLA	38920-38920	CASCILLA	39097-39097	LOUISE
38610-38610	BLUE MOUNTAIN	38753-38753	INVERNESS	38921-38921	CHARLESTON	39098-39098	LUDLOW
38611-38611	BYHALIA	38754-38754	ISOLA	38922-38922	COFFEEVILLE	39107-39107	MC ADAMS
38614-38614	CLARKSDALE	38756-38756	LELAND	38923-38923	COILA	39108-39108	MC COOL
38617-38617	COAHOMA	38758-38758	MATTSON	38924-38924	CRUGER	39109-39109	MADDEN
38618-38618	COLDWATER	38759-38759	MERIGOLD	38925-38925	DUCK HILL	39110-39110	MADISON
38619-38619	COMO	38760-38760	METCALFE	38926-38926	ELLIOTT	39111-39111	MAGEE
38620-38620	COURTLAND	38761-38761	MOORHEAD	38927-38927	ENID	39112-39112	SANATORIUM
38621-38621	CRENSHAW	38762-38762	MOUND BAYOU	38928-38928	GLENDORA	39113-39113	MAYERSVILLE
38622-38622	CROWDER	38763-38763	NITTA YUMA	38929-38929	GORE SPRINGS	39114-39114	MENDENHALL
38623-38623	DARLING	38764-38764	PACE	38930-38935	GREENWOOD	39115-39115	MIDNIGHT
38625-38625	DUMAS	38765-38765	PANTHER BURN	38940-38940	HOLCOMB	39116-39116	MIZE
38626-38626	DUNDEE	38767-38767	RENA LARA	38941-38941	ITTA BENA	39117-39117	MORTON
38627-38627	ETTA	38768-38768	ROME	38943-38943	MC CARLEY	39119-39119	MOUNT OLIVE
38628-38628	FALCON	38769-38769	ROSEDALE	38944-38944	MINTER CITY	39120-39122	NATCHEZ
38629-38629	FALKNER	38771-38771	RULEVILLE	38945-38945	MONEY	39130-39130	MADISON
38630-38630	FARRELL	38772-38772	SCOTT	38946-38946	MORGAN CITY	39140-39140	NEWHEBRON
38631-38631	FRIARS POINT	38773-38773	SHAW	38947-38947	NORTH CARROLLTON	39144-39144	PATTISON
38632-38632	HERNANDO	38774-38774	SHELBY	38948-38948	OAKLAND	39145-39145	PELAHATCHIE
38633-38633	HICKORY FLAT	38776-38776	STONEVILLE	38949-38949	PARIS	39146-39146	PICKENS
38634-38635	HOLLY SPRINGS	38778-38778	SUNFLOWER	38950-38950	PHILIPP	39148-39148	PINEY WOODS
38637-38637	HORN LAKE	38780-38780	WAYSIDE	38951-38951	PITTSBORO	39149-39149	PINOLA
38638-38638	INDEPENDENCE	38781-38781	WINSTONVILLE	38952-38952	SCHLATER	39150-39150	PORT GIBSON
38639-38639	JONESTOWN	38782-38782	WINTERVILLE	38953-38953	SCOBEY	39151-39151	PUCKETT
38641-38641	LAKE CORMORANT	38801-38803	TUPELO	38954-38954	SIDON	39152-39152	PULASKI
38642-38642	LAMAR	38820-38820	ALGOMA	38955-38955	SLATE SPRING	39153-39153	RALEIGH
38643-38643	LAMBERT	38821-38821	AMORY	38957-38957	SUMNER	39154-39154	RAYMOND
38644-38644	LULA	38824-38824	BALDWYN	38958-38958	SWAN LAKE	39156-39156	REDWOOD
38645-38645	LYON	38825-38825	BECKER	38959-38959	SWIFTOWN	39157-39158	RIDGELAND
38646-38646	MARKS	38826-38826	BELDEN	38960-38960	TIE PLANT	39159-39159	ROLLING FORK
38647-38647	MICHIGAN CITY	38827-38827	BELMONT	38961-38961	TILLATOBA	39160-39160	SALLIS
38649-38649	MOUNT PLEASANT	38828-38828	BLUE SPRINGS	38962-38962	TIPPO	39161-39161	SANDHILL
38650-38650	MYRTLE	38829-38829	BOONEVILLE	38963-38963	TUTWILER	39162-39162	SATARTIA
38651-38651	NESBIT	38833-38833	BURNSVILLE	38964-38964	VANCE	39163-39163	SHARON
38652-38652	NEW ALBANY	38834-38835	CORINTH	38965-38965	WATER VALLEY	39165-39165	SIBLEY
38654-38654	OLIVE BRANCH	38838-38838	DENNIS	38966-38966	WEBB	39166-39166	SILVER CITY
38655-38655	OXFORD	38839-38839	DERMA	38967-38967	WINONA	39167-39167	STAR
38658-38658	POPE	38841-38841	ECRU	39038-39038	BELZONI	39168-39168	TAYLORSVILLE
38659-38659	POTTS CAMP	38843-38843	FULTON	39039-39039	BENTON	39169-39169	TCHULA
38661-38661	RED BANKS	38844-38844	GATTMAN	39040-39040	BENTONIA	39170-39170	TERRY
38663-38663	RIPLEY	38846-38846	GLEN	39041-39041	BOLTON	39171-39171	THOMASTOWN
38664-38664	ROBINSONVILLE	38847-38847	GOLDEN	39042-39043	BRANDON	39173-39173	TINSLEY
38665-38665	SARAH	38848-38848	GREENWOOD SPRINGS	39044-39044	BRAXTON	39174-39174	TOUGALOO
38666-38666	SARDIS	38849-38849	GUNTOWN	39045-39045	CAMDEN	39175-39175	UTICA
38668-38668	SENATOBIA	38850-38850	HOULKA	39046-39046	CANTON	39176-39176	VAIDEN
38669-38669	SHERARD	38851-38851	HOUSTON	39047-39047	BRANDON	39177-39177	VALLEY PARK
38670-38670	SLEDGE	38852-38852	IUKA	39051-39051	CARTHAGE	39179-39179	VAUGHAN
38671-38671	SOUTHAVEN	38854-38854	MC CONDY	39054-39054	CARY	39180-39182	VICKSBURG
38673-38673	TAYLOR	38855-38855	MANTACHIE	39056-39056	CLINTON	39189-39189	WALNUT GROVE
38674-38674	TIPLERSVILLE	38856-38856	MARIETTA	39057-39057	CONEHATTA	39190-39190	WASHINGTON
38675-38675	TULA	38857-38857	MOOREVILLE	39058-39058	CLINTON	39191-39191	WESSON
38676-38676	TUNICA	38858-38858	NETTLETON	39059-39059	CRYSTAL SPRINGS	39192-39192	WEST
38677-38677	UNIVERSITY	38859-38859	NEW SITE	39060-39060	CLINTON	39193-39193	WHITFIELD
38679-38679	VICTORIA	38860-38860	OKOLONA	39061-39061	DELTA CITY	39194-39194	YAZOO CITY
38680-38680	WALLS	38862-38862	PLANTERSVILLE	39062-39062	D LO	39200-39298	JACKSON
38683-38683	WALNUT	38863-38863	PONTOTOC	39063-39063	DURANT	39301-39309	MERIDIAN
38685-38685	WATERFORD	38864-38864	RANDOLPH	39066-39066	EDWARDS	39320-39320	BAILEY
38686-38686	WALLS	38865-38865	RIENZI	39067-39067	ETHEL	39322-39322	BUCKATUNNA
38701-38704	GREENVILLE	38866-38866	SALTILLO	39069-39069	FAYETTE	39323-39323	CHUNKY
38720-38720	ALLIGATOR	38868-38868	SHANNON	39071-39071	FLORA	39324-39324	CLARA
38721-38721	ANGUILLA	38869-38869	SHERMAN	39072-39072	POCAHONTAS	39325-39325	COLLINSVILLE
38722-38722	ARCOLA	38870-38870	SMITHVILLE	39073-39073	FLORENCE	39326-39326	DALEVILLE
38723-38723	AVON	38871-38871	THAXTON	39074-39074	FOREST	39327-39327	DECATUR
38725-38725	BENOIT	38873-38873	TISHOMINGO	39077-39077	GALLMAN	39328-39328	DE KALB
38726-38726	BEULAH	38874-38874	TOCCOPOLA	39078-39078	GEORGETOWN	39330-39330	ENTERPRISE
38730-38730	BOYLE	38875-38875	TREBLOC	39079-39079	GOODMAN	39332-39332	HICKORY
38731-38731	CHATHAM	38876-38876	TREMONT	39080-39080	HARPERVILLE	39335-39335	LAUDERDALE
38732-38733	CLEVELAND	38877-38877	VAN VLEET	39081-39081	HARRISTON	39336-39336	LAWRENCE
38736-38736	DODDSVILLE	38878-38878	VARDAMAN	39082-39082	HARRISVILLE	39337-39337	LITTLE ROCK
38737-38737	DREW	38879-38879	VERONA	39083-39083	HAZLEHURST	39338-39338	LOUIN
38738-38738	PARCHMAN	38880-38880	WHEELER	39086-39086	HERMANVILLE	39339-39339	LOUISVILLE
38739-38739	DUBLIN	38901-38902	GRENADA	39087-39087	HILLSBORO	39341-39341	MACON
38740-38740	DUNCAN	38912-38912	AVALON	39088-39088	HOLLY BLUFF	39342-39342	MARION
38744-38744	GLEN ALLAN	38913-38913	BANNER	39090-39090	KOSCIUSKO	39345-39345	NEWTON

Zip Range	City	Zip Range	City	Zip Range	City	Zip Range	City
39346-39346	NOXAPATER	39456-39456	MC LAIN	39564-39566	OCEAN SPRINGS	39668-39668	UNION CHURCH
39347-39347	PACHUTA	39457-39457	MC NEILL	39567-39569	PASCAGOULA	39669-39669	WOODVILLE
39348-39348	PAULDING	39459-39459	MOSELLE	39571-39571	PASS CHRISTIAN	39701-39710	COLUMBUS
39350-39350	PHILADELPHIA	39460-39460	MOSS	39572-39572	PEARLINGTON	39730-39730	ABERDEEN
39352-39352	PORTERVILLE	39461-39461	NEELY	39573-39573	PERKINSTON	39735-39735	ACKERMAN
39354-39354	PRESTON	39462-39462	NEW AUGUSTA	39574-39574	SAUCIER	39736-39736	ARTESIA
39355-39355	QUITMAN	39463-39463	NICHOLSON	39576-39576	WAVELAND	39737-39737	BELLEFONTAINE
39356-39356	ROSE HILL	39464-39464	OVETT	39577-39577	WIGGINS	39739-39739	BROOKSVILLE
39358-39358	SCOOBA	39465-39465	PETAL	39581-39595	PASCAGOULA	39740-39740	CALEDONIA
39359-39359	SEBASTOPOL	39466-39466	PICAYUNE	39601-39603	BROOKHAVEN	39741-39741	CEDARBLUFF
39360-39360	SHUBUTA	39470-39470	POPLARVILLE	39629-39629	BOGUE CHITTO	39743-39743	CRAWFORD
39361-39361	SHUQUALAK	39474-39474	PRENTISS	39630-39630	BUDE	39744-39744	EUPORA
39362-39362	STATE LINE	39475-39475	PURVIS	39631-39631	CENTREVILLE	39745-39745	FRENCH CAMP
39363-39363	STONEWALL	39476-39476	RICHTON	39632-39632	CHATAWA	39746-39746	HAMILTON
39364-39364	TOOMSUBA	39477-39477	SANDERSVILLE	39633-39633	CROSBY	39747-39747	KILMICHAEL
39365-39365	UNION	39478-39478	SANDY HOOK	39635-39635	FERNWOOD	39750-39750	MABEN
39366-39366	VOSSBURG	39479-39479	SEMINARY	39638-39638	GLOSTER	39751-39751	MANTEE
39367-39367	WAYNESBORO	39480-39480	SOSO	39641-39641	JAYESS	39752-39752	MATHISTON
39400-39407	HATTIESBURG	39481-39481	STRINGER	39643-39643	KOKOMO	39753-39753	MAYHEW
39421-39421	BASSFIELD	39482-39482	SUMRALL	39645-39645	LIBERTY	39754-39754	MONTPELIER
39422-39422	BAY SPRINGS	39483-39483	FOXWORTH	39647-39647	MC CALL CREEK	39755-39755	PHEBA
39423-39423	BEAUMONT	39500-39507	GULFPORT	39648-39649	MC COMB	39756-39756	PRAIRIE
39425-39425	BROOKLYN	39520-39522	BAY SAINT LOUIS	39652-39652	MAGNOLIA	39759-39760	STARKVILLE
39426-39426	CARRIERE	39525-39525	DIAMONDHEAD	39653-39653	MEADVILLE	39762-39762	MISSISSIPPI STATE
39427-39427	CARSON	39529-39529	BAY SAINT LOUIS	39654-39654	MONTICELLO	39766-39766	STEENS
39428-39428	COLLINS	39530-39535	BILOXI	39656-39656	OAK VALE	39767-39767	STEWART
39429-39429	COLUMBIA	39552-39552	ESCATAWPA	39657-39657	OSYKA	39769-39769	STURGIS
39436-39436	EASTABUCHIE	39553-39553	GAUTIER	39661-39661	ROXIE	39771-39771	WALTHALL
39437-39437	ELLISVILLE	39555-39555	HURLEY	39662-39662	RUTH	39772-39772	WEIR
39439-39439	HEIDELBERG	39556-39556	KILN	39663-39663	SILVER CREEK	39773-39773	WEST POINT
39440-39442	LAUREL	39558-39558	LAKESHORE	39664-39664	SMITHDALE	39776-39776	WOODLAND
39451-39451	LEAKESVILLE	39560-39560	LONG BEACH	39665-39665	SONTAG		
39452-39452	LUCEDALE	39561-39561	MC HENRY	39666-39666	SUMMIT		
39455-39455	LUMBERTON	39562-39563	MOSS POINT	39667-39667	TYLERTOWN		

Missouri

General Help Numbers:

Governor's Office
PO Box 720
Jefferson City, MO 65102-0720
www.gov.state.mo.us

573-751-3222
Fax 573-751-1495
8AM-5PM

Attorney General's Office
PO Box 899
Jefferson City, MO 65102
www.ago.state.mo.us

573-751-3321
Fax 573-751-0774
8AM-5PM

State Court Administrator
2112 Industrial Drive - PO Box 104480
Jefferson City, MO 65110
www.osca.state.mo.us

573-751-4377
Fax 573-751-5540
8AM-5PM

State Archives
Archives Division
PO Box 1747
Jefferson City, MO 65102-1747 8-5 M-F (till 9PM on Th
http://mosl.sos.state.mo.us/rec-man/arch.html

573-751-3280
Fax 573-526-7333

State Specifics:

Capital: Jefferson City
                            Cole County

Time Zone: CST

Number of Counties: 114

Population: 5,468,338

Web Site: www.state.mo.us

State Agencies

Criminal Records

Missouri State Highway Patrol, Criminal Record & Identification Division, PO Box 568, Jefferson City, MO 65102-0568 (Courier: 1510 E Elm St, Jefferson City, MO 65102); 573-526-6153, 573-751-9382 (Fax), 8AM-5PM.

Indexing & Storage: Records are available from 1970 on. It takes 3 weeks before new records are available for inquiry. Records are indexed on inhouse computer.

Searching: Only convictions are reported. Include the following in your request-full name, date of birth, sex, race, Social Security Number.

Access by: mail, in person.

Fee & Payment: The search fee is $5.00 per individual for a name search. Searches by fingerprint cost $14.00 each. Fee payee: State of Missouri. Prepayment required. Personal checks accepted. No credit cards accepted.

Mail search: Turnaround time: 3 weeks. No self addressed stamped envelope is required.

In person search: Turnaround time is while you wait for one search only.

Corporation Records
Fictitious Name
Limited Partnership Records
Assumed Name
Trademarks/Servicemarks
Limited Liability Company Records

Secretary of State, Corporation Services, PO Box 778, Jefferson City, MO 65102 (Courier: 600 W Main, Jefferson City, MO 65101); 573-751-4153, 573-751-5841 (Fax), 8AM-5PM.

http://mosl.sos.state.mo.us

Note: Trademarks and servicemarks are handled by the Commissions Division within Sec. of State and can be reached at 573-751-4756.

Indexing & Storage: Records are available from the 1800s. New records are available for inquiry immediately. Records are indexed on microfilm, inhouse computer, hard copy.

Searching: Include the following in your request-full name of business, specific records that you need copies of. In addition to the articles of incorporation, corporation records include the following information: Annual Reports, Officers, Directors, DBAs, Prior (merged) names, Inactive and Reserved names.

Access by: mail, phone, fax, in person, online.

Fee & Payment: An uncertified copy of a record is $.50 per page, a certified copy of a record is $10.00 certification fee plus $.50 per page. The fee for an officers and directors list is $10.00. A Good Standing is $10.00. A trademark or servicemark search is $5.00. Fee payee: Secretary of State. Prepayment required. They will invoice. Personal checks accepted. Credit cards accepted: Mastercard, Visa.

Mail search: Turnaround time: 2-3 days. No self addressed stamped envelope is required.

Phone search: No fee for telephone request. Status information is given over the phone at no charge.

Fax search: Same criteria as mail searching. Records are returned by mail.

In person search: Results are returned by mail.

Online search: Searching can be done from the Internet site. The corporate name, the agent name or the charter number is required to search. The site will indicate the currency of the data. Many business entity type searches are available.

Uniform Commercial Code

UCC Division, Secretary of State, PO Box 1159, Jefferson City, MO 65102 (Courier: 600 W Main St, Rm 302, Jefferson City, MO 65101); 573-751-2360, 573-522-2057 (Fax), 8AM-5PM.

Indexing & Storage: Records are available from 1965. Records are on microfiche from 7-1-80-present.

Searching: Use search request form UCC-11. Please note that all tax liens are filed at the county level only. Include the following in your request-debtor name.

Access by: mail, phone, in person.

Fee & Payment: Fees: Information request - $13.00; Information and copy request - $26.00 (including 10 copies.) Copies cost $.50 per page after the first 10. UCC-3's are not listed on the summary; order copies to review them. Fee payee: Secretary of State. Prepayment required. Personal checks accepted. Credit cards accepted: Mastercard, Visa.

Mail search: Turnaround time: 2 weeks. A self addressed stamped envelope is requested.

Phone search: General information is available without charge.

In person search: You may request information in person.

Other access: The agency will release information for bulk purchase, call for procedures and pricing.

Federal Tax Liens
State Tax Liens

Records not maintained by a state level agency.

Note: All tax liens are filed at the county level.

Sales Tax Registrations

Records not maintained by a state level agency.

Note: This agency will neither confirm nor supply any information. They suggest to check at the city level. This agency will provide no information. Confidential information is only released to owners or corporate officers registered with the Department.

Birth Certificates

Department of Health, Bureau of Vital Records, PO Box 570, Jefferson City, MO 65102-0570 (Courier: 930 Wildwood, Jefferson City, MO 65109); 573-751-6387, 573-751-6400 (Message Number), 573-526-3846 (Fax), 8AM-5PM.

www.health.state.mo.us

Indexing & Storage: Records are available from 1910 on. New records are available for inquiry immediately. Records are indexed on microfiche, inhouse computer.

Searching: Records are only released to person of record or legal representative of immediate family member. Must have a signed release form from person of record or immediate family member for investigative purposes. Include the following in your request-full name, names of parents, mother's maiden name, date of birth, place of birth, relationship to person of record, reason for information request.

Access by: mail, phone, in person.

Fee & Payment: Search fee is $10.00 per 5 years searched. Fee is charged regardless if record is found. Emergency requests using a credit card pay an additional $4.95 fee. Fee payee: Missouri Department of Health. Prepayment required. Personal checks accepted. Credit cards accepted: Mastercard, Visa, AmEx, Discover.

Mail search: Turnaround time: 2-3 weeks. No self addressed stamped envelope is required.

Phone search: This service is only available for emergencies.

In person search: Turnaround time 10 minutes.

Death Records

Department of Health, Bureau of Vital Records, PO Box 570, Jefferson City, MO 65102-0570 (Courier: 930 Wildwood, Jefferson City, MO 65109); 573-751-6370, 573-751-6400 (Message Number), 573-526-3846 (Fax), 8AM-5PM.

www.health.state.mo.us

Indexing & Storage: Records are available from 1910 on. New records are available for inquiry immediately. Records are indexed on microfiche, inhouse computer.

Searching: Records are only released to legal representative of person of record or immediate family member. Must have a signed release form from immediate family member for investigative purposes. Include the following in your request-

full name, date of death, place of death, relationship to person of record, reason for information request.

Access by: mail, in person.

Fee & Payment: The $10.00 search fee is for 5 years searched. Use of credit card is additional $4.95. Fee payee: Missouri Department of Health. Prepayment required. Personal checks accepted.

Mail search: Turnaround time: 2-3 weeks. No self addressed stamped envelope is required.

In person search: Turnaround time 10 minutes.

Expedited service: Expedited service is available for mail and phone searches. This is for emergency use only. The additional fee is $14.95 for regular mail (includes credit card use) or $25.45 for express shipping.

Marriage Certificates
Divorce Records

Department of Health, Bureau of Vital Records, PO Box 570, Jefferson City, MO 65102-0570 (Courier: 930 Wildwood, Jefferson City, MO 65109); 573-751-6382, 573-751-6400 (Message Number), 573-526-3846 (Fax), 8AM-5PM.

www.health.state.mo.us

Note: Actual marriage and divorce records are found at county of issue. This agency will issue a certificate of statement only.

Indexing & Storage: Records are available from July 1, 1948-present on microfiche.

Searching: Include names, year of occurrence and county in your request.

Access by: mail, in person.

Fee & Payment: The fee is $10.00 for each 5 years searched. Use of credit card is additional $4.95. Fee payee: Missouri Department of Health. Prepayment required. Personal checks accepted.

Mail search: Turnaround time: 1-2 weeks. No self addressed stamped envelope is required.

In person search: The agency personnel do the searching.

Expedited service: Expedited service is available for fax searches. Add $14.95 for regular mail and $25.95 for overnight (includes credit card fee).

Workers' Compensation Records

Labor & Industrial Relations Department, Workers Compensation Division, PO Box 58, Jefferson City, MO 65102-0058 (Courier: 3315 W Truman Blvd, Jefferson City, MO 65101); 573-751-4231, 573-751-2012 (Fax), 8AM-4:30PM.

www.dolir.state.mo.us

Indexing & Storage: Records are available from 1945. Records are computerized since 1994. Records are indexed on inhouse computer.

Searching: Report of injury and medical records released only with a release form. All other records are open. Include the following in your request-claimant name, Social Security Number, date of accident.

Access by: mail, fax, in person.

Fee & Payment: The search fee is $2.00. Fee payee: Workers Compensation Division. Personal checks accepted. No credit cards accepted.

Mail search: Turnaround time: 1-2 days. No self addressed stamped envelope is required.

Fax search: The initial fax must include a written request for the search. Turnaround time is 1-2 days.

In person search: To search in person, you must be party to the case in question or possess written authorization.

Driver Records

Department of Revenue, Driver License Bureau, PO Box 200, Jefferson City, MO 65105-0200 (Courier: Harry S Truman Bldg, 301 W High St, Room 470, Jefferson City, MO 65105); 573-751-4300, 573-526-4769 (Fax), 7:45AM-4:45PM.

www.dor.state.mo.us/dmv

Note: Copies of tickets are available from the same address. Requests must be in writing, include the name, DOB, license number, and specific violation information. The cost is $3.75 per ticket.

Indexing & Storage: Records are available for 5 years for moving violations and suspensions, permanent for DWI's. Zero point violations are not shown on the record. Accidents are stored in the state computer, but are not shown on the driving record, unless suspension/revocation action taken.

Searching: The state complies with DPPA. Casual requesters can obtain records without personal information.

Access by: mail, phone, fax, in person, online.

Fee & Payment: The fee is $1.25 per record for walk-in or mail-in requests. The fee for online retrieval is $1.25 per record plus network line charges. Fee payee: Department of Revenue. Prepayment required. Cashier's check and money orders preferred. Personal checks accepted. No credit cards accepted.

Mail search: Turnaround time: 2 days. A self addressed stamped envelope is requested.

Phone search: Search costs $1.50 per page. Phone-in service is available for pre-approved, established accounts. Call the number above for more information.

Fax search: Fax ordering-retrieval is available. Same criteria as phone requesting with an additional $.50 fee.

In person search: You may request information in person.

Online search: Online access costs $1.25 per record. Online inquiries can be put in Missouri's "mailbox" any time of the day. These inquiries are then picked up at 2 AM the following morning, and the resulting MVR's are sent back to each customer's "mailbox" approximately two hours later.

Other access: The tape-to-tape process has been replaced by the online system. The entire license file can be purchased, with updates. Call 573-751-5579 for more information.

Vehicle Ownership
Vehicle Identification
Boat & Vessel Ownership
Boat & Vessel Registration

Department of Revenue, Division of Motor Vehicles, PO Box 100, Jefferson City, MO 65105-0100 (Courier: Harry S Truman Bldg, 301 W High St, Jefferson City, MO 65105); 573-526-3669, 573-751-7060 (Fax), 7:45AM-4:45PM.

www.dor.state.mo.us/mvdl/default.htm

Note: Lien information shows on the title records.

Indexing & Storage: Records are available from 1968-present. Records are indexed on microfiche from 1968-present, and microfilm from 1981-present. Records include boats and mobile homes. All motorized boats 12 ft or longer must be titled and registered.

Searching: Ownership and vehicle information is available with no restrictions to access, if request is of a legal nature. Casual request must have consent of subject to obtain records that contain personal information. Current registration/title records are on computer. Records are purged from the computer files after 2 years of no activity. However, the records will remain on microfiche.

Access by: mail, phone, fax, in person.

Fee & Payment: The fee for a record search is $4.50 and a complete title history is $8.00. There is an additional $3.00 for certification. Fee payee: Department of Revenue. Prepayment required. Pre-approved accounts may be billed. Personal checks accepted. No credit cards accepted.

Mail search: Turnaround time: 2-4 weeks.

Phone search: The state offers a phone-in service for title verification and lien holder information ONLY for dealers and lienholders. The fee is $1.50 per record. For more information, call 573-526-3669.

Fax search: To have results returned by fax costs an additional $.50 per page.

In person search: You may request records in person.

Other access: Missouri has an extensive range of records and information available on magnetic tape, labels or paper. Besides offering license, vehicle, title, dealer, and marine records, specific public report data is also available.

Accident Reports

Missouri Highway Patrol, Traffic Division, PO Box 568, Jefferson City, MO 65102-0568 (Courier: 1510 E Elm St, Jefferson City, MO 65102); 573-526-6113, 573-751-9921 (Fax), 8AM-5PM.

www.mshp.state.mo,us

Indexing & Storage: Records are available for 5 years to present on computer. Records are indexed on an in-house computer. Records are on microfilm from 1941.

Searching: Record requests must be in writing. Generally, these records are open to the public. Include the following in your request-full name, date of accident, location of accident. There is no telephone searching, but you can call to determine if an accident is on file.

Access by: mail, in person.

Fee & Payment: At present, due to restrictions imposed by legislation, the $5.00 fee for reports has not been implemented.

Mail search: Turnaround time: 3-4 working days. A self addressed stamped envelope is requested.

In person search: Turnaround time is immediate.

Legislation-Current/Pending
Legislation-Passed

Legislative Library, 117A State Capitol, Jefferson City, MO 65101; 573-751-4633 (Bill Status Only), 8:30AM-4:30PM.

www.moga.state.mo.us

Note: Sessions are from January to May.

Indexing & Storage: Records are available from 1993-present on computer, from 1909-1972 and 1985-1999 on microfiche, and from 1973-1984 in books. Records are indexed on microfiche, books (volumes).

Searching: Include the following in your request-bill number, year.

Access by: mail, phone, in person, online.

Mail search: Turnaround time: 1 week to 10 days. No self addressed stamped envelope is required. No fee for mail request.

Phone search: No fee for telephone request. If the requests involves much time/paper, it will be refused.

In person search: No fee for request.

Online search: The web site offers access to bills and statutes. One can search or track bills by key words, bill number, or sponsers.

Voter Registration
Access to Records is Restricted

Secretary of State, Division of Elections, PO Box 1767, Jefferson City, MO 65102; 573-751-2301, 573-526-3242 (Fax), 8AM-5PM.

http://mosl.sos.state.mo.us

Note: The state will neither permit individual look-ups nor sell the records for commercial purposes. Records are sold in various media formats for political purposes. Individual look-ups can be done at the county level by the County Clerks.

GED Certificates

GED Office, PO Box 480, Jefferson City, MO 65102; 573-751-3504, 8AM-4:30PM.

www.dese.state.mo.us/divvoced/ged

Indexing & Storage: It takes 3-4 weeks before new records are available for inquiry.

Searching: Include the following in your request-signed release, date of birth, Social Security Number. The year and location of the test are very helpful and should also be included in the request.

Access by: mail, in person.

Fee & Payment: The fee is $2.00 for either a verification or a transcript. Fee payee: Treasurer, State of Missouri. Prepayment required. Personal checks accepted.

Mail search: Turnaround time: same day. No self addressed stamped envelope is required.

In person search: $2.00 fee per request.

Hunting License Information
Fishing License Information

Conservation Department, Fiscal Services, PO Box 180, Jefferson City, MO 65102-0180 (Courier: 2901 W Truman Blvd, Jefferson City, MO 65102); 573-751-4115, 573-751-4864 (Fax), 8AM-Noon; 1PM-5PM.

www.conservation.state.mo.us

Indexing & Storage: Records are available for most recent years. Records are computerized since 3/1/96. Prior to that date, records must be searched in boxes, by vendor account number. Records are indexed on inhouse computer, hard copy.

Searching: Records are only released to the permitee. Otherwise, they are not released until the reason for the request is reviewed by the Department's General Counsel. Names and addresses may be released, if request is approved.

Include the following in your request-full name. For older records, you will need the permittee's name, date of birth, and type of permit. The records are in the receipt books that were assigned to vendors and are in boxes in no particular order.

Access by: in person.

Fee & Payment: Prepayment required. Fee payee: Conservation Department. Price is based upon type of service provided. Personal checks accepted. Credit cards accepted: Mastercard, Visa.

No self addressed stamped envelope is required. No searching by mail.

In person search: There is a "time" charge for your searches. Call ahead of time for an appointment before searches.

Other access: Mailing lists of the hunting and fishing permit vendors are available. The cost is about $700.

Licenses Searchable Online

Architect #02	www.ecodev.state.mo.us/pr/ftp4.htm
Athletic Trainer #28	www.ecodev.state.mo.us/pr/healingdown.html
Audiologist (Clinical) #16	www.ecodev.state.mo.us/pr/healingdown.html
Barber #03	www.ecodev.state.mo.us/pr/ftp4.htm
Barber Instructor #03	www.ecodev.state.mo.us/pr/ftp4.htm
Barber Schools #03	www.ecodev.state.mo.us/pr/ftp4.htm
Barber Shop #03	www.ecodev.state.mo.us/pr/ftp4.htm
Chiropractor #04	www.ecodev.state.mo.us/pr/ftp4.htm
Combined Speech/Clinical Audiologist #16	www.ecodev.state.mo.us/pr/healingdown.html
Cosmetologist #05	www.ecodev.state.mo.us/pr/ftp4.htm
Cosmetology Instructor #05	www.ecodev.state.mo.us/pr/ftp4.htm
Cosmetology School #05	www.ecodev.state.mo.us/pr/ftp4.htm
Cosmetology Shop #05	www.ecodev.state.mo.us/pr/ftp4.htm
Dental Hygienist #17	www.ecodev.state.mo.us/pr/ftp4.htm
Dentist #17	www.ecodev.state.mo.us/pr/ftp4.htm
Drug Distribution #09	www.ecodev.state.mo.us/pr/ftp4.htm
Embalmer #06	www.ecodev.state.mo.us/pr/ftp4.htm
Engineer #02	www.ecodev.state.mo.us/pr/ftp4.htm
Funeral Director #06	www.ecodev.state.mo.us/pr/ftp4.htm
Funeral Establishment #06	www.ecodev.state.mo.us/pr/ftp4.htm
Funeral Preneed Provider #06	www.ecodev.state.mo.us/pr/ftp4.htm
Funeral Preneed Seller #06	www.ecodev.state.mo.us/pr/ftp4.htm
Interpreter for the Deaf #46	www.ecodev.state.mo.us/pr/ftp4.htm
Landscape Architect #26	www.ecodev.state.mo.us/pr/ftp4.htm
Landscape Architect Corporation & Partnership #26	www.ecodev.state.mo.us/pr/ftp4.htm
Manicurist #05	www.ecodev.state.mo.us/pr/ftp4.htm
Medical Doctor #11	www.ecodev.state.mo.us/pr/healingdown.html
Nurse #07	www.ecodev.state.mo.us/pr/nursingdown.html
Nurse-LPN #07	www.ecodev.state.mo.us/pr/nursingdown.html
Occupational Therapist #41	www.ecodev.state.mo.us/pr/occupdown.html
Occupational Therapist Assistant #41	www.ecodev.state.mo.us/pr/occupdown.html
Optometrist #08	www.ecodev.state.mo.us/pr/optometristdown.html
Osteopathic Physician #11	www.ecodev.state.mo.us/pr/healingdown.html
Pharmacist/Pharmacy Intern #09	www.ecodev.state.mo.us/pr/pharmacy/search.htm
Pharmacy #09	www.ecodev.state.mo.us/pr/pharmacy/phesearch.htm
Physical Therapist #11	www.ecodev.state.mo.us/pr/healingdown.html
Physician Assistant #11	www.ecodev.state.mo.us/pr/healingdown.html
Podiatrist #10	www.ecodev.state.mo.us/pr/ftp4.htm
Podiatrist Temporary #10	www.ecodev.state.mo.us/pr/ftp4.htm
Podiatrist/Ankle #10	www.ecodev.state.mo.us/pr/ftp4.htm
Professional Counselor #23	www.ecodev.state.mo.us/pr/counselorsdown.html
Professional Nurse #07	www.ecodev.state.mo.us/pr/nursingdown.html
Psychologist #36	www.ecodev.state.mo.us/pr/ftp4.htm
Public Accountant Partnership #01	www.ecodev.state.mo.us/pr/ftp4.htm
Public Accountant-CPA #01	www.ecodev.state.mo.us/pr/ftp4.htm
Real Estate Appraiser #14	www.ecodev.state.mo.us/pr/rea/search.htm
Real Estate Broker #35	www.ecodev.state.mo.us/pr
Real Estate Sales Agent #35	www.ecodev.state.mo.us/pr
Respiratory Care Practitioner #42	www.ecodev.state.mo.us/pr/ftp4.htm
Social Worker (Clinical) #15	www.ecodev.state.mo.us/pr/ftp4.htm
Speech Pathologist/Audiologist #16	www.ecodev.state.mo.us/pr/healingdown.html
Surveyor #02	www.ecodev.state.mo.us/pr/ftp4.htm
Veterinarian #31	www.ecodev.state.mo.us/pr/ftp4.htm
Veterinary Technician #31	www.ecodev.state.mo.us/pr/ftp4.htm

Licensing Quick Finder

Architect #02	573-751-0047	Barber Instructor #03	573-751-0805	Child Care Facility #29	573-751-2450
Associate in Training #39	573-751-9211	Barber Schools #03	573-751-0805	Chiropractor #04	573-751-2104
Athletic Trainer #28	573-751-0171	Barber Shop #03	573-751-0805	Combined Speech/Clinical Audiologist #16	
Attorney #40	573-635-4128	Boxer #44	573-751-0243		573-751-0171
Audiologist (Clinical) #16	573-751-0171	Cemetery (Endowed Care Cemetery) #25		Cosmetologist #05	573-751-1052
Barber #03	573-751-0805		573-751-0849	Cosmetology Instructor #05	573-751-1052

Cosmetology School #05....................573-751-1052
Cosmetology Shop #05 573-751-1052
Court Reporter #12 573-751-4144
Dental Hygienist #17 573-751-0040
Dental Specialist #17..........................573-751-0040
Dentist #17 573-751-0040
Drug Distribution #09..........................573-751-0091
Embalmer #06 573-751-0813
Emergency Medical Technician (Basic) #19
....573-751-6356
Employment Agency #45.....................573-751-0239
Engineer #02 573-751-0047
Funeral Director #06...........................573-751-0813
Funeral Establishment #06 573-751-0813
Funeral Preneed Provider #06 573-751-0813
Funeral Preneed Seller #06 573-751-0813
Gaming Supply #30.............................573-526-4092
Gaming-Occupational Licenses I & II #30
....573-526-4092
Gaming-Property (Boat) #30...............573-526-4092
Geologist #47......................................573-526-7625
Horse Racing #30 573-526-4083
Insurance Agent/Broker #20 573-751-3518
Interpreter for the Deaf #46 573-526-7787
Investment Advisor #34.......................573-751-4136
Landfill Operator #37..........................573-751-5401
Landscape Architect #26 573-751-0039

Landscape Architect Corporation & Partnership #26
....573-751-0039
Liquor Control #21..............................573-751-2333
Manicurist #05 573-751-1052
Marriage & Family Therapist #43 573-751-0870
Martial Artist #44 573-751-0243
Medical Doctor #11 573-751-0108
Notary Public #33................................573-751-2783
Nurse #07 573-751-0681
Nurse-LPN #07...................................573-751-0681
Nursing Home Administrator #32 573-751-3511
Occupational Therapist #41 573-751-0877
Occupational Therapist Assistant #41
....573-751-0877
Optometrist #08 573-751-0814
Osteopathic Physician #11 573-751-0108
Pesticide Applicator #18 573-751-5504
Pesticide Dealer #18 573-751-5504
Pesticide Technician #18.....................573-751-9298
Pharmacist/Pharmacy Intern #09 573-751-0091
Pharmacy #09.....................................573-751-0091
Physical Therapist #11 573-751-0171
Physician Assistant #11.......................573-751-0171
Podiatrist #10......................................573-751-0873
Podiatrist Temporary #10.....................573-751-0873
Podiatrist/Ankle #10............................573-751-0873
Prevention Specialist #39 573-751-9211

Professional Counselor #23.................573-751-0018
Professional Nurse #07 573-751-0681
Psychologist #36.................................573-751-0099
Public Accountant Partnership #01 573-751-0012
Public Accountant-CPA #01.................573-751-0012
Real Estate Appraiser #14 573-751-0038
Real Estate Broker #35 573-751-2628
Real Estate Sales Agent #35 573-751-2628
Respiratory Care Practitioner #42 573-522-2864
School Counselor #24..........................573-751-4234
School Librarian #24 573-751-4234
School Principal #24............................573-751-4234
School Superintendent #24 573-751-4234
Securities Agent #34 573-751-4136
Securities Broker/Dealer #34 573-751-4136
Social Worker (Clinical) #15.................573-751-0885
Speech Pathologist/Audiologist #16 573-751-0171
Substance Abuse Counselor #39..........573-751-9211
Surveyor #02 573-751-0047
Teacher #24..573-751-4234
Veterinarian #31.................................573-751-0031
Veterinary Technician #31 573-751-0031
Waste Water System Operator #38.......573-526-6627
Water Supply Operator #38 573-526-6627
Wrestler #44 573-751-0243

Licensing Agency Information

01 Board of Accountancy, PO Box 613 (3605 Missouri Blvd), Jefferson City, MO 65102-0613; 573-751-1052, Fax: 573-751-0890.

www.ecodev.state.mo.us/pr/account

02 Engineers & Land Survey, Board of Architects, PO Box 184 (3605 Missouri Blvd, #380), Jefferson City, MO 65102; 573-751-0047, Fax: 573-751-8046.
www.ecodev.state.mo.us/pr/moapels

Direct URL to search licenses: www.ecodev.state.mo.us/pr/ftp4.htm

03 Board of Barber Examiners, PO Box 1335 (3605 Missouri Blvd), Jefferson City, MO 65102-1335; 573-751-0805, Fax: 573-751-8167.
www.ecodev.state.mo.us/pr/barber

Direct URL to search licenses: www.ecodev.state.mo.us/pr/ftp4.htm The online search URL is used to download the list of active licensees. Adobe Acrobat Reader software ineeded to open the downloaded files. To obtain the Acrobat Reader software, visit www.ecodev.state.mo.us/download/instructions.htm .

04 Board of Chiropractic Examiners, PO Box 672 (3605 Missouri Blvd), Jefferson City, MO 65102-0672; 573-751-2104, Fax: 573-751-0735.
www.ecodev.state.mo.us/pr/chiro

Direct URL to search licenses: www.ecodev.state.mo.us/pr/ftp4.htm

05 Board of Cosmetology, PO Box 1062 (3605 Missouri Blvd), Jefferson City, MO 65102; 573-751-1052, Fax: 573-751-8167.

www.ecodev.state.mo.us/pr/cosmo

06 Board of Embalmers & Funeral Directors, PO Box 423 (3605 Missouri Blvd), Jefferson City, MO 65102-0625; 573-751-0813, Fax: 573-751-1155.
www.ecodev.state.mo.us/pr/embalm

Direct URL to search licenses: www.ecodev.state.mo.us/pr/ftp4.htm

07 Board of Nursing, PO Box 656 (3605 Missouri Blvd), Jefferson City, MO 65102; 573-751-0681, Fax: 573-751-0075.

www.ecodev.state.mo.us/pr/nursing
Direct URL to search licenses: www.ecodev.state.mo.us/pr/nursingdown.htm

08 Board of Optometry, PO Box 1335 (PO Box 1335 (3605 Missouri Blvd)), Jefferson City, MO 65102-0423; 573-751-0814, Fax: 573-751-0735.
www.ecodev.state.mo.us/pr/optom

Direct URL to search licenses: www.ecodev.state.mo.us/pr/optometristdown.html You can search online using alphabetical list.

09 Board of Pharmacy, PO Box 625 (3605 Missouri Blvd), Jefferson City, MO 65102; 573-751-3464, Fax: 573-526-2831.
www.ecodev.state.mo.us/pr/pharmacy

Direct URL to search licenses: www.ecodev.state.mo.us/pr/pharmacy/phsearch.htm You can search online using name, pharmacy name, street, city, ZIP Code, and disciplinary status.

10 Board of Podiatric Medicine, PO Box 423 (3605 Missouri Blvd), Jefferson City, MO 65102; 573-751-0873, Fax: 573-751-1155.
www.ecodev.state.mo.us/pr/podiatry

Direct URL to search licenses: www.ecodev.state.mo.us/pr/ftp4.htm

11 Board of Registration for Healing Arts, PO Box 4 (3605 Missouri Blvd), Jefferson City, MO 65102; 573-751-0098, Fax: 573-751-3166.
www.ecodev.state.mo.us/pr/healarts

Direct URL to search licenses: www.ecodev.state.mo.us/pr/healingdown.html

14 Commission of Real Estate Appraisers, PO Box 1335 (3605 Missouri Blvd), Jefferson City, MO 65102; 573-751-0038, Fax: 573-526-2831.
www.ecodev.state.mo.us/pr/rea

Direct URL to search licenses: www.ecodev.state.mo.us/pr/rea/search.htm You can search online using license number, name, business name, city, ZIP Code, and classification.

15 Division of Professional Registration, Committee for Licensed Clinical Social Workers, PO Box 1335 (3605 Missouri Blvd), Jefferson

City, MO 65102; 573-751-0085, Fax: 573-751-7670.
www.ecodev.state.mo.us/pr/social

Direct URL to search licenses: www.ecodev.state.mo.us/pr/ftp4.htm You can search online using www.state.mo.us/boards/cgi/boards.cgi?FUNCTION=LIST.

16 Committee of Speech Pathology & Audiology, PO Box 423 (3605 Missouri Blvd), Jefferson City, MO 65102; 573-751-0098, Fax: 573-751-3166.
www.ecodev.state.mo.us/pr/healarts/

Direct URL to search licenses: www.ecodev.state.mo.us/pr/healingdown.html

17 Dental Board, PO Box 1367 (3605 Missouri Blvd), Jefferson City, MO 65102; 573-751-0040, Fax: 573-751-8216.
www.ecodev.state.mo.us/pr/dental

Direct URL to search licenses: www.ecodev.state.mo.us/pr/ftp4.htm

18 Department of Agriculture, Division of Plant Industries, Bureau of Pesticide, PO Box 630 (1616 Missouri Blvd), Jefferson City, MO 65102; 573-751-2462, Fax: 573-751-0005.

www.mda.state.mo.us/d.htm

19 Department of Health, Emergency Medical Services, PO Box 570 (PO Box 570), Jefferson City, MO 65102-0570; 573-751-6356, Fax: 573-526-4102.

20 Department of Insurance, Licensing Section, PO Box 690 (PO Box 690), Jefferson City, MO 65102-0690; 573-751-4126, Fax: 573-526-3416.

www.insurance.state.mo.us

21 Department of Public Safety, Division of Liquor Control, PO Box 837 (Truman Bldg, Rm 870), Jefferson City, MO 65102-0837; 573-751-5445, Fax: 573-526-4540.

www.mdlc.state.mo.us

23 Division of Professional Regulation, Committee for Professional Counselors, PO Box 1335 (PO Box 1335 (3605 Missouri Blvd)), Jefferson City, MO 65102-1335; 573-751-0018, Fax: 573-526-3489.

www.ecodev.state.mo.us/pr/counselr/

Direct URL to search licenses: www.ecodev.state.mo.us/pr/counselorsdown.html

24 Education, Elementary & Secondary Instruction, PO Box 480 (205 Jefferson St), Jefferson City, MO 65102-0480; 573-751-4234, Fax: 573-751-1179.

25 Endowed Care Cemeteries, PO Box 1335 (3605 Missouri Blvd), Jefferson City, MO 65102-1335; 573-751-0849, Fax: 573-751-0878.

www.ecodev.state.mo.us/pr/endowed

26 Landscape Architectural Council, PO Box 1335 (3605 Missouri Blvd), Jefferson City, MO 65102-1339; 573-751-0039, Fax: 573-751-2831.

www.ecodev.state.mo.us/pr/landarch

29 Department of Health, Bureau of Child Care Safety & Licensure, PO Box 570 (PO Box 570), Jefferson City, MO 65102-0119; 573-635-4128, Fax: 573-635-2811.

30 Gaming Commission, 3417 Knipp Dr, Jefferson City, MO 65109; 573-526-4080, Fax: 573-526-4080.

www.dps.state.mo.us/mgc/index.htm

31 Veterinary Medical Board, PO Box 633 (3605 Missouri Blvd), Jefferson City, MO 65102-0633; 573-751-0031, Fax: 573-751-3856.

www.ecodev.state.mo.us/pr/vet

Direct URL to search licenses: www.ecodev.state.mo.us/pr/ftp4.htm

32 Board of Nursing Home Administrators, PO Box 1337 (615 Howerton Ct), Jefferson City, MO 65102; 573-751-3511, Fax: 573-573-4314.

33 Office of Secretary of State, PO Box 778 (PO Box 784), Jefferson City, MO 65102; 573-751-0018, Fax: 573-526-3489.

http://mosl.sos.state.mo.us/

34 Secretary of State, Securities Division, 1600 W Main St, Jefferson City, MO 65101; 573-751-4136, Fax: 573-526-3124.

35 Real Estate Commission, PO Box 1339 (PO Box 1339 (3605 Missouri Blvd)), Jefferson City, MO 65102-1339; 573-751-2628, Fax: 573-751-2777.

www.ecodev.state.mo.us/pr/restate/default.htm

Direct URL to search licenses: www.ecodev.state.mo.us/pr You can search online using downloadable lists

36 Committee of Psychology, PO Box 1335 (3605 Missouri Blvd), Jefferson City, MO 65102-1335; 573-751-0099, Fax: 573-526-3489.

www.ecodev.state.mo.us/pr/psych

37 Department of Natural Resources, Div of Environmental Quality, Solid Waste Mgmt, PO Box 176 (205 Jefferson St), Jefferson City, MO 65102-1335; 573-751-0805, Fax: 573-526-8782.

38 Department of Natural Resources, Technical Assistance Program, PO Box 176 (1659B Elm St), Jefferson City, MO 65102-0570; 573-526-6627, Fax: 573-526-5808.

39 Abuse Counselors Certification Board, PO Box 1250 (1706 E Elm), Jefferson City, MO 65102; 573-751-9211, Fax: 573-526-3489.

www.modmh.state.mo.us/msaccb

40 The Missouri Bar, PO Box 119 (326 Monroe St), Jefferson City, MO 65102-0119; 573-635-4128, Fax: 573-635-2811.

42 Board for Respiratory Care, PO Box 1335 (3605 Missouri Blvd), Jefferson City, MO 65102-1335; 573-522-5864, Fax: 573-526-4176.

www.ecodev.state.mo.us/pr/mbrc

Direct URL to search licenses: www.ecodev.state.mo.us/pr/ftp4.htm

43 Committee of Marital & Family Therapists, PO Box 1335 (3605 Missouri Blvd), Jefferson City, MO 65102-1335; 573-751-0870, Fax: 573-526-3489.

www.ecodev.state.mo.us/pr/mft

44 Office of Athletics, PO Box 1335 (3605 Missouri Blvd), Jefferson City, MO 65102-1335; 573-751-0243, Fax: 573-751-5649.

www.ecodev.state.mo.us/pr/athletic

45 Office of Employment Agencies, PO Box 1335 (3605 Missouri Blvd), Jefferson City, MO 65102; 573-751-0239, Fax: 573-751-4176.

www.ecodev.state.mo.us/pr/employ

46 Committee of Interpreters, PO Box 1335 (PO Box 1335 (3605 Missouri Blvd)), Jefferson City, MO 65102-1335; 573-526-7787, Fax: 573-526-3489.

www.ecodev.state.mo.us/pr/inter

Direct URL to search licenses: www.ecodev.state.mo.us/pr/ftp4.htm

47 Board of Geologist Registration, PO Box 1335 (3605 Missouri Blvd, PO Box 1335), Jefferson City, MO 65102; 573-526-7625, Fax: 573-526-3489.

www.ecodev.state.mo.us/pr/geo

41 Division of Professional Registration, Board of Occupational Therapy, PO Box 1335 (PO Box 1335 (3605 Missouri Blvd, 65109)), Jefferson City, MO 65102-1335; 573-751-0877, Fax: 573-526-3489.

www.ecodev.state.mo.us/pr/octherap

The following list indicates the district and division name for each county in the state. If the district or division name of the bankruptcy court is different from the civil/criminal court, it appears in parentheses.

County/Court Cross Reference

County	District	Division
Adair	Eastern	Hannibal (St Louis)
Andrew	Western	St Joseph (Kansas City - Western)
Atchison	Western	St Joseph (Kansas City - Western)
Audrain	Eastern	Hannibal (St Louis)
Barry	Western	Joplin-Southwestern (Kansas City)
Barton	Western	Joplin-Southwestern (Kansas City)
Bates	Western	Kansas City - Western
Benton	Western	Jefferson City-Central (Kansas City)
Bollinger	Eastern	Cape Girardeau (St Louis)
Boone	Western	Jefferson City-Central (Kansas City)
Buchanan	Western	St Joseph (Kansas City - Western)
Butler	Eastern	Cape Girardeau (St Louis)
Caldwell	Western	St Joseph (Kansas City - Western)
Callaway	Western	Jefferson City-Central (Kansas City)
Camden	Western	Jefferson City-Central (Kansas City)
Cape Girardeau	Eastern	Cape Girardeau (St Louis)
Carroll	Western	Kansas City - Western
Carter	Eastern	Cape Girardeau (St Louis)
Cass	Western	Kansas City - Western
Cedar	Western	Springfield-Southern (Kansas City)
Chariton	Eastern	Hannibal (St Louis)
Christian	Western	Springfield-Southern (Kansas City)
Clark	Eastern	Hannibal (St Louis)
Clay	Western	Kansas City - Western
Clinton	Western	St Joseph (Kansas City - Western)
Cole	Western	Jefferson City-Central (Kansas City)
Cooper	Western	Jefferson City-Central (Kansas City)
Crawford	Eastern	St Louis
Dade	Western	Springfield-Southern (Kansas City)
Dallas	Western	Springfield-Southern (Kansas City)
Daviess	Western	St Joseph (Kansas City - Western)
De Kalb	Western	St Joseph (Kansas City - Western)
Dent	Eastern	St Louis
Douglas	Western	Springfield-Southern ((Kansas City)
Dunklin	Eastern	Cape Girardeau (St Louis)
Franklin	Eastern	St Louis
Gasconade	Eastern	St Louis
Gentry	Western	St Joseph (Kansas City - Western)
Greene	Western	Springfield-Southern (Kansas City)
Grundy	Western	St Joseph (Kansas City - Western)
Harrison	Western	St Joseph (Kansas City - Western)
Henry	Western	Kansas City - Western
Hickory	Western	Jefferson City-Central (Kansas City)
Holt	Western	St Joseph (Kansas City - Western)
Howard	Western	Jefferson City-Central (Kansas City)
Howell	Western	Springfield-Southern (Kansas City)
Iron	Eastern	St Louis
Jackson	Western	Kansas City – Western
Jasper	Western	Joplin-Southwestern (Kansas City)
Jefferson	Eastern	St Louis
Johnson	Western	Kansas City - Western
Knox	Eastern	Hannibal (St Louis)
Laclede	Western	Springfield-Southern (Kansas City
Lafayette	Western	Kansas City - Western
Lawrence	Western	Joplin-Southwestern (Kansas City)
Lewis	Eastern	Hannibal (St Louis)
Lincoln	Eastern	St Louis
Linn	Eastern	Hannibal (St Louis)
Livingston	Western	St Joseph (Kansas City - Western)
Macon	Eastern	Hannibal (St Louis)
Madison	Eastern	Cape Girardeau (St Louis)
Maries	Eastern	St Louis
Marion	Eastern	Hannibal (St Louis)
McDonald	Western	Joplin-Southwestern (Kansas City)
Mercer	Western	St Joseph (Kansas City - Western)
Miller	Western	Jefferson City-Central (Kansas City)
Mississippi	Eastern	Cape Girardeau (St Louis)
Moniteau	Western	Jefferson City-Central (Kansas City)
Monroe	Eastern	Hannibal (St Louis)
Montgomery	Eastern	Hannibal (St Louis)
Morgan	Western	Jefferson City-Central (Kansas City)
New Madrid	Eastern	Cape Girardeau (St Louis)
Newton	Western	Joplin-Southwestern (Kansas City)
Nodaway	Western	St Joseph (Kansas City - Western)
Oregon	Western	Springfield-Southern (Kansas City)
Osage	Western	Jefferson City-Central (Kansas City)
Ozark	Western	Springfield-Southern (Kansas City)
Pemiscot	Eastern	Cape Girardeau (St Louis)
Perry	Eastern	Cape Girardeau (St Louis)
Pettis	Western	Jefferson City-Central (Kansas City)
Phelps	Eastern	St Louis
Pike	Eastern	Hannibal (St Louis)
Platte	Western	St Joseph (Kansas City - Western)
Polk	Western	Springfield-Southern (Kansas City)
Pulaski	Western	Springfield-Southern (Kansas City)
Putnam	Western	St Joseph (Kansas City - Western)
Ralls	Eastern	Hannibal (St Louis)
Randolph	Eastern	Hannibal (St Louis)
Ray	Western	Kansas City - Western)
Reynolds	Eastern	Cape Girardeau (St Louis)
Ripley	Eastern	Cape Girardeau (St Louis)
Saline	Western	Kansas City - Western
Schuyler	Eastern	Hannibal (St Louis)
Scotland	Eastern	Hannibal (St Louis)
Scott	Eastern	Cape Girardeau (St Louis)
Shannon	Eastern	Cape Girardeau (St Louis)
Shelby	Eastern	Hannibal (St Louis)
St. Charles	Eastern	St Louis
St. Clair	Western	Kansas City - Western
St. Francois	Eastern	St Louis
St. Louis	Eastern	St Louis
St. Louis City City	Eastern	St Louis
Ste. Genevieve	Eastern	St Louis
Stoddard	Eastern	Cape Girardeau (St Louis)
Stone	Western	Joplin-Southwestern (Kansas City)
Sullivan	Western	St Joseph (Kansas City - Western)
Taney	Western	Springfield-Southern (Kansas City)
Texas	Western	Springfield-Southern (Kansas City)
Vernon	Western	Joplin-Southwestern (Kansas City)
Warren	Eastern	St Louis
Washington	Eastern	St Louis
Wayne	Eastern	Cape Girardeau (St Louis)
Webster	Western	Springfield-Southern (Kansas City)
Worth	Western	St Joseph (Kansas City - Western)
Wright	Western	Springfield-Southern (Kansas City)

US District Court

Eastern District of Missouri

Cape Girardeau Division 339 Broadway, Room 240, Cape Girardeau, MO 63701, 573-335-8538, Fax: 573-335-0379.

www.moed.uscourts.gov

Counties: Bollinger, Butler, Cape Girardeau, Carter, Dunklin, Madison, Mississippi, New Madrid, Pemiscot, Perry, Reynolds, Ripley, Scott, Shannon, Stoddard, Wayne.

Indexing & Storage: Cases are indexed by defendant and plaintiff as well as by case number. New cases are available in the index 1-2 days after filing date. Both computer and card indexes are maintained. Computerized records are available from January 1, 1992. Open records are located at this court.

Fee & Payment: The fee is $15.00 per item (one party name or case number). Payment may be made by money order, cashier check, personal check. Prepayment is required. Payee: Clerk, US District Court. Certification fee: $5.00 per document. Copy fee: $.50 per page.

Phone Search: Only docket information is available by phone. An automated voice case information service (VCIS) is not available.

Mail Search: A stamped self addressed envelope is not required.

In Person Search: In person searching is available.

PACER: Sign-up number is 800-676-6856. Access fee is $.60 per minute. Toll-free access: 800-533-8105. Local access: 314-539-3857. Case records are available back to 1992. Records are never purged. New records are available online after 4-5 days. PACER is available on the Internet at http://pacer.moed.uscourts.gov.

Hannibal Division c/o St Louis Division, Room 260, 1114 Market St, St Louis, MO 63101, 314-539-2315, Fax: 314-539-2929.

www.moed.uscourts.gov

Counties: Adair, Audrain, Chariton, Clark, Knox, Lewis, Linn, Macon, Marion, Monroe, Montgomery, Pike, Ralls, Randolph, Schuyler, Scotland, Shelby.

Indexing & Storage: Cases are indexed by as well as by case number. New cases are available in the index after filing date. Open records are located at the Division.

Fee & Payment: The fee is no charge per item (one party name or case number). Payment may be made by money order, cashier check. Business checks are not accepted. Personal checks are not accepted.

Phone Search: An automated voice case information service (VCIS) is not available.

In Person Search: In person searching is available.

PACER: Sign-up number is 800-676-6856. Access fee is $.60 per minute. Toll-free access: 800-533-8105. Local access: 314-539-3857. Case records are available back to 1992. Records are never purged. New records are available online after 4-5 days. PACER is available on the Internet at http://pacer.moed.uscourts.gov.

St Louis Division Room 260, 1114 Market St, St Louis, MO 63101, 314-539-2315, Fax: 314-539-2929.

www.moed.uscourts.gov

Counties: Crawford, Dent, Franklin, Gasconade, Iron, Jefferson, Lincoln, Maries, Phelps, St. Charles, Ste. Genevieve, St. Francois, St. Louis, Warren, Washington, City of St. Louis.

Indexing & Storage: Cases are indexed by defendant and plaintiff as well as by case number. New cases are available in the index immediately after filing date. A computer index is maintained. Open records are located at this court.

Fee & Payment: The fee is $15.00 per item (one party name or case number). Payment may be made by money order, cashier check, personal check. Prepayment is required. Payee: Clerk, US District Court. Certification fee: $5.00 per document. Copy fee: $.50 per page.

Phone Search: Only docket information is available by phone. An automated voice case information service (VCIS) is not available.

Mail Search: A stamped self addressed envelope is not required.

In Person Search: In person searching is available.

PACER: Sign-up number is 800-676-6856. Access fee is $.60 per minute. Toll-free access: 800-533-8105. Local access: 314-539-3857. Case records are available back to 1992. Records are never purged. New records are available online after 4-5 days. PACER is available on the Internet at http://pacer.moed.uscourts.gov.

US Bankruptcy Court

Eastern District of Missouri

St Louis Division 7th Floor, 211 N Broadway, St Louis, MO 63102-2734, 314-425-4222, Fax: 314-425-4063.

www.moeb.uscourts.gov

Counties: Adair, Audrain, Bollinger, Butler, Cape Girardeau, Carter, Chariton, Clark, Crawford, Dent, Dunklin, Franklin, Gasconade, Iron, Jefferson, Knox, Lewis, Lincoln, Linn, Macon, Madison, Maries, Marion, Mississippi, Monroe, Montgomery, New Madrid, Pemiscot, Perry, Phelps, Pike, Ralls, Randolph, Reynolds, Ripley, Schuyler, Scotland, Scott, Shannon, Shelby, St. Charles, St. Francois, St. Louis, St.Louis City, Ste. Genevieve, Stoddard, Warren, Washington, Wayne.

Indexing & Storage: Cases are indexed by debtor as well as by case number. New cases are available in the index 24 hours after filing date. A computer index is maintained. Open records are located at this court.

Fee & Payment: The fee is $15.00 per item (one party name or case number). Payment may be made by money order, cashier check, personal check. Prepayment is required. Payee: Clerk, US Bankruptcy Court. Certification fee: $5.00 per document. Copy fee: $.50 per page.

Phone Search: Docket information is available by phone. An automated voice case information service (VCIS) is available. Call VCIS at 888-223-6431 or 314-425-4054.

Mail Search: A stamped self addressed envelope is not required.

In Person Search: In person searching is available.

PACER: Sign-up number is 800-676-6856. Access fee is $.60 per minute. Toll-free access: 888-577-1668. Local access: 314-425-6935. Case records are available back to January 1991. Records are purged every six months. New civil records are available online after 1 day. PACER is available online at http://pacer.moeb.uscourts.gov.

US District Court

Western District of Missouri

Jefferson City-Central Division 131 W High St, Jefferson City, MO 65101, 573-636-4015, Fax: 573-636-3456.

Counties: Benton, Boone, Callaway, Camden, Cole, Cooper, Hickory, Howard, Miller, Moniteau, Morgan, Osage, Pettis.

Indexing & Storage: Cases are indexed by defendant and plaintiff as well as by case number. New cases are available in the index 1-2 days after filing date. A computer index is maintained. Open records are located at this court.

Fee & Payment: The fee is $15.00 per item (one party name or case number). Payment may be made by money order, cashier check, personal check. Prepayment is required. Payee: Clerk, US District Court. Certification fee: $5.00 per document. Copy fee: $.50 per page.

Phone Search: Only docket information is available by phone. An automated voice case information service (VCIS) is not available.

Mail Search: Always enclose a stamped self addressed envelope.

In Person Search: In person searching is available.

PACER: Sign-up number is 800-676-6856. Access fee is $.60 per minute. Toll-free access: 888-205-2527. Local access: 816-512-5110. Case records are available back to May 1, 1989. Records are purged as deemed necessary. New records are available online after 1 day. PACER is available online at http://pacer.mowd.uscourts.gov.

Electronic Filing: Only law firms and practioners may file cases electronically. Anyone may search online; however, the search only includes cases which have been filed electronically. To conduct a search, visit http://ecf.mowd.uscourts.gov/cgi-bin/PublicCaseFiled-Rpt.pl. Electronic filing information is available online at http://ecf.mowd.uscourts.gov

Joplin-Southwestern Division c/o Kansas City Division, Charles Evans Whitttaker Courthouse, 400 E 9th St, Kansas City, MO 64106, 816-512-5000, Fax: 816-512-5078.

Counties: Barry, Barton, Jasper, Lawrence, McDonald, Newton, Stone, Vernon.

Indexing & Storage: Cases are indexed by defendant and plaintiff as well as by case number. New cases are available in the index after filing date. Open records are located at the Division.

Fee & Payment: The fee is no charge per item (one party name or case number). Payment may be made by money order, cashier check. Business checks are not accepted. Personal checks are not accepted.

Phone Search: Searching is not available by phone.

In Person Search: In person searching is available.

PACER: Sign-up number is 800-676-6856. Access fee is $.60 per minute. Toll-free access: 888-205-2527. Local access: 816-512-5110. Case records are available back to May 1, 1989. Records are purged as deemed necessary. New records are available online after 1 day. PACER is available online at http://pacer.mowd.uscourts.gov.

Electronic Filing: Only law firms and practioners may file cases electronically. Anyone may search online; however, the search only includes cases which have been filed electronically. To conduct a search, visit http://ecf.mowd.uscourts.gov/cgi-bin/PublicCaseFiled-Rpt.pl Electronic filing information is available online at http://ecf.mowd.uscourts.gov

Kansas City-Western Division Clerk of Court, 201 US Courthouse, 811 Grand Ave, Kansas City, MO 64106, 816-426-2811, Fax: 816-426-2819.

Counties: Bates, Carroll, Cass, Clay, Henry, Jackson, Johnson, Lafayette, Ray, St. Clair, Saline.

Indexing & Storage: Cases are indexed by defendant and plaintiff as well as by case number. New cases are available in the index 1-2 days after filing date. Records are indexed on computer and microfiche. Open records are located at this court.

Fee & Payment: The fee is $15.00 per item (one party name or case number). Payment may be made by money order, cashier check, personal check. Prepayment is required. Payee: US District Court Clerk. Certification fee: $5.00 per document. Copy fee: $.50 per page.

Phone Search: Only docket information is available by phone. An automated voice case information service (VCIS) is not available.

Fax Search: Will accept fax requests.

Mail Search: A stamped self addressed envelope is not required.

In Person Search: In person searching is available.

PACER: Sign-up number is 800-676-6856. Access fee is $.60 per minute. Toll-free access: 888-205-2527. Local access: 816-512-5110. Case records are available back to May 1, 1989. Records are purged as deemed necessary. New records are available online after 1 day. PACER is available online at http://pacer.mowd.uscourts.gov.

Electronic Filing: Only law firms and practioners may file cases electronically. Anyone may search online; however, the search only includes cases which have been filed electronically. To conduct a search, visit http://ecf.mowd.uscourts.gov/cgi-bin/PublicCaseFiled-Rpt.pl Electronic filing information is available online at http://ecf.mowd.uscourts.gov

Springfield-Southern Division 222 N John Q Hammons Pkwy, Suite 1400, Springfield, MO 65806, 417-865-3869, Fax: 417-865-7719.

Counties: Cedar, Christian, Dade, Dallas, Douglas, Greene, Howell, Laclede, Oregon, Ozark, Polk, Pulaski, Taney, Texas, Webster, Wright.

Indexing & Storage: Cases are indexed by defendant and plaintiff as well as by case number. New cases are available in the index immediately after filing date. A computer index is maintained. Open records are located at this court.

Fee & Payment: The fee is $15.00 per item (one party name or case number). Payment may be made by money order, cashier check, personal check. Prepayment is required. Payee: Clerk, US District Court. Certification fee: $5.00 per document. Copy fee: $.50 per page.

Phone Search: Only docket information is available by phone. An automated voice case information service (VCIS) is not available.

Mail Search: Always enclose a stamped self addressed envelope.

In Person Search: In person searching is available.

PACER: Sign-up number is 800-676-6856. Access fee is $.60 per minute. Toll-free access: 888-205-2527. Local access: 816-512-5110. Case records are available back to May 1, 1989. Records are purged as deemed necessary. New records are available online after 1 day. PACER is available online at http://pacer.mowd.uscourts.gov.

Electronic Filing: Only law firms and practioners may file cases electronically. Anyone may search online; however, the search only includes cases which have been filed electronically. To conduct a search, visit http://ecf.mowd.uscourts.gov/cgi-bin/PublicCaseFiled-Rpt.pl Electronic filing information is available online at http://ecf.mowd.uscourts.gov

St Joseph Division PO Box 387, 201 S 8th St, St Joseph, MO 64501, Fax: 816-279-0177.

Counties: Andrew, Atchison, Buchanan, Caldwell, Clinton, Daviess, De Kalb, Gentry, Grundy, Harrison, Holt, Livingston, Mercer, Nodaway, Platte, Putnam, Sullivan, Worth.

Indexing & Storage: Cases are indexed by defendant and plaintiff as well as by case number. New cases are available in the index immediately after filing date. A computer index is maintained. Open records are located at this court.

Fee & Payment: The fee is $15.00 per item (one party name or case number). Payment may be made by money order, cashier check, personal check. Prepayment is required. Payee: Clerk, US District Court. Certification fee: $5.00 per document. Copy fee: $.50 per page.

Phone Search: Only docket information is available by phone. An automated voice case information service (VCIS) is not available.

Mail Search: A stamped self addressed envelope is not required.

In Person Search: In person searching is available.

PACER: Sign-up number is 800-676-6856. Access fee is $.60 per minute. Toll-free access:

888-205-2527. Local access: 816-512-5110. Case records are available back to May 1, 1989. Records are purged as deemed necessary. New records are available online after 1 day. PACER is available online at http://pacer.mowd.uscourts.gov.

Electronic Filing: Only law firms and practioners may file cases electronically. Anyone may search online; however, the search only includes cases which have been filed electronically. To conduct a search, visit http://ecf.mowd.uscourts.gov/cgi-bin/PublicCaseFiled-Rpt.pl Electronic filing information is available online at http://ecf.mowd.uscourts.gov

US Bankruptcy Court
Western District of Missouri

Kansas City-Western Division Room 913, 811 Grand Ave, Kansas City, MO 64106, 816-426-3321, Fax: 816-426-3364.

Counties: Andrew, Atchison, Barry, Barton, Bates, Benton, Boone, Buchanan, Caldwell, Callaway, Camden, Carroll, Cass, Cedar, Christian, Clay, Clinton, Cole, Cooper, Dade, Dallas, Daviess, De Kalb, Douglas, Gentry, Greene, Grundy, Harrison, Henry, Hickory, Holt,Howard, Howell, Jackson, Jasper, Johnson, Laclede, Lafayette, Lawrence, Livingston, McDonald, Mercer, Miller, Moniteau, Morgan, Newton, Nodaway, Oregon, Osage, Ozark, Pettis, Platte, Polk, Pulaski, Putnam, Ray, Saline, St. Clair, Sullivan, Taney, Texas,Vernon, Webster, Worth, Wright.

Indexing & Storage: Cases are indexed by debtor and creditors as well as by case number. New cases are available in the index 24 hours after filing date. A computer index is maintained. Older records are indexed on microfiche. Open records are located at this court. District wide searches are available from June 1989 from this division.

Fee & Payment: The fee is $15.00 per item (one party name or case number). Payment may be made by money order, cashier check, personal check. Prepayment is required. Payee: Clerk, US Bankruptcy Court. Certification fee: $5.00 per document. Copy fee: $.50 per page. You are allowed to make your own copies. These copies cost $.10 per page. There is no search fee for in person searchers.

Phone Search: Use VCIS for docket information. In addition to numbers given, call 816-426-2913 for information on cases closed prior to October 1995. An automated voice case information service (VCIS) is available. Call VCIS at 888-205-2527 or 816-426-5822.

Mail Search: Always enclose a stamped self addressed envelope.

In Person Search: In person searching is available.

PACER: Sign-up number is 800-676-6856. PACER is available on the Internet at http://pacer.mowb.uscourts.gov/bc/index.html.

Court	Jurisdiction	No. of Courts	How Organized
Circuit Courts*	General	114	45 Circuits
Associate Circuit Courts*	Limited	114	45 Circuits
Combined Courts*		7	
Probate Courts*	Probate	5	
Municipal Courts	Municipal	406	
Family Courts	Special	8	

* Profiled in this Sourcebook.

Court	CIVIL								
	Tort	Contract	Real Estate	Min. Claim	Max. Claim	Small Claims	Estate	Eviction	Domestic Relations
Circuit Courts*	X	X	X	$25,000	No Max				X
Associate Circuit Courts*	X	X	X	$0	$25,000	$3000		X	
Municipal Courts									
Probate Courts*							X		
Family Courts									X

Court	CRIMINAL				
	Felony	Misdemeanor	DWI/DUI	Preliminary Hearing	Juvenile
Circuit Courts*	X				X
Associate Circuit Courts*		X	X	X	
Probate Courts*					
Family Courts					X

ADMINISTRATION   State Court Administrator, 2112 Industrial Dr., PO Box 104480, Jefferson City, MO, 65109; 573-751-4377, Fax: 573-751-5540. www.osca.state.mo.us

COURT STRUCTURE   The Ciircuit Court is the court of general jurisdiction (113 courts in 45 circuits). There are Assouciate Circuit Courts with limited jurisdiction and some counties have Combined Courts. Municipal Courts only have jurisdiction over traffic and ordinance violations.

ONLINE ACCESS   Casenet, a limited but growing online system, is available at http://casenet.osca.state.mo.us/casenet/. The system includes eight counties as well as the Eastern, Western, and Southern Apellate Courts. Cases can be searched by case number, filing date, or litigant name.

ADDITIONAL INFORMATION   While the Missouri State Statutes set the Civil Case limit at $25,000 for the Associate Courts, and over $25,000 for the Circuit Courts, a great many Missouri County Courts have adopted their own Local Court Rules regarding civil cases and the monetary limits. Presumably, Local Court's Rules are setup to allow the county to choose which court - Circuit or Associate - to send a case. This may depend on the court's case load, but generally, the cases are assigned more by "the nature of the case" and less by the monetary amount involved. Often, Local Court Rules are found where both the Circuit and the Associate Court are located in the same building, or share the same offices and perhaps the same phones. A solution for court record searches is to use this source to find a telephone number of a County's Court Clerk, and call to determine the court location of the case.

Adair County

Circuit Court PO Box 690, Kirksville, MO 63501; 660-665-2552; Fax: 660-665-3420. Hours: 8AM-5PM (CST). *Felony, Misdemeanor, Civil Actions Over $45,000.*

Civil Records: Access: Fax, mail, in person. Only the court conducts in person searches; visitors may not. Search fee: $5.00 per name. Required to search: name, years to search. Civil cases indexed by defendant, plaintiff. Civil records on computer since 1991, prior on index cards. **Criminal Records:** Access: In person only. Court does not conduct in person searches; visitors must perform searches for themselves. Search fee: No criminal searches performed by court. Required to search: name, years to search. Criminal records on computer since 1991, prior on index cards. All written requests referred to State Highway Patrol. **General Information:** No juvenile, mental, expunged, sealed, dismissed or suspended records released. Turnaround time 2 weeks. Copy fee: $.10 per page. Certification fee: $1.00. Fee payee: Circuit Clerk. Personal checks accepted. Prepayment is required. Fax notes: $.50 per page. No fee for faxing results to 800 number.

Associate Circuit Court Courthouse, Kirksville, MO 63501; 660-665-3877; Fax: 660-785-3222. Hours: 8AM-5PM (CST).

Misdemeanor, Civil Actions Under $25,000, Eviction, Small Claims, Probate.

Civil Records: Access: Phone, fax, mail, in person. Only the court conducts in person searches; visitors may not. No search fee. Required to search: name, years to search. Civil cases indexed by defendant, plaintiff. Probate records on microfilm since 1840. **Criminal Records:** Access: Phone, fax, mail, in person. Only the court conducts in person searches; visitors may not. No search fee. Required to search: name, years to search, DOB, SSN. Criminal records on computer since 1994; prior records in files. Signed release required for closed cases. **General Information:** No juvenile, mental, expunged, sealed, dismissed or suspended imposition of case records released. SASE required. Turnaround time 1 day. Copy fee: $.25 per page. Certification fee: No certification fee. Fee payee: Associate Circuit Court. Personal checks accepted. Prepayment is required. Fax notes: $1.50 per page.

Andrew County

Circuit Court PO Box 208 Division I, Savannah, MO 64485; 816-324-4221; Fax: 816-324-5667. Hours: 8AM-5PM (CST). *Felony, Misdemeanor, Civil Actions Over $45,000.*

Civil Records: Access: Phone, fax, mail, in person. Both court and visitors may perform in person searches. No search fee. Required to search: name, years to search. Civil cases indexed by defendant, plaintiff. Civil records on index cards since 1976, archived since 1850. **Criminal Records:** Access: Phone, fax, mail, in person. Both court and visitors may perform in person searches. No search fee. Required to search: name, years to search; also helpful-DOB. Criminal records on computer since mid-1993. **General Information:** No juvenile, mental, expunged, sealed, dismissed or suspended imposition of sentence records released. Turnaround time 1-2 days. Copy fee: $.25 per page. Certification fee: $2.50. Fee payee: Andrew County Circuit Clerk. Personal checks accepted. Prepayment is required.

Associate Circuit Court PO Box 49, Savannah, MO 64485; 816-324-3921; Fax: 816-324-5667. Hours: 8AM-5PM (CST). *Misdemeanor, Civil Actions Under $45,000, Eviction, Small Claims, Probate.*

Civil Records: Access: Mail, in person. Both court and visitors may perform in person searches. No search fee. Required to search: name, years to search. Civil cases indexed by defendant, plaintiff. Civil records on card file, archived from 1950. **Criminal Records:** Access: Mail, in person. Both court and visitors may perform in person searches. No search fee. Required to search: name, years to search. Criminal records on computer since mid-1993. **General Information:** No juvenile, mental, expunged, sealed, dismissed or suspended imposition of sentence records released. SASE required. Turnaround time varies. Copy fee: $.50 per page. Certification fee: $2.50 plus additional pages for $.50 each. Fee payee: Associate Circuit Court. Personal checks accepted. Prepayment is required.

Atchison County

Circuit Court PO Box 280, Rock Port, MO 64482; 660-744-2707; Fax: 660-744-5705. Hours: 8:30AM-4:30PM (CST). *Felony, Misdemeanor, Civil Actions Over $25,000.*

Civil Records: Access: Mail, in person. Both court and visitors may perform in person searches.

Search fee: No civil searches performed by court. Required to search: name, years to search. Civil cases indexed by defendant, plaintiff. Civil records on index books, and archived from 1845. **Criminal Records:** Access: Mail, in person. Both court and visitors may perform in person searches. Search fee: $4.00 per name. Required to search: name, years to search. Criminal records on index books, and archived from 1845. **General Information:** No juvenile, mental, expunged, sealed, dismissed or suspended imposition of sentence records released. Turnaround time 1 day. Copy fee: $1.00 per page. Certification fee: $1.00. Fee payee: Circuit Clerk. Personal checks accepted. Prepayment is required.

Associate Division PO Box 187, Rock Port, MO 64482; 660-744-2700; Fax: 660-744-5705. Hours: 8AM-4:30PM (CST). *Misdemeanor, Civil Actions Under $25,000, Eviction, Small Claims, Probate.*

Civil Records: Access: Fax, mail, in person. Both court and visitors may perform in person searches. Search fee: $4.00 per name. Required to search: name, years to search; also helpful-address. Civil cases indexed by defendant, plaintiff. Civil records on books and cardex system, archived since 1845. **Criminal Records:** Access: Fax, mail, in person. Both court and visitors may perform in person searches. Search fee: $4.00 per name. Required to search: name, years to search; also helpful-address, DOB, SSN, offense. Criminal records on computer since mid 1980s; prior on books and cardex system. **General Information:** No juvenile, mental, expunged, sealed, dismissed or suspended imposition of sentence records released. SASE required. Turnaround time 7 days. Copy fee: $1.00 per page. Certification fee: $1.50. Fee payee: Circuit Court Division II. Personal checks accepted. Prepayment is required. Fax notes: $2.00 per page.

Audrain County

Circuit Court Courthouse, 101 N Jefferson, Mexico, MO 65265; 573-473-5840; Fax: 573-581-3237. Hours: 8AM-5PM (CST). *Felony, Misdemeanor, Civil Actions Over $25,000.*

www.audrain-county.org

Civil Records: Access: In person only. Court does not conduct in person searches; visitors must perform searches for themselves. Search fee: No civil searches performed by court. Required to search: name, years to search. Civil cases indexed by defendant, plaintiff. Civil records on computer since 8/92, prior on index cards, older records archived at Genealogy Club in Mexico, MO. **Criminal Records:** Access: In person only. Court does not conduct in person searches; visitors must perform searches for themselves. Search fee: No criminal searches performed by court. Required to search: name, years to search. Criminal records on computer since 8/92, stored for 25 years on site then archived (back to 1800s). **General Information:** No juvenile, mental, expunged, sealed, dismissed or suspended imposition of sentence records released. Copy fee: $.25 per page. Certification fee: $1.50. Fee payee: Circuit Clerk. Prepayment is required.

Associate Circuit Court Courthouse, 101 N Jefferson, Rm 205, Mexico, MO 65265; 573-473-5850; Probate phone:573-473-5854; Fax: 573-581-3237. Hours: 8AM-5PM (CST). *Misdemeanor, Civil Actions Under $25,000, Eviction, Small Claims, Probate.*

Civil Records: Access: Mail, in person. Both court and visitors may perform in person searches.

No search fee. Required to search: name, years to search. Civil cases indexed by defendant, plaintiff. Civil records on computer since 9/93, prior on cards, archived to 1800s. **Criminal Records:** Access: Mail, in person. Only the court conducts in person searches; visitors may not. No search fee. Required to search: name, years to search, DOB, SSN, signed release. Criminal records on computer since 9/93, prior on cards, archived to 1800s. **General Information:** No juvenile, mental, expunged, sealed, dismissed or suspended imposition of sentence records released. Turnaround time 1 week. Copy fee: $.15 per page. Certification fee: $1.50 first page, $1.00 each additional. Fee payee: Circuit Court Division II. Only cashiers checks and money orders accepted. Prepayment is required.

Barry County

Circuit Court Barry County Courthouse, 700 Main, Ste 1, Cassville, MO 65625; 417-847-2361. Hours: 8AM-4PM (CST). *Felony, Misdemeanor, Civil Actions Over $25,000.*

Civil Records: Access: Mail, in person. Both court and visitors may perform in person searches. Search fee: $4.00 per name. Required to search: name, years to search. Civil cases indexed by defendant, plaintiff. Civil records on index cards, archived since mid-1800s. **Criminal Records:** Access: Mail, in person. Both court and visitors may perform in person searches. Search fee: $4.00 per name. Required to search: name, years to search. Criminal records on index cards, archived since mid-1800s. **General Information:** No juvenile, mental expunged, sealed, dismissed or suspended imposition of sentence records released. SASE required. Turnaround time 1-3 days. Copy fee: $.25 per page. Certification fee: $1.00. Fee payee: Circuit Clerk. Personal checks accepted. Prepayment is required.

Associate Circuit Court Barry County Courthouse, Suite H, Cassville, MO 65625;; Civil phone:417-847-2127; Criminal phone:417-847-2127. Hours: 7:30AM-4PM (CST). *Misdemeanor, Civil Actions Under $25,000, Eviction, Small Claims, Probate.*

Civil Records: Access: Mail, in person. Both court and visitors may perform in person searches. No search fee. Required to search: name, years to search. Civil cases indexed by defendant, plaintiff. Civil records on index cards since 1982; prior records on index books to mid 1800s. **Criminal Records:** Access: Mail, in person. Both court and visitors may perform in person searches. No search fee. Required to search: name, years to search. Criminal records on computer since 1996; prior records on index books to mid 1800s. **General Information:** No juvenile, mental, expunged, sealed, dismissed or suspended imposton of sentence records released. Turnaround time 1-3 days. Copy fee: $.50 per page. Certification fee: No certification fee. Fee payee: Barry County. Personal checks accepted. Prepayment is required.

Barton County

Circuit Court Courthouse, 1007 Broadway, Lamar, MO 64759; 417-682-2444/5754; Fax: 417-682-2960. Hours: 8AM-4:30PM (CST). *Felony, Misdemeanor, Civil, Eviction, Small Claims, Probate.*

http://casenet.osca.state.mo.us/casenet

Civil Records: Access: Mail, online, in person. Both court and visitors may perform in person searches. No search fee. Required to search: name, years to search; also helpful-address. Civil cases indexed by defendant, plaintiff. Civil records on computer since 1993; prior from 1865 on books or archived. Free access at htp://casenet.state.mo.us/casenet. **Criminal Records:** Access: Mail, remote online, in person. Both court and visitors may perform in person searches. No search fee. Required to search: name, years to search; also helpful-address, DOB, SSN. Criminal records on computer since 1993; prior from 1865 on books or archived. Same online as civil. **General Information:** No juvenile, mental, expunged, dismissed, or suspended imposition of sentence records released. SASE required. Turnaround time 1 week. Copy fee: $1.00 per page. Certification fee: $1.50. Fee payee: Circuit Court. Personal checks accepted. Prepayment is required. Fax notes: Fee to fax is $2.00 per document.

Bates County

Circuit Court Bates County Courthouse, Butler, MO 64730; 660-679-5171; Fax: 660-679-4446. Hours: 8AM-4:30PM (CST). *Felony, Misdemeanor, Civil Actions Over $25,000.*

Civil Records: Access: Fax, mail, in person. Both court and visitors may perform in person searches. No search fee. Required to search: name, years to search. Civil cases indexed by defendant, plaintiff. Civil records on computer since 9/1/92, prior on books since 1858. **Criminal Records:** Access: Fax, mail, in person. Both court and visitors may perform in person searches. No search fee. Required to search: name, years to search. Criminal records on computer since 9/1/92, prior on books since 1858. **General Information:** No juvenile, mental, expunged, dismissed, or suspended imposition of sentence records released. SASE required. Turnaround time varies. Copy fee: $.25 per page. Certification fee: $1.50. Fee payee: Circuit Court. Only cashiers checks and money orders accepted. Prepayment is required. Fax notes: No fee to fax results.

Associate Circuit Court Courthouse, Butler, MO 64730; 660-679-3311. Hours: 8:30AM-4PM (CST). *Misdemeanor, Civil Actions Under $25,000, Eviction, Small Claims, Probate.*

Civil Records: Access: Mail, in person. Both court and visitors may perform in person searches. No search fee. Required to search: name, years to search. Civil cases indexed by defendant, plaintiff. Civil records on index cards (unsure of starting date). **Criminal Records:** Access: Mail, in person. Only the court conducts in person searches; visitors may not. No search fee. Required to search: name, years to search, DOB; also helpful-SSN. Criminal records on computer since 1992, prior on index cards. **General Information:** No juvenile, mental, expunged, dismissed, or suspended imposition of sentence records released. SASE required. Turnaround time 1 week. Copy fee: $.50 per page. Certification fee: $1.50. Fee payee: Associate Circuit Court. Only cashiers checks and money orders accepted.

Benton County

Circuit Court PO Box 37, Warsaw, MO 65355; 660-438-7712; Fax: 660-438-5755. Hours: 8AM-4:30PM (CST). *Felony, Misdemeanor, Civil Actions Over $25,000.*

www.bigfoot.com/~circuit30

Civil Records: Access: In person only. Court does not conduct in person searches; visitors must perform searches for themselves. Search fee: No civil searches performed by court. Required to search: name, years to search. Civil cases indexed

by defendant, plaintiff. Civil records on computer since 1993, prior on index cards since 1800. **Criminal Records:** Access: In person only. Court does not conduct in person searches; visitors must perform searches for themselves. Search fee: No criminal searches performed by court. Required to search: name, years to search. Criminal records on computer since 1993, prior on index cards since 1800. The court will onlyt indicate if subject is on probation or has open case. For criminal searches contact Jefferson City Highway Patrol. **General Information:** No juvenile, mental, expunged, dismissed, or suspended imposition of sentence records released. Copy fee: $1.00 for first page, $.25 each addl. Certification fee: $2.50. Fee payee: Clerk of Circuit Court. Personal checks accepted. Prepayment is required.

Associate Circuit Court PO Box 37, Warsaw, MO 65355-0037; 660-438-6231. Hours: 8AM-4:30PM (CST). *Misdemeanor, Civil Actions Under $25,000, Eviction, Small Claims, Probate.*

www.bigfoot.com/~circuit30

Civil Records: Access: Mail, in person. Court does not conduct in person searches; visitors must perform searches for themselves. Search fee: No civil searches performed by court. Required to search: name, years to search. Civil cases indexed by defendant, plaintiff. Civil records on computer since 1994, in case files and judgment index cards prior. Will do searches as time permits. **Criminal Records:** Access: Mail, in person. Court does not conduct in person searches; visitors must perform searches for themselves. Search fee: No criminal searches performed by court. Required to search: name, years to search. Criminal records on computer since 1994. Will do searches only if time permits. **General Information:** No juvenile, mental, expunged, dismissed, or suspended imposition of sentence records released. Copy fee: $.50 per page. Certification fee: $1.50. Fee payee: Associate Circuit Court. Personal checks accepted. Prepayment is required.

Bollinger County

Circuit Court PO Box 949, Marble Hill, MO 63764; 573-238-2710; Fax: 573-238-2773. Hours: 8AM-4PM (CST). *Felony, Misdemeanor, Civil Actions Over $25,000.*

Civil Records: Access: Mail, in person. Only the court conducts in person searches; visitors may not. No search fee. Required to search: name, years to search. Civil cases indexed by defendant, plaintiff. Civil records on computer since 1990, prior on index cards 1976-1990. **Criminal Records:** Access: Mail, in person. Only the court conducts in person searches; visitors may not. No search fee. Required to search: name, years to search. Criminal records on computer since 1990, prior on index cards 1976-1990. **General Information:** No juvenile, mental, expunged, dismissed, or suspended imposition of sentence records released. SASE requried. Turnaround time 1 day to 1 week. Copy fee: $1.00 for first page, $.50 each addl. Certification fee: $2.00. Fee payee: Circuit Clerk and Recorder's Office. Personal checks accepted. Prepayment is required.

Associate Circuit Court PO Box 1040, Marble Hill, MO 63764-1040; 573-238-2730; Fax: 573-238-4511. Hours: 8AM-4PM (CST). *Misdemeanor, Civil Actions Under $25,000, Eviction, Small Claims, Probate.*

Civil Records: Access: In person only. Court does not conduct in person searches; visitors must perform searches for themselves. Search fee: No civil searches performed by court. Required to

search: name, years to search. Civil cases indexed by defendant, plaintiff. Civil records on computer since 1994, prior on books, archived to 1890. **Criminal Records:** Access: In person only. Court does not conduct in person searches; visitors must perform searches for themselves. Search fee: No criminal searches performed by court. Required to search: name, years to search. Criminal records on computer since 1994, prior on books, archived to 1890. **General Information:** No juvenile, mental, expunged, dismissed, or suspended imposition of sentence records released. Copy fee: $1.00 per page. Certification fee: $1.50. Fee payee: Circuit Court Division IV. Personal checks accepted. Prepayment is required.

Boone County

Circuit Court 705 E Walnut, Columbia, MO 65201; 573-886-4000; Fax: 573-886-4044. Hours: 8AM-5PM (CST). *Felony, Misdemeanor, Civil, Eviction, Small Claims, Probate.*

http://casenet.osca.state.mo.us/casenet

Civil Records: Access: Phone, mail, online, in person. Both court and visitors may perform in person searches. No search fee. Required to search: name, years to search. Civil cases indexed by defendant, plaintiff. Civil records on computer for recent cases, others on books. Free access at http://casenet.osca.state.mo.us/casenet. **Criminal Records:** Access: Remote online, in person. Court does not conduct in person searches; visitors must perform searches for themselves. Search fee: No criminal searches performed by court. Required to search: name, years to search, DOB. Criminal records on computer for recent cases, others on books. Free internet access is available, see civil records above. **General Information:** No juvenile, mental,paternity, expunged, dismissed, or suspended imposition of sentence records released. SASE required. Turnaround time varies. Copy fee: $.25 per page. Certification fee: $1.00. Fee payee: Boone County Circuit Clerk. Business checks accepted. Prepayment is required. Public access terminal is available.

Buchanan County

Circuit Court 411 Jules St, Rm 331, St Joseph, MO 64501; 816-271-1462; Fax: 816-271-1538. Hours: 8AM-5PM (CST). *Felony, Misdemeanor, Civil, Eviction, Small Claims.*

Civil Records: Access: In person only. Court does not conduct in person searches; visitors must perform searches for themselves. Search fee: No civil searches performed by court. Required to search: name, years to search. Civil cases indexed by defendant, plaintiff. Civil records on computer since 2/92, on index cards since 1976, prior archived. **Criminal Records:** Access: In person only. Court does not conduct in person searches; visitors must perform searches for themselves. Search fee: No criminal searches performed by court. Required to search: name, years to search. Criminal records on computer since 2/92, on index cards since 1976, prior archived. **General Information:** No juvenile, mental, expunged, dismissed, or suspended imposition of sentence records released. Copy fee: $.25 per page. Certification fee: $2.50. Fee payee: Buchanan Circuit Court. Personal checks accepted. Public access terminal is available.

Probate Court Buchanan County Courthouse, 411 Jules St, Room 333, St Joseph, MO 64501; 816-271-1477; Fax: 816-271-1538. Hours: 8AM-5PM (CST). *Probate.*

plaintiff. Probate records archived since 1803. **Criminal Records:** Access: Mail, in person. Only the court conducts in person searches; visitors may not. No search fee. Required to search: name, years to search. Criminal records archived since 1947. **General Information:** No juvenile, mental, expunged, dismissed, or suspended imposition of sentence records released. Turnaround time 1-2 weeks. No copy fee. Certification fee: No certification fee. Fee payee: Associate Circuit Court Division #2. Prepayment is required.

Newton County

Circuit Court PO Box 130, Neosho, MO 64850; 417-451-8257; Fax: 417-451-8298. Hours: 8:30AM-5PM (CST). *Felony, Misdemeanor, Civil Actions Over $25,000.*

Civil Records: Access: Phone, fax, mail, in person. Only the court conducts in person searches; visitors may not. No search fee. Required to search: name, years to search. Civil cases indexed by defendant, plaintiff. Civil records on computer since 1991, prior on index cards and books. **Criminal Records:** Access: Phone, fax, mail, in person. Only the court conducts in person searches; visitors may not. No search fee. Required to search: name, years to search; also helpful-DOB, SSN. Criminal records on computer since 1991, prior on index cards and books. **General Information:** No juvenile, mental, expunged, dismissed, or suspended imposition of sentence records released. SASE required. Turnaround time 1-2 days. Copy fee: $.25 per page. Certification fee: $1.00. Fee payee: Newton County Circuit Clerk. Business checks accepted. Copy fees may be billed. Fax notes: $2.00 per page.

Associate Circuit Court PO Box 170, Neosho, MO 64850; 417-451-8212; Fax: 417-451-8272. Hours: 8AM-5PM (CST). *Misdemeanor, Civil Actions Under $45,000, Eviction, Small Claims, Probate.*

Civil Records: Access: Phone, mail, in person. Both court and visitors may perform in person searches. No search fee. Required to search: name, years to search. Civil cases indexed by defendant, plaintiff. Civil records on computer since 1989, prior on index cards. **Criminal Records:** Access: Phone, mail, in person. Both court and visitors may perform in person searches. No search fee. Required to search: name, years to search, DOB. Criminal records on computer since 1989, prior on index cards. **General Information:** No juvenile, mental, expunged, dismissed, or suspended imposition of sentence records released. SASE requried. Turnaround time 1 week. Copy fee: $.25 per page. Certification fee: $1.00. Fee payee: Associate Circuit Court-Division II. Business checks accepted. Prepayment is required.

Nodaway County

Circuit Court PO Box 218, Maryville, MO 64468; 660-582-5431; Fax: 660-582-5499. Hours: 8AM-4:30PM (CST). *Felony, Misdemeanor, Civil Actions Over $25,000.*

Civil Records: Access: Fax, mail, in person. Both court and visitors may perform in person searches. Search fee: $5.00 per name. Required to search: name, years to search. Civil cases indexed by defendant, plaintiff. Civil records on computer since 5/91, archived since 1845. **Criminal Records:** Access: Fax, mail, in person. Both court and visitors may perform in person searches. No search fee. Required to search: name, years to search, DOB, SSN, signed release. Criminal records on computer since 5/91, archived since 1845. **General Information:** No juvenile, mental, expunged, dismissed, or suspended imposition of sentence records released. SASE required. Turnaround time same day. Copy fee: $1.00 per page. Certification fee: $1.00. Fee payee: Circuit Clerk. Personal checks accepted. Prepayment is required. Fax notes: $1.00 per page.

Associate Circuit Court Courthouse Annex, 303 N Market, Maryville, MO 64468; 660-582-2531; Fax: 660-582-2047. Hours: 8AM-4:30PM (CST). *Misdemeanor, Civil Actions Under $45,000, Eviction, Small Claims, Probate.*

Civil Records: Access: Mail, in person. Only the court conducts in person searches; visitors may not. Search fee: $5.00. Required to search: name, years to search. Civil cases indexed by defendant, plaintiff. Civil records on computer since 1981, archived since 1845. **Criminal Records:** Access: Mail, in person. Only the court conducts in person searches; visitors may not. Search fee: $5.00. Required to search: name, years to search. Criminal records on computer since 1981, archived since 1845. **General Information:** No juvenile, mental, expunged, dismissed, or suspended imposition of sentence records released. SASE required. Turnaround time 2 days. Copy fee: $.50 per page. Certification fee: $1.50. Fee payee: Circuit Court Associate Division. Business checks accepted. Prepayment is required.

Oregon County

Circuit Court PO Box 406, Alton, MO 65606; 417-778-7460; Fax: 417-778-6641. Hours: 8AM-4PM (CST). *Felony, Misdemeanor, Civil Actions Over $45,000.*

Civil Records: Access: Phone, fax, mail, in person. Both court and visitors may perform in person searches. No search fee. Required to search: name, years to search; also helpful-address. Civil cases indexed by defendant, plaintiff. Civil records on books. **Criminal Records:** Access: Phone, fax, mail, in person. Both court and visitors may perform in person searches. No search fee. Required to search: name, years to search; also helpful-DOB, SSN. Criminal records on books. **General Information:** No juvenile, mental, expunged, dismissed, or suspended imposition of sentence records released. SASE required. Turnaround time 1-2 days. Copy fee: $.50 per page. Certification fee: $2.00. Fee payee: Circuit Court. Personal checks accepted. Prepayment is required. Fax notes: $1.00 for first page, $.50 each addl.

Associate Circuit Court PO Box 211, Alton, MO 65606; 417-778-7461; Fax: 417-778-6209. Hours: 8:00AM-4:00PM (CST). *Misdemeanor, Civil Actions Under $45,000, Eviction, Small Claims, Probate.*

Civil Records: Access: Mail, in person. Both court and visitors may perform in person searches. No search fee. Required to search: name, years to search. Civil cases indexed by defendant, plaintiff. Civil records on index cards, archived since 1850. **Criminal Records:** Access: Mail, in person. Both court and visitors may perform in person searches. No search fee. Required to search: name, years to search. Criminal records on computer since 3/11/92, prior on files. **General Information:** No juvenile, mental, expunged, dismissed, or suspended imposition of sentence records released. SASE not required. Turnaround time varies. Copy fee: $1.00 per page. Certification fee: $2.00. Fee payee: Associate Circuit Court. Business checks accepted. Prepayment is required.

Osage County

Circuit Court PO Box 825, Linn, MO 65051; 573-897-3114 573-897-2136 (Assoc Div). Hours: 8AM-4:30PM (CST). *Felony, Misdemeanor, Civil Actions Over $45,000.*

Civil Records: Access: Phone, mail, in person. Both court and visitors may perform in person searches. No search fee. Required to search: name, years to search. Civil cases indexed by defendant, plaintiff. Civil records on index cards and books. **Criminal Records:** Access: Phone, mail, in person. Both court and visitors may perform in person searches. No search fee. Required to search: name, years to search, DOB; also helpful-SSN. Criminal records on index cards and books. **General Information:** No juvenile, mental, expunged, dismissed, or suspended imposition of sentence records released. SASE required. Turnaround time ASAP. Copy fee: $.50 per page. $1.00 minimum. Certification fee: $2.00. Fee payee: Circuit Clerk. Personal checks accepted. Prepayment is required. Fax notes: Fee to fax results is $1.00 per page.

Associate Circuit Court PO Box 470, Linn, MO 65051; 573-897-2136; Fax: 573-897-2285. Hours: 8AM-4:30PM (CST). *Misdemeanor, Civil Actions Under $25,000, Eviction, Small Claims, Probate.*

Civil Records: Access: Phone, mail, in person. Only the court conducts in person searches; visitors may not. No search fee. Required to search: name, years to search. Civil cases indexed by defendant, plaintiff. Civil records on index cards. **Criminal Records:** Access: Phone, mail, in person. Only the court conducts in person searches; visitors may not. No search fee. Required to search: name, years to search, DOB; also helpful-SSN. Criminal records on index cards. **General Information:** No juvenile, mental, expunged, dismissed, or suspended imposition of sentence records released. SASE not required. Turnaround time 2 weeks. Copy fee: $.25 per page. Certification fee: $2.00. Fee payee: Osage County Circuit Court-Associate Division. Personal checks accepted. Prepayment is required.

Ozark County

Circuit Court PO Box 36, Gainesville, MO 65655; 417-679-4232; Fax: 417-679-4554. Hours: 8AM-Noon, 1-5PM (CST). *Felony, Misdemeanor, Civil Actions Over $45,000.*

Civil Records: Access: Mail, in person. No search fee. Required to search: name, years to search. Civil cases indexed by defendant, plaintiff. Civil records on index cards since 1979, archived since 1841. **Criminal Records:** Access: Mail, in person. Only the court conducts in person searches; visitors may not. No search fee. Required to search: name, years to search, DOB; also helpful-SSN. Criminal records on index cards since 1979, archived since 1841. **General Information:** No juvenile, mental, expunged, dismissed, or suspended imposition of sentence records released. SASE requested. Turnaround time 10 days-2 weeks. Copy fee: $1.00 per page. Certification fee: $1.50. Fee payee: Ozark County Circuit Court. Personal checks accepted. Prepayment is required.

Associate Circuit Court PO Box 278, Gainesville, MO 65655; 417-679-4611; Fax: 417-679-2099. Hours: 8AM-4:30PM (CST). *Misdemeanor, Civil Actions Under $25,000, Eviction, Small Claims, Probate.*

Civil Records: Access: Fax, mail, in person. Both court and visitors may perform in person searches.

No search fee. Required to search: name, years to search. Civil cases indexed by defendant, plaintiff. Civil records on case files. **Criminal Records:** Access: Fax, mail, in person. Both court and visitors may perform in person searches. No search fee. Required to search: name, years to search, DOB, signed release; also helpful-SSN. Criminal records on computer since 1990. **General Information:** No juvenile, mental, expunged, dismissed, or suspended imposition of sentence records released. SASE required. Turnaround time 2 weeks. Copy fee: $1.00 per page. Certification fee: $1.50. Fee payee: Associate Circuit Court. Personal checks accepted. Prepayment is required. Fax notes: $1.00 per page.

Pemiscot County

Circuit Court County Courthouse, PO Box 34, Caruthersville, MO 63830; 573-333-0182. Hours: 7:30AM-4:30PM (CST). *Felony, Misdemeanor, Civil Actions Over $45,000.*

Civil Records: Access: In person only. Court does not conduct in person searches; visitors must perform searches for themselves. Search fee: No civil searches performed by court. Required to search: name, years to search. Civil cases indexed by defendant, plaintiff. Civil records on index cards since 1979, prior on books. **Criminal Records:** Access: In person only. Court does not conduct in person searches; visitors must perform searches for themselves. Search fee: No criminal searches performed by court. Required to search: name, years to search. Criminal records on index cards since 1979, prior on books. **General Information:** No juvenile, mental, expunged, dismissed, or suspended imposition of sentence records released. Copy fee: $.25 per page. Certification fee: No certification fee. Fee payee: Pemiscot County Treasurer. Personal checks accepted.

Associate Circuit Court County Courthouse, PO Drawer 228, Caruthersville, MO 63830; 573-333-2784. Hours: 7:30AM-4:30PM (CST). *Misdemeanor, Civil Actions Under $45,000, Eviction, Small Claims, Probate.*

Civil Records: Access: Mail, in person. Both court and visitors may perform in person searches. No search fee. Required to search: name, years to search. Civil cases indexed by defendant, plaintiff. Civil records on index cards since 1979, prior on books. **Criminal Records:** Access: Mail, in person. Both court and visitors may perform in person searches. No search fee. Required to search: name, years to search. Criminal records on computer since 5/90, on index cards from 1979-1990, prior on books. **General Information:** No juvenile, mental, expunged, dismissed, or suspended imposition of sentence records released. SASE required. Turnaround time varies. Copy fee: $1.00 per page. Certification fee: No certification fee. Fee payee: Pemiscot County Clerk. Only cashiers checks and money orders accepted. Prepayment is required.

Perry County

Circuit Court 15 W Saint Maries St, Perryville, MO 63775-1399; 573-547-6581; Fax: 573-547-9323. Hours: 8AM-5PM (CST). *Felony, Misdemeanor, Civil Actions Over $25,000.*

Civil Records: Access: Fax, mail, in person. Both court and visitors may perform in person searches. No search fee. Required to search: name, years to search. Civil cases indexed by defendant, plaintiff. Civil records on computer since 1991, prior on index cards. **Criminal Records:** Access: Fax, mail, in person. Both court and visitors may

perform in person searches. No search fee. Required to search: name, years to search. Criminal records on computer since 1991, prior on index cards. **General Information:** No juvenile, mental, paternity, expunged, dismissed, or suspended imposition of sentence records released. SASE requried. Turnaround time 3 days. Copy fee: $1.00 for first page, $.50 each addl. Certification fee: $1.00. Fee payee: Perry County Circuit Clerk. Personal checks accepted. Prepayment is required. Public access terminal is available. Fax notes: No fee to fax results.

Associate Circuit Court 15 W Saint Maries, Suite 3, Perryville, MO 63775-1399; 573-547-7861; Fax: 573-547-9323. Hours: 8AM-5PM (CST). *Misdemeanor, Civil Actions Under $25,000, Eviction, Small Claims, Probate.*

Civil Records: Access: Mail, in person. Only the court conducts in person searches; visitors may not. No search fee. Required to search: name, years to search; also helpful-address. Civil cases indexed by defendant, plaintiff. Civil records on computer since 1994, prior on index cards. **Criminal Records:** Access: Mail, in person. Only the court conducts in person searches; visitors may not. No search fee. Required to search: name, years to search, DOB; also helpful-address, SSN. Criminal records on computer since 1994, prior on index cards. **General Information:** No juvenile, mental, expunged, dismissed, or suspended imposition of sentence records released. SASE required. Turnaround time varies. Copy fee: $.50 per page. Certification fee: $1.50 plus $1.00 per page. Fee payee: Circuit Court Division 6. Only cashiers checks and money orders accepted. Prepayment is required. Public access terminal is available.

Pettis County

Circuit Court PO Box 804, Sedalia, MO 65302-0804; 660-826-0617; Fax: 660-827-8637. Hours: 8AM-5PM (CST). *Felony, Misdemeanor, Civil Actions Over $45,000.*

Civil Records: Access: Phone, fax, mail, in person. Both court and visitors may perform in person searches. No search fee. Required to search: name, years to search. Civil cases indexed by defendant, plaintiff. Civil records on index books since 9/75, prior on judgement books. **Criminal Records:** Access: Phone, fax, mail, in person. Both court and visitors may perform in person searches. No search fee. Required to search: name, years to search, DOB. Criminal records on computer since 1993, prior on index cards since 9/75. **General Information:** No juvenile, mental, expunged, dismissed, or suspended imposition of sentence records released. SASE requried. Turnaround time 1-2 days. Copy fee: $.15 per page. Certification fee: $1.50. Fee payee: Pettis County Circuit Clerk. Personal checks accepted. Fax notes: $2.50 for first page, $1.50 each addl.

Associate Circuit Court 415 S Ohio, Sedalia, MO 65301; 660-826-4699; Fax: 660-827-8637. Hours: 8:30AM-5PM (CST). *Misdemeanor, Civil Actions Under $45,000, Eviction, Small Claims.*

Civil Records: Access: Fax, mail, in person. Both court and visitors may perform in person searches. No search fee. Required to search: name, years to search. Civil cases indexed by defendant, plaintiff. Civil records on index cards since 1975, prior on judgement books. **Criminal Records:** Access: Fax, mail, in person. Both court and visitors may perform in person searches. No search fee.

Required to search: name, years to search. Criminal records on computer since 1993, on index cards from 1975-1993, prior on judgement books. **General Information:** No juvenile, mental, expunged, dismissed, or suspended imposition of sentence records released. SASE required. Turnaround time 1-2 weeks. Copy fee: $.25 per page. Certification fee: $1.50. Fee payee: Circuit Court Division 6. Only cashiers checks and money orders accepted.

Probate Court 415 S. Ohio, Sedalia, MO 65301; 660-826-0368; Fax: 660-827-8637. Hours: 8:30AM-4:30PM (CST). *Probate.*

Phelps County

Circuit & Associate Court 200 N Main St, Rolla, MO 65401; 573-364-1891 X200; Fax: 573-364-1419. Hours: 8AM-5PM (CST). *Felony, Misdemeanor, Civil, Small Claims, Eviction, Probate.*

Civil Records: Access: Fax, mail, in person. Only the court conducts in person searches; visitors may not. No search fee. Required to search: name, years to search. Civil cases indexed by defendant, plaintiff. Civil records on computer since 1991. **Criminal Records:** Access: Fax, mail, in person. Only the court conducts in person searches; visitors may not. No search fee. Required to search: name, years to search. Criminal records on computer since 1991. **General Information:** No juvenile, mental, expunged or dismissed records released. SASE required. Turnaround time 1 week. Copy fee: $.20 per page. Certification fee: $1.00. Fee payee: Circuit Clerk. Personal checks accepted. no out-of-state checks accepted. Copy fees may be billed. Fax notes: $.50 per page.

Phelps County Courthouse 200 N Main, PO Box 1550, Rolla, MO 65401; 573-364-1891 X251. Hours: 8AM-Noon, 1-5PM (CST). *Probate.*

Pike County

Circuit Court 115 W Main, Bowling Green, MO 63334; 573-324-3112. Hours: 8AM-4:30PM (CST). *Felony, Misdemeanor, Civil Actions Over $45,000.*

Civil Records: Access: Mail, in person. Both court and visitors may perform in person searches. No search fee. Required to search: name, years to search; also helpful-address. Civil cases indexed by defendant, plaintiff. Civil records on index cards since 1977, prior on books. **Criminal Records:** Access: In person only. Court does not conduct in person searches; visitors must perform searches for themselves. No search fee. Required to search: name, years to search; also helpful-DOB. Criminal records on index cards since 1977, prior on books. The Circuit Clerks will provide a from to mail requests to the State Patrol. **General Information:** No juvenile, mental, expunged, dismissed, or suspended imposition of sentence records released. SASE required. Turnaround time 1-2 days. Copy fee: $.25 per page. Certification fee: $1.00. Fee payee: Pike County Circuit Clerk. Personal checks accepted.

Associate Circuit Court 115 W Main, Bowling Green, MO 63334; 573-324-5582; Fax: 573-324-6297. Hours: 8AM-4:30PM (CST). *Misdemeanor, Civil Actions Under $25,000, Eviction, Small Claims, Probate.*

Civil Records: Access: Phone, mail, fax, in person. Both court and visitors may perform in person searches. No search fee. Required to search: name, years to search. Civil cases indexed by defendant, plaintiff. Civil records on index cards since 1979, archived since 1819. **Criminal**

Records: Access: Phone, mail, fax, in person. Only the court conducts in person searches; visitors may not. No search fee. Required to search: name, years to search; also helpful-DOB. Criminal records on index cards since 1979, archived since 1819. **General Information:** No juvenile, mental, expunged, dismissed, or suspended imposition of sentence records released. SASE requried. Turnaround time 3-7 days. Copy fee: $.50 per page. Certification fee: $1.50. Fee payee: Associate Circuit or Probate Court. Business checks accepted. Prepayment is required.

Platte County

Circuit Court 328 Main St, #5, Platte City, MO 64079; 816-858-2232; Fax: 816-858-3392. Hours: 8AM-5PM (CST). *Felony, Misdemeanor, Civil Actions Over $45,000.*

http://casenet.osca.state.mo.us/casenet

Civil Records: Access: Mail, online, in person. Both court and visitors may perform in person searches. No search fee. Required to search: name, years to search. Civil cases indexed by defendant, plaintiff. Civil records on computer since 10/91. Free access at http://casenet.osca.state.mo.us/casenet. **Criminal Records:** Access: Mail, remote online, in person. Both court and visitors may perform in person searches. No search fee. Required to search: name, years to search, DOB; also helpful-SSN. Criminal records on computer since 10/91. Free access at http://casenet.osca.state.mo.us/casenet. **General Information:** No juvenile, mental, expunged, dismissed, or suspended imposition of sentence records released. SASE required. Turnaround time 2-3 days. Copy fee: $.25 per page. Certification fee: $1.00. Fee payee: Platte County Circuit Clerk. Only cashiers checks and money orders accepted. Prepayment is required. Public access terminal is available.

Associate Circuit Court 328 Main St, Box 5CH, Platte City, MO 64079; 816-858-2232; Fax: 816-858-3392. Hours: 8AM-5PM (CST). *Misdemeanor, Civil Actions Under $25,000, Eviction, Small Claims.*

http://casenet.osca.state.mo.us/casenet

Civil Records: Access: Mail, online, in person. Both court and visitors may perform in person searches. No search fee. Required to search: name, years to search. Civil cases indexed by defendant, plaintiff. Civil records on computer since 10/91, prior on index cards. Free access at http://casenet.state.mo.us/casenet. **Criminal Records:** Access: Mail, remote online, in person. Both court and visitors may perform in person searches. No search fee. Required to search: name, years to search, DOB; also helpful-SSN. Criminal records on computer since 10/91, prior on index cards. See civil for online access. **General Information:** No juvenile, mental, expunged, dismissed, or suspended imposition of sentence records released. SASE requried. Turnaround time 1-3 days. Copy fee: $.25 per page. Certification fee: $1.00. Fee payee: Circuit Clerk. Only cashiers checks and money orders accepted. Prepayment is required. Public access terminal is available.

Probate Court 415 Third St, #95, Platte City, MO 64079; 816-858-2232 X3438; Fax: 816-858-3392. Hours: 8AM-5PM (CST). *Probate.*

Polk County

Circuit Court 102 E Broadway, Rm 14, Bolivar, MO 65613; 417-326-4912; Fax: 417-326-4194. Hours: 8AM-5PM (CST). *Felony, Misdemeanor, Civil Actions Over $45,000.*

Civil Records: Access: Fax, mail, in person. Both court and visitors may perform in person searches. Search fee: $5.00 per name. Required to search: name, years to search. Civil cases indexed by defendant, plaintiff. Civil records on computer since 1991, prior on card index since 1979. **Criminal Records:** Access: Fax, mail, in person. Only the court conducts in person searches; visitors may not. Search fee: $5.00 per name. Required to search: name, years to search. Criminal records on computer since 1991, prior on card index since 1979. **General Information:** No juvenile, mental, expunged, dismissed, or suspended imposition of sentence records released. SASE required. Turnaround time 1 week. Copy fee: $.25 per page. Certification fee: $2.00. Fee payee: Circuit Clerk. Personal checks accepted. Fax notes: $3.00 for first page, $.25 each addl.

Associate Circuit Court Courthouse, Rm 7, Bolivar, MO 65613; 417-326-4921; Fax: 417-326-5238. Hours: 8:00AM-5:00PM (CST). *Misdemeanor, Civil Actions Under $25,000, Eviction, Small Claims, Probate.*

Civil Records: Access: Phone, mail, in person. Only the court conducts in person searches; visitors may not. No search fee. Required to search: name, years to search; also helpful-case number. Civil cases indexed by defendant, plaintiff. Civil records on index cards since 1950s, prior on books. **Criminal Records:** Access: Phone, mail, in person. Only the court conducts in person searches; visitors may not. No search fee. Required to search: name, years to search; also helpful-case number. Criminal records on index cards since 1950s, prior on books. **General Information:** No juvenile, mental, expunged, dismissed, or suspended imposition of sentence records released. SASE required. Turnaround time 1 week. Copy fee: $.25 per page. Certification fee: $1.50. Fee payee: Associate Circuit Court. Only cashiers checks and money orders accepted. Prepayment is required.

Pulaski County

Circuit & Associate Circuit Courts 301 Historic Rt 66 E, Suite 202, Waynesville, MO 65583; 573-774-4755; Fax: 573-774-6967. Hours: 8AM-4:30PM (CST). *Felony, Misdemeanor, Civil, Eviction, Small Claims.*

Civil Records: Access: In person only. Court does not conduct in person searches; visitors must perform searches for themselves. Search fee: No civil searches performed by court. Required to search: name, years to search; also helpful-address. Civil cases indexed by defendant, plaintiff. Civil records on computer since 1990, prior on books since 1903. **Criminal Records:** Access: Fax, mail, in person. Both court and visitors may perform in person searches. No search fee. Required to search: name, years to search; also helpful-DOB, SSN. Criminal records on computer since 1990, prior on books since 1903. **General Information:** No juvenile, mental, paternity, expunged, dismissed, or suspended imposition of sentence records released. SASE requested. Turnaround time 1 day. Copy fee: $.25 per page. Certification fee: $2.00. Fee payee: Circuit Clerk. Business checks accepted. Prepayment is required. Public access terminal is available. Fax notes: No fee to fax results. Will only fax to 800 numbers.

Probate Court 301 Historic 66 East, Suite 316, Waynesville, MO 65583; 573-774-4784; Fax: 573-774-6673. *Probate.*

Putnam County

Circuit Court Courthouse Rm 202, Unionville, MO 63565; 660-947-2071; Fax: 660-947-2320 Div I; 947-7348 Div II. Hours: 8AM-12; 1PM-5PM (CST). *Felony, Misdemeanor, Civil Actions Over $45,000.*

Civil Records: Access: Mail, in person. Both court and visitors may perform in person searches. No search fee. Required to search: name, years to search. Civil cases indexed by defendant, plaintiff. Civil records on index cards since late 1970s. **Criminal Records:** Access: Mail, in person. Both court and visitors may perform in person searches. No search fee. Required to search: name, years to search. Criminal records on index cards since late 1970s. **General Information:** No juvenile, mental, expunged, dismissed, or suspended imposition of sentence records released. SASE required. Turnaround time same day. Copy fee: $.25 per page. Certification fee: $1.00. Fee payee: Circuit Clerk. Business checks accepted. Prepayment is required.

Associate Circuit Court Courthouse Rm 101, Unionville, MO 63565; 660-947-2117; Fax: 660-947-7348. Hours: 9AM-5PM (CST). *Misdemeanor, Civil Actions Under $45,000, Eviction, Small Claims, Probate.*

Civil Records: Access: Mail, in person. Both court and visitors may perform in person searches. No search fee. Required to search: name, years to search. Civil cases indexed by defendant, plaintiff. Civil records on computer since 1994, prior on books. **Criminal Records:** Access: Mail, in person. Only the court conducts in person searches; visitors may not. No search fee. Required to search: name, years to search. Criminal records on computer since 1994, prior on books. **General Information:** No juvenile, mental, expunged, dismissed, or suspended imposition of sentence records released. SASE required. Turnaround time 30-60 days. Copy fee: $1.00 per page. Certification fee: $1.50. Fee payee: Associate Circuit Court. Only cashiers checks and money orders accepted. Prepayment is required.

Ralls County

Circuit Court PO Box 444, New London, MO 63459; 573-985-5631. Hours: 8:30AM-4:30PM (CST). *Felony, Misdemeanor, Civil Actions Over $45,000.*

Civil Records: Access: Mail, in person. Only the court conducts in person searches; visitors may not. No search fee. Required to search: name, years to search. Civil cases indexed by defendant, plaintiff. Civil records on index cards since 1976, prior on books. **Criminal Records:** Access: Mail, in person. Only the court conducts in person searches; visitors may not. No search fee. Required to search: name, years to search, signed release. Criminal records on index cards since 1976, prior on books. **General Information:** No juvenile, mental, expunged, dismissed, or suspended imposition of sentence records released. SASE required. Turnaround time varies. Copy fee: $.25 per page. Certification fee: $1.00. Fee payee: Ralls County Circuit Clerk. Personal checks accepted. Prepayment is required.

Associate Circuit Court PO Box 466, New London, MO 63459; 573-985-5641; Fax: 573-985-3446. Hours: 8:00AM-4:30PM (CST). *Misdemeanor, Civil Actions Under $25,000, Eviction, Small Claims, Probate.*

Civil Records: Access: Phone, mail, in person. Both court and visitors may perform in person searches. Search fee: $5.00 per name. Required to search: name, years to search. Civil cases indexed by defendant, plaintiff. Civil records on index cards since 1979, prior on record books. **Criminal Records:** Access: Phone, mail, in person. Both court and visitors may perform in person searches. Search fee: $5.00 per name. Required to search: name, years to search, signed release. Criminal records on index cards since 1979, prior on record books. **General Information:** No juvenile, mental, expunged, dismissed, or suspended imposition of sentence records released. SASE required. Turnaround time 1-2 weeks, geneaology turnaround time varies. Copy fee: $.25 per page. Certification fee: $1.50. Fee payee: Associate Circuit Court. Personal checks accepted. Prepayment is required.

Randolph County

Circuit Court 223 N Williams, Moberly, MO 65270; 660-263-4474; Fax: 660-263-5966. Hours: 8AM-4:30PM (CST). *Felony, Misdemeanor, Civil Actions Over $45,000.*

Civil Records: Access: Fax, mail, in person. Both court and visitors may perform in person searches. No search fee. Required to search: name, years to search, address. Civil cases indexed by defendant, plaintiff. Civil records on index cards since 1975, prior on record books. **Criminal Records:** Access: Fax, mail, in person. Both court and visitors may perform in person searches. No search fee. Required to search: name, years to search, address, DOB; also helpful-SSN. Criminal records on computer since 1994, prior on index books. **General Information:** No juvenile, mental, expunged, dismissed, or suspended imposition of sentence records released. SASE required. Turnaround time 1 week. Copy fee: $1.00 per page. Certification fee: $1.50. Fee payee: Randolph County Circuit Clerk. Personal checks accepted. Fax notes: $4.00 per page.

Associate Circuit Court 223 N Williams, Moberly, MO 65270; 660-263-4450; Fax: 660-263-1007. Hours: 8AM-4:30PM (CST). *Misdemeanor, Civil Actions Under $45,000, Eviction, Small Claims, Probate.*

Civil Records: Access: Mail, in person. Only the court conducts in person searches; visitors may not. No search fee. Required to search: name, years to search. Civil cases indexed by defendant, plaintiff. Civil records on index cards since 1979, prior on books. **Criminal Records:** Access: Mail, in person. Only the court conducts in person searches; visitors may not. No search fee. Required to search: name, years to search. Criminal records on computer since 1994, prior on index cards and books. **General Information:** No juvenile, mental, expunged, dismissed, or suspended imposition of sentence records released. SASE required. Turnaround time 3-5 days or up to 2 weeks if office busy. Copy fee: $.20 per page. Certification fee: $1.50. Fee payee: Associate Circuit Court. Personal checks accepted.

Ray County

Circuit Court PO Box 594, Richmond, MO 64085; 816-776-3377; Fax: 816-776-6016. Hours: 8AM-4PM (CST). *Felony, Misdemeanor, Civil Actions Over $45,000.*

www.osca.state.mo.us/circuits/index.nsf/County+/ +Ray

Civil Records: Access: Phone, fax, mail, in person. Only the court conducts in person searches; visitors may not. No search fee. Required to search: name, years to search. Civil cases indexed by defendant, plaintiff. Civil records on index cards since 1977, prior on judgment books. **Criminal Records:** Access: Phone, fax, mail, in person. Only the court conducts in person searches; visitors may not. No search fee. Required to search: name, years to search; also helpful-DOB, SSN. Criminal records on index cards since 1977, prior on judgment books. **General Information:** No juvenile, mental, expunged, dismissed, or suspended imposition of sentence records released. SASE required. Turnaround time varies. Copy fee: $.25 per page. Certification fee: $2.50. Fee payee: Ray County Circuit Clerk. Business checks accepted. Prepayment is required. Fax notes: $1.00 per page.

Associate Circuit Court Ray County Courthouse, 100 W Main St, Richmond, MO 64085-1710; 660-776-2335; Fax: 660-776-2185. Hours: 8AM-4PM (CST). *Misdemeanor, Civil Actions Under $25,000, Eviction, Small Claims, Probate.*

Civil Records: Access: Fax, mail, in person. Only the court conducts in person searches; visitors may not. No search fee. Required to search: name; also helpful-years to search. Civil cases indexed by defendant, plaintiff. Civil records on index cards since 1979, prior on books. **Criminal Records:** Access: Fax, mail, in person. Only the court conducts in person searches; visitors may not. No search fee. Required to search: name, DOB; also helpful-years to search, SSN. Criminal records on index cards since 1979, prior on books. **General Information:** No juvenile, mental, expunged, dismissed, or suspended imposition of sentence records released. SASE required. Turnaround time varies. Copy fee: $.20 per page. Certification fee: $1.50. Fee payee: Associate Circuit Court. Business checks accepted. Prepayment is required. Fax notes: No fee to fax results.

Reynolds County

Circuit Court PO Box 76, Centerville, MO 63633; 573-648-2494 X44; Fax: 573-648-2296. Hours: 8AM-4PM (CST). *Felony, Misdemeanor, Civil Actions Over $45,000.*

Civil Records: Access: Mail, in person. Both court and visitors may perform in person searches. No search fee. Required to search: name, years to search. Civil cases indexed by defendant, plaintiff. Civil records on cards and books, archived since 1872. **Criminal Records:** Access: Phone, mail, in person. Both court and visitors may perform in person searches. No search fee. Required to search: name, years to search. Criminal records on cards and books, archived since 1872. **General Information:** No juvenile, mental, expunged, dismissed, or suspended imposition of sentence records released. SASE required. Turnaround time 2 days. Copy fee: $1.00 per page. Certification fee: $2.00. Fee payee: Randy L Cowin. Personal checks accepted. Prepayment is required.

Associate Circuit Court PO Box 39, Centerville, MO 63633; 573-648-2494 X41; Fax: 573-648-2296. Hours: 8AM-4PM (CST). *Misdemeanor, Civil Actions Under $45,000, Eviction, Small Claims, Probate.*

Civil Records: Access: Phone, mail, in person. Both court and visitors may perform in person searches. No search fee. Required to search: name, years to search. Civil cases indexed by defendant, plaintiff. Civil records on index cards and files (probate books). **Criminal Records:** Access: Phone, mail, in person. Both court and visitors

may perform in person searches. No search fee. Required to search: name, years to search. Criminal records on index cards and files (probate books). **General Information:** No juvenile, mental, expunged, dismissed, or suspended imposition of sentence records released. SASE not required. Turnaround time 1 day, phone turnaround time same day. Copy fee: $1.00 per page. Certification fee: $2.00. Fee payee: Associate Circuit Court. Personal checks accepted.

Ripley County

Circuit Court Courthouse, Doniphan, MO 63935; 573-996-2818; Fax: 573-996-5014. Hours: 8AM-4PM (CST). *Felony, Misdemeanor, Civil Actions Over $25,000.*

Civil Records: Access: Phone, fax, mail, in person. Both court and visitors may perform in person searches. Search fee: $5.00 per name. Required to search: name, years to search. Civil cases indexed by defendant, plaintiff. Civil records on cards and books since 1976, archived since 1850s. **Criminal Records:** Access: Fax, mail, in person. Both court and visitors may perform in person searches. Search fee: $5.00 per name. Required to search: name, years to search, DOB. Criminal records on cards and books since 1976, archived since 1850s. **General Information:** No juvenile, mental, expunged, dismissed, or suspended imposition of sentence records released. SASE required. Turnaround time same day. Copy fee: $3.00 per page. Certification fee: $2.00 if done by in-person searcher, otherwise certification is included in the search fee. Fee payee: Circuit Clerk. Personal checks accepted. Prepayment is required.

Associate Circuit Court 100 Court Sq, Courthouse, Doniphan, MO 63935; 573-996-2013; Fax: 573-996-5014. Hours: 8AM-4PM (CST). *Misdemeanor, Civil Actions Under $25,000, Eviction, Small Claims, Probate.*

Civil Records: Access: Phone, fax, mail, in person. Both court and visitors may perform in person searches. No search fee. Required to search: name, years to search. Civil cases indexed by defendant, plaintiff. Civil records on index cards since 1984, prior on books. **Criminal Records:** Access: Phone, mail, in person. Both court and visitors may perform in person searches. No search fee. Required to search: name, years to search; also helpful-DOB, SSN. Criminal records on index cards since 1984, prior on books. **General Information:** No juvenile, mental, expunged, dismissed, or suspended imposition of sentence records released. SASE required. Turnaround time 1 week. Copy fee: $.25 per page. Certification fee: $1.00. Fee payee: Circuit Court Division II. Only cashiers checks and money orders accepted.

Saline County

Circuit Court PO Box 597, Marshall, MO 65340; 660-886-2300. Hours: 8:00AM-5:00PM (CST). *Felony, Misdemeanor, Civil Actions Over $45,000.*

Civil Records: Access: Mail, in person. Both court and visitors may perform in person searches. No search fee. Required to search: name, years to search. Civil cases indexed by defendant, plaintiff. Civil records on index cards since 1974, prior on books since 1820. **Criminal Records:** Access: Mail, in person. Both court and visitors may perform in person searches. No search fee. Required to search: name, years to search. Criminal records on index cards since 1974, prior on books since 1820. **General Information:** No juvenile, mental, expunged, dismissed, or suspended imposition of sentence records released. SASE requried. Turnaround time 1 week. Copy fee: $.25 per page. Certification fee: $1.50. Fee payee: Saline County Circuit Court. Personal checks accepted. Copy fees may be billed.

Associate Circuit Court PO Box 751, Marshall, MO 65340; 660-886-6988; Fax: 660-886-2919. Hours: 8AM-5PM (CST). *Misdemeanor, Civil Actions Under $25,000, Eviction, Small Claims.*

Civil Records: Access: Phone, mail, in person. Only the court conducts in person searches; visitors may not. No search fee. Required to search: name, years to search. Civil cases indexed by defendant, plaintiff. Civil records on index cards since 1979, prior on books. **Criminal Records:** Access: Phone, mail, in person. Only the court conducts in person searches; visitors may not. No search fee. Required to search: name, years to search. Criminal records on computer since 1993, prior on cards and books. **General Information:** No juvenile, mental, expunged, dismissed, or suspended imposition of sentence records released. SASE requried. Turnaround time 1-2 days. No copy fee. Certification fee: No certification fee.

Schuyler County

Circuit Court PO Box 186, Lancaster, MO 63548; 660-457-3784; Fax: 660-457-3016. Hours: 8AM-4PM (CST). *Felony, Misdemeanor, Civil Actions Over $45,000.*

Civil Records: Access: Mail, in person. Both court and visitors may perform in person searches. Search fee: $14.00 per name. Required to search: name, years to search. Civil cases indexed by defendant, plaintiff. Civil records on index cards & books. **Criminal Records:** Access: Mail, in person. Both court and visitors may perform in person searches. Search fee: $14.00 per name. Required to search: name, years to search. Criminal records on index cards & books. **General Information:** No juvenile, mental, expunged, dismissed, or suspended imposition of sentence records released. SASE required. Turnaround time 1-2 days. Copy fee: $1.00 per page. Certification fee: $1.00. Fee payee: Schuyler County Circuit Clerk. Personal checks accepted. Prepayment is required. Fax notes: Fee to fax is $2.00 plus $1.00 each page.

Associate Circuit Court Box 158, Lancaster, MO 63548; 660-457-3755; Fax: 660-457-3016. Hours: 8:15AM-4PM (CST). *Misdemeanor, Civil Actions Under $45,000, Eviction, Small Claims, Probate.*

Civil Records: Access: Mail, in person. Both court and visitors may perform in person searches. Search fee: $5.00 per name. Required to search: name, years to search. Civil cases indexed by defendant, plaintiff. Civil records on index cards since 1976. **Criminal Records:** Access: Mail, in person. Both court and visitors may perform in person searches. Search fee: $5.00 per name. Required to search: name, years to search. Criminal records on computer since 5/92, prior on index cards. **General Information:** No juvenile, mental, expunged, dismissed, or suspended imposition of sentence records released. SASE requried. Turnaround time 4 days. Copy fee: $.25 per page. Certification fee: $1.50. Fee payee: Associate Circuit Court. Business checks accepted. Prepayment is required.

Scotland County

Circuit Court 117 S Market St #106, Memphis, MO 63555; 660-465-8605; Fax: 660-465-8673. Hours: 9AM-4PM (CST). *Felony, Misdemeanor, Civil Actions Over $45,000.*

Civil Records: Access: Mail, in person. Both court and visitors may perform in person searches. No search fee. Required to search: name, years to search. Civil cases indexed by defendant, plaintiff. Civil records on index cards since 1979, prior on books. Only judgements on computer. **Criminal Records:** Access: Mail, in person. Both court and visitors may perform in person searches. No search fee. Required to search: name, years to search, DOB, signed release; also helpful-address. Criminal records on index cards since 1979, prior on books. Only judgements on computer. **General Information:** No juvenile, mental, expunged, dismissed, or suspended imposition of sentence records released. SASE required. Turnaround time same day. Copy fee: $.25 per page. Certification fee: $2.50. Fee payee: Scotland County Circuit Clerk. Personal checks accepted. Prepayment is required.

Associate Circuit Court Courthouse, Rm 102, 117 S Market, Memphis, MO 63555; 660-465-2404; Fax: 660-465-8673. Hours: 8AM-4:30PM (CST). *Misdemeanor, Civil Actions Under $25,000, Eviction, Small Claims, Probate.*

Civil Records: Access: Phone, mail, in person. Both court and visitors may perform in person searches. No search fee. Required to search: name, years to search. Civil cases indexed by defendant, plaintiff. Civil records on computer since 1986, prior on cards and books. **Criminal Records:** Access: Phone, mail, in person. Both court and visitors may perform in person searches. No search fee. Required to search: name, years to search. Criminal records on computer since 1986, prior on cards and books. **General Information:** No juvenile, mental, expunged, dismissed, or suspended imposition of sentence records released. SASE required. Turnaround time ASAP. Copy fee: $.25 per page. Certification fee: $1.50 plus $1.00 per page. Fee payee: Info provided on bill. Personal checks accepted.

Scott County

Circuit Court PO Box 277, Benton, MO 63736; 573-545-3596; Fax: 573-545-3597. Hours: 8:30AM-12, 1-5PM (CST). *Felony, Misdemeanor, Civil Actions Over $25,000.*

Civil Records: Access: Fax, mail, in person. Both court and visitors may perform in person searches. No search fee. Required to search: name, years to search. Civil cases indexed by defendant, plaintiff. Civil records on computer since 1991, prior on index cards and books. **Criminal Records:** Access: In person only. Court does not conduct in person searches; visitors must perform searches for themselves. Search fee: No criminal searches performed by court. Required to search: name, years to search, DOB, SSN. Criminal records on computer since 1991, prior on index cards and books. **General Information:** No juvenile, mental, expunged, dismissed, or suspended imposition of sentence records released. SASE required. Turnaround time 2 days-1 week. Copy fee: $1.00 for first page, $.25 each addl. Certification fee: $3.00. Fee payee: Pam Glastetter, Circuit Clerk. Personal checks accepted. Prepayment is required. Public access terminal is available.

Associate Circuit Court PO Box 249, Benton, MO 63736; 573-545-3576; Fax: 573-545-4231. Hours: 8AM-5PM (CST). *Misdemeanor, Civil Actions Under $45,000, Eviction, Small Claims, Probate.*

Civil Records: Access: Phone, mail, in person. No search fee. Required to search: name, years to search. Civil cases indexed by defendant, plaintiff. Civil records on index cards and books. **Criminal Records:** Access: Phone, mail, in person. Court does not conduct in person searches; visitors must perform searches for themselves. No search fee. Required to search: name, years to search. Criminal records on index cards and books. **General Information:** No juvenile, mental, expunged, dismissed, or suspended imposition of sentence records released. SASE required. Turnaround time varies. No copy fee. Certification fee: No certification fee. Only cashiers checks and money orders accepted. Prepayment is required.

Shannon County

Circuit Court PO Box 148, Eminence, MO 65466; 573-226-3315; Fax: 573-226-5321. Hours: 8AM-4:30PM (CST). *Felony, Misdemeanor, Civil Actions Over $45,000.*

Civil Records: Access: Mail, in person. Only the court conducts in person searches; visitors may not. No search fee. Required to search: name, years to search. Civil cases indexed by defendant, plaintiff. Civil records on index cards and books. Record index searchable on computer back to 1980. **Criminal Records:** Access: Mail, in person. Only the court conducts in person searches; visitors may not. No search fee. Required to search: name, years to search, offense. Criminal records on index cards and books. Record index searchable on computer back to 1980. **General Information:** No juvenile, mental, expunged, dismissed, or suspended imposition of sentence records released. SASE requried. Turnaround time 1 week. Copy fee: $.25 per page. Certification fee: $2.00. Fee payee: Shannon County Circuit Clerk. Personal checks accepted. Prepayment is required.

Associate Circuit Court PO Box 845, Eminence, MO 65466-0845; 573-226-5515; Fax: 573-226-3239. Hours: 8AM-4:30PM (CST). *Misdemeanor, Civil Actions Under $45,000, Eviction, Small Claims, Probate.*

Civil Records: Access: Mail, in person. Only the court conducts in person searches; visitors may not. Search fee: $10.00 per name. Required to search: name, years to search. Civil cases indexed by defendant, plaintiff. Civil records on index cards since 1979, archived since 1881. **Criminal Records:** Access: Mail, in person. Only the court conducts in person searches; visitors may not. Search fee: $10.00 per name. Required to search: name, years to search. Criminal records on computer since 1992. **General Information:** No juvenile, mental, expunged, dismissed, or suspended imposition of sentence records released. SASE required. Turnaround time 1 week. Copy fee: $.25 per page. Certification fee: $3.00. Fee payee: Associate Circuit Court. Personal checks accepted. Prepayment is required.

Shelby County

Circuit Court PO Box 176, Shelbyville, MO 63469; 573-633-2151; Fax: 573-633-1004. Hours: 8AM-4:30PM (CST). *Felony, Misdemeanor, Civil Actions Over $45,000.*

Civil Records: Access: Mail, in person. Both court and visitors may perform in person searches. No search fee. Required to search: name, years to search. Civil cases indexed by defendant, plaintiff. Civil records on index cards since 1975, prior on books since 1835. **Criminal Records:** Access: Mail, in person. Both court and visitors may perform in person searches. No search fee. Required to search: name, years to search. Criminal records on index cards since 1975, prior on books since 1835. **General Information:** No juvenile, mental, expunged, dismissed, or suspended imposition of sentence records released. SASE required. Turnaround time 1 day. Copy fee: $.25 per page. Certification fee: $2.00. Fee payee: Shelby County Circuit Clerk. Personal checks accepted. Prepayment is required.

Associate Circuit Court PO Box 206, Shelbyville, MO 63469; 573-633-2251; Fax: 573-633-2142. Hours: 8AM-4:30PM (CST). *Misdemeanor, Civil Actions Under $25,000, Eviction, Small Claims, Probate.*

Civil Records: Access: Fax, mail, in person. Both court and visitors may perform in person searches. No search fee. Required to search: name, years to search. Civil cases indexed by defendant, plaintiff. Civil records on index cards, archived from 1845 to 1950. **Criminal Records:** Access: Phone, fax, mail, in person. Both court and visitors may perform in person searches. No search fee. Required to search: name, years to search, DOB. Criminal records on index cards, archived from 1845 to 1950. **General Information:** No juvenile, mental, expunged, dismissed, or suspended imposition of sentence records released. SASE not required. Turnaround time 2 weeks. Copy fee: $.25 per page. Certification fee: $1.00. Fee payee: Probate Court or Associate Circuit Court. Personal checks accepted. Fax notes: No fee to fax results.

St. Charles County

Circuit Court 300 N 2nd St, St. Charles, MO 63301; 636-949-7900 X3098; Fax: 636-949-7390. Hours: 8:30AM-5PM (CST). *Felony, Misdemeanor, Civil Actions Over $25,000.*

Civil Records: Access: Mail, online, in person. Both court and visitors may perform in person searches. No search fee. Required to search: name, years to search. Civil cases indexed by defendant, plaintiff. Civil records on index cards since 1971, prior on books; judgment records (A-M) on computer since 1987. Free access at http://casebet.osca.state.mo.us/casenet. **Criminal Records:** Access: Remote online, in person. Court does not conduct in person searches; visitors must perform searches for themselves. Search fee: No criminal searches performed by court. Required to search: name, years to search; also helpful-DOB. Criminal records on index cards since 1971, prior on books; judgment records (A-M) on computer since 1987. Clerk refers all record requests to the Sheriff or Highway Patrol. Free online access at http://casenet.osca.state.mo.us/casenet. **General Information:** No juvenile, mental, expunged, dismissed, or suspended imposition of sentence records released. SASE required. Turnaround time varies. Copy fee: $.25 per page. Certification fee: $1.00. Fee payee: St. Charles Circuit Clerk. Personal checks accepted. Prepayment is required. Public access terminal is available.

Associate Circuit Court 300 N 2nd, Suite 436, St. Charles, MO 63301; 636-949-3043. Hours: 8:30AM-5:00PM (CST). *Civil Actions Under $25,000, Eviction, Small Claims, Probate.*

http://casenet.osca.state.mo.us/casenet

Civil Records: Access: online, in person. Court does not conduct in person searches; visitors must perform searches for themselves. Search fee: No

civil searches performed by court. Required to search: name, years to search. Civil cases indexed by defendant, plaintiff. Civil records on computer since 1988 (judgements only), prior on index cards and books. Free access at http://casenet.state.mo.us/casenet. **General Information:** SASE required. Turnaround time varies. Copy fee: $.25 per page. Certification fee: No certification fee. Fee payee: Associate Circuit Court. Only cashiers checks and money orders accepted. Prepayment is required.

St. Clair County

Circuit & Associate Circuit Courts PO Box 493, Osceola, MO 64776; 417-646-2226; Fax: 417-646-2401. Hours: 8AM-4:30PM (CST). *Felony, Misdemeanor, Civil, Eviction, Small Claims, Probate.*

Civil Records: Access: Mail, in person. Both court and visitors may perform in person searches. Search fee: $2.00 per name. Required to search: name, years to search. Civil cases indexed by defendant, plaintiff. Civil records on computer since 1991 for judgments, on index cards since 1980, prior records on index books. **Criminal Records:** Access: Mail, in person. Both court and visitors may perform in person searches. Search fee: $2.00 per name. Required to search: name, years to search, DOB. Criminal records on computer since 1991, on index cards since 1980, prior records on index books. **General Information:** No juvenile, mental, expunged, dismissed, or suspended imposition of sentence records released. SASE required. Turnaround time 1-2 days. No copy fee. Certification fee: $1.50. Fee payee: St Clair County Circuit Clerk. Personal checks accepted. Prepayment is required.

St. Francois County

Circuit Court, Division I & II 1 N Washington, 3rd Floor, Farmington, MO 63640; 573-756-4551; Fax: 573-756-3733. Hours: 8AM-5PM (CST). *Felony, Misdemeanor, Civil Actions Over $25,000.*

Civil Records: Access: Fax, mail, in person. Both court and visitors may perform in person searches. No search fee. Required to search: name, years to search. Civil cases indexed by defendant, plaintiff. Civil records on computer since 6/90, on microfiche since 1970, archived since 1821. **Criminal Records:** Access: Fax, mail, in person. Both court and visitors may perform in person searches. No search fee. Required to search: name, years to search; also helpful-DOB, SSN. Criminal records on computer since 3/1/93. **General Information:** No juvenile, mental, expunged, dismissed, or suspended imposition of sentence records released. SASE required. Turnaround time 1-2 weeks. Copy fee: $.25 per page. Certification fee: $1.50. Fee payee: Clerk of Circuit Court. Business checks accepted. Public access terminal is available.

Associate Circuit Court County Courthouse, 2nd Fl, 1 N. Washington, Rm 202, Farmington, MO 63640; 573-756-5755; Fax: 573-756-8173. Hours: 8AM-5PM (CST). *Misdemeanor, Civil Actions Under $25,000, Eviction, Small Claims, Probate.*

Civil Records: Access: Mail, in person. Only the court conducts in person searches; visitors may not. No search fee. Required to search: name, years to search. Civil cases indexed by defendant, plaintiff. Civil records on index cards since 1979, archived since 1947. **Criminal Records:** Access: Mail, in person. Only the court conducts in person searches; visitors may not. No search fee.

Required to search: name, years to search. Criminal records on computer. **General Information:** No juvenile, mental, expunged, dismissed, or suspended imposition of sentence records released. SASE not required. No copy fee. Certification fee: No certification fee. Fee payee: Circuit Court Division II. Business checks accepted.

St. Louis County

Circuit Court of St. Louis County 7900 Carondolet, Clayton, MO 63105-1766; 314-615-8029; Fax: 314-615-8739. Hours: 8AM-5PM (CST). *Felony, Misdemeanor, Civil.*

Civil Records: Access: Phone, fax, mail, in person. Both court and visitors may perform in person searches. No search fee. Required to search: name, years to search; also helpful-address. Civil cases indexed by defendant, plaintiff. Civil records on computer since 1978, prior on index cards. Permanent records on microfiche since 1978, earlier in books. Case files archived for 25 years. **Criminal Records:** Access: Phone, fax, mail, in person. Both court and visitors may perform in person searches. No search fee. Required to search: name, years to search; also helpful-address, DOB, SSN. Criminal records on computer since 1978, prior on index cards. Permanent records on microfiche since 1978, earlier in books. Case files archived for 25 years. **General Information:** No juvenile, paternity, mental, expunged, dismissed, or suspended imposition of sentence records released. SASE not requried. Turnaround time up to 5 days. Copy fee: $.30 per page. Certification fee: $1.50 plus $.30 per page after first. Fee payee: Circuit Clerk. Personal checks accepted. Prepayment is required. Public access terminal is available.

Associate Circuit - Civil Division 7900 Carondolet, Clayton, MO 63105; 314-615-8090; Probate phone:314-615-2629; Fax: 314-615-2689. Hours: 8AM-5PM (CST). *Civil Actions Under $25,000, Eviction, Small Claims, Probate.*

Civil Records: Access: Phone, mail, in person. Both court and visitors may perform in person searches. No search fee. Required to search: name, years to search. Civil cases indexed by defendant, plaintiff. Civil records on computer since 1986, prior on cards. **General Information:** No juvenile, mental, expunged, dismissed, paternity, suspended imposition of sentence records released. SASE required. Turnaround time 1 week. Copy fee: $.30 per page. Certification fee: $1.50. Fee payee: Circuit Clerk-Civil Division. Personal checks accepted. Prepayment is required. Public access terminal is available.

Associate Circuit Court - Criminal Division 7900 Carondolet, Clayton, MO 63105; 314-889-2675; Fax: 314-889-2689. *Misdemeanor.* **Criminal Records:** Access: Mail, in person. Both court and visitors may perform in person searches. No search fee. Required to search: name, years to search, DOB, offense, date of offense. Criminal records on computer since 1986. **General Information:** No juvenile, mental, expunged, dismissed, or suspended imposition of sentence records released. SASE required. Turnaround time varies. Copy fee: $.30 per page. Certification fee: $1.50. Fee payee: Circuit Clerk. Personal checks accepted. Prepayment is required. Public access terminal is available.

St. Louis City

Circuit & Associate Circuit Courts 10 N Tucker, Civil Courts Bldg, St Louis, MO 63101;

314-622-4405; Fax: 314-622-4537. Hours: 8:00AM-5:00PM (CST). *Civil, Eviction, Small Claims, Probate.*

Civil Records: Access: Mail, online, in person. No search fee. Required to search: name, years to search. Civil cases indexed by defendant, plaintiff. Civil records on computer since 1/80, on index cards since early 1800s. Remote access is through MoBar Net and is open only to attorneys. Call 314-535-1950 for more information. **General Information:** No sealed or confidential records released. SASE required. Turnaround time usually 1 week. Copy fee: $.50 per page. Certification fee: $3.50. Fee payee: City of St. Louis Circuit Clerk. Only cashiers checks and money orders accepted. Prepayment is required. Public access terminal is available.

City of St Louis Circuit Court 1320 Market, St Louis, MO 63103; 314-622-4582; Fax: 314-622-3202. Hours: 8AM-5PM (CST). *Felony, Misdemeanor.* **Criminal Records:** Access: In person only. Both court and visitors may perform in person searches. No search fee. Required to search: name, years to search, DOB, signed release; also helpful-address, SSN. Criminal records on computer since 1990 for misdemeanor; since 1992 for felony. **General Information:** No juvenile, mental, expunged, dismissed, or suspended imposition of sentence records released. SASE required. Copy fee: $.50 per page. Certification fee: $3.50. Fee payee: City of St. Louis Circuit Clerk. Business checks accepted. Prepayment is required.

Ste. Genevieve County

Circuit Court 55 S 3rd, Rm 23, Ste Genevieve, MO 63670; 573-883-2705; Fax: 573-883-9351. Hours: 8AM-5PM (CST). *Felony, Misdemeanor, Civil Actions Over $25,000.*

Civil Records: Access: In person only. Court does not conduct in person searches; visitors must perform searches for themselves. Search fee: No civil searches performed by court. Required to search: name, years to search. Civil cases indexed by defendant, plaintiff. Civil records on books since early 1800s, recent civil records computerized. **Criminal Records:** Access: In person only. Court does not conduct in person searches; visitors must perform searches for themselves. Search fee: No criminal searches performed by court. Required to search: name, years to search. Criminal Record indexes on books, not computerized. **General Information:** No juvenile, mental, expunged, paternity, dismissed, or suspended imposition of sentence records released. Copy fee: $1.00 per page. Certification fee: $1.50. Fee payee: St Genevieve County Circuit Clerk. Business checks accepted. Prepayment is required. Public access terminal is available.

Associate Circuit Court 3rd and Market, Ste Genevieve, MO 63670; 573-883-2265; Fax: 573-883-9351. Hours: 8AM-5PM (CST). *Misdemeanor, Civil Actions Under $45,000, Eviction, Small Claims, Probate.*

Civil Records: Access: In person only. Court does not conduct in person searches; visitors must perform searches for themselves. Search fee: No civil searches performed by court. Required to search: name, years to search. Civil cases indexed by defendant, plaintiff. Civil records on books. **Criminal Records:** Access: In person only. Court does not conduct in person searches; visitors must perform searches for themselves. Search fee: No criminal searches performed by court. Required to

search: name, years to search. Criminal records on books. **General Information:** No juvenile, mental, expunged, dismissed, or suspended imposition of sentence records released. Copy fee: $1.00 per page. Certification fee: $2.50. Only cashiers checks and money orders accepted.

Stoddard County

Circuit Court PO Box 30, Bloomfield, MO 63825; 573-568-4640; Fax: 573-568-2271. Hours: 8:30AM-4:30PM (CST). *Felony, Misdemeanor, Civil Actions Over $45,000.*

Civil Records: Access: Fax, mail, in person. Both court and visitors may perform in person searches. No search fee. Required to search: name, years to search. Civil cases indexed by defendant, plaintiff. Civil records on computer since 1991, prior on cards and books. **Criminal Records:** Access: Fax, mail, in person. Both court and visitors may perform in person searches. No search fee. Required to search: name, years to search; also helpful-DOB, SSN. Criminal records on computer since 1991, prior on cards and books. **General Information:** No juvenile, mental, expunged, dismissed, or suspended imposition of sentence records released. SASE required. Turnaround time 1 day. Copy fee: $.10 per page. Certification fee: $1.50. Fee payee: Stoddard County Circuit Clerk. Personal checks accepted.

Division III & Probate PO Box 518, Bloomfield, MO 63825; 573-568-2181; Fax: 573-568-3229. Hours: 7:30AM-4PM (CST). *Civil Actions Under $25,000, Eviction, Small Claims, Probate.*

Associate Circuit Court - Criminal Division II PO Box 218, Bloomfield, MO 63825; 573-568-4671; Fax: 573-568-2299. Hours: 8:30AM-4:30PM (CST). *Misdemeanor.* **Criminal Records:** Access: In person only. Court does not conduct in person searches; visitors must perform searches for themselves. Search fee: No criminal searches performed by court. Required to search: name, years to search. Criminal records on index cards, traffic on computer since 1994. **General Information:** No juvenile, mental, expunged, dismissed, or suspended imposition of sentence records released. No copy fee. Certification fee: No certification fee. Fee payee: Stoddard County. Personal checks accepted. Prepayment is required.

Stone County

Circuit Court PO Box 18, Galena, MO 65656; 417-357-6114; 417-357-6115 child support; Fax: 417-357-6163. Hours: 7:30AM-4PM (CST). *Felony, Misdemeanor, Civil Actions Over $25,000.*

Civil Records: Access: Phone, fax, mail, in person. Both court and visitors may perform in person searches. No search fee. Required to search: name, years to search. Civil cases indexed by defendant, plaintiff. Civil records on cards and books, archived since 1852. **Criminal Records:** Access: Phone, fax, mail, in person. Both court and visitors may perform in person searches. No search fee. Required to search: name, years to search; also helpful-DOB, SSN. Criminal records on cards and books, archived since 1852. **General Information:** No juvenile, mental, expunged, dismissed, or suspended imposition of sentence records released. SASE required. Turnaround time 1 week. Copy fee: $.25 per page. Certification fee: $1.00. Fee payee: Circuit Court. Personal checks accepted. Fax notes: $3.00 per page.

Circuit Court-Division II & III PO Box 186, Galena, MO 65656; 417-357-6511; Fax: 417-357-

6163. Hours: 7:30AM-4PM (CST). *Misdemeanor, Civil Actions Under $25,000, Eviction, Small Claims, Probate.*

Civil Records: Access: Phone, fax, mail, in person. Both court and visitors may perform in person searches. No search fee. Required to search: name, years to search; also helpful-address. Civil cases indexed by defendant, plaintiff. Civil records on index cards since 1979, prior on log sheets. **Criminal Records:** Access: Phone, fax, mail, in person. Both court and visitors may perform in person searches. No search fee. Required to search: name, years to search, signed release; also helpful-address, DOB, SSN. Criminal records on computer and microfiche. **General Information:** No juvenile, mental, expunged, dismissed, or suspended imposition of sentence records released. SASE required. Turnaround time 2-3 weeks. Copy fee: $.25 per page. Certification fee: $2.50. Fee payee: Circuit Court Division II. Only cashiers checks and money orders accepted. Prepayment is required. Fax notes: $3.00 per page.

Sullivan County

Circuit Court Courthouse, Milan, MO 63556-1358; 660-265-4717; Fax: 660-265-5071. Hours: 9:00AM-4:30PM (CST). *Felony, Misdemeanor, Civil Actions Over $45,000.*

Civil Records: Access: In person only. Court does not conduct in person searches; visitors must perform searches for themselves. Search fee: No civil searches performed by court. Required to search: name, years to search. Civil cases indexed by defendant, plaintiff. Civil records on index cards since 1979, prior on books. **Criminal Records:** Access: In person only. Court does not conduct in person searches; visitors must perform searches for themselves. Search fee: No criminal searches performed by court. Required to search: name, years to search; also helpful-DOB, SSN. Criminal records on index cards since 1979, prior on books. **General Information:** No juvenile, mental, expunged, dismissed, or suspended imposition of sentence records released. Copy fee: $.25 per page. Certification fee: $1.50. Fee payee: Consolidated Circuit Court of Sullivan County. Personal checks accepted. Prepayment is required.

Associate Circuit Court Courthouse, Milan, MO 63556; 660-265-3303; Fax: 660-265-4711. Hours: 9AM-4:30PM (CST). *Misdemeanor, Civil Actions Under $45,000, Eviction, Small Claims, Probate.*

Civil Records: Access: In person only. Both court and visitors may perform in person searches. No search fee. Required to search: name, years to search. Civil cases indexed by defendant, plaintiff. Civil records on index cards and books. **Criminal Records:** Access: In person only. Both court and visitors may perform in person searches. No search fee. Required to search: name, years to search. Criminal records on computer since 5/93. **General Information:** No juvenile, mental, expunged, dismissed, or suspended imposition of sentence records released. Certification fee: $1.50. Fee payee: Associate Circuit Court. Personal checks accepted. Prepayment is required.

Taney County

Circuit Court PO Box 335, Forsyth, MO 65653; 417-546-7230; Fax: 417-546-6133. Hours: 8AM-5PM (CST). *Felony, Misdemeanor, Civil Actions Over $45,000.*

Civil Records: Access: Mail, in person. Both court and visitors may perform in person searches. Search fee: $4.00 per name. Required to search:

name, years to search. Civil cases indexed by defendant, plaintiff. Civil records on computer since 1/95, prior on index cards and books since 1885. **Criminal Records:** Access: Mail, in person. Both court and visitors may perform in person searches. Search fee: $4.00 per name. Required to search: name, years to search, DOB; also helpful-SSN. Criminal records on computer since 1/95, prior on index cards and books since 1885. **General Information:** No juvenile, mental, expunged, dismissed, or suspended imposition of sentence records released. SASE helpful. Copy fee: $.25 per page. Certification fee: $1.50. Fee payee: Circuit Clerk. Personal checks accepted. Prepayment is required. Public access terminal is available.

Associate Circuit Court PO Box 129, Forsyth, MO 65653; 417-546-7212; Fax: 417-546-4513. Hours: 8AM-5PM (CST). *Misdemeanor, Civil Actions Under $25,000, Eviction, Small Claims, Probate.*

Civil Records: Access: Mail, in person. Only the court conducts in person searches; visitors may not. Search fee: $4.00 per name. Required to search: name, years to search. Civil cases indexed by defendant, plaintiff. Civil records on computer since 1984, prior on cards and books. **Criminal Records:** Access: Mail, in person. Only the court conducts in person searches; visitors may not. Search fee: $4.00 per name. Required to search: name, years to search, DOB, SSN. Criminal records on computer since 1984, prior on cards and books. **General Information:** No juvenile, mental, expunged, dismissed, or suspended imposition of sentence records released. SASE required. Turnaround time 2 days. Copy fee: $.25 per page. Certification fee: $1.50. Fee payee: Associate Circuit Court. Personal checks accepted. Prepayment is required.

Texas County

Circuit Court 210 N Grand, Houston, MO 65483; 417-967-3742; Fax: 417-967-4220. Hours: 8AM-5PM (CST). *Felony, Misdemeanor, Civil Actions Over $45,000.*

Civil Records: Access: In person only. Both court and visitors may perform in person searches. No search fee. Required to search: name, years to search. Civil cases indexed by defendant, plaintiff. Civil records on index books since 1900s. **Criminal Records:** Access: In person only. Both court and visitors may perform in person searches. No search fee. Required to search: name, years to search. Criminal records on index books since 1900s. **General Information:** No juvenile, mental, expunged, dismissed, or suspended imposition of sentence records released. Copy fee: $1.00 per page. Certification fee: $2.00. Fee payee: Texas County Circuit Clerk. Personal checks accepted. Prepayment is required.

Associate Circuit Court County Courthouse, 210 N Grand, Rm 205, Houston, MO 65483; 417-967-3663; Fax: 417-967-4128. Hours: 8AM-5PM (CST). *Misdemeanor, Civil Actions Under $45,000, Eviction, Small Claims, Probate.*

Civil Records: Access: Phone, fax, mail, in person. Only the court conducts in person searches; visitors may not. No search fee. Required to search: name, years to search. Civil cases indexed by defendant, plaintiff. Civil records on index cards since 1979, prior on cards and books. **Criminal Records:** Access: Phone, fax, mail, in person. Only the court conducts in person searches; visitors may not. No search fee. Required to search: name, years to search.

Criminal records on index cards since 1979, prior on cards and books. **General Information:** No juvenile, mental, expunged, dismissed, or suspended imposition of sentence records released. SASE required. Turnaround time 7-10 days, phone turnaround time immediate. Copy fee: $1.00 per page. Certification fee: $1.50. Fee payee: Associate Circuit Court. Business checks accepted. Fax notes: $2.00 for first page, $.50 each addl.

Vernon County

Circuit Court Courthouse, 3rd Fl, Nevada, MO 64772; 417-448-2525; Fax: 417-448-2512. Hours: 8AM-4:30PM (CST). *Felony, Misdemeanor, Civil Actions Over $45,000.*

Civil Records: Access: Fax, mail, in person. Both court and visitors may perform in person searches. Search fee: $5.00 per name. Required to search: name, years to search. Civil cases indexed by defendant, plaintiff. Civil records on computer since 7/94, prior on index cards (judgments only). **Criminal Records:** Access: Fax, mail, in person. Both court and visitors may perform in person searches. Search fee: $5.00 per name. Required to search: name, years to search; also helpful-DOB, SSN. Criminal records on computer since 7/94, prior on index cards (judgments only). **General Information:** No juvenile, mental, expunged, dismissed, or suspended imposition of sentence records released. SASE required. Turnaround time varies. Copy fee: $.20 per page. Certification fee: $1.50. Fee payee: Vernon County Circuit Clerk. Personal checks accepted. Prepayment is required. Fax notes: $1.00 per page.

Associate Circuit Court County Courthouse, Nevada, MO 64772; 417-448-2550; Fax: 417-448-2512. Hours: 8:30AM-4:30PM (CST). *Misdemeanor, Civil Actions Under $25,000, Eviction, Small Claims, Probate.*

Civil Records: Access: Fax, mail, in person. Both court and visitors may perform in person searches. Search fee: $5.00 per name. Required to search: name, years to search. Civil cases indexed by defendant, plaintiff. Civil records on computer since 1990, on index cards since 1979, prior on index books. **Criminal Records:** Access: Mail, in person. Both court and visitors may perform in person searches. Search fee: $5.00 per name. Required to search: name, years to search; also helpful-DOB, SSN. Criminal records on computer since 1990, on index cards since 1979, prior on index books. **General Information:** No juvenile, mental, expunged, dismissed, or suspended imposition of sentence records released. SASE required. Turnaround time 1-2 weeks. Copy fee: $.20 per page. Certification fee: $1.50. Fee payee: Circuit Court. Personal checks accepted. Prepayment is required. Fax notes: $1.00 per page.

Warren County

Circuit Court 104 W Main, Warrenton, MO 63383; 636-456-3363; Fax: 636-456-2422. Hours: 8AM-4:30PM (CST). *Felony, Misdemeanor, Civil Actions Over $45,000.*

http://casenet.asca.state.mo.us/casenet

Civil Records: Access: online, in person. Court does not conduct in person searches; visitors must perform searches for themselves. Search fee: No civil searches performed by court. Required to search: name, years to search. Civil cases indexed by defendant, plaintiff. Civil records on index cards since 1976, prior on books. Free access at http://casenet.osca.state.mo.us/casenet. **Criminal Records:** Access: Remote online, in person. Court does not conduct in person searches; visitors must

perform searches for themselves. Search fee: No criminal searches performed by court. Required to search: name, years to search. Criminal records on index cards since 1976, prior on books. Free internet access if available, see civil records above. **General Information:** No juvenile, mental, expunged, dismissed, or suspended imposition of sentence records released. Copy fee: $.25 per page. Certification fee: $1.00. Fee payee: Warren County Circuit Clerk. Business checks accepted. Prepayment is required.

Associate Circuit Court Warren County Courthouse, 104 W Main, Warrenton, MO 63383; 636-456-3375; Fax: 636-456-2422. Hours: 8:30AM-4:30PM (CST). *Misdemeanor, Civil Actions Under $25,000, Eviction, Small Claims, Probate.*

http://casenet.asca.state.mo.us/casenet

Civil Records: Access: Phone, fax, mail, online, in person. Both court and visitors may perform in person searches. No search fee. Required to search: name, years to search. Civil cases indexed by defendant, plaintiff. Civil records on index cards since 1979, prior on books. Free access at http://casenet.osca.state.mo.us/casenet. **Criminal Records:** Access: Phone, fax, mail, remote online, in person. Only the court conducts in person searches; visitors may not. No search fee. Required to search: name, years to search; also helpful-DOB, SSN. Criminal records on computer since 2/92, on cards since 1979, prior on books. See civil for online access mode. **General Information:** No juvenile, mental, expunged, dismissed, or suspended imposition of sentence records released. SASE not requried. Turnaround time 1 week. Copy fee: $.25 per page. Certification fee: $1.50 plus $1.00 per page. Fee payee: Associate Circuit Clerk. Personal checks accepted. Prepayment is required. Fax notes: $1.00 per page.

Washington County

Circuit Court PO Box 216, Potosi, MO 63664; 573-438-4171; Fax: 573-438-7900. Hours: 8AM-5PM (CST). *Felony, Misdemeanor, Civil Actions Over $45,000.*

Civil Records: Access: Mail, in person. Both court and visitors may perform in person searches. No search fee. Required to search: name, years to search. Civil cases indexed by defendant, plaintiff. Civil records on index cards since 1976, prior on books. **Criminal Records:** Access: Mail, in person. Both court and visitors may perform in person searches. No search fee. Required to search: name, years to search. Criminal records on index cards since 1976, prior on books. **General Information:** No juvenile, mental, expunged, dismissed, or suspended imposition of sentence records released. SASE requried. Turnaround time 1-2 days. Copy fee: $.50 per page. Certification fee: $2.00. Fee payee: Washington County Circuit Clerk. Personal checks accepted. Prepayment is required.

Associate Circuit Court 102 N Missouri St, Potosi, MO 63664; 573-438-3691; Fax: 573-438-7900. Hours: 8AM-5PM (CST). *Misdemeanor, Civil Actions Under $45,000, Eviction, Small Claims, Probate.*

Civil Records: Access: Phone, fax, mail, in person. Both court and visitors may perform in person searches. No search fee. Required to search: name, years to search. Civil cases indexed by defendant, plaintiff. Civil records on index cards since 1976. **Criminal Records:** Access: Phone, fax, mail, in person. Both court and visitors may perform in person searches. No search fee. Required to search: name, years to search; also helpful-DOB, SSN. Criminal records on index cards since 1976. **General Information:** No juvenile, mental, expunged, dismissed, or suspended imposition of sentence records released. SASE required. Turnaround time 1 week. Copy fee: $.50 per page. Certification fee: No certification fee. Fee payee: Associate Circuit Clerk. Personal checks accepted. Prepayment is required.

Wayne County

Circuit Court PO Box 78, Greenville, MO 63944; 573-224-3014; Fax: 573-224-3015. Hours: 8:30AM-4:30PM (CST). *Felony, Misdemeanor, Civil Actions Over $45,000.*

Civil Records: Access: Mail, in person. Both court and visitors may perform in person searches. Search fee: $14.00 per name. Required to search: name, years to search. Civil cases indexed by defendant, plaintiff. Civil records on index cards since 1978, prior on books. **Criminal Records:** Access: Mail, in person. Both court and visitors may perform in person searches. Search fee: $14.00 per name. Required to search: name, years to search; also helpful-DOB. Criminal records on index cards since 1978, prior on books. **General Information:** No juvenile, mental, expunged, dismissed, or suspended imposition of sentence records released. SASE required. Turnaround time 1 week. Copy fee: $.25 per page. Certification fee: $1.00. Fee payee: Wayne County Circuit Clerk. Personal checks accepted. Prepayment is required.

Associate Circuit Court PO Box 47, Greenville, MO 63944; 573-224-3052; Fax: 573-224-3225. Hours: 8:30AM-4:30PM (CST). *Misdemeanor, Civil Actions Under $45,000, Eviction, Small Claims, Probate.*

Civil Records: Access: Phone, fax, mail, in person. Both court and visitors may perform in person searches. No search fee. Required to search: name, years to search. Civil cases indexed by defendant, plaintiff. Civil records on index cards since 1979. **Criminal Records:** Access: Phone, fax, mail, in person. Only the court conducts in person searches; visitors may not. No search fee. Required to search: name, years to search, DOB; also helpful-SSN. Criminal records on computer since 1992, prior on index cards. **General Information:** No juvenile, mental, expunged, dismissed, or suspended imposition of sentence records released. SASE required. Turnaround time 1 day. Copy fee: $.25 per page. Certification fee: $1.50 per page. Fee payee: Associate Circuit Court. Personal checks accepted. Fax notes: $.50 per page.

Webster County

Circuit Court PO Box 529, Marshfield, MO 65706; 417-859-2006; Fax: 417-468-3786. Hours: 8AM-5PM (CST). *Felony, Misdemeanor, Civil Actions Over $25,000.*

Civil Records: Access: Fax, mail, in person. Both court and visitors may perform in person searches. No search fee. Required to search: name, years to search. Civil cases indexed by defendant, plaintiff.

Civil records on computer since 1976 (judgment index). **Criminal Records:** Access: Fax, mail, in person. Only the court conducts in person searches; visitors may not. No search fee. Required to search: name, years to search, DOB. Criminal records on computer since 1976 (judgment index). **General Information:** No juvenile, mental, expunged, dismissed, or suspended imposition of sentence records released. SASE required. Turnaround time 1 day. Copy fee: $.15 per page. Certification fee: $2.00. Fee payee: Webster County Circuit Clerk. Personal checks accepted. Public access terminal is available. Public Access Terminal Note: Judgments only. Fax notes: $2.00 per page.

Associate Circuit Court Courthouse, Marshfield, MO 65706; 417-859-2041; Fax: 417-859-6265. Hours: 8AM-4:30PM (CST). *Misdemeanor, Civil Actions Under $45,000, Eviction, Small Claims, Probate.*

Civil Records: Access: Phone, fax, mail, in person. Only the court conducts in person searches; visitors may not. No search fee. Required to search: name, years to search. Civil cases indexed by defendant, plaintiff. Civil records on computer since 1992; prior records on index cards since 1980 & on books. **Criminal Records:** Access: Mail, in person. Only the court conducts in person searches; visitors may not. No search fee. Required to search: name, years to search; also helpful-DOB, SSN. Criminal records on computer since 1992. **General Information:** No juvenile, mental, expunged, dismissed, or suspended imposition of sentence records released. SASE required. Turnaround time varies. Copy fee: $1.00 per page. Certification fee: $1.50. Fee payee: Associate Circuit Court. Only cashiers checks and money orders accepted. Prepayment is required.

Worth County

Circuit Court PO Box 340, Grant City, MO 64456; 660-564-2210; Fax: 660-564-2432. Hours: 8:30AM-4:30PM (CST). *Felony, Misdemeanor, Civil Actions Over $45,000.*

Civil Records: Access: Mail, in person. Both court and visitors may perform in person searches. Search fee: $14.00 per name. Required to search: name, years to search. Civil cases indexed by defendant, plaintiff. Civil records on computer since 1990, prior on index cards. **Criminal Records:** Access: Mail, in person. Both court and visitors may perform in person searches. Search fee: $14.00 per name. Required to search: name, years to search. Criminal records on computer since 1990, prior on index cards. **General Information:** No juvenile, mental, expunged, dismissed, or suspended imposition of sentence records released. SASE required. Turnaround time same day. Copy fee: $.20 per page. Certification fee: $2.50. Fee payee: Worth County Circuit Clerk. Personal checks accepted. Prepayment is required.

Associate Circuit Court PO Box 428, Grant City, MO 64456; 660-564-2152; Fax: 660-564-2432. Hours: 9AM-4:30PM (CST). *Misdemeanor, Civil Actions Under $45,000, Eviction, Small Claims, Probate.*

Civil Records: Access: In person only. Court does not conduct in person searches; visitors must perform searches for themselves. Search fee: No civil searches performed by court. Required to search: name, years to search. Civil cases indexed by defendant, plaintiff. Civil records on index cards since 1979, prior on index books. **Criminal Records:** Access: Mail, in person. Both court and visitors may perform in person searches. No search fee. Required to search: name, years to search. Criminal records on index cards since 1979, prior on index books. **General Information:** No juvenile, mental, expunged, dismissed, or suspended imposition of sentence records released. SASE requried. Turnaround time varies. Copy fee: $1.00 per page. Certification fee: $2.50. Fee payee: Associate Circuit Court. Personal checks accepted. Prepayment is required.

Wright County

Circuit Court PO Box 39, Hartville, MO 65667; 417-741-7121; Fax: 417-741-7504. Hours: 8AM-4:30PM (CST). *Felony, Misdemeanor, Civil Actions Over $45,000.*

Civil Records: Access: Mail, in person. Both court and visitors may perform in person searches. No search fee. Required to search: name, years to search. Civil cases indexed by defendant, plaintiff. Civil records on index cards since 1979, prior on books. **Criminal Records:** Access: Mail, in person. Both court and visitors may perform in person searches. No search fee. Required to search: name, years to search. Criminal records on index cards since 1979, prior on books. **General Information:** No juvenile, mental, expunged, dismissed, or suspended imposition of sentence records released. SASE not required. Turnaround time 1 day. Copy fee: $.25 per page. Certification fee: $2.00. Fee payee: Wright County Circuit Clerk. Personal checks accepted. Prepayment is required.

Associate Circuit Court PO Box 58, Hartville, MO 65667; 417-741-6450; Fax: 417-741-7504. Hours: 8AM-4:30PM (CST). *Misdemeanor, Civil Actions Under $25,000, Eviction, Small Claims, Probate.*

Civil Records: Access: Phone, fax, mail, in person. Only the court conducts in person searches; visitors may not. No search fee. Required to search: name, years to search. Civil cases indexed by defendant, plaintiff. Civil records on index cards since 1979, prior on books. **Criminal Records:** Access: Phone, fax, mail, in person. Only the court conducts in person searches; visitors may not. No search fee. Required to search: name, years to search; also helpful-DOB, SSN. Criminal records on computer since 1989, prior on on cards and books. **General Information:** No juvenile, mental, expunged, or dismissed records released. SASE requried. Turnaround time 1 week. Copy fee: $.25 per page. Certification fee: $1.00. Fee payee: Associate Circuit Court. Only cashiers checks and money orders accepted. Fax notes: $1.00 per page.

ORGANIZATION 114 counties and **one independent city**, 115 recording offices. The recording officer is. Recorder of Deeds. The **City of St. Louis** has its own recording office. See the City/County Locator section at the end of this chapter for ZIP Codes that cover both the city and county of St. Louis. The entire state is in the Central Time Zone (CST).

REAL ESTATE RECORDS A few counties will perform real estate searches. Copy and certification fees vary.

UCC RECORDS This is a **dual filing state**. Financing statements are filed both at the state level and with the Recorder of Deeds, except for consumer goods, farm related and real estate related filings, which are filed only with the Recorder. All but one county will perform UCC searches. Use search request form UCC-11. Search fees are usually $14.00 per debtor name without copies and $28.00 with copies. Copies usually cost $.50 per page.

TAX LIEN RECORDS All federal and state tax liens are filed with the county Recorder of Deeds. They are usually indexed together. Some counties will perform tax lien searches. Search and copy fees vary widely.

OTHER LIENS Mechanics, judgment, child support.

Adair County
County Recorder of Deeds, Courthouse, 106 W. Washington St., Kirksville, MO 63501. 660-665-3890. Fax: 660-785-3212.

Andrew County
County Recorder of Deeds, P.O Box 208, Savannah, MO 64485. 816-324-4221. Fax: 816-324-5667.

Atchison County
County Recorder of Deeds, Box 280, Rock Port, MO 64482. 660-744-2707. Fax: 660-744-5705.

Audrain County
County Recorder of Deeds, Room 105, Audrain County Courthouse, 101 N. Jefferson, Mexico, MO 65265. 573-473-5830. Fax: 573-581-2380.

Barry County
County Recorder of Deeds, Courthouse, Cassville, MO 65625. 417-847-2914.

Barton County
County Recorder of Deeds, Courthouse, Room 107, 1004 Gulf, Lamar, MO 64759. 417-682-2110.

Bates County
County Recorder of Deeds, Box 186, Butler, MO 64730. 660-679-3611.

Benton County
County Recorder of Deeds, P.O. Box 37, Warsaw, MO 65355. 660-438-5732. Fax: 660-438-3652.

Bollinger County
County Recorder of Deeds, Box 949, Marble Hill, MO 63764. 573-238-2710. Fax: 573-238-2773.

Boone County
County Recorder of Deeds, Boone County Gov't Center, 801 E. Walnut, Rm 132, Columbia, MO 65201-7728. 573-886-4355. Fax: 573-886-4359.

Buchanan County
County Recorder of Deeds, 411 Jules Streets, Courthouse, St. Joseph, MO 64501-1789. 816-271-1437. Fax: 816-271-1582.

Butler County
County Recorder of Deeds, 100 N. Main Street, Courthouse, Poplar Bluff, MO 63901. 573-686-8086.

Caldwell County
County Recorder of Deeds, P.O. Box 86, Kingston, MO 64650. 816-586-3080. Fax: 816-586-2705.

Callaway County
County Recorder of Deeds, PO Box 406, Fulton, MO 65251. 573-642-0787.

Camden County
County Recorder of Deeds, P.O. Box 740, Camdenton, MO 65020. 573-346-4440. Fax: 573-346-5422.

Cape Girardeau County
County Recorder of Deeds, P.O. Box 248, Jackson, MO 63755. 573-243-8123. Fax: 573-243-8124.

Carroll County
County Recorder of Deeds, P.O. Box 245, Carrollton, MO 64633. 660-542-1466. Fax: 660-542-1444.

Carter County
County Recorder of Deeds, P.O. Box 578, Van Buren, MO 63965. 573-323-4513. Fax: 573-323-8577.

Cass County
County Recorder of Deeds, 102 East Wall Street, Cass County Court House, Harrisonville, MO 64701. 816-380-1510. Fax: 816-380-5136.
Online Access: Real Estate, Liens. Access to Cass County online records requires a $250 monthly fee plus $.10 per minute after 50 minutes usage. The system operates 24 hours daily. Records date back to 1990. Images are viewable and can be printed, $1.00 per image For information, contact John Kohler at 816-380-1510. A fax back service is available for $1.00 per page.

Cedar County
County Recorder of Deeds, P.O. Box 665, Stockton, MO 65785. 417-276-6700x246. Fax: 417-276-5001.

Chariton County
County Recorder of Deeds, P.O. Box 112, Keytesville, MO 65261. 660-288-3602. Fax: 660-288-3602.

Christian County
County Recorder of Deeds, P.O. Box 278, Ozark, MO 65721. 417-581-6372. Fax: 417-581-0391.

Clark County
County Recorder of Deeds, 111 East Court, Courthouse, Kahoka, MO 63445. 660-727-3292. Fax: 660-727-1051.

Clay County
County Recorder of Deeds, P.O. Box 238, Liberty, MO 64069. 816-792-7641.

Clinton County
County Recorder of Deeds, P.O. Box 275, Plattsburg, MO 64477. 816-539-3719. Fax: 816-539-3893.

Cole County
County Recorder of Deeds, P.O. Box 353, Jefferson City, MO 65102. 573-634-9115.

Cooper County
County Recorder of Deeds, 200 Main Street, Courthouse - Room 26, Boonville, MO 65233-1276. 660-882-2232. Fax: 660-882-2043.

Crawford County
County Recorder of Deeds, P.O. Box 177, Steelville, MO 65565. 573-775-5048. Fax: 573-775-3365.

Dade County
County Recorder of Deeds, Courthouse, Greenfield, MO 65661. 417-637-5373. Fax: 417-637-5055.

Dallas County
County Recorder of Deeds, P.O. Box 373, Buffalo, MO 65622. 417-345-2242. Fax: 417-345-5539.

Daviess County
County Recorder of Deeds, P.O. Box 337, Gallatin, MO 64640. 660-663-2932. Fax: 660-663-3376.

De Kalb County
County Recorder of Deeds, P.O. Box 248, Maysville, MO 64469-0248. 816-449-2602. Fax: 816-449-2440.

Dent County
County Recorder of Deeds, 112 East 5th Street, Salem, MO 65560-1444. 573-729-3931. Fax: 573-729-9414.

Douglas County
County Recorder of Deeds, P.O. Box 249, Ava, MO 65608. 417-683-4713. Fax: 417-683-3100.

Dunklin County
County Recorder of Deeds, P.O. Box 389, Kennett, MO 63857. 573-888-3468.

Franklin County
County Recorder of Deeds, P.O. Box 391, Union, MO 63084. 636-583-6367. Fax: 636-583-6367.

Gasconade County
County Recorder of Deeds, 119 E.1st St., Room 6, Hermann, MO 65041-1182. 573-486-2632. Fax: 573-486-3693.

Gentry County
County Recorder of Deeds, P.O. Box 27, Albany, MO 64402. 660-726-3618. Fax: 660-726-4102.

Greene County
County Recorder of Deeds, 940 Boonville, Room 100, Springfield, MO 65802. 417-868-4068. Fax: 417-868-4807.

Grundy County
County Recorder of Deeds, P.O. Box 196, Trenton, MO 64683. 660-359-5409.

Harrison County
County Recorder of Deeds, P.O. Box 189, Bethany, MO 64424. 660-425-6425. Fax: 660-425-3772.

Henry County
County Recorder of Deeds, 100 W. Franklin #4, Courthouse, Clinton, MO 64735. 660-885-6963. Fax: 660-885-2264.

Hickory County
County Recorder of Deeds, P.O. Box 101, Hermitage, MO 65668. 417-745-6421. Fax: 417-745-6670.

Holt County
County Recorder of Deeds, P.O. Box 318, Oregon, MO 64473. 660-446-3301.

Howard County
County Recorder of Deeds, 1 Courthouse Square, Fayette, MO 65248. 660-248-2194. Fax: 660-248-1075.

Howell County
County Recorder of Deeds, P.O. Box 1011, West Plains, MO 65775. 417-256-3750.

Iron County
County Recorder of Deeds, P.O. Box 24, Ironton, MO 63650. 573-546-2811. Fax: 573-546-2166.

Jackson County (Kansas City)
County Recorder of Deeds, 415 East 12th Street, Room 104, Kansas City, MO 64106. 816-881-3192. Fax: 816-881-3719.
Online Access: Property. Property owner records on the Kansas City Neighborhood Network are available free on the Internet at www.kcmo-net.org/cgi-bin/db2www/realform.d2w/report.

Jasper County
County Recorder of Deeds, P.O. Box 387, Carthage, MO 64836-0387. 417-358-0432.

Jefferson County
County Recorder of Deeds, P.O. Box 100, Hillsboro, MO 63050. 636-797-5414.

Johnson County
County Recorder of Deeds, P.O. Box 32, Warrensburg, MO 64093. 660-747-6811.

Knox County
County Recorder of Deeds, P.O. Box 116, Edina, MO 63537. 660-397-2305. Fax: 660-397-3331.

Laclede County
County Recorder of Deeds, Main Courthouse, 200 North Adams, Lebanon, MO 65536-3046. 417-532-4011. Fax: 417-532-3852.

Lafayette County
County Recorder of Deeds, P.O. Box 416, Lexington, MO 64067. 660-259-6178. Fax: 660-259-2918.

Lawrence County
County Recorder of Deeds, P.O. Box 449, Mount Vernon, MO 65712. 417-466-2670. Fax: 417-466-4995.

Lewis County
County Recorder of Deeds, P.O. Box 97, Monticello, MO 63457-0097. 573-767-5440. Fax: 573-767-5378.

Lincoln County
County Recorder of Deeds, 201 Main Street, Troy, MO 63379. 636-528-6300. Fax: 636-528-2665.

Linn County
County Recorder of Deeds, P.O. Box 151, Linneus, MO 64653. 660-895-5216. Fax: 660-895-5533.

Livingston County
County Recorder of Deeds, Courthouse, Suite 6, 700 Webster St., Chillicothe, MO 64601. 660-646-0166.

Macon County
County Recorder of Deeds, P.O. Box 382, Macon, MO 63552. 660-385-2732. Fax: 660-385-4235.

Madison County
County Recorder of Deeds, P.O. Box 470, Fredericktown, MO 63645-0470. 573-783-2102. Fax: 573-783-2715.

Maries County
County Recorder of Deeds, P.O. Box 213, Vienna, MO 65582. 573-422-3338. Fax: 573-422-3269.

Marion County
County Recorder of Deeds, P.O. Box 392, Palmyra, MO 63461. 573-769-2550. Fax: 573-769-6012.

McDonald County
County Recorder of Deeds, P.O. Box 157, Pineville, MO 64856. 417-223-7523. Fax: 417-223-4125.

Mercer County
County Recorder of Deeds, Courthouse, Princeton, MO 64673. 660-748-4335. Fax: 660-748-3180.

Miller County
County Recorder of Deeds, P.O. Box 11, Tuscumbia, MO 65082. 573-369-2911. Fax: 573-369-2910.

Mississippi County
County Recorder of Deeds, 313 E. Main, East Prairie, MO 63845. 573-683-2146. Fax: 573-649-2284.
Online Access: Tax Assessor Records. Fee based service provides Mississippi County Tax record information. User ID and password required. Direct questions via email to: question@jdirs.com.

Moniteau County
County Recorder of Deeds, 200 East Main Street, California, MO 65018. 573-796-2071. Fax: 573-796-2591.

Monroe County
County Recorder of Deeds, P.O. Box 227, Paris, MO 65275. 660-327-5204. Fax: 660-327-5781.

Montgomery County
County Recorder of Deeds, 211 East 3rd Street, Montgomery City, MO 63361. 573-564-3157. Fax: 573-564-3914.

Morgan County
County Recorder of Deeds, 100 Newton Street, Courthouse, Versailles, MO 65084. 573-378-4029. Fax: 573-378-6431.

New Madrid County
County Recorder of Deeds, P.O. Box 217, New Madrid, MO 63869. 573-748-5146.

Newton County
County Recorder of Deeds, P.O. Box 130, Neosho, MO 64850-0130. 417-451-8224. Fax: 417-451-8273.

Nodaway County
County Recorder of Deeds, 305 N. Main, Room 104, Maryville, MO 64468. 660-582-5711. Fax: 660-582-5282.

Oregon County
County Recorder of Deeds, P.O. Box 406, Alton, MO 65606. 417-778-7460. Fax: 417-778-7206.

Osage County
County Recorder of Deeds, P.O. Box 825, Linn, MO 65051-0825. 573-897-3114.

Ozark County
County Recorder of Deeds, P.O. Box 36, Gainesville, MO 65655. 417-679-4232. Fax: 417-679-4554.

Pemiscot County
County Recorder of Deeds, Courthouse, 610 Ward Ave., Caruthersville, MO 63830. 573-333-2204.

Perry County
County Recorder of Deeds, 15 West Ste. Marie Street, Suite 1, Perryville, MO 63775. 573-547-1611. Fax: 573-547-2637.

Pettis County
County Recorder of Deeds, 415 South Ohio, Sedalia, MO 65301. 660-826-1136. Fax: 660-827-8637.

Phelps County
County Recorder of Deeds, Courthouse, 200 N. Main, Rolla, MO 65401. 573-364-1891. Fax: 573-364-1419.

Pike County
County Recorder of Deeds, 115 West Main Street, Bowling Green, MO 63334. 573-324-5567.

Platte County
County Recorder of Deeds, 415 3rd St., Suite 70, Platte City, MO 64079. 816-858-3323. Fax: 816-858-2379.

Polk County
County Recorder of Deeds, 102 E. Broadway, Courthouse, Bolivar, MO 65613-1502. 417-326-4924. Fax: 417-326-4194.

Pulaski County
County Recorder of Deeds, 301 Historic Route 66, Courthouse Suite 202, Waynesville, MO 65583. 573-774-4760. Fax: 573-774-6967.

Putnam County
County Recorder of Deeds, Courthouse, Room 202, Unionville, MO 63565-1659. 660-947-2071. Fax: 660-947-2320.

Ralls County
County Recorder of Deeds, P.O. Box 444, New London, MO 63459-0444. 573-985-5631.

Randolph County
County Recorder of Deeds, 110 S. Main St., Courthouse, Huntsville, MO 65259. 660-277-4718. Fax: 660-277-3246.

Ray County
County Recorder of Deeds, P.O. Box 167, Richmond, MO 64085. 660-776-4500.

Reynolds County
County Recorder of Deeds, P.O. Box 76, Centerville, MO 63633-0076. 573-648-2494. Fax: 573-648-2296.

Ripley County
County Recorder of Deeds, 100 Courthouse Square, Suite 3, Doniphan, MO 63935. 573-996-2818. Fax: 573-966-5014.

Saline County
County Recorder of Deeds, Courthouse, Room 206, Marshall, MO 65340. 660-886-2677. Fax: 660-886-2603.

Schuyler County
County Recorder of Deeds, P.O. Box 186, Lancaster, MO 63548. 660-457-3784. Fax: 660-457-3016.

Scotland County
County Recorder of Deeds, 117 South Market St., Ste 106, Memphis, MO 63555-1449. 660-465-8605. Fax: 660-465-8673.

Scott County
County Recorder of Deeds, P.O. Box 78, Benton, MO 63736. 573-545-3551.

Shannon County
County Recorder of Deeds, P.O. Box 148, Eminence, MO 65466. 573-226-3315. Fax: 573-226-5321.

Shelby County
County Recorder of Deeds, P.O. Box 176, Shelbyville, MO 63469. 573-633-2151. Fax: 573-633-1004.

St. Charles County
County Recorder of Deeds, P.O. Box 99, St. Charles, MO 63302-0099. 636-949-7508. Fax: 636-949-7512. www.win.org/library
Online Access: Assessor. Records on the St. Charles County Property Assessment database are available free on the Web at www.win.org/library/library_office/assessment.

St. Clair County
County Circuit Clerk, P.O. Box 493, Osceola, MO 64776-0493. 417-646-2226. Fax: 417-646-2401.

St. Francois County
County Recorder of Deeds, Courthouse, Farmington, MO 63640. 573-756-2323.

St. Louis City
City Recorder, Tucker & Market Streets, City Hall Room 127, St. Louis, MO 63103. 314-622-4328. Fax: 314-622-4175.

St. Louis County
County Recorder of Deeds, 41 S. Central Ave., 4th Floor, Clayton, MO 63105. 314-889-2185.

Ste. Genevieve County
County Recorder of Deeds, 3rd Street, Court House, Ste. Genevieve, MO 63670. 573-883-2706. Fax: 573-883-5312.

Stoddard County
County Recorder of Deeds, P.O. Box 217, Bloomfield, MO 63825-0217. 573-568-3444. Fax: 573-568-2545.

Stone County
County Recorder of Deeds, P.O. Box 18, Galena, MO 65656. 417-357-6362. Fax: 417-357-8131.

Sullivan County
County Recorder of Deeds, Courthouse, Milan, MO 63556. 660-265-3630. Fax: 660-265-5071.

Taney County
County Recorder of Deeds, P.O. Box 335, Forsyth, MO 65653. 417-546-6132.

Texas County
County Recorder of Deeds, 210 North Grand, P.O. Box 237, Houston, MO 65483. 417-967-3742. Fax: 417-967-4220.

Vernon County
County Recorder of Deeds, Courthouse, Nevada, MO 64772. 417-448-2520.

Warren County
County Recorder of Deeds, 104 West Boone's Lick Rd., Warrenton, MO 63383. 636-456-9800.

Washington County
County Recorder of Deeds, P.O. Box 216, Potosi, MO 63664-0216. 573-438-5023. Fax: 573-438-7900.

Wayne County
County Recorder of Deeds, P.O. Box 187A, Greenville, MO 63944. 573-224-3221. Fax: 573-224-3225.

Webster County
County Recorder of Deeds, P.O. Box 529, Marshfield, MO 65706. 417-468-2173. Fax: 417-468-3786.

Worth County
County Recorder of Deeds, Box 340, Grant City, MO 64456. 660-564-2210. Fax: 660-564-2432.

Wright County
County Recorder of Deeds, P.O. Box 39, Hartville, MO 65667. 417-741-7322. Fax: 417-741-7504.

You will usually be able to find the city name in the City/County Cross Reference below. In that case, it is a simple matter to determine the county from the cross reference. However, only the official US Postal Service city names are included in this index. There are an additional 40,000 place names that people use in their addresses. Therefore, we have also included a ZIP/City Cross Reference immediately following the City/County Cross Reference.

If you know the ZIP Code but the city name does not appear in the City/County Cross Reference index, look up the ZIP Code in the ZIP/City Cross Reference, find the city name, then look up the city name in the City/County Cross Reference. For example, you want to know the county for an address of Menands, NY 12204. There is no "Menands" in the City/County Cross Reference. The ZIP/City Cross Reference shows that ZIP Codes 12201-12288 are for the city of Albany. Looking back in the City/County Cross Reference, Albany is in Albany County.

City/County Cross Reference

ADRIAN (64720) Bates(99), Cass(1)
ADVANCE (63730) Stoddard(79), Cape Girardeau(16), Bollinger(4)
AGENCY Buchanan
ALBA Jasper
ALBANY Gentry
ALDRICH (65601) Polk(82), Dade(17)
ALEXANDRIA Clark
ALLENDALE Worth
ALLENTON St. Louis
ALMA Lafayette
ALTAMONT Daviess
ALTENBURG (63732) Cape Girardeau(82), Perry(18)
ALTON Oregon
AMAZONIA Andrew
AMITY De Kalb
AMORET Bates
AMSTERDAM Bates
ANABEL Macon
ANDERSON McDonald
ANNADA Pike
ANNAPOLIS (63620) Iron(60), Madison(33), Reynolds(8)
ANNISTON Mississippi
APPLETON CITY (64724) St. Clair(92), Bates(8)
ARBELA (63432) Scotland(88), Clark(12)
ARBYRD Dunklin
ARCADIA (63621) Iron(69), Madison(31)
ARCHIE (64725) Cass(94), Bates(6)
ARCOLA (65603) Dade(97), Cedar(3)
ARGYLE (65001) Maries(70), Osage(30)
ARMSTRONG (65230) Howard(97), Randolph(3)
ARNOLD Jefferson
ARROW ROCK Saline
ASBURY (64832) Barton(61), Jasper(39)
ASH GROVE (65604) Greene(61), Lawrence(38), Dade(2)
ASHBURN Pike
ASHLAND Boone
ATLANTA Macon
AUGUSTA St. Charles
AURORA (65605) Lawrence(91), Barry(9)
AUXVASSE Callaway
AVA (65608) Douglas(90), Taney(10)
AVALON Livingston
AVILLA Jasper
BAKERSFIELD (65609) Ozark(76), Howell(24)
BALLWIN St. Louis
BARING (63531) Knox(60), Scotland(40)
BARNARD (64423) Nodaway(99), Andrew(1)
BARNETT (65011) Morgan(93), Moniteau(7)
BARNHART Jefferson
BATES CITY (64011) Lafayette(51), Cass(41), Johnson(8)
BEAUFORT Franklin
BELGRADE Washington

BELL CITY (63735) Stoddard(94), Scott(6)
BELLE (65013) Maries(67), Osage(33)
BELLEVIEW (63623) Iron(97), Reynolds(3)
BELLFLOWER (63333) Montgomery(97), Lincoln(3)
BELTON Cass
BENDAVIS Texas
BENTON Scott
BENTON CITY Audrain
BERGER Franklin
BERNIE (63822) Stoddard(98), Dunklin(2)
BERTRAND (63823) Mississippi(95), Scott(5)
BETHANY Harrison
BETHEL Shelby
BEULAH (65436) Phelps(87), Texas(9), Pulaski(3)
BEVIER Macon
BILLINGS (65610) Christian(90), Stone(5), Greene(4), Lawrence(2)
BIRCH TREE (65438) Shannon(81), Oregon(19)
BISMARCK (63624) St. Francois(90), Washington(6), Iron(3)
BIXBY Iron
BLACK (63625) Reynolds(88), Iron(12)
BLACKBURN (65321) Saline(88), Lafayette(12)
BLACKWATER Cooper
BLACKWELL (63626) St. Francois(69), Washington(31)
BLAIRSTOWN Henry
BLAND (65014) Gasconade(85), Osage(12), Maries(3)
BLODGETT Scott
BLOOMFIELD Stoddard
BLOOMSDALE (63627) Ste. Genevieve(89), Jefferson(11)
BLUE EYE (65611) Stone(87), Taney(13)
BLUE SPRINGS Jackson
BLYTHEDALE Harrison
BOGARD Carroll
BOIS D ARC (65612) Greene(91), Lawrence(9)
BOLCKOW (64427) Andrew(94), Nodaway(6)
BOLIVAR Polk
BONNE TERRE (63628) St. Francois(96), Ste. Genevieve(2), Washington(1)
BONNOTS MILL Osage
BOONVILLE Cooper
BOSS (65440) Dent(57), Reynolds(33), Iron(10)
BOSWORTH Carroll
BOURBON (99999) Crawford(98), Washington(1)
BOWLING GREEN (63334) Pike(98), Lincoln(2)
BRADLEYVILLE (65614) Taney(92), Christian(8)
BRAGG CITY Pemiscot
BRAGGADOCIO Pemiscot

BRANDSVILLE Howell
BRANSON (65616) Taney(97), Stone(3)
BRANSON Taney
BRASHEAR (63533) Adair(98), Knox(2)
BRAYMER (64624) Caldwell(83), Ray(12), Carroll(4)
BRAZEAU Perry
BRECKENRIDGE (64625) Caldwell(84), Daviess(10), Livingston(6)
BRIAR Ripley
BRIDGETON St. Louis
BRIGHTON Polk
BRINKTOWN Maries
BRIXEY Ozark
BRONAUGH (64728) Vernon(72), Barton(28)
BROOKFIELD (64628) Linn(98), Chariton(2)
BROOKLINE STATION (65619) Greene(96), Christian(4)
BROSELEY Butler
BROWNING (64630) Linn(84), Sullivan(16)
BROWNWOOD Stoddard
BRUMLEY Miller
BRUNER (65620) Christian(98), Douglas(2)
BRUNSWICK Chariton
BUCKLIN (64631) Linn(84), Macon(16)
BUCKNER Jackson
BUCYRUS Texas
BUFFALO (65622) Dallas(97), Polk(3)
BUNCETON Cooper
BUNKER (63629) Reynolds(65), Dent(26), Shannon(9)
BURFORDVILLE Cape Girardeau
BURLINGTON JUNCTION (64428) Nodaway(95), Atchison(5)
BUTLER Bates
BUTTERFIELD Barry
CABOOL (65689) Howell(57), Texas(40), Douglas(3)
CADET Washington
CAINSVILLE (64632) Harrison(76), Mercer(24)
CAIRO Randolph
CALEDONIA Washington
CALHOUN Henry
CALIFORNIA (65018) Moniteau(95), Cooper(5)
CALLAO Macon
CAMDEN (64017) Ray(92), Lafayette(8)
CAMDEN POINT Platte
CAMDENTON Camden
CAMERON (64429) Clinton(69), De Kalb(26), Caldwell(3), Daviess(2)
CAMPBELL Dunklin
CANALOU New Madrid
CANTON (63435) Lewis(93), Clark(7)
CAPE FAIR Stone
CAPE GIRARDEAU Cape Girardeau
CAPLINGER MILLS Cedar
CARDWELL Dunklin
CARL JUNCTION Jasper

CARROLLTON Carroll
CARTERVILLE Jasper
CARTHAGE Jasper
CARUTHERSVILLE Pemiscot
CASCADE Wayne
CASSVILLE Barry
CATAWISSA (63015) Franklin(80), Jefferson(20)
CATRON (63833) New Madrid(67), Stoddard(33)
CAULFIELD (65626) Howell(72), Ozark(28)
CEDAR CITY Callaway
CEDAR HILL Jefferson
CEDARCREEK Taney
CENSUS BUREAU Boone
CENTER Ralls
CENTERTOWN (65023) Cole(89), Moniteau(11)
CENTERVIEW Johnson
CENTERVILLE Reynolds
CENTRALIA (65240) Boone(78), Audrain(20), Callaway(1)
CHADWICK (65629) Christian(98), Taney(2)
CHAFFEE (63740) Scott(95), Cape Girardeau(6)
CHAMOIS Osage
CHARLESTON (63834) Mississippi(95), Scott(5)
CHERRYVILLE Crawford
CHESTERFIELD St. Louis
CHESTNUTRIDGE Christian
CHILHOWEE (64733) Johnson(71), Henry(27), Jackson(3)
CHILLICOTHE Livingston
CHULA (64635) Livingston(61), Linn(29), Grundy(10)
CLARENCE (63437) Shelby(91), Macon(7), Monroe(2)
CLARK (65243) Boone(43), Audrain(31), Randolph(16), Howard(9), Monroe(2)
CLARKSBURG (65025) Cooper(50), Moniteau(50)
CLARKSDALE (64430) De Kalb(96), Andrew(4)
CLARKSVILLE Pike
CLARKTON (63837) Dunklin(98), New Madrid(2)
CLEARMONT (64431) Nodaway(99), Daviess(1)
CLEVELAND Cass
CLEVER Christian
CLIFTON HILL (65244) Randolph(96), Chariton(4)
CLIMAX SPRINGS (65324) Camden(98), Benton(2)
CLINTON (64735) Henry(99), Benton(1)
CLUBB Wayne
CLYDE Nodaway
COATSVILLE (63535) Schuyler(54), Putnam(22), Cole(14), Audrain(11)

COFFEY (64636) Daviess(89), Harrison(11)
COLE CAMP (65325) Benton(95), Pettis(4), Morgan(2)
COLLINS St. Clair
COLUMBIA (65202) Boone(98), Callaway(2)
COLUMBIA Boone
COMMERCE Scott
CONCEPTION Nodaway
CONCEPTION JUNCTION Nodaway
CONCORDIA (64020) Lafayette(89), Johnson(9), Saline(1)
CONRAN New Madrid
CONTEL CORPORATION St. Charles
CONWAY (65632) Laclede(72), Webster(14), Dallas(14)
COOK STATION (65449) Crawford(97), Phelps(3)
COOTER Pemiscot
CORDER Lafayette
CORNING Holt
COSBY Andrew
COTTLEVILLE St. Charles
COUCH Oregon
COWGILL (64637) Caldwell(86), Ray(14)
CRAIG Holt
CRANE (65633) Stone(88), Barry(12)
CREIGHTON (64739) Henry(78), Cass(22)
CROCKER (65452) Pulaski(97), Miller(3)
CROSS TIMBERS (65634) Hickory(94), Benton(5), Camden(2)
CRYSTAL CITY Jefferson
CUBA (65453) Crawford(99), Gasconade(1)
CURRYVILLE Pike
DADEVILLE Dade
DAISY Cape Girardeau
DALTON Chariton
DARLINGTON Gentry
DAVISVILLE Crawford
DAWN (64638) Livingston(71), Carroll(29)
DE KALB (64440) Howell(72), Buchanan(27), Platte(1)
DE SOTO Jefferson
DE WITT Carroll
DEARBORN Platte
DEEPWATER (64740) Henry(86), St. Clair(14)
DEERFIELD Vernon
DEERING Pemiscot
DEFIANCE St. Charles
DELTA Cape Girardeau
DENVER (64441) Worth(65), Gentry(35)
DES ARC (63636) Iron(68), Madison(26), Wayne(6)
DEVILS ELBOW (65457) Pulaski(90), Phelps(11)
DEXTER Stoddard
DIAMOND (64840) Newton(98), Jasper(3)
DIGGINS Webster
DITTMER Jefferson
DIXON (65459) Pulaski(83), Maries(10), Miller(5), Phelps(2)
DOE RUN St. Francois
DONIPHAN (63935) Ripley(98), Carter(1)
DORA (65637) Ozark(63), Howell(25), Douglas(12)
DOVER Lafayette
DOWNING (63536) Schuyler(67), Scotland(34)
DREXEL (64742) Cass(78), Bates(22)
DRURY (65638) Douglas(90), Ozark(11)
DUDLEY Stoddard
DUENWEG Jasper
DUKE (65461) Phelps(94), Pulaski(6)
DUNNEGAN (65640) Polk(90), Cedar(10)
DURHAM (63438) Marion(65), Lewis(35)
DUTCHTOWN Cape Girardeau
DUTZOW Warren
EAGLE ROCK Barry
EAGLEVILLE Harrison

EARTH CITY St. Louis
EAST LYNNE Cass
EAST PRAIRIE Mississippi
EASTON Buchanan
EDGAR SPRINGS (65462) Phelps(97), Dent(3)
EDGERTON (64444) Platte(93), Buchanan(7)
EDINA Knox
EDWARDS (65326) Benton(63), Camden(36), Hickory(1)
EL DORADO SPRINGS (64744) Cedar(86), Vernon(8), St. Clair(6)
ELDON (65026) Miller(96), Morgan(4)
ELDRIDGE (65463) Laclede(99), Dallas(1)
ELK CREEK Texas
ELKLAND (65644) Webster(51), Dallas(49)
ELLINGTON (63638) Reynolds(93), Shannon(5), Carter(2)
ELLSINORE (63937) Carter(83), Butler(16)
ELMER Macon
ELMO Nodaway
ELSBERRY (63343) Lincoln(97), Pike(4)
EMDEN (63439) Marion(52), Shelby(48)
EMINENCE Shannon
EMMA Lafayette
EOLIA (63344) Pike(60), Lincoln(40)
ESSEX Stoddard
ETHEL Macon
ETTERVILLE Miller
EUDORA Polk
EUGENE (65032) Cole(89), Miller(11)
EUNICE Texas
EUREKA (63025) St. Louis(67), Jefferson(33)
EVERTON (65646) Dade(62), Lawrence(38)
EWING (63440) Marion(51), Lewis(47), Shelby(2)
EXCELLO Macon
EXCELSIOR SPRINGS (64024) Clay(77), Ray(23)
EXETER (65647) Barry(78), Newton(20), McDonald(2)
FAGUS Butler
FAIR GROVE (65648) Greene(88), Dallas(8), Webster(2), Polk(2)
FAIR PLAY (65649) Polk(82), Cedar(18)
FAIRDEALING Ripley
FAIRFAX (64446) Atchison(90), Holt(10)
FAIRPORT De Kalb
FAIRVIEW (64842) Newton(98), Barry(2)
FALCON (65470) Wright(71), Laclede(29)
FARBER Audrain
FARLEY Platte
FARMINGTON (63640) St. Francois(97), Ste. Genevieve(3)
FARRAR Perry
FAUCETT Buchanan
FAYETTE Howard
FENTON (63026) St. Louis(52), Jefferson(49)
FENTON St. Louis
FESTUS (63028) Jefferson(94), Ste. Genevieve(6)
FILLMORE Andrew
FISK Butler
FLEMINGTON (65650) Polk(69), Hickory(31)
FLETCHER (63030) Jefferson(82), Washington(19)
FLINTHILL St. Charles
FLORENCE Morgan
FLORISSANT St. Louis
FOLEY Lincoln
FORDLAND (65652) Webster(82), Christian(14), Douglas(5)
FOREST CITY Holt
FORISTELL (63348) St. Charles(64), Warren(33), Lincoln(3)
FORSYTH (65653) Taney(98), Christian(2)
FORT LEONARD WOOD Pulaski

FORTESCUE Holt
FORTUNA (65034) Morgan(55), Moniteau(45)
FOSTER Bates
FRANKFORD (63441) Pike(98), Ralls(2)
FRANKLIN Howard
FREDERICKTOWN (63645) Madison(97), St. Francois(2), Ste. Genevieve(1)
FREEBURG Osage
FREEMAN Cass
FREISTATT Lawrence
FREMONT (63941) Carter(68), Oregon(24), Ripley(8)
FRENCH VILLAGE (63036) St. Francois(74), Ste. Genevieve(26)
FRIEDHEIM Cape Girardeau
FROHNA Perry
FULTON Callaway
GAINESVILLE Ozark
GALENA (65656) Stone(95), Barry(4), Christian(1)
GALLATIN Daviess
GALT (64641) Grundy(92), Sullivan(8)
GARDEN CITY Cass
GARRISON (65657) Christian(98), Taney(2)
GASCONADE Gasconade
GATEWOOD (63942) Ripley(80), Oregon(20)
GENTRY Gentry
GERALD Franklin
GIBBS Adair
GIBSON Dunklin
GIDEON (63848) New Madrid(65), Pemiscot(35)
GILLIAM Saline
GILMAN CITY (64642) Harrison(85), Grundy(8), Daviess(7)
GIPSY Bollinger
GLASGOW (65254) Howard(96), Chariton(4)
GLENALLEN Bollinger
GLENCOE St. Louis
GLENWOOD Schuyler
GLOVER Iron
GOBLER (63849) Pemiscot(65), Dunklin(35)
GOLDEN Barry
GOLDEN CITY (64748) Barton(54), Jasper(27), Dade(16), Lawrence(3)
GOODMAN (64843) McDonald(66), Newton(34)
GOODSON Polk
GORDONVILLE Cape Girardeau
GORIN (63543) Scotland(96), Knox(3), Clark(1)
GOWER (64454) Clinton(51), Buchanan(49)
GRAFF (65660) Wright(95), Texas(5)
GRAHAM (64455) Nodaway(89), Andrew(11)
GRAIN VALLEY Jackson
GRANBY Newton
GRANDIN (63943) Carter(81), Ripley(19)
GRANDVIEW Jackson
GRANGER Scotland
GRANT CITY (64456) Worth(98), Harrison(2)
GRASSY Bollinger
GRAVOIS MILLS (65037) Morgan(93), Camden(7)
GRAY SUMMIT Franklin
GRAYRIDGE Stoddard
GREEN CASTLE (63544) Sullivan(50), Adair(43), Putnam(7)
GREEN CITY Sullivan
GREEN RIDGE Pettis
GREENFIELD Dade
GREENTOP (63546) Adair(64), Schuyler(34), Scotland(3)
GREENVILLE Wayne

GREENWOOD (64034) Jackson(91), Cass(9)
GROVER St. Louis
GROVESPRING (65662) Wright(79), Laclede(20)
GRUBVILLE (63041) Franklin(76), Jefferson(24)
GUILFORD (64457) Nodaway(90), Andrew(10)
HALE (64643) Carroll(63), Livingston(37)
HALF WAY Polk
HALLSVILLE Boone
HALLTOWN Lawrence
HAMILTON (64644) Caldwell(97), Daviess(3)
HANNIBAL (63401) Marion(93), Ralls(7)
HARDENVILLE Ozark
HARDIN (64035) Ray(99), Carroll(1)
HARRIS (64645) Sullivan(73), Mercer(28)
HARRISBURG (65256) Boone(82), Howard(18)
HARRISONVILLE Cass
HARTSBURG (65039) Boone(86), Callaway(14)
HARTSHORN (65479) Texas(69), Shannon(31)
HARTVILLE Wright
HARVIELL (63945) Butler(92), Ripley(8)
HARWOOD (64750) Vernon(97), St. Clair(3)
HATFIELD (64458) Harrison(96), Worth(4)
HAWK POINT (63349) Lincoln(98), Warren(2)
HAYTI Pemiscot
HAZELWOOD St. Louis
HELENA Andrew
HEMATITE Jefferson
HENLEY (65040) Cole(97), Miller(3)
HENRIETTA Ray
HERCULANEUM Jefferson
HERMANN (65041) Gasconade(84), Montgomery(14), Warren(1)
HERMANN Montgomery
HERMITAGE Hickory
HIGBEE (65257) Randolph(60), Howard(41)
HIGGINSVILLE Lafayette
HIGH HILL Montgomery
HIGH POINT Moniteau
HIGH RIDGE (63049) Jefferson(98), St. Louis(2)
HIGHLANDVILLE (65669) Christian(94), Stone(6)
HILLSBORO Jefferson
HIRAM Wayne
HOLCOMB (63852) Dunklin(97), Pemiscot(3)
HOLDEN Johnson
HOLLAND (63853) Pemiscot(93), Dunklin(7)
HOLLIDAY Monroe
HOLLISTER Taney
HOLT (64048) Clay(92), Clinton(8)
HOLTS SUMMIT Callaway
HOPKINS Nodaway
HORNERSVILLE Dunklin
HORTON Vernon
HOUSE SPRINGS Jefferson
HOUSTON Texas
HOUSTONIA (65333) Pettis(98), Saline(2)
HUGGINS Texas
HUGHESVILLE Pettis
HUMANSVILLE (65674) Polk(73), Cedar(20), Hickory(4), St. Clair(3)
HUME (64752) Bates(73), Vernon(27)
HUMPHREYS (64646) Sullivan(77), Linn(23)
HUNNEWELL (63443) Marion(50), Shelby(32), Monroe(19)
HUNTSVILLE Randolph
HURDLAND (63547) Knox(90), Adair(10)
HURLEY Stone

WARDELL (63879) Pemiscot(96), New Madrid(4)
WARRENSBURG Johnson
WARRENTON (63383) Warren(98), Lincoln(2)
WARSAW (65355) Benton(99), Hickory(1)
WASHBURN (65772) Barry(86), McDonald(14)
WASHINGTON Franklin
WASOLA (65773) Ozark(99), Douglas(1)
WATSON Atchison
WAVERLY (64096) Lafayette(98), Saline(2)
WAYLAND Clark
WAYNESVILLE Pulaski
WEATHERBY (64497) De Kalb(82), Daviess(18)
WEAUBLEAU (65774) Hickory(87), St. Clair(14)

WEBB CITY Jasper
WELLINGTON Lafayette
WELLSVILLE (63384) Montgomery(89), Audrain(9), Callaway(2)
WENTWORTH (64873) Lawrence(80), Newton(20)
WENTZVILLE St. Charles
WESCO Crawford
WEST ALTON St. Charles
WEST PLAINS Howell
WESTBORO Atchison
WESTON Platte
WESTPHALIA Osage
WHEATLAND Hickory
WHEATON Barry
WHEELING (64688) Linn(55), Livingston(45)
WHITEMAN AIR FORCE BASE Johnson

WHITEOAK Dunklin
WHITESIDE Lincoln
WHITEWATER (63785) Cape Girardeau(99), Bollinger(1)
WILLARD (65781) Greene(99), Polk(2)
WILLIAMSBURG Callaway
WILLIAMSTOWN (63473) Lewis(56), Clark(44)
WILLIAMSVILLE (63967) Wayne(70), Butler(30)
WILLOW SPRINGS (65793) Howell(96), Texas(5)
WINDSOR (65360) Henry(56), Pettis(29), Johnson(10), Benton(5)
WINDYVILLE Dallas
WINFIELD Lincoln
WINIGAN (63566) Linn(90), Sullivan(10)
WINONA (65588) Shannon(93), Oregon(7)

WINSTON Daviess
WITTENBERG Perry
WOLF ISLAND Mississippi
WOOLDRIDGE (65287) Cooper(82), Moniteau(18)
WORTH (64499) Worth(94), Gentry(6)
WORTHINGTON (63567) Putnam(89), Morgan(12)
WRIGHT CITY (63390) Warren(88), Lincoln(12)
WYACONDA (63474) Clark(93), Scotland(5), Lewis(1)
WYATT Mississippi
YUKON Texas
ZALMA (63787) Bollinger(94), Wayne(6)
ZALMA Bollinger
ZANONI Ozark

ZIP/City Cross Reference

ZIP	City	ZIP	City	ZIP	City	ZIP	City
63001-63001	ALLENTON	63099-63099	FENTON	63439-63439	EMDEN	63560-63560	POLLOCK
63005-63006	CHESTERFIELD	63101-63199	SAINT LOUIS	63440-63440	EWING	63561-63561	QUEEN CITY
63010-63010	ARNOLD	63301-63304	SAINT CHARLES	63441-63441	FRANKFORD	63563-63563	RUTLEDGE
63011-63011	BALLWIN	63330-63330	ANNADA	63442-63442	GRANGER	63565-63565	UNIONVILLE
63012-63012	BARNHART	63332-63332	AUGUSTA	63443-63443	HUNNEWELL	63566-63566	WINIGAN
63013-63013	BEAUFORT	63333-63333	BELLFLOWER	63445-63445	KAHOKA	63567-63567	WORTHINGTON
63014-63014	BERGER	63334-63334	BOWLING GREEN	63446-63446	KNOX CITY	63601-63601	PARK HILLS
63015-63015	CATAWISSA	63336-63336	CLARKSVILLE	63447-63447	LA BELLE	63620-63620	ANNAPOLIS
63016-63016	CEDAR HILL	63338-63338	COTTLEVILLE	63448-63448	LA GRANGE	63621-63621	ARCADIA
63017-63017	CHESTERFIELD	63339-63339	CURRYVILLE	63450-63450	LENTNER	63622-63622	BELGRADE
63019-63019	CRYSTAL CITY	63341-63341	DEFIANCE	63451-63451	LEONARD	63623-63623	BELLEVIEW
63020-63020	DE SOTO	63342-63342	DUTZOW	63452-63452	LEWISTOWN	63624-63624	BISMARCK
63021-63022	BALLWIN	63343-63343	ELSBERRY	63453-63453	LURAY	63625-63625	BLACK
63023-63023	DITTMER	63344-63344	EOLIA	63454-63454	MAYWOOD	63626-63626	BLACKWELL
63024-63024	BALLWIN	63345-63345	FARBER	63456-63456	MONROE CITY	63627-63627	BLOOMSDALE
63025-63025	EUREKA	63346-63346	FLINTHILL	63457-63457	MONTICELLO	63628-63628	BONNE TERRE
63026-63026	FENTON	63347-63347	FOLEY	63458-63458	NEWARK	63629-63629	BUNKER
63028-63028	FESTUS	63348-63348	FORISTELL	63459-63459	NEW LONDON	63630-63630	CADET
63030-63030	FLETCHER	63349-63349	HAWK POINT	63460-63460	NOVELTY	63631-63631	CALEDONIA
63031-63034	FLORISSANT	63350-63350	HIGH HILL	63461-63461	PALMYRA	63632-63632	CASCADE
63036-63036	FRENCH VILLAGE	63351-63351	JONESBURG	63462-63462	PERRY	63633-63633	CENTERVILLE
63037-63037	GERALD	63352-63352	LADDONIA	63463-63463	PHILADELPHIA	63636-63636	DES ARC
63038-63038	GLENCOE	63353-63353	LOUISIANA	63464-63464	PLEVNA	63637-63637	DOE RUN
63039-63039	GRAY SUMMIT	63357-63357	MARTHASVILLE	63465-63465	REVERE	63638-63638	ELLINGTON
63040-63040	GROVER	63359-63359	MIDDLETOWN	63466-63466	SAINT PATRICK	63640-63640	FARMINGTON
63041-63041	GRUBVILLE	63361-63361	MONTGOMERY CITY	63467-63467	SAVERTON	63645-63645	FREDERICKTOWN
63042-63042	HAZELWOOD	63362-63362	MOSCOW MILLS	63468-63468	SHELBINA	63646-63646	GLOVER
63043-63043	MARYLAND HEIGHTS	63363-63363	NEW FLORENCE	63469-63469	SHELBYVILLE	63648-63648	IRONDALE
63044-63044	BRIDGETON	63364-63364	NEW HARTFORD	63470-63470	STEFFENVILLE	63650-63650	IRONTON
63045-63045	EARTH CITY	63365-63365	NEW MELLE	63471-63471	TAYLOR	63651-63651	KNOB LICK
63047-63047	HEMATITE	63366-63366	O FALLON	63472-63472	WAYLAND	63653-63653	LEADWOOD
63048-63048	HERCULANEUM	63367-63367	LAKE SAINT LOUIS	63473-63473	WILLIAMSTOWN	63654-63654	LESTERVILLE
63049-63049	HIGH RIDGE	63369-63369	OLD MONROE	63474-63474	WYACONDA	63655-63655	MARQUAND
63050-63050	HILLSBORO	63370-63370	OLNEY	63501-63501	KIRKSVILLE	63656-63656	MIDDLE BROOK
63051-63051	HOUSE SPRINGS	63371-63371	PAYNESVILLE	63530-63530	ATLANTA	63660-63660	MINERAL POINT
63052-63052	IMPERIAL	63373-63373	PORTAGE DES SIOUX	63531-63531	BARING	63661-63661	NEW OFFENBURG
63053-63053	KIMMSWICK	63376-63376	SAINT PETERS	63532-63532	BEVIER	63662-63662	PATTON
63055-63055	LABADIE	63377-63377	SILEX	63533-63533	BRASHEAR	63663-63663	PILOT KNOB
63056-63056	LESLIE	63378-63378	TRELOAR	63534-63534	CALLAO	63664-63664	POTOSI
63057-63057	LIGUORI	63379-63379	TROY	63535-63535	COATSVILLE	63665-63665	REDFORD
63060-63060	LONEDELL	63381-63381	TRUXTON	63536-63536	DOWNING	63666-63666	REYNOLDS
63061-63061	LUEBBERING	63382-63382	VANDALIA	63537-63537	EDINA	63670-63670	SAINTE GENEVIEVE
63065-63065	MAPAVILLE	63383-63383	WARRENTON	63538-63538	ELMER	63673-63673	SAINT MARY
63066-63066	MORSE MILL	63384-63384	WELLSVILLE	63539-63539	ETHEL	63674-63674	TIFF
63068-63068	NEW HAVEN	63385-63385	WENTZVILLE	63540-63540	GIBBS	63675-63675	VULCAN
63069-63069	PACIFIC	63386-63386	WEST ALTON	63541-63541	GLENWOOD	63701-63705	CAPE GIRARDEAU
63070-63070	PEVELY	63387-63387	WHITESIDE	63543-63543	GORIN	63730-63730	ADVANCE
63071-63071	RICHWOODS	63388-63388	WILLIAMSBURG	63544-63544	GREEN CASTLE	63732-63732	ALTENBURG
63072-63072	ROBERTSVILLE	63389-63389	WINFIELD	63545-63545	GREEN CITY	63735-63735	BELL CITY
63073-63073	SAINT ALBANS	63390-63390	WRIGHT CITY	63546-63546	GREENTOP	63736-63736	BENTON
63074-63074	SAINT ANN	63401-63401	HANNIBAL	63547-63547	HURDLAND	63737-63737	BRAZEAU
63077-63077	SAINT CLAIR	63430-63430	ALEXANDRIA	63548-63548	LANCASTER	63738-63738	BROWNWOOD
63079-63079	STANTON	63431-63431	ANABEL	63549-63549	LA PLATA	63739-63739	BURFORDVILLE
63080-63080	SULLIVAN	63432-63432	ARBELA	63551-63551	LIVONIA	63740-63740	CHAFFEE
63084-63084	UNION	63433-63433	ASHBURN	63552-63552	MACON	63742-63742	COMMERCE
63087-63087	VALLES MINES	63434-63434	BETHEL	63555-63555	MEMPHIS	63743-63743	DAISY
63088-63088	VALLEY PARK	63435-63435	CANTON	63556-63556	MILAN	63744-63744	DELTA
63089-63089	VILLA RIDGE	63436-63436	CENTER	63557-63557	NEW BOSTON	63745-63745	DUTCHTOWN
63090-63090	WASHINGTON	63437-63437	CLARENCE	63558-63558	NEW CAMBRIA	63746-63746	FARRAR
63091-63091	ROSEBUD	63438-63438	DURHAM	63559-63559	NOVINGER	63747-63747	FRIEDHEIM

Zip	City	Zip	City	Zip	City	Zip	City
63748-63748	FROHNA	63936-63936	DUDLEY	64402-64402	ALBANY	64632-64632	CAINSVILLE
63750-63750	GIPSY	63937-63937	ELLSINORE	64420-64420	ALLENDALE	64633-64633	CARROLLTON
63751-63751	GLENALLEN	63938-63938	FAGUS	64421-64421	AMAZONIA	64635-64635	CHULA
63752-63752	GORDONVILLE	63939-63939	FAIRDEALING	64422-64422	AMITY	64636-64636	COFFEY
63753-63753	GRASSY	63940-63940	FISK	64423-64423	BARNARD	64637-64637	COWGILL
63755-63755	JACKSON	63941-63941	FREMONT	64424-64424	BETHANY	64638-64638	DAWN
63758-63758	KELSO	63942-63942	GATEWOOD	64426-64426	BLYTHEDALE	64639-64639	DE WITT
63760-63760	LEOPOLD	63943-63943	GRANDIN	64427-64427	BOLCKOW	64640-64640	GALLATIN
63763-63763	MC GEE	63944-63944	GREENVILLE	64428-64428	BURLINGTON JUNCTION	64641-64641	GALT
63764-63764	MARBLE HILL	63945-63945	HARVIELL	64429-64429	CAMERON	64642-64642	GILMAN CITY
63766-63766	MILLERSVILLE	63947-63947	HIRAM	64430-64430	CLARKSDALE	64643-64643	HALE
63767-63767	MORLEY	63950-63950	LODI	64431-64431	CLEARMONT	64644-64644	HAMILTON
63769-63769	OAK RIDGE	63951-63951	LOWNDES	64432-64432	CLYDE	64645-64645	HARRIS
63770-63770	OLD APPLETON	63952-63952	MILL SPRING	64433-64433	CONCEPTION	64646-64646	HUMPHREYS
63771-63771	ORAN	63953-63953	NAYLOR	64434-64434	CONCEPTION JUNCTION	64647-64647	JAMESON
63772-63772	PAINTON	63954-63954	NEELYVILLE	64436-64436	COSBY	64648-64648	JAMESPORT
63774-63774	PERKINS	63955-63955	OXLY	64437-64437	CRAIG	64649-64649	KIDDER
63775-63775	PERRYVILLE	63956-63956	PATTERSON	64438-64438	DARLINGTON	64650-64650	KINGSTON
63776-63776	MC BRIDE	63957-63957	PIEDMONT	64439-64439	DEARBORN	64651-64651	LACLEDE
63779-63779	POCAHONTAS	63960-63960	PUXICO	64440-64440	DE KALB	64652-64652	LAREDO
63780-63780	SCOTT CITY	63961-63961	QULIN	64441-64441	DENVER	64653-64653	LINNEUS
63781-63781	SEDGEWICKVILLE	63962-63962	ROMBAUER	64442-64442	EAGLEVILLE	64654-64654	LOCK SPRINGS
63782-63782	STURDIVANT	63963-63963	SHOOK	64443-64443	EASTON	64655-64655	LUCERNE
63783-63783	UNIONTOWN	63964-63964	SILVA	64444-64444	EDGERTON	64656-64656	LUDLOW
63784-63784	VANDUSER	63965-63965	VAN BUREN	64445-64445	ELMO	64657-64657	MC FALL
63785-63785	WHITEWATER	63966-63966	WAPPAPELLO	64446-64446	FAIRFAX	64658-64658	MARCELINE
63787-63787	ZALMA	63967-63967	WILLIAMSVILLE	64447-64447	FAIRPORT	64659-64659	MEADVILLE
63801-63801	SIKESTON	64001-64001	ALMA	64448-64448	FAUCETT	64660-64660	MENDON
63820-63820	ANNISTON	64011-64011	BATES CITY	64449-64449	FILLMORE	64661-64661	MERCER
63821-63821	ARBYRD	64012-64012	BELTON	64451-64451	FOREST CITY	64664-64664	MOORESVILLE
63822-63822	BERNIE	64013-64015	BLUE SPRINGS	64453-64453	GENTRY	64665-64665	MOUNT MORIAH
63823-63823	BERTRAND	64016-64016	BUCKNER	64454-64454	GOWER	64667-64667	NEWTOWN
63824-63824	BLODGETT	64017-64017	CAMDEN	64455-64455	GRAHAM	64668-64668	NORBORNE
63825-63825	BLOOMFIELD	64018-64018	CAMDEN POINT	64456-64456	GRANT CITY	64670-64670	PATTONSBURG
63826-63826	BRAGGADOCIO	64019-64019	CENTERVIEW	64457-64457	GUILFORD	64671-64671	POLO
63827-63827	BRAGG CITY	64020-64020	CONCORDIA	64458-64458	HATFIELD	64672-64672	POWERSVILLE
63828-63828	CANALOU	64021-64021	CORDER	64459-64459	HELENA	64673-64673	PRINCETON
63829-63829	CARDWELL	64022-64022	DOVER	64461-64461	HOPKINS	64674-64674	PURDIN
63830-63830	CARUTHERSVILLE	64024-64024	EXCELSIOR SPRINGS	64463-64463	KING CITY	64676-64676	ROTHVILLE
63833-63833	CATRON	64028-64028	FARLEY	64465-64465	LATHROP	64679-64679	SPICKARD
63834-63834	CHARLESTON	64029-64029	GRAIN VALLEY	64466-64466	MAITLAND	64680-64680	STET
63837-63837	CLARKTON	64030-64030	GRANDVIEW	64467-64467	MARTINSVILLE	64681-64681	SUMNER
63838-63838	CONRAN	64034-64034	GREENWOOD	64468-64468	MARYVILLE	64682-64682	TINA
63839-63839	COOTER	64035-64035	HARDIN	64469-64469	MAYSVILLE	64683-64683	TRENTON
63840-63840	DEERING	64036-64036	HENRIETTA	64470-64470	MOUND CITY	64686-64686	UTICA
63841-63841	DEXTER	64037-64037	HIGGINSVILLE	64471-64471	NEW HAMPTON	64687-64687	WAKENDA
63845-63845	EAST PRAIRIE	64040-64040	HOLDEN	64473-64473	OREGON	64688-64688	WHEELING
63846-63846	ESSEX	64048-64048	HOLT	64474-64474	OSBORN	64689-64689	WINSTON
63847-63847	GIBSON	64050-64058	INDEPENDENCE	64475-64475	PARNELL	64701-64701	HARRISONVILLE
63848-63848	GIDEON	64060-64060	KEARNEY	64476-64476	PICKERING	64720-64720	ADRIAN
63849-63849	GOBLER	64061-64061	KINGSVILLE	64477-64477	PLATTSBURG	64722-64722	AMORET
63850-63850	GRAYRIDGE	64062-64062	LAWSON	64478-64478	QUITMAN	64723-64723	AMSTERDAM
63851-63851	HAYTI	64063-64065	LEES SUMMIT	64479-64479	RAVENWOOD	64724-64724	APPLETON CITY
63852-63852	HOLCOMB	64066-64066	LEVASY	64480-64480	REA	64725-64725	ARCHIE
63853-63853	HOLLAND	64067-64067	LEXINGTON	64481-64481	RIDGEWAY	64726-64726	BLAIRSTOWN
63855-63855	HORNERSVILLE	64068-64069	LIBERTY	64482-64482	ROCK PORT	64728-64728	BRONAUGH
63857-63857	KENNETT	64070-64070	LONE JACK	64483-64483	ROSENDALE	64730-64730	BUTLER
63860-63860	KEWANEE	64071-64071	MAYVIEW	64484-64484	RUSHVILLE	64733-64733	CHILHOWEE
63862-63862	LILBOURN	64072-64072	MISSOURI CITY	64485-64485	SAVANNAH	64734-64734	CLEVELAND
63863-63863	MALDEN	64073-64073	MOSBY	64486-64486	SHERIDAN	64735-64735	CLINTON
63866-63866	MARSTON	64074-64074	NAPOLEON	64487-64487	SKIDMORE	64738-64738	COLLINS
63867-63867	MATTHEWS	64075-64075	OAK GROVE	64489-64489	STANBERRY	64739-64739	CREIGHTON
63868-63868	MOREHOUSE	64076-64076	ODESSA	64490-64490	STEWARTSVILLE	64740-64740	DEEPWATER
63869-63869	NEW MADRID	64077-64077	ORRICK	64491-64491	TARKIO	64741-64741	DEERFIELD
63870-63870	PARMA	64078-64078	PECULIAR	64492-64492	TRIMBLE	64742-64742	DREXEL
63871-63871	PASCOLA	64079-64079	PLATTE CITY	64493-64493	TURNEY	64743-64743	EAST LYNNE
63873-63873	PORTAGEVILLE	64080-64080	PLEASANT HILL	64494-64494	UNION STAR	64744-64744	EL DORADO SPRINGS
63874-63874	RISCO	64081-64082	LEES SUMMIT	64496-64496	WATSON	64745-64745	FOSTER
63875-63875	RIVES	64083-64083	RAYMORE	64497-64497	WEATHERBY	64746-64746	FREEMAN
63876-63876	SENATH	64084-64084	RAYVILLE	64498-64498	WESTBORO	64747-64747	GARDEN CITY
63877-63877	STEELE	64085-64085	RICHMOND	64499-64499	WORTH	64748-64748	GOLDEN CITY
63878-63878	TALLAPOOSA	64086-64086	LEES SUMMIT	64501-64508	SAINT JOSEPH	64750-64750	HARWOOD
63879-63879	WARDELL	64088-64088	SIBLEY	64601-64601	CHILLICOTHE	64751-64751	HORTON
63880-63880	WHITEOAK	64089-64089	SMITHVILLE	64620-64620	ALTAMONT	64752-64752	HUME
63881-63881	WOLF ISLAND	64090-64090	STRASBURG	64621-64621	AVALON	64755-64755	JASPER
63882-63882	WYATT	64092-64092	WALDRON	64622-64622	BOGARD	64756-64756	JERICO SPRINGS
63901-63902	POPLAR BLUFF	64093-64093	WARRENSBURG	64623-64623	BOSWORTH	64759-64759	LAMAR
63931-63931	BRIAR	64096-64096	WAVERLY	64624-64624	BRAYMER	64761-64761	LEETON
63932-63932	BROSELEY	64097-64097	WELLINGTON	64625-64625	BRECKENRIDGE	64762-64762	LIBERAL
63933-63933	CAMPBELL	64098-64098	WESTON	64628-64628	BROOKFIELD	64763-64763	LOWRY CITY
63934-63934	CLUBB	64101-64199	KANSAS CITY	64630-64630	BROWNING	64765-64765	METZ
63935-63935	DONIPHAN	64401-64401	AGENCY	64631-64631	BUCKLIN	64766-64766	MILFORD

ZIP	City	ZIP	City	ZIP	City	ZIP	City
64767-64767	MILO	65049-65049	LAKE OZARK	65324-65324	CLIMAX SPRINGS	65583-65583	WAYNESVILLE
64769-64769	MINDENMINES	65050-65050	LATHAM	65325-65325	COLE CAMP	65586-65586	WESCO
64770-64770	MONTROSE	65051-65051	LINN	65326-65326	EDWARDS	65588-65588	WINONA
64771-64771	MOUNDVILLE	65052-65052	LINN CREEK	65327-65327	EMMA	65589-65589	YUKON
64772-64772	NEVADA	65053-65053	LOHMAN	65329-65329	FLORENCE	65590-65590	LONG LANE
64776-64776	OSCEOLA	65054-65054	LOOSE CREEK	65330-65330	GILLIAM	65591-65591	MONTREAL
64777-64777	PASSAIC	65055-65055	MC GIRK	65332-65332	GREEN RIDGE	65601-65601	ALDRICH
64778-64778	RICHARDS	65058-65058	META	65333-65333	HOUSTONIA	65603-65603	ARCOLA
64779-64779	RICH HILL	65059-65059	MOKANE	65334-65334	HUGHESVILLE	65604-65604	ASH GROVE
64780-64780	ROCKVILLE	65061-65061	MORRISON	65335-65335	IONIA	65605-65605	AURORA
64781-64781	ROSCOE	65062-65062	MOUNT STERLING	65336-65336	KNOB NOSTER	65606-65606	ALTON
64783-64783	SCHELL CITY	65063-65063	NEW BLOOMFIELD	65337-65337	LA MONTE	65607-65607	CAPLINGER MILLS
64784-64784	SHELDON	65064-65064	OLEAN	65338-65338	LINCOLN	65608-65608	AVA
64788-64788	URICH	65065-65065	OSAGE BEACH	65339-65339	MALTA BEND	65609-65609	BAKERSFIELD
64789-64789	VISTA	65066-65066	OWENSVILLE	65340-65340	MARSHALL	65610-65610	BILLINGS
64790-64790	WALKER	65067-65067	PORTLAND	65344-65344	MIAMI	65611-65611	BLUE EYE
64801-64804	JOPLIN	65068-65068	PRAIRIE HOME	65345-65345	MORA	65612-65612	BOIS D ARC
64830-64830	ALBA	65069-65069	RHINELAND	65347-65347	NELSON	65613-65613	BOLIVAR
64831-64831	ANDERSON	65072-65072	ROCKY MOUNT	65348-65348	OTTERVILLE	65614-65614	BRADLEYVILLE
64832-64832	ASBURY	65074-65074	RUSSELLVILLE	65349-65349	SLATER	65615-65616	BRANSON
64833-64833	AVILLA	65075-65075	SAINT ELIZABETH	65350-65350	SMITHTON	65617-65617	BRIGHTON
64834-64834	CARL JUNCTION	65076-65076	SAINT THOMAS	65351-65351	SWEET SPRINGS	65618-65618	BRIXEY
64835-64835	CARTERVILLE	65077-65077	STEEDMAN	65354-65354	SYRACUSE	65619-65619	BROOKLINE STATION
64836-64836	CARTHAGE	65078-65078	STOVER	65355-65355	WARSAW	65620-65620	BRUNER
64840-64840	DIAMOND	65079-65079	SUNRISE BEACH	65360-65360	WINDSOR	65622-65622	BUFFALO
64841-64841	DUENWEG	65080-65080	TEBBETTS	65401-65409	ROLLA	65623-65623	BUTTERFIELD
64842-64842	FAIRVIEW	65081-65081	TIPTON	65433-65433	BENDAVIS	65624-65624	CAPE FAIR
64843-64843	GOODMAN	65082-65082	TUSCUMBIA	65436-65436	BEULAH	65625-65625	CASSVILLE
64844-64844	GRANBY	65083-65083	ULMAN	65438-65438	BIRCH TREE	65626-65626	CAULFIELD
64847-64847	LANAGAN	65084-65084	VERSAILLES	65439-65439	BIXBY	65627-65627	CEDARCREEK
64848-64848	LA RUSSELL	65085-65085	WESTPHALIA	65440-65440	BOSS	65629-65629	CHADWICK
64849-64849	NECK CITY	65101-65111	JEFFERSON CITY	65441-65441	BOURBON	65630-65630	CHESTNUTRIDGE
64850-64850	NEOSHO	65201-65218	COLUMBIA	65443-65443	BRINKTOWN	65631-65631	CLEVER
64853-64853	NEWTONIA	65230-65230	ARMSTRONG	65444-65444	BUCYRUS	65632-65632	CONWAY
64854-64854	NOEL	65231-65231	AUXVASSE	65446-65446	CHERRYVILLE	65633-65633	CRANE
64855-64855	ORONOGO	65232-65232	BENTON CITY	65449-65449	COOK STATION	65634-65634	CROSS TIMBERS
64856-64856	PINEVILLE	65233-65233	BOONVILLE	65452-65452	CROCKER	65635-65635	DADEVILLE
64857-64857	PURCELL	65236-65236	BRUNSWICK	65453-65453	CUBA	65636-65636	DIGGINS
64858-64858	RACINE	65237-65237	BUNCETON	65456-65456	DAVISVILLE	65637-65637	DORA
64859-64859	REEDS	65239-65239	CAIRO	65457-65457	DEVILS ELBOW	65638-65638	DRURY
64861-64861	ROCKY COMFORT	65240-65240	CENTRALIA	65459-65459	DIXON	65640-65640	DUNNEGAN
64862-64862	SARCOXIE	65243-65243	CLARK	65461-65461	DUKE	65641-65641	EAGLE ROCK
64863-64863	SOUTH WEST CITY	65244-65244	CLIFTON HILL	65462-65462	EDGAR SPRINGS	65644-65644	ELKLAND
64864-64864	SAGINAW	65246-65246	DALTON	65463-65463	ELDRIDGE	65645-65645	EUDORA
64865-64865	SENECA	65247-65247	EXCELLO	65464-65464	ELK CREEK	65646-65646	EVERTON
64866-64866	STARK CITY	65248-65248	FAYETTE	65466-65466	EMINENCE	65647-65647	EXETER
64867-64867	STELLA	65250-65250	FRANKLIN	65468-65468	EUNICE	65648-65648	FAIR GROVE
64868-64868	TIFF CITY	65251-65251	FULTON	65470-65470	FALCON	65649-65649	FAIR PLAY
64869-64869	WACO	65254-65254	GLASGOW	65473-65473	FORT LEONARD WOOD	65650-65650	FLEMINGTON
64870-64870	WEBB CITY	65255-65255	HALLSVILLE	65479-65479	HARTSHORN	65652-65652	FORDLAND
64873-64873	WENTWORTH	65256-65256	HARRISBURG	65483-65483	HOUSTON	65653-65653	FORSYTH
64874-64874	WHEATON	65257-65257	HIGBEE	65484-65484	HUGGINS	65654-65654	FREISTATT
64944-64999	KANSAS CITY	65258-65258	HOLLIDAY	65486-65486	IBERIA	65655-65655	GAINESVILLE
65001-65001	ARGYLE	65259-65259	HUNTSVILLE	65501-65501	JADWIN	65656-65656	GALENA
65010-65010	ASHLAND	65260-65260	JACKSONVILLE	65529-65529	JEROME	65657-65657	GARRISON
65011-65011	BARNETT	65261-65261	KEYTESVILLE	65532-65532	LAKE SPRING	65658-65658	GOLDEN
65013-65013	BELLE	65262-65262	KINGDOM CITY	65534-65534	LAQUEY	65659-65659	GOODSON
65014-65014	BLAND	65263-65263	MADISON	65535-65535	LEASBURG	65660-65660	GRAFF
65016-65016	BONNOTS MILL	65264-65264	MARTINSBURG	65536-65536	LEBANON	65661-65661	GREENFIELD
65017-65017	BRUMLEY	65265-65265	MEXICO	65540-65540	LECOMA	65662-65662	GROVESPRING
65018-65018	CALIFORNIA	65270-65270	MOBERLY	65541-65541	LENOX	65663-65663	HALF WAY
65020-65020	CAMDENTON	65274-65274	NEW FRANKLIN	65542-65542	LICKING	65664-65664	HALLTOWN
65022-65022	CEDAR CITY	65275-65275	PARIS	65543-65543	LYNCHBURG	65666-65666	HARDENVILLE
65023-65023	CENTERTOWN	65276-65276	PILOT GROVE	65546-65546	MONTIER	65667-65667	HARTVILLE
65024-65024	CHAMOIS	65278-65278	RENICK	65548-65548	MOUNTAIN VIEW	65668-65668	HERMITAGE
65025-65025	CLARKSBURG	65279-65279	ROCHEPORT	65550-65550	NEWBURG	65669-65669	HIGHLANDVILLE
65026-65026	ELDON	65280-65280	RUSH HILL	65552-65552	PLATO	65672-65673	HOLLISTER
65031-65031	ETTERVILLE	65281-65281	SALISBURY	65555-65555	RAYMONDVILLE	65674-65674	HUMANSVILLE
65032-65032	EUGENE	65282-65282	SANTA FE	65556-65556	RICHLAND	65675-65675	HURLEY
65034-65034	FORTUNA	65283-65283	STOUTSVILLE	65557-65557	ROBY	65676-65676	ISABELLA
65035-65035	FREEBURG	65284-65284	STURGEON	65559-65559	SAINT JAMES	65679-65679	KIRBYVILLE
65036-65036	GASCONADE	65285-65285	THOMPSON	65560-65560	SALEM	65680-65680	KISSEE MILLS
65037-65037	GRAVOIS MILLS	65286-65286	TRIPLETT	65564-65564	SOLO	65681-65681	LAMPE
65038-65038	LAURIE	65287-65287	WOOLDRIDGE	65565-65565	STEELVILLE	65682-65682	LOCKWOOD
65039-65039	HARTSBURG	65299-65299	MID MISSOURI	65566-65566	VIBURNUM	65685-65685	LOUISBURG
65040-65040	HENLEY	65301-65302	SEDALIA	65567-65567	STOUTLAND	65686-65686	KIMBERLING CITY
65041-65041	HERMANN	65305-65305	WHITEMAN AIR FORCE BASE	65570-65570	SUCCESS	65688-65688	BRANDSVILLE
65042-65042	HIGH POINT			65571-65571	SUMMERSVILLE	65689-65689	CABOOL
65043-65043	HOLTS SUMMIT	65320-65320	ARROW ROCK	65572-65572	SWEDEBORG	65690-65690	COUCH
65046-65046	JAMESTOWN	65321-65321	BLACKBURN	65573-65573	TERESITA	65692-65692	KOSHKONONG
65047-65047	KAISER	65322-65322	BLACKWATER	65580-65580	VICHY	65701-65701	MC CLURG
65048-65048	KOELTZTOWN	65323-65323	CALHOUN	65582-65582	VIENNA	65702-65702	MACOMB

65704-65704 MANSFIELD	65727-65727 POLK	65752-65752 SOUTH GREENFIELD	65773-65773 WASOLA
65705-65705 MARIONVILLE	65728-65728 PONCE DE LEON	65753-65753 SPARTA	65774-65774 WEAUBLEAU
65706-65706 MARSHFIELD	65729-65729 PONTIAC	65754-65754 SPOKANE	65775-65775 WEST PLAINS
65707-65707 MILLER	65730-65730 POWELL	65755-65755 SQUIRES	65776-65776 SOUTH FORK
65708-65708 MONETT	65731-65731 POWERSITE	65756-65756 STOTTS CITY	65777-65777 MOODY
65710-65710 MORRISVILLE	65732-65732 PRESTON	65757-65757 STRAFFORD	65778-65778 MYRTLE
65711-65711 MOUNTAIN GROVE	65733-65733 PROTEM	65759-65759 TANEYVILLE	65779-65779 WHEATLAND
65712-65712 MOUNT VERNON	65734-65734 PURDY	65760-65760 TECUMSEH	65781-65781 WILLARD
65713-65713 NIANGUA	65735-65735 QUINCY	65761-65761 THEODOSIA	65783-65783 WINDYVILLE
65714-65714 NIXA	65737-65737 REEDS SPRING	65762-65762 THORNFIELD	65784-65784 ZANONI
65715-65715 NOBLE	65738-65738 REPUBLIC	65764-65764 TUNAS	65785-65785 STOCKTON
65717-65717 NORWOOD	65739-65739 RIDGEDALE	65765-65765 TURNERS	65786-65786 MACKS CREEK
65720-65720 OLDFIELD	65740-65740 ROCKAWAY BEACH	65766-65766 UDALL	65787-65787 ROACH
65721-65721 OZARK	65741-65741 ROCKBRIDGE	65767-65767 URBANA	65788-65788 PEACE VALLEY
65722-65722 PHILLIPSBURG	65742-65742 ROGERSVILLE	65768-65768 VANZANT	65789-65789 POMONA
65723-65723 PIERCE CITY	65744-65744 RUETER	65769-65769 VERONA	65790-65790 POTTERSVILLE
65724-65724 PITTSBURG	65745-65745 SELIGMAN	65770-65770 WALNUT GROVE	65791-65791 THAYER
65725-65725 PLEASANT HOPE	65746-65746 SEYMOUR	65771-65771 WALNUT SHADE	65793-65793 WILLOW SPRINGS
65726-65726 POINT LOOKOUT	65747-65747 SHELL KNOB	65772-65772 WASHBURN	65801-65899 SPRINGFIELD

Montana

General Help Numbers:

Governor's Office
PO Box 200801, State Capitol   406-444-3111
Helena, MT 59620-0801   Fax 406-444-5529
www.state.mt.us/governor/governor.htm   8AM-5PM

Attorney General's Office
PO Box 201401   406-444-2026
Helena, MT 59620   Fax 406-444-3549
www.doj.state.mt.us/ago/index.htm   8AM-5PM

State Court Administrator
PO Box 203002   406-444-2621
Helena, MT 59620-3002   Fax 406-444-0834
www.lawlibrary.state.mt.us   8AM-5PM

State Archives
Library/Archives Division   406-444-2694
PO Box 201201, 225 N Roberts St   Fax 406-444-2696
Helena, MT 59620-1201   8AM-5PM M-F
www.his.state.mt.us 9AM-4:30PM 1st SA of each month

State Specifics:

Capital: Helena
          Lewis and Clark County

Time Zone: MST

Number of Counties: 56

Population: 882,799

Web Site: www.mt.gov

State Agencies

Criminal Records

Department of Justice, Criminal History Records Program, PO Box 201417, Helena, MT 59620-1417; 406-444-3625, 406-444-0689 (Fax), 8AM-5PM.

Indexing & Storage: Records are available from 1950's on and are computerized. It takes four days before new records are available for inquiry.

Searching: All felonies, and misdemeanors for the past 5 years, are reported on convictions. Include the following in your request-name, date of birth, Social Security Number, any aliases. The following data is not released: pending cases or dismissals.

Access by: mail, fax, in person.

Fee & Payment: The fee is $5.00 per individual. Fee payee: Criminal History Records Program. Prepayment required. Personal checks accepted. No credit cards accepted.

Mail search: Turnaround time: 2 days. A self addressed stamped envelope is requested.

Fax search: If request is returned by fax, an additional $2.00 fee is charged, regardless the number of names.

In person search: Turnaround time is usually immediate.

Corporation Records
Limited Liability Company Records
Fictitious Name
Limited Partnerships
Assumed Name
Trademarks/Servicemarks

Business Services Bureau, Secretary of State, PO Box 202801, Helena, MT 59620-2801 (Courier: State Capitol, Room 225, Helena, MT 59620); 406-444-3665, 406-444-3976 (Fax), 8AM-5PM.

www.state.mt.us/sos

Indexing & Storage: Records are available from the 1860s. New records are available for inquiry immediately. Records are indexed on inhouse computer.

Searching: Include the following in your request-full name of business, specific records that you need copies of. In addition to the articles of incorporation, corporation records include the following information: Annual Reports, Officers, Directors, DBAs, Prior (merged) names, Inactive and Reserved names.

Access by: mail, phone, fax, in person.

Fee & Payment: There is no search fee, copies are 4.50 each, certification is $2.00 per document. Fee payee: Secretary of State. Prepayment required. Prepaid accounts may be established. Personal checks accepted. No credit cards accepted.

Mail search: Turnaround time: 2 weeks. A self addressed stamped envelope is requested.

Phone search: Limit of three requests per call.

Fax search: Fax requests are accepted for prepaid accounts at a cost of $3.00 for up to 10 pages and $.25 per additional page. Turnaround time is 1 week.

In person search: Searching is available in person.

Other access: Lists of the new corporations per month are available.

Expedited service: Expedited service is available for mail, phone and in person searches. Turnaround time: 1 day. Add $20.00 per search.

Uniform Commercial Code
Federal Tax Liens

Business Services Bureau, Secretary of State, PO Box 202801, Helena, MT 59620-2801 (Courier: 100 N Park, 2nd Fl, Helena, MT 59620); 406-444-3665, 406-444-3976 (Fax), 8AM-5PM.

www.state.mt.us/sos

Indexing & Storage: Records are available from 1965, indexed on computer and on microfiche. Terminated or expired financing statements are not available with the exception of notices of federal tax liens. It takes one day before new records are available for inquiry.

Searching: Use search request form UCC-11. The search includes notice of federal tax liens on businesses and individuals. All state tax liens are filed at the county level. Include the following in your request-debtor exact name and any fictitious names.

Access by: mail, fax, in person, online.

Fee & Payment: The search fee is $7.00 per debtor name, copies are $.50 per page. Fee payee: Secretary of State. Prepayment required. The state will accept prepaid accounts. Personal checks accepted. No credit cards accepted.

Mail search: Turnaround time: 3-5 days. A self addressed stamped envelope is requested.

Fax search: Same fees and turnaround time apply.

In person search: Searching is available in person.

Online search: The online system costs $25 per month plus $.50 per page if copies of filed documents are requested. A prepaid account is required. The system is open 24 hours daily.

Other access: The agency offers farm bill filings lists on a monthly basis for $5.00 per product. A CD-Rom for Farm Products is available for $20.00.

Expedited service: Expedited service is available for fax searches. Turnaround time: 1-2 days. Add $20.00 per document.

State Tax Liens
Records not maintained by a state level agency.

Note: Records are at the county level.

%%MT717-A%%
Sales Tax Registrations
State does not impose sales tax.

Birth Certificates

Montana Department of Health, Vital Records, PO Box 4210, Helena, MT 59604 (Courier: 111 N Sanders, Rm 209, Helena, MT 59601); 406-444-4228, 406-444-1803 (Fax), 8AM-5PM.

Indexing & Storage: Records are available from 1907 on. It takes 3 months before new records are available for inquiry.

Searching: Must be able to show direct and tangible interest of records. The decision if you can get copies of records will be up to the staff of the Vital Records department. Include the following in your request-full name, names of parents, mother's maiden name, date of birth, place of birth, relationship to person of record, reason for information request. Must include copy of guardianship papers, if you are guardian. All requesters must include photo ID and phone number.

Access by: mail, fax, in person.

Fee & Payment: The search fee is $10.00. Add $5.00 for using a credit card. The search fee is per 5 years searched. Fee payee: Montana Vital Records. Prepayment required. Personal checks accepted. Credit cards accepted: Mastercard, Visa, AmEx, Discover.

Mail search: Turnaround time: 10 days. No self addressed stamped envelope is required. Search costs $10.00 for each name in request.

Fax search: Must use credit card for additional $5.00.

In person search: Search costs $10.00 for each name in request. Turnaround time same day.

Expedited service: Expedited service is available for mail and phone searches. Turnaround time: overnight delivery. Add $11.00 per package for Fed Ex return or $11.75 per package for Express Mail return plus the $5.00 credit card fee and the $10.00 search fee.

Death Records

Montana Department of Health, Vital Records, PO Box 4210, Helena, MT 59604 (Courier: 111 N Sanders, Rm 209, Helena, MT 59601); 406-444-4228, 406-444-1803 (Fax), 8AM-5PM.

Indexing & Storage: Records are available from 1907 on. It takes 3 months before new records are available for inquiry.

Searching: Records are open. Include the following in your request-full name, date of death, place of death, relationship to person of record, reason for information request. Requesters should include a copy of picture ID and phone number.

Access by: mail, fax, in person.

Fee & Payment: The search fee is $10.00. Add $5.00 for using a credit card. The search fee is per 5 years searched. Fee payee: Montana Vital Records. Prepayment required. Personal checks accepted. Credit cards accepted: Mastercard, Visa, AmEx, Discover.

Mail search: Turnaround time: 10 days. Search costs $10.00 for each name in request.

Fax search: Must use credit card.

In person search: Search costs $10.00 for each name in request. Turnaround time same day.

Expedited service: Expedited service is available for mail and phone searches. Turnaround time: overnight delivery. Add $11.00 per document for Fed Ex return and $11.75 per document for Express Mail return, plus the search and credit card fee.

Marriage Certificates
Divorce Records
Records not maintained by a state level agency.

Note: Marriage and divorce records are found at county of issue. The State is required by law to maintain an index of these records. The index is from 1943 to present. The State can direct you to the correct county for a fee of $10.00 per 5 years searched.

Workers' Compensation
Records

Montana State Fund, PO Box 4759, Helena, MT 59604-4759 (Courier: 5 S. Last Chance Gulch, Helena, MT 59601); 406-444-6500, 406-444-7796 (Fax), 8AM-5PM.

http://stfund.state.mt.us

Indexing & Storage: Records are available from mid 1980's to 1995 on microfiche. Records 1996 forward are computerized.

Searching: Put request in writing, including reason for the request. They will determine whether the request is legitimate, unless you include a signed release form. Include the following in your request-claimant name, Social Security Number, date of accident, employer.

Access by: mail, fax, in person.

Fee & Payment: Copy fees are $.35 per page if from computer, $.50 per page if from microfiche. There is no search fee. Fee payee: Montana State Fund. Personal checks accepted. No credit cards accepted.

Mail search: Turnaround time: 7 days. No self addressed stamped envelope is required.

Fax search: Same criteria as mail searches.

In person search: One may request information in person.

Driver Records

Motor Vehicle Division, Driver's Services, PO Box 201430, Helena, MT 59620-1430 (Courier: Records Unit, 303 N Roberts, Room 262, Helena, MT 59620); 406-444-4590, 406-444-1631 (Fax), 8AM-5PM.

www.doj.state.mt.us

Note: Copies of tickets are available from the same address; requests must be in writing.

Indexing & Storage: Records are available for lifetime. For suspensions the time varies according to violation-90 days to indefinite and 6 years for an unsatisfied judgment. Note this is availability; records are stored indefinitely. It takes 5-10 days before new records are available for inquiry.

Searching: Anyone may order a driving record; however, personal information including address, SSN, photo, and medical information is not released.Opt out is not necessary. The driver's full name, DOB, and/or license number is required.

Access by: mail, phone, fax, in person.

Fee & Payment: The fee is $4.00 per three year record history and $10.00 for a certified history. Fee payee: Motor Vehicle Division Prepayment required. Billing or draw accounts available. Personal checks accepted. No credit cards accepted.

Mail search: Turnaround time: 3 days. Requests must be in writing, stating purpose and on letterhead.A self addressed stamped envelope is requested.

Phone search: Accounts must be pre-paid.

Fax search: Established pre-paid accounts may fax requests and receive results for an additional $2.00 per record.

In person search: Up to 5 records may be requested in person for immediate delivery at a Montana Driver Exam Station. There are 16 stations in the state that will provide driving records. ID must be provided.

Other access: Magnetic tape overnight batch retrieval is available for higher volume users.

Vehicle Ownership
Vehicle Identification
Boat & Vessel Ownership
Boat & Vessel Registration

Department of Justice, Title and Registration Bureau, 1032 Buckskin Drive, Deer Lodge, MT 59722; 406-846-6000, 406-846-6039 (Fax), 8AM-5PM.

Note: Lien information appears on the title record.

Indexing & Storage: Records are available from 1976-present on microfiche. Watercraft data is available from 1988. It takes 5-10 days before new records are available for inquiry.

Searching: Casual requesters may not obtain records without consent of the subject subject. Items required for search could include full name, VIN, plate number, or title number.

Access by: mail, phone, fax, in person.

Fee & Payment: The fee is $6.00 per vehicle/vessel or name search. Fee payee: Title and Registration Bureau. Prepayment required. Personal checks accepted. No credit cards accepted.

Mail search: Turnaround time: 5-7 days. Requests must be in writing and signed; using letterhead or the state form is suggested.No self addressed stamped envelope is required.

Phone search: Phone-in accounts have to be pre-approved and must carry a "bank account" with the Bureau.

Fax search: Fee is $6.00 for the first page and a $1.00 for each additional page. Turnaround time is 5-7 days.

In person search: Searching is available in person.

Other access: Bulk or batch ordering of registration information is available on tape, disk, or paper. The user must fill out a specific form, which gives the user the capability of customization. For further information, contact the Registrar at address above.

Accident Reports

Montana Highway Patrol, Accident Records, 2550 Prospect Ave, Helena, MT 59620-1419; 406-444-3278, 406-444-4169 (Fax), 8AM-5PM.

Note: Digital images are available with previous year's data.

Indexing & Storage: Records are available for 10 years to present. Computer indexing since 1991. Digital images are available starting with the year 1995. It takes 10-14 days after the accident before new records are available for inquiry.

Searching: Records are only released to persons involved in accident, or an attorney involved in the case. Insurance representatives must have signed authority. Witness statements are only released with a signed authorization from the witness. Include the following in your request-location of accident, date of accident, full name.

Access by: mail, phone, in person.

Fee & Payment: The fee is $2.00 per report. Fee payee: Montana Highway Patrol. Prepayment required. Personal checks accepted. No credit cards accepted.

Mail search: Turnaround time: 3-4 working days. Requests must be submitted in writing following guidelines mentioned above.No self addressed stamped envelope is required.

Phone search: The agency will only release names over the phone of people involved in crash.

In person search: Records will be released if proper authorization is shown.

Other access: Statistics, but not reports, are available.

Legislation-Current/Pending
Legislation-Passed

State Legislature of Montana, State Capitol, PO Box 201706, Helena, MT 59620-1706; 406-444-3064, 406-444-3036 (Fax), 8AM-5PM.

www.leg.state.mt.us

Indexing & Storage: Records are available from 1983-present, on computer since 1997 and on microfiche 1987-1997.

Searching: Include the following in your request-bill number, year.

Access by: mail, phone, in person, online.

Fee & Payment: Copy fee is $.15 per page. Fee payee: Montana Legislative Services Division.

Personal checks accepted. No credit cards accepted.

Mail search: Turnaround time: variable. No self addressed stamped envelope is required. No fee for mail request.

Phone search: No fee for telephone request.

In person search: No fee for request. No cash will be accepted.

Online search: Information is available on the Internet. Committee minutes for 1999 forward are available on the Internet. Exhibits from 1999 forward are available on CD-ROM.

Other access: Current session bills and resolutions are available on CD-ROM for $150; other products include the Montana Code, House and Senate Journals, and Annotations, among others.

Voter Registration

Secretary of State, Election Records, PO Box 202801, Helena, MT 59620; 406-444-4732, 406-444-3976 (Fax), 8AM-5PM.

www.state.mt.us/sos

Note: Searching by state personnel depends on the voter file system workload.

Indexing & Storage: Records are available from 1998 (new centralized system). Counties will update the state database 3 times during a 2 year election cycle. Therefore, it is suggested to also search at the county level.

Searching: The following data is not released: Social Security Numbers.

Access by: mail, phone, fax, in person.

Fee & Payment: There are no fees at this time.

Mail search: Turnaround time: 2-4 days. No self addressed stamped envelope is required.

Phone search: Searching is available by phone.

Fax search: Fax searching available.

In person search: Searching is available in person.

Other access: The state database can be purchased on disk or CD-ROM. Cost depends on sort parameters. For more information, contact Joe Kerwin.

GED Certificates

Office of Public Instruction, GED Program, PO Box 202501, Helena, MT 59620-2501; 406-444-4438, 406-444-1373 (Fax), 7AM-4PM.

Indexing & Storage: It takes three weeks before new records are available for inquiry.

Searching: The agency will not issue duplicate diplomas. To search, all of the following are required: a signed release, name, approximate year of test, date of birth, social security number, and city of test. Please include a self-addressed stamped envelope.

Access by: mail, in person.

Fee & Payment: There is no fee for either a verification or transcript.

Mail search: Turnaround time 1 week.A self addressed stamped envelope is requested.

In person search: No fee for request. Turnaround time same day.

Hunting License Information
Fishing License Information

Fish, Wildlife & Parks Department, Department of Fish & Wildlife, PO Box 200701, Helena, MT 59620-0701 (Courier: 1420 E 6th Ave, Helena, MT 59620); 406-444-2950, 406-444-4952 (Fax), 8AM-5PM.

http://fwp.state.mt.us

Indexing & Storage: Records are available from 1976 for the special resident and non-resident permits and the general permits go back for 5 years. Records are computerized for the current year, prior on microfiche. Records are indexed on inhouse computer, microfiche.

Searching: State law restricts distribution of license lists. The agency will only verify if a person has purchased a license. Include the following in your request-full name, date of birth, Social Security Number. The following data is not released: phone numbers.

Access by: mail, phone, in person.

Fee & Payment: There is no search fee.

Mail search: Turnaround time: 1 week. A self addressed stamped envelope is requested.

Phone search: Searching is available by phone.

In person search: Searching is available in person.

Licenses Searchable Online

NOTE: In Montana, there are very few web sites in Montana designed to search licenses. However, they do accept e-mail search requests. The e-mail addresses for such requests are listed here.

Architect #05	compolarc@state.mt.us
Barber #02	compolbar@state.mt.us
Barber Instructor #02	compolbar@state.mt.us
Chemical Dependency Counselor #19	compolcdc@state.mt.us
Dental Assistant #05	compolden@state.mt.us
Dental Hygienist #05	compolden@state.mt.us
Dentist #05	compolden@state.mt.us
Denturist #05	compolden@state.mt.us
Nurse-RN & LPN #32	compolnur@state.mt.us
Nursing #32	compolnur@state.mt.us
Occupational Therapist #21	compolotp@mt.gov
Pharmacist #07	compolpha@state.mt.us
Radiologic Technologist #21	compolrts@state.mt.us
Respiratory Care Practitioner #21	compolrcp@state.mt.us
Sanitarian #21	compolsan@state.mt.us
Speech Pathologist/Audiologist #21	compolslp@state.mt.us
Underground Storage Tank Inspector #42	www.deq.state.mt.us/rem/tsb/ess/enfLicensedComplianceInspectors.pdf
Underground Storage Tank Installer/Remover #42	www.deq.state.mt.us/rem/tsb/ess/installation_closure.htm

Licensing Quick Finder

Acupuncturist #33	406-444-4284	
Adoption Agency #30	406-444-6587	
Advisor Representative #37	406-444-2040	
Appraiser #14	406-841-2386	
Architect #05	406-841-2390	
Asbestos Abatement Worker #25	406-444-3490	
Asbestos Management Planner #25	406-444-3490	
Athletic Event #03	406-841-2393	
Attorney #16	406-444-3858	
Barber #02	406-841-2333	
Barber Instructor #02	406-841-2333	
Boxer/Boxing Promoter #03	406-841-2393	
Calcutta #28	406-444-1971	
Card Contractor #28	406-444-1971	
Card Dealer #28	406-444-1971	
Card Tournament #28	406-444-1971	
Casino Night #28	406-444-1971	
Chemical Dependency Counselor #19	406-444-2827	
Child Care Agency #30	406-444-6587	
Chiropractor #03	406-841-2393	
Construction Blaster #18	406-841-2351	
Contractor #36	406-444-7734	
Cosmetologist #02	406-841-2333	
Day Care Center #26	406-444-2012	
Dental Assistant #05	406-841-2390	
Dental Hygienist #05	406-841-2390	
Dentist #05	406-841-2390	
Denturist #05	406-841-2390	
Dietitian #33	406-444-9395	
Electrician #39	406-841-2328	
Electrologist #02	406-841-2333	
Emergency Medical Technician #33	406-444-4284	
Engineer #10	406-841-2367	
Esthetician #02	406-841-2333	
Foster Care Home #30	406-444-6587	
Foster Care Program #30	406-444-6587	
Funeral Director #03	406-841-2393	
Fur/Hide Dealer #27	406-444-4558	
Gambling Operator #28	406-444-1971	
Gaming Manufacturer/Distributor #28	406-444-1971	
Hairstylist #21	406-444-4288	
Hearing Aid Dispenser #03	406-841-2395	
Horse Racing #22	406-444-4287	
Insurance Adjuster #37	406-444-2040	
Insurance Agent #37	406-444-2040	
Jockey #22	406-444-4287	
Land Surveyor #10	406-841-2367	
Landscape Architect #03	406-841-2395	
Lay Midwife #01	406-841-2394	
Live Card Table #28	406-444-1971	
Lobbyist #23	406-444-2942	
Lottery Retailer #23	406-444-5825	
Manicurist #02	406-841-2333	
Manicurist (Manager/Operator) #02	406-444-4288	
Medical Doctor #33	406-444-4284	
Milk & Cream Tester #29	406-444-5202	
Milk & Cream Weigher, Grader, Sampler #29	406-444-5202	
Mortician #03	406-841-2333	
Naturopathic Physician #01	406-841-2394	
Notary Public #35	406-444-5379	
Nurse-RN & LPN #32	406-444-2071	
Nurseryman #20	406-444-5400	
Nursing #32	406-444-2071	
Nutritionist #33	406-444-4284	
Occupational Therapist #21	406-444-3091	
Osteopath #33	406-444-4284	
Outfitter #06	406-444-3738	
Pesticide Applicator #20	406-444-5400	
Pesticide Dealer #20	406-444-5400	
Pharmacist #07	406-841-2356	
Physical Therapist #09	406-841-2387	
Physician Assistant #33	406-444-4284	
Plumber #08	406-841-2328	
Podiatrist #33	406-444-4284	
Private Investigator #09	406-841-2387	
Private Security Guard #09	406-841-2387	
Property Manager #15	406-444-2961	
Psychologist #11	406-841-2394	
Public Accountant #12	406-841-2388	
Radiologic Technologist #21	406-444-3091	
Real Estate Broker #15	406-444-2961	
Real Estate Salesperson #15	406-444-2961	
Respiratory Care Practitioner #21	406-444-3091	
Sanitarian #21	406-444-3091	
School Guidance Counselor #34	406-444-3150	
School Librarian #34	406-444-3150	
School Principal #34	406-444-3150	
School Superintendent #34	406-444-3150	
Securities Broker/Salesperson #38	406-444-2040	
Security Guard #21	406-444-4288	
Septic Tank Cleaner #25	406-444-4400	
Shorthand Reporter #31	406-721-1143	
Social Worker #21	406-444-4288	
Solicitor/Advisor #37	406-444-2040	
Speech Pathologist/Audiologist #21	406-444-3091	
Surveyor #10	406-841-2367	
Taxidermist #27	406-444-4558	
Teacher #34	406-444-3150	
Timeshare Broker/Salesperson #15	406-444-2961	
Underground Storage Tank Inspector #42	406-444-1420	
Underground Storage Tank Installer/Remover #42	406-444-1420	
Veterinarian #11	406-841-2394	
Video Gambling Machine #28	406-444-1971	
Water & Sewage Plant Operator #25	406-444-4400	
Weather Modifier #40	406-444-6601	
Wrester #03	406-841-2393	
Youth Group Home #30	406-444-6587	

Licensing Agency Information

01 Board of Alternative Health Care, Division of Professional and Occupational Licensing, PO Box 200513 (301 S Park, 4th Fl), Helena, MT 59620-0513; 406-841-2394, Fax: 406-841-2305.

02 Board of Barbers & Cosmetologists, Division of Professional and Occupational Licensing, PO Box 200513 (301 S Park, 4th Fl), Helena, MT 59620-0513; 406-841-2333, Fax: 406-841-2305.

www.com.state.mt.us/License/POL/pol_boards/bar_board/board_page.htm

03 Board: Chiropractor, Funerary, Hearing, Lanscape Architect, Athletic Events, Division of Professional and Occupational Licensing, PO Box 200513 (301 S Park, 4th Fl, #428), Helena, MT 59620-0513; 406-841-2393, Fax: 406-841-2305.

http://commerce.state.mt.us/LICENSE/pol/index.htm

05 Board: Dentistry, Architects, Division of Professional and Occupational Licensing, PO Box 200513 (301 S Park), Helena, MT 59620-0513; 406-841-2390, Fax: 406-841-2305.

www.com.state.mt.us/License/POL/index.htm

06 Board of Outfitters, Divison of Professional and Occupational Licensing, PO Box 200513 (301 S Park, 4th Fl), Helena, MT 59620-0513; 406-444-5983, Fax: 406-444-1667.

MT07 Board of Pharmacy & Optometry, Division of Professional and Occupational Licensing, PO Box 200513 (301 S Park, 4th Fl), Helena, MT 59620-0513; 406-841-2394, Fax: 406-841-2343.

www.com.state.mt.us/license/POL

Direct URL to search licenses: www.arbo.org/nodb2000/licsearch.asp You can search online using nationaol database by name, city or state.

MT08 Plumbing and Electrical Board, Division of Professional and Occupational Licensing, PO Box 200513 (301 S Park, 4th Fl), Helena, MT 59620-0513; 406-841-2328, Fax: 406-841-2305.

MT09 Board of Private Security Patrol Officers & Invest, Board of Physical Therapy Examiners, PO Box 200513 (301 S Park, 4th Fl), Helena, MT 59620-0513; 406-841-2387, Fax: 406-841-2305.

MT10 Board of Professional Engineers & Land Surveyors, Division of Professional and Occupational Licensing, PO Box 200513 (301 S Park, 4th Fl), Helena, MT 59620-0513; 406-841-2367, Fax: 406-841-2309.

www.state.mt.us/doa/aed/aeinfo.html

MT11 Veterinary Board, Board of Psychologists, PO Box 200513 (301 S Park, 4th Fl), Helena, MT 59620-0513; 406-841-2394, Fax: 406-841-2305.

www.com.mt.gov/license/pol/pol_boards/vet_board/contacts.htm

MT12 Board of Public Accountants, PO Box 200513 (301 South Park (PO Box 200513)), Helena, MT 59620-0513; 406-841-2388, Fax: 406-841-2309.

www.com.state.mt.us/license/POL

14 Board of Real Estate Appraisers, PO Box 200513 (301 S Park Ave), Helena, MT 59620-0513; 406-841-2386, Fax: 406-841-2305.

www.com.state.mt.us/LICENSE/pol/pol_boards/rea_board/board_page.htm

15 Board of Realty Regulation, Division of Professional and Occupational Licensing, PO Box 200513 (PO Box 200513 (301 S. Park)), Helena, MT 59620-0513; 406-444-2961, Fax: 406-841-2323.

www.com.state.mt.us/LICENSE/pol/pol_boards/rre_board/board_page.htm

16 Clerk of Superior Court, State Bar of Montana, 215 N Sanders, RM 323 Justice Bldg, Helena, MT 59620; 406-444-3858, Fax: 406-444-5705.

www.montanabar.org

18 Construction Blasters, Division of Professional and Occupational Licensing, PO Box 200513 (301 S Park), Helena, MT 59620-0513; 406-841-2351, Fax: 406-841-2309.

www.com.mt.gov/license/pol/licensing_boards.htm

19 Chemical Dependency Counselors Board, Division of Professional & Occupational Licensing, PO Box 200513 (301 S Park), Helena, MT 59620-0513; 406-444-2827, Fax: 406-841-2305.

www.com.state.mt.us/license/POL/pol_boards/cdc_board/board_page.htm

MT20 Department of Agriculture, PO Box 200201, Helena, MT 59620; 406-444-5400, Fax: 406-444-7336.

MT21 Department of Commerce, Licensing Boards, PO Box 200513 (301 South Park, 4th Fl), Helena, MT 59620-0513; 406-841-2300, Fax: 406-841-2305.

www.com.state.mt.us/License/POL/index.htm

MT22 Department of Commerce, Board of Horse Racing, PO Box 200513 (1424 9th Av), Helena, MT 59620-0512; 406-444-4287, Fax: 406-444-4305.

www.com.mt.gov/license/horse/index.htm

MT23 Department of Commerce, Montana Lottery, PO Box 200544, Helena, MT 59620-0544; 406-444-5825, Fax: 406-444-5830.

MT25 Department of Environmental Quality, Permitting & Compliance Division, PO Box 200901 (1520 E 6th Ave), Helena, MT 59620-0901; 406-444-2544, Fax: 406-444-1374.

www.deq.state.mt.us

MT26 Department of Health & Human Services, Quality Assurance Division, PO Box 202953 (PO Box 202953), Helena, MT 59620; 406-444-2012, Fax: 406-444-1742.

www.dphhs.mt.gov

MT27 Department of Fish, Wildlife & Parks, Licensing/Data Bureau, 1420 E 6th Ave, Helena, MT 59620-0701; 406-444-4558, Fax: 406-444-4952.

MT28 Department of Justice, Gambling Control Division, PO Box 201424 (2687 Airport Rd), Helena, MT 59620-1424; 406-444-1971, Fax: 406-444-9157.

www.doj.mt.gov

MT29 Department of Livestock, PO Box 202001, Helena, MT 59620; 406-444-5202, Fax: 406-444-1929.

MT30 Department of Public Health Human Services, Research & Planning Bureau, PO Box 204001 (48 N Last Chance Gulch), Helena, MT 59620-4001; 406-444-6587, Fax: 406-444-5956.

www.dphhs.mt.gov

MT31 Jeffries Court Reporting Inc., 161 S Mt Ave #C, Missoula, MT 59801; 406-721-1143, Fax: 406-728-0888.

MT32 Board of Nursing, Division of Professional & Occupational Licensing, PO Box 200513 (301 S Park), Helena, MT 59620-0513; 406-444-2071, Fax: 406-4841-2343.

www.com.state.mt.us/License/POL/pol_boards/nur_board/board_page.htm

MT33 Board of Medical Examiners, 21 N Last Chance Gulch, Helena, MT 59620-0513; 406-444-4284, Fax: 406-444-9396.

MT35 Certification Division, Office of Public Instruction, PO Box 1043, Helena, MT 59620-2501; 406-444-3095, Fax: 406-444-2893.

http://161.7.114.15/OPI/opi.html

MT36 Public Contractors Licensing, PO Box PO Box 8011 (PO Box 8011), Helena, MT 59604; 406-444-7734, Fax: 406-444-3465.

www.state.mt.gov.sos

Direct URL to search licenses: www.state.mt.us You can search online using name At State main site, click on Government Agencies, Then Labor & Industry, then Employer Information, then Construction Contractors and download the alphabetical list.

MT37 Insurance Division, State Auditor's Office, PO Box 200513, Helena, MT 59604-4009; 406-444-2040.

MT38 Securities Division, State Auditor's Office, PO Box PO Box 4009 (PO Box 4009), Helena, MT 59604-4009; 406-444-2040, Fax: 406-444-5558.

www.mt.gov/sao/lic.htm

MT40 Dept. of Natural Resoruces & Conservation, Water Resources Division, PO Box 200544 (48 N Last Chance Gulch), Helena, MT 59620-1601; 406-444-6601, Fax: 406-444-0533.

MT42 Department of Environmental Quality, Remediation Division, PO Box 200901 (2209 Phoenix Ave), Helena, MT 59620-0901; 406-444-1420, Fax: 406-444-1901.

www.deq.state.mt.us/rem

Direct URL to search licenses: www.deq.state.mt.us/rem/tsb/ess/ess.htm You can search online using alphabetized lists.

The following list indicates the district and division name for each county in the state. If the district or division name of the bankruptcy court is different from the civil/criminal court, it appears in parentheses.

County/Court Cross. Reference

County	Court	County	Court
Beaverhead	Butte	Meagher	Helena (Butte)
Big Horn	Billings (Butte)	Mineral	Missoula (Butte)
Blaine	Great Falls (Butte)	Missoula	Missoula (Butte)
Broadwater	Helena (Butte)	Musselshell	Billings (Butte)
Carbon	Billings (Butte)	Park	Billings (Butte)
Carter	Billings (Butte)	Petroleum	Billings (Butte)
Cascade	Great Falls (Butte)	Phillips	Billings (Butte)
Chouteau	Great Falls (Butte)	Pondera	Great Falls (Butte)
Custer	Billings (Butte)	Powder River	Billings (Butte)
Daniels	Billings (Butte)	Powell	Helena (Butte)
Dawson	Billings (Butte)	Prairie	Billings (Butte)
Deer Lodge	Butte	Ravalli	Missoula (Butte)
Fallon	Billings (Butte)	Richland	Billings (Butte)
Fergus	Great Falls (Butte)	Roosevelt	Billings (Butte)
Flathead	Missoula (Butte)	Rosebud	Billings (Butte)
Gallatin	Butte	Sanders	Missoula (Butte)
Garfield	Billings (Butte)	Sheridan	Billings (Butte)
Glacier	Great Falls (Butte)	Silver Bow	Butte
Golden Valley	Billings (Butte)	Stillwater	Billings (Butte)
Granite	Missoula (Butte)	Sweet Grass	Billings (Butte)
Hill	Great Falls (Butte)	Teton	Great Falls (Butte)
Jefferson	Helena (Butte)	Toole	Great Falls (Butte)
Judith Basin	Great Falls (Butte)	Treasure	Billings (Butte)
Lake	Missoula (Butte)	Valley	Billings (Butte)
Lewis and Clark	Helena (Butte)	Wheatland	Billings (Butte)
Liberty	Great Falls (Butte)	Wibaux	Billings (Butte)
Lincoln	Missoula (Butte)	Yellowstone	Billings (Butte)
Madison	Butte	Yellowstone Nat. Park (part)	Billings (Butte)
McCone	Billings (Butte)		

US District Court

District of Montana

Billings Division Clerk, Room 5405, Federal Bldg, 316 N 26th St, Billings, MT 59101, 406-247-7000, Fax: 406-247-7008.

Counties: Big Horn, Carbon, Carter, Custer, Dawson, Fallon, Garfield, Golden Valley, McCone, Musselshell, Park, Petroleum, Powder River, Prairie, Richland, Rosebud, Stillwater, Sweet Grass, Treasure, Wheatland,Wibaux, Yellowstone, Yellowstone National Park.

Indexing & Storage: Cases are indexed by defendant and plaintiff as well as by case number. New cases are available in the index 1 week after filing date. A computer index is maintained. Open records are located at this court.

Fee & Payment: The fee is $25.00 per item (one party name or case number). Payment may be made by money order, cashier check, personal check. Prepayment is required. Payee: Clerk, US District Court. Certification fee: $5.00 per document. Copy fee: $.50 per page. You are allowed to make your own copies. These copies cost $.10 per page.

Phone Search: Only docket information is available by phone. An automated voice case information service (VCIS) is not available.

Fax Search: The fee is $15.00.

Mail Search: A stamped self addressed envelope is not required.

In Person Search: In person searching is available.

PACER: Sign-up number is 800-676-6856. Access fee is $.60 per minute. Toll-free access: 800-305-5235. Local access: 406-452-9851. Case records are available back to 1992. Records are never purged. New records are available online after 5 days.

Butte Division Room 273, Federal Bldg, Butte, MT 59701, 406-782-0432, Fax: 406-782-0537.

Counties: Beaverhead, Deer Lodge, Gallatin, Madison, Silver Bow.

Indexing & Storage: Cases are indexed by defendant and plaintiff as well as by case number. New cases are available in the index 1 week after filing date. A computer index is maintained. Open records are located at this court.

Fee & Payment: The fee is $15.00 per item (one party name or case number). Payment may be made by money order, cashier check, personal check. Prepayment is required. Payee: Clerk, US District Court. Certification fee: $5.00 per document. Copy fee: $.50 per page. You are allowed to make your own copies. These copies cost $.10 per page.

Phone Search: Searching is not available by phone.

Fax Search: Will accept fax requests if search fee paid in advance.

Mail Search: A stamped self addressed envelope is not required.

In Person Search: In person searching is available.

PACER: Sign-up number is 800-676-6856. Access fee is $.60 per minute. Toll-free access: 800-305-5235. Local access: 406-452-9851. Case records are available back to 1992. Records are never purged. New records are available online after 5 days.

Great Falls Division Clerk, PO Box 2186, Great Falls, MT 59403 (Courier Address: 215 1st Ave N, Great Falls, MT 59401), 406-727-1922, Fax: 406-727-7648.

Counties: Blaine, Cascade, Chouteau, Daniels, Fergus, Glacier, Hill, Judith Basin, Liberty, Phillips, Pondera, Roosevelt, Sheridan, Teton, Toole, Valley.

Indexing & Storage: Cases are indexed by defendant and plaintiff as well as by case number. New cases are available in the index immediately after filing date. A computer index is maintained. Open records are located at this court. District wide searches are available for all information from this division.

Fee & Payment: The fee is $15.00 per item (one party name or case number). Payment may be made by money order, cashier check, personal check. Prepayment required. Payee: Clerk, US District Court. Certification fee: $5.00 per document. Copy fee: $.50 per page.

Phone Search: Only docket information available by case number. An automated voice case information service (VCIS) is not available.

Mail Search: Always enclose a stamped self addressed envelope.

In Person Search: In person searching is available.

PACER: Sign-up number is 800-676-6856. Access fee is $.60 per minute. Toll-free access: 800-305-5235. Local access: 406-452-9851. Case records are available back to 1992. Records are never purged. New records are available online after 5 days.

Helena Division Federal Bldg, Drawer 10015, Helena, MT 59626 (Courier Address: Room 542, 301 S Park Ave, Helena, MT 59626), 406-441-1355, Fax: 406-441-1357.

Counties: Broadwater, Jefferson, Lewis and Clark, Meagher, Powell.

Indexing & Storage: Cases are indexed by defendant and plaintiff as well as by case number. New cases are available in the index same day if possible after filing date. Both computer and card indexes are maintained. Open records are located at this court. Cases filed in the Missoula division prior to January 1997 are held here.

Fee & Payment: The fee is $15.00 per item (one party name or case number). Payment may be made by money order, cashier check, personal check. Prepayment is required. Payee: Clerk, US District Court. Certification fee: $5.00 per document. Copy fee: $.50 per page.

Phone Search: Information by phone is limited. An automated voice case information service (VCIS) is not available.

Mail Search: Always enclose a stamped self addressed envelope.

In Person Search: In person searching is available.

PACER: Sign-up number is 800-676-6856. Access fee is $.60 per minute. Toll-free access: 800-305-5235. Local access: 406-452-9851. Case records are available back to 1992. Records are never purged. New records are available online after 5 days.

Missoula Division Russell Smith Courthouse, PO Box 8537, Missoula, MT 59807 (Courier Address: 201 E Broadway, Missoula, MT 59802), 406-542-7260, Fax: 406-542-7272.

Counties: Flathead, Granite, Lake, Lincoln, Mineral, Missoula, Ravalli, Sanders.

Indexing & Storage: Cases are indexed by defendant and plaintiff as well as by case number. New cases are available in the index 1-2 days after filing date. A computer index is maintained. Open records are located at this court. Cases in this district originate here; after closing they are held here rather than being sent to a Federal Records Center.

Fee & Payment: The fee is $15.00 per item (one party name or case number). Payment may be made by money order, cashier check, personal check. Prepayment required except for attorneys. Court will fax results for a $5.00 fee. Payee: Clerk, US District Court. Certification fee: $5.00 per document. Copy fee: $.50 per page.

Phone Search: Docket information is available by phone. An automated voice case information service (VCIS) is not available.

Mail Search: A stamped self addressed envelope is not required.

In Person Search: In person searching is available.

PACER: Sign-up number is 800-676-6856. Access fee is $.60 per minute. Toll-free access: 800-305-5235. Local access: 406-452-9851. Case records are available back to 1992. Records are never purged. New records are available online after 5 days.

US Bankruptcy Court

District of Montana

Butte Division PO Box 689, Butte, MT 59703 (Courier Address: 303 Federal Bldg, 400 N Main St, Butte, MT 59703), 406-782-3354, Fax: 406-782-0537.

www.mtb.uscourts.gov

Counties: All counties in Montana.

Indexing & Storage: Cases are indexed by debtor as well as by case number. New cases are available in the index immediately after filing date. A computer index is maintained. Open records are located at this court.

Fee & Payment: The fee is $15.00 per item (one party name or case number). Payment may be made by money order, cashier check, personal check. Debtor's checks are not accepted. Payee: Clerk, US Bankruptcy Court. Certification fee: $5.00 per document. Copy fee: $.50 per page.

Phone Search: Only docket information is available by phone. An automated voice case information service (VCIS) is available. Call VCIS at 888-879-0071 or 406-782-1060.

Fax Search: Will accept fax searches. Will fax results at $1.00 per page.

Mail Search: A stamped self addressed envelope is not required.

In Person Search: In person searching is available.

PACER: Sign-up number is 800-676-6856. Access fee is $.60 per minute. Toll-free access: 800-716-4305. Local access: 406-782-1051. Use of PC Anywhere v4.0 suggested. Case records are available back to 1986. New civil records are available online after 1 day.

Court	Jurisdiction	No. of Courts	How Organized
District Courts*	General	56	21 Districts
Limited Jurisdiction Courts*	Limited	66	56 Counties
City Courts	Limited	83	
Municipal Court	Municipal	1	
Water Courts	Special		4 Divisions
Workers' Compensation Court	Special	1	

* Profiled in this Sourcebook.

Court	CIVIL								
	Tort	Contract	Real Estate	Min. Claim	Max. Claim	Small Claims	Estate	Eviction	Domestic Relations
District Courts*	X	X	X	$5000-7000	No Max		X		X
Limited Jurisdiction Courts*	X	X	X	$0	$5000-7000	$3000		X	
City Courts	X	X	X	$0	$5000				
Municipal Court	X	X	X	$0	$5000	$3000			
Water Courts			X						
Workers' Compensation Court									

Court	CRIMINAL				
	Felony	Misdemeanor	DWI/DUI	Preliminary Hearing	Juvenile
District Courts*	X				X
Limited Jurisdiction Courts*		X	X		
City Courts		X	X		
Municipal Court		X	X		
Water Courts					
Workers' Compensation Court					

ADMINISTRATION Court Administrator, Justice Building, 215 N Sanders, Room 315 (PO Box 203002), Helena, MT, 59620; 406-444-2621, Fax: 406-444-0834.

COURT STRUCTURE The District Courts have no maximum amount for civil judgment cases. Most district courts handle civil over $7,000; there are exceptions that handle a civil minimum of $5000. Limited Jusridiction Courts, which are also known as Justice Courts, may handle civil actions under $7000. The Small Claims limit is $3000. Many Montana Justices of the Peace maintain case record indexes on their personal PCs, which does speed the retrieval process.

ONLINE ACCESS There is no statewide internal or external online computer system available. Those courts with computer systems use them for internal purposes only.

Beaverhead County

District Court Beaverhead County Courthouse, 2 S Pacific St, Dillon, MT 59725; 406-683-5831; Fax: 406-683-6473. Hours: 8AM-5PM (MST). *Felony, Civil Actions Over $5,000, Eviction, Probate.*

Civil Records: Access: Fax, mail, in person. Both court and visitors may perform in person searches. Search fee: $.50 per name per year. Maximum fee-$25.00. Required to search: name, years to search.

Civil cases indexed by defendant, plaintiff. Civil records in books, a few records are on computer. For fax, send fax copy of check for fee. **Criminal Records:** Access: Fax, mail, in person. Both court and visitors may perform in person searches. Search fee: $.50 per name per year. Maximum fee-$25.00. Required to search: name, years to search. Criminal records in books, a few records are on computer. For fax, send fax copy of check for fee. **General Information:** No adoption, juvenile, sanity, paternity or dismissed criminal records

released. SASE required. Turnaround time 1-2 days. Copy fee: $.50 per page. $.25 per page after first 5. Certification fee: $2.00. Fee payee: Clerk of Court. Personal checks accepted. Prepayment is required. Public access terminal is available. Fax notes: $1.00 per page.

Beaverhead County Justice Court PO Box 107, Lima, MT 59739; 406-276-3741. Hours: 3:30-6PM (MST). *Misdemeanor, Civil Actions Under $7,000, Eviction, Small Claims.*

Dillon Justice Court 2 S Pacific, Cluster #16, Dillon, MT 59725; 406-683-2383; Fax: 406-683-5776. Hours: 8AM-Noon (MST). *Misdemeanor, Civil Actions Under $7,000, Eviction, Small Claims.*

Big Horn County

District Court 121 West 3rd St #221, PO Box 908, Hardin, MT 59034; 406-665-9750; Fax: 406-665-9755. Hours: 8AM-5PM (MST). *Felony, Civil Actions Over $7,000, Eviction, Probate.*

Civil Records: Access: Phone, fax, mail, in person. Both court and visitors may perform in person searches. Search fee: $.50 per name per year. Maximum fee-$25.00. Required to search: name, years to search; also helpful-address. Civil cases indexed by defendant, plaintiff. Civil records in books and on microfilm. **Criminal Records:** Access: Phone, fax, mail, in person. Both court and visitors may perform in person searches. Search fee: $.50 per name per year. Maximum fee-$25.00. Required to search: name, years to search; also helpful-address, DOB. Criminal records in books and on microfilm. Signed release required for confidential information. **General Information:** No adoption, sanity, pre-sentence, psychiatric evaluation, depednent & neglected, or confidential criminal justice records released. SASE not required. Turnaround time same day. Copy fee: $.50 per page. $.25 per page after first 5. Certification fee: $2.00. Fee payee: Clerk of Court. Personal checks accepted. Will bill government agencies. Public access terminal is available. Fax notes: $1.00 per page.

Justice Court PO Box 908, Hardin, MT 59034; 406-665-9760; Fax: 406-665-3101. Hours: 8AM-5PM (MST). *Misdemeanor, Civil Actions Under $7,000, Eviction, Small Claims.*

Blaine County

District Court PO Box 969, Chinook, MT 59523; 406-357-3230; Fax: 406-357-2199. Hours: 8AM-5PM (MST). *Felony, Civil Actions Over $5,000, Eviction, Probate.*

Civil Records: Access: Fax, mail, in person. Both court and visitors may perform in person searches. Search fee: $.50 per name per year. Maximum fee-$25.00. Required to search: name, years to search. Civil cases indexed by defendant, plaintiff. Civil records in books from 1912. **Criminal Records:** Access: Fax, mail, in person. Both court and visitors may perform in person searches. Search fee: $.50 per name per year. Maximum fee-$25.00. Required to search: name, years to search, signed release. Criminal records in books from 1912. **General Information:** No adoption, juvenile or sanity records released. SASE required. Turnaround time same day. Copy fee: $.50 per page. $.25 per page after first 5. Certification fee: $2.00. Fee payee: Clerk of Court. Personal checks accepted. Prepayment is required. Fax notes: $1.00 per page.

Chinook Justice Court PO Box 1266, Chinook, MT 59523; 406-357-2335. Hours: 8AM-3PM M,W,F; 9AM-3PM T,Th (MST). *Misdemeanor, Civil Actions Under $7,000, Eviction, Small Claims.*

Broadwater County

District Court 515 Broadway, Townsend, MT 59644; 406-266-3418; Fax: 406-266-4720. Hours: 8AM-Noon, 1-5PM (MST). *Felony, Civil Actions Over $5,000, Eviction, Probate.*

Civil Records: Access: Phone, fax, mail, in person. Both court and visitors may perform in person searches. Search fee: $.50 per name per year. Maximum fee-$25.00. Required to search: name, years to search. Civil records on microfiche and archives. **Criminal Records:** Access: Phone, fax, mail, in person. Both court and visitors may perform in person searches. Search fee: $.50 per name per year. Maximum fee-$25.00. Required to search: name, years to search. Criminal records on microfiche and archives. **General Information:** No adoption, juvenile or sanity records released. SASE required. Turnaround time same day. Copy fee: $.50 per page. $.25 per page after first 5. Certification fee: $2.00. Fee payee: Clerk of Court. Personal checks accepted. Prepayment is required.

Limited Jurisdiction Court 515 Broadway, Townsend, MT 59644; 406-266-9231; Fax: 406-266-4720. Hours: 8AM-5PM (MST). *Misdemeanor, Civil Actions Under $7,000, Eviction, Small Claims.*

Carbon County

District Court PO Box 948, Red Lodge, MT 59068; 406-446-1225; Fax: 406-446-1911. Hours: 8AM-5PM (MST). *Felony, Civil, Probate.*

Note: Also, this court holds youth, adoption and sanity records

Civil Records: Access: Phone, fax, mail, in person. Both court and visitors may perform in person searches. Search fee: $.50 per name per year. Maximum fee-$25.00. Required to search: name, years to search. Civil cases indexed by defendant, plaintiff. Civil records on docket books from 1895. **Criminal Records:** Access: Fax, mail, in person. Only the court conducts in person searches; visitors may not. Search fee: $.50 per name per year. Maximum fee-$25.00. Required to search: name, years to search. Criminal records on docket books from 1895. **General Information:** No adoption, juvenile or sanity records released. SASE required. Turnaround time 1-2 days. Copy fee: $.50 per page. $.25 per page after first 5. Certification fee: $2.00. Fee payee: Clerk of Court. Personal checks accepted. Prepayment is required. Fax notes: $1.00 per page.

Carbon County Justice Court PO Box 2, Red Lodge, MT 59068; 406-446-1440; Fax: 406-446-1911. Hours: 8AM-5PM (MST). *Misdemeanor, Civil Actions Under $7,000, Eviction, Small Claims.*

Joliet City Court PO Box 210, Joliet, MT 59041; 406-962-3133. Hours: 8AM-1PM on 1st, 2nd &3rd Wed of month (MST). *Misdemeanor, Civil Actions Under $7,000.*

Carter County

District Court PO Box 322, Ekalaka, MT 59324; 406-775-8714; Fax: 406-775-8730. Hours: 8AM-5PM (MST). *Felony, Civil Actions Over $5,000, Eviction, Probate.*

Civil Records: Access: Fax, mail, in person. Both court and visitors may perform in person searches. Search fee: $.50 per name per year. Maximum fee-$25.00. Required to search: name, years to search. Civil cases indexed by defendant, plaintiff. Civil records in books from 1917. **Criminal Records:** Access: Fax, mail, in person. Only the court conducts in person searches; visitors may not. Search fee: $.50 per name per year. Maximum fee-$25.00. Required to search: name, years to search, signed release; also helpful-SSN. Criminal records in books from 1917. **General Information:** No adoption, juvenile or sanity records released. SASE required. Turnaround time 1-2 days, same to next day for phone requests. Copy fee: $.50 per page. $.25 per page after first 5. Certification fee:

$2.00. Fee payee: Clerk of Court. Personal checks accepted. Prepayment is required. Fax notes: $1.00 per page.

Limited Jurisdiction Court PO Box 72, Ekalaka, MT 59324-0072; 406-775-8754; Fax: 406-775-8714. Hours: 8AM-5PM TH (MST). *Misdemeanor, Civil Actions Under $7,000, Eviction, Small Claims.*

Note: 1st & 3rd Thurs of month here, 2nd & 4th Thurs of month in Alzada (406-775-8749)

Cascade County

District Court County Courthouse, 415 2nd Ave North, Great Falls, MT 59401; 406-454-6780. Hours: 8AM-5PM (MST). *Felony, Civil Actions Over $5,000, Probate.*

Civil Records: Access: Phone, mail, in person. Both court and visitors may perform in person searches. Search fee: $.50 per name per year. Maximum fee-$25.00. Required to search: name, years to search. Civil cases indexed by defendant, plaintiff. Civil records on computer from 1987. **Criminal Records:** Access: Phone, mail, in person. Both court and visitors may perform in person searches. Search fee: $.50 per name per year. Maximum fee-$25.00. Required to search: name, years to search, DOB, SSN. Criminal records on computer from 1987. **General Information:** No adoption or sanity records released. SASE required. Turnaround time 1-2 days. Copy fee: $.50 per page. $.25 per page after first 5. Certification fee: $2.00. Fee payee: Clerk of Court. Business checks accepted. Prepayment is required. Public access terminal is available.

Cascade Justice Court Cascade County Courthouse, 415 2nd Ave N, Great Falls, MT 59401; 406-454-6870; Fax: 406-454-6877. Hours: 8AM-5PM (MST). *Misdemeanor, Civil Actions Under $7,000, Eviction, Small Claims.*

Chouteau County

District Court PO Box 459, Ft Benton, MT 59442; 406-622-5024; Fax: 406-622-3028. Hours: 8AM-5PM (MST). *Felony, Civil Actions Over $5,000, Eviction, Probate.*

Civil Records: Access: Phone, fax, mail, in person. Both court and visitors may perform in person searches. Search fee: $.50 per name per year. Maximum fee-$25.00. Required to search: name, years to search. Civil cases indexed by defendant, plaintiff. Civil records on books from 1886. **Criminal Records:** Access: Fax, mail, in person. Both court and visitors may perform in person searches. Search fee: $.50 per name per year. Maximum fee-$25.00. Required to search: name, years to search. Criminal records on books from 1886. **General Information:** No adoption, paternity, juvenile or sanity records released. SASE required. Turnaround time 1 day. Copy fee: $.50 per page. $.25 per page after first 5. Certification fee: $2.00. Fee payee: Clerk of Court. Business checks accepted. Prepayment is required. Public access terminal is available. Fax notes: $2.00 for first page, $1.00 each addl.

Big Sandy Justice Court PO Box 234, Big Sandy, MT 59520; 406-378-2203; Fax: 406-378-2378. Hours: 1-5PM Th (MST). *Misdemeanor, Civil Actions Under $7,000, Eviction, Small Claims.*

Ft Benton Justice Court PO Box 459, Ft Benton, MT 59442; 406-622-5502; Fax: 406-622-3815. Hours: 8AM-4PM M,T,W (MST). *Misdemeanor, Civil Actions Under $7,000, Eviction, Small Claims.*

Custer County

District Court 1010 Main, Miles City, MT 59301-3419; 406-233-3326; Fax: 406-233-3451. Hours: 8AM-5PM (MST). *Felony, Civil Actions Over $5,000, Eviction, Probate.*

Civil Records: Access: Mail, in person. Both court and visitors may perform in person searches. Search fee: $.50 per name per year. Maximum fee-$25.00. Required to search: name, years to search. Civil cases indexed by defendant, plaintiff. Civil records in books. **Criminal Records:** Access: Mail, in person. Both court and visitors may perform in person searches. Search fee: $.50 per name per year. Maximum fee-$25.00. Required to search: name, years to search. Criminal records in books. **General Information:** No dependent & neglected, juvenile or sanity records released. SASE required. Turnaround time 1-2 days. Copy fee: $.50 per page. $.25 per page after first 5. Certification fee: $2.00. Fee payee: Clerk of District Court. Personal checks accepted. Prepayment is required.

Limited Jurisdiction Court 1010 Main St, Miles City, MT 59301; 406-233-3408; Fax: 406-233-3452. Hours: 8AM-5PM (MST). *Misdemeanor, Civil Actions Under $7,000, Eviction, Small Claims.*

Daniels County

District Court PO Box 67, Scobey, MT 59263; 406-487-2651. Hours: 8AM-5PM (MST). *Felony, Civil Actions Over $5,000, Eviction, Probate.*

Civil Records: Access: Phone, mail, in person. Both court and visitors may perform in person searches. Search fee: $.50 per name per year. Maximum fee-$25.00. Required to search: name, years to search. Civil cases indexed by defendant, plaintiff. Civil records on books since 1920. **Criminal Records:** Access: Phone, mail, in person. Both court and visitors may perform in person searches. Search fee: $.50 per name per year. Maximum fee-$25.00. Required to search: name, years to search. Criminal records on books since 1920. **General Information:** No adoption, juvenile or sanity records released. SASE required. Turnaround time 1-2 days. Copy fee: $.50 per document. Add $.25 per page after first 5. Certification fee: $2.00. Fee payee: Clerk of Court. Personal checks accepted. Prepayment is required.

Limited Jurisdiction Court Daniels County Courthouse, Scobey, MT 59263; 406-487-5432; Fax: 406-487-5432. Hours: 8AM-5PM (MST). *Misdemeanor, Civil Actions Under $7,000, Eviction, Small Claims.*

Dawson County

District Court 207 W Bell, Glendive, MT 59330; 406-377-3967; Fax: 406-377-7280. Hours: 8AM-5PM (MST). *Felony, Civil Actions Over $5,000, Eviction, Probate.*

Civil Records: Access: Mail, in person. Both court and visitors may perform in person searches. Search fee: $.50 per name per year. Maximum fee-$25.00. Required to search: name, years to search. Civil cases indexed by defendant, plaintiff. Civil records on computer from 1991, on card index prior. **Criminal Records:** Access: Mail, in person. Only the court conducts in person searches; visitors may not. Search fee: $.50 per name per year. Maximum fee-$25.00. Required to search: name, years to search, DOB, SSN. Criminal records on computer from 1991, on card index prior. **General Information:** No adoption, juvenile, sanity or expunged records released.

SASE required. Turnaround time same day. Copy fee: $.50 per page. $.25 per page after first 5. Certification fee: $2.00. Fee payee: Justice Court. Only cashiers checks and money orders accepted. Prepayment is required.

Limited Jurisdiction Court 207 W Towne, Glendive, MT 59330; 406-377-5425; Fax: 406-377-2022. Hours: 8AM-5PM (MST). *Misdemeanor, Civil Actions Under $7,000, Eviction, Small Claims.*

Deer Lodge County

District Court 800 S Main, Anaconda, MT 59711; 406-563-4040; Fax: 406-563-4001. Hours: 8AM-5PM (MST). *Felony, Civil Actions Over $5,000, Eviction, Probate.*

Civil Records: Access: Mail, in person. Only the court conducts in person searches; visitors may not. Search fee: $.50 per name per year. Maximum fee-$25.00. Required to search: name, years to search. Civil cases indexed by defendant, plaintiff. Civil records in archives and index books. **Criminal Records:** Access: Mail, in person. Only the court conducts in person searches; visitors may not. Search fee: $.50 per name per year. Maximum fee-$25.00. Required to search: name, years to search. Criminal records in archives and index books. **General Information:** No adoption, juvenile or sanity records released. SASE required. Turnaround time 2-3 days. Copy fee: $.50 per page. $.25 per page after first 5. Certification fee: $2.00. Fee payee: Clerk of Court. Personal checks accepted.

Limited Jurisdiction Court 800 S Main, Anaconda, MT 59711; 406-563-4025; Fax: 406-563-4028. Hours: 8AM-5PM (MST). *Misdemeanor, Civil Actions Under $7,000, Eviction, Small Claims.*

Fallon County

District Court PO Box 1521, Baker, MT 59313; 406-778-7114; Fax: 406-778-2815. Hours: 8AM-5PM (MST). *Felony, Civil Actions Over $5,000, Eviction, Probate.*

Civil Records: Access: Mail, in person. Both court and visitors may perform in person searches. Search fee: $.50 per name per year. Maximum fee-$25.00. Required to search: name, years to search, address. Civil cases indexed by defendant, plaintiff. Civil records in books. **Criminal Records:** Access: Mail, in person. Both court and visitors may perform in person searches. Search fee: $.50 per name per year. Maximum fee-$25.00. Required to search: name, years to search. Criminal records in books. **General Information:** No confidential records released. SASE required. Turnaround time same day. Copy fee: $.50 per page. $.25 per page after first 5. Certification fee: $2.00. Fee payee: Clerk of Court. Personal checks accepted. Prepayment is required.

Limited Jurisdiction Court Box 846, Baker, MT 59313; 406-778-7128; Fax: 406-778-7128. Hours: 11:00AM-4:00PM T,W,Th (MST). *Misdemeanor, Civil Actions Under $7,000, Eviction, Small Claims.*

Fergus County

District Court PO Box 1074, Lewistown, MT 59457; 406-538-5026; Fax: 406-538-6076. Hours: 8AM-5PM (MST). *Felony, Civil Actions Over $7,000, Eviction, Probate.*

Civil Records: Access: Phone, fax, mail, in person. Both court and visitors may perform in person searches. Search fee: $.50 per name per year. Maximum fee-$25.00. Required to search:

name, years to search. Civil cases indexed by defendant, plaintiff. Civil records on docket books, microfiche. **Criminal Records:** Access: Phone, fax, mail, in person. Both court and visitors may perform in person searches. Search fee: $.50 per name per year. Maximum fee-$25.00. Required to search: name, years to search. Criminal records on docket books, microfiche. **General Information:** No adoption, juvenile, sanity or expunged records released. SASE required. Turnaround time 1 day. Copy fee: $.50 per page. $.25 per page after first 5. Certification fee: $2.00. Fee payee: Clerk of Court. Personal checks accepted. Prepayment is required. Fax notes: $1.00 per page.

Limited Jurisdiction Court 121 8th Ave South, Lewistown, MT 59457; 406-538-5418; Fax: 406-538-3860. Hours: 9AM-4PM (MST). *Misdemeanor, Civil Actions Under $7,000, Eviction, Small Claims.*

Flathead County

District Court 800 S Main, Kalispell, MT 59901; 406-758-5660. Hours: 8AM-5PM (MST). *Felony, Civil Actions Over $5,000, Eviction, Probate.*

www.co.flathead.mt.us/distrct/index.html

Civil Records: Access: Phone, mail, in person. Both court and visitors may perform in person searches. Search fee: $.50 per name per year. Maximum fee-$25.00. Required to search: name, years to search. Civil cases indexed by defendant, plaintiff. Civil records on computer since 1/1/93. **Criminal Records:** Access: Phone, mail, in person. Only the court conducts in person searches; visitors may not. Search fee: $.50 per name per year. Maximum fee-$25.00. Required to search: name, years to search. Criminal records on computer since 1/1/93. **General Information:** No adoption, domestic relations, (some) criminal or sanity records released (all considered confidential). SASE required. Turnaround time 1 week. Certification fee: $2.00. Fee payee: Clerk of Court. Personal checks accepted. Prepayment is required. Public access terminal is available.

Limited Jurisdiction Court 800 S Main St, Kalispell, MT 59901; 406-758-5643; Fax: 406-758-5642. Hours: 8AM-5PM (MST). *Misdemeanor, Civil Actions Under $7,000, Eviction, Small Claims.*

www.co.flathead.mt.us/justice/index.html

Gallatin County

District Court 615 S 16th, Rm 302, Bozeman, MT 59715; 406-582-2165; Fax: 406-582-2176. Hours: 8AM-5PM (MST). *Felony, Civil Actions Over $7,000, Eviction, Probate.*

Civil Records: Access: Mail, in person. Both court and visitors may perform in person searches. Search fee: $.50 per name per year. Maximum fee-$25.00. Required to search: name, years to search. Civil cases indexed by defendant, plaintiff. Civil records on computer and docket books, back to 1891. **Criminal Records:** Access: Mail, in person. Both court and visitors may perform in person searches. Search fee: $.50 per name per year. Maximum fee-$25.00. Required to search: name, years to search. Criminal records on computer and docket books, back to 1891. **General Information:** No adoption, juvenile or sanity records released. SASE required. Turnaround time same day. Copy fee: $.50 per page. $.25 per page after first 5. Certification fee: $2.00. Fee payee: Clerk of Court. Personal checks accepted. Prepayment is required.

Belgrade Justice & City Court 91 E Central, Belgrade, MT 59714; 406-388-3774; Fax: 406-388-3779. Hours: 8AM-Noon M,W,F (MST). *Misdemeanor, Civil Actions Under $7,000, Eviction, Small Claims.*

Bozeman Justice Court 615 S 16th St, Bozeman, MT 59715; 406-582-2191; Fax: 406-582-2041. Hours: 8AM-5PM (MST). *Misdemeanor, Civil Actions Under $7,000, Eviction, Small Claims.*

Garfield County

District Court PO Box 8, Jordan, MT 59337; 406-557-6254; Fax: 406-557-2625. Hours: 8AM-5PM (MST). *Felony, Civil Actions Over $5,000, Eviction, Probate.*

Civil Records: Access: Phone, mail, in person. Both court and visitors may perform in person searches. Search fee: $.50 per name per year. Maximum fee-$25.00. Required to search: name, years to search. Civil cases indexed by plaintiff. Civil records in books from early 1900s. Some records lost due to fire in December, 1997. **Criminal Records:** Access: Phone, mail, in person. Both court and visitors may perform in person searches. Search fee: $.50 per name per year. Maximum fee-$25.00. Required to search: name, years to search; also helpful-DOB. Criminal records in books from early 1900s. Some records lost due to fire in December, 1997. **General Information:** No adoption, juvenile or sanity records released. SASE required. Turnaround time 1 week. Copy fee: $.50 per page. $.25 per page after first 5. Certification fee: $2.00. Fee payee: Clerk of Court. Personal checks accepted. Prepayment is required.

Limited Jurisdiction Court PO Box 482, Jordan, MT 59337; 406-557-2733; Fax: 406-557-2735. Hours: 8AM-5PM Wed (MST). *Misdemeanor, Civil Actions Under $7,000, Eviction, Small Claims.*

Glacier County

District Court 512 E Main St, Cut Bank, MT 59427; 406-873-5063 X36; Fax: 406-873-5627. Hours: 8AM-5PM (MST). *Felony, Civil, Eviction, Probate.*

Civil Records: Access: Phone, fax, mail, in person. Both court and visitors may perform in person searches. Search fee: $.50 per name per year. Maximum fee-$25.00. Required to search: name, years to search. Civil cases indexed by defendant, plaintiff. Civil records in books from 1919. **Criminal Records:** Access: Fax, mail, in person. Both court and visitors may perform in person searches. Search fee: $.50 per name per year. Maximum fee-$25.00. Required to search: name, years to search; also helpful-DOB, SSN. Criminal records in books from 1919. Written request required. **General Information:** No adoption, juvenile, sanity or paternity records released without court order. SASE required. Turnaround time usually same day, 2-3 hours for phone requests, depending on workload. Copy fee: $.50 per page. $.25 per page after first 5. Certification fee: $2.00. Fee payee: Clerk of District Court. Personal checks accepted. Prepayment is required. Fax notes: $1.00 per page.

Limited Jurisdiction Court 512 E Main St, Cut Bank, MT 59427; 406-873-5063 X39; Fax: 406-873-4218. Hours: 8AM-Noon, 1-5PM (MST). *Misdemeanor, Civil Actions Under $7,000, Eviction, Small Claims.*

Golden Valley County

District Court PO Box 10, Ryegate, MT 59074; 406-568-2231; Fax: 406-568-2598. Hours: 8AM-5PM (MST). *Felony, Civil Actions Over $5,000, Eviction, Probate.*

Civil Records: Access: Fax, mail, in person. Search fee: $.50 per name per year. Maximum fee-$25.00. Required to search: name, years to search. Civil cases indexed by defendant, plaintiff. Civil records on books. **Criminal Records:** Access: Fax, mail, in person. Only the court conducts in person searches; visitors may not. Search fee: $.50 per name per year. Maximum fee-$25.00. Required to search: name, years to search. Criminal records on books. **General Information:** No adoption, juvenile or sanity records released. SASE required. Turnaround time 2-3 days. Copy fee: $.50 per page. $.25 per page after first 5. Certification fee: $2.00. Fee payee: Clerk of Court. Personal checks accepted. Prepayment is required. Fax notes: $1.00 per page; no fee to a toll-free number.

Limited Jurisdiction Court PO Box 10, Ryegate, MT 59074; 406-568-2272; Fax: 406-568-2598. Hours: 10AM-2PM Tues (MST). *Misdemeanor, Civil Actions Under $7,000, Eviction, Small Claims.*

Granite County

District Court PO Box 399, Philipsburg, MT 59858-0399; 406-859-3712; Fax: 406-859-3817. Hours: 8AM-Noon, 1-5PM (MST). *Felony, Civil Actions Over $5,000, Eviction, Probate.*

Civil Records: Access: Phone, fax, mail, in person. Both court and visitors may perform in person searches. Search fee: $.50 per name per year. Maximum fee-$25.00. Required to search: name, years to search. Civil cases indexed by defendant, plaintiff. Civil records on docket books since 1893. **Criminal Records:** Access: Phone, fax, mail, in person. Both court and visitors may perform in person searches. Search fee: $.50 per name per year. Maximum fee-$25.00. Required to search: name, years to search. Criminal records on docket books since 1893. **General Information:** No adoption, juvenile or sanity records released. SASE required. Turnaround time 1-4 days. Copy fee: $.50 per page. $.25 per page after first 5. Certification fee: $2.00. Fee payee: Clerk of Court. Personal checks accepted. Prepayment is required.

Drummond Justice Court PO Box 159, Drummond, MT 59832; 406-288-3446; Fax: 406-288-3050. Hours: 9AM-4PM M,W,F (MST). *Misdemeanor, Civil Actions Under $7,000, Eviction, Small Claims.*

Philipsburg Justice Court PO Box 356, Philipsburg, MT 59858; 406-859-3006; Fax: 406-859-3817. Hours: 11AM-Noon, 1-5PM M,W,F (MST). *Misdemeanor, Civil Actions Under $7,000, Eviction, Small Claims.*

Hill County

District Court Hill County Courthouse, Havre, MT 59501; 406-265-5481 X224; Fax: 406-265-1273. Hours: 8AM-5PM (MST). *Felony, Civil Actions Over $5,000, Eviction, Probate.*

Civil Records: Access: Phone, fax, mail, in person. Both court and visitors may perform in person searches. Search fee: $.50 per name per year. Maximum fee-$25.00. Required to search: name, years to search. Civil cases indexed by defendant, plaintiff. Civil records on computer since 1985; prior records on docket books. Maiden name helpful in searching. **Criminal Records:**

Access: Fax, mail, in person. Both court and visitors may perform in person searches. Search fee: $.50 per name per year. Maximum fee-$25.00. Required to search: name, years to search; also helpful-maiden name. Criminal records on computer since 1988; prior records on docket books. **General Information:** No adoption, juvenile, paternity, sanity records released. SASE required. Turnaround time 2-3 days. Copy fee: $.50 per page. $.25 per page after first 5. Certification fee: $2.00. Fee payee: Clerk of Court. Business checks accepted. Prepayment is required. Public access terminal is available. Fax notes: $1.00 per page.

Limited Jurisdiction Court Hill County Courthouse, Havre, MT 59501; 406-265-5481 X240; Fax: 406-265-5487. Hours: 8AM-4PM (MST). *Misdemeanor, Civil Actions Under $7,000, Eviction, Small Claims.*

Jefferson County

District Court PO Box H, Boulder, MT 59632; 406-225-4041 & 4042; Fax: 406-225-4149. Hours: 8AM-Noon, 1-5PM (MST). *Felony, Civil Actions Over $7,000, Eviction, Probate.*

Civil Records: Access: Mail, in person. Both court and visitors may perform in person searches. Search fee: $.50 per name per year. Maximum fee-$25.00. Required to search: name, years to search. Civil cases indexed by defendant, plaintiff. Civil records on computer since 1992, on microfilm since 1925. **Criminal Records:** Access: Mail, in person. Both court and visitors may perform in person searches. Search fee: $.50 per name per year. Maximum fee-$25.00. Required to search: name, years to search. Criminal records on computer since 1992, on microfilm since 1925. **General Information:** Juvenile, sanity or adoption records not released. SASE required. Turnaround time same day. Copy fee: $.50 per page. $.25 per page after first 5. Certification fee: $2.00. Fee payee: Clerk of Court. Personal checks accepted. Prepayment is required. Public access terminal is available.

Limited Jurisdiction Court PO Box H, Boulder, MT 59632; 406-225-4055. Hours: 8AM-5PM (MST). *Misdemeanor, Civil Actions Under $7,000, Eviction, Small Claims.*

Judith Basin County

District Court PO Box 307, Stanford, MT 59479; 406-566-2277 X113; Fax: 406-566-2211. Hours: 8AM-5PM (MST). *Felony, Civil Actions Over $5,000, Eviction, Probate.*

Civil Records: Access: Phone, mail, in person. Both court and visitors may perform in person searches. Search fee: $.50 per name per year. Maximum fee-$25.00. Required to search: name, years to search. Civil cases indexed by defendant, plaintiff. Civil records on books. **Criminal Records:** Access: Phone, mail, in person. Both court and visitors may perform in person searches. Search fee: $.50 per name per year. Maximum fee-$25.00. Required to search: name, years to search, signed release. Criminal records on books. **General Information:** No adoption, sanity records released. SASE required. Turnaround time 10 days. Copy fee: $.50 per page. $.25 per page after first 5. Certification fee: $2.00. Fee payee: Clerk of Court. Business checks accepted. Prepayment is required.

Hobson Justice Court PO Box 276, Hobson, MT 59452; 406-423-5503. Hours: 4:30-9:30PM M-Th (MST). *Misdemeanor, Civil Actions Under $7,000, Eviction, Small Claims.*

Stanford Justice Court PO Box 339, Stanford, MT 59479; 406-566-2277 X117. Hours: 9AM-Noon M,W,F (MST). *Misdemeanor, Civil Actions Under $7,000, Eviction, Small Claims.*

Lake County

District Court 106 4th Ave E, Polson, MT 59860; 406-883-7254; Fax: 406-883-7343. Hours: 8AM-5PM (MST). *Felony, Civil Actions Over $7,000, Probate.*

Civil Records: Access: Phone, fax, mail, in person. Both court and visitors may perform in person searches. Search fee: $.50 per name per year. Maximum fee-$25.00. Required to search: name, years to search. Civil cases indexed by defendant, plaintiff. Civil records on books since 1923. **Criminal Records:** Access: Phone, fax, mail, in person. Both court and visitors may perform in person searches. Search fee: $.50 per name per year. Maximum fee-$25.00. Required to search: name, years to search, DOB, SSN. Criminal records on books since 1923. **General Information:** No adoption, juvenile, sanity or expunged records released. SASE required. Turnaround time 3 days; 2 hours for phone requests. Copy fee: $.50 per page. $.25 per page after first 5. Certification fee: $2.00. Fee payee: Clerk of Court. Business checks accepted. Prepayment is required. Public access terminal is available. Fax notes: $1.00 per page.

Limited Jurisdiction Court 106 4th Ave E, Polson, MT 59860; 406-883-7258; Fax: 406-883-7343. Hours: 8AM-5PM (MST). *Misdemeanor, Civil Actions Under $7,000, Eviction, Small Claims.*

Lewis and Clark County

District Court 228 Broadway, PO Box 158, Helena, MT 59624; 406-447-8216; Fax: 406-447-8275. Hours: 8AM-5PM *Felony, Civil Actions Over $5,000, Eviction, Probate, Small Claims.*

www.co.lewis-clark.mt.us

Civil Records: Access: Fax, mail, online, in person. Both court and visitors may perform in person searches. Search fee: $.50 per name per year. Maximum fee-$25.00. Required to search: name, years to search. Civil cases indexed by defendant, plaintiff. Civil records on computer since 9/90, microfilm prior to 01/89. Will accept e-mail requests to jwright@co.lewis-clark.mt.us. **Criminal Records:** Access: Fax, mail, remote online, in person. Both court and visitors may perform in person searches. Search fee: $.50 per name per year. Maximum fee-$25.00. Required to search: name, years to search. Criminal records on computer since 1/93, microfilm prior to 1/90. Will accept e-mail requests to jwright@co.lewis-clark.mt.us. **General Information:** No adoption, juvenile or sanity records released. SASE required. Turnaround time 2 days. Copy fee: $.50 per page. $.25 per page after first 5. Certification fee: $2.00. Fee payee: Clerk of Court. Personal checks accepted. Prepayment is required. Public access terminal is available. Fax notes: $1.00 per page.

Limited Jurisdiction Court 228 Broadway, Helena, MT 59623; 406-447-8202; Fax: 406-447-8269. Hours: 8AM-5PM *Misdemeanor, Civil Actions Under $7,000, Eviction, Small Claims.*

Liberty County

District Court PO Box 549, Chester, MT 59522; 406-759-5615; Fax: 406-759-5996. Hours: 8AM-5PM (MST). *Felony, Civil Actions Over $5,000, Eviction, Probate.*

Civil Records: Access: Phone, mail, in person. Only the court conducts in person searches; visitors may not. Search fee: $.50 per name per year. Maximum fee-$25.00. Required to search: name, years to search, address. Civil cases indexed by defendant, plaintiff. Civil records on books since 1920. **Criminal Records:** Access: Phone, mail, in person. Both court and visitors may perform in person searches. Search fee: $.50 per name per year. Maximum fee-$25.00. Required to search: name, years to search, signed release. Criminal records on books since 1920. **General Information:** No adoption, juvenile or sanity records released. SASE required. Turnaround time 2-3 days. Copy fee: $.50 per page. $.25 per page after first 5. Certification fee: $2.00. Fee payee: Clerk of Court. Personal checks accepted. Prepayment is required.

Limited Jurisdiction Court PO Box K, Chester, MT 59522; 406-759-5172; Fax: 406-759-5395. Hours: 9AM-5PM Tues (MST). *Misdemeanor, Civil Actions Under $7,000, Eviction, Small Claims.*

Lincoln County

District Court 512 California Ave, Libby, MT 59923; 406-293-7781; Fax: 406-293-9816. Hours: 8AM-5PM (MST). *Felony, Civil Actions Over $5,000, Eviction, Probate.*

Civil Records: Access: Mail, in person. Both court and visitors may perform in person searches. Search fee: $3.00 per name for ten year search; $.50 each addl year with $25.00 maximum. Required to search: name, years to search. Civil cases indexed by defendant, plaintiff. Civil records on computer from 1991, prior on docket books. **Criminal Records:** Access: Mail, in person. Both court and visitors may perform in person searches. Search fee: $3.00 per name. Fee is for 10 year search. Maximum fee $25.00. Required to search: name, years to search, DOB. Criminal records on computer from 1991, prior on docket books. **General Information:** No adoption, juvenile or sanity records released. SASE required. Turnaround time 1 week. Copy fee: $.50 per page. $.25 per page after first 5. Certification fee: $2.00. Fee payee: Clerk of Court. Personal checks accepted. Prepayment is required.

Eureka Justice Court #2 Highway 93 North, Eureka, MT 59917; 406-296-2622; Fax: 406-296-3829. Hours: 8AM-5M M-W (MST). *Misdemeanor, Civil Actions Under $7,000, Eviction, Small Claims.*

Libby Justice Court #1 418 Mineral Ave, Libby, MT 59923; 406-293-7781 X236; Fax: 406-293-5948. Hours: 8AM-5PM (MST). *Misdemeanor, Civil Actions Under $7,000, Eviction, Small Claims.*

Madison County

District Court PO Box 185, Virginia City, MT 59755; 406-843-4230; Fax: 406-843-5207. Hours: 8AM-5PM (MST). *Felony, Civil Actions Over $5,000, Eviction, Probate.*

Civil Records: Access: Fax, mail, in person. Both court and visitors may perform in person searches. Search fee: $.50 per name per year. Maximum fee-$25.00. Required to search: name, years to search. Civil cases indexed by defendant, plaintiff. Civil records on books since 1864. **Criminal Records:** Access: Fax, mail, in person. Only the court conducts in person searches; visitors may not. Search fee: $.50 per name per year. Maximum fee-$25.00. Required to search: name, years to search. Criminal records on books since 1864. **General**

Information: No adoption, juvenile or sanity records released. SASE required. Turnaround time 1 week. Copy fee: $.50 per page. $.25 per page after first 5. Certification fee: $2.00. Fee payee: Clerk of Court. Personal checks accepted. Prepayment is required. Fax notes: $4.00 for first page, $1.00 each addl.

Limited Jurisdiction Court PO Box 277, Virginia City, MT 59755; 406-843-4230; Fax: 406-843-5517. Hours: 8AM-5PM (MST). *Misdemeanor, Civil Actions Under $7,000, Eviction, Small Claims.*

McCone County

District Court PO Box 199, Circle, MT 59215; 406-485-3410; Fax: 406-485-3410. Hours: 8AM-5PM (MST). *Felony, Civil Actions Over $5,000, Eviction, Probate.*

Civil Records: Access: Mail, in person. Only the court conducts in person searches; visitors may not. Search fee: $.50 per name per year. Maximum fee-$25.00. Required to search: name, years to search. Civil cases indexed by defendant, plaintiff. Civil records in books from 1919. **Criminal Records:** Access: Mail, in person. Only the court conducts in person searches; visitors may not. Search fee: $.50 per name per year. Maximum fee-$25.00. Required to search: name, years to search. Criminal records in books and microfilm since 1919. **General Information:** No adoption, juvenile, sanity or mental health records released. SASE required. Turnaround time 1-2 days. Copy fee: $.50 per page. $.25 per page after first 5. Certification fee: $2.00. Fee payee: Clerk of Court. Personal checks accepted. Prepayment is required.

Limited Jurisdiction Court PO Box 24, Circle, MT 59215; 406-485-3548. Hours: 2-5PM Wed (MST). *Misdemeanor, Civil Actions Under $7,000, Eviction, Small Claims.*

Meagher County

District Court PO Box 443, White Sulphur Springs, MT 59645; 406-547-3612 Ext110; Fax: 406-547-3388. Hours: 8AM-5PM (MST). *Felony, Civil Actions Over $5,000, Eviction, Probate.*

Civil Records: Access: Phone, mail, in person. Both court and visitors may perform in person searches. Search fee: $.50 per name per year. Maximum fee-$25.00. Required to search: name, years to search. Civil cases indexed by defendant, plaintiff. Civil records on docket books or microfiche. **Criminal Records:** Access: Phone, mail, in person. Both court and visitors may perform in person searches. Search fee: $.50 per name per year. Maximum fee-$25.00. Required to search: name, years to search. Criminal records on docket books or microfiche. **General Information:** No adoption, juvenile or sanity records released. SASE required. Turnaround time 3 days. Copy fee: $.50 per page. $.25 per page after first 5. Certification fee: $2.00. Fee payee: Clerk of Court. Personal checks accepted.

Limited Jurisdiction Court Justice Court, W. Main St., White Sulphur Springs, MT 59645; 406-547-3954 X115; Fax: 406-547-3388. Hours: 8AM-5PM T-Th (MST). *Misdemeanor, Civil Actions Under $7,000, Eviction, Small Claims.*

Mineral County

District Court PO Box 129, Superior, MT 59872; 406-822-3538; Fax: 406-822-3579. Hours: 8AM-Noon,1-5PM (MST). *Felony, Civil Actions Over $5,000, Probate.*

Civil Records: Access: Phone, fax, mail, in person. Both court and visitors may perform in person searches. Search fee: $.50 per name per year. Maximum fee-$25.00. Required to search: name, years to search. Civil cases indexed by defendant, plaintiff. Civil records on docket books from 1914, records are computerized since 1990. **Criminal Records:** Access: Phone, fax, mail, in person. Both court and visitors may perform in person searches. Search fee: $.50 per name per year. Maximum fee-$25.00. Required to search: name, years to search. Criminal records on docket books from 1914, records are computerized since 1990. **General Information:** No adoption, sanity records released. SASE required. Turnaround time same day after payment received. Copy fee: $.50 per page. $.25 per page after first 5. Certification fee: $2.00. Fee payee: Clerk of Court. Personal checks accepted. Prepayment is required. Fax notes: $5.00 per document.

Limited Jurisdiction Court PO Box 658, Superior, MT 59872; 406-822-3550; Fax: 406-822-3579. Hours: 8AM-5PM (MST). *Misdemeanor, Civil Actions Under $7,000, Eviction, Small Claims.*

Missoula County

District Court 200 W Broadway, Missoula, MT 59802; 406-523-4780 X3523; Fax: 406-523-4899. Hours: 8AM-5PM (MST). *Felony, Civil Actions Over $5,000, Probate.*

Civil Records: Access: Fax, mail, in person. Both court and visitors may perform in person searches. Search fee: $.50 per name per year. Maximum fee-$25.00. Required to search: name, years to search. Civil cases indexed by defendant, plaintiff. Civil records on computer from 10/89, microfilm from 1970s, archived to late 1800s. **Criminal Records:** Access: Fax, mail, in person. Both court and visitors may perform in person searches. Search fee: $.50 per name per year. Maximum fee-$25.00. Required to search: name, years to search. Criminal records on computer from 10/89, microfilm from 1970s, archived to late 1800s. **General Information:** No adoption, juvenile, sealed, expunged or pre-sentence psychiatric records released. SASE not required. Turnaround time up to 2 weeks. Copy fee: $.50 per page. $.25 per page after first 5. Certification fee: $2.00. Fee payee: Clerk of Court. Personal checks accepted. Credit cards accepted: Visa, Mastercard. Prepayment is required. Public access terminal is available. Fax notes: $2.00 per document. No fee if returning on toll free line g each add'l pg. Fax fee payment must be made by credit card.

Limited Jurisdiction Court, Dept 1 200 W Broadway, Missoula County Courthouse, Missoula, MT 59802; 406-721-2703; Fax: 406-721-4043. Hours: 8AM-5PM (MST). *Misdemeanor, Civil Actions Under $7,000, Eviction, Small Claims.*

Musselshell County

District Court PO Box 357, Roundup, MT 59072; 406-323-1413; Fax: 406-323-1710. Hours: 8AM-5PM (MST). *Felony, Civil Actions Over $5,000, Eviction, Probate.*

Civil Records: Access: Mail, in person. Both court and visitors may perform in person searches. Search fee: $.50 per name per year. Maximum fee-$25.00. Required to search: name, years to search. Civil cases indexed by defendant, plaintiff. Civil records on docket books from 1911. **Criminal Records:** Access: Mail, in person. Both court and visitors may perform in person searches. Search fee: $.50 per name per year. Maximum fee-$25.00. Required to search: name, years to search.

Criminal records on docket books from 1911. **General Information:** No adoption, (some) juvenile or sanity records released. SASE required. Turnaround time 2-3 days. Copy fee: $.50 per page. $.25 per page after first 5. Certification fee: $2.00. Fee payee: Clerk of Court. Personal checks accepted. Prepayment is required.

Limited Jurisdiction Court PO Box 660, Roundup, MT 59072; 406-323-1078; Fax: 406-323-3452. Hours: 9AM-Noon (MST). *Misdemeanor, Civil Actions Under $7,000, Eviction, Small Claims.*

Park County

District Court PO Box 437, Livingston, MT 59047; 406-222-4125; Fax: 406-222-4128. Hours: 8AM-5PM (MST). *Felony, Civil Actions Over $7,000, Eviction, Probate.*

Civil Records: Access: Phone, mail, in person. Both court and visitors may perform in person searches. Search fee: $.50 per name per year. Maximum fee-$25.00. Required to search: name, years to search. Civil cases indexed by defendant, plaintiff. Civil records on computer, microfiche, and docket books from 1889 to present. **Criminal Records:** Access: Phone, mail, in person. Both court and visitors may perform in person searches. Search fee: $.50 per name per year. Maximum fee-$25.00. Required to search: name, years to search. Criminal records on computer, microfiche, and docket books from 1889 to present. **General Information:** No adoption, juvenile or sanity records released. SASE not required. Turnaround time 1-2 days for all requests. Copy fee: $.50 per page. $.25 per page after first 5. Certification fee: $2.00. Fee payee: Clerk of Court. Personal checks accepted. Prepayment is required. Public access terminal is available.

Limited Jurisdiction Court 414 E Callender, Livingston, MT 59047; 406-222-4169/4171; Fax: 406-222-4103. Hours: 8AM-5PM (MST). *Misdemeanor, Civil Actions Under $7,000, Eviction, Small Claims.*

Petroleum County

District Court PO Box 226, Winnett, MT 59087; 406-429-5311; Fax: 406-429-6328. Hours: 8AM-5PM (MST). *Felony, Civil Actions Over $5,000, Eviction, Probate.*

Civil Records: Access: Phone, mail, in person. Both court and visitors may perform in person searches. Search fee: $.50 per name per year. Maximum fee-$25.00. Required to search: name, years to search. Civil cases indexed by defendant, plaintiff. Civil records on docket books from 1924. **Criminal Records:** Access: Phone, mail, in person. Only the court conducts in person searches; visitors may not. Search fee: $.50 per name per year. Maximum fee-$25.00. Required to search: name, years to search. Criminal records on docket books from 1924. **General Information:** No adoption, juvenile or sanity records released. SASE required. Turnaround time 1 day. Copy fee: $.50 per page. $.25 per page after first 5. Certification fee: $2.00. Fee payee: Clerk of Court. Personal checks accepted. Prepayment is required.

Limited Jurisdiction Court PO Box 223, Winnett, MT 59087; 406-429-5311; Fax: 406-429-6328. Hours: 9AM-Noon Th (MST). *Misdemeanor, Civil Actions Under $7,000, Eviction, Small Claims.*

Phillips County

District Court PO Box 530, Malta, MT 59538; 406-654-1023; Fax: 406-654-1023. Hours: 8AM-5PM (MST). *Felony, Civil Actions Over $5,000, Eviction, Probate.*

Civil Records: Access: Phone, fax, mail, in person. Only the court conducts in person searches; visitors may not. Search fee: $.50 per name per year. Maximum fee-$25.00. Required to search: name, years to search; also helpful-address. Civil cases indexed by defendant, plaintiff. Civil records on computer, books, microfilm back to 1915. **Criminal Records:** Access: Mail, in person. Only the court conducts in person searches; visitors may not. Search fee: $.50 per name per year. Maximum fee-$25.00. Required to search: name, years to search, signed release; also helpful-address. Criminal records on computer, books, microfilm back to 1915. **General Information:** No adoption, juvenile or sanity records released. SASE required. Turnaround time 1-2 days. Copy fee: $.50 per page. $.25 per page after first 5. Certification fee: $2.00. Fee payee: Clerk of Court. Personal checks accepted. Prepayment is required. Fax notes: There is a $5.00 fee to return by fax, unless a toll free line is used.

Limited Jurisdiction Court PO Box 1396, Malta, MT 59538; 406-654-1118; Fax: 406-654-1213. Hours: 10AM-4PM M-Th (MST). *Misdemeanor, Civil Actions Under $7,000, Eviction, Small Claims.*

Pondera County

District Court 20 Fourth Ave SW, Conrad, MT 59425; 406-278-4026; Fax: 406-278-4081. Hours: 8AM-5PM (MST). *Felony, Civil Actions Over $5,000, Eviction, Probate.*

Civil Records: Access: Fax, mail, in person. Both court and visitors may perform in person searches. Search fee: $.50 per name per year. Maximum fee-$25.00. Required to search: name, years to search. Civil cases indexed by defendant, plaintiff. Civil records on docket books from 1919. **Criminal Records:** Access: Fax, mail, in person. Both court and visitors may perform in person searches. Search fee: $.50 per name per year. Maximum fee-$25.00. Required to search: name, years to search. Criminal records on docket books from 1919. **General Information:** No adoption or sanity records released. SASE required. Turnaround time 2-3 days. Copy fee: $.50 per page. $.25 per page after first 5. Certification fee: $2.00. Fee payee: Clerk of Court. Personal checks accepted. Prepayment is required. Fax notes: Fax fee: $.50 1st 5 pages, $.25 each additional page. $1.00 for cover page.

Limited Jurisdiction Court 20 Fourth Ave SW, Conrad, MT 59425; 406-278-4030; Fax: 406-278-4070. Hours: 9AM-4PM (MST). *Misdemeanor, Civil Actions Under $7,000, Eviction, Small Claims.*

Powder River County

District Court PO Box 239, Broadus, MT 59317; 406-436-2320; Fax: 406-436-2325. Hours: 8AM-Noon, 1-5PM (MST). *Felony, Civil Actions Over $5,000, Eviction, Probate.*

Civil Records: Access: Fax, mail, in person. Both court and visitors may perform in person searches. Search fee: $.50 per name per year. Maximum fee-$25.00. Required to search: name, years to search. Civil cases indexed by defendant, plaintiff. Civil records on computer since 1993, microfiche since 1974, and books since 1919. **Criminal Records:**

Access: Fax, mail, in person. Both court and visitors may perform in person searches. Search fee: $.50 per name per year. Maximum fee-$25.00. Required to search: name, years to search. Criminal records on computer since 1993, microfiche since 1974, and books since 1919. **General Information:** No adoption, juvenile, sanity, dismissed criminal records released. SASE required. Turnaround time same day if pre-paid. Copy fee: $.50 per page. $.25 per page after first 5. Certification fee: $2.00. Fee payee: Clerk of Court. Only cashiers checks and money orders accepted. Prepayment is required. Fax notes: Fee to fax is $.50 per page.

Limited Jurisdiction Court PO Box 488, Broadus, MT 59317; 406-436-2503; Fax: 406-436-2866. Hours: 9AM-3:30PM M-Th (MST). *Misdemeanor, Civil Actions Under $7,000, Eviction, Small Claims.*

Powell County

District Court 409 Missouri Ave, Deer Lodge, MT 59722; 406-846-3680 X234/235; Fax: 406-846-2784. Hours: 8AM-5PM (MST). *Felony, Civil Actions Over $5,000, Eviction, Probate.*

Civil Records: Access: Mail, in person. Both court and visitors may perform in person searches. Search fee: $.50 per name per year. Maximum fee-$25.00. Required to search: name, years to search. Civil cases indexed by defendant, plaintiff. Civil records on docket books since turn of century, on computer since 1996. **Criminal Records:** Access: Mail, in person. Both court and visitors may perform in person searches. Search fee: $.50 per name per year. Maximum fee-$25.00. Required to search: name, years to search, DOB, SSN. Criminal records on docket books since turn of century, on computer since 1996. **General Information:** No adoption, juvenile or sanity records released. SASE required. Turnaround time 2-3 days, immediately over phone. Copy fee: $.50 per page. $.25 per page after first 5. Certification fee: $2.00. Fee payee: Clerk of Court. Personal checks accepted. Prepayment is required.

Limited Jurisdiction Court 409 Missouri, Powell County Courthouse, Deer Lodge, MT 59722; 406-846-3680 X40. Hours: 8AM-5PM (MST). *Misdemeanor, Civil Actions Under $7,000, Eviction, Small Claims.*

Prairie County

District Court PO Box 125, Terry, MT 59349; 406-635-5575. Hours: 8AM-5PM (MST). *Felony, Civil Actions Over $5,000, Eviction, Probate.*

Civil Records: Access: Mail, in person. Both court and visitors may perform in person searches. Search fee: $.50 per name. Maximum fee-$25.00. Required to search: name, years to search. Civil cases indexed by defendant, plaintiff. Civil records on books since 1915. **Criminal Records:** Access: Mail, in person. Both court and visitors may perform in person searches. Search fee: $.50 per name. Maximum fee-$25.00. Required to search: name, years to search, DOB, SSN. Criminal records on books since 1915. **General Information:** No adoption, juvenile or sanity records released. SASE required. Turnaround time 5 days. Copy fee: $.25 per page. Certification fee: $2.00. Fee payee: Clerk of Court. Personal checks accepted.

Limited Jurisdiction Court PO Box 40, Terry, MT 59349; 406-635-4466; Fax: 406-635-5580. Hours: 1-2PM (MST). *Misdemeanor, Civil Actions Under $7,000, Eviction, Small Claims.*

Ravalli County

District Court Ravalli County Courthouse, Box 5014, Hamilton, MT 59840; 406-375-6214; Fax: 406-375-6327. Hours: 8AM-5PM (MST). *Felony, Civil Actions Over $7,000, Probate.*

Civil Records: Access: Fax, mail, in person. Both court and visitors may perform in person searches. Search fee: $.50 per name per year. Maximum fee-$25.00. Required to search: name, years to search. Civil cases indexed by defendant, plaintiff. Civil records on microfiche (1989), docket books (1914). **Criminal Records:** Access: Fax, mail, in person. Both court and visitors may perform in person searches. Search fee: $.50 per name per year. Maximum fee-$25.00. Required to search: name, years to search. Criminal records on microfiche (1989), docket books (1914). **General Information:** No adoption, juvenile, psychological, medical or expunged records released. SASE required. Turnaround time 4-5 days. Copy fee: $.50 per page. $.25 per page after first 5. Certification fee: $2.00. Fee payee: Clerk of Court. Personal checks accepted. Prepayment is required. Fax notes: $1.00 per page.

Limited Jurisdiction Court Courthouse Box 5023, Hamilton, MT 59840; 406-375-6252; Fax: 406-375-6383. Hours: 8AM-5PM (MST). *Misdemeanor, Civil Actions Under $7,000, Eviction, Small Claims.*

Richland County

District Court 201 W Main, Sidney, MT 59270; 406-482-6945; Fax: 406-482-3731. Hours: 8AM-5PM (MST). *Felony, Civil Actions Over $5,000, Eviction, Probate.*

Civil Records: Access: Phone, fax, mail, in person. Both court and visitors may perform in person searches. Search fee: $.50 per name per year. Maximum fee-$25.00. Required to search: name, years to search. Civil cases indexed by defendant, plaintiff. Civil records in books since 1914. **Criminal Records:** Access: Phone, fax, mail, in person. Both court and visitors may perform in person searches. Search fee: $.50 per name per year. Maximum fee-$25.00. Required to search: name, years to search. Criminal records in books since 1914. **General Information:** No adoption, juvenile, paternity, sanity, dismissed or expunged records released. SASE required. Turnaround time 1-3 days. Copy fee: $.50 per page. $.25 per page after first 5. Certification fee: $2.00. Fee payee: Clerk of Court. Personal checks accepted. Prepayment is required. Fax notes: $1.00 per page.

Limited Jurisdiction Court 123 W Main, Sidney, MT 59270; 406-433-2815; Fax: 406-433-6885. Hours: 8AM-5PM (MST). *Misdemeanor, Civil Actions Under $7,000, Eviction, Small Claims.*

Roosevelt County

District Court County Courthouse, Wolf Point, MT 59201; 406-653-6266; Fax: 406-653-6203. Hours: 8AM-5PM (MST). *Felony, Civil Actions Over $5,000, Eviction, Probate.*

Civil Records: Access: Fax, mail, in person. Only the court conducts in person searches; visitors may not. Search fee: $.50 per name per year. Maximum fee-$25.00. Required to search: name, years to search. Civil cases indexed by defendant, plaintiff. Civil records on books and microfiche. **Criminal Records:** Access: Fax, mail, in person. Only the court conducts in person searches; visitors may not. Search fee: $.50 per name per year. Maximum

fee-$25.00. Required to search: name, years to search; also helpful-DOB. Criminal records on books and microfiche. **General Information:** No adoption, juvenile or sanity records released. SASE required. Turnaround time 2-3 days after receipt of payment. Copy fee: $.50 per page. $.25 per page after first 5. Certification fee: $2.00. Fee payee: Clerk of Court. Personal checks accepted. Prepayment is required. Fax notes: $3.00 for first page, $.50 each addl.

Culbertson Justice Court Post #2 PO Box 421, Culbertson, MT 59218; 406-787-6607; Fax: 406-787-6607. Hours: 9AM-3PM M-Th (MST). *Misdemeanor, Civil Actions Under $7,000, Eviction, Small Claims.*

Wolf Point Justice Court Post #1 County Courthouse, 400 Second Ave. S., Wolf Point, MT 59201; 406-653-6261; Fax: 406-653-6203. Hours: 8AM-1PM M-Th; 8AM-Noon Fri. (MST). *Misdemeanor, Civil Actions Under $7,000, Eviction, Small Claims.*

Rosebud County

District Court PO Box 48, Forsyth, MT 59327; 406-356-7322; Fax: 406-356-7551. Hours: 8AM-5PM (MST). *Felony, Civil Actions Over $5,000, Eviction, Probate.*

Civil Records: Access: Fax, mail, in person. Only the court conducts in person searches; visitors may not. Search fee: $.50 per name per year. Maximum fee-$25.00, written requests only. Required to search: name, years to search. Civil cases indexed by defendant, plaintiff. Civil records in books, on microfiche. **Criminal Records:** Access: Mail, in person. Only the court conducts in person searches; visitors may not. Search fee: $.50 per name per year. Maximum fee-$25.00, written requests only. Required to search: name, years to search, signed release. Criminal records in books, on microfiche. **General Information:** No adoption, juvenile, sanity or sealed records released. SASE required. Turnaround time 2 days. Copy fee: $.50 per page. $.25 per page after first 5. Certification fee: $2.00. Fee payee: Clerk of Court. Personal checks accepted. Prepayment is required. Fax notes: No fee to fax results.

Limited Jurisdiction Court #1 Rosebud County Courthouse, PO Box 504, Forsyth, MT 59327; 406-356-2638; Fax: 406-356-7551. Hours: 8AM-5PM (MST). *Misdemeanor, Civil Actions Under $7,000, Eviction, Small Claims.*

Limited Jurisdiction Court #2 PO Box 575, Colstrip, MT 59323; 406-748-2934; Fax: 406-748-4832. Hours: 8AM-5PM; Ashland 2nd & 4th Wed 1PM (MST). *Misdemeanor, Civil Actions Under $7,000, Eviction, Small Claims.*

Sanders County

District Court PO Box 519, Thompson Falls, MT 59873; 406-827-4316; Fax: 406-827-0094. Hours: 8AM-5PM (MST). *Felony, Civil Actions Over $5,000, Eviction, Probate.*

Civil Records: Access: Mail, in person. Both court and visitors may perform in person searches. Search fee: $.50 per name per year. Maximum fee-$25.00. Required to search: name, years to search. Civil cases indexed by defendant, plaintiff. Civil records on docket books since 1906. **Criminal Records:** Access: Mail, in person. Both court and visitors may perform in person searches. Search fee: $.50 per name per year. Maximum fee-$25.00. Required to search: name, years to search, DOB, SSN, signed release. Criminal records on docket books since 1906. **General Information:** No adoption, juvenile, sanity or pre-sentence

Licenses Searchable Online

Alcohol/Drug Testing #30...www.hhs.state.ne.us/lis/lis.asp
Architect #02...www.nol.org/home/NBOP/roster.html
Asbestos #30..www.hhs.state.ne.us/lis/lis.asp
Athletic Trainer #30..www.hhs.state.ne.us/lis/lis.asp
Attorney #32...www.nebar.com/directory/dir.asp
Bank #31..www.ndbf.org/banks.htm
Chiropractor #30...www.hhs.state.ne.us/lis/lis.asp
Collection Agency #26..www.nol.org/home/SOS/Collections/col-agn.htm
Cosmetology Salon #30..www.hhs.state.ne.us/lis/lis.asp
Cosmetology School #30...www.hhs.state.ne.us/lis/lis.asp
Credit Union #31...www.ndbf.org/culist.htm
Debt Management Agency #26.................................www.nol.org/home/SOS/Collections/debtlist.htm
Delayed Deposit Service #31...................................www.ndbf.org/ddslist.htm
Dental Hygienist #30...www.hhs.state.ne.us/lis/lis.asp
Dentist #30...www.hhs.state.ne.us/lis/lis.asp
Engineer #02..www.nol.org/home/NBOP/roster.html
Environmental Health Specialist #30........................www.hhs.state.ne.us/lis/lis.asp
Funeral Establishment #30......................................www.hhs.state.ne.us/lis/lis.asp
Health Clinic & Emergency Medical Care #30...........www.hhs.state.ne.us/lis/lis.asp
Hearing Aid Dispenser/Fitter #30.............................www.hhs.state.ne.us/lis/lis.asp
Investment Advisor #11...www.ndbf.org/secsearch.htm
Investment Advisor Representative #11.....................www.ndbf.org/secsearch.htm
Massage Therapy School #30..................................www.hhs.state.ne.us/lis/lis.asp
Medical Nutrition Therapy #30.................................www.hhs.state.ne.us/lis/lis.asp
Mental Health Center #30..www.hhs.state.ne.us/lis/lis.asp
Nurse #30...www.hhs.state.ne.us/lis/lis.asp
Nursing Home #30..www.hhs.state.ne.us/lis/lis.asp
Occupational Therapist #30.....................................www.hhs.state.ne.us/lis/lis.asp
Optometrist #30..www.hhs.state.ne.us/lis/lis.asp
Pharmacist #30...www.hhs.state.ne.us/lis/lis.asp
Pharmacy #30...www.hhs.state.ne.us/lis/lis.asp
Physical Therapist #30..www.hhs.state.ne.us/lis/lis.asp
Physician #30..www.hhs.state.ne.us/lis/lis.asp
Physician Assistant #30..www.hhs.state.ne.us/lis/lis.asp
Plainclothes Investigator #26...................................www.nol.org/home/SOS/Privatedetectives/pilist.htm
Podiatrist #30...www.hhs.state.ne.us/lis/lis.asp
Polygraph Examiner, Private #26.............................www.nol.org/home/SOS/Polygraph/polypri.htm
Polygraph Examiner, Public #26..............................www.nol.org/home/SOS/Polygraph/polypub.htm
Private Detective #26..www.nol.org/home/SOS/Privatedetectives/pdlist.htm
Psychologist #30...www.hhs.state.ne.us/lis/lis.asp
Radiographer #30..www.hhs.state.ne.us/lis/lis.asp
Real Estate Appraiser #22.......................................http://dbdec.nrc.state.ne.us/appraiser/docs/list.html
Respiratory Care #30..www.hhs.state.ne.us/lis/lis.asp
Securities Agent #11...www.ndbf.org/secsearch.htm
Securities Broker/Dealer #11...................................www.ndbf.org/secsearch.htm
Swimming Pool Operator #30...................................www.hhs.state.ne.us/lis/lis.asp
Vendor (Liquor) #19..www.nol.org/home/NLCC/nlccsearch.html
Veterinarian #30..www.hhs.state.ne.us/lis/lis.asp
Voice Stress Examiner #26......................................www.nol.org/home/SOS/Polygraph/voice.htm
Water Operator #30...www.hhs.state.ne.us/lis/lis.asp

Licensing Quick Finder

Abstractor #04 402-471-2383
Aerial Applicator #10 402-471-2371
Air Conditioning/Heating #12 402-441-7508
Alcohol/Drug Testing #30 402-471-2118
Amusement Ride Inspector #21 402-471-2031
Animal Technician #30 402-471-2118
Architect #02 402-471-2021
Attorney #32 402-471-3731
Auctioneer #06 402-441-7437
Bank #31 402-471-2171
Barber #01 402-471-2051

Boarding Home #30 402-471-2115
Boiler & Pressure Inspector #16 402-471-4721
Boxer #28 402-471-2009
Boxing Promoter #28 402-471-2009
Center for Develop. Disabled #30 ... 402-471-2115
Child Caring/Placing Agency #15 ... 402-471-9138
Collection Agency #26 402-471-2555
Contractor #21 402-595-3189
Contractor (Building) #12 402-441-6456
Cosmetology Salon #30 402-471-2115
Cosmetology School #30 402-471-2115

Credit Union #31 402-471-2171
Debt Management Agency #26 402-471-2555
Delayed Deposit Service #31 402-471-2171
Dental Anesthesia Permit #30 402-471-2118
Dental Hygienist #30 402-471-2118
Dentist #30 402-471-2118
Domiciliary Facility #30 402-471-2115
Drug Distributor, Wholesale #30 ... 402-471-2118
Drug Wholesale Facility #30 402-471-2115
Educational Media Specialist #13 ... 402-471-0739
Electrician #29 402-471-3550

Electrologist #15	402-471-2117
Elevator Inspection Manager #21	402-471-8674
Elevator Inspector #21	402-471-8674
Embalmer #15	402-471-2115
Employment Agency #21	402-471-2230
Engineer #02	402-471-2021
Esthetician #15	402-471-2117
Exterminator #18	402-437-5080
Farm Labor Contractor #21	402-471-2230
Fire Protection Sprinkler Contractor #12	402-441-6456
Foster/Group Home #15	402-471-9138
Funeral Director #15	402-471-2115
Funeral Establishment #30	402-471-2115
General Contractor #12	402-471-5729
Health Clinic & Emergency Care #30	402-471-2115
Hearing Assessment (EIPA) #09	402-471-3593
Home Health Agency #30	402-471-2115
Hospital #30	402-471-2115
Insurance Agency #14	402-471-4913
Insurance Agent #14	402-471-4913
Insurance Broker #14	402-471-4913
Insurance Company #14	402-471-4913
Insurance Consultant #14	402-471-4913
Interpreter for Hearing Impaired #09	402-471-3593
Investment Advisor #11	402-471-3445
Landscape Architect #23	402-471-2021
Law Enforcement Officer #20	308-385-6030

Lobbyist #08	402-471-2608
Local Anesthesia Certification #30	402-471-2118
Marriage & Family Therapist #15	402-471-9138
Massage Establishment #30	402-471-2115
Massage Therapy School #30	402-471-2115
Mental Health Center #30	402-471-2115
Notary Public #27	402-471-2558
Nursing Education Program #30	402-471-2115
Nursing Home #30	402-471-2115
Nursing Home Administrator #15	402-471-2115
Optometrist #30	402-471-2118
Osteopatchic Physician #30	402-471-2118
Pawnborker #06	402-441-7437
Pharmacist #30	402-471-2118
Pharmacy #30	402-471-2115
Pharmacy, Mail Order #30	402-471-2115
Physician #30	402-471-2118
Physician Assistant #30	402-471-2118
Plainclothes Investigator #26	402-471-2384
Plumber Journeyman #07	402-466-5154
Podiatrist #30	402-471-2118
Polygraph Examiner, Private #26	402-471-4070
Polygraph Examiner, Public #26	402-471-4070
Private Detective #26	402-471-2384
Public Accountant-CPA #05	402-471-3595
Quality Assurance Screening-Test #09	402-471-3593
Racing #24	402-471-4155

Radiographer #30	402-471-2118
Real Estate Appraiser #22	402-471-9015
Real Estate Broker #25	402-471-2004
Real Estate Salesperson #25	402-471-2004
Residential Care Facility #30	402-471-2115
Sanitarian #17	402-471-0515
School Administrator/Supervisor #13	402-471-0739
School Nurse #13	402-471-0739
Secondhand Jewelry Dealer #06	402-441-7437
Securities Agent #11	402-471-3445
Securities Broker/Dealer #11	402-471-3445
Skin Care Salon #30	402-471-2115
Social Worker #15	402-471-9138
Speech-Language Pathologist #15	402-471-9138
Substance Abuse Treatment #30	402-471-2115
Surveyor #03	402-471-2566
Taxi Driver/Chauffeur #06	402-441-7437
Teacher #13	402-471-0739
Utilization Review Agent #14	402-471-4913
Vendor (Liquor) #19	402-471-2571
Veterinarian #30	402-471-2118
Veterinary Technician #15	402-471-2118
Voice Stress Examiner #26	402-471-4070
Water Treatment Plant Operator #17	402-471-0515
Well Driller/Pump Installer #17	402-471-0515
Wrestler #28	402-471-2009

Licensing Agency Information

01 Board of Barber Examiners, PO Box 94723 (301 Centennial Mall S, 6th Fl), Lincoln, NE 68509-4723; 402-471-2051.

02 Board of Examiners for Engineers & Architects, PO Box 94751 (PO Box 95165, 301 Centennial Mall S 6th Fl), Lincoln, NE 68509-4751; 402-471-2021, Fax: 402-471-0787.
www.nol.org/home/NBOP

03 Board of Examiners for Land Surveyors, 555 N Cotner Blvd LL, Lincoln, NE 68505; 402-471-2566, Fax: 402-471-3057.

04 Board of Examiners or Abstractors, PO Box 949444 (301 Centennial Mall S), Lincoln, NE 68509-4944; 402-471-2383.

05 Board of Public Accountancy, PO Box 94725 (301 Centennial Mall S, 3rd Fl), Lincoln, NE 68509-4725; 402-471-3595, Fax: 402-471-4484.
www.nol.org/home/BPA

06 City Clerk's Office, 555 S 10th St, Lincoln, NE 68508; 402-441-7437, Fax: 402-441-8325.
http://interlinc.ci.lincoln.ne.us

07 City Codes Administration, PO Box 95026 (555 S 10th St), Lincoln, NE 68508; 402-466-5154.

08 Clerk of the Legislature, PO Box 94604 (PO Box 94604), Lincoln, NE 68509-4604; 402-471-2608, Fax: 402-471-2126.
www.unicam.state.ne.us

09 Commission for the Deaf & Hard of Hearing, 4600 Valley Rd #420, Lincoln, NE 68510-4844; 402-471-3593, Fax: 402-471-3067.
www.nol.org/home/NCDHH

10 Department of Aeronautics, PO Box 82088 (3431 Aviation Rd #150 (68524)), Lincoln, NE 68501; 402-471-2371, Fax: 402-471-2906.
www.nol.org/home/NDOA

11 Department of Banking & Finance, Bureau of Securities, PO Box 95006 (PO Box 95006 (1200 "N" Street, Suite 311)), Lincoln, NE 68509-5006; 402-471-3445.
www.ndbf.org/sec.htm

12 Department of Building & Safety, 555 S 10th St, Lincoln, NE 68508; 402-441-7791, Fax: 402-471-8214.

13 Department of Education, Teacher Accreditation/Certification Division, PO Box 94987 (301 Centennial Mall S 6th Fl), Lincoln, NE 68509-4987; 402-471-0739, Fax: 402-471-9735.
www.nde.state.ne.us/TCERT/TCERT.html

14 Department of Insurance, PO Box 95024 (641 O St #400), Lincoln, NE 68508-3639; 402-471-2201, Fax: 402-471-6559.
www.nol.org/home/NDOI

15 Department of Health & Human Services, Credentialing & Licensing, PO Box 95026 (PO Box 95044 (301 Centennial Mall S, 5th Fl)), Lincoln, NE 68509; 402-471-9138, Fax: 402-471-9435.
www.hhs.state.ne.us/reg/regindex.htm

16 Division of Safety, Boiler Section, PO Box 95024 (PO Box 95024), Lincoln, NE 68509; 402-471-4721, Fax: 402-471-5039.
www.dol.state.ne.us/safety/boiler.htm

17 Drinking Water & Environmental Sanitation Division, PO Box 95007 (301 Centennial Mall S), Lincoln, NE 68509; 402-471-2541, Fax: 402-471-6436.

18 Environmental Protection Agency, 100 Centennial Mall N, Lincoln, NE 68508; 402-437-5080.

19 Liquor Control Commission, PO Box 95046 (301 Centennial Mall S, 5th Fl), Lincoln, NE 68509-5046; 402-471-2571, Fax: 402-471-2814.
www.nol.org/home/NLCC

20 Crime Commission, 3600 N Academy Rd, Grand Island, NE 68801; 308-385-6030, Fax: 308-385-6032.
www.nol.org/home/crimecom

21 Department of Labor, PO Box 94608 (State Capitol, #2300), Lincoln, NE 68509; 402-471-2230, Fax: 402-471-5039.
www.dol.state.ne.us

22 Real Estate Appraiser Board, PO Box 95066 (PO Box 95066), Lincoln, NE 68509-4963; 402-471-9015, Fax: 402-471-9017.
http://dbdec.nrc.state.ne.us/appraiser

23 Board of Landscape Architects, PO Box 95165, Lincoln, NE 68509-5165; 402-471-2021, Fax: 402-471-0787.

24 Racing Commission, PO Box 95014 (301 Centennial Mall S 4th Fl), Lincoln, NE 68509-5014; 402-471-4155, Fax: 402-471-2339.

25 Real Estate Commission, PO Box 94751 (301 Centennial Mall S, 6th Fl), Lincoln, NE 68509-4667; 402-471-2004, Fax: 402-471-4492.
http://www.nol.org/home/NREC/index.htm

26 Secretary of State, State Capitol Rm 2300, PO Box 94743 (PO Box 94608), Lincoln, NE 68509-4608; 402-471-2554, Fax: 402-471-3237.
www.nol.org/home/SOS

27 Secretary of State, Notary Division, PO Box 95104 (Rm 1301 State Capitol Bldg), Lincoln, NE 68509-5104; 402-471-2558, Fax: 402-471-4429.
www.nol.org/home/SOS/Notary/notary.htm

28 Athletic Commission, PO Box 94743 (301 Centennial Mall S, 3rd Fl), Lincoln, NE 68509-4743; 402-471-2009, Fax: 402-471-2009.

29 Electrical Division, PO Box 95066 (1791 Bodwell Rd), Lincoln, NE 68509-5066; 402-471-3550, Fax: 402-471-4297.

30 Department of Regulation & Licensure, Credentialing Division, PO Box 95007 (PO Box 95007), Lincoln, NE 68509-5007; 402-471-2115, Fax: 402-471-3577.
www.hhs.state.ne.us/crl/crlindex.htm

31 Department of Banking and Finance, Financial Institutions Divison, PO Box 95006 (1200 "N" Street, Suite 311), Lincoln, NE 68509-5006; 402-471-2171.
www.ndbf.org/fin.htm

32 Supreme Court, State Capitol, Rm 2413, Lincoln, NE 68509; 402-471-3731.

The following list indicates the district and division name for each county in the state. If the district or division name of the bankruptcy court is different from the civil/criminal court, it appears in parentheses.

County/Court Cross Reference

County	Court		County	Court
Adams	Lincoln		Jefferson	Lincoln
Antelope	Lincoln		Johnson	Lincoln
Arthur	North Platte		Kearney	Lincoln
Banner	North Platte		Keith	North Platte
Blaine	North Platte		Keya Paha	North Platte
Boone	Lincoln		Kimball	North Platte
Box Butte	North Platte		Knox	Omaha
Boyd	Lincoln		Lancaster	Lincoln
Brown	North Platte		Lincoln	North Platte
Buffalo	Lincoln		Logan	North Platte
Burt	Omaha		Loup	North Platte
Butler	Lincoln		Madison	Lincoln
Cass	Lincoln		McPherson	North Platte
Cedar	Omaha		Merrick	Lincoln
Chase	North Platte		Morrill	North Platte
Cherry	North Platte		Nance	Lincoln
Cheyenne	North Platte		Nemaha	Lincoln
Clay	Lincoln		Nuckolls	Lincoln
Colfax	Lincoln		Otoe	Lincoln
Cuming	Omaha		Pawnee	Lincoln
Custer	North Platte		Perkins	North Platte
Dakota	Omaha		Phelps	Lincoln
Dawes	North Platte		Pierce	Omaha
Dawson	North Platte		Platte	Lincoln
Deuel	North Platte		Polk	Lincoln
Dixon	Omaha		Red Willow	North Platte
Dodge	Omaha		Richardson	Lincoln
Douglas	Omaha		Rock	North Platte
Dundy	North Platte		Saline	Lincoln
Fillmore	Lincoln		Sarpy	Omaha
Franklin	Lincoln		Saunders	Lincoln
Frontier	North Platte		Scotts. Bluff	North Platte
Furnas	North Platte		Seward	Lincoln
Gage	Lincoln		Sheridan	North Platte
Garden	North Platte		Sherman	Lincoln
Garfield	North Platte		Sioux	North Platte
Gosper	North Platte		Stanton	Omaha
Grant	North Platte		Thayer	Lincoln
Greeley	Lincoln		Thomas	North Platte
Hall	Lincoln		Thurston	Omaha
Hamilton	Lincoln		Valley	North Platte
Harlan	Lincoln		Washington	Omaha
Hayes	North Platte		Wayne	Omaha
Hitchcock	North Platte		Webster	Lincoln
Holt	Lincoln		Wheeler	Lincoln
Hooker	North Platte		York	Lincoln
Howard	Lincoln			

US District Court

District of Nebraska

Lincoln Division PO Box 83468, Lincoln, NE 68501 (Courier Address: 593 Federal Bldg, 100 Centennial Mall N, Lincoln, NE 68508), 402-437-5225, Fax: 402-437-5651.

www.ned.uscourts.gov

Counties: Nebraska cases may be filed in any of the three courts at the option of the attorney, except that filings in the North Platte Division must be during trial session.

Indexing & Storage: Cases are indexed by defendant and plaintiff as well as by case number. New cases are available in the index 1-2 days after filing date. Both computer and card indexes are maintained. Open records are located at this court.

Fee & Payment: The fee is $15.00 per item (one party name or case number). Payment may be made by money order, cashier check, personal check. Prepayment is required. Payee: Clerk, US District Court. Certification fee: $5.00 per document. Copy fee: $.50 per page.

Phone Search: Only docket information available by telephone. An automated voice case information service (VCIS) is not available.

Mail Search: Always enclose a stamped self addressed envelope.

In Person Search: In person searching is available.

PACER: Sign-up number is 800-676-6856. Access fee is $.60 per minute. Toll-free access: 800-252-9724. Local access: 402-221-4797. Case records are available back to late 1990. Records are purged every year. New records are available online after 2 days. PACER is available on the Internet at http://pacer.ned.uscourts.gov.

North Platte Division c/o Lincoln Division, PO Box 83468, Lincoln, NE 68501 (Courier Address: 593 Federal Bldg, 100 Centennial Mall N, Lincoln, NE 68508), 402-437-5225, Fax: 402-437-5651.

www.ned.uscourts.gov

Counties: Nebraska cases may be filed in any of the three courts at the option of the attorney, except that filings in the North Platte Division must be during trial session. Some case records may be in the Omaha Division as well as the Lincoln Division.

Indexing & Storage: Cases are indexed by defendant and plaintiff as well as by case number. New cases are available in the index 1-2 days after filing date. Records can also be located at Omaha or Lincoln, depending on the judge assigned. Open records are located at the Division.

Fee & Payment: The fee is $15.00 per item (one party name or case number). Payment may be made by money order, cashier check, personal check. Payee: Clerk, US District Court. Copy fee: $.50 per page. You are allowed to make your own copies. These copies cost $.50 per page.

Phone Search: An automated voice case information service (VCIS) is not available.

In Person Search: In person searching is available.

PACER: Sign-up number is 800-676-6856. Access fee is $.60 per minute. Toll-free access: 800-252-9724. Local access: 402-221-4797. Case

records are available back to late 1990. Records are purged every year. New records are available online after 2 days. PACER is available on the Internet at http://pacer.ned.uscourts.gov.

Omaha Division PO Box 129, DTS, Omaha, NE 68101 (Courier Address: Room 9000, 215 N 17th St, Omaha, NE 68101), 402-221-4761, Fax: 402-221-3160.

www.ned.uscourts.gov

Counties: Nebraska cases may be filed in any of the three courts at the option of the attorney, except that filings in the North Platte Division must be during trial session.

Indexing & Storage: Cases are indexed by defendant and plaintiff as well as by case number. New cases are available in the index 1-2 days after filing date. Both computer and card indexes are maintained. Open records are located at this court.

Fee & Payment: The fee is $15.00 per item (one party name or case number). Payment may be made by money order, cashier check, personal check. Prepayment is required. Payee: Clerk, US District Court. Certification fee: $5.00 per document. Copy fee: $.50 per page.

Phone Search: Searching is not available by phone.

Mail Search: Always enclose a stamped self addressed envelope.

In Person Search: In person searching is available.

PACER: Sign-up number is 800-676-6856. Access fee is $.60 per minute. Toll-free access: 800-252-9724. Local access: 402-221-4797. Case records are available back to late 1990. Records are purged every year. New records are available online after 2 days. PACER is available on the Internet at http://pacer.ned.uscourts.gov.

US Bankruptcy Court

District of Nebraska

Lincoln Division 460 Federal Bldg, 100 Centennial Mall N, Lincoln, NE 68508, 402-437-5100, Fax: 402-437-5454.

Counties: Adams, Antelope, Boone, Boyd, Buffalo, Butler, Cass, Clay, Colfax, Fillmore, Franklin, Gage, Greeley, Hall, Hamilton, Harlan, Holt, Howard, Jefferson, Johnson, Kearney, Lancaster, Madison, Merrick, Nance, Nemaha, Nuckolls, Otoe, Pawnee, Phelps, Platte,Polk, Richardson, Saline, Saunders, Seward, Sherman, Thayer, Webster, Wheeler, York. Cases from the North Platte Division may also be assigned here.

Indexing & Storage: Cases are indexed by as well as by case number. New cases are available in the index within 1 day after filing date. All debtor names are indexed for files from 9/89 to the present. A computer index is maintained. Open records are located at this court. District wide searches are available from this division. This court maintains records for the main bankruptcy office in Omaha.

Fee & Payment: The fee is $15.00 per item (one party name or case number). Payment may be made by money order, cashier check, personal check. Prepayment is required. Debtor's checks are not accepted. Payee: Clerk, US Bankrutpcy Court. Certification fee: $5.00 per document. Copy fee: $.50 per page.

Phone Search: Only the debtor's name, case number, date filed, 341 information and date discharged and closed will be released. An automated voice case information service (VCIS) is available. Call VCIS at 800-829-0112 or 402-221-3757.

Mail Search: A stamped self addressed envelope is not required.

In Person Search: In person searching is available.

PACER: Sign-up number is 800-676-6856. Access fee is $.60 per minute. Toll-free access: 800-788-0656. Local access: 402-221-4882. Case records are available back to September 1989. Records are purged every six months. New civil records are available online after 3 days. PACER is available online at http://pacer.neb.uscourts.gov.

North Platte Division c/o Omaha Division, PO Box 428, DTS, Omaha, NE 68101-0428 (Courier Address: Room 8400, 215 N 17th St, Omaha, NE 68102), 402-221-4687.

Counties: Arthur, Banner, Blaine, Box Butte, Brown, Chase, Cherry, Cheyenne, Custer, Dawes, Dawson, Deuel, Dundy, Frontier, Furnas, Garden, Garfield, Gosper, Grant, Hayes, Hitchcock, Hooker, Keith, Keya Paha, Kimball, Lincoln, Logan, Loup, McPherson, Morrill,Perkins, Red Willow, Rock, Scotts Bluff, Sheridan, Sioux, Thomas, Valley. Cases may be randomly allocated to Omaha or Lincoln.

Indexing & Storage: Cases are indexed by as well as by case number. New cases are available in the index 1 day after filing date. Open records are located at the Division. Case records may also be in the Lincoln Division (Lancaster County).

Fee & Payment: The fee is no charge per item (one party name or case number). Payment may be made by money order, cashier check. Business checks are not accepted. Personal checks are not accepted.

Phone Search: An automated voice case information service (VCIS) is available. Call VCIS at 800-829-0112 or 402-221-3757.

Mail Search: A stamped self addressed envelope is not required.

In Person Search: In person searching is available.

PACER: Sign-up number is 800-676-6856. Access fee is $.60 per minute. Toll-free access: 800-788-0656. Local access: 402-221-4882. Case records are available back to September 1989. Records are purged every six months. New civil records are available online after 3 days. PACER is available online at http://pacer.neb.uscourts.gov.

Omaha Division PO Box 428, DTS, Omaha, NE 68101-4281 (Courier Address: Room 8400, 215 N 17th St, Omaha, NE 68102), 402-221-4687.

Counties: Burt, Cedar, Cuming, Dakota, Dixon, Dodge, Douglas, Knox, Pierce, Sarpy, Stanton, Thurston, Washington, Wayne.

Indexing & Storage: Cases are indexed by debtor and creditors as well as by case number. New cases are available in the index 24 hours after filing date. A computer index is maintained. Open records are located at this court.

Fee & Payment: The fee is $15.00 per item (one party name or case number). Payment may be made by money order, cashier check, personal check. Prepayment is required. Payee: Clerk, US Bankruptcy Court. Certification fee: $5.00 per document. Copy fee: $.50 per page.

Phone Search: Only docket information is available by phone. An automated voice case information service (VCIS) is available. Call VCIS at 800-829-0112 or 402-221-3757.

Mail Search: Always enclose a stamped self addressed envelope.

In Person Search: In person searching is available.

PACER: Sign-up number is 800-676-6856. Access fee is $.60 per minute. Toll-free access: 800-788-0656. Local access: 402-221-4882. Case records are available back to September 1989. Records are purged every six months. New civil records are available online after 3 days. PACER is available online at http://pacer.neb.uscourts.gov.

`Court	Jurisdiction	No. of Courts	How Organized
District Courts*	General	92	12 Districts
County Courts*	Limited	93	11 Districts
Juvenile Courts	Special	3	3 Counties
Workers' Compensation Court	Special	1	

* Profiled in this Sourcebook.

Court	CIVIL								
	Tort	Contract	Real Estate	Min. Claim	Max. Claim	Small Claims	Estate	Eviction	Domestic Relations
District Courts*	X	X	X	$15,000	No Max				X
County Courts*	X	X	X	$0	$15,000	$1800	X	X	X
Juvenile Courts									
Workers' Compensation Court									

Court	CRIMINAL				
	Felony	Misdemeanor	DWI/DUI	Preliminary Hearing	Juvenile
District Courts*	X				
County Courts*		X	X	X	X
Juvenile Courts					X
Workers' Compensation Court					

ADMINISTRATION   Court Administrator, PO Box 98910, Lincoln, NE, 68509-8910; 402-471-2643, Fax: 402-471-2197. http://court.nol.org

COURT STRUCTURE   The District Court is the court of general jurisdiction. The County Court is limited to $15,000 in civil judgment matters. The number of judicial districts went from 21 to the current 12 in July 1992.

County Courts have juvenile jurisdiction in all but 3 counties. Douglas, Lancaster, and Sarpy counties have separate Juvenile Courts. Probate is handled by County Courts. Many have records on microfiche back to the mid/late 1800s.

ONLINE ACCESS   Implementation of a statewide, internal online access system is underway. The goal is statewide access by the end of year 2000, except, however, Douglas County which has opted out of this system. All internal online courts allow public access at their offices. Douglas county offers remote online. Remote access by the public for all the courts will be considered in the future.

ADDITIONAL INFORMATION   Most Nebraska courts require the public to do their own in-person searches and will not respond to written search requests. The State Attorney General has recommended that courts not perform searches because of the time involved and concerns over possible legal liability.

📖 📖 📖 📖 📖 📖

Adams County

District Court PO Box 9, Hastings, NE 68902; 402-461-7264; Fax: 402-461-7269. Hours: 8:30AM-5PM (CST). *Felony, Civil Actions Over $15,000.*

Civil Records: Access: In person only. Court does not conduct in person searches; visitors must perform searches for themselves. Search fee: No civil searches performed by court. Required to search: name, years to search. Civil cases indexed by defendant, plaintiff. Civil records on microfiche from 1800s, 5 yrs on index cards, on docket books from 1800s. **Criminal Records:** Access: In person only. Court does not conduct in person searches; visitors must perform searches for themselves. Search fee: No criminal searches performed by court. Required to search: name, years to search. Criminal records on microfiche from 1800s, 5 yrs on index cards, on docket books from 1800s. **General Information:** No juvenile, search warrants or mental health records released. Copy fee: $.25 per page. Certification fee: $1.00.

Adams County Court PO Box 95, Hastings, NE 68902-0095; 402-461-7143; Fax: 402-461-7144. Hours: 8AM-5PM (CST). *Misdemeanor, Civil Actions Under $15,000, Eviction, Small Claims, Probate.*

Civil Records: Access: In person only. Court does not conduct in person searches; visitors must perform searches for themselves. Search fee: No civil searches performed by court. Required to search: name, years to search; also helpful-address. Civil cases indexed by defendant. Civil records on index cards and files from 1970s. **Criminal Records:** Access: In person only. Court does not conduct in person searches; visitors must perform searches for themselves. Search fee: No criminal searches performed by court. Required to search: name, years to search; also helpful-DOB, SSN. Criminal records on index cards and files from 1970s. **General Information:** No adoption or juvenile records released. Copy fee: $.25 per page. Certification fee: $1.00. Fee payee: Adams County Court. Business checks accepted. Prepayment is required. Public access terminal is available.

Antelope County

District Court PO Box 45, Neligh, NE 68756; 402-887-4508; Fax: 402-887-4870. Hours: 8:30AM-5PM (CST). *Felony, Civil Actions Over $15,000.*

Civil Records: Access: In person only. Court does not conduct in person searches; visitors must perform searches for themselves. Search fee: No civil searches performed by court. Required to search: name, years to search. Civil cases indexed by defendant, plaintiff. Civil records on index books from 1872. **Criminal Records:** Access: In person only. Court does not conduct in person searches; visitors must perform searches for themselves. Search fee: No criminal searches performed by court. Required to search: name, years to search. Criminal records on index books from 1872. **General Information:** No juvenile, sealed, search warrants, or mental health record released. Copy fee: $.25 per page. Certification fee: $1.00. Fee payee: Clerk of District Court. Personal checks accepted. Public access terminal is available. Fax notes: $1.00 per page.

Antelope County Court 501 Main, Neligh, NE 68756; 402-887-4650; Fax: 402-887-4160. Hours: 8:30AM-5PM (CST). *Misdemeanor, Civil Actions Under $15,000, Eviction, Small Claims, Probate.*

Civil Records: Access: In person only. Court does not conduct in person searches; visitors must perform searches for themselves. Search fee: No civil searches performed by court. Required to search: name, years to search. Civil cases indexed by defendant, plaintiff. Civil records on computer from 1994, probate on microfiche from 1800s, civil and small claims indexed from 1983. **Criminal Records:** Access: In person only. Court does not conduct in person searches; visitors must perform searches for themselves. Search fee: No criminal searches performed by court. Required to search: name, years to search, DOB, signed release; also helpful-SSN. Criminal index on computer from 1994, indexed from 1800s. **General Information:** No adoption, or sealed records released. Copy fee: $.25 per page. Certification fee: $1.00 plus $.25 per page. Fee payee: Antelope County Court. Personal checks accepted. Prepayment is required.

Arthur County

District & County Court PO Box 126, Arthur, NE 69121; 308-764-2203; Fax: 308-764-2216. Hours: 8AM-4PM (MST). *Felony, Misdemeanor, Civil, Eviction, Small Claims, Probate.*

Civil Records: Access: Phone, fax, mail, in person. Both court and visitors may perform in

person searches. No search fee. Required to search: name, years to search. Civil cases indexed by defendant, plaintiff. Civil records on index books from 1987, on docket books from 1913. **Criminal Records:** Access: Phone, fax, mail, in person. Both court and visitors may perform in person searches. No search fee. Required to search: name, years to search. Criminal records on index books from 1987, on docket books from 1913. **General Information:** No search warrants, juvenile, adoption, hental health, or sealed records released. SASE required. Turnaround time 1-2 days. Copy fee: $.20 per page. Certification fee: $1.00. Fee payee: Arthur County Clerk. Personal checks accepted. Fax notes: $1.00 per page. Incoming fax fee $.25.

Banner County

District Court PO Box 67, Harrisburg, NE 69345; 308-436-5265; Fax: 308-436-4180. Hours: 8AM-5PM (MST). *Felony, Civil Actions Over $15,000.*

Civil Records: Access: Fax, mail, in person. Both court and visitors may perform in person searches. Search fee: $3.00 per name. Required to search: name, years to search; also helpful-address. Civil cases indexed by defendant, plaintiff. Civil records on docket books from 1800s. **Criminal Records:** Access: Fax, mail, in person. Both court and visitors may perform in person searches. Search fee: $3.00 per name. Required to search: name, years to search, DOB; also helpful-address. Criminal records on docket books from 1800s. **General Information:** No search warrants, mental health, or sealed records released. SASE required. Turnaround time 5-7 days. Copy fee: $.25 per page. Certification fee: $1.00. Fee payee: Banner County Clerk. Personal checks accepted. Prepayment is required. Fax notes: $1.00 per page.

Banner County Court PO Box 67, Harrisburg, NE 69345; 308-436-5268; Fax: 308-436-4180. Hours: 8AM-Noon, 1-5PM (MST). *Misdemeanor, Civil Actions Under $15,000, Eviction, Small Claims, Probate.*

Civil Records: Access: Fax, mail, in person. Both court and visitors may perform in person searches. No search fee. Required to search: name, years to search. Civil cases indexed by defendant, plaintiff. Civil records on register of action cards from 1992, prior on docket books. **Criminal Records:** Access: Fax, mail, in person. Both court and visitors may perform in person searches. No search fee. Required to search: name, years to search, signed release; also helpful-address, DOB. Criminal records on register of action cards from 1992, prior on docket books. **General Information:** No adoption, sealed records released. SASE required. Turnaround time 1-2 days. Copy fee: $.25 per page. Certification fee: $1.00. Fee payee: Banner County Court. Personal checks accepted. Fax notes: $3.00 for first page, $1.00 each addl.

Blaine County

District Court Lincoln Ave, Box 136, Brewster, NE 68821; 308-547-2222; Fax: 308-547-2228. Hours: 8AM-4PM (CST). *Felony, Civil Actions Over $15,000.*

Civil Records: Access: Fax, mail, in person. Only the court conducts in person searches; visitors may not. No search fee. Required to search: name, years to search. Civil cases indexed by defendant, plaintiff. Civil records on index books from late 1800s. **Criminal Records:** Access: Fax, mail, in person. Only the court conducts in person searches; visitors may not. No search fee.

Required to search: name, years to search, DOB. Criminal records on index books from late 1800s. **General Information:** No search warrants, mental health, or sealed records released. SASE required. Turnaround time 1-2 days. Copy fee: $.25 per page. Certification fee: $1.50. Fee payee: Blaine County Clerk. Personal checks accepted. Prepayment is required. Fax notes: $1.00 per page.

Blaine County Court Lincoln Ave, Box 123, Brewster, NE 68821; 308-547-2225; Fax: 308-547-2228. Hours: 8AM-4PM (CST). *Misdemeanor, Civil Actions Under $15,000, Eviction, Small Claims, Probate.*

Civil Records: Access: Phone, fax, mail, in person. Only the court conducts in person searches; visitors may not. No search fee. Required to search: name, years to search; also helpful-address. Civil cases indexed by defendant, plaintiff. Civil records on index books from 1960. on microfiche prior to 1960. **Criminal Records:** Access: Phone, fax, mail, in person. Only the court conducts in person searches; visitors may not. No search fee. Required to search: name, years to search; also helpful-address, DOB, SSN. Criminal records on index books from 1960. on microfiche prior to 1960. **General Information:** No juvenile, adoption, or sealed records released. SASE required. Turnaround time 2 days. Copy fee: $.25 per page. Certification fee: $1.25. Fee payee: Blaine County Court. Personal checks accepted. Prepayment is required. Fax notes: $1.00 per page.

Boone County

District Court 222 Fourth St, Albion, NE 68620; 402-395-2057; Fax: 402-395-6592. Hours: 8:30AM-5PM (CST). *Felony, Civil Actions Over $15,000.*

Civil Records: Access: Phone, fax, mail, in person. Both court and visitors may perform in person searches. No search fee. Required to search: name, years to search. Civil cases indexed by defendant, plaintiff. Civil records in general index and dockets from 1800s. **Criminal Records:** Access: Phone, fax, mail, in person. Both court and visitors may perform in person searches. No search fee. Required to search: name, years to search; also helpful-DOB. Criminal records in general index and dockets from 1800s. **General Information:** No search warrants, mental health, or sealed records released. SASE required. Turnaround time 2-3 days. Copy fee: $.25 per page. Certification fee: $1.00. Fee payee: Clerk of District Court. Personal checks accepted. Prepayment is required. Fax notes: $3.00 for first page, $1.00 each addl.

Boone County Court 222 S 4th St, Albion, NE 68620; 402-395-6184; Fax: 402-395-6592. Hours: 8AM-5PM (CST). *Misdemeanor, Civil Actions Under $15,000, Eviction, Small Claims, Probate.*

Civil Records: Access: Fax, mail, in person. Both court and visitors may perform in person searches. No search fee. Required to search: name, years to search. Civil cases indexed by defendant, plaintiff. Civil records on general index and docket books from late 1800s, probate on microfiche from 1970. **Criminal Records:** Access: Fax, mail, in person. Both court and visitors may perform in person searches. No search fee. Required to search: name, years to search; also helpful-DOB. Criminal records on general index and docket books from late 1800s, probate on microfiche from 1970. **General Information:** No adoption, or sealed records released. SASE required. Turnaround time 1-2 days. SASE required for large requests. Copy fee: $.25 per page. Certification fee: $1.00. Fee payee: Clerk of County Court. Personal checks accepted. Fax notes: No fee to fax results.

Box Butte County

District Court 515 Box Butte Suite 300, Alliance, NE 69301; 308-762-6293; Fax: 308-762-7703. Hours: 9AM-5PM (MST). *Felony, Civil Actions Over $15,000.*

Civil Records: Access: In person only. Court does not conduct in person searches; visitors must perform searches for themselves. Search fee: No civil searches performed by court. Required to search: name, years to search. Civil cases indexed by defendant, plaintiff. Civil records on general index and docekt books from late 1800s. **Criminal Records:** Access: In person only. Court does not conduct in person searches; visitors must perform searches for themselves. Search fee: No criminal searches performed by court. Required to search: name, years to search. Criminal records on general index and docekt books from late 1800s. **General Information:** No search warrants, mental health, or sealed records released. Copy fee: $.25 per page. Certification fee: $1.00.

Box Butte County Court PO Box 613, Alliance, NE 69301; 308-762-6800; Fax: 308-762-6802. Hours: 8:30AM-5PM (MST). *Misdemeanor, Civil Actions Under $15,000, Eviction, Small Claims, Probate.*

Civil Records: Access: Phone, fax, mail, in person. Both court and visitors may perform in person searches. No search fee. Required to search: name, years to search. Civil cases indexed by defendant, plaintiff. Civil records on microfiche for 10 years, on index cards to docket books from late 1800s. **Criminal Records:** Access: Phone, fax, mail, in person. Both court and visitors may perform in person searches. No search fee. Required to search: name, years to search, DOB. Criminal records on microfiche for 10 years, on index cards to docket books from late 1800s. **General Information:** No juvenile, adoption, or sealed records released. SASE required. Turnaround time 5-10 days. Copy fee: $.25 per page. Certification fee: $1.00. Fee payee: Box Butte County Court. Personal checks accepted. Fax notes: No fee to fax results.

Boyd County

District Court PO Box 26, Butte, NE 68722; 402-775-2391; Fax: 402-775-2146. Hours: 8:45AM-5PM (CST). *Felony, Civil Actions Over $15,000.*

Civil Records: Access: Mail, in person. Both court and visitors may perform in person searches. Search fee: $3.00 per name. Required to search: name, years to search, address. Civil cases indexed by defendant, plaintiff. Civil records on general index and docket books from late 1800s. **Criminal Records:** Access: Mail, in person. Both court and visitors may perform in person searches. Search fee: $3.00 per name. Required to search: name, years to search, address. Criminal records on general index and docket books from late 1800s. **General Information:** No search warrants, mental health, or sealed records released. SASE required. Turnaround time 3-4 days. Copy fee: $.25 per page. Certification fee: $1.50. Fee payee: Boyd County Clerk. Personal checks accepted. Prepayment is required.

Boyd County Court PO Box 396, Butte, NE 68722; 402-775-2211; Fax: 402-775-2146. Hours: 8AM-5PM W,Th (CST). *Misdemeanor, Civil Actions Under $15,000, Eviction, Small Claims, Probate.*

Civil Records: Access: Phone, fax, mail, in person. Both court and visitors may perform in person searches. No search fee. Required to search: name, years to search; also helpful-address. Civil cases indexed by defendant, plaintiff. Civil records on general index and docket books from late 1800s. **Criminal Records:** Access: Phone, fax, mail, in person. Both court and visitors may perform in person searches. No search fee. Required to search: name, years to search; also helpful-address, DOB, SSN. Criminal records on general index and docket books from late 1800s. **General Information:** No adoption, juvenile, or sealed records released. SASE required. Turnaround time 2 weeks. Copy fee: $.25 per page. Certification fee: $1.00. Fee payee: Boyd County Court. Personal checks accepted. Prepayment is required. Fax notes: $3.00 for first page, $1.00 each addl.

Brown County

District Court 148 W Fourth St, Ainsworth, NE 69210; 402-387-2705; Fax: 402-387-0918. Hours: 8AM-5PM (CST). *Felony, Civil Actions Over $15,000.*

Civil Records: Access: Phone, fax, mail, in person. Both court and visitors may perform in person searches. No search fee. Required to search: name, years to search; also helpful-address. Civil cases indexed by defendant, plaintiff. Civil records on general index and docket books from late 1800s. **Criminal Records:** Access: Phone, fax, mail, in person. Both court and visitors may perform in person searches. No search fee. Required to search: name, years to search, signed release; also helpful-address, DOB, SSN. Criminal records on general index and docket books from late 1800s. **General Information:** No search warrants, mental health, or sealed records released. SASE required. Turnaround time 3-4 days. Copy fee: $.25 per page. Certification fee: $2.00. Fee payee: Clerk of District Court, Brown County. Personal checks accepted. Fax notes: $3.00 for first page, $1.00 each addl.

Brown County Court 148 W Fourth St, Ainsworth, NE 69210; 402-387-2864; Fax: 402-387-0918. Hours: 8AM-5PM (CST). *Misdemeanor, Civil Actions Under $15,000, Eviction, Small Claims, Probate.*

Civil Records: Access: Mail, in person. Both court and visitors may perform in person searches. No search fee. Required to search: name, years to search. Civil cases indexed by defendant, plaintiff. Civil records in boxes in office. **Criminal Records:** Access: Mail, in person. Both court and visitors may perform in person searches. No search fee. Required to search: name, years to search, DOB. Criminal records in boxes in office. **General Information:** No adoption, juvenile, or sealed records released. SASE required. Copy fee: $.25 per page. Certification fee: $1.00. Fee payee: Brown County Court. Personal checks accepted. Prepayment is required. Public access terminal is available.

Buffalo County

District Court PO Box 520, Kearney, NE 68848; 308-236-1246; Fax: 308-233-3693. Hours: 8AM-5PM (CST). *Felony, Civil Actions Over $15,000.*

Civil Records: Access: Mail, in person. Both court and visitors may perform in person searches. No search fee. Required to search: name, years to search; also helpful-address. Civil cases indexed by defendant, plaintiff. Civil records on computer from 1993, on microfiche through 1991, on books from 1800s. **Criminal Records:** Access: In person only. Court does not conduct in person searches; visitors must perform searches for themselves. Search fee: No criminal searches performed by court. Required to search: name, years to search; also helpful-DOB, SSN. Criminal records on computer from 1993, on microfiche through 1991, on books from 1800s. **General Information:** No juvenile, mental health, search warrants or sealed records released. SASE required. Turnaround time 1 week. Copy fee: $.50 per page. Certification fee: $1.00. Fee payee: Clerk of District Court. Business checks accepted. Prepayment is required. Public access terminal is available.

Buffalo County Court PO Box 520, Kearney, NE 68848; 308-236-1228; Fax: 308-236-1243. Hours: 8AM-5PM (CST). *Misdemeanor, Civil Actions Under $15,000, Eviction, Small Claims, Probate.*

Civil Records: Access: In person only. Court does not conduct in person searches; visitors must perform searches for themselves. Search fee: No civil searches performed by court. Required to search: name, years to search. Civil cases indexed by defendant, plaintiff. Civil records on computer from 4/94, on microfiche, general index, and docket books from late 1800s. **Criminal Records:** Access: In person only. Court does not conduct in person searches; visitors must perform searches for themselves. Search fee: No criminal searches performed by court. Required to search: name, years to search. Criminal records on computer from 4/94, on microfiche, general index, and docket books from late 1800s. **General Information:** No adoption, or sealed records released. Copy fee: $.25 per page. Certification fee: $1.00. Fee payee: County Court. Personal checks accepted. Prepayment is required. Public access terminal is available.

Burt County

District Court 111 N 13th St, Tekamah, NE 68061; 402-374-2605; Fax: 402-374-2746. Hours: 8AM-4:30PM (CST). *Felony, Civil Actions Over $15,000.*

Civil Records: Access: Mail, in person. Both court and visitors may perform in person searches. No search fee. Required to search: name, years to search. Civil cases indexed by defendant, plaintiff. Civil records on books from 1800s. **Criminal Records:** Access: Mail, in person. Both court and visitors may perform in person searches. No search fee. Required to search: name, years to search; also helpful-DOB, SSN. Criminal records on books from 1800s. **General Information:** No mental health records released. SASE required. Copy fee: $.50 per page. Certification fee: $2.00. Fee payee: Clerk of District Court. Personal checks accepted.

Burt County Court 111 N 13th St, PO Box 87, Tekamah, NE 68061; 402-374-2950; Fax: 402-374-2951. Hours: 8AM-4:30PM (CST). *Misdemeanor, Civil Actions Under $15,000, Eviction, Small Claims, Probate.*

Civil Records: Access: In person only. Court does not conduct in person searches; visitors must perform searches for themselves. Search fee: No civil searches performed by court. Required to search: name, years to search, address. Civil cases indexed by defendant, plaintiff. Civil records on index cards. **Criminal Records:** Access: In person only. Court does not conduct in person searches; visitors must perform searches for themselves.

Search fee: No criminal searches performed by court. Required to search: name, years to search, address, DOB, SSN, signed release. Criminal records on index cards. **General Information:** No adoption records released. Copy fee: $.25 per page. Certification fee: $1.25. Fee payee: County Court. Personal checks accepted. Prepayment is required.

Butler County

District Court 451 5th St, David City, NE 68632-1666; 402-367-7460; Fax: 402-367-3249. Hours: 8:30AM-5PM (CST). *Felony, Civil Actions Over $15,000.*

Civil Records: Access: Phone, fax, mail, in person. Both court and visitors may perform in person searches. Search fee: $2.00 per name. Required to search: name, years to search. Civil cases indexed by defendant, plaintiff. Civil records on books. **Criminal Records:** Access: Phone, fax, mail, in person. Both court and visitors may perform in person searches. Search fee: $2.00 per name. Required to search: name, years to search; also helpful-DOB, SSN. Criminal records on books. **General Information:** No juvenile, mental health or protection order records released. SASE required. Turnaround time 1-2 days. Copy fee: $.10 per page. Certification fee: $1.50. Fee payee: District Court. Personal checks accepted. Fax notes: No fee to fax results.

Butler County Court 451 5th St, David City, NE 68632-1666; 402-367-7480; Fax: 402-367-3249. Hours: 8AM-Noon, 1-5PM (CST). *Misdemeanor, Civil Actions Under $15,000, Eviction, Small Claims, Probate.*

Civil Records: Access: In person only. Court does not conduct in person searches; visitors must perform searches for themselves. No search fee. Required to search: name, years to search. Civil cases indexed by defendant, plaintiff. Civil records on docket books from late 1800s, probate on microfiche. They can refer requestors to parties who perform searches at the court. **Criminal Records:** Access: In person only. Court does not conduct in person searches; visitors must perform searches for themselves. No search fee. Required to search: name, years to search; also helpful-DOB. Criminal records on docket books from late 1800s, probate on microfiche. They can refer requestors to parties who perform searches at the court. **General Information:** No adoption records released. Some juvenile requires signed release. Copy fee: $.25 per page. Certification fee: $1.00. Fee payee: Butler County Court. Personal checks accepted. Fax notes: $3.00 for first page, $1.00 each add'l.

Cass County

District Court Cass County Courthouse, 346 Main Street, Plattsmouth, NE 68048; 402-296-9339; Fax: 402-296-9345. Hours: 8AM-5PM (CST). *Felony, Civil Actions Over $15,000.*

Civil Records: Access: In person only. Court does not conduct in person searches; visitors must perform searches for themselves. Search fee: No civil searches performed by court. Required to search: name, years to search. Civil cases indexed by defendant, plaintiff. Civil records on index books from 1860s, index on computer since 09/97. **Criminal Records:** Access: In person only. Court does not conduct in person searches; visitors must perform searches for themselves. Search fee: No criminal searches performed by court. Required to search: name, years to search. Criminal records on index books from 1860s, index on computer since 09/97. **General Information:** Copy fee: $.25 per page. Certification fee: $1.50. Fee payee: Clerk of District Court. Public access terminal is available.

Cass County Court Cass County Courthouse, Plattsmouth, NE 68048; 402-296-9334. Hours: 8AM-5PM (CST). *Misdemeanor, Civil Actions Under $15,000, Eviction, Small Claims, Probate.*

Civil Records: Access: In person only. Court does not conduct in person searches; visitors must perform searches for themselves. Search fee: No civil searches performed by court. Required to search: name, years to search. Civil cases indexed by defendant, plaintiff. Civil records on index cards for 5 years then sent to Capital for storage. **Criminal Records:** Access: In person only. Court does not conduct in person searches; visitors must perform searches for themselves. Search fee: No criminal searches performed by court. Required to search: name, years to search. Criminal records on computer since 1/97. **General Information:** Copy fee: $.25 per page. Certification fee: $1.00. Fee payee: Cass County Court. No personal checks accepted. Prepayment is required.

Cedar County

District Court PO Box 796, Hartington, NE 68739-0796; 402-254-6957; Fax: 402-254-6954. Hours: 8AM-5PM (CST). *Felony, Civil Actions Over $15,000.*

Civil Records: Access: In person only. Court does not conduct in person searches; visitors must perform searches for themselves. Search fee: No civil searches performed by court. Required to search: name, years to search. Civil cases indexed by defendant, plaintiff. Civil records in books from 1890. **Criminal Records:** Access: In person only. Court does not conduct in person searches; visitors must perform searches for themselves. Search fee: No criminal searches performed by court. Required to search: name, years to search; also helpful-SSN. Criminal records in books from 1890. **General Information:** No mental health records released. Copy fee: $.25 per page. Certification fee: $1.00. Fee payee: District Court. Prepayment is required.

Cedar County Court 101 S Broadway Ave, Hartington, NE 68739; 402-254-7441; Fax: 402-254-6954. Hours: 8AM-5PM (CST). *Misdemeanor, Civil Actions Under $15,000, Eviction, Small Claims, Probate.*

Civil Records: Access: In person only. Court does not conduct in person searches; visitors must perform searches for themselves. Search fee: No civil searches performed by court. Required to search: name, years to search. Civil cases indexed by defendant. Civil records on general index, docket books 15 years; some on microfiche. **Criminal Records:** Access: In person only. Court does not conduct in person searches; visitors must perform searches for themselves. Search fee: No criminal searches performed by court. Required to search: name, years to search, offense; also helpful-DOB. Criminal records on general index, docket books for 18 years; some on microfiche. **General Information:** No juvenile or judge sealed records released. Copy fee: $.25 per page. Certification fee: $1.00. Fee payee: Cedar County Court. Personal checks accepted. Prepayment is required.

Chase County

District Court PO Box 1299, Imperial, NE 69033; 308-882-5266; Fax: 308-882-5390. Hours: 8AM-4PM (MST). *Felony, Civil Actions Over $15,000.*

Civil Records: Access: Phone, fax, mail, in person. Both court and visitors may perform in person searches. Search fee: $5.00 per name. Required to search: name, years to search. Civil cases indexed by defendant, plaintiff. Civil records general index, docket books from early 1900s. **Criminal Records:** Access: Phone, fax, mail, in person. Both court and visitors may perform in person searches. Search fee: $5.00 per name. Required to search: name, years to search; also helpful-DOB, SSN. Criminal records general index, docket books from early 1900s. **General Information:** No restrictions. SASE required. Turnaround time 5 days. Copy fee: $.25 per page. Certification fee: $1.50. Fee payee: Chase County Clerk. Personal checks accepted. Prepayment is required. Fax notes: $1.00 per page.

Chase County Court PO Box 1299, Imperial, NE 69033; 308-882-4690; Fax: 308-882-5679. Hours: 7:30AM-4:30PM (MST). *Misdemeanor, Civil Actions Under $15,000, Eviction, Small Claims, Probate.*

Civil Records: Access: Phone, mail, in person. No search fee. Required to search: name, years to search. Civil records on general index, docket books from 1910; prior incomplete. Some probate on microfiche. **Criminal Records:** Access: Phone, mail, in person. Both court and visitors may perform in person searches. No search fee. Required to search: name, years to search, DOB. Criminal records on general index, docket books from 1910; prior incomplete. Some probate on microfiche. **General Information:** No adoption, juvenile. SASE required. Turnaround time 1 day. Copy fee: $.25 per page. Certification fee: $1.00. Fee payee: Chase County Court. Personal checks accepted. Prepayment is required.

Cherry County

District Court 365 N Main St, Valentine, NE 69201; 402-376-1840; Fax: 402-376-3830. Hours: 8:30AM-4:30PM (MST). *Felony, Civil Actions Over $15,000.*

Civil Records: Access: In person only. Court does not conduct in person searches; visitors must perform searches for themselves. Search fee: No civil searches performed by court. Required to search: name, years to search; also helpful-address. Civil cases indexed by defendant, plaintiff. Civil records on index books from late 1800s. Fax & mail access limited to partial search to confirm: if case was filed, case #, title & date of filing. **Criminal Records:** Access: In person only. Court does not conduct in person searches; visitors must perform searches for themselves. Search fee: No criminal searches performed by court. Required to search: name, years to search. Criminal records on index books from late 1800s. Same as civil. **General Information:** No juvenile records released. Copy fee: $.25 per page. Certification fee: $1.00. Fee payee: Clerk of District Court. Personal checks accepted. Public access terminal is available.

Cherry County Court 365 N Main St, Valentine, NE 69201; 402-376-2590; Fax: 402-376-3830. Hours: 8AM-5PM (MST). *Misdemeanor, Civil Actions Under $15,000, Eviction, Small Claims, Probate.*

Civil Records: Access: In person only. Court does not conduct in person searches; visitors must perform searches for themselves. Search fee: No civil searches performed by court. Required to search: name, years to search. Civil cases indexed by defendant. Civil records on docket card file from 1986, general index prior from late 1800s.

Criminal Records: Access: In person only. Court does not conduct in person searches; visitors must perform searches for themselves. Search fee: No criminal searches performed by court. Required to search: name, years to search, DOB. Criminal records on docket card file from 1986, general index prior from late 1800s. **General Information:** No adoption records released. Juvenile released only to parties involved. Copy fee: $.25 per page. Certification fee: $1.25. Fee payee: Cherry County Court. Personal checks accepted.

Cheyenne County

District Court PO Box 217, Sidney, NE 69162; 308-254-2814; Fax: 308-254-4293. Hours: 8AM-Noon,1-5PM (MST). *Felony, Civil Actions Over $15,000.*

Civil Records: Access: In person only. Court does not conduct in person searches; visitors must perform searches for themselves. Search fee: No civil searches performed by court. Required to search: name, years to search. Civil cases indexed by defendant, plaintiff. Civil records on general index, docket books going back to late 1800s, on computer since 09/98. **Criminal Records:** Access: In person only. Court does not conduct in person searches; visitors must perform searches for themselves. Search fee: No criminal searches performed by court. Required to search: name, years to search; also helpful-DOB, SSN. Criminal records on general index, docket books going back to late 1800s, on computer since 09/98. **General Information:** No mental health or search warrants released. Copy fee: $.25 per page. Certification fee: $2.00. Fee payee: Clerk of District Court. Personal checks accepted. All fees can be billed to attorneys.

Cheyenne County Court 1000 10th Ave, Sidney, NE 69162; 308-254-2929; Fax: 308-254-4641 permission to use required. Hours: 8AM-5PM (MST). *Misdemeanor, Civil Actions Under $15,000, Eviction, Small Claims, Probate.*

Civil Records: Access: Mail, in person. Both court and visitors may perform in person searches. No search fee. Required to search: name, years to search. Civil cases indexed by defendant, plaintiff. Civil records on index books from late 1800s. Fax access requires special permission. **Criminal Records:** Access: Mail, in person. Both court and visitors may perform in person searches. No search fee. Required to search: name, years to search; also helpful-DOB. Criminal records on index books from late 1800s. **General Information:** No adoption, juvenile, confidential records released. SASE required. Turnaround time within 1 week. Copy fee: $.25 per page. Certification fee: $1.00. Fee payee: Cheyenne County Court. Personal checks accepted. Prepayment is required.

Clay County

District Court 111 W Fairfield St, Clay Center, NE 68933; 402-762-3595; Fax: 402-762-3250. Hours: 8:30AM-5PM (CST). *Felony, Civil Actions Over $15,000.*

Civil Records: Access: In person only. Court does not conduct in person searches; visitors must perform searches for themselves. Search fee: No civil searches performed by court. Required to search: name; also helpful-years to search. Civil cases indexed by defendant, plaintiff. Civil records on index books from late 1800s, on microfiche from 1986. **Criminal Records:** Access: In person only. Court does not conduct in person searches; visitors must perform searches for themselves. Search fee: No criminal searches performed by

court. Required to search: name, DOB; also helpful-years to search, SSN. Criminal records on index books from late 1800s, on microfiche from 1986. **General Information:** No mental health records released. Copy fee: $.25 per page. Certification fee: $1.00. Fee payee: Clerk of District Court. Personal checks accepted.

Clay County Court 111 W Fairfield St, Clay Center, NE 68933; 402-762-3651; Fax: 402-762-3250. Hours: 8:30AM-5PM (CST). *Misdemeanor, Civil Actions Under $15,000, Eviction, Small Claims, Probate.*

Civil Records: Access: In person only. Court does not conduct in person searches; visitors must perform searches for themselves. Search fee: No civil searches performed by court. Required to search: name, years to search. Civil cases indexed by defendant. Civil records in index books from late 1800s. **Criminal Records:** Access: In person only. Court does not conduct in person searches; visitors must perform searches for themselves. Search fee: No criminal searches performed by court. Required to search: name, years to search; also helpful-DOB, SSN. Criminal records in index books from late 1800s. **General Information:** No adoption or juvenile records released. Copy fee: $.25 per page. Certification fee: $1.00. Fee payee: Clay County. Personal checks accepted.

Colfax County

District Court 411 E 11th St, PO Box 429, Schuyler, NE 68661; 402-352-8506; Fax: 402-352-2847. Hours: 8:30AM-5PM (CST). *Felony, Civil Actions Over $15,000.*

Civil Records: Access: In person only. Court does not conduct in person searches; visitors must perform searches for themselves. Search fee: No civil searches performed by court. Required to search: name, years to search; also helpful-address. Civil cases indexed by defendant, plaintiff. Civil records on index books and general index from 1880. **Criminal Records:** Access: In person only. Court does not conduct in person searches; visitors must perform searches for themselves. Search fee: No criminal searches performed by court. Required to search: name, years to search; also helpful-address, DOB, SSN. Criminal records on index books and general index from 1880. **General Information:** No juvenile or mental health records released. Copy fee: $.25 per page. Certification fee: $2.00. Fee payee: Clerk of District Court. Business checks accepted. Will take personal check if local. Prepayment is required. Public access terminal is available.

Colfax County Court 411 E 11th St, Box 191, Schuyler, NE 68661; 402-352-8511; Fax: 402-352-8535. Hours: 8AM-5PM (CST). *Misdemeanor, Civil Actions Under $15,000, Eviction, Small Claims, Probate.*

Civil Records: Access: In person only. Court does not conduct in person searches; visitors must perform searches for themselves. Search fee: No civil searches performed by court. Required to search: name, years to search. Civil cases indexed by defendant, plaintiff. Civil records on index books from 1880s. **Criminal Records:** Access: In person only. Court does not conduct in person searches; visitors must perform searches for themselves. Search fee: No criminal searches performed by court. Required to search: name, years to search; also helpful-DOB, SSN. Criminal records on index books from 1880s. **General Information:** No juvenile records released. Copy fee: $.25 per page. Certification fee: $1.00. Fee

payee: Colfax County Court. Personal checks accepted. Prepayment is required.

Cuming County

District Court 200 S Lincoln, Rm 200, West Point, NE 68788; 402-372-6004; Fax: 402-372-6017. Hours: 8:30AM-4:30PM (CST). *Felony, Civil Actions Over $15,000.*

Civil Records: Access: In person only. Court does not conduct in person searches; visitors must perform searches for themselves. Search fee: No civil searches performed by court. Required to search: name, years to search. Civil cases indexed by defendant, plaintiff. Civil records in books from 1939. **Criminal Records:** Access: In person only. Court does not conduct in person searches; visitors must perform searches for themselves. Search fee: No criminal searches performed by court. Required to search: name, years to search. Criminal records in books from 1939. **General Information:** No mental health records released. Copy fee: $.15 per page. Certification fee: $1.00. No personal checks accepted.

Cuming County Court 200 S Lincoln, Rm 103, West Point, NE 68788; 402-372-6003; Fax: 402-372-6017 (District Court). Hours: 8:30AM-4:30PM (CST). *Misdemeanor, Civil Actions Under $15,000, Eviction, Small Claims, Probate.*

Civil Records: Access: In person only. Court does not conduct in person searches; visitors must perform searches for themselves. Search fee: No civil searches performed by court. Required to search: name, years to search. Civil cases indexed by defendant, plaintiff. Civil records on index books. **Criminal Records:** Access: In person only. Court does not conduct in person searches; visitors must perform searches for themselves. Search fee: No criminal searches performed by court. Required to search: name, years to search; also helpful-DOB, SSN. Criminal records on index books. **General Information:** No mental health records releaased. Copy fee: $.25 per page. Certification fee: $1.00. Personal checks accepted. ID required for payment by check. Prepayment is required.

Custer County

District Court 431 S 10th Ave, Broken Bow, NE 68822; 308-872-2121; Fax: 308-872-5826. Hours: 9AM-5PM (CST). *Felony, Civil Actions Over $15,000.*

Civil Records: Access: Phone, fax, mail, in person. Both court and visitors may perform in person searches. No search fee. Required to search: name, years to search; also helpful-address. Civil cases indexed by defendant, plaintiff. Civil records on index books and docket books from late 1800s. **Criminal Records:** Access: Phone, fax, mail, in person. Both court and visitors may perform in person searches. No search fee. Required to search: name, years to search; also helpful-address, DOB, SSN. Criminal records on index books and docket books from late 1800s. **General Information:** No adoption, juvenile records released. SASE required. Turnaround time 3-4 days. Copy fee: $.25 per page. Certification fee: $1.00. Fee payee: Clerk of District Court. Business checks accepted. Prepayment is required. Fax notes: $3.00 per page.

Custer County Court 431 South 10th Ave, Broken Bow, NE 68822; 308-872-5761; Fax: 308-872-6052. Hours: 8AM-12 1-5PM (CST). *Misdemeanor, Civil Actions Under $15,000, Eviction, Small Claims, Probate.*

Civil Records: Access: In person only. Court does not conduct in person searches; visitors must perform searches for themselves. Search fee: No civil searches performed by court. Required to search: name, years to search. Civil cases indexed by defendant, plaintiff. Civil records on index books from 1988, probate from 1986, balance are archived. **Criminal Records:** Access: In person only. Court does not conduct in person searches; visitors must perform searches for themselves. Search fee: No criminal searches performed by court. Required to search: name, years to search. Criminal records on index books from 1988, probate from 1986, balance are archived. **General Information:** No adoption or juvenile records released. Copy fee: $.25 per page. Certification fee: $1.00. Fee payee: Custer County Court. Personal checks accepted. Prepayment is required.

Dakota County

District Court PO Box 66, Dakota City, NE 68731; 402-987-2114; Fax: 402-987-2117. Hours: 8AM-4:30PM (CST). *Felony, Civil Actions Over $15,000.*

Civil Records: Access: In person only. Court does not conduct in person searches; visitors must perform searches for themselves. Search fee: No civil searches performed by court. Required to search: name, years to search. Civil cases indexed by defendant, plaintiff. Civil records on index books from 1985, prior records archived at NE State Historical Society, Lincoln, NE. **Criminal Records:** Access: In person only. Court does not conduct in person searches; visitors must perform searches for themselves. Search fee: No criminal searches performed by court. Required to search: name, years to search. Criminal records on index books from 1985, prior records archived at NE State Historical Society, Lincoln, NE. **General Information:** No juvenile or mental health records released. Copy fee: $.25 per page. Certification fee: $1.00. Fee payee: Clerk of District Court. Personal checks accepted.

Dakota County Court PO Box 385, Dakota City, NE 68731; 402-987-2145; Fax: 402-987-2185. Hours: 8AM-4:30PM (CST). *Misdemeanor, Civil Actions Under $15,000, Eviction, Small Claims, Probate.*

Civil Records: Access: In person only. Court does not conduct in person searches; visitors must perform searches for themselves. Search fee: No civil searches performed by court. Required to search: name, years to search. Civil cases indexed by defendant, plaintiff. Civil records on index books from late 1800s. **Criminal Records:** Access: In person only. Court does not conduct in person searches; visitors must perform searches for themselves. Search fee: No criminal searches performed by court. Required to search: name, years to search. Criminal records on index books from late 1800s. **General Information:** No adoption or juvenile records released. Copy fee: $.25 per page. Certification fee: $1.00. Fee payee: Dakota County Court. Business checks accepted. Prepayment is required. Public access terminal is available.

Dawes County

District Court PO Box 630, Chadron, NE 69337; 308-432-0109; Fax: 308-432-0110. Hours: 8:30AM-4:30PM (MST). *Felony, Civil Actions Over $15,000.*

Civil Records: Access: In person only. Court does not conduct in person searches; visitors must perform searches for themselves. Search fee: No civil searches performed by court. Required to search: name, years to search. Civil cases indexed by defendant, plaintiff. Civil records on general index, docket books from 1886. **Criminal Records:** Access: In person only. Court does not conduct in person searches; visitors must perform searches for themselves. Search fee: No criminal searches performed by court. Required to search: name, years to search. Criminal records on general index, docket books from 1886. **General Information:** No mental health records released. Copy fee: $.25 per page. Certification fee: $1.00. Fee payee: Clerk of District Court. Personal checks accepted.

Dawes County Court PO Box 806, Chadron, NE 69337; 308-432-0116; Fax: 308-432-0110. Hours: 7:30AM-4:30PM (MST). *Misdemeanor, Civil Actions Under $15,000, Eviction, Small Claims, Probate.*

Civil Records: Access: In person only. Court does not conduct in person searches; visitors must perform searches for themselves. Search fee: No civil searches performed by court. Required to search: name, years to search. Civil cases indexed by defendant, plaintiff. Civil records on case cards, case files kept since 1892. **Criminal Records:** Access: In person only. Court does not conduct in person searches; visitors must perform searches for themselves. Search fee: No criminal searches performed by court. Required to search: name, years to search, DOB; also helpful-address. Criminal records on case cards, case files kept since 1892. **General Information:** No confidential records released. No copy fee. Certification fee: $1.00. Fee payee: Dawes County Court. Personal checks accepted. Prepayment is required.

Dawson County

District Court PO Box 429, Lexington, NE 68850; 308-324-4261; Fax: 308-324-3374. Hours: 8AM-5PM (CST). *Felony, Civil Actions Over $15,000.*

Civil Records: Access: In person only. Court does not conduct in person searches; visitors must perform searches for themselves. Search fee: No civil searches performed by court. Required to search: name, years to search. Civil cases indexed by defendant, plaintiff. recent records on microfiche, some older records on microfilm, index books date to late 1800s. **Criminal Records:** Access: In person only. Court does not conduct in person searches; visitors must perform searches for themselves. Search fee: No criminal searches performed by court. Required to search: name, years to search. recent records on microfiche, some older records on microfilm, index books date to late 1800s. **General Information:** No juvenile or mental health records released. Copy fee: $.25 per page. Certification fee: $1.00. Fee payee: Clerk of District Court. Personal checks accepted. Prepayment is required.

Dawson County Court 700 N Washington St, Lexington, NE 68850; 308-324-5606. Hours: 8AM-5PM (CST). *Misdemeanor, Civil Actions Under $15,000, Eviction, Small Claims, Probate.*

Civil Records: Access: In person only. Court does not conduct in person searches; visitors must perform searches for themselves. Search fee: No civil searches performed by court. Required to search: name, years to search; also helpful-address. Civil cases indexed by defendant, plaintiff. Civil records on books from late 1800s, docket books from 1980. **Criminal Records:** Access: In person only. Court does not conduct in person searches; visitors must perform searches for themselves.

Search fee: No criminal searches performed by court. Required to search: name, years to search, offense; also helpful-address, DOB, SSN. Criminal records on books from late 1800s, docket books from 1980. **General Information:** No adoption or juvenile records released. Copy fee: $.25 per page. Certification fee: $3.00 plus $1.00 each additional page. Fee payee: Dawson County Court. Personal checks accepted. Credit cards accepted: Visa, Mastercard. Prepayment is required.

Deuel County

District Court PO Box 327, Chappell, NE 69129; 308-874-3308; Fax: 308-874-3472. Hours: 8AM-4PM (MST). *Felony, Civil Actions Over $15,000.*

Civil Records: Access: Phone, fax, mail, in person. Both court and visitors may perform in person searches. No search fee. Required to search: name; also helpful-years to search. Civil cases indexed by defendant, plaintiff. Civil records on general index and docket books form late 1800s. **Criminal Records:** Access: Phone, fax, mail, in person. Both court and visitors may perform in person searches. No search fee. Required to search: name; also helpful-years to search, DOB, SSN. Criminal records on general index and docket books form late 1800s. **General Information:** No mental health or service discharge records released. SASE required. Turnaround time 1 week. Copy fee: $.50 per page. Only $.25 if you make the copy. Certification fee: $1.00. Fee payee: Clerk of District Court. Personal checks accepted. Prepayment is required. Fax notes: No fee to fax results.

Deuel County Court PO Box 514, Chappell, NE 69129; 308-874-2909; Fax: 308-874-2994. Hours: 8AM-4PM (MST). *Misdemeanor, Civil Actions Under $15,000, Eviction, Small Claims, Probate.*

Civil Records: Access: Mail, in person. Both court and visitors may perform in person searches. No search fee. Required to search: name, years to search. Civil cases indexed by defendant, plaintiff. Civil records on index cards. **Criminal Records:** Access: Mail, in person. Both court and visitors may perform in person searches. No search fee. Required to search: name, years to search, DOB, signed release. Criminal records on index cards. **General Information:** No juvenile records released. SASE required. Turnaround time 3-4 days. Copy fee: $.25 per page. Certification fee: $1.00. Fee payee: Deuel County Court. No personal checks accepted. Prepayment is required.

Dixon County

District Court PO Box 395, Ponca, NE 68770; 402-755-2881; Fax: 402-755-2632. Hours: 8AM-Noon, 1-5PM (CST). *Felony, Civil Actions Over $15,000.*

Civil Records: Access: In person only. Court does not conduct in person searches; visitors must perform searches for themselves. Search fee: No civil searches performed by court. Required to search: name, years to search. Civil cases indexed by defendant, plaintiff. Civil records on books from 1876. **Criminal Records:** Access: In person only. Court does not conduct in person searches; visitors must perform searches for themselves. Search fee: No criminal searches performed by court. Required to search: name, years to search. Criminal records on books from 1876. **General Information:** No mental health records released. Copy fee: $.25 per page. Certification fee: $1.00. Fee payee: Clerk of District Court. Personal checks accepted. Will bill copy fees.

Dixon County Court PO Box 497, Ponca, NE 68770; 402-755-2355; Fax: 402-755-2632. Hours: 8AM-4:30PM (CST). *Misdemeanor, Civil Actions Under $15,000, Eviction, Small Claims, Probate.*

Civil Records: Access: In person only. Court does not conduct in person searches; visitors must perform searches for themselves. Search fee: No civil searches performed by court. Required to search: name, years to search. Civil cases indexed by defendant, plaintiff. Civil records in files, cards from 1987, prior in dockets from 1876. **Criminal Records:** Access: In person only. Court does not conduct in person searches; visitors must perform searches for themselves. Search fee: No criminal searches performed by court. Required to search: name, years to search, DOB. Criminal records in files, cards from 1987, prior in dockets from 1876. **General Information:** No adoption or juvenile records released. Copy fee: $.25 per page. Certification fee: $1.00. Fee payee: Dixon County Court. Personal checks accepted.

Dodge County

District Court PO Box 1237, Fremont, NE 68026; 402-727-2780; Fax: 402-727-2773. Hours: 8:30AM-4:30PM (CST). *Felony, Civil Actions Over $15,000.*

Civil Records: Access: In person only. Court does not conduct in person searches; visitors must perform searches for themselves. Search fee: No civil searches performed by court. Required to search: name, years to search. Civil cases indexed by defendant, plaintiff. Civil records on general index, docket books from late 1800s. **Criminal Records:** Access: In person only. Court does not conduct in person searches; visitors must perform searches for themselves. Search fee: No criminal searches performed by court. Required to search: name, years to search. Criminal records on general index, docket books from late 1800s. **General Information:** No mental health records released. Copy fee: $.25 per page. Certification fee: $1.50. Fee payee: District Court. Personal checks accepted. Prepayment is required.

Dodge County Court 428 N Broad St, Fremont, NE 68025; 402-727-2755; Fax: 402-727-2762. Hours: 8AM-5PM (CST). *Misdemeanor, Civil Actions Under $15,000, Eviction, Small Claims, Probate.*

Civil Records: Access: In person only. Both court and visitors may perform in person searches. Search fee: No civil searches performed by court. Required to search: name, years to search. Civil cases indexed by defendant. Civil records on general index, docket books from early 1900s. Probate on microfiche from early 1900s. **Criminal Records:** Access: In person only. Court does not conduct in person searches; visitors must perform searches for themselves. Search fee: No criminal searches performed by court. Required to search: name, years to search; also helpful-DOB, SSN. Criminal records on general index, docket books from early 1900s. Probate on microfiche from early 1900s. **General Information:** No adoption or juvenile records released. Copy fee: $.25 per page. Certification fee: $1.00. Fee payee: Dodge County Court. Personal checks accepted. Prepayment is required. Fax notes: Fee to fax is $3.00 for 1st page; $1.00 each add'l.

Douglas County

District Court 1701 Farnam, Hall of Justice, Rm 300, Omaha, NE 68183; 402-444-7018.

Hours: 8:30AM-4:30PM (CST). *Felony, Civil Actions Over $15,000.*

Civil Records: Access: Mail, in person. Both court and visitors may perform in person searches. Search fee: $5.00 per name. Required to search: name, years to search; also helpful-address. Civil cases indexed by defendant, plaintiff. Civil records on computer from 1980, on books back to late 1800s. **Criminal Records:** Access: Mail, in person. Court does not conduct in person searches; visitors must perform searches for themselves. Search fee: $5.00 per name. Required to search: name, years to search; also helpful-address, DOB, SSN. Criminal records on computer from 1980, on books back to late 1800s. **General Information:** No juvenile records released. SASE required. Turnaround time 1-2 days. Copy fee: $.50 per page. $1.00 minimum. Add $.50 postage fee. Certification fee: $3.50 for 1-5 pages, then $15.50 per page. Fee payee: Clerk of District Court. Personal checks accepted. Prepayment is required. Public access terminal is available.

Douglas County Court 1819 Farnam, #F03, Omaha, NE 68183;; Civil phone:402-444-5425; Criminal phone:402-444-5425. Hours: 8AM-4:30PM (CST). *Misdemeanor, Civil Actions Under $15,000, Eviction, Small Claims, Probate.*

Civil Records: Access: Phone, mail, online, in person. Both court and visitors may perform in person searches. Search fee: No civil searches performed by court. Required to search: name, years to search. Civil cases indexed by defendant, plaintiff. Civil records on computer from 1987 (small claims), from 1983 (civil). Civil records are purged after about 20 years. Online access is $25 per month for the first 250 transations and $.10 per per transaction thereafter. The system is open 24 hours daily and can be searched by name or case number. Call Jo Williams at 402-444-7705 for more information. **Criminal Records:** Access: Mail, in person. Both court and visitors may perform in person searches. Search fee: No criminal searches performed by court. Required to search: name, years to search; also helpful-DOB. Criminal records on computer from 1987 (small claims), from 1983 (civil). Civil records are purged after about 20 years. **General Information:** SASE required. Copy fee: $.25 per page. Certification fee: $1.00. Fee payee: Douglas County Court. Personal checks accepted. Prepayment is required. Public access terminal is available.

Dundy County

District Court PO Box 506, Benkelman, NE 69021; 308-423-2058. Hours: 8AM-5PM (MST). *Felony, Civil Actions Over $15,000.*

Civil Records: Access: Phone, mail, in person. Both court and visitors may perform in person searches. No search fee. Required to search: name, years to search; also helpful-address. Civil cases indexed by defendant, plaintiff. Civil records on index books from late 1800s. **Criminal Records:** Access: Phone, mail, in person. Both court and visitors may perform in person searches. No search fee. Required to search: name, years to search; also helpful-address, DOB, SSN. Criminal records on index books from late 1800s. **General Information:** No juvenile records released. SASE required. Turnaround time 1-2 days. Copy fee: $.50 per page. Certification fee: $1.00. Fee payee: Clerk of District Court. Personal checks accepted. Prepayment is required.

Dundy County Court PO Box 377, Benkelman, NE 69021; 308-423-2374. Hours:

8AM-4:30PM (MST). *Misdemeanor, Civil Actions Under $15,000, Eviction, Small Claims, Probate.*

Civil Records: Access: Phone, mail, in person. Only the court conducts in person searches; visitors may not. No search fee. Required to search: name, years to search. Civil cases indexed by defendant, plaintiff. Civil records on general index, docket books from late 1800s; some probate, civil on microfiche. **Criminal Records:** Access: Phone, mail, in person. Only the court conducts in person searches; visitors may not. No search fee. Required to search: name, years to search, DOB, signed release; also helpful-address. Criminal records on general index, docket books from late 1800s; some probate, civil on microfiche. **General Information:** No adoption or juvenile records released. SASE required. Turnaround time 3-4 days. Copy fee: $.25 per page. Certification fee: $1.00. Fee payee: Dundy County Court. Business checks accepted. Prepayment is required.

Fillmore County

Fillmore County District Court PO Box 147, Geneva, NE 68361-0147; 402-759-3811; Fax: 402-759-4440. Hours: 8AM-Noon, 1-5PM (CST). *Felony, Civil Actions Over $15,000.*

Civil Records: Access: Phone, fax, mail, in person. Both court and visitors may perform in person searches. No search fee. Required to search: name, years to search. Civil cases indexed by defendant, plaintiff. Civil records on index books to late 1800s, last 10 years on microfiche. **Criminal Records:** Access: Phone, fax, mail, in person. Both court and visitors may perform in person searches. No search fee. Required to search: name, years to search. Criminal records on index books to late 1800s, last 10 years on microfiche. **General Information:** No juvenile or mental health records released. SASE required. Turnaround time 1-5 days, 1 day for phone and FAX. Copy fee: $.35 per page. Certification fee: $1.00. Fee payee: Clerk of District Court. Personal checks accepted. Will bill fax & copy fees. Fax notes: $2.00 for first page, $1.00 each addl.

Fillmore County Court PO Box 66, Geneva, NE 68361; 402-759-3514; Fax: 402-759-4440. Hours: 8AM-5PM (CST). *Misdemeanor, Civil Actions Under $15,000, Eviction, Small Claims, Probate.*

Civil Records: Access: Fax, mail, in person. Both court and visitors may perform in person searches. No search fee. Required to search: name, years to search. Civil cases indexed by defendant, plaintiff. Civil records on general index, docket books from late 1800s; probate on microfiche. **Criminal Records:** Access: Fax, mail, in person. Both court and visitors may perform in person searches. No search fee. Required to search: name, years to search. Criminal records on general index, docket books from late 1800s; probate on microfiche. **General Information:** No adoption or juvenile records released. SASE required. Turnaround time 7-8 days. Copy fee: $.25 per page. Certification fee: $1.25. Fee payee: County Court. Personal checks accepted. Prepayment is required. Fax notes: $2.00 for first page, $1.00 each addl.

Franklin County

District Court PO Box 146, Franklin, NE 68939; 308-425-6202; Fax: 308-425-6289. Hours: 8:30AM-4:30PM (CST). *Felony, Civil Actions Over $15,000.*

Civil Records: Access: In person only. Court does not conduct in person searches; visitors must perform searches for themselves. Search fee: No civil searches performed by court. Required to search: name, years to search. Civil cases indexed by defendant, plaintiff. Civil records on index books back to turn of century. **Criminal Records:** Access: In person only. Court does not conduct in person searches; visitors must perform searches for themselves. Search fee: No criminal searches performed by court. Required to search: name, years to search. Criminal records on index books back to turn of century. **General Information:** No adoption or juvenile records released. Copy fee: $.25 per page. Certification fee: $1.00. Fee payee: Clerk of District Court or County Clerk. Personal checks accepted. Prepayment is required.

Franklin County Court PO Box 174, Franklin, NE 68939; 308-425-6288; Fax: 308-425-6289. Hours: 8:30AM-4:30PM M-F (CST). *Misdemeanor, Civil Actions Under $15,000, Eviction, Small Claims, Probate.*

Civil Records: Access: Mail, in person. Both court and visitors may perform in person searches. No search fee. Required to search: name, years to search. Civil cases indexed by defendant, plaintiff. Civil records on docket cards since 1988, prior on docket books. **Criminal Records:** Access: Mail, in person. Both court and visitors may perform in person searches. No search fee. Required to search: name, years to search. Criminal records on docket cards since 1988, prior on docket books. **General Information:** No juvenile, adoption records released. SASE required. Turnaround time 2 days. Copy fee: $.25 per page. Certification fee: $1.00. Fee payee: Franklin County Court. Personal checks accepted.

Frontier County

District Court PO Box 40, Stockville, NE 69042; 308-367-8641; Fax: 308-367-8730. Hours: 9AM-4:30PM (CST). *Felony, Civil Actions Over $15,000.*

Civil Records: Access: Mail, in person. Both court and visitors may perform in person searches. No search fee. Required to search: name, years to search. Civil cases indexed by defendant, plaintiff. Civil records on general index, docket books from late 1800s. **Criminal Records:** Access: Mail, in person. Both court and visitors may perform in person searches. No search fee. Required to search: name, years to search, DOB, signed release. Criminal records on general index, docket books from late 1800s. **General Information:** SASE required. Turnaround time 5 days. Copy fee: $.25 per page. Certification fee: $1.00. Fee payee: Clerk of District Court. Only cashiers checks and money orders accepted. Prepayment is required.

Frontier County Court PO Box 38, Stockville, NE 69042; 308-367-8629; Fax: 308-367-8730. Hours: 9AM-4:30PM (CST). *Misdemeanor, Civil Actions Under $15,000, Eviction, Small Claims, Probate.*

Civil Records: Access: Fax, mail, in person. Only the court conducts in person searches; visitors may not. No search fee. Required to search: name, years to search. Civil cases indexed by plaintiff. Civil records on general index, docket books from late 1800s, no computerization. **Criminal Records:** Access: Fax, mail, in person. Only the court conducts in person searches; visitors may not. No search fee. Required to search: name, years to search, DOB, signed release. Criminal records on general index, docket books from late

1800s, no computerization. **General Information:** No adoption or juvenile records released. SASE required. Turnaround time 5 days. Copy fee: $.25 per page. Certification fee: $1.00. Fee payee: County Court. Only cashiers checks and money orders accepted. Prepayment is required. Fax notes: $3.00 per page.

Furnas County

District Court PO Box 413, Beaver City, NE 68926; 308-268-4015; Fax: 308-268-2345. Hours: 10AM-Noon, 1-3PM (CST). *Felony, Civil Actions Over $15,000.*

Civil Records: Access: Mail, in person. Both court and visitors may perform in person searches. No search fee. Required to search: name, years to search. Civil cases indexed by defendant, plaintiff. Civil records in general index books and files from late 1800s. **Criminal Records:** Access: Mail, in person. Both court and visitors may perform in person searches. No search fee. Required to search: name, years to search. Criminal records in general index books and files from late 1800s. **General Information:** No mental health records released. SASE required. Turnaround time 3-4 days. Copy fee: $.25 per page. Certification fee: $1.00. Fee payee: Clerk of District Court. Personal checks accepted.

Furnas County Court 912 R St (PO Box 373), Beaver City, NE 68926; 308-268-4025. Hours: 8AM-4PM (CST). *Misdemeanor, Civil Actions Under $15,000, Eviction, Small Claims, Probate.*

Civil Records: Access: In person only. Court does not conduct in person searches; visitors must perform searches for themselves. Search fee: No civil searches performed by court. Required to search: name, years to search. Civil cases indexed by defendant, plaintiff. Civil records on card system from 1984, docket books back to late 1800s. **Criminal Records:** Access: In person only. Court does not conduct in person searches; visitors must perform searches for themselves. Search fee: No criminal searches performed by court. Required to search: name, years to search; also helpful-DOB. Criminal records on card system from 1984, docket books back to late 1800s. **General Information:** No adoption, juvenile or sealed records released. Copy fee: $.25 per page. Certification fee: $1.00. Plus $.25 per page. Fee payee: County Court. Personal checks accepted.

Gage County

District Court PO Box 845, Beatrice, NE 68310; 402-223-1332; Fax: 402-223-1313. Hours: 8AM-5PM (CST). *Felony, Civil Actions Over $15,000.*

Civil Records: Access: Mail, in person. Both court and visitors may perform in person searches. No search fee. Required to search: name, years to search. Civil cases indexed by defendant, plaintiff. Civil records on index books from late 1800s. **Criminal Records:** Access: Mail, in person. Both court and visitors may perform in person searches. No search fee. Required to search: name, years to search, DOB. Criminal records on index books from late 1800s. **General Information:** No juvenile or mental health records released. SASE required. Turnaround time up to 7-10 days. Copy fee: $.25 per page. Certification fee: $1.00. Fee payee: Clerk of District Court. Personal checks accepted. Prepayment is required.

Gage County Court PO Box 219, Beatrice, NE 68310; 402-223-1323. Hours: 8AM-5PM

(CST). *Misdemeanor, Civil Actions Under $15,000, Eviction, Small Claims, Probate.*

Civil Records: Access: Mail, in person. Both court and visitors may perform in person searches. No search fee. Required to search: name, years to search. Civil cases indexed by defendant, plaintiff. probate records from 1860, probate on microfiche. Contact court before faxing. **Criminal Records:** Access: Mail, in person. Both court and visitors may perform in person searches. No search fee. Required to search: name, years to search; also helpful-DOB. probate records from 1860, probate on microfiche. Contact court before faxing. **General Information:** No adoption or juvenile records released. SASE required. Turnaround time 1-3 weeks. Copy fee: $.25 per page. Certification fee: $1.00. Fee payee: Gage County Court. Personal checks accepted. Prepayment is required.

Garden County

District Court PO Box 486, Oshkosh, NE 69154; 308-772-3924; Fax: 308-772-4143. Hours: 8AM-4PM (MST). *Felony, Civil Actions Over $15,000.*

Civil Records: Access: Fax, mail, in person. Both court and visitors may perform in person searches. No search fee. Required to search: name, years to search. Civil cases indexed by defendant, plaintiff. Civil records in files, docket books back to 1910. **Criminal Records:** Access: Fax, mail, in person. Both court and visitors may perform in person searches. No search fee. Required to search: name, years to search. Criminal records in files, docket books back to 1910. **General Information:** No confidential records released. SASE required. Turnaround time same day. Copy fee: $.50 per page. Certification fee: $1.50 per page. Fee payee: Clerk of District Court. Personal checks accepted. Prepayment is required. Fax notes: $2.00 for first page, $1.00 each addl.

Garden County Court PO Box 465, Oshkosh, NE 69154; 308-772-3696. Hours: 8AM-4PM (MST). *Misdemeanor, Civil Actions Under $15,000, Eviction, Small Claims, Probate.*

Civil Records: Access: In person only. Court does not conduct in person searches; visitors must perform searches for themselves. Search fee: No civil searches performed by court. Required to search: name, years to search. Civil cases indexed by defendant, plaintiff. Civil records on general index, docket books from 1910. Phone access limited to short searches. **Criminal Records:** Access: In person only. Court does not conduct in person searches; visitors must perform searches for themselves. Search fee: No criminal searches performed by court. Required to search: name, years to search. Criminal records on general index, docket books from 1910. Same as civil. **General Information:** No adoption or juvenile records released. Copy fee: $.25 per page. Certification fee: $1.00. Fee payee: Garden County Court. Personal checks accepted. Prepayment is required.

Garfield County

District Court PO Box 218, Burwell, NE 68823; 308-346-4161. Hours: 9AM-5PM (CST). *Felony, Civil Actions Over $15,000.*

Civil Records: Access: Mail, in person. Both court and visitors may perform in person searches. No search fee. Required to search: name, years to search; also helpful-address. Civil cases indexed by defendant, plaintiff. Civil records on index books from 1885. **Criminal Records:** Access: Mail, in person. Both court and visitors may perform in person searches. No search fee.

Required to search: name, years to search; also helpful-address, DOB, SSN. Criminal records on index books from 1885. **General Information:** SASE required. Turnaround time 3-4 days. Copy fee: $.25 per page. Certification fee: $1.50. Fee payee: Clerk of District Court. Personal checks accepted. Prepayment is required.

Garfield County Court PO Box 431, Burwell, NE 68823; 308-346-4123; Fax: 308-346-5064. Hours: 9AM-4PM (CST). *Misdemeanor, Civil Actions Under $15,000, Eviction, Small Claims, Probate.*

Civil Records: Access: Fax, mail, in person. Both court and visitors may perform in person searches. No search fee. Required to search: name, years to search. Civil cases indexed by defendant. Civil records on index books, from 1885 (probate), 25 years for civil. **Criminal Records:** Access: Fax, mail, in person. Both court and visitors may perform in person searches. No search fee. Required to search: name, years to search. Criminal record keeping back for 25 years. **General Information:** No juvenile records released. SASE required. Turnaround time within 5 days. Copy fee: $.25 per page. Certification fee: $1.00. Fee payee: County Court. Personal checks accepted. Prepayment is required. Fax notes: $3.00 for first page, $1.00 each addl.

Gosper County

District Court PO Box 136, Elwood, NE 68937; 308-785-2611. Hours: 8:30AM-4:30PM (CST). *Felony, Civil Actions Over $15,000.*

Civil Records: Access: In person only. Court does not conduct in person searches; visitors must perform searches for themselves. Search fee: No civil searches performed by court. Required to search: name, years to search. Civil cases indexed by defendant, plaintiff. Civil records in general index books since late 1800s. **Criminal Records:** Access: In person only. Court does not conduct in person searches; visitors must perform searches for themselves. Search fee: No criminal searches performed by court. Required to search: name, years to search; also helpful-DOB. Criminal records in general index books since late 1800s. **General Information:** No juvenile records or search warrants released. Copy fee: $.25 per page. Certification fee: $1.00. Fee payee: Clerk of District Court. Personal checks accepted. Prepayment is required.

Gosper County Court PO Box 55, Elwood, NE 68937; 308-785-2531; Fax: 308-785-2036 (call before faxing). Hours: 8:30AM-4:30PM (CST). *Misdemeanor, Civil Actions Under $15,000, Eviction, Small Claims, Probate.*

Civil Records: Access: In person only. Court does not conduct in person searches; visitors must perform searches for themselves. Search fee: No civil searches performed by court. Required to search: name, years to search. Civil cases indexed by defendant, plaintiff. Civil records on index cards, docket books kept for 10 years (civil), to late 1800s (probate). Mail access limited to short searches. **Criminal Records:** Access: In person only. Court does not conduct in person searches; visitors must perform searches for themselves. Search fee: No criminal searches performed by court. Required to search: name, years to search, DOB. Criminal record keeping back for 10 years. **General Information:** No adoption or juvenile records released. Copy fee: $.25 per page. Certification fee: $1.00. Fee payee: Gosper County Court. Personal checks accepted. Out of state checks not accepted. Prepayment is required.

Grant County

District Court PO Box 139, Hyannis, NE 69350; 308-458-2488; Fax: 308-458-2485. Hours: 8AM-4PM (MST). *Felony, Civil Actions Over $15,000.*

Civil Records: Access: Fax, mail, in person. Both court and visitors may perform in person searches. No search fee. Required to search: name, years to search. Civil cases indexed by defendant, plaintiff. Civil records on index books from 1888. **Criminal Records:** Access: Fax, mail, in person. Both court and visitors may perform in person searches. No search fee. Required to search: name, years to search. Criminal records on index books from 1888. **General Information:** No mental health records released. SASE required. Turnaround time 3-4 days. Copy fee: $.20 per page. Certification fee: $1.50. Fee payee: Grant County Clerk. Personal checks accepted. Prepayment is required. Fax notes: $.20 per page.

Grant County Court PO Box 97, Hyannis, NE 69350; 308-458-2433; Fax: 308-458-2283 (Sheriff). Hours: 8AM-4PM (MST). *Misdemeanor, Civil Actions Under $15,000, Eviction, Small Claims, Probate.*

Civil Records: Access: Phone, mail, in person. Both court and visitors may perform in person searches. No search fee. Required to search: name, years to search; also helpful-address. Civil cases indexed by defendant, plaintiff. Civil records in files, docket books from 1888. **Criminal Records:** Access: Phone, mail, in person. Both court and visitors may perform in person searches. No search fee. Required to search: name, years to search, DOB; also helpful-address, SSN. Criminal records in files, docket books from 1888. **General Information:** No adoption records released. SASE not required. Turnaround time 7 days, limited phone searching immediate. Copy fee: $.20 per page. Certification fee: $1.50. Fee payee: Grant County Court. Personal checks accepted.

Greeley County

District Court PO Box 287, Greeley, NE 68842; 308-428-3625; Fax: 308-428-6500. Hours: 8AM-4PM (CST). *Felony, Civil Actions Over $15,000.*

Civil Records: Access: Mail, in person. Only the court conducts in person searches; visitors may not. No search fee. Required to search: name, years to search, address. Civil cases indexed by defendant, plaintiff. Civil records on general index books from late 1800s. **Criminal Records:** Access: Mail, in person. Only the court conducts in person searches; visitors may not. No search fee. Required to search: name, years to search, DOB, signed release. Criminal records on general index books from late 1800s. **General Information:** No mental health records released. SASE required. Turnaround time 1 day. Copy fee: $.25 per page. Certification fee: $1.50. Fee payee: Clerk of District Court. Only cashiers checks and money orders accepted. Prepayment is required.

Greeley County Court PO Box 302, Greeley, NE 68842; 308-428-2705; Fax: 308-428-6500. Hours: 8AM-5PM (CST). *Misdemeanor, Civil Actions Under $15,000, Eviction, Small Claims, Probate.*

Civil Records: Access: In person only. Court does not conduct in person searches; visitors must perform searches for themselves. Search fee: No civil searches performed by court. Required to search: name, years to search. Civil cases indexed by defendant, plaintiff. Civil records on index

cards, kept from late 1800s. **Criminal Records:** Access: In person only. Court does not conduct in person searches; visitors must perform searches for themselves. Search fee: No criminal searches performed by court. Required to search: name, years to search. Criminal records on index cards, kept from late 1800s. **General Information:** No adoption records released. Copy fee: $.25 per page. Certification fee: $1.00. Fee payee: County Court. Only cashiers checks and money orders accepted. Prepayment is required.

Hall County

District Court PO Box 1926, Grand Island, NE 68802; 308-385-5144; Fax: 308-385-5110. Hours: 8AM-5PM (CST). *Felony, Civil Actions Over $15,000.*

Civil Records: Access: Mail, in person. Both court and visitors may perform in person searches. No search fee. Required to search: name, years to search. Civil cases indexed by defendant, plaintiff. Many records on computer since 1985, some on microfilm, original index books back to late 1800s. **Criminal Records:** Access: Mail, in person. Both court and visitors may perform in person searches. No search fee. Required to search: name, years to search. Many records on computer since 1985, some on microfilm, original index books back to late 1800s. **General Information:** No mental health records released. SASE required. Turnaround time 3-4 days. Copy fee: $.20 per page. Certification fee: $2.00. Fee payee: Clerk of District Court. Personal checks accepted. Prepayment is required. Public access terminal is available.

Hall County Court 111 W 1st Suite 1, Grand Island, NE 68801; 308-385-5135. Hours: 8AM-4:30PM (CST). *Misdemeanor, Civil Actions Under $15,000, Eviction, Small Claims, Probate.*

Civil Records: Access: In person only. Court does not conduct in person searches; visitors must perform searches for themselves. Search fee: No civil searches performed by court. Required to search: name, years to search. Civil cases indexed by defendant. Civil records on index books. **Criminal Records:** Access: In person only. Court does not conduct in person searches; visitors must perform searches for themselves. Search fee: No criminal searches performed by court. Required to search: name, years to search, DOB. Criminal records on index books. **General Information:** No confidential records released. Copy fee: $.25 per page. Certification fee: $1.00. Fee payee: County Court. Personal checks accepted. Prepayment is required. Public access terminal is available.

Hamilton County

District Court PO Box 201, Aurora, NE 68818-0201; 402-694-3533; Fax: 402-694-2250. Hours: 8AM-5PM (CST). *Felony, Civil Actions Over $15,000.*

Civil Records: Access: In person only. Both court and visitors may perform in person searches. No search fee. Required to search: name, years to search. Civil cases indexed by defendant, plaintiff. Civil records on index books and files from late 1800s. **Criminal Records:** Access: In person only. Both court and visitors may perform in person searches. No search fee. Required to search: name, years to search. Criminal records on index books and files from late 1800s. **General Information:** No mental health board hearing records released. Copy fee: $.25 per page. Certification fee: $1.00. Fee payee: Clerk of District Court. Personal checks accepted. Prepayment is required.

Hamilton County Court PO Box 323, Aurora, NE 68818; 402-694-6188; Fax: 402-694-2250. *Misdemeanor, Civil Actions Under $15,000, Eviction, Small Claims, Probate.*

Civil Records: Access: In person only. Court does not conduct in person searches; visitors must perform searches for themselves. Search fee: No civil searches performed by court. Required to search: name, years to search. Civil cases indexed by defendant, plaintiff. Civil records computerized since 1998, older on docket cards, probate on microfiche from late 1800s. **Criminal Records:** Access: In person only. Court does not conduct in person searches; visitors must perform searches for themselves. Search fee: No criminal searches performed by court. Required to search: name, years to search. computerized since 1997. **General Information:** No adoption records released. Copy fee: $.25 per page. Certification fee: $1.00. Fee payee: Hamilton County Court. Personal checks accepted. Credit cards accepted: Visa, Mastercard. Prepayment is required. Public access terminal is available.

Harlan County

District Court PO Box 698, Alma, NE 68920; 308-928-2173; Fax: 308-928-2170. Hours: 8:30AM-4:30PM (CST). *Felony, Civil Actions Over $15,000.*

Civil Records: Access: Phone, mail, in person. Both court and visitors may perform in person searches. Search fee: $5.00 per name. Required to search: name, years to search. Civil cases indexed by defendant, plaintiff. Civil records on books and in files from late 1800s. **Criminal Records:** Access: Phone, mail, in person. Both court and visitors may perform in person searches. Search fee: $5.00 per name. Required to search: name, years to search. Criminal records on books and in files from late 1800s. **General Information:** No juvenile records released. SASE not required. Turnaround time 1 day. Copy fee: $.25 per page. Certification fee: $3.00. Fee payee: Clerk of District Court. Personal checks accepted.

Harlan County Court PO Box 379, Alma, NE 68920; 308-928-2179; Fax: 308-928-2170. Hours: 8:30AM-4:30PM (CST). *Misdemeanor, Civil Actions Under $15,000, Eviction, Small Claims, Probate.*

Civil Records: Access: In person only. Court does not conduct in person searches; visitors must perform searches for themselves. Search fee: No civil searches performed by court. Required to search: name, years to search; also helpful-address. Civil cases indexed by defendant. Civil records on index cards, back to late 1800s. **Criminal Records:** Access: In person only. Court does not conduct in person searches; visitors must perform searches for themselves. Search fee: No criminal searches performed by court. Search limited to two. Required to search: name, years to search; also helpful-address, DOB, SSN. Criminal records on index cards, back to late 1800s. **General Information:** No adoption records released. Limited access to juvenile records. Copy fee: $.25 per page. Certification fee: $1.00. Fee payee: County Court. Business checks accepted. Prepayment is required. Public access terminal is available. Public Access Terminal Note: CD rom legal research only.

Hayes County

District Court PO Box 370, Hayes Center, NE 69032; 308-286-3413; Fax: 308-286-3208. Hours:

8AM-4PM (CST). *Felony, Civil Actions Over $15,000.*

Civil Records: Access: Fax, mail, in person. Both court and visitors may perform in person searches. No search fee. Required to search: name; also helpful-years to search, address. Civil cases indexed by defendant, plaintiff. Civil records on index books back to late 1800s. **Criminal Records:** Access: Fax, mail, in person. Both court and visitors may perform in person searches. No search fee. Required to search: name; also helpful-years to search, address, DOB, SSN. Criminal records on index books back to late 1800s. **General Information:** No sealed records released. SASE required. Turnaround time 2 days. Copy fee: $.25 per page. Certification fee: $4.00. Fee payee: Clerk of District Court. Personal checks accepted. Prepayment is required.

Hayes County Court PO Box 370, Hayes Center, NE 69032; 308-286-3315. Hours: 9AM-Noon, 1-4PM Tuesday (Clerk's hours) (CST). *Misdemeanor, Civil Actions Under $15,000, Eviction, Small Claims, Probate.*

Civil Records: Access: Phone, mail, in person. Both court and visitors may perform in person searches. No search fee. Required to search: name, years to search. Civil cases indexed by defendant, plaintiff. Civil records on general index books and files back to late 1800s. **Criminal Records:** Access: Phone, mail, in person. Both court and visitors may perform in person searches. No search fee. Required to search: name, years to search, DOB. Criminal records on general index books and files back to late 1800s. **General Information:** No juvenile or adoption records released. SASE required. Turnaround time 1 week. Copy fee: $.25 per page. Certification fee: $1.00. Fee payee: County Court. Personal checks accepted. Prepayment is required.

Hitchcock County

District Court PO Box 248, Trenton, NE 69044; 308-334-5646; Fax: 308-334-5398. Hours: 8:30AM-4PM (CST). *Felony, Civil Actions Over $15,000.*

Civil Records: Access: Phone, fax, mail, in person. Both court and visitors may perform in person searches. No search fee. Required to search: name, years to search. Civil cases indexed by defendant, plaintiff. Civil records on books from late 1800s. **Criminal Records:** Access: Phone, fax, mail, in person. Both court and visitors may perform in person searches. No search fee. Required to search: name, years to search. Criminal records on books from late 1800s. **General Information:** No sealed records released. SASE required. Turnaround time 2 days. Copy fee: $.25 per page. Certification fee: $1.00. Fee payee: Clerk of District Court. Personal checks accepted. Prepayment is required. Fax notes: $3.00 for first page, $1.50 each addl.

Hitchcock County Court PO Box 366, Trenton, NE 69044; 308-334-5383. Hours: 8:30AM-4PM (CST). *Misdemeanor, Civil Actions Under $15,000, Eviction, Small Claims, Probate.*

Civil Records: Access: Phone, mail, in person. Both court and visitors may perform in person searches. No search fee. Required to search: name, years to search. Civil cases indexed by defendant, plaintiff. Civil records on docket books, cards back to late 1800s. **Criminal Records:** Access: Phone, mail, in person. Both court and visitors may perform in person searches. No search fee. Required to search: name, years to search, DOB. Criminal records on docket books, cards back to

late 1800s. **General Information:** No adoption or juvenile records released. SASE required. Turnaround time 2 weeks, limited phone searching same day. Copy fee: $.25 per page. Certification fee: $1.00. Fee payee: County Court. Personal checks accepted. Prepayment is required.

Holt County

District Court PO Box 755, O'Neill, NE 68763; 402-336-2840; Fax: 402-336-3601. Hours: 8AM-4:30PM (CST). *Felony, Civil Actions Over $15,000.*

Civil Records: Access: Phone, fax, mail, in person. Both court and visitors may perform in person searches. No search fee. Required to search: name, years to search; also helpful-address. Civil cases indexed by defendant, plaintiff. Civil records on docket books and general index books since late 1800s. **Criminal Records:** Access: Phone, fax, mail, in person. Both court and visitors may perform in person searches. No search fee. Required to search: name, years to search. Criminal records on docket books and general index books since late 1800s. **General Information:** No juvenile or mental health records released. SASE required. Turnaround time 1 week or less. Copy fee: $.25 per page. Certification fee: $1.00. Fee payee: Clerk of District Court. Personal checks accepted. Fax notes: $3.00 for first page, $1.00 each addl.

Holt County Court 204 N 4th St, O'Neill, NE 68763; 402-336-1662; Fax: 402-336-1663. Hours: 8AM-4:30PM (CST). *Misdemeanor, Civil Actions Under $15,000, Eviction, Small Claims, Probate.*

Civil Records: Access: Mail, in person. Both court and visitors may perform in person searches. No search fee. Required to search: name, years to search. Civil cases indexed by defendant. Civil records in files for 15 years, probate kept longer. **Criminal Records:** Access: Mail, in person. Both court and visitors may perform in person searches. No search fee. Required to search: name, years to search, DOB. Criminal records in files for 15 years, probate kept longer. **General Information:** No adoption records released. SASE required. Turnaround time 1 week. Copy fee: $.25 per page. Certification fee: $1.25. Fee payee: Holt County Court. Personal checks accepted. Prepayment is required.

Hooker County

District Court PO Box 184, Mullen, NE 69152; 308-546-2244; Fax: 308-546-2490. Hours: 8:30AM-Noon, 1-4:30PM (MST). *Felony, Civil Actions Over $15,000.*

Civil Records: Access: Phone, fax, mail, in person. Court does not conduct in person searches; visitors must perform searches for themselves. No search fee. Required to search: name, years to search. Civil cases indexed by defendant, plaintiff. Civil records on index books since late 1800s. **Criminal Records:** Access: Phone, fax, mail, in person. Court does not conduct in person searches; visitors must perform searches for themselves. No search fee. Required to search: name, years to search. Criminal records on index books since late 1800s. **General Information:** No mental health records released. SASE required. Turnaround time 3-4 days. Copy fee: $1.00 per page. Certification fee: $1.50. Fee payee: Clerk of District Court. Personal checks accepted. Prepayment is required. Fax notes: $2.00 for first page, $1.00 each addl.

Hooker County Court PO Box 184, Mullen, NE 69152; 308-546-2249; Fax: 308-546-2490 (Sheriff). Hours: 8:30AM-4:30PM (MST).

Misdemeanor, Civil Actions Under $15,000, Eviction, Small Claims, Probate.

Civil Records: Access: Fax, mail, in person. Both court and visitors may perform in person searches. No search fee. Required to search: name, years to search. Civil cases indexed by defendant, plaintiff. Civil records on index cards and books from late 1800s. **Criminal Records:** Access: Fax, mail, in person. Both court and visitors may perform in person searches. No search fee. Required to search: name, years to search; also helpful-DOB, SSN. Criminal records on index cards and books from late 1800s. **General Information:** No adoption or juvenile records released. SASE required. Turnaround time 3-4 days. Copy fee: $.25 per page. Certification fee: $1.00. Fee payee: County Court. Business checks accepted. Prepayment is required. Fax notes: No fee to fax results.

Howard County

District Court PO Box 25, St Paul, NE 68873; 308-754-4343; Fax: 308-754-4727. Hours: 8AM-5PM (CST). *Felony, Civil Actions Over $15,000.*

Civil Records: Access: Mail, in person. Both court and visitors may perform in person searches. No search fee. Required to search: name, years to search. Civil cases indexed by defendant, plaintiff. Civil records on microfiche from 1986, books prior. **Criminal Records:** Access: Mail, in person. Both court and visitors may perform in person searches. No search fee. Required to search: name, years to search, DOB. Criminal records on microfiche from 1986, books prior. **General Information:** No pending case records released. SASE required. Turnaround time 1-2 days. Copy fee: $.25 per page. Certification fee: $4.00. Fee payee: Clerk of District Court. Personal checks accepted. Prepayment is required.

Howard County Court 612 Indian St Suite #6, St Paul, NE 68873; 308-754-4192. Hours: 8AM-5PM (CST). *Misdemeanor, Civil Actions Under $15,000, Eviction, Small Claims, Probate.*

Civil Records: Access: In person only. Court does not conduct in person searches; visitors must perform searches for themselves. Search fee: No civil searches performed by court. Required to search: name, years to search. Civil cases indexed by defendant. Civil records on docket cards since 1982. **Criminal Records:** Access: In person only. Court does not conduct in person searches; visitors must perform searches for themselves. Search fee: No criminal searches performed by court. Required to search: name, years to search; also helpful-DOB. Criminal records on docket cards since 1982. **General Information:** Copy fee: $.25 per page. Certification fee: $1.00. Fee payee: Howard County Court. Business checks accepted. Prepayment is required.

Jefferson County

District Court Jefferson County Courthouse, 411 Fourth Street, Fairbury, NE 68352; 402-729-2019; Fax: 402-729-2016. Hours: 9AM-5PM (CST). *Felony, Civil Actions Over $15,000.*

Civil Records: Access: Fax, mail, in person. Both court and visitors may perform in person searches. No search fee. Required to search: name, years to search; also helpful-address. Civil cases indexed by defendant, plaintiff. Civil records on index books from 1870s. **Criminal Records:** Access: Fax, mail, in person. Both court and visitors may perform in person searches. No search fee. Required to search: name, years to search. Criminal records on index books from 1870s. This

office will not verify a DOB or SSN on individuals. **General Information:** No mental health records released. SASE required. Turnaround time 1-2 days. Increases to 10 days if paying by personal check. Copy fee: $.50 per page. Certification fee: $1.00. Fee payee: Clerk of District Court. Personal checks accepted. Prepayment is required. Public access terminal is available. Fax notes: $2.00 per document.

Jefferson County Court 411 Fourth St, Fairbury, NE 68352; 402-729-2312; Fax: 402-729-2016. Hours: 8AM-Noon, 1-5PM (CST). *Misdemeanor, Civil Actions Under $15,000, Eviction, Small Claims, Probate.*

Civil Records: Access: Mail, in person. Both court and visitors may perform in person searches. No search fee. Required to search: name, years to search. Civil cases indexed by defendant, plaintiff. Civil records on cards from 1988, prior on docket books. **Criminal Records:** Access: Mail, in person. Both court and visitors may perform in person searches. No search fee. Required to search: name, years to search, DOB. Criminal records on cards from 1988, prior on docket books. **General Information:** No adoption or sealed records released. SASE required. Turnaround time varies. Copy fee: $.25 per page. Certification fee: $1.00. Fee payee: County Court. Personal checks accepted. Prepayment is required.

Johnson County

District Court PO Box 416, Tecumseh, NE 68450; 402-335-2871; Fax: 402-335-3975. Hours: 8AM-Noon, 1-4:30PM (CST). *Felony, Civil Actions Over $15,000.*

Civil Records: Access: Fax, mail, in person. Both court and visitors may perform in person searches. No search fee. Required to search: name, years to search. Civil cases indexed by defendant, plaintiff. Civil records on index and docket books from late 1800s, microfiche back 7 years. **Criminal Records:** Access: Fax, mail, in person. Both court and visitors may perform in person searches. No search fee. Required to search: name, years to search. Criminal records on index and docket books from late 1800s, microfiche back 7 years. **General Information:** No juvenile records released. SASE required. Turnaround time 3-4 days. Copy fee: $.25 per page. Certification fee: $1.00. Fee payee: Clerk of District Court. Personal checks accepted. Prepayment is required. Fax notes: $2.00 per document.

Johnson County Court PO Box 285, Tecumseh, NE 68450; 402-335-3050; Fax: 402-335-3070. Hours: 8AM-4:30PM (CST). *Misdemeanor, Civil Actions Under $15,000, Eviction, Small Claims, Probate.*

Note: The court is in the process of computerizing their records

Civil Records: Access: In person only. Court does not conduct in person searches; visitors must perform searches for themselves. No search fee. Required to search: name, years to search; also helpful-address. Civil cases indexed by defendant, plaintiff. Civil records on index cards back 15 years, microfiche back to late 1800s for probate. **Criminal Records:** Access: In person only. Court does not conduct in person searches; visitors must perform searches for themselves. Search fee: No criminal searches performed by court. Required to search: name, years to search, DOB, signed release; also helpful-address, SSN. Criminal records on index cards back 15 years, microfiche back to late 1800s for probate. **General Information:** No adoption or juvenile records

released. Copy fee: $.25 per page. Certification fee: $1.00. Fee payee: County Court. Personal checks accepted. Prepayment is required.

Kearney County

District Court PO Box 208, Minden, NE 68959; 308-832-1742; Fax: 308-832-0636. Hours: 8:30AM-5PM (CST). *Felony, Civil Actions Over $15,000.*

Civil Records: Access: In person only. Court does not conduct in person searches; visitors must perform searches for themselves. Search fee: No civil searches performed by court. Required to search: name, years to search. Civil cases indexed by defendant, plaintiff. All records on microfilm since 1800s. Mail access available to attorneys only. **Criminal Records:** Access: In person only. Court does not conduct in person searches; visitors must perform searches for themselves. Search fee: No criminal searches performed by court. Required to search: name, years to search. All records on microfilm since 1800s. **General Information:** No mental health records released. Copy fee: $.25 per page. Certification fee: $1.50. Fee payee: Clerk of District Court. Personal checks accepted. Prepayment is required. Public access terminal is available. Public Access Terminal Note: For records since 09/01/98.

Kearney County Court PO Box 377, Minden, NE 68959; 308-832-2719; Fax: 308-832-0636. Hours: 8:30AM-5PM (CST). *Misdemeanor, Civil Actions Under $15,000, Eviction, Small Claims, Probate.*

Civil Records: Access: In person only. Court does not conduct in person searches; visitors must perform searches for themselves. Search fee: No civil searches performed by court. Required to search: name, years to search. Civil cases indexed by defendant. Civil records computerized since 10/99, rest on index cards, some probate on microfiche. **Criminal Records:** Access: In person only. Court does not conduct in person searches; visitors must perform searches for themselves. Search fee: No criminal searches performed by court. Required to search: name, years to search. Criminal records computerized since 03/97. **General Information:** Copy fee: $.25 per page. Certification fee: $1.00. Fee payee: Kearney County Court. Personal checks accepted. Prepayment is required.

Keith County

District Court PO Box 686, Ogallala, NE 69153; 308-284-3849; Fax: 308-284-3978. Hours: 8AM-4PM (MST). *Felony, Civil Actions Over $15,000.*

Civil Records: Access: Fax, mail, in person. Both court and visitors may perform in person searches. No search fee. Required to search: name, years to search. Civil cases indexed by defendant, plaintiff. Civil records on index books from late 1800s. **Criminal Records:** Access: Fax, mail, in person. Both court and visitors may perform in person searches. No search fee. Required to search: name, years to search, DOB. Criminal records on index books from late 1800s. **General Information:** No juvenile or mental health records released. SASE not required. Turnaround time 2-3 days. Copy fee: $.25 per page. Certification fee: $1.00. Fee payee: Clerk of District Court. Personal checks accepted. Fax notes: No fee to fax results. Fees incurred for long distance calls.

Keith County Court PO Box 358, Ogallala, NE 69153; 308-284-3693; Fax: 308-284-6825. Hours: 8AM-5PM M-Th; 7AM-4PM F (MST).

Misdemeanor, Civil Actions Under $15,000, Eviction, Small Claims, Probate.

Civil Records: Access: In person only. Court does not conduct in person searches; visitors must perform searches for themselves. Search fee: No civil searches performed by court. Required to search: name, years to search. Civil cases indexed by defendant, plaintiff. Civil records on index cards, files. **Criminal Records:** Access: In person only. Court does not conduct in person searches; visitors must perform searches for themselves. Search fee: No criminal searches performed by court. Required to search: name, years to search. Criminal records on index cards, files. **General Information:** No adoption records released. Copy fee: $.25 per page. Certification fee: $1.00. Fee payee: County Court. Local checks only. Public access terminal is available.

Keya Paha County

District Court PO Box 349, Springview, NE 68778; 402-497-3791; Fax: 402-497-3799. Hours: 8AM-5PM (CST). *Felony, Civil Actions Over $15,000.*

Civil Records: Access: Fax, mail, in person. Both court and visitors may perform in person searches. No search fee. Required to search: name, years to search. Civil cases indexed by defendant, plaintiff. Civil records on microfiche 7-9 years, on docket books since late 1800s. **Criminal Records:** Access: Fax, mail, in person. Both court and visitors may perform in person searches. No search fee. Required to search: name, years to search. Criminal records on microfiche 7-9 years, on docket books since late 1800s. **General Information:** No confidential records released. SASE required. Turnaround time 3-4 days. Copy fee: $.25 per page. Legal Size Copy Fee: $.30 per page. Certification fee: $4.00. Fee payee: Clerk of District Court. Personal checks accepted. Prepayment is required. Fax notes: $2.00 for first page, $1.00 each addl.

Keya Paha County Court PO Box 275, Springview, NE 68778; 402-497-3021. Hours: 8AM-Noon M; 8AM-4:30PM Th,F (CST). *Misdemeanor, Civil Actions Under $15,000, Eviction, Small Claims, Probate.*

Civil Records: Access: In person only. Court does not conduct in person searches; visitors must perform searches for themselves. Search fee: No civil searches performed by court. Required to search: name, years to search; also helpful-address. Civil cases indexed by defendant, plaintiff. Civil records in index books and files, many records on microfiche, back to late 1800s. **Criminal Records:** Access: In person only. Court does not conduct in person searches; visitors must perform searches for themselves. Search fee: No criminal searches performed by court. Required to search: name, years to search; also helpful-address, DOB, SSN. Criminal records in index books and files, many records on microfiche, back to late 1800s. **General Information:** No juvenile records released. Copy fee: $.25 per page. Certification fee: $1.25. Fee payee: County Clerk. Personal checks accepted.

Kimball County

District Court 114 E 3rd St, Kimball, NE 69145; 308-235-3591; Fax: 308-235-3654. Hours: 8AM-5PM M-Th, 8AM-4PM F (MST). *Felony, Civil Actions Over $15,000.*

Civil Records: Access: In person only. Court does not conduct in person searches; visitors must perform searches for themselves. Search fee: No civil searches performed by court. Required to search: name, years to search. Civil cases indexed by defendant, plaintiff. Civil records on microfiche from 1960 forward, prior in books from early 1900s, computerized since 11/97. **Criminal Records:** Access: In person only. Court does not conduct in person searches; visitors must perform searches for themselves. Search fee: No criminal searches performed by court. Required to search: name, years to search; also helpful-DOB. Criminal records on microfiche from 1960 forward, prior in books from early 1900s, computerized since 11/97. **General Information:** No mental health records released. Copy fee: $1.00 per page. Certification fee: $1.50. Fee payee: Clerk of District Court. Personal checks accepted. Prepayment is required. Public access terminal is available.

Kimball County Court 114 E 3rd St, Kimball, NE 69145; 308-235-2831. Hours: 8AM-5PM (MST). *Misdemeanor, Civil Actions Under $15,000, Small Claims, Probate.*

Civil Records: Access: In person only. Court does not conduct in person searches; visitors must perform searches for themselves. Search fee: No civil searches performed by court. Required to search: name, years to search. Civil cases indexed by defendant, plaintiff. Civil records on index cards and original files. **Criminal Records:** Access: In person only. Court does not conduct in person searches; visitors must perform searches for themselves. Search fee: No criminal searches performed by court. Required to search: name, years to search. Criminal records on index cards and original files. **General Information:** Copy fee: The court reports that photocopying is not available. Certification fee: $1.25. Fee payee: County Court. Only cashiers checks and money orders accepted. Prepayment is required.

Knox County

District Court PO Box 126, Center, NE 68724; 402-288-4484; Fax: 402-288-4275. Hours: 8:30AM-4:30PM (CST). *Felony, Civil Actions Over $15,000.*

Civil Records: Access: In person only. Court does not conduct in person searches; visitors must perform searches for themselves. Search fee: No civil searches performed by court. Required to search: name, years to search. Civil cases indexed by defendant, plaintiff. Civil records on index books from late 1800s. **Criminal Records:** Access: In person only. Court does not conduct in person searches; visitors must perform searches for themselves. Search fee: No criminal searches performed by court. Required to search: name, years to search; also helpful-DOB. Criminal records on index books from late 1800s. **General Information:** No mental health records released. Copy fee: $.25 per page. Certification fee: $1.00. Fee payee: Clerk of District Court. Personal checks accepted.

Knox County Court PO Box 125, Center, NE 68724; 402-288-4277; Fax: 402-288-4275. Hours: 8:30AM-4:30PM (CST). *Misdemeanor, Civil Actions Under $15,000, Eviction, Small Claims, Probate.*

Civil Records: Access: In person only. Court does not conduct in person searches; visitors must perform searches for themselves. Search fee: No civil searches performed by court. Required to search: name, years to search. Civil cases indexed by defendant, plaintiff. Civil records on index cards and general docket books from late 1800s. **Criminal Records:** Access: In person only. Court does not conduct in person searches; visitors must perform searches for themselves. Search fee: No criminal searches performed by court. Required to search: name, years to search; also helpful-DOB. Criminal records on index cards and general docket books from late 1800s. **General Information:** No adoption records released. Copy fee: $.25 per page. Certification fee: $1.00. Fee payee: County Court. Personal checks accepted. Prepayment is required.

Lancaster County

District Court 575 S Tenth St, Lincoln, NE 68508-2810; 402-441-7328; Fax: 402-441-6190. Hours: 8AM-4:30PM (CST). *Felony, Civil Actions Over $15,000.*

www.ci.lincoln.ne.us/cnty/discrt/index.htm

Civil Records: Access: Phone, mail, in person. Both court and visitors may perform in person searches. No search fee. Required to search: name, years to search. Civil cases indexed by defendant, plaintiff. Civil records on computer from 1985, microfiche from 1900s, docket books from 1800s. **Criminal Records:** Access: Phone, mail, in person. Both court and visitors may perform in person searches. No search fee. Required to search: name, years to search, DOB. Criminal records on computer from 1985, microfiche from 1900s, docket books from 1800s. **General Information:** No juvenile, mental health or grand jury records released. SASE required. Turnaround time 1 week. Copy fee: $.25 per page. Certification fee: $1.00. Fee payee: Clerk of District Court. Personal checks accepted. Prepayment is required. Public access terminal is available.

Lancaster County Court 575 S 10th, Lincoln, NE 68508; 402-441-7295. Hours: 8AM-4:30PM (CST). *Misdemeanor, Civil Actions Under $15,000, Eviction, Small Claims, Probate.*

www.ci.lincoln.ne.us/cnty/discrt/index.htm

Civil Records: Access: In person only. Court does not conduct in person searches; visitors must perform searches for themselves. Search fee: No civil searches performed by court. Required to search: name, years to search. Civil cases indexed by defendant, plaintiff. Civil records on index books back to 1968, computerized since 11/98. **Criminal Records:** Access: In person only. Court does not conduct in person searches; visitors must perform searches for themselves. Search fee: No criminal searches performed by court. Required to search: name, years to search; also helpful-DOB. Criminal records on computer since 2/95; prior records are avilable if the case number is known. **General Information:** No adoption records released. Copy fee: $.25 per page. Certification fee: $1.00. Fee payee: County Court. Personal checks accepted. Credit cards accepted: Visa, Mastercard. $3.00 service charge. Prepayment is required. Public access terminal is available. Public Access Terminal Note: Criminal only.

Lincoln County

District Court (301 N Jeffers Third Floor), PO Box 1616, North Platte, NE 69103-1616; 308-534-4350 X301 & X303. Hours: 8AM-5PM (CST). *Felony, Civil Actions Over $15,000.*

Civil Records: Access: In person only. Court does not conduct in person searches; visitors must perform searches for themselves. Search fee: No civil searches performed by court. Required to search: name, years to search. Civil cases indexed by defendant, plaintiff. Civil records on computer from 1979, books from 1866. **Criminal Records:** Access: In person only. Court does not conduct in person searches; visitors must perform searches for themselves. Search fee: No criminal searches performed by court. Required to search: name, years to search. Criminal records on computer from 1979, books from 1866. **General Information:** No sealed, court ordered or mental health records released. Copy fee: $.25 per page. Certification fee: $1.00. Fee payee: Clerk of District Court. Personal checks accepted. Prepayment is required.

Lincoln County Court PO Box 519, North Platte, NE 69103; 308-534-4350; Fax: 308-534-6468. Hours: 8AM-5PM (CST). *Misdemeanor, Civil Actions Under $15,000, Eviction, Small Claims, Probate.*

Civil Records: Access: In person only. Court does not conduct in person searches; visitors must perform searches for themselves. Search fee: No civil searches performed by court. Required to search: name, years to search. Civil cases indexed by defendant, plaintiff. Civil records kept on index books back 20-25 years. **Criminal Records:** Access: In person only. Court does not conduct in person searches; visitors must perform searches for themselves. Search fee: No criminal searches performed by court. Required to search: name, years to search, DOB. Criminal records on computer since 04/97. **General Information:** No adoption records released. Copy fee: $.25 per page. Certification fee: $1.00. Fee payee: County Court. Personal checks accepted. Credit cards accepted: Visa, Mastercard, Discover. $3.00 service charge. Prepayment is required. Public access terminal is available.

Logan County

District Court PO Box 8, Stapleton, NE 69163; 308-636-2311. Hours: 8:30AM-4:30PM M-Th; 8:30AM-4PM F (CST). *Felony, Civil Actions Over $15,000.*

Civil Records: Access: Mail, in person. Both court and visitors may perform in person searches. No search fee. Required to search: name, years to search. Civil cases indexed by defendant, plaintiff. Civil records on docket books. **Criminal Records:** Access: Mail, in person. Both court and visitors may perform in person searches. No search fee. Required to search: name, years to search. Criminal records on docket books. **General Information:** Turnaround time same day. Copy fee: $.25 per page. Certification fee: $1.00. Fee payee: Clerk of the District Court. Personal checks accepted. Prepayment is required.

Logan County Court PO Box 8, Stapleton, NE 69163; 308-636-2677. Hours: 8AM-Noon, 1-4:30PM M-Th; 8:30AM-Noon, 1-4PM F (CST). *Misdemeanor, Civil Actions Under $15,000, Eviction, Small Claims, Probate.*

Civil Records: Access: Fax, mail, in person. Both court and visitors may perform in person searches. No search fee. Required to search: name, years to search; also helpful-address. Civil cases indexed by defendant, plaintiff. Civil records on docket books since 1837. **Criminal Records:** Access: Fax, mail, in person. Both court and visitors may perform in person searches. No search fee. Required to search: name, years to search, signed release; also helpful-DOB. Criminal records on docket books since 1837. **General Information:** Adoption and juvenile records are not released. SASE required. Turnaround time 3-4 days. Copy fee: $.25 per page. Certification fee: $1.00. Fee payee: County Court. Personal checks accepted. Prepayment is required. Fax notes: $3.00 for first page, $1.00 each addl.

Loup County

District Court PO Box 146, Taylor, NE 68879; 308-942-6035; Fax: 308-942-6015. Hours: 8:30AM-4:30PM M-Th, 8:30AM-Noon F (CST). *Felony, Civil Actions Over $15,000.*

Civil Records: Access: In person only. Court does not conduct in person searches; visitors must perform searches for themselves. Search fee: No civil searches performed by court. Required to search: name, years to search. Civil cases indexed by defendant, plaintiff. Civil records in index books from late 1800s. **Criminal Records:** Access: In person only. Court does not conduct in person searches; visitors must perform searches for themselves. Search fee: No criminal searches performed by court. Required to search: name, years to search; also helpful-address, DOB, SSN. Criminal records in index books from late 1800s. **General Information:** No juvenile or adoption records released. Copy fee: $.25 per page. Certification fee: $1.00. Fee payee: Clerk of District Court. Personal checks accepted. Prepayment is required.

Loup County Court PO Box 146, Taylor, NE 68879; 308-942-6035; Fax: 308-942-6015. Hours: 8:30AM-4:30PM M-Th, 8:30AM-Noon F (CST). *Misdemeanor, Civil Actions Under $15,000, Eviction, Small Claims, Probate.*

Civil Records: Access: In person only. Court does not conduct in person searches; visitors must perform searches for themselves. Search fee: No civil searches performed by court. Required to search: name, years to search. Civil cases indexed by defendant, plaintiff. Civil records on index books since late 1800s. Some records have been filmed and forwarded to state archives. **Criminal Records:** Access: In person only. Court does not conduct in person searches; visitors must perform searches for themselves. Search fee: No criminal searches performed by court. Required to search: name, years to search. Criminal records on index books since late 1800s. Some records have been filmed and forwarded to state archives. **General Information:** Copy fee: $.25 per page. Certification fee: $1.00. Fee payee: County Court. Personal checks accepted. Prepayment is required.

Madison County

District Court PO Box 249, Madison, NE 68748; 402-454-3311 X140; Fax: 402-454-6528. Hours: 8AM-5PM (CST). *Felony, Civil Actions Over $15,000.*

Civil Records: Access: In person only. Court does not conduct in person searches; visitors must perform searches for themselves. Search fee: No civil searches performed by court. Required to search: name, years to search. Civil cases indexed by defendant, plaintiff. Civil records on microfiche from late 1970s, prior on docket books from 1800s. **Criminal Records:** Access: In person only. Court does not conduct in person searches; visitors must perform searches for themselves. Search fee: No criminal searches performed by court. Required to search: name, years to search. Criminal records on microfiche from late 1970s, prior on docket books from 1800s. **General Information:** No mental health records released. Copy fee: $.25 per page. Certification fee: $1.50. Fee payee: Clerk of District Court. Personal checks accepted.

Madison County Court PO Box 230, Madison, NE 68748; 402-454-3311 X143; Fax: 402-454-3438. Hours: 8:30AM-5PM (CST).

Misdemeanor, Civil Actions Under $15,000, Eviction, Small Claims, Probate.

Civil Records: Access: In person only. Court does not conduct in person searches; visitors must perform searches for themselves. Search fee: No civil searches performed by court. Required to search: name, years to search. Civil cases indexed by defendant, plaintiff. Civil records on computer since 1986, prior on docket book, cards. **Criminal Records:** Access: In person only. Court does not conduct in person searches; visitors must perform searches for themselves. Search fee: No criminal searches performed by court. Required to search: name, years to search, DOB. Criminal records on computer from 1986. **General Information:** No adoption records released. Copy fee: $.25 per page. Certification fee: $1.00. Fee payee: Madison County Court. Personal checks accepted. Prepayment is required.

McPherson County

District Court PO Box 122, Tryon, NE 69167; 308-587-2363; Fax: 308-587-2363 (Call first). Hours: 8:30AM-4:30PM (CST). *Felony, Civil Actions Over $15,000.*

Civil Records: Access: Fax, mail, in person. Both court and visitors may perform in person searches. No search fee. Required to search: name, years to search; also helpful-address. Civil cases indexed by defendant, plaintiff. Civil records on index books since late 1800s. **Criminal Records:** Access: Fax, mail, in person. Both court and visitors may perform in person searches. No search fee. Required to search: name, years to search; also helpful-address, DOB, SSN. Criminal records on index books since late 1800s. **General Information:** No adoption records released. SASE required. Turnaround time 3-4 days. Copy fee: $.50 per page. Certification fee: $1.50. Fee payee: Clerk of District Court. Business checks accepted. Prepayment is required. Fax notes: $2.00 for first page, $1.00 each addl.

McPherson County Court PO Box 122, Tryon, NE 69167; 308-587-2363; Fax: 308-587-2363. Hours: 8:30AM-Noon, 1-4:30PM (CST). *Misdemeanor, Civil Actions Under $15,000, Eviction, Small Claims, Probate.*

Civil Records: Access: Fax, mail, in person. Both court and visitors may perform in person searches. No search fee. Required to search: name, years to search; also helpful-address. Civil cases indexed by defendant, plaintiff. Civil records computerized since 06/99, rest on index cards, are not computerized. **Criminal Records:** Access: Fax, mail, in person. Both court and visitors may perform in person searches. No search fee. Required to search: name, years to search, signed release; also helpful-address, DOB. Criminal records computerized since 08/98. **General Information:** Adoption and juvenile records are not released. SASE required. Turnaround time 3-4 days. Copy fee: $.25 per page. Certification fee: $1.00. Fee payee: County Court. Personal checks accepted. Prepayment is required. Fax notes: $3.00 for first page, $1.00 each addl.

Merrick County

District Court PO Box 27, Central City, NE 68826; 308-946-2461; Fax: 308-946-3692. Hours: 8AM-5PM (CST). *Felony, Civil Actions Over $15,000.*

Civil Records: Access: In person only. Court does not conduct in person searches; visitors must perform searches for themselves. Search fee: No civil searches performed by court. Required to

search: name, years to search. Civil cases indexed by defendant, plaintiff. Civil records on index books from 1860. **Criminal Records:** Access: In person only. Court does not conduct in person searches; visitors must perform searches for themselves. Search fee: No criminal searches performed by court. Required to search: name, years to search, signed release. Criminal records on index books from 1860. **General Information:** No probation or mental health records released. Copy fee: $.25 per page. Certification fee: $1.00. Fee payee: Clerk of District Court. Personal checks accepted.

Merrick County Court County Courthouse, PO Box 27, Central City, NE 68826; 308-946-2812. Hours: 8AM-5PM (CST). *Misdemeanor, Civil Actions Under $15,000, Eviction, Small Claims, Probate.*

Civil Records: Access: online, in person. Court does not conduct in person searches; visitors must perform searches for themselves. Search fee: No civil searches performed by court. Required to search: name, years to search. Civil cases indexed by defendant, plaintiff. Civil records on index books from 1860. Remote online access available through Court Administrator's Office. **Criminal Records:** Access: Remote online, in person. Court does not conduct in person searches; visitors must perform searches for themselves. Search fee: No criminal searches performed by court. Required to search: name, years to search; also helpful-DOB. Criminal records on index books from 1860. Remote online available through Court Administrator's Office. **General Information:** No financial affidavits or sealed records released. Copy fee: $.25 per page. Certification fee: $1.00. Fee payee: County Court. Personal checks accepted. Prepayment is required.

Morrill County

District Court PO Box 824, Bridgeport, NE 69336; 308-262-1261; Fax: 308-262-1799. Hours: 8AM-Noon, 1-4:30PM (MST). *Felony, Civil Actions Over $15,000.*

Civil Records: Access: Phone, fax, mail, in person. Both court and visitors may perform in person searches. Search fee: $5.00 per hour. Required to search: name, years to search. Civil cases indexed by defendant, plaintiff. Civil records on microfilm, books dating back to late 1800s. **Criminal Records:** Access: Phone, fax, mail, in person. Both court and visitors may perform in person searches. Search fee: $5.00 per hour. Required to search: name, years to search. Criminal records on microfilm, books dating back to late 1800s. **General Information:** No mental health records released. SASE required. Turnaround time 2-3 days. Copy fee: $.25 per page. Certification fee: $1.00. Fee payee: Clerk of District Court. Personal checks accepted. Prepayment is required. Public access terminal is available. Fax notes: $3.25 for first page, $.25 each addl.

Morrill County Court PO Box 418, Bridgeport, NE 69336; 308-262-0812. Hours: 8AM-4:30PM (MST). *Misdemeanor, Civil Actions Under $15,000, Eviction, Small Claims, Probate.*

Civil Records: Access: In person only. Court does not conduct in person searches; visitors must perform searches for themselves. Search fee: No civil searches performed by court. Required to search: name, years to search. Civil cases indexed by defendant, plaintiff. Civil records on index books to 1908; probate on microfiche. **Criminal**

Records: Access: In person only. Court does not conduct in person searches; visitors must perform searches for themselves. Search fee: No criminal searches performed by court. Required to search: name, years to search. Criminal records on index books to 1908; probate on microfiche. **General Information:** No adoption records released. No copy fee. Certification fee: $1.00. Fee payee: County Court. Personal checks accepted. Prepayment is required.

Nance County

District Court PO Box 338, Fullerton, NE 68638; 308-536-2365; Fax: 308-536-2742. Hours: 8AM-5PM (CST). *Felony, Civil Actions Over $15,000.*

Civil Records: Access: Phone, fax, mail, in person. Both court and visitors may perform in person searches. No search fee. Required to search: name, years to search; also helpful-address. Civil cases indexed by defendant, plaintiff. Civil records on index books from late 1800s. **Criminal Records:** Access: Phone, fax, mail, in person. Both court and visitors may perform in person searches. No search fee. Required to search: name, years to search; also helpful-address, DOB, SSN. Criminal records on index books from late 1800s. **General Information:** No mental health records released. SASE required. Turnaround time 2 days. Copy fee: $.25 per page. Certification fee: $1.00. Fee payee: Clerk of District Court. Personal checks accepted. Prepayment is required. Fax notes: $1.50 per page.

Nance County Court PO Box 837, Fullerton, NE 68638; 308-536-2675; Fax: 308-536-2742. Hours: 8AM-5PM (CST). *Misdemeanor, Civil Actions Under $15,000, Eviction, Small Claims, Probate.*

Civil Records: Access: Mail, in person. Both court and visitors may perform in person searches. No search fee. Required to search: name, years to search; also helpful-address. Civil cases indexed by defendant, plaintiff. Civil records on index cards since late 1800s, probate on microfilm. **Criminal Records:** Access: Mail, in person. Both court and visitors may perform in person searches. No search fee. Required to search: name, years to search; also helpful-address, DOB. Criminal records on index cards since late 1800s, probate on microfilm. **General Information:** No juvenile, psychological reports or adoption records released. SASE required. Turnaround time 1-2 days. Copy fee: $.25 per page. Certification fee: $1.00. Fee payee: County Court. Personal checks accepted. Prepayment is required.

Nemaha County

District Court 1824 N St, Auburn, NE 68305; 402-274-3616; Fax: 402-274-4478. Hours: 8AM-5PM (CST). *Felony, Civil Actions Over $15,000.*

Civil Records: Access: In person only. Both court and visitors may perform in person searches. Court will search on a time available basis No search fee. Required to search: name, years to search; also helpful-address. Civil cases indexed by defendant, plaintiff. Civil records on general index and docket books since the late 1800s. **Criminal Records:** Access: In person only. Both court and visitors may perform in person searches. Court will search on a time available basis No search fee. Required to search: name, years to search; also helpful-address, DOB, SSN. Criminal records on general index and docket books since the late 1800s. **General Information:** No mental, juvenile records released. Copy fee: $.25 per page. Certification fee: $1.00. Fee payee: Clerk of

District Court. Personal checks accepted. Prepayment is required.

Nemaha County Court 1824 N St, Auburn, NE 68305; 402-274-3008; Fax: 402-274-4605. Hours: 8AM-Noon, 1-5PM (CST). *Misdemeanor, Civil Actions Under $15,000, Eviction, Small Claims, Probate.*

Note: This court also handles adoption, juvenile, and preliminary felony hearings

Civil Records: Access: In person only. Court does not conduct in person searches; visitors must perform searches for themselves. Search fee: No civil searches performed by court. Required to search: name, years to search. Civil cases indexed by defendant, plaintiff. Civil records on index books since late 1800s. **Criminal Records:** Access: In person only. Court does not conduct in person searches; visitors must perform searches for themselves. Search fee: No criminal searches performed by court. Required to search: name, years to search; also helpful-DOB, SSN. Criminal records on index books since late 1800s. **General Information:** No adoption records released. Copy fee: $.25 per page. Certification fee: $1.00. Fee payee: Clerk of County Court. Personal checks accepted.

Nuckolls County

District Court PO Box 362, Nelson, NE 68961; 402-225-4341; Fax: 402-225-2373. Hours: 8:30AM-4:30PM (CST). *Felony, Civil Actions Over $15,000.*

Civil Records: Access: In person only. Court does not conduct in person searches; visitors must perform searches for themselves. Search fee: No civil searches performed by court. Required to search: name, years to search. Civil cases indexed by defendant, plaintiff. Civil records on index books since late 1800s. Search services not available to employment agencies. **Criminal Records:** Access: In person only. Court does not conduct in person searches; visitors must perform searches for themselves. Search fee: No criminal searches performed by court. Required to search: name, years to search. Criminal records on index books since late 1800s. **General Information:** Copy fee: $.25 per page. Certification fee: $1.00. Fee payee: Clerk of District Court. Personal checks accepted. Prepayment is required.

Nuckolls County Court PO Box 372, Nelson, NE 68961; 402-225-2371; Fax: 402-225-2371. Hours: 8AM-4:30PM (CST). *Misdemeanor, Civil Actions Under $15,000, Eviction, Small Claims, Probate.*

Civil Records: Access: In person only. Court does not conduct in person searches; visitors must perform searches for themselves. Search fee: No civil searches performed by court. Required to search: name, years to search. Civil cases indexed by defendant, plaintiff. Civil records on index cards, probate on microfilm. Mail access limited to short searches. **Criminal Records:** Access: In person only. Court does not conduct in person searches; visitors must perform searches for themselves. Search fee: No criminal searches performed by court. Required to search: name, years to search. Criminal records on index cards, probate on microfilm. **General Information:** No adoption or juvenile records released. Copy fee: $.25 per page. Certification fee: $1.00. Fee payee: County Court. Personal checks accepted. Prepayment is required.

69217-69217	LONG PINE	69335-69335	BINGHAM	69347-69347	HAY SPRINGS	69356-69356	MINATARE
69218-69218	MERRIMAN	69336-69336	BRIDGEPORT	69348-69348	HEMINGFORD	69357-69357	MITCHELL
69219-69219	NENZEL	69337-69337	CHADRON	69349-69349	HENRY	69358-69358	MORRILL
69220-69220	SPARKS	69339-69339	CRAWFORD	69350-69350	HYANNIS	69360-69360	RUSHVILLE
69221-69221	WOOD LAKE	69340-69340	ELLSWORTH	69351-69351	LAKESIDE	69361-69363	SCOTTSBLUFF
69301-69301	ALLIANCE	69341-69341	GERING	69352-69352	LYMAN	69365-69365	WHITECLAY
69331-69331	ANGORA	69343-69343	GORDON	69353-69353	MCGREW	69366-69366	WHITMAN
69333-69333	ASHBY	69345-69345	HARRISBURG	69354-69354	MARSLAND	69367-69367	WHITNEY
69334-69334	BAYARD	69346-69346	HARRISON	69355-69355	MELBETA		

General Help Numbers:

Governor's Office
Capitol Building   775-684-5670
Carson City, NV 89710   Fax 775-684-5683
www.state.nv.us/gov/gov.htm   8AM-5PM

Attorney General's Office
100 N Carson St   775-684-1100
Carson City, NV 89710   Fax 775-684-1108
http://ag.state.nv.us   8AM-5PM

State Court Administrator
Administrative Office of the Courts   775-684-1700
201 S Carson St, #250   Fax 775-684-1723
Carson City, NV 89701-4702   8AM-5PM
www.state.nv.us/elec_judicial.html

State Archives
100 N Stewart St   775-684-3360
Carson City, NV 89701-4285   Fax 775-684-3330
http://dmla.clan.lib.nv.us/docs/nsla   8AM-5PM M-F

State Specifics:

Capital:	Carson City
	Carson City County
Time Zone:	PST
Number of Counties:	17
Number of Filing Locations:	17
Population:	1,809,253
Web Site:	www.state.nv.us

State Agencies

Criminal Records

Nevada Highway Patrol, Record & ID Services, 808 W Nye Lane, Carson City, NV 89703; 775-687-1600, 775-687-1843 (Fax), 8AM-5PM.

Indexing & Storage: Records are available from 1987 and are on computer.

Searching: This repository has maintains all "fingerprintable charges" meaning essentially all felony records and misdemeanor offenses like DUI and domestic violence. They will not release an arrest record without a disposition, unless a waiver is submitted. Include the following in your request-set of fingerprints, signed release, full name. DOB, SS#, sex and race are helpful. The following data is not released: sealed records or juvenile records.

Access by: mail, in person.

Fee & Payment: The search fee is $15.00 per individual. Fee payee: Nevada Highway Patrol. Prepayment required. Money order or cashier's check preferred. No credit cards accepted.

Mail search: Turnaround time: 10 days. No self addressed stamped envelope is required.

In person search: Records are still returned by mail.

Assumed Name
Fictitious Name

Records not maintained by a state level agency.

Note: Records are at the county level.

Corporation Records
Limited Partnerships
Limited Liability Company Records
Limited Partnership Records

Secretary of State, Records, 101 N Carson, #3, Carson City, NV 89701-4786; 775-684-5708, 702-486-2880 (Las Vegas Ofc.:), 702-486-2888 (Las Vegas Ofc fax:), 775-684-5725 (Fax), 8AM-5PM.

www.sos.state.nv.us

Note: File are here, but records can also be looked up on computer at the Las Vegas office (555 E Washington Ave., #2900, Las Vegas, NV 89101). To get forms, use their Document-on-Demand System 800-583-9486.

Indexing & Storage: Records are available since inception of laws. Old, inactive records are purged from computer and archived. New records are available for inquiry immediately. Records are indexed on microfiche, inhouse computer.

Searching: Fax searching is available only for state government agencies. Include the following in your request-full name of business, corporation file number. In addition to the articles of incorporation, corporation records include the following information: Annual Lists of Officers & Directors, Prior (merged) names, Inactive and Reserved names, and Resident Agent names.

Access by: mail, phone, in person, online.

Fee & Payment: The search fee is $20.00. The certification fee is $10.00. Copy fees are $1.00 per page. There are set fees for certain specific documents that range from $10.00-$25.00. Fee payee: Secretary of State. Prepayment required. Personal checks accepted. Credit cards accepted: Mastercard, Visa.

Mail search: Turnaround time: 1-2 weeks. No self addressed stamped envelope is required.

Phone search: Staff will give status for corporations and partnerships, corporate officer names, and trademark information.

In person search: Information requests are available.

Online search: Online access is offered on the Internet site for no charge. You can search by corporate name, resident agent, corporate officers, or by file number.

Expedited service: Expedited service is available for mail, phone and in person searches. There is a $25.00 fee for overnight service of copies if 1-10 pages, and $50.00 if over 10 pages.

Trademarks/Servicemarks

Secretary of State, Corporate Expedite Office, 555 E. Washington Ave, #2900, Las Vegas, NV 89101;, 702-486-2885, 702-486-2888 (Fax), 8AM-5PM.

www.sos.state.nv.us

Note: Trademark files are kept here; however, they are on the same computer system as the Carson City office. They can do all of the same searches on corporate records as Carson City, except for making copies of actual documents in files.

Indexing & Storage: Records are available since inception.

Searching: The same search requirements apply here as in Carson City.

Access by: mail, phone, fax, in person.

Fee & Payment: Certified copies of trademarks are $10.00. Fee payee: NV Secretary of State. Prepayment required. Personal checks accepted. No credit cards accepted.

Mail search: Turnaround time: 1-2 weeks.

Phone search: Limited information is offered over the phone.

Fax search: Turnaround time is 1-2 weeks.

In person search: Searching is available in person.

Uniform Commercial Code
Federal Tax Liens
State Tax Liens

UCC Department, Secretary of State, 220 N Carson St, Carson City, NV 89701-4201; 775-684-5708, 775-684-5630 (Fax), 8AM-5PM.

www.sos.state.nv.us

Note: At present, the only material about UCC on the web site is a form download. The agency plans a more extensive site in the future.

Indexing & Storage: Records are available from 1967 on both computer and microfilm.

Searching: Use search request form UCC-3. A search of federal tax liens must be requested separately. Tax liens on individuals are filed at the county level, on businesses here. Since there is no state income tax, most state liens are on unemployment withholding. Include the following in your request-debtor name.

Access by: mail, fax, in person, online.

Fee & Payment: Fees: approved form - $15.00 per debtor name; other forms - $20.00 per debtor name. Copies cost $1.00 per page. Fee payee: Secretary of State. Prepayment required. Personal checks accepted. Credit cards accepted: Mastercard, Visa.

Mail search: Turnaround time: 3-5 days. A self addressed stamped envelope is requested.

Fax search: See Expedited Services.

In person search: You may request information in person.

Online search: This is a PC dial-up system. The fee is $24.50 per hour or $10.75 per hour on an 800 number for unlimited access. There is a $50.00 minimum deposit. The system is up from 7 AM to 5 PM. Call 775-684-5704 and ask for Tom Horton.

Expedited service: Expedited service is available for mail, phone and fax searches. Turnaround time: 1 day. Add $25.00 per name.

Sales Tax Registrations
State does not impose sales tax.

Birth Certificates

Nevada Department of Health, Office of Vital Statistics, 505 E King St, Rm 102, Carson City, NV 89701-4749; 775-684-4242, 775-684-4280 (Message Phone), 775-684-4156 (Fax), 8AM-4PM.

Indexing & Storage: Records are available from 1911-present. It takes 30 days of filing before new records are available for inquiry. Records are indexed on microfiche, index cards, inhouse computer, hard copy.

Searching: Birth and death records are considered confidential and not open to the general public. Include the following in your request-full name, names of parents, mother's maiden name, date of birth, place of birth, relationship to person of record, reason for information request. Parents' names are a must to get record.

Access by: mail, phone, fax, in person.

Fee & Payment: The fee for a verification only is $8.00. For a certified copy the fee is $11.00. If you wish to purchase using a credit card, there is an additional $5.00 fee. Fee payee: Office of Vital Statistics. Prepayment required. Personal checks accepted. Credit cards accepted: Mastercard, Visa, AmEx, Discover.

Mail search: Turnaround time: 2-3 days. No self addressed stamped envelope is required.

Phone search: You must use a credit card.

Fax search: You must use a credit card.

In person search: Turnaround time 20 minutes.

Expedited service: Expedited service is available for mail, phone and fax searches. The overnight fee is $15.50. Use of credit card required.

Death Records

Nevada Department of Health, Office of Vital Statistics, 505 E King St, Rm 102, Carson City, NV 89701-4749; 775-684-4242, 775-684-4280 (Message Phone), 775-684-4156 (Fax), 8AM-4PM.

Indexing & Storage: Records are available from 1911 on. It takes 30 days of filing before new records are available for inquiry. Records are indexed on microfiche, index cards, inhouse computer, hard copy.

Searching: Records are considered confidential, need to state relationship. However, a verification printout with name, date, and location is available to the public. Include the following in your request-full name, date of death, place of death, relationship to person of record, reason for information request.

Access by: mail, phone, fax, in person.

Fee & Payment: The fee for a verification only is $8.00. A certified copy is $8.00. There is an additional $5.00 fee if using a credit card. Fee payee: Office of Vital Statistics. Prepayment required. Personal checks accepted. Credit cards accepted: Mastercard, Visa, AmEx, Discover.

Mail search: Turnaround time: 5-10 working days. No self addressed stamped envelope is required.

Phone search: Use of credit card required.

Fax search: Same search criteria.

In person search: Turnaround time is 20 minutes.

Expedited service: Expedited service is available for mail, phone and fax searches. Records are sent overnight at expense of requester, usually $15.50. A credit card is required.

Marriage Certificates
Divorce Records

Access to Records is Restricted

Nevada Department of Health, Office of Vital Statistics, 505 E King St, Rm 102, Carson City, NV 89701-4749; 775-684-4481.

Note: Marriage and Divorce records are found at county of issue. However, the agency has an index and will relate the county and date of the event. The fee is $8.00. Call (775) 684-4242.

Workers' Compensation Records

Employers Insurance Co of NV, Workers Compensation Records, 515 E Musser St, Carson City, NV 89714; 775-886-1000, 8AM-5PM.

www.employersinsco.com

Note: Effective 01/01/00, the state of Nevada privitized the business of workers' compensation insurance. The state agency formally named State Industrial Insurance System became a private company. This company holds the records from the state agency.

Indexing & Storage: Records are available from 1940's on. It takes 1 week before new records are available for inquiry. Records are indexed on microfilm, inhouse computer, file folders.

Searching: Must have a signed release form from claimant and you must specify what you want from the file. Older records are kept on microfilm, the records on the in-house computer are for general information only. Include the following in your request-claimant name, Social Security Number, claim number, date of accident.

Access by: mail, fax, in person.

Fee & Payment: Fee is $.20 per page if copies are over 20 pages. Fee payee: Employers Insurance CO of NV. Personal checks accepted. No credit cards accepted.

Mail search: Turnaround time: 30 days. A self addressed stamped envelope is requested.

Fax search: Same criteria as mail searches.

In person search: By going in person, you will only reduce the mail time.

Driver Records

Department of Motor Vehicles and Public Safety, Records Section, 555 Wright Way, Carson City, NV 89711-0250; 775-684-4590, 800-992-7945 (In-state), 8AM-5PM.

Note: Copies of citations may be obtained at the same address. There is no fee when requesting your own citation, otherwise the fee is $8.

Indexing & Storage: Records are available for 3 years. Non-moving violations are not listed on the driving record for non-CDL drivers. Nevada complies with the Driver's Privacy Protection Act, so personal information is available only to specific users. Records are computer indexed since 1980.

Searching: Authorized users may establish an account by completing the appropriate application. Call 775-684-4590-request an application. The driver's license number, or name and DOB are needed for a request. The SSN is helpful for searching, but will not be released on the record. Accidents do not appear on the record.

Access by: mail, phone.

Fee & Payment: The fee is $5.00 per record. Fee payee: Nevada Department of Motor Vehicles. Prepayment required. Personal checks accepted. No credit cards accepted.

Mail search: Turnaround time: 10 days. Your request must be on department approved forms.No self addressed stamped envelope is required.

Phone search: Phone-in requesters must be pre-approved, are assigned a five-digit account number and can request up to five records at one time over the phone. Call 775-684-4590 for more information. There is an in-state toll free line at 800-992-7945.

Other access: Overnight magnetic tape requesting is available for high volume users.

Vehicle Ownership
Vehicle Identification

Department of Motor Vehicles and Public Safety, Motor Vehicle Record Section, 555 Wright Way, Carson City, NV 89711-0250; 775-684-4590, 775-684-4740 (Fax), 8AM-5PM.

www.state.nv.us/dmv_ps

Indexing & Storage: Records are available for the present on computer and on microfilm back to 1980. Nevada enacted its version of the Driver's Privacy Protection Act, restricting access to certain permissible users. Forms are available at the web site.

Searching: Social Security Numbers, withdrawal action, accidents, and information connected to a license plate are not released to the general public.

Access by: mail, phone.

Fee & Payment: The cost is $5.00 per record. Fee payee: Nevada Department of Motor Vehicles. Prepayment required. Personal checks accepted. No credit cards accepted.

Mail search: Turnaround time: 10 days. Be sure to give as much specific information as possible. Your request must be on department-approved forms.No self addressed stamped envelope is required.

Phone search: Phone-in service is offered in the same manner as driving record requests.

Other access: Database is available for sale to permissible users under DPPA at costs varying from $500-$2,500.

Accident Reports

Department of Motor Vehicles, Highway Patrol Division, 555 Wright Way, Carson City, NV 89711; 775-684-4870, 775-684-4879 (Fax), 8AM-5PM.

www.state.nv.us/dmv_ps/psdivisions.htm

Indexing & Storage: Records are available from 1995-1997 at this office. Records are computer indexed. Records are indexed on inhouse computer.

Searching: Requests must be in writing. You may use the department's form. Include the following in your request-full name, date of accident, location of accident, report number. For any accidents after 1997, the reports will be found at a regional office (Las Vegas 702-486-4100; Reno 775-688-2500; or Elko 775-738-8035) associated with where the accidents occurred. Call for further information.

Access by: mail, fax, in person.

Fee & Payment: The fee is $3.50 per report (up to 10 pages), and report(s) will not be mailed until payment has been received. Fee payee: Nevada Highway Patrol. Prepayment required. Personal checks accepted. No credit cards accepted.

Mail search: Turnaround time: 3 days. A self addressed stamped envelope is requested.

Fax search: Fax searching available.

In person search: Turnaround time is immediate if the record is on file.

Boat & Vessel Ownership
Boat & Vessel Registration

Division of Wildlife, Boat Registration, 1100 Valley Rd, Reno, NV 89512-2815; 775-688-1511, 8AM-5PM M-F.

www.state.nv.us/cnr/nvwildlife

Indexing & Storage: Records are available from 1972-the present and are indexed on computer. All boats must be registered.

Searching: To search, one of the following is required: hull ID #, boat #, or name. The following data is not released: Social Security Numbers.

Access by: mail, in person.

Fee & Payment: The fee is $5.00 per boat or person, which includes 1 computer print-out. Photocopies cost $1.00 per page. Fee payee: NDOW. Prepayment required. Cash is accepted from in person searchers only. No credit cards accepted.

Mail search: Turnaround time: 4 days. No self addressed stamped envelope is required.

In person search: Turnaround time can be immediate if search is not lengthy.

Other access: Information is available on magnetic tape, labels, and printed lists. Fees depend on media type, can be up to $750.

Legislation-Current/Pending
Legislation-Passed

Nevada Legislature, 401 S Carson St, Carson City, NV 89701-4747; 775-684-6827 (Bill Status Only), 775-684-6800 (Main Number), 775-684-6835 (Publications), 775-684-6600 (Fax), 8AM-5PM.

www.leg.state.nv.us

Note: If you want to order copies, call the publications number.

Indexing & Storage: Records are available from 1915-present. Records are computer indexed from 1985-present, and on microfiche from 1967-present.

Searching: Include the following in your request-bill number, year.

Access by: mail, phone, fax, in person, online.

Fee & Payment: No charge for one or two bills. If you request more than two, the fee varies by page numbers requested, You may request any search by mail or telephone. The agency will determine fee, but will not release copies until paid. Fee payee: Legislative Council Bureau. Prepayment required. Personal checks accepted. Credit cards accepted: Mastercard, Visa.

Mail search: Turnaround time: 1-2 days. Information requests are available.No self addressed stamped envelope is required.

Phone search: You may request bills by phone.

Fax search: Turnaround time is generally in 1-2 days.

In person search: You may request bills in person.

Online search: Bills and bill status information is available via this agency's web site. Legislative bills, hearings, journals are searchable online for years 1997, 1999, and 2001.

Expedited service: Expedited service is available for mail and phone searches. You must provide an account number with a shipper.

Voter Registration

Records not maintained by a state level agency.

Note: Records are open to the public at the county level. All data is released except for SSNs.

GED Certificates

Department of Education, State GED Administration, 700 E 5th Street, Carson City, NV 89701; 775-687-9104, 775-687-9114 (Fax), 8AM-5PM.

Searching: Include the following in your request-signed release, date of birth, Social Security Number. There is a possibility that this office may not have the tests results, so it is important to also submit the location and year of the test.

Access by: mail, phone, fax, in person.

Fee & Payment: There is no fee.

Mail search: Turnaround time: 7-10 days.

Phone search: Verifications only.

Fax search: Same criteria as mail searching.

In person search: Searching is available in person.

Hunting License Information
Fishing License Information

Division of Wildlife, 1100 Valley Rd, Reno, NV 89512-2815; 775-688-1500, 775-688-1595 (Fax), 8AM-12; 1PM-5PM.

www.state.nv.us/cnr/ndwildlife

Indexing & Storage: Records are available from 1976-1992 on microfiche; from 1993-present on computer.

Searching: Include the following in your request-full name, date of birth, Social Security Number. The following data is not released: Social Security Numbers or telephone numbers.

Access by: mail.

Fee & Payment: The fee is $5.00 per name per year searched. Fee payee: Wildlife Department. Prepayment required. No credit cards accepted.

Mail search: Turnaround time: 3-4 working days. No self addressed stamped envelope is required.

Other access: The Division offers mailing lists of licensees for $270.00.

Licenses Searchable Online

Architect #02	www.state.nv.us/nsbaidrd/adact1.htm
Chiropractor #03	www.state.nv.us/chirobd/dcactive.htm
Dental Hygienist #04	http://nvdentalboard.org/databaseRDH.html
Dentist #04	http://nvdentalboard.org/databaseDDS.html
Engineer #19	http://nevada7.natinfo.net/boe/rost_home.htm
Interior Designer #02	www.state.nv.us/nsbaidrd/idact2.htm
Optometrist #05	www.arbo.org/nodb2000/licsearch.asp
Residential Designer #02	www.state.nv.us/nsbaidrd/rdact1.htm
Surveyor #19	http://nevada7.natinfo.net/boe/rost_home.htm

Licensing Quick Finder

Acupuncturist #14 ... 702-359-7025
Adult Day Care #22 ... 775-687-4475
Adult Group Care #22 ... 775-687-4475
Aesthetician #38 ... 702-486-6542
Alcohol & Drug Abuse Center #22 ... 775-687-4475
Alcohol & Drug Abuse Counselor #22 ... 775-687-4475
Ambulance Attendant #22 ... 775-687-4475
Ambulance Permit #22 ... 775-687-4475
Ambulatory Surgical Center #22 ... 775-687-4475
Animal Technician #21 ... 775-688-1788
Appraiser (MVD) #24 ... 702-486-4009
Architect #02 ... 702-486-7300
Athletic Promoter (Professional & Amateur) #35 ... 702-486-2575
Attorney #44 ... 702-382-2200
Auditor #01 ... 775-786-0231
Barber #45 ... 702-456-4769
Blood Gas Technician #22 ... 775-687-4475
Blood Gas Technologist #22 ... 775-687-4475
Boxer #35 ... 702-486-2575
Bus Driver #25 ... 775-684-4590
Carpentry Contractor #46 ... 702-486-1100
Casino General Manager #36 ... 775-687-6520
Cemetery #07 ... 702-646-6860
Chiropractor #03 ... 775-688-1919
Claims Adjuster #24 ... 702-486-4009
Clinical Laboratory Technologist #22 ... 775-687-4475
Cosmetologist #38 ... 702-486-6542
Crematorium #07 ... 702-646-6860
Dental Hygienist #04 ... 702-486-7044
Dentist #04 ... 702-486-7044
Director (Medical Laboratory) #22 ... 775-687-4475
Drug Wholesalers/Distributor #16 ... 775-322-0691
Electrologist #38 ... 702-486-6542
Embalmer #07 ... 702-646-6860
Emergency Medical Technician #22 ... 775-687-4475
Engineer #19 ... 775-688-1231
Environmental Health Specialist #42 ... 775-328-2422
ESRD #22 ... 775-687-4475
Euthanasia Technician #21 ... 775-688-1788
Exempt Laboratory #22 ... 775-687-4475
Financial Advisor (Investment Advisor) #40 ... 702-486-2440
First Responder EMT #22 ... 775-687-4475
Fishing Guide #26 ... 775-688-1541
Floor & Carpet Layer #46 ... 702-486-1100
Funeral Director #07 ... 702-646-6860
Fur Dealer #26 ... 775-688-1541
Gaming #36 ... 775-687-6570
Gaming License (By Company) #36 ... 775-687-6570
General Supervisory Medical Technology #22 ... 775-687-4475
Glazier Contractor #46 ... 702-486-1100
Groundskeeper/Gardener #28 ... 775-688-1182x243
Hair Stylist (Designer) #38 ... 702-486-6542
Hearing Aid Specialist #08 ... 702-571-9000
Heating & Air Conditioning Mechanic #46 ... 702-486-1100

Histotechnologist #22 ... 775-687-4475
Histologic Technician #22 ... 775-687-4475
Home Health Agency #22 ... 775-687-4475
Homeopathic Assistant #09 ... 702-258-5487
Homeopathic Physician #09 ... 702-258-5487
Homeopathic Practitioner, Advanced #09 ... 702-258-5487
Hospice #22 ... 775-687-4475
Hospital #22 ... 775-687-4475
IC Emergency Center #22 ... 775-687-4475
Independent Center for Emergency Care #22 ... 775-687-4475
Insulation Installer Contractor #46 ... 702-486-1100
Insurance Agent #24 ... 702-486-4009
Interior Designer #02 ... 702-486-7300
Intermediate Care Facility for Mentally Retarded #22 ... 775-687-4475
Intermedical Care Facility #22 ... 775-687-4475
Investment Advisor #40 ... 702-486-2440
Kickboxer #35 ... 702-486-2575
K-Nine Handler #39 ... 775-684-1147
Laboratory Assistant/Blood Gas Assistant #22 ... 775-687-4475
Landscape Architect #10 ... 775-626-0604
Licensed Laboratory #22 ... 775-687-4475
Limited Dealer #34 ... 702-486-4590
Limited Servicemen #34 ... 702-486-4590
Liquefied Petroleum Gas Distribution (LPG) #33 ... 775-687-4890
Liquefied Petroleum Gas Technician (LPG) #33 ... 775-687-4890
Lobbyist #27 ... 775-684-6800
Manicurist #38 ... 702-486-6542
Manufacturer or Distributor of Gaming Device #36 ... 775-687-6570
Marriage & Family Therapist #32 ... 702-486-7388
Medical Doctor #11 ... 775-688-2559
Medical Laboratory #22 ... 775-687-4475
Medical Technician #22 ... 775-687-4475
Mobile Home Dealer #34 ... 702-486-4590
Mobile Home Installer #34 ... 702-486-4590
Mobile Home Manufacturer #34 ... 702-486-4590
Mobile Home Salesman #34 ... 702-486-4590
Mobile Home Servicemen #34 ... 702-486-4590
Monitor Well Driller #30 ... 775-687-3861
Notary Public #41 ... 775-684-5749
Nurse #16 ... 775-322-0691
Nursing Facility #22 ... 775-687-4475
Nursing Home Administrator #49 ... 702-486-5445
Nursing Pool Operator #22 ... 775-687-4475
Occupational Therapist/Assistant #12 ... 775-857-1700
Office Laboratory Assistant #22 ... 775-687-4475
Optician #05 ... 775-345-1444
Optician, Apprentice #05 ... 775-345-1444
Optometrist #05 ... 775-883-8367
Osteopathic Physician #15 ... 702-732-2147
Osteopathic Physician Assistant #15 ... 702-732-2147
Painter #46 ... 702-486-1100

Painter/Paper Hanger #46 ... 702-486-1100
Pathologist Assistant #22 ... 775-687-4475
Pest Control #28 ... 775-688-1182x252
Pharmacist #16 ... 775-322-0691
Pharmacy #16 ... 775-322-0691
Pharmacy Technician #16 ... 775-322-0691
Physical Therapist #17 ... 702-876-5535
Physical Therapist Assistant #17 ... 702-876-5535
Physician Assistant #11 ... 775-688-2559
Plasterer/Drywall Installer #46 ... 702-486-1100
Plumber #46 ... 702-486-1100
Podiatrist #18 ... 775-829-8066
Polygraph Examiner #39 ... 775-684-1147
Private Investigator #39 ... 775-684-1147
Private Patrol Company #39 ... 775-684-1147
Private Patrol Man #39 ... 775-684-1147
Process Server #39 ... 775-684-1147
Program Administrator #47 ... 702-687-9200
Psychologist #20 ... 775-688-1268
Public Accountant-CPA #01 ... 775-786-0231
Public Sanitarian #42 ... 775-328-2418
Racing #37 ... 775-687-6500
Real Estate Broker #50 ... 702-486-4033
Real Estate Salesperson #50 ... 702-486-4033
Rebuilder #34 ... 702-486-4590
Referee/Judge/Timekeeper #35 ... 702-486-2575
Registered Laboratory Certification #22 ... 775-687-4475
Rehabilitation Service #22 ... 775-687-4475
Repossessor #39 ... 775-684-1147
Residential Designer #02 ... 702-486-7300
Restricted Use Pesticide #28 ... 775-688-1182x251
Ring Announcer #35 ... 702-486-2575
Roofer #46 ... 702-486-1100
Rotary Driller #29 ... 775-687-3861
Rural Health Clinic #22 ... 775-687-4475
School Administrator #47 ... 702-687-9200
School Counselor #47 ... 702-687-9200
School Librarian #47 ... 702-687-9200
Scientific Collection #26 ... 775-688-1541
Securities Branch Office #40 ... 702-486-2440
Securities Broker/Dealer #40 ... 702-486-2440
Securities Registration #40 ... 702-486-2440
Securities Sales Representative #40 ... 702-486-2440
Shorthand Reporter #23 ... 702-384-1663
Skilled Nursing Facility #22 ... 775-687-4475
Slot Route Operator #36 ... 775-687-6570
Social Worker #06 ... 702-486-2555
Speech Pathologist/Audiologist #31 ... 702-857-3500
Surveyor #19 ... 775-688-1231
Taxi Driver #48 ... 702-486-6532
Teacher #47 ... 702-687-9200
Veterinarian #21 ... 775-688-1788
Water Well Driller #30 ... 775-687-3861
Wrestler #35 ... 702-486-2575

Licensing Agency Information

01 Board of Accountancy, 200 S Virginia St, #670, Reno, NV 89501; 775-786-0231, Fax: 775-786-0234.

www.state.nv.us/accountancy

02 Interior & Residential Design, Board of Architecture, 2080 E Flamingo Rd, #225, Las Vegas, NV 89119; 702-486-7300, Fax: 702-486-7304.

www.state.nv.us/nsbaidrd/

Direct URL to search licenses: www.state.nv.us/nsbaidrd/ You can search online using alphabetical lists

03 Board of Chiropractic Examiners, 4600 Kietzke Ln, M, #245, Reno, NV 89502; 775-688-1919, Fax: 775-688-1920.

www.state.nv.us/chirobd

Direct URL to search licenses: www.state.nv.us/chirobd/dcactive.htm You can search online using name. The online searching is not up-to-date. When checked in 1999, the site only offered data from 1998.

04 Board of Dental Examiners, 2295 Renaissance Dr, #B, Las Vegas, NV 89119-6171; 800-337-3926 or 702-486-7044, Fax: 702-486-7046.

http://nvdentalboard.org

Direct URL to search licenses: http://nvdentalboard.org/DatabaseIndex.html You can search online using search the alphabetical list

05 Board of Dispensing Opticians, PO Box 1824 (PO Box 1824), Carson City, NV 89702; 775-883-8367, Fax: 775-883-1938.

www.state.nv.us/optometry

06 Board of Examiners for Social Workers, 4600 Kietzke Ln, Bldg C, Rm 121, Reno, NV 89502; 775-688-2555, Fax: 775-688-2557.

07 Board of Funeral Directors & Embalmers, 4894 Lone Mt Rd PMB186, Las Vegas, NV 89130; 702-646-6860, Fax: 702-648-5858.

08 Board of Hearing Aid Specialists, PO Box 195 (PO Box 18068), Reno, NV 89511-0068; 702-571-9000.

09 Board of Homeopathic Medical Examiners, PO Box 34329 (PO Box 34329), Las Vegas, NV 89133; 702-258-5487, Fax: 702-258-5487.

10 Board of Landscape Architecture, PO Box 517801 (PO Box 51780), Sparks, NV 89435; 775-626-0604, Fax: 775-626-0604.

11 Board of Medical Examiners, PO Box 7238 (1105 Terminal Way, #301), Reno, NV 89510; 775-688-2559, Fax: 775-688-2321.

www.state.nv.us/medical

12 Board of Occupational Therapy, PO Box 70220 (PO Box 70220), Reno, NV 89570-0220; 775-857-1700, Fax: 775-857-2121.

www.nvot.org

14 Board of Oriental Medicine, 1860 Renata Cir, North Las Vegas, NV 89030; 702-642-3322.

15 Board of Osteopathic Medicine, 2950 E Flamingo, #E-3, Las Vegas, NV 89121; 702-732-2147.

16 Board of Pharmacy, 555 Double Eagle Ct #1100, Reno, NV 89511-8991; 775-322-0691, Fax: 775-322-0895.

www.state.nv.us/pharmacy

17 Board of Physical Therapy Examiners, PO Box 81467 (PO Box 81467), Las Vegas, NV 89180-1467; 702-876-5535, Fax: 702-876-2097.

18 Board of Podiatry, PO Box 12215, Reno, NV 89510-2215; 775-829-8066, Fax: 775-829-8069.

www.state.nv.us/podiatry

19 Board of Professional Engineers & Land Surveyors, 1755 E Plumb Ln, #135, Reno, NV 89502; 775-688-1231, Fax: 775-688-2991.

www.state.nv.us./boe

Direct URL to search licenses: http://nevada7.natinfo.net/boe/rost_home.htm You can search online using name.

20 Board of Psychological Examiners, PO Box 2286 (275 Hill St, #246), Reno, NV 89505-2286; 775-688-1268, Fax: 775-688-1272.

21 Board of Veterinary Medical Examiners, 4600 Kietzke, Bldg O, #265, Reno, NV 89502; 775-688-1788, Fax: 775-688-1808.

www.state.nv.us/vet

22 Bureau of Licensure & Certification, Medical Laboratory Services, 1550 College Parkway #158, Carson City, NV 89710; 775-687-4475, Fax: 775-687-6588.

23 Certified Court Reporters Board, PO Box 237 (3355 Spring Mountain Rd #2), Las Vegas, NV 89102-8631; 702-384-1663.

24 Department of Business & Industry, Insurance Division, 2501 E Sahara Ave, #302, Las Vegas, NV 89104; 702-486-4009, Fax: 702-486-4007.

www.state.nv.us/b&i/id

25 Department of Motor Vehicles & Public Safety, Records Section, 555 Wright Way, Carson City, NV 89711-0250; 775-684-4590.

26 Department of Wildlife, Law Enforcement, PO Box 10678 (1100 Valley Rd), Reno, NV 89520; 775-688-1530, Fax: 775-688-1551.

www.state.nv.us/cnr/nvwildlife.

27 Director of Legislative Counsel Bureau, 401 S Carson, Carson City, NV 89701-4747; 775-684-6800, Fax: 775-684-6600.

www.leg.state.nv.us/lcb/admin/lobbyist.htm

28 Department of Agriculture, Pest Control Licensing Division, 350 Capitol Hill, Reno, NV 89502-2923; 775-688-1180, Fax: 775-688-1178.

www.state.nv.us/b&i/ad/chem/index.htm

29 Division of Water Resources, 555 Wright Way, Carson City, NV 89706-0818; 775-687-4380, Fax: 775-687-6972.

30 Division of Water Resources, Well Drillers' Advisory Board, 123 W Nye Ln, Capitol Complex Rm 246, Carson City, NV 89706-0818; 775-687-4380, Fax: 775-687-6972.

31 Examiners for Audiology & Speech Pathology, Department of Speech Pathology & Audiology, PO Box 35469 (PO Box 35469), Las Vegas, NV 89133; 702-784-4887, Fax: 702-857-2121.

32 Board of Examiners of Marriage & Family Therapists, PO Box 72758 (PO Box 72758), Las Vegas, NV 89170; 702-486-7388, Fax: 702-434-7181.

33 Liquefied Petroleum Gas Regulation Board, PO Box 338 (PO Box 338), Carson City, NV 89702; 775-687-4890, Fax: 775-687-3956.

34 Attn: Gisele Jordan, Licensing Officer, Manufactured Housing Division, 2501 E Sahara Ave, #205, Las Vegas, NV 89104; 702-486-4135, Fax: 702-486-4309.

35 Athletic Commission, 555 E Washington St #1500, Las Vegas, NV 89101; 702-486-2575, Fax: 702-486-2577.

www.state.nv.us/b&i/ac

36 Tax & License Division, Gaming Control Board, PO Box 8004 (PO Box 8003), Carson City, NV 89702; 775-486-2000, Fax: 775-687-5817.

www.state.nv.us/gaming

37 Gaming Control Board, Enforcement Division, PO Box 8003, Carson City, NV 89702; 775-687-6500.

www.state.nv.us/gaming

38 Board of Cosmetology, 1785 E Sahara Ave, #255, Las Vegas, NV 89104; 702-486-6542, Fax: 702-369-8064.

39 Office of the Attorney General, Private Investigators Licensing Board, 100 N Carson St, Carson City, NV 89701; 775-684-1147, Fax: 775-684-1108.

http://aq.state.nv.us/pilb

40 Office of the Secretary of State, Securities Division, 555 E Washington Av #5200, Las Vegas, NV 89101; 702-486-2440, Fax: 702-486-2454.

www.sos.state.nv.us/securities

41 Office of the Secretary of State, 101 N Carson St, Carson City, NV 89710-4786; 775-684-5708, Fax: 775-684-5725.

http://sos.state.nv.us/notary/

42 Registration of Public Health Sanitarians, c/o Washoe County District Health Department, PO Box 1130 (PO Box 1130), Reno, NV 89520; 775-328-2434, Fax: 775-328-6176.

44 State Bar of Nevada, 600 E Charleston Blvd, Las Vegas, NV 89104; 702-382-2200, Fax: 702-385-2878.

www.nvbar.org

45 Barbers' Health & Sanitation Board, 4710 E Flamingo Rd, Las Vegas, NV 89121; 702-731-1966, Fax: 702-456-1948.

46 Contractors' Board, 4220 S Maryland Pky, Bldg D, #800, Las Vegas, NV 89119; 702-688-1141, Fax: 702-486-1190.

47 Department of Education Licensure, 1820 E Sahara, #205, Las Vegas, NV 89104; 702-687-3115, Fax: 702-687-9101.

www.ccsd.net/HRD/NVDOE

48 Taxicab Authority, 1785 E Sahara Ave #200, Las Vegas, NV 89104; 702-486-6532, Fax: 702-486-7350.

www.state.nv.us/b&i/ta

49 Board of Examiners for Long Term Care Administrators, 6010 W Cheyenne Ave #970, Las Vegas, NV 89108; 702-486-5445.

50 Department of Business & Industry, Real Estate Division, 2501 E Sahara Ave, Las Vegas, NV 89158; 702-486-4033.

The following list indicates the district and division name for each county in the state. If the district or division name of the bankruptcy court is different from the civil/criminal court, it appears in parentheses.

County/Court Cross Reference

Carson City	Reno (Reno-Northern)	Lincoln	Las Vegas
Churchill	Reno (Reno-Northern)	Lyon	Reno (Reno-Northern)
Clark	Las Vegas	Mineral	Reno (Reno-Northern)
Douglas	Reno (Reno-Northern)	Nye	Las Vegas
Elko	Reno (Reno-Northern)	Pershing	Reno (Reno-Northern)
Esmeralda	Las Vegas	Storey	Reno (Reno-Northern)
Eureka	Reno (Reno-Northern)	Washoe	Reno (Reno-Northern)
Humboldt	Reno (Reno-Northern)	White Pine	Reno (Reno-Northern)
Lander	Reno (Reno-Northern)		

US District Court

District of Nevada

Las Vegas Division Room 4425, 300 Las Vegas Blvd S, Las Vegas, NV 89101, 702-388-6351.

www.nvd.uscourts.gov

Counties: Clark, Esmeralda, Lincoln, Nye.

Indexing & Storage: Cases are indexed by defendant and plaintiff as well as by case number. New cases are available in the index 2 weeks after filing date. A computer index is maintained. Open records are located at this court.

Fee & Payment: The fee is $15.00 per item (one party name or case number). Payment may be made by money order, cashier check, personal check. Prepayment is required. Payee: Clerk, US District Court. Certification fee: $5.00 per document. Copy fee: $.50 per page.

Phone Search: Only docket information available by phone. An automated voice case information service (VCIS) is not available.

Mail Search: A stamped self addressed envelope is not required.

In Person Search: In person searching is available.

PACER: There is no PACER access to this court.

Reno Division Room 301, 400 S Virginia St, Reno, NV 89501, 775-686-5800, Fax: 702-686-5851.

www.nvd.uscourts.gov

Counties: Carson City, Churchill, Douglas, Elko, Eureka, Humboldt, Lander, Lyon, Mineral, Pershing, Storey, Washoe, White Pine.

Indexing & Storage: Cases are indexed by defendant and plaintiff as well as by case number. New cases are available in the index 1-2 days after filing date. A computer index is maintained. Records are also indexed on microfiche. Open records are located at this court.

Fee & Payment: The fee is $15.00 per item (one party name or case number). Payment may be made by money order, cashier check, personal check. Prepayment is required. Payee: Clerk, US District Court. Certification fee: $5.00 per document. Copy fee: $.50 per page.

Phone Search: Only docket information available by phone. An automated voice case information service (VCIS) is not available.

Fax Search: The cost for a fax search is $15.00 per name to be certified. Will fax results for $.50 per page prepaid.

Mail Search: A stamped self addressed envelope is not required.

In Person Search: In person searching is available.

PACER: There is no PACER access to this court.

US Bankruptcy Court

District of Nevada

Las Vegas Division Room 2130, 300 Las Vegas Blvd S, Las Vegas, NV 89101, 702-388-6257.

www.nvb.uscourts.gov

Counties: Clark, Esmeralda, Lincoln, Nye.

Indexing & Storage: Cases are indexed by debtor as well as by case number. New cases are available in the index 24 hours after filing date. Both computer and card indexes are maintained. Open records are located at this court.

Fee & Payment: The fee is $15.00 per item (one party name or case number). Payment may be made by money order, cashier check, personal check. Debtor's checks are not accepted. Payee: Clerk, US Bankruptcy Court. Certification fee: $5.00 per document. Copy fee: $.50 per page. You are allowed to make your own copies. These copies cost $.25 per page.

Phone Search: An automated voice case information service (VCIS) is available. Call VCIS at 800-314-3436 or 702-388-6708.

Mail Search: Always enclose a stamped self addressed envelope.

In Person Search: In person searching is available.

PACER: Sign-up number is 800-676-6856. Access fee is $.60 per minute. Case records are available back to September 1993. Records are purged every 16 months. New civil records are available online after 1 day. PACER is available on the Internet at http://pacer.nvb.uscourts.gov.

Other Online Access: You can search records on the Internet using RACER. Currently the system is free and requires free registration. Simply visit http://207.221.188.71/wconnect/wc.dll?usbc_racer~main.

Reno-Northern Division Room 1109, 300 Booth St, Reno, NV 89509, 775-784-5559.

www.nvb.uscourts.gov

Counties: Carson City, Churchill, Douglas, Elko, Eureka, Humboldt, Lander, Lyon, Mineral, Pershing, Storey, Washoe, White Pine.

Indexing & Storage: Cases are indexed by debtor as well as by case number. New cases are available in the index 24 hours after filing date. A computer index is maintained. Open records are located at this court.

Fee & Payment: The fee is $15.00 per item (one party name or case number). Payment may be made by money order, cashier check, personal check. Debtor's checks are not accepted. Payee: Clerk, US Bankruptcy Court. Certification fee: $5.00 per document. Copy fee: $.50 per page.

Phone Search: An automated voice case information service (VCIS) is available. Call VCIS at 800-314-3436 or 702-388-6708.

Mail Search: Always enclose a stamped self addressed envelope.

In Person Search: In person searching is available.

PACER: Sign-up number is 800-676-6856. Access fee is $.60 per minute. Case records are available back to September 1993. Records are purged every 16 months. New civil records are available online after 1 day. PACER is available on the Internet at http://pacer.nvb.uscourts.gov.

Other Online Access: You can search records on the Internet using RACER. Currently the system is free and requires free registration. Simply visit http://207.221.188.71/wconnect/wc.dll?usbc_racer~main.

Court	Jurisdiction	No. of Courts	How Organized
District Courts*	General	17	9 Districts
Justice Courts*	Limited	56	56 Towns
Municipal Courts	Municipal	19	19 Incorporated Cities/Towns

* Profiled in this Sourcebook.

Court	CIVIL								
	Tort	Contract	Real Estate	Min. Claim	Max. Claim	Small Claims	Estate	Eviction	Domestic Relations
District Courts*	X	X	X	$7500	No Max		X		X
Justice Courts*	X	X	X	$0	$7500	$3500		X	
Municipal Courts	X	X	X	$0	$3500	$3500			

Court	CRIMINAL				
	Felony	Misdemeanor	DWI/DUI	Preliminary Hearing	Juvenile
District Courts*	X	X	X		X
Justice Courts*		X	X	X	
Municipal Courts					

ADMINISTRATION

Supreme Court of Nevada, Administrative Office of the Courts, Capitol Complex, 201 S Carson St, Carson City, NV, 89701; 775-684-1700, Fax: 775-684-1723.

COURT STRUCTURE

There are 17 District Courts within 9 judicial districts. The 56 Justice Courts are named for the township of jurisdiction. Probate is handled by the District Courts.

ONLINE ACCESS

Some Nevada Courts have internal online computer systems, but only Clark County has online access available to the public. A statewide court automation system has been with implemented, but there are no plans to make this system available to the public.

ADDITIONAL INFORMATION

Many Nevada Justice Courts are small and have very few records. Their hours of operation vary widely and contact is difficult. It is recommended that requesters call ahead for information prior to submitting a written request or attempting an in-person retrieval.

Carson City County

1st Judicial District Court 885 E Musser St #3031, Carson City, NV 89701-4775; 775-887-2082; Fax: 775-887-2177. Hours: 9AM-5PM (PST). *Felony, Misdemeanor, Civil Actions Over $7,500, Probate.*

Civil Records: Access: Mail, in person. Only the court conducts in person searches; visitors may not. Search fee: $1.00 per name per year. Required to search: name, years to search. Civil cases indexed by defendant, plaintiff. Civil records on computer from 1988, on microfiche and archives from beginning of court. **Criminal Records:** Access: Mail, in person. Only the court conducts in person searches; visitors may not. Search fee: $1.00 per name per year. Required to search: name, years to search. Criminal records on computer from 1988, on microfiche and archives from beginning of court. **General Information:** No sealed or juvenile records released. SASE required. Turnaround time 2-7 days. Copy fee: $1.00 per page. Certification fee: $5.00. Fee payee: Carson City. Personal checks accepted. Personal check accepted with check guarantee card only. Prepayment is required.

Justice Court Dept II 885 E Musser St, #7, Carson City, NV 89701; 775-887-2275; Fax: 775-887-2297. Hours: 8:30AM-5PM (PST). *Civil Actions Under $7,500, Eviction, Small Claims.*

Civil Records: Access: Phone, fax, mail, in person. Only the court conducts in person searches; visitors may not. Search fee: $1.00 per name per year. Required to search: name, years to search. Civil cases indexed by defendant, plaintiff. Civil records on computer alpha from 1991, on docket books with proceedings back to 1989. **General Information:** No sealed, sexual victims, juvenile records released. SASE required. Turnaround time 1 week. Copy fee: $.30 per page. Certification fee: $3.00. Fee payee: Carson City. Personal checks accepted. Prepayment is required.

Justice Court Dept I 885 E Musser St #2007, Carson City, NV 89701-4775; 775-887-2121; Fax: 775-887-2297. Hours: 9AM-4PM M-W/9AM-5PM Th/9AM-3:30PM F (PST). *Misdemeanor.*

Criminal Records: Access: Phone, fax, mail, in person. Both court and visitors may perform in person searches. Search fee: $1.00 per name per year. Required to search: name, years to search. Criminal records on computer alpha from 1991, on docket books with proceedings back to 1952. **General Information:** No sealed, sexual victims, juvenile records released. SASE required. Turnaround time 1 week. Copy fee: $1.00 per page. Certification fee: $2.00. Fee payee: Carson City. Personal checks accepted. Prepayment is required. Public access terminal is available.

Churchill County

3rd Judicial District Court 73 N Maine St, Ste B, Fallon, NV 89406; 775-423-6080; Fax: 775-423-8578. Hours: 8AM-Noon, 1-5PM (PST). *Felony, Misdemeanor, Civil Actions Over $7,500, Probate.*

Civil Records: Access: Fax, mail, in person. Only the court conducts in person searches; visitors may not. Search fee: $1.00 per name per year. Required to search: name, years to search. Civil cases indexed by defendant, plaintiff. Civil records on computer from 1990, prior on books, microfiche. **Criminal Records:** Access: Fax, mail, in person. Only the court conducts in person searches; visitors may not. Search fee: $1.00 per name per year. Required to search: name, years to search, DOB; also helpful-SSN. Criminal records on computer from 1990, prior on books, microfiche. **General Information:** No juvenile, adoption or sealed records released. SASE required. Turnaround time 1-2 day. Copy fee: $1.00 per page. Certification fee: $5.00. Fee payee: Office of Court Clerk. Personal checks accepted. Prepayment is required. Fax notes: No fee to fax results. local or toll free numbers only.

Justice Court 73 N Maine St #C, Fallon, NV 89406; 775-423-2845; Fax: 775-423-0472. Hours: 8AM-Noon, 1-5PM (PST). *Misdemeanor, Civil Actions Under $7,500, Eviction, Small Claims.*

Civil Records: Access: Mail, in person. Both court and visitors may perform in person searches. Search fee: $1.00 per name per year. Required to search: name, years to search. Civil cases indexed by defendant, plaintiff. Civil records on computer from 1987, prior on microfiche. **Criminal Records:** Access: Mail, in person. Both court and visitors may perform in person searches. Search fee: $1.00 per name per year. Required to search: name, years to search, DOB. Criminal records on computer from 1987, prior on microfiche. **General Information:** No sealed records released. SASE not required. Turnaround time 1 day. Copy fee: $.30 per page. Certification fee: $3.00. Fee payee: Justice Court. Personal checks accepted. Credit cards accepted: Visa, Mastercard. Prepayment is required.

Clark County

8th Judicial District Court 200 S 3rd (PO Box 551601), Las Vegas, NV 89155; 702-455-3156; Fax: 702-455-4929. Hours: 8AM-5PM (PST). *Felony, Misdemeanor, Civil Actions Over $7,500, Probate.*

http://co.clark.nv.us

Civil Records: Access: Mail, online, in person. Only the court conducts in person searches; visitors may not. Search fee: $1.00 per name per year. Fee is per case type. Required to search: name, years to search. Civil cases indexed by defendant, plaintiff. Civil records on computer from 11/90, prior records on microfilm. Free searching via the Internet at http://courtgate.coca.co.clark.nv.us:8490. Search by case number or party name. Probate also available. **Criminal Records:** Access: Mail, remote online, in person. Only the court conducts in person searches; visitors may not. Search fee: $1.00 per name per year. Fee is per case type. Required to search: name, years to search. Criminal records on computer from 11/90, prior records on microfilm. Free record searching via the Internet by name or case number, see civil remarks for url. **General Information:** No sealed records released. SASE required. Turnaround time 10 working days. Copy fee: $1.00 per page. Certification fee: $3.00. Fee payee: County Clerk's Office. Personal checks accepted. Prepayment is required.

Boulder Township Justice Court 505 Avenue G, Boulder City, NV 89005; 702-455-8000; Fax: 702-455-8003. Hours: 7:30AM-5PM (PST). *Misdemeanor, Civil Actions Under $7,500, Eviction, Small Claims.*

Civil Records: Access: Fax, mail, in person. Both court and visitors may perform in person searches. Search fee: $1.00 per name per year. Required to search: name, years to search; also helpful-address. Civil cases indexed by defendant. Civil records on microfiche varies depending on subject. **Criminal Records:** Access: Fax, mail, in person. Only the court conducts in person searches; visitors may not. Search fee: $1.00 per name per year. Required to search: name, years to search, DOB, date of offense; also helpful-SSN. Criminal records on microfiche varies depending on subject. **General Information:** No financial records released. SASE required. Turnaround time 1 week. Copy fee: $.30 per page. Certification fee: $3.00. Fee payee: Justice Court. Personal checks accepted. Prepayment is required.

Bunkerville Justice Court 190 W Virgin St, Bunkerville, NV 89007; 702-346-5711; Fax: 702-346-7212. Hours: 7AM-5PM M-Th (PST). *Misdemeanor, Civil Actions Under $7,500, Eviction, Small Claims.*

Civil Records: Access: Phone, fax, mail, in person. Only the court conducts in person searches; visitors may not. Search fee: $1.00 per name per year. Required to search: name, years to search. Civil cases indexed by plaintiff. Civil records (citations) on computer from 1991, on docket books. **Criminal Records:** Access: Phone, fax, mail, in person. Only the court conducts in person searches; visitors may not. Search fee: $1.00 per name per year. Required to search: name, years to search, DOB; also helpful-SSN. Criminal records (citations) on computer from 1991, on docket books. **General Information:** No sealed or confidential records released. SASE required. Turnaround time 2 weeks. Copy fee: $.30 per page. Certification fee: $3.00. Fee payee: Bunkerville Justice Court. Only cashiers checks and money orders accepted. Prepayment is required.

Goodsprings Township Jean Justice Court 1 Main St (PO Box 19155), Jean, NV 89019; 702-874-1405; Fax: 702-874-1612. Hours: 7AM-5PM M-Th (PST). *Misdemeanor, Civil Actions Under $7,500, Eviction, Small Claims.*

Civil Records: Access: Phone, fax, mail, in person. Only the court conducts in person searches; visitors may not. Search fee: $1.00 per name per year. Required to search: name, years to search. Civil cases indexed by defendant, plaintiff. Civil records on computer for 6 months, file reports from 1990. **Criminal Records:** Access: Phone, fax, mail, in person. Only the court conducts in person searches; visitors may not. Search fee: $1.00 per name per year. Required to search: name, years to search, DOB; also helpful-SSN. Criminal records on computer for 6 months, file reports from 1990. **General Information:** No sealed records released. SASE required. Turnaround time within 2-3 days. Copy fee: $.25 per page. Certification fee: $2.00. Fee payee: Jean Justice Court. Business checks accepted.

Henderson Township Justice 243 Water St, Henderson, NV 89015; 702-455-7951; Fax: 702-455-7935. Hours: 7AM-6PM M-Th (PST). *Misdemeanor, Civil Actions Under $7,500, Eviction, Small Claims.*

Civil Records: Access: Mail, in person. Only the court conducts in person searches; visitors may not. Search fee: $1.00 per name per year. Required to search: name, years to search. Civil cases indexed by defendant. Civil records on index cards and docket books. Evictions kept for 2 years; civil and small claims for 6 years. **Criminal Records:** Access: Mail, in person. Only the court conducts in person searches; visitors may not. Search fee: $1.00 per name per year. Required to search: name, years to search, DOB; also helpful-SSN. Criminal records on index cards and docket books. Evictions kept for 2 years; civil and small claims for 6 years. **General Information:** SASE required. Turnaround time 2 weeks. Copy fee: $.30 per page. Certification fee: $3.00. Fee payee: Henderson Justice Court. Personal checks accepted. Prepayment is required.

Las Vegas Township Justice 200 S 3rd, 2nd Fl, PO Box 552511, Las Vegas, NV 89155-2511; 702-455-4435; Fax: 702-455-4529. Hours: 8AM-5PM (PST). *Misdemeanor, Civil Actions Under $7,500, Eviction, Small Claims.*

www.co.clark.nv.us/juscourt/welcome.htm

Note: Calendars are available online at the website

Civil Records: Access: Phone, fax, mail, in person. Both court and visitors may perform in person searches. Search fee: $1.00 per name per year. Required to search: name, years to search. Civil cases indexed by defendant, plaintiff. Civil records on computer since 1994. **Criminal Records:** Access: Phone, fax, mail, in person. Only the court conducts in person searches; visitors may not. Search fee: $1.00 per name per year. Required to search: name, years to search; also helpful-DOB, SSN. Criminal records on computer. **General Information:** No sealed, confidential or judge's notes records released. SASE required. Turnaround time 2 weeks. Copy fee: $.30 per page. Certification fee: $3.00. Fee payee: Justice Court, Las Vegas Township. Personal checks accepted. Prepayment is required.

Laughlin Township Justice Court 101 Civic Way #2, Laughlin, NV 89029; 702-298-4622; Fax: 702-298-7508. Hours: 8AM-5PM (PST). *Misdemeanor, Civil Actions Under $7,000, Eviction, Small Claims.*

Civil Records: Access: Fax, mail, in person. Search fee: $1.00 per name per year. Required to search: name, years to search. Civil cases indexed by defendant, plaintiff. Civil records on docket book by name and case number. **Criminal Records:** Access: Fax, mail, in person. Only the court conducts in person searches; visitors may not. Search fee: $1.00 per name per year. Required to search: name, years to search, DOB. Criminal records on computer from 1990, prior in files and must be cross referenced. **General Information:** No sealed records released. SASE required. Turnaround time 2 weeks. Copy fee: $.30 per page. Certification fee: $3.00. Fee payee: Laughlin Justice Court. Personal checks accepted. Prepayment is required.

Mesquite Township Justice Court PO Box 1209, Mesquite, NV 89024; 702-346-5298; Fax: 702-346-7319. Hours: 8AM-5PM M,T; 8AM-Noon F (PST). *Misdemeanor, Civil Actions Under $7,500, Eviction, Small Claims.*

Civil Records: Access: Phone, mail, in person. Only the court conducts in person searches; visitors may not. Search fee: $1.00 per name per year. Required to search: name, years to search. Civil cases indexed by defendant. Civil records in files. None available prior to 1989. **Criminal Records:** Access: Mail, in person. Only the court conducts in person searches; visitors may not. Search fee: $1.00 per name per year. Required to search: name, years to search, DOB; also helpful-SSN. Criminal records in files. None available prior to 1989. **General Information:** No sealed records released. SASE not required. Turnaround time approx 1-2 weeks. Copy fee: $.30 per page. Certification fee: $3.00. Fee payee: Mesquite Justice Court. Only cashiers checks and money orders accepted. Prepayment is required.

Moapa Township Justice Court 1340 E Com Hwy, PO Box 280, Moapa, NV 89025; 702-864-2333; Fax: 702-864-2585. Hours: 8AM-5PM M-Th (PST). *Misdemeanor, Civil Actions Under $7,500, Eviction, Small Claims.*

Civil Records: Access: Fax, mail, in person. Only the court conducts in person searches; visitors may not. Search fee: $1.00 per name per year. Required to search: name, years to search. Civil cases indexed by defendant, plaintiff. Civil records on computer from 10/90, prior records on index cards and docket books. Archives flooded in 1980s.

Criminal Records: Access: Fax, mail, in person. Only the court conducts in person searches; visitors may not. Search fee: $1.00 per name per year. Required to search: name, years to search; also helpful-DOB, SSN. Criminal records on computer from 10/90, prior records on index cards and docket books. Archives flooded in 1980s. **General Information:** No sealed records released. SASE required. Turnaround time 1-5 days. Copy fee: $.25 per page. Certification fee: $3.00. Fee payee: Moapa Township Justice Court. Personal checks accepted. Prepayment is required. Fax notes: No fee to fax results.

Moapa Valley Township Justice Court

320 N Moapa Valley Blvd, Overton, NV 89040; 702-397-2840; Fax: 702-397-2842. Hours: 6:30AM-4:30PM M-Th (PST). *Misdemeanor, Civil Actions Under $7,500, Eviction, Small Claims.*

Civil Records: Access: Mail, in person. Only the court conducts in person searches; visitors may not. Search fee: $1.00 per name per year. Required to search: name, years to search. Civil cases indexed by defendant, plaintiff. Civil records on computer from 1991, prior on docket books. **Criminal Records:** Access: Mail, in person. Only the court conducts in person searches; visitors may not. Search fee: $1.00 per name per year. Required to search: name, years to search, DOB; also helpful-SSN. Criminal records on computer from 1991, prior on docket books. **General Information:** No sealed records released. SASE required. Turnaround time approx 1-2 weeks. Copy fee: $.25 per page. Certification fee: $3.00. Fee payee: Moapa Valley Justice Court. Personal checks accepted. Prepayment is required.

North Las Vegas Township Justice

2428 N Martin L King Blvd, N Las Vegas, NV 89032-3700; 702-455-7802; Civil phone:702-455-7801; Fax: 702-455-7831. Hours: 8:30AM-5PM (PST). *Misdemeanor, Civil Actions Under $7,500, Eviction, Small Claims.*

Note: Judge must approve all search requests

Civil Records: Access: Phone, in person. Court does not conduct in person searches; visitors must perform searches for themselves. Search fee: No civil searches performed by court. Required to search: name, years to search. Civil cases indexed by defendant, plaintiff. Civil records on docket books, microfilm. **Criminal Records:** Access: Phone, mail, in person. Only the court conducts in person searches; visitors may not. Search fee: $1.00 per name per year. Required to search: name, years to search, DOB, SSN. Criminal records on docket books, microfilm. **General Information:** SASE required. Turnaround time 1-10 days. Copy fee: $.30 per page. Certification fee: $3.00. Fee payee: Clark Justice Court. Personal checks accepted. Personbal check accepted with bank card. Prepayment is required.

Searchlight Township Justice

PO Box 815, Searchlight, NV 89046; 702-297-1252; Fax: 702-297-1022. Hours: 7AM-5:30PM M-Th (PST). *Misdemeanor, Civil Actions Under $7,500, Eviction, Small Claims.*

Civil Records: Access: Fax, mail, in person. Only the court conducts in person searches; visitors may not. Search fee: $1.00 per name per year. Required to search: name, years to search. Civil cases indexed by defendant, plaintiff. Civil records on computer from 1988, prior to 1988 filed by case number. **Criminal Records:** Access: Fax, mail, in person. Only the court conducts in person searches; visitors may not. Search fee: $1.00 per

name per year. Required to search: name, years to search, DOB; also helpful-SSN. Criminal records on computer from 1988, prior to 1988 filed by case number. **General Information:** No sealed records released. SASE required. Turnaround time 1-2 weeks. Copy fee: $1.00 per page. Certification fee: $2.00. Fee payee: Searchlight Justice Court. Personal checks accepted. Prepayment is required.

Douglas County

9th Judicial District Court

Box 218, Minden, NV 89423; 775-782-9820; Fax: 775-782-9954. Hours: 8AM-5PM (PST). *Felony, Civil Actions Over $7,500, Probate.*

http://cltr.co.douglas.nv.us/CourtClerk/courtideas/courtclerkhome.htm

Note: Misdemeanors are handled by the East Fork Justice Court

Civil Records: Access: Mail, in person. Only the court conducts in person searches; visitors may not. Search fee: $1.00 per name per year. Required to search: name, years to search. Civil cases indexed by defendant, plaintiff. Civil records on index cards from 1962, docket books prior to 1962, archived from mid-1850s. **Criminal Records:** Access: Mail, in person. Only the court conducts in person searches; visitors may not. Search fee: $1.00 per name per year. Required to search: name, years to search, DOB. Criminal records on index cards from 1962, docket books prior to 1962, archived from mid-1850s. **General Information:** No sealed records released. SASE required. Turnaround time 1 week. Copy fee: $1.00 per page. Certification fee: $3.00. Fee payee: Douglas County Court Clerk. Business checks accepted. Prepayment is required.

E Fork Justice Court

PO Box 218, Minden, NV 89423; 775-782-9955; Fax: 775-782-9947. Hours: 8AM-5PM (PST). *Misdemeanor, Civil Actions Under $7,500, Eviction, Small Claims.*

Civil Records: Access: Mail, in person. Only the court conducts in person searches; visitors may not. Search fee: $1.00 per name per year. Required to search: name, years to search. Civil cases indexed by defendant, plaintiff. **Criminal Records:** Access: Mail, in person. Only the court conducts in person searches; visitors may not. Search fee: $1.00 per name per year. Required to search: name, years to search. **General Information:** No sealed records released. SASE required. Turnaround time 2-4 days. Copy fee: $.30 per page. Certification fee: $3.00. Fee payee: E Fork Justice Court. Personal checks accepted. Prepayment is required.

Tahoe Justice Court

PO Box 7169, Stateline, NV 89449; 775-588-8100; Fax: 775-588-6844. Hours: 9AM-5PM (PST). *Misdemeanor, Civil Actions Under $7,500, Eviction, Small Claims.*

Civil Records: Access: Phone, mail, in person. Only the court conducts in person searches; visitors may not. Search fee: $1.00 per name per year. Required to search: name, years to search. Civil cases indexed by defendant, plaintiff. Civil records on index cards from 1985, prior records on docket books to 1/1/81. Prior to 1/1/81, records destroyed, but are in docket books. **Criminal Records:** Access: Phone, mail, in person. Only the court conducts in person searches; visitors may not. Search fee: $1.00 per name per year. Required to search: name, years to search, DOB. Criminal records prior to 1/1/81 records are destoyed, are in process of placing on computer. **General Information:** No sealed records released. SASE required. Turnaround time 2 weeks. Copy fee: $.25

per page. Certification fee: $3.00 per page. Fee payee: Tahoe Justice Court. Personal checks accepted. Credit cards accepted: Visa, Mastercard. Prepayment is required.

Elko County

4th Judicial District Court

571 Idaho St, 3rd Flr, Elko, NV 89801; 775-753-4600; Fax: 775-753-4610. Hours: 9AM-5PM (PST). *Felony, Gross Misdemeanor, Civil Actions Over $7,500, Probate.*

Civil Records: Access: Phone, mail, in person. Both court and visitors may perform in person searches. Search fee: $1.00 per name per year. Fee is for years prior to 10/01/91. Required to search: name, years to search. Civil cases indexed by defendant, plaintiff. Civil records on computer from 1991, on microfilm. **Criminal Records:** Access: Phone, mail, in person. Both court and visitors may perform in person searches. Search fee: $1.00 per name per year. Fee is for years prior to 1980. Required to search: name, years to search. Criminal records go back 10 years, primarily on microfilm prior (including probate). **General Information:** No sealed records released. SASE required. Turnaround time 1 day. Copy fee: $1.00 per page. Certification fee: $3.00. Fee payee: Elko County Clerk. Personal checks accepted. Prepayment is required.

Carlin Justice Court

PO Box 789, Carlin, NV 89822; 775-754-6321; Fax: 775-754-6893. Hours: 8AM-5PM (PST). *Misdemeanor, Civil Actions Under $7,500, Eviction, Small Claims.*

Civil Records: Access: Mail, in person. Both court and visitors may perform in person searches. Search fee: $1.00 per name per year. Required to search: name, years to search. Civil cases indexed by defendant, plaintiff. Civil records on computer starting in 1994, prior are in books. **Criminal Records:** Access: Mail, in person. Only the court conducts in person searches; visitors may not. Search fee: $1.00 per name per year. Required to search: name, years to search, DOB, SSN. Criminal records on computer starting in 1994, prior are in books. **General Information:** SASE required. Turnaround time 1 week. Copy fee: $.30 per page. Certification fee: $3.00. Fee payee: Carlin Court. Personal checks accepted. Prepayment is required.

Eastline Justice Court

PO Box 2300, West Wendover, NV 89883; 775-664-2305; Fax: 775-664-2979. Hours: 9AM-4PM (PST). *Misdemeanor, Civil Actions Under $7,500, Eviction, Small Claims.*

Civil Records: Access: Mail, in person. Only the court conducts in person searches; visitors may not. Search fee: $1.00 per name per year. Required to search: name, years to search. Civil cases indexed by defendant. Civil records on computer from 1992, prior on index, docket book. **Criminal Records:** Access: Mail, in person. Only the court conducts in person searches; visitors may not. Search fee: $1.00 per name per year. Required to search: name, years to search; also helpful-DOB. Criminal records on computer from 1992, prior on index, docket book. **General Information:** No open case records released. SASE required. Turnaround time 1 week. Copy fee: $.25 per page. Certification fee: $3.00. Fee payee: Eastline Justice Court. Only cashiers checks and money orders accepted. Prepayment is required.

Elko Justice Court

PO Box 176, Elko, NV 89803; 775-738-8403; Fax: 775-738-8416. Hours: 9AM-Noon, 1-5PM (PST). *Misdemeanor, Civil Actions Under $7,500, Eviction, Small Claims.*

Note: There is a small Justice Court located in Tecoma Township at PO Box 8, Montello, NV 89830, 775-776-2544

Civil Records: Access: Fax, mail, in person. Both court and visitors may perform in person searches. Search fee: $1.00 per name per year. Fee is per court. Required to search: name, years to search. Civil cases indexed by defendant, plaintiff. Civil records on computer after 1994, on docket books after 1970s, prior in county archives. **Criminal Records:** Access: Mail, in person. Both the court and visitors may conduct searches. Search fee: $1.00 per name per year. Fee is per court. Required to search: name, years to search; DOB or SSN also required. Criminal records on computer after 1994, on docket books after 1970s, prior in county archives. **General Information:** No confidential evaluations or sealed records released. SASE required. Turnaround time 7-10 days. Copy fee: $.30 per page. Certification fee: $3.00. Fee payee: Elko Justice Court. Personal checks accepted. Prepayment is required.

Jackpot Justice Court PO Box 229, Jackpot, NV 89825; 775-755-2456; Fax: 775-755-2727. Hours: 9AM-Noon, 1-5PM (PST). *Misdemeanor, Civil Actions Under $7,500, Eviction, Small Claims.*

Civil Records: Access: Mail, in person. Only the court conducts in person searches; visitors may not. Search fee: $1.00 per name per year. Required to search: name, years to search. Civil cases indexed by defendant. Civil records on docket books per year. **Criminal Records:** Access: Fax, mail, in person. Only the court conducts in person searches; visitors may not. Search fee: $1.00 per name per year. Required to search: name, years to search, DOB. Criminal records on docket books per year. **General Information:** SASE required. Turnaround time 1 week. Copy fee: $.25 per page. Certification fee: $3.00. Fee payee: Jackpot Justice Court. Business checks accepted. Fax notes: No fee to fax results.

Jarbidge Justice Court PO Box 26001, Jarbidge, NV 89826-2001; 775-488-2331. *Misdemeanor, Civil Actions Under $7,500, Eviction, Small Claims.*

Note: This is "unincorporated ghost town." No criminal or civil cases in more than 20 years. Mostly marriages, fish and game violations. Only 40 year round residents here

Civil Records: Access: In person only. Court does not conduct in person searches; visitors must perform searches for themselves. Search fee: No civil searches performed by court. Required to search: name, years to search. **Criminal Records:** Access: In person only. Court does not conduct in person searches; visitors must perform searches for themselves. Search fee: No criminal searches performed by court. Required to search: name, years to search. **General Information:**.

Mountain City Justice Court PO Box 116, Mountain City, NV 89831; 775-763-6699. *Misdemeanor, Civil Actions Under $7,500, Eviction, Small Claims.*

Note: New records held in Elko Justice Court; older ones may soon be transferred also. Limited cases heard here. Phone listed is sheriff's office. Only 49 people living here

Civil Records: Access: Mail, in person. Both court and visitors may perform in person searches. No search fee. Required to search: name, years to search. Civil cases indexed by defendant. **Criminal Records:** Access: Mail, in person. Both court and visitors may perform in person searches.

No search fee. Required to search: name, years to search, DOB. **General Information:** SASE required. Copy fee: $.25 per page. Certification fee: $2.00.

Wells Justice Municipal Court PO Box 297, Wells, NV 89835; 775-752-3726; Fax: 775-752-3363. Hours: 9AM-Noon, 1-5PM (PST). *Misdemeanor, Civil Actions Under $7,500, Eviction, Small Claims.*

Civil Records: Access: Mail, in person. Only the court conducts in person searches; visitors may not. Search fee: $1.00 per name per year. Required to search: name, years to search. Civil cases indexed by defendant, plaintiff. Civil records on computer from 1989, prior on docket books. In person access may require fee for clerical assistance. **Criminal Records:** Access: Mail, in person. Only the court conducts in person searches; visitors may not. Search fee: $1.00 per name per year. Required to search: name, years to search; also helpful-DOB, SSN. Criminal records on computer from 1989, prior on docket books. Same as civil. **General Information:** No pending, confidential records released. SASE required. Turnaround time 2 weeks. Copy fee: $.25 per page. Certification fee: $3.00. Fee payee: Wells Justice Court. Personal checks accepted. Prepayment is required.

Esmeralda County

5th Judicial District Court PO Box 547, Goldfield, NV 89013; 775-485-6367; Fax: 775-485-6376. Hours: 8AM-5PM (PST). *Felony, Misdemeanor, Civil Actions Over $7,500, Probate.*

Note: E-mail address is escdct@sierra.net.

Civil Records: Access: Fax, mail, in person, e-mail. Both court and visitors may perform in person searches. Search fee: $1.00 per name per year. Required to search: name, years to search. Civil cases indexed by defendant, plaintiff. Civil records on docket books from 1800s. **Criminal Records:** Access: Fax, mail, in person, e-mail. Both court and visitors may perform in person searches. Search fee: $1.00 per name per year. Required to search: name, years to search. Criminal records on docket books from 1800s. **General Information:** No juvenile or pre-sentence records released. SASE required. Turnaround time 2 weeks. Copy fee: $1.00 per page. Certification fee: $3.00. Fee payee: Esmeralda County Clerk. Personal checks accepted. Credit cards accepted: Visa and MasterCard. Prepayment is required. Fax notes: Fee to fax results is $1.00 per page.

Esmeralda Justice Court PO Box 370, Goldfield, NV 89013; 775-485-6359; Fax: 775-485-3462. Hours: 8AM-5PM (PST). *Misdemeanor, Civil Actions Under $7,500, Eviction, Small Claims.*

Civil Records: Access: Phone, fax, mail, in person. Only the court conducts in person searches; visitors may not. Search fee: $1.00 per name per year. Required to search: name, years to search. Civil cases indexed by plaintiff. Civil records on docket books for 6 years. **Criminal Records:** Access: Phone, fax, mail, in person. Only the court conducts in person searches; visitors may not. Search fee: $1.00 per name per year. Required to search: name, years to search. Criminal records on docket books for 6 years. **General Information:** No sealed records released. SASE required. Turnaround time 1 day. Copy fee: $.30 per page. Certification fee: $3.00. Fee payee: Justice Court. Only cashiers checks and money

orders accepted. Prepayment is required. Fax notes: $1.00 per page.

Eureka County

7th Judicial District Court PO Box 677, Eureka, NV 89316; 775-237-5262; Fax: 775-237-6015. Hours: 8AM-Noon, 1-5PM (PST). *Felony, Misdemeanor, Civil Actions Over $7,500, Probate.*

Civil Records: Access: Phone, fax, mail, in person. Both court and visitors may perform in person searches. Search fee: $1.00 per name per year. Required to search: name, years to search. Civil cases indexed by defendant, plaintiff. Civil records archived from 1873. Public can search docket books. **Criminal Records:** Access: Phone, fax, mail, in person. Both court and visitors may perform in person searches. Search fee: $1.00 per name per year. Required to search: name, years to search. Criminal records archived from 1873. Public can search docket books. **General Information:** No juvenile, sealed records released. SASE required. Turnaround time 1 day. Copy fee: $1.00 per page. Certification fee: $3.00. Fee payee: Eureka County Clerk. Personal checks accepted. Prepayment is required.

Beowawe Justice Court PO Box 211338, Crescent Valley, NV 89821; 775-468-0244; Fax: 775-468-0323. Hours: 8AM-5PM (PST). *Misdemeanor, Civil Actions Under $7,500, Eviction, Small Claims.*

Civil Records: Access: Mail, in person. Only the court conducts in person searches; visitors may not. Search fee: $1.00 per name per year. Required to search: name, years to search. Civil cases indexed by plaintiff. Civil records on docket books. **Criminal Records:** Access: Mail, in person. Only the court conducts in person searches; visitors may not. Search fee: $1.00 per name per year. Required to search: name, years to search. Criminal records on docket books. **General Information:** SASE required. Copy fee: $.30 per page. Certification fee: $3.00. Fee payee: Beowawe Justice Court. Only cashiers checks and money orders accepted. Prepayment is required.

Eureka Justice Court PO Box 496, Eureka, NV 89316; 775-237-5540; Fax: 775-237-6016. Hours: 8AM-Noon, 1-5PM (PST). *Misdemeanor, Civil Actions Under $7,500, Eviction, Small Claims.*

Civil Records: Access: Phone, mail, in person. Only the court conducts in person searches; visitors may not. No search fee. Required to search: name, years to search. Civil cases indexed by defendant, plaintiff. Civil records on computer since 1995; on docket books, archived from 1940. **Criminal Records:** Access: Phone, mail, in person. Only the court conducts in person searches; visitors may not. No search fee. Required to search: name, years to search. Criminal records on computer since 1995; on docket books, archived from 1940. **General Information:** SASE required. Turnaround time 2 days. Copy fee: $.50 per page. Certification fee: $3.00. Fee payee: Eureka Justice Court. Only cashiers checks and money orders accepted. Prepayment is required.

Humboldt County

6th Judicial District Court 50 W Fifth St, Winnemucca, NV 89445; 775-623-6343; Fax: 775-623-6309. Hours: 8AM-5PM (PST). *Felony, Misdemeanor, Civil Actions Over $7,500, Probate.*

Civil Records: Access: Phone, fax, mail, in person. Both court and visitors may perform in person searches. Search fee: $1.00 per name per year. Required to search: name, years to search. Civil cases indexed by defendant, plaintiff. Civil records on computer from 1984, on microfiche from 1900. **Criminal Records:** Access: Phone, fax, mail, in person. Both court and visitors may perform in person searches. Search fee: $1.00 per name per year. Required to search: name, years to search. Criminal records on computer from 1984, on microfiche from 1900. **General Information:** No adoption, sealed records released. SASE required. Turnaround time 1 day, immediate if on computer and requested by phone. Copy fee: $1.00 per page. Certification fee: $3.00. Fee payee: Humboldt County Clerk. Personal checks accepted. Prepayment is required. Public access terminal is available.

Union Justice Court PO Box 1218, Winnemucca, NV 89446; 775-623-6377; Fax: 775-623-6439. Hours: 7AM-5PM (PST). *Misdemeanor, Civil Actions Under $7,500, Eviction, Small Claims.*

Civil Records: Access: Fax, mail, in person. Only the court conducts in person searches; visitors may not. Search fee: $1.00 per name per year; minimum of $7.00. Required to search: name, years to search; also helpful-address. Civil cases indexed by defendant, plaintiff. Civil records on computer from 1988, prior on docket books. **Criminal Records:** Access: Fax, mail, in person. Only the court conducts in person searches; visitors may not. Search fee: $1.00 per name per year; minimum of $7.00. Required to search: name, years to search; also helpful-address, DOB, SSN. Criminal records on computer from 1988. **General Information:** SASE required. Turnaround time 1-2 days. Certification fee: $3.00. Fee payee: Justice Court. Personal checks accepted. Prepayment is required. Fax notes: No fee to fax results.

Lander County

6th Judicial District Court 315 S Humboldt, Battle Mountain, NV 89820; 775-635-5738; Fax: 775-635-5761. Hours: 8AM-5PM (PST). *Felony, Misdemeanor, Civil Actions Over $7,500, Probate.*

Civil Records: Access: Phone, fax, mail, in person. Only the court conducts in person searches; visitors may not. No search fee. Required to search: name, years to search. Civil cases indexed by defendant, plaintiff. Civil records on computer from 1992, on index from 1986-1990, on microfiche until 1985, prior records on docket books. **Criminal Records:** Access: Phone, fax, mail, in person. Only the court conducts in person searches; visitors may not. No search fee. Required to search: name, years to search. Criminal records on computer from 1992, on index from 1986-1990, on microfiche until 1985, prior records on docket books. **General Information:** No juvenile, sealed records released. SASE required. Turnaround time 7 days. Copy fee: $1.00 per page. Certification fee: $5.00. Fee payee: Lander County Clerk. Personal checks accepted. Fax notes: $1.00 per page.

Argenta Justice Court 315 S Humboldt, Battle Mountain, NV 89820; 775-635-5151; Fax: 775-635-0604. Hours: 8AM-5PM (PST). *Misdemeanor, Civil Actions Under $7,500, Eviction, Small Claims.*

Civil Records: Access: Phone, fax, mail, in person. Only the court conducts in person searches; visitors may not. Search fee: $1.00 per name per year. Required to search: name, years to search. Civil cases indexed by defendant, plaintiff. Civil records on computer from 1988, prior on docket books. **Criminal Records:** Access: Phone, fax, mail, in person. Only the court conducts in person searches; visitors may not. Search fee: $1.00 per name per year. Required to search: name, years to search; also helpful-DOB, SSN. Criminal records on computer from 1988, prior on docket books. **General Information:** No unserved search warrant records released. SASE required. Turnaround time 1 day. Copy fee: $.25 per page. Certification fee: $2.50 per page. Fee payee: Argenta Justice Court. Only cashiers checks and money orders accepted. Fax notes: $1.00 per page.

Austin Justice Court PO Box 100, Austin, NV 89310; 775-964-2380; Fax: 775-964-2327. Hours: 8AM-5PM M, 8AM-Noon T-Th (PST). *Misdemeanor, Civil Actions Under $7,500, Eviction, Small Claims.*

Note: No fees for requests from government agencies.

Civil Records: Access: Phone, mail, fax, in person. Only the court conducts in person searches; visitors may not. Search fee: $1.00 per name per year. Required to search: name, years to search. Civil cases indexed by defendant, plaintiff. Civil records on docket books. **Criminal Records:** Access: Phone, mail, fax, in person. Only the court conducts in person searches; visitors may not. Search fee: $1.00 per name per year. Required to search: name, years to search. Criminal records on computer from 1988. **General Information:** SASE required. Turnaround time 1 week. Copy fee: $.25 per page. Certification fee: $1.00 per page. Fee payee: Austin Justice Court. Prepayment is required.

Lincoln County

7th Judicial District Court PO Box 90, Pioche, NV 89043; 775-962-5390; Fax: 702-962-5180. Hours: 9AM-5PM (PST). *Felony, Misdemeanor, Civil Actions Over $7,500, Probate.*

Civil Records: Access: Mail, in person. Both court and visitors may perform in person searches. Search fee: $1.00 per name per year. Required to search: name, years to search. Civil cases indexed by defendant, plaintiff. Civil records on docket books from 1855 and are not computerized. **Criminal Records:** Access: Mail, in person. Both court and visitors may perform in person searches. Search fee: $1.00 per name per year. Required to search: name, years to search. Criminal records on docket books from 1855 and are not computerized. **General Information:** No juvenile, sealed records released. SASE not required. Turnaround time 2-3 days. Copy fee: $1.00 per page. Certification fee: $5.00. Fee payee: Lincoln County Clerk. Personal checks accepted. Prepayment is required.

Meadow Valley Justice Court PO Box 36, Pioche, NV 89043; 775-962-5140; Fax: 775-962-5877. Hours: 9AM-5PM (PST). *Misdemeanor, Civil Actions Under $7,500, Eviction, Small Claims.*

Civil Records: Access: Phone, fax, mail, in person. Only the court conducts in person searches; visitors may not. Search fee: $1.00 per name per year. Required to search: name, years to search. Civil cases indexed by defendant, plaintiff. Civil records archived from 1982, on docket books. **Criminal Records:** Access: Phone, fax, mail, in person. Only the court conducts in person searches; visitors may not. Search fee: $1.00 per name per year. Required to search: name, years to search. Criminal records are all originals. **General Information:** Juvenile records are not released. SASE required. Turnaround time 1-5 days. Copy fee: $1.00 per page. Certification fee: No certification fee. Fee payee: Meadow Valley Justice Court. Personal checks accepted. Prepayment is required. Fax notes: $3.00 for first page, $1.00 each addl.

Pahranagat Valley Justice Court PO Box 449, Alamo, NV 89001; 775-725-3357; Fax: 775-725-3566. Hours: 9AM-5PM (PST). *Misdemeanor, Civil Actions Under $7,500, Eviction, Small Claims.*

Civil Records: Access: Fax, mail, in person. Only the court conducts in person searches; visitors may not. No search fee. Required to search: name, years to search. Civil cases indexed by defendant. Civil records on docket books. **Criminal Records:** Access: Fax, mail, in person. Only the court conducts in person searches; visitors may not. No search fee. Required to search: name, years to search. Criminal records on docket books. **General Information:** No personal notes released. SASE required. Turnaround time 1-3 days. Copy fee: $.25 per page. Certification fee: $1.00 per page. Fee payee: Pahranagat Valley Justice Court. Personal checks accepted. Prepayment is required. Fax notes: No fee to fax results.

Lyon County

3rd Judicial District Court PO Box 816, Yerington, NV 89447; 775-463-6503; Fax: 775-463-6575. Hours: 8AM-5PM (PST). *Felony, Misdemeanor, Civil Actions Over $7,500, Probate.*

Civil Records: Access: Phone, mail, in person. Only the court conducts in person searches; visitors may not. Search fee: $1.00 per name per year. Required to search: name, years to search. Civil cases indexed by defendant, plaintiff. Civil records on computer from 1989. **Criminal Records:** Access: Phone, mail, in person. Only the court conducts in person searches; visitors may not. Search fee: $1.00 per name per year. Required to search: name, years to search. Criminal records on computer from 1985. **General Information:** No adoption, juvenile or sealed records released. SASE required. Turnaround time 1 week for mail requests, immediate for phone requests if on computer. Copy fee: $.25 per page. Certification fee: $3.00. Fee payee: Lyon County Clerk. Personal checks accepted. Prepayment is required.

Dayton Township Justice Court PO Box 490, Dayton, NV 89403; 775-246-6233; Fax: 775-246-6203. Hours: 8AM-5PM (PST). *Misdemeanor, Civil Actions Under $7,500, Eviction, Small Claims.*

Civil Records: Access: Phone, fax, mail, in person. Only the court conducts in person searches; visitors may not. Search fee: $1.00 per name per year. Required to search: name, years to search. Civil cases indexed by defendant, plaintiff. Civil records on computer from 1991, prior on docket books by year. **Criminal Records:** Access: Phone, fax, mail, in person. Only the court conducts in person searches; visitors may not. Search fee: $1.00 per name per year. Required to search: name, years to search. Criminal records on computer from 1991, prior on docket books by year. **General Information:** No sealed records released. SASE required. Turnaround time within 1 week. Copy fee: $.25 per page. Certification fee: $3.00. Fee payee: Dayton Township Justice Court. Personal checks accepted. Prepayment is required. Fax notes: No fee to fax results.

Fernley Justice Court PO Box 497, Fernley, NV 89408; 775-575-3355; Fax: 775-575-3359. Hours: 8AM-5PM (PST). *Misdemeanor, Civil Actions Under $7,500, Eviction, Small Claims.*

Civil Records: Access: Phone, mail, in person. Only the court conducts in person searches; visitors may not. Search fee: $1.00 per name per year. Required to search: name, years to search. Civil cases indexed by defendant, plaintiff. Civil records on computer from 1992, prior on docket books. **Criminal Records:** Access: Phone, mail, in person. Only the court conducts in person searches; visitors may not. Search fee: $1.00 per name per year. Required to search: name, years to search; also helpful-SSN. Criminal records on computer from 1992, prior on docket books. **General Information:** No police reports or sealed records released. SASE required. Turnaround time 1 week. Copy fee: $.30 per page. Certification fee: $2.00. Fee payee: Fernley Justice Court. Personal checks accepted. Out of state checks not accepted. Prepayment is required.

Mason Valley Justice Court 30 Nevin Way, Yerington, NV 89447; 775-463-6639; Fax: 775-463-6610. Hours: 8AM-5PM (PST). *Misdemeanor, Civil Actions Under $7,500, Eviction, Small Claims.*

Civil Records: Access: Phone, mail, in person. Only the court conducts in person searches; visitors may not. Search fee: $1.00 per name per year. Required to search: name, years to search. Civil cases indexed by defendant, plaintiff. Civil records on computer from 1988, archives from 1900s. **Criminal Records:** Access: Phone, mail, in person. Only the court conducts in person searches; visitors may not. Search fee: $1.00 per name per year. Required to search: name, years to search; also helpful-DOB, SSN. Criminal records on computer from 1988, archives from 1900s. **General Information:** No police, sheriff reports released. SASE required. Turnaround time 3 days, immediate for phone requests. Copy fee: $.25 per page. Certification fee: $3.00. Fee payee: Mason Valley Justice Court. Personal checks accepted. Prepayment is required.

Smith Valley Justice Court PO Box 141, Smith, NV 89430; 775-465-2313; Fax: 775-465-2153. Hours: 8AM-Noon Tues & Fri or by appointment (PST). *Misdemeanor, Civil Actions Under $10,000, Eviction, Small Claims.*

Civil Records: Access: Phone, fax, mail, in person. Only the court conducts in person searches; visitors may not. No search fee. Required to search: name, years to search; also helpful-address. Civil cases indexed by defendant, plaintiff. Civil records on computer from 1994, prior in docket books. **Criminal Records:** Access: Phone, mail, in person. Only the court conducts in person searches; visitors may not. No search fee. Required to search: name, years to search; also helpful-address, DOB, SSN. Criminal records on computer from 1994, prior in docket books. **General Information:** SASE required. Turnaround time 1-2 weeks. Copy fee: $.30 per page. Certification fee: $3.00. Fee payee: Smith

Valley Justice Court. Personal checks accepted. Prepayment is required.

Mineral County

5th Judicial District Court PO Box 1450, Hawthorne, NV 89415; 775-945-2446; Fax: 775-945-0706. Hours: 8AM-5PM (PST). *Felony, Misdemeanor, Civil Actions Over $7,500, Probate.*

Civil Records: Access: Phone, fax, mail, in person. Both court and visitors may perform in person searches. Search fee: $1.00 per name per year. Required to search: name, years to search. Civil cases indexed by defendant, plaintiff. Civil records on computer. **Criminal Records:** Access: Phone, fax, mail, in person. Both court and visitors may perform in person searches. Search fee: $1.00 per name per year. Required to search: name, years to search. Criminal records on computer. **General Information:** No juvenile records released. SASE required. Turnaround time 1 day. Copy fee: $1.00 per page. Certification fee: $3.00. Fee payee: Mineral County Clerk. Personal checks accepted. Prepayment is required. Fax notes: $1.50 per page.

Hawthorne Justice Court PO Box 1660, Hawthorne, NV 89415; 775-945-3859; Fax: 775-945-0700. Hours: 8AM-5PM (PST). *Misdemeanor, Civil Actions Under $7,500, Eviction, Small Claims.*

Civil Records: Access: Phone, mail, in person. Both court and visitors may perform in person searches. No search fee. Required to search: name, years to search. Civil cases indexed by defendant. Civil records on computer from 1994, prior on docket books. **Criminal Records:** Access: Phone, mail, in person. Both court and visitors may perform in person searches. No search fee. Required to search: name, years to search. Criminal records on computer from 1992. **General Information:** No pending case or sealed records released. SASE required. Turnaround time 1-5 days. Copy fee: $.25 per page. Legal Size Copy Fee: $1.00 per page. Certification fee: No certification fee. Fee payee: Hawthorne Justice Court. Personal checks accepted.

Mina Justice Court PO Box 415, Mina, NV 89422; 775-573-2547; Fax: 775-573-2244. Hours: 9AM-Noon, 2-4PM (PST). *Misdemeanor, Civil Actions Under $7,500, Eviction, Small Claims.*

Civil Records: Access: Phone, mail, in person. Only the court conducts in person searches; visitors may not. No search fee. Required to search: name, years to search. Civil cases indexed by plaintiff. Civil records on docket books. **Criminal Records:** Access: Phone, mail, in person. Only the court conducts in person searches; visitors may not. No search fee. Required to search: name, years to search. Criminal records on docket books. **General Information:** No sealed records released. SASE required. Turnaround time 1 day. Copy fee: $.50 for first page, $.25 each addl. Certification fee: No certification fee. Fee payee: Mina Justice Court. Personal checks accepted. Prepayment is required.

Schurz Justice Court PO Box 265, Schurz, NV 89427; 775-773-2241; Fax: 775-773-2030. Hours: 9AM-4PM Fri only (PST). *Misdemeanor, Civil Actions Under $7,500, Eviction, Small Claims.*

Civil Records: Access: Mail, in person. Only the court conducts in person searches; visitors may not. No search fee. Required to search: name, years to search. Civil cases indexed by defendant. Civil records on docket books. **Criminal Records:**

Access: Mail, in person. Only the court conducts in person searches; visitors may not. No search fee. Required to search: name, years to search. Criminal records on docket books. **General Information:** Will release all records considered public. SASE not required. Turnaround time 1-5 days. Copy fee: $.25 per page. Certification fee: No certification fee. Fee payee: Schurz Justice Court. Personal checks accepted. Credit cards accepted.

Nye County

5th Judicial District Court PO Box 1031, Tonopah, NV 89049; 775-482-8131; Fax: 775-482-8133. Hours: 8AM-5PM (PST). *Felony, Misdemeanor, Civil Actions Over $7,500, Probate.*

Civil Records: Access: Phone, fax, mail, in person. Search fee: $1.00 per name per year. Required to search: name, years to search. Civil records on computer from 1991, on docket books from 1800s, many are microfilmed. **Criminal Records:** Access: Phone, fax, mail, in person. Only the court conducts in person searches; visitors may not. Search fee: $1.00 per name per year. Required to search: name, years to search. Criminal records on computer from 1991, on docket books from 1800s, many are microfilmed. **General Information:** No adoptions or juvenile records released. SASE required. Turnaround time 1 day. Copy fee: $1.00 per page. Certification fee: $3.00. Fee payee: Nye County Clerk. Business checks accepted. In-state personal checks accepted. Prepayment is required. Payment required if more than $15.00. Public access terminal is available. Fax notes: $2.00 for first page, $1.00 each addl.

Beatty Justice Court PO Box 805, Beatty, NV 89003; 775-553-2951; Fax: 775-553-2136. Hours: 8AM-5PM (PST). *Misdemeanor, Civil Actions Under $7,500, Eviction, Small Claims.*

Civil Records: Access: Phone, mail, in person. Only the court conducts in person searches; visitors may not. Search fee: $1.00 per name per year. Computer printouts on all civil actions (no way to segregate samll claims or evictions) is $.50 per page. Required to search: name, years to search. Civil cases indexed by defendant, plaintiff. Civil records on computer from 1991, archived from 1950s, some on docket books. **Criminal Records:** Access: Phone, mail, in person. Only the court conducts in person searches; visitors may not. Search fee: $1.00 per name per year. Required to search: name, years to search, DOB. Criminal records on computer from 1989. **General Information:** No sealed, confidential records released. SASE required. Turnaround time 1 week for mail requests, same day for phone requests when possible. Copy fee: $.30 per page. Certification fee: $3.00. Fee payee: Beatty Justice Court. Personal checks accepted. Prepayment is required.

Gabbs Justice Court PO Box 533, Gabbs, NV 89409; 775-285-2379; Fax: 775-285-4263. Hours: 9AM-4PM M-Th (PST). *Misdemeanor, Civil Actions Under $7,500, Eviction, Small Claims.*

Civil Records: Access: Phone, mail, in person. Only the court conducts in person searches; visitors may not. Search fee: $1.00 per name per year. Required to search: name, years to search. Civil cases indexed by plaintiff. Civil records on computer from 1993, archived from 1950s, some on docket books. **Criminal Records:** Access: Phone, mail, in person. Only the court conducts in person searches; visitors may not. Search fee: $1.00 per name per year. Required to search: name, years to search, DOB, offense, date of offense; also helpful-SSN. Criminal records on computer from 1993, archived from 1950s, some on docket books. **General Information:** No juvenile records released. SASE required. Turnaround time same day. Copy fee: $1.00 per page. Certification fee: No certification fee. Fee payee: Gabbs Justice Court. Personal checks accepted.

Tonopah Justice Court PO Box 1151, Tonopah, NV 89049; 775-482-8155. Hours: 8AM-Noon, 1-5PM (PST). *Misdemeanor, Civil Actions Under $7,500, Eviction, Small Claims.*

Civil Records: Access: Phone, mail, in person. Only the court conducts in person searches; visitors may not. Search fee: $1.00 per name per year. Required to search: name, years to search. Civil cases indexed by plaintiff. Civil records on computer from 1992, on archives from 1950s, some on docket books. **Criminal Records:** Access: Phone, mail, in person. Only the court conducts in person searches; visitors may not. Search fee: $1.00 per name per year. Required to search: name, years to search, offense, date of offense; also helpful-DOB, SSN. Criminal records on computer from 1992, on archives from 1950s, some on docket books. **General Information:** SASE required. Turnaround time 1-2 weeks. Copy fee: $.30 per page. Certification fee: $3.00 per certification. Fee payee: Tonopah Justice Court. Business checks accepted.

Pershing County

6th Judicial District Court PO Box 820, Lovelock, NV 89419; 775-273-2410; Fax: 775-273-2434. Hours: 9AM-5PM (PST). *Felony, Civil Actions Over $7,500, Probate.*

Note: Misdemeanors are handled by the Lake Justice Court

Civil Records: Access: Phone, fax, mail, in person. Only the court conducts in person searches; visitors may not. Search fee: $1.00 per name per year. Required to search: name, years to search. Civil cases indexed by defendant, plaintiff. Civil records on computer from 1992, microfilmed from 1919-1938, books from 1919. **Criminal Records:** Access: Phone, fax, mail, in person. Only the court conducts in person searches; visitors may not. Search fee: $1.00 per name per year. Required to search: name, years to search. Criminal records on computer from 1992, microfilmed from 1919-1938, books from 1919. **General Information:** No adoption, juvenile or sealed records released. SASE required. Turnaround time 1-3 days. Copy fee: $1.00 per page. Certification fee: $3.00. Fee payee: Pershing County Clerk. Personal checks accepted. Prepayment is required. Fax notes: No fee to fax results.

Lake Township Justice Court PO Box 8, Lovelock, NV 89419; 775-273-2753; Fax: 775-273-0416. Hours: 8AM-5PM (PST). *Misdemeanor, Civil Actions Under $7,500, Eviction, Small Claims.*

Civil Records: Access: Phone, mail, in person. Only the court conducts in person searches; visitors may not. Search fee: $1.00 per name per year. Required to search: name, years to search; also helpful-address. Civil cases indexed by defendant, plaintiff. Civil records on computer from 1988, on docket books prior. **Criminal Records:** Access: Phone, mail, in person. Only the court conducts in person searches; visitors may

not. Search fee: $1.00 per name per year. Required to search: name, years to search; also helpful-DOB. Criminal records on computer from 1988, on docket books prior. **General Information:** No sealed, driver's history or highway patrol records released. SASE required. Turnaround time 2 days, 30 minutes for phone requests for records prior to 1988. Copy fee: $.25 per page. Certification fee: $3.00. Fee payee: Lake Township Justice Court. Personal checks accepted. For payment by check proof of ID required.

Storey County

1st Judicial District Court PO Drawer D, Virginia City, NV 89440; 775-847-0969; Fax: 775-847-0949. Hours: 9AM-5PM (PST). *Felony, Misdemeanor, Civil Actions Over $7,500, Probate.*

Civil Records: Access: Phone, mail, in person. Both court and visitors may perform in person searches. Search fee: $1.00 per name per year. Required to search: name, years to search. Civil cases indexed by defendant, plaintiff. Civil records on computer since 1992; prior years on books. Search by phone only if paid in advance. **Criminal Records:** Access: Phone, mail, in person. Both court and visitors may perform in person searches. Search fee: $1.00 per name per year. Required to search: name, years to search; also helpful-DOB, SSN. Criminal records on computer since 1992; prior years on books. Search by phone only if pre-paid. **General Information:** No juvenile or sealed records released. SASE required. Turnaround time 1 week, 5 minutes for phone requests when possible. Copy fee: $1.00 per page. Certification fee: $5.00. Fee payee: Storey County Clerk. Personal checks accepted. Prepayment is required.

Virginia City Justice Court PO Box 674, Virginia City, NV 89440; 775-847-0962; Fax: 775-847-0915. Hours: 9AM-5PM (PST). *Misdemeanor, Civil Actions Under $7,500, Eviction, Small Claims.*

Civil Records: Access: Phone, mail, in person. Both court and visitors may perform in person searches. Search fee: $1.00 per name per year. Required to search: name, years to search. Civil cases indexed by defendant, plaintiff. Civil records retained for 7 years, some on docket books. **Criminal Records:** Access: Phone, mail, in person. Both court and visitors may perform in person searches. Search fee: $1.00 per name per year. Required to search: name, years to search, DOB; also helpful-SSN. Criminal records on computer since 1988. **General Information:** SASE required. Turnaround time 1 week. Copy fee: $.25 per page. Certification fee: $3.00. Fee payee: Justice Court. Personal checks accepted. Prepayment is required.

Washoe County

2nd Judicial District Court PO Box 11130, Reno, NV 89520; 775-328-3110; Fax: 775-328-3515. Hours: 8AM-5PM (PST). *Felony, Misdemeanor, Civil Actions Over $7,500, Probate.*

Civil Records: Access: Mail, in person. Both court and visitors may perform in person searches. Search fee: $1.00 per name per year. Required to search: name, years to search. Civil cases indexed by defendant, plaintiff. Civil records on computer from 1984, microfiche from 1983, archives from 1920. Phone access limited to computer records. **Criminal Records:** Access: Mail, in person. Both court and visitors may perform in person searches. Search fee: $1.00 per name per year. Required to search: name, years to search. Criminal records on

computer from 1984, microfiche from 1983, archives from 1920. Phone access limited to computer records. **General Information:** No sealed or juvenile records released. SASE required. Turnaround time 2 weeks, immediately if by phone and on computer. Copy fee: $1.00 per page. Certification fee: $3.00. Fee payee: Washoe County Clerk. Business checks accepted. Prepayment is required. Public access terminal is available.

Reno Justice Court PO Box 30083, Reno, NV 89520; 775-325-6501; Criminal phone:; Fax: 775-325-6510. Hours: 8AM-5PM (PST). *Misdemeanor, Civil Actions Under $7,500, Eviction, Small Claims.*

Civil Records: Access: Phone, mail, in person. Both court and visitors may perform in person searches. Search fee: $1.00 per name per year. Required to search: name, years to search. Civil cases indexed by defendant. Civil records archived from 1982, on docket books. For mail access call first. Court will send form to be filled out & returned with payment. **Criminal Records:** Access: Phone, mail, in person. Only the court conducts in person searches; visitors may not. Search fee: $1.00 per name per year. Required to search: name, years to search; also helpful-DOB, SSN, aliases. Criminal records archived from 1982, on docket books. Same as civil. **General Information:** No sealed records released. SASE required. Turnaround time 2-5 days. Copy fee: $.25 per page. Certification fee: No certification fee. Certification fee is $3.00 per page. Fee payee: Reno Justice Court. Only cashiers checks and money orders accepted.

Sparks Justice Court 630 Greenbrae Dr, Sparks, NV 89431; 775-352-3000. Hours: 8AM-5PM (PST). *Misdemeanor, Civil Actions Under $7,500, Eviction, Small Claims.*

Civil Records: Access: Mail, in person. Only the court conducts in person searches; visitors may not. Search fee: $1.00 per name per year. Required to search: name, years to search. Civil cases indexed by defendant, plaintiff. Civil records on computer last 4 years, prior in books and on cards. **Criminal Records:** Access: Mail, in person. Only the court conducts in person searches; visitors may not. Search fee: $1.00 per name per year. Required to search: name, years to search; also helpful-DOB, SSN. Criminal records on computer last 4 years, prior in books and on cards. **General Information:** Turnaround time 1-3 days. Copy fee: $1.00 per document. Certification fee: $3.00. Fee payee: Justice Court. Personal checks accepted. For payment by check guarantee card required. Prepayment is required.

White Pine County

7th Judicial District Court PO Box 659, Ely, NV 89301; 775-289-2341; Fax: 775-289-2544. Hours: 9AM-5PM (PST). *Felony, Misdemeanor, Civil Actions Over $7,500, Probate.*

Civil Records: Access: Phone, fax, mail, in person. Search fee: $1.00 per name. Required to search: name, years to search. Civil cases indexed by defendant, plaintiff. Civil records on computer from 1991, some on dockets. **Criminal Records:** Access: Phone, fax, mail, in person. Only the court conducts in person searches; visitors may not. Search fee: $1.00 per name. Required to search: name, years to search. Criminal records on computer from 1991, some on dockets. **General Information:** No juvenile or sealed records released. SASE required. Turnaround time 2 days,

8AM-4PM (EST). *Misdemeanor, Civil Actions Under $25,000, Eviction, Small Claims.*

Civil Records: Access: Mail, in person. Only the court conducts in person searches; visitors may not. Search fee: $10.00 fee for electronic search up to 10 names, $25.00 for 10+ names. Manual search is $25.00 per name. Required to search: name, years to search. Civil cases indexed by defendant, plaintiff. Civil records on computer from 3/92, kept in files prior. **Criminal Records:** Access: Mail, in person. Only the court conducts in person searches; visitors may not. Search fee: Same fee structure as civil. Required to search: name, years to search, DOB; also helpful-SSN. Criminal records on computer from 3/92, kept in files prior. **General Information:** No sealed, juvenile, mental health, expunged or dismissed records released. SASE required. Turnaround time 2 weeks. Copy fee: $.50 per page. Certification fee: $1.00. Fee payee: Goffstown District Court. Personal checks accepted. Prepayment is required.

Hillsborough District Court PO Box 763, Hillsborough, NH 03244; 603-464-5811. Hours: 8AM-3:30PM (EST). *Misdemeanor, Civil Actions Under $25,000, Eviction, Small Claims.*

Civil Records: Access: Mail, in person. Only the court conducts in person searches; visitors may not. Search fee: Research fees will vary, call first. Required to search: name, years to search. Civil cases indexed by defendant, plaintiff. Civil records on computer from 1994, on index cards from 1980, index books from 1960. Appointment required for in person searching. **Criminal Records:** Access: Mail, in person. Only the court conducts in person searches; visitors may not. Search fee: Research fees will vary, call first. Required to search: name, years to ...DOB; also helpful-SSN. Criminal records ...uter from 1994, on index cards from 19.., index books from 1960. **General Information:** No adoptions, sealed, juvenile, mental health, expunged or dismissed records released. SASE required. Turnaround time 1 week. Copy fee: $.50 per page. Certification fee: $5.00. Fee payee: Hillsborough District Court. Personal checks accepted. Prepayment is required.

Manchester District Court PO Box 456, Manchester, NH 03105; 603-624-6510. Hours: 8AM-4PM (EST). *Misdemeanor, Civil Actions Under $25,000, Eviction, Small Claims.*

Civil Records: Access: Mail, in person. Only the court conducts in person searches; visitors may not. Search fee: $10.00 per request up to 10 names or $25.00 per request over 10. Manual searches $25.00 per hour. Required to search: name, years to search, DOB; also helpful-address. Civil cases indexed by defendant, plaintiff. Civil records on computer from 6/92, on index cards from 1960. **Criminal Records:** Access: Mail, in person. Only the court conducts in person searches; visitors may not. Search fee: $10.00 per request up to 10 names or $25.00 per request over 10. Manual searches $25.00 per hour. Required to search: name, years to search, DOB; also helpful-address. Criminal records on computer from 6/92, on index cards from 1960. **General Information:** No adoptions, sealed, juvenile, mental health, expunged or dismissed records released. SASE required. Turnaround time 2 weeks. Copy fee: $.50 per page. Certification fee: $1.00. Fee payee: Manchester District Court. Personal checks accepted.

Merrimack District Court PO Box 324, Merrimack, NH 03054-0324; 603-424-9916. Hours: 8:30AM-3PM (EST). *Misdemeanor, Civil Actions Under $25,000, Eviction, Small Claims.*

Civil Records: Access: Mail, in person. Only the court conducts in person searches; visitors may not. Search fee: $25 per hour for manual searches. For electronic, $10 for up to first 9 names or $25 for first 25 names, then hour rate. Required to search: name, years to search. Civil cases indexed by defendant, plaintiff. Civil records on computer from 7/92, on index cards from 1970, index books in archives at Concord. **Criminal Records:** Access: Mail, in person. Both court and visitors may perform in person searches. Search fee: Same as civil. Required to search: name, years to search; also helpful-DOB. Criminal records on computer from 7/92, on index cards from 1970, index books in archives at Concord. **General Information:** No adoptions, sealed, juvenile, mental health, expunged or dismissed records released. SASE required. Turnaround time 1-2 days. Copy fee: $.50 per page. Certification fee: $5.00. Fee payee: Merrimack District Court. Personal checks accepted. Prepayment is required.

Milford District Court PO Box 148, Amherst, NH 03031; 603-673-2900. Hours: 8AM-4PM (EST). *Misdemeanor, Civil Actions Under $25,000, Eviction, Small Claims.*

Civil Records: Access: Mail, in person. Only the court conducts in person searches; visitors may not. Search fee: See state introduction for standard state search fees. Required to search: name, years to search. Civil cases indexed by defendant, plaintiff. Civil records on computer from 08/92, on index cards from 1950s, prior records may or may not be at old courthouse. **Criminal Records:** Access: Mail, in person. Only the court conducts in person searches; visitors may not. Search fee: See state introduction for standard state search fees. Required to search: name, years to search; also helpful-DOB, SSN. Criminal records on computer from 08/92, on index cards from 1950s, prior records may or may not be at old courthouse. **General Information:** No adoptions, sealed, juvenile, mental health, expunged or dismissed records released. SASE required. Turnaround time 10 days. Copy fee: $.50 per page. Certification fee: $5.00. Fee payee: Milford District Court. Personal checks accepted. Credit cards accepted: Visa, Mastercard. Prepayment is required.

Nashua District Court Walnut St Oval, Nashua, NH 03060; 603-880-3333. Hours: 8AM-4PM (EST). *Misdemeanor, Civil Actions Under $25,000, Eviction, Small Claims.*

Civil Records: Access: Mail, in person. Only the court conducts in person searches; visitors may not. Search fee: Records prior to 08/92 are $25.00; after are $10.00. Required to search: name, years to search. Civil cases indexed by defendant, plaintiff. Civil records on computer from 1993, index cards from 1982. All requests must be in writing. **Criminal Records:** Access: Mail, in person. Only the court conducts in person searches; visitors may not. Search fee: Same fees as civil. Required to search: name, years to search; also helpful-DOB, SSN. Criminal records on computer from August 1992, index cards from 1982. All requests must be in writing. **General Information:** No adoptions, sealed, juvenile, mental health, expunged records released. SASE required. Turnaround time 10 days. Copy fee: $.50 per page. Certification fee: $5.00. Fee payee: Nashua District Court. Personal checks accepted. Prepayment is required.

Probate Court PO Box P, Nashua, NH 03061-6015; 603-882-1231; Fax: 603-882-1620. Hours: 8AM-4PM (EST). *Probate.*

Merrimack County

Superior Court PO Box 2880, Concord, NH 03302-2880; 603-225-5501. Hours: 8:30AM-4PM (EST). *Felony, Civil Actions Over $1,500.*

Civil Records: Access: Mail, in person. Only the court conducts in person searches; visitors may not. No search fee. Required to search: name, years to search. Civil cases indexed by defendant, plaintiff. Civil records on computer from 1983, index cards from 1950, index books from 1800s; organized 1823. **Criminal Records:** Access: Phone, mail, in person. Only the court conducts in person searches; visitors may not. No search fee. Required to search: name, years to search, DOB; also helpful-SSN. Criminal records on computer since 1984. **General Information:** No adoptions, sealed, juvenile, mental health, expunged or dismissed records released. SASE required. Turnaround time 2-3 days. Copy fee: $.50 per page. Certification fee: $5.00. Fee payee: Merrimack Superior Court. Personal checks accepted. Prepayment is required.

Concord District Court 32 Clinton St, PO Box 3420, Concord, NH 03302-3420; 603-271-6400. Hours: 8AM-4PM; Drive-up hours: 8AM-4:30PM (EST). *Misdemeanor, Civil Actions Under $25,000, Eviction, Small Claims.*

Note: The former Pittsfield District Court has been combined with this court

Civil Records: Access: Mail, in person. Only the court conducts in person searches; visitors may not. Search fee: $10 for less than 10 electronic searches or $25 per hour. Required to search: name, years to search. Civil cases indexed by defendant, plaintiff. Civil records on computer from 1989, index cards from 1978, docket books from 1800. **Criminal Records:** Access: Mail, in person. Only the court conducts in person searches; visitors may not. Search fee: See state introduction for standard search fees. Required to search: name, years to search, DOB. Criminal records on computer from 1989, index cards from 1978, docket books from 1800. **General Information:** No adoptions, sealed, juvenile, mental health, expunged or dismissed records released. SASE required. Turnaround time 10 days. Copy fee: $.50 per page. Certification fee: $1.00. Fee payee: Concord District Court. Personal checks accepted. Prepayment is required.

Franklin District Court 7 Hancock Terrace, Franklin, NH 03235; 603-934-3290. Hours: 8AM-4PM (EST). *Misdemeanor, Civil Actions Under $25,000, Eviction, Small Claims.*

Civil Records: Access: Mail, in person. Only the court conducts in person searches; visitors may not. Search fee: $10.00 per name. Required to search: name, years to search. Civil cases indexed by plaintiff. Civil records on computer from 1/91, index cards from 1/80, index books from 1960s. **Criminal Records:** Access: Mail, in person. Only the court conducts in person searches; visitors may not. Search fee: $10.00 per name. Required to search: name, years to search; also helpful-DOB, SSN. Criminal records on computer from 1/91, index cards from 1/80, index books from 1960s. **General Information:** No adoptions, sealed, juvenile, mental health, expunged or dismissed records released. SASE required. Turnaround time 2-3 days. No copy fee. Certification fee: $1.00 per page. Fee payee: Franklin District Court. Personal checks accepted. Prepayment is required.

Henniker District Court 2 Depot St, Henniker, NH 03242; 603-428-3214. Hours: 8AM-4PM (EST). *Misdemeanor, Civil Actions Under $25,000, Eviction, Small Claims.*

Civil Records: Access: Mail, in person. Only the court conducts in person searches; visitors may not. Search fee: See state introduction for standard search fees. Required to search: name, years to search. Civil cases indexed by defendant, plaintiff. Civil records on index cards from 1988, index books from 1960s. **Criminal Records:** Access: Mail, in person. Only the court conducts in person searches; visitors may not. Search fee: See state introduction for standard search fees. Required to search: name, years to search; also helpful-DOB, SSN. Criminal records on index cards from 1988, index books from 1960s. **General Information:** No adoptions, sealed, juvenile, mental health, expunged or dismissed records released. SASE required. Turnaround time can take as long as 6 weeks. Copy fee: $.50 per page. Certification fee: $5.00. Fee payee: Henniker District Court. Personal checks accepted. Prepayment is required.

Hooksett District Court 101 Merrimack, Hooksett, NH 03106; 603-485-9901. Hours: 8:30AM-4PM (EST). *Misdemeanor, Civil Actions Under $25,000, Eviction, Small Claims.*

Civil Records: Access: Mail, in person. Only the court conducts in person searches; visitors may not. Search fee: Fee for electronic searching is $10.00 per name if less than 10 names submitted; 10 or more names are $25.00 each. Manual research is charged at $25.00 per hour. Browse screens are $.50 per page (bilk case info). Required to search: name, years to search. Civil cases indexed by defendant, plaintiff. Civil records on computer from 1993, on index cards from 1980, index books from 1975. All requests must be in writing. **Criminal Records:** Access: Mail, in person. Only the court conducts in person searches; visitors may not. Search fee: Same fees as civil. Required to search: name, years to search; also helpful-DOB, SSN. Criminal records on computer from 1993, on index cards from 1980, index books from 1975. **General Information:** No sealed, juvenile, mental health, expunged or dismissed records released. SASE required. Turnaround time 1-2 months. Copy fee: $.50 per page. Certification fee: $5.00. Fee payee: Hooksett District Court. Personal checks accepted. Prepayment is required.

New London District Court PO Box 1966, New London, NH 03257; 603-526-6519. Hours: 8:30AM-4PM (EST). *Misdemeanor, Civil Actions Under $25,000, Eviction, Small Claims.*

Civil Records: Access: Mail, in person. Only the court conducts in person searches; visitors may not. Search fee: 1-10 names is $10.00; 11-24 names is $25.00; 25+ names is $25.00 per hour. Required to search: name, years to search. Civil cases indexed by defendant, plaintiff. Civil records on computer from 1993, on index cards from 1980, index books from 1800s. An appointment is necessary before performing an in person search. **Criminal Records:** Access: Mail, in person. Only the court conducts in person searches; visitors may not. Search fee: Same fees as civil. Required to search: name, years to search; also helpful-DOB, SSN. Criminal records on computer from 1993, on index cards from 1980, index books from 1800s. An appointment is necessary before performing an in person search. **General Information:** No adoptions, sealed, juvenile, mental health, expunged or dismissed records released. SASE required. Turnaround time 1-2 days. Copy fee:

$.50 per page. Certification fee: $1.00. Fee payee: New London District Court. Personal checks accepted. Prepayment is required.

Probate Court 163 N Main St, Concord, NH 03301; 603-224-9589. Hours: 8AM-4:30PM (EST). *Probate.*

Rockingham County

Superior Court PO Box 1258, Kingston, NH 03848-1258; 603-642-5256. Hours: 8AM-4PM (EST). *Felony, Civil Actions Over $1,500.*

Civil Records: Access: In person only. Only the court conducts in person searches; visitors may not. Search fee: No civil searches performed by court. Required to search: name, years to search. Civil cases indexed by defendant, plaintiff. Civil records on computer from 1988, index cards from 1920, organized 1769. **Criminal Records:** Access: In person only. Only the court conducts in person searches; visitors may not. Search fee: No criminal searches performed by court. Required to search: name, years to search; also helpful-DOB, SSN. Criminal records on computer from 1988, index cards from 1920, organized 1769. **General Information:** No sealed, juvenile, mental health, expunged, annulled records released. Copy fee: $.50 if court makes the copy, $.25 if visitor makes the copy. Certification fee: $5.00. Fee payee: Clerk Superior Court. Personal checks accepted. Prepayment is required.

Auburn District Court 5 Priscilla Lane, Auburn, NH 03032; 603-624-2265; Criminal phone:. Hours: 8AM-4PM (EST). *Misdemeanor, Civil Actions Under $25,000, Eviction, Small Claims.*

Civil Records: Access: Mail, in person. Only the court conducts in person searches; visitors may not. Search fee: The search fee is $25.00 per hour. Required to search: name, years to search; also helpful-address. Civil cases indexed by defendant, plaintiff. Civil records on computer from 5/92, index cards from 1980, index books from 1968. **Criminal Records:** Access: Mail, in person. Only the court conducts in person searches; visitors may not. Search fee: The search fee is $25.00 per hour. Required to search: name, years to search, DOB, signed release. Criminal records on computer from 5/92, index cards from 1980, index books from 1968. **General Information:** No adoptions, sealed, juvenile, mental health, expunged or dismissed records released. SASE required. Turnaround time 3 days. Copy fee: $.50 per page. Certification fee: $5.00. Fee payee: Auburn District Court. Personal checks accepted. Prepayment is required.

Derry District Court 10 Manning St, Derry, NH 03038; 603-434-4676. Hours: 8AM-4PM (EST). *Misdemeanor, Civil Actions Under $25,000, Eviction, Small Claims.*

Civil Records: Access: Phone, mail, in person. Only the court conducts in person searches; visitors may not. Search fee: A $10.00 fee applies for all computer searches for up to 10 names. If searching over 10 names in the computer, the fee is $25.00. For lengthy computer searches, the fee is $25.00 per hour. All index book searches are $25.00 per hour. Required to search: name, years to search. Civil cases indexed by defendant, plaintiff. Civil records on computer from 10/92, on index cards prior. **Criminal Records:** Access: Phone, mail, in person. Only the court conducts in person searches; visitors may not. Search fee: Same as civil. Required to search: name, years to search; also helpful-DOB, SSN. Criminal records on computer from 10/92, on index cards prior.

General Information: No adoptions, sealed, juvenile, mental health, expunged, dismissed or annulment records released. SASE required. Turnaround time 1 week. Copy fee: $.50 per page. Certification fee: $5.00. Fee payee: Derry District Court. Personal checks accepted. Prepayment is required.

Exeter District Court PO Box 394, Exeter, NH 03833; 603-772-2931. Hours: 8AM-4PM (EST). *Misdemeanor, Civil Actions Under $25,000, Eviction, Small Claims.*

Civil Records: Access: Mail, in person. Only the court conducts in person searches; visitors may not. Search fee: See state introduction for standard search fees. Required to search: name, years to search; also helpful-address. Civil cases indexed by defendant, plaintiff. Civil records on computer from 1991. **Criminal Records:** Access: Mail, in person. Both court and visitors may perform in person searches. Search fee: See state introduction for standard search fees. Required to search: name, years to search, DOB, signed release. Criminal records on computer from 1991. **General Information:** No adoptions, sealed, juvenile, mental health, expunged or dismissed records released. SASE required. Turnaround time 3 days. Copy fee: $.50 per page. Certification fee: $5.00. Fee payee: Exeter District Court. Personal checks accepted. Prepayment is required.

Hampton District Court PO Box 10, Hampton, NH 03843-0010; 603-926-8117. Hours: 8AM-4PM (EST). *Misdemeanor, Civil Actions Under $25,000, Eviction, Small Claims.*

Civil Records: Access: Mail, in person. Only the court conducts in person searches; visitors may not. Search fee: A $10.00 fee applies for all computer searches for up to 10 names. If searching over 10 names in the computer, the fee is $25.00. For lengthy computer searches, the fee is $25.00 per hour. All index book searches are $25.00 per hour. Required to search: name, years to search. Civil cases indexed by defendant. Civil records on computer from 4/91, index cards from 1979, index books from 1900s. **Criminal Records:** Access: Mail, in person. Only the court conducts in person searches; visitors may not. Search fee: Same fees as civil. Required to search: name, years to search; also helpful-DOB, SSN. Criminal records on computer from 4/91, index cards from 1979, index books from 1900s. **General Information:** No adoptions, sealed, juvenile, mental health, expunged or dismissed records released. SASE required. Turnaround time 1 week. No copy fee. Certification fee: $5.00. Fee payee: Hampton District Court. Personal checks accepted. Prepayment is required.

Plaistow District Court PO Box 129, Plaistow, NH 03865; 603-382-4651; Fax: 603-382-4952. Hours: 8AM-4PM (EST). *Misdemeanor, Civil Actions Under $25,000, Eviction, Small Claims.*

Civil Records: Access: Mail, in person. Only the court conducts in person searches; visitors may not. Search fee: $10.00 1-9 names; $25.00 10 or more names. $25.00 per hour manual search fee. Required to search: name, years to search. Civil cases indexed by defendant, plaintiff. Civil records on computer from 7/91, index cards from 1980, index books from 1960s. **Criminal Records:** Access: Mail, in person. Only the court conducts in person searches; visitors may not. Search fee: $10.00 1-9 names; $25.00 10 or more names. $25.00 per hour manual search fee. Required to search: name, years to search, DOB. Criminal records on computer from 7/91, index cards from

1980, index books from 1960s. **General Information:** No adoptions, sealed, juvenile, mental health, expunged or dismissed records released. SASE required. Turnaround time 2-3 days. Copy fee: $.50 per page. Certification fee: $5.00. Fee payee: Plaistow District Court. Personal checks accepted. Prepayment is required.

Portsmouth District Court 111 Parrott Ave, Portsmouth, NH 03801; 603-431-2192. Hours: 8AM-4PM (EST). *Misdemeanor, Civil Actions Under $25,000, Eviction, Small Claims.*

Civil Records: Access: Mail, in person. Only the court conducts in person searches; visitors may not. Search fee: $10.00 if computerized search (after 1992), otherwise $35.00. Required to search: name, years to search. Civil cases indexed by defendant, plaintiff. Civil records on computer from 04/92, docket cards from 1980, index books from 1960s. **Criminal Records:** Access: Mail, in person. Only the court conducts in person searches; visitors may not. Search fee: Same fees as civil. Required to search: name, years to search; also helpful-DOB, SSN. Criminal records on computer from 04/92, docket cards from 1980, index books from 1960s. **General Information:** No adoptions, sealed, juvenile, mental health, expunged or dismissed records released. SASE required. Turnaround time 2-3 days. Copy fee: $.50 per page. Certification fee: $1.00 per page. Fee payee: Portsmouth District Court. Personal checks accepted. Prepayment is required.

Salem District Court 35 Geremonty Dr, Salem, NH 03079; 603-893-4483. Hours: 8AM-4PM (EST). *Misdemeanor, Civil Actions Under $25,000, Eviction, Small Claims.*

Civil Records: Access: Mail, in person. Search fee: Fee varies based on number of names per request. Required to search: name, years to search. Civil cases indexed by defendant, plaintiff. Civil records on computer from 4/92, docket cards from 1980, docket books from 1950. An appointment is necessary before performing an in person search. **Criminal Records:** Access: Mail, in person. Only the court conducts in person searches; visitors may not. Search fee: Fee varies based on number of names per request. Required to search: name, years to search, DOB. Criminal records on computer from 4/92, docket cards from 1980, docket books from 1950. **General Information:** No adoptions, sealed, juvenile, mental health, expunged or dismissed records released. SASE required. Turnaround time 2-3 week. Copy fee: $.50 per page. Certification fee: $1.00. Fee payee: Salem District Court. Personal checks accepted. Prepayment is required.

Probate Court PO Box 789, Kingston, NH 03848; 603-642-7117. Hours: 8AM-4PM (EST). *Probate.*

Strafford County

Superior Court PO Box 799, Dover, NH 03821-0799; 603-742-3065. Hours: 8:30AM-4:30PM (EST). *Felony, Civil Actions Over $1,500.*

Civil Records: Access: Mail, in person. Only the court conducts in person searches; visitors may not. No search fee. Required to search: name, years to search. Civil cases indexed by defendant, plaintiff. Civil records on computer from 3/89, index cards from 1970, index books from 1900s, organized 1769. **Criminal Records:** Access: Mail, in person. Only the court conducts in person searches; visitors may not. No search fee. Required to search: name, years to search; also helpful-DOB, SSN. Criminal records on computer

from 3/89, index cards from 1970, index books from 1900s, organized 1769. **General Information:** No sealed, juvenile, mental health, expunged or dismissed records released. SASE required. Turnaround time 1 week. Copy fee: $.50 per page. Certification fee: $5.00. Fee payee: Superior Court Clerk. Personal checks accepted. Prepayment is required.

Dover District Court 25 St Thomas St, Dover, NH 03820; 603-742-7202. Hours: 8AM-4PM (EST). *Misdemeanor, Civil Actions Under $20,000, Eviction, Small Claims.*

Civil Records: Access: Mail, in person. Only the court conducts in person searches; visitors may not. Search fee: $10.00 per name. Required to search: name, years to search. Civil cases indexed by defendant, plaintiff. Civil records on computer from 1993, on index cards from 1980, index books from 1970. **Criminal Records:** Access: Mail, in person. Only the court conducts in person searches; visitors may not. Search fee: $10.00 per name. Required to search: name, years to search, DOB. Criminal records on computer from 1993, on index cards from 1980, index books from 1970. **General Information:** No adoptions, sealed, juvenile, mental health, expunged or dismissed records released. SASE required. Turnaround time 1-2 days. Copy fee: $.50 per page. Certification fee: $5.00. Fee payee: Dover District Court. Personal checks accepted. Prepayment is required.

Durham District Court 1 Main Street, Durham, NH 03824; 603-868-2323. Hours: 8:30AM-4PM (EST). *Misdemeanor, Civil Actions Under $25,000, Eviction, Small Claims.*

Civil Records: Access: Mail, in person. Only the court conducts in person searches; visitors may not. Search fee: See state introduction for standard search fee. Required to search: name, years to search. Civil cases indexed by defendant, plaintiff. Civil records on computer from 1/91, index cards from 1980, index books from 1945. **Criminal Records:** Access: Mail, in person. Only the court conducts in person searches; visitors may not. Search fee: See state introduction for standard search fee. Required to search: name, years to search; also helpful-DOB, SSN. Criminal records on computer from 1/91, index cards from 1980, index books from 1945. **General Information:** No adoptions, sealed, juvenile, mental health, expunged or dismissed records released. SASE required. Turnaround time 4 days. Copy fee: $.50 per page. Certification fee: $5.00. Fee payee: Durham District Court. Personal checks accepted. Prepayment is required.

Rochester District Court 76 N Main St, Rochester, NH 03866; 603-332-3516. Hours: 8AM-4:30PM (EST). *Misdemeanor, Civil Actions Under $25,000, Eviction, Small Claims.*

Civil Records: Access: Mail, in person. Only the court conducts in person searches; visitors may not. Search fee: If on computer, $10 for up to 10 names, $25.00 if over 10 names. If manual, then 25.00. Required to search: name, years to search. Civil cases indexed by defendant, plaintiff. Civil records on computer from 1989, index cards from 7/80, index books from 1960s. **Criminal Records:** Access: Mail, in person. Only the court conducts in person searches; visitors may not. Search fee: Same fees as civil. Required to search: name, years to search; also helpful-DOB. Criminal records on computer from 1989, index cards from 7/80, index books from 1960s. **General Information:** No adoptions, sealed, juvenile, mental health, expunged or dismissed records released. SASE required. Turnaround time 1 week.

Copy fee: $.50 per page. Certification fee: $5.00. Fee payee: Rochester District Court. Only cashiers checks and money orders accepted. Prepayment is required.

Somersworth District Court 2 Pleasant St, Somersworth, NH 03878-2543; 603-692-5967; Fax: 603-692-5752. Hours: 8AM-5:30PM (EST). *Misdemeanor, Civil Actions Under $25,000, Eviction, Small Claims.*

Note: The first 3 Tuesdays of the month the court is open until 8:30PM

Civil Records: Access: Phone, mail, in person. Only the court conducts in person searches; visitors may not. Search fee: Fee is based on type of search. See state introduction. Required to search: name, years to search. Civil cases indexed by defendant, plaintiff. Civil records on computer from 1993, on index cards from 1981, index books from 1960s. **Criminal Records:** Access: Phone, mail, in person. Only the court conducts in person searches; visitors may not. Search fee: Fee is based on type of search. See state introduction. Required to search: name, years to search, DOB. Criminal records on computer from 1993, on index cards from 1981, index books from 1960s. **General Information:** No adoptions, sealed, juvenile, mental health, expunged or dismissed records released. SASE required. Turnaround time 7-10 days. Copy fee: $.50 per page. No fee for computer printouts. Certification fee: $5.00. Fee payee: Somersworth District Court. Personal checks accepted. Credit cards accepted. Prepayment is required.

Probate Court PO Box 799, Dover, NH 03821-0799; 603-742-2550. Hours: 8AM-4:30PM (EST). *Probate.*

Sullivan County

Superior Court 22 Main St, Newport, NH 03773; 603-863-3450. Hours: 8AM-4:30PM (EST). *Felony, Civil Actions Over $1,500.*

Civil Records: Access: Mail, in person. Only the court conducts in person searches; visitors may not. No search fee. Required to search: name, years to search. Civil cases indexed by defendant, plaintiff. Civil records on computer from 1992, on index cards from 1980s, index books from 1800s. **Criminal Records:** Access: Mail, in person. Only the court conducts in person searches; visitors may not. No search fee. Required to search: name, years to search, DOB. Criminal records on computer from 1992, on index cards from 1980s, index books from 1800s. **General Information:** No adoptions, sealed, juvenile, mental health, expunged or dismissed records released. SASE required. Turnaround time 1 week. Copy fee: $.50 per page. Certification fee: $5.00. Fee payee: Sullivan County Superior Court. Personal checks accepted. Prepayment is required.

Claremont District Court PO Box 313, Claremont, NH 03743; 603-542-6064. Hours: 8AM-4PM (EST). *Misdemeanor, Civil Actions Under $25,000, Eviction, Small Claims.*

Civil Records: Access: Phone, mail, in person. Only the court conducts in person searches; visitors may not. Search fee: $10.00 1992 to present. $35.00 prior to 1992. Required to search: name, years to search. Civil cases indexed by defendant, plaintiff. Civil records on computer from 10/92, on index cards from 1980, index books from 1960. **Criminal Records:** Access: Phone, mail, in person. Only the court conducts in person searches; visitors may not. Search fee: $10.00 1992 to present. $35.00 prior to 1992.

Required to search: name, years to search, DOB. Criminal records on computer from 10/92, on index cards from 1980, index books from 1960. **General Information:** No adoptions, sealed, juvenile, mental health, expunged or dismissed records released. SASE required. Turnaround time 1 week. Copy fee: $.50 per page. Certification fee: $5.00. Fee payee: Claremont District Court. Personal checks accepted. Prepayment is required.

Newport District Court PO Box 581, Newport, NH 03773; 603-863-1832. Hours: 8AM-4PM (EST). *Misdemeanor, Civil Actions Under $25,000, Eviction, Small Claims.*

Civil Records: Access: Phone, mail, in person. Only the court conducts in person searches; visitors may not. Search fee: $25.00 per hour. Required to search: name, years to search. Civil cases indexed by defendant, plaintiff. Civil records on computer from 1993, on index cards from 1980, index books from 1960s. **Criminal Records:** Access: Phone, mail, in person. Only the court conducts in person searches; visitors may not. Search fee: $25.00 per hour. Required to search:

name, years to search, DOB. Criminal records on computer from 1993, on index cards from 1980, index books from 1960s. **General Information:** No adoptions, sealed, juvenile, mental health, expunged or dismissed records released. SASE required. Turnaround time 2-3 days. Copy fee: $.50 per page. Certification fee: $1.00. Fee payee: Newport District Court. Personal checks accepted. Prepayment is required.

Probate Court PO Box 417, Newport, NH 03773; 603-863-3150. Hours: 8AM-4:30PM (EST). *Probate.*

ORGANIZATION

238 cities/towns and 10 counties, 10 recording offices and 242 UCC filing offices. The recording officers are Town/City Clerk (UCC) and Register of Deeds (real estate only). Each town/city profile indicates the county in which the town/city is located. **Be careful to distinguish the following names that are identical for both a town/city and a county**—Grafton, Hillsborough, Merrimack, Strafford, and Sullivan. Many towns are so small that their mailing addresses are within another town. The following unincorporated towns do **not** have a Town Clerk, so all liens are located at the corresponding county: Cambridge (Coos), Dicksville (Coos), Green's Grant (Coos), Hale's Location (Carroll), Millsfield (Coos), and Wentworth's Location (Coos). The entire state is in the Eastern Time Zone (EST).

REAL ESTATE RECORDS

Real estate transactions are recorded at the county level, and property taxes are handled at the town/city level. Local town real estate ownership and assessment records are usually located at the Selectman's Office. Each town/city profile indicates the county in which the town/city is located. Most counties will **not** perform real estate searches. Copy fees vary. Certification fees generally are $2.00 per document.

UCC RECORDS

This is a **dual filing state**. Financing statements are filed at the state level and with the Town/City Clerk, except for consumer goods and farm related collateral, which are filed only with the Town/City Clerk, and real estate related collateral, which are filed with the county Register of Deeds. Most recording offices will perform UCC searches. Use search request form UCC-11. Search fees are usually $5.00 per debtor name using the standard UCC-11 request form and $7.00 using a non-standard form. Copy fees are usually $.75 per page.

TAX LIEN RECORDS

Federal and state tax liens on personal property of businesses are filed with the Secretary of State. Other federal and state tax liens on personal property are filed with the Town/City Clerk. Federal and state tax liens on real property are filed with the county Register of Deeds. There is wide variation in indexing and searching practices among the recording offices. Where a search fee of $7.00 is indicated, it refers to a non-standard request form such as a letter.

OTHER LIENS

Condominium, town tax, mechanics, welfare.

Belknap County
County Register of Deeds, P.O. Box 1343, Laconia, NH 03247-1343. 603-527-5420. Fax: 603-527-5429.

Berlin City
City Clerk, 168 Main Street, City Hall, Berlin, NH 03570. 603-752-2340. Fax: 603-752-8586.

Carroll County
County Register of Deeds, P.O. Box 163, Ossipee, NH 03864-0163. 603-539-4872. Fax: 603-539-5239.

Cheshire County
County Register of Deeds, 33 West Street, Keene, NH 03431. 603-352-0403. Fax: 603-352-7678.

Claremont City
City Clerk, City Hall - Finance Office, 58 Tremont Square, Claremont, NH 03743. 603-542-7001. Fax: 603-542-7014.

Concord City
City Clerk, 41 Green Street, Room 2, Concord, NH 03301-4255. 603-225-8500. Fax: 603-228-2724.
Online Access: Assessor. Records on the City of Concord Assessor's database are available free on the Internet at http://140.239.211.227/concordnh. User ID is required; registration is free.

Coos County
County Register of Deeds, Coos County Courthouse, 55 School St, Suite 103, Lancaster, NH 03584. 603-788-2392. Fax: 603-788-4291.

Dover City
City Clerk, 288 Central Avenue, City Hall, Dover, NH 03820. 603-743-6021. Fax: 603-790-6322.

Franklin City
City Clerk, 316 Central Street, Franklin, NH 03235. 603-934-3109.

Grafton County
County Register of Deeds, RR 1, Box 65B, North Haverhill, NH 03774-9700. 603-787-6921. Fax: 603-787-2363.
Online Access: Real Estate, Liens. Access to Grafton County records requires a $100 set up fee plus $40 monthly. Two years of data are kept on the system; prior years are on CD-ROM. System operates 24 hours daily and supports a baud rate of 9,600. Lending agency information is available For information, contact Carol Elliot at 603-787-6921. A fax back service available for instate only; first page is $4.00, second $3.00; adn'l are $2.00.

Hillsborough County
County Register of Deeds, P.O. Box 370, Nashua, NH 03061-0370. 603-882-6933. Fax: 603-594-4137.

Keene City
City Clerk, 3 Washington Street, Keene, NH 03431. 603-352-0133. Fax: 603-357-9884.

Laconia City
City Clerk, P.O. Box 489, Laconia, NH 03247. 603-527-1265. Fax: 603-524-1520.

Lebanon City
City Clerk, 51 North Park Street, Lebanon, NH 03766. 603-448-3054. Fax: 603-448-4891.
Online Access: Assessor. Records on the Assessor's Taxpayer Information System database are available free online at http://140.239.211.227/lebanonnh. Search by street name & number, map/block/lot/unit, or account number.

Manchester City
City Clerk, One City Hall Plaza, Manchester, NH 03101. 603-624-6455. Fax: 603-624-6481.

Merrimack County
County Register of Deeds, P.O. Box 248, Concord, NH 03302-0248. 603-228-0101. Fax: 603-226-0868. www.nhdeeds.com
Online Access: real estate. Search free on the Internet. Records available from 1960 to present month.

Nashua City
City Clerk, 229 Main Street, Nashua, NH 03061-2019. 603-594-3305. Fax: 603-594-3451.

Portsmouth City
City Clerk, P.O. Box 628, Portsmouth, NH 03802-0628. 603-431-2000. Fax: 603-427-1526.

Rochester City
City Clerk, 31 Wakefield Street, City Hall, Rochester, NH 03867-1917. 603-332-2130. Fax: 603-335-7565.

Rockingham County
County Register of Deeds, P.O. Box 896, Kingston, NH 03848. 603-642-5526. Fax: 603-642-8548.

Somersworth City
City Clerk, 157 Main Street, Somersworth, NH 03878-3192. 603-692-4262. Fax: 603-692-7338.

Strafford County
County Register of Deeds, P.O. Box 799, Dover, NH 03820. 603-742-1741. Fax: 603-749-5130.

Sullivan County
County Register of Deeds, P.O. Box 448, Newport, NH 03773. 603-863-2110. Fax: 603-863-0013.

You will usually be able to find the city name in the City/County Cross Reference below. In that case, it is a simple matter to determine the county from the cross reference. However, only the official US Postal Service city names are included in this index. There are an additional 40,000 place names that people use in their addresses. Therefore, we have also included a ZIP/City Cross Reference immediately following the City/County Cross Reference.

If you know the ZIP Code but the city name does not appear in the City/County Cross Reference index, look up the ZIP Code in the ZIP/City Cross Reference, find the city name, then look up the city name in the City/County Cross Reference. For example, you want to know the county for an address of Menands, NY 12204. There is no "Menands" in the City/County Cross Reference. The ZIP/City Cross Reference shows that ZIP Codes 12201-12288 are for the city of Albany. Looking back in the City/County Cross Reference, Albany is in Albany County.

City/County Cross Reference

ACWORTH Sullivan
ALSTEAD Cheshire
ALTON Belknap
ALTON BAY Belknap
AMHERST Hillsborough
ANDOVER Merrimack
ANTRIM Hillsborough
ASHLAND Grafton
ASHUELOT Cheshire
ATKINSON Rockingham
AUBURN Rockingham
BARNSTEAD Belknap
BARRINGTON Strafford
BARTLETT Carroll
BATH Grafton
BEDFORD Hillsborough
BELMONT Belknap
BENNINGTON Hillsborough
BERLIN Coos
BETHLEHEM Grafton
BOW Merrimack
BRADFORD Merrimack
BRETTON WOODS Coos
BRISTOL Grafton
BROOKLINE Hillsborough
CAMPTON Grafton
CANAAN Grafton
CANDIA Rockingham
CANTERBURY Merrimack
CENTER BARNSTEAD Belknap
CENTER CONWAY Carroll
CENTER HARBOR Belknap
CENTER OSSIPEE Carroll
CENTER SANDWICH Carroll
CENTER STRAFFORD Strafford
CENTER TUFTONBORO Carroll
CHARLESTOWN Sullivan
CHESTER Rockingham
CHESTERFIELD Cheshire
CHOCORUA Carroll
CLAREMONT Sullivan
COLEBROOK Coos
CONCORD Merrimack
CONTOOCOOK Merrimack
CONWAY Carroll
CORNISH Sullivan
CORNISH FLAT Sullivan
DANBURY Merrimack
DANVILLE Rockingham
DEERFIELD Rockingham
DERRY Rockingham
DOVER Strafford
DREWSVILLE Cheshire
DUBLIN Cheshire
DURHAM Strafford
EAST ANDOVER Merrimack
EAST CANDIA Rockingham
EAST DERRY Rockingham
EAST HAMPSTEAD Rockingham
EAST HEBRON Grafton
EAST KINGSTON Rockingham
EAST WAKEFIELD Carroll
EATON CENTER Carroll
ELKINS Merrimack

ENFIELD (03748) Grafton(98), Sullivan(2)
ENFIELD CENTER Grafton
EPPING Rockingham
EPSOM Merrimack
ERROL Coos
ETNA Grafton
EXETER Rockingham
FARMINGTON Strafford
FITZWILLIAM Cheshire
FRANCESTOWN Hillsborough
FRANCONIA Grafton
FRANKLIN Merrimack
FREEDOM Carroll
FREMONT Rockingham
GEORGES MILLS Sullivan
GILMANTON Belknap
GILMANTON IRON WORKS Belknap
GILSUM Cheshire
GLEN Carroll
GLENCLIFF Grafton
GOFFSTOWN (03045) Hillsborough(87),
   Merrimack(13)
GORHAM Coos
GOSHEN Sullivan
GRAFTON Grafton
GRANTHAM Sullivan
GREENFIELD Hillsborough
GREENLAND Rockingham
GREENVILLE Hillsborough
GROVETON Coos
GUILD Sullivan
HAMPSTEAD Rockingham
HAMPTON Rockingham
HAMPTON FALLS Rockingham
HANCOCK Hillsborough
HANOVER Grafton
HARRISVILLE Cheshire
HAVERHILL Grafton
HEBRON Grafton
HENNIKER (03242) Merrimack(98),
   Hillsborough(2)
HILL (03243) Merrimack(95), Grafton(5)
HILLSBORO (03244) Hillsborough(98),
   Sullivan(2)
HINSDALE Cheshire
HOLDERNESS Grafton
HOLLIS Hillsborough
HOOKSETT Merrimack
HUDSON Hillsborough
INTERVALE Carroll
JACKSON Carroll
JAFFREY Cheshire
JEFFERSON Coos
KEARSARGE Carroll
KEENE Cheshire
KINGSTON Rockingham
LACONIA Belknap
LANCASTER Coos
LEBANON Grafton
LEMPSTER Sullivan
LINCOLN Grafton
LISBON Grafton
LITCHFIELD Hillsborough
LITTLETON Grafton

LOCHMERE Belknap
LONDONDERRY Rockingham
LYME Grafton
LYME CENTER Grafton
LYNDEBOROUGH Hillsborough
MADISON Carroll
MANCHESTER Hillsborough
MARLBOROUGH Cheshire
MARLOW Cheshire
MEADOWS Coos
MELVIN VILLAGE Carroll
MEREDITH Belknap
MERIDEN Sullivan
MERRIMACK Hillsborough
MILAN Coos
MILFORD Hillsborough
MILTON Strafford
MILTON MILLS Strafford
MIRROR LAKE Carroll
MONROE Grafton
MONT VERNON Hillsborough
MOULTONBOROUGH Carroll
MOUNT SUNAPEE Merrimack
MOUNT WASHINGTON Coos
MUNSONVILLE Cheshire
NASHUA Hillsborough
NEW BOSTON Hillsborough
NEW CASTLE Rockingham
NEW DURHAM Strafford
NEW HAMPTON Belknap
NEW IPSWICH Hillsborough
NEW LONDON (03257) Merrimack(98),
   Sullivan(2)
NEWBURY Merrimack
NEWFIELDS Rockingham
NEWMARKET Rockingham
NEWPORT Sullivan
NEWTON Rockingham
NEWTON JUNCTION Rockingham
NORTH CONWAY Carroll
NORTH HAMPTON Rockingham
NORTH HAVERHILL Grafton
NORTH SALEM Rockingham
NORTH SANDWICH Carroll
NORTH STRATFORD Coos
NORTH SUTTON Merrimack
NORTH WALPOLE Cheshire
NORTH WOODSTOCK Grafton
NORTHWOOD Rockingham
NOTTINGHAM Rockingham
ORFORD Grafton
OSSIPEE Carroll
PELHAM Hillsborough
PETERBOROUGH Hillsborough
PIERMONT Grafton
PIKE Grafton
PITTSBURG Coos
PITTSFIELD Merrimack
PLAINFIELD Sullivan
PLAISTOW Rockingham
PLYMOUTH Grafton
PORTSMOUTH Rockingham
RAYMOND Rockingham
RINDGE Cheshire

ROCHESTER Strafford
ROLLINSFORD Strafford
RUMNEY Grafton
RYE Rockingham
RYE BEACH Rockingham
SALEM Rockingham
SALISBURY Merrimack
SANBORNTON Belknap
SANBORNVILLE Carroll
SANDOWN Rockingham
SEABROOK Rockingham
SILVER LAKE Carroll
SOMERSWORTH Strafford
SOUTH ACWORTH Sullivan
SOUTH EFFINGHAM Carroll
SOUTH NEWBURY Merrimack
SOUTH SUTTON Merrimack
SOUTH TAMWORTH Carroll
SPOFFORD Cheshire
SPRINGFIELD Sullivan
STINSON LAKE Grafton
STODDARD Cheshire
STRAFFORD Strafford
STRATHAM Rockingham
SULLIVAN Cheshire
SUNAPEE Sullivan
SUNCOOK Merrimack
SWANZEY Cheshire
TAMWORTH Carroll
TEMPLE Hillsborough
TILTON (03276) Belknap(59),
   Merrimack(41)
TROY Cheshire
TWIN MOUNTAIN Coos
UNION (03887) Strafford(74), Carroll(26)
WALPOLE Cheshire
WARNER Merrimack
WARREN Grafton
WASHINGTON Sullivan
WATERVILLE VALLEY Grafton
WEARE Hillsborough
WENTWORTH Grafton
WEST CHESTERFIELD Cheshire
WEST LEBANON Grafton
WEST NOTTINGHAM Rockingham
WEST OSSIPEE Carroll
WEST PETERBOROUGH Hillsborough
WEST STEWARTSTOWN Coos
WEST SWANZEY Cheshire
WESTMORELAND Cheshire
WHITEFIELD Coos
WILMOT Merrimack
WILTON Hillsborough
WINCHESTER Cheshire
WINDHAM Rockingham
WINNISQUAM Belknap
WOLFEBORO Carroll
WOLFEBORO FALLS Carroll
WONALANCET Carroll
WOODSTOCK Grafton
WOODSVILLE Grafton

ZIP/City Cross Reference

ZIP	City	ZIP	City	ZIP	City	ZIP	City
00210-00215	PORTSMOUTH	03244-03244	HILLSBORO	03470-03470	WINCHESTER	03812-03812	BARTLETT
03031-03031	AMHERST	03245-03245	HOLDERNESS	03561-03561	LITTLETON	03813-03813	CENTER CONWAY
03032-03032	AUBURN	03246-03247	LACONIA	03570-03570	BERLIN	03814-03814	CENTER OSSIPEE
03033-03033	BROOKLINE	03251-03251	LINCOLN	03574-03574	BETHLEHEM	03815-03815	CENTER STRAFFORD
03034-03034	CANDIA	03252-03252	LOCHMERE	03575-03575	BRETTON WOODS	03816-03816	CENTER TUFTONBORO
03036-03036	CHESTER	03253-03253	MEREDITH	03576-03576	COLEBROOK	03817-03817	CHOCORUA
03037-03037	DEERFIELD	03254-03254	MOULTONBOROUGH	03579-03579	ERROL	03818-03818	CONWAY
03038-03038	DERRY	03255-03255	NEWBURY	03580-03580	FRANCONIA	03819-03819	DANVILLE
03040-03040	EAST CANDIA	03256-03256	NEW HAMPTON	03581-03581	GORHAM	03820-03822	DOVER
03041-03041	EAST DERRY	03257-03257	NEW LONDON	03582-03582	GROVETON	03824-03824	DURHAM
03042-03042	EPPING	03259-03259	NORTH SANDWICH	03583-03583	JEFFERSON	03825-03825	BARRINGTON
03043-03043	FRANCESTOWN	03260-03260	NORTH SUTTON	03584-03584	LANCASTER	03826-03826	EAST HAMPSTEAD
03044-03044	FREMONT	03261-03261	NORTHWOOD	03585-03585	LISBON	03827-03827	EAST KINGSTON
03045-03045	GOFFSTOWN	03262-03262	NORTH WOODSTOCK	03587-03587	MEADOWS	03830-03830	EAST WAKEFIELD
03047-03047	GREENFIELD	03263-03263	PITTSFIELD	03588-03588	MILAN	03832-03832	EATON CENTER
03048-03048	GREENVILLE	03264-03264	PLYMOUTH	03589-03589	MOUNT WASHINGTON	03833-03833	EXETER
03049-03049	HOLLIS	03266-03266	RUMNEY	03590-03590	NORTH STRATFORD	03835-03835	FARMINGTON
03051-03051	HUDSON	03268-03268	SALISBURY	03592-03592	PITTSBURG	03836-03836	FREEDOM
03052-03052	LITCHFIELD	03269-03269	SANBORNTON	03595-03595	TWIN MOUNTAIN	03837-03837	GILMANTON IRON
03053-03053	LONDONDERRY	03272-03272	SOUTH NEWBURY	03597-03597	WEST STEWARTSTOWN		WORKS
03054-03054	MERRIMACK	03273-03273	SOUTH SUTTON	03598-03598	WHITEFIELD	03838-03838	GLEN
03055-03055	MILFORD	03274-03274	STINSON LAKE	03601-03601	ACWORTH	03839-03839	ROCHESTER
03057-03057	MONT VERNON	03275-03275	SUNCOOK	03602-03602	ALSTEAD	03840-03840	GREENLAND
03060-03063	NASHUA	03276-03276	TILTON	03603-03603	CHARLESTOWN	03841-03841	HAMPSTEAD
03070-03070	NEW BOSTON	03278-03278	WARNER	03604-03604	DREWSVILLE	03842-03843	HAMPTON
03071-03071	NEW IPSWICH	03279-03279	WARREN	03605-03605	LEMPSTER	03844-03844	HAMPTON FALLS
03073-03073	NORTH SALEM	03280-03280	WASHINGTON	03607-03607	SOUTH ACWORTH	03845-03845	INTERVALE
03076-03076	PELHAM	03281-03281	WEARE	03608-03608	WALPOLE	03846-03846	JACKSON
03077-03077	RAYMOND	03282-03282	WENTWORTH	03609-03609	NORTH WALPOLE	03847-03847	KEARSARGE
03079-03079	SALEM	03284-03284	SPRINGFIELD	03740-03740	BATH	03848-03848	KINGSTON
03082-03082	LYNDEBOROUGH	03287-03287	WILMOT	03741-03741	CANAAN	03849-03849	MADISON
03084-03084	TEMPLE	03289-03289	WINNISQUAM	03743-03743	CLAREMONT	03850-03850	MELVIN VILLAGE
03086-03086	WILTON	03290-03290	NOTTINGHAM	03745-03745	CORNISH	03851-03851	MILTON
03087-03087	WINDHAM	03291-03291	WEST NOTTINGHAM	03746-03746	CORNISH FLAT	03852-03852	MILTON MILLS
03101-03105	MANCHESTER	03293-03293	WOODSTOCK	03748-03748	ENFIELD	03853-03853	MIRROR LAKE
03106-03106	HOOKSETT	03301-03303	CONCORD	03749-03749	ENFIELD CENTER	03854-03854	NEW CASTLE
03107-03109	MANCHESTER	03304-03304	BOW	03750-03750	ETNA	03855-03855	NEW DURHAM
03110-03110	BEDFORD	03305-03305	CONCORD	03751-03751	GEORGES MILLS	03856-03856	NEWFIELDS
03111-03111	MANCHESTER	03431-03435	KEENE	03752-03752	GOSHEN	03857-03857	NEWMARKET
03215-03215	WATERVILLE VALLEY	03440-03440	ANTRIM	03753-03753	GRANTHAM	03858-03858	NEWTON
03216-03216	ANDOVER	03441-03441	ASHUELOT	03754-03754	GUILD	03859-03859	NEWTON JUNCTION
03217-03217	ASHLAND	03442-03442	BENNINGTON	03755-03755	HANOVER	03860-03860	NORTH CONWAY
03218-03218	BARNSTEAD	03443-03443	CHESTERFIELD	03756-03756	LEBANON	03862-03862	NORTH HAMPTON
03220-03220	BELMONT	03444-03444	DUBLIN	03765-03765	HAVERHILL	03864-03864	OSSIPEE
03221-03221	BRADFORD	03445-03445	SULLIVAN	03766-03766	LEBANON	03865-03865	PLAISTOW
03222-03222	BRISTOL	03446-03446	SWANZEY	03768-03768	LYME	03866-03868	ROCHESTER
03223-03223	CAMPTON	03447-03447	FITZWILLIAM	03769-03769	LYME CENTER	03869-03869	ROLLINSFORD
03224-03224	CANTERBURY	03448-03448	GILSUM	03770-03770	MERIDEN	03870-03870	RYE
03225-03225	CENTER BARNSTEAD	03449-03449	HANCOCK	03771-03771	MONROE	03871-03871	RYE BEACH
03226-03226	CENTER HARBOR	03450-03450	HARRISVILLE	03772-03772	MOUNT SUNAPEE	03872-03872	SANBORNVILLE
03227-03227	CENTER SANDWICH	03451-03451	HINSDALE	03773-03773	NEWPORT	03873-03873	SANDOWN
03229-03229	CONTOOCOOK	03452-03452	JAFFREY	03774-03774	NORTH HAVERHILL	03874-03874	SEABROOK
03230-03230	DANBURY	03455-03455	MARLBOROUGH	03777-03777	ORFORD	03875-03875	SILVER LAKE
03231-03231	EAST ANDOVER	03456-03456	MARLOW	03779-03779	PIERMONT	03878-03878	SOMERSWORTH
03232-03232	EAST HEBRON	03457-03457	MUNSONVILLE	03780-03780	PIKE	03882-03882	SOUTH EFFINGHAM
03233-03233	ELKINS	03458-03458	PETERBOROUGH	03781-03781	PLAINFIELD	03883-03883	SOUTH TAMWORTH
03234-03234	EPSOM	03461-03461	RINDGE	03782-03782	SUNAPEE	03884-03884	STRAFFORD
03235-03235	FRANKLIN	03462-03462	SPOFFORD	03784-03784	WEST LEBANON	03885-03885	STRATHAM
03237-03237	GILMANTON	03464-03464	STODDARD	03785-03785	WOODSVILLE	03886-03886	TAMWORTH
03238-03238	GLENCLIFF	03465-03465	TROY	03801-03804	PORTSMOUTH	03887-03887	UNION
03240-03240	GRAFTON	03466-03466	WEST CHESTERFIELD	03805-03805	ROLLINSFORD	03890-03890	WEST OSSIPEE
03241-03241	HEBRON	03467-03467	WESTMORELAND	03809-03809	ALTON	03894-03894	WOLFEBORO
03242-03242	HENNIKER	03468-03468	WEST PETERBOROUGH	03810-03810	ALTON BAY	03896-03896	WOLFEBORO FALLS
03243-03243	HILL	03469-03469	WEST SWANZEY	03811-03811	ATKINSON	03897-03897	WONALANCET

New Jersey

General Help Numbers:

Governor's Office
PO Box 001, 125 W State St
Trenton, NJ 08625-0001
www.state.nj.us/governor

609-292-6000
Fax 609-292-3454
8:30AM-4:30PM

Attorney General's Office
Law & Public Safety Department
PO Box 080, 25 Market St
Trenton, NJ 08625-0080
www.state.nj.us/lps

609-292-8740
Fax 609-292-3508
8:30AM-5PM

State Court Administrator
RJH Justice Complex
PO Box 037, Courts Bldg, 7th Floor
Trenton, NJ 08625
www.judiciary.state.nj.us/admin.htm

609-984-0275
Fax 609-984-6968
8:30AM-4:30PM

State Archives
PO Box 307, 225 W. State Street, L2
Trenton, NJ 08625-0307
www.state.nj.us/state/darm/archives.html

609-633-8334
Fax 609-396-2454

State Specifics:

Capital: Trenton
                          Mercer County

Time Zone: EST

Number of Counties: 21

Population: 8,143,412

Web Site: www.state.nj.us

State Agencies

Criminal Records

Division of State Police, Records and Identification Section, PO Box 7068, West Trenton, NJ 08628-0068; 609-882-2000 x2878, 609-530-5780 (Fax), 9AM-5PM.

www.state.nj.us/njsp

Note: For requesters not living in the state, it is advised to contact a NJ-based investigator to obtain the record.

Searching: Criminal records are not open to the public, but can be obtained by NJ employers, NJ volunteer organizations, NJ private investigators, NJ attorney firms, and the subject. Include the following in your request-date of birth, Social Security Number, set of fingerprints. The name must match exactly. All requesters, except attorney firms, must submit Form 212 B which must be signed by the subject. Attorney firms do not need the subject's signature.

Access by: mail, in person.

Fee & Payment: The fee is $15.00 for a name check and $25.00 for a full check with fingerprints. Fee payee: Division of State Police-SBI. Prepayment required. No credit cards accepted.

Mail search: Turnaround time: 5-10 working days.

In person search: Searching is available in person.

Corporation Records
Limited Liability Company Records
Fictitious Name
Limited Partnerships

Division of Revenue, Business Support Services Bureau, PO 308, Trenton, NJ 08625 (Courier: 225 W State St, 3rd Fl, Trenton, NJ 08608); 609-292-9292, 8:30AM-5:00PM.

www.state.nj.us/njbgs

Indexing & Storage: Records are available from inception of laws. New records are available for

911

inquiry immediately. Records are indexed on inhouse computer.

Searching: Include the following in your request- full name of business. In addition to the articles of incorporation, corporation records include the following information: Annual Reports, Officers, Directors, Prior (merged) names, Inactive and Reserved names. Assumed names are located at the county level.

Access by: mail, phone, in person, online.

Fee & Payment: A status report is $5.00. Copies are $1.00 per page (except LLC, then $10.00 first and $2.00 each additional). There is a $25.00 ($15.00 if non-profit) fee to certify a document. A Good Standing is $25.00. Fee payee: Treasurer, State of NJ Prepayment required. Ongoing requesters may set up a pre-paid account. Call 609-633-8255 for more information. Personal checks accepted. Credit cards accepted: Mastercard, Visa, Discover, AMEX

Mail search: Turnaround time: 2-3 weeks.

Phone search: This is considered expedited service.

In person search: You can look at 3 records per day for no fee. Copies can be provided. The turnaround time is over 1 week.

Online search: Records are available from the New Jersey Business Gateway Service (NJBGS) web site at www.state.nj.us/njbgs. There is no fee to browse the site to locate a name; however fees are involved for copies or status reports.

Expedited service: Expedited service is available for phone and in person searches. Turnaround time: 8.5 business hours. Add $10.00 per search. Records may be picked up the next day.

Trademarks/Servicemarks

Department of Treasury, Trademark Division, PO Box 453, Trenton, NJ 08625-0453 (Courier: 225 W State St, 3rd Floor, Trenton, NJ 08608); 609-633-8259, 8AM-5PM.

Indexing & Storage: Records are available from the inception of the Division. It takes 2-3 days before new records are available for inquiry. Records are indexed on computer.

Searching: Include the following in your request- trademark/servicemark name, name of owner, date of application. Information returned includes name and address of owner and date of filing.

Access by: mail, in person.

Fee & Payment: Search fee is $25.00 for up to 3 names, which includes copy costs. Fee payee: NJ State Treasurer. Prepayment required. Personal checks accepted. No credit cards accepted.

Mail search: Turnaround time: 1 week. No self addressed stamped envelope is required.

In person search: You can take the request in person, but they return the records by mail unless expedited service is requested.

Uniform Commercial Code

UCC Section, Secretary of State, PO 303, Trenton, NJ 08625 (Courier: 225 West State St, Trenton, NJ 08608); 609-292-9292, 8AM-5PM.

www.state.nj.us/njbgs

Note: The state plans to place the Index on the Internet in 2001. Fees will be involved.

Indexing & Storage: Records are indexed on inhouse computer.

Searching: Use search request form UCC-11. Federal tax liens are filed at the county level. State tax liens follow two rules: certificates of debt are filed in Superior Court at Trenton; a warrant of execution is filed at the county level. Include the following in your request-debtor name, address.

Access by: mail, fax, in person.

Fee & Payment: The fee is $25.00 for a search certificate per debtor name, $25.00 for certification of any document, copies are $1.00 per page. Fee payee: Secretary of State. Prepayment required. Regular requesters can set up a pre-paid account, call 609-530-6424. Personal checks accepted. Credit cards accepted: Mastercard, Visa.

Mail search: Turnaround time: 2 weeks. A self addressed stamped envelope is requested.

Fax search: You can order using a credit card; however, results will be mailed or available for pickup by a courier.

In person search: Information is mailed, unless you pay the $10.00 expedite fee for 24 hour service.

Expedited service: Expedited service is available for mail and phone searches. Turnaround time: same day if possible. Add $10.00 per name. This is not available for mail-in requests.

Federal Tax Liens
State Tax Liens

Records not maintained by a state level agency.

Note: Federal tax liens are filed at the county clerk or register of deeds. All state "docketed judgments" are filed at the superior court in Trenton. "Certificates of Debt" are filed at the respective county superior court.

Sales Tax Registrations

Records not maintained by a state level agency.

Note: Sales tax information is considered confidential. The only way to verify if an entity has a license is to ask to look at the certificate at the place of business, per Joan Bench, Chief of Taxpayer Services Branch.

Birth Certificates

Department of Health, Bureau of Vital Statistics, PO Box 370, Trenton, NJ 08625-0370 (Courier: S Warren St, Room 504, Health & Agriculture Building, Trenton, NJ 08625); 609-292-4087, 609-633-2860 (Credit Card Requests), 609-392-4292 (Fax), 9AM-5PM.

www.state.nj.us/health/vital/vital.htm

Indexing & Storage: Records are available from 1878-present. New records are available for inquiry immediately. Records are indexed on microfiche.

Searching: The general public is denied access to records. You must include the county in your request if it is regarding events before 1903. Include the following in your request-full name, names of parents, mother's maiden name, date of birth, place of birth.

Access by: mail, phone, fax, in person.

Fee & Payment: The fee is $4.00 per record. Add $2.00 per copy for additional copies. Add $1.00 per year for each additional year searched. The fee for using a credit card is $8.95. Fee payee: New Jersey Department of Health & Senior Services. Prepayment required. Personal checks accepted. Credit cards accepted: Mastercard, Visa, AmEx, Discover.

Mail search: Turnaround time: 3-4 weeks. No self addressed stamped envelope is required.

Phone search: Must use a credit card. The hours are 8AM to 3PM.

Fax search: Same criteria as phone searching.

In person search: Turnaround time 2 hours.

Expedited service: Expedited service is available for fax searches. Turnaround time: 2-3 days. Add fee of overnight carrier ($14.75) if used, plus credit card fee.

Death Records

Department of Health, Bureau of Vital Statistics, PO Box 370, Trenton, NJ 08625-0370 (Courier: S Warren St, Room 504, Health & Agriculture Building, Trenton, NJ 08625); 609-292-4087, 609-633-2860 (Credit Card Requests), 609-392-4292 (Fax), 9AM-4PM.

www.state.nj.us/health

Indexing & Storage: Records are available from 1878-present. It takes the 10th of the following month before new records are available for inquiry. Records are indexed on microfiche.

Searching: Cause of death, unless immediate family, is not released. Only those with a legal interest may obtain a record. Include the following in your request-full name, date of death, place of death, Social Security Number.

Access by: mail, phone, fax, in person.

Fee & Payment: The fee is $4.00 per record. Add $2.00 per copy for additional copies. Add $1.00 per year for each additional year searched. Add $8.95 if credit card is used. Fee payee: NJ Department of Health and Senior Services. Prepayment required. Personal checks accepted. Credit cards accepted: Mastercard, Visa, AmEx, Discover.

Mail search: Turnaround time: 1 month. No self addressed stamped envelope is required.

Phone search: Must use a credit card.

Fax search: Same criteria as phone, turnaround time is 10-15 days.

In person search: Turnaround time 2 hours.

Expedited service: Expedited service is available for mail, phone and fax searches. Turnaround time: 2-3 days. Add carrier fee of $14.75 plus the $8.95 credit card fee.

Marriage Certificates

Department of Health, Bureau of Vital Statistics, PO Box 370, Trenton, NJ 08625-0370 (Courier: S Warren St, Room 504, Health & Agriculture Building, Trenton, NJ 08625); 609-292-4087, 609-633-2860 (Credit Card Requests), 609-392-4292 (Fax), 8:45AM-5PM.

ww.state.nj.us/health

Indexing & Storage: Records are available from 1878-present. New records are available for inquiry immediately. Records are indexed on microfiche.

Searching: The general public is denied access to the records. You must include the county in your request if it is regarding events before 1903. Include the following in your request-names of husband and wife, date of marriage, place or county of marriage.

Access by: mail, phone, fax, in person.

Fee & Payment: The fee is $4.00 per record. Add $2.00 per copy for additional copies. Add $1.00 per year for each additional year searched. The fee to use a credit card is $8.95. Fee payee: New Jersey Department of Health. Prepayment required. Personal checks accepted. Credit cards accepted: Mastercard, Visa, AmEx, Discover.

Mail search: Turnaround time: 3-4 weeks. No self addressed stamped envelope is required.

Phone search: Must use a credit card. The hours are from 8AM to 3PM.

Fax search: Same criteria as phone searches.

In person search: Turnaround time 2 hours.

Expedited service: Expedited service is available for fax searches. Turnaround time: 2-3 days. Add $14.75 carrier fees for overnight shipping and the $8.95 credit card fee.

Divorce Records

Clerk of Superior Court, Records Center, PO Box 967, Trenton, NJ 08625-0967 (Courier: Corner of Jerser & Tremont Streets, Building #2, Trenton, NJ 08625); 609-777-0092, 609-777-0094 (Fax), 8:30AM-4PM.

Indexing & Storage: Records are available until 9/89. Records after 1989 must be obtained from the Family Division Court in county of occurrence.

Searching: Also provide married name, unless maiden name was used during the marraige. Information on cases that are impounded is not released. Include the following in your request-names of husband and wife, date of divorce, year divorce case began, docket number (if known). No copies are made and no records are retrieved after 3:30PM.

Access by: mail, fax, in person.

Fee & Payment: There is no search fee, but there is a $10.00 certification fee. Fee payee: Clerk of Superior Court. Prepayment required. If you are not sure how many pages the results or your request will be, you may send a blank check with "Not to exceed $25.00" written in the memo. Personal checks accepted. No credit cards accepted.

Mail search: Turnaround time: 2-3 weeks. Mail is the preferred request method.A self addressed stamped envelope is requested.

Fax search: Requesters must be pre-approved to fax, and only written information is faxed back. Attorneys with charge accounts with the Superior Court can receive copies, without the seal of the court, via fax.

In person search: Turnaround time: while you wait. The Clerk's Office recommends that you not come to the office in person except for emergency requests.

Workers' Compensation Records

Labor Department, Division of Workers Compensation, John Fitch Plaza, PO Box 381, Trenton, NJ 08625 (Courier: Labor Building, 6th Floor, John Fitch Plaza, Trenton, NJ 08625); 609-292-6026, 609-984-3924 (Fax), 8:30AM-4:30PM.

www.state.nj.us/labor/wc/Default.htm

Indexing & Storage: Records are available for 40 years, then are purged. New records are available for inquiry immediately. Records are indexed on inhouse computer.

Searching: Use Form WC-147 if you want copies of a case. This does not require signature of claimant. Records are open. Include the following in your request-claimant name, Social Security Number, date of accident.

Access by: mail, in person.

Fee & Payment: There is no search fee. The copy fee is $.75 each for first 10 pages; $.50 each for next 10; and $.25 per page over 20. Fee payee: Division of Workers Compensation. Prepayment required. Personal checks accepted. No credit cards accepted.

Mail search: Turnaround time: 4-6 weeks. If request is just to know if the person has a claim, the turnaround time is same day.A self addressed stamped envelope is requested.

In person search: Turnaround time is same day.

Driver Records

Motor Vehicle Services, Driver History Abstract Unit, PO Box 142, Trenton, NJ 08666; 609-292-6500, 888-486-3339 (In-state only), 609-292-7500 (Suspensions), 8AM-5PM.

www.state.nj.us/mvs

Note: Copies of tickets are not kept on file and must be obtained from the municipal courts.

Indexing & Storage: Records are available for five years for the public (complete history for attorneys). Non-moving violations are not reported on the record. Accidents are reported, but fault is not shown. The driver's address is provided on the record. It takes 3 days to 2 weeks normally before new records are available for inquiry.

Searching: Access of driving records is strict, release to casual requesters is prohibited. The driver's license number should be submitted with all requests. The full name, DOB, sex, and eye color are also helpful. The following data is not released: Social Security Numbers or medical records.

Access by: mail, in person, online.

Fee & Payment: The current fee is $10.00 for mail-in or walk-in requests, $2.00 for magnetic tape requests, and $2.00 per record using control cards (200 minimum purchase) Fee payee: Motor Vehicle Services. Prepayment required. Personal checks accepted. No credit cards accepted.

Mail search: Turnaround time: 2 weeks. Batches of 100 or more requested can be submitted on customized format cards at a cost of $2.00 per record.A self addressed stamped envelope is requested.

In person search: Driving records can obtained at any one of the four Regional Service Centers - Deptford, Wayne, Eatontown, and Trenton.

Online search: Fee is $4.00 per record. Access is limited to insurance, bus and trucking companies, parking authorities, and approved vendors. There is a minimum of 100 requests per quarter. For more information, call 609-984-7771.

Other access: Most high volume requesters use the magnetic tape method to obtain overnight records at $2.00 per request (minimum 500 requests) or purchase control cards at $2.00 (100 purchased at a time, used whenever).

Vehicle Ownership
Vehicle Identification
Boat & Vessel Ownership
Boat & Vessel Registration

Motor Vehicle Services, Certified Information Unit, PO Box 146, Trenton, NJ 08666; 609-292-6500, 888-486-3339 (In-state), 8AM-5PM.

www.state.nj.us/mvs

Note: Lien records must be ordered from Special Titles at Motor Vehicle Services, CN-017 (Zip is 08666-0017). Lien records are on the complete title history, or can be purchased at $5.00 for each lien history search.

Indexing & Storage: Records are available from 1986 for most records. All boats 12 ft and over must be titled and registered. All motorized boats and sailboats under 12 ft must be registered. It takes 3 days to 3 weeks normally before new records are available for inquiry.

Searching: SSNs and medical information are not currently released and more restrictions are forthcoming. Casual requesters cannot obtain records. A special request form is required for ownership searches. Also, this agency maintains records on mobile homes.

Access by: mail, online.

Fee & Payment: The fee is $8.00 per record non-certified and $10.00 certified and take 1-2 weeks to process. A lien history search is $5.00 for each lien. A complete title history costs $10.50 and can take as long as 12 weeks to obtain. Fee payee: Motor Vehicle Services. Prepayment required. Personal checks accepted. No credit cards accepted.

Mail search: Requests must be submitted on Form ISM/DO-11A for registration requests and on Form ISM/DO-22A for title record requests.A self addressed stamped envelope is requested.

Online search: Limited online access is available for insurance companies, bus and trucking companies, highway/parking authorities, and approved vendors for these businesses. Participation requires a minimum of 100 requests per calendar quarter at $4.00 per request. Call 609-684-7771 for more information.

Other access: Tape-to-tape capability is available for volume users at $2.00 per record. There is no standard program for massive or customized bulk look-ups. Each request is looked at on an individual basis. Records are not sold for commercial or political reasons.

Accident Reports

New Jersey State Police, Criminal Justice Records Bureau, PO Box 7068, West Trenton, NJ 08628-0068; 609-882-2000 x2234, 8AM-5PM.

www.state.nj.us/lps/njsp/index.html

Indexing & Storage: Records are available for 6 years. Records are computer indexed. It takes 2 weeks before new records are available for inquiry.

Searching: Fatal accident information is not available until it has been released from the County Prosecutor. Include the following in your request-location of accident, date of accident, full name.

Access by: mail.

Fee & Payment: Fees: $10.00 for first 3 pages and $2.00 for each additional page with a maximum fee of $16.00. Fee payee: New Jersey State Police Department. Prepayment required. Personal checks accepted. No credit cards accepted.

Mail search: Turnaround time: 3 weeks. A self addressed stamped envelope is requested.

Legislation-Current/Pending
Legislation-Passed

New Jersey State Legislature, State House Annex, PO Box 068, Room B01, Trenton, NJ 08625-0068; 609-292-4840 (Bill Status Only), 609-292-6395 (Copy Room), 800-792-8630 (In State Only), 609-777-2440 (Fax), 8:30AM-5PM.

www.njleg.state.nj.us

Note: Older bills may be found at the State Law Library.

Indexing & Storage: Records are available for current session only. Records have been indexed on computer since 1994.

Searching: Include the following in your request-bill number.

Access by: mail, phone, fax, in person, online.

Fee & Payment: There is no search fee.

Mail search: Turnaround time: same day. For mail searches, provide bill number with the year or sponsor with accurate bill description.No self addressed stamped envelope is required.

Phone search: Searching is available by phone.

Fax search: Fax searching available.

In person search: For in person searches, please provide bill number with year or sponsor with accurate bill description.

Online search: The web site is a good source of information about bills. All statutes are online, also.

Voter Registration
Records not maintained by a state level agency.

Note: The Commissioner of Registration maintains these records at the county level. Although these county agencies may permit individual look-ups, records may may only be purchased for political purposes.

GED Certificates

GED Office, PO Box 500, Trenton, NJ 08625-0500; 609-777-1050.

www.state.nj.us/njded/students/ged

Searching: GED Information Request Form is required and can be obtained by calling the Office of Specialized Populations at 609-777-1050. To search, all of the following is required: a signed release, name, date/year of test, Social Security Number, and city of test. Records are not maintained for persons tested at federal correctional institutions.

Access by: mail, in person.

Fee & Payment: The fee is $5.00 for a verification or a copy of the transcript. Fee payee: Commissioner of Education. Prepayment required. Money orders and business checks are accepted. No credit cards accepted.

Mail search: Turnaround time: 2-3 days.

In person search: Searching is available in person.

Hunting License Information
Fishing License Information
Records not maintained by a state level agency.

Note: They do not have a central database. You must contact the vendor where the license was purchased.

Superior Court-Civil Division 2 Broad St, Elizabeth, NJ 07207; 908-659-4176; Fax: 908-659-4185. Hours: 8:30AM-4:30PM (EST). *Civil Actions Over $10,000.*

Civil Records: Access: Phone, mail, online, in person. Only the court conducts in person searches; visitors may not. No search fee. Required to search: name, years to search. Civil cases indexed by defendant, plaintiff. Civil records on computer from 1988, prior records archived in Trenton NJ. See state introduction for information on how to sign up for online access. **General Information:** No sealed, expunged, dismissed, judges notes, PSI's, or discovery packets records released. Turnaround time varies. Copy fee: $.75 per page for the first ten pages, $.50 per page for the next ten, and $.25 per page thereafter. Certification fee: $5.00. Fee payee: Clerk of Superior Court. Personal checks accepted. Prepayment is required. Public access terminal is available.

Special Civil Part 2 Broad St, Elizabeth, NJ 07207; 908-659-3637/8. Hours: 8:30AM-4:30PM (EST). *Civil Actions Under $10,000, Eviction, Small Claims.*

Civil Records: Access: Phone, mail, online, in person. Both court and visitors may perform in person searches. No search fee. Required to search: name, years to search. Civil cases indexed by defendant, plaintiff. Civil records on computer from 1993, on index books 1965, prior archived. See state introduction for information on how to sign up for online access. Phone access limited to info after 11/93. **General Information:** No adoptions, sealed, juvenile, expunged, dismissed, or mental illness records released. Turnaround time varies. Copy fee: $.75 per page. Fee is for first 10 pages, $.50 per page next 10; each add'l $.25. Certification fee: $5.00. Fee payee: Special Civil Part. Personal checks accepted. Prepayment is required.

Warren County

Warren County Superior Court Criminal Case Management Division, PO Box 900, Belvidere, NJ 07823; 908-475-6990; Fax: 908-475-6982. Hours: 8:30AM-4:30PM (EST). *Felony.* **Criminal Records:** Access: Mail, in person. Only the court conducts in person searches; visitors may not. Search fee: $6.00 per name. Required to search: name, years to search, DOB; also helpful-SSN. Criminal records on computer from 1990, prior on index cards. **General Information:** No sealed, expunged, dismissed, judges notes, PSI's, or discovery packets records released. Turnaround time 2 days. Copy fee: $1.50 per page. Certification fee: $3.00. Fee payee: State of New Jersey Judiciary. Personal checks accepted. Prepayment is required.

Superior Court-Civil Division PO Box 900, Belvidere, NJ 07823; 908-475-6140. Hours: 8:30AM-4:30PM (EST). *Civil Actions Over $10,000, Probate.*

Civil Records: Access: Mail, online, in person. Only the court conducts in person searches; visitors may not. No search fee. Required to search: name, years to search. Civil cases indexed by defendant, plaintiff. Civil records on computer from 1990, prior on index cards. See state introduction for information on how to sign up for online access. **General Information:** No sealed, expunged, dismissed, judges notes, PSIs, or discovery packets records released. Turnaround time 2 days. Copy fee: $.75 fee per page for first 10 pages; $.50 per page next 10; each add'l $.10. Certification fee: Certification is free for 1st page, next 5 pgs $5.00; each add'l pg $.75. Fee payee: Superior Court of New Jersey. Personal checks accepted. Prepayment is required. Public access terminal is available.

Special Civil Part 314 2nd St, PO Box 900, Belvidere, NJ 07823; 908-475-6140. Hours: 8:30AM-4:30PM (EST). *Civil Actions Under $10,000, Eviction, Small Claims.*

Civil Records: Access: Mail, online, in person. Only the court conducts in person searches; visitors may not. No search fee. Required to search: name, years to search. Civil cases indexed by defendant, plaintiff. Civil records on computer from 10/91, prior on index books from 1951. See state introduction for information on how to sign up for online access. In person access requires an appointment. **General Information:** No adoptions, sealed, juvenile, expunged, dismissed, or mental illness records released. SASE required. Turnaround time 2-3 days. Copy fee: $.75 per page for the first ten pages, $.50 per page for the second ten pages, and $.25 per page thereafter. Certification fee: No certification fee. Fee payee: Clerk of Special Civil Part. Personal checks accepted. Prepayment is required. Public access terminal is available.

ORGANIZATION

21 counties, 21 recording offices. The recording officer title varies depending upon the county. It is either Register of Deeds or County Clerk. The Clerk of Circuit Court records the equivalent of some state tax liens. The entire state is in the Eastern Time Zone (EST).

REAL ESTATE RECORDS

No counties will provide real estate searches. Copy and certification fees vary. Assessment and tax offices are at the municipal level.

UCC RECORDS

Financing statements are filed at the state level, except for consumer goods, farm related and real estate related collateral, which are filed only with the County Clerk. Only 12 recording offices will perform UCC searches. Use search request form UCC-11. Search fees are usually $25.00 per debtor name and copy fees vary.

TAX LIEN RECORDS

All federal tax liens are filed with the County Clerk/Register of Deeds and are indexed separately from all other liens. State tax liens comprise two categories—certificates of debt are filed with the Clerk of Superior Court (some, called docketed judgments are filed specifically with the Trenton court), and warrants of execution are filed with the County Clerk/Register of Deeds. Few counties will provide tax lien searches.

OTHER LIENS

Judgment, mechanics, bail bond.

Atlantic County
County Clerk, 5901 Main Street, Courthouse-CN 2005, Mays Landing, NJ 08330-1797. 609-625-4011. Fax: 609-625-4738.

Bergen County
County Clerk, Justice Center Room 214, 10 Main St., Hackensack, NJ 07601-7000. 201-646-2291.

Burlington County
County Clerk, P.O. Box 6000, Mount Holly, NJ 08060. 609-265-5180. Fax: 609-265-0696.

Camden County
County Register of Deeds, Courthouse Room 102, 520 Market Street, Camden, NJ 08102-1375. 856-225-5300. Fax: 856-225-5316.

Cape May County
County Clerk, P.O. Box 5000, Cape May Court House, NJ 08210-5000. 609-465-1010. Fax: 609-465-8625.

Cumberland County
County Clerk, P.O. Box 716, Bridgeton, NJ 08302. 856-453-4864. Fax: 856-455-1410.

Essex County
County Register of Deeds, 465 Martin Luther King Boulevard, Hall of Records, Room 130, Newark, NJ 07102. 973-621-4960. Fax: 973-621-6114. www.essexregister.com/

Gloucester County
County Clerk, P.O. Box 129, Woodbury, NJ 08096-0129. 856-853-3230. Fax: 856-853-3327.

Hudson County
County Register of Deeds, 595 Newark Ave, Room 105, Jersey City, NJ 07306. 201-795-6571. Fax: 201-795-5179.

Hunterdon County
County Clerk, 71 Main Street, Hall of Records, Flemington, NJ 08822. 908-788-1221. Fax: 908-782-4068.

Mercer County
County Clerk, 209 South Broad Street, Courthouse, Room 100, Trenton, NJ 08650. 609-989-6466. Fax: 609-989-1111.

Middlesex County
County Clerk, P.O. Box 1110, New Brunswick, NJ 08903. 732-745-3204.

Monmouth County
County Clerk, Hall of Records, Main Street, Room 102, Freehold, NJ 07728. 732-431-7321.

Morris County
County Clerk, P.O. Box 315, Morristown, NJ 07963-0315. 973-285-6135. Fax: 973-285-5231.

Ocean County
County Clerk, P.O. Box 2191, Toms River, NJ 08754. 732-929-2110. Fax: 732-349-4336. www.oceancountyclerk.com
Online Access: Property tax, real estate. Records on the County Clerk database are available free on the Internet at www.oceancountyclerk.com/search.htm. Search by parties, document or instrument type, or township.

Passaic County
County Register of Deeds, 77 Hamilton Street, Courthouse, Paterson, NJ 07505. 973-881-4777.

Salem County
County Clerk, 92 Market Street, Salem, NJ 08079-1911. 856-935-7510x8218. Fax: 856-935-8882.

Somerset County
County Clerk, P.O. Box 3000, Somerville, NJ 08876. 908-231-7006.

Sussex County
County Clerk, 4 Park Place, Hall of Records, Newton, NJ 07860-1795. 973-579-0900. Fax: 973-383-7493. www.sussexcountyclerk.com/recording.html

Union County
County Register of Deeds, 2 Broad Street, Courthouse, Room 115, Elizabeth, NJ 07207. 908-527-4787. Fax: 908-558-2589. www.unioncountynj.org/constit/clerk/record.html

Warren County
County Clerk, 413 Second Street, Courthouse, Belvidere, NJ 07823-1500. 908-475-6211.

You will usually be able to find the city name in the City/County Cross Reference below. In that case, it is a simple matter to determine the county from the cross reference. However, only the official US Postal Service city names are included in this index. There are an additional 40,000 place names that people use in their addresses. Therefore, we have also included a ZIP/City Cross Reference immediately following the City/County Cross Reference.

If you know the ZIP Code but the city name does not appear in the City/County Cross Reference index, look up the ZIP Code in the ZIP/City Cross Reference, find the city name, then look up the city name in the City/County Cross Reference. For example, you want to know the county for an address of Menands, NY 12204. There is no "Menands" in the City/County Cross Reference. The ZIP/City Cross Reference shows that ZIP Codes 12201-12288 are for the city of Albany. Looking back in the City/County Cross Reference, Albany is in Albany County.

City/County Cross Reference

ABSECON Atlantic
ADELPHIA Monmouth
ALLAMUCHY Warren
ALLENDALE Bergen
ALLENHURST Monmouth
ALLENTOWN (08501) Monmouth(65), Mercer(19), Burlington(16)
ALLENWOOD Monmouth
ALLOWAY Salem
ALPINE Bergen
ANDOVER Sussex
ANNANDALE Hunterdon
ASBURY (08802) Hunterdon(71), Warren(29)
ASBURY PARK Monmouth
ATCO (08004) Camden(85), Burlington(15)
ATLANTIC CITY Atlantic
ATLANTIC HIGHLANDS Monmouth
AUDUBON Camden
AUGUSTA Sussex
AVALON Cape May
AVENEL Middlesex
AVON BY THE SEA Monmouth
BAPTISTOWN Hunterdon
BARNEGAT Ocean
BARNEGAT LIGHT Ocean
BARRINGTON Camden
BASKING RIDGE Somerset
BAYONNE Hudson
BAYVILLE Ocean
BEACH HAVEN Ocean
BEACHWOOD Ocean
BEDMINSTER Somerset
BELFORD Monmouth
BELLE MEAD Somerset
BELLEVILLE Essex
BELLMAWR Camden
BELMAR Monmouth
BELVIDERE Warren
BERGENFIELD Bergen
BERKELEY HEIGHTS Union
BERLIN Camden
BERNARDSVILLE Somerset
BEVERLY Burlington
BIRMINGHAM Burlington
BLACKWOOD (08012) Camden(56), Gloucester(45)
BLAIRSTOWN Warren
BLAWENBURG Somerset
BLOOMFIELD Essex
BLOOMINGDALE Passaic
BLOOMSBURY (08804) Warren(94), Hunterdon(6)
BOGOTA Bergen
BOONTON Morris
BORDENTOWN Burlington
BOUND BROOK Somerset
BRADLEY BEACH Monmouth
BRANCHVILLE (07826) Sussex(92), Morris(9)
BRANCHVILLE Sussex
BRICK Ocean

BRIDGEPORT Gloucester
BRIDGETON (08302) Cumberland(94), Salem(6)
BRIDGEWATER Somerset
BRIELLE Monmouth
BRIGANTINE Atlantic
BROADWAY Warren
BROOKSIDE Morris
BROWNS MILLS Burlington
BUDD LAKE Morris
BUENA Atlantic
BURLINGTON Burlington
BUTLER Morris
BUTTZVILLE Warren
CALDWELL Essex
CALIFON (07830) Hunterdon(90), Morris(9), Warren(1)
CAMDEN Camden
CAPE MAY Cape May
CAPE MAY COURT HOUSE Cape May
CAPE MAY POINT Cape May
CARLSTADT Bergen
CARTERET Middlesex
CEDAR BROOK Camden
CEDAR GROVE Essex
CEDAR KNOLLS Morris
CEDARVILLE Cumberland
CHANGEWATER Warren
CHATHAM Morris
CHATSWORTH Burlington
CHERRY HILL Camden
CHESTER Morris
CLARK Union
CLARKSBORO Gloucester
CLARKSBURG (99999) Monmouth(99), Ocean(1)
CLAYTON Gloucester
CLEMENTON Camden
CLIFFSIDE PARK Bergen
CLIFFWOOD Monmouth
CLIFTON Passaic
CLINTON Hunterdon
CLOSTER Bergen
COLLINGSWOOD Camden
COLOGNE Atlantic
COLONIA Middlesex
COLTS NECK Monmouth
COLUMBIA Warren
COLUMBUS Burlington
COOKSTOWN Burlington
CRANBURY (08512) Middlesex(72), Mercer(29)
CRANBURY Middlesex
CRANFORD Union
CREAMRIDGE (08514) Monmouth(70), Ocean(30)
CRESSKILL Bergen
CROSSWICKS Burlington
DAYTON Middlesex
DEAL Monmouth
DEEPWATER Salem
DEERFIELD STREET Cumberland

DELAWARE Warren
DELMONT Cumberland
DEMAREST Bergen
DENNISVILLE Cape May
DENVILLE Morris
DIVIDING CREEK Cumberland
DORCHESTER Cumberland
DOROTHY Atlantic
DOVER Morris
DUMONT Bergen
DUNELLEN (08812) Somerset(52), Middlesex(48)
EAST BRUNSWICK Middlesex
EAST HANOVER Morris
EAST ORANGE Essex
EAST RUTHERFORD Bergen
EATONTOWN Monmouth
EDGEWATER Bergen
EDISON Middlesex
EGG HARBOR CITY (08215) Atlantic(99), Burlington(1)
EGG HARBOR TOWNSHIP Atlantic
ELIZABETH Union
ELMER Salem
ELMWOOD PARK Bergen
ELWOOD Atlantic
EMERSON Bergen
ENGLEWOOD Bergen
ENGLEWOOD CLIFFS Bergen
ENGLISHTOWN Monmouth
ESSEX FELLS Essex
ESTELL MANOR Atlantic
EWAN Gloucester
FAIR HAVEN Monmouth
FAIR LAWN Bergen
FAIRFIELD Essex
FAIRTON Cumberland
FAIRVIEW Bergen
FANWOOD Union
FAR HILLS (07931) Somerset(83), Morris(17)
FARMINGDALE Monmouth
FLAGTOWN Somerset
FLANDERS Morris
FLEMINGTON Hunterdon
FLORENCE Burlington
FLORHAM PARK Morris
FORDS Middlesex
FORKED RIVER Ocean
FORT LEE Bergen
FORT MONMOUTH Monmouth
FORTESCUE Cumberland
FRANKLIN Sussex
FRANKLIN LAKES Bergen
FRANKLIN PARK Somerset
FRANKLINVILLE Gloucester
FREEHOLD Monmouth
FRENCHTOWN Hunterdon
GARFIELD Bergen
GARWOOD Union
GIBBSBORO Camden
GIBBSTOWN Gloucester

GILLETTE Morris
GLADSTONE Somerset
GLASSBORO Gloucester
GLASSER Sussex
GLEN GARDNER Hunterdon
GLEN RIDGE Essex
GLEN ROCK Bergen
GLENDORA Camden
GLENWOOD Sussex
GLOUCESTER CITY Camden
GOSHEN Cape May
GREAT MEADOWS Warren
GREEN CREEK Cape May
GREEN VILLAGE Morris
GREENDELL Sussex
GREENWICH Cumberland
GRENLOCH Gloucester
HACKENSACK Bergen
HACKETTSTOWN (07840) Warren(83), Morris(17)
HADDON HEIGHTS Camden
HADDONFIELD Camden
HAINESPORT Burlington
HALEDON Passaic
HAMBURG Sussex
HAMMONTON (08037) Atlantic(83), Camden(18)
HAMPTON Hunterdon
HANCOCKS BRIDGE Salem
HARRINGTON PARK Bergen
HARRISON Hudson
HARRISONVILLE Gloucester
HASBROUCK HEIGHTS Bergen
HASKELL Passaic
HAWORTH Bergen
HAWTHORNE Passaic
HAZLET Monmouth
HEISLERVILLE Cumberland
HELMETTA Middlesex
HEWITT Passaic
HIBERNIA Morris
HIGH BRIDGE Hunterdon
HIGHLAND LAKES Sussex
HIGHLAND PARK Middlesex
HIGHLANDS Monmouth
HIGHTSTOWN (08520) Mercer(97), Middlesex(2), Monmouth(1)
HILLSDALE Bergen
HILLSIDE Union
HO HO KUS Bergen
HOBOKEN Hudson
HOLMDEL Monmouth
HOPATCONG Sussex
HOPE Warren
HOPEWELL (08525) Mercer(93), Hunterdon(7)
HOWELL Monmouth
IMLAYSTOWN Monmouth
IRONIA Morris
IRVINGTON Essex
ISELIN Middlesex
ISLAND HEIGHTS Ocean

JACKSON Ocean
JAMESBURG Middlesex
JERSEY CITY Hudson
JOBSTOWN Burlington
JOHNSONBURG Warren
JULIUSTOWN Burlington
KEANSBURG Monmouth
KEARNY Hudson
KEASBEY Middlesex
KENDALL PARK Middlesex
KENILWORTH Union
KENVIL Morris
KEYPORT (07735) Monmouth(92),
  Middlesex(8)
KINGSTON Somerset
KIRKWOOD VOORHEES Camden
LAFAYETTE Sussex
LAKE HIAWATHA Morris
LAKE HOPATCONG Morris
LAKEHURST Ocean
LAKEWOOD Ocean
LAMBERTVILLE (08530) Hunterdon(96),
  Mercer(4)
LANDING Morris
LANDISVILLE Atlantic
LANOKA HARBOR Ocean
LAVALLETTE Ocean
LAWNSIDE Camden
LAYTON Sussex
LEBANON Hunterdon
LEDGEWOOD Morris
LEEDS POINT Atlantic
LEESBURG Cumberland
LEONARDO Monmouth
LEONIA Bergen
LIBERTY CORNER Somerset
LINCOLN PARK Morris
LINCROFT Monmouth
LINDEN Union
LINWOOD Atlantic
LITTLE FALLS Passaic
LITTLE FERRY Bergen
LITTLE SILVER Monmouth
LITTLE YORK Hunterdon
LIVINGSTON Essex
LODI Bergen
LONG BRANCH Monmouth
LONG VALLEY Morris
LONGPORT Atlantic
LUMBERTON Burlington
LYNDHURST Bergen
LYONS Somerset
MADISON Morris
MAGNOLIA Camden
MAHWAH Bergen
MALAGA Gloucester
MANAHAWKIN Ocean
MANASQUAN Monmouth
MANTOLOKING Ocean
MANTUA Gloucester
MANVILLE Somerset
MAPLE SHADE Burlington
MAPLEWOOD Essex
MARGATE CITY Atlantic
MARLBORO Monmouth
MARLTON Burlington
MARMORA Cape May
MARTINSVILLE Somerset
MATAWAN (07747) Monmouth(82),
  Middlesex(18)
MAURICETOWN Cumberland
MAYS LANDING Atlantic
MAYWOOD Bergen
MC AFEE Sussex
MEDFORD Burlington
MENDHAM Morris
MERCHANTVILLE Camden
METUCHEN Middlesex
MICKLETON Gloucester
MIDDLESEX Middlesex
MIDDLETOWN Monmouth
MIDDLEVILLE Sussex

MIDLAND PARK Bergen
MILFORD Hunterdon
MILLBURN Essex
MILLINGTON Morris
MILLTOWN Middlesex
MILLVILLE Cumberland
MILMAY (08340) Cumberland(52),
  Atlantic(48)
MINE HILL Morris
MINOTOLA Atlantic
MIZPAH Atlantic
MONMOUTH BEACH Monmouth
MONMOUTH JUNCTION Middlesex
MONROEVILLE (08343) Gloucester(69),
  Salem(31)
MONTAGUE (07827) Sussex(98), Morris(2)
MONTCLAIR (07043) Essex(97),
  Passaic(3)
MONTCLAIR Essex
MONTVALE Bergen
MONTVILLE Morris
MOONACHIE Bergen
MOORESTOWN Burlington
MORGANVILLE Monmouth
MORRIS PLAINS Morris
MORRISTOWN Morris
MOUNT ARLINGTON Morris
MOUNT EPHRAIM Camden
MOUNT FREEDOM Morris
MOUNT HOLLY Burlington
MOUNT LAUREL Burlington
MOUNT ROYAL Gloucester
MOUNT TABOR Morris
MOUNTAIN LAKES Morris
MOUNTAINSIDE Union
MULLICA HILL Gloucester
MUSICAL HERITAGE Monmouth
NATIONAL PARK Gloucester
NAVESINK Monmouth
NEPTUNE Monmouth
NESHANIC STATION Somerset
NETCONG Morris
NEW BRUNSWICK Middlesex
NEW EGYPT Ocean
NEW GRETNA Burlington
NEW LISBON Burlington
NEW MILFORD Bergen
NEW PROVIDENCE Union
NEW VERNON Morris
NEWARK Essex
NEWFIELD (08344) Gloucester(72),
  Cumberland(15), Salem(10), Atlantic(3)
NEWFOUNDLAND Passaic
NEWPORT Cumberland
NEWTON Sussex
NEWTONVILLE Atlantic
NORMA Salem
NORMANDY BEACH Ocean
NORTH ARLINGTON Bergen
NORTH BERGEN Hudson
NORTH BRUNSWICK Middlesex
NORTHFIELD Atlantic
NORTHVALE Bergen
NORWOOD Bergen
NUTLEY Essex
OAK RIDGE (07438) Passaic(78),
  Morris(22)
OAKHURST Monmouth
OAKLAND Bergen
OAKLYN Camden
OCEAN CITY Cape May
OCEAN GATE Ocean
OCEAN GROVE Monmouth
OCEAN VIEW Cape May
OCEANPORT Monmouth
OCEANVILLE Atlantic
OGDENSBURG Sussex
OLD BRIDGE Middlesex
OLDWICK Hunterdon
ORADELL Bergen
ORANGE Essex
OXFORD Warren

PALISADES PARK Bergen
PALMYRA Burlington
PARAMUS Bergen
PARK RIDGE Bergen
PARLIN Middlesex
PARSIPPANY Morris
PASSAIC Passaic
PATERSON Passaic
PAULSBORO Gloucester
PEAPACK Somerset
PEDRICKTOWN Salem
PEMBERTON Burlington
PENNINGTON Mercer
PENNS GROVE Salem
PENNSAUKEN Camden
PENNSVILLE Salem
PEQUANNOCK Morris
PERRINEVILLE (08535) Monmouth(88),
  Ocean(12)
PERTH AMBOY Middlesex
PHILLIPSBURG Warren
PICATINNY ARSENAL Morris
PINE BEACH Ocean
PINE BROOK Morris
PISCATAWAY Middlesex
PITMAN Gloucester
PITTSTOWN Hunterdon
PLAINFIELD (07060) Union(55),
  Somerset(45)
PLAINFIELD (07062) Union(92),
  Somerset(8)
PLAINFIELD (07063) Union(71),
  Somerset(29)
PLAINFIELD Union
PLAINSBORO Middlesex
PLEASANTVILLE Atlantic
PLUCKEMIN Somerset
POINT PLEASANT BEACH Ocean
POMONA Atlantic
POMPTON LAKES Passaic
POMPTON PLAINS Morris
PORT ELIZABETH Cumberland
PORT MONMOUTH Monmouth
PORT MURRAY Warren
PORT NORRIS Cumberland
PORT READING Middlesex
PORT REPUBLIC Atlantic
POTTERSVILLE Hunterdon
PRINCETON (08540) Mercer(75),
  Middlesex(13), Somerset(12)
PRINCETON Mercer
PRINCETON JUNCTION Mercer
QUAKERTOWN Hunterdon
QUINTON Salem
RAHWAY Union
RAMSEY Bergen
RANCOCAS Burlington
RANDOLPH Morris
RARITAN Somerset
READINGTON Hunterdon
RED BANK Monmouth
RICHLAND Atlantic
RICHWOOD Gloucester
RIDGEFIELD Bergen
RIDGEFIELD PARK Bergen
RIDGEWOOD Bergen
RINGOES Hunterdon
RINGWOOD Passaic
RIO GRANDE Cape May
RIVER EDGE Bergen
RIVERDALE Morris
RIVERSIDE Burlington
RIVERTON Burlington
ROCHELLE PARK Bergen
ROCKAWAY Morris
ROCKY HILL Somerset
ROEBLING Burlington
ROOSEVELT Monmouth
ROSELAND Essex
ROSELLE Union
ROSELLE PARK Union
ROSEMONT Hunterdon

ROSENHAYN Cumberland
RUMSON Monmouth
RUNNEMEDE Camden
RUTHERFORD Bergen
SADDLE BROOK Bergen
SADDLE RIVER Bergen
SALEM Salem
SAYREVILLE Middlesex
SCHOOLEYS MOUNTAIN Morris
SCOTCH PLAINS Union
SEA GIRT Monmouth
SEA ISLE CITY Cape May
SEASIDE HEIGHTS Ocean
SEASIDE PARK Ocean
SECAUCUS Hudson
SERGEANTSVILLE Hunterdon
SEWAREN Middlesex
SEWELL Gloucester
SHILOH Cumberland
SHORT HILLS Essex
SHREWSBURY Monmouth
SICKLERVILLE (08081) Camden(97),
  Gloucester(4)
SKILLMAN (08558) Somerset(99),
  Mercer(1)
SOMERDALE Camden
SOMERS POINT Atlantic
SOMERSET Somerset
SOMERVILLE Somerset
SOUTH AMBOY Middlesex
SOUTH BOUND BROOK Somerset
SOUTH DENNIS Cape May
SOUTH HACKENSACK Bergen
SOUTH ORANGE Essex
SOUTH PLAINFIELD Middlesex
SOUTH RIVER Middlesex
SOUTH SEAVILLE Cape May
SPARTA Sussex
SPOTSWOOD Middlesex
SPRING LAKE Monmouth
SPRINGFIELD Union
STANHOPE Sussex
STANTON Hunterdon
STEWARTSVILLE Warren
STILLWATER Sussex
STIRLING Morris
STOCKHOLM (07460) Sussex(94),
  Morris(4), Passaic(2)
STOCKTON Hunterdon
STONE HARBOR Cape May
STRATFORD Camden
STRATHMERE Cape May
SUCCASUNNA Morris
SUMMIT Union
SUSSEX Sussex
SWARTSWOOD Sussex
SWEDESBORO (08085) Gloucester(97),
  Salem(3)
TEANECK Bergen
TENAFLY Bergen
TENNENT Monmouth
TETERBORO Bergen
THOROFARE Gloucester
THREE BRIDGES Hunterdon
TITUSVILLE Mercer
TOMS RIVER Ocean
TOTOWA Passaic
TOWACO Morris
TRANQUILITY Sussex
TRENTON (08620) Mercer(86),
  Burlington(14)
TRENTON (08691) Mercer(96),
  Monmouth(4)
TRENTON Burlington
TRENTON Mercer
TUCKAHOE Cape May
TUCKERTON (08087) Ocean(94),
  Burlington(6)
UNION Union
UNION CITY Hudson
VAUXHALL Union
VENTNOR CITY Atlantic

VERNON Sussex	WARETOWN Ocean	WESTVILLE Gloucester	WINDSOR Mercer
VERONA Essex	WARREN Somerset	WESTWOOD Bergen	WINSLOW Camden
VIENNA Warren	WASHINGTON Warren	WHARTON Morris	WOOD RIDGE Bergen
VILLAS Cape May	WATERFORD WORKS Camden	WHIPPANY Morris	WOODBINE (08270) Cape May(89),
VINCENTOWN Burlington	WAYNE Passaic	WHITEHOUSE Hunterdon	Atlantic(12)
VINELAND (08360) Cumberland(90),	WENONAH Gloucester	WHITEHOUSE STATION Hunterdon	WOODBRIDGE Middlesex
Atlantic(6), Gloucester(4)	WEST BERLIN Camden	WHITESBORO Cape May	WOODBURY Gloucester
VINELAND Cumberland	WEST CREEK Ocean	WHITING Ocean	WOODBURY HEIGHTS Gloucester
VOORHEES Camden	WEST LONG BRANCH Monmouth	WICKATUNK Monmouth	WOODSTOWN Salem
WALDWICK Bergen	WEST MILFORD Passaic	WILDWOOD Cape May	WRIGHTSTOWN Burlington
WALLINGTON Bergen	WEST NEW YORK Hudson	WILLIAMSTOWN (08094) Gloucester(89),	WYCKOFF Bergen
WALLPACK CENTER Sussex	WEST ORANGE Essex	Atlantic(11)	ZAREPHATH Somerset
WANAQUE Passaic	WESTFIELD Union	WILLINGBORO Burlington	

ZIP/City Cross Reference

07001-07001	AVENEL	07090-07091	WESTFIELD	07543-07544	PATERSON	07735-07735	KEYPORT
07002-07002	BAYONNE	07092-07092	MOUNTAINSIDE	07601-07602	HACKENSACK	07737-07737	LEONARDO
07003-07003	BLOOMFIELD	07093-07093	WEST NEW YORK	07603-07603	BOGOTA	07738-07738	LINCROFT
07004-07004	FAIRFIELD	07094-07094	SECAUCUS	07604-07604	HASBROUCK HEIGHTS	07739-07739	LITTLE SILVER
07005-07005	BOONTON	07095-07095	WOODBRIDGE	07605-07605	LEONIA	07740-07740	LONG BRANCH
07006-07007	CALDWELL	07096-07096	SECAUCUS	07606-07606	SOUTH HACKENSACK	07746-07746	MARLBORO
07008-07008	CARTERET	07097-07097	JERSEY CITY	07607-07607	MAYWOOD	07747-07747	MATAWAN
07009-07009	CEDAR GROVE	07099-07099	KEARNY	07608-07608	TETERBORO	07748-07748	MIDDLETOWN
07010-07010	CLIFFSIDE PARK	07101-07108	NEWARK	07620-07620	ALPINE	07750-07750	MONMOUTH BEACH
07011-07015	CLIFTON	07109-07109	BELLEVILLE	07621-07621	BERGENFIELD	07751-07751	MORGANVILLE
07016-07016	CRANFORD	07110-07110	NUTLEY	07624-07624	CLOSTER	07752-07752	NAVESINK
07017-07019	EAST ORANGE	07111-07111	IRVINGTON	07626-07626	CRESSKILL	07753-07754	NEPTUNE
07020-07020	EDGEWATER	07112-07199	NEWARK	07627-07627	DEMAREST	07755-07755	OAKHURST
07021-07021	ESSEX FELLS	07201-07202	ELIZABETH	07628-07628	DUMONT	07756-07756	OCEAN GROVE
07022-07022	FAIRVIEW	07203-07203	ROSELLE	07630-07630	EMERSON	07757-07757	OCEANPORT
07023-07023	FANWOOD	07204-07204	ROSELLE PARK	07631-07631	ENGLEWOOD	07758-07758	PORT MONMOUTH
07024-07024	FORT LEE	07205-07205	HILLSIDE	07632-07632	ENGLEWOOD CLIFFS	07760-07760	RUMSON
07026-07026	GARFIELD	07206-07216	ELIZABETH	07640-07640	HARRINGTON PARK	07762-07762	SPRING LAKE
07027-07027	GARWOOD	07302-07399	JERSEY CITY	07641-07641	HAWORTH	07763-07763	TENNENT
07028-07028	GLEN RIDGE	07401-07401	ALLENDALE	07642-07642	HILLSDALE	07764-07764	WEST LONG BRANCH
07029-07029	HARRISON	07403-07403	BLOOMINGDALE	07643-07643	LITTLE FERRY	07765-07765	WICKATUNK
07030-07030	HOBOKEN	07405-07405	BUTLER	07644-07644	LODI	07777-07777	HOLMDEL
07031-07031	NORTH ARLINGTON	07407-07407	ELMWOOD PARK	07645-07645	MONTVALE	07799-07799	EATONTOWN
07032-07032	KEARNY	07410-07410	FAIR LAWN	07646-07646	NEW MILFORD	07801-07802	DOVER
07033-07033	KENILWORTH	07416-07416	FRANKLIN	07647-07647	NORTHVALE	07803-07803	MINE HILL
07034-07034	LAKE HIAWATHA	07417-07417	FRANKLIN LAKES	07648-07648	NORWOOD	07806-07806	PICATINNY ARSENAL
07035-07035	LINCOLN PARK	07418-07418	GLENWOOD	07649-07649	ORADELL	07820-07820	ALLAMUCHY
07036-07036	LINDEN	07419-07419	HAMBURG	07650-07650	PALISADES PARK	07821-07821	ANDOVER
07039-07039	LIVINGSTON	07420-07420	HASKELL	07652-07653	PARAMUS	07822-07822	AUGUSTA
07040-07040	MAPLEWOOD	07421-07421	HEWITT	07656-07656	PARK RIDGE	07823-07823	BELVIDERE
07041-07041	MILLBURN	07422-07422	HIGHLAND LAKES	07657-07657	RIDGEFIELD	07825-07825	BLAIRSTOWN
07042-07043	MONTCLAIR	07423-07423	HO HO KUS	07660-07660	RIDGEFIELD PARK	07826-07826	BRANCHVILLE
07044-07044	VERONA	07424-07424	LITTLE FALLS	07661-07661	RIVER EDGE	07827-07827	MONTAGUE
07045-07045	MONTVILLE	07428-07428	MC AFEE	07662-07662	ROCHELLE PARK	07828-07828	BUDD LAKE
07046-07046	MOUNTAIN LAKES	07430-07430	MAHWAH	07663-07663	SADDLE BROOK	07829-07829	BUTTZVILLE
07047-07047	NORTH BERGEN	07432-07432	MIDLAND PARK	07666-07666	TEANECK	07830-07830	CALIFON
07050-07051	ORANGE	07435-07435	NEWFOUNDLAND	07670-07670	TENAFLY	07831-07831	CHANGEWATER
07052-07052	WEST ORANGE	07436-07436	OAKLAND	07675-07675	WESTWOOD	07832-07832	COLUMBIA
07054-07054	PARSIPPANY	07438-07438	OAK RIDGE	07688-07688	TEANECK	07833-07833	DELAWARE
07055-07055	PASSAIC	07439-07439	OGDENSBURG	07701-07701	RED BANK	07834-07834	DENVILLE
07057-07057	WALLINGTON	07440-07440	PEQUANNOCK	07702-07702	SHREWSBURY	07836-07836	FLANDERS
07058-07058	PINE BROOK	07442-07442	POMPTON LAKES	07703-07703	FORT MONMOUTH	07837-07837	GLASSER
07059-07059	WARREN	07444-07444	POMPTON PLAINS	07704-07704	FAIR HAVEN	07838-07838	GREAT MEADOWS
07060-07063	PLAINFIELD	07446-07446	RAMSEY	07709-07709	ALLENHURST	07839-07839	GREENDELL
07064-07064	PORT READING	07450-07451	RIDGEWOOD	07710-07710	ADELPHIA	07840-07840	HACKETTSTOWN
07065-07065	RAHWAY	07452-07452	GLEN ROCK	07711-07711	ALLENHURST	07842-07842	HIBERNIA
07066-07066	CLARK	07456-07456	RINGWOOD	07712-07712	ASBURY PARK	07843-07843	HOPATCONG
07067-07067	COLONIA	07457-07457	RIVERDALE	07715-07715	BELMAR	07844-07844	HOPE
07068-07068	ROSELAND	07458-07458	SADDLE RIVER	07716-07716	ATLANTIC HIGHLANDS	07845-07845	IRONIA
07070-07070	RUTHERFORD	07460-07460	STOCKHOLM	07717-07717	AVON BY THE SEA	07846-07846	JOHNSONBURG
07071-07071	LYNDHURST	07461-07461	SUSSEX	07718-07718	BELFORD	07847-07847	KENVIL
07072-07072	CARLSTADT	07462-07462	VERNON	07719-07719	BELMAR	07848-07848	LAFAYETTE
07073-07073	EAST RUTHERFORD	07463-07463	WALDWICK	07720-07720	BRADLEY BEACH	07849-07849	LAKE HOPATCONG
07074-07074	MOONACHIE	07465-07465	WANAQUE	07721-07721	CLIFFWOOD	07850-07850	LANDING
07075-07075	WOOD RIDGE	07470-07477	WAYNE	07722-07722	COLTS NECK	07851-07851	LAYTON
07076-07076	SCOTCH PLAINS	07480-07480	WEST MILFORD	07723-07723	DEAL	07852-07852	LEDGEWOOD
07077-07077	SEWAREN	07481-07481	WYCKOFF	07724-07724	EATONTOWN	07853-07853	LONG VALLEY
07078-07078	SHORT HILLS	07495-07498	MAHWAH	07726-07726	ENGLISHTOWN	07855-07855	MIDDLEVILLE
07079-07079	SOUTH ORANGE	07501-07505	PATERSON	07727-07727	FARMINGDALE	07856-07856	MOUNT ARLINGTON
07080-07080	SOUTH PLAINFIELD	07506-07507	HAWTHORNE	07728-07728	FREEHOLD	07857-07857	NETCONG
07081-07081	SPRINGFIELD	07508-07508	HALEDON	07730-07730	HAZLET	07860-07860	NEWTON
07082-07082	TOWACO	07509-07511	PATERSON	07731-07731	HOWELL	07863-07863	OXFORD
07083-07083	UNION	07511-07512	TOTOWA	07732-07732	HIGHLANDS	07865-07865	PORT MURRAY
07087-07087	UNION CITY	07513-07533	PATERSON	07733-07733	HOLMDEL	07866-07866	ROCKAWAY
07088-07088	VAUXHALL	07538-07538	HALEDON	07734-07734	KEANSBURG	07869-07869	RANDOLPH

ZIP	Place	ZIP	Place	ZIP	Place	ZIP	Place
07870-07870	SCHOOLEYS MOUNTAIN	08046-08046	WILLINGBORO	08241-08241	PORT REPUBLIC	08555-08555	ROOSEVELT
07871-07871	SPARTA	08048-08048	LUMBERTON	08242-08242	RIO GRANDE	08556-08556	ROSEMONT
07874-07874	STANHOPE	08049-08049	MAGNOLIA	08243-08243	SEA ISLE CITY	08557-08557	SERGEANTSVILLE
07875-07875	STILLWATER	08050-08050	MANAHAWKIN	08244-08244	SOMERS POINT	08558-08558	SKILLMAN
07876-07876	SUCCASUNNA	08051-08051	MANTUA	08245-08245	SOUTH DENNIS	08559-08559	STOCKTON
07877-07877	SWARTSWOOD	08052-08052	MAPLE SHADE	08246-08246	SOUTH SEAVILLE	08560-08560	TITUSVILLE
07878-07878	MOUNT TABOR	08053-08053	MARLTON	08247-08247	STONE HARBOR	08561-08561	WINDSOR
07879-07879	TRANQUILITY	08054-08054	MOUNT LAUREL	08248-08248	STRATHMERE	08562-08562	WRIGHTSTOWN
07880-07880	VIENNA	08055-08055	MEDFORD	08250-08250	TUCKAHOE	08570-08570	CRANBURY
07881-07881	WALLPACK CENTER	08056-08056	MICKLETON	08251-08251	VILLAS	08601-08695	TRENTON
07882-07882	WASHINGTON	08057-08057	MOORESTOWN	08252-08252	WHITESBORO	08701-08701	LAKEWOOD
07885-07885	WHARTON	08059-08059	MOUNT EPHRAIM	08260-08260	WILDWOOD	08720-08720	ALLENWOOD
07890-07890	BRANCHVILLE	08060-08060	MOUNT HOLLY	08270-08270	WOODBINE	08721-08721	BAYVILLE
07901-07902	SUMMIT	08061-08061	MOUNT ROYAL	08302-08302	BRIDGETON	08722-08722	BEACHWOOD
07920-07920	BASKING RIDGE	08062-08062	MULLICA HILL	08310-08310	BUENA	08723-08724	BRICK
07921-07921	BEDMINSTER	08063-08063	NATIONAL PARK	08311-08311	CEDARVILLE	08730-08730	BRIELLE
07922-07922	BERKELEY HEIGHTS	08064-08064	NEW LISBON	08312-08312	CLAYTON	08731-08731	FORKED RIVER
07924-07924	BERNARDSVILLE	08065-08065	PALMYRA	08313-08313	DEERFIELD STREET	08732-08732	ISLAND HEIGHTS
07926-07926	BROOKSIDE	08066-08066	PAULSBORO	08314-08314	DELMONT	08733-08733	LAKEHURST
07927-07927	CEDAR KNOLLS	08067-08067	PEDRICKTOWN	08315-08315	DIVIDING CREEK	08734-08734	LANOKA HARBOR
07928-07928	CHATHAM	08068-08068	PEMBERTON	08316-08316	DORCHESTER	08735-08735	LAVALLETTE
07930-07930	CHESTER	08069-08069	PENNS GROVE	08317-08317	DOROTHY	08736-08736	MANASQUAN
07931-07931	FAR HILLS	08070-08070	PENNSVILLE	08318-08318	ELMER	08738-08738	MANTOLOKING
07932-07932	FLORHAM PARK	08071-08071	PITMAN	08319-08319	ESTELL MANOR	08739-08739	NORMANDY BEACH
07933-07933	GILLETTE	08072-08072	QUINTON	08320-08320	FAIRTON	08740-08740	OCEAN GATE
07934-07934	GLADSTONE	08073-08073	RANCOCAS	08321-08321	FORTESCUE	08741-08741	PINE BEACH
07935-07935	GREEN VILLAGE	08074-08074	RICHWOOD	08322-08322	FRANKLINVILLE	08742-08742	POINT PLEASANT BEACH
07936-07936	EAST HANOVER	08075-08075	RIVERSIDE	08323-08323	GREENWICH		
07938-07938	LIBERTY CORNER	08076-08077	RIVERTON	08324-08324	HEISLERVILLE	08750-08750	SEA GIRT
07939-07939	LYONS	08078-08078	RUNNEMEDE	08326-08326	LANDISVILLE	08751-08751	SEASIDE HEIGHTS
07940-07940	MADISON	08079-08079	SALEM	08327-08327	LEESBURG	08752-08752	SEASIDE PARK
07945-07945	MENDHAM	08080-08080	SEWELL	08328-08328	MALAGA	08753-08757	TOMS RIVER
07946-07946	MILLINGTON	08081-08081	SICKLERVILLE	08329-08329	MAURICETOWN	08758-08758	WARETOWN
07950-07950	MORRIS PLAINS	08083-08083	SOMERDALE	08330-08330	MAYS LANDING	08759-08759	WHITING
07960-07963	MORRISTOWN	08084-08084	STRATFORD	08332-08332	MILLVILLE	08801-08801	ANNANDALE
07970-07970	MOUNT FREEDOM	08085-08085	SWEDESBORO	08340-08340	MILMAY	08802-08802	ASBURY
07974-07974	NEW PROVIDENCE	08086-08086	THOROFARE	08341-08341	MINOTOLA	08803-08803	BAPTISTOWN
07976-07976	NEW VERNON	08087-08087	TUCKERTON	08342-08342	MIZPAH	08804-08804	BLOOMSBURY
07977-07977	PEAPACK	08088-08088	VINCENTOWN	08343-08343	MONROEVILLE	08805-08805	BOUND BROOK
07978-07978	PLUCKEMIN	08089-08089	WATERFORD WORKS	08344-08344	NEWFIELD	08807-08807	BRIDGEWATER
07979-07979	POTTERSVILLE	08090-08090	WENONAH	08345-08345	NEWPORT	08808-08808	BROADWAY
07980-07980	STIRLING	08091-08091	WEST BERLIN	08346-08346	NEWTONVILLE	08809-08809	CLINTON
07981-07999	WHIPPANY	08092-08092	WEST CREEK	08347-08347	NORMA	08810-08810	DAYTON
08001-08001	ALLOWAY	08093-08093	WESTVILLE	08348-08348	PORT ELIZABETH	08812-08812	DUNELLEN
08002-08003	CHERRY HILL	08094-08094	WILLIAMSTOWN	08349-08349	PORT NORRIS	08816-08816	EAST BRUNSWICK
08004-08004	ATCO	08095-08095	WINSLOW	08350-08350	RICHLAND	08817-08820	EDISON
08005-08005	BARNEGAT	08096-08096	WOODBURY	08352-08352	ROSENHAYN	08821-08821	FLAGTOWN
08006-08006	BARNEGAT LIGHT	08097-08097	WOODBURY HEIGHTS	08353-08353	SHILOH	08822-08822	FLEMINGTON
08007-08007	BARRINGTON	08098-08098	WOODSTOWN	08358-08358	CHERRY HILL	08823-08823	FRANKLIN PARK
08008-08008	BEACH HAVEN	08099-08099	BELLMAWR	08360-08362	VINELAND	08824-08824	KENDALL PARK
08009-08009	BERLIN	08101-08105	CAMDEN	08370-08370	RIVERSIDE	08825-08825	FRENCHTOWN
08010-08010	BEVERLY	08106-08106	AUDUBON	08401-08401	ATLANTIC CITY	08826-08826	GLEN GARDNER
08011-08011	BIRMINGHAM	08107-08107	OAKLYN	08402-08402	MARGATE CITY	08827-08827	HAMPTON
08012-08012	BLACKWOOD	08108-08108	COLLINGSWOOD	08403-08403	LONGPORT	08828-08828	HELMETTA
08014-08014	BRIDGEPORT	08109-08109	MERCHANTVILLE	08404-08405	ATLANTIC CITY	08829-08829	HIGH BRIDGE
08015-08015	BROWNS MILLS	08110-08110	PENNSAUKEN	08406-08406	VENTNOR CITY	08830-08830	ISELIN
08016-08016	BURLINGTON	08201-08201	ABSECON	08411-08411	ATLANTIC CITY	08831-08831	JAMESBURG
08018-08018	CEDAR BROOK	08202-08202	AVALON	08501-08501	ALLENTOWN	08832-08832	KEASBEY
08019-08019	CHATSWORTH	08203-08203	BRIGANTINE	08502-08502	BELLE MEAD	08833-08833	LEBANON
08020-08020	CLARKSBORO	08204-08204	CAPE MAY	08504-08504	BLAWENBURG	08834-08834	LITTLE YORK
08021-08021	CLEMENTON	08210-08210	CAPE MAY COURT HOUSE	08505-08505	BORDENTOWN	08835-08835	MANVILLE
08022-08022	COLUMBUS			08510-08510	CLARKSBURG	08836-08836	MARTINSVILLE
08023-08023	DEEPWATER	08212-08212	CAPE MAY POINT	08511-08511	COOKSTOWN	08837-08837	EDISON
08025-08025	EWAN	08213-08213	COLOGNE	08512-08512	CRANBURY	08840-08840	METUCHEN
08026-08026	GIBBSBORO	08214-08214	DENNISVILLE	08514-08514	CREAMRIDGE	08846-08846	MIDDLESEX
08027-08027	GIBBSTOWN	08215-08215	EGG HARBOR CITY	08515-08515	CROSSWICKS	08848-08848	MILFORD
08028-08028	GLASSBORO	08217-08217	ELWOOD	08518-08518	FLORENCE	08850-08850	MILLTOWN
08029-08029	GLENDORA	08218-08218	GOSHEN	08520-08520	HIGHTSTOWN	08852-08852	MONMOUTH JUNCTION
08030-08030	GLOUCESTER CITY	08219-08219	GREEN CREEK	08525-08525	HOPEWELL	08853-08853	NESHANIC STATION
08031-08031	BELLMAWR	08220-08220	LEEDS POINT	08526-08526	IMLAYSTOWN	08854-08854	PISCATAWAY
08032-08032	GRENLOCH	08221-08222	LINWOOD	08527-08527	JACKSON	08857-08857	OLD BRIDGE
08033-08033	HADDONFIELD	08223-08223	MARMORA	08528-08528	KINGSTON	08858-08858	OLDWICK
08034-08034	CHERRY HILL	08224-08224	NEW GRETNA	08530-08530	LAMBERTVILLE	08859-08859	PARLIN
08035-08035	HADDON HEIGHTS	08225-08225	NORTHFIELD	08533-08533	NEW EGYPT	08861-08862	PERTH AMBOY
08036-08036	HAINESPORT	08226-08226	OCEAN CITY	08534-08534	PENNINGTON	08863-08863	FORDS
08037-08037	HAMMONTON	08227-08227	LINWOOD	08535-08535	PERRINEVILLE	08865-08865	PHILLIPSBURG
08038-08038	HANCOCKS BRIDGE	08230-08230	OCEAN VIEW	08536-08536	PLAINSBORO	08867-08867	PITTSTOWN
08039-08039	HARRISONVILLE	08231-08231	OCEANVILLE	08540-08544	PRINCETON	08868-08868	QUAKERTOWN
08041-08041	JOBSTOWN	08232-08233	PLEASANTVILLE	08550-08550	PRINCETON JUNCTION	08869-08869	RARITAN
08042-08042	JULIUSTOWN	08234-08234	EGG HARBOR TOWNSHIP	08551-08551	RINGOES	08870-08870	READINGTON
08043-08043	VOORHEES			08553-08553	ROCKY HILL	08871-08872	SAYREVILLE
08045-08045	LAWNSIDE	08240-08240	POMONA	08554-08554	ROEBLING	08873-08875	SOMERSET

08876-08876	SOMERVILLE	08884-08884	SPOTSWOOD	08889-08889	WHITEHOUSE STATION
08877-08877	SOUTH RIVER	08885-08885	STANTON	08890-08890	ZAREPHATH
08878-08879	SOUTH AMBOY	08886-08886	STEWARTSVILLE	08896-08896	RARITAN
08880-08880	SOUTH BOUND BROOK	08887-08887	THREE BRIDGES	08899-08899	EDISON
08882-08882	SOUTH RIVER	08888-08888	WHITEHOUSE	08901-08901	NEW BRUNSWICK

08902-08902	NORTH BRUNSWICK
08903-08903	NEW BRUNSWICK
08904-08904	HIGHLAND PARK
08905-08989	NEW BRUNSWICK

New Mexico

General Help Numbers:

Governor's Office
State Capitol, Room 400   505-827-3000
Santa Fe, NM 87503   Fax 505-827-3026
www.governor.state.nm.us   8AM-5PM

Attorney General's Office
PO Drawer 1508   505-827-6000
Santa Fe, NM 87504-1508   Fax 505-827-5826
www.ago.state.nm.us   8AM-5PM

State Court Administrator
237 Don Gaspar, Rm 25   505-827-4800
Santa Fe, NM 87501   Fax 505-827-4246
www.nmcourts.com   8AM-5PM

State Archives
1205 Camino Carols Rey   505-476-7908
Santa Fe, NM 87505   Fax 505-476-7909
www.state.nm.us/cpr   8AM-5PM

State Specifics:

Capital:	Santa Fe
	Santa Fe County
Time Zone:	MST
Number of Counties:	33
Population:	1,739,844
Web Site:	www.state.nm.us

State Agencies

Criminal Records

Department of Public Safety, Records Bureau, PO Box 1628, Santa Fe, NM 87504-1628 (Courier: 4491 Cerrillos Rd, Santa Fe, NM 87504); 505-827-9181, 505-827-3388 (Fax), 8AM-5PM.

Indexing & Storage: Records are available from 1935 on. It takes 2-4 weeks before new records are available for inquiry. Records are indexed on inhouse computer.

Searching: Must have a notarized signed release from person of record authorizing the State of New Mexico to release records to requester. Except for law enforcement officials, specify which records you want. Juvenile records are not released. Include the following in your request-date of birth, Social Security Number, full name.

Access by: mail, in person.

Fee & Payment: The fee is $7.00 per individual. Fee payee: Department of Public Safety. Prepayment required. Must use cashiers check or money order. No credit cards accepted.

Mail search: Turnaround time: 1-2 weeks. A self addressed stamped envelope is requested.

In person search: Searching is available in person.

Corporation Records
Limited Liability Company Records

New Mexico Public Regulation Commission, Corporate Department, PO Box 1269, Santa Fe, NM 87504-1269 (Courier: 1120 Paseo de Peralta, Pera Bldg 4th Fl, Rm 413, Santa Fe, NM 87501); 505-827-4502 (Main Number), 800-947-4722 (In-state Only), 505-827-4510 (Good Standing), 505-827-4513 (Copy Request), 505-827-4387 (Fax), 8AM-12:00: 1PM-5PM.

www.nmprc.state.nm.us

Note: For Charter Requirement Information call 505-827-4511.

Indexing & Storage: Records are available for all entities. Records are indexed on microfilm.

Searching: Include the following in your request- full name of business. In addition to the articles of incorporation, corporation records include the following information: Annual Reports, Officers, Directors, Prior (merged) names, Inactive, Registered and Reserved names. The following data is not released: financial information.

Access by: mail, phone, fax, in person, online.

Fee & Payment: There is no charge for a computer printout. minimum fees are $10.00 for for-profit companies or domestic LLCs and a $5.00 for non-profit companies. Certification fee is $25.00, except for non-profits which is $10.00. Copies are $1.00 per page. Fee payee: Public Regulation Commission Payment is due in 10 days. Personal checks accepted. No credit cards accepted.

Mail search: Turnaround time: 2 days. A self addressed stamped envelope is requested.

Phone search: Limited information is given over the phone.

Fax search: Information can be requested by fax, but is returned by mail in 3-5 days.

In person search: Call is to schedule viewing time for microfilm.

Online search: There is no charge to view records online at www.nmprc.state.nm.us/ftq.htm. Records can be searched by company name or by director name.

Other access: The state makes the database available on electronic format using a 3480 tape cartridge.

Trademarks/Servicemarks Trade Names

Secretary of State, Trademarks Division, State Capitol North, Santa Fe, NM 87503; 505-827-3600, 505-827-3611 (Fax), 8AM-5PM.

www.sos.state.nm.us

Note: Effective July 1, 1997, New Mexico no longer registers trade names. However, the agency will do searches for records on file.

Indexing & Storage: Records are available from 1980-present. It takes 1-2 days before new records are available for inquiry. Records are indexed on inhouse computer.

Searching: Include the following in your request- trademark/servicemark name. Include your full name, address and telephone number.

Access by: mail, phone, fax, in person.

Fee & Payment: Prepayment required. Fee payee: Secretary of State. Personal checks accepted.

Mail search: Turnaround time: 2-3 days. No self addressed stamped envelope is required. No fee for mail request.

Phone search: They will do a computer search and will give you the information over the phone for no fee.

Fax search: There is no fee. Turnaround time: 24 hours.

In person search: No fee for request. Turnaround time is usually immediate.

Other access: Monthly listings are available at $.10 per trademark/service mark record.

Uniform Commercial Code

UCC Division, Secretary of State, State Capitol North, Santa Fe, NM 87503; 505-827-3610, 505-827-3611 (Fax), 8AM-5PM.

www.sos.state.nm.us/ucc/ucchome.htm

Note: This agency will not conduct in-person searches. You must come in yourself, hire a local search company, or conduct your search at the agency web site.

Indexing & Storage: Records are available from 1965. It takes 24 hours before new records are available for inquiry.

Searching: Please note that all tax liens are filed at the county level. The system does not give information on collateral.

Access by: in person, online.

Fee & Payment: Copies are $1.00 per page plus $3.00 if certification requested. Fee payee: Secretary of State. Prepayment required. Personal checks accepted. No credit cards accepted. No self addressed stamped envelope is required.

In person search: You may use their in-house computer by appointment only. Call 505-827-3614. You may view documents for free.

Online search: The web site permits searches and a form to use to order copies of filings.

Federal Tax Liens
State Tax Liens
Records not maintained by a state level agency.

Note: Records are filed with the Clerk at the county level.

Sales Tax Registrations

Taxation & Revenue Department, Tax Administrative Services Division, PO Box 630, Santa Fe, NM 87504-0630 (Courier: Montoya Bldg, 1100 S St Francis Drive, Santa Fe, NM 87501); 505-827-0700, 505-827-0469 (Fax), 8AM-5PM.

www.state.nm.us/tax

Indexing & Storage: Records are available from 1988.

Searching: This agency will only confirm that a business is registered and active. They will provide no other information. The business name is required, the permit number and federal ID are optional.

Access by: mail, phone, in person.

Fee & Payment: There is no search fee, copies are $.05 per page

Mail search: Turnaround time: 6-12 weeks. A self addressed stamped envelope is requested.

Phone search: Searching is available by phone.

In person search: Searching is available in person.

Birth Certificates

Department of Health, Bureau of Vital Records, PO Box 26111, Santa Fe, NM 87502 (Courier: 1105 South St Francis Dr, Santa Fe, NM 87502); 505-827-0121, 505-827-2338 (Information), 505-984-1048 (Fax), 8AM-5:00PM (Counter Service: 9AM-4PM).

www.health.state.nm.us

Note: All requesters must sign and date the request. It is a felony to obtain a record fraudulently.

Indexing & Storage: Records are available from 1920 on. New records are available for inquiry immediately. Records are indexed on microfiche, inhouse computer.

Searching: Records available only to immediate family members or those demonstrating legal tangible interest in the desired record. Sealed records (e.g. adoptions and paternity) are unavailable. Include the following in your request- full name, names of parents, mother's maiden name, date of birth, place of birth, relationship to person of record, reason for information request. Signature of requester and physical & mailing addresses are required.

Access by: mail, phone, fax, in person.

Fee & Payment: The search fee is $10.00 per record. There is an additional $10.00 fee if you order by phone or by fax for use of a credit card. Fee payee: NM Vital Records. Prepayment required. Personal checks accepted. Credit cards accepted: Mastercard, Visa, AmEx, Discover.

Mail search: Turnaround time: 3 weeks. No self addressed stamped envelope is required.

Phone search: Searching is available by phone.

Fax search: Same criteria as phone searches.

In person search: Turnaround time is usually less than 1/2 hour.

Expedited service: Expedited service is available for mail, phone and fax searches. Turnaround time: 24 hours. Use of credit card required for additional fee. Add $13.25 for delivery service.

Death Records

Department of Health, Bureau of Vital Records, PO Box 26111, Santa Fe, NM 87502 (Courier: 1105 South St Francis Dr, Santa Fe, NM 87502); 505-827-0121, 505827-2338 (Information), 505-984-1048 (Fax), 8AM-5PM (Counter Service: 9AM-4PM).

www.health.state.nm.us

Indexing & Storage: Records are available from 1920-present. New records are available for inquiry immediately. Records are indexed on microfiche, inhouse computer.

Searching: Only immediate family member or a person with tangible interest can receive record. Include the following in your request-full name, date of death, place of death, Social Security Number, relationship to person of record, reason for information request. Age at death and name of mortuary must also be included for search.

Access by: mail, phone, fax, in person.

Fee & Payment: The fee is $5.00 per record. An additional fee may be charged if required information is not submitted. Use of credit card is an additional $10.00. Fee payee: NM Vital Records. Prepayment required. Credit cards are only used for phone and fax ordering. Personal checks accepted. Credit cards accepted: Mastercard, Visa, AmEx, Discover.

Mail search: Turnaround time: 3-4 weeks. No self addressed stamped envelope is required.

Phone search: You must use a credit card.

Fax search: Same criteria as phone searches.

In person search: Turnaround time is usually 1 hour or less.

Expedited service: Expedited service is available for mail, phone and fax searches. Turnaround time: 24 hours. Use of credit card required. Delivery fee is $13.25 minimum.

Marriage Certificates
Divorce Records

Records not maintained by a state level agency.

Note: Marriage and Divorce records are found at county of issue.

Workers' Compensation Records

Access to Records is Restricted

Workers Compensation Administration, PO Box 27198, Albuquerque, NM 87125-7198 (Courier: 2410 Centre Ave, SE, Albuquerque, NM 87106); 505-841-6000, 800-255-7965 (In-State Toll Free), 505-841-6060 (Fax), 8AM-5PM.

http://www.state.nm.us/wca

Note: Records are restricted to only those involved in the case. The subject must write the agency, provide proof of ID with a driver's license, and request the record, and pay a copy fee of $.25 per page.

Driver Records

Motor Vehicle Division, Driver Services Bureau, PO Box 1028, Santa Fe, NM 87504-1028 (Courier: Joseph M. Montoya Bldg, 1100 S St. Francis Dr, 2nd Floor, Santa Fe, NM 87504); 505-827-2234, 505-827-2267 (Fax), 8AM-5PM.

www.state.nm.us/tax/mvd

Note: Copies of tickets may be obtained from the same address. There is no fee.

Indexing & Storage: Records are available for 3 years for moving violations; 25 years DWIs. Accidents are not reported on the record and neither are violations less than 10 mph over the limit in 55 or 65 zones. The driver's address is included on the record. It takes 30-40 days before new records are available for inquiry.

Searching: The law lists 9 permissable user groups and permits release of records with written consent. Purchasers may not use the information for direct mail solicitation or resell the reports after usage. The full name, DOB and either the license number or Social Security Number is required when ordering. The following data is not released: Social Security Numbers, addresses or date of birth.

Access by: mail, in person, online.

Fee & Payment: There is no fee for mail or walk-in requests. Fee payee: Motor Vehicle Division. Prepayment required. Personal checks accepted. No credit cards accepted.

Mail search: Turnaround time: 3-5 days. No fee for manual search. A self addressed stamped envelope is requested.

In person search: No fee for manual search. Up to 2 requests can be processed while you wait, the rest must be in writing and left overnight.

Online search: New Mexico Technet is the state authorized vendor for access. The costs are $2.50 per record for interactive, $1.50 per record for batch, plus a $.25 per minute network fee. The system is open 24 hours a day, batch requesters must wait 24 hours. Call 505-345-6555 for more information.

Vehicle Ownership
Vehicle Identification
Boat & Vessel Ownership
Boat & Vessel Registration

Motor Vehicle Division, Vehicle Services Bureau, PO Box 1028, Santa Fe, NM 87504-1028 (Courier: Joseph M. Montoya Bldg, 1100 S St. Francis Dr, 2nd Floor, Santa Fe, NM 87504); 505-827-4636, 505-827-1004, 505-827-0395 (Fax), 8AM-5PM.

www.state.nm.us/tax/mvd

Indexing & Storage: Records are available for a minimum of 3 years on boats and 6 years on vehicles. All motorized boats, sailboats, and jet skis must be both titled and registered if over 10 ft, and only registered if 10 ft or less. It takes 30 days before new records are available for inquiry.

Searching: Authorized requesters are restricted to 9 user groups and must sign a contract that states purpose of request and subsequent use. Requesters may not use ownership and vehicle information to create a resellable database. The following data is not released: addresses, Social Security Numbers or date of birth.

Access by: mail, in person, online.

Fee & Payment: There are no fees for mail or in person requests. A vehicle history search (microfilm) goes back 6 years. Fee payee: Department of Motor Vehicles. Prepayment required. Personal checks accepted. No credit cards accepted.

Mail search: Turnaround time: 3-4 weeks. A self addressed stamped envelope is requested.

In person search: Up to ten requests will be processed while you wait.

Online search: Records are available, for authorized users, from the state's designated vendor New Mexico Technet. Cost is $2.50 per record plus a $.25 per minute network charge. There is a $35.00 set-up fee, also. Call 505-345-6555 for more information.

Other access: Bulk requests for vehicle or ownership information must be approved by the Director's office. Once a sale is made, further resale is prohibited.

Accident Reports

Department of Public Safety, Records, PO Box 1628, Santa Fe, NM 87504-1628 (Courier: New Mexico State Police Complex, 4491 Cerrillos Rd, Santa Fe, NM 87504); 505-827-9300, 505-827-3396 (Fax), 8AM-5PM.

Indexing & Storage: Records are available 2 years to present in-house (on computer) and up to 10 years archived (25 years for fatalities). It takes 15 days before new records are available for inquiry.

Searching: Arrest information is not released. Include the following in your request-full name, date of accident, county, location of accident.

Access by: mail, phone, in person.

Fee & Payment: The fee is $1.00 per page. There is no fee for a no record found. There is no fee charged for persons directly involved in the accident. Fee payee: Department of Public Safety. Prepayment required. Personal checks accepted. No credit cards accepted.

Mail search: Turnaround time: 3-5 days. A self addressed stamped envelope is requested.

Phone search: No fee for telephone request.

In person search: Turnaround time is immediate for the last two years.

Legislation-Current/Pending
Legislation-Passed

Legislative Council Service, State Capitol Bldg, Room 411, Santa Fe, NM 87501; 505-986-4600, 505-986-4350 (Bill Room During Session Only), 505-986-4610 (Fax), 8AM-5PM.

http://legis.state.nm.us

Note: Signed laws of the current year can be obtained from the Secretary of State's Office at 505-827-3600. Searchers are encouraged to use the web.

Indexing & Storage: Records are available for current back four years, online. The current session meets starting the third Tuesday in January. Sessions are 60 days in odd-numbered years and 30 days in even-numbered years.

Searching: Submit bill number or topic to search. Records on computer.

Access by: mail, phone, in person, online.

Fee & Payment: Depending on the extent of the search, the agency may charge for copies. There is no search fee. Fee payee: New Mexico State Legislature. Personal checks accepted. No credit cards accepted.

Mail search: Turnaround time: variable.

Phone search: Limited searching is available during session.

In person search: You may request bills in person.

Online search: The Internet site is a complete source of information about bills and legislators. There ares also links to other NM state agencies and NM statutes.

Other access: Subscription purchase for the complete file of current session is available. However, your must request your subscription by mid-session.

Voter Registration

Access to Records is Restricted

Secretary of State, Bureau of Elections, State Capitol Annex, Ste 300, Santa Fe, NM 87503; 505-827-3620, 505-827-4954 (Fax), 8AM-5PM.

Note: Individual look-ups must be done at the county level. This agency will sell its database, but for restricted purposes only (not for commercial purposes).

GED Certificates

Department of Education, GED Testing Program, 300 Don Gaspar, Rm 124, Santa Fe, NM 87501-2786; 505-827-6702, 505-827-6616 (Fax), 8AM-5PM.

http://sde.state.nm.us

Searching: The SSN, DOB, and year of test are needed for a verification. A signed release is needed for a copy of a transcript.

Access by: mail, fax, in person.

Fee & Payment: There are no fees.

Mail search: Turnaround time: 2 weeks. No self addressed stamped envelope is required.

Fax search: Same criteria as mail searching.

In person search: Searching is available in person.

Hunting License Information
Fishing License Information

NM Dept of Game & Fish, PO Box 25112, Santa Fe, NM 87504 (Courier: Villagra Bldg, 408 Galisto St, Santa Fe, NM 87501); 505-827-7911, 800-862-9310, 505-827-7915 (Fax), 8AM-12PM; 1PM-5PM.

www.gmfsh.state.nm.us

Indexing & Storage: Records are available for last season only. Records are indexed on hard copy.

Searching: Include the following in your request-name.

Access by: in person.

Fee & Payment: Fee is $60 per hours plus $.25 per copy. Fee payee: NM Dept of Fish & Game.

In person search: You may do the search yourself for no fee.

Licenses Searchable Online

Architect #17	www.nmbea.org/People/Aroster.htm
Clinical Nurse Specialist #19	www.state.nm.us/nursing/lookup.html
Contractor #13	www.newmexlicense.org/pub/index.cfm
Engineer #44	www.state.nm.us/pepsboard/roster.htm
Hemodialysis Technician #19	www.state.nm.us/nursing/lookup.html
Journeyman #13	www.newmexlicense.org/pub/index.cfm
Liquefied Petroleum Gas (LPG) #30	www.newmexlicense.org/pub/index.cfm
Lobbyist #32	http://web.state.nm.us/LOBBY/LOB.htm
LP Gas Licensee #13	www.newmexlicense.org/pub/index.cfm
LPN #19	www.state.nm.us/nursing/lookup.html
Medication Aide #19	www.state.nm.us/nursing/lookup.html
Nurse #19	www.state.nm.us/nursing/lookup.html
Nurse Anesthetist #19	www.state.nm.us/nursing/lookup.html
Nurse-RN #19	www.state.nm.us/nursing/lookup.html
Optometrist #40	OptometryBd@state.nm.us (e-mail verification requests are accepted)
Psychologist #37	www.rld.state.nm.us/b&c/psychology/lcnssrch.asp
Surveyor #44	www.state.nm.us/pepsboard/roster.htm

Licensing Quick Finder

Acupuncturist #26	505-476-7081
Animal Pregnancy Diagnosis #55	505-841-9112
Architect #17	505-827-6375
Art Therapist #57	505-827-7554
Artificial Inseminator #55	505-841-9112
Athletic Promoter #39	505-827-7172
Athletic Trainer #01	505-476-7098
Attorney #20	505-271-9706
Audiologist #29	505-827-7554
Audiologist #11	505-476-7098
Bank #51	505-827-7100
Barber #02	505-476-7110
Boiler Operator Journeyman #33	505-884-5850
Boxer #39	505-827-7172
Boxer Manager #39	505-827-7172
Boxing Judge #39	505-827-7172
Boxing Timekeeper #39	505-827-7172
Broker #52	505-827-7070
Broker Dealer #32	505-827-7140
Chiropractor #03	505-827-7120
Clinical Nurse Specialist #19	505-841-8340
Collection Agency #51	505-827-7100
Collection Agency Manager #47	505-827-7100
Collection Agency Manager #51	505-827-7100
Consumer Credit #51	505-827-7100
Consumer Loan #51	505-827-7100
Contractor #13	505-827-7030
Cosmetologist #02	505-476-7110
Credit Union #51	505-827-7100
Crematory #12	505-476-7100
Dental Assistant #04	505-476-7125
Dental Hygienist #04	505-476-7125
Dentist #04	505-476-7125
Dietitian/Nutritionist #08	505-476-7127
Direct Disposer #12	505-476-7100
Electrologist #02	505-827-7550
Electrophysician #02	505-476-7110
Emergency Medical Technician #22	505-476-7000
Endowed/Perpetual Care Cemetery #51	505-827-7100
Engineer #44	505-827-7561
Escrow Company #51	505-827-7100
Esthetician #02	505-476-7110
Fireworks Distributor Class C or Class B #54	505-827-3761
Fireworks Vendor (Retailers, Wholesalers) #54	505-827-3761
Funeral Director #12	505-476-7100
Funeral Home #12	505-476-7100
Gambling (Non-profit) #14	505-827-7088
General Real Estate Appraiser #49	505-476-7096
Hearing Aid Specialist #11	505-476-7098
Hemodialysis Technician #19	505-841-8340
Insurance Agent #23	505-827-4349
Interior Designer #25	505-476-7077
Investment Advisor #32	505-827-7140
Investment Advisor/Representative #48	505-827-7140
Journeyman #13	505-827-7030
Landscape Architect #18	505-476-7077
Liquefied Petroleum Gas (LPG) #30	505-884-5850
Liquor Distributor #14	505-827-7066
LP Gas Licensee #13	505-827-7030
LPN #19	505-841-8340
Manicurist #02	505-476-7110
Manufactured Housing Dealer #52	505-827-7070
Manufactured Housing Installer/Repairman #52	505-827-7070
Manufactured Housing Manufacturer #52	505-827-7070
Manufactured Housing Salesperson #52	505-827-7070
Manufacturer 1.4G Fireworks #54	505-827-3761
Marriage/Family Therapist #57	505-476-7100
Massage Instructor #05	505-827-7013
Massage School #05	505-827-7013
Massage Therapist #05	505-827-7013
Mechanic #31	505-827-7030
Medical Doctor #36	505-827-6784
Medical Researcher #41	505-841-9102
Medical Wholesale Company #41	505-841-9102
Medication Aide #19	505-841-8340
Mental Health Counselor #57	505-476-7100
Midwife #34	505-476-8586
Midwife (CNM) #34	505-476-8586
Money Order Company #51	505-827-7100
Mortgage Company/Loan Brokers #51	505-827-7100
Motor Vehicle Sales Finance Company #51	505-827-7100
Non-Residential Pharmacy #41	505-841-9102
Notary Public #53	505-827-3605
Nuclear Medicine Technologist #38	505-827-1870
Nurse #19	505-841-8340
Nurse Anesthetist #19	505-841-8340
Nurse-RN #19	505-841-8340
Nursing Home Administrator #06	505-827-7121
Nutrition & Dietetic #04	505-476-7125
Occupational Therapist #27	505-476-7085
Occupational Therapist Assistant #27	505-476-7085
Optometrist #40	505-827-7121
Osteopathic Physician #07	505-476-7120
Pest Management Consultant #21	505-646-2133
Pesticide Applicator #21	505-646-2133
Pesticide Dealer #21	505-646-2133
Pesticide Operator #21	505-646-2133
Pharmacist #41	505-841-9102
Physical Therapist #28	505-476-7085
Physical Therapist Assistant #28	505-476-7085
Physician #41	505-841-9102
Physician Assistant #36	505-827-6784
Podiatrist #42	505-827-7120
Polygraph Examiner #43	505-476-7080
Polygrapher #09	505-827-7172
Private Investigator #09	505-827-7172
Private Investigator #43	505-476-7080
Private Patrol Operator #43	505-476-7080
Provisional Social Worker #10	505-476-7100
Psychologist #37	505-476-7077
Psychologist Associate #37	505-476-7077
Public Accountant-CPA #35	505-841-9108
Racing #45	505-841-6400
Radiation Therapy Technologist #38	505-827-1870
Radiologic Technologist #38	505-827-1870
Real Estate Agent #46	505-841-9120
Real Estate Appraiser #49	505-476-7096
Real Estate Broker #46	505-841-9120
Residential Real Estate Appraiser #49	505-476-7096
Respiratory Care Therapist #56	505-476-7121
School Administrator #24	505-827-6587
School Counselor #24	505-827-6587
Securities Broker/Dealer #48	505-827-7140
Securities Division Agent #32	505-827-7140
Securities Sales Representative #48	505-827-7140
Security Guard #43	505-476-7080
Security Sales Representative #32	505-827-7140
Shorthand Reporter #16	505-797-6000
SLP #11	505-476-7098
Social Worker (LBSW) #10	505-476-7100
Social Worker (LI) #10	505-476-7100
Social Worker (LM) #10	505-476-7100
Speech-Language Pathologist #29	505-827-7554
Speech-Language Pathologist #11	505-476-7098
Substance Abuse Counselor #57	505-476-7100
Substance Abuse Intern #57	505-476-7100
Surveyor #44	505-827-7561
Teacher #24	505-827-6587
Veterinarian #55	505-841-9112
Veterinary Facility #55	505-841-9112
Veterinary Technician #55	505-841-9112
Waste Water Systems Operator #38	505-827-2836

Licensing Agency Information

01 Administrative Services Division, Athletic Trainers Board, PO Box 25101 (POB 25101), Santa Fe, NM 87504; 505-476-7100.

www.state.nm.us/rld/b&c/athletic%20trainers%20board.htm

02 Administrative Services Division, Board of Barbers & Cosmetologists, PO Box 25101, 2055 S. Pacheco St, Santa Fe, NM 87504; 505-476-7110, Fax: 505-476-7118.

www.rld.state.nm.us/b&c/barber_and_cosmetologist_board.htm

03 Administrative Services Division, Board of Chiropractic Examiners, PO Box 25101 (PO Box 25101), Santa Fe, NM 87504; 505-476-7120, Fax: 505-476-7095.

www.rld.state.nm.us/b&c/chiropractic_examiners_board.htm

04 Administrative Services Division, Board of Dental Health Care, PO Box 25101 (PO Box 25101), Santa Fe, NM 87504; 505-476-7125, Fax: 505-476-7095.

www.rld.state.nm.us/b&c/dental/index.htm

05 Administrative Services Division, Board of Massage Therapy, 725 St Michael's Dr, Santa Fe, NM 87501; 505-476-7089, Fax: 505-827-7095.

www.rld.state.nm.us/b&c/massage/index.htm

06 Regulation and Licensing Department, Nursing Home Administrators Board, PO Box 25101 (PO Box 25101 (2055 Pacheco St, #400)), Santa Fe, NM 87504; 505-476-7121, Fax: 505-827-7095.

www.rld.state.nm.us/b&c/nhab/index.htm

07 Administrative Services Division, Board of Osteopathic Medical Examiners, PO Box 25101 (725 St Michael's Dr), Santa Fe, NM 87504; 505-476-7120, Fax: 505-476-7095.

www.rld.state.nm.us/b&c/osteopathic_examiners_board.htm

08 Administrative Services Division, Nutrition & Dietetics Practice Board, PO Box 25101 (2055 S Pacheco #400), Santa Fe, NM 87504; 505-476-7127, Fax: 505-476-7095.

09 Regulation & Licensing Department, Private Investigators Board, 725 St Michael's Dr, Santa Fe, NM 87501; 505-476-7100.

www.rld.state.nm.us/b&c/private_investigators_board.htm

10 Regulation & Licensing Dept, Social Work Examiners Board, PO Box 25101, Santa Fe, NM 87504; 505-476-7100, Fax: 505-827-7548.

www.rld.state.nm.us/b&c/social_work_examiners_board.htm

11 Regulation & Licensing Department, Speech, Language, Audiology, & Hearing Aid Board, PO Box 25101, Santa Fe, NM 87504; 505-476-7100, Fax: 505-476-7094.

www.state.nm.us/rld/b&c/hearing%20aid%20board.htm

12 Regulation & Licensing Department, Thanatopractice Board, PO Box 25101 (725 St Michael's Dr), Santa Fe, NM 87501; 505-476-7100, Fax: 505-827-7095.

www.rld.state.nm.us/b&c/thanato/thanatopractice%20board.htm

13 Regulation & Licensing Department, Construction Industries Division, 1650 University Blvd NE #201, Sante Fe, NM 87102-1731; 505-827-7030, Fax: 505-765-5670.

http://rld.state.nm.us/cid

Direct URL to search licenses: www.newmexlicense.org/pub/index.cfm You can search online using name

14 Alcohol Gaming Division, 725 St. Michaels Dr, Santa Fe, NM 87505-7605; 505-827-7088, Fax: 505-827-7168.

www.state.nm.us/rld/rld_agd.html

16 Board Governing Recording of Judicial Proceedings, PO Box 25883 (PO Box 25883), Albuquerque, NM 87125; 505-797-6000, Fax: 505-843-8765.

17 Board of Examiners for Architects, PO Box 509, Santa Fe, NM 87504; 505-827-6375, Fax: 505-827-6373.

www.nmbea.org

Direct URL to search licenses: www.nmbea.org/People/Aroster.htm You can search online using registration #, name, city, or state

18 Board of Landscape Architects, PO Box 25101 (2055 South Pacheco #400 (PO Box 25101)), Santa Fe, NM 87504; 505-476-7077, Fax: 505-476-7087.

19 Board of Nursing, 4206-A Lousiana Blvd NE, Albuquerque, NM 87109; 505-841-8340, Fax: 505-841-8347.

www.state.nm.us/nursing

Direct URL to search licenses: www.state.nm.us/nursing/lookup.html You can search online using name, SSN, license #, or certificate #.

20 Board of Bar Examiners, 9420 Indian School NE, Albuquerque, NM 87112; 505-271-9706, Fax: 505-271-9768.

21 Department of Agriculture, Pesticide Management Bureau, MSC 3AQ, PO Box 30005 (PO Box 30005), Las Cruces, NM 88003-8005; 505-646-2133, Fax: 505-646-5977.

http://nmdaweb.nmsu.edu/AES/PEST/tconlic.htm

22 Department of Health, Injury Prevention & EMS Bureau, PO Box 26110 (PO Box 26110), Santa Fe, NM 87502-6110; 505-476-7000, Fax: 505-476-7010.

23 Department of Insurance, Licensing Division, PO Drawer 1269, Santa Fe, NM 87504; 505-827-4349, Fax: 505-827-4734.

24 Education Department, Professional Licensure, 300 Don Gaspar, Education Bldg, Santa Fe, NM 87501-2786; 505-827-6587, Fax: 505-827-6696.

25 Board of Interior Design, 2055 South Pacheco St #400 (PO Box 25101), Santa Fe, NM 87504; 505-476-7077, Fax: 505-827-7087.

www.rld.state.nm.us/b&c/interior_design_board.htm

26 Regulation & Licensing Department, Acupuncture & Oriental Medicine Board, PO Box 25101 (2055 S Pacheco St #400), Santa Fe, NM 87505; 505-476-7081, Fax: 505-476-7095.

www.rld.state.nm.us/b&c/acupunture_oriental_medicine-bd.htm

27 Regulation & Licensing Department, Occupational Therapy Board, PO Box 25101 (725 St Michael's Dr), Santa Fe, NM 87504; 505-476-7085, Fax: 505-476-7086.

www.rld.state.nm.us/b&c/otb/index.htm

28 Regulation & Licensing Department, Physical Therapy Board, PO Box 25101 (2055 S Pacheco #400), Santa Fe, NM 87505; 505-476-7085, Fax: 505-476-7086.

www.rld.state.nm.us/b&c/ptb/index.htm

30 Licensing Boards, 3311 Candelaria NE #C, Albuquerque, NM 87107; 505-884-5850, Fax: 505-883-7696.

31 Licensing Boards, 725 St Michaels Dr, Santa Fe, NM 87503-.

32 Licensing Boards, 725 St Michael's Dr, Santa Fe, NM 87505; 505-827-7140, Fax: 505-984-0617.

33 Boiler Operator Journeyman Licensing Board, 3311 Candelaria NE #C, Albuquerque, NM 87107; 505-884-5850, Fax: 505-883-7696.

34 Maternal Health program, 525 Camino De Los Marquez #1, Santa Fe, NM 87501; 505-476-8586, Fax: 505-476-8620.

35 Regulation & Licensing Department, Board of Accountancy, 1650 University Blvd, #400A, Albuquerque, NM 87102; 505-841-9108, Fax: 505-841-9113.

www.state.nm.us/rld/b&c/accountancy/board%20of%20accountancy.htm

36 Board of Medical Examiners, 491 Old Sante Fe Trail, Lamy Bldg, 2nd Fl, Santa Fe, NM 87501; 505-827-5022, Fax: 505-827-7377.

www.nmbeme.org

37 Board of Psychologist Examiners, PO Box 25101 (PO Box 25101, 2055 South Pacheco St #400), Santa Fe, NM 87504; 505-476-7100, Fax: 505-827-7017.

www.rld.state.nm.us/b&c/psychology

Direct URL to search licenses: www.rld.state.nm.us/b&c/psychology You can search online using name, city, state

38 Environment Department, Licensing & Registration Section, PO Box 26110 (PO Box 26110), Santa Fe, NM 87505-6110; 505-827-1870, Fax: 505-827-1544.

39 Regulation & Licensing Department, Athletic Commission, PO Box 25101 (PO Box 25101), Santa Fe, NM 87504; 505-827-7080, Fax: 505-827-7095.

www.state.nm.us/rld/b&c/athletic%20commission.htm

40 Regulation and Licensing Department, Board of Examiners in Optometry, PO Box 25101 (PO Box 25101 (2055 South Pacheco Street)), Santa Fe, NM 87504; 505-476-7121, Fax: 505-476-7095.

www.rld.state.nm.us/b&c/optometry/index.htm

Direct URL to search licenses: www.arbo.org/nodb2000/licsearch.asp You can search online using national database by name, city or state.

41 Administrative Services Division, Pharmacy Board, 1650 University Blvd, Albuquerque, NM 87102; 505-841-9102, Fax: 505-841-9113.

www.state.nm.us/pharmacy

42 Regulation & Licensing Department, Podiatry Board, PO Box 25101 (2055 S Pacheco St. #400), Santa Fe, NM 87504; 505-476-7120, Fax: 505-827-7095.

www.rld.state.nm.us/b&c/podiatry_board.htm

43 Polygraph Examiners Bureau, Department of Regulation & Licensing, PO Box 25101 (PO Box

25101), Santa Fe, NM 87504; 505-476-7080, Fax: 505-476-7095.

www.rld.state.nm.us/b&c/otb/index.htm

44 Professional Engineers & Surveyors Board, 1010 Marquez Pl, Santa Fe, NM 87501; 505-827-7561, Fax: 505-827-7566.
www.state.nm.us/pepsboard

Direct URL to search licenses: www.state.nm.us/pepsboard/roster.htm You can search online using name. When checked in 1999, the online search page was only current as of November 1998.

45 Racing Commission, PO Box 8576 (300 San Mateo Blvd NE, #110), Albuquerque, NM 87198; 505-841-6400, Fax: 505-841-6400.

www.state.nm.us/src

46 Regulation & Licensing Department, Real Estate Commission, 1650 University Blvd, #490, Albuquerque, NM 87102; 505-841-9120, Fax: 505-276-0725.

www.state.nm.us/nmrec

48 Regulation & Licensing Department, Securities Division, PO Box 25101 (PO Box 25101), Santa Fe, NM 87504; 505-827-7140, Fax: 505-984-0617.

www.rld.state.nm.us/sec/index.htm

49 Regulation & Licensing Department, Real Estate Appraisers Board, POB 25101 (2055 S. Pacheco St), Santa Fe, NM 87504; 505-476-7096, Fax: 505-827-7096.

www.rld.state.nm.us/b&c/real_estate_appraisers_board.htm

51 Regulation & Licensing Department, Financial Institutions Department, PO Box 26110 (PO Box 26110), Santa Fe, NM 87501; 505-827-7110, Fax: 505-827-7107.

www.state.nm.us/rld/rld_fid.html

52 Regulation & Licensing Department, Manufactured Housing Division, 725 St Michael's Dr, Santa Fe, NM 87501; 505-827-7070, Fax: 505-827-7074.

www.rld.state.nm.us/mhd/index.htm

53 Secretary of State, Notary Public, PO Box 509 (State Capitol North), Santa Fe, NM 87503; 505-827-3600, Fax: 505-827-3611.

www.sos.state.nm.us

54 State Fire Marshal, Public Regulation Commission, PO Box 1269 (PO Drawer 1269), Santa Fe, NM 87504; 505-827-3761, Fax: 505-827-3778.

55 Veterinary Medicine Board, 1650 University Blvd NE, Albuquerque, NM 87102; 505-841-9112, Fax: 505-841-9113.

56 Repiratory Care Advisory Board, Regulation & Licensing Department, PO Box 25101 (PO Box 25101 (2055 Pacheco St, #400)), Santa Fe, NM 87504; 505-476-7121, Fax: 505-476-7095.

www.rld.state.nm.us/b&c/rcb/index.htm

57 Regulation & Licensing Department, Counseling & Therapy Practice Board, 1599 St Francis Dr, PO Box 25101, Sante Fe, NM 87504; 505-476-7100.

www.state.nm.us/rld/b&c/counseling/counseling%20and%20therapy%20practice%20board.htm

The following list indicates the district and division name for each county in the state. If the district or division name of the bankruptcy court is different from the civil/criminal court, it appears in parentheses.

County/Court Cross Reference

Bernalillo	Albuquerque	McKinley	Albuquerque
Catron	Albuquerque	Mora	Albuquerque
Chaves	Albuquerque	Otero	Albuquerque
Cibola	Albuquerque	Quay	Albuquerque
Colfax	Albuquerque	Rio Arriba	Albuquerque
Curry	Albuquerque	Roosevelt	Albuquerque
De Baca	Albuquerque	San Juan	Albuquerque
Dona Ana	Albuquerque	San Miguel	Albuquerque
Eddy	Albuquerque	Sandoval	Albuquerque
Grant	Albuquerque	Santa Fe	Albuquerque
Guadalupe	Albuquerque	Sierra	Albuquerque
Harding	Albuquerque	Socorro	Albuquerque
Hidalgo	Albuquerque	Taos	Albuquerque
Lea	Albuquerque	Torrance	Albuquerque
Lincoln	Albuquerque	Union	Albuquerque
Los Alamos	Albuquerque	Valencia	Albuquerque
Luna	Albuquerque		

US District Court

District of New Mexico

Albuquerque Division 333 Lomas Blvd NW #270, Albuquerque, NM 87102-2274, 505-348-2000, Fax: 505-348-2028.

www.nmcourt.fed.us

Counties: All counties in New Mexico. Cases may be assigned to any of its three divisions.

Indexing & Storage: Cases are indexed by defendant and plaintiff as well as by case number. New cases are available in the index within 2 days after filing date. Inquirer's phone number and the years to search are required to search for a record. Records from 1990 to the present can be searched by the plaintiff's name. Prior records can be searched by defendant or case number. A computer index is maintained. Open records are located at this court.

Fee & Payment: The fee is $15.00 per item (one party name or case number). Payment may be made by money order, cashier check, personal check. Copies are made through a copy service only. They charge $.15 per page. Prepayment is required. Payee: Clerk, US District Court. Certification fee: $5.00 per document. Copy fee: $.35 per page.

Phone Search: Only docket information available by phone. An automated voice case information service (VCIS) is not available.

Mail Search: A stamped self addressed envelope is not required.

In Person Search: In person searching is available.

PACER: Sign-up number is 800-676-6856. Access fee is $.60 per minute. Case records are available back to 1990. Records are purged every six months. New records are available online after 2 weeks.

Electronic Filing: See Internet site for information about electronic filing. You must register to use the system. Electronic filing information is available online at www.nmcourt.fed.us/dcdocs (Click on ACE Filing)

US Bankruptcy Court

District of New Mexico

Albuquerque Division PO Box 546, Albuquerque, NM 87103 (Courier Address: 3rd Floor, Room 314, 421 Gold Ave SW, Albuquerque, NM 87102), 505-348-2500, Fax: 505-348-2473.

www.nmcourt.fed.us

Counties: All counties in New Mexico.

Indexing & Storage: Cases are indexed by debtor as well as by case number. New cases are available in the index 24 hours after filing date. Both computer and card indexes are maintained. Card indexes are maintained on cases filed prior to May 26, 1987. Cases filed after that date are indexed in the computer. Open records are located at this court.

Fee & Payment: The fee is $15.00 per item (one party name or case number). Payment may be made by money order, cashier check, personal check, Visa or Mastercard. Prepayment is required. Debtor's checks are not accepted. Payee: Clerk, US Bankruptcy Court. Certification fee: $5.00 per document. Copy fee: $.50 per page.

Phone Search: Index, docket and claim information will be released over the phone. An automated voice case information service (VCIS) is available. Call VCIS at 888-435-7822 or 505-248-6536.

Fax Search: The fee is $15.00 and must be prepaid.

Mail Search: Fee will be charged only when a case file search is required. Always enclose a stamped self addressed envelope.

In Person Search: In person searching is available.

PACER: Sign-up number is 800-676-6856. Access fee is $.60 per minute. Toll-free access: 888-821-8813. Local access: 505-248-6518. Case records are available back to July 1, 1991. New civil records are available online after 1 day.

Court	Jurisdiction	No. of Courts	How Organized
District Courts*	General	30	13 Districts
Magistrate Courts*	Limited	48	32 Magistrate Districts
Metropolitan Court of Bernalillo County*	Municipal	1	
Municipal Courts	Municipal	82	
Probate Courts	Probate	30	33 Counties

* Profiled in this Sourcebook.

Court	CIVIL								
	Tort	Contract	Real Estate	Min. Claim	Max. Claim	Small Claims	Estate	Eviction	Domestic Relations
District Courts*	X	X	X	$0	No Max		X		X
Magistrate Courts*	X	X	X	$0	$7500	$5000		X	
Metropolitan Court of Bernalillo County*	X	X	X	$0	$5000	$5000			
Municipal Courts									
Probate Courts*							X		

Court	CRIMINAL				
	Felony	Misdemeanor	DWI/DUI	Preliminary Hearing	Juvenile
District Courts*	X				X
Magistrate Courts*		X	X	X	
Metropolitan Court of Bernalillo County*		X	X	X	
Municipal Courts					
Probate Courts*					

ADMINISTRATION
Administrative Office of the Courts, Supreme Court Building Room 25, Santa Fe, NM, 87503; 505-827-4800, Fax: 505-827-7549. www.nmcourts.com

COURT STRUCTURE
The 30 District Courts in 13 districts are the courts of general jurisdiction. Magistrate Courts handle cases up to $7,500. The Bernalillo Metropolitan Court has jurisdiction in cases up to $5000. The County Clerks handle "informal" (uncontested) probate cases, and the District Courts handle "formal" (contested) probate cases.

ONLINE ACCESS
The www.nmcourts.com web site offers free access to District and Magistrate Court case information. In general, records are available from June 1997 forward.

Also, a commercial online service is available for the Metropolitan Court of Bernalillo County. There is a $35.00 set up fee, a connect time fee based on usage. The system is available 24 hours a day. Call 505-345-6555 for more information.

ADDITIONAL INFORMATION
There are some "shared" courts in New Mexico, with one county handling cases arising in another. Records are held at the location(s) indicated in the text.

All magistrate courts and the Bernalillo Metropolitan Court have public access terminals to access civil records only.

Bernalillo County

2nd Judicial District Court PO Box 488, Albuquerque, NM 87103; 505-841-7425 (Administration); Civil phone:505-841-7437; Criminal phone:505-841-7437; Probate phone:505-841-7404; Fax: 505-841-7446. Hours: 8AM-5PM (MST). *Felony, Civil, Probate.*

www.cabq.gov/cjnet/dst2alb

Civil Records: Access: Mail, online, in person. Both court and visitors may perform in person searches. Search fee: $1.50 per name. Required to search: name, years to search. Civil cases indexed by defendant, plaintiff. Civil records on computer from 1984, prior on docket books/microfiche. Online access to civil records from 1997 forward is available free on the Internet at www.nmcourts.com/disclaim.htm. **Criminal Records:** Access: Mail, remote online, in person.

Both court and visitors may perform in person searches. Search fee: $1.50 per name. Required to search: name, years to search; also helpful-DOB, SSN. Criminal records on computer from 1979, prior on docket books/microfiche. Online access to criminal records is the same as civil, see above. **General Information:** No sequestered or juvenile records released. SASE required. Turnaround time up to 10 days. Copy fee: $.35 per page. Certification fee: $1.50. Fee payee: Clerk of the

Court. Only cashiers checks and money orders accepted. Prepayment is required.

Metropolitan Court 401 Roma NW, Albuquerque, NM 87102; 505-841-8110/841-8142; Fax: 505-841-8192. Hours: 8AM-5PM (MST). *Misdemeanor, Civil Actions Under $5,000, Eviction, Small Claims.*

Civil Records: Access: Phone, fax, mail, online, in person. Both court and visitors may perform in person searches. No search fee. Required to search: name, years to search. Civil cases indexed by defendant, plaintiff. Civil records on computer from 1987. Max. 5 years back except uncollected judgements which stay open 14 years from date of judgement. Online access is available through New Mexico Technet on the Internet at www.technet.nm.nte/menu/metro-ct.htm.. There is a $35 setup fee and a per minute usage fee. Search by name, case number, SSN or arrext number. Call 505-345-6555 for information. **Criminal Records:** Access: Phone, fax, mail, remote online, in person. Both court and visitors may perform in person searches. No search fee. Required to search: name, SSN; also helpful-DOB. Criminal records on computer from 1983. For online access, see civil records. **General Information:** No pre-sentence reports, psychological evaluations, confidential records released. SASE required. Turnaround time 5-10 days. Copy fee: $.50 per page. Computer printouts are $1.00 per page. Certification fee: $1.50. Fee payee: Metro Court. Personal checks accepted. Credit cards accepted: Visa, AmEx. Prepayment is required. Public access terminal is available. Public Access Terminal Note: Civil only.

County Clerk #1 Civic Plaza NW, 6th Fl, Albuquerque, NM 87102; 505-768-4247. Hours: 8AM-4:30PM (MST). *Probate.*

Catron County

7th Judicial District Court PO Drawer 1129, Socorro, NM 87801; 505-835-0050; Fax: 505-838-5217. Hours: 8AM-4PM (MST). *Felony, Civil, Probate.*

Note: This court is also responsible for Socorro County.

Civil Records: Access: Phone, mail, online, in person. Both court and visitors may perform in person searches. No search fee. Required to search: name, years to search. Civil cases indexed by defendant, plaintiff. Civil records on microfiche and hard copies from 1912. Access to records from 1997 forward is free on the Internet at www.nmcourts.com/disclaim.htm. **Criminal Records:** Access: Phone, mail, remote online, in person. Both court and visitors may perform in person searches. No search fee. Required to search: name, years to search. Criminal records on microfiche and hard copies from 1912. For online access, see civil records. **General Information:** No sequestered records released. SASE required. Turnaround time 1 day. Copy fee: $.35 per page. Certification fee: $1.50. Fee payee: District Court Clerk. Business checks accepted. Prepayment is required.

Quemado Magistrate Court PO Box 283, Quemado, NM 87829; 505-773-4604; Fax: 505-773-4688. Hours: 8AM-5PM (MST). *Misdemeanor, Civil Actions Under $7,500, Eviction, Small Claims.*

Reserve Magistrate Court PO Box 447, Reserve, NM 87830; 505-533-6474; Fax: 505-533-6623. Hours: 8AM-5PM (MST). *Misdemeanor, Civil Actions Under $7,500, Eviction, Small Claims.*

County Clerk PO Box I, Socorro, NM 87801; 505-835-0423. Hours: 8AM-5PM (MST). *Probate.*

Chaves County

5th Judicial District Court Box 1776, Roswell, NM 88202; 505-622-2212; Fax: 505-624-9510. Hours: 8AM-Noon,1-5PM (MST). *Felony, Civil, Probate.*

www.fifthdistrictcourt.com

Civil Records: Access: Mail, online, in person. Both court and visitors may perform in person searches. No search fee. Required to search: name, years to search. Civil cases indexed by defendant, plaintiff. Civil records on computer from 1996, on microfiche and archived from 1891. Access to records from 1997 forward is free on the Internet at www.nmcourts.com/disclaim.htm. **Criminal Records:** Access: Mail, remote online, in person. Both court and visitors may perform in person searches. No search fee. Required to search: name, years to search, DOB, aliases; also helpful-SSN. Criminal records on computer from 1996, on microfiche and archived from 1891. For online access, see civil records. **General Information:** No sequestered records released. SASE required. Turnaround time 1-3 days. Copy fee: $.35 per page. Certification fee: $1.50. Fee payee: District Court Clerk. Only cashiers checks and money orders accepted. Prepayment is required. Public access terminal is available.

Magistrate Court 200 E 4th St, Roswell, NM 88201; 505-624-6088; Fax: 505-624-6092. Hours: 8AM-4PM (MST). *Misdemeanor, Civil Actions Under $7,500, Eviction, Small Claims.*

www.nmcourts.com/disclaim.htm

County Clerk Box 820, Roswell, NM 88201; 505-624-6614; Fax: 505-624-6523. Hours: 7AM-5PM (MST). *Probate.*

Cibola County

13th Judicial District Court Box 758, Grants, NM 87020; 505-287-8831; Fax: 505-285-5755. Hours: 8AM-4PM (MST). *Felony, Civil, Probate.*

Civil Records: Access: Mail, online, in person. Both court and visitors may perform in person searches. No search fee. Required to search: name, years to search. Civil cases indexed by defendant, plaintiff. Civil records on microfiche from 1981; prior to 1981 belong to Valencia County. Access to records from 1997 forward is free on the Internet at www.nmcourts.com/disclaim.htm. **Criminal Records:** Access: Mail, remote online, in person. Both court and visitors may perform in person searches. No search fee. Required to search: name, years to search. Criminal records on microfiche from 1981; prior to 1981 belong to Valencia County. For online access, see civil records. **General Information:** No sequestered records released. Turnaround time 2-3 days. Copy fee: $.35 per page. Certification fee: $1.50. Fee payee: District Court Clerk. Business checks accepted. Prepayment is required. Public access terminal is available.

Magistrate Court 515 W High, PO Box 130, Grants, NM 87020; 505-285-4605. Hours: 8AM-4PM (MST). *Misdemeanor, Civil Actions Under $7,500, Eviction, Small Claims.*

County Clerk 515 W. High, PO Box 19, Grants, NM 87020; 505-285-2535; Fax: 505-285-5434. Hours: 8AM-5PM (MST). *Probate.*

Colfax County

8th Judicial District Court Box 160, Raton, NM 87740; 505-445-5585; Fax: 505-445-2626. Hours: 8AM-4PM (MST). *Felony, Civil, Probate.*

Civil Records: Access: Phone, mail, online, in person. Both court and visitors may perform in person searches. No search fee. Required to search: name, years to search. Civil cases indexed by defendant, plaintiff. Civil records archived from 1912. Access to records from 1997 forward is free at www.nmcourts.com/disclaim.htm. **Criminal Records:** Access: Phone, mail, remote online, in person. Both court and visitors may perform in person searches. No search fee. Required to search: name, years to search; also helpful-DOB, SSN. Criminal records archived from 1912. For online access, see civil records. **General Information:** No adoption, mental, guardianship, children's cases (neglect & child in need of supervision) records released. SASE required. Turnaround time 1 week. Copy fee: $.35 per page. Certification fee: $1.50. Fee payee: District Court. Business checks accepted.

Cimarron Magistrate Court PO Drawer 367, Highway 21, Cimarron, NM 87714; 505-376-2634. *Misdemeanor, Civil Actions Under $7,500, Eviction, Small Claims.*

Raton Magistrate Court PO Box 68, Raton, NM 87740; 505-445-2220; Fax: 505-445-8966. Hours: 8AM-5PM (MST). *Misdemeanor, Civil Actions Under $7,500, Eviction, Small Claims.*

Springer Magistrate Court 300 Colbert Ave. PO Box 778, Springer, NM 87747; 505-483-2417; Fax: 505-483-0127. Hours: 8AM-Noon, 1-5PM (MST). *Misdemeanor, Civil Actions Under $7,500, Eviction, Small Claims.*

County Clerk PO Box 159, Raton, NM 87740; 505-445-5551; Fax: 505-445-4031. Hours: 8AM-5PM (MST). *Probate.*

Curry County

9th Judicial District Court Curry County Courthouse, 700 N Main, #11, Clovis, NM 88101; 505-762-9148; Fax: 505-763-5160. Hours: 8AM-4PM (MST). *Felony, Civil, Probate.*

Civil Records: Access: online, in person. Court does not conduct in person searches; visitors must perform searches for themselves. Search fee: No civil searches performed by court. Required to search: name, years to search, address. Civil cases indexed by defendant, plaintiff. Civil records on computer from 1986, on microfiche and archived from 1910. Access to records from 1997 forward is free at www.nmcourts.com/disclaim.htm. **Criminal Records:** Access: Remote online, in person. Court does not conduct in person searches; visitors must perform searches for themselves. Search fee: No criminal searches performed by court. Required to search: name, years to search; also helpful-SSN. Criminal records on computer from 1986, on microfiche and archived from 1910. For online access, see civil records. **General Information:** No adoptions, insanity, sequestered, neglect or abuse released. Copy fee: $.35 per page. Certification fee: $1.50. Fee payee: 9th Judicial District Court. Only cashiers checks and money orders accepted. Prepayment is required.

Magistrate Court 900 Main St, Clovis, NM 88101; 505-762-3766; Fax: 505-769-1437. Hours:

8AM-4PM (MST). *Misdemeanor, Civil Actions Under $7,500, Eviction, Small Claims.*

De Baca County

10th Judicial District Court Box 910, Ft. Sumner, NM 88119; 505-355-2896; Fax: 505-355-2896. Hours: 8AM-4:30PM (MST). *Felony, Civil, Probate.*

Civil Records: Access: Phone, mail, online, in person. Only the court conducts in person searches; visitors may not. No search fee. Required to search: name, years to search. Civil cases indexed by defendant, plaintiff. Civil records on index cards and docket books archived from 1917. Internet access to records from 1997 forward is free at www.nmcourts.com/disclaim.htm. **Criminal Records:** Access: Phone, mail, remote online, in person. Only the court conducts in person searches; visitors may not. No search fee. Required to search: name, years to search. Criminal records on index cards and docket books archived from 1917. For online access, see civil records. **General Information:** No mental, adoptions, or juvenile released. SASE required. Turnaround time 2 days. Copy fee: $.35 per page. Certification fee: $1.50. Fee payee: District Court. Only cashiers checks and money orders accepted. Prepayment is required.

Magistrate Court Box 24, Ft Sumner, NM 88119; 505-355-7371; Fax: 505-355-7149. Hours: 8AM-5PM (MST). *Misdemeanor, Civil Actions Under $7,500, Eviction, Small Claims.*

County Clerk 514 Ave C, PO Box 347, Ft. Sumner, NM 88119; 505-355-2601; Fax: 505-355-2441. Hours: 8AM-Noon, 1-4:30PM (MST). *Probate.*

Dona Ana County

3rd Judicial District Court 201 W Picacho, Suite A, Las Cruces, NM 88005; 505-523-8200; Fax: 505-523-8290. Hours: 8AM-Noon, 1-5PM (MST). *Felony, Civil, Probate.*

Civil Records: Access: Mail, online, in person. Both court and visitors may perform in person searches. Search fee: $1.50 per name. Required to search: name, years to search. Civil cases indexed by defendant, plaintiff. Civil records on computer from 1986, on microfiche and archived from 1912. Access to records from 1997 forward is free on the Internet at www.nmcourts.com/disclaim.htm. **Criminal Records:** Access: Mail, remote online, in person. Both court and visitors may perform in person searches. Search fee: $1.50 per name. Required to search: name, years to search; also helpful-DOB, SSN. Criminal records on computer from 1986, on microfiche and archived from 1912. For online access, see civil records. **General Information:** No adoption, mental health, or juvenile released. SASE required. Turnaround time 2-3 days. Copy fee: $.35 per page. Certification fee: $1.50. Fee payee: 3rd Judicial District. Only cashiers checks and money orders accepted. Prepayment is required. Public access terminal is available.

Anthony Magistrate Court PO Box 1259, Anthony, NM 88021; 505-233-3147. Hours: 8AM-Noon, 1-5PM (MST). *Misdemeanor, Civil Actions Under $7,500, Eviction, Small Claims.*

Las Cruces Magistrate Court 151 N Church, Las Cruces, NM 88001; 505-524-2814; Fax: 505-525-2951. Hours: 8AM-Noon, 1-5PM (MST). *Misdemeanor, Civil Actions Under $7,500, Eviction, Small Claims.*

County Clerk 251 W Amador, Los Cruces, NM 88005; 505-647-7419; Fax: 505-647-7464. Hours: 8AM-5PM (MST). *Probate.*

Eddy County

5th Judicial District Court Box 1838, Carlsbad, NM 88221; 505-885-4740; Fax: 505-887-7095. Hours: 8AM-Noon, 1-5PM (MST). *Felony, Civil, Probate.*

www.fifthdistrictcourt.com

Civil Records: Access: Phone, mail, online, in person. Both court and visitors may perform in person searches. No search fee. Required to search: name, years to search. Civil cases indexed by defendant. Civil records on computer from 1986, microfiche from 1900s. Access to records from 1997 forward is free on the Internet at www.nmcourts.com/disclaim.htm, or via the court web site above. **Criminal Records:** Access: Phone, mail, remote online, in person. Both court and visitors may perform in person searches. No search fee. Required to search: name, years to search. Criminal records on computer from 1986, microfiche from 1900s. For online access, see civil records. **General Information:** No adoption, SS case w/children, or guardianship released. SASE required. Turnaround time 1 day. Copy fee: $.35 per page. Certification fee: $1.50. Fee payee: District Court Clerk. Only cashiers checks and money orders accepted. Law firm checks only. Prepayment is required.

Artesia Magistrate Court 611 Mahone Dr Ste A, Artesia, NM 88210; 505-746-2481; Fax: 505-746-6763. Hours: 8AM-4PM (MST). *Misdemeanor, Civil Actions Under $7,500, Eviction, Small Claims.*

www.nmcourts.com/disclaim.htm

Carlsbad Magistrate Court 302 N Main St, Carlsbad, NM 88220; 505-885-3218; Fax: 505-887-3460. Hours: 8AM-4PM (MST). *Felony, Misdemeanor, Civil Actions Under $7,500, Eviction, Small Claims.*

County Clerk Eddy County Probate Judge, Rm 100, PO Box 850, Carlsbad, NM 88221; 505-885-4008; Fax: 505-887-1039. Hours: 8AM-5PM (MST). *Probate.*

Grant County

6th Judicial District Court Box 2339, Silver City, NM 88062; 505-538-3250; Fax: 505-588-5439. Hours: 8AM-5PM (MST). *Felony, Civil, Probate.*

Civil Records: Access: Fax, mail, online, in person. Both court and visitors may perform in person searches. Search fee: $3.00 per name. Required to search: name, years to search. Civil cases indexed by defendant, plaintiff. Civil records on microfiche from 1912-1977, on books from 1977. Internet access to records from 1997 forward is free at www.nmcourts.com/disclaim.htm. **Criminal Records:** Access: Fax, mail, remote online, in person. Both court and visitors may perform in person searches. Search fee: $3.00 per name. Required to search: name, years to search. Criminal records on microfiche from 1912-1977, on books from 1977. For online access, see civil records. **General Information:** No adoptions or abuse records released. SASE required. Turnaround time 1 day. Copy fee: $.35 per page. Certification fee: $1.50. Fee payee: District Court Clerk. Only cashiers checks and money orders accepted. Prepayment is required. Fax notes: No fee to fax results. Must be toll free number.

Bayard Magistrate Court PO Box 125, Bayard, NM 88023; 505-537-3402; Fax: 505-537-7365. Hours: 8AM-5PM (MST). *Misdemeanor, Civil Actions Under $7,500, Eviction, Small Claims.*

Silver City Magistrate Court 1620 E Pine St, Silver City, NM 88061; 505-538-3811; Fax: 505-538-8079. Hours: 8AM-5PM; Public hours 9AM-4PM (MST). *Misdemeanor, Civil Actions Under $7,500, Eviction, Small Claims.*

www.nmcourts.com/disclaim.htm

County Clerk Box 898, Silver City, NM 88061; 505-538-2979; Fax: 505-538-8926. Hours: 8AM-5PM (MST). *Probate.*

Guadalupe County

4th Judicial District Court 420 Parker Ave Suite #5, Guadalupe County Courthouse, Santa Rosa, NM 88435; 505-472-3888; Fax: 505-472-3888. Hours: 8AM-5PM (MST). *Felony, Civil, Probate.*

Civil Records: Access: online, in person. Court does not conduct in person searches; visitors must perform searches for themselves. Search fee: No civil searches performed by court. Required to search: name, years to search. Civil cases indexed by defendant, plaintiff. Civil records on docket books from 1912. Access to records from 1997 forward is free on the Internet at www.nmcourts.com/disclaim.htm. **Criminal Records:** Access: Remote online, in person. Court does not conduct in person searches; visitors must perform searches for themselves. Search fee: No criminal searches performed by court. Required to search: name, years to search, DOB; also helpful-SSN. Criminal records on docket books from 1912. For online access, see civil records. **General Information:** No adoption, insanity, juvenile, guardianship records released. Copy fee: $.35 per page. Certification fee: $1.50. Fee payee: District Court Clerk Office. Only cashiers checks and money orders accepted.

Santa Rosa Magistrate Court 603 Parker Ave, Santa Rosa, NM 88435; 505-472-3237. Hours: 8AM-Noon, 1-5PM (MST). *Misdemeanor, Civil Actions Under $7,500, Eviction, Small Claims.*

Vaughn Magistrate Court PO Box 246, Vaughn, NM 88353; 505-584-2345. Hours: 8AM-Noon, 1-5PM (MST). *Misdemeanor, Civil Actions Under $7,500, Eviction, Small Claims.*

County Clerk 420 Parker Ave, Courthouse, Santa Rosa, NM 88435; 505-472-3791; Fax: 505-472-3735. Hours: 8AM-5PM (MST). *Probate.*

Harding County

10th Judicial District Court Box 1002, Mosquero, NM 87733; 505-673-2252; Fax: 505-673-2252. Hours: 9AM-3PM M-W,F (MST). *Felony, Civil, Probate.*

Civil Records: Access: Phone, fax, mail, online, in person. No search fee. Required to search: name; also helpful-years to search. Civil cases indexed by defendant, plaintiff. Civil records on books from 1927, will have records available on microfiche. Internet access to records from 1997 forward is free at www.nmcourts.com/disclaim.htm. **Criminal Records:** Access: Phone, fax, mail, remote online, in person. Court does not conduct in person searches; visitors must perform searches for themselves. No search fee. Required to search: name, DOB, SSN; also helpful-years to search. Criminal records on books from 1927, will have records available on microfiche. For online access, see civil records. **General Information:** No adoption records released. SASE required. Turnaround time 1 week. Copy fee: $.35 per page. Certification fee: $1.50. Fee payee: District Court Clerk. Business checks accepted. Prepayment is required. Fax notes: $2.00 for first page, $1.00 each addl.

Magistrate Court Box 9, Roy, NM 87743; 505-485-2549; Fax: 505-485-2407. Hours: 8AM-4:30PM (MST). *Misdemeanor, Civil Actions Under $7,500, Eviction, Small Claims.*

County Clerk County Clerk, Box 1002, Mosquero, NM 87733; 505-673-2301; Fax: 505-673-2922. Hours: 8AM-5PM (MST). *Probate.*

Hidalgo County

6th Judicial District Court PO 608, Lordsburg, NM 88045; 505-542-3411; Fax: 505-542-3481. Hours: 8AM-Noon, 1-5PM (MST). *Felony, Civil, Probate.*

Civil Records: Access: Phone, mail, online, in person. Only the court conducts in person searches; visitors may not. No search fee. Required to search: name, years to search. Civil cases indexed by defendant, plaintiff. Civil records on microfiche and archived from 1920. Access to records from 1997 forward is free on the Internet at www.nmcourts.com/disclaim.htm. **Criminal Records:** Access: Phone, mail, remote online, in person. Only the court conducts in person searches; visitors may not. No search fee. Required to search: name, years to search. Criminal records on microfiche and archived from 1920. For online access, see civil records. **General Information:** No juvenile or adoption records released. SASE required. Turnaround time 3-5 days. Copy fee: $.35 per page. Certification fee: $1.50. Fee payee: District Court Clerk. Business checks accepted.

Magistrate Court 420 Wabash Ave, Lordsburg, NM 88045; 505-542-3582. Hours: 8AM-5PM (MST). *Misdemeanor, Civil Actions Under $7,500, Eviction, Small Claims.*

www.nmcourts.com/disclaim.htm

County Clerk 300 S Shakespeare, Lordsburg, NM 88045; 505-542-9213; Fax: 505-542-3193. Hours: 9AM-Noon (MST). *Probate.*

Lea County

5th Judicial District Court 100 N. Main, Box 6C, Lovington, NM 88260; 505-396-8571; Fax: 505-396-2428. Hours: 8AM-5PM (MST). *Felony, Civil, Probate.*

www.fifthdistrictcourt.com

Civil Records: Access: Fax, mail, online, in person. Both court and visitors may perform in person searches. No search fee. Required to search: name, years to search. Civil cases indexed by defendant, plaintiff. Civil records on computer from 1990, on microfiche from 1912. Court refers search requests to a private researcher. Access to records from 1997 forward is free on the Internet at www.nmcourts.com/disclose.htm. **Criminal Records:** Access: Fax, mail, remote online, in person. Both court and visitors may perform in person searches. No search fee. Required to search: name, years to search. Criminal records on computer from 1990, on microfiche from 1912. Court refers searches to a private researcher. For online access, see civil records. **General Information:** No adoptions, mental, abuse records released. SASE required. Turnaround time 1-3 days. Copy fee: $.35 per page. Certification fee: $1.50. Fee payee: District Court Clerk. Only

cashiers checks and money orders accepted. Prepayment is required. Public access terminal is available.

Eunice Magistrate Court PO Box 240, Eunice, NM 88231; 505-394-3368; Fax: 505-394-3335. *Misdemeanor, Civil Actions Under $7,500, Eviction, Small Claims.*

Hobbs Magistrate Court 2110 N Alto Dr, Hobbs, NM 88240-3455; 505-397-3621; Fax: 505-393-9121. Hours: 8AM-4PM (MST). *Misdemeanor, Civil Actions Under $7,500, Eviction, Small Claims.*

www.nmcourts.com/disclaim.htm

Lovington Magistrate Court 100 W Central, Suite D, Lovington, NM 88260; 505-396-6677; Fax: 505-396-6163. Hours: 8AM-4PM (MST). *Misdemeanor, Civil Actions Under $7,500, Eviction, Small Claims.*

www.nmcourts.com/disclaim.htm

Tatum Magistrate Court PO Box 918, Tatum, NM 88267; 505-398-5300; Fax: 505-398-5310. Hours: 8AM-4PM (MST). *Misdemeanor, Civil Actions Under $7,500, Eviction, Small Claims.*

County Clerk Box 1507, Lovington, NM 88260; 505-396-8531; Fax: 505-396-3293. Hours: 8AM-5PM (MST). *Probate.*

Lincoln County

12th Judicial District Court Box 725, Carrizozo, NM 88301; 505-648-2432; Fax: 505-648-2581. Hours: 8AM-5PM (MST). *Felony, Civil, Probate.*

Civil Records: Access: online, in person. Court does not conduct in person searches; visitors must perform searches for themselves. Search fee: No civil searches performed by court. Required to search: name, years to search. Civil cases indexed by defendant, plaintiff. Civil records on computer from 1991, docket books from 1960, microfiche to 1960. The court will refer searches to a private researcher. Access to records from 1997 forward is free at www.nmcourts.com/disclose.htm. **Criminal Records:** Access: Remote online, in person. Court does not conduct in person searches; visitors must perform searches for themselves. Search fee: No criminal searches performed by court. Required to search: name, years to search. Criminal records on computer from 1991, docket books from 1960, microfiche to 1960. The court will refer all search requests to a private researcher. For online access, see civil records. **General Information:** No juvenile, adoption, or mental records released. Copy fee: $.35 per page. Certification fee: $1.50. Fee payee: District Court Clerk. Business checks accepted. Prepayment is required. Public access terminal is available.

Ruidoso Magistrate Court 301 W Highway 70 #2, Ruidoso, NM 88345; 505-378-7022; Fax: 505-378-8508. Hours: 8AM-4PM (MST). *Misdemeanor, Civil Actions Under $7,500, Eviction, Small Claims.*

County Clerk PO Box 338, Carrizozo, NM 88301; 505-648-2394; Fax: 505-648-2576. Hours: 8AM-5PM (MST). *Probate.*

Note: This court will not do searches

Los Alamos County

1st Judicial District Court, NM;.

http://firstdistrictcourt.com

Note: All civil and criminal cases handled by Santa Fe District Court.

Magistrate Court 1319 Trinity Dr, Los Alamos, NM 87544; 505-662-2727; Fax: 505-661-6258. Hours: 8AM-5PM (MST). *Misdemeanor, Civil Actions Under $7,500, Eviction, Small Claims.*

County Clerk PO Box 30, Los Alamos, NM 87544; 505-662-8010; Fax: 505-662-8008. Hours: 8AM-5PM (MST). *Probate.*

Luna County

6th Judicial District Court Luna County Courthouse Room 40, Deming, NM 88030; 505-546-9611; Fax: 505-546-0971. Hours: 8AM-4PM (MST). *Felony, Civil, Probate.*

www.nmcourts.com

Civil Records: Access: Mail, online, in person. Both court and visitors may perform in person searches. Search fee: $5.00 per name. Required to search: name, years to search. Civil cases indexed by defendant, plaintiff. Civil records on microfiche from 1911. Access to records from 1997 forward is free at www.nmcourts.com/disclaim.htm. **Criminal Records:** Access: Mail, remote online, in person. Both court and visitors may perform in person searches. Search fee: $5.00 per name. Required to search: name, years to search. Criminal records on microfiche from 1911. For online access, see civil records. **General Information:** No adoptions, mental, sequestered or juvenile records released. SASE required. Turnaround time 5 days. Copy fee: $.35 per page. Certification fee: $1.50. Only cashiers checks and money orders accepted. Prepayment is required. Fax notes: $.35 per page.

Magistrate Court 912 S Silver St, Deming, NM 88030; 505-546-9321; Fax: 505-546-4896. Hours: 8AM-Noon, 1-5PM (MST). *Misdemeanor, Civil Actions Under $7,500, Eviction, Small Claims.*

www.nmcourts.com/disclaim.htm

County Clerk PO Box 1838, Deming, NM 88031; 505-546-0491; Fax: 505-546-4708. Hours: 8AM-5PM (MST). *Probate.*

McKinley County

11th Judicial District Court 201 W. Hill, Room 4, Gallup, NM 87301; 505-863-6816; Fax: 505-722-9172. Hours: 8AM-Noon, 1-5PM (MST). *Felony, Civil, Probate.*

Civil Records: Access: Phone, mail, online, in person. Both court and visitors may perform in person searches. No search fee. Required to search: name, years to search. Civil cases indexed by defendant, plaintiff. Civil records on computer from 1989, on microfiche from 1923. One name only by phone. Access to records from 1997 forward is free on the Internet at www.nmcourts.com/disclaim.htm. **Criminal Records:** Access: Phone, mail, remote online, in person. Both court and visitors may perform in person searches. No search fee. Required to search: name, years to search, DOB; also helpful-SSN. Criminal records on computer from 1989, on microfiche from 1923. One name only by phone. For online access, see civil records. **General Information:** No adoption or juvenile records released. SASE required. Turnaround time 3-5 days. Copy fee: $.35 per page. Certification fee: $1.50. Fee payee: McKinley County District Court. No personal checks accepted. Prepayment is required.

Magistrate Court 285 S Boardman Dr, Gallup, NM 87301; 505-722-6636. Hours: 8AM-

4PM (MST). *Misdemeanor, Civil Actions Under $7,500, Eviction, Small Claims.*

County Clerk PO Box 1268, Gallup, NM 87305; 505-863-6866; Fax: 505-863-1419. Hours: 8AM-5PM (MST). *Probate.*

Mora County

4th Judicial District Court PO Box 1540, Las Vegas, NM 87701; 505-425-7281; Fax: 505-425-6307. Hours: 8AM-Noon, 1-5PM (MST). *Felony, Civil, Probate.*

Civil Records: Access: online, in person. Court does not conduct in person searches; visitors must perform searches for themselves. Search fee: No civil searches performed by court. Required to search: name, years to search. Civil cases indexed by defendant, plaintiff. Civil records on microfiche from 1912, archived before 1912. Access to records from 1997 forward is free on the Internet at www.nmcourts.com/disclaim.htm. **Criminal Records:** Access: Remote online, in person. Court does not conduct in person searches; visitors must perform searches for themselves. Search fee: No criminal searches performed by court. Required to search: name, years to search. Criminal records on microfiche from 1912, archived before 1912. For online access, see civil records. **General Information:** No adoptions, insanity, or juvenile records released. Copy fee: $.35 per page. Certification fee: $1.50. Fee payee: 4th Judicial District Court. Only cashiers checks and money orders accepted. Prepayment is required.

Magistrate Court 1927 7th Street, Las Vegas, NM 87701-4957; 505-425-5204. Hours: 8AM-4PM (closed for lunch) (MST). *Misdemeanor, Civil Actions Under $7,500, Eviction, Small Claims.*

Probate Court PO Box 36, Mora, NM 87732; 505-387-5702. Hours: 8AM-5PM (MST). *Probate.*

Otero County

12th Judicial District Court 1000 New York Ave, Rm 209, Alamogordo, NM 88310-6940; 505-437-7310; Fax: 505-434-8886. Hours: 8AM-5PM (MST). *Felony, Civil, Probate.*

Civil Records: Access: online, in person. Court does not conduct in person searches; visitors must perform searches for themselves. Search fee: No civil searches performed by court. Required to search: name, years to search. Civil cases indexed by defendant, plaintiff. Civil records on computer from 1991, on microfiche from 1926. Phone & mail access limited to 5 names each. Access to records from 1997 forward is free on the Internet at www.nmcourts.com/disclose.htm. **Criminal Records:** Access: Remote online, in person. Court does not conduct in person searches; visitors must perform searches for themselves. Search fee: No criminal searches performed by court. Required to search: name, years to search. Criminal records on computer from 1991, on microfiche from 1926. Phone & mail access limited to 5 names each. For online access, see civil records. **General Information:** No sealed, adoption records released. Copy fee: $.35 per page. Certification fee: $1.50. Fee payee: District Court. Only cashiers checks and money orders accepted. Prepayment is required.

Magistrate Court 263 Robert H Bradley Dr, Alamogordo, NM 88310-8288; 505-437-9000; Fax: 505-439-1365. Hours: 8AM-4PM (MST). *Misdemeanor, Civil Actions Under $7,500, Eviction, Small Claims.*

County Clerk 1000 New York Ave, Rm 108, Alamogordo, NM 88310-6932; 505-437-4942; Fax: 505-443-2922. Hours: 7:30AM-6PM (MST). *Probate.*

Quay County

10th Judicial District Court Box 1067, Tucumcari, NM 88401; 505-461-2764; Fax: 505-461-4498. Hours: 8AM-5PM (MST). *Felony, Civil, Probate.*

Civil Records: Access: Phone, fax, mail, online, in person. Both court and visitors may perform in person searches. No search fee. Required to search: name, years to search. Civil cases indexed by defendant, plaintiff. Civil records on hard copy file from 1976 to present, on microfiche from 1912 to 1986, archived from 1911. Access to records from 1997 forward is free on the Internet at www.nmcourts.com/disclaim.htm. **Criminal Records:** Access: Phone, fax, mail, remote online, in person. Both court and visitors may perform in person searches. No search fee. Required to search: name; also helpful-years to search, DOB, SSN. Criminal records on hard copy file from 1976 to present, on microfiche from 1912 to 1986, archived from 1911. For online access, see civil records. **General Information:** No adoptions, juvenile, insanity records released. SASE required. Turnaround time same day. Copy fee: $.35 per page. Certification fee: $1.50. Fee payee: District Court Clerk. Only cashiers checks and money orders accepted. Fax notes: $2.00 for first page, $1.00 each addl.

Tucumcari Magistrate Court PO Box 1301, Tucumcari, NM 88401; 505-461-1700; Fax: 505-461-4522. Hours: 8AM-Noon, 1-5PM (MST). *Misdemeanor, Civil Actions Under $7,500, Eviction, Small Claims.*

Note: San Jon Magistrate Court (closed) records are found here.

County Clerk 3000 S Third St, PO Box 1225, Tucumcari, NM 88401; 505-461-0510; Fax: 505-461-0513. Hours: 8AM-5PM (MST). *Probate.*

Rio Arriba County

1st Judicial District Court, NM;.

http://firstdistrictcourt.com

Note: All civil and criminal cases handled by Santa Fe District Court.

Rio Arriba Magistrate Court-Division 1 PO Box 538, Chama, NM 87520; 505-756-2278. Hours: 8AM-Noon, 1-5PM (MST). *Misdemeanor, Civil Actions Under $7,500, Eviction, Small Claims.*

Rio Arriba Magistrate Court-Division 2 410 Paseo de Onate, Espanola, NM 87532; 505-753-2532. Hours: 8AM-4PM (MST). *Misdemeanor, Civil Actions Under $7,500, Eviction, Small Claims.*

County Clerk PO Box 158, Tierra Amarilla, NM 87575; 505-588-7724; Fax: 505-588-7418. Hours: 8AM-5PM (MST). *Probate.*

Roosevelt County

9th Judicial District Court 109 West 1st St, Suite 207, Portales, NM 88130; 505-356-4463; Fax: 505-359-2140. Hours: 8AM-4PM (MST). *Felony, Civil, Probate.*

Civil Records: Access: online, in person. Court does not conduct in person searches; visitors must perform searches for themselves. Search fee: No civil searches performed by court. Required to search: name, years to search. Civil cases indexed

by defendant, plaintiff. Civil records on microfiche from 1912, archived before 1912. Access to records from 1997 forward is free on the Internet at www.nmcourts.com/disclaim.htm. **Criminal Records:** Access: Remote online, in person. Court does not conduct in person searches; visitors must perform searches for themselves. Search fee: No criminal searches performed by court. Required to search: name, years to search. Criminal records on microfiche from 1912, archived before 1912. For online access, see civil records. **General Information:** No adoption, guardianship, insanity records released. Copy fee: $.35 per page. Certification fee: $1.50. Fee payee: 9th Judicial District Court. Only cashiers checks and money orders accepted. Prepayment is required.

Magistrate Court 42427 US Hwy 70, Portales, NM 88130; 505-356-8569; Fax: 505-359-6883. Hours: 8AM-4PM (MST). *Misdemeanor, Civil Actions Under $7,500, Eviction, Small Claims.*

www.nmcourts.com/disclaim.htm

County Clerk Roosevelt County Courthouse, 109 W First, Portales, NM 88130; 505-356-8562; Fax: 505-356-3560. Hours: 8AM-5PM (MST). *Probate.*

San Juan County

11th Judicial District Court 103 S. Oliver, Aztec, NM 87410; 505-334-6151; Fax: 505-334-1940. Hours: 8AM-Noon, 1-5PM (MST). *Felony, Civil, Probate.*

Civil Records: Access: online, in person. Court does not conduct in person searches; visitors must perform searches for themselves. Search fee: No civil searches performed by court. Required to search: name, years to search; also helpful-address. Civil cases indexed by defendant, plaintiff. Civil records on computer from 1982, on microfiche from 1900s, on cards from 1800s. Access to records from 1997 forward is free on the Internet at www.nmcourts.com/disclaim.htm. **Criminal Records:** Access: Remote online, in person. Court does not conduct in person searches; visitors must perform searches for themselves. Search fee: No criminal searches performed by court. Required to search: name, years to search, DOB; also helpful-address, SSN. Criminal records on computer from 1982, on microfiche from 1900s, on cards from 1800s. For online access, see civil records. **General Information:** No adoptions, insanity, sealed, expunged records released. Copy fee: $.35 per page. Certification fee: $1.50 per page. Fee payee: Eleventh District Court. No personal or out-of-state checks accepted. Prepayment is required. Public access terminal is available.

Aztec Magistrate Court 101 S Oliver Dr Ste 1, Aztec, NM 87410; 505-334-9479. Hours: 8AM-Noon, 1-5PM (MST). *Misdemeanor, Civil Actions Under $7,500, Eviction, Small Claims.*

Farmington Magistrate Court 950 W Apache St, Farmington, NM 87401; 505-326-4338; Fax: 505-325-2618. Hours: 8AM-4PM (MST). *Misdemeanor, Civil Actions Under $7,500, Eviction, Small Claims.*

www.nmcourts.com/disclaim.htm

County Clerk PO Box 550, Aztec, NM 87410; 505-334-9471; Fax: 505-334-3635. Hours: 7AM-5:30PM (MST). *Probate.*

San Miguel County

4th Judicial District Court PO Box 1540, Las Vegas, NM 87701; 505-425-7281; Fax: 505-425-6307. Hours: 8AM-Noon, 1-5PM (MST). *Felony, Civil, Probate.*

Note: Also handles cases for Mora County

Civil Records: Access: Phone, mail, online, in person. Court does not conduct in person searches; visitors must perform searches for themselves. Search fee: No civil searches performed by court. Required to search: name, years to search. Civil cases indexed by defendant, plaintiff. Civil records on microfiche from 1912, archived before 1912. Access to records from 1997 forward is free on the Internet at www.nmcourts.com/disclaim.htm. **Criminal Records:** Access: Remote online, in person. Court does not conduct in person searches; visitors must perform searches for themselves. Search fee: No criminal searches performed by court. Required to search: name, years to search. Criminal records on microfiche from 1912, archived before 1912. For online access, see civil records. **General Information:** No adoptions, insanity, juvenile records released. SASE required. Turnaround time 2 days. Copy fee: $.35 per page. Certification fee: $1.50. Fee payee: 4th Judicial District Court Clerk. Only cashiers checks and money orders accepted.

Magistrate Court 1927 7th St, Las Vegas, NM 87701-4957; 505-425-5204; Fax: 505-425-0422. Hours: 8AM-4PM (MST). *Misdemeanor, Civil Actions Under $7,500, Eviction, Small Claims.*

County Clerk San Miguel County Clerk, 500 W. National Av, Las Vegas, NM 87701; 505-425-9331; Fax: 505-454-7199. Hours: 8AM-Noon, 1-5PM (MST). *Probate.*

Sandoval County

13th Judicial District Court 110 Avenida De Justicia, Bernalillo, NM 87004; 505-867-2376. Hours: 8AM-Noon, 1-5PM (MST). *Felony, Civil, Probate.*

Civil Records: Access: Fax, mail, online, in person. Both court and visitors may perform in person searches. No search fee. Required to search: name, years to search. Civil cases indexed by defendant, plaintiff. Civil records indexed on microfiche. Access to records from 1997 forward is free at www.nmcourts.com/disclaim.htm. **Criminal Records:** Access: Fax, mail, remote online, in person. Both court and visitors may perform in person searches. Search fee: up to 2 names $5.00; 3-10 names $10.00; 11+ names $20.00. Required to search: name, years to search. Criminal records on computer since 11/96. For online access, see civil records. **General Information:** No sequestered, juvenile, probate or guardianship records released. Turnaround time 1-2 days. Copy fee: $.35 per page. Microfilm copies $.50 per page (1991 and prior). Certification fee: $1.50. Fee payee: 13th Judicial District Court. Business checks accepted. Fax notes: $5.00 for first page, $1.00 each addl.

Bernalillo Magistrate Court PO Box 818, Bernalillo, NM 87004; 505-867-5202. Hours: 8AM-4PM (MST). *Misdemeanor, Civil Actions Under $7,500, Eviction, Small Claims.*

Cuba Magistrate Court 16B Cordova St, Cuba, NM 87013; 505-289-3519; Fax: 505-289-3013. Hours: 8AM-Noon, 1-5PM (MST). *Misdemeanor, Civil Actions Under $7,500, Eviction, Small Claims.*

County Clerk PO Box 40, Bernalillo, NM 87004; 505-867-7572; Fax: 505-771-8610. Hours: 8AM-5PM (MST). *Probate.*

Santa Fe County

1st Judicial District Court Box 2268, Santa Fe, NM 87504; 505-476-0189; Fax: 505-827-7998. Hours: 8AM-4PM (MST). *Felony, Civil, Probate.*

http://firstdistrictcourt.com

Note: Because this court also handles the counties of Los Alamos and Rio Arriba, you must indicate which county you are searching.

Civil Records: Access: Phone, mail, online, in person. Both court and visitors may perform in person searches. Search fee: Search fee: $10.00 minimum if more than 5 names requested or to search docket books. Required to search: name, years to search. Civil cases indexed by defendant, plaintiff. Civil records on computer from 1986, older records on docket books. Access to court records from 1997 forward is available free on the Internet at www.nmcourts.com/disclaim.htm. **General Information:** No adoption, juvenile, mental or abuse records released. SASE required. Turnaround time 2 days. Copy fee: $.35 per page. Certification fee: $1.50. Fee payee: District Court. Business checks accepted. Prepayment is required. Public access terminal is available.

Magistrate Court Rte 11, Box 21M, Pojoaque, NM 87501; 505-455-7938; Fax: 505-455-3053. Hours: 8AM-Noon,1-5PM (MST). *Misdemeanor, Civil Actions Under $7,500, Eviction, Small Claims.*

County Clerk Box 276, Santa Fe, NM 87504; 505-986-6279; Fax: 505-986-6362. Hours: 8AM-5PM (MST). *Probate.*

Sierra County

7th Judicial District Court PO Box 3009, Truth or Consequences, NM 87901; 505-894-7167; Fax: 505-894-7168. Hours: 8AM-4PM (MST). *Felony, Civil, Probate.*

Civil Records: Access: Fax, mail, online, in person. Only the court conducts in person searches; visitors may not. No search fee. Required to search: name, years to search, address. Civil cases indexed by defendant, plaintiff. Civil records on microfiche from 1920, archived before 1920. Access to records from 1997 forward is free at www.nmcourts.com/disclaim.htm. **Criminal Records:** Access: Fax, mail, remote online, in person. Only the court conducts in person searches; visitors may not. No search fee. Required to search: name, years to search, address, SSN. Criminal records on microfiche from 1920, archived before 1920. For online access, see civil records. **General Information:** No adoptions, insanity, juvenile, guardianship records released. SASE required. Turnaround time 2 days. Copy fee: $.35 per page. Certification fee: $1.50. Fee payee: Sierra County District Court. Only cashiers checks and money orders accepted. Prepayment is required. Public access terminal is available.

Magistrate Court 155 W Barton, Truth or Consequences, NM 87901; 505-894-3051; Fax: 505-894-0476. Hours: 8AM-4PM (MST). *Misdemeanor, Civil Actions Under $7,500, Eviction, Small Claims.*

County Clerk 311 Date St., Truth or Consequences, NM 87901; 505-894-2840; Probate phone:505-894-4416; Fax: 505-894-2516. Hours: 8AM-5PM (MST). *Probate.*

Socorro County

7th Judicial District Court

Note: All civil and criminal cases are handled by Catron District Court.

Magistrate Court 404 Park St, Socorro, NM 87801; 505-835-2500. Hours: 8AM-Noon, 1-5PM (MST). *Misdemeanor, Civil Actions Under $7,500, Eviction, Small Claims.*

County Clerk 200 Church St, Socorro, NM 87801; 505-835-0423; Fax: 505-835-1043. Hours: 8AM-5PM (MST). *Probate.*

Taos County

8th Judicial District Court 105 Albright St Ste H, Taos, NM 87571; 505-758-3173; Fax: 505-751-1281. Hours: 8AM-4PM (MST). *Felony, Civil, Probate.*

Civil Records: Access: Mail, fax, online, in person. Court does not conduct in person searches; visitors must perform searches for themselves. Search fee: No civil searches performed by court. Required to search: name, years to search. Civil cases indexed by defendant, plaintiff. Civil records on computer since 1993, books since 1912, microfiche from 1912-1950. Access to records from 1997 forward is free on the Internet at www.nmcourts.com/disclaim.htm. **Criminal Records:** Access: Mail, fax, remote online, in person. Court does not conduct in person searches; visitors must perform searches for themselves. Search fee: No criminal searches performed by court. Required to search: name, years to search; also helpful-DOB, SSN. Criminal records on computer since 1993, books since 1912, microfiche from 1912-1950. For online access, see civil records. **General Information:** No adoption, juvenile, abuse or sequestered case records released. SASE required. Turnaround time 2 days. Copy fee: $.35 per page. Certification fee: $1.50. Fee payee: District Court. Only cashiers checks and money orders accepted. Prepayment is required. Public access terminal is available.

Questa Magistrate Court PO Box 586, Questa, NM 87556; 505-586-0761; Fax: 505-586-0428. Hours: 8AM-Noon,1-5PM (MST). *Misdemeanor, Civil Actions Under $7,500, Eviction, Small Claims.*

Taos Magistrate Court Box 1121, Taos, NM 87571; 505-758-4030; Fax: 505-751-0983. Hours: 8AM-4PM (MST). *Misdemeanor, Civil Actions Under $7,500, Eviction, Small Claims.*

County Clerk 105 Albright, Suite D, Taos, NM 87551; 505-758-8266; Fax: 505-751-3391. Hours: 8AM-5PM (MST). *Probate.*

Torrance County

7th Judicial District Court County Courthouse, PO Box 78, Estancia, NM 87016; 505-384-2974; Fax: 505-384-2229. Hours: 8AM-4PM (MST). *Felony, Civil, Probate.*

www.nmcourts.com/disclaim.htm

Civil Records: Access: Mail, online, in person. Both court and visitors may perform in person searches. No search fee. Required to search: name, years to search. Civil cases indexed by defendant, plaintiff. Civil records on hard copy until filmed, microfiche from 1912. Access to records from 1997 forward is free on the Internet at www.nmcourts.com/disclaim.htm. **Criminal Records:** Access: Mail, remote online, in person. Only the court conducts in person searches; visitors may not. No search fee. Required to search: name, years to search; also helpful-SSN,

DOB. Criminal records on hard copy until filmed, microfiche from 1912. For online access, see civil records. **General Information:** No juvenile, neglect, adoption, mental health records released. SASE required. Turnaround time 1 day. Copy fee: $.35 per page. Certification fee: $1.50. Fee payee: Seventh Judicial District Court. Only cashiers checks and money orders accepted. Prepayment is required.

Moriarty Magistrate Court PO Box 2027, Moriarty, NM 87035; 505-832-4476; Fax: 505-832-1563. Hours: 8AM-4PM (MST). *Misdemeanor, Civil Actions Under $7,500, Eviction, Small Claims.*

County Clerk PO Box 48, Estancia, NM 87016; 505-384-2221; Fax: 505-384-4080. Hours: 8AM-Noon, 1-5PM (MST). *Probate.*

Union County

8th Judicial District Court Box 310, Clayton, NM 88415; 505-374-9577; Fax: 505-374-2089. Hours: 8AM-Noon, 1-5PM (MST). *Felony, Civil, Probate.*

Civil Records: Access: Mail, online, in person. Both court and visitors may perform in person searches. No search fee. Required to search: name, years to search. Civil cases indexed by defendant, plaintiff. Civil records on cards from 1981. Access to records from 1997 forward is free on the Internet at www.nmcourts.com/disclaim.htm. **Criminal Records:** Access: Mail, remote online,

in person. Both court and visitors may perform in person searches. No search fee. Required to search: name, years to search. Criminal records on docket sheets from 1981. For online access, see civil records. **General Information:** No adoption, juvenile records released. SASE required. Turnaround time 1-2 days. Copy fee: $.35 per page. Certification fee: $1.50. Fee payee: Clerk of District Court. Only cashiers checks and money orders accepted. Prepayment is required.

Magistrate Court 836 Main Street, Clayton, NM 88415; 505-374-9472; Fax: 505-374-9368. Hours: 8AM-Noon, 1-5PM (MST). *Misdemeanor, Civil Actions Under $7,500, Eviction, Small Claims.*

County Clerk PO Box 430, Clayton, NM 88415; 505-374-9491; Fax: 505-374-2763. Hours: 9AM-Noon, 1-5PM (MST). *Probate.*

Valencia County

13th Judicial District Court Box 1089, Los Lunas, NM 87031; 505-865-4291; Fax: 505-865-8801. Hours: 8AM-5PM (MST). *Felony, Civil, Probate.*

Civil Records: Access: Fax, mail, online, in person. Both court and visitors may perform in person searches. Search fee: $5.00 for up to 2 names, $10.00 for 3-10 names. Required to search: name, years to search. Civil cases indexed by defendant, plaintiff. Civil records on microfiche from 1915. Access to records from 1997 forward

is free at www.nmcourts.com/disclaim.htm. **Criminal Records:** Access: Mail, remote online, in person. Both court and visitors may perform in person searches. Search fee: $5.00 fee for 2 names, $10.00 for 3-10 names. Required to search: name, years to search. Criminal records on microfiche from 1915. For online access, see civil records. **General Information:** No adoptions or juvenile records released. SASE required. Turnaround time 2 days. Copy fee: $.35 per page. Certification fee: $1.50. Fee payee: 13th Judicial District Court. Only cashiers checks and money orders accepted. Public access terminal is available. Fax notes: Fax fees: $2.50 in-state; $5.00 out-of-state.

Belen Magistrate Court 237 N Main St, Belen, NM 87002; 505-864-7509; Fax: 505-864-9532. Hours: 8AM-Noon,1-5PM (MST). *Misdemeanor, Civil Actions Under $7,500, Eviction, Small Claims.*

Los Lunas Magistrate Court 121 SE Don Diego, Los Lunas, NM 87031; 505-865-4637. Hours: 8AM-4PM (MST). *Misdemeanor, Civil Actions Under $7,500, Eviction, Small Claims.*

County Clerk PO Box 939, Los Lunas, NM 87031; 505-866-2073; Fax: 505-866-2023. Hours: 8AM-4:30PM (MST). *Probate.*

ORGANIZATION   33 counties, 33 recording offices. The recording officer is County Clerk. Most counties maintain a grantor/grantee index and a miscellaneous index. The entire state is in the Mountain Time Zone (MST).

UCC RECORDS   Financing statements are filed at the state level, except for consumer goods, farm related and real estate related collateral, which are filed only with the County Clerk. Only a few recording offices will perform UCC searches. Use search request form UCC-11. Search and copy fees vary.

TAX LIEN RECORDS   All federal and state tax liens are filed with the County Clerk. Most counties will **not** provide tax lien searches.

REAL ESTATE RECORDS   Most counties will **not** perform real estate searches. Copy and certification fees vary.

OTHER LIENS   Judgment, mechanics, lis pendens, contractors, hospital.

Bernalillo County

County Clerk, P.O. Box 542, Albuquerque, NM 87103-0542. 505-768-4141. Fax: 505-768-4631.
www.berncotreasurer.com
Online Access: Asesssor. Records on the Bernalillo County Records Search page are available free on the Internet at www.berncotreasurer.com/ProcessSearch.asp?cmd=NewSearch.

Catron County

County Clerk, P.O. Box 197, Reserve, NM 87830-0197. 505-533-6400. Fax: 505-533-6400.

Chaves County

County Clerk, Box 580, Roswell, NM 88202-0580. 505-624-6614. Fax: 505-624-6523.

Cibola County

County Clerk, P.O. Box 190, Grants, NM 87020. 505-287-9431. Fax: 505-285-5434.

Colfax County

County Clerk, P.O. Box 159, Raton, NM 87740-0159. 505-445-5551. Fax: 505-445-4031.

Curry County

County Clerk, P.O. Box 1168, Clovis, NM 88102-1168. 505-763-5591. Fax: 505-763-4232.

De Baca County

County Clerk, P.O. Box 347, Fort Sumner, NM 88119. 505-355-2601. Fax: 505-355-2441.

Dona Ana County

County Clerk, 251 West Amador, Room 103, Las Cruces, NM 88005-2893. 505-647-7421. Fax: 505-647-7464.
www.co.dona-ana.nm.us
Online Access: Real Estate, Assessor. Records on Dona Ana County Real Property database are available free on the Internet at www.co.dona-ana.nm.us/assr/txparcel.html. Records date back to 1990.

Eddy County

County Clerk, 101 W. Greene St., Room 312, Carlsbad, NM 88220. 505-885-3383. Fax: 505-234-1793.

Grant County

County Clerk, P.O. Box 898, Silver City, NM 88062. 505-538-2979. Fax: 505-538-8926.

Guadalupe County

County Clerk, 420 Parker Avenue, Courthouse-Suite 1, Santa Rosa, NM 88435. 505-472-3791. Fax: 505-472-3735.

Harding County

County Clerk, P.O. Box 1002, Mosquero, NM 87733-1002. 505-673-2301. Fax: 505-673-2922.

Hidalgo County

County Clerk, 300 Shakespeare Street, Lordsburg, NM 88045. 505-542-9213.

Lea County

County Clerk, P.O. Box 1507, Lovington, NM 88260. 505-396-8531. Fax: 505-396-3293.

Lincoln County

County Clerk, P.O. Box 338, Carrizozo, NM 88301. 505-648-2394. Fax: 505-648-2576.

Los Alamos County

County Clerk, P.O. Box 30, Los Alamos, NM 87544. 505-662-8010.

Luna County

County Clerk, P.O. Box 1838, Deming, NM 88031-1838. 505-546-0491. Fax: 505-546-4708.

McKinley County

County Clerk, P.O. Box 1268, Gallup, NM 87301. 505-863-6866.

Mora County

County Clerk, P.O. Box 360, Mora, NM 87732-0360. 505-387-2448. Fax: 505-387-9023.

Otero County

County Clerk, 1000 New York Avenue, Room 108, Alamogordo, NM 88310-6932. 505-437-4942. Fax: 505-443-2922.

Quay County

County Clerk, P.O. Box 1225, Tucumcari, NM 88401-1225. 505-461-0510. Fax: 505-461-0513.

Rio Arriba County

County Clerk, P.O. Box 158, Tierra Amarilla, NM 87575. 505-588-7724.

Roosevelt County

County Clerk, 101 West First, Portales, NM 88130. 505-356-8562. Fax: 505-356-8562.

San Juan County

County Clerk, P.O. Box 550, Aztec, NM 87410. 505-334-9471. Fax: 505-334-3635.

San Miguel County

County Clerk, Courthouse, Las Vegas, NM 87701. 505-425-9331. Fax: 505-425-7019.

Sandoval County

County Clerk, P.O. Box 40, Bernalillo, NM 87004. 505-867-7572. Fax: 505-771-8610.

Santa Fe County

County Clerk, P.O. Box 1985, Santa Fe, NM 87504-1985. 505-986-6280. Fax: 505-995-2767.
Online Access: Real Estate, Liens. Access to Santa Fe County online records requires a $20 monthly fee and $5 per hour of use. The system operates 24 hours daily and support baud rates up to 9,600. Records date back to 1990. Lending agency information is available For information, contact Mary Quintana at 505-995-2782.

Sierra County

County Clerk, 311 Date Street, Truth or Consequences, NM 87901. 505-894-2840. Fax: 505-894-2516.

Socorro County

County Clerk, P.O. Box I, Socorro, NM 87801. 505-835-3263. Fax: 505-835-1043.

Taos County

County Clerk, 105 Albright Street, Suite D, Taos, NM 87571-. 505-751-8654. Fax: 505-751-8637.

Torrance County

County Clerk, P.O. Box 48, Estancia, NM 87016. 505-384-2221. Fax: 505-384-4080.

Union County

County Clerk, P.O. Box 430, Clayton, NM 88415. 505-374-9491. Fax: 505-374-2763.

Valencia County

County Clerk, P.O. Box 969, Los Lunas, NM 87031. 505-866-2073. Fax: 505-866-2023.

You will usually be able to find the city name in the City/County Cross Reference below. In that case, it is a simple matter to determine the county from the cross reference. However, only the official US Postal Service city names are included in this index. There are an additional 40,000 place names that people use in their addresses. Therefore, we have also included a ZIP/City Cross Reference immediately following the City/County Cross Reference.

If you know the ZIP Code but the city name does not appear in the City/County Cross Reference index, look up the ZIP Code in the ZIP/City Cross Reference, find the city name, then look up the city name in the City/County Cross Reference. For example, you want to know the county for an address of Menands, NY 12204. There is no "Menands" in the City/County Cross Reference. The ZIP/City Cross Reference shows that ZIP Codes 12201-12288 are for the city of Albany. Looking back in the City/County Cross Reference, Albany is in Albany County.

City/County Cross Reference

ABIQUIU Rio Arriba
ALAMOGORDO Otero
ALBUQUERQUE (87114) Bernalillo(99), Sandoval(1)
ALBUQUERQUE Bernalillo
ALCALDE Rio Arriba
ALGODONES Sandoval
ALTO Lincoln
AMALIA Taos
AMISTAD Union
ANGEL FIRE Colfax
ANIMAS Hidalgo
ANTHONY (88021) Dona Ana(87), Otero(13)
ANTON CHICO Guadalupe
ARAGON Catron
ARENAS VALLEY Grant
ARREY Sierra
ARROYO HONDO Taos
ARROYO SECO Taos
ARTESIA Eddy
AZTEC San Juan
BARD Quay
BAYARD Grant
BELEN Valencia
BELL RANCH San Miguel
BELLVIEW Curry
BENT Otero
BERINO Dona Ana
BERNALILLO Sandoval
BINGHAM Socorro
BLANCO San Juan
BLOOMFIELD San Juan
BOSQUE (87006) Socorro(87), Valencia(13)
BOSQUE FARMS (87068) Bernalillo(99), Valencia(2)
BRIMHALL McKinley
BROADVIEW (88112) Curry(92), Quay(8)
BUCKHORN Grant
BUENA VISTA Mora
BUEYEROS Harding
CABALLO Sierra
CANJILON Rio Arriba
CANNON AFB Curry
CANONES Rio Arriba
CAPITAN Lincoln
CAPROCK Lea
CAPULIN Union
CARLSBAD Eddy
CARRIZOZO (88301) Lincoln(77), Torrance(23)
CARSON Taos
CASA BLANCA Cibola
CAUSEY Roosevelt
CEBOLLA Rio Arriba
CEDAR CREST Bernalillo
CEDARVALE Torrance
CERRILLOS Santa Fe
CERRO Taos
CHACON Mora
CHAMA Rio Arriba
CHAMBERINO Dona Ana
CHAMISAL Taos
CHIMAYO Rio Arriba
CHURCH ROCK McKinley

CIMARRON Colfax
CLAUNCH Socorro
CLAYTON Union
CLEVELAND Mora
CLIFF Grant
CLINES CORNERS Torrance
CLOUDCROFT Otero
CLOVIS Curry
COCHITI LAKE Sandoval
COCHITI PUEBLO Sandoval
COLUMBUS Luna
CONCHAS DAM San Miguel
CONTINENTAL DIVIDE McKinley
CORDOVA Rio Arriba
CORONA Lincoln
CORRALES Sandoval
COSTILLA Taos
COUNSELOR Sandoval
COYOTE Rio Arriba
CROSSROADS Lea
CROWNPOINT McKinley
CUBA Sandoval
CUBERO Cibola
CUCHILLO Sierra
CUERVO Guadalupe
DATIL Catron
DEMING Luna
DERRY Sierra
DES MOINES Union
DEXTER Chaves
DIXON Rio Arriba
DONA ANA Dona Ana
DORA Roosevelt
DULCE Rio Arriba
DURAN Torrance
EAGLE NEST Colfax
EDGEWOOD Santa Fe
EL PRADO Taos
EL RITO Rio Arriba
ELEPHANT BUTTE Sierra
ELIDA (88116) Roosevelt(97), Chaves(4)
EMBUDO Rio Arriba
ENCINO Torrance
ESPANOLA Rio Arriba
ESTANCIA Torrance
EUNICE Lea
FAIRACRES Dona Ana
FARMINGTON San Juan
FAYWOOD Grant
FENCE LAKE Cibola
FLORA VISTA San Juan
FLOYD (88118) Roosevelt(94), Curry(6)
FLYING H Chaves
FOLSOM Union
FORT BAYARD Grant
FORT STANTON Lincoln
FORT SUMNER De Baca
FORT WINGATE McKinley
FRUITLAND San Juan
GALLINA Rio Arriba
GALLUP McKinley
GALLUP San Juan
GAMERCO McKinley
GARFIELD Dona Ana
GARITA San Miguel
GILA Grant
GLADSTONE Union

GLENCOE Lincoln
GLENRIO Quay
GLENWOOD Catron
GLORIETA Santa Fe
GONZALES RANCH San Miguel
GRADY (88120) Quay(82), Curry(18)
GRANTS Cibola
GRENVILLE Union
GUADALUPITA Mora
HACHITA Grant
HAGERMAN Chaves
HANOVER Grant
HATCH Dona Ana
HERNANDEZ Rio Arriba
HIGH ROLLS MOUNTAIN PARK Otero
HILLSBORO Sierra
HOBBS Lea
HOLLOMAN AIR FORCE BASE Otero
HOLMAN Mora
HONDO Lincoln
HOPE (88250) Chaves(61), Eddy(40)
HOUSE Quay
HURLEY Grant
ILFELD San Miguel
ISLETA Bernalillo
JAL Lea
JAMESTOWN (87347) McKinley(80), Valencia(20)
JARALES Valencia
JEMEZ PUEBLO Sandoval
JEMEZ SPRINGS Sandoval
KENNA Roosevelt
KIRTLAND San Juan
KIRTLAND AFB Bernalillo
LA JARA Sandoval
LA JOYA Socorro
LA LOMA Guadalupe
LA LUZ Otero
LA MADERA Rio Arriba
LA MESA Dona Ana
LA PLATA San Juan
LAGUNA Cibola
LAKE ARTHUR (88253) Chaves(97), Eddy(3)
LAKEWOOD Eddy
LAMY Santa Fe
LAS CRUCES Dona Ana
LAS TABLAS Rio Arriba
LAS VEGAS San Miguel
LEDOUX Mora
LEMITAR Socorro
LINCOLN Lincoln
LINDRITH Rio Arriba
LINGO Roosevelt
LLANO Taos
LOCO HILLS Eddy
LOGAN Quay
LORDSBURG Hidalgo
LOS ALAMOS Los Alamos
LOS LUNAS Valencia
LOS OJOS Rio Arriba
LOVING Eddy
LOVINGTON Lea
LUMBERTON Rio Arriba
LUNA Catron
MAGDALENA Socorro
MALAGA Eddy

MALJAMAR Lea
MAXWELL Colfax
MAYHILL (88339) Otero(81), Chaves(19)
MC ALISTER Quay
MC DONALD Lea
MC INTOSH Torrance
MEDANALES Rio Arriba
MELROSE (88124) Curry(79), Quay(13), Roosevelt(8)
MENTMORE McKinley
MESCALERO Otero
MESILLA Dona Ana
MESILLA PARK Dona Ana
MESQUITE Dona Ana
MEXICAN SPRINGS McKinley
MIAMI Colfax
MILAN Cibola
MILLS Harding
MILNESAND Roosevelt
MIMBRES Grant
MONTEZUMA San Miguel
MONTICELLO Sierra
MONUMENT Lea
MORA Mora
MORIARTY Torrance
MOSQUERO Harding
MOUNT DORA Union
MOUNTAINAIR Torrance
MULE CREEK Grant
NAGEEZI San Juan
NARA VISA Quay
NAVAJO (87328) McKinley(79), San Juan(21)
NAVAJO DAM San Juan
NEW LAGUNA Cibola
NEWCOMB San Juan
NEWKIRK Guadalupe
NOGAL Lincoln
OCATE Mora
OIL CENTER Lea
OJO CALIENTE Taos
OJO FELIZ Mora
OJO SARCO Rio Arriba
ORGAN Dona Ana
OROGRANDE Otero
PAGUATE Cibola
PECOS San Miguel
PENA BLANCA Sandoval
PENASCO Taos
PEP Roosevelt
PERALTA (87042) Valencia(93), Bernalillo(7)
PETACA Rio Arriba
PICACHO Lincoln
PIE TOWN Catron
PINEHILL Cibola
PINON (88344) Chaves(87), Otero(13)
PINOS ALTOS Grant
PLACITAS Sandoval
PLAYAS Hidalgo
POLVADERA Socorro
PONDEROSA Sandoval
PORTALES Roosevelt
PREWITT McKinley
PUEBLO OF ACOMA Valencia
QUAY Quay
QUEMADO Catron

QUESTA Taos
RADIUM SPRINGS Dona Ana
RAINSVILLE Mora
RAMAH (87321) Cibola(54), McKinley(46)
RANCHOS DE TAOS Taos
RATON Colfax
RED RIVER Taos
REDROCK Grant
REGINA Sandoval
REHOBOTH McKinley
RESERVE Catron
RIBERA San Miguel
RINCON Dona Ana
RIO RANCHO Bernalillo
RIO RANCHO Sandoval
ROCIADA (87742) Mora(63), San Miguel(38)
RODARTE Taos
RODEO Hidalgo
ROGERS Roosevelt
ROSWELL Chaves
ROWE San Miguel
ROY Harding
RUIDOSO Lincoln
RUIDOSO DOWNS Lincoln
RUTHERON Rio Arriba
SACRAMENTO Otero
SAINT VRAIN Curry
SALEM Dona Ana
SAN ACACIA Socorro

SAN ANTONIO Socorro
SAN CRISTOBAL Taos
SAN FIDEL Cibola
SAN JON Quay
SAN JOSE San Miguel
SAN JUAN PUEBLO Rio Arriba
SAN MATEO Cibola
SAN MIGUEL Dona Ana
SAN PATRICIO Lincoln
SAN RAFAEL Cibola
SAN YSIDRO Sandoval
SANDIA PARK (87047) Bernalillo(52), Santa Fe(48)
SANOSTEE (87461) San Juan(83), McKinley(17)
SANTA CLARA Grant
SANTA CRUZ Santa Fe
SANTA FE Santa Fe
SANTA ROSA Guadalupe
SANTA TERESA Dona Ana
SANTO DOMINGO PUEBLO Sandoval
SAPELLO San Miguel
SEBOYETA Cibola
SEDAN Union
SENA San Miguel
SENECA Union
SERAFINA San Miguel
SHEEP SPRINGS San Juan
SHIPROCK San Juan
SILVER CITY Grant

SMITH LAKE McKinley
SOCORRO Socorro
SOLANO Harding
SPRINGER Colfax
STANLEY Santa Fe
STEAD Union
SUNLAND PARK Dona Ana
SUNSPOT Otero
TAIBAN (88134) Roosevelt(42), De Baca(37), Quay(21)
TAJIQUE Torrance
TAOS Taos
TAOS SKI VALLEY Taos
TATUM Lea
TERERRO San Miguel
TESUQUE Santa Fe
TEXICO Curry
THOREAU McKinley
TIERRA AMARILLA Rio Arriba
TIJERAS Bernalillo
TIMBERON Otero
TINNIE Lincoln
TOHATCHI (87325) McKinley(93), San Juan(7)
TOME Valencia
TORREON Torrance
TRAMPAS Taos
TREMENTINA San Miguel
TRES PIEDRAS Taos
TRUCHAS Rio Arriba

TRUTH OR CONSEQUENCES Sierra
TUCUMCARI Quay
TULAROSA Otero
TYRONE Grant
UTE PARK Colfax
VADITO Taos
VADO Dona Ana
VALDEZ Taos
VALLECITOS Rio Arriba
VALMORA Mora
VANADIUM Grant
VANDERWAGEN McKinley
VAUGHN Guadalupe
VEGUITA Socorro
VELARDE Rio Arriba
VILLANUEVA San Miguel
WAGON MOUND Mora
WATERFLOW San Juan
WATROUS Mora
WEED Otero
WHITE SANDS MISSILE RANGE Dona Ana
WHITES CITY Eddy
WILLARD Torrance
WILLIAMSBURG Sierra
WINSTON Sierra
YATAHEY McKinley
YESO De Baca
YOUNGSVILLE Rio Arriba
ZUNI McKinley

ZIP/City Cross Reference

ZIP	City	ZIP	City	ZIP	City	ZIP	City
87001-87001	ALGODONES	87060-87060	TOME	87499-87499	FARMINGTON	87576-87576	TRAMPAS
87002-87002	BELEN	87061-87061	TORREON	87500-87509	SANTA FE	87577-87577	TRES PIEDRAS
87004-87004	BERNALILLO	87062-87062	VEGUITA	87510-87510	ABIQUIU	87578-87578	TRUCHAS
87005-87005	BLUEWATER	87063-87063	WILLARD	87511-87511	ALCALDE	87579-87579	VADITO
87006-87006	BOSQUE	87064-87064	YOUNGSVILLE	87512-87512	AMALIA	87580-87580	VALDEZ
87007-87007	CASA BLANCA	87068-87068	BOSQUE FARMS	87513-87513	ARROYO HONDO	87581-87581	VALLECITOS
87008-87008	CEDAR CREST	87070-87070	CLINES CORNERS	87514-87514	ARROYO SECO	87582-87582	VELARDE
87009-87009	CEDARVALE	87072-87072	COCHITI PUEBLO	87515-87515	CANJILON	87583-87583	VILLANUEVA
87010-87010	CERRILLOS	87083-87083	COCHITI LAKE	87516-87516	CANONES	87592-87594	SANTA FE
87011-87011	CLAUNCH	87101-87116	ALBUQUERQUE	87517-87517	CARSON	87701-87701	LAS VEGAS
87012-87012	COYOTE	87117-87117	KIRTLAND AFB	87518-87518	CEBOLLA	87710-87710	ANGEL FIRE
87013-87013	CUBA	87118-87123	ALBUQUERQUE	87519-87519	CERRO	87711-87711	ANTON CHICO
87014-87014	CUBERO	87124-87124	RIO RANCHO	87520-87520	CHAMA	87712-87712	BUENA VISTA
87015-87015	EDGEWOOD	87125-87158	ALBUQUERQUE	87521-87521	CHAMISAL	87713-87713	CHACON
87016-87016	ESTANCIA	87174-87174	RIO RANCHO	87522-87522	CHIMAYO	87714-87714	CIMARRON
87017-87017	GALLINA	87176-87201	ALBUQUERQUE	87523-87523	CORDOVA	87715-87715	CLEVELAND
87018-87018	COUNSELOR	87300-87305	GALLUP	87524-87524	COSTILLA	87718-87718	EAGLE NEST
87020-87020	GRANTS	87310-87310	BRIMHALL	87525-87525	TAOS SKI VALLEY	87722-87722	GUADALUPITA
87021-87021	MILAN	87311-87311	CHURCH ROCK	87527-87527	DIXON	87723-87723	HOLMAN
87022-87022	ISLETA	87312-87312	CONTINENTAL DIVIDE	87528-87528	DULCE	87724-87724	LA LOMA
87023-87023	JARALES	87313-87313	CROWNPOINT	87529-87529	EL PRADO	87728-87728	MAXWELL
87024-87024	JEMEZ PUEBLO	87315-87315	FENCE LAKE	87530-87530	EL RITO	87729-87729	MIAMI
87025-87025	JEMEZ SPRINGS	87316-87316	FORT WINGATE	87531-87531	EMBUDO	87730-87730	MILLS
87026-87026	LAGUNA	87317-87317	GAMERCO	87532-87533	ESPANOLA	87731-87731	MONTEZUMA
87027-87027	LA JARA	87319-87319	MENTMORE	87535-87535	GLORIETA	87732-87732	MORA
87028-87028	LA JOYA	87320-87320	MEXICAN SPRINGS	87537-87537	HERNANDEZ	87733-87733	MOSQUERO
87029-87029	LINDRITH	87321-87321	RAMAH	87538-87538	ILFELD	87734-87734	OCATE
87031-87031	LOS LUNAS	87322-87322	REHOBOTH	87539-87539	LA MADERA	87735-87735	OJO FELIZ
87032-87032	MC INTOSH	87323-87323	THOREAU	87540-87540	LAMY	87736-87736	RAINSVILLE
87034-87034	PUEBLO OF ACOMA	87325-87325	TOHATCHI	87543-87543	LLANO	87740-87740	RATON
87035-87035	MORIARTY	87326-87326	VANDERWAGEN	87544-87545	LOS ALAMOS	87742-87742	ROCIADA
87036-87036	MOUNTAINAIR	87327-87327	ZUNI	87548-87548	MEDANALES	87743-87743	ROY
87037-87037	NAGEEZI	87328-87328	NAVAJO	87549-87549	OJO CALIENTE	87745-87745	SAPELLO
87038-87038	NEW LAGUNA	87347-87347	JAMESTOWN	87551-87551	LOS OJOS	87746-87746	SOLANO
87040-87040	PAGUATE	87357-87357	PINEHILL	87552-87552	PECOS	87747-87747	SPRINGER
87041-87041	PENA BLANCA	87364-87364	SHEEP SPRINGS	87553-87553	PENASCO	87749-87749	UTE PARK
87042-87042	PERALTA	87365-87365	SMITH LAKE	87554-87554	PETACA	87750-87750	VALMORA
87043-87043	PLACITAS	87375-87375	YATAHEY	87556-87556	QUESTA	87752-87752	WAGON MOUND
87044-87044	PONDEROSA	87401-87402	FARMINGTON	87557-87557	RANCHOS DE TAOS	87753-87753	WATROUS
87045-87045	PREWITT	87410-87410	AZTEC	87558-87558	RED RIVER	87801-87801	SOCORRO
87046-87046	REGINA	87412-87412	BLANCO	87560-87560	RIBERA	87820-87820	ARAGON
87047-87047	SANDIA PARK	87413-87413	BLOOMFIELD	87562-87562	ROWE	87821-87821	DATIL
87048-87048	CORRALES	87415-87415	FLORA VISTA	87564-87564	SAN CRISTOBAL	87823-87823	LEMITAR
87049-87049	SAN FIDEL	87416-87416	FRUITLAND	87565-87565	SAN JOSE	87824-87824	LUNA
87051-87051	SAN RAFAEL	87417-87417	KIRTLAND	87566-87566	SAN JUAN PUEBLO	87825-87825	MAGDALENA
87052-87052	SANTO DOMINGO PUEBLO	87418-87418	LA PLATA	87567-87567	SANTA CRUZ	87827-87827	PIE TOWN
		87419-87419	NAVAJO DAM	87569-87569	SERAFINA	87828-87828	POLVADERA
87053-87053	SAN YSIDRO	87420-87420	SHIPROCK	87571-87571	TAOS	87829-87829	QUEMADO
87056-87056	STANLEY	87421-87421	WATERFLOW	87573-87573	TERERRO	87830-87830	RESERVE
87057-87057	TAJIQUE	87455-87455	NEWCOMB	87574-87574	TESUQUE	87831-87831	SAN ACACIA
87059-87059	TIJERAS	87461-87461	SANOSTEE	87575-87575	TIERRA AMARILLA	87832-87832	SAN ANTONIO

87901-87901	TRUTH OR CONSEQUENCES	88043-88043	HURLEY	88201-88202	ROSWELL	88341-88341	NOGAL
87930-87930	ARREY	88044-88044	LA MESA	88210-88211	ARTESIA	88342-88342	OROGRANDE
87931-87931	CABALLO	88045-88045	LORDSBURG	88213-88213	CAPROCK	88343-88343	PICACHO
87933-87933	DERRY	88046-88046	MESILLA	88220-88221	CARLSBAD	88344-88344	PINON
87935-87935	ELEPHANT BUTTE	88047-88047	MESILLA PARK	88230-88230	DEXTER	88345-88345	RUIDOSO
87936-87936	GARFIELD	88048-88048	MESQUITE	88231-88231	EUNICE	88346-88346	RUIDOSO DOWNS
87937-87937	HATCH	88049-88049	MIMBRES	88232-88232	HAGERMAN	88347-88347	SACRAMENTO
87939-87939	MONTICELLO	88051-88051	MULE CREEK	88240-88244	HOBBS	88348-88348	SAN PATRICIO
87940-87940	RINCON	88052-88052	ORGAN	88250-88250	HOPE	88349-88349	SUNSPOT
87941-87941	SALEM	88053-88053	PINOS ALTOS	88252-88252	JAL	88350-88350	TIMBERON
87942-87942	WILLIAMSBURG	88054-88054	RADIUM SPRINGS	88253-88253	LAKE ARTHUR	88351-88351	TINNIE
87943-87943	WINSTON	88055-88055	REDROCK	88254-88254	LAKEWOOD	88352-88352	TULAROSA
88001-88001	LAS CRUCES	88056-88056	RODEO	88255-88255	LOCO HILLS	88353-88353	VAUGHN
88002-88002	WHITE SANDS MISSILE RANGE	88058-88058	SAN MIGUEL	88256-88256	LOVING	88354-88354	WEED
		88061-88062	SILVER CITY	88260-88260	LOVINGTON	88355-88355	RUIDOSO
88003-88006	LAS CRUCES	88063-88063	SUNLAND PARK	88262-88262	MC DONALD	88401-88401	TUCUMCARI
88008-88008	SANTA TERESA	88065-88065	TYRONE	88263-88263	MALAGA	88410-88410	AMISTAD
88009-88009	PLAYAS	88072-88072	VADO	88264-88264	MALJAMAR	88411-88411	BARD
88011-88012	LAS CRUCES	88101-88102	CLOVIS	88265-88265	MONUMENT	88414-88414	CAPULIN
88020-88020	ANIMAS	88103-88103	CANNON AFB	88267-88267	TATUM	88415-88415	CLAYTON
88021-88021	ANTHONY	88112-88112	BROADVIEW	88268-88268	WHITES CITY	88416-88416	CONCHAS DAM
88022-88022	ARENAS VALLEY	88113-88113	CAUSEY	88301-88301	CARRIZOZO	88417-88417	CUERVO
88023-88023	BAYARD	88114-88114	CROSSROADS	88310-88311	ALAMOGORDO	88418-88418	DES MOINES
88024-88024	BERINO	88115-88115	DORA	88312-88312	ALTO	88419-88419	FOLSOM
88025-88025	BUCKHORN	88116-88116	ELIDA	88314-88314	BENT	88421-88421	GARITA
88026-88026	SANTA CLARA	88118-88118	FLOYD	88316-88316	CAPITAN	88422-88422	GLADSTONE
88027-88027	CHAMBERINO	88119-88119	FORT SUMNER	88317-88317	CLOUDCROFT	88424-88424	GRENVILLE
88028-88028	CLIFF	88120-88120	GRADY	88318-88318	CORONA	88426-88426	LOGAN
88029-88029	COLUMBUS	88121-88121	HOUSE	88321-88321	ENCINO	88427-88427	MC ALISTER
88030-88031	DEMING	88122-88122	KENNA	88323-88323	FORT STANTON	88429-88429	MOUNT DORA
88032-88032	DONA ANA	88123-88123	LINGO	88324-88324	GLENCOE	88430-88430	NARA VISA
88033-88033	FAIRACRES	88124-88124	MELROSE	88325-88325	HIGH ROLLS MOUNTAIN PARK	88431-88431	NEWKIRK
88034-88034	FAYWOOD	88125-88125	MILNESAND			88433-88433	QUAY
88036-88036	FORT BAYARD	88126-88126	PEP	88330-88330	HOLLOMAN AIR FORCE BASE	88434-88434	SAN JON
88038-88038	GILA	88130-88130	PORTALES			88435-88435	SANTA ROSA
88039-88039	GLENWOOD	88132-88132	ROGERS	88336-88336	HONDO	88436-88436	SEDAN
88040-88040	HACHITA	88133-88133	SAINT VRAIN	88337-88337	LA LUZ	88437-88437	SENECA
88041-88041	HANOVER	88134-88134	TAIBAN	88338-88338	LINCOLN	88439-88439	TREMENTINA
88042-88042	HILLSBORO	88135-88135	TEXICO	88339-88339	MAYHILL	88441-88441	BELL RANCH
		88136-88136	YESO	88340-88340	MESCALERO		

New York

General Help Numbers:

Governor's Office
Executive Chamber, State Capitol   518-474-8390
Albany, NY 12224   Fax 518-474-8390
www.state.ny.us/governor   9AM-5PM

Attorney General's Office
State Capitol   518-474-7330
Albany, NY 12224-0341   Fax 518-473-9909
www.oag.state.ny.us   9AM-5:30PM

State Court Administrator
Empire State Plaza   518-473-1196
Agency Bldg #4, Suite 2001   Fax 518-473-6860
Albany, NY 12223   9AM-5PM
www.courts.state.ny.us

State Archives
Empire State Plaza   518-474-8955
Cultural Education Center Rm 11D40 Fax 518-473-9985
Albany, NY 12230   9AM-5PM
www.sara.nysed.gov

State Specifics:

Capital: Albany
                                  Albany County

Time Zone: EST

Number of Counties: 62

Population: 18,196,601

Web Site: www.state.ny.us

State Agencies

Criminal Records

Access to Records is Restricted

Division of Criminal Justice Services, 4 Tower Place, Albany, NY 12203; 518-457-6043, 518-457-6550 (Fax), 8AM-5PM.

www.criminaljustice.state.ny.us

One may order their own record from this agency. Submit fingerprint card and $25.00. Records are released by court order, subpoena or to person of record only. Also, the New York State Office of Court Administration (address below) will perform an electronic search for criminal history information from a database of criminal case records from the boroughs and counties of Bronx, Dutchess, Erie, Kings, Nassau, New York, Orange, Putnam, Queens, Richmond, Rockland, Suffolk and Westchester. A separate form is required for each county to be searched. The request must include complete name and date of birth, and, for mail requests, be accompanied by two (2) self addressed stamped return envelopes. The fee, payable by check, is $16.00 per name per county. Mail and in person requests go to: Office of Court Administration, Criminal History Search, 25 Beaver St, 8th Floor, New York, NY 10004. The public must search other counties at the county court level.

Corporation Records
Limited Partnership Records
Limited Liability Company Records
Limited Liability Partnerships

Division of Corporations, Department of State, 41 State St, Albany, NY 12231; 518-473-2492 (General Information), 900-835-2677 (Corporate Searches), 518-474-1418 (Fax), 8AM-4:30PM.

www.dos.state.ny.us

Note: Information available includes date of incorporation, subsequent filings, status, principle business location, registered agent, service of process address, number and type of stock shares entitled to issue, and biennial statements w/addresses.

Indexing & Storage: Records are available from inception. Information on active entities is automated. Records entities inactive prior to 1978 are not automated and require additional research. New records are available for inquiry immediately.

Searching: All data is considered public information. Include the following in your request-full name of business.

Access by: mail, phone, in person, online.

Fee & Payment: There is no fee for basic information up to 5 names. Over 5 names, the fee is $5.00 per name. For documents, the certification fee is $10.00, $25.00 if SOS seal is required. The fee is $5.00 for every name availability checked. Fee payee: New York Department of State. Prepayment required. Payments over $500 must be by certified check or money order. Personal checks accepted. No credit cards accepted.

Mail search: Turnaround time: 1 week. A self addressed stamped envelope is requested.

Phone search: Call 1-900-TEL-CORP. You may search up to 5 names per call for a flat rate charge of $4.00 per call.

In person search: This is considered expedited service, extra fees apply. The general public may obtain copies of documents while they wait.

Online search: A commercial account can be set up for Internet access. Fee is $.75 per transaction through a drawdown account. There is an extensive amount of information available. Search the web at http://wdb.dos.state.ny.us/corp_public/corp_wdb.corp_search_inputs.show. Includes corporations, limited partnerships, limited liability companies/partnerships. Updated weekly and does not contain historical data.

Other access: You may submit an e-mail search request at corporations@dos.state.ny.us.

Trademarks/Servicemarks

Department of State, Miscellaneous Records, 41 State St, Albany, NY 12231; 518-474-4770, 518-473-0730 (Fax), 8:30AM-4:30PM.

Indexing & Storage: Records are available for past 10 years. It takes 1-2 days before new records are available for inquiry.

Searching: Searches are only done on registered marks, not on pending marks. You need to provide written description of design or features of the mark.

Access by: mail, phone, fax, in person.

Fee & Payment: The first two requests by mail, fax, or phone are free. Additional requests cost $5.00 per search. Fee payee: New York Department of State. Prepayment required. Payments of more than $500.00 must be certified check or money order; personal checks accepted for amounts less than $500.00 Personal checks accepted. No credit cards accepted.

Mail search: Turnaround time: 2-3 days. A self addressed stamped envelope is requested.

Phone search: Limited verification information is available.

Fax search: Turnaround time: 2-3 days.

In person search: No fee for request. You can request 1 search in person.

Other access: New marks can be photocopied and sent out on a regular monthly basis. Fees are determined by numbers of marks.

Uniform Commercial Code
Federal Tax Liens
State Tax Liens

UCC Division, Department of State, 41 State Street, Albany, NY 12231; 518-474-4763, 8AM-4:30PM.

www.dos.state.ny.us/corp/uccfaq.html

Indexing & Storage: Records are available from 1964. Records are computerized from 1/96. Records are indexed on computer, microfilm.

Searching: Use search request form UCC-11. Federal tax liens on businesses will be included. Lists of state tax liens (warrants) are available, but must be searched separately on premises. Federal tax liens on individuals are filed at the county level. Include the following in your request-debtor name. It is suggested for written requests that the form be 5" x 8" or use a UCC-11.

Access by: mail, in person.

Fee & Payment: UCC search is $7.00 per debtor name, one name per form. Individual debtor names should list addresses. The copy fee is $1.50 per page. You can search state tax liens, in person, at no charge. Fee payee: Secretary of State. Prepayment required. Personal checks accepted. No credit cards accepted.

Mail search: Turnaround time: 2 days. No self addressed stamped envelope is required.

In person search: You may request information in person.

Other access: The state offers its database for sale on microfilm.

Sales Tax Registrations

Sales Tax Registration Bureau, WA Harriman Campus, Building 8, Rm 408, Albany, NY 12227; 518-457-0259, 518-457-0453 (Fax), 7AM-5PM.

Indexing & Storage: Records are available for current records only. Records are computerized since 1970.

Searching: This agency will confirm that a business is registered and release the legal name and physical address. Include the following in your request-business name. They will also search by tax permit number or federal tax number.

Access by: mail, phone, fax, in person.

Mail search: Turnaround time: 2-3 weeks. A self addressed stamped envelope is requested. No fee for mail request.

Phone search: No fee for telephone request.

Fax search: Fax searching available.

In person search: No fee for request.

Birth Certificates

Vital Records Section, Certification Unit, 733 Broadway, Albany, NY 12237-0023; 518-474-3038, 518-474-3077, 518-474-9168 (Fax), 8:30AM-4:30PM.

www.health.state.ny.us

Note: For records from New York City information, see that profile.

Indexing & Storage: Records are available from 1881 on. New records are available for inquiry immediately. Records are indexed on microfiche, inhouse computer.

Searching: May only obtain your own or a dependent child's records, without notorized release. They will not return records to a PO Box or an "in care of." Include the following in your request-full name, names of parents, mother's maiden name, date of birth, place of birth, relationship to person of record, reason for information request.

Access by: mail, phone, fax, in person.

Fee & Payment: The fee is $15.00 per name per record for a 3-year search. Fee payee: New York State Department of Health. Prepayment required. Personal checks accepted. Credit cards accepted: Mastercard, Visa, AmEx, Discover.

Mail search: Turnaround time: 2-3 months. Turnaround time will be 2 weeks if you send your request by Express Mail. A self addressed stamped envelope is requested.

Phone search: Use of a credit card is required, there is an additional $5.00 fee. Turnaround time is 1 week.

Fax search: Same criteria as phone searches, use 518-432-6286.

In person search: Results are still returned by mail.

Expedited service: Expedited service is available for mail, phone and fax searches. Add $5.00 for use of credit card and $10.50 for express delivery.

Death Records

Vital Records Section, certification Unit, 733 Broadway, Albany, NY 12237-0023; 518-474-3038, 518-474-3077, 518-474-9168 (Fax), 8:30AM-4:30PM.

www.health.state.ny.us

Note: For New York City, see the separate entry.

Indexing & Storage: Records are available from 1880 on. New records are available for inquiry immediately. Records are indexed on microfiche, inhouse computer.

Searching: You must show cause why record is needed on letterhead, if not member of the immediate family. Include the following in your request-full name, date of death, place of death, relationship to person of record, reason for information request.

Access by: mail, in person.

Fee & Payment: The fee is $15.00 per record. Use of credit card adds $5.00. Fee payee: New York State Department of Health. Prepayment required. Personal checks accepted. Credit cards accepted: Mastercard, Visa, AmEx, Discover.

Mail search: Turnaround time: 2-3 months. If request is sent by express mail, turnaround time shortened to 2 weeks. A self addressed stamped envelope is requested.

In person search: Turnaround time shortened by mail time only.

Expedited service: Expedited service is available for mail, phone and fax searches. Use of credit card is required, add $10.50 for overnight delivery.

Marriage Certificates

Vital Records Section, Certification Unit, 733 Broadway, Albany, NY 12237-0023; 518-474-3038, 518-474-3077, 8:30AM-4:30PM.

www.health.state.ny.us

Note: For New York City information, see the separate entry.

Indexing & Storage: Records are available from 1881 on. New records are available for inquiry immediately. Records are indexed on microfiche, inhouse computer.

Searching: Must have a notarized release form from persons of record or immediate family member for investigative purposes. Include the following in your request-names of husband and wife, date of marriage, place or county of marriage, relationship to person of record, reason for information request, wife's maiden name.

Access by: mail, in person.

Fee & Payment: The fee is $5.00 per record (for 1-3 years, additional years cost more). Also, there is a $5.00 fee to use a credit card. Fee payee: New York State Department of Health. Prepayment required. Personal checks accepted. Credit cards accepted: Mastercard, Visa, AmEx, Discover.

Mail search: Turnaround time: 2-3 months. Turnaround time is 2 weeks if request is sent by overnight express mail.A self addressed stamped envelope is requested.

In person search: Turnaround time shortened by mail time only.

Expedited service: Expedited service is available for mail, phone and fax searches. Add credit card fee and express delivery fee ($10.50).

Divorce Records

Vital Records Section, Certification Unit, 733 Broadway, Albany, NY 12237-0023; 518-474-3038, 518-474-3077, 8:30AM-4:30PM.

www.health.state.ny.us

Note: For New York City information, see the separate entry.

Indexing & Storage: Records are available from 1963 on. New records are available for inquiry immediately. Records are indexed on microfiche, inhouse computer.

Searching: If you are not a party to the divorce you must have a court order to obtain records or show legal cause. Include the following in your request-names of husband and wife, date of divorce, place of divorce, relationship to person of record, reason for information request.

Access by: mail, in person.

Fee & Payment: The fee is $15.00 for searching 1994-present; $25.00 for 1975-1994; $35 for search from 1963-1994. Add $5.00 for use of credit card. Fee payee: New York State Department of Health. Prepayment required. Personal checks accepted. Credit cards accepted: Mastercard, Visa, AmEx, Discover.

Mail search: Turnaround time: 2-3 months. A self addressed stamped envelope is requested.

In person search: Turnaround time shortened by mail time only.

Expedited service: Expedited service is available for mail, phone and fax searches. Plus $5.00 for using a credit card and $10.50 for express delivery.

Birth Certificate-New York City
Death Records-New York City

Department of Health, Bureau of Vital Records, 125 Worth St, Rm 133, New York, NY 10013; 212-788-4520, 212-442-1999, 212-962-6105 (Fax), 9AM-4PM.

www.ci.nyc.ny.us/html/doh/html/vr/vr.html

Indexing & Storage: Records are available from 1910-present for birth and from 1949 forward for death. For prior records, call Municipal Archives at 212-566-5292. It takes 2 months before new records are available for inquiry. Records are indexed on microfiche, inhouse computer.

Searching: Must have a notarized signed release form from immediate family member. Include a copy of your photo ID. Include the following in your request-full name, date of birth, date of death, place of birth, place of death, reason for information request, name of the hospital. Parents' names are also required, mother's maiden name for birth.

Access by: mail, phone, fax, in person.

Fee & Payment: The fee is $15.00 per record plus $5.00 if using a credit card. Only those parties appearing on the birth record may order via a credit card. All other parties must order by mail or in-person and show cause or reason for the request. Fee payee: Department of Health. Prepayment required. Personal checks accepted. Credit cards accepted: Mastercard, Visa, AmEx, Discover.

Mail search: Allow 3-4 weeks for a birth record and 8-10 weeks for a death record.A self addressed stamped envelope is requested.

Phone search: Birth only. Use of credit card is required. Turnaround time is 5-7 days.

Fax search: Same criteria as phone searching.

In person search: Turnaround time is usually while you wait.

Expedited service: Expedited service is available for fax searches. Turnaround time: 1-2 days. Add $11.00 for delivery service. The $15.00 search fee and $5.00 credit card fee must also be included.

Marriage Certificate-New York City

City Clerk's Office, Department of Records & Information Services, 1 Centre Street, Rm 252, New York, NY 10007; 212-669-8898, 9AM-4:30PM M-TH; 9AM-1PM F.

Note: Records from 1908-1929 can be obtained from the Municipal Archives at 212-788-8580. Records from 1995 forward can be obtained from the City Clerk's Borough Office. Call this office for further information.

Indexing & Storage: Records are available from 1930-1994.

Searching: Current records are not public information and are only available to the parties involved or legal representatives.

Access by: mail, in person.

Fee & Payment: Search fee of $15.00 incudes certification. Each additional is $10.00. Multiple year searches may be more costly, depending on extent of request. Fee payee: City Clerk. Prepayment required. Personal checks accepted.

Mail search: Turnaround time: 1 week.

In person search: Searching is available in person.

Divorce Records-New York City

New York County Clerk's Office, Division of Old Records, 60 Centre Street, Rm 141, New York City, NY 10007; 212-374-4376, 9AM-3PM, M-F.

Note: Records of divorces from 1979-1991 can be found at 31 Chambers St, Room 703. This is open Tuesdays and Thursdays from 9-1 and 2-5. Call for specific details.

Indexing & Storage: Records are available from 1955-1970 on index cards, computerized since 1971.

Searching: Manhattan records are limited by statute to parties or attorneys of record or with notarized authorization by party involved.

Access by: mail, in person.

Fee & Payment: Fee is $8.00 for the search and a certified copy. Fee payee: New York County Clerk. Prepayment required. On site requests require cash; mail requests require postal money order or certified check. No credit cards accepted.

Mail search: Turnaround time: 2 weeks.

In person search: You may make copies at $.25 per page. Go to basement, either room 103 or room 141 and bring identification.

Workers' Compensation Records

NY Workers' Compensation Board, Director of Claims Office, 180 Livingston St, Room 400, Brooklyn, NY 11248; 718-802-6621, 718-834-2116 (Fax), 9AM-5PM.

www.wcb.state.ny.us

Note: File copies of records are not released for employment purposes, even with a signed release.

Indexing & Storage: Records are available for up to 18 years after the case is closed. Older records are destroyed. New records are available for inquiry immediately. Records are indexed on inhouse computer.

Searching: Must have a notarized release from claimant naming requesting party and stating the purpose for which information is going to be used to access case files. Include the following in your request-claimant name, Social Security Number, claim number, date of accident.

Access by: mail, in person.

Fee & Payment: There is a $10.00 "mailing and handling fee" but no search fee. Copies are $.25 each. Fee payee: Workers' Compensation Board. Prepayment required. Personal checks accepted. No credit cards accepted.

Mail search: Turnaround time: 2 weeks. No self addressed stamped envelope is required.

In person search: Turnaround time is while you wait.

Driver Records

Department of Motor Vehicles, MV-15 Processing, 6 Empire State Plaza, Room 430, Albany, NY 12228; 518-474-0774, 8AM-5PM.

www.nydmv.state.ny.us

Note: Copies of tickets may be purchased from the same address for a fee of $6.00 per ticket.

Indexing & Storage: Records are available for 3 years in addition to the current year for moving violations, 10 years for DWIs, and indefinitely for open (4 years for closed) suspensions. Most non-moving violations are not shown on record. It takes a few days after conviction before new records are available for inquiry. Records are normally destroyed after 5 years from expiration.

Searching: New York restricts the release of personal information on driving records to casual requesters. The driver's license number (ID#), name, and DOB are required when ordering a record.

Access by: mail, phone, in person, online.

Fee & Payment: The fee is $5.00 per record search, $4.00 if online or by tape. Fee payee: Department of Motor Vehicles. Prepayment required. Escrow accounts can be set up for high volume users. Personal checks accepted. No credit cards accepted.

Mail search: Turnaround time: 4-6 weeks. Form MV-15 is required when ordering.A self addressed stamped envelope is requested.

Phone search: Only drivers wishing to obtain their own record may call. The DL# or name, DOB and sex are required when ordered. Payment by a credit card is required and an additional $5.00 is charged.

In person search: Records can be ordered from most any county-operated motor vehicle office and at the state offices in Albany. A photo ID of the requester and use of Form MV-14C is required.

Online search: NY has implemented a "Dial-In Inquiry" system which enables customers to obtain data online 24 hours a day. The DL# or name, DOB and sex are required to retrieve. If the DOB and sex are not entered, the system defaults to a limited group of 5 records. The fee is $5.00 per record. For more information, call 518-474-4293.

Other access: Tape-to-tape ordering is available. For more information call (518) 474-0606.

Vehicle Ownership
Vehicle Identification
Boat & Vessel Ownership
Boat & Vessel Registration

Department of Motor Vehicles, MV-15 Processing, 6 Empire State Plaza, Room 430, Albany, NY 12228; 518-474-0710, 518-474-8510, 8AM-5PM.

www.nydmv.state.ny.us

Indexing & Storage: Records are available for a minimum of 4 years on computer. All motorized vessels must be registered, titles are not issued. New records are available for inquiry immediately.

Searching: Generally, vehicle and ownership information is available. However, accessed is restricted in adherence to the Drivers' Privacy Protection Act and casual requesters cannot obtain records.

Access by: mail, in person, online.

Fee & Payment: Mail requests are $5.00 per record, online inquiries are $4.00 per record. Fee payee: Commissioner of Motor Vehicles. Prepayment required. For information regarding deposit accounts, call 518-474-4293. Personal checks accepted. No credit cards accepted.

Mail search: Turnaround time: 4-6 weeks. A self addressed stamped envelope is requested.

In person search: Results are returned by mail.

Online search: New York offers plate, VIN and ownership data through the same network discussed in the Driving Records Section. The system is interactive and open 24 hours a day, with the exception of 10 hours on Sunday. The fee is $5.00 per record. Call 518-474-4293 for more information.

Other access: New York also offers a tape to diskette search of registration information at $4.00 per record. There is no bulk list retrieval offered at lesser prices; however, a contracted vendor may sell data. Call 518-474-0606 for more information.

Accident Reports

DMV Certified Document Center, Accident Report Section, Empire State Plaza, Swan St Bldg, Albany, NY 12228; 518-474-0710, 8AM-4:30PM.

www.nysdmv.com

Indexing & Storage: Records are available for 4 years to present. It takes 120 days after date of accident before new records are available for inquiry. Records are indexed on inhouse computer.

Searching: Records are open to the public, but request must be in writing. Use of Form MV-198C is suggested. Release of records is restricted based on the Drivers' Privacy Protection Act. Include the following in your request-date of accident, location of accident, full name. Provide driver's address, if known.

Access by: mail, in person.

Fee & Payment: Fees: $5.00 per search and $15.00 per accident report. Express mail is given priority. Fee payee: Commissioner of Motor Vehicle. Prepayment required. Personal checks accepted. No credit cards accepted.

Mail search: Turnaround time: 4-6 weeks. No self addressed stamped envelope is required.

In person search: Turnaround time is next day pickup.

Legislation-Current/Pending
Legislation-Passed

NY Senate Document Room, State Capitol, State Street Rm 317, Albany, NY 12247;, 518-455-2312 (Senate Document Room), 518-455-3216 (Calls Without Bill Numbers), 518-455-5164 (Assembly Document Room), 9AM-5PM.

www.senate.state.ny.us

Note: Prior session bills may be found at the State Library, 518-474-5355.

Indexing & Storage: Records are available for current session only. Records are indexed on computer.

Searching: Include the following in your request-bill number. The law section number or description can be helpful.

Access by: mail, phone, in person, online.

Fee & Payment: There is no search fee.

Mail search: Turnaround time: same day. No self addressed stamped envelope is required.

Phone search: Searching is available by phone.

In person search: research materials are available if bill number is not known.

Online search: Both the Senate (senate.state.ny.us) and the Assembly (assembly.state.ny.us) have web sites to search for a bill or specific bill text. A much more complete system is the LRS online system. This offers complete state statutes, agency rules and regulations, bill text, bill status, summaries, and more. For more information, call Barbara Lett at 800-356-6566.

Voter Registration
Records not maintained by a state level agency.

Note: Records may only be viewed or purchased at the county level. Purchases are restricted for political purposes only.

GED Certificates

NY State Education Dept, GED Testing, PO Box 7348, Albany, NY 12224-0348; 518-474-5906, 518-474-3041 (Fax), 10AM-12PM, 1PM-3PM M-F.

Searching: To search, all of the following is required: full name, SSN, and date of birth. If the subject was tested prior to 1985, include the address, year of test, and location.

Access by: mail, phone, fax.

Fee & Payment: There is no fee for verification. Copies of transcripts are $4.00 each. Copies of diplomas are $10.00 each. Fee payee: NY State Education Dept. Prepayment required. Money orders are accepted. No credit cards accepted.

Mail search: Turnaround time: 1 week. Turnaround time: 1 week.No self addressed stamped envelope is required.

Phone search: Automated phone verifications can be accomplished for records that are from 1985-the present.

Fax search: Same criteria as mail searching.

Hunting License Information
Fishing License Information
Records not maintained by a state level agency.

Note: They do not have a central database. Only vendors have the names and addresses.

Licenses Searchable Online

Acupuncturist/Assistant #19	www.nysed.gov/dpls/opnme.html
Architect #19	www.nysed.gov/dpls/opnme.html
Athletic Trainer #19	www.nysed.gov/dpls/opnme.html
Attorney #18	www.courts.state.ny.us/webdb/wdbcgi.exe/apps/INTERNETDB.attyreghome.show
Audiologist #19	www.nysed.gov/dpls/opnme.html
Chiropractor #19	www.nysed.gov/dpls/opnme.html
Court Reporter #19	www.nysed.gov/dpls/opnme.html
Dental Assistant #19	www.nysed.gov/dpls/opnme.html
Dental Hygienist #19	www.nysed.gov/dpls/opnme.html
Dentist #19	www.nysed.gov/dpls/opnme.html
Dietitian #19	www.nysed.gov/dpls/opnme.html
Engineer #19	www.nysed.gov/dpls/opnme.html
HMO #12	www.ins.state.ny.us/tocol4.htm
Insurance Company #12	www.ins.state.ny.us/tocol4.htm
Interior Designer #19	www.nysed.gov/dpls/opnme.html
Landscape Architect #19	www.nysed.gov/dpls/opnme.html
Lobbyist #16	www.nylobby.state.ny.us/lobbysearch.html
Massage Therapist #19	www.nysed.gov/dpls/opnme.html
Medical Doctor #19	www.nysed.gov/dpls/opnme.html
Midwife #19	www.nysed.gov/dpls/opnme.html
Nurse #19	www.nysed.gov/dpls/opnme.html
Nurse-LPN #19	www.nysed.gov/dpls/opnme.html
Nutritionist #19	www.nysed.gov/dpls/opnme.html
Occupational Therapist/Assistant #19	www.nysed.gov/dpls/opnme.html
Ophthalmic Dispenser #19	www.nysed.gov/dpls/opnme.html
Optometrist #19	www.nysed.gov/dpls/opnme.html
Pharmacist #19	www.nysed.gov/dpls/opnme.html
Physical Therapist/Assistant #19	www.nysed.gov/dpls/opnme.html
Physician #19	www.nysed.gov/dpls/opnme.html
Physician Assistant #19	www.nysed.gov/dpls/opnme.html
Podiatrist #19	www.nysed.gov/dpls/opnme.html
Psychologist #19	www.nysed.gov/dpls/opnme.html
Public Accountant-CPA #19	www.nysed.gov/dpls/opnme.html
Respiratory Therapist/Therapy Technician #19	www.nysed.gov/dpls/opnme.html
RPN #19	www.nysed.gov/dpls/opnme.html
Social Worker #19	www.nysed.gov/dpls/opnme.html
Specialist Assistant #19	www.nysed.gov/dpls/opnme.html
Speech Pathologist/Audiologist #19	www.nysed.gov/dpls/opnme.html
Surveyor #19	www.nysed.gov/dpls/opnme.html
Veterinarian #19	www.nysed.gov/dpls/opnme.html

Licensing Quick Finder

Acupuncturist/Assistant #19 518-474-3817	Dental Assistant #19 518-474-3817	Landscape Architect #19 518-474-3817
Apartment Information Vendor #10 518-474-4429	Dental Hygienist #19 518-474-3817	Lobbyist #16 518-474-7126
Apartment Manager/Vendor & Agent #10 518-474-4429	Dentist #19 518-474-3817	Massage Therapist #19 518-474-3817
	Dietitian #19 518-474-3817	Medical Doctor #19 518-474-3817
Apartment Sharing Agent #10 518-474-4429	Emergency Medical Technician-Paramedic #07 518-402-0985	Midwife #19 518-474-3817
Architect #19 518-474-3817		Mobil Laser Operator #09 518-457-2735
Armored Car/Car Carrier #10 518-474-4429	Engineer #19 518-474-3817	Nail Technology #10 518-474-4429
Asbestos Handler #09 518-457-2735	Esthetics Specialist #10 518-474-4429	Natural Hair Styling #10 518-474-4429
Athletic Trainer #19 518-474-3817	Fishing Guide #03 518-457-5740	Notary Public #10 518-474-4429
Attorney #18 212-428-2800	Franchise Sales #01 212-416-8222	Nurse #19 518-474-3817
Audiologist #19 518-474-3817	Funeral Director #06 518-402-0785	Nurse-LPN #19 518-474-3817
Bail Bond Agent #12 518-474-6630	Funeral Home #06 518-402-0785	Nurses Aide #05 518-474-3817
Barber #10 518-474-4429	Games of Chance Registration #10 518-474-4429	Nursing Home Administrator #05 518-474-3817
Blaster #09 518-457-2735	Guide #03 518-457-5740	Nutritionist #19 518-474-3817
Boiler Inspector #08 518-457-2722	Health Club #10 518-474-4429	Occupational Therapist/Assistant #19 518-474-3817
Casino Employee #15 ..... 518-453-8460 X2	Hearing Aid Dealer #10 518-474-4429	Off Track Betting #15 ..... 518-453-8460 X2
Charitable Gaming #15 ..... 518-453-8460 X2	Hiking Guide #03 518-457-5740	Ophthalmic Dispenser #19 518-474-3817
Chiropractor #19 518-474-3817	Hunting Guide #03 518-457-5740	Optometrist #19 518-474-3817
Collection Agency #11 702-687-4259	Insurance Agent/Consultant/Broker #12 518-474-6630	Pesticide Applicator #02 518-457-7482
Commercial Applicator #02 518-457-7482		Pesticide Distributor #02 518-457-7482
Cosmetologist #10 518-474-4429	Insurance Appraiser #12 518-474-6630	Pet Cemetery #10 518-474-4429
Court Reporter #19 518-474-3817	Interior Designer #19 518-474-3817	Pharmacist #19 518-474-3817
Crane Operator #09 518-457-2735	Investment Advisor #01 212-416-8222	Physical Therapist/Assistant #19 518-474-3817

Physician #19 518-474-3817
Physician Assistant #19.......................518-474-3817
Podiatrist #19...518-474-3817
Private Investigator #10.......................518-474-4429
Psychologist #19....................................518-474-3817
Public Accountant-CPA #19.................518-474-3817
Race Track #15..............................518-453-8460 X2
Racing #15......................................518-453-8460 X2
Radiologic Technologist #14.................518-402-7580
Radiotherapy Technologist #14............518-402-7580
Real Estate Salesperson/Broker/Appraiser #10
....518-474-4429
Respiratory Therapist/Therapy Technician #19
....518-474-3817

Restricted Pesticide Distributor #02 518-457-7482
RPN #19..518-474-3817
School Administrator/Supervisor #17 518-474-3901
School Counselor #17 518-474-3901
School Media Specialist #17 518-474-3901
Securities Broker/Dealer #01 212-416-8222
Securities Salesperson #01 212-416-8222
Security & Fire Alarm Installer #10........518-474-4429
Security Guard #10 518-474-4429
Short Hand Reporter #19.......................518-474-3817
Social Worker #19..................................518-474-3817
Specialist Assistant #19........................518-474-3817
Speech Pathologist/Audiologist #19......518-474-3817
Surveyor #19 518-474-3817

Teacher #17..518-474-3901
Theatrical Syndication #01 212-416-8222
Upholsters & Bedding Industry #10.......518-474-4429
Veterinarian #19....................................518-474-3817
Veterinary Technician #19.....................518-474-3901
Waste Water Treatment Plant Operator #04
....518-457-5968
Watch Dog/Patrol Agency #10...............518-474-4429
Watch Guard or Patrol Agency #10.......518-474-4429
Water Treatment Plant Operator #13 518-458-6755
White Water Rafting Guide #03 518-457-5740

Licensing Agency Information

01 Bureau of Investor Protection & Securities, 120 Broadway, 23rd Floor, New York, NY 10271; 212-416-8222, Fax: 212-416-8816.

www.oag.state.ny.us

02 Department of Environmental Conservation, Bureau of Pesticide & Radiation, 50 Wolf Rd #498, Albany, NY 12233-7254; 518-457-7482, Fax: 518-485-8366.

www.dec.state.ny.us/website/dcs/permits_level2.html

03 Department of Environmental Conservation, Division of Forest Protection & Fire Mgmt., 50 Wolf Rd Rm 440C, Albany, NY 12233-2560; 518-457-5740, Fax: 518-485-8458.

www.dec.state.ny.us/website/protection/rangers/frguid6.html

04 Department of Environmental Conservation, Division of Water, Bureau of Watershed Compliance, 50 Wolf Rd Rm 340, Albany, NY 12233-3506; 518-457-5968, Fax: 518-457-7038.

www.dec.state.ny.us

05 Board of Examiners of Nursing Home Administrators, Bureau of Proffessional Credentialling, 161 Delaware Av, Delmar, NY 10254; 518-478-1060.

06 Department of Health, Bureau of Funeral Directing, 433 River St #303, Troy, NY 12180-2299; 518-402-0785, Fax: 518-402-0784.

07 Department of Health, Emergency Medical Services, 433 River St, Troy, NY 12180; 518-402-0996, Fax: 518-402-0985.

www.health.state.ny.us

08 Department of Labor, Boiler Safety Bureau, Bldg 12, Rm 165, Albany, NY 12240-0102; 518-457-2722, Fax: 518-485-9077.

09 Department of Labor, License & Certificate Unit, State Campus, Bldg 12 Rm 133, Albany, NY 12240; 518-457-2735, Fax: 518-457-8452.

10 Department of State, Division of Licensing Services, 84 Holland Ave, Albany, NY 12208-3490; 518-474-4429, Fax: 518-473-6648.

www.dos.state.ny.us/lcns/licensing.html

12 Insurance Department, Licensing Bureau Agency, Empire State Plaza, Bldg 1, Albany, NY 12257; 518-474-6630.

www.ins.state.ny.us

13 Department of Health, Bureau of Public Water Supply Protection, 150 Broadway #8, Albany, NY 12204-2719; 518-458-6731, Fax: 518-458-6732.

14 Department of Health, Bureau of Environmental Radiation Protection, Flanigan Sq Room 530, 547 River St, Troy, NY 12180-2216; 518-402-7580, Fax: 518-402-7554.

15 Racing & Wagering Board, 1 Watervliet Av Extension #2, Albany, NY 12206; 518-453-8460 X2, Fax: 518-453-8492.

www.racing.state.ny.us

16 Temporary Commission on Lobbying, Agency Bldg #2, 17th Fl, Albany, NY 12223-1254; 518-474-7126, Fax: 518-473-6492.

www.nylobby.state.ny.us

Direct URL to search licenses: www.nylobby.state.ny.us/lobbysearch.html You can search online using lobbyist, client, business nature, city, income level, and expense level.

17 Office of Teaching, Education Bldg, Albany, NY 12234; 518-474-3901, Fax: 518-473-0271.

www.nysed.gov/tcert/homepage.htm

18 Unified Court System, Attorney Registration Unit, PO Box 2806 (PO Box 2806, Church Street Station), New York, NY 10008; 212-428-2800, Fax: 212-428-2804.

www.courts.state.ny.us

Direct URL to search licenses: www.courts.state.ny.us/webdb/wdbcgi.exe/apps/INTERNETDB.attyreghome.show You can search online using name.

19 Education Department, Office of the Professions, Cultural Education Ctr, Empire State Plaza, Albany, NY 12230; 518-474-3817 attendant available 9-11:45AM and 12:45-4:30PM ESTTDD 518-473-1426 wwwnysedgov/dpls/opnmehtml.
www.nysed.gov/prof

Direct URL to search licenses: www.nysed.gov/dpls/opnme.html You can search online using name and license number.

The following list indicates the district and division name for each county in the state. If the district or division name of the bankruptcy court is different from the civil/criminal court, it appears in parentheses.

County/Court Cross Reference

Albany	Northern	Albany
Allegany	Western	Buffalo
Bronx	Southern	New York City (New York)
Broome	Northern	Binghamton (Utica)
Cattaraugus	Western	Buffalo
Cayuga	Northern	Syracuse (Utica)
Chautauqua	Western	Buffalo
Chemung	Western	Rochester
Chenango	Northern	Binghamton (Utica)
Clinton	Northern	Albany
Columbia	Northern (Southern)	Albany (Poughkeepsie)
Cortland	Northern	Syracuse (Utica)
Delaware	Northern	Binghamton (Utica)
Dutchess	Southern	White Plains (Poughkeepsie)
Erie	Western	Buffalo
Essex	Northern	Albany
Franklin	Northern	Binghamton (Albany)
Fulton	Northern	Syracuse (Albany)
Genesee	Western	Buffalo
Greene	Northern (Southern)	Albany (Poughkeepsie)
Hamilton	Northern	Syracuse (Utica)
Herkimer	Northern	Syracuse (Utica)
Jefferson	Northern	Binghamton (Albany)
Kings	Eastern	Brooklyn
Lewis	Northern	Binghamton (Utica)
Livingston	Western	Rochester
Madison	Northern	Syracuse (Utica)
Monroe	Western	Rochester
Montgomery	Northern	Syracuse (Albany)
Nassau	Eastern	Brooklyn (Westbury)
New York	Southern	New York City (New York)
Niagara	Western	Buffalo
Oneida	Northern	Utica
Onondaga	Northern	Syracuse (Utica)
Ontario	Western	Rochester
Orange	Southern	White Plains (Poughkeepsie)
Orleans	Western	Buffalo
Oswego	Northern	Syracuse (Utica)
Otsego	Northern	Binghamton (Utica)
Putnam	Southern	White Plains (Poughkeepsie)
Queens	Eastern	Brooklyn
Rensselaer	Northern	Albany
Richmond	Eastern	Brooklyn
Rockland	Southern	White Plains
Saratoga	Northern	Albany
Schenectady	Northern	Albany
Schoharie	Northern	Albany
Schuyler	Western	Rochester
Seneca	Western	Rochester
St. Lawrence	Northern	Binghamton (Albany)
Steuben	Western	Rochester
Suffolk	Eastern	Hauppauge
Sullivan	Southern	White Plains (Poughkeepsie)
Tioga	Northern	Binghamton (Utica)
Tompkins	Northern	Syracuse (Utica)
Ulster	Northern (Southern)	Albany (Poughkeepsie)
Warren	Northern	Albany
Washington	Northern	Albany
Wayne	Western	Rochester
Westchester	Southern	White Plains
Wyoming	Western	Buffalo
Yates	Western	Rochester

US District Court

Eastern District of New York

Brooklyn Division Brooklyn Courthouse, 225 Cadman Plaza E, Room 130, Brooklyn, NY 11201, 718-260-2600.

www.nyed.uscourts.gov

Counties: Kings, Queens, Richmond. Cases from Nassau and Suffolk may also be heard here.

Indexing & Storage: Cases are indexed by defendant and plaintiff as well as by case number. New cases are available in the index 2 days after filing date. A computer index is maintained. Open records are located at this court.

Fee & Payment: The fee is $15.00 per item (one party name or case number). Payment may be made by money order, cashier check, personal check. Prepayment is required. Payee: Clerk, US District Court. Certification fee: $5.00 per document. Copy fee: $.50 per page. You are allowed to make your own copies. These copies cost $.25 per page.

Phone Search: Searching is not available by phone.

Mail Search: A stamped self addressed envelope is not required.

In Person Search: In person searching is available.

PACER: Sign-up number is 800-676-6856. Access fee is $.60 per minute. Toll-free access: 888-331-4965. Local access: 718-246-2494. Case records are available back to January 1, 1990. Records are never purged. New records are available online after 1 day. PACER is available on the Internet at http://pacer.nyed.uscourts.gov.

Electronic Filing: Only law firms and practitioners may file cases electronically. Anyone can search online; however only cases filed electronically are included in the search. To search, visit http://ecf.nyed.uscourts.gov/cgi-bin/PublicCaseFiled-Rpt.pl. Electronic filing information is available online at http://ecf.nyed.uscourts.gov

Hauppauge Division 300 Rabro Dr, Hauppauge, NY 11788, 516-582-1100, Fax: 516-582-1417.

www.nyed.uscourts.gov

Counties: Suffolk.

Indexing & Storage: Cases are indexed by defendant and plaintiff as well as by case number. New cases are available in the index 2 days after filing date. Both computer and card indexes are maintained. Indexes and files are available here from 1987 on. Open records are located at this court.

Fee & Payment: The fee is $15.00 per item (one party name or case number). Payment may be made by money order, cashier check, personal check. Prepayment is required. Payee: Clerk, US District Court. Certification fee: $5.00 per document. Copy fee: $.50 per page. You are allowed to make your own copies. These copies cost $.25 per page.

Phone Search: Some limited docket information is available by phone. An automated voice case information service (VCIS) is not available.

Fax Search: Fax requests may only be made for a few names at most. Regular fees apply to fax requests.

Mail Search: Always enclose a stamped self addressed envelope.

In Person Search: In person searching is available.

PACER: Sign-up number is 800-676-6856. Access fee is $.60 per minute. Toll-free access: 888-331-4965. Local access: 718-246-2494. Case records are available back to January 1, 1990. Records are never purged. New records are available online after 1 day. PACER is available on the Internet at http://pacer.nyed.uscourts.gov.

Electronic Filing: Only law firms and practitioners may file cases electronically. Anyone can search online; however only cases filed electronically are included in the search. To search, visit http://ecf.nyed.uscourts.gov/cgi-bin/PublicCaseFiled-Rpt.pl. Electronic filing information is available online at http://ecf.nyed.uscourts.gov

US Bankruptcy Court

Eastern District of New York

Brooklyn Division 75 Clinton St, Brooklyn, NY 11201, 718-330-2188.

Counties: Kings, Queens, Richmond. Kings and Queens County Chapter 11 cases may also be assigned to Westbury. Other Queens County cases may be assigned to Westbury Division. Nassau County Chapter 11 cases may be assigned here.

Indexing & Storage: Cases are indexed by debtor as well as by case number. New cases are available in the index 1 day after filing date. Older cases are indexed on microfiche. A computer index is maintained. Open records are located at this court.

Fee & Payment: The fee is $15.00 per item (one party name or case number). Payment may be made by money order, cashier check, business check. Personal checks are not accepted. Prepayment is required. Payee: Clerk, US Bankruptcy Court. Certification fee: $5.00 per document. Copy fee: $.50 per page. You are allowed to make your own copies. These copies cost $.10 per page.

Phone Search: Only docket information is available by phone. An automated voice case information service (VCIS) is available. Call VCIS at 800-252-2537 or 718-852-5726.

Mail Search: A stamped self addressed envelope is not required.

In Person Search: In person searching is available.

PACER: Sign-up number is 800-676-6856. Access fee is $.60 per minute. Toll-free access: 800-263-7790. Local access: 718-488-7012. Case records are available back to 1991. Records are purged every year. New civil records are available online after 3 days. PACER is available on the Internet at http://pacer.nyeb.uscourts.gov.

Hauppauge Division 601 Veterans Memorial Hwy, Hauppauge, NY 11788, 631-361-8038.

Counties: Suffolk. Suffolk County Chapter 11 cases may also be assigned to Westbury Division. Nassau County Chapter 11 cases may be assigned here. Other cases for western Suffolk County may also be assigned to Westbury Division.

Indexing & Storage: Cases are indexed by debtor as well as by case number. New cases are available in the index 1-2 days after filing date. A computer index is maintained. Open records are located at this court.

Fee & Payment: The fee is $15.00 per item (one party name or case number). Payment may be made by money order, cashier check, personal check. Prepayment is required. Debtor's checks are not accepted. Enclose a FedEx package for expedited service. Payee: Clerk, US Bankruptcy Court. Certification fee: $5.00 per document. Copy fee: $.50 per page. You are allowed to make your own copies. These copies cost $.10 per page.

Phone Search: Basic docket information only available by phone. An automated voice case information service (VCIS) is available. Call VCIS at 800-252-2537 or 718-852-5726.

Mail Search: A stamped self addressed envelope is not required.

In Person Search: In person searching is available.

PACER: Sign-up number is 800-676-6856. Access fee is $.60 per minute. Toll-free access: 800-263-7790. Local access: 718-488-7012. Case records are available back to 1991. Records are purged every year. New civil records are available online after 3 days. PACER is available on the Internet at http://pacer.nyeb.uscourts.gov.

Westbury Division 1635 Privado Rd, Westbury, NY 11590, 516-832-8801.

Counties: Nassau. Chapter 11 cases for Nassau County may also be assigned to the Brooklyn or Hauppauge Divisions. Kings and Suffolk County Chapter 11 cases may be assigned here. Any Queens County cases may be assigned here. Non-Chapter 11 cases from westernSuffolk County may also be assigned here.

Indexing & Storage: Cases are indexed by debtor as well as by case number. New cases are available in the index 48 hours after filing date. Both computer and card indexes are maintained. Open records are located at this court.

Fee & Payment: The fee is $15.00 per item (one party name or case number). Payment may be made by money order, cashier check, personal check. Prepayment is required. Payee: Clerk, US Bankruptcy Court. Certification fee: $5.00 per document. Copy fee: $.50 per page. You are allowed to make your own copies. These copies cost $.10 per page.

Phone Search: Docket information is available by phone. An automated voice case information service (VCIS) is available. Call VCIS at 800-252-2537 or 718-852-5726.

Mail Search: Always enclose a stamped self addressed envelope.

In Person Search: In person searching is available.

PACER: Sign-up number is 800-676-6856. Access fee is $.60 per minute. Toll-free access: 800-263-7790. Local access: 718-488-7012. Case records are available back to 1991. Records are purged every year. New civil records are available online after 3 days. PACER is available on the Internet at http://pacer.nyeb.uscourts.gov.

US District Court

Northern District of New York

Albany Division 345 Broadway, Room 222, James T Foley Courthouse, Albany, NY 12207-2924, 518-257-1800.

www.nynd.uscourts.gov

Counties: Albany, Clinton, Columbia, Essex, Greene, Rensselaer, Saratoga, Schenectady, Schoharie, Ulster, Warren, Washington.

Indexing & Storage: Cases are indexed by defendant and plaintiff as well as by case number. New cases are available in the index 1 day after filing date. Case indexes are available on computer terminal in any of the divisions in the Northern District. Both computer and card indexes are maintained. Open records are located at this court.

Fee & Payment: The fee is $15.00 per item (one party name or case number). Payment may be made by money order, cashier check, personal check. Prepayment is required. Payee: Clerk, US District Court. Certification fee: $5.00 per document. Copy fee: $.50 per page.

Phone Search: Searching is not available by phone.

Mail Search: A stamped self addressed envelope is not required.

In Person Search: In person searching is available.

PACER: Sign-up number is 800-676-6856. Access fee is $.60 per minute. Toll-free access: 800-480-7525. Local access: 315-448-0537. Case records are available back to June 1991. New records are available online after 2 days.

Binghamton Division 15 Henry St, Binghamton, NY 13901, 607-773-2893.

www.nynd.uscourts.gov

Counties: Broome, Chenango, Delaware, Franklin, Jefferson, Lewis, Otsego, St. Lawrence, Tioga.

Indexing & Storage: Cases are indexed by defendant and plaintiff as well as by case number. New cases are available in the index 1 day after filing date. A computer index is maintained. Open records are located at this court.

Fee & Payment: The fee is $15.00 per item (one party name or case number). Payment may be made by money order, cashier check, personal check. Prepayment is required. Payee: Clerk, US District Court. Certification fee: $5.00 per document. Copy fee: $.50 per page.

Phone Search: Only docket information is available by phone.

Mail Search: Always enclose a stamped self addressed envelope.

In Person Search: In person searching is available.

PACER: Sign-up number is 800-676-6856. Access fee is $.60 per minute. Toll-free access: 800-480-7525. Local access: 315-448-0537. Case records are available back to June 1991. New records are available online after 2 days.

Syracuse Division PO Box 7367, Syracuse, NY 13261-7367 (Courier Address: 100 S Clinton St, #7367, Syracuse, NY 13261), 315-234-8500.

www.nynd.uscourts.gov

Counties: Cayuga, Cortland, Fulton, Hamilton, Herkimer, Madison, Montgomery, Onondaga, Oswego, Tompkins.

Indexing & Storage: Cases are indexed by defendant and plaintiff as well as by case number. New cases are available in the index 1 day after filing date. A computer index is maintained. Open records are located at this court.

Fee & Payment: The fee is $15.00 per item (one party name or case number). Payment may be made by money order, cashier check, personal check. Prepayment is required. Credit cards accepted in person only. Payee: Clerk, US District Court. Certification fee: $5.00 per document. Copy fee: $.50 per page.

Phone Search: Only docket information is available by phone.

Mail Search: Always enclose a stamped self addressed envelope.

In Person Search: In person searching is available.

PACER: Sign-up number is 800-676-6856. Access fee is \$.60 per minute. Toll-free access: 800-480-7525. Local access: 315-448-0537. Case records are available back to June 1991. New records are available online after 2 days.

Utica Division Alexander Pirnie Bldg, 10 Broad St, Utica, NY 13501, 315-793-8151.

www.nynd.uscourts.gov

Counties: Oneida.

Indexing & Storage: Cases are indexed by defendant and plaintiff as well as by case number. New cases are available in the index 1 day after filing date. Indexes are on computer starting in 1991 and on cards prior to that. Open records are located at this court. Closed case records from the other three Northern district courts were assembled here before going to the New York Federal Records Center. Starting in 1995, Albany and Binghamton and Syracuse are no longer sending their records to Utica.

Fee & Payment: The fee is \$15.00 per item (one party name or case number). Payment may be made by money order, cashier check, business check. Personal checks are not accepted. Prepayment is required. Payee: Clerk, US District Court. Certification fee: \$5.00 per document. Copy fee: \$.50 per page.

Phone Search: Information from the computer for 1991 forward is available by phone. An automated voice case information service (VCIS) is not available.

Mail Search: A stamped self addressed envelope is not required.

In Person Search: In person searching is available.

PACER: Sign-up number is 800-676-6856. Access fee is \$.60 per minute. Toll-free access: 800-480-7525. Local access: 315-448-0537. Case records are available back to June 1991. New records are available online after 2 days.

US Bankruptcy Court

Northern District of New York

Albany Division James T Foley Courthouse, 445 Broadway #330, Albany, NY 12207, 518-257-1661.

www.nynb.uscourts.gov

Counties: Albany, Clinton, Essex, Franklin, Fulton, Jefferson, Montgomery, Rensselaer, Saratoga, Schenectady, Schoharie, St. Lawrence, Warren, Washington.

Indexing & Storage: Cases are indexed by debtor as well as by case number. New cases are available in the index 48 hours after filing date. Both computer and card indexes are maintained. Open records are located at this court. As of January 1, 1995, Jefferson and St. Lawrence Counties moved to Albany Division from Utica, while Broome, Chenango, Delaware, Otsego, Tioga and Tompkins Counties moved to Utica Division from Albany.

Fee & Payment: The fee is \$15.00 per item (one party name or case number). Payment may be made by money order, cashier check. Business checks are not accepted, Visa or Mastercard. Personal checks are not accepted. Prepayment is required. Credit cards are only accepted from in-person searchers. Payee:

Clerk, US Bankruptcy Court. Certification fee: \$5.00 per document. Copy fee: \$.25 per page.

Phone Search: Only docket information is available by phone. An automated voice case information service (VCIS) is available. Call VCIS at 800-206-1952 or.

Mail Search: If a case number is not known, the turnaround time may be as long as 5 days after the request is received. Always enclose a stamped self addressed envelope.

In Person Search: In person searching is available.

PACER: Sign-up number is 800-676-6856. Access fee is \$.60 per minute. Toll-free access: 800-390-8432. Local access: 518-431-0175. Case records are available back to 1992. New civil records are available online after 48 hours.

Other Online Access: A system called CHASER is available on the Internet at http://pacer.nynb.uscourts.gov/bc/chs.html.

Utica Division Room 230, 10 Broad St, Utica, NY 13501, 315-793-8101, Fax: 315-793-8128.

www.nynb.uscourts.gov

Counties: Broome, Cayuga, Chenango, Cortland, Delaware, Hamilton, Herkimer, Lewis, Madison, Oneida, Onondaga, Otsego, Oswego, Tioga, Tompkins.

Indexing & Storage: Cases are indexed by debtor as well as by case number. New cases are available in the index 24 hours after filing date. Both computer and card indexes are maintained. Open records are located at this court. As of January 1, 1995, Jefferson and St. Lawrence Counties moved to Albany Division from Utica, while Broome, Chenango, Delaware, Otsego, Tioga and Tompkins Counties moved to Utica Division from Albany.

Fee & Payment: The fee is \$15.00 per item (one party name or case number). Payment may be made by money order, cashier check, personal check. Debtor's checks are not accepted. Payee: Clerk, US Bankruptcy Court. Certification fee: \$5.00 per document. Copy fee: \$.50 per page.

Phone Search: Only docket information is available by phone. An automated voice case information service (VCIS) is available. Call VCIS at 800-206-1952 or.

Mail Search: A stamped self addressed envelope is not required.

In Person Search: In person searching is available.

PACER: Sign-up number is 800-676-6856. Access fee is \$.60 per minute. Toll-free access: 800-390-8432. Local access: 518-431-0175. Case records are available back to 1992. New civil records are available online after 48 hours.

Other Online Access: A system called CHASER is available on the Internet at http://pacer.nynb.uscourts.gov/bc/chs.html.

US District Court

Southern District of New York

New York City Division 500 Pearl St, New York, NY 10007, 212-805-0136.

www.nysd.uscourts.gov

Counties: Bronx, New York. Some cases from the counties in the White Plains Division are also assigned to the New York Division.

Indexing & Storage: Cases are indexed by defendant and plaintiff as well as by case number. New cases are available in the index 2 days after filing date. A computer index is maintained. Open records are located at this court.

Fee & Payment: The fee is \$15.00 per item (one party name or case number). Payment may be made by money order, cashier check. Business checks are not accepted. Personal checks are not accepted. Prepayment is required. Payee: Clerk of Court, S.D.N.Y. Certification fee: \$5.00 per document. Copy fee: \$.50 per page. You are allowed to make your own copies. These copies cost Not Applicable per page.

Phone Search: Only docket information is available by phone.

Mail Search: Always enclose a stamped self addressed envelope.

In Person Search: In person searching is available.

PACER: Sign-up number is 800-676-6856. Access fee is \$.60 per minute. Case records are available back to early 1990. Records are purged every six months. New records are available online after 1 day.

Opinions Online: Selected rulings are searchable online using CourtWeb. To download and view copies of rulings you must have Adobe Acrobat Reader. Court opinions are available online at www.nysd.uscourts.gov/courtweb

White Plains Division 300 Quarropas St, White Plains, NY 10601, 914-390-4000.

www.nysd.uscourts.gov

Counties: Dutchess, Orange, Putnam, Rockland, Sullivan, Westchester. Some cases may be assigned to New York Division.

Indexing & Storage: Cases are indexed by defendant and plaintiff as well as by case number. New cases are available in the index 2 days after filing date. A computer index is maintained. Indexes have been automated since 1983. Open records are located at this court.

Fee & Payment: The fee is \$15.00 per item (one party name or case number). Payment may be made by money order, cashier check. Business checks are not accepted. Personal checks are not accepted. Prepayment is required. Attorney checks are accepted. Payee: Clerk of Court, S.D.N.Y. Certification fee: \$5.00 per document. Copy fee: \$.50 per page. You are allowed to make your own copies. These copies cost \$.15 per page.

Phone Search: Searching is not available by phone.

Mail Search: Always enclose a stamped self addressed envelope.

In Person Search: In person searching is available.

PACER: Sign-up number is 800-676-6856. Access fee is \$.60 per minute. Case records are available back to early 1990. Records are purged every six months. New records are available online after 1 day.

Opinions Online: Selected rulings are searchable online using CourtWeb. To download and view copies of rulings you must have Adobe Acrobat Reader. Court opinions are available online at www.nysd.uscourts.gov/courtweb

US Bankruptcy Court

Southern District of New York

New York Division Room 534, 1 Bowling Green, New York, NY 10004-1408, 212-668-2870.

www.nysb.uscourts.gov

Counties: Bronx, New York.

Indexing & Storage: Cases are indexed by debtor as well as by case number. New cases are available in the index 1-3 days after filing date. Both computer and card indexes are maintained. Open records are located at this court.

Fee & Payment: The fee is $15.00 per item (one party name or case number). Payment may be made by money order, cashier check, business check. Personal checks are not accepted. Prepayment is required. Payee: Clerk, US Bankruptcy Court. Certification fee: $5.00 per document. Copy fee: $.50 per page. You are allowed to make your own copies. These copies cost $.25 per page.

Phone Search: Over the phone, this court will only provide whether a case is pending. A copy service is available at 212-480-0737 if you have the case number. An automated voice case information service (VCIS) is available.

Mail Search: A stamped self addressed envelope is not required.

In Person Search: In person searching is available.

PACER: Sign-up number is 800-676-6856. Access fee is $.60 per minute. Case records are available back to June 1991. Records are purged every six months. New civil records are available online after 2 days. PACER is available on the Internet at http://pacer.nysb.uscourts.gov.

Electronic Filing: Only law firms and practitioners may file cases electronically. Anyone can search online; however only cases filed electronically are included in the search. To search, visit http://ecf.nysb.uscourts.gov/cgi-bin/PublicCaseFiled-Rpt.pl. Electronic filing information is available online at http://ecf.nysb.uscourts.gov

Poughkeepsie Division 176 Church St, Poughkeepsie, NY 12601, 914-452-4200, Fax: 914-452-8375.

www.nysb.uscourts.gov

Counties: Columbia, Dutchess, Greene, Orange, Putnam, Sullivan, Ulster.

Indexing & Storage: Cases are indexed by debtor as well as by case number. New cases are available in the index 1-3 days after filing date. Both computer and card indexes are maintained. Open records are located at this court.

Fee & Payment: The fee is $15.00 per item (one party name or case number). Payment may be made by money order, cashier check, business check. Personal checks are not accepted. Prepayment is required. Payee: Clerk, US Bankruptcy Court. Certification fee: $5.00 per document. Copy fee: $.50 per page. You are allowed to make your own copies. These copies cost $.15 per page.

Phone Search: Over the phone, this court will only reveal whether the case is pending. An automated voice case information service (VCIS) is available.

Mail Search: A stamped self addressed envelope is not required.

In Person Search: In person searching is available.

PACER: Sign-up number is 800-676-6856. Access fee is $.60 per minute. Case records are available back to June 1991. Records are purged every six months. New civil records are available online after 2 days. PACER is available on the Internet at http://pacer.nysb.uscourts.gov.

Electronic Filing: Only law firms and practitioners may file cases electronically. Anyone can search online; however only cases filed electronically are included in the search. To search, visit http://ecf.nysb.uscourts.gov/cgi-bin/PublicCaseFiled-Rpt.pl. Electronic filing information is available online at http://ecf.nysb.uscourts.gov

White Plains Division 300 Quarropas St, White Plains, NY 10601, 914-390-4060.

www.nysb.uscourts.gov

Counties: Rockland, Westchester.

Indexing & Storage: Cases are indexed by debtor as well as by case number. New cases are available in the index 1-3 days after filing date. Both computer and card indexes are maintained. Records are also indexed on microfiche. Open records are located at this court. District wide searches are available for cases from 1991 from this court.

Fee & Payment: The fee is $15.00 per item (one party name or case number). Payment may be made by money order, business check. Personal checks are not accepted. Prepayment is required. Checks and credit cards are not accepted from debtors. Payee: Clerk, US Bankruptcy Court. Certification fee: $5.00 per document. Copy fee: $.50 per page. You are allowed to make your own copies. These copies cost $.15 per page. Visa and MasterCard are only accepted for in person searches.

Phone Search: Over the phone, this court will only reveal whether the case is pending. An automated voice case information service (VCIS) is available.

Mail Search: Always enclose a stamped self addressed envelope.

In Person Search: In person searching is available.

PACER: Sign-up number is 800-676-6856. Access fee is $.60 per minute. Case records are available back to June 1991. Records are purged every six months. New civil records are available online after 2 days. PACER is available on the Internet at http://pacer.nysb.uscourts.gov.

Electronic Filing: Only law firms and practitioners may file cases electronically. Anyone can search online; however only cases filed electronically are included in the search. To search, visit http://ecf.nysb.uscourts.gov/cgi-bin/PublicCaseFiled-Rpt.pl. Electronic filing information is available online at http://ecf.nysb.uscourts.gov

US District Court

Western District of New York

Buffalo Division Room 304, 68 Court St, Buffalo, NY 14202, 716-551-4211, Fax: 716-551-4850.

www.nywd.uscourts.gov

Counties: Allegany, Cattaraugus, Chautauqua, Erie, Genesee, Niagara, Orleans, Wyoming. Prior to 1982, this division included what is now the Rochester Division.

Indexing & Storage: Cases are indexed by defendant and plaintiff as well as by case number. New cases are available in the index 2 days after filing date. A computer index is maintained. Open records are located at this court.

Fee & Payment: The fee is $15.00 per item (one party name or case number). Payment may be made by money order, cashier check, personal check. Prepayment is required. Payee: Clerk, US District Court. Certification fee: $5.00 per document. Copy fee: $.50 per page.

Phone Search: Searching is not available by phone.

Mail Search: A stamped self addressed envelope is not required.

In Person Search: In person searching is available.

PACER: Sign-up number is 800-676-6856. Access fee is $.60 per minute. Toll-free access: 877-233-5848. Local access: 716-551-3333. Case records are available back to 1992. Records are never purged. New civil records are available online after 1 day. New criminal records are available online after 2 days. PACER is available on the Internet at http://pacer.nywd.uscourts.gov.

Rochester Division Room 2120, 100 State St, Rochester, NY 14614, 716-263-6263, Fax: 716-263-3178.

www.nywd.uscourts.gov

Counties: Chemung, Livingston, Monroe, Ontario, Schuyler, Seneca, Steuben, Wayne, Yates.

Indexing & Storage: Cases are indexed by defendant and plaintiff as well as by case number. New cases are available in the index 1 day after filing date. A computer index is maintained. Open records are located at this court. This division was established in 1981. Cases closed from 1996 to present are also held here. Earlier case records and indexes are held in the Buffalo Division (Erie County).

Fee & Payment: The fee is $15.00 per item (one party name or case number). Payment may be made by money order, cashier check, personal check. Prepayment is required. Payee: Clerk, US District Court. Certification fee: $5.00 per document. Copy fee: $.50 per page.

Phone Search: Simple docket information available by phone. An automated voice case information service (VCIS) is not available.

Fax Search: Fees for fax requests depend on the nature of the search. Call for more information. Will fax results. Call for instructions.

Mail Search: Mail searches including years prior to 1982 will be forwarded to the Buffalo Division. A stamped self addressed envelope is not required.

In Person Search: In person searching is available.

PACER: Sign-up number is 800-676-6856. Access fee is $.60 per minute. Toll-free access: 877-233-5848. Local access: 716-551-3333. Case records are available back to 1992. Records are never purged. New civil records are available online after 1 day. New criminal records are available online after 2 days. PACER is available on the Internet at http://pacer.nywd.uscourts.gov.

US Bankruptcy Court

Western District of New York

Buffalo Division Olympic Towers, 300 Pearl St #250, Buffalo, NY 14202-2501, 716-551-4130.

www.nywb.uscourts.gov

Counties: Allegany, Cattaraugus, Chautauqua, Erie, Genesee, Niagara, Orleans, Wyoming.

Indexing & Storage: Cases are indexed by debtor as well as by case number. New cases are available in the index 24 hours after filing date. Both computer and card indexes are maintained. Open records are located at this court.

Fee & Payment: The fee is $15.00 per item (one party name or case number). Payment may be made by money order, cashier check, business check. Personal checks are not accepted. Prepayment is required. Payee: Clerk, US Bankruptcy Court. Certification fee: $5.00 per document. Copy fee: $.50 per page.

Phone Search: Only docket information is available by phone. An automated voice case information service (VCIS) is available. Call VCIS at 800-776-9578 or 716-551-5311.

Mail Search: Always enclose a stamped self addressed envelope.

In Person Search: In person searching is available.

PACER: Sign-up number is 800-676-6856. Access fee is $.60 per minute. Toll-free access: 800-450-8052. Local access: 716-551-3152, 716-551-3153, 716-551-3154, 716-551-3155. Case records are available back to August 1987. Records are never purged. New civil records are available online after 1 day. PACER is available on the Internet at http://pacer.nywb.uscourts.gov.

Rochester Division Room 1220, 100 State St, Rochester, NY 14614, 716-263-3148.

www.nywb.uscourts.gov

Counties: Chemung, Livingston, Monroe, Ontario, Schuyler, Seneca, Steuben, Wayne, Yates.

Indexing & Storage: Cases are indexed by debtor as well as by case number. New cases are available in the index 24 hours after filing date. A computer index is maintained. Records are also indexed on microfiche. Open records are located at this court. District wide searches are available for information from August 1, 1987 from this division.

Fee & Payment: The fee is $15.00 per item (one party name or case number). Payment may be made by money order, cashier check, business check. Personal checks are not accepted. Prepayment is required. The SASE should be large enough to hold all copies and have sufficient postage to send them. Payee: Clerk, US Bankruptcy Court. Certification fee: $5.00 per document. Copy fee: $.50 per page.

Phone Search: Only docket information is available by phone. An automated voice case information service (VCIS) is available. Call VCIS at 800-776-9578 or 716-551-5311.

Mail Search: Always enclose a stamped self addressed envelope.

In Person Search: In person searching is available.

PACER: Sign-up number is 800-676-6856. Access fee is $.60 per minute. Toll-free access: 800-450-8052. Local access: 716-551-3152, 716-551-3153, 716-551-3154, 716-551-3155. Case records are available back to August 1987. Records are never purged. New civil records are available online after 1 day. PACER is available on the Internet at http://pacer.nywb.uscourts.gov.

Court	Jurisdiction	No. of Courts	How Organized
Supreme Courts*	General	11	12 Districts
County Courts*	General	2	57 Counties
Combined Courts*	General	57	
City Courts*	Limited	61	61 Cities
District Courts*	Limited	10	Nassau, Suffolk
Civil /Criminal Courts of the City of New York*	Municipal	6	
Town and Village Justice Courts	Municipal	1269	
Surrogates' Courts*	Probate	62	62 Counties and Boroughs
Court of Claims	Limited	1	
Family Courts	Special	62	62 Counties and Boroughs

* Profiled in this Sourcebook.

Court	CIVIL								
	Tort	Contract	Real Estate	Min. Claim	Max. Claim	Small Claims	Estate	Eviction	Domestic Relations
Supreme Courts*	X	X	X	$25,000	No Max				X
County Courts*	X	X	X	$0	$25,000				
City Courts*	X	X	X	$0	$15,000	$3000		X	
District Courts*	X	X	X	$0	$15,000	$3000		X	
Civil /Criminal Courts of the City of New York*	X	X	X	$0	$25,000	$3000		X	
Town and Village Justice Courts	X	X	X	$0	$3000	$3000			
Surrogates' Courts*							X		X
Court of Claims	X	X	X	$0	No Max				
Family Courts									X

Court	CRIMINAL				
	Felony	Misdemeanor	DWI/DUI	Preliminary Hearing	Juvenile
Supreme Courts*	X				
County Courts*				X	
City Courts*	X	X	X	X	
District Courts*		X	X	X	
Civil /Criminal Courts of the City of New York*		X	X	X	
Town and Village Justice Courts		X	X	X	
Surrogates' Courts*					
Court of Claims					
Family Courts					X

ADMINISTRATION   Office of Administration, Empire State Plaza, Agency Plaza #4, Suite 2001, Albany, NY, 12223; 518-473-1196, Fax: 518-473-6860. www.courts.state.ny.us

COURT STRUCTURE   New York State has two sites for Administration; in addition to the Albany address above, there is a New York City office at this address: Office of Administration, 25 Beaver St, New York NY 10004, and telephone: 212-428-2100.

"Supreme Courts" are the highest trial courts in the state, equivalent to Circuit or District Courts in other states; they are not appeals courts. Many New York City courts are indexed by plaintiff only. After 1992 the small claims limit was raised from $2,000 to $3,000.

Records for Supreme and County Courts are maintained by County Clerks. In most counties, the address for the clerk is the same as for the court. Exceptions are noted in the court profiles.

CRIMINAL COURTS

The New York State Office of Court Administration (address below) will perform an electronic search for criminal history information from a database of criminal case records from the boroughs and counties of Bronx, Dutchess, Erie, Kings, Nassau, New York, Orange, Putnam, Queens, Richmond, Rockland, Suffolk and Westchester. The request must include complete name and date of birth, and, for mail requests, be accompanied by two (2) self addressed stamped return envelopes. The fee, payable by check, is $16.00 per name per county.

Mail and in person requests go to

Office of Court Administration
Criminal History Search
25 Beaver St, 8th Floor
New York, NY 10004

You may obtain copies of any case dispositions found from the applicable county court.

ONLINE ACCESS

Civil case information from the 13 largest counties is available through DataCase, a database index of civil case information publicly available at terminals located at Supreme and County courts. In addition to the civil case index, DataCase also includes judgment docket and lien information, New York County Clerk system data, and the New York State attorney registration file. Remote access is also available at a fee of $1.00 per minute. Call 800-494-8981 for more remote access information.

ADDITIONAL INFORMATION

Supreme and County Court records are generally maintained in the County Clerk's Office, which outside of New York City may index civil cases by defendant, whereas the court itself maintains only a plaintiff index.

Fees for Supreme and County Courts are generally as follows: $5.00 per 2 year search per name for a manual search, and $16.00 per name for a computer or OCA search; $.50 per page (minimum $1.00) for copies; and $4.00 for certification. City Courts charge $5.00 for certification. Effective 4-95, no New York court will accept credit cards for any transaction.

Albany County

Supreme & County Court Courthouse Rm 128, 16 Eagle St, Albany, NY 12207; 518-487-5118; Fax: 518-487-5099. Hours: 9AM-5PM (EST). *Felony, Civil.*

www.albanycounty.com/clerk

Civil Records: Access: Mail, in person. Both court and visitors may perform in person searches. Search fee: $5.00 per name. Fee is for each two years requested. Required to search: name, years to search. Civil cases indexed by defendant, plaintiff. Civil records on computer from 1981, prior in books. **Criminal Records:** Access: Mail, in person. Both court and visitors may perform in person searches. Search fee: $5.00 per name. Fee is per two years requested. Required to search: name, years to search, DOB. Criminal records on computer from 1981, prior in books. Search requests must be in writing. **General Information:** No sealed, expunged, adoption, sex offense, juvenile, mental health or divorce records released. SASE appreciated. Turnaround time 1-3 days. Copy fee: $.50 per page. Certification fee: $1.00. Minimum $4.00. Fee payee: County Clerk. Personal checks accepted. Prepayment is required.

Albany City Court - Civil Part City Hall Rm 209, Albany, NY 12207; 518-434-5115; Fax: 518-434-5034. Hours: 8:30AM-5PM (EST). *Civil Actions Under $15,000, Eviction, Small Claims.*

Civil Records: Access: Mail, in person. Only the court conducts in person searches; visitors may not. No search fee. Required to search: name, years to search. Civil cases indexed by plaintiff. Civil records on computer from 1993, prior in books. **General Information:** No code enforcement records released. SASE required. Turnaround time varies. Copy fee: $1.00 for first page, $.50 each addl. Certification fee: $5.00. Fee payee: Albany City Court. Business checks accepted.

Albany City Court - Misdemeanors Morton & Broad St, Albany, NY 12202; 518-462-6714; Fax: 518-447-8778. Hours: 8AM-4PM (EST). *Misdemeanor.* **Criminal Records:** Access: Phone, mail, in person. Only the court conducts in person searches; visitors may not. Search fee: $5.00 per name. Required to search: name, years to search, DOB, SSN, signed release. Criminal records on computer since mid-'93, on index cards prior. **General Information:** No sealed, expunged, adoption, sex offense, juvenile, or mental health records released without a signed release from the party. SASE required. Turnaround time 5 Days. Copy fee: $.50 per page. Certification fee: $4.00. Fee payee: Albany City Court Criminal Part. Business checks accepted. Prepayment is required.

Cohoes City Court 97 Mohawk St, PO Box 678, Cohoes, NY 12047-0678;; Civil phone:518-233-2133; Criminal phone:518-233-2133. Hours: 8AM-4PM (EST). *Misdemeanor, Civil Actions Under $15,000, Eviction, Small Claims.*

Civil Records: Access: Mail, in person. Only the court conducts in person searches; visitors may not. Search fee: $16.00 per name. Required to search: name, years to search. Civil cases indexed by defendant, plaintiff. Civil records on computer from 1/95, prior in books, on cards. **Criminal Records:** Access: Mail, in person. Only the court conducts in person searches; visitors may not. Search fee: $16.00 per name. Required to search: name, years to search, DOB; also helpful-SSN. Criminal records on computer from 1/95, prior in books, on cards. **General Information:** No sealed or expunged records released. SASE required. Turnaround time 2 weeks. Copy fee: $.25 per page. Certification fee: $5.00. Fee payee: City Court. Only cashiers checks and money orders accepted. Prepayment is required.

Watervliet City Court 15th & Broadway, Watervliet, NY 12189; 518-270-3803; Fax: 518-270-3812. Hours: 8AM-3PM (EST). *Misdemeanor, Civil Actions Under $15,000, Eviction, Small Claims.*

Civil Records: Access: Mail, in person. Only the court conducts in person searches; visitors may not. Search fee: $5.00 per name. Required to search: name, years to search. Civil cases indexed by plaintiff. Civil records on computer from 1991, prior on index cards. **Criminal Records:** Access: Mail, in person. Only the court conducts in person searches; visitors may not. Search fee: $5.00 per name. Required to search: name, years to search. Criminal records on computer from 1991, prior on index cards. **General Information:** SASE required. Turnaround time 1-2 weeks. Copy fee: $5.00 per page. Certification fee: $5.00. Fee payee: City Court. Business checks accepted. Prepayment is required.

Surrogate Court Courthouse, 16 Eagle St, Albany, NY 12207; 518-487-5393. Hours: 9AM-5PM (EST). *Probate.*

Note: Search fee is $25.00 for up to 25 year search, $70 over

Allegany County

Supreme & County Court 7 Court Street, Belmont, NY 14813; 716-268-5813; Fax: 716-268-7090. Hours: 9AM-5PM (EST). *Felony, Civil.*

Civil Records: Access: Phone, mail, in person. Only the court conducts in person searches; visitors may not. No search fee. Required to search: name, years to search. Civil cases indexed by defendant. Civil records with the County Court books, all in books, no computer. **Criminal Records:** Access: Fax, mail, in person. Only the court conducts in person searches; visitors may not. No search fee. Required to search: name, years to search, DOB. Criminal records with the Supreme Court, no computer, all in books. **General Information:** No youth offender or sealed records released. SASE required. Turnaround time 7-10 days. Copy fee: $1.00 per page. Fee payee: Joseph Presutti, County Clerk. Personal checks accepted. Prepayment is required. Fax notes: No fee to fax results. Will fax to toll free numbers only.

Surrogate Court Courthouse, 7 Court St, Belmont, NY 14813; 716-268-5815; Fax: 716-268-7090. Hours: 9AM-5PM Sept-May; 8:30AM-4PM June-Aug (EST). *Probate.*

Bronx County

Supreme Court - Civil Division 851 Grand Concourse, Bronx, NY 10451; 718-590-3641; Fax: 718-590-8122. Hours: 9AM-5PM (EST). *Civil Actions Over $25,000.*

Civil Records: Access: Mail, in person. Both court and visitors may perform in person searches. Search fee: $5.00 per name. Fee is for each 2 years searched. Required to search: name, years to search. Civil cases indexed by defendant, plaintiff. Civil records on computer since 1995; prior records on microfilm. **General Information:** No marriage or divorce records released. SASE required. Turnaround time 7-10 days. Copy fee: $.75 per page. Certification fee: $5.00. Fee payee: Bronx County Clerk. Only cashiers checks and money orders accepted. Prepayment is required. Public access terminal is available.

Supreme Court-Criminal Division 215 E 161st St, Bronx, NY 10451; 718-417-3149. Hours: 9:30AM-4:30PM, Closed 12-2 (EST). *Felony.* **Criminal Records:** Access: Mail, in person. Only the court conducts in person searches; visitors may not. Search fee: $16.00 per name. Fee is per county searched. Required to search: name, years to search, DOB. Criminal records on computer from 1977, prior on microfiche. **General Information:** No sealed, expunged, juvenile or sex offense records released. SASE required. Copy

fee: $.75 per page. Certification fee: $5.00. Fee payee: Bronx County Clerk. Only cashiers checks and money orders accepted. Prepayment is required.

Civil Court of the City of New York - Bronx Branch 851 Grand Concourse, Bronx, NY 10451; 718-590-3601. Hours: 9AM-5PM (EST). *Civil Actions Under $25,000, Eviction, Small Claims.*

Civil Records: Access: In person only. Court does not conduct in person searches; visitors must perform searches for themselves. Search fee: No civil searches performed by court. Required to search: name, years to search. Civil cases indexed by defendant, plaintiff. Civil records in books, on file cards. Records archived after five years, requiring 3-5 days to requisition. **General Information:** Copy fee: $.25 per page. Certification fee: $5.00. Fee payee: County Clerk. Business checks accepted.

Surrogate Court 851 Grand Concourse, Bronx, NY 10451; 718-590-4515; Fax: 718-537-5158. Hours: 9AM-5PM (EST). *Probate.*

Broome County

Supreme & County Court PO Box 2062, Binghamton, NY 13902; 607-778-2448/2451; Fax: 607-778-6426. Hours: 9AM-5PM (EST). *Felony, Civil.*

Civil Records: Access: Fax, mail, in person. Both court and visitors may perform in person searches. Search fee: $5.00 per name. Fee is per 2 years searched. Required to search: name, years to search. Civil cases indexed by defendant, plaintiff. Civil records on computer from 1985, prior in books. **Criminal Records:** Access: Fax, mail, in person. Both court and visitors may perform in person searches. Search fee: $5.00 per name. Fee is per 2 years searched, 10 year maximum. Required to search: name, years to search, DOB. Criminal records on computer from 1985, prior in books. **General Information:** No sealed or youthful offender records released. SASE required. Turnaround time 3-5 days. Copy fee: $.50 per page. $1.00 minimum. Certification fee: $4.00. Fee payee: County Clerk. Personal checks accepted. No personal checks over $1000.00. Prepayment is required. Public access terminal is available. Fax notes: $1.00 per page.

Binghamton City Court Governmental Plaza, Binghamton, NY 13901; 607-772-7006; Fax: 607-772-7041. Hours: 9AM-5PM (EST). *Misdemeanor, Civil Actions Under $15,000, Eviction, Small Claims.*

Civil Records: Access: Mail, in person. Both court and visitors may perform in person searches. Search fee: $5.00 per name. Fee is for manual search prior to 1991. Required to search: name, years to search. Civil cases indexed by defendant. Civil records on computer from 1977, prior in books, index cards. In person searching only for 04/21/99 forward. **Criminal Records:** Access: Mail, in person. Only the court conducts in person searches; visitors may not. Search fee: $5.00 fee for manual search prior to 1991; electronic search $16.00 (pending or disposed) 1990 to present. Required to search: name, years to search, DOB. Criminal records on computer from 1990. **General Information:** No sealed records released. SASE required. Turnaround time 1-2 weeks. Copy fee: $.50 per page. $1.00 minimum. Certification fee: $5.00. per certificate. Fee payee: Binghamton City Court. Only cashiers checks and money orders accepted. Prepayment is required. Public access

terminal is available. Public Access Terminal Note: For civil only, from 1996.

Surrogate Court Courthouse, 92 Court St, Rm 109, Binghamton, NY 13901; 607-778-2111; Fax: 607-778-2308. Hours: 9AM-5PM (EST). *Probate.*

Note: $25 search fee

Cattaraugus County

Supreme & County Court 303 Court St, Little Valley, NY 14755; 716-938-9111; Fax: 716-938-6413. Hours: 9AM-5PM (EST). *Felony, Civil.*

Civil Records: Access: Mail, in person. Both court and visitors may perform in person searches. Search fee: $5.00 per name. Fee is per 2 years searched. Required to search: name, years to search. Civil cases indexed by defendant, plaintiff. Civil records on computer from 1989, prior in books, index cards from 1900. **Criminal Records:** Access: Phone, mail, in person. Both court and visitors may perform in person searches. Search fee: $5.00 per name. Fee is per 2 years searched. Required to search: name, years to search, DOB. Criminal records on computer from 1989, prior in books, index cards from 1900. **General Information:** No sealed or youthful offender records released. SASE not required. Turnaround time 2-3 days. Copy fee: $1.00 per page. Certification fee: $4.00. Fee payee: County Clerk. Business checks accepted. Prepayment is required. Public access terminal is available.

Olean City Court PO Box 631, Olean, NY 14760; 716-376-5620; Fax: 716-376-5623. Hours: 8:30AM-4:30PM (EST). *Misdemeanor, Civil Actions Under $15,000, Eviction, Small Claims.*

Civil Records: Access: Mail, in person. Only the court conducts in person searches; visitors may not. Search fee: $5.00 per name. Required to search: name, years to search. Civil cases indexed by defendant. Civil records on docket books. **Criminal Records:** Access: Mail, in person. Only the court conducts in person searches; visitors may not. Search fee: $5.00 per name. Required to search: name, years to search, DOB. Criminal records on computer from 1990, prior in books. **General Information:** No sealed or youthful offender records released. SASE required. Turnaround time 2 days. Certification fee: $5.00. Fee payee: City Court. Business checks accepted. Prepayment is required.

Salamanca City Court Municipal Center, 225 Wildwood, Salamanca, NY 14779; 716-945-4153. Hours: 8AM-4PM (EST). *Misdemeanor, Civil Actions Under $15,000, Eviction, Small Claims.*

Civil Records: Access: Mail, in person. Only the court conducts in person searches; visitors may not. Search fee: $5.00 per name. Required to search: name, years to search. Civil cases indexed by defendant. Civil records on dockets from 1930s. **Criminal Records:** Access: Mail, in person. Only the court conducts in person searches; visitors may not. Search fee: $5.00 per name. Required to search: name, years to search, DOB. Criminal records on dockets from 1930s. **General Information:** No sealed records released. SASE required. Turnaround time 1-2 weeks. Fee payee: Salamanca City Court. No personal checks accepted. Prepayment is required.

Surrogate Court 303 Court St, Little Valley, NY 14755; 716-938-9111; Fax: 716-938-6983. Hours: 9AM-5PM (EST). *Probate.*

Note: Public can search, but if court has to search there is a fee

Cayuga County

Supreme & County Court 160 Genesee St, Auburn, NY 13021-3424; 315-253-1271; Fax: 315-253-1586. Hours: 9AM-5PM Sept-June; 8AM-4PM July-Aug (EST). *Felony, Civil.*

Note: The court is located at 154 Genesee Street

Civil Records: Access: Mail, in person. Both court and visitors may perform in person searches. Search fee: $5.00 per name. Required to search: name, years to search. Civil cases indexed by defendant, plaintiff. Civil records on computer from 1986, prior in books. **Criminal Records:** Access: Mail, in person. Both court and visitors may perform in person searches. Search fee: $16.00 per name. Required to search: name, years to search, DOB. names are computerized since 1930. **General Information:** No sealed records released. SASE required. Turnaround time 1 day. Copy fee: $.50 per page. Certification fee: $4.00 plus $.50 per page after first 8. Fee payee: County Clerk. Personal checks accepted. Prepayment is required. Public access terminal is available.

Auburn City Court 153 Genesee St, Auburn, NY 13021-3434; 315-253-1570; Fax: 315-253-1085. Hours: 8AM-4PM (EST). *Misdemeanor, Civil Actions Under $15,000, Eviction, Small Claims.*

Civil Records: Access: Mail, in person. Only the court conducts in person searches; visitors may not. Search fee: Electronic searh is $16.00, extra years are $5.00. Required to search: name, years to search. Civil cases indexed by defendant. Civil records on computer from 1986. **Criminal Records:** Access: Mail, in person. Only the court conducts in person searches; visitors may not. Search fee: Electronic search is $16.00, extra years are $5.00 per 2 years. Required to search: name, years to search, DOB. Criminal records on computer from 1986. **General Information:** No sealed, expunged, adoption, sex offense, juvenile or mental health records released. SASE required. Turnaround time 3 days. Certification fee: $5.00. Fee payee: City Court. Only cashiers checks and money orders accepted. Prepayment is required.

Surrogate Court Courthouse, 154 Genesee St, Auburn, NY 13021-3471; 315-255-4316; Fax: 315-255-4322. Hours: 8:30AM-4:30PM; Summer hours 8AM-4:00PM (EST). *Probate.*

www.courts.state.ny.us/www/jd7/cayuga_surrogate.htm

Chautauqua County

Supreme & County Court - Civil Records PO Box 170, Mayville, NY 14757; 716-753-4331. Hours: 9AM-5PM/Summer 8:30AM-4:30PM (EST). *Civil.*

Civil Records: Access: Mail, in person. Only the court conducts in person searches; visitors may not. No search fee. Required to search: name, years to search. Civil cases indexed by plaintiff. Civil records in docket books, on cards. **General Information:** No sealed records released. SASE required. Turnaround time 1-2 days. Copy fee: $4.00. Add $1.00 per page after first 4. Certification fee: No certification fee. Fee payee: Chautauqua County Clerk. Personal checks accepted. Prepayment is required.

Supreme & County Court-Criminal Records Courthouse, PO Box 190, Mayville, NY 14757; 716-753-4331; Fax: 716-753-4993. Hours: 9AM-5PM/Summer 8:30AM-4:30PM (EST). *Felony.* **Criminal Records:** Access: Mail, in person. Only the court conducts in person searches; visitors may not. Search fee: $16.00 per name. Also, a Certificate of Conviction can be ordered for $5.00. Required to search: name, years to search, DOB, signed release. Criminal records are available electronically from 01-01-87. Be advised that all requests without a DOB will be returned. **General Information:** No sealed records released. SASE required. Turnaround time 1-2 days. Copy fee: $4.00. Add $1.00 per page after first 4. Certification fee: No certification fee. Fee payee: County Clerk. Prepayment is required.

Dunkirk City Court City Hall, 342 Central Ave, Dunkirk, NY 14048; 716-366-2055; Fax: 716-366-3622. Hours: 9AM-5PM (EST). *Misdemeanor, Civil Actions Under $15,000, Eviction, Small Claims.*

Civil Records: Access: Mail, in person. Only the court conducts in person searches; visitors may not. Search fee: $16.00 per name. Required to search: name, years to search. Civil cases indexed by defendant. Civil records on computer from 1992, prior in books. **Criminal Records:** Access: Mail, in person. Only the court conducts in person searches; visitors may not. Search fee: $16.00 per name. Required to search: name, years to search, DOB. Criminal records on computer from 1992, prior in books. **General Information:** No sealed, expunged, adoption, sex offense, juvenile or mental health records released. SASE required. Turnaround time 1 week. Copy fee: $.50 per page. Certification fee: $5.00. Fee payee: Dunkirk City Court. Only cashiers checks and money orders accepted. Prepayment is required.

Jamestown City Court City Hall, Jamestown, NY 14701; 716-483-7561/7562; Fax: 716-483-7519. Hours: 9AM-5PM (EST). *Misdemeanor, Civil Actions Under $15,000, Eviction, Small Claims.*

Civil Records: Access: Fax, mail, in person. Both court and visitors may perform in person searches. No search fee. Required to search: name, years to search. Civil cases indexed by defendant. Civil records on computer from 1989, prior in books. **Criminal Records:** Access: Fax, mail, in person. Only the court conducts in person searches; visitors may not. Search fee: $5.00 per name. Fee is for 2 year search, or $16.00 for automated search. Required to search: name, years to search, DOB, signed release; also helpful-address, SSN. Criminal records on computer from 1989, prior in books. **General Information:** No sealed records released. SASE required. Turnaround time 1 week. Copy fee: $1.00 per page. Certification fee: $5.00. Fee payee: City Court. Business checks accepted. Prepayment is required.

Surrogate Court Gerace Office Bldg, Rm 231 (PO Box C), 3 N Erie St, Mayville, NY 14757; 716-753-4339; Fax: 716-753-4600. Hours: 9AM-5PM (EST). *Probate.*

Chemung County

Supreme & County Court - Civil Records 210 Lake St, Elmira, NY 14901; 607-737-2920; Fax: 607-737-2897. Hours: 8:30AM-4:30PM (EST). *Civil.*

Civil Records: Access: Mail, in person. Only the court conducts in person searches; visitors may not. Search fee: $5.00 per name. Fee is per 2 years searched. Required to search: name, years to search. Civil cases indexed by defendant, plaintiff. Civil records on computer from 1994, prior in books. **General Information:** No sealed, divorce or adoption records released. SASE required. Turnaround time 4-6 weeks. Copy fee: $.50 per page. $1.00 minimum. Certification fee: $4.00 plus $1.00 per page after first 4. Fee payee: County Clerk. Personal checks accepted. Prepayment is required. Public access terminal is available. Public Access Terminal Note: For land records only from 1991 forward.

Supreme & County Court-Criminal Records PO Box 588, Elmira, NY 14902-0588; 607-737-2844. Hours: 8:30AM-4:30PM (EST). *Felony.* **Criminal Records:** Access: Phone, mail, in person. Only the court conducts in person searches; visitors may not. Search fee: $5.00 for every 2 years searched or $20.00 for a seven year search. Searches with both maiden and married names are considered two searches. Required to search: name, years to search, DOB, SSN, signed release. Criminal records in docket books. **General Information:** No sealed, divorce or adoption records released. SASE required. Turnaround time 4-6 weeks. Copy fee: $.25 per page. Certification fee: $5.00. Fee payee: County Clerk. Personal checks accepted. Prepayment is required.

Elmira City Court 317 E Church St, Elmira, NY 14901-2790; 607-737-5681; Fax: 607-737-5820. Hours: 8AM-4PM (EST). *Misdemeanor, Civil Actions Under $15,000, Eviction, Small Claims.*

Civil Records: Access: Mail, in person. Only the court conducts in person searches; visitors may not. Search fee: $16.00 per name. Required to search: name, years to search. Civil cases indexed by defendant. Civil records on computer since 1997; prior records on index cards. **Criminal Records:** Access: Mail, in person. Only the court conducts in person searches; visitors may not. Search fee: $16.00 per name. Required to search: name, years to search, DOB; also helpful-SSN. Criminal records on computer from 1982. **General Information:** No sealed records released. SASE required. Turnaround time 3-5 days. Copy fee: $1.00 per page. Certification fee: $5.00. Fee payee: Elmira City Court. Personal checks accepted. Prepayment is required. Public access terminal is available. Public Access Terminal Note: Look-up only civil records.

Surrogate Court 224 Lake St, Elmira, NY 14901; 607-737-2946/2819; Fax: 607-737-2874. Hours: 9AM-5PM (EST). *Probate.*

Chenango County

Supreme & County Court County Office Bldg, Norwich, NY 13815-1676; 607-337-1450. Hours: 8:30AM-5PM (EST). *Felony, Civil.*

Civil Records: Access: Mail, in person. Both court and visitors may perform in person searches. Search fee: $5.00 per name. Fee is per 2 years searched. Required to search: name, years to search. Civil cases indexed by defendant, plaintiff. Civil records on computer from 1994, prior in books since 1880. **Criminal Records:** Access: Mail, in person. Both court and visitors may perform in person searches. Search fee: $5.00 per name. Fee is per 2 years searched. Required to search: name, years to search, DOB. Criminal records in docket books. **General Information:** No sealed, expunged, adoption, sex offense, juvenile or mental health records released. SASE required. Turnaround time 2 days. Copy fee: $.50 per page. $1.00 minimum. Certification fee: Certification fee is $1.00 per pg, $4.00 minimum. Fee payee: County Clerk. Personal checks accepted. Prepayment is required. Public access terminal is available.

Norwich City Court 1 Court Plaza, Norwich, NY 13815; 607-334-1224; Fax: 607-334-8494. Hours: 8:30AM-4:30PM (EST). *Misdemeanor, Civil Actions Under $15,000, Eviction, Small Claims.*

Civil Records: Access: Fax, mail, in person. Both court and visitors may perform in person searches. Search fee: $16.00 per name. Required to search: name, years to search. Civil cases indexed by defendant. Civil records on computer from 1986, prior in books. **Criminal Records:** Access: Fax, mail, in person. Both court and visitors may perform in person searches. Search fee: $16.00 per name. Required to search: name, years to search, DOB, signed release. Criminal records on computer from 1986, prior in books. **General Information:** No sealed, expunged, adoption, sex offense, juvenile or mental health records released. SASE required. Turnaround time 1 week. Certification fee: $5.00. Fee payee: City Court. Business checks accepted. Prepayment is required.

Surrogate Court County Office Bldg, 5 Court St, Norwich, NY 13815; 607-337-1822/1827; Fax: 607-337-1834. Hours: 9AM-Noon, 1-5PM (EST). *Probate.*

Clinton County

Supreme & County Court County Government Center, 137 Margaret St, Plattsburgh, NY 12901; 518-565-4715; Fax: 518-565-4708. Hours: 9AM-5PM (EST). *Felony, Civil.*

Civil Records: Access: In person only. Court does not conduct in person searches; visitors must perform searches for themselves. Search fee: No civil searches performed by court. Required to search: name, years to search. Civil cases indexed by defendant. Civil records in docket books. **Criminal Records:** Access: Mail, in person. Both court and visitors may perform in person searches. Search fee: $16.00 per name. Required to search: name, years to search, DOB. Criminal records on computer from 1986, prior in dcoket books. **General Information:** No sealed or sex case records released. SASE required. Turnaround time 3-4 days. Copy fee: $.50 per page. Certification fee: Certification $4.00 up to 4 pages, then $1.00 per additional page. Fee payee: County Clerk. Personal checks accepted. Prepayment is required.

Plattsburg City Court 41 City Hall Pl, Plattsburgh, NY 12901; 518-563-7870; Fax: 518-563-3124. Hours: 8AM-4PM (EST). *Misdemeanor, Civil Actions Under $15,000, Eviction, Small Claims.*

Civil Records: Access: Mail, in person. Only the court conducts in person searches; visitors may not. Search fee: $16.00 for computerized search. Required to search: name, years to search. Civil cases indexed by defendant. Civil records on computer from 1986, prior in books. **Criminal Records:** Access: Mail, in person. Only the court conducts in person searches; visitors may not. Search fee: $16.00 per name. Required to search: name, years to search, DOB. Criminal records on computer from 1986, prior in books. **General Information:** No sealed records released. SASE required. Turnaround time same day. Copy fee: $1.00 per page. Certification fee: $5.00. Fee payee: City Court. Only cashiers checks and money orders accepted. Prepayment is required.

Surrogate Court 137 Margaret St, Plattsburgh, NY 12901-2933; 518-565-4630; Fax: 518-565-4769. Hours: 9AM-5PM (EST). *Probate.*

Columbia County

Supreme & County Court 560 Warren Street, Hudson, NY 12534; 518-828-3339; Fax: 518-828-5299. Hours: 9AM-5PM (EST). *Felony, Civil.*

Note: Note that the Supreme and county courts are actually located at 401 Union in Hudson, but records for both courts are located at the County Clerk's Office as listed above

Civil Records: Access: Mail, in person. Both court and visitors may perform in person searches. Search fee: $5.00 per name. Fee is per 2 years searched. Required to search: name, years to search. Civil cases indexed by defendant. Civil records on computer from 1993, prior on cards to 1985. **Criminal Records:** Access: Mail, in person. Both court and visitors may perform in person searches. Search fee: $5.00 per name. Required to search: name, years to search, DOB. Criminal records on computer from 1993, prior on cards to 1985. **General Information:** No sealed records released. SASE required. Turnaround time 1 week. Copy fee: $.25 per page. Certification fee: $4.00. Fee payee: County Clerk. Personal checks accepted. Prepayment is required. Public access terminal is available.

Hudson City Court 429 Warren St, Hudson, NY 12534; 518-828-3100; Fax: 518-828-3628. Hours: 8AM-4PM (EST). *Misdemeanor, Civil Actions Under $15,000, Eviction, Small Claims.*

Civil Records: Access: Fax, mail, in person. Only the court conducts in person searches; visitors may not. Search fee: $5.00 per name. per every two years. Required to search: name, years to search; also helpful-address. Civil cases indexed by defendant, plaintiff. Civil records on computer from 1991, prior in books. **Criminal Records:** Access: Fax, mail, in person. Only the court conducts in person searches; visitors may not. Search fee: $5.00 per name. per every two years. Required to search: name, years to search, DOB. Criminal records on computer from 1991, prior in books. **General Information:** No sealed, expunged, adoption, sex offense, juvenile or mental health records released. SASE required. Turnaround time 1 week. Copy fee: $.25 per page. Certification fee: $5.00. Fee payee: City Court. Business checks accepted. Prepayment is required.

Surrogate Court Courthouse, 401 Union St, Hudson, NY 12534; 518-828-0414; Fax: 518-828-1603. Hours: 9AM-5PM (EST). *Probate.*

Cortland County

Supreme & County Court 46 Greenbush St, Ste 301, Cortland, NY 13045; 607-753-5010; Civil phone:607-753-5021; Criminal phone:607-753-5021; Fax: 607-756-3409. Hours: 9AM-5PM (EST). *Felony, Civil.*

Civil Records: Access: Mail, in person. Both court and visitors may perform in person searches. Search fee: $5.00 per name. per 2 year search. Required to search: name, years to search. Civil cases indexed by defendant, plaintiff. Civil records on computer from 5/94, prior in books. **Criminal Records:** Access: Mail, in person. Only the court conducts in person searches; visitors may not. Search fee: $5.00 per name. per 2 year search. Required to search: name, years to search, DOB. Criminal records on computer from 1986, prior in books. **General Information:** No sealed or youthful offender records released. SASE required. Turnaround time 1 day. Copy fee: $.50 per page. Certification fee: $1.00. Minimum $4.00.

Fee payee: County Clerk. Personal checks accepted. Prepayment is required.

Cortland City Court 25 Court St, Cortland, NY 13045; 607-753-1811; Fax: 607-753-9932. Hours: 8:30AM-4:30PM (EST). *Misdemeanor, Civil Actions Under $15,000, Eviction, Small Claims.*

Civil Records: Access: Mail, in person. Only the court conducts in person searches; visitors may not. Search fee: $5.00 per name. Required to search: name, years to search. Civil cases indexed by defendant. Civil records on computer from 1985, prior in books. **Criminal Records:** Access: Mail, in person. Only the court conducts in person searches; visitors may not. Search fee: $5.00 per name. $16.00 for electronic search. Required to search: name, years to search, DOB. Criminal records on computer from 1985, prior in books. **General Information:** No sealed records released. SASE required. Turnaround time 10 days. Copy fee: $.50 per page. Certification fee: $5.00. Fee payee: City Court. Only cashiers checks and money orders accepted. Prepayment is required.

Surrogate Court 46 Greenbush St, Ste 301, Cortland, NY 13045; 607-753-5355. Hours: 9AM-5PM (EST). *Probate.*

Delaware County

Supreme & County Court 3 Court St, Delhi, NY 13753; 607-746-2131; Fax: 607-746-3253. Hours: 9AM-5PM (EST). *Felony, Civil.*

Civil Records: Access: Mail, in person. Both court and visitors may perform in person searches. Search fee: $5.00 per name. Required to search: name, years to search. Civil cases indexed by defendant, plaintiff. Civil records in books. **Criminal Records:** Access: Mail, in person. Both court and visitors may perform in person searches. Search fee: $5.00 per name. Required to search: name, years to search, DOB. Criminal records in books. **General Information:** No sealed records released. SASE required. Turnaround time 2 days. Copy fee: $.50 per page. Certification fee: Certification $4.00 for up to 4 pages, then $1.00 per page. Fee payee: County Clerk. Personal checks accepted. Prepayment is required.

Surrogate Court 3 Court St, Delhi, NY 13753; 607-746-2126; Fax: 607-746-3253. *Probate.*

Dutchess County

Supreme & County Court 22 Market St, Poughkeepsie, NY 12601-3203; 845-486-2125; Fax: 845-486-2138. Hours: 9AM-5PM (EST). *Felony, Civil.*

Note: Criminal index computer search available at OCA. See state introduction

Civil Records: Access: In person only. Court does not conduct in person searches; visitors must perform searches for themselves. Search fee: No civil searches performed by court. Required to search: name, years to search. Civil cases indexed by defendant, plaintiff. Civil records on computer from 1986, prior in books. **Criminal Records:** Access: Mail, in person. Both court and visitors may perform in person searches. Search fee: $5.00 per name. Fee is per 2 years or part thereof (convictions only). Required to search: name, years to search. Criminal records on computer from 1987. **General Information:** No sealed or youthful offender records released. SASE required. Turnaround time 2 weeks. Copy fee: $5.00 per document. Certification fee: $4.00 plus $.50 per page after first 8 in person. $6.00 per document by mail. $5.00 for assumed name, if in person. Fee payee: Dutchess County Clerk. Personal checks accepted. Prepayment is required. Public access terminal is available.

Beacon City Court One Municipal Plaza, #2, Beacon, NY 12508; 845-838-5030; Fax: 845-838-5041. Hours: 8AM-4PM (EST). *Misdemeanor, Civil Actions Under $15,000, Eviction, Small Claims.*

Civil Records: Access: Mail, in person. Both court and visitors may perform in person searches. Search fee: $16.00 per name. Required to search: name, years to search. Civil cases indexed by defendant, plaintiff. Civil records on computer from 1996, prior in books and cards. **Criminal Records:** Access: Mail, in person. Only the court conducts in person searches; visitors may not. Search fee: $16.00 per name. Required to search: name, years to search, DOB, SSN, signed release. Criminal records computerized since 1990. **General Information:** No sealed or youthful offender records released. SASE required. Turnaround time 3-4 days. Copy fee: $.75 per page. Certification fee: $5.00. Fee payee: City Court of Beacon. Only cashiers checks and money orders accepted. Prepayment is required.

Poughkeepsie City Court Civic Center Plaza, PO Box 300, Poughkeepsie, NY 12601; 845-451-4091; Fax: 845-451-4094. Hours: 8AM-4PM (EST). *Misdemeanor, Civil Actions Under $15,000, Eviction, Small Claims.*

Civil Records: Access: Mail, in person. Both court and visitors may perform in person searches. Search fee: $16.00 per name. $5.00 for certificate of disposition. Required to search: name, years to search. Civil cases indexed by defendant. Civil records on computer from 1993. **Criminal Records:** Access: Mail, in person. Both court and visitors may perform in person searches. Search fee: $16.00 per name. $5.00 per certified disposition. Required to search: name, years to search, DOB, signed release. Criminal records on computer from 1990. **General Information:** No sealed, expunged, adoption, sex offense, juvenile or mental health records released. SASE required. Turnaround time 1 week. Copy fee: $.50 per page. Certification fee: $5.00. Fee payee: Poughkeepsie City Court. Only cashiers checks and money orders accepted. Prepayment is required.

Surrogate Court 10 Market St, Poughkeepsie, NY 12601; 845-486-2235; Fax: 845-486-2234. Hours: 9AM-5PM (EST). *Probate.*

Erie County

Supreme & County Court 25 Delaware Ave, Buffalo, NY 14202;; Civil phone:716-858-7766; Criminal phone:716-858-7766; Fax: 716-858-6550. Hours: 9AM-5PM (EST). *Felony, Civil.*

Note: Criminal index available from OCA. See state introduction

Civil Records: Access: Mail, in person. Both court and visitors may perform in person searches. Search fee: $5.00 per name. Fee is per 2 years searched. Required to search: name, years to search. Civil cases indexed by defendant, plaintiff. Civil records on computer from 1993, prior in books. Plaintiffs indexed starting in 1993. **Criminal Records:** Access: Mail, in person. Both court and visitors may perform in person searches. Search fee: $5.00 per name. Fee is per 2 years searched. Required to search: name, years to search. Civil records on computer from 1993, prior in books. Plaintiffs indexed starting in 1993. **General Information:** No sealed records released.

SASE required. Turnaround time 3-4 days. Copy fee: $1.00 per page. Certification fee: $4.00. Fee payee: County Clerk. Personal checks accepted. Prepayment is required. Public access terminal is available.

Buffalo City Court 50 Delaware Ave, Buffalo, NY 14202; 716-847-8200; Fax: 716-847-8257. Hours: 9AM-5PM (EST). *Misdemeanor, Civil Actions Under $15,000, Eviction, Small Claims.*

Civil Records: Access: Mail, in person. Both court and visitors may perform in person searches. Search fee: $5.00 per name. Required to search: name, years to search. Civil cases indexed by defendant, plaintiff. Civil records in books, some records computerized since 1983. **Criminal Records:** Access: Mail, in person. Only the court conducts in person searches; visitors may not. Search fee: $5.00 per name. Required to search: name, years to search, DOB; also helpful-date of offense. Criminal records in books, some records computerized since 1983. **General Information:** No sealed or youthful offender records released. SASE required. Turnaround time 3 days. Copy fee: $1.00 per page. Certification fee: $5.00. Fee payee: City Court. Business checks accepted. Prepayment is required.

Lackawanna City Court 714 Ridge Rd, Rm 225, Lackawanna, NY 14218; 716-827-6486; Fax: 716-827-1874. Hours: 8:30AM-4:30PM (EST). *Misdemeanor, Civil Actions Under $15,000, Eviction, Small Claims.*

Civil Records: Access: Mail, in person. Both court and visitors may perform in person searches. Search fee: $16.00 per name. Required to search: name; also helpful-years to search. Civil cases indexed by defendant. Civil records on computer from 1994, prior on docket books. Mail access available to government agencies only. **Criminal Records:** Access: Mail, in person. Only the court conducts in person searches; visitors may not. Search fee: $16.00 per name. Required to search: name; also helpful-years to search, DOB. Criminal records on computer from 1994, prior on docket books. Mail access available to government agencies only. **General Information:** No sealed or youthful offender records released. SASE required. Turnaround time 2-3 days. Copy fee: $1.00 per page. Certification fee: $5.00. Fee payee: City Court. Only cashiers checks and money orders accepted. Prepayment is required.

Tonawanda City Court 200 Niagara St, Tonawanda, NY 14150; 716-693-3484; Fax: 716-693-1612. Hours: 9AM-4PM (EST). *Misdemeanor, Civil Actions Under $15,000, Eviction, Small Claims.*

Civil Records: Access: Mail, in person. Only the court conducts in person searches; visitors may not. Search fee: $5.00 per name. Required to search: name, years to search. Civil cases indexed by defendant, plaintiff. Civil records on computer since 1997, prior on index cards, in books. **Criminal Records:** Access: Mail, in person. Only the court conducts in person searches; visitors may not. Search fee: $5.00 per name. Required to search: name, years to search, DOB, SSN, signed release. Criminal records on computer since 1997, prior on index cards, in books. **General Information:** No sealed records released. SASE not required. Turnaround time 3-5 days. Copy fee: $1.00 per page. Certification fee: $5.00. Fee payee: City Court of Tonawanda. Business checks accepted. Prepayment is required.

Surrogate Court 92 Franklin St, Buffalo, NY 14202; 716-854-7867; Fax: 716-853-3741. Hours: 9AM-5PM (EST). *Probate.*

Essex County

Supreme & County Courts Essex County Government Center, Court St, PO Box 217, Elizabethtown, NY 12932; 518-873-3370; Civil phone:518-873-3600; Criminal phone:518-873-3600; Fax: 518-873-3376. Hours: 8:30AM-5PM (EST). *Felony, Civil.*

Civil Records: Access: Mail, in person. Both court and visitors may perform in person searches. No search fee. Required to search: name, years to search. Civil cases indexed by defendant, plaintiff. Civil records on computer from 11/93, prior in books. **Criminal Records:** Access: Mail, in person. Both court and visitors may perform in person searches. Search fee: Two types of searches available-manual since 1956 at $5.00 per name per each two years, and computer at $16.00 per name. Call for copy of special form to compute fee and submit with payment. Required to search: name, years to search, DOB. Criminal records on computer from 1950s, prior in books. **General Information:** No sealed or youthful offender records released. SASE required. Turnaround time same day. Copy fee: $.50 per page. Certification fee: $1.00. Minimum $4.00. Fee payee: Essex County Clerk. Personal checks accepted. Prepayment is required.

Surrogate Court 100 Court St, PO Box 505, Elizabethtown, NY 12932; 518-873-3384. Hours: 9AM-5PM (EST). *Probate.*

Franklin County

Supreme & County Court 63 W Main St, Malone, NY 12953-1817; 518-481-1748. Hours: 9AM-5PM (EST). *Felony, Civil.*

Civil Records: Access: Mail, in person. Both court and visitors may perform in person searches. Search fee: $5.00 per name per year. Fee is per name per 2 years. Required to search: name, years to search. Civil cases indexed by defendant. Civil records on computer from 1990, prior in file folders in Clerk's office. **Criminal Records:** Access: Mail, in person. Both court and visitors may perform in person searches. Search fee: $5.00 per name per year. Fee is per 2 years. Required to search: name, years to search, DOB. Criminal records on computer from 1990. **General Information:** No sealed or youthful offender records released. SASE required. Turnaround time 1 week. Copy fee: $.50 per page. Certification fee: $4.00. Fee payee: County Clerk. Personal checks accepted.

Surrogate Court Courthouse, 63 W Main St, Malone, NY 12953-1817; 518-481-1736 & 1737. Hours: 9AM-5PM Sept-May; 8AM-4PM June-Aug (EST). *Probate.*

Fulton County

Supreme & County Court 223 West Main St, County Bldg, Johnstown, NY 12095; 518-736-5539; Fax: 518-762-5078. Hours: 9AM-5PM (EST). *Felony, Civil.*

Civil Records: Access: Mail, in person. Both court and visitors may perform in person searches. Search fee: $16.00 per name. Fee is $5.00 for in person searching, if record found. Required to search: name, years to search. Civil cases indexed by defendant, plaintiff. Civil records in file folders. **Criminal Records:** Access: Mail, in person. Only the court conducts in person searches; visitors may not. Search fee: $16.00 per name. Fee is $5.00 for in person searching, if record is found. Required to search: name, years to search, DOB. Criminal records in file folders. **General Information:** No sealed, expunged, adoption, sex offense, juvenile or mental health records released. SASE required. Turnaround time 1 week. Copy fee: $1.00 per page. $.15 per page self service. Certification fee: $4.00. Fee payee: County Clerk. Business checks accepted. Prepayment is required.

Gloversville City Court City Hall, Frontage Rd, Gloversville, NY 12078; 518-773-4527; Fax: 518-773-4599. Hours: 8AM-4PM (EST). *Misdemeanor, Civil Actions Under $15,000, Eviction, Small Claims.*

Civil Records: Access: Mail, in person. Only the court conducts in person searches; visitors may not. Search fee: $16.00 per name. Required to search: name, years to search. Civil cases indexed by plaintiff. Civil records in books. **Criminal Records:** Access: Mail, in person. Only the court conducts in person searches; visitors may not. Search fee: $16.00 per name. Required to search: name, years to search, DOB. Criminal records in books. **General Information:** No sealed, youthful offender or sex abuse case records released. SASE required. Turnaround time 2 weeks. Copy fee: $.50. There is a $1.00 minimum. Certification fee: $5.00. Fee payee: Gloversville City Court. Only cashiers checks and money orders accepted. Prepayment is required.

Johnstown City Court City Hall, Johnstown, NY 12095; 518-762-0007; Fax: 518-762-2720. Hours: 8AM-4PM (EST). *Misdemeanor, Civil Actions Under $15,000, Eviction, Small Claims.*

Civil Records: Access: Mail, in person. Only the court conducts in person searches; visitors may not. Search fee: $16.00 per name. Required to search: name, years to search. Civil cases indexed by plaintiff. Civil records in file folders. **Criminal Records:** Access: Mail, in person. Only the court conducts in person searches; visitors may not. Search fee: $16.00 per name. Required to search: name, years to search, DOB. Criminal records on computer from 1986. **General Information:** No sealed or youthful offender records released. SASE required. Turnaround time 1 month. Copy fee: $.50 per page. Certification fee: $5.00. Fee payee: City Court. Only cashiers checks and money orders accepted. Prepayment is required.

Surrogate Court 223 West Main St, Johnstown, NY 12095; 518-762-0685; Fax: 518-762-6372. Hours: 8AM-5PM (8AM-4PM July-August) (EST). *Probate.*

Genesee County

Supreme & County Courts PO Box 379, Batavia, NY 14021-0379; 716-344-2550 X2242; Fax: 716-344-8521. Hours: 8:30AM-5PM (EST). *Felony, Civil.*

Note: All records maintained at County Clerk's office, PO Box 379, Batavia, NY 14021

Civil Records: Access: Mail, in person. Both court and visitors may perform in person searches. Search fee: $5.00 per five year period. Required to search: name, years to search; also helpful-address. Civil cases indexed by defendant, plaintiff. Civil records in books from 1802, computerized since 1995. **Criminal Records:** Access: Fax, mail, in person. Both court and visitors may perform in person searches. Search fee: $5.00 per five year period. Required to search: name, years to search, DOB; also helpful-SSN. Criminal records in books from 1802, computerized since 1995. **General**

Information: No sealed, expunged, adoption, sex offense, juvenile or mental health records released. SASE required. Turnaround time 1-3 days. Copy fee: $1.00 for first page, $.50 each addl. Certification fee: $4.00 plus $.50 per page in excess of 8 pages. Fee payee: County Clerk. Personal checks accepted. Prepayment is required. Public access terminal is available. Fax notes: $5.00 per document.

Batavia City Court Genesee County Courts Facility, 1 W Main St, Batavia, NY 14020; 716-344-2550 X2416, 2417, 2418; Fax: 716-344-8556. Hours: 9AM-5PM (EST). *Misdemeanor, Civil Actions Under $15,000, Eviction, Small Claims.*

Civil Records: Access: Fax, mail, in person. Both court and visitors may perform in person searches. Search fee: $5.00 per name. Required to search: name, years to search. Civil cases indexed by plaintiff. Civil records on computer from 1993, in books from 1970. **Criminal Records:** Access: Fax, mail, in person. Only the court conducts in person searches; visitors may not. Search fee: $16.00 per name. Required to search: name, years to search, DOB. Criminal records on computer from 1993, in books from 1970. **General Information:** No sealed, expunged, sex offense or mental health records released. SASE required. Turnaround time 1-3 days. Copy fee: $.50 per page. Certification fee: $5.00. Fee payee: City Court. Only cashiers checks and money orders accepted. Prepayment is required.

Surrogate Court 1 West Main St, Batavia, NY 14020; 716-344-2550 X237; Fax: 716-344-8517. Hours: 9AM-5PM (EST). *Probate.*

Note: $25.00 search fee

Greene County

Supreme & County Court Courthouse, 320 Main St, Catskill, NY 12414; 518-943-2230; Fax: 518-943-7763. Hours: 9AM-5PM (EST). *Felony, Misdemeanor, Civil.*

Civil Records: Access: Phone, fax, mail, in person. Both court and visitors may perform in person searches. No search fee. Required to search: name, years to search. Civil cases indexed by defendant, plaintiff. Civil records in file folder, computerized since 06/13/97. **Criminal Records:** Access: Fax, mail, in person. Only the court conducts in person searches; visitors may not. Search fee: $17.50 per name. Required to search: name, years to search, DOB. Criminal records on index cards. Address requests to the County Clerk's office. **General Information:** No sealed or youthful offender records released. SASE required. Turnaround time 1 week. Copy fee: $1.00 per page. Certification fee: $5.00. Fee payee: County Clerk. Personal checks accepted. Prepayment is required. Public access terminal is available. Fax notes: $1.00 per document.

Surrogate Court Courthouse, 320 Main St, Catskill, NY 12414; 518-943-2484; Fax: 518-943-4372. Hours: 9AM-5PM (EST). *Probate.*

Hamilton County

Supreme & County Court Courthouse, Route 8, Box 204, Lake Pleasant, NY 12108; 518-548-7111. Hours: 8:30AM-4:30PM (EST). *Felony, Civil.*

Civil Records: Access: Mail, in person. Only the court conducts in person searches; visitors may not. No search fee. Required to search: name, years to search. Civil cases indexed by defendant. Civil records on index cards, in books. **Criminal Records:** Access: Mail, in person. Only the court

conducts in person searches; visitors may not. Search fee: $5.00 per name. Fee is per two years searched. Required to search: name, years to search, DOB. Criminal records on index cards, in books. Request must be in writing. **General Information:** No sealed or youthful offender records released. SASE not required. Turnaround time 2-3 days. Copy fee: $.50 per page. $1.00 minimum. Certification fee: $1.00 per page; $4.00 minimum. Fee payee: Hamilton County Clerk. Personal checks accepted. Prepayment is required.

Surrogate Court Hamilton County Ofc. Bldg, White Birch Lane, Indian Lake, NY 12842; 518-648-5411; Fax: 518-648-6286. Hours: 8:30AM-4:30PM (EST). *Probate.*

Herkimer County

Supreme & County Court 301 N Washington Street, Herkimer County Office Bldg, Herkimer, NY 13350-1993; 315-867-1209; Fax: 315-866-1802. Hours: 9AM-5PM Sept-May; 8:30AM-4PM June-Aug (EST). *Felony, Civil.*

Civil Records: Access: Phone, mail, in person. Only the court conducts in person searches; visitors may not. Search fee: $5.00 per name. Search is per 2 year period. Required to search: name, years to search. Civil cases indexed by defendant, plaintiff. Civil records on index books since 1800s. **Criminal Records:** Access: Phone, mail, in person. Only the court conducts in person searches; visitors may not. Search fee: $5.00 per name. Required to search: name, years to search, DOB. Criminal records on index books since 1800s. **General Information:** No sealed, expunged, adoption, sex offense, juvenile or mental health records released. SASE required. Turnaround time varies. Copy fee: $1.00 for first page, $.50 each addl. Certification fee: $1.00 per page, $4.00 minimum. Fee payee: County Clerk. Personal checks accepted. Prepayment is required.

Little Falls City Court 659 E Main St, Little Falls, NY 13365; 315-823-1690; Fax: 315-823-1623. Hours: 8:30AM-4:30PM (EST). *Misdemeanor, Civil Actions Under $15,000, Eviction, Small Claims.*

Civil Records: Access: Mail, in person. Search fee: $5.00 per name. Required to search: name, years to search. Civil cases indexed by defendant. Civil records in books, files. **Criminal Records:** Access: Mail, in person. Only the court conducts in person searches; visitors may not. Search fee: $5.00 per name. Required to search: name, years to search, DOB. Criminal records in books, files. **General Information:** No sealed, expunged, adoption, sex offense, juvenile or mental health records released. SASE required. Turnaround time 1 week. Certification fee: $5.00. Fee payee: City Court. Only cashiers checks and money orders accepted. Prepayment is required.

Surrogate Court 301 N Washington St #5548, Herkimer, NY 13350; 315-867-1170. Hours: 9AM-5PM Sept-May; 8:30AM-4PM June-Aug (EST). *Probate.*

Jefferson County

Supreme & County Court Jefferson County Clerk's Office-Court Records, 175 Arsenal St, County Building, Watertown, NY 13601-3783; 315-785-3200; Fax: 315-785-5048. Hours: 9AM-5PM Sept-June; 8:30AM-4PM July-Aug (EST). *Felony, Civil.*

www.sunyjefferson.edu/jc

Civil Records: Access: In person only. Both court and visitors may perform in person searches.

Search fee: No civil searches performed by court. Required to search: name, years to search. Civil cases indexed by defendant, plaintiff. Civil records on computer from 1992 (by first defendant name only); prior in books from 1805. **Criminal Records:** Access: Mail, in person. Both court and visitors may perform in person searches. Search fee: $5.00 per name. Fee is per 2 years searched. Required to search: name, years to search, DOB, signed release. Criminal records on computer from 1992 (by first defendant name only); prior in books from 1805. **General Information:** No sealed, expunged, adoption, sex offense, juvenile or mental health records released. SASE required. Turnaround time 1 week. Copy fee: $.50 per page. The minimum copy fee is $1.00. Certification fee: $4.00. Plus $1.00 per page. Fee payee: County Clerk of Jefferson County. Personal checks accepted. Prepayment is required. Public access terminal is available.

Watertown City Court Municipal Bldg, 245 Washington St, Watertown, NY 13601; 315-785-7785; Fax: 315-785-7818. Hours: 9AM-5PM (EST). *Misdemeanor, Civil Actions Under $15,000, Eviction, Small Claims.*

Civil Records: Access: Mail, in person. Only the court conducts in person searches; visitors may not. Search fee: $5.00 per name. Fee is per name & docket. Required to search: name, years to search. Civil cases indexed by defendant. Civil records in docket books. **Criminal Records:** Access: Mail, in person. Only the court conducts in person searches; visitors may not. Search fee: $16.00 per name. Required to search: name, years to search, DOB. Criminal records in docket books. **General Information:** No sealed records released. SASE required. Turnaround time same day. Copy fee: $.50 per page. Certification fee: $5.00. Fee payee: City Court. Only cashiers checks and money orders accepted. Prepayment is required.

Surrogate Court County Office Bldg, 7th Flr, 175 Arsenal St, Watertown, NY 13601-2562; 315-785-3019; Fax: 315-785-5194. Hours: 9AM-5PM Sept-May; 8:30AM-4PM June-Aug (EST). *Probate.*

Kings County

Supreme Court -- Civil Division 360 Adams St, Brooklyn, NY 11201; 718-643-5894; Fax: 718-643-8187. Hours: 9AM-5PM (EST). *Civil Actions Over $25,000.*

Civil Records: Access: In person only. Court does not conduct in person searches; visitors must perform searches for themselves. Search fee: No civil searches performed by court. Required to search: name, years to search. Civil cases indexed by defendant. Civil records on computer, in books, on microfiche. Picture ID required. **General Information:** No sealed, expunged, adoption, sex offense, juvenile or mental health records released. Copy fee: $.75 per page. Certification fee: $5.00. Fee payee: County Clerk. Only cashiers checks and money orders accepted. Prepayment is required. Public access terminal is available.

Supreme   Court-Criminal 120 Schermerhorn St, Brooklyn, NY 11210; 212-428-2810; Fax: 212-417-5856. Hours: 9:30AM-4:30PM (EST). *Felony, Misdemeanor.* **Criminal Records:** Access: In person only. Only the court conducts in person searches; visitors may not. Search fee: $16.00 per name. Fee is per county. Required to search: name, DOB, signed release. Criminal records on computer from 1976, prior on index. **General Information:** No sealed, sex offense or youthful offender records released.

SASE required. Turnaround time 1-3 days. Copy fee: Included in search fee. Certification fee: Included in search fee. Fee payee: Office of Court Administration.   Personal   checks   accepted. Prepayment is required.

Civil Court of the City of New York - Kings Branch 141 Livingston St, Brooklyn, NY 11201; 718-643-5069/643-8133 Clerk. Hours: 9AM-5PM (EST). *Civil Actions Under $25,000, Eviction, Small Claims.*

Civil Records: Access: In person only. Court does not conduct in person searches; visitors must perform searches for themselves. Search fee: No civil searches performed by court. Required to search: name, years to search. Civil cases indexed by plaintiff. Civil records on computer from 1987 for small claims, 1990 for tenant/landlord, and from January 1998 for civil. **General Information:** All records public. Copy fee: $.15 public copying machine fee. Certification fee: $5.00. Fee payee: NYC Civil Court. Only cashiers checks and money orders accepted. Prepayment is required. Public access terminal is available. Public Access Terminal Note: Landlord & Tenant, civil, and small claims since 1998.

Surrogate Court 2 Johnson St, Brooklyn, NY 11201; 718-643-5262. Hours: 9AM-5PM (EST). *Probate.*

Lewis County

Supreme & County Court Courthouse, PO Box 232, Lowville, NY 13367; 315-376-5333; Fax: 315-376-3768. Hours: 8:30AM-4:30PM (EST). *Felony, Civil.*

Civil Records: Access: Mail, in person. Both court and visitors may perform in person searches. Search fee: $10.00 per name. Required to search: name, years to search. Civil cases indexed by defendant. Civil records on index cards from 1935. **Criminal Records:** Access: Mail, in person. Both court and visitors may perform in person searches. Search fee: $10.00 per name. Required to search: name, years to search. Criminal records on index cards from 1935. **General Information:** No sealed, youthful offender or sex abuse case records released. SASE required. Turnaround time 2 days. Copy fee: $.50 per page. Certification fee: $4.00. Fee payee: County Clerk. Personal checks accepted. Prepayment is required.

Surrogate Court Courthouse, 7660 State St, Lowville, NY 13367; 315-376-5344; Fax: 315-376-4145. Hours: 8:30AM-4:30PM (EST). *Probate.*

Note: Fee is $25 for under 25 years to $70 for over 70 years

Livingston County

Supreme & County Court 6 Court St, Rm 201, Geneseo, NY 14454; 716-243-7010. Hours: 8:30AM-4:30PM Oct-May; 8AM-4PM June-Sept (EST). *Felony, Civil.*

Civil Records: Access: Mail, in person. Both court and visitors may perform in person searches. Search fee: $2.50 per name per year. Required to search: name, years to search. Civil cases indexed by defendant, plaintiff. Civil records on computer since 1996. Plaintiff index available only on computer searches. **Criminal Records:** Access: Mail, in person. Both court and visitors may perform in person searches. Search fee: $2.50 per name per year. Required to search: name, years to search. Criminal records on computer since 1996. Plaintiff index available only on computer searches. **General Information:** No sealed or

youthful offender records released. SASE required. Turnaround time same day. Copy fee: $.50 per page. Certification fee: $4.00 plus $.50 per page after first 4. Fee payee: County Clerk. Personal checks accepted. Prepayment is required. Public access terminal is available.

Surrogate Court 2 Court St, Geneseo, NY 14454; 716-243-7095; Fax: 716-243-7583. Hours: 9AM-5PM (EST). *Probate.*

Madison County

Supreme & County Court County Office Bldg, PO Box 668, Wampsville, NY 13163; 315-366-2261; Fax: 315-366-2615. Hours: 9AM-5PM (EST). *Felony, Civil.*

Civil Records: Access: Mail, in person. Both court and visitors may perform in person searches. Search fee: $5.00 per name. Fee is per 5 years searched. Required to search: name, years to search. Civil cases indexed by defendant. Judgment records on computer from 1997, prior in books. **Criminal Records:** Access: Mail, in person. Both court and visitors may perform in person searches. Search fee: $5.00 per name. Per 5 years. Required to search: name, years to search, DOB. Criminal records on coumputer to 1989, previous years in books. **General Information:** No sealed, expunged, adoption, sex offense, juvenile or mental health records released. SASE required. Turnaround time 2 days. Copy fee: $1.00 for first page, $.50 each addl. Certification fee: $1.00. Minimum $4.00. Fee payee: County Clerk. Personal checks accepted. Prepayment is required.

Oneida City Court 109 N Main St, Oneida, NY 13421; 315-363-1310; Fax: 315-363-3230. Hours: 8:30AM-4:30PM (EST). *Misdemeanor, Civil Actions Under $15,000, Eviction, Small Claims.*

Civil Records: Access: Mail, in person. Only the court conducts in person searches; visitors may not. Search fee: $5.00 per name. Fee is for search prior to 1990, other years $16.00 per name. Required to search: name, years to search. Civil cases indexed by plaintiff. Civil records on computer from 1990, prior in books from 1980s. **Criminal Records:** Access: Mail, in person. Only the court conducts in person searches; visitors may not. Search fee: $16 fee is for 1989 forward; searches prior to 1989 are $5.00 per name. Required to search: name, years to search, DOB. Criminal records on computer from 1989. **General Information:** No sealed, expunged, sex offense, mental health or youthful offenders records released. SASE required. Turnaround time 1-2 days. Copy fee: $.50 per page. Certification fee: $5.00. Fee payee: City Court. Personal checks accepted. Prepayment is required.

Surrogate Court County Courthouse, North Court st, Wampsville, NY 13163; 315-366-2392; Fax: 315-366-2539. Hours: 9AM-5PM (EST). *Probate.*

Monroe County

Supreme & County Court County Office Bldg, 39 Main Street West, Rochester, NY 14614; 716-428-5151; Fax: 716-428-4698. Hours: 9AM-5PM (EST). *Felony, Civil.*

Civil Records: Access: Fax, mail, online, in person. Both court and visitors may perform in person searches. Search fee: $5.00 per name. Fee is per 2 years searched. Required to search: name, years to search. Civil cases indexed by defendant. Civil records on computer since 6/93, prior in books. The online system is open 7am to 7pm daily. No special software is need. Access is $.50

Orange County

County Clerk, 255-275 Main Street, Goshen, NY 10924. 845-291-2690. Fax: 845-291-2691.

Orleans County

County Clerk, 3 South Main Street, Courthouse Square, Albion, NY 14411-1498. 716-589-5334. Fax: 716-589-0181.

Oswego County

County Clerk, 46 East Bridge Street, Oswego, NY 13126. 315-349-8385. Fax: 315-343-8383.

Otsego County

County Clerk, P.O. Box 710, Cooperstown, NY 13326-0710. 607-547-4278. Fax: 607-547-7544.

Putnam County

County Clerk, 40 Gleneida Ave., Carmel, NY 10512. 845-225-3641. Fax: 845-228-0231.

Queens County

City Register, 144-06 94th Ave., Jamaica, NY 11435. 718-298-7000.

Online Access: Real Estate, Liens, Tax Assessor Records. Access to Queens County online records (including Boroughs of Brooklyn, Queens, Staten Island, Bronx and Manhattan) requires a $250 monthly fee and $5 per transaction fee. Records are kept 2-5 years. The system operates from 9AM-5PM M-F For information, contact Richard Reskin at 718-935-6523.

Rensselaer County

County Clerk, Courthouse, Congress & 2nd Street, Troy, NY 12180. 518-270-4080.

Richmond County

County Clerk, 18 Richmond Terrace, County Courthouse, Staten Island, NY 10301-1990. 718-390-5386.

Rockland County

County Clerk, 27 New Hempstead Road, New City, NY 10956. 845-638-5354. Fax: 845-638-5647.

Online Access: Real Estate, Liens. Access to Rockland County online records requires a $250 set up fee which includes software. There is also a monthly $150 minimum fee for use. The system is available 24 hours daily. Images back to 6/96 are viewable, and more are being added For information, contact Paul Pipearto at 914-638-5221. System includes criminal index since 1982 plus civil judgments, real estate records, tax

warrants. Case file pages can be ordered and faxed back.

Saratoga County

County Clerk, 40 McMaster Street, Ballston Spa, NY 12020. 518-885-2213. Fax: 518-884-4726.

Schenectady County

County Clerk, 620 State Street, Schenectady, NY 12305-2114. 518-388-4220. Fax: 518-388-4224. www.scpl.org

Online Access: Assessor. Records on the Schenectady County Property Assessments database are available free on the Internet at www.scpl.org/assessments. Includes records for City of Schenectady, Towns of Glenville and Nisayuna, and Village of Scotia. More planned.

Schoharie County

County Clerk, P.O. Box 549, Schoharie, NY 12157. 518-295-8316. Fax: 518-295-8338.

Schuyler County

County Clerk, 105 Ninth Street Unit 8, County Office Building, Watkins Glen, NY 14891. 607-535-8133.

Seneca County

County Clerk, 1 DiPronio Drive, Waterloo, NY 13165. 315-539-5655. Fax: 315-539-3789.

St. Lawrence County

County Clerk, 48 Court Street, Canton, NY 13617-1198. 315-379-2237. Fax: 315-379-2302.

Steuben County

County Clerk, 3 East Pulteney Square, County Office Building, Bath, NY 14810. 607-776-9631x3210. Fax: 607-776-7158.

www.pennynet.org/erwin

Online Access: Assessor. Records on the Town of Erwin Final Real Property Assessment Roll are available free on the Internet at www.penny.org/erwin/er95tax.htm. Village of Painted Post has not accepted this tax roll, thus the Erwin Assessment Roll does not apply to Painted Post.

Suffolk County

County Clerk, 310 Center Drive, Riverhead, NY 11901-3392. 631-852-2038. Fax: 631-852-2004.

Sullivan County

County Clerk, P.O. Box 5012, Monticello, NY 12701. 845-794-3000x3152.

Tioga County

County Clerk, P.O. Box 307, Owego, NY 13827. 607-687-8660. Fax: 607-687-4612.

Tompkins County

County Clerk, 320 North Tioga Street, Ithaca, NY 14850-4284. 607-274-5432.

Ulster County

County Clerk, P.O. Box 1800, Kingston, NY 12402-0800. 845-340-3288. Fax: 845-340-3299.

Online Access: Real Estate, Liens. Access to Ulster County online records requires a $25 monthly fee and a commitment to one year of service. Also, a $.05 per minute of use fee applies. Records date back to 1984. System operates 24 hours daily and supports baud rates of 9,600-28.8 For information, contact Valerie Harris at 914-340-5300. Lending agency information is available. Also, the Ulster County Parcel Viewer at http://216.132.131.214/ulster/ provides free access to tax parcel information. Search by GIS map, parcel ID #, street name, municipality, or selected criteria.

Warren County

County Clerk, Municipal Center, 1340 State Route 9, Lake George, NY 12845. 518-761-6426. Fax: 518-761-6551.

Washington County

County Clerk, 383 Broadway, Bldg A, Fort Edward, NY 12828. 518-746-2170. Fax: 518-746-2166.

Wayne County

County Clerk, P.O. Box 608, Lyons, NY 14489-0608. 315-946-5971. Fax: 315-946-5978.

Westchester County

County Clerk, 110 Dr. Martin Luther King Jr. Blvd., White Plains, NY 10601. 914-285-3098. Fax: 914-285-3172.

Wyoming County

County Clerk, P.O. Box 70, Warsaw, NY 14569-0070. 716-786-8810. Fax: 716-786-3703.

Yates County

County Clerk, 110 Court Street, Penn Yan, NY 14527. 315-536-5120. Fax: 315-536-5545.

You will usually be able to find the city name in the City/County Cross Reference below. In that case, it is a simple matter to determine the county from the cross reference. However, only the official US Postal Service city names are included in this index. There are an additional 40,000 place names that people use in their addresses. Therefore, we have also included a ZIP/City Cross Reference immediately following the City/County Cross Reference.

If you know the ZIP Code but the city name does not appear in the City/County Cross Reference index, look up the ZIP Code in the ZIP/City Cross Reference, find the city name, then look up the city name in the City/County Cross Reference. For example, you want to know the county for an address of Menands, NY 12204. There is no "Menands" in the City/County Cross Reference. The ZIP/City Cross Reference shows that ZIP Codes 12201-12288 are for the city of Albany. Looking back in the City/County Cross Reference, Albany is in Albany County.

City/County Cross Reference

ACCORD Ulster
ACRA Greene
ADAMS Jefferson
ADAMS BASIN Monroe
ADAMS CENTER Jefferson
ADDISON Steuben
ADIRONDACK Warren
AFTON (13730) Broome(51), Chenango(49)
AKRON (14001) Erie(92), Niagara(4), Genesee(4)
ALABAMA Genesee
ALBANY Albany
ALBERTSON Nassau
ALBION Orleans
ALCOVE Albany
ALDEN (14004) Erie(93), Wyoming(6), Genesee(2)
ALDER CREEK Oneida
ALEXANDER Genesee
ALEXANDRIA BAY Jefferson
ALFRED Allegany
ALFRED STATION (14803) Allegany(89), Steuben(11)
ALLEGANY Cattaraugus
ALLENTOWN Allegany
ALMA Allegany
ALMOND Allegany
ALPINE Schuyler
ALPLAUS Schenectady
ALTAMONT Albany
ALTMAR Oswego
ALTON Wayne
ALTONA Clinton
AMAGANSETT Suffolk
AMAWALK Westchester
AMENIA Dutchess
AMITYVILLE Suffolk
AMSTERDAM (12010) Montgomery(94), Schenectady(4), Fulton(1)
ANCRAM Columbia
ANCRAMDALE Columbia
ANDES Delaware
ANDOVER (14806) Allegany(84), Steuben(16)
ANGELICA Allegany
ANGOLA Erie
ANNANDALE ON HUDSON Dutchess
ANTWERP (13608) Jefferson(88), St. Lawrence(12)
APALACHIN Tioga
APO
APPLETON Niagara
APULIA STATION Onondaga
AQUEBOGUE Suffolk
ARCADE (14009) Wyoming(90), Cattaraugus(10)
ARDEN Orange
ARDSLEY Westchester
ARDSLEY ON HUDSON Westchester
ARGYLE Washington
ARKPORT (14807) Steuben(79), Allegany(21)

ARKVILLE (12406) Delaware(65), Ulster(36)
ARMONK Westchester
ASHLAND Greene
ASHVILLE Chautauqua
ATHENS Greene
ATHOL Warren
ATHOL SPRINGS Erie
ATLANTA Steuben
ATLANTIC BEACH Nassau
ATTICA (14011) Wyoming(91), Genesee(9)
AU SABLE FORKS (12912) Clinton(96), Essex(4)
AUBURN Cayuga
AURIESVILLE Montgomery
AURORA Cayuga
AUSTERLITZ Columbia
AVA Oneida
AVERILL PARK Rensselaer
AVOCA Steuben
AVON Livingston
BABYLON Suffolk
BAINBRIDGE (13733) Chenango(97), Delaware(2), Otsego(2)
BAKERS MILLS Warren
BALDWIN Nassau
BALDWIN PLACE (10505) Westchester(71), Putnam(29)
BALDWINSVILLE Onondaga
BALLSTON LAKE Saratoga
BALLSTON SPA Saratoga
BALMAT St. Lawrence
BANGALL Dutchess
BANGOR Franklin
BARKER (14012) Niagara(95), Orleans(5)
BARNEVELD Oneida
BARRYTOWN Dutchess
BARRYVILLE Sullivan
BARTON Tioga
BASOM Genesee
BATAVIA Genesee
BATH Steuben
BAY SHORE Suffolk
BAYPORT Suffolk
BAYVILLE Nassau
BEACON Dutchess
BEAR MOUNTAIN Rockland
BEARSVILLE Ulster
BEAVER DAMS (14812) Schuyler(44), Chemung(33), Steuben(23)
BEAVER FALLS Lewis
BEDFORD Westchester
BEDFORD HILLS Westchester
BELFAST Allegany
BELLEVILLE Jefferson
BELLMORE Nassau
BELLONA Yates
BELLPORT Suffolk
BELLVALE Orange
BELMONT Allegany
BEMUS POINT Chautauqua
BERGEN (14416) Genesee(90), Monroe(10)

BERKSHIRE (13736) Tioga(89), Tompkins(6), Broome(5)
BERLIN Rensselaer
BERNE (12023) Albany(94), Schoharie(6)
BERNHARDS BAY Oswego
BETHEL Sullivan
BETHPAGE Nassau
BIBLE SCHOOL PARK Broome
BIG FLATS (14814) Chemung(86), Steuben(14)
BIG INDIAN Ulster
BILLINGS Dutchess
BINGHAMTON Broome
BLACK CREEK Allegany
BLACK RIVER Jefferson
BLAUVELT Rockland
BLISS (14024) Wyoming(90), Allegany(10)
BLODGETT MILLS Cortland
BLOOMFIELD Ontario
BLOOMING GROVE Orange
BLOOMINGBURG (12721) Sullivan(92), Orange(8)
BLOOMINGDALE (12913) Essex(75), Franklin(26)
BLOOMINGTON Ulster
BLOOMVILLE Delaware
BLOSSVALE Oneida
BLUE MOUNTAIN LAKE Hamilton
BLUE POINT Suffolk
BOHEMIA Suffolk
BOICEVILLE Ulster
BOLIVAR Allegany
BOLTON LANDING Warren
BOMBAY (12914) Franklin(96), St. Lawrence(4)
BOONVILLE (13309) Oneida(95), Lewis(5)
BOSTON Erie
BOUCKVILLE Madison
BOUQUET Essex
BOVINA CENTER Delaware
BOWMANSVILLE Erie
BRADFORD (14815) Schuyler(66), Steuben(34)
BRAINARD Rensselaer
BRAINARDSVILLE Franklin
BRANCHPORT (14418) Yates(91), Steuben(10)
BRANT Erie
BRANT LAKE Warren
BRANTINGHAM Lewis
BRASHER FALLS St. Lawrence
BREESPORT Chemung
BRENTWOOD Suffolk
BREWERTON Onondaga
BREWSTER (10509) Putnam(98), Westchester(2)
BRIARCLIFF MANOR Westchester
BRIDGEHAMPTON Suffolk
BRIDGEPORT (13030) Onondaga(79), Madison(21)
BRIDGEWATER Oneida
BRIER HILL St. Lawrence
BRIGHTWATERS Suffolk

BROADALBIN (12025) Fulton(97), Saratoga(3)
BROCKPORT Monroe
BROCTON Chautauqua
BRONX Bronx
BRONX New York
BRONXVILLE Westchester
BROOKFIELD Madison
BROOKHAVEN Suffolk
BROOKLYN Kings
BROOKTONDALE (14817) Tompkins(94), Tioga(6)
BROOKVIEW Rensselaer
BROWNVILLE Jefferson
BRUSHTON Franklin
BUCHANAN Westchester
BUFFALO Erie
BULLVILLE Orange
BURDETT Schuyler
BURKE Franklin
BURLINGHAM Sullivan
BURLINGTON FLATS Otsego
BURNT HILLS (12027) Saratoga(81), Schenectady(19)
BURT Niagara
BUSKIRK (12028) Rensselaer(94), Washington(6)
BYRON (14422) Genesee(98), Orleans(2)
CADYVILLE Clinton
CAIRO Greene
CALCIUM Jefferson
CALEDONIA (14423) Livingston(98), Monroe(2)
CALLICOON Sullivan
CALLICOON CENTER Sullivan
CALVERTON Suffolk
CAMBRIDGE Washington
CAMDEN (13316) Oneida(98), Lewis(1)
CAMERON Steuben
CAMERON MILLS Steuben
CAMILLUS Onondaga
CAMPBELL Steuben
CAMPBELL HALL Orange
CANAAN Columbia
CANAJOHARIE Montgomery
CANANDAIGUA Ontario
CANASERAGA (14822) Allegany(88), Livingston(12)
CANASTOTA Madison
CANDOR Tioga
CANEADEA Allegany
CANISTEO Steuben
CANTON St. Lawrence
CAPE VINCENT Jefferson
CARLE PLACE Nassau
CARLISLE Schoharie
CARMEL Putnam
CAROGA LAKE Fulton
CARTHAGE (13619) Jefferson(81), St. Lawrence(11), Lewis(8)
CASSADAGA Chautauqua
CASSVILLE Oneida
CASTILE Wyoming
CASTLE CREEK Broome

CASTLE POINT Dutchess
CASTLETON ON HUDSON Rensselaer
CASTORLAND Lewis
CATO Cayuga
CATSKILL Greene
CATTARAUGUS Cattaraugus
CAYUGA Cayuga
CAYUTA (14824) Schuyler(70),
   Chemung(30)
CAZENOVIA (13035) Madison(96),
   Onondaga(4)
CEDARHURST Nassau
CELORON Chautauqua
CEMENTON Greene
CENTER MORICHES Suffolk
CENTEREACH Suffolk
CENTERPORT Suffolk
CENTERVILLE Allegany
CENTRAL BRIDGE Schoharie
CENTRAL ISLIP Suffolk
CENTRAL SQUARE Oswego
CENTRAL VALLEY Orange
CERES Allegany
CHADWICKS Oneida
CHAFFEE (14030) Erie(77),
   Cattaraugus(18), Wyoming(5)
CHAMPLAIN Clinton
CHAPPAQUA Westchester
CHARLOTTEVILLE (12036) Schoharie(77),
   Otsego(23)
CHASE MILLS St. Lawrence
CHATEAUGAY Franklin
CHATHAM Columbia
CHAUMONT Jefferson
CHAUTAUQUA Chautauqua
CHAZY Clinton
CHELSEA Dutchess
CHEMUNG Chemung
CHENANGO BRIDGE Broome
CHENANGO FORKS (13746) Broome(73),
   Chenango(27)
CHERRY CREEK Chautauqua
CHERRY PLAIN Rensselaer
CHERRY VALLEY Otsego
CHESTER Orange
CHESTERTOWN Warren
CHICHESTER Ulster
CHILDWOLD St. Lawrence
CHIPPEWA BAY St. Lawrence
CHITTENANGO Madison
CHURCHVILLE Monroe
CHURUBUSCO Clinton
CICERO Onondaga
CINCINNATUS (13040) Cortland(97),
   Chenango(3)
CIRCLEVILLE Orange
CLARENCE Erie
CLARENCE CENTER (14032) Erie(98),
   Niagara(2)
CLARENDON Orleans
CLARK MILLS Oneida
CLARKSON Monroe
CLARKSVILLE Albany
CLARYVILLE (12725) Ulster(60),
   Sullivan(41)
CLAVERACK Columbia
CLAY Onondaga
CLAYTON Jefferson
CLAYVILLE (13322) Herkimer(81),
   Oneida(19)
CLEMONS Washington
CLEVELAND (13042) Oswego(92),
   Oneida(8)
CLEVERDALE Warren
CLIFTON PARK Saratoga
CLIFTON SPRINGS Ontario
CLIMAX Greene
CLINTON Oneida
CLINTON CORNERS Dutchess
CLINTONDALE Ulster
CLOCKVILLE Madison
CLYDE (14433) Wayne(95), Seneca(5)

CLYMER Chautauqua
COBLESKILL Schoharie
COCHECTON (12726) Sullivan(99),
   Delaware(2)
COCHECTON CENTER Sullivan
COEYMANS Albany
COEYMANS HOLLOW (12046)
   Albany(98), Greene(2)
COHOCTON Steuben
COHOES Albany
COLD BROOK Herkimer
COLD SPRING Putnam
COLD SPRING HARBOR Suffolk
COLDEN Erie
COLLIERSVILLE Otsego
COLLINS Erie
COLLINS CENTER Erie
COLTON St. Lawrence
COLUMBIAVILLE Columbia
COMMACK Suffolk
COMSTOCK Washington
CONESUS Livingston
CONEWANGO VALLEY (14726)
   Cattaraugus(89), Chautauqua(11)
CONGERS Rockland
CONKLIN Broome
CONNELLY Ulster
CONSTABLE Franklin
CONSTABLEVILLE Lewis
CONSTANTIA Oswego
COOPERS PLAINS Steuben
COOPERSTOWN Otsego
COPAKE Columbia
COPAKE FALLS Columbia
COPENHAGEN (13626) Lewis(90),
   Jefferson(10)
COPIAGUE Suffolk
CORAM Suffolk
CORBETTSVILLE Broome
CORFU (14036) Genesee(98), Erie(2)
CORINTH Saratoga
CORNING (14830) Steuben(99),
   Chemung(1)
CORNING Steuben
CORNWALL Orange
CORNWALL ON HUDSON Orange
CORNWALLVILLE Greene
CORTLAND (13045) Cortland(97),
   Tompkins(2), Cayuga(1)
COSSAYUNA Washington
COTTEKILL Ulster
COWLESVILLE (14037) Wyoming(77),
   Erie(23)
COXSACKIE Greene
CRAGSMOOR Ulster
CRANBERRY LAKE St. Lawrence
CRARYVILLE Columbia
CRITTENDEN Erie
CROGHAN Lewis
CROMPOND Westchester
CROPSEYVILLE Rensselaer
CROSS RIVER Westchester
CROTON FALLS Westchester
CROTON ON HUDSON Westchester
CROWN POINT Essex
CUBA (14727) Allegany(80),
   Cattaraugus(20)
CUDDEBACKVILLE Orange
CUTCHOGUE Suffolk
CUYLER (13050) Cortland(96),
   Onondaga(5)
DALE Wyoming
DALTON (14836) Livingston(60),
   Allegany(41)
DANNEMORA Clinton
DANSVILLE (14437) Livingston(91),
   Steuben(9)
DARIEN CENTER (14040) Genesee(87),
   Wyoming(13)
DAVENPORT (13750) Delaware(98),
   Otsego(2)
DAVENPORT CENTER Delaware

DAYTON Cattaraugus
DE KALB JUNCTION St. Lawrence
DE LANCEY Delaware
DE PEYSTER St. Lawrence
DE RUYTER (13052) Madison(70),
   Chenango(27), Onondaga(3)
DEANSBORO Oneida
DEER PARK Suffolk
DEER RIVER Lewis
DEFERIET Jefferson
DELANSON (12053) Schenectady(81),
   Albany(16), Schoharie(3)
DELEVAN Cattaraugus
DELHI Delaware
DELMAR Albany
DELPHI FALLS Onondaga
DENMARK Lewis
DENVER Delaware
DEPAUVILLE Jefferson
DEPEW Erie
DEPOSIT (13754) Broome(58),
   Delaware(42)
DERBY Erie
DEWITTVILLE Chautauqua
DEXTER Jefferson
DIAMOND POINT Warren
DICKINSON CENTER (12930)
   Franklin(95), St. Lawrence(5)
DOBBS FERRY Westchester
DOLGEVILLE (13329) Herkimer(87),
   Fulton(13)
DORMANSVILLE Albany
DOVER PLAINS Dutchess
DOWNSVILLE Delaware
DRESDEN Yates
DRYDEN (13053) Tompkins(83),
   Cortland(17)
DUANESBURG Schenectady
DUNDEE (14837) Yates(76), Schuyler(22),
   Steuben(2)
DUNKIRK Chautauqua
DURHAM Greene
DURHAMVILLE Oneida
EAGLE BAY Herkimer
EAGLE BRIDGE (12057) Rensselaer(80),
   Washington(20)
EAGLE HARBOR Orleans
EARLTON Greene
EARLVILLE (13332) Chenango(52),
   Madison(48)
EAST AMHERST Erie
EAST AURORA Erie
EAST BERNE Albany
EAST BETHANY (14054) Genesee(91),
   Wyoming(9)
EAST BLOOMFIELD Ontario
EAST BRANCH Delaware
EAST CHATHAM Columbia
EAST CONCORD Erie
EAST DURHAM Greene
EAST FREETOWN Cortland
EAST GREENBUSH Rensselaer
EAST GREENWICH Washington
EAST HAMPTON Suffolk
EAST HOMER Cortland
EAST ISLIP Suffolk
EAST JEWETT Greene
EAST MARION Suffolk
EAST MEADOW Nassau
EAST MEREDITH Delaware
EAST MORICHES Suffolk
EAST NASSAU (12062) Columbia(87),
   Rensselaer(13)
EAST NORTHPORT Suffolk
EAST NORWICH Nassau
EAST OTTO Cattaraugus
EAST PALMYRA Wayne
EAST PEMBROKE Genesee
EAST PHARSALIA Chenango
EAST QUOGUE Suffolk
EAST RANDOLPH Cattaraugus
EAST ROCHESTER Monroe

EAST ROCKAWAY Nassau
EAST SCHODACK Rensselaer
EAST SETAUKET Suffolk
EAST SPRINGFIELD Otsego
EAST SYRACUSE Onondaga
EAST WILLIAMSON Wayne
EAST WORCESTER Otsego
EASTCHESTER Westchester
EASTPORT Suffolk
EATON Madison
EDEN Erie
EDMESTON Otsego
EDWARDS St. Lawrence
ELBA (14058) Genesee(95), Orleans(5)
ELBRIDGE (13060) Onondaga(97),
   Cayuga(3)
ELDRED Sullivan
ELIZABETHTOWN Essex
ELIZAVILLE Columbia
ELKA PARK Greene
ELLENBURG Clinton
ELLENBURG CENTER Clinton
ELLENBURG DEPOT Clinton
ELLENVILLE Ulster
ELLICOTTVILLE Cattaraugus
ELLINGTON Chautauqua
ELLISBURG Jefferson
ELMA Erie
ELMIRA Chemung
ELMONT Nassau
ELMSFORD Westchester
ENDICOTT (13760) Broome(88), Tioga(12)
ENDICOTT Broome
ENDWELL Broome
ERIEVILLE Madison
ERIN Chemung
ESOPUS Ulster
ESPERANCE (12066) Montgomery(85),
   Schoharie(12), Schenectady(3)
ESSEX Essex
ETNA Tompkins
EVANS MILLS Jefferson
FABIUS Onondaga
FAIR HAVEN (13064) Oswego(94),
   Onondaga(6)
FAIRFIELD Herkimer
FAIRPORT Monroe
FALCONER Chautauqua
FALLSBURG Sullivan
FANCHER Orleans
FAR ROCKAWAY Queens
FARMERSVILLE STATION (14060)
   Allegany(55), Cattaraugus(45)
FARMINGDALE (11735) Nassau(72),
   Suffolk(28)
FARMINGDALE Nassau
FARMINGTON Ontario
FARMINGVILLE Suffolk
FARNHAM Erie
FAYETTE Seneca
FAYETTEVILLE Onondaga
FELTS MILLS Jefferson
FERNDALE Sullivan
FEURA BUSH Albany
FILLMORE Allegany
FINDLEY LAKE Chautauqua
FINE St. Lawrence
FISHERS Ontario
FISHERS ISLAND Suffolk
FISHERS LANDING Jefferson
FISHKILL Dutchess
FISHS EDDY Delaware
FLEISCHMANNS (12430) Delaware(78),
   Greene(22)
FLORAL PARK Nassau
FLORAL PARK Queens
FLORIDA Orange
FLUSHING Queens
FLY CREEK Otsego
FONDA (12068) Montgomery(98), Fulton(2)
FORESTBURGH Sullivan

FORESTPORT (13338) Oneida(97), Herkimer(3)
FORESTVILLE Chautauqua
FORT ANN Washington
FORT COVINGTON Franklin
FORT DRUM Jefferson
FORT EDWARD (12828) Washington(77), Saratoga(23)
FORT HUNTER Montgomery
FORT JACKSON St. Lawrence
FORT JOHNSON (12070) Montgomery(84), Fulton(16)
FORT MONTGOMERY Orange
FORT PLAIN (13339) Montgomery(72), Herkimer(17), Fulton(11)
FPO
FRANKFORT Herkimer
FRANKLIN Delaware
FRANKLIN SPRINGS Oneida
FRANKLIN SQUARE Nassau
FRANKLINVILLE (14737) Cattaraugus(99), Allegany(1)
FREDONIA Chautauqua
FREEDOM (14065) Cattaraugus(54), Allegany(46)
FREEHOLD Greene
FREEPORT Nassau
FREEVILLE Tompkins
FREMONT CENTER Sullivan
FREWSBURG (14738) Chautauqua(91), Cattaraugus(9)
FRIENDSHIP Allegany
FULTON Oswego
FULTONHAM Schoharie
FULTONVILLE Montgomery
GABRIELS Franklin
GAINESVILLE Wyoming
GALLUPVILLE Schoharie
GALWAY Saratoga
GANSEVOORT Saratoga
GARDEN CITY Nassau
GARDINER Ulster
GARNERVILLE Rockland
GARRATTSVILLE Otsego
GARRISON Putnam
GASPORT Niagara
GENESEO Livingston
GENEVA (14456) Ontario(94), Seneca(6)
GENOA Cayuga
GEORGETOWN (13072) Madison(89), Chenango(12)
GEORGETOWN Chenango
GERMANTOWN Columbia
GERRY Chautauqua
GETZVILLE Erie
GHENT Columbia
GILBERTSVILLE Otsego
GILBOA Schoharie
GLASCO Ulster
GLEN AUBREY Broome
GLEN COVE Nassau
GLEN HEAD Nassau
GLEN OAKS Queens
GLEN SPEY Sullivan
GLEN WILD Sullivan
GLENFIELD Lewis
GLENFORD Ulster
GLENHAM Dutchess
GLENMONT Albany
GLENS FALLS Warren
GLENWOOD Erie
GLENWOOD LANDING Nassau
GLOVERSVILLE Fulton
GODEFFROY Orange
GOLDENS BRIDGE Westchester
GORHAM Ontario
GOSHEN Orange
GOUVERNEUR St. Lawrence
GOWANDA (14070) Cattaraugus(59), Erie(42)
GRAFTON Rensselaer

GRAHAMSVILLE (12740) Sullivan(87), Ulster(13)
GRAND GORGE Delaware
GRAND ISLAND Erie
GRANITE SPRINGS Westchester
GRANVILLE Washington
GREAT BEND Jefferson
GREAT NECK Nassau
GREAT RIVER Suffolk
GREAT VALLEY Cattaraugus
GREENE (13778) Chenango(82), Broome(18)
GREENFIELD CENTER Saratoga
GREENFIELD PARK Ulster
GREENHURST Chautauqua
GREENLAWN Suffolk
GREENPORT Suffolk
GREENVALE Nassau
GREENVILLE (12083) Greene(81), Albany(19)
GREENWICH Washington
GREENWOOD Steuben
GREENWOOD LAKE Orange
GREIG Lewis
GROTON (13073) Tompkins(99), Cayuga(1)
GROVELAND Livingston
GUILDERLAND Albany
GUILDERLAND CENTER Albany
GUILFORD Chenango
HADLEY (12835) Saratoga(98), Warren(2)
HAGAMAN (12086) Montgomery(95), Fulton(3), Saratoga(2)
HAGUE (99999) Warren(99), Essex(1)
HAILESBORO St. Lawrence
HAINES FALLS Greene
HALCOTTSVILLE Delaware
HALL Ontario
HAMBURG Erie
HAMDEN Delaware
HAMILTON Madison
HAMLIN (14464) Monroe(97), Orleans(3)
HAMMOND St. Lawrence
HAMMONDSPORT (14840) Steuben(97), Schuyler(3)
HAMPTON Washington
HAMPTON BAYS Suffolk
HANCOCK Delaware
HANKINS Sullivan
HANNACROIX (12087) Greene(94), Albany(6)
HANNAWA FALLS St. Lawrence
HANNIBAL Oswego
HARFORD Cortland
HARPERSFIELD Delaware
HARPURSVILLE (13787) Broome(89), Chenango(12)
HARRIMAN Orange
HARRIS Sullivan
HARRISON Westchester
HARRISVILLE (13648) St. Lawrence(65), Lewis(35)
HARTFORD Washington
HARTSDALE Westchester
HARTWICK Otsego
HARTWICK SEMINARY Otsego
HASTINGS Oswego
HASTINGS ON HUDSON Westchester
HAUPPAUGE Suffolk
HAVERSTRAW Rockland
HAWTHORNE Westchester
HECTOR Schuyler
HELENA St. Lawrence
HELMUTH Erie
HEMLOCK (14466) Ontario(60), Livingston(40)
HEMPSTEAD Nassau
HENDERSON Jefferson
HENDERSON HARBOR Jefferson
HENRIETTA Monroe
HENSONVILLE Greene
HERKIMER Herkimer

HERMON St. Lawrence
HEUVELTON St. Lawrence
HEWLETT Nassau
HICKSVILLE Nassau
HIGH FALLS Ulster
HIGHLAND Ulster
HIGHLAND FALLS Orange
HIGHLAND LAKE Sullivan
HIGHLAND MILLS Orange
HIGHMOUNT Ulster
HILLBURN Rockland
HILLSDALE Columbia
HILTON Monroe
HIMROD Yates
HINCKLEY Oneida
HINSDALE Cattaraugus
HOBART Delaware
HOFFMEISTER Hamilton
HOGANSBURG Franklin
HOLBROOK Suffolk
HOLLAND Erie
HOLLAND PATENT Oneida
HOLLEY (14470) Orleans(97), Monroe(3)
HOLLOWVILLE Columbia
HOLMES (12531) Dutchess(74), Putnam(26)
HOLTSVILLE Suffolk
HOMER Cortland
HONEOYE Ontario
HONEOYE FALLS (14472) Monroe(91), Livingston(7), Ontario(3)
HOOSICK Rensselaer
HOOSICK FALLS Rensselaer
HOPEWELL JUNCTION (12533) Dutchess(99), Putnam(1)
HOPKINTON St. Lawrence
HORNELL Steuben
HORSEHEADS Chemung
HORTONVILLE Sullivan
HOUGHTON Allegany
HOWELLS Orange
HOWES CAVE Schoharie
HUBBARDSVILLE Madison
HUDSON Columbia
HUDSON FALLS Washington
HUGHSONVILLE Dutchess
HUGUENOT Orange
HULETTS LANDING Washington
HUME Allegany
HUNT (14846) Livingston(77), Allegany(23)
HUNTER Greene
HUNTINGTON Suffolk
HUNTINGTON STATION Suffolk
HURLEY Ulster
HURLEYVILLE Sullivan
HYDE PARK Dutchess
ILION Herkimer
INDIAN LAKE Hamilton
INDUSTRY Monroe
INLET Hamilton
INTERLAKEN Seneca
INWOOD Nassau
INWOOD Queens
IONIA (14475) Ontario(90), Monroe(11)
IRVING (14081) Chautauqua(54), Erie(44), Cattaraugus(2)
IRVINGTON Westchester
ISLAND PARK Nassau
ISLIP Suffolk
ISLIP TERRACE Suffolk
ITHACA Tompkins
JACKSONVILLE Tompkins
JAMAICA Queens
JAMESPORT Suffolk
JAMESTOWN Chautauqua
JAMESVILLE Onondaga
JASPER Steuben
JAVA CENTER Wyoming
JAVA VILLAGE Wyoming
JAY Essex
JEFFERSON (12093) Schoharie(73), Delaware(27)

JEFFERSON VALLEY Westchester
JEFFERSONVILLE Sullivan
JERICHO Nassau
JEWETT Greene
JOHNSBURG Warren
JOHNSON Orange
JOHNSON CITY Broome
JOHNSONVILLE (12094) Rensselaer(99), Washington(1)
JOHNSTOWN (12095) Fulton(99), Montgomery(1)
JORDAN Onondaga
JORDANVILLE (13361) Herkimer(98), Otsego(2)
KANONA Steuben
KATONAH Westchester
KATTSKILL BAY (12844) Warren(78), Washington(22)
KAUNEONGA LAKE Sullivan
KEENE Essex
KEENE VALLEY Essex
KEESEVILLE (12944) Clinton(85), Essex(15)
KEESEVILLE Clinton
KENDALL (14476) Orleans(96), Monroe(4)
KENNEDY (14747) Chautauqua(89), Cattaraugus(11)
KENOZA LAKE Sullivan
KENT Orleans
KERHONKSON Ulster
KEUKA PARK Yates
KIAMESHA LAKE Sullivan
KILL BUCK Cattaraugus
KILLAWOG Broome
KINDERHOOK Columbia
KING FERRY Cayuga
KINGS PARK Suffolk
KINGSTON Ulster
KIRKVILLE (13082) Onondaga(53), Madison(47)
KIRKWOOD Broome
KNAPP CREEK Cattaraugus
KNOWLESVILLE Orleans
KNOX Albany
KNOXBORO Oneida
LA FARGEVILLE Jefferson
LA FAYETTE Onondaga
LACONA Oswego
LAGRANGEVILLE Dutchess
LAKE CLEAR Franklin
LAKE GEORGE Warren
LAKE GROVE Suffolk
LAKE HILL Ulster
LAKE HUNTINGTON Sullivan
LAKE KATRINE Ulster
LAKE LUZERNE Warren
LAKE PEEKSKILL Putnam
LAKE PLACID Essex
LAKE PLEASANT Hamilton
LAKE VIEW Erie
LAKEMONT Yates
LAKEVILLE Livingston
LAKEWOOD Chautauqua
LANCASTER Erie
LANESVILLE Greene
LANSING Tompkins
LARCHMONT Westchester
LATHAM Albany
LAUREL Suffolk
LAURENS Otsego
LAWRENCE Nassau
LAWRENCEVILLE St. Lawrence
LAWTONS Erie
LAWYERSVILLE Schoharie
LE ROY (14482) Genesee(96), Livingston(3)
LEBANON Madison
LEBANON SPRINGS Columbia
LEE CENTER Oneida
LEEDS Greene
LEICESTER (14481) Livingston(99), Wyoming(1)

LEON Cattaraugus
LEONARDSVILLE Madison
LEVITTOWN Nassau
LEW BEACH (12753) Ulster(58), Sullivan(38), Delaware(4)
LEWIS Essex
LEWISTON Niagara
LEXINGTON Greene
LIBERTY Sullivan
LILY DALE Chautauqua
LIMA (14485) Livingston(95), Ontario(5)
LIMERICK Jefferson
LIMESTONE Cattaraugus
LINCOLNDALE Westchester
LINDENHURST Suffolk
LINDLEY Steuben
LINWOOD Genesee
LISBON St. Lawrence
LISLE Broome
LITTLE FALLS Herkimer
LITTLE GENESEE Allegany
LITTLE VALLEY Cattaraugus
LITTLE YORK Cortland
LIVERPOOL Onondaga
LIVINGSTON Columbia
LIVINGSTON MANOR (12758) Sullivan(93), Ulster(7)
LIVONIA (14487) Livingston(92), Ontario(8)
LIVONIA CENTER Livingston
LOCH SHELDRAKE Sullivan
LOCKE (13092) Tompkins(64), Cayuga(36)
LOCKPORT Niagara
LOCKWOOD (14859) Tioga(60), Chemung(40)
LOCUST VALLEY Nassau
LODI Seneca
LONG BEACH Nassau
LONG EDDY (12760) Sullivan(63), Delaware(37)
LONG ISLAND CITY Queens
LONG LAKE Hamilton
LORRAINE Jefferson
LOWMAN Chemung
LOWVILLE Lewis
LYCOMING Oswego
LYNBROOK Nassau
LYNDONVILLE (14098) Orleans(98), Niagara(2)
LYON MOUNTAIN (12952) Clinton(98), Essex(2)
LYON MOUNTAIN (12955) Clinton(98), Franklin(3)
LYONS (14489) Wayne(95), Ontario(3), Seneca(2)
LYONS FALLS Lewis
LYSANDER Onondaga
MACEDON (14502) Wayne(97), Monroe(3)
MACHIAS Cattaraugus
MADISON (13402) Madison(80), Oneida(20)
MADRID St. Lawrence
MAHOPAC (10541) Putnam(99), Westchester(1)
MAHOPAC FALLS Putnam
MAINE Broome
MALDEN BRIDGE Columbia
MALDEN ON HUDSON Ulster
MALLORY Oswego
MALONE Franklin
MALVERNE Nassau
MAMARONECK Westchester
MANCHESTER Ontario
MANHASSET Nassau
MANLIUS Onondaga
MANNSVILLE (13661) Jefferson(98), Oswego(2)
MANORVILLE Suffolk
MAPLE SPRINGS Chautauqua
MAPLE VIEW Oswego
MAPLECREST Greene
MARATHON (13803) Cortland(92), Broome(8)

MARCELLUS Onondaga
MARCY Oneida
MARGARETVILLE Delaware
MARIETTA Onondaga
MARILLA Erie
MARION Wayne
MARLBORO (12542) Ulster(94), Orange(6)
MARTINSBURG Lewis
MARTVILLE (13111) Cayuga(88), Oswego(12)
MARYKNOLL Westchester
MARYLAND Otsego
MASONVILLE Delaware
MASSAPEQUA Nassau
MASSAPEQUA PARK Nassau
MASSENA St. Lawrence
MASTIC Suffolk
MASTIC BEACH Suffolk
MATTITUCK Suffolk
MATTYDALE Onondaga
MAYBROOK Orange
MAYFIELD Fulton
MAYVILLE Chautauqua
MC CONNELLSVILLE Oneida
MC DONOUGH Chenango
MC GRAW Cortland
MC LEAN Tompkins
MECHANICVILLE (12118) Saratoga(97), Rensselaer(3)
MECKLENBURG Schuyler
MEDFORD Suffolk
MEDINA Orleans
MEDUSA Albany
MELLENVILLE Columbia
MELROSE Rensselaer
MELVILLE Suffolk
MEMPHIS Onondaga
MENDON Monroe
MERIDALE Delaware
MERIDIAN Cayuga
MERRICK Nassau
MEXICO Oswego
MID HUDSON Orange
MID ISLAND Suffolk
MIDDLE FALLS Washington
MIDDLE GRANVILLE Washington
MIDDLE GROVE Saratoga
MIDDLE ISLAND Suffolk
MIDDLEBURGH (12122) Albany(54), Schoharie(47)
MIDDLEPORT (14105) Niagara(94), Orleans(4), Genesee(2)
MIDDLESEX Yates
MIDDLETOWN Orange
MIDDLEVILLE Herkimer
MILFORD Otsego
MILL NECK Nassau
MILLBROOK Dutchess
MILLER PLACE Suffolk
MILLERTON (12546) Dutchess(91), Columbia(9)
MILLPORT (14864) Chemung(81), Schuyler(19)
MILLWOOD Westchester
MILTON Ulster
MINEOLA Nassau
MINERVA Essex
MINETTO Oswego
MINEVILLE Essex
MINOA Onondaga
MODEL CITY Niagara
MODENA Ulster
MOHAWK Herkimer
MOHEGAN LAKE Westchester
MOIRA Franklin
MONGAUP VALLEY Sullivan
MONROE Orange
MONSEY Rockland
MONTAUK Suffolk
MONTEZUMA Cayuga
MONTGOMERY Orange
MONTICELLO Sullivan

MONTOUR FALLS Schuyler
MONTROSE Westchester
MOOERS Clinton
MOOERS FORKS Clinton
MORAVIA Cayuga
MORIAH Essex
MORIAH CENTER Essex
MORICHES Suffolk
MORRIS Otsego
MORRISONVILLE Clinton
MORRISTOWN St. Lawrence
MORRISVILLE Madison
MORTON Orleans
MOTTVILLE Onondaga
MOUNT KISCO Westchester
MOUNT MARION Ulster
MOUNT MORRIS Livingston
MOUNT SINAI Suffolk
MOUNT TREMPER Ulster
MOUNT UPTON (13809) Chenango(72), Otsego(28)
MOUNT VERNON Westchester
MOUNT VISION Otsego
MOUNTAIN DALE Sullivan
MOUNTAINVILLE Orange
MUMFORD Monroe
MUNNSVILLE Madison
NANUET Rockland
NAPANOCH Ulster
NAPLES (14512) Ontario(74), Yates(22), Steuben(4)
NARROWSBURG Sullivan
NASSAU Rensselaer
NATURAL BRIDGE (13665) Jefferson(64), Lewis(36)
NEDROW Onondaga
NELLISTON Montgomery
NESCONSET Suffolk
NEVERSINK Sullivan
NEW BALTIMORE Greene
NEW BERLIN Chenango
NEW CITY Rockland
NEW HAMPTON Orange
NEW HARTFORD Oneida
NEW HAVEN Oswego
NEW HYDE PARK Nassau
NEW KINGSTON Delaware
NEW LEBANON Columbia
NEW LISBON Otsego
NEW MILFORD Orange
NEW PALTZ Ulster
NEW ROCHELLE Westchester
NEW RUSSIA Essex
NEW SUFFOLK Suffolk
NEW WINDSOR Orange
NEW WOODSTOCK (13122) Onondaga(59), Madison(41)
NEW YORK New York
NEW YORK MILLS Oneida
NEWARK (14513) Wayne(98), Ontario(2)
NEWARK VALLEY (13811) Tioga(94), Broome(6)
NEWBURGH Orange
NEWCOMB Essex
NEWFANE Niagara
NEWFIELD Tompkins
NEWPORT Herkimer
NEWTON FALLS St. Lawrence
NEWTONVILLE Albany
NIAGARA FALLS Niagara
NIAGARA UNIVERSITY Niagara
NICHOLS Tioga
NICHOLVILLE St. Lawrence
NINEVEH (13813) Broome(86), Chenango(14)
NIOBE Chautauqua
NIVERVILLE Columbia
NORFOLK St. Lawrence
NORTH BABYLON Suffolk
NORTH BANGOR Franklin
NORTH BAY Oneida
NORTH BLENHEIM Schoharie

NORTH BOSTON Erie
NORTH BRANCH Sullivan
NORTH BROOKFIELD Madison
NORTH CHATHAM Columbia
NORTH CHILI Monroe
NORTH CLYMER Chautauqua
NORTH COHOCTON Steuben
NORTH COLLINS Erie
NORTH CREEK Warren
NORTH EVANS Erie
NORTH GRANVILLE Washington
NORTH GREECE Monroe
NORTH HOOSICK Rensselaer
NORTH HUDSON Essex
NORTH JAVA Wyoming
NORTH LAWRENCE (12967) St. Lawrence(98), Franklin(2)
NORTH NORWICH Chenango
NORTH PITCHER Chenango
NORTH RIVER Warren
NORTH ROSE Wayne
NORTH SALEM Westchester
NORTH TONAWANDA Niagara
NORTHPORT Suffolk
NORTHVILLE Fulton
NORTON HILL Greene
NORWICH Chenango
NORWOOD St. Lawrence
NUNDA Livingston
NYACK Rockland
OAK HILL Greene
OAKDALE Suffolk
OAKFIELD (99999) Genesee(99), Orleans(1)
OAKS CORNERS Ontario
OBERNBURG Sullivan
OCEAN BEACH Suffolk
OCEANSIDE Nassau
ODESSA Schuyler
OGDENSBURG St. Lawrence
OLCOTT Niagara
OLD BETHPAGE Nassau
OLD CHATHAM Columbia
OLD FORGE Herkimer
OLD WESTBURY Nassau
OLEAN Cattaraugus
OLIVEBRIDGE Ulster
OLIVEREA Ulster
OLMSTEDVILLE (12857) Essex(92), Warren(9)
ONCHIOTA Franklin
ONEIDA (13421) Madison(90), Oneida(10)
ONEONTA (13820) Otsego(90), Delaware(10)
ONTARIO (14519) Wayne(96), Monroe(4)
ONTARIO CENTER Wayne
ORAN Onondaga
ORANGEBURG Rockland
ORCHARD PARK Erie
ORIENT Suffolk
ORISKANY Oneida
ORISKANY FALLS Oneida
ORWELL Oswego
OSSINING Westchester
OSWEGATCHIE St. Lawrence
OSWEGO Oswego
OTEGO (13825) Otsego(98), Delaware(2)
OTISVILLE Orange
OTTO Cattaraugus
OUAQUAGA Broome
OVID Seneca
OWASCO Cayuga
OWEGO Tioga
OWLS HEAD Franklin
OXBOW Jefferson
OXFORD Chenango
OYSTER BAY Nassau
PAINTED POST (14870) Steuben(97), Schuyler(3)
PALATINE BRIDGE Montgomery
PALENVILLE Greene
PALISADES Rockland

PALMYRA (14522) Wayne(90), Ontario(10)
PANAMA Chautauqua
PARADOX Essex
PARIS Oneida
PARISH Oswego
PARISHVILLE St. Lawrence
PARKSVILLE Sullivan
PATCHOGUE Suffolk
PATTERSON (12563) Putnam(99), Dutchess(1)
PATTERSONVILLE Schenectady
PAUL SMITHS Franklin
PAVILION (14525) Genesee(60), Wyoming(34), Livingston(6)
PAWLING Dutchess
PEARL RIVER Rockland
PECONIC Suffolk
PEEKSKILL Westchester
PELHAM Westchester
PENFIELD Monroe
PENN YAN Yates
PENNELLVILLE Oswego
PERKINSVILLE Steuben
PERRY Wyoming
PERRYSBURG Cattaraugus
PERRYVILLE Madison
PERU Clinton
PETERBORO Madison
PETERSBURG Rensselaer
PHELPS (14532) Ontario(95), Seneca(5)
PHILADELPHIA Jefferson
PHILLIPSPORT Sullivan
PHILMONT Columbia
PHOENICIA Ulster
PHOENIX (13135) Oswego(91), Onondaga(9)
PIERCEFIELD St. Lawrence
PIERMONT Rockland
PIERREPONT MANOR Jefferson
PIFFARD Livingston
PIKE Wyoming
PINE BUSH (12566) Ulster(58), Orange(40), Sullivan(2)
PINE CITY (14871) Chemung(85), Steuben(16)
PINE HILL (12465) Ulster(94), Delaware(6)
PINE ISLAND Orange
PINE PLAINS (12567) Dutchess(88), Columbia(13)
PINE VALLEY Chemung
PISECO Hamilton
PITCHER (13136) Chenango(98), Cortland(2)
PITTSFORD Monroe
PLAINVIEW Nassau
PLAINVILLE Onondaga
PLATTEKILL Ulster
PLATTSBURGH Clinton
PLEASANT VALLEY Dutchess
PLEASANTVILLE Westchester
PLESSIS Jefferson
PLYMOUTH Chenango
POESTENKILL Rensselaer
POINT LOOKOUT Nassau
POLAND (13431) Herkimer(77), Oneida(23)
POMONA Rockland
POMPEY Onondaga
POND EDDY Sullivan
POOLVILLE Madison
POPLAR RIDGE Cayuga
PORT BYRON Cayuga
PORT CHESTER Westchester
PORT CRANE Broome
PORT EWEN Ulster
PORT GIBSON Ontario
PORT HENRY Essex
PORT JEFFERSON Suffolk
PORT JEFFERSON STATION Suffolk
PORT JERVIS Orange
PORT KENT Essex
PORT LEYDEN Lewis

PORT WASHINGTON Nassau
PORTAGEVILLE (14536) Wyoming(73), Allegany(27)
PORTER CORNERS Saratoga
PORTLAND Chautauqua
PORTLANDVILLE Otsego
PORTVILLE (14770) Cattaraugus(76), Allegany(24)
POTSDAM St. Lawrence
POTTERSVILLE Warren
POUGHKEEPSIE Dutchess
POUGHQUAG Dutchess
POUND RIDGE Westchester
PRATTS HOLLOW Madison
PRATTSBURGH (14873) Steuben(99), Yates(1)
PRATTSVILLE (12468) Greene(97), Delaware(3)
PREBLE (13141) Cortland(57), Onondaga(43)
PRESTON HOLLOW (12469) Albany(87), Schoharie(11), Greene(2)
PROSPECT Oneida
PULASKI Oswego
PULTENEY Steuben
PULTNEYVILLE Wayne
PURCHASE Westchester
PURDYS Westchester
PURLING Greene
PUTNAM STATION (12861) Washington(95), Essex(5)
PUTNAM VALLEY (10579) Putnam(99), Westchester(1)
PYRITES St. Lawrence
QUAKER STREET Schenectady
QUEENSBURY Warren
QUOGUE Suffolk
RAINBOW LAKE Franklin
RANDOLPH Cattaraugus
RANSOMVILLE Niagara
RAQUETTE LAKE Hamilton
RAVENA (12143) Albany(99), Greene(2)
RAY BROOK Essex
RAYMONDVILLE St. Lawrence
READING CENTER Schuyler
RED CREEK (13143) Wayne(96), Cayuga(3)
RED HOOK (12571) Dutchess(96), Columbia(4)
REDFIELD (13437) Oswego(98), Lewis(2)
REDFORD Clinton
REDWOOD (13679) Jefferson(95), St. Lawrence(5)
REMSEN (13438) Oneida(97), Herkimer(3)
REMSENBURG Suffolk
RENSSELAER Rensselaer
RENSSELAER FALLS St. Lawrence
RENSSELAERVILLE Albany
RETSOF Livingston
REXFORD (12148) Saratoga(96), Schenectady(4)
REXVILLE (14877) Steuben(98), Allegany(2)
RHINEBECK Dutchess
RHINECLIFF Dutchess
RICHBURG Allegany
RICHFIELD SPRINGS (13439) Otsego(86), Herkimer(14)
RICHFORD (13835) Tioga(56), Broome(31), Cortland(13)
RICHLAND Oswego
RICHMONDVILLE (12149) Schoharie(94), Otsego(6)
RICHVILLE St. Lawrence
RIDGE Suffolk
RIFTON Ulster
RIPARIUS Warren
RIPLEY Chautauqua
RIVERHEAD Suffolk
ROCHESTER Monroe
ROCK CITY FALLS Saratoga
ROCK HILL Sullivan

ROCK STREAM (14878) Schuyler(71), Yates(29)
ROCK TAVERN Orange
ROCKLAND M P C Rockland
ROCKVILLE CENTRE Nassau
ROCKY POINT Suffolk
RODMAN (13682) Jefferson(96), Lewis(4)
RODMAN Lewis
ROME Oneida
ROMULUS Seneca
RONKONKOMA Suffolk
ROOSEVELT Nassau
ROOSEVELTOWN St. Lawrence
ROSCOE (12776) Sullivan(71), Delaware(29)
ROSE Wayne
ROSEBOOM Otsego
ROSENDALE Ulster
ROSLYN Nassau
ROSLYN HEIGHTS Nassau
ROSSBURG Allegany
ROTTERDAM JUNCTION Schenectady
ROUND LAKE Saratoga
ROUND TOP Greene
ROUSES POINT Clinton
ROXBURY Delaware
RUBY Ulster
RUSH Monroe
RUSHFORD Allegany
RUSHVILLE (14544) Yates(55), Ontario(45)
RUSSELL St. Lawrence
RYE Westchester
SABAEL Hamilton
SACKETS HARBOR Jefferson
SAG HARBOR Suffolk
SAGAPONACK Suffolk
SAINT BONAVENTURE Cattaraugus
SAINT JAMES Suffolk
SAINT JOHNSVILLE (13452) Montgomery(91), Fulton(9)
SAINT REGIS FALLS (12980) Franklin(94), St. Lawrence(6)
SALAMANCA Cattaraugus
SALEM (12865) Washington(95), Albany(5)
SALISBURY CENTER Herkimer
SALISBURY MILLS Orange
SALT POINT Dutchess
SANBORN Niagara
SAND LAKE Rensselaer
SANDUSKY Cattaraugus
SANDY CREEK Oswego
SANGERFIELD Oneida
SARANAC Clinton
SARANAC LAKE (12983) Franklin(79), Essex(21)
SARANAC LAKE Franklin
SARATOGA SPRINGS Saratoga
SARDINIA Erie
SAUGERTIES Ulster
SAUQUOIT (13456) Oneida(97), Herkimer(3)
SAVANNAH Wayne
SAVONA Steuben
SAYVILLE Suffolk
SCARSDALE Westchester
SCHAGHTICOKE (12154) Rensselaer(95), Washington(5)
SCHENECTADY (12302) Schenectady(98), Saratoga(2)
SCHENECTADY (12303) Schenectady(69), Albany(31)
SCHENECTADY (12304) Schenectady(89), Albany(11)
SCHENECTADY (12309) Schenectady(93), Albany(7)
SCHENECTADY Schenectady
SCHENEVUS (12155) Otsego(86), Delaware(14)
SCHODACK LANDING (12156) Rensselaer(90), Columbia(10)
SCHOHARIE Schoharie

SCHROON LAKE (12870) Essex(92), Warren(8)
SCHUYLER FALLS Clinton
SCHUYLER LAKE Otsego
SCHUYLERVILLE Saratoga
SCIO Allegany
SCIPIO CENTER Cayuga
SCOTTSBURG Livingston
SCOTTSVILLE Monroe
SEA CLIFF Nassau
SEAFORD Nassau
SELDEN Suffolk
SELKIRK Albany
SENECA CASTLE Ontario
SENECA FALLS Seneca
SENNETT Cayuga
SEVERANCE Essex
SHANDAKEN (12480) Ulster(96), Greene(4)
SHARON SPRINGS (13459) Schoharie(93), Montgomery(5), Otsego(2)
SHEDS Madison
SHELTER ISLAND Suffolk
SHELTER ISLAND HEIGHTS Suffolk
SHENOROCK Westchester
SHERBURNE (13460) Chenango(99), Madison(1)
SHERIDAN Chautauqua
SHERMAN Chautauqua
SHERRILL Oneida
SHINHOPPLE Delaware
SHIRLEY Suffolk
SHOKAN Ulster
SHOREHAM Suffolk
SHORTSVILLE Ontario
SHRUB OAK Westchester
SHUSHAN Washington
SIDNEY (13838) Delaware(96), Otsego(4)
SIDNEY CENTER Delaware
SILVER BAY Warren
SILVER CREEK Chautauqua
SILVER LAKE Wyoming
SILVER SPRINGS Wyoming
SINCLAIRVILLE Chautauqua
SKANEATELES (13152) Onondaga(93), Cayuga(7)
SKANEATELES FALLS Onondaga
SLATE HILL Orange
SLATERVILLE SPRINGS Tompkins
SLINGERLANDS Albany
SLOANSVILLE Schoharie
SLOATSBURG Rockland
SMALLWOOD Sullivan
SMITHBORO Tioga
SMITHTOWN Suffolk
SMITHVILLE FLATS (13841) Cortland(53), Chenango(40), Broome(7)
SMYRNA Chenango
SODUS Wayne
SODUS CENTER Wayne
SODUS POINT Wayne
SOLSVILLE Madison
SOMERS Westchester
SONYEA Livingston
SOUND BEACH Suffolk
SOUTH BETHLEHEM Albany
SOUTH BUTLER Wayne
SOUTH BYRON Genesee
SOUTH CAIRO Greene
SOUTH COLTON St. Lawrence
SOUTH DAYTON (14138) Cattaraugus(63), Chautauqua(37)
SOUTH EDMESTON Otsego
SOUTH FALLSBURG Sullivan
SOUTH GLENS FALLS Saratoga
SOUTH JAMESPORT Suffolk
SOUTH KORTRIGHT Delaware
SOUTH LIMA Livingston
SOUTH NEW BERLIN (13843) Chenango(66), Otsego(34)
SOUTH OTSELIC Chenango

SOUTH PLYMOUTH Chenango
SOUTH RUTLAND Jefferson
SOUTH SALEM Westchester
SOUTH SCHODACK Rensselaer
SOUTH WALES Erie
SOUTH WESTERLO Albany
SOUTHAMPTON Suffolk
SOUTHFIELDS Orange
SOUTHOLD Suffolk
SPARKILL Rockland
SPARROW BUSH (12780) Orange(89),
   Sullivan(11)
SPECULATOR Hamilton
SPENCER (14883) Tioga(79),
   Tompkins(21)
SPENCERPORT Monroe
SPENCERTOWN Columbia
SPEONK Suffolk
SPRAKERS Montgomery
SPRING BROOK Erie
SPRING GLEN Ulster
SPRING VALLEY Rockland
SPRINGFIELD CENTER Otsego
SPRINGVILLE (14141) Erie(94),
   Cattaraugus(6)
SPRINGWATER (14560) Ontario(51),
   Livingston(49)
STAATSBURG Dutchess
STAFFORD Genesee
STAMFORD (12167) Delaware(74),
   Schoharie(26)
STANFORDVILLE Dutchess
STANLEY (14561) Ontario(95), Yates(6)
STAR LAKE St. Lawrence
STATEN ISLAND Richmond
STEAMBURG Cattaraugus
STELLA NIAGARA Niagara
STEPHENTOWN Rensselaer
STERLING Cayuga
STERLING FOREST Orange
STILLWATER Saratoga
STITTVILLE Oneida
STOCKTON Chautauqua
STONE RIDGE Ulster
STONY BROOK Suffolk
STONY CREEK Warren
STONY POINT Rockland
STORMVILLE (12582) Dutchess(98),
   Putnam(2)
STOTTVILLE Columbia
STOW Chautauqua
STRATFORD (13470) Fulton(97),
   Herkimer(3)
STRYKERSVILLE (14145) Wyoming(92),
   Erie(8)
STUYVESANT Columbia
STUYVESANT FALLS Columbia
SUFFERN Rockland
SUGAR LOAF Orange
SUMMIT Schoharie
SUMMITVILLE Sullivan
SUNDOWN Ulster
SURPRISE Greene
SWAIN Allegany
SWAN LAKE Sullivan
SYLVAN BEACH Oneida
SYOSSET Nassau
SYRACUSE Onondaga
TABERG Oneida
TALLMAN Rockland
TANNERSVILLE Greene
TAPPAN Rockland
TARRYTOWN Westchester
THENDARA Herkimer

THERESA Jefferson
THIELLS Rockland
THOMPSON RIDGE Orange
THOMPSONVILLE Sullivan
THORNWOOD Westchester
THOUSAND ISLAND PARK Jefferson
THREE MILE BAY Jefferson
TICONDEROGA Essex
TILLSON Ulster
TIOGA CENTER Tioga
TIVOLI (12583) Dutchess(62),
   Columbia(39)
TOMKINS COVE Rockland
TONAWANDA Erie
TREADWELL Delaware
TRIBES HILL Montgomery
TROUPSBURG Steuben
TROUT CREEK Delaware
TROY Albany
TROY Rensselaer
TRUMANSBURG (14886) Tompkins(62),
   Schuyler(26), Seneca(12)
TRUXTON Cortland
TUCKAHOE Westchester
TULLY (13159) Onondaga(71),
   Cortland(29)
TUNNEL Broome
TUPPER LAKE (12986) Franklin(97), St.
   Lawrence(3)
TURIN Lewis
TUXEDO PARK Orange
TYRONE Schuyler
ULSTER PARK Ulster
UNADILLA (13849) Otsego(81),
   Delaware(19)
UNION HILL Wayne
UNION SPRINGS Cayuga
UNIONDALE Nassau
UNIONVILLE Orange
UPPER JAY Essex
UPTON Suffolk
UTICA (13501) Oneida(99), Herkimer(1)
UTICA Oneida
VAILS GATE Orange
VALATIE Columbia
VALHALLA Westchester
VALLEY COTTAGE Rockland
VALLEY FALLS (12185) Rensselaer(96),
   Washington(4)
VALLEY STREAM Nassau
VALOIS (14888) Schuyler(83), Seneca(17)
VAN BUREN POINT Chautauqua
VAN ETTEN (14889) Chemung(89),
   Schuyler(6), Tioga(5)
VAN HORNESVILLE (13475)
   Herkimer(65), Otsego(35)
VARYSBURG Wyoming
VERBANK Dutchess
VERMONTVILLE Franklin
VERNON Oneida
VERNON CENTER Oneida
VERONA Oneida
VERONA BEACH Oneida
VERPLANCK Westchester
VERSAILLES Cattaraugus
VESTAL Broome
VICTOR (14564) Ontario(97), Monroe(3)
VICTORY MILLS Saratoga
VOORHEESVILLE Albany
WACCABUC Westchester
WADDINGTON St. Lawrence
WADHAMS Essex
WADING RIVER Suffolk
WAINSCOTT Suffolk

WALDEN Orange
WALES CENTER Erie
WALKER VALLEY Ulster
WALLKILL (12589) Ulster(77), Orange(23)
WALTON Delaware
WALWORTH Wayne
WAMPSVILLE Madison
WANAKENA St. Lawrence
WANTAGH Nassau
WAPPINGERS FALLS Dutchess
WARNERS Onondaga
WARNERVILLE Schoharie
WARRENSBURG Warren
WARSAW Wyoming
WARWICK Orange
WASHINGTON MILLS Oneida
WASHINGTONVILLE Orange
WASSAIC Dutchess
WATER MILL Suffolk
WATERFORD Saratoga
WATERLOO Seneca
WATERPORT Orleans
WATERTOWN Jefferson
WATERVILLE (13480) Oneida(98),
   Madison(2)
WATERVLIET Albany
WATKINS GLEN Schuyler
WAVERLY (14892) Tioga(92), Chemung(8)
WAWARSING Ulster
WAYLAND (14572) Steuben(79),
   Livingston(21)
WAYNE Schuyler
WEBSTER Monroe
WEBSTER CROSSING Livingston
WEEDSPORT Cayuga
WELLESLEY ISLAND Jefferson
WELLS Hamilton
WELLS BRIDGE (13859) Otsego(95),
   Delaware(5)
WELLSBURG Chemung
WELLSVILLE Allegany
WEST BABYLON Suffolk
WEST BLOOMFIELD Ontario
WEST BURLINGTON Otsego
WEST CAMP Ulster
WEST CHAZY Clinton
WEST CLARKSVILLE Allegany
WEST COPAKE Columbia
WEST COXSACKIE Greene
WEST DANBY Tompkins
WEST DAVENPORT Delaware
WEST EATON Madison
WEST EDMESTON (13485) Madison(63),
   Otsego(34), Chenango(3)
WEST EXETER Otsego
WEST FALLS Erie
WEST FULTON Schoharie
WEST HARRISON Westchester
WEST HAVERSTRAW Rockland
WEST HEMPSTEAD Nassau
WEST HENRIETTA Monroe
WEST HURLEY Ulster
WEST ISLIP Suffolk
WEST KILL Greene
WEST LEBANON Columbia
WEST LEYDEN (13489) Lewis(98),
   Oneida(2)
WEST MONROE Oswego
WEST NYACK Rockland
WEST ONEONTA Otsego
WEST PARK Ulster
WEST POINT Orange
WEST SAND LAKE Rensselaer
WEST SAYVILLE Suffolk

WEST SHOKAN Ulster
WEST STOCKHOLM St. Lawrence
WEST VALLEY Cattaraugus
WEST WINFIELD (13491) Herkimer(87),
   Otsego(9), Oneida(3)
WESTBROOKVILLE Sullivan
WESTBURY Nassau
WESTDALE (13483) Oneida(97),
   Oswego(3)
WESTERLO Albany
WESTERN Oneida
WESTERNVILLE Oneida
WESTFIELD Chautauqua
WESTFORD Otsego
WESTHAMPTON Suffolk
WESTHAMPTON BEACH Suffolk
WESTMORELAND Oneida
WESTONS MILLS Cattaraugus
WESTPORT Essex
WESTTOWN Orange
WEVERTOWN Warren
WHIPPLEVILLE Franklin
WHITE LAKE Sullivan
WHITE PLAINS Westchester
WHITE SULPHUR SPRINGS Sullivan
WHITEHALL Washington
WHITESBORO Oneida
WHITESVILLE (14897) Allegany(95),
   Steuben(5)
WHITNEY POINT (99999) Broome(99),
   Cortland(1)
WILLARD Seneca
WILLET (13863) Cortland(97), Broome(1),
   Chenango(1)
WILLIAMSON Wayne
WILLIAMSTOWN Oswego
WILLISTON PARK Nassau
WILLOW Ulster
WILLSBORO Essex
WILLSEYVILLE (13864) Tioga(70),
   Tompkins(30)
WILMINGTON (12997) Essex(87),
   Saratoga(13)
WILSON Niagara
WINDHAM Greene
WINDSOR Broome
WINGDALE Dutchess
WINTHROP St. Lawrence
WITHERBEE Essex
WOLCOTT Wayne
WOODBOURNE (12788) Sullivan(98),
   Ulster(2)
WOODBURY Nassau
WOODGATE Oneida
WOODHULL Steuben
WOODMERE Nassau
WOODRIDGE Sullivan
WOODSTOCK Ulster
WOODVILLE Jefferson
WORCESTER Otsego
WURTSBORO Sullivan
WYANDANCH Suffolk
WYNANTSKILL Rensselaer
WYOMING (14591) Wyoming(88),
   Genesee(13)
YAPHANK Suffolk
YONKERS Westchester
YORK Livingston
YORKSHIRE Cattaraugus
YORKTOWN HEIGHTS Westchester
YORKVILLE Oneida
YOUNGSTOWN Niagara
YOUNGSVILLE Sullivan
YULAN Sullivan

ZIP/City Cross Reference

00401-00401	PLEASANTVILLE	10451-10499	BRONX	10505-10505	BALDWIN PLACE	10511-10511	BUCHANAN
00501-00544	HOLTSVILLE	10501-10501	AMAWALK	10506-10506	BEDFORD	10512-10512	CARMEL
06390-06390	FISHERS ISLAND	10502-10502	ARDSLEY	10507-10507	BEDFORD HILLS	10514-10514	CHAPPAQUA
10001-10292	NEW YORK	10503-10503	ARDSLEY ON HUDSON	10509-10509	BREWSTER	10516-10516	COLD SPRING
10301-10314	STATEN ISLAND	10504-10504	ARMONK	10510-10510	BRIARCLIFF MANOR	10517-10517	CROMPOND

10518-10518	CROSS RIVER	10933-10933	JOHNSON	11569-11569	POINT LOOKOUT	11775-11775	MELVILLE
10519-10519	CROTON FALLS	10940-10943	MIDDLETOWN	11570-11571	ROCKVILLE CENTRE	11776-11776	PORT JEFFERSON
10520-10521	CROTON ON HUDSON	10950-10950	MONROE	11572-11572	OCEANSIDE		STATION
10522-10522	DOBBS FERRY	10951-10951	ROCKLAND M P C	11575-11575	ROOSEVELT	11777-11777	PORT JEFFERSON
10523-10523	ELMSFORD	10952-10952	MONSEY	11576-11576	ROSLYN	11778-11778	ROCKY POINT
10524-10524	GARRISON	10953-10953	MOUNTAINVILLE	11577-11577	ROSLYN HEIGHTS	11779-11779	RONKONKOMA
10526-10526	GOLDENS BRIDGE	10954-10954	NANUET	11579-11579	SEA CLIFF	11780-11780	SAINT JAMES
10527-10527	GRANITE SPRINGS	10956-10956	NEW CITY	11580-11583	VALLEY STREAM	11782-11782	SAYVILLE
10528-10528	HARRISON	10958-10958	NEW HAMPTON	11588-11588	UNIONDALE	11783-11783	SEAFORD
10530-10530	HARTSDALE	10959-10959	NEW MILFORD	11590-11590	WESTBURY	11784-11784	SELDEN
10532-10532	HAWTHORNE	10960-10960	NYACK	11592-11592	ROCKVILLE CENTRE	11786-11786	SHOREHAM
10533-10533	IRVINGTON	10962-10962	ORANGEBURG	11593-11595	WESTBURY	11787-11787	SMITHTOWN
10535-10535	JEFFERSON VALLEY	10963-10963	OTISVILLE	11596-11596	WILLISTON PARK	11788-11788	HAUPPAUGE
10536-10536	KATONAH	10964-10964	PALISADES	11597-11597	WESTBURY	11789-11789	SOUND BEACH
10537-10537	LAKE PEEKSKILL	10965-10965	PEARL RIVER	11598-11598	WOODMERE	11790-11790	STONY BROOK
10538-10538	LARCHMONT	10968-10968	PIERMONT	11599-11599	GARDEN CITY	11791-11791	SYOSSET
10540-10540	LINCOLNDALE	10969-10969	PINE ISLAND	11690-11695	FAR ROCKAWAY	11792-11792	WADING RIVER
10541-10541	MAHOPAC	10970-10970	POMONA	11696-11696	INWOOD	11793-11793	WANTAGH
10542-10542	MAHOPAC FALLS	10973-10973	SLATE HILL	11697-11697	FAR ROCKAWAY	11794-11794	STONY BROOK
10543-10543	MAMARONECK	10974-10974	SLOATSBURG	11701-11701	AMITYVILLE	11795-11795	WEST ISLIP
10545-10545	MARYKNOLL	10975-10975	SOUTHFIELDS	11702-11702	BABYLON	11796-11796	WEST SAYVILLE
10546-10546	MILLWOOD	10976-10976	SPARKILL	11703-11703	NORTH BABYLON	11797-11797	WOODBURY
10547-10547	MOHEGAN LAKE	10977-10977	SPRING VALLEY	11704-11704	WEST BABYLON	11798-11798	WYANDANCH
10548-10548	MONTROSE	10979-10979	STERLING FOREST	11705-11705	BAYPORT	11801-11802	HICKSVILLE
10549-10549	MOUNT KISCO	10980-10980	STONY POINT	11706-11706	BAY SHORE	11803-11803	PLAINVIEW
10550-10559	MOUNT VERNON	10981-10981	SUGAR LOAF	11707-11707	WEST BABYLON	11804-11804	OLD BETHPAGE
10560-10560	NORTH SALEM	10982-10982	TALLMAN	11708-11708	AMITYVILLE	11805-11805	MID ISLAND
10562-10562	OSSINING	10983-10983	TAPPAN	11709-11709	BAYVILLE	11815-11819	HICKSVILLE
10566-10566	PEEKSKILL	10984-10984	THIELLS	11710-11710	BELLMORE	11853-11853	JERICHO
10570-10572	PLEASANTVILLE	10985-10985	THOMPSON RIDGE	11713-11713	BELLPORT	11854-11855	HICKSVILLE
10573-10573	PORT CHESTER	10986-10986	TOMKINS COVE	11714-11714	BETHPAGE	11901-11901	RIVERHEAD
10576-10576	POUND RIDGE	10987-10987	TUXEDO PARK	11715-11715	BLUE POINT	11930-11930	AMAGANSETT
10577-10577	PURCHASE	10988-10988	UNIONVILLE	11716-11716	BOHEMIA	11931-11931	AQUEBOGUE
10578-10578	PURDYS	10989-10989	VALLEY COTTAGE	11717-11717	BRENTWOOD	11932-11932	BRIDGEHAMPTON
10579-10579	PUTNAM VALLEY	10990-10990	WARWICK	11718-11718	BRIGHTWATERS	11933-11933	CALVERTON
10580-10581	RYE	10992-10992	WASHINGTONVILLE	11719-11719	BROOKHAVEN	11934-11934	CENTER MORICHES
10583-10583	SCARSDALE	10993-10993	WEST HAVERSTRAW	11720-11720	CENTEREACH	11935-11935	CUTCHOGUE
10587-10587	SHENOROCK	10994-10995	WEST NYACK	11721-11721	CENTERPORT	11937-11937	EAST HAMPTON
10588-10588	SHRUB OAK	10996-10997	WEST POINT	11722-11722	CENTRAL ISLIP	11939-11939	EAST MARION
10589-10589	SOMERS	10998-10998	WESTTOWN	11724-11724	COLD SPRING HARBOR	11940-11940	EAST MORICHES
10590-10590	SOUTH SALEM	11001-11002	FLORAL PARK	11725-11725	COMMACK	11941-11941	EASTPORT
10591-10592	TARRYTOWN	11003-11003	ELMONT	11726-11726	COPIAGUE	11942-11942	EAST QUOGUE
10594-10594	THORNWOOD	11004-11004	GLEN OAKS	11727-11727	CORAM	11944-11944	GREENPORT
10595-10595	VALHALLA	11005-11005	FLORAL PARK	11729-11729	DEER PARK	11946-11946	HAMPTON BAYS
10596-10596	VERPLANCK	11010-11010	FRANKLIN SQUARE	11730-11730	EAST ISLIP	11947-11947	JAMESPORT
10597-10597	WACCABUC	11020-11027	GREAT NECK	11731-11731	EAST NORTHPORT	11948-11948	LAUREL
10598-10598	YORKTOWN HEIGHTS	11030-11030	MANHASSET	11732-11732	EAST NORWICH	11949-11949	MANORVILLE
10601-10603	WHITE PLAINS	11040-11044	NEW HYDE PARK	11733-11733	EAST SETAUKET	11950-11950	MASTIC
10604-10604	WEST HARRISON	11050-11055	PORT WASHINGTON	11735-11737	FARMINGDALE	11951-11951	MASTIC BEACH
10605-10650	WHITE PLAINS	11096-11096	INWOOD	11738-11738	FARMINGVILLE	11952-11952	MATTITUCK
10701-10705	YONKERS	11099-11099	NEW HYDE PARK	11739-11739	GREAT RIVER	11953-11953	MIDDLE ISLAND
10706-10706	HASTINGS ON HUDSON	11101-11120	LONG ISLAND CITY	11740-11740	GREENLAWN	11954-11954	MONTAUK
10707-10707	TUCKAHOE	11201-11256	BROOKLYN	11741-11741	HOLBROOK	11955-11955	MORICHES
10708-10708	BRONXVILLE	11351-11390	FLUSHING	11742-11742	HOLTSVILLE	11956-11956	NEW SUFFOLK
10709-10709	EASTCHESTER	11402-11499	JAMAICA	11743-11743	HUNTINGTON	11957-11957	ORIENT
10710-10710	YONKERS	11501-11501	MINEOLA	11745-11745	SMITHTOWN	11958-11958	PECONIC
10801-10802	NEW ROCHELLE	11507-11507	ALBERTSON	11746-11746	HUNTINGTON STATION	11959-11959	QUOGUE
10803-10803	PELHAM	11509-11509	ATLANTIC BEACH	11747-11747	MELVILLE	11960-11960	REMSENBURG
10804-10805	NEW ROCHELLE	11510-11510	BALDWIN	11749-11749	FARMINGVILLE	11961-11961	RIDGE
10901-10901	SUFFERN	11514-11514	CARLE PLACE	11750-11750	HUNTINGTON STATION	11962-11962	SAGAPONACK
10910-10910	ARDEN	11516-11516	CEDARHURST	11751-11751	ISLIP	11963-11963	SAG HARBOR
10911-10911	BEAR MOUNTAIN	11518-11518	EAST ROCKAWAY	11752-11752	ISLIP TERRACE	11964-11964	SHELTER ISLAND
10912-10912	BELLVALE	11520-11520	FREEPORT	11753-11753	JERICHO	11965-11965	SHELTER ISLAND
10913-10913	BLAUVELT	11530-11536	GARDEN CITY	11754-11754	KINGS PARK		HEIGHTS
10914-10914	BLOOMING GROVE	11542-11542	GLEN COVE	11755-11755	LAKE GROVE	11967-11967	SHIRLEY
10915-10915	BULLVILLE	11545-11545	GLEN HEAD	11756-11756	LEVITTOWN	11968-11969	SOUTHAMPTON
10916-10916	CAMPBELL HALL	11547-11547	GLENWOOD LANDING	11757-11757	LINDENHURST	11970-11970	SOUTH JAMESPORT
10917-10917	CENTRAL VALLEY	11548-11548	GREENVALE	11758-11758	MASSAPEQUA	11971-11971	SOUTHOLD
10918-10918	CHESTER	11549-11551	HEMPSTEAD	11760-11760	HAUPPAUGE	11972-11972	SPEONK
10919-10919	CIRCLEVILLE	11552-11552	WEST HEMPSTEAD	11762-11762	MASSAPEQUA PARK	11973-11973	UPTON
10920-10920	CONGERS	11553-11553	UNIONDALE	11763-11763	MEDFORD	11975-11975	WAINSCOTT
10921-10921	FLORIDA	11554-11554	EAST MEADOW	11764-11764	MILLER PLACE	11976-11976	WATER MILL
10922-10922	FORT MONTGOMERY	11555-11556	UNIONDALE	11765-11765	MILL NECK	11977-11977	WESTHAMPTON
10923-10923	GARNERVILLE	11557-11557	HEWLETT	11766-11766	MOUNT SINAI	11978-11978	WESTHAMPTON BEACH
10924-10924	GOSHEN	11558-11558	ISLAND PARK	11767-11767	NESCONSET	11980-11980	YAPHANK
10925-10925	GREENWOOD LAKE	11559-11559	LAWRENCE	11768-11768	NORTHPORT	12007-12007	ALCOVE
10926-10926	HARRIMAN	11560-11560	LOCUST VALLEY	11769-11769	OAKDALE	12008-12008	ALPLAUS
10927-10927	HAVERSTRAW	11561-11561	LONG BEACH	11770-11770	OCEAN BEACH	12009-12009	ALTAMONT
10928-10928	HIGHLAND FALLS	11563-11564	LYNBROOK	11771-11771	OYSTER BAY	12010-12010	AMSTERDAM
10930-10930	HIGHLAND MILLS	11565-11565	MALVERNE	11772-11772	PATCHOGUE	12015-12015	ATHENS
10931-10931	HILLBURN	11566-11566	MERRICK	11773-11773	SYOSSET	12016-12016	AURIESVILLE
10932-10932	HOWELLS	11568-11568	OLD WESTBURY	11774-11774	FARMINGDALE	12017-12017	AUSTERLITZ

Zip	Place	Zip	Place	Zip	Place	Zip	Place
12018-12018	AVERILL PARK	12132-12132	NORTH CHATHAM	12434-12434	GRAND GORGE	12530-12530	HOLLOWVILLE
12019-12019	BALLSTON LAKE	12133-12133	NORTH HOOSICK	12435-12435	GREENFIELD PARK	12531-12531	HOLMES
12020-12020	BALLSTON SPA	12134-12134	NORTHVILLE	12436-12436	HAINES FALLS	12533-12533	HOPEWELL JUNCTION
12022-12022	BERLIN	12136-12136	OLD CHATHAM	12438-12438	HALCOTTSVILLE	12534-12534	HUDSON
12023-12023	BERNE	12137-12137	PATTERSONVILLE	12439-12439	HENSONVILLE	12537-12537	HUGHSONVILLE
12024-12024	BRAINARD	12138-12138	PETERSBURG	12440-12440	HIGH FALLS	12538-12538	HYDE PARK
12025-12025	BROADALBIN	12139-12139	PISECO	12441-12441	HIGHMOUNT	12540-12540	LAGRANGEVILLE
12027-12027	BURNT HILLS	12140-12140	POESTENKILL	12442-12442	HUNTER	12541-12541	LIVINGSTON
12028-12028	BUSKIRK	12141-12141	QUAKER STREET	12443-12443	HURLEY	12542-12542	MARLBORO
12029-12029	CANAAN	12143-12143	RAVENA	12444-12444	JEWETT	12543-12543	MAYBROOK
12031-12031	CARLISLE	12144-12144	RENSSELAER	12446-12446	KERHONKSON	12544-12544	MELLENVILLE
12032-12032	CAROGA LAKE	12147-12147	RENSSELAERVILLE	12448-12448	LAKE HILL	12545-12545	MILLBROOK
12033-12033	CASTLETON ON HUDSON	12148-12148	REXFORD	12449-12449	LAKE KATRINE	12546-12546	MILLERTON
		12149-12149	RICHMONDVILLE	12450-12450	LANESVILLE	12547-12547	MILTON
12035-12035	CENTRAL BRIDGE	12150-12150	ROTTERDAM JUNCTION	12451-12451	LEEDS	12548-12548	MODENA
12036-12036	CHARLOTTEVILLE	12151-12151	ROUND LAKE	12452-12452	LEXINGTON	12549-12549	MONTGOMERY
12037-12037	CHATHAM	12153-12153	SAND LAKE	12453-12453	MALDEN ON HUDSON	12550-12552	NEWBURGH
12040-12040	CHERRY PLAIN	12154-12154	SCHAGHTICOKE	12454-12454	MAPLECREST	12553-12553	NEW WINDSOR
12041-12041	CLARKSVILLE	12155-12155	SCHENEVUS	12455-12455	MARGARETVILLE	12555-12555	MID HUDSON
12042-12042	CLIMAX	12156-12156	SCHODACK LANDING	12456-12456	MOUNT MARION	12561-12561	NEW PALTZ
12043-12043	COBLESKILL	12157-12157	SCHOHARIE	12457-12457	MOUNT TREMPER	12563-12563	PATTERSON
12045-12045	COEYMANS	12158-12158	SELKIRK	12458-12458	NAPANOCH	12564-12564	PAWLING
12046-12046	COEYMANS HOLLOW	12159-12159	SLINGERLANDS	12459-12459	NEW KINGSTON	12565-12565	PHILMONT
12047-12047	COHOES	12160-12160	SLOANSVILLE	12460-12460	OAK HILL	12566-12566	PINE BUSH
12050-12050	COLUMBIAVILLE	12161-12161	SOUTH BETHLEHEM	12461-12461	OLIVEBRIDGE	12567-12567	PINE PLAINS
12051-12051	COXSACKIE	12162-12162	SOUTH SCHODACK	12463-12463	PALENVILLE	12568-12568	PLATTEKILL
12052-12052	CROPSEYVILLE	12164-12164	SPECULATOR	12464-12464	PHOENICIA	12569-12569	PLEASANT VALLEY
12053-12053	DELANSON	12165-12165	SPENCERTOWN	12465-12465	PINE HILL	12570-12570	POUGHQUAG
12054-12054	DELMAR	12166-12166	SPRAKERS	12466-12466	PORT EWEN	12571-12571	RED HOOK
12055-12055	DORMANSVILLE	12167-12167	STAMFORD	12468-12468	PRATTSVILLE	12572-12572	RHINEBECK
12056-12056	DUANESBURG	12168-12169	STEPHENTOWN	12469-12469	PRESTON HOLLOW	12574-12574	RHINECLIFF
12057-12057	EAGLE BRIDGE	12170-12170	STILLWATER	12470-12470	PURLING	12575-12575	ROCK TAVERN
12058-12058	EARLTON	12172-12172	STOTTVILLE	12471-12471	RIFTON	12577-12577	SALISBURY MILLS
12059-12059	EAST BERNE	12173-12173	STUYVESANT	12472-12472	ROSENDALE	12578-12578	SALT POINT
12060-12060	EAST CHATHAM	12174-12174	STUYVESANT FALLS	12473-12473	ROUND TOP	12580-12580	STAATSBURG
12061-12061	EAST GREENBUSH	12175-12175	SUMMIT	12474-12474	ROXBURY	12581-12581	STANFORDVILLE
12062-12062	EAST NASSAU	12176-12176	SURPRISE	12475-12475	RUBY	12582-12582	STORMVILLE
12063-12063	EAST SCHODACK	12177-12177	TRIBES HILL	12477-12477	SAUGERTIES	12583-12583	TIVOLI
12064-12064	EAST WORCESTER	12179-12183	TROY	12480-12480	SHANDAKEN	12584-12584	VAILS GATE
12065-12065	CLIFTON PARK	12184-12184	VALATIE	12481-12481	SHOKAN	12585-12585	VERBANK
12066-12066	ESPERANCE	12185-12185	VALLEY FALLS	12482-12482	SOUTH CAIRO	12586-12586	WALDEN
12067-12067	FEURA BUSH	12186-12186	VOORHEESVILLE	12483-12483	SPRING GLEN	12588-12588	WALKER VALLEY
12068-12068	FONDA	12187-12187	WARNERVILLE	12484-12484	STONE RIDGE	12589-12589	WALLKILL
12069-12069	FORT HUNTER	12188-12188	WATERFORD	12485-12485	TANNERSVILLE	12590-12590	WAPPINGERS FALLS
12070-12070	FORT JOHNSON	12189-12189	WATERVLIET	12486-12486	TILLSON	12592-12592	WASSAIC
12071-12071	FULTONHAM	12190-12190	WELLS	12487-12487	ULSTER PARK	12593-12593	WEST COPAKE
12072-12072	FULTONVILLE	12192-12192	WEST COXSACKIE	12489-12489	WAWARSING	12594-12594	WINGDALE
12073-12073	GALLUPVILLE	12193-12193	WESTERLO	12490-12490	WEST CAMP	12601-12604	POUGHKEEPSIE
12074-12074	GALWAY	12194-12194	WEST FULTON	12491-12491	WEST HURLEY	12701-12701	MONTICELLO
12075-12075	GHENT	12195-12195	WEST LEBANON	12492-12492	WEST KILL	12719-12719	BARRYVILLE
12076-12076	GILBOA	12196-12196	WEST SAND LAKE	12493-12493	WEST PARK	12720-12720	BETHEL
12077-12077	GLENMONT	12197-12197	WORCESTER	12494-12494	WEST SHOKAN	12721-12721	BLOOMINGBURG
12078-12078	GLOVERSVILLE	12198-12198	WYNANTSKILL	12495-12495	WILLOW	12722-12722	BURLINGHAM
12082-12082	GRAFTON	12201-12288	ALBANY	12496-12496	WINDHAM	12723-12723	CALLICOON
12083-12083	GREENVILLE	12301-12345	SCHENECTADY	12498-12498	WOODSTOCK	12724-12724	CALLICOON CENTER
12084-12084	GUILDERLAND	12401-12402	KINGSTON	12501-12501	AMENIA	12725-12725	CLARYVILLE
12085-12085	GUILDERLAND CENTER	12404-12404	ACCORD	12502-12502	ANCRAM	12726-12726	COCHECTON
12086-12086	HAGAMAN	12405-12405	ACRA	12503-12503	ANCRAMDALE	12727-12727	COCHECTON CENTER
12087-12087	HANNACROIX	12406-12406	ARKVILLE	12504-12504	ANNANDALE ON HUDSON	12729-12729	CUDDEBACKVILLE
12089-12089	HOOSICK	12407-12407	ASHLAND			12732-12732	ELDRED
12090-12090	HOOSICK FALLS	12409-12409	BEARSVILLE	12506-12506	BANGALL	12733-12733	FALLSBURG
12092-12092	HOWES CAVE	12410-12410	BIG INDIAN	12507-12507	BARRYTOWN	12734-12734	FERNDALE
12093-12093	JEFFERSON	12411-12411	BLOOMINGTON	12508-12508	BEACON	12736-12736	FREMONT CENTER
12094-12094	JOHNSONVILLE	12412-12412	BOICEVILLE	12510-12510	BILLINGS	12737-12737	GLEN SPEY
12095-12095	JOHNSTOWN	12413-12413	CAIRO	12511-12511	CASTLE POINT	12738-12738	GLEN WILD
12106-12106	KINDERHOOK	12414-12414	CATSKILL	12512-12512	CHELSEA	12739-12739	GODEFFROY
12107-12107	KNOX	12416-12416	CHICHESTER	12513-12513	CLAVERACK	12740-12740	GRAHAMSVILLE
12108-12108	LAKE PLEASANT	12417-12417	CONNELLY	12514-12514	CLINTON CORNERS	12741-12741	HANKINS
12110-12111	LATHAM	12418-12418	CORNWALLVILLE	12515-12515	CLINTONDALE	12742-12742	HARRIS
12115-12115	MALDEN BRIDGE	12419-12419	COTTEKILL	12516-12516	COPAKE	12743-12743	HIGHLAND LAKE
12116-12116	MARYLAND	12420-12420	CRAGSMOOR	12517-12517	COPAKE FALLS	12745-12745	HORTONVILLE
12117-12117	MAYFIELD	12421-12421	DENVER	12518-12518	CORNWALL	12746-12746	HUGUENOT
12118-12118	MECHANICVILLE	12422-12422	DURHAM	12520-12520	CORNWALL ON HUDSON	12747-12747	HURLEYVILLE
12120-12120	MEDUSA	12423-12423	EAST DURHAM	12521-12521	CRARYVILLE	12748-12748	JEFFERSONVILLE
12121-12121	MELROSE	12424-12424	EAST JEWETT	12522-12522	DOVER PLAINS	12749-12749	KAUNEONGA LAKE
12122-12122	MIDDLEBURGH	12427-12427	ELKA PARK	12523-12523	ELIZAVILLE	12750-12750	KENOZA LAKE
12123-12123	NASSAU	12428-12428	ELLENVILLE	12524-12524	FISHKILL	12751-12751	KIAMESHA LAKE
12124-12124	NEW BALTIMORE	12429-12429	ESOPUS	12525-12525	GARDINER	12752-12752	LAKE HUNTINGTON
12125-12125	NEW LEBANON	12430-12430	FLEISCHMANNS	12526-12526	GERMANTOWN	12754-12754	LIBERTY
12128-12128	NEWTONVILLE	12431-12431	FREEHOLD	12527-12527	GLENHAM	12758-12758	LIVINGSTON MANOR
12130-12130	NIVERVILLE	12432-12432	GLASCO	12528-12528	HIGHLAND	12759-12759	LOCH SHELDRAKE
12131-12131	NORTH BLENHEIM	12433-12433	GLENFORD	12529-12529	HILLSDALE	12760-12760	LONG EDDY

12762-12762	MONGAUP VALLEY	12865-12865	SALEM	12993-12993	WESTPORT
12763-12763	MOUNTAIN DALE	12866-12866	SARATOGA SPRINGS	12995-12995	WHIPPLEVILLE
12764-12764	NARROWSBURG	12870-12870	SCHROON LAKE	12996-12996	WILLSBORO
12765-12765	NEVERSINK	12871-12871	SCHUYLERVILLE	12997-12997	WILMINGTON
12766-12766	NORTH BRANCH	12872-12872	SEVERANCE	12998-12998	WITHERBEE
12767-12767	OBERNBURG	12873-12873	SHUSHAN	13020-13020	APULIA STATION
12768-12768	PARKSVILLE	12874-12874	SILVER BAY	13021-13024	AUBURN
12769-12769	PHILLIPSPORT	12878-12878	STONY CREEK	13026-13026	AURORA
12770-12770	POND EDDY	12879-12879	NEWCOMB	13027-13027	BALDWINSVILLE
12771-12771	PORT JERVIS	12883-12883	TICONDEROGA	13028-13028	BERNHARDS BAY
12775-12775	ROCK HILL	12884-12884	VICTORY MILLS	13029-13029	BREWERTON
12776-12776	ROSCOE	12885-12885	WARRENSBURG	13030-13030	BRIDGEPORT
12777-12777	FORESTBURGH	12886-12886	WEVERTOWN	13031-13031	CAMILLUS
12778-12778	SMALLWOOD	12887-12887	WHITEHALL	13032-13032	CANASTOTA
12779-12779	SOUTH FALLSBURG	12901-12903	PLATTSBURGH	13033-13033	CATO
12780-12780	SPARROW BUSH	12910-12910	ALTONA	13034-13034	CAYUGA
12781-12781	SUMMITVILLE	12911-12911	KEESEVILLE	13035-13035	CAZENOVIA
12782-12782	SUNDOWN	12912-12912	AU SABLE FORKS	13036-13036	CENTRAL SQUARE
12783-12783	SWAN LAKE	12913-12913	BLOOMINGDALE	13037-13037	CHITTENANGO
12784-12784	THOMPSONVILLE	12914-12914	BOMBAY	13039-13039	CICERO
12785-12785	WESTBROOKVILLE	12915-12915	BRAINARDSVILLE	13040-13040	CINCINNATUS
12786-12786	WHITE LAKE	12916-12916	BRUSHTON	13041-13041	CLAY
12787-12787	WHITE SULPHUR SPRINGS	12917-12917	BURKE	13042-13042	CLEVELAND
		12918-12918	CADYVILLE	13043-13043	CLOCKVILLE
12788-12788	WOODBOURNE	12919-12919	CHAMPLAIN	13044-13044	CONSTANTIA
12789-12789	WOODRIDGE	12920-12920	CHATEAUGAY	13045-13045	CORTLAND
12790-12790	WURTSBORO	12921-12921	CHAZY	13051-13051	DELPHI FALLS
12791-12791	YOUNGSVILLE	12922-12922	CHILDWOLD	13052-13052	DE RUYTER
12792-12792	YULAN	12923-12923	CHURUBUSCO	13053-13053	DRYDEN
12801-12801	GLENS FALLS	12924-12924	KEESEVILLE	13054-13054	DURHAMVILLE
12803-12803	SOUTH GLENS FALLS	12926-12926	CONSTABLE	13056-13056	EAST HOMER
12804-12804	QUEENSBURY	12927-12927	CRANBERRY LAKE	13057-13057	EAST SYRACUSE
12808-12808	ADIRONDACK	12928-12928	CROWN POINT	13060-13060	ELBRIDGE
12809-12809	ARGYLE	12929-12929	DANNEMORA	13061-13061	ERIEVILLE
12810-12810	ATHOL	12930-12930	DICKINSON CENTER	13062-13062	ETNA
12811-12811	BAKERS MILLS	12932-12932	ELIZABETHTOWN	13063-13063	FABIUS
12812-12812	BLUE MOUNTAIN LAKE	12933-12933	ELLENBURG	13064-13064	FAIR HAVEN
12814-12814	BOLTON LANDING	12934-12934	ELLENBURG CENTER	13065-13065	FAYETTE
12815-12815	BRANT LAKE	12935-12935	ELLENBURG DEPOT	13066-13066	FAYETTEVILLE
12816-12816	CAMBRIDGE	12936-12936	ESSEX	13068-13068	FREEVILLE
12817-12817	CHESTERTOWN	12937-12937	FORT COVINGTON	13069-13069	FULTON
12819-12819	CLEMONS	12939-12939	GABRIELS	13071-13071	GENOA
12820-12820	CLEVERDALE	12941-12941	JAY	13072-13072	GEORGETOWN
12821-12821	COMSTOCK	12942-12942	KEENE	13073-13073	GROTON
12822-12822	CORINTH	12943-12943	KEENE VALLEY	13074-13074	HANNIBAL
12823-12823	COSSAYUNA	12944-12944	KEESEVILLE	13076-13076	HASTINGS
12824-12824	DIAMOND POINT	12945-12945	LAKE CLEAR	13077-13077	HOMER
12827-12827	FORT ANN	12946-12946	LAKE PLACID	13078-13078	JAMESVILLE
12828-12828	FORT EDWARD	12949-12949	LAWRENCEVILLE	13080-13080	JORDAN
12831-12831	GANSEVOORT	12950-12950	LEWIS	13081-13081	KING FERRY
12832-12832	GRANVILLE	12952-12952	LYON MOUNTAIN	13082-13082	KIRKVILLE
12833-12833	GREENFIELD CENTER	12953-12953	MALONE	13083-13083	LACONA
12834-12834	GREENWICH	12955-12955	LYON MOUNTAIN	13084-13084	LA FAYETTE
12835-12835	HADLEY	12956-12956	MINEVILLE	13087-13087	LITTLE YORK
12836-12836	HAGUE	12957-12957	MOIRA	13088-13090	LIVERPOOL
12837-12837	HAMPTON	12958-12958	MOOERS	13092-13092	LOCKE
12838-12838	HARTFORD	12959-12959	MOOERS FORKS	13093-13093	LYCOMING
12839-12839	HUDSON FALLS	12960-12960	MORIAH	13101-13101	MC GRAW
12841-12841	HULETTS LANDING	12961-12961	MORIAH CENTER	13102-13102	MC LEAN
12842-12842	INDIAN LAKE	12962-12962	MORRISONVILLE	13103-13103	MALLORY
12843-12843	JOHNSBURG	12964-12964	NEW RUSSIA	13104-13104	MANLIUS
12844-12844	KATTSKILL BAY	12965-12965	NICHOLVILLE	13107-13107	MAPLE VIEW
12845-12845	LAKE GEORGE	12966-12966	NORTH BANGOR	13108-13108	MARCELLUS
12846-12846	LAKE LUZERNE	12967-12967	NORTH LAWRENCE	13110-13110	MARIETTA
12847-12847	LONG LAKE	12969-12969	OWLS HEAD	13111-13111	MARTVILLE
12848-12848	MIDDLE FALLS	12970-12970	PAUL SMITHS	13112-13112	MEMPHIS
12849-12849	MIDDLE GRANVILLE	12972-12972	PERU	13113-13113	MERIDIAN
12850-12850	MIDDLE GROVE	12973-12973	PIERCEFIELD	13114-13114	MEXICO
12851-12851	MINERVA	12974-12974	PORT HENRY	13115-13115	MINETTO
12852-12852	NEWCOMB	12975-12975	PORT KENT	13116-13116	MINOA
12853-12853	NORTH CREEK	12976-12976	RAINBOW LAKE	13117-13117	MONTEZUMA
12854-12854	NORTH GRANVILLE	12977-12977	RAY BROOK	13118-13118	MORAVIA
12855-12855	NORTH HUDSON	12978-12978	REDFORD	13119-13119	MOTTVILLE
12856-12856	NORTH RIVER	12979-12979	ROUSES POINT	13120-13120	NEDROW
12857-12857	OLMSTEDVILLE	12980-12980	SAINT REGIS FALLS	13121-13121	NEW HAVEN
12858-12858	PARADOX	12981-12981	SARANAC	13122-13122	NEW WOODSTOCK
12859-12859	PORTER CORNERS	12983-12983	SARANAC LAKE	13123-13123	NORTH BAY
12860-12860	POTTERSVILLE	12985-12985	SCHUYLER FALLS	13124-13124	NORTH PITCHER
12861-12861	PUTNAM STATION	12986-12986	TUPPER LAKE	13126-13126	OSWEGO
12862-12862	RIPARIUS	12987-12987	UPPER JAY	13129-13129	GEORGETOWN
12863-12863	ROCK CITY FALLS	12989-12989	VERMONTVILLE	13131-13131	PARISH
12864-12864	SABAEL	12992-12992	WEST CHAZY	13132-13132	PENNELLVILLE

13134-13134	PETERBORO
13135-13135	PHOENIX
13136-13136	PITCHER
13137-13137	PLAINVILLE
13138-13138	POMPEY
13139-13139	POPLAR RIDGE
13140-13140	PORT BYRON
13141-13141	PREBLE
13142-13142	PULASKI
13143-13143	RED CREEK
13144-13144	RICHLAND
13145-13145	SANDY CREEK
13146-13146	SAVANNAH
13147-13147	SCIPIO CENTER
13148-13148	SENECA FALLS
13152-13152	SKANEATELES
13153-13153	SKANEATELES FALLS
13154-13154	SOUTH BUTLER
13155-13155	SOUTH OTSELIC
13156-13156	STERLING
13157-13157	SYLVAN BEACH
13158-13158	TRUXTON
13159-13159	TULLY
13160-13160	UNION SPRINGS
13162-13162	VERONA BEACH
13163-13163	WAMPSVILLE
13164-13164	WARNERS
13165-13165	WATERLOO
13166-13166	WEEDSPORT
13167-13167	WEST MONROE
13201-13210	SYRACUSE
13211-13211	MATTYDALE
13212-13290	SYRACUSE
13301-13301	ALDER CREEK
13302-13302	ALTMAR
13303-13303	AVA
13304-13304	BARNEVELD
13305-13305	BEAVER FALLS
13308-13308	BLOSSVALE
13309-13309	BOONVILLE
13310-13310	BOUCKVILLE
13312-13312	BRANTINGHAM
13313-13313	BRIDGEWATER
13314-13314	BROOKFIELD
13315-13315	BURLINGTON FLATS
13316-13316	CAMDEN
13317-13317	CANAJOHARIE
13318-13318	CASSVILLE
13319-13319	CHADWICKS
13320-13320	CHERRY VALLEY
13321-13321	CLARK MILLS
13322-13322	CLAYVILLE
13323-13323	CLINTON
13324-13324	COLD BROOK
13325-13325	CONSTABLEVILLE
13326-13326	COOPERSTOWN
13327-13327	CROGHAN
13328-13328	DEANSBORO
13329-13329	DOLGEVILLE
13331-13331	EAGLE BAY
13332-13332	EARLVILLE
13333-13333	EAST SPRINGFIELD
13334-13334	EATON
13335-13335	EDMESTON
13337-13337	FLY CREEK
13338-13338	FORESTPORT
13339-13339	FORT PLAIN
13340-13340	FRANKFORT
13341-13341	FRANKLIN SPRINGS
13342-13342	GARRATTSVILLE
13343-13343	GLENFIELD
13345-13345	GREIG
13346-13346	HAMILTON
13348-13348	HARTWICK
13350-13350	HERKIMER
13352-13352	HINCKLEY
13353-13353	HOFFMEISTER
13354-13354	HOLLAND PATENT
13355-13355	HUBBARDSVILLE
13357-13357	ILION
13360-13360	INLET
13361-13361	JORDANVILLE

ZIP	City
13362-13362	KNOXBORO
13363-13363	LEE CENTER
13364-13364	LEONARDSVILLE
13365-13365	LITTLE FALLS
13367-13367	LOWVILLE
13368-13368	LYONS FALLS
13401-13401	MC CONNELLSVILLE
13402-13402	MADISON
13403-13403	MARCY
13404-13404	MARTINSBURG
13406-13406	MIDDLEVILLE
13407-13407	MOHAWK
13408-13408	MORRISVILLE
13409-13409	MUNNSVILLE
13410-13410	NELLISTON
13411-13411	NEW BERLIN
13413-13413	NEW HARTFORD
13415-13415	NEW LISBON
13416-13416	NEWPORT
13417-13417	NEW YORK MILLS
13418-13418	NORTH BROOKFIELD
13420-13420	OLD FORGE
13421-13421	ONEIDA
13424-13424	ORISKANY
13425-13425	ORISKANY FALLS
13426-13426	ORWELL
13428-13428	PALATINE BRIDGE
13431-13431	POLAND
13433-13433	PORT LEYDEN
13435-13435	PROSPECT
13436-13436	RAQUETTE LAKE
13437-13437	REDFIELD
13438-13438	REMSEN
13439-13439	RICHFIELD SPRINGS
13440-13449	ROME
13450-13450	ROSEBOOM
13452-13452	SAINT JOHNSVILLE
13454-13454	SALISBURY CENTER
13455-13455	SANGERFIELD
13456-13456	SAUQUOIT
13457-13457	SCHUYLER LAKE
13459-13459	SHARON SPRINGS
13460-13460	SHERBURNE
13461-13461	SHERRILL
13464-13464	SMYRNA
13465-13465	SOLSVILLE
13468-13468	SPRINGFIELD CENTER
13469-13469	STITTVILLE
13470-13470	STRATFORD
13471-13471	TABERG
13472-13472	THENDARA
13473-13473	TURIN
13475-13475	VAN HORNESVILLE
13476-13476	VERNON
13477-13477	VERNON CENTER
13478-13478	VERONA
13479-13479	WASHINGTON MILLS
13480-13480	WATERVILLE
13482-13482	WEST BURLINGTON
13483-13483	WESTDALE
13484-13484	WEST EATON
13485-13485	WEST EDMESTON
13486-13486	WESTERNVILLE
13488-13488	WESTFORD
13489-13489	WEST LEYDEN
13490-13490	WESTMORELAND
13491-13491	WEST WINFIELD
13492-13492	WHITESBORO
13493-13493	WILLIAMSTOWN
13494-13494	WOODGATE
13495-13495	YORKVILLE
13501-13599	UTICA
13601-13601	WATERTOWN
13602-13602	FORT DRUM
13603-13603	WATERTOWN
13605-13605	ADAMS
13606-13606	ADAMS CENTER
13607-13607	ALEXANDRIA BAY
13608-13608	ANTWERP
13610-13610	RODMAN
13611-13611	BELLEVILLE
13612-13612	BLACK RIVER
13613-13613	BRASHER FALLS
13614-13614	BRIER HILL
13615-13615	BROWNVILLE
13616-13616	CALCIUM
13617-13617	CANTON
13618-13618	CAPE VINCENT
13619-13619	CARTHAGE
13620-13620	CASTORLAND
13621-13621	CHASE MILLS
13622-13622	CHAUMONT
13623-13623	CHIPPEWA BAY
13624-13624	CLAYTON
13625-13625	COLTON
13626-13626	COPENHAGEN
13627-13627	DEER RIVER
13628-13628	DEFERIET
13630-13630	DE KALB JUNCTION
13631-13631	DENMARK
13632-13632	DEPAUVILLE
13633-13633	DE PEYSTER
13634-13634	DEXTER
13635-13635	EDWARDS
13636-13636	ELLISBURG
13637-13637	EVANS MILLS
13638-13638	FELTS MILLS
13639-13639	FINE
13640-13640	WELLESLEY ISLAND
13641-13641	FISHERS LANDING
13642-13642	GOUVERNEUR
13643-13643	GREAT BEND
13645-13645	HAILESBORO
13646-13646	HAMMOND
13647-13647	HANNAWA FALLS
13648-13648	HARRISVILLE
13649-13649	HELENA
13650-13650	HENDERSON
13651-13651	HENDERSON HARBOR
13652-13652	HERMON
13654-13654	HEUVELTON
13655-13655	HOGANSBURG
13656-13656	LA FARGEVILLE
13657-13657	LIMERICK
13658-13658	LISBON
13659-13659	LORRAINE
13660-13660	MADRID
13661-13661	MANNSVILLE
13662-13662	MASSENA
13664-13664	MORRISTOWN
13665-13665	NATURAL BRIDGE
13666-13666	NEWTON FALLS
13667-13667	NORFOLK
13668-13668	NORWOOD
13669-13669	OGDENSBURG
13670-13670	OSWEGATCHIE
13671-13671	OXBOW
13672-13672	PARISHVILLE
13673-13673	PHILADELPHIA
13674-13674	PIERREPONT MANOR
13675-13675	PLESSIS
13676-13676	POTSDAM
13677-13677	PYRITES
13678-13678	RAYMONDVILLE
13679-13679	REDWOOD
13680-13680	RENSSELAER FALLS
13681-13681	RICHVILLE
13682-13682	RODMAN
13683-13683	ROOSEVELTOWN
13684-13684	RUSSELL
13685-13685	SACKETS HARBOR
13687-13687	SOUTH COLTON
13688-13688	SOUTH RUTLAND
13690-13690	STAR LAKE
13691-13691	THERESA
13692-13692	THOUSAND ISLAND PARK
13693-13693	THREE MILE BAY
13694-13694	WADDINGTON
13695-13695	WANAKENA
13696-13696	WEST STOCKHOLM
13697-13697	WINTHROP
13699-13699	POTSDAM
13730-13730	AFTON
13731-13731	ANDES
13732-13732	APALACHIN
13733-13733	BAINBRIDGE
13734-13734	BARTON
13736-13736	BERKSHIRE
13737-13737	BIBLE SCHOOL PARK
13738-13738	BLODGETT MILLS
13739-13739	BLOOMVILLE
13740-13740	BOVINA CENTER
13743-13743	CANDOR
13744-13744	CASTLE CREEK
13745-13745	CHENANGO BRIDGE
13746-13746	CHENANGO FORKS
13747-13747	COLLIERSVILLE
13748-13748	CONKLIN
13749-13749	CORBETTSVILLE
13750-13750	DAVENPORT
13751-13751	DAVENPORT CENTER
13752-13752	DE LANCEY
13753-13753	DELHI
13754-13754	DEPOSIT
13755-13755	DOWNSVILLE
13756-13756	EAST BRANCH
13757-13757	EAST MEREDITH
13758-13758	EAST PHARSALIA
13760-13761	ENDICOTT
13762-13762	ENDWELL
13763-13763	ENDICOTT
13774-13774	FISHS EDDY
13775-13775	FRANKLIN
13776-13776	GILBERTSVILLE
13777-13777	GLEN AUBREY
13778-13778	GREENE
13780-13780	GUILFORD
13782-13782	HAMDEN
13783-13783	HANCOCK
13784-13784	HARFORD
13786-13786	HARPERSFIELD
13787-13787	HARPURSVILLE
13788-13788	HOBART
13790-13790	JOHNSON CITY
13794-13794	KILLAWOG
13795-13795	KIRKWOOD
13796-13796	LAURENS
13797-13797	LISLE
13801-13801	MC DONOUGH
13802-13802	MAINE
13803-13803	MARATHON
13804-13804	MASONVILLE
13806-13806	MERIDALE
13807-13807	MILFORD
13808-13808	MORRIS
13809-13809	MOUNT UPTON
13810-13810	MOUNT VISION
13811-13811	NEWARK VALLEY
13812-13812	NICHOLS
13813-13813	NINEVEH
13814-13814	NORTH NORWICH
13815-13815	NORWICH
13820-13820	ONEONTA
13825-13825	OTEGO
13826-13826	OUAQUAGA
13827-13827	OWEGO
13830-13830	OXFORD
13832-13832	PLYMOUTH
13833-13833	PORT CRANE
13834-13834	PORTLANDVILLE
13835-13835	RICHFORD
13837-13837	SHINHOPPLE
13838-13838	SIDNEY
13839-13839	SIDNEY CENTER
13840-13840	SMITHBORO
13841-13841	SMITHVILLE FLATS
13842-13842	SOUTH KORTRIGHT
13843-13843	SOUTH NEW BERLIN
13844-13844	SOUTH PLYMOUTH
13845-13845	TIOGA CENTER
13846-13846	TREADWELL
13847-13847	TROUT CREEK
13848-13848	TUNNEL
13849-13849	UNADILLA
13850-13851	VESTAL
13856-13856	WALTON
13859-13859	WELLS BRIDGE
13860-13860	WEST DAVENPORT
13861-13861	WEST ONEONTA
13862-13862	WHITNEY POINT
13863-13863	WILLET
13864-13864	WILLSEYVILLE
13865-13865	WINDSOR
13901-13905	BINGHAMTON
14001-14001	AKRON
14003-14003	ALABAMA
14004-14004	ALDEN
14005-14005	ALEXANDER
14006-14006	ANGOLA
14008-14008	APPLETON
14009-14009	ARCADE
14010-14010	ATHOL SPRINGS
14011-14011	ATTICA
14012-14012	BARKER
14013-14013	BASOM
14020-14021	BATAVIA
14024-14024	BLISS
14025-14025	BOSTON
14026-14026	BOWMANSVILLE
14027-14027	BRANT
14028-14028	BURT
14029-14029	CENTERVILLE
14030-14030	CHAFFEE
14031-14031	CLARENCE
14032-14032	CLARENCE CENTER
14033-14033	COLDEN
14034-14034	COLLINS
14035-14035	COLLINS CENTER
14036-14036	CORFU
14037-14037	COWLESVILLE
14038-14038	CRITTENDEN
14039-14039	DALE
14040-14040	DARIEN CENTER
14041-14041	DAYTON
14042-14042	DELEVAN
14043-14043	DEPEW
14047-14047	DERBY
14048-14048	DUNKIRK
14051-14051	EAST AMHERST
14052-14052	EAST AURORA
14054-14054	EAST BETHANY
14055-14055	EAST CONCORD
14056-14056	EAST PEMBROKE
14057-14057	EDEN
14058-14058	ELBA
14059-14059	ELMA
14060-14060	FARMERSVILLE STATION
14061-14061	FARNHAM
14062-14062	FORESTVILLE
14063-14063	FREDONIA
14065-14065	FREEDOM
14066-14066	GAINESVILLE
14067-14067	GASPORT
14068-14068	GETZVILLE
14069-14069	GLENWOOD
14070-14070	GOWANDA
14072-14072	GRAND ISLAND
14075-14075	HAMBURG
14080-14080	HOLLAND
14081-14081	IRVING
14082-14082	JAVA CENTER
14083-14083	JAVA VILLAGE
14085-14085	LAKE VIEW
14086-14086	LANCASTER
14091-14091	LAWTONS
14092-14092	LEWISTON
14094-14095	LOCKPORT
14098-14098	LYNDONVILLE
14101-14101	MACHIAS
14102-14102	MARILLA
14103-14103	MEDINA
14105-14105	MIDDLEPORT
14107-14107	MODEL CITY
14108-14108	NEWFANE
14109-14109	NIAGARA UNIVERSITY
14110-14110	NORTH BOSTON

14111-14111	NORTH COLLINS	14475-14475	IONIA	14592-14592	YORK	14805-14805	ALPINE
14112-14112	NORTH EVANS	14476-14476	KENDALL	14601-14694	ROCHESTER	14806-14806	ANDOVER
14113-14113	NORTH JAVA	14477-14477	KENT	14701-14704	JAMESTOWN	14807-14807	ARKPORT
14120-14120	NORTH TONAWANDA	14478-14478	KEUKA PARK	14706-14706	ALLEGANY	14808-14808	ATLANTA
14125-14125	OAKFIELD	14479-14479	KNOWLESVILLE	14707-14707	ALLENTOWN	14809-14809	AVOCA
14126-14126	OLCOTT	14480-14480	LAKEVILLE	14708-14708	ALMA	14810-14810	BATH
14127-14127	ORCHARD PARK	14481-14481	LEICESTER	14709-14709	ANGELICA	14812-14812	BEAVER DAMS
14129-14129	PERRYSBURG	14482-14482	LE ROY	14710-14710	ASHVILLE	14813-14813	BELMONT
14130-14130	PIKE	14485-14485	LIMA	14711-14711	BELFAST	14814-14814	BIG FLATS
14131-14131	RANSOMVILLE	14486-14486	LINWOOD	14712-14712	BEMUS POINT	14815-14815	BRADFORD
14132-14132	SANBORN	14487-14487	LIVONIA	14714-14714	BLACK CREEK	14816-14816	BREESPORT
14133-14133	SANDUSKY	14488-14488	LIVONIA CENTER	14715-14715	BOLIVAR	14817-14817	BROOKTONDALE
14134-14134	SARDINIA	14489-14489	LYONS	14716-14716	BROCTON	14818-14818	BURDETT
14135-14135	SHERIDAN	14502-14502	MACEDON	14717-14717	CANEADEA	14819-14819	CAMERON
14136-14136	SILVER CREEK	14504-14504	MANCHESTER	14718-14718	CASSADAGA	14820-14820	CAMERON MILLS
14138-14138	SOUTH DAYTON	14505-14505	MARION	14719-14719	CATTARAUGUS	14821-14821	CAMPBELL
14139-14139	SOUTH WALES	14506-14506	MENDON	14720-14720	CELORON	14822-14822	CANASERAGA
14140-14140	SPRING BROOK	14507-14507	MIDDLESEX	14721-14721	CERES	14823-14823	CANISTEO
14141-14141	SPRINGVILLE	14508-14508	MORTON	14722-14722	CHAUTAUQUA	14824-14824	CAYUTA
14143-14143	STAFFORD	14510-14510	MOUNT MORRIS	14723-14723	CHERRY CREEK	14825-14825	CHEMUNG
14144-14144	STELLA NIAGARA	14511-14511	MUMFORD	14724-14724	CLYMER	14826-14826	COHOCTON
14145-14145	STRYKERSVILLE	14512-14512	NAPLES	14726-14726	CONEWANGO VALLEY	14827-14827	COOPERS PLAINS
14150-14151	TONAWANDA	14513-14513	NEWARK	14727-14727	CUBA	14830-14831	CORNING
14166-14166	VAN BUREN POINT	14514-14514	NORTH CHILI	14728-14728	DEWITTVILLE	14836-14836	DALTON
14167-14167	VARYSBURG	14515-14515	NORTH GREECE	14729-14729	EAST OTTO	14837-14837	DUNDEE
14168-14168	VERSAILLES	14516-14516	NORTH ROSE	14730-14730	EAST RANDOLPH	14838-14838	ERIN
14169-14169	WALES CENTER	14517-14517	NUNDA	14731-14731	ELLICOTTVILLE	14839-14839	GREENWOOD
14170-14170	WEST FALLS	14518-14518	OAKS CORNERS	14732-14732	ELLINGTON	14840-14840	HAMMONDSPORT
14171-14171	WEST VALLEY	14519-14519	ONTARIO	14733-14733	FALCONER	14841-14841	HECTOR
14172-14172	WILSON	14520-14520	ONTARIO CENTER	14735-14735	FILLMORE	14842-14842	HIMROD
14173-14173	YORKSHIRE	14521-14521	OVID	14736-14736	FINDLEY LAKE	14843-14843	HORNELL
14174-14174	YOUNGSTOWN	14522-14522	PALMYRA	14737-14737	FRANKLINVILLE	14844-14845	HORSEHEADS
14201-14280	BUFFALO	14525-14525	PAVILION	14738-14738	FREWSBURG	14846-14846	HUNT
14301-14305	NIAGARA FALLS	14526-14526	PENFIELD	14739-14739	FRIENDSHIP	14847-14847	INTERLAKEN
14410-14410	ADAMS BASIN	14527-14527	PENN YAN	14740-14740	GERRY	14850-14853	ITHACA
14411-14411	ALBION	14529-14529	PERKINSVILLE	14741-14741	GREAT VALLEY	14854-14854	JACKSONVILLE
14413-14413	ALTON	14530-14530	PERRY	14742-14742	GREENHURST	14855-14855	JASPER
14414-14414	AVON	14532-14532	PHELPS	14743-14743	HINSDALE	14856-14856	KANONA
14415-14415	BELLONA	14533-14533	PIFFARD	14744-14744	HOUGHTON	14857-14857	LAKEMONT
14416-14416	BERGEN	14534-14534	PITTSFORD	14745-14745	HUME	14858-14858	LINDLEY
14418-14418	BRANCHPORT	14536-14536	PORTAGEVILLE	14747-14747	KENNEDY	14859-14859	LOCKWOOD
14420-14420	BROCKPORT	14537-14537	PORT GIBSON	14748-14748	KILL BUCK	14860-14860	LODI
14422-14422	BYRON	14538-14538	PULTNEYVILLE	14750-14750	LAKEWOOD	14861-14861	LOWMAN
14423-14423	CALEDONIA	14539-14539	RETSOF	14751-14751	LEON	14863-14863	MECKLENBURG
14424-14424	CANANDAIGUA	14541-14541	ROMULUS	14752-14752	LILY DALE	14864-14864	MILLPORT
14425-14425	FARMINGTON	14542-14542	ROSE	14753-14753	LIMESTONE	14865-14865	MONTOUR FALLS
14427-14427	CASTILE	14543-14543	RUSH	14754-14754	LITTLE GENESEE	14867-14867	NEWFIELD
14428-14428	CHURCHVILLE	14544-14544	RUSHVILLE	14755-14755	LITTLE VALLEY	14869-14869	ODESSA
14429-14429	CLARENDON	14545-14545	SCOTTSBURG	14756-14756	MAPLE SPRINGS	14870-14870	PAINTED POST
14430-14430	CLARKSON	14546-14546	SCOTTSVILLE	14757-14757	MAYVILLE	14871-14871	PINE CITY
14432-14432	CLIFTON SPRINGS	14547-14547	SENECA CASTLE	14758-14758	NIOBE	14872-14872	PINE VALLEY
14433-14433	CLYDE	14548-14548	SHORTSVILLE	14759-14759	NORTH CLYMER	14873-14873	PRATTSBURGH
14435-14435	CONESUS	14549-14549	SILVER LAKE	14760-14760	OLEAN	14874-14874	PULTENEY
14437-14437	DANSVILLE	14550-14550	SILVER SPRINGS	14766-14766	OTTO	14876-14876	READING CENTER
14441-14441	DRESDEN	14551-14551	SODUS	14767-14767	PANAMA	14877-14877	REXVILLE
14443-14443	EAST BLOOMFIELD	14555-14555	SODUS POINT	14769-14769	PORTLAND	14878-14878	ROCK STREAM
14444-14444	EAST PALMYRA	14556-14556	SONYEA	14770-14770	PORTVILLE	14879-14879	SAVONA
14445-14445	EAST ROCHESTER	14557-14557	SOUTH BYRON	14772-14772	RANDOLPH	14880-14880	SCIO
14449-14449	EAST WILLIAMSON	14558-14558	SOUTH LIMA	14774-14774	RICHBURG	14881-14881	SLATERVILLE SPRINGS
14450-14450	FAIRPORT	14559-14559	SPENCERPORT	14775-14775	RIPLEY	14882-14882	LANSING
14452-14452	FANCHER	14560-14560	SPRINGWATER	14776-14776	ROSSBURG	14883-14883	SPENCER
14453-14453	FISHERS	14561-14561	STANLEY	14777-14777	RUSHFORD	14884-14884	SWAIN
14454-14454	GENESEO	14563-14563	UNION HILL	14778-14778	SAINT BONAVENTURE	14885-14885	TROUPSBURG
14456-14456	GENEVA	14564-14564	VICTOR	14779-14779	SALAMANCA	14886-14886	TRUMANSBURG
14461-14461	GORHAM	14568-14568	WALWORTH	14781-14781	SHERMAN	14887-14887	TYRONE
14462-14462	GROVELAND	14569-14569	WARSAW	14782-14782	SINCLAIRVILLE	14888-14888	VALOIS
14463-14463	HALL	14571-14571	WATERPORT	14783-14783	STEAMBURG	14889-14889	VAN ETTEN
14464-14464	HAMLIN	14572-14572	WAYLAND	14784-14784	STOCKTON	14891-14891	WATKINS GLEN
14466-14466	HEMLOCK	14580-14580	WEBSTER	14785-14785	STOW	14892-14892	WAVERLY
14467-14467	HENRIETTA	14584-14584	WEBSTER CROSSING	14786-14786	WEST CLARKSVILLE	14893-14893	WAYNE
14468-14468	HILTON	14585-14585	WEST BLOOMFIELD	14787-14787	WESTFIELD	14894-14894	WELLSBURG
14469-14469	BLOOMFIELD	14586-14586	WEST HENRIETTA	14788-14788	WESTONS MILLS	14895-14895	WELLSVILLE
14470-14470	HOLLEY	14588-14588	WILLARD	14801-14801	ADDISON	14897-14897	WHITESVILLE
14471-14471	HONEOYE	14589-14589	WILLIAMSON	14802-14802	ALFRED	14898-14898	WOODHULL
14472-14472	HONEOYE FALLS	14590-14590	WOLCOTT	14803-14803	ALFRED STATION	14901-14975	ELMIRA
14474-14474	INDUSTRY	14591-14591	WYOMING	14804-14804	ALMOND		

North Carolina

General Help Numbers:

Governor's Office

20301 Mail Service Center	919-733-4240
Raleigh, NC 27699-0301	Fax 919-715-3175
www.governor.state.nc.us	8AM-6PM

Attorney General's Office

Justice Department	919-716-6400
PO Box 629	Fax 919-716-6750
Raleigh, NC 27602-0629	8AM-5PM
www.jus.state.nc.us	

State Court Administrator

2 E Morgan St, Justice Bldg, 4th Floor	919-733-7107
Raleigh, NC 27602	Fax 919-715-5779
www.aoc.state.nc.us/www/public/html/aoc.htm	8AM-5PM

State Archives

Archives & History Division	919-733-3952
109 E Jones St	Fax 919-733-1354
Raleigh, NC 27601-2807	8AM-5:30PM TU-F, 9-5 SA
www.ah.dcr.state.nc.us	

State Specifics:

Capital:	Raleigh
	Wake County
Time Zone:	EST
Number of Counties:	100
Population:	7,425,183
Web Site:	www.state.nc.us

State Agencies

Criminal Records

Access to Records is Restricted

State Bureau of Investigation, Identification Section, 407 N Blount St, Raleigh, NC 27601-1009; 919-662-4500 x300, 919-662-4380 (Fax), 7:30AM-5PM.

Note: Employers or screening companies are denied access unless subject is in the health or child care business. Contact agency for proper paperwork. Record access is limited to criminal justice and other government agencies authorized by law.

Corporation Records
Limited Partnerships
Limited Liability Company Records
Trademarks/Servicemarks

Secretary of State, Corporations Section, PO Box 29622, Raleigh, NC 27626-0622 (Courier: 2 S Salisbury, Raleigh, NC 27603); 919-807-2251 (Corporations), 919-807-2164 (Trademarks), 919-807-2039 (Fax), 8AM-5PM.

www.secretary.state.nc.us

Note: DBAs, Fictitious Names and Assumed Name records are found at the county Register of Deeds offices.

Indexing & Storage: Records are available from 1800's on. Most information is available on the computer database and on the agency's website. New records are available for inquiry immediately.

Searching: Information is open to the public. Include the following in your request-full name of business. Information contained in filings includes officers' names and addresses; registered agent; principal office; date of incorporation; and nature of the business.

Access by: mail, phone, fax, in person, online.

Fee & Payment: There is no search fee. Copies are $1.00 per page. Certification is $5.00. Fee payee: Secretary of State. Prepayment required. They will invoice except for in person searching. Personal checks accepted. No credit cards accepted.

Mail search: Expect 6-10 day turnaround time for corporation documents, 2-3 day turnaroundtime for trademark documents.

Phone search: There is no fee to do simple searches over the phone.

Fax search: They will invoice.

In person search: Turnaround time is immediate. There is a public access terminal to view records.

Online search: Access is currently vailable through a dial-up system. There is an initial registration fee of $185 and a charge of $.02 each time the "enter key" is pushed. To register, call Bonnie Elek at (919) 807-2196. Also, the web site offers a free search of status and registered agent by corporation name. The trademark database is not available online.

Other access: The state makes database information available for purchase, contact Bonnie Elek at number above.

Uniform Commercial Code Federal Tax Liens

UCC Division, Secretary of State,, Raleigh, NC 27626-0622 (Courier: 2 South Salisbury St, Raleigh, NC 27603-5909); 919-807-2111, 919-807-2120 (Fax), 7:30AM-5PM.

www.secretary.state.nc.us/ucc

Indexing & Storage: Records are available from 1967. Records are computerized since 1985.

Searching: Use search request form UCC-11. The search includes federal tax liens on businesses since 1985 if you request (add $5.00). You may search federal tax liens separately. Federal tax liens on individuals and all state tax liens are filed at Superior Courts. Include the following in your request-debtor name. Name will be searched as submitted; name variation printouts will be given.

Access by: mail, in person, online.

Fee & Payment: As of Sept. 1, 2000, the search fee is $30.00 per debtor name. Copies are $1.00 per page if done by the staff or $.25 if done by yourself in person. Certification is $6.25 for the first page and $1.00 for each additional. Fee payee: Secretary of State. Prepayment required. Prepayment is required. Underpayment requests will be rejected. Personal checks accepted. No credit cards accepted.

Mail search: Turnaround time: 3 days. A self addressed stamped envelope is requested.

In person search: Searching is available in person.

Online search: Free access is available at http://ucc.secstate.state.nc.us. Search by ID number or debtor name. The state is preparing to offer a FTP system for ongoing commercial requesters. Call 919-807-2196 for more information.

Other access: The UCC or tax lien database can be purchased on microfilm. Updates can be purchased on either a weekly or monthly basis. For a packet, call 919-807-2196.

State Tax Liens

Records not maintained by a state level agency.

Note: Tax lien data is found at the county level.

Sales Tax Registrations

Access to Records is Restricted

Revenue Department, Sales & Use Tax Division, PO Box 25000, Raleigh, NC 27640 (Courier: 501 N Wilmington Street, Raleigh, NC 27604); 919-733-3661, 919-715-6086 (Fax), 8AM-5PM.

www.dor.state.us/dor

Note: This agency refuses to release any information about registrants, but will validate a number if presented with one.

Birth Certificates

Center for health Statistics, Vital Records Branch, 1903 Mail Service Center, Raleigh, NC 27699-1903; 919-733-3526, 800-669-8310 (Credit Card Orders), 919-829-1359 (Fax), 8AM-4PM.

www.schs.state.nc.us/SCHS

Note: Anyone can order an non-certified copy of a record. Only family members can order a certified copy. The fee is the same.

Indexing & Storage: Records are available from 1913-present. Prior to 1913, the state did not keep records of births. It takes 90 days after birth before new records are available for inquiry. Records are indexed on microfiche, inhouse computer.

Searching: Investigative searches are permitted, but only non-certified copies are provided. Otherwise, requester must state relationship to subject and why record is needed. Include the following in your request-full name, names of parents, mother's maiden name, date of birth, place of birth. The following data is not released: adoption records or medical records.

Access by: mail, phone, fax, in person.

Fee & Payment: Search fee is $10.00 per 5 years searched. Add $5.00 for using a credit card. Add $5.00 per copy for additional copies. Fee payee: North Carolina Vital Records. Prepayment required. Credit cards accepted for expedited service only. Personal checks accepted. Credit cards accepted: Mastercard, Visa.

Mail search: Turnaround time: 2 weeks. No self addressed stamped envelope is required.

Phone search: See expedited service.

Fax search: See expedited service.

In person search: Turnaround time is 30 minutes.

Expedited service: Expedited service is available for credit card searches. Turnaround time: overnight delivery. Total fee is $42.95 and includes overnight delivery.

Death Records

Dept of Environment, Health & Natural Resources, Vital Records Section, 1903 Mail Service Center, Raleigh, NC 27699-1903; 919-733-3526, 919-829-1359 (Fax), 8AM-4PM.

www.schs.state.nc.us/SCHS

Note: Non-certified records may be obtained by the public; certified copies can only be purchased by family members. The fee is the same for either record.

Indexing & Storage: Records are available from 1930-present. It takes 90 days after death before new records are available for inquiry. Records are indexed on microfiche, inhouse computer.

Searching: Investigative searches are permitted, but only non-certified copies are provided. Include the following in your request-full name, date of death, place of death. Social Security Number is helpful.

Access by: mail, phone, fax, in person.

Fee & Payment: The search fee is $10.00 for each 5 years searched. Add $5.00 for using a credit card. Add $5.00 per copy for additional copies. Fee payee: North Carolina Vital Records. Prepayment required. Credit cards accepted for fax and phone service only. Personal checks accepted. Credit cards accepted: Mastercard, Visa, AmEx, Discover.

Mail search: Turnaround time: 2 weeks. No self addressed stamped envelope is required.

Phone search: See expedited service.

Fax search: See expedited service.

In person search: Turnaround time 30 minutes.

Expedited service: Expedited service is available for fax searches. Total fee is $42.95 and includes overnight delivery.

Marriage Certificates

Dept of Environment, Health & Natural Resources, Vital Records Section, 1903 Mail Service Center, Raleigh, NC 27699-1903; 919-733-3526, 919-829-1359 (Fax), 8AM-4PM.

www.schs.state.nc.us/SCHS

Note: Non-certified copies may be purchased by the public. Certified copies can be obtained by family members. The fee is the same for either report.

Indexing & Storage: Records are available from 1962-present. New records are available for inquiry immediately. Records are indexed on microfiche, inhouse computer.

Searching: Investigative searches are permitted, but only non-certified copies are provided. Include the following in your request-names of husband and wife, date of marriage, place or county of marriage.

Access by: mail, phone, fax, in person.

Fee & Payment: The search fee is $10.00 for each 5 years searched. Add $5.00 for using a credit card. Add $5.00 per copy for additional copies. Fee payee: North Carolina Vital Records. Prepayment required. Personal checks accepted. Credit cards accepted: Mastercard, Visa, AmEx, Discover.

Mail search: Turnaround time: 2 weeks. No self addressed stamped envelope is required.

Phone search: See expedited service.

Fax search: See expedited service.

In person search: Turnaround time 30 minutes.

Expedited service: Expedited service is available for fax searches. Total fee is $42.95 and includes overnight delivery.

Divorce Records

Dept of Environment, Health & Natural Resources, Vital Records Section, 1903 Mail Service Center, Raleigh, NC 27699-1903; 919-733-3526, 919-829-1359 (Fax), 8AM-4PM.

www.schs.state.nc.us/SCHS

Note: Non-certified copies are available to the public, certified copies to family members. The fee is the same for either report.

Indexing & Storage: Records are available from 1958-present. New records are available for inquiry immediately. Records are indexed on microfiche, inhouse computer.

Searching: Investigative searches are permitted, but only non-certified copies are provided. Include the following in your request-names of husband and wife, date of divorce, place of divorce, case number (if known).

Access by: mail, phone, in person.

Fee & Payment: The search fee is $10.00 for each 5 years searched. Add $5.00 for using a credit card. Add $5.00 per copy for additional copies. Fee payee: North Carolina Vital Records. Prepayment required. Personal checks accepted. Credit cards accepted: Mastercard, Visa, AmEx, Discover.

Mail search: Turnaround time: 2 weeks. No self addressed stamped envelope is required.

Phone search: See expedited service.

In person search: Turnaround time is 30 minutes.

Expedited service: Expedited service is available for fax searches. Total fee is $42.95 and includes overnight delivery.

Workers' Compensation Records

NC Industrial Commission, Dobbs Bldg, 430 N Salisbury-6th floor, Raleigh, NC 27611; 919-733-1989, 8AM-5PM.

www.comp.state.nc.us

Indexing & Storage: Records are available from 1980.

Searching: Searches require a signed release or statement of purpose of request on letterhead. Only parties to claim will be allowed access. Records may not be used for pre-employment screening.

Access by: mail, in person.

Fee & Payment: There is no search fee. There is no copy fee unless the file is over 20 pages, then the fee is $1.00 per page (over 20). Fee payee: NC Industrial Commission. Personal checks accepted. No credit cards accepted.

Mail search: Turnaround time: 2-3 days.

In person search: Generally turnaround time is immediate, unless the case is closed and records must be researched.

Driver Records

Division of Motor Vehicles, Driver's License Section, 1100 New Bern Ave, Raleigh, NC 27697; 919-715-7000, 8AM-5PM.

www.dmv.dot.state.nc.us

Note: Copies of tickets may be purchased from the same address for a fee of $5.00 per ticket.

Indexing & Storage: Records are available for 5 years or more for moving violations, 10 years or more for DWIs and suspensions. Records of surrendered licenses are kept for one year after the expiration date. North Carolina utilizes two point systems-one for the DMV, one for insurance purposes. It takes 30 days or less before new records are available for inquiry.

Searching: Large volume users are pre-approved and must file a certificate with the state. Form DL-DPPA-1 is required. Casual requesters can obtain records, but no personal information is released. Include the following in your request-driver's license number, full name, date of birth. Some search modes will look at the driver's license number first, then the name and DOB as a secondary search. Online requesters must have the license number to search. The following data is not released: medical information.

Access by: mail, in person, online.

Fee & Payment: The current fee is $5.00 per record. Certified records are an additional $2.00. Fee payee: Division of Motor Vehicles. Prepayment required. Personal checks accepted. No credit cards accepted.

Mail search: Turnaround time: 7 business days. No self addressed stamped envelope is required.

In person search: Up to 2 requests will be processed across the counter; the rest are available the next day.

Online search: To qualify for online availability, a client must be an insurance agent or insurance company support organization. The mode is interactive and is open from 7 AM to 10 PM. The DL# and name are needed when ordering. Records are $5.00 each. A minimum $500 security deposit is required.

Other access: Magnetic tape for high volume batch users is available. Requests must be pre-paid.

Vehicle Ownership
Vehicle Identification

Division of Motor Vehicles, Registration/Correspondence Unit, 1100 New Bern Ave, Rm 100, Raleigh, NC 27697-0001; 919-715-7000, 8AM-5PM.

www.dmv.dot.state.nc.us

Indexing & Storage: Records are available from their first records for title records (on microfilm). Computer records are purged periodically according to plate activity. Records are maintained for mobile homes and boat trailers, also.

Searching: State complies with DPPA. Casual requesters receive records without personal information. Effective 01/01/00, only vehicle owners who have opted in, will be placed on marketing list requests.

Access by: mail, in person.

Fee & Payment: The fee is $1.00 per record (includes lien data) or $5.00 for a certified record. Fee payee: Department of Motor Vehicles. Prepayment required. Personal checks accepted. No credit cards accepted.

Mail search: Turnaround time: 3 days. The use of Form MVR-605A is helpful. The requests require the requester's signature.A self addressed stamped envelope is requested.

In person search: Turnaround time is while you wait if you have the correct authorization.

Other access: North Carolina offers a bulk retrieval of ownership and registration information on magnetic tape. A written request specifying the purpose and details of the request is required. For more information, call 913-250-4230.

Accident Reports

Division of Motor Vehicles, Traffic Records Section, 1100 New Bern Ave, Annex Bldg Rm 112, Raleigh, NC 27697; 919-733-7250, 919-733-9605 (Fax), 8AM-5PM.

www.dmv.dot.state.nc.us/trafficrecords/faq

Indexing & Storage: Records are available from 1986-present on computer, from 1990-present on microfiche. Hard copies are available from 1992.

Searching: Records are not released on minor drivers. Using Form TR-67A, the requester should submit at least one of the names of the participants, the county of occurence, date of occurence, and the exception under which he/she qualifies to receive personal information in accordance with DPPA.

Access by: mail, fax, in person.

Fee & Payment: The fee is $4.00 for a certified copy or no cost for a non-certified copy. Fee payee: Division of Motor Vehicles. Prepayment required. Charge accounts are not required to pre-pay. Personal checks accepted. No credit cards accepted.

Mail search: Turnaround time: 3 days. A self addressed stamped envelope is requested.

Fax search: Results may be returned by fax for a chrage of $2.00 per report. This is only for ongoing requesters and a deposit is required.

In person search: Turnaround time is immediate if the record is available.

Other access: Bulk file purchase is available.

Boat & Vessel Ownership
Boat & Vessel Registration

North Carolina Wildlife Resources Commission, Vessel Registration & Titling, 4709 Mail Service Center, Raleigh, NC 27699-1709; 800-628-3773, 919-662-4379 (Fax), 8AM-5PM.

www.state.nc.us/Wildlife

Indexing & Storage: Records are available from 1970 and are computerized. This is an optional title state. Lien information will show if the vessel is titled. All motorized boats and and sailboats over 14 ft must be registered.

Searching: Submit the name or registration number or hull number.

Access by: mail, fax.

Fee & Payment: There is no search fee.

Mail search: Turnaround time: 1-2 weeks. No self addressed stamped envelope is required.

Fax search: Turnaround time is several days.

Other access: The agency sells a CD-ROM disk with registration information for $10.00 per disk.

Legislation-Current/Pending
Legislation-Passed

North Carolina General Assembly, State Legislative Bldg, 16 W. Jones Street, 1st Fl, Raleigh, NC 27603; 919-733-7779 (Bill Numbers), 919-733-3270 (Archives), 919-733-5648 (Order Desk), 8:30AM-5:30PM.

www.ncleg.net

Note: To get a copy of a bill, you must have a bill number first.

Indexing & Storage: Records are available for current and prior sessions only. Records are computer indexed since 1985, and are indexed on microfiche from 1969-1984.

Searching: Can search by 10 fields including bill number and subject.

Access by: mail, phone, in person, online.

Fee & Payment: There is no search fee, but copies are $.20 each. Fee payee: North Carolina General Assembly. Prepayment required. Money is only needed for the copy machine. Personal checks accepted. No credit cards accepted.

Mail search: Turnaround time: variable. They will invoice.No self addressed stamped envelope is required.

Phone search: Searches by phone are limited to between 5 and 8 bills depending on workload.

In person search: Turnaround time is immediate.

Online search: The Internet site has copies of biils, status, and state statutes.

Other access: This agency will mail lists of bills on computer printouts.

Voter Registration

Access to Records is Restricted

State Board of Elections, PO Box 2169, Raliegh, NC 27602-2169; 919-733-7173, 919-715-0125 (Fax), 8AM-5PM.

www.sboe.state.nc.us/BOE

Note: There is no statewide system, although one will be in place sometime in 2001. Records are open to the public and currently must be accessed at the county level through the County Director of Elections.

GED Certificates

Department of Community Colleges, GED Office, 5024 Mail Service Center, Raleigh, NC 27699-5024; 919-733-7051 x744, 919-715-5796 (Fax), 8AM-4PM.

Indexing & Storage: Records are available from 09/78.

Searching: Include the following in your request-signed release, Social Security Number, date of birth. The year of the test is helpful.

Access by: mail, phone, in person.

Fee & Payment: The fee for a transcript copy is $3.00, there is no fee for merely a verification or a duplicate diploma. Fee payee: GED Office. Prepayment required. Personal checks accepted. No credit cards accepted.

Mail search: Turnaround time: 1 week.

Phone search: Only records after 09/78 can be verified by phone.

In person search: No fee for request.

Hunting License Information
Fishing License Information

Access to Records is Restricted

Wildlife Resource Commission, Archdale Bldg, 512 N Salisbury Street, Raleigh, NC 27604-0118; 919-662-4370, 919-662-4381 (Fax), 8AM-5PM.

www.state.nc.us/wildlife

Note: They only maintain a database of lifetime license holders and consider the information to be confidential and not available to the general public.

Licenses Searchable Online

Architect #03.. www.ncbarch.org/cgi-ncbarch/ncbarch_licdb/ncbarch/architects/query_form
Banking Division #17.. www.banking.state.nc.us/banks.htm
Check Cashers #17... www.banking.state.nc.us/checkcas.htm
Chiropractor #41.. www.ncchiroboard.org/public/licensed_chiros.html
Consumer Financers #17 .... www.banking.state.nc.us/cf.htm
Electrical Contractor/Inspector #06........................ www.ncbeec.org/LicSearch.asp
Engineer #48... www.afiniti.com/cgi-afiniti/ncbels_licdb/ncbels/engineers/query_form
Fire Sprinkler Contractor/Inspector #31.................... www.nclicensing.org/OnlineReg.htm
Heating Contractor #31..................................... www.nclicensing.org/OnlineReg.htm
Lobbyist #51 .... www.secretary.state.nc.us/lobbyists/Lsearch.asp
Medical Doctor/Physician #47 .... www.docboard.org/nc/df/ncsearch.htm
Mortgage Division #17...................................... www.banking.state.nc.us/mbb.htm
Nurse #08 .... www.docboard.org/nc/df/ncsearch.htm
Nurse-LPN #08 .... www.docboard.org/nc/df/ncsearch.htm
Occupational Therapist #09................................. www.ncbot.org/fpdb/otimport.html
Occupational Therapist Assistant #09....................... www.ncbot.org/fpdb/otimport.html
Optometrist #18 .... www.iabopt.org/Nodb2000/LicSearch.asp
Osteopathic Physician #47 .... www.docboard.org/nc/df/ncsearch.htm
Physician Assistant #47 .... www.docboard.org/nc/df/ncsearch.htm
Plumber #31.. www.nclicensing.org/OnlineReg.htm
Provisional Occupational Therapist/Assistant #09..... www.ncbot.org/fpdb/otimport.html
Public Accountant-CPA #37 .... http://ndsips01.sips.state.nc.us/cpabd/search_the_database.htm
Real Estate Broker #39 .... www.realtor.org/realtortemplates/membership_search/search.cfm
Real Estate Dealer #39 .... www.realtor.org/realtortemplates/membership_search/search.cfm
Surveyor #48... www.afiniti.com/cgi-afiniti/ncbels_licdb/ncbels/surveyors/query_form

Licensing Quick Finder

Acupuncturist #40	919-773-0530
Alarm Installer #01	919-662-4387
Alarm System Business License #01	919-662-4459
Alcoholic Beveral Control #20	919-779-0700
Ambulance Attendant #21	919-733-2285
Amusement Device #24	919-807-2770
Architect #03	919-733-9544
Armed Security Guard #38	919-662-4387
Athletic Agent #51	919-807-2156
Attorney #45	919-828-4886
Auctioneer #02	919-981-5066
Bail Bond Runner #23	919-733-2200
Bank #27	919-508-5973
Banking Division #17	919-733-3016
Barber #04	919-715-1159
Barber Inspector #04	919-715-1159
Barber Instructor #04	919-715-1159
Barber, Apprentice #04	919-715-1159
Bingo Registration #21	919-733-3029
Boiler/Pressure Vessel Inspector #24	919-807-2760
Bondsman #23	919-733-2200
Building Inspector #23	919-733-3901
Cemetery #19	919-981-2536
Cemetery Salesperson #19	919-981-2536
Charitable/Sponsor Organization #52	919-807-2214
Check Cashers #17	919-733-3016
Chiropractor #41	704-782-0111
Consumer Financers #17	919-733-3016
Cosmetologist #55	919-850-2793
Counselor #13	919-515-2244
Crematory #07	919-733-9380
Day Care Administrator #21	919-622-4499
Day Care Center Teacher #21	919-622-4499
Dental Hygienist #42	919-781-4901
Dentist #42	919-781-4901
DME (Rx Device) #11	919-942-4454
EDM #21	919-733-2285
Electrical Contractor/Inspector #06	919-733-9042
Electrologist #35	336-574-1414
Electrologist Instructor #35	336-574-1414
Elevator Inspector #24	919-807-2770
Embalmer #07	919-733-9380
Emergency Medical Service #21	919-733-2285
Emergency Medical Technician #21	919-733-2285
Engineer #48	919-781-9499
Family Therapist #57	336-724-1288
Fire Sprinkler Contractor/Inspector #31	919-875-3612
Firearms Trainer #38	919-662-4387
Fundraiser Consultants/Solicitor #52	919-807-2214
Funeral Director #07	919-733-9380
Funeral Home/Chapel #07	919-733-9380
Funeral Service #07	919-733-9380
General Contractor #32	919-571-4183
Geologist #46	919-850-9669
Guard Dog Service #53	919-662-4387
Hearing Aid Dispenser/Fitter #43	910-715-8750
Heating Contractor #31	919-875-3612
Hospital #21	919-733-7461
Insurance Agent #23	919-733-7487
Insurance Company #23	919-733-7487
Investment Advisor #27	919-733-3924
Investment Representative #26	919-733-3924
Investment Representative Advisor #26	919-733-3924
Jailer #56	919-716-6460
Landscape Architect #44	919-850-9088
Licensure #21	919-733-1610
Lobbyist #51	919-807-2156
Manicurist #54	919-850-2793
Manicurist Instructor #55	919-850-2793
Marriage & Family Therapist #33	336-724-1288
Medical Doctor/Physician #47	919-326-1100
Medical Program Director #21	919-715-1872
Medical Responder #21	919-733-2285
Mortgage Division #17	919-733-3016
Notary #58	919-733-3406
Nurse #08	919-782-3211
Nurse-LPN #08	919-782-3211
Nursing Home #21	919-733-7461
Nursing Home Administrator #05	919-571-4164
Occupational Therapist #09	919-832-1380
Occupational Therapist Assistant #09	919-832-1380
Optician #10	919-733-9321
Optometrist #18	919-285-3160
Osteopathic Physician #47	919-326-1100
Paramedic #21	919-733-2285
Pesticide Applicator #16	919-733-3556
Pesticide Consultant #16	919-733-3556
Pesticide Dealer #16	919-733-3556
Pharmacist #11	919-942-4454
Pharmacy #11	919-942-4454
Physical Therapist #49	919-490-6393
Physician Assistant #47	919-326-1100
Physician-Pharmacy #11	919-942-4454
Plumber #31	919-875-3612
Podiatrist #12	919-468-8055
Polygraph Examiner #38	919-662-4387
Pre-need Seller #07	919-733-9380
Private Investigator #38	919-662-4387
Provisional Occupational Therapist/Assistant #09	919-832-1380
Psychological Associate #36	828-262-2258
Psychologist #36	828-262-2258
Public Accountant-CPA #37	919-733-4222
Public Librarian #28	919-733-2570
Real Estate Broker #39	919-733-9580
Real Estate Dealer #39	919-733-9580
Sanitarian #14	919-212-2000
Shorthand Reporter #29	919-733-7107
Social Worker #15	336-625-1679
Solicitor #21	919-733-4510
Solid Waste Facility Operator #34	919-733-0379
Speech Pathologist/Audiologist #30	336-272-1828
Surveyor #48	919-781-9499
Taxidermist #25	919-733-4984
Veterinarian #50	919-733-7689
Veterinary Technician #50	919-733-7689
Waste Water Treatment Plant Operator #34	919-733-0379

Licensing Agency Information

01 Alarm Systems Licensing Board, 18 W Colony Pl, #120, Raleigh, NC 27626; 919-662-4387, Fax: 919-662-4459.

www.jus.state.nc.us/justice/pps/aslmain.htm

02 Auctioneer Licensing Board, 1001 Navajo Dr #105, Raleigh, NC 27609-7318; 919-981-5066, Fax: 919-981-5069.

03 Board of Architecture, PO Box 10834 (127 Hargett St #304), Raleigh, NC 27601; 919-733-9544, Fax: 919-733-1272.

www.ncbarch.org

Direct URL to search licenses: www.ncbarch.org/cgi-ncbarch/ncbarch_licdb/ ncbarch/architects/query_form You can search online using personal name, firm name, license number, license status, city, state and ZIP Code. Or, at the main website, click on "Directory." You can also search for architect license applicants as well as licensed firms.

04 Board of Barber Examiners, 2321 Crabtree Blvd #110, Raleigh, NC 27604-2260; 919-715-1159, Fax: 919-715-4669.

05 Board of Examiners for Nursing Home Administrators, 3733 National Drive #228, Raleigh, NC 27612; 919-571-4164, Fax: 919-571-4166.

06 Division of Enviornmental Health, Public Water Supply Section, Board of Examiners of Electrical Contractors, PO Box 27687 (PO Box 27687), Raleigh, NC 27609-7554; 919-733-9042, Fax: 919-733-6105.

www.ncbeec.org

Direct URL to search licenses: www.ncbeec.org/LicSearch.asp You can search online using license number, qualifier's name, licensee's name, city, state, ZIP Code and license class.

07 Board of Mortuary Science, PO Box 27368 (2123 Crabtree Blvd #100), Raleigh, NC 27604; 919-733-9380, Fax: 919-733-8271.

www.ncbms.org

08 Board of Nursing, PO Box 2129 (PO Box 2129), Raleigh, NC 27602; 919-782-3211, Fax: 919-781-9461.

www.ncbon.com

Direct URL to search licenses: www.docboard.org/nc/df/ncsearch.htm You can search online using name.

09 Board of Occupational Therapy, PO Box 2280 (PO Box 2280), Raleigh, NC 27602; 919-832-1380, Fax: 919-833-1059.

www.ncbot.org

Direct URL to search licenses: www.ncbot.org/fpdb/otimport.html

10 Board of Opticians, PO Box 25336 (PO Box 25336), Raleigh, NC 27611-5336; 919-733-9321, Fax: 919-733-0040.

11 Board of Pharmacy, PO Box 459 (PO Box 459), Carrboro, NC 27510-0459; 919-942-4454, Fax: 919-967-5757.

www.nbop.org

12 Board of Podiatry Examiners, PO Box 1088 (PO Box 3914), Cary, NC 27519-3914; 919-468-8055, Fax: 919-468-4209.

13 Board of Registered Practicing Counselors, PO Box 21005 (893 Hwy 70 W #202), Garner, NC 27529; 919-661-0820, Fax: 919-779-5642.

www.ncblpc.org

14 Board of Sanitarian Examiners, 5025 Harbour Towne Dr, Raleigh, NC 27604; 919-212-2000, Fax: 919-212-2000.

15 Certification Board for Social Workers, PO Box 1043 (PO Box 1043), Asheboro, NC 27204; 336-625-1679, Fax: 336-625-1680.

www.nccbsw.org

16 Department of Agriculture, Pesticide Section, PO Box 27647 (PO Box 27647), Raleigh, NC 27611; 919-733-3556, Fax: 919-733-9796.

www.agr.state.nc.us

Direct URL to search licenses: www.agr.state.nc.us/license.htm

17 Department of Commerce, 4309 Mail Service Center (702 Oberlin Rd #400), Raleigh, NC 27699; 919-733-3016, Fax: 919-733-6918.

www.banking.state.nc.us

Direct URL to search licenses: www.banking.state.nc.us

18 Board of Examiners in Optometry, 109 N. Graham Street, Wallace, NC 28466; 910-285-3160, Fax: 910-285-4546.

www.ncoptometry.org/

Direct URL to search licenses: www.iabopt.org/Nodb2000/LicSearch.asp You can search online using national database by name, city or state.

19 Department of Commerce, 1000 Navaho Dr GL-2, Raleigh, NC 27609; 919-981-2536, Fax: 919-981-2538.

20 Department of Commerce, Alcoholic Beverage Control Commission, 4307 Mail Service Center, Raleigh, NC 27699-4307; 919-779-0700, Fax: 919-661-5927.

21 Department of Health & Human Services, 2702 Mail Service Center (701 Barbour Drive), Raleigh, NC 27699-2707; 919-733-2285, Fax: 919-733-7021.

www.dhhs.state.nc.us/

23 Department of Insurance, Special Svcs Division, PO Box 26387, 430 N Salisbury St, Raleigh, NC 27611; 919-733-7487, Fax: 919-715-3794.

24 Department of Labor, 4 W Edenton St, Labor Bldg, Raleigh, NC 27601-1092; 919-733-7394, Fax: 919-662-3588.

www.dol.state.nc.us

25 Department of Natural Resources & Community Dev, PO Box 12827 (512 N Salisbury St), Raleigh, NC 27604-1188; 919-733-4984.

26 Department of State, Securities Division, 300 N Salisbury #404, Raleigh, NC 27603; 919-733-3924, Fax: 919-821-0818.

www.state.nc.us/secstate

27 Department of State Treasurer, Investment & Banking Division, 300 N Salisbury St, Raleigh, NC 27603-5909; 919-733-3924, Fax: 919-733-6918.

28 Division of State Library, Department of Cultural Resources, 109 E Jones St, Raleigh, NC 27601-2807; 919-733-2570, Fax: 919-733-8714.

http://web.dcr.state.nc.us/divisions/library.html

29 Examiners for Court Reporting Standards & Testing, PO Box 2448 (PO Box 2448), Raleigh, NC 27602; 919-733-7107, Fax: 919-715-5779.

30 Examiners for Speech Pathologists & Audiologists, PO Box 16885 (PO Box 16885), Greensboro, NC 27416-0885; 336-272-1828, Fax: 336-272-4353.

31 Board of Examiners of Plumbing, Heating & Fire Sprinkler Contractors, 3801 Wake Forest Rd #201, Raleigh, NC 27609; 919-875-3612, Fax: 919-875-3616.

www.nclicensing.org

Direct URL to search licenses: www.nclicensing.org/OnlineReg.htm You can search online using personal name, business name, and license number.

32 Licensing Board for General Contractors, PO Box 29500 (PO Box 29500), Raleigh, NC 27612; 919-571-4183, Fax: 919-571-4703.

http://ncbia.org/mbr_serv/boards/gen_con/gen_con .htm

33 Marital & Family Therapy Certification Board, 1001 S Marshall St #5, Winston-Salem, NC 27101-5893; 336-724-1288, Fax: 336-777-3601.

34 Water Treatment Facility Operators, Certification Board, PO Box 27687 (1635 Mail Service Center), Raleigh, NC 27699-1635; 919-733-0379, Fax: 919-715-2726.

35 Board of Electrolysis Examiners, PO Box 10834 (PO Box 13626), Greensboro, NC 27415-3626; 336-574-1414, Fax: 336-574-1414.

36 Psychology Board, 895 State Farm Road #101, Boone, NC 28607; 828-262-2258, Fax: 828-265-8611.

37 Board of CPA Examiners, PO Box 12827 (PO Box 12827), Raleigh, NC 27605-2827; 919-733-4222.

www.cpaboard.state.nc.us

Direct URL to search licenses: www.cpaboard.state.nc.us/licendir.htm

38 Private Protective Services Board, PO Box 29500 (895 State Farm Road, #102), Raleigh, NC 27626-0500; 919-662-4387, Fax: 919-662-4459.

www.jus.state.nc.us/pps/pps.htm

39 Real Estate Commission, PO Box 27368 (1313 Navaho Dr), Raleigh, NC 27609-7460; 919-733-9580, Fax: 919-872-0038.

Direct URL to search licenses: www.realtor.org/realtortemplates/membership_ search/search.cfm You can search online using agent name, firm name, city, county, speciality and board name.

40 Acupuncture Licensing Board, 893 US Highway 70 West, Garner, NC 27529; 919-773-0530, Fax: 919-779-5642.

www.covecreek.org

41 Board of Chiropractic Examiners, 174 Church St N, Concord, NC 28025; 704-782-0111.

www.ncchiroboard.org

Direct URL to search licenses: www.ncchiroboard.org/public/licensed_chiros.html

42 Board of Dental Examiners, PO Box 32270 (PO Box 32270 (37 National Dr, Spe. 221)), Raleigh, NC 27622-2270; 919-781-4901, Fax: 919-571-4197.

www.ncdentalboard.org

43 Board of Hearing Aid Dispensers & Fitters, 401 Oberlin Rd #101, Raleigh, NC 27605; 919-715-8750, Fax: 919-715-8774.

44 Board of Landscape Architecture, PO Box 26852 (3733 Benson Dr (27609)), Raleigh, NC 27609; 919-850-9088, Fax: 919-872-1598.

45 Board of Law Examiners, PO Box 2946 (208 Fayetteville St Mall), Raleigh, NC 27602; 919-828-4886, Fax: 919-828-2251.

46 Board of Licensing Geologists, PO Box 27402 (PO Box 27402), Raleigh, NC 27611; 919-850-9669, Fax: 919-872-1598.

47 Board of Medical Examiners, PO Box 20007 (PO Box 20007 (1201 Front St, 27609)), Raleigh, NC 27619; 919-326-1100, Fax: 919-326-1130. www.docboard.org

Direct URL to search licenses: www.docboard.org/nc/df/ncsearch.htm You can search online using name

48 Board of Registration for Prof Engineers & Land Surveyors, 310 W Mill Brook Rd, Raleigh, NC 27609; 919-841-4000, Fax: 919-841-4012. www.ncbels.org

Direct URL to search licenses: www.memberbase.com/ncbels/public/searchdb.asp You can search online using name, license number, city, state, ZIP Code, county and status.

49 Examining Committee of Physical Therapy, 18 W Colony Pl #120, Durham, NC 27705; 919-490-6393, Fax: 919-490-5106. www.ncptboard.org

Direct URL to search licenses: www.ncptboard.org/search.asp You can search online using name or license number

50 Veterinary Medical Board, PO Box 12587 (PO Box 12587), Raleigh, NC 27605; 919-733-7689.

51 Secretary of State, Lobbyist Registration, 2 N Salisbury St (PO Box 29622), Raleigh, NC 27626-0622; 919-807-2156, Fax: 919-807-2160. www.secstate.state.nc.us/

Direct URL to search licenses: www.secretary.state.nc.us/lobbyists/Lsearch.asp You can search online using lobbyist name, principal, and year

52 Secretary of State, Solicitation Licensing Section, PO Box 29622 (PO Box 29622), Raleigh, NC 27626-0525; 919-807-2214, Fax: 919-807-2220.

Direct URL to search licenses: www.state.nc.us/secstate.sls/default

53 Private Protective Svcs Board, PO Box 29500, 3320 Old Garnder Rd, Raleigh, NC 27626; 919-662-4387.

54 Board of Cosmetic Arts, 1110 Navaho Dr, Raleigh, NC 27609; 919-580-2793.

55 Board of Cosmetic Arts, 1110 Navaho Dr, Raleigh, Dr 27609; 919-580-2793.

56 Department of Justice, Attorney General's Office, Sheriff's Standard Division, PO Drawer 629, Raleigh, NC 27602; 919-716-6460.

57 Marital & Family Therapy Licensure Board, 1001 S Marshall St #5, Winston-Salem, NC 27101; 336-724-1288.

58 Secretary of State, Notary Division, 300 N Salisbury St, Raleigh, NC 27603-5909; 919-733-3406.

The following list indicates the district and division name for each county in the state. If the district or division name of the bankruptcy court is different from the civil/criminal court, it appears in parentheses.

County/Court Cross Reference

County	District	Division
Alamance	Middle	Greensboro
Alexander	Western	Statesville (Charlotte)
Alleghany	Western	Statesville (Charlotte)
Anson	Western	Charlotte
Ashe	Western	Statesville (Charlotte)
Avery	Western	Asheville (Charlotte)
Beaufort	Eastern	Greenville-Eastern (Wilson)
Bertie	Eastern	Elizabeth City (Wilson)
Bladen	Eastern	Wilmington (Wilson)
Brunswick	Eastern	Wilmington (Wilson)
Buncombe	Western	Asheville (Charlotte)
Burke	Western	Shelby (Charlotte)
Cabarrus	Middle	Greensboro
Caldwell	Western	Statesville (Charlotte)
Camden	Eastern	Elizabeth City (Wilson)
Carteret	Eastern	Greenville-Eastern (Wilson)
Caswell	Middle	Greensboro
Catawba	Western	Statesville (Charlotte)
Chatham	Middle	Greensboro
Cherokee	Western	Bryson City (Charlotte)
Chowan	Eastern	Elizabeth City (Wilson)
Clay	Western	Bryson City (Charlotte)
Cleveland	Western	Shelby (Charlotte)
Columbus	Eastern	Wilmington (Wilson)
Craven	Eastern	Greenville-Eastern (Wilson)
Cumberland	Eastern	Greenville-Eastern (Wilson)
Currituck	Eastern	Elizabeth City (Wilson)
Dare	Eastern	Elizabeth City (Wilson)
Davidson	Middle	Greensboro (Winston-Salem)
Davie	Middle	Greensboro
Duplin	Eastern	Wilmington (Wilson)
Durham	Middle	Greensboro
Edgecombe	Eastern	Raleigh (Wilson)
Forsyth	Middle	Greensboro (Winston-Salem)
Franklin	Eastern	Raleigh
Gaston	Western	Charlotte
Gates	Eastern	Elizabeth City (Wilson)
Graham	Western	Bryson City (Charlotte)
Granville	Eastern	Raleigh
Greene	Eastern	Greenville-Eastern (Wilson)
Guilford	Middle	Greensboro
Halifax	Eastern	Greenville-Eastern (Wilson)
Harnett	Eastern	Raleigh
Haywood	Western	Asheville (Charlotte)
Henderson	Western	Asheville (Charlotte)
Hertford	Eastern	Elizabeth City (Wilson)
Hoke	Middle	Greensboro
Hyde	Eastern	Greenville-Eastern (Wilson)
Iredell	Western	Statesville (Charlotte)
Jackson	Western	Bryson City (Charlotte)
Johnston	Eastern	Raleigh
Jones	Eastern	Greenville-Eastern (Wilson)
Lee	Middle	Greensboro
Lenoir	Eastern	Greenville-Eastern (Wilson)
Lincoln	Western	Statesville (Charlotte)
Macon	Western	Bryson City (Charlotte)
Madison	Western	Asheville (Charlotte)
Martin	Eastern	Greenville-Eastern (Wilson)
McDowell	Western	Shelby (Charlotte)
Mecklenburg	Western	Charlotte
Mitchell	Western	Asheville (Charlotte)
Montgomery	Middle	Greensboro
Moore	Middle	Greensboro
Nash	Eastern	Raleigh (Wilson)
New Hanover	Eastern	Wilmington (Wilson)
Northampton	Eastern	Elizabeth City (Wilson)
Onslow	Eastern	Wilmington (Wilson)
Orange	Middle	Greensboro
Pamlico	Eastern	Greenville-Eastern (Wilson)
Pasquotank	Eastern	Elizabeth City (Wilson)
Pender	Eastern	Wilmington (Wilson)
Perquimans	Eastern	Elizabeth City (Wilson)
Person	Middle	Greensboro
Pitt	Eastern	Greenville-Eastern (Wilson)
Polk	Western	Shelby (Charlotte)
Randolph	Middle	Greensboro
Richmond	Middle	Greensboro
Robeson	Eastern	Wilmington (Wilson)
Rockingham	Middle	Greensboro
Rowan	Middle	Greensboro
Rutherford	Western	Shelby (Charlotte)
Sampson	Eastern	Wilmington (Wilson)
Scotland	Middle	Greensboro
Stanly	Middle	Greensboro
Stokes	Middle	Greensboro (Winston-Salem)
Surry	Middle	Greensboro (Winston-Salem)
Swain	Western	Bryson City (Charlotte)
Transylvania	Western	Asheville (Charlotte)
Tyrrell	Eastern	Elizabeth City (Wilson)
Union	Western	Charlotte
Vance	Eastern	Raleigh
Wake	Eastern	Raleigh
Warren	Eastern	Raleigh
Washington	Eastern	Elizabeth City (Wilson)
Watauga	Western	Statesville (Charlotte)
Wayne	Eastern	Raleigh (Wilson)
Wilkes	Western	Statesville (Charlotte)
Wilson	Eastern	Raleigh (Wilson)
Yadkin	Middle	Greensboro (Winston-Salem)
Yancey	Western	Asheville (Charlotte)

US District Court

Eastern District of North Carolina

Elizabeth City Division c/o Raleigh Division, PO Box 25670, Raleigh, NC 27611 (Courier Address: Room 574, 310 New Bern Ave, Raleigh, NC 27601), 919-856-4370.

www.nced.uscourts.gov

Counties: Bertie, Camden, Chowan, Currituck, Dare, Gates, Hertford, Northampton, Pasquotank, Perquimans, Tyrrell, Washington.

Indexing & Storage: Cases are indexed by as well as by case number. New cases are available in the index after filing date. Open records are located at the Division.

Fee & Payment: The fee is $15.00 per item (one party name or case number). Payment may be made by money order, cashier check, personal check.

Phone Search: An automated voice case information service (VCIS) is not available.

In Person Search: In person searching is available.

PACER: Sign-up number is 800-676-6856. Access fee is $.60 per minute. Toll-free access: 800-995-0313. Local access: 919-856-4768. Case records are available back to 1989. Records are purged when deemed necessary. New records are available online after 3 days.

Greenville-Eastern Division Room 209, 201 S Evans St, Greenville, NC 27858-1137, 252-830-6009, Fax: 919-830-2793.

www.nced.uscourts.gov

Counties: Beaufort, Carteret, Craven, Edgecombe, Greene, Halifax, Hyde, Jones, Lenoir, Martin, Pamlico, Pitt.

Indexing & Storage: Cases are indexed by defendant and plaintiff as well as by case number. New cases are available in the index same day if possible after filing date. A computer index is maintained. Open records are located at this court. Civil records are retained for 2 years. All criminal records after 1979 are forwarded to Raleigh.

Fee & Payment: The fee is $15.00 per item (one party name or case number). Payment may be made by money order, cashier check, business check. In state personal checks are also accepted. Prepayment is required. Payee: Clerk, US District Court. Certification fee: $5.00 per document. Copy fee: $.50 per page. You are allowed to make your own copies. These copies cost $.50 per page.

Phone Search: Only limited docket information is available by phone. An automated voice case information service (VCIS) is not available.

Mail Search: Always enclose a stamped self addressed envelope.

In Person Search: In person searching is available.

PACER: Sign-up number is 800-676-6856. Access fee is $.60 per minute. Toll-free access: 800-995-0313. Local access: 919-856-4768. Case records are available back to 1989. Records are purged when deemed necessary. New records are available online after 3 days.

Raleigh Division Clerk's Office, PO Box 25670, Raleigh, NC 27611 (Courier Address: Room 574, 310 New Bern Ave, Raleigh, NC 27601), 919-856-4370, Fax: 919-856-4160.

www.nced.uscourts.gov

Counties: Cumberland, Franklin, Granville, Harnett, Johnston, Nash, Vance, Wake, Warren, Wayne, Wilson.

Indexing & Storage: Cases are indexed by defendant and plaintiff as well as by case number. New cases are available in the index 1 day after filing date. Records from a former office in Fayetteville that handled Cumberland and Harnett counties are maintained here. Both computer and card indexes are maintained. Open records are located at this court. District wide searches are available after 1979 for criminal records through this court.

Fee & Payment: The fee is $15.00 per item (one party name or case number). Payment may be made by money order, cashier check, business check. In state personal checks are also accepted. Prepayment is required. Payee: Clerk, US District Court. Certification fee: $5.00 per document. Copy fee: $.50 per page.

Phone Search: Only docket information is available by phone. An automated voice case information service (VCIS) is not available.

Mail Search: A stamped self addressed envelope is not required.

In Person Search: In person searching is available.

PACER: Sign-up number is 800-676-6856. Access fee is $.60 per minute. Toll-free access: 800-995-0313. Local access: 919-856-4768. Case records are available back to 1989. Records are purged when deemed necessary. New records are available online after 3 days.

Wilmington Division PO Box 338, Wilmington, NC 28402 (Courier Address: Room 239, 2 Princess St, Wilmington, NC 28401), 910-815-4663, Fax: 910-815-4518.

www.nced.uscourts.gov

Counties: Bladen, Brunswick, Columbus, Duplin, New Hanover, Onslow, Pender, Robeson, Sampson.

Indexing & Storage: Cases are indexed by defendant and plaintiff as well as by case number. New cases are available in the index within 1 day after filing date. Both computer and card indexes are maintained. Open records are located at this court. Closed civil records are retained for 2 years. All criminal records after 1979 are located in Raleigh.

Fee & Payment: The fee is $15.00 per item (one party name or case number). Payment may be made by money order, cashier check, personal check. Prepayment is required. Payee: Clerk, US District Court. Certification fee: $5.00 per document. Copy fee: $.50 per page. You are allowed to make your own copies. These copies cost $.50 per page.

Phone Search: Phone searches are only available for information from 1992 to the present. An automated voice case information service (VCIS) is not available.

Mail Search: A stamped self addressed envelope is not required.

In Person Search: In person searching is available.

PACER: Sign-up number is 800-676-6856. Access fee is $.60 per minute. Toll-free access: 800-995-0313. Local access: 919-856-4768. Case records are available back to 1989. Records are

purged when deemed necessary. New records are available online after 3 days.

US Bankruptcy Court

Eastern District of North Carolina

Raleigh Division PO Box 1441, Raleigh, NC 27602 (Courier Address: Room 209, Century Station Bldg, 300 Fayetteville St Mall, Raleigh, NC 27602), 919-856-4752.

www.nceb.uscourts.gov

Counties: Franklin, Granville, Harnett, Johnston, Vance, Wake, Warren.

Indexing & Storage: Cases are indexed by debtor as well as by case number. New cases are available in the index 1 day after filing date. A computer index is maintained. Open records are located at this court.

Fee & Payment: The fee is $15.00 per item (one party name or case number). Payment may be made by money order, cashier check, business check, Visa or Mastercard. Personal checks are not accepted. Credit cards are accepted from companies only. Prepayment is required. Payee: Clerk, US Bankruptcy Court. Certification fee: $5.00 per document. Copy fee: $.50 per page. You are allowed to make your own copies. These copies cost $.25 per page.

Phone Search: An automated voice case information service (VCIS) is available. Call VCIS at 888-513-9765 or 252-234-7655.

Mail Search: Always enclose a stamped self addressed envelope.

In Person Search: In person searching is available.

PACER: Sign-up number is 800-676-6856. Access fee is $.60 per minute. Toll-free access: 800-565-2105. Local access:. Use of PC Anywhere v4.0 suggested. Case records are available back to 1992. Records are purged two years. New civil records are available online after 1 day.

Other Online Access: RACER is available on the Intenet at http://pacer.nceb.uscourts.gov.

Wilson Division PO Drawer 2807, Wilson, NC 27894-2807 (Courier Address: The Thomas Milton Moore Bldg, 1760 Parkwood Blvd, Wilson, NC 27894), 252-237-0248.

www.nceb.uscourts.gov

Counties: Beaufort, Bertie, Bladen, Brunswick, Camden, Carteret, Chowan, Columbus, Craven, Cumberland, Currituck, Dare, Duplin, Edgecombe, Gates, Greene, Halifax, Hertford, Hyde, Jones, Lenoir, Martin, Nash, New Hanover, Northampton, Onslow, Pamlico, Pasquotank,Pender, Perquimans, Pitt, Robeson, Sampson, Tyrrell, Washington, Wayne, Wilson.

Indexing & Storage: Cases are indexed by debtor as well as by case number. New cases are available in the index 1 day after filing date. A computer index is maintained. Open records are located at this court.

Fee & Payment: The fee is $15.00 per item (one party name or case number). Payment may be made by money order, cashier check, business check, Visa or Mastercard. Personal checks are not accepted. Prepayment is required. Payee: Clerk, US Bankruptcy Court. Certification fee: $5.00 per document. Copy fee: $.50 per page. You are

allowed to make your own copies. These copies cost $.25 per page.

Phone Search: Only major dates such as the 341 date, discharge date and entry date will be released. An automated voice case information service (VCIS) is available. Call VCIS at 888-513-9765 or 252-234-7655.

Mail Search: Always enclose a stamped self addressed envelope.

In Person Search: In person searching is available.

PACER: Sign-up number is 800-676-6856. Access fee is $.60 per minute. Toll-free access: 800-564-2104. Local access: 252-243-1766. Use of PC Anywhere v4.0 suggested. Case records are available back to 1976. Records are never purged. New civil records are available online after 1 day.

Other Online Access: RACER is available on the Intenet at http://pacer.nceb.uscourts.gov.

US District Court

Middle District of North Carolina

Greensboro Division Clerk's Office, PO Box 2708, Greensboro, NC 27402 (Courier Address: Room 311, 324 W Market St, Greensboro, NC 27401), 336-332-6000.

www.ncmd.uscourts.gov

Counties: Alamance, Cabarrus, Caswell, Chatham, Davidson, Davie, Durham, Forsyth, Guilford, Hoke, Lee, Montgomery, Moore, Orange, Person, Randolph, Richmond, Rockingham, Rowan, Scotland, Stanly, Stokes, Surry, Yadkin.

Indexing & Storage: Cases are indexed by defendant and plaintiff as well as by case number. New cases are available in the index 1 day after filing date. Both computer and card indexes are maintained. Open records are located at this court. All other divisions in this district have been abolished as of July 1997.

Fee & Payment: The fee is $15.00 per item (one party name or case number). Payment may be made by money order, cashier check, business check. In state personal checks are also accepted. Prepayment is required. Payee: Clerk, US District Court. Certification fee: $5.00 per document. Copy fee: $.50 per page.

Phone Search: Only docket information is available by case number over the phone.

Mail Search: A stamped self addressed envelope is not required.

In Person Search: In person searching is available.

PACER: Sign-up number is 800-676-6856. Access fee is $.60 per minute. Toll-free access: 800-372-8820. Local access: 336-332-6010. Case records are available back to September 1991. Records are never purged. New records are available online after 2 days. PACER is available on the Internet at http://pacer.ncmd.uscourts.gov.

US Bankruptcy Court

Middle District of North Carolina

Greensboro Division PO Box 26100, Greensboro, NC 27420-6100 (Courier Address: 101 S Edgeworth St, Greensboro, NC 27401), 336-333-5647.

www.ncmb.uscourts.gov

Counties: Alamance, Cabarrus, Caswell, Chatham, Davidson, Davie, Durham, Guilford, Hoke, Lee, Montgomery, Moore, Orange, Person, Randolph, Richmond, Rockingham, Rowan, Scotland, Stanly.

Indexing & Storage: Cases are indexed by debtor as well as by case number. New cases are available in the index 1-2 days after filing date. A computer index is maintained. Only pre-BANCAP cases (cases filed prior to 7/17/89) are indexed on a separate computer program. Open records are located at this court. District wide searches are available for information on cases filed after July 17, 1989 from this division on their VCIS system.

Fee & Payment: The fee is $15.00 per item (one party name or case number). Payment may be made by money order, cashier check, personal check. Prepayment is required. Debtor's checks are not accepted. Payee: Clerk, US Bankruptcy Court. Certification fee: $5.00 per document. Copy fee: $.50 per page.

Phone Search: Only the name of the debtor, case number, date filed, trustee and attorney for the debtor will be released over the phone. An automated voice case information service (VCIS) is available. Call VCIS at 888-319-0455 or 336-333-5532.

Mail Search: Always enclose a stamped self addressed envelope.

In Person Search: In person searching is available.

PACER: Sign-up number is 800-676-6856. Access fee is $.60 per minute. Toll-free access: 800-417-3571. Local access: 336-333-5389. Case records are available back to 1992. Records are purged every two years. New civil records are available online after 1 day. PACER is available on the Internet at http://pacer.ncmb.uscourts.gov.

Winston-Salem Division 226 S Liberty St, Winston-Salem, NC 27101, 336-631-5340.

www.ncmb.uscourts.gov

Counties: Forsyth, Stokes, Surry, Yadkin.

Indexing & Storage: Cases are indexed by debtor as well as by case number. New cases are available in the index 2 days after filing date. Both computer and card indexes are maintained. Open records are located at this court.

Fee & Payment: The fee is $15.00 per item (one party name or case number). Payment may be made by money order, cashier check, personal check. Prepayment is required. Debtor's checks are not accepted. Payee: Clerk, US Bankruptcy Court. Certification fee: $5.00 per document. Copy fee: $.50 per page.

Phone Search: Basic docket information only is available by phone. An automated voice case information service (VCIS) is available. Call VCIS at 888-319-0455 or 336-333-5532.

Mail Search: Always enclose a stamped self addressed envelope.

In Person Search: In person searching is available.

PACER: Sign-up number is 800-676-6856. Access fee is $.60 per minute. Toll-free access: 800-417-3571. Local access: 336-333-5389. Case records are available back to 1992. Records are purged every two years. New civil records are available online after 1 day. PACER is available on the Internet at http://pacer.ncmb.uscourts.gov.

US District Court

Western District of North Carolina

Asheville Division Clerk of the Court, Room 309, US Courthouse Bldg, 100 Otis St, Asheville, NC 28801-2611, 828-771-7200, Fax: 828-271-4343.

www.ncwd.uscourts.gov

Counties: Avery, Buncombe, Haywood, Henderson, Madison, Mitchell, Transylvania, Yancey.

Indexing & Storage: Cases are indexed by defendant and plaintiff as well as by case number. New cases are available in the index 1 day after filing date. Both computer and card indexes are maintained. Not all records are entered on the in house automated system. Open records are located at this court. This office also handles records for the Bryson City and Shelby Divisions.

Fee & Payment: The fee is $15.00 per item (one party name or case number). Payment may be made by money order, cashier check, personal check. Prepayment is required. Payee: Clerk, US District Court. Certification fee: $5.00 per document. Copy fee: $.50 per page. You are allowed to make your own copies. These copies cost $.50 per page.

Phone Search: Only docket information is available by phone. An automated voice case information service (VCIS) is not available.

Mail Search: Always enclose a stamped self addressed envelope.

In Person Search: In person searching is available.

PACER: Sign-up number is 800-676-6856. Toll-free access: 888-509-2865. Local access: 704-350-7426. Case records are available back to 1991. New records are available online after 2 days. PACER is available on the Internet at http://pacer.ncwd.uscourts.gov.

Bryson City Division c/o Asheville Division, Clerk of the Court, Room 309, US Courthouse, 100 Otis St, Asheville, NC 28801-2611, 828-771-7200.

www.ncwd.uscourts.gov

Counties: Cherokee, Clay, Graham, Jackson, Macon, Swain.

Indexing & Storage: Cases are indexed by as well as by case number. New cases are available in the index after filing date. Open records are located at the Division.

Fee & Payment: The fee is no charge per item (one party name or case number). Payment may be made by money order, cashier check. Business checks are not accepted. Personal checks are not accepted.

Phone Search: An automated voice case information service (VCIS) is not available.

In Person Search: In person searching is available.

PACER: Sign-up number is 800-676-6856. Toll-free access: 888-509-2865. Local access: 704-350-7426. Case records are available back to 1991. New records are available online after 2 days. As of May 1, 2000, PACER is available on the Internet at http://pacer.ncwd.uscourts.gov.

Other Online Access: You can search cases online at http://208.141.47.221/dc/search.html. You can search using case number, name and/or filing date. This service is only available for documents filed AFTER 03/01/99. The service is currently free to use.

Charlotte Division Clerk, Room 210, 401 W Trade St, Charlotte, NC 28202, 704-350-7400.

www.ncwd.uscourts.gov

Counties: Anson, Gaston, Mecklenburg, Union.

Indexing & Storage: Cases are indexed by defendant and plaintiff as well as by case number. New cases are available in the index 1-2 days after filing date. A computer index is maintained. Open records are located at this court. District wide searches are available for records from 1950 forward from this court.

Fee & Payment: The fee is $15.00 per item (one party name or case number). Payment may be made by money order, cashier check, personal check. Prepayment is required. Payee: Clerk, US District Court. Certification fee: $5.00 per document. Copy fee: $.50 per page.

Phone Search: Only docket information is available by phone.

Mail Search: A stamped self addressed envelope is not required.

In Person Search: In person searching is available.

PACER: Sign-up number is 800-676-6856. Toll-free access: 888-509-2865. Local access: 704-350-7426. Case records are available back to 1991. New records are available online after 2 days.

Other Online Access: You can search cases online at http://208.141.47.221/dc/search.html. You can search using case number, name and/or filing date. This service is only available for documents filed AFTER 03/01/99. The service is currently free to use.

Shelby Division c/o Asheville Division, Clerk of the Court, Room 309, US Courthouse, 100 Otis St, Asheville, NC 28801-2611, 828-771-7200.

www.ncwd.uscourts.gov

Counties: Burke, Cleveland, McDowell, Polk, Rutherford.

Indexing & Storage: Cases are indexed by as well as by case number. New cases are available in the index after filing date. Open records are located at the Division.

Fee & Payment: The fee is no charge per item (one party name or case number). Payment may be made by money order, cashier check. Business checks are not accepted. Personal checks are not accepted.

Phone Search: Searching is not available by phone.

In Person Search: In person searching is available.

PACER: Sign-up number is 800-676-6856. Toll-free access: 888-509-2865. Local access: 704-350-7426. Case records are available back to 1991. New records are available online after 2 days. PACER is available on the Internet at http://pacer.ncwd.uscourts.gov.

Statesville Division PO Box 466, Statesville, NC 28687 (Courier Address: Room 205, 200 W Broad St, Statesville, NC 28687), 704-873-7112, Fax: 704-873-0903.

www.ncwd.uscourts.gov

Counties: Alexander, Alleghany, Ashe, Caldwell, Catawba, Iredell, Lincoln, Watauga, Wilkes.

Indexing & Storage: Cases are indexed by defendant and plaintiff as well as by case number. New cases are available in the index 2 days after filing date. Both computer and card indexes are maintained. Open records are located at this court.

Fee & Payment: The fee is $15.00 per item (one party name or case number). Payment may be made by money order, cashier check, personal check. Prepayment is required. Payee: Clerk, US District Court. Certification fee: $5.00 per document. Copy fee: $.50 per page. You are allowed to make your own copies. These copies cost Not Applicable per page.

Phone Search: Only docket information is available by phone. An automated voice case information service (VCIS) is not available.

Mail Search: A stamped self addressed envelope is not required.

In Person Search: In person searching is available.

PACER: Sign-up number is 800-676-6856. Toll-free access: 888-509-2865. Local access: 704-350-7426. Case records are available back to 1991. New records are available online after 2 days. PACER is available on the Internet at http://pacer.ncwd.uscourts.gov.

US Bankruptcy Court
Western District of North Carolina

Charlotte Division 401 W Trade St, Charlotte, NC 28202, 704-350-7500.

www.ncbankruptcy.org

Counties: Alexander, Alleghany, Anson, Ashe, Avery, Buncombe, Burke, Caldwell, Catawba, Cherokee, Clay, Cleveland, Gaston, Graham, Haywood, Henderson, Iredell, Jackson, Lincoln, Macon, Madison, McDowell, Mecklenburg, Mitchell, Polk, Rutherford, Swain, Transylvania, Union, Watauga, Wilkes, Yancey.

Indexing & Storage: Cases are indexed by debtor as well as by case number. New cases are available in the index 1-2 days after filing date. A computer index is maintained. Open records are located at this court.

Fee & Payment: The fee is $15.00 per item (one party name or case number). Payment may be made by money order, cashier check, business check. Personal checks are not accepted. Prepayment is required. Debtor's checks are not accepted. Payee: Clerk, US Bankruptcy Court. Certification fee: $5.00 per document. Copy fee: $.50 per page.

Phone Search: Only docket information available by telephone. An automated voice case information service (VCIS) is available. Call VCIS at 800-884-9868 or 704-350-7505.

Mail Search: Always enclose a stamped self addressed envelope.

In Person Search: In person searching is available.

PACER: Sign-up number is 800-676-6856. Access fee is $.60 per minute. Toll-free access: 800-324-5614. Local access: 704-344-6121, 704-344-6122, 705-344-6123, 705-344-6124. Case records are available back to 1992. Records are purged every 2 years. New civil records are available online after 1 day.

Other Online Access: You can search records using the Internet. Searching is currently free. Visit www.ncbankruptcy.org/view.html to search. You can search for creditors at www.ncbankruptcy.org/creditor.htm.

Court	Jurisdiction	No. of Courts	How Organized
Superior Courts*	General	0	34 Districts
District Courts*	Limited	0	34 Districts
Combined Courts*		100	

* Profiled in this Sourcebook.

Court	CIVIL								
	Tort	Contract	Real Estate	Min. Claim	Max. Claim	Small Claims	Es-tate	Eviction	Domestic Relations
Superior Courts*	X	X	X	$10,000	No Max				X
District Courts*	X	X	X	$0	$10,000	3000		X	X

Court	CRIMINAL				
	Felony	Misdemeanor	DWI/DUI	Preliminary Hearing	Juvenile
Superior Courts*	X				
District Courts*		X	X	X	X

ADMINISTRATION Administrative Office of the Courts, Justice Bldg, 2 E Morgan St, Raleigh, NC, 27602; 919-733-7107, Fax: 919-715-5779. www.aoc.state.nc.us

COURT STRUCTURE The Superior Court is the court of general jurisdiction, the District Court is limited. The counties combine the courts, thus searching is done through one court, not two, within the county

ONLINE ACCESS The web site offers free access to the active criminal calendar, on a county by county basis or statewide. Historical information is not available.

ADDITIONAL INFORMATION Many courts recommend that civil searches be done in person or by a retriever and that only criminal searches be requested in writing (for a $5.00 search fee). Many courts have archived their records prior to 1968 in the Raleigh State Archives, 919-733-5722.

Alamance County

Superior-District Court 212 West Elm St, Suite 105, Graham, NC 27253; 336-570-6867. Hours: 8AM-5PM (EST). *Felony, Misdemeanor.*

www.aoc.state.nc.us/www/public/courts/alamance.html

Criminal Records: Access: Mail, remote online, in person. Both court and visitors may perform in person searches. Search fee: $5.00 per name. Required to search: name, years to search, DOB; also helpful-address, SSN. Criminal records on computer since 1985, on index cards back to 1975. Search the active Criminal Calendar by defendant name at the web site. **General Information:** No sealed cases, juvenile, sex offenders, or dismissed records released. Turnaround time 1 week. Copy fee: $1.00 for first page, $.25 each addl. Certification fee: $2.00. Fee payee: Clerk of Superior Court. Only cashiers checks and money orders accepted. Prepayment is required. Public access terminal is available.

Superior-District Court, Civil 1 Court Square, Graham, NC 27253; 336-570-6865. Hours: 8AM-5PM (EST). *Civil, Eviction, Small Claims, Probate.*

Civil Records: Access: In person only. Court does not conduct in person searches; visitors must perform searches for themselves. Search fee: No civil searches performed by court. Required to

search: name, years to search. Civil cases indexed by defendant, plaintiff. Civil Records computerized since 1985, prior indexed on books. **General Information:** No adoptions, sealed cases, juvenile, sex offenders, or mental records released. Copy fee: $1.00 for first page, $.25 each addl. Certification fee: $2.00.

Alexander County

Superior-District Court PO Box 100, Taylorsville, NC 28681; 828-632-2215; Fax: 828-632-3550. Hours: 8AM-5PM (EST). *Felony, Misdemeanor, Civil, Eviction, Small Claims, Probate.*

www.aoc.state.nc.us/www/public/courts/alexander.htm

Civil Records: Access: Mail, in person. Both court and visitors may perform in person searches. Search fee: $5.00 per name. Required to search: name, years to search, address. Civil cases indexed by defendant, plaintiff. Civil records on computer since Oct. 1989, prior on books. **Criminal Records:** Access: Mail, remote online, in person. Both court and visitors may perform in person searches. Search fee: $5.00 per name. Required to search: name, years to search, address, DOB, SSN. Criminal records on computer since Oct. 1989, prior on books. Search the active Criminal Calendar by defendant name at the web site. **General Information:** No adoptions, sealed cases, juvenile, sex offenders, mental, expunged records

released. SASE required. Turnaround time 1-3 days. Copy fee: $.25 per page. Certification fee: $2.00. Fee payee: Clerk of Superior Court. Business checks accepted. Prepayment is required. Public access terminal is available.

Alleghany County

Superior-District Court PO Box 61, Sparta, NC 28675; 336-372-8949; Fax: 336-372-4899. Hours: 8AM-5PM (EST). *Felony, Misdemeanor, Civil, Eviction, Small Claims, Probate.*

www.aoc.state.nc.us/www/public/courts/alleghany.html

Civil Records: Access: Fax, mail, in person. Both court and visitors may perform in person searches. Search fee: $5.00 per name. Required to search: name, years to search; also helpful-address. Civil cases indexed by defendant, plaintiff. Civil records on computer from Nov. 1988, index books. **Criminal Records:** Access: Fax, mail, remote online, in person. Only the court conducts in person searches; visitors may not. Search fee: $5.00 per name. Required to search: name, years to search, DOB; also helpful-address, SSN. Criminal records on computer from Nov. 1988, index books. Search the active Criminal Calendar by defendant name at the web site. **General Information:** No adoptions, sealed cases, juvenile, sex offenders, mental or expunged records released. SASE required. Turnaround time 2 days. Copy fee: $1.00 for first page, $.25 each addl.

Certification fee: $2.00. Fee payee: Clerk of Superior Court. Business checks accepted. Prepayment is required. Fax notes: $4.00 per page.

Anson County

Superior-District Court PO Box 1064 (114 N Greene St), Wadesboro, NC 28170; 704-694-2314; Fax: 704-695-1161. Hours: 8AM-5PM (EST). *Felony, Misdemeanor, Civil, Eviction, Small Claims, Probate.*

www.aoc.state.nc.us/www/public/courts/anson.htm

Civil Records: Access: Mail, in person. Court does not conduct in person searches; visitors must perform searches for themselves. Search fee: $5.00 per name. Required to search: name, years to search. Civil cases indexed by defendant, plaintiff. Civil records on computer since Oct. 1989, in books prior. **Criminal Records:** Access: Mail, remote online, in person. Only the court conducts in person searches; visitors may not. Search fee: $5.00 per name. Required to search: name, years to search, DOB; also helpful-SSN. Criminal records on computer since 10/89, on microfilm 1982-89, in books prior. Search the active Criminal Calendar by defendant name at the web site. **General Information:** No adoptions, sealed cases, juvenile, mental, or expunged records released. SASE required. Turnaround time 2-5 days. Copy fee: $1.00 for first page, $.25 each addl. Certification fee: $2.00. Fee payee: Clerk of Superior Court. Business checks accepted. Prepayment is required. Public access terminal is available. Public Access Terminal Note: Estates & Special Proceedings only.

Ashe County

Superior-District Court PO Box 95, Jefferson, NC 28640; 336-246-5641; Fax: 336-246-4276. Hours: 8AM-5PM (EST). *Felony, Misdemeanor, Civil, Eviction, Small Claims, Probate.*

www.aoc.state.nc.us/www/public/courts/ashe.html

Civil Records: Access: Mail, in person. Both court and visitors may perform in person searches. Search fee: $5.00 per name. Required to search: name, years to search. Civil cases indexed by defendant, plaintiff. Civil records on computer from 12/89, on index books back to 1900s. **Criminal Records:** Access: Mail, remote online, in person. Both court and visitors may perform in person searches. Search fee: $5.00 per name. Required to search: name, years to search. Criminal records on computer from 12/89, on index books back to 1900s. Court will search records after 1988; visitors or researchers must search themselves for records prior to 1988. Search the active Criminal Calendar by defendant name at the web site. **General Information:** No adoptions, sealed cases, juvenile, sex offenders, mental or expunged records released. Turnaround time 1-3 days. Copy fee: $1.00 for first page, $.25 each addl. Certification fee: $2.00. Fee payee: Clerk of Superior Court. Only cashiers checks and money orders accepted. Public access terminal is available.

Avery County

Superior-District Court PO Box 115, Newland, NC 28657; 828-733-2900; Fax: 828-733-8410. Hours: 8AM-4:30PM (EST). *Felony, Misdemeanor, Civil, Eviction, Small Claims, Probate.*

www.aoc.state.nc.us/www/public/courts/avery.htm

Civil Records: Access: Mail, in person. Only the court conducts in person searches; visitors may

not. Search fee: $5.00 per name. Required to search: name, years to search; also helpful-address. Civil cases indexed by defendant, plaintiff. Civil records on computer since 1988, on index books to 1912. **Criminal Records:** Access: Mail, remote online, in person. Only the court conducts in person searches; visitors may not. Search fee: $5.00 per name. Required to search: name, years to search; also helpful-address. Criminal records on computer from 11/88; on cards and books back to 1968. Search the active Criminal Calendar by defendant name at the web site. **General Information:** No adoptions, sealed cases, juvenile, sex offenders, mental or expunged records released. Turnaround time 2-3 days. Copy fee: $.25 per page. Certification fee: $2.00. Fee payee: Clerk of Superior Court. Only cashiers checks and money orders accepted. Will bill copy fees.

Beaufort County

Superior-District Court PO Box 1403, Washington, NC 27889; 919-946-5184. Hours: 8:30AM-5:30PM (EST). *Felony, Misdemeanor, Civil, Eviction, Small Claims, Probate.*

www.aoc.state.nc.us/www/public/courts/beaufort. html

Civil Records: Access: In person only. Court does not conduct in person searches; visitors must perform searches for themselves. Search fee: No civil searches performed by court. Required to search: name, years to search, address. Civil cases indexed by defendant, plaintiff. Civil records on computer since 6/87, docket books to 1800s. **Criminal Records:** Access: Mail, remote online, in person. Both court and visitors may perform in person searches. Search fee: $5.00 per name. Required to search: name, years to search, address, DOB, SSN. Criminal records on computer since 6/87, docket books to 1800s. Search the active Criminal Calendar by defendant name at the web site. **General Information:** No adoptions, sealed cases, juvenile, sex offenders, mental or expunged records released. Turnaround time 5 days. Copy fee: $1.00 for first page, $.25 each addl. Certification fee: $2.00. Fee payee: Clerk of Superior Court. Business checks accepted. Public access terminal is available.

Bertie County

Superior-District Court PO Box 370, Windsor, NC 27983; 252-794-3039; Fax: 252-794-2482. Hours: 8AM-5PM (EST). *Felony, Misdemeanor, Civil, Eviction, Small Claims, Probate.*

www.aoc.state.nc.us/www/public/courts/bertie.html

Civil Records: Access: In person only. Court does not conduct in person searches; visitors must perform searches for themselves. Search fee: No civil searches performed by court. Required to search: name, years to search. Civil cases indexed by defendant, plaintiff. Civil records on computer from 3/89, prior on books to 1968. **Criminal Records:** Access: Mail, remote online, in person. Both court and visitors may perform in person searches. Search fee: $5.00 per name. Required to search: name, years to search, DOB; also helpful-address, SSN. Criminal records on computer from 3/89, prior on books to 1968. Search the active Criminal Calendar by defendant name at the web site. **General Information:** No adoptions, sealed cases, juvenile, mental, expunged records released. SASE requested. Turnaround time 1-2 days. Copy fee: $1.00 for first page, $.25 each addl. Certification fee: Court will not certify any in-person searches, otherise $5.00. Fee payee: Clerk of Superior Court. Only cashiers checks and

money orders accepted. Prepayment is required. Public access terminal is available.

Bladen County

Superior-District Court PO Box 2619, Elizabethtown, NC 28337; 910-862-2143. Hours: 8:30AM-5PM (EST). *Felony, Misdemeanor, Civil, Eviction, Small Claims, Probate.*

www.aoc.state.nc.us/www/public/courts/bladen.html

Civil Records: Access: In person only. Court does not conduct in person searches; visitors must perform searches for themselves. Search fee: No civil searches performed by court. Required to search: name, years to search. Civil cases indexed by defendant, plaintiff. Civil records on computer since 1989, prior on judgement books back to 1896 (fire). **Criminal Records:** Access: Mail, remote online, in person. Both court and visitors may perform in person searches. Search fee: $5.00 per name. Required to search: name, years to search, DOB. Criminal records on computer from 5/89, on books to 1968. Search the active Criminal Calendar by defendant name at the web site. **General Information:** No adoptions, sealed cases, juvenile, sex offenders, mental or expunged records released. Turnaround time 5 days. Copy fee: $1.00 for first page, $.25 each addl. Certification fee: $2.00. Fee payee: Clerk of Superior Court. Only cashiers checks and money orders accepted. Prepayment is required. Public access terminal is available.

Brunswick County

Superior-District Court PO Box 127, Bolivia, NC 28422; 910-253-8502; Fax: 910-253-7652. Hours: 8:30AM-5:00PM (EST). *Felony, Misdemeanor, Civil, Eviction, Small Claims, Probate.*

www.aoc.state.nc.us/www/public/courts/ brunswick.html

Civil Records: Access: In person only. Court does not conduct in person searches; visitors must perform searches for themselves. Search fee: No civil searches performed by court. Required to search: name, years to search. Civil cases indexed by defendant, plaintiff. Civil records on computer since 1989, prior on books to 1968. **Criminal Records:** Access: Mail, remote online, in person. Both court and visitors may perform in person searches. Search fee: $5.00 per name. Required to search: name, years to search. Criminal records on computer since 1989, prior on books to 1968. Search the active Criminal Calendar by defendant name at the web site. **General Information:** No adoptions, sealed cases, juvenile, sex offenders, mental or expunged records. Turnaround time 1-2 days. Copy fee: $1.00 for first page, $.25 each addl. Certification fee: $1.00. Fee payee: Clerk of Court. Business checks accepted. Prepayment is required.

Buncombe County

Superior-District Court 60 Court Plaza, Asheville, NC 28801-3519; 828-232-2605; Fax: 828-251-6257. Hours: 8:30AM-5PM (EST). *Felony, Misdemeanor, Civil, Eviction, Small Claims, Probate.*

www.aoc.state.nc.us/www/public/courts/ buncombe.html

Civil Records: Access: Mail, in person. Both court and visitors may perform in person searches. Search fee: $5.00 per name. Required to search: name, years to search. Civil cases indexed by defendant, plaintiff. Civil records on computer since 1/89; on books or dockets to 1832; judgment books in archives. **Criminal Records:** Access: Mail, remote online, in person. Both court and visitors may perform in person searches. Search fee: $5.00 per name. Required to search: name, years to search, DOB. Criminal records on computer since 1/89; on books or dockets to 1832; judgment books in archives. Search the active Criminal Calendar by defendant name at the web site. **General Information:** No adoptions, sealed cases, juvenile, sex offenders, mental or expunged records required. SASE required. Turnaround time 1 week. Copy fee: $1.00 for first page, $.25 each addl. Certification fee: $2.00. Fee payee: Clerk of Court. Only cashiers checks and money orders accepted. Prepayment is required. Public access terminal is available.

Burke County

Superior-District Court PO Box 796, Morganton, NC 28680; 828-432-2800; Fax: 828-438-5460. Hours: 8AM-5PM (EST). *Felony, Misdemeanor, Civil, Eviction, Small Claims, Probate.*

www.aoc.state.nc.us/www/public/courts/burke.html

Civil Records: Access: Fax, mail, in person. Both court and visitors may perform in person searches. Search fee: $5.00 per name. Required to search: name, years to search; also helpful-address. Civil cases indexed by defendant, plaintiff. Civil records on computer since 10/88, on index books to 1890s. **Criminal Records:** Access: Fax, mail, remote online, in person. Both court and visitors may perform in person searches. Search fee: $5.00 per name. Required to search: name, years to search, DOB; also helpful-address, SSN. Criminal records on computer since 6/86, on cards or books back to 1900s. Search the active Criminal Calendar by defendant name at the web site. **General Information:** No adoptions, sealed cases, juvenile, sex offenders, mental or expunged records released. SASE required. Turnaround time 1-2 days. Copy fee: $1.00 for first page, $.25 each addl. Certification fee: $2.00. Fee payee: Clerk of Court. Business checks accepted. Prepayment is required. Public access terminal is available. Fax notes: $3.00 per document.

Cabarrus County

Superior-District Court PO Box 70, Concord, NC 28026-0070; 704-786-4137 (Estates & Special Proceed); Civil phone:704-786-4201; Criminal phone:704-786-4201. Hours: 8:30AM-5PM (EST). *Felony, Misdemeanor, Civil, Eviction, Small Claims, Probate.*

www.aoc.state.nc.us/www/public/courts/cabarrus.htm

Civil Records: Access: In person only. Court does not conduct in person searches; visitors must perform searches for themselves. Search fee: No civil searches performed by court. Required to search: name, years to search; also helpful-address. Civil cases indexed by defendant, plaintiff. Civil records on computer since 1/89, prior on books. **Criminal Records:** Access: Mail, remote online, in person. Both court and visitors may perform in person searches. Search fee: $5.00 per name. Required to search: name; also helpful-address, DOB, SSN, maiden name. Criminal records computerized since 01/85. Search the active Criminal Calendar by defendant name at the web site. **General Information:** No adoptions, sealed cases, juvenile, sex offenders, mental or expunged records released. Turnaround time 2-3 days. Copy fee: $1.00 for first page, $.25 each addl. Certification fee: $2.00. Fee payee: Clerk of Superior Court. Only cashiers checks and money

orders accepted. Prepayment is required. Public access terminal is available.

Caldwell County

Superior-District Court PO Box 1376, Lenoir, NC 28645; 828-757-1375; Fax: 828-757-1479. Hours: 8AM-5PM (EST). *Felony, Misdemeanor, Civil, Eviction, Small Claims, Probate.*

www.aoc.state.nc.us/www/public/courts/caldwell.html

Civil Records: Access: Fax, mail, in person. Both court and visitors may perform in person searches. Search fee: $5.00 per name. Required to search: name, years to search. Civil cases indexed by defendant, plaintiff. Civil records on computer since Nov. 1988, prior on books to 1849. **Criminal Records:** Access: Fax, mail, remote online, in person. Both court and visitors may perform in person searches. Search fee: $5.00 per name. Required to search: name, years to search; also helpful-address, DOB, SSN. Criminal records on computer from 8/86, prior in books to 1966. Search the active Criminal Calendar by defendant name at the web site. **General Information:** No adoptions, sealed cases, juvenile, sex offenders, mental or expunged records released. Turnaround time 1-2 days. Copy fee: $1.00 for first page, $.25 each addl. Certification fee: Certification is included in search fee, if do it yourself then $2.00. Fee payee: Clerk of Superior Court. Only cashiers checks and money orders accepted. Prepayment is required. Public access terminal is available. Fax notes: $1.00 for first page, $.25 each addl.

Camden County

Superior-District Court PO Box 219, Camden, NC 27921; 252-331-4871; Fax: 252-331-4827. Hours: 8AM-5PM (EST). *Felony, Misdemeanor, Civil, Eviction, Small Claims, Probate.*

www.aoc.state.nc.us/www/public/courts/camden.html

Civil Records: Access: In person only. Court does not conduct in person searches; visitors must perform searches for themselves. Search fee: $5.00 per name. Required to search: name, years to search. Civil cases indexed by defendant, plaintiff. Civil records on computer since Nov. 27 1989, prior on index books to 1966. **Criminal Records:** Access: Mail, remote online, in person. Both court and visitors may perform in person searches. Search fee: $5.00 per name. Required to search: name, years to search, DOB. Criminal records on computer since Nov. 27 1989, prior on index books to 1966. Search the active Criminal Calendar by defendant name at the web site. **General Information:** No adoptions, sealed cases, juvenile, sex offenders, mental or expunged records released. Turnaround time 1-2 days. Copy fee: $1.00 for first page, $.25 each addl. Certification fee: $2.00 if you do search, otherwise is included in search fee. Fee payee: Clerk of Superior Court. Business checks accepted. Prepayment is required. Public access terminal is available.

Carteret County

Superior-District Court, Carteret County Courthouse Square, Beaufort, NC 28516; 252-728-8500; Fax: 252-728-6502. Hours: 8AM-5PM (EST). *Felony, Misdemeanor, Civil, Eviction, Small Claims, Probate.*

www.aoc.state.nc.us/www/public/courts/carteret.html

Civil Records: Access: In person only. Court does not conduct in person searches; visitors must

perform searches for themselves. Search fee: No civil searches performed by court. Required to search: name, years to search. Civil cases indexed by defendant, plaintiff. Civil records on computer since 1988, prior on books to 1800s. **Criminal Records:** Access: Mail, remote online, in person. Both court and visitors may perform in person searches. Search fee: $5.00 per name. Required to search: name, years to search; also helpful-address, DOB, SSN. Criminal records on computer to 1/87, prior on cards and books to 1800s. Call first. Search the active Criminal Calendar by defendant name at the web site. **General Information:** No adoptions, sealed cases, juvenile, sex offenders, mental or expunged records released. Turnaround time 1-2 days. Copy fee: $1.00 for first page, $.25 each addl. Certification fee: $2.00. Fee payee: Clerk of Superior Court. Business checks accepted. Prepayment is required. Public access terminal is available.

Caswell County

Superior-District Court PO Drawer 790, Yanceyville, NC 27379; 336-694-4171; Fax: 336-694-7338. Hours: 8AM-5PM (EST). *Felony, Misdemeanor, Civil, Eviction, Small Claims, Probate.*

www.aoc.state.nc.us/www/public/courts/caswell.html

Civil Records: Access: In person only. Court does not conduct in person searches; visitors must perform searches for themselves. Search fee: No civil searches performed by court. Required to search: name, years to search. Civil cases indexed by defendant, plaintiff. Civil records on computer from 3/89 to present, on index books back to 1970, prior records in civil summons book. **Criminal Records:** Access: Mail, remote online, in person. Both court and visitors may perform in person searches. Search fee: $5.00 per name. Required to search: name, years to search, DOB; also helpful-address. Criminal records on computer since 5/88, prior on books and cards. Search the active Criminal Calendar by defendant name at the web site. **General Information:** No adoptions, sealed cases, juvenile, mental or expunged records released. SASE helpful. Turnaround time 1-2 days. Copy fee: $1.00 for first page, $.25 each addl. Certification fee: $2.00. Fee payee: Clerk of Superior Court. Business checks accepted. Prepayment is required. Public access terminal is available.

Catawba County

Superior-District Court PO Box 790, Newton, NC 28658; 828-464-5216. Hours: 8AM-5PM (EST). *Felony, Misdemeanor, Civil, Eviction, Small Claims, Probate.*

www.aoc.state.nc.us/www/public/courts/catawba.html

Civil Records: Access: In person only. Court does not conduct in person searches; visitors must perform searches for themselves. Search fee: No civil searches performed by court. Required to search: name, years to search. Civil cases indexed by defendant, plaintiff. Civil records on computer since Mar. 1988, prior on books. **Criminal Records:** Access: Mail, remote online, in person. Both court and visitors may perform in person searches. Search fee: $5.00 per name. Required to search: name, years to search, DOB. Criminal records on computer since 4/85, on books to 1966, archived prior. Search the active Criminal Calendar by defendant name at the web site. **General Information:** No adoptions, sealed cases, juvenile, sex offenders, mental or expunged records released. SASE required. Turnaround time 5 days. Copy fee: $1.00 for first page, $.25 each addl. Certification fee: $2.00. Fee payee: Clerk of Court. Only cashiers checks and money orders accepted. Prepayment is required. Public access terminal is available.

Chatham County

Superior-District Court PO Box 369, Pittsboro, NC 27312; 919-542-3240; Fax: 919-542-1402. Hours: 8AM-5PM (EST). *Felony, Misdemeanor, Civil, Eviction, Small Claims, Probate.*

www.aoc.state.nc.us/www/public/courts/chatham.html

Civil Records: Access: Phone, mail, in person. Both court and visitors may perform in person searches. Search fee: $5.00 per name. Required to search: name, years to search. Civil cases indexed by defendant, plaintiff. Civil records on computer since 4/89, prior on books, archived 1968 back in Raleigh. **Criminal Records:** Access: Mail, remote online, in person. Both court and visitors may perform in person searches. Search fee: $5.00 per name. Required to search: name, years to search; also helpful-address, DOB, SSN. Criminal records on computer since 7/87, prior on books or cards to 1968. Search the active Criminal Calendar by defendant name at the web site. **General Information:** No adoptions, sealed cases, juvenile, sex offenders, mental or expunged records released. Turnaround time 1 day. Copy fee: $1.00 for first page, $.25 each addl. Certification fee: $2.00. Fee payee: Clerk of Superior Court. Personal checks accepted. Prepayment is required. Public access terminal is available.

Cherokee County

Superior-District Court 75 Peachtree St, Rm 201, Murphy, NC 28906; 828-837-2522. Hours: 8AM-5PM (EST). *Felony, Misdemeanor, Civil, Eviction, Small Claims, Probate.*

www.aoc.state.nc.us/www/public/courts/cherokee.html

Civil Records: Access: Mail, in person. Both court and visitors may perform in person searches. Search fee: $5.00 per name. Required to search: name, years to search, address. Civil cases indexed by defendant, plaintiff. Civil records on computer since 5/89, on index books to 1867. **Criminal Records:** Access: Mail, remote online, in person. Only the court conducts in person searches; visitors may not. Search fee: $5.00 per name. Required to search: name, years to search, DOB. Criminal records on computer since 5/89, index cards to 1985, index books to 1966. Search the active Criminal Calendar by defendant name at the web site. There is no public access terminal for searching criminal records. **General Information:** No adoptions, sealed cases, juvenile or mental records released. SASE required. Turnaround time 1-2 days. Copy fee: $1.00 for first page, $.25 each addl. Certification fee: $2.00. Fee payee: Clerk of Superior Court. No personal checks accepted. Public access terminal is available.

Chowan County

Superior-District Court N.C. Courier Box 106319, PO Box 588, Edenton, NC 27932; 252-482-2323; Fax: 252-482-2190. Hours: 9AM-5PM (EST). *Felony, Misdemeanor, Civil, Eviction, Small Claims, Probate.*

www.aoc.state.nc.us/www/public/courts/chowan.html

Civil Records: Access: In person only. Court does not conduct in person searches; visitors must perform searches for themselves. Search fee: No civil searches performed by court. Required to

search: name, years to search; also helpful-address. Civil cases indexed by defendant, plaintiff. Civil records on computer since 1990, prior on books to 1800s. **Criminal Records:** Access: Mail, remote online, in person. Both court and visitors may perform in person searches. Search fee: $5.00 per name. Required to search: name, years to search, DOB; also helpful-address, SSN. Criminal records on computer from 1/90, prior as civil. Search the active Criminal Calendar by defendant name at the web site. **General Information:** No adoptions, sealed cases, juvenile, sex offenders, mental or expunged records released. SASE requested. Turnaround time 3-5 days. Copy fee: $1.00 for first page, $.25 each addl. Certification fee: $2.50. Fee payee: Clerk of Superior Court. Only cashiers checks and money orders accepted. Prepayment is required. Public access terminal is available.

Clay County

Superior-District Court PO Box 506, Hayesville, NC 28904; 828-389-8334; Fax: 828-389-3329. Hours: 8AM-5PM (EST). *Felony, Misdemeanor, Civil, Eviction, Small Claims, Probate.*

www.aoc.state.nc.us/www/public/courts/clay.html

Civil Records: Access: Fax, mail, in person. Only the court conducts in person searches; visitors may not. Search fee: $5.00 per name. Required to search: name, years to search; also helpful-address. Civil cases indexed by defendant, plaintiff. Civil records on computer since 1989, on books since 1888. **Criminal Records:** Access: Fax, mail, remote online, in person. Only the court conducts in person searches; visitors may not. Search fee: $5.00 per name. Required to search: name, years to search; also helpful-address, DOB, SSN. Criminal records on computer since 1989, on books since 1888. Search the active Criminal Calendar by defendant name at the web site. **General Information:** No adoptions, sealed cases, juvenile, sex offenders, mental or expunged records released. Turnaround time 1-2 days. Copy fee: $1.00 for first page, $.25 each addl. Certification fee: $2.00. Fee payee: Clerk of Court. Business checks accepted. Prepayment is required. Public access terminal is available. Public Access Terminal Note: Aavailable for civil only. Fax notes: No fee to fax results.

Cleveland County

Superior-District Court 100 Justice Place, Shelby, NC 28150; 704-484-4851; Fax: 704-480-5487. Hours: 8AM-5PM (EST). *Felony, Misdemeanor, Civil, Eviction, Small Claims, Probate.*

www.aoc.state.nc.us/www/public/courts/cleveland.html

Civil Records: Access: In person only. Court does not conduct in person searches; visitors must perform searches for themselves. Search fee: No civil searches performed by court. Required to search: name, years to search; also helpful-address. Civil cases indexed by defendant, plaintiff. Civil records on computer since 1988, books to 1968, archived prior. **Criminal Records:** Access: Fax, mail, remote online, in person. Both court and visitors may perform in person searches. Search fee: $5.00 per name. Required to search: name, years to search, DOB; also helpful-address, SSN. Criminal records on computer since 6/86, on books to 1972, archived prior. Search the active Criminal Calendar by defendant name at the web site. **General Information:** No adoptions, sealed cases, juvenile, sex offenders, mental or expunged records released. SASE requested. Turnaround

time 1-2 days. Copy fee: $1.00 for first page, $.25 each addl. Certification fee: $2.00. Fee payee: Clerk of Superior Court. No out-of-state checks accepted. Prepayment is required. Public access terminal is available. Fax notes: $1.00 for first page, $.25 each addl.

Columbus County

Superior-District Court PO Box 1587, Whiteville, NC 28472; 910-641-3000; Fax: 910-641-3027. Hours: 8AM-5PM (EST). *Felony, Misdemeanor, Civil, Eviction, Small Claims, Probate.*

www.aoc.state.nc.us/www/public/courts/columbus.html

Civil Records: Access: Phone, mail, in person. Court does not conduct in person searches; visitors must perform searches for themselves. Search fee: No civil searches performed by court. Required to search: name, years to search; also helpful-address. Civil cases indexed by defendant, plaintiff. Civil records on computer from 5/89, prior on books to 1968. **Criminal Records:** Access: Phone, mail, in person. Both court and visitors may perform in person searches. Search fee: $5.00 per name. Required to search: name, years to search, DOB; also helpful-address, SSN. Criminal records on computer from 6/87, prior on books or cards to 1968. Search the active Criminal Calendar by defendant name at the web site. **General Information:** No adoptions, sealed, juvenile, tax offender, mental, expunged or dismissed. SASE required. Turnaround time 2-5 days. Copy fee: $1.00 per page. Certification fee: $2.00. Fee payee: Clerk of Superior Court. Only cashiers checks and money orders accepted. Prepayment is required. Public access terminal is available.

Craven County

Superior-District Court PO Box 1187, New Bern, NC 28563; 252-514-4774; Fax: 252-514-4891. Hours: 8AM-5PM (EST). *Felony, Misdemeanor, Civil, Eviction, Small Claims, Probate.*

www.aoc.state.nc.us/www/public/courts/craven.htm

Civil Records: Access: Mail, in person. Both court and visitors may perform in person searches. Search fee: $5.00 per name. Required to search: name, years to search; also helpful-address. Civil cases indexed by defendant, plaintiff. Civil records on computer from 10/88, prior to 1968 are archived. **Criminal Records:** Access: Mail, remote online, in person. Both court and visitors may perform in person searches. Search fee: $5.00 per name. Required to search: name, years to search, DOB; also helpful-address, SSN. Criminal records on computer since 1/87, prior on books and cards to 1968. Search the active Criminal Calendar by defendant name at the web site. **General Information:** No adoptions, sealed cases, juvenile, sex offenders, mental, expunged, or dismissed. SASE required. Turnaround time 1-2 days. Copy fee: $1.00 for first page, $.25 each addl. Certification fee: $2.00. Fee payee: Clerk of Superior Court. Only cashiers checks and money orders accepted. Prepayment is required. Public access terminal is available.

Cumberland County

Superior-District Court PO Box 363, Fayetteville, NC 28302;; Civil phone:910-678-2909; Criminal phone:910-678-2909. Hours: 8:30AM-5PM (EST). *Felony, Misdemeanor, Civil, Eviction, Small Claims, Probate.*

www.aoc.state.nc.us/data/district12

Civil Records: Access: Mail, in person. Both court and visitors may perform in person searches. Search fee: $5.00 per name. Required to search: name, years to search; also helpful-address. Civil cases indexed by defendant, plaintiff. Civil records on computer since 1988, books back to 1956. **Criminal Records:** Access: Mail, remote online, in person. Both court and visitors may perform in person searches. Search fee: $5.00 per name. Required to search: name, years to search; also helpful-address, DOB, SSN. Criminal records on computer since 5/82, books and cards to 1920s. Search the active Criminal Calendar by defendant name at the web site. **General Information:** No adoptions, sealed cases, juvenile, sex offenders, mental or expunged records released. Turnaround time 2 weeks. Copy fee: $2.00 per page. Certification fee: Included in search fee, unless in-person then $2.00. Fee payee: Clerk of Superior Court. Business checks accepted. Prepayment is required. Public access terminal is available.

Currituck County

Superior-District Court PO Box 175, Currituck, NC 27929; 252-232-2010; Fax: 252-232-3722. Hours: 8AM-5PM (EST). *Felony, Misdemeanor, Civil, Eviction, Small Claims, Probate.*

www.aoc.state.nc.us/www/public/courts/currituck. html

Civil Records: Access: Fax, mail, in person. Both court and visitors may perform in person searches. Search fee: $5.00 per name. Required to search: name, years to search. Civil cases indexed by defendant, plaintiff. Civil records on computer since 11/27/89, books to 1968, prior archived. **Criminal Records:** Access: Fax, mail, remote online, in person. Both court and visitors may perform in person searches. Search fee: $5.00 per name. Required to search: name, years to search, DOB. Criminal records on computer since 11/27/89, books to 1968, prior archived. Search the active Criminal Calendar by defendant name at the web site. **General Information:** No adoptions, sealed cases, juvenile, sex offenders, mental or expunged records released. Copy fee: $1.00 for first page, $.25 each addl. Certification fee: $2.00. Fee payee: Clerk of Superior Court. Only cashiers checks and money orders accepted. Prepayment is required. Public access terminal is available.

Dare County

Superior-District Court PO Box 1849, Manteo, NC 27954; 252-473-2950; Fax: 252-473-1620. Hours: 8:30AM-5PM (EST). *Felony, Misdemeanor, Civil, Eviction, Small Claims, Probate.*

www.aoc.state.nc.us/www/public/courts/dare.htm

Civil Records: Access: Mail, in person. Both court and visitors may perform in person searches. Search fee: $5.00 per name. Required to search: name, years to search; also helpful-address. Civil cases indexed by defendant, plaintiff. Civil records on computer since 1985, on books to 1968. **Criminal Records:** Access: Mail, remote online, in person. Both court and visitors may perform in person searches. Search fee: $5.00 per name. Required to search: name, years to search, DOB; also helpful-SSN. Criminal records on computer since 1987, on books and cards to 1968. Search the active Criminal Calendar by defendant name at the web site. **General Information:** No adoptions, sealed cases, juvenile, sex offenders, mental or expunged records released. Turnaround time 2 days. Copy fee: $1.00 for first page, $.25 each addl. Certification fee: $2.00. Fee payee: Superior

District Court. Business checks accepted. Out of state business checks not accepted. Prepayment is required. Public access terminal is available.

Davidson County

Superior-District Court PO Box 1064, Lexington, NC 27293-1064;; Civil phone:336-249-0351; Criminal phone:336-249-0351; Fax: 336-249-6951. Hours: 8AM-5PM (EST). *Felony, Misdemeanor, Civil, Eviction, Small Claims, Probate.*

www.aoc.state.nc.us/www/public/courts/davidson. html

Civil Records: Access: In person only. Court does not conduct in person searches; visitors must perform searches for themselves. Search fee: No civil searches performed by court. Required to search: name, years to search; also helpful-address. Civil cases indexed by defendant, plaintiff. Civil records on computer since 5/16/88, prior on books. **Criminal Records:** Access: Mail, remote online, in person. Both court and visitors may perform in person searches. Search fee: $5.00 per name. Required to search: name, years to search; also helpful-address, DOB, SSN. Criminal records on computer since 10/85, on books and cards to 1952. Search the active Criminal Calendar by defendant name at the web site. **General Information:** No adoptions, sealed cases, juvenile, sex offenders, mental or expunged records released. SASE requested. Turnaround time 2-3 days. Copy fee: $1.00 for first page, $.25 each addl. Certification fee: $2.00. Fee payee: Clerk of Superior Court. Business checks accepted. Prepayment is required. Public access terminal is available.

Davie County

Superior-District Court 140 S Main St, Mocksville, NC 27028;; Civil phone:336-751-3507; Criminal phone:336-751-3507; Fax: 336-751-4720. Hours: 8:30AM-5PM (EST). *Felony, Misdemeanor, Civil, Eviction, Small Claims, Probate.*

www.aoc.state.nc.us/www/public/courts/davie.html

Civil Records: Access: Mail, in person. Both court and visitors may perform in person searches. Search fee: $5.00 per name. Required to search: name, years to search. Civil cases indexed by defendant, plaintiff. Civil records on computer since Oct. 1989, on books to 1970. **Criminal Records:** Access: Mail, remote online, in person. Both court and visitors may perform in person searches. Search fee: $5.00 per name. Required to search: name, years to search, DOB. Criminal records on computer since Oct. 1989, on books to 1970. Search the active Criminal Calendar by defendant name at the web site. **General Information:** No adoptions, sealed cases, juvenile, sex offenders, mental or expunged records released. SASE required. Turnaround time 5 days. Copy fee: $1.00 for first page, $.25 each addl. Certification fee: $2.00. Fee payee: Clerk of Superior Court. Personal checks accepted. Prepayment is required. Public access terminal is available.

Duplin County

Superior-District Court PO Box 189, Kenansville, NC 28349;; Civil phone:910-296-1686; Criminal phone:910-296-1686; Fax: 910-296-2310. Hours: 8AM-5PM (EST). *Felony, Misdemeanor, Civil, Eviction, Small Claims, Probate.*

www.aoc.state.nc.us/www/public/courts/duplin.htm

Civil Records: Access: Phone, fax, mail, in person. Only the court conducts in person searches; visitors may not. Search fee: $5.00 per name. Required to search: name, years to search. Civil cases indexed by defendant, plaintiff. Civil records on computer since 1989, prior on books to early 1900s. **Criminal Records:** Access: Phone, fax, mail, remote online, in person. Only the court conducts in person searches; visitors may not. Search fee: $5.00 per name. Required to search: name, years to search, DOB. Criminal records on computer since 5/88, on cards and books to 1927. Search the active Criminal Calendar by defendant name at the web site. **General Information:** No adoptions, sealed cases, juvenile, sex offenders, mental or expunged records released. Turnaround time 1-2 days. Copy fee: $1.00 for first page, $.25 each addl. Certification fee: $2.00. Fee payee: Clerk of Superior Court. Personal checks accepted. Prepayment is required. Public access terminal is available.

Durham County

Superior-District Court 201 E Main St, Durham, NC 27702;; Civil phone:919-560-6823; Criminal phone:919-560-6823. Hours: 8:30AM-5PM (EST). *Felony, Misdemeanor, Civil, Eviction, Small Claims, Probate.*

www.aoc.state.nc.us/www/public/courts/durham.htm

Civil Records: Access: In person only. Court does not conduct in person searches; visitors must perform searches for themselves. Search fee: No civil searches performed by court. Required to search: name, years to search; also helpful-address. Civil cases indexed by defendant, plaintiff. Civil records on computer since 1/88, on books to late 1800s. **Criminal Records:** Access: Mail, remote online, in person. Both court and visitors may perform in person searches. Search fee: $5.00 per name. Required to search: name, years to search, DOB; also helpful-address. Criminal records on microfiche since 1982, prior on books to 1979. Search the active Criminal Calendar by defendant name at the web site. **General Information:** No adoptions, sealed cases, juvenile, sex offenders, mental or expunged records released. SASE required. Turnaround time 3-4 days. Copy fee: $1.00 for first page, $.25 each addl. Certification fee: Certification is $2.00 for civil, but is included in search fee for criminal. Fee payee: Clerk of Superior Court. Only cashiers checks and money orders accepted. Prepayment is required. Public access terminal is available.

Edgecombe County

Superior-District Court PO Drawer 9, Tarboro, NC 27886;; Civil phone:919-823-6161; Criminal phone:919-823-6161; Fax: 919-823-1278. Hours: 8AM-5PM (EST). *Felony, Misdemeanor, Civil, Eviction, Small Claims, Probate.*

www.aoc.state.nc.us/www/public/courts/ edgecombe.htm

Civil Records: Access: In person only. Court does not conduct in person searches; visitors must perform searches for themselves. Search fee: No civil searches performed by court. Required to search: name, years to search, address. Civil cases indexed by defendant, plaintiff. Civil records on computer since 1988, prior on books to 1945, files to 1968. **Criminal Records:** Access: Mail, remote online, in person. Both court and visitors may perform in person searches. Search fee: $5.00 per name. Required to search: name, years to search, DOB, SSN; also helpful-address. Criminal records on computer since 4/87, on books and cards to

1900s. Search the active Criminal Calendar by defendant name at the web site. **General Information:** No adoptions, sealed cases, juvenile, sex offenders, mental or expunged records required. Turnaround time 1-2 days. Copy fee: $1.00 for first page, $.25 each addl. Certification fee: $2.00. Fee payee: Clerk of Superior Court. Business checks accepted. Public access terminal is available.

Forsyth County

Superior-District Court PO Box 20099, Winston Salem, NC 27120-0099; 336-761-2250; Civil phone:336-761-2340; Criminal phone:336-761-2340; Fax: 336-761-2018. Hours: 8AM-5PM (EST). *Felony, Misdemeanor, Civil, Eviction, Small Claims, Probate.*

www.aoc.state.nc.us/www/public/courts/forsyth.html

Civil Records: Access: Mail, in person. Both court and visitors may perform in person searches. Search fee: $5.00 per name. Required to search: name, years to search. Civil cases indexed by defendant, plaintiff. Civil records on computer since April 1988, prior on books to 1968, on microfiche prior. **Criminal Records:** Access: Mail, remote online, in person. Both court and visitors may perform in person searches. Search fee: $5.00 per name. Required to search: name, years to search, DOB. Criminal records on computer since April 1988, prior on books to 1968, on microfiche prior. Search the active Criminal Calendar by defendant name at the web site. **General Information:** No adoptions, sealed cases, juvenile, sex offenders, mental or expunged records released. SASE required. Turnaround time 1-2 days. Copy fee: $1.00 for first page, $.25 each addl. Certification fee: $2.00. Fee payee: Clerk of Superior Court. Business checks accepted. Prepayment is required. Public access terminal is available.

Franklin County

Superior-District Court 102 S Main St, Louisburg, NC 27549; 919-496-5104; Fax: 919-496-0407. Hours: 8:30AM-5PM (EST). *Felony, Misdemeanor, Civil, Eviction, Small Claims, Probate.*

www.aoc.state.nc.us/www/public/courts/franklin.html

Civil Records: Access: Fax, mail, in person. Both court and visitors may perform in person searches. Search fee: $5.00 per name. Required to search: name, years to search; also helpful-address. Civil cases indexed by defendant, plaintiff. Civil records on computer since June 1989, prior on books. **Criminal Records:** Access: Fax, mail, in person. Both court and visitors may perform in person searches. Search fee: $5.00 per name. Required to search: name, years to search, DOB; also helpful-address. Criminal records on computer since 1980, on index books back to 1968. Search the active Criminal Calendar by defendant name at the web site. **General Information:** No adoptions, sealed cases, juvenile, mental or expunged records released. SASE requested. Turnaround time 1-2 days. Copy fee: $1.00 for first page, $.25 each addl. Certification fee: $2.00. Fee payee: Clerk of Superior Court. Personal checks accepted. Prepayment is required. Public access terminal is available.

Gaston County

Superior-District Court PO Box 340, Gastonia, NC 28053; 704-852-3100. Hours: 8AM-5PM (EST). *Felony, Misdemeanor, Civil, Eviction, Small Claims, Probate.*

www.aoc.state.nc.us/www/public/courts/gaston.htm

Civil Records: Access: In person only. Court does not conduct in person searches; visitors must perform searches for themselves. Search fee: No civil searches performed by court. Required to search: name, years to search; also helpful-address. Civil cases indexed by defendant, plaintiff. Civil records on computer since 1988, prior on books to 1891. **Criminal Records:** Access: Mail, remote online, in person. Both court and visitors may perform in person searches. Search fee: $5.00 per name. Required to search: name, address, DOB; also helpful-years to search, SSN. Criminal records on criminal to 1/83, on books and cards to 1973. Search the active Criminal Calendar by defendant name at the web site. **General Information:** No adoptions, sealed cases, juvenile, sex offenders, mental or expunged records released. Turnaround time 1-2 days. Copy fee: $1.00 for first page, $.25 each addl. Certification fee: $2.00. Fee payee: Clerk of Superior Court. Only cashiers checks and money orders accepted. No out of state checks. Prepayment is required. Public access terminal is available.

Gates County

Superior-District Court PO Box 31, Gatesville, NC 27938; 252-357-1365; Fax: 252-357-1047. Hours: 8AM-5PM (EST). *Felony, Misdemeanor, Civil, Eviction, Small Claims, Probate.*

www.aoc.state.nc.us/www/public/courts/gates.html

Civil Records: Access: In person only. Court does not conduct in person searches; visitors must perform searches for themselves. Search fee: No civil searches performed by court. Required to search: name, years to search; also helpful-address. Civil cases indexed by defendant, plaintiff. Civil records on computer since 1990, prior on books to 1966. **Criminal Records:** Access: Mail, remote online, in person. Only the court conducts in person searches; visitors may not. Search fee: $5.00 per name. Required to search: name, years to search, DOB; also helpful-address, SSN. Criminal records on computer since 1990, prior on books to 1966. Search the active Criminal Calendar by defendant name at the web site. **General Information:** No adoptions, sealed cases, juvenile, sex offenders, mental or expunged records released. Turnaround time 1-2 days. Copy fee: $1.00 for first page, $.25 each addl. Certification fee: Included in search fee. Fee payee: Clerk of Superior Court. Business checks accepted. Prepayment is required. Public access terminal is available. Public Access Terminal Note: Available for civil only.

Graham County

Superior-District Court PO Box 1179, Robbinsville, NC 28771; 828-479-7986; Civil phone:828-479-7986 X7974; Criminal phone:828-479-7986 X7974; Fax: 828-479-6417. Hours: 8AM-5PM M-Th; 8AM-4:30PM Fri (EST). *Felony, Misdemeanor, Civil, Eviction, Small Claims, Probate.*

www.aoc.state.nc.us/www/public/courts/graham.html

Civil Records: Access: In person only. Court does not conduct in person searches; visitors must perform searches for themselves. Search fee: No civil searches performed by court. Required to search: name, years to search. Civil cases indexed by defendant, plaintiff. Civil records on computer since 1989, on books since 1920s. **Criminal Records:** Access: Mail, remote online, in person. Both court and visitors may perform in person

searches. Search fee: $5.00 per name. Required to search: name, years to search; also helpful-address, DOB, SSN. Criminal records on computer since 1984, on books to 1920s. Search the active Criminal Calendar by defendant name at the web site. **General Information:** No adoptions, sealed cases, juvenile, sex offenders, mental or expunged records released. SASE required. Turnaround time 3-5 days. Copy fee: $1.00 for first page, $.25 each addl. Certification fee: $2.00. Fee payee: Clerk of Superior Court. Only cashiers checks and money orders accepted. Prepayment is required. Public access terminal is available.

Granville County

Superior-District Court Courthouse, 101 Main Street, Oxford, NC 27565; 919-693-2649; Fax: 919-693-8944. *Felony, Misdemeanor, Civil, Eviction, Small Claims, Probate.*

www.aoc.state.nc.us/www/public/courts/granville.html

Civil Records: Access: Phone, mail, in person. Search fee: $5.00 per name. Required to search: name, years to search; also helpful-address. Civil cases indexed by defendant, plaintiff. Civil records on computer since June 12, 1989, on books to 1968, prior files destroyed. **Criminal Records:** Access: Phone, mail, remote online, in person. Both court and visitors may perform in person searches. Search fee: $5.00 per name. Required to search: name, years to search, DOB; also helpful-address. Criminal records on computer since Feb. 29, 1988, prior on books on cards to 1968. Search the active Criminal Calendar by defendant name at the web site. **General Information:** No adoptions, sealed cases, juvenile, mental or expunged records released. SASE would be helpful. Turnaround time 1 day. Copy fee: $1.00 for first page, $.25 each addl. Certification fee: $2.00. Fee payee: Clerk of Superior Court. Personal checks accepted. Prepayment is required. Public access terminal is available.

Greene County

Superior-District Court PO Box 675, Snow Hill, NC 28580; 252-747-3505. Hours: 8AM-5PM (EST). *Felony, Misdemeanor, Civil, Eviction, Small Claims, Probate.*

www.aoc.state.nc.us/www/public/courts/greene.htm

Civil Records: Access: In person only. Court does not conduct in person searches; visitors must perform searches for themselves. Search fee: No civil searches performed by court. Required to search: name, years to search; also helpful-address. Civil cases indexed by defendant, plaintiff. Civil records on computer since Oct. 1989, prior on books to 1865. **Criminal Records:** Access: Mail, remote online, in person. Both court and visitors may perform in person searches. Search fee: $5.00 per name. Required to search: name, years to search; also helpful-address, DOB, SSN. Criminal records on computer since Oct. 1989, prior on books to 1865. Search the active Criminal Calendar by defendant name at the web site. **General Information:** No adoptions, sealed cases, juvenile, sex offenders, mental or expunged records released. Turnaround time 1-2 days. Copy fee: $1.00 for first page, $.25 each addl. Certification fee: Included in search fee, unless in-person then $2.00. Fee payee: Clerk of Superior Court. Business checks accepted. Prepayment is required. Public access terminal is available.

Guilford County

Superior-District Court 201 S Eugene, PO Box 3008, Greensboro, NC 27402;; Civil phone:336-574-4305; Criminal phone:336-574-4305; Fax: 336-334-5020. Hours: 8:30AM-5PM (EST). *Felony, Misdemeanor, Civil, Eviction, Small Claims, Probate.*

www.aoc.state.nc.us/www/public/courts/guilford.html

Civil Records: Access: In person only. Court does not conduct in person searches; visitors must perform searches for themselves. Search fee: No civil searches performed by court. Required to search: name, years to search; also helpful-address. Civil cases indexed by defendant, plaintiff. Civil records on computer since 9/88, on books to late 1800s. **Criminal Records:** Access: Mail, remote online, in person. Both court and visitors may perform in person searches. Search fee: $5.00 per name. Required to search: name, years to search; also helpful-address, DOB, SSN. Criminal records on computer since 5/83, on cards and books to late 1800s. Search the active Criminal Calendar by defendant name at the web site. **General Information:** No adoptions, sealed cases, juvenile, sex offenders, mental or expunged records released. SASE required. Turnaround time 1 week. Copy fee: $1.00 for first page, $.25 each addl. Certification fee: $2.00. Fee payee: Clerk of Superior Court. Business checks accepted. Prepayment is required. Public access terminal is available.

Halifax County

Superior-District Court PO Box 66, Halifax, NC 27839; 252-583-5061; Fax: 252-583-1005. Hours: 8:30AM-5PM (EST). *Felony, Misdemeanor, Civil, Eviction, Small Claims, Probate.*

www.aoc.state.nc.us/data/halifax/index.html

Civil Records: Access: In person only. Court does not conduct in person searches; visitors must perform searches for themselves. Search fee: No civil searches performed by court. Required to search: name, years to search; also helpful-address. Civil cases indexed by defendant, plaintiff. Civil records on computer since 1988, on books to 1968, prior archived. **Criminal Records:** Access: Mail, remote online, in person. Both court and visitors may perform in person searches. Search fee: $5.00 per name. Required to search: name, years to search; also helpful-address, DOB, SSN. Criminal records on computer since 1988, on books to 1968, prior archived. Search the active Criminal Calendar by defendant name at the web site. **General Information:** No adoptions, sealed cases, juvenile, sex offenders, mental or expunged records released. Turnaround time 1-2 days. Copy fee: $1.00 for first page, $.25 each addl. Certification fee: $2.00. Fee payee: Clerk of Superior Court. Business checks accepted. Prepayment is required. Public access terminal is available. Public Access Terminal Note: Available for civil only.

Harnett County

Superior-District Court PO Box 849, Lillington, NC 27546; 910-893-5164; Civil phone:910-893-4961; Criminal phone:910-893-4961; Fax: 910-893-3683. Hours: 8:15AM-5:15PM (EST). *Felony, Misdemeanor, Civil, Eviction, Small Claims, Probate.*

www.aoc.state.nc.us/www/public/courts/harnett.html

Civil Records: Access: In person only. Court does not conduct in person searches; visitors must perform searches for themselves. Search fee: No civil searches performed by court. Required to search: name, years to search; also helpful-address. Civil cases indexed by defendant, plaintiff. Civil records on computer since April 17, 1989, prior on books from 1938. **Criminal Records:** Access: Mail, remote online, in person. Both court and visitors may perform in person searches. Search fee: $5.00 per name. Required to search: name, years to search; also helpful-address, DOB, SSN. Criminal records on computer since 5/87, on books from 1968. Search the active Criminal Calendar by defendant name at the web site. **General Information:** No adoptions, sealed cases, juvenile, mental or expunged records released. SASE required. Turnaround time 1 week-10 days. Copy fee: $1.00 for first page, $.25 each addl. Certification fee: $2.00. Fee payee: Clerk of Superior Court. Only cashiers checks and money orders accepted. Prepayment is required. Public access terminal is available.

Haywood County

Superior-District Court 215 N. Main, Waynesville, NC 28786; 828-456-3540; Fax: 828-456-4937. Hours: 8:30AM-5PM (EST). *Felony, Misdemeanor, Civil, Eviction, Small Claims, Probate.*

www.aoc.state.nc.us/www/public/courts/haywood.html

Civil Records: Access: In person only. Court does not conduct in person searches; visitors must perform searches for themselves. Search fee: No civil searches performed by court. Required to search: name, years to search; also helpful-address. Civil cases indexed by defendant, plaintiff. Civil records on computer since Oct. 13, 1988, prior on books to 1955. **Criminal Records:** Access: Mail, remote online, in person. Both court and visitors may perform in person searches. Search fee: $5.00 per name. Required to search: name, years to search, DOB; also helpful-address, SSN. Criminal records on computer from 5/87, on books or cards from 1800s. Search the active Criminal Calendar by defendant name at the web site. **General Information:** No adoptions, sealed cases, juvenile, sex offenders, mental or expunged records released. Turnaround time 1-2 days. Copy fee: $1.00 for first page, $.25 each addl. Certification fee: Included in search fee, unless do it yourself, then $1.00 first page and $.25 each additional. Fee payee: Clerk of Superior Court. Only cashiers checks and money orders accepted. Prepayment is required. Public access terminal is available.

Henderson County

Superior-District Court PO Box 965, Hendersonville, NC 28793;; Civil phone:828-697-4851; Criminal phone:828-697-4851. Hours: 8:30AM-5PM (EST). *Felony, Misdemeanor, Civil, Eviction, Small Claims, Probate.*

www.aoc.state.nc.us/www/public/courts/henderson.html

Civil Records: Access: Mail, in person. Both court and visitors may perform in person searches. Search fee: $5.00 per name. Required to search: name, years to search; also helpful-address. Civil cases indexed by defendant, plaintiff. Civil records on computer since 1988, prior on books to 1968. **Criminal Records:** Access: Mail, remote online, in person. Both court and visitors may perform in person searches. Search fee: $5.00 per name. Required to search: name, years to search; also helpful-address, DOB, SSN. Criminal records on computer since 09/89, prior on books to 1968. Search the active Criminal Calendar by defendant

name at the web site. **General Information:** No adoptions, sealed cases, juvenile, sex offenders, mental or expunged records released. SASE not required. Turnaround time 1 week. Copy fee: $.25 per page. Certification fee: $2.00. Fee payee: Clerk of Superior Court. Personal checks accepted. Prepayment is required. Public access terminal is available.

Hertford County

Superior-District Court PO Box 86, Winton, NC 27986; 252-358-7845; Fax: 252-358-0793. Hours: 8AM-5PM (EST). *Felony, Misdemeanor, Civil, Eviction, Small Claims, Probate.*

www.aoc.state.nc.us/www/public/courts/hertford.html

Civil Records: Access: In person only. Court does not conduct in person searches; visitors must perform searches for themselves. Search fee: No civil searches performed by court. Required to search: name, years to search; also helpful-address. Civil cases indexed by defendant, plaintiff. Civil records on computer since April, 1989, prior on index cards to 1968. **Criminal Records:** Access: Mail, remote online, in person. Both court and visitors may perform in person searches. Search fee: $5.00 per name. Required to search: name, years to search, DOB; also helpful-address, SSN. Criminal records on computer since April, 1989, prior on index cards to 1968. Search the active Criminal Calendar by defendant name at the web site. **General Information:** No adoptions, sealed cases, juvenile, sex offenders, mental or expunged records released. Turnaround time 1-2 days. Copy fee: $1.00 for first page, $.25 each addl. Certification fee: Included in search fee, unless do it yourself then $2.00. Fee payee: Clerk of Superior Court. Only cashiers checks and money orders accepted. Local personal checks accepted. Prepayment is required. Public access terminal is available.

Hoke County

Superior-District Court PO Drawer 1569, Raeford, NC 28376; 910-875-3728; Fax: 910-904-1708. Hours: 8:30AM-5PM (EST). *Felony, Misdemeanor, Civil, Eviction, Small Claims, Probate.*

www.aoc.state.nc.us/www/public/courts/hoke.html

Civil Records: Access: In person only. Court does not conduct in person searches; visitors must perform searches for themselves. Search fee: No civil searches performed by court. Required to search: name, years to search; also helpful-address. Civil cases indexed by defendant, plaintiff. Civil records on computer since 10/89, on books to 1967. **Criminal Records:** Access: Mail, remote online, in person. Only the court conducts in person searches; visitors may not. Search fee: $5.00 per name. Required to search: name, years to search, DOB; also helpful-address, SSN. Criminal records on computer since 10/89, on books to 1967. Search the active Criminal Calendar by defendant name at the web site. **General Information:** No adoptions, sealed cases, juvenile, mental or expunged records released. SASE required. Turnaround time 1-2 days. Copy fee: $1.00 for first page, $.25 each addl. Certification fee: $2.00. Fee payee: Clerk of Superior Court. Business checks accepted. Prepayment is required. Public access terminal is available.

Hyde County

Superior-District Court PO Box 337, Swanquarter, NC 27885; 919-926-4101; Fax: 919-926-1002. Hours: 8:30AM-5:30PM (EST). *Felony, Misdemeanor, Civil, Eviction, Small Claims, Probate.*

www.aoc.state.nc.us/www/public/courts/hyde.html

Note: Phone requesting only for general inquires

Civil Records: Access: Phone, mail, in person. Both court and visitors may perform in person searches. Search fee: $5.00 per name. Required to search: name, years to search. Civil cases indexed by defendant, plaintiff. Civil records on computer since 7/89, on books to 1968. **Criminal Records:** Access: Phone, mail, remote online, in person. Only the court conducts in person searches; visitors may not. Search fee: $5.00 per name. Required to search: name, years to search. Criminal records on computer since 7/89, on books to 1968. Search the active Criminal Calendar by defendant name at the web site. **General Information:** No adoptions, sealed cases, juvenile, sex offenders, mental or expunged records released. SASE required. Turnaround time 2 days, phone searches 15 minutes. Copy fee: $1.00 for first page, $.25 each addl. Certification fee: $2.00. Fee payee: Clerk of Superior Court. Only cashiers checks and money orders accepted. Prepayment is required. Public access terminal is available. Public Access Terminal Note: Civil only.

Iredell County

Superior-District Court PO Box 186, Statesville, NC 28687;; Civil phone:704-878-4306; Criminal phone:704-878-4306; Fax: 704-878-3261. Hours: 8AM-5PM (EST). *Felony, Misdemeanor, Civil, Eviction, Small Claims, Probate.*

www.aoc.state.nc.us/www/public/courts/iredell.htm

Civil Records: Access: Mail, in person. Both court and visitors may perform in person searches. Search fee: $5.00 per name. Required to search: name, years to search. Civil cases indexed by defendant, plaintiff. Civil records on computer since 1986, in books since, 1786, on microfiche since 1939. **Criminal Records:** Access: Mail, remote online, in person. Both court and visitors may perform in person searches. Search fee: $5.00 per name. Required to search: name, years to search, DOB. Criminal records on computer since 9/85, prior on books and cards to 1970. Search the active Criminal Calendar by defendant name at the web site. **General Information:** No adoptions, sealed cases, juvenile, sex offenders, mental or expunged records released. SASE required. Turnaround time 2 days. Copy fee: $1.00 for first page, $.25 each addl. Certification fee: $2.00. Fee payee: Clerk of Superior Court. Only cashiers checks and money orders accepted. Prepayment is required. Public access terminal is available.

Jackson County

Superior-District Court 401 Grindstaff Cove Rd, Sylva, NC 28779; 828-586-7512; Fax: 828-586-9009. Hours: 8:30AM-5PM (EST). *Felony, Misdemeanor, Civil, Eviction, Small Claims, Probate.*

www.aoc.state.nc.us/www/public/courts/jackson.html

Civil Records: Access: In person only. Court does not conduct in person searches; visitors must perform searches for themselves. Search fee: No civil searches performed by court. Required to search: name, years to search; also helpful-address. Civil cases indexed by defendant, plaintiff. Civil

records on computer since May 29, 1989, prior on books from 1966. **Criminal Records:** Access: Mail, remote online, in person. Both court and visitors may perform in person searches. Search fee: $5.00 per name. Required to search: name, years to search, DOB; also helpful-address, SSN. Criminal records on computer since May 29, 1989, prior on books from 1966. Search the active Criminal Calendar by defendant name at the web site. **General Information:** No adoptions, sealed cases, juvenile, mental or expunged records released. SASE required. Turnaround time 1-2 days. Copy fee: $1.00 for first page, $.25 each addl. Certification fee: $2.00. Fee payee: Clerk of Superior Court. Only cashiers checks and M.O.s accepted. Prepayment is required. Public access terminal is available. Public Access Terminal Note: Available for civil only.

Johnston County

Superior-District Court PO Box 297, Smithfield, NC 27577; 919-934-3192; Fax: 919-934-5857. Hours: 8AM-5PM (EST). *Felony, Misdemeanor, Civil, Eviction, Small Claims, Probate.*

www.aoc.state.nc.us/www/public/courts/johnston.html

Civil Records: Access: In person only. Court does not conduct in person searches; visitors must perform searches for themselves. Search fee: No civil searches performed by court. Required to search: name, years to search; also helpful-address. Civil cases indexed by defendant, plaintiff. Civil records on computer since 1989, prior on books to 1930s. **Criminal Records:** Access: Mail, remote online, in person. Both court and visitors may perform in person searches. Search fee: $5.00 per name. Required to search: name, DOB; also helpful-years to search, address, SSN. Criminal records on computer from 5/86, prior on books and cards to 1968. Search the active Criminal Calendar by defendant name at the web site. **General Information:** No adoptions, sealed cases, juvenile, sex offenders, mental or expunged records released. SASE requested. Turnaround time 1-2 days. Copy fee: $1.00 for first page, $.25 each addl. Certification fee: $2.00. Fee payee: Clerk of Superior Court. Business checks accepted. Prepayment is required. Public access terminal is available.

Jones County

Superior-District Court PO Box 280, Trenton, NC 28585; 252-448-7351; Fax: 252-448-1607. Hours: 8AM-5PM (EST). *Felony, Misdemeanor, Civil, Eviction, Small Claims, Probate.*

www.aoc.state.nc.us/www/public/courts/jones.html

Civil Records: Access: Mail, in person. Both court and visitors may perform in person searches. Search fee: $5.00 per name. Required to search: name, years to search. Civil cases indexed by defendant, plaintiff. Civil records on computer since 1989, prior on microfilm. **Criminal Records:** Access: Mail, remote online, in person. Both court and visitors may perform in person searches. Search fee: $5.00 per name. Required to search: name, years to search, DOB. Criminal records on computer since 1989, prior on microfilm. Search the active Criminal Calendar by defendant name at the web site. **General Information:** No adoptions, sealed cases, juvenile, sex offenders, mental or expunged records released. SASE required. Turnaround time 5 days. Copy fee: $1.00 for first page, $.25 each addl. Certification fee: $2.00. Fee payee: Clerk of Court.

Only cashiers checks and money orders accepted. Prepayment is required. Public access terminal is available.

Lee County

Superior-District Court PO Box 4209, Sanford, NC 27331; 919-708-4400; Fax: 919-775-3483. Hours: 8AM-5PM (EST). *Felony, Misdemeanor, Civil, Eviction, Small Claims, Probate.*

www.aoc.state.nc.us/www/public/courts/lee.html

Civil Records: Access: Mail, in person. Both court and visitors may perform in person searches. Search fee: $5.00 per name. Required to search: name, years to search; also helpful-address. Civil cases indexed by defendant, plaintiff. Civil records on computer since 1989, prior on books to 1967. **Criminal Records:** Access: Mail, remote online, in person. Both court and visitors may perform in person searches. Search fee: $5.00 per name. Required to search: name, years to search, DOB. Criminal records on computer since 1989, prior on books to 1967. Search the active Criminal Calendar by defendant name at the web site. **General Information:** No adoptions, sealed cases, juvenile, sex offenders, mental or expunged records released. Turnaround time 1-3 days. Copy fee: $1.00 for first page, $.25 each addl. Certification fee: $2.00. Fee payee: Clerk of Superior Court. Only cashiers checks and money orders accepted. Prepayment is required. Public access terminal is available.

Lenoir County

Superior-District Court PO Box 68, Kinston, NC 28502-0068; 252-527-6231; Fax: 252-527-9154. Hours: 8AM-5PM (EST). *Felony, Misdemeanor, Civil, Eviction, Small Claims, Probate.*

www.aoc.state.nc.us/www/public/courts/lenoir.htm

Civil Records: Access: In person only. Both court and visitors may perform in person searches. No search fee. Required to search: name, years to search; also helpful-address. Civil cases indexed by defendant, plaintiff. Civil records on computer since Oct. 24, 1988, prior on books to 1900s, prior destroyed due to fire. **Criminal Records:** Access: Mail, remote online, in person. Both court and visitors may perform in person searches. Search fee: $5.00 per name. Required to search: name, years to search, DOB; also helpful-address. Criminal records on computer since 8/86, prior records on books and cards to 1925. Search the active Criminal Calendar by defendant name at the web site. **General Information:** No adoptions, sealed cases, juvenile, sex offenders, mental or expunged records released. SASE required. Turnaround time 1-2 days. Copy fee: $1.00 for first page, $.25 each addl. Certification fee: Included in search fee, unless do it yourself then $2.00. Fee payee: Clerk of Superior Court. Only cashiers checks and money orders accepted. Prepayment is required. Public access terminal is available.

Lincoln County

Superior-District Court PO Box 8, Lincolnton, NC 28093; 704-736-8566; Fax: 704-736-8718. Hours: 8AM-5PM (EST). *Felony, Misdemeanor, Civil, Eviction, Small Claims, Probate.*

www.aoc.state.nc.us/www/public/courts/lincoln.htm

Civil Records: Access: In person only. Court does not conduct in person searches; visitors must perform searches for themselves. Search fee: No civil searches performed by court. Required to search: name, years to search. Civil cases indexed by defendant, plaintiff. Civil records on computer since 1988, in books since 1920s, on microfiche since 1988. **Criminal Records:** Access: Mail, remote online, in person. Both court and visitors may perform in person searches. Search fee: $5.00 per name. Required to search: name, years to search, DOB. Criminal records on computer since 1986, prior on books and cards to 1968. Search the active Criminal Calendar by defendant name at the web site. **General Information:** No adoptions, sealed cases, juvenile, sex offenders, mental or expunged records released. SASE required. Turnaround time 2 days to 1 week. Copy fee: $1.00 for first page, $.25 each addl. Certification fee: $2.00. Fee payee: Clerk of Court. Business checks accepted. Prepayment is required. Public access terminal is available.

Macon County

Superior-District Court PO Box 288, Franklin, NC 28744; 828-349-2000; Fax: 828-369-2515. Hours: 8:30AM-5PM (EST). *Felony, Misdemeanor, Civil, Eviction, Small Claims, Probate.*

www.aoc.state.nc.us/www/public/courts/macon.html

Civil Records: Access: In person only. Court does not conduct in person searches; visitors must perform searches for themselves. Search fee: No civil searches performed by court. Required to search: name, years to search; also helpful-address. Civil cases indexed by defendant, plaintiff. Civil records on computer since May 1989, prior on books to 1968. **Criminal Records:** Access: Mail, remote online, in person. Only the court conducts in person searches; visitors may not. Search fee: $5.00 per name. Required to search: name, DOB; also helpful-years to search, address. Criminal records on computer since May 1989, prior on books to 1968. Search the active Criminal Calendar by defendant name at the web site. **General Information:** No adoptions, sealed cases, juvenile, sex offenders, mental or expunged records released. Turnaround time 1-2 days. Copy fee: $.25 per page. Certification fee: No certification fee. Fee payee: Clerk of Superior Court. Local personal checks accepted. Prepayment is required. Public access terminal is available. Public Access Terminal Note: Available for civil only.

Madison County

Superior-District Court PO Box 217, Marshall, NC 28753; 828-649-2531; Fax: 828-649-2829. Hours: 8AM-5PM (EST). *Felony, Misdemeanor, Civil, Eviction, Small Claims, Probate.*

www.aoc.state.nc.us/www/public/courts/madison.htm

Civil Records: Access: In person only. Court does not conduct in person searches; visitors must perform searches for themselves. Search fee: No civil searches performed by court. Required to search: name, years to search; also helpful-address. Civil cases indexed by defendant, plaintiff. Civil records on computer since 10/88, prior on books to 1968. **Criminal Records:** Access: Mail, remote online, in person. Only the court conducts in person searches; visitors may not. Search fee: $5.00 per name. Required to search: name, DOB; also helpful-years to search. Criminal records on computer since 10/88, prior on books to 1968. Search the active Criminal Calendar by defendant name at the web site. **General Information:** No adoptions, sealed cases, juvenile, sex offenders, mental, expunged, or dismissed records released.

Turnaround time 1-2 days. Copy fee: $1.00 for first page, $.25 each addl. Certification fee: $2.00. Fee payee: Clerk of Superior Court. Only cashiers checks and money orders accepted. Prepayment is required. Public access terminal is available.

Martin County

Superior-District Court PO Box 807, Williamston, NC 27892; 252-792-2515; Fax: 252-792-6668. Hours: 8AM-5PM (EST). *Felony, Misdemeanor, Civil, Eviction, Small Claims, Probate.*

www.aoc.state.nc.us/www/public/courts/martin.html

Civil Records: Access: Mail, in person. Both court and visitors may perform in person searches. Search fee: $5.00 per name. Required to search: name, years to search, address. Civil cases indexed by defendant, plaintiff. Civil records on computer since 1989, in books since 1968. **Criminal Records:** Access: Mail, remote online, in person. Both court and visitors may perform in person searches. Search fee: $5.00 per name. Required to search: name, years to search, address, DOB; also helpful-SSN. Criminal records on computer since 1989, in books since 1968. Search the active Criminal Calendar by defendant name at the web site. **General Information:** No adoptions, sealed cases, juvenile, mental or expunged records released. SASE required. Turnaround time 1 week. Copy fee: $1.00 for first page, $.25 each addl. Certification fee: $2.00. Fee payee: Clerk of Court. Only cashiers checks and money orders accepted. Prepayment is required. Public access terminal is available.

McDowell County

Superior-District Court PO Drawer 729, Marion, NC 28752; 828-652-7717; Fax: 828-659-2641. Hours: 8:30AM-5PM (EST). *Felony, Misdemeanor, Civil, Eviction, Small Claims, Probate.*

www.aoc.state.nc.us/www/public/courts/mcdowell.html

Civil Records: Access: Mail, in person. Both court and visitors may perform in person searches. No search fee. Required to search: name, years to search; also helpful-address. Civil cases indexed by defendant, plaintiff. Civil records on computer since 11/88, prior on books to 1930. **Criminal Records:** Access: Mail, remote online, in person. Both court and visitors may perform in person searches. Search fee: $5.00 per name. Required to search: name, DOB; also helpful-years to search, address, SSN. Criminal records on computer since Oct. 1987, prior on books to 1968. Search the active Criminal Calendar by defendant name at the web site. **General Information:** No adoptions, sealed cases, juvenile, sex offenders, mental or expunged records released. SASE required. Turnaround time 1-2 days. Copy fee: $1.00 for first page, $.25 each addl. Certification fee: $2.00. Fee payee: Clerk of Superior Court. Business checks accepted. Prepayment is required. Public access terminal is available.

Mecklenburg County

Superior-District Court 800 E 4th St, PO Box 37971, Charlotte, NC 28237;; Civil phone:704-347-7814; Criminal phone:704-347-7814. Hours: 8AM-5PM (EST). *Felony, Misdemeanor, Civil, Eviction, Small Claims, Probate.*

www.aoc.state.nc.us/www/public/courts/mecklenburg.htm

Civil Records: Access: In person only. Court does not conduct in person searches; visitors must perform searches for themselves. Search fee: No civil searches performed by court. Required to search: name. Civil cases indexed by defendant, plaintiff. Civil records on computer since April 1988, prior on books to 1940s. **Criminal Records:** Access: Mail, remote online, in person. Both court and visitors may perform in person searches. Search fee: $5.00 per name. Required to search: name, years to search, address, DOB; also helpful-SSN. Criminal records on computer from 1/83, prior on cards and books to 1930s. Search the active Criminal Calendar by defendant name at the web site. **General Information:** No adoptions, sealed cases, juvenile, sex offenders, mental or expunged records released. SASE requested. Turnaround time 1-2 days. Copy fee: $1.00 for first page, $.25 each addl. Certification fee: $2.00. Fee payee: Clerk of Superior Court. Only cashiers checks and money orders accepted. Public access terminal is available.

Mitchell County

Superior-District Court PO Box 402, Bakersville, NC 28705; 828-688-2161; Fax: 828-688-2168. Hours: 8:30AM-5PM (EST). *Felony, Misdemeanor, Civil, Eviction, Small Claims, Probate.*

www.aoc.state.nc.us/www/public/courts/mitchell.htm

Civil Records: Access: Mail, in person. Both court and visitors may perform in person searches. Search fee: $5.00 per name. Required to search: name, years to search; also helpful-address. Civil cases indexed by defendant, plaintiff. Civil records on computer since 1988, prior on books since 1968. **Criminal Records:** Access: Mail, remote online, in person. Only the court conducts in person searches; visitors may not. Search fee: $5.00 per name. Required to search: name, years to search, DOB, SSN; also helpful-address. Criminal records on computer since 1988, prior on books since 1968. Search the active Criminal Calendar by defendant name at the web site. **General Information:** No adoptions, sealed cases, juvenile, sex offenders, mental or expunged records released. SASE required. Turnaround time 1-2 days. Copy fee: $1.00 for first page, $.25 each addl. Certification fee: $2.00. Fee payee: Superior-District Court. Business checks accepted. Prepayment is required. Public access terminal is available. Public Access Terminal Note: Civil only.

Montgomery County

Superior-District Court PO Box 527, Troy, NC 27371; 910-576-4211; Fax: 910-576-5020. Hours: 8AM-5PM (EST). *Felony, Misdemeanor, Civil, Eviction, Small Claims, Probate.*

www.aoc.state.nc.us/www/public/courts/montgomery.html

Civil Records: Access: Phone, fax, mail, in person. Both court and visitors may perform in person searches. Search fee: $5.00 per name. Required to search: name, years to search. Civil cases indexed by defendant, plaintiff. Civil records on computer since April 1989, on books to 170, archived in Raleigh to 1843, prior records destroyed in fire. **Criminal Records:** Access: Phone, fax, mail, remote online, in person. Both court and visitors may perform in person searches. Search fee: $5.00 per name. Required to search: name, years to search, address, DOB, signed release. Criminal records on computer since April 1989, on books to 170, archived in Raleigh to 1843, prior records destroyed in fire. Search the active Criminal Calendar by defendant name at the web site. **General Information:** No adoptions, sealed cases, juvenile, sex offenders, mental or expunged records released. Turnaround time 1-2 days. Copy fee: $.25 per page. Certification fee: $2.00. Fee payee: Clerk of Superior Court. Only cashiers checks and money orders accepted. Prepayment is required. Public access terminal is available. Fax notes: No fee to fax results. Faxing available for civil only.

Moore County

Superior-District Court PO Box 936, Carthage, NC 28327; 910-947-2396; Fax: 910-947-1444. Hours: 8AM-5PM (EST). *Felony, Misdemeanor, Civil, Eviction, Small Claims, Probate.*

www.aoc.state.nc.us/www/public/courts/moore.html

Civil Records: Access: Mail, in person. Both court and visitors may perform in person searches. Search fee: $5.00 per name. Required to search: name, years to search. Civil cases indexed by defendant, plaintiff. Civil records on computer since March 1989, prior on books to 1968, older records in basement. **Criminal Records:** Access: Mail, remote online, in person. Only the court conducts in person searches; visitors may not. Search fee: $5.00 per name. Required to search: name, years to search, DOB, signed release; also helpful-address, SSN. Criminal records on computer since March 1989, prior on books to 1968, older records in basement. Search the active Criminal Calendar by defendant name at the web site. **General Information:** No adoptions, sealed cases, juvenile, sex offenders, mental or expunged records released. Turnaround time 2-4 days. Copy fee: $1.00 for first page, $.25 each addl. Certification fee: $2.00. Fee payee: Clerk of Superior Court. Only cashiers checks and money orders accepted. Prepayment is required. Public access terminal is available.

Nash County

Superior-District Court PO Box 759, Nashville, NC 27856;; Civil phone:252-459-4081; Criminal phone:252-459-4081; Fax: 252-459-6050. Hours: 8AM-5PM (EST). *Felony, Misdemeanor, Civil, Eviction, Small Claims, Probate.*

www.aoc.state.nc.us/www/public/courts/nash.html

Civil Records: Access: Mail, in person. Both court and visitors may perform in person searches. No search fee. Required to search: name, years to search; also helpful-address. Civil cases indexed by defendant, plaintiff. Civil records on computer since 6/88, prior in books to 1988. **Criminal Records:** Access: Mail, remote online, in person. Both court and visitors may perform in person searches. Search fee: $5.00 per name. Required to search: name, years to search, DOB; also helpful-address. Criminal records on computer since 5/80, prior on books and cards dating back to late 1800s. Search the active Criminal Calendar by defendant name at the web site. **General Information:** No adoptions, sealed cases, juvenile, mental or expunged records released. SASE required. Turnaround time 1 week. Copy fee: $1.00 for first page, $.25 each addl. Certification fee: $2.00. Fee payee: Rachel M Joyner, CSC. Only cashiers checks and money orders accepted. Prepayment is required. Public access terminal is available. Public Access Terminal Note: Criminal & Civil.

New Hanover County

Superior-District Court PO Box 2023, Wilmington, NC 28402; 910-341-4430; Criminal

phone:; Fax: 910-251-2676. Hours: 8AM-5PM (EST). *Felony, Misdemeanor, Civil, Eviction, Small Claims, Probate.*

www.aoc.state.nc.us/www/public/courts/new_hanover.html

Civil Records: Access: In person only. Court does not conduct in person searches; visitors must perform searches for themselves. Search fee: No civil searches performed by court. Required to search: name, years to search; also helpful-address. Civil cases indexed by defendant, plaintiff. Civil records on computer since 1988, on books to late 1800s. **Criminal Records:** Access: Mail, remote online, in person. Both court and visitors may perform in person searches. Search fee: $5.00 per name. Required to search: name, years to search, DOB; also helpful-address, SSN. Criminal records on computer since 11/83, prior on books and files to late 1800s. Search the active Criminal Calendar by defendant name at the web site. **General Information:** No adoptions, sealed cases, juvenile, sex offenders, mental or expunged records released. SASE required. Turnaround time 1-2 days. Copy fee: $1.00 for first page, $.25 each addl. Certification fee: $2.50. Fee payee: Clerk of Superior Court. Only cashiers checks and money orders accepted. Prepayment is required. Public access terminal is available.

Northampton County

Superior-District Court PO Box 217, Jackson, NC 27845; 252-534-1631; Fax: 252-534-1308. Hours: 8:30AM-5PM (EST). *Felony, Misdemeanor, Civil, Eviction, Small Claims, Probate.*

www.aoc.state.nc.us/www/public/courts/northampton.html

Civil Records: Access: Mail, in person. Search fee: $5.00 per name. Required to search: name, years to search; also helpful-address. Civil cases indexed by defendant, plaintiff. Civil records on computer since 1989, prior on books to 1968. **Criminal Records:** Access: Mail, remote online, in person. Both court and visitors may perform in person searches. Search fee: $5.00 per name. Required to search: name, years to search, DOB; also helpful-address. Criminal records on computer since 1989, prior on books to 1968. Search the active Criminal Calendar by defendant name at the web site. **General Information:** No adoptions, sealed cases, juvenile, sex offenders, mental or expunged records released. Turnaround time is 3-10 days. Copy fee: $1.00 for first page, $.25 each addl. Certification fee: $2.00. Fee payee: Clerk of Superior Court. Business checks accepted. Prepayment is required. Public access terminal is available.

Onslow County

Superior-District Court 625 Court St, Jacksonville, NC 28540; 910-455-4458. Hours: 8AM-5PM (EST). *Felony, Misdemeanor, Civil, Eviction, Small Claims, Probate.*

www.aoc.state.nc.us/www/public/courts/onslow.htm

Civil Records: Access: In person only. Court does not conduct in person searches; visitors must perform searches for themselves. Search fee: No civil searches performed by court. Required to search: name, years to search; also helpful-address. Civil cases indexed by defendant, plaintiff. Civil records on computer since 1988, prior on books to 1920s. **Criminal Records:** Access: Mail, remote online, in person. Both court and visitors may perform in person searches. Search fee: $5.00 per name. Required to search: name, years to search,

DOB; also helpful-address, SSN. Criminal records on computer since 2/83, prior on books to 1920s. Search the active Criminal Calendar by defendant name at the web site. **General Information:** No adoptions, sealed cases, juvenile, sex offenders, mental or expunged records released. Turnaround time 1-2 days. Copy fee: $1.00 for first page, $.25 each addl. Certification fee: $2.00. Fee payee: Clerk of Superior Court. Business checks required. Public access terminal is available.

Orange County

Superior-District Court 106 E Margaret Lane, Hillsborough, NC 27278; 919-732-8181 X2210; Fax: 919-644-3043. Hours: 8AM-5PM (EST). *Felony, Misdemeanor, Civil, Eviction, Small Claims, Probate.*

www.aoc.state.nc.us/www/public/courts/orange.htm

Civil Records: Access: Mail, in person. Both court and visitors may perform in person searches. Search fee: $5.00 per name. Required to search: name, years to search; also helpful-address. Civil cases indexed by defendant, plaintiff. Civil records on computer since May 1989, prior on books to early 1800s. **Criminal Records:** Access: Mail, remote online, in person. Both court and visitors may perform in person searches. Search fee: $5.00 per name. Required to search: name, years to search, DOB; also helpful-address, SSN, race, sex. computer records go to 3/87. Search the active Criminal Calendar by defendant name at the web site. **General Information:** No adoptions, sealed cases, juvenile, sex offenders, mental or expunged records released. SASE required. Turnaround time 1-3 days. Copy fee: $1.00 for first page, $.25 each addl. Certification fee: $2.00. Fee payee: Clerk of Superior Court. Business checks accepted. Prepayment is required. Public access terminal is available. Public Access Terminal Note: Criminal & Civil.

Pamlico County

Superior-District Court PO Box 38, Bayboro, NC 28515; 252-745-6000; Fax: 252-745-6018. Hours: 8AM-5PM (EST). *Felony, Misdemeanor, Civil, Eviction, Small Claims, Probate.*

www.aoc.state.nc.us/www/public/courts/pamlico.html

Civil Records: Access: Mail, in person. Both court and visitors may perform in person searches. Search fee: $5.00 per name. Required to search: name, years to search, address. Civil cases indexed by defendant, plaintiff. Civil records on computer since 9/84, prior on books to 1968. **Criminal Records:** Access: Mail, remote online, in person. Only the court conducts in person searches; visitors may not. Search fee: $5.00 per name. Required to search: name, years to search, DOB. Criminal records on computer since 9/84, prior on books to 1968. Search the active Criminal Calendar by defendant name at the web site. **General Information:** No adoptions, sealed cases, juvenile, sex offenders, mental or expunged records released. SASE required. Turnaround time 1-2 days. Copy fee: $1.00 for first page, $.25 each addl. Certification fee: $2.00. Fee payee: Clerk of Court. Only cashiers checks and money orders accepted. Prepayment is required. Public access terminal is available.

Pasquotank County

Superior-District Court PO Box 449, Elizabeth City, NC 27907-0449; 252-331-4751. Hours: 8AM-5PM (EST). *Felony, Misdemeanor, Civil, Eviction, Small Claims, Probate.*

www.aoc.state.nc.us/www/public/courts/
pasquotank.html

Civil Records: Access: In person only. Court does not conduct in person searches; visitors must perform searches for themselves. Search fee: No civil searches performed by court. Required to search: name, years to search; also helpful-address. Civil cases indexed by defendant, plaintiff. Civil records on computer since March 6, 1989, books prior to 1800s (some in Raleigh). **Criminal Records:** Access: Mail, remote online, in person. Both court and visitors may perform in person searches. Search fee: $5.00 per name. Required to search: name, years to search, DOB; also helpful-address, SSN, race, sex. Criminal records on computer since 4/88, prior on books and microfiche. Search the active Criminal Calendar by defendant name at the web site. **General Information:** No adoptions, sealed cases, juvenile, sex offenders, mental or expunged records released. Turnaround time 2 days. Copy fee: $1.00 for first page, $.25 each addl. Certification fee: Included in search fee, court must do search. Fee payee: Clerk of Superior Court. Business checks accepted. Prepayment is required. Public access terminal is available.

Pender County

Superior-District Court PO Box 308, Burgaw, NC 28425; 910-259-1229; Fax: 910-259-1292. Hours: 8AM-5PM (EST). *Felony, Misdemeanor, Civil, Eviction, Small Claims, Probate.*

www.aoc.state.nc.us/www/public/courts/pender.html

Civil Records: Access: In person only. Court does not conduct in person searches; visitors must perform searches for themselves. Search fee: No civil searches performed by court. Required to search: name, years to search; also helpful-address. Civil cases indexed by defendant, plaintiff. Civil records on computer since 9/89, prior in books from 1968. **Criminal Records:** Access: Fax, mail, remote online, in person. Only the court conducts in person searches; visitors may not. Search fee: $5.00 per name. Required to search: name, years to search, DOB; also helpful-address, SSN. Criminal records on computer since 9/89, prior in books from 1968. Search the active Criminal Calendar by defendant name at the web site. **General Information:** No adoptions, sealed cases, juvenile, sex offenders, mental or expunged records released. Turnaround time 1 week. Copy fee: $1.00 for first page, $.25 each addl. Certification fee: Included in search fee, unless do it yourself then $2.00. Fee payee: Clerk of Superior Court. Business checks accepted. Prepayment is required. Public access terminal is available. Fax notes: $1.00 for first page, $.25 each addl.

Perquimans County

Superior-District Court PO Box 33, Hertford, NC 27944; 252-426-1505. Hours: 8AM-5PM (EST). *Felony, Misdemeanor, Civil, Eviction, Small Claims, Probate.*

www.aoc.state.nc.us/www/public/courts/
perquimans.html

Civil Records: Access: In person only. Court does not conduct in person searches; visitors must perform searches for themselves. Search fee: No civil searches performed by court. Required to search: name, years to search. Civil cases indexed by defendant, plaintiff. Civil records on computer since 1989, prior in books to 1966, rest archived and must be serached in person only. **Criminal**

Records: Access: Mail, remote online, in person. Both court and visitors may perform in person searches. Search fee: $5.00 per name. Required to search: name, years to search, DOB. Criminal records on computer since 1989, prior in books to 1966, rest archived and must be serached in person only. Search the active Criminal Calendar by defendant name at the web site. **General Information:** No adoptions, sealed cases, juvenile, sex offenders, mental or expunged records released. Turnaround time 1-2 days. Copy fee: $1.00 for first page, $.25 each addl. Certification fee: $2.00. Fee payee: Clerk of Superior Court. Only cashiers checks and money orders accepted. Prepayment is required.

Person County

Superior-District Court 105 S Main St, Roxboro, NC 27573;; Civil phone:336-597-0554; Criminal phone:336-597-0554; Fax: 336-597-0568. Hours: 8:30AM-5PM (EST). *Felony, Misdemeanor, Civil, Eviction, Small Claims, Probate.*

www.aoc.state.nc.us/www/public/courts/person.html

Civil Records: Access: In person only. Both court and visitors may perform in person searches. No search fee. Required to search: name, years to search. Civil cases indexed by defendant, plaintiff. Civil records on microfiche since 4/89, prior in index books to 1968. **Criminal Records:** Access: Mail, remote online, in person. Both court and visitors may perform in person searches. Search fee: $5.00 per name. Required to search: name, years to search, DOB. Criminal records on computer since 3/88, index cards and books prior to 1968. Search the active Criminal Calendar by defendant name at the web site. **General Information:** No adoptions, sealed cases, juvenile, sex offenders, mental or expunged records released. SASE required. Turnaround time 1-2 days. Copy fee: $1.00 for first page, $.25 each addl. Certification fee: Included in search fee, unless do it yourself then $2.00. Fee payee: Clerk of Superior Court. Business checks accepted. Public access terminal is available.

Pitt County

Superior-District Court PO Box 6067, Greenville, NC 27834; 252-830-6400; Civil phone:252-830-6420; Criminal phone:252-830-6420; Fax: 252-830-3144. Hours: 8AM-5PM (EST). *Felony, Misdemeanor, Civil, Eviction, Small Claims, Probate.*

www.aoc.state.nc.us/www/public/courts/pitt.htm

Civil Records: Access: In person only. Court does not conduct in person searches; visitors must perform searches for themselves. Search fee: No civil searches performed by court. Required to search: name, years to search; also helpful-address. Civil cases indexed by defendant, plaintiff. Civil records on computer since 1988, on books to 1968. **Criminal Records:** Access: Mail, remote online, in person. Both court and visitors may perform in person searches. Search fee: $5.00 per name. Required to search: name, years to search, DOB; also helpful-address, SSN. Criminal records on computer since 2/85, on books and cards to early 1900s. Search the active Criminal Calendar by defendant name at the web site. **General Information:** No adoptions, sealed cases, juvenile, sex offenders, mental or expunged records released. Turnaround time 1-2 days. Copy fee: $1.00 for first page, $.25 each addl. Certification fee: $2.00. Fee payee: Clerk of Court. Business checks accepted. Prepayment is required. Public access terminal is available.

Polk County

Superior-District Court PO Box 38, Columbus, NC 28722; 828-894-8231; Fax: 828-894-5752. Hours: 8AM-5PM (EST). *Felony, Misdemeanor, Civil, Eviction, Small Claims, Probate.*

www.aoc.state.nc.us/www/public/courts/polk.html

Civil Records: Access: Mail, in person. Both court and visitors may perform in person searches. Search fee: $5.00 per name. Required to search: name, years to search. Civil cases indexed by defendant, plaintiff. Civil records on computer since 5/89, prior on books to 1968. **Criminal Records:** Access: Mail, remote online, in person. Only the court conducts in person searches; visitors may not. Search fee: $5.00 per name. Required to search: name, years to search, DOB. Criminal records on computer since 5/89, prior on books to 1968. Search the active Criminal Calendar by defendant name at the web site. **General Information:** No adoptions, sealed cases, juvenile, sex offenders, mental, expunged or dismissed records released. SASE required. Turnaround time 1-2 days. Copy fee: $1.00 for first page, $.25 each addl. Certification fee: $2.00. Fee payee: Clerk of Superior Court. Business checks accepted. Prepayment is required.

Randolph County

Superior-District Court PO Box 1925, Asheboro, NC 27204-1925;; Civil phone:336-318-6750; Criminal phone:336-318-6750; Fax: 336-318-6709. Hours: 8AM-5PM (EST). *Felony, Misdemeanor, Civil, Eviction, Small Claims, Probate.*

www.aoc.state.nc.us/www/public/courts/
randolph.htm

Civil Records: Access: In person only. Court does not conduct in person searches; visitors must perform searches for themselves. Search fee: No civil searches performed by court. Required to search: name, years to search. Civil cases indexed by defendant, plaintiff. Civil records on computer since 02/89, prior on books to 1800s. **Criminal Records:** Access: Mail, remote online, in person. Only the court conducts in person searches; visitors may not. Search fee: $5.00 per name. Required to search: name, years to search, address, DOB. Criminal records on computer since 06/85, prior on books and cards from 1970 to 1981. Microfilm from 1981 to 06/85. Search the active Criminal Calendar by defendant name at the web site. **General Information:** No adoptions, sealed cases, juvenile, sex offenders, mental or expunged records released. SASE required. Turnaround time 1-2 days. Copy fee: $1.00 for first page, $.25 each addl. Certification fee: $2.00. Fee payee: Clerk of Superior Court. Only cashiers checks and money orders accepted. Prepayment is required. Public access terminal is available. Public Access Terminal Note: Civil only.

Richmond County

Superior-District Court PO Box 724, Rockingham, NC 28380;; Civil phone:910-997-9102; Criminal phone:910-997-9102; Fax: 910-997-9126. Hours: 8AM-5PM (EST). *Felony, Misdemeanor, Civil, Eviction, Small Claims, Probate.*

www.aoc.state.nc.us/www/public/courts/richmond.htm

Civil Records: Access: In person only. Court does not conduct in person searches; visitors must perform searches for themselves. Search fee: No civil searches performed by court. Required to

search: name, years to search; also helpful-address. Civil cases indexed by defendant, plaintiff. Civil records on computer since 4/89, prior on books since 1968. **Criminal Records:** Access: Mail, remote online, in person. Both court and visitors may perform in person searches. Search fee: $5.00 per name. Required to search: name, years to search, DOB; also helpful-address, SSN. Criminal records on computer since 1977, cards to 1977, books to 1940, prior archived. Search the active Criminal Calendar by defendant name at the web site. **General Information:** No adoptions, sealed cases, juvenile, sex offenders, mental or expunged records released. SASE required. Turnaround time 1-2 days. Copy fee: $1.00 for first page, $.25 each addl. Certification fee: $2.00. Fee payee: Clerk of Superior Court. Business checks accepted. Prepayment is required. Public access terminal is available.

Robeson County

Superior-District Court PO Box 1084, Lumberton, NC 28358; 910-737-5035; Civil phone:910-671-3372; Criminal phone:910-671-3372; Fax: 910-618-5598. Hours: 8:30AM-5PM (EST). *Felony, Misdemeanor, Civil, Eviction, Small Claims, Probate.*

www.aoc.state.nc.us/www/public/courts/robeson.html

Civil Records: Access: In person. Court does not conduct searches; visitors must perform searches for themselves. No search fee. Required to search: name, years to search; also helpful-address. Civil cases indexed by defendant, plaintiff. Civil records on computer since 1988, prior on books since 1966. **Criminal Records:** Access: Mail, remote online, in person. Both court and visitors may perform in person searches. Search fee: $5.00 per name. Required to search: name, years to search; also helpful-address, DOB. Criminal records on computer since 1983, index books prior. Search the active Criminal Calendar by defendant name at the web site. **General Information:** No adoptions, sealed cases, juvenile, sex offenders, mental or expunged records released. SASE required. Turnaround time 1-2 days. Copy fee: $1.00 for first page, $.25 each addl. Certification fee: $2.00. Fee payee: Clerk of Superior Court. Business checks accepted. Prepayment is required. Public access terminal is available.

Rockingham County

Superior-District Court PO Box 127, Wentworth, NC 27375; 336-342-8700. Hours: 8AM-5PM (EST). *Felony, Misdemeanor, Civil, Eviction, Small Claims, Probate.*

www.aoc.state.nc.us/www/public/courts/rockingham.html

Civil Records: Access: In person only. Both court and visitors may perform in person searches. Search fee: $5.00 per name. Required to search: name, years to search. Civil cases indexed by defendant, plaintiff. Civil records on computer since 2/89, prior on books. **Criminal Records:** Access: Mail, remote online, in person. Both court and visitors may perform in person searches. Search fee: No criminal searches performed by court. Required to search: name, years to search, DOB. Criminal records on computer since 5/85, prior on cards and books. Search the active Criminal Calendar by defendant name at the web site. **General Information:** No adoptions, sealed cases, juvenile, sex offenders, mental or expunged records released. Turnaround time 1-2 days. Copy fee: $1.00 for first page, $.25 each addl. Certification fee: $2.00. Fee payee: Clerk of Superior Court. Only cashiers checks and money

orders accepted. Prepayment is required. Public access terminal is available.

Rowan County

Superior-District Court PO Box 4599, 210 N Main St, Salisbury, NC 28144; 704-639-7505. Hours: 8AM-5PM (EST). *Felony, Misdemeanor, Civil, Eviction, Small Claims, Probate.*

www.aoc.state.nc.us/www/public/courts/rowan.html

Civil Records: Access: In person only. Both court and visitors may perform in person searches. No search fee. Required to search: name, years to search; also helpful-address. Civil cases indexed by defendant, plaintiff. Civil records on computer since 1989, prior on books to 1800s. **Criminal Records:** Access: Mail, remote online, in person. Both court and visitors may perform in person searches. Search fee: $5.00 per name. Required to search: name, DOB; also helpful-years to search, address, SSN. Criminal records on computer from 5/85, prior on books and cards to 1970. Search the active Criminal Calendar by defendant name at the web site. **General Information:** No adoptions, sealed cases, juvenile, sex offenders, mental or expunged records released. Turnaround time 1-3 days. Copy fee: $1.00 for first page, $.25 each addl. Certification fee: Included in search fee, unless do it yourself then $2.00. Fee payee: Clerk of Superior Court. Business checks accepted. Prepayment is required.

Rutherford County

Superior-District Court PO Box 630, Rutherfordton, NC 28139;; Civil phone:828-286-9136; Criminal phone:828-286-9136; Fax: 828-286-4322. Hours: 8:30AM-5PM (EST). *Felony, Misdemeanor, Civil, Eviction, Small Claims, Probate.*

www.aoc.state.nc.us/www/public/courts/rutherford.htm

Civil Records: Access: In person only. Court does not conduct in person searches; visitors must perform searches for themselves. Search fee: No civil searches performed by court. Required to search: name, years to search; also helpful-address. Civil cases indexed by defendant, plaintiff. Civil records on computer Oct. 1988, prior on books, some records to 1700s. **Criminal Records:** Access: Mail, remote online, in person. Both court and visitors may perform in person searches. Search fee: $5.00 per name. Required to search: name, years to search, DOB; also helpful-address, SSN. Criminal records on computer since 6/87, prior on microfiche and books dating to 1800s. Search the active Criminal Calendar by defendant name at the web site. **General Information:** No adoptions, sealed cases, juvenile, sex offenders, mental or expunged records released. Turnaround time 1-2 days. Copy fee: $1.00 for first page, $.25 each addl. Certification fee: $2.00. Fee payee: Clerk of Superior Court. Business checks accepted. Prepayment is required. Public access terminal is available.

Sampson County

Superior-District Court Courthouse, Clinton, NC 28328; 910-592-5191; Civil phone:910-592-5192; Criminal phone:910-592-5192; Fax: 910-592-5502. Hours: 8AM-5PM (EST). *Felony, Misdemeanor, Civil, Eviction, Small Claims, Probate.*

www.aoc.state.nc.us/www/public/courts/sampson.html

Civil Records: Access: In person only. Court does not conduct in person searches; visitors must

perform searches for themselves. Search fee: No civil searches performed by court. Required to search: name, years to search; also helpful-address. Civil cases indexed by defendant, plaintiff. Civil records on computer since 1989, prior on books. **Criminal Records:** Access: Phone, mail, remote online, in person. Both court and visitors may perform in person searches. Search fee: $5.00 per name. Required to search: name, years to search, DOB; also helpful-address, SSN. Criminal records on computer since 7/87, prior on books. Search the active Criminal Calendar by defendant name at the web site. **General Information:** No adoptions, sealed cases, juvenile, sex offenders, mental or expunged records released. SASE requested. Turnaround time 1-2 days. Copy fee: $1.00 for first page, $.25 each addl. Certification fee: $2.00. Fee payee: Clerk of Superior Court. Personal checks accepted. Prepayment is required. Public access terminal is available.

Scotland County

Superior-District Court PO Box 769, Laurinburg, NC 28353; 910-277-3240. Hours: 8:30AM-5PM (EST). *Felony, Misdemeanor, Civil, Eviction, Small Claims, Probate.*

www.aoc.state.nc.us/www/public/courts/scotland.html

Civil Records: Access: Mail, in person. Both court and visitors may perform in person searches. Search fee: $5.00 per name. Required to search: name, years to search. Civil cases indexed by defendant, plaintiff. Civil records on computer since 1988, in books since 1966, on microfiche since 1984. **Criminal Records:** Access: Mail, remote online, in person. Only the court conducts in person searches; visitors may not. Search fee: $5.00 per name. Required to search: name, years to search, DOB. Criminal records on computer since 1988, in books since 1966, on microfiche since 1984. Search the active Criminal Calendar by defendant name at the web site. **General Information:** No adoptions, sealed cases, juvenile, sex offenders, mental or expunged records released. SASE required. Turnaround time 1-2 days. Copy fee: $1.00 for first page, $.25 each addl. Certification fee: $2.00. Fee payee: Clerk of Court. Only cashiers checks and money orders accepted. Prepayment is required. Public access terminal is available.

Stanly County

Superior-District Court PO Box 668, Albemarle, NC 28002-0668; 704-982-2161; Fax: 704-982-8107. Hours: 8:30AM-5PM (EST). *Felony, Misdemeanor, Civil, Eviction, Small Claims, Probate.*

www.aoc.state.nc.us/www/public/courts/stanly.htm

Civil Records: Access: In person only. Court does not conduct in person searches; visitors must perform searches for themselves. Search fee: No civil searches performed by court. Required to search: name, years to search; also helpful-address. Civil cases indexed by defendant, plaintiff. Civil records on computer since 1989, books to 1968. **Criminal Records:** Access: Mail, remote online, in person. Both court and visitors may perform in person searches. Search fee: $5.00 per name. Required to search: name, years to search, DOB; also helpful-address, SSN. Criminal records on computer since 1989, books to 1968. Search the active Criminal Calendar by defendant name at the web site. **General Information:** No adoptions, sealed cases, juvenile, sex offenders, mental or expunged records released. SASE required. Turnaround time 1-2 days. Copy fee: $1.00 for first page, $.25 each addl. Certification fee: $2.00. Fee payee: Clerk of Superior Court. Only cashiers checks and money orders accepted. Prepayment is required. Public access terminal is available.

Stokes County

Superior-District Court PO Box 256, Danbury, NC 27016; 336-593-2416. Hours: 8AM-5PM (EST). *Felony, Misdemeanor, Civil, Eviction, Small Claims, Probate.*

www.aoc.state.nc.us/www/public/courts/stokes.html

Civil Records: Access: In person only. Court does not conduct in person searches; visitors must perform searches for themselves. Search fee: No civil searches performed by court. Required to search: name, years to search; also helpful-address. Civil cases indexed by defendant, plaintiff. Civil records on computer since 1988, prior on books to early 1900s. Civil background checks not performed. **Criminal Records:** Access: Mail, remote online, in person. Both court and visitors may perform in person searches. Search fee: $5.00 per name. Required to search: name, years to search; also helpful-address, DOB. Criminal records on computer since 1988, prior on books to early 1900s. Search the active Criminal Calendar by defendant name at the web site. **General Information:** No adoptions, sealed cases, juvenile, sex offenders, mental or expunged records released. SASE required. Turnaround time 1 week. Copy fee: $1.00 for first page, $.25 each addl. Certification fee: Included in search fee, unless do it yourself then $2.00. Fee payee: Clerk of Superior Court. Only cashiers checks and money orders accepted. Prepayment is required. Public access terminal is available.

Surry County

Superior-District Court PO Box 345, Dobson, NC 27017; 336-386-8131; Fax: 336-386-9879. Hours: 8AM-5PM (EST). *Felony, Misdemeanor, Civil, Eviction, Small Claims, Probate.*

www.aoc.state.nc.us/www/public/courts/surry.html

Civil Records: Access: In person only. Court does not conduct in person searches; visitors must perform searches for themselves. Search fee: No civil searches performed by court. Required to search: name, years to search; also helpful-address. Civil cases indexed by defendant, plaintiff. Civil records on computer since 10/88, on books to 1970, must know township for prior. **Criminal Records:** Access: Mail, remote online, in person. Both court and visitors may perform in person searches. Search fee: $5.00 per name. Required to search: name, years to search, DOB. Criminal records on computer since 10/88, on books to 1970, must know township for prior. Search the active Criminal Calendar by defendant name at the web site. **General Information:** No adoptions, sealed cases, juvenile, sex offenders, mental or expunged records released. SASE required. Turnaround time 1-2 days. Copy fee: $1.00 for first page, $.25 each addl. Certification fee: $2.00. Fee payee: Clerk of Superior Court. Business checks accepted. Prepayment is required. Public access terminal is available.

Swain County

Superior-District Court PO Box 1397, Bryson City, NC 28713; 828-488-2288; Fax: 828-488-9360. Hours: 8:30AM-5PM (EST). *Felony, Misdemeanor, Civil, Eviction, Small Claims, Probate.*

www.aoc.state.nc.us/www/public/courts/swain.html

Civil Records: Access: Mail, in person. Both court and visitors may perform in person searches. Search fee: $5.00 per name. Required to search: name, years to search. Civil cases indexed by defendant, plaintiff. Civil records on computer since May 1989, prior on books to 1966. **Criminal Records:** Access: Mail, remote online, in person. Only the court conducts in person searches; visitors may not. Search fee: $5.00 per name. Required to search: name, years to search, DOB. Criminal records on computer since May 1989, prior on books to 1966. Search the active Criminal Calendar by defendant name at the web site. **General Information:** No adoptions, sealed cases, juvenile, sex offenders, mental or expunged records released. SASE requested. Turnaround time 1-2 days. Copy fee: $1.00 for first page, $.25 each addl. Certification fee: $2.00. Fee payee: Clerk of Superior Court. Only cashiers checks and money orders accepted. Prepayment is required. Public access terminal is available. Public Access Terminal Note: Civil only.

Transylvania County

Superior-District Court 12 E Main St, Brevard, NC 28712; 828-884-3120; Fax: 828-883-2161. Hours: 8AM-5PM (EST). *Felony, Misdemeanor, Civil, Eviction, Small Claims, Probate.*

www.aoc.state.nc.us/www/public/courts/transylvania.html

Civil Records: Access: In person only. Court does not conduct in person searches; visitors must perform searches for themselves. Search fee: No civil searches performed by court. Required to search: name, years to search; also helpful-address. Civil cases indexed by defendant, plaintiff. Civil records on computer from 6/89, on books 1968-1989. **Criminal Records:** Access: Mail, remote online, in person. Court does not conduct in person searches; visitors must perform searches for themselves. Search fee: $5.00 per name. Fee is for certified record check. Required to search: name, years to search, DOB; also helpful-address, SSN. Criminal records on computer from 6/89, on books 1968-1989. Search the active Criminal Calendar by defendant name at the web site. **General Information:** No adoptions, sealed cases, juvenile, mental or expunged records released. SASE required. Turnaround time 1-3 days. Copy fee: $1.00 for first page, $.25 each addl. Certification fee: $2.00. Fee payee: Clerk of Superior Court. Personal checks accepted. Prepayment is required.

Tyrrell County

Superior-District Court PO Box 406, Columbia, NC 27925; 252-796-6281; Fax: 252-796-0008. Hours: 8:30AM-5PM (EST). *Felony, Misdemeanor, Civil, Eviction, Small Claims, Probate.*

www.aoc.state.nc.us/www/public/courts/tyrrell.html

Civil Records: Access: In person only. Court does not conduct in person searches; visitors must perform searches for themselves. Search fee: No civil searches performed by court. Required to search: name, years to search; also helpful-address. Civil cases indexed by defendant, plaintiff. Civil records on computer since 10/89, prior on books to 1968. **Criminal Records:** Access: Mail, remote online, in person. Both court and visitors may perform in person searches. Search fee: $5.00 per name. Required to search: name, years to search, DOB; also helpful-address, SSN. Criminal records on computer since 10/89, prior on books to 1968. Search the active Criminal Calendar by defendant name at the web site. **General Information:** No

adoptions, sealed cases, juvenile, sex offenders, mental records expunged. Turnaround time 1-2 days. Copy fee: $1.00 for first page, $.25 each addl. Certification fee: $2.00. Fee payee: Clerk of Superior Court. Business checks accepted. Prepayment is required. Public access terminal is available.

Union County

Superior-District Court PO Box 5038, Monroe, NC 28111; 704-283-4313. Hours: 8AM-5PM (EST). *Felony, Misdemeanor, Civil, Eviction, Small Claims, Probate.*

www.aoc.state.nc.us/www/public/courts/union.htm

Civil Records: Access: In person only. Court does not conduct in person searches; visitors must perform searches for themselves. Search fee: No civil searches performed by court. Required to search: name, years to search; also helpful-address. Civil cases indexed by defendant, plaintiff. Civil records on computer since 1987, prior on books to 1968. **Criminal Records:** Access: Mail, remote online, in person. Both court and visitors may perform in person searches. Search fee: $5.00 per name. Required to search: name, years to search; also helpful-address, DOB, SSN. Criminal record on computer since 1987; prior on books to 1968. Search the active Criminal Calendar by defendant name at the web site. **General Information:** No adoptions, sealed cases, juvenile, sex offenders, mental or expunged records released. Turnaround time 1-2 days. Copy fee: $1.00 for first page, $.25 each addl. Certification fee: Included in copy fee or search fee. Fee payee: Clerk of Superior Court. Only cashiers checks and money orders accepted. Local business checks only. Prepayment is required. Public access terminal is available.

Vance County

Superior-District Court 122 Young St, Henderson, NC 27536; 919-492-0031. Hours: 8AM-5PM (EST). *Felony, Misdemeanor, Civil, Eviction, Small Claims, Probate.*

www.aoc.state.nc.us/www/public/courts/vance.html

Civil Records: Access: In person only. Court does not conduct in person searches; visitors must perform searches for themselves. Search fee: No civil searches performed by court. Required to search: name, years to search; also helpful-address. Civil cases indexed by defendant, plaintiff. Civil records on computer since 1989, prior on books to 1881. **Criminal Records:** Access: Mail, remote online, in person. Both court and visitors may perform in person searches. Search fee: $5.00 per name. Required to search: name, years to search, address, DOB; also helpful-SSN. Criminal records on computer to 12/80, prior on books and cards to 1881. Search the active Criminal Calendar by defendant name at the web site. **General Information:** No adoptions, sealed cases, juvenile, sex offenders, mental or expunged records released. Turnaround time 1-2 days. Copy fee: $1.00 for first page, $.25 each addl. Certification fee: Included in search fee, unless do it yourself then $2.00. Fee payee: Clerk of Superior Court. Business checks accepted. Prepayment is required. Public access terminal is available.

Wake County

Superior-District Court PO Box 351, Raleigh, NC 27602; 919-755-4105; Civil phone:919-755-4108; Criminal phone:919-755-4108. Hours: 8:30AM-5:00PM (EST). *Felony, Misdemeanor, Civil, Eviction, Small Claims, Probate.*

www.aoc.state.nc.us/www/public/courts/wake.htm

Civil Records: Access: In person only. Court does not conduct in person searches; visitors must perform searches for themselves. Search fee: No civil searches performed by court. Required to search: name, years to search. Civil cases indexed by defendant, plaintiff. Civil records on computer since 1988, prior on books to 1920s. **Criminal Records:** Access: Mail, remote online, in person. Both court and visitors may perform in person searches. Search fee: $5.00 per name. Required to search: name, years to search. Criminal records on computer from 5/82, prior on books and cards from 1968. Search the active Criminal Calendar by defendant name at the web site. **General Information:** No adoptions, sealed cases, juvenile, sex offenders, mental or expunged records released. Turnaround time 1-2 days. Copy fee: $1.00 for first page, $.25 each addl. Certification fee: $2.00. Fee payee: Clerk of Superior Court. Business checks accepted. Public access terminal is available.

Warren County

Superior-District Court PO Box 709, Warrenton, NC 27589; 252-257-3261; Fax: 252-257-5529. Hours: 8:30AM-5PM (EST). *Felony, Misdemeanor, Civil, Eviction, Small Claims, Probate.*

www.aoc.state.nc.us/www/public/courts/warren.htm

Civil Records: Access: In person only. Court does not conduct in person searches; visitors must perform searches for themselves. Search fee: No civil searches performed by court. Required to search: name, years to search. Civil cases indexed by defendant, plaintiff. Civil records on computer since 1989, prior on books to 1968. **Criminal Records:** Access: Mail, remote online, in person. Both court and visitors may perform in person searches. Search fee: $5.00 per name. Required to search: name, years to search, DOB. Criminal records on computer from 5/81, prior on books as civil. Search the active Criminal Calendar by defendant name at the web site. **General Information:** No adoptions, sealed cases, juvenile, sex offenders, mental or expunged records released. Turnaround time 1-2 days. Copy fee: $1.00 for first page, $.25 each addl. Certification fee: $2.00. Fee payee: Clerk of Superior Court. Business checks accepted. Prepayment is required.

Washington County

Superior-District Court PO Box 901, Plymouth, NC 27962; 252-793-3013; Fax: 252-793-1081. Hours: 8AM-5PM (EST). *Felony, Misdemeanor, Civil, Eviction, Small Claims, Probate.*

www.aoc.state.nc.us/www/public/courts/
washington.html

Civil Records: Access: In person only. Court does not conduct in person searches; visitors must perform searches for themselves. Search fee: No civil searches performed by court. Required to search: name, years to search. Civil cases indexed by defendant, plaintiff. Civil records on computer since 12/89, prior on books. **Criminal Records:** Access: Mail, remote online, in person. Both court and visitors may perform in person searches. Search fee: $5.00 per name. Required to search: name, years to search; also helpful-address, DOB, SSN. Criminal records on computer since 12/89, prior on books. Search the active Criminal Calendar by defendant name at the web site. **General Information:** No adoptions, sealed, juvenile, mental health, expunged or dismissed

records released. SASE required. Turnaround time 2-3 days. Copy fee: $1.00 for first page, $.25 each addl. Certification fee: $2.00. Fee payee: Clerk of Court. Business checks accepted. Prepayment is required. Public access terminal is available.

Watauga County

Superior-District Court Courthouse Suite 13, 842 West King St, Boone, NC 28607-3525; 828-265-5364; Fax: 828-262-5753. Hours: 8AM-5PM (EST). *Felony, Misdemeanor, Civil, Eviction, Small Claims, Probate.*

www.aoc.state.nc.us/www/public/courts/watauga.htm

Civil Records: Access: Mail, in person. Both court and visitors may perform in person searches. Search fee: $5.00 per name. Required to search: name, years to search. Civil cases indexed by defendant, plaintiff. Civil records on computer since 12/5/88, on books to 1872, prior destroyed by fire. **Criminal Records:** Access: Mail, remote online, in person. Both court and visitors may perform in person searches. Search fee: $5.00 per name. Required to search: name, years to search, DOB. Criminal records on computer from 11/88, prior on cards and books to 1968. Search the active Criminal Calendar by defendant name at the web site. **General Information:** No adoptions, sealed, juvenile, sex offenders, mental, expunged or dismissed records released. SASE requested. Turnaround time 1-2 days. Copy fee: $1.00 for first page, $.25 each addl. Certification fee: $2.00. Fee payee: Clerk of Court. Only cashiers checks and money orders accepted. Public access terminal is available.

Wayne County

Superior-District Court PO Box 267, Goldsboro, NC 27530;; Civil phone:919-731-7919; Criminal phone:919-731-7919; Fax: 919-731-2037. Hours: 8AM-5PM (EST). *Felony, Misdemeanor, Civil, Eviction, Small Claims, Probate.*

www.aoc.state.nc.us/www/public/courts/wayne.htm

Civil Records: Access: In person. Court does not conduct searches; visitors must perform searches for themselves. No search fee. Required to search: name, years to search; also helpful-address. Civil cases indexed by defendant, plaintiff. Civil records on computer since 7-18-88, on books since 1968, open to public prior. The court will not do a search unless book and page number or a year of judgment given. **Criminal Records:** Access: Mail, remote online, in person. Both court and visitors may perform in person searches. Search fee: $5.00 per name. Required to search: name, years to search, DOB; also helpful-address, SSN, aliases. Criminal records on computer since 7-18-88, on books since 1968, open to public prior. Search the active Criminal Calendar by defendant name at the web site. **General Information:** No adoptions, sealed, juvenile, sex offenders, mental, expunged or dismissed. SASE requested. Turnaround time 1-2 days. Copy fee: $1.00 for first page, $.25 each addl. Certification fee: $2.00. Fee payee: Clerk of Superior Court. Business checks accepted. Prepayment is required. Public access terminal is available.

Wilkes County

Superior-District Court 500 Courthouse Drive, #1115, Wilkesboro, NC 28697;; Civil phone:336-667-1201; Criminal phone:336-667-1201; Fax: 336-667-1985. Hours: 8AM-5PM (EST). *Felony, Misdemeanor, Civil, Eviction, Small Claims, Probate.*

www.aoc.state.nc.us/www/public/courts/wilkes.htm

Civil Records: Access: In person only. Court does not conduct in person searches; visitors must perform searches for themselves. Search fee: No civil searches performed by court. Required to search: name, years to search. Civil cases indexed by defendant, plaintiff. Civil records on computer since 12/88, prior on books to early 1900s. **Criminal Records:** Access: Mail, remote online, in person. Only the court conducts in person searches; visitors may not. Search fee: $5.00 per name. Required to search: name, years to search, DOB; also helpful-address. Criminal records on computer since 12/88, prior on books to early 1900s. Search the active Criminal Calendar by defendant name at the web site. **General Information:** No adoptions, sealed cases, juvenile, sex offenders, mental or expunged records released. SASE requested. Turnaround time 1-2 days. Copy fee: $1.00 for first page, $.25 each addl. Certification fee: $2.00. Fee payee: Clerk of Superior Court. Only cashiers checks and money orders accepted. Prepayment is required. Public access terminal is available.

Wilson County

Superior-District Court PO Box 1608, Wilson, NC 27894;; Civil phone:252-291-7502; Criminal phone:252-291-7502; Fax: 252-291-8049 (Criminal) 291-8635 (Civil). Hours: 9AM-5PM (EST). *Felony, Misdemeanor, Civil, Eviction, Small Claims, Probate.*

www.aoc.state.nc.us/www/public/courts/wilson.html

Civil Records: Access: In person only. Court does not conduct in person searches; visitors must perform searches for themselves. Search fee: No civil searches performed by court. Required to search: name, years to search; also helpful-address. Civil cases indexed by defendant, plaintiff. Civil records on computer since 8/88, prior on books to 1968, public viewing from 1915 to 1968. **Criminal Records:** Access: Mail, remote online, in person. Both court and visitors may perform in person searches. Search fee: $5.00 per name. Required to search: name, years to search, DOB; also helpful-address, SSN. Criminal records on computer since 5/86, Index cards to 9/76, books to 1918. Search the active Criminal Calendar by defendant name at the web site. **General Information:** No adoptions, sealed cases, juvenile, sex offenders, mental, or expunged records released. SASE requested. Turnaround time 2-4 days. Copy fee: $1.00 for first page, $.25 each addl. Certification fee: $2.00. Fee payee: Clerk of Court. Only cashiers checks and money orders accepted. In-state personal checks accepted. Prepayment is required. Public access terminal is available.

Yadkin County

Superior-District Court PO Box 95, Yadkinville, NC 27055; 336-679-8838; Fax: 336-679-4378. Hours: 8AM-5PM (EST). *Felony, Misdemeanor, Civil, Eviction, Small Claims, Probate.*

www.aoc.state.nc.us/www/public/courts/yadkin.htm

Civil Records: Access: In person only. Court does not conduct in person searches; visitors must perform searches for themselves. Search fee: No civil searches performed by court. Required to search: name, years to search; also helpful-address. Civil cases indexed by defendant, plaintiff. Civil records on computer since 8/89, prior on books to 1970. **Criminal Records:** Access: Mail, remote online, in person. Both court and visitors may perform in person searches. Search fee: $5.00 per name. Required to search: name, years to search, DOB; also helpful-address. Criminal records on computer since 8/89, prior on books to 1970. Search the active Criminal Calendar by defendant name at the web site. **General Information:** No adoptions, sealed cases, juvenile, sex offenders, mental or expunged records released. SASE required. Turnaround time 1-2 days. Copy fee: $1.00 for first page, $.25 each addl. Certification fee: $2.00. Fee payee: Clerk of Superior Court. Business checks accepted. Prepayment is required. Public access terminal is available.

Yancey County

Superior-District Court 110 Town Square, Burnsville, NC 28714; 828-682-2122. Hours: 8:30AM-5PM (EST). *Felony, Misdemeanor, Civil, Eviction, Small Claims, Probate.*

www.aoc.state.nc.us/www/public/courts/yancey.htm

Civil Records: Access: In person only. Court does not conduct in person searches; visitors must perform searches for themselves. Search fee: No civil searches performed by court. Required to search: name, years to search; also helpful-address. Civil cases indexed by defendant, plaintiff. Civil records on computer since 1988, prior on books. **Criminal Records:** Access: Mail, remote online, in person. Only the court conducts in person

searches; visitors may not. Search fee: $5.00 per name. Required to search: name, years to search, DOB; also helpful-address, SSN. Criminal records on computer since 1988, prior on books. Search the active Criminal Calendar by defendant name at the web site. **General Information:** No adoptions, sealed cases, juvenile, sex offenders, mental, expunged or dismissed records released. Turnaround time depends on ease of access, can take up to 2 weeks. Copy fee: $1.00 for first page, $.25 each addl. Certification fee: $2.00. Fee payee: Clerk of Superior Court. Business checks accepted. Prepayment is required. Public access terminal is available. Public Access Terminal Note: Civil only.

ORGANIZATION 100 counties, 100 recording offices. The recording officers are Register of Deeds and Clerk of Superior Court (tax liens). The entire state is in the Eastern Time Zone (EST).

REAL ESTATE RECORDS Counties will **not** perform real estate searches. Copy fees are usually $1.00 per page. Certification usually costs $3.00 for the first page and $1.00 for each additional page of a document.

UCC RECORDS This is a **dual filing state**. Financing statements are filed both at the state level and with the Register of Deeds, except for consumer goods, farm related and real estate related collateral. All counties will perform UCC searches. Use search request form UCC-11. Search fees are usually $15.00 per debtor name. Copies usually cost $1.00 per page.

TAX LIEN RECORDS Federal tax liens on personal property of businesses are filed with the Secretary of State. Other federal and all state tax liens are filed with the county Clerk of Superior Court, **not** with the Register of Deeds. (Oddly, even tax liens on real property are also filed with the Clerk of Superior Court, **not** with the Register of Deeds.) Refer to the county courts section for information about North Carolina Superior Courts.

OTHER LIENS Judgment, mechanics (all at Clerk of Superior Court).

Alamance County
County Register of Deeds, P.O. Box 837, Graham, NC 27253. 336-570-6565.

Alexander County
County Register of Deeds, 201 First Street SW, Suite 1, Taylorsville, NC 28681-2504. 828-632-3152. Fax: 828-632-1119.

Alleghany County
County Register of Deeds, P.O. Box 186, Sparta, NC 28675. 336-372-4342. Fax: 336-372-2061.

Anson County
County Register of Deeds, P.O. Box 352, Wadesboro, NC 28170-0352. 704-694-3212. Fax: 704-694-6135.

Ashe County
County Register of Deeds, P.O. Box 367, Jefferson, NC 28640-0367. 336-246-1841.
www.andassoc.com/gismaps
Online Access: Assessor, Real Estate. Records on the Ashe County Tax Parcel Information System are available free on the Internet at www.andassoc.com/gimaps/Aplus/Aplus.htm. Click on the map area - zoom in to find the parcel on the map, or use the search fields.

Avery County
County Register of Deeds, P.O. Box 87, Newland, NC 28657. 704-733-8260.

Beaufort County
County Register of Deeds, P.O. Box 514, Washington, NC 27889. 252-946-2323.

Bertie County
County Register of Deeds, P.O. Box 340, Windsor, NC 27983. 252-794-5309. Fax: 252-794-5327.

Bladen County
County Register of Deeds, P.O. Box 247, Elizabethtown, NC 28337. 910-862-6710. Fax: 910-862-6716.

Brunswick County
County Register of Deeds, P.O. Box 87, Bolivia, NC 28422-0087. 910-253-2690. Fax: 910-253-2703.

Buncombe County
County Register of Deeds, 60 Court Plaza, Room 110, Asheville, NC 28801-3563. 828-250-4300. Fax: 828-255-5829.
www.propex.com:1200/pex_web/owa/kiaa$.startup
Online Access: Assessor, Real Estate. Property tax data for Buncombe Count is available free on the Internet at a private company web site.

Burke County
County Register of Deeds, P.O. Box 936, Morganton, NC 28680. 828-438-5450. Fax: 828-438-5463.
Online Access: Real Estate.

Cabarrus County
County Register of Deeds, P.O. Box 707, Concord, NC 28026. 704-788-8112. Fax: 704-788-9898.
www.co.cabarrus.nc.us
Online Access: Assessor, Real Estate. Records on the Cabarrus County GIS Public Access database are available free on the Internet at www.co.cabarrus.nc.us/Pages/GIS.html. Click on the map area; zoom in to find the parcel on the map, or go directly to the "query section" & click on "find" Database contains owner, year built, ZIP Code, sales data, values, legal description, real ID, zoning, deed book, parcel number, tax maps, school district.

Caldwell County
County Register of Deeds, 905 West Avenue N.W., County Office Building, Lenoir, NC 28645. 828-757-1399. Fax: 828-757-1294.
http://maps.co.caldwell.nc.us
Online Access: Assessor, Real Estate. Parcels, property records, flood plains, streets, and election district records are available on the Caldwell County Geographic Information System on the Internet for no fee. Click on "Start Spatial-Data Explorer".

Camden County
County Register of Deeds, P.O. Box 190, Camden, NC 27921. 252-335-4077.

Carteret County
County Register of Deeds, Courthouse Square, Beaufort, NC 28516-1898. 252-728-8474. Fax: 252-728-7693.

Caswell County
County Register of Deeds, P.O. Box 98, Yanceyville, NC 27379. 336-694-4193. Fax: 336-694-1405.

Catawba County
County Register of Deeds, P.O. Box 65, Newton, NC 28658-0065. 828-465-1573.
www.gis.catawba.nc.us
Online Access: Assessor, Real Estate. Records on the Catawba County Geographic Information System database are available free on the Internet at www.gi.catawba.nc.us/maps/public.htm. Click on map area; zoom in to find the parcel on the map, or search in the query fields.

Chatham County
County Register of Deeds, P.O. Box 756, Pittsboro, NC 27312. 919-542-8235.

Cherokee County
County Register of Deeds, 75 Peachtree St., Suite 102, Murphy, NC 28906. 828-837-2613. Fax: 828-837-8414.

Chowan County
County Register of Deeds, P.O. Box 487, Edenton, NC 27932-0487. 252-482-2619.

Clay County
County Register of Deeds, P.O. Box 118, Hayesville, NC 28904. 828-389-0087. Fax: 828-389-9749.

Cleveland County
County Register of Deeds, P.O. Box 1210, Shelby, NC 28151-1210. 704-484-4834. Fax: 704-484-4909.

Columbus County
County Register of Deeds, P.O. Box 1086, Whiteville, NC 28472-1086. 910-640-6625. Fax: 910-640-2547.

Craven County
County Register of Deeds, 406 Craven Street, New Bern, NC 28560. 252-636-6617. Fax: 252-636-1937.

Cumberland County
County Register of Deeds, P.O. 2039, Fayetteville, NC 28302-2039. 910-678-7718. Fax: 910-323-1456.
www.ccrod.org/

Currituck County
County Register of Deeds, P.O. Box 71, Currituck, NC 27929. 252-232-3297. Fax: 252-232-3906.

Dare County
County Register of Deeds, P.O. Box 70, Manteo, NC 27954. 252-473-3438.
www.co.dare.nc.us
Online Access: Assessor, Real Estate. Records on the Dare County Property Inquiry database are available free on the Internet at www.co.dare.nc.us/interactive/setup.htm.

Davidson County
County Register of Deeds, P.O. Box 464, Lexington, NC 27293-0464. 336-242-2150. Fax: 336-238-2318.
www.co.davidson.nc.us
Online Access: Assessor, Real Estate. Records on the Davidson County Tax Department database are available free on the Internet at www.co.davidson.nc.us/asp/taxsearch.asp. Provides owner, property, and deed information, also legal description, zoning and property values.

Davie County
County Register of Deeds, 123 South Main Street, Mocksville, NC 27028. 336-634-2513.

Duplin County
County Register of Deeds, P.O. Box 970, Kenansville, NC 28349. 910-296-2108. Fax: 910-296-2344.

Durham County
County Register of Deeds, P.O. Box 1107, Durham, NC 27702. 919-560-0494. Fax: 919-560-0497.
http://199.72.142.253
Online Access: Assessor, Real Estate. Tax parcel, voting district, flood zones records are available on the Durham Spatial Data Explorer GIS site for no fee. Click on "Start: I understand and Accept the Limits of Data Accuracy".

Edgecombe County
County Register of Deeds, P.O. Box 386, Tarboro, NC 27886. 252-641-7924. Fax: 252-641-1771.

Forsyth County
County Register of Deeds, P.O. Box 20639, Winston-Salem, NC 27120-0639. 336-727-2903. Fax: 336-727-2341.

Franklin County
County Register of Deeds, P.O. Box 545, Louisburg, NC 27549-0545. 919-496-3500. Fax: 919-496-1457.

Gaston County
County Register of Deeds, P.O. Box 1578, Gastonia, NC 28053. 704-862-7681. Fax: 704-862-7519.

Gates County
County Register of Deeds, P.O. Box 471, Gatesville, NC 27938-0471. 252-357-0850. Fax: 252-357-0850.

Graham County
County Register of Deeds, P.O. Box 406, Robbinsville, NC 28771-0406. 828-479-7971. Fax: 828-479-7988.

Granville County
County Register of Deeds, P.O. Box 427, Oxford, NC 27565. 919-693-6314. Fax: 919-603-1345.

Greene County
County Register of Deeds, P.O. Box 86, Snow Hill, NC 28580. 252-747-3620.

Guilford County
County Register of Deeds, P.O. Box 1467, High Point, NC 27261-1467. 336-884-7931.

Halifax County
County Register of Deeds, P.O. Box 67, Halifax, NC 27839-0067. 252-583-2101. Fax: 252-583-1273.

Harnett County
County Register of Deeds, P.O. Box 279, Lillington, NC 27546. 910-893-7540. Fax: 910-814-3841.
Online access: Real estate. Harnett County offers real estate and property tax information available free on the Internet on the GIS map server web site at www.roktech.net/harnett/index.html. Search the map or by parcel #m, account #, PIN # or name.

Haywood County
County Register of Deeds, Courthouse, 215 N. Main St., Waynesville, NC 28786. 828-452-6635. Fax: 828-452-6762.
www.undersys.com/haywood/haywood.html
Online Access: Real Estate. Records on the Haywood County Land Records Search database are available free on the Internet. Search will result in a map showing the parcel(s) selected and owner, parcel nubmer, and deed book & page information on the parcel(s).

Henderson County
County Register of Deeds, Suite 129, 200 N. Grove St., Hendersonville, NC 28792. 704-697-4901.

Hertford County
County Register of Deeds, P.O. Box 36, Winton, NC 27986. 252-358-7850. Fax: 252-358-7806.

Hoke County
County Register of Deeds, 304 N. Main St., Raeford, NC 28376. 910-875-2035. Fax: 910-875-9515.

Hyde County
County Register of Deeds, P.O. Box 294, Swanquarter, NC 27885. 252-926-3011. Fax: 252-926-3082.

Iredell County
County Register of Deeds, P.O. Box 904, Statesville, NC 28687. 704-872-7468. Fax: 704-878-3055.

Jackson County
County Register of Deeds, 401 Grindstaff Cove Rd., Sylva, NC 28779. 828-586-7530. Fax: 828-586-6879.

Johnston County
County Register of Deeds, Box 118, Smithfield, NC 27577. 919-989-5164.

Jones County
County Register of Deeds, P.O. Box 189, Trenton, NC 28585-0189. 252-448-2551. Fax: 252-448-1357.

Lee County
County Register of Deeds, P.O. Box 2040, Sanford, NC 27331-2040. 919-774-4821. Fax: 919-774-5063.

Lenoir County
County Register of Deeds, P.O. Box 3289, Kinston, NC 28502. 252-559-6420. Fax: 252-523-6139.

Lincoln County
County Register of Deeds, P.O. Box 218, Lincolnton, NC 28093-0218. 704-736-8530. Fax: 704-732-9049.

Macon County
County Register of Deeds, 5 West Main Street, Franklin, NC 28734. 828-349-2095. Fax: 828-369-6382.

Madison County
County Register of Deeds, P.O. Box 66, Marshall, NC 28753. 828-649-3131.

Martin County
County Register of Deeds, P.O. Box 348, Williamston, NC 27892. 252-792-1683. Fax: 252-792-1684.

McDowell County
County Register of Deeds, 1 South Main Street, Courthouse, Marion, NC 28752-3992. 828-652-4727. Fax: 828-652-4727.

Mecklenburg County
County Register of Deeds, 720 East 4th Street, Ste. 100, Charlotte, NC 28202. 704-336-2443. Fax: 704-336-7699.
Online Access: Real Estate. Mecklenburg County offers real estate and property tax information available free on the Internet on the GIS map server web site at http://maps.co.mecklenburg.nc.us/taxgis/disclaimer.htm

Mitchell County
County Register of Deeds, P.O. Box 82, Bakersville, NC 28705-0082. 828-688-2139. Fax: 828-688-3666.

Montgomery County
County Register of Deeds, P.O. Box 695, Troy, NC 27371-0695. 910-576-4271. Fax: 910-576-2209.

Moore County
County Register of Deeds, P.O. Box 1210, Carthage, NC 28327. 910-947-6370. Fax: 910-947-6396.

Nash County
County Register of Deeds, P.O. Box 974, Nashville, NC 27856. 252-459-9836. Fax: 252-459-9889.

New Hanover County
County Register of Deeds, 316 Princess Street, Room 216, Wilmington, NC 28401. 910-341-4530. Fax: 910-341-4323.

Northampton County
County Register of Deeds, P.O. Box 128, Jackson, NC 27845. 252-534-2511.

Onslow County
County Register of Deeds, 109 Old Bridge Street, Jacksonville, NC 28540. 910-347-3451.

Orange County
County Register of Deeds, P.O. Box 8181, Hillsborough, NC 27278-8181. 919-732-8181. Fax: 919-644-3015.

Pamlico County
County Register of Deeds, P.O. Box 433, Bayboro, NC 28515. 252-745-4421.

Pasquotank County
County Register of Deeds, P.O. Box 154, Elizabeth City, NC 27907-0154. 252-335-4367. Fax: 252-335-5106.

Pender County
County Register of Deeds, P.O. Box 43, Burgaw, NC 28425. 910-259-1225. Fax: 910-259-1299.

Perquimans County
County Register of Deeds, P.O. Box 74, Hertford, NC 27944. 252-426-5660. Fax: 252-426-7443.

Person County
County Register of Deeds, Courthouse Square, Roxboro, NC 27573. 336-597-1733.

Pitt County
County Register of Deeds, P.O. Box 35, Greenville, NC 27835-0035. 252-830-4128.

Polk County
County Register of Deeds, P.O. Box 308, Columbus, NC 28722. 828-894-8450. Fax: 828-894-5781.

Randolph County
County Register of Deeds, P.O. Box 4066, Asheboro, NC 27204. 336-318-6960.

Richmond County
County Register of Deeds, 114 E Franklin St., Suite 101, Rockingham, NC 28379-3601. 910-997-8250. Fax: 910-997-8499.

Robeson County
County Register of Deeds, Box 22 Courthouse-Room 102, Lumberton, NC 28358. 910-671-3046. Fax: 910-671-3041.

Rockingham County
County Register of Deeds, P.O. Box 56, Wentworth, NC 27375-0056. 336-342-8820.

Rowan County
County Register of Deeds, P.O. Box 2568, Salisbury, NC 28145. 704-638-3102.

Rutherford County
County Register of Deeds, P.O. Box 551, Rutherfordton, NC 28139. 828-287-6155. Fax: 828-287-6470.

Sampson County
County Register of Deeds, P.O. Box 256, Clinton, NC 28329. 910-592-8026. Fax: 910-592-1803.

Scotland County
County Register of Deeds, P.O. Box 769, Laurinburg, NC 28353. 910-277-2575. Fax: 910-277-3133.

Stanly County
County Register of Deeds, P.O. Box 97, Albemarle, NC 28002-0097. 704-986-3640.
www.webgis.net/stanly
Online Access: Real Estate. Records on the Stanly County Property database are available free on the Internet. On the main page, click on "Continue on to GIS". Click on the map area and zoom in to find the parcel, or use the "Search" field Provides parcel ID and tax numbers, owner, address, year, land and building values.

Stokes County
County Register of Deeds, P.O. Box 67, Danbury, NC 27016. 336-593-2811. Fax: 336-593-9360.

Surry County
County Register of Deeds, P.O. Box 303, Dobson, NC 27017-0303. 336-401-8150. Fax: 336-401-8151.

Swain County
County Register of Deeds, P.O. Box 1183, Bryson City, NC 28713. 828-488-9273. Fax: 828-488-6947.

Phone search: Searching is available by phone.

Fax search: Results can be faxed, mailed, or phoned.

In person search: Turnaround time is usually immediate.

Online search: There is a free public inquiry system on the home page. One can also search lottery hunting permit applications.

Other access: A printed list is available of all registered vessels.

Legislation-Current/Pending Legislation-Passed

North Dakota Legislative Council, State Capitol, 600 E Boulevard Ave, Bismarck, ND 58505; 701-328-2916, 701-328-2900 (Secretary of State), 701-328-2992 (Sec of State fax), 8AM-5PM.

www.state.nd.us/lr

Note: Copies of "enrolled bills" are found at the Secretary of State's office; search fee is $1.00 for each 4 pages. The legislature meets every odd year.

Indexing & Storage: Records are available from 1889 on. Records are on microfiche from 1969-1997, and computerized from 1997 forward. Records are indexed on inhouse computer, hard copy.

Searching: Include the following in your request-bill number.

Access by: mail, phone, fax, in person, online.

Fee & Payment: Fees is $1.00 for each 4 pages (through Sec of State). Fee payee: Secretary of State. Prepayment required. Personal checks accepted. Credit cards accepted: Mastercard, Visa, Discover.

Mail search: Turnaround time: 1-2 days. No self addressed stamped envelope is required.

Phone search: You may call for information.

Fax search: Fax to Secretary of State.

In person search: You may request information in person.

Online search: Their Internet site offers an extensive array of legislative information at no charge, including proposed and enacted legislation since 1997. Also, one may e-mail requests for information.

Voter Registration

Records not maintained by a state level agency.

Note: Records are maintained at the county level by the County Auditors. Records are open to the public.

GED Certificates

Department of Public Instruction, GED Testing, 600 E Blvd Ave, Bismarck, ND 58505-0440; 701-328-2393, 701-328-4770 (Fax), 8AM-4:30PM.

www.dpi.state.nd.us

Searching: A verification will only verify that a test was taken, but not if the subject passed the test. Include the following in your request-signed release, Social Security Number, date of birth.

Access by: mail, fax, in person, online.

Fee & Payment: There is no fee for a verification and a $2.00 fee for a copy of a transcript. Fee payee: Dept of Public Instruction. Prepayment required. Personal checks accepted. No credit cards accepted.

Mail search: Turnaround time: 1 week. No self addressed stamped envelope is required.

Fax search: Used only for verification.

In person search: Searching is available in person.

Online search: One may request records via e-mail at JMarcell@mail.dpi.state.nd.us. There is no fee, unless a transcript is ordered.

Hunting License Information
Fishing License Information

ND Game & Fish Department, 100 N Bismarck Expressway, Bismarck, ND 58501-5095; 701-328-6300, 701-328-6335 (Licensing), 701-328-6352 (Fax), 8AM-5PM.

www.state.nd.us/gnf

Indexing & Storage: Records are available from 1992 on computer. Big Game Lottery Permits are only available for the current season. Records are indexed on inhouse computer.

Searching: Include the following in your request-full name, date of birth, Social Security Number. This agency also registers boats.

Access by: mail, fax, in person, online.

Fee & Payment: There is no search fee.

Mail search: Turnaround time: 1-3 days. A self addressed stamped envelope is requested.

Fax search: Same criteria as mail searches.

In person search: You can go in and access their records. They also make the boat registrations available.

Online search: One can search to see if a person has been choosen (lottery) for a specific hunt or passed hunter safety.

Other access: They sell mailing lists. Call Paul Schadewald at 701-328-6328 for more information.

Licenses Searchable Online

Asbestos Abatement Contractor #27	www.health.state.nd.us/ndhd/environ/ee/rad/asb/
Asbestos Abatement Inspector/Monitor #27	www.health.state.nd.us/ndhd/environ/ee/rad/asb/
Asbestos Abatement Project Planner #27	www.health.state.nd.us/ndhd/environ/ee/rad/asb/
Asbestos Abatement Supervisor #27	www.health.state.nd.us/ndhd/environ/ee/rad/asb/
Asbestos Worker/Designer #27	www.health.state.nd.us/ndhd/environ/ee/rad/asb/
Attorney #41	www.court.state.nd.us/court/lawyers/index/frameset.htm
Bank #20	www.state.nd.us/bank/Bank%20List.htm
Collection Agency #20	www.state.nd.us/bank/Collection%20Agencies.htm
Consumer Finance Company #20	www.state.nd.us/bank/Finance%20Companies.htm
Contractor/General Contractor #39	www.state.nd.us/sec/contractorsearch.htm
Credit Union #20	www.state.nd.us/bank/Credit%20Union%20List.htm
Livestock Agent #19	www.state.nd.us/agr/agents.html
Livestock Auction Market #19	www.state.nd.us/agr/markets.html
Livestock Dealer #19	www.state.nd.us/agr/dealers.html
Lobbyist #39	www.state.nd.us/sec/lobbyistregmnu.htm
Money Broker Company #20	www.state.nd.us/bank/Money%20Brokers.htm
Optometrist #49	http://home.ctctel.com/ndsbopt/ods.htm
Pesticide Applicator #19	www.ag.ndsu.nodak.edu/aginfo/pesticid/cert_info.htm
Pesticide Dealer #19	www.ag.ndsu.nodak.edu/aginfo/pesticid/cert_info.htm
Public Accountant-CPA #42	http://soc01.accountingnet.com/society_common/nd/members/mem_search.asp
Pulbic Accounting Firms #42	http://soc01.accountingnet.com/society_common/nd/members/mem_search.asp
Trust Company #20	www.state.nd.us/bank/Trust%20Companies.htm

Licensing Quick Finder

Abstractor #01	701-947-2446
Abstractor Company #01	701-947-2446
Addiction Counselor #04	701-255-1439
Adoption Service #22	701-328-4805
Aerial Applicator #30	701-328-9650
Aircraft Dealer #30	701-328-9650
Aircraft Registration #30	701-328-9650
Alcoholic Beverage Control #03	701-328-2329
Architect #43	701-223-3184
Asbestos Abatement #27	701-328-5188
Asbestos Worker/Designer #27	701-328-5188
Athletic Trainer #05	701-857-5286
Attorney #41	701-328-4201
Auction Clerk #34	701-328-2400
Auctioneer #34	701-328-2400
Bank #20	701-328-9933
Barber #06	701-523-3327
Barber Shop #06	701-523-3327
Boxer #38	701-328-3665
Boxing #38	701-328-3665
Charitable Solicitation #39	701-328-3665
Check Seller #20	701-328-9933
Chiropractor #07	701-352-1690
Collection Agency #20	701-328-9933
Consumer Finance Company #20	701-328-9933
Contractor/General Contractor #39	701-328-3665
Corporate Broker #28	701-328-3548
Cosmetologist #08	701-224-9800
Cosmetologist Instructor #08	701-224-9800
Credit Union #20	701-328-9933
Crematorium #44	701-662-2511
Day Care Service #22	701-328-4809
Debt Collector #20	701-328-9933
Debt Collector/Collection Agency #20	701-328-9933
Dental Assistant #10	701-224-1815
Dental Hygienist #10	701-224-1815
Dentist #10	701-224-1815
Dietitian/Nutritionist #11	701-746-9171
Electrician #25	701-328-9522
Electrician Apprentice #25	701-328-9522
Embalmer #44	701-662-2511
Employment Agency#23	701-328-2660
Engineer #36	701-258-0786
Engineer/Land Surveyor Combo #36	701-258-0786
Esthetician/Manicurist #08	701-224-9800
Fireworks (Wholesale) #03	701-328-2329
Fishing Guide #26	701-328-6300
Foster Care Program #22	701-328-3587
Funeral Director #44	701-662-2511
Funeral Home #44	701-662-2511
Gaming #03	701-328-2329
Gaming Distributor #03	701-328-2329
Gaming Manufacturer #03	701-328-2329
Hearing Aid Dealer/Fitter #45	701-222-0201
Hunting Guide #26	701-328-6300
Hunting/Fishing Guide Combo #26	701-328-6300
Insurance Agency #28	701-328-3548
Insurance Agent #28	701-328-3548
Insurance Broker #28	701-328-3548
Investment Advisor #40	701-328-2910
Kickboxer #38	701-328-3665
Laboratory Clinician #53	701-224-1815
Land Surveyor #36	701-258-0786
Livestock Agent #19	701-328-4756
Livestock Auction Market #19	701-328-4756
Livestock Dealer #19	701-328-4756
Lobbyist #39	701-328-3665
Massage Therapist #46	701-255-1525
Medical Doctor #47	701-328-6500
Money Broker Company #20	701-328-9933
Monitoring Well Contractor #50	701-328-2754
Mortician #44	701-662-2511
Notary Public #39	701-328-2901
Nurse Assistant #31	701-328-9780
Nurse-LPN #31	701-328-9777
Nurse-RN #31	701-328-9777
Nursing Home Administrator #13	701-222-4867
Nutritionist #11	701-746-9171
Occupational Therapist #48	701-250-0847
Oil & Gas Broker #40	701-328-2910
Oil & Gas Wellhead Welder #40	701-328-2910
Optometrist #49	701-225-9333
Osteopathic Physician #47	701-328-6500
Pesticide Applicator #19	701-231-7180
Pesticide Dealer #19	701-231-7180
Pharmacist #14	701-328-9535
Pharmacy #14	701-328-9535
Physical Therapist/Assistant #51	701-352-0125
Physician Assistant #47	701-328-6500
Plumber Apprentice #32	701-328-9977
Plumber Journeyman #32	701-328-9977
Plumber Master #32	701-328-9977
Podiatrist #15	701-258-8120
Polygraph Examiner #03	701-328-2329
Private Investigation Agency #33	701-222-3063
Private Investigator #33	701-222-3063
Professional Counselor #09	701-667-5969
Professional Fund Raiser #39	701-328-3665
Psychologist #16	701-777-2044
Public Accountant-CPA #42	701-775-7100
Pulbic Accounting Firms #42	701-775-7100
Racing #03	701-328-4633
Real Estate Agent #35	701-328-9749
Real Estate Broker #35	701-328-9749
Respiratory Care Practitioner #37	701-222-1564
School Counselor/Designate #24	701-328-2260
School Media Specialist #24	701-328-2260
School Principal/Assistant #24	701-328-2260
School Superintendent/Assistant #24	701-328-2260
Securities Agent #40	701-328-2910
Securities Dealer #40	701-328-2910
Security Employee #33	701-222-2063
Security Providers & Providers #33	701-222-3063
Sewer & Water Contractor #32	701-328-9977
Social Worker #18	701-222-0255
Soil Classifier #17	701-225-3381
Speech-Language Pathologist/Audiologist #12	701-777-4421
Taxidermist #26	701-328-6300
Teacher #24	701-328-2260
Tobacco (Retail) #03	701-328-2329
Tobacco (Wholesale) #03	701-328-2329
Transient Merchant #03	701-328-2329
Trust Company #20	701-328-9933
Veterinarian #29	701-328-9540
Veterinary Technician #29	701-328-9540
Waste Water System Operator #21	701-328-6628
Water Conditioning Contractor #32	701-328-9977
Water Distribution System Operator #21	701-328-6628
Water Well Driller #50	701-328-2754
Water Well Pump & Pitless Unit #50	701-328-2754
Weather Modifier #02	701-328-2788
Wholesale Drug Manufacturer #14	701-328-9535

Licensing Agency Information

01 Abstractors Board of Examiners, PO Box 551 (PO Box 551), New Rockford, ND 58356; 701-947-2446, Fax: 701-947-2443.

www.health.state.nd.us/gov/boards/boards_query.asp?Board_ID=1

02 Atmospheric Resource Board, Water Commission, 900 E Boulevard Ave, Bismarck, ND 58505; 701-328-4940, Fax: 701-328-4749.

http://water.swc.state.ns.us

03 Attorney General's Office, Licensing Division, 600 E Boulevard Ave, Dept 125, Bismarck, ND 58505-0240; 701-328-2210, Fax: 701-328-3535.

www.ag.state.nd.us/buslic/bli.html

04 Board of Addiction Counseling Examiners, PO Box 975, Bismarck, ND 58502-0975; 701-255-1439, Fax: 701-224-9824.

05 Pat Hubel, Board of Athletic Trainers, PO Box 5020 (PO Box 5020), Minot, ND 58702; 701-857-5286, Fax: 701-857-5694.

06 Board of Barber Examiners, PO Box 885 (PO Box 885), Bowman, ND 58623; 701-523-3327, Fax: 701-574-3126.

07 c/o Jerry Blanchard, Board of Chiropractic Examiners, PO Box 185 (PO Box 185), Grafton, ND 58237; 701-352-1690, Fax: 701-352-2258.

08 Board of Cosmetology, PO Box 2177 (PO Box 2177), Bismarck, ND 58502; 701-224-9800, Fax: 701-222-8756.

09 Board of Counselor Examiners, PO Box 2735 (2112 10th Av SE), Mandan, ND 58554-5066; 701-667-5969.

www.sendit.nodak.edu/ndbce

10 Board of Dental Examiners, PO Box 7246 (PO Box 7246), Bismarck, ND 58507-7246; 701-224-1815, Fax: 701-224-9824.

www.nddentalboard.org

11 Board of Dietetic Practice, PO Box 6142 (PO Box 6142), Grand Forks, ND 58206-6142; 701-777-2539, Fax: 701-777-3268.

12 Board of Examiners in Audiology/Speech Pathology, 720 4th St N, Fargo, ND 58122; 701-777-4421, Fax: 701-777-4365.

13 Board of Examiners in Nursing Home Adminstrators, 1900 N 11th St, Bismarck, ND 58501-1914; 701-222-4867, Fax: 701-223-0977.

14 Board of Pharmacy, PO Box 1354 (PO Box 1354), Bismarck, ND 58502-1354; 701-328-9535, Fax: 701-258-9312.

15 Dr. Hofsommer, Board of Podiatric Medicine, 2631 12th Ave S, Fargo, ND 58103-2354; 701-258-8120.

16 University of North Dakota - Psychology Department, Board of Psychologist Examiners, PO Box 8380 (PO Box 8380), Grand Forks, ND 58202-8380; 701-777-2044, Fax: 701-777-3454.

www.health.state.nd.us/gov/boards/boards.htm

17 Board of Registry for Professional Soil Classifier, 2493 4th Ave W, Dickinson, ND 58601; 701-225-3381.

18 Board of Social Worker Examiners, PO Box 914 (PO Box 914), Bismarck, ND 58502-0914; 701-224-1815, Fax: 701-224-9824.

www.aptnd.com/ndbswe

19 Department of Agriculture, 600 E Boulevard Ave,Dept 602, Bismarck, ND 58505-0020; 701-328-2231, Fax: 701-328-4567.

www.state.nd.us/agr

Direct URL to search licenses: www.state.nd.us/agr You can search online using name

20 Department of Banking & Financial Institutions, 2000 Schaefer St #G, Bismarck, ND 58501-1204; 701-328-9933, Fax: 701-328-9955.

www.state.nd.us/bank

21 Department of Health, Municipal Facilities, 1200 Missouri Av, Bismarck, ND 58506-5520; 701-328-6628, Fax: 701-328-6206.

22 Department of Human Services, Children & Family Services, 600 E Boulevard Ave, Bismarck, ND 58505-0250; 701-328-2210, Fax: 701-328-2359.

23 Department of Labor, 600 E Blvd Ave, Dept 406, Bismarck, ND 58505-0340; 701-328-2660, Fax: 701-328-2031.

www.state.nd.us/labor

24 Department of Public Instruction, 600 E Boulevard Ave, 1st Fl-Judicial Wing, Bismarck, ND 58505-0440; 701-328-2260, Fax: 701-328-2461.

www.dpi.state.ns.us

25 Electrical Board, PO Box 857 (PO Box 857), Bismarck, ND 58502; 701-328-9522, Fax: 701-328-9524.

26 Game & Fish Department, 100 N Bismarck Exprwy, Bismarck, ND 58501-5095; 701-328-6300, Fax: 701-328-6352.

www.state.ns.us/gnf

27 Department of Health, Asbestos Control Program, PO Box 5520 (1200 Missouri Ave), Bismarck, ND 58506-5520; 701-328-5188, Fax: 701-328-5200.
www.health.state.nd.us/ndhd/environ/ee/rad/asb/

28 Insurance Department, 600 E Boulevard Ave, Capitol Bldg, 1st Fl, Bismarck, ND 58505-0320; 701-328-2440, Fax: 701-328-4880.

www.state.nd.us/ndins/prodinfo/license.html

29 Veterinarian Examining Board, PO Box 5001, Bismarck, ND 58502-5001; 701-328-9540, Fax: 701-224-0435.

30 Aeronautics Commission, PO Box 5020 (314 E Thayer), Bismarck, ND 58502-5020; 701-328-9650, Fax: 701-328-9656.

www.state.nd.us/ndaero

31 Board of Nursing, 919 S 7th St #504, Bismarck, ND 58504-5881; 701-328-9777, Fax: 701-328-9785.

www.ndbon.org

32 Plumbing Board, 204 W Thayer Av, Bismarck, ND 58501; 701-328-9977, Fax: 701-328-9979.

33 Private Investigation & Security Board, Private Investigators Licensing, 513 E Bismarck Expy, #5, Bismarck, ND 58504-6577; 701-222-3063, Fax: 701-222-3063.

34 Public Service Commission, 600 E Boulevard Ave, Dept 408, Bismarck, ND 58505-0480; 701-328-2400, Fax: 701-328-2410.

http://pc6.psc.state.nd.us/psc/license/license.htm

35 Real Estate Commission, PO Box 727 (PO Box 727), Bismarck, ND 58502-0727; 701-328-9749, Fax: 701-328-9750.

36 Registration for Prof. Engineers & Land Surveyors, PO Box 1357 (PO Box 1357), Bismarck, ND 58502-1357; 701-258-0786, Fax: 701-258-7471.

37 Respiratory Care Examining Board, PO Box 2223 (PO Box 2223), Bismarck, ND 58502; 701-222-1564, Fax: 701-255-9149.

38 Secretary of State, Licensing Division, 600 E Blvd Ave, Dept 108, Bismarck, ND 58505-0040; 701-328-2900, Fax: 701-328-1690.

www.state.nd.us/sec

39 Secretary of State, Licensing Division, 600 East Blvd Av, Dept 108, Bismarck, ND 58505-0500; 701-328-3665, Fax: 701-328-1690.
www.state.nd.us/sec

40 Securities Commissioner, 600 E Blvd Ave, Dept 414, State Capitol, 5th Fl, Bismarck, ND 58505-0510; 701-328-2910, Fax: 701-255-3113.

www.state.nd.us/securities

41 Bar Board, 600 E Boulevard Ave, Dept. 180, Bismarck, ND 58505-0530; 701-328-4201, Fax: 701-328-4480.
www.court.state.nd.us

42 Board of Accountancy, 2701 S Columbia Rd, Grand Forks, ND 58201-6029; 800-532-5904, Fax: 701-775-7430.

www.state.nd.us/ndsba

43 Board of Architects, 419 E Brandon Dr, Bismarck, ND 58501-0410; 701-223-3184, Fax: 701-223-8154.

44 Board of Funeral Service, PO Box 633 (PO Box 633), Devil's Lake, ND 58201; 701-662-2511, Fax: 701-662-2501.

45 Board of Hearing Instrument Dispensers, PO Box 1458 (PO Box 1458), Jamestown, ND 58402; 701-222-0201, Fax: 701-258-9652.

46 Richard Radspinner, Board of Massage, 104 Georgia, Bismarck, ND 58504; 701-255-1525.

47 Board of Medical Examiners, 418 E. Broadway #12, Bismarck, ND 58501; 701-328-6500, Fax: 701-328-6505.
www.ndbomex.com

48 Board of Occupational Therapy Practice, PO Box 4005 (PO Box 4005), Bismarck, ND 58502-4005; 701-250-0847, Fax: 701-224-9824.

www.aptnd.com/ndsbot

49 Board of Optometry, 341 1st St E, Dickinson, ND 58601; 701-483-9141, Fax: 701-483-9501.
http://home.ctctel.com/~ndsbopt

50 Board of Water Well Contractors, 900 E Boulevard Ave, Bismarck, ND 58505; 701-328-2754, Fax: 701-328-3696.

51 Examining Committee of Physical Therapists, PO Box 69 (PO Box 69), Grafton, ND 58237; 701-352-0125, Fax: 701-352-3093.

53 Board of Clinical Laboratory Practice, PO Box 4103 (PO Box 4103), Bismarck, ND 58502-4103; 701-224-1815, Fax: 701-224-9824.

The following list indicates the district and division name for each county in the state. If the district or division name of the bankruptcy court is different from the civil/criminal court, it appears in parentheses.

County/Court Cross Reference

Adams	Bismarck-Southwestern (Fargo)
Barnes	Fargo-Southeastern (Fargo)
Benson	Grand Forks-Northeastern (Fargo)
Billings	Bismarck-Southwestern (Fargo)
Bottineau	Minot-Northwestern (Fargo)
Bowman	Bismarck-Southwestern (Fargo)
Burke	Minot-Northwestern (Fargo)
Burleigh	Bismarck-Southwestern (Fargo)
Cass	Fargo-Southeastern (Fargo)
Cavalier	Grand Forks-Northeastern (Fargo)
Dickey	Fargo-Southeastern (Fargo)
Divide	Minot-Northwestern (Fargo)
Dunn	Bismarck-Southwestern (Fargo)
Eddy	Fargo-Southeastern (Fargo)
Emmons	Bismarck-Southwestern (Fargo)
Foster	Fargo-Southeastern (Fargo)
Golden Valley	Bismarck-Southwestern (Fargo)
Grand Forks	Grand Forks-Northeastern (Fargo)
Grant	Bismarck-Southwestern (Fargo)
Griggs	Fargo-Southeastern (Fargo)
Hettinger	Bismarck-Southwestern (Fargo)
Kidder	Bismarck-Southwestern (Fargo)
La Moure	Fargo-Southeastern (Fargo)
Logan	Bismarck-Southwestern (Fargo)
McHenry	Minot-Northwestern (Fargo)
McIntosh	Bismarck-Southwestern (Fargo)
McKenzie	Minot-Northwestern (Fargo)
McLean	Bismarck-Southwestern (Fargo)
Mercer	Bismarck-Southwestern (Fargo)
Morton	Bismarck-Southwestern (Fargo)
Mountrail	Minot-Northwestern (Fargo)
Nelson	Grand Forks-Northeastern (Fargo)
Oliver	Bismarck-Southwestern (Fargo)
Pembina	Grand Forks-Northeastern (Fargo)
Pierce	Minot-Northwestern (Fargo)
Ramsey	Grand Forks-Northeastern (Fargo)
Ransom	Fargo-Southeastern (Fargo)
Renville	Minot-Northwestern (Fargo)
Richland	Fargo-Southeastern (Fargo)
Rolette	Minot-Northwestern (Fargo)
Sargent	Fargo-Southeastern (Fargo)
Sheridan	Minot-Northwestern (Fargo)
Sioux	Bismarck-Southwestern (Fargo)
Slope	Bismarck-Southwestern (Fargo)
Stark	Bismarck-Southwestern (Fargo)
Steele	Fargo-Southeastern (Fargo)
Stutsman	Fargo-Southeastern (Fargo)
Towner	Grand Forks-Northeastern (Fargo)
Traill	Grand Forks-Northeastern (Fargo)
Walsh	Grand Forks-Northeastern (Fargo)
Ward	Minot-Northwestern (Fargo)
Wells	Minot-Northwestern (Fargo)
Williams	Minot-Northwestern (Fargo)

US District Court

District of North Dakota

Bismarck-Southwestern Division PO Box 1193, Bismarck, ND 58502 (Courier Address: 220 E Rosser Ave, Room 476, Bismarck, ND 58501), 701-530-2300, Fax: 701-530-2312.

www.ndd.uscourts.gov

Counties: Adams, Billings, Bowman, Burleigh, Dunn, Emmons, Golden Valley, Grant, Hettinger, Kidder, Logan, McIntosh, McLean, Mercer, Morton, Oliver, Sioux, Slope, Stark.

Indexing & Storage: Cases are indexed by defendant and plaintiff as well as by case number. New cases are available in the index 24 hours after filing date. A computer index is maintained. Records are on computer and stored as hard copy records. Open records are located at this court.

Fee & Payment: The fee is $15.00 per item (one party name or case number). Payment may be made by money order, cashier check, in-state business check. In state personal checks are also accepted. Court will bill for copies. Payee: Clerk, US District Court. Certification fee: $5.00 per document. Copy fee: $.50 per page.

Phone Search: Only docket information is available by phone. An automated voice case information service (VCIS) is not available.

Mail Search: A stamped self addressed envelope is not required.

In Person Search: In person searching is available.

PACER: Sign-up number is 800-676-6856. Access fee is $.60 per minute. Toll-free access: 800-407-4453. Local access: 701-530-2367. Case records are available back to October 1990. Records are never purged. New records are available online after 1 day.

Fargo-Southeastern Division PO Box 870, Fargo, ND 58107 (Courier Address: 655 1st Ave N, Fargo, ND 58102), 701-297-7000, Fax: 701-297-7005.

www.ndd.uscourts.gov

Counties: Barnes, Cass, Dickey, Eddy, Foster, Griggs, La Moure, Ransom, Richland, Sargent, Steele, Stutsman. Rolette County cases prior to 1995 may be located here.

Indexing & Storage: Cases are indexed by defendant and plaintiff as well as by case number. New cases are available in the index 1 day after filing date. Both computer and card indexes are maintained. Civil cases prior to 10/90 are on index cards as well as all criminal records. Current records are on computer and stored as hard copy records. Open records are located at this court.

Fee & Payment: The fee is $15.00 per item (one party name or case number). Payment may be made by money order, cashier check, in-state business check. In state personal checks are also accepted. Prepayment is required. Payee: Clerk, US District Court. Certification fee: $5.00 per document. Copy fee: $.50 per page.

Phone Search: Only docket information is available by phone. An automated voice case information service (VCIS) is not available.

Fax Search: Will accept fax search request, but results are held until payment received. Will fax results at $.50 per page paid in advance.

Mail Search: A stamped self addressed envelope is not required.

In Person Search: In person searching is available.

PACER: Sign-up number is 800-676-6856. Access fee is $.60 per minute. Toll-free access: 800-407-4453. Local access: 701-530-2367. Case records are available back to October 1990. Records are never purged. New records are available online after 1 day.

Grand Forks-Northeastern Division c/o Fargo-Southeastern Division, 102 N 4th St, Grand Forks, ND 58201 (Courier Address: 655 1st Ave N, Fargo, ND 58102), 701-772-0511, Fax: 701-746-7544.

www.ndd.uscourts.gov

Counties: Benson, Cavalier, Grand Forks, Nelson, Pembina, Ramsey, Towner, Traill, Walsh.

Indexing & Storage: Cases are indexed by as well as by case number. New cases are available in the index after filing date. Open records are located at the Division.

Fee & Payment: The fee is no charge per item (one party name or case number). Payment may be made by money order, cashier check. Business checks are not accepted. Personal checks are not accepted.

Phone Search: Searching is not available by phone.

In Person Search: In person searching is available.

PACER: Sign-up number is 800-676-6856. Access fee is $.60 per minute. Toll-free access: 800-407-4453. Local access: 701-530-2367. Case records are available back to October 1990. Records are never purged. New records are available online after 1 day.

Minot-Northwestern Division c/o

Bismarck Division, PO Box 1193, Bismarck, ND 58502 (Courier Address: 100 1st St SW, Minot, ND 58701), 701-839-6251, Fax: 701-838-3267.

www.ndd.uscourts.gov

Counties: Bottineau, Burke, Divide, McHenry, McKenzie, Mountrail, Pierce, Renville, Rolette, Sheridan, Ward, Wells, Williams. Case records from Rolette County prior to 1995 may be located in Fargo-Southeastern Division.

Indexing & Storage: Cases are indexed by as well as by case number. New cases are available in the index after filing date. Open records are located at the Division.

Fee & Payment: The fee is no charge per item (one party name or case number). Payment may be made by money order, cashier check. Business checks are not accepted. Personal checks are not accepted.

Phone Search: An automated voice case information service (VCIS) is not available.

In Person Search: In person searching is available.

PACER: Sign-up number is 800-676-6856. Access fee is $.60 per minute. Toll-free access: 800-407-4453. Local access: 701-530-2367. Case records are available back to October 1990. Records are never purged. New records are available online after 1 day.

US Bankruptcy Court
District of North Dakota

Fargo Division 655 1st Ave N #210, Fargo, ND 58102-4932 (Courier Address: Room 236, Federal Bldg & US Courthouse, Fargo, ND 58102), 701-297-7104.

www.ndb.uscourts.gov

Counties: All counties in North Dakota.

Indexing & Storage: Cases are indexed by debtor as well as by case number. New cases are available in the index 1 day after filing date. A computer index is maintained. Open records are located at this court.

Fee & Payment: The fee is $15.00 per item (one party name or case number). Payment may be made by money order, cashier check, business check. Personal checks are not accepted. Prepayment is required. Exemplification costs $10.00 per document. The court will FAX in an emergency for $.50 per page sending or receiving. Payee: Clerk, US Bankruptcy Court. Certification fee: $5.00 per document. Copy fee: $.50 per page.

Phone Search: Only docket information available by telephone. An automated voice case information service (VCIS) is available.

Mail Search: A stamped self addressed envelope is not required.

In Person Search: In person searching is available.

PACER: Sign-up number is 800-676-6856. Access fee is $.60 per minute. Toll-free access: 800-810-4092. Local access: 701-297-7164. Case records are available back to 1990. New civil records are available online after 1 day. PACER is available online at http://pacer.okwd.uscourts.gov.

Court	Jurisdiction	No. of Courts	How Organized
District Courts*	General	53	7 Judicial Districts
Municipal Courts	Municipal	76	76 Cities

* Profiled in this Sourcebook.

CIVIL									
Court	Tort	Contract	Real Estate	Min. Claim	Max. Claim	Small Claims	Estate	Eviction	Domestic Relations
District Courts*	X	X	X	$0	No Max	$5000	X	X	X
Municipal Courts									

CRIMINAL					
Court	Felony	Misdemeanor	DWI/DUI	Preliminary Hearing	Juvenile
District Courts*	X	X	X	X	X
Municipal Courts			X		

ADMINISTRATION   Court Administrator, North Dakota Supreme Court, 600 E Blvd, 1st Floor Judicial Wing, Bismarck, ND, 58505-0530; 701-328-4216, Fax: 701-328-4480. www.ndcourts.com or www.court.state.nd.us

COURT STRUCTURE   In 1995, the County Courts were merged with the District Courts across the entire state. County court records are maintained by the 53 District Courts in the 7 judicial districts. We recommend stating "include all County Court cases" in search requests. There are 76 Municipal Courts that handle traffic cases.

ONLINE ACCESS   A statewide computer system for internal purposes is in operation in most counties. You may now search North Dakota Supreme Court dockets and opinions at www.ndcourts.com. Search by docket number, party name, or anything else that may appear in the text. Records are from 1991 forward. E-mail notification of new opinions is also available.

ADDITIONAL INFORMATION   In Summer, 1997, the standard search fee in District Courts increased to $10.00 per name, and the certification fee increased to $10.00 per document. Copy fees remain at $.50 per page, but many courts charge only $.25.

Adams County

Southwest Judicial District Court 602 Adams Ave, PO Box 469, Hettinger, ND 58639; 701-567-2460; Fax: 701-567-2910. Hours: 8:30AM-5PM (MST). *Felony, Misdemeanor, Civil, Eviction, Small Claims, Probate.*

Civil Records: Access: Phone, fax, mail, in person. Only the court conducts in person searches; visitors may not. Search fee: $10.00 per name. Required to search: name, years to search; also helpful-address. Civil cases indexed by defendant, plaintiff. Civil records on index cards from 1990, on docket books in vault from 1900s. **Criminal Records:** Access: Phone, fax, mail, in person. Only the court conducts in person searches; visitors may not. Search fee: $10.00 per name. Required to search: name, years to search, DOB; also helpful-address. Criminal records on index cards from 1990, on docket books in vault from 1900s. **General Information:** No adoptions, sealed, juvenile, mental health, expunged or dismissed records released. SASE required. Turnaround time 1-2 days. Copy fee: $.25 per page. Certification fee: $5.00. Fee payee: Clerk of District Court. Personal checks accepted. Prepayment is required. Fax notes: Fax fee is $5.00 first 2 pages, $.50 each additional page.

Barnes County

Southeast Judicial District Court PO Box 774, Valley City, ND 58072; 701-845-8512; Fax: 701-845-1341. Hours: 8AM-5PM (CST). *Felony, Misdemeanor, Civil, Eviction, Small Claims, Probate.*

Civil Records: Access: Phone, fax, mail, in person. Only the court conducts in person searches; visitors may not. Search fee: $10.00 per name. Required to search: name, years to search; also helpful-address. Civil cases indexed by defendant, plaintiff. Civil records on index books from early 1900s. **Criminal Records:** Access: Phone, fax, mail, in person. Only the court conducts in person searches; visitors may not. Search fee: $10.00 per name. Required to search: name, years to search; also helpful-address, DOB, SSN. Criminal records on index books from early 1900s. **General Information:** No adoptions, paternity, sealed, juvenile, mental health, expunged or dismissed records released. SASE required. Turnaround time 1-2 days. Copy fee: $.25 per page. Certification fee: $10.00. $5.00 for second copy. Fee payee: Clerk of District Court. Personal checks accepted. Prepayment is required. Fax notes: $10.00 per document.

Benson County

Northeast Judicial District Court PO Box 213, Minnewaukan, ND 58351; 701-473-5345; Fax: 701-473-5571. Hours: 8:30AM-4:30PM (CST). *Felony, Misdemeanor, Civil, Eviction, Small Claims, Probate.*

Civil Records: Access: Phone, fax, mail, in person. Only the court conducts in person searches; visitors may not. Search fee: $10.00 per name. Fee is for written confirmation. Required to search: name, years to search; also helpful-address. Civil cases indexed by defendant, plaintiff. Civil records on docket books and index books from early 1900s, on index cards from 6/10/91. **Criminal Records:** Access: Phone, fax, mail, in person. Only the court conducts in person searches; visitors may not. Search fee: $10.00 per name. Fee is for written confirmation. Required to search: name, years to search, DOB, signed release; also helpful-address. Criminal records on docket books and index books from early 1900s, on index cards from 6/10/91. Signed release required for juvenile cases. **General Information:** No adoptions, sealed, juvenile, mental health, expunged or dismissed records released. SASE not required. Turnaround time 5 days. Copy fee: $1.00 per page. Certification fee: $10.00. Fee payee: Benson County Court. Personal checks accepted. Prepayment is required. Fax notes: $1.00 per page.

Billings County

Southwest Judicial District Court PO Box 138, Medora, ND 58645; 701-623-4492; Fax: 701-623-4896. Hours: 9AM-Noon, 1-5PM (MST). *Felony, Misdemeanor, Civil, Eviction, Small Claims, Probate.*

Civil Records: Access: Fax, mail, in person. Both court and visitors may perform in person searches. Search fee: $10.00 per name. Required to search: name, years to search; also helpful-address. Civil cases indexed by defendant, plaintiff. Civil records on index cards from 1986, on index books from 1800s. **Criminal Records:** Access: Fax, mail, in person. Both court and visitors may perform in person searches. Search fee: $10.00 per name. Required to search: name, years to search; also helpful-address, DOB, SSN. Criminal records in books. **General Information:** No adoptions, sealed, juvenile, mental health, expunged or dismissed records released. SASE required. Turnaround time 2-3 days. Copy fee: $.25 per page. Certification fee: $10.00 plus $5.00 each add'l page. Fee payee: Clerk of District Court. Personal checks accepted. Prepayment is required. Fax notes: Fax fee $2.00 1st 4 pages, $.50 each additional page.

Bottineau County

Northeast Judicial District Court 314 W 5th St, Bottineau, ND 58318; 701-228-3983; Fax: 701-228-2336. *Felony, Misdemeanor, Civil, Eviction, Small Claims, Probate.*

Civil Records: Access: Phone, fax, mail, in person. Only the court conducts in person searches; visitors may not. Search fee: $10.00 per name. Required to search: name, years to search; also helpful-address. Civil cases indexed by defendant, plaintiff. Civil records on index cards from 1987, on docket books from 1972. **Criminal Records:** Access: Phone, fax, mail, in person. Only the court conducts in person searches; visitors may not. Search fee: $10.00 per name. Required to search: name, years to search; also helpful-address, DOB, SSN. Criminal records on docket books from 1885. **General Information:** No adoptions, paternity, sealed, juvenile, mental health, expunged or dismissed records released. SASE required. Turnaround time 1 day. Copy fee: $.20 per page. Certification fee: $10.00. Fee payee: Clerk of the Court. Personal checks accepted. Prepayment is required. Fax notes: $4.00 for first page, $2.00 each addl.

Bowman County

Southwest Judicial District Court PO Box 379, Bowman, ND 58623; 701-523-3450; Fax: 701-523-5443. Hours: 8:30AM-Noon, 1-5PM (MST). *Felony, Misdemeanor, Civil, Eviction, Small Claims, Probate.*

Civil Records: Access: Phone, mail, in person. Both court and visitors may perform in person searches. Search fee: $10.00 per name. Required to search: name, years to search; also helpful-address. Civil cases indexed by defendant, plaintiff. Civil records on microfiche from 1978, on dockets from 1907. **Criminal Records:** Access: Mail, in person. Both court and visitors may perform in person searches. Search fee: $10.00 per name. Required to search: name, years to search, DOB; also helpful-address. Criminal records on microfiche from 1978, on dockets from 1907. **General Information:** No adoptions, sealed, juvenile, mental health, expunged or dismissed records released. SASE required. Turnaround time 1-2 days. Copy fee: $1.00 per page. Certification fee:

$10.00. Fee payee: Clerk of Court. Personal checks accepted. Prepayment is required.

Burke County

Northwest Judicial District Court PO Box 219, Bowbells, ND 58721; 701-377-2718; Fax: 701-377-2020. Hours: 8:30AM-Noon, 1-5 PM (CST). *Felony, Misdemeanor, Civil, Eviction, Small Claims, Probate.*

Civil Records: Access: Phone, fax, mail, in person. Both court and visitors may perform in person searches. Search fee: $5.00 if a written reply is required. Required to search: name, years to search; also helpful-address. Civil cases indexed by defendant, plaintiff. Civil records for county civil, probate, and district from 1910, county criminal and small claims from 1980. **Criminal Records:** Access: Phone, fax, mail, in person. Both court and visitors may perform in person searches. Search fee: $5.00 if a written reply is required. Required to search: name, years to search; also helpful-address, DOB, SSN. Criminal records for county civil, probate, and district from 1910, county criminal and small claims from 1980. **General Information:** No adoptions, sealed, juvenile, mental health, expunged or dismissed records released. SASE not required. Turnaround time 1-3 days. Copy fee: $.50 per page. Certification fee: $10.00. Fee payee: Clerk of Court. Personal checks accepted. Prepayment is required. Fax notes: $2.00 for first page, $1.00 each addl.

Burleigh County

South Central Judicial District Court PO Box 1055, Bismarck, ND 58502; 701-222-6690; Fax: 701-221-3756. Hours: 8AM-5PM (CST). *Felony, Misdemeanor, Civil, Eviction, Small Claims, Probate.*

Civil Records: Access: Mail, in person. Both court and visitors may perform in person searches. Search fee: $10.00 per name. Required to search: name; also helpful-years to search. Civil cases indexed by defendant, plaintiff. Civil records on computer from 1/91 in books from early 1900s. **Criminal Records:** Access: Mail, in person. Both court and visitors may perform in person searches. Search fee: $10.00 per name. Required to search: name; also helpful-years to search, address, DOB, SSN. Criminal records on computer from 1/91 in books from early 1900s. **General Information:** No adoptions, sealed, juvenile, mental health, expunged or dismissed records released. SASE required. Turnaround time 1-2 days. Copy fee: $.20 per page. Certification fee: $10.00 plus $5.00 each add'l copy of same document, if needed. Fee payee: Clerk of Court. Personal checks accepted. Prepayment is required. Public access terminal is available.

Cass County

East Central Judicial District Court 211 South 9th St, Fargo, ND 58108; 701-241-5645; Fax: 701-241-5636. Hours: 8AM-5PM (CST). *Felony, Misdemeanor, Civil, Eviction, Small Claims, Probate.*

Civil Records: Access: Mail, in person. Only the court conducts in person searches; visitors may not. Search fee: $10.00 per name. Required to search: name, years to search; also helpful-address. Civil cases indexed by defendant, plaintiff. Civil records on computer from 1988, on index books from late 1800s. **Criminal Records:** Access: Mail, in person. Only the court conducts in person searches; visitors may not. Search fee: $10.00 per name. Required to search: name, years to search;

also helpful-address, DOB, SSN. Criminal records on computer from 1988, on index cards from 1980. **General Information:** No adoptions, sealed, juvenile, mental health, expunged or dismissed records released. SASE required. Turnaround time 3-5 days. Copy fee: $.25 per page. $1.00 minimum. Certification fee: $10.00. Fee payee: Clerk of District Court. Personal checks accepted. Prepayment is required.

Cavalier County

Northeast Judicial District Court 901 Third St, Langdon, ND 58249; 701-256-2124; Fax: 701-256-2124. Hours: 8:30AM-4:30PM (CST). *Felony, Misdemeanor, Civil, Eviction, Small Claims, Probate.*

Civil Records: Access: Phone, fax, mail, in person. Only the court conducts in person searches; visitors may not. Search fee: $10.00 per name. Required to search: name, years to search; also helpful-address. Civil cases indexed by defendant, plaintiff. Civil records going on computer, prior stored. **Criminal Records:** Access: Phone, fax, mail, in person. Only the court conducts in person searches; visitors may not. Search fee: $10.00 per name. Required to search: name, years to search; also helpful-address, DOB, SSN. Criminal records for District Court on index books from 1937, for County Court on index books from 1983, prior stored. **General Information:** No adoptions, sealed, juvenile, mental health, expunged or dismissed records released. SASE required. Turnaround time 1 week. Copy fee: $.25 per page. Certification fee: $10.00. Fee payee: Clerk of Court. Personal checks accepted. Prepayment is required. Fax notes: No fee to fax results.

Dickey County

Southeast Judicial District Court PO Box 336, Ellendale, ND 58436; 701-349-3249 X4; Fax: 701-349-3560. Hours: 9AM-Noon, 1-5PM (CST). *Felony, Misdemeanor, Civil, Eviction, Small Claims, Probate.*

Civil Records: Access: Mail, in person. Only the court conducts in person searches; visitors may not. Search fee: $10.00 per name. Required to search: name, years to search; also helpful-address. Civil cases indexed by defendant, plaintiff. Civil records on index books from 1983, probate on index books from 1800s. Old district court records have no index and are very hard to find. **Criminal Records:** Access: Mail, in person. Only the court conducts in person searches; visitors may not. Search fee: $10.00 per name. Required to search: name, years to search, DOB; also helpful-address. Criminal records on index books from 1983, probate on index books from 1800s. Old district court records have no index and are very hard to find. **General Information:** No adoptions, sealed, juvenile, mental health, expunged or dismissed records released. SASE not required. Turnaround time 1-2 days. Copy fee: $.25 per page. Certification fee: $10.00. Fee payee: Clerk of Court. Personal checks accepted. Prepayment is required.

Divide County

Northwest Judicial District Court PO Box 68, Crosby, ND 58730; 701-965-6831; Fax: 701-965-6943. Hours: 8:30AM-Noon, 1-5PM (CST). *Felony, Misdemeanor, Civil, Eviction, Small Claims, Probate.*

Civil Records: Access: Phone, fax, mail, in person. Only the court conducts in person searches; visitors may not. Search fee: $10.00 per name. Required to search: name, years to search; also helpful-address. Civil cases indexed by defendant, plaintiff. Civil records on index books from 1910. Visitor can check for judgments. **Criminal Records:** Access: Phone, fax, mail, in person. Only the court conducts in person searches; visitors may not. Search fee: $10.00 per name. Required to search: name, years to search; also helpful-address, DOB, SSN. Criminal records on index books from 1910. **General Information:** No adoptions, sealed, juvenile, mental health, expunged or dismissed records released. SASE required. Turnaround time 1-2 days. Copy fee: $.25 per page. $1.00 minimum. Certification fee: Included in search fee. Fee payee: Clerk of District Court. Personal checks accepted. Prepayment is required. Fax notes: $3.00 for first page, $1.00 each addl. There is also a charge of $1.00 per incoming fax page.

Dunn County

District Court PO Box 136, Manning, ND 58642-0136; 701-573-4447; Fax: 701-573-4444. Hours: 8AM-Noon,12:30-4:30PM (MST). *Felony, Misdemeanor, Civil, Small Claims, Probate.*

Civil Records: Access: Fax, mail, in person. Only the court conducts in person searches; visitors may not. Search fee: $10.00 per name. Required to search: name, years to search; also helpful-address. Civil cases indexed by defendant, plaintiff. Civil records on plaintiff/defendant index cards from 1988, on docket books from 1900s, on computer since 01/97. Fax requests must fax copy of the check to be mailed. **Criminal Records:** Access: Fax, mail, in person. Only the court conducts in person searches; visitors may not. Search fee: $10.00 per name. Required to search: name, years to search, DOB; also helpful-address, SSN. Criminal records on plaintiff/defendant index cards from 1988, on docket books from 1900s, on computer since 01/97. Fax requesters must fax copy of the check, which can be mailed. **General Information:** Adoptions, paternity, juvenile, mental health, deferred impositions, and termination of parental rights are restricted access files. SASE not required. Turnaround time 2 days. Copy fee: $2.00 for first page, $.50 each addl. Certification fee: $10.00. Fee payee: Dunn County Clerk of Court. Personal checks accepted. In state personal checks accepted. Prepayment is required. Public access terminal is available. Fax notes: $2.00 for first page, $1.00 each addl.

Eddy County

Southeast Judicial District Court 524 Central Ave, New Rockford, ND 58356; 701-947-2813; Fax: 701-947-2067. Hours: 8AM-4PM (CST). *Felony, Misdemeanor, Civil, Eviction, Small Claims, Probate.*

Civil Records: Access: Fax, mail, in person. Only the court conducts in person searches; visitors may not. Search fee: $10.00 per name. Required to search: name, years to search; also helpful-address. Civil cases indexed by defendant, plaintiff. Civil records on index cards from 4/92, on index books from early 1900s. All requests must be in writing. **Criminal Records:** Access: Fax, mail, in person. Only the court conducts in person searches; visitors may not. Search fee: $10.00 per name. Required to search: name, years to search; also helpful-address, DOB, SSN. Criminal records on index cards from 4/92, on index books from early 1900s. All requests must be in writing. **General Information:** No adoptions, sealed, juvenile, mental health, expunged or dismissed records released. SASE required. Turnaround time 1-2

days. Copy fee: $1.00 per document. Certification fee: $10.00. Fee payee: Eddy County District Court. Personal checks accepted. Fax notes: Fax fee $4.00 1st 3 pages, $1.00 each additional page.

Emmons County

South Central Judicial District Court PO Box 905, Linton, ND 58552; 701-254-4812; Fax: 701-254-4012. Hours: 8:30AM-Noon, 1-5PM (CST). *Felony, Misdemeanor, Civil, Eviction, Small Claims, Probate.*

Civil Records: Access: Fax, mail, in person. Only the court conducts in person searches; visitors may not. Search fee: $10.00 per name. Required to search: name, years to search; also helpful-address. Civil cases indexed by defendant, plaintiff. Civil records on index cards from 1988, on index books from 1914. **Criminal Records:** Access: Fax, mail, in person. Only the court conducts in person searches; visitors may not. Search fee: $10.00 per name. Required to search: name, years to search; also helpful-address, DOB, SSN. Criminal records on index books frm 1983, prior records not available. **General Information:** No adoptions, sealed, juvenile, mental health, expunged or dismissed records released. SASE required. Turnaround time 1-2 days. Copy fee: $.20 per page. Certification fee: $10.00. Fee payee: Clerk of Courts. Personal checks accepted. Prepayment is required. Fax notes: $3.00 for first page, $1.00 each addl.

Foster County

Southeast Judicial District Court PO Box 257, Carrington, ND 58421; 701-652-1001; Fax: 701-652-2173. Hours: 8:30AM-4:30PM (CST). *Felony, Misdemeanor, Civil, Eviction, Small Claims, Probate.*

Civil Records: Access: Mail, in person. Both court and visitors may perform in person searches. Search fee: $10.00 per name if court performs search. Required to search: name, years to search; also helpful-address. Civil cases indexed by defendant, plaintiff. Civil records on index books from early 1900s. **Criminal Records:** Access: Mail, in person. Both court and visitors may perform in person searches. Search fee: $10.00 per name if court performs search. Required to search: name, years to search, DOB; also helpful-address. Criminal records on index books from early 1900s. **General Information:** No adoptions, sealed, juvenile, mental health, expunged or dismissed records released. SASE required. Turnaround time 1-2 days. Copy fee: $1.00 per page. Certification fee: $10.00. Fee payee: Clerk of Courts. Personal checks accepted. Prepayment is required. Fax notes: $3.00 per document.

Golden Valley County

Southwest Judicial District Court PO Box 9, Beach, ND 58621-0009; 701-872-4352; Fax: 701-872-4383. Hours: 8-Noon, 1-4PM (MST). *Felony, Misdemeanor, Civil, Eviction, Small Claims, Probate.*

Civil Records: Access: Fax, mail, in person. Only the court conducts in person searches; visitors may not. Search fee: $10.00 per name. Required to search: name, years to search; also helpful-address. Civil cases indexed by defendant, plaintiff. Civil records on index cards from 1987, on index books from 1913 to 1960. From 1960 to 1987, records are hard to find; there is no indexing and files are filed by number. Fax request must include copy of check. **Criminal Records:** Access: Fax, mail, in person. Only the court conducts in person searches; visitors may not. Search fee: $10.00 per

name. Required to search: name, years to search, DOB; also helpful-address, SSN. Criminal records on index cards from 1987, on index books from 1913 to 1960. From 1960 to 1987, records are hard to find; there is no indexing and files are filed by number. Fax request must include copy of check. **General Information:** No adoptions, sealed, juvenile, mental health, expunged or dismissed records released. SASE required. Turnaround time 3-4 days. Copy fee: $.50 per page. Certification fee: $10.00. Fee payee: Clerk of Court. Personal checks accepted. Prepayment is required. Fax notes: $1.00 per page.

Grand Forks County

Northeast Central Judicial District Court PO Box 5939, Grand Forks, ND 58206-5939; 701-780-8214. Hours: 8AM-5PM (CST). *Felony, Misdemeanor, Civil, Eviction, Small Claims, Probate.*

Civil Records: Access: Mail, in person. Only the court conducts in person searches; visitors may not. Search fee: $10.00 per name. Required to search: name, years to search; also helpful-address. Civil cases indexed by defendant, plaintiff. Civil records on computer from 10/91, on index books from early 1900s. **Criminal Records:** Access: Mail, in person. Only the court conducts in person searches; visitors may not. Search fee: $10.00 per name. Required to search: name, years to search, DOB, signed release; also helpful-address. Criminal records on computer from 10/91, on index books from early 1900s. **General Information:** No adoptions, sealed, juvenile, mental health, expunged or dismissed records released. SASE required. Turnaround time 1-2 days. Copy fee: $.25 per page. Certification fee: $10.00. Fee payee: Clerk of District Court. Personal checks accepted. Prepayment is required. Public access terminal is available.

Grant County

South Central Judicial District Court PO Box 258, Carson, ND 58529; 701-622-3615; Fax: 701-622-3717. Hours: 8AM-Noon, 12:30-4PM (MST). *Felony, Misdemeanor, Civil, Eviction, Small Claims, Probate.*

Civil Records: Access: Phone, fax, mail, in person. Both court and visitors may perform in person searches. Search fee: $10.00 per name. Required to search: name, years to search; also helpful-address. Civil cases indexed by defendant, plaintiff. Civil records on index cards from 1990, on docket books in vault from 1900s. **Criminal Records:** Access: Phone, fax, mail, in person. Both court and visitors may perform in person searches. Search fee: $10.00 per name. Required to search: name, years to search; also helpful-address, DOB, SSN. Criminal records on index cards from 1990, on docket books in vault from 1900s. **General Information:** No adoptions, sealed, juvenile, mental health, expunged or dismissed records released. SASE not required. Turnaround time 1 day. Copy fee: $.25 per page. Certification fee: $10.00. Fee payee: Clerk of Grant County Court. Personal checks accepted. Prepayment is required. Fax notes: $3.00 per document.

Griggs County

Southeast Judicial District Court PO Box 326, Cooperstown, ND 58425; 701-797-2772; Fax: 701-797-3587. Hours: 8AM-Noon, 1-4:30PM (CST). *Felony, Misdemeanor, Civil, Eviction, Small Claims, Probate.*

Civil Records: Access: Phone, fax, mail, in person. Both court and visitors may perform in person searches. Search fee: $10.00 per name. Required to search: name, years to search; also helpful-address. Civil cases indexed by defendant, plaintiff. Civil records on docket books from 1890 for District and 1983 for County. Phone access discouraged. **Criminal Records:** Access: Phone, fax, mail, in person. Both court and visitors may perform in person searches. Search fee: $10.00 per name. Required to search: name, years to search; also helpful-address, DOB, SSN. Criminal records on docket books from 1890 for District and 1983 for County. Phone access discouraged. **General Information:** No adoptions, sealed, juvenile, mental health, expunged or dismissed records released. SASE required. Turnaround time 1-2 days. Copy fee: $.25 per page. Certification fee: $10.00 plus $5.00 each add'l pg of same document. Fee payee: Clerk of Courts. Personal checks accepted. Prepayment is required. Fax notes: $3.00 for first page, $1.00 each addl. Incoming fax, $1.00 1st page, $.50 each aditional page. Free for attorneys.

Hettinger County

Southwest Judicial District Court PO Box 668, Mott, ND 58646; 701-824-2645; Fax: 701-824-2717. Hours: 8AM-Noon, 1-4:30PM (MST). *Felony, Misdemeanor, Civil, Eviction, Small Claims, Probate.*

Civil Records: Access: Phone, fax, mail, in person. Only the court conducts in person searches; visitors may not. Search fee: $10.00 per name. Required to search: name, years to search; also helpful-address. Civil cases indexed by defendant, plaintiff. Civil records on index cards from 1987, on index books from 1908. **Criminal Records:** Access: Phone, fax, mail, in person. Only the court conducts in person searches; visitors may not. Search fee: $10.00 per name. Required to search: name, years to search, DOB; also helpful-address. Criminal records on index cards from 1987, on index books from 1908. **General Information:** No adoptions, sealed, juvenile, mental health, expunged or dismissed records released. SASE required. Turnaround time 1 day. Copy fee: $.50 per page. Certification fee: $10.00. Fee payee: Hettinger Court Clerk. Personal checks accepted. Prepayment is required. Fax notes: $3.00 per document. Fee is for up to 20 pages.

Kidder County

District Court PO Box 66, Steele, ND 58482; 701-475-2632; Fax: 701-475-2202. Hours: 9AM-5PM (CST). *Felony, Misdemeanor, Civil, Eviction, Small Claims, Probate.*

Civil Records: Access: Fax, mail, in person. Only the court conducts in person searches; visitors may not. Search fee: $10.00 per name. Required to search: name, years to search; also helpful-address. Civil cases indexed by defendant, plaintiff. Civil records on index book from 1900s. **Criminal Records:** Access: In person only. Court does not conduct in person searches; visitors must perform searches for themselves. Search fee: No criminal searches performed by court. Required to search: name, years to search, DOB; also helpful-address. **General Information:** No adoptions, sealed, juvenile, mental health, expunged or dismissed records released. SASE required. Turnaround time 1-2 days. Copy fee: $1.00 per page. Certification fee: $10.00. Fee payee: Clerk of Court. Personal checks accepted. Prepayment is required. Fax notes: Fee to fax is $3.00 per page.

La Moure County

Southeast Judicial District Court PO Box 128, LaMoure, ND 58458; 701-883-5193; Fax: 701-883-5304. Hours: 9AM-Noon, 1-5PM (CST). *Felony, Misdemeanor, Civil, Eviction, Small Claims, Probate.*

Civil Records: Access: Phone, fax, mail, in person. Both court and visitors may perform in person searches. Search fee: $10.00 per name. Required to search: name, years to search; also helpful-address. Civil cases indexed by defendant, plaintiff. Civil records on docket books from 1800s. **Criminal Records:** Access: Phone, fax, mail, in person. Both court and visitors may perform in person searches. Search fee: $10.00 per name. Required to search: name, years to search, DOB; also helpful-address. Criminal records on docket books from 1800s. **General Information:** No adoptions, sealed, juvenile, mental health, expunged or dismissed records released. SASE required. Turnaround time 1 day. Copy fee: $.25 for first page, $.10 each addl. Certification fee: $10.00. Fee payee: Clerk of Court. Personal checks accepted. Prepayment is required. Fax notes: $3.00 per document.

Logan County

South Central Judicial District Court PO Box 6, Napoleon, ND 58561; 701-754-2751; Fax: 701-754-2270. Hours: 8:30AM-4:30PM (CST). *Felony, Misdemeanor, Civil, Eviction, Small Claims, Probate.*

Civil Records: Access: Fax, mail, in person. Both court and visitors may perform in person searches. Search fee: $10.00 per name. Required to search: name, years to search; also helpful-address. Civil cases indexed by defendant, plaintiff. Civil records on index books from 1884. **Criminal Records:** Access: Fax, mail, in person. Both court and visitors may perform in person searches. Search fee: $10.00 per name. Required to search: name, years to search, DOB; also helpful-address. Criminal records on index books from 1884. **General Information:** No adoptions, sealed, juvenile, mental health, expunged or dismissed records released. SASE required. Turnaround time 1-2 days. Copy fee: $1.00 per page. Certification fee: $10.00. Fee payee: Clerk of Court. Business checks accepted. Prepayment is required. Fax notes: Fee to fax is $3.00 for first page, $1.00 each add'l.

McHenry County

Northeast Judicial District Court PO Box 147, Towner, ND 58788; 701-537-5729; Fax: 701-537-5969. Hours: 8AM-4:30PM (CST). *Felony, Misdemeanor, Civil, Eviction, Small Claims, Probate.*

Civil Records: Access: Phone, fax, mail, in person. Both court and visitors may perform in person searches. Search fee: $10.00 per name. Required to search: name, years to search; also helpful-address. Civil cases indexed by defendant, plaintiff. Civil records on index cards from 1991, on index books from 1905. **Criminal Records:** Access: Phone, fax, mail, in person. Both court and visitors may perform in person searches. Search fee: $10.00 per name. Required to search: name, years to search; also helpful-address, DOB, SSN. Criminal records on index cards from 1991, on index books from 1905. **General Information:** No adoptions, sealed, juvenile, mental health, expunged or dismissed records released. SASE required. Turnaround time 1-2 days. Copy fee: $.25 per page. Certification fee: $10.00. Fee

payee: Clerk of Courts. Personal checks accepted. Prepayment is required. Fax notes: $1.00 for first page, $.25 each addl.

McIntosh County

South Central Judicial District Court PO Box 179, Ashley, ND 58413; 701-288-3450; Fax: 701-288-3671. Hours: 8AM-4:30PM (CST). *Felony, Misdemeanor, Civil, Eviction, Small Claims, Probate.*

Civil Records: Access: Phone, fax, mail, in person. Court does not conduct in person searches; visitors must perform searches for themselves. Search fee: $10.00 per name. Required to search: name, years to search; also helpful-address. Civil cases indexed by defendant, plaintiff. Civil records on index cards from 1987, on index books from 1930s. **Criminal Records:** Access: Phone, fax, mail, in person. Both court and visitors may perform in person searches. Search fee: $10.00 per name. Required to search: name, years to search, DOB; also helpful-address. Criminal records on index cards from 1987, on index books from 1930s. **General Information:** No adoptions, sealed, juvenile, mental health, expunged or dismissed records released. SASE not required. Turnaround time 1-2 days. Copy fee: $.25 per page. Certification fee: $10.00. Fee payee: Clerk of Court. Only cashiers checks and money orders accepted. Prepayment is required.

McKenzie County

Northwest District Court PO Box 524, Watford City, ND 58854; 701-842-3452; Fax: 701-842-3916. Hours: 8:30AM-Noon, 1-5PM (CST). *Felony, Misdemeanor, Civil, Eviction, Small Claims, Probate.*

Civil Records: Access: Phone, fax, mail, in person. Both court and visitors may perform in person searches. Search fee: $10.00 per name. Required to search: name, years to search; also helpful-address. Civil cases indexed by defendant, plaintiff. Civil records on computer since 01/96. **Criminal Records:** Access: Phone, fax, mail, in person. Only the court conducts in person searches; visitors may not. Search fee: $10.00 per name. Required to search: name, years to search, DOB; also helpful-address. Criminal records on computer since 12/87. **General Information:** No adoptions, juvenile, mental health, expunged or dismissed records released. SASE required. Turnaround time 1-2 days. Copy fee: $.50 per page. Certification fee: $10.00. Fee payee: Clerk of Court, McKenzie County. Personal checks accepted. Prepayment is required. Fax notes: $2.00 per page.

McLean County

South Central Judicial District Court PO Box 1108, Washburn, ND 58577; 701-462-8541; Fax: 701-462-8212. Hours: 8AM-Noon, 12:30-4:30PM (CST). *Felony, Misdemeanor, Civil, Eviction, Small Claims, Probate.*

Civil Records: Access: Mail, in person. Both court and visitors may perform in person searches. Search fee: $10.00 per name. Required to search: name, years to search; also helpful-address. Civil cases indexed by defendant, plaintiff. Civil records on index books from early 1900s. **Criminal Records:** Access: Mail, in person. Both court and visitors may perform in person searches. Search fee: $10.00 per name. Required to search: name, years to search, DOB; also helpful-address, SSN. Criminal records on index cards from 1983, on index books from early 1900s. **General Information:** No adoptions, sealed, juvenile, mental health, expunged or defereed imposition dismissed records released. SASE required. Turnaround time 1-2 days. Copy fee: $.25 per page. Certification fee: $10.00. Fee payee: Clerk of Courts. Personal checks accepted. Prepayment is required.

Mercer County

District Court PO Box 39, Stanton, ND 58571; 701-745-3262; Fax: 701-745-3364. Hours: 8AM-4PM (MST). *Felony, Misdemeanor, Civil, Eviction, Small Claims, Probate.*

Civil Records: Access: Fax, mail, in person. Both court and visitors may perform in person searches. Search fee: $10.00 per name. Required to search: name, years to search; also helpful-address. Civil cases indexed by defendant, plaintiff. Civil records on index cards from 1979, on index books from 1889. **Criminal Records:** Access: Fax, mail, in person. Both court and visitors may perform in person searches. Search fee: $10.00 per name. Required to search: name, years to search, signed release; also helpful-address, DOB, SSN. Criminal records on index cards from 1979, on index books from 1889. **General Information:** No adoptions, sealed, juvenile, mental health, expunged or dismissed records released. SASE required. Turnaround time 1-2 days. Copy fee: $.25 per page. Certification fee: $10.00. Fee payee: Mercer County Clerk of Court. Personal checks accepted. Prepayment is required. Fax notes: $5.00 per document.

Morton County

South Central Judicial District Court 210 2nd Ave NW, Mandan, ND 58554; 701-667-3358. Hours: 8AM-5PM (MST). *Felony, Misdemeanor, Civil, Eviction, Small Claims, Probate.*

Civil Records: Access: Mail, in person. Only the court conducts in person searches; visitors may not. Search fee: $10.00 per name. Fee is for written search request. Required to search: name, years to search; also helpful-address. Civil cases indexed by defendant, plaintiff. Civil records on computer from 10/91, on index books from 1800s. **Criminal Records:** Access: Mail, in person. Only the court conducts in person searches; visitors may not. Search fee: $10.00 per name. Fee is for written search request. Required to search: name, years to search, DOB; also helpful-address. Criminal records on computer from 10/91, on index books from 1800s. **General Information:** No adoptions, sealed, juvenile, mental health, expunged or dismissed records released. SASE required. Turnaround time 1-2 days. Copy fee: $5.00 per document. Certification fee: $10.00. Fee payee: Clerk of District Court. Personal checks accepted. Prepayment is required.

Mountrail County

Northwest Judicial District Court PO Box 69, Stanley, ND 58784; 701-628-2915; Fax: 701-628-3975. Hours: 8:30AM-4:30PM (CST). *Felony, Misdemeanor, Civil, Eviction, Small Claims, Probate.*

Note: E-mail serch requests can be sent to debbien@nwjd.court.state.nd.us

Civil Records: Access: Phone, fax, mail, in person, e-mail. Only the court conducts in person searches; visitors may not. Search fee: $10.00 per name. Fee is for written search. Required to search: name, years to search; also helpful-address. Civil cases indexed by defendant, plaintiff. Civil records on index books from 1909. **Criminal Records:** Access: Phone, fax, mail, in person, e-

mail. Only the court conducts in person searches; visitors may not. Search fee: $10.00 per name. Fee is for written search. Required to search: name, years to search, DOB; also helpful-address, SSN. Criminal records on index books from 1909. **General Information:** No adoptions, sealed, juvenile, mental health, expunged or dismissed records released. SASE not required. Turnaround time 1-2 days. Copy fee: $.25 per page. Certification fee: $10.00. Fee payee: Clerk of District Court. Personal checks accepted. Prepayment is required. Fax notes: No fee to fax results.

Nelson County

Northeast Central Judicial District Court PO Box 565, Lakota, ND 58344; 701-247-2462; Fax: 701-247-2412. Hours: 8:30AM-5PM (CST). *Felony, Misdemeanor, Civil, Eviction, Small Claims, Probate.*

Note: Will accept e-mail record requests at rstevens@pioneer.state.nd.us

Civil Records: Access: Phone, fax, mail, in person. Both court and visitors may perform in person searches. Search fee: $10.00 per name. Required to search: name, years to search; also helpful-address. Civil cases indexed by defendant, plaintiff. Civil records on index books from 1883. **Criminal Records:** Access: Phone, fax, mail, in person. Only the court conducts in person searches; visitors may not. Search fee: $10.00 per name. Required to search: name, years to search, DOB; also helpful-address, SSN. Criminal records on index books from 1883. **General Information:** No adoptions, sealed, juvenile, mental health, expunged or dismissed records released. SASE required. Turnaround time 1-2 days. Copy fee: $1.00 per page. Certification fee: $10.00. Fee payee: Clerk of Courts. Personal checks accepted. Prepayment is required. Fax notes: $3.00 per document.

Oliver County

South Central Judicial District Court Box 125, Center, ND 58530; 701-794-8777; Fax: 701-794-3476. Hours: 8AM-4PM (CST). *Felony, Misdemeanor, Civil, Eviction, Small Claims, Probate.*

Civil Records: Access: Phone, fax, mail, in person. Only the court conducts in person searches; visitors may not. Search fee: $10.00 per name. Required to search: name, years to search; also helpful-address. Civil cases indexed by defendant. Civil records on docket books from 1900s. **Criminal Records:** Access: Phone, fax, mail, in person. Only the court conducts in person searches; visitors may not. Search fee: $10.00 per name. Required to search: name, years to search, DOB; also helpful-address. Criminal records on docket books from 1900s. **General Information:** No adoptions, sealed, juvenile, mental health, expunged or dismissed records released. SASE required. Turnaround time 1-2 days. Copy fee: $.25 per page. Certification fee: $10.00. Fee payee: Clerk of Court. Personal checks accepted. Prepayment is required. Fax notes: $1.00 for first page, $.50 each addl.

Pembina County

Pembina County District Court 301 Dakota St West #6, Cavalier, ND 58220-4100; 701-265-4275; Fax: 701-265-4876. Hours: 8:30AM-5PM (CST). *Felony, Misdemeanor, Civil, Eviction, Small Claims, Probate.*

Civil Records: Access: Phone, fax, mail, in person. Only the court conducts in person

searches; visitors may not. Search fee: $10.00 per name. Required to search: name, years to search; also helpful-address. Civil cases indexed by defendant, plaintiff. Civil records on index books from 1880s. **Criminal Records:** Access: Phone, fax, mail, in person. Only the court conducts in person searches; visitors may not. Search fee: $10.00 per name. Required to search: name, years to search, DOB; also helpful-address, SSN. Felony records kept for 21 years, misdemeanor for 15 years. **General Information:** No adoptions, sealed, juvenile, mental health, expunged or dismissed records released. SASE not required. Turnaround time 1-2 days. Copy fee: $.25 per page. Certification fee: $10.00. Fee payee: Pembina County Clerk of Court. Personal checks accepted. Prepayment is required. Fax notes: $5.00 per document.

Pierce County

Northeast Judicial District Court 240 SE 2nd St, Rugby, ND 58368; 701-776-6161; Fax: 701-776-5707. Hours: 9AM-5PM (CST). *Felony, Misdemeanor, Civil, Eviction, Small Claims, Probate.*

Civil Records: Access: Phone, fax, mail, in person. Only the court conducts in person searches; visitors may not. Search fee: $10.00 per name. Required to search: name, years to search; also helpful-address. Civil cases indexed by defendant, plaintiff. Civil records on index cards from 1986, on index books and docket books from early 1900s. **Criminal Records:** Access: Phone, fax, mail, in person. Only the court conducts in person searches; visitors may not. Search fee: $10.00 per name. Required to search: name, years to search, DOB; also helpful-address, SSN. Criminal records on index cards from 1986, on index books and docket books from early 1900s. **General Information:** No adoptions, sealed, juvenile, mental health, expunged or dismissed records released. SASE required. Turnaround time 1-2 days. Copy fee: $.25 per page. Certification fee: $10.00. Fee payee: Clerk of Courts. Personal checks accepted. Prepayment is required. Fax notes: $5.00 per document.

Ramsey County

District Court 524 4th Ave #4, Devils Lake, ND 58301; 701-662-7066; Fax: 701-662-7063. Hours: 8AM-5PM (CST). *Felony, Misdemeanor, Civil, Eviction, Small Claims, Probate.*

Civil Records: Access: Fax, mail, in person. Only the court conducts in person searches; visitors may not. Search fee: $10.00 per name. Required to search: name; also helpful-years to search. Civil cases indexed by defendant, plaintiff. Civil records on index cards from 1985, on index books from early 1900s. **Criminal Records:** Access: Fax, mail, in person. Only the court conducts in person searches; visitors may not. Search fee: $10.00 per name. Required to search: name; also helpful-years to search, address, DOB, SSN. Criminal records on index cards from 1985, on index books from early 1900s. **General Information:** No adoptions, sealed, juvenile, mental health, expunged or dismissed records released. SASE required. Turnaround time 1-2 days. Copy fee: $.50 per page. Certification fee: $10.00. Fee payee: Clerk of Courts. Personal checks accepted. Prepayment is required. Fax notes: No fee to fax results. Fax only available to businesses.

Ransom County

Southeast Judicial District Court PO

Box 626, Lisbon, ND 58054; 701-683-5823 X120; Fax: 701-683-5827. Hours: 8:30AM-5PM (CST). *Felony, Misdemeanor, Civil, Eviction, Small Claims, Probate.*

Civil Records: Access: Phone, fax, mail, in person. Both court and visitors may perform in person searches. Search fee: $10.00 per name. Required to search: name, years to search; also helpful-address. Civil cases indexed by defendant, plaintiff. Civil records on docket books from 1967. **Criminal Records:** Access: Phone, fax, mail, in person. Both court and visitors may perform in person searches. Search fee: $10.00 per name. Required to search: name, years to search, DOB; also helpful-address. Criminal records on index books from 1930s. **General Information:** No adoptions, sealed, juvenile, mental health, expunged or dismissed records released. SASE required. Turnaround time 3-4 days. Copy fee: $.20 per page. Certification fee: $10.00. Fee payee: Clerk of Court. Personal checks accepted. Prepayment is required. Fax notes: No fee to fax results.

Renville County

Northeast Judicial District Court PO

Box 68, Mohall, ND 58761; 701-756-6398; Fax: 701-756-6398. Hours: 9AM-4:30PM (CST). *Felony, Misdemeanor, Civil, Eviction, Small Claims, Probate.*

Civil Records: Access: Fax, mail, in person. Both court and visitors may perform in person searches. Search fee: $5.00 per name. Required to search: name, years to search; also helpful-address. Civil cases indexed by defendant, plaintiff. Civil records on index books from 1910. **Criminal Records:** Access: Fax, mail, in person. Both court and visitors may perform in person searches. Search fee: $5.00 per name. Required to search: name, years to search, DOB; also helpful-address. Criminal records on computer from 1/88, on index books from 1910 but not reliable before 1940. **General Information:** No adoptions, sealed, juvenile, mental health, expunged or dismissed records released. SASE required. Turnaround time 1-2 days. Copy fee: $1.00 per page. Certification fee: $10.00. Fee payee: Clerk of Courts. Personal checks accepted. Prepayment is required. Fax notes: $3.00 for first page, $1.00 each addl.

Richland County

Southeast Judicial District Court 418

2nd Ave North, Wahpeton, ND 58074; 701-642-7818; Fax: 701-671-1512. Hours: 8AM-5PM (CST). *Felony, Misdemeanor, Civil, Eviction, Small Claims, Probate.*

Civil Records: Access: Mail, in person. Only the court conducts in person searches; visitors may not. Search fee: $10.00 per name. Required to search: name, years to search; also helpful-address. Civil cases indexed by defendant. Civil records on index cards from 1985, on docket books from late 1800s, but not very accurate. Plaintiff and defendant names required to search. **Criminal Records:** Access: Mail, in person. Only the court conducts in person searches; visitors may not. Search fee: $10.00 per name. Required to search: name, years to search, DOB, SSN; also helpful-address. Criminal records on docket books from late 1800s but not very accurate. **General Information:** No adoptions, sealed, juvenile, mental health, expunged or dismissed records released. SASE required. Turnaround time 1-2

days. Copy fee: $.25 per page. Certification fee: $10.00. Fee payee: Clerk of District Court. Personal checks accepted. Prepayment is required.

Rolette County

Northeast Judicial District Court PO

Box 460, Rolla, ND 58367; 701-477-3816; Fax: 701-477-5770. Hours: 8:30AM-4:30PM (CST). *Felony, Misdemeanor, Civil, Eviction, Small Claims, Probate.*

Civil Records: Access: Phone, fax, mail, in person. Only the court conducts in person searches; visitors may not. Search fee: $10.00 per name. Required to search: name, years to search; also helpful-address. Civil cases indexed by defendant, plaintiff. Civil records on dockets from 1970. Prior to 1970, records hard to find and not very accurate. **Criminal Records:** Access: Phone, fax, mail, in person. Only the court conducts in person searches; visitors may not. Search fee: $10.00 per name. Required to search: name, years to search; also helpful-address, DOB, SSN. Criminal records on dockets from 1970. Prior to 1970, records hard to find and not very accurate. **General Information:** No adoptions, sealed, juvenile, mental health, expunged or dismissed records released. SASE required. Turnaround time 1-2 days. Copy fee: $.50 per page. Certification fee: $10.00. Fee payee: Clerk of Court. Business checks accepted. Prepayment is required. Fax notes: $5.00 per document.

Sargent County

Southeast Judicial District Court 355

Main St (PO Box 176), Forman, ND 58032; 701-724-6241 X215-216; Fax: 701-724-6244. Hours: 9AM-Noon, 12:30-4:30PM (CST). *Felony, Misdemeanor, Civil, Eviction, Small Claims, Probate.*

Civil Records: Access: Phone, fax, mail, in person. Both court and visitors may perform in person searches. Search fee: $10.00 per name. Required to search: name, years to search; also helpful-address. Civil cases indexed by defendant. Civil records on books from early 1800s. **Criminal Records:** Access: Phone, fax, mail, in person. Both court and visitors may perform in person searches. Search fee: $10.00 per name. Required to search: name, years to search, DOB; also helpful-address. Criminal records on books from early 1800s. **General Information:** No adoptions, sealed, juvenile, mental health, expunged or dismissed records released. SASE not required. Turnaround time 1-2 days. Copy fee: $.10 per page. Certification fee: $10.00. Fee payee: Clerk of Court. Personal checks accepted. Prepayment is required. Fax notes: $3.00 for first page, $1.00 each addl.

Sheridan County

South Central Judicial District Court

PO Box 636, McClusky, ND 58463; 701-363-2207; Fax: 701-363-2953. Hours: 9AM-Noon, 1-5PM (CST). *Felony, Misdemeanor, Civil, Eviction, Small Claims, Probate.*

Civil Records: Access: Mail, in person. Both court and visitors may perform in person searches. Search fee: $10.00 per name. Required to search: name, years to search; also helpful-address. Civil cases indexed by defendant, plaintiff. Civil records on index books from 1909. **Criminal Records:** Access: Mail, in person. Both court and visitors may perform in person searches. Search fee: $10.00 per name. Required to search: name, years to search, signed release; also helpful-address, DOB, SSN. Criminal records on index books from

1909. **General Information:** No adoptions, sealed, juvenile, mental health, expunged or dismissed records released. SASE not required. Turnaround time 1-2 days. Copy fee: $.25 per page. Certification fee: $10.00. Fee payee: Clerk of District Court. Business checks accepted. Prepayment is required.

Sioux County

South Central Judicial District Court

Box L, Fort Yates, ND 58538; 701-854-3853; Fax: 701-854-3854. Hours: 9AM-5PM (CST). *Felony, Misdemeanor, Civil, Eviction, Small Claims, Probate.*

Civil Records: Access: Phone, fax, mail, in person. Both court and visitors may perform in person searches. Search fee: $10.00 per name per year. Required to search: name, years to search; also helpful-address. Civil cases indexed by defendant, plaintiff. Civil records on index books from 1914. **Criminal Records:** Access: Phone, fax, mail, in person. Both court and visitors may perform in person searches. Search fee: $10.00 per name per year. Required to search: name, years to search; also helpful-address, DOB, SSN. Criminal records on index books from 1914. **General Information:** No adoptions, sealed, juvenile, mental health, expunged or dismissed records released. SASE required. Turnaround time 1-2 days. Copy fee: $.50 per page. Certification fee: $10.00. Fee payee: Clerk of Court. Personal checks accepted. All fees may be billed.

Slope County

Southwest Judicial District Court PO

Box JJ, Amidon, ND 58620; 701-879-6275; Fax: 701-879-6278. Hours: 9AM-5PM (MST). *Felony, Misdemeanor, Civil, Eviction, Small Claims, Probate.*

Civil Records: Access: Fax, mail, in person. Both court and visitors may perform in person searches. Search fee: $10.00 per name. Required to search: name, years to search; also helpful-address. Civil cases indexed by defendant, plaintiff. Civil records on index cards from 1989. **Criminal Records:** Access: Fax, mail, in person. Both court and visitors may perform in person searches. Search fee: $10.00 per name. Required to search: name, years to search, DOB; also helpful-address. Criminal records on index books from 1915. **General Information:** No adoptions, sealed, juvenile, mental health, expunged or dismissed records released. SASE required. Turnaround time 1-2 days. Copy fee: $.25 per page. Certification fee: $10.00. Fee payee: Clerk of Court. Personal checks accepted. Prepayment is required. Fax notes: $3.00 per document.

Stark County

District Court PO Box 130, Dickinson, ND

58602;; Civil phone:701-264-7636; Criminal phone:701-264-7636; Fax: 701-264-7640. Hours: 7AM-5PM (MST). *Felony, Misdemeanor, Civil, Eviction, Small Claims, Probate.*

Civil Records: Access: Mail, in person. Both court and visitors may perform in person searches. Search fee: $10.00 per name. Required to search: name, years to search. Civil cases indexed by defendant, plaintiff. Civil records on computer since 1/92, index cards since 1800s. **Criminal Records:** Access: Mail, in person. Both court and visitors may perform in person searches. Search fee: $10.00 per name. Required to search: name, years to search, DOB; also helpful-SSN. Criminal records on computer since 1/92, index cards since 1800s. **General Information:** No adoptions, sealed, juvenile, mental health, expunged or dismissed records. SASE required. Turnaround time 1-2 days. Copy fee: $.25 per page. Certification fee: $10.00. Fee payee: Clerk of Court. Personal checks accepted. Prepayment is required. Public access terminal is available.

Steele County

East Central Judicial District Court PO
Box 296, Finley, ND 58230; 701-524-2152; Fax: 701-524-1325. Hours: 8AM-Noon; 1-4:30PM (CST). *Felony, Misdemeanor, Civil, Eviction, Small Claims, Probate.*

Civil Records: Access: Mail, in person. Only the court conducts in person searches; visitors may not. Search fee: $10.00 per name. Required to search: name, years to search; also helpful-address. Civil cases indexed by defendant, plaintiff. Civil records on docket books from approx 1894. **Criminal Records:** Access: Mail, in person. Only the court conducts in person searches; visitors may not. Search fee: $10.00 per name. Required to search: name, years to search, DOB, signed release; also helpful-address. Criminal records on docket books from approx 1894. **General Information:** No adoptions, sealed, juvenile, mental health, expunged or dismissed records released. SASE required. Turnaround time 1-2 days. Copy fee: $1.00 per page. Certification fee: $10.00. Fee payee: Clerk of Court. Business checks accepted. Prepayment is required.

Stutsman County

Southeast Judicial District Court 511
2nd Ave SE, Jamestown, ND 58401; 701-252-9042; Fax: 701-251-1006. Hours: 8AM-5PM (CST). *Felony, Misdemeanor, Civil, Eviction, Small Claims, Probate.*

Civil Records: Access: Mail, in person. Only the court conducts in person searches; visitors may not. Search fee: $10.00 per name. Required to search: name, years to search; also helpful-address. Civil records on computer from 1/87, on index books from 1800s. **Criminal Records:** Access: Mail, in person. Only the court conducts in person searches; visitors may not. Search fee: $10.00 per name. Required to search: name, years to search, DOB; also helpful-address. Criminal records on computer from 1/96, on index books from 1800s. **General Information:** No adoptions, sealed, juvenile, mental health, expunged or dismissed records released. SASE required. Turnaround time 1-2 days. Copy fee: $.25 per page. Certification fee: $10.00. Fee payee: Clerk of Court. Personal checks accepted. Prepayment is required.

Towner County

Northeast Judicial District Court Box
517, Cando, ND 58324; 701-968-4340 Ext 3; Fax: 701-968-4344. Hours: 8:30AM-5PM (CST). *Felony, Misdemeanor, Civil, Eviction, Small Claims, Probate.*

Civil Records: Access: Phone, fax, mail, in person. Only the court conducts in person searches; visitors may not. Search fee: $10.00 per name. Required to search: name, years to search; also helpful-address. Civil cases indexed by defendant, plaintiff. Civil records on index books from 1800s. **Criminal Records:** Access: Phone, fax, mail, in person. Only the court conducts in person searches; visitors may not. Search fee:

$10.00 per name. Required to search: name, years to search; also helpful-address, DOB, SSN. Criminal records on index books from 1800s. **General Information:** No adoptions, sealed, juvenile, mental health, expunged or dismissed records released. SASE required. Turnaround time 1-2 days. Copy fee: $.50 per page. Certification fee: $10.00 plus $5.00 per copy. Fee payee: Clerk of District Court. Personal checks accepted. Prepayment is required. Fax notes: $3.00 per document.

Traill County

East Central Judicial District Court PO
Box 805, Hillsboro, ND 58045; 701-436-4454; Fax: 701-436-5124. Hours: 8AM-4:30PM (CST). *Felony, Misdemeanor, Civil, Eviction, Small Claims, Probate.*

Civil Records: Access: Phone, fax, mail, in person. Only the court conducts in person searches; visitors may not. Search fee: $10.00 per name. Required to search: name, years to search; also helpful-address. Civil cases indexed by defendant, plaintiff. Civil records on index books from 1800s. **Criminal Records:** Access: Phone, fax, mail, in person. Only the court conducts in person searches; visitors may not. Search fee: $10.00 per name. Required to search: name, years to search; also helpful-address, DOB, SSN. Criminal records on index books from 1800s. **General Information:** No adoptions, sealed, juvenile, mental health, expunged or dismissed records released. SASE required. Turnaround time 1-2 days. Copy fee: $.25 per page. Certification fee: $10.00. Fee payee: Clerk of Court. Personal checks accepted. Prepayment is required. Fax notes: $1.00 per page.

Walsh County

Northeast Judicial District Court 600
Cooper Ave, Grafton, ND 58237; 701-352-0350; Fax: 701-352-1104. Hours: 8:30AM-5PM (CST). *Felony, Misdemeanor, Civil, Eviction, Small Claims, Probate.*

Civil Records: Access: Phone, fax, mail, in person. Both court and visitors may perform in person searches. Search fee: $10.00 per name. Required to search: name, years to search; also helpful-address. Civil cases indexed by defendant, plaintiff. Civil records on index books from early 1900s. **Criminal Records:** Access: Phone, fax, mail, in person. Only the court conducts in person searches; visitors may not. Search fee: $10.00 per name. Required to search: name, years to search, DOB; also helpful-address, SSN. Criminal records on index books from early 1900s. **General Information:** No adoptions, sealed, juvenile, mental health, expunged or dismissed records released. SASE required. Turnaround time 5-10 days. Copy fee: $.25 per page. Certification fee: $5.00. Fee payee: Clerk of Court. Personal checks accepted. Prepayment is required.

Ward County

Northwest Judicial District Court PO
Box 5005, Minot, ND 58702-5005; 701-857-6460; Fax: 701-857-6468. Hours: 8AM-4:30PM (CST). *Felony, Misdemeanor, Civil, Eviction, Small Claims, Probate.*

Civil Records: Access: Mail, in person. Both court and visitors may perform in person searches.

Search fee: $10.00 per name. Required to search: name, years to search; also helpful-address. Civil cases indexed by defendant, plaintiff. Civil records on index cards from 1990, on index books from 1800s. **Criminal Records:** Access: Mail, in person. Both court and visitors may perform in person searches. Search fee: $10.00 per name. Required to search: name, years to search; also helpful-address, DOB, SSN. Criminal records on index cards from 1990, on index books from 1800s. **General Information:** No adoptions, sealed, juvenile, mental health, expunged or dismissed records released. SASE not required. Turnaround time 5 days. Copy fee: $.25 per page. Certification fee: $10.00. Fee payee: Clerk of District Court. Business checks accepted. Prepayment is required.

Wells County

Southeast Judicial District Court PO
Box 596, Fessenden, ND 58438; 701-547-3122; Fax: 701-547-3719. Hours: 8AM-4:30PM (CST). *Felony, Misdemeanor, Civil, Eviction, Small Claims, Probate.*

Civil Records: Access: Mail, in person. Only the court conducts in person searches; visitors may not. Search fee: $10.00 per name. Required to search: name, years to search; also helpful-address. Civil cases indexed by defendant, plaintiff. Civil records on index books. **Criminal Records:** Access: Mail, in person. Only the court conducts in person searches; visitors may not. Search fee: $10.00 per name. Required to search: name, years to search; also helpful-address, DOB, SSN. Criminal records on index books from 1980. **General Information:** No adoptions, sealed, juvenile, mental health, expunged or dismissed records released. SASE required. Turnaround time 1-2 days. Copy fee: $1.00 per document. Certification fee: $10.00 plus $2.00 each page after first. Fee payee: District Court. Personal checks accepted. Prepayment is required.

Williams County

Northwest Judicial District Court PO
Box 2047, Williston, ND 58802; 701-572-1720; Fax: 701-572-1760. Hours: 9AM-5PM (CST). *Felony, Misdemeanor, Civil, Eviction, Small Claims, Probate.*

Civil Records: Access: Mail, in person. Both court and visitors may perform in person searches. Search fee: $10.00 per name. Required to search: name, years to search; also helpful-address. Civil cases indexed by defendant, plaintiff. Civil records computerized since 1/98, on index cards from 1/92, on index books from 1899. **Criminal Records:** Access: Mail, in person. Both court and visitors may perform in person searches. Search fee: $10.00 per name. Required to search: name, years to search; also helpful-address, DOB, SSN. Criminal records computerized since 1/98, on index cards from 1/92, on index books from 1899. **General Information:** No adoptions, sealed, juvenile, mental health, expunged or dismissed records released. SASE required. Turnaround time 1-2 days. Copy fee: $2.00 fee for first 10 pages, add $.10 per page thereafter. Certification fee: $10.00. Fee payee: Clerk of Court. Personal checks accepted. Prepayment is required.

ORGANIZATION	53 counties, 53 recording offices. The recording officer is the Register of Deeds. The entire state is in the Central Time Zone (CST).
REAL ESTATE RECORDS	Some counties will perform real estate searches by name or by legal description. Copy fees are usually $1.00 per page. Certified copies usually cost $5.00 for the first page and $2.00 for each additional page. Copies may be faxed.
UCC RECORDS	Financing statements may be filed either at the state level or with any Register of Deeds, except for real estate related collateral, which are filed only with the Register of Deeds. All counties access a **statewide computer database** of filings and will perform UCC searches. Use search request form UCC-11. Various search options are available, including by federal tax identification number or Social Security number The search with copies costs $7.00 per debtor name, including three pages of copies and $1.00 per additional page. Copies may be faxed for an additional fee of $3.00.
TAX LIEN RECORDS	Federal tax liens on personal property of businesses are filed with the Secretary of State. Other federal and all state tax liens are filed with the county Register of Deeds. All counties will perform tax lien searches. Some counties automatically include business federal tax liens as part of a UCC search because they appear on the statewide database. (**Be careful**—federal tax liens on **individuals** may only be in the county lien books, not on the statewide system.) Separate searches are usually available at $5.00-7.00 per name. Copy fees vary. Copies may be faxed.
OTHER LIENS	Mechanics, judgment, hospital, repair, egg cutter.

Adams County
County Register of Deeds, P.O. Box 469, Hettinger, ND 58639-0469. 701-567-2460. Fax: 701-567-2910.

Barnes County
County Register of Deeds, P.O. Box 684, Valley City, ND 58072. 701-845-8506. Fax: 701-845-8538.

Benson County
County Register of Deeds, P.O. Box 193, Minnewaukan, ND 58351. 701-473-5332. Fax: 701-473-5571.

Billings County
County Register of Deeds, P.O. Box 138, Medora, ND 58645-0138. 701-623-4491. Fax: 701-623-4896.

Bottineau County
County Register of Deeds, 314 West 5th Street, Bottineau, ND 58318-1265. 701-228-2786. Fax: 701-228-3658.

Bowman County
County Register of Deeds, P.O. Box 379, Bowman, ND 58623. 701-523-3450. Fax: 701-523-5443.

Burke County
County Register of Deeds, P.O. Box 219, Bowbells, ND 58721-0219. 701-377-2818. Fax: 701-377-2020.

Burleigh County
County Register of Deeds, P.O. Box 5518, Bismarck, ND 58506-5518. 701-222-6749. Fax: 701-222-6717.

Cass County
County Register of Deeds, P.O. Box 2806, Fargo, ND 58108-2806. 701-241-5620. Fax: 701-241-5621.

Cavalier County
County Register of Deeds, 901 3rd Street, Langdon, ND 58249. 701-256-2136. Fax: 701-256-2566.

Dickey County
County Register of Deeds, P.O. Box 148, Ellendale, ND 58436. 701-349-3029. Fax: 701-349-4639.

Divide County
County Register of Deeds, P.O. Box 68, Crosby, ND 58730. 701-965-6661. Fax: 701-965-6943.

Dunn County
County Register of Deeds, P.O. Box 106, Manning, ND 58642-0106. 701-573-4443. Fax: 701-573-4444.

Eddy County
County Register of Deeds, 524 Central Avenue, New Rockford, ND 58356-1698. 701-947-2813. Fax: 701-947-2067.

Emmons County
County Register of Deeds, P.O. Box 905, Linton, ND 58552. 701-254-4812. Fax: 701-254-4012.

Foster County
County Register of Deeds, P.O. Box 257, Carrington, ND 58421. 701-652-2491. Fax: 701-652-2173.

Golden Valley County
County Register of Deeds, P.O. Box 130, Beach, ND 58621-0130. 701-872-3713. Fax: 701-872-4383.

Grand Forks County
County Register of Deeds, P.O. Box 5066, Grand Forks, ND 58206. 701-780-8261. Fax: 701-780-8212.

Grant County
County Register of Deeds, P.O. Box 258, Carson, ND 58529. 701-622-3544. Fax: 701-622-3717.

Griggs County
County Register of Deeds, P.O. Box 237, Cooperstown, ND 58425. 701-797-2771. Fax: 701-797-3587.

Hettinger County
County Register of Deeds, P.O. Box 668, Mott, ND 58646. 701-824-2545. Fax: 701-824-2717.

Kidder County
County Register of Deeds, P.O. Box 66, Steele, ND 58482. 701-475-2632. Fax: 701-475-2202.

La Moure County
County Register of Deeds, P.O. Box 128, La Moure, ND 58458-0128. 701-883-5304. Fax: 701-883-5304.

Logan County
County Register of Deeds, P.O. Box 6, Napoleon, ND 58561-0006. 701-754-2751. Fax: 701-754-2270.

McHenry County
County Register of Deeds, P.O. Box 149, Towner, ND 58788. 701-537-5634. Fax: 701-537-5969.

McIntosh County
County Register of Deeds, P.O. Box 179, Ashley, ND 58413. 701-288-3589. Fax: 701-288-3671.

McKenzie County
County Register of Deeds, P.O. Box 523, Watford City, ND 58854. 701-842-3453. Fax: 701-842-3902.

McLean County
County Register of Deeds, P.O. Box 1108, Washburn, ND 58577-1108. 701-462-8541x225-6. Fax: 701-462-3633.

Mercer County
County Register of Deeds, P.O. Box 39, Stanton, ND 58571. 701-745-3272. Fax: 701-745-3364.

Morton County
County Register of Deeds, 210 2nd Avenue, Mandan, ND 58554. 701-667-3305. Fax: 701-667-3453.

Mountrail County
County Register of Deeds, P.O. Box 69, Stanley, ND 58784. 701-628-2945. Fax: 701-628-2276.

Nelson County
County Register of Deeds, P.O. Box 565, Lakota, ND 58344. 701-247-2433. Fax: 701-247-2412.

Oliver County
County Register of Deeds, P.O. Box 125, Center, ND 58530-0125. 701-794-8777. Fax: 701-794-3476.

Pembina County
County Register of Deeds, 301 Dakota Street W. 10, Cavalier, ND 58220. 701-265-4373. Fax: 701-265-4876.

Pierce County
County Register of Deeds, 240 S.E. 2nd Street, Rugby, ND 58368. 701-776-5206. Fax: 701-776-5707.

Ramsey County
County Register of Deeds, 524 4th Avenue #30, Devils Lake, ND 58301. 701-662-7018. Fax: 701-662-7093.

Ransom County
County Register of Deeds, P.O. Box 666, Lisbon, ND 58054-0666. 701-683-5823. Fax: 701-683-5827.

Renville County
County Register of Deeds, P.O. Box 68, Mohall, ND 58761-0068. 701-756-6398. Fax: 701-756-6398. www.renvillecounty.org/

Richland County
County Register of Deeds, 418 2nd Avenue North, Courthouse, Wahpeton, ND 58075-4400. 701-642-7800. Fax: 701-642-7820.

Rolette County
County Register of Deeds, P.O. Box 276, Rolla, ND 58367. 701-477-3166. Fax: 701-477-5770.

Sargent County
County Register of Deeds, P.O. Box 176, Forman, ND 58032-0176. 701-724-6241. Fax: 701-724-6244.

Sheridan County
County Register of Deeds, P.O. Box 668, McClusky, ND 58463-0668. 701-363-2207. Fax: 701-363-2953.

Sioux County

County Register of Deeds, P.O. Box L, Fort Yates, ND 58538. 701-854-3853. Fax: 701-854-3854.

Slope County

County Register of Deeds, P.O. Box JJ, Amidon, ND 58620-0445. 701-879-6275. Fax: 701-879-6278.

Stark County

County Register of Deeds, P.O. Box 130, Dickinson, ND 58601. 701-264-7645. Fax: 701-264-7628.

Steele County

County Register of Deeds, P.O. Box 296, Finley, ND 58230. 701-524-2152. Fax: 701-524-1325.

Stutsman County

County Register of Deeds, 511 2nd Avenue S.E., Courthouse, Jamestown, ND 58401. 701-252-9034. Fax: 701-251-1603.

Towner County

County Register of Deeds, P.O. Box 517, Cando, ND 58324. 701-968-4343. Fax: 701-968-4344.

Traill County

County Register of Deeds, P.O. Box 399, Hillsboro, ND 58045. 701-436-4457. Fax: 701-436-4457.

Walsh County

County Register of Deeds, 600 Cooper Avenue, Courthouse, Grafton, ND 58237. 701-352-2380. Fax: 701-352-3340.

Ward County

County Register of Deeds, 315 S.E. Third Street, Courthouse, Minot, ND 58705-5005. 701-857-6410. Fax: 701-857-6414.

Wells County

County Register of Deeds, P.O. Box 125, Fessenden, ND 58438-0125. 701-547-3141. Fax: 701-547-3719.

Williams County

County Register of Deeds, P.O. Box 2047, Williston, ND 58802-2047. 701-572-1740. Fax: 701-572-1759.

You will usually be able to find the city name in the City/County Cross Reference below. In that case, it is a simple matter to determine the county from the cross reference. However, only the official US Postal Service city names are included in this index. There are an additional 40,000 place names that people use in their addresses. Therefore, we have also included a ZIP/City Cross Reference immediately following the City/County Cross Reference.

If you know the ZIP Code but the city name does not appear in the City/County Cross Reference index, look up the ZIP Code in the ZIP/City Cross Reference, find the city name, then look up the city name in the City/County Cross Reference. For example, you want to know the county for an address of Menands, NY 12204. There is no "Menands" in the City/County Cross Reference. The ZIP/City Cross Reference shows that ZIP Codes 12201-12288 are for the city of Albany. Looking back in the City/County Cross Reference, Albany is in Albany County.

City/County Cross Reference

ABERCROMBIE Richland
ABSARAKA Cass
ADAMS Walsh
AGATE Rolette
ALAMO (58830) Williams(77), Divide(23)
ALEXANDER McKenzie
ALFRED La Moure
ALICE Cass
ALMONT (58520) Morton(72), Grant(28)
ALSEN Cavalier
AMBROSE Divide
AMENIA Cass
AMIDON Slope
ANAMOOSE (58710) McHenry(55),
    Sheridan(26), Pierce(18)
ANETA (58212) Nelson(70), Griggs(20),
    Grand Forks(8), Steele(3)
ANTLER Bottineau
ARDOCH (58213) Walsh(66), Grand
    Forks(34)
ARENA (58412) Burleigh(99), Kidder(1)
ARGUSVILLE Cass
ARNEGARD McKenzie
ARTHUR Cass
ARVILLA Grand Forks
ASHLEY (58413) McIntosh(93), Dickey(7)
AYR Cass
BALDWIN Burleigh
BALFOUR McHenry
BALTA Pierce
BANTRY McHenry
BARNEY Richland
BARTON Pierce
BATHGATE Pembina
BEACH (58621) Golden Valley(99),
    McKenzie(1)
BELCOURT Rolette
BELFIELD (58622) Stark(64), Billings(36)
BENEDICT (58716) McLean(79), Ward(21)
BERLIN (58415) La Moure(98), Dickey(2)
BERTHOLD (58718) Ward(73),
    Mountrail(25), Renville(2)
BEULAH (58523) Mercer(98), Oliver(2)
BINFORD (58416) Griggs(96), Nelson(4)
BISBEE (58317) Towner(85), Rolette(8),
    Pierce(7)
BISMARCK Burleigh
BLAISDELL Mountrail
BLANCHARD Traill
BOTTINEAU Bottineau
BOWBELLS (58721) Burke(95), Ward(5)
BOWBELLS Burke
BOWDON (58418) Wells(98), Kidder(2)
BOWMAN (58623) Bowman(95), Slope(5)
BRADDOCK (58524) Emmons(74),
    Burleigh(14), Kidder(12)
BREMEN Wells
BRINSMADE Benson
BROCKET (58321) Nelson(38), Walsh(37),
    Ramsey(26)
BUCHANAN Stutsman
BUFFALO Cass
BURLINGTON Ward
BUTTE (58723) McLean(92), Sheridan(8)

BUXTON Traill
CALEDONIA Traill
CALVIN (58323) Cavalier(82), Towner(18)
CANDO Towner
CANNON BALL Sioux
CARPIO (58725) Ward(52), Renville(48)
CARRINGTON (58421) Foster(95),
    Stutsman(2), Wells(2), Eddy(1)
CARSON Grant
CARTWRIGHT McKenzie
CASSELTON Cass
CATHAY Wells
CAVALIER Pembina
CAYUGA Sargent
CENTER Oliver
CHAFFEE Cass
CHASELEY (58423) Wells(93), Kidder(7)
CHRISTINE (58015) Richland(98), Cass(2)
CHURCHS FERRY (58325) Ramsey(57),
    Benson(43)
CLEVELAND Stutsman
CLIFFORD (58016) Traill(66), Steele(34)
COGSWELL Sargent
COLEHARBOR McLean
COLFAX Richland
COLUMBUS Burke
COOPERSTOWN (99999) Griggs(99),
    Steele(1)
COURTENAY (58426) Stutsman(98),
    Foster(2)
CRARY Ramsey
CROSBY Divide
CRYSTAL Pembina
CRYSTAL SPRINGS Kidder
CUMMINGS Traill
DAHLEN (58224) Nelson(93), Walsh(7)
DAVENPORT Cass
DAWSON Kidder
DAZEY (58429) Barnes(98), Griggs(2)
DEERING (58731) McHenry(96), Ward(4)
DENHOFF Sheridan
DES LACS Ward
DEVILS LAKE Ramsey
DICKEY La Moure
DICKINSON (58601) Stark(98), Dunn(2)
DICKINSON Stark
DODGE (58625) Dunn(75), Mercer(25)
DONNYBROOK (58734) Ward(46),
    Mountrail(38), Renville(15)
DOUGLAS (58735) Ward(51), McLean(49)
DOYON Ramsey
DRAKE (58736) McHenry(86),
    Sheridan(14)
DRAYTON (58225) Pembina(77),
    Walsh(23)
DRISCOLL (58532) Burleigh(83),
    Kidder(17)
DUNN CENTER Dunn
DUNSEITH (58329) Rolette(82),
    Bottineau(18)
ECKELSON Barnes
EDGELEY (58433) La Moure(90),
    Dickey(10)

EDINBURG (58227) Walsh(65),
    Pembina(31), Cavalier(4)
EDMORE (58330) Ramsey(89), Walsh(9),
    Cavalier(3)
EGELAND Towner
ELGIN Grant
ELLENDALE Dickey
EMERADO Grand Forks
ENDERLIN (58027) Ransom(75),
    Cass(19), Barnes(6)
EPPING Williams
ERIE Cass
ESMOND (58332) Benson(75), Pierce(25)
FAIRDALE (58229) Walsh(90), Cavalier(9)
FAIRFIELD Billings
FAIRMOUNT Richland
FARGO Cass
FESSENDEN Wells
FINGAL (58031) Barnes(61), Cass(39)
FINLEY Steele
FLASHER (58535) Morton(81), Grant(19)
FLAXTON Burke
FORBES Dickey
FORDVILLE (58231) Walsh(79), Grand
    Forks(21)
FOREST RIVER (58233) Walsh(92), Grand
    Forks(8)
FORMAN Sargent
FORT RANSOM (58033) Ransom(98), La
    Moure(2)
FORT RICE Morton
FORT TOTTEN Benson
FORT YATES Sioux
FORTUNA Divide
FOXHOLM Ward
FREDONIA (58440) Logan(71),
    McIntosh(29)
FULLERTON Dickey
GACKLE (58442) Logan(85), Stutsman(15)
GALESBURG (58035) Traill(56), Cass(29),
    Steele(15)
GARDENA Bottineau
GARDNER Cass
GARRISON McLean
GILBY Grand Forks
GLADSTONE (58630) Stark(87), Dunn(13)
GLASSTON Pembina
GLEN ULLIN (58631) Morton(82),
    Grant(12), Mercer(5), Oliver(1)
GLENBURN (58740) Renville(68),
    Ward(28), McHenry(2), Bottineau(2)
GLENFIELD (58443) Foster(99), Griggs(1)
GOLDEN VALLEY Mercer
GOLVA Golden Valley
GOODRICH (58444) Sheridan(96),
    Burleigh(4)
GRACE CITY (58445) Foster(85), Eddy(16)
GRAFTON Walsh
GRAND FORKS Grand Forks
GRAND FORKS AFB Grand Forks
GRANDIN (58038) Cass(74), Traill(26)
GRANVILLE McHenry
GRASSY BUTTE (58634) McKenzie(92),
    Billings(8)

GREAT BEND Richland
GRENORA (58845) Williams(82),
    Divide(18)
GUELPH Dickey
GWINNER Sargent
HAGUE Emmons
HALLIDAY (58636) Dunn(97), Mercer(3)
HAMBERG Wells
HAMILTON Pembina
HAMPDEN (58338) Ramsey(70),
    Cavalier(30)
HANKINSON Richland
HANNAFORD (58448) Griggs(98),
    Barnes(2)
HANNAH Cavalier
HANSBORO Towner
HARVEY (58341) Wells(87), Pierce(11)
HARWOOD Cass
HATTON (58240) Traill(72), Steele(17),
    Grand Forks(11)
HAVANA Sargent
HAZELTON Emmons
HAZEN (58545) Mercer(95), Oliver(5)
HEATON (58450) Wells(87), Kidder(13)
HEBRON (58638) Morton(77), Mercer(9),
    Stark(9), Dunn(4), Grant(2)
HEIMDAL Wells
HENSEL Pembina
HENSLER Oliver
HETTINGER Adams
HILLSBORO Traill
HOOPLE (58243) Walsh(92), Pembina(8)
HOPE (58046) Steele(80), Barnes(16),
    Cass(4)
HORACE Cass
HUNTER (58048) Cass(96), Traill(5)
HURDSFIELD (58451) Wells(97),
    Sheridan(4)
INKSTER (58244) Grand Forks(94),
    Walsh(6)
JAMESTOWN Stutsman
JESSIE Griggs
JOLIETTE Pembina
JUD (58454) La Moure(80), Stutsman(20)
KARLSRUHE McHenry
KATHRYN (58049) Barnes(77),
    Ransom(17), La Moure(6)
KEENE McKenzie
KENMARE (58746) Ward(77), Burke(13),
    Renville(11)
KENSAL (58455) Stutsman(73), Foster(27)
KIEF (58747) Sheridan(82), McHenry(18)
KILLDEER (58640) Dunn(99), McKenzie(1)
KINDRED (58051) Cass(79), Richland(22)
KINTYRE (58549) Emmons(66),
    Logan(32), Kidder(2)
KNOX Benson
KRAMER (58748) Bottineau(93),
    McHenry(7)
KULM (58456) La Moure(77), Dickey(17),
    McIntosh(7)
LAKOTA (58344) Nelson(98), Ramsey(2)
LAMOURE (58458) La Moure(99),
    Dickey(1)

LANGDON Cavalier
LANKIN Walsh
LANSFORD (58750) Bottineau(61), Renville(40)
LARIMORE Grand Forks
LAWTON (58345) Walsh(60), Ramsey(40)
LEEDS (58346) Benson(93), Towner(6), Pierce(2)
LEFOR Stark
LEHR (58460) McIntosh(55), Logan(45)
LEITH Grant
LEONARD (58052) Cass(80), Richland(16), Ransom(4)
LIDGERWOOD (58053) Richland(86), Sargent(14)
LIGNITE Burke
LINTON Emmons
LISBON Ransom
LITCHVILLE (58461) Barnes(75), La Moure(26)
LUVERNE (58056) Barnes(59), Steele(30), Griggs(11)
MADDOCK (58348) Benson(86), Wells(14)
MAIDA Cavalier
MAKOTI (58756) Ward(79), Mountrail(17), McLean(4)
MANDAN Morton
MANDAREE (58757) McKenzie(53), Dunn(48)
MANFRED Wells
MANNING (58642) Dunn(85), Billings(15)
MANTADOR Richland
MANVEL Grand Forks
MAPLETON Cass
MARION (58466) La Moure(77), Barnes(21), Stutsman(2)
MARMARTH (58643) Slope(68), Bowman(32)
MARSHALL Dunn
MARTIN (58758) Sheridan(66), Wells(17), Pierce(17)
MAX (58759) Ward(57), McLean(43)
MAXBASS Bottineau
MAYVILLE Traill
MCCANNA Grand Forks
MCCLUSKY Sheridan
MCGREGOR (58755) Williams(71), Divide(16), Burke(13)
MCHENRY (58464) Foster(51), Eddy(46), Griggs(2)
MCKENZIE Burleigh
MCLEOD (58057) Richland(73), Ransom(27)
MCVILLE Nelson
MEDINA (58467) Stutsman(96), Kidder(4)
MEDORA (58645) Billings(92), Golden Valley(8)
MEKINOCK Grand Forks
MENOKEN Burleigh
MERCER (58559) McLean(87), Sheridan(13)
MERRICOURT Dickey
MICHIGAN Nelson

MILNOR (58060) Sargent(81), Ransom(19)
MILTON (58260) Cavalier(88), Walsh(12)
MINNEWAUKAN (58351) Benson(91), Ramsey(9)
MINOT Ward
MINOT AFB Ward
MINTO Walsh
MOFFIT (58560) Burleigh(81), Emmons(19)
MOHALL (58761) Renville(71), Bottineau(29)
MONANGO Dickey
MONTPELIER (58472) Stutsman(66), La Moure(34)
MOORETON Richland
MOTT (58646) Hettinger(98), Adams(2)
MOUNTAIN (58262) Pembina(94), Cavalier(6)
MUNICH (58352) Cavalier(96), Towner(4)
MYLO Rolette
NAPOLEON Logan
NECHE Pembina
NEKOMA Cavalier
NEW ENGLAND (58647) Hettinger(74), Slope(18), Stark(8)
NEW LEIPZIG (58562) Grant(91), Hettinger(8), Adams(1)
NEW ROCKFORD (58356) Eddy(94), Wells(4), Foster(2)
NEW SALEM (58563) Morton(82), Oliver(17)
NEW TOWN (58763) Mountrail(90), McKenzie(10)
NEWBURG (58762) Bottineau(80), McHenry(20)
NIAGARA (58266) Grand Forks(75), Nelson(26)
NOME (58062) Barnes(80), Ransom(20)
NOONAN Divide
NORTHWOOD (58267) Grand Forks(99), Steele(1)
NORWICH (58768) McHenry(55), Ward(45)
OAKES (58474) Dickey(97), Sargent(3)
OBERON Benson
ORISKA Barnes
ORRIN Pierce
OSNABROCK Cavalier
OVERLY Bottineau
PAGE (58064) Cass(89), Barnes(9), Steele(2)
PALERMO Mountrail
PARK RIVER Walsh
PARSHALL (58770) Mountrail(82), McLean(18)
PEKIN Nelson
PEMBINA Pembina
PENN Ramsey
PERTH (58363) Towner(80), Rolette(20)
PETERSBURG Nelson
PETTIBONE (58475) Kidder(90), Stutsman(10)
PILLSBURY Barnes
PINGREE Stutsman

PISEK Walsh
PLAZA (58771) Mountrail(78), Ward(20), McLean(3)
PORTAL Burke
PORTLAND (58274) Traill(85), Steele(15)
POWERS LAKE (58773) Burke(73), Mountrail(28)
RALEIGH Grant
RAY Williams
REEDER (58649) Adams(62), Hettinger(29)
REGAN Burleigh
REGENT (58650) Hettinger(96), Adams(5)
REYNOLDS (58275) Grand Forks(67), Traill(33)
RHAME (58651) Bowman(63), Slope(37)
RICHARDTON (58652) Stark(93), Dunn(7)
RIVERDALE McLean
ROBINSON Kidder
ROCKLAKE Towner
ROGERS Barnes
ROLETTE (58366) Rolette(96), Pierce(4)
ROLLA (58367) Rolette(94), Towner(6)
ROSEGLEN McLean
ROSS Mountrail
RUGBY (58368) Pierce(96), McHenry(3), Benson(1)
RUSO (58778) McLean(95), McHenry(5)
RUTLAND Sargent
RYDER (58779) McLean(57), Ward(44)
SAINT ANTHONY Morton
SAINT JOHN Rolette
SAINT MICHAEL Benson
SAINT THOMAS Pembina
SANBORN Barnes
SARLES (58372) Cavalier(65), Towner(35)
SAWYER Ward
SCRANTON (58653) Bowman(88), Slope(12)
SELFRIDGE (58568) Sioux(98), Grant(2)
SELZ Pierce
SENTINEL BUTTE (58654) Golden Valley(56), Slope(45)
SHARON Steele
SHELDON (58068) Ransom(99), Cass(1)
SHERWOOD (58782) Renville(96), Bottineau(5)
SHEYENNE (58374) Eddy(69), Benson(19), Wells(12)
SHIELDS Grant
SOLEN (58570) Morton(79), Sioux(21)
SOURIS Bottineau
SOUTH HEART Stark
SPIRITWOOD (58481) Stutsman(53), Barnes(47)
STANLEY (58784) Mountrail(94), Burke(6)
STANTON (58571) Mercer(74), Oliver(26)
STARKWEATHER (58377) Ramsey(83), Cavalier(9), Towner(7)
STEELE Kidder
STERLING Burleigh
STIRUM (58069) Sargent(95), Ransom(5)
STRASBURG Emmons

STREETER (58483) Stutsman(71), Logan(23), Kidder(7)
SURREY Ward
SUTTON (58484) Griggs(63), Foster(37)
SYKESTON (58486) Wells(94), Stutsman(6)
TAPPEN Kidder
TAYLOR (58656) Stark(90), Dunn(11)
THOMPSON Grand Forks
TIOGA (58852) Williams(90), Mountrail(11)
TOKIO Benson
TOLLEY (58787) Renville(98), Ward(2)
TOLNA (58380) Nelson(47), Eddy(45), Benson(8)
TOWER CITY (58071) Cass(81), Barnes(20)
TOWNER (58788) McHenry(95), Pierce(5)
TRENTON Williams
TROTTERS Golden Valley
TURTLE LAKE McLean
TUTTLE Kidder
UNDERWOOD McLean
UNION Cavalier
UPHAM (58789) McHenry(93), Bottineau(7)
VALLEY CITY Barnes
VELVA (58790) McHenry(91), Ward(9)
VENTURIA McIntosh
VERONA (58490) La Moure(87), Ransom(13)
VOLTAIRE McHenry
WAHPETON Richland
WALCOTT Richland
WALES Cavalier
WALHALLA (58282) Pembina(91), Cavalier(9)
WARWICK (58381) Eddy(74), Benson(26)
WASHBURN McLean
WATFORD CITY McKenzie
WEBSTER Ramsey
WEST FARGO Cass
WESTHOPE Bottineau
WHEATLAND Cass
WHITE EARTH (58794) Mountrail(99), Williams(2)
WILDROSE (58795) Williams(70), Divide(30)
WILLISTON Williams
WILLOW CITY (58384) Bottineau(61), Pierce(22), McHenry(11), Rolette(6)
WILTON (58579) McLean(53), Burleigh(48)
WIMBLEDON (58492) Barnes(81), Stutsman(13), Griggs(5)
WING Burleigh
WISHEK (58495) McIntosh(85), Logan(15)
WOLFORD (58385) Pierce(94), Rolette(6)
WOODWORTH Stutsman
WYNDMERE Richland
YORK (58386) Benson(54), Pierce(46)
YPSILANTI (58497) Stutsman(94), Barnes(6)
ZAHL (58856) Williams(84), Divide(16)
ZAP Mercer
ZEELAND McIntosh

ZIP/City Cross Reference

58001-58001	ABERCROMBIE
58002-58002	ABSARAKA
58004-58004	AMENIA
58005-58005	ARGUSVILLE
58006-58006	ARTHUR
58007-58007	AYR
58008-58008	BARNEY
58009-58009	BLANCHARD
58011-58011	BUFFALO
58012-58012	CASSELTON
58013-58013	CAYUGA
58014-58014	CHAFFEE
58015-58015	CHRISTINE
58016-58016	CLIFFORD
58017-58017	COGSWELL
58018-58018	COLFAX
58021-58021	DAVENPORT
58027-58027	ENDERLIN
58029-58029	ERIE
58030-58030	FAIRMOUNT
58031-58031	FINGAL
58032-58032	FORMAN
58033-58033	FORT RANSOM
58035-58035	GALESBURG
58036-58036	GARDNER
58038-58038	GRANDIN
58039-58039	GREAT BEND
58040-58040	GWINNER
58041-58041	HANKINSON
58042-58042	HARWOOD
58043-58043	HAVANA
58045-58045	HILLSBORO
58046-58046	HOPE
58047-58047	HORACE
58048-58048	HUNTER
58049-58049	KATHRYN
58051-58051	KINDRED
58052-58052	LEONARD
58053-58053	LIDGERWOOD
58054-58054	LISBON
58056-58056	LUVERNE
58057-58057	MCLEOD
58058-58058	MANTADOR
58059-58059	MAPLETON
58060-58060	MILNOR
58061-58061	MOORETON
58062-58062	NOME
58063-58063	ORISKA
58064-58064	PAGE
58065-58065	PILLSBURY
58067-58067	RUTLAND
58068-58068	SHELDON
58069-58069	STIRUM
58071-58071	TOWER CITY
58072-58072	VALLEY CITY
58074-58076	WAHPETON
58077-58077	WALCOTT
58078-58078	WEST FARGO
58079-58079	WHEATLAND
58081-58081	WYNDMERE

Zip Range	City	Zip Range	City	Zip Range	City	Zip Range	City
58102-58126	FARGO	58344-58344	LAKOTA	58486-58486	SYKESTON	58655-58655	SOUTH HEART
58201-58203	GRAND FORKS	58345-58345	LAWTON	58487-58487	TAPPEN	58656-58656	TAYLOR
58204-58205	GRAND FORKS AFB	58346-58346	LEEDS	58488-58488	TUTTLE	58701-58703	MINOT
58206-58208	GRAND FORKS	58348-58348	MADDOCK	58489-58489	VENTURIA	58704-58705	MINOT AFB
58210-58210	ADAMS	58351-58351	MINNEWAUKAN	58490-58490	VERONA	58707-58707	MINOT
58212-58212	ANETA	58352-58352	MUNICH	58492-58492	WIMBLEDON	58710-58710	ANAMOOSE
58213-58213	ARDOCH	58353-58353	MYLO	58494-58494	WING	58711-58711	ANTLER
58214-58214	ARVILLA	58355-58355	NEKOMA	58495-58495	WISHEK	58712-58712	BALFOUR
58216-58216	BATHGATE	58356-58356	NEW ROCKFORD	58496-58496	WOODWORTH	58713-58713	BANTRY
58218-58218	BUXTON	58357-58357	OBERON	58497-58497	YPSILANTI	58716-58716	BENEDICT
58219-58219	CALEDONIA	58359-58359	ORRIN	58501-58507	BISMARCK	58718-58718	BERTHOLD
58220-58220	CAVALIER	58361-58361	PEKIN	58520-58520	ALMONT	58721-58721	BOWBELLS
58222-58222	CRYSTAL	58362-58362	PENN	58521-58521	BALDWIN	58722-58722	BURLINGTON
58223-58223	CUMMINGS	58363-58363	PERTH	58523-58523	BEULAH	58723-58723	BUTTE
58224-58224	DAHLEN	58365-58365	ROCKLAKE	58524-58524	BRADDOCK	58725-58725	CARPIO
58225-58225	DRAYTON	58366-58366	ROLETTE	58528-58528	CANNON BALL	58727-58727	COLUMBUS
58227-58227	EDINBURG	58367-58367	ROLLA	58529-58529	CARSON	58730-58730	CROSBY
58228-58228	EMERADO	58368-58368	RUGBY	58530-58530	CENTER	58731-58731	DEERING
58229-58229	FAIRDALE	58369-58369	SAINT JOHN	58531-58531	COLEHARBOR	58733-58733	DES LACS
58230-58230	FINLEY	58370-58370	SAINT MICHAEL	58532-58532	DRISCOLL	58734-58734	DONNYBROOK
58231-58231	FORDVILLE	58372-58372	SARLES	58533-58533	ELGIN	58735-58735	DOUGLAS
58233-58233	FOREST RIVER	58374-58374	SHEYENNE	58535-58535	FLASHER	58736-58736	DRAKE
58235-58235	GILBY	58377-58377	STARKWEATHER	58538-58538	FORT YATES	58737-58737	FLAXTON
58236-58236	GLASSTON	58379-58379	TOKIO	58540-58540	GARRISON	58740-58740	GLENBURN
58237-58237	GRAFTON	58380-58380	TOLNA	58541-58541	GOLDEN VALLEY	58741-58741	GRANVILLE
58238-58238	HAMILTON	58381-58381	WARWICK	58542-58542	HAGUE	58744-58744	KARLSRUHE
58239-58239	HANNAH	58382-58382	WEBSTER	58544-58544	HAZELTON	58746-58746	KENMARE
58240-58240	HATTON	58384-58384	WILLOW CITY	58545-58545	HAZEN	58747-58747	KIEF
58241-58241	HENSEL	58385-58385	WOLFORD	58549-58549	KINTYRE	58748-58748	KRAMER
58243-58243	HOOPLE	58386-58386	YORK	58552-58552	LINTON	58750-58750	LANSFORD
58244-58244	INKSTER	58401-58405	JAMESTOWN	58553-58553	MCKENZIE	58752-58752	LIGNITE
58249-58249	LANGDON	58413-58413	ASHLEY	58554-58554	MANDAN	58755-58755	MCGREGOR
58250-58250	LANKIN	58415-58415	BERLIN	58558-58558	MENOKEN	58756-58756	MAKOTI
58251-58251	LARIMORE	58416-58416	BINFORD	58559-58559	MERCER	58757-58757	MANDAREE
58254-58254	MCVILLE	58418-58418	BOWDON	58560-58560	MOFFIT	58758-58758	MARTIN
58255-58255	MAIDA	58420-58420	BUCHANAN	58561-58561	NAPOLEON	58759-58759	MAX
58256-58256	MANVEL	58421-58421	CARRINGTON	58562-58562	NEW LEIPZIG	58760-58760	MAXBASS
58257-58257	MAYVILLE	58422-58422	CATHAY	58563-58563	NEW SALEM	58761-58761	MOHALL
58258-58258	MEKINOCK	58423-58423	CHASELEY	58564-58564	RALEIGH	58762-58762	NEWBURG
58259-58259	MICHIGAN	58424-58424	CLEVELAND	58565-58565	RIVERDALE	58763-58763	NEW TOWN
58260-58260	MILTON	58425-58425	COOPERSTOWN	58566-58566	SAINT ANTHONY	58765-58765	NOONAN
58261-58261	MINTO	58426-58426	COURTENAY	58568-58568	SELFRIDGE	58768-58768	NORWICH
58262-58262	MOUNTAIN	58428-58428	DAWSON	58569-58569	SHIELDS	58769-58769	PALERMO
58265-58265	NECHE	58429-58429	DAZEY	58570-58570	SOLEN	58770-58770	PARSHALL
58266-58266	NIAGARA	58430-58430	DENHOFF	58571-58571	STANTON	58771-58771	PLAZA
58267-58267	NORTHWOOD	58431-58431	DICKEY	58572-58572	STERLING	58772-58772	PORTAL
58269-58269	OSNABROCK	58432-58432	ECKELSON	58573-58573	STRASBURG	58773-58773	POWERS LAKE
58270-58270	PARK RIVER	58433-58433	EDGELEY	58575-58575	TURTLE LAKE	58775-58775	ROSEGLEN
58271-58271	PEMBINA	58436-58436	ELLENDALE	58576-58576	UNDERWOOD	58776-58776	ROSS
58272-58272	PETERSBURG	58438-58438	FESSENDEN	58577-58577	WASHBURN	58778-58778	RUSO
58273-58273	PISEK	58439-58439	FORBES	58579-58579	WILTON	58779-58779	RYDER
58274-58274	PORTLAND	58440-58440	FREDONIA	58580-58580	ZAP	58781-58781	SAWYER
58275-58275	REYNOLDS	58441-58441	FULLERTON	58581-58581	ZEELAND	58782-58782	SHERWOOD
58276-58276	SAINT THOMAS	58442-58442	GACKLE	58601-58602	DICKINSON	58783-58783	SOURIS
58277-58277	SHARON	58443-58443	GLENFIELD	58620-58620	AMIDON	58784-58784	STANLEY
58278-58278	THOMPSON	58444-58444	GOODRICH	58621-58621	BEACH	58785-58785	SURREY
58281-58281	WALES	58445-58445	GRACE CITY	58622-58622	BELFIELD	58787-58787	TOLLEY
58282-58282	WALHALLA	58448-58448	HANNAFORD	58623-58623	BOWMAN	58788-58788	TOWNER
58301-58301	DEVILS LAKE	58451-58451	HURDSFIELD	58625-58625	DODGE	58789-58789	UPHAM
58310-58310	AGATE	58452-58452	JESSIE	58626-58626	DUNN CENTER	58790-58790	VELVA
58311-58311	ALSEN	58454-58454	JUD	58627-58627	FAIRFIELD	58792-58792	VOLTAIRE
58313-58313	BALTA	58455-58455	KENSAL	58630-58630	GLADSTONE	58793-58793	WESTHOPE
58316-58316	BELCOURT	58456-58456	KULM	58631-58631	GLEN ULLIN	58794-58794	WHITE EARTH
58317-58317	BISBEE	58458-58458	LAMOURE	58632-58632	GOLVA	58795-58795	WILDROSE
58318-58318	BOTTINEAU	58460-58460	LEHR	58634-58634	GRASSY BUTTE	58801-58802	WILLISTON
58319-58319	BREMEN	58461-58461	LITCHVILLE	58636-58636	HALLIDAY	58830-58830	ALAMO
58320-58320	BRINSMADE	58463-58463	MCCLUSKY	58638-58638	HEBRON	58831-58831	ALEXANDER
58321-58321	BROCKET	58464-58464	MCHENRY	58639-58639	HETTINGER	58833-58833	AMBROSE
58323-58323	CALVIN	58466-58466	MARION	58640-58640	KILLDEER	58835-58835	ARNEGARD
58324-58324	CANDO	58467-58467	MEDINA	58641-58641	LEFOR	58838-58838	CARTWRIGHT
58325-58325	CHURCHS FERRY	58472-58472	MONTPELIER	58642-58642	MANNING	58843-58843	EPPING
58327-58327	CRARY	58474-58474	OAKES	58643-58643	MARMARTH	58844-58844	FORTUNA
58329-58329	DUNSEITH	58475-58475	PETTIBONE	58644-58644	MARSHALL	58845-58845	GRENORA
58330-58330	EDMORE	58476-58476	PINGREE	58645-58645	MEDORA	58847-58847	KEENE
58331-58331	EGELAND	58477-58477	REGAN	58646-58646	MOTT	58849-58849	RAY
58332-58332	ESMOND	58478-58478	ROBINSON	58647-58647	NEW ENGLAND	58852-58852	TIOGA
58335-58335	FORT TOTTEN	58479-58479	ROGERS	58649-58649	REEDER	58853-58853	TRENTON
58337-58337	HAMBERG	58480-58480	SANBORN	58650-58650	REGENT	58854-58854	WATFORD CITY
58338-58338	HAMPDEN	58481-58481	SPIRITWOOD	58651-58651	RHAME	58856-58856	ZAHL
58339-58339	HANSBORO	58482-58482	STEELE	58652-58652	RICHARDTON		
58341-58341	HARVEY	58483-58483	STREETER	58653-58653	SCRANTON		
58343-58343	KNOX	58484-58484	SUTTON	58654-58654	SENTINEL BUTTE		

General Help Numbers:

Governor's Office
77 S High St, 30th Floor   614-466-3555
Columbus, OH 43215   Fax 614-466-9354
www.state.oh.us/gov   8AM-5PM

Attorney General's Office
State office Tower   614-466-4320
30 E Broad St, 17th Floor   Fax 614-644-6135
Columbus, OH 43215-3428   8AM-5PM
www.ag.state.oh.us

State Court Administrator
Supreme Court of Ohio   614-466-2653
30 E Broad St, 3rd Floor   Fax 614-752-8736
Columbus, OH 43266-0419   8AM-5PM
www.sconet.state.oh.us

State Archives
Archives/Library   614-297-2300
1982 Velma Ave   Fax 614-297-2546
Columbus, OH 43211-2497   9AM-5PM TH-SA: 10-5 SU
www.ohiohistory.org/ar_tools.html

State Specifics:

Capital:	Columbus Franklin County
Time Zone:	EST
Number of Counties:	88
Population:	11,256,654
Web Site:	www.state.oh.us

State Agencies

Criminal Records

Ohio Bureau of Investigation, Civilian Background Section, PO Box 365, London, OH 43140 (Courier: 1560 State Rte 56, London, OH 43140); 740-845-2000 (General Info), 740-845-2375 (Civilian Background Cks), 740-845-2633 (Fax), 8AM-4:45PM.

www.webcheck.ag.state.oh.us

Note: The state has an innovative system over the web for electronic transfer of firngerprints.

Indexing & Storage: Records are available from 1921 on. Records from 1972 on are computerized.

Searching: Must have a signed, witnessed release from person of record. Must also have a full set of fingerprints with the release form. They will not release arrests without dispositions. Information required is the FP card, waiver, name, DOB and SSN.

Access by: mail.

Fee & Payment: The search fee is $15.00 per record. Fee payee: Treasurer - State of Ohio. Prepayment required. No credit cards accepted.

Mail search: Turnaround time: 30 days. No self addressed stamped envelope is required.

Corporation Records
Fictitious Name
Limited Partnership Records
Assumed Name
Trademarks/Servicemarks
Limited Liability Company
Records

Secretary of State, Attn: Customer Service, 30 E Broad St, 14th Floor, Columbus, OH 43266-0418; 877-767-3453, 614-466-3910, 614-466-3899 (Fax), 8AM-5PM.

www.state.oh.us/sos

Note: Information regarding officers is available from the Department of Taxation at 614-438-5339.

Indexing & Storage: Records are available from the 1800's. New records are available for inquiry immediately. Records are indexed on microfilm, index cards, inhouse computer.

Searching: Include the following in your request-full name of business. In addition to the articles of incorporation, corporation records include the following information: Annual Reports, Prior (merged) names, Inactive and Reserved names.

Access by: mail, phone, fax, in person, online.

Fee & Payment: There is no search fee or a fee for certification of a document. Copy fees are no charges up to 34 pages, $1.05 for the 35th, and $.03 per copy thereafter. Good Standings are $5.00 each. There is no fee for a corporate printout of limited information. Fee payee: Secretary of State. Prepayment required. Personal checks accepted. No credit cards accepted.

Mail search: Turnaround time: 3-5 days. No self addressed stamped envelope is required.

Phone search: They will release limited information over the phone.

Fax search: No fee, turnaround time is 3-5 days.

In person search: There is no fee to look at records.

Online search: The agency has a free Internet search available for a number of business and corporation records, also includes UCC and campaign finance.

Other access: The state makes the database available for purchase, call for details.

Expedited service: Expedited service is available for mail and phone searches. Turnaround time: 1 day. Add $10.00 per page.

Uniform Commercial Code

UCC Division, 14th Floor, Secretary of State, 30 E Broad St, State Office Tower, Columbus, OH 43215; 877-767-3453, 614-466-3126, 614-466-2892 (Fax), 8AM-5PM.

www.state.oh.us/sos

Indexing & Storage: Records are available for only current or active filings. Records are indexed on inhouse computer.

Searching: Use search form UCC-11. All tax liens are filed at the county level. Include the following in your request-debtor name. Be sure to include the words "any and all addresses" in your search request.

Access by: mail, phone, in person, online.

Fee & Payment: The search fee is $9.00 per debtor name plus $1.00 for each filing listed. Copy charges are: first 34 pages free, page 35 is $1.05, and each additional page is $.03. There is no search fee if the file # and date of recording is given. Fee payee: Secretary of State. Prepayment required. Personal checks accepted. No credit cards accepted.

Mail search: Turnaround time: 2 weeks.

Phone search: Calls are limited to 10 filings, 3 debtor names per call. There is no charge for verbal information.

In person search: Searching is available in person.

Online search: The Internet site offers free online access to records.

Other access: The complete database is available on magnetic tape on a $335 per week basis.

Expedited service: Expedited service is available for mail and phone searches. Turnaround time: 3-5 days. Add $10.00 per debtor name.

Federal Tax Liens
State Tax Liens
Records not maintained by a state level agency.

Note: Records are not housed by a state agency. You must secure from the local county recorder offices.

Sales Tax Registrations
Access to Records is Restricted

Taxation Department, Sale & Use Tax Division, 30 E Broad St, 20th Floor, Columbus, OH 43215; 614-466-7351, 888-405-4039, 614-466-4977 (Fax), 8AM-5PM M-F.

http://www.state.oh.us/tax

Note: This agency refuses to release any information about registrants.

Birth Certificates

Ohio Department of Health, Bureau of Vital Statistics, PO Box 15098, Columbus, OH 43215-0098 (Courier: 35 E Chestnut, 6th Floor, Columbus, OH 43215); 614-466-2531, 614-466-6604 (Fax), 7:45AM-4:30PM.

www.odh.state.oh.us/Birth/birthmain.htm

Indexing & Storage: Records are available from 1908-present. Records are indexed using microfiche and books. It takes 6 months before new records are available for inquiry.

Searching: Include the following in your request-full name, names of parents, mother's maiden name, date of birth, place of birth.

Access by: mail, in person.

Fee & Payment: The fee is $3.00 per name covering a ten year search. If a certified copy is needed, the fee is $9.00. Uncertified copies are $.03 per page plus postage. Fee payee: Treasurer,

State of Ohio Prepayment required. Credit card use only for expedited service. Personal checks accepted. Credit cards accepted: Mastercard, Visa, AmEx, Discover.

Mail search: Turnaround time: 4-6 weeks. No self addressed stamped envelope is required.

In person search: Turnaround time 7-10 days.

Expedited service: Expedited service is available for fax searches at (877) 553-2439. Turnaround time: 5 days.

Death Records

Ohio Department of Health, Bureau of Vital Statistics, PO Box 15098, Columbus, OH 43215-0098 (Courier: 35 E Chestnut, 6th Floor, Columbus, OH 43215); 614-466-2531, 614-466-6604 (Fax), 7:45AM-4:30PM.

www.odh.state.oh.us/Birth/birthmain.htm

Indexing & Storage: Records are available from 1945-present. Death records from 1908-1944 are found at Ohio Historical Society, 1982 Velma Ave, Columbus, OH 43211. Records prior to 1908 are located at the county level.

Searching: Requests must be in writing. Include the following in your request-full name, date of death, place of death.

Access by: mail, fax, in person, online.

Fee & Payment: The fee is $9.00 for a certified copy. The search includes a ten year period. There is an additional $3.00 for each 10 years searched. Uncertified copies are $.03 per page plus postage. Fee payee: Treasurer, State of Ohio. Prepayment required. Credit cards only accepted for expedited service. Personal checks accepted. Credit cards accepted: Mastercard, Visa, AmEx, Discover.

Mail search: Turnaround time: 4-6 weeks. No self addressed stamped envelope is required.

Fax search: See expedited service below.

In person search: Turnaround time is 7-10 days.

Online search: The Ohio Historical Society Death Certificate Index Searchable Database at www.ohiohistory.org/dindex/search.cfm permits searching by name, county, index. Data is available from 1913-1937 only.

Expedited service: Expedited service is available for fax searches at (877) 553-2439 Turnaround time: 5 days. This is available from VitalChek. The fee is $26.75 which includes use of credit card and express delivery.

Marriage Certificates
Divorce Records
Records not maintained by a state level agency.

Note: Marriage and Divorce records are found at county of issue. Marriage or Divorce abstracts (basic information) are available through the state website:
www.odh.state.oh.us/Birth/vr_marriag.htm   or www.odh.state.oh.us/Birth/vr_divor.htm.

Workers' Compensation Records

Bureau of Workers Compensation, Customer Assistance, 30 W Spring St, Fl 10, Columbus, OH 43215-2241; 800-644-6292, 614-752-4732 (Fax), 7:30AM-5:30PM.

www.ohiobwc.com

Indexing & Storage: Records are available for the past 10 years. Records are indexed on inhouse computer. Records are normally destroyed after 10 years if records are inactive.

Searching: All information is public except injured worker medical report and information pertaining to the employer's financial condition. Include the following in your request-claimant name, Social Security Number. Claim number is helpful. All requests must be in writing.

Access by: mail, phone, fax, in person.

Fee & Payment: There is no search fee, copy fee is $.25 per page. Fee payee: Ohio Bureau of Workers Compensation. Prepayment required. Personal checks accepted. No credit cards accepted.

Mail search: Turnaround time: 1 week. A self addressed stamped envelope is requested.

Phone search: They will provide the information immediately unless file is lengthy or excessive.

Fax search: Service is available with a 24 hour turnaround time.

In person search: Call for location of records before going in because there are 22 different office locations.

Other access: Bulk data is released to approved accounts; however, the legal department must approve requesters. The agency has general information available on a web site.

Driver Records

Department of Public Safety, Bureau of Motor Vehicles, 1970 W Broad St, Columbus, OH 43223-1102; 614-752-7600, 8AM-5:30PM M-T-W; 8AM-4:30PM TH-F.

www.ohio.gov/odps

Note: Copies of tickets are available from the Bureau of Motor Vehicles, Transcript Records, PO Box 16520, Columbus 43266-0020. The fee is $1.00 per page.

Indexing & Storage: Records are available for 5 years for moving violations, DWI's and suspensions. Records are purged from public view after 7 years; insurance laws require 36 months of availability. It takes 2-5 weeks before new records are available for inquiry.

Searching: SSNs are not released unless provided by requester (except government agency requesters). Bulk requesters must sign "Agreement for the Sale of Information." Casual requesters cannot obtain records without consent. Include the following in your request-driver's license number, full name, date of birth, Social Security Number. Driver's address is included as part of the search report for permissible requesters, except for requests received from California. The following data is not released: mental health records.

Access by: mail, phone, in person, online.

Fee & Payment: The fee is $2.00 per record for non-CDL (commercial drivers) and $3.00 per

record for CDL. You can purchase a license status record for $2.00. Fee payee: Treasurer, State of Ohio. Prepayment required. Personal checks accepted. No credit cards accepted.

Mail search: Turnaround time: 1-3 days. A self addressed stamped envelope is requested.

Phone search: Pre-approved accounts may order by phone. There is a $100.00 deposit.

In person search: Up to eight records will be processed while you wait.

Online search: The system is called "Defender System" and is suggested for requesters who order 100 or more motor vehicle reports per day in batch mode. Turnaround is in 4-8 hours. The DL# or SSN and name are needed when ordering. For more information, call 614-752-7692.

Other access: Overnight magnetic tape service is available for larger accounts.

Vehicle Ownership
Vehicle Identification

Bureau of Motor Vehicles, Motor Vehicle Title Records, 1970 W Broad St, Columbus, OH 43223-1102; 614-752-7671, 614-752-8929 (Fax), 8AM-5:30PM M-T-W; 8AM-4:30PM TH-F.

www.state.oh.us/odps/division/bmv/bmv/html

Indexing & Storage: Records are available for the current year plus four. It takes 2-5 days normally before new records are available for inquiry.

Searching: Bulk requesters must sign an "Agreement for the Sale of Information." The Social Security Number will not be provided unless included on request. Casual requesters cannot obtain records without consent. Lien information is not recorded on vehicle registration records in Ohio. The following data is not released: Social Security Numbers.

Access by: mail, in person, online.

Fee & Payment: The fee is $2.00 or each record searched. Fee payee: Treasurer, State of Ohio. Prepayment required. Personal checks accepted. No credit cards accepted.

Mail search: Turnaround time: 1-3 days. A self addressed stamped envelope is requested.

In person search: There may be a limit on the number of requests processed immediately, most are not available until the next day.

Online search: Ohio offers online access through AAMVAnet. All requesters must comply with a contractual agreement prior to release of data, which complies with DPPA regulations. Call 614-752-7692 for more information.

Accident Reports

Department of Public Safety, Central Records Unit, PO Box 182074, Columbus, OH 43218-2074; 614-752-1593, 614-644-9749 (Fax), 8AM-4:45PM.

Indexing & Storage: Records are available for 5 years to present. Records are indexed on computer. It takes 2-5 weeks before new records are available for inquiry.

Searching: Include the following in your request-full name, date of accident. Submitting the driver's license number or SSN is very helpful. The following data is not released: Social Security Numbers.

Access by: mail, in person.

Fee & Payment: The fee is $3.00 per record. There is a charge for a no record found. Fee payee: Department of Public Safety. Prepayment required. Personal checks accepted. No credit cards accepted.

Mail search: Turnaround time: 2-3 days.

In person search: Turnaround time is immediate if the record is on file.

Boat & Vessel Ownership
Boat & Vessel Registration

Natural Resources Department, Division of Watercraft, 4435 Fountain Square Dr Bldg A, Columbus, OH 43224-1300; 614-265-6480, 614-267-8883 (Fax), 8AM-5PM.

www.dnr.state.oh.us/odnr/watercraft

Indexing & Storage: Records are available from 1960-the present. Records are indexed on computer for the last 3 years. Any boat operated on public waters must be registered. All boats 14 ft or longer or having a 10+ hp motor must be titled.

Searching: To search, one of the following is required: name, hull ID #, registration #, or serial #. The following data is not released: Social Security Numbers.

Access by: mail, phone, fax, in person.

Fee & Payment: There is no search fee for registration records. There is a $2.00 fee for a title search. Fee payee: Division of Watercraft. Prepayment required. Personal checks accepted. No credit cards accepted.

Mail search: Turnaround time: 2-4 days. No self addressed stamped envelope is required.

Phone search: There is a limit of five names per call for registration information.

Fax search: Same criteria as mail searching.

In person search: Searching is available in person.

Legislation-Current/Pending
Legislation-Passed

Ohio House of Representatives, 77 S High Street, Columbus, OH 43266 (Courier: Ohio Senate, State House, Columbus, OH 43215); 614-466-8842 (In-State Only), 614-466-9745 (Out-of-State), 614-466-3357 (Clerk's Office), 614-644-8744 (Fax), 8:30AM-5PM.

www.legislature.state.oh.us

Note: Note the two addresses for the different bodies.

Indexing & Storage: Records are available from 1888-present on microfiche and are computerized since 1990. Bills for the years 1888-1990 are available on microfilm at many libraries in Ohio.

Searching: Include the following in your request-bill number.

Access by: mail, phone, fax, in person, online.

Fee & Payment: There is no search fee.

Mail search: Turnaround time: 1-2 days.

Phone search: Searching is available by phone.

Fax search: Searching is available by fax.

In person search: Searching is available in person.

Online search: Web site has bill text and status.

Other access: E-mail requests are accepted.

Voter Registration

Secretary of State, Elections Division, 180 E Broad St, 15th Fl, Columbus, OH 43215; 614-466-2585, 614-752-4360 (Fax), 8AM-5PM.

www.state.oh.us/sos

Indexing & Storage: Records are available for 6 years.

Searching: The state suggests that all individual requests be done at the county Board of Elections.

Access by: mail, in person.

Fee & Payment: There is no fee. Fee payee: Secretary of State. Prepayment required. No credit cards accepted.

Mail search: Turnaround time: 1 week to 10 days. No self addressed stamped envelope is required.

In person search: The state is not prepared to handle look-ups, but will assist as necessary.

Other access: Records may be purchased in a variety of formats. Lists are arranged in alpha order within precinct, unless otherwise indicated. For further information, contact Christine Moore at (614) 466-8895.

GED Certificates

Department of Education, State GED Office, 65 S Front Street, Room 210, Columbus, OH 43215-4183; 614-466-4868, 614-752-9445 (Fax), 8-4:45.

www.ode.ohio.gov/www/ae/ae_ged.html

Searching: Include the following in your request- date of birth, Social Security Number, signed release.

Access by: fax, in person.

Fee & Payment: There is no fee for a verification, a $5.00 fee for a copy of a transcript. Fee payee: OH Dept of Education. Prepayment required. No credit cards accepted. No self addressed stamped envelope is required.

Fax search: Same criteria as mail searching.

In person search: Searching is available in person.

Hunting License Information
Fishing License Information
Records not maintained by a state level agency.

Note: They do not have a central database. Only vendors have the names and addresses, which are kept for one year.

Licenses Searchable Online

Accounting Firm #01	www.state.oh.us/acc/search.html
Architect #02	www.state.oh.us/scripts/arc/query.asp
Barber School #26	www.state.oh.us/brb/barbsch.htm
Chiropractor #09	http://156.63.245.111/index.html
Clinical Nurse Specialist #06	www.state.oh.us/scripts/nur/query.asp
Coil Cleaner #27	www.state.oh.us/com/liquor/liquor13.htm
Cosmetic Therapist #28	www.state.oh.us/scripts/med/license/Query.stm
Counselor #11	www.state.oh.us/scripts/csw/query.asp
Dental Assistant Radiologist #33	www.state.oh.us/scripts/den/query.stm
Dental Hygienist #33	www.state.oh.us/scripts/den/query.stm
Dentist #33	www.state.oh.us/scripts/den/query.stm
Engineer #23	www.peps.state.oh.us
Executive Agency Lobbyist #30	www.jlec-olig.state.oh.us/agent_search_form.cfm
Landscape Architect #02	www.state.oh.us/scripts/arc/query.asp
Legislative Agent #30	www.jlec-olig.state.oh.us/agent_search_form.cfm
Legislative Lobbyist #30	www.jlec-olig.state.oh.us/agent_search_form.cfm
Liquor Distributor #27	www.state.oh.us/com/liquor/liquor14.htm
Liquor License #27	www.state.oh.us/com/liquor/phone.txt
Lottery Retailer #35	www.ohiolottery.com/frameset/games/retailer.html
Massage Therapist #28	www.state.oh.us/scripts/med/license/Query.stm
Medical Doctor #28	www.state.oh.us/scripts/med/license/Query.stm
Nurse Anesthetist #06	www.state.oh.us/scripts/nur/query.asp
Nurse Midwife #06	www.state.oh.us/scripts/nur/query.asp
Nurse Practioner #06	www.state.oh.us/scripts/nur/query.asp
Nurse-RN & LPN #06	www.state.oh.us/scripts/nur/query.asp
Optometrist #37	www.state.oh.us/scripts/opt/query.asp
Optometrist-Diagnostic #37	www.state.oh.us/scripts/opt/query.asp
Optometrist-Therapeutic #37	www.state.oh.us/scripts/opt/query.asp
Osteopathic Doctor #28	www.state.oh.us/scripts/med/license/Query.stm
Physician Assistant #28	www.state.oh.us/scripts/med/license/Query.stm
Podiatrist #28	www.state.oh.us/scripts/med/license/Query.stm
Psychologist #36	www2.state.oh.us/psy/query.asp
Public Accountant-CPA #01	www.state.oh.us/acc/search.html
Respiratory Therapist #42	www.state.oh.us/scripts/rsp/query.asp
Respiratory Therapist Student #42	www.state.oh.us/scripts/rsp/query.asp
School Psychologist #36	www2.state.oh.us/psy/query.asp
Social Worker #11	www.state.oh.us/scripts/csw/query.asp
Surveyor #23	www.peps.state.oh.us

Licensing Quick Finder

Accounting Firm #01	614-466-4135
Adoption Agency #19	614-466-3438
Adult Care Home #18	614-466-7713
Airline Liquor #27	614-644-2360
Architect #02	614-466-2316
Athletic Trainer #29	614-466-3774
Attorney #44	614-644-1553
Auctioneer #15	614-466-4130
Audiologist #08	614-466-3145
Audiologist Aide #08	614-466-3145
Backflow Prevention Assemblies Inspector #34	614-644-2248
Bank #13	614-728-8400
Bank #17	614-728-8400
Barber #26	614-466-5003
Barber Instructor #26	614-466-5003
Barber School #26	614-466-5003
Barber Shop #26	614-466-5003
Bedding/Furniture Dealer #38	614-644-2233
Bedding/Furniture Distributor#38	614-644-2233
Bedding/Furniture Manufacturer#38	614-644-2233
Bedding/Furniture Renovator#38	614-644-2233
Boiler Inspector #34	614-644-2248
Boiler Operator #34	614-644-2248
Boxer #32	330-742-5120

Boxing Event #32	330-742-5120
Boxing Inspector #32	330-742-5120
Boxing Judge #32	330-742-5120
Boxing Manager/Trainer/Second #32	330-742-5120
Boxing Official #32	330-742-5120
Boxing Physician #32	330-742-5120
Boxing Promoter/Matchmaker #32	330-742-5120
Boxing Referee #32	330-742-5120
Building Inspector #03	614-644-2613
Building Official #03	614-644-2613
Cemetery #15	216-787-3100
Check Cashing Service #17	614-728-8400
Check Lending Service #17	614-728-8400
Child Day Care Facility #19	614-466-3822
Children's Residential Center #19	614-466-3438
Children's Services Agency #19	614-466-3438
Chiropractor #09	614-644-7032
Clinical Nurse Specialist #06	614-952-3980
Coil Cleaner #27	614-644-2360
Consumer Finance Company #17	614-728-8400
Cosmetic Therapist #28	614-466-3934
Cosmetologist/Managing Cosmetologist #04	614-644-3834
Cosmetology/Manicuring/Esthetician Instructor #04	614-644-3834

Counselor #11	614-466-0912
Credit Service Organization #13	614-466-2221
Credit Union #13	614-466-2221or728-8400
Crematory #05	614-466-4252
Dairy Farm #12	614-466-5550
Dental Assistant Radiologist #33	614-466-2580
Dental Hygienist #33	614-466-2580
Dentist #33	614-466-2580
Dietitian #31	614-466-3291
Drug Wholesaler/Distributor #07	614-466-4143
Electrical Safety Inspector #03	614-644-2613
Electrical Safety Trainee #03	614-644-2613
Elevator Inspector #38	614-644-2233
Embalmer #05	614-466-4252
Emergency Medical Technician #22	614-466-9447
EMT Instructor #22	614-466-9447
Engineer #23	614-466-3650
Engineered Extinguishing Equipment Inspector #34	614-644-2223
Esthetician/Managing Esthetician #04	614-644-3834
Executive Agency Lobbyist #30	614-728-5100
Explosives #34	614-752-7133
Family Foster Home #19	614-466-3438
Fire Alarm & Detection Inspector #34	614-644-2223
Firefighter #22	614-466-9447

Fire Extinguisher Inspector #34 614-644-2223	Nurse Practioner #06 614-952-3980	Real Estate Mortgage Broker #13 614-466-2221
Firefighter Instructor #22 614-466-9447	Nurse-RN & LPN #06 614-952-3980	Real Estate Sales Agent #15 614-466-4100
Fireworks Assistant #34 614-752-7133	Nursing Home #18 614-466-7713	Residential Care #18 614-466-7713
Fireworks Exhibitor #34 614-752-7133	Nursing Home Administrator #18 614-466-5114	Residential Parenting Organization #19
Fishing Guide #21 419-625-8062	Occupational Therapist/Assistant #29	614-466-3438
Foreign Real Estate Property #15 614-466-4100	614-466-3774	Respiratory Therapist #42 614-752-9218
Funeral Director #05............................614-466-4252	Ocularist #39.......................................614-466-9707	Respiratory Therapist Student #42........614-752-9218
Funeral Home #05 614-466-4252	Ocularist Apprentice #39 614-466-9707	Savings & Loan Association #17...........614-728-8400
Health Care Facility #18 614-466-7713	Operators of Group Home #19...............614-466-3438	Savings Bank #17 614-728-8400
Hearing Aid Dealer/Fitter #25 614-466-5215	Optical Dispenser #39 614-466-9707	School Administrator #43 614-466-3593
Horse Facility #41 614-466-2757	Optician #39...614-466-9707	School Counselor #43 614-466-3593
Horse Owner #41 614-466-2757	Optician, Apprentice #39 614-466-9707	School Principal #43.............................614-466-3593
Hotels/Motel #34 614-752-7133	Optometrist #37....................................614-466-5115	School Psychologist #36 614-466-8808
Independent Living Arranger #19 614-466-3438	Optometrist-Diagnostic #37 614-466-5115	Scientific Collecting Permit #21............614-265-6666
Insurance Agent #20............................614-644-2665	Optometrist-Therapeutic #37 614-466-5115	Securities Dealer #16 614-644-7381
Insurance Solicitor #20........................614-644-2665	Osteopathic Doctor #28 614-466-3934	Securities Salesperson #16 614-644-7381
Investment Advisor #16 614-644-7381	Pawn Shop #13.....................................614-466-2221	Security Guard #15 614-466-4130
Investment Advisor Representative #16	Pawnbroker #13....................................614-466-2221	Social Worker #11 614-466-0912
....614-644-7381	Pawnbrokers #17 614-728-8400	Solid Waste Facility Operator #24.........614-644-2621
Landscape Architect #02 614-466-2316	Pesticide Applicator #40 614-728-6987	Speech Pathologist Aide #08 614-466-3145
Legislative Agent #30 614-728-5100	Pesticide Dealer #40 614-728-6987	Speech Pathologist/Audiologist #08 614-466-3145
Legislative Lobbyist #30 614-728-5100	Pesticide Operator #40 614-728-6987	Sprinkler Inspector #03 614-644-2613
Liquor Distributor #27...........................614-644-2360	Pharmacist #07 614-466-4143	Sprinkler Equipment Inspector #34 614-644-2223
Liquor License #27...............................614-644-2360	Pharmacy Company #07 614-466-4143	Sprinkler, Fire Alarm, & Hazardous Designer #03
Lottery Retailer #35.............................216-787-3200	Pharmacy Dispensary #07.....................614-466-4143	614-644-2613
Manicurist/Managing Manicurist #04 614-644-3834	Physical Therapist/Assistant #29 614-466-3774	Stationary Steam #34............................614-644-2004
Massage Therapist #28 614-466-3934	Physician Assistant #28.........................614-466-3934	Steam Engineer #34..............................614-644-2248
Mechanical Inspector #03.....................614-644-2613	Plan Examiner #03................................614-644-2613	Surveyor #23 614-466-3650
Medical Doctor #28 614-466-3934	Podiatrist #28 614-466-3934	Teacher/Teacher's Aide #43..................614-466-3593
Milk Hauler/Tester #12 614-466-5550	Precious Metal Dealer #17 614-728-8400	Track Personnel, Trainers, etc. #41 614-466-2757
Milk Plant #12 614-466-5550	Precious Metals Dealer #13...................614-466-2221	Travel Agent #34...................................614-752-7133
Milk Processor/Producer #12 614-466-5550	Premium Finance Company #13 614-466-2221	Travel Agent/Tour Promoter #34...........614-752-7133
Milk Sampler #12 614-466-5550	Pressure Piping Inspect. #34 614-644-2248	Treasurer & Business Manager #43.......614-466-3593
Mortgage Broker #17............................614-728-8400	Private Investigator #15........................614-466-4130	Underground Storage Tank #34............614-836-7881
Mortgage Loan Act #13 614-466-2221	Psychologist #36 614-466-8808	Underground Storage Tank Inspector #34
Non Resident Insurance Broker #20 614-644-2665	Public Accountant-CPA #01..................614-752-8248	614-836-7881
Non-resident Broker #20 614-644-2665	Public Adjuster #20 614-644-2665	Underground Storage Tank Installer #34
Notary Public #10.................................614-466-2566	Racing #41 614-466-2757	614-836-7881
Nurse Anesthetist #06 614-952-3980	Real Estate Appraiser #15....................216-787-3100	Veterinarian #45...................................614-644-5281
Nurse Midwife #06 614-952-3980	Real Estate Broker #15 614-466-4100	Veterinary Technician #45....................614-644-5281

Licensing Agency Information

01 Accountancy Board of Ohio, 77 S High St, 18th Fl, Columbus, OH 43266-0301; 614-466-4135, Fax: 614-466-2628.
www.state.oh.us/acc

Direct URL to search licenses: www.state.oh.us/acc/search.html You can search online using name or license #

02 Architects Board of Ohio, 77 S High St, 16th Fl, Columbus, OH 43266-0303; 614-466-2316, Fax: 614-644-9048.
www.state.oh.us/arc

Direct URL to search licenses: www.state.oh.us/scripts/arc/query.asp You can search online using name and license number.

03 Board of Building Standards, PO Box 4009 (6606 Tussing Rd), Reynoldsburg, OH 43068-9009; 614-644-2613, Fax: 614-644-3147.
www.com.state.oh.us/dic/Default.htm

04 Board of Cosmetology, 1010 Sland Mall, Columbus, OH 43207-4041; 614-466-3834, Fax: 614-644-6880.
www.state.oh.us/cos An online search system is planned. Once available, the web address will be www.state.oh.us/cos/licensedb.htm.

05 Board of Embalmers & Funeral Directors of Ohio, 77 S High St, 16th Fl, Columbus, OH 43266; 614-466-4252, Fax: 614-728-6825.
www.ohio.gov/fun

06 Board of Nursing, 17 S High St #400, Columbus, OH 43215; 614-466-3947, Fax: 614-466-0388.

www.state.oh.us/nvr

Direct URL to search licenses: www.state.oh.us/nvr You can search online using SSN, license number.

07 Board of Pharmacy, 77 S High St, 17th Fl, Columbus, OH 43266-0320; 614-466-4143, Fax: 614-752-4836.

www.ohio.gov/pharmacy

08 Board of Speech Pathology & Audiology, 77 S High St, 16th Fl, Columbus, OH 43266-0324; 614-466-3145, Fax: 614-995-2286.

09 Chiropractic Board, 77 S High St, 16th Fl, Columbus, OH 43266-0542; 614-644-7032, Fax: 614-752-2539.
www.state.oh.us/chr

Direct URL to search licenses: http://156.63.245.111/index.html You can search online using name, license #, city, state, zip No Online searches

10 Commission Clerk, 77 S High St, 19th Fl, Columbus, OH 43215; 614-466-2566.

11 Counselor & Social Worker Board, 77 S High St, 16th Fl, Columbus, OH 43266-0340; 614-466-0912, Fax: 614-728-7790.
www.state.oh.us/csw

Direct URL to search licenses: www.state.oh.us/scripts/csw/query.asp You can search online using name and license number.

12 Department of Agriculture, 8995 E Main St, Reynoldsburg, OH 43068-3399; 614-466-5550, Fax: 614-728-2652.

www.state.oh.us/agr

15 Department of Commerce, Division of Real Estate & Professional Licensing, 77 S High St, 20th Fl, Columbus, OH 43266-0547; 614-466-4130, Fax: 614-466-0584.

www.com.state.oh.us/real

16 Department of Commerce, Division of Securities, 77 S High St, 22nd Fl, Columbus, OH 43215-0548; 614-644-7381, Fax: 614-466-3316.

www.securities.state.oh.us

17 Department of Commerce, Division of Financial Institutions, 77 S High St, 21st Fl, Columbus, OH 43266-0121; 614-466-2221, Fax: 614-466-1631.

www.com.state.oh.us/dfi/default.htm

18 Department of Health, PO Box 118 (246 N High St), Columbus, OH 43266-0118; 614-466-5114, Fax: 614-466-0271.

www.odh.state.oh.us

19 Department of Human Services, 65 E State St, 2nd Fl, Columbus, OH 43215; 614-466-3438, Fax: 614-728-9682; 614-752-2580.

www.oh.state.oh.us/odhs/oapl

20 Department of Insurance, 2100 Stella Ct, Columbus, OH 43215-1067; 614-644-2665, Fax: 614-644-3475.

www.ohio.gov/ins

21 Department of Natural Resources, 1840 Belcher Dr, Columbus, OH 43224; 614-265-7040, Fax: 614-262-1143.

www.dnr.state.oh.us

22 Department of Public Safety, PO Box 182073 (1970 W Broad St), Columbus, OH 43218-2073; 614-466-9447, Fax: 614-466-9461.

www.state.oh.us/odps

23 Engineers & Surveyors Board, 77 S High St, 16th Fl, Columbus, OH 43266-0314; 614-466-3650, Fax: 614-728-3059.

www.peps.state.oh.us

Direct URL to search licenses: www.peps.state.oh.us/sbdefault.htm You can search online using name, company name, license number and county.

24 Hazardous Waste Facility Board, PO Box 1049 (1800 WaterMark Dr), Columbus, OH 43216-1049; 614-644-3020, Fax: 614-728-5315.

www.epd.state.oh.us/DSIWM

25 Hearing Aid Dealers & Fitters Board, PO Box 118 (246 N High St), Columbus, OH 43266-0118; 614-466-5215, Fax: 614-466-0271.

26 Licensing Boards, 77 S High St, 16th Fl, Columbus, OH 43266-0304; 614-466-5003, Fax: 614-644-8112.

www.state.oh.us/brb

27 Division of Liquor Control, 6606 Tussing Rd, Reynoldsburg, OH 43068-9005; 614-644-2360, Fax: 614-644-2480.

www.state.oh.us/com/liquor/liquor.htm

28 Medical Board of Ohio, 77 S High St, 17th Fl, Columbus, OH 43266-0315; 614-466-3934, Fax: 614-728-5946.

www.state.oh.us/med

Direct URL to search licenses: www.state.oh.us/scripts/med/license/Query.stm You can search online using name and license number.

29 OT, PT, 77 S High St, 16th Fl, Columbus, OH 43266-0317; 614-466-3774, Fax: 614-644-8112.

www.state.oh.us/pyt

30 Office of Legislative Inspector General, 50 W Broad St, #1308, Columbus, OH 43215-3365; 614-728-5100, Fax: 614-728-5074.

www.jlec-olig.state.oh.us

Direct URL to search licenses: www.jlec-olig.state.oh.us/agent_search_form.cfm You can search online using name.

31 Board of Dietetics, 77 S High St, 18th Fl, Columbus, OH 43266-0337; 614-466-3291, Fax: 614-728-0723.

www.state.oh.us/obd

32 Boxing Commission, 2545 Belmont Ave, Union Square Plaza, Youngstown, OH 44505; 330-742-5120, Fax: 330-742-2571.

33 Dental Board, 77 S High St, 18th Fl, Columbus, OH 43266-0306; 614-466-2580, Fax: 614-752-8995.

www.state.oh.us/den

Direct URL to search licenses: www.state.oh.us/scripts/den/query.stm You can search online using name, license number, and SSN.

34 Ohio Department of Commerce, PO Box 4009 (6606 Tussing Rd), Reynoldsburg, OH 43068-9009; 614-644-2223, Fax: 614-644-2428.

35 Lottery Commission, 615 W Superior Ave, NW Frank J. Lausche Bldg, Cleveland, OH 44113; 216-787-3200, Fax: 216-787-3718.

www.ohiolottery.com

Direct URL to search licenses: www.ohiolottery.com/frameset/games/retailer.html You can search online using name, city, ZIP Code, and county.

36 Board of Psychology, 77 S High St, 18th Fl, Columbus, OH 43266-0321; 614-466-8808, Fax: 614-728-7081.

www.state.oh.us/psy

Direct URL to search licenses: www2.state.oh.us/psy/query.asp You can search online using licensee name or license number. If "SP" is part of a license number, that indicates a "school psychologist."

37 Board of Optometry, 77 S High St, 16th Fl, Columbus, OH 43266-0318; 614-466-5115, Fax: 614-644-3937.

www.state.oh.us/opt

Direct URL to search licenses: www.state.oh.us/scripts/opt/query.asp You can search online using name.

38 Operations & Maintenance, PO Box 4009 (6606 Tussing Rd), Reynoldsburg, OH 43068-9009; 614-644-2233, Fax: 614-644-2428.

www.state.oh.us/com/fin/index.htm

39 Optical Dispensers Board, 77 S High St, 16th Fl, Columbus, OH 43266-0328; 614-466-9707, Fax: 614-995-5392.

www.state.oh.us/odb

40 Pesticide Regulations, 8995 E Main St, Reynoldsburg, OH 43068-3399; 614-728-6200, Fax: 614-728-4235.

www.state.oh.us/agr

41 Racing Commission, 77 S High St, 18th Fl, Columbus, OH 43266-0416; 614-466-2757, Fax: 614-466-1900.

42 Respiratory Care Board, 77 S High St, 16th Fl, Columbus, OH 43266-0777; 614-752-9218, Fax: 614-728-8691.

www.state.oh.us/rsp

Direct URL to search licenses: www.state.oh.us/scripts/rsp/query.asp You can search online using name

43 Department of Education, 65 S Front St, Rm 412, Columbus, OH 43215-4183; 614-466-3593, Fax: 614-466-1999.

www.ode.ohio.gov/www/tc/teacher.html

44 Supreme Court, 30 E Broad St, Columbus, OH 43266-0419; 614-644-1553, Fax: 614-728-0930.

45 Veterinary Medical Board, 77 S High St, 16th Fl, Columbus, OH 43266-0116; 614-644-5281, Fax: 614-644-9038.

The following list indicates the district and division name for each county in the state. If the district or division name of the bankruptcy court is different from the civil/criminal court, it appears in parentheses.

County/Court Cross Reference

County	District	Division
Adams	Southern	Cincinnati
Allen	Northern	Toledo
Ashland	Northern	Cleveland (Canton)
Ashtabula	Northern	Cleveland (Youngstown)
Athens	Southern	Columbus
Auglaize	Northern	Toledo
Belmont	Southern	Columbus
Brown	Southern	Cincinnati
Butler	Southern	Cincinnati (Dayton)
Carroll	Northern	Akron (Canton)
Champaign	Southern	Dayton
Clark	Southern	Dayton
Clermont	Southern	Cincinnati
Clinton	Southern	Cincinnati (Dayton)
Columbiana	Northern	Youngstown
Coshocton	Southern	Columbus
Crawford	Northern	Cleveland (Canton)
Cuyahoga	Northern	Cleveland
Darke	Southern	Dayton
Defiance	Northern	Toledo
Delaware	Southern	Columbus
Erie	Northern	Toledo
Fairfield	Southern	Columbus
Fayette	Southern	Columbus
Franklin	Southern	Columbus
Fulton	Northern	Toledo
Gallia	Southern	Columbus
Geauga	Northern	Cleveland
Greene	Southern	Dayton
Guernsey	Southern	Columbus
Hamilton	Southern	Cincinnati
Hancock	Northern	Toledo
Hardin	Northern	Toledo
Harrison	Southern	Columbus
Henry	Northern	Toledo
Highland	Southern	Cincinnati
Hocking	Southern	Columbus
Holmes	Northern	Akron (Canton)
Huron	Northern	Toledo
Jackson	Southern	Columbus
Jefferson	Southern	Columbus
Knox	Southern	Columbus
Lake	Northern	Cleveland
Lawrence	Southern	Cincinnati
Licking	Southern	Columbus
Logan	Southern	Columbus
Lorain	Northern	Cleveland
Lucas	Northern	Toledo
Madison	Southern	Columbus
Mahoning	Northern	Youngstown
Marion	Northern	Toledo
Medina	Northern	Cleveland (Akron)
Meigs	Southern	Columbus
Mercer	Northern	Toledo
Miami	Southern	Dayton
Monroe	Southern	Columbus
Montgomery	Southern	Dayton
Morgan	Southern	Columbus
Morrow	Southern	Columbus
Muskingum	Southern	Columbus
Noble	Southern	Columbus
Ottawa	Northern	Toledo
Paulding	Northern	Toledo
Perry	Southern	Columbus
Pickaway	Southern	Columbus
Pike	Southern	Columbus
Portage	Northern	Akron
Preble	Southern	Dayton
Putnam	Northern	Toledo
Richland	Northern	Cleveland (Canton)
Ross	Southern	Columbus
Sandusky	Northern	Toledo
Scioto	Southern	Cincinnati
Seneca	Northern	Toledo
Shelby	Southern	Dayton
Stark	Northern	Akron (Canton)
Summit	Northern	Akron
Trumbull	Northern	Youngstown
Tuscarawas	Northern	Akron (Canton)
Union	Southern	Columbus
Van Wert	Northern	Toledo
Vinton	Southern	Columbus
Warren	Southern	Cincinnati (Dayton)
Washington	Southern	Columbus
Wayne	Northern	Akron (Canton)
Williams	Northern	Toledo
Wood	Northern	Toledo
Wyandot	Northern	Toledo

US District Court

Northern District of Ohio

Akron Division 568 Federal Bldg, 2 S Main St, Akron, OH 44308, 330-375-5407.

www.ohnd.uscourts.gov

Counties: Carroll, Holmes, Portage, Stark, Summit, Tuscarawas, Wayne. Cases filed prior to 1995 for counties in the Youngstown Division may be located here.

Indexing & Storage: Cases are indexed by defendant and plaintiff as well as by case number. New cases are available in the index immediately after filing date. A computer index is maintained. Open records are located at this court. Open cases may be located in another division in this district, depending on the judge assigned.

Fee & Payment: The fee is $15.00 per item (one party name or case number). Payment may be made by money order, cashier check, personal check. Prepayment is required. Payee: Clerk, US District Court. Certification fee: $5.00 per document. Copy fee: $.50 per page.

Phone Search: Only docket information is available by phone. An automated voice case information service (VCIS) is not available.

Mail Search: Always enclose a stamped self addressed envelope.

In Person Search: In person searching is available.

PACER: Sign-up number is 800-676-6856. Access fee is $.60 per minute. Toll-free access: 800-673-4409. Local access: 216-522-3669. Many cases prior to the indicated dates are also online. Case records are available back to January 1, 1990. Records are never purged. New records are available online after 1 day. PACER is available on the Internet at http://pacer.ohnd.uscourts.gov.

Electronic Filing: Only law firms and practictioners may file cases electronically. Anyone can search online; however, the search results only include cases which were filed electronically. To search, visit http://ecf.ohnd.uscourts.gov/cgi-bin/ PublicCaseFiled-Rpt.pl. Electronic filing information is available online at http://ecf.ohnd.uscourts.gov

Cleveland Division 201 Superior Ave, NE, Cleveland, OH 44114, 216-522-4355, Fax: 216-522-2140.

Counties: Ashland, Ashtabula, Crawford, Cuyahoga, Geauga, Lake, Lorain, Medina, Richland. Cases prior to July 1995 for the counties of Ashland, Crawford, Medina and Richland are located in the Akron Division. Cases filed prior to 1995 from the counties in theYoungstown Division may be located here.

Indexing & Storage: Cases are indexed by defendant and plaintiff as well as by case number. New cases are available in the index immediately after filing date. A computer index is maintained. Open records are located at this court. Open cases may be located in other divisions in this district, depending on the judge assigned.

Fee & Payment: The fee is $15.00 per item (one party name or case number). Payment may be made by money order, cashier check, personal check. Prepayment is required. Payee: Clerk, US District Court. Certification fee: $5.00 per document. Copy fee: $.50 per page. You are allowed to make your own copies. These copies cost $.25 per page.

Phone Search: Only docket information is available by phone. An automated voice case information service (VCIS) is not available.

Mail Search: A stamped self addressed envelope is not required.

In Person Search: In person searching is available.

PACER: Sign-up number is 800-676-6856. Access fee is $.60 per minute. Toll-free access: 800-673-4409. Local access: 216-522-3669. Many cases prior to the indicated dates are also online. Case records are available back to January 1, 1990. Records are never purged. New records are available online after 1 day. PACER is available on the Internet at http://pacer.ohnd.uscourts.gov.

Electronic Filing: Only law firms and practictioners may file cases electronically. Anyone can search online; however, the search results only include cases which were filed electronically. To search, visit http://ecf.ohnd.uscourts.gov/cgi-bin/PublicCaseFiled-Rpt.pl. Electronic filing information is available online at http://ecf.ohnd.uscourts.gov

Toledo Division 114 US Courthouse, 1716 Spielbusch, Toledo, OH 43624, 419-259-6412.

www.ohnd.uscourts.gov

Counties: Allen, Auglaize, Defiance, Erie, Fulton, Hancock, Hardin, Henry, Huron, Lucas, Marion, Mercer, Ottawa, Paulding, Putnam, Sandusky, Seneca, Van Wert, Williams, Wood, Wyandot.

Indexing & Storage: Cases are indexed by defendant and plaintiff as well as by case number. New cases are available in the index within 1 day after filing date. A computer index is maintained. Open records are located at this court.

Fee & Payment: The fee is $15.00 per item (one party name or case number). Payment may be made by money order, cashier check, personal check. Prepayment is required. Payee: Clerk, US District Court. Certification fee: $5.00 per document. Copy fee: $.50 per page.

Phone Search: Only docket information is available by phone. An automated voice case information service (VCIS) is not available.

Mail Search: Always enclose a stamped self addressed envelope.

In Person Search: In person searching is available.

PACER: Sign-up number is 800-676-6856. Access fee is $.60 per minute. Toll-free access: 800-673-4409. Local access: 216-522-3669. Many cases prior to the indicated dates are also online. Case records are available back to January 1, 1990. Records are never purged. New records are available online after 1 day. PACER is available on the Internet at http://pacer.ohnd.uscourts.gov.

Electronic Filing: Only law firms and practictioners may file cases electronically. Anyone can search online; however, the search results only include cases which were filed electronically. To search, visit http://ecf.ohnd.uscourts.gov/cgi-bin/PublicCaseFiled-Rpt.pl. Electronic filing information is available online at http://ecf.ohnd.uscourts.gov

Youngstown Division 337 Federal Bldg, 125 Market St, Youngstown, OH 44503-1787, 330-746-1726, Fax: 330-746-2027.

www.ohnd.uscourts.gov

Counties: Columbiana, Mahoning, Trumbull. This division was reactivated in the middle of 1995. Older cases will be found in Akron or Cleveland.

Indexing & Storage: Cases are indexed by defendant and plaintiff as well as by case number. New cases are available in the index immediately after filing date. A computer index is maintained. Open records are located at this court. Open cases may also be located in other divisions in this district, depending upon the judge assigned.

Fee & Payment: The fee is $15.00 per item (one party name or case number). Payment may be made by money order, cashier check, personal check. Prepayment is required. Payee: Clerk, US District Court. Certification fee: $5.00 per document. Copy fee: $.50 per page.

Phone Search: Only docket information is available by phone. An automated voice case information service (VCIS) is not available.

Fax Search: Prepayment is required for all fax requests.

Mail Search: Always enclose a stamped self addressed envelope.

In Person Search: In person searching is available.

PACER: Sign-up number is 800-676-6856. Access fee is $.60 per minute. Toll-free access: 800-673-4409. Local access: 216-522-3669. Many cases prior to the indicated dates are also online. Case records are available back to January 1, 1990. Records are never purged. New records are available online after 1 day. PACER is available on the Internet at http://pacer.ohnd.uscourts.gov.

Electronic Filing: Only law firms and practictioners may file cases electronically. Anyone can search online; however, the search results only include cases which were filed electronically. To search, visit http://ecf.ohnd.uscourts.gov/cgi-bin/ PublicCaseFiled-Rpt.pl. Electronic filing information is available online at http://ecf.obnd.uscourts.gov

US Bankruptcy Court
Northern District of Ohio

Akron Division 455 Federal Bldg, 2 S Main, Akron, OH 44308, 330-375-5840.

www.ohnb.uscourts.gov

Counties: Medina, Portage, Summit.

Indexing & Storage: Cases are indexed by debtor as well as by case number. New cases are available in the index 1-2 days after filing date. Both computer and card indexes are maintained. Open records are located at this court. Case records closed before 1993 were sent to the Chicago Federal Records Center. In Spring 1995, the 1994 closed cases were sent to Dayton.

Fee & Payment: The fee is $15.00 per item (one party name or case number). Payment may be made by money order, cashier check, personal check, Visa or Mastercard. Prepayment is required. Payee: Clerk, US Bankruptcy Court. Certification fee: $5.00 per document. Copy fee: $.50 per page. You are allowed to make your own copies. These copies cost $.25 per page.

Phone Search: An automated voice case information service (VCIS) is available. Call VCIS at 800-898-6899 or 330-489-4731.

Mail Search: Always enclose a stamped self addressed envelope.

In Person Search: In person searching is available.

PACER: Sign-up number is 800-676-6856. Access fee is $.60 per minute. Toll-free access: 800-579-5735. Local access: 330-489-4779. Case records are available back to January 1985. Records are purged only up to September 1990. New civil records are available online after 2 days.

Canton Division Frank T Bow Federal Bldg, 201 Cleveland Ave SW, Canton, OH 44702, 330-489-4426, Fax: 330-489-4434.

www.ohnb.uscourts.gov

Counties: Ashland, Carroll, Crawford, Holmes, Richland, Stark, Tuscarawas, Wayne.

Indexing & Storage: Cases are indexed by debtor as well as by case number. New cases are available in the index 48 hours after filing date. A computer index is maintained. Records are indexed on computer from 1985 to the present. Records are indexed on index cards from 1982 to 1984, and also journalized in books from 1984 to 1990. Open records are located at this court. Prior to 1995, closed case records were sent to the Chicago Federal Records Center.

Fee & Payment: The fee is $15.00 per item (one party name or case number). Payment may be made by money order, cashier check, personal check, Visa or Mastercard. Prepayment is required. Debtor's checks are not accepted. Payee: Clerk, US Bankruptcy Court. Certification fee: $5.00 per document. Copy fee: $.50 per page. You are allowed to make your own copies. These copies cost $.25 per page.

Phone Search: An automated voice case information service (VCIS) is available. Call VCIS at 800-898-6899 or 330-489-4731.

Fax Search: Will accept fax search request, but will not process until fee is received.

Mail Search: Always enclose a stamped self addressed envelope.

In Person Search: In person searching is available.

PACER: Sign-up number is 800-676-6856. Access fee is $.60 per minute. Toll-free access: 800-579-5735. Local access: 330-489-4779. Case records are available back to January 1985. Records are purged only up to September 1990. New civil records are available online after 2 days.

Cleveland Division Key Tower, Room 3001, 127 Public Square, Cleveland, OH 44114, 216-522-4373.

www.ohnb.uscourts.gov

Counties: Cuyahoga, Geauga, Lake, Lorain.

Indexing & Storage: Cases are indexed by debtor as well as by case number. New cases are available in the index 2 days after filing date. Both computer and card indexes are maintained. Records are also indexed on microfiche. Open records are located at this court. Prior to 1995, closed case records were sent to the Chicago Federal Records Center.

Fee & Payment: The fee is $15.00 per item (one party name or case number). Payment may be made by money order, personal check. Debtor's checks are not accepted. Payee: Clerk, US Bankruptcy Court. Certification fee: $5.00 per document. Copy fee: $.50 per page.

Phone Search: An automated voice case information service (VCIS) is available. Call VCIS at 800-898-6899 or 330-489-4731.

Mail Search: Always enclose a stamped self addressed envelope.

In Person Search: In person searching is available.

PACER: Sign-up number is 800-676-6856. Access fee is $.60 per minute. Toll-free access: 800-579-5735. Local access: 330-489-4779. Case records are available back to January 1985. Records are purged only up to September 1990. New civil records are available online after 2 days.

Toledo Division Room 411, 1716 Spielbusch Ave, Toledo, OH 43624, 419-259-6440.

www.ohnb.uscourts.gov

Counties: Allen, Auglaize, Defiance, Erie, Fulton, Hancock, Hardin, Henry, Huron, Lucas, Marion, Mercer, Ottawa, Paulding, Putnam, Sandusky, Seneca, Van Wert, Williams, Wood, Wyandot.

Indexing & Storage: Cases are indexed by debtor as well as by case number. New cases are available in the index 24 hours after filing date. A computer index is maintained. Open records are located at this court. Prior to 1995, closed case records were sent to the Chicago Federal Records Center.

Fee & Payment: The fee is $15.00 per item (one party name or case number). Payment may be made by money order, cashier check, business check, Visa or Mastercard. Personal checks are not accepted. Prepayment is required. Payee: Clerk, US Bankruptcy Court. Certification fee: $5.00 per document. Copy fee: $.50 per page.

Phone Search: An automated voice case information service (VCIS) is available. Call VCIS at 800-898-6899 or 330-489-4731.

Mail Search: Always enclose a stamped self addressed envelope.

In Person Search: In person searching is available.

PACER: Sign-up number is 800-676-6856. Access fee is $.60 per minute. Toll-free access: 800-579-5735. Local access: 330-489-4779. Case records are available back to January 1985. Records are purged only up to September 1990. New civil records are available online after 2 days.

Youngstown Division PO Box 147, Youngstown, OH 44501 (Courier Address: 125 Market St, #210, Youngstown, OH 44503), 330-746-7027.

www.ohnb.uscourts.gov

Counties: Ashtabula, Columbiana, Mahoning, Trumbull.

Indexing & Storage: Cases are indexed by debtor and creditors as well as by case number. New cases are available in the index 24 hours after filing date. A card index is maintained. Open records are located at this court. Prior to 1995, closed cases were sent to the Chicago Federal Records Center. Now case records are sent to the Dayton Federal Records Center every few years.

Fee & Payment: The fee is $15.00 per item (one party name or case number). Payment may be made by money order, cashier check, business check, Visa or Mastercard. Personal checks are not accepted. Prepayment is required. Payee: Clerk, US Bankruptcy Court. Certification fee: $5.00 per document. Copy fee: $.50 per page.

Phone Search: An automated voice case information service (VCIS) is available. Call VCIS at 800-898-6899 or 330-489-4731.

Mail Search: A stamped self addressed envelope is not required.

In Person Search: In person searching is available.

PACER: Sign-up number is 800-676-6856. Access fee is $.60 per minute. Toll-free access: 800-579-5735. Local access: 330-489-4779. Case records are available back to January 1985. Records are purged only up to September 1990. New civil records are available online after 2 days.

US District Court

Southern District of Ohio

Cincinnati Division Clerk, US District Court, 324 Potter Stewart Courthouse, 100 E 5th St, Cincinnati, OH 45202, 513-564-7500, Fax: 513-564-7505.

Counties: Adams, Brown, Butler, Clermont, Clinton, Hamilton, Highland, Lawrence, Scioto, Warren.

Indexing & Storage: Cases are indexed by defendant and plaintiff as well as by case number. New cases are available in the index immediately after filing date. A computer index is maintained. Open records are located at this court.

Fee & Payment: The fee is $15.00 per item (one party name or case number). Payment may be made by money order, cashier check, personal check. Prepayment is required. Give FedEx account number for expedited copy delivery.

Payee: Clerk, US District Court. Certification fee: $5.00 per document. Copy fee: $.50 per page.

Phone Search: Only docket information is available by phone. An automated voice case information service (VCIS) is not available.

Mail Search: A stamped self addressed envelope is not required.

In Person Search: In person searching is available.

PACER: Sign-up number is 800-676-6856. Access fee is $1.00 per minute. Toll-free access: 800-710-4939. Local access: 614-469-6990, 614-469-7460. Case records are available back to June January 1994. Records are never purged. New records are available online after 1 day. PACER is available on the Internet at http://pacer.ohsd.uscourts.gov.

Columbus Division Office of the clerk, Room 260, 85 Marconi Blvd, Columbus, OH 43215, 614-719-3000, Fax: 614-469-5953.

Counties: Athens, Belmont, Coshocton, Delaware, Fairfield, Fayette, Franklin, Gallia, Guernsey, Harrison, Hocking, Jackson, Jefferson, Knox, Licking, Logan, Madison, Meigs, Monroe, Morgan, Morrow, Muskingum, Noble, Perry, Pickaway, Pike, Ross, Union, Vinton, Washington.

Indexing & Storage: Cases are indexed by defendant and plaintiff as well as by case number. New cases are available in the index 1-2 days after filing date. Both computer and card indexes are maintained. Records are also indexed on microfiche back to 1982. Open records are located at this court. District wide searches are available from this division.

Fee & Payment: The fee is $15.00 per item (one party name or case number). Payment may be made by money order, cashier check, business check. Personal checks are not accepted. Prepayment is required. Payee: Clerk, US District Court. Certification fee: $5.00 per document. Copy fee: $.50 per page.

Phone Search: Only docket information is available by phone. An automated voice case information service (VCIS) is not available.

Mail Search: Always enclose a stamped self addressed envelope.

In Person Search: In person searching is available.

PACER: Sign-up number is 800-676-6856. Access fee is $1.00 per minute. Toll-free access: 800-710-4939. Local access: 614-469-6990, 614-469-7460. Case records are available back to June January 1994. Records are never purged. New records are available online after 1 day. PACER is available online at http://pacer.ohsd.uscourts.gov.

Dayton Division Federal Bldg, 200 W 2nd, Room 712, Dayton, OH 45402, 937-512-1400.

Counties: Champaign, Clark, Darke, Greene, Miami, Montgomery, Preble, Shelby.

Indexing & Storage: Cases are indexed by defendant and plaintiff as well as by case number. New cases are available in the index 1 day after filing date. Both computer and card indexes are maintained. Records are also indexed on microfiche. The computer is only valid for cases that were open and pending from 1/90 to present. A view box is available to the public for cases filed for the present day that have not been entered into the computer. Open records are located at this court.

Fee & Payment: The fee is $15.00 per item (one party name or case number). Payment may be made by money order, cashier check, business check. Personal checks are not accepted. Prepayment is required. The Clerk's office will not respond to telephone requests that involve copywork. The searcher must provide a wide envelope for return of documents or, if documents are bulky, the searcher must provide access for bulk mailing. Payee: Clerk, US District Court. Certification fee: $5.00 per document. Copy fee: $.50 per page.

Phone Search: Over the phone, this court will only reveal whether a case has been filed. An automated voice case information service (VCIS) is not available.

Mail Search: Always enclose a stamped self addressed envelope.

In Person Search: In person searching is available.

PACER: Sign-up number is 800-676-6856. Access fee is $1.00 per minute. Toll-free access: 800-710-4939. Local access: 614-469-6990, 614-469-7460. Case records are available back to June January 1994. Records are never purged. New records are available online after 1 day. PACER is available online at http://pacer.ohsd.uscourts.gov.

US Bankruptcy Court

Southern District of Ohio

Cincinnati Division Atrium Two, Suite 800, 221 E Fourth St, Cincinnati, OH 45202, 513-684-2572.

Counties: Adams, Brown, Clermont, Hamilton, Highland, Lawrence, Scioto and a part of Butler.

Indexing & Storage: Cases are indexed by debtor as well as by case number. New cases are available in the index 2 days after filing date. A computer index is maintained. Open records are located at this court. Prior to 1993, closed case records were sent to the Chicago Federal Records Center.

Fee & Payment: The fee is $15.00 per item (one party name or case number). Payment may be made by money order, cashier check. Business checks are not accepted, Visa or Mastercard.

Personal checks are not accepted. Credit cards are accepted only from law firms. Debtor checks are not accepted. Payee: Clerk, US Bankruptcy Court. Certification fee: $5.00 per document. Copy fee: $.50 per page.

Phone Search: Only docket information is available by phone. An automated voice case information service (VCIS) is available. Call VCIS at 800-726-1004 or 937-225-2544.

Mail Search: Always enclose a stamped self addressed envelope.

In Person Search: In person searching is available.

PACER: Sign-up number is 800-676-6856. Access fee is $.60 per minute. Toll-free access: 800-793-7003. Local access: 937-225-7561. Case records are available back to 1990. Records are purged every six months. New civil records are available online after 1 day. PACER is available on the Internet at http://pacer.ohsb.uscourts.gov.

Columbus Division 170 N High St, Columbus, OH 43215, 614-469-6638.

Counties: Athens, Belmont, Coshocton, Delaware, Fairfield, Fayette, Franklin, Gallia, Guernsey, Harrison, Hocking, Jackson, Jefferson, Knox, Licking, Logan, Madison, Meigs, Monroe, Morgan, Morrow, Muskingum, Noble, Perry, Pickaway, Pike, Ross, Union, Vinton,Washington.

Indexing & Storage: Cases are indexed by as well as by case number. New cases are available in the index within 1 day after filing date. A computer index is maintained. Open records are located at this court. Prior to 1993, closed cases were sent to the Chicago Federal Records Facility.

Fee & Payment: The fee is $15.00 per item (one party name or case number). Payment may be made by money order, cashier check, business check. Personal checks are not accepted. Debtor's checks are not accepted. Payee: Clerk, US Bankruptcy Court. Certification fee: $5.00 per document. Copy fee: $.50 per page.

Phone Search: An automated voice case information service (VCIS) is available. Call VCIS at 800-726-1006 or 513-225-2562.

Mail Search: A stamped self addressed envelope is not required.

In Person Search: In person searching is available.

PACER: Sign-up number is 800-676-6856. Access fee is $.60 per minute. Toll-free access: 800-793-7003. Local access: 937-225-7561. Case records are available back to 1990. Records are purged every six months. New civil records are available online after 1 day. PACER is available on the Internet at http://pacer.ohsb.uscourts.gov.

Dayton Division 120 W 3rd St, Dayton, OH 45402, 937-225-2516.

Counties: Butler, Champaign, Clark, Clinton, Darke, Greene, Miami, Montgomery, Preble, Shelby, Warren; parts of Butler County are handled by Cincinnati Division.

Indexing & Storage: Cases are indexed by debtor as well as by case number. New cases are available in the index within 1 day after filing date. Both computer and card indexes are maintained. Open records are located at this court. Cases closed before June 1991 were sent to the Chicago Federal Records Facility.

Fee & Payment: The fee is $15.00 per item (one party name or case number). Payment may be made by money order, cashier check, in-state business check. Personal checks are not accepted. Debtor's checks are not accepted. Payee: Clerk, US Bankruptcy Court. Certification fee: $5.00 per document. Copy fee: $.50 per page.

Phone Search: Only docket information is available by phone. An automated voice case information service (VCIS) is available. Call VCIS at 800-726-1004 or 937-225-2544.

Mail Search: Always enclose a stamped self addressed envelope.

In Person Search: In person searching is available.

PACER: Sign-up number is 800-676-6856. Access fee is $.60 per minute. Toll-free access: 800-793-7003. Local access: 937-225-7561. Case records are available back to 1990. Records are purged every six months. New civil records are available online after 1 day. PACER is available on the Internet at http://pacer.ohsb.uscourts.gov.

Court	Jurisdiction	No. of Courts	How Organized
Court of Common Pleas*	General	88	
County Courts*	Limited	49	
Municipal Courts*	Municipal	99	
Combined County/Municipal*		19	
Mayors Courts	Municipal	428	
Court of Claims	Special	1	

* Profiled in this Sourcebook.

	CIVIL								
Court	Tort	Contract	Real Estate	Min. Claim	Max. Claim	Small Claims	Estate	Eviction	Domestic Relations
Court of Common Pleas*	X	X	X	$3000/ $10,000	No Max		X		X
County Courts*	X	X	X	$0	$15,000	$3000		X	
Municipal Courts*	X	X	X	$0	$15,000	$3000		X	
Mayors Courts									
Court of Claims					No Max				

	CRIMINAL				
Court	Felony	Misdemeanor	DWI/DUI	Preliminary Hearing	Juvenile
Court of Common Pleas*	X				X
County Courts*		X	X	X	
Municipal Courts*		X	X	X	
Mayors Courts		X	X		
Court of Claims					

ADMINISTRATION Administrative Director, Supreme Court of Ohio, 30 E Broad St, 3rd Fl, Columbus, OH, 43266-0419; 614-466-2653, Fax: 614-752-8736. www.sconet.state.oh.us

COURT STRUCTURE The Court of Common Pleas is the general jurisdiction court and County Courts have limited jurisdiction. Effective July 1, 1997, the dollar limits for civil cases in County and Municipal Courts were raised as follows: County Court - from $3,000 to $15,000; Municipal Court - from $10,000 to $15,000. In addition the small claims limit was raised from $2,000 to $3,000. Probate courts are separate from the Court of Common Pleas, but Probate Court phone numbers are given with that court in each county.

ONLINE ACCESS There is no statewide computer system, but a number of counties offer online access.

Adams County

Common Pleas Court 110 W Main, Rm 207, West Union, OH 45693; 937-544-2344; Probate phone:937-544-2368; Fax: 937-544-8911. Hours: 8:30AM-4PM (EST). *Felony, Civil Actions Over $3,000, Probate.*

Civil Records: Access: In person only. Court does not conduct in person searches; visitors must perform searches for themselves. Search fee: No civil searches performed by court. Required to search: name, years to search. Civil cases indexed by defendant, plaintiff. Civil records on computer from April, 93, prior in books, archived from 1910. **Criminal Records:** Access: In person only.

Court does not conduct in person searches; visitors must perform searches for themselves. Search fee: No criminal searches performed by court. Required to search: name, years to search, signed release; also helpful-DOB, SSN. Criminal records on computer from April, 93, prior in books, archived from 1910. **General Information:** Copy fee: $.25 per page. Certification fee: $1.00. Fee payee: Clerk of Court. Personal checks accepted. Prepayment is required. Public access terminal is available.

County Court 110 W Main, Rm 25, West Union, OH 45693; 937-544-2011; Fax: 937-544-

8911. Hours: 8AM-4PM (EST). *Misdemeanor, Civil Actions Under $15,000, Small Claims.*

Civil Records: Access: Mail, in person. Both court and visitors may perform in person searches. Search fee: $10.00 per name. Required to search: name, years to search. Civil cases indexed by defendant, plaintiff. Civil records on computer from April, 93, index from 1958, prior on dockets and microfilm. **Criminal Records:** Access: Mail, in person. Both court and visitors may perform in person searches. Search fee: $10.00 per name. Required to search: name, years to search; also helpful-SSN. Criminal records on computer from April, 93, index from 1958, prior on dockets and microfilm. **General Information:** SASE required.

Turnaround time 1-2 days. Copy fee: $.50 per page. Certification fee: $1.00. Fee payee: Adams County Court. Business checks accepted. Prepayment is required. Public access terminal is available.

Allen County

Common Pleas Court PO Box 1243, Lima, OH 45802; 419-228-3700; Fax: 419-222-8427. Hours: 8AM-4:30PM (EST). *Felony, Civil Actions Over $15,000, Probate.*

Note: Probate is a separate court

Civil Records: Access: Fax, mail, in person. Both court and visitors may perform in person searches. No search fee. Required to search: name; also helpful-years to search, address. Civil cases indexed by defendant, plaintiff. Civil records on computer from 1982, in books and archived prior. **Criminal Records:** Access: Fax, mail, in person. Both court and visitors may perform in person searches. Search fee: No criminal searches performed by court. Required to search: name, years to search; also helpful-address, DOB, SSN. Criminal records on computer from 1982, in books and archived prior. **General Information:** No secret indictment records released. SASE required. Turnaround time 1-2 days. Copy fee: $1.00 for first page, $.25 each addl. Certification fee: $3.00. Fee payee: Clerk of Court. Personal checks accepted. Prepayment is required. Public access terminal is available. Fax notes: $3.00 for first page, $1.00 each addl.

Lima Municipal Court 109 N Union St (PO Box 1529), Lima, OH 45802; 419-221-5275; Fax: 419-228-2305. Hours: 8AM-5PM (EST). *Misdemeanor, Civil Actions Under $15,000, Eviction, Small Claims.*

www.bright.net/~limamuni

Civil Records: Access: Phone, fax, mail, in person. Both court and visitors may perform in person searches. No search fee. Required to search: name, years to search; also helpful-address. Civil cases indexed by defendant, plaintiff. Civil records on computer from April, 90, microfilm from 1975, books and archived prior. **Criminal Records:** Access: Phone, fax, mail, in person. Both court and visitors may perform in person searches. No search fee. Required to search: name, years to search; also helpful-address, DOB, SSN. Criminal records on computer from April, 90, microfilm from 1975, books and archived prior. **General Information:** SASE required. Turnaround time same day. Copy fee: $.25 per page. Certification fee: $2.00. Fee payee: Clerk of Court. Business checks accepted. Credit cards accepted: Visa, Mastercard. Prepayment is required. Public access terminal is available. Fax notes: No fee to fax results. Local or toll free faxing only.

Ashland County

Common Pleas Court 142 W 2nd St, Ashland, OH 44805; 419-289-0000. Hours: 8AM-4PM (EST). *Felony, Civil Actions Over $10,000, Probate.*

Civil Records: Access: In person only. Court does not conduct in person searches; visitors must perform searches for themselves. Search fee: No civil searches performed by court. Required to search: name, years to search. Civil cases indexed by defendant, plaintiff. Civil records in books and index from 1800s. **Criminal Records:** Access: Mail, in person. Both court and visitors may perform in person searches. Search fee: $10.00 per name. Required to search: name, years to search,

DOB; also helpful-SSN. Criminal records in books and index from 1800s. **General Information:** SASE not required. Turnaround time 1-2 days. Copy fee: $.25 per page. Computer printout copies: $1.00 per page. Certification fee: No certification fee. Fee payee: Clerk of Court. Personal checks accepted. Prepayment is required. Public access terminal is available.

Ashland Municipal Court PO Box 385, Ashland, OH 44805; 419-289-8137; Fax: 419-289-8545. Hours: 8AM-5PM (EST). *Misdemeanor, Civil Actions Under $15,000, Eviction, Small Claims.*

www.ashland-ohio.com

Civil Records: Access: Mail, in person. Both court and visitors may perform in person searches. No search fee. Required to search: name, years to search. Civil cases indexed by defendant, plaintiff. Civil records on docket books from 1952. **Criminal Records:** Access: Mail, in person. Both court and visitors may perform in person searches. No search fee. Required to search: name, years to search, SSN. Criminal records on docket books from 1952. **General Information:** SASE required. Turnaround time 1-3 days. Copy fee: $1.00 per page. Certification fee: $1.00. Fee payee: Municipal Court. Personal checks accepted. Prepayment is required.

Ashtabula County

Common Pleas Court 25 W Jefferson St, Jefferson, OH 44047; 440-576-3637; Probate phone:440-576-3451; Fax: 440-576-2819. Hours: 8AM-4:30PM (EST). *Felony, Civil Actions Over $10,000, Probate.*

Civil Records: Access: In person only. Court does not conduct in person searches; visitors must perform searches for themselves. Search fee: No civil searches performed by court. Required to search: name, years to search; also helpful-address. Civil cases indexed by defendant, plaintiff. Civil records on computer from May, 93, in books back to the 1800s. **Criminal Records:** Access: In person only. Court does not conduct in person searches; visitors must perform searches for themselves. Search fee: No criminal searches performed by court. Required to search: name, years to search; also helpful-address, DOB, SSN. Criminal records on computer from May, 93, in books back to the 1800s. **General Information:** No expungments released. Copy fee: $.50 per page. Certification fee: $1.00. Fee payee: Clerk of Court. Personal checks accepted. Prepayment is required. Public access terminal is available.

County Court Eastern Division 25 W Jefferson St, Jefferson, OH 44047; 440-576-3617. Hours: 8AM-4:30PM (EST). *Misdemeanor, Civil Actions Under $15,000, Small Claims.*

Civil Records: Access: Mail, in person. Both court and visitors may perform in person searches. No search fee. Required to search: name, years to search. Civil cases indexed by defendant, plaintiff. Civil records in books and on compuetr since 01/09/95. **Criminal Records:** Access: Mail, in person. Both court and visitors may perform in person searches. No search fee. Required to search: name, years to search, SSN; also helpful-DOB. Criminal records in books and on compuetr since 01/09/95. **General Information:** SASE required. Turnaround time 1-2 days. Copy fee: $.50 per page. Certification fee: $1.50. Fee payee: Eastern County Court. Only cashiers checks and money orders accepted. Prepayment is required. Public access terminal is available.

County Court Western Division 117 W Main St, Geneva, OH 44041; 440-466-1184; Fax: 440-466-7171. Hours: 8AM-4:30PM (EST). *Misdemeanor, Civil Actions Under $15,000, Small Claims.*

Civil Records: Access: In person only. Court does not conduct in person searches; visitors must perform searches for themselves. Search fee: No civil searches performed by court. Required to search: name, years to search. Civil cases indexed by defendant, plaintiff. Civil records on computer since 1995; prior records on docket books. **Criminal Records:** Access: In person only. Court does not conduct in person searches; visitors must perform searches for themselves. Search fee: No criminal searches performed by court. Required to search: name, years to search, DOB, SSN, signed release. Criminal records on computer since 1995; prior records on docket books. **General Information:** No confidential records released. Copy fee: $.50 per page. Certification fee: $.50 per page. Fee payee: Western County Court. Only cashiers checks and money orders accepted. Prepayment is required. Public access terminal is available.

Ashtabula Municipal Court 110 W 44th St, Ashtabula, OH 44004; 440-992-7110; Fax: 440-998-5786. Hours: 8AM-4:30PM (EST). *Misdemeanor, Civil Actions Under $15,000, Eviction, Small Claims.*

Note: 440-992-7109 gives a directory

Civil Records: Access: In person only. Court does not conduct in person searches; visitors must perform searches for themselves. Search fee: No civil searches performed by court. Required to search: name, years to search. Civil cases indexed by defendant, plaintiff. Civil records on computer from 1988, books back to 1971. **Criminal Records:** Access: In person only. Court does not conduct in person searches; visitors must perform searches for themselves. Search fee: No criminal searches performed by court. Required to search: name, years to search, DOB, SSN, signed release. Criminal records on computer from 1988, books back to 1971. **General Information:** No expunged records released. Copy fee: $.10 per page. Certification fee: $5.00. Fee payee: Municipal Court. Personal checks accepted. Prepayment is required. Public access terminal is available.

Athens County

Common Pleas Court PO Box 290, Athens, OH 45701-0290; 740-592-3242; Probate phone:740-592-3251. Hours: 8AM-4PM (EST). *Felony, Civil Actions Over $10,000, Probate.*

Civil Records: Access: In person only. Court does not conduct in person searches; visitors must perform searches for themselves. Search fee: No civil searches performed by court. Required to search: name, years to search; also helpful-address. Civil cases indexed by defendant, plaintiff. Civil records on computer from January, 92, prior in books. **Criminal Records:** Access: In person only. Court does not conduct in person searches; visitors must perform searches for themselves. Search fee: No criminal searches performed by court. Required to search: name, years to search; also helpful-address, DOB, SSN. Criminal records on computer from January, 92, prior in books. **General Information:** Copy fee: $1.00 per page. Certification fee: $1.00. Fee payee: Clerk of Court. Business checks accepted. Prepayment is required. Public access terminal is available.

Athens Municipal Court City Hall, 8 East Washington St, Athens, OH 45701; 740-592-3328; Fax: 740-592-3331. Hours: 8AM-4PM (EST). *Misdemeanor, Civil Actions Under $15,000, Eviction, Small Claims.*

Civil Records: Access: In person only. Court does not conduct in person searches; visitors must perform searches for themselves. Search fee: No civil searches performed by court. Required to search: name, years to search; also helpful-address. Civil cases indexed by defendant, plaintiff. Civil records on computer from 1994, prior in books. **Criminal Records:** Access: In person only. Court does not conduct in person searches; visitors must perform searches for themselves. Search fee: No criminal searches performed by court. Required to search: name, years to search; also helpful-address, DOB, SSN. Criminal records on computer from 1994, prior in books. **General Information:** No expunged or sealed records released. Copy fee: $.50 per page. Certification fee: $1.00. Fee payee: ACMC. Personal checks accepted. Credit cards accepted: Visa, Mastercard. Prepayment is required. Public access terminal is available.

Auglaize County

Common Pleas Court PO Box 409, Wapakoneta, OH 45895; 419-738-4219; Probate phone:419-738-7710. Hours: 8AM-4:30PM (EST). *Felony, Civil Actions Over $10,000, Probate.*

Civil Records: Access: In person only. Court does not conduct in person searches; visitors must perform searches for themselves. Search fee: No civil searches performed by court. Required to search: name, years to search; also helpful-address. Civil cases indexed by defendant, plaintiff. Civil records on dockets from 1860, computerized since 02/00. **Criminal Records:** Access: In person only. Court does not conduct in person searches; visitors must perform searches for themselves. Search fee: No criminal searches performed by court. Required to search: name, years to search; also helpful-address, DOB, SSN. Criminal records on dockets from 1860, computerized since 02/00. **General Information:** Copy fee: $.50 per page. Certification fee: $1.00. Fee payee: Clerk of Court. Personal checks accepted. Prepayment is required.

Auglaize County Municipal Court PO Box 409, Wapakoneta, OH 45895; 419-738-2923. Hours: 8AM-4:30PM (EST). *Misdemeanor, Civil Actions Under $15,000, Eviction, Small Claims.*

Civil Records: Access: In person only. Court does not conduct in person searches; visitors must perform searches for themselves. Search fee: No civil searches performed by court. Required to search: name, years to search; also helpful-address. Civil cases indexed by defendant, plaintiff. Civil records on computer from April, 1994, docket back to 1976. **Criminal Records:** Access: In person only. Court does not conduct in person searches; visitors must perform searches for themselves. Search fee: No criminal searches performed by court. Required to search: name, years to search, signed release; also helpful-address, DOB, SSN. Criminal records on computer from October, 1993, docket back to 1976. **General Information:** No records released. Copy fee: $.50 per page. Certification fee: $1.00. Fee payee: Clerk of Court. Personal checks accepted. Prepayment is required. Public access terminal is available.

Belmont County

Common Pleas Court Main St, Courthouse, St Clairsville, OH 43950; 740-695-2121; Probate phone:740-695-2121 X202. Hours: 8:30AM-

4:30PM (EST). *Felony, Civil Actions Over $3,000, Probate.*

Civil Records: Access: Mail, in person. Both court and visitors may perform in person searches. Search fee: $3.00 per name. Required to search: name, years to search. Civil cases indexed by defendant, plaintiff. Civil records in books, archived from 1896. Recent records are computerized. **Criminal Records:** Access: Mail, in person. Both court and visitors may perform in person searches. Search fee: $3.00 per name. Required to search: name, years to search. Criminal records in books, archived from 1896. Recent records are computerized. **General Information:** No secret criminal records released. SASE required. Turnaround time 1 day. Copy fee: $1.00 per page. Certification fee: $5.00. Fee payee: Clerk of Court. Personal checks accepted. Prepayment is required. Public access terminal is available.

County Court Eastern Division 400 W 26th St, Bellaire, OH 43906; 740-676-4490. Hours: 8AM-4PM (EST). *Misdemeanor, Civil Actions Under $15,000, Small Claims.*

Civil Records: Access: Mail, in person. Both court and visitors may perform in person searches. No search fee. Required to search: name, years to search. Civil cases indexed by defendant, plaintiff. Civil records on computer from September, 94, books back to 1950s. Mail access available to attorneys only. **Criminal Records:** Access: Mail, in person. Both court and visitors may perform in person searches. No search fee. Required to search: name, years to search; also helpful-DOB, SSN. Criminal records on computer from September, 94, books back to 1950s. **General Information:** No sealed or confidential records released. SASE required. Copy fee: $1.00 per page. Certification fee: No certification fee. Fee payee: Eastern Division. Only cashiers checks and money orders accepted. Prepayment is required. Public access terminal is available.

County Court Northern Division PO Box 40, Martins Ferry, OH 43935; 740-633-3147; Fax: 740-633-6631. Hours: 8AM-4PM (EST). *Misdemeanor, Civil Actions Under $15,000, Small Claims.*

Civil Records: Access: Mail, in person. Both court and visitors may perform in person searches. No search fee. Required to search: name, years to search. Civil cases indexed by defendant, plaintiff. Civil records on computer from June, 1994, books back to 1950s. **Criminal Records:** Access: Mail, in person. Both court and visitors may perform in person searches. No search fee. Required to search: name, years to search, DOB; also helpful-SSN. Criminal records on computer from June, 1994, books back to 1950s. **General Information:** SASE not required. Turnaround time 5-7 days. No copy fee. Certification fee: No certification fee. Fee payee: Clerk of Court, Northern Division. Only cashiers checks and money orders accepted. Prepayment is required. Public access terminal is available.

County Court Western Division 147 W Main St, St Clairsville, OH 43950; 740-695-2875; Fax: 740-695-7285. Hours: 8AM-4PM (EST). *Misdemeanor, Civil Actions Under $15,000, Small Claims.*

Civil Records: Access: Fax, mail, in person. Both court and visitors may perform in person searches. No search fee. Required to search: name, years to search, address. Civil cases indexed by defendant, plaintiff. Civil records on computer from 1994,

books back to 1950s. **Criminal Records:** Access: Fax, mail, in person. Both court and visitors may perform in person searches. No search fee. Required to search: name, years to search, address, DOB, SSN. Criminal records on computer from 1994, books back to 1950s. **General Information:** Pending case information not released. SASE required. Turnaround time 1 week. Copy fee: $1.00 per page. Certification fee: $1.00. Fee payee: Western Division Court. Only cashiers checks and money orders accepted. Prepayment is required. Public access terminal is available. Fax notes: No fee to fax results.

Brown County

Common Pleas Court 101 S Main, Georgetown, OH 45121; 937-378-3100; Probate phone:937-378-6549. Hours: 8AM-4PM (EST). *Felony, Civil Actions Over $3,000, Probate.*

Civil Records: Access: Mail, in person. Both court and visitors may perform in person searches. No search fee. Required to search: name, years to search; also helpful-address. Civil cases indexed by defendant, plaintiff. Civil records on computer since 1995, in books back to 1860s. **Criminal Records:** Access: Mail, in person. Both court and visitors may perform in person searches. No search fee. Required to search: name, years to search; also helpful-address, DOB, SSN. Criminal records on computer since 1995, in books back to 1860s. **General Information:** No criminal expungment records released. SASE required. Turnaround time same day. Copy fee: $.25 per page. Certification fee: $1.00. Fee payee: Clerk of Court. Personal checks accepted. Prepayment is required. Public access terminal is available.

County Court 770 Mount Orab Pike, Georgetown, OH 45121; 937-378-6358; Fax: 937-378-2462. Hours: 8AM-4PM (EST). *Misdemeanor, Civil Actions Under $15,000, Eviction, Small Claims.*

Civil Records: Access: Mail, in person. Both court and visitors may perform in person searches. No search fee. Required to search: name, years to search. Civil cases indexed by defendant, plaintiff. Civil records in books back to 1958, computerized since 1995. **Criminal Records:** Access: Mail, in person. Both court and visitors may perform in person searches. No search fee. Required to search: name, years to search, DOB; also helpful-SSN. Criminal records in books back to 1958, computerized since 1995. **General Information:** SASE required. Copy fee: $.25. Certification fee: No certification. Fee payee: Brown County Court. Only cashiers checks and money orders accepted. Prepayment is required. Public access terminal is available.

Butler County

Common Pleas Court 101 High St, Hamilton, OH 45011; 513-887-3996; Probate phone:513-887-3296; Fax: 513-887-3089. Hours: 8:30AM-4:30PM (EST). *Felony, Civil Actions Over $3,000, Probate.*

http://38.155.160.5/pa/pa.urd/pamw6500.display

Civil Records: Access: online, in person. Court does not conduct in person searches; visitors must perform searches for themselves. Search fee: No civil searches performed by court. Required to search: name, years to search. Civil cases indexed by defendant, plaintiff. Civil records on computer from 1988, prior in books. Online access to Butler County Clerk of Courts recrods is available free on the Courtview 2000 Court Records search page at http://38.155.160.5/pa/pa.urd/pamw6500.display.

Search by name, dates, or case # and type. **Criminal Records:** Access: Remote online, in person. Court does not conduct in person searches; visitors must perform searches for themselves. Search fee: No criminal searches performed by court. Required to search: name, years to search, DOB; also helpful-SSN. Criminal records on computer from 1988, prior in books. See civil records for online access information. **General Information:** Copy fee: $.25 per page. Certification fee: $2.00. Fee payee: Clerk of Court. Personal checks accepted. Public access terminal is available.

County Court Area #1
118 West High, Oxford, OH 45056; 513-523-4748; Fax: 513-523-4737. Hours: 8:30AM-4:30PM (EST). *Misdemeanor, Civil Actions Under $15,000, Small Claims.*

Civil Records: Access: Phone, mail, in person. Both court and visitors may perform in person searches. No search fee. Required to search: name, years to search. Civil cases indexed by defendant, plaintiff. Civil records on index back to 1983. **Criminal Records:** Access: Phone, mail, in person. Both court and visitors may perform in person searches. No search fee. Required to search: name, years to search, DOB. Criminal records on index back to 1983. **General Information:** No sealed records released. SASE required. Turnaround time 1-5 days. No copy fee. Certification fee: No certification fee.

County Court Area #2
Butler County Courthouse, 101 High St, 3rd Fl, Hamilton, OH 45011; 513-887-3459. Hours: 8AM-5PM (EST). *Misdemeanor, Civil Actions Under $15,000, Small Claims.*

Civil Records: Access: Phone, in person. Court does not conduct in person searches; visitors must perform searches for themselves. Search fee: No civil searches performed by court. Required to search: name, years to search. Civil cases indexed by defendant, plaintiff. Civil records on computer from 1993, books back to 1983. **Criminal Records:** Access: Phone, in person. Court does not conduct in person searches; visitors must perform searches for themselves. Search fee: No criminal searches performed by court. Required to search: name, years to search. Criminal records on computer from 1993, books back to 1983. **General Information:** No sealed records released. No copy fee. Certification fee: No certification fee. Only cashiers checks and money orders accepted. Prepayment is required. Public access terminal is available.

County Court Area #3
9113 Cincinnati, Dayton Rd, West Chester, OH 45069; 513-867-5070; Fax: 513-777-0558. Hours: 8:30AM-4:30PM (EST). *Misdemeanor, Civil Actions Under $15,000, Small Claims.*

Civil Records: Access: Mail, in person. Both court and visitors may perform in person searches. No search fee. Required to search: name, years to search. Civil cases indexed by defendant, plaintiff. Civil records on computer from 1993, books back to 1983. **Criminal Records:** Access: Mail, in person. Both court and visitors may perform in person searches. No search fee. Required to search: name, years to search. Criminal records on computer from 1993, books back to 1983. **General Information:** SASE required. Turnaround time 2-3 days. No copy fee. Certification fee: $1.00. Fee payee: Area #3 Court. Personal checks accepted. Prepayment is required.

Carroll County

Common Pleas Court
PO Box 367, Carrollton, OH 44615; 330-627-4886; Probate phone:216-627-2323; Fax: 330-627-6734. Hours: 8AM-4PM (EST). *Felony, Civil Actions Over $15,000, Probate.*

Civil Records: Access: Mail, in person. Both court and visitors may perform in person searches. No search fee. Required to search: name, years to search. Civil cases indexed by defendant, plaintiff. Civil records in books back to 1900s. **Criminal Records:** Access: In person only. Court does not conduct in person searches; visitors must perform searches for themselves. Search fee: No criminal searches performed by court. Required to search: name, years to search; also helpful-DOB, SSN. Criminal records in books back to 1900s. **General Information:** SASE required. Turnaround time 1 day. Copy fee: $.50 per page. Certification fee: $1.00. Fee payee: Clerk of Court. Personal checks accepted. Prepayment is required.

County Court
Courthouse, 3rd Fl, Carrollton, OH 44615; 330-627-5049; Fax: 330-627-3662. Hours: 8AM-4PM (EST). *Misdemeanor, Civil Actions Under $15,000, Small Claims.*

Civil Records: Access: Mail, in person. Both court and visitors may perform in person searches. No search fee. Required to search: name, years to search. Civil cases indexed by defendant, plaintiff. Civil records in books from 1958. **Criminal Records:** Access: Mail, in person. Both court and visitors may perform in person searches. No search fee. Required to search: name, years to search, DOB; also helpful-SSN. Criminal records in books from 1958. **General Information:** No confidential records released. SASE required. Turnaround time 1-2 weeks. Copy fee: $.50 per page. Certification fee: $2.00. Fee payee: Carroll County Court. Personal checks accepted. Prepayment is required.

Champaign County

Common Pleas Court
200 N Main St, Urbana, OH 43078; 937-653-2746; Probate phone:937-652-2108. Hours: 8AM-4PM (EST). *Felony, Civil Actions Over $10,000, Probate.*

Note: Probate is separate court at phone number given

Civil Records: Access: Phone, mail, in person. Court does not conduct in person searches; visitors must perform searches for themselves. Search fee: No civil searches performed by court. Required to search: name, years to search. Civil cases indexed by defendant, plaintiff. Civil records on computer from 06/92, books back to late 1800'. Will only do phone or mail searches with a case number. **Criminal Records:** Access: Phone, mail, in person. Court does not conduct in person searches; visitors must perform searches for themselves. No search fee. Required to search: name, years to search, DOB, SSN, signed release. Criminal records on computer from 06/92, books back to late 1800'. Will only do mail or phone searches with a case number. **General Information:** All records are public. SASE required. Copy fee: $.25 per page. Certification fee: $5.00. Fee payee: Clerk of Court. Personal checks accepted. Personal checks over $10.00 not accepted. Prepayment is required. Public access terminal is available.

Champaign County Municipal Court
PO Box 85, Urbana, OH 43078; 937-653-7376. Hours: 8AM-4PM (EST). *Misdemeanor, Civil Actions Under $15,000, Eviction, Small Claims.*

Civil Records: Access: Mail, in person. Both court and visitors may perform in person searches.

No search fee. Required to search: name, years to search. Civil cases indexed by defendant, plaintiff. Civil records on computer from June, 93, books back to late 1800s. **Criminal Records:** Access: Mail, in person. Both court and visitors may perform in person searches. No search fee. Required to search: name, years to search; also helpful-DOB, SSN. Criminal records on computer from June, 93, books back to late 1800s. **General Information:** No sealed records released. SASE required. Turnaround time 2-3 days. Copy fee: $.25 per page. Certification fee: $2.50. Fee payee: Municipal Court. Only cashiers checks and money orders accepted. Prepayment is required.

Clark County

Common Pleas Court
101 N Limestone St, Springfield, OH 45502; 937-328-2458; 937-328-4648 (Domestic); Fax: 937-328-2436. Hours: 8AM-4:30PM (EST). *Felony, Civil Actions Over $10,000, Probate.*

Civil Records: Access: In person only. Court does not conduct in person searches; visitors must perform searches for themselves. Search fee: No civil searches performed by court. Required to search: name, years to search. Civil cases indexed by defendant. Civil records in index books. **Criminal Records:** Access: In person only. Court does not conduct in person searches; visitors must perform searches for themselves. Search fee: No criminal searches performed by court. Required to search: name, years to search. Criminal records in index books. **General Information:** Copy fee: $1.00 per page. Certification fee: $1.00. Fee payee: Clerk of Court. Business checks accepted. Prepayment is required. Public access terminal is available.

Clark County Municipal Court
50 E Columbia St, Springfield, OH 45502; 937-328-3700. Hours: 8AM-5PM (EST). *Misdemeanor, Civil Actions Under $15,000, Eviction, Small Claims.*

Civil Records: Access: Mail, in person. Both court and visitors may perform in person searches. No search fee. Required to search: name, years to search. Civil cases indexed by defendant, plaintiff. Civil records on computer from 1991. **Criminal Records:** Access: Mail, in person. Both court and visitors may perform in person searches. No search fee. Required to search: name, years to search; also helpful-DOB, SSN. Criminal records on computer since 3/90. **General Information:** SASE required. Turnaround time 2-3 days. Copy fee: $.50 per page. Certification fee: $1.00. Fee payee: Clerk of Court. Personal checks accepted. Prepayment is required. Public access terminal is available.

Clermont County

Common Pleas Court
270 Main St, Batavia, OH 45103; 513-732-7130; Probate phone:513-732-7243; Fax: 513-732-7050. Hours: 8:30AM-4:30PM (EST). *Felony, Civil Actions Over $10,000, Probate.*

Note: Online service is planned for late 2000.

Civil Records: Access: In person only. Court does not conduct in person searches; visitors must perform searches for themselves. Search fee: No civil searches performed by court. Required to search: name, years to search; also helpful-address. Civil cases indexed by defendant, plaintiff. Civil records on computer from 1987, some on microfiche from 1920s, index books from 1959. **Criminal Records:** Access: In person only. Court does not conduct in person searches; visitors must perform searches for themselves. Search fee: No criminal searches performed by court. Required to search: name, years to search, DOB; also helpful-address, SSN. Criminal records on computer from 1987, some on microfiche from 1920s, index books from 1959. The clerk refers criminal record resquests to the Sheriff (513-732-7500) who will do searches for $5.00 per name. **General Information:** Copy fee: $.10 per page. Certification fee: $1.00 per page. Fee payee: Clerk of Court. Business checks accepted. Prepayment is required. Public access terminal is available.

Clermont County Municipal Court
289 Main St, Batavia, OH 45103;; Civil phone:513-732-7292; Criminal phone:513-732-7292. Hours: 8:30AM-4:30PM (EST). *Misdemeanor, Civil Actions Under $15,000, Eviction, Small Claims.*

Civil Records: Access: Mail, in person. Court does not conduct in person searches; visitors must perform searches for themselves. No search fee. Required to search: name, years to search. Civil cases indexed by defendant, plaintiff. Civil records in books and microfiche from 1965, docket books back to 1800s. **Criminal Records:** Access: Mail, in person. Court does not conduct in person searches; visitors must perform searches for themselves. No search fee. Required to search: name, years to search, DOB; also helpful-SSN. Criminal records in books and microfiche from 1965, docket books back to 1800s. **General Information:** SASE required. Copy fee: $.25 per page. Certification fee: $1.00. Fee payee: Clerk of Court. Only cashiers checks and money orders accepted. Prepayment is required.

Clinton County

Common Pleas Court 46 S South St, Wilmington, OH 45177; 937-382-2316; Probate phone:937-382-2280; Fax: 937-383-3455. Hours: 7:30AM-4:30PM (EST). *Felony, Civil Actions Over $15,000, Probate.*

Note: Probate fax is 937-383-1158; hours are 8AM-4:30PM

Civil Records: Access: Fax, mail, in person. Both court and visitors may perform in person searches. No search fee. Required to search: name, years to search; also helpful-address. Civil cases indexed by defendant, plaintiff. Civil records on computer since 1995; prior in books back to 1810. **Criminal Records:** Access: Mail, in person. Both court and visitors may perform in person searches. Search fee: $5.00 per name. Required to search: name, years to search, DOD, SSN; also helpful-address. Criminal records on computer since 1995; prior in books back to 1810. **General Information:** No confidential records released. SASE required. Turnaround time 1 week. Copy fee: $.25 per page. Certification fee: $1.00. Fee payee: Clerk of Court. Personal checks accepted. Prepayment is required. Public access terminal is available.

Clinton County Municipal Court
69 N South St, Wilmington, OH 45177; 937-382-8985; Fax: 937-383-0130. Hours: 8AM-3:30PM (EST). *Misdemeanor, Civil Actions Under $15,000, Eviction, Small Claims.*

Civil Records: Access: Phone, mail, in person. Both court and visitors may perform in person searches. No search fee. Required to search: name, years to search. Civil cases indexed by defendant, plaintiff. Civil records in books from 1961. **Criminal Records:** Access: Phone, mail, in person. Both court and visitors may perform in person searches. No search fee. Required to search: name, years to search, DOB; also helpful-SSN. Criminal records in books from 1961. **General Information:** SASE required.

Turnaround time 1 day. Copy fee: $.25 per page after 10 pages. Certification fee: No certification fee. Fee payee: Clerk of Court. Only cashiers checks and money orders accepted.

Columbiana County

Common Pleas Court 105 S Market St, Lisbon, OH 44432; 330-424-7777; Fax: 330-424-3960. Hours: 8AM-4:30PM (EST). *Felony, Civil Actions Over $10,000, Probate.*

Civil Records: Access: In person only. Court does not conduct in person searches; visitors must perform searches for themselves. Search fee: No civil searches performed by court. Required to search: name, years to search; also helpful-address. Civil cases indexed by defendant, plaintiff. Civil records on computer since 1993; prior in books from 1968, archived back to 1800s. **Criminal Records:** Access: In person only. Court does not conduct in person searches; visitors must perform searches for themselves. Search fee: No criminal searches performed by court. Required to search: name, years to search, DOB; also helpful-address, SSN. Criminal records on computer since 1993; prior in books from 1968, archived back to 1800s. **General Information:** No secret indictment records released. Copy fee: $.50 per page. Certification fee: $1.00. Fee payee: Clerk of Court. Personal checks accepted. Prepayment is required. Public access terminal is available.

County Court Eastern Area
31 North Market St, East Palestine, OH 44413; 330-426-3774; Fax: 330-426-6328. Hours: 8AM-12, 1PM-4PM (EST). *Misdemeanor, Civil Actions Under $15,000, Small Claims.*

Civil Records: Access: Mail, in person. Both court and visitors may perform in person searches. No search fee. Required to search: name, years to search. Civil cases indexed by defendant, plaintiff. Civil records in books from 1950s, archived from 1800s, recent records computerized. **Criminal Records:** Access: Mail, in person. Both court and visitors may perform in person searches. No search fee. Required to search: name, years to search. Criminal records in books from 1950s, archived from 1800s, recent records computerized. **General Information:** SASE required. Turnaround time 1 day. Copy fee: $.25 per page. Certification fee: $1.00. Fee payee: Clerk of Court. Only cashiers checks and money orders accepted. Prepayment is required. Public access terminal is available.

County Court Northwest Area
130 Penn Ave, Salem, OH 44460; 330-332-0297. Hours: 8AM-4PM (EST). *Misdemeanor, Civil Actions Under $15,000, Small Claims.*

Civil Records: Access: Mail, in person. Both court and visitors may perform in person searches. No search fee. Required to search: name, years to search. Civil cases indexed by defendant, plaintiff. Civil records in books from 1950s, archived from 1800s, computerized since 11/94. **Criminal Records:** Access: Mail, in person. Both court and visitors may perform in person searches. No search fee. Required to search: name, years to search; also helpful-DOB. Criminal records in books from 1950s, archived from 1800s, computerized since 11/94. **General Information:** SASE required. Turnaround time 2-3 days. Copy fee: $.25 per page. Certification fee: $1.00. Fee payee: Northwest Area Court. Only cashiers checks and money orders accepted. Prepayment is required. Public access terminal is available.

County Court Southwest Area
41 N Park Ave, Lisbon, OH 44432; 330-424-5326; Fax: 330-424-6658. Hours: 8AM-4PM (EST).

Misdemeanor, Civil Actions Under $15,000, Small Claims.

Civil Records: Access: In person only. Court does not conduct in person searches; visitors must perform searches for themselves. Search fee: No civil searches performed by court. Required to search: name, years to search. Civil cases indexed by defendant, plaintiff. Civil records in books from 1950s, archived back to 1800s. **Criminal Records:** Access: Mail, in person. Both court and visitors may perform in person searches. No search fee. Required to search: name, years to search; also helpful-DOB, SSN. Criminal records in books from 1950s, archived back to 1800s. **General Information:** No expungement records released. SASE required. Turnaround time 1 week. Copy fee: $.50 per page. Certification fee: $1.00. Fee payee: Southwest Court. Only cashiers checks and money orders accepted. Prepayment is required. Public access terminal is available.

East Liverpool Municipal Court
126 W 6th St, East Liverpool, OH 43920; 330-385-5151; Fax: 330-385-1566. Hours: 8AM-4PM (EST). *Misdemeanor, Civil Actions Under $15,000, Eviction, Small Claims.*

Civil Records: Access: Phone, fax, mail, in person. Both court and visitors may perform in person searches. No search fee. Required to search: name, years to search. Civil cases indexed by defendant, plaintiff. Civil records in books from 1968, archived back to 1800s, computerized since 11/92. **Criminal Records:** Access: Phone, fax, mail, in person. Both court and visitors may perform in person searches. No search fee. Required to search: name, years to search, signed release; also helpful-DOB, SSN. Criminal records in books from 1968, archived back to 1800s, computerized since 11/92. **General Information:** No expungment records released. SASE required. Turnaround time 1-2 days. Copy fee: $.10 per page. Certification fee: $3.00. Fee payee: East Liverpool Municipal Court. Business checks accepted. Prepayment is required. Public access terminal is available. Fax notes: No fee to fax results.

Coshocton County

Common Pleas Court 318 Main St, Coshocton, OH 43812; 740-622-1456; Probate phone:740-622-1837. Hours: 8AM-4PM (EST). *Felony, Civil Actions Over $10,000, Probate.*

Civil Records: Access: Mail, in person. Both court and visitors may perform in person searches. No search fee. Required to search: name, years to search. Civil cases indexed by defendant, plaintiff. Civil records in books, microfilm back to 1985, archived back to 1800s. **Criminal Records:** Access: Mail, in person. Both court and visitors may perform in person searches. No search fee. Required to search: name, years to search, DOB; also helpful-SSN. Criminal records in books, microfilm back to 1985, archived back to 1800s. **General Information:** No expunged records released. SASE not required. Turnaround time 2 days. Copy fee: $.25 per page. Certification fee: $1.00. Fee payee: Clerk of Court. Personal checks accepted. Prepayment is required.

Coshocton Municipal Court
760 Chesnut St, Coshocton, OH 43812; 740-622-2871; Fax: 740-623-5928. Hours: 8AM-4:30PM M-W,F; 8AM-Noon Th (EST). *Misdemeanor, Civil Actions Under $15,000, Eviction, Small Claims.*

Civil Records: Access: Phone, fax, mail, in person. Both court and visitors may perform in person searches. No search fee. Required to search: name, years to search. Civil cases indexed by defendant, plaintiff. Civil records on computer from 1989, books back to 1952. **Criminal Records:** Access: Phone, fax, mail, in person. Both court and visitors may perform in person searches. No search fee. Required to search: name, years to search; also helpful-DOB, SSN. Criminal records on computer from 1989, books back to 1952. **General Information:** No expunged records released. SASE required. Turnaround time same day. Copy fee: $.50 per page. Certification fee: $1.00. Fee payee: Clerk of Court. Personal checks accepted. Prepayment is required. Public access terminal is available. Fax notes: No fee to fax results.

Crawford County

Common Pleas Court PO Box 470, Bucyrus, OH 44820; 419-562-2766; Probate phone:419-562-8891; Fax: 419-562-8011. Hours: 8:30AM-4:30PM (EST). *Felony, Civil Actions Over $3,000, Probate.*

Civil Records: Access: Mail, in person. Both court and visitors may perform in person searches. Search fee: $5.00 per name. Required to search: name, years to search; also helpful-address. Civil cases indexed by defendant, plaintiff. Civil records on computer from 1990, some on microfiche and index books from 1800s. **Criminal Records:** Access: Mail, in person. Both court and visitors may perform in person searches. Search fee: $5.00 per name. Required to search: name, years to search, notarized release; also helpful-address, DOB, SSN. Criminal records on computer from 1990, some on microfiche and index books from 1800s. **General Information:** No divorce investigations. SASE required. Turnaround time 1-2 days. Certification fee: $1.00. Fee payee: Clerk of Court. Personal checks accepted. Prepayment is required. Public access terminal is available.

Crawford County Municipal Court PO Box 550, Bucyrus, OH 44820; 419-562-2731. Hours: 8:30AM-4:30PM (EST). *Misdemeanor, Civil Actions Under $15,000, Eviction, Small Claims.*

Civil Records: Access: Mail, in person. Both court and visitors may perform in person searches. No search fee. Required to search: name, years to search. Civil cases indexed by defendant, plaintiff. Civil records in books back to 1978. **Criminal Records:** Access: Mail, in person. Both court and visitors may perform in person searches. No search fee. Required to search: name, years to search. Criminal records in books back to 1978. **General Information:** No counseling report records released. SASE not required. Turnaround time within 1 week. Copy fee: $.10 per page. Certification fee: $2.00. Business checks accepted. Crawford county business checks accepted. Prepayment is required. Public access terminal is available.

Crawford County Municipal Court Eastern Division 301 Harding Way East, Galion, OH 44833; 419-468-6819; Fax: 419-468-6828. Hours: 8:30AM-4:30PM (EST). *Misdemeanor, Civil Actions Under $15,000, Eviction, Small Claims.*

Civil Records: Access: Mail, in person. Both court and visitors may perform in person searches. No search fee. Required to search: name, years to search. Civil cases indexed by defendant, plaintiff. Civil records in books back to 1800s. **Criminal Records:** Access: Mail, in person. Both court and visitors may perform in person searches. No search fee. Required to search: name, years to search,

DOB, SSN, signed release. Criminal records in books back to 1800s. **General Information:** SASE required. Turnaround time 2-3 days. Copy fee: $.25 per page. Certification fee: $3.00. Fee payee: Municipal Court. Only cashiers checks and money orders accepted. Prepayment is required.

Cuyahoga County

Common Pleas Court-General Div 1200 Ontario St, Cleveland, OH 44113; 216-443-8560; Civil phone:216-443-7966; Criminal phone:216-443-7966; Probate phone:216-443-8764; Fax: 216-443-5424. Hours: 8:30AM-4:30PM (EST). *Felony, Civil Actions Over $10,000, Probate.*

www.cuyahoga.oh.us

Note: Probate is a separate division with separate records and personnel

Civil Records: Access: Phone, mail, in person. Both court and visitors may perform in person searches. No search fee. Required to search: name, years to search; also helpful-address. Civil cases indexed by defendant, plaintiff. Civil records on index and dockets from 1968, archived from 1800s. Address mail requests to Gerald Fuerst, 1st Floor, Index Dept. **Criminal Records:** Access: In person only. Court does not conduct in person searches; visitors must perform searches for themselves. Search fee: No criminal searches performed by court. Required to search: name, years to search; also helpful-address, DOB, SSN. Criminal records on index and dockets from 1968, archived from 1800s. Address mail requests to Criminal Dept, 2nd Floor. **General Information:** No expungments or sealed records released. SASE required. Copy fee: $.25 per page. Certification fee: $1.00 per page. Fee payee: Clerk of Court. Business checks accepted. Prepayment is required. Public access terminal is available.

Cleveland Municipal Court - Civil Division 1200 Ontario St, Cleveland, OH 44113; 216-664-4870; Fax: 216-664-4065. Hours: 8AM-3:50PM (EST). *Civil Actions Under $15,000, Eviction, Small Claims.*

Civil Records: Access: Fax, mail, in person. Both court and visitors may perform in person searches. No search fee. Required to search: name, years to search; also helpful-address. Civil cases indexed by defendant, plaintiff. Civil records on computer from 1988, docket books and index from 1950s, prior archived. **General Information:** SASE required. Turnaround time 2 days. Copy fee: $.25 per page. Certification fee: $1.00. Fee payee: Municipal Court. Personal checks accepted. Prepayment is required. Public access terminal is available.

Cleveland Municipal Court -Criminal Division 1200 Ontario St, Cleveland, OH 44113; 216-664-4790. Hours: 8AM-3:50PM (EST). *Misdemeanor.* **Criminal Records:** Access: Mail, in person. Both court and visitors may perform in person searches. No search fee. Required to search: name, years to search, DOB, SSN, signed release. Criminal records on computer since 1988, on books to 1950s, archived prior. **General Information:** No adoption or juvenile records released. SASE required. Turnaround time 3-4 days. Copy fee: $.25 per page. Certification fee: $3.00. Fee payee: Municipal Court. Personal checks accepted. Prepayment is required

Bedford Municipal Court 65 Columbus Rd, Bedford, OH 44146; 440-232-3420; Fax: 440-232-2510. Hours: 8:30AM-4:30PM (EST). *Misdemeanor, Civil Actions Under $15,000, Eviction, Small Claims.*

Civil Records: Access: Fax, mail, in person. Both court and visitors may perform in person searches. No search fee. Required to search: name, years to search. Civil cases indexed by defendant, plaintiff. Civil records on computer from 1985, docket books and index from 1970s, prior archived. **Criminal Records:** Access: Fax, mail, in person. Both court and visitors may perform in person searches. No search fee. Required to search: name, years to search, signed release. Criminal records on computer from 1985, docket books and index from 1970s, prior archived. **General Information:** SASE required. Turnaround time 3 days. Copy fee: $.50 per page. Certification fee: $2.00. Fee payee: Municipal Court. Only cashiers checks and money orders accepted. Prepayment is required. Fax notes: No fee to fax results.

Berea Municipal Court 11 Berea Commons, Berea, OH 44017; 440-826-5860; Fax: 440-891-3387. Hours: 8AM-4:30PM (EST). *Misdemeanor, Civil Actions Under $15,000, Eviction, Small Claims.*

Civil Records: Access: Mail, in person. Both court and visitors may perform in person searches. No search fee. Required to search: name, years to search. Civil cases indexed by defendant, plaintiff. Civil records on computer from 1991, prior in books and archived. **Criminal Records:** Access: Phone, fax, mail, in person. Both court and visitors may perform in person searches. Search fee: $5.00 per name. Required to search: name, years to search; also helpful-address, DOB. Criminal records on computer from 1991, prior in books and archived. **General Information:** No probation records released. SASE required. Turnaround time 1 week-10 days. Copy fee: $1.00 per page. Certification fee: $5.00. Fee payee: Berea Municipal Court. Personal checks accepted. Credit cards accepted: Visa, Mastercard. Prepayment is required. Public access terminal is available. Fax notes: No fee to fax results.

Cleveland Heights Municipal Court 40 Severence Circle, Cleveland Heights, OH 44118; 216-291-4901; Fax: 216-291-2459. Hours: 8AM-5PM (EST). *Misdemeanor, Civil Actions Under $15,000, Eviction, Small Claims.*

www.clevelandheightscourt.com

Civil Records: Access: online, in person. Court does not conduct in person searches; visitors must perform searches for themselves. Search fee: No civil searches performed by court. Required to search: name, years to search; also helpful-address. Civil cases indexed by defendant, plaintiff. Civil records on computer from 1990, prior in books to 1970s. Online, available for attorneys, is free. Call 216-291-3418 for details. **Criminal Records:** Access: Remote online, in person. Court does not conduct in person searches; visitors must perform searches for themselves. Search fee: No criminal searches performed by court. Required to search: name, years to search; also helpful-address, DOB, SSN. Criminal records on computer from 1990, prior in books to 1970s. same as civil. **General Information:** No expungements or search warrant records released. Copy fee: $1.00 per page. Certification fee: $3.00. Fee payee: Municipal Court. Personal checks accepted. Credit cards accepted: Visa, Mastercard. Visa, MC in person only. Prepayment is required. Public access terminal is available.

East Cleveland Municipal Court 14340 Euclid Ave, East Cleveland, OH 44112; 216-681-2021/2022. Hours: 8:30AM-4:30PM (EST). *Misdemeanor, Civil Actions Under $15,000, Eviction, Small Claims.*

Civil Records: Access: In person only. Court does not conduct in person searches; visitors must perform searches for themselves. Search fee: No civil searches performed by court. Required to search: name, years to search. Civil cases indexed by defendant, plaintiff. Civil records on computer from 1989, docket books and index from 1950s, prior archived. **Criminal Records:** Access: Mail, in person. Court does not conduct in person searches; visitors must perform searches for themselves. Search fee: No criminal searches performed by court. Required to search: name, years to search, DOB, SSN, signed release; also helpful-address. Criminal records on computer from 1989, docket books and index from 1950s, prior archived. Address mail requests to Police Record Room. **General Information:** SASE required. Turnaround time 1-2 weeks. Copy fee: $1.00 per page. Certification fee: $3.00. Fee payee: Municipal Court. Personal checks accepted. Prepayment is required.

Euclid Municipal Court 555 E 222 St, Euclid, OH 44123-2099; 216-289-2888. Hours: 8:30AM-4:30PM (EST). *Misdemeanor, Civil Actions Under $15,000, Eviction, Small Claims.*

Civil Records: Access: Mail, in person. Both court and visitors may perform in person searches. Search fee: $5.00 per name. Required to search: name, years to search. Civil cases indexed by defendant, plaintiff. Civil records on computer from 1995, docket books and index from 1950s, prior archived. **Criminal Records:** Access: Mail, in person. Both court and visitors may perform in person searches. Search fee: $5.00 per name. Required to search: name, years to search, DOB; also helpful-address, SSN. Criminal records on computer from 1995, docket books and index from 1950s, prior archived. **General Information:** No expunged records released. SASE required. Turnaround time 1 week. Copy fee: $1.00 per page. Certification fee: $5.00. Fee payee: Municipal Court. Personal checks accepted. Prepayment is required.

Garfield Heights Municipal Court 5555 Turney Rd, Garfield Heights, OH 44125; 216-475-1900. Hours: 8:30AM-4:30PM (EST). *Misdemeanor, Civil Actions Under $15,000, Eviction, Small Claims.*

Civil Records: Access: Phone, mail, in person. Both court and visitors may perform in person searches. No search fee. Required to search: name, years to search; also helpful-address. Civil cases indexed by defendant, plaintiff. Civil records on computer from 11/91, docket books and index from 1950s, prior archived. Phone access depends on age of case. **Criminal Records:** Access: Phone, mail, in person. Both court and visitors may perform in person searches. No search fee. Required to search: name, years to search; also helpful-address, DOB, SSN. Criminal records on computer from 11/91, docket books and index from 1950s, prior archived. **General Information:** No expunged records released. SASE required. Turnaround time 2 weeks. Copy fee: $1.00 per page. Certification fee: $2.00. Fee payee: Municipal Court. Personal checks accepted. Prepayment is required.

Lakewood Municipal Court 12650 Detroit Ave, Lakewood, OH 44107; 216-529-6700; Fax: 216-529-7687. Hours: 8AM-5PM (EST). *Misdemeanor, Civil Actions Under $15,000, Eviction, Small Claims.*

Civil Records: Access: Fax, mail, in person. Both court and visitors may perform in person searches. No search fee. Required to search: name, years to

search; also helpful-address. Civil cases indexed by defendant, plaintiff. Civil records on computer from 1983, prior in books. **Criminal Records:** Access: Fax, mail, in person. Both court and visitors may perform in person searches. No search fee. Required to search: name, years to search; also helpful-address, DOB, SSN. Criminal records on computer since 1983, prior in books. **General Information:** No confidential records released. SASE required. Turnaround time 1 week. Copy fee: $.25 per page. Certification fee: $3.00. Fee payee: Municipal Court. Personal checks accepted. Prepayment is required. Public access terminal is available. Fax notes: No fee to fax results. Local faxing only.

Lyndhurst Municipal Court 5301 Mayfield Rd, Lyndhurst, OH 44124; 216-461-6500. Hours: 8:30AM-5PM (EST). *Misdemeanor, Civil Actions Under $15,000, Eviction, Small Claims.*

Civil Records: Access: Mail, in person. Both court and visitors may perform in person searches. No search fee. Required to search: name, years to search; also helpful-address. Civil cases indexed by defendant, plaintiff. Civil records on computer from 1991, prior in books. **Criminal Records:** Access: Mail, in person. Both court and visitors may perform in person searches. No search fee. Required to search: name, years to search, signed release; also helpful-address, DOB, SSN. Criminal records on computer from 1991, prior in books. **General Information:** SASE required. Turnaround time 1 week. Copy fee: $1.00 per page. Certification fee: $2.00 per page. Fee payee: Municipal Court. Personal checks accepted. Prepayment is required.

Parma Municipal Court 5750 W 54th St, Parma, OH 44129; 440-884-4000; Fax: 440-885-8937. Hours: 8:30AM-4:30PM (EST). *Misdemeanor, Civil Actions Under $15,000, Eviction, Small Claims.*

Note: The court is making changes to block the SSN from appearing on record requests

Civil Records: Access: Phone, fax, mail, in person. Both court and visitors may perform in person searches. Search fee: No civil searches performed by court. Required to search: name, years to search; also helpful-address. Civil cases indexed by defendant, plaintiff. Civil records on computer from 1993, prior in books. **Criminal Records:** Access: Phone, fax, mail, in person. Both court and visitors may perform in person searches. Search fee: No criminal searches performed by court. Required to search: name, years to search, DOB; also helpful-address, SSN. Criminal records on computer from 1993, prior in books. **General Information:** SASE required. Turnaround time up to 1 week. Copy fee: $.50 per page. Certification fee: $1.00. Fee payee: Municipal Court. Personal checks accepted. Prepayment is required.

Rocky River Municipal Court 21012 Hilliard Blvd, Rocky River, OH 44116; 440-333-0066; Fax: 440-356-5613. Hours: 8:30AM-4:30PM (EST). *Misdemeanor, Civil Actions Under $15,000, Eviction, Small Claims.*

Civil Records: Access: Phone, fax, mail, in person. Both court and visitors may perform in person searches. No search fee. Required to search: name, years to search. Civil cases indexed by defendant, plaintiff. Civil records on computer from 1988, prior in books. **Criminal Records:** Access: Phone, fax, mail, in person. Both court and visitors may perform in person searches. No search fee. Required to search: name, years to

search; also helpful-DOB, SSN. Criminal records on computer from 1988, prior in books. **General Information:** No pre-trial criminal records released. SASE required. Turnaround time 2 days. Copy fee: $.10 per page. Certification fee: $5.00. Fee payee: Municipal Court. Personal checks accepted. Prepayment is required. Public access terminal is available.

Shaker Heights Municipal Court 3355 Lee Rd, Shaker Heights, OH 44120; 216-491-1300; Fax: 216-491-1314. Hours: 8:30AM-5PM (EST). *Misdemeanor, Civil Actions Under $15,000, Eviction, Small Claims.*

Civil Records: Access: Mail, in person. Both court and visitors may perform in person searches. No search fee. Required to search: name, years to search; also helpful-address. Civil cases indexed by defendant, plaintiff. Civil records on computer from 06/86, prior in books. **Criminal Records:** Access: Phone, mail, in person. Both court and visitors may perform in person searches. Search fee: No search fee. Complete dockets $10.00. Required to search: name, years to search, SSN; also helpful-address, DOB. Criminal records on computer from 06/86, prior in books. Phone access limited to gov't agencies. **General Information:** No medical or LEADS print-out records released. SASE required. Turnaround time 2 days. Copy fee: $.50 per page. Certification fee: $5.00. Fee payee: Shaker Heights Municipal Court. Personal checks accepted. Credit cards accepted: Visa, Mastercard. Visa, MC accepted in person only. Prepayment is required. Public access terminal is available.

South Euclid Municipal Court 1349 S Green Rd, South Euclid, OH 44121; 216-381-0400; Fax: 216-381-1195. Hours: 8:30AM-5PM (EST). *Misdemeanor, Civil Actions Under $15,000, Eviction, Small Claims.*

Civil Records: Access: Mail, in person. Both court and visitors may perform in person searches. No search fee. Required to search: name, years to search; also helpful-address. Civil cases indexed by defendant, plaintiff. Civil records on computer since 10/97; prior in books. **Criminal Records:** Access: Mail, in person. Both court and visitors may perform in person searches. No search fee. Required to search: name, years to search; also helpful-address, DOB, SSN. Criminal records on computer since 10/97; prior in books. **General Information:** SASE required. Turnaround time 1 week. Copy fee: No charge until at least 10 pages, then $.10 per copy. Certification fee: $1.00 per page. Fee payee: Clerk of Court, South Euclid Muicipal Court. Personal checks accepted. Prepayment is required. Public access terminal is available.

Darke County

Common Pleas Court Courthouse, Greenville, OH 45331; 937-547-7335; Probate phone:937-547-7345; Fax: 937-547-7305. Hours: 8:30AM-4:30PM (EST). *Felony, Civil Actions Over $3,000, Probate.*

Note: Probate is a separate court located at 300 Garst Ave at the number given

Civil Records: Access: Mail, in person. Both court and visitors may perform in person searches. Search fee: $5.00 per name. Required to search: name, years to search. Civil cases indexed by defendant, plaintiff. Civil records in books to 1832, on microfiche from 1940s. **Criminal Records:** Access: Mail, in person. Both court and visitors may perform in person searches. Search fee: $5.00 per name. Required to search: name, years to search. Criminal records in books to 1832, on microfiche from 1940s. **General Information:** No secret indictment records released. SASE required. Turnaround time 1-2 days. Copy fee: $.25 per page. Certification fee: $1.00. Fee payee: Clerk of Court. Business checks accepted. Prepayment is required. Public access terminal is available.

County Court Courthouse, Greenville, OH 45331-1990; 937-547-7340; Fax: 937-547-7378. Hours: 8:30AM-4:30PM (EST). *Misdemeanor, Civil Actions Under $15,000, Small Claims.*

Civil Records: Access: Mail, in person. Both court and visitors may perform in person searches. Search fee: $5.00 per name. Required to search: name, years to search. Civil cases indexed by defendant, plaintiff. Civil records in books since 1959. **Criminal Records:** Access: Mail, in person. Both court and visitors may perform in person searches. Search fee: $5.00 per name. Required to search: name, years to search, DOB; also helpful-SSN. Criminal records in books since 1959. **General Information:** No sealed or confidential records released. SASE required. Turnaround time 1 week. Copy fee: $.25 per page. Certification fee: $1.00. Fee payee: Clerk of Court, Darke County. Only cashiers checks and money orders accepted. Credit cards accepted: Visa, Mastercard. Prepayment is required. Public access terminal is available.

Defiance County

Common Pleas Court PO Box 716, Defiance, OH 43512; 419-782-1936; Probate phone:419-782-4181. Hours: 8:30AM-4:30PM (EST). *Felony, Civil Actions Over $10,000, Probate.*

Civil Records: Access: Fax, mail, in person. Court does not conduct in person searches; visitors must perform searches for themselves. Search fee: No civil searches performed by court. Required to search: name, years to search; also helpful-address. Civil cases indexed by defendant, plaintiff. Civil Records on computer since 1995. Most recent records are kept here, usually up to 10 years. **Criminal Records:** Access: Fax, mail, in person. Court does not conduct in person searches; visitors must perform searches for themselves. Search fee: No criminal searches performed by court. Required to search: name, years to search; also helpful-address, DOB, SSN. Criminal records on computer since 1995; prior records on docket books. **General Information:** SASE required. Copy fee: $.25 per page. Certification fee: $1.00. Fee payee: Clerk of Court. Personal checks accepted. Prepayment is required. Public access terminal is available. Fax notes: $3.00 for first page, $1.00 each addl.

Defiance Municipal Court 324 Perry St, Defiance, OH 43512; 419-782-5756; Civil phone:419-782-4092; Fax: 419-782-2018. Hours: 8AM-5PM (EST). *Misdemeanor, Civil Actions Under $15,000, Eviction, Small Claims.*

Civil Records: Access: Mail, in person. Both court and visitors may perform in person searches. Search fee: $8.00 per name. Fee only for records prior to 1989. Required to search: name, years to search. Civil cases indexed by defendant, plaintiff. Civil records on computer from 10/89, prior in books. **Criminal Records:** Access: Mail, in person. Both court and visitors may perform in person searches. Search fee: $8.00 per name. Fee only for records prior to 1989. Required to search: name, years to search; also helpful-address, DOB, SSN. Criminal records on computer from 10/89,

prior in books. **General Information:** No confidential records released. SASE required. Turnaround time 14 days. Copy fee: $.50 per page. Certification fee: $1.00. Fee payee: Municipal Court. Personal checks accepted. Credit cards accepted. Prepayment is required. Public access terminal is available.

Delaware County

Common Pleas Court 91 N Sandusky, Delaware, OH 43015; 740-368-1850; Probate phone:740-368-1880; Fax: 740-368-1849. Hours: 8:30AM-4:30PM (EST). *Felony, Civil Actions Over $10,000, Probate.*

Civil Records: Access: Mail, in person. Both court and visitors may perform in person searches. No search fee. Required to search: name, years to search; also helpful-address. Civil cases indexed by defendant, plaintiff. Civil records on computer from 1992, prior books go back ro 1800s. **Criminal Records:** Access: Mail, in person. Both court and visitors may perform in person searches. No search fee. Required to search: name, years to search, DOB; also helpful-address, SSN. Criminal records on computer from 1992, prior books go back ro 1800s. **General Information:** No grand jury proceedings or expungement records released. SASE required. Turnaround time 1-2 days. Copy fee: $.25 per page. Certification fee: $1.00. Fee payee: Clerk of Court. Personal checks accepted. Prepayment is required. Public access terminal is available.

Delaware Municipal Court 70 N Union St, Delaware, OH 43015; 740-363-1296/548-6707; Fax: 740-368-1583. Hours: 8AM-4:45PM (EST). *Misdemeanor, Civil Actions Under $15,000, Eviction, Small Claims.*

www.municipalcourt.org

Civil Records: Access: Phone, mail, in person. Both court and visitors may perform in person searches. Search fee: $5.00 per name. Fee is per 5 years searched. Required to search: name, years to search. Civil cases indexed by defendant, plaintiff. Civil records on computer from 1990, prior in books. **Criminal Records:** Access: Phone, mail, in person. Both court and visitors may perform in person searches. No search fee. Required to search: name, years to search, DOB; also helpful-SSN. Criminal records on computer from 1990, prior in books. **General Information:** No assessment results or probation records released. SASE required. Turnaround time 1-2 weeks. Copy fee: $.25 per page. No certification fee. Fee payee: Delaware Municipal Court. Personal checks accepted. Delaware County checks accepted. Prepayment is required. Public access terminal is available.

Erie County

Common Pleas Court 323 Columbus Ave, Sandusky, OH 44870; 419-627-7705; Probate phone:419-627-7759; Fax: 419-627-6873. Hours: 8AM-4PM M-Th/8AM-5PM F (EST). *Felony, Civil Actions Over $10,000, Probate.*

Civil Records: Access: In person only. Court does not conduct in person searches; visitors must perform searches for themselves. Search fee: No civil searches performed by court. Required to search: name, years to search. Civil cases indexed by defendant, plaintiff. Civil records on books. **Criminal Records:** Access: In person only. Court does not conduct in person searches; visitors must perform searches for themselves. Search fee: No criminal searches performed by court. Required to search: name, years to search, DOB, SSN, signed

release. Criminal records on books. **General Information:** Passports and expungements not released. Copy fee: $.25 per page. Certification fee: $5.00. Fee payee: Clerk of Court. Personal checks accepted. Prepayment is required.

Erie County Court 150 W Mason Rd, Milan, OH 44846; 419-499-4689; Fax: 419-499-3300. Hours: 8AM-4PM (EST). *Misdemeanor, Civil Actions Under $15,000, Small Claims.*

Civil Records: Access: Phone, mail, in person. Both court and visitors may perform in person searches. No search fee. Required to search: name, years to search; also helpful-address. Civil cases indexed by defendant, plaintiff. Civil records on computer from 1990, microfiche back to 1982, index books from 1950s. **Criminal Records:** Access: Phone, mail, in person. Both court and visitors may perform in person searches. No search fee. Required to search: name, years to search; also helpful-address, DOB. Criminal records on computer from 1990, microfiche back to 1982, index books from 1950s. **General Information:** No sealed records released. SASE required. Turnaround time 3-4 days. Copy fee: $.15 per page. Certification fee: No certification fee. Fee payee: County Court. Business checks accepted. Prepayment is required.

Sandusky Municipal Court 222 Meigs St, Sandusky, OH 44870; 419-627-5926; Civil phone:419-627-5917; Criminal phone:419-627-5917; Fax: 419-627-5950. Hours: 7AM-4PM (EST). *Misdemeanor, Civil Actions Under $15,000, Eviction, Small Claims.*

Civil Records: Access: Phone, fax, mail, in person. Both court and visitors may perform in person searches. No search fee. Required to search: name, years to search. Civil cases indexed by defendant, plaintiff. Civil records on computer from 1987, prior in books. **Criminal Records:** Access: Phone, fax, mail, in person. Both court and visitors may perform in person searches. No search fee. Required to search: name, years to search, DOB; also helpful-SSN. Criminal records on computer from 1987, prior in books. **General Information:** No pending, (some) crimes of violence records, or expunged records released. SASE requested. Turnaround time 1-2 days. Copy fee: $.25 per page. Certification fee: $2.00. Fee payee: Sandusky Municipal Court. Personal checks accepted. Public access terminal is available.

Vermilion Municipal Court 687 Delatur St, Vermilion, OH 44089; 440-967-6543; Fax: 440-967-1467. Hours: 8AM-4PM (EST). *Misdemeanor, Civil Actions Under $15,000, Eviction, Small Claims.*

Civil Records: Access: Fax, mail, in person. Both court and visitors may perform in person searches. No search fee. Required to search: name, years to search. Civil cases indexed by defendant, plaintiff. Civil records on computer from 1992, prior in books. **Criminal Records:** Access: Fax, mail, in person. Both court and visitors may perform in person searches. No search fee. Required to search: name, years to search, DOB; also helpful-SSN. Criminal records on computer from 1992, prior in books. **General Information:** SASE required. Turnaround time 1-5 days. Copy fee: $1.00 per page. The fee is for a computer printout. Certification fee: $2.00. Fee payee: Vermilion Municipal Court. Only cashiers checks and money orders accepted. Credit cards accepted: Visa, Mastercard. Prepayment is required. Public access terminal is available.

Fairfield County

Common Pleas Court 224 E Main, 2nd Flr, Lancaster, OH 43130-0370; 740-687-7030; Probate phone:740-687-7093. Hours: 8AM-4PM (EST). *Felony, Civil Actions Over $10,000, Probate.*

Civil Records: Access: Phone, mail, in person. Both court and visitors may perform in person searches. No search fee. Required to search: name, years to search; also helpful-address. Civil cases indexed by defendant, plaintiff. Civil records on computer from 10/93, in books to 1970, prior archived to 1800s. **Criminal Records:** Access: Phone, mail, in person. Both court and visitors may perform in person searches. No search fee. Required to search: name, years to search; also helpful-address, DOB, SSN. Criminal records on computer from 10/93, in books to 1970, prior archived to 1800s. **General Information:** No adoption or juvenile records released. SASE required. Turnaround time 1 week. Copy fee: $.50 per page. Certification fee: $5.00. Fee payee: Clerk of Court. Personal checks accepted. Credit cards accepted: Visa. Credit cards not accepted over the phone. Prepayment is required. Public access terminal is available.

Fairfield County Municipal Court PO Box 2390, Lancaster, OH 43130; 740-687-6621. Hours: 8AM-4PM (EST). *Misdemeanor, Civil Actions Under $15,000, Eviction, Small Claims.*

Civil Records: Access: Mail, in person. Both court and visitors may perform in person searches. No search fee. Required to search: name, years to search. Civil cases indexed by defendant, plaintiff. Civil records on computer from 1990, prior in books. **Criminal Records:** Access: Mail, in person. Both court and visitors may perform in person searches. No search fee. Required to search: name, years to search. Criminal records on computer from 1989, prior in books. **General Information:** SASE required. Turnaround time 2 days. No copy fee. Certification fee: $1.00. Fee payee: Fairfiled County Court. Personal checks accepted. Prepayment is required. Public access terminal is available.

Fayette County

Common Pleas Court 110 E Court St, Washington Court House, OH 43160; 740-335-6371; Probate phone:740-335-0640. Hours: 9AM-4PM (EST). *Felony, Civil Actions Over $10,000, Probate.*

Note: Probate is a separate court at number given

Civil Records: Access: Mail, in person. Both court and visitors may perform in person searches. Search fee: $3.00 per name. Required to search: name, years to search. Civil cases indexed by defendant, plaintiff. Civil records on computer from 1992, prior in books to 1800s. **Criminal Records:** Access: Mail, in person. Both court and visitors may perform in person searches. Search fee: $3.00 per name. Required to search: name, years to search, DOB, SSN. Criminal records on computer from 1992, prior in books to 1800s. **General Information:** No records released. SASE required. Turnaround time varies. Copy fee: $1.00 per page. Certification fee: $1.00. Fee payee: Clerk of Court. Personal checks accepted. Prepayment is required. Public access terminal is available.

Municipal Court Washington Courthouse, 119 N Main St, Washington Court House, OH 43160; 740-636-2350; Fax: 740-636-2359. Hours: 8AM-4PM (EST). *Misdemeanor, Civil Actions Under $15,000, Eviction, Small Claims.*

Civil Records: Access: Mail, in person. Both court and visitors may perform in person searches. No search fee. Required to search: name, years to search. Civil cases indexed by defendant, plaintiff. Civil records on computer from 1990, prior in books to 1950s. **Criminal Records:** Access: Mail, in person. Both court and visitors may perform in person searches. No search fee. Required to search: name, years to search, DOB; also helpful-SSN. Criminal records on computer from 1990, prior in books to 1950s. **General Information:** No records protected by the privacy act released. SASE required. Turnaround time 1 week. No copy fee. Certification fee: $5.00. Fee payee: Clerk of Court. Only cashiers checks and money orders accepted. Prepayment is required. Public access terminal is available.

Franklin County

Common Pleas Court 369 S High St, Columbus, OH 43215-6311;; Civil phone:614-462-3621; Criminal phone:614-462-3621; Probate phone:614-462-3894; Fax: 614-462-4325 Civil; 614-462-6661 Crim. Hours: 8AM-5PM (EST). *Felony, Civil Actions Over $15,000, Probate.*

www.franklincountyclerk.com

Civil Records: Access: online, in person. Court does not conduct in person searches; visitors must perform searches for themselves. No search fee. Required to search: name, years to search. Civil cases indexed by defendant, plaintiff. Access records via the web site. **Criminal Records:** Access: Mail, in person. Both court and visitors may perform in person searches. Search fee: $4.00 per name. Required to search: name, years to search. **General Information:** No psych, adoption or estate tax records released. SASE required. Turnaround time to 7 days. Copy fee: First 20 pages free, then $.25 per page. Certification fee: $1.00 per page. Fee payee: Franklin County Probate Court (Civil); Clerk of Court (Criminal). Only cashiers checks and money orders accepted. Prepayment is required. Public access terminal is available.

Franklin County Municipal Court - Civil Division 375 S High St, 3rd Flr, Columbus, OH 43215; 614-645-7220; Civil phone:614-645-8161; Criminal phone:614-645-8161; Fax: 614-645-6919. Hours: 8AM-5PM (EST). *Civil Actions Under $15,000, Eviction, Small Claims.*

www.fcmcclerk.com

Civil Records: Access: Phone, fax, mail, online, in person. Both court and visitors may perform in person searches. No search fee. Required to search: name, years to search. Civil cases indexed by defendant, plaintiff. Civil records on computer from 1992, prior in books to 1970s. This court offers free Internet access to their civil records. **General Information:** No sealed or expunged records released. SASE required. Turnaround time 2-3 days. Copy fee: Fisrt 20 copies are free, then $.05 each. Certification fee: $1.00. Fee payee: Franklin County Municipal Court. Personal checks accepted. Credit cards accepted: Visa, Mastercard, Discover. Prepayment is required. Public access terminal is available.

Franklin County Municipal Court 375 S High St, 2nd Flr, Columbus, OH 43215; 614-645-8186; Civil phone:614-645-7220. Hours: Open 24 hours a day (EST). *Misdemeanor.*

www.fcmcclerk.com **Criminal Records:** Access: Mail, remote online, in person. Both court and visitors may perform in person searches. No search

fee. Required to search: name, years to search; also helpful-DOB, SSN. same as civil. Records are available from the Internet site, see civil records, above. **General Information:** No sealed or expunged records released. SASE required. Turnaround time 2 days. Copy fee: $.25 per page. Certification fee: $1.00. Fee payee: Franklin County Municipal Court. Personal checks accepted. Credit cards accepted: Visa, Mastercard. Prepayment is required. Public access terminal is available.

Fulton County

Common Pleas Court 210 S Fulton, Wauseon, OH 43567; 419-337-9230; Probate phone:419-337-9242. Hours: 8:30AM-4:30PM (EST). *Felony, Civil Actions Over $3,000, Probate.*

Civil Records: Access: In person only. Court does not conduct in person searches; visitors must perform searches for themselves. Search fee: No civil searches performed by court. Required to search: name, years to search. Civil cases indexed by defendant, plaintiff. Civil records on computer from 9/88, prior in books to 1968, archived to 1800s. **Criminal Records:** Access: In person only. Court does not conduct in person searches; visitors must perform searches for themselves. Search fee: No criminal searches performed by court. Required to search: name, years to search, DOB; also helpful-SSN. Criminal records on computer from 9/88, prior in books to 1968, archived to 1800s. **General Information:** Copy fee: $.25 per page. Certification fee: $1.00 per page. Fee payee: Mary Gype Clerk of Court. Personal checks accepted. Prepayment is required. Public access terminal is available.

County Court Eastern District 128 N Main St, Swanton, OH 43558; 419-826-5636; Fax: 419-825-3324. Hours: 8:30AM-4:30PM (EST). *Misdemeanor, Civil Actions Under $15,000, Small Claims.*

Civil Records: Access: Mail, in person. Both court and visitors may perform in person searches. No search fee. Required to search: name, years to search. Civil cases indexed by defendant, plaintiff. Civil records on computer from 1988, prior in books. **Criminal Records:** Access: Mail, in person. Both court and visitors may perform in person searches. No search fee. Required to search: name, years to search, DOB. Criminal records on computer from 1988, prior in books. **General Information:** No pending case records released. SASE required. Turnaround time 2 weeks. No copy fee. Must supply own paper for copies. Certification fee: No certification fee. Fee payee: County Court Eastern District. Only cashiers checks and money orders accepted. Prepayment is required.

County Court Western District 224 S Fulton St, Wauseon, OH 43567; 419-337-9212; Fax: 419-337-9286. Hours: 8:30AM-4:30PM (EST). *Misdemeanor, Civil Actions Under $15,000, Small Claims.*

Civil Records: Access: Mail, in person. Both court and visitors may perform in person searches. No search fee. Required to search: name, years to search. Civil cases indexed by defendant, plaintiff. Civil records on computer from 1989, prior in books. In-person searchers should call first; Tuesdays are court day and computers in use. **Criminal Records:** Access: Mail, in person. Both court and visitors may perform in person searches. No search fee. Required to search: name, years to search, DOB; also helpful-SSN. Criminal records on computer after 1988, indexed by name and DOB. In-person searchers should call first; be aware Tuesdays are busy and hard to get on computer to search. **General Information:** No pending case records released. SASE required. Turnaround time 2-3 days. Copy fee: $.10 per page. Certification fee: $1.00. Fee payee: County Court Western District. Personal checks accepted. Public access terminal is available.

Gallia County

Common Pleas Court - Gallia County Courthouse 18 Locust St, Rm 1290, Gallipolis, OH 45631-1290; 740-446-4612 x223; Probate phone:740-446-4612 x240; Fax: 740-441-2094. Hours: 8AM-4PM (EST). *Felony, Civil Actions Over $10,000, Probate.*

Civil Records: Access: In person only. Court does not conduct in person searches; visitors must perform searches for themselves. Search fee: No civil searches performed by court. Required to search: name, years to search. Civil cases indexed by defendant, plaintiff. Civil records on computer from 7/91, in books to 1968, archived to 1800s. Will fax copies for $1.00 per page if pre-paid. **Criminal Records:** Access: In person only. Court does not conduct in person searches; visitors must perform searches for themselves. Search fee: No criminal searches performed by court. Required to search: name, years to search. Criminal records on computer from 7/91, in books to 1968, archived to 1800s. Will fax copies for $1.00 per page if pre-paid. **General Information:** No records released. Copy fee: $.25 per page. Certification fee: $1.00. Fee payee: Clerk of Court. Personal checks accepted. Prepayment is required. Public access terminal is available.

Gallipolis Municipal Court 518 2nd Ave, Gallipolis, OH 45631; 614-446-9400; Fax: 614-446-2070. Hours: 9AM-4:30PM (EST). *Misdemeanor, Civil Actions Under $15,000, Eviction, Small Claims.*

Civil Records: Access: Phone, mail, in person. Both court and visitors may perform in person searches. No search fee. Required to search: name, years to search; also helpful-address. Civil cases indexed by defendant, plaintiff. Civil records on computer from 8/93, prior in books. **Criminal Records:** Access: Phone, mail, in person. Both court and visitors may perform in person searches. No search fee. Required to search: name, years to search; also helpful-address, DOB, SSN. Criminal records on computer from 8/93, prior in books. **General Information:** No expunged records released. SASE required. Turnaround time 1 week. Copy fee: $.25 per page. Certification fee: $1.00. Fee payee: Municipal Court. Personal checks accepted. Prepayment is required. Public access terminal is available.

Geauga County

Common Pleas Court 100 Short Court, Chardon, OH 44024; 440-285-2222 X2380; Probate phone:440-285-2222 X2000; Fax: 440-286-2127. Hours: 8AM-4:30PM (EST). *Felony, Civil Actions Over $10,000, Probate.*

Civil Records: Access: In person only. Court does not conduct in person searches; visitors must perform searches for themselves. Search fee: No civil searches performed by court. Required to search: name, years to search. Civil cases indexed by defendant, plaintiff. Civil records on computer from 1990, in books from 1968, prior archived. **Criminal Records:** Access: In person only. Court does not conduct in person searches; visitors must

perform searches for themselves. Search fee: No criminal searches performed by court. Required to search: name, years to search. Criminal records on computer from 1990, in books from 1968, prior archived. **General Information:** no sealed records released. Copy fee: $.25 per page. Certification fee: $1.00. Fee payee: Clerk of Court. Personal checks accepted. Prepayment is required. Public access terminal is available.

Chardon Municipal Court 111 Water St, Chardon, OH 44024; 440-286-2670/2684; Fax: 440-286-2679. Hours: 8AM-4:30PM (EST). *Misdemeanor, Civil Actions Under $15,000, Eviction, Small Claims.*

Civil Records: Access: Mail, in person. Both court and visitors may perform in person searches. No search fee. Required to search: name, years to search; also helpful-address. Civil cases indexed by defendant, plaintiff. Civil records on computer from 1990, prior in books. **Criminal Records:** Access: Mail, in person. Both court and visitors may perform in person searches. No search fee. Required to search: name, years to search; also helpful-address, DOB, SSN. Criminal records on computer from 1990, prior in books. **General Information:** No expunged records released. SASE required. Turnaround time 2-4 days. Copy fee: $1.00 per page. Certification fee: $1.50. Fee payee: Chardon Municipal Court. Personal checks accepted. Credit cards accepted: Visa, Mastercard. Accepted for criminal only. Prepayment is required. Public access terminal is available. Public Access Terminal Note: Available 8AM-11:30AM, 1:30-4:30PM. Two hour maximum.

Greene County

Common Pleas Court 45 N Detroit St (PO Box 156), Xenia, OH 45385; 937-376-5292; Probate phone:937-376-5280; Fax: 937-376-5309. Hours: 8AM-4PM (EST). *Felony, Civil Actions Over $10,000, Probate.*

Civil Records: Access: In person only. Court does not conduct in person searches; visitors must perform searches for themselves. Search fee: No civil searches performed by court. Required to search: name, years to search. Civil cases indexed by defendant, plaintiff. Civil records on computer from 1982, prior in books and on microfiche. **Criminal Records:** Access: In person only. Court does not conduct in person searches; visitors must perform searches for themselves. Search fee: No criminal searches performed by court. Required to search: name, years to search, DOB, SSN. Criminal records on computer from 1982, prior in books and on microfiche. **General Information:** No sealed records released. Copy fee: $.25 per page. Certification fee: $1.00. Fee payee: Clerk of Court. Personal checks accepted. Credit cards accepted: Visa, Mastercard. Prepayment is required. Public access terminal is available.

Fairborn Municipal Court 44 W Hebble Ave, Fairborn, OH 45324; 937-754-3040; Civil phone:937-754-3044; Criminal phone:937-754-3044; Fax: 937-879-4422. Hours: 7:30AM-4:30PM (EST). *Misdemeanor, Civil Actions Under $20,000, Eviction, Small Claims.*

Civil Records: Access: Mail, in person. Both court and visitors may perform in person searches. No search fee. Required to search: name, years to search; also helpful-address. Civil cases indexed by defendant, plaintiff. Civil records on computer from mid 1990, prior in books. **Criminal Records:** Access: Mail, in person. Both court and visitors may perform in person searches. No search fee. Required to search: name, years to search,

SSN; also helpful-address, DOB. Criminal records on computer from mid 1990, prior in books. **General Information:** SASE required. Turnaround time 1 week. Copy fee: $.25 per page. Certification fee: $2.00. Fee payee: Municipal Court. Personal checks accepted. Prepayment is required.

Xenia Municipal Court 101 N Detroit, Xenia, OH 45385; 937-376-7294; 376-7297 (Civil Clerk); Fax: 937-376-7288. Hours: 8AM-4:30PM (EST). *Misdemeanor, Civil Actions Under $15,000, Eviction, Small Claims.*

Civil Records: Access: Fax, mail, in person. Both court and visitors may perform in person searches. No search fee. Required to search: name, years to search; also helpful-address. Civil cases indexed by defendant, plaintiff. Civil records on computer from 1994, prior in books to 1960s. **Criminal Records:** Access: Fax, mail, in person. Both court and visitors may perform in person searches. No search fee. Required to search: name, years to search; also helpful-address, DOB, SSN. Criminal records on computer from 1994, prior in books to 1960s. **General Information:** No search warrant records released. SASE required. Copy fee: $.10 per page. Certification fee: $2.00. Fee payee: Municipal Court. Business checks accepted. Credit cards accepted: Visa, Mastercard. Visa, MC. Prepayment is required. Public access terminal is available. Fax notes: No fee to fax results.

Guernsey County

Common Pleas Court 801 E Wheeling Ave D-300, Cambridge, OH 43725; 740-432-9230; Probate phone:740-432-9262; Fax: 740-432-7807. Hours: 8:30AM-4PM (EST). *Felony, Civil Actions Over $10,000, Probate.*

Note: Probate is a separte division with separate records and personnel

Civil Records: Access: In person only. Court does not conduct in person searches; visitors must perform searches for themselves. Search fee: No civil searches performed by court. Required to search: name, years to search. Civil cases indexed by defendant, plaintiff. Civil records on computer from 1990, prior in books, archived to 1800s. **Criminal Records:** Access: In person only. Court does not conduct in person searches; visitors must perform searches for themselves. Search fee: No criminal searches performed by court. Required to search: name, years to search, DOB, SSN, signed release. Criminal records on computer from 1990, prior in books, archived to 1800s. **General Information:** No expunged records released. Copy fee: $.25 per page. Certification fee: $5.00. Fee payee: Clerk of Court. Personal checks accepted. Prepayment is required. Public access terminal is available.

Cambridge Municipal Court 134 Southgate Parkway, Cambridge, OH 43725; 740-439-5585 x40; Fax: 740-439-5666. Hours: 8:30AM-4:30PM (EST). *Misdemeanor, Civil Actions Under $15,000, Eviction, Small Claims.*

Civil Records: Access: Phone, mail, in person. Both court and visitors may perform in person searches. No search fee. Required to search: name, years to search; also helpful-address. Civil cases indexed by defendant, plaintiff. Civil records on computer from 1988, prior in books. **Criminal Records:** Access: Mail, in person. Court does not conduct in person searches; visitors must perform searches for themselves. No search fee. Required to search: name, years to search, DOB, SSN; also helpful-address. Criminal records on computer from 1988, prior in books. **General Information:**

No confidential records released. SASE required. Turnaround time 3-5 days. Copy fee: $1.00 per page. Certification fee: $2.00. Fee payee: Cambridge Municipal Court. Personal checks accepted. Credit cards accepted: Visa, Mastercard. Prepayment is required. Public access terminal is available.

Hamilton County

Common Pleas Court 1000 Main St, Room 315, Cincinnati, OH 45202;; Civil phone:513-632-8245; Criminal phone:513-632-8245; Probate phone:513-946-3580; Fax: 513-632-7216. Hours: 8AM-4PM (EST). *Felony, Civil Actions Over $10,000, Probate.*

www.courtclerk.org

Note: Probate is separate court at telephone number given

Civil Records: Access: Phone, fax, mail, online, in person. Both court and visitors may perform in person searches. No search fee. Required to search: name, years to search. Civil cases indexed by defendant, plaintiff. Civil records indexed on computer since 1960s, prior in books and files. Access is free from the Internet site. Civil index goes back to 1991. **Criminal Records:** Access: Fax, mail, remote online, in person. Both court and visitors may perform in person searches. No search fee. Required to search: name, years to search, signed release; also helpful-DOB, SSN. Criminal records indexed on computer since 1960s, prior in books and files. Access is free from the Internet site. Criminal index goes back to 1986. **General Information:** Criminal histories not released. SASE required. Turnaround time 2-3 days. Copy fee: Fees vary by storage media of original. Certification fee: $1.00. Fee payee: Clerk of Court. Personal checks accepted. Credit cards accepted. Prepayment is required. Public access terminal is available.

Hamilton County Municipal Court 1000 Main St, Cincinnati, OH 45202; 513-632-8891; Fax: 513-632-7325. Hours: 8AM-4PM (EST). *Civil Actions Under $15,000, Eviction, Small Claims.*

www.courtclerk.org

Civil Records: Access: Phone, fax, mail, online, in person. Both court and visitors may perform in person searches. No search fee. Required to search: name; also helpful-years to search. Civil cases indexed by defendant, plaintiff. Civil records on computer from 1989, prior in books. Access is free from the Internet. **General Information:** No expungement records released. Turnaround time 5 days. Copy fee: $.25 per page. $4.00 for docket sheet (civil). Certification fee: $5.00. Fee payee: Clerk of Courts. Personal checks accepted. Credit cards accepted: Visa, Mastercard. Prepayment is required. Public access terminal is available. Fax notes: No fee to fax results.

Hancock County

Common Pleas Court 300 S Main St, Findlay, OH 45840; 419-424-7037; Probate phone:419-424-7079. Hours: 8:30AM-4:30PM (EST). *Felony, Civil Actions Over $10,000, Probate.*

Civil Records: Access: Mail, in person. Both court and visitors may perform in person searches. Search fee: $10.00 per name. Required to search: name, years to search. Civil cases indexed by defendant, plaintiff. Civil records on computer from 1985, microfiche from 1974, dockets archived to 1800s. **Criminal Records:** Access: Mail, in person. Both court and visitors may

perform in person searches. Search fee: $10.00 per name. Required to search: name, years to search. Criminal records on computer from 1985, microfiche from 1974, dockets archived to 1800s. **General Information:** No home investigations, medical records released. SASE required. Turnaround time 1-2 days. Copy fee: $1.00 for first page, $.25 each addl. Certification fee: $1.00. Fee payee: Clerk of Court. Personal checks accepted. Prepayment is required. Public access terminal is available.

Findlay Municipal Court PO Box 826, Findlay, OH 45839; 419-424-7141; Fax: 419-424-7803. Hours: 8AM-5PM (EST). *Misdemeanor, Civil Actions Under $15,000, Eviction, Small Claims.*

Civil Records: Access: Mail, in person. Both court and visitors may perform in person searches. Search fee: $2.00 per name. Required to search: name, years to search. Civil cases indexed by defendant, plaintiff. Civil records on computer from 1984. **Criminal Records:** Access: Mail, in person. Both court and visitors may perform in person searches. Search fee: $2.00 per name. Required to search: name, years to search, DOB, SSN. Criminal records on computer from 1984. **General Information:** SASE required. Copy fee: $.25 per page. Certification fee: $1.00. Fee payee: Findlay Municipal Court. Only cashiers checks and money orders accepted. Local (Hancock County) personal checks accepted. Credit cards accepted: Visa, Mastercard. Prepayment is required. Public access terminal is available.

Hardin County

Common Pleas Court Courthouse, Ste 310, Kenton, OH 43326; 419-674-2278; Probate phone:419-674-2230; Fax:419-674-2273. Hours: 8:30AM-4PM M-Th; 8:30AM-6PM F (EST). *Felony, Civil Actions Over $10,000, Probate.*

Civil Records: Access: Mail, in person. Both court and visitors may perform in person searches. No search fee. Required to search: name, years to search. Civil cases indexed by defendant, plaintiff. Current records on computer as of 1/95. **Criminal Records:** Access: Mail, in person. Both court and visitors may perform in person searches. No search fee. Required to search: name, years to search, DOB, signed release; also helpful-SSN. Current records on computer as of 1/95. **General Information:** SASE required. Turnaround time 2-4 days. Copy fee: $.25 per page. Certified copies $1.00 per page. Certification fee: $1.00. Fee payee: Clerk of Court. No personal checks accepted. Prepayment is required. Public access terminal is available.

Hardin County Municipal Court PO Box 250, Kenton, OH 43326; 419-674-4362; Fax: 419-674-4096. Hours: 8:30AM-4PM (EST). *Misdemeanor, Civil Actions Under $15,000, Eviction, Small Claims.*

Civil Records: Access: Mail, in person. Both court and visitors may perform in person searches. Search fee: $5.00. Required to search: name, years to search. Civil cases indexed by defendant, plaintiff. Civil records on computer since 1989, prior on books. **Criminal Records:** Access: Mail, in person. Both court and visitors may perform in person searches. Search fee: $5.00. Required to search: name, years to search; also helpful-SSN. Criminal records on computer since 1989, prior on books. **General Information:** SASE required. Turnaround time 1-2 days. Copy fee: $.25 per page. Certification fee: $2.00. Fee payee: Hardin County Municipal Court. Business checks

accepted. Prepayment is required. Public access terminal is available.

Harrison County

Common Pleas Court 100 W Market, Cadiz, OH 43907; 740-942-8863; Fax: 740-942-4693. Hours: 8:30AM-4:30PM (EST). *Felony, Civil Actions Over $3,000, Probate.*

Civil Records: Access: Phone, fax, mail, in person. Both court and visitors may perform in person searches. No search fee. Required to search: name, years to search; also helpful-address. Civil cases indexed by defendant, plaintiff. Civil records on computer since 1994, in books back to 1800s. **Criminal Records:** Access: In person only. Court does not conduct in person searches; visitors must perform searches for themselves. Search fee: No criminal searches performed by court. Required to search: name, years to search; also helpful-address, DOB, SSN. Criminal records on computer since 1994, in books back to 1800s. **General Information:** No secret records released. SASE required. Turnaround time 1-2 days. Copy fee: $1.00 per page. Certification fee: $1.00. Fee payee: Clerk of Court. Personal checks accepted. Prepayment is required. Public access terminal is available. Fax notes: $1.00 per page.

Harrison County Court Courthouse, 100 W Market St, Cadiz, OH 43907; 740-942-8865; Fax: 740-942-4693. Hours: 8:00AM-4:30PM (EST). *Misdemeanor, Civil Actions Under $15,000, Small Claims.*

Civil Records: Access: In person only. Court does not conduct in person searches; visitors must perform searches for themselves. Search fee: No civil searches performed by court. Required to search: name, years to search. Civil cases indexed by defendant, plaintiff. Civil records in books. **Criminal Records:** Access: In person only. Court does not conduct in person searches; visitors must perform searches for themselves. Search fee: No criminal searches performed by court. Required to search: name, years to search, DOB; also helpful-SSN. Criminal records in books. **General Information:** Copy fee: $.25 per page. Certification fee: $1.00. Fee payee: Harrison County Court. Only cashiers checks and money orders accepted. Prepayment is required.

Henry County

Common Pleas Court PO Box 71, Napoleon, OH 43545; 419-592-5886; Probate phone:419-592-7771; Fax: 419-592-4575. Hours: 8:30AM-4:30PM (EST). *Felony, Civil Actions Over $10,000, Probate.*

Note: Probate Court's address is PO Box 70, fax is 419-599-0803

Civil Records: Access: Fax, mail, in person. Both court and visitors may perform in person searches. No search fee. Required to search: name, years to search. Civil cases indexed by defendant, plaintiff. Civil records on computer from 10/94, prior in books. **Criminal Records:** Access: Fax, mail, in person. Both court and visitors may perform in person searches. No search fee. Required to search: name, years to search. Criminal records on computer from 10/94, prior in books. **General Information:** No adoption or mental records released. SASE required. Turnaround time 2 days. Copy fee: $1.00 per page. Certification fee: $1.00. Fee payee: Clerk of Court. Personal checks accepted. Prepayment is required. Fax notes: $3.00 for first page, $1.00 each addl.

Napoleon Municipal Court PO Box 502, Napoleon, OH 43545; 419-592-2851; Fax: 419-

592-1805. Hours: 8AM-5PM (EST). *Misdemeanor, Civil Actions Under $15,000, Eviction, Small Claims.*

Civil Records: Access: Phone, fax, mail, in person. Both court and visitors may perform in person searches. No search fee. Required to search: name, years to search. Civil cases indexed by defendant, plaintiff. Civil records on computer from 1990, prior in books. **Criminal Records:** Access: Phone, fax, mail, in person. Both court and visitors may perform in person searches. No search fee. Required to search: name, years to search, DOB; also helpful-SSN. Criminal records on computer from 1990, prior in books. **General Information:** No alcohol treatment records released. SASE required. Turnaround time 1-2 days. Copy fee: $.75 per page. Certification fee: $1.00. Fee payee: Clerk of Court. Personal checks accepted. Credit cards accepted: Visa, Mastercard. Public access terminal is available.

Highland County

Common Pleas Court PO Box 821, Hillsboro, OH 45133; 937-393-9957; Probate phone:937-393-9981; Fax: 937-393-6878. Hours: 8AM-4:30PM (EST). *Felony, Civil Actions Over $10,000, Probate.*

Note: Probate is a separate court

Civil Records: Access: Mail, in person. Both court and visitors may perform in person searches. No search fee. Required to search; also helpful-address. Civil cases indexed by defendant, plaintiff. Civil records in books sine 1800s. **Criminal Records:** Access: Mail, in person. Both court and visitors may perform in person searches. No search fee. Required to search: name, years to search, DOB, signed release; also helpful-SSN. Criminal records in books sine 1800s. **General Information:** no sealed records released. SASE required. Turnaround time same day. Copy fee: $.10 per page. Certification fee: $1.00 per page. Fee payee: Clerk of Court. Personal checks accepted. Public access terminal is available.

Hillsboro County Municipal Court 108 Governor Trimble Pl, Hillsboro, OH 45133; 937-393-3022; Fax: 937-393-3273. Hours: 7AM-3:30PM M,T,Th,F; 7AM-Noon W (EST). *Misdemeanor, Civil Actions Under $15,000, Eviction, Small Claims.*

Civil Records: Access: Phone, fax, mail, in person. Only the court conducts in person searches; visitors may not. No search fee. Required to search: name, years to search. Civil cases indexed by defendant, plaintiff. Civil records on computer from 1991, prior in books. **Criminal Records:** Access: Phone, fax, mail, in person. Only the court conducts in person searches; visitors may not. No search fee. Required to search: name, years to search. Criminal records on computer from 1991, prior in books. **General Information:** No expunged records released. Turnaround time 1-2 days. Copy fee: $.25 per page. Certification fee: No certification fee. Fee payee: Hillsboro Municipal Court. Personal checks accepted. Prepayment is required. Fax notes: No fee to fax results. local or toll free calls only.

Hocking County

Common Pleas Court PO Box 108, Logan, OH 43138; 740-385-2616; Probate phone:740-385-3022; Fax: 740-385-1822. Hours: 8:30AM-4PM (EST). *Felony, Civil Actions Over $10,000, Probate.*

Note: Probate is a separate court at the number given

Civil Records: Access: Phone, fax, mail, in person. Both court and visitors may perform in person searches. No search fee. Required to search: name, years to search; also helpful-address. Civil cases indexed by defendant. Civil records on computer since 1996, in books to late 1800s. **Criminal Records:** Access: Phone, fax, mail, in person. Both court and visitors may perform in person searches. No search fee. Required to search: name, years to search; also helpful-address, DOB, SSN. Criminal records date back to 1980 on docket books. **General Information:** No secret records released. SASE required. Turnaround time 1-2 days. Copy fee: $1.00 per page. Certification fee: $1.00. Fee payee: Clerk of Court. Business checks accepted. Prepayment is required. Public access terminal is available. Fax notes: $1.00 per page.

Hocking County Municipal Court 1 E Main St (PO Box 950), Logan, OH 43138-1278; 740-385-2250. Hours: 8:30AM-4PM (EST). *Misdemeanor, Civil Actions Under $15,000, Eviction, Small Claims.*

Civil Records: Access: Mail, in person. Both court and visitors may perform in person searches. No search fee. Required to search: name, years to search. Civil cases indexed by defendant, plaintiff. Civil records on computer from 1989, prior in books. **Criminal Records:** Access: Mail, in person. Both court and visitors may perform in person searches. No search fee. Required to search: name, years to search, DOB, SSN, signed release. Criminal records on computer from 1989, prior in books. **General Information:** SASE required. Turnaround time 1-2 days. Copy fee: $.50 per page. Certification fee: $1.00. Fee payee: Municipal Court. Personal checks accepted.

Holmes County

Common Pleas Court 1 E Jackson St #301, Millersburg, OH 44654; 330-674-1876; Probate phone:330-674-5841; Fax: 330-674-0289. Hours: 8:30AM-4:30PM (EST). *Felony, Civil Actions Over $10,000, Probate.*

Note: Juvenile and probate court at suite 201

Civil Records: Access: Fax, mail, in person. Both court and visitors may perform in person searches. Search fee: $5.00 per name. Required to search: name, years to search; also helpful-address. Civil cases indexed by defendant, plaintiff. Civil records on computer from 6/30/94, prior in books. **Criminal Records:** Access: Fax, mail, in person. Both court and visitors may perform in person searches. Search fee: $5.00 per name. Required to search: name, years to search; also helpful-address, DOB, SSN. Criminal records on computer from 6/30/94, prior in books. **General Information:** No court order, expunged records released. SASE required. Turnaround time 1-2 days. Copy fee: $1.00 per page. Certification fee: $1.00. Fee payee: Clerk of Court. Personal checks accepted. Prepayment is required. Public access terminal is available. Fax notes: $2.00 for first page, $1.00 each addl.

County Court 1 E Jackson St, Ste 101, Millersburg, OH 44654; 330-674-4901; Fax: 330-674-5514. Hours: 8:30AM-4:30PM (EST). *Misdemeanor, Civil Actions Under $15,000, Small Claims.*

Civil Records: Access: Phone, fax, mail, in person. Both court and visitors may perform in person searches. Search fee: $1.00 per name. Required to search: name, years to search. Civil

cases indexed by defendant, plaintiff. Civil records in books going back to 1813. Phone & fax access limited to 1 name. **Criminal Records:** Access: Phone, fax, mail, in person. Both court and visitors may perform in person searches. Search fee: $1.00 per name. Required to search: name, years to search. Criminal records in books going back to 1813. Same as civil. **General Information:** No search warrant records released. SASE required. Turnaround time 2-5 days. Copy fee: $.25 per page. Certification fee: $1.00 per page. Fee payee: Holmes County Court. Personal checks accepted. Prepayment is required. Public access terminal is available.

Huron County

Common Pleas Court 2 E Main St, Norwalk, OH 44857; 419-668-5113; Probate phone:419-668-4383; Fax: 419-663-4048. Hours: 8AM-4:30PM (EST). *Felony, Civil Actions Over $10,000, Probate.*

Note: Probate is separate court at phone number given

Civil Records: Access: Fax, mail, in person. Both court and visitors may perform in person searches. Search fee: $1.00 per name. Required to search: name, years to search; also helpful-address. Civil cases indexed by defendant, plaintiff. Civil records on computer from 1989, prior in books and on microfiche. **Criminal Records:** Access: Fax, mail, in person. Both court and visitors may perform in person searches. Search fee: $1.00 per name. Required to search: name, years to search, offense, date of offense; also helpful-address, DOB, SSN. Criminal records on computer since 1989, records from 1985 to present in actual files, 1930 to 1985 on microfiche. **General Information:** No secret records released. SASE required. Turnaround time 2 days. Copy fee: $.25 per page. Certification fee: $1.00. Fee payee: Clerk of Court. Personal checks accepted. Prepayment is required. Public access terminal is available. Fax notes: No fee to fax results.

Bellevue Municipal Court 117 N Sandusky, PO Box 305, Bellevue, OH 44811; 419-483-5880; Fax: 419-484-8060. Hours: 8:30AM-4:30PM (EST). *Misdemeanor, Civil Actions Under $15,000, Eviction, Small Claims.*

Civil Records: Access: Phone, mail, in person. Both court and visitors may perform in person searches. No search fee. Required to search: name, years to search. Civil cases indexed by defendant, plaintiff. Civil records on index from 1988, prior in books. Will only do phone searching if not busy. **Criminal Records:** Access: Phone, mail, in person. Both court and visitors may perform in person searches. No search fee. Required to search: name, years to search, DOB; also helpful-SSN. Criminal records on computer from 8/93. Court searches back to 8/93 only. Use an abstractor to go back further. **General Information:** SASE required. Turnaround time 3-7 days. Copy fee: $.25 per page. Certification fee: $1.00. Fee payee: Bellevue Municipal Court. Only cashiers checks and money orders accepted.

Norwalk Municipal Court 45 N Linwood, Norwalk, OH 44857; 419-663-6750; Fax: 419-663-6749. Hours: 8:30AM-4:30PM (EST). *Misdemeanor, Civil Actions Under $15,000, Eviction, Small Claims.*

Civil Records: Access: Fax, mail, in person. Both court and visitors may perform in person searches. Search fee: $1.00 per name. Required to search: name, years to search; also helpful-address. Civil cases indexed by defendant, plaintiff. Civil records on computer from 7/88. **Criminal Records:** Access: Fax, mail, in person. Both court and visitors may perform in person searches. Search fee: $1.00 per name. Required to search: name, years to search, DOB, SSN; also helpful-address. Criminal records on computer from 7/88. **General Information:** SASE not required. Turnaround time 2-7 days. Copy fee: $.25 per page. Certification fee: $1.00 per page. Fee payee: Municipal Court. Personal checks accepted. Prepayment is required. Public access terminal is available. Fax notes: $1.00 per page.

Jackson County

Common Pleas Court 226 Main St, Jackson, OH 45640; 740-286-2006; Probate phone:740-286-1401; Fax: 740-286-4061. Hours: 8AM-4PM (EST). *Felony, Civil Actions Over $10,000, Probate.*

Civil Records: Access: Mail, in person. Both court and visitors may perform in person searches. No search fee. Required to search: name, years to search; also helpful-address. Civil cases indexed by defendant, plaintiff. Civil records in books from late 1800s, computerized since 06/20/97. **Criminal Records:** Access: Mail, in person. Both court and visitors may perform in person searches. Search fee: No search fee. Searches only performed in emergency situations. Required to search: name, years to search; also helpful-address, DOB, SSN. Criminal records on books from 1980, computerized since 06/20/97. **General Information:** No juvenile or search warrant record released. SASE required. Turnaround time varies. Copy fee: $.50 per page. Certification fee: $1.00. Fee payee: Clerk of Court. Personal checks accepted. Prepayment is required.

Jackson County Municipal Court 226 Main St, Jackson, OH 45640-1764; 740-286-2718; Fax: 740-286-4061. Hours: 8AM-4PM (EST). *Misdemeanor, Civil Actions Under $15,000, Eviction, Small Claims.*

Civil Records: Access: In person only. Court does not conduct in person searches; visitors must perform searches for themselves. Search fee: No civil searches performed by court. Required to search: name, years to search. Civil cases indexed by defendant, plaintiff. Civil records in books readily available for 8-10 years, prior archived. **Criminal Records:** Access: In person only. Court does not conduct in person searches; visitors must perform searches for themselves. Search fee: No criminal searches performed by court. Required to search: name, years to search, DOB, SSN. Criminal records in books readily available for 8-10 years, prior archived. **General Information:** No victim records released. Copy fee: $.50 per page. Certification fee: No certification fee. Fee payee: Clerk of Municipal Court. Only cashiers checks and money orders accepted. Prepayment is required. Public access terminal is available.

Jefferson County

Common Pleas Court 301 Market St (PO Box 1326), Steubenville, OH 43952; 740-283-8583. Hours: 8:30AM-4:30PM (EST). *Felony, Civil Actions Over $500, Probate.*

www.uov.net/jeffcodp/index.htm

Note: Probate is at PO Box 649 and can be reached at 740-283-8653

Civil Records: Access: In person only. Court does not conduct in person searches; visitors must perform searches for themselves. Search fee: No civil searches performed by court. Required to search: name, years to search. Civil cases indexed

by defendant, plaintiff. Civil records on books for 10 years or so, prior archived. **Criminal Records:** Access: Mail, in person. Both court and visitors may perform in person searches. Search fee: $5.00 per name. Required to search: name, years to search, DOB, offense, date of offense. Criminal records on books for 10 years or so, prior archived. **General Information:** No sealed records released. SASE required. Turnaround time 1-2 days. Copy fee: $.10 per page. Certification fee: $1.00. Fee payee: Jefferson County Clerk of Courts. Business checks accepted. Prepayment is required. Public access terminal is available.

County Court #1 1007 Franklin Ave, Toronto, OH 43964; 740-537-2020. Hours: 8:30AM-4:30PM (EST). *Misdemeanor, Civil Actions Under $15,000, Small Claims.*

Civil Records: Access: Mail, in person. Both court and visitors may perform in person searches. Search fee: $5.00 per name. Required to search: name, years to search. Civil cases indexed by defendant, plaintiff. Civil records in books, dating from 1813. **Criminal Records:** Access: Mail, in person. Both court and visitors may perform in person searches. Search fee: $5.00 per name. Required to search: name, years to search. Criminal records in books, dating from 1813. **General Information:** All records are public. SASE required. Turnaround time 1-2 days. No copy fee. Certification fee: No certification fee. Fee payee: Jefferson County Court #1. Only cashiers checks and money orders accepted.

County Court #2 PO Box 2207, Wintersville, OH 43953; 740-264-7644. Hours: 8:30AM-4PM (EST). *Misdemeanor, Civil Actions Under $15,000, Small Claims.*

Civil Records: Access: Mail, in person. Both court and visitors may perform in person searches. Search fee: $5.00 per name. Required to search: name, years to search. Civil cases indexed by defendant, plaintiff. Civil records in books from 1950s, prior archived. **Criminal Records:** Access: Mail, in person. Both court and visitors may perform in person searches. Search fee: $5.00 per name. Required to search: name, years to search. Criminal records in books from 1950s, prior archived. **General Information:** SASE required. Turnaround time 1-2 days. Copy fee: $.25 per page. Certification fee: $1.00 per page. Fee payee: County Court #2. Only cashiers checks and money orders accepted. Prepayment is required.

County Court #3 PO Box 495, Dillonvale, OH 43917; 740-769-2903. Hours: 8AM-4PM (EST). *Misdemeanor, Civil Actions Under $15,000, Small Claims.*

Civil Records: Access: Mail, in person. Both court and visitors may perform in person searches. No search fee. Required to search: name, years to search. Civil cases indexed by defendant, plaintiff. Civil records on computer from 1998, prior on microfiche. **Criminal Records:** Access: Mail, in person. Both court and visitors may perform in person searches. No search fee. Required to search: name, years to search, DOB; also helpful-SSN. Criminal records on computer from 1998, prior on microfiche. **General Information:** SASE required. Turnaround time 1-2 days. Copy fee: $1.00 per page. Certification fee: $1.00. Fee payee: County Court #3. Only cashiers checks and money orders accepted. Prepayment is required.

Steubenville Municipal Court 123 S 3rd St, Steubenville, OH 43952; 740-283-6020; Fax: 740-283-6167. Hours: 8:30AM-4PM (EST).

Misdemeanor, Civil Actions Under $15,000, Eviction, Small Claims.

Civil Records: Access: Mail, in person. Both court and visitors may perform in person searches. No search fee. Required to search: name, years to search; also helpful-address. Civil cases indexed by defendant, plaintiff. Civil records on computer from 1991, prior in books. **Criminal Records:** Access: Mail, in person. Both court and visitors may perform in person searches. No search fee. Required to search: name, years to search; also helpful-address, DOB, SSN. Criminal records on computer from 1991, prior in books. **General Information:** No expunged records released. SASE required. Turnaround time 1-5 days. Copy fee: $1.00 per page. Certification fee: $2.00. Fee payee: Steubenville Municipal Court. Only cashiers checks and money orders accepted. Prepayment is required. Public access terminal is available.

Knox County

Common Pleas Court 111 E High St, Mt Vernon, OH 43050; 740-393-6788; Probate phone:740-393-6797. Hours: 8AM-4PM, til 6PM on Wed (EST). *Felony, Civil Actions Over $10,000, Probate.*

Civil Records: Access: In person only. Court does not conduct in person searches; visitors must perform searches for themselves. Search fee: No civil searches performed by court. Required to search: name, years to search. Civil cases indexed by defendant, plaintiff. Civil records on computer since 9/86, on microfilm from 1960, prior archived. **Criminal Records:** Access: In person only. Court does not conduct in person searches; visitors must perform searches for themselves. Search fee: No criminal searches performed by court. Required to search: name, years to search, DOB, SSN, signed release. Criminal records on computer since 9/86, on microfilm from 1960, prior archived. **General Information:** Copy fee: $.25 per page. Certification fee: $5.00. Fee payee: Common Pleas Court. Personal checks accepted.

Mount Vernon Municipal Court 5 North Gay St, Mount Vernon, OH 43050; 740-393-9510; Fax: 740-393-5349. Hours: 8AM-4PM (EST). *Misdemeanor, Civil Actions Under $15,000, Eviction, Small Claims.*

Civil Records: Access: Mail, in person. Both court and visitors may perform in person searches. No search fee. Required to search: name, years to search. Civil cases indexed by defendant, plaintiff. Civil records on computer from 06/89, prior in books. **Criminal Records:** Access: Phone, mail, in person. Both court and visitors may perform in person searches. No search fee. Required to search: name, years to search. Criminal records on computer from 06/89, prior in books. **General Information:** SASE required. Turnaround time 1 week. No copy fee. Certification fee: No certification fee. Fee payee: Mount Vernon Municipal Court. Personal checks accepted. Credit cards accepted in some cases.

Lake County

Common Pleas Court PO Box 490, Painesville, OH 44077; 440-350-2658; Probate phone:440-350-2624. Hours: 8AM-4:30PM (EST). *Felony, Civil Actions Over $10,000, Probate.*

www.lakecountyohio.org/clerk

Civil Records: Access: In person only. Court does not conduct in person searches; visitors must perform searches for themselves. Search fee: No civil searches performed by court. Required to

Business checks accepted. Prepayment is required. Public access terminal is available.

Trumbull County

Common Pleas Court 160 High St, Warren, OH 44481; 330-675-2557; Probate phone:330-675-2521. Hours: 8:30AM-4:30PM (EST). *Felony, Civil Actions Over $10,000, Probate.*

Civil Records: Access: Mail, in person. Both court and visitors may perform in person searches. Search fee: $5.00 per name. Required to search: name, years to search. Civil cases indexed by defendant, plaintiff. Civil records indexed in books from 1977, archived from 1800s. **Criminal Records:** Access: Mail, in person. Both court and visitors may perform in person searches. Search fee: $5.00 per name. Required to search: name, years to search, DOB, SSN, signed release. Criminal records indexed in books from 1977, archived from 1800s. **General Information:** No secret or sealed records released. SASE required. Turnaround time 1 week. Copy fee: $.10 per page. Certification fee: $1.00. Fee payee: Clerk of Court. Business checks accepted. Prepayment is required. Public access terminal is available.

Trumbull County Court Central 180 N Mecca St, Cortland, OH 44410; 330-637-5023; Fax: 330-637-5021. Hours: 8AM-4PM (EST). *Misdemeanor, Civil Actions Under $15,000, Eviction, Small Claims.*

Civil Records: Access: Phone, fax, mail, in person. Both court and visitors may perform in person searches. No search fee. Required to search: name, years to search. **Criminal Records:** Access: Phone, fax, mail, in person. Both court and visitors may perform in person searches. No search fee. Required to search: name, years to search; also helpful-DOB, SSN. same as civil. **General Information:** Turnaround time is 1-2 days. Copy fee: $.25 per page. Certification fee: $2.00 per page. Fee payee: Trumbull County Court Central. Personal checks accepted. Credit cards accepted: Visa, Mastercard. In person only. Prepayment is required. Public access terminal is available. Fax notes: No fee to fax results. Local calls only.

Trumbull County Court East 7130 Brookwood Dr, Brookfield, OH 44403; 330-448-1726; Fax: 330-448-6310. Hours: 8:30AM-4:30PM (EST). *Misdemeanor, Civil Under $15,000, Eviction, Small Claims.*

Civil Records: Access: Phone, fax, mail, in person. Both court and visitors may perform in person searches. No search fee. Required to search: name, years to search. **Criminal Records:** Access: Phone, fax, mail, in person. Both court and visitors may perform in person searches. No search fee. Required to search: name, years to search; also helpful-DOB, SSN. Criminal Records in docket books since 1990, computerized since 1994. **General Information:** Turnaround time 1-2 days. Copy fee: $.25 per page. Certification fee: No certification fee. Fee payee: Trumbull County Court East. Personal checks accepted. Credit cards accepted: Visa, Mastercard. Prepayment is required. Public access terminal is available. Fax notes: No fee to fax results. Local calls only.

Girard Municipal Court City Hall, 100 W Main St, Girard, OH 44420-2522;; Civil phone:330-545-3177; Criminal phone:330-545-3177; Fax: 330-545-7045. Hours: 8AM-4PM (EST). *Misdemeanor, Civil Actions Under $15,000, Eviction, Small Claims.*

Note: Traffic Records at 330-545-3049

Civil Records: Access: Fax, mail, in person. Both court and visitors may perform in person searches. No search fee. Required to search: name, years to search. Civil cases indexed by defendant, plaintiff. Civil records on books since 1964, computerized since 09/96. **Criminal Records:** Access: Fax, mail, in person. Both court and visitors may perform in person searches. No search fee. Required to search: name, years to search; also helpful-DOB, SSN. Criminal records on books since 1964, computerized since 09/96. **General Information:** Turnaround time 1 week. Copy fee: $1.00 per page. Certification fee: $10.00 per page. Fee payee: Girard Municipal Court. Business checks accepted. Prepayment is required. Public access terminal is available. Fax notes: No fee to fax results.

Newton Falls Municipal Court 19 N Canal St, Newton Falls, OH 44444-1302; 330-872-0302; Fax: 330-872-3899. Hours: 8AM-4:30PM (EST). *Misdemeanor, Civil Actions Under $15,000, Eviction, Small Claims.*

Civil Records: Access: Fax, mail, in person. Both court and visitors may perform in person searches. No search fee. Required to search: name, years to search. Civil cases indexed by defendant, plaintiff. Civil records in books since 1970, computerized since 1992. **Criminal Records:** Access: Fax, mail, in person. Both court and visitors may perform in person searches. No search fee. Required to search: name, years to search; also helpful-DOB, SSN. Criminal records in books since 1970, computerized since 1992. **General Information:** Copy fee: $.10 per page. Certification fee: $2.50. Fee payee: Newton Falls Municipal Court. Only cashiers checks and money orders accepted. Prepayment is required. Fax notes: No fee to fax results. Local calls only.

Niles Municipal Court 15 East St, Niles, OH 44446-5051; 330-652-5863; Fax: 330-544-9025. Hours: 8AM-4PM (EST). *Misdemeanor, Civil Actions Under $15,000, Eviction, Small Claims.*

Civil Records: Access: Fax, mail, in person. Both court and visitors may perform in person searches. Search fee: $10.00 per name. Required to search: name, years to search. Civil cases indexed by defendant, plaintiff. Civil records on comupter since 10/96, in books since 1990, in storage from 1930. **Criminal Records:** Access: Fax, mail, in person. Both court and visitors may perform in person searches. Search fee: $10.00 per name. Required to search: name, years to search; also helpful-DOB, SSN. Criminal records on comupter since 10/96, in books since 1990, in storage from 1930. **General Information:** Turnaround time will vary. Copy fee: $.25 per page. Certification fee: $1.00 per page. Fee payee: Niles Municipal Court. Only cashiers checks and money orders accepted. Prepayment is required. Public access terminal is available. Fax notes: No fee to fax results. Local calls only.

Warren Municipal Court 141 South St SE (PO Box 1550), Warren, OH 44482;; Civil phone:330-841-2527; Criminal phone:330-841-2527; Fax: 330-841-2760. Hours: 8AM-4:30PM (EST). *Misdemeanor, Civil Actions Under $15,000, Eviction, Small Claims.*

Civil Records: Access: Fax, mail, in person. Both court and visitors may perform in person searches. No search fee. Required to search: name, years to search; also helpful-address. Civil cases indexed by defendant, plaintiff. Civil records on computer since 1995; prior in books to 1978. **Criminal Records:** Access: Fax, mail, in person. Both court and visitors may perform in person searches. No

search fee. Required to search: name, years to search, DOB, SSN, signed release; also helpful-address. Criminal records on computer since 1995; prior in books to 1978. **General Information:** No open case records released. SASE required. Turnaround time to 1-5 days. Copy fee: $.25 per page. Certification fee: $1.00. Is per page and includes copy fee. Fee payee: Warren Municipal Court. Personal checks accepted. Credit cards accepted: Visa, Mastercard. Prepayment is required. Public access terminal is available. Fax notes: No fee to fax results.

Tuscarawas County

Common Pleas Court 125 E High (PO Box 628), New Philadelphia, OH 44663; 330-364-8811 X243; Fax: 330-343-4682. Hours: 8AM-4:30PM (EST). *Felony, Civil Actions Over $15,000, Probate.*

Note: Probate is a separate court

Civil Records: Access: In person only. Court does not conduct in person searches; visitors must perform searches for themselves. Search fee: No civil searches performed by court. Required to search: name, years to search; also helpful-address. Civil cases indexed by defendant, plaintiff. Civil records on computer from 1987, prior in books to 1808, archived prior. **Criminal Records:** Access: In person only. Court does not conduct in person searches; visitors must perform searches for themselves. Search fee: No criminal searches performed by court. Required to search: name, years to search; also helpful-address, DOB, SSN. Criminal records on computer from 1987, prior in books to 1808, archived prior. **General Information:** Copy fee: $.10 per page. Certification fee: $1.00 per page. Fee payee: Clerk of Court. Personal checks accepted. Credit cards accepted: Visa, Mastercard. Visa, MC. Prepayment is required. Public access terminal is available.

County Court 220 E 3rd, Uhrichsville, OH 44683; 740-922-4795; Fax: 740-922-7020. Hours: 8AM-4:30PM (EST). *Misdemeanor, Civil Actions Under $15,000, Small Claims.*

Note: Probation Office phone: 740-922-3653 & 922-4360. Probation Office hours: 8AM-4:30PM

Civil Records: Access: Fax, mail, in person. Both court and visitors may perform in person searches. No search fee. Required to search: name, years to search. Civil cases indexed by defendant, plaintiff. Civil records on computer from 2/94, prior in books. **Criminal Records:** Access: Fax, mail, in person. Both court and visitors may perform in person searches. No search fee. Required to search: name, years to search, DOB; also helpful-SSN. Criminal records on computer from 2/94, prior in books. **General Information:** No confidential records released. SASE required. Turnaround time 1-2 days. Copy fee: $1.00 per page. Certification fee: No certification fee. Fee payee: Tuscarawas County Court. Personal checks accepted. Tuscarawas County personal checks accepted. Prepayment is required. Public access terminal is available. Fax notes: No fee to fax results. Local faxing only.

New Philadelphia Municipal Court 166 E High Ave, New Philadelphia, OH 44663; 330-364-4491; Fax: 330-364-6885. Hours: 8AM-4PM (EST). *Misdemeanor, Civil Actions Under $15,000, Eviction, Small Claims.*

Civil Records: Access: Mail, in person. Both court and visitors may perform in person searches. No search fee. Required to search: name, years to search. Civil cases indexed by defendant, plaintiff.

Civil records on computer from 4/91, prior in books to 1976. **Criminal Records:** Access: Mail, in person. Both court and visitors may perform in person searches. No search fee. Required to search: name, years to search. Criminal records on computer from 4/91, prior in books to 1976. **General Information:** SASE required. Turnaround time 1-2 days. Copy fee: $1.00 per page. $.25 per page after first 5. Certification fee: $3.00. Fee payee: Municipal Court. Personal checks accepted. Credit cards accepted: Visa, Mastercard. Prepayment is required.

Union County

Common Pleas Court County Courthouse, 215 W 5th, PO Box 605, Marysville, OH 43040; 937-645-3006; Fax: 937-645-3162. Hours: 8:30AM-4PM (EST). *Felony, Civil Actions Over $10,000, Probate.*

Civil Records: Access: In person only. Court does not conduct in person searches; visitors must perform searches for themselves. Search fee: No civil searches performed by court. Required to search: name, years to search; also helpful-address. Civil cases indexed by defendant, plaintiff. Civil records on computer from 1990, prior in books back to 1800s. **Criminal Records:** Access: Mail, in person. Both court and visitors may perform in person searches. Search fee: $5.00 per name. Required to search: name, years to search; also helpful-address, DOB, SSN. Criminal records on computer from 1990, prior in books back to 1800s. **General Information:** Turnaround time 2 days. Copy fee: $.50 per page. Certification fee: $2.00. Fee payee: Clerk of Court. Only cashiers checks and money orders accepted. Prepayment is required. Public access terminal is available.

Marysville Municipal Court 125 East 6th Street, Marysville, OH 43040; 937-644-9102; Fax: 937-644-1228. Hours: 8AM-4PM (EST). *Misdemeanor, Civil Actions Under $15,000, Eviction, Small Claims.*

www.munict.ci.marysville.oh.us

Civil Records: Access: Phone, fax, mail, in person. Both court and visitors may perform in person searches. No search fee. Required to search: name, years to search. Civil cases indexed by defendant, plaintiff. Civil records on computer from 1989, prior on microfilm. **Criminal Records:** Access: Phone, fax, mail, in person. Both court and visitors may perform in person searches. No search fee. Required to search: name, years to search; also helpful-SSN. Criminal records on computer from 1989, prior on microfilm. **General Information:** No probation records released. SASE required. Turnaround time 1-2 days. No copy fee. Certification fee: No certification fee. Fee payee: Marysville Municipal Court. Personal checks accepted. Union County personal checks accepted. Credit cards accepted: Visa, Mastercard. Public access terminal is available. Fax notes: No fee to fax results.

Van Wert County

Common Pleas Court PO Box 366, 121 E Main St, Van Wert, OH 45891; 419-238-1022; Probate phone:419-238-0027; Fax: 419-238-4760. Hours: 8AM-4PM (EST). *Felony, Civil Actions Over $10,000, Probate.*

www.vwcommonpleas.org

Civil Records: Access: In person only. Court does not conduct in person searches; visitors must perform searches for themselves. Search fee: No civil searches performed by court. Required to search: name, years to search. Civil cases indexed

by defendant, plaintiff. Some early years on microfiche, have docket books and files, indexed on computer since 05/98. **Criminal Records:** Access: In person only. Court does not conduct in person searches; visitors must perform searches for themselves. Search fee: No criminal searches performed by court. Required to search: name, years to search; also helpful-address, DOB, SSN. Some early years on microfiche, have docket books and files, indexed on computer since 05/98. **General Information:** All records public. Copy fee: $.15 per page. Certification fee: $1.00. Fee payee: Clerk of Court. Personal checks accepted. Prepayment is required. Public access terminal is available. Public Access Terminal Note: records available from 05/98.

Van Wert Municipal Court 124 S Market, Van Wert, OH 45891; 419-238-5767. Hours: 8AM-4PM (EST). *Misdemeanor, Civil Actions Under $15,000, Eviction, Small Claims.*

Civil Records: Access: Mail, in person. Both court and visitors may perform in person searches. No search fee. Required to search: name, years to search. Civil cases indexed by defendant, plaintiff. Civil records on computer from 1989. **Criminal Records:** Access: Mail, in person. Both court and visitors may perform in person searches. No search fee. Required to search: name, years to search; also helpful-SSN. Criminal records on computer from 1989. **General Information:** SASE required. Turnaround time 1-2 days. Copy fee: $1.00 per page. Certification fee: $1.00. Fee payee: Municipal Court. Personal checks accepted. Prepayment is required.

Vinton County

Common Pleas Court County Courthouse, 100 E Main St, McArthur, OH 45651; 740-596-3001; Probate phone:740-596-3438; Fax: 740-596-3001. Hours: 8:30AM-4PM M-F (EST). *Felony, Civil Actions Over $3,000, Probate.*

Civil Records: Access: Mail, in person. Both court and visitors may perform in person searches. No search fee. Required to search: name, years to search. Civil cases indexed by defendant, plaintiff. Civil records in books since 1850. **Criminal Records:** Access: Mail, in person. Both court and visitors may perform in person searches. No search fee. Required to search: name, years to search; also helpful-DOB, SSN. Criminal records in books since 1850. **General Information:** No sealed records released. SASE required. Turnaround time 2-3 days. Copy fee: $.25 per page. Certification fee: $2.00. Fee payee: Clerk of Court. Personal checks accepted. Prepayment is required.

Vinton County Court County Courthouse, McArthur, OH 45651; 740-596-5000; Fax: 740-596-9721. Hours: 8:30AM-4PM (EST). *Misdemeanor, Civil Actions Under $15,000, Small Claims.*

Civil Records: Access: Phone, mail, in person. Both court and visitors may perform in person searches. No search fee. Required to search: name, years to search. Civil cases indexed by defendant, plaintiff. Civil records in books from 1980s, archived from 1800s. **Criminal Records:** Access: Phone, mail, in person. Both court and visitors may perform in person searches. No search fee. Required to search: name, years to search, DOB; also helpful-SSN. Criminal records in books from 1980s, archived from 1800s. **General Information:** SASE required. Turnaround time 1-2 days. No copy fee. Certification fee: No certification fee. Fee payee: Vinton County Court.

Only cashiers checks and money orders accepted. Prepayment is required.

Warren County

Common Pleas Court PO Box 238, Lebanon, OH 45036; 513-695-1120; Probate phone:513-695-1180; Fax: 513-695-2965. Hours: 8:30AM-4:30PM (EST). *Felony, Civil Actions Over $3,000, Probate.*

Civil Records: Access: Phone, mail, in person. Both court and visitors may perform in person searches. Search fee: $4.00 per name. Required to search: name, years to search. Civil cases indexed by defendant, plaintiff. Civil records on computer from 1974, archived from 1850. **Criminal Records:** Access: Mail, in person. Both court and visitors may perform in person searches. Search fee: $4.00 per name. Required to search: name, years to search, DOB; also helpful-SSN. Criminal records on computer from 1974, archived from 1850. **General Information:** SASE required. Turnaround time 1-4 days. Copy fee: $.20 per page. Certification fee: $1.00. Fee payee: Clerk of Court. Personal checks accepted. Prepayment is required. Public access terminal is available.

County Court 550 Justice Dr, Lebanon, OH 45036; 513-933-1370. Hours: 8AM-4:30PM (EST). *Misdemeanor, Civil Actions Under $15,000, Small Claims.*

Civil Records: Access: Phone, mail, in person. Both court and visitors may perform in person searches. No search fee. Required to search: name, years to search; also helpful-address. Civil cases indexed by defendant, plaintiff. Civil records on computer from 1990, prior in books. No in person searches on Thursdays. **Criminal Records:** Access: Mail, in person. Both court and visitors may perform in person searches. No search fee. Required to search: name, years to search, DOB, SSN; also helpful-address. Criminal records on computer from 1990, prior in books. No in person searches on Thursdays. **General Information:** SASE required. Turnaround time 1-2 weeks. Copy fee: $.50 per page. Certification fee: No certification fee. Warren County checks accepted. Credit cards accepted: Visa, Mastercard. Prepayment is required. Public access terminal is available.

Franklin Municipal Court 35 E 4th Street, Franklin, OH 45006-2484; 513-746-2858; Fax: 513-743-7751. Hours: 8:30AM-5PM (EST). *Misdemeanor, Civil Actions Under $15,000, Eviction, Small Claims.*

Civil Records: Access: Phone, fax, mail, in person. Both court and visitors may perform in person searches. No search fee. Required to search: name, years to search. Civil cases indexed by defendant, plaintiff. Civil records in books since 1955, computerized since 1990. **Criminal Records:** Access: Phone, fax, mail, in person. Both court and visitors may perform in person searches. No search fee. Required to search: name, years to search; also helpful-DOB, SSN. Criminal records in books since 1955, computerized since 1990. **General Information:** Turnaround time 1-2 days. Copy fee: $.50 per page. Certification fee: $1.00. Fee payee: Franklin Municipal Court. Personal checks accepted. Credit cards accepted: Visa, Mastercard. In person only. Prepayment is required. Fax notes: No fee to fax results. Local calls only.

Lebanon Muncipal Court City Building, Lebanon, OH 45036-1777; 513-932-7210; Fax: 513-933-7212. Hours: 8AM-4PM (EST). *Misdemeanor, Civil Actions, Eviction, Small Claims.*

Civil Records: Access: Fax, mail, in person. Both court and visitors may perform in person searches. No search fee. Required to search: name, years to search. Civil cases indexed by defendant, plaintiff. Civil records on books since 1956, computerized since 1990. **Criminal Records:** Access: Fax, mail, in person. Both court and visitors may perform in person searches. No search fee. Required to search: name, years to search; also helpful-DOB, SSN. Criminal records on books since 1956, computerized since 1990. **General Information:** Turnaround time 2 days. Copy fee: No fee for first 6 pages, then $.50 per page. Certification fee: No certification fee. Fee payee: Lebanon Municipal Court. Personal checks accepted. Credit cards accepted: Visa, Mastercard. Only for criminal record searching, not civil. Prepayment is required. Public access terminal is available. Fax notes: No fee to fax results. Local calls only.

Mason Municipal Court 200 W Main St, Mason, OH 45040-1620; 513-398-7901; Fax: 513-459-8085. Hours: 7:30AM-4PM (EST). *Misdemeanor, Civil Actions Under $15,000, Eviction, Small Claims.*

Civil Records: Access: Phone, fax, mail, in person. Both court and visitors may perform in person searches. Search fee: $25.00 per name. Required to search: name, years to search. Civil cases indexed by defendant, plaintiff. Civil records in docket books since 1985, computerized since 1988. **Criminal Records:** Access: Phone, fax, mail, in person. Both court and visitors may perform in person searches. Search fee: $25.00 per name. Required to search: name, years to search; also helpful-SSN. Criminal records in docket books since 1985, computerized since 1988. **General Information:** Turnaround time 1-2 weeks. Copy fee: $1.00 per page. Certification fee: $3.00 per page. Fee payee: Mason Municipal Court. Only cashiers checks and money orders accepted. Credit cards accepted: Visa, Mastercard. In person criminal searching only. Prepayment is required. Fax notes: No fee to fax results. Local calls only.

Washington County

Common Pleas Court 205 Putnam St, Marietta, OH 45750; 740-373-6623; Probate phone:740-373-6623. Hours: 8AM-4:15PM (EST). *Felony, Civil Actions Over $10,000, Probate.*

Civil Records: Access: In person only. Court does not conduct in person searches; visitors must perform searches for themselves. Search fee: No civil searches performed by court. Required to search: name, years to search. Civil cases indexed by defendant, plaintiff. Civil records on computer since 1985, microfilm to 1977, index in books prior. **Criminal Records:** Access: In person only. Court does not conduct in person searches; visitors must perform searches for themselves. Search fee: No criminal searches performed by court. Required to search: name, years to search. Criminal records on computer since 1985, microfilm to 1977, index in books prior. **General Information:** No sealed, expunged records released. Copy fee: $.25 per page. Certification fee: $1.00. Fee payee: Clerk of Court. Personal checks accepted. Public access terminal is available.

Marietta Municipal Court PO Box 615, Marietta, OH 45750; 740-373-4474; Fax: 740-373-2547. Hours: 8AM-5PM (EST). *Misdemeanor, Civil Actions Under $15,000, Eviction, Small Claims.*

www.mariettacourt.com

Civil Records: Access: Phone, mail, in person. Both court and visitors may perform in person searches. No search fee. Required to search: name, years to search. Civil cases indexed by defendant, plaintiff. Civil records on computer from 11/91, prior in books. **Criminal Records:** Access: Phone, mail, in person. Both court and visitors may perform in person searches. No search fee. Required to search: name, years to search. Criminal records on computer from 11/91, prior in books. **General Information:** SASE required. Turnaround time 1 week. Copy fee: $.25 per page. Certification fee: $1.50. Fee payee: Municipal Court. Personal checks accepted. Prepayment is required. Public access terminal is available.

Wayne County

Common Pleas Court PO Box 507, Wooster, OH 44691; 330-287-5590; Probate phone:330-287-5575; Fax: 330-287-5416. Hours: 8AM-4:30PM (EST). *Felony, Civil Actions Over $15,000, Probate.*

Note: Probate is a separate court at number given

Civil Records: Access: Phone, mail, in person. Both court and visitors may perform in person searches. No search fee. Required to search: name, years to search. Civil cases indexed by defendant, plaintiff. Civil records on computer since 1995, in books to 1800s. No name searches are performed by mail. **Criminal Records:** Access: Phone, mail, in person. Both court and visitors may perform in person searches. No search fee. Required to search: name, years to search. Criminal records on computer since 1995, in books to 1800s. No name searches are performed by mail. **General Information:** No grand jury indictment records released. SASE required. Turnaround time 1-5 days. Copy fee: $.25 per page. Certification fee: $1.00. Fee payee: Clerk of Court. Personal checks accepted. Prepayment is required. Public access terminal is available.

Wayne County Municipal Court 538 N Market St, Wooster, OH 44691; 330-287-5650; Fax: 330-263-4043. Hours: 8AM-4:30PM (EST). *Misdemeanor, Civil Actions Under $15,000, Eviction, Small Claims.*

Civil Records: Access: In person only. Court does not conduct in person searches; visitors must perform searches for themselves. Search fee: No civil searches performed by court. Required to search: name, years to search. Civil cases indexed by defendant, plaintiff. Civil records are partly on computer from 9/94, in books from 1975. **Criminal Records:** Access: In person only. Court does not conduct in person searches; visitors must perform searches for themselves. Search fee: No criminal searches performed by court. Required to search: name, years to search, offense, date of offense. Criminal records are partly on computer from 9/94, in books from 1975. **General Information:** Copy fee: $.10 per page. Certification fee: $1.00. Fee payee: Wayne County Municipal Court. In state personal checks accepted. Prepayment is required. Public access terminal is available.

Williams County

Common Pleas Court 1 Courthouse Square, Bryan, OH 43506; 419-636-1551; Probate

phone:419-636-1548; Fax: 419-636-7877. Hours: 8:30AM-4:30PM (EST). *Felony, Civil Actions Over $10,000, Probate.*

Civil Records: Access: Phone, fax, mail, in person. Both court and visitors may perform in person searches. No search fee. Required to search: name, years to search. Civil cases indexed by defendant, plaintiff. Civil records on computer from 1988, in books archived from 1930. **Criminal Records:** Access: In person only. Court does not conduct in person searches; visitors must perform searches for themselves. Search fee: No criminal searches performed by court. Required to search: name, years to search. Criminal records on computer from 1988, prior in books archived from 1930. **General Information:** No expunged records released. SASE required. Turnaround time 1-2 days. Copy fee: $.50 per page. Certification fee: $1.00 per page. Fee payee: Clerk of Court. Personal checks accepted. Prepayment is required. Public access terminal is available.

Bryan Municipal Court 516 E High, PO Box 546, Bryan, OH 43506; 419-636-6939; Fax: 419-636-3417. Hours: 8:30AM-4:30PM (EST). *Misdemeanor, Civil Actions Under $15,000, Eviction, Small Claims.*

Civil Records: Access: Fax, mail, in person. Both court and visitors may perform in person searches. Search fee: $1.00 per name. Required to search: name, years to search. Civil cases indexed by defendant, plaintiff. Civil records on computer from 1988, prior in books to 1966, indexed prior. **Criminal Records:** Access: Fax, mail, in person. Both court and visitors may perform in person searches. Search fee: $1.00 per name. Required to search: name, years to search, DOB; also helpful-SSN. Criminal records on computer from 1988, prior in books to 1966, indexed prior. **General Information:** SASE required. Turnaround time 5 days. Copy fee: $4.00. Flat fee for first 5 pages, then $1.00 per page. Certification fee: $2.00. Fee payee: Municipal Court. Personal checks accepted. Credit cards accepted: Visa, Mastercard. Prepayment is required. Public access terminal is available. Fax notes: $2.00.

Wood County

Common Pleas Court Courthouse Square, Bowling Green, OH 43402; 419-354-9280; Probate phone:419-354-9230; Fax: 419-354-9241. Hours: 8:30AM-4:30PM (EST). *Felony, Civil Actions Over $10,000, Probate.*

Note: Probate record searching and copy fees are differnt than those listed for civil and criminal records

Civil Records: Access: Phone, fax, mail, in person. Both court and visitors may perform in person searches. Search fee: $3.00 per name. Required to search: name, years to search. Civil cases indexed by defendant, plaintiff. Civil records on computer from 7/90, in books and on microfilm from 1980, docket books, journals & microfilm back to 1800s. **Criminal Records:** Access: Phone, fax, mail, in person. Both court and visitors may perform in person searches. Search fee: $3.00 per name. Required to search: name, years to search; also helpful-SSN. Criminal records on computer from 7/90, in books and on microfilm from 1980, docket books, journals & microfilm back to 1800s. **General Information:** No adoption commitment, parental rights, juvenile, mental illness records released. SASE required. Turnaround time same day. Copy fee: $.25 per page first 25 pages, $.10 thereafter. Certification fee: $1.00. Fee payee: Clerk of Court. Business checks accepted.

Personal checks accepted for amounts under 420.00. Prepayment is required. Public access terminal is available. Fax notes: No fee to fax results.

Bowling Green Municipal Court PO
Box 326, Bowling Green, OH 43402; 419-352-5263; Fax: 419-352-9407. Hours: 8:30AM-4:30PM (EST). *Misdemeanor, Civil Actions Under $15,000, Eviction, Small Claims.*

Civil Records: Access: Phone, fax, mail, in person. Both court and visitors may perform in person searches. No search fee. Required to search: name, years to search. Civil cases indexed by defendant, plaintiff. Civil records on computer from 1988. **Criminal Records:** Access: Phone, fax, mail, in person. Both court and visitors may perform in person searches. No search fee. Required to search: name, years to search, DOB; also helpful-SSN. Criminal records on computer from 1988. **General Information:** SASE required. Turnaround time 3 days. Copy fee: $.50 per page. Certification fee: No certification fee. Fee payee: Municipal Court. Personal checks accepted. Credit cards accepted: Visa, Mastercard. Fax notes: No fee to fax results. Local faxing only.

Perrysburg Municipal Court 300 Walnut,
Perrysburg, OH 43551; 419-872-7900; Fax: 419-872-7905. Hours: 8AM-4:30PM (EST). *Misdemeanor, Civil Actions Under $15,000, Eviction, Small Claims.*

Civil Records: Access: Phone, fax, mail, online, in person. Both court and visitors may perform in person searches. Search fee: $3.00 per name. Fee is $15.00 to look in closed, stored files. Required to search: name, years to search; also helpful-

address. Civil cases indexed by defendant, plaintiff. Civil records on computer from 1989, prior in books to 1982, archived from 1972. Contact Judy Daquano at 419-872-7906 for information about remote access. Access is free using up to 14.4 modem speed. Civil and crimnal indexes go back to 1988. The system is open 24 hours daily. **Criminal Records:** Access: Phone, fax, mail, remote online, in person. Both court and visitors may perform in person searches. Search fee: $3.00 per name. Fee is $15.00 to look in closed, stored files. Required to search: name, years to search; also helpful-DOB, SSN. Criminal records on computer from 1989, prior in books to 1982, archived from 1972. For online access information see civil records. **General Information:** No expunged records released. SASE required. Turnaround time 2 days. Copy fee: $.10 per page. Certification fee: $3.00. Fee payee: Municipal Court. Personal checks accepted. Credit cards accepted: Visa, Mastercard. Not accepted over the phone. Prepayment is required. Public access terminal is available. Fax notes: $5.00 per document.

Wyandot County

Common Pleas Court 109 S Sandusky Ave, Upper Sandusky, OH 43351; 419-294-1432; Probate phone:419-294-2302. Hours: 8:30AM-4:30PM (EST). *Felony, Civil Actions Over $10,000, Probate.*

Civil Records: Access: Fax, mail, in person. No search fee. Required to search: name, years to search. Civil cases indexed by defendant, plaintiff. Civil records on computer from 1990, prior in books from late 1800s. **Criminal Records:**

Access: Fax, mail, in person. Both court and visitors may perform in person searches. No search fee. Required to search: name, years to search; also helpful-SSN. Criminal records on computer from 1990, prior in books from late 1800s. **General Information:** SASE required. Turnaround time 1-2 days. Copy fee: $.25 per page. Certification fee: $1.00 per page. Fee payee: Clerk of Court. Personal checks accepted. Prepayment is required. Public access terminal is available. Fax notes: $1.00 per page.

Upper Sandusky Municipal Court 119 N
7th St, Upper Sandusky, OH 43351; 419-294-3354; Fax: 419-09-04747. Hours: 8AM-4:30PM (EST). *Misdemeanor, Civil Actions Under $15,000, Eviction, Small Claims.*

Civil Records: Access: Mail, in person. Both court and visitors may perform in person searches. Search fee: $10.00 per name. Required to search: name, years to search. Civil cases indexed by defendant, plaintiff. Civil records on computer from 5/90, prior in books. **Criminal Records:** Access: Mail, in person. Both court and visitors may perform in person searches. Search fee: $10.00 per name. Required to search: name, years to search; also helpful-SSN. Criminal records on computer from 5/90, prior in books. **General Information:** No sealed records released. SASE required. Turnaround time 1-2 days. Copy fee: $.50 per page. Certification fee: $1.00. Fee payee: Upper Sandusky. Personal checks accepted. Credit cards accepted: Visa, Mastercard. Not accepted over the phone. Prepayment is required. Public access terminal is available.

ORGANIZATION   88 counties, 88 recording offices. The recording officer is County Recorder and Clerk of Common Pleas Court (state tax liens). The entire state is in the Eastern Time Zone (EST).

REAL ESTATE RECORDS   Counties will **not** perform real estate searches. Copy fees are usually $1.00 per page. Certification usually costs $.50 per document. Tax records are located at the Auditor's Office.

UCC RECORDS   This is a **dual filing state**. Financing statements are filed both at the state level and with the County Recorder, except for consumer goods, farm related and real estate related collateral, which are filed only with the County Recorder. All counties will perform UCC searches. Use search request form UCC-11. Search fees are usually $9.00 per debtor name. Copies usually cost $1.00 per page.

TAX LIEN RECORDS   All federal tax liens are filed with the County Recorder. All state tax liens are filed with the Clerk of Common Pleas Court. Federal tax liens are filed in the "Official Records" of each county. Most counties will **not** perform a federal tax lien search.

OTHER LIENS   Mechanics, workers compensation, judgment.

Adams County
County Recorder, 110 West Main, Courthouse, West Union, OH 45693. 937-544-2513. Fax: 937-544-5051.

Allen County
County Recorder, P.O. Box 1243, Lima, OH 45802. 419-223-8517.

Ashland County
County Recorder, Courthouse, 142 W. 2nd St., Ashland, OH 44805-2193. 419-282-4238. Fax: 419-281-5715.
Online Access: Auditor/Assessor. Records on the Ashland County Auditor's database are available free on the Internet at www.ashlandcoauditor.org/ashland208/landrover.asp.

Ashtabula County
County Recorder, 25 West Jefferson Street, Jefferson, OH 44047. 440-576-3762. Fax: 440-576-3231.

Athens County
County Recorder, Room 236, 15 South Court, Athens, OH 45701. 740-592-3228. Fax: 740-592-3229.

Auglaize County
County Recorder, Courthouse, Suite 101, 201 S. Willipie St., Wapakoneta, OH 45895-1972. 419-738-4318. Fax: 419-738-4115.

Belmont County
County Recorder, Courthouse, Room 105, 101 Main St., St. Clairsville, OH 43950. 740-699-2140.

Brown County
County Recorder, P.O. Box 149, Georgetown, OH 45121. 937-378-6478. Fax: 937-378-2848.

Butler County
County Recorder, 130 High Street, Hamilton, OH 45011. 513-887-3191. Fax: 513-887-3198.

Carroll County
County Recorder, P.O. Box 550, Carrollton, OH 44615-0550. 330-627-4545. Fax: 330-627-4295.

Champaign County
County Recorder, 200 North Main Street, Urbana, OH 43078-1679. 937-652-2263. Fax: 937-652-1515.

Clark County
County Recorder, P.O. Box 1406, Springfield, OH 45501. 937-328-2445. Fax: 937-328-4620.

Clermont County
County Recorder, 101 E. Main Street, Batavia, OH 45103-2958. 513-732-7236. Fax: 513-732-7891.

Clinton County
County Recorder, 46 S. South Street, Courthouse, Wilmington, OH 45177. 937-382-2067. Fax: 937-383-6653.

Columbiana County
County Recorder, County Courthouse, Room 104, 105 South Market St., Lisbon, OH 44432. 330-424-9517x641. Fax: 330-424-5067.

Coshocton County
County Recorder, P.O. Box 817, Coshocton, OH 43812. 740-622-2817. Fax: 740-622-0190.

Crawford County
County Recorder, P.O. Box 788, Bucyrus, OH 44820-0788. 419-562-6961. Fax: 419-562-6061.

Cuyahoga County
County Recorder, 1219 Ontario Street, Room 220, Cleveland, OH 44113. 216-443-7314. Fax: 216-443-8193.

Darke County
County Recorder, 504 South Broadway, Courthouse, Greenville, OH 45331. 937-547-7390.

Defiance County
County Recorder, 221 Clinton Street, Courthouse, Defiance, OH 43512. 419-782-4741. Fax: 419-782-3421.

Delaware County
County Recorder, 91 North Sandusky Street, Courthouse, Delaware, OH 43015. 740-368-1835. www.co.delaware.oh.us
Online Access: Auditor/Assessor. Records on the Delaware Appraisal Land Information System Project (DALIS) maps for the Delaware County Auditor database are available free onthe Internet. At main site, click on "GIS mapping" in the lefthand menu bar, then select a search method Once parcel is identified on the map, click on "identify" then on parcel map to get parcel information, values, sales, and building information.

Erie County
County Recorder, Erie County Office Bldg, Room 225, 247 Columbus Ave., Sandusky, OH 44870-2635. 419-627-7686. Fax: 419-627-6639.

Fairfield County
County Recorder, P.O. Box 2420, Lancaster, OH 43130-5420. 740-687-7100. Fax: 740-687-7104.

Fayette County
County Recorder, 110 East Court Street, Courthouse Building, Washington Court House, OH 43160-1393. 740-335-1770. Fax: 740-333-3530.

Franklin County
County Recorder, 373 S. High Street, 18th Floor, Columbus, OH 43215-6307. 614-462-3930. Fax: 614-462-4312.
http://198.234.34.195/auditor
Online Access: Auditor/Assessor. Geographic Information records on the Franklin County Auditor database are available free on the Internet at http://198.234.34.206/search.html.

Fulton County
County Recorder, Courthouse, Room 103, 210 S. Fulton St., Wauseon, OH 43567. 419-337-9232. Fax: 419-337-9282.

Gallia County
County Recorder, 18 Locust Street, Room 1265, Gallipolis, OH 45631-1265. 740-446-4612x248. Fax: 740-446-4804.

Geauga County
County Recorder, 231 Main Street, Courthouse Annex, Chardon, OH 44024-1299. 440-285-2222x3680.

Greene County
County Recorder, P.O. Box 100, Xenia, OH 45385-0100. 937-376-5270. Fax: 937-376-5386.
www.co.greene.oh.us/recorder.htm
Online Access: Real Estate, Auditor. Records on the Greene County Internet Map Server are available free on the Internet at www.co.greene.oh.us/gismapserver.htm. Click on "Click here to enter. Server Site #1". Data includes owner, address, valuation, taxes, sales data, and parcel ID #.

Guernsey County
County Recorder, Courthouse D-202, Wheeling Avenue, Cambridge, OH 43725. 740-432-9275.

Hamilton County
County Recorder, 138 East Court Street, Room 101-A, Cincinnati, OH 45202. 513-946-4588. Fax: 513-946-4577.
www.hcro.org
Online Access: Real Estate, Liens. Access to Hamilton County online records requires a $100 escrow account, plus $1 per connection and $.30 per minute. The system operates 6:30AM to 10:30PM daily and support baud rates up to 9,600. Records date back to 6/1988 For information, contact Vicky Jones at 513-946-4571. Lending agency information is available.

Hancock County
County Recorder, 300 South Main Street, Courthouse, Findlay, OH 45840. 419-424-7091. Fax: 419-424-7828.

Hardin County
County Recorder, One Courthouse Square, Suite 220, Kenton, OH 43326. 419-674-2250. Fax: 419-675-2802.

Harrison County
County Recorder, 100 West Market Street, Courthouse, Cadiz, OH 43907. 740-942-8869. Fax: 740-942-4693.

Henry County
County Recorder, Courthouse, Room 202, 660 North Perry St., Napoleon, OH 43545-1747. 419-592-1766. Fax: 419-592-1652.

Highland County
County Recorder, P.O. Box 804, Hillsboro, OH 45133. 937-393-9954. Fax: 937-393-5855.

Hocking County
County Recorder, P.O. Box 949, Logan, OH 43138-0949. 740-385-2031. Fax: 740-385-0377.

Holmes County
County Recorder, P.O. Box 213, Millersburg, OH 44654. 330-674-5916.

Huron County
County Recorder, P.O. Box 354, Norwalk, OH 44857. 419-668-1916. Fax: 419-663-4052.

Jackson County
County Recorder, 226 E. Main St., Courthouse, Suite 1, Jackson, OH 45640. 740-286-1919.

Jefferson County
County Recorder, Jefferson County Recorder 301 Market St., Steubenville, OH 43952. 740-283-8566.

Knox County
County Recorder, 106 East High Street, Mount Vernon, OH 43050. 740-393-6755.

Lake County
County Recorder, P.O. Box 490, Painesville, OH 44077-0490. 440-350-2510. Fax: 440-350-5940.

Lawrence County
County Recorder, P.O. Box 77, Ironton, OH 45638. 740-533-4314. Fax: 740-533-4411.

Online Access: Real Estate, Liens. Access to Lawrence County online records requires a $600-700 set up fee, plus $150 monthly fee. The system operates 24 hours daily and supports baud rates up to 28.8. Mortgage records date back to 1988 and deeds back to 1986; UCC liens back to 1989 For information, contact Kim Estep or Sue Deeds at 740-533-4314. Lending agency info available. Federal tax liens are online; state are with Court Clerk.

Licking County
County Recorder, P.O. Box 548, Newark, OH 43058-0548. 740-349-6061. Fax: 740-349-1415.

Logan County
County Recorder, 100 South Madriver, Suite A, Bellefontaine, OH 43311-2075. 937-599-7201. Fax: 937-599-7287.

Online Access: Auditor/Assessor. Records on the Logan County Auditor database are available free on the Internet at www2.logan.oh.us/logan208/LandRover.asp. Click on "Real Estate Search" in the left hand menu.

Lorain County
County Recorder, 226 Middle Avenue, Elyria, OH 44035-5643. 440-329-5148. Fax: 440-329-5199.

Online Access: Real Estate, Liens, Auditor/Assessor. Two access methods are available. Access to Lorain County online records require no set up fee and you receive two free months, then monthly charges are $10 for two hours, plus $.10 per minute of use. The online system operates 24 hours daily and supports baud rates up to 14.4. Records go back to 5/1992. Lending agency information is available. For information, contact Rich Barrett at 440-329-5413. Property tax records on the Lorain County. Auditor database are available free on the Internet at www.loraincountyauditor.org/lorain208/landrover.asp.

Lucas County
County Recorder, 1 Government Center #700, Jackson Street, Toledo, OH 43604. 419-245-4400.
ww.co.lucas.oh.us
Online Access: Assessor/Auditor. Records on the Lucas County Auditor's Real Estate Information System Online database are available free on the Internet at www.co.lucas.oh.us/real_estate/aries_online/logon.asp. User ID is required; registration is free.

Madison County
County Recorder, Courthouse, Room 40, 1 N. Main St., London, OH 43140. 740-852-1854.

Mahoning County
County Recorder, P.O. Box 928, Youngstown, OH 44501. 330-740-2345. Fax: 330-740-2006.
www.mahoningcountyauditor.org
Online Access: Assessor/Auditor, Real Estate. Property and sales records on the Mahoning County Taxpayer site ae available free on the Internet at www.mahoningcountyauditor.org@maho208/LandRover.asp.

Marion County
County Recorder, 171 E. Center St., Marion, OH 43302-3089. 740-387-4521. Fax: 740-383-1190.

Medina County
County Recorder, County Administration Bldg, 144 N. Broadway, Medina, OH 44256-2295. 330-725-9782.
www.medinacountyauditor.org
Online Access: Assessor/Auditor, Real Estate. Real porperty records on the Medina County Auditor database are available free on the Internet at http://222.medinacountyauditor.org/ftax2.htm.

Meigs County
County Recorder, 100 East Second Street, Courthouse, Pomeroy, OH 45769. 740-992-3806. Fax: 740-992-2867.

Mercer County
County Recorder, 101 North Main Street, Courthouse Square-Room 203, Celina, OH 45822. 419-586-4232. Fax: 419-586-3541.
www.mercercountyohio.org
Online Access: Auditor/Assessor, Real Estate. Records on the Mercer County Auditor - Real Estate Department database are available free on the Internet at www.mercercountyohio.org/auditor/RealEstate/PcardInq/category.htm.

Miami County
County Recorder, P.O. Box 653, Troy, OH 45373. 937-332-6893. Fax: 937-332-6806.

Monroe County
County Recorder, P.O. Box 152, Woodsfield, OH 43793-0152. 740-472-5264.

Montgomery County
County Recorder, P.O. Box 972, Dayton, OH 45422. 937-225-4282. Fax: 937-225-5980.

Morgan County
County Recorder, 19 East Main Street, McConnelsville, OH 43756. 740-962-4051. Fax: 740-962-3364.

Morrow County
County Recorder, 48 East High Street, Mount Gilead, OH 43338. 419-947-3060. Fax: 419-947-3709.

Muskingum County
County Recorder, P.O. Box 2333, Zanesville, OH 43702-2333. 740-455-7107. Fax: 740-455-7943.

Noble County
County Recorder, 260 Courthouse, Room 2E, Caldwell, OH 43724. 740-732-4319.

Ottawa County
County Recorder, 315 Madison Street, Room 204, Port Clinton, OH 43452. 419-734-6730. Fax: 419-734-6919.

Paulding County
County Sorcerder, Courthouse, 115 N. Williams St., Paulding, OH 45879. 419-399-8275. Fax: 419-399-2862.

Perry County
County Recorder, P.O. Box 147, New Lexington, OH 43764. 740-342-2494.

Pickaway County
County Recorder, 207 South Court Street, Circleville, OH 43113. 740-474-5826. Fax: 740-477-6361.

Pike County
County Recorder, Courthouse, 100 E. 2nd St., Waverly, OH 45690. 740-947-2622. Fax: 740-947-7997.

Portage County
County Recorder, 449 South Meridian Street, Ravenna, OH 44266. 330-297-3554. Fax: 330-297-7349.

Preble County
County Recorder, P.O. Box 371, Eaton, OH 45320-0371. 937-456-8173.

Putnam County
County Recorder, 245 East Main Street, Courthouse - Suite 202, Ottawa, OH 45875-1959. 419-523-6490. Fax: 419-523-4403.

Richland County
County Recorder, 50 Park Avenue East, Mansfield, OH 44902. 419-774-5599. Fax: 419-774-5603.

Ross County
County Recorder, P.O. Box 6162, Chillicothe, OH 45601. 740-702-3000. Fax: 740-702-3006.

Sandusky County
County Recorder, 100 N. Park Ave., Courthouse, Fremont, OH 43420-2477. 419-334-6226.

Scioto County
County Recorder, 602 7th Street, Room 110, Portsmouth, OH 45662-3950. 740-355-8304. Fax: 740-353-7358.

Seneca County
County Recorder, 103 South Washington Street, Room 7, Tiffin, OH 44883-2352. 419-447-4434.

Shelby County
County Recorder, 129 East Court Street, Shelby County Annex, Sidney, OH 45365. 937-498-7270. Fax: 937-498-7272.

Stark County
County Recorder, 110 Central Plaza South, Suite 170, Canton, OH 44702-1409. 330-438-0441x13953. Fax: 330-438-0394.

Summit County
County Recorder, 175 South Main Street, Akron, OH 44308-1355. 330-643-2717.

Online Access: Auditor/Assessor. Property tax records from the Summit County Auditor are available free on the Internet at www.summitoh.net:85/summit/pawsmain.html.

Trumbull County
County Recorder, 160 High Street N.W., Warren, OH 44481. 330-675-2401. Fax: 330-675-2404.

Online Access: Auditor/Assessor. Records on the Trumbull County Auditor Real Estate web site are available free online at www.co.auditor.trumbull.oh.us/trumv208/LandRover.asp. Click on "Press here to start. property search" to enter the database query page.

Tuscarawas County
County Recorder, 125 East High Avenue, New Philadelphia, OH 44663. 330-364-8811.

Union County
County Recorder, 233 West Sixth St., Marysville, OH 43040. 937-645-3032. Fax: 937-642-3397.

Van Wert County

County Recorder, 121 East Main Street, Courthouse - Room 206, Van Wert, OH 45891-1729. 419-238-2558. Fax: 419-238-5410.

Vinton County

County Recorder, P.O. Box 11, McArthur, OH 45651. 740-596-4314.

Warren County

County Recorder, 320 East Silver Street, Lebanon, OH 45036-1887. 513-695-1382. Fax: 513-695-2949.

Washington County

County Recorder, 205 Putnam Street, Courthouse, Marietta, OH 45750. 740-373-6623. Fax: 740-373-9643.

Wayne County

County Recorder, 428 West Liberty Street, Wooster, OH 44691-5097. 330-287-5460. Fax: 330-287-5685.

Williams County

County Recorder, 1 Courthouse Square, Bryan, OH 43506. 419-636-3259.

Wood County

County Recorder, 1 Courthouse Square, Bowling Green, OH 43402-2427. 419-354-9140.

Wyandot County

County Recorder, Courthouse, 109 S. Sandusky Ave., Upper Sandusky, OH 43351. 419-294-1442. Fax: 419-294-6405.

You will usually be able to find the city name in the City/County Cross Reference below. In that case, it is a simple matter to determine the county from the cross reference. However, only the official US Postal Service city names are included in this index. There are an additional 40,000 place names that people use in their addresses. Therefore, we have also included a ZIP/City Cross Reference immediately following the City/County Cross Reference.

If you know the ZIP Code but the city name does not appear in the City/County Cross Reference index, look up the ZIP Code in the ZIP/City Cross Reference, find the city name, then look up the city name in the City/County Cross Reference. For example, you want to know the county for an address of Menands, NY 12204. There is no "Menands" in the City/County Cross Reference. The ZIP/City Cross Reference shows that ZIP Codes 12201-12288 are for the city of Albany. Looking back in the City/County Cross Reference, Albany is in Albany County.

City/County Cross Reference

ABERDEEN Brown
ADA (45810) Hardin(95), Hancock(3), Allen(2)
ADAMSVILLE Muskingum
ADDYSTON Hamilton
ADELPHI Ross
ADENA (43901) Jefferson(74), Harrison(16), Belmont(10)
ADRIAN Seneca
AKRON Summit
ALBANY (45710) Athens(54), Vinton(26), Meigs(20)
ALEXANDRIA Licking
ALGER (45812) Hardin(95), Allen(3), Paulding(3)
ALLEDONIA Belmont
ALLIANCE (44601) Stark(90), Mahoning(7), Columbiana(3)
ALPHA Greene
ALVADA (44802) Seneca(57), Hancock(42), Wyandot(1)
ALVORDTON Williams
AMANDA (43102) Fairfield(90), Hocking(9), Pickaway(2)
AMELIA Clermont
AMESVILLE (45711) Athens(90), Washington(8), Morgan(2)
AMHERST Lorain
AMLIN Franklin
AMSDEN Seneca
AMSTERDAM (43903) Carroll(77), Jefferson(24)
ANDOVER Ashtabula
ANNA Shelby
ANSONIA Darke
ANTWERP (45813) Paulding(99), Defiance(1)
APPLE CREEK Wayne
ARCADIA Hancock
ARCANUM (45304) Darke(86), Miami(13)
ARCHBOLD (43502) Fulton(91), Henry(9)
ARLINGTON Hancock
ASHLAND Ashland
ASHLEY (43003) Delaware(56), Morrow(44)
ASHTABULA Ashtabula
ASHVILLE Pickaway
ATHENS Athens
ATTICA (44807) Seneca(86), Huron(14)
ATWATER (44201) Portage(97), Stark(3)
AUGUSTA Carroll
AURORA (44202) Portage(86), Summit(11), Geauga(2)
AUSTINBURG Ashtabula
AVA Noble
AVON Lorain
AVON LAKE Lorain
B F GOODRICH CO Summit
BAINBRIDGE (45612) Ross(65), Pike(21), Highland(14)
BAKERSVILLE Coshocton
BALTIC (43804) Holmes(57), Tuscarawas(25), Coshocton(18)
BALTIMORE Fairfield

BANNOCK Belmont
BARBERTON Summit
BARLOW Washington
BARNESVILLE Belmont
BARTLETT Washington
BARTON Belmont
BASCOM Seneca
BATAVIA Clermont
BATH Summit
BAY VILLAGE Cuyahoga
BEACH CITY (44608) Stark(72), Tuscarawas(29)
BEACHWOOD Cuyahoga
BEALLSVILLE (43716) Monroe(75), Belmont(26)
BEAVER (45613) Pike(82), Jackson(18)
BEAVERDAM Allen
BEDFORD Cuyahoga
BELLAIRE Belmont
BELLBROOK Greene
BELLE CENTER (43310) Logan(74), Hardin(26)
BELLE VALLEY Noble
BELLEFONTAINE Logan
BELLEVUE (44811) Huron(43), Sandusky(41), Seneca(11), Erie(6)
BELLVILLE (44813) Richland(85), Knox(8), Morrow(7)
BELMONT Belmont
BELMORE Putnam
BELOIT (44609) Mahoning(60), Columbiana(40)
BELPRE Washington
BENTON RIDGE Hancock
BENTONVILLE Adams
BEREA Cuyahoga
BERGHOLZ (43908) Carroll(53), Jefferson(47)
BERKEY (43504) Lucas(94), Fulton(6)
BERLIN Holmes
BERLIN CENTER Mahoning
BERLIN HEIGHTS Erie
BETHEL Clermont
BETHESDA Belmont
BETTSVILLE Seneca
BEVERLY (45715) Washington(63), Morgan(29), Noble(8)
BIDWELL Gallia
BIG PRAIRIE (44611) Holmes(94), Wayne(6)
BIRMINGHAM Erie
BLACKLICK Franklin
BLADENSBURG Knox
BLAINE Belmont
BLAKESLEE Williams
BLANCHESTER Clinton
BLISSFIELD Coshocton
BLOOMDALE (44817) Wood(93), Hancock(7)
BLOOMINGBURG Fayette
BLOOMINGDALE (43910) Jefferson(97), Harrison(3)
BLOOMVILLE (44818) Seneca(62), Crawford(38)

BLUE CREEK (45616) Adams(84), Scioto(16)
BLUE ROCK (43720) Muskingum(91), Morgan(9)
BLUFFTON (45817) Allen(85), Hancock(14), Putnam(1)
BOLIVAR (44612) Tuscarawas(94), Stark(6)
BOTKINS (45306) Shelby(94), Auglaize(6)
BOURNEVILLE Ross
BOWERSTON (44695) Harrison(54), Carroll(46)
BOWERSVILLE Greene
BOWLING GREEN Wood
BRADFORD (45308) Darke(54), Miami(46)
BRADNER (43406) Wood(90), Sandusky(10)
BRADY LAKE Portage
BRECKSVILLE (44141) Cuyahoga(93), Summit(7)
BREMEN (43107) Fairfield(92), Hocking(5), Perry(3)
BREWSTER Stark
BRICE Franklin
BRIDGEPORT Belmont
BRILLIANT Jefferson
BRINKHAVEN (43006) Coshocton(39), Holmes(39), Knox(22)
BRISTOLVILLE Trumbull
BROADVIEW HEIGHTS Cuyahoga
BROADWAY Union
BROOKFIELD Trumbull
BROOKPARK Cuyahoga
BROOKVILLE (45309) Montgomery(99), Darke(1)
BROWNSVILLE Licking
BRUNSWICK Medina
BRYAN (43506) Williams(97), Defiance(3)
BUCHTEL Athens
BUCKEYE LAKE Licking
BUCKLAND Auglaize
BUCYRUS Crawford
BUFFALO Guernsey
BUFORD Highland
BURBANK (44214) Wayne(83), Medina(17)
BURGHILL Trumbull
BURGOON (43407) Sandusky(98), Seneca(2)
BURKETTSVILLE Mercer
BURTON Geauga
BUTLER (44822) Richland(61), Knox(38)
BYESVILLE Guernsey
CABLE Champaign
CADIZ Harrison
CAIRO Allen
CALDWELL (43724) Noble(98), Morgan(2)
CALEDONIA (43314) Marion(84), Morrow(10), Crawford(6)
CAMBRIDGE Guernsey
CAMDEN Preble
CAMERON Monroe
CAMP DENNISON Hamilton
CAMPBELL Mahoning

CANAL FULTON (44614) Stark(97), Summit(2), Wayne(1)
CANAL WINCHESTER (43110) Fairfield(55), Franklin(44)
CANFIELD Mahoning
CANTON (44720) Stark(93), Summit(8)
CANTON (44730) Stark(99), Carroll(1)
CANTON Stark
CARBON HILL Hocking
CARBONDALE Athens
CARDINGTON (43315) Morrow(93), Marion(7)
CAREY (43316) Wyandot(82), Seneca(16), Hancock(3)
CARROLL Fairfield
CARROLLTON Carroll
CASSTOWN (45312) Miami(98), Champaign(2)
CASTALIA (44824) Erie(98), Sandusky(3)
CATAWBA Clark
CECIL (45821) Paulding(93), Defiance(7)
CEDARVILLE (45314) Greene(97), Clark(3)
CELINA Mercer
CENTERBURG (43011) Knox(57), Morrow(17), Delaware(13), Licking(12)
CHAGRIN FALLS (44022) Cuyahoga(78), Geauga(22)
CHAGRIN FALLS Geauga
CHANDLERSVILLE Muskingum
CHARDON (44024) Geauga(98), Lake(2)
CHARM Holmes
CHATFIELD Crawford
CHAUNCEY Athens
CHERRY FORK Adams
CHESAPEAKE Lawrence
CHESHIRE (45620) Gallia(97), Meigs(3)
CHESTER Meigs
CHESTERHILL (43728) Morgan(92), Athens(8)
CHESTERLAND Geauga
CHESTERVILLE Morrow
CHICKASAW Mercer
CHILLICOTHE Ross
CHILO Clermont
CHIPPEWA LAKE Medina
CHRISTIANSBURG Champaign
CINCINNATI (45241) Hamilton(75), Butler(22), Warren(3)
CINCINNATI (45244) Hamilton(60), Clermont(40)
CINCINNATI (45246) Hamilton(94), Butler(6)
CINCINNATI (45249) Hamilton(97), Warren(3)
CINCINNATI (45255) Hamilton(71), Clermont(29)
CINCINNATI Brown
CINCINNATI Clermont
CINCINNATI Hamilton
CIRCLEVILLE Pickaway
CLARINGTON Monroe
CLARKSBURG (43115) Ross(79), Pickaway(21)

CLARKSVILLE Clinton
CLAY CENTER Ottawa
CLAYTON Montgomery
CLEVELAND Cuyahoga
CLEVES Hamilton
CLIFTON Greene
CLINTON (44216) Summit(88), Stark(11)
CLOVERDALE (45827) Putnam(87), Paulding(13)
CLYDE (43410) Sandusky(97), Seneca(4)
COAL RUN Washington
COALTON Jackson
COLDWATER Mercer
COLERAIN Belmont
COLLEGE CORNER Butler
COLLINS (44826) Huron(85), Erie(16)
COLLINSVILLE Butler
COLTON Henry
COLUMBIA STATION Lorain
COLUMBIANA (44408) Columbiana(87), Mahoning(13)
COLUMBUS Delaware
COLUMBUS Franklin
COLUMBUS GROVE (45830) Putnam(80), Allen(20)
COMMERCIAL POINT Pickaway
CONESVILLE (43811) Coshocton(99), Muskingum(1)
CONNEAUT Ashtabula
CONOVER (45317) Miami(50), Champaign(40), Shelby(10)
CONTINENTAL (45831) Putnam(96), Defiance(2), Paulding(2)
CONVOY (45832) Van Wert(98), Paulding(2)
COOLVILLE (45723) Athens(83), Meigs(14), Washington(3)
CORNING (43730) Perry(98), Morgan(3)
CORTLAND Trumbull
COSHOCTON Coshocton
COVINGTON (45318) Miami(96), Shelby(4)
CREOLA (45622) Vinton(98), Hocking(2)
CRESTLINE (44827) Crawford(99), Richland(1)
CRESTON (44217) Wayne(91), Medina(9)
CROOKSVILLE (43731) Perry(86), Morgan(14)
CROTON (99999) Licking(99), Delaware(1)
CROWN CITY (45623) Gallia(86), Lawrence(14)
CUBA Clinton
CUMBERLAND (43732) Guernsey(74), Noble(17), Muskingum(7), Morgan(2)
CURTICE (43412) Lucas(62), Ottawa(38)
CUSTAR (43511) Wood(77), Henry(23)
CUTLER (45724) Washington(96), Athens(4)
CUYAHOGA FALLS Summit
CYGNET Wood
CYNTHIANA Pike
DALTON (44618) Wayne(92), Stark(8)
DAMASCUS Mahoning
DANVILLE Knox
DAYTON (45424) Montgomery(97), Greene(3)
DAYTON (45431) Montgomery(59), Greene(41)
DAYTON (45432) Greene(52), Montgomery(48)
DAYTON (45433) Greene(97), Montgomery(3)
DAYTON (45434) Greene(99), Montgomery(1)
DAYTON (45440) Montgomery(60), Greene(40)
DAYTON (45458) Montgomery(95), Warren(5)
DAYTON (45459) Montgomery(99), Greene(1)
DAYTON Greene
DAYTON Montgomery

DE GRAFF (43318) Logan(77), Champaign(23)
DECATUR Brown
DEERFIELD Portage
DEERSVILLE Harrison
DEFIANCE (43512) Defiance(96), Paulding(4)
DELAWARE Delaware
DELLROY Carroll
DELPHOS (45833) Allen(56), Van Wert(40), Putnam(4)
DELTA Fulton
DENNISON (44621) Tuscarawas(91), Harrison(8), Carroll(1)
DERBY Pickaway
DERWENT Guernsey
DESHLER (43516) Henry(81), Wood(13), Putnam(4), Hancock(2)
DEXTER CITY Noble
DIAMOND (44412) Portage(77), Mahoning(23)
DILLONVALE (43917) Jefferson(77), Belmont(23)
DOLA Hardin
DONNELSVILLE Clark
DORSET Ashtabula
DOVER Tuscarawas
DOYLESTOWN (99999) Wayne(99), Medina(1)
DRESDEN (43821) Muskingum(85), Coshocton(15)
DUBLIN (43016) Franklin(97), Delaware(2)
DUBLIN (43017) Franklin(87), Delaware(13)
DUNBRIDGE Wood
DUNCAN FALLS Muskingum
DUNDEE (44624) Tuscarawas(57), Holmes(29), Wayne(12), Stark(1)
DUNKIRK (45836) Hardin(99), Hancock(1)
DUPONT Putnam
EAST CLARIDON Geauga
EAST FULTONHAM Muskingum
EAST LIBERTY (43319) Logan(97), Union(3)
EAST LIVERPOOL Columbiana
EAST PALESTINE Columbiana
EAST ROCHESTER (44625) Columbiana(81), Carroll(20)
EAST SPARTA (44626) Stark(95), Tuscarawas(5)
EAST SPRINGFIELD Jefferson
EASTLAKE Lake
EATON Preble
EDGERTON (43517) Williams(80), Defiance(20)
EDISON Morrow
EDON Williams
ELDORADO Preble
ELGIN Van Wert
ELKTON Columbiana
ELLSWORTH Mahoning
ELMORE (43416) Ottawa(89), Sandusky(11)
ELYRIA Lorain
EMPIRE Jefferson
ENGLEWOOD (45322) Montgomery(97), Miami(3)
ENON Clark
ETNA Licking
EUCLID Cuyahoga
EVANSPORT Defiance
FAIRBORN Greene
FAIRFIELD Butler
FAIRPOINT Belmont
FAIRVIEW Guernsey
FARMDALE Trumbull
FARMER Defiance
FARMERSVILLE Montgomery
FAYETTE (43521) Fulton(97), Williams(3)
FAYETTEVILLE (45118) Brown(98), Clermont(2)
FEESBURG Brown

FELICITY Clermont
FINDLAY Hancock
FLAT ROCK Seneca
FLEMING Washington
FLETCHER (45326) Miami(99), Shelby(1)
FLUSHING (43977) Belmont(77), Harrison(23)
FOREST (45843) Hardin(63), Wyandot(19), Hancock(17)
FORT JENNINGS (45844) Putnam(91), Allen(5), Van Wert(4)
FORT LORAMIE (45845) Shelby(94), Auglaize(5), Mercer(1)
FORT RECOVERY (45846) Mercer(88), Darke(12)
FORT SENECA Seneca
FOSTORIA (44830) Seneca(66), Hancock(18), Wood(17)
FOWLER Trumbull
FRANKFORT Ross
FRANKLIN Warren
FRANKLIN FURNACE (45629) Scioto(94), Lawrence(6)
FRAZEYSBURG (43822) Muskingum(60), Licking(21), Coshocton(11), Knox(8)
FREDERICKSBURG (44627) Wayne(66), Holmes(35)
FREDERICKTOWN (43019) Knox(82), Morrow(16), Richland(2)
FREEPORT (43973) Guernsey(52), Harrison(47), Tuscarawas(1)
FREMONT Sandusky
FRESNO (43824) Coshocton(92), Tuscarawas(8)
FRIENDSHIP Scioto
FULTON Morrow
FULTONHAM Muskingum
GALENA Delaware
GALION (43833) Crawford(87), Morrow(9), Richland(4)
GALLIPOLIS Gallia
GALLOWAY (43119) Franklin(94), Madison(6)
GAMBIER Knox
GARRETTSVILLE (44231) Portage(88), Geauga(10), Trumbull(2)
GATES MILLS Cuyahoga
GENEVA (44041) Ashtabula(99), Lake(2)
GENOA (43430) Ottawa(96), Wood(3)
GEORGETOWN Brown
GERMANTOWN (45327) Montgomery(95), Preble(4), Butler(1)
GETTYSBURG Darke
GIBSONBURG (43431) Sandusky(98), Wood(2)
GIRARD Trumbull
GLANDORF Putnam
GLENCOE Belmont
GLENFORD (43739) Perry(64), Licking(36)
GLENMONT (44628) Holmes(63), Knox(37)
GLOUSTER (45732) Athens(89), Morgan(6), Perry(5), Hocking(1)
GNADENHUTTEN Tuscarawas
GOMER Allen
GORDON Darke
GOSHEN Clermont
GRAFTON Lorain
GRAND RAPIDS (43522) Wood(54), Lucas(37), Henry(9)
GRAND RIVER Lake
GRANVILLE Licking
GRATIOT Licking
GRATIS Preble
GRAYSVILLE (45734) Monroe(76), Washington(24)
GRAYTOWN Ottawa
GREEN Summit
GREEN CAMP Marion
GREEN SPRINGS (44836) Seneca(64), Sandusky(36)
GREENFIELD Highland

GREENFORD Mahoning
GREENTOWN Stark
GREENVILLE Darke
GREENWICH (44837) Huron(77), Richland(12), Ashland(10)
GRELTON Henry
GROVE CITY Franklin
GROVEPORT (43125) Franklin(97), Pickaway(3)
GROVEPORT Franklin
GROVER HILL (45849) Paulding(65), Van Wert(33), Putnam(2)
GUYSVILLE (45735) Athens(98), Meigs(2)
GYPSUM Ottawa
HALLSVILLE Ross
HAMDEN Vinton
HAMERSVILLE Brown
HAMILTON Butler
HAMLER Henry
HAMMONDSVILLE (43930) Jefferson(54), Columbiana(46)
HANNIBAL Monroe
HANOVERTON Columbiana
HARBOR VIEW Lucas
HARLEM SPRINGS Carroll
HARPSTER (43323) Wyandot(97), Marion(3)
HARRISBURG Franklin
HARRISON Hamilton
HARRISVILLE Harrison
HARROD (45850) Allen(68), Hardin(22), Auglaize(10)
HARTFORD Trumbull
HARTVILLE (44632) Stark(95), Portage(5)
HARVEYSBURG Warren
HASKINS Wood
HAVERHILL Scioto
HAVILAND Paulding
HAYDENVILLE Hocking
HAYESVILLE Ashland
HEBRON Licking
HELENA Sandusky
HICKSVILLE (43526) Defiance(97), Paulding(4)
HIGGINSPORT Brown
HIGHLAND Highland
HILLIARD Franklin
HILLSBORO Highland
HINCKLEY Medina
HIRAM (44234) Portage(64), Geauga(36)
HOCKINGPORT Athens
HOLGATE (43527) Henry(90), Defiance(11)
HOLLAND Lucas
HOLLANSBURG Darke
HOLLOWAY Belmont
HOLMESVILLE Holmes
HOMER Licking
HOMERVILLE (44235) Medina(98), Ashland(2)
HOMEWORTH (44634) Columbiana(79), Stark(21)
HOOVEN Hamilton
HOPEDALE (43976) Harrison(98), Jefferson(2)
HOPEWELL (43746) Muskingum(88), Licking(12)
HOUSTON Shelby
HOWARD Knox
HOYTVILLE Wood
HUBBARD Trumbull
HUDSON (99999) Summit(99), Portage(1)
HUNTSBURG (44046) Geauga(99), Ashtabula(1)
HUNTSVILLE Logan
HURON Erie
IBERIA Morrow
INDEPENDENCE Cuyahoga
IRONDALE (43932) Jefferson(59), Columbiana(41)
IRONTON (45638) Lawrence(95), Scioto(5)
IRWIN (43029) Union(75), Madison(26)

ISLE SAINT GEORGE Ottawa
JACKSON Jackson
JACKSON Monroe
JACKSON CENTER (45334) Shelby(90),
   Auglaize(5), Logan(5)
JACKSONTOWN Licking
JACKSONVILLE Athens
JACOBSBURG Belmont
JAMESTOWN (45335) Greene(97),
   Fayette(2)
JASPER Pike
JEFFERSON Ashtabula
JEFFERSONVILLE Fayette
JENERA Hancock
JEROMESVILLE (44840) Ashland(98),
   Wayne(2)
JERRY CITY Wood
JERUSALEM (43747) Monroe(64),
   Belmont(36)
JEWELL Defiance
JEWETT (43986) Harrison(93), Carroll(7)
JOHNSTOWN (43031) Licking(98),
   Delaware(2)
JUNCTION CITY Perry
KALIDA Putnam
KANSAS (44841) Seneca(72),
   Sandusky(28)
KEENE Coshocton
KELLEYS ISLAND Erie
KENSINGTON (44427) Columbiana(54),
   Carroll(46)
KENT (44240) Portage(99), Summit(1)
KENT Portage
KENTON Hardin
KERR Gallia
KETTLERSVILLE Shelby
KIDRON Wayne
KILBOURNE Delaware
KILLBUCK (44637) Holmes(87),
   Coshocton(13)
KIMBOLTON (43749) Guernsey(93),
   Coshocton(5), Tuscarawas(2)
KINGS MILLS Warren
KINGSTON (45644) Ross(62),
   Pickaway(38)
KINGSVILLE Ashtabula
KINSMAN (44428) Trumbull(97),
   Ashtabula(4)
KIPLING Guernsey
KIPTON Lorain
KIRBY Wyandot
KIRKERSVILLE Licking
KITTS HILL Lawrence
KUNKLE Williams
LA RUE (43332) Marion(94), Hardin(4),
   Wyandot(2)
LACARNE Ottawa
LAFAYETTE Allen
LAFFERTY Belmont
LAGRANGE Lorain
LAINGS Monroe
LAKE MILTON (99999) Mahoning(99),
   Portage(1)
LAKEMORE Summit
LAKESIDE MARBLEHEAD Ottawa
LAKEVIEW (43331) Logan(95), Auglaize(5)
LAKEVILLE (44638) Holmes(73),
   Ashland(18), Wayne(9)
LAKEWOOD Cuyahoga
LANCASTER Fairfield
LANGSVILLE Meigs
LANSING Belmont
LATHAM Pike
LATTY Paulding
LAURA (45337) Miami(77), Darke(24)
LAURELVILLE (43135) Hocking(71),
   Pickaway(13), Ross(12), Vinton(4)
LEAVITTSBURG Trumbull
LEBANON Warren
LEES CREEK Clinton
LEESBURG (45135) Highland(99),
   Fayette(1)

LEESVILLE Carroll
LEETONIA Columbiana
LEIPSIC (45856) Putnam(97), Henry(2)
LEMOYNE Wood
LEWIS CENTER Delaware
LEWISBURG (45338) Preble(98),
   Montgomery(2)
LEWISTOWN Logan
LEWISVILLE Monroe
LIBERTY CENTER (43532) Henry(90),
   Fulton(7), Lucas(4)
LIMA (45806) Allen(95), Auglaize(6)
LIMA Allen
LIMAVILLE Stark
LINDSEY (43442) Sandusky(95), Ottawa(5)
LISBON Columbiana
LITCHFIELD (44253) Medina(81),
   Lorain(19)
LITHOPOLIS Fairfield
LITTLE HOCKING (45742)
   Washington(94), Athens(6)
LOCKBOURNE (43137) Franklin(58),
   Pickaway(42)
LODI Medina
LOGAN (43138) Hocking(98), Perry(2)
LONDON (99999) Madison(99), Franklin(1)
LONDONDERRY (45647) Ross(58),
   Vinton(42)
LONG BOTTOM Meigs
LORAIN Lorain
LORE CITY Guernsey
LOUDONVILLE (44842) Ashland(91),
   Holmes(9)
LOUISVILLE Stark
LOVELAND (45140) Clermont(91),
   Hamilton(4), Van Wert(3), Warren(1)
LOWELL (45744) Washington(80),
   Noble(18), Morgan(2)
LOWELLVILLE Mahoning
LOWER SALEM (45745) Noble(55),
   Monroe(26), Washington(20)
LUCAS (44843) Richland(94), Ashland(6)
LUCASVILLE (45648) Scioto(67), Pike(33)
LUCASVILLE Scioto
LUCKEY (43443) Wood(97), Sandusky(3)
LUDLOW FALLS Miami
LYNCHBURG (45142) Highland(90),
   Clinton(10)
LYNX Adams
LYONS Fulton
MACEDONIA Summit
MACKSBURG (45746) Washington(67),
   Noble(33)
MADISON Lake
MAGNETIC SPRINGS Union
MAGNOLIA (44643) Stark(43),
   Tuscarawas(38), Carroll(20)
MAINEVILLE (45039) Warren(98),
   Hamilton(2)
MALAGA Monroe
MALINTA Henry
MALTA Morgan
MALVERN Carroll
MANCHESTER Adams
MANSFIELD (44903) Richland(98),
   Morrow(1)
MANSFIELD (44904) Richland(89),
   Morrow(12)
MANSFIELD Richland
MANTUA (44255) Portage(88), Geauga(12)
MAPLE HEIGHTS Cuyahoga
MAPLEWOOD Shelby
MARATHON Clermont
MARENGO (43334) Morrow(96),
   Delaware(4)
MARIA STEIN (45860) Mercer(98),
   Darke(2)
MARIETTA Washington
MARION Marion
MARK CENTER Defiance
MARSHALLVILLE (44645) Wayne(97),
   Stark(3)

MARTEL Marion
MARTIN (43445) Ottawa(63), Lucas(37)
MARTINS FERRY Belmont
MARTINSBURG Knox
MARTINSVILLE Clinton
MARYSVILLE Union
MASON Warren
MASSILLON Stark
MASURY Trumbull
MAUMEE Lucas
MAXIMO Stark
MAYNARD Belmont
MC ARTHUR Vinton
MC CLURE (43534) Henry(98), Wood(2)
MC COMB (45858) Hancock(98),
   Putnam(2)
MC CONNELSVILLE (43756) Morgan(99),
   Muskingum(1)
MC CUTCHENVILLE (44844)
   Wyandot(60), Seneca(40)
MC DERMOTT Scioto
MC DONALD (44437) Trumbull(98),
   Mahoning(3)
MC GUFFEY Hardin
MECHANICSBURG (43044)
   Champaign(82), Clark(12), Madison(6)
MECHANICSTOWN Carroll
MEDINA Medina
MEDWAY Clark
MELMORE Seneca
MELROSE Paulding
MENDON (45862) Mercer(92), Auglaize(8)
MENTOR Lake
MESOPOTAMIA Trumbull
METAMORA Fulton
MIAMISBURG (99999) Montgomery(99),
   Warren(1)
MIAMITOWN Hamilton
MIAMIVILLE Clermont
MIDDLE BASS Ottawa
MIDDLE POINT Van Wert
MIDDLEBRANCH Stark
MIDDLEBURG Logan
MIDDLEFIELD (44062) Geauga(80),
   Trumbull(17), Ashtabula(3)
MIDDLEPORT Meigs
MIDDLETOWN Butler
MIDLAND Clinton
MIDVALE Tuscarawas
MILAN (44846) Erie(94), Huron(6)
MILFORD Clermont
MILFORD CENTER (43045) Union(96),
   Champaign(4)
MILLBURY (43447) Wood(85), Ottawa(16)
MILLEDGEVILLE Fayette
MILLER CITY Putnam
MILLERSBURG (44654) Holmes(97),
   Coshocton(3)
MILLERSPORT (43046) Fairfield(92),
   Licking(8)
MILLFIELD Athens
MILTON CENTER Wood
MINERAL CITY (44656) Tuscarawas(97),
   Carroll(3)
MINERAL RIDGE (44440) Trumbull(82),
   Mahoning(18)
MINERVA (44657) Stark(52), Carroll(34),
   Columbiana(14)
MINFORD Scioto
MINGO Champaign
MINGO JUNCTION Jefferson
MINSTER (45865) Auglaize(77),
   Shelby(22)
MOGADORE (44260) Portage(70),
   Summit(25), Stark(6)
MONCLOVA Lucas
MONROE Butler
MONROEVILLE (44847) Huron(67),
   Erie(33)
MONTEZUMA Mercer
MONTPELIER Williams

MONTVILLE (44064) Geauga(98),
   Ashtabula(2)
MORRAL (43337) Marion(83), Wyandot(17)
MORRISTOWN Belmont
MORROW Warren
MOSCOW Clermont
MOUNT BLANCHARD (45867)
   Hancock(93), Wyandot(7)
MOUNT CORY (45868) Hancock(95),
   Putnam(5)
MOUNT EATON Wayne
MOUNT GILEAD Morrow
MOUNT HOPE Holmes
MOUNT LIBERTY Knox
MOUNT ORAB Brown
MOUNT PERRY (43760) Perry(57),
   Muskingum(39), Licking(5)
MOUNT PLEASANT Jefferson
MOUNT SAINT JOSEPH Hamilton
MOUNT STERLING (43143) Madison(76),
   Pickaway(16), Fayette(8)
MOUNT VERNON Knox
MOUNT VICTORY (43340) Hardin(87),
   Union(13)
MOWRYSTOWN Highland
MOXAHALA Perry
MUNROE FALLS Summit
MURRAY CITY Hocking
NANKIN Ashland
NAPOLEON (43545) Henry(98),
   Defiance(1)
NASHPORT (43830) Muskingum(87),
   Licking(13)
NASHVILLE Holmes
NAVARRE (44662) Stark(97), Wayne(3)
NEAPOLIS Lucas
NEFFS Belmont
NEGLEY Columbiana
NELSONVILLE (45764) Athens(88),
   Hocking(12)
NEVADA (44849) Wyandot(79),
   Crawford(20)
NEVILLE Clermont
NEW ALBANY (43054) Franklin(82),
   Delaware(18)
NEW ATHENS Harrison
NEW BAVARIA (43548) Henry(95),
   Defiance(3), Putnam(2)
NEW BLOOMINGTON Marion
NEW BREMEN (45869) Auglaize(92),
   Mercer(5), Shelby(3)
NEW CARLISLE (45344) Clark(83),
   Miami(13), Montgomery(4)
NEW CONCORD (43762) Muskingum(83),
   Guernsey(17)
NEW HAMPSHIRE Auglaize
NEW HAVEN Huron
NEW HOLLAND (43145) Pickaway(63),
   Fayette(37)
NEW KNOXVILLE (45871) Auglaize(84),
   Shelby(16)
NEW LEBANON Montgomery
NEW LEXINGTON Perry
NEW LONDON (44851) Huron(83),
   Lorain(11), Ashland(5)
NEW MADISON Darke
NEW MARSHFIELD (45766) Athens(87),
   Vinton(13)
NEW MATAMORAS (45767)
   Washington(54), Monroe(46)
NEW MIDDLETOWN Mahoning
NEW PARIS Preble
NEW PHILADELPHIA Tuscarawas
NEW PLYMOUTH (45654) Vinton(78),
   Hocking(22)
NEW RICHMOND Clermont
NEW RIEGEL Seneca
NEW RUMLEY Harrison
NEW SPRINGFIELD (44443)
   Mahoning(95), Columbiana(5)
NEW STRAITSVILLE (43766) Perry(84),
   Hocking(16)

NEW VIENNA (45159) Clinton(96), Highland(4)
NEW WASHINGTON (44854) Crawford(92), Seneca(6), Huron(2)
NEW WATERFORD Columbiana
NEW WESTON Darke
NEWARK Licking
NEWBURY Geauga
NEWCOMERSTOWN (43832) Tuscarawas(86), Coshocton(13), Guernsey(2)
NEWPORT Washington
NEWTON FALLS (44444) Trumbull(93), Portage(5), Mahoning(2)
NEWTONSVILLE Clermont
NEY Defiance
NILES Trumbull
NORTH BALTIMORE (45872) Wood(98), Hancock(2)
NORTH BEND Hamilton
NORTH BENTON (44449) Portage(51), Mahoning(49)
NORTH BLOOMFIELD Trumbull
NORTH FAIRFIELD Huron
NORTH GEORGETOWN Columbiana
NORTH HAMPTON Clark
NORTH JACKSON Mahoning
NORTH KINGSVILLE Ashtabula
NORTH LAWRENCE (44666) Stark(84), Wayne(16)
NORTH LEWISBURG (43060) Champaign(42), Union(40), Logan(18)
NORTH LIMA Mahoning
NORTH OLMSTED Cuyahoga
NORTH RIDGEVILLE Lorain
NORTH ROBINSON Crawford
NORTH ROYALTON Cuyahoga
NORTH STAR Darke
NORTHFIELD Summit
NORTHWOOD Wood
NORWALK (44857) Huron(98), Erie(2)
NORWICH Muskingum
NOVA (44859) Ashland(96), Lorain(4)
NOVELTY Geauga
OAK HARBOR (43449) Ottawa(98), Sandusky(2)
OAK HILL (45656) Jackson(88), Gallia(8), Lawrence(4)
OAKWOOD Paulding
OBERLIN Lorain
OCEOLA Crawford
OHIO CITY Van Wert
OKEANA Butler
OKOLONA Henry
OLD FORT Seneca
OLD WASHINGTON Guernsey
OLMSTED FALLS Cuyahoga
ONTARIO Richland
ORANGEVILLE Trumbull
OREGON Lucas
OREGONIA Warren
ORIENT (43146) Pickaway(74), Franklin(25), Madison(1)
ORRVILLE Wayne
ORWELL (44076) Ashtabula(91), Trumbull(9)
OSGOOD Darke
OSTRANDER (43061) Delaware(80), Union(20)
OTTAWA Putnam
OTTOVILLE Putnam
OTWAY (45657) Scioto(80), Adams(18), Pike(2)
OVERPECK Butler
OWENSVILLE Clermont
OXFORD Butler
PAINESVILLE Lake
PALESTINE Darke
PANDORA (45877) Putnam(94), Allen(5)
PARIS Stark
PARKMAN Geauga

PATASKALA (99999) Licking(98), Franklin(1)
PATRIOT Gallia
PAULDING Paulding
PAYNE Paulding
PEDRO Lawrence
PEEBLES (45660) Adams(88), Pike(10), Highland(2)
PEMBERTON Shelby
PEMBERVILLE Wood
PENINSULA Summit
PERRY Lake
PERRYSBURG Wood
PERRYSVILLE (44864) Ashland(59), Richland(41)
PETERSBURG (44454) Mahoning(86), Columbiana(14)
PETTISVILLE Fulton
PHILLIPSBURG Montgomery
PHILO Muskingum
PICKERINGTON (43147) Fairfield(92), Franklin(7), Licking(1)
PIEDMONT (43983) Belmont(74), Guernsey(23), Harrison(3)
PIERPONT Ashtabula
PIKETON Pike
PINEY FORK Jefferson
PIONEER Williams
PIQUA (45356) Miami(96), Shelby(4)
PITSBURG Darke
PLAIN CITY (43064) Madison(52), Union(46), Franklin(1)
PLAINFIELD Coshocton
PLEASANT CITY (43772) Guernsey(58), Noble(42)
PLEASANT HILL Miami
PLEASANT PLAIN Warren
PLEASANTVILLE (43148) Fairfield(90), Perry(10)
PLYMOUTH (44865) Huron(50), Richland(47), Crawford(4)
POLK Ashland
POMEROY Meigs
PORT CLINTON Ottawa
PORT JEFFERSON Shelby
PORT WASHINGTON (43837) Tuscarawas(96), Guernsey(4)
PORT WILLIAM Clinton
PORTAGE Wood
PORTLAND Meigs
PORTSMOUTH Scioto
POTSDAM Miami
POWELL (43065) Delaware(69), Franklin(32)
POWHATAN POINT (43942) Belmont(93), Monroe(7)
PROCTORVILLE Lawrence
PROSPECT (43342) Marion(89), Delaware(8), Union(3)
PUT IN BAY Ottawa
QUAKER CITY (43773) Guernsey(56), Noble(39), Belmont(3), Monroe(2)
QUINCY (43343) Logan(77), Champaign(13), Shelby(10)
RACINE Meigs
RADCLIFF Vinton
RADNOR Delaware
RANDOLPH Portage
RARDEN (45671) Scioto(66), Pike(21), Adams(9), Fairfield(5)
RAVENNA Portage
RAWSON Hancock
RAY (45672) Vinton(80), Jackson(17), Ross(2)
RAYLAND (43943) Jefferson(95), Belmont(5)
RAYMOND Union
REEDSVILLE Meigs
REESVILLE Clinton
RENO Washington
REPUBLIC Seneca

REYNOLDSBURG (43068) Franklin(85), Licking(13), Fairfield(2)
REYNOLDSBURG Franklin
RICHFIELD Summit
RICHMOND Jefferson
RICHMOND DALE Ross
RICHWOOD (43344) Union(75), Marion(22), Delaware(3)
RIDGEVILLE CORNERS Henry
RIDGEWAY (43345) Logan(50), Hardin(48), Union(2)
RIO GRANDE Gallia
RIPLEY Brown
RISINGSUN (43457) Wood(71), Sandusky(23), Seneca(6)
RITTMAN (44270) Wayne(95), Medina(6)
ROBERTSVILLE Stark
ROCK CAMP Lawrence
ROCK CREEK Ashtabula
ROCKBRIDGE Hocking
ROCKFORD (45882) Mercer(96), Van Wert(4)
ROCKY RIDGE Ottawa
ROCKY RIVER Cuyahoga
ROGERS Columbiana
ROME Ashtabula
ROOTSTOWN Portage
ROSEVILLE (43777) Muskingum(69), Perry(31)
ROSEWOOD Champaign
ROSS Butler
ROSSBURG Darke
ROSSFORD Wood
ROUNDHEAD Hardin
RUDOLPH Wood
RUSHSYLVANIA (43347) Logan(93), Hardin(7)
RUSHVILLE (43150) Fairfield(70), Perry(30)
RUSSELLS POINT Logan
RUSSELLVILLE Brown
RUSSIA (45363) Shelby(96), Darke(4)
RUTLAND Meigs
SABINA Clinton
SAINT CLAIRSVILLE Belmont
SAINT HENRY (45883) Mercer(99), Darke(1)
SAINT JOHNS Auglaize
SAINT LOUISVILLE Licking
SAINT MARYS Auglaize
SAINT PARIS Champaign
SALEM (44460) Columbiana(90), Mahoning(11)
SALESVILLE (43778) Guernsey(96), Noble(4)
SALINEVILLE (43945) Columbiana(69), Carroll(21), Jefferson(10)
SANDUSKY Erie
SANDYVILLE Tuscarawas
SARAHSVILLE Noble
SARDINIA Brown
SARDIS Monroe
SAVANNAH Ashland
SCIO (43988) Harrison(72), Carroll(28)
SCIOTO FURNACE Scioto
SCOTT (45886) Van Wert(55), Paulding(45)
SCOTTOWN (45678) Lawrence(79), Gallia(21)
SEAMAN (45679) Adams(93), Highland(7)
SEBRING Mahoning
SEDALIA Madison
SENECAVILLE (43780) Guernsey(69), Noble(31)
SEVEN MILE Butler
SEVILLE Medina
SHADE (45776) Meigs(51), Athens(49)
SHADYSIDE Belmont
SHANDON Butler
SHARON CENTER Medina
SHARPSBURG Athens
SHAUCK Morrow

SHAWNEE Perry
SHEFFIELD LAKE Lorain
SHELBY (44875) Richland(97), Crawford(3)
SHERRODSVILLE (44675) Carroll(71), Tuscarawas(29)
SHERWOOD (43556) Defiance(98), Paulding(2)
SHILOH (44878) Richland(91), Huron(5), Ashland(3)
SHORT CREEK Harrison
SHREVE (44676) Wayne(81), Holmes(19)
SIDNEY Shelby
SINKING SPRING Highland
SMITHFIELD Jefferson
SMITHVILLE Wayne
SOLON Cuyahoga
SOMERDALE Tuscarawas
SOMERSET Perry
SOMERVILLE Butler
SOUTH BLOOMINGVILLE (43152) Hocking(83), Vinton(17)
SOUTH CHARLESTON (45368) Clark(98), Greene(1)
SOUTH LEBANON Warren
SOUTH POINT Lawrence
SOUTH SALEM Ross
SOUTH SOLON (43153) Madison(74), Fayette(14), Clark(7), Greene(6)
SOUTH VIENNA (45369) Clark(96), Madison(5)
SOUTH WEBSTER Scioto
SOUTHINGTON (44470) Trumbull(99), Portage(1)
SPARTA Morrow
SPENCER (44275) Medina(95), Lorain(5)
SPENCERVILLE (45887) Allen(76), Auglaize(15), Van Wert(7), Mercer(2)
SPRING HILL NURSERIES Miami
SPRING VALLEY (45370) Greene(98), Montgomery(2)
SPRINGBORO Warren
SPRINGFIELD (45502) Clark(98), Champaign(2)
SPRINGFIELD Clark
STAFFORD Monroe
STERLING Wayne
STEUBENVILLE Jefferson
STEWART Athens
STEWARTSVILLE Belmont
STILLWATER Tuscarawas
STOCKDALE Pike
STOCKPORT (43787) Morgan(96), Washington(4)
STOCKPORT Morgan
STONE CREEK (43840) Coshocton(65), Tuscarawas(35)
STONY RIDGE Wood
STOUT (45684) Scioto(68), Adams(32)
STOUTSVILLE (43154) Fairfield(89), Pickaway(11)
STOW Summit
STRASBURG Tuscarawas
STRATTON Jefferson
STREETSBORO Portage
STRONGSVILLE Cuyahoga
STRUTHERS Mahoning
STRYKER (43557) Williams(80), Henry(14), Fulton(6)
SUGAR GROVE (43155) Fairfield(73), Hocking(28)
SUGARCREEK (44681) Tuscarawas(78), Holmes(22)
SULLIVAN (44880) Ashland(84), Lorain(13), Medina(3)
SULPHUR SPRINGS Crawford
SUMMERFIELD (43788) Noble(79), Monroe(21)
SUMMIT STATION Licking
SUMMITVILLE Columbiana
SUNBURY (43074) Delaware(97), Licking(2)

SWANTON (43558) Fulton(70), Lucas(30)
SYCAMORE (44882) Wyandot(64), Crawford(31), Seneca(5)
SYCAMORE VALLEY Monroe
SYLVANIA Lucas
SYRACUSE Meigs
TALLMADGE (44278) Summit(97), Portage(3)
TARLTON Pickaway
TERRACE PARK Hamilton
THE PLAINS Athens
THOMPSON (44086) Geauga(79), Lake(16), Ashtabula(5)
THORNVILLE (43076) Perry(45), Licking(31), Fairfield(25)
THURMAN (45685) Gallia(74), Jackson(26)
THURSTON Fairfield
TIFFIN Seneca
TILTONSVILLE Jefferson
TIPP CITY Miami
TIPPECANOE (44699) Harrison(73), Tuscarawas(25), Guernsey(2)
TIRO Crawford
TOLEDO (43605) Lucas(98), Wood(2)
TOLEDO Lucas
TOLEDO Wood
TONTOGANY Wood
TORCH Athens
TORONTO Jefferson
TREMONT CITY Clark
TRENTON Butler
TRIMBLE Athens
TRINWAY Muskingum
TROY Miami
TUPPERS PLAINS Meigs
TUSCARAWAS Tuscarawas
TWINSBURG Summit
UHRICHSVILLE (44683) Tuscarawas(92), Harrison(8)
UNION CITY Darke
UNION FURNACE Hocking
UNIONPORT Jefferson
UNIONTOWN (44685) Stark(53), Summit(47)
UNIONVILLE Ashtabula
UNIONVILLE CENTER Union
UNIOPOLIS Auglaize
UPPER SANDUSKY Wyandot

URBANA Champaign
UTICA (43080) Licking(70), Knox(30)
VALLEY CITY (44280) Medina(95), Lorain(6)
VAN BUREN (45889) Hancock(97), Wood(3)
VAN WERT Van Wert
VANDALIA Montgomery
VANLUE Hancock
VAUGHNSVILLE Putnam
VENEDOCIA (45894) Van Wert(94), Mercer(5), Allen(1)
VERMILION (44089) Erie(58), Lorain(42)
VERONA Preble
VERSAILLES Darke
VICKERY (43464) Sandusky(78), Erie(22)
VIENNA Trumbull
VINCENT Washington
VINTON (45686) Gallia(94), Vinton(5), Meigs(2)
WADSWORTH Medina
WAKEFIELD Pike
WAKEMAN (44889) Huron(68), Erie(20), Lorain(13)
WALBRIDGE Wood
WALDO (43356) Marion(77), Delaware(17), Morrow(7)
WALHONDING (43843) Coshocton(66), Knox(34)
WALNUT CREEK Holmes
WAPAKONETA (45895) Auglaize(98), Logan(1)
WARNOCK Belmont
WARREN (99999) Trumbull(99), Mahoning(1)
WARSAW (43844) Coshocton(95), Knox(5)
WASHINGTON COURT HOUSE (43160) Fayette(99), Ross(1)
WASHINGTONVILLE Columbiana
WATERFORD (45786) Washington(74), Morgan(26)
WATERLOO (45688) Lawrence(95), Gallia(5)
WATERTOWN Washington
WATERVILLE Lucas
WAUSEON (43567) Fulton(99), Henry(1)
WAVERLY (45690) Pike(92), Ross(8)
WAYLAND Portage

WAYNE Wood
WAYNESBURG (44688) Stark(89), Carroll(11)
WAYNESFIELD (45896) Auglaize(79), Hardin(15), Allen(6)
WAYNESVILLE Warren
WELLINGTON Lorain
WELLSTON Jackson
WELLSVILLE Columbiana
WEST ALEXANDRIA (45381) Preble(96), Montgomery(4)
WEST CHESTER Butler
WEST ELKTON Preble
WEST FARMINGTON (44491) Trumbull(85), Geauga(14), Portage(1)
WEST JEFFERSON Madison
WEST LAFAYETTE Coshocton
WEST LIBERTY (43357) Logan(76), Champaign(24)
WEST MANCHESTER (45382) Preble(78), Darke(22)
WEST MANSFIELD (43358) Logan(59), Union(41)
WEST MILLGROVE Wood
WEST MILTON Miami
WEST POINT Columbiana
WEST PORTSMOUTH Scioto
WEST RUSHVILLE Fairfield
WEST SALEM (44287) Wayne(58), Ashland(35), Medina(7)
WEST UNION Adams
WEST UNITY (43570) Williams(95), Fulton(6)
WESTERVILLE (43081) Franklin(97), Delaware(3)
WESTERVILLE Delaware
WESTERVILLE Franklin
WESTFIELD CENTER Medina
WESTLAKE Cuyahoga
WESTON Wood
WESTVILLE Champaign
WHARTON Wyandot
WHEELERSBURG Scioto
WHIPPLE Washington
WHITE COTTAGE Muskingum
WHITEHOUSE Lucas
WICKLIFFE Lake
WILBERFORCE Greene

WILKESVILLE Vinton
WILLARD Huron
WILLIAMSBURG Clermont
WILLIAMSFIELD Ashtabula
WILLIAMSPORT (43164) Pickaway(94), Ross(6)
WILLIAMSTOWN Hancock
WILLISTON Ottawa
WILLOUGHBY Lake
WILLOW WOOD Lawrence
WILLSHIRE (45898) Van Wert(66), Mercer(34)
WILMINGTON Clinton
WILMOT (44689) Holmes(61), Stark(39)
WINCHESTER (45697) Adams(61), Brown(26), Highland(13)
WINDHAM (44288) Portage(99), Trumbull(1)
WINDSOR (44099) Ashtabula(89), Geauga(11)
WINESBURG Holmes
WINGETT RUN Monroe
WINONA Columbiana
WINTERSVILLE Jefferson
WOLF RUN Jefferson
WOODSFIELD Monroe
WOODSTOCK (43084) Champaign(90), Union(10)
WOODVILLE (43469) Sandusky(94), Ottawa(5), Wood(1)
WOOSTER Wayne
WREN Van Wert
XENIA Greene
YELLOW SPRINGS (45387) Greene(97), Clark(3)
YORKSHIRE (45388) Darke(94), Shelby(3), Mercer(2)
YORKVILLE (43971) Jefferson(62), Belmont(39)
YOUNGSTOWN (44504) Mahoning(96), Trumbull(4)
YOUNGSTOWN (44505) Mahoning(66), Trumbull(34)
YOUNGSTOWN Mahoning
ZALESKI Vinton
ZANESFIELD Logan
ZANESVILLE Muskingum
ZOAR Tuscarawas

ZIP/City Cross Reference

ZIP	City	ZIP	City	ZIP	City	ZIP	City
43001-43001	ALEXANDRIA	43037-43037	MARTINSBURG	43086-43086	WESTERVILLE	43144-43144	MURRAY CITY
43002-43002	AMLIN	43040-43041	MARYSVILLE	43093-43093	NEWARK	43145-43145	NEW HOLLAND
43003-43003	ASHLEY	43044-43044	MECHANICSBURG	43099-43099	BLACKLICK	43146-43146	ORIENT
43004-43004	BLACKLICK	43045-43045	MILFORD CENTER	43101-43101	ADELPHI	43147-43147	PICKERINGTON
43005-43005	BLADENSBURG	43046-43046	MILLERSPORT	43102-43102	AMANDA	43148-43148	PLEASANTVILLE
43006-43006	BRINKHAVEN	43047-43047	MINGO	43103-43103	ASHVILLE	43149-43149	ROCKBRIDGE
43007-43007	BROADWAY	43048-43048	MOUNT LIBERTY	43105-43105	BALTIMORE	43150-43150	RUSHVILLE
43008-43008	BUCKEYE LAKE	43050-43050	MOUNT VERNON	43106-43106	BLOOMINGBURG	43151-43151	SEDALIA
43009-43009	CABLE	43054-43054	NEW ALBANY	43107-43107	BREMEN	43152-43152	SOUTH BLOOMINGVILLE
43010-43010	CATAWBA	43055-43058	NEWARK	43109-43109	BRICE	43153-43153	SOUTH SOLON
43011-43011	CENTERBURG	43060-43060	NORTH LEWISBURG	43110-43110	CANAL WINCHESTER	43154-43154	STOUTSVILLE
43013-43013	CROTON	43061-43061	OSTRANDER	43111-43111	CARBON HILL	43155-43155	SUGAR GROVE
43014-43014	DANVILLE	43062-43062	PATASKALA	43112-43112	CARROLL	43156-43156	TARLTON
43015-43015	DELAWARE	43064-43064	PLAIN CITY	43113-43113	CIRCLEVILLE	43157-43157	THURSTON
43016-43017	DUBLIN	43065-43065	POWELL	43115-43115	CLARKSBURG	43158-43158	UNION FURNACE
43018-43018	ETNA	43066-43066	RADNOR	43116-43116	COMMERCIAL POINT	43160-43160	WASHINGTON COURT HOUSE
43019-43019	FREDERICKTOWN	43067-43067	RAYMOND	43117-43117	DERBY		
43021-43021	GALENA	43068-43068	REYNOLDSBURG	43119-43119	GALLOWAY	43162-43162	WEST JEFFERSON
43022-43022	GAMBIER	43070-43070	ROSEWOOD	43123-43123	GROVE CITY	43163-43163	WEST RUSHVILLE
43023-43023	GRANVILLE	43071-43071	SAINT LOUISVILLE	43125-43125	GROVEPORT	43164-43164	WILLIAMSPORT
43025-43025	HEBRON	43072-43072	SAINT PARIS	43126-43126	HARRISBURG	43199-43199	GROVEPORT
43026-43026	HILLIARD	43073-43073	SUMMIT STATION	43127-43127	HAYDENVILLE	43201-43299	COLUMBUS
43027-43027	HOMER	43074-43074	SUNBURY	43128-43128	JEFFERSONVILLE	43301-43307	MARION
43028-43028	HOWARD	43076-43076	THORNVILLE	43130-43130	LANCASTER	43310-43310	BELLE CENTER
43029-43029	IRWIN	43077-43077	UNIONVILLE CENTER	43135-43135	LAURELVILLE	43311-43311	BELLEFONTAINE
43030-43030	JACKSONTOWN	43078-43078	URBANA	43136-43136	LITHOPOLIS	43314-43314	CALEDONIA
43031-43031	JOHNSTOWN	43080-43080	UTICA	43137-43137	LOCKBOURNE	43315-43315	CARDINGTON
43032-43032	KILBOURNE	43081-43082	WESTERVILLE	43138-43138	LOGAN	43316-43316	CAREY
43033-43033	KIRKERSVILLE	43083-43083	WESTVILLE	43140-43140	LONDON	43317-43317	CHESTERVILLE
43035-43035	LEWIS CENTER	43084-43084	WOODSTOCK	43142-43142	MILLEDGEVILLE	43318-43318	DE GRAFF
43036-43036	MAGNETIC SPRINGS	43085-43085	COLUMBUS	43143-43143	MOUNT STERLING	43319-43319	EAST LIBERTY

ZIP	City	ZIP	City	ZIP	City	ZIP	City
43320-43320	EDISON	43511-43511	CUSTAR	43749-43749	KIMBOLTON	43943-43943	RAYLAND
43321-43321	FULTON	43512-43512	DEFIANCE	43750-43750	KIPLING	43944-43944	RICHMOND
43322-43322	GREEN CAMP	43515-43515	DELTA	43752-43752	LAINGS	43945-43945	SALINEVILLE
43323-43323	HARPSTER	43516-43516	DESHLER	43754-43754	LEWISVILLE	43946-43946	SARDIS
43324-43324	HUNTSVILLE	43517-43517	EDGERTON	43755-43755	LORE CITY	43947-43947	SHADYSIDE
43325-43325	IBERIA	43518-43518	EDON	43756-43756	MC CONNELSVILLE	43948-43948	SMITHFIELD
43326-43326	KENTON	43519-43519	EVANSPORT	43757-43757	MALAGA	43950-43950	SAINT CLAIRSVILLE
43330-43330	KIRBY	43520-43520	FARMER	43758-43758	MALTA	43951-43951	LAFFERTY
43331-43331	LAKEVIEW	43521-43521	FAYETTE	43759-43759	MORRISTOWN	43952-43952	STEUBENVILLE
43332-43332	LA RUE	43522-43522	GRAND RAPIDS	43760-43760	MOUNT PERRY	43953-43953	WINTERSVILLE
43333-43333	LEWISTOWN	43523-43523	GRELTON	43761-43761	MOXAHALA	43960-43960	STEWARTSVILLE
43334-43334	MARENGO	43524-43524	HAMLER	43762-43762	NEW CONCORD	43961-43961	STRATTON
43335-43335	MARTEL	43525-43525	HASKINS	43764-43764	NEW LEXINGTON	43962-43962	SUMMITVILLE
43336-43336	MIDDLEBURG	43526-43526	HICKSVILLE	43766-43766	NEW STRAITSVILLE	43963-43963	TILTONSVILLE
43337-43337	MORRAL	43527-43527	HOLGATE	43767-43767	NORWICH	43964-43964	TORONTO
43338-43338	MOUNT GILEAD	43528-43528	HOLLAND	43768-43768	OLD WASHINGTON	43966-43966	UNIONPORT
43340-43340	MOUNT VICTORY	43529-43529	HOYTVILLE	43771-43771	PHILO	43967-43967	WARNOCK
43341-43341	NEW BLOOMINGTON	43530-43530	JEWELL	43772-43772	PLEASANT CITY	43968-43968	WELLSVILLE
43342-43342	PROSPECT	43531-43531	KUNKLE	43773-43773	QUAKER CITY	43970-43970	WOLF RUN
43343-43343	QUINCY	43532-43532	LIBERTY CENTER	43777-43777	ROSEVILLE	43971-43971	YORKVILLE
43344-43344	RICHWOOD	43533-43533	LYONS	43778-43778	SALESVILLE	43972-43972	BANNOCK
43345-43345	RIDGEWAY	43534-43534	MC CLURE	43779-43779	SARAHSVILLE	43973-43973	FREEPORT
43346-43346	ROUNDHEAD	43535-43535	MALINTA	43780-43780	SENECAVILLE	43974-43974	HARRISVILLE
43347-43347	RUSHSYLVANIA	43536-43536	MARK CENTER	43782-43782	SHAWNEE	43976-43976	HOPEDALE
43348-43348	RUSSELLS POINT	43537-43537	MAUMEE	43783-43783	SOMERSET	43977-43977	FLUSHING
43349-43349	SHAUCK	43540-43540	METAMORA	43786-43786	STAFFORD	43981-43981	NEW ATHENS
43350-43350	SPARTA	43541-43541	MILTON CENTER	43787-43787	STOCKPORT	43983-43983	PIEDMONT
43351-43351	UPPER SANDUSKY	43542-43542	MONCLOVA	43788-43788	SUMMERFIELD	43984-43984	NEW RUMLEY
43356-43356	WALDO	43543-43543	MONTPELIER	43789-43789	SYCAMORE VALLEY	43985-43985	HOLLOWAY
43357-43357	WEST LIBERTY	43545-43545	NAPOLEON	43791-43791	WHITE COTTAGE	43986-43986	JEWETT
43358-43358	WEST MANSFIELD	43547-43547	NEAPOLIS	43793-43793	WOODSFIELD	43988-43988	SCIO
43359-43359	WHARTON	43548-43548	NEW BAVARIA	43802-43802	ADAMSVILLE	43989-43989	SHORT CREEK
43360-43360	ZANESFIELD	43549-43549	NEY	43803-43803	BAKERSVILLE	44001-44001	AMHERST
43402-43403	BOWLING GREEN	43550-43550	OKOLONA	43804-43804	BALTIC	44003-44003	ANDOVER
43406-43406	BRADNER	43551-43552	PERRYSBURG	43805-43805	BLISSFIELD	44004-44005	ASHTABULA
43407-43407	BURGOON	43553-43553	PETTISVILLE	43811-43811	CONESVILLE	44010-44010	AUSTINBURG
43408-43408	CLAY CENTER	43554-43554	PIONEER	43812-43812	COSHOCTON	44011-44011	AVON
43410-43410	CLYDE	43555-43555	RIDGEVILLE CORNERS	43821-43821	DRESDEN	44012-44012	AVON LAKE
43412-43412	CURTICE	43556-43556	SHERWOOD	43822-43822	FRAZEYSBURG	44017-44017	BEREA
43413-43413	CYGNET	43557-43557	STRYKER	43824-43824	FRESNO	44021-44021	BURTON
43414-43414	DUNBRIDGE	43558-43558	SWANTON	43828-43828	KEENE	44022-44023	CHAGRIN FALLS
43416-43416	ELMORE	43560-43560	SYLVANIA	43830-43830	NASHPORT	44024-44024	CHARDON
43420-43420	FREMONT	43565-43565	TONTOGANY	43832-43832	NEWCOMERSTOWN	44026-44026	CHESTERLAND
43430-43430	GENOA	43566-43566	WATERVILLE	43836-43836	PLAINFIELD	44028-44028	COLUMBIA STATION
43431-43431	GIBSONBURG	43567-43567	WAUSEON	43837-43837	PORT WASHINGTON	44030-44030	CONNEAUT
43432-43432	GRAYTOWN	43569-43569	WESTON	43840-43840	STONE CREEK	44032-44032	DORSET
43433-43433	GYPSUM	43570-43570	WEST UNITY	43842-43842	TRINWAY	44033-44033	EAST CLARIDON
43434-43434	HARBOR VIEW	43571-43571	WHITEHOUSE	43843-43843	WALHONDING	44035-44036	ELYRIA
43435-43435	HELENA	43601-43615	TOLEDO	43844-43844	WARSAW	44039-44039	NORTH RIDGEVILLE
43436-43436	ISLE SAINT GEORGE	43616-43616	OREGON	43845-43845	WEST LAFAYETTE	44040-44040	GATES MILLS
43437-43437	JERRY CITY	43617-43617	TOLEDO	43901-43901	ADENA	44041-44041	GENEVA
43438-43438	KELLEYS ISLAND	43618-43618	OREGON	43902-43902	ALLEDONIA	44044-44044	GRAFTON
43439-43439	LACARNE	43619-43619	NORTHWOOD	43903-43903	AMSTERDAM	44045-44045	GRAND RIVER
43440-43440	LAKESIDE MARBLEHEAD	43620-43699	TOLEDO	43905-43905	BARTON	44046-44046	HUNTSBURG
43441-43441	LEMOYNE	43701-43702	ZANESVILLE	43906-43906	BELLAIRE	44047-44047	JEFFERSON
43442-43442	LINDSEY	43711-43711	AVA	43907-43907	CADIZ	44048-44048	KINGSVILLE
43443-43443	LUCKEY	43713-43713	BARNESVILLE	43908-43908	BERGHOLZ	44049-44049	KIPTON
43445-43445	MARTIN	43716-43716	BEALLSVILLE	43909-43909	BLAINE	44050-44050	LAGRANGE
43446-43446	MIDDLE BASS	43717-43717	BELLE VALLEY	43910-43910	BLOOMINGDALE	44052-44053	LORAIN
43447-43447	MILLBURY	43718-43718	BELMONT	43912-43912	BRIDGEPORT	44054-44054	SHEFFIELD LAKE
43449-43449	OAK HARBOR	43719-43719	BETHESDA	43913-43913	BRILLIANT	44055-44055	LORAIN
43450-43450	PEMBERVILLE	43720-43720	BLUE ROCK	43914-43914	CAMERON	44056-44056	MACEDONIA
43451-43451	PORTAGE	43721-43721	BROWNSVILLE	43915-43915	CLARINGTON	44057-44057	MADISON
43452-43452	PORT CLINTON	43722-43722	BUFFALO	43916-43916	COLERAIN	44060-44061	MENTOR
43456-43456	PUT IN BAY	43723-43723	BYESVILLE	43917-43917	DILLONVALE	44062-44062	MIDDLEFIELD
43457-43457	RISINGSUN	43724-43724	CALDWELL	43920-43920	EAST LIVERPOOL	44064-44064	MONTVILLE
43458-43458	ROCKY RIDGE	43725-43725	CAMBRIDGE	43925-43925	EAST SPRINGFIELD	44065-44065	NEWBURY
43460-43460	ROSSFORD	43727-43727	CHANDLERSVILLE	43926-43926	EMPIRE	44067-44067	NORTHFIELD
43462-43462	RUDOLPH	43728-43728	CHESTERHILL	43927-43927	FAIRPOINT	44068-44068	NORTH KINGSVILLE
43463-43463	STONY RIDGE	43730-43730	CORNING	43928-43928	GLENCOE	44070-44070	NORTH OLMSTED
43464-43464	VICKERY	43731-43731	CROOKSVILLE	43930-43930	HAMMONDSVILLE	44072-44073	NOVELTY
43465-43465	WALBRIDGE	43732-43732	CUMBERLAND	43931-43931	HANNIBAL	44074-44074	OBERLIN
43466-43466	WAYNE	43733-43733	DERWENT	43932-43932	IRONDALE	44076-44076	ORWELL
43467-43467	WEST MILLGROVE	43734-43734	DUNCAN FALLS	43933-43933	JACOBSBURG	44077-44077	PAINESVILLE
43468-43468	WILLISTON	43735-43735	EAST FULTONHAM	43934-43934	LANSING	44080-44080	PARKMAN
43469-43469	WOODVILLE	43736-43736	FAIRVIEW	43935-43935	MARTINS FERRY	44081-44081	PERRY
43501-43501	ALVORDTON	43738-43738	FULTONHAM	43937-43937	MAYNARD	44082-44082	PIERPONT
43502-43502	ARCHBOLD	43739-43739	GLENFORD	43938-43938	MINGO JUNCTION	44084-44084	ROCK CREEK
43504-43504	BERKEY	43740-43740	GRATIOT	43939-43939	MOUNT PLEASANT	44085-44085	ROME
43505-43505	BLAKESLEE	43746-43746	HOPEWELL	43940-43940	NEFFS	44086-44086	THOMPSON
43506-43506	BRYAN	43747-43747	JERUSALEM	43941-43941	PINEY FORK	44087-44087	TWINSBURG
43510-43510	COLTON	43748-43748	JUNCTION CITY	43942-43942	POWHATAN POINT	44088-44088	UNIONVILLE

ZIP Range	City	ZIP Range	City	ZIP Range	City	ZIP Range	City
44089-44089	VERMILION	44403-44403	BROOKFIELD	44638-44638	LAKEVILLE	44848-44848	NANKIN
44090-44090	WELLINGTON	44404-44404	BURGHILL	44639-44639	LEESVILLE	44849-44849	NEVADA
44092-44092	WICKLIFFE	44405-44405	CAMPBELL	44640-44640	LIMAVILLE	44850-44850	NEW HAVEN
44093-44093	WILLIAMSFIELD	44406-44406	CANFIELD	44641-44641	LOUISVILLE	44851-44851	NEW LONDON
44094-44094	WILLOUGHBY	44408-44408	COLUMBIANA	44643-44643	MAGNOLIA	44853-44853	NEW RIEGEL
44095-44095	EASTLAKE	44410-44410	CORTLAND	44644-44644	MALVERN	44854-44854	NEW WASHINGTON
44096-44096	WILLOUGHBY	44411-44411	DEERFIELD	44645-44645	MARSHALLVILLE	44855-44855	NORTH FAIRFIELD
44099-44099	WINDSOR	44412-44412	DIAMOND	44646-44648	MASSILLON	44856-44856	NORTH ROBINSON
44101-44106	CLEVELAND	44413-44413	EAST PALESTINE	44650-44650	MAXIMO	44857-44857	NORWALK
44107-44107	LAKEWOOD	44415-44415	ELKTON	44651-44651	MECHANICSTOWN	44859-44859	NOVA
44108-44115	CLEVELAND	44416-44416	ELLSWORTH	44652-44652	MIDDLEBRANCH	44860-44860	OCEOLA
44116-44116	ROCKY RIVER	44417-44417	FARMDALE	44653-44653	MIDVALE	44861-44861	OLD FORT
44117-44117	EUCLID	44418-44418	FOWLER	44654-44654	MILLERSBURG	44862-44862	ONTARIO
44118-44121	CLEVELAND	44420-44420	GIRARD	44656-44656	MINERAL CITY	44864-44864	PERRYSVILLE
44122-44122	BEACHWOOD	44422-44422	GREENFORD	44657-44657	MINERVA	44865-44865	PLYMOUTH
44123-44123	EUCLID	44423-44423	HANOVERTON	44659-44659	MOUNT EATON	44866-44866	POLK
44124-44130	CLEVELAND	44424-44424	HARTFORD	44660-44660	MOUNT HOPE	44867-44867	REPUBLIC
44131-44131	INDEPENDENCE	44425-44425	HUBBARD	44661-44661	NASHVILLE	44870-44871	SANDUSKY
44132-44132	EUCLID	44427-44427	KENSINGTON	44662-44662	NAVARRE	44874-44874	SAVANNAH
44133-44133	NORTH ROYALTON	44428-44428	KINSMAN	44663-44663	NEW PHILADELPHIA	44875-44875	SHELBY
44134-44135	CLEVELAND	44429-44429	LAKE MILTON	44665-44665	NORTH GEORGETOWN	44878-44878	SHILOH
44136-44136	STRONGSVILLE	44430-44430	LEAVITTSBURG	44666-44666	NORTH LAWRENCE	44880-44880	SULLIVAN
44137-44137	MAPLE HEIGHTS	44431-44431	LEETONIA	44667-44667	ORRVILLE	44881-44881	SULPHUR SPRINGS
44138-44138	OLMSTED FALLS	44432-44432	LISBON	44669-44669	PARIS	44882-44882	SYCAMORE
44139-44139	SOLON	44436-44436	LOWELLVILLE	44670-44670	ROBERTSVILLE	44883-44883	TIFFIN
44140-44140	BAY VILLAGE	44437-44437	MC DONALD	44671-44671	SANDYVILLE	44887-44887	TIRO
44141-44141	BRECKSVILLE	44438-44438	MASURY	44672-44672	SEBRING	44888-44888	WILLARD
44142-44142	BROOKPARK	44439-44439	MESOPOTAMIA	44675-44675	SHERRODSVILLE	44889-44889	WAKEMAN
44143-44144	CLEVELAND	44440-44440	MINERAL RIDGE	44676-44676	SHREVE	44890-44890	WILLARD
44145-44145	WESTLAKE	44441-44441	NEGLEY	44677-44677	SMITHVILLE	44901-44999	MANSFIELD
44146-44146	BEDFORD	44442-44442	NEW MIDDLETOWN	44678-44678	SOMERDALE	45001-45001	ADDYSTON
44147-44147	BROADVIEW HEIGHTS	44443-44443	NEW SPRINGFIELD	44679-44679	STILLWATER	45002-45002	CLEVES
44177-44199	CLEVELAND	44444-44444	NEWTON FALLS	44680-44680	STRASBURG	45003-45003	COLLEGE CORNER
44201-44201	ATWATER	44445-44445	NEW WATERFORD	44681-44681	SUGARCREEK	45004-45004	COLLINSVILLE
44202-44202	AURORA	44446-44446	NILES	44682-44682	TUSCARAWAS	45005-45005	FRANKLIN
44203-44203	BARBERTON	44449-44449	NORTH BENTON	44683-44683	UHRICHSVILLE	45011-45013	HAMILTON
44210-44210	BATH	44450-44450	NORTH BLOOMFIELD	44685-44685	UNIONTOWN	45014-45014	FAIRFIELD
44211-44211	BRADY LAKE	44451-44451	NORTH JACKSON	44687-44687	WALNUT CREEK	45015-45015	HAMILTON
44212-44212	BRUNSWICK	44452-44452	NORTH LIMA	44688-44688	WAYNESBURG	45018-45018	FAIRFIELD
44214-44214	BURBANK	44453-44453	ORANGEVILLE	44689-44689	WILMOT	45020-45026	HAMILTON
44215-44215	CHIPPEWA LAKE	44454-44454	PETERSBURG	44690-44690	WINESBURG	45030-45030	HARRISON
44216-44216	CLINTON	44455-44455	ROGERS	44691-44691	WOOSTER	45032-45032	HARVEYSBURG
44217-44217	CRESTON	44460-44460	SALEM	44693-44693	DEERSVILLE	45033-45033	HOOVEN
44221-44223	CUYAHOGA FALLS	44470-44470	SOUTHINGTON	44695-44695	BOWERSTON	45034-45034	KINGS MILLS
44224-44224	STOW	44471-44471	STRUTHERS	44697-44697	ZOAR	45036-45036	LEBANON
44230-44230	DOYLESTOWN	44473-44473	VIENNA	44699-44699	TIPPECANOE	45039-45039	MAINEVILLE
44231-44231	GARRETTSVILLE	44481-44488	WARREN	44701-44799	CANTON	45040-45040	MASON
44232-44232	GREEN	44490-44490	WASHINGTONVILLE	44801-44801	ADRIAN	45041-45041	MIAMITOWN
44233-44233	HINCKLEY	44491-44491	WEST FARMINGTON	44802-44802	ALVADA	45042-45044	MIDDLETOWN
44234-44234	HIRAM	44492-44492	WEST POINT	44803-44803	AMSDEN	45050-45050	MONROE
44235-44235	HOMERVILLE	44493-44493	WINONA	44804-44804	ARCADIA	45051-45051	MOUNT SAINT JOSEPH
44236-44238	HUDSON	44501-44599	YOUNGSTOWN	44805-44805	ASHLAND	45052-45052	NORTH BEND
44240-44240	KENT	44601-44601	ALLIANCE	44807-44807	ATTICA	45053-45053	OKEANA
44241-44241	STREETSBORO	44606-44606	APPLE CREEK	44809-44809	BASCOM	45054-45054	OREGONIA
44242-44243	KENT	44607-44607	AUGUSTA	44811-44811	BELLEVUE	45055-45055	OVERPECK
44250-44250	LAKEMORE	44608-44608	BEACH CITY	44813-44813	BELLVILLE	45056-45056	OXFORD
44251-44251	WESTFIELD CENTER	44609-44609	BELOIT	44814-44814	BERLIN HEIGHTS	45061-45061	ROSS
44253-44253	LITCHFIELD	44610-44610	BERLIN	44815-44815	BETTSVILLE	45062-45062	SEVEN MILE
44254-44254	LODI	44611-44611	BIG PRAIRIE	44816-44816	BIRMINGHAM	45063-45063	SHANDON
44255-44255	MANTUA	44612-44612	BOLIVAR	44817-44817	BLOOMDALE	45064-45064	SOMERVILLE
44256-44258	MEDINA	44613-44613	BREWSTER	44818-44818	BLOOMVILLE	45065-45065	SOUTH LEBANON
44260-44260	MOGADORE	44614-44614	CANAL FULTON	44820-44820	BUCYRUS	45066-45066	SPRINGBORO
44262-44262	MUNROE FALLS	44615-44615	CARROLLTON	44822-44822	BUTLER	45067-45067	TRENTON
44264-44264	PENINSULA	44617-44617	CHARM	44824-44824	CASTALIA	45068-45068	WAYNESVILLE
44265-44265	RANDOLPH	44618-44618	DALTON	44825-44825	CHATFIELD	45069-45069	WEST CHESTER
44266-44266	RAVENNA	44619-44619	DAMASCUS	44826-44826	COLLINS	45070-45070	WEST ELKTON
44270-44270	RITTMAN	44620-44620	DELLROY	44827-44827	CRESTLINE	45071-45071	WEST CHESTER
44272-44272	ROOTSTOWN	44621-44621	DENNISON	44828-44828	FLAT ROCK	45073-45099	MONROE
44273-44273	SEVILLE	44622-44622	DOVER	44830-44830	FOSTORIA	45101-45101	ABERDEEN
44274-44274	SHARON CENTER	44624-44624	DUNDEE	44833-44833	GALION	45102-45102	AMELIA
44275-44275	SPENCER	44625-44625	EAST ROCHESTER	44836-44836	GREEN SPRINGS	45103-45103	BATAVIA
44276-44276	STERLING	44626-44626	EAST SPARTA	44837-44837	GREENWICH	45105-45105	BENTONVILLE
44278-44278	TALLMADGE	44627-44627	FREDERICKSBURG	44838-44838	HAYESVILLE	45106-45106	BETHEL
44280-44280	VALLEY CITY	44628-44628	GLENMONT	44839-44839	HURON	45107-45107	BLANCHESTER
44281-44282	WADSWORTH	44629-44629	GNADENHUTTEN	44840-44840	JEROMESVILLE	45110-45110	BUFORD
44285-44285	WAYLAND	44630-44630	GREENTOWN	44841-44841	KANSAS	45111-45111	CAMP DENNISON
44286-44286	RICHFIELD	44631-44631	HARLEM SPRINGS	44842-44842	LOUDONVILLE	45112-45112	CHILO
44287-44287	WEST SALEM	44632-44632	HARTVILLE	44843-44843	LUCAS	45113-45113	CLARKSVILLE
44288-44288	WINDHAM	44633-44633	HOLMESVILLE	44844-44844	MC CUTCHENVILLE	45114-45114	CUBA
44301-44399	AKRON	44634-44634	HOMEWORTH	44845-44845	MELMORE	45115-45115	DECATUR
44401-44401	BERLIN CENTER	44636-44636	KIDRON	44846-44846	MILAN	45118-45118	FAYETTEVILLE
44402-44402	BRISTOLVILLE	44637-44637	KILLBUCK	44847-44847	MONROEVILLE	45119-45119	FEESBURG

Zip Range	City
45120-45120	FELICITY
45121-45121	GEORGETOWN
45122-45122	GOSHEN
45123-45123	GREENFIELD
45130-45130	HAMERSVILLE
45131-45131	HIGGINSPORT
45132-45132	HIGHLAND
45133-45133	HILLSBORO
45135-45135	LEESBURG
45138-45138	LEES CREEK
45140-45140	LOVELAND
45142-45142	LYNCHBURG
45144-45144	MANCHESTER
45145-45145	MARATHON
45146-45146	MARTINSVILLE
45147-45147	MIAMIVILLE
45148-45148	MIDLAND
45150-45150	MILFORD
45152-45152	MORROW
45153-45153	MOSCOW
45154-45154	MOUNT ORAB
45155-45155	MOWRYSTOWN
45156-45156	NEVILLE
45157-45157	NEW RICHMOND
45158-45158	NEWTONSVILLE
45159-45159	NEW VIENNA
45160-45160	OWENSVILLE
45162-45162	PLEASANT PLAIN
45164-45164	PORT WILLIAM
45165-45165	GREENFIELD
45166-45166	REESVILLE
45167-45167	RIPLEY
45168-45168	RUSSELLVILLE
45169-45169	SABINA
45171-45171	SARDINIA
45172-45172	SINKING SPRING
45174-45174	TERRACE PARK
45176-45176	WILLIAMSBURG
45177-45177	WILMINGTON
45201-45299	CINCINNATI
45301-45301	ALPHA
45302-45302	ANNA
45303-45303	ANSONIA
45304-45304	ARCANUM
45305-45305	BELLBROOK
45306-45306	BOTKINS
45307-45307	BOWERSVILLE
45308-45308	BRADFORD
45309-45309	BROOKVILLE
45310-45310	BURKETTSVILLE
45311-45311	CAMDEN
45312-45312	CASSTOWN
45314-45314	CEDARVILLE
45315-45315	CLAYTON
45316-45316	CLIFTON
45317-45317	CONOVER
45318-45318	COVINGTON
45319-45319	DONNELSVILLE
45320-45320	EATON
45321-45321	ELDORADO
45322-45322	ENGLEWOOD
45323-45323	ENON
45324-45324	FAIRBORN
45325-45325	FARMERSVILLE
45326-45326	FLETCHER
45327-45327	GERMANTOWN
45328-45328	GETTYSBURG
45329-45329	GORDON
45330-45330	GRATIS
45331-45331	GREENVILLE
45332-45332	HOLLANSBURG
45333-45333	HOUSTON
45334-45334	JACKSON CENTER
45335-45335	JAMESTOWN
45336-45336	KETTLERSVILLE
45337-45337	LAURA
45338-45338	LEWISBURG
45339-45339	LUDLOW FALLS
45340-45340	MAPLEWOOD
45341-45341	MEDWAY
45342-45343	MIAMISBURG
45344-45344	NEW CARLISLE
45345-45345	NEW LEBANON
45346-45346	NEW MADISON
45347-45347	NEW PARIS
45348-45348	NEW WESTON
45349-45349	NORTH HAMPTON
45350-45350	NORTH STAR
45351-45351	OSGOOD
45352-45352	PALESTINE
45353-45353	PEMBERTON
45354-45354	PHILLIPSBURG
45356-45356	PIQUA
45358-45358	PITSBURG
45359-45359	PLEASANT HILL
45360-45360	PORT JEFFERSON
45361-45361	POTSDAM
45362-45362	ROSSBURG
45363-45363	RUSSIA
45365-45367	SIDNEY
45368-45368	SOUTH CHARLESTON
45369-45369	SOUTH VIENNA
45370-45370	SPRING VALLEY
45371-45371	TIPP CITY
45372-45372	TREMONT CITY
45373-45374	TROY
45377-45377	VANDALIA
45378-45378	VERONA
45380-45380	VERSAILLES
45381-45381	WEST ALEXANDRIA
45382-45382	WEST MANCHESTER
45383-45383	WEST MILTON
45384-45384	WILBERFORCE
45385-45385	XENIA
45387-45387	YELLOW SPRINGS
45388-45388	YORKSHIRE
45389-45389	CHRISTIANSBURG
45390-45390	UNION CITY
45401-45490	DAYTON
45501-45506	SPRINGFIELD
45601-45601	CHILLICOTHE
45612-45612	BAINBRIDGE
45613-45613	BEAVER
45614-45614	BIDWELL
45616-45616	BLUE CREEK
45617-45617	BOURNEVILLE
45618-45618	CHERRY FORK
45619-45619	CHESAPEAKE
45620-45620	CHESHIRE
45621-45621	COALTON
45622-45622	CREOLA
45623-45623	CROWN CITY
45624-45624	CYNTHIANA
45628-45628	FRANKFORT
45629-45629	FRANKLIN FURNACE
45630-45630	FRIENDSHIP
45631-45631	GALLIPOLIS
45633-45633	HALLSVILLE
45634-45634	HAMDEN
45636-45636	HAVERHILL
45638-45638	IRONTON
45640-45640	JACKSON
45642-45642	JASPER
45643-45643	KERR
45644-45644	KINGSTON
45645-45645	KITTS HILL
45646-45646	LATHAM
45647-45647	LONDONDERRY
45648-45648	LUCASVILLE
45650-45650	LYNX
45651-45651	MC ARTHUR
45652-45652	MC DERMOTT
45653-45653	MINFORD
45654-45654	NEW PLYMOUTH
45656-45656	OAK HILL
45657-45657	OTWAY
45658-45658	PATRIOT
45659-45659	PEDRO
45660-45660	PEEBLES
45661-45661	PIKETON
45662-45662	PORTSMOUTH
45663-45663	WEST PORTSMOUTH
45669-45669	PROCTORVILLE
45671-45671	RARDEN
45672-45672	RAY
45673-45673	RICHMOND DALE
45674-45674	RIO GRANDE
45675-45675	ROCK CAMP
45677-45677	SCIOTO FURNACE
45678-45678	SCOTTOWN
45679-45679	SEAMAN
45680-45680	SOUTH POINT
45681-45681	SOUTH SALEM
45682-45682	SOUTH WEBSTER
45683-45683	STOCKDALE
45684-45684	STOUT
45685-45685	THURMAN
45686-45686	VINTON
45687-45687	WAKEFIELD
45688-45688	WATERLOO
45690-45690	WAVERLY
45692-45692	WELLSTON
45693-45693	WEST UNION
45694-45694	WHEELERSBURG
45695-45695	WILKESVILLE
45696-45696	WILLOW WOOD
45697-45697	WINCHESTER
45698-45698	ZALESKI
45699-45699	LUCASVILLE
45701-45701	ATHENS
45710-45710	ALBANY
45711-45711	AMESVILLE
45712-45712	BARLOW
45713-45713	BARTLETT
45714-45714	BELPRE
45715-45715	BEVERLY
45716-45716	BUCHTEL
45717-45717	CARBONDALE
45719-45719	CHAUNCEY
45720-45720	CHESTER
45721-45721	COAL RUN
45723-45723	COOLVILLE
45724-45724	CUTLER
45727-45727	DEXTER CITY
45729-45729	FLEMING
45732-45732	GLOUSTER
45734-45734	GRAYSVILLE
45735-45735	GUYSVILLE
45739-45739	HOCKINGPORT
45740-45740	JACKSONVILLE
45741-45741	LANGSVILLE
45742-45742	LITTLE HOCKING
45743-45743	LONG BOTTOM
45744-45744	LOWELL
45745-45745	LOWER SALEM
45746-45746	MACKSBURG
45750-45750	MARIETTA
45760-45760	MIDDLEPORT
45761-45761	MILLFIELD
45764-45764	NELSONVILLE
45766-45766	NEW MARSHFIELD
45767-45767	NEW MATAMORAS
45768-45768	NEWPORT
45769-45769	POMEROY
45770-45770	PORTLAND
45771-45771	RACINE
45772-45772	REEDSVILLE
45773-45773	RENO
45775-45775	RUTLAND
45776-45776	SHADE
45777-45777	SHARPSBURG
45778-45778	STEWART
45779-45779	SYRACUSE
45780-45780	THE PLAINS
45781-45781	TORCH
45782-45782	TRIMBLE
45783-45783	TUPPERS PLAINS
45784-45784	VINCENT
45786-45786	WATERFORD
45787-45787	WATERTOWN
45788-45788	WHIPPLE
45789-45789	WINGETT RUN
45801-45807	LIMA
45808-45808	BEAVERDAM
45809-45809	GOMER
45810-45810	ADA
45812-45812	ALGER
45813-45813	ANTWERP
45814-45814	ARLINGTON
45815-45815	BELMORE
45816-45816	BENTON RIDGE
45817-45817	BLUFFTON
45819-45819	BUCKLAND
45820-45820	CAIRO
45821-45821	CECIL
45822-45822	CELINA
45826-45826	CHICKASAW
45827-45827	CLOVERDALE
45828-45828	COLDWATER
45830-45830	COLUMBUS GROVE
45831-45831	CONTINENTAL
45832-45832	CONVOY
45833-45833	DELPHOS
45835-45835	DOLA
45836-45836	DUNKIRK
45837-45837	DUPONT
45838-45838	ELGIN
45839-45840	FINDLAY
45841-45841	JENERA
45843-45843	FOREST
45844-45844	FORT JENNINGS
45845-45845	FORT LORAMIE
45846-45846	FORT RECOVERY
45848-45848	GLANDORF
45849-45849	GROVER HILL
45850-45850	HARROD
45851-45851	HAVILAND
45853-45853	KALIDA
45854-45854	LAFAYETTE
45855-45855	LATTY
45856-45856	LEIPSIC
45858-45858	MC COMB
45859-45859	MC GUFFEY
45860-45860	MARIA STEIN
45861-45861	MELROSE
45862-45862	MENDON
45863-45863	MIDDLE POINT
45864-45864	MILLER CITY
45865-45865	MINSTER
45866-45866	MONTEZUMA
45867-45867	MOUNT BLANCHARD
45868-45868	MOUNT CORY
45869-45869	NEW BREMEN
45870-45870	NEW HAMPSHIRE
45871-45871	NEW KNOXVILLE
45872-45872	NORTH BALTIMORE
45873-45873	OAKWOOD
45874-45874	OHIO CITY
45875-45875	OTTAWA
45876-45876	OTTOVILLE
45877-45877	PANDORA
45879-45879	PAULDING
45880-45880	PAYNE
45881-45881	RAWSON
45882-45882	ROCKFORD
45883-45883	SAINT HENRY
45884-45884	SAINT JOHNS
45885-45885	SAINT MARYS
45886-45886	SCOTT
45887-45887	SPENCERVILLE
45888-45888	UNIOPOLIS
45889-45889	VAN BUREN
45890-45890	VANLUE
45891-45891	VAN WERT
45893-45893	VAUGHNSVILLE
45894-45894	VENEDOCIA
45895-45895	WAPAKONETA
45896-45896	WAYNESFIELD
45897-45897	WILLIAMSTOWN
45898-45898	WILLSHIRE
45899-45899	WREN
45944-45999	CINCINNATI

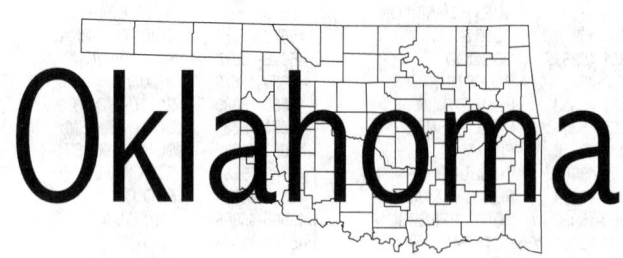

Oklahoma

General Help Numbers:

Governor's Office
State Capitol, Suite 212   405-521-2342
Oklahoma City, OK 73105   Fax 405-521-3317
www.state.ok.us/~governor   8AM-5PM

Attorney General's Office
2300 N Lincoln, #112   405-521-3921
Oklahoma City, OK 73105   Fax 405-521-6246
www.oag.state.ok.us   8:30AM-5PM

State Court Administrator
1915 N Stiles, #305   405-521-2450
Oklahoma City, OK 73105   Fax 405-521-6815
www.oscn.net   8AM-5PM

State Archives
Archives & Records Management Div   405-522-3577
200 NE 18th   Fax 405-525-7804
Oklahoma City, OK 73105-3298   8AM-5PM
www.odl.state.ok.us

State Specifics:

Capital: Oklahoma City
                  Oklahoma County

Time Zone: CST

Number of Counties: 77

Population: 3,358,044

Web Site: www.state.ok.us

State Agencies

Criminal Records

State Bureau of Investigation, Criminal History Reporting, 6600 N Harvey, Bldg 6, #300, Oklahoma City, OK 73116; 405-848-6724, 8AM-5PM.

www.osbi.state.ok.us

Note: A record check request form is available at the web site.

Indexing & Storage: Records are available from 1925 on.

Searching: Arrests with or without dispositions are available if the party was fingerprinted. Computer searches include arrests without dispositions. A DOB or approximate age is mandatory. A SSN, sex or race are helpful and provide a better search, but not required.

Access by: mail, fax, in person.

Fee & Payment: The fee for a computer name search is $15.00. The fee for a fingerprint search is $35.00. Copies are #.25 per page. Fee payee: O.S.B.I. Prepayment required. Credit cards accepted: Mastercard, Visa.

Mail search: Turnaround time: 2 weeks. A self addressed stamped envelope is requested.

Fax search: Use of credit card required.

In person search: Name requests take 20 minutes, fingerprint searches take up to ten days to process.

Corporation Records
Limited Liability Company Records
Limited Partnerships
Trademarks/Servicemarks
Limited Liability Partnerships

Secretary of State, 2300 N Lincoln Blvd, Rm 101, Oklahoma City, OK 73105-4897; 405-521-3911, 900-825-2424 (Corporate Records), 405-521-3771 (Fax), 8AM-5PM.

www.oklaosf.state.ok.us/~sos

Civil Records: Access: Phone, mail, in person. Both court and visitors may perform in person searches. Search fee: $5.00 per name. Required to search: name, years to search. Civil cases indexed by defendant, plaintiff. Civil records in original files from 1907, court is in the process of placing indexes on computer. **Criminal Records:** Access: Phone, mail, in person. Both court and visitors may perform in person searches. Search fee: $5.00 per name. Required to search: name, years to search; also helpful-SSN. Criminal records in original files from 1907, court is in the process of placing indexes on computer. **General Information:** No guardianship or juvenile records released. SASE not required. Turnaround time 2 days. Copy fee: $1.00 for first page, $.50 each addl. Certification fee: $.50. Fee payee: Latimer County Court Clerk. Personal checks accepted. Will bill search fee to law firms. Public access terminal is available.

Le Flore County

16th Judicial District Court PO Box 688, Poteau, OK 74953; 918-647-3181. Hours: 8AM-4:30PM (CST). *Felony, Misdemeanor, Civil, Eviction, Small Claims, Probate.*

Civil Records: Access: Mail, in person. Both court and visitors may perform in person searches. Search fee: $5.00 per name. Required to search: name, years to search. Civil cases indexed by defendant, plaintiff. Civil records on computer since July 1, 1997; prior records archived since 1904 in files and books. **Criminal Records:** Access: Mail, in person. Both court and visitors may perform in person searches. Search fee: $5.00 per name. Required to search: name, years to search; also helpful-SSN. Criminal records on computer since July 1, 1997; prior records archived since 1904 in files and books. **General Information:** No juvenile, adoptions, mental health or guardian records released. SASE required. Turnaround time 1 week. Copy fee: $1.00 for first page, $.50 each addl. Certification fee: $.50. Fee payee: Court Clerk. Personal checks accepted.

Lincoln County

23rd Judicial District Court PO Box 307, Chandler, OK 74834; 405-258-1309. Hours: 8AM-4:30PM (CST). *Felony, Misdemeanor, Civil, Eviction, Small Claims, Probate.*

Civil Records: Access: Mail, in person. Both court and visitors may perform in person searches. Search fee: $5.00 per name. Required to search: name, years to search. Civil cases indexed by defendant, plaintiff. Civil records archived since 1891. **Criminal Records:** Access: Mail, in person. Both court and visitors may perform in person searches. Search fee: $5.00 per name. Required to search: name, years to search, DOB, signed release; also helpful-SSN. Criminal records archived since 1891. **General Information:** No juvenile, adoption or guardianship records released. SASE required. Turnaround time can take 30 days or more. Record searching is a low priority. Copy fee: $1.00 for first page, $.50 each addl. Certification fee: $3.00. Fee payee: Court Clerk. Personal checks accepted. Prepayment is required. Public access terminal is available.

Logan County

9th Judicial District Court 301 E. Harrison, Rm 201, Guthrie, OK 73044; 405-282-0123. Hours: 8:30AM-4:30PM (CST). *Felony, Misdemeanor, Civil, Eviction, Small Claims, Probate.*

Civil Records: Access: Mail, in person. Both court and visitors may perform in person searches. Search fee: $5.00 per name. Required to search: name, years to search. Civil cases indexed by defendant, plaintiff. Civil records on microfiche from 1889. **Criminal Records:** Access: Mail, in person. Both court and visitors may perform in person searches. Search fee: $5.00 per name. Required to search: name, years to search; also helpful-SSN. Criminal records on microfiche from 1889. **General Information:** No juvenile, mental health or adoption records released. SASE required. Turnaround time 2 days. Copy fee: $1.00 for first page, $.50 each addl. Certification fee: $.50. Fee payee: Court Clerk. Personal checks accepted. Prepayment is required.

Love County

20th Judicial District Court 405 W. Main, Marietta, OK 73448; 580-276-2235. Hours: 8AM-4:30PM (CST). *Felony, Misdemeanor, Civil, Eviction, Small Claims, Probate.*

Civil Records: Access: Mail, in person. Both court and visitors may perform in person searches. Search fee: $5.00 per name. Required to search: name, years to search. Civil cases indexed by defendant, plaintiff. Civil records on docket books from 1907. **Criminal Records:** Access: Mail, in person. Both court and visitors may perform in person searches. Search fee: $5.00 per name. Required to search: name, years to search; also helpful-DOB, SSN. Criminal records on docket books from 1907. **General Information:** No juvenile or adoptions records released. SASE required. Turnaround time 1-2 days. Copy fee: $1.00 for first page, $.50 each addl. Certification fee: $.50. Fee payee: Court Clerk. Only cashiers checks and money orders accepted. Prepayment is required.

Major County

4th Judicial District Court 500 E Broadway, Fairview, OK 73737; 580-227-4690 X204. Hours: 8:30AM-4:30PM (CST). *Felony, Misdemeanor, Civil, Eviction, Small Claims, Probate.*

Civil Records: Access: Phone, fax, mail, in person. Both court and visitors may perform in person searches. Search fee: $5.00 per name. Fee is per book. Required to search: name, years to search. Civil cases indexed by defendant, plaintiff. Civil records on docket books from 1907, on microfiche from 1970. **Criminal Records:** Access: Phone, fax, mail, in person. Both court and visitors may perform in person searches. Search fee: $5.00 per name. Fee is per book. Required to search: name, years to search; also helpful-SSN. Criminal records on docket books from 1907, on microfiche from 1970. **General Information:** No juvenile, adoptions or mental records released. SASE required. Turnaround time 3 days. Copy fee: $1.00 for first page, $.50 each addl. Certification fee: $.50. Fee payee: Court Clerk. Personal checks accepted. Attorney's or firms with previous credit paid. Fax notes: $3.00 for first page, $1.00 each addl.

Marshall County

20th Judicial District Court Box 58, Madill, OK 73446; 580-795-3278 X240. Hours: 8:30AM-5PM (CST). *Felony, Misdemeanor, Civil, Eviction, Small Claims, Probate.*

Civil Records: Access: Phone, mail, in person. Both court and visitors may perform in person searches. No search fee. Required to search: name, years to search. Civil cases indexed by defendant,

plaintiff. Civil records on docket books from 1907. **Criminal Records:** Access: Phone, mail, in person. Both court and visitors may perform in person searches. No search fee. Required to search: name, years to search, DOB, SSN, signed release. Criminal records on docket books from 1907. **General Information:** No juvenile, adoptions, mental health or guardianship records released. SASE required. Turnaround time 3 days. Copy fee: $1.00 for first page, $.50 each addl. Certification fee: $3.00. Fee payee: Court Clerk. Personal checks accepted.

Mayes County

12th Judicial District Court Box 867, Pryor, OK 74362; 918-825-0133. Hours: 9AM-5PM (CST). *Felony, Misdemeanor, Civil, Eviction, Small Claims, Probate.*

Civil Records: Access: Phone, mail, in person. Both court and visitors may perform in person searches. Search fee: $1.00 per name per year. Search fee is payable to employee doing research after hours. Required to search: name, years to search. Civil cases indexed by defendant, plaintiff. Civil records archived from 1907 on microfilm. **Criminal Records:** Access: Phone, mail, in person. Both court and visitors may perform in person searches. Search fee: $1.00 per name per year. Search fee is payable to employee doing research after hours. Required to search: name, years to search; also helpful-DOB, SSN. Criminal records archived from 1907 on microfilm. **General Information:** No mental, adoption, most juvenile, and some reports in guardianship records not released. SASE required. Turnaround time 1 week. Copy fee: $1.00 for first page, $.50 each addl. Certification fee: $.50. Fee payee: Clerk of Court. Personal checks accepted. Prepayment is required.

McClain County

21st Judicial District Court 121 N. 2nd Rm 231, Purcell, OK 73080; 405-527-3221. Hours: 8AM-4:30PM (CST). *Felony, Misdemeanor, Civil, Eviction, Small Claims, Probate.*

Civil Records: Access: Mail, in person. Both court and visitors may perform in person searches. Search fee: $10.00 per name. Required to search: name, years to search. Civil cases indexed by defendant, plaintiff. Civil records on docket books and cards from 1907, computerized since 01/97. **Criminal Records:** Access: Mail, in person. Both court and visitors may perform in person searches. Search fee: $10.00 per name. Required to search: name, years to search; also helpful-DOB, SSN. Criminal records kept in individual docket files. **General Information:** No adoptions, mental health or juvenile records released. SASE required. Turnaround time 2 days. Copy fee: $1.00 for first page, $.50 each addl. Certification fee: $.50. Fee payee: Court Clerk. Personal checks accepted. Prepayment is required. Public access terminal is available.

McCurtain County

17th Judicial District Court Box 1378, Idabel, OK 74745; 580-286-3693; Fax: 580-286-7095. Hours: 8AM-4PM (CST). *Felony, Misdemeanor, Civil, Eviction, Small Claims, Probate.*

Civil Records: Access: Phone, fax, mail, in person. Both court and visitors may perform in person searches. Search fee: $5.00 per name. Required to search: name, years to search. Civil cases indexed by defendant, plaintiff. Civil records on docket books from 1907. **Criminal Records:** Access: Phone, fax, mail, in person. Both court and visitors may perform in person searches. Search fee: $5.00. Required to search: name, years to search; also helpful-SSN. Criminal records on docket books from 1907. **General Information:** No adoptions, guardianship or juvenile records released. SASE required. Turnaround time 1 day. Copy fee: $2.00 per page. Certification fee: No certification fee. Fee payee: Court Clerk. Personal checks accepted. Prepayment is required. Public access terminal is available.

McIntosh County

18th Judicial District Court Box 426, Eufaula, OK 74432; 918-689-2282. Hours: 8AM-4PM (CST). *Felony, Misdemeanor, Civil, Eviction, Small Claims, Probate.*

Civil Records: Access: Mail, in person. Both court and visitors may perform in person searches. Search fee: $5.00 per name. Required to search: name, years to search. Civil cases indexed by defendant, plaintiff. Civil records on microfilm since 1907 and computer since 1996. **Criminal Records:** Access: Mail, in person. Both court and visitors may perform in person searches. Search fee: $5.00 per name. Required to search: name, years to search; also helpful-SSN, DOB. Criminal records on microfilm since 1947 and computer since 1996. **General Information:** No adoptions, mental health, guardianship or juvenile records released. SASE required. Turnaround time 3 days. Copy fee: $1.00 for first page, $.50 each addl. Certification fee: $.50. Fee payee: Court. Personal checks accepted. Prepayment is required. Public access terminal is available.

Murray County

20th Judicial District Court Box 578, Sulphur, OK 73086; 580-622-3223. Hours: 8AM-4:30PM, closed for lunch (CST). *Felony, Misdemeanor, Civil, Eviction, Small Claims, Probate.*

Civil Records: Access: Mail, in person. Both court and visitors may perform in person searches. Search fee: $5.00 per name. Required to search: name, years to search; also helpful-DOB. Civil cases indexed by defendant, plaintiff. Civil records on docket books from 1907, from 1973 back records are on microfilm. **Criminal Records:** Access: Mail, in person. Both court and visitors may perform in person searches. Search fee: $5.00 per name. Required to search: name, years to search; also helpful-SSN, DOB. Criminal records on docket books from 1907, from 1973 back records are on microfilm. **General Information:** No mental health, guardianship, juvenile or adoption records released. SASE required. Turnaround time 2 days, immediate if easily accessible. Copy fee: $1.00 for first page, $.50 each addl. Certification fee: $5.00. Fee payee: Murray County Court Clerk. Personal checks accepted. Prepayment is required. Public access terminal is available. Public Access Terminal Note: For records since 1997.

Muskogee County

15th Judicial District Court Box 1350, Muskogee, OK 74402; 918-682-7873. Hours: 8AM-4:30PM (CST). *Felony, Misdemeanor, Civil, Eviction, Small Claims, Probate.*

Civil Records: Access: Mail, in person. Both court and visitors may perform in person searches. Search fee: $10.00 per name. Required to search: name, years to search. Civil cases indexed by defendant, plaintiff. Civil records on docket books

from 1907. **Criminal Records:** Access: Mail, in person. Both court and visitors may perform in person searches. Search fee: $10.00 per name. Required to search: name, years to search, DOB; also helpful-SSN. Criminal records on docket books from 1907. **General Information:** No adoptions, mental health, guardianship or juvenile records released. SASE required. Turnaround time 2-3 days. Copy fee: $1.00 for first page, $.50 each addl. Certification fee: $.50. Fee payee: Court Clerk. Personal checks accepted. Prepayment is required.

Noble County

8th Judicial District Court 300 Courthouse Dr, Box 14, Perry, OK 73077; 580-336-5187. Hours: 8AM-4:30PM (CST). *Felony, Misdemeanor, Civil, Eviction, Small Claims, Probate.*

Civil Records: Access: Mail, in person. Both court and visitors may perform in person searches. Search fee: $5.00 per name. Required to search: name, years to search. Civil cases indexed by defendant, plaintiff. Civil records on microfiche from 1893. **Criminal Records:** Access: Mail, in person. Both court and visitors may perform in person searches. Search fee: $5.00 per name. Required to search: name, years to search, DOB; also helpful-address, SSN. Criminal records on microfiche from 1893. **General Information:** No adoptions, mental health, guardianship or juvenile records released. SASE appreciated. Turnaround time 1 day. Copy fee: $1.00 for first page, $.50 each addl. Certification fee: $.50. Fee payee: Noble County Court Clerk. Personal checks accepted. Prepayment is required. Public access terminal is available.

Nowata County

11th Judicial District Court 229 N. Maple, Nowata, OK 74048; 918-273-0127. Hours: 8AM-4:30PM (CST). *Felony, Misdemeanor, Civil, Eviction, Small Claims, Probate.*

Civil Records: Access: Mail, in person. Both court and visitors may perform in person searches. Search fee: $5.00 per name. Required to search: name, years to search. Civil cases indexed by defendant, plaintiff. Civil records on docket books from 1907. **Criminal Records:** Access: Mail, in person. Both court and visitors may perform in person searches. Search fee: $5.00 per name. Required to search: name, years to search; also helpful-SSN. Criminal records on docket books from 1907. **General Information:** No adoptions, menatl health, guardianship or juvenile records released. SASE requested. Turnaround time 1 day. Copy fee: $1.00 for first page, $.50 each addl. Certification fee: $.50 per page. Fee payee: Court Clerk. Personal checks accepted. Prepayment is required.

Okfuskee County

24th Judicial District Court Box 30, Okemah, OK 74859; 918-623-0525. Hours: 8:30AM-4:30PM (CST). *Felony, Misdemeanor, Civil, Eviction, Small Claims, Probate.*

Civil Records: Access: Mail, in person. Both court and visitors may perform in person searches. Search fee: $5.00 per name. Required to search: name, years to search. Civil cases indexed by defendant, plaintiff. Civil records in files and docket books from 1907. **Criminal Records:** Access: Mail, in person. Both court and visitors may perform in person searches. Search fee: $5.00 per name. Required to search: name, years to search; also helpful-SSN. Criminal records in files

and docket books from 1907. **General Information:** No adoptions, mental health, guardianship or juvenile released. SASE required. Turnaround time 3 day. Copy fee: $1.00 for first page, $.50 each addl. Certification fee: $.50 per page. Fee payee: Court Clerk. Personal checks accepted. Prepayment is required.

Oklahoma County

District Court 320 Robert S. Kerr St, Rm 409, Oklahoma City, OK 73102; 405-713-1705. Hours: 8AM-5PM (CST). *Felony, Misdemeanor, Civil, Eviction, Small Claims, Probate.*

Civil Records: Access: Mail, online, in person. Both court and visitors may perform in person searches. Search fee: Lengthy searches are $5.00 per half hour, otherwise no search fee. Required to search: name, years to search. Civil cases indexed by defendant, plaintiff. Civil records on microfiche from 1980, prior archived. Access to court dockets is available free on the Internet at www.oscn.net/pinpoint3/applications/dockets/start.asp. Search by case number, parties, locations, or citation numbers. **Criminal Records:** Access: Mail, remote online, in person. Both court and visitors may perform in person searches. Search fee: Lengthy searches $5.00 per half hour. Required to search: name, years to search, DOB; also helpful-SSN. Criminal records on microfiche from 1980, prior archived. Online access to court dockets is same as civil, see above. **General Information:** No juvenile, sealed, or expunged records released. SASE required. Turnaround time 5-10 days. Copy fee: $1.00 for first page, $.50 each addl. Certification fee: $.50. Fee payee: District Court Clerk. Personal checks accepted. Prepayment is required. Public access terminal is available.

Okmulgee County

24th Judicial District Court -Henryetta Branch 114 S 4th, Henryetta, OK 74437; 918-652-7142. Hours: 8:30AM-4:30PM (CST). *Felony, Misdemeanor, Civil, Eviction, Small Claims, Probate.*

Note: You must search both courts in this county, records are not co-mingled

Civil Records: Access: Phone, mail, in person. Both court and visitors may perform in person searches. Search fee: $5.00 per name. Required to search: name, years to search. Civil cases indexed by defendant, plaintiff. Civil records on microfiche from 1970. **Criminal Records:** Access: Phone, mail, in person. Both court and visitors may perform in person searches. Search fee: $5.00 per name. Required to search: name, years to search; also helpful-SSN. Criminal records on microfiche from 1970. **General Information:** No expunged or guardianship records released. SASE required. Turnaround time 1-2 days, limited phone searching immediate. Copy fee: $1.00 for first page, $.50 each addl. Certification fee: $5.00. Fee payee: Court Clerk. Business checks accepted. Prepayment is required.

24th Judicial District Court -Okmulgee Branch 314 W 7th, Okmulgee, OK 74447; 918-756-3042. Hours: 8AM-4:30PM (CST). *Felony, Misdemeanor, Civil, Eviction, Small Claims, Probate.*

Civil Records: Access: Phone, mail, in person. Both court and visitors may perform in person searches. Search fee: $5.00 per name. Required to search: name, years to search. Civil cases indexed by defendant, plaintiff. Civil records on microfiche from 1986, archived from 1907. **Criminal**

Records: Access: Phone, mail, in person. Both court and visitors may perform in person searches. Search fee: $5.00 per name. Required to search: name, years to search; also helpful-SSN. Criminal records on microfiche from 1986, archived from 1907. **General Information:** No juvenile, mental health, adoption or guardianship records released. SASE requested. Turnaround time 1-2 days. Copy fee: $1.00 for first page, $.50 each addl. Certification fee: $.50. Fee payee: Linda Beaver Court Clerk. Business checks accepted. Prepayment is required. Public access terminal is available.

Osage County

10th Judicial District Court County Courthouse, 600 Grandview, Pawhuska, OK 74056; 918-287-4104. Hours: 9AM-5PM (CST). *Felony, Misdemeanor, Civil, Eviction, Small Claims, Probate.*

Civil Records: Access: Mail, in person. Both court and visitors may perform in person searches. Search fee: $5.00 per name. Required to search: name, years to search; also helpful-address. Civil cases indexed by defendant, plaintiff. Civil records archived from 1969. **Criminal Records:** Access: Mail, in person. Both court and visitors may perform in person searches. Search fee: $5.00 per name. Required to search: name, years to search; also helpful-address. Criminal records archived from 1969. **General Information:** No juvenile or adoption records released. SASE required. Turnaround time 2 days. Copy fee: $1.00 for first page, $.50 each addl. Certification fee: $.50. Fee payee: Court Clerk. Only cashiers checks and money orders accepted. Prepayment is required. Public access terminal is available.

Ottawa County

13th Judicial District Court 102 E Central Ave, Suite 300, Miami, OK 74354; 918-542-2801. Hours: 9:00AM-5:00PM (CST). *Felony, Misdemeanor, Civil, Eviction, Small Claims, Probate.*

Civil Records: Access: Phone, mail, in person. Both court and visitors may perform in person searches. Search fee: $5.00 per name. Required to search: name, years to search. Civil cases indexed by defendant, plaintiff. Civil records on docket books or cards from 1907, recent records computerized. **Criminal Records:** Access: Mail, in person. Both court and visitors may perform in person searches. Search fee: $5.00. Required to search: name, years to search; also helpful-SSN. Criminal records on docket books or cards from 1907, recent records computerized. **General Information:** No juvenile, mental health, adoption or guardianship records released. SASE required. Turnaround time 1-2 days. Copy fee: $1.00 for first page, $.50 each addl. Certification fee: $.50. Fee payee: Clerk of Court. Business checks accepted. Public access terminal is available. Public Access Terminal Note: &.

Pawnee County

14th Judicial District Court Courthouse, 500 Harrison St, Pawnee, OK 74058; 918-762-2547. Hours: 8AM-4:30PM (CST). *Felony, Misdemeanor, Civil, Eviction, Small Claims, Probate.*

Civil Records: Access: Mail, in person. Both court and visitors may perform in person searches. No search fee. Required to search: name, years to search. Civil cases indexed by defendant, plaintiff. Civil records on microfiche from 1970, also on docket sheets. **Criminal Records:** Access: Mail, in person. Both court and visitors may perform in person searches. No search fee. Required to search: name, years to search; also helpful-SSN. Criminal records on microfiche from 1970, also on docket sheets. **General Information:** No sealed records released. SASE required. Turnaround time 1-3 days. Copy fee: $1.00 for first page, $.50 each addl. Certification fee: $.50. Fee payee: Court Clerk. Personal checks accepted. Prepayment is required. Public access terminal is available.

Payne County

9th Judicial District Court 606 S. Husband Rm 308, Stillwater, OK 74074; 405-372-4774. Hours: 8AM-5PM (CST). *Felony, Misdemeanor, Civil, Eviction, Small Claims, Probate.*

Civil Records: Access: Mail, online, in person. Both court and visitors may perform in person searches. Search fee: $10.00 per name. Fee is for 7 year search. Required to search: name, years to search. Civil cases indexed by defendant, plaintiff. Civil records on docket books from late 1800s, as of 1994 on computer. Access to court dockets is available free on the Internet at www.oscn.net/pinpoint3/applications/dockets/start.asp. Search by case number, parties, locations, or citation numbers. **Criminal Records:** Access: Mail, remote online, in person. Both court and visitors may perform in person searches. Search fee: $10.00 per name. Fee is for 7 year search. Required to search: name, years to search, DOB, SSN, signed release. Criminal records on docket books from late 1800s, as of 1994 on computer. Online access to court dockets is same as civil, see above. **General Information:** No sealed records, juveniles or adoption records released. SASE required. Turnaround time 2 days. Copy fee: $1.00 for first page, $.50 each addl. Certification fee: $3.00. Fee payee: Clerk of Court. Personal checks accepted. Prepayment is required. Public access terminal is available.

Pittsburg County

18th Judicial District Court Box 460, McAlester, OK 74502; 918-423-4859. Hours: 8:30AM-5PM (CST). *Felony, Misdemeanor, Civil, Eviction, Small Claims, Probate.*

Civil Records: Access: Mail, in person. Both court and visitors may perform in person searches. Search fee: $5.00 per name. Required to search: name, years to search. Civil cases indexed by defendant, plaintiff. Civil records on microfiche since 1907. **Criminal Records:** Access: Mail, in person. Both court and visitors may perform in person searches. Search fee: $5.00 per name. Required to search: name, years to search; also helpful-SSN. Criminal records on microfiche since 1907. **General Information:** No juvenile, adoptions, mental health or guardianship records released. SASE required. Turnaround time 1-2 days. Copy fee: $1.00 for first page, $.50 each addl. Certification fee: $.50. Fee payee: Court Clerk. Personal checks accepted. Prepayment is required.

Pontotoc County

22nd Judicial District Court Box 427, Ada, OK 74820; 580-332-5763; Fax: 580-436-5613. Hours: 8AM-5PM (CST). *Felony, Misdemeanor, Civil, Eviction, Small Claims, Probate.*

Civil Records: Access: Phone, mail, in person. Both court and visitors may perform in person searches. No search fee. Required to search: name, years to search. Civil cases indexed by defendant, plaintiff. Civil records on card index from 1907.

Criminal Records: Access: Phone, mail, in person. Both court and visitors may perform in person searches. No search fee. Required to search: name, years to search; also helpful-DOB, SSN. Criminal records on card index from 1907. **General Information:** No juvenile, adoptions, mental health or guardianship records released. SASE required. Turnaround time 2 days. Copy fee: $1.00 for first page, $.50 each addl. Certification fee: $.50. Fee payee: Clerk of Court. Personal checks accepted. Must prepay if out of state. Will bill marriage license fees.

Pottawatomie County

23rd Judicial District Court 325 N. Broadway, Shawnee, OK 74801; 405-273-3624. Hours: 8:30AM-Noon, 1-5 PM (CST). *Felony, Misdemeanor, Civil, Eviction, Small Claims, Probate.*

Civil Records: Access: Mail, in person. Both court and visitors may perform in person searches. Search fee: $5.00 per name. Required to search: name, years to search. Civil cases indexed by defendant, plaintiff. Civil records on computer from 07/97; prior records on book of names from 1892. **Criminal Records:** Access: Mail, in person. Both court and visitors may perform in person searches. Search fee: $5.00 per name. Required to search: name, years to search; also helpful-SSN. Criminal records on computer from 07/97; prior records on book of names from 1892. **General Information:** No juvenile, adoptions, mental health or guardianship records released. SASE not required. Turnaround time 2 weeks or less. Copy fee: $1.00 for first page, $.50 each addl. Certification fee: $.50. Fee payee: Court Clerk. Personal checks accepted. Prepayment is required.

Pushmataha County

17th Judicial District Court Push County Courthouse, Antlers, OK 74523; 580-298-2274. Hours: 8AM-4:30PM (CST). *Felony, Misdemeanor, Civil, Eviction, Small Claims, Probate.*

Civil Records: Access: Mail, in person. Both court and visitors may perform in person searches. Search fee: $5.00 per name. Required to search: name, years to search. Civil cases indexed by defendant, plaintiff. Civil records on docket book from 1907. **Criminal Records:** Access: Mail, in person. Both court and visitors may perform in person searches. Search fee: $5.00 per name. Required to search: name, years to search; also helpful-SSN. Criminal records on docket book from 1907. **General Information:** No juvenile or adoption records released. SASE required. Turnaround time 1 day. Copy fee: $1.00 for first page, $.50 each addl. Certification fee: $.50. Fee payee: Court Clerk. Personal checks accepted. Prepayment is required.

Roger Mills County

2nd Judicial District Court Box 409, Cheyenne, OK 73628; 580-497-3361. Hours: 8AM-Noon, 1-4:30PM (CST). *Felony, Misdemeanor, Civil, Eviction, Small Claims, Probate.*

Civil Records: Access: Phone, mail, in person. Both court and visitors may perform in person searches. No search fee. Required to search: name, years to search. Civil cases indexed by defendant, plaintiff. Civil records on computer since 1992, in books since 1893. **Criminal Records:** Access: Phone, mail, in person. Both court and visitors may perform in person searches. No search fee. Required to search: name, years to search, DOB;

also helpful-SSN. Criminal records on computer since 1992, in books since 1893. **General Information:** No adoption, juvenile, mental health or guardianship records released. SASE required. Turnaround time 1 day. Copy fee: $1.00 for first page, $.50 each addl. Certification fee: $.50. Fee payee: Court Clerk. Personal checks accepted. Prepayment is required. Public access terminal is available.

Rogers County

12th Judicial District Court Box 839, 1219 S Missouri, Claremore, OK 74018; 918-341-5711. Hours: 8AM-4:30PM (CST). *Felony, Misdemeanor, Civil, Eviction, Small Claims, Probate.*

Civil Records: Access: Mail, online, in person. Both court and visitors may perform in person searches. No search fee. Required to search: name, years to search. Civil cases indexed by defendant, plaintiff. Card index for last 7 years, some computerized. Access to court dockets is available free on the Internet at www.oscn.net/pinpoint3/ applications/dockets/start.asp. Search by case number, parties, locations, or citation numbers. **Criminal Records:** Access: Mail, remote online, in person. Both court and visitors may perform in person searches. No search fee. Required to search: name, years to search, DOB; also helpful-SSN. Card index for last 7 years, some computerized. Online access to court dockets is same as civil, see above. **General Information:** No juvenile or adoption records released. SASE required. Turnaround time 1 day. Copy fee: $1.00 for first page, $.50 each addl. Certification fee: $.50. Fee payee: Court Clerk. Personal checks accepted. Prepayment is required. Public access terminal is available.

Seminole County

22nd Judicial District Court -Seminole Branch Box 1320, 401 Main St, Seminole, OK 74868; 405-382-3424. Hours: 8AM-Noon, 1-4PM (CST). *Civil, Small Claims, Probate.*

Note: Criminal records are now maintained at 22nd Judicial District Court, PO Box 130, Wewoka, OK, 405-257-6236.

Civil Records: Access: Phone, mail, in person. Only the court conducts in person searches; visitors may not. Search fee: $5.00 per name. Required to search: name, years to search. Civil cases indexed by defendant, plaintiff. Civil records on index cards from 1931, probate from 1969. **General Information:** SASE required. Turnaround time 1 to 2 days. Copy fee: $1.00 for first page, $.50 each addl. Certification fee: $.50. Fee payee: Court Clerk. Only cashiers checks and money orders accepted. Prepayment is required.

22nd Judicial District Court - Wewoka Branch Box 130, Wewoka, OK 74884; 405-257-6236. Hours: 8AM-4PM (CST). *Felony, Misdemeanor, Civil, Eviction, Small Claims, Probate.*

Civil Records: Access: Mail, in person. Both court and visitors may perform in person searches. Search fee: $5.00 per name. Required to search: name, years to search. Civil cases indexed by defendant, plaintiff. Civil records indexed on computer since 1995; prior records on books. **Criminal Records:** Access: Mail, in person. Both court and visitors may perform in person searches. Search fee: $5.00 per name. Required to search: name, years to search; also helpful-SSN. Criminal records indexed on computer since 1995; prior records on books. They maintain the criminal

records for the Seminole Branch in Seminole, OK. **General Information:** No juvenile or adoption records released. SASE required. Turnaround time 1 day. Copy fee: $1.00 for first page, $.50 each addl. Certification fee: $.50. Fee payee: Court Clerk. Personal checks accepted. Prepayment is required.

Sequoyah County

15th Judicial District Court 120 E Chickasaw, Sallisaw, OK 74955; 918-775-4411. Hours: 8AM-4PM (CST). *Felony, Misdemeanor, Civil, Eviction, Small Claims, Probate.*

Civil Records: Access: Phone, mail, in person. Both court and visitors may perform in person searches. Search fee: $5.00 per name. Required to search: name, years to search. Civil cases indexed by defendant, plaintiff. Civil records in files and dockets from 1907. **Criminal Records:** Access: Phone, mail, in person. Both court and visitors may perform in person searches. Search fee: $5.00 per name. Required to search: name, years to search; also helpful-SSN. Some criminal records on computer since 11/94, rest in files and dockets. **General Information:** No juvenile, adoptions, mental health or guardianship records released. SASE required. Turnaround time 1 week. Copy fee: $1.00 for first page, $.50 each addl. Certification fee: $.50. Fee payee: Court Clerk. Personal checks accepted. Will bill mail requests. Public access terminal is available.

Stephens County

5th Judicial District Court 101 S 11th Rm 301, Duncan, OK 73533; 580-255-8460. Hours: 8:30AM-4:30PM (CST). *Felony, Misdemeanor, Civil, Eviction, Small Claims, Probate.*

Civil Records: Access: Phone, mail, in person. Both court and visitors may perform in person searches. Search fee: $5.00 per name. Required to search: name, years to search. Civil cases indexed by defendant, plaintiff. Civil records on computer from 10/95; prior records on docket books from 1907. **Criminal Records:** Access: Phone, mail, in person. Both court and visitors may perform in person searches. Search fee: $5.00 per name. Required to search: name, years to search; also helpful-address, DOB, SSN. Criminal records on computer from 10/95; prior records on docket books from 1907. **General Information:** No juvenile, adoptions, mental health or guardianship records released. SASE required. Turnaround time 1 day. Copy fee: $1.00 for first page, $.50 each addl. Certification fee: $.50. Fee payee: Stephens County 5th Judicial Court. Personal checks accepted. Prepayment is required. Public access terminal is available.

Texas County

1st Judicial District Court Box 1081, Guymon, OK 73942; 580-338-3003. Hours: 9AM-5PM (CST). *Felony, Misdemeanor, Civil, Eviction, Small Claims, Probate.*

Civil Records: Access: Mail, in person. Both court and visitors may perform in person searches. Search fee: $5.00 per name. Required to search: name, years to search. Civil cases indexed by defendant, plaintiff. Civil records on microfiche from 1976, archived prior, computerized since 03/95. **Criminal Records:** Access: Mail, in person. Both court and visitors may perform in person searches. Search fee: $5.00 per name. Required to search: name, years to search; also helpful-SSN. Criminal records on microfiche from 1976, archived prior, computerized since 03/95. **General Information:** No juvenile, adoptions,

mental health or guardianship records released. SASE required. Turnaround time 5 days, 1 day for phone. Copy fee: $1.00 for first page, $.50 each addl. Certification fee: $.50. Fee payee: Court Clerk. Personal checks accepted. Prepayment is required. Public access terminal is available.

Tillman County

3rd Judicial District Court Box 116, Frederick, OK 73542; 580-335-3023. Hours: 8AM-4PM (CST). *Felony, Misdemeanor, Civil, Eviction, Small Claims, Probate.*

Civil Records: Access: Mail, in person. Both court and visitors may perform in person searches. Search fee: $5.00 per name. Required to search: name, years to search. Civil cases indexed by defendant, plaintiff. Civil records on docket books from 1907. **Criminal Records:** Access: Mail, in person. Both court and visitors may perform in person searches. Search fee: $5.00 per name. Required to search: name, years to search; also helpful-SSN. Criminal records on docket books from 1907. **General Information:** No expunged records released. SASE required. Turnaround time 1 day. Copy fee: $1.00 for first page, $.50 each addl. Copy charge is only if the person does their own search in person. Certification fee: $1.00. Fee payee: District Court. Business checks accepted. Will bill law firms.

Tulsa County

14th Judicial District Court 500 S. Denver, Tulsa, OK 74103-3832; 918-596-5000. Hours: 8:30AM-5PM (CST). *Felony, Misdemeanor, Civil, Eviction, Small Claims, Probate.*

Civil Records: Access: Mail, online, in person. Both court and visitors may perform in person searches. Search fee: $5.00 per name. Required to search: name, years to search. Civil cases indexed by defendant, plaintiff. Civil records on computer from 1984, on microfiche from 1907, archived from 1907. Access to court dockets is available free on the Internet at www.oscn.net/pinpoint3/ applications/dockets/start.asp. Search by case number, parties, locations, or citation numbers. **Criminal Records:** Access: Mail, remote online, in person. Both court and visitors may perform in person searches. Search fee: $5.00 per name. Required to search: name, years to search; also helpful-SSN. Criminal records on computer from 1984, on microfiche from 1907, archived from 1907. Online access to court dockets is same as civil, see above. **General Information:** No juvenile, adoption or guardianship records released. SASE required. Turnaround time 1 week. Copy fee: $1.00 for first page, $.50 each addl. Certification fee: $.50. Fee payee: Court Clerk. Will accept attorney personal checks. Prepayment is required. Public access terminal is available.

Wagoner County

15th Judicial District Court Box 249, Wagoner, OK 74477; 918-485-4508. Hours: 8:00AM-4:30PM (CST). *Felony, Misdemeanor, Civil, Eviction, Small Claims, Probate.*

Civil Records: Access: Mail, in person. Both court and visitors may perform in person searches. Search fee: $5.00 per name. Required to search: name, years to search. Civil cases indexed by defendant, plaintiff. Some records on microfiche from 1991, all on docket books from 1980. **Criminal Records:** Access: Phone, mail, in person. Both court and visitors may perform in person searches. Search fee: $5.00 per name. Required to search: name, years to search; also helpful-SSN. Some records are on microfiche for last 3-4 years, files and dockets to 1907. **General Information:** No juvenile, mental health, adoption or guardianship records released. SASE required. Turnaround time 1-2 days for civil, longer for criminal. Copy fee: $1.00 for first page, $.50 each addl. Certification fee: $.50. Fee payee: Court Clerk. Personal checks accepted. Prepayment is required.

Washington County

11th Judicial District Court 420 S Johnstone, Rm 212, Bartlesville, OK 74003; 918-337-2870; Fax: 918-337-2897. Hours: 8AM-5PM (CST). *Felony, Misdemeanor, Civil, Eviction, Small Claims, Probate.*

Civil Records: Access: Phone, mail, in person. Both court and visitors may perform in person searches. Search fee: $5.00 per name. Required to search: name, years to search. Civil cases indexed by defendant, plaintiff. Civil records on microfiche from 1988, on docket books from 1907. **Criminal Records:** Access: Phone, mail, in person. Both court and visitors may perform in person searches. Search fee: $5.00 per name. Required to search: name, years to search, signed release; also helpful-DOB, SSN. Criminal records on microfiche from 1988, on docket books from 1907. **General Information:** No juvenile, mental health, adoption or guardianship records released. Turnaround time 1-3 days. Copy fee: $1.00 for first page, $.50 each addl. Certification fee: $3.00. Fee payee: Court Clerk. Personal checks accepted. Prepayment is required. Public access terminal is available.

Washita County

3rd Judicial District Court Box 397, Cordell, OK 73632,; 580-832-3836. Hours: 8AM-4PM (CST). *Felony, Misdemeanor, Civil, Small Claims, Probate.*

Civil Records: Access: Mail, in person. Both court and visitors may perform in person searches. Search fee: $5.00 per name. Required to search: name, years to search. Civil cases indexed by defendant, plaintiff. Civil records on computer since 1998; prior records on microfiche from 1980s & on docket books from 1892. **Criminal Records:** Access: Mail, in person. Both court and visitors may perform in person searches. Search fee: $5.00 per name. Required to search: name, years to search; also helpful-DOB, SSN, aliases. Criminal records on computer since 1998; prior records on microfiche from 1980s & on docket books from 1892. **General Information:** No juvenile, mental health, adoption or guardianship records released. SASE required. Turnaround time same day. Copy fee: $1.00 for first page, $.50 each addl. Certification fee: $.50. Fee payee: Court Clerk. Personal checks accepted. Prepayment is required.

Woods County

4th Judicial District Court Box 924, Alva, OK 73717; 580-327-3119. Hours: 9AM-5PM (CST). *Felony, Misdemeanor, Civil, Eviction, Small Claims, Probate.*

Civil Records: Access: Mail, in person. Both court and visitors may perform in person searches. Search fee: $5.00 per name. Required to search: name, years to search. Civil cases indexed by defendant, plaintiff. Civil records on docket books

from 1890. **Criminal Records:** Access: Mail, in person. Both court and visitors may perform in person searches. Search fee: $5.00 per name. Required to search: name, years to search. Criminal records on computer since 1987, on dockets and cards from 1890s. **General Information:** No juvenile, mental health, adoption or guardianship records released. SASE required. Turnaround time 2 days. Copy fee: $1.00 for first page, $.50 each addl. Certification fee: $.50. Fee payee: Clerk of Court. Personal checks accepted. Prepayment is required.

Woodward County

4th Judicial District Court 1600 Main, Woodward, OK 73801; 580-256-3413. Hours: 9AM-5PM (CST). *Felony, Misdemeanor, Civil, Eviction, Small Claims, Probate.*

Civil Records: Access: Mail, in person. Both court and visitors may perform in person searches. Search fee: $5.00 per name. Required to search: name, years to search. Civil cases indexed by defendant, plaintiff. Civil records on docket books from 1890, on microfiche from 1989. **Criminal Records:** Access: Mail, in person. Both court and visitors may perform in person searches. Search fee: $5.00 per name. Required to search: name, years to search; also helpful-DOB, SSN. Criminal records on docket books from 1890, on microfiche from 1989. **General Information:** No mental, juvenile, adoption, guardianship records released. SASE reqired. Turnaround time 1-2 days unless older cases found. Copy fee: $1.00 for first page, $.50 each addl. Certification fee: $.50. $5.00 for whole file. Fee payee: Court Clerk. Personal checks accepted. Prepayment is required.

ORGANIZATION 77 counties, 77 recording offices. The recording officer is County Clerk. The entire state is in the Central Time Zone (CST).

REAL ESTATE RECORDS Many counties will perform real estate searches by legal description. Copy fees are usually $1.00 per page. Certification usually costs $1.00 per document.

UCC RECORDS Financing statements are filed centrally with the County Clerk of Oklahoma County, except for consumer goods, which are dual filed, and farm related and real estate related collateral, which are filed with the County Clerk. All counties will perform UCC searches. Use search request form UCC-4. Search fees are usually $5.00 per debtor name for a written request and $3.00 per name by telephone. Copies usually cost $1.00 per page.

TAX LIEN RECORDS Federal tax liens on personal property of businesses are filed with the County Clerk of Oklahoma County, which is the central filing office for the state. Other federal and all state tax liens are filed with the County Clerk. Usually state and federal tax liens on personal property are filed in separate indexes. Some counties will perform tax lien searches. Search fees vary.

OTHER LIENS Judgment, mechanics, physicians, hospital.

Adair County
County Clerk, P.O. Box 169, Stilwell, OK 74960. 918-696-7198. Fax: 918-696-2603.

Alfalfa County
County Clerk, 300 South Grand, Cherokee, OK 73728. 580-596-3158.

Atoka County
County Clerk, 200 East Court Street, Atoka, OK 74525. 580-889-5157. Fax: 580-889-5063.

Beaver County
County Clerk, P.O. Box 338, Beaver, OK 73932-0338. 580-625-3141. Fax: 580-625-3430.

Beckham County
County Clerk, P.O. Box 428, Sayre, OK 73662-0428. 580-928-3383.

Blaine County
County Clerk, P.O. Box 138, Watonga, OK 73772. 580-623-5890. Fax: 580-623-5009.

Bryan County
County Clerk, P.O. Box 1789, Durant, OK 74702. 580-924-2202. Fax: 580-924-3094.

Caddo County
County Clerk, P.O. Box 68, Anadarko, OK 73005. 405-247-6609. Fax: 405-247-6510.

Canadian County
County Clerk, P.O. Box 458, El Reno, OK 73036. 405-262-1070. Fax: 405-422-2411.
http://164.58.150.126/coclerk/
Online access: Real Estate, Assessor. Records on the Canadian County Register of Deeds database are available free on the Internet at http://164.58.150.126/coclerk/deeds/default.asp. Search by grantor/grantee, subdivision, document # or book & page. Records go back to 1991.

Carter County
County Clerk, P.O. Box 1236, Ardmore, OK 73402. 580-223-8162.

Cherokee County
County Clerk, 213 West Delaware, Room 200, Tahlequah, OK 74464. 918-456-3171. Fax: 918-458-6508.

Choctaw County
County Clerk, Courthouse, 300 E. Duke, Hugo, OK 74743. 580-326-3778. Fax: 580-326-6787.

Cimarron County
County Clerk, P.O. Box 145, Boise City, OK 73933. 580-544-2251. Fax: 580-544-3420.

Cleveland County
County Clerk, 201 South Jones, Room 204, Norman, OK 73069-6099. 405-366-0253. Fax: 405-366-0229.

Coal County
County Clerk, 4 North Main, Suite 1, Coalgate, OK 74538. 580-927-2103. Fax: 580-927-4003.

Comanche County
County Clerk, 315 SW 5th, Room 304, Lawton, OK 73501-4347. 580-355-5214.

Cotton County
County Clerk, 301 North Broadway, Walters, OK 73572. 580-875-3026. Fax: 580-875-3756.

Craig County
County Clerk, P.O. Box 397, Vinita, OK 74301. 918-256-2507. Fax: 918-256-3617.

Creek County
County Clerk, 317 E. Lee, First Floor, Sapulpa, OK 74066. 918-227-6306.

Custer County
County Clerk, P.O. Box 300, Arapaho, OK 73620. 580-323-1221. Fax: 580-323-4421.

Delaware County
County Clerk, P.O. Box 309, Jay, OK 74346. 918-253-4520. Fax: 918-253-8352.

Dewey County
County Clerk, P.O. Box 368, Taloga, OK 73667. 580-328-5361.

Ellis County
County Clerk, P.O. Box 197, Arnett, OK 73832. 580-885-7301. Fax: 580-885-7258.

Garfield County
County Clerk, P.O. Box 1664, Enid, OK 73702-1664. 580-237-0226. Fax: 580-249-5951.

Garvin County
County Clerk, P.O. Box 926, Pauls Valley, OK 73075. 405-238-2772. Fax: 405-238-6283.

Grady County
County Clerk, P.O. Box 1009, Chickasha, OK 73023. 405-224-7388. Fax: 405-222-4506.

Grant County
County Clerk, P.O. Box 167, Medford, OK 73759-0167. 580-395-2274.

Greer County
County Clerk, P.O. Box 207, Mangum, OK 73554. 580-782-3664. Fax: 580-782-3803.

Harmon County
County Clerk, Courthouse, 14 W. Hollis, Hollis, OK 73550. 580-688-3658.

Harper County
County Clerk, P.O. Box 369, Buffalo, OK 73834. 580-735-2012.

Haskell County
County Clerk, 202 East Main, Courthouse, Stigler, OK 74462. 918-967-2884. Fax: 918-967-2885.

Hughes County
County Clerk, 200 North Broadway ST. #5, Holdenville, OK 74848-3400. 405-379-5487.

Jackson County
County Clerk, P.O. Box 515, Altus, OK 73522. 580-482-4070.

Jefferson County
County Clerk, 220 North Main, Courthouse - Room 103, Waurika, OK 73573. 580-228-2029. Fax: 580-228-3418.

Johnston County
County Clerk, 414 West Main, Room 101, Tishomingo, OK 73460. 580-371-3184.

Kay County
County Clerk, P.O. Box 450, Newkirk, OK 74647-0450. 580-362-2537. Fax: 580-362-3300.

Kingfisher County
County Clerk, 101 South Main, Room #3, Kingfisher, OK 73750. 405-375-3887. Fax: 405-375-6033.

Kiowa County
County Clerk, P.O. Box 73, Hobart, OK 73651-0073. 580-726-5286. Fax: 580-726-6033.

Latimer County
County Clerk, 109 North Central, Room 103, Wilburton, OK 74578. 918-465-3543. Fax: 918-465-4001.

Le Flore County
County Clerk, P.O. Box 218, Poteau, OK 74953-0218. 918-647-5738. Fax: 918-647-8930.

Lincoln County
County Clerk, P.O. Box 126, Chandler, OK 74834-0126. 405-258-1264.

Logan County
County Clerk, 301 East Harrison, Suite 102, Guthrie, OK 73044-4999. 405-282-0267.

Love County
County Clerk, 405 West Main, Room 203, Marietta, OK 73448. 580-276-3059.

Major County
County Clerk, P.O. Box 379, Fairview, OK 73737-0379. 580-227-4732. Fax: 580-227-2736.

Marshall County
County Clerk, Marshall County Courthouse, Room 101, Madill, OK 73446. 580-795-3220.

Mayes County
County Clerk, P.O. Box 97, Pryor, OK 74362. 918-825-2426. Fax: 918-825-2913.

McClain County
County Clerk, P.O. Box 629, Purcell, OK 73080-0629. 405-527-3360.

McCurtain County
County Clerk, P.O. Box 1078, Idabel, OK 74745. 580-286-2370.

McIntosh County
County Clerk, P.O. Box 110, Eufaula, OK 74432-0110. 918-689-5419. Fax: 918-689-3385.

Murray County
County Clerk, P.O. Box 442, Sulphur, OK 73086. 580-622-3920. Fax: 580-622-6209.

Muskogee County
County Clerk, P.O. Box 1008, Muskogee, OK 74401. 918-682-7781.

Noble County
County Clerk, 300 Courthouse Dr., Courthouse, Box 11, Room 201, Perry, OK 73077. 580-336-2141. Fax: 580-336-2481.

Nowata County
County Clerk, 229 North Maple, Nowata, OK 74048. 918-273-2480. Fax: 918-273-2481.

Okfuskee County
County Clerk, P.O. Box 108, Okemah, OK 74859-0108. 918-623-1724. Fax: 918-623-0739.

Oklahoma County
County Clerk, 320 Robert S. Kerr Avenue, Courthouse - Room 107, Oklahoma City, OK 73102. 405-278-1538. Fax: 405-278-2241.
www.oklahomacounty.org
Online Access: Real Estate, Assessor, Grantor/Grantee. Records on the Oklahoma County Assessor Records database are available free on the Internet at www.oklahomacounty.org/assessor/disclaimer.htm. Provides real property, business personal property, manufactured housing and farm personal property records At the disclaimer page, click on "Yes" after "I understand and. above statement." At the "Select Type of Search" page, select one of the four options Grantor/Grantee records, real estate, and UCC records on the Oklahoma County Clerk database are available free online at www.oklahomacounty.org/coclerk. Registrar of Deeds search page is www.oklahomacounty.org/clerk/deeds/default.asp.

Okmulgee County
County Clerk, P.O. Box 904, Okmulgee, OK 74447-0904. 918-756-0788. Fax: 918-758-1261.

Osage County
County Clerk, P.O. Box 87, Pawhuska, OK 74056. 918-287-3136.

Ottawa County
County Clerk, 102 E. Central, Suite 203, Miami, OK 74354-7043. 918-542-3332.

Pawnee County
County Clerk, Courthouse, Room 202, 500 Harrison St., Pawnee, OK 74058. 918-762-2732.

Payne County
County Clerk, P.O. Box 7, Stillwater, OK 74076-0007. 405-747-8310.

Pittsburg County
County Clerk, P.O. Box 3304, McAlester, OK 74502. 918-423-6865. Fax: 918-423-7304.

Pontotoc County
County Clerk, P.O. Box 1425, Ada, OK 74820. 580-332-1425. Fax: 580-332-9509.

Pottawatomie County
County Clerk, P.O. Box 576, Shawnee, OK 74802. 405-273-8222. Fax: 405-275-6898.

Pushmataha County
County Clerk, 302 SW 'B', Antlers, OK 74523. 580-298-3626. Fax: 580-298-3626.

Roger Mills County
County Clerk, P.O. Box 708, Cheyenne, OK 73628. 580-497-3395. Fax: 580-497-3488.

Rogers County
County Clerk, P.O. Box 1210, Claremore, OK 74017. 918-341-1860.

Seminole County
County Clerk, P.O. Box 1180, Wewoka, OK 74884. 405-257-2501. Fax: 405-257-6422.

Sequoyah County
County Clerk, 120 East Chickasaw, Sallisaw, OK 74955. 918-775-4516. Fax: 918-775-1218.

Stephens County
County Clerk, 101 S. 11th St., Room 203, Duncan, OK 73533-4758. 580-255-0977. Fax: 580-255-0991.

Texas County
County Clerk, P.O. Box 197, Guymon, OK 73942-0197. 580-338-3141.

Tillman County
County Clerk, P.O. Box 992, Frederick, OK 73542. 580-335-3421. Fax: 580-335-3795.

Tulsa County
County Clerk, 500 South Denver Avenue, County Admin. Bldg.-Room 112, Tulsa, OK 74103-3832. 918-596-5801. Fax: 918-596-5867.

Wagoner County
County Clerk, P.O. Box 156, Wagoner, OK 74477. 918-485-2216. Fax: 918-485-8677.

Washington County
County Clerk, 420 South Johnstone, Room 102, Bartlesville, OK 74003. 918-337-2840. Fax: 918-337-2894.

Washita County
County Clerk, P.O. Box 380, Cordell, OK 73632. 580-832-3548.

Woods County
County Clerk, P.O. Box 386, Alva, OK 73717-0386. 580-327-0998. Fax: 580-327-6230.

Woodward County
County Clerk, 1600 Main Street, Woodward, OK 73801-3051. 580-254-6800.

You will usually be able to find the city name in the City/County Cross Reference below. In that case, it is a simple matter to determine the county from the cross reference. However, only the official US Postal Service city names are included in this index. There are an additional 40,000 place names that people use in their addresses. Therefore, we have also included a ZIP/City Cross Reference immediately following the City/County Cross Reference.

If you know the ZIP Code but the city name does not appear in the City/County Cross Reference index, look up the ZIP Code in the ZIP/City Cross Reference, find the city name, then look up the city name in the City/County Cross Reference. For example, you want to know the county for an address of Menands, NY 12204. There is no "Menands" in the City/County Cross Reference. The ZIP/City Cross Reference shows that ZIP Codes 12201-12288 are for the city of Albany. Looking back in the City/County Cross Reference, Albany is in Albany County.

City/County Cross Reference

ACHILLE Bryan
ADA Pontotoc
ADAIR Mayes
ADAMS Texas
ADDINGTON Jefferson
AFTON (74331) Delaware(72), Ottawa(26), Craig(2)
AGRA (74824) Lincoln(84), Payne(16)
ALBANY Bryan
ALBERT Caddo
ALBION Pushmataha
ALDERSON Pittsburg
ALEX (73002) Grady(89), McClain(12)
ALINE (73716) Alfalfa(57), Woods(36), Major(7)
ALLEN (74825) Pontotoc(69), Hughes(27), Coal(4)
ALTUS Jackson
ALTUS AFB Jackson
ALVA Woods
AMBER Grady
AMES (73718) Major(89), Garfield(9), Kingfisher(2)
AMORITA Alfalfa
ANADARKO Caddo
ANTLERS Pushmataha
APACHE (73006) Caddo(66), Comanche(34)
ARAPAHO Custer
ARCADIA (73007) Oklahoma(64), Logan(36)
ARDMORE Carter
ARKOMA Le Flore
ARNETT (73832) Ellis(90), Woodward(11)
ASHER Pottawatomie
ATOKA Atoka
ATWOOD Hughes
AVANT Osage
BACHE Pittsburg
BALKO Beaver
BARNSDALL Osage
BARTLESVILLE (74003) Washington(90), Osage(10)
BARTLESVILLE Washington
BATTIEST McCurtain
BEAVER Beaver
BEGGS Okmulgee
BENNINGTON Bryan
BESSIE Washita
BETHANY Oklahoma
BETHEL McCurtain
BIG CABIN (74332) Craig(51), Mayes(27), Rogers(21)
BILLINGS (74630) Noble(85), Garfield(15)
BINGER Caddo
BISON Garfield
BIXBY Tulsa
BLACKWELL Kay
BLAIR Jackson
BLANCHARD (73010) McClain(54), Grady(46)
BLANCO Pittsburg

BLOCKER Pittsburg
BLUEJACKET (74333) Ottawa(56), Craig(44)
BOISE CITY Cimarron
BOKCHITO Bryan
BOKOSHE Le Flore
BOLEY Okfuskee
BOSWELL (74727) Choctaw(84), Bryan(10), Atoka(6)
BOWLEGS Seminole
BOWRING Osage
BOYNTON (74422) Muskogee(65), Okmulgee(36)
BRADLEY Grady
BRAGGS Muskogee
BRAMAN Kay
BRAY (73012) McClain(50), Stephens(50)
BRISTOW Creek
BROKEN ARROW (74014) Wagoner(99), Tulsa(1)
BROKEN ARROW Tulsa
BROKEN BOW McCurtain
BROMIDE Johnston
BUFFALO Harper
BUNCH (74931) Adair(67), Cherokee(25), Sequoyah(9)
BURBANK Osage
BURLINGTON Alfalfa
BURNEYVILLE Love
BURNS FLAT Washita
BUTLER Custer
BYARS (74831) McClain(89), Pontotoc(9), Garvin(2)
BYRON Alfalfa
CACHE Comanche
CADDO (74729) Bryan(58), Atoka(42)
CALERA Bryan
CALUMET Canadian
CALVIN Hughes
CAMARGO Dewey
CAMERON Le Flore
CANADIAN Pittsburg
CANEY Atoka
CANTON (73724) Blaine(61), Dewey(39)
CANUTE Washita
CAPRON (73725) Woods(80), Alfalfa(20)
CARDIN Ottawa
CARMEN (73726) Alfalfa(78), Woods(22)
CARNEGIE (73015) Caddo(90), Washita(10)
CARNEY Lincoln
CARRIER Garfield
CARTER Beckham
CARTWRIGHT Bryan
CASHION (73016) Kingfisher(59), Logan(38), Canadian(4)
CASTLE Okfuskee
CATOOSA Rogers
CEMENT (73017) Grady(50), Caddo(46), Comanche(4)
CENTRAHOMA Coal
CHANDLER Lincoln

CHATTANOOGA Comanche
CHECOTAH McIntosh
CHELSEA (74016) Rogers(85), Mayes(7), Nowata(5), Craig(3)
CHEROKEE Alfalfa
CHESTER (73838) Major(90), Woodward(10)
CHEYENNE Roger Mills
CHICKASHA Grady
CHOCTAW Oklahoma
CHOUTEAU (74337) Mayes(90), Wagoner(10)
CLAREMORE Rogers
CLARITA Coal
CLAYTON (74536) Pushmataha(97), Latimer(2), Pittsburg(2)
CLEARVIEW Okfuskee
CLEO SPRINGS (73729) Major(84), Woods(13), Alfalfa(2)
CLEVELAND Pawnee
CLINTON (73601) Custer(98), Washita(3)
COALGATE Coal
COLBERT Bryan
COLCORD Delaware
COLEMAN Johnston
COLLINSVILLE (74021) Tulsa(76), Rogers(20), Washington(4)
COLONY (73021) Washita(66), Caddo(34)
COMANCHE Stephens
COMMERCE Ottawa
CONCHO Canadian
CONNERVILLE Johnston
COOKSON Cherokee
COPAN (74022) Washington(95), Osage(5)
CORDELL Washita
CORN Washita
COUNCIL HILL (74428) McIntosh(59), Muskogee(41)
COUNTYLINE Stephens
COVINGTON Garfield
COWETA Wagoner
COYLE (73027) Logan(66), Payne(34)
CRAWFORD Roger Mills
CRESCENT (73028) Logan(89), Kingfisher(11)
CROMWELL Seminole
CROWDER Pittsburg
CUSHING (74023) Payne(93), Lincoln(7)
CUSTER CITY Custer
CYRIL Caddo
DACOMA (73731) Woods(95), Alfalfa(6)
DAISY (74540) Pushmataha(55), Atoka(46)
DAVENPORT Lincoln
DAVIDSON Tillman
DAVIS (73030) Murray(98), Garvin(3)
DEER CREEK Grant
DELAWARE Nowata
DEPEW (74028) Creek(99), Lincoln(1)
DEWAR Okmulgee
DEWEY Washington
DIBBLE McClain

DILL CITY Washita
DISNEY Mayes
DOUGHERTY Murray
DOUGLAS Garfield
DOVER Kingfisher
DRUMMOND (73735) Garfield(95), Major(5)
DRUMRIGHT (74030) Creek(98), Payne(2)
DUKE Jackson
DUNCAN Stephens
DURANT Bryan
DURHAM Roger Mills
DUSTIN (74839) Hughes(65), Okfuskee(24), McIntosh(11)
EAGLETOWN McCurtain
EAKLY Caddo
EARLSBORO (74840) Seminole(52), Pottawatomie(48)
EDMOND (73003) Oklahoma(87), Logan(13)
EDMOND (73034) Oklahoma(82), Logan(18)
EDMOND Oklahoma
EL RENO Canadian
ELDORADO (73537) Jackson(91), Harmon(9)
ELGIN Comanche
ELK CITY (73644) Beckham(98), Washita(2)
ELK CITY Beckham
ELMER Jackson
ELMORE CITY Garvin
ENID Garfield
ERICK Beckham
EUCHA Delaware
EUFAULA (74432) McIntosh(92), Pittsburg(8)
FAIRFAX Osage
FAIRLAND Ottawa
FAIRMONT Garfield
FAIRVIEW Major
FANSHAWE Le Flore
FARGO (73840) Ellis(65), Woodward(35)
FAXON Comanche
FAY (73646) Blaine(44), Dewey(41), Custer(15)
FELT Cimarron
FINLEY Pushmataha
FITTSTOWN Johnston
FITTSTOWN Pontotoc
FITZHUGH Pontotoc
FLETCHER Comanche
FORGAN Beaver
FORT COBB Caddo
FORT GIBSON (74434) Muskogee(85), Cherokee(8), Wagoner(7)
FORT SILL Comanche
FORT SUPPLY Woodward
FORT TOWSON (74735) Choctaw(73), Pushmataha(27)
FOSS (73647) Washita(84), Custer(16)
FOSTER (73039) Stephens(69), Garvin(31)

FOX Carter
FOYIL Rogers
FRANCIS Pontotoc
FREDERICK Tillman
FREEDOM (73842) Woods(64), Woodward(26), Harper(10)
GAGE (73843) Ellis(96), Beaver(4)
GANS Sequoyah
GARBER Garfield
GARVIN McCurtain
GATE (73844) Beaver(65), Harper(35)
GEARY (73040) Blaine(77), Canadian(23)
GENE AUTRY Carter
GERONIMO Comanche
GLENCOE (74032) Payne(76), Pawnee(15), Noble(8)
GLENPOOL (74033) Tulsa(98), Creek(2)
GOLDEN McCurtain
GOLTRY (73739) Alfalfa(78), Garfield(22)
GOODWELL Texas
GORE (74435) Sequoyah(88), Muskogee(12)
GOTEBO (73041) Kiowa(73), Washita(28)
GOULD Harmon
GOWEN Latimer
GRACEMONT Caddo
GRAHAM Carter
GRANDFIELD Tillman
GRANITE Greer
GRANT Choctaw
GREENFIELD Blaine
GROVE (74344) Delaware(98), Ottawa(1)
GROVE Delaware
GUTHRIE Logan
GUYMON Texas
HAILEYVILLE Pittsburg
HALLETT Pawnee
HAMMON (73650) Roger Mills(76), Custer(24)
HANNA McIntosh
HARDESTY Texas
HARRAH (73045) Oklahoma(70), Lincoln(26), Pottawatomie(4)
HARTSHORNE (74547) Pittsburg(98), Latimer(2)
HASKELL (74436) Muskogee(72), Wagoner(23), Okmulgee(5)
HASTINGS (73548) Stephens(43), Jefferson(30), Cotton(27)
HAWORTH McCurtain
HAYWOOD Pittsburg
HEADRICK Jackson
HEALDTON Carter
HEAVENER Le Flore
HELENA Alfalfa
HENDRIX Bryan
HENNEPIN (73046) Carter(57), Garvin(36), Murray(7)
HENNESSEY (73742) Kingfisher(97), Garfield(3)
HENRYETTA (74437) Okmulgee(99), McIntosh(1)
HILLSDALE Garfield
HINTON (73047) Caddo(73), Canadian(27)
HITCHCOCK (73744) Blaine(92), Kingfisher(8)
HITCHITA McIntosh
HOBART Kiowa
HODGEN Le Flore
HOLDENVILLE (74848) Hughes(98), Seminole(2)
HOLLIS Harmon
HOLLISTER Tillman
HOMINY Osage
HONOBIA (74549) Le Flore(89), Pushmataha(11)
HOOKER Texas
HOPETON Woods
HOWE Le Flore
HOYT Haskell
HUGO Choctaw
HULBERT Cherokee

HUNTER (74640) Garfield(79), Grant(21)
HYDRO (73048) Caddo(52), Custer(30), Blaine(18)
IDABEL McCurtain
INDIAHOMA Comanche
INDIANOLA Pittsburg
INOLA (74036) Rogers(89), Mayes(7), Wagoner(5)
ISABELLA Major
JAY Delaware
JENKS Tulsa
JENNINGS (74038) Pawnee(58), Creek(42)
JET Alfalfa
JONES Oklahoma
KANSAS (74347) Delaware(56), Adair(43)
KAW CITY Kay
KELLYVILLE Creek
KEMP Bryan
KENEFIC (74748) Johnston(59), Atoka(23), Bryan(18)
KENTON Cimarron
KEOTA (74941) Haskell(72), Le Flore(28)
KETCHUM Mayes
KEYES Cimarron
KIEFER Creek
KINGFISHER Kingfisher
KINGSTON Marshall
KINTA Haskell
KIOWA (74553) Pittsburg(70), Atoka(30)
KNOWLES Beaver
KONAWA (74849) Seminole(86), Pottawatomie(14)
KREBS Pittsburg
KREMLIN Garfield
LAHOMA (73754) Garfield(76), Major(22), Alfalfa(2)
LAMAR Hughes
LAMONT (74643) Grant(92), Kay(8)
LANE Atoka
LANGLEY Mayes
LANGSTON Logan
LAVERNE Harper
LAWTON Comanche
LEBANON Marshall
LEEDEY (73654) Dewey(58), Roger Mills(29), Custer(12)
LEFLORE Le Flore
LEHIGH Atoka
LENAPAH Nowata
LEON Love
LEONARD Tulsa
LEQUIRE Haskell
LEXINGTON Cleveland
LINDSAY (73052) Garvin(92), McClain(6), Stephens(1), Grady(1)
LOCO Stephens
LOCUST GROVE (74352) Mayes(77), Sequoyah(10), Wagoner(8), Cherokee(5)
LOGAN Beaver
LONE GROVE Carter
LONE WOLF Kiowa
LONGDALE (73755) Blaine(61), Major(33), Dewey(6)
LOOKEBA Caddo
LOVELAND Tillman
LOYAL Kingfisher
LUCIEN (73757) Garfield(57), Noble(39), McClain(4)
LUTHER (73054) Oklahoma(79), Lincoln(12), Logan(10)
MACOMB Pottawatomie
MADILL Marshall
MANCHESTER (73758) Grant(81), Alfalfa(19)
MANGUM Greer
MANITOU Tillman
MANNFORD (74044) Creek(66), Pawnee(34)
MANNSVILLE Johnston
MARAMEC (74045) Pawnee(97), Payne(4)
MARBLE CITY Sequoyah

MARIETTA Love
MARLAND (74644) Noble(98), Pawnee(2)
MARLOW (73055) Stephens(91), Grady(6), Comanche(3)
MARSHALL (73056) Logan(51), Garfield(40), Kingfisher(9)
MARTHA Jackson
MAUD (74854) Pottawatomie(53), Seminole(47)
MAY Harper
MAYFIELD McClain
MAYSVILLE (73057) Garvin(71), McClain(29)
MAZIE Mayes
MC LOUD (74851) Pottawatomie(76), Lincoln(14), Cleveland(10)
MCALESTER Pittsburg
MCCURTAIN (74944) Haskell(76), Le Flore(24)
MEAD Bryan
MEDFORD Grant
MEDICINE PARK Comanche
MEEKER (74855) Lincoln(88), Pottawatomie(12)
MEERS Comanche
MENO (73760) Major(99), Alfalfa(1)
MERIDIAN Logan
MIAMI Ottawa
MILBURN Johnston
MILFAY Creek
MILL CREEK (74856) Johnston(77), Murray(23)
MILLERTON McCurtain
MINCO (73059) Grady(67), Caddo(29), Canadian(5)
MOFFETT Sequoyah
MONROE Le Flore
MOODYS Cherokee
MOORELAND Woodward
MORRIS Okmulgee
MORRISON (73061) Noble(84), Pawnee(17)
MOUNDS (74047) Creek(41), Tulsa(40), Okmulgee(19)
MOUNTAIN PARK (73559) Kiowa(99), McClain(1)
MOUNTAIN VIEW (73062) Kiowa(99), Comanche(1)
MOYERS Pushmataha
MULDROW Sequoyah
MULHALL (73063) Logan(77), Payne(23)
MUSE Le Flore
MUSKOGEE Muskogee
MUSTANG Canadian
MUTUAL Woodward
NARDIN (74646) Kay(91), Grant(10)
NASH (73761) Grant(93), Garfield(7)
NASHOBA Pushmataha
NEWALLA (74857) Cleveland(69), Oklahoma(30), Pottawatomie(1)
NEWCASTLE McClain
NEWKIRK Kay
NICOMA PARK Oklahoma
NINNEKAH Grady
NOBLE Cleveland
NORMAN (73072) Cleveland(95), McClain(5)
NORMAN Cleveland
NORTH MIAMI Ottawa
NOWATA Nowata
OAKHURST Tulsa
OAKS (74359) Delaware(75), Cherokee(25)
OAKWOOD (73658) Dewey(90), Blaine(10)
OCHELATA Washington
OILTON Creek
OKARCHE (73762) Kingfisher(70), Canadian(30)
OKAY Wagoner
OKEENE (73763) Blaine(95), Major(5)
OKEMAH (74859) Okfuskee(94), Seminole(6)

OKLAHOMA CITY (73159) Oklahoma(94), Canadian(6)
OKLAHOMA CITY (73169) Oklahoma(88), Cleveland(12)
OKLAHOMA CITY (73173) Cleveland(98), Oklahoma(2)
OKLAHOMA CITY Cleveland
OKLAHOMA CITY Oklahoma
OKMULGEE Okmulgee
OKTAHA Muskogee
OLUSTEE Jackson
OMEGA (73764) Blaine(57), Kingfisher(43)
OOLOGAH Rogers
ORLANDO (73073) Noble(38), Logan(32), Payne(22), Garfield(8)
OSAGE Osage
OSCAR Jefferson
OVERBROOK Love
OWASSO (74055) Tulsa(74), Rogers(26)
PADEN Okfuskee
PANAMA Le Flore
PANOLA Latimer
PAOLI (73074) Garvin(80), McClain(20)
PARK HILL Cherokee
PAULS VALLEY Garvin
PAWHUSKA Osage
PAWNEE Pawnee
PEGGS (74452) Cherokee(73), Mayes(27)
PERKINS (74059) Payne(92), Lincoln(7)
PERNELL Garvin
PERRY Noble
PHAROAH Okfuskee
PICHER Ottawa
PICKENS McCurtain
PIEDMONT (73078) Canadian(99), Oklahoma(1)
PITTSBURG (74560) Pittsburg(90), Atoka(10)
PLATTER Bryan
POCASSET (73079) Grady(84), Caddo(15)
POCOLA Le Flore
PONCA CITY (74604) Kay(66), Osage(34)
PONCA CITY Kay
POND CREEK Grant
PORTER Wagoner
PORUM (74455) Muskogee(83), McIntosh(17)
POTEAU Le Flore
PRAGUE (74864) Lincoln(74), Pottawatomie(26)
PRESTON Okmulgee
PROCTOR Adair
PRUE Osage
PRYOR Mayes
PURCELL McClain
PUTNAM (73659) Dewey(96), Custer(2), McClain(2)
QUAPAW Ottawa
QUINTON (74561) Pittsburg(65), Haskell(35)
RALSTON (74650) Osage(60), Pawnee(40)
RAMONA Washington
RANDLETT Cotton
RATLIFF CITY Carter
RATTAN Pushmataha
RAVIA (73455) Johnston(83), Murray(17)
RED OAK Latimer
RED ROCK (74651) Noble(96), Pawnee(4)
REDBIRD Wagoner
RENTIESVILLE McIntosh
REYDON Roger Mills
RINGLING Jefferson
RINGOLD (74754) McCurtain(68), Pushmataha(30), Choctaw(2)
RINGWOOD Major
RIPLEY Payne
ROCKY (73661) Washita(98), Kiowa(2)
ROFF (74865) Pontotoc(66), Murray(26), Garvin(8)
ROLAND Sequoyah
ROOSEVELT (73564) Kiowa(96), Comanche(3)

ROSE (74364) Delaware(43), Cherokee(29), Mayes(28)
ROSSTON (73855) Harper(98), Roger Mills(2)
RUFE McCurtain
RUSH SPRINGS Grady
RYAN Jefferson
S COFFEYVILLE (74072) Nowata(95), Craig(5)
SAINT LOUIS (74866) Pottawatomie(75), Pontotoc(25)
SALINA (74365) Mayes(88), Delaware(12)
SALLISAW Sequoyah
SAND SPRINGS (74063) Tulsa(84), Osage(14), Creek(2)
SAPULPA (74066) Creek(98), Tulsa(2)
SAPULPA Creek
SASAKWA (74867) Seminole(94), Hughes(5)
SAVANNA Pittsburg
SAWYER Choctaw
SAYRE (73662) Beckham(97), Roger Mills(3)
SCHULTER Okmulgee
SEILING (73663) Dewey(89), Major(6), Woodward(5)
SEMINOLE Seminole
SENTINEL Washita
SHADY POINT Le Flore
SHAMROCK Creek
SHARON Woodward
SHATTUCK Ellis
SHAWNEE Pottawatomie
SHIDLER (74652) Osage(96), Kay(4)
SKIATOOK (74070) Osage(52), Tulsa(41), Washington(8)
SLICK Creek
SMITHVILLE (74957) McCurtain(55), Le Flore(45)
SNOW Pushmataha
SNYDER (73566) Kiowa(99), Tillman(1)
SOPER Choctaw
SOUTHARD (73770) Blaine(86), Roger Mills(14)

SPARKS Lincoln
SPAVINAW (74366) Mayes(85), Delaware(15)
SPENCER Oklahoma
SPENCERVILLE (74760) Choctaw(62), Pushmataha(39)
SPERRY (74073) Tulsa(72), Osage(28)
SPIRO Le Flore
SPRINGER (73458) Carter(99), Grady(1)
STERLING (73567) Comanche(89), McClain(11)
STIDHAM McIntosh
STIGLER (74462) Haskell(98), Pittsburg(2)
STILLWATER Payne
STILWELL Adair
STONEWALL (74871) Pontotoc(83), Coal(10), Johnston(8)
STRANG (74367) Mayes(99), Pontotoc(1)
STRATFORD (74872) Garvin(78), Pontotoc(19), McClain(3)
STRINGTOWN Atoka
STROUD (74079) Lincoln(94), Okfuskee(3), Creek(2)
STUART (74570) Hughes(51), Pittsburg(47), Coal(1)
SULPHUR Murray
SWEETWATER Roger Mills
SWINK Choctaw
TAFT Muskogee
TAHLEQUAH Cherokee
TALALA (74080) Rogers(70), Washington(30)
TALIHINA (74571) Latimer(54), Le Flore(41), Pushmataha(5)
TALOGA Dewey
TATUMS Carter
TECUMSEH Pottawatomie
TEMPLE Cotton
TERLTON (74081) Pawnee(88), Creek(13)
TERRAL Jefferson
TEXHOMA (73949) Cimarron(55), Texas(45)
TEXOLA Beckham
THACKERVILLE Love

THOMAS (73669) Custer(95), Blaine(3), Dewey(3)
TIPTON Tillman
TISHOMINGO Johnston
TONKAWA (74653) Kay(99), Noble(1)
TRYON Lincoln
TULLAHASSEE Wagoner
TULSA (74106) Tulsa(92), Osage(8)
TULSA (74108) Tulsa(88), Wagoner(12)
TULSA (74116) Tulsa(59), Rogers(41)
TULSA (74126) Tulsa(91), Osage(9)
TULSA (74127) Tulsa(65), Osage(35)
TULSA (74132) Tulsa(63), Creek(37)
TULSA Creek
TULSA Tulsa
TUPELO Coal
TURPIN (73950) Beaver(82), Texas(18)
TUSKAHOMA (74574) Pushmataha(51), Latimer(49)
TUSSY Carter
TUTTLE Grady
TWIN OAKS Delaware
TYRONE Texas
UNION CITY Canadian
VALLIANT (74764) McCurtain(89), Choctaw(11)
VELMA Stephens
VERA Washington
VERDEN (73092) Grady(72), Caddo(28)
VERNON McIntosh
VIAN Sequoyah
VICI (73859) Dewey(76), Woodward(21), Ellis(3)
VINITA (74301) Craig(91), Mayes(8)
VINSON Harmon
WAGONER Wagoner
WAINWRIGHT Muskogee
WAKITA Grant
WALTERS Cotton
WANETTE (74878) Pottawatomie(84), Cleveland(16)
WANN (74083) Nowata(76), Washington(24)
WAPANUCKA Johnston

WARDVILLE (74576) Atoka(51), Pittsburg(49)
WARNER (74469) Muskogee(95), McIntosh(5)
WASHINGTON McClain
WASHITA Caddo
WATONGA Blaine
WATSON McCurtain
WATTS (74964) Adair(87), Delaware(13)
WAUKOMIS Garfield
WAURIKA Jefferson
WAYNE McClain
WAYNOKA (73860) Woods(91), Major(10)
WEATHERFORD (73096) Custer(97), Washita(2)
WEBBERS FALLS Muskogee
WELCH Craig
WELEETKA (74880) Okfuskee(89), Okmulgee(11)
WELLING Cherokee
WELLSTON (74881) Lincoln(90), Logan(6), Beckham(3)
WELTY Okfuskee
WESTVILLE Adair
WETUMKA (74883) Hughes(95), Okfuskee(5)
WEWOKA Seminole
WHEATLAND Oklahoma
WHITEFIELD Haskell
WHITESBORO Le Flore
WILBURTON Latimer
WILLOW (73673) Greer(80), Beckham(20)
WILSON (73463) Carter(96), Love(4)
WISTER (74966) Le Flore(90), Latimer(11)
WOODWARD Woodward
WRIGHT CITY McCurtain
WYANDOTTE (74370) Ottawa(92), Delaware(8)
WYNNEWOOD Garvin
WYNONA Osage
YALE (74085) Payne(98), Pawnee(1)
YUKON Canadian

ZIP/City Cross Reference

ZIP	City		ZIP	City		ZIP	City		ZIP	City
73001-73001	ALBERT		73036-73036	EL RENO		73075-73075	PAULS VALLEY		73440-73440	LEBANON
73002-73002	ALEX		73038-73038	FORT COBB		73076-73076	PERNELL		73441-73441	LEON
73003-73003	EDMOND		73039-73039	FOSTER		73077-73077	PERRY		73442-73442	LOCO
73004-73004	AMBER		73040-73040	GEARY		73078-73078	PIEDMONT		73443-73443	LONE GROVE
73005-73005	ANADARKO		73041-73041	GOTEBO		73079-73079	POCASSET		73446-73446	MADILL
73006-73006	APACHE		73042-73042	GRACEMONT		73080-73080	PURCELL		73447-73447	MANNSVILLE
73007-73007	ARCADIA		73043-73043	GREENFIELD		73081-73081	RATLIFF CITY		73448-73448	MARIETTA
73008-73008	BETHANY		73044-73044	GUTHRIE		73082-73082	RUSH SPRINGS		73449-73449	MEAD
73009-73009	BINGER		73045-73045	HARRAH		73083-73083	EDMOND		73450-73450	MILBURN
73010-73010	BLANCHARD		73046-73046	HENNEPIN		73084-73084	SPENCER		73453-73453	OVERBROOK
73011-73011	BRADLEY		73047-73047	HINTON		73085-73085	YUKON		73455-73455	RAVIA
73012-73012	BRAY		73048-73048	HYDRO		73086-73086	SULPHUR		73456-73456	RINGLING
73013-73013	EDMOND		73049-73049	JONES		73087-73087	TATUMS		73458-73458	SPRINGER
73014-73014	CALUMET		73050-73050	LANGSTON		73088-73088	TUSSY		73459-73459	THACKERVILLE
73015-73015	CARNEGIE		73051-73051	LEXINGTON		73089-73089	TUTTLE		73460-73460	TISHOMINGO
73016-73016	CASHION		73052-73052	LINDSAY		73090-73090	UNION CITY		73461-73461	WAPANUCKA
73017-73017	CEMENT		73053-73053	LOOKEBA		73091-73091	VELMA		73463-73463	WILSON
73018-73018	CHICKASHA		73054-73054	LUTHER		73092-73092	VERDEN		73501-73502	LAWTON
73019-73019	NORMAN		73055-73055	MARLOW		73093-73093	WASHINGTON		73503-73503	FORT SILL
73020-73020	CHOCTAW		73056-73056	MARSHALL		73094-73094	WASHITA		73505-73507	LAWTON
73021-73021	COLONY		73057-73057	MAYSVILLE		73095-73095	WAYNE		73520-73520	ADDINGTON
73022-73022	CONCHO		73058-73058	MERIDIAN		73096-73096	WEATHERFORD		73521-73522	ALTUS
73023-73023	CHICKASHA		73059-73059	MINCO		73097-73097	WHEATLAND		73523-73523	ALTUS AFB
73024-73024	CORN		73061-73061	MORRISON		73098-73098	WYNNEWOOD		73526-73526	BLAIR
73025-73025	COUNTYLINE		73062-73062	MOUNTAIN VIEW		73099-73099	YUKON		73527-73527	CACHE
73027-73027	COYLE		73063-73063	MULHALL		73101-73199	OKLAHOMA CITY		73528-73528	CHATTANOOGA
73028-73028	CRESCENT		73064-73064	MUSTANG		73401-73403	ARDMORE		73529-73529	COMANCHE
73029-73029	CYRIL		73065-73065	NEWCASTLE		73430-73430	BURNEYVILLE		73530-73530	DAVIDSON
73030-73030	DAVIS		73066-73066	NICOMA PARK		73432-73432	COLEMAN		73531-73531	DEVOL
73031-73031	DIBBLE		73067-73067	NINNEKAH		73434-73435	FOX		73532-73532	DUKE
73032-73032	DOUGHERTY		73068-73068	NOBLE		73436-73436	GENE AUTRY		73533-73536	DUNCAN
73033-73033	EAKLY		73069-73072	NORMAN		73437-73437	GRAHAM		73537-73537	ELDORADO
73034-73034	EDMOND		73073-73073	ORLANDO		73438-73438	HEALDTON		73538-73538	ELGIN
73035-73035	ELMORE CITY		73074-73074	PAOLI		73439-73439	KINGSTON		73539-73539	ELMER

ZIP	City	ZIP	City	ZIP	City	ZIP	City
73540-73540	FAXON	73733-73733	DOUGLAS	74026-74026	DAVENPORT	74401-74403	MUSKOGEE
73541-73541	FLETCHER	73734-73734	DOVER	74027-74027	DELAWARE	74421-74421	BEGGS
73542-73542	FREDERICK	73735-73735	DRUMMOND	74028-74028	DEPEW	74422-74422	BOYNTON
73543-73543	GERONIMO	73736-73736	FAIRMONT	74029-74029	DEWEY	74423-74423	BRAGGS
73544-73544	GOULD	73737-73737	FAIRVIEW	74030-74030	DRUMRIGHT	74425-74425	CANADIAN
73546-73546	GRANDFIELD	73738-73738	GARBER	74031-74031	FOYIL	74426-74426	CHECOTAH
73547-73547	GRANITE	73739-73739	GOLTRY	74032-74032	GLENCOE	74427-74427	COOKSON
73548-73548	HASTINGS	73741-73741	HELENA	74033-74033	GLENPOOL	74428-74428	COUNCIL HILL
73549-73549	HEADRICK	73742-73742	HENNESSEY	74034-74034	HALLETT	74429-74429	COWETA
73550-73550	HOLLIS	73743-73743	HILLSDALE	74035-74035	HOMINY	74430-74430	CROWDER
73551-73551	HOLLISTER	73744-73744	HITCHCOCK	74036-74036	INOLA	74431-74431	DEWAR
73552-73552	INDIAHOMA	73746-73746	HOPETON	74037-74037	JENKS	74432-74432	EUFAULA
73553-73553	LOVELAND	73747-73747	ISABELLA	74038-74038	JENNINGS	74434-74434	FORT GIBSON
73554-73554	MANGUM	73749-73749	JET	74039-74039	KELLYVILLE	74435-74435	GORE
73555-73555	MANITOU	73750-73750	KINGFISHER	74041-74041	KIEFER	74436-74436	HASKELL
73556-73556	MARTHA	73753-73753	KREMLIN	74042-74042	LENAPAH	74437-74437	HENRYETTA
73557-73557	MEDICINE PARK	73754-73754	LAHOMA	74043-74043	LEONARD	74438-74438	HITCHITA
73558-73558	MEERS	73755-73755	LONGDALE	74044-74044	MANNFORD	74440-74440	HOYT
73559-73559	MOUNTAIN PARK	73756-73756	LOYAL	74045-74045	MARAMEC	74441-74441	HULBERT
73560-73560	OLUSTEE	73757-73757	LUCIEN	74046-74046	MILFAY	74442-74442	INDIANOLA
73561-73561	OSCAR	73758-73758	MANCHESTER	74047-74047	MOUNDS	74444-74444	MOODYS
73562-73562	RANDLETT	73759-73759	MEDFORD	74048-74048	NOWATA	74445-74445	MORRIS
73564-73564	ROOSEVELT	73760-73760	MENO	74050-74050	OAKHURST	74446-74446	OKAY
73565-73565	RYAN	73761-73761	NASH	74051-74051	OCHELATA	74447-74447	OKMULGEE
73566-73566	SNYDER	73762-73762	OKARCHE	74052-74052	OILTON	74450-74450	OKTAHA
73567-73567	STERLING	73763-73763	OKEENE	74053-74053	OOLOGAH	74451-74451	PARK HILL
73568-73568	TEMPLE	73764-73764	OMEGA	74054-74054	OSAGE	74452-74452	PEGGS
73569-73569	TERRAL	73766-73766	POND CREEK	74055-74055	OWASSO	74454-74454	PORTER
73570-73570	TIPTON	73768-73768	RINGWOOD	74056-74056	PAWHUSKA	74455-74455	PORUM
73571-73571	VINSON	73770-73770	SOUTHARD	74058-74058	PAWNEE	74456-74456	PRESTON
73572-73572	WALTERS	73771-73771	WAKITA	74059-74059	PERKINS	74457-74457	PROCTOR
73573-73573	WAURIKA	73772-73772	WATONGA	74060-74060	PRUE	74458-74458	REDBIRD
73575-73575	DUNCAN	73773-73773	WAUKOMIS	74061-74061	RAMONA	74459-74459	RENTIESVILLE
73601-73601	CLINTON	73801-73802	WOODWARD	74062-74062	RIPLEY	74460-74460	SCHULTER
73620-73620	ARAPAHO	73832-73832	ARNETT	74063-74063	SAND SPRINGS	74461-74461	STIDHAM
73622-73622	BESSIE	73834-73834	BUFFALO	74066-74067	SAPULPA	74462-74462	STIGLER
73624-73624	BURNS FLAT	73835-73835	CAMARGO	74068-74068	SHAMROCK	74463-74463	TAFT
73625-73625	BUTLER	73838-73838	CHESTER	74070-74070	SKIATOOK	74464-74465	TAHLEQUAH
73626-73626	CANUTE	73840-73840	FARGO	74071-74071	SLICK	74466-74466	TULLAHASSEE
73627-73627	CARTER	73841-73841	FORT SUPPLY	74072-74072	S COFFEYVILLE	74467-74467	WAGONER
73628-73628	CHEYENNE	73842-73842	FREEDOM	74073-74073	SPERRY	74468-74468	WAINWRIGHT
73632-73632	CORDELL	73843-73843	GAGE	74074-74078	STILLWATER	74469-74469	WARNER
73638-73638	CRAWFORD	73844-73844	GATE	74079-74079	STROUD	74470-74470	WEBBERS FALLS
73639-73639	CUSTER CITY	73847-73847	KNOWLES	74080-74080	TALALA	74471-74471	WELLING
73641-73641	DILL CITY	73848-73848	LAVERNE	74081-74081	TERLTON	74472-74472	WHITEFIELD
73642-73642	DURHAM	73851-73851	MAY	74082-74082	VERA	74477-74477	WAGONER
73644-73644	ELK CITY	73852-73852	MOORELAND	74083-74083	WANN	74501-74502	MCALESTER
73645-73645	ERICK	73853-73853	MUTUAL	74084-74084	WYNONA	74521-74521	ALBION
73646-73646	FAY	73855-73855	ROSSTON	74085-74085	YALE	74522-74522	ALDERSON
73647-73647	FOSS	73857-73857	SHARON	74101-74194	TULSA	74523-74523	ANTLERS
73648-73648	ELK CITY	73858-73858	SHATTUCK	74301-74301	VINITA	74525-74525	ATOKA
73650-73650	HAMMON	73859-73859	VICI	74330-74330	ADAIR	74528-74528	BLANCO
73651-73651	HOBART	73860-73860	WAYNOKA	74331-74331	AFTON	74529-74529	BLOCKER
73654-73654	LEEDEY	73901-73901	ADAMS	74332-74332	BIG CABIN	74530-74530	BROMIDE
73655-73655	LONE WOLF	73931-73931	BALKO	74333-74333	BLUEJACKET	74531-74531	CALVIN
73656-73656	MAYFIELD	73932-73932	BEAVER	74335-74335	CARDIN	74533-74533	CANEY
73658-73658	OAKWOOD	73933-73933	BOISE CITY	74337-74337	CHOUTEAU	74534-74534	CENTRAHOMA
73659-73659	PUTNAM	73937-73937	FELT	74338-74338	COLCORD	74535-74535	CLARITA
73660-73660	REYDON	73938-73938	FORGAN	74339-74339	COMMERCE	74536-74536	CLAYTON
73661-73661	ROCKY	73939-73939	GOODWELL	74340-74340	DISNEY	74538-74538	COALGATE
73662-73662	SAYRE	73942-73942	GUYMON	74342-74342	EUCHA	74540-74540	DAISY
73663-73663	SEILING	73944-73944	HARDESTY	74343-74343	FAIRLAND	74542-74542	ATOKA
73664-73664	SENTINEL	73945-73945	HOOKER	74344-74345	GROVE	74543-74543	FINLEY
73666-73666	SWEETWATER	73946-73946	KENTON	74346-74346	JAY	74545-74545	GOWEN
73667-73667	TALOGA	73947-73947	KEYES	74347-74347	KANSAS	74546-74546	HAILEYVILLE
73668-73668	TEXOLA	73949-73949	TEXHOMA	74349-74349	KETCHUM	74547-74547	HARTSHORNE
73669-73669	THOMAS	73950-73950	TURPIN	74350-74350	LANGLEY	74549-74549	HONOBIA
73673-73673	WILLOW	73951-73951	TYRONE	74352-74352	LOCUST GROVE	74552-74552	KINTA
73701-73706	ENID	74001-74001	AVANT	74353-74353	MAZIE	74553-74553	KIOWA
73716-73716	ALINE	74002-74002	BARNSDALL	74354-74355	MIAMI	74554-74554	KREBS
73717-73717	ALVA	74003-74006	BARTLESVILLE	74358-74358	NORTH MIAMI	74555-74555	LANE
73718-73718	AMES	74008-74008	BIXBY	74359-74359	OAKS	74556-74556	LEHIGH
73719-73719	AMORITA	74009-74009	BOWRING	74360-74360	PICHER	74557-74557	MOYERS
73720-73720	BISON	74010-74010	BRISTOW	74361-74362	PRYOR	74558-74558	NASHOBA
73722-73722	BURLINGTON	74011-74014	BROKEN ARROW	74363-74363	QUAPAW	74559-74559	PANOLA
73724-73724	CANTON	74015-74015	CATOOSA	74364-74364	ROSE	74560-74560	PITTSBURG
73726-73726	CARMEN	74016-74016	CHELSEA	74365-74365	SALINA	74561-74561	QUINTON
73727-73727	CARRIER	74017-74018	CLAREMORE	74366-74366	SPAVINAW	74562-74562	RATTAN
73728-73728	CHEROKEE	74020-74020	CLEVELAND	74367-74367	STRANG	74563-74563	RED OAK
73729-73729	CLEO SPRINGS	74021-74021	COLLINSVILLE	74368-74368	TWIN OAKS	74565-74565	SAVANNA
73730-73730	COVINGTON	74022-74022	COPAN	74369-74369	WELCH	74567-74567	SNOW
73731-73731	DACOMA	74023-74023	CUSHING	74370-74370	WYANDOTTE	74569-74569	STRINGTOWN

74570-74570	STUART	74731-74731	CARTWRIGHT	74833-74833	CASTLE	74884-74884	WEWOKA
74571-74571	TALIHINA	74733-74733	COLBERT	74834-74834	CHANDLER	74901-74901	ARKOMA
74572-74572	TUPELO	74734-74734	EAGLETOWN	74836-74836	CONNERVILLE	74902-74902	POCOLA
74574-74574	TUSKAHOMA	74735-74735	FORT TOWSON	74837-74837	CROMWELL	74930-74930	BOKOSHE
74576-74576	WARDVILLE	74736-74736	GARVIN	74839-74839	DUSTIN	74931-74931	BUNCH
74577-74577	WHITESBORO	74737-74737	GOLDEN	74840-74840	EARLSBORO	74932-74932	CAMERON
74578-74578	WILBURTON	74738-74738	GRANT	74842-74842	FITTSTOWN	74935-74935	FANSHAWE
74601-74604	PONCA CITY	74740-74740	HAWORTH	74843-74843	FITZHUGH	74936-74936	GANS
74630-74630	BILLINGS	74741-74741	HENDRIX	74844-74844	FRANCIS	74937-74937	HEAVENER
74631-74631	BLACKWELL	74743-74743	HUGO	74845-74845	HANNA	74939-74939	HODGEN
74632-74632	BRAMAN	74745-74745	IDABEL	74848-74848	HOLDENVILLE	74940-74940	HOWE
74633-74633	BURBANK	74747-74747	KEMP	74849-74849	KONAWA	74941-74941	KEOTA
74636-74636	DEER CREEK	74748-74748	KENEFIC	74850-74850	LAMAR	74942-74942	LEFLORE
74637-74637	FAIRFAX	74750-74750	MILLERTON	74851-74851	MC LOUD	74943-74943	LEQUIRE
74640-74640	HUNTER	74752-74752	PICKENS	74852-74852	MACOMB	74944-74944	MCCURTAIN
74641-74641	KAW CITY	74753-74753	PLATTER	74854-74854	MAUD	74945-74945	MARBLE CITY
74643-74643	LAMONT	74754-74754	RINGOLD	74855-74855	MEEKER	74946-74946	MOFFETT
74644-74644	MARLAND	74755-74755	RUFE	74856-74856	MILL CREEK	74947-74947	MONROE
74646-74646	NARDIN	74756-74756	SAWYER	74857-74857	NEWALLA	74948-74948	MULDROW
74647-74647	NEWKIRK	74759-74759	SOPER	74859-74859	OKEMAH	74949-74949	MUSE
74650-74650	RALSTON	74760-74760	SPENCERVILLE	74860-74860	PADEN	74951-74951	PANAMA
74651-74651	RED ROCK	74761-74761	SWINK	74864-74864	PRAGUE	74953-74953	POTEAU
74652-74652	SHIDLER	74764-74764	VALLIANT	74865-74865	ROFF	74954-74954	ROLAND
74653-74653	TONKAWA	74766-74766	WRIGHT CITY	74866-74866	SAINT LOUIS	74955-74955	SALLISAW
74701-74702	DURANT	74801-74802	SHAWNEE	74867-74867	SASAKWA	74956-74956	SHADY POINT
74720-74720	ACHILLE	74818-74818	SEMINOLE	74868-74868	SEMINOLE	74957-74957	SMITHVILLE
74721-74721	ALBANY	74820-74821	ADA	74869-74869	SPARKS	74959-74959	SPIRO
74722-74722	BATTIEST	74824-74824	AGRA	74871-74871	STONEWALL	74960-74960	STILWELL
74723-74723	BENNINGTON	74825-74825	ALLEN	74872-74872	STRATFORD	74962-74962	VIAN
74724-74724	BETHEL	74826-74826	ASHER	74873-74873	TECUMSEH	74963-74963	WATSON
74726-74726	BOKCHITO	74827-74827	ATWOOD	74875-74875	TRYON	74964-74964	WATTS
74727-74727	BOSWELL	74829-74829	BOLEY	74878-74878	WANETTE	74965-74965	WESTVILLE
74728-74728	BROKEN BOW	74830-74830	BOWLEGS	74880-74880	WELEETKA	74966-74966	WISTER
74729-74729	CADDO	74831-74831	BYARS	74881-74881	WELLSTON		
74730-74730	CALERA	74832-74832	CARNEY	74883-74883	WETUMKA		

General Help Numbers:

Governor's Office
State Capitol Bldg.   503-378-4582
Salem, OR 97310   Fax 503-378-4863
www.governor.state.or.us   8AM-5PM

Attorney General's Office
Department of Justice   503-378-4400
1162 Court St NE   Fax 503-378-4017
Salem, OR 97310   8AM-5PM
www.doj.state.or.us

State Court Administrator
Supreme Court Bldg, 1163 State St   503-986-5500
Salem, OR 97310   Fax 503-986-5503
www.ojd.state.or.us/osca   8AM-5PM

State Archives
Archives Division   503-373-0701
800 Summer St NE   Fax 503-373-0953
Salem, OR 97301   8AM-4:45PM
http://arcweb.sos.state.or.us

State Specifics:

Capital: Salem
Marion County

Time Zone: PST

Number of Counties: 36

Population: 3,316,154

Web Site: www.state.or.us

State Agencies

Criminal Records

Oregon State Police, Unit 11, Identification Services Section, PO Box 4395, Portland, OR 97208-4395 (Courier: 3772 Portland Rd NE, Bldg C, Salem, OR 97303); 503-378-3070, 503-378-2121 (Fax), 8AM-5PM.

www.osp.state.or.us

Indexing & Storage: Records are available from 1941 on and are computerized. Records are indexed on inhouse computer.

Searching: Information will include all convictions and all arrests within the past year without disposition. Include the following in your request-name, date of birth. Submitting the SSN is helpful, but not required. If record exists, person of record will be notified of the request and the record will not be released for 14 additional days.

Access by: mail, fax, online.

Fee & Payment: Fee is $15.00 per individual name. If someone is submitting a search on oneself, the fee is $12.00 and fingerprints are required. $5.00 fee to notarize. Fee payee: Oregon State Police. Prepayment required. Personal checks accepted. No credit cards accepted.

Mail search: Clean records are returned in 7-10 days, records with activity take 3 weeks to return. A self addressed stamped envelope is requested.

Fax search: Requesters must be pre-approved.

Online search: A web based site is available for requesting and receiving criminal records. Use of this site is ONLY for high vol. requesters who must be pre-approved. Results are posted as "No Record" or "In Process" which means a record will be mailed in 14 days. Use the "open records" link to get into the proper site. Call 503-373-1808, ext 230-receive the application, or visit the web site.

Corporation Records
Limited Partnership Records
Trademarks/Servicemarks
Fictitious Name
Assumed Name
Limited Liability Company
Records

Corporation Division, Public Service Building, 255 Capital St NE, #151, Salem, OR 97310-1327; 503-986-2200, 503-378-4381 (Fax), 8AM-5PM.

Indexing & Storage: Records are available on the computer screen for 10 years after inactive. Assumed names are only available for 5 years after inactive. The records prior to 20 years ago are stored in the State Archives back to the 1800's for corporations only. New records are available for inquiry immediately. Records are indexed on microfilm, inhouse computer.

Searching: All information is public record. Include the following in your request-full name of business. In addition to the articles of incorporation, corporation records include the following information: Annual Reports, Prior (merged) names, Articles of Amendment.

Access by: mail, phone, fax, in person, online.

Fee & Payment: There is no search fee. Copies cost $5.00 per business name or $15.00 if certified, otherwise there is a $1.00 fee per business name for a computer printout. A Good Standing certificate is $10.00. Fee payee: Corporation Division. Prepayment required. Personal checks accepted. Credit cards accepted: Mastercard, Visa.

Mail search: Turnaround time: 7-10 days. A self addressed stamped envelope is requested.

Phone search: There is a limit of 3 searches per phone call.

Fax search: Requesters must use a credit card, turnaround time is 5 days or less.

In person search: Turnaround time while you wait.

Online search: A commercial dial-up system is available. Call 503-229-5133 for details. Also, the complete database can be purchased with monthly updates via e-mail, call 503-986-2343.

Other access: A subscription service for new business lists and tapes of the database are available for $15.00 per month or $150.00 for an annual subscription. Call 503-986-2343 for more information.

Expedited service: Expedited service is available for phone and in person searches. Turnaround time: 1 day. They will ship overnight if you supply your shipper's account number. Fax requests are expedited only if phoned in first.

Uniform Commercial Code
Federal Tax Liens
State Tax Liens

UCC Division, Secretary of State, 255 Capitol St NE, Suite 151, Salem, OR 97310-1327; 503-986-2200, 503-373-1166 (Fax), 8AM-5PM.

www.sos.state.or.us/corporation/ucc/ucc.htm

Note: State tax liens on personal property are filed here; state tax liens on real property are filed at the county level.

Indexing & Storage: Records are available from the 1960's on computer and microfiche.

Searching: Use search request form UCC-11. The search includes tax liens filed here. Include the following in your request-debtor name.

Access by: mail, fax, in person, online.

Fee & Payment: The search fee is $10.00 per name. The copy fee is $5.00 per copy per name. The $5.00 copy fee is charged, whether or not copies are found. Microfilm service is $20.00 per reel. Special research projects are $20.00 per hour. Fee payee: Secretary of State. Prepayment required. Personal checks accepted. Credit cards accepted: Mastercard, Visa.

Mail search: Turnaround time: 1-4 days.

Fax search: A credit card is required. Results are mailed.

In person search: Searching is available in person.

Online search: UCC index information can be obtained for free from the web site. You can search by debtor name or by lien number. You can also download forms from here.

Other access: Monthly UCC information can be on diskette or e-mail. Prices start at $15.00 per month or $150.00 annually. For more information, call Program Services at 503-986-2343.

Sales Tax Registrations
State does not impose sales tax.

Birth Certificates

Oregon State Health Division, Vital Records, PO Box 14050, Portland, OR 97293-0050 (Courier: 800 NE Oregon St, #205, Portland, OR 97232); 503-731-4095 (Recorded Message), 503-731-4108, 503-234-8417 (Fax), 8AM-4:30PM.

www.ohd.hr.state.or.us/chs/welcome.htm

Indexing & Storage: Records are available from July 1903-present. There are some delayed filed records with DOBs from 1885-1902. There are no indexes available. Birth indexes prior to 1902 available at the State Archives. It takes 2-4 weeks before new records are available for inquiry.

Searching: Investigative searches must have a signed, notarized release form from person of record or immediate family member, unless record over 100 years old. Records only available to legal guardians & legal representatives with proof of such Include the following in your request-full name, names of parents, mother's maiden name, date of birth, place of birth, relationship to person of record. Must request "long form" if time of birth, hospital or physician's names is needed. The following data is not released: original records of adoption.

Access by: mail, phone, fax, in person.

Fee & Payment: The search fee is $15.00. Add $12 for each additional copy. Fee payee: Oregon Health Division. Prepayment required. Personal checks accepted. Credit cards accepted: Mastercard, Visa, AmEx, Discover.

Mail search: Turnaround time: 2-3 weeks. Express mail requests are handled immediately.No self addressed stamped envelope is required.

Phone search: Fax and phone orders are billed to credit cards and processed the next day. There is an additional $10.00 service fee.

Fax search: Same criteria as phone searching.

In person search: Turnaround time is under 20 minutes.

Expedited service: Expedited service is available for fax and phone searches. Turnaround time: overnight delivery. Orders are charged to credit cards. Fee depends on delivery service.

Death Records

Oregon State Health Division, Vital Records, PO Box 14050, Portland, OR 97293-0050 (Courier: 800 NE Oregon St, #205, Portland, OR 97232); 503-731-4095 (Recorded Message), 503-731-4108, 503-234-8417 (Fax), 8AM-4:30PM.

www.ohd.hr.state.or.us/chs/welcome.htm

Indexing & Storage: Records are available from July 1903-present. It takes 2 ro 4 weeks before new records are available for inquiry.

Searching: Investigative searches must have a signed, notarized release from immediate family member or legal representative or person with a personal property right. After 50 years, a record becomes public record and there are no restrictions. Include the following in your request-full name, date of death, place of death, relationship to person of record, reason for information request. The name of the spouse is helpful. The date of birth is helpful for common names.

Access by: mail, phone, fax, in person.

Fee & Payment: The search fee is $15.00 and additional copies are $12.00 each. Fee payee: Oregon Health Division. Prepayment required. Personal checks accepted. Credit cards accepted: Mastercard, Visa, AmEx, Discover.

Mail search: Turnaround time: 2-3 weeks. Express mail requests are processed immediately.No self addressed stamped envelope is required.

Phone search: Phone and fax orders require use of a credit card and an additional $10.00 service fee. Turnaround time is generally in 24 hours.

Fax search: Same criteria as phone searching.

In person search: Turnaround time is within 20 minutes.

Other access: Indexes are available at many state libraries.

Expedited service: Expedited service is available for fax and phone searches. Turnaround time: overnight delivery. Carrier chosen to return documents determines fees. Use of credit card is required.

Marriage Certificates

Oregon State Health Division, Vital Records, PO Box 14050, Portland, OR 97293-0050 (Courier: 800 NE Oregon St, #205, Portland, OR 97232); 503-731-4095 (Recorded Message), 503-731-4108, 503-234-8417 (Fax), 8AM-4:30PM.

www.ohd.hr.state.or.us/chs/welcome.htm

Indexing & Storage: Records are available from 1906-1925 and 1946-1960 on microfilm, from 1961-1996 on microfiche. It takes 4-8 weeks before new records are available for inquiry.

Searching: Records less than 50 years old are only available to family members, legal representatives or those with a personal or property right. Include the following in your request-names of husband and wife, date of marriage, place or county of marriage. Include daytime phone number and as many identifiers as possible.

Access by: mail, phone, fax, in person.

Fee & Payment: The search fee is $15.00, additional copies $12.00 per record. Fee payee: Oregon Health Division. Prepayment required. Personal checks accepted. Credit cards accepted: Mastercard, Visa, AmEx, Discover.

Mail search: Turnaround time: 2-3 weeks. If request is expressed, it will be answered asap.No self addressed stamped envelope is required.

Phone search: There is an additional $10.00 quick service search fee per telephone or fax order. Use of a credit card is required.

Fax search: Results are sent by mail. Turnaround time is next working day.

In person search: Turnaround time is usually within 20 minutes.

Other access: Many state libraries offer record indexes.

Expedited service: Expedited service is available for mail, phone and fax searches. Turnaround time: overnight delivery. Additional fees will be added, depending on carrier. For mail requests, enclose a prepaid, self-addressed envelope for overnight carrier.

Divorce Records

Oregon State Health Division, Vital Records, Suite 205, PO Box 14050, Portland, OR 97293-0050 (Courier: 800 NE Oregon St, #205, Portland, OR 97232); 503-731-4095 (Recorded Message), 502-731-4108, 503-234-8417 (Fax), 8AM-4:30PM.

www.ohd.hr.state.or.us/chs/welcome.htm

Indexing & Storage: Records are available from 1961-1996 on microfiche and 1906-1924 and 1945-1960 on microfilm. Only certificates of divorce are issued; copies of decrees must be obtained at the county level. It takes 4-8 weeks before new records are available for inquiry.

Searching: Records less than 50 years old are only available to family members, legal representatives and those with a personal or property right. Include the following in your request-date of divorce. Also include names of husband and wife, and reason for request.

Access by: mail, phone, fax, in person.

Fee & Payment: The search fee is $15.00, additional copies are $12.00 each. Fee payee: Oregon Health Division. Prepayment required. Using personal checks (with guarantee card) may delay processing by 2 weeks. For a mail request, enclose a prepaid, self-addressed envelope for overnight carrier. Personal checks accepted. Credit cards accepted: Mastercard, Visa, AmEx, Discover.

Mail search: Turnaround time: 2-3 weeks. Send request by overnight delivery and it will be processed asap.No self addressed stamped envelope is required.

Phone search: There is an additional $10.00 service fee for ordering by fax or phone and you must use a credit card.

Fax search: Results are sent by mail. Turnaround time next working day.

In person search: Turnaround time is usually within 20 minutes.

Other access: Indexes are available in many state libraries.

Expedited service: Expedited service is available for fax and phone searches. Turnaround time: overnight delivery.

Workers' Compensation Records

Department of Consumer & Business Srvs, Workers Compensation Division, 350 Winter Street NE, Salem, OR 97301-3879; 503-947-7818, 503-947-7993 (TTY), 503-945-7630 (Fax), 8AM-5PM M-F.

www.cbs.state.or.us/wcd

Indexing & Storage: Records are available from June 1980 on. Records from 1966-June 1980 are in the State Archives. New records are available for inquiry immediately. Records are indexed on inhouse computer.

Searching: Per ORS 192.502(18), claims records are exempt from public disclosure. Access to records is at the discretion of the Director. In general, those with a legitimate business purpose are granted access. Include the following in your request-claimant name, Social Security Number, claim number. The web site features rules, bulletins, forms, and publications.

Access by: mail, fax, in person.

Fee & Payment: The Department has the authority to charge for staff time and resources for any record request. Records releases only after disclosure requirements are met. Fee payee: DCBS. Prepayment required. Personal checks accepted. No credit cards accepted.

Mail search: Turnaround time: 1-5 days. No self addressed stamped envelope is required.

Fax search: Fax requests are accepted if disclosure requirements are met. Completed report may be mailed back.

In person search: Completed report may need to be mailed back. Turnaround time: 1-5 days.

Driver Records

Driver and Motor Vehicle Services, Record Services, 1905 Lana Ave, NE, Salem, OR 97314; 503-945-5000, 8AM-5PM.

www.odot.state.or.us/dmv

Indexing & Storage: Records are available for 3 or 5 years; major conviction 10 years for moving violations; 3 or 10 years for DUIs; 3 or 5 years after reinstatement for suspensions. Note: Both 3 year and 5 year records are offered. It takes 2-3 weeks normally before new records are available for inquiry.

Searching: Oregon differentiates between "employment" and "non-employment" records. Include the following in your request-full name, date of birth, driver's license number. A driver's license report is available which lists the driver's name, address, date of birth, license number, issue and expiration dates, original business date, restrictions, status, and, if applicable, the ID card expiration date. The following data is not released: medical information.

Access by: mail, phone, fax.

Fee & Payment: Fees: $1.50 for a 3 year non-employment driving record; $2.00 for a 3 year employment driving record; $3.00 for 5 year combination of both records; $1.50 per record for a driver license information report. There is a charge of $1.50 for no record found. Fee payee:

DMV Services. Prepayment required. Personal checks accepted. No credit cards accepted.

Mail search: Turnaround time: 1 day from receipt. No self addressed stamped envelope is required.

Phone search: Oregon offers "DAVE" (DMV's Interactive Voice Response System) which reads information from computer files in a human sounding voice. A variety of records are available on DAVE 24 hours a day. Call 503-945-7950 for more information.

Fax search: Searching is available by fax.

Other access: Magnetic tape ordering is available for high volume batch requesters. The agency will sell its DL file to commercial vendors and has an automated "flag program" for customers with re-occurring name lists. Call 503-945-7950 for more information.

Vehicle Ownership Vehicle Identification

Driver and Motor Vehicle Services, Record Services Unit, 1905 Lana Ave, NE, Salem, OR 97314; 503-945-5000, 503-945-5425 (Fax), 8AM-5PM.

www.odot.state.or.us/dmv

Indexing & Storage: Records are available from 1963-present. Early records are on microfilm. It takes 2-3 weeks from issue before new records are available for inquiry.

Searching: Title and registration ownership records are open to the public, for a fee. By law, only certain entities may receive full records. Casual requesters cannot obtain records with personal information including address, telephone, license number, etc. DOB is helpful. The following data is not released: medical information.

Access by: mail, phone.

Fee & Payment: Vehicle record prints are $4.00, information given orally is $2.50 (to account holders). A complete vehicle title history is $22.50. An insurance information search is $10.00. Generally, $2.50 is charged if no record is found. Fee payee: Driver & Motor Services (DMV). Prepayment required. Personal checks accepted. No credit cards accepted.

Mail search: Turnaround time: 1 day. A self addressed stamped envelope is requested.

Phone search: The automated system called "DAVE" is open 24 hours a day. An account is necessary. Call 503-945-7950 for more information.

Other access: Oregon offers an extensive program to obtain bulk ownership and vehicle information on magnetic tape or paper. Many customized selections are available. Call 503-945-7950 for more information.

Accident Reports

Motor Vehicle Division, Accident Reports & Information, 1905 Lana Ave, NE, Salem, OR 97314; 503-945-5098, 503-945-5267 (Fax), 8AM-5PM.

Indexing & Storage: Records are available for 5 years to present. It takes 2-4 weeks before new records are available for inquiry.

Searching: The report is provided without personal information unless the requester qualifies for personal information under OR law. Qualified

You will usually be able to find the city name in the City/County Cross Reference below. In that case, it is a simple matter to determine the county from the cross reference. However, only the official US Postal Service city names are included in this index. There are an additional 40,000 place names that people use in their addresses. Therefore, we have also included a ZIP/City Cross Reference immediately following the City/County Cross Reference.

If you know the ZIP Code but the city name does not appear in the City/County Cross Reference index, look up the ZIP Code in the ZIP/City Cross Reference, find the city name, then look up the city name in the City/County Cross Reference. For example, you want to know the county for an address of Menands, NY 12204. There is no "Menands" in the City/County Cross Reference. The ZIP/City Cross Reference shows that ZIP Codes 12201-12288 are for the city of Albany. Looking back in the City/County Cross Reference, Albany is in Albany County.

City/County Cross Reference

ADAMS Umatilla
ADEL Lake
ADRIAN Malheur
AGNESS Curry
ALBANY (97321) Linn(87), Benton(13)
ALLEGANY Coos
ALSEA (97324) Benton(92), Lincoln(9)
ALVADORE Lane
AMITY (97101) Yamhill(83), Polk(17)
ANTELOPE Wasco
ARCH CAPE Clatsop
ARLINGTON Gilliam
AROCK Malheur
ASHLAND Jackson
ASHWOOD Jefferson
ASTORIA Clatsop
ATHENA Umatilla
AUMSVILLE Marion
AURORA (97002) Marion(84), Clackamas(16)
AZALEA Douglas
BAKER CITY Baker
BANDON Coos
BANKS Washington
BATES Grant
BAY CITY Tillamook
BEATTY (97621) Klamath(89), Lake(11)
BEAVER Tillamook
BEAVERCREEK Clackamas
BEAVERTON Washington
BEND Deschutes
BLACHLY Lane
BLODGETT (97326) Lincoln(59), Benton(41)
BLUE RIVER Lane
BLY (97622) Klamath(83), Lake(17)
BOARDMAN Morrow
BONANZA Klamath
BORING Clackamas
BRIDAL VEIL Multnomah
BRIDGEPORT Baker
BRIGHTWOOD Clackamas
BROADBENT Coos
BROGAN Malheur
BROOKINGS Curry
BROTHERS Deschutes
BROWNSVILLE Linn
BURNS Harney
BUTTE FALLS Jackson
BUXTON Washington
CAMAS VALLEY Douglas
CAMP SHERMAN Jefferson
CANBY Clackamas
CANNON BEACH Clatsop
CANYON CITY Grant
CANYONVILLE Douglas
CARLTON Yamhill
CASCADE LOCKS (97014) Hood River(80), Multnomah(20)
CASCADIA Linn
CAVE JUNCTION Josephine
CAYUSE Umatilla

CENTRAL POINT Jackson
CHEMULT Klamath
CHESHIRE Lane
CHILOQUIN Klamath
CHRISTMAS VALLEY Lake
CLACKAMAS Clackamas
CLATSKANIE (97016) Columbia(92), Clatsop(8)
CLOVERDALE Tillamook
COLTON Clackamas
COLUMBIA CITY Columbia
CONDON Gilliam
COOS BAY Coos
COQUILLE Coos
CORBETT Multnomah
CORNELIUS Washington
CORVALLIS (97333) Benton(92), Linn(8)
CORVALLIS Benton
COTTAGE GROVE Lane
COVE Union
CRABTREE Linn
CRANE Harney
CRATER LAKE Klamath
CRAWFORDSVILLE Linn
CRESCENT Klamath
CRESCENT LAKE Klamath
CRESWELL Lane
CULP CREEK Lane
CULVER Jefferson
CURTIN Douglas
DAIRY Klamath
DALLAS Polk
DAYS CREEK Douglas
DAYTON Yamhill
DAYVILLE Grant
DEADWOOD Lane
DEER ISLAND Columbia
DEPOE BAY Lincoln
DETROIT Marion
DEXTER Lane
DIAMOND Harney
DILLARD Douglas
DONALD Marion
DORENA Lane
DRAIN Douglas
DREWSEY Harney
DUFUR Wasco
DUNDEE Yamhill
DURKEE Baker
EAGLE CREEK Clackamas
EAGLE POINT Jackson
ECHO Umatilla
EDDYVILLE Lincoln
ELGIN Union
ELKTON Douglas
ELMIRA Lane
ENTERPRISE Wallowa
ESTACADA Clackamas
EUGENE Lane
FAIRVIEW Multnomah
FALL CREEK Lane
FALLS CITY Polk

FIELDS Harney
FLORENCE Lane
FOREST GROVE Washington
FORT KLAMATH (97626) Klamath(75), Lake(25)
FORT ROCK Lake
FOSSIL Wheeler
FOSTER Linn
FOX Grant
FRENCHGLEN Harney
GALES CREEK Washington
GARDINER Douglas
GARIBALDI Tillamook
GASTON (97119) Washington(76), Yamhill(24)
GATES (97346) Marion(68), Linn(32)
GERVAIS Marion
GILCHRIST Klamath
GLADSTONE Clackamas
GLENDALE Douglas
GLENEDEN BEACH Lincoln
GLIDE Douglas
GOLD BEACH Curry
GOLD HILL Jackson
GOVERNMENT CAMP Clackamas
GRAND RONDE (97347) Polk(64), Yamhill(34), Tillamook(2)
GRANTS PASS Josephine
GRASS VALLEY (97029) Wasco(67), Sherman(33)
GREENLEAF Lane
GRESHAM (97080) Multnomah(95), Clackamas(5)
GRESHAM Multnomah
HAINES Baker
HALFWAY Baker
HALSEY Linn
HAMMOND Clatsop
HARPER Malheur
HARRISBURG (97446) Linn(99), Lane(1)
HEBO Tillamook
HELIX Umatilla
HEPPNER Morrow
HEREFORD Baker
HERMISTON Umatilla
HILLSBORO (97123) Washington(96), Yamhill(4)
HILLSBORO (97124) Washington(94), Multnomah(6)
HINES Harney
HOOD RIVER Hood River
HUBBARD (97032) Marion(88), Clackamas(12)
HUNTINGTON (97907) Baker(54), Malheur(47)
IDANHA (97350) Marion(67), Linn(33)
IDLEYLD PARK Douglas
IMBLER Union
IMNAHA Wallowa
INDEPENDENCE Polk
IONE Morrow
IRONSIDE Malheur

IRRIGON Morrow
JACKSONVILLE Jackson
JAMIESON Malheur
JEFFERSON Marion
JOHN DAY Grant
JORDAN VALLEY Malheur
JOSEPH Wallowa
JUNCTION CITY (97448) Lane(99), Benton(1)
JUNTURA Malheur
KEIZER Marion
KENO (97627) Klamath(95), Lake(5)
KENT Sherman
KERBY Josephine
KIMBERLY Grant
KLAMATH FALLS Klamath
LA GRANDE Union
LA PINE (97739) Deschutes(93), Klamath(7)
LAFAYETTE Yamhill
LAKE OSWEGO (97034) Clackamas(99), Multnomah(1)
LAKE OSWEGO (97035) Clackamas(92), Multnomah(6), Washington(2)
LAKESIDE Coos
LAKEVIEW Lake
LANGLOIS Curry
LAWEN Harney
LEBANON Linn
LEXINGTON Morrow
LINCOLN CITY Lincoln
LOGSDEN Lincoln
LONG CREEK Grant
LORANE Lane
LOSTINE Wallowa
LOWELL Lane
LYONS (97358) Linn(75), Marion(25)
MADRAS Jefferson
MALIN Klamath
MANNING Washington
MANZANITA Tillamook
MAPLETON Lane
MARCOLA Lane
MARION Marion
MARYLHURST Clackamas
MAUPIN Wasco
MCMINNVILLE Yamhill
MEACHAM Umatilla
MEDFORD Jackson
MEHAMA Marion
MERLIN Josephine
MERRILL Klamath
MIDLAND Klamath
MIKKALO Gilliam
MILL CITY (97360) Linn(85), Marion(15)
MILTON FREEWATER Umatilla
MITCHELL Wheeler
MOLALLA Clackamas
MONMOUTH (97361) Polk(98), Benton(2)
MONROE Benton
MONUMENT Grant
MORO (97039) Wasco(54), Sherman(46)

MOSIER Wasco
MOUNT ANGEL (97362) Marion(95), Clackamas(5)
MOUNT HOOD PARKDALE Hood River
MOUNT VERNON Grant
MULINO Clackamas
MURPHY Josephine
MYRTLE CREEK Douglas
MYRTLE POINT Coos
NEHALEM (97131) Tillamook(97), Clatsop(4)
NEOTSU Lincoln
NESKOWIN Tillamook
NETARTS Tillamook
NEW PINE CREEK (97635) Lake(50), Morrow(50)
NEWBERG (97132) Yamhill(98), Washington(1)
NEWPORT Lincoln
NORTH BEND Coos
NORTH PLAINS Washington
NORTH POWDER (97867) Union(87), Baker(13)
NORWAY Coos
NOTI Lane
NYSSA Malheur
O BRIEN Josephine
OAKLAND Douglas
OAKRIDGE Lane
OCEANSIDE Tillamook
ODELL Hood River
ONTARIO Malheur
OPHIR Curry
OREGON CITY Clackamas
OTIS (97368) Lincoln(74), Tillamook(26)
OTTER ROCK Lincoln
OXBOW Baker
PACIFIC CITY Tillamook
PAISLEY Lake
PAULINA Crook
PENDLETON Umatilla
PHILOMATH Benton
PHOENIX Jackson
PILOT ROCK Umatilla
PLEASANT HILL Lane
PLUSH Lake
PORT ORFORD Curry

PORTLAND (97206) Multnomah(94), Clackamas(6)
PORTLAND (97219) Multnomah(97), Clackamas(2)
PORTLAND (97229) Washington(83), Multnomah(17)
PORTLAND (97231) Multnomah(90), Washington(7), Columbia(4)
PORTLAND (97236) Multnomah(82), Clackamas(18)
PORTLAND (97266) Multnomah(76), Clackamas(24)
PORTLAND Clackamas
PORTLAND Multnomah
PORTLAND Washington
POST Crook
POWELL BUTTE Crook
POWERS Coos
PRAIRIE CITY Grant
PRINCETON Harney
PRINEVILLE Crook
PROSPECT Jackson
RAINIER Columbia
REDMOND Deschutes
REEDSPORT Douglas
REMOTE Coos
RHODODENDRON Clackamas
RICHLAND Baker
RICKREALL Polk
RIDDLE Douglas
RILEY Harney
RITTER Grant
RIVERSIDE Malheur
ROCKAWAY BEACH Tillamook
ROGUE RIVER Jackson
ROSE LODGE Lincoln
ROSEBURG Douglas
RUFUS Sherman
SAGINAW Lane
SAINT BENEDICT Marion
SAINT HELENS Columbia
SAINT PAUL Marion
SALEM (97304) Polk(98), Yamhill(2)
SALEM Marion
SANDY Clackamas
SCAPPOOSE (97056) Columbia(99), Multnomah(1)

SCIO Linn
SCOTTS MILLS (97375) Marion(94), Clackamas(6)
SCOTTSBURG Douglas
SEAL ROCK Lincoln
SEASIDE Clatsop
SELMA Josephine
SENECA Grant
SHADY COVE Jackson
SHANIKO Wasco
SHEDD Linn
SHERIDAN (97378) Yamhill(85), Polk(15)
SHERWOOD (97140) Washington(71), Clackamas(24), Yamhill(5)
SILETZ Lincoln
SILVER LAKE Lake
SILVERTON Marion
SISTERS (97759) Deschutes(94), Jefferson(6)
SIXES Curry
SOUTH BEACH Lincoln
SPRAGUE RIVER Klamath
SPRAY Wheeler
SPRINGFIELD Lane
STANFIELD Umatilla
STAYTON (97383) Marion(96), Linn(4)
SUBLIMITY Marion
SUMMER LAKE Lake
SUMMERVILLE Union
SUMPTER Baker
SUTHERLIN Douglas
SWEET HOME Linn
SWISSHOME Lane
TALENT Jackson
TANGENT Linn
TENMILE Douglas
TERREBONNE Deschutes
THE DALLES Wasco
THURSTON Lane
TIDEWATER (97390) Lincoln(91), Lane(9)
TILLAMOOK Tillamook
TILLER Douglas
TIMBER Washington
TOLEDO Lincoln
TOLOVANA PARK Clatsop
TRAIL Jackson
TROUTDALE Multnomah

TUALATIN (97062) Washington(85), Clackamas(15)
TURNER Marion
TYGH VALLEY Wasco
UKIAH Umatilla
UMATILLA Umatilla
UMPQUA Douglas
UNION Union
UNITY Baker
VALE Malheur
VENETA Lane
VERNONIA Columbia
VIDA Lane
WALDPORT Lincoln
WALLOWA Wallowa
WALTERVILLE Lane
WALTON Lane
WARM SPRINGS Jefferson
WARREN Columbia
WARRENTON Clatsop
WASCO (97065) Wasco(76), Sherman(24)
WEDDERBURN Curry
WELCHES Clackamas
WEST LINN Clackamas
WESTFALL Malheur
WESTFIR Lane
WESTLAKE Lane
WESTON Umatilla
WHEELER Tillamook
WHITE CITY Jackson
WILBUR Douglas
WILDERVILLE Josephine
WILLAMINA (97396) Yamhill(55), Polk(46)
WILLIAMS Josephine
WILSONVILLE (97070) Clackamas(95), Washington(5)
WINCHESTER Douglas
WINSTON Douglas
WOLF CREEK Josephine
WOODBURN (97071) Marion(97), Clackamas(3)
YACHATS Lincoln
YAMHILL Yamhill
YONCALLA Douglas

ZIP/City Cross Reference

ZIP	City	ZIP	City	ZIP	City	ZIP	City
97001-97001	ANTELOPE	97039-97039	MORO	97106-97106	BANKS	97143-97143	NETARTS
97002-97002	AURORA	97040-97040	MOSIER	97107-97107	BAY CITY	97144-97144	TIMBER
97004-97004	BEAVERCREEK	97041-97041	MOUNT HOOD PARKDALE	97108-97108	BEAVER	97145-97145	TOLOVANA PARK
97005-97008	BEAVERTON			97109-97109	BUXTON	97146-97146	WARRENTON
97009-97009	BORING	97042-97042	MULINO	97110-97110	CANNON BEACH	97147-97147	WHEELER
97010-97010	BRIDAL VEIL	97044-97044	ODELL	97111-97111	CARLTON	97148-97148	YAMHILL
97011-97011	BRIGHTWOOD	97045-97045	OREGON CITY	97112-97112	CLOVERDALE	97149-97149	NESKOWIN
97013-97013	CANBY	97048-97048	RAINIER	97113-97113	CORNELIUS	97201-97299	PORTLAND
97014-97014	CASCADE LOCKS	97049-97049	RHODODENDRON	97114-97114	DAYTON	97301-97306	SALEM
97015-97015	CLACKAMAS	97050-97050	RUFUS	97115-97115	DUNDEE	97307-97307	KEIZER
97016-97016	CLATSKANIE	97051-97051	SAINT HELENS	97116-97116	FOREST GROVE	97308-97314	SALEM
97017-97017	COLTON	97053-97053	WARREN	97117-97117	GALES CREEK	97321-97321	ALBANY
97018-97018	COLUMBIA CITY	97054-97054	DEER ISLAND	97118-97118	GARIBALDI	97324-97324	ALSEA
97019-97019	CORBETT	97055-97055	SANDY	97119-97119	GASTON	97325-97325	AUMSVILLE
97020-97020	DONALD	97056-97056	SCAPPOOSE	97121-97121	HAMMOND	97326-97326	BLODGETT
97021-97021	DUFUR	97057-97057	SHANIKO	97122-97122	HEBO	97327-97327	BROWNSVILLE
97022-97022	EAGLE CREEK	97058-97058	THE DALLES	97123-97124	HILLSBORO	97329-97329	CASCADIA
97023-97023	ESTACADA	97060-97060	TROUTDALE	97125-97125	MANNING	97330-97333	CORVALLIS
97024-97024	FAIRVIEW	97062-97062	TUALATIN	97127-97127	LAFAYETTE	97335-97335	CRABTREE
97026-97026	GERVAIS	97063-97063	TYGH VALLEY	97128-97128	MCMINNVILLE	97336-97336	CRAWFORDSVILLE
97027-97027	GLADSTONE	97064-97064	VERNONIA	97130-97130	MANZANITA	97338-97338	DALLAS
97028-97028	GOVERNMENT CAMP	97065-97065	WASCO	97131-97131	NEHALEM	97339-97339	CORVALLIS
97029-97029	GRASS VALLEY	97067-97067	WELCHES	97132-97132	NEWBERG	97341-97341	DEPOE BAY
97030-97030	GRESHAM	97068-97068	WEST LINN	97133-97133	NORTH PLAINS	97342-97342	DETROIT
97031-97031	HOOD RIVER	97070-97070	WILSONVILLE	97134-97134	OCEANSIDE	97343-97343	EDDYVILLE
97032-97032	HUBBARD	97071-97071	WOODBURN	97135-97135	PACIFIC CITY	97344-97344	FALLS CITY
97033-97033	KENT	97075-97078	BEAVERTON	97136-97136	ROCKAWAY BEACH	97345-97345	FOSTER
97034-97035	LAKE OSWEGO	97080-97080	GRESHAM	97137-97137	SAINT PAUL	97346-97346	GATES
97036-97036	MARYLHURST	97101-97101	AMITY	97138-97138	SEASIDE	97347-97347	GRAND RONDE
97037-97037	MAUPIN	97102-97102	ARCH CAPE	97140-97140	SHERWOOD	97348-97348	HALSEY
97038-97038	MOLALLA	97103-97103	ASTORIA	97141-97141	TILLAMOOK	97350-97350	IDANHA

Zip Range	City	Zip Range	City	Zip Range	City	Zip Range	City
97351-97351	INDEPENDENCE	97439-97439	FLORENCE	97533-97533	MURPHY	97818-97818	BOARDMAN
97352-97352	JEFFERSON	97440-97440	EUGENE	97534-97534	O BRIEN	97819-97819	BRIDGEPORT
97355-97355	LEBANON	97441-97441	GARDINER	97535-97535	PHOENIX	97820-97820	CANYON CITY
97357-97357	LOGSDEN	97442-97442	GLENDALE	97536-97536	PROSPECT	97821-97821	CAYUSE
97358-97358	LYONS	97443-97443	GLIDE	97537-97537	ROGUE RIVER	97823-97823	CONDON
97359-97359	MARION	97444-97444	GOLD BEACH	97538-97538	SELMA	97824-97824	COVE
97360-97360	MILL CITY	97446-97446	HARRISBURG	97539-97539	SHADY COVE	97825-97825	DAYVILLE
97361-97361	MONMOUTH	97447-97447	IDLEYLD PARK	97540-97540	TALENT	97826-97826	ECHO
97362-97362	MOUNT ANGEL	97448-97448	JUNCTION CITY	97541-97541	TRAIL	97827-97827	ELGIN
97364-97364	NEOTSU	97449-97449	LAKESIDE	97543-97543	WILDERVILLE	97828-97828	ENTERPRISE
97365-97365	NEWPORT	97450-97450	LANGLOIS	97544-97544	WILLIAMS	97830-97830	FOSSIL
97366-97366	SOUTH BEACH	97451-97451	LORANE	97601-97603	KLAMATH FALLS	97831-97831	FOX
97367-97367	LINCOLN CITY	97452-97452	LOWELL	97604-97604	CRATER LAKE	97833-97833	HAINES
97368-97368	OTIS	97453-97453	MAPLETON	97620-97620	ADEL	97834-97834	HALFWAY
97369-97369	OTTER ROCK	97454-97454	MARCOLA	97621-97621	BEATTY	97835-97835	HELIX
97370-97370	PHILOMATH	97455-97455	PLEASANT HILL	97622-97622	BLY	97836-97836	HEPPNER
97371-97371	RICKREALL	97456-97456	MONROE	97623-97623	BONANZA	97837-97837	HEREFORD
97372-97372	ROSE LODGE	97457-97457	MYRTLE CREEK	97624-97624	CHILOQUIN	97838-97838	HERMISTON
97373-97373	SAINT BENEDICT	97458-97458	MYRTLE POINT	97625-97625	DAIRY	97839-97839	LEXINGTON
97374-97374	SCIO	97459-97459	NORTH BEND	97626-97626	FORT KLAMATH	97840-97840	OXBOW
97375-97375	SCOTTS MILLS	97460-97460	NORWAY	97627-97627	KENO	97841-97841	IMBLER
97376-97376	SEAL ROCK	97461-97461	NOTI	97630-97630	LAKEVIEW	97842-97842	IMNAHA
97377-97377	SHEDD	97462-97462	OAKLAND	97632-97632	MALIN	97843-97843	IONE
97378-97378	SHERIDAN	97463-97463	OAKRIDGE	97633-97633	MERRILL	97844-97844	IRRIGON
97380-97380	SILETZ	97464-97464	OPHIR	97634-97634	MIDLAND	97845-97845	JOHN DAY
97381-97381	SILVERTON	97465-97465	PORT ORFORD	97635-97635	NEW PINE CREEK	97846-97846	JOSEPH
97383-97383	STAYTON	97466-97466	POWERS	97636-97636	PAISLEY	97848-97848	KIMBERLY
97384-97384	MEHAMA	97467-97467	REEDSPORT	97637-97637	PLUSH	97850-97850	LA GRANDE
97385-97385	SUBLIMITY	97468-97468	REMOTE	97638-97638	SILVER LAKE	97856-97856	LONG CREEK
97386-97386	SWEET HOME	97469-97469	RIDDLE	97639-97639	SPRAGUE RIVER	97857-97857	LOSTINE
97388-97388	GLENEDEN BEACH	97470-97470	ROSEBURG	97640-97640	SUMMER LAKE	97859-97859	MEACHAM
97389-97389	TANGENT	97472-97472	SAGINAW	97641-97641	CHRISTMAS VALLEY	97861-97861	MIKKALO
97390-97390	TIDEWATER	97473-97473	SCOTTSBURG	97701-97709	BEND	97862-97862	MILTON FREEWATER
97391-97391	TOLEDO	97476-97476	SIXES	97710-97710	FIELDS	97864-97864	MONUMENT
97392-97392	TURNER	97477-97478	SPRINGFIELD	97711-97711	ASHWOOD	97865-97865	MOUNT VERNON
97394-97394	WALDPORT	97479-97479	SUTHERLIN	97712-97712	BROTHERS	97867-97867	NORTH POWDER
97396-97396	WILLAMINA	97480-97480	SWISSHOME	97720-97720	BURNS	97868-97868	PILOT ROCK
97401-97405	EUGENE	97481-97481	TENMILE	97721-97721	PRINCETON	97869-97869	PRAIRIE CITY
97406-97406	AGNESS	97482-97482	THURSTON	97722-97722	DIAMOND	97870-97870	RICHLAND
97407-97407	ALLEGANY	97484-97484	TILLER	97730-97730	CAMP SHERMAN	97872-97872	RITTER
97408-97408	EUGENE	97486-97486	UMPQUA	97731-97731	CHEMULT	97873-97873	SENECA
97409-97409	ALVADORE	97487-97487	VENETA	97732-97732	CRANE	97874-97874	SPRAY
97410-97410	AZALEA	97488-97488	VIDA	97733-97733	CRESCENT	97875-97875	STANFIELD
97411-97411	BANDON	97489-97489	WALTERVILLE	97734-97734	CULVER	97876-97876	SUMMERVILLE
97412-97412	BLACHLY	97490-97490	WALTON	97735-97735	FORT ROCK	97877-97877	SUMPTER
97413-97413	BLUE RIVER	97491-97491	WEDDERBURN	97736-97736	FRENCHGLEN	97880-97880	UKIAH
97414-97414	BROADBENT	97492-97492	WESTFIR	97737-97737	GILCHRIST	97882-97882	UMATILLA
97415-97415	BROOKINGS	97493-97493	WESTLAKE	97738-97738	HINES	97883-97883	UNION
97416-97416	CAMAS VALLEY	97494-97494	WILBUR	97739-97739	LA PINE	97884-97884	UNITY
97417-97417	CANYONVILLE	97495-97495	WINCHESTER	97740-97740	LAWEN	97885-97885	WALLOWA
97419-97419	CHESHIRE	97496-97496	WINSTON	97741-97741	MADRAS	97886-97886	WESTON
97420-97420	COOS BAY	97497-97497	WOLF CREEK	97750-97750	MITCHELL	97901-97901	ADRIAN
97423-97423	COQUILLE	97498-97498	YACHATS	97751-97751	PAULINA	97902-97902	AROCK
97424-97424	COTTAGE GROVE	97499-97499	YONCALLA	97752-97752	POST	97903-97903	BROGAN
97425-97425	CRESCENT LAKE	97501-97501	MEDFORD	97753-97753	POWELL BUTTE	97904-97904	DREWSEY
97426-97426	CRESWELL	97502-97502	CENTRAL POINT	97754-97754	PRINEVILLE	97905-97905	DURKEE
97427-97427	CULP CREEK	97503-97503	WHITE CITY	97756-97756	REDMOND	97906-97906	HARPER
97428-97428	CURTIN	97504-97504	MEDFORD	97758-97758	RILEY	97907-97907	HUNTINGTON
97429-97429	DAYS CREEK	97520-97520	ASHLAND	97759-97759	SISTERS	97908-97908	IRONSIDE
97430-97430	DEADWOOD	97522-97522	BUTTE FALLS	97760-97760	TERREBONNE	97909-97909	JAMIESON
97431-97431	DEXTER	97523-97523	CAVE JUNCTION	97761-97761	WARM SPRINGS	97910-97910	JORDAN VALLEY
97432-97432	DILLARD	97524-97524	EAGLE POINT	97801-97801	PENDLETON	97911-97911	JUNTURA
97434-97434	DORENA	97525-97525	GOLD HILL	97810-97810	ADAMS	97913-97913	NYSSA
97435-97435	DRAIN	97526-97528	GRANTS PASS	97812-97812	ARLINGTON	97914-97914	ONTARIO
97436-97436	ELKTON	97530-97530	JACKSONVILLE	97813-97813	ATHENA	97917-97917	RIVERSIDE
97437-97437	ELMIRA	97531-97531	KERBY	97814-97814	BAKER CITY	97918-97918	VALE
97438-97438	FALL CREEK	97532-97532	MERLIN	97817-97817	BATES	97920-97920	WESTFALL

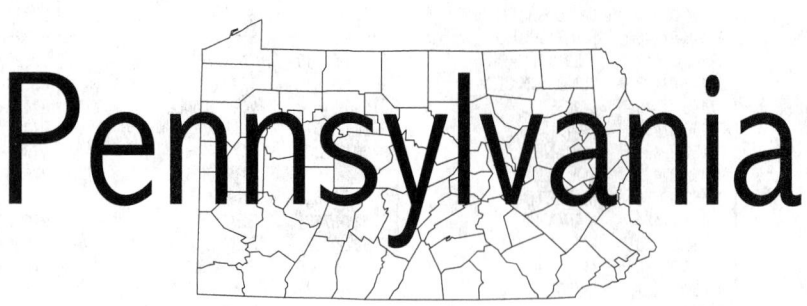

Pennsylvania

General Help Numbers:

Governor's Office
225 Main Capitol Bldg   717-787-2500
Harrisburg, PA 17120   Fax 717-772-8284
www.state.pa.us/PA_Exec/Governor/organization.html

Attorney General's Office
Strawberry Square, 16th Floor   717-787-3391
Harrisburg, PA 17120   Fax 717-787-1190
www.attorneygeneral.gov   8AM-5PM

State Court Administrator
PO Box 719   717-795-2000
Mechanicsburg, PA 17055-0719   Fax 717-795-2050
www.courts.state.pa.us   9AM-5PM

State Archives
Bureau of Archives & History   717-783-3281
PO Box 1026   Fax 717-787-4822
Harrisburg, PA 17108-1026   9AM-4PM TU-F
www.state.pa.us/PA_Exec/Historical_Museum/DAM/
genie1.htm

State Specifics:

Capital:	Harrisburg Dauphin County
Time Zone:	EST
Number of Counties:	67
Population:	11,994,016
Web Site:	www.state.pa.us

State Agencies

Criminal Records

State Police Central Repository, 1800 Elmerton Ave, Harrisburg, PA 17110-9758; 717-783-9973, 717-772-3681 (Fax), 8:15AM-4:15PM.

www.pwp.state.pa.us

Indexing & Storage: Records are available from the 1920s. New records are available for inquiry immediately. Records are indexed on fingerprint cards. Records are normally destroyed after 70 years of age or 3 years after indiviual is confirmed deceased by fingerprints. Records are unavailable after subject has been free of arrest or probation for 10 years following final release from confinement or supervision.

Searching: Must make request on Request Form SP4-164 or the request will be returned. Information will include felony and misdemeanor convictions and open cases less than 3 years old. Include the following in your request-full name, date of birth, Social Security Number, sex, race, any aliases.

Access by: mail, in person.

Fee & Payment: Fee is $10.00 per name search. Fee payee: Commonwealth of Pennsylvania. Prepayment required. No personal checks accepted. No credit cards accepted.

Mail search: Turnaround time: 2-3 weeks. No self addressed stamped envelope is required.

In person search: Turnaround time is 10-13 days.

Corporation Records
Limited Partnership Records
Trademarks/Servicemarks
Fictitious Name
Assumed Name
Limited Liability Company Records
Limited Liability Partnerships

Corporation Bureau, Department of State, PO Box 8722, Harrisburg, PA 17105-8722 (Courier: 308 North Office Bldg, Harrisburg, PA 17120); 717-787-1057, 717-783-2244 (Fax), 8AM-5PM.

www.dos.state.pa.us/corp.htm

Indexing & Storage: Records are available from 1700's on. Records are indexed on computer since the 1800's.

Searching: Include the following in your request-full name of business. Corporation records include: Articles of Incorporation, Officers, Directors, DBAs, Prior (merged) names, Withdrawn and Reserved (120 days) names. Annual Reports on for-profit corporations are not required by the Department of State.

Access by: mail, phone, fax, in person.

Fee & Payment: The search fee is $12.00, copies are $2.00 per page. Fee payee: Department of State. Prepayment required. Ongoing requesters should open a customer deposit account. Personal checks accepted. No credit cards accepted.

Mail search: Turnaround time: 3-5 days. No self addressed stamped envelope is required.

Phone search: No fee for telephone request. They will provide basic information only.

Fax search: You must have an account to have materials returned by fax, same fees as above.

In person search: There are 3 computer terminals available for public use.

Other access: Business lists, UCC on microfilm, and financing statements are available in bulk for $.25 per name.

Expedited service: Expedited service is available for mail and phone searches. Add $52.00 per transaction. If ordered before 1 PM, the record will be available by 5 PM.

Uniform Commercial Code

UCC Division, Department of State, PO Box 8721, Harrisburg, PA 17105-8721 (Courier: North Office Bldg, Rm 308, Harrisburg, PA 17120); 717-787-1057, 717-783-2244 (Fax), 8AM-5PM.

www.dos.state.pa.us/corp.htm

Indexing & Storage: Records are available from 1964-present on microfiche and computer.

Searching: Use search request form UCC-11. All federal and state tax liens are filed at the Prothonotary of each county. Include the following in your request-debtor name.

Access by: mail, fax, in person.

Fee & Payment: The search fee is $12.00 per debtor name, copies cost $2.00 per page. In addition, the agency charges $1.00 per financing statement and statement of assignment reported on an information only listing. Fee payee:

Pennsylvania Department of State. Prepayment required. Deposit accounts are accepted. Personal checks accepted. No credit cards accepted.

Mail search: Turnaround time: 3-5 days. A self addressed stamped envelope is requested.

Fax search: There is an additional $2.00 per page fee if returned by fax. A customer deposit account is required.

In person search: If the search is conducted by the customer, there is no $12.00 search fee.

Other access: Daily computer tapes and copies of microfilm are available. Call the number above for details.

Federal Tax Liens
State Tax Liens

Records not maintained by a state level agency.

Note: All federal and state tax liens are filed at the Prothonotary of each county.

Sales Tax Registrations

Revenue Department, Sales Tax Division, Dept 280905, Harrisburg, PA 17128-0905; 717-783-9360, 717-783-5274 (Fax), 7:30AM-5PM.

www.revenue.state.pa.us

Indexing & Storage: Records are available from 1971-present.

Searching: This agency will only confirm that a business is registered. They will provide no other information. They will only search with a tax permit number.

Access by: mail, phone, fax.

Fee & Payment: There is no search fee.

Mail search: Turnaround time: 2-7 days. A self addressed stamped envelope is requested.

Phone search: Searching is available by phone.

Fax search: Same criteria as mail searches.

Birth Certificates

PA Department of Health, Division of Vital Records, PO Box 1528, New Castle, PA 16103-1528 (Courier: 101 S Mercer St, Room 401, New Castle, PA 16101); 724-656-3100 (Message Phone), 724-652-8951 (Fax), 8AM-4PM.

www.health.state.pa.us

Indexing & Storage: Records are available from 1906-present.

Searching: Must have a signed release form from person of record or immediate family member. Include the following in your request-full name, names of parents, mother's maiden name, date of birth, place of birth, relationship to person of record, reason for information request. Must include daytime phone number.

Access by: mail, phone, fax, in person.

Fee & Payment: The fee is $4.00 per record. Fee payee: Vital Records. Prepayment required. Personal checks accepted. Credit cards not accepted for mail requests. Credit cards accepted: Mastercard, Visa, AmEx, Discover.

Mail search: Turnaround time: 4-6 weeks. Credit cards not accepted for mail requests. A self addressed stamped envelope is requested.

Phone search: Phone requests accepted with a credit card for an additional $7.00 fee. Turnaround time is 2-3 days.

Fax search: Credit card is required for an additional $7.00. Results are mailed in 2-3 days.

In person search: Turnaround time is 1 hour.

Expedited service: Expedited service is available for mail, phone and fax searches. Turnaround time: 2-3 days. Add fees for express delivery, use of credit card required.

Death Records

Department of Health, Division of Vital Records, PO Box 1528, New Castle, PA 16103-1528 (Courier: 101 S Mercer St, Room 401, New Castle, PA 16101); 724-656-3100 (Message Phone), 724-652-8951 (Fax), 8AM-4PM.

www.health.state.pa.us

Indexing & Storage: Records are available from 1906-present. Records are indexed on microfiche, inhouse computer.

Searching: Must have a signed release form from immediate family member. Include the following in your request-full name, date of death, place of death, relationship to person of record, reason for information request. SSN helpful, if known. Include daytime phone number.

Access by: mail, phone, fax, in person.

Fee & Payment: The fee is $3.00 per record. Fee payee: Vital Records. Prepayment required. Personal checks accepted. Credit cards not accepted for mail requests. Credit cards accepted: Mastercard, Visa, AmEx, Discover.

Mail search: Turnaround time: 4-6 weeks. A self addressed stamped envelope is requested.

Phone search: Phone service available with a credit card for an additional $7.00 fee. Turnaround time is 3 days.

Fax search: There is an additional $7.00 fee to use a credit card. Turnaround time is 3 days.

In person search: Turnaround time 1 hour.

Expedited service: Expedited service is available for mail, phone and fax searches. Turnaround time: 2-3 days. Add cost of express delivery, credit card required.

Marriage Certificates
Divorce Records

Records not maintained by a state level agency.

Note: Marriage and divorce records are found at county or Prothonotary of issue.

Workers' Compensation Records

Bureau of Workers' Compensation, Physical Records Section, 1171 S Cameron St, Rm 103, Harrisburg, PA 17104-2501; 717-772-4447, 7:30AM-4PM.

www.dli.state.pa.us

Indexing & Storage: Records are available for past 2-10 years. Records are indexed on inhouse computer.

Searching: Only the party to the record is allowed full access without a subpoena or a signed release.

They will indicate whether they have a record for a person, but will not give any other information to the public. Include the following in your request-claimant name, year, date of accident, Social Security Number.

Access by: mail.

Fee & Payment: No fees invloved for simple requests.

Mail search: Turnaround time: 30 days. No self addressed stamped envelope is required.

Driver Records

Department of Transportation, Driver Record Services, PO Box 68695, Harrisburg, PA 17106-8695 (Courier: 1101 S Front Street, Harrisburg, PA 17104); 717-391-6190, 800-932-4600 (In-state only), 7:30AM-4:30PM.

www.dmv.state.pa.us

Note: Copies of tickets may be purchased from this location for a fee of $5.00 each.

Indexing & Storage: Records are available for minimum of 3 calendar years for moving violations and departmental actions, minimum of 7 years for DWIs, and indefinite for suspensions. Accidents are reported on record as involvement only. The driver's address appears on the record. It takes 60 days from receipt before new records are available for inquiry.

Searching: Casual requesters submit Form DL-503. Large volume requesters must sign an agreement stating the individual authorizations are on file. There is no opt out.The state is in the process of authorizing all customers of MVR provider companies. Include the following in your request-driver's license number, full name, date of birth.

Access by: mail, in person, online.

Fee & Payment: The fee is $5.00 for each record. A 10 year employment record for commercial drivers is available. Fee payee: Department of Transportation. Prepayment required. Personal checks accepted. No credit cards accepted.

Mail search: Turnaround time: 5-7 days. No self addressed stamped envelope is required.

In person search: The state will process one record request while you wait, additional requests are mailed back to the requester.

Online search: The online system is available to high volume requesters only. Call 717-787-7154 for more information. The sale of records over the Internet is strictly forbidden.

Vehicle Ownership
Vehicle Identification

Department of Transportation, Vehicle Record Services, PO Box 68691, Harrisburg, PA 17106-8691 (Courier: 1101 South Front St, Harrisburg, PA 17104); 717-391-6190, 800-932-6000 (In-state), 7:30AM-4:30PM.

www.dmv.state.pa.us

Note: This agency also holds records for unattached mobile homes.

Searching: The requester must sumbit Form DL-135. The state does not authorize the bulk delivery or commercial use of ownership & vehicle information.

Access by: mail.

Fee & Payment: The fee is $5.00 per transaction. Title history may have more than one transaction per vehicle. You can call first to determine the number. There is an additional $5.00 for certification. Fee payee: Department of Transportation. Prepayment required. Personal checks accepted. No credit cards accepted.

Mail search: Turnaround time: 7-10 days. You can order a record in person, but results will be mailed.No self addressed stamped envelope is required.

Other access: Bulk information is not sold for commercial purposes. Certain statistical type user requests will be honored.

Accident Reports

State Police Headquarters, Accident Records Unit, 1800 Elmerton Ave, Harrisburg, PA 17110; 717-783-5516, 8AM-5PM.

www.psp.state.pa.us

Indexing & Storage: Records are available for 10 years to present. It takes 60 days before new records are available for inquiry. Records are indexed on inhouse computer.

Searching: Only those involved, their attorney or insurer may request a copy of the accident report. Include the following in your request-full name, date of accident, claim number. The following data is not released: medical information or expunged records.

Access by: mail.

Fee & Payment: Reports are $8.00 per record. Fee payee: Commonwealth of Pennsylvania. Prepayment required. Personal checks accepted. No credit cards accepted.

Mail search: Turnaround time: 4-6 weeks.

Boat & Vessel Ownership
Boat & Vessel Registration

Access to Records is Restricted

Note: Boat registration and ownership information is not open to the public. Liens are filed at UCC filing locations.

Legislation-Current/Pending
Legislation-Passed

Pennsylvania General Assembly, Main Capitol Bldg, Room 641, Harrisburg, PA 17120; 717-787-2342 (History Room), 717-787-5320 (House Bills), 717-787-6732 (Senate Bills), House-8:30AM-4:30PM/Senate-8:30AM-5PM.

www.legis.state.pa.us

Note: Call the History Room first to get the bill number, print number, and status.

Indexing & Storage: Records are available for current session only. Records are indexed on inhouse computer.

Searching: Include the following in your request-bill number, topic of bill.

Access by: mail, phone, in person, online.

Fee & Payment: There is no search fee.

Mail search: Turnaround time: 2 days. No self addressed stamped envelope is required.

Phone search: They will help with up to 5 bills per phone call.

In person search: Searching is available in person.

Online search: Free access to bill text is available at the Electronic Bill Room found at the web page.

Voter Registration

Records not maintained by a state level agency.

Note: Records are kept at the county level and cannot be sold for commerical purposes.

GED Certificates

Commonwealth Diploma Program, GED Testing, 333 Market St 12th Fl, Harrisburg, PA 17126-0333; 717-787-6747, 8:30AM-4:30PM.

www.paadulted.org

Searching: For all requests the following is required: a signed release, name, approximate year of test, date of birth, Social Security Number, city of test, and a phone number where you can be reached.

Access by: mail.

Fee & Payment: Verifications and copies of transcripts are $3.00 each. The fee is non-refundable. Fee payee: Commonwealth of PA. Prepayment required. Cashier's checks and money orders are accepted. No credit cards or personal checks accepted.

Mail search: Turnaround time: 3-4 weeks. No self addressed stamped envelope is required.

Fishing License Information

Access to Records is Restricted

Fish & Boat Commission, Fishing License Division, PO Box 67000, Harrisburg, PA 17106 (Courier: 3532 Walnut St, Harrisburg, PA 17106); 717-657-4518 (Fishing License Division), 717-787-4250 (Hunting License Division), 717-657-4549 (Fax), 8AM-4PM.

Hunting License Information

Records not maintained by a state level agency.

Note: Hunting license information is not released to the public.

Licenses Searchable Online

Athletic Agent #22 .... www.dos.state.pa.us/sac/agents.html
Bank #04 .... www.state.pa.us/PA_Exec/Banking/resource/bkfrm.pdf
Credit Union #04 .... www.state.pa.us/PA_Exec/Banking/resource/cufrm.pdf
Education Specialist #06 .... http://tcp.ed.state.pa.us/tcsmainJS.asp
Insurance Company #11.. www.insurance.state.pa.us/html/licensed.html
Optometrist #20 .... www.arbo.org/nodb2000/licsearch.asp
Savings Association #04 .... www.state.pa.us/PA_Exec/Banking/resource/safrm.pdf
Trust Company #04.. www.state.pa.us/PA_Exec/Banking/resource/tcfrm.pdf

Licensing Quick Finder

Accelerated Mortgage Payment Provider #04
....717-787-3717
Acupuncturist #20 717-783-1400
Ambulance Service #08.......................717-787-8740
Amphetamine Program #20 717-787-2568
Animal Health Technician #23 717-783-7134
Architect #20...................................717-783-3397
Athletic Agent #22 717-787-5720
Athletic Announcer #22 717-787-5720
Athletic Manager #22 717-787-5720
Athletic Trainer #22 717-787-5720
Attorney #01....................................717-731-7073
Auctioneer #20.................................717-783-3397
Bank #04 717-787-3717
Barber #20.......................................717-783-3402
Boat Registration #13.........................717-705-7940
Boxer #22..717-787-5720
Boxing Judge #22 717-787-5720
Boxing Promoter #22..........................717-787-5720
Boxing Second #22.............................717-787-5720
Check Casher #04 717-787-3717
Child Day Care Facility #12 717-787-8691
Chiropractor #20...............................717-783-7155
Consumer Discount Company #04 717-787-3717
Cosmetologist/Cosmetician #20...........717-783-7130
Credit Services Loan Broker #04 717-787-3717
Credit Union #04 717-787-3717
Debt Collector-Repossessor #04 717-787-3717
Dental Assistant, Expanded Function #18
....717-783-7162
Dental Hygienist #18 717-783-7162
Dentist #18 717-783-7162
Education Specialist #06 717-787-2967
Emergency Medical Technician #08......717-787-8740
Engineer #20 717-783-7049
First Mortgage Banker #04 717-787-3717
First Mortgage Broker & Banker #04 717-787-3717
First Mortgage Limited Broker #04 717-787-3717
First Mortgage Loan Correspondent #04
....717-787-3717
First Responder-EMT #08 717-787-8740
Funeral Director #20...........................717-783-3397
Geologist #20...................................717-783-7049
Harness Racing #03............................717-783-8725

Health Professional #08 717-787-8740
Hearing Aid Dealer #07 717-783-8078
Hearing Aid Fitter #07 717-783-8078
Hearing Aid Fitter Apprentice #07 717-783-8078
Horse Racing #03...............................717-783-8725
Installment Loan Seller #04 717-787-3717
Installment Seller #04.........................717-787-3717
Insurance Agent #11...........................717-787-3840
Insurance Company #11.......................717-787-2735
Insurance Supervisor/Broker #11..........717-787-3840
Investment Adviser #16.......................717-783-4211
Kickboxer #22 717-787-5720
Landscape Architect #20 717-772-8528
Licensing Division #11........................717-787-3840
Liquor Distributor #14.........................717-783-8250
Lobbyist #17....................................717-787-5920
Manicurist #20..................................717-783-7130
Medical Doctor #20............................717-787-2381
Medical Laboratory #10.......................610-363-8500
Midwife #20.....................................717-783-1400
Money Transmitter #04........................717-787-3717
Notary Public #21..............................717-787-5280
Nuclear Medicine Technologist #20 717-787-4858
Nurse #20..717-783-7142
Nursing Home #09 610-594-8041
Nursing Home Administrator #20 717-783-7155
Occupational Therapist/Assistant #20 ...717-783-1389
Optometrist #20 717-783-7155
Osteopathic Physician #20 717-783-4858
Osteopathic Physician Assistant #20 ...717-783-4858
Paramedic #08..................................717-787-8740
Pawnbroker #04................................717-787-3717
Pest Management Consultant #02 717-787-5231 ext2
Pesticide Applicator #02 .... 717-787-5231 ext2
Pesticide Dealer #02 .... 717-787-5231 ext2
Pesticide Technician #02............... 717-787-5231 ext2
Pharmacist #20.................................717-783-7156
Physical Therapist/Assistant #20 717-783-7134
Physician Assistant #20......................717-787-2381
Podiatrist #20...................................717-783-4858
Prehospital RN #08 717-787-8740
Private Investigator #15......................717-255-2692
Private School Staff #06 717-783-8228
Psychologist #23...............................717-783-7134

Public Accountant Corporation #20 717-783-1404
Public Accountant-CPA #20.................717-783-1404
Public Accountant-PA #20 717-783-1404
Public Accounting Partnership #20 717-783-1404
Radiation Therapy Technician #20........717-783-4858
Radiologic Technologist #20................717-783-4858
Real Estate Appraiser #20...................717-783-4866
Real Estate Auctioneer #20 717-783-3658
Real Estate Broker #20 717-783-3658
Real Estate Sales Person #20 717-783-3658
Referee #22 717-787-5720
Residential Appraiser #20....................717-783-4866
Respiratory Care Practitioner #20 717-783-4858
Retail Liquor #14...............................717-787-5428
Sales Finance Company #04 717-787-3717
Savings Association #04 717-787-3717
School Administrator #06.....................717-787-2967
School Intermediate Unit Executive Director #06
....717-787-2967
School Superintendent #06 717-787-2967
School Supervisor #06 717-787-2967
Secondary Mortgage Lender #04..........717-787-3717
Secondary Mortgage Loan Broker #04 ..717-787-3717
Secondary Mortgage Loan Broker Agent #04
....717-787-3717
Securities Agent #16 717-783-4212
Securities Broker/Dealer #16 717-783-4213
Social Worker #20.............................717-783-1389
Speech Pathologist/Audiologist #20 717-783-1389
Sports Physician #22..........................717-787-5720
Surveyor #20 717-783-7049
Teacher #05.....................................717-787-2967
Temporary Hearing Aid Apprentice #07 717-783-8078
Timekeeper #22 717-787-5720
Trust Company #04............................717-787-3717
Vehicle Dealer #19............................717-783-1697
Vehicle Salesperson #19 717-783-1697
Veterinarian #20................................717-783-7134
Veterinary Technician #20 717-783-7134
Wholesale Liquor #14.........................717-787-5428
Wholesale Tablefunder #04 717-787-3717
Wrestling Promoter #22.......................717-787-5720

Licensing Agency Information

01 Administration Office of PA Courts, PO Box 46 (PO Box 46), Camphill, PA 17001-0046; 717-731-7073, Fax: 717-731-7080.

02 Department of Agriculture, 2301 N Cameron St, Harrisburg, PA 17110-9408; 717-772-5231, Fax: 717-783-3275.

www.state.pa.us/PA_Exec/Agriculture/bureaus/plant_industry/index.html

03 Department of Agriculture, 2301 N Cameron St, Agriculture Office Bldg, Harrisburg, PA 17110-9408; 717-787-5196, Fax: 717-787-2271.

www.state.pa.us/govstate.html

04 Department of Banking, 333 Market St, 16th Fl, Harrisburg, PA 17111-2290; 717-787-3717, Fax: 717-787-8773.

www.state.pa.us/PA_Exec/Banking/organiz.htm

06 Department of Education, 333 Market St, 3rd Fl, Harrisburg, PA 17126-0333; 717-787-2967, Fax: 717-783-6736.

www.pde.psu.edu

Direct URL to search licenses: http://tcp.ed.state.pa.us/tcsmainJS.asp You can search online using SSN

07 Department of Health, Bureau of Community Program Licensure & Certification, 132 Kline

Plaza, Harrisburg, PA 17104; 717-783-8078, Fax: 717-787-3188. www.state.pa.us

08 Department of Health, PO Box 90 (PO Box 90), Harrisburg, PA 17108; 717-787-8740, Fax: 717-772-0910.

09 Department of Health, PO Box 500 (PO Box 500), Exton, PA 19341-0500; 610-594-8041, Fax: 610-436-3346.

http://38.240.57.102/nffa/panpha/nurseaid.idc?

10 Department of Health-Bureau of Labs, PO Box 500 (PO Box 500), Exton, PA 19341-0500; 610-363-8500, Fax: 610-436-3346.

www.health.state.pa.us/HPA/labinvst.htm

11 Department of Insurance, 1300 Strawberry Sq, Harrisburg, PA 17120; 717-787-2735, Fax: 717-787-8557.

www.insurance.state.pa.us

Direct URL to search licenses: www.insurance.state.pa.us/html/licensed.html You can search online using alphabetical list for insurance companies

12 Department of Public Welfare, PO Box 2675 (333 Health and Welfare Bldg), Harrisburg, PA 17105-2675; 717-787-8691, Fax: 717-787-1529.

13 Fish & Boat Commission, PO Box 68900 (1601 Elmerton Ave), Harrisburg, PA 17110-9299; 717-705-7940, Fax: 717-705-7931.

www.fish.state.pa.us

14 Liquor Control Board, PO Box 8940 (PO Box 8940), Harrisburg, PA 17105-8940; 717-787-8250, Fax: 717-772-2165.

wwww.lcb.state.pa.us/agency/overview.htm

16 Securities Commission, 1010 N 7th St, Eastgate-2nd Fl, Harrisburg, PA 17102-1410; 717-787-8061, Fax: 717-783-5122.

www.psc.state.pa.us/

17 Secretary of Senate, State Capitol, Main Capitol Bldg, Rm 462, Harrisburg, PA 17120; 717-787-5920.

18 Department of State, Board of Dentistry, PO Box 2649 (PO Box 2649), Harrisburg, PA 17105-2649; 717-783-7162, Fax: 717-787-7769.

www.dos.state.pa.us/bpoa/denbd/mainpage.htm

19 Bureau of Professional & Occupational Affairs, Board of Vehicle Manufacturers, 124 Pine St, Transportation & Safety Bldg, 6th Fl, Harrisburg, PA 17101; 717-783-1697, Fax: 717-787-0250.

www.dos.state.pa.us/bpoa/vehbd.htm   For verifications, call or contact the Board via e-mail at vehicle@pados.dos.state.pa.us.

20 State Department, PO Box 2649 (124 Pine St), Harrisburg, PA 17105-2649; 717-787-8503, Fax: 717-787-7769.

www.dos.state.pa.us/sitemap.html

21 State Department, Elections & Legislation, North Office Bldg, Rm 304, Harrisburg, PA 17120; 717-787-5280, Fax: 717-787-2854.

www.dos.state.pa.us

22 Department of State, Athletic Commission, 116 Pine St, 3rd Fl, Harrisburg, PA 17101; 717-787-5720, Fax: 717-783-0824.

www.dos.state.pa.us/sac/sac.html

23 Department of State, Bureau of Professional & Occupational Affairs, 116 Pine St, Harrisburg, PA 17101; 717-783-7134.

The following list indicates the district and division name for each county in the state. If the district or division name of the bankruptcy court is different from the civil/criminal court, it appears in parentheses.

County/Court Cross Reference

County	District	Division
Adams	Middle	Harrisburg
Allegheny	Western	Pittsburgh
Armstrong	Western	Pittsburgh
Beaver	Western	Pittsburgh
Bedford	Western	Johnstown (Pittsburgh)
Berks	Eastern	Allentown/Reading (Reading)
Blair	Western	Johnstown (Pittsburgh)
Bradford	Middle	Scranton (Wilkes-Barre)
Bucks	Eastern	Philadelphia
Butler	Western	Pittsburgh
Cambria	Western	Johnstown (Pittsburgh)
Cameron	Middle	Williamsport (Wilkes-Barre)
Carbon	Middle	Scranton (Wilkes-Barre)
Centre	Middle	Williamsport (Harrisburg)
Chester	Eastern	Philadelphia
Clarion	Western	Pittsburgh (Erie)
Clearfield	Western	Johnstown (Pittsburgh)
Clinton	Middle	Williamsport (Wilkes-Barre)
Columbia	Middle	Williamsport (Wilkes-Barre)
Crawford	Western	Erie
Cumberland	Middle	Harrisburg
Dauphin	Middle	Harrisburg
Delaware	Eastern	Philadelphia
Elk	Western	Erie
Erie	Western	Erie
Fayette	Western	Pittsburgh
Forest	Western	Erie
Franklin	Middle	Harrisburg
Fulton	Middle	Harrisburg
Greene	Western	Pittsburgh
Huntingdon	Middle	Harrisburg
Indiana	Western	Pittsburgh
Jefferson	Western	Pittsburgh (Erie)
Juniata	Middle	Harrisburg
Lackawanna	Middle	Scranton (Wilkes-Barre)
Lancaster	Eastern	Allentown/Reading (Reading)
Lawrence	Western	Pittsburgh
Lebanon	Middle	Harrisburg
Lehigh	Eastern	Allentown/Reading (Reading)
Luzerne	Middle	Scranton (Wilkes-Barre)
Lycoming	Middle	Williamsport (Wilkes-Barre)
McKean	Western	Erie
Mercer	Western	Pittsburgh (Erie)
Mifflin	Middle	Harrisburg
Monroe	Middle	Scranton (Wilkes-Barre)
Montgomery	Eastern	Philadelphia
Montour	Middle	Williamsport (Harrisburg)
Northampton	Eastern	Allentown/Reading (Reading)
Northumberland	Middle	Williamsport (Harrisburg)
Perry	Middle	Williamsport (Harrisburg)
Philadelphia	Eastern	Philadelphia
Pike	Middle	Scranton (Wilkes-Barre)
Potter	Middle	Williamsport (Wilkes-Barre)
Schuylkill	Eastern	Allentown/Reading (Reading)
Snyder	Middle	Williamsport (Harrisburg)
Somerset	Western	Johnstown (Pittsburgh)
Sullivan	Middle	Williamsport (Wilkes-Barre)
Susquehanna	Middle	Scranton (Wilkes-Barre)
Tioga	Middle	Williamsport (Wilkes-Barre)
Union	Middle	Williamsport (Harrisburg)
Venango	Western	Erie
Warren	Western	Erie
Washington	Western	Pittsburgh
Wayne	Middle	Scranton (Wilkes-Barre)
Westmoreland	Western	Pittsburgh
Wyoming	Middle	Scranton (Wilkes-Barre)
York	Middle	Harrisburg

US District Court

Eastern District of Pennsylvania

Allentown/Reading Division c/o Philadelphia Division, Room 2609, US Courthouse, 601 Market St, Philadelphia, PA 19106-1797, 215-597-7704, Fax: 215-597-6390.

www.paed.uscourts.gov

Counties: Berks, Lancaster, Lehigh, Northampton, Schuylkill.

Indexing & Storage: Cases are indexed by as well as by case number. New cases are available in the index after filing date. Open records are located at the Division.

Fee & Payment: The fee is no charge per item (one party name or case number). Payment may be made by money order, cashier check. Business checks are not accepted. Personal checks are not accepted.

Phone Search: An automated voice case information service (VCIS) is not available.

In Person Search: In person searching is available.

PACER: Sign-up number is 215-597-5710. Access fee is $.60 per minute. Toll-free access: 800-458-2993. Local access: 215-597-0258. Case records are available back to July 1, 1990. Records are never purged. New records are available online after 1 day. PACER is available on the Internet at http://pacer.paed.uscourts.gov.

Electronic Filing: Anyone may submit civil and criminal documents in electronic form; however, you must first fill out the application available on the web site. Electronic filing information is available online at www.paed.uscourts.gov/us01003.shtml

Opinions Online: Court opinions are available online at www.paed.uscourts.gov/contents.shtml

Philadelphia Division Room 2609, US Courthouse, 601 Market St, Philadelphia, PA 19106-1797, 215-597-7704, Fax: 215-597-0303.

www.paed.uscourts.gov

Counties: Bucks, Chester, Delaware, Montgomery, Philadelphia.

Indexing & Storage: Cases are indexed by defendant and plaintiff as well as by case number. New cases are available in the index immediately after filing date. A computer index is maintained. The computer index is from 1990 on. Records are also indexed on microfiche. Indexes by judgment and by nature of suit are also available. Open records are located at this court. District wide searches are available from this division.

Fee & Payment: The fee is $15.00 per item (one party name or case number). Payment may be made by money order, cashier check, personal check, Visa, Mastercard. Payee: Clerk, US District Court. Certification fee: $5.00 per document. Copy fee: $.50 per page.

Phone Search: Docket information available by phone if case number is known. An automated voice case information service (VCIS) is not available.

Fax Search: Will accept fax searches at $15.00 per name. Will fax docket listing at $.50 per page.

Mail Search: Always enclose a stamped self addressed envelope.

In Person Search: In person searching is available.

PACER: Sign-up number is 215-597-5710. Access fee is $.60 per minute. Toll-free access: 800-458-2993. Local access: 215-597-0258. Case records are available back to July 1, 1990. Records are never purged. New records are available online after 1 day. PACER is available on the Internet at http://pacer.paed.uscourts.gov.

Electronic Filing: Anyone may submit civil and criminal documents in electronic form; however, you must first fill out the application available on the web site. To register, dial 215-597-5861. To access the computer, dial 215-597-3773. Electronic filing information is available online at www.paed.uscourts.gov/us01003.shtml

Opinions Online: Call to register. Court opinions are available online at www.paed.uscourts.gov/contents.shtml

US Bankruptcy Court

Eastern District of Pennsylvania

Philadelphia Division 4th Floor, 900 Market St, Philadelphia, PA 19107, 215-408-2800.

www.paeb.uscourts.gov

Counties: Bucks, Chester, Delaware, Montgomery, Philadelphia.

Indexing & Storage: Cases are indexed by debtor and creditors as well as by case number. New cases are available in the index 1 day after filing date. A card index is maintained. A microfiche index is also maintained. Open records are located at this court.

Fee & Payment: The fee is $15.00 per item (one party name or case number). Payment may be made by money order, cashier check, business check, Visa or Mastercard. Personal checks are not accepted. Prepayment is required. Payee: Clerk, US Bankruptcy Court. Certification fee: $5.00 per document. Copy fee: $.50 per page. You are allowed to make your own copies. These copies cost $.25 per page. In person searchers may not search the card index.

Phone Search: An automated voice case information service (VCIS) is available. Call VCIS at 888-584-5853 or 215-597-2244.

Mail Search: Always enclose a stamped self addressed envelope.

In Person Search: In person searching is available.

PACER: Sign-up number is 800-676-6856. Access fee is $.60 per minute. Toll-free access: 888-381-2921. Local access: 215-597-3501. Case records are available back to 1988. Records are purged every 6 months. New civil records are available online after 1 day. PACER is available on the Internet at http://pacer.paeb.uscourts.gov.

Reading Division Suite 300, The Madison, 400 Washington St, Reading, PA 19601, 610-320-5255.

www.paeb.uscourts.gov

Counties: Berks, Lancaster, Lehigh, Northampton, Schuylkill.

Indexing & Storage: Cases are indexed by debtor as well as by case number. New cases are available in the index 1 day after filing date. Both computer and card indexes are maintained. Open records are located at this court.

Fee & Payment: The fee is $15.00 per item (one party name or case number). Payment may be made by money order, cashier check, business check, Visa or Mastercard. Personal checks are not accepted. Prepayment is required. Payee: Clerk, US Bankruptcy Court. Certification fee: $5.00 per document. Copy fee: $.50 per page.

Phone Search: Only docket information is available by phone. An automated voice case information service (VCIS) is available. Call VCIS at 888-584-5853 or 215-597-2244.

Mail Search: Always enclose a stamped self addressed envelope.

In Person Search: In person searching is available.

PACER: Sign-up number is 800-676-6856. Access fee is $.60 per minute. Toll-free access: 888-381-2921. Local access: 215-597-3501. Case records are available back to 1988. Records are purged every 6 months. New civil records are available online after 1 day. PACER is available on the Internet at http://pacer.paeb.uscourts.gov.

US District Court

Middle District of Pennsylvania

Harrisburg Division PO Box 983, Harrisburg, PA 17108-0983 (Courier Address: US Courthouse & Federal Bldg, 228 Walnut St, Harrisburg, PA 17108), 717-221-3920, Fax: 717-221-3959.

www.pamd.uscourts.gov

Counties: Adams, Cumberland, Dauphin, Franklin, Fulton, Huntingdon, Juniata, Lebanon, Mifflin, York.

Indexing & Storage: Cases are indexed by defendant and plaintiff as well as by case number. New cases are available in the index immediately after filing date. Both computer and card indexes are maintained. Open records are located at this court.

Fee & Payment: The fee is $15.00 per item (one party name or case number). Payment may be made by money order, cashier check, personal check, American Express, Visa, Mastercard. Prepayment is required. Payee: Clerk, US District Court. Certification fee: $5.00 per document. Copy fee: $.50 per page.

Phone Search: Only accession numbers for a specific case are available by phone.

Fax Search: Will accept fax search requests for $25.00. The fee is $1.00 per page.

Mail Search: A stamped self addressed envelope is not required.

In Person Search: In person searching is available.

PACER: Sign-up number is 800-676-6856. Access fee is $.60 per minute. Toll-free access: 800-658-8381. Local access: 570-347-8286, 570-341-0569. Case records are available back to May 1989. Records are never purged. New records are available online after 1 day. PACER is available on the Internet at http://pacer.pamd.uscourts.gov.

Scranton Division Clerk's Office, William J Nealon Fedearl Bldg & US Courthouse, PO Box 1148, Scranton, PA 18501 (Courier Address: 235 N Washington Ave, Room 101, Scranton, PA 18503), 570-207-5600, Fax: 717-207-5650.

www.pamd.uscourts.gov

Counties: Bradford, Carbon, Lackawanna, Luzerne, Monroe, Pike, Susquehanna, Wayne, Wyoming.

Indexing & Storage: Cases are indexed by defendant and plaintiff as well as by case number. New cases are available in the index 1 day after filing date. A computer index is maintained. Records are also indexed on microfiche. Records are stored on an in-house computer from 1989. Open records are located at this court. District wide searches are available for information from 1901 from this court.

Fee & Payment: The fee is $15.00 per item (one party name or case number). Payment may be made by money order, cashier check, personal check, Visa, Mastercard. Prepayment is required. Payee: Clerk, US District Court. Certification fee: $5.00 per document. Copy fee: $.50 per page.

Phone Search: Only minimal docket information will be released over the phone. An automated voice case information service (VCIS) is not available.

Fax Search: Will accept fax search with credit card number.

Mail Search: A stamped self addressed envelope is not required.

In Person Search: In person searching is available.

PACER: Sign-up number is 800-676-6856. Access fee is $.60 per minute. Toll-free access: 800-658-8381. Local access: 570-347-8286, 570-341-0569. Case records are available back to May 1989. Records are never purged. New records are available online after 1 day. PACER is available on the Internet at http://pacer.pamd.uscourts.gov.

Williamsport Division PO Box 608, Williamsport, PA 17703 (Courier Address: Federal Bldg, ROom 402, 240 W 3rd St, Williamsport, PA 17701), 570-323-6380, Fax: 717-323-0636.

www.pamd.uscourts.gov

Counties: Cameron, Centre, Clinton, Columbia, Lycoming, Montour, Northumberland, Perry, Potter, Snyder, Sullivan, Tioga, Union.

Indexing & Storage: Cases are indexed by defendant and plaintiff as well as by case number. New cases are available in the index immediately after filing date. A computer index is maintained. Open records are located at this court.

Fee & Payment: The fee is $15.00 per item (one party name or case number). Payment may be made by money order, cashier check, personal check, Visa, Mastercard. Prepayment is required. Payee: Clerk, US District Court. Certification fee: $5.00 per document. Copy fee: $.50 per page.

Phone Search: Only docket information is available by phone. An automated voice case information service (VCIS) is not available.

Fax Search: Fax requests require the original signature and prepayment.

Mail Search: Always enclose a stamped self addressed envelope.

In Person Search: In person searching is available.

PACER: Sign-up number is 800-676-6856. Access fee is $.60 per minute. Toll-free access: 800-658-8381. Local access: 570-347-8286, 570-341-0569. Case records are available back to May 1989. Records are never purged. New records are available online after 1 day. PACER is available on the Internet at http://pacer.pamd.uscourts.gov.

US Bankruptcy Court

Middle District of Pennsylvania

Harrisburg Division PO Box 908, Harrisburg, PA 17108 (Courier Address: 228 Walnut St, 3rd Floor, Harrisburg, PA 17101), 717-901-2800.

www.paeb.uscourts.gov

Counties: Adams, Centre, Cumberland, Dauphin, Franklin, Fulton, Huntingdon, Juniata, Lebanon, Mifflin, Montour, Northumberland, Perry, Schuylkill, Snyder, Union, York.

Indexing & Storage: Cases are indexed by debtor as well as by case number. New cases are available in the index 1 day after filing date. A computer index is maintained. Open records are located at this court.

Fee & Payment: The fee is $15.00 per item (one party name or case number). Payment may be made by money order, cashier check, personal check. Prepayment is required. Debtor's checks are not accepted. Payee: Clerk, US Bankruptcy Court. Certification fee: $5.00 per document. Copy fee: $.50 per page.

Phone Search: Only docket information is available by phone. An automated voice case information service (VCIS) is not available.

Mail Search: Always enclose a stamped self addressed envelope.

In Person Search: In person searching is available.

PACER: Sign-up number is 800-676-6856. Access fee is $.60 per minute. Toll-free access: 800-882-6899. Local access: 717-782-3727. Use of PC Anywhere v4.0 suggested. Case records are available back to August 1986. Records are never purged. New civil records are available online after 1 day. PACER is available on the Internet at http://pacer.paeb.uscourts.gov.

Wilkes-Barre Division Clerk's Office, Max Rosen US Courthouse, 197 S Main St, Wilkes-Barre, PA 18701, 570-826-6450.

www.paeb.uscourts.gov

Counties: Bradford, Cameron, Carbon, Clinton, Columbia, Lackawanna, Luzerne, Lycoming, Monroe, Pike, Potter, Schuylkill, Sullivan, Susquehanna, Tioga, Wayne, Wyoming.

Indexing & Storage: Cases are indexed by debtor as well as by case number. New cases are available in the index 1-3 days after filing date. A computer index is maintained. Open records are located at this court.

Fee & Payment: The fee is $15.00 per item (one party name or case number). Payment may be made by money order, cashier check, personal check. Debtor's checks are not accepted. Make checks payable to the Clerk for services other than copy services; for copies, make checks payable to Louise Cannon Copy Service. Payee: Clerk, US Bankruptcy Court. Certification fee: $5.00 per document. Copy fee: $.50 per page. You are allowed to make your own copies. These copies cost Not Applicable per page.

Phone Search: Phone searches can be done if the name, social security number, or case number is provided. Only docket information will be released. An automated voice case information service (VCIS) is not available.

Mail Search: Always enclose a stamped self addressed envelope.

In Person Search: In person searching is available.

PACER: Sign-up number is 800-676-6856. Access fee is $.60 per minute. Toll-free access: 800-640-3037. Local access: 570-821-4033. Use of PC Anywhere v4.0 suggested. Case records are available back to 1987. New civil records are available online after 1 day. PACER is available on the Internet at http://pacer.paeb.uscourts.gov.

US District Court

Western District of Pennsylvania

Erie Division PO Box 1820, Erie, PA 16507 (Courier Address: 102 US Courthouse, 617 State St, Erie, PA 16501), 814-453-4829.

www.pawd.uscourts.gov

Counties: Crawford, Elk, Erie, Forest, McKean, Venango, Warren.

Indexing & Storage: Cases are indexed by defendant and plaintiff as well as by case number. New cases are available in the index 1 day after filing date. The court prefers that you perform searches through the Pittsburgh Division. Both computer and card indexes are maintained. Open records are located at this court.

Fee & Payment: The fee is $15.00 per item (one party name or case number). Payment may be made by money order, cashier check, personal check, Visa, Mastercard. Prepayment is required. Payee: Clerk, US District Court. Certification fee: $5.00 per document. Copy fee: $.50 per page.

Phone Search: Only the number, caption and attorneys' names will be released over the phone. An automated voice case information service (VCIS) is not available.

Mail Search: Always enclose a stamped self addressed envelope.

In Person Search: In person searching is available.

PACER: Sign-up number is 800-676-6856. Access fee is $.60 per minute. Toll-free access: 800-770-4745. Local access: 412-644-6374. Case records are available back to 1989. Records are never purged. New records are available online after 1 day. PACER is available on the Internet at http://pacer.pawd.uscourts.gov.

Johnstown Division Penn Traffic Bldg, Room 208, 319 Washington St, Johnstown, PA 15901, 814-533-4504, Fax: 814-533-4519.

www.pawd.uscourts.gov

Counties: Bedford, Blair, Cambria, Clearfield, Somerset.

Indexing & Storage: Cases are indexed by defendant and plaintiff as well as by case number. New cases are available in the index 1 day after filing date. Both computer and card indexes are maintained. On computer since June 1992. Card index from 1989 to 1992. Open records are located at this court.

Fee & Payment: The fee is $15.00 per item (one party name or case number). Payment may be made by money order, cashier check, personal check, Visa. Prepayment is required. Payee: Clerk, US District Court. Certification fee: $5.00 per document. Copy fee: $.50 per page.

Phone Search: Only the number, caption and attorneys' names will be released over the phone.

An automated voice case information service (VCIS) is not available.

Mail Search: A stamped self addressed envelope is not required.

In Person Search: In person searching is available.

PACER: Sign-up number is 800-676-6856. Access fee is $.60 per minute. Toll-free access: 800-770-4745. Local access: 412-644-6374. Case records are available back to 1989. Records are never purged. New records are available online after 1 day. PACER is available on the Internet at http://pacer.pawd.uscourts.gov.

Pittsburgh Division US Post Office & Courthouse, Room 829, 7th Ave & Grant St, Pittsburgh, PA 15219, 412-644-3527.

www.pawd.uscourts.gov

Counties: Allegheny, Armstrong, Beaver, Butler, Clarion, Fayette, Greene, Indiana, Jefferson, Lawrence, Mercer, Washington, Westmoreland.

Indexing & Storage: Cases are indexed by defendant and plaintiff as well as by case number. New cases are available in the index 2 days after filing date. Both computer and card indexes are maintained. Open records are located at this court. The Erie and Johnstown Divisions send complete paper copies of case records to Pittsburgh, so that all case records for the District are available here.

Fee & Payment: The fee is $15.00 per item (one party name or case number). Payment may be made by money order, cashier check, personal check, Visa, Mastercard. Prepayment is required. Payee: Clerk, US District Court. Certification fee: $5.00 per document. Copy fee: $.50 per page.

Phone Search: Only docket information is available by phone. An automated voice case information service (VCIS) is not available.

Mail Search: Always enclose a stamped self addressed envelope.

In Person Search: In person searching is available.

PACER: Sign-up number is 800-676-6856. Access fee is $.60 per minute. Toll-free access: 800-770-4745. Local access: 412-644-6374. Case records are available back to 1989. Records are never purged. New records are available online after 1 day. PACER is available on the Internet at http://pacer.pawd.uscourts.gov.

US Bankruptcy Court

Western District of Pennsylvania

Erie Division 717 State St, #501, Erie, PA 16501, 814-453-7580.

www.pawb.uscourts.gov

Counties: Clarion, Crawford, Elk, Erie, Forest, Jefferson, McKean, Mercer, Venango, Warren.

Indexing & Storage: Cases are indexed by debtor as well as by case number. New cases are available in the index 1 day after filing date. A computer index is maintained. Open records are located at this court.

Fee & Payment: The fee is $15.00 per item (one party name or case number). Payment may be made by money order, cashier check, personal check. Prepayment is required. Payee: Clerk, US Bankruptcy Court. Certification fee: $5.00 per document. Copy fee: $.50 per page.

Phone Search: Docket information is available by phone. An automated voice case information service (VCIS) is available.

Mail Search: Always enclose a stamped self addressed envelope.

In Person Search: In person searching is available.

PACER: Sign-up number is 800-676-6856. Access fee is $.60 per minute. Toll-free access: 800-795-2829. Local access: 412-355-2588. Case records are available back to 1991. Records are purged every six months. New civil records are available online after 1 day. PACER is available on the Internet at http://pacer.pawb.uscourts.gov.

Pittsburgh Division 600 Grant St #5414, Pittsburgh, PA 15219-2801, 412-644-2700.

www.pawb.uscourts.gov

Counties: Allegheny, Armstrong, Beaver, Bedford, Blair, Butler, Cambria, Clearfield, Fayette, Greene, Indiana, Lawrence, Somerset, Washington, Westmoreland.

Indexing & Storage: Cases are indexed by debtor as well as by case number. New cases are available in the index 1 day after filing date. A computer index is maintained. Records are also indexed on microfiche. Open records are located at this court. District wide searches are available for information from 1986 from this division.

Fee & Payment: The fee is $15.00 per item (one party name or case number). Payment may be made by money order, personal check. Prepayment is required. Debtor's checks are not accepted. Payee: Clerk, US Bankruptcy Court. Certification fee: $5.00 per document. Copy fee: $.50 per page.

Phone Search: Docket information is available by phone. An automated voice case information service (VCIS) is available.

Mail Search: Always enclose a stamped self addressed envelope.

In Person Search: In person searching is available.

PACER: Sign-up number is 800-676-6856. Access fee is $.60 per minute. Toll-free access: 800-795-2829. Local access: 412-355-2588. Case records are available back to 1991. Records are purged every six months. New civil records are available online after 1 day. PACER is available on the Internet at http://pacer.pawb.uscourts.gov.

Court	Jurisdiction	No. of Courts	How Organized
Court of Common Pleas*	General	103	60 Districts
Philadelphia Municipal Court*	Municipal	1	1st District
Philadelphia Traffic Court	Municipal	1	1st District
Pittsburgh Magistrates Court	Municipal	1	Pittsburgh
Register of Wills*	Probate	67	
District Justice Courts	Limited	549	

* Profiled in this Sourcebook.

Court	CIVIL								
	Tort	Contract	Real Estate	Min. Claim	Max. Claim	Small Claims	Estate	Eviction	Domestic Relations
Court of Common Pleas*	X	X	X	$0	No Max			X	X
Philadelphia Municipal Court*	X	X	X	$0	$5000	$5000		X	X
Philadelphia Traffic Court									
Pittsburgh City Magistrates Court			X	$0	No Max				
Register of Wills*							X		
District Justice Courts	X	X	X	$0	$4000	$8000			

Court	CRIMINAL				
	Felony	Misdemeanor	DWI/DUI	Preliminary Hearing	Juvenile
Court of Common Pleas*	X	X	X		X
Philadelphia Municipal Court*	X	X	X	X	
Philadelphia Traffic Court					
Pittsburgh City Magistrates Court		X	X	X	
Register of Wills*					
District Justice Courts		X	X	X	

ADMINISTRATION
Administrative Office of Pennsylvania Courts, PO Box 719, Mechanicsburg, PA, 17055; 717-795-2000, Fax: 717-795-2050. www.courts.state.pa.us

COURT STRUCTURE
The civil records clerk of the Court of Common Pleas is called the Prothonotary. Small claims cases are, usually, handled by the District Justice Courts/Magistrates. However, all small claims actions are recorded through the Prothonotary Section (civil) of the Court of Common Pleas, which then holds the records. It is not necessary to check with each District Justice Court, but rather to check with the Prothonotary for the county.

Probate is handled by the Register of Wills.

ONLINE ACCESS
Pennsylvania has an online computer system for internal access only to criminal cases for the District Justice Courts, though some courts provide remote online access systems.

ADDITIONAL INFORMATION
Fees vary widely among jurisdictions. Many courts will not conduct searches due to a lack of personnel or, if they do search, turnaround time may be excessively lengthy. Many courts have public access terminals for in-person searches.

Adams County

Court of Common Pleas – Civil 111-117 Baltimore St Rm 104, Gettysburg, PA 17325; 717-334-6781 X285. Hours: 8AM-4:30PM (EST). *Civil, Eviction.*

Civil Records: Access: Mail, in person. Both court and visitors may perform in person searches. No search fee. Required to search: name, years to search. Civil cases indexed by defendant, plaintiff. Civil records on computer from 1988, some microfiche (dates unsure), on index from 1800s. **General Information:** No mental health, sealed records released. SASE required. Turnaround time 1-2 days. Copy fee: $.25 per page. Certification fee: $3.00 plus $1.00 per page. Fee payee: Prothonotary. Personal checks accepted. Prepayment is required. Public access terminal is available.

Court of Common Pleas-Criminal 111-117 Baltimore St, Gettysburg, PA 17325; 717-337-9806. Hours: 8AM-4:30PM (EST). *Felony, Misdemeanor.* **Criminal Records:** Access: Mail, in person. Both court and visitors may perform in person searches. Search fee: $5.00 per name. Required to search: name, years to search, DOB. Criminal records on computer since 1985, on microfiche since 1974, previous records on microfilm. **General Information:** No juvenile records released. SASE required. Turnaround time 1 day. Copy fee: $.25 per page. Certification fee: $5.00. Fee payee: Clerk of Courts. Personal checks accepted. No third party checks. Prepayment is required.

Register of Wills 111-117 Baltimore St Rm 102, Gettysburg, PA 17325; 717-337-9826; Fax: 717-334-1758. Hours: 8AM-4:30PM (EST). *Probate.*

Allegheny County

Court of Common Pleas - Civil City County Bldg, 414 Grant St, First Floor, Pittsburgh, PA 15219; 412-350-4200; Fax: 412-350-5260. Hours: 8:30AM-4:30PM (EST). *Civil, Eviction.*

Civil Records: Access: Mail, in person. Both court and visitors may perform in person searches. Search fee: $25.00 per name. Required to search: name, years to search. Civil cases indexed by defendant, plaintiff. Civil records in card file for 5 years, archived from 1700s. **General Information:** No juvenile records released. SASE required. Turnaround time 10 days. Copy fee: $1.00 per page. Certification fee: $8.00. Fee payee: Prothonotary of Allegheny County. Business checks accepted. Prepayment is required. Business accounts may set up a draw down account. Public access terminal is available.

Court of Common Pleas-Criminal 220 Courthouse, 436 Grant Street, Pittsburgh, PA 15219; 412-355-5378. Hours: 8:30AM-4:30PM (EST). *Felony, Misdemeanor.* **Criminal Records:** Access: Mail, in person. Both court and visitors may perform in person searches. Search fee: $15.00 per name. Required to search: name, years to search, DOB; also helpful-SSN. Criminal records on files, microfilm. **General Information:** All records public. SASE required. Turnaround time 2 days. Copy fee: $.50 per page. Certification fee: $10.00. Fee payee: Clerk of Courts. Personal checks accepted. Prepayment is required.

Register of Wills 414 Grant St, City County Bldg, PIttsburgh, PA 15219; 412-350-4183. Hours: 8:30AM-4:30PM (EST). *Probate.*

www.info.co.alleghany.pa.us

Armstrong County

Court of Common Pleas - Civil 500 E Market St, Kittanning, PA 16201; 724-548-3251; Fax: 724-548-3236. Hours: 8AM-4:30PM (EST). *Civil, Eviction.*

Civil Records: Access: In person only. Court does not conduct in person searches; visitors must perform searches for themselves. Search fee: No civil searches performed by court. Required to search: name, years to search. Civil cases indexed by defendant, plaintiff. Civil records on files, microfiche since 1930. **General Information:** No juvenile, civil committment records released. Copy fee: $1.00 per page. Certification fee: $3.00. Fee payee: Nancy E Heilman, Prothonotary. Personal checks accepted. Prepayment is required. Public access terminal is available.

Court of Common Pleas-Criminal 500 Market St, Kittanning, PA 16201; 724-548-3252. Hours: 8AM-4:30PM (EST). *Felony, Misdemeanor.* **Criminal Records:** Access: Mail, in person. Both court and visitors may perform in person searches. Search fee: $10.00 per name. Required to search: name, years to search; also helpful-DOB, SSN. Criminal records in card file from early 1900s. **General Information:** No juvenile or mental health records released. SASE required. Turnaround time same day. Copy fee: $1.00 per page. Certification fee: $5.00. Fee payee: Clerk of Courts. Personal checks accepted. Prepayment is required. Public access terminal is available.

Register of Wills 500 Market St, Kittanning, PA 16201; 724-548-3256; Fax: 724-548-3236. Hours: 8AM-4:30PM (EST). *Probate.*

Beaver County

Court of Common Pleas - Civil Beaver County Courthouse, 3rd St, Beaver, PA 15009; 724-728-5700. Hours: 8:30AM-4:30PM (EST). *Civil, Eviction.*

Civil Records: Access: Mail, in person. Both court and visitors may perform in person searches. No search fee. Required to search: name, years to search. Civil cases indexed by defendant, plaintiff. Civil records on computer since 1995. **General Information:** No sealed records released. Turnaround time 1 week. Copy fee: $.25 per page. Certification fee: No certification fee. Fee payee: Prothonotary. Personal checks accepted. Prepayment is required. Public access terminal is available.

Court of Common Pleas-Criminal Beaver County Courthouse, 810 3rd St, Beaver, PA 15009; 724-728-5700; Fax: 724-728-8853. Hours: 8:30AM-4:30PM (EST). *Felony, Misdemeanor.* **Criminal Records:** Access: Mail, in person. Both court and visitors may perform in person searches. Search fee: $10.00 per name. Required to search: name, years to search; also helpful-DOB, SSN. Criminal records on computer from 1973, on microfiche since 1802. **General Information:** Records sealed by court order not released. SASE required. Turnaround time 1 week. Copy fee: $.50 per page. Certification fee: $5.00. Fee payee: Clerk of Courts Office. Personal checks accepted. Prepayment is required. Fax notes: $1.00 per page.

Register of Wills Beaver County Courthouse, 3rd St, Beaver, PA 15009; 724-728-5700; Fax: 724-728-9810. Hours: 8:30AM-4:30PM (EST). *Probate.*

Bedford County

Court of Common Pleas - Criminal/Civil Bedford County Courthouse, Bedford, PA 15522; 814-623-4833; Fax: 814-623-4831. Hours: 8:30AM-4:30PM (EST). *Felony, Misdemeanor, Civil, Eviction.*

Civil Records: Access: Mail, in person. Both court and visitors may perform in person searches. Search fee: $12.00 per name. Required to search: name, years to search. Civil cases indexed by defendant, plaintiff. Civil records on file from late 1700s. **Criminal Records:** Access: Mail, in person. Both court and visitors may perform in person searches. Search fee: $10.00 per name. Required to search: name, years to search, DOB. Criminal records on file from late 1700s. **General Information:** No sex related or juvenile released. SASE required. Turnaround time 2 weeks. Copy fee: $.50 per page. Certification fee: $3.00. Fee payee: Prothonotary of Beford County. Personal checks accepted. Prepayment is required.

Register of Wills 200 S Juliana St, Bedford, PA 15522; 814-623-4836; Fax: 814-624-0488. Hours: 8:30AM-4:30PM (EST). *Probate.*

Berks County

Court of Common Pleas - Civil 2nd Floor, 633 Court St, Reading, PA 19601; 610-478-6970; Fax: 610-478-6969. Hours: 8AM-4PM (EST). *Civil, Eviction.*

Civil Records: Access: Fax, mail, online, in person. Both court and visitors may perform in person searches. Search fee: No civil searches performed by court. Required to search: name, years to search. Civil cases indexed by defendant, plaintiff. Civil records partially on microfiche, on manual index files from 1750. Mail access limited to docket information only. The Registry of Wills has a free searchable website at www.berksregofwills.com which includes marriage, estate, birth and death records for the county. The estate and marriage records are current. **General Information:** No mental, sealed records released. SASE required. Turnaround time 1-2 days. Copy fee: $.50 per page. Certification fee: $3.75. Fee payee: Prothonotary. Personal checks accepted. Prepayment is required. Public access terminal is available. Fax notes: $5.00 for first page, $1.00 each addl. For emergency use only.

Court of Common Pleas-Criminal 4th Floor, 633 Court St, Reading, PA 19601; 610-478-6550; Fax: 610-478-6570. Hours: 8AM-5PM (EST). *Felony, Misdemeanor.* **Criminal Records:** Access: In person only. Court does not conduct in person searches; visitors must perform searches for themselves. Search fee: No criminal searches performed by court. Required to search: name, years to search; also helpful-DOB, SSN. Criminal records on computer from 1992, in files from 1988, prior archived. **General Information:** No juvenile records released. Copy fee: $.25 per page. Add $1.00 for each 10 page after first 10. Certification fee: $5.00. Fee payee: Berks County Clerk of Courts. Only cashiers checks and money orders accepted. Credit cards accepted. Accepted for payments on criminal cases only. Public access terminal is available.

Register of Wills 633 Court St 2nd Floor, Reading, PA 19601; 610-478-6600; Fax: 610-478-6251. Hours: 8AM-5PM (EST). *Probate.*

www.berksregofwills.com

Blair County

Court of Common Pleas - Criminal/Civil 412 Allegheny Street, Hollidaysburg, PA 16648; 814-693-3080. Hours: 8AM-4:30PM (EST). *Felony, Misdemeanor, Civil, Eviction.*

Civil Records: Access: In person only. Court does not conduct in person searches; visitors must perform searches for themselves. Search fee: No civil searches performed by court. Required to search: name, years to search. Civil cases indexed by defendant, plaintiff. Civil records on computer from 1989, on index books from 1846 to 1989. **Criminal Records:** Access: Mail, in person. Both court and visitors may perform in person searches. Search fee: $10.00 per name. Required to search: name, years to search, DOB; also helpful-SSN. Criminal records on computer from 1989, on index books from 1846 to 1989. **General Information:** No adoption records released. SASE required. Turnaround time 2 days. Copy fee: $.50 per page. Certification fee: $3.00. Fee payee: Blair County Prothonotary. Personal checks accepted. Prepayment is required. Public access terminal is available.

Register of Wills 423 Allegheny #145, Hollidaysburg, PA 16648-2022; 814-693-3095. Hours: 8AM-4PM (EST). *Probate.*

Bradford County

Court of Common Pleas - Criminal/Civil Courthouse, 301 Main St, Towanda, PA 18848; 570-265-1705. Hours: 9AM-5PM (EST). *Felony, Misdemeanor, Civil, Eviction.*

Civil Records: Access: Mail, in person. Both court and visitors may perform in person searches. Search fee: $5.00 per name. Required to search: name, years to search. Civil cases indexed by defendant, plaintiff. Civil records on computer from 1986, on microfiche from mid 1800s, archived from mid-1940s. **Criminal Records:** Access: Mail, in person. Both court and visitors may perform in person searches. Search fee: $5.00 per name. Required to search: name, years to search, DOB. Criminal records on computer from 1986, on microfiche from mid 1800s, archived from mid-1940s. **General Information:** SASE required. Turnaround time 1-2 days. Copy fee: $.25 per page. Certification fee: $3.00. $5.00 for criminal records. Fee payee: Prothonotary. Personal checks accepted. Prepayment is required. Public access terminal is available.

Register of Wills 301 Main St., Towanda, PA 18848; 570-265-1702. Hours: 9AM-5PM (EST). *Probate.*

Bucks County

Court of Common Pleas - Civil 55 E Court St, Doylestown, PA 18901; 215-348-6191. Hours: 8:15AM-4:15PM (EST). *Civil, Eviction.*

www.buckscounty.org

Civil Records: Access: online, in person. Court does not conduct in person searches; visitors must perform searches for themselves. Search fee: No civil searches performed by court. Required to search: name, years to search. Civil cases indexed by defendant, plaintiff. Civil records on computer from 1980, prior on dockets. Online access requires a Sprint ID ($24). The per minute fee is $.60 with a 2 minute minimum. The system is open 8am to 9pm during the week. Contact Jack Morris at 215-348-6579 for more information. **General Information:** No mental, sealed records

released. Copy fee: $.25 per page. Certification fee: $3.00 per page. Fee payee: Prothonotary. Personal checks accepted. Prepayment is required. Public access terminal is available.

Court of Common Pleas-Criminal Bucks County Courthouse, Doylestown, PA 18901; 215-348-6389; Fax: 215-348-6740. Hours: 8AM-4:30PM (EST). *Felony, Misdemeanor.* **Criminal Records:** Access: Mail, remote online, in person. Both court and visitors may perform in person searches. Search fee: $5.00 per name. Required to search: name, years to search, DOB. Criminal records on computer from 1980, some records on microfiche, on card index from 1932 to 1979. Contact Jack Morris at 215-348-6579 for information about remote access. Fees include $24 annual subscription and $.60 per minute, 2 minute minimum. The system is open 8am to 9pm M-F and 8am to 5pm on weekends. Search by name or case number. **General Information:** No sealed, juvenile or mental records released. SASE required. Turnaround time same day. No copy fee. Certification fee: $5.00. Fee payee: Clerk of Courts Criminal Division. Personal checks accepted. Public access terminal is available.

Register of Wills Bucks County Courthouse, Doylestown, PA 18901; 215-348-6265; Fax: 215-348-6156. Hours: 8:15AM-4:15PM M-F; 8:15AM-7:30PM 1st & 3rd Wed of month (EST). *Probate.*

Butler County

Court of Common Pleas - Civil Butler County Courthouse, PO Box 1208, Butler, PA 16001-1208; 724-284-5214. Hours: 8:30AM-4:30PM (EST). *Civil, Eviction.*

Civil Records: Access: In person. Court does not conduct in person searches; visitors must perform searches for themselves. Search fee: No civil searches performed by court. Required to search: name, years to search. Civil cases indexed by defendant, plaintiff. Civil records on computer from 1993, prior on files. **General Information:** No mental records released. Copy fee: $.25 per page. Certification fee: $3.00. Fee payee: Prothonotary. Personal checks accepted. Prepayment is required. Public access terminal is available.

Court of Common Pleas-Criminal Butler County Courthouse, PO Box 1208, Butler, PA 16003-1208; 724-284-5233; Fax: 724-284-5244. Hours: 8:30AM-4:30PM (EST). *Felony, Misdemeanor.* **Criminal Records:** Access: Mail, remote online, in person. Both court and visitors may perform in person searches. Search fee: $10.00 per name. Required to search: name, DOB; also helpful-years to search, SSN. original records in office for 10 years. Computerized from 1988 to present, prior in Russell Index. Call Infocon Corp. at 814-472-6066 for more information about the remote online system. **General Information:** No mental, sealed, juvenile (16 & under) victim records released. SASE required. Turnaround time 1-2 days. Copy fee: $.25 per page. Certification fee: $5.00 per page. Fee payee: Clerk of Courts. Personal checks accepted. Prepayment is required. Public access terminal is available.

Register of Wills Butler County Courthouse, PO Box 1208, Butler, PA 16003-1208; 724-284-5348; Fax: 724-284-5278. Hours: 8:30AM-4:30PM (EST). *Probate.*

Cambria County

Court of Common Pleas - Civil 200 S Center St, Ebensburg, PA 15931; 814-472-1636; Fax: 814-472-2353. Hours: 9AM-4PM (EST). *Civil, Eviction.*

Civil Records: Access: Mail, in person. Both court and visitors may perform in person searches. No search fee. Required to search: name, years to search. Civil cases indexed by defendant, plaintiff. Civil records on computer from 1/1/94, prior on dockets from 1800s. **General Information:** No divorce or mental records released. SASE requested. Copy fee: $.25 per page. Certification fee: $3.00. Fee payee: Prothonotary. Personal checks accepted. Prepayment is required. Public access terminal is available.

Court of Common Pleas-Criminal Cambria County Courthouse S Center St, Ebensburg, PA 15931; 814-472-1540. Hours: 9AM-4PM (EST). *Felony, Misdemeanor.* **Criminal Records:** Access: Mail, in person. Only the court conducts in person searches; visitors may not. Search fee: $3.00 per name. Required to search: name, years to search, DOB; also helpful-SSN. Criminal records are computerized, indexed from 1800s. **General Information:** No sealed or child victim records released. SASE required. Turnaround time 3 days. Copy fee: $.40 per page. Certification fee: $5.00. Fee payee: Clerk of Court. Personal checks accepted. Third party checks not accepted. Prepayment is required.

Register of Wills 200 S Center St, Ebensburg, PA 15931; 814-472-5440 X1440; Fax: 814-472-0762. Hours: 9AM-4PM (EST). *Probate.*

Cameron County

Court of Common Pleas - Civil Cameron County Courthouse, East 5th St, Emporium, PA 15834; 814-486-3355; Fax: 814-468-0464. Hours: 8:30AM-4:30PM (EST). *Civil, Eviction.*

Civil Records: Access: Phone, fax, mail, in person. Both court and visitors may perform in person searches. Search fee: $15.00 per name. Required to search: name, years to search. Civil cases indexed by defendant, plaintiff. Civil records on computer from 1988, archived from 1860 to present. **General Information:** No adoption, military discharge records released. SASE required. Turnaround time same day. Copy fee: $.50 per page. Certification fee: $5.00. Fee payee: Prothonotary. Personal checks accepted. Credit cards accepted: Visa, Mastercard. Will bill fees with prior permission form Clerk. Public access terminal is available. Fax notes: $1.00 per page.

Court of Common Pleas-Criminal 20 East 5th St, Emporium, PA 15834; 814-486-3349; Fax: 814-486-0464. Hours: 8:30AM-4PM (EST). *Felony, Misdemeanor.* **Criminal Records:** Access: Phone, fax, mail, in person. Both court and visitors may perform in person searches. Search fee: $15.00 per name. Required to search: name, years to search; also helpful-address, DOB, SSN. Criminal records archived from 1860. **General Information:** No juvenile, mental health records released. SASE required. Turnaround time same day. Copy fee: $.50 per page. Certification fee: $5.00. Fee payee: Clerk of Court. Personal checks accepted. Credit cards accepted: Visa, Mastercard. Prepayment is required. Fax notes: $1.00 per page.

Register of Wills Cameron County Courthouse, East 5th St., Emporium, PA 15834; 814-486-3355; Fax: 814-486-0464. Hours: 8:30AM-4PM (EST). *Probate.*

Carbon County

Court of Common Pleas - Civil PO
Box 127, Courthouse, Jim Thorpe, PA 18229; 570-325-2481; Fax: 570-325-8047. Hours: 8:30AM-4:30PM (EST). *Civil, Eviction.*

www.aopc.org/counties/carbon

Civil Records: Access: In person only. Court does not conduct in person searches; visitors must perform searches for themselves. Search fee: No civil searches performed by court. Required to search: name. Civil cases indexed by defendant, plaintiff. Civil records on computer from 1/84, financing statements from 1/87, on microfiche from 1/84, prior archived. **General Information:** No abuse, mental health records released. Copy fee: $1.00 per page. Certification fee: $7.50. Fee payee: Prothonotary of Carbon County. Personal checks accepted. Prepayment is required. Public access terminal is available.

Court of Common Pleas-Criminal
County Courthouse, Jim Thorpe, PA 18229; 570-325-3637; Fax: 570-325-5705. Hours: 8:30AM-4PM (EST). *Felony, Misdemeanor.* **Criminal Records:** Access: Phone, mail, in person. Only the court conducts in person searches; visitors may not. No search fee. Required to search: name, years to search, DOB; also helpful-SSN. Criminal records on computer from 1973, on microfiche from 1800. **General Information:** No juvenile, mental health records released. SASE required. Turnaround time 1 day. Certification fee: $5.00. Fee payee: Clerk of Courts Carbon County. Personal checks accepted.

Register of Wills PO Box 286, Jim Thorpe,
PA 18229; 570-325-2261; Fax: 570-325-5098. Hours: 8:30AM-4:30PM (EST). *Probate.*

Centre County

Court of Common Pleas - Criminal/Civil Centre County Courthouse,
Bellefonte, PA 16823; 814-355-6796. Hours: 8:30AM-5PM (EST). *Felony, Misdemeanor, Civil, Eviction.*

http://countrystore.org/webpages/county/223.htm

Civil Records: Access: Phone, mail, in person. Both court and visitors may perform in person searches. Search fee: $7.00 per name. Required to search: name, years to search. Civil cases indexed by defendant, plaintiff. Civil records on computer from 7-1-94, on card files and docket books from 1986, on microfiche and archived from 1800 to 1986. **Criminal Records:** Access: Phone, mail, in person. Both court and visitors may perform in person searches. Search fee: $7.00 per name. Required to search: name, years to search, DOB. Criminal records on computer from 7-1-94, on card files and docket books from 1986, on microfiche and archived from 1800 to 1986. **General Information:** No sex related, juvenile, mental records released. SASE helpful. Turnaround time 3-5 days. Copy fee: $.50 per page. Certification fee: $4.00. Fee payee: Clerk of Court. Personal checks accepted. Prepayment is required. Public access terminal is available.

Register of Wills Willowbank Office Bldg,
414 Holmes Ave #2, Bellefonte, PA 16823; 814-355-6724. Hours: 8:30AM-5PM (EST). *Probate.*

www.countrystore.org/county/224.htm

Chester County

Court of Common Pleas - Civil 2
North High St, Ste 130, West Chester, PA 19380; 610-344-6300. Hours: 8:30AM-4:30PM (EST). *Civil, Eviction.*

www.chesco.org

Civil Records: Access: online, in person. Court does not conduct in person searches; visitors must perform searches for themselves. Search fee: No civil searches performed by court. Required to search: name, years to search. Civil cases indexed by defendant, plaintiff. Civil records on dockets from 1985 to present, on microfiche from 1981 to 1984, archived from 1700s. Internet access to Chester County countywide records including court records requires a sign-up and credit card payment. Application fee is $50. There is a $10.00 per month minimum (no charge for no activity); and $.10 each transaction beyond 100. Sign-up and/or logon at http://epin.chesco.org/. **General Information:** No sealed records released. Copy fee: $.25 per page. Certification fee: $3.00. Fee payee: Prothonotary. Business checks accepted. b. Prepayment is required. Public access terminal is available.

Court of Common Pleas - Criminal 2
North High St #160, West Chester, PA 19380; 610-344-6135. Hours: 8:30AM-4:30PM (EST). *Felony, Misdemeanor.*

www.chesco.org **Criminal Records:** Access: Mail, remote online, in person. Both court and visitors may perform in person searches. Search fee: $10.00 per name. Required to search: name, years to search; also helpful-DOB. Criminal records on computer and microfiche from mid-70s, archived from the 1700s. Internet access to Chester County countywide records including court records requires a sign-up and credit card payment. Application fee is $50. There is a $10.00 per month minimum (no charge for no activity); and $.10 each transaction beyond 100. Sign-up and/or logon at http://epin.chesco.org/. **General Information:** No juvenile records released. Turnaround time 1 day. Copy fee: $1.00 per page. Certification fee: $5.00. Fee payee: Clerk of Courts. Business checks accepted. Prepayment is required. Public access terminal is available.

Register of Wills 2 North High St, Suite 109,
West Chester, PA 19380-3073; 610-344-6335; Fax: 610-344-6218. Hours: 8:30AM-4:30PM (EST). *Probate.*

Clarion County

Court of Common Pleas - Civil Clarion
County Courthouse, Main St, Clarion, PA 16214; 814-226-1119; Fax: 814-226-8069. Hours: 8:30AM-4:30PM (EST). *Civil, Eviction.*

Civil Records: Access: Phone, fax, mail, in person. Both court and visitors may perform in person searches. Search fee: $10.00 per name. Required to search: name, years to search. Civil cases indexed by defendant, plaintiff. Civil records on computer from mid-1990s, on dockets from 1800s. **General Information:** No juvenile, mental health records released. No copy fee. Certification fee: $5.00. Fee payee: Prothonotary. Personal checks accepted. Prepayment is required. Public access terminal is available. Fax notes: No fee to fax results.

Court of Common Pleas-Criminal
Clarion County Courthouse, Main St, Clarion, PA 16214; 814-226-4000; Fax: 814-226-8069. Hours: 8AM-4:30PM (EST). *Felony, Misdemeanor.*
Criminal Records: Access: Phone, fax, mail, in

person. Both court and visitors may perform in person searches. Search fee: $10.00 per name. Required to search: name, years to search, DOB. Criminal records on computer and microfiche from 1990, on docket books from 1800s. **General Information:** No juvenile, mental health records released. Turnaround time same day. Copy fee: $.50 per page. Certification fee: $5.00. Fee payee: Clerk of Court. Personal checks accepted. Public access terminal is available. Fax notes: No fee to fax results.

Register of Wills Clarion County Courthouse,
Corner of 5th & Main, Clarion, PA 16214; 814-226-4000 X2500; Fax: 814-226-8069. Hours: 8:30AM-4:30PM (EST). *Probate.*

Clearfield County

Court of Common Pleas - Criminal/Civil 1 N 2nd St, Clearfield, PA
16830; 814-765-2641 X1330; Fax: 814-765-7659. Hours: 8:30AM-4PM (EST). *Felony, Misdemeanor, Civil, Eviction.*

Civil Records: Access: Mail, in person. Both court and visitors may perform in person searches. Search fee: $5.00 per name, 5-years seach. Required to search: name, years to search; also helpful-address. Civil cases indexed by defendant, plaintiff. Civil records indexed (Russell System) on dockets from 1820s. **Criminal Records:** Access: Mail, in person. Both court and visitors may perform in person searches. Search fee: $5.00 per name, 5-year search. Required to search: name, years to search, address, DOB, SSN, signed release. Criminal records indexed (Russell System) on dockets from 1820s. **General Information:** No juvenile, sealed or mental health records released. Turnaround time 2 days. Copy fee: $.25 per page. Certification fee: $1.50. Fee payee: Prothonotary. Personal checks accepted. Prepayment is required.

Register of Wills & Clerk of Orphans
Court PO Box 361, Clearfield, PA 16830; 814-765-2641 X1351; Fax: 814-765-6089. Hours: 8:30AM-4PM (EST). *Probate.*

Clinton County

Court of Common Pleas - Criminal/Civil 230 E Water St, Lock Haven,
PA 17745; 570-893-4007. Hours: 8:30AM-5PM (EST). *Felony, Misdemeanor, Civil, Eviction.*

Civil Records: Access: In person only. Court does not conduct in person searches; visitors must perform searches for themselves. Search fee: No civil searches performed by court. Required to search: name, years to search. Civil cases indexed by defendant, plaintiff. Civil records on computer from 1992, on files from 1839. **Criminal Records:** Access: In person only. Court does not conduct in person searches; visitors must perform searches for themselves. Search fee: No criminal searches performed by court. Required to search: name, years to search, DOB, SSN, signed release. Criminal records on computer from 1992, on files from 1839. **General Information:** No sealed, mental health or minor victim abuse cases records released. Copy fee: $.50 per page. Certification fee: $4.00. Fee payee: Clerk of Court or Prothonotary. Personal checks accepted. Will bill Federal Liens fees. Public access terminal is available.

Register of Wills PO Box 943, Lock Haven,
PA 17745; 570-893-4010. Hours: 8:30AM-5PM M,T,Th,F; 8AM-12:30PM Wed (EST). *Probate.*

Columbia County

SASE required. Turnaround time less than one week. Copy fee: $.50 per page. Computer page $1.00 per page. Certification fee: $3.00. Fee payee: Prothonotary. Personal checks accepted. Prepayment is required. Public access terminal is available.

Court of Common Pleas-Criminal Erie County Courthouse, 140 West 6th St, Erie, PA 16501; 814-451-6229; Fax: 814-451-6420. Hours: 8:30AM-4:30PM (EST). *Felony, Misdemeanor.* **Criminal Records:** Access: Mail, in person. Both court and visitors may perform in person searches. Search fee: $10.00 per name. Required to search: name, years to search, DOB. Criminal records on computer from 1992, on docket index from 1951, on files from 1800s. **General Information:** No juvenile or ARD records released. SASE not required. Turnaround time 1 week. Copy fee: $.10 per page. Certification fee: No certification fee. Fee payee: Clerk of Courts. Personal checks accepted. Prepayment is required. Public access terminal is available.

Register of Wills Erie County Courthouse 140 W 6th St, Erie, PA 16501; 814-451-6260. Hours: 8:30AM-4:30PM (EST). *Probate.*

Fayette County

Court of Common Pleas-Civil 61 East Main St, Uniontown, PA 15401; 724-430-1272; Fax: 724-430-4555. Hours: 8AM-4:30PM (EST). *Civil, Eviction.*

Civil Records: Access: Mail, in person. Both court and visitors may perform in person searches. Search fee: $5.00 per name. Required to search: name, years to search. Civil cases indexed by defendant, plaintiff. Civil records on computer from 1992, archived from 1700s. **General Information:** No mental records released. SASE not required. Turnaround time 2 weeks. Copy fee: $.50 per page. Certification fee: $10.00. Fee payee: Prothonotary. Personal checks accepted. Prepayment is required.

Court of Common Pleas-Criminal 61 East Main St, Uniontown, PA 15401; 724-430-1253; Fax: 724-438-8410. Hours: 8AM-4:30PM (EST). *Felony, Misdemeanor.* **Criminal Records:** Access: Fax, mail, in person. Both court and visitors may perform in person searches. Search fee: $10.00 per name; $20.00 for 5-years search; $30.00 for 5-yr. plus. Required to search: name, years to search, DOB; also helpful-SSN. Criminal records on computer from 1993, on files from 1800s. **General Information:** No sex related or juvenile records released. SASE not required. Turnaround time 5-10 days. Copy fee: $.50 per page. Certification fee: $16.50. Fee payee: Clerk of Courts. Personal checks accepted. Prepayment is required. Public access terminal is available. Fax notes: $3.00 per document.

Register of Wills 61 East Main St, Uniontown, PA 15401; 724-430-1206. Hours: 8AM-4:30PM (EST). *Probate.*

Forest County

Court of Common Pleas-Criminal/Civil Forest County Courthouse, PO Box 423, Tionesta, PA 16353; 814-755-3526; Fax: 814-755-8837. Hours: 9AM-4PM (EST). *Felony, Misdemeanor, Civil, Eviction, Probate.*

Note: Includes the Register of Wills

Civil Records: Access: Mail, in person. Both court and visitors may perform in person searches. No search fee. Required to search: name, years to search. Civil cases indexed by defendant, plaintiff.

Civil records on dockets since 1995, archived from 1800s. **Criminal Records:** Access: Mail, in person. Both court and visitors may perform in person searches. Search fee: $10.00 per name. Required to search: name, years to search; also helpful-DOB, SSN. Criminal records on dockets since 1995, archived from 1800s. **General Information:** No adoption records released. SASE required. Turnaround time same day. Copy fee: $2.00 per page. Certification fee: $3.00. Fee payee: Annette M Kiefer. Personal checks accepted. Prepayment is required. Public access terminal is available.

Franklin County

Court of Common Pleas-Civil 157 Lincoln Way East, Chambersburg, PA 17201; 717-261-3858; Fax: 717-264-6772. Hours: 8:30AM-4:30PM (EST). *Civil, Eviction.*

Civil Records: Access: In person only. Court does not conduct in person searches; visitors must perform searches for themselves. Search fee: No civil searches performed by court. Required to search: name, years to search. Civil cases indexed by defendant, plaintiff. Civil records on file from 1985. **General Information:** No mental records released. Copy fee: $1.00 per page. Certification fee: $3.00. Fee payee: Prothonotary or Linda L Beard. Personal checks accepted. Prepayment is required.

Court of Common Pleas-Criminal 157 Lincoln Way East, Chambersburg, PA 17201; 717-261-3805; Fax: 717-261-3896. Hours: 8:30AM-4:30PM (EST). *Felony, Misdemeanor.* **Criminal Records:** Access: Mail, in person. Both court and visitors may perform in person searches. Search fee: $10.00 per name. Required to search: name, years to search, DOB. Criminal records on files for 50 years, archived from 1800s. **General Information:** No juvenile records released. SASE requested. Turnaround time same day. Copy fee: $.25 per page. Certification fee: $5.00. Fee payee: Clerk of Courts. Personal checks accepted. Prepayment is required. Public access terminal is available.

Register of Wills 157 Lincoln Way East, Chambersburg, PA 17201; 717-261-3872; Fax: 717-267-3438. Hours: 8:30AM-4:30PM (EST). *Probate.*

Fulton County

Court of Common Pleas-Criminal/Civil Fulton County Courthouse, 201 N 2nd St, McConnellsburg, PA 17233; 717-485-4212; Fax: 717-485-5568 Attn: Court of Common Pleas. Hours: 8:30AM-4:30PM (EST). *Felony, Misdemeanor, Civil, Eviction.*

Civil Records: Access: Fax, mail, in person. Both court and visitors may perform in person searches. Search fee: $5.00 per name. Required to search: name, years to search. Civil cases indexed by defendant, plaintiff. Civil records on docket index from 1850s. **Criminal Records:** Access: Mail, in person. Both court and visitors may perform in person searches. Search fee: $5.00 per name. Required to search: name, years to search. Criminal records on docket index from 1850s. **General Information:** No juvenile, adoption records released. SASE required. Turnaround time 3-5 days. Copy fee: $.25 per page. Certification fee: $5.00. Fee payee: Prothonotary. Personal checks accepted. Prepayment is required. Public access terminal is available. Fax notes: $5.00 per document.

Register of Wills 201 N 2nd St, McConnellsburg, PA 17233; 717-485-4212; Fax: 717-485-5568. Hours: 8:30AM-4:30PM (EST). *Probate.*

Greene County

Court of Common Pleas Greene County Courthouse, Room 105, Waynesburg, PA 15370; 724-852-5289. Hours: 8:30AM-4:30PM (EST). *Civil, Eviction.*

Civil Records: Access: Mail, in person. Court does not conduct in person searches; visitors must perform searches for themselves. Search fee:. Required to search: name, years to search. Civil cases indexed by defendant, plaintiff. Civil records on index from 1948. **General Information:** No mental health records released. SASE required. Turnaround time 1 week. Copy fee: $.50 per page. Certification fee: $6.00. Fee payee: Prothonotary. Personal checks accepted. Prepayment is required. Public access terminal is available.

Court of Common Pleas-Criminal Greene County Courthouse, Waynesburg, PA 15370; 724-852-5281; Fax: 724-627-4716. Hours: 8:30AM-4:30PM (EST). *Felony, Misdemeanor.* **Criminal Records:** Access: Mail, in person. Both court and visitors may perform in person searches. Search fee: $10.00 per name. Required to search: name, years to search, DOB, signed release; also helpful-SSN. Criminal records on index books from 1940s, on computer since 1996. **General Information:** No juvenile, adoption records released. SASE required. Turnaround time same day. Copy fee: $.50 per page. Certification fee: $5.00. Fee payee: Clerk of Courts. Personal checks accepted. Prepayment is required. Public access terminal is available. Public Access Terminal Note: Limited use only 96 cases.

Register of Wills Greene County Courthouse, 10 E High St, Waynesburg, PA 15370; 724-852-5283. Hours: 8:30AM-4PM (EST). *Probate.*

Huntingdon County

Court of Common Pleas-Criminal/Civil PO Box 39, Courthouse, Huntingdon, PA 16652; 814-643-1610; Fax: 814-643-4172. Hours: 8:30AM-4:30PM (EST). *Felony, Misdemeanor, Civil, Eviction.*

Civil Records: Access: Phone, mail, in person. Both court and visitors may perform in person searches. No search fee. Required to search: name, years to search; also helpful-address. Civil cases indexed by defendant, plaintiff. Civil records on computer from 08/03/92, on dockets from 1700s. **Criminal Records:** Access: Phone, mail, in person. Both court and visitors may perform in person searches. No search fee. Required to search: name, years to search; also helpful-DOB, SSN. Criminal records on computer from 08/03/92, on dockets from 1700s. **General Information:** No juvenile records released. SASE required. Turnaround time 1-2 days. Copy fee: $.25 per page. Certification fee: $4.50. Fee payee: Kay Coons, Prothonotary. Personal checks accepted. Prepayment is required. Public access terminal is available.

Register of Wills Courthouse, 223 Penn St, Huntingdon, PA 16652; 814-643-2740. Hours: 8:30AM-4:30PM (EST). *Probate.*

Indiana County

Court of Common Pleas-Criminal/Civil

County Courthouse, 825 Philadelphia St, Indiana, PA 15701; 724-465-3855/3858; Fax: 724-465-3968. Hours: 8AM-4:30PM (EST). *Felony, Misdemeanor, Civil, Eviction.*

Civil Records: Access: Fax, mail, in person. Both court and visitors may perform in person searches. Search fee: $10.00 per name. Will not conduct judgment searches. Required to search: name, years to search. Civil cases indexed by defendant, plaintiff. Civil records on computer from 1994, prior on index files. **Criminal Records:** Access: Fax, mail, in person. Both court and visitors may perform in person searches. Search fee: $10.00 per name. Required to search: name, years to search, DOB, signed release. Criminal records on computer from 1994, prior on index files. **General Information:** No juvenile, commitment records released. Turnaround time same day. Copy fee: $.25 per page. Certification fee: $3.00. Fee payee: Clerk of Court or Prothonotary. Personal checks accepted. Prepayment is required. Public access terminal is available. Fax notes: $.25 per page.

Register of Wills County Courthouse, 825 Philadelphia St, Indiana, PA 15701; 724-465-3860; Fax: 724-465-3863. Hours: 8AM-4:30PM (EST). *Probate.*

Jefferson County

Court of Common Pleas - Criminal/Civil

Courthouse, 200 Main St, Brookville, PA 15825; 814-849-1606 X225; Fax: 814-849-1607. Hours: 8:30AM-4:30PM (EST). *Felony, Misdemeanor, Civil, Eviction.*

Civil Records: Access: Mail, in person. Both court and visitors may perform in person searches. Search fee: $5.00 per name. Required to search: name, years to search. Civil cases indexed by defendant, plaintiff. Civil records on computer from 1987, all incoming records microfilmed, records from 1823 on microfilm. **Criminal Records:** Access: Mail, in person. Both court and visitors may perform in person searches. Search fee: $5.00 per name. Required to search: name, years to search, DOB; also helpful-SSN. Criminal records on computer from 1987, all incoming records microfilmed, records from 1823 on microfilm. **General Information:** No juvenile, mental health, records released, including criminal cases with a minor as a victim. SASE required. Turnaround time 2 days. Copy fee: $.50 per page. Certification fee: $1.00. Fee payee: Clerk of Courts. Personal checks accepted. Prepayment is required. Public access terminal is available.

Register of Wills Jefferson County Courthouse, 200 Main St, Brookville, PA 15825; 814-849-1610; Fax: 814-849-1612. Hours: 8:30AM-4:30PM (EST). *Probate.*

Juniata County

Court of Common Pleas - Criminal/Civil

Juniata County Courthouse, Mifflintown, PA 17059; 717-436-7715; Fax: 717-436-7734. Hours: 8AM-4:30PM (EST). *Felony, Misdemeanor, Civil, Eviction.*

Civil Records: Access: Mail, in person. Both court and visitors may perform in person searches. Search fee: $5.00 per name. Required to search: name, years to search. Civil cases indexed by defendant, plaintiff. Civil records on computer from 1993, on dockets from 1969, archived from 1700s. **Criminal Records:** Access: Phone, mail, in person. Both court and visitors may perform in

person searches. Search fee: $5.00 per name. Required to search: name, years to search, DOB. Criminal records on computer from 1993, on dockets from 1969, archived from 1700s. **General Information:** No juvenile records released. SASE required. Turnaround time 1 week. Copy fee: $.50 per page. Certification fee: $1.00 per page. Fee payee: Prothonotary or Clerk of Courts. Personal checks accepted. Prepayment is required. Public access terminal is available.

Register of Wills Juniata County Courthouse, PO Box 68, Mifflintown, PA 17059; 717-436-7709; Fax: 717-436-7756. Hours: 8AM-4:30PM M-F, 8AM-12PM Wed (June-Sept) (EST). *Probate.*

Lackawanna County

Court of Common Pleas-Civil

Clerk of Judicial Records, PO Box 133, Scranton, PA 18503; 570-963-6724; Civil phone:717-963-6723. Hours: 9AM-4PM (EST). *Civil, Eviction.*

Civil Records: Access: In person only. Court does not conduct in person searches; visitors must perform searches for themselves. Search fee: No civil searches performed by court. Required to search: name, years to search. Civil cases indexed by defendant, plaintiff. Civil records computerized since 09/01/95, dockets from 1920s, archived from 1800s. Case number is required. **General Information:** No juvenile records released. Copy fee: $.25 if self service; $.50 if done by Clerk; $1.00 for mail requesters first copy, $.50 each add'l. Certification fee: $3.00. Fee payee: Clerk of Judicial Records. Business checks accepted. Prepayment is required. Public access terminal is available.

Court of Common Pleas-Criminal

Lackawanna County Courthouse, Scranton, PA 18503; 570-963-6759; Fax: 570-963-6459. Hours: 9AM-4PM (EST). *Felony, Misdemeanor.* **Criminal Records:** Access: Mail, in person. Both court and visitors may perform in person searches. Search fee: $10.00 per name. Required to search: name, years to search, DOB, SSN. Criminal records computerized since 10/01/95, on dockets from 1983, archived from 1878, indexed by defendant only. **General Information:** No juvenile records released. SASE required. Turnaround time 1-2 days. Copy fee: $.25 per page. Certification fee: $5.00. Fee payee: Clerk of Judical Records. Business checks accepted. Prepayment is required. Public access terminal is available.

Register of Wills Registrar of Wills, County Courthouse, 200 N Washington Ave, Scranton, PA 18503; 570-963-6708; Fax: 570-963-6377. Hours: 9AM-4PM (EST). *Probate.*

Lancaster County

Court of Common Pleas - Civil

50 N Duke St, PO Box 83480, Lancaster, PA 17608-3480; 717-299-8282; Fax: 717-293-7210. Hours: 8:30AM-5PM (EST). *Civil, Eviction.*

http://www.co.lancaster.pa.us/directory.htm#judicial

Civil Records: Access: Phone, fax, mail, online, in person. Both court and visitors may perform in person searches. Search fee: $5.00 per name. Required to search: name, years to search; also helpful-address. Civil cases indexed by defendant, plaintiff. Civil records on computer from 7/87, in files from 1987, judgments on dockets from 1800s, others archived from 1800s. Online access is available 8am to 6pm M-Sat. There is a monthly fee of $25 and a per minute fee of $.18. Search by

name or case number. Call Nancy malloy at 717-299-8252 for more information. **General Information:** No naturalization records released. SASE required. Turnaround time 2-3 days. Copy fee: $1.00 per page. Certification fee: $3.00. Fee payee: Prothonotary. Business checks accepted. Prepayment is required. Public access terminal is available. Fax notes: $2.00 for first page, $1.00 each addl. Fee higher for out of state faxing.

Court of Common Pleas-Criminal

50 North Duke St, Lancaster, PA 17602; 717-299-8275. Hours: 8:30AM-5PM (EST). *Felony, Misdemeanor.* **Criminal Records:** Access: Mail, in person. Both court and visitors may perform in person searches. Search fee: $10.00 per name. Required to search: name, years to search. Criminal records on computer from 1988, archived from 1901. **General Information:** No juvenile records released. SASE required. Turnaround time 2 days. Copy fee: $.50 per copy or $1.00 for docket page including disposition; however, there is no copy fee if court does the search. Certification fee: $5.00. Fee payee: Clerk of Courts. Only cashiers checks and money orders accepted. Prepayment is required. Public access terminal is available.

Register of Wills 50 N. Duke St., Lancaster, PA 17602; 717-299-8243; Fax: 717-295-3522. Hours: 8:30AM-5PM (EST). *Probate.*

www.co.lancaster.pa.us/wills.htm

Lawrence County

Court of Common Pleas - Criminal/Civil

430 Court St, New Castle, PA 16101-3593; 724-656-2143; Fax: 724-656-1988. Hours: 8AM-4PM (EST). *Felony, Misdemeanor, Civil, Eviction.*

Civil Records: Access: Fax, mail, in person. Both court and visitors may perform in person searches. Search fee: $10.00 per name. Required to search: name, years to search. Civil cases indexed by defendant, plaintiff. Civil records on computer from 1987, on Russell Index from 1937. **Criminal Records:** Access: Fax, mail, in person. Both court and visitors may perform in person searches. Search fee: $10.00 per name. Required to search: name, years to search, signed release; also helpful-DOB, SSN. Criminal records on computer from 1987, on Russell Index from 1937. **General Information:** No adoption, juvenile, impounded, or juvenile sex crime victim records released. SASE requested. Turnaround time ASAP. Copy fee: $.50 per page. Certification fee: $1.50. Fee payee: Prothonotary. Business checks accepted. Prepayment is required. Fax notes: No fee to fax results. Fax Fee: Local $1.00 plus $.50 per pg; Long distance $3.00 plus $.50 per pg.

Register of Wills 430 Court St, New Castle, PA 16101-3593; 724-656-2128/2159; Fax: 724-656-1966. Hours: 8AM-4PM (EST). *Probate.* **General Information:**. Fee payee: Register of Wills, Lawrence County. Prepayment is required. Public access terminal is available.

Lebanon County

Court of Common Pleas - Civil

Municipal Bldg, Rm 104, 400 S 8th St, Lebanon, PA 17042; 717-274-2801 X2208. Hours: 8:30AM-4:30PM (EST). *Civil, Eviction.*

Civil Records: Access: In person only. Court does not conduct in person searches; visitors must perform searches for themselves. Search fee: No civil searches performed by court. Required to search: name, years to search; also helpful-address. Civil cases indexed by defendant, plaintiff. Civil records on computer from 1985, on files from 1883. Docket number required for phone access. **General Information:** No mental health records released. Copy fee: $.50 per page. Certification fee: $8.00. Fee payee: Prothonotary. Personal checks accepted. Prepayment is required. Public access terminal is available.

Court of Common Pleas-Criminal
Municipal Bldg, 400 S 8th St, Lebanon, PA 17042; 717-274-2801 X2247. Hours: 8:30AM-4:30PM (EST). *Felony, Misdemeanor.* **Criminal Records:** Access: Phone, mail, in person. Both court and visitors may perform in person searches. Search fee: $10.00 per name. Required to search: name, years to search. Criminal records on computer from 1986, indexed from 1800s. Action number required for phone access. **General Information:** No juvenile records released. SASE required. Turnaround time varies. Copy fee: $.50 per page. Certification fee: $5.00. Fee payee: Clerk of Court. Personal checks accepted. Prepayment is required. Public access terminal is available.

Register of Wills Municipal Bldg, Rm 105, 400 S 8th St, Lebanon, PA 17042; 717-274-2801 X2215; Fax: 717-274-8094. Hours: 8:30AM-4:30PM (EST). *Probate.*

Lehigh County
Court of Common Pleas - Civil Division
455 W Hamilton St, Allentown, PA 18101-1614; 610-782-3148; Fax: 610-770-3840. Hours: 8:30AM-4:30PM (EST). *Civil, Eviction.*

Civil Records: Access: online, in person. Court does not conduct in person searches; visitors must perform searches for themselves. No search fee. Required to search: name, years to search. Civil cases indexed by defendant, plaintiff. Civil records on computer since 1985, on microfilm from 1812, some in books. All types of county records, including criminal cases and real estate records are available online. The system is open 24 hours daily; there is a monthly fee. Call Lehigh Cty Computer Svcs Dept at 610-782-3286 for more information. **General Information:** No sealed, confidential, or impounded records released. Copy fee: $.50 per page; docket printout $3.00. Certification fee: $3.00. Fee payee: Clerk of Courts-Civil. Personal checks accepted. Public access terminal is available.

Court of Common Pleas-Criminal
455 W Hamilton St, Allentown, PA 18101-1614; 610-782-3077; Fax: 610-770-6797. Hours: 8:30AM-4:30PM (EST). *Felony, Misdemeanor.* **Criminal Records:** Access: Fax, mail, remote online, in person. Both court and visitors may perform in person searches. Search fee: $10.00 per name. Fee includes copy of certified docket. Required to search: name, years to search, DOB. Criminal records on computer from 1990, on alpha index from 1962 to 1990, on microfilm from 1812. Online access is available 24 hours daily. There is a monthly usage fee. Search by name or case number. Call Lehigh Cty Computer Svcs Dept at 610-782-3286 for more information. **General Information:** No juvenile or impounded records released. SASE required. Turnaround time 1 week. Copy fee: $.50. Docket printout mailed $2.00. Certification fee: $5.00. Fee payee: Clerk of Courts-Criminal. Personal checks accepted. Prepayment is required. Public access terminal is available. Fax notes: No fee to fax results.

Register of Wills 455 W Hamilton, Allentown, PA 18101-1614; 610-820-3170; Fax: 610-820-3439. Hours: 8AM-4PM (EST). *Probate.*

Luzerne County
Court of Common Pleas - Civil
200 N River St, Wilkes Barre, PA 18711-1001; 570-825-1745; Fax: 570-825-1757. Hours: 9AM-4:30PM (EST). *Civil, Eviction.*

Civil Records: Access: Phone, mail, in person. Both court and visitors may perform in person searches. Search fee: $15.75 per name for 5 years, $1.50 each add'l year, and $1.50 each reference cited. Required to search: name, years to search, address. Civil cases indexed by defendant, plaintiff. Civil records partially on microfiche and archives, on dockets from 1935. **General Information:** No mental, sealed records released. SASE required. Turnaround time 3 days. Copy fee: $1.00 per page. Certification fee: $4.75. Fee payee: Prothonotary. Personal checks accepted. Credit cards accepted: Visa, Mastercard, AmEx. Prepayment is required.

Court of Common Pleas-Criminal
200 N River St, Wilkes Barre, PA 18711; 570-825-1585; Fax: 570-825-1843. Hours: 8AM-4:30PM (EST). *Felony, Misdemeanor.* **Criminal Records:** Access: Phone, fax, mail, in person. Both court and visitors may perform in person searches. Search fee: $10.00 per name. Required to search: name, years to search, DOB. Criminal records on computer, microfiche and archived from 1989, on files from 1972. Records from 1933 to 1959 destroyed in flood. **General Information:** No "M" number (confidential custody case) records released. SASE not required. Turnaround time 1-2 days. Copy fee: $.25 per page. Certification fee: $5.00. Fee payee: Clerk of Courts. Personal checks accepted. Credit cards accepted: Visa, Mastercard, Discover. Prepayment is required. Fax notes: No fee to fax results.

Register of Wills 200 N River St, Wilkes Barre, PA 18711; 570-825-1672. Hours: 9AM-4:30PM (EST). *Probate.*

Lycoming County
Court of Common Pleas-Criminal/Civil
48 W 3rd St, Williamsport, PA 17701; 570-327-2251. Hours: 8:30AM-5PM (EST). *Felony, Misdemeanor, Civil, Eviction.*

Civil Records: Access: In person only. Court does not conduct in person searches; visitors must perform searches for themselves. Search fee: No civil searches performed by court. Required to search: name, years to search; also helpful-address. Civil cases indexed by defendant, plaintiff. Civil records on computer from 1983, on dockets from 1795. **Criminal Records:** Access: Mail, in person. Both court and visitors may perform in person searches. Search fee: $10.00 per name. Required to search: name, years to search, DOB; also helpful-address. Criminal records on computer from 1910. **General Information:** No juvenile, cases involving minors, mental records released. SASE required. Turnaround time same day. Copy fee: $.50 per page. Certification fee: $5.00. Fee payee: Prothonotary. Personal checks accepted. Prepayment is required. Public access terminal is available.

Register of Wills Lycoming Co Courthouse, 48 W 3rd St, Williamsport, PA 17701; 570-327-2258. Hours: 8:30AM-5PM (EST). *Probate.*

McKean County
Court of Common Pleas-Criminal & Civil
PO Box 273, Smethport, PA 16749; 814-887-3270; Fax: 814-887-3219. Hours: 8:30AM-4:30PM (EST). *Felony, Misdemeanor, Civil, Eviction.*

Civil Records: Access: Phone, fax, mail, in person. Both court and visitors may perform in person searches. Search fee: $12.00 per name. Required to search: name, years to search. Civil cases indexed by defendant, plaintiff. Civil records on computer since 1994, on microfiche from 1952 to 1962, on dockets from 1872. **Criminal Records:** Access: Mail, in person. Both court and visitors may perform in person searches. Search fee: $10.00 per name. Required to search: name, years to search, DOB. Criminal records on computer since 1994, on dockets from 1872. **General Information:** No sex related, juvenile, mental health records released. SASE required. Turnaround time same day. Copy fee: $.50 per page. Computer search copy fee: $1.00 per page. Certification fee: $3.50. Fee payee: Prothonotary or Clerk of Courts. Personal checks accepted. Prepayment is required. Public access terminal is available. Fax notes: $2.00 per page.

Register of Wills PO Box 202, Smethport, PA 16749-0202; 814-887-3260; Fax: 814-887-2712. Hours: 8:30AM-4:30PM (EST). *Probate.*

Mercer County
Court of Common Pleas - Civil
105 Mercer County Courthouse, Mercer, PA 16137; 724-662-3800. Hours: 8:30AM-4:30PM (EST). *Civil, Eviction.*

Civil Records: Access: Mail, in person. Both court and visitors may perform in person searches. Search fee: $5.00 per name. Required to search: name, years to search. Civil cases indexed by defendant, plaintiff. Civil records on computer since 1994; prior records on dockets from 1930s, archived from 1700s. Include SSN and DOB in your search. **General Information:** No mental, sealed records released. SASE required. Turnaround time 1-2 days. Copy fee: $.25 per page. Certification fee: $3.00. Fee payee: Prothonotary or Clerk of Courts. Business checks accepted. Prepayment is required. Public access terminal is available.

Court of Common Pleas-Criminal
112 Mercer County Courthouse, Mercer, PA 16137; 724-662-3800 X2248. Hours: 8:30AM-4:30PM (EST). *Felony, Misdemeanor.* **Criminal Records:** Access: Mail, in person. Both court and visitors may perform in person searches. Search fee: $10.00 per name. Required to search: name, years to search, DOB, signed release; also helpful-SSN. Criminal records on computer since 1993, indexed since 1920, on files from 1980. **General Information:** No juvenile records released. SASE required. Turnaround time 1 day. Copy fee: $1.00 for first page, $.50 each addl. Certification fee: $5.00. Fee payee: Clerk of Courts. Personal checks accepted. Prepayment is required. Public access terminal is available.

Register of Wills 112 Mercer County Courthouse, Mercer, PA 16137; 724-662-3800 X2253; Fax: 724-662-1530. Hours: 8:30AM-4:30PM (EST). *Probate.*

Mifflin County
Court of Common Pleas-Criminal & Civil
20 N Wayne St, Lewistown, PA 17044; 717-248-8146; Fax: 717-248-5275. Hours: 8AM-4:30PM (EST). *Felony, Misdemeanor, Civil, Eviction.*

Civil Records: Access: In person only. Court does not conduct in person searches; visitors must perform searches for themselves. Search fee: No civil searches performed by court. Required to search: name, years to search. Civil cases indexed by defendant, plaintiff. Civil records on computer from 1993, on microfiche from 1971-1989, prior on books. **Criminal Records:** Access: In person only. Court does not conduct in person searches; visitors must perform searches for themselves. Search fee: No criminal searches performed by court. Required to search: name, years to search. Criminal records on computer from 1993, on microfiche from 1971-1989, prior on books. **General Information:** No juvenile, mental health records released. Copy fee: $.50 per page. Certification fee: $4.50. Fee payee: Clerk of Courts. Personal checks accepted. Prepayment is required. Public access terminal is available. Fax notes: Will fax back if fees are prepaid.

Register of Wills 20 N. Wayne St., Lewistown, PA 17044; 717-242-1449. Hours: 8AM-4:30PM M-F (EST). *Probate.*

Monroe County

Court of Common Pleas - Civil Monroe County Courthouse, Stroudsburg, PA 18360; 570-420-3570. Hours: 8:30AM-4:30PM (EST). *Civil, Eviction.*

Civil Records: Access: Mail, in person. Both court and visitors may perform in person searches. Search fee: $5.00 per name. Required to search: name, years to search. Civil cases indexed by defendant, plaintiff. Civil records indexed on computer 1986 to present, prior in dockets. **General Information:** No juvenile records released. SASE not required. Turnaround time 1 day. Copy fee: $.50 per page. Certification fee: $3.00. Fee payee: Monroe County Prothonotary. Only cashiers checks and money orders accepted. Prepayment is required. Public access terminal is available.

Court of Common Pleas-Criminal Monroe County Courthouse Rm 312, Stroudsburg, PA 18360-2190; 570-517-3385. Hours: 8:30AM-4:30PM (EST). *Felony, Misdemeanor.* **Criminal Records:** Access: Mail, in person. Both court and visitors may perform in person searches. Search fee: $5.00 per name. Required to search: name, years to search; also helpful-address, DOB, SSN. Criminal records on computer since 1995; prior on dockets. **General Information:** No sex related, juvenile, adoption records released. SASE not required. Turnaround time 1 day. Copy fee: $1.00 per page. Certification fee: $10.00. Fee payee: Clerk of Court. Only cashiers checks and money orders accepted. Prepayment is required. Public access terminal is available.

Register of Wills Monroe County Courthouse, Stroudsburg, PA 18360; 570-517-3359; Fax: 570-420-3537. Hours: 8:30AM-4:30PM (EST). *Probate.*

Montgomery County

Court of Common Pleas - Civil PO Box 311, Airy & Swede St, Norristown, PA 19404-0311; 610-278-3360. Hours: 8:30AM-4:15PM (EST). *Civil, Eviction.*

www.montcopa.org

Civil Records: Access: online, in person. Court does not conduct in person searches; visitors must perform searches for themselves. Search fee: No civil searches performed by court. Required to search: name, years to search. Civil cases indexed by defendant, plaintiff. Civil records on computer from 4/82, on microfilm from 1800s. Court and other records are available free on the Internet at www1.montcopa.org/. The system is experimental

and may or may not be adapted full time. A pay service, offering remote dial-up, is also available. For info, call the helpdesk at 610-292-4931. There is a $10 registration fee plus $.15 per minute of usage. **General Information:** No mental health, divorce, sealed records released. SASE required. Copy fee: $.25 per page. Certification fee: $4.50. Fee payee: Prothonotary. Personal checks accepted. Prepayment is required. Public access terminal is available.

Court of Common Pleas-Criminal PO Box 311, Airy & Swede St, Norristown, PA 19404-0311; 610-278-3346; Fax: 610-278-5188. Hours: 8:30AM-4:15PM (EST). *Felony, Misdemeanor.*

www.montcopa.org **Criminal Records:** Access: Mail, remote online, in person. Both court and visitors may perform in person searches. Search fee: $10.00 per name. Required to search: name, years to search, DOB. Criminal records on computer from 10/84, prior archived and on microfiche. Court and other records are available free on the Internet at www1.montcopa.org/. The system is experimental and may or may not be adapted full time. A pay service, offering remote dial-up, is also available. For info, call the helpdesk at 610-292-4931. There is a $10 registration fee plus $.15 per minute of usage. **General Information:** No impounded, sealed records released. SASE required. Turnaround time 5 days, FAX turnaround 1 day. Copy fee: $1.00 per page. Certification fee: $10.00. Fee payee: Clerk of Courts. Business checks accepted. Credit cards accepted: Visa, Mastercard, Discover. Accepted in person only. Prepayment is required. Public access terminal is available.

Montgomery County Register in Wills, Clerk of Orphan's Court Airy & Swede St, PO Box 311, Norristown, PA 19404; 610-278-3400; Fax: 610-278-3240. Hours: 8:30AM-4:15PM (EST). *Probate.*

www.montcopa.org

Montour County

Court of Common Pleas-Criminal & Civil Montour County Courthouse, 29 Mill St, Danville, PA 17821; 570-271-3010; Fax: 570-271-3088. Hours: 9AM-4PM (EST). *Felony, Misdemeanor, Civil, Eviction.*

Civil Records: Access: Phone, fax, mail, in person. Both court and visitors may perform in person searches. Search fee: $10.00 per name. Required to search: name, years to search. Civil cases indexed by defendant, plaintiff. Civil records on books since 1991, on microfiche since 1939, actual files kept for 20 years. **Criminal Records:** Access: Phone, fax, mail, in person. Both court and visitors may perform in person searches. Search fee: $10.00 per name. Required to search: name, years to search, DOB, SSN. Criminal records on books since 1991, on microfiche since 1939, actual files kept for 20 years. **General Information:** No sex related, juvenile or adoption records released. SASE required. Turnaround time 1-2 days. Copy fee: $.50 per page. Certification fee: $3.00. Fee payee: Prothonotary. Personal checks accepted. Prepayment is required. Public access terminal is available.

Register of Wills 29 Mill St, Danville, PA 17821; 570-271-3012; Fax: 570-271-3071. Hours: 9AM-4PM (EST). *Probate.*

Northampton County

Court of Common Pleas - Civil Gov't Center, 669 Washington St Rm 207, Easton, PA 18042-7498; 610-559-3060. Hours: 8:30AM-4:30PM (EST). *Civil, Eviction.*

Civil Records: Access: In person only. Court does not conduct in person searches; visitors must perform searches for themselves. Search fee: No civil searches performed by court. Required to search: name, years to search; also helpful-address. Civil cases indexed by defendant, plaintiff. Civil records on computer since 1/85 (Civil) and 2/90 (Judgments). **General Information:** No impounded or PSA abuse records released. Copy fee: $1.00 per page. Certification fee: $4.75. Fee payee: Clerk of Court-Civil or Prothonotary's Office. Business checks accepted. Local personal check, certified check accepted. Prepayment is required. Public access terminal is available.

Court of Common Pleas-Criminal 669 Washington St, Easton, PA 18042-7494; 610-559-3000 X2114; Fax: 610-262-4391. Hours: 8:30AM-4:30PM (EST). *Felony, Misdemeanor.* **Criminal Records:** Access: Fax, mail, in person. Both court and visitors may perform in person searches. Search fee: $5.00 per name. Required to search: name, years to search, DOB; also helpful-SSN. Criminal records on computer from 1984, on files from 1800s. **General Information:** No juvenile, expunged records released. SASE not required. Turnaround time same day. Copy fee: $.50 per page. Certification fee: $5.00. Fee payee: Criminal Division. Business checks accepted. Credit cards accepted: Visa, Mastercard. Prepayment is required. Fax notes: No fee to fax results.

Register of Wills Governnment Center, 669 Washington St, Easton, PA 18042; 610-559-3094; Fax: 610-559-3735. Hours: 8:30AM-4:30PM (EST). *Probate.*

Northumberland County

Court of Common Pleas - Civil County Courthouse, 201 Market St, Rm #7, Sunbury, PA 17801-3468; 570-988-4151. Hours: 9AM-5PM M; 9AM-4:30PM T-F (EST). *Civil, Eviction.*

Civil Records: Access: Mail, in person. Both court and visitors may perform in person searches. Search fee: $7.00 per name. Required to search: name, years to search. Civil cases indexed by defendant, plaintiff. Civil records on file from 1772. **General Information:** No adult abuse, involuntary treatment records released. SASE required. Turnaround time 1-2 days. Copy fee: $1.00 2st page; $.25. Each add'l. Certification fee: $4.00. Fee payee: Northumberland Prothonotary. Business checks accepted. Prepayment is required.

Court of Common Pleas-Criminal County Courthouse, 201 Market St, Rm 7, Sunbury, PA 17801-3468; 570-988-4148. Hours: 9AM-5PM M; 9AM-4:30PM T-F (EST). *Felony, Misdemeanor.* **Criminal Records:** Access: Mail, in person. Both court and visitors may perform in person searches. Search fee: $10.00 per name. Required to search: name, years to search, DOB; also helpful-SSN. Criminal records indexed in office from 1945, on dockets from 1772, archived from 1700s to 1945. **General Information:** No juvenile records released. SASE required. Turnaround time 1-2 days. Copy fee: $1.00 for first page, $.25 each addl. First copy for in person requests is $.25. Certification fee: $4.00 plus $1.00 each additional page. Fee payee: Clerk of Courts Office. Personal checks accepted. Prepayment is required. Public access terminal is available.

Register of Wills County Courthouse, 201 Market St, Sunbury, PA 17801; 570-988-4143. Hours: 9AM-4:30PM (EST). *Probate.*

Perry County

Court of Common Pleas-Criminal & Civil PO Box 325, New Bloomfield, PA 17068; 717-582-2131 X240. Hours: 8AM-4PM (EST). *Felony, Misdemeanor, Civil, Eviction.*

Civil Records: Access: Phone, fax, mail, in person. Both court and visitors may perform in person searches. Search fee: $10.00 per name. Required to search: name, years to search. Civil cases indexed by defendant, plaintiff. Civil records on dockets from 1800s. Fax access requires pre-approval. Criminal Records: Access: Phone, fax, mail, in person. Both court and visitors may perform in person searches. Search fee: $10.00 per name. Required to search: name, years to search; also helpful-DOB, SSN. Criminal records on dockets from 1950. Same as civil. General Information: No juvenile records released. SASE required. Turnaround time 1 week, phone turnaround immediate. Copy fee: $.40 per page. Certification fee: $5.00. Fee payee: Prothonotary or Clerk of Courts. Personal checks accepted. Will bill to attorneys & abstract companies upon approval. Fax notes: No fee to fax results.

Register of Wills PO Box 223, New Bloomfield, PA 17068; 717-582-2131; Fax: 717-582-8570. Hours: 8AM-4PM (EST). *Probate.*

Philadelphia County

Court of Common Pleas - Civil First Judicial District of PA, Room 284, City Hall, Philadelphia, PA 19107; 215-686-6656; Fax: 215-567-7380. Hours: 9AM-5PM (EST). *Civil.*

http://dns2.phila.gov:8080

Civil Records: Access: Mail, online, in person. Both court and visitors may perform in person searches. Search fee: $35.00 per name. Required to search: name, years to search. Civil cases indexed by defendant, plaintiff. Civil records on computer from 1/82 to present, archived on files from 1700s to 1982. The Internet site provides free access to name searches, judgment searches and docket information. General Information: No mental health, divorce, abuse, adoption records released. SASE required. Turnaround time 1-5 days. Copy fee: $.50 per page. Certification fee: $30.00. Fee payee: Prothonotary. Business checks accepted. Prepayment is required. Public access terminal is available.

Clerk of Quarter Session 1301 Filbert St Ste 10, Philadelphia, PA 19107; 215-683-7700 X01 & X02. Hours: 8AM-5PM (EST). *Felony, Misdemeanor.* Criminal Records: Access: Mail, in person. Both court and visitors may perform in person searches. Search fee: $10.00 per name. Required to search: name, years to search, DOB, signed release; also helpful-address, SSN, race, sex. Criminal records on computer and microfiche from 1969, archived from 1800s. General Information: No sealed, grand jury, mental records released. SASE required. Turnaround time 1-2. Copy fee: $.25 per page. Certification fee: $12.50. Fee payee: Clerk of Quarter Sessions. Business checks accepted. Prepayment is required.

Municipal Court 34 S 11th St, 5th floor, Philadelphia, PA 19107; 215-686-7997; Fax: 215-569-9254. Hours: 9AM-5PM (EST). *Felony, Misdemeanor, Civil Actions Under $10,000, Eviction.*

Note: Court has jurisdiction over certain criminal offenses with jail terms up to five years

Civil Records: Access: Mail, in person. Only the court conducts in person searches; visitors may not. No search fee. Required to search: name, years to search, address. Civil cases indexed by defendant, plaintiff. Civil records on computer from 1969. Include SSN and DOB if possible. Criminal Records: Access: Mail, in person. Only the court conducts in person searches; visitors may not. No search fee. Required to search: name, years to search, address, DOB, signed release. Civil records on computer from 1969. General Information: SASE required. Turnaround time 1-5 days. Copy fee: $.50 per page. Certification fee: $3.00. Fee payee: Prothonotary. Only cashiers checks and money orders accepted. Prepayment is required.

Register of Wills City Hall Rm 180, Philadelphia, PA 19107; 215-686-6250/6282; Fax: 215-686-6293. Hours: 8:30AM-4:30PM (EST). *Probate.*

Pike County

Court of Common Pleas-Criminal & Civil 412 Broad St, Milford, PA 18337; 570-296-7231. Hours: 8:30AM-4:30PM (EST). *Felony, Misdemeanor, Civil, Eviction.*

Civil Records: Access: Phone, mail, in person. Both court and visitors may perform in person searches. Search fee: No civil searches performed by court. Required to search: name, years to search. Civil cases indexed by defendant, plaintiff. Civil records on files for 100 yrs, computerized since 1995. The court will only do searches from 01/95 forward. Criminal Records: Access: Phone, mail, in person. Both court and visitors may perform in person searches. Search fee: $10.00 per name. Required to search: name, years to search. Criminal records on files for 100 yrs, computerized since 1995. The court will only do searches from 01/95 forward. General Information: No juvenile, adoption, sealed records released. SASE required. Turnaround time varies. Copy fee: $.25 per page. Certification fee: $2.50 per page. Fee payee: Prothonotary. Personal checks accepted. Personal checks not exceeding $25.00 accepted. Prepayment is required. Public access terminal is available.

Register of Wills 506 Broad St, Milford, PA 18337; 570-296-3508. Hours: 8:30AM-4:30PM (EST). *Probate.*

Potter County

Court of Common Pleas-Criminal & Civil 1 E 2nd St Rm 23, Coudersport, PA 16915; 814-274-9740; Fax: 814-274-8284. Hours: 8:30AM-4:30PM (EST). *Felony, Misdemeanor, Civil, Eviction.*

Civil Records: Access: Phone, fax, mail, in person. Both court and visitors may perform in person searches. Search fee: $5.00 per name. Required to search: name, years to search. Civil cases indexed by defendant, plaintiff. Civil records on dockets from early 1900s to present. Criminal Records: Access: Phone, fax, mail, in person. Both court and visitors may perform in person searches. Search fee: $5.00 per name. Required to search: name, years to search. Criminal records on card index from 1983. General Information: No juvenile records released. SASE required. Turnaround time 2 weeks, phone turnaround immediate (unless lengthy search). Copy fee: $.25 per page. Certification fee: $3.00. Fee payee: Prothonotary or Clerk of Courts. Personal checks

accepted. Prepayment is required. Fax notes: No fee to fax results.

Register of Wills 1 E 2nd St, Coudersport, PA 16915; 814-274-8370. Hours: 8:30AM-4:30PM (EST). *Probate.*

Schuylkill County

Court of Common Pleas - Civil 401 N 2nd St, Pottsville, PA 17901-2528; 570-628-1270; Fax: 570-628-1261. Hours: 9AM-4PM (EST). *Civil, Eviction.*

Civil Records: Access: Mail, in person. Both court and visitors may perform in person searches. Search fee: $5.00 per name. Required to search: name, years to search. Civil cases indexed by defendant, plaintiff. Civil records (suits) on computer from 1989, judgements on dockets from 1800s. General Information: No master reports or sealed records released. SASE requested. Turnaround time 1 day. Copy fee: $.25 per page. Certification fee: $3.00 per page. Fee payee: Prothonotary. Personal checks accepted. Will bill copy fees. Public access terminal is available.

Court of Common Pleas-Criminal 410 N 2nd St, Pottsville, PA 17901; 570-622-5570 X1133; Fax: 570-628-1143. Hours: 9AM-4PM (EST). *Felony, Misdemeanor.* Criminal Records: Access: Fax, mail, in person. Both court and visitors may perform in person searches. Search fee: $10.00 per name. Required to search: name, years to search, DOB; also helpful-SSN. Criminal records on computer from 4/88, on dockets from 1800s. General Information: No juvenile records released. SASE not required. Turnaround time same day. Copy fee: $.25 per page. Certification fee: $5.00. Fee payee: Clerk of Courts. Business checks accepted. Prepayment is required. Fax notes: No fee to fax results.

Register of Wills Courthouse 401 N 2nd St, Pottsville, PA 17901-2520; 570-628-1377; Fax: 570-628-1384. Hours: 9AM-4PM (EST). *Probate.*

Snyder County

Court of Common Pleas-Criminal & Civil Snyder County Courthouse, PO Box 217, Middleburg, PA 17842; 570-837-4202. Hours: 8:30AM-4PM (EST). *Felony, Misdemeanor, Civil, Eviction.*

Civil Records: Access: Mail, in person. Both court and visitors may perform in person searches. Search fee: $10.00 per name. Required to search: name, years to search. Civil cases indexed by defendant, plaintiff. Civil records on dockets from 1800s, some on microfilm. Criminal Records: Access: Mail, in person. Both court and visitors may perform in person searches. Search fee: $10.00 per name. Required to search: name, years to search. Criminal records on dockets from 1800s, some on microfilm. General Information: No juvenile records released. SASE required. Turnaround time 2 days. Copy fee: $.40 per page. Certification fee: $4.00. Fee payee: Prothonotary or Clerk of Courts. Personal checks accepted. Prepayment is required.

Register of Wills County Courthouse, PO Box 217, Middleburg, PA 17842; 570-837-4224. Hours: 8:30AM-4PM (EST). *Probate.*

Somerset County

Court of Common Pleas – Civil 111 E Union St Suite 190, Somerset, PA 15501-0586; 814-445-1428; Fax: 814-445-7991. Hours: 8:30AM-4PM (EST). *Civil, Eviction.*

Civil Records: Access: Phone, fax, mail, in person. Both court and visitors may perform in person searches. Search fee: $12.00 per name. Required to search: name, years to search. Civil cases indexed by defendant, plaintiff. Civil records on computer from 1/92, on microfiche from 1920 to 1972, on dockets (Russell System for all other years prior to 1992). Hard copy must follow fax request. **General Information:** No commitment records relased. SASE required. Turnaround time 2-3 days. Copy fee: $.25 per page. Certification fee: $2.00. Fee payee: Prothonotary of Somerset Co. Business checks accepted. Prepayment is required. Public access terminal is available. Fax notes: $.25 per page.

Court of Common Pleas-Criminal 111 E Union St Suite 180, Somerset, PA 15501; 814-445-1435. Hours: 8:30AM-4PM (EST). *Felony, Misdemeanor.* **Criminal Records:** Access: Phone, mail, in person. Both court and visitors may perform in person searches. Search fee: $5.00 per name. Required to search: name, years to search, DOB; also helpful-SSN. Criminal records on microfilm from 1920, archive dates uncertain. **General Information:** No impounded records released. SASE not required. Turnaround time same day, phone turnaround immediate. Copy fee: $.50 per copy. Certification fee: $1.00. Fee payee: Clerk of Courts. Personal checks accepted. Will bill copy fees.

Register of Wills 111 E Union St Suite 170, Somerset, PA 15501-0586; 814-445-1548; Fax: 814-445-7991. Hours: 8:30AM-4PM (EST). *Probate.*

Sullivan County

Court of Common Pleas-Criminal & Civil Main Street, Laporte, PA 18626; 570-946-7351; Probate phone:570-946-7351; Fax: 570-946-4213. Hours: 8:30AM-4PM (EST). *Felony, Misdemeanor, Civil, Eviction, Probate.*

Note: Includes the Register of Wills

Civil Records: Access: Mail, in person. Both court and visitors may perform in person searches. Search fee: No civil searches performed by court. Required to search: name, years to search. Civil cases indexed by defendant, plaintiff. Civil records on dockets from 1847 to present. **Criminal Records:** Access: Mail, in person. Court does not conduct in person searches; visitors must perform searches for themselves. Search fee: No criminal searches performed by court. Required to search: name, years to search; also helpful-SSN. Criminal records on dockets from 1847 to present. **General Information:** No juvenile records released. SASE required. Turnaround time same day. Copy fee: $2.00 per page. Certification fee: $3.00 per page. Fee payee: Prothonotary or Clerk of Courts. Personal checks accepted. Prepayment is required.

Susquehanna County

Court of Common Pleas - Civil Susquehanna Courthouse, PO Box 218, Montrose, PA 18801; 570-278-4600 X120. Hours: 8:30AM-4:30PM (EST). *Civil, Eviction.*

Civil Records: Access: Mail, in person. Both court and visitors may perform in person searches. Search fee: $5.00 per name. Required to search: name, years to search. Civil cases indexed by defendant, plaintiff. Civil records on dockets from 1800s. **General Information:** No juvenile records released. SASE required. Turnaround time same day. Copy fee: $1.00 per page. Certification fee: $3.00. Fee payee: Prothonotary. Personal checks accepted. Prepayment is required.

Court of Common Pleas-Criminal Susquehanna Courthouse, PO Box 218, Montrose, PA 18801; 570-278-4600 X321. Hours: 8:30AM-4:30PM (EST). *Felony, Misdemeanor.* **Criminal Records:** Access: Mail, in person. Both court and visitors may perform in person searches. Search fee: $5.00 per name. Required to search: name, years to search; also helpful-DOB, SSN. Criminal records on dockets from 1800s, archived from 1971, computerized since 08/96. **General Information:** No juvenile records released. SASE required. Turnaround time same day. Copy fee: $1.00 per page. Certification fee: $3.00. Fee payee: Clerk of Courts. Personal checks accepted. Prepayment is required. Public access terminal is available.

Register of Wills Susquehanna County Courthouse, PO Box 218, Montrose, PA 18801; 570-278-4600 X112; Fax: 570-278-9268. Hours: 8:30AM-4:30PM (EST). *Probate.*

Tioga County

Court of Common Pleas-Criminal & Civil 116 Main St, Wellsboro, PA 16901; 570-724-9281. Hours: 9AM-4:30PM (EST). *Felony, Misdemeanor, Civil, Eviction.*

Civil Records: Access: In person only. Court does not conduct in person searches; visitors must perform searches for themselves. Search fee: No civil searches performed by court. Required to search: name. Civil cases indexed by defendant. Civil records on dockets from 1827. **Criminal Records:** Access: Mail, in person. Both court and visitors may perform in person searches. Search fee: $5.00 per name per year. Required to search: name, years to search. Criminal records on dockets from 1827. **General Information:** No mental health, juvenile, abuse (14 or younger) records released. SASE required. Turnaround time same day when possible. Copy fee: $.25 per page. Certification fee: $4.50. Fee payee: Tioga County Prothonotary. Personal checks accepted. Prepayment is required.

Register of Wills 116 Main St, Wellsboro, PA 16901; 570-724-9260. Hours: 9AM-4:30PM (EST). *Probate.*

Union County

Court of Common Pleas-Criminal & Civil 103 S 2nd St, Lewisburg, PA 17837; 570-524-8751. Hours: 8:30AM-4:30PM (EST). *Felony, Misdemeanor, Civil, Eviction.*

Civil Records: Access: Phone, mail, in person. Both court and visitors may perform in person searches. No search fee. Required to search: name, years to search. Civil cases indexed by defendant, plaintiff. Civil records on computer from 1988, on microfiche (orphans court 1813 to 1988, marriage 1885 to 1998), on dockets from 1800s to 1988. **Criminal Records:** Access: Phone, mail, in person. Both court and visitors may perform in person searches. No search fee. Required to search: name, years to search. Criminal records on computer from 1988, on microfiche (orphans court 1813 to 1988, marriage 1885 to 1998), on dockets from 1800s to 1988. **General Information:** No juvenile records released. SASE required. Turnaround time same day. Copy fee: $.25 per page. Certification fee: $1.00. Fee payee: Prothonotary or Clerk of Courts. Personal checks accepted. Prepayment is required. Public access terminal is available.

Register of Wills 103 S 2nd St, Lewisburg, PA 17837-1996; 570-524-8761. Hours: 8:30AM-4:30PM (EST). *Probate.*

Venango County

Court of Common Pleas-Criminal & Civil Venango County Courthouse, Franklin, PA 16323; 814-432-9577; Fax: 814-432-9569. Hours: 8:30AM-4:30PM (EST). *Felony, Misdemeanor, Civil, Eviction.*

Civil Records: Access: Mail, in person. Both court and visitors may perform in person searches. Search fee: $5.00 per name. Required to search: name, years to search. Civil cases indexed by defendant, plaintiff. Civil records on computer from 1993, on dockets from 1800s. **Criminal Records:** Access: Mail, in person. Both court and visitors may perform in person searches. Search fee: $5.00 per name. Required to search: name, years to search, DOB; also helpful-SSN. Criminal records on computer from 1993, on dockets from 1800s. **General Information:** No juvenile records released. SASE required. Turnaround time same day. Copy fee: $.50 per page. Certification fee: $7.00. Fee payee: Peggy L Miller, Clerk of Courts. Personal checks accepted. Prepayment is required. Public access terminal is available.

Register of Wills/Recorder of Deeds 1168 Liberty St, Franklin, PA 16323; 814-432-9534; Fax: 814-432-9569. Hours: 8:30AM-4:30PM (EST). *Probate.*

Warren County

Court of Common Pleas-Criminal & Civil 4th & Market St, Warren, PA 16365; 814-728-3530; Fax: 814-728-3452. Hours: 8:30AM-4:30PM (EST). *Felony, Misdemeanor, Civil, Eviction.*

http://users.penn.com/~wrncourt

Civil Records: Access: Fax, mail, in person. Both court and visitors may perform in person searches. Search fee: $20.00 per name. Required to search: name, years to search. Civil cases indexed by defendant, plaintiff. Civil records on computer from 1987, on dockets from 1800s. **Criminal Records:** Access: Fax, mail, in person. Both court and visitors may perform in person searches. Search fee: $20.00 per name. Required to search: name, years to search; also helpful-DOB. Criminal records on computer from 1987, on dockets from 1800s. **General Information:** No juvenile records released. SASE reuqired. Turnaround time 2 days. Copy fee: $1.00 per page. Certification fee: $4.00. Fee payee: Prothonotary or Clerk of Courts. Business checks accepted. Prepayment is required. Fax notes: No fee to fax results.

Register of Wills Courthouse, 204 4th Ave, Warren, PA 16365; 814-728-3430. Hours: 8:30AM-4:30PM (EST). *Probate.*

Washington County

Court of Common Pleas -- Civil 1 S Main St Suite 1001, Washington, PA 15301; 724-228-6770. Hours: 9AM-4:30PM (EST). *Civil, Eviction.*

Civil Records: Access: In person only. Court does not conduct in person searches; visitors must perform searches for themselves. Search fee: No civil searches performed by court. Required to search: name, years to search. Civil cases indexed by defendant, plaintiff. Civil records on computer from 1987, prior on dockets to 1800s. Online access is open 24 hours daily, there are no fees. Probate, divorce and criminal records are also available. Call Sally Michalski at 724-228-6797 for more information. **General Information:** Copy fee: $1.50 per page. Certification fee: $4.50. Fee payee: Prothonotary. Only cashiers checks and money orders accepted. Checks from attorneys accepted. Prepayment is required. Public access terminal is available.

Court of Common Pleas-Criminal

Courthouse Ste 1005, 1 S Main St, Washington, PA 15301; 724-228-6787; Fax: 724-228-6890. Hours: 9AM-4:30PM (EST). *Felony, Misdemeanor.*

www.co.washington.pa.us/ **Criminal Records:** Access: Mail, remote online, in person. Both court and visitors may perform in person searches. Search fee: $10.00 per name. Required to search: name, years to search, DOB; also helpful-address, SSN. Criminal records on computer since 10/87, prior on dockets, archived from 1800s. **General Information:** No juvenile records released. SASE required. Turnaround time over 1 week. Copy fee: $.50 per page. Certification fee: $8.00. Fee payee: Clerk of Courts. Personal checks accepted. Prepayment is required.

Register of Wills Courthouse, 1 S Main St Suite 1002, Washington, PA 15301; 724-228-6775. Hours: 9AM-4:30PM (EST). *Probate.*

Wayne County

Court of Common Pleas-Criminal & Civil

925 Court St, Honesdale, PA 18431; 570-253-5970 X200; Fax: 570-253-0687. Hours: 8:30AM-4:30PM (EST). *Felony, Misdemeanor, Civil, Eviction.*

Civil Records: Access: In person only. Court does not conduct in person searches; visitors must perform searches for themselves. Search fee: No civil searches performed by court. Required to search: name, years to search. Civil cases indexed by defendant, plaintiff. Civil records on daily docket entries, computerized since 1996. **Criminal Records:** Access: In person only. Court does not conduct in person searches; visitors must perform searches for themselves. Search fee: No criminal searches performed by court. Required to search: name, years to search. Criminal records on daily docket entries, computerized since 1996. **General Information:** Juvenile records not released. Copy fee: $.50 per page. Certification fee: No certification fee. Personal checks accepted. Prepayment is required. Public access terminal is available.

Register of Wills 925 Court St, Honesdale, PA 18431; 570-253-5970 X212. Hours: 8:30AM-4:30PM (EST). *Probate.*

Westmoreland County

Court of Common Pleas - Civil

Courthouse Sq, Rm 501, PO Box 1630, Greensburg, PA 15601-1168; 724-830-3500; Fax: 724-830-3517. Hours: 8:30AM-4PM (EST). *Civil, Eviction.*

Civil Records: Access: online, in person. Court does not conduct in person searches; visitors must perform searches for themselves. Search fee: No civil searches performed by court. Required to search: name, years to search. Civil cases indexed by defendant, plaintiff. Civil records on computer from 9/85, on dockets from 1700s. The online system costs $100 setup plus $20 per month minimum fee. The system includes civil, criminal, prothonotary indexes, and recorder information. For information, call 724-830-3874. **General Information:** No final divorce, mental health records released. Copy fee: $.50 per page. Computer print out: $1.00 per page. Certification fee: $4.75. Fee payee: Prothonotary. Business checks accepted. Prepayment is required. Public access terminal is available.

Court of Common Pleas-Criminal

Criminal Division, 203 Courthouse Square, Greensburg, PA 15601-1168; 724-830-3734; Fax: 724-830-3472/850-3979. Hours: 8:30AM-4PM (EST). *Felony, Misdemeanor.* **Criminal Records:** Access: Fax, mail, remote online, in person. Both court and visitors may perform in person searches. Search fee: $10.00 per name. Required to search: name, years to search, signed release; also helpful-DOB, SSN. Criminal records on computer from 1941, on microfiche from 1793 to 1950, archived from 1773. Online access is open 24 hours daily. The $100 setup fee includes software, the minimum monthly fee is $20. Records are available from 1992 forward. For more information, call Phil Svesnik at 724-830-3874. **General Information:** No juvenile records released. SASE not required. Turnaround time 1 day. Copy fee: $.50 per page. Computer copy $.50 per page. Certification fee: $5.00. Fee payee: Clerk of Courts. Personal checks accepted. Attorney's check accepted. Prepayment is required. Public access terminal is available. Fax notes: $10.00 per document.

Register of Wills 2 N Main St, #301, Greensburg, PA 15601; 724-830-3177; Fax: 724-850-3976. Hours: 8:30AM-4PM (EST). *Probate.*

Wyoming County

Court of Common Pleas - Criminal & Civil

Wyoming County Courthouse, Tunkhannock, PA 18657; 570-836-3200 X232-234. Hours: 8:30AM-4PM (EST). *Felony, Misdemeanor, Civil, Eviction.*

Civil Records: Access: In person only. Court does not conduct in person searches; visitors must perform searches for themselves. Search fee: No civil searches performed by court. Required to search: name, years to search. Civil cases indexed by defendant, plaintiff. Civil records on dockets from 1800s. **Criminal Records:** Access: In person only. Court does not conduct in person searches; visitors must perform searches for themselves. Search fee: No criminal searches performed by court. Required to search: name, years to search; also helpful-DOB. Criminal records on dockets from 1800s. **General Information:** No juvenile records released. Copy fee: $.25 per page. Certification fee: $7.00. Fee payee: Prothonotary or Clerk of Courts. Personal checks accepted. Prepayment is required. Public access terminal is available.

Register of Wills County Courthouse, 1 Courthouse Sq, Tunkhannock, PA 18657; 570-836-3200 X235. Hours: 8:30AM-4PM (EST). *Probate.*

York County

Court of Common Pleas - Civil

York County Courthouse, 28E Market St, York, PA 17401; 717-771-9611. Hours: 8:30AM-4:30PM (EST). *Civil.*

Civil Records: Access: online, in person. Court does not conduct searches; visitors must perform searches for themselves. No search fee. Required to search: name, years to search. Civil cases indexed by defendant, plaintiff. Civil records on computer from mid-1988, on dockets from 1800s, archived from mid-1700s. The online system is available from 4am to 1am, M-F. The setup fee is $200.00 and the access fee is $.75 per minute. For further information, call Greg McCoy at 717-771-9235. **General Information:** No mental health records released. SASE required. Turnaround time 1 day. Copy fee: $1.00 per page. Certification fee: $4.50. Fee payee: Prothonotary. Only cashiers checks and money orders accepted. Prepayment is required. Public access terminal is available.

Court of Common Pleas-Criminal

York County Courthouse 28 E Market St, York, PA 17401; 717-771-9612; Fax: 717-771-9096. Hours: 8:30AM-4:30PM (EST). *Felony, Misdemeanor.* **Criminal Records:** Access: Fax, mail, remote online, in person. Both court and visitors may perform in person searches. Search fee: $5.00 per name. Required to search: name, years to search. Criminal records on computer from 1987, on dockets from 1942, archived from 1700s. Online access is available for criminal records from mid-1988 forward. The system is $.75 per minute plus a $200.00 setup fee. For more information, call 717-771-9321. **General Information:** No sex crime, juvenile records released. SASE required. Turnaround time 1-2 weeks. Copy fee: $.25 per page. Certification fee: $5.00. Fee payee: Clerk of Courts. Personal checks accepted. Prepayment is required. Public access terminal is available. Fax notes: No fee to fax results.

Register of Wills York County Courthouse 28 E Market St, York, PA 17401; 570-771-9263; Fax: 570-771-4678. Hours: 8:30AM-4:15PM (EST). *Probate.*

ORGANIZATION   67 counties, 67 recording offices and 134 UCC filing offices. Each county has two different recording offices: the Prothonotary —their term for "Clerk"—accepts UCC and tax lien filings, and the Recorder of Deeds maintains real estate records. The entire state is in the Eastern Time Zone (EST).

REAL ESTATE RECORDS   County Recorders of Deeds will **not** perform real estate searches. Copy fees and certification fees vary.

UCC RECORDS   This is a **dual filing state**. Financing statements are filed both at the state level and with the Prothonotary, except for real estate related collateral, which are filed with the Recorder of Deeds. Some county offices will **not** perform UCC searches. Use search request form UCC-11. Search fees are usually $57.50 per debtor name. Copies usually cost $.50-$2.00 per page. Counties also charge $5.00 per financing statement found on a search.

TAX LIEN RECORDS   All federal and state tax liens on personal property and on real property are filed with the Prothonotary. Usually, tax liens on personal property are filed in the judgment index of the Prothonotary. Some Prothonotaries will perform tax lien searches. Search fees are usually $5.00 per name.

OTHER LIENS   Judgment, municipal, mechanics.

Adams County Recorder

County Recorder of Deeds, 111-117 Baltimore Street, County Courthouse Room 102, Gettysburg, PA 17325. 717-334-6781.

Allegheny County Recorder

County Recorder of Deeds, 101 County Office Building, 542 Forbes Avenue, Pittsburgh, PA 15219-2947. 412-350-4226. Fax: 412-350-6877.

Armstrong County Recorder

County Recorder of Deeds, County Courthouse, 500 Market St., Kittanning, PA 16201-1495. 724-548-3256. Fax: 724-548-3236.

Beaver County Recorder

County Recorder of Deeds, 3rd Street, County Courthouse, Beaver, PA 15009. 724-728-5700. Fax: 724-728-3630.

Bedford County Recorder

County Recorder of Deeds, 200 South Juliana Street, County Courthouse, Bedford, PA 15522. 814-623-4836. Fax: 814-624-0488.

Berks County Recorder

County Recorder of Deeds, 633 Court St., 3rd Floor, Reading, PA 19601. 610-478-3380. Fax: 610-478-3359.

Blair County Recorder

County Recorder of Deeds, 423 Allegheny St., Suite 145, Hollidaysburg, PA 16648. 814-693-3096.

Bradford County Recorder

County Recorder of Deeds, 301 Main Street, Courthouse, Towanda, PA 18848. 570-265-1702. Fax: 570-265-1721.

Bucks County Recorder

County Recorder of Deeds, Courthouse, 55 E. Court St., Doylestown, PA 18901-4367. 215-348-6209.
Online Access: Real Estate, Liens, Tax Assessor Records. Access to Bucks County records requires a Sprint ID number and payment of $24 annual Sprint fee, plus $.60 per minute of use. Records date back to 1980. The system operates 8AM-9PM M-F and 8AM-5PM S-S; system supports baud rates up to 9,600 For information, contact Jack Morris at 215-348-6579. Lending agency and Register of Wills data is available.

Butler County Recorder

County Recorder of Deeds, P.O. Box 1208, Butler, PA 16003-1208. 724-284-5340. Fax: 724-285-9099.

Cambria County Recorder

County Recorder of Deeds, Cambria County Courthouse, 200 S. Center St., Ebensburg, PA 15931. 814-472-1470. Fax: 814-472-1412.

Cameron County Recorder

County Recorder of Deeds, 20 E. 5th Street, Emporium, PA 15834. 814-486-3349. Fax: 814-486-0464.

Carbon County Recorder

County Recorder of Deeds, P.O. Box 87, Jim Thorpe, PA 18229. 570-325-2651.

Centre County Recorder

County Recorder of Deeds, 414 Holmes Ave. #1, Bellefonte, PA 16823. 814-355-6801. Fax: 814-355-8680.

Chester County Recorder

County Recorder of Deeds, Suite 100, 235 West Market St., West Chester, PA 19382-2616. 610-344-6330. Fax: 610-344-6408.
www.chesco.org
Online Access: Assessor, Real Estate, Marriage. Assessor, real estate, marriage, court and other records from the County Clerk are available by Internet subscription at http://epin.chesco.org. Application fee is $50.00; there is a $10 monthly minimum (100 transactions) and $.10 each over 100. Payment is by Visa or MC.

Clarion County Recorder

County Recorder of Deeds, Courthouse, Corner of 5th Ave. & Main St., Clarion, PA 16214. 814-226-4000x2500. Fax: 814-226-8069.

Clearfield County Recorder

County Recorder of Deeds, P.O. Box 361, Clearfield, PA 16830. 814-765-2641. Fax: 814-765-6089.

Clinton County Recorder

County Recorder of Deeds, P.O. Box 943, Lock Haven, PA 17745. 570-893-4010.

Columbia County Recorder

County Recorder of Deeds, P.O. Box 380, Bloomsburg, PA 17815. 570-389-5632. Fax: 570-389-5636.

Crawford County Recorder

County Recorder of Deeds, Courthouse, 903 Diamond Park, Meadville, PA 16335. 814-333-7339. Fax: 814-337-5296.

Cumberland County Recorder

County Recorder of Deeds, County Courthouse, 1 Courthouse Square, Carlisle, PA 17013. 717-240-6370. Fax: 717-240-6490.

Dauphin County Recorder

County Recorder of Deeds, P.O. Box 12000, Harrisburg, PA 17108. 717-255-2802. Fax: 717-257-1521.

Delaware County Recorder

County Recorder of Deeds, 201 W. Front Street, Room 107, Government Center Building, Media, PA 19063. 610-891-4148.
Online Access: Real Estate, Tax Assessor Records. Access to Delaware County online records is free by dialing 610-566-1507. The system operates 24 hours daily. Records go back to 1990 For information, contact Data Processing at 610-891-4675.

Elk County Recorder

County Recorder of Deeds, P.O. Box 314, Ridgway, PA 15853-0314. 814-776-5349. Fax: 814-776-5379.

Erie County Recorder

County Recorder of Deeds, P.O. Box 1849, Erie, PA 16507-0849. 814-451-6246. Fax: 814-451-6213.

Fayette County Recorder

County Recorder of Deeds, 61 East Main Street, Courthouse, Uniontown, PA 15401-3389. 724-430-1238. Fax: 724-430-1238.

Forest County Recorder

County Recorder of Deeds, P.O. Box 423, Tionesta, PA 16353. 814-755-3526. Fax: 814-755-8837.

Franklin County Recorder

County Recorder of Deeds, 157 Lincoln Way East, Chambersburg, PA 17201. 717-264-4125. Fax: 717-267-3438.

Fulton County Recorder

County Recorder of Deeds, 201 North Second Street, Fulton County Courthouse, McConnellsburg, PA 17233-1198. 717-485-4212.

Greene County Recorder

County Recorder of Deeds, Courthouse, Waynesburg, PA 15370. 724-852-5283.

Huntingdon County Recorder

County Recorder of Deeds, 223 Penn Street, Courthouse, Huntingdon, PA 16652. 814-643-2740.

Indiana County Recorder

County Recorder of Deeds, 825 Philadelphia Street, Courthouse, Indiana, PA 15701. 724-465-3860. Fax: 724-465-3863.

Jefferson County Recorder

County Recorder of Deeds, 200 Main Street, Courthouse, Brookville, PA 15825. 814-849-1610. Fax: 814-849-1612.

Juniata County Recorder

County Recorder of Deeds, P.O. Box 68, Mifflintown, PA 17059. 717-436-7709. Fax: 717-436-7756.

Lackawanna County Recorder

County Recorder of Deeds, 200 North Washington, Courthouse, Scranton, PA 18503. 570-963-6775.

Lancaster County Recorder

County Recorder of Deeds, 50 North Duke Street, Lancaster, PA 17602. 717-299-8238.
www.co.lancaster.pa.us
Online Access: Real Estate, Liens, Tax Assessor Records. Two online resources are available. Access to Lancaster County online records requires $25 monthly plus $.18 per minute of use. This system holds 5 years

data. It uses Windows. System operates 8AM-6PM M-S and supports baud rates up to 56k For information, contact Nancy Malloy at 717-299-8252. Lending agency and Register of Wills information is available Assessor records on the County GIS Department database are available free on the Internet at www.co.lancaster.pa.us/GIS/disclaimer.html. Click on "Lancaster. Search" then choose municipality; then "Go." Search by parcel #, owner name, address, or map.

Lawrence County Recorder
County Recorder of Deeds, 430 Court Street, Government Center, New Castle, PA 16101. 412-656-2127. Fax: 412-656-1966.

Lebanon County Recorder
County Recorder of Deeds, 400 South 8th Street, Room 107, Lebanon, PA 17042. 717-274-2801.

Lehigh County Recorder
County Recorder of Deeds, 455 W. Hamilton Street, Allentown, PA 18101. 610-782-3162. Fax: 610-820-2039.

Luzerne County Recorder
County Recorder of Deeds, 200 North River Street, Courthouse, Wilkes-Barre, PA 18711. 570-825-1641.

Lycoming County Recorder
County Recorder of Deeds, 48 West Third Street, Williamsport, PA 17701. 570-327-2263. Fax: 570-327-2511.

McKean County Recorder
County Recorder of Deeds, P.O. Box 3426, Smethport, PA 16749. 814-887-3253. Fax: 814-887-7766.

Mercer County Recorder
County Recorder of Deeds, Box 109 Courthouse, Mercer, PA 16137. 412-662-3800x2274. Fax: 412-662-2096.

Mifflin County Recorder
County Recorder of Deeds, 20 North Wayne Street, Lewistown, PA 17044. 717-242-1449. Fax: 717-248-3695.

Monroe County Recorder
County Recorder of Deeds, 7th & Monroe Street, Courthouse, Stroudsburg, PA 18360-2185. 570-420-3530. Fax: 570-420-3537.

Montgomery County Recorder
County Recorder of Deeds, P.O. Box 311, Norristown, PA 19404-0311. 610-278-3289. Fax: 610-278-3869.
www.montcopa.org
Online Access: Real Estate, Liens, Tax Assessor Records. Two onlines sources are available. Access to Montgomery County online records requires a $10 sign up fee plus $.15 per minute of use. Records date back to 1990. The system operates 24 hours daily and supports.

baud rates up to 14.4 For information or to sign up, contact Berkheimer Assoc. at 800-360-8989. Lending agency and prothonotary information are available on the system Records on the Montgomery County PIR database are also available free on the Internet at www.montcopa.org/reassessment/boahome0.htm. Click on "Instructions" to learn how to use the search features, then search by parcel #, name, address, or municipality.

Montour County Recorder
County Recorder of Deeds, 29 Mill Street, Courthouse, Danville, PA 17821. 570-271-3012. Fax: 570-271-3071.

Northampton County Recorder
County Recorder of Deeds, 669 Washington Streets, Government Center, Easton, PA 18042. 610-559-3077. Fax: 610-559-3103.

Northumberland County Recorder
County Recorder of Deeds, 2nd & Market Streets, Court House, Sunbury, PA 17801. 570-988-4140.

Perry County Recorder
County Recorder of Deeds, P.O. Box 223, New Bloomfield, PA 17068. 717-582-2131.

Philadelphia County Recorder
County Recorder of Deeds, Broad & Market Streets, City Hall Room 153, Philadelphia, PA 19107. 215-686-2260.

Pike County Recorder
County Recorder of Deeds, 506 Broad Street, Milford, PA 18337. 570-296-3508.

Potter County Recorder
County Recorder of Deeds, Courthouse, Room 20, Coudersport, PA 16915. 814-274-8370.

Schuylkill County Recorder
County Recorder of Deeds, 401 N. Second St., Pottsville, PA 17901. 570-628-1480.

Snyder County Recorder
County Recorder of Deeds, P.O. Box 217, Middleburg, PA 17842-0217. 570-837-4225. Fax: 570-837-4299.

Somerset County Recorder
County Recorder of Deeds, 111 E. Main St., Suite 140, Somerset, PA 15501. 814-445-2160.

Sullivan County Recorder
County Recorder of Deeds, Main Street, Courthouse, Laporte, PA 18626. 570-946-7351.

Susquehanna County Recorder
County Recorder of Deeds, P.O. Box 218, Montrose, PA 18801. 570-278-4600x112/3. Fax: 570-278-9268.

Tioga County Recorder
County Recorder of Deeds, 116 Main Street, Courthouse, Wellsboro, PA 16901. 570-724-9260.

Union County Recorder
County Recorder of Deeds, 103 South 2nd Street, Courthouse, Lewisburg, PA 17837-1996. 570-524-8761.

Venango County Recorder
County Recorder of Deeds, P.O. Box 831, Franklin, PA 16323. 814-432-9539. Fax: 814-432-9569.

Warren County Recorder
County Recorder of Deeds, 4th & Market Streets, Courthouse, Warren, PA 16365. 814-723-7550.

Washington County Recorder
County Recorder of Deeds, Washington County Courthouse, 1 South Main St., Room 1006, Washington, PA 15301. 412-228-6806. Fax: 412-228-6737.
Online Access: Real Estate, Liens, Tax Assessor Records. Access to Washington County online records is available 24 hours daily and the system supports baud rates to 56K. Records date back to 1952. Lending agency and Register of Wills info is available, but tax lien information is kept by Prothonotary's office For information, contact Jack Welty at 724-228-6766.

Wayne County Recorder
County Recorder of Deeds, 925 Court Street, Honesdale, PA 18431-1996. 570-253-5970x212.

Westmoreland County Recorder
County Recorder of Deeds, P.O. Box 160, Greensburg, PA 15601. 724-830-3526. Fax: 724-832-8757.
Online Access: Real Estate, Liens. Access to Westmoreland County online records requires a $100 set up fee and $20 monthly, plus $.50 per minute after 40 minutes of use. Records date back to 1957. System operates 24 hours daily and supports baud rates up to 19.2 For information, contact Phil Svesnik at 724-830-3874. No tax lien information is available, only UCC liens.

Wyoming County Recorder
County Recorder of Deeds, 1 Courthouse Square, Tunkhannock, PA 18657. 717-836-3200x235-6.

York County Recorder
County Recorder of Deeds, 28 East Market Street, York, PA 17401. 717-771-9608. Fax: 717-771-9582.

You will usually be able to find the city name in the City/County Cross Reference below. In that case, it is a simple matter to determine the county from the cross reference. However, only the official US Postal Service city names are included in this index. There are an additional 40,000 place names that people use in their addresses. Therefore, we have also included a ZIP/City Cross Reference immediately following the City/County Cross Reference.

If you know the ZIP Code but the city name does not appear in the City/County Cross Reference index, look up the ZIP Code in the ZIP/City Cross Reference, find the city name, then look up the city name in the City/County Cross Reference. For example, you want to know the county for an address of Menands, NY 12204. There is no "Menands" in the City/County Cross Reference. The ZIP/City Cross Reference shows that ZIP Codes 12201-12288 are for the city of Albany. Looking back in the City/County Cross Reference, Albany is in Albany County.

City/County Cross Reference

AARONSBURG Centre
ABBOTTSTOWN (17301) Adams(71), York(29)
ABINGTON Montgomery
ACKERMANVILLE Northampton
ACME Westmoreland
ACOSTA Somerset
ADAH Fayette
ADAMSBURG Westmoreland
ADAMSTOWN Lancaster
ADAMSVILLE (16110) Crawford(91), Mercer(9)
ADDISON Somerset
ADRIAN Armstrong
AIRVILLE York
AKRON Lancaster
ALBA Bradford
ALBION (16401) Erie(91), Crawford(9)
ALBION Erie
ALBRIGHTSVILLE (18210) Carbon(87), Monroe(13)
ALBURTIS (18011) Berks(62), Lehigh(38)
ALDENVILLE Wayne
ALEPPO Greene
ALEXANDRIA Huntingdon
ALIQUIPPA Beaver
ALLENPORT Washington
ALLENSVILLE (17002) Mifflin(88), Huntingdon(12)
ALLENTOWN Lehigh
ALLENWOOD (17810) Union(51), Lycoming(49)
ALLISON Fayette
ALLISON PARK Allegheny
ALLPORT Clearfield
ALTOONA Blair
ALUM BANK Bedford
ALVERDA Indiana
ALVERTON Westmoreland
AMBERSON Franklin
AMBLER Montgomery
AMBRIDGE (15003) Beaver(95), Allegheny(5)
AMITY Washington
ANALOMINK Monroe
ANDREAS (18211) Schuylkill(87), Carbon(13)
ANITA Jefferson
ANNVILLE Lebanon
ANTES FORT Lycoming
APOLLO (15613) Armstrong(52), Westmoreland(48)
AQUASHICOLA Carbon
ARCADIA Indiana
ARCHBALD Lackawanna
ARCOLA Montgomery
ARDARA Westmoreland
ARDMORE (19003) Montgomery(64), Delaware(36)
ARENDTSVILLE Adams
ARISTES Columbia
ARMAGH Indiana

ARMBRUST Westmoreland
ARNOT Tioga
ARONA Westmoreland
ARTEMAS (17211) Bedford(94), Fulton(6)
ASHFIELD Carbon
ASHLAND Schuylkill
ASHVILLE (16613) Cambria(99), Blair(1)
ASPERS Adams
ASTON Delaware
ATGLEN (19310) Chester(98), Lancaster(2)
ATHENS Bradford
ATLANTIC Crawford
ATLASBURG Washington
AUBURN Schuylkill
AUDUBON Montgomery
AULTMAN Indiana
AUSTIN (16720) Potter(84), Cameron(12), McKean(4)
AVELLA Washington
AVIS Clinton
AVONDALE Chester
AVONMORE Westmoreland
BADEN (15005) Beaver(88), Allegheny(12)
BAINBRIDGE Lancaster
BAIRDFORD Allegheny
BAKERS SUMMIT Bedford
BAKERSTOWN Allegheny
BALA CYNWYD Montgomery
BALLY Berks
BANGOR Northampton
BARNESBORO (15714) Cambria(96), Indiana(5)
BARNESVILLE Schuylkill
BART Lancaster
BARTO (19504) Montgomery(58), Berks(42)
BARTONSVILLE Monroe
BATH Northampton
BAUSMAN Lancaster
BEACH HAVEN Luzerne
BEACH LAKE (18405) Wayne(92), Pike(8)
BEALLSVILLE Washington
BEAR CREEK Luzerne
BEAR LAKE Warren
BEAVER Beaver
BEAVER FALLS Beaver
BEAVER MEADOWS (18216) Carbon(52), Luzerne(48)
BEAVER SPRINGS Snyder
BEAVERDALE Cambria
BEAVERTOWN Snyder
BECCARIA Clearfield
BECHTELSVILLE (19505) Montgomery(79), Berks(21)
BEDFORD Bedford
BEDMINSTER Bucks
BEECH CREEK (16822) Clinton(81), Centre(19)
BELLE VERNON (15012) Fayette(55), Westmoreland(43), Washington(1)
BELLEFONTE Centre

BELLEVILLE Mifflin
BELLWOOD Blair
BELSANO Cambria
BENDERSVILLE Adams
BENEZETT Elk
BENSALEM Bucks
BENTLEYVILLE Washington
BENTON (17814) Columbia(77), Luzerne(17), Sullivan(4), Lycoming(3)
BERLIN Somerset
BERNVILLE Berks
BERRYSBURG Dauphin
BERWICK (18603) Columbia(85), Luzerne(15)
BERWYN (99999) Chester(99), Delaware(1)
BESSEMER Lawrence
BETHEL Berks
BETHEL PARK Allegheny
BETHLEHEM (18015) Northampton(74), Lehigh(26)
BETHLEHEM (18017) Northampton(93), Lehigh(7)
BETHLEHEM (18018) Lehigh(57), Northampton(43)
BETHLEHEM Lehigh
BETHLEHEM Northampton
BEYER Indiana
BIG COVE TANNERY Fulton
BIG RUN Jefferson
BIGLER Clearfield
BIGLERVILLE (17307) Adams(99), Cumberland(1)
BIRCHRUNVILLE Chester
BIRD IN HAND Lancaster
BIRDSBORO Berks
BLACK LICK Indiana
BLAIN Perry
BLAIRS MILLS Huntingdon
BLAIRSVILLE (15717) Indiana(91), Westmoreland(9)
BLAKESLEE Monroe
BLANCHARD Centre
BLANDBURG Cambria
BLANDON Berks
BLOOMING GLEN Bucks
BLOOMSBURG Columbia
BLOSSBURG Tioga
BLUE BALL Lancaster
BLUE BELL Montgomery
BLUE RIDGE SUMMIT Franklin
BOALSBURG Centre
BOBTOWN Greene
BODINES Lycoming
BOILING SPRINGS Cumberland
BOLIVAR Westmoreland
BOSWELL Somerset
BOVARD Westmoreland
BOWERS Berks
BOWMANSDALE Cumberland
BOWMANSTOWN Carbon
BOWMANSVILLE Lancaster

BOYERS Butler
BOYERTOWN (19512) Berks(95), Montgomery(6)
BOYNTON Somerset
BRACKENRIDGE Allegheny
BRACKNEY Susquehanna
BRADDOCK Allegheny
BRADENVILLE Westmoreland
BRADFORD McKean
BRADFORDWOODS Allegheny
BRANCHDALE Schuylkill
BRANCHTON Butler
BRANDAMORE Chester
BRANDY CAMP Elk
BRAVE Greene
BREEZEWOOD (15533) Bedford(99), Fulton(1)
BREINIGSVILLE Lehigh
BRIDGEPORT Montgomery
BRIDGEVILLE (15017) Allegheny(94), Washington(6)
BRIER HILL Fayette
BRISBIN Clearfield
BRISTOL Bucks
BROAD TOP Huntingdon
BROCKPORT (15823) Elk(69), Jefferson(31)
BROCKTON Schuylkill
BROCKWAY (15824) Jefferson(99), Clearfield(2)
BRODHEADSVILLE Monroe
BROGUE York
BROOKHAVEN Delaware
BROOKLYN Susquehanna
BROOKVILLE Jefferson
BROOMALL Delaware
BROWNFIELD Fayette
BROWNSTOWN Lancaster
BROWNSVILLE (15417) Fayette(63), Washington(37)
BRUIN Butler
BRUSH VALLEY Indiana
BRYN ATHYN Montgomery
BRYN MAWR (19010) Delaware(53), Montgomery(47)
BUCK HILL FALLS Monroe
BUCKINGHAM Bucks
BUENA VISTA Allegheny
BUFFALO MILLS (15534) Somerset(90), Bedford(11)
BULGER Washington
BUNOLA Allegheny
BURGETTSTOWN Washington
BURLINGTON Bradford
BURNHAM Mifflin
BURNSIDE Clearfield
BURNT CABINS (17215) Fulton(75), Huntingdon(25)
BUSHKILL Pike
BUTLER Butler
BYRNEDALE Elk
CABOT (16023) Butler(99), Armstrong(1)

Corporation Records
Fictitious Name
Limited Partnerships
Limited Liability Company Records
Limited Liability Partnerships
Not For Profit Entities

Secretary of State, Corporations Division, 100 N Main St, Providence, RI 02903-1335; 401-222-3040, 401-222-1356 (Fax), 8:30AM-4:30PM.

www.sec.state.ri.us

Indexing & Storage: Records are available from the beginning of the Division. Records are computerized since 1984. It takes less than one day before new records are available for inquiry. Records are indexed on an inhouse computer.

Searching: Include the following in your request-full name of business.

Access by: mail, phone, fax, in person, online.

Fee & Payment: The copy fee is $.15 per page. Certification costs $5.00 per document plus copy fees. There is no search fee. Fee payee: Secretary of State. Prepayment required. Personal checks accepted. No credit cards accepted.

Mail search: Turnaround time: variable. No self addressed stamped envelope is required.

Phone search: They will give date of incorporation, registered agent, one officer, status, and whether domestic or foreign.

Fax search: Same criteria as searching by mail.

In person search: Searching is available in person.

Online search: Search both active and inactive entities through the web "Corporations Database Page" at www.corps.state.ri.us. Forms are also available from the web site.

Other access: The corporation database may be purchased on CD.

Trademarks/Servicemarks

Secretary of State, Trademark Section, 100 N Main St, Providence, RI 02903-1335; 401-222-1487, 401-222-3879 (Fax), 8:30AM-4:30PM.

www.sec.state.ri.us

Indexing & Storage: Records are available from the beginning of the Division. It takes less than one day before new records are available for inquiry.

Searching: All records are open to the public. Include the following in your request-trademark/servicemark name, registration number and applicant name, if known.

Access by: mail, phone, fax.

Fee & Payment: There is no search fee. The copy fee is $.15 per page.

Mail search: Turnaround time: 3-5 days. No self addressed stamped envelope is required.

Phone search: No fee for telephone request. Limited verification information available.

Fax search: Fax searching available.

Uniform Commercial Code

UCC Division, Secretary of State, 100 North Main St, Providence, RI 02903; 401-222-2249, 8:30AM-4:30PM.

www.state.ri.us/corporations

Indexing & Storage: Records are indexed on hard copy.

Searching: Use search request form UCC-11. All tax liens are filed at the city/town level. Include the following in your request-debtor name.

Access by: mail, phone, in person.

Fee & Payment: The search fee is $5.00 per name, copies are $.15 each. Fee payee: Secretary of State. Prepayment required. Personal checks accepted. No credit cards accepted.

Mail search: Turnaround time: 5-10 working days.

Phone search: No fee for telephone request. Limited data is available by phone.

In person search: If you do the search yourself, there is no search fee.

Federal Tax Liens
State Tax Liens

Records not maintained by a state level agency.

Note: All records are located at the county level.

Sales Tax Registrations

Taxation Division, Sales & Use Tax Office, One Capitol Hill, Providence, RI 02908-5890; 401-222-2937, 401-222-6006 (Fax), 8:30AM-4PM.

www.tax.state.ri.us

Indexing & Storage: Records are available from the 1960's. All current permits are on the computer, all inactive records are kept on microfiche.

Searching: This agency will only confirm that a business is registered. They will provide no other information. Include the following in your request-business name. They will also search by tax permit number.

Access by: mail, phone, fax, in person.

Fee & Payment: There is no search fee nor a copy fee, unless extensive documents are requested.

Mail search: Turnaround time: 7-10 days. A self addressed stamped envelope is requested.

Phone search: Searching is available by phone.

Fax search: Same criteria as mail searching.

In person search: It will take 24 hours for a response.

Birth Certificates

State Department of Health, Division of Vital Records, 3 Capitol Hill, Room 101, Providence, RI 02908-5097; 401-222-2812, 401-222-2811, 8:30AM-4:30PM.

Indexing & Storage: Records are available from 1900-present. New records are available for inquiry immediately. Records are indexed on microfiche, inhouse computer.

Searching: Investigative searches must have a signed release form from person of record or immediate family member. Include the following

in your request-full name, names of parents, mother's maiden name, date of birth, place of birth.

Access by: mail, phone, in person.

Fee & Payment: The fee is $15.00 for 2 years searched and $.50 for each additional year. Fee payee: General Treasurer, State of Rhode Island. Prepayment required. Credit cards for emergencies only. Personal checks accepted. Credit cards accepted: Mastercard, Visa, AmEx, Discover.

Mail search: Turnaround time: 4-6 weeks. A self addressed stamped envelope is requested.

Phone search: This is for emergency, expedited needs only.

In person search: Turnaround time while you wait.

Expedited service: Expedited service is available for mail and phone searches. For a 1 week service, mark "rush" on envelope and send in an extra $5.00. For emergencies, add an additional $5.00 for using a credit card and $15.50 for shipping.

Death Records

State Department of Health, Division of Vital Records, 3 Capitol Hill, Room 101, Providence, RI 02908-5097; 401-222-2812, 401-222-2811, 8:30AM-4:30PM;.

Indexing & Storage: Records are available from 1950-present. For records from 1853-1949, contact RI Archives at 401-222-2353. New records are available for inquiry immediately. Records are indexed on microfiche, inhouse computer.

Searching: Investigative searches must have a signed release from immediate family member. Include the following in your request-full name, date of death, place of death, names of parents, mother's maiden name. Any other identifying information is helpful.

Access by: mail, phone, in person.

Fee & Payment: The fee is $15.00 for 2 years searched and $.50 for each additional year. Fee payee: General Treasurer, State of Rhode Island. Prepayment required. Credit cards are for emergency use only. Personal checks accepted. Credit cards accepted: Mastercard, Visa, AmEx, Discover.

Mail search: Turnaround time: 4-6 weeks. A self addressed stamped envelope is requested.

Phone search: See expedited services.

In person search: Searching is available in person.

Expedited service: Expedited service is available for mail and phone searches. You must mark "RUSH" on the outside of the envelope and enclose an extra $5.00, if you want 1 week turnaround time. For true emergencies, you can phone in. Add $5.00 fee for use of credit card and provide return express pre-paid package.

Marriage Certificates

State Department of Health, Division of Vital Records, 3 Capitol Hill, Room 101, Providence, RI 02908-5097; 401-222-2812, 401-222-2811, 8:30AM-4:30PM M-F;.

Indexing & Storage: Records are available from 1900-present. New records are available for inquiry immediately. Records are indexed on microfiche, inhouse computer.

Searching: Investigative searches must have a signed release form from persons of record or immediate family member. Include the following in your request-names of husband and wife, date of marriage, place or county of marriage, wife's maiden name.

Access by: mail, phone, in person.

Fee & Payment: The search fee is $15.00 for 2 years searched and $.50 for each additional year. Fee payee: General Treasurer, State of Rhode Island. Prepayment required. Credit card use is for emergencies only. Personal checks accepted. Credit cards accepted: Mastercard, Visa, AmEx, Discover.

Mail search: Turnaround time: 4-6 weeks. A self addressed stamped envelope is requested.

Phone search: See expedited services.

In person search: Searching is available in person.

Expedited service: Expedited service is available for mail and phone searches. For 1 week turnaround, send an extra $5.00 and mark "RUSH" on the outside of the envelope. For true emergencies, you can order by phone. Add $5.00 fee for use of credit card and provide return express pre-paid package.

Divorce Records

Records not maintained by a state level agency.

Note: Divorce records are found at one of the 4 county Family Courts.

Workers' Compensation Records

Department of Labor & Training, Division of Workers' Compensation, PO Box 20190, Cranston, RI 02920 (Courier: 1511 Pontiac Ave, Cranston, RI 02920); 401-462-8100, 8:30AM-4PM.

www.dlt.state.ri.us

Indexing & Storage: Records are available from 1950s. New records are available for inquiry immediately. Records are indexed on inhouse computer.

Searching: Records are not available for employment screening. A first report of injury is not public, by law. Records are released to claimant, attorneys, employer and insurer only if connected to case. Include the following in your request-claimant name, Social Security Number, file number (if known), reason for information request, specific records that you need copies of. Records of insurance carrier coverage only are available for no charge by phone or mail. The following data is not released: medical records.

Access by: mail, in person.

Fee & Payment: The search fee is $15 per hour. Copies are $.15 per page. There is a $.40 per page fee for return by fax. Fee payee: Department of Labor. Prepayment is required for first time requesters. Personal checks accepted. No credit cards accepted.

Mail search: Turnaround time: 1-2 weeks. A self addressed stamped envelope is requested.

In person search: Proof of identity is required.

Driver Records

Division of Motor Vehicles, Driving Record Clerk, Operator Control, 286 Main Street, Pawtucket, RI 02860; 401-588-3010, 8:30AM-4:30PM.

www.dmv.state.ri.us

Note: Copies of tickets may be obtained without fee by writing to the Traffic Tribunal at the address listed above.

Indexing & Storage: Records are available for 3 years for accidents and moving violations, 5 years for alcohol-related violations or suspensions, 3 years after reinstatement for suspensions. Surrendered licenses are purged 3 years after expiration. It takes 20 days after received from courts before new records are available for inquiry.

Searching: Information is not made available for the purpose of commercial solicitation or trade. A description of proposed use must be submitted in advance for departmental approval of high volume requesters. Include the following in your request-driver's license number, full name, date of birth. The following data is not released: Social Security Numbers.

Access by: mail, in person.

Fee & Payment: The fee is $16 per record request. This is the highest fee in the nation for a driving record. Fee payee: Division of Motor Vehicles. Prepayment required. Personal checks accepted. No credit cards accepted.

Mail search: Turnaround time: 1 week. A self addressed stamped envelope is requested.

In person search: Although you may request a record in person, results must be picked up the next day or mailed back.

Other access: Rhode Island offers a tape retrieval system for high volume users.

Vehicle Ownership
Vehicle Identification

Registry of Motor Vehicles, c/o Registration Files, 286 Main Street, Pawtucket, RI 02860; 401-588-3020 x2552, 8:30AM-3:30PM.

www.dmv.state.ri.us

Indexing & Storage: Records are available for 3 years for title information, for 10 years for registration information. It takes 20 days from issue before new records are available for inquiry.

Searching: Request must be in writing and the purpose stated. Records will not be released for commercial or solicitation purposes. Casual requesters cannot obtain records.

Access by: mail, in person.

Fee & Payment: The fee is $10.00 per record request. The state will release lien information. There is a full charge for a no record found request. Fee payee: Registry of Motor Vehicles. Prepayment required. Personal checks accepted. No credit cards accepted.

Mail search: Turnaround time: 1 week. A self addressed stamped envelope is requested.

In person search: Records are not released in person, but are mailed.

Other access: Bulk retrieval of vehicle and ownership information is limited to statistical purposes.

Accident Reports

Rhode Island State Police, Accident Record Division, 311 Danielson Pike, North Scituate, RI 02857; 401-444-1143, 401-444-1133 (Fax), 10AM-4PM M,T,TH,F.

Indexing & Storage: Records are available for the past 2 years plus the current year. Accidents before that are stored in archives. Hard copy files are indexed. It takes 7-14 days before new records are available for inquiry.

Searching: Include the following in your request-reason for information request, full name, date of accident, location of accident.

Access by: mail, phone, in person.

Fee & Payment: The fee is $5.00 per record. Fee payee: Treasurer - State of Rhode Island. Prepayment required. Personal checks accepted. No credit cards accepted.

Mail search: Turnaround time: 1 week. A self addressed stamped envelope is requested.

Phone search: No fee for telephone request. The office will let a requester know if a report is available, but information will not be given over the phone.

In person search: Same day processing is available, provided report has been received.

Boat & Vessel Ownership
Boat & Vessel Registration

Dept of Environmental Managment, Office of Boat Registration, 235 Promenade, Rm 360, Providence, RI 02908; 401-222-6647, 401-222-1181 (Fax), 8:30AM-3:30PM M-F.

www.state.ri.us/dem

Indexing & Storage: Records are available from the late 1970s to the present. Records are computer indexed for the last 3 years. This is a title state, lien information shows on the title record. All boats over 14 ft must be titled and registered.

Searching: All requests must be in writing on the agency's request form. Call or write for the form. Records cannot be purchased for solicitation or commercial purposes. The name or registration number or RI number is needed for a request.

Access by: mail, in person.

Fee & Payment: There is no fee.

Mail search: Turnaround time: 1-2 weeks. No self addressed stamped envelope is required.

In person search: No fee for request. Turnaround time varies.

Legislation-Current/Pending
Legislation-Passed

Secretary of State, State House, Room 38, Public Information Center, Providence, RI 02903; 401-222-3983 (Bill Status Only), 401-222-2473 (State Library), 401-222-1356 (Fax), 8:30AM-4:30PM.

www.sec.state.ri.us

Note: All bills are available at the State Law Library. Current session bills are available from the office of Public Information.

Indexing & Storage: Records are available for current session only.

Searching: One may search by bill number, subject, word, sponser, etc.

Access by: mail, phone, fax, in person, online.

Fee & Payment: Copies are made by the Office of Public Information, $.15 per page. There is no search fee.

Mail search: No self addressed stamped envelope is required.

Phone search: Searching is available by phone.

Fax search: Fax searching available.

In person search: There are public access terminals available.

Online search: The site search http://dirac.rilin.state.ri.us/BillStatus/webclass1.asp provides two excellent means to search enactments and measures by keywords or bill numbers.

Voter Registration

Records not maintained by a state level agency.

Note: The Local Board of Canvassers keeps records at the town and city level. Although records are open, they may not be purchased for commercial purposes.

GED Certificates

Department of Education, GED Testing, 255 Westminster, Providence, RI 02908; 401-222-4600 x2181, 7:30AM-4PM.

Searching: Include the following in your request- Social Security Number, date of birth. A signed release is also required for a verification or transcript copy.

Access by: mail, phone, in person.

Fee & Payment: The fee for a transcript is $3.00 or duplicate diploma. There is no fee for a verification. Fee payee: General Treasurer, State of Rhode Island. Prepayment required. Personal checks accepted. No credit cards accepted.

Mail search: Turnaround time: 1 week. No self addressed stamped envelope is required.

Phone search: Limited data is available.

In person search: Searching is available in person.

Hunting License Information
Fishing License Information

RI DEM, Boat Registration & Licensing, 235 Promenade, Providence, RI 02908; 401-222-3576 (License Issue Only), 401-222-1181 (Fax), 8:30AM-3:30PM.

www.state.ri.us/dem

Indexing & Storage: Records are available for the current year only. Agents have hard copies.

Searching: Although all records are considered open, commercial use of the records is not permitted. Include the following in your request- date of application, date of birth, address. Also, include where purchased. Requests must be in writing.

Access by: mail, phone, fax, in person.

Fee & Payment: There is no fee for a short search or confirmation. Otherwise, for extensive searches the rate $15.00 per hour. Fee payee: RI DEM. Prepayment required. Personal checks accepted. No credit cards accepted.

Mail search: Turnaround time: 1 week to 10 days.

Phone search: They will confirm only.

Fax search: Same criteria as mail searches.

In person search: They will return by mail.

Licenses Searchable Online

Cable Installer #04 .... www.crb.state.ri.us/contract.htm
Chimney Sweep #04 .... www.crb.state.ri.us/contract.htm
Medical Doctor #24 .... www.docboard.org/ri/df/search.htm
Notary Public #15 .... www.sec.state.ri.us/notaries/notaries.htm
Optometrist #13 .... www.arbo.org/nodb2000/licsearch.asp
Osteopathic Physician #13 .... www.docboard.org/ri/df/search.htm
Residential Building Contractor #04 .... www.crb.state.ri.us/contract.htm
Security Alarm Installer #04 .... www.crb.state.ri.us/contract.htm
Underground Sprinkler Installer #04 .... www.crb.state.ri.us/contract.htm

Licensing Quick Finder

Acupuncturist #13 401-222-2827
Arborist #10 401-647-3367
Architect #05 401-222-2565
Asbestos Abatement Worker #13 401-222-3601
Athletic Trainer #13 401-222-2827
Attorney #21 401-222-3272
Auctioneer #11 401-222-3857
Audiologist #13 401-222-2827
Bank #05 401-222-2405
Barber #13 401-222-2827
Barber Instructor #13 401-222-2827
Barber Shop #13 401-222-2827
Beekeeper #09 401-222-2781
Blaster #19 401-294-0861
Bondsman #18 401-222-3212
Boxer #05 401-222-6541
Burglar Alarm Agent #11 401-222-3857
Cable Installer #04 401-222-1268
Cattle Dealer #09 401-222-2781
Chemical Dependency Professional/Supervisor #06
.... 401-233-2215
Chimney Sweep #04 401-222-1268
Chiropractor #13 401-222-2827
Clinical Histologic Technician #07 401-222-2827
Clinical Lab Scientist #07 401-222-2877
Clinical Lab Scientist/Election Microscopy #07
.... 401-222-2827
Clinical Lab Scientist-Cytogenetic #07 .. 401-222-2827
Clinical Lab Technician #07 401-222-2827
Coaching Certificate #16 401-222-2675
Controlled Substances Wholesaler #03
.... 401-222-2837
Court Reporter #18 401-222-3215
Cytotechnologist #13 401-222-2827
Dental Hygienist #13 401-222-2151
Dentist #13 401-222-2151
Dietitian/Nutritionist #13 401-222-2827
Electrician #08 401-462-8527
Electrologist #13 401-222-2827
Elevator Inspector #08 401-462-8527
Elevator Mechanic #08 401-462-8527
Embalmer #13 401-222-2827
Emergency Medical Technician #13 401-222-2401
Engineer #02 401-222-2038
Esthetician #13 401-222-2827
Facility Designer #09 401-222-6820
Family Day Care Home Provider #22 401-222-4741
Family Group Day Care Home Provider #22
.... 401-222-4741
Fire Alarm Installer #19 401-294-0861
Fire Extinguisher Installer/Service #19 .. 401-294-0861
Fireworks Shooter #19 401-294-0861

Fisher, Commercial #09 401-222-6647
Funeral Director #13 401-222-2827
Fur Buyer #09 401-222-6647
Hairdresser #13 401-222-2827
Hairdresser Instructor #13 401-222-2827
Hearing Aid Dispenser #13 401-222-2827
Hoisting Engineer #08 401-462-8527
Hypodermic Needles & Syringes #03 ... 401-222-2837
Insurance Adjuster #05 401-222-2223
Insurance Appraiser #05 401-222-2223
Insurance Broker #05 401-222-2223
Insurance Producer #05 401-222-2223
Insurance Solicitor #05 401-222-2223
Investment Advisor #05 401-222-3048
Journeyman Plumber #13 401-222-2827
Landscape Architect #02 401-222-2038
Landscaper #05 401-222-2565
Lifeguard #12 401-222-2632
Liquor Control #05 401-222-2562
Lobbyist #15 401-222-1487
Manicuring Shop #13 401-222-2827
Manicurist #13 401-222-2827
Marriage Therapist #13 401-222-2827
Master Plumber #13 401-222-2827
Medical Doctor #24 401-222-3855
Mental Health Counselor #13 401-222-2827
Midwife #13 401-222-2827
Money & Mortgage Broker #05 401-222-2405
Non-residence Pharmacy #03 401-222-2837
Notary Public #15 401-222-1487
Nuclear Medicine Technologist #13 401-222-2827
Nurse #13 401-222-3835
Nurse-LPN #13 401-222-2827
Nurseryman #09 401-222-2781
Nursing Assistant #13 401-222-2827
Nursing Home Administrator #13 401-222-2827
Occupational Therapist #13 401-222-2827
Optician #13 401-222-2827
Optometrist #13 401-222-2827
Osteopathic Physician #13 401-222-3855
Park Ranger #12 401-222-2632
Pesticide Applicator #09 401-222-2781
Pharmacist #03 401-222-2837
Pharmacy #03 401-222-2837
Pharmacy Technician #03 401-222-2837
Physical Therapist #13 401-222-2827
Physical Therapist Assistant #13 401-222-2827
Physician Assistant #13 401-222-2827
Physicians Controlled Substance #03 ... 401-222-2837
Pipefitter #08 401-462-8527
Plumber #08 401-462-8527
Podiatrist #13 401-222-2827

Prevention Specialist/Supervisor #06 ... 401-233-2215
Prosthetist #13 401-222-2827
Psychologist #13 401-222-2827
Public Accountant-CPA #01 401-222-3185
Pyrotechnic Operator #19 401-294-0861
Radiographer #13 401-222-2827
Reading Specialist #16 401-222-2675
Real Estate Appraiser #05 401-222-2255
Real Estate Broker #05 401-222-2255
Real Estate Salesperson #05 401-222-2255
Recognized Clinical Sueprvisors #06 ... 401-233-2215
Refrigeration Technician #08 401-462-8527
Residential Building Contractor #04 401-222-1268
Respiratory Care Practitioner #13 401-222-2827
Sanitarian #13 401-222-2827
School Guidance Counselor #16 401-222-2675
School Principal #16 401-222-2675
School Psychologist #16 401-222-2675
School Social Worker #16 401-222-2675
School Superintendent #16 401-222-2675
School Supervisor #16 401-222-2675
Securities Broker/Dealer #05 401-222-3048
Securities Broker/Dealer Sales Representative #05
.... 401-222-3048
Securities Sales Rep. #05 401-222-3048
Security Alarm Installer #04 401-222-1268
Sewage Disposal System Installer #09
.... 401-222-6820
Sheet Metal Technician #08 401-462-8527
Sheet Metal Worker #08 401-462-8527
Ship Pilot #20 401-783-5551
Social Worker #13 401-222-2827
Speech Pathologist #13 401-222-2827
Surveyor #05 401-222-2565
Surveyor Firm #02 401-222-2038
Tattoo Artist #13 401-222-2827
Teacher #16 401-222-2675
Telecommunications Technician #08 401-462-8527
Trapper #09 401-222-6647
Travel Agent #05 401-222-3857
Underground Sprinkler Installer #04 401-222-1268
Vendor Employee #05 401-222-2405
Veterinarian #13 401-222-2827
Waste Water Treatment Plant Operator #09
.... 401-222-6820
Wildlife Propagator #09 401-222-6647
Wildlife Rehabilitator #23 401-222-1267
Woods Operator #10 401-647-3367
Wrestler #05 401-222-6541

Licensing Agency Information

01 Board of Accountancy, 233 Richmond St, #236, Providence, RI 02903-4236; 401-222-3185, Fax: 401-222-6654.

03 Board of Pharmacy, 3 Capitol Hill, Rm 205, Providence, RI 02908; 401-222-2837, Fax: 401-222-2158.

04 Contractors' Registration Board, 1 Capitol Hill, 2nd Fl, Providence, RI 02908; 401-222-1270, Fax: 401-222-2599. www.crb.state.ri.us

Direct URL to search licenses: www.crb.state.ri.us/contract.htm You can search online using name or registration #

05 Business Regulation Department, Division of Commercial Licensing & Regulation, 233 Richmond St, Providence, RI 02903-4232; 401-222-3048.

06 Certification of Chemical Dependency Professionals, 345 Waterman Ave, Smithfield, RI 02917; 401-233-2215, Fax: 401-233-0690.

07 Clinical Laboratory Advisory Board, 3 Capitol Hill, Rm 104, Providence, RI 02908; 401-222-2827, Fax: 401-222-1272.

08 Department of Labor & Training, Division of Prof. Regulation - Bldg #70, PO Box 20247 (1511 Pontiac Av), Providence, RI 02920-0943; 401-462-8527, Fax: 401-462-8528.

09 Department of Environmental Management, 235 Promenade St, #260, Providence, RI 02908-5767; 401-222-4700, Fax: 401-222-6177.

10 Division of Forest Environment, 1037 Hartford Pike, North Scituate, RI 02857; 401-647-3367, Fax: 401-647-3590.

11 Division of Licensing & Consumer Protection, 233 Richmond St, Providence, RI 02903; 401-222-3857.

12 Division of Parks & Recreation, 2321 Hartford Ave, Johnston, RI 02919; 401-222-2632, Fax: 401-934-0610.

www.riparks.com/employment.htm

13 Health Department, Professional Regulation Division, 3 Capitol Hill, Providence, RI 02908-5097; 401-222-2827, Fax: 401-222-1272.

www.health.state.ri.us

15 Office of Secretary of State, 100 N Main St, Providence, RI 02903; 401-222-2249, Fax: 401-222-3879.

16 Office of Teacher Certification, 255 Wminster St, Providence, RI 02903; 401-222-4600, Fax: 401-222-2048.

18 Superior Court, 250 Benefit St, Rm 533, Providence, RI 02903; 401-222-3212, Fax: 401-272-4645.

19 State Fire Marshall's Office, 24 Conway Ave, Quansit-Davisville Industrial Park, North Kingston, RI 02852; 401-294-0861, Fax: 401-295-9092.

20 Pilotage Commission, 301 Great Island Rd, Galilee, RI 02882; 401-783-5551, Fax: 401-783-7285.

21 Supreme Court, Board of Bar Examiners, 250 Benefit St, Providence, RI 02903; 401-222-3272, Fax: 401-222-3599.

www.courts.state.ri.us/supreme/barex.html

22 Department of Children, Youth & Famillies, 610 Mt. Pleasant Ave, Providence, RI 02908; 401-222-4741.

23 Department of Environmental Management, Division of Fish & Wildlife, Box 218, West Kingston, RI 02892; 401-222-1267.

24 Department of Health, 3 Capitol Hill Rm 205, Providence, RI 02908; 401-222-3855, Fax: 401-222-2158.

The following list indicates the district and division name for each county in the state. If the district or division name of the bankruptcy court is different from the civil/criminal court, it appears in parentheses.

County/Court Cross Reference

Bristol .... Providence
Kent .... Providence
Newport .... Providence
Providence .... Providence
Washington .... Providence

US District Court

District of Rhode Island

Providence Division Clerk's Office, Two Exchange Terrace, Federal Bldg, Providence, RI 02903, 401-752-7200, Fax: 401-752-7247.

Counties: All counties in Rhode Island.

Indexing & Storage: Cases are indexed by defendant and plaintiff as well as by case number. New cases are available in the index 1-2 days after filing date. Both computer and card indexes are maintained. Computer indexing is since 1991. Anything prior to that is maintained on card index. Open records are located at this court. District wide searches are available from this court.

Fee & Payment: The fee is $15.00 per item (one party name or case number). Payment may be made by money order, cashier check, personal check. Prepayment is required. Payee: Clerk, US District Court. Certification fee: $5.00 per document. Copy fee: $.50 per page. You are allowed to make your own copies. These copies cost $.25 per page. Naturalization records are at the Federal Records Center in Waltham, MA.

Phone Search: Only the case number or name will be released over the phone. An automated voice case information service (VCIS) is not available.

Mail Search: Always enclose a stamped self addressed envelope.

In Person Search: In person searching is available.

PACER: Sign-up number is 800-676-6856. Access fee is $.60 per minute. Toll-free access: 888-421-6861. Local access: 401-528-5145. Case records are available back to December 1988. Records are never purged. New records are available online after 2 days.

US Bankruptcy Court

District of Rhode Island

Providence Division 6th Floor, 380 Westminster Mall, Providence, RI 02903, 401-528-4477, Fax: 401-528-4470.

www.rib.uscourts.gov

Counties: All counties in Rhode Island.

Indexing & Storage: Cases are indexed by debtor and creditors as well as by case number. New cases are available in the index 1 day after filing date. A computer index is maintained. Open records are located at this court.

Fee & Payment: The fee is $15.00 per item (one party name or case number). Payment may be made by money order, cashier check, personal check, Visa or Mastercard. Prepayment is required. Checks from debtors not accepted. Payee: Clerk, US Bankruptcy Court. Certification fee: $5.00 per document. Copy fee: $.50 per page. You are allowed to make your own copies. These copies cost $.20 per page.

Phone Search: Only docket information is available by phone. An automated voice case information service (VCIS) is available. Call VCIS at 800-843-2841 or 401-528-4476.

Fax Search: The fees for a fax request are the same as for a mail request. The fee is $15.00 per item.

Mail Search: Always enclose a stamped self addressed envelope.

In Person Search: In person searching is available.

PACER: Sign-up number is 800-676-6856. Access fee is $.60 per minute. Toll-free access: 800-610-9310. Local access: 401-528-4062. Case records are available back to 1990. Records are purged every three years. New civil records are available online after 1 day. PACER is available on the Internet at http://204.17.81.145/cgi-bin/webbill/bkplog.html.

Court	Jurisdiction	No. of Courts	How Organized
Superior Courts*	General	5	4 Divisions
District Courts*	Limited	4	6 Divisions
Municipal Courts	Municipal	14	
Probate Courts*	Probate	39	39 Cities/ Towns
Family Courts	Special	4	4 Divisions
Workers' Compensation Court	Special	1	

* Profiled in this Sourcebook.

CIVIL									
Court	Tort	Contract	Real Estate	Min. Claim	Max. Claim	Small Claims	Estate	Eviction	Domestic Relations
Superior Courts*	X	X	X	$5000	No Max				
District Courts*	X	X	X	$1500	$10,000	$1500		X	
Municipal Courts									
Probate Courts*							X		
Family Courts									X
Workers' Compensation Court									

CRIMINAL					
Court	Felony	Misdemeanor	DWI/DUI	Preliminary Hearing	Juvenile
Superior Courts*	X				
District Courts*		X	X	X	
Municipal Courts					
Probate Courts*					
Family Courts					X
Workers' Compensation Court					

ADMINISTRATION   Court Administrator, Supreme Court, 250 Benefit St, Providence, RI, 02903; 401-222-3272, Fax: 401-222-3599. www.courts.state.ri.us

COURT STRUCTURE   Rhode Island has five counties, but only four Superior/District Court Locations (2nd, 3rd, 4th, and 6th Districts). Bristol and Providence counties are completely merged at the Providence location. Civil claims between $5000 and $10,000 may be filed in either Superior or District Court at the discretion of the filer. Probate is handled by the Town Clerk at the 39 cities and towns across Rhode Island.

ONLINE ACCESS   The Superior (civil, domestic, family) and Appellate courts are online internally for court perosnnel only.

There are plans to place criminal record data on the Internet. For more information, call Edward Plunkett at 401-222-3000.

Bristol County

Superior & District Courts, RI;.

Note: All civil and criminal cases handled by the Providence County courts.

Barrington Town Hall 283 County Road, Barrington, RI 02806; 401-247-1900; Fax: Call first. Hours: 8:30AM-4:30PM (EST). *Probate.*

Bristol Town Hall 10 Court Street, Bristol, RI 02809; 401-253-7000; Fax: 401-253-3080. Hours: 8:30AM-4PM (EST). *Probate.*

Warren Town Hall 514 Main Street, Warren, RI 02885; 401-245-7340; Fax: 401-245-7421. Hours: 9AM-4PM (EST). *Probate.*

Kent County

Superior Court 222 Quaker Lane, Warwick, RI 02886-0107; 401-822-1311. Hours: 8:30AM-4:30PM (EST). *Felony, Civil Actions Over $10,000.*

Civil Records: Access: In person only. Court does not conduct in person searches; visitors must perform searches for themselves. Search fee: No civil searches performed by court. Required to search: name, years to search. Civil cases indexed by defendant, plaintiff. Civil records on computer from 1987. **Criminal Records:** Access: In person only. Court does not conduct in person searches; visitors must perform searches for themselves. Search fee: No criminal searches performed by court. Required to search: name, years to search, signed release; also helpful-DOB. Criminal records on computer from 1987. **General Information:** No adoption, confidential or sealed records released. Copy fee: $.50 per page. Certification fee: $3.00. Fee payee: Clerk of Superior Court. Personal checks accepted. Prepayment is required. Public access terminal is available. Public Access Terminal Note: records available from 1997.

3rd Division District Court 222 Quaker Lane, Warwick, RI 02886-0107; 401-822-1771. Hours: 8:30AM-4:30PM (EST). *Misdemeanor, Civil Actions Under $10,000, Eviction, Small Claims.*

Civil Records: Access: In person only. Court does not conduct in person searches; visitors must perform searches for themselves. Search fee: No civil searches performed by court. Required to search: name, years to search. Civil cases indexed by defendant, plaintiff. Civil records for 1995-1997 on index cards. Archives stored at Rhode Island Judicial Records Center, 1 Hill St, Pawtucket, RI 02860, 401-277-3249. Records destroyed after 10 years, but remain in docket books. **Criminal Records:** Access: In person only. Court does not conduct in person searches; visitors must perform searches for themselves. Search fee: No criminal searches performed by court. Required to search: name, years to search, DOB, signed release. Criminal records for 1995-1997 on index cards. Archives stored at Rhode Island Judicial Records Center. Records destroyed after 10 years, but remain in docket books. **General Information:** No mental or sealed records released. Copy fee: $.50 per page. Certification fee: $3.00. Fee payee: 3rd District Court. Personal checks accepted. Credit cards accepted: Visa, AmEx. Prepayment is required.

Coventry Town Hall 1670 Flat River Road, Coventry, RI 02816; 401-822-9174; Fax: 401-822-9132. Hours: 8:30AM-4:30PM (EST). *Probate.*

East Greenwich Town Hall 125 Main St, East Greenwich, RI 02818; 401-886-8603; Fax: 401-886-8625. Hours: 8:30AM-4:30PM (EST). *Probate.*

Warwick City Hall 3275 Post Road, Warwick, RI 02886; 401-738-2000; Fax: 401-738-6639. Hours: 8:30AM-4:30PM (EST). *Probate.*

West Greenwich Town Hall 280 Victory Highway, West Greenwich, RI 02817; 401-397-5016; Fax: 401-392-3805. Hours: 9AM-4PM M,T,Th,F; 9AM-4PM, 7-9PM W (EST). *Probate.*

West Warwick Town Hall 1170 Main Street, West Warwick, RI 02893-4829; 401-822-9201; Fax: 401-822-9266. Hours: 8:30AM-4:30PM; 8:30AM-4PM June 1st-Labor Day (EST). *Probate.*

Newport County

Superior Court Florence K Murray Judicial Complex, 45 Washington Sq, Newport, RI 02840; 401-841-8330. Hours: 8:30AM-4:30PM (July and August till 4PM) (EST). *Felony, Civil Actions Over $10,000.*

Civil Records: Access: Mail, in person. Both court and visitors may perform in person searches. No search fee. Required to search: name, years to search. Civil cases indexed by defendant, plaintiff. Civil records on computer from 1989. Prior records archived at Rhode Island Records Center. **Criminal Records:** Access: Mail, in person. Both court and visitors may perform in person searches. No search fee. Required to search: name, years to search, DOB. Criminal records on computer from 1983, index from 1968. Prior records archived at Records Center. **General Information:** No child molestation or sexual assault records released. SASE required. Turnaround time 1 day. Copy fee: $.50 per page. Certification fee: $1.00. Fee payee: Clerk Superior Court. Personal checks accepted. Prepayment is required. Public access terminal is available.

2nd District Court 45 Washington Square, Newport, RI 02840; 401-841-8350. Hours: 8:30AM-4:30PM (4PM-summer months) (EST). *Misdemeanor, Civil Actions Under $10,000, Eviction, Small Claims.*

Civil Records: Access: In person only. Court does not conduct in person searches; visitors must perform searches for themselves. Search fee: No civil searches performed by court. Required to search: name, years to search. Civil cases indexed by defendant, plaintiff. Civil records on index cards for past 3 years, prior archived at Pawtucket Judicial Records Center. **Criminal Records:** Access: In person only. Both court and visitors may perform in person searches. Search fee: No criminal searches performed by court. Required to search: name. **General Information:** No juvenile, family court, sealed, expunged or ordered by judge or adoption records released. Copy fee: $.25 per page. Certification fee: $1.00. Fee payee: 2nd District Court. Personal checks accepted. Prepayment is required.

Jamestown Town Hall 93 Narragansett Avenue, Jamestown, RI 02835; 401-423-7200; Fax: 401-423-7230. Hours: 8AM-4:30PM (EST). *Probate.*

Little Compton Town Hall 40 Commons, PO Box 226, Little Compton, RI 02837; 401-635-4400; Fax: 401-635-2470. Hours: 8AM-4PM (EST). *Probate.*

Middletown Town Hall 350 East Main Road, Middletown, RI 02842; 401-847-0009; Fax: 401-845-0400. Hours: 9AM-5PM (EST). *Probate.*

Newport City Hall 43 Broadway, Newport, RI 02840; 401-846-9600; Fax: 401-849-8757. Hours: 8:30AM-4:30PM (EST). *Probate.*

Portsmouth Town Hall 2200 East Main Road, PO Box 115, Portsmouth, RI 02871; 401-683-2101. Hours: 9AM-4:30PM (EST). *Probate.*

Tiverton Town Hall 343 Highland Road, Tiverton, RI 02878; 401-625-6700; Fax: 401-624-8640. Hours: 8:30AM-4PM (EST). *Probate.*

Providence County

Providence/Bristol Superior Court 250 Benefit St, Providence, RI 02903; 401-222-3250. Hours: 8:30AM-4:30PM (EST). *Felony, Civil Actions Over $10,000.*

Civil Records: Access: In person only. Court does not conduct in person searches; visitors must perform searches for themselves. Search fee: No civil searches performed by court. Required to search: name, years to search. Civil cases indexed by defendant, plaintiff. Civil records on computer since 1983. **Criminal Records:** Access: In person only. Court does not conduct in person searches; visitors must perform searches for themselves. Search fee: No criminal searches performed by court. Required to search: name, years to search, DOB. Criminal records on computer since 1983. **General Information:** No adoption, confidential or sealed records released. Copy fee: $.15 per page. Certification fee: No certification fee. Fee payee: Providence Superior Court. Personal checks accepted. Prepayment is required. Public access terminal is available.

6th Division District Court 1 Dorrance Plaza 2nd Floor, Providence, RI 02903; 401-222-6710. Hours: 8:30AM-4:30PM (EST). *Misdemeanor, Civil Actions Under $10,000, Eviction, Small Claims.*

Civil Records: Access: Mail, in person. Both court and visitors may perform in person searches. No search fee. Required to search: name, years to search. Civil cases indexed by defendant, plaintiff. Civil records on card files to present. Phone access limited to one name. **Criminal Records:** Access: Mail, in person. Both court and visitors may perform in person searches. No search fee. Required to search: name, years to search. Criminal records for misdemeanor on computer from 1989. Phone requests limited to one name. **General Information:** No adoption, confidential or sealed records released. SASE required. Turnaround time varies. Copy fee: $.50 per page. Certification fee: $1.00. Fee payee: 6th Division District Court. Personal checks accepted. Prepayment is required.

Burrillville Town Hall 105 Harrisville Main Street, Harrisville, RI 02830; 401-568-4300; Fax: 401-568-0490. Hours: 8:30AM-4:30PM (EST). *Probate.*

Central Falls City Hall 580 Broad Street, Central Falls, RI 02863; 401-727-7400; Fax: 401-727-7476. Hours: 8:30AM-4:30PM (EST). *Probate.*

Cranston City Hall 869 Park Avenue, Cranston, RI 02910; 401-461-1000; Fax: 401-461-9650. Hours: 8:30AM-4:30PM (EST). *Probate.*

Cumberland Town Hall 45 Broad Street, PO Box 7, Cumberland, RI 02864; 401-728-2400; Fax: 401-724-1103. Hours: 8:30AM-4:30PM (EST). *Probate.*

East Providence City Hall 145 Taunton Avenue, East Providence, RI 02914; 401-435-7500; Fax: 401-438-7501. Hours: 8AM-4PM (EST). *Probate.*

Foster Town Hall 181 Howard Hill Road, Foster, RI 02825; 401-392-9200; Fax: 401-397-9736. Hours: 9AM-4PM (EST). *Probate.*

Glocester Town Hall 1145 Putnam Pike, Glocester/ Chepachet, RI 02814; 401-568-6206; Fax: 401-568-5850. Hours: 8AM-4:30PM (EST). *Probate.*

Johnston Town Hall 1385 Hartford Avenue, Johnston, RI 02919; 401-351-6618/401-553-8830 (Direct Phone); Fax: 401-553-8835. Hours: 9AM-4:30PM (EST). *Probate.*

Lincoln Town Hall 100 Old River Road, Lincoln, RI 02865; 401-333-1100; Fax: 401-333-3648. Hours: 9AM-4:30PM (EST). *Probate.*

North Providence Town Hall 2000 Smith Street, North Providence, RI 02911; 401-232-0900; Fax: 401-233-1409. Hours: 8:30AM-4:30PM (EST). *Probate.*

North Smithfield Town Hall 1 Main Street, Slatersville, RI 02876; 401-767-2200; Fax: 401-766-0016. Hours: 8AM-4PM (EST). *Probate.*

Pawtucket City Hall 137 Roosevelt Avenue, Pawtucket, RI 02860; 401-728-0500; Fax: 401-728-8932. Hours: 8:30AM-4:30PM (EST). *Probate.*

Providence City Hall 25 Dorrance Street, Providence, RI 02903; 401-421-7740; Fax: 401-861-6208. Hours: 8:45AM-4:15PM (EST). *Probate.*

Scituate Town Hall 195 Danielson Pike, PO Box 328, North Scituate, RI 02857; 401-647-7466; Fax: Call first. Hours: 9AM-4PM (EST). *Probate.*

Smithfield Town Hall 64 Farnum Pike, Smithfield, RI 02917; 401-233-1000; Fax: 401-232-7244. Hours: 9AM-4PM (EST). *Probate.*

Woonsocket City Hall 169 Main Street, Woonsocket, RI 02895; 401-762-6400; Fax: 401-765-0022. Hours: 8:30AM-4PM (EST). *Probate.*

Washington County

Superior Court 4800 Towerhill Rd, Wakefield, RI 02879; 401-782-4121. Hours: 8:30AM-4:30PM (Sept-June) 8:30AM-4PM (July & Aug) (EST). *Felony, Civil Actions Over $10,000.*

Civil Records: Access: Phone, mail, in person. Both court and visitors may perform in person searches. No search fee. Required to search: name, years to search. Civil cases indexed by defendant, plaintiff. Civil records on computer from 1984, on index prior to 1984. Archived at Record Center, 401-277-3249. Phone requests taken only after 3PM. **Criminal Records:** Access: Mail, in person. Both court and visitors may perform in person searches. No search fee. Required to search: name, years to search; also helpful-DOB. Criminal records on computer from 1984, on index prior to 1984. Archived at Record Center, 401-277-3249. **General Information:** No confidential or sealed records released. SASE required. Turnaround time 1 week. Copy fee: $.15 per page. Certification fee: $3.00. Fee payee: Washington Superior Court. Personal checks accepted.

4th District Court 4800 Towerhill Rd, Wakefield, RI 02879; 401-782-4131. Hours: 8:30AM-4:30PM (EST). *Misdemeanor, Civil Actions Under $10,000, Eviction, Small Claims.*

Civil Records: Access: In person only. Court does not conduct in person searches; visitors must perform searches for themselves. Search fee: No civil searches performed by court. Required to search: name, years to search. Civil cases indexed by defendant, plaintiff. Civil records on index cards. **Criminal Records:** Access: In person only. Court does not conduct in person searches; visitors must perform searches for themselves. Search fee: No criminal searches performed by court. Required to search: name, years to search; also helpful-DOB. Criminal records available on computer beginning in 1996. **General Information:** No family court records released.

Copy fee: $.50 per page. Certification fee: $1.00. Fee payee: Court Clerk. Personal checks accepted. Prepayment is required. Public access terminal is available.

Charlestown Town Hall 4540 South County Trail, Charlestown, RI 02813; 401-364-1200; Fax: 401-364-1238. Hours: 8:30AM-4:30PM (EST). *Probate.*

Exeter Town Hall 675 Ten Rod Road, Exeter, RI 02822; 401-294-3891; Fax: 401-295-1248. Hours: 9AM-4PM (EST). *Probate.*

Hopkinton Town Hall 1 Town House Road, Hopkinton, RI 02833; 401-377-7777; Fax: 401-377-7788. Hours: 8:30AM-4:30PM or by appointment (EST). *Probate.*

Narragansett Town Hall 25 Fifth Avenue, Narragansett, RI 02882; 401-789-1044 X621; Fax: 401-783-9637. Hours: 8:30AM-4:30PM (EST). *Probate.*

New Shoreham Town Hall Old Town Road, PO Drawer 220, Block Island, RI 02807; 401-466-3200; Fax: 401-466-3219. Hours: 9AM-3PM (EST). *Probate.*

North Kingstown Town Hall 80 Boston Neck Road, North Kingstown, RI 02852-5762; 401-294-3331; Fax: 401-885-7373. Hours: 8:30AM-4:30PM (EST). *Probate.*

www.northkingstown.org

Richmond Town Hall 5 Richmond Townhouse Rd., Wyoming, RI 02898; 401-539-2497; Fax: 401-539-1089. Hours: 9AM-4PM, 6-7:30PM M; 9AM-4PM T-F (EST). *Probate.*

South Kingstown Town Hall 180 High Street, Wakefield, RI 02879; 401-789-9331; Fax: 401-789-5280. Hours: 8:30AM-4:30PM (EST). *Probate.*

Westerly Town Hall 45 Broad Street, Westerly, RI 02891; 401-348-2500; Fax: 401-348-2571. Hours: 8:30AM-4:30PM (EST). *Probate.*

ORGANIZATION	5 counties and 39 towns, 39 recording offices. The recording officer is Town/City Clerk (Recorder of Deeds). The Town/City Clerk usually also serves as. Recorder of Deeds. **There is no county administration in Rhode Island.** The entire state is in the Eastern Time Zone (EST).
REAL ESTATE RECORDS	Towns will **not** perform real estate searches. Copy fees are usually $1.50 per page. Certification usually costs $3.00 per document.
UCC RECORDS	Financing statements are filed at the state level, except for farm related and real estate related collateral, which are filed with the Town/City Clerk. Most recording offices will **not** perform UCC searches. Use search request form UCC-11. Copy fees are usually $1.50 per page. Certification usually costs $3.00 per document.
TAX LIEN RECORDS	All federal and state tax liens on personal property and on real property are filed with the Recorder of Deeds. Towns will **not** perform tax lien searches.
OTHER LIENS	Mechanics, municipal, lis pendens.

Barrington Town

Town Clerk, 283 County Road, Town Hall, Barrington, RI 02806. 401-247-1900.

Bristol County

There is no real estate recording at the county level in Rhode Island. You must determine the city or town where the property is located.

Bristol Town

Town Clerk, 10 Court Street, Town Hall, Bristol, RI 02809. 401-253-7000.

Burrillville Town

Town Clerk, 105 Harrisville Main Street, Town Hall, Harrisville, RI 02830-1499. 401-568-4300. Fax: 401-568-0490.

Central Falls City

City Clerk, 580 Broad Street, City Hall, Central Falls, RI 02863. 401-727-7400. Fax: 401-727-7476.

Charlestown Town

Town Clerk, 4540 South County Trail, Charlestown, RI 02813. 401-364-1200. Fax: 401-364-1238.

Coventry Town

Town Clerk, 1670 Flat River Road, Town Hall, Coventry, RI 02816-8911. 401-822-9174. Fax: 401-822-9132.

Cranston City

City Clerk, 869 Park Avenue, City Hall, Cranston, RI 02910. 401-461-1000x3130.

Cumberland Town

Town Clerk, P.O. Box 7, Cumberland, RI 02864-0808. 401-728-2400. Fax: 401-724-1103.

East Greenwich Town

Town Clerk, P.O. Box 111, East Greenwich, RI 02818. 401-886-8603. Fax: 401-886-8625.

East Providence City

City Clerk, 145 Taunton Avenue, City Hall, East Providence, RI 02914. 401-435-7500. Fax: 401-435-7501.

Exeter Town

Town Clerk, 675 Ten Rod Road, Town Hall, Exeter, RI 02822. 401-294-3891. Fax: 401-295-1248.
Online Access: Assessor. Property Tax Records on the Town of Exeter Assessor's database are available free on the Internet at http://140.239.211.227/Exeter_ri. User ID number is required; registration is free.

Foster Town

Town Clerk, 181 Howard Hill Road, Town Hall, Foster, RI 02825-1227. 401-392-9200. Fax: 401-392-9201.

Glocester Town

Town Clerk, P.O. Drawer B, Glocester/ Chepachet, RI 02814-0702. 401-568-6206. Fax: 401-568-5850.

Hopkinton Town

Town Clerk, 1 Town House Road, Town Hall, Hopkinton, RI 02833. 401-377-7777. Fax: 401-377-7788.

Jamestown Town

Town Clerk, 93 Narragansett Avenue, Town Hall, Jamestown, RI 02835. 401-423-7200. Fax: 401-423-7230.

Johnston Town

Town Clerk, 1385 Hartford Avenue, Town Hall, Johnston, RI 02919. 401-351-6618. Fax: 401-331-4271.

Kent County

There is no real estate recording at the county level in Rhode Island. You must determine the town or city where the property is located.

Lincoln Town

Town Clerk, P.O. Box 100, Lincoln, RI 02865. 401-333-1100. Fax: 401-333-3648.

Little Compton Town

Town Clerk, P.O. Box 226, Little Compton, RI 02837-0226. 401-635-4400. Fax: 401-635-2470.

Middletown Town

Town Clerk, 350 East Main Road, Town Hall, Middletown, RI 02842. 401-847-0009. Fax: 401-848-0500.
Online Access: Assessor. Property records on the Assessor's database are available on the Internet at http://140.239.211.227/middletownri. User ID number is required is required to access the full database. Non-registered users can access a limited set of data.

Narragansett Town

Town Clerk, 25 Fifth Avenue, Town Hall, Narragansett, RI 02882. 401-789-1044. Fax: 401-783-9637.

New Shoreham Town

Town Clerk, P.O. Drawer 220, Block Island, RI 02807. 401-466-3200. Fax: 401-466-3219.

Newport City

City Clerk, 43 Broadway, Town Hall, Newport, RI 02840-2798. 401-846-9600.

Newport County

There is no real estate recording at the county level in Rhode Island. You must determine the town or city where the property is located.

North Kingstown Town

Town Clerk, 80 Boston Neck Road, Town Hall, North Kingstown, RI 02852. 401-294-3331. Fax: 401-885-7373.

North Providence Town

Town Clerk, 2000 Smith Street, Town Hall, North Providence, RI 02911. 401-232-0900. Fax: 401-233-1409.

North Smithfield Town

Town Clerk, 1 Main Street, Town Hall, Slatersville, RI 02876. 401-767-2200. Fax: 401-766-0016.

Pawtucket City

City Clerk, 137 Roosevelt Avenue, City Hall, Pawtucket, RI 02860. 401-728-0500. Fax: 401-728-8932.

Portsmouth Town

Town Clerk, P.O. Box 155, Portsmouth, RI 02871. 401-683-2101.

Providence City

City Clerk, 25 Dorrance Street, City Hall, Providence, RI 02903. 401-421-7740x312.

Providence County

There is no real estate recording at the county level in Rhode Island. You must determine the proper town or city based on property location.

Richmond Town

Town Clerk, 5 Richmond Townhouse Rd., Town Hall, Wyoming, RI 02898. 401-539-2497. Fax: 401-539-1089.

Scituate Town

Town Clerk, PO Box 328, North Scituate, RI 02857-0328. 401-647-2822.

Smithfield Town

Town Clerk, 64 Farnum Pike, Town Hall, Esmond, RI 02917. 401-233-1000. Fax: 401-232-7244.

South Kingstown Town

Town Clerk, P.O. Box 31, Wakefield, RI 02880. 401-789-9331.

Tiverton Town

Town Clerk, 343 Highland Road, Town Hall, Tiverton, RI 02878. 401-625-6700. Fax: 401-624-8640.

Warren Town

Town Clerk, 514 Main Street, Town Hall, Warren, RI 02885. 401-245-7340. Fax: 401-245-7421.

Warwick City

City Clerk, 3275 Post Road, Warwick, RI 02886. 401-738-2000. Fax: 401-738-6639.

Washington County

There is no real estate recording at the county level in Rhode Island. You must determine the town or city where the property is located.

West Greenwich Town

Town Clerk, 280 Victory Highway, Town Hall, West Greenwich, RI 02817. 401-397-5016. Fax: 401-392-3805.

West Warwick Town

Town Clerk, 1170 Main Street, Town Hall, West Warwick, RI 02893-4829. 401-822-0859. Fax: 401-822-9266.

Westerly Town

Town Clerk, 45 Broad Street, Town Hall, Westerly, RI 02891. 401-348-2500. Fax: 401-348-2571.

Woonsocket City

City Clerk, 169 Main Street, City Hall, Woonsocket, RI 02895. 401-762-6400. Fax: 401-765-4569.

You will usually be able to find the city name in the City/County Cross Reference below. In that case, it is a simple matter to determine the county from the cross reference. However, only the official US Postal Service city names are included in this index. There are an additional 40,000 place names that people use in their addresses. Therefore, we have also included a ZIP/City Cross Reference immediately following the City/County Cross Reference.

If you know the ZIP Code but the city name does not appear in the City/County Cross Reference index, look up the ZIP Code in the ZIP/City Cross Reference, find the city name, then look up the city name in the City/County Cross Reference. For example, you want to know the county for an address of Menands, NY 12204. There is no "Menands" in the City/County Cross Reference. The ZIP/City Cross Reference shows that ZIP Codes 12201-12288 are for the city of Albany. Looking back in the City/County Cross Reference, Albany is in Albany County.

City/County Cross Reference

ADAMSVILLE Newport	EXETER Washington	MANVILLE Providence	RUMFORD Providence
ALBION Providence	FISKEVILLE Providence	MAPLEVILLE Providence	SAUNDERSTOWN Washington
ASHAWAY Washington	FORESTDALE Providence	MIDDLETOWN Newport	SHANNOCK Washington
BARRINGTON Bristol	FOSTER Providence	NARRAGANSETT Washington	SLATERSVILLE Providence
BLOCK ISLAND Washington	GLENDALE Providence	NEWPORT Newport	SLOCUM Washington
BRADFORD Washington	GREENE Kent	NORTH KINGSTOWN Washington	SMITHFIELD Providence
BRISTOL Bristol	GREENVILLE Providence	NORTH PROVIDENCE Providence	TIVERTON Newport
CAROLINA Washington	HARMONY Providence	NORTH SCITUATE Providence	WAKEFIELD Washington
CENTRAL FALLS Providence	HARRISVILLE Providence	NORTH SMITHFIELD Providence	WARREN Bristol
CHARLESTOWN Washington	HOPE Providence	OAKLAND Providence	WARWICK Kent
CHEPACHET Providence	HOPE VALLEY Washington	PASCOAG Providence	WEST GREENWICH Kent
CLAYVILLE Providence	HOPKINTON Washington	PAWTUCKET Providence	WEST KINGSTON Washington
COVENTRY Kent	JAMESTOWN Newport	PEACE DALE Washington	WEST WARWICK Kent
CRANSTON Providence	JOHNSTON Providence	PORTSMOUTH Newport	WESTERLY Washington
CUMBERLAND Providence	KENYON Washington	PROVIDENCE Providence	WOOD RIVER JUNCTION Washington
EAST GREENWICH Kent	KINGSTON Washington	PRUDENCE ISLAND Bristol	WOONSOCKET Providence
EAST PROVIDENCE Providence	LINCOLN Providence	RIVERSIDE Providence	WYOMING Washington
ESCOHEAG Washington	LITTLE COMPTON Newport	ROCKVILLE Washington	

ZIP/City Cross Reference

02801-02801	ADAMSVILLE	02827-02827	GREENE	02863-02863	CENTRAL FALLS	02893-02893	WEST WARWICK
02802-02802	ALBION	02828-02828	GREENVILLE	02864-02864	CUMBERLAND	02894-02894	WOOD RIVER JUNCTION
02804-02804	ASHAWAY	02829-02829	HARMONY	02865-02865	LINCOLN	02895-02895	WOONSOCKET
02806-02806	BARRINGTON	02830-02830	HARRISVILLE	02871-02871	PORTSMOUTH	02896-02896	NORTH SMITHFIELD
02807-02807	BLOCK ISLAND	02831-02831	HOPE	02872-02872	PRUDENCE ISLAND	02898-02898	WYOMING
02808-02808	BRADFORD	02832-02832	HOPE VALLEY	02873-02873	ROCKVILLE	02901-02909	PROVIDENCE
02809-02809	BRISTOL	02833-02833	HOPKINTON	02874-02874	SAUNDERSTOWN	02910-02910	CRANSTON
02812-02812	CAROLINA	02835-02835	JAMESTOWN	02875-02875	SHANNOCK	02911-02911	NORTH PROVIDENCE
02813-02813	CHARLESTOWN	02836-02836	KENYON	02876-02876	SLATERSVILLE	02912-02912	PROVIDENCE
02814-02814	CHEPACHET	02837-02837	LITTLE COMPTON	02877-02877	SLOCUM	02914-02914	EAST PROVIDENCE
02815-02815	CLAYVILLE	02838-02838	MANVILLE	02878-02878	TIVERTON	02915-02915	RIVERSIDE
02816-02816	COVENTRY	02839-02839	MAPLEVILLE	02879-02880	WAKEFIELD	02916-02916	RUMFORD
02817-02817	WEST GREENWICH	02840-02841	NEWPORT	02881-02881	KINGSTON	02917-02917	SMITHFIELD
02818-02818	EAST GREENWICH	02842-02842	MIDDLETOWN	02882-02882	NARRAGANSETT	02918-02918	PROVIDENCE
02822-02822	EXETER	02852-02854	NORTH KINGSTOWN	02883-02883	PEACE DALE	02919-02919	JOHNSTON
02823-02823	FISKEVILLE	02857-02857	NORTH SCITUATE	02885-02885	WARREN	02920-02921	CRANSTON
02824-02824	FORESTDALE	02858-02858	OAKLAND	02886-02889	WARWICK	02940-02940	PROVIDENCE
02825-02825	FOSTER	02859-02859	PASCOAG	02891-02891	WESTERLY		
02826-02826	GLENDALE	02860-02862	PAWTUCKET	02892-02892	WEST KINGSTON		

South Carolina

General Help Numbers:

Governor's Office
PO Box 11829
Columbia, SC 29211
www.state.sc.us/governor

803-734-9400
Fax 803-734-9413
8AM-6PM

Attorney General's Office
PO Box 11549
Columbia, SC 29211
www.scattorneygeneral.org

803-734-3970
Fax 803-734-4323
8:30AM-5:30PM

State Court Administrator
1015 Sumter St, 2nd Floor
Columbia, SC 29201
www.judicial.state.sc.us

803-734-1800
Fax 803-734-1821
8:30AM-5PM M-F

State Archives
8301 Parklane Rd
Columbia, SC 29223
www.state.sc.us/scdah

803-896-6100
Fax 803-896-6198
9AM-9PM TU-FR, 9-6 SA

State Specifics:

Capital:	Columbia
	Richland County
Time Zone:	EST
Number of Counties:	46
Population:	3,885,736
Web Site:	www.state.sc.us

State Agencies

Criminal Records

South Carolina Law Enforcement Division (SLED), Criminal Records Section, PO Box 21398, Columbia, SC 29221 (Courier: 440 Broad River Rd, Columbia, SC 29210); 803-896-7043, 803-896-7022 (Fax), 8:30AM-5PM.

www.sled.state.sc.us

Indexing & Storage: Records are available for many years. New records are available for inquiry immediately. Records are indexed on inhouse computer.

Searching: Criminal records are open without restrictions. Include the following in your request- full name, any aliases, date of birth, sex, race. The SSN is optional.

Access by: mail, in person, online.

Fee & Payment: The search fee is $25.00 per individual. The fee is $8.00 for non-profit organizations, pre-approval is required. Fee payee: SLED. Prepayment required. Business and company checks are accepted. No credit cards accepted.

Mail search: Turnaround time: 5-7 days. The will return by overnight delivery service if prepaid and materials provided.A self addressed stamped envelope is requested.

In person search: Turnaround time is within minutes.

Online search: SLED offers commercial access to criminal record history from 1960 forward on the web site. Fees are $25.00 per screening or $8.00 if

for a charitable organization. Credit card ordering accepted. Visit the web site or call 803-896-7219 for details.

Fictitious Name
Assumed Name
Trade Names

Records not maintained by a state level agency.

Note: Records are found at the county level.

Corporation Records
Trademarks/Servicemarks
Limited Partnerships
Limited Liability Company Records

Corporation Division, Capitol Complex, PO Box 11350, Columbia, SC 29211 (Courier: Edgar A. Brown Bldg, Room 525, Columbia, SC 29201); 803-734-2158, 803-734-2164 (Fax), 8:30PM-5PM.

Note: Trademarks and service marks are not on the computer but are in this department.

Indexing & Storage: Records are available from 1800's on. In house computer records are from 1985 on. Older records are stored at the State Archives. New records are available for inquiry immediately. Records are indexed on microfilm, inhouse computer.

Searching: Include the following in your request-full name of business. In addition to the articles of incorporation, corporation records include the following information: Prior (merged) names, Inactive and Reserved names. Annual Reports, Officer and Directors are kept in the State Department of Revenue.

Access by: mail, phone, in person, online.

Fee & Payment: Fees: $1.00 per page for the first document and $.50 per page for each additional document. If record is to be certifed, then fee is $3.00 for first page. Fee payee: Secretary of State. Prepayment required. Personal checks accepted. No credit cards accepted.

Mail search: Turnaround time: 1-2 days. A self addressed stamped envelope is requested.

Phone search: No fee for telephone request. They will provide basic information only.

In person search: Information requests are available.

Online search: Their program is called Direct Access. Information available includes corporate names, registered agents & addresses, date of original filings, and dates of admendments or merger filings. The system is open 24 hours daily and there are no fees. The system permits the retrieval of documents by fax return. For more information, call Jody Steigerwalt at 803-734-2345.

Annual Reports
Directors and Officers

Department of Revenue, Office Services/Records, 301 Gervias St, Columbia, SC 29201; 803-898-5751, 803-898-5888 (Fax), 8:30AM-5PM.

Indexing & Storage: Records are available from 1990 on. Records are indexed on inhouse computer, hard copy.

Searching: Information on partnerships and on taxes is not public. Include the following in your request-full name of business.

Access by: mail, phone, fax, in person.

Fee & Payment: Fees: $2.63 per year for annual reports. Fee payee: South Carolina Department of Revenue. Prepayment required. Personal checks accepted. No credit cards accepted.

Mail search: Turnaround time: 1 week. A self addressed stamped envelope is requested.

Phone search: No fee for up to 2 corporations. They will give officers and registered agent information.

Fax search: Turnaround is usually in 1 day.

In person search: You may request information in person, but will not receive copies the same day.

Uniform Commercial Code

UCC Division, Secretary of State, PO Box 11350, Columbia, SC 29211 (Courier: Edgar Brown Bldg, 1205 Pendelton St #525, Columbia, SC 29201); 803-734-1961, 803-734-2164 (Fax), 8:30AM-5PM.

www.scsos.com/ucc.htm

Indexing & Storage: Records are available from 1968. Records are computerized since 1985.

Searching: Use search request Form UCC-4 for in-state and UCC-11 for out-of-state. All tax liens are filed at the county level. Include the following in your request-debtor name.

Access by: mail, phone, fax, in person, online.

Fee & Payment: Fees are $5.00 for the first debtor name and $2.00 for each additional name on a request. However, there is no $5.00 search fee if file number given. Copies are $2.00 per financing statement, plus $1.00 for each page of attachments. Fee payee: Secretary of State. Prepayment required. Personal checks accepted. No credit cards accepted.

Mail search: Turnaround time: 5-10 days. A self addressed stamped envelope is requested.

Phone search: No fee for telephone request. The staff will look-up file numbers at no charge.

Fax search: There is an additional $5.00 fee for faxing in and $10.00 fee for faxing back.

In person search: You may request information in person.

Online search: "Direct Access" is open 24 hours daily, there are no fees. Inquiry is by debtor name. The system provides for copies to be faxed automatically. Call 803-734-2345 for registration information.

Federal Tax Liens
State Tax Liens
Records not maintained by a state level agency.
Note: Tax lien data is found at the county level.

Sales Tax Registrations

Revenue Department, Sales Tax Registration Section, PO Box 125, Columbia, SC 29214 (Courier: 301 Gervais St, Columbia, SC 29214); 803-898-5872, 803-898-5888 (Fax), 8:30AM-4:45PM.

www.dor.state.sc.us

Indexing & Storage: Records are available for 4-5 years, then are archived on hard copy. Records are indexed on inhouse computer.

Searching: This agency will only confirm that a business is registered. They will provide no other information. Include the following in your request-business name. They can also search by tax permit number, owner name, or federal ID.

Access by: mail, phone, fax, in person.

Mail search: Turnaround time: 7 days. A self addressed stamped envelope is requested. No fee for mail request.

Phone search: No fee for telephone request.

Fax search: Fax searching available.

In person search: No fee for request.

Birth Certificates

South Carolina DHEC, Vital Records, 2600 Bull St, Columbia, SC 29201; 803-898-3630, 803-898-3631 (Order Line), 803-799-0301 (Fax), 8:30AM-4:30PM.

Note: A "short form" wallet size birth certificate can be obtained from the county of issue. This form will not show parent names.

Indexing & Storage: Records are available from January 1, 1915-present. It takes 2 months before new records are available for inquiry. Records are indexed on microfiche, inhouse computer.

Searching: Records will only be released to the registrant (if 18 or older), parents, guardian or legal representative. Include the following in your request-full name, names of parents, mother's maiden name, date of birth, place of birth. Two types of certificates are issued: wallet-size; photocopy certification (actual birth certificate).

Access by: mail, phone, fax, in person.

Fee & Payment: The fee is $12.00 per name. Add $3.00 per copy for additional copies. Add $5.00 for use of credit card. Fee payee: DHEC. Prepayment required. Credit cards accepted for phone and fax requests only. Personal checks accepted. Credit cards accepted: Mastercard, Visa, AmEx, Discover.

Mail search: Turnaround time: 3-4 weeks. No self addressed stamped envelope is required.

Phone search: Phone requests are accepted, using a credit card. See expedited service.

Fax search: Same criteria as phone searches. Is considered expedited.

In person search: Turnaround time is within 1 hour.

Expedited service: Expedited service is available for mail, phone and fax searches. To have search "expedited" to a 3-4 day turnaround, fee is an extra $5.00 and must use a credit card for add'l $5.00. Overnight shipping is $11.00.

Death Records

South Carolina DHEC, Vital Records, 2600 Bull St, Columbia, SC 29201; 803-898-3630, 803-898-3631 (Order Line), 803-799-0301 (Fax), 8:30AM-4:30PM.

Indexing & Storage: Records are available from January 1, 1915-date. New records are available for inquiry immediately. Records are indexed on microfiche, inhouse computer.

Searching: Copies are available to those who show a direct, tangible interest in a determination of a personal or property right. If less than 5 years, records are at county also. Include the following in your request-full name, date of death, place of death.

Access by: mail, phone, fax, in person.

Fee & Payment: The search fee is $12.00 per name. Add $3.00 per copy for additional copies. Add $5.00 for use of credit card. Fee payee: DHEC. Prepayment required. Credit cards accepted for phone and fax requests only. Personal checks accepted. Credit cards accepted: Mastercard, Visa, AmEx, Discover.

Mail search: Turnaround time: 3-4 weeks. No self addressed stamped envelope is required.

Phone search: Phone requests are accepted, using a credit card. See expedited service.

Fax search: See expedited service.

In person search: Turnaround time within 1 hour.

Expedited service: Expedited service is available for mail, phone and fax searches. To have the request expedited (3-4 days turnaround), fee is $5.00. To use a credit card there is an additional $5.00 fee. Overnight shipping is $11.00.

Marriage Certificates

South Carolina DHEC, Vital Records, 2600 Bull St, Columbia, SC 29201; 803-898-3630, 803-898-3631 (Order Line), 803-799-0301 (Fax), 8:30AM-4:30PM.

Note: Copies may also be obtained from the Probate Judge in the county where license was issued.

Indexing & Storage: Records are available from July 1, 1950-present. New records are available for inquiry immediately. Records are indexed on microfiche, inhouse computer.

Searching: Records are released only to the subjects, their adult children, former or present spouses and legal representatives. Others may obtain a statement of marriage date and place. Include the following in your request-names of husband and wife, date of marriage, place or county of marriage.

Access by: mail, phone, fax, in person.

Fee & Payment: The search fee is $12.00 per name, add $3.00 for each additional copy. Use of credit card is additional $5.00. Fee payee: DHEC. Prepayment required. Credit cards accepted for phone and fax searches only. Personal checks accepted. Credit cards accepted: Mastercard, Visa, AmEx, Discover.

Mail search: Turnaround time: 3 weeks. No self addressed stamped envelope is required.

Phone search: Phone requests are accepted, using a credit card. See expedited service.

Fax search: See expedited service.

In person search: Turnaround time within 1 hour.

Expedited service: Expedited service is available for mail, phone and fax searches. To have request expedited is an additional $5.00 plus $5.00 credit card fee. Overnight delivery is $11.00.

Divorce Records

South Carolina DHEC, Vital Records, 2600 Bull St, Columbia, SC 29201; 803-898-3630, 803-898-3631 (Order Line), 803-799-0301 (Fax), 8:30AM-4:30PM.

Indexing & Storage: Records are available from July 1, 1962-present. New records are available for inquiry immediately. Records are indexed on microfiche, inhouse computer.

Searching: Records are available only to the parties, their adult children, a present or former spouse, and their legal representatives. Others may obtain a statement of the date and county of the event. Include the following in your request-names

of husband and wife, date of divorce, place of divorce.

Access by: mail, phone, fax, in person.

Fee & Payment: The fee is $12.00 per name. Add $3.00 per copy for additional copies. Use of credit card is $5.00. Fee payee: DHEC. Prepayment required. Credit cards accepted for phone and fax requests only. Personal checks accepted. Credit cards accepted: Mastercard, Visa, AmEx, Discover.

Mail search: Turnaround time: 3 weeks. No self addressed stamped envelope is required.

Phone search: Phone requests are accepted, using a credit card. See expedited service.

Fax search: See expedited service.

In person search: Turnaround time within 1 hour.

Expedited service: Expedited service is available for mail, phone and fax searches. The fee for expedited service of 3-4 days turnaround time is $5.00. Use of a credit card is an additional $5.00. Overnight shipping is $11.00.

Workers' Compensation Records

Workers Compensation Commission, PO Box 1715, Columbia, SC 29202 (Courier: 1612 Marion St, Columbia, SC 29201); 803-737-5700, 803-737-5768 (Fax), 8:30AM-5PM.

www.state.sc.us/wcc

Indexing & Storage: Records are available from 1983 on the computer. Some of the older records are at this office and the rest are at the State Archives. Call office first for location of records. New records are available for inquiry immediately. Records are indexed on inhouse computer, books (volumes). Records are normally destroyed after 5 years after closing.

Searching: Must have a signed release form from claimant and you must specify what records you want. Include the following in your request-claimant name, Social Security Number, date of accident.

Access by: mail, fax, in person.

Fee & Payment: The search fee is $6.00 per record and includes a computer printout. File copies cost $20.00 for the first up to 20 pages and $.50 for each additional page. Fee payee: SC Workers Compensation Commission. Prepayment required. Personal checks accepted. No credit cards accepted.

Mail search: Turnaround time: 1 week. A self addressed stamped envelope is requested.

Fax search: You can request by fax, but reply is sent by mail, same turnaround time.

In person search: Records are still returned by mail.

Driver License Information Driver Records

Division of Motor Vehicles, Driver Records Section, PO Box 100178, Columbia, SC 29202-3178 (Courier: 955 Park St, Columbia, SC 29201); 803-737-4000, 803-737-1077 (Fax), 8:30AM-5PM.

www.state.sc.us/dps/dmv

Note: Copies of tickets are available from this department for a fee of $2.00 per record.

Indexing & Storage: Records are available for up to 10 years for moving violations, DWIs and suspensions. Records provided to the public are limited to 3 or 10 years. The state will show moving violations regardless of whether the fine was not paid and license suspended. It takes 1-4 weeks before new records are available for inquiry.

Searching: Identification card information is confidential by statute. Driving records are open; however, personal information is not released. The driver's license number, full name and DOB are required to order a record. The following data is not released: Social Security Numbers or personal information (height, weight, sex, eye color, etc.).

Access by: mail, in person, online.

Fee & Payment: The fee is $2.00 per record request. Fee payee: Department of Public Safety. Prepayment required. Personal checks accepted. No credit cards accepted.

Mail search: Turnaround time: 3 days. Fee and return address must be submitted with each request.No self addressed stamped envelope is required.

In person search: Most DMV Branch offices in the state will process up to 10 records while you wait.

Online search: The online system offers basic driver data, for a 3 year or a 10 year record. This is a single inquiry process. Network charges will be incurred as well as initial set-up and a security deposit. The system is up between 8 AM and 7 PM. Access is through the AAMVAnet (IBMIN), which requesters much "join." Call Libby Thomason for further information.

Other access: Magnetic tape and cassette batch processing is available. The agency, also, will sell all or portions of its driver license file in bulk format.

Vehicle Ownership Vehicle Identification

Division of Motor Vehicles, Title and Registration Records Section, PO Box 1498, Columbia, SC 29216 (Courier: 955 Park St, Columbia, SC 29201); 803-737-4000, 8:30AM-5PM.

www.state.sc.us/dps/dmv

Note: For Registration, use PO Box address with ZIP 29216-0036; use ZIP 29216-0024 for Titles.

Indexing & Storage: Records are available for 10 years for titles, 3 years for registration. The index to the records is computerized since 1984. It takes one day before new records are available for inquiry.

Searching: Information regarding the name, address and telephone number will not be released to the public, unless the requester completes form provided by department. Information is not provided to casual requesters. Requesters must be in compliance with DPPA.

Access by: mail, phone, fax, in person.

Fee & Payment: The fee is $2.00 per record request for all records, including lien information, except for odometer records which are $3.00 per request. Fee payee: Department of Public Safety. Prepayment required. A deposit account is available for ongoing requesters by mail or phone. Personal checks accepted. No credit cards accepted.

Mail search: Turnaround time: 3 days. No self addressed stamped envelope is required.

Phone search: Telephone searching is available for pre-approved, ongoing requesters. A deposit is required.

Fax search: This is only available to pre-approved, ongoing requesters. A deposit is required.

In person search: You may search in person.

Other access: South Carolina offers a variety of bulk retrieval programs where permitted by law. The maximum amount of records that can be retrieved is 100,000. For more information, call Titles or Registration at 803-737-4000.

Expedited service: Expedited service is available for fax searches. Turnaround time: 1-2 days. Must have a deposit account. The fax number is 803-737-2299.

Accident Reports

Accident Reports, PO Box 100178, Columbia, SC 29202-3178 (Courier: 955 Park St, Columbia, SC 29201); 803-737-4000, 803-737-4483 (Fax), 8:30AM-5PM.

Indexing & Storage: Records are available for 10 years to present. The records are indexed on computer. It takes one week after receipt from enforcement agency before new records are available for inquiry. Records are indexed on inhouse computer.

Searching: Must have full name of all the drivers involved in the accident. Include the following in your request-full name, date of accident, driver's license number, county.

Access by: mail, phone, in person.

Fee & Payment: The fees are $3.00 for accident research and $2.00 for insurance research. You may call to find out if record is on file. Fee payee: Department of Public Safety. Ongoing requesters may open an account with a $100.00 deposit and then will be billed monthly. Personal checks accepted. No credit cards accepted.

Mail search: Turnaround time: 7-10 days. Information requests are available.A self addressed stamped envelope is requested.

Phone search: Five records per day may be requested with a pre-approved account.

In person search: Records will be processed while you wait.

Boat & Vessel Ownership
Boat & Vessel Registration

Dept of Natural Resources, Registration & Titles, PO Box 167, Columbia, SC 29202; 803-734-3857, 803-734-4138 (Fax), 8:30AM-5PM.

www.dnr.state.sc.us

Indexing & Storage: Records are available from 1958-present. Active records remain on computer

as long as they are active. Inactive records are put on microfiche seven years after becoming inactive.

Searching: All motorized boats must be titled and registered. All sailboats must be titled, and if used with propulsion then registered. To search, one of the following is required: name and address, hull ID #, title #, or SC (serial) #. The following data is not released: Social Security Numbers.

Access by: mail, fax, in person.

Fee & Payment: The search fee for all types of searches is $3.00 per record. Fee payee: SC Dept of Natural Resources. Prepayment required. Personal checks accepted. No credit cards accepted.

Mail search: Turnaround time: 15-20 days. No self addressed stamped envelope is required.

Fax search: Fax requests must be prepaid.

In person search: Turnaround time is usually same day.

Other access: Bulk data is available. The fee is $200 for up to 20,000 records, then $10 for each 1,000 additional records.

Legislation-Current/Pending
Legislation-Passed

South Carolina Legislature, 937 Assembly Street, Rm 220, Columbia, SC 29201; 803-734-2060, 803-734-2145 (Older Bills), 9AM-5PM.

www.leginfo.state.sc.us

Note: Older passed bills are found at the Legislative Council on the 2nd floor, 803-734-2145.

Indexing & Storage: Records are available for current session only. The session is a 2 year session. Records are indexed on microfiche.

Searching: Include the following in your request-bill number.

Access by: mail, phone, fax, in person, online.

Fee & Payment: There is no fee unless the bill is long. They will compute the charge. Fee payee: South Carolina Legislative Printing. They will invoice. Personal checks accepted. No credit cards accepted.

Mail search: Turnaround time: variable. Information requests are available.No self addressed stamped envelope is required.

Phone search: You may call for copies of bills.

Fax search: Fax searching available.

In person search: Searching is available in person.

Online search: Bill text and status data can be found at the web site.

Voter Registration

State Election Commission, Records, PO Box 5987, Columbia, SC 29205; 803-734-9060, 803-734-9366 (Fax), 8:30AM-5PM.

www.state.sc.us/scsec

Indexing & Storage: Records are available for all active records.

Searching: Records are open to the public. To search, provide the name with the county or DOB. The following data is not released: Social Security Numbers.

Access by: mail, phone, fax, in person.

Fee & Payment: There is no search fee unless extensive time involved. Copies are $.20 each. Fee payee: State Election Commission. Prepayment required. No credit cards accepted.

Mail search: Turnaround time: 1-2 days.

Phone search: Searching is available by phone.

Fax search: Same criteria as mail searching.

In person search: Searching is available in person.

Other access: Lists, labels, diskettes, and magnetic tapes are available with a variety of sort features. The minimum charge varies from $75-$160 depending on the media.

GED Certificates

GED Testing Office, 402 Rutledge Bldg, 1429 Senate St, Columbia, SC 29201; 803-734-8347, 803-734-8336 (Fax), 8:30AM-5PM M-F.

www.state.sc.us/sde

Searching: To search, all of the following is required: a signed release, name, and Social Security Number. If known, the year of test is also helpful.

Access by: mail, fax.

Fee & Payment: There is no fee for a verifcation. There is a $5.00 fee for a copy of a transcript by mail, $3.00 if by fax. Fee payee: SC Dept of Education. Prepayment required. Cash and money orders are accepted. No credit cards accepted.

Mail search: Turnaround time: 1-3 days.No self addressed stamped envelope is required.

Fax search: A verification can be returned by fax within a day.

Hunting License Information
Fishing License Information

Records not maintained by a state level agency.

Note: They do not have a central database. Licenses are kept on file within the License Division by the county and agent where the license was sold.

Licenses Searchable Online

Accounting Practitioner-AP #02 .... http://167.7.126.243/Lookup/Cpa.asp
Animal Health Technician #43 .... http://167.7.126.243/lookup/vet.asp
Architect #03.. http://167.7.126.243/Lookup/Architects.asp
Architecture Partnership/Corporation #03................. http://167.7.126.243/Lookup/Architects.asp
Attorney #48 .... www.scbar.org/lawyer_directory.asp
Auctioneer #50... http://167.7.126.243/Lookup/Auctioneers.asp
Audiologist #22.. http://167.7.126.243/Lookup/Speech.asp
Barber #47 .... http://167.7.126.243/lookup/barbers.asp
Barber Instructor #47.. http://167.7.126.243/lookup/barbers.asp
Burglar Alarm Contractor #24 .... www.llr.state.sc.us/dss/burglar.asp
Chiropractor #04... http://167.7.126.243/lookup/Chiropractic.asp
Contractor, General & Mechanical #24 .... http://167.7.126.243/Lookup/Contractors.asp
Cosmetologist #05.. http://167.7.126.243/lookup/cosmetology.asp
Dentist #06... http://167.7.126.243/Lookup/Dentistry.asp
Engineer #07... http://167.7.126.243/Lookup/Engineers.asp
Forester #38.. http://167.7.126.243/Lookup/Foresters.asp
Geologist #20.. http://167.7.126.243/Lookup/Geologists.asp
Landscape Architect #40 .... www.dnr.state.sc.us/water/envaff/prolicense/prolicense.html
Lobbyist #37 .... www.lpitr.state.sc.us/reports/ethrpt.htm
Manicurist #05... http://167.7.126.243/lookup/barbers.asp
Manufactured House Manufacturer #41 .... http://167.7.126.243/Lookup/Mh.asp
Marriage & Family Therapist #08 .... http://167.7.126.243/lookup/Counselors.asp
Master Hair Care Specialist #47 .... http://167.7.126.243/lookup/barbers.asp
Medical Doctor #39 .... http://167.7.126.243/Lookup/Physicians.asp
Nurse #12 .... http://167.7.126.243/lookup/nurses.asp
Nurse-LPN #12 .... http://167.7.126.243/lookup/nurses.asp
Occupational Therapist/Assistant #13..................... http://167.7.126.243/Lookup/OT.asp
Optician #14.. http://167.7.126.243/Lookup/Opticians.asp
Optometrist #09 .... http://167.7.126.243/Lookup/Optometry.asp
Pharmacist/Pharmacy Store #15 .... www.llr.state.sc.us/dss/pharm.asp
Physical Therapist #16 .... http://167.7.126.243/Lookup/PT.asp
Podiatrist #17.. http://167.7.126.243/Lookup/Podiatry.asp
Professional Counselor #08.................................. http://167.7.126.243/lookup/Counselors.asp
Psycho-Educational Specialist #08......................... http://167.7.126.243/lookup/Counselors.asp
Psychologist #18.. http://167.7.126.243/Lookup/SW.asp
Public Accountant-CPA #02 .... http://167.7.126.243/Lookup/Cpa.asp
Public Accountant-PA #02 .... http://167.7.126.243/Lookup/Cpa.asp
Residential Home Builder #45................................ http://167.7.126.243/Lookup/ResidentialBuilders.asp
Shampoo Assistant #47 .... http://167.7.126.243/lookup/barbers.asp
Social Worker #21 .... http://167.7.126.243/Lookup/SW.asp
Soil Classifier #40 .... www.dnr.state.sc.us/water/envaff/prolicense/prolicense.html
Speech-Language Pathologist #22.......................... http://167.7.126.243/Lookup/Speech.asp
Surveyor #07... http://167.7.126.243/Lookup/Engineers.asp
Veterinarian #43... http://167.7.126.243/lookup/vet.asp

Licensing Quick Finder

Accounting Practitioner-AP #02 803-896-4492
Acupuncturist #39 803-896-4500
Agricultural Dealer & Handler #25..........803-737-9696
Alcoholic Beverage Control #34.............803-898-5864
Amusement Ride #46..........................803-734-9711
Animal Health Technician #43 803-896-4598
Architect #03.....................................803-896-4408
Architecture Partnership/Corporation #03
....803-896-4408
Athletic Trainer #49 803-896-4498
Attorney #48 803-799-6653
Auctioneer #50...................................803-896-4853
Audiologist #22..................................803-896-4650
Barber #47 803-896-4588
Barber Apprentice #47.........................803-896-4588
Barber Instructor #47...........................803-896-4588
Boxer #49 803-896-4498
Burglar Alarm Contractor #24 803-896-4686

Butterfat Testers #25...........................803-737-9700
Chiropractor #04 803-896-4587
Community Residential Care #32............803-896-4544
Contact Lens License #14 803-896-4681
Contractor, General & Mechanical #24
....803-896-4686
Cosmetologist #05..............................803-896-4494
Cosmetology Instructor/school #05 803-896-4494
Dental Hygienist #06...........................803-896-4599
Dental Specialist #06...........................803-896-4599
Dental Technician #06..........................803-896-4599
Dentist #06 803-896-4599
Electrician #42 803-933-1209
Elevator Service #46 803-734-9711
Embalmer #11....................................803-896-4497
Emergency Medical Technician #27.........803-737-7204
EMS (Ambulance Co) #27 803-737-7204
Engineer #07 803-896-4422

Esthetician #05 803-896-4494
Feed Manufacturers & Products #25.......803-737-9700
Financial Institution #10.......................803-734-2001
Forester #38 803-896-4498
Funeral Director #11............................803-896-4497
Funeral Home #11 803-896-4497
Geologist #20.....................................803-896-4497
Hearing Aid Dispenser/Fitter #29 803-737-7370
Heating & Air/Gas Fitting #42 803-933-1209
Insurance Agent #31 803-737-5757
Investment Advisor #01 803-734-9916
Landscape Architect #40 803-734-9100
Lobbyist #37 803-253-4192
Manicurist #05 803-896-4494
Manufactured House Manufacturer #41
....803-896-4682
Marriage & Family Therapist #08 803-896-4655
Master Hair Care Specialist #47 803-896-4588

Medical Doctor #39	803-896-4500
Midwife #29	803-737-7370
Municipal Solid Waste Landfill Operator #30	803-896-4207
Nurse #12	803-896-4550
Nurse-LPN #12	803-896-4550
Nursing Home Administrator #32	803-896-4544
Occupational Therapist/Assistant #13	803-896-4683
Optician #14	803-896-4681
Optician, Apprentice #14	803-896-4681
Optometrist #09	803-869-4679
Osteopathic Physician #39	803-896-4500
Percolation Test Technician #36	803-896-4430
Pesticide Applicator #33	803-646-2155
Pesticide Dealer #33	803-646-2155
Pharmacist/Pharmacy Store #15	803-896-4700
Physical Therapist #16	803-896-4655
Physician Assistant #39	803-896-4500
Pilot #35	803-896-6280
Plumbing #42	803-933-1209
Podiatrist #17	803-896-4685
Polygraph Examiner #51	803-896-7292

Private Detective #51	803-737-9000
Professional Counselor #08	803-896-4655
Property Manager #44	803-896-4400
Psycho-Educational Specialist #08	803-896-4655
Psychologist #18	803-896-4661
Public Accountant-CPA #02	803-896-4492
Public Accountant-PA #02	803-896-4492
Pyrotechnic Technician #19	803-896-4420
Real Estate Appraiser #44	803-896-4400
Real Estate Broker #44	803-896-4400
Residential Home Builder #45	803-896-4688
Respiratory Care Practitioner #39	803-896-4500
Sanitarian #28	803-935-7958
School Guidance Counselor #26	803-898-3224
School Media Communications Specialist #26	803-896-3224
School Principal/Supervisor #26	803-896-3224
School Superintendent #26	803-896-3224
Securities Agent #01	803-734-9916
Securities Broker/Dealer #01	803-734-9916
Seed Salesman #25	803-737-9690
Shampoo Assistant #47	803-896-4588

Sheet Metal & Pipefitting #42	803-933-1209
Social Worker #21	803-896-4665
Soil Classifier #40	803-734-9100
Specialty Contractor #45	803-896-4688
Speech Pathologist/Audiologist #19	803-896-4650
Speech-Language Pathologist #22	803-896-4650
Sprinkler Systems Contractor #24	803-896-4686
Surveyor #07	803-896-4422
Swimming Pool/Spa Operator #36	803-896-4430
Teacher #26	803-896-3224
Times Share and Land Sales People #44	803-896-4400
Veterinarian #43	803-896-4598
Waste Water Treatment Plant Operator #36	803-896-4430
Water Treatment #36	803-896-4430
Weighmaster #025	803-737-9696
Well Driller #36	803-896-4430
Wrestler #49	803-896-4498

Licensing Agency Information

01 Attorney Generals Office, Securities Division, PO Box 11549 (PO Box 11549 (1000 Assembly St, Rembert C. Dennis Building)), Columbia, SC 29211-1549; 803-734-9916, Fax: 803-734-0032.

www.scsecurities.org/brokerdealer.html

02 Department of Labor, Licensing & Regulation, Board of Accountancy, PO Box 11329 (PO Box 11329 (3600 Forest Dr, #101)), Columbia, SC 29211; 803-896-4492, Fax: 803-896-4554.
www.llr.state.sc.us/bac.htm

Direct URL to search licenses: http://167.7.126.243/Lookup/Cpa.asp You can search online using last name, license #

03 Department of Labor, Licensing & Regulation, Board of Architectural Examiners, PO Box 11419 (110 Centerview Dr, #201), Columbia, SC 29211; 803-896-4408, Fax: 803-734-4410.
www.llr.state.sc.us/boards.htm

Direct URL to search licenses: www.llr.state.sc.us/dss/dss_menu.htm You can search online using last name, license #, city

04 Department of Labor, Licensing & Regulation, Division of Chiropractic Examiners, PO Box 11329 (PO Box 11329), Columbia, SC 29211-1329; 803-896-4587, Fax: 803-896-4719.
www.llr.state.sc.us/bce.htm

Direct URL to search licenses: http://167.7.126.243/lookup/Chiropractic.asp You can search online using last name, license #

05 Department of Labor, Licensing & Regulation, Board of Cosmetology, PO Box 11329 (PO Box 11329), Columbia, SC 29211-1329; 803-896-4494, Fax: 803-896-4484.
www.llr.state.sc.us/boc.htm

Direct URL to search licenses: http://167.7.126.243/lookup/cosmetology.asp You can search online using name or license # See also Board of Barber examiners for Shampoo Assistants and master Hair Care Specialist

06 Department of Labor, Licensing & Regulation, Board of Dentistry, PO Box 11329 (PO Box 11329), Columbia, SC 29211-1329; 803-896-4599, Fax: 803-896-4596.
www.llr.state.sc.us/denlic.htm

Direct URL to search licenses: http://167.7.126.243/Lookup/Dentistry.asp You can search online using name, license #

07 Department of Labor, Licensing & Regulation, Board of Prof. Engineers & Land Surveyors, PO Box 11597 (PO Box 11597), Columbia, SC 29211-1597; 803- 896-4422, Fax: 803-896-4427.

www.llr.state.sc.us/bpe.htm

08 Department of Labor, Licensing & Regulation, Board of Examiners of Prof. Counselors / Family Therapists, PO Box 11329 (PO Box 11329), Columbia, SC 29211; 803-896-4655, Fax: 803-896-4719.
www.llr.state.sc.us/bel.htm

Direct URL to search licenses: http://167.7.126.243/lookup/Counselors.asp You can search online using name, license #

09 Department of Labor, Licensing & Regulation, Board of Examiners in Optometry, PO Box 11329 (PO Box 11329 (110 Centerview Dr.)), Columbia, SC 29211-1329; 803-896-4679, Fax: 803-896-4719.
www.llr.state.sc.us/beop.htm

Direct URL to search licenses: http://167.7.126.243/Lookup/Optometry.asp You can search online using name or license #

10 Board of Financial Institutions, PO Box 12549 (PO Box 12549), Columbia, SC 29201; 803-734-2001, Fax: 803-734-2013.

www.llr.sc.edu/boards.htm

11 Department of Labor, Licensing & Regulation, Board of Funeral Service, PO Box 11329 (PO Box 11329), Columbia, SC 29211-1329; 803-896-4497, Fax: 803-896-4554.

www.llr.state.sc.us/bfs.htm

12 Department of Labor, Licensing & Regulation, Board of Nursing, PO Box 11329 (110 Centerview Dr, #202), Columbia, SC 29211-1329; 803-896-4550, Fax: 803-896-4525.
www.llr.state.sc.us/bon.htm

Direct URL to search licenses: http://167.7.126.243/lookup/nurses.asp You can search online using last name. License #

13 Department of Labor, Licensing & Regulation, Board of Occupational Therapy, PO Box 11329 (PO Box 11329 (110 Centerview Dr, Kingstree Bldg, 29210)), Columbia, SC 29211; 803-896-4683, Fax: 803-896-4719.
www.llr.state.sc.us/bot.htm

Direct URL to search licenses: http://167.7.126.243/Lookup/OT.asp You can search online using name, city, license #

14 Department of Labor, Licensing & Regulation, Board of Opticianry Examiners, PO Box 11329 (PO Box 11329 (110 Centerview Dr.)), Columbia, SC 29211-1329; 803-896-4681, Fax: 803-896-4719.
www.llr.state.sc.us/beo.htm

Direct URL to search licenses: www.llr.state.sc.us/dss/dss_menu.htm You can search online using agency select, then search by name

15 Department of Labor, Licensing & Regulation, Board of Pharmacy, PO Box 11927 (110 Centerview Dr, Kingstree Bldg, #306), Columbia, SC 29211-1927; 803-896-4700, Fax: 803-896-4596.
www.llr.state.sc.us/bop.htm

Direct URL to search licenses: www.llr.state.sc.us/dss/pharm.asp You can search online using name or license #

16 Department of Labor, Licensing & Regulation, Board of Physical Therapy Examiners, PO Box 11329 (PO Box 11329 (110 Centerview Dr, 29210)), Columbia, SC 29211; 803-896-4655, Fax: 803-896-4719.
www.llr.state.sc.us/bpte.htm

Direct URL to search licenses: http://167.7.126.243/Lookup/PT.asp You can search online using last name, city, license #

17 Department of Labor, Licensing & Regulation, Board of Podiatry Examiners, PO Box 11289 (PO Box 11289), Columbia, SC 29211-1289; 803-896-4685, Fax: 803-896-4515.
www.llr.state.sc.us/podb.htm

Direct URL to search licenses: http://167.7.126.243/Lookup/Podiatry.asp You can search online using name or license #

18 Department of Labor, Licensing & Regulation, Board of Examiners in Psychology, PO Box 11329 (PO Box 11329), Columbia, SC 29211-1329; 803-896-4664, Fax: 803-896-4687.
www.llr.state.sc.us

Direct URL to search licenses: www.llr.state.sc.us/dss/social/asp You can search online using name, city, license number.

19 Department of Labor, Licensing & Regulation, Board of Pyrotechnic Safety, PO Box 11329 (PO Box 11329), Columbia, SC 29211-1329; 803-896-4420, Fax: 803-896-4431.

www.llr.state.sc.us/bpyro.htm

20 Department of Labor, Licensing & Regulation, Board of Registration for Geologists, PO Box 11329 (PO Box 11329), Columbia, SC 29211-1329; 803-896-4494 or 803-896-4497, Fax: 803-896-4484.
www.llr.state.sc.us/brg.htm

Direct URL to search licenses: http://167.7.126.243/Lookup/Geologists.asp You can search online using name or license #

21 Department of Labor, Licensing & Regulation, Board of Social Work Examiners, PO Box 11329 (PO Box 11329), Columbia, SC 29211-1329; 803-896-4665, Fax: 803-896-4687.
www.llr.state.sc.us/bosw.htm

Direct URL to search licenses: http://167.7.126.243/Lookup/SW.asp You can search online using name, city, licence number.

22 Department of Labor, Licensing & Regulation, Board of Speech-Language Pathology & Audiology, PO Box 11329 (PO Box 11329 (110 Centerview Dr, 29210)), Columbia, SC 29211-1329; 803-896-4650, Fax: 803-896-4719.
www.llr.state.sc.us/path.htm

Direct URL to search licenses: http://167.7.126.243/Lookup/Speech.asp You can search online using name or license #

24 Department of Labor, Licensing & Regulation, Contractor's Licensing Board, PO Box 11329 (PO Box 11329), Columbia, SC 29211-1329; 803-896-4686, Fax: 803-896-4364.
www.llr.state.sc.us/contrctr/clb.htm

Direct URL to search licenses: www.llr.state.sc.us/dss/dss_menu.htm You can search online using company or individual name.

25 Department of Agriculture, PO Box 11280 (PO Box 11280), Columbia, SC 29211; 803-734-2210, Fax: 803-734-2192.

26 Department of Education, 1429 Senate St, Columbia, SC 29201; 803-734-8466, Fax: 803-734-2873.
www.llr.sc.edu/boards.htm

27 Department of Health & Environmental Control, 2600 Bull St, Columbia, SC 29201; 803-737-7204, Fax: 803-737-7212.

28 Department of Health & Environmental Control, 2600 Bull St, Columbia, SC 29201; 803-935-7958, Fax: 803-935-7825.

29 Department of Health & Environmental Control, 2600 Bull St, Columbia, SC 29201; 803-737-7370, Fax: 803-737-7212.
www.state.sc.us/dhec

30 Department of Health & Environmental Control, 2600 Bull St, Columbia, SC 29201; 803-896-4000, Fax: 803-896-4001.

31 Department of Insurance, PO Box 100105 (PO Box 100105), Columbia, SC 29202-3105; 803-737-6095, Fax: 803-737-6232.
www.state.sc.us/doi

32 Department of Labor, Licensing & Regulation, Board of Long Term care Administrators, PO Box 11329, Columbia, SC 29211; 803-896-4544, Fax: 803-896-4555.
www.llr.state.sc.us/boards.htm

33 Department of Pesticide Regulation, 511 Winghouse Rd, Pendleton, SC 29670; 864-646-2155, Fax: 864-646-2179.

34 Department of Revenue & Taxation, PO Box 125 (PO Box 125), Columbia, SC 29214; 803-898-5864, Fax: 803-898-5899.

35 Division of Aeronautics, PO Box 280068 (PO Box 280068), Columbia, SC 29228-0068; 803-896-6270, Fax: 803-896-6277.

36 Department of Labor, Licensing & Regulation, Environmental Certification Board, PO Box 11329 (PO Box 11329), Columbia, SC 29211; 803-896-4430, Fax: 803-896-4424.
www.llr.state.sc.us/boards.htm

Direct URL to search licenses: www.llr.state.sc.us/ecb.htm

37 Ethics Commission, PO Box 11926 (5000 Thurmond Mall #250), Columbia, SC 29201; 803-253-4193, Fax: 803-253-7539.
www.state.sc.us/ethics.htm

Direct URL to search licenses: www.lpitr.state.sc.us/reports/ethrpt.htm

38 Department of Labor, Licensing & Regulation, Board of Registration for Foresters, PO Box 11329 (PO Box 11329), Columbia, SC 29211-1329; 803-896-4498, Fax: 803-896-4595.
www.llr.state.sc.us/brf.htm

Direct URL to search licenses: www.llr.state.sc.us/dss/dss_menu.htm You can search online using agency select, then search by name

39 Department of Labor, Licensing & Regulation, Board of Medical Examiners, PO Box 11289 (PO Box 11289), Columbia, SC 29211-1289; 803-896-4500, Fax: 803-896-4515.
www.llr.state.sc.us/me.htm

Direct URL to search licenses: www.llr.state.sc.us/dss/dss_menu.htm You can search online using medical board, name

40 Department of Natural Resources, Land, Water & Conservation Div., Licensing Program, 2221 Devine St, #222, Columbia, SC 29205-2474; 803-734-9100, Fax: 803-734-9200.
www.dnr.state.sc.us

Direct URL to search licenses: www.dnr.state.sc.us/water/envaff/prolicense/prolicense.html

41 Department of Labor, Licensing & Regulation, Manufactured Housing Board, PO Box 11329 (PO Box 11329 (110 Centerview Dr #102, 29210)), Columbia, SC 29211-1329; 803-896-4682, Fax: 803-896-4814.
www.llr.state.sc.us/mhb.htm

Direct URL to search licenses: www.llr.state.sc.us/dss/dss_menu.htm

42 Municipal Association of South Carolina, PO Box 12109 (1411 Gervais St), Columbia, SC 29211-2109; 803-933-1209, Fax: 803-933-1299.
http://masc.state.sc.us

43 Department of Labor, Licensing & Regulation, Board of Veterinary Medical Examiners, PO Box 11329, Columbia, SC 29211-1329; 803-896-4598, Fax: 803-896-4719.
www.llr.state.sc.us/bov.htm

Direct URL to search licenses: http://167.7.126.243/lookup/vet.asp You can search online using name or license #

44 Real Estate Commission, PO Box 11847 (PO Box 11847), Columbia, SC 29211-1847; 803-896-4400, Fax: 803-896-4404.
www.llr.state.sc.us/rec.htm

45 Department of Labor, Licensing & Regulation, Residential Home Builders Commission, PO Box 11329 (PO Box 11329), Columbia, SC 29211-1329; 803-896-4688, Fax: 803-896-4656.
www.llr.state.sc.us/boards.htm

46 Department of Labor, Licensing & Regulation, PO Box 11329 (PO Box 11329), Columbia, SC 29211-1329; 803-734-9711, Fax: 803-737-9119.
www.llr.state.sc.us/

47 Department of Labor, Licensing & Regulation, Board of Barber Examiners, PO Box 11329 (PO Box 11329), Columbia, SC 29211-1329; 803-896-4588, Fax: 803-896-4484.
www.llr.state.sc.us/bar.htm

Direct URL to search licenses: http://167.7.126.243/lookup/barbers.asp You can search online using name or license #

48 Supreme Court, PO Box 608 (950 Taylor St), Columbia, SC 29202; 803-799-6653, Fax: 803-799-4118.

49 Department of Labor, Licensing & Regulation, Athletic Commission, PO Box 11329 (PO Box 11329), Columbia, SC 29211; 803-896-4498, Fax: 803-896-4595.
www.llr.state.sc.us/ac.htm

50 Department of Labor, Licensing & Regulation, Auctioneer's Commission, PO Box 11329 (PO Box 11329), Columbia, SC 29211-1329; 803-896-4853, Fax: 803-896-4595.
www.llr.state.sc.us/auc.htm

Direct URL to search licenses: www.llr.state.sc.us/dss/dss_menu.htm You can search online using Auctioneers, name

51 Law Enforcement Division, 4400 Broad River Rd, Columbia, SC 29210; 803-737-9000, Fax: 803-896-7041.

The following list indicates the district and division name for each county in the state. If the district or division name of the bankruptcy court is different from the civil/criminal court, it appears in parentheses.

County/Court Cross Reference

Abbeville	Greenwood (Columbia)
Aiken	Greenwood (Columbia)
Allendale	Greenwood (Columbia)
Anderson	Anderson (Columbia)
Bamberg	Greenwood (Columbia)
Barnwell	Greenwood (Columbia)
Beaufort	Beaufort (Columbia)
Berkeley	Charleston (Columbia)
Calhoun	Greenwood (Columbia)
Charleston	Charleston (Columbia)
Cherokee	Spartanburg (Columbia)
Chester	Spartanburg (Columbia)
Chesterfield	Florence (Columbia)
Clarendon	Charleston (Columbia)
Colleton	Charleston (Columbia)
Darlington	Florence (Columbia)
Dillon	Florence (Columbia)
Dorchester	Charleston (Columbia)
Edgefield	Greenwood (Columbia)
Fairfield	Greenwood (Columbia)
Florence	Florence (Columbia)
Georgetown	Charleston (Columbia)
Greenville	Greenville (Columbia)
Greenwood	Greenwood (Columbia)
Hampton	Beaufort (Columbia)
Horry	Florence (Columbia)
Jasper	Beaufort (Columbia)
Kershaw	Columbia
Lancaster	Greenwood (Columbia)
Laurens	Greenville (Columbia)
Lee	Columbia
Lexington	Columbia
Marion	Florence (Columbia)
Marlboro	Florence (Columbia)
McCormick	Greenwood (Columbia)
Newberry	Greenwood (Columbia)
Oconee	Anderson (Columbia)
Orangeburg	Greenwood (Columbia)
Pickens	Anderson (Columbia)
Richland	Columbia
Saluda	Greenwood (Columbia)
Spartanburg	Spartanburg (Columbia)
Sumter	Columbia
Union	Spartanburg (Columbia)
Williamsburg	Florence (Columbia)
York	Spartanburg (Columbia)

US District Court

District of South Carolina

Anderson Division c/o Greenville Division, PO Box 10768, Greenville, SC 29603 (Courier Address: 300 E Washington St, Greenville, SC 29601), 864-241-2700.

www.scd.uscourts.gov

Counties: Anderson, Oconee, Pickens.

Indexing & Storage: Cases are indexed by as well as by case number. New cases are available in the index after filing date. Open records are located at the Division.

Fee & Payment: The fee is no charge per item (one party name or case number). Payment may be made by money order, cashier check. Business checks are not accepted. Personal checks are not accepted.

Phone Search: An automated voice case information service (VCIS) is not available.

In Person Search: In person searching is available.

PACER: Sign-up number is 800-676-6856. Access fee is $.60 per minute. Toll-free access: 800-831-6162. Local access: 803-765-5871. Case records are available back to January 1990. Records are never purged. New records are available online after 1 day. PACER is available on the Internet at http://pacer.scd.uscourts.gov.

Opinions Online: Court opinions are available online at www.law.sc.edu/dsc/dsc.htm

Beaufort Division c/o Charleston Division, PO Box 835, Charleston, SC 29402 (Courier

Address: 85 Broad St, Hollings Judicial Center, Charleston, SC 29401), 843-579-1401, Fax: 803-579-1402.

www.scd.uscourts.gov

Counties: Beaufort, Hampton, Jasper.

Indexing & Storage: Cases are indexed by as well as by case number. New cases are available in the index after filing date. Open records are located at the Division. Civil records are sent to Federal Records Center 1 year after case close. Criminal records are sent 5 years after case close.

Fee & Payment: The fee is no charge per item (one party name or case number). Payment may be made by money order, cashier check. Business checks are not accepted. Personal checks are not accepted.

Phone Search: An automated voice case information service (VCIS) is not available.

In Person Search: In person searching is available.

PACER: Sign-up number is 800-676-6856. Access fee is $.60 per minute. Toll-free access: 800-831-6162. Local access: 803-765-5871. Case records are available back to January 1990. Records are never purged. New records are available online after 1 day. PACER is available on the Internet at http://pacer.scd.uscourts.gov.

Opinions Online: Court opinions are available online at www.law.sc.edu/dsc/dsc.htm

Charleston Division PO Box 835, Charleston, SC 29402 (Courier Address: 85 Broad St, Hollings Judicial Center, Charleston, SC 29401), 843-579-1401, Fax: 803-579-1402.

www.scd.uscourts.gov

Counties: Berkeley, Charleston, Clarendon, Colleton, Dorchester, Georgetown.

Indexing & Storage: Cases are indexed by defendant and plaintiff as well as by case number. New cases are available in the index 1-2 days after filing date. A computer index is maintained. Older records are indexed on cards and microfiche. Open records are located at this court. District wide searches are available for information from 1980 from this court.

Fee & Payment: The fee is $15.00 per item (one party name or case number). Payment may be made by money order, cashier check, personal check. Prepayment is required. Payee: US District Court. Certification fee: $5.00 per document. Copy fee: $.50 per page.

Phone Search: Only docket information is available by phone. An automated voice case information service (VCIS) is not available.

Mail Search: Always enclose a stamped self addressed envelope.

In Person Search: In person searching is available.

PACER: Sign-up number is 800-676-6856. Access fee is $.60 per minute. Toll-free access: 800-831-6162. Local access: 803-765-5871. Case records are available back to January 1990. Records are never purged. New records are available online after 1 day. PACER is available on the Internet at http://pacer.scd.uscourts.gov.

Opinions Online: Court opinions are available online at www.law.sc.edu/dsc/dsc.htm

Columbia Division 1845 Assembly St, Columbia, SC 29201, 803-765-5816.

www.scd.uscourts.gov

Counties: Kershaw, Lee, Lexington, Richland, Sumter.

ORGANIZATION 46 counties, 46 recording offices. The recording officer is. Register of Mesne Conveyances or Clerk of Court (varies by county). The entire state is in the Eastern Time Zone (EST).

REAL ESTATE RECORDS Most counties will **not** perform real estate searches. Copy and certification fees vary. The Assessor keeps tax records.

UCC RECORDS Financing statements are filed at the state level, except for consumer goods, farm related and real estate related collateral, which are filed with the Register. All recording offices will perform UCC searches. Use search request form UCC-4. Searches fees are usually $5.00 per debtor name. Copy fees are usually $1.00 per page.

TAX LIEN RECORDS All federal and state tax liens on personal property and on real property are filed with the Register of Mesne Conveyances (Clerk of Court). Some counties will perform tax lien searches. Search fees and copy fees vary.

Abbeville County
Clerk of Court, P.O. Box 99, Abbeville, SC 29620. 864-459-5074.

Aiken County
County Register of Mesne Conveyances, P.O. Box 537, Aiken, SC 29802-0537. 803-642-2072.

Allendale County
Clerk of Court, P.O. Box 126, Allendale, SC 29810. 803-584-2737. Fax: 803-584-7058.

Anderson County
County Register of Mesne Conveyances, P.O. Box 8002, Anderson, SC 29622. 864-260-4054. Fax: 864-260-4443.

Bamberg County
Clerk of Court, P.O. Box 150, Bamberg, SC 29003. 803-245-3025. Fax: 803-245-3088.

Barnwell County
Clerk of Court, P.O. Box 723, Barnwell, SC 29812-0723. 803-541-1020. Fax: 803-541-1025.

Beaufort County
County Register of Mesne Conveyances, P.O. Drawer 1197, Beaufort, SC 29901-1197. 843-470-2700. Fax: 843-470-2709.

Berkeley County
County Register of Mesne Conveyances, 223 North Live Oak Drive, Moncks Corner, SC 29461. 843-719-4084. Fax: 843-719-4139.

Calhoun County
Clerk of Court, 302 S. F.R. Huff Drive, St. Matthews, SC 29135. 803-874-3524. Fax: 803-874-1942.

Charleston County
County Register of Mesne Conveyances, P.O. Box 726, Charleston, SC 29402. 843-723-6780. Fax: 843-720-2210.

Cherokee County
Clerk of Court, P.O. Drawer 2289, Gaffney, SC 29342. 864-487-2571. Fax: 864-487-2754.

Chester County
Clerk of Court, P.O. Drawer 580, Chester, SC 29706. 803-385-2605. Fax: 803-581-7975.

Chesterfield County
Clerk of Court, P.O. Box 529, Chesterfield, SC 29709. 843-623-2574. Fax: 843-623-3945.

Clarendon County
Clerk of Court, P.O. Drawer E, Manning, SC 29102. 803-435-4443. Fax: 803-435-8258.

Colleton County
Clerk of Court, P.O. Box 620, Walterboro, SC 29488-0028. 843-549-5791. Fax: 843-549-2875.

Darlington County
Clerk of Court, P.O. Box 1177, Darlington, SC 29540. 843-398-4330. Fax: 843-398-4172.

Dillon County
Clerk of Court, P.O. Drawer 1220, Dillon, SC 29536. 843-774-1425. Fax: 843-774-1443.

Dorchester County
County Register of Mesne Conveyances, P.O. Box 38, St. George, SC 29477. 843-563-0106. Fax: 843-563-0277.

Edgefield County
Clerk of Court, P.O. Box 34, Edgefield, SC 29824. 803-637-4080. Fax: 803-637-4117.

Fairfield County
Clerk of Court, P.O. Drawer 299, Winnsboro, SC 29180. 803-635-1411.

Florence County
Clerk of Court, MSC-E City/County Complex, Florence, SC 29501. 843-665-3031. Fax: 843-665-3097.

Georgetown County
Clerk of Court, P.O. Drawer 1270, Georgetown, SC 29442. 843-527-6315.

Greenville County
County Register of Mesne Conveyances, 301 University Ridge, County Square Suite 1300, Greenville, SC 29601-3655. 864-467-7240. Fax: 864-467-7107.

Greenwood County
Clerk of Court, Courthouse, 528 Monument St., Greenwood, SC 29646. 864-942-8551.
www.akanda.com/grnwood
Online Access: Real Estate. Records on the Greenwood County Parcel Search database are available free on the Internet at www.akanda.com/grnwood/Search/search.htm. All county property is listed with details. An interactive map is included.

Hampton County
Clerk of Court, Courthouse Square, Elm Street, Hampton, SC 29924. 803-943-7510. Fax: 803-943-7596.

Horry County
County Register of Mesne Conveyances, P.O. Box 470, Conway, SC 29528. 843-248-1252. Fax: 843-248-1566.

Jasper County
Clerk of Court, P.O. Box 248, Ridgeland, SC 29936. 843-726-7710. Fax: 843-726-7782.

Kershaw County
Clerk of Court, P.O. Box 1557, Camden, SC 29020-1557. 803-425-1500. Fax: 803-425-1505.

Lancaster County
Clerk of Court, P.O. Box 1809, Lancaster, SC 29721. 803-285-1581. Fax: 803-416-9388.

Laurens County
Clerk of Court, P.O. Box 287, Laurens, SC 29360. 864-984-3538.

Lee County
Clerk of Court, P.O. Box 387, Bishopville, SC 29010. 803-484-5341. Fax: 803-484-5043.

Lexington County
County Register of Mesne Conveyances, 212 South Lake Drive, Lexington, SC 29072. 803-359-8404. Fax: 803-359-8189.

Marion County
Clerk of Court, P.O. Box 295, Marion, SC 29571. 843-423-8240. Fax: 843-423-8306.

Marlboro County
Clerk of Court, P.O. Drawer 996, Bennettsville, SC 29512. 843-479-5613. Fax: 843-479-5640.

McCormick County
Clerk of Court, 133 South Mine Street, Courthouse, Room 102, McCormick, SC 29835. 864-465-2195. Fax: 864-465-0071.

Newberry County
Clerk of Court, P.O. Box 278, Newberry, SC 29108. 803-321-2110. Fax: 803-321-2111.

Oconee County
Clerk of Court, P.O. Box 678, Walhalla, SC 29691. 864-638-4280.

Orangeburg County
County Register of Mesne Conveyances, Box 9000, Orangeburg, SC 29116-9000. 803-533-6236. Fax: 803-534-3848.

Pickens County
Clerk of Court, 222 McDaniel Ave. B-5, Pickens, SC 29671. 864-898-5868. Fax: 864-898-5924.

Richland County
County Register of Mesne Conveyances, P.O. Box 192, Columbia, SC 29202. 803-748-4800. Fax: 803-748-4807.

Saluda County
Clerk of Court, Courthouse, Saluda, SC 29138. 864-445-3303. Fax: 864-445-3772.

Spartanburg County
County Register of Mesne Conveyances, 366 North Church Street, County Administrative Offices, Spartanburg, SC 29303. 864-596-2514.

Sumter County
County Register of Mesne Conveyances, Courthouse, Room 202, 141 N. Main St., Sumter, SC 29150. 803-436-2177.

Union County
Clerk of Court, P.O. Box 200, Union, SC 29379. 864-429-1630. Fax: 864-429-1715.

Williamsburg County
Clerk of Court, P.O. Box 86, Kingstree, SC 29556. 843-354-6855. Fax: 843-354-5813.

York County
Clerk of Court, P.O. Box 649, York, SC 29745. 803-684-8510.

The Sourcebook to Public Record Information

County Locator - South Carolina

You will usually be able to find the city name in the City/County Cross Reference below. In that case, it is a simple matter to determine the county from the cross reference. However, only the official US Postal Service city names are included in this index. There are an additional 40,000 place names that people use in their addresses. Therefore, we have also included a ZIP/City Cross Reference immediately following the City/County Cross Reference.

If you know the ZIP Code but the city name does not appear in the City/County Cross Reference index, look up the ZIP Code in the ZIP/City Cross Reference, find the city name, then look up the city name in the City/County Cross Reference. For example, you want to know the county for an address of Menands, NY 12204. There is no "Menands" in the City/County Cross Reference. The ZIP/City Cross Reference shows that ZIP Codes 12201-12288 are for the city of Albany. Looking back in the City/County Cross Reference, Albany is in Albany County.

City/County Cross Reference

ABBEVILLE Abbeville
ADAMS RUN (29426) Charleston(76), Dorchester(24)
AIKEN Aiken
ALCOLU (29001) Clarendon(55), Sumter(45)
ALLENDALE Allendale
ANDERSON Anderson
ANDREWS (29510) Georgetown(75), Williamsburg(24)
ARCADIA Spartanburg
AWENDAW Charleston
AYNOR Horry
BALLENTINE Richland
BAMBERG Bamberg
BARNWELL Barnwell
BATESBURG (29006) Lexington(60), Aiken(20), Saluda(20)
BATH Aiken
BEAUFORT Beaufort
BEECH ISLAND Aiken
BELTON (29627) Anderson(94), Greenville(6)
BENNETTSVILLE Marlboro
BETHERA Berkeley
BETHUNE (29009) Kershaw(93), Chesterfield(4), Lee(4)
BISHOPVILLE (29010) Lee(99), Kershaw(2)
BLACKSBURG Cherokee
BLACKSTOCK (29014) Chester(70), Fairfield(30)
BLACKVILLE (29817) Barnwell(99), Bamberg(1)
BLAIR Fairfield
BLENHEIM Marlboro
BLUFFTON Beaufort
BLYTHEWOOD (29016) Richland(99), Fairfield(1)
BONNEAU Berkeley
BORDEN Sumter
BOWLING GREEN (29703) York(88), Cherokee(13)
BOWMAN (29018) Orangeburg(92), Dorchester(8)
BRADLEY (29819) Greenwood(98), McCormick(2)
BRANCHVILLE (29432) Orangeburg(86), Bamberg(7), Dorchester(7)
BRUNSON Hampton
BUFFALO Union
CADES (29518) Williamsburg(98), Clarendon(2)
CALHOUN FALLS (29628) Abbeville(98), McCormick(2)
CAMDEN (29020) Kershaw(98), Lee(2)
CAMERON (29030) Orangeburg(62), Calhoun(38)
CAMPOBELLO (29322) Spartanburg(98), Greenville(2)
CANADYS Colleton

CARLISLE (29031) Union(61), Chester(36), Fairfield(3)
CASSATT (29032) Kershaw(92), Lee(8)
CATAWBA York
CAYCE Lexington
CENTENARY Marion
CENTRAL (29630) Pickens(92), Anderson(8)
CHAPIN (29036) Lexington(74), Richland(21), Newberry(5)
CHAPPELLS (29037) Newberry(86), Saluda(12), Laurens(2)
CHARLESTON (29406) Charleston(75), Berkeley(25)
CHARLESTON (29414) Charleston(99), Dorchester(1)
CHARLESTON (29418) Charleston(78), Dorchester(22)
CHARLESTON (29420) Dorchester(53), Charleston(47)
CHARLESTON Berkeley
CHARLESTON Charleston
CHARLESTON AFB Charleston
CHERAW Chesterfield
CHEROKEE FALLS Cherokee
CHESNEE (29323) Spartanburg(88), Cherokee(12)
CHESTER Chester
CHESTERFIELD Chesterfield
CLARKS HILL (29821) McCormick(90), Edgefield(10)
CLEARWATER Aiken
CLEMSON Pickens
CLEVELAND (29635) Greenville(72), Pickens(28)
CLIFTON Spartanburg
CLINTON Laurens
CLIO (29525) Marlboro(98), Dillon(2)
CLOVER York
COLUMBIA (29210) Richland(70), Lexington(30)
COLUMBIA (29212) Lexington(89), Richland(11)
COLUMBIA Lexington
COLUMBIA Richland
CONESTEE Greenville
CONVERSE Spartanburg
CONWAY Horry
COOSAWATCHIE Jasper
COPE Orangeburg
CORDESVILLE Berkeley
CORDOVA Orangeburg
COTTAGEVILLE Colleton
COWARD Florence
COWPENS (29330) Spartanburg(65), Cherokee(35)
CROCKETVILLE Hampton
CROSS (29436) Berkeley(96), Orangeburg(4)
CROSS ANCHOR Spartanburg
CROSS HILL Laurens
DALE Beaufort

DALZELL (29040) Sumter(91), Lee(9)
DARLINGTON Darlington
DAUFUSKIE ISLAND Beaufort
DAVIS STATION Clarendon
DENMARK Bamberg
DILLON Dillon
DONALDS (29638) Abbeville(88), Greenwood(12)
DORCHESTER Dorchester
DRAYTON Spartanburg
DUE WEST Abbeville
DUNCAN Spartanburg
EARLY BRANCH (29916) Hampton(57), Jasper(43)
EASLEY (29642) Pickens(69), Anderson(31)
EASLEY Pickens
EASTOVER Richland
EDGEFIELD Edgefield
EDGEMOOR Chester
EDISTO ISLAND (29438) Colleton(60), Charleston(40)
EFFINGHAM Florence
EHRHARDT (29081) Bamberg(79), Colleton(21)
ELGIN (29045) Kershaw(60), Richland(39), Fairfield(1)
ELKO Barnwell
ELLIOTT Lee
ELLOREE (29047) Orangeburg(77), Calhoun(23)
ENOREE (29335) Spartanburg(86), Union(8), Laurens(7)
ESTILL Hampton
EUTAWVILLE Orangeburg
FAIR PLAY (29643) Oconee(80), Anderson(20)
FAIRFAX (29827) Allendale(96), Hampton(4)
FAIRFOREST Spartanburg
FINGERVILLE Spartanburg
FLORENCE (29501) Florence(91), Darlington(9)
FLORENCE Florence
FLOYD DALE Dillon
FOLLY BEACH Charleston
FORK Dillon
FORT LAWN Chester
FORT MILL (29715) York(98), Lancaster(2)
FORT MILL York
FOUNTAIN INN (29644) Greenville(61), Laurens(39)
FURMAN Hampton
GABLE (29051) Sumter(81), Clarendon(19)
GADSDEN Richland
GAFFNEY Cherokee
GALIVANTS FERRY Horry
GARNETT (29922) Hampton(57), Jasper(43)
GASTON (29053) Lexington(92), Calhoun(8)
GEORGETOWN Georgetown

GIFFORD Hampton
GILBERT Lexington
GLENDALE Spartanburg
GLOVERVILLE Aiken
GOOSE CREEK Berkeley
GRAMLING Spartanburg
GRANITEVILLE Aiken
GRAY COURT Laurens
GREAT FALLS (29055) Chester(91), Fairfield(9)
GREELEYVILLE (29056) Williamsburg(90), Clarendon(10)
GREEN POND Colleton
GREEN SEA Horry
GREENVILLE (29611) Greenville(95), Anderson(3), Pickens(2)
GREENVILLE Greenville
GREENWOOD (29649) Greenwood(99), Abbeville(1)
GREENWOOD Greenwood
GREER (29650) Greenville(99), Spartanburg(1)
GREER (29651) Greenville(52), Spartanburg(48)
GREER Greenville
GRESHAM Marion
GROVER Dorchester
HAMER Dillon
HAMPTON Hampton
HARDEEVILLE (29927) Jasper(99), Beaufort(1)
HARLEYVILLE Dorchester
HARTSVILLE (29550) Darlington(95), Chesterfield(4), Lee(1)
HARTSVILLE Darlington
HEATH SPRINGS (29058) Lancaster(94), Kershaw(6)
HEMINGWAY (29554) Georgetown(78), Williamsburg(20), Florence(2)
HICKORY GROVE York
HILDA Barnwell
HILTON HEAD ISLAND Beaufort
HODGES (29653) Greenwood(91), Abbeville(9)
HODGES Greenwood
HOLLY HILL (29059) Orangeburg(97), Berkeley(4)
HOLLYWOOD Charleston
HONEA PATH (29654) Anderson(59), Abbeville(32), Greenville(8), Laurens(2)
HOPKINS Richland
HORATIO Sumter
HUGER Berkeley
INMAN Spartanburg
IRMO (29063) Richland(92), Lexington(8)
ISLANDTON Colleton
ISLE OF PALMS Charleston
IVA (29655) Anderson(56), Abbeville(44)
JACKSON Aiken
JACKSONBORO Colleton
JAMESTOWN Berkeley
JEFFERSON Chesterfield

JENKINSVILLE Fairfield
JOANNA Laurens
JOHNS ISLAND Charleston
JOHNSONVILLE (29555) Florence(99),
 Williamsburg(1)
JOHNSTON (29832) Edgefield(93),
 Saluda(7)
JONESVILLE Union
KERSHAW (29067) Lancaster(74),
 Kershaw(26)
KINARDS (29355) Newberry(79),
 Laurens(22)
KINGS CREEK Cherokee
KINGSTREE Williamsburg
KLINE Barnwell
LA FRANCE Anderson
LADSON (29456) Berkeley(45),
 Dorchester(35), Charleston(20)
LAKE CITY (29560) Florence(91),
 Williamsburg(6), Clarendon(3)
LAKE VIEW Dillon
LAMAR (29069) Darlington(96), Lee(5)
LANCASTER Lancaster
LANDO Chester
LANDRUM (29356) Spartanburg(60),
 Greenville(40)
LANE Williamsburg
LANGLEY Aiken
LATTA (29565) Dillon(87), Marion(11),
 Marlboro(2)
LAURENS Laurens
LEESVILLE (29070) Lexington(84),
 Saluda(16)
LEXINGTON Lexington
LIBERTY (29657) Pickens(88),
 Anderson(13)
LIBERTY HILL Kershaw
LITTLE MOUNTAIN (29075) Newberry(80),
 Richland(13), Lexington(7)
LITTLE RIVER Horry
LITTLE ROCK Dillon
LIVINGSTON Orangeburg
LOBECO Beaufort
LOCKHART Union
LODGE (29082) Colleton(92), Bamberg(8)
LONE STAR Calhoun
LONG CREEK Oconee
LONGS Horry
LORIS Horry
LOWNDESVILLE Abbeville
LUGOFF (29078) Kershaw(96), Richland(4)
LURAY (29932) Hampton(52),
 Allendale(48)
LYDIA Darlington
LYMAN Spartanburg
LYNCHBURG (29080) Sumter(76), Lee(24)
MANNING (99999) Clarendon(99),
 Sumter(1)
MARIETTA (29661) Greenville(76),
 Pickens(24)
MARION Marion
MARTIN (29836) Allendale(89),
 Barnwell(11)
MAULDIN Greenville
MAYESVILLE (29104) Sumter(77), Lee(23)
MAYO Spartanburg
MC BEE (29101) Darlington(54),
 Chesterfield(28), Chester(19)
MC CLELLANVILLE Charleston
MC COLL Marlboro
MC CONNELLS York
MC CORMICK McCormick
MILEY Hampton

MINTURN Dillon
MODOC (29838) McCormick(82),
 Edgefield(18)
MONCKS CORNER Berkeley
MONETTA (29105) Aiken(77), Saluda(23)
MONTICELLO Fairfield
MONTMORENCI Aiken
MOORE Spartanburg
MOUNT CARMEL McCormick
MOUNT CROGHAN Chesterfield
MOUNT PLEASANT Charleston
MOUNTAIN REST Oconee
MOUNTVILLE Laurens
MULLINS Marion
MURRELLS INLET (29576) Horry(53),
 Georgetown(47)
MYRTLE BEACH Horry
NEESES Orangeburg
NESMITH Williamsburg
NEW ELLENTON Aiken
NEW ZION (29111) Clarendon(93),
 Williamsburg(7)
NEWBERRY Newberry
NEWRY Oconee
NICHOLS (29581) Horry(87), Dillon(11),
 Marion(3)
NINETY SIX (29666) Greenwood(98),
 Saluda(2)
NORRIS Pickens
NORTH (29112) Orangeburg(95),
 Lexington(3), Calhoun(2)
NORTH AUGUSTA (29860) Edgefield(67),
 Aiken(33)
NORTH AUGUSTA Aiken
NORTH MYRTLE BEACH (29598)
 Horry(94), Florence(6)
NORTH MYRTLE BEACH Horry
NORWAY Orangeburg
OLANTA (29114) Florence(56),
 Sumter(43), Clarendon(1)
OLAR (29843) Bamberg(51), Barnwell(49)
ORANGEBURG (29118) Orangeburg(99),
 Calhoun(1)
ORANGEBURG Orangeburg
PACOLET (29372) Spartanburg(70),
 Union(16), Cherokee(14)
PACOLET MILLS Spartanburg
PAGELAND Chesterfield
PAMPLICO Florence
PARKSVILLE McCormick
PATRICK Chesterfield
PAULINE (29374) Spartanburg(94),
 Union(6)
PAWLEYS ISLAND Georgetown
PEAK Newberry
PELION Lexington
PELZER (29669) Anderson(67),
 Greenville(33)
PENDLETON (29670) Anderson(99),
 Pickens(1)
PERRY Aiken
PICKENS Pickens
PIEDMONT (29673) Greenville(50),
 Anderson(50)
PINELAND (29934) Jasper(79),
 Hampton(21)
PINEVILLE Berkeley
PINEWOOD (29125) Sumter(65),
 Clarendon(35)
PINOPOLIS Berkeley
PLUM BRANCH (29845) McCormick(97),
 Edgefield(3)
POMARIA Newberry

PORT ROYAL Beaufort
POSTON Florence
PROSPERITY (29127) Newberry(98),
 Saluda(2)
RAINS Marion
RAVENEL (29470) Charleston(87),
 Dorchester(13)
REEVESVILLE Dorchester
REIDVILLE Spartanburg
REMBERT (29128) Sumter(86),
 Kershaw(8), Lee(6)
RICHBURG Chester
RICHLAND Oconee
RIDGE SPRING (29129) Aiken(51),
 Saluda(36), Edgefield(13)
RIDGELAND (29936) Jasper(88),
 Beaufort(12)
RIDGEVILLE (29472) Dorchester(62),
 Colleton(22), Berkeley(16)
RIDGEWAY (29130) Fairfield(51),
 Kershaw(44), Richland(5)
RIMINI (29131) Sumter(65), Clarendon(35)
RION Fairfield
ROCK HILL York
ROEBUCK Spartanburg
ROUND O Colleton
ROWESVILLE Orangeburg
RUBY Chesterfield
RUFFIN Colleton
RUSSELLVILLE Berkeley
SAINT GEORGE Dorchester
SAINT HELENA ISLAND Beaufort
SAINT MATTHEWS (29135) Calhoun(95),
 Orangeburg(5)
SAINT STEPHEN Berkeley
SALEM Oconee
SALLEY (29137) Aiken(84),
 Orangeburg(16)
SALTERS Williamsburg
SALUDA (29138) Saluda(94),
 Greenwood(4), Aiken(2)
SANDY SPRINGS Anderson
SANTEE Orangeburg
SARDINIA Clarendon
SCOTIA Hampton
SCRANTON Florence
SEABROOK Beaufort
SELLERS (29592) Dillon(81), Marion(19)
SENECA Oconee
SHARON York
SHAW A F B Sumter
SHELDON Beaufort
SILVERSTREET Newberry
SIMPSONVILLE Greenville
SIX MILE Pickens
SLATER Greenville
SMOAKS (29481) Colleton(94),
 Bamberg(6)
SMYRNA York
SOCIETY HILL (29593) Darlington(89),
 Chesterfield(11)
SPARTANBURG (29307) Spartanburg(97),
 Cherokee(3)
SPARTANBURG Spartanburg
SPRINGFIELD (29146) Orangeburg(73),
 Aiken(27)
STARR Anderson
STARTEX Spartanburg
STATE PARK Richland
SULLIVANS ISLAND Charleston
SUMMERTON Clarendon
SUMMERVILLE (29483) Dorchester(70),
 Berkeley(30)

SUMMERVILLE (29485) Dorchester(90),
 Charleston(10)
SUMMERVILLE Dorchester
SUMTER (29153) Sumter(96), Lee(4)
SUMTER Sumter
SUNSET Pickens
SWANSEA (29160) Lexington(67),
 Calhoun(32), Orangeburg(1)
SYCAMORE Allendale
TAMASSEE Oconee
TATUM Marlboro
TAYLORS Greenville
TIGERVILLE Greenville
TILLMAN Jasper
TIMMONSVILLE (29161) Florence(81),
 Darlington(19)
TOWNVILLE (29689) Anderson(89),
 Oconee(11)
TRAVELERS REST Greenville
TRENTON (29847) Edgefield(54),
 Aiken(46)
TRIO Williamsburg
TROY (29848) Greenwood(88),
 McCormick(10), Saluda(2)
TURBEVILLE (29162) Clarendon(99),
 Sumter(2)
ULMER (29849) Allendale(83),
 Barnwell(17)
UNA Spartanburg
UNION Union
VAN WYCK Lancaster
VANCE Orangeburg
VARNVILLE (29944) Hampton(93),
 Jasper(7)
VAUCLUSE Aiken
WADMALAW ISLAND Charleston
WAGENER Aiken
WALHALLA Oconee
WALLACE Marlboro
WALTERBORO Colleton
WARD Saluda
WARE SHOALS (29692) Greenwood(42),
 Laurens(41), Abbeville(17)
WARRENVILLE Aiken
WATERLOO Laurens
WEDGEFIELD Sumter
WELLFORD Spartanburg
WEST COLUMBIA Lexington
WEST UNION Oconee
WESTMINSTER Oconee
WESTVILLE Kershaw
WHITE OAK Fairfield
WHITE ROCK Richland
WHITE STONE Spartanburg
WHITMIRE (29178) Newberry(82),
 Union(17), Laurens(1)
WILLIAMS Colleton
WILLIAMSTON Anderson
WILLISTON (29853) Barnwell(53),
 Aiken(47)
WINDSOR Aiken
WINNSBORO (29180) Fairfield(94),
 Richland(6)
WISACKY Lee
WOODRUFF (29388) Spartanburg(98),
 Laurens(2)
YEMASSEE (29945) Colleton(61),
 Beaufort(24), Hampton(9), Jasper(6)
YORK York

ZIP/City Cross Reference

29001-29001	ALCOLU		29010-29010	BISHOPVILLE		29020-29020	CAMDEN		29036-29036	CHAPIN
29002-29002	BALLENTINE		29014-29014	BLACKSTOCK		29030-29030	CAMERON		29037-29037	CHAPPELLS
29003-29003	BAMBERG		29015-29015	BLAIR		29031-29031	CARLISLE		29038-29038	COPE
29006-29006	BATESBURG		29016-29016	BLYTHEWOOD		29032-29032	CASSATT		29039-29039	CORDOVA
29009-29009	BETHUNE		29018-29018	BOWMAN		29033-29033	CAYCE		29040-29040	DALZELL

ZIP Range	City	ZIP Range	City	ZIP Range	City	ZIP Range	City
29041-29041	DAVIS STATION	29322-29322	CAMPOBELLO	29482-29482	SULLIVANS ISLAND	29656-29656	LA FRANCE
29042-29042	DENMARK	29323-29323	CHESNEE	29483-29485	SUMMERVILLE	29657-29657	LIBERTY
29044-29044	EASTOVER	29324-29324	CLIFTON	29487-29487	WADMALAW ISLAND	29658-29658	LONG CREEK
29045-29045	ELGIN	29325-29325	CLINTON	29488-29488	WALTERBORO	29659-29659	LOWNDESVILLE
29046-29046	ELLIOTT	29329-29329	CONVERSE	29492-29492	CHARLESTON	29661-29661	MARIETTA
29047-29047	ELLOREE	29330-29330	COWPENS	29493-29493	WILLIAMS	29662-29662	MAULDIN
29048-29048	EUTAWVILLE	29331-29331	CROSS ANCHOR	29501-29506	FLORENCE	29664-29664	MOUNTAIN REST
29051-29051	GABLE	29332-29332	CROSS HILL	29510-29510	ANDREWS	29665-29665	NEWRY
29052-29052	GADSDEN	29333-29333	DRAYTON	29511-29511	AYNOR	29666-29666	NINETY SIX
29053-29053	GASTON	29334-29334	DUNCAN	29512-29512	BENNETTSVILLE	29667-29667	NORRIS
29054-29054	GILBERT	29335-29335	ENOREE	29516-29516	BLENHEIM	29669-29669	PELZER
29055-29055	GREAT FALLS	29336-29336	FAIRFOREST	29518-29518	CADES	29670-29670	PENDLETON
29056-29056	GREELEYVILLE	29338-29338	FINGERVILLE	29519-29519	CENTENARY	29671-29671	PICKENS
29058-29058	HEATH SPRINGS	29340-29342	GAFFNEY	29520-29520	CHERAW	29672-29672	SENECA
29059-29059	HOLLY HILL	29346-29346	GLENDALE	29525-29525	CLIO	29673-29673	PIEDMONT
29061-29061	HOPKINS	29348-29348	GRAMLING	29526-29528	CONWAY	29675-29675	RICHLAND
29062-29062	HORATIO	29349-29349	INMAN	29530-29530	COWARD	29676-29676	SALEM
29063-29063	IRMO	29351-29351	JOANNA	29532-29532	DARLINGTON	29677-29677	SANDY SPRINGS
29065-29065	JENKINSVILLE	29353-29353	JONESVILLE	29536-29536	DILLON	29678-29679	SENECA
29067-29067	KERSHAW	29355-29355	KINARDS	29540-29540	DARLINGTON	29680-29681	SIMPSONVILLE
29069-29069	LAMAR	29356-29356	LANDRUM	29541-29541	EFFINGHAM	29682-29682	SIX MILE
29070-29070	LEESVILLE	29360-29360	LAURENS	29542-29542	FLOYD DALE	29683-29683	SLATER
29071-29073	LEXINGTON	29364-29364	LOCKHART	29543-29543	FORK	29684-29684	STARR
29074-29074	LIBERTY HILL	29365-29365	LYMAN	29544-29544	GALIVANTS FERRY	29685-29685	SUNSET
29075-29075	LITTLE MOUNTAIN	29368-29368	MAYO	29545-29545	GREEN SEA	29686-29686	TAMASSEE
29078-29078	LUGOFF	29369-29369	MOORE	29546-29546	GRESHAM	29687-29687	TAYLORS
29079-29079	LYDIA	29370-29370	MOUNTVILLE	29547-29547	HAMER	29688-29688	TIGERVILLE
29080-29080	LYNCHBURG	29372-29372	PACOLET	29550-29551	HARTSVILLE	29689-29689	TOWNVILLE
29081-29081	EHRHARDT	29373-29373	PACOLET MILLS	29554-29554	HEMINGWAY	29690-29690	TRAVELERS REST
29082-29082	LODGE	29374-29374	PAULINE	29555-29555	JOHNSONVILLE	29691-29691	WALHALLA
29101-29101	MC BEE	29375-29375	REIDVILLE	29556-29556	KINGSTREE	29692-29692	WARE SHOALS
29102-29102	MANNING	29376-29376	ROEBUCK	29560-29560	LAKE CITY	29693-29693	WESTMINSTER
29104-29104	MAYESVILLE	29377-29377	STARTEX	29563-29563	LAKE VIEW	29695-29695	HODGES
29105-29105	MONETTA	29378-29378	UNA	29564-29564	LANE	29696-29696	WEST UNION
29106-29106	MONTICELLO	29379-29379	UNION	29565-29565	LATTA	29697-29697	WILLIAMSTON
29107-29107	NEESES	29384-29384	WATERLOO	29566-29566	LITTLE RIVER	29698-29698	GREENVILLE
29108-29108	NEWBERRY	29385-29385	WELLFORD	29567-29567	LITTLE ROCK	29702-29702	BLACKSBURG
29111-29111	NEW ZION	29386-29386	WHITE STONE	29568-29568	LONGS	29703-29703	BOWLING GREEN
29112-29112	NORTH	29388-29388	WOODRUFF	29569-29569	LORIS	29704-29704	CATAWBA
29113-29113	NORWAY	29390-29391	DUNCAN	29570-29570	MC COLL	29706-29706	CHESTER
29114-29114	OLANTA	29401-29403	CHARLESTON	29571-29571	MARION	29709-29709	CHESTERFIELD
29115-29118	ORANGEBURG	29404-29404	CHARLESTON AFB	29572-29572	MYRTLE BEACH	29710-29710	CLOVER
29122-29122	PEAK	29405-29425	CHARLESTON	29573-29573	MINTURN	29712-29712	EDGEMOOR
29123-29123	PELION	29426-29426	ADAMS RUN	29574-29574	MULLINS	29714-29714	FORT LAWN
29124-29124	PERRY	29429-29429	AWENDAW	29575-29575	MYRTLE BEACH	29715-29716	FORT MILL
29125-29125	PINEWOOD	29430-29430	BETHERA	29576-29576	MURRELLS INLET	29717-29717	HICKORY GROVE
29126-29126	POMARIA	29431-29431	BONNEAU	29577-29579	MYRTLE BEACH	29718-29718	JEFFERSON
29127-29127	PROSPERITY	29432-29432	BRANCHVILLE	29580-29580	NESMITH	29719-29719	KINGS CREEK
29128-29128	REMBERT	29433-29433	CANADYS	29581-29581	NICHOLS	29720-29722	LANCASTER
29129-29129	RIDGE SPRING	29434-29434	CORDESVILLE	29582-29582	NORTH MYRTLE BEACH	29724-29724	LANDO
29130-29130	RIDGEWAY	29435-29435	COTTAGEVILLE	29583-29583	PAMPLICO	29726-29726	MC CONNELLS
29132-29132	RION	29436-29436	CROSS	29584-29584	PATRICK	29727-29727	MOUNT CROGHAN
29133-29133	ROWESVILLE	29437-29437	DORCHESTER	29585-29585	PAWLEYS ISLAND	29728-29728	PAGELAND
29135-29135	SAINT MATTHEWS	29438-29438	EDISTO ISLAND	29587-29587	MYRTLE BEACH	29729-29729	RICHBURG
29137-29137	SALLEY	29439-29439	FOLLY BEACH	29589-29589	RAINS	29730-29734	ROCK HILL
29138-29138	SALUDA	29440-29442	GEORGETOWN	29590-29590	SALTERS	29741-29741	RUBY
29142-29142	SANTEE	29445-29445	GOOSE CREEK	29591-29591	SCRANTON	29742-29742	SHARON
29143-29143	SARDINIA	29446-29446	GREEN POND	29592-29592	SELLERS	29743-29743	SMYRNA
29145-29145	SILVERSTREET	29447-29447	GROVER	29593-29593	SOCIETY HILL	29744-29744	VAN WYCK
29146-29146	SPRINGFIELD	29448-29448	HARLEYVILLE	29594-29594	TATUM	29745-29745	YORK
29147-29147	STATE PARK	29449-29449	HOLLYWOOD	29596-29596	WALLACE	29801-29808	AIKEN
29148-29148	SUMMERTON	29450-29450	HUGER	29597-29598	NORTH MYRTLE BEACH	29809-29809	NEW ELLENTON
29150-29151	SUMTER	29451-29451	ISLE OF PALMS	29601-29617	GREENVILLE	29810-29810	ALLENDALE
29152-29152	SHAW A F B	29452-29452	JACKSONBORO	29620-29620	ABBEVILLE	29812-29812	BARNWELL
29153-29154	SUMTER	29453-29453	JAMESTOWN	29621-29626	ANDERSON	29813-29813	HILDA
29160-29160	SWANSEA	29455-29455	JOHNS ISLAND	29627-29627	BELTON	29814-29814	KLINE
29161-29161	TIMMONSVILLE	29456-29456	LADSON	29628-29628	CALHOUN FALLS	29816-29816	BATH
29162-29162	TURBEVILLE	29457-29457	JOHNS ISLAND	29630-29630	CENTRAL	29817-29817	BLACKVILLE
29163-29163	VANCE	29458-29458	MC CLELLANVILLE	29631-29634	CLEMSON	29819-29819	BRADLEY
29164-29164	WAGENER	29461-29461	MONCKS CORNER	29635-29635	CLEVELAND	29821-29821	CLARKS HILL
29166-29166	WARD	29464-29465	MOUNT PLEASANT	29636-29636	CONESTEE	29822-29822	CLEARWATER
29168-29168	WEDGEFIELD	29468-29468	PINEVILLE	29638-29638	DONALDS	29824-29824	EDGEFIELD
29169-29172	WEST COLUMBIA	29469-29469	PINOPOLIS	29639-29639	DUE WEST	29826-29826	ELKO
29175-29175	WESTVILLE	29470-29470	RAVENEL	29640-29642	EASLEY	29827-29827	FAIRFAX
29176-29176	WHITE OAK	29471-29471	REEVESVILLE	29643-29643	FAIR PLAY	29828-29828	GLOVERVILLE
29177-29177	WHITE ROCK	29472-29472	RIDGEVILLE	29644-29644	FOUNTAIN INN	29829-29829	GRANITEVILLE
29178-29178	WHITMIRE	29474-29474	ROUND O	29645-29645	GRAY COURT	29831-29831	JACKSON
29180-29180	WINNSBORO	29475-29475	RUFFIN	29646-29649	GREENWOOD	29832-29832	JOHNSTON
29201-29292	COLUMBIA	29476-29476	RUSSELLVILLE	29650-29652	GREER	29834-29834	LANGLEY
29301-29319	SPARTANBURG	29477-29477	SAINT GEORGE	29653-29653	HODGES	29835-29835	MC CORMICK
29320-29320	ARCADIA	29479-29479	SAINT STEPHEN	29654-29654	HONEA PATH	29836-29836	MARTIN
29321-29321	BUFFALO	29481-29481	SMOAKS	29655-29655	IVA	29838-29838	MODOC

29839-29839	MONTMORENCI	29851-29851	WARRENVILLE	29916-29916	EARLY BRANCH	29932-29932	LURAY
29840-29840	MOUNT CARMEL	29853-29853	WILLISTON	29918-29918	ESTILL	29933-29933	MILEY
29841-29841	NORTH AUGUSTA	29856-29856	WINDSOR	29920-29920	SAINT HELENA ISLAND	29934-29934	PINELAND
29842-29842	BEECH ISLAND	29860-29861	NORTH AUGUSTA	29921-29921	FURMAN	29935-29935	PORT ROYAL
29843-29843	OLAR	29899-29899	MC CORMICK	29922-29922	GARNETT	29936-29936	RIDGELAND
29844-29844	PARKSVILLE	29901-29906	BEAUFORT	29923-29923	GIFFORD	29938-29938	HILTON HEAD ISLAND
29845-29845	PLUM BRANCH	29910-29910	BLUFFTON	29924-29924	HAMPTON	29939-29939	SCOTIA
29846-29846	SYCAMORE	29911-29911	BRUNSON	29925-29926	HILTON HEAD ISLAND	29940-29940	SEABROOK
29847-29847	TRENTON	29912-29912	COOSAWATCHIE	29927-29927	HARDEEVILLE	29941-29941	SHELDON
29848-29848	TROY	29913-29913	CROCKETVILLE	29928-29928	HILTON HEAD ISLAND	29943-29943	TILLMAN
29849-29849	ULMER	29914-29914	DALE	29929-29929	ISLANDTON	29944-29944	VARNVILLE
29850-29850	VAUCLUSE	29915-29915	DAUFUSKIE ISLAND	29931-29931	LOBECO	29945-29945	YEMASSEE

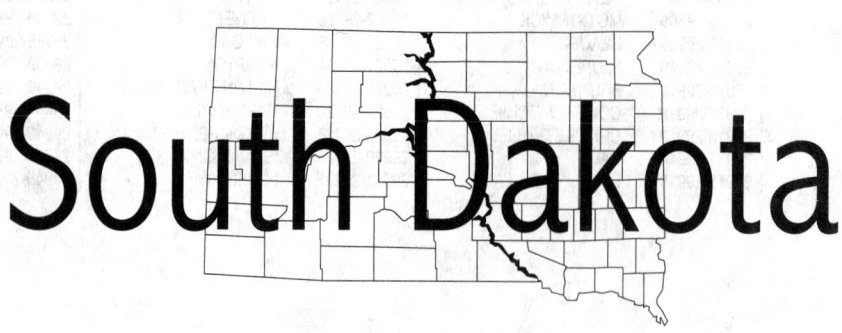

South Dakota

General Help Numbers:

Governor's Office
State Capitol, 500 E Capitol Ave   605-773-3212
Pierre, SD 57501-5070   Fax 605-773-4711
www.state.sd.us/governor/index.htm   8AM-5PM

Attorney General's Office
State Capitol, 500 E Capitol Ave   605-773-3215
Pierre, SD 57501-5070   Fax 605-773-4106
www.state.sd.us/attorney/attorney.html   8AM-5PM

State Court Administrator
State Capitol Bldg   605-773-3474
500 E Capitol Ave   Fax 605-773-5627
Pierre, SD 57501   8AM-5PM
www.state.sd.us/state/judicial

State Archives
Cultural Heritage Center/State Archives   605-773-3804
900 Governors Dr   Fax 605-773-6041
Pierre, SD 57501-2217   9AM-4:30PM
www.state.sd.us/deca/cultural/archives.htm

State Specifics:

Capital: Pierre
Hughes County

Time Zone: CST*
* South Dakota's eighteen western-most counties are MST: They are: Bennett, Butte, Corson, Custer, Dewey, Fall River, Haakon, Harding, Jackson, Lawrence, Meade, Mellette, Pennington, Perkins, Shannon, Stanley, Todd, Ziebach,

Number of Counties: 66

Population: 733,133

Web Site: www.state.sd.us

State Agencies

Criminal Records

Division of Criminal Investigation, Office of Attorney General, 500 E Capitol, Pierre, SD 57501-5070; 605-773-3331, 605-773-4629 (Fax), 8AM-5PM.

www.state.sd.us/attorney/attorney.html

Note: The state Court Administrator's Office has a statewide database of criminal record information from the state's circuit courts. For more information about setting up a commercial account, contact Jill Smith at 605-773-3474.

Indexing & Storage: Records are available for 10 years for misdemeanors and lifetime for felonies. Records are indexed on inhouse computer.

Searching: Include the following in your request- date of birth, full name, set of fingerprints. The form requires identifying information: color of hair and eyes, height, weight, date of birth, Social Security Number. The following data is not released: juvenile records, minor traffic violations or out-of-state or federal charges.

Access by: mail.

Fee & Payment: The fee is $15.00 per name. Fee payee: Division of Criminal Investigation.

Prepayment required. Personal checks accepted. No credit cards accepted.

Mail search: Turnaround time: 5-10 working days. Upon receipt of those requirements, they will conduct a search of their files and supply a copy of any criminal history that is found or a statement that there is no criminal history.A self addressed stamped envelope is requested.

Fictitious Name
Assumed Name

Records not maintained by a state level agency.

Note: Records are located at the county level.

Corporation Records
Limited Partnerships
Limited Liability Company Records
Trademarks/Servicemarks

Corporation Division, Secretary of State, 500 E Capitol Ave, Suite B-05, Pierre, SD 57501-5070; 605-773-4845, 605-773-4550 (Fax), 8AM-5PM.

www.state.sd.us/sos/sos.htm

Indexing & Storage: Records are available from the founding of the state. New records are available for inquiry immediately. Records are indexed on microfiche, inhouse computer.

Searching: Include the following in your request-full name of business. In addition to the articles of incorporation, corporation records include the following information: Annual Reports, Officers, Directors, Prior (merged) names, Inactive and Reserved names.

Access by: mail, phone, in person.

Fee & Payment: There is no fee for a general search. A Certificate of Good Standing is available for a fee of $10.00. Copies are $1.00 per page, add $5.00 for certification. Fee payee: Secretary of State. Prepayment required. Personal checks accepted. Credit cards accepted: Mastercard, Visa.

Mail search: Turnaround time: 1-3 days. A self addressed stamped envelope is requested.

Phone search: They will provide basic information only.

In person search: Turnaround time is immediate.

Expedited service: Expedited service is available for mail and phone searches. Add $10.00 per request.

Uniform Commercial Code
Federal Tax Liens

UCC Division, Secretary of State, 500 East Capitol, Pierre, SD 57501-5077; 605-773-4422, 605-773-4550 (Fax), 8AM-5PM.

www.state.sd.us/sos/sos.htm

Indexing & Storage: Records are available for all active records. Records are indexed on computer.

Searching: Use search request form UCC-11. The search includes federal tax liens on businesses. Federal tax liens on businesses and all state tax liens on individuals are filed at the county level. Include the following in your request-debtor name.

Access by: mail, phone, fax, in person, online.

Fee & Payment: The fee is $10.00 per debtor name, copies are $1.00 per page. Fee payee: Secretary of State. Prepayment required. Credit cards accepted: Mastercard, Visa.

Mail search: Turnaround time: 1-2 days. A self addressed stamped envelope is requested.

Phone search: Limited information is given over the phone. Reports can be ordered.

Fax search: Use of a credit card is required.

In person search: Searching is available in person.

Online search: Online access costs $240.00 per year plus a transaction charge over 200 keystrokes per month. Prepayment is required. The system is open 24 hours per day. Place request in writing to set up an account. The agency is considering an Internet site in the future, but does offer Dakota Fast File whicha allows users to file and review their own filings via the web.

Expedited service: Expedited service is available for mail, phone and fax searches. Turnaround time: 1 day. Add $10.00 per debtor name.

State Tax Liens

Records not maintained by a state level agency.

Note: Records are filed at the county level.

Sales Tax Registrations

Revenue Department, Business Tax Division, 445 E Capitol, Pierre, SD 57501-3100; 605-773-3311, 605-773-5129 (Fax), 8AM-5PM.

www.state.sd.us/revenue

Indexing & Storage: Records are available from 1990 on computer. Records have been placed on microfilm from 1970-1996.

Searching: This agency will only confirm if a business is registered and licensed. They will provide no other information. Include the following in your request-business name. Also search by tax permit number or owner name.

Access by: mail, phone, fax, in person.

Mail search: Turnaround time: 2-3 weeks. A self addressed stamped envelope is requested. No fee for mail request.

Phone search: No fee for telephone request.

Fax search: There is no fee, turnaround time is 2-3 weeks.

In person search: No fee for request. Usually requests can be processed while you wait.

Birth Certificates

South Dakota Department of Health, Vital Records, 600 E Capitol, Pierre, SD 57501-2536; 605-773-4961, 8AM-5PM.

www.state.sd.us/doh/VitalRec/index.htm

Indexing & Storage: Records are available from 1905-present. It takes Current before new records are available for inquiry.

Searching: Include the following in your request-full name, names of parents, mother's maiden name, date of birth, place of birth. Any county Register of Deeds can provide a computer generated birth certificate for the same fee. The following data is not released: sealed records.

Access by: mail, phone, in person, online.

Fee & Payment: The fee is $10.00. Use of a credit card is an additional $10.00 expedited fee. Fee payee: South Dakota Department of Health. Prepayment required. Personal checks accepted. Credit cards accepted: Mastercard, Visa, AmEx, Discover.

Mail search: Turnaround time: 2-3 days. No self addressed stamped envelope is required.

Phone search: You must use a credit card, considered expeditied service.

In person search: Turnaround time 30 minutes.

Online search: You can search free at the web site for birth records over 100 years old. You can order recent (less than 100 years) birth records at the web site, for a fee.

Expedited service: Expedited service is available for web and phone searches. Turnaround time: overnight delivery. Add $16.00 for delivery. Use of credit card required.

Death Records

South Dakota Department of Health, Vital Records, 600 E Capitol, Pierre, SD 57501-2536; 605-773-4961, 8AM-5PM.

www.state.sd.us/doh/VitalRec/index.htm

Indexing & Storage: Records are available from 1905-present. New records are available for inquiry immediately.

Searching: Include the following in your request-full name, date of death, place of death. The following data is not released: sealed records.

Access by: mail, phone, in person, online.

Fee & Payment: The fee is $10.00 per record. There is an additional $10.00 fee is a credit card is used. Fee payee: South Dakota Department of Health. Prepayment required. Personal checks accepted. Credit cards accepted: Mastercard, Visa, AmEx, Discover.

Mail search: Turnaround time: 2-3 days. No self addressed stamped envelope is required.

Phone search: You must use a credit card.

In person search: Turnaround time is 30 minutes.

Online search: Records may be ordered online at the web site.

Expedited service: Expedited service is available for mail and phone searches. Turnaround time: overnight delivery. Add $16.00 for delivery and fee for credit card use.

Marriage Certificates

South Dakota Department of Health, Vital Records, 600 E Capitol, Pierre, SD 57501-2536; 605-773-4961, 8AM-5PM.

www.state.sd.us/doh/VitalRec/index.htm

Indexing & Storage: Records are available from 1905-present. New records are available for inquiry immediately.

Searching: Include the following in your request-names of husband and wife, date of marriage, place or county of marriage. Also include wife's maiden name. The following data is not released: sealed records.

Access by: mail, phone, in person, online.

Fee & Payment: The fee is $7.00 per record. There is an additional $10.00 fee if a credit card is used. Fee payee: South Dakota Department of Health. Prepayment required. Personal checks accepted. Credit cards accepted: Mastercard, Visa, AmEx, Discover.

Mail search: Turnaround time: 2-3 days. No self addressed stamped envelope is required.

Phone search: You must use a credit card.

In person search: Turnaround time is 30 minutes.

Online search: Records may be ordered online at the web site.

Expedited service: Expedited service is available for mail and phone searches. Turnaround time: overnight delivery. Add $16.00 for express delivery. Use of credit card is required.

Divorce Records

South Dakota Department of Health, Vital Records, 600 E Capitol, Pierre, SD 57501-2536; 605-773-4961, 8AM-5PM.

www.state.sd.us/doh/VitalRec/index.htm

Indexing & Storage: Records are available from 1905-present. New records are available for inquiry immediately.

Searching: Include the following in your request-names of husband and wife, date of divorce, place of divorce. The following data is not released: sealed records.

Access by: mail, phone, in person, online.

Fee & Payment: The fee is $7.00 per record. There is an additional $10.00 fee if a credit card is used. Fee payee: South Dakota Department of Health. Prepayment required. Personal checks accepted. Credit cards accepted: Mastercard, Visa, AmEx, Discover.

Mail search: Turnaround time: 2-3 days. No self addressed stamped envelope is required.

Phone search: You must use a credit card.

In person search: Turnaround time 30 minutes.

Online search: records may be ordered at the web site.

Expedited service: Expedited service is available for mail and phone searches. Turnaround time: overnight delivery. Add $16.00 for express delivery, also use of credit card is required.

Workers' Compensation Records

Labor Department, Workers Compensation Division, 700 Governors Dr, Pierre, SD 57501; 605-773-3681, 605-773-4211 (Fax), 8AM-5PM.

www.state.sd.us/dol/dol.htm

Indexing & Storage: Records are available from 1982. New records are available for inquiry immediately. Records are indexed on inhouse computer.

Searching: Must have a signed release form from the claimant. Must also specify which records you are requesting. A computer search will only go back to July 1989. Fraud reports and sealed files are not released. Include the following in your request-claimant name, Social Security Number, date of accident.

Access by: mail, in person.

Fee & Payment: Search fee is $20.00, copies are included. Fee payee: Division of Labor Management. Prepayment required. Personal checks accepted. No credit cards accepted.

Mail search: Turnaround time: 1 week. A self addressed stamped envelope is requested.

In person search: By going in person you will only eliminate the mail time.

Driver Records

Dept of Commerce & Regulation, Office of Driver Licensing, 118 W Capitol, Pierre, SD 57501; 605-773-6883, 605-773-3018 (Fax), 8AM-5PM.

www.state.sd.us/dcr/dl/sddriver.htm

Note: Ticket information is maintained at the local courts, not at the state.

Indexing & Storage: Records are available for 3 years for moving violations and DWIs. Speeding violations less than 10 mph over and out-of-state speeding violations (except for commercial drivers), suspensions and revocations are not listed on the record. It takes 1-3 weeks before new records are available for inquiry.

Searching: Casual requesters can only obtain records with the written permission of the subjects. All other requesters must certify for what reason they are obtaining the information. Include the following in your request-full name, date of birth. A secondary search will be done with the license number if no record is found on the name search. The following data is not released: Social Security Numbers.

Access by: mail, phone, in person, online.

Fee & Payment: The fee is $4.00 per record. The agency charges sales tax, if record request comes from a South Dakota address. Fee payee: Dept of Commerce and Regulation. Prepayment required. Personal checks accepted. No credit cards accepted.

Mail search: Turnaround time: 48 hours. A self addressed stamped envelope is requested.

Phone search: Pre-approved accounts may order via the telephone.

In person search: Turnaround time while you wait.

Online search: The system is open for batch requests 24 hours a day. There is a minimum of 250 requests. It generally takes 10 minutes to process a batch. The current fee is $4.00 per record and there are some start-up costs. For more information, call 605-773-6883.

Other access: Lists are available to the insurance industry.

Vehicle Ownership
Vehicle Identification
Boat & Vessel Ownership
Boat & Vessel Registration

Division of Motor Vehicles, Information Section, 445 E Capitol Ave, Pierre, SD 57501-3100; 605-773-3541, 605-773-5129 (Fax), 8AM-5PM.

www.state.sd.us/revenue/motorvcl.htm

Indexing & Storage: Records are available for 20 years to present. The DMV took over the registration and title process for boats in 1992. All boats (except canoes and inflatables) over 12 ft in length must be titled and registered. Motorized boats 12 foot and under need to be registered. It takes 2 weeks before new records are available for inquiry.

Searching: The state requires all requests for vehicle related records be on the Division Form. Casual requesters can only obtain information with written permission of the subject. All requests must be in writing.

Access by: mail, in person.

Fee & Payment: The fee for VIN, plate, owner, title, or lien searches is $2.00 per record. A title history is $5.00 Fee payee: Division of Motor Vehicles. Prepayment required. Personal checks accepted. No credit cards accepted.

Mail search: Turnaround time: 1 day to 1 week. Must provide details regarding the reasons for requesting the information.A self addressed stamped envelope is requested.

In person search: You may request records in person, but the request must be in writing on the Division Form.

Accident Reports

Department of Transportation, Accident Records, 700 E. Broadway, Pierre, SD 57501-2586; 605-773-3868, 605-773-4870 (Fax), 8AM-5PM.

Indexing & Storage: Records are available for 10 years to present. It takes 2 weeks from receipt from law enforcement agency before new records are available for inquiry.

Searching: Include the following in your request-full name, date of accident, location of accident.

Access by: mail, in person.

Fee & Payment: The fee is $4.00 per record. Fee payee: Accident Records. Prepayment required. Personal checks accepted. No credit cards accepted.

Mail search: Turnaround time: 5 days. A self addressed stamped envelope is requested.

In person search: Normal turnaround time is immediate if the record is on file.

Legislation-Current/Pending
Legislation-Passed

South Dakota Legislature, Capitol Bldg - Legislative Research Council, 500 E Capitol Ave, Pierre, SD 57501; 605-773-3251, 605-773-4576 (Fax), 8AM-5PM.

http://legis.state.sd.us

Note: Signed bills are found at the Secretary of State's office, 605-773-3537. Pending legislation may be obtained here during the session.

Indexing & Storage: Records are available from 1951 on.

Searching: Search by bill number, subject, sponsor or by keyword.

Access by: mail, phone, in person, online.

Fee & Payment: Fees are not charged for documents, unless one purchases a subscription to all the bills or journals.

Mail search: Turnaround time: same day. Single copies of legislation can be requested by mail.No self addressed stamped envelope is required.

Phone search: You may order bills by phone.

In person search: Searching is available in person.

Online search: Information is available at their web site at no charge. The site is very thorough and has enrolled version of bills.

Voter Registration

Records not maintained by a state level agency.

Note: The county auditors hold records. There are no restrictions on usage.

GED Certificates

Department of Education, GED Testing, 700 Governors Drive, Pierre, SD 57501-2291; 605-773-4463, 605-773-4236 (Fax), 8AM-5PM.

Searching: The SSN, approximate date of test and DOB are needed to verify a record. In addition, a signed release is required for a copy of a transcript.

Access by: mail, fax, in person.

Mail search: Turnaround time: 1 day. No self addressed stamped envelope is required. No fee for mail request.

Fax search: Results will available in 1 hour.

In person search: No fee for request. You can wait for results.

Hunting License Information
Fishing License Information

Game, Fish & Parks Department, License Division, 412 W Missouri, Pierre, SD 57501; 605-773-3926, 605-773-5842 (Fax), 8AM-5PM.

www.state.sd.us/gfp

Indexing & Storage: Records are available for current and previous years only.

Searching: Requests must be in writing. They will release address data. The DOB and address are helpful.

Access by: mail, in person.

Fee & Payment: The fee depends on the extent of the names and the search. The state refuses to quote a price at this time. Fee payee: Dept of game & Fish. Prepayment required. Personal checks accepted. No credit cards accepted.

Mail search: Turnaround time: 1-2 days.

In person search: Searching is available in person.

Other access: Mailing lists are available. There is a $75.00 set up fee $75.00 per 1000 names, with a minimum of $90.00. They have records for big game licensees.

Licenses Searchable Online

Animal Remedy #19	www.state.sd.us/doa/databases/index.cfm
Architect #23	www.state.sd.us/dcr/engineer/Roster/index.cfm
Assessor #23	www.state.sd.us/dcr/engineer/Roster/index.cfm
Auctioneer #28	www.state.sd.us/state/executive/dcr/realestate/roster/index.cfm
Chiropractor #05	prill@mitchell.com
Counselor #06	www.state.sd.us./state/executive/dcr/counselor/roster.htm
Engineer #23	www.state.sd.us/dcr/engineer/Roster/index.cfm
Engineer-Petroleum Environmental #23	www.state.sd.us/dcr/engineer/Roster/index.cfm
Fertilizer #19	www.state.sd.us/doa/databases/index.cfm
Home Inspector #28	www.state.sd.us/state/executive/dcr/realestate/roster/index.cfm
Landscape Architect #23	www.state.sd.us/dcr/engineer/Roster/index.cfm
Marriage & Family Counselor #06	www.state.sd.us./state/executive/dcr/counselor/roster.htm
Optometrist #09	www.arbo.org/nodb2000/licsearch.asp
Pesticide Applicator #19	www.state.sd.us/doa/databases/commercial/index.cfm
Pesticide Dealer #19	www.state.sd.us/doa/databases/commercial/index.cfm
Petroleum Release Remedictor #23	www.state.sd.us/dcr/engineer/Roster/index.cfm
Plumber #34	www.state.sd.us/dcr/plumbing/
Real Estate Broker #28	www.state.sd.us/state/executive/dcr/realestate/roster/index.cfm
Real Estate Property Manager #28	www.state.sd.us/state/executive/dcr/realestate/roster/index.cfm
Real Estate Salesperson #28	www.state.sd.us/state/executive/dcr/realestate/roster/index.cfm
Real Estate Time Share #28	www.state.sd.us/state/executive/dcr/realestate/roster/index.cfm
Remediator #23	www.state.sd.us/dcr/engineer/Roster/index.cfm
Surveyor #23	www.state.sd.us/dcr/engineer/Roster/index.cfm
Waste Water Collection System Operator #12	www.state.sd.us/denr/databases/operator/index.cfm
Waste Water Treatment Plant Operator #12	www.state.sd.us/denr/databases/operator/index.cfm
Water Distributor #12	www.state.sd.us/denr/databases/operator/index.cfm

Licensing Quick Finder

Abstractor #01	605-869-2269
Acupuncturist #05	605-343-7440
Alcoholic Beverage Distributor #21	605-773-3311
Ambulance #20	605-773-4031
Animal Remedy #19	605-773-4432
Appliance Contractor #34	605-773-3429
Architect #23	605-394-2510
Asbestos Abatement Worker #36	605-773-5559
Assessor #23	605-394-2510
Athletic Trainer #10	605-334-8343
Attorney #32	605-224-7554
Auctioneer #28	605-773-3600
Audiologist #30	605-642-1600
Bail Bond Agent #37	605-773-3513
Bank #02	605-773-3421
Barber #04	605-224-6281
Barber Shop #04	605-224-6281
Brokerage Firm #31	605-733-4013
Bus Driver #17	605-773-6511
Business Opportunities Broker #31	605-733-4823
Chiropractor #05	605-343-7440
Cigarette Wholesaler #21	605-773-3311
Clinical Nurse Specialist #11	605-362-2760
Cosmetologist #18	605-773-6193
Cosmetology Instructor #18	605-773-6193
Cosmetology Salon #18	605-773-6193
Counselor #06	605-331-2927
Court/Shorthand Reporter #38	605-773-3474
Dental Assistant #07	605-224-1282
Dental Hygienist #07	605-224-1282
Dentist #07	605-224-1282
Dietitian/Nutritionist #10	605-334-8343
Electrical Inspector #33	605-773-3573
Electrician #33	605-773-3573
Emergency Medical Technician #20	605-773-4031
Engineer #23	605-394-2510
Estetician #18	605-773-6193
Fertilizer #19	605-773-4432
Franchise Sales #31	605-733-4823
Funeral Director/Embalmer #29	605-642-1600
Funeral Establishment #29	605-642-1600
Funeral Service #15	605-642-1600
Gaming #24	605-773-6050
Hearing Aid Dispenser #30	605-642-1600
Home Inspector #28	605-773-3600
Insurance Agent #17	605-773-6511
Investment Advisor #31	605-733-4013
Landscape Architect #23	605-394-2510
Law Enforcement Officer #25	605-773-3584
Livestock Dealer #16	605-773-3321
Loan Production #02	605-773-3421
Lobbyist #27	605-773-5666
Marriage & Family Counselor #06	605-331-2927
Medical Assistant #10	605-334-8343
Medical Doctor #10	605-334-8343
Milk Grader/Hauler/Tester #19	605-773-4294
Mobile Home Contractor #34	605-773-3429
Money Lending License #02	605-773-3421
Money Order Business #02	605-773-3421
Mortgage Broker #02	605-773-3421
Mortgage Lender #02	605-773-3421
Nail Salon #18	605-773-6193
Nail Technician/Manicurist #18	605-773-6193
Notary Public #27	605-773-5666
Nurse #11	605-362-2760
Nurse Anesthetist #11	605-362-2760
Nurse Midwife #11	605-362-2760
Nurse-RN #11	605-362-2760
Nurses' Aide #08	605-339-2071
Nursing Home Administrator #08	605-331-5040
Occupational Therapist/Assistant #10	605-334-8343
Optometrist #09	605-347-2136
Osteopathic Physician #10	605-334-8343
Paramedic #20	605-773-4031
Pesticide Applicator #19	605-773-4432
Pesticide Dealer #19	605-773-4432
Petroleum Release Remedictor #23	605-394-2510
Pharmacist/Pharmacy #13	605-362-2737
Physical Therapist/Assistant #10	605-334-8343
Physician/Medical Assistant #10	605-334-8343
Plumber #34	605-773-3429
Podiatrist #14	605-642-1600
Polygraph Examiner #25	605-773-3584
Psychologist #26	605-642-1600
Public Accountant-CPA #03	605-367-5770
Racing #24	605-773-6050
Radiologist #05	605-343-7440
Radiology #07	605-224-1282
Real Estate Broker #28	605-773-3600
Real Estate Property Manager #28	605-773-3600
Real Estate Salesperson #28	605-773-3600
Real Estate Time Share #28	605-773-3600
Remediator #23	605-394-2510
Respiratory Care Practitioner #10	605-334-8343
Salon #18	605-773-6193
School Bus Driver #17	605-773-6511
School Counselor #22	605-773-3553
School Principal #22	605-773-3553
School Superintendent #22	605-773-3553
Securities Agent/Broker/Dealer #31	605-733-4013
Sewage & Water Installation Contractor/Installer #34	605-773-3429
Social Worker #15	605-642-1600
Surveyor #23	605-394-2510
Teacher #22	605-773-3553
Truck Driver #17	605-773-6511
Veterinarian #16	605-773-3321
Veterinary Corporation #16	605-773-3321
Veterinary Technician #16	605-773-3321
Waste Water Collection System Operator #12	605-773-4208
Waste Water Treatment Plant Operator #12	605-773-4208
Water Conditioning Plumbing Installer #34	605-773-3429
Water Distributor #12	605-773-4208
Water Treatment Operator #39	605-773-4208
Well Driller #36	605-773-5559
Wholesaler (of prescription/non-prescription drugs) #13	605-362-2737

Licensing Agency Information

01 Abstractors Board of Examiners, PO Box 187 (PO Box 187), Kennebec, SD 57544-0187; 605-869-2269, Fax: 605-869-2269.

www.state.sd.us/state/executive/dcr/abstractors/abst-hom.htm

02 Department of Commerce & Regulation, Division of Banking, 217 1/2 W Missouri, Pierre, SD 57501-4590; 605-773-3421, Fax: 605-773-5367.

www.state.sd.us/dcr/bank

03 Board of Accountancy, 301 E 14th St, #200, Sioux Falls, SD 57104-5022; 605-367-5770, Fax: 605-367-5773.

www.state.sd.us/state/executive/dcr/accountancy/acc-home.htm

04 Board of Barber Examiners, PO Box 1115 (PO Box 1115), Pierre, SD 57501-1115; 605-224-6281, Fax: 605-224-6060.

www.state.sd.us/state/executive/dcr/barber/barber-h.htm

05 Board of Chiropractic Examiners, 1406 Mt Rushmore Road, Rapid City, SD 57701; 605-343-7440, Fax: 605-342-7868.

www.state.sd.us/dcr/chiropractic

Direct URL to search licenses: prill@mitchell.com You can search online using downloadble form at main internet site

06 Board of Counselor Examiners, PO Box 1822 (PO Box 1822), Sioux Falls, SD 57101-1822; 605-331-2927, Fax: 605-331-2043.

www.state.sd.us/state/executive/dcr/counselor/couns-ho.htm

Direct URL to search licenses: www.state.sd.us./state/executive/dcr/counselor/roster.htm

07 Board of Dentistry, PO Box 1037 (106 W Capitol, #7), Pierre, SD 57501; 605-224-1282, Fax: 605-224-7426.

www.state.sd.us/state/executive/dcr/dentistry/dent-hom.htm

08 Board of Examiners for Nursing Home Administrators, PO Box 632 (PO Box 632), Sioux Falls, SD 57101-0632; 605-331-5040, Fax: 605-331-2043.

www.state.sd.us/state/executive/dcr/nursinghome/nurhom-h.hml

09 Board of Examiners in Optometry, PO Box 370 (PO Box 370), Sturgis, SD 57785-0370; 605-347-2136, Fax: 605-347-5823.

www.state.sd.us/state/executive/dcr/optometry/optom-ho.htm

Direct URL to search licenses: www.arbo.org/nodb2000/licsearch.asp You can search online using national database by name, city or state.

10 Board of Medical & Osteopathic Examiners, 1323 S Minnesota Ave, Sioux Falls, SD 57105-0685; 605-334-8343, Fax: 605-336-0270.

11 Board of Nursing, 4300 S Louise Ave, Sioux Falls, SD 57106-3124; 605-362-2760, Fax: 605-362-2768.

www.state.sd.us/dcr/nursing/nurs-hom.htm

12 Board of Operator Certification, 523 E Capitol Ave, Foss Bldg, Pierre, SD 57501; 605-773-3754, Fax: 605-773-5286.

www.state.sd.us/opercert

Direct URL to search licenses: www.state.sd.us/denr/databases/operator/index.cfm You can search online using name, type of certificate, employer name, and region of state.

13 Board of Pharmacy, 4305 S Louise Ave, #104, Sioux Falls, SD 57106-3115; 605-362-2737, Fax: 605-362-2738.

www.state.sd.us/state/executive/dcr/pharmacy/pharm-ho.htm

14 Board of Podiatry Examiners, 135 E Illinois, #214, Spearfish, SD 57783; 605-642-1600, Fax: 605-642-1756.

www.state.sd.us/dcr/podiatry/pod-home.htm

15 Board of Social Work Examiners, 135 E Illinois, #214, Spearfish, SD 57783; 605-642-1600, Fax: 605-642-1756.

www.state.sd.us/state/executive/dcr/socialwork/soc-hom.htm

16 Board of Veterinary Medical Examiners, 411 S Fort St, Pierre, SD 57501-4503; 605-773-3321, Fax: 605-773-5459.

www.state.sd.us/state/executive/dcr/veterinary/vet-hom.htm

17 Department of Commerce & Regulation, 118 W Capitol Ave, Pierre, SD 57501; 605-733-6511.

18 Cosmetology Commission, 500 E Capitol, Pierre, SD 57501-5070; 605-773-6193, Fax: 605-773-7175.

www.state.sd.us/state/executive/dcr/cosmo/

19 Department of Agriculture, 523 E Capitol, Foss Bldg, Pierre, SD 57501-3182; 605-773-3375, Fax: 605-773-3481.

www.state.sd.us/doa/dos

20 Department of Health, 600 E Capitol Ave, Pierre, SD 57501-3185; 605-773-4031, Fax: 605-773-5904.

www.state.sd.us/doh/ems

21 Department of Revenue, 445 E Capitol Ave, Pierre, SD 57501-3185; 605-773-3311, Fax: 605-773-5129.

www.state.sd.us/state/executive/revenue

22 Education & Cultural Affairs Department, Office of Policy & Accountability, 700 Governors Dr, Pierre, SD 57501-2291; 605-773-3553, Fax: 605-773-6139.

www.state.sd.us/deca

23 Engineering, Board of Technical Professions, 2040 W Main St, #304, Rapid City, SD 57702-2447; 605-394-2510, Fax: 605-395-2509.

www.state.sd.us/dcr/engineer

Direct URL to search licenses: www.state.sd.us/dcr/engineer/Roster/index.cfm You can search online using last name, profession, license number, or business.

24 Gaming Commission, 118 W Capitol, Pierre, SD 57501-5070; 605-773-6050, Fax: 605-773-6053.

www.state.sd.us/state/executive/dcr/gaming-hom/gam.htm

25 Law Enforcement Standards & Training Commission, Division of Criminal Justice Training Center, Pierre, SD 57501; 605-773-3584, Fax: 605-773-4629.

27 Office of Secretary of State, 500 E Capitol Ave, State Capitol Bldg, #204, Pierre, SD 57501-5070; 605-773-3537, Fax: 605-773-6580.

28 Real Estate Commission, 118 W Capitol, Pierre, SD 57501; 605-773-3600, Fax: 605-773-4356.

www.state.sd.us/state/executive/dcr/realestate/Real-hom.htm

Direct URL to search licenses: www.state.sd.us/state/executive/dcr/realestate/roster/index.cfm You can search online using name, city, state, firm name, and license type.

29 Board of Funeral Services, PO Box 654 (135 E Illinois, #214), Spearfish, SD 57783; 605-642-1600, Fax: 605-642-1756.

www.state.sd.us/state/executive/dcr/funeral/fun-hom.htm

30 Board of Licensing, 135 E Illinois Way, Spearfish, SD 57783-0654; 605-642-1600, Fax: 605-642-1756.

www.state.sd.us/state/executive/dcr/hearing/hear-hom.htm

31 Division of Securities, 118 W Capitol Ave, Pierre, SD 57501-2017; 605-773-4823, Fax: 605-773-5953.

www.state.sd.us/dcr/securities/security.htm

32 State Bar, 222 E Capitol Ave, Pierre, SD 57501-2596; 605-224-7554, Fax: 605-224-0282.

www.sdbar.org

33 Electrical Commission, 118 W Capitol, Pierre, SD 57501-5070; 605-773-3573, Fax: 605-773-6213.

www.state.sd.us/state/executive/dcr/dcr.html

34 Plumbing Commission, 118 W Capitol Ave, Pierre, SD 57501; 605-773-3429, Fax: 605-773-5405.

www.state.sd.us/der/plumbing

Direct URL to search licenses: www.state.sd.us/dcr/plumbing/ Online searching availble after October, 2000

35 Healthcare Administration, Nurses Aide Testing, 804 N Western Av, Souix Falls, SD 57104-2098; 605-339-2071, Fax: 605-339-1354.

36 Department of Environment & Natural Resources, Division of Environmental Svcs, 523 E Capitol Ave, Pierre, SD 57501-3182; 605-773-5559.

37 Division of Insurance, 910 E Sioux Ave, Pierre, SD 57501; 605-773-3513.

38 Supreme Court, Unified Judicial Court Administrators Office, Capitol Bldg, 500 E Capitol, Pierre, SD 57501; 605-773-3474.

39 Department of Environment & Natural Resources, Division of Environmental Svcs, Drinking Water Program, 523 E Capitol Ave, Pierre, SD 57501; 605-773-4208.

The following list indicates the district and division name for each county in the state. If the district or division name of the bankruptcy court is different from the civil/criminal court, it appears in parentheses.

County/Court Cross Reference

County	Court		County	Court
Aurora	Sioux Falls		Hyde	Pierre
Beadle	Sioux Falls		Jackson	Pierre
Bennett	Rapid City (Pierre)		Jerauld	Pierre
Bon Homme	Sioux Falls		Jones	Pierre
Brookings	Sioux Falls		Kingsbury	Sioux Falls
Brown	Aberdeen (Pierre)		Lake	Sioux Falls
Brule	Sioux Falls		Lawrence	Rapid City (Pierre)
Buffalo	Pierre		Lincoln	Sioux Falls
Butte	Aberdeen (Pierre)		Lyman	Pierre
Campbell	Aberdeen (Pierre)		Marshall	Aberdeen (Pierre)
Charles Mix	Sioux Falls		McCook	Sioux Falls
Clark	Aberdeen (Pierre)		McPherson	Aberdeen (Pierre)
Clay	Sioux Falls		Meade	Rapid City (Pierre)
Codington	Aberdeen (Pierre)		Mellette	Pierre
Corson	Aberdeen (Pierre)		Miner	Sioux Falls
Custer	Rapid City (Pierre)		Minnehaha	Sioux Falls
Davison	Sioux Falls		Moody	Sioux Falls
Day	Aberdeen (Pierre)		Pennington	Rapid City (Pierre)
Deuel	Aberdeen (Pierre)		Perkins	Rapid City (Pierre)
Dewey	Pierre		Potter	Pierre
Douglas	Sioux Falls		Roberts	Aberdeen (Pierre)
Edmunds	Aberdeen (Pierre)		Sanborn	Sioux Falls
Fall River	Rapid City (Pierre)		Shannon	Rapid City (Pierre)
Faulk	Pierre		Spink	Aberdeen (Pierre)
Grant	Aberdeen (Pierre)		Stanley	Pierre
Gregory	Pierre		Sully	Pierre
Haakon	Pierre		Todd	Pierre
Hamlin	Aberdeen (Pierre)		Tripp	Pierre
Hand	Pierre		Turner	Sioux Falls
Hanson	Sioux Falls		Union	Sioux Falls
Harding	Rapid City (Pierre)		Walworth	Aberdeen (Pierre)
Hughes	Pierre		Yankton	Sioux Falls
Hutchinson	Sioux Falls		Ziebach	Pierre

US District Court

District of South Dakota

Aberdeen Division c/o Pierre Division, Federal Bldg & Courthouse, 225 S Pierre St, Room 405, Pierre, SD 57501, 605-224-5849, Fax: 605-224-0806.

www.sdd.uscourts.gov

Counties: Brown, Butte, Campbell, Clark, Codington, Corson, Day, Deuel, Edmunds, Grant, Hamlin, McPherson, Marshall, Roberts, Spink, Walworth. Judge Battey's closed case records are located at the Rapid City Division.

Indexing & Storage: Cases are indexed by as well as by case number. New cases are available in the index after filing date. Open records are located at the Division.

Fee & Payment: The fee is no charge per item (one party name or case number). Payment may be made by money order, cashier check. Business checks are not accepted. Personal checks are not accepted.

Phone Search: An automated voice case information service (VCIS) is not available.

In Person Search: In person searching is available.

PACER: Sign-up number is 800-676-6856. Access fee is $.60 per minute. Case records are available back to 1991. Records are purged every six months. New records are available online after 1 day. PACER is available on the Internet at http://pacer.sdd.uscourts.gov.

Opinions Online: Court opinions are available online at www.sdbar.org/opinions/dsindex.htm

Other Online Access: You can search records on the Internet using RACER. Currently the system is free and requires free registration. Simply visit http://207.222.24.8/wconnect/wc.dll?usdc_racer~main.

Pierre Division Federal Bldg & Courthouse, Room 405, 225 S Pierre St, Pierre, SD 57501, 605-224-5849, Fax: 605-224-0806.

www.sdd.uscourts.gov

Counties: Buffalo, Dewey, Faulk, Gregory, Haakon, Hand, Hughes, Hyde, Jackson, Jerauld, Jones, Lyman, Mellette, Potter, Stanley, Sully, Todd, Tripp, Ziebach.

Indexing & Storage: Cases are indexed by defendant and plaintiff as well as by case number. New cases are available in the index 1 day after filing date. Both computer and card indexes are maintained. Open records are located at this court.

Fee & Payment: The fee is $15.00 per item (one party name or case number). Payment may be made by money order, cashier check, personal check. Prepayment is required. Payee: Clerk, US District Court. Certification fee: $5.00 per document. Copy fee: $.50 per page.

Phone Search: Only docket information is available by phone. An automated voice case information service (VCIS) is not available.

Fax Search: Will accept fax for a price quote only.

Mail Search: Always enclose a stamped self addressed envelope.

In Person Search: In person searching is available.

PACER: Sign-up number is 800-676-6856. Access fee is $.60 per minute. Case records are available back to 1991. Records are purged every six months. New records are available online after 1 day. PACER is available on the Internet at http://pacer.sdd.uscourts.gov.

Opinions Online: Court opinions are available online at www.sdbar.org/opinions/dsindex.htm

Other Online Access: You can search records on the Internet using RACER. Currently the system is free and requires free registration. Simply visit http://207.222.24.8/wconnect/wc.dll?usdc_racer~main.

Rapid City Division Clerk's Office, Room 302, 515 9th St, Rapid City, SD 57701, 605-342-3066.

www.sdd.uscourts.gov

Counties: Bennett, Custer, Fall River, Harding, Lawrence, Meade, Pennington, Perkins, Shannon. Judge Battey's closed cases are located here.

Indexing & Storage: Cases are indexed by defendant and plaintiff as well as by case number. New cases are available in the index 24 hours after filing date. Both computer and card indexes are maintained. Open records are located at this court.

Fee & Payment: The fee is $15.00 per item (one party name or case number). Payment may be made by money order, cashier check, business check. Personal checks are not accepted. Prepayment is required. Payee: Clerk, US District Court. Certification fee: $5.00 per document. Copy fee: $.50 per page.

Phone Search: Only docket information available by telephone. An automated voice case information service (VCIS) is not available.

Mail Search: A stamped self addressed envelope is not required.

In Person Search: In person searching is available.

PACER: Sign-up number is 800-676-6856. Access fee is $.60 per minute. Case records are available back to 1991. Records are purged every six months. New records are available online after 1 day. PACER is available on the Internet at http://pacer.sdd.uscourts.gov.

Opinions Online: Court opinions are available online at www.sdbar.org/opinions/dsindex.htm

Other Online Access: You can search records on the Internet using RACER. Currently the system is free and requires free registration. Simply visit http://207.222.24.8/wconnect/wc.dll?usdc_racer~main.

Sioux Falls Division Room 128, US Courthouse, 400 S Phillips Ave, Sioux Falls, SD 57104-6851, 605-330-4447, Fax: 605-330-4312.

www.sdd.uscourts.gov

Counties: Aurora, Beadle, Bon Homme, Brookings, Brule, Charles Mix, Clay, Davison, Douglas, Hanson, Hutchinson, Kingsbury, Lake, Lincoln, McCook, Miner, Minnehaha, Moody, Sanborn, Turner, Union, Yankton.

Indexing & Storage: Cases are indexed by defendant and plaintiff as well as by case number. New cases are available in the index 1 day after

filing date. Both computer and card indexes are maintained. Open records are located at this court.

Fee & Payment: The fee is $15.00 per item (one party name or case number). Payment may be made by money order, cashier check, personal check. Prepayment is required. Payee: Clerk, US District Court. Certification fee: $5.00 per document. Copy fee: $.50 per page.

Phone Search: Only docket information for civil cases will be released over the phone. An automated voice case information service (VCIS) is not available.

Fax Search: To send a fax request, you must set up an account with the court. The fee for a fax request is $15.00 per name and $1.50 per page sent. The fee is $1.50 per page sent.

Mail Search: Always enclose a stamped self addressed envelope.

In Person Search: In person searching is available.

PACER: Sign-up number is 800-676-6856. Access fee is $.60 per minute. Case records are available back to 1991. Records are purged every six months. New records are available online after 1 day. PACER is available on the Internet at http://pacer.sdd.uscourts.gov.

Opinions Online: Court opinions are available online at www.sdbar.org/opinions/dsindex.htm

Other Online Access: You can search records on the Internet using RACER. Currently the system is free and requires free registration. Simply visit http://207.222.24.8/wconnect/wc.dll?usdc_racer~main.

US Bankruptcy Court

District of South Dakota

Pierre Division Clerk, Room 203, Federal Bldg, 225 S Pierre St, Pierre, SD 57501, 605-224-6013, Fax: 605-224-9808.

www.sdb.uscourts.gov

Counties: Bennett, Brown, Buffalo, Butte, Campbell, Clark, Codington, Corson, Custer, Day, Deuel, Dewey, Edmunds, Fall River, Faulk, Grant, Gregory, Haakon, Hamlin, Hand, Harding, Hughes, Hyde, Jackson, Jerauld, Jones, Lawrence, Lyman, Marshall, McPherson, Meade,Mellette, Pennington, Perkins, Potter, Roberts, Shannon, Spink, Stanley, Sully, Todd, Tripp, Walworth, Ziebach.

Indexing & Storage: Cases are indexed by debtor and creditors as well as by case number. New cases are available in the index immediately after filing date. A computer index is maintained. Open records are located at this court. District wide searches are available for information from 10/1/91 from this court.

Fee & Payment: The fee is $15.00 per item (one party name or case number). Payment may be made by money order, cashier check, in-state business check. Personal checks are not accepted.

Prepayment is required. Payee: Clerk, US Bankruptcy Court. Certification fee: $5.00 per document. Copy fee: $.50 per page.

Phone Search: Only docket information is available by phone. An automated voice case information service (VCIS) is available. Call VCIS at 800-768-6218 or 605-330-4559.

Fax Search: Will accept fax searches. Will fax docket listings at no extra charge.

Mail Search: Always enclose a stamped self addressed envelope.

In Person Search: In person searching is available.

PACER: Sign-up number is 800-676-6856. Access fee is $.60 per minute. Toll-free access: 800-261-3167. Local access: 605-330-4342. Case records are available back to October 1, 1991. Records are never purged. New civil records are available online after 1 day. PACER is available on the Internet at http://pacer.sdb.uscourts.gov.

Sioux Falls Division PO Box 5060, Sioux Falls, SD 57117-5060 (Courier Address: Room 104, 400 S Phillips Ave, Sioux Falls, SD 57102), 605-330-4541, Fax: 605-330-4548.

www.sdb.uscourts.gov

Counties: Aurora, Beadle, Bon Homme, Brookings, Brule, Charles Mix, Clay, Davison, Douglas, Hanson, Hutchinson, Kingsbury, Lake, Lincoln, McCook, Miner, Minnehaha, Moody, Sanborn, Turner, Union, Yankton.

Indexing & Storage: Cases are indexed by debtor and creditors as well as by case number. New cases are available in the index 1 day after filing date. A computer index is maintained. Open records are located at this court. District wide searches are available for information from 10/1/91 from this court.

Fee & Payment: The fee is $15.00 per item (one party name or case number). Payment may be made by money order, cashier check, in-state business check. Personal checks are not accepted. Prepayment is required. Payee: Clerk, US Bankruptcy Court. Certification fee: $5.00 per document. Copy fee: $.50 per page.

Phone Search: Only docket information is available by phone. An automated voice case information service (VCIS) is available. Call VCIS at 800-768-6218 or 605-330-4559.

Fax Search: Will accept fax search at $15.00 fee. Will fax docket listing at no extra charge.

Mail Search: Always enclose a stamped self addressed envelope.

In Person Search: In person searching is available.

PACER: Sign-up number is 800-676-6856. Access fee is $.60 per minute. Toll-free access: 800-261-3167. Local access: 605-330-4342. Case records are available back to October 1, 1991. Records are never purged. New civil records are available online after 1 day. PACER is available on the Internet at http://pacer.sdb.uscourts.gov.

Court	Jurisdiction	No. of Courts	How Organized
Circuit Courts	General	66	7 Circuits
Magistrate Courts		66	

* Profiled in this Sourcebook.

Court	CIVIL								
	Tort	Contract	Real Estate	Min. Claim	Max. Claim	Small Claims	Estate	Eviction	Domestic Relations
Circuit Courts	X	X	X	$0	No Max	$8000	X	X	X
Magistrate Courts				$0	$10,000	$8000	X	X	X

Court	CRIMINAL				
	Felony	Misdemeanor	DWI/DUI	Preliminary Hearing	Juvenile
Circuit Courts	X	X	X	X	X
Magistrate Courts		X	X	X	

ADMINISTRATION   State Court Administrator, State Capitol Building, 500 E Capitol Av, Pierre, SD, 57501; 605-773-3474, Fax: 605-773-5627. www.state.sd.us/state/judicial

COURT STRUCTURE   South Dakota has a statewide criminal record search database, administrated by the State Court Administrator's Office in Pierre. All criminal record information from July 1, 1989 forward, statewide, is contained in the database. To facilitate quicker access for the public, the state has designated 10 county record centers to process all mail or ongoing commercial accounts' criminal record requests. All mail requests are forwarded to, and commercial account requests are assigned to one of 10 specific county court clerks for processing a statewide search. Note that walk-in requesters seeking a single or minimum of requests may still obtain a record from their local county court. 6 counties (Buffalo, Campbell, Corson, Dewey, McPherson, & Ziebach) do not have computer terminals in-house. Criminal records from these 6 counties are entered into the database by court personnel at another location.

The fee is $15.00 per record. State authorized commercial accounts may order and receive records by fax, there is an additional $5.00 fee unless a non-toll free line is used.

Requesters who wish to set up a commercial account are directed to contact Jill Smith at the Court Administrator's Office in Pierre at the address mentioned above.

The state re-aligned their circuits from 8 to 7 effective June, 2000.

ONLINE ACCESS   There is no statewide online access computer system currently available. Larger courts are being placed on computer systems at a rate of 4 to 5 courts per year. Access is intended for internal use only. Smaller courts place their information on computer cards that are later sent to Pierre for input by the state office.

ADDITIONAL INFORMATION   Most South Dakota courts do not allow the public to perform searches, but rather require the court clerk to do them for a fee of $15.00 per name (increased from $5.00 as of July 1, 1997). A special Record Search Request Form must be used. Searches will be returned with a disclaimer stating that the clerk is not responsible for the completeness of the search. Clerks are not required to respond to telephone or Fax requests. Many courts are not open all day so they prefer written requests.

Aurora County

Circuit Court PO Box 366, Plankinton, SD 57368; 605-942-7165; Fax: 605-942-7751. Hours: 8AM-Noon, 1-5PM (CST). *Felony, Misdemeanor, Civil, Eviction, Small Claims, Probate.*

Civil Records: Access: Fax, mail, in person. Both court and visitors may perform in person searches. Search fee: $15.00 per name. Required to search: name, years to search; also helpful-address. Civil cases indexed by defendant, plaintiff. Civil records on manual index since 1879, some computerized since 1988. **Criminal Records:** Access: Fax, mail, in person. Only the court conducts in person searches; visitors may not. Search fee: $15.00 per name. Required to search: name, years to search, signed release; also helpful-address, DOB, SSN. Criminal records are computerized since 07/89 on a statewide system. Mail requests are forwarded to Miner County for processing. **General Information:** No juvenile, sealed, dismissed, adoption or mental health records released. SASE required. Turnaround time 1 day. Copy fee: $.20 per page. Certification fee: $2.00. Fee payee: Aurora County Clerk of Court. Business checks accepted. Prepayment is required. Fax notes: $1.00 per page to fax back, $5.00 minimum.

Beadle County

Circuit Court PO Box 1358, Huron, SD 57350; 605-353-7165. Hours: 8AM-5PM (CST). *Felony, Misdemeanor, Civil, Eviction, Small Claims, Probate.*

Civil Records: Access: Mail, in person. Only the court conducts in person searches; visitors may not. Search fee: $15.00 per name. Required to search: name, years to search. Civil cases indexed by defendant, plaintiff. Civil records on computer from 1990 (limited), cards from 1900. Not for public use. **Criminal Records:** Access: Mail, in person. Only the court conducts in person searches; visitors may not. Search fee: $15.00 per name. Required to search: name, years to search, DOB; also helpful-SSN. Criminal records are computerized since 07/89 on a statewide system. Mail requests are forwarded to Hand County for processing. **General Information:** No juvenile, sealed, dismissed, adoption, or mental health records released. Turnaround time up to 2 weeks. Copy fee: $.20 per page. Certification fee: $2.00. Fee payee: Beadle County Clerk of Court. Personal checks accepted. Out of state checks not accepted. Prepayment is required.

Bennett County

Circuit Court PO Box 281, Martin, SD 57551; 605-685-6969. Hours: 8AM-4:30PM (MST). *Felony, Misdemeanor, Civil, Eviction, Small Claims, Probate.*

Civil Records: Access: Mail, in person. Only the court conducts in person searches; visitors may not. Search fee: $15.00 per name. Required to search: name, years to search; also helpful-address. Civil cases indexed by defendant, plaintiff. Civil records on index from 1912. **Criminal Records:** Access: Mail, in person. Only the court conducts in person searches; visitors may not. Search fee: $15.00 per name. Required to search: name, years to search, DOB; also helpful-address. Criminal records are computerized since 07/89 on a statewide system. All mail requests are forwarded to Potter County for processing. **General Information:** No juvenile, sealed, dismissed, or mental health records released. SASE required. Turnaround time 48 hours. Application form available. Copy fee: $.25 for first page, $.10 each addl. Certification fee: $3.00. Fee payee: Bennett County Clerk of Courts. Business checks accepted. Prepayment is required.

Bon Homme County

Circuit Court PO Box 6, Tyndall, SD 57066; 605-589-4215; Fax: 605-589-4209. Hours: 8AM-4:30PM (CST). *Felony, Misdemeanor, Civil, Eviction, Small Claims, Probate.*

Civil Records: Access: Fax, mail, in person. Both court and visitors may perform in person searches. Search fee: $15.00 per name. Required to search: name, years to search; also helpful-address. Civil cases indexed by defendant, plaintiff. Civil records on alpha index books from 1877. Requests should be in writing. **Criminal Records:** Access: Mail, in person. Only the court conducts in person searches; visitors may not. Search fee: $15.00 per name. Required to search: name, years to search, DOB, signed release; also helpful-address, SSN. Criminal records are computerized since 07/89 on a statewide system. All mail requests are forwarded to Douglas County for processing. **General Information:** No juvenile, sealed, dismissed, or mental health records released. SASE required. Turnaround time 3 days to 1 week. Copy fee: $.25 per page. Certification fee: $2.00. Fee payee: Bon Homme County Clerk of Court. Personal checks accepted. Prepayment is required. Fax notes: $1.00 per page. $5.00 minimum, unless call is local or toll free.

Brookings County

Circuit Court 314 6th Ave, Brookings, SD 57006; 605-688-4200; Fax: 605-688-4952. Hours: 8AM-5PM (CST). *Felony, Misdemeanor, Civil, Eviction, Small Claims, Probate.*

Civil Records: Access: Mail, in person. Only the court conducts in person searches; visitors may not. Search fee: $15.00 per name. Required to search: name, years to search; also helpful-address. Civil cases indexed by defendant, plaintiff. Civil records on alpha index books from 1900s. **Criminal Records:** Access: Mail, in person. Only the court conducts in person searches; visitors may not. Search fee: $15.00 per name. Required to search: name, years to search, DOB; also helpful-address, SSN. Criminal records on computer since July 1989 on a statewide system. Alll mail requests are forwarded to Hand County for processing. **General Information:** No juvenile, sealed, dismissed, or mental health records released. SASE required. Turnaround time 3 days.

Copy fee: $.20 per page. Certification fee: $2.00. Fee payee: Brookings County Clerk of Court. Only cashiers checks and money orders accepted. Prepayment is required.

Brown County

Circuit Court 101 1st Ave SE, Aberdeen, SD 57401; 605-626-2451; Fax: 605-626-2491. Hours: 8AM-5PM (CST). *Felony, Misdemeanor, Civil, Eviction, Small Claims, Probate.*

Civil Records: Access: Mail, in person. Both court and visitors may perform in person searches. Search fee: $15.00 per name. Required to search: name, years to search; also helpful-address. Civil cases indexed by defendant, plaintiff. Civil records on registers from 1975 (misdemeanor), registers from 1900s (civil). **Criminal Records:** Access: Mail, in person. Only the court conducts in person searches; visitors may not. Search fee: $15.00 per name. Required to search: name, years to search; also helpful-address, DOB, SSN. Criminal records on computer since 07/89 on a statewide system. All mail requests are forwarded to Edmunds County for processing. **General Information:** No juvenile, sealed, dismissed, or mental health records released. SASE required. Turnaround time 1-3 days. Copy fee: $.20 per page. Certification fee: $2.00. Fee payee: Brown County Clerk of Court. Personal checks accepted. Prepayment is required.

Brule County

Circuit Court 300 S Courtland #111, Chamberlain, SD 57325-1599; 605-734-5443; Fax: 605-734-5443. Hours: 8AM-Noon, 1-5PM (CST). *Felony, Misdemeanor, Civil, Eviction, Small Claims, Probate.*

Civil Records: Access: Fax, mail, in person. Both court and visitors may perform in person searches. Search fee: $15.00 per name. Required to search: name, years to search; also helpful-address. Civil cases indexed by defendant, plaintiff. Civil records on index books or docket books from 1875. **Criminal Records:** Access: Fax, mail, in person. Only the court conducts in person searches; visitors may not. Search fee: $15.00 per name. Required to search: name, years to search, DOB; also helpful-address, SSN. Criminal records on computer since July 1989 on a statewide system. All mail requests are forwarded to Miner County for processing. Fax requests accepted for commercial acounts only and are forwarded as well. **General Information:** No juvenile, sealed, dismissed, or mental health records released. SASE required. Turnaround time 3-5 days. Copy fee: $.25 per page. Certification fee: $2.00. Fee payee: Brule County Clerk of Court. Personal checks accepted. Prepayment is required. Fax notes: $1.00 per page. $5.00 minimum.

Buffalo County

Circuit Court PO Box 148, Gann Valley, SD 57341; 605-293-3234; Fax: 605-293-3240. Hours: 9AM-Noon (CST). *Felony, Misdemeanor, Civil, Eviction, Small Claims, Probate.*

Civil Records: Access: Mail, in person. Only the court conducts in person searches; visitors may not. Search fee: $15.00 per name. Required to search: name, years to search; also helpful-address. Civil cases indexed by defendant, plaintiff. All data on alpha index from 1915. **Criminal Records:** Access: Mail, in person. Only the court conducts in person searches; visitors may not. Search fee: $15.00 per name. Required to search: name, years to search, DOB; also helpful-address, SSN. Criminal records are on books, but

computerized on the statewide computer system since 07/89. This office does not have a computer hook-up. All mail requests are forwared to Miner County for processing. **General Information:** No juvenile, sealed, dismissed, or mental health records released. SASE required. Turnaround time 1 week. Copy fee: $.20 per page. Certification fee: $2.00. Fee payee: Buffalo County Clerk of Court. Personal checks accepted. Prepayment is required.

Butte County

Circuit Court PO Box 237, Belle Fourche, SD 57717; 605-892-2516; Fax: 605-892-2836. Hours: 8AM-Noon, 1-5PM (MST). *Felony, Misdemeanor, Civil, Eviction, Small Claims, Probate.*

Civil Records: Access: Mail, in person. Only the court conducts in person searches; visitors may not. Search fee: $15.00 per name. Required to search: name, years to search; also helpful-address. Civil cases indexed by defendant, plaintiff. All data on alpha index from 1900s. **Criminal Records:** Access: Mail, in person. Only the court conducts in person searches; visitors may not. Search fee: $15.00 per name. Required to search: name, years to search; also helpful-address. Criminal records on computer since 07/89 on a statewide system. All mail requests are forwarded to Lawrence County for processing. **General Information:** No juvenile, sealed, dismissed, or mental health records released. SASE required. Turnaround time varies. Copy fee: $.20 per page. Certification fee: $2.00. Fee payee: Butte County Clerk of Court. Personal checks accepted. Prepayment is required.

Campbell County

Circuit Court PO Box 146, Mound City, SD 57646; 605-955-3536; Fax: 605-955-3308. Hours: 8AM-Noon T-W-F (CST). *Felony, Misdemeanor, Civil, Small Claims, Probate.*

Civil Records: Access: Mail, in person. Both court and visitors may perform in person searches. Search fee: $15.00 per name. Required to search: name, years to search; also helpful-address. Civil cases indexed by defendant, plaintiff. All data on alpha index from 1800s. **Criminal Records:** Access: Mail, in person. Only the court conducts in person searches; visitors may not. Search fee: $15.00 per name. Required to search: name, years to search, DOB; also helpful-address, SSN. although records are computerized at the state level, this office has records and indices on paper. All mail requests are forwarded to Edmunds County for processing. **General Information:** No juvenile, sealed, dismissed, or mental health records released. SASE required. Turnaround time varies. Copy fee: $.10 per page. Certification fee: $2.00. Fee payee: Campbell County Clerk of Court. Only cashiers checks and money orders accepted. Prepayment is required.

Charles Mix County

Circuit Court PO Box 640, Lake Andes, SD 57356; 605-487-7511; Fax: 605-487-7547. Hours: 8AM-4:30PM (CST). *Felony, Misdemeanor, Civil, Eviction, Small Claims, Probate.*

Civil Records: Access: Fax, mail, in person. Both court and visitors may perform in person searches. Search fee: $15.00 per name. Required to search: name, years to search; also helpful-address. Civil cases indexed by defendant, plaintiff. Civil records on alpha index books from 1917. **Criminal Records:** Access: Fax, mail, in person. Only the court conducts in person searches; visitors may not. Search fee: $15.00 per name. Required to

Tennessee

General Help Numbers:

Governor's Office
State Capitol, 1st Floor
Nashville, TN 37243-0001
www.state.tn.us/governor

615-741-2001
Fax 615-532-9711
8AM-5PM

Attorney General's Office
425 5th Ave North
Nashville, TN 37243-0497
www.attorneygeneral.state.tn.us

615-741-3491
Fax 615-741-2009
8AM-4:30PM

State Court Administrator
Nashville City Center
511 Union St, Suite 600
Nashville, TN 37243-0607
www.tsc.state.tn.us

615-741-2687
Fax 615-741-6285
8AM-4:30PM

State Archives
State Library & Archives Division
403 7th Ave N
Nashville, TN 37243-0312
www.state.tn.us/sos/statelib/techsvs

615-741-7996
Fax 615-741-6471
8AM-6PM M-SA

State Specifics:

Capital:
Nashville
Davidson County

Time Zone: CST*
* Tennessee's twenty-nine eastern-most counties are EST: They are: Anderson, Blount, Bradley, Campbell, Carter, Claiborne, Cocke, Grainger, Greene, Hamilton, Hancock, Hawkins, Jefferson, Johnson, Knox, Loudon, McMinn, Meigs, Monroe, Morgan, Polk, Rhea, Roane, Scott, Sevier, Sullivan, Unicoi, Union, Washington.

Number of Counties: 95

Population: 5,483,535

Web Site: www.state.tn.us

State Agencies

Criminal Records

Access to Records is Restricted

Tennessee Bureau of Investigation, Records and Identification Unit, 1148 Foster Ave, Menzler-Nix Bldg, Nashville, TN 37210; 615-741-0430, 24 hours daily.

Note: The record database is not open to the general public or employers. It can only be accessed by those who have specific authorization per state law.

Corporation Records
Limited Partnership Records
Fictitious Name
Assumed Name
Limited Liability Company Records

Division of Business Svcs; Corporations, Department of State, 312 Eighth Ave. N, 6th Fl, Nashville, TN 37243; 615-741-2286, 615-741-7310 (Fax), 8AM-4:30PM.

www.state.tn.us/sos

Indexing & Storage: Records are available from 1875-present. Records are computerized and are on microfilm from 1979. Records are indexed on inhouse computer.

Searching: All information is considered public record. Include the following in your request-full name of business. In addition to the articles of incorporation, corporation records include the following information: Annual Reports, Officers, Directors, DBAs (assumed names only), Prior (merged) names, Inactive and Reserved names.

Access by: mail, phone, in person.

Fee & Payment: Certification costs $20.00. Corp., LLC, LP, and LLP records cost $20.00 per copy, which includes certification. Fee payee: Secretary of State. Prepayment required. Personal checks accepted. No credit cards accepted.

Mail search: Turnaround time: 1-3 days. Certificates are usually processed in 1 day.No self addressed stamped envelope is required.

Phone search: Limited information is given over the phone. Requests for certificates must be in writing.

In person search: Turnaround time is immediate unless certified documents are ordered which are ready the next day.

Other access: Some data can be purchased in bulk or list format. Call 615-532-9007 for more details.

Trademarks/Servicemarks Trade Names

Secretary of State, Trademarks/Tradenames Division, James K. Polk Bldg, Nashville, TN 37243-0306; 615-741-0531, 615-741-7310 (Fax), 8AM-4:30PM.

www.state.tn.us/sos

Indexing & Storage: Records are available from the 1950s to present. It takes 2-3 days before new records are available for inquiry. Records are indexed on microfilm.

Searching: Include the following in your request-trademark/servicemark name, name of owner, date of application.

Access by: mail, phone, in person.

Fee & Payment: Prepayment required. Fee payee: Secretary of State. Personal checks accepted. No credit cards accepted.

Mail search: Turnaround time: 1-3 days. A self addressed stamped envelope is requested. No fee for mail request. Copies cost $.50 per page.

Phone search: No fee for telephone request.

In person search: No fee for request. Copies cost $.50 per page. Turnaround time is while you wait.

Other access: The agency will provide a file update every three months for $.50 per page. Requests must be in writing.

Uniform Commercial Code State Tax Liens Federal Tax Liens

Division 0f Business Services, Secretary of State, 312 Eighth Ave N, 6th Fl, Nashville, TN 37243; 615-741-3276, 615-741-7310 (Fax), 8AM-4:30PM.

www.state.tn.us/sos

Indexing & Storage: Records are available from 1964. Records are computerized from 03/01/96.

Searching: Use search request form UCC-11. Federal tax liens are filed at the county level. Include the following in your request-debtor name.

Access by: mail, in person.

Fee & Payment: The fee is $15.00 per document, copies are $1.00 per page. Fee payee: Secretary of State. Prepayment required. Personal checks accepted. No credit cards accepted.

Mail search: Turnaround time: 1-2 days. A self addressed stamped envelope is requested.

In person search: The results are mailed in 3-5 days.

Sales Tax Registrations
Access to Records is Restricted

Revenue Department, Tax Enforcement Division, Andrew Jackson Bldg, 500 Deaderick St, Nashville, TN 37242-0100; 615-741-7071, 615-532-6339 (Fax), 8AM-4:30PM.

Note: This agency refuses to make any information about registrants available.

Birth Certificates

Tennessee Department of Health, Office of Vital Records, 421 5th Ave North, 1st floor, Nashville, TN 37247; 615-741-1763, 615-741-0778 (Credit card order), 615-726-2559 (Fax), 8AM-4PM.

www.state.tn.us/health/vr

Indexing & Storage: Records are available from 1914-present. For birth records prior to 1914, contact the State Library and Archives at 615-741-2764. Short forms are only available since 1949. New records are available for inquiry immediately. Records are indexed on index cards, inhouse computer.

Searching: Must have a signed release form from person of record or immediate family member for certified copy. Medical and health information is not released. Include the following in your request-full name, names of parents, mother's maiden name, date of birth, place of birth, relationship to person of record. Daytime phone helpful.

Access by: mail, phone, fax, in person, online.

Fee & Payment: $10.00 for the long (copy of actual certificate) form; $5.00 for the short computerized form. Add $2.00 per name per copy for additional copies. Fee payee: Tennessee Vital Records. Prepayment required. Personal checks accepted. Credit cards accepted: Mastercard, Visa, AmEx, Discover.

Mail search: Turnaround time: 2-3 weeks. No self addressed stamped envelope is required.

Phone search: You must use credit cards with fax or phone requests. There is an additional $10.00 fee. Phone service is available from 8AM to 4PM.

Fax search: Fax requests are handled like phone requests.

In person search: Available while you wait.

Online search: Records may be ordered from the web site, but are returned by mail.

Expedited service: Expedited service is available for fax or online searches. Turnaround time: 1 day. Phone and fax records ordered by credit card, for $10.00 extra, can be returned overnight for an additional fee.

Death Records

Tennessee Department of Health, Office of Vital Records, 421 5th Ave North, 1st floor, Nashville, TN 37247; 615-741-1763, 615-741-0778 (Credit card order), 615-726-2559 (Fax), 8AM-4PM.

www.state.tn.us/health/vr

Indexing & Storage: Records are available for 50 years. Previous records are at the State Archives at 615-726-2559. New records are available for inquiry immediately. Records are indexed on index cards, inhouse computer.

Searching: Must have a signed release form from immediate family member. Cause of death is restricted to immediate family members or their representatives and must be specifically requested. Include the following in your request-full name, names of parents, mother's maiden name, date of death, place of death, reason for information request, relationship to person of record. Daytime phone helpful.

Access by: mail, phone, fax, in person, online.

Fee & Payment: The fee is $5.00 per name. Fee payee: Tennessee Vital Records. Prepayment required. Personal checks accepted. Credit cards accepted: Mastercard, Visa, AmEx, Discover.

Mail search: Turnaround time: 2-3 weeks. No self addressed stamped envelope is required.

Phone search: You must use a credit card for an additional fee of $10.00. Turnaround time is one day.

Fax search: Same criteria as phone requests.

In person search: Searching is available in person.

Online search: Records may be ordered online but are returned by mail.

Expedited service: Expedited service is available for fax or online searches. Turnaround time: 24 hours. Add $10.00 per request. For credit card orders only. Add fees for overnight shipping.

Marriage Certificates

Tennessee Department of Health, Office of Vital Records, 421 5th Ave North, 1st floor, Nashville, TN 37247; 615-741-1763, 615-741-0778 (Credit card order), 615-726-2559 (Fax), 8AM-4PM.

www.state.tn.us/health/vr

Indexing & Storage: Records are available for 50 years. It takes 1 month before new records are available for inquiry. Records are indexed on index cards, inhouse computer.

Searching: Must have a signed release form from persons of record or immediate family member for certified copy. Information on race or previous marriages is only released for statistical purposes. Include the following in your request-names of husband and wife, date of marriage, place or county of marriage.

Access by: mail, phone, fax, in person, online.

Fee & Payment: The search fee is $10.00. Add $2.00 for each additional copy. Fee payee: Tennessee Vital Records. Prepayment required. Personal checks accepted. Credit cards accepted: Mastercard, Visa, AmEx, Discover.

Mail search: Turnaround time: 2-3 weeks. No self addressed stamped envelope is required.

Phone search: You must use a credit card for an additional $10.00 fee. Records are processed in 24 hours.

Fax search: Same criteria as phone searching.

In person search: Searching is available in person.

Online search: Records may be ordered from the web site, but are returned by mail.

Expedited service: Expedited service is available for fax or online searches. Turnaround time: 24 hours. Add $10.00 per name. You must use a credit card. Add fees if overnight shipping desired.

Divorce Records

Tennessee Department of Health, Office of Vital Records, 421 5th Ave North, 1st floor, Nashville, TN 37247-0460; 615-741-1763, 615-741-0778 (Credit card order), 615-726-2559 (Fax), 8AM-4PM.

www.state.tn.us/health/vr

Indexing & Storage: Records are available for 50 years. New records are available for inquiry immediately. Records are indexed on index cards, inhouse computer.

Searching: Must have a signed release form from person of record or immediate family member. Information on previous marriages and education is released for statistical use only. Include the following in your request-names of husband and wife, date of divorce, place of divorce.

Access by: mail, phone, fax, in person, online.

Fee & Payment: The search fee is $10.00. There is an additional $2 charge for an extra copy. Fee payee: Tennessee Vital Records. Prepayment required. Personal checks accepted. Credit cards accepted: Mastercard, Visa, AmEx, Discover.

Mail search: Turnaround time: 2-3 weeks. No self addressed stamped envelope is required.

Phone search: You must use a credit card and there is an additional fee of $10.00. Records are processed in one day.

Fax search: Same criteria as phone searching.

In person search: Orders in by 10:30AM are available that same day at 3PM, otherwise next day at 3PM.

Online search: Records may be ordered online, but are returned by mail.

Expedited service: Expedited service is available for fax or online searches. Turnaround time: 24 hours. Add $10.00 per request. This requires use of credit card. Add fees if overnight delivery is desired.

Workers' Compensation Records

Tennessee Department of Labor, Workers Compensation Division, 710 James Robertson Pwy, 2nd Floor, Nashville, TN 37243-0661; 615-741-2395, 615-532-1468 (Fax), 8AM-4:30PM.

Indexing & Storage: Records are available from 09/91 on computer, from 1987-present on microfiche. Prior records are maintained on index cards.

Searching: Unless you have a signed authorization from the injured party or are an attorney representing the injured party, a court order is required to obtain records. This information is not considered public record; however, they'll tell if a claim is on file. The SSN, company name, date of injury, and claim # is required for searching records after 1987, prior record searching requires the name of the company involved.

Access by: mail, fax, in person.

Fee & Payment: The search fee is $5.00, copy fee is $.25 per page. Fee payee: State of Tennessee Treasurer. Prepayment required. Personal checks accepted. No credit cards accepted.

Mail search: Turnaround time: within 2 weeks. They will invoice you for copies and postage.No self addressed stamped envelope is required.

Fax search: This will not effect turnaround time.

In person search: Records are still returned in 2 weeks, but you can pick them up.

Driver Records

Dept. of Safety, Financial Responsibility Section, Attn: Driving Records, 1150 Foster Ave, Nashville, TN 37210; 615-741-3954, 8AM-4:30PM.

www.state.tn.us/safety

Note: Tickets are available from this office for a $5.00 fee per record.

Indexing & Storage: Records are available for past 3 years for convictions, if valid; 7 years if the license is suspended, restricted, or revoked. It takes 30 days or more before new records are available for inquiry.

Searching: Tennessee passed legislation similar to DPPA. Casual requesters must have written notarized authorization to receive record information with address data if subject opted out. The driver's license number and last name or DOB are needed when ordering.

Access by: mail, in person.

Fee & Payment: The fee is $5.00 per record. Fee payee: Tennessee Department of Safety. Prepayment required. Certified checks or money orders are preferred. Mastercard & Visa accepted in person only.

Mail search: Turnaround time: 2 weeks. No self addressed stamped envelope is required.

In person search: Up to 10 requests will be processed while you wait at this location or at offices in Nashville, Memphis, Knoxville, Chattanooga, and various Driver License Testing Centers.

Other access: Magnetic tape retrieval is available for high volume users. Purchase of the DL file is available for approved requesters.

Vehicle Ownership
Vehicle Identification

Titling and Registration Division, Information Unit, 44 Vantage Way #160, Nashville, TN 37243-8050; 615-741-3101 (Titles), 8AM-4:30PM.

www.state.tn.us/safety

Indexing & Storage: Records are available for 5 years to present. It takes 12 weeks before new records are available for inquiry.

Searching: Records are not released to casual requesters without consent (Form SF-1189). Include the following in your request-make or yr or VIN, purpose of request, notarized form, copy of requester's photo ID.

Access by: mail, in person.

Fee & Payment: The fee is $1.00 for name or plate searches, $5.00 for current title data, and $15.00 for a complete title history. Fee payee: Titling and Registration. Prepayment required. Personal checks accepted. No credit cards accepted.

Mail search: Turnaround time: 2-4 weeks. A self addressed stamped envelope is requested.

In person search: Turnaround time is while you wait, unless photocopy of actual document is required. The office closes at 4PM for walk-in customers. Photo ID required.

Accident Reports

Financial Responsibility Section, Records Unit, 1150 Foster Avenue, Nashville, TN 37210; 615-741-3954, 8AM-4:30PM.

www.state.tn.us/safety

Note: Also, you can obtain accident reports from the investigating agency.

Indexing & Storage: Records are available for 3 years to present. It takes 30 days before new records are available for inquiry.

Searching: Include the following in your request-full name, date of accident, location of accident. Also, include the county of the accident and DL of driver(s).

Access by: mail, in person.

Fee & Payment: The fee is $4.00 per record copy. Fee payee: Tennessee Department of Safety. Prepayment required. Agency prefers money orders and certified checks. Personal checks not accpeted. Mastercard & Visa accpeted for in person only.

Mail search: Turnaround time: 2 weeks. No self addressed stamped envelope is required.

In person search: Turnaround time is generally while you wait.

Boat & Vessel Ownership
Boat & Vessel Registration

Wildlife Resources Agency, Boating Division, PO Box 40747, Nashville, TN 37204; 615-781-6500, 615-741-4606 (Fax), 8AM-4:30PM.

www.state.tn.us/twra

Note: All liens are filed with the Secretary of State.

Indexing & Storage: Records are available for the past 3 years. Records are indexed on computer. The state does not issue titles. All motorized boats and all sailboats must be registered. It takes 30 days before new records are available for inquiry.

Searching: To search, one of the following is required: Tennessee ID #, hull id #, name, or SSN.

Access by: mail, phone, fax, in person.

Fee & Payment: There is no fee to do 1 or 2 searches; however, large lists may incur a charge.

Mail search: Turnaround time: 2 days. No self addressed stamped envelope is required.

Phone search: Whether a phone search will be performed depends on how busy the personnel is at the time of the call. Phone searches are only verbal verifications and require a Tennessee ID # to search.

Fax search: Turnaround time is 2 days. Results will be sent by mail.

In person search: Turnaround time is usually immediate, when staff available.

Other access: Records can be purchased in bulk. There is a minimum $272.50 fee if on labels and $240.00 minimum fee if on tape. Call Paulette Fuqua at 615-781-6500 for more details.

Legislation-Current/Pending
Legislation-Passed

Tennessee General Assembly, Office of Legislative Information Services, Rachel Jackson Bldg, 1st Floor, Nashville, TN 37243; 615-741-3511 (Status), 615-741-0927 (Bill Room), 8AM-4:30PM.

www.legislature.state.tn.us

Indexing & Storage: Records are available for the current and past session only. Earlier records are maintained in the State Library & Archives.

Searching: Include the following in your request-bill number, topic of bill.

Access by: mail, phone, in person, online.

Fee & Payment: No fee to search, copy fee is $.25 per page. Fee payee: State of Tennessee. Personal checks accepted. No credit cards accepted.

Mail search: Turnaround time: same day. No self addressed stamped envelope is required.

Phone search: You may call for information.

In person search: You may request information in person.

Online search: Bill information can be viewed at the Internet site. The Tennessee Code is also available from the web page.

Voter Registration
Records not maintained by a state level agency.

Note: Records are held by the Administrator of Elections at the county level. Records can only be purchased for political related purposes.

GED Certificates

Department of Education, GED Records - Johnson Tower, 710 James Robertson Parkway, 2nd Fl, Nashville, TN 37243-0387; 615-741-7054, 615-532-4899 (Fax), 8AM-4:30PM.

Searching: Include the following in your request-date of birth, Social Security Number, signed release. Year diploma issued also helpful.

Access by: mail, fax, in person.

Fee & Payment: There is no fee for a verification.

Mail search: Turnaround time: 7-10 working days. No self addressed stamped envelope is required.

Fax search: Turnaround time is generally in 3 days.

In person search: Searching is available in person.

Hunting License Information
Fishing License Information
Access to Records is Restricted

Wildlife Resources Agency, Sportsman License Division, PO Box 40747, Nashville, TN 37204; 615-781-6585, 615-741-4606 (Fax), 8AM-4:30PM.

Note: There is not a central database of hunting or fishing licenses. You must contact the vendor where the license was sold. The Sportman License Division (615-781-6585) does hold information on 45,000 sportsman licenses (boating, etc).

Licenses Searchable Online

Accounting Firm #03 .... www.state.tn.us/cgi-bin/commerce/roster2.pl
Alarm Contractor #03 .... www.state.tn.us/cgi-bin/commerce/roster2.pl
Architect #03 .... www.state.tn.us/cgi-bin/commerce/roster2.pl
Auctioneer #03 .... www.state.tn.us/cgi-bin/commerce/roster2.pl
Auctioneer Firm #03 .... www.state.tn.us/cgi-bin/commerce/roster2.pl
Barber #03 .... www.state.tn.us/cgi-bin/commerce/roster2.pl
Barber School #03 .... www.state.tn.us/cgi-bin/commerce/roster2.pl
Barber Shop #03 .... www.state.tn.us/cgi-bin/commerce/roster2.pl
Barber Technician #03 .... www.state.tn.us/cgi-bin/commerce/roster2.pl
Boxing & Racing #03 .... www.state.tn.us/cgi-bin/commerce/roster2.pl
Collection Agent #03 .... www.state.tn.us/cgi-bin/commerce/roster2.pl
Collections Manager #03 .... www.state.tn.us/cgi-bin/commerce/roster2.pl
Contractor #03 .... www.state.tn.us/cgi-bin/commerce/roster2.pl
Cosmetologist #03 .... www.state.tn.us/cgi-bin/commerce/roster2.pl
Cosmetology School #03 .... www.state.tn.us/cgi-bin/commerce/roster2.pl
Cosmetology Shop #03 .... www.state.tn.us/cgi-bin/commerce/roster2.pl
Embalmer #03 .... www.state.tn.us/cgi-bin/commerce/roster2.pl
Engineer #03 .... www.state.tn.us/cgi-bin/commerce/roster2.pl
Funeral & Burial Apprentice #03 .... www.state.tn.us/cgi-bin/commerce/roster2.pl
Funeral & Burial Cemetery #03 .... www.state.tn.us/cgi-bin/commerce/roster2.pl
Funeral & Burial Director #03 .... www.state.tn.us/cgi-bin/commerce/roster2.pl
Funeral & Burial Establishment #03 .... www.state.tn.us/cgi-bin/commerce/roster2.pl
Geologist #03 .... www.state.tn.us/cgi-bin/commerce/roster2.pl
Home Improvement #03 .... www.state.tn.us/cgi-bin/commerce/roster2.pl
Insurance Agent #03 .... www.state.tn.us/cgi-bin/commerce/roster2.pl
Insurance Firm #03 .... www.state.tn.us/cgi-bin/commerce/roster2.pl
Interior Designer #03 .... www.state.tn.us/cgi-bin/commerce/roster2.pl
Landscape Architect #03 .... www.state.tn.us/cgi-bin/commerce/roster2.pl
Landscape Architect Firm #03 .... www.state.tn.us/cgi-bin/commerce/roster2.pl
Motor Vehicle Auction #03 .... www.state.tn.us/cgi-bin/commerce/roster2.pl
Motor Vehicle Dealer #03 .... www.state.tn.us/cgi-bin/commerce/roster2.pl
Motor Vehicle Salesperson #03 .... www.state.tn.us/cgi-bin/commerce/roster2.pl
Nursery #11 .... www.state.tn.us/agriculture/regulate/regulat1.html
Nursery Plant Dealer #11 .... www.state.tn.us/agriculture/regulate/regulat1.html
Optometrist #07 .... www.arbo.org/nodb2000/licsearch.asp
Personnel Leasing #03 .... www.state.tn.us/cgi-bin/commerce/roster2.pl
Pharmacist #03 .... www.state.tn.us/cgi-bin/commerce/roster2.pl
Pharmacy #03 .... www.state.tn.us/cgi-bin/commerce/roster2.pl
Pharmacy Researcher #03 .... www.state.tn.us/cgi-bin/commerce/roster2.pl
Polygraph Examiner #03 .... www.state.tn.us/cgi-bin/commerce/roster2.pl
Private Investigative Company #03 .... www.state.tn.us/cgi-bin/commerce/roster2.pl
Private Investigator #03 .... www.state.tn.us/cgi-bin/commerce/roster2.pl
Public Accountant-CPA #03 .... www.state.tn.us/cgi-bin/commerce/roster2.pl
Race Track #03 .... www.state.tn.us/cgi-bin/commerce/roster2.pl
Real Estate Appraiser #03 .... www.state.tn.us/cgi-bin/commerce/roster2.pl
Real Estate Broker #03 .... www.state.tn.us/cgi-bin/commerce/roster2.pl
Real Estate Firm #03 .... www.state.tn.us/cgi-bin/commerce/roster2.pl
Real Estate Sales Agent #03 .... www.state.tn.us/cgi-bin/commerce/roster2.pl
Security Company #03 .... www.state.tn.us/cgi-bin/commerce/roster2.pl
Security Guard #03 .... www.state.tn.us/cgi-bin/commerce/roster2.pl
Security Trainer #03 .... www.state.tn.us/cgi-bin/commerce/roster2.pl
Time Share Agent #03 .... www.state.tn.us/cgi-bin/commerce/roster2.pl

Licensing Quick Finder

Accounting Firm #03 615-741-9771	Auctioneer #03............615-741-3226	Chiropractor #06 615-532-3202
Aesthetician #03 615-741-2515	Auctioneer Firm #03............615-741-9771	Clinical Lab Technician #06 615-532-3202
Alarm Contractor #03 615-741-9771	Barber #03............615-741-9771	Collection Agent #03 615-741-1741
Alcohol & Drug Abuse Counselor #06 ...615-532-5097	Barber School #03............615-741-9771	Collections Manager #03 615-741-9771
Animal/Livestock Dealer #11 615-837-5183	Barber Shop #03............615-741-9771	Contractor #03 615-741-8307
Architect #03............615-741-3221	Barber Technician #03 615-741-9771	Cosmetologist #03 615-741-2515
Athletic Trainer #06 615-532-3202	Boiler Operator #08............901-385-5077	Cosmetology School #03............615-741-9771
Attorney #12 615-741-3234	Boxing & Racing #03............615-741-9771	Cosmetology Shop #03 615-741-9771

Court Reporter/Stenographer #02	423-756-0221
Dental Assistant #06	615-532-3202
Dental Hygienist #06	615-532-3202
Dentist #06	615-532-3202
Dietitian/Nutritionist #06	615-532-3202
Disciplinary Tracking #07	615-532-3202
Dispensing Optician #07	615-532-3202
Electrologist #03	615-741-2515
Electrology #07	615-532-3202
Elevator Inspector #15	615-741-2123
Embalmer #03	615-741-9771
Emergency Medical Service #07	615-532-3202
Engineer #03	615-741-3221
Environmentalist #07	615-532-3202
Fire Protection Sprinkler System Contractor #03	615-741-7190
Funeral & Burial Apprentice #03	615-741-9771
Funeral & Burial Cemetery #03	615-741-9771
Funeral & Burial Director #03	615-741-9771
Funeral & Burial Establishment #03	615-741-2895
Geologist #03	615-741-3611
Geologist #03	615-741-9771
Health Care Facility #07	615-532-3202
Hearing Aid Dispenser #07	615-532-3202
Home Improvement #03	615-741-9771
Insurance Agent #03	615-741-9771
Insurance Firm #03	615-741-9771
Interior Designer #03	615-741-9771
Investigation #07	615-532-3202
Investment Advisor #03	615-741-2947
Landscape Architect #03	615-741-3221
Landscape Architect Firm #03	615-741-9771
Liquor Control #01	615-741-1602
Lobbyist #10	615-741-7959
Manicurist #03	615-741-2515
Marital & Family Therapist #06	615-532-5133
Massage Therapist #06	615-532-5083
Medical Doctor #06	615-532-3202
Medical Laboratory Personnel #06	615-532-3202
Milk Tester/Sampler #11	615-837-5177
Motor Vehicle Auction #03	615-741-9771
Motor Vehicle Dealer #03	615-741-9771
Motor Vehicle Salesperson #03	615-741-9771
Notary Public #09	615-741-3699
Nurse-RN & LPN #07	615-532-3202
Nursery #11	615-837-5338
Nursery Plant Dealer #11	615-837-5338
Nursing Home Administrator #07	615-532-3202
Occupational Therapist/Assistant #07	615-532-3202
Optometrist #07	615-532-3202
Osteopathic Physician #06	615-532-3202
Personnel Leasing #03	615-741-9771
Pest Control Operator #11	615-837-5135
Pharmacist #03	615-741-9771
Pharmacy #03	615-741-9771
Pharmacy Researcher #03	615-741-9771
Physical Therapist/Assistant #07	615-532-3202
Physician Assistant #06	615-532-3202
Plumber #08	901-385-5077
Podiatrist #06	615-532-3202
Polygraph Examiner #03	615-741-9771
Private Investigative Company #03	615-741-9771
Private Investigator #03	615-741-9771
Private Security Guard #03	615-741-4827
Professional Counselor & Marriage/Family Therapist #07	615-532-3202
Psychologist #07	615-532-3202
Public Accountant-CPA #03	615-741-2550
Public Weigher (Bulk Products, Aggregates) #11	615-837-5109
Race Track #03	615-741-9771
Radiation Therapy Technician #06	615-532-3202
Radiologic Technologist #06	615-532-3202
Real Estate Appraiser #03	615-741-9771
Real Estate Broker #03	615-741-9771
Real Estate Firm #03	615-741-9771
Real Estate Sales Agent #03	615-741-1831
Refrigeration #08	901-385-5077
Respiratory Care Practitioner #06	615-532-3202
School Administrative Supervisor #05	615-532-4885
School Counselor #05	615-532-4885
School Librarian #05	615-532-4885
Securities Agent #03	615-741-2947
Securities Broker/Dealer #03	615-741-2947
Security Company #03	615-741-9771
Security Guard #03	615-741-9771
Security Trainer #03	615-741-9771
Service Technician (Weigh Scales) #11	615-837-5109
Shampoo Technician #03	615-741-2515
Shorthand Reporter #02	423-756-0221
Social Worker #07	615-532-3202
Speech Pathologist/Audiologist #07	615-532-3202
Surveyor #03	615-741-3611
Tattoo Artist/Apprentice #14	615-741-7206
Teacher #05	615-532-4885
Time Share Agent #03	615-741-2273
Veterinarian #07	615-532-3202
Water Treatment Plant Operator #13	615-898-8090
Weighmaster #11	615-837-5109
X-ray Operator #06	615-532-3202
X-ray Technologist #06	615-532-6280

Licensing Agency Information

01 Alcoholic Beverage Commission, 226 Capitol Blvd Bldg, #300, Nashville, TN 37243-0755; 615-741-1602, Fax: 615-741-0847.

03 Department of Commerce & Insurance, 500 James Robertson Pky, 2nd Fl, Nashville, TN 37243; 615-741-9771, Fax: 615-532-2965.
www.state.tn.us/commerce

Direct URL to search licenses: www.state.tn.us/cgi-bin/commerce/roster2.pl

05 Department of Education, 710 James Robertson Pky, Andrew Johnson Tower, 5th Fl, Nashville, TN 37243-0377; 615-532-4885, Fax: 615-532-1448.
www.state.tn.us/education/lic_home.htm

06 Department of Health, 425 5th Ave N, Cordell Hull Bldg 1st Fl, Nashville, TN 37247-1010; 615-532-3202.
www.state.tn.us/health

07 Department of Health, 283 Plus Park Blvd, Nashville, TN 37247-1010; 615-532-3202.
http://170.142.76.180/bmf-bin/BMFproflist.pl You can check for disciplinary actions against of any of the licensed professionals of this agency by visiting http://170.142.76.180/cgi-bin/licensure.pl.

08 Mechanical Licensing Board, 6465 Mullins Station Rd, Memphis, TN 38134; 901-385-5054, Fax: 901-385-5198.

09 Office of Secretary of State, James K Polk Bldg, #1800, Nashville, TN 37243-0306; 615-741-3699, Fax: 615-741-7310.
www.state.tn.us/sos/sos.htm

10 Registry of Election Finance, 404 James Robertson Pky, #1614, Nashville, TN 37243; 615-741-7959, Fax: 615-532-8902.

11 Department of Agriculture, PO Box 40627 (Melrose Station), Nashville, TN 37204; 615-837-5120, Fax: 615-837-5335.
www.state.tn.us/agriculture

12 Board of Law Examiners, 706 Church St, #100, Nashville, TN 37243-0740; 615-741-3234, Fax: 615-741-5867.
www.state.tn.us/lawexaminers

13 Water & Wastewater Certification Program, 2022 Blanton Dr, Fleming Training Ctr, Murfreesboro, TN 37129; 615-898-8090.

14 Department of Health, Division of General Environmental Health, 415 5th Ave N, Cordell Hull Bldg 6th Fl, Nashville, TN 37247-3901; 615-741-7206.

15 Department of Labor, Boiler & Elevator Division, Board of Boiler Rules, 710 James Robertson Pky, Andrew Johnson Tower 4th Fl, Nashville, TN 37243; 615-741-2123.

The following list indicates the district and division name for each county in the state. If the district or division name of the bankruptcy court is different from the civil/criminal court, it appears in parentheses.

County/Court Cross Reference

County	District	Division
Anderson	Eastern	Knoxville
Bedford	Eastern	Winchester (Chattanooga)
Benton	Western	Jackson
Bledsoe	Eastern	Chattanooga
Blount	Eastern	Knoxville
Bradley	Eastern	Chattanooga
Campbell	Eastern	Knoxville
Cannon	Middle	Nashville
Carroll	Western	Jackson
Carter	Eastern	Greeneville (Knoxville)
Cheatham	Middle	Nashville
Chester	Western	Jackson
Claiborne	Eastern	Knoxville
Clay	Middle	Cookeville (Nashville)
Cocke	Eastern	Greeneville (Knoxville)
Coffee	Eastern	Winchester (Chattanooga)
Crockett	Western	Jackson
Cumberland	Middle	Cookeville (Nashville)
Davidson	Middle	Nashville
De Kalb	Middle	Cookeville (Nashville)
Decatur	Western	Jackson
Dickson	Middle	Nashville
Dyer	Western	Memphis
Fayette	Western	Memphis
Fentress	Middle	Cookeville (Nashville)
Franklin	Eastern	Winchester (Chattanooga)
Gibson	Western	Jackson
Giles	Middle	Columbia (Nashville)
Grainger	Eastern	Knoxville
Greene	Eastern	Greeneville (Knoxville)
Grundy	Eastern	Winchester (Chattanooga)
Hamblen	Eastern	Greeneville (Knoxville)
Hamilton	Eastern	Chattanooga
Hancock	Eastern	Greeneville (Knoxville)
Hardeman	Western	Jackson
Hardin	Western	Jackson
Hawkins	Eastern	Greeneville (Knoxville)
Haywood	Western	Jackson
Henderson	Western	Jackson
Henry	Western	Jackson
Hickman	Middle	Columbia (Nashville)
Houston	Middle	Nashville
Humphreys	Middle	Nashville
Jackson	Middle	Cookeville (Nashville)
Jefferson	Eastern	Knoxville
Johnson	Eastern	Greeneville (Knoxville)
Knox	Eastern	Knoxville
Lake	Western	Jackson
Lauderdale	Western	Memphis
Lawrence	Middle	Columbia (Nashville)
Lewis	Middle	Columbia (Nashville)
Lincoln	Eastern	Winchester (Chattanooga)
Loudon	Eastern	Knoxville
Macon	Middle	Cookeville (Nashville)
Madison	Western	Jackson
Marion	Eastern	Chattanooga
Marshall	Middle	Columbia (Nashville)
Maury	Middle	Columbia (Nashville)
McMinn	Eastern	Chattanooga
McNairy	Western	Jackson
Meigs	Eastern	Chattanooga
Monroe	Eastern	Knoxville
Montgomery	Middle	Nashville
Moore	Eastern	Winchester (Chattanooga)
Morgan	Eastern	Knoxville
Obion	Western	Jackson
Overton	Middle	Cookeville (Nashville)
Perry	Western	Jackson
Pickett	Middle	Cookeville (Nashville)
Polk	Eastern	Chattanooga
Putnam	Middle	Cookeville (Nashville)
Rhea	Eastern	Chattanooga
Roane	Eastern	Knoxville
Robertson	Middle	Nashville
Rutherford	Middle	Nashville
Scott	Eastern	Knoxville
Sequatchie	Eastern	Chattanooga
Sevier	Eastern	Knoxville
Shelby	Western	Memphis
Smith	Middle	Cookeville (Nashville)
Stewart	Middle	Nashville
Sullivan	Eastern	Greeneville (Knoxville)
Sumner	Middle	Nashville
Tipton	Western	Memphis
Trousdale	Middle	Nashville
Unicoi	Eastern	Greeneville (Knoxville)
Union	Eastern	Knoxville
Van Buren	Eastern	Winchester (Chattanooga)
Warren	Eastern	Winchester (Chattanooga)
Washington	Eastern	Greeneville (Knoxville)
Wayne	Middle	Columbia (Nashville)
Weakley	Western	Jackson
White	Middle	Cookeville (Nashville)
Williamson	Middle	Nashville
Wilson	Middle	Nashville

US District Court

Eastern District of Tennessee

Chattanooga Division Clerk's Office, PO Box 591, Chattanooga, TN 37401 (Courier Address: Room 309, 900 Georgia Ave, Chattanooga, TN 37402), 423-752-5200.

Counties: Bledsoe, Bradley, Hamilton, McMinn, Marion, Meigs, Polk, Rhea, Sequatchie.

Indexing & Storage: Cases are indexed by defendant and plaintiff as well as by case number. New cases are available in the index 1-2 days after filing date. Both computer and card indexes are maintained. Open records are located at this court.

Fee & Payment: The fee is $15.00 per item (one party name or case number). Payment may be made by money order, cashier check, personal check. Prepayment is required. Payee: Clerk, US District Court. Certification fee: $5.00 per document. Copy fee: $.50 per page.

Phone Search: Only docket information available by telephone. An automated voice case information service (VCIS) is not available.

Mail Search: Always enclose a stamped self addressed envelope.

In Person Search: In person searching is available.

PACER: Sign-up number is 800-676-6856. Toll-free access: 800-869-1265. Local access: 423-545-4647. Case records are available back to 1994. Records are never purged. New records are available online after 1 day. PACER is available on the Internet at http://pacer.tned.uscourts.gov.

Greeneville Division 101 Summer St W, Greenville, TN 37743, 423-639-3105.

Counties: Carter, Cocke, Greene, Hamblen, Hancock, Hawkins, Johnson, Sullivan, Unicoi, Washington.

Indexing & Storage: Cases are indexed by defendant and plaintiff as well as by case number. New cases are available in the index immediately after filing date. Both computer and card indexes are maintained. Open records are located at this court.

Fee & Payment: The fee is $15.00 per item (one party name or case number). Payment may be made by money order, cashier check, personal check. Prepayment is required. Payee: Clerk, US District Court. Certification fee: $5.00 per document. Copy fee: $.50 per page.

Phone Search: Only docket information is available by phone. An automated voice case information service (VCIS) is not available.

Mail Search: A stamped self addressed envelope is not required.

In Person Search: In person searching is available.

PACER: Sign-up number is 800-676-6856. Toll-free access: 800-869-1265. Local access: 423-545-4647. Case records are available back to 1994. Records are never purged. New records are available online after 1 day. PACER is available on the Internet at http://pacer.tned.uscourts.gov.

Knoxville Division Clerk's Office, 800 Market St, Knoxville, TN 37902, 865-545-4228.

Counties: Anderson, Blount, Campbell, Claiborne, Grainger, Jefferson, Knox, Loudon, Monroe, Morgan, Roane, Scott, Sevier, Union.

Indexing & Storage: Cases are indexed by defendant and plaintiff as well as by case number. New cases are available in the index 1-2 days after filing date. Both computer and card indexes are maintained. Computerized index as of June 1, 1992. Index cards prior to June 1, 1992. Open records are located at this court.

Fee & Payment: The fee is $15.00 per item (one party name or case number). Payment may be made by money order, cashier check, personal check. Prepayment is required. Payee: Clerk, US District Court. Certification fee: $5.00 per document. Copy fee: $.50 per page.

Phone Search: Only docket information is available by phone. An automated voice case information service (VCIS) is not available.

Mail Search: A stamped self addressed envelope is not required.

In Person Search: In person searching is available.

PACER: Sign-up number is 800-676-6856. Toll-free access: 800-869-1265. Local access: 423-545-4647. Case records are available back to 1994. Records are never purged. New records are available online after 1 day. PACER is available on the Internet at http://pacer.ohsd.uscourts.gov.

Winchester Division PO Box 459, Winchester, TN 37398 (Courier Address: 200 S Jefferson St, Room 201, Winchester, TN 37397), 931-967-1444.

Counties: Bedford, Coffee, Franklin, Grundy, Lincoln, Moore, Van Buren, Warren.

Indexing & Storage: Cases are indexed by defendant and plaintiff as well as by case number. New cases are available in the index 1-2 days after filing date. A computer index is maintained. Open records are located at this court. Office has just begun maintaining records in 1997.

Fee & Payment: The fee is $15.00 per item (one party name or case number). Payment may be made by money order, cashier check, personal check. Prepayment is required. Payee: Clerk, US District Court. Certification fee: $5.00 per document. Copy fee: $.50 per page.

Phone Search: Only docket information available by telephone. An automated voice case information service (VCIS) is not available.

Mail Search: Always enclose a stamped self addressed envelope.

In Person Search: In person searching is available.

PACER: Sign-up number is 800-676-6856. Toll-free access: 800-869-1265. Local access: 423-545-4647. Case records are available back to 1994. Records are never purged. New records are available online after 1 day. PACER is available on the Internet at http://pacer.tned.uscourts.gov.

US Bankruptcy Court

Eastern District of Tennessee

Chattanooga Division Historic US Courthouse, 31 E 11th St, Chattanooga, TN 37402, 423-752-5163.

www.tneb.uscourts.gov

Counties: Bedford, Bledsoe, Bradley, Coffee, Franklin, Grundy, Hamilton, Lincoln, Marion, McMinn, Meigs, Moore, Polk, Rhea, Sequatchie, Van Buren, Warren.

Indexing & Storage: Cases are indexed by debtor and creditors as well as by case number. New cases are available in the index 2 days after filing date. The court needs the name of the debtor and to obtain positive identification, a social security number or address is needed. A computer index is maintained. Open records are located at this court.

Fee & Payment: The fee is $15.00 per item (one party name or case number). Payment may be made by money order, cashier check, business check. Personal checks are not accepted. Will invoice for copy fees only. Payee: US Bankruptcy Court. Certification fee: $5.00 per document. Copy fee: $.50 per page.

Phone Search: The court will only confirm bankruptcy filings over the phone and will only honor up to three requests per phone call per day. An automated voice case information service (VCIS) is available. Call VCIS at 800-767-1512 or 423-752-5272.

Mail Search: A stamped self addressed envelope is not required.

In Person Search: In person searching is available.

PACER: Sign-up number is 800-676-6856. Access fee is $.60 per minute. Toll-free access: 888-833-9512. Local access: 423-752-5131, 423-752-5133, 423-752-5134, 423-752-5135, 423-752-5136, 423-752-5137. Case records are available back to January 1986. Records are purged as deemed necessary. New civil records are available online after 1 day. PACER is available on the Internet at http://pacer.tneb.uscourts.gov.

Knoxville Division 800 Market St #330, Howard H Baker Jr US Courthouse, Knoxville, TN 37902, 423-545-4279.

www.tneb.uscourts.gov

Counties: Anderson, Blount, Campbell, Carter, Claiborne, Cocke, Grainger, Greene, Hamblen, Hancock, Hawkins, Jefferson, Johnson, Knox, Loudon, Monroe, Morgan, Roane, Scott, Sevier, Sullivan, Unicoi, Union, Washington.

Indexing & Storage: Cases are indexed by debtor as well as by case number. New cases are available in the index 2-3 days after filing date. Both computer and card indexes are maintained. Open records are located at this court. District wide searches are possible for limited information from 1/86 from this court.

Fee & Payment: The fee is $15.00 per item (one party name or case number). Payment may be made by money order, cashier check, personal check. Prepayment is required. Payee: Clerk, US Bankruptcy Court. Certification fee: $5.00 per document. Copy fee: $.50 per page.

Phone Search: The court will only confirm debtor names, SSN, address, attorney, trustee, chapter filed, date of filing, date of discharge/dismissal, date case closed, in addition to limited information regarding motions, hearings, etc. An automated voice case information service (VCIS) is available. Call VCIS at 800-767-1512 or 423-752-5272.

Mail Search: Always enclose a stamped self addressed envelope.

In Person Search: In person searching is available.

PACER: Sign-up number is 800-676-6856. Access fee is $.60 per minute. Toll-free access: 888-833-9512. Local access: 423-752-5131, 423-752-5133, 423-752-5134, 423-752-5135, 423-752-5136, 423-752-5137. Case records are available back to January 1986. Records are purged as deemed necessary. New civil records are available online after 1 day. PACER is available on the Internet at http://pacer.tneb.uscourts.gov.

US District Court
Middle District of Tennessee

Columbia Division c/o Nashville Division, 800 US Courthouse, 801 Broadway, Nashville, TN 37203, 615-736-5498.

Counties: Giles, Hickman, Lawrence, Lewis, Marshall, Maury, Wayne.

Indexing & Storage: Cases are indexed by as well as by case number. New cases are available in the index after filing date. Open records are located at the Division.

Fee & Payment: The fee is no charge per item (one party name or case number). Payment may be made by money order, cashier check. Business checks are not accepted. Personal checks are not accepted.

Phone Search: An automated voice case information service (VCIS) is not available.

In Person Search: In person searching is available.

PACER: Sign-up number is 800-676-6856. Access fee is $.60 per minute. Toll-free access: 800-458-2994. Local access: 615-736-7164. Case records are available back three years. Records are purged every year. New records are available online after 1 day. PACER is available on the Internet at http://pacer.tnmd.uscourts.gov.

Cookeville Division c/o Nashville Division, 800 US Courthouse, 801 Broadway, Nashville, TN 37203, 615-736-5498, Fax: 615-736-7488.

Counties: Clay, Cumberland, De Kalb, Fentress, Jackson, Macon, Overton, Pickett, Putnam, Smith, White.

Indexing & Storage: Cases are indexed by defendant and plaintiff as well as by case number. New cases are available in the index 1 month after filing date. A computer index is maintained. Records are also indexed on microfiche. Open records are located at the Division.

Fee & Payment: The fee is $15.00 per item (one party name or case number). Payment may be made by money order, cashier check, business check. Personal checks are not accepted. Prepayment is required. Payee: Clerk, US District Court. Certification fee: $5.00 per document. Copy fee: $.50 per page.

Phone Search: Only docket information is available by phone. An automated voice case information service (VCIS) is not available.

Mail Search: Always enclose a stamped self addressed envelope.

In Person Search: In person searching is available.

PACER: Sign-up number is 800-676-6856. Access fee is $.60 per minute. Toll-free access: 800-458-2994. Local access: 615-736-7164. Case records are available back three years. Records are purged every year. New records are available online after 1 day. PACER is available on the Internet at http://pacer.tnmd.uscourts.gov.

Nashville Division 800 US Courthouse, 801 Broadway, Nashville, TN 37203, 615-736-5498, Fax: 615-736-7488.

Counties: Cannon, Cheatham, Davidson, Dickson, Houston, Humphreys, Montgomery, Robertson, Rutherford, Stewart, Sumner, Trousdale, Williamson, Wilson.

Indexing & Storage: Cases are indexed by defendant and plaintiff as well as by case number. New cases are available in the index immediately after filing date. A computer index is maintained. Records are also indexed on microfiche. Open records are located at this court.

Fee & Payment: The fee is $15.00 per item (one party name or case number). Payment may be made by money order, cashier check, personal check. Prepayment is required. Payee: Clerk, US District Court. Certification fee: $5.00 per document. Copy fee: $.50 per page.

Phone Search: Only docket information is available by phone. An automated voice case information service (VCIS) is not available.

Fax Search: Will accept fax search at $15.00 per name.

Mail Search: A stamped self addressed envelope is not required.

In Person Search: In person searching is available.

PACER: Sign-up number is 800-676-6856. Access fee is $.60 per minute. Toll-free access: 800-458-2994. Local access: 615-736-7164. Case records are available back three years. Records are purged every year. New records are available online after 1 day. PACER is available on the Internet at http://pacer.tnmd.uscourts.gov.

US Bankruptcy Court
Middle District of Tennessee

Nashville Division PO Box 24890, Nashville, TN 37202-4890 (Courier Address: Customs House, Room 200, 701 Broadway, Nashville, TN 37203), 615-736-5584.

www.tnmb.uscourts.gov

Counties: Cannon, Cheatham, Clay, Cumberland, Davidson, De Kalb, Dickson, Fentress, Giles, Hickman, Houston, Humphreys, Jackson, Lawrence, Lewis, Macon, Marshall, Maury, Montgomery, Overton, Pickett, Putnam, Robertson, Rutherford, Smith, Stewart, Sumner, Trousdale, Wayne, White, Williamson, Wilson.

Indexing & Storage: Cases are indexed by debtor as well as by case number. New cases are available in the index 24 hours after filing date. Both computer and card indexes are maintained. Open records are located at this court.

Fee & Payment: The fee is $15.00 per item (one party name or case number). Payment may be made by money order, cashier check, business check. Personal checks are not accepted. Prepayment is required. Payee: Clerk, US Bankruptcy Court. Certification fee: $5.00 per document. Copy fee: $.50 per page.

Phone Search: Only docket information is available by phone. An automated voice case information service (VCIS) is available. Call VCIS at 800-767-1512 or 423-752-5272.

Mail Search: Always enclose a stamped self addressed envelope.

In Person Search: In person searching is available.

PACER: Sign-up number is 615-736-5577. Access fee is $.60 per minute. Case records are available back to September 1989. Records are never purged. New civil records are available online after 1 day. PACER is available on the Internet at http://pacer.tnmb.uscourts.gov.

Other Online Access: You can search all cases on the Internet clicking on "Database Access" and then choosing "NIBS case information" from the pop-up menu on the main page.

US District Court
Western District of Tennessee

Jackson Division Rm 26, US Courthouse 262, 111 S Highland, Jackson, TN 38301, 901-421-9200, Fax: 901-421-9210.

www.tnwd.uscourts.gov

Counties: Benton, Carroll, Chester, Crockett, Decatur, Gibson, Hardeman, Hardin, Haywood, Henderson, Henry, Lake, McNairy, Madison, Obion, Perry, Weakley.

Indexing & Storage: Cases are indexed by defendant and plaintiff as well as by case number. New cases are available in the index 1-2 days after filing date. A computer index is maintained. Open records are located at this court.

Fee & Payment: The fee is $15.00 per item (one party name or case number). Payment may be made by money order, cashier check, personal check, Visa, Mastercard. Prepayment is required. Payee: Clerk, US District Court. Certification fee: $5.00 per document. Copy fee: $.50 per page.

Phone Search: Only docket information is available by phone. An automated voice case information service (VCIS) is not available.

Mail Search: Always enclose a stamped self addressed envelope.

In Person Search: In person searching is available.

PACER: Sign-up number is 800-676-6856. Access fee is $.60 per minute. Toll-free access: 800-407-4456. Local access: 901-495-1259. Case records are available back to 1993. Records are purged as deemed necessary. New records are available online after 2 days.

Memphis Division Federal Bldg, Room 242, 167 N Main, Memphis, TN 38103, 901-495-1200, Fax: 901-495-1250.

www.tnwd.uscourts.gov

Counties: Dyer, Fayette, Lauderdale, Shelby, Tipton.

Indexing & Storage: Cases are indexed by defendant and plaintiff as well as by case number. New cases are available in the index 1-2 days after filing date. A computer index is maintained. Open records are located at this court.

Fee & Payment: The fee is $15.00 per item (one party name or case number). Payment may be made by money order, cashier check, personal check, Visa, Mastercard. Prepayment is required. Payee: Clerk, US District Court. Certification fee: $5.00 per document. Copy fee: $.50 per page.

Phone Search: Only docket information is available by phone. An automated voice case information service (VCIS) is not available.

Fax Search: Will accept fax searches with credit card number. Will fax docket listings at $.50 per page.

Mail Search: Always enclose a stamped self addressed envelope.

In Person Search: In person searching is available.

PACER: Sign-up number is 800-676-6856. Access fee is $.60 per minute. Toll-free access: 800-407-4456. Local access: 901-495-1259. Case records are available back to 1993. Records are purged as deemed necessary. New records are available online after 2 days.

US Bankruptcy Court

Western District of Tennessee

Jackson Division Room 107, 111 S Highland Ave, Jackson, TN 38301, 901-421-9300.

www.tnwb.uscourts.gov

Counties: Benton, Carroll, Chester, Crockett, Decatur, Gibson, Hardeman, Hardin, Haywood, Henderson, Henry, Lake, Madison, McNairy, Obion, Perry, Weakley.

Indexing & Storage: Cases are indexed by debtor as well as by case number. New cases are available in the index 1-2 days after filing date. A computer index is maintained. Open records are located at this court.

Fee & Payment: The fee is $15.00 per item (one party name or case number). Payment may be made by money order, cashier check, business check. Personal checks are not accepted. Prepayment is required. A search fee is charged only when certification of the search is issued. Payee: US Bankruptcy Court. Copy fee: $.50 per page.

Phone Search: Only docket information is available by phone. An automated voice case information service (VCIS) is available. Call VCIS at 888-381-4961 or 901-328-3622.

Mail Search: A stamped self addressed envelope is not required.

In Person Search: In person searching is available.

PACER: Sign-up number is 800-676-6856. Access fee is $.60 per minute. Toll-free access: 800-406-0190. Local access: 901-544-4336. Case records are available back to 1989. Records are never purged. New civil records are available online after 2 days.

Memphis Division Suite 413, 200 Jefferson Ave, Memphis, TN 38103, 901-328-3500, Fax: 901-328-3500.

www.tnwb.uscourts.gov

Counties: Dyer, Fayette, Lauderdale, Shelby, Tipton.

Indexing & Storage: Cases are indexed by debtor as well as by case number. New cases are available in the index 2 days after filing date. A computer index is maintained. Open records are located at this court.

Fee & Payment: The fee is $15.00 per item (one party name or case number). Payment may be made by money order, cashier check, business check. Personal checks are not accepted. Prepayment is required. In general, if the cost of copies exceeds the amount of the check, the court will bill for the excess by mail. Payee: Clerk, US Bankruptcy Court. Certification fee: $5.00 per document. Copy fee: $.50 per page.

Phone Search: Only docket information is available by phone. An automated voice case information service (VCIS) is available. Call VCIS at 888-381-4961 or 901-328-3622.

Mail Search: A stamped self addressed envelope is not required.

In Person Search: In person searching is available.

PACER: Sign-up number is 800-676-6856. Access fee is $.60 per minute. Toll-free access: 800-406-0190. Local access: 901-544-4336. Case records are available back to 1989. Records are never purged. New civil records are available online after 2 days.

Court	Jurisdiction	No. of Courts	How Organized
Circuit Courts*	General	15	31 Districts
Criminal Courts*	General	0	31 Districts
Chancery Courts*	General	87	31 Districts
General Sessions Courts*	Limited	16	
Combined Circuit/ General Sessions*		87	
Municipal Courts	Municipal	300	
Probate Courts*	Probate	4	
Juvenile Courts	Special	19	

* Profiled in this Sourcebook.

Court	CIVIL								
	Tort	Contract	Real Estate	Min. Claim	Max. Claim	Small Claims	Estate	Eviction	Domestic Relations
Circuit Courts*	X	X	X	$0	No Max				X
Criminal Courts*									
Chancery Courts*	X	X	X	$0	No Max		X		X
General Sessions Courts*	X	X	X	$0	$15,000	$4000	X		X
Municipal Courts									
Probate Courts*							X		
Juvenile Courts									X

Court	CRIMINAL				
	Felony	Misdemeanor	DWI/DUI	Preliminary Hearing	Juvenile
Circuit Courts*	X	X	X		
Criminal Courts*	X				
Chancery Courts*					
General Sessions Courts*		X	X	X	X
Municipal Courts		X	X		
Probate Courts*					
Juvenile Courts					X

ADMINISTRATION Administrative Office of the Courts, 511 Union St (Nashville City Center) #600, Nashville, TN, 37243-0607; 615-741-2687, Fax: 615-741-6285. www.tsc.state.tn.us

COURT STRUCTURE Criminal cases are handled by the Circuit Courts and General Sessions Courts. All General Sessions Courts have raised the maximum civil case limit to $15,000 from $10,000. The Chancery Courts, in addition to handling probate, also hear certain types of equitable civil cases. Combined courts vary by county, and the counties of Davidson, Hamilton, Knox, and Shelby have separate Criminal Courts.

Probate is handled in the Chancery or County Courts, except in Shelby and Davidson Counties where it is handled by the Probate Court.

ONLINE ACCESS There is currently no statewide, online computer system available, internal or external. The Tennessee Administrative Office of Courts (AOC) has provided computers and CD-ROM readers to state judges, and a computerization project (named TnCIS) to implement statewide court automation started in January 1997.

Anderson County

7th District Circuit Court & General Sessions 100 Main St, Clinton, TN 37716; 865-457-5400. Hours: 8AM-4:30PM (EST). *Felony, Misdemeanor, Civil, Eviction, Small Claims.*

Civil Records: Access: In person only. Court does not conduct in person searches; visitors must perform searches for themselves. Search fee: No civil searches performed by court. Required to search: name, years to search. Civil cases indexed by defendant, plaintiff. Civil records on computer from 1988, archived from 1947. **Criminal Records:** Access: In person only. Court does not conduct in person searches; visitors must perform searches for themselves. Search fee: No criminal searches performed by court. Required to search: name, years to search, DOB, SSN. Criminal records on computer from 1988, archived from 1947. **General Information:** No juvenile records released. Copy fee: $1.00 per page. Certification fee: $4.00. Fee payee: Circuit Court Clerk or General Sessions Clerk. Personal checks accepted. Prepayment is required. Public access terminal is available.

Chancery Court Anderson County Courthouse, PO Box 501, Clinton, TN 37717; 865-457-5400; Fax: 865-457-4828. Hours: 8:30AM-4:30PM (EST). *Civil, Probate.*

Civil Records: Access: Phone, mail, in person. Both court and visitors may perform in person searches. Search fee: No civil searches performed by court. Required to search: name, years to search. Civil cases indexed by defendant, plaintiff. Civil records 1992 to present, prior records on another system. **General Information:** No adoption or mental health records released. Copy fee: $2.00 for first page, $1.00 each addl. Certification fee: $4.00. Fee payee: Clerk and Master. Personal checks accepted. Prepayment is required.

Bedford County

17th District Circuit Court & General Sessions 1 Public Sq, Suite 200, Shelbyville, TN 37160; 931-684-3223. Hours: 8AM-4PM M-Th, 8AM-5PM Fri (CST). *Felony, Misdemeanor, Civil, Eviction, Small Claims.*

Civil Records: Access: In person only. Court does not conduct in person searches; visitors must perform searches for themselves. Search fee: No civil searches performed by court. Required to search: name, years to search. Civil cases indexed by defendant, plaintiff. Civil records on archives and books from 1934. **Criminal Records:** Access: In person only. Court does not conduct in person searches; visitors must perform searches for themselves. Search fee: No criminal searches performed by court. Required to search: name, years to search, DOB; also helpful-SSN. Criminal records on archives and books from 1934. **General Information:** No juvenile, adoptions, mental health, expunged or sealed records released. Certification fee: $1.50. Fee payee: Thomas Smith, Clerk. Personal checks accepted. Prepayment is required.

Chancery Court Chancery Court, 1 Public Sq, Suite 302, Shelbyville, TN 37160; 931-684-1672. Hours: 8AM-4PM M-Th, 8AM-5PM Fri (CST). *Civil, Probate.*

Civil Records: Access: In person only. Court does not conduct in person searches; visitors must perform searches for themselves. Search fee: No civil searches performed by court. Required to

search: name, years to search. Civil cases indexed by defendant, plaintiff. Civil records on books from 9/82 (probate), prior records back to 1800s filed in county clerk's office. **General Information:** No adoption records released. Turnaround time same day. Copy fee: $.50 per page. Certification fee: $5.00. Fee payee: Clerk and Master. Personal checks accepted. Prepayment is required.

Benton County

24th District Circuit Court, General Sessions & Juvenile 1 East Court Sq Rm 207, Camden, TN 38320; 901-584-6711; Fax: 901-584-0475. Hours: 8AM-4PM M-Th; 8AM-5PM F (CST). *Felony, Misdemeanor, Civil, Eviction, Small Claims.*

Civil Records: Access: In person only. Both court and visitors may perform in person searches. No search fee. Required to search: name, years to search. Civil cases indexed by defendant, plaintiff. Civil records computerized since 1995. Public can only use docket books to search, older records archived to 1800s. **Criminal Records:** Access: In person only. Both court and visitors may perform in person searches. No search fee. Required to search: name, years to search. Criminal records computerized since 1995. Public can only use docket books to search, older records archived to 1800s. **General Information:** No juvenile records released without judge approval. Copy fee: $1.00 per page. Certification fee: $3.00. Fee payee: Circuit Court Clerk or General Session. Business checks accepted. Prepayment is required.

Chancery Court 1 E Court Sq, Courthouse Rm 206, Camden, TN 38320; 901-584-4435; Fax: 901-584-5956. Hours: 8AM-4PM M-Th; 8AM-5PM F (CST). *Civil, Probate.*

Civil Records: Access: In person only. Court does not conduct in person searches; visitors must perform searches for themselves. Search fee: No civil searches performed by court. Required to search: name, years to search. Civil cases indexed by defendant, plaintiff. Civil records in books since 1880. **General Information:** No adoption or sealed records released. Certification fee: $3.00. Fee payee: Clerk & Master. No personal checks accepted. Prepayment is required. Public access terminal is available.

Bledsoe County

12th District Circuit Court & General Sessions PO Box 455, Pikeville, TN 37367; 423-447-6488; Fax: 423-447-6856. Hours: 8AM-4PM (CST). *Felony, Misdemeanor, Civil, Eviction, Small Claims.*

Civil Records: Access: In person only. Court does not conduct in person searches; visitors must perform searches for themselves. Search fee: No civil searches performed by court. Required to search: name, years to search. Civil cases indexed by plaintiff. Civil records archived from 1920 in books. **Criminal Records:** Access: In person only. Court does not conduct in person searches; visitors must perform searches for themselves. Search fee: No criminal searches performed by court. Required to search: name, years to search. Criminal records archived from 1920 in books. **General Information:** No juvenile records released. Certification fee: No certification fee. Prepayment is required.

Chancery Court PO Box 413, Pikeville, TN 37367; 423-447-2484; Fax: 423-447-6856. Hours: 8AM-4PM (CST). *Civil, Probate.*

Civil Records: Access: Phone, fax, mail, in person. Both court and visitors may perform in person searches. No search fee. Required to search: name, years to search. Civil cases indexed by defendant, plaintiff. Civil records on books since 1856. **General Information:** No juvenile or adoption records released. Turnaround time 3 days. Copy fee: $1.00 per page. Certification fee: $2.00 per page. Fee payee: Bledsoe County Clerk and Master. Personal checks accepted. Fax notes: $1.00 per page.

Blount County

5th District Circuit Court & General Sessions 926 E Lamar Alexander Pkwy, Maryville, TN 37804-6201; 865-273-5400; Fax: 865-273-5411. Hours: 8AM-4:30PM (EST). *Felony, Misdemeanor, Civil, Eviction, Small Claims.*

Civil Records: Access: Mail, in person. Both court and visitors may perform in person searches. Search fee: $15.00 per name. Required to search: name, years to search. Civil cases indexed by defendant, plaintiff. Civil records archived in books since court started, on computer but no dates given. **Criminal Records:** Access: Mail, in person. Both court and visitors may perform in person searches. Search fee: $15.00 per name. Required to search: name, years to search. Criminal records archived in books since court started, on computer but no dates given. **General Information:** No juvenile records released. Turnaround time 3-6 days. Copy fee: $1.00 per page. Certification fee: $4.00. Fee payee: Circuit Court Clerk or General Session. Business checks accepted. Prepayment is required.

Circuit Court 926 E Lamar Alexander Parkway, Maryville, TN 37804; 865-273-5400; Probate phone:865; Fax: 865-273-5411. Hours: 8AM-4:30PM (EST). *Misdemeanor, Civil, Probate.*

Note: Probate is at the County Court located at 345 Court Street.

Civil Records: Access: Mail, in person. Both court and visitors may perform in person searches. Search fee: $15.00 per name. Required to search: name, years to search. Civil cases indexed by defendant. Civil records on books. **Criminal Records:** Access: Mail, in person. Both court and visitors may perform in person searches. Search fee: $15.00 per name. Required to search: name, years to search. Criminal records on books. **General Information:** No juvenile records released. Copy fee: $1.00 per page. Certification fee: $2.00. Fee payee: Circuit Court Clerk. Only cashiers checks and money orders accepted. Prepayment is required.

Bradley County

10th District Criminal, Circuit, & General Sessions Court Courthouse, Rm 205, 155 N Ocoee St, Cleveland, TN 37311-5068; 423-476-0692; Fax: 423-476-0488. Hours: 8:30AM-4:30PM M-Th, 8:30AM-5PM Fri (EST). *Felony, Misdemeanor, Civil, Eviction, Small Claims.*

Civil Records: Access: Mail, in person. Both court and visitors may perform in person searches. Search fee: $25.00 per name. Required to search: name, years to search. Civil cases indexed by defendant, plaintiff. Civil records archived from 1955, on computer from 1990. **Criminal Records:** Access: Mail, in person. Both court and visitors may perform in person searches. Search fee: $25.00 per name. Required to search: name, years to search, DOB; also helpful-SSN. Criminal records archived from 1955, on computer from 1990. **General Information:** No juvenile records released. Turnaround time 10 days. Copy fee: $.30 per page. Certification fee: $10.00. Fee payee: Circuit Court Clerk or General Session. Personal checks accepted. Prepayment is required. Public access terminal is available.

Chancery Court Chancery Court, 155 N. Ocoee St, Cleveland, TN 37311; 423-476-0526. Hours: 8:30AM-4:30PM M-Th, 8:30AM-5PM Fri (EST). *Civil, Probate.*

Civil Records: Access: Mail, in person. Both court and visitors may perform in person searches. No search fee. Required to search: name, years to search. Civil cases indexed by defendant, plaintiff. Civil records filed in books. **General Information:** No adoption records released. Turnaround time same day. Copy fee: $.25 per page. Certification fee: $5.00. Fee payee: Clerk and Master. Personal checks accepted.

Campbell County

8th District Criminal, Circuit, & General Sessions Court PO Box 26, Jacksboro, TN 37757; 423-562-2624. Hours: 8AM-4:30PM (EST). *Felony, Misdemeanor, Civil, Eviction, Small Claims.*

Civil Records: Access: Mail, in person. Both court and visitors may perform in person searches. No search fee. Required to search: name, years to search. Civil cases indexed by defendant, plaintiff. Civil records on computer since 1991. On microfiche from 1987 and archived since court started located at La Follette Library, La Follette, TN 37766. **Criminal Records:** Access: Mail, in person. Both court and visitors may perform in person searches. No search fee. Required to search: name, years to search, DOB, SSN. Criminal records on computer since 1991. On microfiche from 1987 and archived since court started located at La Follette Library, La Follette, TN 37766. **General Information:** No juvenile, adoption and judicial hospitalization records released. Turnaround time depends on type of search. Copy fee: $1.00 per page. Certification fee: $3.00. Fee payee: Circuit Court Clerk or General Session. Business checks accepted. Prepayment is required.

Chancery Court PO Box 182, Jacksboro, TN 37757; 423-562-3496. Hours: 8AM-4:30PM (EST). *Civil, Probate.*

Civil Records: Access: In person only. Court does not conduct in person searches; visitors must perform searches for themselves. Search fee: No civil searches performed by court. Required to search: name, years to search. Civil cases indexed by defendant, plaintiff. Civil records filed in books, microfiche available at LaFollette Library. **General Information:** No adoption records released. SASE preferred. Turnaround time 1-2 days. Copy fee: $1.00 per page. Certification fee: $3.00. Fee payee: Clerk and Master. Business checks accepted.

Cannon County

16th District Circuit Court & General Sessions County Courthouse Public Sq, Woodbury, TN 37190; 615-563-4461; Fax: 615-563-6391. Hours: 8AM-4:30PM M,T,Th,F; 8AM-Noon Wed (CST). *Felony, Misdemeanor, Civil, Eviction, Small Claims.*

Civil Records: Access: In person only. Court does not conduct in person searches; visitors must perform searches for themselves. Search fee: No civil searches performed by court. Required to

search: name, years to search. Civil cases indexed by defendant, plaintiff. Civil records archived on books from 1980s. **Criminal Records:** Access: In person only. Court does not conduct in person searches; visitors must perform searches for themselves. Search fee: $6.00 per name. Required to search: name, years to search, DOB. Criminal records archived on books from 1980s. **General Information:** No juvenile records released. Copy fee: $1.00 per page. Certification fee: $3.00. Fee payee: Circuit Court Clerk or General Session. Personal checks accepted. Prepayment is required.

County Court County Courthouse Public Square, Woodbury, TN 37190; 615-563-4278/5936; Fax: 615-563-5696. Hours: 8AM-4PM M,T,Th,F; 8AM-Noon Sat (CST). *Probate.*

Carroll County

24th District Circuit Court & General Sessions PO Box 587, Huntingdon, TN 38344; 901-986-1931. Hours: 8AM-4PM (CST). *Felony, Misdemeanor, Civil, Eviction, Small Claims.*

Civil Records: Access: In person only. Court does not conduct in person searches; visitors must perform searches for themselves. Search fee: No civil searches performed by court. Required to search: name, years to search. Civil cases indexed by defendant, plaintiff. Civil records archived from 1800s, on computer from 1988. **Criminal Records:** Access: In person only. Court does not conduct in person searches; visitors must perform searches for themselves. Search fee: No criminal searches performed by court. Required to search: name, years to search, DOB. Criminal records archived from 1800s, on computer from 1988. **General Information:** Copy fee: $.50 per page. No copies by mail. Certification fee: No certification fee. Fee payee: Circuit Court Clerk or General Session. Only cashiers checks and money orders accepted. Prepayment is required. Public access terminal is available.

Chancery Court PO Box 886, Huntingdon, TN 38344; 901-986-1920. Hours: 8AM-4PM (CST). *Civil, Probate.*

Civil Records: Access: Mail, in person. Both court and visitors may perform in person searches. Search fee: $5.00 per name. Required to search: name, years to search. Civil cases indexed by defendant, plaintiff. Civil records on computer since 6/88, prior records on books. **General Information:** No adoption or sealed documents released. SASE required ($.52 postage). Turnaround time 5-10 days. Copy fee: $1.00 per page and $3.00 per document. Certification fee: $6.00. Fee payee: Clerk and Master. No out-of-state checks, money orders and cashiers checks accepted. Prepayment is required.

Carter County

1st District Criminal, Circuit, & General Sessions Court Carter County Justice Center, 900 E Elk Ave, Elizabethton, TN 37643; 423-542-1835; Fax: 423-542-3742. Hours: 8AM-5PM (EST). *Felony, Misdemeanor, Civil, Eviction, Small Claims.*

Civil Records: Access: In person only. Court does not conduct in person searches; visitors must perform searches for themselves. Search fee: No civil searches performed by court. Required to search: name, years to search. Civil cases indexed by defendant, plaintiff. Civil records archived from 1800s (partial lost in fire), on computer from 4-92. **Criminal Records:** Access: In person only. Court does not conduct in person searches; visitors must perform searches for themselves. Search fee: No

criminal searches performed by court. Required to search: name, years to search. Criminal records archived from 1800s (partial lost in fire), on computer from 4-92. **General Information:** No juvenile, psychiatric or expunged records released. Certification fee: $4.00. Fee payee: Circuit Court Clerk or General Session. Personal checks accepted. Prepayment is required. Public access terminal is available.

County Court 801 E Elk, Elizabethton, TN 37643; 423-542-1814; Fax: 423-547-1502. Hours: 8AM-5PM (EST). *Probate.*

Cheatham County

23rd District Circuit Court & General Sessions 100 Public Sq, Ashland City, TN 37015; 615-792-3272; Civil phone:615-792-4866; Fax: 615-792-3203. Hours: 8AM-4PM (CST). *Felony, Misdemeanor, Civil, Eviction, Small Claims.*

Note: Circuit Court is room 225, General sessions is in room 223

Civil Records: Access: Phone, mail, in person. Both court and visitors may perform in person searches. Search fee: $5.00 per name. Required to search: name, years to search. Civil cases indexed by defendant, plaintiff. Civil records archived on books from 1946 in office, since court started in storage and on computer from 1990. **Criminal Records:** Access: Phone, mail, in person. Both court and visitors may perform in person searches. Search fee: $5.00 per name. Required to search: name, years to search. Criminal records archived on books from 1946 in office, since court started in storage and on computer from 1990. **General Information:** No juvenile records released. SASE required. Turnaround time 2-3 days. Copy fee: $2.50 per document. Certification fee: $5.00. Fee payee: Circuit Court, or General Sessions Clerk. Business checks accepted. Prepayment is required.

Chancery Court Clerk & Master, Suite 106, Ashland City, TN 37015; 615-792-4620. Hours: 8AM-4PM (CST). *Civil, Probate.*

Civil Records: Access: In person only. Court does not conduct in person searches; visitors must perform searches for themselves. Search fee: No civil searches performed by court. Required to search: name, years to search. Civil cases indexed by defendant, plaintiff. Civil records on computer. **General Information:** No adoption records released. SASE required. Turnaround time same day. Copy fee: $1.00 per page. Certification fee: $2.00. Fee payee: Chancery Court. Personal checks accepted. Prepayment is required.

Chester County

26th District Circuit Court & General Sessions PO Box 133, Henderson, TN 38340; 901-989-2454. Hours: 8AM-4PM (CST). *Felony, Misdemeanor, Civil, Eviction, Small Claims.*

Civil Records: Access: Phone, fax, mail, in person. Both court and visitors may perform in person searches. No search fee. Required to search: name, years to search. Civil cases indexed by defendant, plaintiff. Civil records in books and archived from 1892. **Criminal Records:** Access: Phone, mail, in person. Both court and visitors may perform in person searches. No search fee. Required to search: name, years to search, DOB. Criminal records in books and archived from 1892. **General Information:** No juvenile records released. Turnaround time 2 days. Copy fee: $1.00 per page. Certification fee: No certification fee. Fee payee: Circuit Court, or General Sessions Clerk. Prepayment is required.

Chancery Court Clerk & Master, PO Box 262, Henderson, TN 38340; 901-989-7171; Fax: 901-989-7176. Hours: 8AM-4PM (CST). *Civil, Probate.*

Civil Records: Access: In person only. Court does not conduct in person searches; visitors must perform searches for themselves. Search fee: No civil searches performed by court. Required to search: name, years to search. Civil cases indexed by defendant, plaintiff. Civil records on books. **General Information:** No adoption or sealed records released. Certification fee: $5.00. Fee payee: Clerk and Master. Personal checks accepted.

Claiborne County

8th District Criminal, Circuit, & General Sessions Court PO Drawer 570, Tazewell, TN 37879; 423-626-8181; Fax: 423-626-5631. Hours: 8:30AM-4PM M-F, 8:30AM-Noon Sat (EST). *Felony, Misdemeanor, Civil, Eviction, Small Claims.*

Civil Records: Access: Mail, in person. Both court and visitors may perform in person searches. Search fee: $10.00 per name. Required to search: name, years to search. Civil cases indexed by defendant, plaintiff. Civil records archived since 1932. **Criminal Records:** Access: Mail, in person. Both court and visitors may perform in person searches. Search fee: $10.00 per name. Required to search: name, years to search. Criminal records archived since 1932. **General Information:** No adoption records released. SASE required. Turnaround time 2-3 days. Copy fee: $.25 per page. Certification fee: $5.00. Fee payee: Circuit Court Clerk or General Sessions. Business checks accepted. In-state personal checks accepted. Prepayment is required.

Chancery Court PO Drawer G, Tazewell, TN 37879; 423-626-3284. Hours: 8:30AM-Noon, 1-4PM (EST). *Civil, Probate.*

Civil Records: Access: Mail, in person. Both court and visitors may perform in person searches. No search fee. Required to search: name, years to search. Civil cases indexed by defendant, plaintiff. Civil records kept on books. **General Information:** No adoption records released. Turnaround time 1-2 days. Copy fee: $.25 per page. Certification fee: $5.00. Fee payee: Clerk and Master. Personal checks accepted. Prepayment is required.

Clay County

13th District Criminal, Circuit, & General Sessions Court PO Box 749, Celina, TN 38551; 931-243-2557. Hours: 8AM-4PM (CST). *Felony, Misdemeanor, Civil, Eviction, Small Claims.*

Civil Records: Access: In person only. Court does not conduct in person searches; visitors must perform searches for themselves. Search fee: No civil searches performed by court. Required to search: name, years to search. Civil cases indexed by defendant, plaintiff. Civil records archived from early 1900s, on microfiche from 1986. **Criminal Records:** Access: In person only. Court does not conduct in person searches; visitors must perform searches for themselves. Search fee: No criminal searches performed by court. Required to search: name, years to search; also helpful-SSN. Criminal records archived from early 1900s, on microfiche from 1986. **General Information:** No juvenile records released. Copy fee: $.25 per page. Certification fee: No certification fee. Fee payee:

Circuit Court, or General Sessions Clerk. Personal checks accepted. Prepayment is required.

Chancery Court PO Box 332, Celina, TN 38551; 931-243-3145. Hours: 8AM-4PM M,T,Th,F; 8AM-Noon W (CST). *Civil, Probate.*

Civil Records: Access: Mail, in person. Both court and visitors may perform in person searches. No search fee. Required to search: name, years to search. Civil cases indexed by defendant, plaintiff. Civil records on books. **General Information:** No juvenile records released. Turnaround time 1 week. Copy fee: $1.00 per page. Certification fee: No certification fee. Fee payee: Clerk & Master. Personal checks accepted. Prepayment is required.

Cocke County

4th District Circuit Court 111 Court Ave Rm 201, Newport, TN 37821; 423-623-6124; Fax: 423-625-3889. Hours: 8:30AM-5PM (EST). *Felony, Misdemeanor, Civil Actions Over $15,000.*

Civil Records: Access: Mail, in person. Both court and visitors may perform in person searches. Search fee: $3.00 per name. Required to search: name, years to search. Civil cases indexed by defendant, plaintiff. Civil records archived from late 1800s. **Criminal Records:** Access: Mail, in person. Both court and visitors may perform in person searches. Search fee: $3.00 per name. Required to search: name, years to search. Criminal records archived from late 1800s. **General Information:** No divorce or sealed records released. SASE not required. Turnaround time ASAP. Copy fee: $.25 per page. Certification fee: $5.00. Fee payee: Circuit Court. Personal checks accepted.

General Sessions 111 Court Ave, Newport, TN 37821; 423-623-8619; Fax: 423-623-9808. Hours: 8AM-4PM (EST). *Misdemeanor, Civil Actions Under $15,000, Eviction, Small Claims.*

Civil Records: Access: Phone, mail, in person. Both court and visitors may perform in person searches. Search fee: $3.00 per name. Required to search: name, years to search. Civil cases indexed by defendant, plaintiff. Civil records on books. **Criminal Records:** Access: Phone, mail, in person. Both court and visitors may perform in person searches. Search fee: $3.00 per name. Required to search: name, years to search. Criminal records on books. **General Information:** No juvenile records released. SASE required. Turnaround time varies. Copy fee: $3.00 per document. Certification fee: $3.00. Fee payee: General Sessions Court. Business checks accepted. Prepayment is required.

Chancery Court Courthouse Annex, 360 E Main St, Suite 103, Newport, TN 37821; 423-623-3321; Fax: 423-625-3642. Hours: 8AM-4:30PM (EST). *Civil, Probate.*

Civil Records: Access: Phone, mail, in person. Only the court conducts in person searches; visitors may not. No search fee. Required to search: name, years to search. Civil cases indexed by defendant, plaintiff. Civil records on computer since 1980, on books from 1930. **General Information:** No sealed records released. Turnaround time 1 week. Copy fee: $1.00 per document. Certification fee: $3.00. Fee payee: Chancery Court, Clerk and Master. Personal checks accepted. Prepayment is required.

Coffee County

14th District Circuit Court & General Sessions PO Box 629, Manchester, TN 37349;

931-723-5110. Hours: 8AM-4:30PM (CST). *Felony, Misdemeanor, Civil, Eviction, Small Claims.*

Civil Records: Access: Mail, in person. Both court and visitors may perform in person searches. Search fee: July 1, 1996 to present is $5.00; 10 year check is $10.00; beyond 10 years add $5.00 per year. Required to search: name, years to search. Civil cases indexed by defendant, plaintiff. Civil records archived from late 1800s, indexed chronologically by court date. **Criminal Records:** Access: Mail, in person. Both court and visitors may perform in person searches. Search fee: Same fees as civil. Required to search: name, years to search, DOB; also helpful-SSN. Criminal records archived from late 1800s, indexed chronologically by court date. **General Information:** No juvenile record released. Turnaround time 1 week. Copy fee: $1.00 per page. Certification fee: $3.50. Fee payee: General Sessions Clerk. Personal checks accepted. Prepayment is required.

Chancery Court 101 W. Fort St, Box 5, Manchester, TN 37355; 931-723-5132. Hours: 8AM-4:30PM (CST). *Civil, Probate.*

Civil Records: Access: Mail, in person. Both court and visitors may perform in person searches. No search fee. Required to search: name, years to search. Civil cases indexed by defendant, plaintiff. Civil records on books after 1980, before 1980 filed in County Clerk's Office. **General Information:** No juvenile or adoption records released. Copy fee: $.50 per page. Certification fee: $2.00. Fee payee: Chancery Court. Personal checks accepted. Prepayment is required.

Crockett County

Circuit Court & General Sessions 1 South Bell St, Ste 6 Courthouse, Alamo, TN 38001; 901-696-5462; Fax: 901-696-2605. Hours: 8AM-4PM (CST). *Felony, Misdemeanor, Civil, Eviction, Small Claims.*

Civil Records: Access: Mail, in person. Both court and visitors may perform in person searches. Search fee: $10.00 per name. Required to search: name, years to search. Civil cases indexed by defendant, plaintiff. Civil records archived since court started, records prior to 1986 on docket books. All requests must be in writing. **Criminal Records:** Access: Mail, in person. Both court and visitors may perform in person searches. Search fee: $10.00 per name. Required to search: name, years to search. Criminal records on docket books, on computer from 1993. All requests must be in writing. **General Information:** No adoption or mental records released. SASE requested. Turnaround time 1-2 days. Copy fee: $1.00 per page. Certification fee: $6.00. Fee payee: Circuit Court, or General Sessions Clerk. Business checks accepted. Prepayment is required. Public access terminal is available.

Chancery Court 1 South Bells St, Suite 5, Alamo, TN 38001; 901-696-5458; Fax: 901-696-3028. Hours: 8AM-4PM (CST). *Civil, Probate.*

Civil Records: Access: Mail, in person. Both court and visitors may perform in person searches. No search fee. Required to search: name, years to search. Civil cases indexed by defendant, plaintiff. Civil records on books. **General Information:** No adoption records released. SASE required. Turnaround time 1-3 days. Copy fee: $1.00 per page. Certification fee: $3.00. Plus $1.00 per page. Fee payee: Chancery Court Clerk. Personal checks accepted. Prepayment is required.

Cumberland County

13th District Criminal, Circuit, & General Sessions Court 2 N Main St, Suite 302, Crossville, TN 38555; 931-484-6647; Fax: 931-456-5013. Hours: 8AM-4PM (CST). *Felony, Misdemeanor, Civil, Eviction, Small Claims.*

Civil Records: Access: In person only. Court does not conduct in person searches; visitors must perform searches for themselves. Search fee: No civil searches performed by court. Required to search: name, years to search. Civil cases indexed by defendant, plaintiff. Civil records archived on books from 1940s approx. **Criminal Records:** Access: In person only. Court does not conduct in person searches; visitors must perform searches for themselves. Search fee: No criminal searches performed by court. Required to search: name, years to search, DOB; also helpful-SSN. Criminal records archived on books from 1940s approx. **General Information:** No sealed records released. Certification fee: No certification fee. Only cashiers checks and money orders accepted. Prepayment is required. Public access terminal is available.

Chancery Court 2 N Main St, Suite 101, Crossville, TN 38555-4583; 931-484-4731. Hours: 8AM-4PM (CST). *Civil, Probate.*

Civil Records: Access: Mail, in person. Only the court conducts in person searches; visitors may not. No search fee. Required to search: name, years to search. Civil cases indexed by defendant, plaintiff. Civil records on computer since 1991, on books since 1900s. **General Information:** No juvenile, adoption records released. SASE requested. Turnaround time 2 days. Copy fee: $.50 per page. Certification fee: $1.00 per page. Fee payee: Clerk and Master. Personal checks accepted. Prepayment is required.

Davidson County

20th District Criminal Court Metro Courthouse, Rm 305, Nashville, TN 37201; 615-862-5600; Fax: 615-862-5676. Hours: 8AM-4PM (CST). *Felony, Misdemeanor.*

www.nashville.org.ccrt **Criminal Records:** Access: Mail, remote online, in person. Both court and visitors may perform in person searches. Search fee: $10.00 per name. Required to search: name, years to search, DOB, signed release; also helpful-SSN, race. The web site has a link to a free criminal court inquiry system. Search by case number, attorney or defendant. **General Information:** No records unauthorized by statutes released. SASE required. Turnaround time 2-3 days. Copy fee: $.25 per page. Certification fee: $6.00. Fee payee: Circuit Court Clerk. Personal checks accepted. Credit cards accepted: Visa, Mastercard, Discover. Visa, MC, Discover. Prepayment is required.

Circuit Court 506 Metro Courthouse, Nashville, TN 37201; 615-862-5181. Hours: 8AM-4:30PM (CST). *Civil.*

www.nashville.org/cir

Civil Records: Access: Mail, in person. Both court and visitors may perform in person searches. No search fee. Required to search: name, years to search. Civil cases indexed by defendant, plaintiff. Civil records archived on books from 1800s, on computer from 1974. **General Information:** No juvenile or adoption records released. Turnaround time 2-3 days. Copy fee: $.50 per page. Certification fee: $2.00 per page. Fee payee: Circuit Court Clerk. Prepayment is required. Public access terminal is available.

General Sessions Court 100 James Robinson Parkway, Ben West Bldg Room 2, Nashville, TN 37201; 615-862-5195; Fax: 615-862-5924. Hours: 8AM-4:30PM (CST). *Civil Actions Under $5,000, Eviction, Small Claims.*

Civil Records: Access: In person only. Court does not conduct in person searches; visitors must perform searches for themselves. Search fee: No civil searches performed by court. Required to search: name, years to search. **General Information:** No juvenile records released. Copy fee: $1.00 per page. Certification fee: $3.00 per page. Fee payee: General Sessions Court Clerk. Personal checks accepted. Credit cards accepted: Visa, Discover. Prepayment is required. Public access terminal is available.

Probate Court 408 Metro Courthouse #105, Nashville, TN 37201; 615-862-5980; Fax: 615-862-5994. Hours: 8AM-4:30 (CST). *Probate.*

De Kalb County

13th District Criminal, Circuit, & General Sessions Court 1 Public Sq, Rm 303, Smithville, TN 37166; 615-597-5711. Hours: 8AM-4:30PM M,T,W,Th; 8AM-5PM Fri (CST). *Felony, Misdemeanor, Civil, Eviction, Small Claims.*

Civil Records: Access: In person only. Both court and visitors may perform in person searches. Search fee: $5.00 per name. Required to search: name, years to search. Civil cases indexed by defendant, plaintiff. Civil records archived in office last 10 years. Prior to 1982, records are not very accurate because of fire. **Criminal Records:** Access: In person only. Court does not conduct in person searches; visitors must perform searches for themselves. Search fee: No criminal searches performed by court. Required to search: name, years to search, DOB; also helpful-SSN. Criminal records archived in office last 10 years. Prior to 1982, records are not very accurate because of fire. **General Information:** No juvenile records released. Copy fee: $1.00 per page. Certification fee: $6.00. Fee payee: Circuit Court, or General Sessions Clerk. Personal checks accepted. Prepayment is required.

Chancery Court 1 Public Square, Rm 302, Smithville, TN 37166; 615-597-4360. Hours: 8AM-4PM (CST). *Civil, Probate.*

Civil Records: Access: In person only. Court does not conduct in person searches; visitors must perform searches for themselves. Search fee: No civil searches performed by court. Required to search: name, years to search. Civil cases indexed by defendant, plaintiff. Civil records on books. **General Information:** No adoption, juvenile records released. Copy fee: $1.00 per page. Certification fee: $6.00. Fee payee: Clerk and Master. Personal checks accepted. Prepayment is required.

Decatur County

24th District Circuit Court & General Sessions PO Box 488, Decaturville, TN 38329; 901-852-3125; Fax: 901-852-2130. Hours: 8AM-4PM M,T,Th,F; 8AM-Noon W & Sat (CST). *Felony, Misdemeanor, Civil, Eviction, Small Claims.*

Civil Records: Access: In person only. Court does not conduct in person searches; visitors must perform searches for themselves. Search fee: No civil searches performed by court. Required to search: name, years to search. Civil cases indexed by defendant, plaintiff. Civil records archived on

books from 1927. **Criminal Records:** Access: In person only. Court does not conduct in person searches; visitors must perform searches for themselves. Search fee: No criminal searches performed by court. Required to search: name, years to search, DOB, SSN, signed release. Criminal records archived on books from 1927. **General Information:** No adoption records released. No copy fee. Certification fee: No certification fee. Fee payee: Circuit Court. Business checks accepted. Prepayment is required.

Chancery Court Clerk & Master, Decaturville, TN 38329; 901-852-3422; Fax: 901-852-2130. Hours: 9M-4PM M,T,Th,F; 9AM-Noon Sat (CST). *Civil, Probate.*

Civil Records: Access: In person only. Court does not conduct in person searches; visitors must perform searches for themselves. Search fee: No civil searches performed by court. Required to search: name, years to search. Civil cases indexed by plaintiff. Probate records in books since 1869 for probate, civil records in books since 1958. **General Information:** No adoption records released. SASE required. Turnaround time 2 days. Copy fee: $.25 per page. Certification fee: $2.00. Fee payee: Elizabeth Carpenter, Clerk and Master. Personal checks accepted.

Dickson County

23rd District Circuit Court Court Square, PO Box 220, Charlotte, TN 37036; 615-789-7010; Probate phone:615-789-4171; Fax: 615-789-7018. Hours: 8AM-4PM (CST). *Felony, Misdemeanor, Civil Actions Over $15,000.*

Civil Records: Access: Phone, fax, mail, in person. Both court and visitors may perform in person searches. Search fee: $6.00 per name. Required to search: name, years to search. Civil cases indexed by defendant, plaintiff. Civil records archived from 1800s, on computer from 1986, some records back to 1974. **Criminal Records:** Access: Phone, fax, mail, in person. Both court and visitors may perform in person searches. Search fee: $6.00 per name. Required to search: name, years to search; also helpful-DOB. Criminal records archived from 1800s, on computer from 1986, some records back to 1974. **General Information:** No adoption records released. SASE required. Turnaround time 1 day. Copy fee: $.25 per page. Certification fee: $2.00. Fee payee: Circuit Court Clerk. Personal checks accepted. Prepayment is required. Public access terminal is available. Fax notes: $6.00 per document.

General Sessions PO Box 217, Charlotte, TN 37036; 615-789-5414; Fax: 615-789-3456. Hours: 8AM-4PM (CST). *Civil Actions Under $15,000, Eviction, Small Claims.*

Civil Records: Access: Phone, mail, in person. Both court and visitors may perform in person searches. Search fee: $6.00. Required to search: name, years to search. Civil cases indexed by defendant. Civil records archived since court began, on computer from Aug 1991. **General Information:** No sealed or expunged records released. SASE required. Turnaround time 2-3 days. Copy fee: $.50 per page. Certification fee: $3.00. Fee payee: General Sessions. Personal checks accepted. Prepayment is required.

County Court Court Square, PO Box 220, Charlotte, TN 37036; 615-789-4171. Hours: 8AM-4PM (CST). *Probate.*

Dyer County

29th District Circuit Court & General Sessions PO Box 1360, Dyersburg, TN 38025; 901-286-7809; Fax: 901-286-3580. Hours: 8:30AM-4:30PM (CST). *Felony, Misdemeanor, Civil, Eviction, Small Claims.*

Civil Records: Access: Mail, in person. Both court and visitors may perform in person searches. Search fee: $25.00 per name. Required to search: name, years to search. Civil cases indexed by defendant, plaintiff. Civil records archived since 1990. **Criminal Records:** Access: Mail, in person. Both court and visitors may perform in person searches. Search fee: $25.00 per name. Required to search: name, years to search, DOB, SSN. Criminal records archived since 1990. **General Information:** No juvenile records released. SASE not required. Turnaround time 1 week. No copy fee. Certification fee: No certification fee. Fee payee: Circuit Court, or General Sessions Clerk. Personal checks accepted. Prepayment is required. Public access terminal is available.

Chancery Court PO Box 1360, Dyersburg, TN 38024; 901-286-7818; Fax: 901-286-7812. Hours: 8:30AM-4:30PM M-Th, 8:30AM-5PM Fri (CST). *Civil, Probate.*

Civil Records: Access: Mail, in person. Both court and visitors may perform in person searches. No search fee. Required to search: name, years to search. Civil cases indexed by defendant, plaintiff. Civil records on books. **General Information:** No adoption, juvenile records released. SASE requested. Turnaround time 1 week. Copy fee: $.50 per page. Certification fee: $1.00. Fee payee: Chancery Court Clerk. Personal checks accepted. Prepayment is required.

Fayette County

25th District Circuit Court & General Sessions PO Box 670, Somerville, TN 38068; 901-465-5205; Fax: 901-465-5215. Hours: 9AM-5PM (CST). *Felony, Misdemeanor, Civil, Eviction, Small Claims.*

Civil Records: Access: Mail, in person. Both court and visitors may perform in person searches. Search fee: $10.00 per name per year. Fee is per year for General Sessions. Required to search: name, years to search. Civil cases indexed by defendant, plaintiff. Civil records on computer since 1991, prior records archived since court began, some older records destroyed by fire. **Criminal Records:** Access: Mail, in person. Both court and visitors may perform in person searches. Search fee: $10.00 per name per year. Fee is per year for General Sessions. Required to search: name, years to search. Criminal records on computer since 1991, prior records archived since court began, some older records destroyed by fire. **General Information:** No adoption or sealed records released. SASE required. Turnaround time 2-5 days to search books, immediate for computer records. Copy fee: $.25 per page. Certification fee: $6.00. Fee payee: Circuit Court, or General Sessions Clerk. Personal checks accepted. Prepayment is required.

Chancery Court PO Drawer 220, Somerville, TN 38068; 901-465-5220; Fax: 901-465-5215. Hours: 9AM-5PM (CST). *Civil, Probate.*

Civil Records: Access: In person only. Court does not conduct in person searches; visitors must perform searches for themselves. Search fee: No civil searches performed by court. Required to search: name, years to search. Civil cases indexed by defendant, plaintiff. Civil records on computer

since 10/92; on books. **General Information:** No adoption records released. Copy fee: $1.00 per page. Certification fee: $4.00 plus $2.00 per page. Fee payee: Clerk and Master. Personal checks accepted.

Fentress County

8th District Criminal, Circuit & General Sessions Court PO Box 699, Jamestown, TN 38556; 931-879-7919. Hours: 8AM-4PM M-F; 8AM-Noon Sat (CST). *Felony, Misdemeanor, Civil, Eviction, Small Claims.*

Civil Records: Access: Mail, in person. Both court and visitors may perform in person searches. Search fee: $25.00 per name. Required to search: name, years to search. Civil cases indexed by defendant, plaintiff. Civil records archived from 1800s. **Criminal Records:** Access: Mail, in person. Both court and visitors may perform in person searches. Search fee: $25.00 per name. Required to search: name, years to search, DOB, SSN. Criminal records archived from 1800s. **General Information:** No juvenile records released. SASE required. Turnaround time 5 days. Copy fee: $.25 per page. Certification fee: $2.00. Fee payee: Circuit Court Clerk or General Session. Personal checks accepted.

Chancery Court PO Box 66, Jamestown, TN 38556; 931-879-8615; Fax: 931-879-4236. Hours: 9AM-5PM M,T,Th,F; 9AM-Noon Wed (CST). *Civil, Probate.*

Civil Records: Access: Mail, in person. Both court and visitors may perform in person searches. No search fee. Required to search: name, years to search. Civil cases indexed by defendant, plaintiff. Civil records in books. **General Information:** No sealed or adoption records released. Turnaround time 1-5 days. Copy fee: $.25 per page. Certification fee: $4.00. Fee payee: Clerk and Master. Personal checks accepted. Prepayment is required.

Franklin County

12th District Circuit Court & General Sessions 1 South Jefferson St, Winchester, TN 37398; 931-967-2923; Fax: 931-962-1479. Hours: 8AM-4:30PM (CST). *Felony, Misdemeanor, Civil, Eviction, Small Claims.*

Civil Records: Access: Mail, in person. Both court and visitors may perform in person searches. Search fee: $10.00 per name. Required to search: name, years to search. Civil cases indexed by defendant, plaintiff. Civil records archived on docket books from 1940s, on computer since mid 1991. **Criminal Records:** Access: Mail, in person. Both court and visitors may perform in person searches. Search fee: $10.00 per name. Required to search: name, years to search, DOB; also helpful-SSN. Criminal records archived on docket books from 1940s, on computer since mid 1991. **General Information:** No juvenile records released. Turnaround time 1 week. Copy fee: $.25 per page. Certification fee: $4.00. Fee payee: Circuit Court Clerk or General Session. Business checks accepted. Public access terminal is available.

County Court 1 South Jefferson St, Winchester, TN 37398; 931-962-1485; Fax: 931-962-3394. Hours: 8AM-4:30PM; *AM-Noon Sat (CST). *Probate.*

Gibson County

28th District Circuit Court & General Sessions 295 N College, PO Box 147, Trenton, TN 38382; 901-855-7615; Fax: 901-855-7676.

Hours: 8AM-4:30PM (CST). *Felony, Misdemeanor, Civil, Eviction, Small Claims.*

Civil Records: Access: Fax, mail, in person. Both court and visitors may perform in person searches. Search fee: $5.00 per name. Required to search: name, years to search; also helpful-address. Civil cases indexed by defendant, plaintiff. Civil recordsd archived in vault mid 1800s, in office since 1982. On computer since 1990. **Criminal Records:** Access: Fax, mail, in person. Both court and visitors may perform in person searches. Search fee: $5.00 per name. Required to search: name, years to search; also helpful-address, DOB, SSN. Criminal recordsd archived in vault mid 1800s, in office since 1982. On computer since 1990. **General Information:** No adoption or expunged records released. SASE requested. Turnaround time 1-3 days. Copy fee: $.25 per page. $3.00 maximum fee. Certification fee: $5.00. Fee payee: Circuit Court Clerk. Business checks accepted. In-state checks accepted. Public access terminal is available. Fax notes: No fee to fax results.

Chancery Court Clerk & Master, PO Box 290, Trenton, TN 38382; 901-855-7639; Fax: 901-855-7655. Hours: 8AM-4:30PM (CST). *Civil, Probate.*

Civil Records: Access: In person only. Court does not conduct in person searches; visitors must perform searches for themselves. Search fee: No civil searches performed by court. Required to search: name, years to search. Civil cases indexed by defendant, plaintiff. Filed records in this office since 9/82, prior records filed in County Clerk's office. **General Information:** No adoption, commitment records released. SASE required. Turnaround time 1 week. Copy fee: $1.00 per page. Certification fee: $4.00. Fee payee: Clerk & Master. Personal checks accepted. Prepayment is required.

Giles County

22nd District Circuit Court & General Sessions PO Box 678, Pulaski, TN 38478; 931-363-5311; Fax: 931-424-4790. Hours: 8AM-4PM (CST). *Felony, Misdemeanor, Civil, Eviction, Small Claims.*

Civil Records: Access: Mail, in person. Both court and visitors may perform in person searches. Search fee: $20.00 per name. Fee applies only to pre-1990 searches. Required to search: name, years to search. Civil cases indexed by defendant, plaintiff. Civil records on computer from 1/90, remaining records filed in docket books. **Criminal Records:** Access: Mail, in person. Both court and visitors may perform in person searches. Search fee: $20.00 per name. Fee applies only to pre-1990 searches. Required to search: name, years to search, DOB; also helpful-SSN. Criminal records on computer from 1/90, remaining records filed in docket books. **General Information:** No juvenile records released. SASE required. Turnaround time 1 week. Copy fee: $.25 per page. Certification fee: $6.00. Fee payee: Circuit Court Clerk. Prepayment is required. Public access terminal is available.

County Court PO Box 678, Pulaski, TN 38478; 931-363-1509; Fax: 931-424-6101. Hours: 8AM-4PM M-F (CST). *Probate.*

Grainger County

4th District Circuit Court & General Sessions PO Box 157, Rutledge, TN 37861; 865-828-3605; Fax: 423-828-3339. Hours: 8:30AM-4:30PM (EST). *Felony, Misdemeanor, Civil, Eviction, Small Claims.*

Civil Records: Access: In person only. Court does not conduct in person searches; visitors must perform searches for themselves. Search fee: No civil searches performed by court. Required to search: name, years to search. Civil cases indexed by defendant, plaintiff. Civil records archived from 1977 in office. **Criminal Records:** Access: In person only. Court does not conduct in person searches; visitors must perform searches for themselves. Search fee: $4.00 per name. Required to search: name, years to search, DOB, SSN. Criminal records archived from 1977 in office. **General Information:** No sealed records released. Copy fee: $4.00 per page. Certification fee: $4.00. Fee payee: Circuit Court Clerk. Business checks accepted. Prepayment is required.

Chancery Court Clerk & Master, Rutledge, TN 37861; 865-828-8436; Fax: 865-828-8714. Hours: 8:30AM-4:30PM M,T,Th,F, 8:30AM-Noon Wed (EST). *Civil, Probate.*

Civil Records: Access: Mail, in person. Both court and visitors may perform in person searches. No search fee. Required to search: name, years to search. Civil cases indexed by defendant, plaintiff. Civil records on books. **General Information:** No adoption records released. SASE requested. Turnaround time varies. Copy fee: $1.00 per page. Certification fee: $1.00. Fee payee: Clerk & Master. Personal checks accepted. Prepayment is required.

Greene County

3rd District Criminal, Circuit & General Sessions Court 101 S Main, Geene County Courthouse, Suite 302, Greeneville, TN 37743; 423-798-1760; Fax: 423-798-1763. Hours: 8AM-4:30PM (EST). *Felony, Misdemeanor, Civil, Eviction, Small Claims.*

Civil Records: Access: In person only. Court does not conduct in person searches; visitors must perform searches for themselves. Search fee: No civil searches performed by court. Required to search: name, years to search. Civil cases indexed by defendant, plaintiff. Civil records archived since court started, on computer from end of 1990. **Criminal Records:** Access: In person only. Court does not conduct in person searches; visitors must perform searches for themselves. Search fee: No criminal searches performed by court. Required to search: name, years to search. Criminal records archived since court started, on computer from end of 1990. **General Information:** No adoption records released. Copy fee: $1.00 per page. Certification fee: $3.00. Fee payee: Circuit Court Clerk. Personal checks accepted. Prepayment is required.

County Court 204 N Cutler St, #200, County Court Annex, Greeneville, TN 37745; 423-798-1708; Fax: 423-798-1822. Hours: 8AM-4:30PM (EST). *Probate.*

Grundy County

12th District Circuit Court & General Sessions PO Box 161, Altamont, TN 37301; 931-692-3368; Fax: 931-692-2414. Hours: 8AM-4PM M,T,Th,F; 8AM-Noon W (CST). *Felony, Misdemeanor, Civil, Eviction, Small Claims.*

Civil Records: Access: Mail, in person. Both court and visitors may perform in person searches. Search fee: $10.00 per name. Fee is per court. Required to search: name, years to search. Civil cases indexed by defendant, plaintiff. Civil records on computer since 1993, prior records in books to 1990. Before 1990 on microfiche since 1868. **Criminal Records:** Access: Mail, in person. Both

court and visitors may perform in person searches. Search fee: $10.00 per name. Fee is per court. Required to search: name, years to search, DOB; also helpful-SSN. Criminal records on computer since 1993, prior records in books to 1990. Before 1990 on microfiche since 1868. **General Information:** No juvenile records released. Turnaround time 5 days. Copy fee: $1.00 per page. Certification fee: $5.00. Fee payee: Circuit Court Clerk. Personal checks accepted. Prepayment is required.

Chancery Court PO Box 174, Altamont, TN 37301; 931-692-3455; Fax: 931-692-4125. Hours: 8AM-4PM M,T,Th,F; 8AM-Noon Wed & Sat (CST). *Civil, Probate.*

Civil Records: Access: Phone, mail, in person. Both court and visitors may perform in person searches. Search fee: $5.00 per name. Required to search: name, years to search. Civil cases indexed by defendant, plaintiff. Civil records on computer since 1993, prior records on books. **General Information:** No adoption records released. SASE requested. Turnaround time 5 days. Copy fee: $.25 per page. Certification fee: $2.00. Fee payee: Clerk & Master. Personal checks accepted. Prepayment is required.

Hamblen County

3rd District, Criminal, Circuit & General Sessions Court 510 Allison St, Morristown, TN 37814; 423-586-5640; Fax: 423-585-2764. Hours: 8AM-4PM M-Th, 8AM-5PM Fri, 9-11:30AM Sat (CST). *Felony, Misdemeanor, Civil, Eviction, Small Claims.*

Civil Records: Access: Mail, in person. Both court and visitors may perform in person searches. Search fee: $5.00 per name. Required to search: name, years to search. Civil cases indexed by defendant, plaintiff. Civil records archived from early 1900s, on computer from 1989. **Criminal Records:** Access: Mail, in person. Both court and visitors may perform in person searches. Search fee: $5.00 per name. Required to search: name, years to search, DOB; also helpful-SSN. Criminal records archived from early 1900s, on computer from 1989. **General Information:** No adoption records released. SASE required. Turnaround time 1 day. Copy fee: $.25 per page. Certification fee: $4.00. Fee payee: Circuit Court Clerk or General Sessions. Personal checks accepted. Prepayment is required.

Chancery Court 511 West 2nd North St, Morristown, TN 37814; 423-586-9112; Fax: 423-587-9798. Hours: 8AM-4PM M-Th; 8AM-4:30PM F (CST). *Civil.*

Civil Records: Access: Phone, fax, mail, in person. Both court and visitors may perform in person searches. No search fee. Required to search: name, years to search. Civil cases indexed by defendant, plaintiff. Civil records on computer from 1979; prior on books. **General Information:** No adoption records released. Turnaround time 3-5 days. Copy fee: $.50 per page. Certification fee: $2.00. Fee payee: Clerk & Master. Only cashiers checks and money orders accepted. Prepayment is required. Fax notes: $1.00 per page.

Hamilton County

11th District General Sessions Civil Division, 600 Market St, Room 111, Chattanooga, TN 37402; 423-209-7630; Fax: 423-209-7631. Hours: 7AM-4PM (EST). *Civil Actions Under $15,000, Eviction, Small Claims.*

www.hamiltontn.gov/courts/sessions/default.htm

Civil Records: Access: Phone, mail, in person. Both court and visitors may perform in person searches. No search fee. Required to search: name, years to search. Civil cases indexed by defendant, plaintiff. Civil records archived on docket books, on computer from 6/1985. **General Information:** No mental health records released. Turnaround time 3-4 days. Copy fee: $1.00 per page. Certification fee: $4.00. Fee payee: Sessions Court Clerk. Personal checks accepted. Prepayment is required. Public access terminal is available.

11th Judicial District Circuit Court Room 500 Courthouse, 625 Georgia Ave, Chattanooga, TN 37402; 423-209-6700. Hours: 8AM-4PM (EST). *Civil Actions Over $15,000.*

www.hamiltontn.gov

Civil Records: Access: Mail, in person. Both court and visitors may perform in person searches. Search fee: $5.00. Required to search: name, years to search. Civil cases indexed by defendant, plaintiff. Civil records archived from 1900s, on computer from 7/89. Court minutes are on microfiche. **General Information:** No adoptions or judicial hospitalization records released. Turnaround time 1 week. Copy fee: $2.00 per page. Certification fee: $4.00. Fee payee: Circuit Court Clerk. Personal checks accepted. Prepayment is required. Public access terminal is available.

11th District Criminal Court 600 Market St, Room 102, Chattanooga, TN 37402; 423-209-7500; Fax: 423-209-7501. Hours: 8AM-4PM (EST). *Felony, Misdemeanor.* **Criminal Records:** Access: Mail, in person. Both court and visitors may perform in person searches. Search fee: $10.00 per name. Required to search: name, years to search, DOB, signed release; also helpful-SSN. Criminal records on computer since 1985, prior records in books. **General Information:** No juvenile records released. Turnaround time 1 week. Copy fee: $1.00 per page. Certification fee: $2.00. Fee payee: Circuit Court Clerk. Personal checks accepted. Prepayment is required. Public access terminal is available.

Chancery Court Chancery Court, Clerk & Master, Room 300, Chattanooga, TN 37402; 423-209-6615; Fax: 423-209-6601. Hours: 8AM-4PM (EST). *Civil, Probate.*

www.hamilton.gov/courts/clerkmaster

Civil Records: Access: Phone, mail, in person. Both court and visitors may perform in person searches. No search fee. Required to search: name, years to search. Civil cases indexed by defendant, plaintiff. Civil records on index cards from 1919, on dockets from 6/56, microfilm: wills since 1862, inventories since 1911, settlements since 1869, bonds and letters since 1878. **General Information:** No mental health, adoption records released. SASE required. Turnaround time 2-3 days. Copy fee: $1.00 per page. Certification fee: $4.00 plus $2.00 per page. Fee payee: Hamilton County Clerk and Master. Personal checks accepted. Prepayment is required. Public access terminal is available. Fax notes: $1.00 per page.

Hancock County

3rd District, Criminal, Circuit & General Sessions Court PO Box 347, Sneedville, TN 37869; 423-733-2954; Fax: 423-733-2119. Hours: 8AM-4PM (EST). *Felony, Misdemeanor, Civil, Eviction, Small Claims.*

Civil Records: Access: Mail, in person. Both court and visitors may perform in person searches. Search fee: $4.00 per name. Required to search:

name, years to search. Civil cases indexed by plaintiff. Civil records archived on books from 1934. **Criminal Records:** Access: Mail, in person. Both court and visitors may perform in person searches. Search fee: $4.00 per name. Required to search: name, years to search, DOB; also helpful-SSN. Criminal records archived on books from 1934. **General Information:** No juvenile records released. Turnaround time 3-4 days. Copy fee: $.25 per page. Certification fee: $3.00. Fee payee: Circuit Court Clerk. Personal checks accepted. Prepayment is required. Public access terminal is available.

Chancery Court PO Box 277, Sneedville, TN 37869; 423-733-4524; Fax: 423-733-2762. Hours: 9AM-4PM (EST). *Civil, Probate.*

Civil Records: Access: Mail, in person. Both court and visitors may perform in person searches. No search fee. Required to search: name, years to search. Civil cases indexed by defendant, plaintiff. Civil records on books. **General Information:** No adoption records released. SASE requested. Turnaround time 2 days. Copy fee: $.50 per page. Certification fee: $1.00. Fee payee: Clerk & Master. Personal checks accepted. Prepayment is required.

Hardeman County

25th District Circuit Court & General Sessions Courthouse, 100 N Main, Bolivar, TN 38008; 901-658-6524; Fax: 901-658-4584. Hours: 8:30AM-4:30PM M-Th, 8AM-5PM Fri (CST). *Felony, Misdemeanor, Civil, Eviction, Small Claims.*

Civil Records: Access: In person only. Court does not conduct in person searches; visitors must perform searches for themselves. Search fee: No civil searches performed by court. Required to search: name, years to search. Civil cases indexed by defendant, plaintiff. Civil records on computer since 12/92, archived General Sessions from 1960 and Circuit from 1800s. **Criminal Records:** Access: In person only. Court does not conduct in person searches; visitors must perform searches for themselves. Search fee: No criminal searches performed by court. Required to search: name, years to search, DOB, SSN, signed release. Criminal records on computer since 12/92, archived General Sessions from 1960 and Circuit from 1800s. **General Information:** No juvenile records releaased. Copy fee: $1.00 per page. Certification fee: $4.00. Fee payee: Circuit Court Clerk. Only cashiers checks and money orders accepted. Hardeman county personal checks accepted. Prepayment is required.

Chancery Court PO Box 45, Bolivar, TN 38008; 901-658-3142; Fax: 901-658-4580. Hours: 8:30AM-4:30PM M-Th, 8:30AM-5PM Fri (CST). *Civil, Probate.*

Civil Records: Access: Mail, in person. Both court and visitors may perform in person searches. No search fee. Required to search: name, years to search. Civil cases indexed by defendant, plaintiff. Civil records on books. **General Information:** No mental health, adoption records released. SASE requested. Turnaround time 1 day. Copy fee: $.25 per page. Additional fee for postage. Certification fee: $2.00 plus $1.00 per page. Fee payee: Chancery Court Clerk. Business checks accepted. Prepayment is required. Public access terminal is available.

Hardin County

24th District Circuit Court & General Sessions 601 Main St, Savannah, TN 38372;

901-925-3583; Fax: 901-926-2955. Hours: 8AM-4:30PM M,T,Th,F, 8AM-Noon Wed (CST). *Felony, Misdemeanor, Civil, Eviction, Small Claims.*

Civil Records: Access: In person only. Court does not conduct in person searches; visitors must perform searches for themselves. Search fee: No civil searches performed by court. Required to search: name, years to search. Civil cases indexed by defendant, plaintiff. Civil records archived on books and on microfiche from 1800s, on computer from 1996. **Criminal Records:** Access: In person only. Court does not conduct in person searches; visitors must perform searches for themselves. Search fee: No criminal searches performed by court. Required to search: name, years to search. Criminal records archived on books and on microfiche from 1800s, on computer from 1996. **General Information:** No juvenile records released. Certification fee: $5.00. Fee payee: Circuit Court Clerk. Hardin county personal checks accepted. Prepayment is required.

County Court 601 Main St, Savannah, TN 38372; 901-925-3921. Hours: 8AM-4:30PM M,T,TH,F, 8AM-12PM Wed & Sat (CST). *Probate.*

Hawkins County

3rd District Criminal, Circuit & General Sessions Court PO Box 9, Rogersville, TN 37857; 423-272-3397; Fax: 423-272-9646. Hours: 8AM-4PM (EST). *Felony, Misdemeanor, Civil, Eviction, Small Claims.*

Civil Records: Access: In person only. Court does not conduct in person searches; visitors must perform searches for themselves. Search fee: No civil searches performed by court. Required to search: name, years to search. Civil cases indexed by defendant, plaintiff. Civil records archived on books from 1800s. **Criminal Records:** Access: In person only. Court does not conduct in person searches; visitors must perform searches for themselves. Search fee: No criminal searches performed by court. Required to search: name, years to search. Criminal records archived on books from 1800s. **General Information:** No juvenile records released. Copy fee: $1.00 per page. Certification fee: $4.00. Fee payee: Circuit Court Clerk. No personal checks accepted.

Chancery Court PO Box 908, Rogersville, TN 37857; 423-272-8150. Hours: 8AM-4PM (EST). *Civil, Probate.*

Civil Records: Access: In person only. Court does not conduct in person searches; visitors must perform searches for themselves. Search fee: No civil searches performed by court. Required to search: name, years to search. Civil cases indexed by defendant, plaintiff. Civil records on index books from 1927 to present. **General Information:** No adoption records released. Copy fee: $1.00 per page. Certification fee: $2.00. Fee payee: Hawkins County Clerk and Master. Personal checks accepted. Prepayment is required.

Haywood County

28th District Circuit Court & General Sessions 1 N Washington Ave, Brownsville, TN 38012; 901-772-1112; Fax: 901-772-3864. Hours: 8:30AM-5PM (CST). *Felony, Misdemeanor, Civil, Eviction, Small Claims.*

Civil Records: Access: Phone, mail, in person. Both court and visitors may perform in person searches. No search fee. Required to search: name, years to search. Civil cases indexed by defendant, plaintiff. Civil records on computer since 1993,

prior archived since the 1800s. **Criminal Records:** Access: Phone, mail, in person. Both court and visitors may perform in person searches. No search fee. Required to search: name, years to search, DOB; also helpful-SSN. Criminal records on computer since 1993, prior archived since the 1800s. **General Information:** No juvenile records released. Turnaround time dependent upon search. Copy fee: $1.00 per page. Certification fee: $3.50. Fee payee: Circuit Court Clerk. Personal checks accepted. Prepayment is required.

Chancery Court 1 N Washington, PO Box 356, Brownsville, TN 38012; 901-772-0122; Fax: 901-772-3864. Hours: 8:30AM-5PM (CST). *Civil, Probate.*

Civil Records: Access: In person only. Court does not conduct in person searches; visitors must perform searches for themselves. Search fee: No civil searches performed by court. Required to search: name, years to search. Civil cases indexed by defendant, plaintiff. Probate records on books since 9/82; other records go back to 1800s. **General Information:** No adoption or sealed records released. Turnaround time 2 days. Copy fee: $1.00 per page. Certification fee: $5.00. Fee payee: Chancery Court. Personal checks accepted. Prepayment is required.

Henderson County

26th District Circuit Court & General Sessions Henderson County Courthouse, Lexington, TN 38351; 901-968-2031; Fax: 901-967-9441 (criminal). Hours: 8AM-4:30PM M,T,Th,F (CST). *Felony, Misdemeanor, Civil, Eviction, Small Claims.*

Civil Records: Access: Phone, fax, mail, in person. Both court and visitors may perform in person searches. Search fee: $6.00 per name. Required to search: name, years to search. Civil cases indexed by defendant, plaintiff. Civil records on cards or books, archived from 1800s. Phone access limited to 4 years. **Criminal Records:** Access: Phone, fax, mail, in person. Both court and visitors may perform in person searches. Search fee: $6.00 per name. Required to search: name, years to search. Criminal records on cards or books, archived from 1800s. Phone access limited to 4 years. **General Information:** No sealed indictment records released. SASE required. Turnaround time 1-2 weeks. Copy fee: $1.00 per page. Certification fee: $4.00. Fee payee: Circuit Court Clerk. Personal checks accepted. Prepayment is required. Public access terminal is available. Fax notes: $10.00 per document.

Chancery Court 17 Monroe Rm 2, 2nd Fl, Lexington, TN 38351; 901-968-2801; Fax: 901-967-5380. Hours: 8AM-4:30PM (till noon on Wed) (CST). *Civil, Probate.*

Civil Records: Access: In person only. Court does not conduct in person searches; visitors must perform searches for themselves. Search fee: No civil searches performed by court. Required to search: name, years to search. Civil cases indexed by defendant, plaintiff. Civil records on books. **General Information:** No confidential adoption records released. SASE required. Turnaround time dependent on search length. Copy fee: $2.00 per page. Certification fee: $2.00. Fee payee: Chancery Court. Only cashiers checks and money orders accepted. Prepayment is required.

Henry County

24th District Circuit Court & General Sessions
PO Box 429, Paris, TN 38242; 901-642-0461. Hours: 8AM-4:30PM (CST). *Felony, Misdemeanor, Civil, Eviction, Small Claims.*

Civil Records: Access: Phone, mail, in person. Both court and visitors may perform in person searches. No search fee. Required to search: name, years to search. Civil cases indexed by defendant, plaintiff. Civil records archived from 1820s (you search) or 1900s (they search); General Sessions on computer from 1991. **Criminal Records:** Access: Phone, mail, in person. Both court and visitors may perform in person searches. No search fee. Required to search: name, years to search, DOB; also helpful-SSN. Criminal records archived from 1820s (you search) or 1900s (they search); General Sessions on computer from 1991. **General Information:** No juvenile records released. Turnaround time 1-2 weeks. Copy fee: $.25 per page. Certification fee: $2.00. Fee payee: Circuit Court Clerk or General Sessions. Personal checks accepted.

County Court PO Box 24, Paris, TN 38242; 901-642-2412; Fax: 901-644-0947. Hours: 8AM-4:30PM (CST). *Probate.*

Hickman County

21st District Circuit Court & General Sessions
104 College Ave #204, Centerville, TN 37033; 931-729-2211; Fax: 931-729-6141. Hours: 8AM-4PM (CST). *Felony, Misdemeanor, Civil, Eviction, Small Claims.*

Civil Records: Access: In person only. Court does not conduct in person searches; visitors must perform searches for themselves. Search fee: No civil searches performed by court. Required to search: name, years to search. Civil cases indexed by defendant, plaintiff. Civil records on computer since 1991, prior records on books. **Criminal Records:** Access: In person only. Court does not conduct in person searches; visitors must perform searches for themselves. Search fee: No criminal searches performed by court. Required to search: name, years to search. Criminal records on computer since 1991, prior records on books. **General Information:** No juvenile records released. Copy fee: $1.00 per page. Certification fee: $5.00. Fee payee: Circuit Court Clerk. No personal checks accepted. Prepayment is required.

Chancery Court 104 College Ave #202, Centerville, TN 37033; 931-729-2522; Fax: 931-729-6141. Hours: 8AM-4PM (CST). *Civil, Probate.*

Civil Records: Access: Mail, in person. Both court and visitors may perform in person searches. No search fee. Required to search: name, years to search. Civil cases indexed by defendant, plaintiff. Civil records on books since 1965. **General Information:** No confidential or adoption records released. SASE requested. Turnaround time 1 week. Copy fee: $.25 per page. Certification fee: $3.00. Fee payee: Clerk & Master. Personal checks accepted.

Houston County

23rd District Circuit Court & General Sessions
PO Box 403, Erin, TN 37061; 931-289-4673; Fax: 931-289-5182. Hours: 8AM-4:30PM (CST). *Felony, Misdemeanor, Civil, Eviction, Small Claims.*

Civil Records: Access: Phone, fax, mail, in person. Only the court conducts in person searches; visitors may not. Search fee: $5.00 per name. Required to search: name, years to search. Civil cases indexed by defendant, plaintiff. Civil records archived from 1930s in books. **Criminal Records:** Access: Phone, fax, mail, in person. Only the court conducts in person searches; visitors may not. Search fee: $5.00 per name. Required to search: name, years to search; also helpful-SSN. Criminal records archived from 1930s in books. **General Information:** No juvenile records released. SASE required. Turnaround time 1-2 days. Copy fee: $.25 per page. Certification fee: $3.50. Fee payee: Circuit Court Clerk. Personal checks accepted. Prepayment is required.

Chancery Court PO Box 332, Erin, TN 37061; 931-289-3870; Fax: 931-289-5679. Hours: 8AM-4PM (CST). *Civil, Probate.*

Civil Records: Access: Mail, in person. Both court and visitors may perform in person searches. No search fee. Required to search: name, years to search. Civil cases indexed by defendant, plaintiff. Civil records on books. **General Information:** No adoption records released. Turnaround time 2 days. Copy fee: $.25 per page. Certification fee: $3.50. Fee payee: Clerk & Master. Personal checks accepted. Prepayment is required.

Humphreys County

23rd District Circuit Court & General Sessions
Room 106, Waverly, TN 37185; 931-296-2461; Fax: 931-296-1651. Hours: 8AM-4:30PM (CST). *Felony, Misdemeanor, Civil, Eviction, Small Claims.*

Civil Records: Access: Phone, mail, in person. Both court and visitors may perform in person searches. Search fee: $1.00 per name per year. If more than 15 years, the fee is a flat $25.00. Required to search: name, years to search. Civil cases indexed by defendant, plaintiff. Civil records archived from early 1900s, on computer from approximately 1988. **Criminal Records:** Access: Phone, mail, in person. Both court and visitors may perform in person searches. Search fee: $1.00 per name per year. If more than 15 years, the fee is a flat $25.00. Required to search: name, years to search, DOB, SSN, signed release. Criminal records archived from early 1900s, on computer from approximately 1988. **General Information:** No expunged records released. SASE required. Turnaround time same day. Copy fee: $.25 per page. Certification fee: $2.00 for the document seal plus $2.00 per page. Fee payee: Stephanie Caudle, Deputy Clerk. Business checks accepted. Prepayment is required.

County Court Clerk, Room 2 Courthouse Annex, Waverly, TN 37185; 931-296-7671; Fax: 931-296-5011. Hours: 8AM-4:30PM (CST). *Probate.*

Jackson County

15th District Criminal, Circuit & General Sessions Court
PO Box 205, Gainesboro, TN 38562; 931-268-9314; Fax: 931-268-4555. Hours: 8AM-4PM M,T,Th,F; 8AM-3PM W; 8AM-Noon Sat (CST). *Felony, Misdemeanor, Civil, Eviction, Small Claims.*

Civil Records: Access: Phone, fax, mail, in person. Both court and visitors may perform in person searches. Search fee: $5.00 per name. Required to search: name, years to search. Civil cases indexed by defendant, plaintiff. Civil records archived from 1900s in books. **Criminal Records:** Access: Phone, fax, mail, in person. Both court and visitors may perform in person searches. Search fee: $5.00 per name. Required to search: name, years to search, DOB; also helpful-SSN. Criminal records archived from 1900s in books. **General Information:** No juvenile records released. SASE required. Turnaround time 1 week. Copy fee: $.50 per page. Certification fee: $5.00. Fee payee: Circuit Court Clerk. Business checks accepted. Prepayment is required.

Chancery Court PO Box 733, Gainesboro, TN 38562-0733; 931-268-9216; Fax: 931-268-9060. Hours: 8AM-4PM M,T,Th,F; 8AM-3PM W (CST). *Probate.*

www.jacksonco.com

Jefferson County

4th District Circuit Court & General Sessions
PO Box 671, Dandridge, TN 37725; 865-397-2786; Fax: 865-397-4894. Hours: 8AM-4PM M-F; 8-11AM Sat (EST). *Felony, Misdemeanor, Civil, Eviction, Small Claims.*

Civil Records: Access: Mail, in person. Both court and visitors may perform in person searches. No search fee. Required to search: name, years to search. Civil cases indexed by defendant, plaintiff. Civil records archived from early 1900s on books. **Criminal Records:** Access: Mail, in person. Both court and visitors may perform in person searches. No search fee. Required to search: name, years to search, DOB, SSN, signed release. Criminal records archived from early 1900s on books. **General Information:** No adoption or juvenile records released. Turnaround time 1 week. Copy fee: $.15 per page. Certification fee: $3.00. Copy fee included in cert fee. Fee payee: Circuit Court Clerk. Personal checks accepted.

County Court PO Box 710, Dandridge, TN 37725; 865-397-2935; Fax: 865-397-3839. Hours: 8AM-4PM M-F, 8AM-11PM Sat (EST). *Probate.*

Johnson County

1st District Criminal, Circuit & General Sessions Court
PO Box 73, Mountain City, TN 37683; 423-727-9012; Fax: 423-727-7047. Hours: 8:30AM-5PM (EST). *Felony, Misdemeanor, Civil, Eviction, Small Claims.*

Civil Records: Access: Phone, mail, in person. Both court and visitors may perform in person searches. Search fee: $5.00 per name. Required to search: name, years to search. Civil cases indexed by defendant, plaintiff. Civil records in docket books, sessions 1976, criminal & circuit 1800s. **Criminal Records:** Access: Phone, mail, in person. Both court and visitors may perform in person searches. Search fee: $5.00 per name. Required to search: name, years to search, DOB. Civil records in docket books, sessions 1976, criminal & circuit 1800s. **General Information:** No adoption, expunged or juvenile records released. SASE required. Turnaround time 2-3 days. Copy fee: $2.00 per page. Certification fee: $2.00. Fee payee: Circuit Court Clerk. Only cashiers checks and money orders accepted. Prepayment is required.

Chancery Court PO Box 196, Mountain City, TN 37683; 423-727-7853; Fax: 423-727-7047. Hours: 8:30AM-5PM (EST). *Civil, Probate.*

Civil Records: Access: Mail, in person. Both court and visitors may perform in person searches. No search fee. Required to search: name, years to search. Civil cases indexed by defendant, plaintiff. Civil records on books and files. **General Information:** No adoption records released. SASE required. Turnaround time same day. Copy fee: $1.00 per page. Certification fee: $2.00 plus $2.00 per page. Fee payee: Clerk & Master. Only cashiers checks and money orders accepted. Prepayment is required.

Knox County

Circuit Court 400 Main Ave, Room M-30, PO Box 379, Knoxville, TN 37901; 865-215-2400; Fax: 865-215-4251. Hours: 8AM-5PM (EST). *Civil Actions Over $10,000.*

Civil Records: Access: Phone, fax, mail, in person. Both court and visitors may perform in person searches. No search fee. Required to search: name, years to search. Civil cases indexed by defendant, plaintiff. Civil records on computer from 1986, prior records archived and on microfilm. **General Information:** No adoption or sealed records released. Turnaround time 2-3 days. Copy fee: $.25 per page. Certification fee: $2.00. Fee payee: Circuit Court Clerk. Personal checks accepted.

General Sessions 400 Main Ave, Suite M84, Knoxville, TN 37902; 865-215-2518. Hours: 8AM-5PM (4:30 on F) (EST). *Civil Actions Under $15,000, Eviction, Small Claims.*

Civil Records: Access: Mail, in person. Both court and visitors may perform in person searches. No search fee. Required to search: name, years to search. Civil cases indexed by defendant, plaintiff. Civil records on books. **General Information:** No juvenile or adoption records released. Turnaround time 1 week. Copy fee: $1.50 per page. Certification fee: $3.50. Fee payee: General Sessions Court. Personal checks accepted. Credit cards accepted: Visa, Mastercard. Prepayment is required.

6th District Criminal Court 400 Main Ave, Room 149, Knoxville, TN 37902; 865-215-2492; Fax: 865-215-4291. Hours: 8AM-5PM M-Th; 8AM-4:30PM F (EST). *Felony, Misdemeanor.*
Criminal Records: Access: Fax, mail, in person. Only the court conducts in person searches; visitors may not. Search fee: $5.00 per name. Required to search: name, years to search, DOB; also helpful-address, SSN. Criminal records on computer, on books from 1980. **General Information:** No sealed records released. SASE not required. Turnaround time 48 hours. Copy fee: $2.00 per page. Certification fee: $2.00. Fee payee: Criminal Court Clerk. Personal checks accepted. Prepayment is required. Fax notes: $2.00 for first page, $1.00 each addl.

Chancery Court 400 Main Ave, Knoxville, TN 37902; 865-215-2555 (Chancery); Probate phone:865-215-2389; Fax: 865-215-2920. Hours: 8AM-4:30PM (EST). *Civil, Probate.*

Civil Records: Access: Phone, fax, mail, in person. Court does not conduct in person searches; visitors must perform searches for themselves. Search fee: No civil searches performed by court. Required to search: name, years to search. Civil cases indexed by defendant, plaintiff. Civil records on computer since 1978, prior records on books. **General Information:** No commitment or adoption records released. Turnaround time 1-2 days. Copy fee: $1.00 per page. Certification fee: $2.00. Fee payee: Chancery or Probate Court. Personal checks accepted. Prepayment is required. Fax notes: $1.00 per page.

Lake County

29th District Circuit Court & General Sessions 227 Church St, PO Box 11, Tiptonville, TN 38079; 901-253-7137; Fax: 901-253-9815. Hours: 8AM-4PM M-W & F; 8AM-Noon Th (CST). *Felony, Misdemeanor, Civil, Eviction, Small Claims.*

Civil Records: Access: In person only. Court does not conduct in person searches; visitors must perform searches for themselves. Search fee: No civil searches performed by court. Required to search: name, years to search. Civil cases indexed by defendant, plaintiff. Civil records archived on books in office up to 30 yrs, vault records before 1960. **Criminal Records:** Access: In person only. Court does not conduct in person searches; visitors must perform searches for themselves. No search fee. Required to search: name, years to search, DOB; also helpful-SSN. Criminal records archived on books in office up to 30 yrs, vault records before 1960. **General Information:** No sealed records released. Copy fee: $1.00 per page. Certification fee: $3.00. Fee payee: Circuit Court Clerk. Personal checks accepted.

Chancery Court PO Box 12, Tiptonville, TN 38079; 901-253-8926. Hours: 9AM-4PM M-W & F, 8AM-Noon Th (CST). *Civil, Probate.*

Civil Records: Access: Mail, in person. Both court and visitors may perform in person searches. No search fee. Required to search: name, years to search. Civil cases indexed by defendant. Civil records on books and files from 1984, prior records filed in county clerks office. **General Information:** Turnaround time 3-5 days. Copy fee: $.50 per page. Certification fee: $4.00. Fee payee: Clerk and Master. Personal checks accepted. Prepayment is required.

Lauderdale County

25th District Circuit Court Lauderdale County Justice Center, 675 Hwy 51 S, PO Box 509, Ripley, TN 38063; 901-635-0101; Fax: 901-635-0583. Hours: 8AM-4:30PM (CST). *Felony, Misdemeanor, Civil Actions Over $15,000.*

Civil Records: Access: Mail, in person. Both court and visitors may perform in person searches. Search fee: $10.00 per name. Required to search: name, years to search. Civil cases indexed by defendant, plaintiff. Civil records archived on books from 1800s to 1992, on computer since 1992. **Criminal Records:** Access: Mail, in person. Both court and visitors may perform in person searches. Search fee: $10.00 per name. Required to search: name, years to search; also helpful-DOB, SSN. Criminal records archived on books from 1800s to 1992, on computer since 1992. **General Information:** No sealed or adoption records released. SASE required. Turnaround time 2-3 days. Copy fee: $1.00 per page. Certification fee: $10.00. Fee payee: Circuit Court Clerk. Business checks accepted. Prepayment is required. Public access terminal is available.

General Sessions Court PO Box 509, Ripley, TN 38063; 901-635-2572; Fax: 901-635-9682. Hours: 8AM-4:30PM (CST). *Civil Actions Under $15,000, Eviction, Small Claims.*

Civil Records: Access: Mail, in person. Both court and visitors may perform in person searches. Search fee: $10.00 per name. Required to search: name, years to search. Civil cases indexed by defendant, plaintiff. Civil records on computer since 1992, records prior to 1984 on docket books. **General Information:** No confidential records released. SASE required. Turnaround time 2-3 days. Copy fee: $1.00 per page. Certification fee: $5.00. Fee payee: General Sessions. Business checks accepted. Prepayment is required. Public access terminal is available.

County Court Courthouse, 100 Court Sq, Ripley, TN 38063; 901-635-2561. Hours: 8AM-4:30PM M,T,Th,F; 8AM-Noon W & Sat (CST). *Probate.*

Lawrence County

22nd District Circuit Court & General Sessions NBU #12 240 W Gaines, Lawrenceburg, TN 38464; 931-762-4398; Fax: 931-766-2219. Hours: 8AM-4:30PM (CST). *Felony, Misdemeanor, Civil, Eviction, Small Claims.*

Civil Records: Access: In person only. Court does not conduct in person searches; visitors must perform searches for themselves. Search fee: No civil searches performed by court. Required to search: name, years to search. Civil cases indexed by defendant, plaintiff. Civil records archived on books since court started in 1940s. **Criminal Records:** Access: In person only. Court does not conduct in person searches; visitors must perform searches for themselves. Search fee: No criminal searches performed by court. Required to search: name, years to search, DOB, SSN. Criminal records archived on books since court started in 1940s. **General Information:** No expunged records released. Certification fee: $5.00. Fee payee: Circuit Court Clerk. Business checks accepted. Prepayment is required. Public access terminal is available.

County Court 240 Gaines St, NBU #12, Lawrenceburg, TN 38464; 931-762-7700. Hours: 8AM-4:30PM (CST). *Civil, Probate.*

Civil Records: Access: In person only. Court does not conduct in person searches; visitors must perform searches for themselves. Search fee: No civil searches performed by court. Required to search: name, years to search. Civil cases indexed by defendant, plaintiff. Civil records on books. **General Information:** No juvenile or adoption records released. Certification fee: $2.00. Fee payee: Circuit Court Clerk. Personal checks accepted. Prepayment is required.

Lewis County

21st Judicial District Circuit Court & General Sessions Courthouse 110 Park Avenue N, Rm 201, Hohenwald, TN 38462; 931-796-3724; Fax: 931-796-6010. Hours: 8AM-4:30PM (CST). *Felony, Misdemeanor, Civil, Eviction, Small Claims.*

Civil Records: Access: In person only. Court does not conduct in person searches; visitors must perform searches for themselves. Search fee: No civil searches performed by court. Required to search: name, years to search. Civil cases indexed by defendant, plaintiff. Civil records archived 15 years in office, 1800s in vault. **Criminal Records:** Access: In person only. Court does not conduct in person searches; visitors must perform searches for themselves. Search fee: No criminal searches performed by court. Required to search: name, years to search; also helpful-SSN. Criminal records archived 15 years in office, 1800s in vault. **General Information:** No juvenile, adoption records released. Copy fee: $1.00 per page. Certification fee: $2.00 per document plus $2.00 per page. Fee payee: Circuit Court Clerk. Personal checks accepted.

Chancery Court Lewis County Courthouse, 110 Park Ave N, Rm 208, Hohenwald, TN 38462; 931-796-3734; Fax: 931-796-6010. Hours: 8AM-4:30PM (CST). *Civil, Probate.*

Civil Records: Access: Phone, mail, in person. Both court and visitors may perform in person searches. No search fee. Required to search: name, years to search. Civil cases indexed by defendant, plaintiff. Civil records on computer since 10/94, prior records on books. **General Information:** No juvenile or adoption records released. Copy fee: $1.00 per page. Certification fee: $2.00. Fee payee: Clerk & Master. Personal checks accepted. Prepayment is required.

Lincoln County

17th Judicial District Circuit Court & General Sessions 112 Main Ave S, Rm 203, Fayetteville, TN 37334; 931-433-2334; Fax: 931-438-1577. Hours: 8AM-4PM (CST). *Felony, Misdemeanor, Civil, Eviction, Small Claims.*

Civil Records: Access: Phone, fax, mail, in person. Both court and visitors may perform in person searches. Search fee: $10.00 per name. Fee is for 5 years. Add $1.00 for each add'l year. Required to search: name, years to search. Civil cases indexed by defendant, plaintiff. Civil records archived on books since court started. **Criminal Records:** Access: Phone, fax, mail, in person. Both court and visitors may perform in person searches. Search fee: $10.00 per name. Fee is for 5 years. Add $1.00 for each add'l year. Required to search: name, years to search, DOB. Criminal records archived on books since court started. **General Information:** No probation records released. SASE required. Turnaround time 1-2 days. Copy fee: $1.00 per page. Certification fee: $4.00. Fee payee: Circuit Court Clerk. Business checks accepted. Fax notes: $2.00 per page.

Chancery Court 112 Main Ave, Rm B109, Fayetteville, TN 37334; 931-433-1482; Fax: 931-433-9979. Hours: 8AM-4PM (CST). *Civil, Probate.*

Civil Records: Access: In person only. Court does not conduct in person searches; visitors must perform searches for themselves. Search fee: No civil searches performed by court. Required to search: name, years to search. Civil cases indexed by defendant, plaintiff. Civil records archived on books. **General Information:** No adoption, divorce records released. Certification fee: $4.00. Fee payee: Clerk & Master. Personal checks accepted.

Loudon County

9th District Criminal & Circuit Court PO Box 160, Loudon, TN 37774; 865-458-2042; Fax: 865-458-2043. Hours: 8AM-4:30PM (EST). *Felony, Misdemeanor, Civil, Eviction, Small Claims.*

Note: General Sessions & Juvenile Court located at 12680 Hwy 11 W Suite 3, Lenoir City, TN 37771, 423-986-3505

Civil Records: Access: Mail, in person. Both court and visitors may perform in person searches. Search fee: $5.00 per name. Required to search: name, years to search. Civil cases indexed by defendant, plaintiff. Civil records archived from 1800s on books, on computer from Aug 1990. **Criminal Records:** Access: Mail, in person. Both court and visitors may perform in person searches. Search fee: $5.00 per name. Required to search: name, years to search. Criminal records archived from 1800s on books, on computer from Aug 1990. **General Information:** No juvenile, adoption records released. SASE requested. Turnaround time 2-4 days. Copy fee: $1.00 per page. Certification fee: $2.00. Fee payee: Circuit Court or general Sessions Court. Only cashiers checks and money orders accepted. Prepayment is required.

County Court 101 Mulberry St #200, Loudon, TN 37774; 865-458-2726; Fax: 865-458-9891. Hours: 8AM-5:30PM Mon, 8AM-4:30PM T-F (EST). *Probate.*

Macon County

15th District Criminal, Circuit, & General Sessions Court County Court Clerk, Rm 202, Lafayette, TN 37083; 615-666-2354; Fax: 615-666-3001. Hours: 8AM-4:30PM M-Th; 8AM-5PM F (CST). *Felony, Misdemeanor, Civil, Eviction, Small Claims.*

Civil Records: Access: In person only. Court does not conduct in person searches; visitors must perform searches for themselves. Search fee: No civil searches performed by court. Required to search: name, years to search. Civil cases indexed by defendant, plaintiff. Civil records archived in office from 1975, rest in records room from 1914. **Criminal Records:** Access: In person only. Court does not conduct in person searches; visitors must perform searches for themselves. Search fee: No criminal searches performed by court. Required to search: name, years to search, DOB; also helpful-SSN. Criminal records archived in office from 1975, rest in records room from 1914. **General Information:** No juvenile or adoption records released. Copy fee: $1.00 per page. Certification fee: $2.00. Fee payee: Circuit Court Clerk. Personal checks accepted. Prepayment is required.

County Court County Court Clerk, Rm 104, Lafayette, TN 37083; 615-666-2333; Fax: 615-666-5323. Hours: 8AM-4:30PM M-W, Closed Thu, 8AM-5PM Fri, 8AM-1:30PM Sat (CST). *Probate.*

Madison County

26th District Circuit Court 515 S Liberty St, Jackson, TN 38301; 901-423-6035. Hours: 8AM-4PM (CST). *Felony, Misdemeanor, Civil Actions Over $15,000.*

Civil Records: Access: In person only. Court does not conduct in person searches; visitors must perform searches for themselves. Search fee: No civil searches performed by court. Required to search: name, years to search. Civil cases indexed by defendant, plaintiff. Civil records archived on books in office from 1963, rest are located elsewhere. **Criminal Records:** Access: In person only. Court does not conduct in person searches; visitors must perform searches for themselves. Search fee: No criminal searches performed by court. Required to search: name, years to search; also helpful-DOB, SSN. Criminal records computerized since 1995, on books from 1965. **General Information:** No sealed records released. Copy fee: $.50 per page. Searcher can bring own paper then no charges for copies. Certification fee: $5.00. Fee payee: Circuit Court Clerk. Only cashiers checks and money orders accepted. Prepayment is required. Public access terminal is available.

General Sessions 515 S Liberty St, Jackson, TN 38301; 901-423-6041. Hours: 8AM-4PM (CST). *Civil Actions Under $15,000, Eviction, Small Claims.*

Civil Records: Access: Mail, in person. Both court and visitors may perform in person searches. No search fee. Required to search: name, years to search. Civil cases indexed by defendant, plaintiff. Civil records computerized since 04/98, archived on books in office from 1982, rest stored elsewhere from 1950s. **General Information:** Turnaround time 1 week. Copy fee: $1.50 per page. Certification fee: $4.00. Fee payee: General Sessions Court. Only cashiers checks and money orders accepted.

Probate Division, General Sessions Division II 110 Irby St, PO Box 1504, Jackson,

TN 38302-1504; 901-988-3025; Fax: 901-422-6044. Hours: 8:30-12, 1-4PM (CST). *Probate.*

Marion County

12th District Circuit Court & General Sessions PO Box 789, Courthouse Sq, Jasper, TN 37347; 423-942-2134; Fax: 423-942-4160. Hours: 8AM-4PM (CST). *Felony, Misdemeanor, Civil, Eviction, Small Claims.*

Civil Records: Access: Phone, mail, in person. Both court and visitors may perform in person searches. No search fee. Required to search: name, years to search. Civil cases indexed by defendant, plaintiff. Civil records on computer from 1988, prior records archived on books and microfiche since 1922. **Criminal Records:** Access: Phone, mail, in person. Both court and visitors may perform in person searches. No search fee. Required to search: name, years to search, DOB; also helpful-SSN. Criminal records on computer from 1988, prior records archived on books and microfiche since 1922. **General Information:** No adoption records released. Turnaround time 1 week. Copy fee: $3.00 per page. Certification fee: $3.00. Fee payee: Circuit Court Clerk. Personal checks accepted. Public access terminal is available.

Chancery Court PO Box 789, Jasper, TN 37347; 423-942-2601; Fax: 423-942-0291. Hours: 8AM-4PM (CST). *Civil, Probate.*

Civil Records: Access: Mail, in person. Both court and visitors may perform in person searches. No search fee. Required to search: name, years to search. Civil cases indexed by defendant, plaintiff. Civil records on computer since 07/94, prior records on books. **General Information:** No adoption records released. SASE requested. Turnaround time 1 day. Copy fee: $.50 per page. Certification fee: $3.00. Fee payee: Clerk and Master. Personal checks accepted. Prepayment is required.

Marshall County

17th District Circuit Court & General Sessions Courthouse, Lewisburg, TN 37091; 931-359-0536; Fax: 931-359-0543. Hours: 8AM-4PM (CST). *Felony, Misdemeanor, Civil, Eviction, Small Claims.*

Civil Records: Access: In person only. Court does not conduct in person searches; visitors must perform searches for themselves. Search fee: No civil searches performed by court. Required to search: name, years to search. Civil cases indexed by plaintiff. Civil records archived on books, but no date specified. **Criminal Records:** Access: In person only. Court does not conduct in person searches; visitors must perform searches for themselves. Search fee: No criminal searches performed by court. Required to search: name, years to search; also helpful-DOB, SSN. Criminal records in docket books. **General Information:** No adoption records released. Copy fee: $1.00 per page. Certification fee: $3.00. Fee payee: Circuit Court Clerk. Personal checks accepted. Prepayment is required.

County Court 1107 Courthouse Annex, Lewisburg, TN 37091; 931-359-2181; Fax: 931-359-0543. Hours: 8AM-4PM (CST). *Probate.*

Maury County

Circuit Court & General Sessions Maury County Courthouse, 41 Public Square, Columbia, TN 38401; 931-381-3690; Fax: 931-381-5614. Hours: 8:30AM-4PM M,T,Th,F; 8:30AM-Noon W & Sat (CST). *Felony,*

Misdemeanor, Civil, Eviction, Small Claims, Probate.

Civil Records: Access: Phone, fax, mail, in person. Both court and visitors may perform in person searches. No search fee. Required to search: name, years to search. Civil cases indexed by defendant, plaintiff. Civil records on books since 1984. **Criminal Records:** Access: Phone, fax, mail, in person. Both court and visitors may perform in person searches. No search fee. Required to search: name, years to search, DOB; also helpful-SSN. Criminal records on computer since 1990. **General Information:** No juvenile records released. Turnaround time 1 week. Copy fee: $1.00 per page. Certification fee: $6.00. Fee payee: Circuit Court Clerk. Personal checks accepted. Public access terminal is available. Fax notes: $1.00 per page.

McMinn County

10th District Criminal, Circuit & General Sessions Court PO Box 506, Athens, TN 37303; 423-745-1923; Fax: 423-745-1642. Hours: 8:30AM-4PM (EST). *Felony, Misdemeanor, Civil, Eviction, Small Claims, Probate.*

Civil Records: Access: Phone, fax, mail, in person. Both court and visitors may perform in person searches. Search fee: $3.00 per name. Required to search: name, years to search; also helpful-address. Civil cases indexed by defendant, plaintiff. Civil records archived approximately 20 years. Phone access is limited to three names. **Criminal Records:** Access: Phone, fax, mail, in person. Both court and visitors may perform in person searches. Search fee: $3.00. Required to search: name, years to search, DOB; also helpful-address. Criminal records archived approximately 20 years. Phone access is limited to three names. **General Information:** No juvenile, adoption records released. Turnaround time 5-10 days. Copy fee: $2.00 per page. Certification fee: $4.00. Fee payee: Circuit Court Clerk. Business checks accepted. Fax notes: $2.00 per page.

McNairy County

25th District Circuit Court & General Sessions 300 Industrial Drive, Selmer, TN 38375; 901-645-1015; Fax: 901-645-1003. Hours: 8AM-4:30PM M-F; 8AM-Noon Sat (CST). *Felony, Misdemeanor, Civil, Eviction, Small Claims.*

Civil Records: Access: Mail, in person. Both court and visitors may perform in person searches. Search fee: $5.00 per name. Required to search: name, years to search. Civil cases indexed by defendant, plaintiff. Civil records archived on docket books since 1966. **Criminal Records:** Access: Mail, in person. Both court and visitors may perform in person searches. Search fee: $5.00 per name. Required to search: name, years to search, DOB, SSN. Criminal records archived on docket books since 1966. **General Information:** No juvenile records released. Turnaround time 1-2 days. Copy fee: $.25 per page. Certification fee: $3.00. Fee payee: Circuit Court Clerk. Personal checks accepted. Prepayment is required. Public access terminal is available.

Chancery Court Chancery Court, Clerk & Master, Courthouse, Rm 205, Selmer, TN 38375; 901-645-5446; Fax: 901-645-3656. Hours: 8AM-4PM M,T,Th,F; Closed W (CST). *Civil, Probate.*

Civil Records: Access: In person only. Court does not conduct in person searches; visitors must perform searches for themselves. Search fee: No

civil searches performed by court. Required to search: name, years to search. Civil cases indexed by defendant, plaintiff. Civil records on books. **General Information:** No adoption records released. Copy fee: $.50. Certification fee: No certification fee. Fee payee: Clerk & Master. Personal checks accepted.

Meigs County

9th District Criminal, Circuit & General Sessions Court PO Box 205, Decatur, TN 37322; 423-334-5821; Fax: 423-334-4819. Hours: 8AM-5PM M,T,Th,F; 8AM-12PM Sat (EST). *Felony, Misdemeanor, Civil, Eviction, Small Claims.*

Civil Records: Access: Mail, in person. Both court and visitors may perform in person searches. Search fee: $10.00 per name. Required to search: name, years to search. Civil cases indexed by defendant, plaintiff. Civil records archived in office from 1930s, records in storage go further. They refer all name searches to an outside agency. **Criminal Records:** Access: Mail, in person. Both court and visitors may perform in person searches. Search fee: $10.00 per name. Required to search: name, years to search. Criminal records archived in office from 1930s, records in storage go further. They refer all name searches to an outside agency. **General Information:** No juvenile records released. SASE requested. Turnaround time 24 hours. Copy fee: $.25 per page. Certification fee: $5.00. Fee payee: Circuit Court Clerk. Personal checks accepted. Prepayment is required.

Chancery Court PO Box 5, Decatur, TN 37322; 423-334-5243. Hours: 8AM-5PM M,T,Th,F; 8:30AM-Noon Wed (EST). *Civil, Probate.*

Civil Records: Access: In person only. Court does not conduct in person searches; visitors must perform searches for themselves. Search fee: No civil searches performed by court. Required to search: name, years to search. Civil cases indexed by defendant, plaintiff. Civil records on dockets since 1940. **General Information:** No adoption records released. Copy fee: $.25 per page. Certification fee: $5.50. Fee payee: Meigs County Chancery Court. Personal checks accepted. Prepayment is required.

Monroe County

10th District, Circuit & General Sessions Court 105 College St, Madisonville, TN 37354; 423-442-2396; Fax: 423-442-9538. Hours: 8AM-4:30PM (EST). *Felony, Misdemeanor, Civil, Eviction, Small Claims.*

Civil Records: Access: Mail, in person. Both court and visitors may perform in person searches. Search fee: $10.00 per name. Required to search: name, years to search. Civil cases indexed by defendant, plaintiff. Civil records on computer since 1991, records on books in office for 10 years, unspecified prior to then. **Criminal Records:** Access: Mail, in person. Both court and visitors may perform in person searches. Search fee: $10.00 per name. Required to search: name, years to search. Criminal records on computer since 1991, records on books in office for 10 years, unspecified prior to then. **General Information:** No juvenile records released. Turnaround time 2 days. Copy fee: $1.00 per page. Certification fee: $4.00. Fee payee: Circuit Court Clerk. Personal checks accepted. Prepayment is required.

Chancery Court PO Box 56, Madisonville, TN 37354; 423-442-2644; Probate phone:423-442-

4573; Fax: 423-420-0048. Hours: 8:30AM-4:30PM (EST). *Civil, Probate.*

Civil Records: Access: Mail, in person. Both court and visitors may perform in person searches. No search fee. Required to search: name, years to search. Civil cases indexed by defendant. Civil records on computer since 93, prior records on books. **General Information:** No adoption, sealed records released. SASE requested. Turnaround time 2-3 days. Copy fee: $2.00 per page. Certification fee: $4.00. Fee payee: Chancery Court. Personal checks accepted. Prepayment is required.

Montgomery County

19th District Circuit Court PO Box 384, Clarksville, TN 37041-0384; 931-648-5700; Fax: 931-648-5731. Hours: 8:30AM-4:30PM (CST). *Felony, Civil Actions Over $10,000.*

Civil Records: Access: In person only. Court does not conduct in person searches; visitors must perform searches for themselves. Search fee: No civil searches performed by court. Required to search: name, years to search. Civil cases indexed by defendant, plaintiff. Civil records archived on books in office from 1970s, on microfiche from 1950s. **Criminal Records:** Access: In person only. Court does not conduct in person searches; visitors must perform searches for themselves. Search fee: No criminal searches performed by court. Required to search: name, years to search, DOB, signed release; also helpful-SSN. Criminal records on computer since 1997; prior records archived on books from 1970s & on microfiche from 1950s. **General Information:** No juvenile records released. Copy fee: $.50 per page. Certification fee: $6.00. Fee payee: Circuit Court Clerk. Business checks accepted. Prepayment is required.

General Sessions 120 Commerce St, Clarksville, TN 37040;; Civil phone:931-648-5769; Criminal phone:931-648-5769. Hours: 8:30AM-4:30PM (CST). *Misdemeanor, Civil Actions Under $15,000, Eviction, Small Claims.*

Civil Records: Access: Fax, mail, in person. Both court and visitors may perform in person searches. No search fee. Required to search: name, years to search. Civil cases indexed by defendant, plaintiff. Civil records on books, archived but data not given. **Criminal Records:** Access: Fax, mail, in person. Both court and visitors may perform in person searches. No search fee. Required to search: name, years to search, DOB; also helpful-SSN. Criminal records on books, archived but data not given. **General Information:** No records released. Turnaround time 1-2 weeks. Copy fee: $.50 per page. Certification fee: $6.00. Fee payee: General Sessions Court. Business checks accepted. Prepayment is required. Public access terminal is available. Fax notes: $2.00 per page.

Chancery Court Chancery Court, Clerk & Master, Montgomery County Courthouse, Clarksville, TN 37040; 931-648-5703. Hours: 8AM-4:30PM (CST). *Civil, Probate.*

Civil Records: Access: In person only. Court does not conduct in person searches; visitors must perform searches for themselves. Search fee: No civil searches performed by court. Required to search: name, years to search. Civil cases indexed by defendant, plaintiff. Civil records on books and microfilm. **General Information:** No adoption or sealed records released. Copy fee: $1.00 per page. Certification fee: $2.00. Fee payee: Clerk & Master. Business checks accepted. Prepayment is required. Public access terminal is available.

Moore County

17th District Circuit Court & General Sessions Courthouse, PO Box 206, Lynchburg, TN 37352; 931-759-7208; Fax: 931-759-5673. Hours: 8AM-4:30PM MTWF; 8AM-Noon Sat (CST). *Felony, Misdemeanor, Civil, Eviction, Small Claims.*

Civil Records: Access: Mail, in person. Both court and visitors may perform in person searches. Search fee: $5.00 per name. Required to search: name, years to search. Civil cases indexed by defendant, plaintiff. Civil records archived to 1862, on docket books and microfiche from 1862 to 1980s. **Criminal Records:** Access: Mail, in person. Both court and visitors may perform in person searches. Search fee: $5.00 per name. Required to search: name, years to search. Criminal records archived to 1862, on docket books and microfiche from 1862 to 1980s. **General Information:** No juvenile records released. SASE required. Turnaround time 7-10 days. Copy fee: $2.00 per page. Certification fee: $2.00. Fee payee: Circuit Court Clerk. Only cashiers checks and money orders accepted. Prepayment is required.

Chancery Court PO Box 206, Lynchburg, TN 37352; 931-759-7028; Fax: 931-759-7028. Hours: 8AM-4:30PM M-W,F; 8AM-Noon Sat (CST). *Civil, Probate.*

Civil Records: Access: In person only. Court does not conduct in person searches; visitors must perform searches for themselves. Search fee: No civil searches performed by court. Required to search: name, years to search. Civil cases indexed by plaintiff. Civil records on books. **General Information:** No adoption or sealed records released. Copy fee: $.50 per page. Certification fee: $5.00. Fee payee: Clerk and Master. Only cashiers checks and money orders accepted. Prepayment is required.

Morgan County

9th District Criminal, Circuit & General Sessions Court PO Box 163, Wartburg, TN 37887; 423-346-3503. Hours: 8AM-4PM (EST). *Felony, Misdemeanor, Civil, Eviction, Small Claims.*

Civil Records: Access: In person only. Court does not conduct in person searches; visitors must perform searches for themselves. Search fee: No civil searches performed by court. Required to search: name, years to search. Civil cases indexed by defendant, plaintiff. Civil records archived on books from 1855. **Criminal Records:** Access: In person only. Court does not conduct in person searches; visitors must perform searches for themselves. Search fee: No criminal searches performed by court. Required to search: name, years to search, SSN; also helpful-DOB. Criminal records archived on books from 1855. **General Information:** No sealed records released. Copy fee: $1.00 per page. Certification fee: $6.00. Fee payee: Circuit Court Clerk. Only cashiers checks and money orders accepted. Prepayment is required.

Chancery Court PO Box 789, Wartburg, TN 37887; 423-346-3881. Hours: 8AM-4PM (EST). *Civil, Probate.*

Civil Records: Access: Phone, mail, in person. Both court and visitors may perform in person searches. No search fee. Required to search: name, years to search. Civil cases indexed by defendant, plaintiff. Civil records in books since 1883, on microfiche since 1939. **General Information:** No

adoption or conservatorship records released. SASE required. Turnaround time 1-8 days. Copy fee: $.50 per page. Certification fee: $10.00. Fee payee: Clerk & Master. Personal checks accepted. Prepayment is required.

Obion County

27th District Circuit Court 7 Court House Square, Union City, TN 38261; 901-885-1372; Fax: 901-885-7515. Hours: 8:30AM-4:30PM (CST). *Felony, Misdemeanor, Civil Actions Over $10,000.*

Civil Records: Access: Mail, in person. Both court and visitors may perform in person searches. Search fee: $5.00 per name. Required to search: name, years to search. Civil cases indexed by defendant, plaintiff. Civil records for criminal archived on books from 1969, civil on books from 1974, rest are located elsewhere. **Criminal Records:** Access: Phone, mail, in person. Both court and visitors may perform in person searches. Search fee: $5.00. Misdemeanor records are $5.00 per year. Required to search: name, years to search, DOB, SSN. Criminal records for criminal archived on books from 1969, civil on books from 1974, rest are located elsewhere. **General Information:** No adoption records released. SASE required. Turnaround time 2 days. Copy fee: $1.00 per page. Certification fee: $4.00. Fee payee: Circuit Court. Business checks accepted. Prepayment is required.

General Sessions 9 Bill Burnett Circle, Union City, TN 38281-0236; 901-885-1811; Fax: 901-885-7515. Hours: 9AM-4PM (CST). *Civil Actions Under $15,000, Eviction, Small Claims.*

Civil Records: Access: Mail, in person. Both court and visitors may perform in person searches. Search fee: $5.00 5 years & under; $10.00 over 5 years. Required to search: name. Civil cases indexed by defendant, plaintiff. Civil records kept in office for last 10 years. **General Information:** No juvenile or adoption records released. SASE required. Turnaround time 2 days. Copy fee: $1.00 per page. Certification fee: $4.00. Fee payee: Circuit Court Clerk. Personal checks accepted. Prepayment is required.

Chancery Court PO Box 187, Union City, TN 38281; 901-885-2562; Fax: 901-885-7515. Hours: 8:30AM-4:30PM (CST). *Civil, Probate.*

Civil Records: Access: Phone, mail, in person. Both court and visitors may perform in person searches. No search fee. Required to search: name, years to search. Civil cases indexed by defendant, plaintiff. Civil records (probate) from 9/82 on books in Chancery office, prior records on books in County Clerk's office. **General Information:** No adoption or sealed records released. Copy fee: $1.00 per page. Certification fee: $2.00 per page plus $4.00 to certify. Fee payee: Clerk and Master. Personal checks accepted. Prepayment is required.

Overton County

13th District Criminal, Circuit & General Sessions Court Overton County Courthouse, 100 E Court Sq, Livingston, TN 38570; 931-823-2312; Fax: 931-823-9728. Hours: 8AM-4:30PM M,T,Th,F, 8AM-Noon Wed & Sat (CST). *Felony, Misdemeanor, Civil, Eviction, Small Claims.*

Civil Records: Access: Mail, in person. Both court and visitors may perform in person searches. No search fee. Required to search: name, years to search. Civil cases indexed by defendant, plaintiff. Civil records archived on books from late 1800s. **Criminal Records:** Access: Mail, in person. Both

court and visitors may perform in person searches. No search fee. Required to search: name, years to search, DOB, SSN, signed release. Criminal records archived on books from late 1800s. **General Information:** No juvenile records released. Turnaround time 3-5 days. Copy fee: $.25 per page. Certification fee: $5.00. Fee payee: Circuit Court Clerk. Business checks accepted. Prepayment is required.

County Court Courthouse Annex, University St, Livingston, TN 38570; 931-823-2631; Fax: 931-823-7036. Hours: 8AM-4:30PM M,T,Th,F; 8AM-Noon W & Sat (CST). *Probate.*

Perry County

21st District Circuit Court & General Sessions PO Box 91, Linden, TN 37096; 931-589-2218. Hours: 8AM-4PM (CST). *Felony, Misdemeanor, Civil, Eviction, Small Claims.*

Civil Records: Access: Mail, in person. Both court and visitors may perform in person searches. No search fee. Required to search: name, years to search. Civil cases indexed by defendant, plaintiff. Civil records archived on books from 1941, on microfiche (limited) at library. **Criminal Records:** Access: Mail, in person. Both court and visitors may perform in person searches. No search fee. Required to search: name, years to search, DOB, SSN. Criminal records archived on books from 1941, on microfiche (limited) at library. **General Information:** No adoption records released. SASE required. Turnaround time 2-3 days. Copy fee: $.25 per page. Certification fee: $4.00. Fee payee: Circuit Court Clerk. Personal checks accepted.

Chancery Court PO Box 251, Linden, TN 37096; 931-589-2217; Fax: 931-589-2350. Hours: 8AM-4PM (CST). *Civil, Probate.*

Civil Records: Access: In person only. Court does not conduct in person searches; visitors must perform searches for themselves. Search fee: No civil searches performed by court. Required to search: name, years to search. Civil cases indexed by defendant, plaintiff. Civil records (probate) on books from 1982, prior records in County Clerks office. **General Information:** No adoption records released. SASE required. Copy fee: $1.50 per page. Certification fee: $5.00. Fee payee: Clerk and Master. Local checks accepted. Prepayment is required.

Pickett County

13th District, Criminal, Circuit & General Sessions Court PO Box 5, Byrdstown, TN 38549; 931-864-3958; Fax: 931-864-6885. Hours: 8AM-4PM (CST). *Felony, Misdemeanor, Civil, Eviction, Small Claims.*

Civil Records: Access: Mail, in person. Both court and visitors may perform in person searches. No search fee. Required to search: name, years to search. Civil cases indexed by defendant. Civil records archived on books but not specific. **Criminal Records:** Access: Mail, in person. Both court and visitors may perform in person searches. No search fee. Required to search: name, years to search; also helpful-SSN. Criminal records not computerized, all on books. **General Information:** No adoption or juvenile records released. Turnaround time 3-4 days. Copy fee: $.25 per page. Certification fee: $4.00. Fee payee: Circuit Court Clerk. Personal checks accepted.

County Court PO Box 5 Courthoue Square, Byrdstown, TN 38549; 931-864-3879. Hours: 8AM-4PM M,T,Th,F, 8AM-Noon W & Sat (CST). *Probate.*

Polk County

10th District Criminal, Circuit & General Sessions Court PO Box 256, Benton, TN 37307; 423-338-4524; Fax: 423-338-4558. Hours: 8:30AM-4:30PM M-F; 9AM-Noon Sat (EST). *Felony, Misdemeanor, Civil, Eviction, Small Claims.*

Civil Records: Access: Mail, in person. Both court and visitors may perform in person searches. Search fee: $5.00 per name. Required to search: name, years to search. Civil cases indexed by defendant, plaintiff. Civil records archived from 1936. **Criminal Records:** Access: Mail, in person. Both court and visitors may perform in person searches. Search fee: $5.00 per name. Required to search: name, years to search, DOB, SSN. Criminal records archived from 1936. **General Information:** No juvenile records released. SASE requested. Turnaround time 3 days. Copy fee: $5.00 per document. Certification fee: Certification fee varies according to document size. Fee payee: Circuit Court Clerk. Personal checks accepted. Prepayment is required.

Chancery Court PO Drawer L, Benton, TN 37307; 423-338-4522; Fax: 423-338-4553. Hours: 8:30AM-4:30PM M-F, 8:30AM-Noon Sat (EST). *Civil, Probate.*

Civil Records: Access: Mail, in person. Both court and visitors may perform in person searches. Search fee: $5.00 per name. Fee varies by document. Required to search: name, years to search. Civil cases indexed by defendant, plaintiff. Civil records on books. **General Information:** No adoption records released. Copy fee: $1.00 per page. Certification fee: $5.50. Fee payee: Chancery Court. Personal checks accepted.

Putnam County

13th District Criminal, Circuit & General Sessions Court 421 E Spring St, 1C-49A, Cookeville, TN 38501; 931-528-1508. Hours: 8AM-4PM (CST). *Felony, Misdemeanor, Civil, Eviction, Small Claims.*

Civil Records: Access: Mail, in person. Both court and visitors may perform in person searches. No search fee. Required to search: name, years to search. Civil cases indexed by defendant, plaintiff. Civil records archived in office from 1980s, unknown before then. **Criminal Records:** Access: Mail, in person. Both court and visitors may perform in person searches. No search fee. Required to search: name, years to search; also helpful-SSN. Criminal records not computerized. **General Information:** No juvenile or adoption records released. Turnaround time 3-5 days. Copy fee: $.25 per page. Certification fee: $4.00. Fee payee: Circuit Court Clerk. Business checks accepted. Prepayment is required.

County Court PO Box 220, Cookeville, TN 38503-0220; 931-526-7106; Fax: 931-372-8201. Hours: 8AM-4:30PM (CST). *Probate.*

Rhea County

12th District Circuit & General Sessions Court 1475 Market St Rm 200, Dayton, TN 37321; 423-775-7805; Probate phone:423-775-7806; Fax: 423-775-7895. Hours: 8AM-4:30PM (EST). *Felony, Misdemeanor, Civil, Eviction, Small Claims, Probate.*

Civil Records: Access: In person only. Court does not conduct in person searches; visitors must perform searches for themselves. Search fee: No civil searches performed by court. Required to search: name, years to search. Civil cases indexed by defendant, plaintiff. Civil records in docket books. **Criminal Records:** Access: In person only. Court does not conduct in person searches; visitors must perform searches for themselves. Search fee: No criminal searches performed by court. Required to search: name, years to search, DOB; also helpful-SSN. Criminal records in docket books. **General Information:** No adoption records released. Certification fee: $4.50. Fee payee: Circuit Court Clerk. Personal checks accepted. Prepayment is required.

Roane County

9th District Criminal, Circuit, & General Sessions Court PO Box 73, Kingston, TN 37763; 865-376-2390; Fax: 865-376-4458. Hours: 8:30AM-6PM Mon; 8:30AM-4:30PM T-F (EST). *Felony, Misdemeanor, Civil, Eviction, Small Claims.*

Note: General Sessions phone is 865-376-5584, their records are separate

Civil Records: Access: Mail, in person. Both court and visitors may perform in person searches. Search fee: $5.00 per name. Required to search: name, years to search. Civil cases indexed by defendant, plaintiff. Civil records archived since court started, General Sessions and Circuit are on computer since 1991. **Criminal Records:** Access: Mail, in person. Both court and visitors may perform in person searches. Search fee: $5.00 per name. Required to search: name, years to search, DOB. Criminal records archived since court started, General Sessions and Circuit are on computer since 1991. **General Information:** No adoption, expunged records released. SASE required. Turnaround time 2-3 days. Copy fee: $.25 per page. Certification fee: $5.00. Fee payee: Circuit Court Clerk. Business checks accepted. Prepayment is required.

Chancery Court PO Box 402, Kingston, TN 37763; 865-376-2487; Fax: 865-376-4318. Hours: 8:30AM-6PM Mon, 8:30AM-4:30PM T-F (EST). *Civil, Probate.*

Civil Records: Access: Phone, mail, in person. Both court and visitors may perform in person searches. No search fee. Required to search: name, years to search. Civil cases indexed by defendant, plaintiff. Civil records on books, tax records on computer since 1982. **General Information:** No adoption records released. SASE not required. Turnaround time same day. Copy fee: $.50 per page. Certification fee: $2.00. Fee payee: Clerk and Master. Personal checks accepted.

Robertson County

19th District Circuit Court & General Sessions Room 200, Springfield, TN 37172; 615-382-2324; Fax: 615-384-8246. Hours: 8AM-4:30PM (CST). *Felony, Misdemeanor, Civil, Eviction, Small Claims.*

Civil Records: Access: Phone, fax, mail, in person. Both court and visitors may perform in person searches. Search fee: $5.00 per name. Required to search: name, years to search. Civil cases indexed by defendant, plaintiff. Civil records archived in office from 1980s, archived from 1800s located elsewhere. **Criminal Records:** Access: Phone, fax, mail, in person. Both court and visitors may perform in person searches. Search fee: $5.00 per name. Required to search: name, years to search; also helpful-DOB, SSN. Criminal records archived in office from 1980s, archived from 1800s located elsewhere. No long distance outgoing faxing. **General Information:** No sealed records released. SASE required.

Turnaround time 15 days. Copy fee: $.25 per page. Certification fee: $5.00. Fee payee: Circuit Court Clerk. Personal checks accepted. Prepayment is required. Public access terminal is available.

Chancery Court 101 Robertson, County Courthouse, Springfield, TN 37172; 615-384-5650. Hours: 8:30AM-4:30PM (CST). *Civil, Probate.*

Civil Records: Access: Mail, in person. Both court and visitors may perform in person searches. No search fee. Required to search: name, years to search. Civil cases indexed by defendant, plaintiff. Civil records in books since 1982, all chancery records on books. **General Information:** No adoption records released. SASE required. Turnaround time 1-2 days. Copy fee: $1.00 per page. Certification fee: $2.00. Fee payee: Clerk & Master. Personal checks accepted. Prepayment is required.

Rutherford County

16th District Circuit Court Room 201, Murfreesboro, TN 37130;; Civil phone:615-898-7820; Criminal phone:615-898-7820; Fax: 615-849-9553. Hours: 8AM-4:15PM (CST). *Felony, Misdemeanor, Civil Actions Over $15,000.*

Civil Records: Access: In person only. Court does not conduct in person searches; visitors must perform searches for themselves. Search fee: No civil searches performed by court. Required to search: name, years to search. Civil cases indexed by defendant, plaintiff. Civil records archived since court started, criminal on computer since 1990. **Criminal Records:** Access: In person only. Court does not conduct in person searches; visitors must perform searches for themselves. Search fee: No criminal searches performed by court. Required to search: name, years to search, DOB, signed release; also helpful-SSN. Criminal records archived since court started, criminal on computer since 1990. **General Information:** No expunged, sealed criminal records released. Copy fee: $1.00 per page. Certification fee: $2.00 per page to certify. Fee payee: Circuit Court Clerk. Personal checks accepted. Public access terminal is available.

General Sessions Court Judicial Bldg, Room 101, Murfreesboro, TN 37130; 615-898-7831; Fax: 615-898-7835. Hours: 8AM-4:15PM (CST). *Civil Actions Under $10,000, Eviction, Small Claims.*

Civil Records: Access: In person only. Court does not conduct in person searches; visitors must perform searches for themselves. Search fee: No civil searches performed by court. Required to search: name, years to search. Civil cases indexed by defendant, plaintiff. Civil records archived but not specified, on computer from 07/90. **General Information:** No juvenile records released. Copy fee: $1.00 per page. Certification fee: $4.00. Fee payee: General Sessions Court. Personal checks accepted. Prepayment is required. Public access terminal is available.

County Court 319 N Maple St, Murfreesboro, TN 37130; 615-898-7798; Fax: 615-898-7830. Hours: 8AM-4PM M-Th; 8AM-5PM F (CST). *Probate.*

Scott County

8th District Criminal, Circuit, & General Sessions Court PO Box 330, Huntsville, TN 37756; 423-663-2440. Hours: 8AM-4:30PM (EST). *Felony, Misdemeanor, Civil, Eviction, Small Claims, Probate.*

following data is not released: Social Security Numbers.

Access by: mail, online.

Fee & Payment: The current fee for VIN and plate checks is $2.30 per record. If you want to do a title search on an RV or mobile home (either attached or unattached), the fee is $5.75 or $6.75 certified. Fee payee: Department of Transportation. Prepayment required. Personal checks accepted. No credit cards accepted.

Mail search: Turnaround time: 7-10 days. A self addressed stamped envelope is requested.

Online search: Online access is available for pre-approved accounts. A $200 deposit is required, there is a $23 charge per month and $.12 fee per inquiry. Searching by name is not permitted. For more information, contact Production Data Control.

Other access: The state offers tape cartridge retrieval for customized searches or based on the entire database. Weekly updates are available. There are approximately 32,000,000 records in the database.

Accident Reports

Texas Department of Public Safety, Accident Records Bureau, PO Box 15999, Austin, TX 78761-5999 (Courier: 5805 N Lamar Blvd, Austin, TX 78752); 512-424-2600, 8AM-5PM.

www.txdps.state.tx.us

Indexing & Storage: Records are available for 10 years to present. It takes 30 days before new records are available for inquiry.

Searching: Accident reports investigated by DPS are open to the public; however, the driver reports are confidential. Those copies may only be provided to the driver who submitted and signed the report. Items required to search include two or more of following: full name of any person involved, specific city/county location, and date of incident.

Access by: mail, in person.

Fee & Payment: Fees: $4.00 per uncertified report and $6.00 per certified report. There is a $4.00 charge for a no record found search. Fee payee: Texas Department of Public Safety. Prepayment required. Personal checks accepted. No credit cards accepted.

Mail search: Turnaround time: 4-6 weeks. No self addressed stamped envelope is required.

In person search: Up to 5 requests will be processed immediately.

Boat & Vessel Ownership
Boat & Vessel Registration

Parks & Wildlife Dept, 4200 Smith School Rd, Austin, TX 78744; 512-389-4828, 800-262-8755, 8AM-5PM.

www.tpwd.state.tx.us/boat/boat.htm

Indexing & Storage: Records are available from 1976-1988 for titled boats, then from 1989-present

for all boats. Records are indexed on computer. All motorized boats must be registered and titled. All sailboats 14 ft and over must be registered and titled. Lien data shows on all reports.

Searching: The written request must include: name & address of requestor, TX #, motor # and/or serial numbers, and the statement "The use of the information obtained will be for lawful purposes."

Access by: mail, in person.

Fee & Payment: There is a $1.50 fee for a record check and a $6.00 fee for a complete history from microfilm. Fee payee: TX Parks & Wildlife Dept. Prepayment required. Personal checks accepted. No credit cards accepted.

Mail search: Turnaround time: 2-3 weeks. Turnaround time is often longer in the summer.No self addressed stamped envelope is required.

In person search: Histories are returned by mail.

Other access: Records are released in bulk format; however, requesters are screened for lawful purpose. The agency requires a copy of any item mailed or distributed as a result of purchase. media includes tape, labels, and printed lists.

Legislation-Current/Pending
Legislation-Passed

Legislative Reference Library, PO Box 12488, Austin, TX 78711-2488 (Courier: State Capitol Building, 2N.3, 1100 Congress, Austin, TX 78701); 512-463-1252 (Bill Status), 512-463-0252 (Senate Bill Copies), 512-463-1144 (House Bill Copies), 512-475-4626 (Fax), 8AM-5PM.

www.lrl.state.tx.us

Note: They ask that you call first to obtain location of bills. The sessions meet in odd number years from January through May.

Indexing & Storage: Records are available from the beginning of the Legislature in the Library. Records are computerized since 1989 and are on microfiche from 1973-1980.

Searching: Include the following in your request-bill number, year.

Access by: mail, fax, in person, online.

Fee & Payment: There is no search fee. There is no copy fee if under 10 pages; if over it is $.20 per page plus any shipping costs. Will express ship with requester's proper account number of the shipping company. Fee payee: Legislative Reference Library. Prepayment required. Business checks or money orders are preferred. No credit cards accepted.

Mail search: Turnaround time: variable. No self addressed stamped envelope is required.

Fax search: Result will be returned by fax if under 10 pages.

In person search: Searching is available in person.

Online search: The web is a thorough searching site of bills and status.

Voter Registration
Access to Records is Restricted

Secretary of State, Elections Division, PO Box 12060, Austin, TX 78711-2060; 800-252-8683, 512-475-2811 (Fax), 8AM-5PM.

www.sos.state.tx.us

Note: To do individual look-ups, one must go to the Tax Assessor-Collector at the county level Records are open. The state will sell the entire database, for non-commercial purposes, in a variety of media and sort formats.

GED Certificates

Texas Education Association, GED Records, 1701 N Congress Ave, Austin, TX 78701-1494; 512-463-9292, 512-305-9493 (Fax), 7AM-6PM.

www.tea.state.tx.us/ged

Searching: To search, either the name and date of birth or the Social Security Number is required.

Access by: mail, phone, fax, in person.

Fee & Payment: There is no fee for verification or transcripts. However, if the subject did not pay the GED fees and the record is prior to 1994, a fee may be charged to the requester,

Mail search: Turnaround time: 1-2 days. No self addressed stamped envelope is required.

Phone search: Verifications are available by phone.

Fax search: Fax requests require a signed release. Turnaround time: Same day.

In person search: Searching is available in person.

Hunting License Information
Fishing License Information

Parks & Wildlife Department, License Section, 4200 Smith School Rd, Austin, TX 78744; 512-389-4820, 512-389-4330 (Fax), 8AM-5PM.

www.tpwd.state.tx.us

Indexing & Storage: Records are available from 1979 season forward and are computerized.

Searching: All requests must be in writing on their form (if request is for someone other than self). They will release address, status, and date of issue. Include the driver's license number and/or SSN.

Access by: mail, fax.

Fee & Payment: There is no fee.

Mail search: Turnaround time: 1-3 days.

Fax search: Up to 5 names can be requested by fax. Results are mailed unless you have a toll free fax number.

Other access: The license database is for sale. For fees and procedures call 512-389-8069.

Licenses Searchable Online

Audiologist #22..www.tdh.state.tx.us/hcqs/plc/speech.htm
Banks, State Chartered #01 ....www.banking.state.tx.us/asp/lookup.asp
Barber School #02..www.tsbbe.state.tx.us/schoolr.htm
Chiropractor #25...www.tbce.state.tx.us
Currency Exchange #01 ....www.banking.state.tx.us/saudits/cexlicen.htm
Dental Hygienist #23 ....www.tsbde.state.tx.us/dbsearch
Dental Laboratory #23 ....www.tsbde.state.tx.us/dbsearch
Dentist #23..www.tsbde.state.tx.us/dbsearch
Dietitian #22...www.tdh.state.tx.us/hcqs/plc/dtrost.txt
ECA #27 ....http://160.42.108.3/ems_web/blh_html_page1.htm
Emergency Medical Technician #27.................http://160.42.108.3/ems_web/blh_html_page1.htm
Fire Alarm System Contractor #53...................www.tdi.state.tx.us/fire/indexfm.html
Fire Extinguisher Contractor #53.....................www.tdi.state.tx.us/fire/indexfm.html
Fire Protection Sprinkler System Contractor #53.......www.tdi.state.tx.us/fire/indexfm.html
Fireworks Display #53 ....www.tdi.state.tx.us/fire/indexfm.html
Health Facility #17..www.ecptote.state.tx.us/serv/verification/ftverif.taf
Hearing Instrument Dispenser/Fitter #22 ....www.tdh.state.tx.us/hcqs/plc/fdhi.htm
Insurance Adjuster #48.....................................www.tdi.state.tx.us/general/forms.html
Insurance Agency #48.......................................www.tdi.state.tx.us/general/forms.html
Insurance Agent #48...www.tdi.state.tx.us/general/forms.html
Insurance Company #48....................................www.tdi.state.tx.us/general/forms.html
Marriage & Family Therapist #31 ....www.tdh.state.tx.us/hcqs/plc/mft.htm#rosters
Massage Therapist #28 ....www.tdh.state.tx.us/hcqs/plc/mtrost.txt
Massage Therapy Establishment #28 ....www.tdh.state.tx.us/hcqs/plc/mtroste.txt
Massage Therapy School #28 ....www.tdh.state.tx.us/hcqs/plc/mtrosts.txt
Massage Therapy School Instructor #28...........www.tdh.state.tx.us/hcqs/plc/mtrosti.txt
Medical Doctor #30 ....www.docboard.org/tx/df/txsearch.htm
Medical Physicist #26.......................................www.tdh.state.tx.us/hcqs/plc/mprost.txt
Occupational Therapist/Assistant #17..............www.ecptote.state.tx.us/serv/verification/otverif.taf
Optometrist #51 ....www.arbo.org/nodb2000/licsearch.asp
Orthotics/Prosthetics Facility #26 ....www.tdh.state.tx.us/hcqs/plc/op_fac.htm
Orthotist/Prosthetist #26..................................www.tdh.state.tx.us/hcqs/plc/oprost.txt
Paramedic #27..http://160.42.108.3/ems_web/blh_html_page1.htm
Perpetual Care Cemetery #01 ....www.banking.state.tx.us/saudits/pcc-list.htm
Pharmacist #24...www.tsbp.state.tx.us/dbsearch/pht_search.asp
Pharmacy #24..www.tsbp.state.tx.us/dbsearch/phy_search.asp
Physical Therapist/Assistant #17......................www.ecptote.state.tx.us/serv/verification/ptverif.taf
Prepaid Funeral Permit Holder #01 ....www.banking.state.tx.us/saudits/pfc-list.htm
Professional Counselor #41..............................www.tdh.state.tx.us/hcqs/plc/lpcrost.txt
Radiologic Technologist #25 ....www.tdh.state.tx.us/hcqs/plc/mrtrost.txt
Radiology Technician #26.................................www.tdh.state.tx.us/hcqs/plc/mrtrost.txt
Real Estate Broker #52 ....www.trec.state.tx.us/core/mig.ctc
Real Estate Inspector #52 ....www.trec.state.tx.us/core/mig.ctc
Real Estate Salesperson #52 ....www.trec.state.tx.us/core/mig.ctc
Respiratory Care Practitioner #29 ....www.tdh.state.tx.us/hcqs/plc/rcrost.txt
Sale of Checks #01 ....www.banking.state.tx.us/saudits/soclicen.htm
Sex Offender Treatment Provider #26...............www.tdh.state.tx.us/hcqs/plc/cs.htm
Social Worker #26..www.tdh.state.tx.us/hcqs/plc/lsw/lsw_default.htm#roster
Speech-Language Pathologist #22....................www.tdh.state.tx.us/hcqs/plc/speech.htm
Temporary Massage Therapist #28....................www.tdh.state.tx.us/hcqs/plc/mtrostt.txt
Trust Company #01...www.banking.state.tx.us/review/trust.htm

Licensing Quick Finder

Acupuncturist #30 512-305-7030
Agricultural Seed Dealer #11 979-542-3691
Agricultural Specialities/Perishable #11.512-463-7604
Air Conditioning/Refrigeration Contractor #14
................................512-463-6599
Alcoholic Beverage Distributor #46 512-451-0231
Alcoholic Beverage Manufacturer #46...512-451-0231
Alcoholic Beverage Retailer #46 512-451-0231
Appraiser #47 512-465-3950

Architect #61............................512-305-9000
Asbestos Abatement Contractor #12.....512-834-6600
Asbestos Air Monitoring Technician #12
................................512-834-6600
Asbestos Consultant/Inspector #12.......512-834-6600
Asbestos Management Planner #12 512-834-6600
Asbestos Worker #12.......................512-834-6600
Athletic Agent #38...........................512-475-1769
Athletic Trainer #21 512-834-6615

Attorney #40 512-463-1463
Auctioneer #14...........................512-463-6599
Audiologist #22 512-834-6627
Audiology Assistant #25 512-834-6627
Banks, State Chartered #01................512-475-1300
Barber #02................................512-305-8475
Barber School #02 512-305-8475
Barber Shop #02.............................512-305-8475
Beauty Shop #08 512-454-4674

Boiler Inspector #14 800-722-7843
Boiler Installer #14 800-722-7843
Boxing/Combative Sports #14 512-463-5101
Career Counselor #14 512-463-6599
Child Care Administrator #49 512-438-3269
Chiropractor #25 512-305-6700
Contact Lens Dispenser #26...................512-834-4515
Cosmetologist #08 512-454-4674
County Librarian #44 512-463-5466
Court Reporter #09 512-463-1630
Currency Exchange #01 512-475-1290
Day Care Center #49 512-438-3269
Dental Assistant #23 512-463-6400
Dental Hygienist #23 512-434-6400
Dental Laboratory #23 512-463-6400
Dentist #23 512-463-6400
Dietitian #22 512-834-6601
Dog Racing #36 512-833-6697
ECA #27 512-834-6700
Embalmer #15 512-936-2474
Embalmer/Embalming Facility #15........512-936-2474
Emergency Medical Technician #27......512-834-6700
Engineer #05 512-440-7723
Engineering Firms #05 512-440-7723
Facility #49 512-438-3269
Family Home Day Care #49....................512-438-3269
Fire Alarm System Contractor #53........512-305-7931
Fire Extinguisher Contractor #53...........512-305-7931
Fire Inspector #56 512-918-7100
Fire Investigator #56.............................512-918-7100
Fire Protection Sprinkler System Contractor #53
....512-305-7931
Fire Suppression Specialist #56.............512-918-7100
Firefighter #56......................................512-918-7100
Fireworks Display #53 512-305-7931
Fish Farmer #11....................................512-463-7602
Fishing Guide #45 512-389-4818
Funeral Director #15.............................512-936-2474
Funeral Facility #15 512-936-2474
Health Facility #17................................512-305-6900
Health Related Registry #26 512-834-6602
Hearing Instrument Dispenser/Fitter #22
....512-834-6784
Home Equity & Secondary Mortgage Lenders #07
....512-936-7600
Home Health Agency #26 512-834-6646
Horse Racing #36 512-833-6697
Industrialized Housing #14 512-463-7353
Insurance Adjuster #48.........................512-322-3503
Insurance Agency #48..........................512-322-3503
Insurance Agent #48 512-322-3503
Insurance Company #48 512-322-3507
Interior Designer #61............................512-305-9000

Interpreter for the Deaf #06 512-407-3250
Investment Advisor #39.........................512-305-8332
Irrigator #57 512-239-6719
Laboratory Certification #25...................512-463-6400
Landscape Architect #61 512-305-9000
Law Enforcement Officer #58 512-936-7700
Lead Abatement Project Designer #55
....512-834-6612
Lead Abatement Worker #55.................512-834-6612
Lead Firm #55......................................512-834-6612
Lead Inspector #55 512-834-6612
Lead Risk Assessor #55 512-834-6612
Lead Supervisor #55.............................512-834-6612
Lead Training Program Providers #55....512-834-6612
Licensed Service Company #11 512-462-1441
Licensed Specialist in School Psychology #19
....512-305-7700
Loan Company #07...............................512-936-7600
Lobbyist #50 512-463-5800
LP Gas Technician #11 512-462-1441
Manicurist #02 512-305-8475
Manicurist Shop #02.............................512-305-8475
Marriage & Family Therapist #31 512-834-6657
Massage Therapist #28 512-834-6616
Massage Therapy Establishment #28 ...512-834-6616
Massage Therapy School #28 512-834-6616
Massage Therapy School Instructor #28
....512-834-6616
Medical Doctor #30 512-305-7030
Medical Laboratory Practicioner #22.....512-834-6602
Medical Physicist #26............................512-834-6655
Medication Aide #13 512-231-5827
Midwife, Direct Entry #25......................512-458-7700
Notary Public #33.................................512-463-5705
Nurse Aide #13 512-231-5829
Nurse, Advance Practice #25 512-305-7400
Nurse-RN #25......................................512-231-5829
Nursing Facility Administrator #13.........512-231-5825
Nursing Home Administrator #32 512-231-5825
Occupational Therapist/Assistant #17 ...512-305-6900
Optician #26...512-834-6661
Optometrist #51 512-305-8500
Orthotics/Prosthetics Facility #26 512-834-4520
Orthotist/Prosthetist #26 512-834-4520
Paramedic #27.....................................512-834-6700
Pawn Shop #07.....................................512-936-7600
Perfusionist #26 512-834-6751
Perpetual Care Cemetery #01 512-475-1290
Personal Employment Service #14 512-463-6599
Pesticide Applicator #10 512-463-7476
Pesticide Dealer #10 512-463-7476
Pharmacist #24 512-305-8000
Pharmacy #24......................................512-305-8000

Physical Therapist/Assistant #17 512-305-6900
Physician Assistant30 512-305-7030
Plumber #03 512-458-2145
Plumber Journeyman #03......................512-458-2145
Plumbing Inspector #03.........................512-458-2145
Podiatrist #20 512-305-7000
Polygraph Examiner #34 512-424-2058
Prepaid Funeral Permit Holder #01 512-475-1290
Private Investigator #35.........................512-463-5545
Private Security Agency #35..................512-463-5545
Professional Counselor #41 512-834-6658
Property Tax Consultant #14 512-463-6599
Psychological Associate #19 512-305-7700
Psychologist #19 512-305-7700
Psychologist Associate #25 512-305-7700
Public Accountant-CPA #43...................512-305-7853
Public Weigher #11 512-463-7607
Radiologic Technologist #25 512-834-6617
Radiology Technician #26 512-834-6617
Real Estate Broker #52 512-459-6544
Real Estate Inspector #52 512-459-6544
Real Estate Salesperson #52 512-459-6544
Residential Day Care #49......................512-438-3269
Respiratory Care Practitioner #29 512-834-6637
Sale of Checks #01 512-475-1290
Sanitarian #22......................................512-834-6635
Sanitation Code Enforcement Officers #22
....512-834-6635
Savings & Loan Association #37...........512-475-1350
Savings Bank #37 512-475-1350
Securities Broker #39 512-305-8332
Securities Dealer #39 512-305-8332
Securities Salesperson/Agent #39 512-305-8332
Sex Offender Treatment Provider #26...512-834-4530
Shorthand Reporter #09 512-463-1630
Social Worker #26 512-719-3521
Specialist in School Psychology #25 512-305-7700
Speech-Language Pathologist #22 512-834-6627
Staff Leasing #14 512-475-2896
Surveyor #04 512-452-9427
Talent Agency #14 512-463-6599
Tax Professional/Appraiser #59 512-305-7300
Teacher #42...512-469-3000
Temporary Common Worker #14...........512-463-6599
Temporary Massage Therapist #28.......512-834-6616
Transportation Service Provider #54 512-465-3500
Trust Company #01...............................512-475-1300
Underground Storage Tank Installer #60
....512-239-2191
Veterinarian #18...................................512-305-7555
Water Well & Pump Installer #14 512-463-7880
Wig Specialist #02................................512-305-8475

Licensing Agency Information

01 Banking Department, 2601 N Lamar Blvd, Austin, TX 78705-4294; 512-475-1300, Fax: 512-475-1313.
www.banking.state.tx.us
Direct URL to search licenses: www.banking.state.tx.us/asp/lookup.asp You can search online using alphabetical lists

02 Board of Barber Examiners, 333 Guadalupe, #2-110, Austin, TX 78701; 512-305-8475, Fax: 512-305-6800.
www.tsbbe.state.tx.us Cost of bulk record request is estimated based on amount of information requested.

03 Board of Plumbing Examiners, PO Box 4200 (929 E 41st (78765)), Austin, TX 78765-4200; 512-458-2145, Fax: 512-450-0637.

04 Board of Professional Land Surveying, 7701 N Lamar, #400, Austin, TX 78752; 512-452-9427.

05 Board of Registration for Professional Engineers, PO Box 18329 (1917 IH35 S (78760)), Austin, TX 78741; 512-440-7723, Fax: 512-442-1414.
www.tbpe.state.tx.us Licensing data may be availabe online at the web site as early as October, 2000.

06 Commission for the Deaf & Hard of Hearing, PO Box 12904 (4800 N Lamar Blvd, #310), Austin, TX 78711; 512-407-3250 Voice; 512-407-3251 TTY, Fax: 512-451-9316.
http://link.tsl.texas.gov/tx/TCDHH

07 Office of Consumer Credit Commissioner, 2601 N Lamar Blvd, Austin, TX 78705-4207; 512-936-2600, Fax: 512-936-7610.
www.occc.state.tx.us

08 Cosmetology Commission, PO Box 26700 (5717 Balcones Dr (78755-0700)), Austin, TX 78731; 512-454-4674, Fax: 512-454-0339.

09 Court Reporter Certification Board, PO Box 131131 (PO Box 131131), Austin, TX 78711-3131; 512-463-1630, Fax: 512-463-1117.
www.link.tsl.state.tx.us/tx/CRCB

10 Department of Agriculture, Pesticide Program, PO Box 12847 (1700 Congress Ave), Austin, TX 78711; 512-463-7476, Fax: 512-475-1618.
www.agr.state.tx.us/pesticide/index.html

11 Department of Agriculture, PO Box 12847 (1700 N Congress, Stephen F Austin Bldg), Austin, TX 78711; 512-463-7476, Fax: 512-463-7582.
www.agr.state.tx.us

12 Department of Health, Asbestos Programs Branch, 1100 W 49th St, Austin, TX 78756; 512-834-6600, Fax: 512-834-6644.
www.tdh.state.tx.us/beh/asbmain.htm

13 Department of Human Services, PO Box 149030 (Mail Code Y979), Austin, TX 78714-9030; 512-231-5800, Fax: 512-834-6764.

www.dhs.state.tx.us

14 Department of Licensing & Regulation, PO Box 12157 (PO Box 12157), Austin, TX 78711-2157; 512-463-6599, Fax: 512-475-2854.

www.license.state.tx.us

15 Funeral Service Commission, 510 S Congress Ave, #206, Austin, TX 78704; 512-936-2474, Fax: 512-479-5064.

17 Executive Council on Physical Therapy & Occupational Therapy Examiners, 333 Guadalupe St, Tower 2, #510, Austin, TX 78701; 512-305-6900, Fax: 512-305-6951.

www.ecptote.state.tx.us

18 Health Department, 333 Guadalupe, Tower 2, #330, Austin, TX 78701-3998; 512-305-7555, Fax: 512-305-7556.

http://link.tsl.state.tx.us/tx/BVME

19 Board of Examiners of Psychologists, 333 Guadalupe, #2-450, Austin, TX 78701; 512-305-7700, Fax: 512-305-7701.

www.tsbep.state.tx.us

20 Board of Podiatric Medical Examiners, 333 Guadalupe, #2-320, Austin, TX 78701; 512-305-7000, Fax: 512-305-7003.

21 Health Department, Advisory Board of Athletic Trainers, 1100 W 49th St, Austin, TX 78756; 512-834-6615, Fax: 512-834-6677.

www.tdh.state.tx.us/hcqs/plc/at.htm

22 Health Department, Professional Licensure & Certification, 1100 W 49th St, Austin, TX 78756-3183; 512-834-6635, Fax: 512-834-6707.
www.tdh.state.tx.us/license.htm

Direct URL to search licenses: www.tdh.state.tx.us/license.htm

23 Health Department, 333 Guadalupe, Tower 3, #800, Austin, TX 78701; 512-463-6400, Fax: 512-463-7452.

www.tsbde.state.tx.us

24 Health Department, Board of Pharmacy, 333 Guadalupe, Tower 3, #600, Box 21, Austin, TX 78701-3942; 512-305-8000, Fax: 512-305-8082.
www.tsbp.state.tx.us

Direct URL to search licenses: www.tsbp.state.tx.us/dbsearch/index.htm You can search online using status, license number, name, city, county, and ZIP Code.

25 Health Department, 323 Guadalupe, Tower 3, #825, Austin, TX 78701; 512-458-7111, Fax: 512-305-6705.

www.tdh.state.tx.us

26 Health Department, 1100 W 49th St, Austin, TX 78756; 512-834-6658, Fax: 512-834-6789.
www.tdh.state.tx.us/hfl/hfl-web.htm

Direct URL to search licenses: www.tdh.state.tx.us/license.htm

27 Health Department, Bureau of Emergency Management, 1100 W 49th St, Austin, TX 78756; 512-458-6700, Fax: 512-834-6736.
www.tdh.state.tx.us/hcqs/ems/emshome.htm

Direct URL to search licenses: http://160.42.108.3/ems_web/lh_html_page1.htm You can search online using name and/or city

28 Health Department, Professional Licensure & Certification, 1100 W 49th St, Austin, TX 78756; 512-834-6616, Fax: 512-834-6677.

www.tdh.state.tx.us/hcqs/plc/massage.htm

29 Health Department, Professional Licensure & Certification, 1100 W 49th St, Austin, TX 78756; 512-834-6628, Fax: 512-834-6677.

www.tdh.state.tx.us/hcqs/plc/resp.htm

30 Health Department, 333 Guadalupe, Tower 3, #610, Austin, TX 78701; 512-305-7010, Fax: 512-834-7006.
www.tsbme.state.tx.us

Direct URL to search licenses: www.docboard.org/tx/df/txsearch.htm You can search online using name.

31 Health Department, Professional Licensure & Certification, 1100 W 49th St, Austin, TX 78756; 512-834-6628, Fax: 512-834-6677.
www.tdh.state.tx.us/hcqs/plc/mft.htm

Direct URL to search licenses: www.tdh.state.tx.us/license.htm You can search online using alphabetical lists

32 Health Department, PO Box 149030 (PO Box 149030), Austin, TX 78714; 512-231-5825.

33 Office of Secretary of State, PO Box 13375 (1019 Brazos, Rm 214), Austin, TX 78711-2887; 512-463-5705.

www.sos.state.tx.us

34 Polygraph Examiner Board, PO Box 4087 (PO Box 4087), Austin, TX 78773-4087; 512-424-2058, Fax: 512-424-5739.

www.tsl.state.tx.us

35 Private Investigators/Security Agencies Board, PO Box 13509 (Capitol Station), Austin, TX 78711; 512-463-5545, Fax: 512-452-2041 512-707-2041Lic Division.

link.tsl.state.tx.us/TBPI

36 Racing Commission, 8505 Cross Park Dr, #110, Austin, TX 78754; 512-833-6699, Fax: 512-833-6907.

www.txrc6.txrc.state.tx.us

37 Savings & Loan Department, 2601 N Lamar Blvd, #201, Austin, TX 78705-4241; 112-475-1350, Fax: 512-475-1360.

link.tsl.state.tx.us/tx/TSLD

38 Secretary of State, PO Box 12887 (PO Box 12887), Austin, TX 78711-2887; 512-475-1769, Fax: 512-475-2815.

www.sos.state.tx.us

39 Securities Board, 200 E 10th St, 5th Fl, Austin, TX 78701; 512-305-8300, Fax: 512-305-8310.

www.ssb.state.tx.us

40 State Bar of Texas, PO Box 12487 (1414 Colorado, #300), Austin, TX 78701-1627; 512-463-1463 x1383, Fax: 512-462-1475.

www.sbot.org

41 Board of Examiners for Professional Counselors, 1100 W 49th St, Austin, TX 78756; 512-834-6658, Fax: 512-834-6789.

www.tdh.state.tx.us/hcqs/plc/lpc.htm

42 Board for Educator Certification, 1001 Trinity, Austin, TX 78701-2603; 512-469-3000, Fax: 512-469-3016.

www.sbec.state.tx.us

43 Board of Public Accountancy, 333 Guadalupe St, Tower III, #900, Austin, TX 78701; 512-305-7800, Fax: 512-505-7875.

www.tsbpa.state.tx.us

44 Library & Archives Commission, PO Box 12927 (1201 Brazos), Austin, TX 78711-2927; 512-463-5466, Fax: 512-463-8800.

www.tsl.state.tx.us

45 State Parks & Wildlife Department, 4200 Smith School Rd, Austin, TX 78744; 512-389-4818, Fax: 512-389-4349.

www.tpwd.state.tx.us

46 Alcoholic Beverage Commission, 7600 Chevy Chase Dr, #550, Austin, TX 78752; 512-451-0231, Fax: 512-451-0240.

www.tabc.state.tx

47 Appraisers Licensing & Certification Board, 1101 Camino La Costa, Austin, TX 78752; 512-465-3950, Fax: 512-465-3953.

www.talcb.capnet.state.tx.us

48 Department of Insurance, PO Box 149104 (333 Guadalupe), Austin, TX 78701; 512-463-6169, Fax: 512-475-2025.
www.tdi.state.tx.us

Direct URL to search licenses: www.tdi.state.tx.us/general/forms.html You can search online using downloadable lists

49 Department of Protective & Regulatory Services, 701 W 51st St, #E-550, Austin, TX 78714-9030; 512-438-4800, Fax: 512-438-3848.

www.tdprs.state.tx.us

50 Ethics Commission, PO Box 12070 (PO Box 12070), Austin, TX 78711-2070; 512-463-5800, Fax: 512-463-5777.
www.ethics.state.tx.us

Direct URL to search licenses: http://www.ethics.state.tx.us/filinginfo/loblists.htm

51 Optometry Board, 333 Guadalupe St, #2-420, Austin, TX 78701-3942; 512-305-8500, Fax: 512-305-8501.

www.tded.state.tx.us/guide/REGULATORYBODIES.html

Direct URL to search licenses: www.arbo.org/nodb2000/licsearch.asp You can search online using national database by name, city or state.

52 Real Estate Commission, PO Box 12188 (PO Box 12188), Austin, TX 78711-2188; 512-459-6544, Fax: 512-465-3698.
www.trec.state.tx.us

Direct URL to search licenses: www.trec.state.tx.us/core/mig.ctc You can search online using name and license number.

53 State Fire Marshal, 333 Guadalupe, Austin, TX 78701; 512-305-7900, Fax: 512-305-7922.
www.tdi.state.tx.us/fire/indexfm.html

Direct URL to search licenses: www.tdi.state.tx.us/fire/indexfm.html You can search online using self-extracting agent lists include name, license number, type, issue date, expiration date, and mailing address, and telephone information

54 Department of Transportation, 125 E 11th St, Austin, TX 78701; 512-465-3500.

55 Department of Health, Toxic Substances Control Division, Environmental Lead Branch, 1100 W 49th St, Austin, TX 78756-3199; 512-834-6612, Fax: 512-834-6644.

www.tdh.state.tx.us/beh/web.htm

56 Commission on Fire Protection, 12675 Research Blvd, PO Box 2286, Austin, TX 78768-2286; 512-918-7100, Fax: 512-239-4917.

www.tcfp.state.tx.us

57 Natural Resource Conservation Commission, PO Box 13087-MC178, Austin, TX 78711-3087; 512-239-6719.

58 Commission on Law Enforcement Officer, 1033 La Posada #240, Austin, TX 78752; 512-936-7700.

59 Board of Tax Professional Examiners, 333 Guadalupe St, Tower II #520, Austin, TX 78701; 512-305-7300.

60 Natural Resource Conservation Commission, PO Box 13087, Austin, TX 78711-3087; 512-239-2191.

61 Board of Architectural Examiners, 333 Guadalupe #2-350, Austin, TX 78701-3942; 512-305-9000.

The following list indicates the district and division name for each county in the state. If the district or division name of the bankruptcy court is different from the civil/criminal court, it appears in parentheses.

County/Court Cross Reference

County	District	Division
Anderson	Eastern	Tyler
Andrews	Western	Midland (Midland/Odessa)
Angelina	Eastern	Texarkana (Beaumont)
Aransas	Southern	Corpus Christi
Archer	Northern	Wichita Falls
Armstrong	Northern	Amarillo
Atascosa	Western	San Antonio
Austin	Southern	Houston
Bailey	Northern	Lubbock
Bandera	Western	San Antonio
Bastrop	Western	Austin
Baylor	Northern	Wichita Falls
Bee	Southern	Corpus Christi
Bell	Western	Waco
Bexar	Western	San Antonio
Blanco	Western	Austin
Borden	Northern	Lubbock
Bosque	Western	Waco
Bowie	Eastern	Texarkana
Brazoria	Southern	Galveston (Houston)
Brazos	Southern	Houston
Brewster	Western	Pecos (Midland/Odessa)
Briscoe	Northern	Amarillo
Brooks	Southern	Corpus Christi
Brown	Northern	San Angelo (Lubbock)
Burleson	Western	Austin
Burnet	Western	Austin
Caldwell	Western	Austin
Calhoun	Southern	Victoria (Corpus Christi)
Callahan	Northern	Abilene (Lubbock)
Cameron	Southern	Brownsville (Corpus Christi)
Camp	Eastern	Marshall
Carson	Northern	Amarillo
Cass	Eastern	Marshall
Castro	Northern	Amarillo
Chambers	Southern	Galveston (Houston)
Cherokee	Eastern	Tyler
Childress	Northern	Amarillo
Clay	Northern	Wichita Falls
Cochran	Northern	Lubbock
Coke	Northern	San Angelo (Lubbock)
Coleman	Northern	San Angelo (Lubbock)
Collin	Eastern	Sherman (Plano)
Collingsworth	Northern	Amarillo
Colorado	Southern	Houston
Comal	Western	San Antonio
Comanche	Northern	Fort Worth
Concho	Northern	San Angelo (Lubbock)
Cooke	Eastern	Sherman (Plano)
Coryell	Western	Waco
Cottle	Northern	Wichita Falls
Crane	Western	Midland (Midland/Odessa)
Crockett	Northern	San Angelo (Lubbock)
Crosby	Northern	Lubbock
Culberson	Western	Pecos (Midland/Odessa)
Dallam	Northern	Amarillo
Dallas	Northern	Dallas
Dawson	Northern	Lubbock
De Witt	Southern	Victoria (Houston)
Deaf Smith	Northern	Amarillo
Delta	Eastern	Sherman (Plano)
Denton	Eastern	Sherman (Plano)
Dickens	Northern	Lubbock
Dimmit	Western	San Antonio
Donley	Northern	Amarillo
Duval	Southern	Corpus Christi
Eastland	Northern	Abilene (Lubbock)
Ector	Western	Midland (Midland/Odessa)
Edwards	Western	Del Rio (San Antonio)
El Paso	Western	El Paso
Ellis	Northern	Dallas
Erath	Northern	Fort Worth
Falls	Western	Waco
Fannin	Eastern	Sherman (Plano)
Fayette	Southern	Houston
Fisher	Northern	Abilene (Lubbock)
Floyd	Northern	Lubbock
Foard	Northern	Wichita Falls
Fort Bend	Southern	Houston
Franklin	Eastern	Texarkana
Freestone	Western	Waco
Frio	Western	San Antonio
Gaines	Northern	Lubbock
Galveston	Southern	Galveston (Houston)
Garza	Northern	Lubbock
Gillespie	Western	Austin
Glasscock	Northern	San Angelo (Lubbock)
Goliad	Southern	Victoria (Corpus Christi)
Gonzales	Western	San Antonio
Gray	Northern	Amarillo
Grayson	Eastern	Sherman (Plano)
Gregg	Eastern	Tyler
Grimes	Southern	Houston
Guadalupe	Western	San Antonio
Hale	Northern	Lubbock
Hall	Northern	Amarillo
Hamilton	Western	Waco
Hansford	Northern	Amarillo
Hardeman	Northern	Wichita Falls
Hardin	Eastern	Beaumont
Harris	Southern	Houston
Harrison	Eastern	Marshall
Hartley	Northern	Amarillo
Haskell	Northern	Abilene (Lubbock)
Hays	Western	Austin
Hemphill	Northern	Amarillo
Henderson	Eastern	Tyler
Hidalgo	Southern	McAllen (Corpus Christi)
Hill	Western	Waco
Hockley	Northern	Lubbock
Hood	Northern	Fort Worth
Hopkins	Eastern	Sherman (Plano)
Houston	Eastern	Texarkana (Beaumont)
Howard	Northern	Abilene (Lubbock)
Hudspeth	Western	Pecos (Midland/Odessa)
Hunt	Northern	Dallas
Hutchinson	Northern	Amarillo
Irion	Northern	San Angelo (Lubbock)
Jack	Northern	Fort Worth
Jackson	Southern	Victoria (Corpus Christi)

County	District	Court
Jasper	Eastern	Beaumont
Jeff Davis	Western	Pecos (Midland/Odessa)
Jefferson	Eastern	Beaumont
Jim Hogg	Southern	Laredo (Houston)
Jim Wells	Southern	Corpus Christi
Johnson	Northern	Dallas
Jones	Northern	Abilene (Lubbock)
Karnes	Western	San Antonio
Kaufman	Northern	Dallas
Kendall	Western	San Antonio
Kenedy	Southern	Corpus Christi
Kent	Northern	Lubbock
Kerr	Western	San Antonio
Kimble	Western	Austin
King	Northern	Wichita Falls
Kinney	Western	Del Rio (San Antonio)
Kleberg	Southern	Corpus Christi
Knox	Northern	Wichita Falls
La Salle	Southern	Laredo (Corpus Christi)
Lamar	Eastern	Sherman (Plano)
Lamb	Northern	Lubbock
Lampasas	Western	Austin
Lavaca	Southern	Victoria (Houston)
Lee	Western	Austin
Leon	Western	Waco
Liberty	Eastern	Beaumont
Limestone	Western	Waco
Lipscomb	Northern	Amarillo
Live Oak	Southern	Corpus Christi
Llano	Western	Austin
Loving	Western	Pecos (Midland/Odessa)
Lubbock	Northern	Lubbock
Lynn	Northern	Lubbock
Madison	Southern	Houston
Marion	Eastern	Marshall
Martin	Western	Midland (Midland/Odessa)
Mason	Western	Austin
Matagorda	Southern	Galveston (Houston)
Maverick	Western	Del Rio (San Antonio)
McCulloch	Western	Austin
McLennan	Western	Waco
McMullen	Southern	Laredo (Houston)
Medina	Western	San Antonio
Menard	Northern	San Angelo (Lubbock)
Midland	Western	Midland (Midland/Odessa)
Milam	Western	Waco
Mills	Northern	San Angelo (Lubbock)
Mitchell	Northern	Abilene (Lubbock)
Montague	Northern	Wichita Falls
Montgomery	Southern	Houston
Moore	Northern	Amarillo
Morris	Eastern	Marshall
Motley	Northern	Lubbock
Nacogdoches	Eastern	Texarkana (Beaumont)
Navarro	Northern	Dallas
Newton	Eastern	Beaumont
Nolan	Northern	Abilene (Lubbock)
Nueces	Southern	Corpus Christi
Ochiltree	Northern	Amarillo
Oldham	Northern	Amarillo
Orange	Eastern	Beaumont
Palo Pinto	Northern	Fort Worth
Panola	Eastern	Tyler
Parker	Northern	Fort Worth
Parmer	Northern	Amarillo
Pecos	Western	Pecos (Midland/Odessa)
Polk	Eastern	Texarkana (Beaumont)
Potter	Northern	Amarillo
Presidio	Western	Pecos (Midland/Odessa)
Rains	Eastern	Tyler
Randall	Northern	Amarillo
Reagan	Northern	San Angelo (Lubbock)
Real	Western	San Antonio
Red River	Eastern	Sherman (Plano)
Reeves	Western	Pecos (Midland/Odessa)
Refugio	Southern	Victoria (Corpus Christi)
Roberts	Northern	Amarillo
Robertson	Western	Waco
Rockwall	Northern	Dallas
Runnels	Northern	San Angelo (Lubbock)
Rusk	Eastern	Tyler
Sabine	Eastern	Texarkana (Beaumont)
San Augustine	Eastern	Texarkana (Beaumont)
San Jacinto	Southern	Houston
San Patricio	Southern	Corpus Christi
San Saba	Western	Austin
Schleicher	Northern	San Angelo (Lubbock)
Scurry	Northern	Lubbock
Shackelford	Northern	Abilene (Lubbock)
Shelby	Eastern	Texarkana (Beaumont)
Sherman	Northern	Amarillo
Smith	Eastern	Tyler
Somervell	Western	Waco
Starr	Southern	McAllen (Corpus Christi)
Stephens	Northern	Abilene (Lubbock)
Sterling	Northern	San Angelo (Lubbock)
Stonewall	Northern	Abilene (Lubbock)
Sutton	Northern	San Angelo (Lubbock)
Swisher	Northern	Amarillo
Tarrant	Northern	Fort Worth
Taylor	Northern	Abilene (Lubbock)
Terrell	Western	Del Rio (San Antonio)
Terry	Northern	Lubbock
Throckmorton	Northern	Abilene (Lubbock)
Titus	Eastern	Texarkana
Tom Green	Northern	San Angelo (Lubbock)
Travis	Western	Austin
Trinity	Eastern	Texarkana (Beaumont)
Tyler	Eastern	Texarkana (Beaumont)
Upshur	Eastern	Marshall
Upton	Western	Midland (Midland/Odessa)
Uvalde	Western	Del Rio (San Antonio)
Val Verde	Western	Del Rio (San Antonio)
Van Zandt	Eastern	Tyler
Victoria	Southern	Victoria (Corpus Christi)
Walker	Southern	Houston
Waller	Southern	Houston
Ward	Western	Pecos (Midland/Odessa)
Washington	Western	Austin
Webb	Southern	Laredo (Houston)
Wharton	Southern	Houston
Wheeler	Northern	Amarillo
Wichita	Northern	Wichita Falls
Wilbarger	Northern	Wichita Falls
Willacy	Southern	Brownsville (Corpus Christi)
Williamson	Western	Austin
Wilson	Western	San Antonio
Winkler	Western	Pecos (Midland/Odessa)
Wise	Northern	Fort Worth
Wood	Eastern	Tyler
Yoakum	Northern	Lubbock
Young	Northern	Wichita Falls
Zapata	Southern	Laredo (Houston)
Zavala	Western	Del Rio (San Antonio)

US District Court

Eastern District of Texas

Beaumont Division PO Box 3507, Beaumont, TX 77704 (Courier Address: Room 104, 300 Willow, Beaumont, TX 77701), 409-654-7000.

www.txed.uscourts.gov

Counties: Delta*, Fannin*, Hardin, Hopkins*, Jasper, Jefferson, Lamar*, Liberty, Newton, Orange, Red River. Counties marked with an asterisk are called the Paris Division, whos case records are maintained here.

Indexing & Storage: Cases are indexed by defendant and plaintiff as well as by case number. New cases are available in the index immediately after filing date. A computer index is maintained. Records are also indexed on microfiche. Open records are located at this court. District wide searches are available for records from 3/86 from this division. This division maintains records for the Paris Division also.

Fee & Payment: The fee is $15.00 per item (one party name or case number). Payment may be made by money order, cashier check, personal check. Prepayment is required. Payee: Clerk, US District Court. Certification fee: $5.00 per document. Copy fee: $.50 per page. You are allowed to make your own copies. These copies cost $.25 per page. Copies are made from a public copy machine. Certified search requests are $25.00.

Phone Search: Only docket information is available by phone. An automated voice case information service (VCIS) is not available.

Mail Search: A stamped self addressed envelope is not required.

In Person Search: In person searching is available.

PACER: Sign-up number is 800-676-6856. Access fee is $.60 per minute. Toll-free access: 888-837-7816. Local access: 903-590-1104. Case records are available back to 1992. Records are purged once per year. New records are available online after 1 day. PACER is available on the Internet at http://pacer.txed.uscourts.gov.

Marshall Division PO Box 1499, Marshall, TX 75671-1499 (Courier Address: 100 E Houston, Marshall, TX 75670), 903-935-2912, Fax: 903-938-2651.

www.txed.uscourts.gov

Counties: Camp, Cass, Harrison, Marion, Morris, Upshur.

Indexing & Storage: Cases are indexed by defendant and plaintiff as well as by case number. New cases are available in the index 1 day after filing date. Both computer and card indexes are maintained. Records are also indexed on microfiche. Open records are located at this court.

Fee & Payment: The fee is $15.00 per item (one party name or case number). Payment may be made by money order, cashier check, personal check. Prepayment is required. Payee: US District Court. Certification fee: $5.00 per document. Copy fee: $.50 per page. You are allowed to make your own copies. These copies cost $.50 per page.

Phone Search: Only docket information is available by phone. An automated voice case information service (VCIS) is not available.

Mail Search: Always enclose a stamped self addressed envelope.

In Person Search: In person searching is available.

PACER: Sign-up number is 800-676-6856. Access fee is $.60 per minute. Toll-free access: 888-837-7816. Local access: 903-590-1104. Case records are available back to 1992. Records are purged once per year. New records are available online after 1 day. PACER is available on the Internet at http://pacer.txed.uscourts.gov.

Sherman Division 101 E Pecan St, Sherman, TX 75090, 903-892-2921.

www.txed.uscourts.gov

Counties: Collin, Cooke, Denton, Grayson.

Indexing & Storage: Cases are indexed by defendant and plaintiff as well as by case number. New cases are available in the index 1 day after filing date. Both computer and card indexes are maintained. Records are also indexed on microfiche. Open records are located at this court. District wide searches are available from this division.

Fee & Payment: The fee is $15.00 per item (one party name or case number). Payment may be made by money order, cashier check, personal check. Prepayment is required. Payee: Clerk, US District Court. Certification fee: $5.00 per document. Copy fee: $.50 per page.

Phone Search: Docket information available by phone. An automated voice case information service (VCIS) is not available.

Mail Search: Always enclose a stamped self addressed envelope.

In Person Search: In person searching is available.

PACER: Sign-up number is 800-676-6856. Access fee is $.60 per minute. Toll-free access: 888-837-7816. Local access: 903-590-1104. Case records are available back to 1992. Records are purged once per year. New records are available online after 1 day. PACER is available on the Internet at http://pacer.txed.uscourts.gov.

Texarkana Division Clerk's Office, 500 State Line Ave, Room 301, Texarkana, TX 75501, 903-794-8561, Fax: 903-794-0600.

www.txed.uscourts.gov

Counties: Angelina, Bowie, Franklin, Houston, Nacogdoches, Polk, Sabine, San Augustine, Shelby, Titus, Trinity, Tyler.

Indexing & Storage: Cases are indexed by defendant and plaintiff as well as by case number. New cases are available in the index 1-2 days after filing date. Both computer and card indexes are maintained. Records are also indexed on microfiche. Open records are located at this court. There is no set time when cases are sent to the Fort Worth Federal Records Center.

Fee & Payment: The fee is $15.00 per item (one party name or case number). Payment may be made by money order, cashier check, personal check. Prepayment is required. Payee: Clerk, US District Court. Certification fee: $5.00 per document. Copy fee: $.50 per page.

Phone Search: An automated voice case information service (VCIS) is not available.

Mail Search: Always enclose a stamped self addressed envelope.

In Person Search: In person searching is available.

PACER: Sign-up number is 800-676-6856. Access fee is $.60 per minute. Toll-free access: 888-837-7816. Local access: 903-590-1104. Case records are available back to 1992. Records are purged once per year. New records are available online after 1 day. PACER is available on the Internet at http://pacer.txed.uscourts.gov.

Tyler Division Clerk, Room 106, 211 W Ferguson, Tyler, TX 75702, 903-590-1000.

www.txed.uscourts.gov

Counties: Anderson, Cherokee, Gregg, Henderson, Panola, Rains, Rusk, Smith, Van Zandt, Wood.

Indexing & Storage: Cases are indexed by defendant and plaintiff as well as by case number. New cases are available in the index 1-2 days after filing date. Both computer and card indexes are maintained. Records are also indexed on microfiche. Open records are located at this court. There is no set time when cases are sent to the Fort Worth Federal Records Center.

Fee & Payment: The fee is $15.00 per item (one party name or case number). Payment may be made by money order, cashier check, personal check. Prepayment is required. Payee: Clerk, US District Court. Certification fee: $5.00 per document. Copy fee: $.50 per page. You are allowed to make your own copies. These copies cost $.25 per page.

Phone Search: Only docket information is available by phone. An automated voice case information service (VCIS) is not available.

Mail Search: A stamped self addressed envelope is not required.

In Person Search: In person searching is available.

PACER: Sign-up number is 800-676-6856. Access fee is $.60 per minute. Toll-free access: 888-837-7816. Local access: 903-590-1104. Case records are available back to 1992. Records are purged once per year. New records are available online after 1 day. PACER is available on the Internet at http://pacer.txed.uscourts.gov.

US Bankruptcy Court

Eastern District of Texas

Beaumont Division Suite 100, 300 Willow, Beaumont, TX 77701, 409-839-2617.

www.txeb.uscourts.gov

Counties: Angelina, Hardin, Houston, Jasper, Jefferson, Liberty, Nacogdoches, Newton, Orange, Polk, Sabine, San Augustine, Shelby, Trinity, Tyler.

Indexing & Storage: Cases are indexed by debtor as well as by case number. New cases are available in the index 1 day after filing date. A computer index is maintained. Open records are located at this court.

Fee & Payment: The fee is $15.00 per item (one party name or case number). Payment may be made by money order, cashier check, personal check. Prepayment is required. Debtor's checks are not accepted. Payee: Clerk, US Bankruptcy Court. Certification fee: $5.00 per document. Copy fee: $.50 per page. You are allowed to make your own copies. These copies cost $.25 per page. The searcher must fill out a card with their phone number, the date and the case number.

Phone Search: Only docket information is available by phone. An automated voice case information service (VCIS) is available. Call VCIS at 800-466-1694 or 903-590-1217.

Mail Search: Always enclose a stamped self addressed envelope.

In Person Search: In person searching is available.

PACER: Sign-up number is 800-676-6856. Access fee is $.60 per minute. Toll-free access: 800-466-1681. Local access: 903-590-1220. Case records are available back to 1989. Records are purged every six months. New civil records are available online after 1 day. PACER is available on the Internet at http://pacer.txeb.uscourts.gov.

Marshall Division c/o Tyler Division, 200 E Ferguson, Tyler, TX 75702, 903-590-1212, Fax: 903-590-1226.

www.txeb.uscourts.gov

Counties: Camp, Cass, Harrison, Marion, Morris, Upshur.

Indexing & Storage: Cases are indexed by as well as by case number. New cases are available in the index after filing date. Open records are located at the Division.

Fee & Payment: The fee is no charge per item (one party name or case number). Payment may be made by money order, cashier check. Business checks are not accepted. Personal checks are not accepted.

Phone Search: An automated voice case information service (VCIS) is available. Call VCIS at 800-466-1694 or 903-590-1217.

In Person Search: In person searching is available.

PACER: Sign-up number is 800-676-6856. Access fee is $.60 per minute. Toll-free access: 800-466-1681. Local access: 903-590-1220. Case records are available back to 1989. Records are purged every six months. New civil records are available online after 1 day. PACER is available on the Internet at http://pacer.txeb.uscourts.gov.

Plano Division Suite 300B, 660 N Central Expressway, Plano, TX 75074, 972-509-1240, Fax: 972-509-1245.

www.txeb.uscourts.gov

Counties: Collin, Cooke, Delta, Denton, Fannin, Grayson, Hopkins, Lamar, Red River.

Indexing & Storage: Cases are indexed by debtor and creditors as well as by case number. New cases are available in the index 24 hours after filing date. A computer index is maintained. Open records are located at this court.

Fee & Payment: The fee is $15.00 per item (one party name or case number). Payment may be made by money order, cashier check, personal check. Prepayment is required. Payee: Clerk, US Bankruptcy Court. Certification fee: $5.00 per document. Copy fee: $.50 per page. You are allowed to make your own copies. These copies cost $.25 per page.

Phone Search: Only docket information is available by phone. An automated voice case information service (VCIS) is available. Call VCIS at 800-466-1694 or 903-590-1217.

Mail Search: Always enclose a stamped self addressed envelope.

In Person Search: In person searching is available.

PACER: Sign-up number is 800-676-6856. Access fee is $.60 per minute. Toll-free access: 800-466-1681. Local access: 903-590-1220. Case records are available back to 1989. Records are purged every six months. New civil records are available online after 1 day.

Texarkana Division c/o Plano Division, Suite 300B, 660 N Central Expressway, Plano, TX 75074, 972-509-1240, Fax: 972-509-1245.

www.txeb.uscourts.gov

Counties: Bowie, Franklin, Titus.

Indexing & Storage: Cases are indexed by as well as by case number. New cases are available in the index after filing date. Open records are located at the Division.

Fee & Payment: The fee is no charge per item (one party name or case number). Payment may be made by money order, cashier check. Business checks are not accepted. Personal checks are not accepted.

Phone Search: An automated voice case information service (VCIS) is available. Call VCIS at 800-466-1694 or 903-590-1217.

In Person Search: In person searching is available.

PACER: Sign-up number is 800-676-6856. Access fee is $.60 per minute. Toll-free access: 800-466-1681. Local access: 903-590-1220. Case records are available back to 1989. Records are purged every six months. New civil records are available online after 1 day.

Tyler Division 200 E Ferguson, 2nd Floor, Tyler, TX 75702, 903-590-1212, Fax: 903-590-1226.

www.txeb.uscourts.gov

Counties: Anderson, Cherokee, Gregg, Henderson, Panola, Rains, Rusk, Smith, Van Zandt, Wood.

Indexing & Storage: Cases are indexed by debtor as well as by case number. New cases are available in the index 1 day after filing date. Both computer and card indexes are maintained. Records are also indexed on microfiche. Card index is only for cases prior to October 1987. Open records are located at this court. District wide searches are available for information from 10/87 from this court. This court maintains automated case records and all finance records for the other divisions in this district.

Fee & Payment: The fee is $15.00 per item (one party name or case number). Payment may be made by money order, cashier check, personal check. Prepayment is required. Payee: Clerk, US Bankruptcy Court. Certification fee: $5.00 per document. Copy fee: $.50 per page. You are allowed to make your own copies. These copies cost $.25 per page.

Phone Search: This court will answer questions pertaining to information not available from VCIS. An automated voice case information service (VCIS) is available. Call VCIS at 800-466-1694 or 903-590-1217.

Mail Search: A stamped self addressed envelope is not required.

In Person Search: In person searching is available.

PACER: Sign-up number is 800-676-6856. Access fee is $.60 per minute. Toll-free access: 800-466-1681. Local access: 903-590-1220. Case

records are available back to 1989. Records are purged every six months. New civil records are available online after 1 day. PACER is available on the Internet at http://pacer.txeb.uscourts.gov.

US District Court

Northern District of Texas

Abilene Division PO Box 1218, Abilene, TX 79604 (Courier Address: Room 2008, 341 Pine St, Abilene, TX 79601), 915-677-6311.

www.txnd.uscourts.gov

Counties: Callahan, Eastland, Fisher, Haskell, Howard, Jones, Mitchell, Nolan, Shackelford, Stephens, Stonewall, Taylor, Throckmorton.

Indexing & Storage: Cases are indexed by defendant and plaintiff as well as by case number. New cases are available in the index 2 days after filing date. Both computer and card indexes are maintained. A computer index is planned for early 1996. Open records are located at this court. District wide searches can be conducted from this court for information from 1983.

Fee & Payment: The fee is $15.00 per item (one party name or case number). Payment may be made by money order, cashier check, personal check. Prepayment is required. Payee: Clerk, US District Court. Certification fee: $5.00 per document. Copy fee: $.50 per page.

Phone Search: Only a name or case number will be released over the phone. An automated voice case information service (VCIS) is not available.

Mail Search: A stamped self addressed envelope is not required.

In Person Search: In person searching is available.

PACER: Sign-up number is 800-676-6856. Access fee is $.60 per minute. Toll-free access: 800-684-2393. Local access: 214-767-8918. Case records are available back to June 1991. Records are purged once per year. New records are available online after 1 day. PACER is available on the Internet at https://pacer.txnd.uscourts.gov.

Amarillo Division 205 E 5th St, Amarillo, TX 79101, 806-324-2352.

www.txnd.uscourts.gov

Counties: Armstrong, Briscoe, Carson, Castro, Childress, Collingsworth, Dallam, Deaf Smith, Donley, Gray, Hall, Hansford, Hartley, Hemphill, Hutchinson, Lipscomb, Moore, Ochiltree, Oldham, Parmer, Potter, Randall, Roberts, Sherman, Swisher, Wheeler.

Indexing & Storage: Cases are indexed by defendant and plaintiff as well as by case number. New cases are available in the index immediately after filing date. Both computer and card indexes are maintained. Records are also indexed on microfiche. Open records are located at this court.

Fee & Payment: The fee is $15.00 per item (one party name or case number). Payment may be made by money order, cashier check, personal check. Prepayment is required. Payee: Clerk, US District Court. Certification fee: $5.00 per document. Copy fee: $.50 per page.

Phone Search: No party information is released over the phone. Only pleadings are released over the phone. An automated voice case information service (VCIS) is not available.

Mail Search: A stamped self addressed envelope is not required.

In Person Search: In person searching is available.

PACER: Sign-up number is 800-676-6856. Access fee is $.60 per minute. Toll-free access: 800-684-2393. Local access: 214-767-8918. Case records are available back to June 1991. Records are purged once per year. New records are available online after 1 day. PACER is available on the Internet at https://pacer.txnd.uscourts.gov.

Dallas Division Room 14A20, 1100
Commerce St, Dallas, TX 75242, 214-753-2200.

www.txnd.uscourts.gov

Counties: Dallas, Ellis, Hunt, Johnson, Kaufman, Navarro, Rockwall.

Indexing & Storage: Cases are indexed by defendant and plaintiff as well as by case number. New cases are available in the index 2 days after filing date. A computer index is maintained. Computer index goes back to 1990 for the entire district. Records are also indexed on microfiche since 1957. Open records are located at this court. District wide searches are available for information from 1957 forward from this division.

Fee & Payment: The fee is $15.00 per item (one party name or case number). Payment may be made by money order, cashier check, personal check, Visa, Mastercard. Prepayment is required. Payee: Clerk, US District Court. Certification fee: $5.00 per document. Copy fee: $.50 per page. You are allowed to make your own copies. These copies cost $.25 per page.

Phone Search: Only computerized docket information will be released over the phone. An automated voice case information service (VCIS) is not available.

Mail Search: Always enclose a stamped self addressed envelope.

In Person Search: In person searching is available.

PACER: Sign-up number is 800-676-6856. Access fee is $.60 per minute. Toll-free access: 800-684-2393. Local access: 214-767-8918. Case records are available back to June 1991. Records are purged once per year. New records are available online after 1 day. PACER is available on the Internet at https://pacer.txnd.uscourts.gov.

Fort Worth Division Clerk's Office, 501 W
Tenth St, Room 310, Fort Worth, TX 76102, 817-978-3132.

www.txnd.uscourts.gov

Counties: Comanche, Erath, Hood, Jack, Palo Pinto, Parker, Tarrant, Wise.

Indexing & Storage: Cases are indexed by defendant and plaintiff as well as by case number. New cases are available in the index 1 day after filing date. A computer index is maintained. Computer records go back to 1990 for civil cases and 1993 for criminal cases. Records are also indexed on microfiche. Open records are located at this court. District wide searches for information from 1957 are available from this court.

Fee & Payment: The fee is $15.00 per item (one party name or case number). Payment may be made by money order, cashier check, personal check. Prepayment is required. Payee: Clerk, US District Court. Certification fee: $5.00 per document. Copy fee: $.50 per page. You are allowed to make your own copies. These copies cost $.25 per page.

Phone Search: The court will only release minimal information about a case when the caller already has a case number. They will not search for case numbers over the phone. An automated voice case information service (VCIS) is not available.

Mail Search: A stamped self addressed envelope is not required.

In Person Search: In person searching is available.

PACER: Sign-up number is 800-676-6856. Access fee is $.60 per minute. Toll-free access: 800-684-2393. Local access: 214-767-8918. Case records are available back to June 1991. Records are purged once per year. New records are available online after 1 day. PACER is available on the Internet at https://pacer.txnd.uscourts.gov.

Lubbock Division Clerk, Room 209, 1205
Texas Ave, Lubbock, TX 79401, 806-472-7624.

www.txnd.uscourts.gov

Counties: Bailey, Borden, Cochran, Crosby, Dawson, Dickens, Floyd, Gaines, Garza, Hale, Hockley, Kent, Lamb, Lubbock, Lynn, Motley, Scurry, Terry, Yoakum.

Indexing & Storage: Cases are indexed by defendant and plaintiff as well as by case number. New cases are available in the index 1 day after filing date. Both computer and card indexes are maintained. Records are also indexed on microfiche. Open records are located at this court. No records have been sent to the Federal Records Center.

Fee & Payment: The fee is $15.00 per item (one party name or case number). Payment may be made by money order, cashier check, personal check. Prepayment is required. Payee: Clerk, US District Court. Certification fee: $5.00 per document. Copy fee: $.50 per page.

Phone Search: An automated voice case information service (VCIS) is not available.

Mail Search: Always enclose a stamped self addressed envelope.

In Person Search: In person searching is available.

PACER: Sign-up number is 800-676-6856. Access fee is $.60 per minute. Toll-free access: 800-684-2393. Local access: 214-767-8918. Case records are available back to June 1991. Records are purged once per year. New records are available online after 1 day. PACER is available on the Internet at https://pacer.txnd.uscourts.gov.

San Angelo Division Clerk's Office, Room
202, 33 E Twohig, San Angelo, TX 76903, 915-655-4506, Fax: 915-658-6826.

www.txnd.uscourts.gov

Counties: Brown, Coke, Coleman, Concho, Crockett, Glasscock, Irion, Menard, Mills, Reagan, Runnels, Schleicher, Sterling, Sutton, Tom Green.

Indexing & Storage: Cases are indexed by defendant and plaintiff as well as by case number. New cases are available in the index immediately after filing date. A card index is maintained. Records are also indexed on microfiche. Open records are located at this court. Civil records are retained for 3 years. Criminal records are retained for 7 to 8 years.

Fee & Payment: The fee is $15.00 per item (one party name or case number). Payment may be made by money order, cashier check, personal check. Prepayment is required. Payee: Clerk, US

District Court. Certification fee: $5.00 per document. Copy fee: $.50 per page.

Phone Search: Only docket information available by telephone. An automated voice case information service (VCIS) is not available.

Fax Search: Fax requests cost the same as mail requests and require prepayment.

Mail Search: Always enclose a stamped self addressed envelope.

In Person Search: In person searching is available.

PACER: Sign-up number is 800-676-6856. Access fee is $.60 per minute. Toll-free access: 800-684-2393. Local access: 214-767-8918. Case records are available back to June 1991. Records are purged once per year. New records are available online after 1 day. PACER is available on the Internet at https://pacer.txnd.uscourts.gov.

Wichita Falls Division PO Box 1234,
Wichita Falls, TX 76307 (Courier Address: Room 203, 1000 Lamar, Wichita Falls, TX 76301), 940-767-1902, Fax: 940-767-2526.

www.txnd.uscourts.gov

Counties: Archer, Baylor, Clay, Cottle, Foard, Hardeman, King, Knox, Montague, Wichita, Wilbarger, Young.

Indexing & Storage: Cases are indexed by defendant and plaintiff as well as by case number. New cases are available in the index immediately after filing date. A card index is maintained. Records are also indexed on microfiche. Open records are located at this court.

Fee & Payment: The fee is $15.00 per item (one party name or case number). Payment may be made by money order, cashier check, personal check. Prepayment is required. Payee: Clerk, US District Court. Certification fee: $5.00 per document. Copy fee: $.50 per page.

Phone Search: Only docket information is available by phone. An automated voice case information service (VCIS) is not available.

Fax Search: Will accept fax for price quote only.

Mail Search: Always enclose a stamped self addressed envelope.

In Person Search: In person searching is available.

PACER: Sign-up number is 800-676-6856. Access fee is $.60 per minute. Toll-free access: 800-684-2393. Local access: 214-767-8918. Case records are available back to June 1991. Records are purged once per year. New records are available online after 1 day. PACER is available on the Internet at https://pacer.txnd.uscourts.gov.

US Bankruptcy Court

Northern District of Texas

Amarillo Division PO Box 15960, Amarillo,
TX 79105 (Courier Address: 624 Polk St, Suite 100, Amarillo, TX 79101), 806-324-2302.

www.txnb.uscourts.gov

Counties: Armstrong, Briscoe, Carson, Castro, Childress, Collingsworth, Dallam, Deaf Smith, Donley, Gray, Hall, Hansford, Hartley, Hemphill, Hutchinson, Lipscomb, Moore, Ochiltree, Oldham, Parmer, Potter, Randall, Roberts, Sherman, Swisher, Wheeler.

Indexing & Storage: Cases are indexed by debtor as well as by case number. New cases are available in the index immediately after filing date. Both computer and card indexes are maintained. Card index available prio to June 1988. Open records are located at this court.

Fee & Payment: The fee is $15.00 per item (one party name or case number). Payment may be made by money order, cashier check, business check. Personal checks are not accepted. Prepayment is required. Law firm checks are accepted. Payee: Clerk, US Bankruptcy Court. Certification fee: $5.00 per document. Copy fee: $.50 per page. You are allowed to make your own copies. These copies cost $.50 per page. The search fee is required should the court have to pull the file and count pages and the fee is $15.00 per case file. The court does not charge to do a name search.

Phone Search: Only docket information is available by phone. An automated voice case information service (VCIS) is available. Call VCIS at 800-886-9008 or 214-753-2128.

Mail Search: Always enclose a stamped self addressed envelope.

In Person Search: In person searching is available.

PACER: Sign-up number is 800-676-6856. Access fee is $.60 per minute. Toll-free access: 888-225-1738. Local access: 214-753-2134. You can search PACER using the Internet at https://pacer.txnb.uscourts.gov. Case records are available back to 1994. Records are purged every six months. New civil records are available online after 1 day. PACER is available on the Internet at https://pacer.txnb.uscourts.gov.

Dallas Division 1100 Commerce St, Suite 12A24, Dallas, TX 75242-1496, 214-753-2000.

www.txnb.uscourts.gov

Counties: Dallas, Ellis, Hunt, Johnson, Kaufman, Navarro, Rockwall.

Indexing & Storage: Cases are indexed by debtor and creditors as well as by case number. New cases are available in the index 1-2 days after filing date. Both computer and card indexes are maintained. Open records are located at this court. District wide searches are available for records from 8/92 to the present from this division. This court maintains records for the Wichita Falls Division.

Fee & Payment: The fee is $15.00 per item (one party name or case number). Payment may be made by money order. Business checks are not accepted. Personal checks are not accepted. There is no search fee for searching docket sheets or claim registers. Prepayment is required. Payee: Clerk, US Bankruptcy Court. Certification fee: $5.00 per document. Copy fee: $.50 per page.

Phone Search: Only docket information is available by phone. An automated voice case information service (VCIS) is available. Call VCIS at 800-886-9008 or 214-753-2128.

Mail Search: Always enclose a stamped self addressed envelope.

In Person Search: In person searching is available.

PACER: Sign-up number is 800-676-6856. Access fee is $.60 per minute. Toll-free access: 888-225-1738. Local access: 214-753-2134. You can search PACER using the Internet at https://pacer.txnb.uscourts.gov. Case records are available back to 1994. Records are purged every

six months. New civil records are available online after 1 day. PACER is available on the Internet at https://pacer.txnb.uscourts.gov.

Fort Worth Division 501 W 10th, Suite 147, Fort Worth, TX 76102, 817-333-6000, Fax: 817-333-6001.

www.txnb.uscourts.gov

Counties: Comanche, Erath, Hood, Jack, Palo Pinto, Parker, Tarrant, Wise.

Indexing & Storage: Cases are indexed by debtor as well as by case number. New cases are available in the index 1-2 days after filing date. Both computer and card indexes are maintained. Records up to 1986 are on index cards. Complete August 1, 1992 through the present are indexed on computer. From 1987 to August 1, 1992, records are indexed manually. Open records are located at this court. Closed cases are held in house as long as there is space to store them. They are sent opnce at year end to the Fort Worth Federal Records Center.

Fee & Payment: The fee is $15.00 per item (one party name or case number). Payment may be made by money order, cashier check, personal check. Prepayment is required. Debtor's checks are not accepted. Payee: Clerk, US Bankruptcy Court. Certification fee: $5.00 per document. Copy fee: $.50 per page. You are allowed to make your own copies. These copies cost $.25 per page.

Phone Search: Only docket information is available by phone. A record can be searched over the phone by debtor's name for records from 1987 to the present. An automated voice case information service (VCIS) is available. Call VCIS at 800-886-9008 or 214-753-2128.

Mail Search: Always enclose a stamped self addressed envelope.

In Person Search: In person searching is available.

PACER: Sign-up number is 800-676-6856. Access fee is $.60 per minute. Toll-free access: 888-225-1738. Local access: 214-753-2134. You can search PACER using the Internet at https://pacer.txnb.uscourts.gov. Case records are available back to 1994. Records are purged every six months. New civil records are available online after 1 day. PACER is available on the Internet at https://pacer.txnb.uscourts.gov.

Lubbock Division 306 Federal Bldg, 1205 Texas Ave, Lubbock, TX 79401-4002, 806-472-5000.

www.txnb.uscourts.gov

Counties: Bailey, Borden, Brown, Callahan, Cochran, Cooke, Coleman, Concho, Crockett, Crosby, Dawson, Dickens, Eastland, Fisher, Floyd, Gaines, Garza, Glasscock, Hale, Haskell, Hockley, Howard, Irion, Jones, Kent, Lamb, Lubbock, Lynn, Menard, Mills, Mitchell, Motley, Nolan, Reagan, Runnels, Schleicher, Scurry, Shackelford, Stephens, Sterling, Stonewall, Sutton, Taylor, Terry, Throckmorton, Tom Green, Yoakum.

Indexing & Storage: Cases are indexed by debtor as well as by case number. New cases are available in the index 1-2 days after filing date. A computer index is maintained. Open records are located at this court.

Fee & Payment: The fee is $15.00 per item (one party name or case number). Payment may be made by money order, cashier check, business check. Personal checks are not accepted. Prepayment is required. Debtor's checks are not accepted. Payee: Clerk, US Bankruptcy Court.

Certification fee: $5.00 per document. Copy fee: $.50 per page.

Phone Search: Only docket information is available by phone. A record can be searched over the phone by debtor's name for records from 1987 to the present. An automated voice case information service (VCIS) is available. Call VCIS at 800-886-9008 or 214-753-2128.

Mail Search: Always enclose a stamped self addressed envelope.

In Person Search: In person searching is available.

PACER: Sign-up number is 800-676-6856. Access fee is $.60 per minute. Toll-free access: 888-225-1738. Local access: 214-753-2134. You can search PACER using the Internet at https://pacer.txnb.uscourts.gov. Case records are available back to 1994. Records are purged every six months. New civil records are available online after 1 day. PACER is available on the Internet at https://pacer.txnb.uscourts.gov.

Wichita Falls Division c/o Dallas Division, Suite 12A24, 1100 Commerce St, Dallas, TX 75242-1496, 214-753-2000.

www.txnb.uscourts.gov

Counties: Archer, Baylor, Clay, Cottle, Foard, Hardeman, King, Knox, Montague, Wichita, Wilbarger, Young.

Indexing & Storage: Cases are indexed by as well as by case number. New cases are available in the index after filing date. Open records are located at the Division.

Fee & Payment: The fee is no charge per item (one party name or case number). Payment may be made by money order, cashier check. Business checks are not accepted. Personal checks are not accepted.

Phone Search: An automated voice case information service (VCIS) is available. Call VCIS at 800-886-9008 or 214-753-2128.

In Person Search: In person searching is available.

PACER: Sign-up number is 800-676-6856. Access fee is $.60 per minute. Toll-free access: 888-225-1738. Local access: 214-753-2134. You can search PACER using the Internet at https://pacer.txnb.uscourts.gov. Case records are available back to 1994. Records are purged every six months. New civil records are available online after 1 day. PACER is available on the Internet at https://pacer.txnb.uscourts.gov.

US District Court

Southern District of Texas

Brownsville Division 600 E Harrison St Rm 101, Brownsville, TX 78520-7114 (Courier Address: Use mail address for courier delivery., 600 E Harrison St #101,), 956-548-2500, Fax: 956-548-2598.

www.txs.uscourts.gov

Counties: Cameron, Willacy.

Indexing & Storage: Cases are indexed by defendant and plaintiff as well as by case number. New cases are available in the index 2 days after filing date. Both computer and card indexes are maintained. Records are also indexed on microfiche. Open records are located at this court.

Fee & Payment: The fee is $15.00 per item (one party name or case number). Payment may be made by money order, cashier check, personal check. Prepayment is required. Payee: Clerk, US District Court. Certification fee: $5.00 per document. Copy fee: $.50 per page.

Phone Search: Only docket information is available by phone. An automated voice case information service (VCIS) is not available.

Mail Search: Always enclose a stamped self addressed envelope.

In Person Search: In person searching is available.

PACER: Sign-up number is 800-676-8856. Access fee is $.60 per minute. Toll-free access: 800-998-9037. Local access: 713-250-5046. Case records are available back to June 1990. Records are purged every six months. New records are available online after 1 day. PACER is available on the Internet at http://pacer.txs.uscourts.gov.

Corpus Christi Division Clerk's Office, 521 Starr St, Corpus Christi, TX 78401, 361-888-3142.

www.txs.uscourts.gov

Counties: Aransas, Bee, Brooks, Duval, Jim Wells, Kenedy, Kleberg, Live Oak, Nueces, San Patricio.

Indexing & Storage: Cases are indexed by defendant and plaintiff as well as by case number. New cases are available in the index 3 to 5 days after filing date. A computer index is maintained. Records are also indexed on microfiche. Open records are located at this court.

Fee & Payment: The fee is $15.00 per item (one party name or case number). Payment may be made by money order, cashier check, personal check. Prepayment is required. Payee: Clerk, US District Court. Certification fee: $5.00 per document. Copy fee: $.50 per page.

Phone Search: Searching is not available by phone.

Mail Search: Always enclose a stamped self addressed envelope.

In Person Search: In person searching is available.

PACER: Sign-up number is 800-676-8856. Access fee is $.60 per minute. Toll-free access: 800-998-9037. Local access: 713-250-5046. Case records are available back to June 1990. Records are purged every six months. New records are available online after 1 day. PACER is available on the Internet at http://pacer.txs.uscourts.gov.

Galveston Division Clerk's Office, PO Drawer 2300, Galveston, TX 77553 (Courier Address: 601 Rosenberg, Room 411, Galveston, TX 77550), 409-766-3530.

www.txs.uscourts.gov

Counties: Brazoria, Chambers, Galveston, Matagorda.

Indexing & Storage: Cases are indexed by defendant and plaintiff as well as by case number. New cases are available in the index 1 day after filing date. Both computer and card indexes are maintained. Records are also indexed on microfiche. Open records are located at this court.

Fee & Payment: The fee is $15.00 per item (one party name or case number). Payment may be made by money order, cashier check, business check. Personal checks are not accepted. Prepayment is required. Payee: Clerk, US District Court. Certification fee: $5.00 per document. Copy

fee: $.50 per page. You are allowed to make your own copies. These copies cost $.50 per page.

Phone Search: Only the status of the case and the trial settings will be released over the phone. An automated voice case information service (VCIS) is not available.

Mail Search: Always enclose a stamped self addressed envelope.

In Person Search: In person searching is available.

PACER: Sign-up number is 800-676-8856. Access fee is $.60 per minute. Toll-free access: 800-998-9037. Local access: 713-250-5046. Case records are available back to June 1990. Records are purged every six months. New records are available online after 1 day. PACER is available on the Internet at http://pacer.txs.uscourts.gov.

Houston Division PO Box 61010, Houston, TX 77208 (Courier Address: Room 1217, 515 Rusk, Houston, TX 77002), 713-250-5500.

www.txs.uscourts.gov

Counties: Austin, Brazos, Colorado, Fayette, Fort Bend, Grimes, Harris, Madison, Montgomery, San Jacinto, Walker, Waller, Wharton.

Indexing & Storage: Cases are indexed by defendant and plaintiff as well as by case number. New cases are available in the index 2 days after filing date. Mail searches must be coordinated through the court's copy service (IKON). Call 713-236-0903. They charge $8.12 per search plus $.29 per page for copies. Both computer and card indexes are maintained. Records are also indexed on microfiche. Open records are located at this court. District wide searches are available for information from 1979 forward from this court. Criminal docketing for the district is performed in Houston.

Fee & Payment: The fee is $15.00 per item (one party name or case number). Payment may be made by money order, cashier check, personal check. Prepayment is required. Payee: Clerk, US District Court. Certification fee: $5.00 per document. Copy fee: $.50 per page.

Phone Search: Searching is not available by phone.

In Person Search: In person searching is available.

PACER: Sign-up number is 800-676-8856. Access fee is $.60 per minute. Toll-free access: 800-998-9037. Local access: 713-250-5046. Case records are available back to June 1990. Records are purged every six months. New records are available online after 1 day. PACER is available on the Internet at http://pacer.txs.uscourts.gov.

Laredo Division PO Box 597, Laredo, TX 78042-0597 (Courier Address: Room 319, 1300 Matamoros, Laredo, TX 78040), 956-723-3542, Fax: 956-726-2289.

www.txs.uscourts.gov

Counties: Jim Hogg, La Salle, McMullen, Webb, Zapata.

Indexing & Storage: Cases are indexed by defendant and plaintiff as well as by case number. New cases are available in the index immediately after filing date. The style of the case is needed to search. A computer index is maintained. Open records are located at this court.

Fee & Payment: The fee is $15.00 per item (one party name or case number). Payment may be made by cashier check. Business checks are not accepted. Personal checks are not accepted. Payee:

Clerk, US District Court. Certification fee: $5.00 per document. Copy fee: $.50 per page.

Phone Search: Searching is not available by phone.

Mail Search: A stamped self addressed envelope is not required.

In Person Search: In person searching is available.

PACER: Sign-up number is 800-676-8856. Access fee is $.60 per minute. Toll-free access: 800-998-9037. Local access: 713-250-5046. Case records are available back to June 1990. Records are purged every six months. New records are available online after 1 day. PACER is available on the Internet at http://pacer.txs.uscourts.gov.

McAllen Division Suite 1011, 1701 W Business Hwy 83, McAllen, TX 78501, 956-618-8065.

www.txs.uscourts.gov

Counties: Hidalgo, Starr.

Indexing & Storage: Cases are indexed by defendant and plaintiff as well as by case number. New cases are available in the index 1 day after filing date. Both computer and card indexes are maintained. Open records are located at this court. This court has only been in operation for about 4 years. They have sent no records to the Fort Worth Federal Records Center.

Fee & Payment: The fee is $15.00 per item (one party name or case number). Payment may be made by money order, cashier check, business check. Personal checks are not accepted. Prepayment is required. Payee: Clerk, US District Court. Certification fee: $5.00 per document. Copy fee: $.50 per page.

Phone Search: Only docket information available by phone. An automated voice case information service (VCIS) is not available.

Mail Search: Always enclose a stamped self addressed envelope.

In Person Search: In person searching is available.

PACER: Sign-up number is 800-676-8856. Access fee is $.60 per minute. Toll-free access: 800-998-9037. Local access: 713-250-5046. Case records are available back to June 1990. Records are purged every six months. New records are available online after 1 day. PACER is available on the Internet at http://pacer.txs.uscourts.gov.

Victoria Division Clerk US District Court, PO Box 1638, Victoria, TX 77902 (Courier Address: Room 406, 312 S Main, Victoria, TX 77901), 361-788-5000.

www.txs.uscourts.gov

Counties: Calhoun, De Witt, Goliad, Jackson, Lavaca, Refugio, Victoria.

Indexing & Storage: Cases are indexed by defendant and plaintiff as well as by case number. New cases are available in the index 2 days after filing date. Both computer and card indexes are maintained. Open records are located at this court.

Fee & Payment: The fee is $15.00 per item (one party name or case number). Payment may be made by money order, cashier check, personal check. Prepayment is required. Payee: Clerk, US District Court. Certification fee: $5.00 per document. Copy fee: $.50 per page. You are allowed to make your own copies. These copies cost $.50 per page.

Phone Search: Only docket information is available by phone. An automated voice case information service (VCIS) is not available.

Mail Search: Always enclose a stamped self addressed envelope.

In Person Search: In person searching is available.

PACER: Sign-up number is 800-676-6856. Access fee is $.60 per minute. Toll-free access: 800-998-9037. Local access: 713-250-5046. Case records are available back to June 1990. Records are purged every six months. New records are available online after 1 day. PACER is available on the Internet at http://pacer.txs.uscourts.gov.

US Bankruptcy Court

Southern District of Texas

Corpus Christi Division Room 113, 615 Leopard St, Corpus Christi, TX 78476, 361-888-3484.

www.txs.uscourts.gov

Counties: Aransas, Bee, Brooks, Calhoun, Cameron, Duval, Goliad, Hidalgo, Jackson, Jim Wells, Kenedy, Kleberg, Lavaca, Live Oak, Nueces, Refugio, San Patricio, Starr, Victoria, Willacy.Files from Brownsville, Corpus Christi, and McAllen are maintained here.

Indexing & Storage: Cases are indexed by debtor as well as by case number. New cases are available in the index 1-2 days after filing date. A computer index is maintained. Records are also indexed on microfiche. Open records are located at this court. Until further notice as of 9/1/97, this office will continue to hold case records for the Victoria Division.

Fee & Payment: The fee is $15.00 per item (one party name or case number). Payment may be made by money order, cashier check, personal check. Prepayment is required. Payee: Clerk, US Bankruptcy Court. Certification fee: $5.00 per document. Copy fee: $.50 per page. You are allowed to make your own copies. These copies cost $.25 per page. There are dollar and coin-operated copiers available for public use.

Phone Search: An automated voice case information service (VCIS) is available. Call VCIS at 800-745-4459 or 713-250-5049.

Mail Search: Always enclose a stamped self addressed envelope.

In Person Search: In person searching is available.

PACER: Sign-up number is 800-676-6856. Access fee is $.60 per minute. Toll-free access: 800-998-9037. Local access: 713-250-5046. Case records are available back to June 1, 1991. Records are purged every six months. New civil records are available online after 1-3 days. PACER is available on the Internet at http://pacer.txs.uscourts.gov.

Houston Division Room 1217, 515 Rusk Ave, Houston, TX 77002, 713-250-5500.

www.txs.uscourts.gov

Counties: Austin, Brazoria, Brazos, Chambers, Colorado, De Witt, Fayette, Fort Bend, Galveston, Grimes, Harris, Jim Hogg*, La Salle*, Madison, Matagorda, McMullen*, Montgomery, San Jacinto, Walker,Waller, Wharton, Webb* Zapata*.

Open case records for the counties marked with an asterisk are being moved to the Laredo Division.

Indexing & Storage: Cases are indexed by debtor as well as by case number. New cases are available in the index 1-2 days after filing date. Both computer and card indexes are maintained. Records are also indexed on microfiche. Open records are located at this court. Some case files are maintained here from as early as 1978. Case files for the new Laredo Division are being moved to 1300 Matamoros, Laredo, TX 78040, 956-726-2236 as of 9/1/97.

Fee & Payment: The fee is $15.00 per item (one party name or case number). Payment may be made by money order, cashier check, personal check. Prepayment is required. Payee: Clerk, US Bankruptcy Court. Certification fee: $5.00 per document. Copy fee: $.50 per page.

Phone Search: Only docket information is available by phone. An automated voice case information service (VCIS) is available. Call VCIS at 800-745-4459 or 713-250-5049.

Mail Search: Always enclose a stamped self addressed envelope.

In Person Search: In person searching is available.

PACER: Sign-up number is 800-676-6856. Access fee is $.60 per minute. Toll-free access: 800-998-9037. Local access: 713-250-5046. Case records are available back to June 1, 1991. Records are purged every six months. New civil records are available online after 1-3 days. PACER is available on the Internet at http://pacer.txs.uscourts.gov.

San Antonio Division PO Box 1439, San Antonio, TX 78295 (Courier Address: 615 E Houston St, San Antonio, TX 78205), 210-472-6720, Fax: 210-472-5916.

Counties: Atascosa, Bandera, Bexar, Comal, Dimmit, Edwards, Frio, Gonzales, Guadalupe, Karnes, Kendall, Kerr, Kinney, Maverick, Medina, Real, Terrell, Uvalde, Val Verde, Wilson, Zavala.

Indexing & Storage: Cases are indexed by debtor as well as by case number. New cases are available in the index 24 hours after filing date. A computer index is maintained. Open records are located at this court. District wide searches are available for records within a 10 year span from this division.

Fee & Payment: The fee is $15.00 per item (one party name or case number). Payment may be made by cashier check. Business checks are not accepted, American Express, Visa, or Mastercard. Personal checks are not accepted. You are allowed to make your own copies. These copies cost $.35 per page. There is a copy service on site.

Phone Search: An automated voice case information service (VCIS) is not available. Call VCIS at 888-436-7477 or 210-472-4023.

Mail Search: Always enclose a stamped self addressed envelope.

In Person Search: In person searching is available.

PACER: Sign-up number is 800-676-6856. Access fee is $.60 per minute. Toll-free access: 888-372-5708. Local access: 210-472-6262. Case records are available back to May 1, 1987. Records are purged every 6-8 months. New civil records are available online after 1 day.

US District Court

Western District of Texas

Austin Division Room 130, 200 W 8th St, Austin, TX 78701, 512-916-5896.

www.txwd.uscourts.gov

Counties: Bastrop, Blanco, Burleson, Burnet, Caldwell, Gillespie, Hays, Kimble, Lampasas, Lee, Llano, McCulloch, Mason, San Saba, Travis, Washington, Williamson.

Indexing & Storage: Cases are indexed by defendant and plaintiff as well as by case number. New cases are available in the index 1 day after filing date. A computer index is maintained. Records are also indexed on microfiche. Open records are located at this court.

Fee & Payment: The fee is $15.00 per item (one party name or case number). Payment may be made by money order, cashier check, personal check. Prepayment is required. Payee: Clerk, US District Court. Certification fee: $5.00 per document. Copy fee: $.50 per page. You are allowed to make your own copies. These copies cost $.35 per page.

Phone Search: Only docket information is available by phone. The caller must have the case number. An automated voice case information service (VCIS) is not available.

Mail Search: Always enclose a stamped self addressed envelope.

In Person Search: In person searching is available.

PACER: Sign-up number is 800-676-6856. Access fee is $.60 per minute. Toll-free access: 888-869-6365. Local access: 210-472-5256. Case records are available back to 1994. Records are purged every six months. New records are available online after 1 day. PACER is available on the Internet at http://pacer.txwd.uscourts.gov.

Del Rio Division Room L100, 111 E Broadway, Del Rio, TX 78840, 830-703-2054.

www.txwd.uscourts.gov

Counties: Edwards, Kinney, Maverick, Terrell, Uvalde, Val Verde, Zavala.

Indexing & Storage: Cases are indexed by defendant and plaintiff as well as by case number. New cases are available in the index 1 month after filing date. A computer index is maintained. Open records are located at this court.

Fee & Payment: The fee is $15.00 per item (one party name or case number). Payment may be made by money order, cashier check, personal check. Prepayment is required. Payee: Clerk, US District Court. Certification fee: $5.00 per document. Copy fee: $.50 per page.

Phone Search: Only docket information is available by phone. An automated voice case information service (VCIS) is not available.

Mail Search: Always enclose a stamped self addressed envelope.

In Person Search: In person searching is available.

PACER: Sign-up number is 800-676-6856. Access fee is $.60 per minute. Toll-free access: 888-869-6365. Local access: 210-472-5256. Case records are available back to 1994. Records are purged every six months. New records are available online after 1 day. PACER is available on the Internet at http://pacer.txwd.uscourts.gov.

El Paso Division US District Clerk's Office, Room 350, 511 E San Antonio, El Paso, TX 79901, 915-534-6725.

www.txwd.uscourts.gov

Counties: El Paso.

Indexing & Storage: Cases are indexed by defendant and plaintiff as well as by case number. New cases are available in the index 1-2 days after filing date. Both computer and card indexes are maintained. Microfiche also available. Open records are located at this court.

Fee & Payment: The fee is $15.00 per item (one party name or case number). Payment may be made by money order, cashier check, personal check. Prepayment is required. Payee: Clerk, US District Court. Certification fee: $5.00 per document. Copy fee: $.50 per page. You are allowed to make your own copies. These copies cost $.25 per page.

Phone Search: Only docket information is available by phone. An automated voice case information service (VCIS) is not available.

Mail Search: Always enclose a stamped self addressed envelope.

In Person Search: In person searching is available.

PACER: Sign-up number is 800-676-6856. Access fee is $.60 per minute. Toll-free access: 888-869-6365. Local access: 210-472-5256. Case records are available back to 1994. Records are purged every six months. New records are available online after 1 day. PACER is available on the Internet at http://pacer.txwd.uscourts.gov.

Midland Division Clerk, US District Court, 200 E Wall St, Rm 107, Midland, TX 79701, 915-686-4001.

www.txwd.uscourts.gov

Counties: Andrews, Crane, Ector, Martin, Midland, Upton.

Indexing & Storage: Cases are indexed by defendant and plaintiff as well as by case number. New cases are available in the index immediately after filing date. Both computer and card indexes are maintained. Records are also indexed on microfiche. Open records are located at this court.

Fee & Payment: The fee is $15.00 per item (one party name or case number). Payment may be made by money order, cashier check, personal check. Prepayment is required. Payee: Clerk, US District Court. Certification fee: $5.00 per document. Copy fee: $.50 per page. You are allowed to make your own copies. These copies cost $.25 per page. To do your own copies, you must bring your own change. They will not provide change.

Phone Search: Most information will be released over the phone. An automated voice case information service (VCIS) is not available.

Mail Search: Always enclose a stamped self addressed envelope.

In Person Search: In person searching is available.

PACER: Sign-up number is 800-676-6856. Access fee is $.60 per minute. Toll-free access: 888-869-6365. Local access: 210-472-5256. Case records are available back to 1994. Records are purged every six months. New records are available online after 1 day. PACER is available on the Internet at http://pacer.txwd.uscourts.gov.

Pecos Division US Courthouse, 410 S Cedar St, Pecos, TX 79772, 915-445-4228.

www.txwd.uscourts.gov

Counties: Brewster, Culberson, Hudspeth, Jeff Davis, Loving, Pecos, Presidio, Reeves, Ward, Winkler.

Indexing & Storage: Cases are indexed by defendant and plaintiff as well as by case number. New cases are available in the index immediately after filing date. A card index is maintained. Open records are located at this court.

Fee & Payment: The fee is $15.00 per item (one party name or case number). Payment may be made by money order, cashier check, personal check. Prepayment is required. Debtor's checks are not accepted. Payee: Clerk, US District Court. Certification fee: $5.00 per document. Copy fee: $.50 per page. You are allowed to make your own copies. These copies cost $.25 per page.

Phone Search: Searching is not available by phone.

Mail Search: Always enclose a stamped self addressed envelope.

In Person Search: In person searching is available.

PACER: Sign-up number is 800-676-6856. Access fee is $.60 per minute. Toll-free access: 888-869-6365. Local access: 210-472-5256. Case records are available back to 1994. Records are purged every six months. New records are available online after 1 day. PACER is available on the Internet at http://pacer.txwd.uscourts.gov.

San Antonio Division US Clerk's Office, 655 E Durango, Suite G-65, San Antonio, TX 78206, 210-472-6550.

www.txwd.uscourts.gov

Counties: Atascosa, Bandera, Bexar, Comal, Dimmit, Frio, Gonzales, Guadalupe, Karnes, Kendall, Kerr, Medina, Real, Wilson.

Indexing & Storage: Cases are indexed by defendant and plaintiff as well as by case number. New cases are available in the index 1-2 days after filing date. A computer index is maintained. Records are also indexed on microfiche. Open records are located at this court.

Fee & Payment: The fee is $15.00 per item (one party name or case number). Payment may be made by money order, cashier check, personal check. Prepayment is required. Payee: Clerk, US District Court. Certification fee: $5.00 per document. Copy fee: $.50 per page. You are allowed to make your own copies. These copies cost $.35 per page.

Phone Search: Only docket information is available by phone. An automated voice case information service (VCIS) is not available.

Mail Search: Always enclose a stamped self addressed envelope.

In Person Search: In person searching is available.

PACER: Sign-up number is 800-676-6856. Access fee is $.60 per minute. Toll-free access: 888-869-6365. Local access: 210-472-5256. Case records are available back to 1994. Records are purged every six months. New records are available online after 1 day. PACER is available on the Internet at http://pacer.txwd.uscourts.gov.

Waco Division Clerk, PO Box 608, Waco, TX 76703 (Courier Address: Room 303, 800 Franklin, Waco, TX 76701), 254-750-1501.

www.txwd.uscourts.gov

Counties: Bell, Bosque, Coryell, Falls, Freestone, Hamilton, Hill, Leon, Limestone, McLennan, Milam, Robertson, Somervell.

Indexing & Storage: Cases are indexed by defendant and plaintiff as well as by case number. New cases are available in the index 1-2 days after filing date. A card index is maintained. Open records are located at this court.

Fee & Payment: The fee is $15.00 per item (one party name or case number). Payment may be made by money order, cashier check, personal check. Prepayment is required. Payee: Clerk, US District Court. Certification fee: $5.00 per document. Copy fee: $.50 per page. You are allowed to make your own copies. These copies cost $.25 per page.

Phone Search: Only docket information is available by phone. An automated voice case information service (VCIS) is not available.

Mail Search: Always enclose a stamped self addressed envelope.

In Person Search: In person searching is available.

PACER: Sign-up number is 800-676-6856. Access fee is $.60 per minute. Toll-free access: 888-869-6365. Local access: 210-472-5256. Case records are available back to 1994. Records are purged every six months. New records are available online after 1 day. PACER is available on the Internet at http://pacer.txwd.uscourts.gov.

US Bankruptcy Court

Western District of Texas

Austin Division Homer Thornberry Judicial Bldg, 903 San Antonio, Room 322, Austin, TX 78701, 512-916-5237.

www.txwb.uscourts.gov

Counties: Bastrop, Blanco, Burleson, Burnet, Caldwell, Gillespie, Hays, Kimble, Lampasas, Lee, Llano, Mason, McCulloch, San Saba, Travis, Washington, Williamson.

Indexing & Storage: Cases are indexed by debtor and creditors as well as by case number. New cases are available in the index 24 hours after filing date. A computer index is maintained. Records are also indexed on microfiche. Open records are located at this court.

Fee & Payment: The fee is $15.00 per item (one party name or case number). Payment may be made by money order, cashier check, personal check, Visa or Mastercard. Prepayment is required. Debtor's checks are not accepted. Payee: US Bankruptcy Court. Certification fee: $5.00 per document. Copy fee: $.50 per page. You are allowed to make your own copies. These copies cost $.25 per page. Xerox copy service available in lobby. Fee is $.25 per page plus tax.

Phone Search: Only docket information is available by phone. An automated voice case information service (VCIS) is available. Call VCIS at 888-436-7477 or 210-472-4023.

Mail Search: Always enclose a stamped self addressed envelope.

County Court PO Box 250, Waxahachie, TX 75168; 972-923-5070. Hours: 8AM-4:45PM (CST). *Misdemeanor, Civil, Probate.*

Civil Records: Access: Mail, in person. Both court and visitors may perform in person searches. Search fee: $10.00 per name. Fee is per 5 year period. Required to search: name, years to search. Civil cases indexed by defendant, plaintiff. Civil records on computer in 1995. **Criminal Records:** Access: Mail, in person. Both court and visitors may perform in person searches. Search fee: $10.00 per name. Fee is per 5 year period. Required to search: name, years to search. Criminal records on computer since 1992, index books from 1965. **General Information:** No juvenile, mental, sealed, or adoption records released. SASE required. Turnaround time 1-5 days. Copy fee: $1.00 per page. Certification fee: $5.00. Fee payee: Ellis County Clerk. Personal checks accepted. Prepayment is required. Public access terminal is available.

Erath County

District Court 112 W College, Courthouse Annex, Stephenville, TX 76401; 254-965-1486; Fax: 254-965-7156. Hours: 8AM-Noon, 1-5PM (CST). *Felony, Civil.*

Civil Records: Access: Mail, in person. Both court and visitors may perform in person searches. Search fee: $5.00 per name. Fee is per name per search. Required to search: name, years to search. Civil cases indexed by defendant, plaintiff. Civil records on computer last 10 years, index books and archived from 1900. **Criminal Records:** Access: Mail, in person. Both court and visitors may perform in person searches. Search fee: $5.00 per name. Required to search: name, years to search, DOB; also helpful-SSN. Criminal records on computer last 10 years, index books and archived from 1900. **General Information:** No juvenile, mental, sealed, or adoption records released. SASE required. Turnaround time 1-2 days. Copy fee: $1.00 per page. Certification fee: $5.00. Fee payee: District Clerk. Personal checks accepted. Prepayment is required.

County Court Erath County Courthouse, Stephenville, TX 76401; 254-965-1482. Hours: 8AM-Noon, 1-5PM (CST). *Misdemeanor, Civil, Probate.*

Civil Records: Access: Mail, in person. Both court and visitors may perform in person searches. Search fee: $5.00 per name. Required to search: name, years to search. Civil cases indexed by defendant, plaintiff. Civil records on computer since 1993, index books since 1970. **Criminal Records:** Access: Mail, in person. Both court and visitors may perform in person searches. Search fee: $5.00 per name. Required to search: name, years to search, DOB. Criminal records on computer since 1993, index books from 1960. **General Information:** No juvenile, mental, sealed, or adoption records released. SASE required. Turnaround time 1 week. Copy fee: $1.00 per page. Certification fee: $5.00. Fee payee: County Clerk. Personal checks accepted. Prepayment is required.

Falls County

District Court 3rd Floor, PO Box 229, Marlin, TX 76661; 254-883-1419(district); 883-1408(county). Hours: 8AM-Noon, 1-5PM (CST). *Felony, Civil.*

Civil Records: Access: Mail, in person. Both court and visitors may perform in person searches. Search fee: $5.00 per name. Required to search:

name, years to search. Civil cases indexed by defendant, plaintiff. Civil records in index books. **Criminal Records:** Access: Mail, in person. Both court and visitors may perform in person searches. Search fee: $5.00 per name. Required to search: name, years to search; also helpful-DOB. Criminal records in index books. **General Information:** No juvenile, mental, sealed, child support or adoption records released. SASE required. Turnaround time 1-5 days. Copy fee: $1.00 per page. Certification fee: No certification fee. Fee payee: District Clerk. Personal checks accepted. Prepayment is required.

County Court PO Box 458, Marlin, TX 76661; 254-883-1408. Hours: 8AM-5PM (CST). *Misdemeanor, Civil, Probate.*

Civil Records: Access: Phone, mail, in person. Both court and visitors may perform in person searches. Search fee: $5.00 per name. Required to search: name, years to search. Civil cases indexed by defendant, plaintiff. Civil records in index books from 1985. Phone search only available if fee prepaid. **Criminal Records:** Access: Phone, mail, in person. Both court and visitors may perform in person searches. Search fee: $5.00 per name. Required to search: name, years to search. Criminal records in index books from 1985. Phone search only available if fee prepaid. **General Information:** No juvenile, mental, sealed, or adoption records released. SASE required. Turnaround time 1 day. Copy fee: $1.00 per page. Certification fee: $5.00. Fee payee: County Clerk. Business checks accepted. Local personal and business checks accepted. Prepayment is required.

Fannin County

District Court Fannin County Courthouse Ste 201, Bonham, TX 75418; 903-583-7459 X33; Fax: 903-640-1826. Hours: 8AM-Noon, 1-5PM (CST). *Felony, Civil.*

Civil Records: Access: Fax, mail, in person. Both court and visitors may perform in person searches. Search fee: $5.00 per name. Required to search: name, years to search. Civil cases indexed by defendant, plaintiff. Civil records in index books, archived from 1865. **Criminal Records:** Access: Fax, mail, in person. Both court and visitors may perform in person searches. Search fee: $5.00 per name. Fee is for felonies only. Required to search: name, years to search, address, DOB, SSN. Criminal records on computer from 1985, books from 1975, archived from 1865. **General Information:** No juvenile, mental, sealed, or adoption records released. SASE required. Turnaround time 2 days. Copy fee: $1.00 per page. Certification fee: No certification fee. Fee payee: District Clerk, Fannin County. Personal checks accepted. Prepayment is required. Fax notes: No fee to fax results. Fax available to 800 numbers only.

County Court County Courthouse, 101 E Sam Rayburn Ste 102, Bonham, TX 75418; 903-583-7486; Fax: 903-583-7811. Hours: 8AM-5PM (CST). *Misdemeanor, Civil, Probate.*

Civil Records: Access: Phone, mail, in person. Both court and visitors may perform in person searches. Search fee: $5.00 per name. Required to search: name, years to search. Civil cases indexed by defendant, plaintiff. Civil records in index books. **Criminal Records:** Access: Phone, mail, in person. Both court and visitors may perform in person searches. Search fee: $5.00 per name. Required to search: name, years to search. Criminal records in index books. Phone search limited to 1 year. **General Information:** No juvenile, mental, sealed, or adoption records

released. SASE required. Turnaround time 1 day. Copy fee: $1.00 per page. Certification fee: $5.00. Fee payee: County Clerk. Personal checks accepted. Prepayment is required.

Fayette County

District Court Fayette County Courthouse, 151 N Washington, La Grange, TX 78945; 979-968-3548; Fax: 979-968-8621. Hours: 8AM-5PM (CST). *Felony, Civil.*

Civil Records: Access: Mail, in person. Both court and visitors may perform in person searches. Search fee: $5.00 per name. Required to search: name, years to search. Civil cases indexed by defendant, plaintiff. Civil records in index books. **Criminal Records:** Access: Mail, in person. Both court and visitors may perform in person searches. Search fee: $5.00 per name. Required to search: name, years to search. Criminal records in index books. **General Information:** No juvenile, mental, sealed, or adoption records released. SASE required. Turnaround time 2-3 days. Copy fee: $1.00 per page. Certification fee: $2.00. Fee payee: Fayette County District Clerk. Personal checks accepted. Prepayment is required.

County Court PO Box 59, La Grange, TX 78945; 979-968-3251. Hours: 8AM-5PM (CST). *Misdemeanor, Civil, Probate.*

Civil Records: Access: Phone, mail, in person. Both court and visitors may perform in person searches. Search fee: $5.00 per name. Required to search: name, years to search. Civil cases indexed by defendant, plaintiff. Civil records in index books, archived from 1970. **Criminal Records:** Access: Phone, mail, in person. Both court and visitors may perform in person searches. Search fee: $5.00 per name. Required to search: name, years to search. Criminal records on computer from 1980, index books prior. **General Information:** No juvenile, mental, sealed, or adoption records released. SASE required. Turnaround time 1 day. Copy fee: $1.00 per page. Certification fee: $5.00 plus $1.00 per page. Fee payee: County Clerk. Personal checks accepted. Prepayment is required.

Fisher County

32nd District Court PO Box 88, Roby, TX 79543; 915-776-2279; Fax: 915-776-2815. Hours: 8AM-5PM (CST). *Felony, Civil.*

Civil Records: Access: Mail, in person. Both court and visitors may perform in person searches. Search fee: $10.00 per name. Required to search: name, years to search; also helpful-address. Civil cases indexed by defendant, plaintiff. Civil records in index books from 1886. **Criminal Records:** Access: Mail, in person. Both court and visitors may perform in person searches. Search fee: $10.00 per name. Required to search: name, years to search, signed release; also helpful-address, DOB. Criminal records in index books from 1886. **General Information:** No juvenile, mental, sealed, or adoption records released. SASE required. Turnaround time 1-2 days. Copy fee: $1.00 per page. Certification fee: $1.00. Fee payee: District Clerk. Business checks accepted. Prepayment is required.

County Court Box 368, Roby, TX 79543-0368; 915-776-2401. Hours: 8AM-Noon, 1-5PM (CST). *Misdemeanor, Civil, Probate.*

Civil Records: Access: Mail, in person. Both court and visitors may perform in person searches. Search fee: $5.00 per name. Required to search: name, years to search. Civil cases indexed by defendant, plaintiff. Civil records on computer from 1991, index books from 1880. **Criminal Records:** Access: Mail, in person. Both court and visitors may perform in person searches. Search fee: $5.00 per name. Required to search: name, years to search, signed release, offense. Criminal records on computer from from 1989, index books from 1880. **General Information:** No juvenile, mental, sealed, or adoption records released. SASE required. Turnaround time 1 day. Copy fee: $1.00 per page. Certification fee: $5.00. Fee payee: Fisher County Clerk. Personal checks accepted. Prepayment is required.

Floyd County

District Court PO Box 67, Floydada, TX 79235; 806-983-4923. Hours: 8:30AM-Noon, 1-4:45PM (CST). *Felony, Civil.*

Civil Records: Access: Phone, mail, in person. Both court and visitors may perform in person searches. Search fee: $5.00 per name. Required to search: name, years to search. Civil cases indexed by defendant, plaintiff. Civil records in index books from early 1900s. **Criminal Records:** Access: Mail, in person. Both court and visitors may perform in person searches. Search fee: $5.00 per name. Required to search: name, years to search. Criminal records in index books from early 1900s. **General Information:** No juvenile, mental, sealed, or adoption records released. SASE required. Turnaround time 1 day. Copy fee: $.25 per page. Certification fee: $1.00. Fee payee: District Clerk. Personal checks accepted. Prepayment is required.

County Court Courthouse, Rm 101, Main Street, Floydada, TX 79235; 806-983-4900. Hours: 8:30AM-Noon, 1-5PM (CST). *Misdemeanor, Civil, Probate.*

Civil Records: Access: Phone, mail, in person. Both court and visitors may perform in person searches. Search fee: $10.00 per name. Required to search: name, years to search. Civil cases indexed by defendant, plaintiff. Civil records in index books from 1897. **Criminal Records:** Access: Phone, mail, in person. Both court and visitors may perform in person searches. Search fee: $10.00 per name. Required to search: name, years to search, DOB. Criminal records in index books from 1897. **General Information:** No juvenile, mental, sealed, or adoption records released. SASE not required. Turnaround time 1-5 days. Copy fee: $1.00 per page. Certification fee: $5.00. Fee payee: County Clerk. Personal checks accepted. Prepayment is required.

Foard County

District & County Court PO Box 539, Crowell, TX 79227; 940-684-1365. Hours: 9AM-4:30PM (CST). *Felony, Misdemeanor, Civil, Eviction, Probate.*

Civil Records: Access: Mail, in person. Both court and visitors may perform in person searches. Search fee: $10.00 per name. Required to search: name, years to search. Civil cases indexed by defendant, plaintiff. Civil records in index books from 1910. **Criminal Records:** Access: Mail, in person. Both court and visitors may perform in person searches. Search fee: $10.00 per name. Required to search: name, years to search, DOB. Criminal records in index books from 1910. **General Information:** No juvenile, mental, sealed, or adoption records released. SASE required. Turnaround time varies. Copy fee: $1.00 per page. Certification fee: $5.00. Fee payee: District or County Clerk. Personal checks accepted. Prepayment is required.

Fort Bend County

District Court 301 Jackson, Richmond, TX 77469; 281-341-4515; Civil phone:281-341-4562; Criminal phone:281-341-4562; Fax: 281-341-4519. Hours: 8AM-5PM (CST). *Felony, Civil.*

www.co.fort-bend.tx.us/distclerk/index.html

Note: Physical court location is 401 Jackson

Civil Records: Access: Phone, mail, online, in person. Both court and visitors may perform in person searches. Search fee: $5.00 per name. Required to search: name, years to search. Civil cases indexed by defendant, plaintiff. Civil records on computer from 1991, index books from early 1900s. Online searching available through a 900 number service. The access fee is $.55 per minute plus a deposit. Call 281-341-4522 for information. **Criminal Records:** Access: Phone, mail, remote online, in person. Both court and visitors may perform in person searches. Search fee: $5.00 per name. Required to search: name, years to search, DOB, SSN. Criminal records on computer from 1981, index books from early 1900s. Criminal records from 1987 are available on the same online system described in civil records. **General Information:** No juvenile, mental, sealed, termination or adoption records released. SASE required. Turnaround time 2-3 weeks. Copy fee: $.50 per page. Include $1.00 for postage. Fee for microfilm copies $1.00 1st page, $.25 each additional page. Certification fee: No certification. Fee payee: District Clerk. Personal checks accepted. For legal ease account info call 281-341-4508. Prepayment is required. Public access terminal is available. Public Access Terminal Note: Located at 401 Jackson, Rm 100, Richmond, TX 77469.

County Court 301 Jackson St, Richmond, TX 77469; 281-341-8685; Fax: 281-341-4520. Hours: 8AM-4PM (CST). *Misdemeanor, Civil, Probate.*

www.co.fort-bend.tx.us

Note: Plans are to have the record index on the Internet by 03/00

Civil Records: Access: Mail, online, in person. Both court and visitors may perform in person searches. Search fee: $10.00 per name. Search fee is for each type record to be searched. Required to search: name, years to search. Civil cases indexed by defendant, plaintiff. Civil records on computer from 1986, microfiche from 1983-1994, 1994 optical imaged. Index only pre-1994. **Criminal Records:** Access: Mail, remote online, in person. Both court and visitors may perform in person searches. Search fee: $10.00 per name. A search fee for each type record to be searched required. Required to search: name, years to search, DOB. Criminal records on computer from 1983, microfiche from 1983-1994, 1994 optical imaged. Index only pre-1994. **General Information:** No juvenile, mental, sealed, or adoption records released. SASE not required. Turnaround time 1-2 days. Copy fee: $1.00 per page. Certification fee: $5.00. Fee payee: County Clerk. Personal checks accepted. Credit cards accepted: Visa, Mastercard. Prepayment is required. Public access terminal is available.

Franklin County

District Court PO Box 68, Mount Vernon, TX 75457; 903-537-4786. Hours: 8AM-5PM (CST). *Felony, Civil.*

Civil Records: Access: Mail, in person. Both court and visitors may perform in person searches. Search fee: $5.00 per name. Required to search: name, years to search. Civil cases indexed by

defendant, plaintiff. Civil records on computer from 1987, on microfiche from 1986, index books from 1800s. **Criminal Records:** Access: Mail, in person. Both court and visitors may perform in person searches. Search fee: $5.00 per name. Required to search: name, years to search; also helpful-DOB, SSN. Criminal records on computer from 1987, on microfiche from 1986, index books from 1800s. **General Information:** No juvenile, mental, sealed, or adoption records released. SASE required. Turnaround time 1 day. Copy fee: $1.00 per page. Certification fee: $5.00. Fee payee: District Clerk. Personal checks accepted. Prepayment is required.

County Court PO Box 68, Mount Vernon, TX 75457; 903-537-4252; Fax: 903-537-2418. Hours: 8AM-5PM (CST). *Misdemeanor, Civil, Probate.*

Civil Records: Access: Mail, in person. Both court and visitors may perform in person searches. Search fee: $5.00 per name. Required to search: name, years to search. Civil cases indexed by defendant, plaintiff. Civil records on computer from 1987, index books from 1847. **Criminal Records:** Access: Mail, in person. Both court and visitors may perform in person searches. Search fee: $5.00 per name. Required to search: name, years to search. Criminal records on computer from 1987, index books from 1847. **General Information:** No juvenile, mental, sealed, or adoption records released. SASE required. Turnaround time 1 day. Copy fee: $1.00 per page. Certification fee: $5.00 plus $1.00 per page. Fee payee: County Clerk. Personal checks accepted. Prepayment is required.

Freestone County

District Court PO Box 722, Fairfield, TX 75840; 903-389-2534. Hours: 8AM-5PM (CST). *Felony, Civil.*

Civil Records: Access: Mail, in person. Both court and visitors may perform in person searches. Search fee: $5.00 per name. Required to search: name, years to search. Civil cases indexed by defendant, plaintiff. Civil records in index books from 1800s. **Criminal Records:** Access: Mail, in person. Both court and visitors may perform in person searches. Search fee: $5.00 per name. Required to search: name, years to search. Criminal records in index books from 1800s. **General Information:** No juvenile, mental, sealed, or adoption records released. SASE required. Turnaround time 1 day. Copy fee: $1.00 per page. Certification fee: $1.00. Fee payee: District Clerk. Personal checks accepted.

County Court PO Box 1017, Fairfield, TX 75840; 903-389-2635. Hours: 8AM-5PM (CST). *Misdemeanor, Civil, Probate.*

Civil Records: Access: Mail, in person. Both court and visitors may perform in person searches. Search fee: $5.00 per name. Required to search: name, years to search. Civil cases indexed by defendant, plaintiff. Civil records in index books from 1967. **Criminal Records:** Access: Mail, in person. Both court and visitors may perform in person searches. Search fee: $5.00 per name. Required to search: name, years to search. Criminal records in index books from 1967. **General Information:** No juvenile, mental, sealed, or adoption records released. SASE required. Turnaround time 2 days. Copy fee: $1.00 per page. Certification fee: $5.00. Fee payee: Freestone County Clerk. Personal checks accepted. Prepayment is required.

Frio County

District Court 500 E San Antonio Box 8, Pearsall, TX 78061; 830-334-8073; Fax: 830-334-0047. Hours: 8AM-5PM (CST). *Felony, Civil.*

Civil Records: Access: Mail, in person. Both court and visitors may perform in person searches. Search fee: $5.00 per name. Required to search: name, years to search; also helpful-address. Civil cases indexed by defendant, plaintiff. Civil records in index books from 1890s. **Criminal Records:** Access: Mail, in person. Both court and visitors may perform in person searches. Search fee: $5.00 per name. Required to search: name, years to search, DOB; also helpful-address. Criminal records in index books from 1890s. **General Information:** No juvenile, mental, sealed, or adoption records released. SASE required. Turnaround time 2-3 days. Copy fee: $1.00 per page. Certification fee: $1.00. Fee payee: District Clerk. Business checks accepted. Prepayment is required.

County Court 500 E San Antonio St #6, Pearsall, TX 78061; 830-334-2214; Fax: 830-334-0021. Hours: 8AM-5PM (CST). *Misdemeanor, Civil, Probate.*

Civil Records: Access: Fax, mail, in person. Both court and visitors may perform in person searches. Search fee: $5.00 per name. Required to search: name, years to search. Civil cases indexed by defendant, plaintiff. Civil records in index books from 1876. **Criminal Records:** Access: Fax, mail, in person. Both court and visitors may perform in person searches. Search fee: $5.00 per name. Required to search: name, years to search. Criminal records in index books from 1876. **General Information:** No juvenile, mental, sealed, or adoption records released. SASE required. Turnaround time 2-4 days. Copy fee: $1.00 per page. Certification fee: $5.00. Fee payee: County Clerk. Personal checks accepted. Prepayment is required. Fax notes: $2.00 per page.

Gaines County

District Court 101 S Main Rm 213, Seminole, TX 79360; 915-758-4013; Fax: 915-758-4036. Hours: 8AM-Noon, 1-5PM (CST). *Felony, Civil.*

Civil Records: Access: Phone, mail, in person. Only the court conducts in person searches; visitors may not. Search fee: $5.00 per name. Required to search: name, years to search. Civil cases indexed by defendant, plaintiff. Civil records on computer from 1980, index books from 1900s. **Criminal Records:** Access: Phone, mail, in person. Only the court conducts in person searches; visitors may not. Search fee: $5.00 per name. Required to search: name, years to search. Criminal records on computer from 1980, index books from 1900s. **General Information:** No juvenile, mental, sealed, or adoption records released. SASE required. Turnaround time 1 day. Copy fee: $1.00 per page. Certification fee: No certification fee. Fee payee: District Clerk. Personal checks accepted. Prepayment is required.

County Court 101 S Main Rm 107, Seminole, TX 79360; 915-758-4003. Hours: 8AM-5PM (CST). *Misdemeanor, Civil, Probate.*

Civil Records: Access: Mail, in person. Both court and visitors may perform in person searches. No search fee. Required to search: name, years to search. Civil cases indexed by defendant, plaintiff. **Criminal Records:** Access: Mail, in person. Both court and visitors may perform in person searches. No search fee. Required to search: name, years to search. **General Information:** No juvenile,

mental, sealed, or adoption records released. SASE required. Turnaround time 1 day. Copy fee: $1.00 per page. Certification fee: $1.00. Fee payee: County Clerk. Personal checks accepted. Prepayment is required.

Galveston County

District Court 722 Moody St Rm 404, Galveston, TX 77550; 409-766-2424; Fax: 409-766-2292. Hours: 8AM-5PM (CST). *Felony, Civil.*

Civil Records: Access: Fax, mail, in person. Search fee: $5.00 per name. Required to search: name, years to search. Civil cases indexed by defendant, plaintiff. Civil records on computer from 1982, on microfiche from 1982, archived from 1849. Fax access is only allowed with prepaid accounts. **Criminal Records:** Access: Fax, mail, in person. Both court and visitors may perform in person searches. Search fee: $5.00 per name. Required to search: name, years to search, DOB. Criminal records on computer from 1982, on microfiche from 1982, archived from 1849. **General Information:** No juvenile, mental, sealed, or adoption records released. SASE required. Turnaround time 2-5 days. Copy fee: $1.00 per page. Certification fee: $1.00. Fee payee: District Clerk. Personal checks accepted. Prepayment is required. Public access terminal is available.

County Court PO Box 2450, Galveston, TX 77553-2450;; Civil phone:409-766-2203; Criminal phone:409-766-2203; Probate phone:409-766-2022. Hours: 8AM-5PM (CST). *Misdemeanor, Civil, Probate.*

Civil Records: Access: Mail, online, in person. Both court and visitors may perform in person searches. Search fee: $5.00 per name. Required to search: name, years to search. Civil cases indexed by defendant, plaintiff. Civil records on computer from 1984, index books from 1942. A $200 escrow account is required to open online access. The fee is $.25 per minute. The system is available 24 hours daily and gives fax back capability. For more information about GCNET call Robert Dickinson at 409-770-5115. **Criminal Records:** Access: Mail, remote online, in person. Both court and visitors may perform in person searches. Search fee: $5.00 per name. Required to search: name, years to search, DOB. Criminal records on computer from 1984, index books from 1942. Online access is through the GCNET systems as described in civil records. **General Information:** No juvenile, mental, sealed, or adoption records released. SASE required. Turnaround time 1-2 days. Copy fee: $1.00 per page. Certification fee: $5.00. Fee payee: County Clerk. Personal checks accepted. Checks are accepted with mail requests only. Prepayment is required. Public access terminal is available.

Probate Court PO Box 2450, Galveston, TX 77553-2450; 409-766-2202. Hours: 8AM-5PM (CST). *Probate.*

Garza County

District & County Court PO Box 366, Post, TX 79356; 806-495-4430; Fax: 806-495-4431. Hours: 8AM-Noon,1-5PM (CST). *Felony, Misdemeanor, Civil, Eviction, Probate.*

Civil Records: Access: Mail, in person. Both court and visitors may perform in person searches. Search fee: $5.00 per name. Required to search: name, years to search. Civil cases indexed by defendant, plaintiff. Civil records on index books. **Criminal Records:** Access: Mail, in person. Both

court and visitors may perform in person searches. Search fee: $5.00 per name. Required to search: name, years to search. Criminal records on index books. **General Information:** No criminal records released. Turnaround time 2-3 days. Copy fee: $1.00 per page. Certification fee: $5.00. Fee payee: District or County Clerk. Personal checks accepted. Prepayment is required.

Gillespie County

District Court 101 W Main Rm 204, Fredericksburg, TX 78624; 830-997-6517. Hours: Public hours 8AM-Noon, 1-4PM (CST). *Felony, Civil.*

Civil Records: Access: Mail, in person. Both court and visitors may perform in person searches. Search fee: $5.00 per name. Required to search: name, years to search. Civil cases indexed by defendant, plaintiff. Civil records in index books from 1800s. Index #1 from 1800s-1927, Index #2 from 1927-1988, Index #3 from 1989-present. **Criminal Records:** Access: Mail, in person. Both court and visitors may perform in person searches. Search fee: $5.00 per name. Required to search: name, years to search; also helpful-DOB, SSN. Criminal records in index books from 1800s. Index #1 from 1800s-1927, Index #2 from 1927-1988, Index #3 from 1989-present. **General Information:** No juvenile, mental, sealed, or adoption records released. SASE required. Turnaround time 1-2 days. Copy fee: $1.00 for first page, $.25 each addl. Certification fee: $1.00 per page. Fee payee: Gillespie County District Clerk. Personal checks accepted. Prepayment is required.

County Court 101 W Main Unit #13, Fredericksburg, TX 78624; 830-997-6515; Fax: 830-997-9958. Hours: 8AM-4PM (CST). *Misdemeanor, Civil, Probate.*

Civil Records: Access: Mail, in person. Both court and visitors may perform in person searches. Search fee: $5.00 per name. Required to search: name, years to search; also helpful-address. Civil cases indexed by defendant, plaintiff. Civil records on computer from 1988, on microfiche from 1990, index books from 1900s. **Criminal Records:** Access: Mail, in person. Both court and visitors may perform in person searches. Search fee: $5.00 per name. Required to search: name, years to search, aliases; also helpful-DOB, SSN. Criminal records on computer from 1988, on microfiche from 1990, index books from 1900s. **General Information:** No juvenile, mental, sealed, or adoption record released. SASE required. Turnaround time 1-2 days. Copy fee: $1.00 per page. Certification fee: $10.00. Fee payee: Debbie Wahl County Clerk. No out-of-town checks accepted. Prepayment is required.

Glasscock County

District & County Court PO Box 190, 117 E Currie, Garden City, TX 79739; 915-354-2371. Hours: 8AM-4PM (CST). *Felony, Misdemeanor, Civil, Probate.*

Civil Records: Access: Mail, in person. Both court and visitors may perform in person searches. Search fee: $10.00 per name. Required to search: name, years to search. Civil cases indexed by defendant, plaintiff. Civil records in index books from 1893. **Criminal Records:** Access: Mail, in person. Both court and visitors may perform in person searches. Search fee: $10.00 per name. Required to search: name, years to search, signed release. Criminal records in index books from 1893. **General Information:** No juvenile, mental, or adoption records released. SASE required.

Turnaround time 2 days. Copy fee: $1.00 per page. Certification fee: $5.00. Fee payee: District or County Clerk. Personal checks accepted. Prepayment is required.

Goliad County

District & County Court PO Box 50127, North Courthouse Square, Goliad, TX 77963; 361-645-2443/3294; Fax: 361-645-3858. Hours: 8AM-5PM (CST). *Felony, Misdemeanor, Civil, Probate.*

Civil Records: Access: Mail, fax, in person. Both court and visitors may perform in person searches. Search fee: $5.00 per name. Fee is per court. Required to search: name, years to search; also helpful-address. Civil cases indexed by defendant, plaintiff. Civil records on computer since 1983 (real property only), on microfiche and index books from 1870. **Criminal Records:** Access: Mail, fax, in person. Both court and visitors may perform in person searches. Search fee: $5.00 per name. Fee is per court. Required to search: name, years to search; also helpful-address, DOB, SSN, offense. Criminal records on microfiche and index books from 1870. **General Information:** No juvenile, mental, sealed, or adoption records released. SASE not required. Turnaround time 1-2 days. Copy fee: $1.00 per page. Certification fee: Certification: Fee is $5.00 for County Court; $1.00 for District Court. Plus $1.00 per page. Fee payee: Goliad County/District Clerk. Personal checks accepted. Prepayment is required.

Gonzales County

District Court PO Box 34, Gonzales, TX 78629-0034; 830-672-2326; Fax: 830-672-9313. Hours: 8AM-Noon 1-5PM (CST). *Felony, Civil.*

Civil Records: Access: Phone, fax, mail, in person. Both court and visitors may perform in person searches. Search fee: $5.00 per name. Required to search: name, years to search; also helpful-address. Civil cases indexed by defendant, plaintiff. Civil records on computer from 1991, index books from 1800s. **Criminal Records:** Access: Phone, fax, mail, in person. Both court and visitors may perform in person searches. Search fee: $5.00 per name. Required to search: name, years to search; also helpful-address, DOB, SSN. Criminal records on computer from 1991, index books from 1800s. **General Information:** No juvenile, mental, sealed, or adoption records released. SASE required. Turnaround time 1-2 days. Copy fee: $1.00 per page. Certification fee: No certification fee. Fee payee: District Clerk. Personal checks accepted. Fax notes: $5.00 for first page, $1.00 each addl.

County Court PO Box 77, Gonzales, TX 78629; 830-672-2801; Fax: 830-672-2636. Hours: 8AM-5PM (CST). *Misdemeanor, Civil, Probate.*

Civil Records: Access: Fax, mail, in person. Both court and visitors may perform in person searches. Search fee: $5.00 per name. Required to search: name, years to search. Civil cases indexed by defendant, plaintiff. Civil records on computer since 1993, original jackets since 1975, index books from 1900s. **Criminal Records:** Access: Mail, in person. Both court and visitors may perform in person searches. Search fee: $5.00 per name. Required to search: name, years to search, offense, date of offense. Criminal records on computer since 1993, original jackets, index books from 1900s. **General Information:** No mental or drug dependant commitment records released. SASE required. Turnaround time 1-2 days. Copy fee: $1.00 per page. Certification fee: $5.00. Fee

payee: County Clerk. Personal checks accepted. Prepayment is required. Fax notes: $5.00.

Gray County

District Court PO Box 1139, Pampa, TX 79066-1139; 806-669-8010; Fax: 806-669-8053. Hours: 8:30AM-5PM (CST). *Felony, Civil.*

Civil Records: Access: Fax, mail, in person. Both court and visitors may perform in person searches. Search fee: $5.00 per name. Required to search: name, years to search. Civil cases indexed by defendant, plaintiff. Civil records on computer from 1965, index books from 1910. All requests must be in writing. **Criminal Records:** Access: Fax, mail, in person. Both court and visitors may perform in person searches. Search fee: $5.00 per name. Required to search: name, years to search; also helpful-DOB, SSN. Criminal records on computer from 1930. All requests must be in writing. **General Information:** No juvenile, mental, sealed, or adoption records released. SASE required. Turnaround time 1-2 days. Copy fee: $.25 per page. Certification fee: $1.00 per page. Fee payee: District Clerk. Personal checks accepted. Prepayment is required. Fax notes: $1.00 per page.

County & Probate COurt PO Box 1902, Pampa, TX 79066-1902; 806-669-8004; Fax: 806-669-8054. Hours: 8:30AM-5PM (CST). *Misdemeanor, Civil, Probate.*

Grayson County

District Court 200 S Crockett Rm 120-A, Sherman, TX 75090; 903-813-4352. Hours: 8AM-5PM (CST). *Felony, Civil.*

Civil Records: Access: Mail, in person. Both court and visitors may perform in person searches. Search fee: $5.00 per name. Required to search: name, years to search. Civil cases indexed by defendant, plaintiff. Civil records on computer from 1988, microfilm since 1939, index books since 1900s. **Criminal Records:** Access: Mail, in person. Both court and visitors may perform in person searches. Search fee: $5.00 per name. Required to search: name, years to search, DOB; also helpful-SSN. Criminal records on compter since 1988, microfilm since 1939, index books since 1900s. **General Information:** No juvenile, mental, sealed, expunction or adoption records released. SASE required. Turnaround time 1-2 days. Copy fee: $1.00 per page. Certification fee: $2.00. Fee payee: District Clerk. Personal checks accepted. Prepayment is required. Public access terminal is available.

County Court 200 S Crockett, Sherman, TX 75090; 903-813-4336; Fax: 903-892-8300. Hours: 8AM-5PM (CST). *Misdemeanor, Civil, Probate.*

www.co.grayson.tx.us

Civil Records: Access: Mail, in person, online. Both court and visitors may perform in person searches. Search fee: $5.00 per name. Required to search: name, years to search. Civil cases indexed by defendant, plaintiff. Civil records on computer since 1992, index books since 1952. **Criminal Records:** Access: Mail, in person, online. Both court and visitors may perform in person searches. Search fee: $5.00 per name. Required to search: name, years to search, also helpful-DOB, SSN. Criminal records on computer from 1982. **General Information:** No juvenile, mental, sealed, or adoption records released. SASE required. Turnaround time 1-2 days. Copy fee: $1.00 per page. Certification fee: $5.00. Fee payee: County Clerk. Personal checks accepted. Prepayment is

required. Public access terminal is available. Fax notes: Will fax results if prepaid.

Gregg County

District Court PO Box 711, Longview, TX 75606; 903-237-2663. Hours: 8AM-5PM (CST). *Felony, Civil.*

Civil Records: Access: Phone, fax, mail, in person. Both court and visitors may perform in person searches. Search fee: $5.00 per name. Required to search: name, years to search. Civil cases indexed by defendant, plaintiff. Civil records on computer from 1977, index books from 1873. **Criminal Records:** Access: Phone, fax, mail, in person. Both court and visitors may perform in person searches. Search fee: $5.00 per name. Required to search: name, years to search. Criminal records on computer from 1977, index books from 1873. **General Information:** No juvenile, mental, sealed, or adoption records released. SASE required. Turnaround time 1-2 days. Copy fee: $1.00 per page. Certification fee: No certification fee. Fee payee: District Clerk. Only cashiers checks and money orders accepted. Prepayment is required. Fax notes: $1.00 per page.

County Court PO Box 3049, Longview, TX 75606; 903-236-8430. Hours: 8AM-5PM (CST). *Misdemeanor, Civil, Probate.*

Civil Records: Access: Mail, in person. Both court and visitors may perform in person searches. Search fee: $5.00 per name. Required to search: name, years to search. Civil cases indexed by defendant, plaintiff. Civil records on computer from 1983, index books after 1983. **Criminal Records:** Access: Mail, in person. Both court and visitors may perform in person searches. Search fee: $5.00 per name. Required to search: name, years to search. Criminal records on computer from 1983, index books after 1983. **General Information:** No juvenile, mental, sealed, or adoption records released. SASE required. Turnaround time 1 week. Copy fee: $1.00 per page. Certification fee: $5.00. Fee payee: Gregg County Clerk. Personal checks accepted. Prepayment is required.

Grimes County

District Court PO Box 234, Anderson, TX 77830; 936-873-2111; Fax: 936-873-2415. Hours: 8AM-4:45PM (CST). *Felony, Civil.*

Civil Records: Access: Phone, fax, mail, in person. Both court and visitors may perform in person searches. Search fee: $5.00 per name. Required to search: name, years to search. Civil cases indexed by defendant, plaintiff. Civil records on computer from 1990, index books from 1800s. **Criminal Records:** Access: Phone, fax, mail, in person. Both court and visitors may perform in person searches. Search fee: $5.00 per name. Required to search: name, years to search, DOB, SSN. Criminal records on computer from 1990, index books from 1800s. **General Information:** No juvenile, mental, sealed, or adoption records released. SASE not required. Turnaround time 1-2 days. Copy fee: $1.00 per page. Certification fee: $1.00. Fee payee: District Clerk. Personal checks accepted. Prepayment is required.

County Court PO Box 209, Anderson, TX 77830; 936-873-2111. Hours: 8AM-4:45PM (CST). *Misdemeanor, Civil, Probate.*

Civil Records: Access: Mail, in person. Only the court conducts in person searches; visitors may not. Search fee: $5.00 per name. Required to search: name, years to search. Civil cases indexed by defendant, plaintiff. Civil records in index books from 1850. **Criminal Records:** Access: Mail, in person. Only the court conducts in person searches; visitors may not. Search fee: $5.00 per name. Required to search: name, years to search, offense, date of offense. Criminal records in index books from 1850. **General Information:** No juvenile, mental, sealed, or adoption records released. SASE required. Turnaround time 1-2 days. Copy fee: $1.00 per page. Certification fee: $5.00. Fee payee: County Clerk. Personal checks accepted.

Guadalupe County

District Court 101 E Court St, Seguin, TX 78155; 830-303-4188; Fax: 830-379-1943. Hours: 8AM-5PM (CST). *Felony, Civil.*

Civil Records: Access: In person only. Court does not conduct in person searches; visitors must perform searches for themselves. Search fee: No civil searches performed by court. Required to search: name, years to search. Civil cases indexed by defendant, plaintiff. Civil records on computer from 1991, index books from 1900s. **Criminal Records:** Access: In person only. Court does not conduct in person searches; visitors must perform searches for themselves. Search fee: No criminal searches performed by court. Required to search: name, years to search, DOB; also helpful-SSN. Criminal records on computer from 1987, index books from 1900s. **General Information:** No juvenile, mental, sealed, or adoption records released. Copy fee: $.20 per page. Certification fee: $1.00 per page. Fee payee: District Clerk. Personal checks accepted. Credit cards accepted: Visa, Mastercard, AmEx. Prepayment is required. Public access terminal is available.

County Court 101 E Court St, Seguin, TX 78155; 830-303-4188 X266,234,232; Fax: 830-372-1206. Hours: 8AM-4:30PM (CST). *Misdemeanor, Civil, Probate.*

Civil Records: Access: Mail, in person. Both court and visitors may perform in person searches. Search fee: $5.00 per name. Required to search: name, years to search. Civil cases indexed by defendant, plaintiff. Civil records on computer from 1990, index books from 1968. **Criminal Records:** Access: Mail, in person. Both court and visitors may perform in person searches. Search fee: $5.00 per name. Required to search: name, years to search, DOB; also helpful-SSN. Criminal records on computer from 1990, index books from 1968. **General Information:** No juvenile, mental, sealed, or adoption records released. SASE required. Turnaround time 5 days. Copy fee: $1.00 per page. Certification fee: $5.00. Fee payee: County Clerk. Personal checks accepted. Checks accepted for civil fees. Prepayment is required. Public access terminal is available.

Hale County

District Court 500 Broadway #200, Plainview, TX 79072-8050; 806-291-5226; Fax: 806-291-5206. Hours: 8AM-Noon; 1-5PM (CST). *Felony, Civil.*

Civil Records: Access: Phone, mail, in person. Both court and visitors may perform in person searches. Search fee: $5.00 per name. Required to search: name, years to search. Civil cases indexed by defendant, plaintiff. Civil records on computer since 1989, index cards from 1975. **Criminal Records:** Access: Phone, mail, in person. Both court and visitors may perform in person searches. Search fee: $5.00 per name. Required to search: name, years to search, DOB; also helpful-SSN. Criminal records on computer since 1989, index cards from 1975. **General Information:** No

juvenile, mental, sealed, or adoption records released. SASE required. Turnaround time 1-2 days. Copy fee: $1.00 1st 4 pages, $.25 each additional page. Certification fee: $1.00. Fee payee: District Clerk. Personal checks accepted. Prepayment is required.

County Court 500 Broadway #140, Plainview, TX 79072-8030; 806-291-5261; Fax: 806-291-9810. Hours: 8AM-Noon, 1-5PM (CST). *Misdemeanor, Civil, Probate.*

Civil Records: Access: Mail, in person. Both court and visitors may perform in person searches. Search fee: $5.00 per name. Required to search: name, years to search, address. Civil cases indexed by defendant, plaintiff. Civil records in index books from 1800s. **Criminal Records:** Access: Mail, in person. Both court and visitors may perform in person searches. Search fee: $5.00 per name. Required to search: name, years to search, DOB. Criminal records in index books from 1800s. **General Information:** No juvenile, mental, sealed, or adoption records released. SASE not required. Turnaround time 1-2 days. Copy fee: $1.00 per page. Certification fee: $5.00. Fee payee: County Clerk. Personal checks accepted. Checks accepted except for birth/death. Prepayment is required. Public access terminal is available.

Hall County

District & County Court County Courthouse, Memphis, TX 79245; 806-259-2627; Fax: 806-259-5078. Hours: 8:30AM-Noon; 1-5PM (CST). *Felony, Misdemeanor, Civil, Eviction, Probate.*

Civil Records: Access: Phone, mail, in person. Both court and visitors may perform in person searches. Search fee: $10.00 per name. Required to search: name, years to search. Civil cases indexed by defendant, plaintiff. Civil records on computer from 1992, index books from 1890. **Criminal Records:** Access: Phone, mail, in person. Both court and visitors may perform in person searches. Search fee: $10.00 per name. Required to search: name, years to search, offense. Criminal records on computer from 1992, index books from 1890. **General Information:** No juvenile, mental, sealed, or adoption records released. SASE required. Turnaround time 1-2 days. Copy fee: $1.00 per page. Certification fee: $5.00. Fee payee: Hall County Clerk. Personal checks accepted. Prepayment is required.

Hamilton County

District Court County Courthouse, Hamilton, TX 76531; 254-386-3417; Fax: 254-386-8610. Hours: 8AM-5PM M-Th; 8AM-4:30PM F (CST). *Felony, Civil.*

Civil Records: Access: Fax, mail, in person. Both court and visitors may perform in person searches. Search fee: $5.00 per name. Required to search: name, years to search. Civil cases indexed by defendant, plaintiff. Civil records in index books. **Criminal Records:** Access: Fax, mail, in person. Both court and visitors may perform in person searches. Search fee: $5.00 per name. Required to search: name, years to search. Criminal records in index books. **General Information:** No juvenile, mental, sealed, or adoption records released. SASE required. Turnaround time 2-4 days. Copy fee: $1.00 per page. Certification fee: $2.00. Fee payee: District Clerk. Personal checks accepted. Fax notes: No fee to fax results.

County Court County Courthouse, Hamilton, TX 76531; 254-386-3518; Fax: 254-386-8727.

Hours: 8AM-5PM (CST). *Misdemeanor, Civil, Probate.*

Civil Records: Access: Mail, in person. Both court and visitors may perform in person searches. Search fee: $5.00 per name. Required to search: name, years to search. Civil cases indexed by defendant, plaintiff. Civil records in index books. **Criminal Records:** Access: Mail, in person. Both court and visitors may perform in person searches. Search fee: $5.00 per name. Required to search: name, years to search. Criminal records in index books. **General Information:** No juvenile, mental, sealed, or adoption records released. SASE required. Turnaround time 1-2 days. Copy fee: $1.00 per page. Certification fee: $1.00. Fee payee: County Clerk. Personal checks accepted. Prepayment is required.

Hansford County

District & County Court PO Box 397, Spearman, TX 79081; 806-659-4110; Fax: 806-659-4168. Hours: 8:00AM-5PM (CST). *Felony, Misdemeanor, Civil, Eviction, Probate.*

Civil Records: Access: Phone, fax, mail, in person. Both court and visitors may perform in person searches. Search fee: $5.00 per name. Required to search: name, years to search. Civil cases indexed by defendant, plaintiff. Civil records on computer from 01/82, index books from 1900s. **Criminal Records:** Access: Phone, fax, mail, in person. Both court and visitors may perform in person searches. Search fee: $5.00 per name. Required to search: name, years to search; also helpful-DOB, SSN. Criminal records on computer since 06/92. **General Information:** No juvenile, mental, sealed, or adoption records released. SASE required. Turnaround time 1-2 days. Copy fee: $1.00 per page. Certification fee: $2.00 for District Court records; $5.00 for County Court records. Fee payee: District/County Clerk. Personal checks accepted. Public access terminal is available. Fax notes: $4.00 for first page, $1.00 each addl.

Hardeman County

District & County Court PO Box 30, Quanah, TX 79252; 940-663-2901. Hours: 8:30AM-5PM (CST). *Felony, Misdemeanor, Civil, Eviction, Probate.*

Civil Records: Access: Mail, in person. Both court and visitors may perform in person searches. Search fee: $10.00 per name. Required to search: name, years to search. Civil cases indexed by defendant, plaintiff. Civil records in index books from 1900s. **Criminal Records:** Access: Mail, in person. Both court and visitors may perform in person searches. Search fee: $10.00 per name. Required to search: name, years to search. Criminal records in index books from 1900s. **General Information:** No juvenile, mental, sealed, or adoption records released. SASE required. Turnaround time 1-2 days. Copy fee: $1.00 per page. Certification fee: $5.00. Fee payee: District Clerk. Personal checks accepted. Prepayment is required.

Hardin County

District Court PO Box 2997, Kountze, TX 77625; 409-246-5150. Hours: 8AM-4PM (CST). *Felony, Civil.*

Civil Records: Access: Phone, mail, in person. Both court and visitors may perform in person searches. Search fee: $5.00 per name. Required to search: name, years to search. Civil cases indexed by defendant, plaintiff. Civil records in index books since 1920. **Criminal Records:** Access: Phone, mail, in person. Both court and visitors may perform in person searches. Search fee: $5.00 per name. Required to search: name, years to search. Criminal records in index books since 1920. **General Information:** No juvenile, mental, sealed, or adoption records released. SASE required. Turnaround time 1-2 days. Copy fee: $1.00 per page. Certification fee: $2.00. Fee payee: District Clerk. Business checks accepted. Prepayment is required.

County Court PO Box 38, Kountze, TX 77625; 409-246-5185. Hours: 8AM-5PM (CST). *Misdemeanor, Civil, Probate.*

Civil Records: Access: Mail, in person. Both court and visitors may perform in person searches. Search fee: $5.00 per name. Required to search: name, years to search. Civil cases indexed by defendant, plaintiff. Civil records in index books since 1850. **Criminal Records:** Access: Mail, in person. Both court and visitors may perform in person searches. Search fee: $5.00 per name. Required to search: name, years to search. Criminal records on computer since 1992, index books from 1850. **General Information:** No juvenile, mental, sealed, or adoption records released. SASE not required. Turnaround time 1-2 days. Copy fee: $1.00 per page. Certification fee: $5.00. Fee payee: Hardin County Clerk. Personal checks accepted. Prepayment is required.

Harris County

District Court PO Box 4651, Houston, TX 77210;; Civil phone:713-755-5711; Criminal phone:713-755-5711; Fax: 713-755-5480 (civil). Hours: 8AM-5PM (CST). *Felony, Civil Over $100,000.*

www.hcdistrictclerk.com

Civil Records: Access: Phone, fax, mail, online, in person. Both court and visitors may perform in person searches. Search fee: $5.00 per name. Required to search: name, years to search. Civil cases indexed by defendant, plaintiff. Civil records on computer from 1969, microfiche from 1900s. Online access is a commercial fee site and requires a deposit of $150 or $300 for both criminal and civil. Access is private dial up or via the Internet. The system is open 24 hours daily. For information, visit the web site or call (713) 755-7815. Fax requesters must be pre-approved. **Criminal Records:** Access: Phone, mail, remote online, in person. Both court and visitors may perform in person searches. Search fee: $5.00 per name. Required to search: name, years to search, DOB; also helpful-SSN. Criminal records on computer since 1976, microfiche from 1900s. The same online access criteria described in civil applies. In addition, Internet access is available to qualified JIMs subscribers at www.co.harris.tx.us/subscriber/cb/submenu.htm. Records include felonies and A & B class misdemeanors. **General Information:** No juvenile, mental, sealed, or adoption records released. SASE required. Turnaround time 2 days. Copy fee: $1.00 per page. Fax requesters must be pre-approved Certification fee: $1.00. Fee payee: District Clerk, Harris County. Business checks accepted. Business check accepted from attorney with TX Bar Card number, corporate or company check with Harris Co address. Prepayment is required. Public access terminal is available. Fax notes: Fax service available to those with escrow account.

County Court , PO Box 1525, Houston, TX 77251-1525; 713-755-6421, 888-545-5577. Hours: 8AM-4:30PM (CST). *Civil Under $100,000.*

www.hcdistrictclerk.com

Civil Records: Access: Mail, online, in person. Both court and visitors may perform in person searches. Search fee: $5.00 per name. Required to search: name, years to search. Civil cases indexed by defendant, plaintiff. Civil records on computer and microfiche from 1963. Online access is by subscription only. There is a setup fee, deposit and monthly minimum fees of $25 (based on $.05 per minute). The system is open 24 hours daily and also includes probate, misdemeanor and traffic. For further information, call Laura Yanes at 817-884-3202, or (713) 755-7815. Civil court general information is available at www.ccl.co.harris.tx.us/civil/default.htm. **General Information:** No juvenile, mental, sealed, or adoption records released. SASE required. Turnaround time 24-48 hours. Copy fee: $1.00 per page. Certification fee: $5.00. Fee payee: Tarrant County Clerk. Business checks accepted. Credit cards accepted: Visa, Mastercard. Prepayment is required. Public access terminal is available.

Probate Court 1115 Congress, 6th Floor, Houston, TX 77002; 713-755-6084; Fax: 713-755-4349. Hours: 6AM-5PM (CST). *Probate.*

Note: Probate dockets available through the Harris County online system. Call (713) 755-7815 for information

Harrison County

71st District Court PO Box 1119, Marshall, TX 75671-1119; 903-935-4845. Hours: 8AM-5PM (CST). *Felony, Civil.*

www.co.harrison.tx.us

Civil Records: Access: Mail, in person. Both court and visitors may perform in person searches. Search fee: $5.00 per name. Required to search: name, years to search; also helpful-address. Civil cases indexed by defendant, plaintiff. Civil records on computer from 1988, index books from 1845. **Criminal Records:** Access: Mail, in person. Both court and visitors may perform in person searches. Search fee: $5.00 per name. Required to search: name, years to search, DOB; also helpful-address, SSN. Criminal records on computer from 1988, index books from 1845. **General Information:** No juvenile, mental, sealed, or adoption records released. SASE required. Turnaround time 1-2 days. Copy fee: $1.00 per page. Certification fee: No certification fee. Fee payee: Harrison County District Clerk. Personal checks accepted. Prepayment is required. Public access terminal is available.

County Court PO Box 1365, Marshall, TX 75671; 903-935-4858. Hours: 8AM-5PM (CST). *Misdemeanor, Civil, Probate.*

Civil Records: Access: Mail, in person. Both court and visitors may perform in person searches. Search fee: $5.00 per name. Required to search: name, years to search. Civil cases indexed by defendant, plaintiff. Civil records in docket books from 1800. **Criminal Records:** Access: Mail, in person. Both court and visitors may perform in person searches. Search fee: $5.00 per name. Required to search: name, years to search, DOB. Criminal records in docket books from 1800. **General Information:** No juvenile, mental, sealed, birth, death or adoption records released. SASE not required. Turnaround time 10 days. Copy fee: $1.00 per page. Certification fee: $5.00 plus $1.00 per page. Fee payee: County Clerk. Personal checks accepted. In state checks only. Prepayment is required.

Hartley County

District & County Court PO Box Q, Channing, TX 79018; 806-235-3582; Fax: 806-235-2316. Hours: 8:30AM-Noon, 1-5PM (CST). *Felony, Misdemeanor, Civil, Eviction, Probate.*

Civil Records: Access: Mail, in person. Both court and visitors may perform in person searches. Search fee: $5.00 per name. Charge is for each book searched. Required to search: name, years to search. Civil cases indexed by defendant, plaintiff. Civil records on computer from 1992, index books from 1900s. Results can be faxed if pre-paid and local call. **Criminal Records:** Access: Mail, in person. Both court and visitors may perform in person searches. Search fee: $5.00 per name. Required to search: name, years to search, DOB. Criminal records on computer from 1992, index books from 1900s. Results can be faxed if pre-paid and local call. **General Information:** No juvenile, mental, sealed, or adoption records released. SASE required. Turnaround time 1-2 days. Copy fee: $1.00 per page. Certification fee: $5.00. Fee payee: Hartley County Clerk. Personal checks accepted. Prepayment is required.

Haskell County

District Court PO Box 27, Haskell, TX 79521; 940-864-2030. Hours: 8AM-Noon, 1-5PM M-Th; 8AM-4:30PM F (CST). *Felony, Civil.*

Civil Records: Access: Mail, in person. Both court and visitors may perform in person searches. Search fee: $5.00 per name. Required to search: name, years to search. Civil cases indexed by defendant, plaintiff. Civil records on computer from 1992, index books from 1896. **Criminal Records:** Access: Mail, in person. Both court and visitors may perform in person searches. Search fee: $5.00 per name. Required to search: name, years to search, signed release. Criminal records on computer from 1992, index books from 1896. **General Information:** No juvenile, mental, sealed, or adoption records released. SASE required. Turnaround time 1-2 days. Copy fee: $1.00 per page. Certification fee: $1.00. Fee payee: District Clerk. Business checks accepted. In-state checks accepted. Prepayment is required.

County Court PO Box 725, Haskell, TX 79521; 940-864-2451. Hours: 8AM-Noon, 1-5PM (CST). *Misdemeanor, Civil, Probate.*

Civil Records: Access: Phone, fax, mail, in person. Both court and visitors may perform in person searches. Search fee: $5.00 per name. Required to search: name, years to search. Civil cases indexed by defendant, plaintiff. Civil records in index books from 1903. **Criminal Records:** Access: Phone, fax, mail, in person. Both court and visitors may perform in person searches. Search fee: $5.00 per name. Required to search: name, years to search. Criminal records in index books from 1903. **General Information:** No juvenile, mental, sealed, or adoption records released. SASE required. Turnaround time 1-2 days. Copy fee: $1.00 per page. Certification fee: $5.00. Fee payee: County Clerk. Personal checks accepted. Prepayment is required. Fax notes: $2.00 per page.

Hays County

District Court 110 E Martin Luther King, Suite 123, San Marcos, TX 78666; 512-393-7660; Fax: 512-393-7674. Hours: 8AM-5PM (CST). *Felony, Civil.*

www.co.hays.tx.us

Civil Records: Access: Phone, mail, in person. Both court and visitors may perform in person searches. Search fee: $5.00 per name. Required to search: name, years to search. Civil cases indexed by defendant, plaintiff. Civil records on computer from 1987, index books from 1890s. **Criminal Records:** Access: Phone, mail, in person. Both court and visitors may perform in person searches. Search fee: $5.00 per name. Required to search: name, years to search; also helpful-DOB, SSN. Criminal records on computer from 1987, index books from 1890s. **General Information:** No sealed or adoption records released. SASE required. Turnaround time 1-5 days. Copy fee: $.50 per page. Certification fee: $1.00 plus $1.00 per page. Fee payee: District Clerk. Personal checks accepted. Prepayment is required. Public access terminal is available.

County Court Justice Center, 110 E Martin L King Dr, San Marcos, TX 78666; 512-393-7738; Fax: 512-393-7735. Hours: 8AM-5PM (CST). *Misdemeanor, Civil, Probate.*

www.co.hays.tx.us

Civil Records: Access: Mail, in person. Both court and visitors may perform in person searches. Search fee: $5.00 per name. Required to search: name, years to search. Civil cases indexed by defendant, plaintiff. Civil records on computer from 1988, index books from 1848. **Criminal Records:** Access: Mail, in person. Both court and visitors may perform in person searches. Search fee: $5.00 per name. Required to search: name, years to search, DOB. Criminal records on computer from 1987, index books from 1848. **General Information:** No juvenile, mental, sealed, or adoption records released. SASE not required. Turnaround time 1-2 weeks. Copy fee: $1.00 per page. Certification fee: $5.00. Fee payee: Hays County Clerk. Personal checks accepted. Prepayment is required. Public access terminal is available.

Hemphill County

District & County Court PO Box 867, Canadian, TX 79014; 806-323-6212. Hours: 8AM-5PM (CST). *Felony, Misdemeanor, Civil, Eviction, Probate.*

Civil Records: Access: Mail, in person. Both court and visitors may perform in person searches. Search fee: $10.00 per name. Required to search: name, years to search. Civil cases indexed by defendant, plaintiff. Civil records in index books from 1890s. **Criminal Records:** Access: Mail, in person. Both court and visitors may perform in person searches. Search fee: $10.00 per name. Required to search: name, years to search. Criminal records in index books from 1890s. **General Information:** No juvenile, mental, sealed, or adoption records released. SASE required. Turnaround time 1-2 days. Copy fee: $1.00 per page. Certification fee: $5.00 per page. Fee payee: Hemphill County Clerk. Personal checks accepted. Prepayment is required.

Henderson County

District Court Henderson County Courthouse, Athens, TX 75751; 903-675-6115. Hours: 8AM-5PM (CST). *Felony, Civil.*

Civil Records: Access: Mail, in person. Both court and visitors may perform in person searches. Search fee: $5.00 per name. Required to search: name, years to search. Civil cases indexed by defendant, plaintiff. Civil records on computer from 1987, index books from 1849. **Criminal Records:** Access: Mail, in person. Both court and

visitors may perform in person searches. Search fee: $5.00 per name. Required to search: name, years to search, DOB; also helpful-SSN. Criminal records on computer from 1987, index books from 1849. **General Information:** No juvenile, mental, sealed, or adoption records released. SASE required. Turnaround time 1-2 days. Copy fee: $1.00 per page. Certification fee: $2.00. Fee payee: District Clerk. Personal checks accepted. Prepayment is required.

County Court PO Box 632, Athens, TX 75751; 903-675-6140. Hours: 8AM-5PM (CST). *Misdemeanor, Civil, Probate.*

Civil Records: Access: Mail, in person. Both court and visitors may perform in person searches. Search fee: $10.00 per name. Required to search: name, years to search. Civil cases indexed by defendant, plaintiff. Civil records on computer from 1990, index books from 1900s. **Criminal Records:** Access: Mail, in person. Both court and visitors may perform in person searches. Search fee: $10.00 per name. Required to search: name, years to search, DOB, SSN. Criminal records on computer from 1984, index books from 1900s. **General Information:** No juvenile, mental, sealed, or adoption records released. SASE required. Turnaround time 1-2 weeks. Copy fee: $1.00 per page. Fee is for civil; no fee for criminal. Certification fee: No certification fee. Fee payee: County Clerk. Personal checks accepted. Prepayment is required.

Hidalgo County

District Court 100 N Closner, Box 87, Edinburg, TX 78540; 956-318-2200. Hours: 8AM-5PM (CST). *Felony, Civil.*

Civil Records: Access: Mail, in person. Only the court conducts in person searches; visitors may not. Search fee: $5.00 per name. Required to search: name, years to search. Civil cases indexed by defendant, plaintiff. Civil records on computer from 1987. **Criminal Records:** Access: Mail, in person. Only the court conducts in person searches; visitors may not. Search fee: $5.00 per name. Required to search: name, years to search, DOB. Criminal records on computer from 1987. **General Information:** No juvenile, mental, sealed, or adoption records released. SASE required. Turnaround time 1-2 days. Copy fee: $1.00 per page. Certification fee: $1.00. Fee payee: District Clerk. Business checks accepted. Prepayment is required.

County Court PO Box 58, Edinburg, TX 78540; 956-318-2100. Hours: 7:30AM-5:30PM (CST). *Misdemeanor, Civil, Probate.*

Civil Records: Access: Mail, in person. Both court and visitors may perform in person searches. Search fee: $5.00 per name. Required to search: name, years to search. Civil cases indexed by defendant, plaintiff. Civil records on computer from 1985, index books before 1985. **Criminal Records:** Access: Mail, in person. Both court and visitors may perform in person searches. Search fee: $5.00 per name. Required to search: name, years to search. Criminal records on computer from 1985, index books after 1985. **General Information:** No juvenile, mental, sealed, or adoption records released. SASE required. Turnaround time 1-2 days. Copy fee: $1.00 per page. Certification fee: $6.00. Fee payee: County Clerk. Business checks accepted. Prepayment is required. Public access terminal is available. Public Access Terminal Note: Criminal only.

Hill County

District Court PO Box 634, Hillsboro, TX 76645; 254-582-4042. Hours: 8AM-5PM (CST). *Felony, Civil.*

Civil Records: Access: Mail, in person. Both court and visitors may perform in person searches. Search fee: $5.00 per name. Required to search: name, years to search. Civil cases indexed by defendant, plaintiff. Civil records on optical imaging from September, 1993, on computer from 1991, microfilm from 1930s to 1950s, index books from 1900s. **Criminal Records:** Access: Mail, in person. Both court and visitors may perform in person searches. Search fee: $5.00 per name. Required to search: name, years to search; also helpful-DOB, SSN. Criminal records on optical imaging from September, 1993, on computer from 1989, microfilm from 1930s to 1950s, index books from 1900s. **General Information:** No juvenile, mental, sealed, or adoption records released. SASE required. Turnaround time 1-2 days. Copy fee: $1.00 per page. Certification fee: $1.00. Fee payee: District Clerk. Personal checks accepted. Prepayment is required.

County Court PO Box 398, Hillsboro, TX 76645; 254-582-4030. Hours: 8AM-5PM (CST). *Misdemeanor, Probate.* **General Information:** Turnaround time 1-2 days. Fee payee: County Clerk. Prepayment is required.

Hockley County

District Court 802 Houston St, Ste 316, Levelland, TX 79336; 806-894-8527; Fax: 806-894-3891. Hours: 9AM-5PM (CST). *Felony, Civil.*

Civil Records: Access: Phone, mail, in person. Both court and visitors may perform in person searches. Search fee: $5.00 per name. Required to search: name, years to search. Civil cases indexed by defendant, plaintiff. Civil records on computer from 1992, archived from 1929. **Criminal Records:** Access: Phone, mail, in person. Both court and visitors may perform in person searches. Search fee: $5.00 per name. Required to search: name, years to search. Criminal records on computer from 1992, archived from 1929. **General Information:** No juvenile, mental, sealed, or adoption records released. SASE required. Turnaround time 1-2 days. Copy fee: $1.00 per page. Certification fee: $2.00. Fee payee: District Clerk. Personal checks accepted. Prepayment is required.

County Court County Courthouse, 802 Houston St Ste 213, Levelland, TX 79336; 806-894-3185. Hours: 9AM-5PM (CST). *Misdemeanor, Civil, Probate.*

Civil Records: Access: Mail, in person. Both court and visitors may perform in person searches. No search fee. Required to search: name, years to search. Civil cases indexed by defendant, plaintiff. Civil records on computer from 1992, index books from 1925. **Criminal Records:** Access: Mail, in person. Both court and visitors may perform in person searches. No search fee. Required to search: name, years to search; also helpful-DOB. Criminal records on computer from 1992, index books from 1925. **General Information:** No juvenile, mental, sealed, or adoption records released. SASE required. Turnaround time 1-2 days. Copy fee: $1.00 per page. Certification fee: $5.00. Fee payee: Hockley County Clerk. Personal checks accepted.

Hood County

District Court County Courthouse, Granbury, TX 76048; 817-579-3236; Fax: 817-579-3239. Hours: 8AM-5PM (CST). *Felony, Civil.*

Civil Records: Access: Mail, in person. Both court and visitors may perform in person searches. Search fee: $5.00 per name. Required to search: name, years to search. Civil cases indexed by defendant, plaintiff. Civil records on computer and microfiche from 1983, index books before 1983. **Criminal Records:** Access: Mail, in person. Both court and visitors may perform in person searches. Search fee: $5.00 per name. Required to search: name, years to search, DOB, SSN, signed release. Criminal records on computer and microfiche from 1983, index books before 1983. **General Information:** No juvenile, mental, sealed, or adoption records released. SASE required. Turnaround time 1-2 days. Copy fee: $1.00 per page. Certification fee: $1.00. Fee payee: District Clerk. Personal checks accepted. Prepayment is required.

County Court PO Box 339, Granbury, TX 76048; 817-579-3222; Fax: 817-579-3227. Hours: 8AM-5PM (CST). *Misdemeanor, Civil, Probate.*

Civil Records: Access: Mail, in person. Both court and visitors may perform in person searches. Search fee: $5.00 per name. Required to search: name, years to search. Civil cases indexed by defendant, plaintiff. Civil records in index books. **Criminal Records:** Access: Mail, in person. Both court and visitors may perform in person searches. Search fee: $5.00 per name. Required to search: name, years to search; also helpful-DOB. Criminal records on computer and microfiche from 1982, index books before 1982. **General Information:** No juvenile, mental, or adoption records released. SASE required. Turnaround time 1 day. Copy fee: $1.00 per page. Certification fee: $5.00. Fee payee: Hood County Clerk. Personal checks accepted. Prepayment is required. Public access terminal is available.

Hopkins County

District Court PO Box 391, Sulphur Springs, TX 75482; 903-438-4081. Hours: 8AM-5PM (CST). *Felony, Civil.*

Civil Records: Access: Mail, in person. Both court and visitors may perform in person searches. Search fee: $5.00 per name. Required to search: name, years to search. Civil cases indexed by defendant, plaintiff. Civil records on computer from 1987, index books from 1840, archived from 1890. **Criminal Records:** Access: Mail, in person. Both court and visitors may perform in person searches. Search fee: $5.00 per name. Required to search: name, years to search. Criminal records on computer from 1987, index books from 1840, archived from 1890. **General Information:** No juvenile, mental, sealed, or adoption records released. SASE required. Turnaround time 2 days. Copy fee: $1.00 per page. Certification fee: $2.00. Fee payee: District Clerk. Personal checks accepted. Prepayment is required.

County Court PO Box 288, Sulphur Springs, TX 75483; 903-438-4074; Fax: 903-438-4007. Hours: 8AM-5PM (CST). *Misdemeanor, Civil, Probate.*

Civil Records: Access: Mail, in person. Both court and visitors may perform in person searches. Search fee: $5.00 per name. Required to search: name, years to search. Civil cases indexed by defendant, plaintiff. Civil records on computer since 1992, index books from 1846. **Criminal**

Records: Access: Mail, in person. Both court and visitors may perform in person searches. Search fee: $5.00 per name. Required to search: name, years to search. Criminal records on computer from 1992, index books from 1846. **General Information:** No juvenile, mental, sealed, or adoption records released. SASE required. Turnaround time 1-2 days. Copy fee: $1.00 per page. Certification fee: $5.00. Fee payee: County Clerk. Personal checks accepted. Prepayment is required.

Houston County

District Court County Courthouse, 410 E Houston, PO Box 1186, Crockett, TX 75835; 936-544-3255; Fax: 936-544-9523. Hours: 8AM-5PM (CST). *Felony, Civil.*

Civil Records: Access: Fax, mail, in person. Both court and visitors may perform in person searches. Search fee: $5.00 per name. Required to search: name, years to search. Civil cases indexed by plaintiff. Civil records on computer from 10/99, index books since 1800s. **Criminal Records:** Access: Fax, mail, in person. Both court and visitors may perform in person searches. Search fee: $5.00 per name. Required to search: name, years to search, signed release; also helpful-DOB, SSN. Criminal records on computer since 10/99, index books since 1800s. **General Information:** No juvenile, mental, sealed, or adoption records released. SASE required. Turnaround time 1-2 days. Copy fee: $1.00 per page. Certification fee: No certification fee. Fee payee: District Clerk. Personal checks accepted. Prepayment is required. Fax notes: $3.50 for first page, $.50 each addl.

County Court PO Box 370, Crockett, TX 75835; 936-544-3255; Fax: 936-544-8053. Hours: 8AM-4:30 (CST). *Misdemeanor, Civil, Probate.*

Civil Records: Access: Mail, in person. Both court and visitors may perform in person searches. Search fee: $5.00 per name. Required to search: name, years to search. Civil cases indexed by defendant, plaintiff. Civil records on computer since November, 1991 (civil), microfiche since 1983, index books since 1881 (probate). **Criminal Records:** Access: Mail, in person. Both court and visitors may perform in person searches. Search fee: $5.00 per name. Required to search: name, years to search. Criminal records on computer since November, 1991, index books since 1881. **General Information:** No juvenile, mental, sealed, or adoption records released. SASE not required. Turnaround time 1-2 days. Copy fee: $1.00 per page. Certification fee: $5.00. Fee payee: County Clerk. Personal checks accepted. Prepayment is required.

Howard County

District Court PO Box 2138, Big Spring, TX 79721; 915-264-2223; Fax: 915-264-2256. Hours: 8AM-5PM (CST). *Felony, Civil.*

Civil Records: Access: Mail, in person. Both court and visitors may perform in person searches. Search fee: $5.00 per name. Required to search: name, years to search. Civil cases indexed by defendant, plaintiff. Civil records on computer from 1990, index books from 1881. **Criminal Records:** Access: Mail, in person. Both court and visitors may perform in person searches. Search fee: $5.00 per name. Required to search: name, years to search. Criminal records on computer from 1990, index books from 1881. **General Information:** No juvenile, mental, sealed or adoption records released. SASE required. Turnaround time 1-2 days. Copy fee: $1.00 per page. Certification fee: $1.00. Fee payee: District

Clerk. Personal checks accepted. Prepayment is required.

County Court PO Box 1468, Big Spring, TX 79721; 915-264-2213; Fax: 915-264-2215. Hours: 8AM-5PM (CST). *Misdemeanor, Civil, Probate.*

Civil Records: Access: Phone, mail, in person. Both court and visitors may perform in person searches. Search fee: $5.00 per name. Required to search: name, years to search. Civil cases indexed by defendant, plaintiff. Civil records in index books since 1881. **Criminal Records:** Access: Phone, mail, in person. Both court and visitors may perform in person searches. Search fee: $5.00 per name. Required to search: name, years to search. Criminal records in index books since 1881. **General Information:** No juvenile, mental, sealed, or adoption records released. SASE not required. Turnaround time 1-2 days. Copy fee: $1.00 per page. Certification fee: $5.00. Fee payee: County Clerk. Business checks accepted. Prepayment is required. Fax notes: $5.00 per document.

Hudspeth County

District & County Court PO Drawer 58, Sierra Blanca, TX 79851; 915-369-2301; Fax: 915-369-3005. Hours: 8AM-5PM (MST). *Felony, Misdemeanor, Civil, Eviction, Probate.*

Civil Records: Access: Phone, fax, mail, in person. Both court and visitors may perform in person searches. Search fee: $5.00 per name. Required to search: name, years to search. Civil cases indexed by defendant, plaintiff. Civil records in index books from 1900s. **Criminal Records:** Access: Phone, fax, mail, in person. Both court and visitors may perform in person searches. Search fee: $5.00 per name. Required to search: name, years to search. Criminal records in index books from 1900s. **General Information:** No juvenile, mental, sealed, or adoption records released. SASE required. Turnaround time 1-2 days. Copy fee: $1.00 per page. Certification fee: $5.00. Fee payee: District/County Clerk. Personal checks accepted. Prepayment is required. Fax notes: $1.00 per page.

Hunt County

District Court PO Box 1437, Greenville, TX 75403; 903-408-4172. Hours: 8AM-5PM (CST). *Felony, Civil.*

Civil Records: Access: Mail, in person. Both court and visitors may perform in person searches. Search fee: $5.00 per name. Required to search: name, years to search. Civil cases indexed by defendant, plaintiff. Civil records on computer from 1992, microfiche from 1973, index books from 1900s. **Criminal Records:** Access: Mail, in person. Both court and visitors may perform in person searches. Search fee: $5.00 per name. Required to search: name, years to search, DOB. Criminal records on computer from 1992, microfilm from 1973, index books from 1900s. **General Information:** No juvenile, sealed, or adoption records released. SASE required. Turnaround time 1-2 days. Copy fee: $1.00 per page. Certification fee: $1.00. Fee payee: District Clerk. Personal checks accepted. Prepayment is required. Public access terminal is available.

County Court PO Box 1316, Greenville, TX 75403-1316; 903-408-4130. Hours: 8AM-5PM (CST). *Misdemeanor, Civil, Probate.*

Civil Records: Access: Mail, in person. Both court and visitors may perform in person searches. Search fee: $5.00 per name. Required to search: name, years to search. Civil cases indexed by

defendant, plaintiff. Civil records on computer since 1986, index books from 1940; on microfilm prior to 1986. **Criminal Records:** Access: Mail, in person. Both court and visitors may perform in person searches. Search fee: $5.00 per name. Required to search: name, years to search, DOB. Criminal records on computer since 1986, index books from 1940; on microfilm prior to 1986. **General Information:** No juvenile, mental, sealed, or adoption records released. SASE required. Turnaround time 1-2 days. Copy fee: $1.00 per page. Certification fee: $5.00. Fee payee: County Clerk. Personal checks accepted. Prepayment is required. Public access terminal is available.

Hutchinson County

District Court PO Box 580, Stinnett, TX 79083; 806-878-4017; Fax: 806-878-4023 (District Judge Office). Hours: 9AM-5PM (CST). *Felony, Civil.*

Civil Records: Access: Mail, in person. Both court and visitors may perform in person searches. Search fee: $5.00 per name. Required to search: name, years to search. Civil cases indexed by defendant, plaintiff. Civil records on computer from 1988, docket books from 1920. **Criminal Records:** Access: Mail, in person. Both court and visitors may perform in person searches. Search fee: $5.00 per name. Required to search: name, years to search, signed release; also helpful-DOB, SSN. Criminal records on computer from 1988, docket books from 1920. **General Information:** No juvenile, mental, sealed, or adoption records released. SASE required. Turnaround time 2 days. Copy fee: $.25 per page. $1.00 minimum. Certification fee: $1.00 per page. Fee payee: District Clerk. Personal checks accepted. Prepayment is required.

County Court PO Box 1186, Stinnett, TX 79083; 806-878-4002. Hours: 9AM-5PM (CST). *Misdemeanor, Civil, Probate.*

Civil Records: Access: Mail, in person. Both court and visitors may perform in person searches. Search fee: $5.00 per name. Required to search: name, years to search. Civil cases indexed by defendant, plaintiff. Civil records in index books from 1900s. **Criminal Records:** Access: Mail, in person. Both court and visitors may perform in person searches. Search fee: $5.00 per name. Required to search: name, years to search, signed release. Criminal records on computer since 1990, index books from 1900s. **General Information:** No juvenile, mental, sealed, or adoption records released. SASE not required. Turnaround time 2 days. Copy fee: $1.00 per page. Certification fee: $5.00. Fee payee: Carol Ann Herbst, Hutchinson County Clerk. Business checks accepted. Prepayment is required.

Irion County

District & County Court PO Box 736, Mertzon, TX 76941-0736; 915-835-2421; Fax: 915-835-2008. Hours: 8AM-5PM (CST). *Felony, Misdemeanor, Civil, Eviction, Probate.*

Civil Records: Access: Mail, in person. Both court and visitors may perform in person searches. Search fee: $5.00 per name. Fee is per court. Required to search: name, years to search. Civil cases indexed by defendant, plaintiff. Civil records in index books from 1886. **Criminal Records:** Access: Mail, in person. Both court and visitors may perform in person searches. Search fee: $5.00 per name. Fee is per court. Required to search: name, years to search; also helpful-DOB, SSN. Criminal records on index books from 1886.

General Information: No juvenile, mental, or sealed records released. SASE required. Turnaround time 5-20 days. Copy fee: $1.00 per page. Certification fee: $1.00. County Court certification fee $5.00. Fee payee: District/County Clerk. Personal checks accepted. Prepayment is required. Fax notes: $1.00 per page.

Jack County

District Court 100 Main, County Courthouse, Jacksboro, TX 76458; 940-567-2141; Fax: 940-567-2696. Hours: 8AM-5PM (CST). *Felony, Civil.*

Civil Records: Access: Mail, in person. Only the court conducts in person searches; visitors may not. Search fee: $10.00 per name. Required to search: name, years to search. Civil cases indexed by defendant, plaintiff. Civil records in index books from 1857. **Criminal Records:** Access: Mail, in person. Only the court conducts in person searches; visitors may not. Search fee: $10.00 per name. Required to search: name, years to search. Criminal records in index books from 1857. **General Information:** No juvenile, mental, sealed, or adoption records released. SASE required. Turnaround time 2 days. Copy fee: $.50 per page. Certification fee: $1.00. Fee payee: Jack County District Clerk. Personal checks accepted. Prepayment is required.

County Court 100 Main, Jacksboro, TX 76458; 940-567-2111. Hours: 8AM-5PM (CST). *Misdemeanor, Civil, Probate.*

Civil Records: Access: Phone, mail, in person. Both court and visitors may perform in person searches. Search fee: $5.00 per name. Required to search: name, years to search. Civil cases indexed by defendant, plaintiff. Civil records in index books from 1856. **Criminal Records:** Access: Phone, mail, in person. Both court and visitors may perform in person searches. Search fee: $5.00 per name. Required to search: name, years to search. Criminal records in index books from 1856. **General Information:** No juvenile, mental, sealed, or adoption records released. SASE required. Turnaround time 1-2 days. Copy fee: $1.00 per page. Certification fee: $5.00. Fee payee: Jack County Clerk. Personal checks accepted. Prepayment is required.

Jackson County

District Court 115 W Main Rm 203, Edna, TX 77957; 361-782-3812. Hours: 8AM-5PM (CST). *Felony, Civil.*

Civil Records: Access: Phone, mail, in person. Both court and visitors may perform in person searches. Search fee: $5.00 per name. Required to search: name, years to search. Civil cases indexed by defendant, plaintiff. Civil records in index books from 1850. **Criminal Records:** Access: Phone, mail, in person. Both court and visitors may perform in person searches. Search fee: $5.00 per name. Required to search: name, years to search. Criminal records on microfiche from 1981, index books from 1850. **General Information:** No juvenile, mental, sealed, or adoption records released. SASE required. Turnaround time 1-2 days. Copy fee: $1.00 per page. Certification fee: $1.00. Fee payee: District Clerk. Personal checks accepted. Prepayment is required.

County Court 115 W Main Rm101, Edna, TX 77957; 361-782-3563. Hours: 8AM-5PM (CST). *Misdemeanor, Civil, Probate.*

Civil Records: Access: Mail, in person. Both court and visitors may perform in person searches. Search fee: $5.00 per name. Required to search:

name, years to search. Civil cases indexed by defendant, plaintiff. Civil records in index books from 1900s. **Criminal Records:** Access: Mail, in person. Both court and visitors may perform in person searches. Search fee: $5.00 per name. Required to search: name, years to search, DOB, offense, date of offense. Criminal records in index books from 1900s. **General Information:** No juvenile, mental, sealed, or adoption records released. SASE not required. Turnaround time 1-2 days. Copy fee: $1.00 per page. Certification fee: $5.00. Fee payee: County Clerk. Personal checks accepted. Prepayment is required.

Jasper County

District Court County Courthouse #202, PO Box 2088, Jasper, TX 75951; 409-384-2721. Hours: 8AM-4:30PM (CST). *Felony, Civil.*

Civil Records: Access: Mail, in person. Only the court conducts in person searches; visitors may not. Search fee: $5.00 per name. Required to search: name, years to search. Civil cases indexed by defendant, plaintiff. Civil records on computer since 1991, index books and microfilm since 1850s. **Criminal Records:** Access: Mail, in person. Only the court conducts in person searches; visitors may not. Search fee: $5.00 per name. Required to search: name, years to search. Criminal records on computer since 12/96; index books and microfilm since 1850s. **General Information:** No juvenile, mental, sealed, or adoption records released. SASE required. Turnaround time 1-2 days. Copy fee: $1.00 for first page, $.50 each addl. Certification fee: No certification. Fee payee: District Clerk/Court. Personal checks accepted. Prepayment is required.

County Court Rm 103, Courthouse, Main at Lamar, PO Box 2070, Jasper, TX 75951; 409-384-9481; Fax: 409-384-7198. Hours: 8AM-5PM (CST). *Misdemeanor, Civil, Probate.*

Civil Records: Access: Mail, in person. Both court and visitors may perform in person searches. Search fee: $10.00 per name. There is no fee if you do the search yourself. Required to search: name, years to search. Civil cases indexed by defendant, plaintiff. Civil records in index books. **Criminal Records:** Access: Mail, in person. Both court and visitors may perform in person searches. Search fee: $10.00 per name. Thewre is no fee if you do the search yourself. Required to search: name, years to search, DOB; also helpful-SSN. Criminal records in index books. **General Information:** No juvenile, mental, sealed, or adoption records released. SASE not required. Turnaround time 1 day. Copy fee: $1.00 per page. Certification fee: $5.00. Fee payee: Debbie Newman County Clerk. Personal checks accepted. Personal checks require drivers license. Prepayment is required.

Jeff Davis County

District & County Court PO Box 398, Fort Davis, TX 79734; 915-426-3251; Fax: 915-426-3760. Hours: 9AM-Noon, 1-5PM (CST). *Felony, Misdemeanor, Civil, Eviction, Probate.*

Civil Records: Access: Mail, in person. Both court and visitors may perform in person searches. Search fee: $5.00 per name. Required to search: name, years to search. Civil cases indexed by defendant, plaintiff. Civil records in index books. **Criminal Records:** Access: Mail, in person. Both court and visitors may perform in person searches. Search fee: $5.00 per name. Required to search: name, years to search. Criminal records in index books. **General Information:** No juvenile, mental, sealed, or adoption records released. SASE required. Turnaround time 2 days. Copy fee: $1.00

per page. Certification fee: $5.00. Fee payee: County Clerk. Personal checks accepted. Prepayment is required.

Jefferson County

District Court PO Box 3707, Beaumont, TX 77704; 409-835-8580; Fax: 409-835-8527. Hours: 8AM-5PM (CST). *Felony, Civil.*

www.co.jefferson.tx.us

Civil Records: Access: Mail, in person. Both court and visitors may perform in person searches. Search fee: $5.00 per name. Required to search: name, years to search. Civil cases indexed by defendant, plaintiff. Civil records on computer and index books since 1940s. Search results are not certified unless done by the court itself. **Criminal Records:** Access: Mail, in person. Both court and visitors may perform in person searches. Search fee: $5.00 per name. Required to search: name, years to search; also helpful-DOB, SSN. Criminal records on computer and index books since 1940s. **General Information:** No juvenile, mental, sealed, or adoption records released. SASE required. Turnaround time 2-4 days. Copy fee: $1.00 per page. Certification fee: $1.00. Fee payee: District Clerk. Personal checks accepted. Prepayment is required. Public access terminal is available. Public Access Terminal Note: Civil, Family & E-file on selected cases.

County Court PO Box 1151, Beaumont, TX 77704; 409-835-8479; Fax: 409-839-2394. Hours: 8AM-5PM (CST). *Misdemeanor, Civil, Probate.*

Civil Records: Access: Fax, mail, in person. Both court and visitors may perform in person searches. Search fee: $5.00 per name. Required to search: name, years to search. Civil cases indexed by defendant, plaintiff. Civil records on computer since 11/01/95, index books prior. **Criminal Records:** Access: Fax, mail, in person. Both court and visitors may perform in person searches. Search fee: $5.00 per name. Required to search: name, years to search, DOB. Criminal records on computer since 02/25/91, index books prior. **General Information:** No juvenile, mental, sealed, or adoption records released. SASE required. Turnaround time 1 day. Copy fee: $1.00 per page. Certification fee: $5.00. Fee payee: County Clerk. Personal checks accepted. Prepayment is required. Public access terminal is available. Fax notes: $3.00 for first page, $.50 each addl.

Jim Hogg County

District & County Court PO Box 878, Hebbronville, TX 78361; 361-527-4031; Fax: 361-527-5843. Hours: 9AM-5PM (CST). *Felony, Misdemeanor, Civil, Eviction, Probate.*

Civil Records: Access: Mail, in person. Both court and visitors may perform in person searches. Search fee: $15.00 per name. Required to search: name, years to search. Civil cases indexed by defendant, plaintiff. Civil records in index books. **Criminal Records:** Access: Mail, in person. Both court and visitors may perform in person searches. Search fee: $15.00 per name. Required to search: name, years to search. Criminal records in index books. **General Information:** No juvenile, mental, sealed, or adoption records released. SASE required. Turnaround time 2-4 days. Copy fee: $1.00 per page. Certification fee: $5.00. Fee payee: District Clerk. Personal checks accepted. Prepayment is required.

Jim Wells County

79th District Court PO Drawer 2219, Alice, TX 78333; 361-668-5717. Hours: 8AM-Noon, 1-5PM (CST). *Felony, Civil.*

Civil Records: Access: Mail, in person. Both court and visitors may perform in person searches. Search fee: $5.00 per name. Required to search: name, years to search. Civil cases indexed by defendant, plaintiff. Civil records on computer since 1992, index books since 1912. **Criminal Records:** Access: Mail, in person. Both court and visitors may perform in person searches. Search fee: $5.00 per name. Required to search: name, years to search; also helpful-SSN. Criminal records on computer since 1992, index books since 1912. **General Information:** No juvenile, mental, sealed, or adoption records released. SASE required. Turnaround time 2 days. Copy fee: $1.00 per page. Certification fee: $2.00. Fee payee: District Clerk. Personal checks accepted. Prepayment is required.

County Court PO Box 1459, 200 N Almond, Alice, TX 78333; 361-668-5702. Hours: 8:30AM-Noon, 1-5PM (CST). *Misdemeanor, Civil, Probate.*

Civil Records: Access: Phone, mail, in person. Both court and visitors may perform in person searches. Search fee: $10.00 per name. Required to search: name, years to search. Civil cases indexed by defendant, plaintiff. Civil records in index books. **Criminal Records:** Access: Phone, mail, in person. Both court and visitors may perform in person searches. Search fee: $10.00 per name. Required to search: name, years to search, address, DOB. Criminal records on computer since 1986, index books also. **General Information:** No juvenile, mental, sealed, or adoption records released. SASE not required. Turnaround time 1 day. Copy fee: $1.00 per page. Certification fee: $5.00. Fee payee: County Clerk. Personal checks accepted. Prepayment is required.

Johnson County

District Court PO Box 495, Cleburne, TX 76033-0495; 817-556-6300; Fax: 817-556-6120. Hours: 8AM-5PM (CST). *Felony, Civil.*

Civil Records: Access: Fax, mail, in person. Both court and visitors may perform in person searches. Search fee: $5.00 per name. Required to search: name; also helpful-years to search. Civil cases indexed by defendant, plaintiff. Civil records on computer from 1989, index books also. **Criminal Records:** Access: Fax, mail, in person. Both court and visitors may perform in person searches. Search fee: $5.00 per name. Required to search: name; also helpful-years to search, aliases. Criminal records on computer from 1989, index books also. **General Information:** No juvenile, mental, sealed, or adoption records released. SASE required. Turnaround time 2-4 days. Copy fee: $.50 per page. Certification fee: $1.00. Fee payee: District Clerk. Business checks accepted. Prepayment is required. Public access terminal is available.

County Court Room 104, PO Box 662, Cleburne, TX 76033-0662; 817-556-6300. Hours: 8AM-Noon, 1-4:30PM (CST). *Misdemeanor, Civil, Probate.*

Civil Records: Access: Mail, in person. Both court and visitors may perform in person searches. Search fee: $5.00 per name. Required to search: name, years to search. Civil cases indexed by defendant, plaintiff. Civil records on computer since 1988, index books after 1988. **Criminal**

Records: Access: Mail, in person. Both court and visitors may perform in person searches. Search fee: $5.00 per name. Required to search: name, years to search. Criminal records on computer since 1988, index books after 1988. **General Information:** No juvenile, mental, sealed, or adoption records released. SASE required. Turnaround time 1-2 days. Copy fee: $1.00 per page. Certification fee: $5.00. Fee payee: County Clerk. Business checks accepted. Prepayment is required. Public access terminal is available.

Jones County

District Court PO Box 308, Anson, TX 79501; 915-823-3731; Fax: 915-823-3513 (Attn: Nona Carter). Hours: 8AM-5PM (CST). *Felony, Misdemeanor, Civil.*

Civil Records: Access: Mail, in person. Both court and visitors may perform in person searches. Search fee: $5.00 per name. Required to search: name, years to search. Civil cases indexed by defendant, plaintiff. Civil records on computer since 1990, index books since 1881. **Criminal Records:** Access: Mail, in person. Both court and visitors may perform in person searches. Search fee: $5.00 per name. Required to search: name, years to search, DOB. Criminal records on computer since 1986, index books since 1881. **General Information:** No juvenile, mental, sealed, or adoption records released. SASE required. Turnaround time same day. Copy fee: $1.00 per page. Certification fee: $2.00. Fee payee: Nona Carter, District Clerk. Personal checks accepted. Can set up deposit account. Prepayment is required.

Karnes County

District Court County Courthouse, 101 N Panna Maria Ave, Karnes City, TX 78118-2930; 830-780-2562; Fax: 830-780-3227. Hours: 8AM-Noon, 1-5PM (CST). *Felony, Civil.*

Civil Records: Access: Mail, in person. Both court and visitors may perform in person searches. Search fee: $5.00 per name. Required to search: name, years to search. Civil cases indexed by defendant, plaintiff. Civil records in index books. **Criminal Records:** Access: Mail, in person. Both court and visitors may perform in person searches. Search fee: $5.00 per name. Required to search: name, years to search. Criminal records in index books. **General Information:** No juvenile, mental, sealed, or adoption records released. SASE required. Turnaround time 1-2 days. Copy fee: $1.00 per page. Certification fee: $2.00. Fee payee: District Clerk. Personal checks accepted. Prepayment is required.

County Court 101 N Panna Maria Ave #9 Courthouse, Karnes City, TX 78118-2929; 830-780-3938; Fax: 830-780-4576. Hours: 8AM-5PM (CST). *Misdemeanor, Civil, Probate.*

Civil Records: Access: Mail, in person. Both court and visitors may perform in person searches. Search fee: $10.00 per name. Required to search: name, years to search. Civil cases indexed by defendant, plaintiff. Civil records in index books, no compuerization. **Criminal Records:** Access: Mail, in person. Both court and visitors may perform in person searches. Search fee: $10.00 per name. Required to search: name, years to search. Criminal records in index books, no compuerization. **General Information:** No juvenile, mental, sealed, or adoption records released. SASE required. Turnaround time 2 days. Copy fee: $1.00 per page. Certification fee: $5.00. Fee payee: Elizabeth Swize, County Clerk. Personal checks accepted. Prepayment is required.

Kaufman County

District Court County Courthouse, Kaufman, TX 75142; 972-932-4331. Hours: 8AM-5PM (CST). *Felony, Civil.*

Civil Records: Access: Mail, in person. Both court and visitors may perform in person searches. Search fee: $5.00 per name. Required to search: name, years to search. Civil cases indexed by defendant, plaintiff. Civil records on computer from 1849. **Criminal Records:** Access: Mail, in person. Both court and visitors may perform in person searches. Search fee: $5.00 per name. Required to search: name, years to search. Criminal records on computer from 1849. **General Information:** No sealed, or adoption records released. SASE required. Turnaround time up to 1 week. Copy fee: $1.00 per page. Certification fee: $1.00. Fee payee: Kaufman Distric Clerk. Personal checks accepted. Prepayment is required.

County Court County Courthouse, Kaufman, TX 75142; 972-932-4331. Hours: 8AM-5PM (CST). *Misdemeanor, Civil, Probate.*

Civil Records: Access: Mail, in person. Only the court conducts in person searches; visitors may not. Search fee: $5.00 per name. Required to search: name, years to search. Civil cases indexed by defendant, plaintiff. Civil records on computer from 1985, index books before 1985. **Criminal Records:** Access: Mail, in person. Only the court conducts in person searches; visitors may not. Search fee: $5.00 per name. Required to search: name, years to search. Criminal records on computer from 1985, index books before 1985. **General Information:** No juvenile, mental, sealed, or adoption records released. SASE required. Turnaround time 1-2 days. Copy fee: $1.00 per page. Certification fee: $5.00. Fee payee: County Clerk. Personal checks accepted. Prepayment is required.

Kendall County

District Court 201 E. San Antonia, #201, Boerne, TX 78006; 830-249-9343. Hours: 8AM-Noon, 1-5PM (CST). *Felony, Civil.*

Civil Records: Access: Mail, in person. Both court and visitors may perform in person searches. Search fee: $5.00 per name. Required to search: name, years to search. Civil cases indexed by defendant, plaintiff. Civil records in index books. **Criminal Records:** Access: Mail, in person. Both court and visitors may perform in person searches. Search fee: $5.00 per name. Required to search: name, years to search; also helpful-DOB, SSN. Criminal records in index books. **General Information:** No juvenile, mental, sealed, or adoption records released. SASE required. Turnaround time 2-4 days. Copy fee: $.50 per page. Certification fee: $1.00 per page. Fee payee: District Clerk. Personal checks accepted. Prepayment is required.

County Court 204 E San Antonio #127, Boerne, TX 78006; 830-249-9343; Fax: 830-249-3472. Hours: 8AM-5PM (CST). *Misdemeanor, Civil, Probate.*

Civil Records: Access: Mail, in person. Both court and visitors may perform in person searches. Search fee: $10.00 per name. Required to search: name, years to search. Civil cases indexed by defendant, plaintiff. Civil records in index books. **Criminal Records:** Access: Mail, in person. Both court and visitors may perform in person searches. Search fee: $10.00 per name. Required to search: name, years to search. Criminal records in index books. **General Information:** No juvenile,

mental, sealed, or adoption records released. SASE required. Turnaround time 2-4 days. Copy fee: $1.00 per page. Certification fee: $5.00. Fee payee: County Clerk. Personal checks accepted. Prepayment is required.

Kenedy County

District & County Court PO Box 227, Sarita, TX 78385; 361-294-5220; Fax: 361-294-5218. Hours: 8:30AM-Noon, 1PM-4:30PM (CST). *Felony, Misdemeanor, Civil, Eviction, Probate.*

Civil Records: Access: Mail, in person. Both court and visitors may perform in person searches. Search fee: $5.00 per name. Required to search: name, years to search. Civil cases indexed by defendant, plaintiff. Civil records on microfilm since 1991, minute books since 1921. **Criminal Records:** Access: Mail, in person. Both court and visitors may perform in person searches. Search fee: $5.00 per name. Required to search: name, years to search. Criminal records on microfilm since 1991, minute books since 1921. **General Information:** No juvenile, mental, sealed, or adoption records released. SASE not required. Turnaround time 5 days. Copy fee: $1.00 per page. Certification fee: $5.00. Fee payee: District/County Clerk. Personal checks accepted. Prepayment is required.

Kent County

District & County Court PO Box 9, Jayton, TX 79528; 806-237-3881; Fax: 806-237-2632. Hours: 8:30AM-Noon, 1-5PM (CST). *Felony, Misdemeanor, Civil, Eviction, Probate.*

Civil Records: Access: Mail, in person. Both court and visitors may perform in person searches. Search fee: $5.00 per name. Required to search: name, years to search. Civil cases indexed by defendant, plaintiff. Civil records in index books. **Criminal Records:** Access: Mail, in person. Both court and visitors may perform in person searches. Search fee: $5.00 per name. Required to search: name, years to search. Criminal records in index books. **General Information:** No juvenile, mental, sealed, or adoption records released. SASE required. Turnaround time as soon as possible. Copy fee: $1.00 per page. Certification fee: $5.00 plus $1.00 per page. Fee payee: County Clerk. Only cashiers checks and money orders accepted. Prepayment is required.

Kerr County

District Court 700 Main, County Courthouse, Kerrville, TX 78028; 830-792-2281. Hours: 8AM-5PM (CST). *Felony, Civil.*

Civil Records: Access: Mail, in person. Both court and visitors may perform in person searches. Search fee: $5.00 per name. Required to search: name, years to search. Civil cases indexed by defendant, plaintiff. Civil records on computer from late 1991, index books after 1991. **Criminal Records:** Access: Mail, in person. Both court and visitors may perform in person searches. Search fee: $5.00 per name. Required to search: name, years to search, DOB, SSN. Criminal records on computer from late 1991, index books after 1991. **General Information:** No juvenile, mental, sealed, or adoption records released. SASE required. Turnaround time 2-4 days. Copy fee: $1.00 per page. Certification fee: $1.00. Fee payee: District Clerk. Personal checks accepted. 1989. Prepayment is required.

County Court & County Court at Law
700 Main St, #122, Kerrville, TX 78028-5389; 830-792-2255; Probate phone:830-792-2298; Fax:

830-792-2274. Hours: 8AM-5PM (CST). *Misdemeanor, Civil, Probate.*

Civil Records: Access: Phone, mail, fax, in person. Both court and visitors may perform in person searches. Search fee: $5.00 per name. Required to search: name, years to search. Civil cases indexed by defendant, plaintiff. Civil records on computer since 1988, microfiche since 1985, index books prior to 1985. **Criminal Records:** Access: Phone, mail, fax, in person. Both court and visitors may perform in person searches. Search fee: $5.00 per name. Required to search: name, years to search, DOB; also helpful: SSN. Criminal records on computer since 1988, microfiche since 1985, index books prior to 1985. **General Information:** No juvenile, mental, sealed, or adoption records released. SASE not required. Turnaround time 3 days. Copy fee: $1.00 per page. Certification fee: $5.00. Fee payee: Kerr County Clerk. Only cashiers checks and money orders accepted. Prepayment is required. Public access terminal is available. Fax notes: $2.00 1st page; $1.00 each add'l.

Kimble County

District & County Court 501 Main St, Junction, TX 76849; 915-446-3353; Fax: 915-446-2986. Hours: 8AM-Noon, 1-5PM (CST). *Felony, Misdemeanor, Civil, Probate.*

Civil Records: Access: Mail, in person. Both court and visitors may perform in person searches. Search fee: $5.00 per name. Required to search: name, years to search. Civil cases indexed by defendant, plaintiff. Civil records in index books (records are micro-filmed for security only). **Criminal Records:** Access: Mail, in person. Both court and visitors may perform in person searches. Search fee: $5.00 per name. Required to search: name, years to search, DOB. Criminal records in index books (records are micro-filmed for security only). **General Information:** No juvenile, mental, sealed, or adoption records released. SASE not required. Turnaround time 3-4 days. Copy fee: $1.00 per page. Certification fee: $5.00. Fee payee: Kimble County/District Clerk. Personal checks accepted. Prepayment is required.

King County

District & County Court PO Box 135, Guthrie, TX 79236; 806-596-4412; Fax: 806-596-4664. Hours: 9AM-Noon, 1-5PM (CST). *Felony, Misdemeanor, Civil, Eviction, Probate.*

Civil Records: Access: Mail, in person. Both court and visitors may perform in person searches. Search fee: $5.00 per name. Required to search: name, years to search. Civil cases indexed by defendant, plaintiff. Civil records in index books. **Criminal Records:** Access: Mail, in person. Both court and visitors may perform in person searches. Search fee: $5.00 per name. Required to search: name, years to search; also helpful-DOB. Criminal records in index books. **General Information:** No juvenile, mental, sealed, or adoption records released. SASE required. Turnaround time 2-4 days. Copy fee: $1.00 per page. Certification fee: $5.00. Fee payee: District Clerk. Personal checks accepted. Prepayment is required.

Kinney County

District & County Court PO Drawer 9, Brackettville, TX 78832; 830-563-2521; Fax: 830-563-2644. Hours: 8AM-5PM (CST). *Felony, Misdemeanor, Civil, Probate.*

Civil Records: Access: Phone, fax, mail, in person. Both court and visitors may perform in person searches. Search fee: $10.00 per name.

Required to search: name, years to search. Civil cases indexed by defendant, plaintiff. Civil records in index books. **Criminal Records:** Access: Phone, fax, mail, in person. Both court and visitors may perform in person searches. Search fee: $10.00 per name. Required to search: name, years to search. Criminal records in index books. **General Information:** No juvenile, mental, sealed, or adoption records released. SASE required. Turnaround time 1 week. Copy fee: $1.00 per page. Certification fee: Certification fee: $5.00 County; $1.00 District. Fee payee: County & District Clerk. Personal checks accepted. Prepayment is required. Fax notes: $3.00 for 1st page; $2.00 each add'l.

Kleberg County

District & County Court at Law PO Box 312, Kingsville, TX 78364-0312; 361-595-8561; Fax: 361-595-8525. Hours: 8AM-Noon, 1-5 PM (CST). *Felony, Civil.*

Civil Records: Access: Phone, fax, mail, in person. Both court and visitors may perform in person searches. Search fee: $5.00 per name. Required to search: name, years to search. Civil cases indexed by defendant, plaintiff. Civil records in index books since 1916. **Criminal Records:** Access: Phone, fax, mail, in person. Both court and visitors may perform in person searches. Search fee: $5.00 per name. Required to search: name, years to search; also helpful-DOB, SSN. Criminal records in index books since 1916. **General Information:** No sealed or adoption records released. SASE required. Turnaround time 2-3 days. Copy fee: $1.00 per page. Certification fee: $1.00. Fee payee: District Clerk. Personal checks accepted. (local personal checks only). Prepayment is required. Fax notes: $5.00 per document. Incoming fax fee $1.00.

County Court-Criminal PO Box 1327, Kingsville, TX 78364; 361-595-8548. Hours: 8AM-5PM (CST). *Misdemeanor, Probate.*

Note: Court also handles civil cases dealing with occupational licenses and bond forfeitures. **Criminal Records:** Access: Mail, in person. Both court and visitors may perform in person searches. Search fee: $5.00 per name. Required to search: name, years to search, DOB. Criminal records on computer since 1994, index books since 1913. **General Information:** No juvenile or mental records released. SASE required. Turnaround time same day. Copy fee: $1.00 per page. Certification fee: $5.00. Fee payee: Klebert County Clerk. Business checks accepted. Prepayment is required.

Knox County

District & County Court PO Box 196, Benjamin, TX 79505; 940-454-2441. Hours: 8AM-Noon, 1-5PM (CST). *Felony, Misdemeanor, Civil, Eviction, Probate.*

Civil Records: Access: Mail, in person. Both court and visitors may perform in person searches. Search fee: $10.00 per name. Required to search: name, years to search. Civil cases indexed by defendant, plaintiff. Civil records in index books. **Criminal Records:** Access: Mail, in person. Both court and visitors may perform in person searches. Search fee: $5.00 for a misdemeanor search; $5.00 for a felony search. Required to search: name, years to search. Criminal records in index books. **General Information:** No juvenile, mental, sealed, or adoption records released. SASE required. Turnaround time 1 day. Copy fee: $1.00 per page. Certification fee: $5.00. Fee payee: District/County Clerk. Personal checks accepted. Prepayment is required.

La Salle County

District Court PO Box 340, Cotulla, TX 78014; 830-879-2421. Hours: 8AM-5PM (CST). *Felony, Civil.*

Civil Records: Access: Mail, in person. Both court and visitors may perform in person searches. Search fee: $5.00 per name. Required to search: name, years to search. Civil cases indexed by defendant, plaintiff. Civil records in index books. **Criminal Records:** Access: Mail, in person. Both court and visitors may perform in person searches. Search fee: $5.00 per name. Required to search: name, years to search. Criminal records in index books. **General Information:** No juvenile, mental, sealed, or adoption records released. SASE required. Turnaround time 1-2 days. Copy fee: $1.00 per page. Certification fee: $5.00. Fee payee: District Clerk. Personal checks accepted. Prepayment is required.

District & County Courts PO Box 340, Cotulla, TX 78014; 830-879-2117; Fax: 830-879-2933. Hours: 8AM-5PM (CST). *Misdemeanor, Civil, Eviction, Probate.*

Civil Records: Access: Mail, in person. Both court and visitors may perform in person searches. Search fee: $5.00 per name. Required to search: name, years to search. Civil cases indexed by defendant, plaintiff. Civil records on computer since 1994, prior on index books. **Criminal Records:** Access: Mail, in person. Both court and visitors may perform in person searches. Search fee: $5.00 per name. Required to search: name, years to search. Criminal records on computer since 1994, prior on index books. **General Information:** No juvenile, mental, sealed, or adoption records released. SASE required. Turnaround time 1-2 days. Copy fee: $1.00 per page. Certification fee: $5.00. Fee payee: County Clerk. Personal checks accepted. Prepayment is required.

Lamar County

District Court 119 N Main Rm 306, Paris, TX 75460; 903-737-2427. Hours: 8AM-5PM (CST). *Felony, Civil.*

Civil Records: Access: Mail, in person. Both court and visitors may perform in person searches. Search fee: $5.00 per name. Required to search: name, years to search. Civil cases indexed by defendant, plaintiff. Civil records on computer since January, 1994, index books prior to 1994. **Criminal Records:** Access: Mail, in person. Both court and visitors may perform in person searches. Search fee: $5.00 per name. Required to search: name, years to search. Criminal records on computer since January, 1994, index books prior to 1994. **General Information:** No juvenile, mental, sealed, or adoption records released. SASE required. Turnaround time 1-2 days. Copy fee: $1.00 per page. Certification fee: No certification fee. Fee payee: District Clerk. Personal checks accepted. Prepayment is required. Public access terminal is available.

County Court 119 N Main, Paris, TX 75460; 903-737-2420. Hours: 8AM-5PM (CST). *Misdemeanor, Civil, Probate.*

Civil Records: Access: Phone, fax, mail, in person. Both court and visitors may perform in person searches. Search fee: $10.00 per name. Required to search: name, years to search. Civil cases indexed by defendant, plaintiff. Civil records in index books since 1913. **Criminal Records:** Access: Phone, fax, mail, in person. Both court and visitors may perform in person searches.

Search fee: $5.00 per name. Required to search: name, years to search. Criminal records on computer since 1988, index books since 1913. **General Information:** No juvenile, mental, sealed, or adoption records released. SASE not required. Turnaround time 2-3 days. Copy fee: $1.00 per page. Certification fee: $1.00. Fee payee: County Clerk. Business checks accepted. Personal checks must be local. Prepayment is required.

Lamb County

District Court 100 6th Rm 212, Courthouse, Littlefield, TX 79339; 806-385-4222. Hours: 8:30AM-Noon, 1-5PM (CST). *Felony, Civil.*

Civil Records: Access: Mail, in person. Both court and visitors may perform in person searches. Search fee: $5.00 per name. Required to search: name, years to search. Civil cases indexed by defendant, plaintiff. Civil records on computer since 1995. **Criminal Records:** Access: Mail, in person. Both court and visitors may perform in person searches. Search fee: $10.00 per name. Required to search: name, years to search. Criminal records in index books. **General Information:** No juvenile, mental, sealed, or adoption records released. SASE required. Turnaround time 2-3 days. Copy fee: $1.00 per page. Certification fee: $1.00 per page. Fee payee: District Court. Personal checks accepted. Prepayment is required.

County Court County Courthouse, Rm 103, Box 3, Littlefield, TX 79339-3366; 806-385-4222 X214; Fax: 806-385-6485. Hours: 8AM-5PM (CST). *Misdemeanor, Civil, Probate.*

Civil Records: Access: Mail, in person. Both court and visitors may perform in person searches. Search fee: $5.00 per name. Required to search: name, years to search. Civil cases indexed by defendant, plaintiff. Civil records in index books. **Criminal Records:** Access: Mail, in person. Both court and visitors may perform in person searches. Search fee: $5.00 per name. Required to search: name, years to search; also helpful-DOB, SSN. Criminal records in index books. **General Information:** No juvenile, mental, sealed, or adoption records released. SASE required. Turnaround time 1-2 days. Copy fee: $1.00 per page. Certification fee: $5.00. Fee payee: Lamb County Clerk. Personal checks accepted. Prepayment is required.

Lampasas County

District Court PO Box 327, Lampasas, TX 76550; 512-556-8271 X22; Fax: 512-556-8270. Hours: 8AM-5PM (CST). *Felony, Civil.*

Civil Records: Access: Mail, in person. Both court and visitors may perform in person searches. Search fee: $5.00 per name. Required to search: name, years to search. Civil cases indexed by defendant, plaintiff. Civil records in index books. **Criminal Records:** Access: Mail, in person. Both court and visitors may perform in person searches. Search fee: $5.00 per name. Required to search: name, years to search. Criminal records in index books. **General Information:** No juvenile, mental, sealed, or adoption records released. SASE required. Turnaround time 2-4 days. Copy fee: $1.00 per page. Certification fee: $2.00. Fee payee: District Clerk. Business checks accepted. Prepayment is required.

County Court PO Box 347, Lampasas, TX 76550; 512-556-8271 X37. Hours: 8AM-5PM (CST). *Misdemeanor, Civil, Probate.*

Civil Records: Access: Mail, in person. Both court and visitors may perform in person searches. Search fee: $5.00 per name. Required to search: name, years to search. Civil cases indexed by defendant, plaintiff. Civil records in index books. **Criminal Records:** Access: Mail, in person. Both court and visitors may perform in person searches. Search fee: $5.00 per name. Required to search: name, years to search; also helpful-DOB, SSN. Criminal records in index books. **General Information:** No juvenile, mental, sealed, or adoption records released. SASE required. Turnaround time 1-2 days. Copy fee: $1.00 per page. Certification fee: $5.00. Fee payee: County Clerk. Personal checks accepted. Checks must be in state. Prepayment is required. Public access terminal is available.

Lavaca County

District Court PO Box 306, Hallettsville, TX 77964; 361-798-2351. Hours: 8AM-Noon, 1-5PM (CST). *Felony, Civil.*

Civil Records: Access: Phone, mail, in person. Both court and visitors may perform in person searches. Search fee: $5.00 per name. Required to search: name, years to search. Civil cases indexed by defendant, plaintiff. Civil records in index books from 1847. Information released to attorneys only. **Criminal Records:** Access: Mail, in person. Both court and visitors may perform in person searches. Search fee: $5.00 per name. Required to search: name, years to search. Criminal records in index books from 1847. Information released to law enforcement only. **General Information:** No juvenile, Department of Human Services, adoptions and expunction records released. SASE required. Turnaround time same day. Copy fee: $1.00 per page. Certification fee: $2.00. Fee payee: Lavaca County District Clerk. Personal checks accepted. Prepayment is required.

County Court PO Box 326, Hallettsville, TX 77964; 361-798-3612. Hours: 8AM-5PM (CST). *Misdemeanor, Civil, Probate.*

Civil Records: Access: Mail, in person. Both court and visitors may perform in person searches. Search fee: $5.00 per name. Required to search: name, years to search; also helpful-address. Civil cases indexed by defendant, plaintiff. Civil records in index books. **Criminal Records:** Access: Mail, in person. Both court and visitors may perform in person searches. Search fee: $5.00 per name. Required to search: name, years to search; also helpful-address, DOB. Criminal records in index books. **General Information:** No juvenile, mental, sealed or adoption released. SASE not required. Turnaround time same day as received. Copy fee: $1.00 per page. Certification fee: $5.00. Fee payee: County Clerk. Personal checks accepted. Prepayment is required.

Lee County

District Court PO Box 176, Giddings, TX 78942; 979-542-2947; Fax: 979-542-2444. Hours: 8AM-Noon, 1-5PM (CST). *Felony, Civil.*

Civil Records: Access: Mail, in person. Both court and visitors may perform in person searches. Search fee: $5.00 per name. Required to search: name, years to search. Civil cases indexed by defendant, plaintiff. Civil records on index books from 1800s. **Criminal Records:** Access: Mail, in person. Both court and visitors may perform in person searches. Search fee: $5.00 per name. Required to search: name, years to search; also helpful-DOB, SSN. Criminal records on computer since 1989. **General Information:** No juvenile or

adoption records released. Turnaround time 1-2 days. Copy fee: $1.00 per page. Certification fee: $2.00. Fee payee: District Clerk, Lee County. Personal checks accepted. Prepayment is required.

County Court PO Box 419, Giddings, TX 78942; 979-542-3684; Fax: 979-542-2623. Hours: 8AM-5PM (CST). *Misdemeanor, Civil, Probate.*

Civil Records: Access: Mail, in person. Both court and visitors may perform in person searches. Search fee: $5.00 per name. Required to search: name, years to search. Civil cases indexed by defendant, plaintiff. Civil records in index books since 1874 (beginning 1995 on computer). **Criminal Records:** Access: Mail, in person. Both court and visitors may perform in person searches. Search fee: $5.00 per name. Required to search: name, years to search. Criminal records on computer since 1992, index books since 1874. **General Information:** No juvenile, mental, sealed or adoption records released. SASE required. Turnaround time 1-3 days. Copy fee: $1.00 per page. Certification fee: $5.00. Fee payee: County Clerk. Personal checks accepted. Prepayment is required.

Leon County

District Court PO Box 39, Centerville, TX 75833; 903-536-2227. Hours: 8AM-5PM (CST). *Felony, Civil.*

Civil Records: Access: Mail, in person. Both court and visitors may perform in person searches. Search fee: $5.00 per name. Required to search: name, years to search. Civil cases indexed by defendant, plaintiff. Civil records in index books. **Criminal Records:** Access: Mail, in person. Only the court conducts in person searches; visitors may not. Search fee: $5.00 per name. Required to search: name, years to search. Criminal records in index books. **General Information:** No juvenile, mental, sealed, or adoption records released. SASE required. Turnaround time 2-4 days. Copy fee: $1.00 per page. Certification fee: $2.00. Fee payee: District Clerk. Personal checks accepted. Prepayment is required.

County Court PO Box 98, Centerville, TX 75833; 903-536-2352. Hours: 8AM-5PM (CST). *Misdemeanor, Civil, Probate.*

Civil Records: Access: Mail, in person. Both court and visitors may perform in person searches. Search fee: $5.00 per name. Required to search: name, years to search. Civil cases indexed by defendant, plaintiff. Civil records in index books. **Criminal Records:** Access: Mail, in person. Both court and visitors may perform in person searches. Search fee: $5.00 per name. Required to search: name, years to search, signed release. Criminal records in index books. **General Information:** No juvenile, mental, sealed, or adoption records released. SASE not required. Turnaround time 1-3 days. Copy fee: $1.00 per page. Certification fee: $5.00. Fee payee: Leon County Clerk. Business checks accepted. Personal checks accepted in person only. Prepayment is required.

Liberty County

District Court 1923 Sam Houston Rm 303, Liberty, TX 77575; 936-336-4600. Hours: 8AM-Noon, 1-5PM (CST). *Felony, Civil.*

Civil Records: Access: Mail, in person. Both court and visitors may perform in person searches. Search fee: $5.00 per name. Required to search: name, years to search. Civil cases indexed by defendant, plaintiff. Civil records on computer since 1994, index books prior. **Criminal Records:** Access: Mail, in person. Both court and visitors

may perform in person searches. Search fee: $5.00 per name. Required to search: name, years to search. Criminal records on computer since 1994, index books prior. **General Information:** No juvenile, mental, sealed, or adoption records released. SASE required. Turnaround time 2-4 days. Copy fee: $1.00 per page. Certification fee: $2.00. Fee payee: District Clerk. Personal checks accepted. Prepayment is required.

County Court PO Box 369, Liberty, TX 77575; 936-336-4670. Hours: 8AM-5PM (CST). *Misdemeanor, Civil, Probate.*

Civil Records: Access: Mail, in person. Both court and visitors may perform in person searches. Search fee: $5.00 per name. Required to search: name, years to search. Civil cases indexed by defendant, plaintiff. Civil records in index books. **Criminal Records:** Access: Mail, in person. Both court and visitors may perform in person searches. Search fee: $5.00 per name. Required to search: name, years to search, DOB, SSN. Criminal records in index books. **General Information:** No juvenile, mental, sealed, or adoption records released. SASE required. Turnaround time 2-4 days. Copy fee: $1.00 per page. Certification fee: $5.00. Fee payee: County Clerk. Business checks accepted. Personal checks accepted in person only. Prepayment is required.

Limestone County

District Court PO Box 230, Groesbeck, TX 76642; 254-729-3206; Fax: 254-729-2960. Hours: 8AM-5PM (CST). *Felony, Civil.*

Civil Records: Access: Phone, fax, mail, in person. Both court and visitors may perform in person searches. Search fee: $5.00 per name. Required to search: name, years to search. Civil cases indexed by defendant, plaintiff. Civil records on computer since September 1990, index books since 1883. **Criminal Records:** Access: Phone, fax, mail, in person. Both court and visitors may perform in person searches. Search fee: $5.00 per name. Required to search: name, years to search, DOB; also helpful-SSN. Criminal records on computer since September 1990, index books since 1911. **General Information:** No juvenile, mental, sealed, or adoption records released. SASE not required. Turnaround time 1 week. Copy fee: $1.00 per document or $.50 per single page. Certification fee: $2.00. Fee payee: District Clerk. Personal checks accepted. Fax notes: $1.00 for first page, $.25 each addl. No lengthy faxes.

County Court PO Box 350, Groesbeck, TX 76642; 254-729-5504; Fax: 254-729-2951. Hours: 8AM-5PM (CST). *Misdemeanor, Civil, Probate.*

Civil Records: Access: Mail, in person. Both court and visitors may perform in person searches. Search fee: $5.00 per name. Required to search: name, years to search. Civil cases indexed by defendant, plaintiff. Civil records in index books. **Criminal Records:** Access: Mail, in person. Both court and visitors may perform in person searches. Search fee: $10.00 per name. Required to search: name, years to search. Criminal records in index books. **General Information:** No juvenile, mental, sealed, or adoption records released. SASE not required. Turnaround time 2 days. Copy fee: $1.00 per page. Certification fee: $5.00. Fee payee: Limestone County Clerk. Personal checks accepted. Prepayment is required. Public access terminal is available.

Lipscomb County

District & County Court PO Box 70, Lipscomb, TX 79056; 806-862-3091; Fax: 806-862-3004. Hours: 8:30AM-Noon, 1-5PM (CST). *Felony, Misdemeanor, Civil, Eviction, Probate.*

Civil Records: Access: Fax, mail, in person. Both court and visitors may perform in person searches. Search fee: $5.00 per name. Required to search: name. Civil cases indexed by defendant, plaintiff. Civil records in index books since 1887. **Criminal Records:** Access: Fax, mail, in person. Both court and visitors may perform in person searches. Search fee: $5.00 per name. Required to search: name; also helpful-DOB. Criminal records in index books since 1887. **General Information:** No juvenile, mental, sealed, or adoption records released. SASE not required. Turnaround time 2 days. Copy fee: $1.00 per page. Certification fee: $5.00. Fee payee: County Clerk. Personal checks accepted. Prepayment is required. Fax notes: $1.00 for first page, $.50 each addl.

Live Oak County

District Court PO Drawer O, George West, TX 78022; 361-449-2733 X105. Hours: 8AM-5PM (CST). *Felony, Civil.*

Civil Records: Access: Mail, in person. Both court and visitors may perform in person searches. Search fee: $10.00 per name. Required to search: name, years to search. Civil cases indexed by defendant, plaintiff. Civil records in index books and microfiche since 1850s. **Criminal Records:** Access: Mail, in person. Both court and visitors may perform in person searches. Search fee: $10.00 per name. Required to search: name, years to search, DOB; also helpful-SSN. Criminal records in index books and microfiche since 1850s. **General Information:** No juvenile, mental, sealed, or adoption records released. SASE required. Turnaround time 1-2 days. Copy fee: $1.00 per page. Certification fee: $1.00. Fee payee: District Clerk. Personal checks accepted. Prepayment is required.

County Court PO Box 280, George West, TX 78022; 361-449-2733 X3. Hours: 8AM-5PM (CST). *Misdemeanor, Civil, Probate.*

Civil Records: Access: Mail, in person. Both court and visitors may perform in person searches. Search fee: $10.00 per name. Required to search: name, years to search. Civil cases indexed by defendant, plaintiff. Civil records in index books. **Criminal Records:** Access: Mail, in person. Both court and visitors may perform in person searches. Search fee: $10.00 per name. Required to search: name, years to search. Criminal records in index books. **General Information:** No juvenile, mental, sealed, or adoption records released. SASE required. Turnaround time 1-2 days. Copy fee: $1.00 per page. Certification fee: $5.00. Fee payee: County Clerk. Personal checks accepted. Prepayment is required.

Llano County

District Clerk PO Box 877, Llano, TX 78643-0877; 915-247-5036; Fax: 915-247-2446. Hours: 8AM-4:30PM (CST). *Felony, Civil.*

Civil Records: Access: Mail, in person. Both court and visitors may perform in person searches. Search fee: $5.00 per name. Fee is per 5 year period. Required to search: name, years to search. Civil cases indexed by defendant, plaintiff. Civil records in index books. **Criminal Records:** Access: Mail, in person. Both court and visitors may perform in person searches. Search fee: $5.00 per name. Fee is per 5 year period. Required to

search: name, years to search. Criminal records in index books. **General Information:** No juvenile, mental, sealed, or adoption records released. SASE required. Turnaround time 1-3 days. Copy fee: $1.00 per page. Certification fee: $1.00 per page. Fee payee: Llano County District Clerk. Personal checks accepted. Credit cards accepted: Visa, Mastercard. 5% handling fee charged. Prepayment is required.

County Court PO Box 40, Llano, TX 78643-0040; 915-247-4455. Hours: 8AM-4:30PM (CST). *Misdemeanor, Civil, Probate.*

Civil Records: Access: Phone, mail, in person. Both court and visitors may perform in person searches. Search fee: $5.00 per name. Required to search: name, years to search. Civil cases indexed by defendant, plaintiff. Civil records on computer since 1985, index books prior. **Criminal Records:** Access: Phone, mail, in person. Both court and visitors may perform in person searches. Search fee: $5.00 per name. Required to search: name, years to search; also helpful-DOB. Criminal records on computer since 1985, index books prior. **General Information:** No juvenile, mental, sealed, or adoption records released. SASE not required. Turnaround time 2-4 days. Copy fee: $1.00 per page. Certification fee: $5.00. Fee payee: County Clerk. Personal checks accepted.

Loving County

District & County Court PO Box 194, Mentone, TX 79754; 915-377-2441; Fax: 915-377-2701. Hours: 9AM-Noon, 1-5PM (CST). *Felony, Misdemeanor, Civil, Eviction, Probate.*

Civil Records: Access: Fax, mail, in person. Both court and visitors may perform in person searches. Search fee: $5.00 per name. Required to search: name, years to search. Civil cases indexed by defendant, plaintiff. Civil records in index books. **Criminal Records:** Access: Fax, mail, in person. Both court and visitors may perform in person searches. Search fee: $5.00 per name. Required to search: name, years to search. Criminal records in index books. **General Information:** No juvenile, mental, sealed, or adoption records released. SASE required. Turnaround time 2 days. Copy fee: $1.00 per page. Certification fee: $5.00. Fee payee: Loving County Clerk. Personal checks accepted. Prepayment is required. Fax notes: $1.50 per page.

Lubbock County

District Court PO Box 10536, Lubbock, TX 79408-3536; 806-775-1623; Fax: 806-775-1382. Hours: 8AM-5PM (CST). *Felony, Civil.*

http://members.tripod.com/districtclerk

Civil Records: Access: Fax, mail, in person. Both court and visitors may perform in person searches. Search fee: $5.00 per name. Required to search: name, years to search. Civil cases indexed by defendant, plaintiff. Civil records on computer since 1991, index books prior. **Criminal Records:** Access: Fax, mail, in person. Both court and visitors may perform in person searches. Search fee: $5.00 per name. Required to search: name, years to search; also helpful-DOB, SSN. Criminal records on computer since 1991, index books prior. **General Information:** No juvenile, mental, sealed, or adoption records released. SASE required. Certification fee: $1.00. Fee payee: District Clerk. Personal checks accepted. Prepayment is required. Public access terminal is available. Fax notes: $5.00 per document.

County Courts Courthouse, Room 207, PO Box 10536, Lubbock, TX 79408; 806-775-1051.

Hours: 8:30AM-5PM (CST). *Misdemeanor, Civil, Probate.*

Civil Records: Access: Mail, in person. Both court and visitors may perform in person searches. Search fee: $10.00 per name. Fee is for each 5 year period. Required to search: name, years to search. Civil cases indexed by defendant, plaintiff. Civil records on computer since 1986, index books prior. **Criminal Records:** Access: Mail, in person. Both court and visitors may perform in person searches. Search fee: $5.00 per name. Fee is for each 5 year period; $7.00 for more than 5 years. Required to search: name, years to search, DOB. Criminal records on computer since 1986, index books prior. **General Information:** No juvenile, mental, sealed, or adoption records released. SASE required. Turnaround time 3-5 days. Copy fee: $1.00 per page. Certification fee: $5.00. Fee payee: County Clerk. Personal checks accepted. Prepayment is required. Public access terminal is available.

Lynn County

District Court PO Box 939, Tahoka, TX 79373; 806-998-4274; Fax: 806-998-4151. Hours: 8:30AM-5PM (CST). *Felony, Civil.*

Civil Records: Access: Fax, mail, in person. Both court and visitors may perform in person searches. Search fee: $5.00 per name. Required to search: name, years to search. Civil cases indexed by defendant, plaintiff. Civil records on computer from 1997, index books from 1916. **Criminal Records:** Access: Fax, mail, in person. Both court and visitors may perform in person searches. Search fee: $5.00 per name. Required to search: name, years to search. Criminal records on computer from 1997, index books from 1916. **General Information:** No juvenile, mental, sealed, or adoption records released. SASE not required. Turnaround time 2 days. Copy fee: $1.00 per page. Certification fee: $1.00 per page. Fee payee: District Clerk. Personal checks accepted. Prepayment is required. Fax notes: $2.00 per page.

County Court PO Box 937, Tahoka, TX 79373; 806-998-4750; Fax: 806-998-4277. Hours: 8:30AM-5PM (CST). *Misdemeanor, Civil, Probate.*

Civil Records: Access: Mail, in person. Both court and visitors may perform in person searches. Search fee: $5.00. Required to search: name, years to search. Civil cases indexed by defendant, plaintiff. Civil records in index books from 1903. **Criminal Records:** Access: Mail, in person. Both court and visitors may perform in person searches. Search fee: $5.00. Required to search: name, years to search. Criminal records in index books from 1903. **General Information:** No juvenile, mental, sealed, or adoption records released. SASE required. Turnaround time 2-4 days. Copy fee: $1.00 per page. Certification fee: $5.00. Fee payee: Lynn County Clerk. Personal checks accepted. Prepayment is required.

Madison County

District Court 101 W Main Rm 226, Madisonville, TX 77864; 936-348-9203. Hours: 8AM-Noon, 1-5PM (CST). *Felony, Civil.*

Civil Records: Access: Mail, in person. Both court and visitors may perform in person searches. Search fee: $5.00 per name. Required to search: name, years to search. Civil cases indexed by defendant, plaintiff. Civil records in index books. **Criminal Records:** Access: Mail, in person. Both court and visitors may perform in person searches. Search fee: $5.00 per name. Required to search:

name, years to search. Criminal records in index books. **General Information:** No juvenile, mental, sealed, or adoption records released. SASE required. Turnaround time 1 day. Copy fee: $1.00 per page. Certification fee: No certification fee. Fee payee: District Clerk. Personal checks accepted. Prepayment is required.

County Court 101 W Main Rm 102, Madisonville, TX 77864; 936-348-2638; Fax: 936-348-5858. Hours: 8AM-5PM (CST). *Misdemeanor, Civil, Probate.*

Civil Records: Access: Mail, in person. Both court and visitors may perform in person searches. Search fee: $10.00 per name. Required to search: name, years to search. Civil cases indexed by defendant. Civil records on computer from 1985, index books prior. **Criminal Records:** Access: Mail, in person. Both court and visitors may perform in person searches. Search fee: $10.00 per name. Required to search: name, years to search. Criminal records on computer from 1985, index books prior. **General Information:** No juvenile, mental, sealed, or adoption records released. SASE required. Turnaround time as soon as fees are paid. Copy fee: $1.00 per page. Certification fee: $5.00. Fee payee: Madison County Clerk. Personal checks accepted. Prepayment is required. Public access terminal is available. Fax notes: Fee to fax back results is $1.00 per page.

Marion County

District Court PO Box 628, Jefferson, TX 75657; 903-665-2441/2013. Hours: 8AM-5PM (CST). *Felony, Civil.*

Civil Records: Access: Mail, in person. Both court and visitors may perform in person searches. Search fee: $5.00 per name. Required to search: name, years to search. Civil cases indexed by defendant, plaintiff. Civil records on computer from 1991, index books up to 1986. **Criminal Records:** Access: Mail, in person. Both court and visitors may perform in person searches. Search fee: $5.00 per name. Required to search: name, years to search. Criminal records on computer from 1991, index books up to 1986. **General Information:** No juvenile, mental, sealed, or adoption records released. SASE required. Turnaround time 1 week. Copy fee: $1.00 per page. Certification fee: No certification fee. Fee payee: District Clerk. Personal checks accepted. Prepayment is required.

County Court PO Box 763, Jefferson, TX 75657; 903-665-3971. Hours: 8AM-Noon, 1-5PM (CST). *Misdemeanor, Probate.* **Criminal Records:** Access: Phone, mail, in person. Both court and visitors may perform in person searches. No search fee. Required to search: name, years to search. Criminal records in index books. **General Information:** No juvenile, mental, sealed, or adoption records released. SASE required. Turnaround time 2-4 days. Copy fee: $1.00 per page. Certification fee: $5.00. Fee payee: County Clerk. Personal checks accepted. Prepayment is required.

Martin County

District & County Court PO Box 906, Stanton, TX 79782; 915-756-3412. Hours: 8AM-Noon, 1-5PM (CST). *Felony, Misdemeanor, Civil, Eviction, Probate.*

Civil Records: Access: Mail, in person. Both court and visitors may perform in person searches. Search fee: $5.00 per name. Required to search: name, years to search. Civil cases indexed by defendant, plaintiff. Civil records in index books.

Criminal Records: Access: Mail, in person. Both court and visitors may perform in person searches. Search fee: $5.00 per name. Required to search: name, years to search. Criminal records in index books. **General Information:** No juvenile, mental, sealed, or adoption records released. SASE required. Turnaround time 2-4 days. Copy fee: $1.00 per page. Certification fee: $5.00. Fee payee: County/District Clerk. Personal checks accepted. Prepayment is required.

Mason County

District & County Court PO Box 702, Mason, TX 76856; 915-347-5253; Fax: 915-347-6868. Hours: 8AM-Noon, 1-4PM (CST). *Felony, Misdemeanor, Civil, Probate.*

Civil Records: Access: Mail, in person. Both court and visitors may perform in person searches. Search fee: $10.00 per name. Required to search: name, years to search. Civil cases indexed by defendant, plaintiff. Civil records in index books. **Criminal Records:** Access: Mail, in person. Both court and visitors may perform in person searches. Search fee: $10.00 per name. Required to search: name, years to search; also helpful-DOB. Criminal records in index books. **General Information:** No juvenile, mental, sealed, or adoption records released. SASE required. Turnaround time 2 days. Copy fee: $1.00 per page. Certification fee: $5.00. Fee payee: County/District Clerk. Personal checks accepted. Prepayment is required.

Matagorda County

District Court 1700 7th St Rm 307, Bay City, TX 77414-5092; 979-244-7621. Hours: 8AM-Noon, 1-5PM (CST). *Felony, Civil.*

Civil Records: Access: Mail, in person. Both court and visitors may perform in person searches. Search fee: $5.00 per name. Required to search: name, years to search. Civil cases indexed by defendant, plaintiff. Civil records in index books and card files. **Criminal Records:** Access: Mail, in person. Both court and visitors may perform in person searches. Search fee: $5.00 per name. Required to search: name, years to search. Criminal records in index books and card files. **General Information:** No juvenile, sealed, or adoption records released. SASE required. Turnaround time 1-2 days. Copy fee: $1.00 per page. Certification fee: $2.00. Fee payee: District Clerk. Personal checks accepted. Prepayment is required.

County Court 1700 7th St Rm 202, Bay City, TX 77414-5094; 979-244-7680; Fax: 979-244-7688. Hours: 8AM-5PM (CST). *Misdemeanor, Civil, Probate.*

Civil Records: Access: Mail, in person. Both court and visitors may perform in person searches. Search fee: $5.00 per name. Required to search: name, years to search. Civil cases indexed by defendant, plaintiff. Civil records on computer from 1994, index books prior. **Criminal Records:** Access: Mail, in person. Both court and visitors may perform in person searches. Search fee: $5.00 per name. Required to search: name, years to search, DOB, SSN. Criminal records on computer from 1994, index books prior. **General Information:** No juvenile, mental, sealed, or adoption records released. SASE required. Turnaround time 1-2 days. Copy fee: $1.00 per page. Certification fee: $5.00. Fee payee: County Clerk. Personal checks accepted. Credit cards accepted: Visa, Mastercard, Discover. MC, Visa, Discover. Prepayment is required. Public access terminal is available.

Maverick County

District Court PO Box 3659, Eagle Pass, TX 78853; 830-773-2629. Hours: 8AM-5PM (CST). *Felony, Civil.*

Civil Records: Access: Mail, in person. Both court and visitors may perform in person searches. Search fee: $5.00 per name. Required to search: name, years to search. Civil cases indexed by defendant, plaintiff. Civil records in index books. **Criminal Records:** Access: Mail, in person. Both court and visitors may perform in person searches. Search fee: $5.00 per name. Required to search: name, years to search. Criminal records in index books. **General Information:** No juvenile, mental, sealed, or adoption records released. SASE required. Turnaround time 2-4 days. Copy fee: $1.00 per page. Certification fee: $1.00. Fee payee: District Clerk. Personal checks accepted. Prepayment is required.

County Court PO Box 4050, Eagle Pass, TX 78853; 830-773-2829. Hours: 8AM-5PM (CST). *Misdemeanor, Civil, Probate.*

Civil Records: Access: Mail, in person. Both court and visitors may perform in person searches. Search fee: $10.00 per name. Required to search: name, years to search. Civil cases indexed by defendant, plaintiff. Civil records on computer since 1984, prior on index books. **Criminal Records:** Access: Mail, in person. Both court and visitors may perform in person searches. Search fee: $10.00 per name. Required to search: name, years to search, DOB, SSN. Criminal records on computer since 1984, prior on index books. **General Information:** No juvenile, mental, sealed, or adoption records released. SASE not required. Turnaround time 1-2 days. Copy fee: $1.00 per page. Certification fee: $5.00. Fee payee: County Clerk. Personal checks accepted. Prepayment is required.

McCulloch County

District Court County Courthouse Rm 205, Brady, TX 76825; 915-597-0733; Fax: 915-597-0606. Hours: 8:30AM-5PM (CST). *Felony, Civil.*

Civil Records: Access: Mail, fax, in person. Both court and visitors may perform in person searches. Search fee: $5.00 per name. Required to search: name, years to search. Civil cases indexed by defendant, plaintiff. Civil records in index books. **Criminal Records:** Access: Mail, fax, in person. Both court and visitors may perform in person searches. Search fee: $5.00 per name. Required to search: name, years to search; also helpful-DOB, SSN. Criminal records in index books. **General Information:** No juvenile, mental, sealed, or adoption records released. SASE required. Turnaround time 2-4 days. Copy fee: $1.00 per page. Certification fee: $2.00. Fee payee: District Clerk. Personal checks accepted. Prepayment is required.

County Court County Courthouse, Brady, TX 76825; 915-597-0733. Hours: 8AM-5PM (CST). *Misdemeanor, Civil, Probate.*

Civil Records: Access: Mail, in person. Both court and visitors may perform in person searches. Search fee: $5.00 per name. Required to search: name, years to search. Civil cases indexed by defendant, plaintiff. Civil records in index books. **Criminal Records:** Access: Mail, in person. Both court and visitors may perform in person searches. Search fee: $5.00 per name. Required to search: name, years to search. Criminal records in index books. **General Information:** No juvenile, mental, sealed, or adoption records released. SASE required. Turnaround time 1-2 days. Copy fee: $1.00 per page. Certification fee: $1.00. Fee payee: County Clerk. Personal checks accepted. Prepayment is required.

McLennan County

District Court PO Box 2451, Waco, TX 76703; 254-757-5054; Civil phone:254-757-5057; Criminal phone:254-757-5057; Fax: 254-757-5060. Hours: 8AM-Noon, 1-5PM *Felony, Civil.*

Civil Records: Access: Fax, mail, in person. Both court and visitors may perform in person searches. Search fee: $5.00 per name. Required to search: name, years to search. Civil cases indexed by defendant, plaintiff. Civil records on computer since 1986, index books from 1850. **Criminal Records:** Access: Fax, mail, in person. Both court and visitors may perform in person searches. Search fee: $5.00 per name. Required to search: name, years to search. Criminal records on computer since 1959, index books from 1850. **General Information:** No juvenile, mental, sealed, or adoption records released. SASE required. Turnaround time 2 days. Copy fee: $1.00 per page. Certification fee: No certification fee. Fee payee: Joe Johnson, District Clerk. Personal checks accepted. Credit cards accepted: Visa, Mastercard. Prepayment is required.

County Court PO Box 1727, Waco, TX 76703; 254-757-5185; Fax: 254-757-5146. Hours: 8AM-5PM (CST). *Misdemeanor, Civil, Probate.*

Civil Records: Access: Mail, in person. Both court and visitors may perform in person searches. Search fee: $5.00 per name. Required to search: name, years to search. Civil cases indexed by defendant, plaintiff. Civil records in index books. **Criminal Records:** Access: Mail, in person. Both court and visitors may perform in person searches. Search fee: $5.00 per name. Required to search: name, years to search; also helpful-DOB, SSN. Criminal records on computer since 1993. **General Information:** No juvenile, mental, sealed, or adoption records released. SASE required. Turnaround time 2-4 days. Copy fee: $1.00 per page. Certification fee: $5.00. Fee payee: County Clerk. Business checks accepted. Prepayment is required.

McMullen County

District & County Court PO Box 235, Tilden, TX 78072; 361-274-3215; Fax: 361-274-3618. Hours: 8AM-4PM (CST). *Felony, Misdemeanor, Civil, Eviction, Probate.*

Civil Records: Access: Mail, in person. Both court and visitors may perform in person searches. Search fee: $5.00 per name. Required to search: name, years to search. Civil cases indexed by defendant, plaintiff. Civil records in index books. **Criminal Records:** Access: Mail, in person. Both court and visitors may perform in person searches. Search fee: $5.00 per name. Required to search: name, years to search. Criminal records in index books. **General Information:** No juvenile, mental, sealed, or adoption records released. SASE required. Turnaround time 2-4 days. Copy fee: $1.00 per page. Certification fee: $5.00. Fee payee: County Clerk. Personal checks accepted. Prepayment is required.

Medina County

District Court County Courthouse Rm 209, Hondo, TX 78861; 830-741-6000. Hours: 8AM-Noon, 1-5PM (CST). *Felony, Civil.*

Civil Records: Access: Phone, mail, in person. Both court and visitors may perform in person

searches. Search fee: $5.00 per name. Required to search: name, years to search. Civil cases indexed by defendant, plaintiff. Civil records on computer since 1990, microfiche from 1849 to 1982, index books since 1849. **Criminal Records:** Access: Phone, mail, in person. Both court and visitors may perform in person searches. Search fee: $5.00 per name. Required to search: name, years to search, DOB. Criminal records on computer since 1990, microfiche from 1849-1982, index books since 1849. **General Information:** No juvenile, mental, sealed, or adoption records released. SASE required. Turnaround time 1 week. Copy fee: $.50 per page. Certification fee: $1.00 per page. Fee payee: District Clerk. Only cashiers checks and money orders accepted. Out-of-state checks not accepted. Prepayment is required. Public access terminal is available.

County Court at Law 1100 16th St, Rm 109, Hondo, TX 78861; 830-741-6041. Hours: 8AM-Noon, 1-5PM (CST). *Misdemeanor, Civil, Probate.*

Civil Records: Access: Phone, mail, in person. Both court and visitors may perform in person searches. Search fee: $5.00 per name. Required to search: name, years to search. Civil cases indexed by defendant, plaintiff. Civil records on computer since late 1993, index books prior. **Criminal Records:** Access: Phone, mail, in person. Both court and visitors may perform in person searches. Search fee: $5.00 per name. Required to search: name, years to search; also helpful-address, DOB, SSN. Criminal records on computer since late 1993, index books prior. **General Information:** No juvenile, mental, or sealed records released. SASE required. Turnaround time 1-2 days. Copy fee: $1.00 per page. Certification fee: $5.00. Fee payee: County Clerk. Personal checks accepted. Prepayment is required.

Menard County

District & County Court PO Box 1028, Menard, TX 76859; 915-396-4682; Fax: 915-396-2047. Hours: 8AM-Noon, 1-5PM (CST). *Felony, Misdemeanor, Civil, Eviction, Probate.*

Civil Records: Access: Fax, mail, in person. Both court and visitors may perform in person searches. Search fee: $9.00 per name. Required to search: name, years to search. Civil cases indexed by defendant, plaintiff. Civil records in index books. **Criminal Records:** Access: Mail, in person. Both court and visitors may perform in person searches. Search fee: $9.00 per name. Required to search: name, years to search. Criminal records in index books. **General Information:** No juvenile, mental, sealed, or adoption records released. SASE required. Turnaround time 2-4 days. Copy fee: $1.00 per page. Certification fee: $5.00. Fee payee: District/County Clerk. Personal checks accepted. Prepayment is required. Fax notes: $1.00 per page.

Midland County

District Court 200 W Wall #301, Midland, TX 79701; 915-688-1107. Hours: 8AM-5PM (CST). *Felony, Civil.*

Civil Records: Access: Mail, in person. Both court and visitors may perform in person searches. Search fee: $5.00 per name. Required to search: name, years to search. Civil cases indexed by defendant, plaintiff. Civil records on computer from July, 1987, index books prior. **Criminal Records:** Access: Mail, in person. Both court and visitors may perform in person searches. Search fee: $5.00 per name. Required to search: name, years to search. Criminal records on computer

from July, 1987, index books prior. **General Information:** No juvenile, mental, sealed, or adoption records released. SASE required. Turnaround time 2 days. Copy fee: $1.00 per page. Certification fee: No certification fee. Fee payee: District Clerk. Business checks accepted. Prepayment is required. Public access terminal is available.

County Court PO Box 211, Midland, TX 79702; 915-688-1070; Fax: 915-688-8973. Hours: 8AM-5PM (CST). *Misdemeanor, Civil, Probate.*

Civil Records: Access: Mail, in person. Both court and visitors may perform in person searches. Search fee: $5.00 per name. Required to search: name; also helpful-years to search, address. Civil cases indexed by defendant, plaintiff. Civil records on computer since 1987, index books since 1885. Probate records on computer since 1887. **Criminal Records:** Access: Mail, in person. Both court and visitors may perform in person searches. Search fee: $5.00 per name. Required to search: name; also helpful-years to search, address, DOB, SSN. Criminal records on computer since 1978, index books since 1885. **General Information:** No juvenile, mental, sealed, or adoption records released. SASE not required. Turnaround time 1-2 days. Copy fee: $1.00 per page. Certification fee: $5.00. Fee payee: County Clerk. Only cashiers checks and money orders accepted. Prepayment is required. Public access terminal is available.

Milam County

District Court PO Box 999, Cameron, TX 76520; 254-697-3952. Hours: 8AM-5PM (CST). *Felony, Civil.*

Civil Records: Access: Mail, in person. Both court and visitors may perform in person searches. Search fee: $5.00 per name. Required to search: name, years to search. Civil cases indexed by defendant, plaintiff. Civil records on microfilm and index books. **Criminal Records:** Access: Mail, in person. Both court and visitors may perform in person searches. Search fee: $5.00 per name. Required to search: name, years to search. Criminal records on microfilm and index books. **General Information:** No juvenile, mental, sealed, or adoption records released. SASE required. Turnaround time same day. Copy fee: $1.00 per page. Certification fee: $1.00. Fee payee: District Clerk. Only cashiers checks and money orders accepted. Prepayment is required.

County Court PO Box 191, Cameron, TX 76520; 254-697-7049; Fax: 254-697-7002. Hours: 8AM-5PM (CST). *Misdemeanor, Civil, Probate.*

Civil Records: Access: Mail, in person. Both court and visitors may perform in person searches. Search fee: $5.00 per name. Required to search: name, years to search. Civil cases indexed by defendant, plaintiff. Civil records in index books. **Criminal Records:** Access: Mail, in person. Both court and visitors may perform in person searches. Search fee: $5.00 per name. Required to search: name, years to search. Criminal records in index books. **General Information:** No juvenile, mental, sealed, or adoption records released. SASE not required. Turnaround time 1-2 days. Copy fee: $1.00 per page. Certification fee: $5.00. Fee payee: Milam County Clerk. Personal checks accepted. Prepayment is required.

Mills County

District & County Court PO Box 646, Goldthwaite, TX 76844; 915-648-2711; Fax: 915-648-2806. Hours: 8AM-Noon, 1-5PM (CST). *Felony, Misdemeanor, Civil, Probate.*

Civil Records: Access: Phone, mail, in person. Both court and visitors may perform in person searches. Search fee: $5.00 per name. Required to search: name, years to search; also helpful-cause number. Civil cases indexed by defendant, plaintiff. Civil records in index books since 1887. **Criminal Records:** Access: Mail, fax, in person. Both court and visitors may perform in person searches. Search fee: $5.00 per name. Required to search: name, years to search, DOB, signed release; also helpful-cause number. Criminal records in index books since 1887. **General Information:** No juvenile, mental, sealed, or adoption records released. SASE required. Turnaround time 1-2 days. Copy fee: $1.00 per page. Certification fee: $5.00. Fee payee: County-District Clerk. Personal checks accepted. Prepayment is required.

Mitchell County

District Court County Courthouse, Colorado City, TX 79512; 915-728-5918. Hours: 8AM-5PM (CST). *Felony, Civil.*

Civil Records: Access: Mail, in person. Both court and visitors may perform in person searches. Search fee: $5.00 per name. Required to search: name, years to search. Civil cases indexed by defendant, plaintiff. Civil records in index books. **Criminal Records:** Access: Mail, in person. Only the court conducts in person searches; visitors may not. Search fee: $5.00 per name. Required to search: name, years to search. Criminal records in index books. **General Information:** No juvenile, mental, sealed, or adoption records released. SASE required. Turnaround time 1 day. Copy fee: $.35 per page. Certification fee: $1.00 per page. Fee payee: District Clerk. Personal checks accepted. Prepayment is required.

County Court 349 Oak St Rm 103, Colorado City, TX 79512; 915-728-3481; Fax: 915-728-5322. Hours: 8AM-Noon, 1-5PM (CST). *Misdemeanor, Civil, Probate.*

Civil Records: Access: Fax, mail, in person. Both court and visitors may perform in person searches. Search fee: $5.00 per name. Required to search: name, years to search. Civil cases indexed by defendant, plaintiff. Criminal records in index books, on computer from 9-1-1998 to present. **Criminal Records:** Access: Fax, mail, in person. Both court and visitors may perform in person searches. Search fee: $5.00 per name. Required to search: name, years to search; also helpful-DOB. Criminal records in index books, on computer from 9-1-1998 to present. **General Information:** No juvenile, mental, sealed, or adoption, commitment records released. Turnaround time 2-4 days. Copy fee: $1.00 per page. Certification fee: $5.00. Fee payee: Mitchell County Clerk. Personal checks accepted. No out of state personal checks. Money order accepted. Prepayment is required. Fax notes: $3.00 for first page, $1.00 each addl.

Montague County

District Court PO Box 155, Montague, TX 76251; 940-894-2571. Hours: 8AM-5PM (CST). *Felony, Civil.*

Civil Records: Access: Mail, in person. Both court and visitors may perform in person searches. Search fee: $5.00 per name. Required to search: name, years to search. Civil cases indexed by defendant, plaintiff. Civil records on computer and index books. **Criminal Records:** Access: Mail, in person. Both court and visitors may perform in person searches. Search fee: $5.00 per name. Required to search: name, years to search. Criminal records on computer and index books. **General Information:** No juvenile, mental, sealed, or adoption records released. SASE required. Turnaround time 2-4 days. Copy fee: $1.00 per page. Certification fee: $5.00. Fee payee: District Clerk. Personal checks accepted. Prepayment is required.

County Court PO Box 77, Montague, TX 76251; 940-894-2461. Hours: 8AM-5PM (CST). *Misdemeanor, Civil, Probate.*

Civil Records: Access: Mail, in person. Both court and visitors may perform in person searches. Search fee: $5.00 per name. Required to search: name, years to search. Civil cases indexed by defendant, plaintiff. Civil records on computer since 1993, index books prior. **Criminal Records:** Access: Mail, in person. Both court and visitors may perform in person searches. Search fee: $5.00 per name. Required to search: name, years to search. Criminal records on computer since 1993, index books prior. **General Information:** No juvenile, mental, sealed, or adoption records released. SASE required. Turnaround time 1-2 days. Copy fee: $1.00 per page. Certification fee: $5.00. Fee payee: County Clerk. Personal checks accepted. Prepayment is required.

Montgomery County

District Court PO Box 2985, Conroe, TX 77305; 936-539-7855. Hours: 8AM-5PM (CST). *Felony, Civil.*

Civil Records: Access: Mail, in person. Both court and visitors may perform in person searches. Search fee: $5.00 per name. Required to search: name, years to search. Civil cases indexed by defendant, plaintiff. Civil records in index books, on computer since 1988. **Criminal Records:** Access: Mail, in person. Both court and visitors may perform in person searches. Search fee: $5.00 per name. Required to search: name, years to search. Criminal records in index books, on computer since 1988. **General Information:** No juvenile, mental, sealed, or adoption records released. SASE not required. Turnaround time 3-6 days. Copy fee: $1.00 per page. Certification fee: No certification fee. Fee payee: Barbara Adamick, District Clerk. Personal checks accepted. Prepayment is required. Public access terminal is available.

County Court PO Box 959, Conroe, TX 77305; 936-539-7885; Fax: 936-760-6990. Hours: 8AM-5PM (CST). *Misdemeanor, Civil, Probate.*

www.co.montgomery.tx.us

Civil Records: Access: Mail, in person. Both court and visitors may perform in person searches. Search fee: $5.00 per name. Required to search: name, years to search. Civil cases indexed by defendant, plaintiff. Civil records on computer and index books. **Criminal Records:** Access: Mail, in person. Both court and visitors may perform in person searches. Search fee: $5.00 per name. Required to search: name, years to search. Criminal records on computer and index books. **General Information:** No juvenile, mental, sealed, or adoption records released. SASE required. Turnaround time 2 days. Copy fee: $1.00 per page. Certification fee: $5.00. Fee payee: County Clerk. Personal checks accepted. Prepayment is required. Public access terminal is available.

Moore County

District Court 715 Dumas Ave #109, Dumas, TX 79029; 806-935-4218; Fax: 806-935-6325. Hours: 8:30AM-5PM (CST). *Felony, Civil.*

Civil Records: Access: Mail, in person. Both court and visitors may perform in person searches. Search fee: $5.00 per name. Required to search: name, years to search. Civil cases indexed by defendant, plaintiff. Civil records on computer, docket books and original files. **Criminal Records:** Access: Mail, in person. Both court and visitors may perform in person searches. Search fee: $5.00 per name. Required to search: name, years to search, DOB; also helpful-SSN. Criminal records on computer, docket books and original files. **General Information:** No juvenile, mental, sealed, or adoption records released. SASE required. Turnaround time 1 day. Copy fee: $1.00 per page. Certification fee: $1.00. Fee payee: District Clerk. Personal checks accepted. Prepayment is required.

County Court 715 Dumas Ave Rm 105, Dumas, TX 79029; 806-935-6164/2009; Fax: 806-935-9004. Hours: 8:30AM-5PM (CST). *Misdemeanor, Civil, Probate.*

Civil Records: Access: Mail, in person. Both court and visitors may perform in person searches. Search fee: $5.00 per name. Required to search: name, years to search. Civil cases indexed by defendant, plaintiff. Civil records in index books. **Criminal Records:** Access: Mail, in person. Both court and visitors may perform in person searches. Search fee: $5.00 per name. Required to search: name, years to search. Criminal records on computer since July, 1987, in index books prior. **General Information:** No juvenile, mental, sealed, or adoption records released. SASE required. Turnaround time 24 hours. Copy fee: $1.00 per page. Certification fee: $5.00. Fee payee: Moore County Clerk. Business checks accepted. Prepayment is required.

Morris County

District Court 500 Brodnax, Daingerfield, TX 75638; 903-645-2321. Hours: 8AM-5PM (CST). *Felony, Civil.*

Civil Records: Access: Mail, in person. Both court and visitors may perform in person searches. Search fee: $5.00 per name. Required to search: name, years to search. Civil cases indexed by defendant, plaintiff. Civil records in index books and file folders. Plaintiff index only for active cases. **Criminal Records:** Access: Mail, in person. Both court and visitors may perform in person searches. Search fee: $5.00 per name. Required to search: name, years to search, DOB. Criminal records in index books and file folders. Plaintiff index only for active cases. **General Information:** No juvenile, mental, sealed, or adoption records released. SASE required. Turnaround time 1 day. Copy fee: $1.00 per page. Certification fee: No certification fee. Fee payee: Morris County District Clerk. Personal checks accepted. Prepayment is required.

County Court 500 Broadnax, Daingerfield, TX 75638; 903-645-3911. Hours: 8AM-5PM (CST). *Misdemeanor, Probate.* **Criminal Records:** Access: Mail, in person. Both court and visitors may perform in person searches. Search fee: $5.00 per name. Required to search: name, years to search. Criminal record on index books. **General Information:** No juvenile, mental, sealed, or adoption records released. SASE not required. Turnaround time 1 day. Copy fee: $1.00 per page.

owner name, address, or property ID number. Search allows you to access owner address, property address, legal description, taxing entities, exemptions, deed, account number, abstract/subdivision, neighborhood, valuation info, and/or building attributes.

Counties with Assessor/tax records online **no fee:**

Anderson	Angelina	Aransas	Atascosa
Austin	Bastrop	Blanco	Brazoria
Brazos	Brown	Burleson	Burnet
Caldwell	Calhoun	Coleman	Comanche
Fannin	Ft. Bend	Gillespie	Hays
Hunt	Kendall	Kerr	Kimble
Lamb	Liberty	Limestone	Llano
Lubbock	Madison	Maverick	Milam
Montgomery	Newton	Nueces	Rockwall
San Jacinto	Somervell	Swisher	Upshur
Victoria	Waller	Washington	Wharton
Wilson	Wood		

Anderson County

County Clerk, 500 North Church Street, Palestine, TX 75801. 903-723-7402.
Online Access: Assessor/Property Tax. See note at beginning of section.

Andrews County

County Clerk, P.O. Box 727, Andrews, TX 79714. 915-524-1426. Fax: 915-524-1473.

Angelina County

County Clerk, P.O. Box 908, Lufkin, TX 75902-0908. 936-634-8339. Fax: 936-634-8460.
Online Access: Assessor/Property Tax. See note at beginning of section.

Aransas County

County Clerk, 301 North Live Oak, Rockport, TX 78382. 361-790-0122.
Online Access: Assessor/Property Tax. See note at beginning of section.

Archer County

County Clerk, P.O. Box 815, Archer City, TX 76351. 940-574-4615.
Online Access: Property Tax. See note at beginning of section.

Armstrong County

County Clerk, P.O. Box 309, Claude, TX 79019-0309. 806-226-2081. Fax: 806-226-2030.

Atascosa County

County Clerk, Circle Drive, Room 6-1, Jourdanton, TX 78026. 830-769-2511.
Online Access: Assessor/Property Tax. See note at beginning of section.

Austin County

County Clerk, 1 East Main, Bellville, TX 77418-1551. 979-865-5911. Fax: 979-865-0336.
Online Access: Assessor/ Property Tax. See note at beginning of section.

Bailey County

County Clerk, 300 South First, Suite 200, Muleshoe, TX 79347. 806-272-3044. Fax: 806-272-3879.

Bandera County

County Clerk, P.O. Box 823, Bandera, TX 78003. 830-796-3332. Fax: 830-796-8323.
Online Access: Property Tax. See note at beginning of section.

Bastrop County

County Clerk, P.O. Box 577, Bastrop, TX 78602. 512-321-4443.
Online Access: Assessor, Property Tax. See note at beginning of section.

Baylor County

County Clerk, P.O. Box 689, Seymour, TX 76380-0689. 940-888-3322.

Bee County

County Clerk, 105 West Corpus Christi Street, Room 103, Beeville, TX 78102. 361-362-3245. Fax: 361-362-3247. Online Access: Property Tax. See note at beginning of section.

Bell County

County Clerk, P.O. Box 480, Belton, TX 76513-0480. 254-933-5171. Fax: 254-933-5176.
www.texastax.com/bell/index.asp
Online Access: Assessor, Property Tax. TexasTax provides two methods of access to Bell County records. Access to "Advanced Search" records requires a login and subscription fee. Subs are allowed in 12, 6, 3 & 1 month increments. Advanced Search includes full data, maps, and Excel spreadsheets For information, see www.texastax.com/bell/subscriptioninfo.asp Records on "Quick Search - FREE" at www.texastax.com/bell/index/asp allows access to these Bell County records: tax ID #, owner, parcel address, deed date, and land value data. Search FREE by tax ID #, address, name, city or appraisal value. View details

Bexar County

County Clerk, Bexar County Courthouse, 100 Dolorosa, Room 108, San Antonio, TX 78205-3083. 210-335-2581. Fax: 210-335-2813.

Blanco County

County Clerk, P.O. Box 65, Johnson City, TX 78636. 830-868-7357.
Online Access: Assessor/Property Tax. See note at beginning of section.

Borden County

County Clerk, P.O. Box 124, Gail, TX 79738-0124. 806-756-4312.

Bosque County

County Clerk, P.O. Box 617, Meridian, TX 76665. 254-435-2201.

Bowie County

County Clerk, P.O.Box 248, New Boston, TX 75570. 903-628-6740. Fax: 903-628-6729.

Brazoria County

County Clerk, 111 East Locust, Suite 200, Angleton, TX 77515-4654. 979-849-5711. Fax: 979-864-1358.
Online Access: Assessor, Property Tax. See note at beginning of section.

Brazos County

County Clerk, 300 East 26th Street, Suite 120, Bryan, TX 77803. 979-361-4132.

Online Access: Assessor, Property Tax. See note at beginning of section.

Brewster County

County Clerk, P.O. Box 119, Alpine, TX 79831. 915-837-3366. Fax: 915-837-1536.

Briscoe County

County Clerk, P.O. Box 555, Silverton, TX 79257. 806-823-2134. Fax: 806-823-2359.

Brooks County

County Clerk, P.O. Box 427, Falfurrias, TX 78355. 361-325-5604. Fax: 361-325-4944.

Brown County

County Clerk, 200 South Broadway, Courthouse, Brownwood, TX 76801. 915-643-2594.
Online Access: Assessor, Property Tax. See note at beginning of section.

Burleson County

County Clerk, P.O. Box 57, Caldwell, TX 77836. 979-567-2329.
Online Access: Assessor, Property Tax. See note at beginning of section.

Burnet County

County Clerk, 220 South Pierce Street, Burnet, TX 78611. 512-756-5406. Fax: 512-756-5410.
Online Access: Assessor, Property Tax. See note at beginning of section.

Caldwell County

County Clerk, P.O. Box 906, Lockhart, TX 78644-0906. 512-398-1804.
Online Access: Assessor, Property Tax. See note at beginning of section.

Calhoun County

County Clerk, 211 South Ann, Port Lavaca, TX 77979. 361-553-4411. Fax: 361-553-4420.
Online Access: Assessor, Property Tax. See note at beginning of section.

Callahan County

County Clerk, 100 W. 4th, Ste. 104, Courthouse, Baird, TX 79504. 915-854-1217. Fax: 915-854-1227.

Cameron County

County Clerk, P.O. Box 2178, Brownsville, TX 78520. 956-544-0815. Fax: 956-554-0813.
Online Access: Property Tax. See note at beginning of section.

Camp County

County Clerk, 126 Church Street, Room 102, Pittsburg, TX 75686. 903-856-2731. Fax: 903-856-0811.

Carson County

County Clerk, P.O. Box 487, Panhandle, TX 79068. 806-537-3873.

Cass County

County Clerk, P.O. Box 449, Linden, TX 75563. 903-756-5071. Fax: 903-756-5732.

Castro County

County Clerk, 100 East Bedford, Room 101, Dimmitt, TX 79027-2643. 806-647-3338.

Chambers County

County Clerk, P.O. Box 728, Anahuac, TX 77514. 409-267-8309. Fax: 409-267-4453.

Online Access: Property Tax. See note at beginning of section.

Cherokee County

County Clerk, P.O. Box 420, Rusk, TX 75785. 903-683-2350. Fax: 903-683-2393.

Childress County

County Clerk, Courthouse Box 4, Childress, TX 79201. 940-937-6143. Fax: 940-937-3479.

Clay County

County Clerk, P.O. Box 548, Henrietta, TX 76365. 940-538-4631. Online Access: Property Tax. See note at beginning of section.

Cochran County

County Clerk, 100 North Main, Courthouse, Morton, TX 79346-2598. 806-266-5450. Fax: 806-266-9027.

Coke County

County Clerk, P.O. Box 150, Robert Lee, TX 76945. 915-453-2631. Fax: 915-453-2297.

Coleman County

County Clerk, P.O. Box 591, Coleman, TX 76834. 915-625-2889.

Online Access: Assessor, Property Tax. See note at beginning of section.

Collin County

County Clerk, 200 South McDonald, Annex "A", Suite 120, McKinney, TX 75069. 972-548-4134.

Online Access: Property Tax. See note at beginning of section.

Collingsworth County

County Clerk, Courthouse, Room 3, 800 West Ave., Wellington, TX 79095. 806-447-2408. Fax: 806-447-5418.

Colorado County

County Clerk, P.O. Box 68, Columbus, TX 78934. 979-732-2155. Fax: 979-732-8852.

Comal County

County Clerk, 100 Main Plaza, Suite 104, New Braunfels, TX 78130. 830-620-5513. Fax: 830-620-3410.

Comanche County

County Clerk, Courthouse, Comanche, TX 76442. 915-356-2655. Fax: 915-356-3710.

Online Access: Assessor/Property Tax. See note at beginning of section.

Concho County

County Clerk, P.O. Box 98, Paint Rock, TX 76866-0098. 915-732-4322. Fax: 915-732-2040.

Cooke County

County Clerk, Courthouse, Gainesville, TX 76240. 940-668-5420. Fax: 940-668-5440.

Coryell County

County Clerk, P.O. Box 237, Gatesville, TX 76528. 254-865-5016. Fax: 254-865-8631.

Cottle County

County Clerk, P.O. Box 717, Paducah, TX 79248. 806-492-3823.

Crane County

County Clerk, P.O. Box 578, Crane, TX 79731. 915-558-3581.

Crockett County

County Clerk, P.O. Drawer C, Ozona, TX 76943. 915-392-2022. Fax: 915-392-2675.

Crosby County

County Clerk, P.O. Box 218, Crosbyton, TX 79322. 806-675-2334.

Culberson County

County Clerk, P.O. Box 158, Van Horn, TX 79855. 915-283-2059x32. Fax: 915-283-9234.

Dallam County

County Clerk, P.O. Box 1352, Dalhart, TX 79022. 806-249-4751. Fax: 806-249-2252.

Dallas County

County Clerk, Records Bldg, 2nd Floor, 509 Main St., Dallas, TX 75202-3502. 214-653-7131.

Online Access: Property Tax, Voter Registration. See note at beginning of section. Access to the Dallas County Voter Registration Records is available free at www.openrecords.org/records/voting/dallas_voting. Search by name or partial name.

Dawson County

County Clerk, P.O. Drawer 1268, Lamesa, TX 79331. 806-872-3778. Fax: 806-872-2473.

De Witt County

County Clerk, 307 North Gonzales, Courthouse, Cuero, TX 77954. 361-275-3724. Fax: 361-275-8994.

Deaf Smith County

County Clerk, 235 East 3rd, Room 203, Hereford, TX 79045-5542. 806-363-7077. Fax: 806-363-7007.

Delta County

County Clerk, P.O. Box 455, Cooper, TX 75432. 903-395-4110. Fax: 903-395-2178.

Denton County

County Clerk, P.O. Box 2187, Denton, TX 76202-2187. 940-565-8510.

Online Access: Property Tax. See note at beginning of section.

Dickens County

County Clerk, P.O. Box 120, Dickens, TX 79229. 806-623-5531. Fax: 806-623-5319.

Dimmit County

County Clerk, 103 North 5th Street, Carrizo Springs, TX 78834. 830-876-3569. Fax: 830-876-5036.

Donley County

County Clerk, P.O. Drawer U, Clarendon, TX 79226. 806-874-3436. Fax: 806-874-5146.

Duval County

County Clerk, P.O. Box 248, San Diego, TX 78384. 361-279-3322x271,2.

Eastland County

County Clerk, P.O. Box 110, Eastland, TX 76448-0110. 254-629-1583. Fax: 254-629-8125.

Ector County

County Clerk, P.O. Box 707, Odessa, TX 79760. 915-498-4130. Fax: 915-498-4177.

Edwards County

County Clerk, P.O. Box 184, Rocksprings, TX 78880-0184. 830-683-2235. Fax: 830-683-5376.

El Paso County

County Clerk, 500 E. San Antonio, Room 105, El Paso, TX 79901-2496. 915-546-2074.

Online Access: Assessor, Property Tax. See note at beginning of section.

Ellis County

County Clerk, P.O. Box 250, Waxahachie, TX 75168. 972-923-5070.

Online Access: Property Tax. See note at beginning of section.

Erath County

County Clerk, Courthouse, 100 W. Washington St., Stephenville, TX 76401. 254-965-1482. Fax: 254-965-5732.

Online Access: Property Tax. See note at beginning of section.

Falls County

County Clerk, P.O. Box 458, Marlin, TX 76661. 254-883-1408. Fax: 254-883-1406.

Fannin County

County Clerk, Courthouse, Suite 102, 101 E. Sam Rayburn Dr., Bonham, TX 75418-4346. 903-583-7486. Fax: 903-583-7811.

Online Access: Assessor, Property Tax. See note at beginning of section.

Fayette County

County Clerk, P.O. Box 59, La Grange, TX 78945. 979-968-3251.

Fisher County

County Clerk, P.O. Box 368, Roby, TX 79543-0368. 915-776-2401. Fax: 915-776-2815.

Floyd County

County Clerk, Courthouse, Room 101, 100 Main St., Floydada, TX 79235. 806-983-4900.

Foard County

County Clerk, P.O. Box 539, Crowell, TX 79227. 940-684-1365. Fax: 940-684-1947.

Fort Bend County

County Clerk, 301 Jackson, Hwy 90A, Richmond, TX 77469. 281-341-8685. Fax: 281-341-8669.

Online Access: Real Estate, Liens, Assessor. Various access methods exist. Access to Ft Bend County online records requires a $100 escrow account, $15 monthly fee, plus $.25 per minute of use. System operates 24 hours daily and supports a 14.4 baud rate. Reach Out software required For info, contact Linda Jordan, 281-341-8652. Records date back to 1930s; images to 10/94. Print images for $.50 & $.75. Lending agency info available Also, see notes at beginning of section.

Franklin County

County Clerk, P.O. Box 68, Mount Vernon, TX 75457-0068. 903-537-4252. Fax: 903-537-2418.

Online Access: Property Tax. See note at beginning of section.

Freestone County

County Clerk, P.O. Box 1017, Fairfield, TX 75840. 903-389-2635.

Frio County

County Clerk, 500 E San Antonio Street, # 6, Pearsall, TX 78061. 830-334-2214. Fax: 830-334-4881.

Gaines County

County Clerk, 101 S. Main, Room 107, Seminole, TX 79360. 915-758-4003.

Galveston County

County Clerk, P.O. Box 2450, Galveston, TX 77553-2450. 409-766-2208.

Online Access: Real Estate, Liens, Assessor. Two sources exist. Access to Galveston County online records requires $200 escrow deposit, $25 monthly fee, plus $.25 per minute of use. System operates 8AM-12PM and supports baud rates up to 14.4. Index records date back to 1965; image documents to 1/95 For information, contact Robert Dickinson at 409-770-5115. Reach Out software required. Lending agency information and fax back services are available Also, see note at beginning of section

Garza County
County Clerk, P.O. Box 366, Post, TX 79356-0366. 806-495-4430. Fax: 806-495-4431.

Gillespie County
County Clerk, 101 West Main, Room 109, Unit #13, Fredericksburg, TX 78624. 830-997-6515. Fax: 830-997-9958.
Online Access: Assessor, Property Tax. See note at beginning of section.

Glasscock County
County Clerk, P.O. Box 190, Garden City, TX 79739. 915-354-2371.

Goliad County
County Clerk, P.O. Box 50, Goliad, TX 77963. 361-645-3294. Fax: 361-645-3858.

Gonzales County
County Clerk, P.O. Box 77, Gonzales, TX 78629. 830-672-2801. Fax: 830-672-2636.

Gray County
County Clerk, P.O. Box 1902, Pampa, TX 79066-1902. 806-669-8004. Fax: 806-669-8054.

Grayson County
County Clerk, 100 West Houston #17, Sherman, TX 75090. 903-813-4239. Fax: 903-813-4382.
Online Access: Property Tax. See note at beginning of section.

Gregg County
County Clerk, P.O. Box 3049, Longview, TX 75606. 903-236-8430. Fax: 903-237-2574.
Online Access: Property Tax. See note at beginning of section.

Grimes County
County Clerk, P.O. Box 209, Anderson, TX 77830. 936-873-2111.

Guadalupe County
County Clerk, P.O. Box 990, Seguin, TX 78156-0951. 830-303-4188x236.
Online Access: Property Tax. See note at beginning of section.

Hale County
County Clerk, 500 Broadway #140, Plainview, TX 79072-8030. 806-291-5261. Fax: 806-296-7786.

Hall County
County Clerk, Courthouse, Box 8, Memphis, TX 79245. 806-259-2627. Fax: 806-259-5078.

Hamilton County
County Clerk, Main Street, Courthouse, Hamilton, TX 76531. 254-386-3518. Fax: 254-386-8727.

Hansford County
County Clerk, P.O. Box 397, Spearman, TX 79081. 806-659-4110. Fax: 806-659-4168.

Hardeman County
County Clerk, P.O. Box 30, Quanah, TX 79252-0030. 940-663-2901.

Hardin County
County Clerk, P.O. Box 38, Kountze, TX 77625. 409-246-5185.
Online Access: Property Tax. See note at beginning of section.

Harris County
County Clerk, P.O. Box 1525, Houston, TX 77251-1525. 713-755-6411. Fax: 713-755-8839.
www.tax.co.harris.tx.us
Online Access: Real Estate, Liens, Assessor, Voter. Two sources exist. Access to Harris County online

records requires a $300 deposit and $40 per hour of use. Also, free access to records is available from the web site For information, call Ken Peabody at 713-755-7151 Also, see note at beginning of section.

Harrison County
County Clerk, P.O. Box 1365, Marshall, TX 75671. 903-935-4858.
Online Access: Property Tax. See note at beginning of section.

Hartley County
County Clerk, P.O. Box Q, Channing, TX 79018. 806-235-2603. Fax: 806-235-2316.

Haskell County
County Clerk, P.O. Box 725, Haskell, TX 79521-0725. 940-864-2451. Fax: 940-864-6164.

Hays County
County Clerk, 137 N. Guadalupe, Hays County Records Building, San Marcos, TX 78666. 512-393-7330. Fax: 512-393-7337.
Online Access: Assessor, Property Tax. See note at beginning of section.

Hemphill County
County Clerk, P.O. Box 867, Canadian, TX 79014. 806-323-6212.

Henderson County
County Clerk, P.O. Box 632, Athens, TX 75751-0632. 903-675-6140.
Online Access: Property Tax. See note at beginning of section.

Hidalgo County
County Clerk, P.O. Box 58, Edinburg, TX 78540. 956-318-2100. Fax: 956-318-2105.
Online Access: Assessor, Property Tax. See note at beginning of section.

Hill County
County Clerk, P.O. Box 398, Hillsboro, TX 76645. 254-582-2161.
Online Access: Property Tax. See note at beginning of section.

Hockley County
County Clerk, 800 Houston St., Ste 213, Levelland, TX 79336. 806-894-3185.

Hood County
County Clerk, P.O. Box 339, Granbury, TX 76048-0339. 817-579-3222. Fax: 817-579-3227.
Online Access: Property Tax. See note at beginning of section.

Hopkins County
County Clerk, P.O. Box 288, Sulphur Springs, TX 75483. 903-885-3929. Fax: 903-885-2487.

Houston County
County Clerk, P.O. Box 370, Crockett, TX 75835-0370. 936-544-3255.

Howard County
County Clerk, P.O. Box 1468, Big Spring, TX 79721-1468. 915-264-2213. Fax: 915-264-2215.

Hudspeth County
County Clerk, P.O. Drawer A, Sierra Blanca, TX 79851. 915-369-2301. Fax: 915-369-2361.

Hunt County
County Clerk, P.O. Box 1316, Greenville, TX 75403-1316. 903-408-4130.
Online Access: Assessor, Property Tax. See notes at beginning of section.

Hutchinson County
County Clerk, P.O. Box 1186, Stinnett, TX 79083. 806-878-4002.

Irion County
County Clerk, P.O. Box 736, Mertzon, TX 76941-0736. 915-835-2421. Fax: 915-835-2008.

Jack County
County Clerk, 100 Main Street, Jacksboro, TX 76458. 940-567-2111.
Online Access: Property Tax. See note at beginning of section.

Jackson County
County Clerk, 115 West Main, Room 101, Edna, TX 77957. 361-782-3563.

Jasper County
County Clerk, P.O. Box 2070, Jasper, TX 75951. 409-384-2632. Fax: 409-384-7198.

Jeff Davis County
County Clerk, P.O. Box 398, Fort Davis, TX 79734. 915-426-3251. Fax: 915-426-3760.

Jefferson County
County Clerk, P.O. Box 1151, Beaumont, TX 77704-1151. 409-835-8475. Fax: 409-839-2394.
Online Access: Property Tax. See note at beginning of section.

Jim Hogg County
County Clerk, P.O. Box 878, Hebbronville, TX 78361. 361-527-4031. Fax: 361-527-5843.

Jim Wells County
County Clerk, P.O. Box 1459, Alice, TX 78333. 361-668-5702.

Johnson County
County Clerk, P.O. Box 662, Cleburne, TX 76033-0662. 817-556-6314. Fax: 817-556-6326.
Online Access: Assessor, Property Tax. See note at beginning of section.

Jones County
County Clerk, P.O. Box 552, Anson, TX 79501-0552. 915-823-3762. Fax: 915-823-4223.

Karnes County
County Clerk, 101 North Panna Maria Ave., Courthouse - Suite 9, Karnes City, TX 78118-2929. 830-780-3938. Fax: 830-780-4576.

Kaufman County
County Clerk, Courthouse, Kaufman, TX 75142. 972-932-4331. Fax: 972-932-7628.
Online Access: Assessor, Property Tax. See note at beginning of section.

Kendall County
County Clerk, 201 East San Antonio, Suite 127, Boerne, TX 78006. 830-249-9343. Fax: 830-249-3472.
Online Access: Assessor, Property Tax. See notes at beginning of section.

Kenedy County
County Clerk, P.O. Box 227, Sarita, TX 78385-0227. 361-294-5220. Fax: 361-294-5218.

Kent County
County Clerk, P.O. Box 9, Jayton, TX 79528-0009. 806-237-3881. Fax: 806-237-2632.

Kerr County
County Clerk, Courthouse, Room 122, 700 Main, Kerrville, TX 78028-5389. 830-792-2255. Fax: 830-792-2274.
Online Access: Assessor, Property Tax. See note at beginning of section.

Kimble County
County Clerk, 501 Main Street, Junction, TX 76849. 915-446-3353. Fax: 915-446-2986.
Online Access: Assessor/Property Tax. See note at beginning of section.

King County
County Clerk, P.O. Box 135, Guthrie, TX 79236. 806-596-4412. Fax: 806-596-4664.

Kinney County
County Clerk, P.O. Drawer 9, Brackettville, TX 78832. 830-563-2521. Fax: 830-563-2644.

Kleberg County
County Clerk, P.O. Box 1327, Kingsville, TX 78364-1327. 361-595-8548.
Online Access: Property Tax. See note at beginning of section.

Knox County
County Clerk, P.O. Box 196, Benjamin, TX 79505. 940-454-2441. Fax: 940-454-2022.

La Salle County
County Clerk, P.O. Box 340, Cotulla, TX 78014. 830-879-2117. Fax: 830-879-2933.

Lamar County
County Clerk, Courthouse, 119 N. Main #109, Paris, TX 75460. 903-737-2420.

Lamb County
County Clerk, 100 6th Street, Room 103 Box 3, Littlefield, TX 79339-3366. 806-385-4222x210. Fax: 806-385-6485.
Online Access: Assessor, Property Tax. see note at beginning of section.

Lampasas County
County Clerk, P.O. Box 347, Lampasas, TX 76550. 512-556-8271.

Lavaca County
County Clerk, P.O. Box 326, Hallettsville, TX 77964-0326. 361-798-3612.

Lee County
County Clerk, P.O. Box 419, Giddings, TX 78942. 979-542-3684. Fax: 979-542-2623.

Leon County
County Clerk, P.O. Box 98, Centerville, TX 75833. 903-536-2352. Fax: 903-536-2431.

Liberty County
County Clerk, P.O. Box 369, Liberty, TX 77575. 936-336-4673.
Online Access: Assessor, Property Tax. See note at beginning of section.

Limestone County
County Clerk, P.O. Box 350, Groesbeck, TX 76642. 254-729-5504. Fax: 254-729-2951.
Online Access: Assessor, Property Tax. See note at beginning of section.

Lipscomb County
County Clerk, P.O. Box 70, Lipscomb, TX 79056. 806-862-3091. Fax: 806-862-3004.

Live Oak County
County Clerk, P.O. Box 280, George West, TX 78022. 361-449-2733x3.

Llano County
County Clerk, 107 W. Sandstone, Llano, TX 78643-2318. 915-247-4455. Fax: 915-247-2406.
Online Access: Assessor, Property Tax. See note at beginning of section.

Loving County
County Clerk, P.O. Box 194, Mentone, TX 79754. 915-377-2441. Fax: 915-377-2701.

Lubbock County
County Clerk, P.O. Box 10536, Lubbock, TX 79408-0536. 806-775-1060. Fax: 806-775-1660.
Online Access: Assessor, Property Tax. See note at beginning of section.

Lynn County
County Clerk, P.O. Box 937, Tahoka, TX 79373. 806-998-4750. Fax: 806-998-4151.

Madison County
County Clerk, 101 West Main, Room 102, Madisonville, TX 77864. 936-348-2638. Fax: 936-348-5858.
Online Access: Assessor, Property Tax. See note at beginning of section.

Marion County
County Clerk, P.O. Box 763, Jefferson, TX 75657. 903-665-3971.

Martin County
County Clerk, P.O. Box 906, Stanton, TX 79782. 915-756-3412. Fax: 915-756-2992.

Mason County
County Clerk, P.O. Box 702, Mason, TX 76856-0702. 915-347-5253.

Matagorda County
County Clerk, 1700 7th Street, Room 202, Bay City, TX 77414. 979-244-7680. Fax: 979-244-7688.

Maverick County
County Clerk, P.O. Box 4050, Eagle Pass, TX 78853-4050. 830-773-2829.
Online Access: Assessor, Property Tax. See note at beginning of section.

McCulloch County
County Clerk, Courthouse, Brady, TX 76825. 915-597-0733. Fax: 915-597-1731.

McLennan County
County Clerk, P.O. Box 1727, Waco, TX 76703-1727. 254-757-5078. Fax: 254-757-5146.
Online Access: Property Tax. See note at beginning of section.

McMullen County
County Clerk, P.O. Box 235, Tilden, TX 78072-0235. 361-274-3215. Fax: 361-274-3618.

Medina County
County Clerk, Courthouse, Room 109, 16th St., Hondo, TX 78861. 830-741-6041. Fax: 830-741-6015.

Menard County
County Clerk, P.O. Box 1028, Menard, TX 76859. 915-396-4682. Fax: 915-396-2047.

Midland County
County Clerk, P.O. Box 211, Midland, TX 79702. 915-688-1059. Fax: 915-688-8973.

Milam County
County Clerk, P.O. Box 191, Cameron, TX 76520. 254-697-6596. Fax: 254-697-4433.
Online Access: Assessor/Property Tax. See note at beginning of section.

Mills County
County Clerk, P.O. Box 646, Goldthwaite, TX 76844-0646. 915-648-2711. Fax: 915-648-2806.

Mitchell County
County Clerk, 349 Oak St. #103, Colorado City, TX 79512-6213. 915-728-3481.

Montague County
County Clerk, P.O. Box 77, Montague, TX 76251-0077. 940-894-2461. Fax: 940-894-3110.

Montgomery County
County Clerk, P.O. Box 959, Conroe, TX 77305. 936-539-7893. Fax: 936-760-6990.
Online Access: Assessor, Property Tax. See notes at beginning of section.

Moore County
County Clerk, 715 Dumas Ave., Rm. 105, Dumas, TX 79029. 806-935-2009. Fax: 806-935-9004.

Morris County
County Clerk, 500 Broadnax Street, Daingerfield, TX 75638. 903-645-3911.

Motley County
County Clerk, P.O. Box 66, Matador, TX 79244. 806-347-2621. Fax: 806-347-2220.

Nacogdoches County
County Clerk, 101 West Main, Room 205, Nacogdoches, TX 75961. 936-560-7733.
Online Access: Property Tax. See note at beginning of section.

Navarro County
County Clerk, P.O. Box 423, Corsicana, TX 75151. 903-654-3035.
Online Access: Property Tax. See note at beginning of section.

Newton County
County Clerk, P.O. Box 484, Newton, TX 75966-0484. 409-379-5341. Fax: 409-379-9049.
Online Access: Assessor/Property Tax. See note at beginning of section.
Online Access: Death. Death records in this county may be accessed over the Internet at www.jas.net/~newton/txnewton/deaths/death.htm.

Nolan County
County Clerk, P.O. Drawer 98, Sweetwater, TX 79556-0098. 915-235-2462.

Nueces County
County Clerk, P.O. Box 2627, Corpus Christi, TX 78403. 361-888-0611. Fax: 361-888-0329.
Online Access: Assessor/Property Tax. See note at beginning of section.

Ochiltree County
County Clerk, 511 South Main, Perryton, TX 79070. 806-435-8039. Fax: 806-435-2081.

Oldham County
County Clerk, P.O. Box 360, Vega, TX 79092. 806-267-2667.

Orange County
County Clerk, P.O. Box 1536, Orange, TX 77631-1536. 409-882-7055. Fax: 409-882-0379.

Palo Pinto County
County Clerk, P.O. Box 219, Palo Pinto, TX 76484. 940-659-1277.

Panola County
County Clerk, Sabine & Sycamore, Courthouse Bldg., Room 201, Carthage, TX 75633. 903-693-0302. Fax: 903-693-2726.

Parker County
County Clerk, P.O. Box 819, Weatherford, TX 76086. 817-599-6591.
Online Access: Property Tax. See note at beginning of section.

Parmer County
County Clerk, P.O. Box 356, Farwell, TX 79325. 806-481-3691.

Pecos County
County Clerk, 103 West Callaghan Street, Fort Stockton, TX 79735. 915-336-7555. Fax: 915-336-7557.

Polk County
County Clerk, P.O. Drawer 2119, Livingston, TX 77351. 936-327-6804. Fax: 936-327-6874.

Potter County

County Clerk, P.O. Box 9638, Amarillo, TX 79105. 806-379-2275. Fax: 806-379-2296.

www.prad.org

Online Access: Assessor, Property Tax. Two sources exist. Records on the Potter-Randall Appraisal District database are available free on the Internet at www.prad.org/search.html. Records periodically updated; for current tax information call Potter (806-342-2600) or Randall (806-665-6287) Also see notes at the beginning of section.

Presidio County

County Clerk, P.O. Box 789, Marfa, TX 79843. 915-729-4812. Fax: 915-729-4313.

Rains County

County Clerk, P.O. Box 187, Emory, TX 75440. 903-473-2461.

Randall County

County Clerk, P.O. Box 660, Canyon, TX 79015. 806-655-6330.

www.prad.org

Online Access: Assessor, Property Tax. Two sources exist. Randall County records are combined online with Potter County; see Potter County for access information Also see notes at beginning of section.

Reagan County

County Clerk, P.O. Box 100, Big Lake, TX 76932. 915-884-2442.

Real County

County Clerk, P.O. Box 656, Leakey, TX 78873-0656. 830-232-5202. Fax: 830-232-6040.

Red River County

County Clerk, 200 North Walnut, Courthouse Annex, Clarksville, TX 75426-3075. 903-427-2401.

Reeves County

County Clerk, P.O. Box 867, Pecos, TX 79772. 915-445-5467. Fax: 915-445-5096.

Refugio County

County Clerk, P.O. Box 704, Refugio, TX 78377. 361-526-2233.

Roberts County

County Clerk, P.O. Box 477, Miami, TX 79059-0477. 806-868-2341. Fax: 806-868-3381.

Robertson County

County Clerk, P.O. Box 1029, Franklin, TX 77856. 979-828-4130.

Rockwall County

County Clerk, 1101 Ridge Rd., S-101, Rockwall, TX 75087. 972-882-0220. Fax: 972-882-0229.

Online Access: Assessor, Property Tax. See notes at beginning of section.

Runnels County

County Clerk, P.O. Box 189, Ballinger, TX 76821-0189. 915-365-2720. Fax: 915-365-3408.

Rusk County

County Clerk, P.O. Box 758, Henderson, TX 75653-0758. 903-657-0330

Online Access: Property Tax. See note at beginning of section.

Sabine County

County Clerk, P.O. Drawer 580, Hemphill, TX 75948-0580. 409-787-3786. Fax: 409-787-2044.

San Augustine County

County Clerk, 106 Courthouse, 100 W. Columbia, San Augustine, TX 75972-1335. 936-275-2452. Fax: 936-275-9579.

San Jacinto County

County Clerk, P.O. Box 669, Coldspring, TX 77331. 936-653-2324.

Online Access: Assessor, Property Tax. See note at beginning of section.

San Patricio County

County Clerk, P.O. Box 578, Sinton, TX 78387. 361-364-6290. Fax: 361-364-3825.

Online Access: Property Tax. See note at beginning of section.

San Saba County

County Clerk, 500 East Wallace, San Saba, TX 76877. 915-372-3614. Fax: 915-372-5746.

Schleicher County

County Clerk, P.O. Drawer 580, Eldorado, TX 76936. 915-853-2833. Fax: 915-853-2603.

Scurry County

County Clerk, 1806 25th Street, Suite 300, Snyder, TX 79549-2530. 915-573-5332. Fax: 915-573-7396.

Shackelford County

County Clerk, P.O. Box 247, Albany, TX 76430. 915-762-2232.

Shelby County

County Clerk, P.O. Box 1987, Center, TX 75935. 936-598-6361.

Sherman County

County Clerk, P.O. Box 270, Stratford, TX 79084. 806-366-2371. Fax: 806-366-5670.

Smith County

County Clerk, P.O. Box 1018, Tyler, TX 75710. 903-535-0650. Fax: 903-535-0684.

Online Access: Property Tax. See note at beginning of section.

Somervell County

County Clerk, P.O. Box 1098, Glen Rose, TX 76043. 254-897-4427.

Online Access: Assessor/Property Tax. See note at beginning of section.

Starr County

County Clerk, Courthouse, Rio Grande City, TX 78582. 956-487-2954. Fax: 956-487-6227.

Stephens County

County Clerk, Courthouse, Breckenridge, TX 76424. 254-559-3700.

Sterling County

County Clerk, P.O. Box 55, Sterling City, TX 76951-0055. 915-378-5191.

Stonewall County

County Clerk, P.O. Drawer P, Aspermont, TX 79502. 940-989-2272.

Sutton County

County Clerk, Sutton County Annex, 300 E. Oak, Suite 3, Sonora, TX 76950. 915-387-3815.

Swisher County

County Clerk, Courthouse, 119 S. Maxwell, Tulia, TX 79088. 806-995-3294. Fax: 806-995-4121.

Online Access: Assessor, Property Tax. See note at beginning of section.

Tarrant County

County Clerk, 100 West Weatherford, Courthouse, Room 180, Ft. Worth, TX 76196. 817-884-1550.

Online Access: Property Tax. See note at beginning of section.

Taylor County

County Clerk, P.O. Box 5497, Abilene, TX 79608. 915-674-1202. Fax: 915-674-1279.

Online Access: Assessor, Property Tax. See note at beginning of section.

Terrell County

County Clerk, P.O. Drawer 410, Sanderson, TX 79848. 915-345-2391. Fax: 915-345-2653.

Terry County

County Clerk, 500 West Main, Room 105, Brownfield, TX 79316-4398. 806-637-8551. Fax: 806-637-4874.

Throckmorton County

County Clerk, P.O. Box 309, Throckmorton, TX 76483. 940-849-2501. Fax: 940-849-3220.

Titus County

County Clerk, 100 W. 1 St., 2nd Floor, Suite 204, Mount Pleasant, TX 75455. 903-577-6796. Fax: 903-577-6793.

Tom Green County

County Clerk, 124 West Beauregard, San Angelo, TX 76903-5835. 915-659-3262.

Travis County

County Clerk, P.O. Box 1748, Austin, TX 78701. 512-473-9188. Fax: 512-473-9075.

Online Access: Assessor, Property Tax. See note at beginning of section.

Trinity County

County Clerk, P.O. Box 456, Groveton, TX 75845. 936-642-1208. Fax: 936-642-3004.

Tyler County

County Clerk, 110 W. Bluff, Room 110, Woodville, TX 75979. 409-283-2281.

Online Access: Property Tax. See note at beginning of section.

Upshur County

County Clerk, P.O. Box 730, Gilmer, TX 75644. 903-843-4014.

Online Access: Assessor, Property Tax. See note at beginning of section.

Upton County

County Clerk, P.O. Box 465, Rankin, TX 79778. 915-693-2861. Fax: 915-693-2129.

Uvalde County

County Clerk, P.O. Box 284, Uvalde, TX 78802-0284. 830-278-6614.

Val Verde County

County Clerk, P.O. Box 1267, Del Rio, TX 78841-1267. 830-774-7564.

Van Zandt County

County Clerk, 121 East Dallas St, Courthouse - Room 202, Canton, TX 75103. 903-567-6503. Fax: 903-567-6722.

Online Access: Property Tax. See note at beginning of section.

Victoria County

County Clerk, P.O. Box 2410, Victoria, TX 77902. 361-575-1478. Fax: 361-575-6276.

Online Access: Assessor, Property Tax. See note at beginning of section.

Walker County

County Clerk, P.O. Box 210, Huntsville, TX 77342-0210. 936-436-4922. Fax: 936-436-4930.

Waller County

County Clerk, 836 Austin Street, Room 217, Hempstead, TX 77445. 979-826-7711.

Online Access: Assessor, Property Tax. See note at beginning of section.

Ward County

County Clerk, Corner of 4 & Allen, Monahans, TX 79756. 915-943-3294. Fax: 915-942-6054.

Washington County

County Clerk, 100 East Main, Suite 102, Brenham, TX 77833. 979-277-6200. Fax: 979-277-6278.
Online Access: Assessor, Property Tax. See note at beginning of section.

Webb County

County Clerk, P.O. Box 29, Laredo, TX 78042. 956-721-2640. Fax: 956-721-2288.
Online Access: Property Tax. See note at beginning of section.

Wharton County

County Clerk, P.O. Box 69, Wharton, TX 77488. 979-532-2381.
Online Access: Assessor, Property Tax. See note at beginning of section.

Wheeler County

County Clerk, P.O. Box 465, Wheeler, TX 79096. 806-826-5544. Fax: 806-826-3282.

Wichita County

County Clerk, P.O. Box 1679, Wichita Falls, TX 76307-1679. 940-766-8160.
Online Access: Property Tax. See note at beginning of section.

Wilbarger County

County Clerk, Courthouse, 1700 Main St. #15, Vernon, TX 76384. 940-552-5486.
Online Access: Property Tax. See note at beginning of section.

Willacy County

County Clerk, 540 West Hidalgo Avenue, Courthouse Building, First Floor, Raymondville, TX 78580. 956-689-2710. Fax: 956-689-0937.

Williamson County

County Clerk, P.O. Box 18, Georgetown, TX 78627-0018. 512-943-1515. Fax: 512-943-1616.
Online Access: Property Tax. See note at beginning of section.

Wilson County

County Clerk, P.O. Box 27, Floresville, TX 78114. 830-393-7308.
Online Access: Assessor, Property Tax. See note at beginning of section.

Winkler County

County Clerk, P.O. Box 1007, Kermit, TX 79745. 915-586-3401.

Wise County

County Clerk, P.O. Box 359, Decatur, TX 76234. 940-627-3351. Fax: 940-627-2138.

Online Access: Property Tax. See note at beginning of section.

Wood County

County Clerk, P.O. Box 338, Quitman, TX 75783. 903-763-2711. Fax: 903-763-2902.
Online Access: Assessor, Property Tax. See note at beginning of section.

Yoakum County

County Clerk, P.O. Box 309, Plains, TX 79335. 806-456-2721. Fax: 806-456-2258.

Young County

County Clerk, Young County Courthouse, 516 Fourth St., Room 104, Graham, TX 76450-3063. 940-549-8432.

Zapata County

County Clerk, P.O. Box 789, Zapata, TX 78076. 956-765-9915. Fax: 956-765-9933.
Online Access: Property Tax. See note at beginning of section.

Zavala County

County Clerk, Zavala Courthouse, Crystal City, TX 78839. 830-374-2331. Fax: 830-374-5955.

You will usually be able to find the city name in the City/County Cross Reference below. In that case, it is a simple matter to determine the county from the cross reference. However, only the official US Postal Service city names are included in this index. There are an additional 40,000 place names that people use in their addresses. Therefore, we have also included a ZIP/City Cross Reference immediately following the City/County Cross Reference.

If you know the ZIP Code but the city name does not appear in the City/County Cross Reference index, look up the ZIP Code in the ZIP/City Cross Reference, find the city name, then look up the city name in the City/County Cross Reference. For example, you want to know the county for an address of Menands, NY 12204. There is no "Menands" in the City/County Cross Reference. The ZIP/City Cross Reference shows that ZIP Codes 12201-12288 are for the city of Albany. Looking back in the City/County Cross Reference, Albany is in Albany County.

City/County Cross Reference

ABBOTT (76621) Hill(91), McLennan(9)
ABERNATHY (79311) Hale(73), Lubbock(27)
ABILENE (79601) Taylor(79), Jones(15), Callahan(3), Shackelford(3)
ABILENE (79602) Taylor(94), Callahan(6)
ABILENE Taylor
ACE Polk
ACKERLY Dawson
ADDISON (75001) Dallas(98), Collin(2)
ADKINS (78101) Bexar(75), Wilson(25)
ADRIAN (79001) Deaf Smith(50), Oldham(50)
AFTON Dickens
AGUA DULCE Nueces
AIKEN Floyd
ALAMO Hidalgo
ALANREED Gray
ALBA (75410) Wood(88), Rains(12)
ALBANY Shackelford
ALEDO (76008) Parker(79), Tarrant(21)
ALICE Jim Wells
ALIEF Harris
ALLEN Collin
ALLEYTON Colorado
ALLISON Wheeler
ALPINE Brewster
ALTAIR Colorado
ALTO Cherokee
ALVARADO Johnson
ALVIN (77511) Brazoria(94), Galveston(6)
ALVIN Brazoria
ALVORD Wise
AMARILLO (79103) Potter(77), Randall(23)
AMARILLO (79106) Potter(91), Randall(9)
AMARILLO (79109) Randall(75), Potter(25)
AMARILLO (79118) Randall(95), Potter(6)
AMARILLO (79121) Randall(97), Potter(3)
AMARILLO Potter
AMARILLO Randall
AMHERST Lamb
ANAHUAC Chambers
ANDERSON Grimes
ANDREWS Andrews
ANGLETON Brazoria
ANNA Collin
ANNONA Red River
ANSON Jones
ANTHONY El Paso
ANTON (79313) Hockley(74), Lamb(20), Lubbock(5), Hale(2)
APPLE SPRINGS Trinity
AQUILLA Hill
ARANSAS PASS (78336) San Patricio(77), Aransas(22)
ARANSAS PASS San Patricio
ARCHER CITY Archer
ARGYLE Denton
ARLINGTON Tarrant
ARMSTRONG Kenedy
ARP Smith
ART Mason
ARTESIA WELLS La Salle
ARTHUR CITY Lamar
ASHERTON Dimmit

ASPERMONT Stonewall
ATASCOSA Bexar
ATHENS Henderson
ATLANTA Cass
AUBREY Denton
AUSTIN (78728) Travis(97), Williamson(4)
AUSTIN (78729) Williamson(92), Travis(8)
AUSTIN (78736) Travis(91), Hays(9)
AUSTIN (78737) Hays(53), Travis(47)
AUSTIN (78750) Travis(59), Williamson(41)
AUSTIN Travis
AUSTIN Williamson
AUSTWELL Refugio
AVALON Ellis
AVERY (75554) Red River(88), Bowie(12)
AVINGER (75630) Marion(56), Cass(44)
AXTELL (76624) McLennan(97), Limestone(3)
AZLE (76020) Parker(51), Tarrant(48)
AZLE Parker
BACLIFF Galveston
BAGWELL Red River
BAILEY Fannin
BAIRD Callahan
BALLINGER Runnels
BALMORHEA Reeves
BANDERA Bandera
BANGS (76823) Brown(64), Coleman(36)
BANQUETE Nueces
BARDWELL Ellis
BARKER Harris
BARKSDALE (78828) Edwards(72), Real(28)
BARNHART (76930) Irion(55), Crockett(46)
BARRY (75102) Navarro(97), Ellis(3)
BARSTOW Ward
BARTLETT (76511) Bell(60), Williamson(36), Milam(4)
BASTROP Bastrop
BATESVILLE Zavala
BATSON Hardin
BAY CITY Matagorda
BAYSIDE Refugio
BAYTOWN (77520) Harris(82), Chambers(18)
BAYTOWN (77521) Harris(96), Chambers(4)
BAYTOWN Harris
BEASLEY Fort Bend
BEAUMONT Jefferson
BEBE Gonzales
BECKVILLE Panola
BEDFORD Tarrant
BEDIAS Grimes
BEEVILLE Bee
BELLAIRE Harris
BELLEVUE (76228) Clay(83), Montague(17)
BELLS Grayson
BELLVILLE Austin
BELMONT Gonzales
BELTON Bell
BEN ARNOLD Milam
BEN BOLT Jim Wells
BEN FRANKLIN Delta

BEN WHEELER Van Zandt
BENAVIDES Duval
BEND San Saba
BENJAMIN Knox
BERCLAIR Goliad
BERGHEIM Kendall
BERTRAM Burnet
BIG BEND NATIONAL PARK Brewster
BIG LAKE Reagan
BIG SANDY (75755) Upshur(92), Wood(9)
BIG SPRING (79720) Howard(99), Glasscock(1)
BIG SPRING Howard
BIG WELLS Dimmit
BIGFOOT (78005) Frio(84), Atascosa(16)
BIROME Hill
BISHOP Nueces
BIVINS Cass
BLACKWELL (79506) Nolan(83), Coke(17)
BLANCO (78606) Blanco(84), Comal(16)
BLANKET (76432) Brown(98), Comanche(2)
BLEDSOE Cochran
BLEIBLERVILLE Austin
BLESSING Matagorda
BLOOMBURG Cass
BLOOMING GROVE (76626) Navarro(98), Ellis(2)
BLOOMINGTON Victoria
BLOSSOM Lamar
BLUE RIDGE (75424) Collin(98), Fannin(2)
BLUEGROVE Clay
BLUFF DALE (76433) Hood(83), Somervell(10), Erath(8)
BLUFFTON Llano
BLUM Hill
BOERNE (78006) Kendall(83), Bexar(14), Comal(3)
BOERNE (78015) Bexar(64), Kendall(31), Comal(5)
BOGATA Red River
BOLING Wharton
BON WIER Newton
BONHAM Fannin
BOOKER (79005) Lipscomb(73), Ochiltree(27)
BORGER Hutchinson
BOVINA Parmer
BOWIE (76230) Montague(98), Jack(2)
BOYD (76023) Wise(91), Parker(9)
BOYS RANCH (79010) Potter(75), Oldham(25)
BRACKETTVILLE Kinney
BRADY McCulloch
BRANDON Hill
BRASHEAR Hopkins
BRAZORIA Brazoria
BRECKENRIDGE Stephens
BREMOND (76629) Robertson(87), Falls(13)
BRENHAM Washington
BRIDGE CITY Orange
BRIDGEPORT Wise
BRIGGS Burnet

BRISCOE (79011) Hemphill(66), Wheeler(34)
BROADDUS San Augustine
BRONSON (75930) Sabine(63), San Augustine(37)
BRONTE (76933) Runnels(68), Coke(33)
BROOKELAND (75931) Jasper(52), Sabine(48)
BROOKESMITH (76827) Brown(99), Coleman(2)
BROOKSHIRE (77423) Waller(87), Fort Bend(13)
BROOKSTON Lamar
BROWNFIELD Terry
BROWNSBORO (75756) Henderson(99), Van Zandt(1)
BROWNSVILLE Cameron
BROWNWOOD Brown
BRUCEVILLE (76630) McLennan(96), Falls(5)
BRUNI (78344) Webb(94), Duval(6)
BRYAN (77807) Brazos(89), Robertson(11)
BRYAN (77808) Brazos(92), Robertson(8)
BRYAN Brazos
BRYSON Jack
BUCHANAN DAM Llano
BUCKHOLTS Milam
BUDA (78610) Hays(88), Travis(12)
BUFFALO (75831) Leon(83), Freestone(17)
BUFFALO GAP Taylor
BULA (79320) Bailey(82), Lamb(18)
BULLARD (75757) Smith(83), Cherokee(17)
BULVERDE Comal
BUNA Jasper
BURKBURNETT Wichita
BURKETT Coleman
BURKEVILLE Newton
BURLESON (76028) Johnson(78), Tarrant(22)
BURLESON Johnson
BURLINGTON (76519) Milam(67), Bell(28), Falls(6)
BURNET Burnet
BURTON Washington
BUSHLAND Potter
BYERS Clay
BYNUM Hill
CACTUS Moore
CADDO Stephens
CADDO MILLS Hunt
CALDWELL Burleson
CALL (75933) Newton(68), Jasper(32)
CALLIHAM McMullen
CALVERT Robertson
CAMDEN Polk
CAMERON Milam
CAMP WOOD Real
CAMPBELL Hunt
CAMPBELLTON (78008) Atascosa(91), Live Oak(9)
CANADIAN (79014) Hemphill(99), Lipscomb(1)
CANTON Van Zandt

CANUTILLO El Paso
CANYON Randall
CANYON LAKE Comal
CARBON Eastland
CAREY Childress
CARLSBAD Tom Green
CARLTON Hamilton
CARMINE Fayette
CARRIZO SPRINGS Dimmit
CARROLLTON (75007) Denton(90), Dallas(10)
CARROLLTON Dallas
CARROLLTON Denton
CARTHAGE Panola
CASON Morris
CASTELL (76831) Mason(60), Llano(40)
CASTROVILLE Medina
CAT SPRING (78933) Colorado(97), Austin(3)
CATARINA Dimmit
CAYUGA Anderson
CEDAR CREEK (78612) Bastrop(95), Travis(5)
CEDAR HILL Dallas
CEDAR LANE Matagorda
CEDAR PARK (78613) Williamson(98), Travis(2)
CEDAR PARK Williamson
CEE VEE Cottle
CELESTE (75423) Hunt(97), Fannin(3)
CELINA Collin
CENTER Shelby
CENTER POINT Kerr
CENTERVILLE Leon
CENTRALIA Trinity
CHALK Cottle
CHANDLER Henderson
CHANNELVIEW Harris
CHANNING (79018) Hartley(82), Moore(18)
CHAPMAN RANCH Nueces
CHAPPELL HILL (77426) Washington(87), Austin(13)
CHARLOTTE Atascosa
CHATFIELD Navarro
CHEROKEE (76832) San Saba(99), Llano(1)
CHESTER (75936) Tyler(90), Polk(10)
CHICO Wise
CHICOTA Lamar
CHILDRESS (79201) Childress(98), Hall(1)
CHILLICOTHE (79225) Hardeman(85), Wilbarger(15)
CHILTON Falls
CHINA Jefferson
CHINA SPRING (76633) McLennan(99), Bosque(1)
CHIRENO Nacogdoches
CHRIESMAN Burleson
CHRISTINE Atascosa
CHRISTOVAL (76935) Tom Green(74), Schleicher(26)
CIBOLO (78108) Guadalupe(71), Bexar(28), Comal(1)
CISCO (76437) Eastland(96), Callahan(3), Stephens(1)
CLARENDON (79226) Donley(83), Armstrong(12), Hall(4), Briscoe(2)
CLARKSVILLE Red River
CLAUDE Armstrong
CLAY Burleson
CLAYTON Panola
CLEBURNE Johnson
CLEVELAND (77327) Liberty(43), San Jacinto(29), Montgomery(28)
CLEVELAND Liberty
CLIFTON Bosque
CLINT El Paso
CLUTE Brazoria
CLYDE Callahan
COAHOMA (79511) Howard(95), Borden(5)
COLDSPRING San Jacinto

COLEMAN Coleman
COLLEGE STATION Brazos
COLLEGEPORT Matagorda
COLLEYVILLE Tarrant
COLLINSVILLE (76233) Grayson(72), Cooke(28)
COLMESNEIL Tyler
COLORADO CITY Mitchell
COLUMBUS Colorado
COMANCHE Comanche
COMBES Cameron
COMFORT (78013) Kendall(88), Kerr(12)
COMMERCE Hunt
COMO Hopkins
COMSTOCK Val Verde
CONCAN Uvalde
CONCEPCION Duval
CONCORD (77850) Leon(88), Brazos(13)
CONE Crosby
CONROE Montgomery
CONVERSE Bexar
COOKVILLE Titus
COOLIDGE (76635) Limestone(94), McLennan(6)
COOPER Delta
COPEVILLE Collin
COPPELL Dallas
COPPERAS COVE (76522) Coryell(99), Lampasas(1)
CORPUS CHRISTI Nueces
CORRIGAN Polk
CORSICANA Navarro
COST Gonzales
COTTON CENTER Hale
COTULLA La Salle
COUPLAND (78615) Williamson(89), Travis(11)
COVINGTON Hill
COYANOSA Pecos
CRANDALL Kaufman
CRANE Crane
CRANFILLS GAP (76637) Bosque(92), Hamilton(8)
CRAWFORD McLennan
CRESSON (76035) Hood(59), Parker(35), Johnson(6)
CROCKETT Houston
CROSBY Harris
CROSBYTON Crosby
CROSS PLAINS (76443) Callahan(96), Brown(3)
CROWELL Foard
CROWLEY (76036) Tarrant(72), Johnson(28)
CRYSTAL CITY Zavala
CUERO De Witt
CUMBY Hopkins
CUNEY Cherokee
CUNNINGHAM Lamar
CUSHING (75760) Nacogdoches(94), Rusk(6)
CYPRESS Harris
D HANIS Medina
DAINGERFIELD Morris
DAISETTA Liberty
DALE (78616) Caldwell(94), Bastrop(7)
DALHART (79022) Dallam(73), Hartley(27)
DALLARDSVILLE Polk
DALLAS (75252) Collin(96), Dallas(4)
DALLAS (75287) Collin(52), Denton(47), Dallas(1)
DALLAS Dallas
DAMON (77430) Fort Bend(61), Brazoria(39)
DANBURY Brazoria
DANCIGER Brazoria
DANEVANG Wharton
DARROUZETT Lipscomb
DAVILLA Milam
DAWN Deaf Smith
DAWSON (76639) Navarro(88), McLennan(12)

DAYTON (77535) Liberty(94), Chambers(6)
DE BERRY Panola
DE KALB Bowie
DE LEON Comanche
DE SOTO Dallas
DEANVILLE Burleson
DECATUR Wise
DEER PARK Harris
DEL RIO Edwards
DEL RIO Val Verde
DEL VALLE (78617) Travis(88), Bastrop(12)
DELL CITY Hudspeth
DELMITA (78536) Starr(88), Hidalgo(13)
DENISON Grayson
DENNIS Parker
DENTON Denton
DENVER CITY (79323) Yoakum(97), Gaines(3)
DEPORT Lamar
DESDEMONA (76445) Eastland(90), Comanche(9)
DETROIT (75436) Red River(93), Lamar(7)
DEVERS Liberty
DEVINE Medina
DEWEYVILLE Newton
DIANA (75640) Upshur(71), Harrison(27), Marion(2)
DIBOLL Angelina
DICKENS Dickens
DICKINSON Galveston
DIKE Hopkins
DILLEY Frio
DIME BOX Lee
DIMMITT Castro
DINERO Live Oak
DOBBIN Montgomery
DODD CITY Fannin
DODGE Walker
DODSON (79230) Collingsworth(67), Childress(33)
DONIE (75838) Freestone(60), Limestone(39), Leon(1)
DONNA Hidalgo
DOOLE McCulloch
DOSS Gillespie
DOUCETTE Tyler
DOUGHERTY Floyd
DOUGLASS Nacogdoches
DOUGLASSVILLE Cass
DRIFTWOOD Hays
DRIPPING SPRINGS (78620) Hays(90), Travis(10)
DRISCOLL Nueces
DRYDEN Terrell
DUBLIN (76446) Erath(84), Comanche(16)
DUMAS Moore
DUMONT (79232) Dickens(69), King(31)
DUNCANVILLE Dallas
DUNN Scurry
DYESS AFB Taylor
EAGLE LAKE (77434) Colorado(98), Wharton(2)
EAGLE PASS Maverick
EARLY Brown
EARTH (79031) Lamb(75), Castro(17), Bailey(9)
EAST BERNARD (77435) Wharton(90), Fort Bend(10)
EASTLAND Eastland
EASTON Gregg
ECLETO Karnes
ECTOR Fannin
EDCOUCH Hidalgo
EDDY (76524) McLennan(98), Falls(2)
EDEN Concho
EDGEWOOD Van Zandt
EDINBURG Hidalgo
EDMONSON Hale
EDNA Jackson
EDROY San Patricio
EGYPT Wharton

EL CAMPO Wharton
EL INDIO Maverick
EL PASO (79938) El Paso(98), Hudspeth(2)
EL PASO El Paso
ELBERT Throckmorton
ELECTRA (76360) Wichita(88), Wilbarger(12)
ELGIN (78621) Bastrop(76), Travis(14), Williamson(7), Lee(3)
ELIASVILLE Young
ELKHART (75839) Anderson(99), Houston(1)
ELLINGER Fayette
ELM MOTT McLennan
ELMATON Matagorda
ELMENDORF (78112) Bexar(97), Wilson(3)
ELMO Kaufman
ELSA Hidalgo
ELYSIAN FIELDS Harrison
EMORY (75440) Rains(99), Wood(1)
ENCINAL La Salle
ENCINO Brooks
ENERGY Comanche
ENLOE Delta
ENNIS Ellis
ENOCHS Bailey
EOLA (76937) Tom Green(87), Concho(13)
ERA Cooke
ESTELLINE Hall
ETOILE Nacogdoches
EULESS Tarrant
EUSTACE (75124) Henderson(96), Van Zandt(4)
EVADALE Jasper
EVANT Coryell
FABENS El Paso
FAIRFIELD Freestone
FALCON HEIGHTS Starr
FALFURRIAS (78355) Brooks(96), Jim Wells(4)
FALLS CITY (78113) Wilson(57), Karnes(43)
FANNIN Goliad
FARMERSVILLE (75442) Collin(99), Hunt(1)
FARNSWORTH Ochiltree
FARWELL (79325) Parmer(91), Bailey(9)
FATE Rockwall
FAYETTEVILLE (78940) Fayette(85), Colorado(9), Austin(6)
FENTRESS Caldwell
FERRIS (75125) Ellis(83), Dallas(17)
FIELDTON Lamb
FISCHER (78623) Hays(52), Comal(48)
FLAT Coryell
FLATONIA Fayette
FLINT Smith
FLOMOT (79234) Motley(84), Floyd(16)
FLORENCE (76527) Williamson(97), Bell(2)
FLORESVILLE Wilson
FLOWER MOUND Denton
FLOYDADA (79235) Floyd(97), Crosby(2)
FLUVANNA (79517) Scurry(71), Borden(30)
FLYNN Leon
FOLLETT Lipscomb
FORESTBURG (76239) Montague(85), Cooke(15)
FORNEY (75126) Kaufman(97), Rockwall(3)
FORRESTON Ellis
FORSAN Howard
FORT DAVIS Jeff Davis
FORT HANCOCK Hudspeth
FORT MC KAVETT Menard
FORT STOCKTON Pecos
FORT WORTH (76108) Tarrant(93), Parker(7)

FORT WORTH (76126) Tarrant(88), Parker(12)
FORT WORTH (76177) Tarrant(93), Denton(7)
FORT WORTH (76178) Tarrant(99), Denton(2)
FORT WORTH Tarrant
FOWLERTON (78021) La Salle(63), McMullen(25), Atascosa(13)
FRANCITAS Jackson
FRANKLIN Robertson
FRANKSTON (75763) Henderson(78), Anderson(22)
FRED Tyler
FREDERICKSBURG (78624) Gillespie(75), Kendall(24)
FREDONIA (76842) Mason(96), San Saba(5)
FREEPORT Brazoria
FREER Duval
FRESNO Fort Bend
FRIENDSWOOD (77546) Galveston(67), Harris(32)
FRIENDSWOOD Galveston
FRIONA (79035) Parmer(98), Deaf Smith(2)
FRISCO (75034) Collin(85), Denton(15)
FRISCO (75035) Collin(98), Denton(2)
FRITCH (79036) Hutchinson(95), Carson(5)
FROST (76641) Navarro(98), Ellis(2)
FRUITVALE Van Zandt
FULSHEAR Fort Bend
FULTON Aransas
GAIL Borden
GAINESVILLE Cooke
GALENA PARK Harris
GALLATIN Cherokee
GALVESTON Galveston
GANADO Jackson
GARCIASVILLE Starr
GARDEN CITY (79739) Glasscock(88), Reagan(12)
GARDENDALE Ector
GARLAND (75048) Dallas(90), Collin(10)
GARLAND Dallas
GARRISON (75946) Nacogdoches(54), Rusk(46)
GARWOOD Colorado
GARY (75643) Panola(92), Shelby(8)
GATESVILLE (76528) Coryell(98), Bell(2)
GATESVILLE Coryell
GAUSE Milam
GENEVA Sabine
GEORGE WEST Live Oak
GEORGETOWN Williamson
GERONIMO Guadalupe
GIDDINGS Lee
GILCHRIST Galveston
GILLETT Karnes
GILMER Upshur
GIRARD Kent
GIRVIN Pecos
GLADEWATER (75647) Gregg(59), Upshur(31), Smith(10)
GLEN FLORA Wharton
GLEN ROSE Somervell
GLIDDEN Colorado
GOBER Fannin
GODLEY Johnson
GOLDEN Wood
GOLDSBORO (79519) Taylor(46), Runnels(42), Coleman(12)
GOLDSMITH Ector
GOLDTHWAITE Mills
GOLIAD Goliad
GONZALES Gonzales
GOODFELLOW AFB Tom Green
GOODRICH Polk
GORDON (76453) Palo Pinto(96), Erath(4)
GORDONVILLE Grayson

GOREE (76363) Knox(98), Haskell(1), Throckmorton(1)
GORMAN (76454) Eastland(76), Comanche(25)
GOULDBUSK Coleman
GRAFORD Palo Pinto
GRAHAM Young
GRANBURY (76048) Hood(98), Somervell(2)
GRANBURY (76049) Hood(97), Parker(3)
GRAND PRAIRIE (75050) Dallas(74), Tarrant(26)
GRAND PRAIRIE (75051) Dallas(87), Tarrant(13)
GRAND PRAIRIE (75052) Dallas(68), Tarrant(32)
GRAND PRAIRIE Dallas
GRAND SALINE Van Zandt
GRANDFALLS Ward
GRANDVIEW (76050) Johnson(96), Hill(2), Ellis(2)
GRANGER Williamson
GRAPELAND (75844) Houston(87), Anderson(13)
GRAPEVINE Tarrant
GREENVILLE Hunt
GREENWOOD Wise
GREGORY San Patricio
GROESBECK Limestone
GROOM (79039) Carson(58), Gray(39), Armstrong(2), Donley(2)
GROVES Jefferson
GROVETON Trinity
GRULLA Starr
GRUVER (79040) Hansford(65), Sherman(35)
GUERRA (78360) Jim Hogg(80), Starr(20)
GUNTER Grayson
GUSTINE Comanche
GUTHRIE King
GUY (77444) Fort Bend(72), Brazoria(28)
HALE CENTER (79041) Hale(98), Lamb(3)
HALLETTSVILLE Lavaca
HALLSVILLE Harrison
HALTOM CITY Tarrant
HAMILTON Hamilton
HAMLIN (79520) Jones(95), Fisher(5)
HAMSHIRE (77622) Jefferson(83), Chambers(17)
HANKAMER Chambers
HAPPY (79042) Randall(59), Swisher(28), Castro(8), Armstrong(5)
HARDIN Liberty
HARGILL Hidalgo
HARKER HEIGHTS Bell
HARLETON (75651) Harrison(94), Marion(6)
HARLINGEN Cameron
HARPER (78631) Gillespie(97), Kerr(3)
HARROLD Wilbarger
HART (79043) Castro(92), Lamb(9)
HARTLEY Hartley
HARWOOD (78632) Gonzales(81), Caldwell(19)
HASKELL Haskell
HASLET (76052) Tarrant(90), Denton(6), Wise(4)
HASSE Comanche
HAWKINS Wood
HAWLEY Jones
HEARNE Robertson
HEBBRONVILLE Jim Hogg
HEDLEY Donley
HEIDENHEIMER Bell
HELOTES (78023) Bexar(87), Medina(8), Bandera(5)
HEMPHILL Sabine
HEMPSTEAD Waller
HENDERSON Rusk
HENRIETTA Clay
HEREFORD (79045) Deaf Smith(97), Castro(3)

HERMLEIGH (79526) Scurry(95), Fisher(5)
HEWITT McLennan
HEXT Menard
HICO (76457) Hamilton(87), Erath(13)
HIDALGO Hidalgo
HIGGINS (79046) Lipscomb(72), Hemphill(28)
HIGH ISLAND Galveston
HIGHLANDS Harris
HILLISTER Tyler
HILLSBORO Hill
HITCHCOCK Galveston
HOBSON Karnes
HOCHHEIM De Witt
HOCKLEY (77447) Harris(62), Waller(21), Montgomery(17)
HOLLAND Bell
HOLLIDAY Archer
HONDO Medina
HONEY GROVE Fannin
HOOKS Bowie
HOUSTON (77031) Harris(99), Fort Bend(1)
HOUSTON (77053) Fort Bend(59), Harris(41)
HOUSTON (77083) Harris(59), Fort Bend(41)
HOUSTON (77085) Harris(93), Fort Bend(7)
HOUSTON (77099) Harris(97), Fort Bend(3)
HOUSTON Harris
HOWE Grayson
HUBBARD (76648) Hill(96), Navarro(3), Limestone(1)
HUFFMAN Harris
HUFSMITH Harris
HUGHES SPRINGS (75656) Cass(92), Morris(9)
HULL (77564) Liberty(92), Hardin(8)
HUMBLE (77339) Harris(84), Montgomery(16)
HUMBLE Harris
HUNGERFORD Wharton
HUNT (78024) Kerr(98), Real(2)
HUNTINGTON Angelina
HUNTSVILLE Walker
HURST Tarrant
HUTCHINS Dallas
HUTTO Williamson
HYE Blanco
IDALOU Lubbock
IMPERIAL Pecos
INDUSTRY Austin
INEZ Victoria
INGLESIDE San Patricio
INGRAM Kerr
IOLA Grimes
IOWA PARK Wichita
IRA (79527) Scurry(80), Borden(20)
IRAAN Pecos
IREDELL (76649) Bosque(89), Erath(11)
IRENE Hill
IRVING Dallas
ITALY Ellis
ITASCA Hill
IVANHOE Fannin
JACKSBORO Jack
JACKSONVILLE Cherokee
JARRELL Williamson
JASPER Jasper
JAYTON Kent
JEFFERSON (75657) Marion(93), Cass(6), Harrison(1)
JERMYN Jack
JEWETT (75846) Leon(61), Limestone(39)
JOAQUIN (75954) Shelby(94), Panola(6)
JOHNSON CITY Blanco
JOINERVILLE Rusk
JONESBORO (76538) Coryell(90), Hamilton(10)

JONESVILLE (75659) Harrison(86), Rusk(14)
JOSEPHINE Collin
JOSHUA Johnson
JOURDANTON Atascosa
JUDSON Gregg
JUNCTION Kimble
JUSTICEBURG Garza
JUSTIN Denton
KAMAY Wichita
KARNACK Harrison
KARNES CITY Karnes
KATY (77450) Harris(81), Fort Bend(19)
KATY (77493) Harris(84), Waller(14), Fort Bend(2)
KATY (77494) Fort Bend(78), Harris(19), Waller(3)
KATY Harris
KAUFMAN Kaufman
KEENE Johnson
KELLER Tarrant
KEMAH Galveston
KEMP (75143) Kaufman(71), Henderson(29)
KEMPNER (76539) Coryell(48), Lampasas(43), Bell(6), Burnet(3)
KENDALIA Kendall
KENDLETON Fort Bend
KENEDY Karnes
KENNARD (75847) Houston(91), Trinity(9)
KENNEDALE Tarrant
KENNEY Austin
KERENS Navarro
KERMIT Winkler
KERRICK Dallam
KERRVILLE Kerr
KILDARE Cass
KILGORE (75662) Gregg(94), Rusk(6)
KILGORE Gregg
KILLEEN (76544) Bell(52), Coryell(49)
KILLEEN Bell
KINGSBURY Guadalupe
KINGSLAND Llano
KINGSVILLE Kleberg
KIRBYVILLE Jasper
KIRKLAND Childress
KIRVIN Freestone
KLONDIKE Delta
KNICKERBOCKER Tom Green
KNIPPA Uvalde
KNOTT Howard
KNOX CITY (79529) Knox(98), Haskell(2)
KOPPERL Bosque
KOSSE (76653) Limestone(86), Falls(6), Robertson(5), McLennan(4)
KOUNTZE Hardin
KRESS (79052) Swisher(91), Hale(8)
KRUM Denton
KURTEN Brazos
KYLE (78640) Hays(97), Caldwell(3)
LA BLANCA Hidalgo
LA COSTE (78039) Medina(87), Bexar(13)
LA FERIA Cameron
LA GRANGE Fayette
LA JOYA Hidalgo
LA MARQUE Galveston
LA PORTE Harris
LA PRYOR Zavala
LA SALLE Jackson
LA VERNIA (78121) Wilson(55), Guadalupe(45)
LA VILLA Hidalgo
LA WARD Jackson
LADONIA Fannin
LAIRD HILL Rusk
LAKE CREEK Delta
LAKE DALLAS Denton
LAKE JACKSON Brazoria
LAKEVIEW Hall
LAMESA Dawson
LAMPASAS (76550) Lampasas(98), Burnet(2)

LANCASTER (75146) Dallas(99), Ellis(1)
LANCASTER Dallas
LANE CITY Wharton
LANEVILLE Rusk
LANGTRY Val Verde
LAREDO Webb
LARUE Henderson
LASARA Willacy
LATEXO Houston
LAUGHLIN A F B Val Verde
LAVON Collin
LAWN (79530) Taylor(95), Runnels(5)
LAZBUDDIE Parmer
LEAGUE CITY Galveston
LEAKEY Real
LEANDER (78641) Travis(67), Williamson(33)
LEANDER Travis
LEANDER Williamson
LEDBETTER (78946) Fayette(73), Lee(13), Washington(13)
LEESBURG (75451) Camp(92), Upshur(5), Wood(3)
LEESVILLE Gonzales
LEFORS Gray
LEGGETT Polk
LELIA LAKE Donley
LEMING Atascosa
LENORAH Martin
LEON JUNCTION Coryell
LEONA (75850) Leon(99), Madison(1)
LEONARD (75452) Fannin(49), Collin(35), Hunt(16)
LEROY McLennan
LEVELLAND Hockley
LEWISVILLE Denton
LEXINGTON (78947) Lee(98), Milam(2)
LIBERTY Liberty
LIBERTY HILL (78642) Williamson(98), Burnet(2)
LILLIAN Johnson
LINCOLN Lee
LINDALE Smith
LINDEN Cass
LINDSAY Cooke
LINGLEVILLE Erath
LINN (78563) Hidalgo(78), Starr(22)
LIPAN (76462) Hood(56), Palo Pinto(24), Parker(20)
LIPSCOMB Lipscomb
LISSIE Wharton
LITTLE ELM Denton
LITTLE RIVER Bell
LITTLEFIELD (79339) Lamb(97), Hockley(3)
LIVERPOOL Brazoria
LIVINGSTON Polk
LLANO Llano
LOCKHART Caldwell
LOCKNEY (79241) Floyd(97), Swisher(2)
LODI Marion
LOHN McCulloch
LOLITA Jackson
LOMETA (76853) Lampasas(92), Mills(6), San Saba(2)
LONDON (76854) Kimble(76), Menard(20), Mason(4)
LONE OAK (75453) Hunt(79), Rains(20), Hopkins(2)
LONE STAR (75668) Morris(64), Marion(35), Cass(1)
LONG BRANCH (75669) Panola(95), Rusk(5)
LONG MOTT Calhoun
LONGVIEW (75601) Gregg(93), Harrison(7)
LONGVIEW (75602) Gregg(86), Harrison(14)
LONGVIEW (75603) Gregg(86), Rusk(14)
LONGVIEW (75605) Gregg(99), Harrison(1)
LONGVIEW Gregg

LOOP Gaines
LOPENO Zapata
LORAINE (79532) Mitchell(94), Scurry(4), Nolan(3)
LORENA (76655) McLennan(99), Falls(1)
LORENZO (79343) Crosby(68), Lubbock(32)
LOS EBANOS Hidalgo
LOS FRESNOS Cameron
LOS INDIOS Cameron
LOTT (76656) Falls(99), Bell(1)
LOUISE (77455) Wharton(84), Jackson(15), Colorado(1)
LOVELADY (75851) Houston(96), Trinity(4)
LOVING Young
LOWAKE Concho
LOZANO Cameron
LUBBOCK (79407) Lubbock(94), Hockley(6)
LUBBOCK Lubbock
LUEDERS (79533) Jones(57), Shackelford(39), Haskell(5)
LUFKIN Angelina
LULING (78648) Caldwell(93), Guadalupe(7)
LUMBERTON Hardin
LYFORD (78569) Willacy(93), Hidalgo(7)
LYONS Burleson
LYTLE (78052) Atascosa(68), Medina(23), Bexar(9)
MABANK (75147) Henderson(70), Kaufman(28), Van Zandt(3)
MACDONA Bexar
MADISONVILLE Madison
MAGNOLIA (77355) Montgomery(98), Waller(2)
MAGNOLIA Montgomery
MAGNOLIA SPRINGS Bowie
MAGNOLIA SPRINGS Jasper
MALAKOFF Henderson
MALONE Hill
MANCHACA (78652) Travis(71), Hays(30)
MANOR Travis
MANSFIELD (76063) Tarrant(91), Johnson(9)
MANVEL Brazoria
MAPLE Bailey
MARATHON Brewster
MARBLE FALLS (78654) Burnet(56), Blanco(38), Llano(5), Travis(1)
MARBLE FALLS Burnet
MARFA Presidio
MARIETTA Cass
MARION (78124) Guadalupe(99), Bexar(1)
MARKHAM Matagorda
MARLIN Falls
MARQUEZ Leon
MARSHALL Harrison
MART (76664) McLennan(92), Limestone(7), Falls(1)
MARTINDALE (78655) Caldwell(64), Guadalupe(37)
MARTINSVILLE Nacogdoches
MARYNEAL Nolan
MASON Mason
MASTERSON Moore
MATADOR Motley
MATAGORDA Matagorda
MATHIS (78368) San Patricio(97), Live Oak(3)
MAUD Bowie
MAURICEVILLE Orange
MAXWELL (78656) Caldwell(94), Hays(6)
MAY Brown
MAYDELLE Cherokee
MAYPEARL Ellis
MAYSFIELD Milam
MC CAMEY Upton
MC CAULLEY Fisher
MC COY Atascosa
MC DADE Bastrop

MC GREGOR (76657) McLennan(98), Coryell(2)
MC KINNEY Collin
MC LEOD Cass
MC NEIL Travis
MC QUEENEY Guadalupe
MCADOO (79243) Dickens(54), Crosby(46)
MCALLEN Hidalgo
MCFADDIN Victoria
MCLEAN (79057) Gray(73), Wheeler(21), Donley(6)
MEADOW (79345) Terry(93), Lynn(6), Taylor(1)
MEDINA (78055) Bandera(98), Kerr(2)
MEGARGEL Archer
MELISSA Collin
MELVIN (76858) McCulloch(83), Concho(17)
MEMPHIS (79245) Hall(99), Collingsworth(1)
MENARD (76859) Menard(87), Kimble(14)
MENTONE Loving
MERCEDES Hidalgo
MERETA Tom Green
MERIDIAN Bosque
MERIT Hunt
MERKEL (79536) Taylor(76), Jones(24)
MERTENS (76666) Hill(89), Navarro(11)
MERTZON Irion
MESQUITE Dallas
MEXIA (76667) Limestone(97), Freestone(3)
MEYERSVILLE (77974) De Witt(70), Victoria(30)
MIAMI (79059) Roberts(84), Gray(16)
MICO Medina
MIDFIELD Matagorda
MIDKIFF Upton
MIDLAND Midland
MIDLOTHIAN Ellis
MIDWAY (75852) Madison(82), Walker(12), Leon(6)
MILAM Sabine
MILANO (76556) Milam(98), Burleson(2)
MILES (76861) Tom Green(51), Runnels(47), Concho(2)
MILFORD (76670) Ellis(71), Navarro(25), Hill(4)
MILLERSVIEW Concho
MILLICAN Brazos
MILLSAP (76066) Parker(94), Palo Pinto(6)
MINDEN Rusk
MINEOLA (75773) Wood(86), Smith(14)
MINERAL Bee
MINERAL WELLS (76067) Palo Pinto(97), Parker(3)
MINERAL WELLS Palo Pinto
MINGUS (76463) Erath(60), Palo Pinto(39), Eastland(2)
MIRANDO CITY Webb
MISSION Hidalgo
MISSOURI CITY (77489) Fort Bend(96), Harris(4)
MISSOURI CITY Fort Bend
MOBEETIE (79061) Wheeler(87), Gray(9), Hemphill(4)
MONAHANS Ward
MONT BELVIEU Chambers
MONTAGUE Montague
MONTALBA (75853) Anderson(95), Henderson(5)
MONTGOMERY Montgomery
MOODY (76557) McLennan(68), Bell(31), Coryell(2)
MOORE (78057) Frio(87), Medina(13)
MORAN (76464) Shackelford(82), Stephens(11), Callahan(7)
MORGAN Bosque
MORGAN MILL Erath
MORSE (79062) Hutchinson(71), Hansford(21), Bee(7)
MORTON (79346) Cochran(98), Bailey(2)

MOSCOW Polk
MOULTON Lavaca
MOUND Coryell
MOUNT CALM (76673) Hill(65), Limestone(25), McLennan(10)
MOUNT ENTERPRISE Rusk
MOUNT PLEASANT Titus
MOUNT VERNON Franklin
MOUNTAIN HOME Kerr
MUENSTER Cooke
MULDOON Fayette
MULESHOE (79347) Bailey(92), Parmer(5), Lamb(2)
MULLIN Mills
MUMFORD Robertson
MUNDAY (76371) Knox(98), Haskell(2)
MURCHISON (75778) Henderson(85), Van Zandt(15)
MYRA Cooke
NACOGDOCHES Nacogdoches
NADA Colorado
NAPLES (75568) Morris(63), Cass(37)
NASH Bowie
NATALIA Medina
NAVAL AIR STATION/ JRB Tarrant
NAVASOTA (77868) Grimes(96), Brazos(3)
NAVASOTA Brazos
NAZARETH Castro
NECHES Anderson
NEDERLAND Jefferson
NEEDVILLE Fort Bend
NEMO (76070) Somervell(84), Johnson(16)
NEVADA Collin
NEW BADEN Robertson
NEW BOSTON Bowie
NEW BRAUNFELS (78130) Comal(82), Guadalupe(18)
NEW BRAUNFELS Comal
NEW CANEY Montgomery
NEW DEAL Lubbock
NEW HOME Lynn
NEW LONDON Rusk
NEW SUMMERFIELD Cherokee
NEW ULM (78950) Colorado(98), Austin(3)
NEW WAVERLY (77358) Walker(49), San Jacinto(37), Montgomery(14)
NEWARK Wise
NEWCASTLE (76372) Young(76), Throckmorton(24)
NEWGULF Wharton
NEWPORT Clay
NEWTON (75966) Newton(89), Jasper(11)
NIXON (78140) Gonzales(92), Wilson(5), Guadalupe(3)
NOCONA Montague
NOLAN Nolan
NOLANVILLE Bell
NOME Jefferson
NORDHEIM De Witt
NORMANGEE (77871) Madison(91), Leon(10)
NORMANNA Bee
NORTH HOUSTON Harris
NORTH RICHLAND HILLS Tarrant
NORTH ZULCH (77872) Madison(98), Grimes(2)
NORTON Runnels
NOTREES Ector
NOVICE (79538) Runnels(73), Coleman(27)
NURSERY Victoria
O BRIEN Haskell
OAKHURST San Jacinto
OAKLAND Colorado
OAKVILLE Live Oak
OAKWOOD (75855) Leon(57), Freestone(43)
ODELL Wilbarger
ODEM San Patricio
ODESSA (79765) Ector(54), Midland(46)
ODESSA (79766) Ector(91), Midland(9)
ODESSA Ector

ODONNELL (79351) Dawson(40), Lynn(37), Borden(21), Terry(1)
OGLESBY (76561) Coryell(84), McLennan(16)
OILTON Webb
OKLAUNION Wilbarger
OLD GLORY (79540) Stonewall(96), Haskell(4)
OLD OCEAN Brazoria
OLDEN Eastland
OLMITO Cameron
OLNEY (76374) Young(97), Archer(2)
OLTON (79064) Lamb(82), Hale(18)
OMAHA (75571) Morris(99), Titus(1)
ONALASKA Polk
ORANGE (77632) Orange(98), Newton(2)
ORANGE Orange
ORANGE GROVE Jim Wells
ORANGEFIELD Orange
ORCHARD Fort Bend
ORE CITY (75683) Upshur(59), Marion(40), Harrison(1)
ORLA Reeves
OTTINE Gonzales
OTTO Falls
OVALO (79541) Taylor(90), Callahan(10)
OVERTON (75684) Rusk(79), Smith(21)
OZONA (76943) Crockett(79), Val Verde(21)
PADUCAH (79248) Cottle(85), King(12), Foard(4)
PAIGE (78659) Lee(64), Bastrop(36)
PAINT ROCK Concho
PALACIOS Matagorda
PALESTINE Anderson
PALMER Ellis
PALO PINTO Palo Pinto
PALUXY Hood
PAMPA Gray
PANDORA Wilson
PANHANDLE Carson
PANNA MARIA Karnes
PANOLA Panola
PARADISE Wise
PARIS Lamar
PASADENA Harris
PATTISON Waller
PATTONVILLE Lamar
PAWNEE Bee
PEACOCK Stonewall
PEAR VALLEY McCulloch
PEARLAND (77581) Brazoria(96), Harris(4)
PEARLAND Brazoria
PEARSALL Frio
PEASTER Parker
PECAN GAP Delta
PECOS Reeves
PEGGY Atascosa
PENDLETON Bell
PENELOPE Hill
PENITAS Hidalgo
PENNINGTON (75856) Trinity(65), Houston(35)
PENWELL Ector
PEP (79353) Hockley(86), Cochran(14)
PERRIN (76486) Parker(38), Palo Pinto(38), Jack(24)
PERRY Falls
PERRYTON Ochiltree
PETERSBURG (79250) Hale(48), Lubbock(23), Floyd(18), Crosby(11)
PETROLIA Clay
PETTUS Bee
PETTY Lamar
PFLUGERVILLE Travis
PHARR Hidalgo
PICKTON Hopkins
PIERCE Wharton
PILOT POINT (76258) Denton(96), Grayson(4)
PINEHURST Montgomery
PINELAND Sabine

PIPE CREEK Bandera
PITTSBURG (75686) Camp(88), Titus(6), Upshur(5), Morris(1)
PLACEDO Victoria
PLAINS Yoakum
PLAINVIEW Hale
PLANO (75093) Collin(98), Denton(2)
PLANO Collin
PLANTERSVILLE (77363) Grimes(97), Waller(3)
PLEASANTON Atascosa
PLEDGER Matagorda
PLUM Fayette
POINT Rains
POINT COMFORT Calhoun
POINTBLANK San Jacinto
POLLOK Angelina
PONDER (76259) Denton(99), Wise(1)
PONTOTOC (76869) Mason(50), Llano(25), San Saba(25)
POOLVILLE (76487) Parker(75), Wise(23), Jack(3)
PORT ARANSAS Nueces
PORT ARTHUR Jefferson
PORT BOLIVAR Galveston
PORT ISABEL Cameron
PORT LAVACA Calhoun
PORT MANSFIELD Willacy
PORT NECHES Jefferson
PORT O CONNOR Calhoun
PORTER Montgomery
PORTLAND San Patricio
POST (79356) Garza(96), Lynn(3), Crosby(1)
POTEET Atascosa
POTH Wilson
POTTSBORO Grayson
POTTSVILLE Hamilton
POWDERLY Lamar
POWELL Navarro
POYNOR Henderson
PRAIRIE HILL Limestone
PRAIRIE LEA Caldwell
PRAIRIE VIEW Waller
PREMONT (78375) Jim Wells(98), Duval(2)
PRESIDIO Presidio
PRICE Rusk
PRIDDY Mills
PRINCETON Collin
PROCTOR Comanche
PROGRESO Hidalgo
PROSPER (75078) Collin(97), Denton(3)
PURDON Navarro
PURMELA (76566) Coryell(92), Hamilton(8)
PUTNAM Callahan
PYOTE Ward
QUAIL Collingsworth
QUANAH Hardeman
QUEEN CITY Cass
QUEMADO (78877) Maverick(98), Kinney(2)
QUINLAN (75474) Hunt(97), Kaufman(3)
QUITAQUE (79255) Briscoe(52), Motley(29), Floyd(17), Hall(2)
QUITMAN Wood
RAINBOW Somervell
RALLS Crosby
RANDOLPH Fannin
RANGER (76470) Eastland(86), Stephens(14)
RANKIN Upton
RANSOM CANYON Lubbock
RATCLIFF Houston
RAVENNA Fannin
RAYMONDVILLE Willacy
RAYWOOD Liberty
REAGAN Falls
REALITOS Duval
RED OAK (75154) Ellis(82), Dallas(18)
RED ROCK Bastrop
REDFORD Presidio

REDWATER Bowie
REESE AIR FORCE BASE Lubbock
REFUGIO Refugio
REKLAW (75784) Rusk(52), Cherokee(48)
RHOME Wise
RICE (75155) Navarro(92), Ellis(9)
RICHARDS (77873) Montgomery(94), Grimes(6)
RICHARDSON (75080) Dallas(86), Collin(14)
RICHARDSON (75082) Collin(78), Dallas(22)
RICHARDSON Dallas
RICHLAND Navarro
RICHLAND SPRINGS (76871) San Saba(94), McCulloch(6)
RICHMOND Fort Bend
RIESEL (76682) McLennan(94), Falls(6)
RINGGOLD (76261) Montague(85), Clay(15)
RIO FRIO Real
RIO GRANDE CITY Starr
RIO HONDO Cameron
RIO MEDINA Medina
RIO VISTA (76093) Johnson(96), Hill(4)
RISING STAR (76471) Eastland(87), Brown(10), Comanche(3)
RIVERSIDE Walker
RIVIERA Kleberg
ROANOKE (76262) Denton(58), Tarrant(42)
ROANOKE Denton
ROANS PRAIRIE Grimes
ROARING SPRINGS (79256) Motley(55), Dickens(45)
ROBERT LEE (76945) Coke(84), Tom Green(16)
ROBSTOWN Nueces
ROBY Fisher
ROCHELLE McCulloch
ROCHESTER Haskell
ROCK ISLAND Colorado
ROCKDALE Milam
ROCKLAND Tyler
ROCKPORT Aransas
ROCKSPRINGS Edwards
ROCKWALL (75087) Rockwall(98), Collin(2)
ROCKWOOD Coleman
ROGERS (76569) Bell(94), Milam(6)
ROMA Starr
ROMAYOR Liberty
ROOSEVELT Kimble
ROPESVILLE (79358) Hockley(82), Lubbock(18)
ROSANKY (78953) Bastrop(80), Caldwell(20)
ROSCOE (79545) Nolan(93), Scurry(4), Fisher(2)
ROSEBUD (76570) Falls(87), Milam(11), Bell(2)
ROSENBERG Fort Bend
ROSHARON (77583) Brazoria(77), Fort Bend(23)
ROSS McLennan
ROSSER Kaufman
ROSSTON Cooke
ROTAN (79546) Fisher(98), Stonewall(2)
ROUND MOUNTAIN Blanco
ROUND ROCK (78664) Williamson(98), Travis(2)
ROUND ROCK Williamson
ROUND TOP (78954) Fayette(96), Austin(4)
ROUND TOP Fayette
ROWENA (76875) Runnels(97), Concho(3)
ROWLETT (75088) Dallas(90), Rockwall(10)
ROWLETT Dallas
ROXTON Lamar
ROYALTY Ward
ROYSE CITY (75189) Hunt(56), Collin(45)

RULE (79547) Haskell(96), Stonewall(4)
RULE Haskell
RUNGE (78151) Karnes(93), De Witt(5), Goliad(2)
RUSK Cherokee
RYE Liberty
SABINAL Uvalde
SABINE PASS Jefferson
SACUL Nacogdoches
SADLER Grayson
SAINT HEDWIG Bexar
SAINT JO (76265) Montague(97), Cooke(3)
SALADO Bell
SALINENO Starr
SALT FLAT Hudspeth
SALTILLO Hopkins
SAMNORWOOD Collingsworth
SAN ANGELO (76904) Tom Green(99), Irion(1)
SAN ANGELO Tom Green
SAN ANTONIO (78223) Bexar(95), Wilson(5)
SAN ANTONIO (78253) Bexar(90), Medina(10)
SAN ANTONIO (78264) Bexar(94), Atascosa(6)
SAN ANTONIO (78266) Comal(95), Bexar(5)
SAN ANTONIO Bexar
SAN AUGUSTINE San Augustine
SAN BENITO Cameron
SAN DIEGO (78384) Duval(81), Jim Wells(19)
SAN ELIZARIO El Paso
SAN FELIPE Austin
SAN ISIDRO Starr
SAN JUAN Hidalgo
SAN MARCOS (78666) Hays(93), Guadalupe(6)
SAN MARCOS Hays
SAN PERLITA Willacy
SAN SABA San Saba
SAN YGNACIO Zapata
SANDERSON Terrell
SANDIA (78383) Jim Wells(49), Nueces(40), Live Oak(11)
SANDY Blanco
SANFORD Hutchinson
SANGER Denton
SANTA ANNA Coleman
SANTA ELENA Starr
SANTA FE Galveston
SANTA MARIA Cameron
SANTA ROSA Cameron
SANTO Palo Pinto
SARAGOSA Reeves
SARATOGA Hardin
SARITA Kenedy
SATIN Falls
SAVOY Fannin
SCHERTZ (78154) Guadalupe(90), Bexar(8), Comal(2)
SCHULENBURG (78956) Fayette(95), Lavaca(5)
SCHWERTNER Williamson
SCOTLAND Archer
SCOTTSVILLE Harrison
SCROGGINS (75480) Franklin(98), Wood(2)
SCURRY Kaufman
SEABROOK Harris
SEADRIFT Calhoun
SEAGOVILLE (75159) Dallas(86), Kaufman(14)
SEAGRAVES (79359) Gaines(77), Yoakum(12), Terry(11)
SEALY Austin
SEBASTIAN Willacy
SEGUIN Guadalupe
SELMAN CITY Rusk
SEMINOLE Gaines
SEYMOUR (76380) Baylor(98), Knox(2)

SHAFTER Presidio
SHALLOWATER (79363) Lubbock(94), Hockley(5), Hale(1)
SHAMROCK (79079) Wheeler(95), Collingsworth(6)
SHAMROCK Wheeler
SHEFFIELD Pecos
SHELBYVILLE Shelby
SHEPHERD San Jacinto
SHEPPARD AFB Wichita
SHERIDAN Colorado
SHERMAN Grayson
SHINER (77984) Lavaca(91), Gonzales(9)
SHIRO (77876) Grimes(80), Walker(20)
SIDNEY Comanche
SIERRA BLANCA Hudspeth
SILSBEE (99999) Hardin(99), Tyler(1)
SILVER Coke
SILVERTON (79257) Briscoe(97), Swisher(2), Floyd(1)
SIMMS Bowie
SIMONTON Fort Bend
SINTON (78387) San Patricio(94), Bee(6)
SKELLYTOWN (79080) Hutchinson(68), Carson(33)
SKIDMORE Bee
SLATON (79364) Lubbock(96), Lynn(4)
SLIDELL Wise
SMILEY Gonzales
SMITHVILLE (78957) Bastrop(56), Fayette(44)
SMYER Hockley
SNOOK Burleson
SNYDER Scurry
SOMERSET (78069) Atascosa(74), Bexar(26)
SOMERVILLE Burleson
SONORA Sutton
SOUR LAKE Hardin
SOUTH BEND Young
SOUTH HOUSTON Harris
SOUTH PADRE ISLAND Cameron
SOUTH PLAINS Floyd
SOUTHLAKE Tarrant
SOUTHLAND Garza
SOUTHMAYD Grayson
SPADE Lamb
SPEAKS Lavaca
SPEARMAN (79081) Hansford(97), Hutchinson(2), Ochiltree(1)
SPICEWOOD (78669) Travis(95), Burnet(5)
SPLENDORA (77372) Montgomery(90), Liberty(10)
SPRING Harris
SPRING Montgomery
SPRING BRANCH Comal
SPRINGLAKE (79082) Lamb(88), Castro(12)
SPRINGTOWN (76082) Parker(93), Wise(7)
SPUR (79370) Dickens(94), Crosby(5), Kent(1)
SPURGER (77660) Tyler(96), Hardin(4)
STAFFORD (77477) Fort Bend(89), Harris(11)
STAFFORD Fort Bend
STAMFORD (79503) Jones(92), Haskell(8)
STAMFORD (79553) Jones(94), Haskell(6)
STANTON (79782) Martin(91), Glasscock(9)
STAPLES Guadalupe
STAR Mills
STEPHENVILLE Erath
STERLING CITY (76951) Sterling(97), Glasscock(3)
STINNETT (79083) Hutchinson(77), Moore(23)
STOCKDALE Wilson
STONEWALL (78671) Gillespie(99), Blanco(1)
STOWELL Chambers

STRATFORD (79084) Sherman(96), Dallam(4)
STRAWN (76475) Palo Pinto(79), Eastland(18), Stephens(4)
STREETMAN (75859) Freestone(63), Navarro(37)
SUBLIME Lavaca
SUDAN (79371) Lamb(71), Bailey(29)
SUGAR LAND Fort Bend
SULLIVAN CITY Hidalgo
SULPHUR BLUFF Hopkins
SULPHUR SPRINGS Hopkins
SUMMERFIELD (79085) Castro(79), Parmer(14), Oldham(7)
SUMNER Lamar
SUNDOWN Hockley
SUNNYVALE Dallas
SUNRAY (79086) Moore(69), Sherman(31)
SUNSET (76270) Wise(73), Montague(27)
SUTHERLAND SPRINGS Wilson
SWEENY (77480) Matagorda(91), Brazoria(9)
SWEET HOME Lavaca
SWEETWATER (79556) Nolan(95), Fisher(5)
SYLVESTER (79560) Fisher(93), Jones(7)
TAFT San Patricio
TAHOKA Lynn
TALCO (75487) Franklin(79), Titus(21)
TALPA Coleman
TARPLEY Bandera
TARZAN Martin
TATUM Rusk
TAYLOR Williamson
TEAGUE Freestone
TEHUACANA Limestone
TELEGRAPH (76883) Edwards(67), Kimble(33)
TELEPHONE Fannin
TELFERNER Lavaca
TELL (79259) Childress(63), Hall(37)
TEMPLE Bell
TENAHA (75974) Shelby(65), Panola(35)
TENNESSEE COLONY Anderson
TENNYSON Coke
TERLINGUA Brewster
TERRELL (75160) Kaufman(91), Hunt(9)
TERRELL Kaufman
TEXARKANA Bowie
TEXARKANA Miller
TEXAS CITY Galveston
TEXLINE Dallam
THE COLONY Denton
THICKET Hardin
THOMASTON De Witt
THOMPSONS Fort Bend
THORNDALE (76577) Milam(90), Williamson(10)
THORNTON (76687) Limestone(81), Robertson(19)
THRALL (76578) Williamson(99), Milam(1)
THREE RIVERS Live Oak
THROCKMORTON Throckmorton
TILDEN McMullen
TIMPSON (75975) Shelby(91), Panola(5), Rusk(4)
TIOGA (76271) Grayson(82), Cooke(19)
TIVOLI (77990) Refugio(86), Calhoun(15)
TOKIO (79376) Yoakum(71), Terry(29)
TOLAR Hood
TOM BEAN Grayson
TOMBALL Harris
TORNILLO El Paso
TOW Llano
TOYAH Reeves
TOYAHVALE Reeves
TRENT (79561) Taylor(43), Nolan(36), Fisher(11), Jones(10)
TRENTON Fannin
TRINIDAD Henderson
TRINITY (75862) Trinity(92), Walker(6), Houston(2)

TROUP (75789) Smith(87), Cherokee(13)
TROY (76579) Bell(99), Falls(1)
TRUSCOTT Knox
TULETA Bee
TULIA Swisher
TURKEY (79261) Hall(91), Briscoe(9)
TUSCOLA Taylor
TYE Taylor
TYLER Smith
TYNAN Bee
UMBARGER Randall
UNIVERSAL CITY Bexar
UTOPIA Uvalde
UVALDE Uvalde
VALENTINE (79854) Presidio(53), Jeff Davis(47)
VALERA Coleman
VALLEY MILLS (76689) McLennan(49), Bosque(36), Coryell(16)
VALLEY SPRING Llano
VALLEY VIEW (76272) Cooke(99), Denton(1)
VAN (75790) Van Zandt(87), Smith(13)
VAN ALSTYNE (75495) Grayson(60), Collin(40)
VAN HORN Culberson
VAN VLECK Matagorda
VANCOURT (76955) Tom Green(88), Concho(12)
VANDERBILT Jackson
VANDERPOOL Bandera
VEGA (79092) Deaf Smith(53), Oldham(47)
VENUS (76084) Johnson(67), Ellis(33)
VERA (76383) Knox(91), Baylor(9)
VERIBEST Tom Green
VERNON Wilbarger
VICTORIA (77905) Victoria(96), Goliad(4)
VICTORIA Victoria
VIDOR Orange
VILLAGE MILLS Hardin
VOCA McCulloch
VON ORMY (78073) Bexar(72), Atascosa(28)
VOSS Coleman
VOTAW Hardin
VOTH Jefferson
WACO McLennan
WADSWORTH Matagorda
WAELDER (78959) Gonzales(48), Fayette(43), Bastrop(6), Caldwell(3)
WAKA Ochiltree
WALBURG Williamson
WALL Tom Green
WALLER (77484) Waller(64), Harris(35), Grimes(2)
WALLIS (77485) Austin(52), Fort Bend(48)
WALLISVILLE Chambers
WALNUT SPRINGS (76690) Bosque(88), Somervell(10), Erath(2)
WARDA Fayette
WARING Kendall
WARREN Tyler
WASHINGTON Washington
WASKOM Harrison
WATER VALLEY Tom Green
WAXAHACHIE Ellis
WAYSIDE Armstrong
WEATHERFORD (76087) Parker(96), Hood(4)
WEATHERFORD Parker
WEBSTER Harris
WEESATCHE Goliad
WEIMAR Colorado
WEINERT Haskell
WEIR Williamson
WELCH (79377) Dawson(54), Terry(46)
WELLBORN Brazos
WELLINGTON Collingsworth
WELLMAN Terry
WELLS Cherokee
WESLACO Hidalgo
WEST (76691) McLennan(99), Hill(1)

WEST COLUMBIA Brazoria
WEST POINT Fayette
WESTBROOK Mitchell
WESTHOFF De Witt
WESTMINSTER Collin
WESTON Collin
WHARTON Wharton
WHEELER Wheeler
WHEELOCK (77882) Robertson(80), Brazos(20)
WHITE DEER (79097) Carson(90), Gray(10)
WHITE OAK Gregg
WHITEFACE Cochran
WHITEHOUSE Smith
WHITESBORO (76273) Grayson(79), Cooke(21)
WHITEWRIGHT (75491) Grayson(96), Fannin(4)
WHITHARRAL Hockley
WHITNEY Hill
WHITSETT Live Oak
WHITT (76490) Parker(55), Palo Pinto(46)
WHON Coleman
WICHITA FALLS (76301) Wichita(94), Clay(5), Archer(2)
WICHITA FALLS (76302) Wichita(84), Clay(9), Archer(7)
WICHITA FALLS (76308) Wichita(92), Archer(8)
WICHITA FALLS Wichita
WICKETT Ward
WIERGATE Newton
WILDORADO (79098) Deaf Smith(55), Oldham(26), Randall(13), Potter(5)
WILLIS Montgomery
WILLOW CITY Gillespie
WILLS POINT (75169) Van Zandt(70), Hunt(20), Kaufman(10)
WILMER Dallas
WILSON Lynn
WIMBERLEY Hays
WINCHESTER Fayette
WINDOM Fannin
WINDTHORST (76389) Archer(62), Clay(29), Jack(9)
WINFIELD Titus
WINGATE (79566) Taylor(58), Runnels(38), Nolan(4)
WINK Winkler
WINNIE (77665) Chambers(87), Jefferson(13)
WINNSBORO (75494) Wood(82), Franklin(14), Hopkins(3)
WINONA Smith
WINTERS (79567) Runnels(97), Taylor(3)
WODEN Nacogdoches
WOLFE CITY Hunt
WOLFFORTH (79382) Lubbock(98), Hockley(2)
WOODLAKE Trinity
WOODLAWN Harrison
WOODSBORO Refugio
WOODSON (76491) Throckmorton(96), Stephens(5)
WOODVILLE Tyler
WOODWAY McLennan
WORTHAM (76693) Freestone(77), Navarro(15), Limestone(8)
WRIGHTSBORO Gonzales
WYLIE (75098) Collin(87), Dallas(11), Rockwall(2)
YANCEY Medina
YANTIS Wood
YOAKUM (77995) Lavaca(55), De Witt(43), Victoria(2)
YORKTOWN De Witt
ZAPATA Zapata
ZAVALLA (75980) Angelina(99), Jasper(1)
ZEPHYR (76890) Brown(97), Mills(2)

ZIP/City Cross Reference

ZIP Range	City	ZIP Range	City	ZIP Range	City	ZIP Range	City
73301-73344	AUSTIN	75158-75158	SCURRY	75482-75483	SULPHUR SPRINGS	75692-75692	WASKOM
75001-75001	ADDISON	75159-75159	SEAGOVILLE	75485-75485	WESTMINSTER	75693-75693	WHITE OAK
75002-75002	ALLEN	75160-75161	TERRELL	75486-75486	SUMNER	75694-75694	WOODLAWN
75006-75008	CARROLLTON	75163-75163	TRINIDAD	75487-75487	TALCO	75701-75713	TYLER
75009-75009	CELINA	75164-75164	JOSEPHINE	75488-75488	TELEPHONE	75750-75750	ARP
75010-75011	CARROLLTON	75165-75165	WAXAHACHIE	75489-75489	TOM BEAN	75751-75751	ATHENS
75013-75013	ALLEN	75166-75166	LAVON	75490-75490	TRENTON	75754-75754	BEN WHEELER
75014-75017	IRVING	75167-75168	WAXAHACHIE	75491-75491	WHITEWRIGHT	75755-75755	BIG SANDY
75019-75019	COPPELL	75169-75169	WILLS POINT	75492-75492	WINDOM	75756-75756	BROWNSBORO
75020-75021	DENISON	75172-75172	WILMER	75493-75493	WINFIELD	75757-75757	BULLARD
75023-75026	PLANO	75173-75173	NEVADA	75494-75494	WINNSBORO	75758-75758	CHANDLER
75027-75028	FLOWER MOUND	75180-75181	MESQUITE	75495-75495	VAN ALSTYNE	75759-75759	CUNEY
75029-75029	LEWISVILLE	75182-75182	SUNNYVALE	75496-75496	WOLFE CITY	75760-75760	CUSHING
75030-75030	ROWLETT	75185-75187	MESQUITE	75497-75497	YANTIS	75762-75762	FLINT
75034-75035	FRISCO	75189-75189	ROYSE CITY	75501-75507	TEXARKANA	75763-75763	FRANKSTON
75037-75039	IRVING	75201-75398	DALLAS	75550-75550	ANNONA	75764-75764	GALLATIN
75040-75049	GARLAND	75401-75404	GREENVILLE	75551-75551	ATLANTA	75765-75765	HAWKINS
75050-75054	GRAND PRAIRIE	75407-75407	PRINCETON	75554-75554	AVERY	75766-75766	JACKSONVILLE
75056-75056	THE COLONY	75409-75409	ANNA	75555-75555	BIVINS	75770-75770	LARUE
75057-75057	LEWISVILLE	75410-75410	ALBA	75556-75556	BLOOMBURG	75771-75771	LINDALE
75058-75058	GUNTER	75411-75411	ARTHUR CITY	75558-75558	COOKVILLE	75772-75772	MAYDELLE
75060-75063	IRVING	75412-75412	BAGWELL	75559-75559	DE KALB	75773-75773	MINEOLA
75065-75065	LAKE DALLAS	75413-75413	BAILEY	75560-75560	DOUGLASSVILLE	75778-75778	MURCHISON
75067-75067	LEWISVILLE	75414-75414	BELLS	75561-75561	HOOKS	75779-75779	NECHES
75068-75068	LITTLE ELM	75415-75415	BEN FRANKLIN	75562-75562	KILDARE	75780-75780	NEW SUMMERFIELD
75069-75070	MC KINNEY	75416-75416	BLOSSOM	75563-75563	LINDEN	75782-75782	POYNOR
75074-75075	PLANO	75417-75417	BOGATA	75564-75564	LODI	75783-75783	QUITMAN
75076-75076	POTTSBORO	75418-75418	BONHAM	75565-75565	MC LEOD	75784-75784	REKLAW
75078-75078	PROSPER	75420-75420	BRASHEAR	75566-75566	MARIETTA	75785-75785	RUSK
75080-75083	RICHARDSON	75421-75421	BROOKSTON	75567-75567	MAUD	75788-75788	SACUL
75084-75084	IRVING	75422-75422	CAMPBELL	75568-75568	NAPLES	75789-75789	TROUP
75085-75085	RICHARDSON	75423-75423	CELESTE	75569-75569	NASH	75790-75790	VAN
75086-75086	PLANO	75424-75424	BLUE RIDGE	75570-75570	NEW BOSTON	75791-75791	WHITEHOUSE
75087-75087	ROCKWALL	75425-75425	CHICOTA	75571-75571	OMAHA	75792-75792	WINONA
75088-75088	ROWLETT	75426-75426	CLARKSVILLE	75572-75572	QUEEN CITY	75798-75799	TYLER
75090-75092	SHERMAN	75428-75429	COMMERCE	75573-75573	REDWATER	75801-75802	PALESTINE
75093-75094	PLANO	75431-75431	COMO	75574-75574	SIMMS	75831-75831	BUFFALO
75097-75097	WESTON	75432-75432	COOPER	75599-75599	TEXARKANA	75832-75832	CAYUGA
75098-75098	WYLIE	75433-75433	CUMBY	75601-75615	LONGVIEW	75833-75833	CENTERVILLE
75099-75099	COPPELL	75434-75434	CUNNINGHAM	75630-75630	AVINGER	75834-75834	CENTRALIA
75101-75101	BARDWELL	75435-75435	DEPORT	75631-75631	BECKVILLE	75835-75835	CROCKETT
75102-75102	BARRY	75436-75436	DETROIT	75633-75633	CARTHAGE	75838-75838	DONIE
75103-75103	CANTON	75437-75437	DIKE	75636-75636	CASON	75839-75839	ELKHART
75104-75104	CEDAR HILL	75438-75438	DODD CITY	75637-75637	CLAYTON	75840-75840	FAIRFIELD
75105-75105	CHATFIELD	75439-75439	ECTOR	75638-75638	DAINGERFIELD	75844-75844	GRAPELAND
75106-75106	CEDAR HILL	75440-75440	EMORY	75639-75639	DE BERRY	75845-75845	GROVETON
75110-75110	CORSICANA	75441-75441	ENLOE	75640-75640	DIANA	75846-75846	JEWETT
75114-75114	CRANDALL	75442-75442	FARMERSVILLE	75641-75641	EASTON	75847-75847	KENNARD
75115-75115	DE SOTO	75443-75443	GOBER	75642-75642	ELYSIAN FIELDS	75848-75848	KIRVIN
75116-75116	DUNCANVILLE	75444-75444	GOLDEN	75643-75643	GARY	75849-75849	LATEXO
75117-75117	EDGEWOOD	75446-75446	HONEY GROVE	75644-75644	GILMER	75850-75850	LEONA
75118-75118	ELMO	75447-75447	IVANHOE	75647-75647	GLADEWATER	75851-75851	LOVELADY
75119-75120	ENNIS	75448-75448	KLONDIKE	75650-75650	HALLSVILLE	75852-75852	MIDWAY
75121-75121	COPEVILLE	75449-75449	LADONIA	75651-75651	HARLETON	75853-75853	MONTALBA
75123-75123	DE SOTO	75450-75450	LAKE CREEK	75652-75654	HENDERSON	75855-75855	OAKWOOD
75124-75124	EUSTACE	75451-75451	LEESBURG	75656-75656	HUGHES SPRINGS	75856-75856	PENNINGTON
75125-75125	FERRIS	75452-75452	LEONARD	75657-75657	JEFFERSON	75858-75858	RATCLIFF
75126-75126	FORNEY	75453-75453	LONE OAK	75658-75658	JOINERVILLE	75859-75859	STREETMAN
75127-75127	FRUITVALE	75454-75454	MELISSA	75659-75659	JONESVILLE	75860-75860	TEAGUE
75132-75132	FATE	75455-75456	MOUNT PLEASANT	75660-75660	JUDSON	75861-75861	TENNESSEE COLONY
75134-75134	LANCASTER	75457-75457	MOUNT VERNON	75661-75661	KARNACK	75862-75862	TRINITY
75135-75135	CADDO MILLS	75458-75458	MERIT	75662-75663	KILGORE	75865-75865	WOODLAKE
75137-75138	DUNCANVILLE	75459-75459	HOWE	75666-75666	LAIRD HILL	75880-75880	TENNESSEE COLONY
75140-75140	GRAND SALINE	75460-75462	PARIS	75667-75667	LANEVILLE	75882-75882	PALESTINE
75141-75141	HUTCHINS	75468-75468	PATTONVILLE	75668-75668	LONE STAR	75884-75886	TENNESSEE COLONY
75142-75142	KAUFMAN	75469-75469	PECAN GAP	75669-75669	LONG BRANCH	75901-75915	LUFKIN
75143-75143	KEMP	75470-75470	PETTY	75670-75672	MARSHALL	75925-75925	ALTO
75144-75144	KERENS	75471-75471	PICKTON	75680-75680	MINDEN	75926-75926	APPLE SPRINGS
75146-75146	LANCASTER	75472-75472	POINT	75681-75681	MOUNT ENTERPRISE	75928-75928	BON WIER
75147-75147	MABANK	75473-75473	POWDERLY	75682-75682	NEW LONDON	75929-75929	BROADDUS
75148-75148	MALAKOFF	75474-75474	QUINLAN	75683-75683	ORE CITY	75930-75930	BRONSON
75149-75150	MESQUITE	75475-75475	RANDOLPH	75684-75684	OVERTON	75931-75931	BROOKELAND
75151-75151	CORSICANA	75476-75476	RAVENNA	75685-75685	PANOLA	75932-75932	BURKEVILLE
75152-75152	PALMER	75477-75477	ROXTON	75686-75686	PITTSBURG	75933-75933	CALL
75153-75153	POWELL	75478-75478	SALTILLO	75687-75687	PRICE	75934-75934	CAMDEN
75154-75154	RED OAK	75479-75479	SAVOY	75688-75688	SCOTTSVILLE	75935-75935	CENTER
75155-75155	RICE	75480-75480	SCROGGINS	75689-75689	SELMAN CITY	75936-75936	CHESTER
75157-75157	ROSSER	75481-75481	SULPHUR BLUFF	75691-75691	TATUM	75937-75937	CHIRENO

ZIP Range	City	ZIP Range	City	ZIP Range	City	ZIP Range	City
75938-75938	COLMESNEIL	76129-76179	FORT WORTH	76445-76445	DESDEMONA	76623-76623	AVALON
75939-75939	CORRIGAN	76180-76180	NORTH RICHLAND HILLS	76446-76446	DUBLIN	76624-76624	AXTELL
75941-75941	DIBOLL	76181-76181	FORT WORTH	76448-76448	EASTLAND	76626-76626	BLOOMING GROVE
75942-75942	DOUCETTE	76182-76182	NORTH RICHLAND HILLS	76449-76449	GRAFORD	76627-76627	BLUM
75943-75943	DOUGLASS	76185-76199	FORT WORTH	76450-76450	GRAHAM	76628-76628	BRANDON
75944-75944	ETOILE	76201-76208	DENTON	76452-76452	ENERGY	76629-76629	BREMOND
75946-75946	GARRISON	76225-76225	ALVORD	76453-76453	GORDON	76630-76630	BRUCEVILLE
75947-75947	GENEVA	76226-76226	ARGYLE	76454-76454	GORMAN	76631-76631	BYNUM
75948-75948	HEMPHILL	76227-76227	AUBREY	76455-76455	GUSTINE	76632-76632	CHILTON
75949-75949	HUNTINGTON	76228-76228	BELLEVUE	76457-76457	HICO	76633-76633	CHINA SPRING
75951-75951	JASPER	76230-76230	BOWIE	76458-76458	JACKSBORO	76634-76634	CLIFTON
75954-75954	JOAQUIN	76233-76233	COLLINSVILLE	76459-76459	JERMYN	76635-76635	COOLIDGE
75956-75956	KIRBYVILLE	76234-76234	DECATUR	76460-76460	LOVING	76636-76636	COVINGTON
75958-75958	MARTINSVILLE	76238-76238	ERA	76461-76461	LINGLEVILLE	76637-76637	CRANFILLS GAP
75959-75959	MILAM	76239-76239	FORESTBURG	76462-76462	LIPAN	76638-76638	CRAWFORD
75960-75960	MOSCOW	76240-76241	GAINESVILLE	76463-76463	MINGUS	76639-76639	DAWSON
75961-75964	NACOGDOCHES	76244-76244	KELLER	76464-76464	MORAN	76640-76640	ELM MOTT
75966-75966	NEWTON	76245-76245	GORDONVILLE	76465-76465	MORGAN MILL	76641-76641	FROST
75968-75968	PINELAND	76246-76246	GREENWOOD	76466-76466	OLDEN	76642-76642	GROESBECK
75969-75969	POLLOK	76247-76247	JUSTIN	76467-76467	PALUXY	76643-76643	HEWITT
75972-75972	SAN AUGUSTINE	76248-76248	KELLER	76468-76468	PROCTOR	76645-76645	HILLSBORO
75973-75973	SHELBYVILLE	76249-76249	KRUM	76469-76469	PUTNAM	76648-76648	HUBBARD
75974-75974	TENAHA	76250-76250	LINDSAY	76470-76470	RANGER	76649-76649	IREDELL
75975-75975	TIMPSON	76251-76251	MONTAGUE	76471-76471	RISING STAR	76650-76650	IRENE
75976-75976	WELLS	76252-76252	MUENSTER	76472-76472	SANTO	76651-76651	ITALY
75977-75977	WIERGATE	76253-76253	MYRA	76474-76474	SIDNEY	76652-76652	KOPPERL
75978-75978	WODEN	76255-76255	NOCONA	76475-76475	STRAWN	76653-76653	KOSSE
75979-75979	WOODVILLE	76258-76258	PILOT POINT	76476-76476	TOLAR	76654-76654	LEROY
75980-75980	ZAVALLA	76259-76259	PONDER	76481-76481	SOUTH BEND	76655-76655	LORENA
75990-75990	WOODVILLE	76261-76261	RINGGOLD	76483-76483	THROCKMORTON	76656-76656	LOTT
76001-76007	ARLINGTON	76262-76262	ROANOKE	76484-76484	PALO PINTO	76657-76657	MC GREGOR
76008-76008	ALEDO	76263-76263	ROSSTON	76485-76485	PEASTER	76660-76660	MALONE
76009-76009	ALVARADO	76264-76264	SADLER	76486-76486	PERRIN	76661-76661	MARLIN
76010-76019	ARLINGTON	76265-76265	SAINT JO	76487-76487	POOLVILLE	76664-76664	MART
76020-76020	AZLE	76266-76266	SANGER	76490-76490	WHITT	76665-76665	MERIDIAN
76021-76022	BEDFORD	76267-76267	SLIDELL	76491-76491	WOODSON	76666-76666	MERTENS
76023-76023	BOYD	76268-76268	SOUTHMAYD	76501-76508	TEMPLE	76667-76667	MEXIA
76028-76028	BURLESON	76270-76270	SUNSET	76511-76511	BARTLETT	76670-76670	MILFORD
76031-76033	CLEBURNE	76271-76271	TIOGA	76513-76513	BELTON	76671-76671	MORGAN
76034-76034	COLLEYVILLE	76272-76272	VALLEY VIEW	76518-76518	BUCKHOLTS	76673-76673	MOUNT CALM
76035-76035	CRESSON	76273-76273	WHITESBORO	76519-76519	BURLINGTON	76675-76675	OTTO
76036-76036	CROWLEY	76299-76299	ROANOKE	76520-76520	CAMERON	76676-76676	PENELOPE
76039-76040	EULESS	76301-76310	WICHITA FALLS	76522-76522	COPPERAS COVE	76677-76677	PERRY
76041-76041	FORRESTON	76311-76311	SHEPPARD AFB	76523-76523	DAVILLA	76678-76678	PRAIRIE HILL
76043-76043	GLEN ROSE	76351-76351	ARCHER CITY	76524-76524	EDDY	76679-76679	PURDON
76044-76044	GODLEY	76352-76352	BLUEGROVE	76525-76525	EVANT	76680-76680	REAGAN
76048-76049	GRANBURY	76354-76354	BURKBURNETT	76526-76526	FLAT	76681-76681	RICHLAND
76050-76050	GRANDVIEW	76357-76357	BYERS	76527-76527	FLORENCE	76682-76682	RIESEL
76051-76051	GRAPEVINE	76360-76360	ELECTRA	76528-76528	GATESVILLE	76684-76684	ROSS
76052-76052	HASLET	76363-76363	GOREE	76530-76530	GRANGER	76685-76685	SATIN
76053-76054	HURST	76364-76364	HARROLD	76531-76531	HAMILTON	76686-76686	TEHUACANA
76055-76055	ITASCA	76365-76365	HENRIETTA	76533-76533	HEIDENHEIMER	76687-76687	THORNTON
76058-76058	JOSHUA	76366-76366	HOLLIDAY	76534-76534	HOLLAND	76689-76689	VALLEY MILLS
76059-76059	KEENE	76367-76367	IOWA PARK	76537-76537	JARRELL	76690-76690	WALNUT SPRINGS
76060-76060	KENNEDALE	76369-76369	KAMAY	76538-76538	JONESBORO	76691-76691	WEST
76061-76061	LILLIAN	76370-76370	MEGARGEL	76539-76539	KEMPNER	76692-76692	WHITNEY
76063-76063	MANSFIELD	76371-76371	MUNDAY	76540-76547	KILLEEN	76693-76693	WORTHAM
76064-76064	MAYPEARL	76372-76372	NEWCASTLE	76548-76548	HARKER HEIGHTS	76701-76711	WACO
76065-76065	MIDLOTHIAN	76373-76373	OKLAUNION	76550-76550	LAMPASAS	76712-76712	WOODWAY
76066-76066	MILLSAP	76374-76374	OLNEY	76552-76552	LEON JUNCTION	76714-76799	WACO
76067-76068	MINERAL WELLS	76377-76377	PETROLIA	76554-76554	LITTLE RIVER	76801-76801	BROWNWOOD
76070-76070	NEMO	76379-76379	SCOTLAND	76555-76555	MAYSFIELD	76802-76802	EARLY
76071-76071	NEWARK	76380-76380	SEYMOUR	76556-76556	MILANO	76803-76804	BROWNWOOD
76073-76073	PARADISE	76384-76385	VERNON	76557-76557	MOODY	76820-76820	ART
76077-76077	RAINBOW	76388-76388	WEINERT	76558-76558	MOUND	76821-76821	BALLINGER
76078-76078	RHOME	76389-76389	WINDTHORST	76559-76559	NOLANVILLE	76823-76823	BANGS
76082-76082	SPRINGTOWN	76401-76402	STEPHENVILLE	76561-76561	OGLESBY	76824-76824	BEND
76084-76084	VENUS	76424-76424	BRECKENRIDGE	76564-76564	PENDLETON	76825-76825	BRADY
76086-76088	WEATHERFORD	76426-76426	BRIDGEPORT	76565-76565	POTTSVILLE	76827-76827	BROOKESMITH
76092-76092	SOUTHLAKE	76427-76427	BRYSON	76566-76566	PURMELA	76828-76828	BURKETT
76093-76093	RIO VISTA	76429-76429	CADDO	76567-76567	ROCKDALE	76831-76831	CASTELL
76094-76094	ARLINGTON	76430-76430	ALBANY	76569-76569	ROGERS	76832-76832	CHEROKEE
76095-76095	BEDFORD	76431-76431	CHICO	76570-76570	ROSEBUD	76834-76834	COLEMAN
76096-76096	ARLINGTON	76432-76432	BLANKET	76571-76571	SALADO	76836-76836	DOOLE
76097-76097	BURLESON	76433-76433	BLUFF DALE	76573-76573	SCHWERTNER	76837-76837	EDEN
76098-76098	AZLE	76435-76435	CARBON	76574-76574	TAYLOR	76841-76841	FORT MC KAVETT
76099-76099	GRAPEVINE	76436-76436	CARLTON	76577-76577	THORNDALE	76842-76842	FREDONIA
76101-76116	FORT WORTH	76437-76437	CISCO	76578-76578	THRALL	76844-76844	GOLDTHWAITE
76117-76117	HALTOM CITY	76439-76439	DENNIS	76579-76579	TROY	76845-76845	GOULDBUSK
76118-76126	FORT WORTH	76442-76442	COMANCHE	76596-76599	GATESVILLE	76848-76848	HEXT
76127-76127	NAVAL AIR STATION/ JRB	76443-76443	CROSS PLAINS	76621-76621	ABBOTT	76849-76849	JUNCTION
		76444-76444	DE LEON	76622-76622	AQUILLA	76852-76852	LOHN

Zip Range	City	Zip Range	City	Zip Range	City	Zip Range	City
76853-76853	LOMETA	77367-77367	RIVERSIDE	77484-77484	WALLER	77660-77660	SPURGER
76854-76854	LONDON	77368-77368	ROMAYOR	77485-77485	WALLIS	77661-77661	STOWELL
76855-76855	LOWAKE	77369-77369	RYE	77486-77486	WEST COLUMBIA	77662-77662	VIDOR
76856-76856	MASON	77371-77371	SHEPHERD	77487-77487	SUGAR LAND	77663-77663	VILLAGE MILLS
76857-76857	MAY	77372-77372	SPLENDORA	77488-77488	WHARTON	77664-77664	WARREN
76858-76858	MELVIN	77373-77373	SPRING	77489-77489	MISSOURI CITY	77665-77665	WINNIE
76859-76859	MENARD	77374-77374	THICKET	77491-77494	KATY	77670-77670	VIDOR
76861-76861	MILES	77375-77375	TOMBALL	77496-77496	SUGAR LAND	77701-77708	BEAUMONT
76862-76862	MILLERSVIEW	77376-77376	VOTAW	77497-77497	STAFFORD	77709-77709	VOTH
76864-76864	MULLIN	77377-77377	TOMBALL	77501-77508	PASADENA	77710-77710	BEAUMONT
76865-76865	NORTON	77378-77378	WILLIS	77510-77510	SANTA FE	77711-77711	LUMBERTON
76866-76866	PAINT ROCK	77379-77383	SPRING	77511-77512	ALVIN	77713-77726	BEAUMONT
76867-76867	PEAR VALLEY	77384-77385	CONROE	77514-77514	ANAHUAC	77801-77808	BRYAN
76869-76869	PONTOTOC	77386-77393	SPRING	77515-77516	ANGLETON	77830-77830	ANDERSON
76870-76870	PRIDDY	77396-77396	HUMBLE	77517-77517	SANTA FE	77831-77831	BEDIAS
76871-76871	RICHLAND SPRINGS	77401-77402	BELLAIRE	77518-77518	BACLIFF	77833-77834	BRENHAM
76872-76872	ROCHELLE	77404-77404	BAY CITY	77519-77519	BATSON	77835-77835	BURTON
76873-76873	ROCKWOOD	77406-77406	RICHMOND	77520-77522	BAYTOWN	77836-77836	CALDWELL
76874-76874	ROOSEVELT	77410-77410	CYPRESS	77530-77530	CHANNELVIEW	77837-77837	CALVERT
76875-76875	ROWENA	77411-77411	ALIEF	77531-77531	CLUTE	77838-77838	CHRIESMAN
76877-76877	SAN SABA	77412-77412	ALTAIR	77532-77532	CROSBY	77839-77839	CLAY
76878-76878	SANTA ANNA	77413-77413	BARKER	77533-77533	DAISETTA	77840-77845	COLLEGE STATION
76880-76880	STAR	77414-77414	BAY CITY	77534-77534	DANBURY	77850-77850	CONCORD
76882-76882	TALPA	77415-77415	CEDAR LANE	77535-77535	DAYTON	77852-77852	DEANVILLE
76883-76883	TELEGRAPH	77417-77417	BEASLEY	77536-77536	DEER PARK	77853-77853	DIME BOX
76884-76884	VALERA	77418-77418	BELLVILLE	77537-77538	DEVERS	77855-77855	FLYNN
76885-76885	VALLEY SPRING	77419-77419	BLESSING	77539-77539	DICKINSON	77856-77856	FRANKLIN
76886-76886	VERIBEST	77420-77420	BOLING	77541-77542	FREEPORT	77857-77857	GAUSE
76887-76887	VOCA	77422-77422	BRAZORIA	77545-77545	FRESNO	77859-77859	HEARNE
76888-76888	VOSS	77423-77423	BROOKSHIRE	77546-77546	FRIENDSWOOD	77861-77861	IOLA
76890-76890	ZEPHYR	77426-77426	CHAPPELL HILL	77547-77547	GALENA PARK	77862-77862	KURTEN
76901-76906	SAN ANGELO	77428-77428	COLLEGEPORT	77549-77549	FRIENDSWOOD	77863-77863	LYONS
76908-76908	GOODFELLOW AFB	77429-77429	CYPRESS	77550-77555	GALVESTON	77864-77864	MADISONVILLE
76909-76909	SAN ANGELO	77430-77430	DAMON	77560-77560	HANKAMER	77865-77865	MARQUEZ
76930-76930	BARNHART	77431-77431	DANCIGER	77561-77561	HARDIN	77866-77866	MILLICAN
76932-76932	BIG LAKE	77432-77432	DANEVANG	77562-77562	HIGHLANDS	77867-77867	MUMFORD
76933-76933	BRONTE	77433-77433	CYPRESS	77563-77563	HITCHCOCK	77868-77869	NAVASOTA
76934-76934	CARLSBAD	77434-77434	EAGLE LAKE	77564-77564	HULL	77870-77870	NEW BADEN
76935-76935	CHRISTOVAL	77435-77435	EAST BERNARD	77565-77565	KEMAH	77871-77871	NORMANGEE
76936-76936	ELDORADO	77436-77436	EGYPT	77566-77566	LAKE JACKSON	77872-77872	NORTH ZULCH
76937-76937	EOLA	77437-77437	EL CAMPO	77568-77568	LA MARQUE	77873-77873	RICHARDS
76939-76939	KNICKERBOCKER	77440-77440	ELMATON	77571-77572	LA PORTE	77875-77875	ROANS PRAIRIE
76940-76940	MERETA	77441-77441	FULSHEAR	77573-77574	LEAGUE CITY	77876-77876	SHIRO
76941-76941	MERTZON	77442-77442	GARWOOD	77575-77575	LIBERTY	77878-77878	SNOOK
76943-76943	OZONA	77443-77443	GLEN FLORA	77577-77577	LIVERPOOL	77879-77879	SOMERVILLE
76945-76945	ROBERT LEE	77444-77444	GUY	77578-77578	MANVEL	77880-77880	WASHINGTON
76949-76949	SILVER	77445-77445	HEMPSTEAD	77580-77580	MONT BELVIEU	77881-77881	WELLBORN
76950-76950	SONORA	77446-77446	PRAIRIE VIEW	77581-77581	PEARLAND	77882-77882	WHEELOCK
76951-76951	STERLING CITY	77447-77447	HOCKLEY	77582-77582	RAYWOOD	77901-77905	VICTORIA
76953-76953	TENNYSON	77448-77448	HUNGERFORD	77583-77583	ROSHARON	77950-77950	AUSTWELL
76955-76955	VANCOURT	77449-77450	KATY	77584-77584	PEARLAND	77951-77951	BLOOMINGTON
76957-76957	WALL	77451-77451	KENDLETON	77585-77585	SARATOGA	77954-77954	CUERO
76958-76958	WATER VALLEY	77452-77452	KENNEY	77586-77586	SEABROOK	77957-77957	EDNA
77001-77299	HOUSTON	77453-77453	LANE CITY	77587-77587	SOUTH HOUSTON	77960-77960	FANNIN
77301-77306	CONROE	77454-77454	LISSIE	77588-77588	PEARLAND	77961-77961	FRANCITAS
77315-77315	NORTH HOUSTON	77455-77455	LOUISE	77590-77592	TEXAS CITY	77962-77962	GANADO
77325-77325	HUMBLE	77456-77456	MARKHAM	77597-77597	WALLISVILLE	77963-77963	GOLIAD
77326-77326	ACE	77457-77457	MATAGORDA	77598-77598	WEBSTER	77964-77964	HALLETTSVILLE
77327-77328	CLEVELAND	77458-77458	MIDFIELD	77611-77611	BRIDGE CITY	77967-77967	HOCHHEIM
77331-77331	COLDSPRING	77459-77459	MISSOURI CITY	77612-77612	BUNA	77968-77968	INEZ
77332-77332	DALLARDSVILLE	77460-77460	NADA	77613-77613	CHINA	77969-77969	LA SALLE
77333-77333	DOBBIN	77461-77461	NEEDVILLE	77614-77614	DEWEYVILLE	77970-77970	LA WARD
77334-77334	DODGE	77462-77462	NEWGULF	77615-77615	EVADALE	77971-77971	LOLITA
77335-77335	GOODRICH	77463-77463	OLD OCEAN	77616-77616	FRED	77972-77972	LONG MOTT
77336-77336	HUFFMAN	77464-77464	ORCHARD	77617-77617	GILCHRIST	77973-77973	MCFADDIN
77337-77337	HUFSMITH	77465-77465	PALACIOS	77619-77619	GROVES	77974-77974	MEYERSVILLE
77338-77339	HUMBLE	77466-77466	PATTISON	77622-77622	HAMSHIRE	77975-77975	MOULTON
77340-77344	HUNTSVILLE	77467-77467	PIERCE	77623-77623	HIGH ISLAND	77976-77976	NURSERY
77345-77347	HUMBLE	77468-77468	PLEDGER	77624-77624	HILLISTER	77977-77977	PLACEDO
77348-77349	HUNTSVILLE	77469-77469	RICHMOND	77625-77625	KOUNTZE	77978-77978	POINT COMFORT
77350-77350	LEGGETT	77470-77470	ROCK ISLAND	77626-77626	MAURICEVILLE	77979-77979	PORT LAVACA
77351-77351	LIVINGSTON	77471-77471	ROSENBERG	77627-77627	NEDERLAND	77982-77982	PORT O CONNOR
77353-77355	MAGNOLIA	77473-77473	SAN FELIPE	77629-77629	NOME	77983-77983	SEADRIFT
77356-77356	MONTGOMERY	77474-77474	SEALY	77630-77632	ORANGE	77984-77984	SHINER
77357-77357	NEW CANEY	77475-77475	SHERIDAN	77639-77639	ORANGEFIELD	77985-77985	SPEAKS
77358-77358	NEW WAVERLY	77476-77476	SIMONTON	77640-77643	PORT ARTHUR	77986-77986	SUBLIME
77359-77359	OAKHURST	77477-77477	STAFFORD	77650-77650	PORT BOLIVAR	77987-77987	SWEET HOME
77360-77360	ONALASKA	77478-77479	SUGAR LAND	77651-77651	PORT NECHES	77988-77988	TELFERNER
77362-77362	PINEHURST	77480-77480	SWEENY	77655-77655	SABINE PASS	77989-77989	THOMASTON
77363-77363	PLANTERSVILLE	77481-77481	THOMPSONS	77656-77656	SILSBEE	77990-77990	TIVOLI
77364-77364	POINTBLANK	77482-77482	VAN VLECK	77657-77657	LUMBERTON	77991-77991	VANDERBILT
77365-77365	PORTER	77483-77483	WADSWORTH	77659-77659	SOUR LAKE	77993-77993	WEESATCHE

Code	City	Code	City	Code	City	Code	City
77994-77994	WESTHOFF	78145-78145	PAWNEE	78564-78564	LOPENO	78661-78661	PRAIRIE LEA
77995-77995	YOAKUM	78146-78146	PETTUS	78565-78565	LOS EBANOS	78662-78662	RED ROCK
78001-78001	ARTESIA WELLS	78147-78147	POTH	78566-78566	LOS FRESNOS	78663-78663	ROUND MOUNTAIN
78002-78002	ATASCOSA	78148-78150	UNIVERSAL CITY	78567-78567	LOS INDIOS	78664-78664	ROUND ROCK
78003-78003	BANDERA	78151-78151	RUNGE	78568-78568	LOZANO	78665-78665	SANDY
78004-78004	BERGHEIM	78152-78152	SAINT HEDWIG	78569-78569	LYFORD	78666-78667	SAN MARCOS
78005-78005	BIGFOOT	78154-78154	SCHERTZ	78570-78570	MERCEDES	78669-78669	SPICEWOOD
78006-78006	BOERNE	78155-78156	SEGUIN	78572-78573	MISSION	78670-78670	STAPLES
78007-78007	CALLIHAM	78159-78159	SMILEY	78575-78575	OLMITO	78671-78671	STONEWALL
78008-78008	CAMPBELLTON	78160-78160	STOCKDALE	78576-78576	PENITAS	78672-78672	TOW
78009-78009	CASTROVILLE	78161-78161	SUTHERLAND SPRINGS	78577-78577	PHARR	78673-78673	WALBURG
78010-78010	CENTER POINT	78162-78162	TULETA	78578-78578	PORT ISABEL	78674-78674	WEIR
78011-78011	CHARLOTTE	78163-78163	BULVERDE	78579-78579	PROGRESO	78675-78675	WILLOW CITY
78012-78012	CHRISTINE	78164-78164	YORKTOWN	78580-78580	RAYMONDVILLE	78676-78676	WIMBERLEY
78013-78013	COMFORT	78201-78299	SAN ANTONIO	78582-78582	RIO GRANDE CITY	78677-78677	WRIGHTSBORO
78014-78014	COTULLA	78330-78330	AGUA DULCE	78583-78583	RIO HONDO	78680-78683	ROUND ROCK
78015-78015	BOERNE	78332-78333	ALICE	78584-78584	ROMA	78691-78691	PFLUGERVILLE
78016-78016	DEVINE	78335-78336	ARANSAS PASS	78585-78585	SALINENO	78701-78789	AUSTIN
78017-78017	DILLEY	78338-78338	ARMSTRONG	78586-78586	SAN BENITO	78801-78802	UVALDE
78019-78019	ENCINAL	78339-78339	BANQUETE	78588-78588	SAN ISIDRO	78827-78827	ASHERTON
78021-78021	FOWLERTON	78340-78340	BAYSIDE	78589-78589	SAN JUAN	78828-78828	BARKSDALE
78022-78022	GEORGE WEST	78341-78341	BENAVIDES	78590-78590	SAN PERLITA	78829-78829	BATESVILLE
78023-78023	HELOTES	78342-78342	BEN BOLT	78591-78591	SANTA ELENA	78830-78830	BIG WELLS
78024-78024	HUNT	78343-78343	BISHOP	78592-78592	SANTA MARIA	78832-78832	BRACKETTVILLE
78025-78025	INGRAM	78344-78344	BRUNI	78593-78593	SANTA ROSA	78833-78833	CAMP WOOD
78026-78026	JOURDANTON	78347-78347	CHAPMAN RANCH	78594-78594	SEBASTIAN	78834-78834	CARRIZO SPRINGS
78027-78027	KENDALIA	78349-78349	CONCEPCION	78595-78595	SULLIVAN CITY	78836-78836	CATARINA
78028-78029	KERRVILLE	78350-78350	DINERO	78596-78596	WESLACO	78837-78837	COMSTOCK
78039-78039	LA COSTE	78351-78351	DRISCOLL	78597-78597	SOUTH PADRE ISLAND	78838-78838	CONCAN
78040-78049	LAREDO	78352-78352	EDROY	78598-78598	PORT MANSFIELD	78839-78839	CRYSTAL CITY
78050-78050	LEMING	78353-78353	ENCINO	78599-78599	WESLACO	78840-78842	DEL RIO
78052-78052	LYTLE	78355-78355	FALFURRIAS	78602-78602	BASTROP	78843-78843	LAUGHLIN A F B
78053-78053	MC COY	78357-78357	FREER	78603-78603	BEBE	78847-78847	DEL RIO
78054-78054	MACDONA	78358-78358	FULTON	78604-78604	BELMONT	78850-78850	D HANIS
78055-78055	MEDINA	78359-78359	GREGORY	78605-78605	BERTRAM	78851-78851	DRYDEN
78056-78056	MICO	78360-78360	GUERRA	78606-78606	BLANCO	78852-78853	EAGLE PASS
78057-78057	MOORE	78361-78361	HEBBRONVILLE	78607-78607	BLUFFTON	78860-78860	EL INDIO
78058-78058	MOUNTAIN HOME	78362-78362	INGLESIDE	78608-78608	BRIGGS	78861-78861	HONDO
78059-78059	NATALIA	78363-78364	KINGSVILLE	78609-78609	BUCHANAN DAM	78870-78870	KNIPPA
78060-78060	OAKVILLE	78368-78368	MATHIS	78610-78610	BUDA	78871-78871	LANGTRY
78061-78061	PEARSALL	78369-78369	MIRANDO CITY	78611-78611	BURNET	78872-78872	LA PRYOR
78062-78062	PEGGY	78370-78370	ODEM	78612-78612	CEDAR CREEK	78873-78873	LEAKEY
78063-78063	PIPE CREEK	78371-78371	OILTON	78613-78613	CEDAR PARK	78877-78877	QUEMADO
78064-78064	PLEASANTON	78372-78372	ORANGE GROVE	78614-78614	COST	78879-78879	RIO FRIO
78065-78065	POTEET	78373-78373	PORT ARANSAS	78615-78615	COUPLAND	78880-78880	ROCKSPRINGS
78066-78066	RIO MEDINA	78374-78374	PORTLAND	78616-78616	DALE	78881-78881	SABINAL
78067-78067	SAN YGNACIO	78375-78375	PREMONT	78617-78617	DEL VALLE	78883-78883	TARPLEY
78069-78069	SOMERSET	78376-78376	REALITOS	78618-78618	DOSS	78884-78884	UTOPIA
78070-78070	SPRING BRANCH	78377-78377	REFUGIO	78619-78619	DRIFTWOOD	78885-78885	VANDERPOOL
78071-78071	THREE RIVERS	78379-78379	RIVIERA	78620-78620	DRIPPING SPRINGS	78886-78886	YANCEY
78072-78072	TILDEN	78380-78380	ROBSTOWN	78621-78621	ELGIN	78931-78931	BLEIBLERVILLE
78073-78073	VON ORMY	78381-78382	ROCKPORT	78622-78622	FENTRESS	78932-78932	CARMINE
78074-78074	WARING	78383-78383	SANDIA	78623-78623	FISCHER	78933-78933	CAT SPRING
78075-78075	WHITSETT	78384-78384	SAN DIEGO	78624-78624	FREDERICKSBURG	78934-78934	COLUMBUS
78076-78076	ZAPATA	78385-78385	SARITA	78626-78628	GEORGETOWN	78935-78935	ALLEYTON
78101-78101	ADKINS	78387-78387	SINTON	78629-78629	GONZALES	78938-78938	ELLINGER
78102-78104	BEEVILLE	78389-78389	SKIDMORE	78630-78630	CEDAR PARK	78940-78940	FAYETTEVILLE
78107-78107	BERCLAIR	78390-78390	TAFT	78631-78631	HARPER	78941-78941	FLATONIA
78108-78108	CIBOLO	78391-78391	TYNAN	78632-78632	HARWOOD	78942-78942	GIDDINGS
78109-78109	CONVERSE	78393-78393	WOODSBORO	78634-78634	HUTTO	78943-78943	GLIDDEN
78111-78111	ECLETO	78401-78480	CORPUS CHRISTI	78635-78635	HYE	78944-78944	INDUSTRY
78112-78112	ELMENDORF	78501-78505	MCALLEN	78636-78636	JOHNSON CITY	78945-78945	LA GRANGE
78113-78113	FALLS CITY	78516-78516	ALAMO	78638-78638	KINGSBURY	78946-78946	LEDBETTER
78114-78114	FLORESVILLE	78520-78526	BROWNSVILLE	78639-78639	KINGSLAND	78947-78947	LEXINGTON
78115-78115	GERONIMO	78535-78535	COMBES	78640-78640	KYLE	78948-78948	LINCOLN
78116-78116	GILLETT	78536-78536	DELMITA	78641-78641	LEANDER	78949-78949	MULDOON
78117-78117	HOBSON	78537-78537	DONNA	78642-78642	LIBERTY HILL	78950-78950	NEW ULM
78118-78118	KARNES CITY	78538-78538	EDCOUCH	78643-78643	LLANO	78951-78951	OAKLAND
78119-78119	KENEDY	78539-78540	EDINBURG	78644-78644	LOCKHART	78952-78952	PLUM
78121-78121	LA VERNIA	78543-78543	ELSA	78645-78646	LEANDER	78953-78953	ROSANKY
78122-78122	LEESVILLE	78545-78545	FALCON HEIGHTS	78648-78648	LULING	78954-78954	ROUND TOP
78123-78123	MC QUEENEY	78547-78547	GARCIASVILLE	78650-78650	MC DADE	78956-78956	SCHULENBURG
78124-78124	MARION	78548-78548	GRULLA	78651-78651	MC NEIL	78957-78957	SMITHVILLE
78125-78125	MINERAL	78549-78549	HARGILL	78652-78652	MANCHACA	78959-78959	WAELDER
78130-78132	NEW BRAUNFELS	78550-78553	HARLINGEN	78653-78653	MANOR	78960-78960	WARDA
78133-78133	CANYON LAKE	78557-78557	HIDALGO	78654-78654	MARBLE FALLS	78961-78961	ROUND TOP
78135-78135	NEW BRAUNFELS	78558-78558	LA BLANCA	78655-78655	MARTINDALE	78962-78962	WEIMAR
78140-78140	NIXON	78559-78559	LA FERIA	78656-78656	MAXWELL	78963-78963	WEST POINT
78141-78141	NORDHEIM	78560-78560	LA JOYA	78657-78657	MARBLE FALLS	79001-79001	ADRIAN
78142-78142	NORMANNA	78561-78561	LASARA	78658-78658	OTTINE	79002-79002	ALANREED
78143-78143	PANDORA	78562-78562	LA VILLA	78659-78659	PAIGE	79003-79003	ALLISON
78144-78144	PANNA MARIA	78563-78563	LINN	78660-78660	PFLUGERVILLE	79005-79005	BOOKER

Zip Range	City	Zip Range	City	Zip Range	City	Zip Range	City
79007-79008	BORGER	79220-79220	AFTON	79366-79366	RANSOM CANYON	79701-79712	MIDLAND
79009-79009	BOVINA	79221-79221	AIKEN	79367-79367	SMYER	79713-79713	ACKERLY
79010-79010	BOYS RANCH	79222-79222	CAREY	79369-79369	SPADE	79714-79714	ANDREWS
79011-79011	BRISCOE	79223-79223	CEE VEE	79370-79370	SPUR	79718-79718	BALMORHEA
79012-79012	BUSHLAND	79224-79224	CHALK	79371-79371	SUDAN	79719-79719	BARSTOW
79013-79013	CACTUS	79225-79225	CHILLICOTHE	79372-79372	SUNDOWN	79720-79721	BIG SPRING
79014-79014	CANADIAN	79226-79226	CLARENDON	79373-79373	TAHOKA	79730-79730	COYANOSA
79015-79016	CANYON	79227-79227	CROWELL	79376-79376	TOKIO	79731-79731	CRANE
79018-79018	CHANNING	79229-79229	DICKENS	79377-79377	WELCH	79733-79733	FORSAN
79019-79019	CLAUDE	79230-79230	DODSON	79378-79378	WELLMAN	79734-79734	FORT DAVIS
79021-79021	COTTON CENTER	79231-79231	DOUGHERTY	79379-79379	WHITEFACE	79735-79735	FORT STOCKTON
79022-79022	DALHART	79232-79232	DUMONT	79380-79380	WHITHARRAL	79738-79738	GAIL
79024-79024	DARROUZETT	79233-79233	ESTELLINE	79381-79381	WILSON	79739-79739	GARDEN CITY
79025-79025	DAWN	79234-79234	FLOMOT	79382-79382	WOLFFORTH	79740-79740	GIRVIN
79027-79027	DIMMITT	79235-79235	FLOYDADA	79383-79383	NEW HOME	79741-79741	GOLDSMITH
79029-79029	DUMAS	79236-79236	GUTHRIE	79401-79464	LUBBOCK	79742-79742	GRANDFALLS
79031-79031	EARTH	79237-79237	HEDLEY	79489-79489	REESE AIR FORCE BASE	79743-79743	IMPERIAL
79032-79032	EDMONSON	79238-79238	KIRKLAND	79490-79499	LUBBOCK	79744-79744	IRAAN
79033-79033	FARNSWORTH	79239-79239	LAKEVIEW	79501-79501	ANSON	79745-79745	KERMIT
79034-79034	FOLLETT	79240-79240	LELIA LAKE	79502-79502	ASPERMONT	79748-79748	KNOTT
79035-79035	FRIONA	79241-79241	LOCKNEY	79503-79503	STAMFORD	79749-79749	LENORAH
79036-79036	FRITCH	79243-79243	MCADOO	79504-79504	BAIRD	79752-79752	MC CAMEY
79039-79039	GROOM	79244-79244	MATADOR	79505-79505	BENJAMIN	79754-79754	MENTONE
79040-79040	GRUVER	79245-79245	MEMPHIS	79506-79506	BLACKWELL	79755-79755	MIDKIFF
79041-79041	HALE CENTER	79247-79247	ODELL	79508-79508	BUFFALO GAP	79756-79756	MONAHANS
79042-79042	HAPPY	79248-79248	PADUCAH	79510-79510	CLYDE	79758-79758	GARDENDALE
79043-79043	HART	79250-79250	PETERSBURG	79511-79511	COAHOMA	79759-79759	NOTREES
79044-79044	HARTLEY	79251-79251	QUAIL	79512-79512	COLORADO CITY	79760-79769	ODESSA
79045-79045	HEREFORD	79252-79252	QUANAH	79516-79516	DUNN	79770-79770	ORLA
79046-79046	HIGGINS	79255-79255	QUITAQUE	79517-79517	FLUVANNA	79772-79772	PECOS
79051-79051	KERRICK	79256-79256	ROARING SPRINGS	79518-79518	GIRARD	79776-79776	PENWELL
79052-79052	KRESS	79257-79257	SILVERTON	79519-79519	GOLDSBORO	79777-79777	PYOTE
79053-79053	LAZBUDDIE	79258-79258	SOUTH PLAINS	79520-79520	HAMLIN	79778-79778	RANKIN
79054-79054	LEFORS	79259-79259	TELL	79521-79521	HASKELL	79779-79779	ROYALTY
79056-79056	LIPSCOMB	79261-79261	TURKEY	79525-79525	HAWLEY	79780-79780	SARAGOSA
79057-79057	MCLEAN	79311-79311	ABERNATHY	79526-79526	HERMLEIGH	79781-79781	SHEFFIELD
79058-79058	MASTERSON	79312-79312	AMHERST	79527-79527	IRA	79782-79782	STANTON
79059-79059	MIAMI	79313-79313	ANTON	79528-79528	JAYTON	79783-79783	TARZAN
79061-79061	MOBEETIE	79314-79314	BLEDSOE	79529-79529	KNOX CITY	79785-79785	TOYAH
79062-79062	MORSE	79316-79316	BROWNFIELD	79530-79530	LAWN	79786-79786	TOYAHVALE
79063-79063	NAZARETH	79320-79320	BULA	79532-79532	LORAINE	79788-79788	WICKETT
79064-79064	OLTON	79322-79322	CROSBYTON	79533-79533	LUEDERS	79789-79789	WINK
79065-79066	PAMPA	79323-79323	DENVER CITY	79534-79534	MC CAULLEY	79821-79821	ANTHONY
79068-79068	PANHANDLE	79324-79324	ENOCHS	79535-79535	MARYNEAL	79830-79832	ALPINE
79070-79070	PERRYTON	79325-79325	FARWELL	79536-79536	MERKEL	79834-79834	BIG BEND NATIONAL
79072-79073	PLAINVIEW	79326-79326	FIELDTON	79537-79537	NOLAN		PARK
79077-79077	SAMNORWOOD	79329-79329	IDALOU	79538-79538	NOVICE	79835-79835	CANUTILLO
79078-79078	SANFORD	79330-79330	JUSTICEBURG	79539-79539	O BRIEN	79836-79836	CLINT
79079-79079	SHAMROCK	79331-79331	LAMESA	79540-79540	OLD GLORY	79837-79837	DELL CITY
79080-79080	SKELLYTOWN	79336-79338	LEVELLAND	79541-79541	OVALO	79838-79838	FABENS
79081-79081	SPEARMAN	79339-79339	LITTLEFIELD	79543-79543	ROBY	79839-79839	FORT HANCOCK
79082-79082	SPRINGLAKE	79342-79342	LOOP	79544-79544	ROCHESTER	79842-79842	MARATHON
79083-79083	STINNETT	79343-79343	LORENZO	79545-79545	ROSCOE	79843-79843	MARFA
79084-79084	STRATFORD	79344-79344	MAPLE	79546-79546	ROTAN	79845-79845	PRESIDIO
79085-79085	SUMMERFIELD	79345-79345	MEADOW	79547-79548	RULE	79846-79846	REDFORD
79086-79086	SUNRAY	79346-79346	MORTON	79549-79550	SNYDER	79847-79847	SALT FLAT
79087-79087	TEXLINE	79347-79347	MULESHOE	79553-79553	STAMFORD	79848-79848	SANDERSON
79088-79088	TULIA	79350-79350	NEW DEAL	79556-79556	SWEETWATER	79849-79849	SAN ELIZARIO
79091-79091	UMBARGER	79351-79351	ODONNELL	79560-79560	SYLVESTER	79850-79850	SHAFTER
79092-79092	VEGA	79353-79353	PEP	79561-79561	TRENT	79851-79851	SIERRA BLANCA
79093-79093	WAKA	79355-79355	PLAINS	79562-79562	TUSCOLA	79852-79852	TERLINGUA
79094-79094	WAYSIDE	79356-79356	POST	79563-79563	TYE	79853-79853	TORNILLO
79095-79095	WELLINGTON	79357-79357	RALLS	79565-79565	WESTBROOK	79854-79854	VALENTINE
79096-79096	WHEELER	79358-79358	ROPESVILLE	79566-79566	WINGATE	79855-79855	VAN HORN
79097-79097	WHITE DEER	79359-79359	SEAGRAVES	79567-79567	WINTERS	79901-88595	EL PASO
79098-79098	WILDORADO	79360-79360	SEMINOLE	79601-79606	ABILENE		
79101-79189	AMARILLO	79363-79363	SHALLOWATER	79607-79607	DYESS AFB		
79201-79201	CHILDRESS	79364-79364	SLATON	79608-79699	ABILENE		

General Help Numbers:

Governor's Office
210 State Capitol
Salt Lake City, UT 84114
www.governor.state.ut.us

801-538-1000
Fax 801-538-1528
8AM-5PM

Attorney General's Office
236 State Capitol
Salt Lake City, UT 84114
www.attygen.state.ut.us

801-538-9600
Fax 801-538-1121
8AM-5:30PM

State Court Administrator
450 S State
Salt Lake City, UT 84114
http://courtlink.utcourts.gov

801-578-3800
Fax 801-578-3843
8AM-5PM

State Archives
PO Box 141021
Salt Lake City, UT 84114-1021
www.archives.state.ut.us

801-538-3012
Fax 801-538-3354
8AM-5PM M-F

State Specifics:

Capital: Salt Lake City
                             Salt Lake County

Time Zone: MST

Number of Counties: 29

Population: 2,129,836

Web Site: www.state.ut.us

State Agencies

Criminal Records

Access to Records is Restricted

Bureau of Criminal Identification, Box 148280, Salt Lake City, UT 84114-8280 (Courier: 3888 West 5400 South, Salt Lake City, UT 84119); 801-965-4445, 801-965-4749 (Fax), 8AM-5PM.

Note: Records are not open to the public or employers, unless requesting agency has subpoena or authorization by law. However, one can obtain their own record for $10.00. Employers must access at the county level.

Corporation Records
Limited Liability Company Records
Fictitious Name
Limited Partnership Records
Assumed Name
Trademarks/Servicemarks

Commerce Department, Corporate Division, PO Box 146705, Salt Lake City, UT 84114-6705 (Courier: 160 E 300 S, 2nd fl, Salt Lake City, UT 84111); 801-530-4849 (Call Center), 801-530-6205 (Certified Records), 801-530-6034 (Non-

Certified), 801-530-6363 (Cert. Of Existence), 801-530-6111 (Fax), 8AM-5PM.

www.commerce.state.ut.us

Indexing & Storage: Records are available for active entities only. Records are indexed on inhouse computer and via the Internet.

Searching: Include the following in your request-full name of business. In addition to the articles of incorporation, corporation records include the following information: Annual Reports, Officers, Directors, DBAs, Prior (merged) names and Reserved names.

Access by: mail, phone, fax, in person, online.

Fee & Payment: Certified records are $10.00 per record. Copies are $.30 per page. Fax transmittals are $5.00 for the first page and $1.00 each page after. There are higher fees for other specific reports. Fee payee: State of Utah. Prepayment required. Personal checks accepted. Credit cards accepted: Mastercard, Visa.

Mail search: Turnaround time: 5-10 days. A self addressed stamped envelope is requested. Copies cost $.30 per page.

Phone search: Copies cost $.30 per page. They will answer questions on name availablity, status, agent and officer information.

Fax search: Turnaround time is 5-10 days.

In person search: Copies cost $.30 per page.

Online search: The service provided by e-Utah if available over the Internet, click on "corporations." Basic information (name, address, agent) is free, detailed data is a avaible for minimal fees, but registration is required.

Other access: State allows e-mail access for orders of Certification of Existence at orders@br.state.ut.us.

Expedited service: Expedited service is available. Add $75.00 per business name. Turnaround is 24 hours.

Uniform Commercial Code

Department of Commerce, UCC Division, Box 146705, Salt Lake City, UT 84114-6705 (Courier: 160 E 300 South, Heber M Wells Bldg, 2nd Floor, Salt Lake City, UT 84111); 801-530-4849, 801-530-6438 (Fax), 8AM-5PM.

www.commerce.state.ut.us

Note: 0.

Indexing & Storage: Records are available from 1965. Records are computerized since 1995.

Searching: Use search request form UCC-11. All tax liens are filed at the county level. Include the following in your request-debtor name. File number(s) and/or debtor name(s), name and address of requesting party, and daytime phone number are required.

Access by: mail, fax, in person, online.

Fee & Payment: For a certified search, the fee is $10.00 per file number certified, copies are $.30 per page. For uncertified searches, the fee is only $.30 per page. Fee payee: State of Utah. They will bill for copy charges. Personal checks accepted. Credit cards accepted: Mastercard, Visa.

Mail search: Turnaround time: ten working days. A self addressed stamped envelope is requested.

Fax search: Same fees and turnaround time as mail search apply. They will invoice.

In person search: Searching is available in person.

Online search: User fee is $10.00 per month. There is no additional fee at this time; however, the state is considering a certification fee. The system is open 24 hours daily and is the same system used for corporation records. Call 801-530-6643 for details. The web site also provides details of the "Datashare" program. E-mail requests are accepted at orders@br.state.ut.us.

Other access: Records are available on CD-ROM. Call 801-530-2267 for details.

Expedited service: Expedited service is available for mail and phone searches. Add $75.00 per name. Turnaround time is 24 hours.

Federal Tax Liens
State Tax Liens

Records not maintained by a state level agency.

Note: Records are found at the local level.

Sales Tax Registrations

Tax Commission, Taxpayer Services, 210 N 1950 W, Salt Lake City, UT 84134; 801-297-2200, 801-297-7697 (Fax), 8AM-5PM.

http://www.tax.ex.state.ut.us

Note: General forms and tax law information can be downloaded from the web site.

Indexing & Storage: Records are available for 15 years for business records, for 10 years for individual records.

Searching: Requester must have written consent. This agency will only confirm that a business is registered and active if a tax permit number is provided. They will provide no other information. Records are not accessible by the public; access is limited to the owner(s) of the account(s). You can show power of attorney to access, also. Requests must be in writing.

Access by: mail, in person.

Fee & Payment: Copies are $6.50 per record. Fee payee: Utah Tax Commission. Prepayment required. Personal checks accepted. No credit cards accepted.

Mail search: Turnaround time: 1-2 weeks. No self addressed stamped envelope is required.

In person search: Turnaround time is 24 hours.

Birth Certificates

Department of Health, Bureau of Vital Records, Box 141012, Salt Lake City, UT 84114-1012 (Courier: 288 N 1460 W, Salt Lake City, UT 84114); 801-538-6105, 801-538-6380 (Voice, credit card orders), 801-538-9467 (Fax), 9AM-5PM (walk-in counter closes at 4:30 PM).

http://hlunix.state.ut.us/bvr/home.html

Note: Must have a signed release from person of record or immediate family member.

Indexing & Storage: Records are available from 1905 on. Index computer files go back to 1978. Indexes are not available to the public. New records are available for inquiry immediately.

Searching: At the web site you can download an application at the Forms link on the navigation bar. Follow the instructions on the application and mail it or bring it to the Service Window in-person. Or, you may write a letter. Include the following in your request-full name, names of parents, mother's maiden name, date of birth, place of birth, relationship to person of record, reason for information request. Be sure to sign the request and include a daytime phone number. You may phone, fax or email to request an application form. The following data is not released: medical records.

Access by: mail, phone, fax, in person.

Fee & Payment: Search fee is $12.00; specify a 5-year period to search (add'l 5-year periods are add'l charge of $12.00). Fee is $50.00 if the entire index must be searched. Add $5.00 per name for second copies. Fee payee: Vital Records. Prepayment

required. Personal checks accepted. Credit cards accepted: Mastercard, Visa, AmEx, Discover.

Mail search: Turnaround time: 2-3 weeks. No self addressed stamped envelope is required.

Phone search: See expedited service.

Fax search: See expedited service.

In person search: Turnaround time 15-30 minutes.

Expedited service: Expedited service is available for mail, phone and fax searches. Turnaround time: overnight delivery. You must use a credit card which is an additional $15.00. Overnight return is $14.50 for Fedex or $10.50 express mail.

Death Records

Department of Health, Bureau of Vital Records, Box 141012, Salt Lake City, UT 84114-1012 (Courier: 288 N 1460 W, Salt Lake City, UT 84114); 801-538-6105, 801-538-6380 (Voice, credit card orders), 801-538-9467 (Fax), 9AM-5PM (walk-in counter closes at 4:30 PM).

http://hlunix.state.ut.us/bvr/html/certificates.html

Note: Certificates can be obtained by an immediate family member or with written permission from the immediate family.

Indexing & Storage: Records are available from 1905 on. Index computer files go back since 1978. Indexes are not available to the public. New records are available for inquiry immediately.

Searching: At the web site you can download an application at the Forms link on the navigation bar. Follow the instructions on the application and mail it or bring it to the Service Window in-person. Or, you may write a letter. Include the following in your request-full name, date of death, place of death, relationship to person of record, reason for information request. If you do not know the date of death, include last known date alive. You may phone, fax or email to request an application form.

Access by: mail, phone, fax, in person.

Fee & Payment: Search fee is $9.00, add $5.00 per name for second copies. Fee payee: Vital Records. Prepayment required. Personal checks accepted. Credit cards accepted: Mastercard, Visa, AmEx, Discover.

Mail search: Turnaround time: 2 weeks. No self addressed stamped envelope is required.

Phone search: See expedited service.

Fax search: See expedited service.

In person search: Turnaround time 15-30 minutes.

Expedited service: Expedited service is available for mail, phone and fax searches. Turnaround time: overnight delivery. You must use a credit card which is an additional $15.00. Add $14.50 for Fedex or $10.50 express mail for overnight service.

Marriage Certificates

Records not maintained by a state level agency.

Note: Marriage records not held by the state can be found at the County Recorder in county where marriage took place. Certificates can be obtained by an immediate family member or with written permission from the immediate family. At the web site you can download an application at the Forms link on the navigation bar. Follow the instructions on the application and mail it or bring it to the Service Window in-person. Or, you may write a letter.

Divorce Records

Records not maintained by a state level agency.

Note: Divorce records not held by the state can be found at the Clerk of the Court in the county issuing the decree. Certificates can be obtained from the state by an immediate family member or with written permission from the immediate family. At the web site you can download an application at the Forms link on the navigation bar. Follow the instructions on the application and mail it or birng it to the Service Window in person.

Workers' Compensation Records

Labor Commission, Division of Industrial Accidents, PO Box 146610, Salt Lake City, UT 84114-6610 (Courier: 160 E 300 S, 3rd Floor, Salt Lake City, UT 84114); 801-530-6800, 801-530-6804 (Fax), 8AM-5PM.

Indexing & Storage: Records are available from 1970-1988 on microfiche, form 1989-present on computer.

Searching: Must have a notarized release (less than 90 days old) from claimant stating what records and to whom released. If for employment purposes, please state so with written letter of offer of employment has been made with employer's signature. Include the following in your request- Social Security Number, date of birth. Phone or fax to request form.

Access by: mail, fax, in person.

Fee & Payment: The search fee is $15.00 per name, copies are $.50 per page. Fee payee: Division of Industrial Accidents. Prepayment required. Personal checks accepted. No credit cards accepted.

Mail search: Turnaround time: 2-3 days. Include your telephone number so they can call with the total charge, which must be paid before records are released.No self addressed stamped envelope is required.

Fax search: Prepayment is required.

In person search: Same criteria as mail requests.

Accident Reports

Driver's License Division, Accident Reports Section, PO Box 30560, Salt Lake City, UT 84130-0560 (Courier: 4501 South 2700 West, 3rd Floor South, Salt Lake City, UT 84119); 801-965-4428, 8AM-5PM.

Indexing & Storage: Records are available for 10 years to present and are indexed on microfilm. It takes 2 weeks to 6 months before new records are available for inquiry.

Searching: Include the following in your request- full name, date of accident, location of accident. The following data is not released: medical records, Social Security Numbers or addresses.

Access by: mail, fax, in person.

Fee & Payment: The fee is $5.00 per record. Fee payee: Department of Public Safety. Prepayment required. The state will allow ongoing requesters

to pre-pay with an account. Personal checks accepted. No credit cards accepted.

Mail search: Turnaround time: 2 weeks. A self addressed stamped envelope is requested.

Fax search: Money must be received up front before records can be returned by fax.

In person search: Records will be mailed, or can be picked up if pre-paid.

Driver Records

Department of Public Safety, Driver License Division, Customer Service Section, PO Box 30560, Salt Lake City, UT 84130-0560 (Courier: 4501 South 2700 West, 3rd Floor South, Salt Lake City, UT 84119); 801-965-4437, 801-965-4496 (Fax), 8AM-5PM.

www.dl.state.ut.us

Note: Copies of tickets can be purchased for $5.00 per record. However, if the ticket information came to the state via magnetic tape, the state will refer the requester to the court.

Indexing & Storage: Records are available for 3 years for moving violations, 6 years for DWIs and 3 years for suspensions (alcohol related suspensions are 6 years). Records on commercial drivers are kept for 10 years. It takes 2 weeks to 6 months before new records are available for inquiry.

Searching: Interstate speeding convictions less than 10 mph over are not shown unless there is written consent. Accidents are reported only if driver had citation. Addresses removed from report to comply with DPPA. Requests must comply with DPPA permissible uses. The driver's full name and DOB and/or license number are needed when ordering. Also helpful: SSN. The following data is not released: medical records or addresses.

Access by: mail, in person.

Fee & Payment: The fee is $4.25 per record. Fee payee: Department of Public Safety. Prepayment required. Personal checks accepted. No credit cards accepted.

Mail search: Turnaround time: apx. 1 week. Will FedEx if requester has account or submits pre-paid envelope.A self addressed stamped envelope is requested.

In person search: Up to 10 requests can be processed immediately; any additional requests are available the next day. Driving records can be obtained at any one of 17 branch offices throughout the state.

Other access: Magnetic tape inquiry is available for high volume users. The state will not sell its DL file to commercial vendors.

Vehicle Ownership
Vehicle Identification
Boat & Vessel Ownership
Boat & Vessel Registration

State Tax Commission, Motor Vehicle Records Section, 210 North 1950 West, Salt Lake City, UT 84134; 801-297-3507, 801-297-3578 (Fax), 8AM-5PM.

Indexing & Storage: Records are available from 1979. All boats 1985 or newer must be titled. All motors over 25 HP must be titled. All boats,

except canoes, must be registered. It takes 2 weeks before new records are available for inquiry.

Searching: Access is not open to casual requesters without consent of subject. The name or the vehicle ID or registration number or hull ID is needed to search. The following data is not released: medical records or Social Security Numbers.

Access by: mail, phone, in person.

Fee & Payment: The current fee is $2.00 per record and $6.50 for each microfilm record requested. State has established accounts for dealerships and financial institutions requesting lien-holder information. Fee payee: State Tax Commission. Prepayment required. Personal checks accepted. No credit cards accepted.

Mail search: Turnaround time: 2 days. Boat records can take as long as 1 week to process.A self addressed stamped envelope is requested.

Phone search: Searching is available for pre-approved, established accounts.

In person search: Turnaround time while you wait for small amounts.

Other access: Utah offers a bulk or batch format for obtaining registration information on magnetic tape or paper. A written request stating the purpose of the usage is required. Call 801-297-2700 for further information.

Legislation-Current/Pending
Legislation-Passed

Utah Legislature, Research and General Counsel, 436 State Capitol, Salt Lake City, UT 84114;, 801-538-1588 (Bill Room), 801-538-1032 (Older Passed Bills), 801-538-1712 (Fax), 8AM-5PM.

www.le.state.ut.us

Note: Sessions start 3rd Monday in January.

Indexing & Storage: Records are available from 1980-1989 on microfiche and from 1990 forward on computer.

Searching: Bill room only has current bills. Include the following in your request-bill number, topic of bill.

Access by: mail, phone, fax, in person, online.

Fee & Payment: There is no search fee, copy fee is $.10 per page if over 10 pages. Fee payee: State of Utah. Personal checks accepted. No credit cards accepted.

Mail search: Turnaround time: variable. No self addressed stamped envelope is required.

Phone search: Searching is available by phone.

Fax search: The fee is $1.00 per page.

In person search: It is necessary to call first and make an appointment.

Online search: Web site contains bill information and also the Utah Code.

Voter Registration

Access to Records is Restricted

Office of Lt Governor, Elections Office, 115 State Capitol, Salt Lake City, UT 84114; 801-538-1041, 801-538-1133 (Fax), 8AM-5PM.

www.governor.state.ut.us/elections

Note: Records are at the county clerk offices. Records that have not been secured by the registrant are open to the public; however, the counties will not release the SSN or DL.

GED Certificates

State Office of Education, GED Testing, 250 East 500 South, Salt Lake City, UT 84111; 801-538-7870, 801-538-7868 (Fax), 8AM-5PM.

www.usoe.k12.ut.us/adulted/ged/index.html

Searching: Include the following in your request-Social Security Number, signed release, name at time of testing, current name if different. The following information is not required to search, but is very helpful: date/year of test, date of birth, and city of test.

Access by: mail, phone, fax, in person.

Fee & Payment: There is no fee for verification.

Mail search: Turnaround time: 1-2 days. No self addressed stamped envelope is required.

Phone search: Phone searches require that a signed release is on file or is faxed prior to the phone call.

Fax search: Same criteria as phone searching.

In person search: Searchers should call first.

Hunting License Information
Fishing License Information

Utah Division of Wildlife Resources, PO Box 146301, Salt Lake City, UT 84114-6301 (Courier: 1594 West North Temple, #2110, Salt Lake City, UT 84116); 801-538-4700, 801-538-4709 (Fax), 8AM-5PM.

www.nr.state.ut.us?dwr/dwr.htm

Indexing & Storage: Records are available from 1988 on. the last 3 previous years are kept on computer. Records are indexed on inhouse computer.

Searching: Must use the official request form supplied by this agency. You must show a reasonable purpose in order to obtain information. Include the following in your request-name. DOB and SSN are helpful. The following data is not released: telephone numbers.

Access by: mail.

Fee & Payment: Fees are based upon actual cost of computer time, personnel time plus copy fee of $.25 per page. Fee payee: Utah Division of Wildlife Resources. Prepayment required. Personal checks accepted. No credit cards accepted.

Mail search: Turnaround time: variable. No self addressed stamped envelope is required.

Other access: Draw lists are provided for a small fee at the time of big game drawing.

Licenses Searchable Online

Accounting Firm #05	www.commerce.state.ut.us/dopl/current.htm
Acupuncturist #05	www.commerce.state.ut.us/dopl/current.htm
Alarm Company #05	www.commerce.state.ut.us/dopl/current.htm
Alarm Company Agent #05	www.commerce.state.ut.us/dopl/current.htm
Alarm Response Runner #05	www.commerce.state.ut.us/dopl/current.htm
Analytical Laboratory #05	www.commerce.state.ut.us/dopl/current.htm
Animal Euthanasia Agency #05	www.commerce.state.ut.us/dopl/current.htm
Arbitrator, Alternate Dispute Resolution #05	www.commerce.state.ut.us/dopl/current.htm
Architect #05	www.commerce.state.ut.us/dopl/current.htm
Athletic Judge #05	www.commerce.state.ut.us/dopl/current.htm
Bank #10	www.dfi.state.ut.us/Banks.htm
Boxer #05	www.commerce.state.ut.us/dopl/current.htm
Branch Pharmacy #05	www.commerce.state.ut.us/dopl/current.htm
Building Inspector #05	www.commerce.state.ut.us/dopl/current.htm
Building Inspector Trainee #05	www.commerce.state.ut.us/dopl/current.htm
Chiropractor #05	www.commerce.state.ut.us/dopl/current.htm
Clinical Social Worker #05	www.commerce.state.ut.us/dopl/current.htm
Consumer Lender #10	www.dfi.state.ut.us/reglist1.htm
Contractor #05	www.commerce.state.ut.us/dopl/current.htm
Controlled Substance Precursor Distributor #05	www.commerce.state.ut.us/dopl/current.htm
Cosmetologist/Barber #05	www.commerce.state.ut.us/dopl/current.htm
Cosmetologist/Barber Apprentice #05	www.commerce.state.ut.us/dopl/current.htm
Cosmetologist/Barber Instructor/School #05	www.commerce.state.ut.us/dopl/current.htm
Credit Union #10	www.dfi.state.ut.us/CreditUn.htm
Deception Detection Examiner #05	www.commerce.state.ut.us/dopl/current.htm
Deception Detection Intern #05	www.commerce.state.ut.us/dopl/current.htm
Dental Hygienist #05	www.commerce.state.ut.us/dopl/current.htm
Dental Hygienist with Local Anesthesia #05	www.commerce.state.ut.us/dopl/current.htm
Dentist #05	www.commerce.state.ut.us/dopl/current.htm
Dietitian #05	www.commerce.state.ut.us/dopl/current.htm
Electrician, Apprentice #05	www.commerce.state.ut.us/dopl/current.htm
Electrologist #05	www.commerce.state.ut.us/dopl/current.htm
Employee Leasing Company #05	www.commerce.state.ut.us/dopl/current.htm
Engineer #05	www.commerce.state.ut.us/dopl/current.htm
Environmental Health Specialist #05	www.commerce.state.ut.us/dopl/current.htm
Environmental Health Specialist-In-Training #05	www.commerce.state.ut.us/dopl/current.htm
Escrow Agent #10	www.dfi.state.ut.us/OtherInt.htm
Funeral Service Establishment #05	www.commerce.state.ut.us/dopl/current.htm
General Building Trades #05	www.commerce.state.ut.us/dopl/current.htm
Health Care Assistant #05	www.commerce.state.ut.us/dopl/current.htm
Health Facility Administrator #05	www.commerce.state.ut.us/dopl/current.htm
Hearing Aid Specialist #05	www.commerce.state.ut.us/dopl/current.htm
Hearing Instrument Intern #05	www.commerce.state.ut.us/dopl/current.htm
Hospital Pharmacy #05	www.commerce.state.ut.us/dopl/current.htm
Industrial Loan #10	www.dfi.state.ut.us/ILSlist.htm
Institutional Pharmacy #05	www.commerce.state.ut.us/dopl/current.htm
Journeyman Electrician #05	www.commerce.state.ut.us/dopl/current.htm
Journeyman Plumber #05	www.commerce.state.ut.us/dopl/current.htm
Landscape Architect #05	www.commerce.state.ut.us/dopl/current.htm
Manufactured Housing Dealer & Salesperson #05	www.commerce.state.ut.us/dopl/current.htm
Marriage & Family Therapist #05	www.commerce.state.ut.us/dopl/current.htm
Marriage & Family Therapist Trainee #05	www.commerce.state.ut.us/dopl/current.htm
Massage Apprentice #05	www.commerce.state.ut.us/dopl/current.htm
Massage Technician #05	www.commerce.state.ut.us/dopl/current.htm
Master Electrician #05	www.commerce.state.ut.us/dopl/current.htm
Mediator, Alternate Dispute Resolution #05	www.commerce.state.ut.us/dopl/current.htm
Medical Doctor/Surgeon #05	www.commerce.state.ut.us/dopl/current.htm
Mortgage Lenders #10	www.dfi.state.ut.us/mtglist1.htm
Naturopath #05	www.commerce.state.ut.us/dopl/current.htm
Naturopathic Physician #05	www.commerce.state.ut.us/dopl/current.htm
Negotiator, Alternate Dispute Resolution #05	www.commerce.state.ut.us/dopl/current.htm

Nuclear Pharmacy #05..www.commerce.state.ut.us/dopl/current.htm
Nurse #05 ....www.commerce.state.ut.us/dopl/current.htm
Nurse Midwife #05...www.commerce.state.ut.us/dopl/current.htm
Nurse-LPN #05 ....www.commerce.state.ut.us/dopl/current.htm
Occupational Therapist #05....................................www.commerce.state.ut.us/dopl/current.htm
Occupational Therapist Assistant #05.....................www.commerce.state.ut.us/dopl/current.htm
Optometrist #05 ....www.commerce.state.ut.us/dopl/current.htm
Osteopathic Physician #05......................................www.commerce.state.ut.us/dopl/current.htm
Out-of-State Mail Service Pharmacy #05 ....www.commerce.state.ut.us/dopl/current.htm
Pharmaceutical Administration Facility #05..............www.commerce.state.ut.us/dopl/current.htm
Pharmaceutical Dog Trainer #05.............................www.commerce.state.ut.us/dopl/current.htm
Pharmaceutical Manufacturer #05 ....www.commerce.state.ut.us/dopl/current.htm
Pharmaceutical Researcher #05..............................www.commerce.state.ut.us/dopl/current.htm
Pharmaceutical Teaching Organization #05 ....www.commerce.state.ut.us/dopl/current.htm
Pharmaceutical Wholesaler/Distributor #05..............www.commerce.state.ut.us/dopl/current.htm
Pharmacist #05..www.commerce.state.ut.us/dopl/current.htm
Pharmacist Intern #05 ....www.commerce.state.ut.us/dopl/current.htm
Pharmacy Technician #05 ....www.commerce.state.ut.us/dopl/current.htm
Physical Therapist #05..www.commerce.state.ut.us/dopl/current.htm
Physician Assistant #05..www.commerce.state.ut.us/dopl/current.htm
Plumber, Apprentice #05 ....www.commerce.state.ut.us/dopl/current.htm
Podiatrist #05...www.commerce.state.ut.us/dopl/current.htm
Pre-Need Provider #05 ....www.commerce.state.ut.us/dopl/current.htm
Pre-Need Sales Agent #05 ....www.commerce.state.ut.us/dopl/current.htm
Private Probation Provider #05 ....www.commerce.state.ut.us/dopl/current.htm
Professional Counselor #05.....................................www.commerce.state.ut.us/dopl/current.htm
Professional Counselor Trainee #05 ....www.commerce.state.ut.us/dopl/current.htm
Professional Structural Engineer #05 ....www.commerce.state.ut.us/dopl/current.htm
Psychologist #05..www.commerce.state.ut.us/dopl/current.htm
Public Accountant-Certificate Holder #05................www.commerce.state.ut.us/dopl/current.htm
Public Accountant-CPA #05 ....www.commerce.state.ut.us/dopl/current.htm
Radiology Practical Technician #05 ....www.commerce.state.ut.us/dopl/current.htm
Radiology Technologist #05.....................................www.commerce.state.ut.us/dopl/current.htm
Real Estate Agent #02 ....www.commerce.state.ut.us/re/lists/agntbrkr.txt
Real Estate Appraiser #02.......................................www.commerce.state.ut.us/re/lists/apprais.txt
Real Estate Broker #02 ....www.commerce.state.ut.us/re/lists/agntbrkr.txt
Real Estate Establishment #05................................www.commerce.state.ut.us/dopl/current.htm
Recreational Therapist #05......................................www.commerce.state.ut.us/dopl/current.htm
Recreational Vehicle Dealer #05.............................www.commerce.state.ut.us/dopl/current.htm
Residential Apprentice Plumber #05 ....www.commerce.state.ut.us/dopl/current.htm
Residential Electrician Trainee #05.........................www.commerce.state.ut.us/dopl/current.htm
Residential Journeyman Electrician #05 ....www.commerce.state.ut.us/dopl/current.htm
Residential Journeyman Plumber #05......................www.commerce.state.ut.us/dopl/current.htm
Residential Master Electrician #05...........................www.commerce.state.ut.us/dopl/current.htm
Residential Mortgage Broker #02 ....www.commerce.state.ut.us/re/lists/agntbrkr.txt
Respiratory Care Practitioner #05 ....www.commerce.state.ut.us/dopl/current.htm
Retail Pharmacy #05...www.commerce.state.ut.us/dopl/current.htm
Sanitarian #05..www.commerce.state.ut.us/dopl/current.htm
Savings & Loan #10 ....www.dfi.state.ut.us/FinInst.htm
Security Company #05 ....www.commerce.state.ut.us/dopl/current.htm
Security Officer, Armed Private #05........................www.commerce.state.ut.us/dopl/current.htm
Security Officer, Unarmed Private #05....................www.commerce.state.ut.us/dopl/current.htm
Shorthand Reporter #05 ....www.commerce.state.ut.us/dopl/current.htm
Social Service Aide #05 ....www.commerce.state.ut.us/dopl/current.htm
Social Service Worker #05 ....www.commerce.state.ut.us/dopl/current.htm
Social Work Trainee #05 ....www.commerce.state.ut.us/dopl/current.htm
Social Worker #05..www.commerce.state.ut.us/dopl/current.htm
Speech Pathologist/Audiologist #05........................www.commerce.state.ut.us/dopl/current.htm
Substance Abuse Counselor #05............................www.commerce.state.ut.us/dopl/current.htm
Surveyor #05..www.Soumerce.state.ut.us/dopl/current.htm
Veterinarian #05...www.commerce.state.ut.us/dopl/current.htm
Veterinary Intern #05 ....www.commerce.state.ut.us/dopl/current.htm
Veterinary Pharmaceutical Outlet #05.....................www.commerce.state.ut.us/dopl/current.htm

Licensing Quick Finder

Accounting Firm #05	801-530-6628
Acupuncturist #05	801-530-6628
Alarm Company #05	801-530-6628
Alarm Company Agent #05	801-530-6628
Alarm Response Runner #05	801-530-6628
Analytical Laboratory #05	801-530-6628
Animal Euthanasia Agency #05	801-530-6628
Arbitrator, Alternate Dispute Resolution #05	801-530-6628
Architect #05	801-530-6628
Athletic Judge/Manager/Promoter/Referee #05	801-530-6628
Attorney #09	801-531-9077
Bank #10	801-538-8835
Beekeeper #03	801-538-7184
Boxer #05	801-530-6628
Branch Pharmacy #05	801-530-6628
Brand & Meat Inspection #03	801-538-7161
Building Inspector #05	801-530-6628
Building Inspector Trainee #05	801-530-6628
Burglar Alarm Agent #11	801-965-4484
Bus Driver #11	801-965-4406
Chiropractor #05	801-530-6628
Clinical Social Worker #05	801-530-6628
Consumer Lender #10	801-538-8830
Contractor #05	801-530-6628
Controlled Substance Precursor Distributor #05	801-530-6628
Cosmetologist/Barber #05	801-530-6628
Cosmetologist/Barber Apprentice #05	801-530-6628
Cosmetologist/Barber Instructor #05	801-530-6628
Cosmetologist/Barber School #05	801-530-6628
Credit Union #10	801-538-8840
Deception Detection Examiner #05	801-530-6628
Deception Detection Intern #05	801-530-6628
Dental Hygienist #05	801-530-6628
Dental Hygienist with Local Anesthesia #05	801-530-6628
Dentist #05	801-530-6628
Dietitian #05	801-530-6628
Egg & Poultry #03	801-538-7124
Electrician, Apprentice #05	801-530-6628
Electrologist #05	801-530-6628
Employee Leasing Company #05	801-530-6628
Endowment Care-Cemetery #05	801-530-6628
Engineer #05	801-530-6628
Environmental Health Specialist #05	801-530-6628
Environmental Health Specialist-In-Training #05	801-530-6628
Escrow Agent #10	801-538-8842
Feed #03	801-538-7183
Food & Dairy #03	801-538-7124
Funeral Service Apprentice & Director #05	801-530-6628
Funeral Service Establishment #05	801-530-6628
General Building Trades #05	801-530-6628
Geologist #07	801-537-3300
Grain & Seed #03	801-538-7183

Health Care Assistant #05	801-530-6628
Health Facility Administrator #05	801-530-6628
Hearing Aid Specialist #05	801-530-6628
Hearing Instrument Intern #05	801-530-6628
Hospital Pharmacy #05	801-530-6628
Industrial Loan #10	801-538-8841
Institutional Pharmacy #05	801-530-6628
Insurance Agent #08	801-538-3855
Insurance Establishment #08	801-538-3855
Interpreter for the Deaf #12	801-263-4860
Journeyman Electrician #05	801-530-6628
Journeyman Plumber #05	801-530-6628
Landscape Architect #05	801-530-6628
Liquor Licensing #01	801-977-6800
Manufactured Housing Dealer & Salesperson #05	801-530-6628
Marriage & Family Therapist #05	801-530-6628
Marriage & Family Therapist Trainee #05	801-530-6628
Massage Apprentice #05	801-530-6628
Massage Technician #05	801-530-6628
Master Electrician #05	801-530-6628
Mediator, Alternate Dispute Resolution #05	801-530-6628
Medical Doctor/Surgeon #05	801-530-6628
Mortgage Lenders #10	801-538-8830
Naturopath #05	801-530-6628
Naturopathic Physician #05	801-530-6628
Negotiator, Alternate Dispute Resolution #05	801-530-6628
Notary Public #04	801-530-6078
Nuclear Pharmacy #05	801-530-6628
Nurse #05	801-530-6628
Nurse Midwife #05	801-530-6628
Nurse-LPN #05	801-530-6628
Occupational Therapist #05	801-530-6628
Occupational Therapist Assistant #05	801-530-6628
Optometrist #05	801-530-6628
Osteopathic Physician #05	801-530-6628
Out-of-State Mail Service Pharmacy #05	801-530-6628
Pesticide Dealer/Applicator #03	801-538-7188
Pharmaceutical Administration Facility #05	801-530-6628
Pharmaceutical Dog Trainer #05	801-530-6628
Pharmaceutical Manufacturer #05	801-530-6628
Pharmaceutical Researcher #05	801-530-6628
Pharmaceutical Teaching Organization #05	801-530-6628
Pharmaceutical Wholesaler/Distributor #05	801-530-6628
Pharmacist #05	801-530-6628
Pharmacist Intern #05	801-530-6628
Pharmacy Technician #05	801-530-6628
Physical Therapist #05	801-530-6628
Physician Assistant #05	801-530-6628
Plumber, Apprentice #05	801-530-6628
Podiatrist #05	801-530-6628

Polygraph Examiner #11	801-965-4484
Pre-Need Provider #05	801-530-6628
Pre-Need Sales Agent #05	801-530-6628
Private Probation Provider #05	801-530-6628
Professional Counselor #05	801-530-6628
Professional Counselor Trainee #05	801-530-6628
Professional Structural Engineer #05	801-530-6628
Psychological Assistant #05	801-530-6628
Psychologist #05	801-530-6628
Public Accountant-Certificate Holder #05	801-530-6628
Public Accountant-CPA #05	801-530-6628
Radiology Practical Technician #05	801-530-6628
Radiology Technologist #05	801-530-6628
Real Estate Agent #02	801-530-6747
Real Estate Appraiser #02	801-530-6747
Real Estate Broker #02	801-530-6747
Real Estate Establishment #05	801-530-6628
Recreational Therapist #05	801-530-6628
Recreational Vehicle Dealer #05	801-530-6628
Residential Apprentice Plumber #05	801-530-6628
Residential Electrician Trainee #05	801-530-6628
Residential Journeyman Electrician #05	801-530-6628
Residential Journeyman Plumber #05	801-530-6628
Residential Master Electrician #05	801-530-6628
Residential Mortgage Broker #02	801-530-6747
Respiratory Care Practitioner #05	801-530-6628
Retail Pharmacy #05	801-530-6628
Retail Store (Liquor License) #01	801-977-6800
Sanitarian #05	801-530-6628
Savings & Loan #10	801-538-8842
School Administrator #06	801-538-7751
School Librarian #06	801-538-7751
Securities Broker/Dealer #05	801-530-6628
Security Company #05	801-530-6628
Security Guard #11	801-965-4484
Security Officer, Armed Private #05	801-530-6628
Security Officer, Unarmed Private #05	801-530-6628
Shorthand Reporter #05	801-530-6628
Social Service Aide #05	801-530-6628
Social Service Worker #05	801-530-6628
Social Work Trainee #05	801-530-6628
Social Worker #05	801-530-6628
Speech Pathologist/Audiologist #05	801-530-6628
Substance Abuse Counselor #05	801-530-6628
Surveyor #05	801-530-6628
Taxi Driver/Chauffeur #11	801-965-4406
Teacher #06	801-538-7751
Third Party Payment Issuer #10	801-538-8842
Truck Driver #11	801-965-4406
Veterinarian #05	801-530-6628
Veterinary Intern #05	801-530-6628
Veterinary Pharmaceutical Outlet #05	801-530-6628
Weights & Measures #03	801-538-7158

Licensing Agency Information

01 Alcoholic Beverage Control Department, PO Box 30408 (PO Box 30408), Salt Lake City, UT 84130-0408; 801-977-6800, Fax: 801-977-6888.

www.alcbev.state.ut.us

02 Commerce Department, Real Estate Division, 160 E 300 S, 2nd Fl, Salt Lake City, UT 84145-0806; 801-530-6747, Fax: 801-530-6749.
www.commerce.state.ut.us/re/udre1.htm

Direct URL to search licenses: www.commerce.state.ut.us/re/lists/data.htm You can search online using alphabetical lists

03 Department of Agriculture, PO Box 146500, Salt Lake City, UT 84114-6500; 801-538-7100, Fax: 801-538-7126.

04 Department of Commerce, PO Box 146705 (160 E 300 S), Salt Lake City, UT 84114-6705; 801-530-4849.

http://www.commerce.state.ut.us/corporat/notarypublic.htm

05 Department of Commerce, Division of Occupational & Professional Licensing, PO Box 146741 (PO Box 146741 (160 E 300 S, Heber M Wells Bldg)), Salt Lake City, UT 84114-6741; 801-530-6628, Fax: 801-530-6511.
www.commerce.state.ut.us/web/commerce/DOPL/current.htm

Direct URL to search licenses: www.commerce.state.ut.us/dopl/current.htm You can search online using alphabetical lists.

06 Educator Licensing, Office of Education, 250 E 500 S, Salt Lake City, UT 84111; 801-538-7751, Fax: 801-538-7973.

www.usoe.k12.ut.us

07 Geological Survey Department, PO Box 146100 (PO Box 146100), Salt Lake City, UT 84109-6100; 801-537-3300, Fax: 801-537-3400.

www.commerce.state.ut.us/web/commerce/DOPL/current.htm

08 Insurance Department, 3110 State Office Bldg, Salt Lake City, UT 84114-6901; 801-538-3855, Fax: 801-538-3829.
www.insurance.state.ut.us

Direct URL to search licenses: www.commerce.state.ut.us/web/commerce/DOPL/current.htm Or, from www.insurance.state.ut.us, click on "Industry Services."

09 State Bar Association, 645 S 200 E, Salt Lake City, UT 84111; 801-531-9077, Fax: 801-531-0660.

10 Department of Financial Institutions, PO Box 89 (324 S State, #201), Salt Lake City, UT 84110-0089; 801-538-8830, Fax: 801-538-8894.

www.dfi.state.ut.us/FinInst

11 Department of Public Safety, Office of Regulatory Licensing, 4501 S 2700 W, Salt Lake City, UT 84130-0560; 801-965-4406.

12 Division of Services for the Deaf & Hard of Hearing, Interpreter Svcs, 5709 S 1500 W, Salt Lake City, UT 84123; 801-263-4860.

The following list indicates the district and division name for each county in the state. If the district or division name of the bankruptcy court is different from the civil/criminal court, it appears in parentheses.

County/Court Cross Reference

All counties report to Salt Lake City.

US District Court

District of Utah

Division Clerk's Office, Room 150, 350 S Main St, Salt Lake City, UT 84101, 801-524-6100, Fax: 801-526-1175.

www.utd.uscourts.gov

Counties: All counties in Utah. Although all cases are heard here, the district is divided into Northern and Central Divisions. The Northern Division includes the counties of Box Elder, Cache, Rich, Davis, Morgan and Weber, and the Central Division includes all other counties.

Indexing & Storage: Cases are indexed by defendant and plaintiff as well as by case number. New cases are available in the index 1 day after filing date. A computer index is maintained. Older records are on microfiche. Open records are located at this court.

Fee & Payment: The fee is $15.00 per item (one party name or case number). Payment may be made by money order, cashier check, personal check, Visa, Mastercard. Prepayment is required. Payee: Clerk, US District Court. Certification fee: $5.00 per document. Copy fee: $.50 per page. You are allowed to make your own copies. These copies cost $.15 per page. Public terminals are available.

Phone Search: Only limited information will be released over the telephone. An automated voice case information service (VCIS) is not available.

Mail Search: A stamped self addressed envelope is not required.

In Person Search: In person searching is available.

PACER: Sign-up number is 800-676-6856. Access fee is $.60 per minute. Toll-free access: 800-314-3423. Local access: 801-524-4221. PACER is available on the Internet at http://pacer.utd.uscourts.gov. Case records are available back to July 1, 1989. Records are never purged. New records are available online after 1 day. PACER is available on the Internet at http://pacer.utd.uscourts.gov.

US Bankruptcy Court

District of Utah

Division Clerk of Court, Frank E Moss Courthouse, 350 S Main St, Room 301, Salt Lake City, UT 84101, 801-524-6687, Fax: 801-524-4409.

www.utb.uscourts.gov

Counties: All counties in Utah. Although all cases are handled here, the court divides itself into two divisions. The Northern Division includes the counties of Box Elder, Cache, Rich, Davis, Morgan and Weber, and the Central Division includes the remaining counties. Court is held once per week in Ogden for Northern cases.

Indexing & Storage: Cases are indexed by debtor and creditors as well as by case number. New cases are available in the index as soon as the work load permits after filing date. A computer index is maintained. Open records are located at this court.

Fee & Payment: The fee is $15.00 per item (one party name or case number). Payment may be made by money order, cashier check, personal check. Prepayment is required. Debtor's checks are not accepted. Payee: Clerk, US Bankruptcy Court. Certification fee: $5.00 per document. Copy fee: $.50 per page.

Phone Search: Only docket information is available by phone. An automated voice case information service (VCIS) is available. Call VCIS at 800-733-6740 or 801-524-3107.

Fax Search: The court has a contract with a copy service that will accept fax requests. Call for more information. The court has a contract with a copy service that will fax docket listings for a fee. Call for more information.

Mail Search: Always enclose a stamped self addressed envelope.

In Person Search: In person searching is available.

PACER: Sign-up number is 800-676-6856. Access fee is $.60 per minute. Toll-free access: 800-718-1188. Local access: 801-524-5760. Case records are available back to January 1985. Records are purged after 12 months. New civil records are available online after 2 days or more. PACER is available on the Internet at http://pacer.utb.uscourts.gov.

Opinions Online: Court opinions are available online at www.utb.uscourts.gov/OPINIONS/opin.htm

Court	Jurisdiction	No. of Courts	How Organized
District Courts*	General	41	8 Districts
Justice Courts	Limited	171	171 Cities/ Counties
Juvenile Courts	Special		8 Juvenile Districts

* Profiled in this Sourcebook.

Court	CIVIL								
	Tort	Contract	Real Estate	Min. Claim	Max. Claim	Small Claims	Estate	Eviction	Domestic Relations
District Courts*	X	X	X	$20,000	No Max	$2000	X	X	X
Justice Courts	X	X		$0	$1000	$2000			
Juvenile Courts									

Court	CRIMINAL				
	Felony	Misdemeanor	DWI/DUI	Preliminary Hearing	Juvenile
District Courts*	X	X	X	X	
Justice Courts		X	X		
Juvenile Courts					X

ADMINISTRATION

Court Administrator, 450 S State Street, Salt Lake City, UT, 84114; 801-578-3942, Fax: 801-578-3843. http://courtlink.utcourts.gov

COURT STRUCTURE

There are 41 District Courts in 8 judicial districts. Effective July 1, 1996, all Circuit Courts (the lower court) were combined with the District Courts (the higher court) in each county. It is reported that branch courts in larger counties such as Salt Lake which were formerly Circuit Courts have been elevated to District Courts, with full jurisdiction over felony as well as misdemeanor cases. Therefore, it may be necessary to search for felony records at more courts than prior to July 1, 1996. In written requests to District Courts, we recommend including a statement asking to "include Circuit Court cases in the search" to assure that index records from the former court are checked.

ONLINE ACCESS

Case index information from approximately 98% of all Utah court locations is available through XChange. Those counties not yet included as of October 2000 are Randolph, Junction, Kanob, Loa, Manilla, and Panguitch.

Fees include $25.00 registration and $30.00 per month plus $.10 per minute for usage, over 120 minutes. Information about XChange and the subscription agreement can be found on the Utah Internet site or call the Administrative Office of the Courts at 801-578-3850.

ADDITIONAL INFORMATION

The administrative Office of Courts provdes a search service to the public. One can search on a particular case or the case history of individuals. Requests should be sent to the address listed above or faxed to 801-578-3859. Include the county or geographic region. UT Code Rule 4-202.08 sets fees for record searhes at $21.00 per hour, billed on 15 minute increments, with the first 15 minutes free and the copy fee at $.25 per page.

📖 📖 📖 📖 📖 📖 📖

Beaver County

5th Judicial District Court PO Box 1683, Beaver, UT 84713; 435-438-5309; Fax: 435-438-5395. Hours: 8AM-5PM (MST). *Felony, Misdemeanor, Civil, Eviction, Probate.*

Civil Records: Access: Fax, mail, in person. Both court and visitors may perform in person searches. Search fee: $13.33 per hour. Required to search: name, years to search. Civil cases indexed by defendant, plaintiff. Civil records archived from 1800s, are on computer since 1997. **Criminal Records:** Access: Fax, mail, in person. Both court and visitors may perform in person searches.

Search fee: $10.00 per hour. Required to search: name, years to search. Criminal records archived from 1800s, are on computer since 1997. **General Information:** No adoption, sealed records released. SASE required. Turnaround time 2-7 days. Copy fee: $.25 per page. Certification fee: $2.00 plus $.50 per page. Fee payee: Beaver County Court. Personal checks accepted. Prepayment is required. Fax notes: $.25 per page.

Box Elder County

1st District Court 43 N Main, PO Box 873, Brigham City, UT 84302; 435-734-4600; Fax: 435-734-4610. Hours: 8AM-5PM (MST). *Felony,*

Misdemeanor, Civil, Eviction, Small Claims, Probate.

Civil Records: Access: Fax, mail, online, in person. Both court and visitors may perform in person searches. Search fee: $13.00 per name. Required to search: name, years to search. Civil cases indexed by defendant, plaintiff. Civil records on computer from 3-87, books, microfiche, archived from 1856. Online access available through XChange. See state introduction. **Criminal Records:** Access: Fax, mail, remote online, in person. Both court and visitors may perform in person searches. Search fee: $13.00 per name. Required to search: name, years to search;

also helpful-DOB, SSN. Criminal records on computer from 3-87, books, microfiche, archived from 1856. Online access available through XChange. See state introduction. **General Information:** No adoptions, sealed records released. SASE required. Turnaround time 1 week. Copy fee: $.25 per page. Certification fee: $2.00. Fee payee: 1st District Court. Personal checks accepted. Credit cards accepted: Visa, Mastercard. Prepayment is required. Public access terminal is available. Fax notes: $.50 per page.

Cache County

1st District Court 140 N. 100 W., Logan, UT 84321; 435-750-1300; Fax: 435-750-1355. Hours: 8AM-5PM (MST). *Felony, Misdemeanor, Civil, Eviction, Small Claims, Probate.*

http://courtlink.utcourts.gov/howto/access/index.htm

Civil Records: Access: Phone, mail, online, in person. Both court and visitors may perform in person searches. Search fee: $10.00 per hour. Required to search: name, years to search. Civil cases indexed by defendant, plaintiff. Civil records on computer from 11-87, archived from 1983, microfiche in Salt Lake City. Online access available through XChange. See state introduction. **Criminal Records:** Access: Phone, mail, remote online, in person. Both court and visitors may perform in person searches. Search fee: $10.00 per hour. Required to search: name, years to search; also helpful-DOB, SSN. Criminal records on computer from 11-87, archived from 1983, microfiche in Salt Lake City. Online access available through XChange. See state introduction. **General Information:** No sealed records released. SASE required. Turnaround time 2 weeks. Copy fee: $.25 per page. Certification fee: $2.00 plus $.50 per page. Fee payee: 1st Judicial District. Personal checks accepted. Credit cards accepted: Visa, Mastercard. Credit cards accepted in person only. Prepayment is required. Public access terminal is available. Fax notes: $2.00 per page.

Carbon County

7th District Court 149 E. 100 South, Price, UT 84501; 435-636-3400; Fax: 435-637-7349. Hours: 8AM-5PM (MST). *Felony, Misdemeanor, Civil, Eviction, Small Claims, Probate.*

Civil Records: Access: Phone, mail, online, in person. Both court and visitors may perform in person searches. Search fee: $10.00 per hour. First 20 minutes no charge. Required to search: name, years to search. Civil cases indexed by defendant, plaintiff. Civil records on computer from 1988, on microfiche from 1985, archived prior to 1988. Online access available through XChange. See state introduction. **Criminal Records:** Access: Phone, mail, remote online, in person. Both court and visitors may perform in person searches. Search fee: $10.00 per hour. First 20 minutes no charge. Required to search: name, years to search, DOB; also helpful-SSN. Criminal records on computer from 1988, on microfiche from 1985, archived prior to 1988. Online access available through XChange. See state introduction. **General Information:** No sealed records released. SASE required. Turnaround time 48 hrs after receipt. Copy fee: $.25 per page. Certification fee: $2.00 plus $.50 per page. Fee payee: 7th District Court. Personal checks accepted. Credit cards accepted: Visa. Will bill fax fees. Public access terminal is available.

Daggett County

8th District Court PO Box 219, Manila, UT 84046; 435-784-3154; Fax: 435-784-3335. Hours: 9AM-Noon, 1-5PM (MST). *Felony, Misdemeanor, Civil, Eviction, Probate.*

Civil Records: Access: Fax, mail, in person. Both court and visitors may perform in person searches. No search fee. Required to search: name, years to search. Civil cases indexed by defendant, plaintiff. Civil records archived from 1918. Fax access requires prior approval. **Criminal Records:** Access: Fax, mail, in person. Both court and visitors may perform in person searches. No search fee. Required to search: name, years to search, DOB. Criminal records archived from 1918. Same as civil. **General Information:** No sealed records released. SASE required. Turnaround time 5 days. Signature required. Copy fee: $.25 per page. Certification fee: $2.00 plus $.50 per page. Fee payee: Daggett County. Personal checks accepted. Prepayment is required. Fax notes: $1.00 per page.

Davis County

2nd District Court PO Box 769, Farmington, UT 84025; 801-447-3800; Fax: 801-447-3881. Hours: 8AM-5PM (MST). *Felony, Misdemeanor, Civil, Eviction, Small Claims, Probate.*

Note: Area code changes to 385 after May, 2001

Civil Records: Access: Phone, mail, online, in person. Both court and visitors may perform in person searches. Search fee: $10.00 per hour. First 30 minutes no charge. Required to search: name, years to search. Civil cases indexed by defendant, plaintiff. Civil records on computer from 1989, on microfiche and archived prior to 1989. Online access available through XChange. See state introduction. **Criminal Records:** Access: Phone, mail, remote online, in person. Both court and visitors may perform in person searches. Search fee: $10.00 per hour. First 30 minutes no charge. Required to search: name, years to search; also helpful-SSN. Criminal records on computer from 1989, on microfiche and archived prior to 1989. Online access available through XChange. See state introduction. **General Information:** No adoption, criminal pre-sentence investigation records released. SASE required. Turnaround time 2-3 days. Copy fee: $.25 per page. Certified copies $.50 per page. Certification fee: $2.00. Fee payee: 2nd District Court. Personal checks accepted. Prepayment is required.

2nd District Court - Bountiful Department 805 South Main, Bountiful, UT 84010; 801-397-7008; Fax: 801-397-7010. Hours: 8AM-5PM (MST). *Felony, Misdemeanor, Civil, Eviction, Small Claims, Probate.*

Note: Area code changes to 385 after May, 2001

Civil Records: Access: Phone, mail, online, in person. Both court and visitors may perform in person searches. No search fee. Required to search: name, years to search; also helpful-address. Civil cases indexed by defendant, plaintiff. Civil records on computer since 10/86. For in person searching, call ahead. Online access available through XChange. See state introduction. **Criminal Records:** Access: Phone, mail, remote online, in person. Both court and visitors may perform in person searches. No search fee. Required to search: name, years to search, DOB, signed release. Criminal records on computer since 10/86. For in person searching, call ahead. Online access available through XChange. See state introduction. **General Information:** SASE required. Turnaround time 5 days. Copy fee: $.25

per page. Certification fee: $2.50. Fee payee: District Court. Personal checks accepted. Prepayment is required. Public access terminal is available.

2nd District Court - Layton Department 425 Wasatch Dr, Layton, UT 84041; 801-546-2484; Fax: 801-546-8224. Hours: 8AM-5PM (MST). *Felony, Misdemeanor, Civil, Eviction, Small Claims, Probate.*

Note: Area code changes to 385 after May, 2001

Civil Records: Access: online, in person. Court does not conduct in person searches; visitors must perform searches for themselves. Search fee: No civil searches performed by court. Required to search: name, years to search. Civil cases indexed by defendant, plaintiff. Civil records on computer from 1988, archived from start of court. Computer index alpha and case number, archives by alpha from 1982, prior to 1982 not indexed. Online access available through XChange. See state introduction. **Criminal Records:** Access: Mail, remote online, in person. Both court and visitors may perform in person searches. Search fee: $10.00 for 30 minutes after first 10. Required to search: name, years to search; also helpful-DOB, SSN. Criminal records on computer from 1988, archived from start of court. Computer index alpha and case number, archives by alpha from 1982, prior to 1982 not indexed. Online access available through XChange. See state introduction. **General Information:** No confidential records, probation reports, sealed records released. SASE requested. Turnaround time 1 day. Copy fee: $.25 per page. Certification fee: $2.00. Fee payee: Layton Circuit Court. Personal checks accepted. Public access terminal is available.

Duchesne County

8th District Court PO Box 990, Duchesne, UT 84021; 435-738-2753; Fax: 435-738-2754. Hours: 8AM-5PM (MST). *Felony, Misdemeanor, Civil, Eviction, Small Claims, Probate.*

Civil Records: Access: Mail, online, in person. Both court and visitors may perform in person searches. Search fee: $10.00 per hour. First 20 minutes no charge. Required to search: name, years to search. Civil cases indexed by defendant, plaintiff. Civil records on computer from 1988, civil on microfiche from 1915 to 1980. Online access available through XChange. See state introduction. **Criminal Records:** Access: Mail, remote online, in person. Both court and visitors may perform in person searches. Search fee: $10.00 per hour. First 20 minutes no charge. Required to search: name, years to search, DOB, SSN. Criminal records on computer since 1988; index books back 13 years prior; and earlier archived. Online access available through XChange. See state introduction. **General Information:** No confidential records released. SASE required. Turnaround time 1-5 days. Copy fee: $.25 per page. Certification fee: $2.00. Fee payee: 8th District Court. Personal checks accepted. Prepayment is required. Public access terminal is available.

8th District Court-Roosevelt Department PO Box 1286, Roosevelt, UT 84066; 435-722-0235; Fax: 435-722-0236. Hours: 8AM-5PM (MST). *Felony, Misdemeanor, Civil, Eviction, Probate.*

Civil Records: Access: Mail, online, in person. Both court and visitors may perform in person searches. Search fee: $10.00 per hour. First 20 minutes no charge. Required to search: name, years to search. Civil cases indexed by defendant, plaintiff. Civil records on computer since 1988. Online access available through XChange. See state introduction. **Criminal Records:** Access: Mail, remote online, in person. Both court and visitors may perform in person searches. Search fee: $10.00 per hour. FIrst 20 minutes no charge. Required to search: name, years to search; also helpful-DOB. Criminal records on computer since 1988. Online access available through XChange. See state introduction. **General Information:** No confidential, sealed, expunged or juvenile records released. Turnaround time 2-5 days. Copy fee: $.25 per page. Certification fee: $2.00 plus $.50 per page. Personal checks accepted. Prepayment is required. Public access terminal is available.

Emery County

7th District Court PO Box 635, Castle Dale, UT 84513; 435-636-3400; Fax: 435-637-7349. Hours: 8AM-5PM (MST). *Felony, Misdemeanor, Civil, Eviction, Probate.*

Note: Phone for hearing impaired is 800-992-0172

Civil Records: Access: Phone, fax, mail, online, in person. Only the court conducts in person searches; visitors may not. Search fee: $10.00 per hour. First 20 minutes no charge. Required to search: name, years to search. Civil cases indexed by defendant, plaintiff. Civil records on computer from 1986, microfiche and archived from start of district court. **Criminal Records:** Access: Phone, fax, mail, remote online, in person. Only the court conducts in person searches; visitors may not. Search fee: $10.00 per hour. First 20 minutes no charge. Required to search: name, years to search, DOB, SSN. Criminal records on computer from 1986, microfiche and archived from start of district court. **General Information:** No adoption, sealed records released. SASE required. Turnaround time same day unless large request. Copy fee: $.25 per page. Certification fee: $2.00. Fee payee: 7th District Court. Personal checks accepted. Prepayment is required. Public access terminal is available. Fax notes: $2.00 for first page, $1.00 each addl.

Garfield County

6th District Court PO Box 77, Panguitch, UT 84759; 435-676-8826 X104; Fax: 435-676-8239. Hours: 9AM-5PM (MST). *Felony, Misdemeanor, Civil, Eviction, Small Claims, Probate.*

Civil Records: Access: Fax, mail, in person. Both court and visitors may perform in person searches. Search fee: $13.00 per hour. Required to search: name, years to search. Civil cases indexed by defendant, plaintiff. Civil records archived for 100 years. **Criminal Records:** Access: Fax, mail, in person. Both court and visitors may perform in person searches. Search fee: $13.00 per hour. Required to search: name, years to search. Criminal records archived for 100 years. **General Information:** No adoption records released. SASE not required, but helpful. Turnaround time 1 day. Copy fee: $.25 per page. Certification fee: $2.00 plus $.50 per page. Fee payee: 6th District Court. Personal checks accepted. Prepayment is required. Fax notes: $1.00 for first page, $.50 each addl.

Grand County

7th District Court 125 E. Center, Moab, UT 84532; 435-259-1349; Fax: 435-259-4081. Hours: 8AM-5PM (MST). *Felony, Misdemeanor, Civil, Eviction, Probate.*

Civil Records: Access: Phone, mail, online, in person. Both court and visitors may perform in person searches. No search fee. Required to search: name, years to search. Civil cases indexed

by defendant. District records on computer from spring 1990, Circuit from spring 1989, archived since court started. **Criminal Records:** Access: Phone, mail, remote online, in person. Both court and visitors may perform in person searches. Search fee: No search fee for 1st 20 minutes; $10.00 per hour thereafter. Required to search: name, years to search; also helpful-DOB, SSN. District records on computer from spring 1990, Circuit from spring 1989, archived since court started. **General Information:** No adoption, expunged records released. SASE required. Turnaround time same day. Copy fee: $.25 per page. Certification fee: $2.00 plus $.50 per page. Fee payee: 7th District Court. Personal checks accepted. Credit cards accepted: Visa, Mastercard. Prepayment is required. Public access terminal is available. Fax notes: $2.00 for 1st page; $1.00 each add'l.

Iron County

5th District Court 40 North 100 East, Cedar City, UT 84720; 435-586-7440; Fax: 435-586-4801. Hours: 8AM-5PM (MST). *Felony, Misdemeanor, Civil, Eviction, Small Claims, Probate.*

Note: Hearing location also in Parawon, but records held here

Civil Records: Access: Mail, online, in person. Both court and visitors may perform in person searches. Search fee: Per hour charges vary. Required to search: name. Civil cases indexed by defendant, plaintiff. District records on computer from 4/89, former Circuit Court records on computer from 1987, archived from 1900. **Criminal Records:** Access: Mail, remote online, in person. Both court and visitors may perform in person searches. Search fee: Per hour charge varies. Required to search: name, years to search, DOB, SSN. District records on computer from 4/89, former Circuit Court records on computer from 1987, archived from 1900. **General Information:** No sealed records released. SASE required. Turnaround time 2-3 days. Copy fee: $.50 per page. Certification fee: $2.00. Fee payee: 5th District Court. Personal checks accepted. Prepayment is required. Public access terminal is available.

Juab County

4th District Court 160 N. Main, PO Box 249, Nephi, UT 84648; 435-623-0901; Fax: 435-623-0922. Hours: 8AM-5PM (MST). *Felony, Misdemeanor, Civil, Eviction, Probate.*

Civil Records: Access: Phone, mail, online, in person. Both court and visitors may perform in person searches. Search fee: $13.00 per hour. First 15 minutes are no charge. Required to search: name, years to search. Civil cases indexed by defendant, plaintiff. Civil records on computer from 11/94, archived since court started. Online access available through XChange. See state introduction. **Criminal Records:** Access: Phone, mail, remote online, in person. Both court and visitors may perform in person searches. Search fee: $13.00 per hour. First 15 minutes are no charge. Required to search: name, years to search. Criminal records on computer from 11/94, archived since court started. Online access available through XChange. See state introduction. **General Information:** All records must be viewed in this office. SASE required. Turnaround time 1 week. Copy fee: $.25 per page. Certification fee: $2.00 plus $.50 per page. Fee payee: 4th Circuit or District Court. Personal checks accepted.

Prepayment is required. Public access terminal is available.

Kane County

6th District Court 76 North Main, Kanab, UT 84741; 435-644-2458; Fax: 435-644-2052. Hours: 8AM-5PM (MST). *Felony, Misdemeanor, Civil, Eviction, Small Claims, Probate.*

Civil Records: Access: Phone, fax, mail, in person. Only the court conducts in person searches; visitors may not. Search fee: First 15 minutes of search if free, thereafter $25.00 per hour. Required to search: name, years to search. Civil cases indexed by defendant, plaintiff. Civil records on computer from 1987, archived since court started. **Criminal Records:** Access: Phone, fax, mail, in person. Only the court conducts in person searches; visitors may not. Search fee: First 15 minutes of search if free, thereafter $25.00 per hour. Required to search: name, years to search. Criminal records on computer from 1987, archived since court started. **General Information:** No sealed, expunged records released. SASE requested. Turnaround time 2-3 days. Copy fee: $.25 per page. Certification fee: $2.00. Fee payee: Kane County. Personal checks accepted. Prepayment is required. Fax notes: $2.00 for first page, $1.00 each addl.

Millard County

4th District Court 765 S Highway 99, #6, Fillmore, UT 84631; 435-743-6223; Fax: 435-743-6923. Hours: 8AM-5PM (MST). *Felony, Misdemeanor, Civil, Eviction, Small Claims, Probate.*

Civil Records: Access: Phone, mail, online, in person. Both court and visitors may perform in person searches. Search fee: $10.00 per hour. Required to search: name, years to search. Civil cases indexed by defendant, plaintiff. Civil records on computer from 1988, archived from 1896. Online access available through XChange. See state introduction. **Criminal Records:** Access: Phone, mail, remote online, in person. Both court and visitors may perform in person searches. Search fee: $10.00 per hour. Required to search: name, years to search. Criminal records on computer from 1988, archived from 1896. Online access available through XChange. See state introduction. **General Information:** No pre-sentence, expunged or sealed records released. SASE required. Turnaround time 1 day. Copy fee: $.25 per page. Certification fee: $2.00. Fee payee: 4th District Court. Business checks accepted. Prepayment is required. Public access terminal is available.

Morgan County

2nd District Court PO Box 886, Morgan, UT 84050; 801-845-4020; Fax: 801-829-6176. Hours: 8AM-5PM (MST). *Felony, Misdemeanor, Civil, Eviction, Small Claims, Probate.*

Note: Area code changes to 385 after May, 2001

Civil Records: Access: Phone, fax, mail, online, in person. Both court and visitors may perform in person searches. Search fee: $13.00 per hour. If less than 10 minutes, no charge. Required to search: name, years to search. Civil cases indexed by defendant, plaintiff. Civil records on computer since 1992; on microfiche, books, archived from 1862. Online access available through XChange. See state introduction. **Criminal Records:** Access: Phone, fax, mail, remote online, in person. Both court and visitors may perform in person searches.

Search fee: $13.00 per hour. If less than 10 minutes, no charge. Required to search: name, years to search, DOB; also helpful-SSN. Criminal records on computer since 1992, prior in books. Online access available through XChange. See state introduction. **General Information:** No sealed records released. Turnaround time same day. Copy fee: $.25 per page. Certification fee: $2.00. Fee payee: Morgan District or Circuit Court. Personal checks accepted. Prepayment is required. Public access terminal is available. Fax notes: No fee to fax results.

Piute County

6th District Court PO Box 99, Junction, UT 84740; 435-577-2840; Fax: 435-577-2433. Hours: 9AM-Noon, 1-5PM (MST). *Felony, Misdemeanor, Civil, Eviction, Small Claims, Probate.*

Civil Records: Access: Mail, in person. Both court and visitors may perform in person searches. Search fee: $10.00 per hour. Required to search: name, years to search. Civil cases indexed by defendant, plaintiff. Civil records archived from 1889. **Criminal Records:** Access: Mail, in person. Both court and visitors may perform in person searches. Search fee: $10.00 per hour. Required to search: name, years to search. Criminal records archived from 1889. **General Information:** No sealed records released. SASE required. Turnaround time 2-3 days. Copy fee: $.50 per page. Certification fee: $2.00. Fee payee: Piute County District Court. Personal checks accepted. Search fees may be billed if prior arrangements have been made.

Rich County

1st District Court PO Box 218, Randolph, UT 84064; 435-793-2415; Fax: 435-793-2410. Hours: 9AM-5PM (MST). *Felony, Misdemeanor, Civil, Eviction, Small Claims, Probate.*

Civil Records: Access: Phone, fax, mail, in person. Both court and visitors may perform in person searches. Search fee: $10.00 per hour. Required to search: name, years to search; also helpful-address. Civil cases indexed by defendant, plaintiff. Civil records archived since court started. **Criminal Records:** Access: Phone, fax, mail, in person. Both court and visitors may perform in person searches. Search fee: $10.00 per hour. Required to search: name, years to search; also helpful-address, DOB, SSN. Criminal records archived since court started. **General Information:** No sealed records released. SASE required. Turnaround time 2-3 days. Copy fee: $.25 per page. Certification fee: $2.00. Fee payee: Rich County. Personal checks accepted. Prepayment is required.

Salt Lake County

3rd District Court 450 South State Street, Salt Lake City, UT 84111; 801-238-7300; Fax: 801-238-7404. Hours: 8AM-5PM (MST). *Felony, Misdemeanor, Civil, Eviction, Small Claims, Probate.*

Civil Records: Access: Phone, mail, online, in person. Both court and visitors may perform in person searches. Search fee: $10.00 per hour. First 20 minutes no charge. Required to search: name, years to search. Civil cases indexed by defendant, plaintiff. Civil records on computer from 1988, microfiche from 1940, archived from 1800s. Online access available through XChange. See state introduction. **Criminal Records:** Access: Phone, mail, remote online, in person. Both court and visitors may perform in person searches.

Search fee: $10.00 per hour. First 20 minutes no charge. Required to search: name, years to search, DOB, SSN. Criminal records on computer from 1988, microfiche from 1940, archived from 1800s. Online access available through XChange. See state introduction. **General Information:** No juvenile or adoption records released. Turnaround time 2-3 days. Copy fee: $1.00 per page. Certification fee: $5.00. Fee payee: 3rd District Court. Personal checks accepted. Prepayment is required. Public access terminal is available.

3rd District Court - Murray Department
5022 S. State St, Murray, UT 84107; 801-281-7700; Fax: 801-281-7736. Hours: 8AM-5PM (MST). *Felony, Misdemeanor, Civil, Eviction, Small Claims.*

Civil Records: Access: Fax, mail, online, in person. Both court and visitors may perform in person searches. Search fee: $10.00 per name. Required to search: name, years to search. Civil cases indexed by defendant, plaintiff. Civil records on computer from 1985, archived from 1979. Online access available through XChange. See state introduction. Fax access requires pre-arrangement. **Criminal Records:** Access: Fax, mail, remote online, in person. Both court and visitors may perform in person searches. Search fee: $10.00 per name. Required to search: name, years to search, DOB. Criminal records on computer from 1985, archived from 1979. Same as civil. **General Information:** No sealed records released. SASE required. Turnaround time 1 week. Copy fee: $.25 per page. Certification fee: $2.00 plus $.50 per page. Fee payee: Murray District Court. Personal checks accepted. Prepayment is required. Public access terminal is available. Fax notes: No fee to fax results.

3rd District Court - Salt Lake City
451 South 2nd East, Salt Lake City, UT 84111; 801-238-7480; Fax: 801-238-7396. Hours: 8AM-5PM (MST). *Felony, Misdemeanor, Civil, Eviction, Small Claims, Probate.*

Civil Records: Access: Mail, online, in person. Both court and visitors may perform in person searches. No search fee. Required to search: name, years to search. Civil cases indexed by defendant, plaintiff. Civil records on computer from 1986, archived after satisfaction or dismissal, destroyed prior to 1985. Online access available through XChange. See state introduction. **Criminal Records:** Access: Mail, remote online, in person. Both court and visitors may perform in person searches. Search fee: No search fee. First 20 minutes no charge. Required to search: name, years to search, DOB; also helpful-SSN. Criminal records on computer from 1986, archived after satisfaction or dismissal, destroyed prior to 1985. Online access available through XChange. See state introduction. **General Information:** No confidential records released. Turnaround time 2-3 days. Copy fee: $.50 per page. Certification fee: $2.00. Fee payee: 3rd Circuit Court. Business checks accepted. Credit cards accepted: Visa, Mastercard. Public access terminal is available.

3rd District Court - Sandy Department
210 West 10,000 South, Sandy, UT 84070-3282; 801-565-5714; Fax: 801-565-5703. Hours: 8AM-5PM (MST). *Felony, Misdemeanor, Civil, Eviction, Small Claims, Probate.*

Civil Records: Access: Phone, mail, online, in person. Both court and visitors may perform in person searches. Search fee: $13.00 per hour. Required to search: name, years to search. Civil cases indexed by defendant, plaintiff. Civil records on computer from 1986, civil archived from 1985.

Online access available through XChange. See state introduction. **Criminal Records:** Access: Phone, mail, remote online, in person. Both court and visitors may perform in person searches. Search fee: $13.00 per hour. Required to search: name, years to search. Criminal records on computer from 1986, civil archived from 1985. Online access available through XChange. See state introduction. **General Information:** No police reports, pre-sentence records released. SASE required. Turnaround time 1-2 weeks. Copy fee: $.50 per page. Certification fee: $2.00. Fee payee: 3rd District Court-Sandy Dept. Personal checks accepted. No two-party checks. Credit cards accepted: Visa, Mastercard. Prepayment is required. Public access terminal is available. Public Access Terminal Note: Available by appointment.

3rd District Court - West Valley Department
3636 S. Constitution Blvd, West Valley, UT 84119; 801-982-2400; Fax: 801-967-9857. Hours: 8AM-5PM (MST). *Felony, Misdemeanor, Civil, Eviction, Small Claims, Probate.*

Civil Records: Access: Mail, online, in person. Both court and visitors may perform in person searches. Search fee: $10.00 per hour. Required to search: name, years to search. Civil cases indexed by defendant, plaintiff. Civil records on computer since 1986, archived from 1983. Online access available through XChange. See state introduction. **Criminal Records:** Access: Mail, remote online, in person. Both court and visitors may perform in person searches. Search fee: $10.00 per hour. Required to search: name, years to search. Criminal records on computer since 1986, archived from 1983. Online access available through XChange. See state introduction. **General Information:** No sealed records released. SASE required. Turnaround time 1 week. Copy fee: $.25 per page. Certification fee: $2.00. Fee payee: 3rd District Court. Personal checks accepted. Prepayment required. Public terminal available.

San Juan County

7th District Court PO Box 68, Monticello, UT 84535; 435-587-2122; Fax: 435-587-2372. Hours: 8AM-5PM (MST). *Felony, Misdemeanor, Civil, Eviction, Probate.*

Civil Records: Access: Mail, online, in person. Both court and visitors may perform in person searches. Search fee: $10.00 per hour. Required to search: name, years to search. Civil cases indexed by defendant, plaintiff. Civil records on compter since 1991; on index books from 1919 to 1991. **Criminal Records:** Access: Mail, remote online, in person. Both court and visitors may perform in person searches. Search fee: $10.00 per hour. Required to search: name, years to search. Criminal records on compter since 1991; on index books from 1919 to 1991. **General Information:** No juvenile records released. SASE required. Turnaround time 1 week. Copy fee: $.25 per page. Certification fee: $2.00 plus $.50 per page. Fee payee: 7th District Court. Personal checks accepted. Credit cards accepted: Visa, Mastercard. Visa, MC accepted in person only. Prepayment is required. Public access terminal is available.

Sanpete County

6th District Court 160 N. Main, Manti, UT 84642; 435-835-2131; Fax: 435-835-2135. Hours: 8:30AM-5PM (MST). *Felony, Misdemeanor, Civil, Eviction, Small Claims, Probate.*

Civil Records: Access: Phone, fax, mail, in person. Both court and visitors may perform in person searches. Search fee: $13.00 per hour after first 15 minutes free. Required to search: name, years to search. Civil cases indexed by defendant, plaintiff. Civil records on computer from 1986. **Criminal Records:** Access: Phone, fax, mail, in person. Both court and visitors may perform in person searches. Search fee: $13.00 per hour. Required to search: name, years to search; also helpful-DOB. Criminal records on computer from 1986. **General Information:** No criminal, expunged, or sealed records released. SASE requested. Turnaround time 10 days. Copy fee: $.25 per page. Certification fee: $2.00 plus $.50 per page. Fee payee: 6th District Court. Personal checks accepted. Prepayment is required. Public access terminal is available. Fax notes: $3.50 for first page, $2.50 each addl.

Sevier County

6th District Court 895 E 300 N, Richfield, UT 84701-2345; 435-896-2700; Fax: 435-896-8047. Hours: 8AM-5PM (MST). *Felony, Misdemeanor, Civil, Eviction, Probate.*

Civil Records: Access: Phone, fax, mail, online, in person. Both court and visitors may perform in person searches. Search fee: $10.00 per hour. For search requiring 20 minutes or less, no charge. Required to search: name, years to search. Civil cases indexed by defendant, plaintiff. Circuit on computer from 1989, District on computer from 1991. **Criminal Records:** Access: Phone, fax, mail, remote online, in person. Both court and visitors may perform in person searches. Search fee: $10.00 per hour. Required to search: name, years to search, DOB, SSN. Circuit on computer from 1989, District on computer from 1991. **General Information:** No sealed records released. Turnaround time 2-3 days. Copy fee: $.50 per page. Certification fee: $2.00. Fee payee: 6th District Court. Personal checks accepted. Prepayment is required. Public access terminal is available. Fax notes: $2.00 for first page, $1.00 each addl.

Summit County

3rd District Court PO Box 128, Coalville, UT 84017; 435-336-4451 X3274 & 3202; Fax: 435-336-3030. Hours: 8AM-5PM (MST). *Felony, Misdemeanor, Civil, Eviction, Probate.*

Civil Records: Access: Mail, online, in person. Both court and visitors may perform in person searches. Search fee: $10.00 per hour. Required to search: name, years to search. Civil cases indexed by defendant, plaintiff. All indexes on computer, records archived. Online access available through XChange. See state introduction. **Criminal Records:** Access: Mail, remote online, in person. Both court and visitors may perform in person searches. Search fee: $10.00 per hour. Required to search: name, years to search. All indexes on computer, records archived. Online access available through XChange. See state introduction. **General Information:** No sealed probate records released. SASE required. Turnaround time 2-3 days. Copy fee: $.25 per page. Certification fee: $2.00 plus $.50 each additional page. Fee payee: 3rd District Court. Personal checks accepted. Prepayment is required. Public access terminal is available.

3rd District Court - Park City Department PO Box 1480, 455 Marsac Ave, Park City, UT 84060; 435-645-5211. Hours: 8AM-5PM (MST). *Felony, Misdemeanor, Civil, Eviction, Small Claims.*

Civil Records: Access: Mail, online, in person. Only the court conducts in person searches; visitors may not. Search fee: $10.00 per hour. First 20 minutes no charge. Required to search: name, years to search. Civil cases indexed by defendant, plaintiff. Civil records on computer since 1988. Access available remotely through XChange. See state introduction. **Criminal Records:** Access: Mail, remote online, in person. Only the court conducts in person searches; visitors may not. Search fee: $10.00 per hour. First 20 minutes no charge. Required to search: name, years to search; also helpful-DOB. Criminal records on computer since 1988. Access available remotely through XChange. See state introduction. **General Information:** No sealed, expunged or juvenile records released. Turnaround time 5 days. Copy fee: $.25 per page. Certification fee: $2.00 plus $.50 per page. Fee payee: 3rd District Court. Personal checks accepted. Prepayment is required.

Tooele County

3rd District Court 47 S. Main, Tooele, UT 84074; 435-843-3210; Fax: 435-882-8524. Hours: 8AM-5PM (MST). *Felony, Misdemeanor, Civil, Eviction, Small Claims, Probate.*

Civil Records: Access: Fax, mail, online, in person. Both court and visitors may perform in person searches. Search fee: $10.00 per hour. First 20 minutes no charge. Required to search: name, years to search. Civil cases indexed by defendant, plaintiff. Civil records on computer from 1982, archived since court started. Online access available through XChange. See state introduction. **Criminal Records:** Access: Fax, mail, remote online, in person. Both court and visitors may perform in person searches. Search fee: $10.00 per hour. First 20 minutes no charge. Required to search: name, years to search; also helpful-SSN. Criminal records on computer from 1982, archived since court started. Online access available through XChange. See state introduction. **General Information:** No adoption records released. SASE required. Turnaround time 2-3 days. Copy fee: $.25 per page. Certification fee: $2.00. Fee payee: 3rd District Court. Personal checks accepted. Prepayment is required. Public access terminal is available.

Uintah County

8th District Court PO Box 1015, Vernal, UT 84078; 435-789-7534; Fax: 435-789-0564. Hours: 8AM-5PM (MST). *Felony, Misdemeanor, Civil, Eviction, Probate.*

Civil Records: Access: Mail, online, in person. Both court and visitors may perform in person searches. Search fee: $10.00 per hour. First 20 minutes no charge. Required to search: name, years to search. Civil cases indexed by defendant, plaintiff. Circuit on computer from 1987, everything else from 1989, archived since court started. **Criminal Records:** Access: Mail, remote online, in person. Both court and visitors may perform in person searches. Search fee: $10.00 per hour. First 20 minutes no charge. Required to search: name, years to search. Circuit on computer from 1987, everything else from 1989, archived since court started. **General Information:** No sealed records released. SASE required. Turnaround time 2-3 days. Copy fee: $.25 per page. Certification fee: $2.00 plus $.50 per page. Fee payee: 8th District Court. Personal checks accepted. Prepayment is required. Public access terminal is available.

Utah County

4th District Court 125 North, 100 West, Provo, UT 84601; 801-429-1000; Fax: 801-429-1033. Hours: 8AM-5PM *Felony, Misdemeanor, Civil, Eviction, Small Claims, Probate.*

http://courtlink.utcourts.gov

Note: Area code changes to 385 after May, 2001

Civil Records: Access: Mail, online, in person. Both court and visitors may perform in person searches. Search fee: $13.00 per hour. Required to search: name, years to search. Civil cases indexed by defendant, plaintiff. Civil and probate on computer from 1986, judgements, tax liens, and divorce decrees on microfiche from 1900 to 1975, archived from 1900s. Online access available through XChange. See state introduction. **Criminal Records:** Access: Mail, remote online, in person. Both court and visitors may perform in person searches. Search fee: $13.00 per hour. Required to search: name, years to search, DOB. Felony on computer from 1989. Online access available through XChange. See state introduction. **General Information:** No sealed records released. SASE required. Turnaround time 7-10 days. Copy fee: $.25 per page. Certification fee: $2.00. Fee payee: 4th District Court. Personal checks accepted. Credit cards accepted: Visa, Mastercard. Accepted in person only. Prepayment is required. Public access terminal is available.

4th District Court - Orem Department 97 E Center, Orem, UT 84057; 801-764-5870/5864; Fax: 801-226-5244. Hours: 8AM-5PM (MST). *Misdemeanor, Civil, Eviction, Small Claims.*

Note: Area code changes to 385 after May, 2001

Civil Records: Access: Mail, online, in person. Only the court conducts in person searches; visitors may not. Search fee: $10.00 per hour. First 20 minutes no charge. Required to search: name, years to search. Civil cases indexed by defendant, plaintiff. Civil records on computer since 1988. Access available remotely through XChange. See state introduction. **Criminal Records:** Access: Mail, remote online, in person. Only the court conducts in person searches; visitors may not. Search fee: $10.00 per hour. First 20 minutes no charge. Required to search: name, years to search; also helpful-DOB. Criminal records on computer since 1988. Access available remotely through XChange. See state introduction. **General Information:** No sealed, expunged or confidential records released. Turnaround time 5-7 days. Copy fee: $.25 per page. Certification fee: $2.00 plus $.50 per page. Fee payee: 4th District Court. Personal checks accepted. Credit cards accepted: Visa, Mastercard. Prepayment is required.

4th District Court - Spanish Forks Department 40 S Main St, Spanish Forks, UT 84660; 801-798-8674; Fax: 801-798-1377. Hours: 8AM-5PM (MST). *Felony, Misdemeanor, Civil, Eviction, Small Claims.*

Note: Area code changes to 385 after May, 2001

Civil Records: Access: Phone, fax, mail, online, in person. Both court and visitors may perform in person searches. Search fee: $10.00 per hour. First 20 minutes no charge. Required to search: name, years to search. Civil cases indexed by defendant, plaintiff. Civil records on computer since 1988. Access available remotely through XChange. See state introduction. **Criminal Records:** Access: Phone, fax, mail, remote online, in person. Both court and visitors may perform in person searches. Search fee: $10.00 per hour. First 20 minutes no charge. Required to search: name, years to search; also helpful-DOB. Criminal records on computer since 1988. Access available remotely through XChange. See state introduction. **General Information:** No sealed, expunged or confidential records released. Turnaround time 5-7 days. Copy fee: $.25 per page. Certification fee: $2.00 plus $.50 per page. Fee payee: 4th District Court. Personal checks accepted. Credit cards accepted: Visa, Mastercard. Prepayment is required. Fax notes: No fee to fax results. Fax requires prior arrangement.

4th District Court - American Fork Department

98 N Center St, American Fork, UT 84003-1626; 801-756-9654; Fax: 801-763-0153. Hours: 8AM-5PM (MST). *Misdemeanor, Civil, Eviction, Small Claims.*

Note: Area code changes to 385 after May, 2001

Civil Records: Access: Mail, online, in person. Both court and visitors may perform in person searches. Search fee: $10.00 per hour. First 20 minutes no charge. Required to search: name, years to search. Civil cases indexed by defendant, plaintiff. Civil records on computer since 1988. Access available remotely through XChange. See state introduction. **Criminal Records:** Access: Mail, remote online, in person. Both court and visitors may perform in person searches. Search fee: $10.00 per hour. First 20 minutes no charge. Required to search: name, years to search; also helpful-DOB. Access available remotely through XChange. See state introduction. **General Information:** No sealed, expunged or confidential records released. SASE required. Turnaround time 5-7 days. Copy fee: $.25 per page. Certification fee: $2.00 plus $.50 per page. Fee payee: 4th District Court. Personal checks accepted. Credit cards accepted: Visa, Mastercard. Prepayment is required.

Wasatch County

4th District Court

PO Box 730, Heber City, UT 84032; 435-654-4676; Fax: 435-654-5281. Hours: 8AM-5PM (MST). *Felony, Misdemeanor, Civil, Eviction, Small Claims, Probate.*

Civil Records: Access: Phone, fax, mail, online, in person. Both court and visitors may perform in person searches. No search fee. Required to search: name, years to search. Civil cases indexed by defendant, plaintiff. Civil records on computer since 01/95; records archived since court started. Online access available through XChange. See state introduction. **Criminal Records:** Access: Phone, fax, mail, remote online, in person. Both court and visitors may perform in person searches. No search fee. Required to search: name, years to

search; also helpful-DOB. Criminal records on computer since 01/95; records archived since court started. Online access available through XChange. See state introduction. **General Information:** No adoption records released. SASE required. Turnaround time 1-2 days. Copy fee: $.25 per page. Certification fee: $2.00 plus $.50 per page. Fee payee: 4th District Court. Personal checks accepted. Prepayment is required. Public access terminal is available. Fax notes: No fee to fax results.

Washington County

5th District Court

220 North 200 East, St. George, UT 84770;; Civil phone:435-986-5701; Criminal phone:435-986-5701; Fax: 435-986-5723. Hours: 8AM-5PM (MST). *Felony, Misdemeanor, Civil, Eviction, Small Claims, Probate.*

Civil Records: Access: Mail, online, in person. Both court and visitors may perform in person searches. No search fee. Required to search: name. Civil cases indexed by defendant, plaintiff. District Court records on computer from April, 1990; Circuit Court on computer from 1987. **Criminal Records:** Access: Mail, remote online, in person. Both court and visitors may perform in person searches. No search fee. Required to search: name, years to search. District Court records on computer from April, 1990; Circuit Court on computer from 1987. **General Information:** No mental health, adoption records released. SASE required. Turnaround time 2-3 days. Copy fee: $.25 per page. Certification fee: $2.00 plus $.50 per page. Fee payee: 5th District Court. Personal checks accepted. Credit cards accepted: Visa, Mastercard. Prepayment is required. Public access terminal is available.

Wayne County

6th District Court

PO Box 189, Loa, UT 84747; 435-836-2731; Fax: 435-836-2479. Hours: 9AM-5PM (MST). *Felony, Misdemeanor, Civil, Eviction, Small Claims, Probate.*

Civil Records: Access: Mail, in person. Both court and visitors may perform in person searches. Search fee: $10.00 per hour. Required to search: name, years to search. Civil cases indexed by defendant, plaintiff. Civil records archived since court started. **Criminal Records:** Access: Mail, in person. Both court and visitors may perform in person searches. Search fee: $10.00 per hour. Required to search: name, years to search; also helpful-SSN. Criminal records archived since court started. **General Information:** No sealed records released. SASE required. Turnaround time 2-3 days. Copy fee: $.25 per page. Certification

fee: $2.00 plus $.50 per page. Fee payee: 6th District Court. Personal checks accepted. Prepayment is required.

Weber County

2nd District Court

2525 Grant Ave, Ogden, UT 84401;; Civil phone:801-395-1091; Criminal phone:801-395-1091; Probate phone:801-395-1173. Hours: 8AM-5PM (MST). *Felony, Misdemeanor, Civil, Eviction, Small Claims, Probate.*

Civil Records: Access: Phone, mail, online, in person. Both court and visitors may perform in person searches. Search fee: $13.00 per hour. First 20 minutes no charge. Required to search: name, years to search. Civil cases indexed by defendant, plaintiff. Civil records on computer from 1980, books prior to that. Online access available through XChange. See state introduction. **Criminal Records:** Access: Phone, mail, remote online, in person. Both court and visitors may perform in person searches. Search fee: $13.00 per hour. First 20 minutes no charge. Required to search: name, years to search, DOB, SSN. Criminal records on computer from 1980, books prior to that. Online access available through XChange. See state introduction. **General Information:** No adoption, voluntary commitments, expunged criminal records released. SASE required. Turnaround time 2-9 days. Copy fee: $.25 per page. Certification fee: $2.00. Plus $.50 per page. Fee payee: Ogden District Court. Personal checks accepted. Credit cards accepted: Visa, Mastercard. Prepayment is required. Public access terminal is available.

2nd District Court - Roy Department

5051 South 1900 West, Roy, UT 84067; 801-774-1051; Fax: 801-774-1060. Hours: 8AM-5PM (MST). *Felony, Misdemeanor.*

Note: Area code changes to 385 after May, 2001. Civil and small claims records here only prior to 01/01/90. Newer records maintained in Ogden **Criminal Records:** Access: Mail, remote online, in person. Both court and visitors may perform in person searches. Search fee: $10.00 per hour. First 20 minutes no charge. Required to search: name, years to search, signed release; also helpful-address, DOB. Criminal records on computer since January 1987. **General Information:** No sealed, expunged or juvenile records released. Turnaround time 5 days. Copy fee: $.25 per page. Certification fee: $2.00 plus $.50 per page. Fee payee: Roy District Court. Personal checks accepted. Credit cards accepted: Visa, Mastercard. Prepayment is required.

ORGANIZATION

29 counties 29 recording offices. The recording officers are County Recorder and Clerk of District Court (state tax liens). The entire state is in the Mountain Time Zone (MST).

UCC RECORDS

Financing statements are filed at the state level, except for real estate related collateral, which are filed with the Register of Deeds (and at the state level in certain cases). Filing offices will **not** perform UCC searches. Copy fees vary. Certification usually costs $2.00 per document.

TAX LIEN RECORDS

All federal tax liens are filed with the County Recorder. They do **not** perform searches. All state tax liens are filed with Clerk of District Court, many of which have on-line access. Refer to Utah County Courts section for information about Utah District Courts.

REAL ESTATE RECORDS

County Recorders will **not** perform real estate searches. Copy fees vary, and certification fees are usually $2.00 per document.

Beaver County

County Recorder, P.O. Box 431, Beaver, UT 84713. 435-438-6480. Fax: 435-438-6481.

Box Elder County

County Recorder, 1 South Main, Courthouse, Brigham City, UT 84302-2599. 435-734-2031. Fax: 435-734-2038.

Cache County

County Recorder, 179 North Main Street, Logan, UT 84321. 435-752-5561. Fax: 435-753-7120.

Carbon County

County Recorder, Courthouse Building, 120 East Main, Price, UT 84501. 435-636-3244. Fax: 435-637-6757.

Daggett County

County Recorder, P.O. Box 219, Manila, UT 84046-0219. 435-784-3210. Fax: 435-784-3335.

Davis County

County Recorder, P.O. Box 618, Farmington, UT 84025. 801-451-3225. Fax: 801-451-3111.

Duchesne County

County Recorder, P.O. Drawer 450, Duchesne, UT 84021-0450. 435-738-1160. Fax: 435-738-5522.

Emery County

County Recorder, P.O. Box 698, Castle Dale, UT 84513-0698. 435-381-2414. Fax: 435-381-5529.

Garfield County

County Recorder, P.O. Box 77, Panguitch, UT 84759. 435-676-1112x112. Fax: 435-676-8239.

Grand County

County Recorder, 125 East Center St., Moab, UT 84532. 435-259-1331. Fax: 435-259-2959.

Iron County

County Recorder, P.O. Box 506, Parowan, UT 84761. 435-477-8350.

Juab County

County Recorder, 160 North Main, Nephi, UT 84648. 435-623-3430.

Kane County

County Recorder, 76 North Main #14, Kanab, UT 84741. 435-644-2360.

Millard County

County Recorder, 50 South Main, Fillmore, UT 84631. 435-743-6210. Fax: 435-743-4221.

Morgan County

County Recorder, P.O. Box 886, Morgan, UT 84050. 801-829-3277. Fax: 801-829-6176.

Piute County

County Recorder, P.O. Box 116, Junction, UT 84740. 435-577-2505. Fax: 435-577-2433.

Rich County

County Recorder, P.O. Box 322, Randolph, UT 84064. 435-793-2005.

Salt Lake County

County Recorder, 2001 South State Street, Room N-1600, Salt Lake City, UT 84190-1150. 801-468-3391. www.co.slc.ut.us
Online Access: Assessor, Real Estate. Two sources are available. Assessment records on the Salt Lake County Truth-In-Tax Information web site are available free on the Internet at www.co.slc.ut.us/valnotice. Also, Assessor, real estate, appraisal, abstracts, and GIS mapping are available for a $150.00 fee on the Polaris online system at http://rec.co.slc.ut.us/polaris/default.cfm. Search by GIS, name, property information. Register online or call 801-468-3013.

San Juan County

County Recorder, P.O. Box 789, Monticello, UT 84535. 435-587-3228. Fax: 435-587-2425.

Sanpete County

County Recorder, 160 North Main, Manti, UT 84642. 435-835-2181. Fax: 435-835-2143.

Sevier County

County Recorder, 250 North Main, Richfield, UT 84701. 435-896-9262x210. Fax: 435-896-8888.

Summit County

County Recorder, P.O. Box 128, Coalville, UT 84017. 435-336-3238. Fax: 435-336-3030.

Tooele County

County Recorder, 47 South Main Street, Courthouse, Tooele, UT 84074-2194. 435-843-3180. Fax: 435-882-7317.

Uintah County

County Recorder, 147 East Main St., County Building, Vernal, UT 84078. 435-781-5461. Fax: 435-781-5319.

Utah County

County Recorder, P.O. Box 122, Provo, UT 84603. 801-370-8179. Fax: 801-370-8181.

Wasatch County

County Recorder, 25 North Main, Heber, UT 84032. 435-654-3211.

Washington County

County Recorder, 197 East Tabernacle, St. George, UT 84770. 435-634-5709. Fax: 435-634-5718.

Wayne County

County Recorder, P.O. Box 187, Loa, UT 84747-0187. 435-836-2765. Fax: 435-836-2479.

Weber County

County Recorder, 2380 Washington Blvd, Suite 370, Ogden, UT 84401. 801-399-8441. www.co.weber.ut.us
Online Access: Real Estate. Property records on the Weber County Parcel Search site are available free on Internet: www.co.weber.ut.us/netapps/Parcel/main.htm.

You will usually be able to find the city name in the City/County Cross Reference below. In that case, it is a simple matter to determine the county from the cross reference. However, only the official US Postal Service city names are included in this index. There are an additional 40,000 place names that people use in their addresses. Therefore, we have also included a ZIP/City Cross Reference immediately following the City/County Cross Reference.

If you know the ZIP Code but the city name does not appear in the City/County Cross Reference index, look up the ZIP Code in the ZIP/City Cross Reference, find the city name, then look up the city name in the City/County Cross Reference. For example, you want to know the county for an address of Menands, NY 12204. There is no "Menands" in the City/County Cross Reference. The ZIP/City Cross Reference shows that ZIP Codes 12201-12288 are for the city of Albany. Looking back in the City/County Cross Reference, Albany is in Albany County.

City/County Cross Reference

ALPINE Utah
ALTAMONT Duchesne
ALTON Kane
ALTONAH Duchesne
AMERICAN FORK Utah
ANETH San Juan
ANNABELLA Sevier
ANTIMONY Garfield
AURORA Sevier
AXTELL Sanpete
BEAR RIVER CITY Box Elder
BEAVER Beaver
BERYL Iron
BICKNELL Wayne
BINGHAM CANYON Salt Lake
BLANDING San Juan
BLUEBELL Duchesne
BLUFF San Juan
BONANZA Uintah
BOULDER Garfield
BOUNTIFUL Davis
BRIAN HEAD Iron
BRIDGELAND Duchesne
BRIGHAM CITY Box Elder
BRYCE Garfield
BRYCE CANYON Garfield
CACHE JUNCTION Cache
CANNONVILLE Garfield
CASTLE DALE Emery
CEDAR CITY Iron
CEDAR VALLEY Utah
CENTERFIELD Sanpete
CENTERVILLE Davis
CENTRAL Washington
CHESTER Sanpete
CIRCLEVILLE Piute
CISCO Grand
CLARKSTON Cache
CLAWSON Emery
CLEARFIELD Davis
CLEVELAND Emery
COALVILLE Summit
COLLINSTON Box Elder
CORINNE Box Elder
CORNISH Cache
CROYDON Morgan
DAMMERON VALLEY Washington
DELTA Millard
DEWEYVILLE Box Elder
DRAPER Salt Lake
DUCHESNE Duchesne
DUCK CREEK VILLAGE Kane
DUGWAY Tooele
DUTCH JOHN Daggett
EAST CARBON Carbon
ECHO Summit
EDEN Weber
ELBERTA Utah
ELMO Emery
ELSINORE Sevier
EMERY Emery
ENTERPRISE Washington
EPHRAIM Sanpete
ESCALANTE Garfield
EUREKA Juab

FAIRVIEW (84629) Sanpete(66), Utah(33),
    San Juan(2)
FARMINGTON Davis
FAYETTE Sanpete
FERRON Emery
FIELDING Box Elder
FILLMORE Millard
FORT DUCHESNE Uintah
FOUNTAIN GREEN Sanpete
FRUITLAND Duchesne
GARDEN CITY Rich
GARLAND Box Elder
GARRISON Millard
GLENDALE Kane
GLENWOOD Sevier
GOSHEN Utah
GRANTSVILLE Tooele
GREEN RIVER Emery
GREENVILLE Beaver
GREENWICH (84732) Sevier(71),
    Piute(29)
GROUSE CREEK Box Elder
GUNLOCK Washington
GUNNISON Sanpete
GUSHER Uintah
HANKSVILLE Wayne
HANNA Duchesne
HATCH Garfield
HEBER CITY Wasatch
HELPER Carbon
HENEFER Summit
HENRIEVILLE Garfield
HIAWATHA Carbon
HILDALE Washington
HILL AFB Davis
HINCKLEY Millard
HOLDEN Millard
HONEYVILLE Box Elder
HOOPER (84315) Weber(93), Davis(7)
HOWELL Box Elder
HUNTINGTON Emery
HUNTSVILLE Weber
HURRICANE Washington
HYDE PARK Cache
HYRUM Cache
IBAPAH Tooele
IVINS Washington
JENSEN Uintah
JOSEPH Sevier
JUNCTION Piute
KAMAS Summit
KANAB Kane
KANARRAVILLE Iron
KANOSH Millard
KAYSVILLE Davis
KENILWORTH Carbon
KINGSTON Piute
KOOSHAREM Sevier
LA SAL San Juan
LA VERKIN Washington
LAKE POWELL San Juan
LAKETOWN Rich
LAPOINT Uintah
LAYTON Davis
LEAMINGTON Millard

LEEDS Washington
LEHI Utah
LEVAN Juab
LEWISTON Cache
LINDON Utah
LOA Wayne
LOGAN Cache
LYMAN Wayne
LYNNDYL Millard
MAGNA Salt Lake
MANILA Daggett
MANTI Sanpete
MANTUA Box Elder
MAPLETON Utah
MARYSVALE Piute
MAYFIELD Sanpete
MEADOW Millard
MENDON Cache
MEXICAN HAT San Juan
MIDVALE Salt Lake
MIDWAY Wasatch
MILFORD Beaver
MILLVILLE Cache
MINERSVILLE Beaver
MOAB Grand
MODENA Iron
MONA Juab
MONROE Sevier
MONTEZUMA CREEK San Juan
MONTICELLO San Juan
MONUMENT VALLEY San Juan
MORGAN Morgan
MORONI Sanpete
MOUNT CARMEL Kane
MOUNT PLEASANT Sanpete
MOUNTAIN HOME Duchesne
MYTON (84052) Duchesne(74), Uintah(26)
NEOLA Duchesne
NEPHI Juab
NEW HARMONY Washington
NEWCASTLE Iron
NEWTON Cache
NORTH SALT LAKE Davis
OAK CITY Millard
OAKLEY Summit
OASIS Millard
OGDEN (84405) Weber(91), Davis(9)
OGDEN Weber
ORANGEVILLE Emery
ORDERVILLE Kane
OREM Utah
PANGUITCH Garfield
PARADISE Cache
PARAGONAH Iron
PARK CITY Summit
PARK VALLEY Box Elder
PAROWAN Iron
PAYSON Utah
PEOA Summit
PINE VALLEY Washington
PLEASANT GROVE Utah
PLYMOUTH Box Elder
PORTAGE Box Elder
PRICE Carbon
PROVIDENCE Cache

PROVO Utah
RANDLETT Uintah
RANDOLPH Rich
REDMOND Sevier
RICHFIELD Sevier
RICHMOND Cache
RIVERSIDE Box Elder
RIVERTON Salt Lake
ROCKVILLE Washington
ROOSEVELT (84066) Duchesne(96),
    Uintah(4)
ROY Weber
RUSH VALLEY Tooele
SAINT GEORGE Washington
SALEM Utah
SALINA Sevier
SALT LAKE CITY Salt Lake
SANDY Salt Lake
SANTA CLARA Washington
SANTAQUIN Utah
SCIPIO Millard
SEVIER Sevier
SIGURD Sevier
SMITHFIELD Cache
SNOWVILLE Box Elder
SOUTH JORDAN Salt Lake
SPANISH FORK Utah
SPRING CITY Sanpete
SPRINGDALE (84767) Washington(73),
    Garfield(27)
SPRINGVILLE Utah
STERLING Sanpete
STOCKTON Tooele
SUMMIT Iron
SUNNYSIDE Carbon
SYRACUSE Davis
TABIONA Duchesne
TALMAGE Duchesne
TEASDALE Wayne
THOMPSON Grand
TOOELE Tooele
TOQUERVILLE Washington
TORREY Wayne
TREMONTON Box Elder
TRENTON Cache
TRIDELL Uintah
TROPIC Garfield
VERNAL Uintah
VERNON Tooele
VEYO Washington
VIRGIN Washington
WALES Sanpete
WALLSBURG Wasatch
WASHINGTON Washington
WELLINGTON Carbon
WELLSVILLE Cache
WENDOVER Tooele
WEST JORDAN Salt Lake
WHITEROCKS Uintah
WILLARD Box Elder
WOODRUFF Rich
WOODS CROSS Davis

ZIP/City Cross Reference

ZIP	City	ZIP	City	ZIP	City	ZIP	City
84001-84001	ALTAMONT	84078-84079	VERNAL	84523-84523	FERRON	84714-84714	BERYL
84002-84002	ALTONAH	84080-84080	VERNON	84525-84525	GREEN RIVER	84715-84715	BICKNELL
84003-84003	AMERICAN FORK	84082-84082	WALLSBURG	84526-84526	HELPER	84716-84716	BOULDER
84004-84004	ALPINE	84083-84083	WENDOVER	84527-84527	HIAWATHA	84717-84717	BRYCE CANYON
84006-84006	BINGHAM CANYON	84084-84084	WEST JORDAN	84528-84528	HUNTINGTON	84718-84718	CANNONVILLE
84007-84007	BLUEBELL	84085-84085	WHITEROCKS	84529-84529	KENILWORTH	84719-84719	BRIAN HEAD
84008-84008	BONANZA	84086-84086	WOODRUFF	84530-84530	LA SAL	84720-84721	CEDAR CITY
84010-84011	BOUNTIFUL	84087-84087	WOODS CROSS	84531-84531	MEXICAN HAT	84722-84722	CENTRAL
84013-84013	CEDAR VALLEY	84088-84088	WEST JORDAN	84532-84532	MOAB	84723-84723	CIRCLEVILLE
84014-84014	CENTERVILLE	84090-84094	SANDY	84533-84533	LAKE POWELL	84724-84724	ELSINORE
84015-84016	CLEARFIELD	84095-84095	SOUTH JORDAN	84534-84534	MONTEZUMA CREEK	84725-84725	ENTERPRISE
84017-84017	COALVILLE	84097-84097	OREM	84535-84535	MONTICELLO	84726-84726	ESCALANTE
84018-84018	CROYDON	84098-84098	PARK CITY	84536-84536	MONUMENT VALLEY	84728-84728	GARRISON
84020-84020	DRAPER	84101-84199	SALT LAKE CITY	84537-84537	ORANGEVILLE	84729-84729	GLENDALE
84021-84021	DUCHESNE	84201-84244	OGDEN	84539-84539	SUNNYSIDE	84730-84730	GLENWOOD
84022-84022	DUGWAY	84301-84301	BEAR RIVER CITY	84540-84540	THOMPSON	84731-84731	GREENVILLE
84023-84023	DUTCH JOHN	84302-84302	BRIGHAM CITY	84542-84542	WELLINGTON	84732-84732	GREENWICH
84024-84024	ECHO	84304-84304	CACHE JUNCTION	84601-84606	PROVO	84733-84733	GUNLOCK
84025-84025	FARMINGTON	84305-84305	CLARKSTON	84620-84620	AURORA	84734-84734	HANKSVILLE
84026-84026	FORT DUCHESNE	84306-84306	COLLINSTON	84621-84621	AXTELL	84735-84735	HATCH
84027-84027	FRUITLAND	84307-84307	CORINNE	84622-84622	CENTERFIELD	84736-84736	HENRIEVILLE
84028-84028	GARDEN CITY	84308-84308	CORNISH	84623-84623	CHESTER	84737-84737	HURRICANE
84029-84029	GRANTSVILLE	84309-84309	DEWEYVILLE	84624-84624	DELTA	84738-84738	IVINS
84030-84030	GUSHER	84310-84310	EDEN	84626-84626	ELBERTA	84739-84739	JOSEPH
84031-84031	HANNA	84311-84311	FIELDING	84627-84627	EPHRAIM	84740-84740	JUNCTION
84032-84032	HEBER CITY	84312-84312	GARLAND	84628-84628	EUREKA	84741-84741	KANAB
84033-84033	HENEFER	84313-84313	GROUSE CREEK	84629-84629	FAIRVIEW	84742-84742	KANARRAVILLE
84034-84034	IBAPAH	84314-84314	HONEYVILLE	84630-84630	FAYETTE	84743-84743	KINGSTON
84035-84035	JENSEN	84315-84315	HOOPER	84631-84631	FILLMORE	84744-84744	KOOSHAREM
84036-84036	KAMAS	84316-84316	HOWELL	84632-84632	FOUNTAIN GREEN	84745-84745	LA VERKIN
84037-84037	KAYSVILLE	84317-84317	HUNTSVILLE	84633-84633	GOSHEN	84746-84746	LEEDS
84038-84038	LAKETOWN	84318-84318	HYDE PARK	84634-84634	GUNNISON	84747-84747	LOA
84039-84039	LAPOINT	84319-84319	HYRUM	84635-84635	HINCKLEY	84749-84749	LYMAN
84040-84041	LAYTON	84320-84320	LEWISTON	84636-84636	HOLDEN	84750-84750	MARYSVALE
84042-84042	LINDON	84321-84323	LOGAN	84637-84637	KANOSH	84751-84751	MILFORD
84043-84043	LEHI	84324-84324	MANTUA	84638-84638	LEAMINGTON	84752-84752	MINERSVILLE
84044-84044	MAGNA	84325-84325	MENDON	84639-84639	LEVAN	84753-84753	MODENA
84046-84046	MANILA	84326-84326	MILLVILLE	84640-84640	LYNNDYL	84754-84754	MONROE
84047-84047	MIDVALE	84327-84327	NEWTON	84642-84642	MANTI	84755-84755	MOUNT CARMEL
84049-84049	MIDWAY	84328-84328	PARADISE	84643-84643	MAYFIELD	84756-84756	NEWCASTLE
84050-84050	MORGAN	84329-84329	PARK VALLEY	84644-84644	MEADOW	84757-84757	NEW HARMONY
84051-84051	MOUNTAIN HOME	84330-84330	PLYMOUTH	84645-84645	MONA	84758-84758	ORDERVILLE
84052-84052	MYTON	84331-84331	PORTAGE	84646-84646	MORONI	84759-84759	PANGUITCH
84053-84053	NEOLA	84332-84332	PROVIDENCE	84647-84647	MOUNT PLEASANT	84760-84760	PARAGONAH
84054-84054	NORTH SALT LAKE	84333-84333	RICHMOND	84648-84648	NEPHI	84761-84761	PAROWAN
84055-84055	OAKLEY	84334-84334	RIVERSIDE	84649-84649	OAK CITY	84762-84762	DUCK CREEK VILLAGE
84056-84056	HILL AFB	84335-84335	SMITHFIELD	84650-84650	OASIS	84763-84763	ROCKVILLE
84057-84059	OREM	84336-84336	SNOWVILLE	84651-84651	PAYSON	84764-84764	BRYCE
84060-84060	PARK CITY	84337-84337	TREMONTON	84652-84652	REDMOND	84765-84765	SANTA CLARA
84061-84061	PEOA	84338-84338	TRENTON	84653-84653	SALEM	84766-84766	SEVIER
84062-84062	PLEASANT GROVE	84339-84339	WELLSVILLE	84654-84654	SALINA	84767-84767	SPRINGDALE
84063-84063	RANDLETT	84340-84340	WILLARD	84655-84655	SANTAQUIN	84770-84771	SAINT GEORGE
84064-84064	RANDOLPH	84341-84341	LOGAN	84656-84656	SCIPIO	84772-84772	SUMMIT
84065-84065	RIVERTON	84401-84414	OGDEN	84657-84657	SIGURD	84773-84773	TEASDALE
84066-84066	ROOSEVELT	84501-84501	PRICE	84660-84660	SPANISH FORK	84774-84774	TOQUERVILLE
84067-84067	ROY	84510-84510	ANETH	84662-84662	SPRING CITY	84775-84775	TORREY
84068-84068	PARK CITY	84511-84511	BLANDING	84663-84663	SPRINGVILLE	84776-84776	TROPIC
84069-84069	RUSH VALLEY	84512-84512	BLUFF	84664-84664	MAPLETON	84779-84779	VIRGIN
84070-84070	SANDY	84513-84513	CASTLE DALE	84665-84665	STERLING	84780-84780	WASHINGTON
84071-84071	STOCKTON	84515-84515	CISCO	84667-84667	WALES	84781-84781	PINE VALLEY
84072-84072	TABIONA	84516-84516	CLAWSON	84701-84701	RICHFIELD	84782-84782	VEYO
84073-84073	TALMAGE	84518-84518	CLEVELAND	84710-84710	ALTON	84783-84783	DAMMERON VALLEY
84074-84074	TOOELE	84520-84520	EAST CARBON	84711-84711	ANNABELLA	84784-84784	HILDALE
84075-84075	SYRACUSE	84521-84521	ELMO	84712-84712	ANTIMONY	84790-84790	SAINT GEORGE
84076-84076	TRIDELL	84522-84522	EMERY	84713-84713	BEAVER		

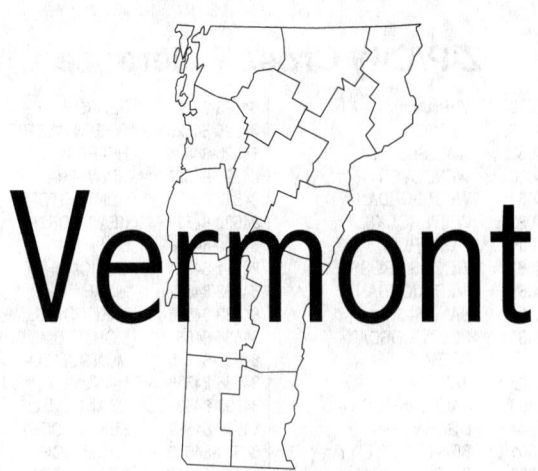

Vermont

General Help Numbers:

Governor's Office
Pavillion Office Bldg   802-828-3333
109 State St   Fax 802-828-3339
Montpelier, VT 05609   7:45AM-4:30PM
www.state.vt.us/governor/index.htm

Attorney General's Office
109 State St   802-828-3171
Montpelier, VT 05609-1001   Fax 802-828-2154
www.state.vt.us/atg   7:45AM-4:30PM

State Court Administrator
Administrative Office of Courts   802-828-3278
111 State St   Fax 802-828-3457
Montpelier, VT 05609-0701   7:45AM-4:30PM
www.state.vt.us/courts/admin.htm

State Archives
State Archives Division   802-828-2308
26 Terrace-Redstone Bldg   Fax 802-828-2496
Montpelier, VT 05609-1103   7:45AM-4:30PM
http://vermont-archives.org

State Specifics:

Capital:	Montpelier
	Washington County
Time Zone:	EST
Number of Counties:	14
Population:	593,740
Web Site:	www.state.vt.us

State Agencies

Criminal Records

Access to Records is Restricted

State Repository, Vermont Criminal Information Center, 103 S. Main St., Waterbury, VT 05671-2101; 802-244-8727, 802-241-5552 (Fax), 8AM-4:30PM.

www.dps.state.vt.us

Note: Records are not available to the public and can only be access by those authorized by law. This includes employers with employees working with children, the elderly, or the disabled. Otherwise, suggest searching at the county level.

Corporation Records
Limited Liability Company Records
Limited Liability Partnerships
Limited Partnerships
Trademarks/Servicemarks

Secretary of State, Corporation Division, 109 State St, Montpelier, VT 05609-1101 (Courier: 81 River St, Heritage Bldg, Montpelier, VT 05602); 802-828-2386, 802-828-2853 (Fax), 7:45AM-4:30PM.

www.sec.state.vt.us/soshome.htm

Indexing & Storage: Records are available from beginning of record keeping. Records are on computer if active. Inactive records are indexed by a card file.

Searching: Include the following in your request-full name of business.

Access by: mail, phone, fax, in person, online.

Fee & Payment: There is no search fee. Copies are $.10 per page or $.25 per page if on microfiche. The fee for certification is $5.00, or $1.00 per page when copies pulled. Fee payee: Secretary of State. Personal checks accepted. No credit cards accepted.

Mail search: Turnaround time: 3-5 days.

Phone search: They will only confirm if business is active.

Fax search: Same criteria as mail searching. They will return a page or two by fax, if local number, otherwise results are mailed.

In person search: Searching is available in person.

Online search: Corporate and trademark records can be accessed from the Internet for no fee. All records are available except for LPs, LLCs, and Farm Product Liens (however, all of these records will eventually be up). Also, the web site offers a "Trade Name Finder."

Other access: There is an option on the Internet to download the entire corporation (and tradename) database.

Uniform Commercial Code

UCC Division, Secretary of State, 81 River St, Drawer 4, Montpelier, VT 05609-1101; 802-828-2386, 802-828-2853 (Fax), 7:45AM-4:30PM.

www.sec.state.vt.us/corps/corpindex.htm

Indexing & Storage: Records are available from 1967. All active records are computerized.

Searching: Use search request form UCC-11. All tax liens are filed at the town/city level. Include the following in your request-debtor name, business name.

Access by: mail, fax, in person, online.

Fee & Payment: Searches are $10.00 per name. The copy fee is $2.00 per page. If there are attachments, they are an additional $5.00 per page. Fee payee: Secretary of State. Personal checks accepted. No credit cards accepted.

Mail search: Turnaround time: 4 days. A self addressed stamped envelope is requested.

Fax search: Same criteria as mail searching.

In person search: Turnaround time depends on workload, may not be immediate.

Online search: Searches are available from the Internet site. You can search by debtor or business name, there is no fee.

Federal Tax Liens
State Tax Liens

Records not maintained by a state level agency.

Note: Records are found at the local town level.

Sales Tax Registrations

Administrative Agency/Tax Department, Business Tax Division, 109 State St, Montpelier, VT 05609-1401; 802-828-2551, 802-828-5787 (Fax), 7:45AM-4:30PM.

Indexing & Storage: Records are available for 4 years on computer database, then records are archived.

Searching: This agency will only confirm that a business is registered. Records are considered confidential. They will provide no other information. Include the following in your request-business name. They will also search by tax permit number, owner name or federal tax ID.

Access by: mail, phone, fax.

Mail search: Turnaround time: 7-10 days. A self addressed stamped envelope is requested. No fee for mail request.

Phone search: No fee for telephone request.

Fax search: Fax searching available.

Birth Certificates

Reference & Research, Vital Records Section, US Rte 2, Drawer 33, Montpelier, VT 05633-7601; 802-828-3286, 802-828-3710 (Fax), 8AM-4PM.

www.bgs.state.vt.us/gsc/pubrec/referen

Note: For records for the past ten years only, contact the Department of Health at 802-863-7300.

Indexing & Storage: Records are available from 1760-1990. New records are available for inquiry immediately. Records are indexed on index cards, inhouse computer.

Searching: The records are open to the public. Include the following in your request-full name, names of parents, mother's maiden name, date of birth, place of birth.

Access by: mail, phone, fax, in person.

Fee & Payment: The search fee is $7.00 per name. Fee payee: VT Vital Records. Prepayment required. Use of credit card is only for expedited service. Personal checks accepted. Credit cards accepted: Mastercard, Visa, AmEx, Discover.

Mail search: Turnaround time: 2-3 days. A self addressed stamped envelope is requested.

Phone search: See expedited service.

Fax search: See expedited service.

In person search: You may view the records for no charge.

Expedited service: Expedited service is available for fax searches. Turnaround time: 1-2 days. Add $5.00 for use of credit card and $15.50 for overnight shipping.

Death Records

Reference & Research, Vital Records, US Rte 2, Drawer 33, Montpelier, VT 05633-7601; 802-828-3286, 8AM-4PM.

www.bgs.state.vt.us/gsc/pubrec/referen

Note: For records up to 10 years old, contact the Department of Health at 802-863-7300.

Indexing & Storage: Records are available from 1760-1990. New records are available for inquiry immediately. Records are indexed on index cards, inhouse computer.

Searching: Records are open to the public. Include the following in your request-full name, date of death, place of death, names of parents.

Access by: mail, phone, in person.

Fee & Payment: The search fee is $7.00 per name. Fee payee: VT Vital Records. Prepayment required. Credit card for expedited service only. Personal checks accepted. No credit cards accepted.

Mail search: Turnaround time: 2-3 days. A self addressed stamped envelope is requested.

Phone search: See expedited service.

In person search: You may view records at no charge.

Marriage Certificates

Reference & Research, Vital Records Section, US Rte 2, Drawer 33, Montpelier, VT 05633-7601; 802-828-3286, 8AM-4PM.

www.bgs.state.vt.us/gsc/pubrec/referen

Note: For records up to 10 years old, contact the VT Department of Health at 802-863-7300.

Indexing & Storage: Records are available from 1760-1990. New records are available for inquiry immediately. Records are indexed on index cards, inhouse computer.

Searching: Records are open. Include the following in your request-names of husband and wife, date of marriage, place or county of marriage, names of parents.

Access by: mail, in person.

Fee & Payment: The search fee is $7.00 per name. Fee payee: VT Vital Records. Prepayment required. Personal checks accepted. No credit cards accepted.

Mail search: Turnaround time: 2-3 days. A self addressed stamped envelope is requested.

In person search: Records may be viewed in person at no charge.

Divorce Records

Research & Reference, Vital Records Section, US Rte 2, Drawer 33, Montpelier, VT 05633-7601; 802-828-3286, 8AM-4PM.

www.bgs.state.vt.us/gsc/pubrec/referen

Note: For records less than 10 years old, contact the VT Department of health at 802-863-7300.

Indexing & Storage: Records are available from 1760-1990. New records are available for inquiry immediately. Records are indexed on index cards, inhouse computer.

Searching: Records are open. Include the following in your request-names of husband and wife, date of divorce, place of divorce.

Access by: mail, in person.

Fee & Payment: The search fee is $7.00 per name. Fee payee: VT Vital Records. Prepayment required. Personal checks accepted. No credit cards accepted.

Mail search: Turnaround time: 2-3 days. A self addressed stamped envelope is requested.

In person search: There is no fee to view records.

Workers' Compensation Records

Labor and Industry, Workers Compensation Division, Drawer 20, Montpelier, VT 05620-3401 (Courier: National Life Bldg, Montpelier, VT 05620); 802-828-2286, 802-828-2195 (Fax), 7:45AM-4:30PM.

www.state.vt.us/labind/wcindex.htm

Indexing & Storage: Records are available from 1995 on. Records prior to 1995 are in the State Archives. New records are available for inquiry immediately. Records are indexed on inhouse computer.

Searching: Must have a signed release from the claimant. You also will get only the employer's first report of injury. Include the following in your request-claimant name, Social Security Number, place of employment at time of accident. The following data is not released: medical records.

Access by: mail, phone, fax, in person.

Fee & Payment: No search fee, copy fee is $.045 per page. Fee payee: State of Vermont. Personal checks accepted. No credit cards accepted.

Mail search: Turnaround time: 2 weeks. A self addressed stamped envelope is requested.

Phone search: No fee for telephone request. They will indicate if there was a first report filed. They will release no additional information.

Fax search: Turnaround time is 2 weeks.

In person search: Turnaround time is while you wait if staff is available.

Driver Records
Driver License Information

Department of Motor Vehicles, DI - Records Unit, 120 State St, Montpelier, VT 05603-0001; 802-828-2050, 802-828-2098 (Fax), 7:45AM-4:30PM.

www.aot.state.vt.us/dmv/dmvhp.htm

Note: This office is closed on Wed. mornings. Ticket information is available from the Vermont Judicial Bureau, PO Box 607, White River Junction, VT 05001, 802-295-8869. There is no charge, but no information is given over the phone.

Indexing & Storage: Records are available for convictions and accidents. Records are sold as 3 year records or as complete (8+ years) records. It takes 5-7 days normally before new records are available for inquiry.

Searching: Written authorization from the subject releases personal information to a requester. Mail or walk-in requesters need the driver's full name and DOB; the license number is optional. Online requesters need only the license number, but the last name and DOB are helpful. The following data is not released: addresses, Social Security Numbers, medical information or personal information (height, weight, sex, eye color, etc.).

Access by: mail, in person, online.

Fee & Payment: Fees: $4.00 for 3 year record; $8.00 for the "complete" record. There is a full charge for a "no record found." Fee payee: Vermont Department of Motor Vehicles. Prepayment required. Personal checks accepted. No credit cards accepted.

Mail search: Turnaround time: 5-7 days. A self addressed stamped envelope is requested.

In person search: Normal turnaround time is while you wait.

Online search: Online access costs $4.00 per 3 year record. The system is called "GovNet." Two methods are offered-single inquiry and batch mode. The system is open 24 hours a day, 7 days a week (except for file maintenance periods). Only the license number is needed when ordering, but it is suggested to submit the name and DOB also.

Other access: The state will sell its license file to approved requesters, but customization is not available.

Accident Reports

Department of Motor Vehicles, Accident Report Section, 120 State St, Montpelier, VT 05603; 802-828-2050, 7:45AM-4PM.

Note: The office is closed Wednesday mornings.

Indexing & Storage: Records are available for 5 years to present. Only records involving damage in excess of $1,000 are reportable. It takes 45 days after the incident before new records are available for inquiry.

Searching: Include the following in your request-full name, date of accident, location of accident. If accident involves a criminal action it may take up to 3 months after accident date to get the report. The following data is not released: Social Security Numbers.

Access by: mail.

Fee & Payment: The fee is $12.00 for the police report and $6.00 for a copy of the individual's report. For insurance information of the accident the fee is $4.00. Fee payee: Vermont Department of Motor Vehicles. Prepayment required. Personal checks accepted. No credit cards accepted.

Mail search: Turnaround time: 3 weeks. A self addressed stamped envelope is requested.

Vehicle Ownership
Vehicle Identification
Boat & Vessel Ownership
Boat & Vessel Registration

Department of Motor Vehicles, Registration & License Information/Records, 120 State St, Montpelier, VT 05603; 802-828-2000, 7:45AM-4:30PM.

www.aot.state.vt.us/dmv/dmvhp.htm

Indexing & Storage: Records are available from 1971-present. Vessel records go back to the late 1970s and are removed after 14 years of inactivity. All motorized boats must be registered. It takes 1-3 weeks before new records are available for inquiry.

Searching: You must have name and DOB or plate # or VIN. To receive personal information, you must include signed release by individual. The following data is not released: Social Security Numbers, residence addresses, bulk information or lists for commercial purposes or medical information.

Access by: mail, in person.

Fee & Payment: Vehicle fees: $4.00 for each group (1-4) of registration records and $15.00 for an ownership (lien) search. There is a full charge for a "no record found." Vessel fees: registration check is $4.00, title search with lien is $7.50. Fee payee: Vermont Department of Motor Vehicles. Prepayment required. Personal checks accepted. No credit cards accepted.

Mail search: Turnaround time: 7-10 days. A self addressed stamped envelope is requested.

In person search: The turnaround time is generally 30 minutes for vehicle records. Vessel records are returned by mail.

Other access: High volume requesters can obtain records via magnetic tape. Bulk release of the database is not available except for statistical purposes. Apply to the Commissioner's Office.

Legislation-Current/Pending
Legislation-Passed

Vermont General Assembly, State House-Legislative Council, 115 State Street, Drawer 33, Montpelier, VT 05633; 802-828-2231, 802-828-2424 (Fax), 8AM-4:30PM.

www.leg.state.vt.us

Indexing & Storage: Records are available from 1940 at Legislative Council. Records are indexed on inhouse computer.

Searching: Include the following in your request-bill number, topic of bill.

Access by: mail, phone, fax, in person, online.

Fee & Payment: There is no fee.

Mail search: Turnaround time: same day. No self addressed stamped envelope is required.

Phone search: Searching is available by phone.

Fax search: Fax searching available.

In person search: No fee for request. A public access terminal is available in the public lobby of the legislature.

Online search: The web site offers access to bill information.

Other access: A subscription service is available for bill text.

Voter Registration
Records not maintained by a state level agency.

Note: There is no statewide database. All records are kept at the municipal level.

GED Certificates

Department of Education, GED Testing, 120 State Street, Montpelier, VT 05620; 802-828-5161, 802-828-3146 (Fax), 8AM-4:30PM.

Searching: Include the following in your request-date of birth, Social Security Number, signed release.

Access by: mail, fax, in person.

Fee & Payment: The fee is $3.00 for a transcript copy. Fee payee: Treasurer, State of Vermont. Prepayment required. No credit cards accepted.

Mail search: Turnaround time: 1 week.

Fax search: Same criteria as mail searching.

In person search: Searching is available in person.

Hunting License Information
Fishing License Information
Records not maintained by a state level agency.

Note: They do maintain a central database on computer. Vendors forward records on a yearly basis (July).

Licenses Searchable Online

Accounting Firm #15 .... www.sec.state.vt.us/seek/lrspseek.htm
Acupuncturist #15 .... www.sec.state.vt.us/seek/lrspseek.htm
Appraiser #12 .... www.sec.state.vt.us/seek/lrspseek.htm
Architect #15 .... www.sec.state.vt.us/seek/lrspseek.htm
Auctioneer #15 .... www.sec.state.vt.us/seek/lrspseek.htm
Barber #15 .... www.sec.state.vt.us/seek/lrspseek.htm
Boxing Manager/Promoter #15 .... www.sec.state.vt.us/seek/lrspseek.htm
Chiropractor #15 .... www.sec.state.vt.us/seek/lrspseek.htm
Cosmetologist #15 .... www.sec.state.vt.us/seek/lrspseek.htm
Dental Assistant #15 .... www.sec.state.vt.us/seek/lrspseek.htm
Dental Hygienist #15 .... www.sec.state.vt.us/seek/lrspseek.htm
Dentist #15 .... www.sec.state.vt.us/seek/lrspseek.htm
Dietitian #15 .... www.sec.state.vt.us/seek/lrspseek.htm
Embalmer #12 .... www.sec.state.vt.us/seek/lrspseek.htm
Engineer #15 .... www.sec.state.vt.us/seek/lrspseek.htm
Esthetician #15 .... www.sec.state.vt.us/seek/lrspseek.htm
Funeral Director #12 .... www.sec.state.vt.us/seek/lrspseek.htm
Hearing Aid Dispenser #15 .... www.sec.state.vt.us/seek/lrspseek.htm
Lobbyist #15 .... www.sec.state.vt.us/seek/lbylseek.htm
Manicurist #15 .... www.sec.state.vt.us/seek/lrspseek.htm
Marriage & Family Therapist #15 .... www.sec.state.vt.us/seek/lrspseek.htm
Medical Doctor/Surgeon #15................. www.docboard.org/vt/df/vtsearch.htm
Mental Health Counselor, Clinical #15 ..... www.sec.state.vt.us/seek/lrspseek.htm
Naturopathic Physician #15 .... www.sec.state.vt.us/seek/lrspseek.htm
Notary Public #13 .... www.sec.state.vt.us/seek/not_seek.htm
Notary Public #15 .... www.sec.state.vt.us/seek/not_seek.htm
Nurse/Nurse Practitioner/LNA #15 .... www.sec.state.vt.us/seek/lrspseek.htm
Nursing Home Administrator #15 .... www.sec.state.vt.us/seek/lrspseek.htm
Occupational Therapist #15 .... www.sec.state.vt.us/seek/lrspseek.htm
Optician #15 .... www.sec.state.vt.us/seek/lrspseek.htm
Optometrist #15 .... www.sec.state.vt.us/seek/lrspseek.htm
Osteopathic Physician #15 .... www.sec.state.vt.us/seek/lrspseek.htm
Pharmacist #15 .... www.sec.state.vt.us/seek/lrspseek.htm
Pharmacy #15 .... www.sec.state.vt.us/seek/lrspseek.htm
Physical Therapist/Assistant #15........... www.sec.state.vt.us/seek/lrspseek.htm
Physician Assistant #15 .... www.docboard.org/vt/df/vtsearch.htm
Podiatrist #15 .... www.docboard.org/vt/df/vtsearch.htm
Private Investigator #15...................... www.sec.state.vt.us/seek/lrspseek.htm
Psychoanalyst #15 .... www.sec.state.vt.us/seek/lrspseek.htm
Psychologist #15 .... www.sec.state.vt.us/seek/lrspseek.htm
Psychotherapist #15 .... www.sec.state.vt.us/seek/lrspseek.htm
Public Accountant-CPA #15 .... www.sec.state.vt.us/seek/lrspseek.htm
Racing Promoter #15 .... www.sec.state.vt.us/seek/lrspseek.htm
Radiologic Technologist #15 .... www.sec.state.vt.us/seek/lrspseek.htm
Real Estate Appraiser #12................... www.sec.state.vt.us/seek/lrspseek.htm
Real Estate Broker/Agent #12 .... www.sec.state.vt.us/seek/lrspseek.htm
Real Estate Salesperson #12 .... www.sec.state.vt.us/seek/lrspseek.htm
Security Guard #15 .... www.sec.state.vt.us/seek/lrspseek.htm
Social Worker, Clinical #15................... www.sec.state.vt.us/seek/lrspseek.htm
Surveyor #15................................... www.sec.state.vt.us/seek/lrspseek.htm
Tattooist #15 .... www.sec.state.vt.us/seek/lrspseek.htm
Veterinarian #15 .... www.sec.state.vt.us/seek/lrspseek.htm

Licensing Quick Finder

Accounting Firm #15 802-828-2363
Acupuncturist #15 802-828-2373
Alcohol & Drug Abuse Counselor #18 ...802-334-4066
Appraiser #12 802-828-3183
Architect #15................................... 802-828-2373
Armed Courier #15 802-828-2837
Asbestos Abatement Contractor/Worker #19
.... 802-863-7231

Attorney #02 802-828-3281
Auctioneer #15................................. 802-828-3183
Barber #15...................................... 802-828-2837
Boiler & Pressure Vessel Inspector #09
.... 802-828-2107
Boxing Manager/Promoter #15 802-828-2363
Chiropractor #15 802-828-2363

Commercial Driving Instructor/School #11
.... 802-828-2114
Cosmetologist #15 802-828-2363
Dealer/Repairer Weighing & Measuring Devices #04
.... 802-244-2436
Dental Assistant #15 802-828-2363
Dental Hygienist #15 802-828-2363
Dentist #15 802-828-2363

Dietitian #15 802-828-2363	Milk & Cream Tester #04 802-244-4510	Racing Promoter #15 802-828-2363
Driver Training Instructor #11 802-828-2114	Naturopathic Physician #15 802-828-2363	Radiologic Technologist #15 802-828-2363
Electrician #08 802-828-2107	Notary Public #15 802-828-2464	Real Estate Appraiser #12 802-828-3183
Embalmer #12 802-828-3183	Nurse/Nurse Practitioner/LNA #15 802-828-2396	Real Estate Broker/Agent #12 802-828-3228
Emergency Care Attendant #07 802-863-7310	Nursing Home Administrator #15 802-828-2363	Real Estate Salesperson #12 802-828-3228
Emergency Medical Technician #07 802-863-7310	Occupational Therapist #15 802-828-2363	Retail Liquor #10 802-828-2339
Engineer #15 802-828-2363	Optician #15 802-828-2363	School Guidance Counselor #06 802-828-2445
Esthetician #15 802-828-2363	Optometrist #15 802-828-2373	School Librarian/Media Specialist #06 ... 802-828-2445
Fire Detection System Installer/Dealer #08	Osteopathic Physician #15 802-828-2373	School Principal #06 802-828-2445
.... 802-828-2107	Peddler #15 802-828-2363	School Superintendent #06 802-828-2445
Funeral Director #12 802-828-3183	Pediatrist #15 802-828-2673	Securities Broker/Dealer #05 802-828-3420
Guard Dog Handler #15 802-828-2363	Pesticide Applicator #04 802-244-2431	Securities Sales Representative #05 802-828-3420
Hearing Aid Dispenser #15 802-828-2363	Pharmacist #15 802-828-2363	Security Guard #15 802-828-2363
Insurance Adjuster #05 802-828-3303	Pharmacy #15 802-828-2363	Social Worker, Clinical #15 802-828-2363
Insurance Agent/Consultant #05 802-828-3303	Photographer, Itinerant #15 802-828-2363	Surveyor #15 802-828-3183
Insurance Appraiser #05 802-828-3303	Physical Therapist/Assistant #15 802-828-2363	Tattooist #15 802-828-2363
Insurance Broker #05 802-828-3303	Physician Assistant #15 802-828-2673	Teacher #06 802-828-2445
Investment Advisor #05 802-828-3420	Plumber #08 802-828-2107	Vehicle Dealer #11 802-828-2038
Issuer Agent #05 802-828-3420	Podiatrist #15 802-828-2363	Vendor-Itinerant #15 802-828-2363
Lightning Rod Installer/Dealer #08 802-828-2107	Polygraph Examiner #03 802-244-8781	Veterinarian #15 802-828-2363
Livestock Dealer #04 802-828-2421	Private Investigator #15 802-828-2363	Vocational Education Teacher #06 802-828-2445
Lobbyist #15 802-828-2464	Psychoanalyst #15 802-828-2373	Waste Water Treatment Facility Operator #01
Lottery Retailer #16 802-479-5686	Psychologist #15 802-828-2373	 802-241-3822
Manicurist #15 802-828-2363	Psychotherapist #15 802-828-2363	Well Driller #01 802-241-3400
Marriage & Family Therapist #15 802-828-2363	Public Accountant-CPA #15 802-828-2363	Wholesale Liquor #10 802-828-2339
Meat Inspection Laboratory #04 802-244-4510	Public Adjuster #05 802-828-3303	
Medical Doctor/Surgeon #15 802-828-2673	Race Driver/Track Personnel #15 802-828-2363	
Mental Health Counselor, Clinical #15 ... 802-828-2363	Racing #17 802-786-5050	

Licensing Agency Information

01 Agency of Natural Resources, 103 S Main St, The Sewing Bldg, Waterbury, VT 05671-0405; 802-241-3822, Fax: 802-241-2596.

02 Board of Bar Examiners, 109 State St, Montpelier, VT 05609-0702; 802-828-3281, Fax: 802-828-3457.

www.state.vt.us/courts

03 Commission of Public Safety, 103 S Main St, Waterbury State Complex, Waterbury, VT 05671-2101; 802-244-8781, Fax: 802-244-1106.

04 Department of Agriculture, Laboratories & Consumer Assurance, 103 S Main St, Waterbury, VT 05671; 802-244-4510, Fax: 802-241-3008.

www.clt.agr.state.us

05 Department of Banking, 89 Main St City Ctr, Drawer 20, Montpelier, VT 05620-3101; 802-828-3420, Fax: 802-828-2896.

www.state.vt.us/bis

06 Department of Education, 120 State St, Montpelier, VT 05620-2501; 802-828-2445, Fax: 802-828-5107.

07 Department of Health, PO Box 70 (108 Cherry St), Burlington, VT 05402; 802-863-7310, Fax: 802-863-7577.

08 Department of Labor & Industry, Drawer 20, National Life Bldg, Montpelier, VT 05620-3401; 802-828-2107, Fax: 802-828-2195.

www.state.vt.us/labind

09 Department of Labor & Industry, 372 Hurricane Ln #102, Williston, VT 05495-2080; 802-658-2199, Fax: 802-863-7410.

10 Department of Liquor Control, PO Drawer 20, Montpelier, VT 05620-4501; 802-828-2339, Fax: 802-828-2803.

www.sec.state.vt.us

11 Department of Motor Vehicles, 120 State St, Montpelier, VT 05603; 802-828-2114, Fax: 802-828-2092.

www.aot.state.vt.us/dmv/dmvhp.htm

12 Real Estate Commission, 81 Riverside St. Heritage Bldg, Montpelier, VT 05609-1106; 802-828-3228, Fax: 802-828-2368.

www.sec.state.vt.us

Direct URL to search licenses: www.sec. state.vt.us/seek/lrspseek.htm You can search online using last name; first name optional. Also, search profession lists.

15 Secretary of State, 109 State St, Montpelier, VT 05609; 802-828-2673, Fax: 802-828-5450.

www.vtprofessionals.org

Direct URL to search licenses: www.sec. state.vt.us/seek/lrspseek.htm You can search online using name.

16 Lottery Commission, PO Box 420 (PO Box 420), South Barre, VT 05670-0429; 802-479-5686, Fax: 802-479-4294.

17 Racing Commission, 128 Merchants Row, Rutland, VT 05701; 802-786-5059, Fax: 802-786-5051.

18 Alcohol & Drug Abuse Certification Board, PO Box 562, Newport, VT 05885; 802-334-4066.

19 Department of Health, Environmental Health, PO Box 70, Burlington, VT 05402; 802-863-7231.

The following list indicates the district and division name for each county in the state. If the district or division name of the bankruptcy court is different from the civil/criminal court, it appears in parentheses.

County/Court Cross Reference

Addison .... Rutland
Bennington .... Rutland
Caledonia .... Burlington (Rutland)
Chittenden .... Burlington (Rutland)
Essex .... Burlington (Rutland)
Franklin .... Burlington (Rutland)
Grand Isle .... Burlington (Rutland)

Lamoille.. Burlington (Rutland)
Orange.. Rutland
Orleans.. Burlington (Rutland)
Rutland.. Rutland
Washington................................... Burlington (Rutland)
Windham... Rutland
Windsor... Rutland

US District Court

District of Vermont

Burlington Division Clerk's Office, PO Box 945, Burlington, VT 05402-0945 (Courier Address: Room 506, 11 Elmwood Ave, Burlington, VT 05401), 802-951-6301.

www.vtd.uscourts.gov

Counties: Caledonia, Chittenden, Essex, Franklin, Grand Isle, Lamoille, Orleans, Washington. However, cases from all counties in the state are assigned randomly to either Burlington or Brattleboro. Brattleboro is a hearing location only, not listed here.

Indexing & Storage: Cases are indexed by defendant and plaintiff as well as by case number. New cases are available in the index 1 working day after filing date. Both computer and card indexes are maintained. New cases filed January 1, 1991 to present are on the automated in house system. Pre-1991 cases are indexed on microfiche or microfilm. Open records are located at this court.

Fee & Payment: The fee is $15.00 per item (one party name or case number). Payment may be made by money order, cashier check, personal check. Prepayment is required. Payee: Clerk, US District Court. Certification fee: $5.00 per document. Copy fee: $.50 per page. You are allowed to make your own copies. These copies cost $.50 per page.

Phone Search: Only general information which can be accessed by computer will be released over the phone. An automated voice case information service (VCIS) is not available.

Mail Search: Always enclose a stamped self addressed envelope.

In Person Search: In person searching is available.

PACER: Sign-up number is 800-676-6856. Access fee is $.60 per minute. Toll-free access: 800-263-9396. Local access: 802-951-6623. Case records are available back to January 1991. Records are never purged. New records are available online after 1 day.

Rutland Division PO Box 607, Rutland, VT 05702-0607 (Courier Address: 151 West St, Rutland, VT 05701), 802-773-0245.

www.vtd.uscourts.gov

Counties: Addison, Bennington, Orange, Rutland, Windsor, Windham. However, cases from all counties in the state are randomly assigned to either Burlington or Brattleboro. Rutland is a hearing location only, not listed here.

Indexing & Storage: Cases are indexed by defendant and plaintiff as well as by case number. New cases are available in the index 1 day after filing date. A computer index is maintained. New cases filed January 1, 1991 to present are on the automated in house system. Pre-1991 cases are indexed on microfiche or microfilm. Open records are located at this court. There is no judge sitting in Rutland itself, but one is in Brattleboro.

Fee & Payment: The fee is $15.00 per item (one party name or case number). Payment may be made by money order, cashier check, personal check. Prepayment is required. Payee: Clerk, US District Court. Certification fee: $5.00 per document. Copy fee: $.50 per page. You are allowed to make your own copies. These copies cost $.50 per page.

Phone Search: Only docket information is available by phone. An automated voice case information service (VCIS) is not available.

Mail Search: Always enclose a stamped self addressed envelope.

In Person Search: In person searching is available.

PACER: Sign-up number is 800-676-6856. Access fee is $.60 per minute. Toll-free access: 800-263-9396. Local access: 802-951-6623. Case records are available back to January 1991. Records are never purged. New records are available online after 1 day.

US Bankruptcy Court

District of Vermont

Rutland Division PO Box 6648, Rutland, VT 05702-6648 (Courier Address: 67 Merchants Row, Rutland, VT 05701), 802-776-2000, Fax: 802-776-2020.

www.vtb.uscourts.gov

Counties: All counties in Vermont.

Indexing & Storage: Cases are indexed by debtor and creditors as well as by case number. New cases are available in the index immediately after filing date. A computer index is maintained. Open records are located at this court.

Fee & Payment: The fee is $15.00 per item (one party name or case number). Payment may be made by money order, cashier check, personal check, Visa or Mastercard. Prepayment is required. Payee: US Bankruptcy Court. Certification fee: $5.00 per document. Copy fee: $.50 per page.

Phone Search: Docket information is available by phone. An automated voice case information service (VCIS) is available. Call VCIS at 800-260-9956 or 802-776-2007.

Fax Search: Will accept fax searches with credit card. Copy fees apply to faxed dockets.

Mail Search: A stamped self addressed envelope is not required.

In Person Search: In person searching is available.

PACER: Sign-up number is 800-676-6856. Access fee is $.60 per minute. Toll-free access: 800-260-9968. Local access: 802-776-2006. Case records are available back to 1992 (limited information prior). Records are never purged. New civil records are available online after 1 day. PACER is available on the Internet at http://pacer.vtb.uscourts.gov.

Court	Jurisdiction	No. of Courts	How Organized
Superior Courts*	General	11	14 Counties
District Courts*	Limited	11	3 Circuits
Combined Courts*		3	
Probate Courts*	Probate	18	
Family Courts	Special	14	14 Counties
Environmental Court	Special	1	

* Profiled in this Sourcebook.

	CIVIL								
Court	Tort	Contract	Real Estate	Min. Claim	Max. Claim	Small Claims	Estate	Eviction	Domestic Relations
Superior Courts*	X	X	X	$0	No Max	$3500		X	
District Courts*									
Probate Courts*							X		
Family Courts									X

	CRIMINAL				
Court	Felony	Misdemeanor	DWI/DUI	Preliminary Hearing	Juvenile
Superior Courts*					
District Courts*	X	X	X	X	
Probate Courts*					
Family Courts					X

ADMINISTRATION

Administrative Office of Courts, Court Administrator, 109 State St, Montpelier, VT, 05609-0701; 802-828-3278, Fax: 802-828-3457. www.state.vt.us/courts

COURT STRUCTURE

As of September, 1996, all small claims came under the jurisdiction of Superior Court, the court of general jurisdiction. All counties have a diversion program in which first offenders go through a process that includes a letter of apology, community service, etc. and, after 2 years, the record is expunged. These records are never released.

There is one Probate Court per county except in the four southern counties (Bennington, Rutland, Windsor, and Windham) which have two each.

The Vermont Traffic and Municipal Ordinance Bureau has jurisdiction over traffic, municipal ordinance, and fish and game.

ONLINE ACCESS

There is no online computer access to the public; however, some courts offer calendar data over the Internet.

ADDITIONAL INFORMATION

There are statewide certification and copy fees, as follows: Certification Fee - $5.00 per document plus copy fee; Copy Fee - $.25 per page with a $1.00 minimum.

📖 📖 📖 📖 📖 📖 📖

Addison County

Superior Court 7 Mahady Ct, Middlebury, VT 05753; 802-388-7741. Hours: 8:30AM-4:30PM (EST). *Civil, Eviction, Small Claims.*

Civil Records: Access: Mail, in person. Only the court conducts in person searches; visitors may not. No search fee. Required to search: name, years to search. Civil cases indexed by defendant, plaintiff. Civil records on index cards and recording books. **General Information:** No sealed or unserved records released. Turnaround time 2-3

days. Copy fee: $.25 per page. Certification fee: $5.00. Fee payee: Addison County Clerk. Personal checks accepted. Credit cards accepted. Prepayment is required.

District Court 7 Mahady Ct, Middlebury, VT 05753; 802-388-4237. Hours: 8AM-4:30PM (EST). *Felony, Misdemeanor.* **Criminal Records:** Access: Phone, mail, in person. Only the court conducts in person searches; visitors may not. Search fee: $1.00 per name. Required to search: name, years to search, DOB. Criminal records on

computer since mid 1991; prior on dockets and index cards. **General Information:** No adoptions, juvenile, sealed, or expunged records released. Turnaround time up to 1 week. Copy fee: $.25 per page. Certification fee: $5.00. Fee payee: Addison District Court. Personal checks accepted. Prepayment is required.

Probate Court 7 Mahady Court, Middlebury, VT 05753; 802-388-2612. Hours: 8AM-4:30PM (EST). *Probate.*

Bennington County

Superior Court 207 South St, PO Box 4157, Bennington, VT 05201; 802-447-2700; Fax: 802-447-2703. Hours: 8AM-4:30PM (EST). *Civil, Eviction, Small Claims.*

Civil Records: Access: Phone, mail, in person. Both court and visitors may perform in person searches. No search fee. Required to search: name, years to search. Civil cases indexed by defendant, plaintiff. Civil records on computer from 1989, index from 1968. **General Information:** No deposition, adoption, juvenile, sealed or expunged records released. Turnaround time 2-3 days. Copy fee: $.25 per page. Certification fee: $5.00. Fee payee: Bennington County. Personal checks accepted. Prepayment is required.

District Court 1 Veterans Memorial Dr, Bennington, VT 05201; 802-447-2727; Fax: 802-447-2750. Hours: 7:45AM-4:30PM (EST). *Felony, Misdemeanor.* **Criminal Records:** Access: Phone, mail, in person. Both court and visitors may perform in person searches. No search fee. Required to search: name, years to search; also helpful-DOB. Criminal records on index cards and docket books. **General Information:** No sealed, diversion case records released. SASE requested. Turnaround time varies. Copy fee: $.25 per page. $1.00 minimum. Certification fee: $5.00. Fee payee: District Court or Vermont District Court. Personal checks accepted. Prepayment is required.

Probate Court-Bennington District 207 South St, PO Box 65, Bennington, VT 05201; 802-447-2705; Fax: 802-447-2703 (Attn: Probate Court). Hours: 9AM-Noon, 1:30-4PM *Probate.*

Probate Court-Manchester District PO Box 446, Manchester, VT 05254; 802-362-1410. Hours: 8AM-Noon, 1-4:20PM *Probate.*

Caledonia County

Superior Court Box 4129, St Johnsbury, VT 05819; 802-748-6600; Fax: 802-748-6603. Hours: 8AM-4:30PM 30PM (EST). *Civil, Eviction, Small Claims.*

Civil Records: Access: Phone, fax, mail, in person. Only the court conducts in person searches; visitors may not. No search fee. Required to search: name, years to search. Civil cases indexed by defendant, plaintiff. Civil records on computer from 1992, in archives before 1985, index from 1985, all other records on index cards. **General Information:** No adoption, juvenile, sealed or expunged records released. SASE requested. Turnaround time 1 week. Copy fee: Superior Court $1.00 minimum; Family Court $.25 per page, $1.00 minimum. Certification fee: $5.00 plus $.25 per page. Fee payee: Caledonia Superior Court. Personal checks accepted. Prepayment is required. Fax notes: $2.00 per page.

District Court 2176 Portland St, St Johnsbury, VT 05819; 802-748-6610; Fax: 802-748-6603. Hours: 8AM-4:30PM (EST). *Felony, Misdemeanor.*

Note: This is a temporary address, prior was 27 Main St **Criminal Records:** Access: Fax, mail, in person. Both court and visitors may perform in person searches. No search fee. Required to search: name, years to search; also helpful-DOB. Criminal records on computer since 1991, prior on index cards. **General Information:** No adoptions, juvenile, sealed or expunged records released. SASE not required. Turnaround time less than a week. Copy fee: $.25 per page. $1.00 minimum. Certification fee: $5.00. Fee payee: Caledonia District Court. Personal checks accepted. Public access terminal is available. Fax notes: $2.00 per page.

Probate Court 27 Main St, PO Box 406, St Johnsbury, VT 05819; 802-748-6605; Fax: 802-748-6603. Hours: 8AM-4:30PM (EST). *Probate.*

Chittenden County

Superior Court 175 Main St.(PO Box 187), Burlington, VT 05402; 802-863-3467. Hours: 8AM-4:30PM (EST). *Civil, Eviction, Small Claims.*

http://vbimail.chaplain.edu.superior

Civil Records: Access: Phone, mail, in person. Only the court conducts in person searches; visitors may not. No search fee. Required to search: name, years to search. Civil cases indexed by defendant, plaintiff. Civil records on computer from 1983, small claims since 1996, prior records on books from 1800s. **General Information:** No adoption, juvenile, sealed or expunged records released. Turnaround time 1 week. Copy fee: $.25 per page. $1.00 minimum. Certification fee: $5.00. Fee payee: Chittenden County Superior Court. Personal checks accepted. Prepayment is required.

District Court 32 Cherry St #300, Burlington, VT 05401; 802-651-1800. Hours: 8AM-4:30PM (EST). *Felony, Misdemeanor.* **Criminal Records:** Access: Mail, in person. Both court and visitors may perform in person searches. No search fee. Required to search: name, years to search; also helpful-DOB. Criminal records on new computer from 6/90, on old computer from 6/85 to 06/90, books by alpha name from 12/69 to 1980, on index cards from 1970. **General Information:** No adoption, juvenile, sealed or expunged records released. Turnaround time 1-2 days. Copy fee: $.25 per page. Certification fee: $5.00. Fee payee: Vermont District Court. Personal checks accepted. Prepayment is required.

Probate Court PO Box 511, Burlington, VT 05402; 802-651-1518. Hours: 8AM-4:30PM (EST). *Probate.*

Essex County

District & Superior Court Box 75, Guildhall, VT 05905; 802-676-3910; Fax: 802-676-3463. Hours: 8AM-4:30PM (EST). *Felony, Misdemeanor, Civil, Eviction, Small Claims.*

Civil Records: Access: Phone, fax, mail, in person. Only the court conducts in person searches; visitors may not. No search fee. Required to search: name, years to search. Civil cases indexed by defendant, plaintiff. Civil records indexed from 1974. **Criminal Records:** Access: Phone, fax, mail, in person. Only the court conducts in person searches; visitors may not. No search fee. Required to search: name, years to search, DOB. Criminal records indexed from 1974. **General Information:** No adoptions, juvenile, sealed or expunged records released. Turnaround time 1 week. Copy fee: $.25 per page. $1.00 minimum. Certification fee: $5.00. Fee payee: Depends on court(superior or district). Only cashiers checks and money orders accepted. Prepayment is required. Fax notes: $1.00 per page.

Probate Court PO Box 426, Island Pond, VT 05846; 802-723-4770. Hours: 8:30AM-Noon, 1-3:30PM (EST). *Probate.*

Franklin County

Superior Court Box 808 Church St, St Albans, VT 05478; 802-524-3863; Fax: 802-524-7996. Hours: 8AM-4:30PM (EST). *Civil, Eviction, Small Claims.*

Civil Records: Access: Phone, fax, mail, in person. Only the court conducts in person searches; visitors may not. No search fee. Required to search: name, years to search. Civil cases indexed by defendant, plaintiff. Civil records on computer since 1996; prior on index cards from 1840. **General Information:** No adoption, juvenile, sealed or expunged records released. SASE required. Turnaround time 1 week. Copy fee: $.25 per page. $1.00 minimum. Certification fee: $5.00. Fee payee: Franklin Superior Court. Personal checks accepted. Prepayment is required. Fax notes: $2.00 per page.

District Court 36 Lake St, St Albans, VT 05478; 802-524-7997; Fax: 802-524-7946. Hours: 8AM-4:30PM (EST). *Felony, Misdemeanor.* **Criminal Records:** Access: Phone, mail, in person. Only the court conducts in person searches; visitors may not. No search fee. Required to search: name, years to search; also helpful-DOB, SSN. Criminal records on computer since 1987. **General Information:** No adoption, juvenile, sealed or expunged records released. Turnaround time 7-10 days. Copy fee: $.25 per page. Certification fee: $5.00. Fee payee: Vermont District Court. Personal checks accepted. Prepayment is required.

Franklin Probate Court 17 Church St, St Albans, VT 05478; 802-524-4112. Hours: 8AM-Noon, 1-4:30PM (EST). *Probate.*

Grand Isle County

District & Superior Court PO Box 7, North Hero, VT 05474; 802-372-8350; Fax: 802-372-3221. Hours: 8AM-4:30PM (EST). *Felony, Misdemeanor, Civil, Eviction, Small Claims.*

Civil Records: Access: Phone, fax, mail, in person. Both court and visitors may perform in person searches. No search fee. Required to search: name, years to search. Civil cases indexed by defendant, plaintiff. Civil records on computer from 1990, on index 1970. **Criminal Records:** Access: Phone, fax, mail, in person. Both court and visitors may perform in person searches. No search fee. Required to search: name, years to search; also helpful-DOB, SSN. Criminal records on computer from 1990, on index from 1979. **General Information:** No adoption, juvenile, sealed or expunged records released. Turnaround time 1-2 days. Copy fee: $.25 per page. $1.00 minimum. Certification fee: $5.00. Fee payee: Grand Isle Superior or District Court. Personal checks accepted. Prepayment is required. Fax notes: $.25 per page.

Probate Court PO Box 7, North Hero, VT 05474; 802-372-8350; Fax: 802-372-3221. Hours: 8AM-4:30PM (EST). *Probate.*

Lamoille County

Superior Court Box 490, Hyde Park, VT 05655; 802-888-2207. Hours: 8AM-4:30PM (EST). *Civil, Eviction, Small Claims.*

Civil Records: Access: Mail, in person. Only the court conducts in person searches; visitors may not. No search fee. Required to search: name, years to search. Civil cases indexed by defendant, plaintiff. Civil records on computer from 1989, index from 1970s. **General Information:** No adoption, juvenile, sealed or expunged records released. SASE required. Turnaround time 1 week. Copy fee: $.25 per page. $1.00 minimum. Certification fee: $5.00. Fee payee: Lamoille Superior Court. Personal checks accepted.

District Court PO Box 489, Hyde Park, VT 05655-0489; 802-888-3887; Fax: 802-888-2591.

Hours: 8AM-4:30PM (EST). *Felony, Misdemeanor.* **Criminal Records:** Access: Fax, mail, in person. Only the court conducts in person searches; visitors may not. No search fee. Required to search: name, DOB; also helpful-years to search. Criminal records on computer since 06/88; prior on index cards. **General Information:** No adoption, juvenile, sealed or expunged records released. SASE required. Turnaround time 3 days if record on-site, 1 week if off-site. Copy fee: $.25 per page. $1.00 minimum. Certification fee: $5.00. Fee payee: Vermont District Court. Personal checks accepted. Prepayment is required. Fax notes: No fee to fax results. They will only fax returns to toll free calls.

Probate Court PO Box 102, Hyde Park, VT 05655-0102; 802-888-3306; Fax: 802-888-1347. Hours: 8AM-12:30, 1-4:30PM (EST). *Probate.*

Orange County

District & Superior Court 5 Court St, Chelsea, VT 05038-9746; 802-685-4870; Fax: 802-685-3246. Hours: 8AM-4:30PM (EST). *Felony, Misdemeanor, Civil, Eviction, Small Claims.*

Civil Records: Access: Fax, mail, in person. Only the court conducts in person searches; visitors may not. No search fee. Required to search: name, years to search; also helpful-address. Civil cases indexed by defendant, plaintiff. Civil records on computer from 7/94, on index from 1967. **Criminal Records:** Access: Phone, fax, mail, in person. Only the court conducts in person searches; visitors may not. No search fee. Required to search: name, years to search, DOB; also helpful-address. Criminal records on computer from 1990, on index from 1967. **General Information:** No adoption, juvenile, sealed or expunged records released. Turnaround time 1 week. Copy fee: $.25 per page. $1.00 minimum. Certification fee: $5.00. Fee payee: Clerk of Court. Personal checks accepted. Prepayment is required. Fax notes: $1.00 per page.

Probate Court-Orange District 5 Court Street, Chelsea, VT 05038-9746; 802-685-4610; Fax: 802-685-3246. Hours: 8AM-Noon, 1-4:30PM (EST). *Probate.*

Note: The Bradford and Randolph Districts were consolidated into this one probate court 6/1/1994.

Orleans County

Superior Court 247 Main St, Newport, VT 05855-5099; 802-334-3344; Fax: 802-334-3385. Hours: 8AM-4:30PM (EST). *Civil, Eviction, Small Claims.*

Civil Records: Access: Phone, fax, mail, in person. Only the court conducts in person searches; visitors may not. No search fee. Required to search: name; also helpful-years to search. Civil cases indexed by defendant, plaintiff. Civil records on computer since 1994; prior records on index from 1800s. **General Information:** No juvenile records released. SASE required. Turnaround time 1 week. Copy fee: $.25 per page. $1.00 minimum. Certification fee: $5.00. Fee payee: Orleans Superior Court. Personal checks accepted. Prepayment is required. Fax notes: $2.00 per page.

District Court 217 Main St, Newport, VT 05855; 802-334-3325. Hours: 8AM-4:30PM (EST). *Felony, Misdemeanor.* **Criminal Records:** Access: Phone, mail, in person. Both court and visitors may perform in person searches. No search fee. Required to search: name, years to search; also helpful-DOB. Criminal records on computer since

01/91; prior on index cards back to 1971. No search requests received by phone will be conducted on Tuesdays. **General Information:** No adoption, juvenile, sealed or expunged records released. SASE required. Turnaround time 1 week. Copy fee: $.25 per page. $1.00 minimum. Certification fee: $5.00. Fee payee: District Court of Vermont. Personal checks accepted. Prepayment is required.

Probate Court 247 Main St, Newport, VT 05855; 802-334-3366. Hours: 8AM-Noon, 1-4:30PM (EST). *Probate.*

Rutland County

Superior Court 83 Center St, Rutland, VT 05701; 802-775-4394. Hours: 8AM-4:30PM (EST). *Civil, Eviction, Small Claims.*

Civil Records: Access: Mail, in person. Only the court conducts in person searches; visitors may not. No search fee. Required to search: name, years to search. Civil cases indexed by defendant, plaintiff. Civil records on computer from 1987, on index from late 1700s. **General Information:** No adoption, juvenile, sealed or expunged records released. SASE required. Turnaround time 1 week. Copy fee: $.25 per page. $1.00 minimum. Certification fee: $5.00. Fee payee: Rutland Superior Court. Personal checks accepted. Prepayment is required.

District Court 92 State St, Rutland, VT 05701-2886; 802-786-5880. Hours: 8AM-4:30PM (EST). *Felony, Misdemeanor.* **Criminal Records:** Access: Phone, mail, in person. Both court and visitors may perform in person searches. No search fee. Required to search: name, years to search, DOB; also helpful-SSN. Criminal records on computer since 1985. **General Information:** No sealed, expunged records released. SASE required. Turnaround time 1 week. Copy fee: $.25 per page. $1.00 minimum. Certification fee: $5.00. Fee payee: District Court of Vermont. Personal checks accepted. Public access terminal is available.

Probate Court-Fair Haven District 3 North Park Place, Fair Haven, VT 05743; 802-265-3380. Hours: 8AM-4PM (EST). *Probate.*

Probate Court-Rutland District 83 Center St, Rutland, VT 05701; 802-775-0114. Hours: 8AM-4:30PM (EST). *Probate.*

Washington County

Superior Court 65 State St, Montpelier, VT 05602-3594; 802-828-2091. Hours: 8AM-4:30PM (EST). *Civil, Eviction, Small Claims.*

Civil Records: Access: Phone, mail, in person. Only the court conducts in person searches; visitors may not. No search fee. Required to search: name, years to search; also helpful-address. Civil cases indexed by defendant, plaintiff. Civil records on computer from 1987, archives from 1900s. **General Information:** No adoption, juvenile or expunged records released. SASE requested. Turnaround time 1-2 days. Copy fee: $.25 per page. $1.00 minimum. Certification fee: $5.00. Fee payee: Washington County Superior Court. Personal checks accepted.

District Court 255 N Main, Barre, VT 05641; 802-479-4252. Hours: 8AM-4:30PM (EST). *Felony, Misdemeanor.* **Criminal Records:** Access: Phone, mail, in person. Both court and visitors may perform in person searches. No search fee. Required to search: name, years to search; also helpful-DOB. Criminal records on computer since 1989; prior records in index form 1970s. **General Information:** No adoption, juvenile, sealed or

expunged records released. SASE requested. Turnaround time 3-5 days. Copy fee: $.25 per page. $1.00 minimum. Certification fee: $5.00. Fee payee: Washington District Court. Personal checks accepted.

Probate Court 10 Elm Street, Montpelier, VT 05601; 802-828-3405. Hours: 8AM-Noon, 1-4:30PM M-Th; 8AM-Noon, 1-4PM F (EST). *Probate.*

Windham County

Superior Court Box 207, Newfane, VT 05345; 802-365-7979; Fax: 802-365-4360. Hours: 9AM-4PM (EST). *Civil, Eviction, Small Claims.*

Civil Records: Access: Phone, fax, mail, in person. Both court and visitors may perform in person searches. No search fee. Required to search: name, years to search. Civil cases indexed by defendant, plaintiff. Civil records on computer from 1994, on index from 1919. Fax available only in emergency. **General Information:** No adoption, juvenile, sealed or expunged records released. SASE required. Turnaround time 1-2 days. Copy fee: $.25 per page. $1.00 minimum. Certification fee: $5.00. Fee payee: Windham Superior Court. Personal checks accepted. Prepayment is required. Fax notes: No fee to fax results.

District Court 30 Putney Rd, Brattleboro, VT 05301; 802-257-2800; Fax: 802-257-2853. Hours: 8AM-4:30PM (EST). *Felony, Misdemeanor.* **Criminal Records:** Access: Phone, fax, mail, in person. Both court and visitors may perform in person searches. No search fee. Required to search: name, years to search; also helpful-address, DOB, SSN. Criminal records on computer since 1990; prior on index cards and docket books. **General Information:** No adoption, juvenile, sealed or expunged records released. SASE requested. Turnaround time 5-7 days. Copy fee: $.25 per page. Certification fee: $5.00. Fee payee: Vermont District Court. Personal checks accepted. Prepayment is required. Fax notes: $.25 per page.

Probate Court - Marlboro District PO Box 523, Brattleboro, VT 05302; 802-257-2898. Hours: 8AM-Noon, 1-4:30PM (EST). *Probate.*

Probate Court - Westminster District PO Box 47, Bellows Falls, VT 05101; 802-463-3019. Hours: 8AM-Noon,1-4:30PM (EST). *Probate.*

Windsor County

Superior Court Box 458, Woodstock, VT 05091; 802-457-2121; Fax: 802-457-3446. Hours: 8AM-4:30PM (EST). *Civil, Eviction, Small Claims.*

Civil Records: Access: Phone, mail, in person. Only the court conducts in person searches; visitors may not. No search fee. Required to search: name, years to search. Civil cases indexed by defendant, plaintiff. Civil records on computer since 1990. **General Information:** No adoption, juvenile, sealed or expunged records released. SASE required. Turnaround time 1-2 weeks. Copy fee: $.25 per page. $1.00 minimum. Certification fee: $5.00. Fee payee: Windsor County Clerk or Windsor Superior Court. Personal checks accepted. Prepayment is required.

District Court Windsor Circuit Unit 1, 82 Railroad Row, White River Junction, VT 05001-1962; 802-295-8865. Hours: 8AM-4:30PM (EST). *Felony, Misdemeanor.* **Criminal Records:** Access: Phone, mail, in person. Only the court conducts in person searches; visitors may not. No search fee. Required to search: name, years to search; also helpful-DOB, SSN. Criminal records on computer from 1989, index from 1968. **General Information:** No adoption, juvenile, sealed or expunged records released. SASE requested. Turnaround time 7 days. Copy fee: $.25 per page. $1.00 minimum. Certification fee: $5.00. Fee payee: Vermont District Court. Personal checks accepted. Prepayment is required.

Probate Court-Hartford District PO Box 275, Woodstock, VT 05091; 802-457-1503; Fax: 802-457-3446. Hours: 8AM-Noon, 1-4:30PM (EST). *Probate.*

Probate Court-Windsor District PO Box 402, North Springfield, VT 05150; 802-886-2284; Fax: 802-886-2285. Hours: 8AM-Noon, 1-4:30PM (EST). *Probate.*

ORGANIZATION   14 counties and 246 towns/cities, 246 recording offices. The recording officer is Town/City Clerk. **There is no county administration in Vermont.** Many towns are so small that their mailing addresses are in different towns. Four towns/cities have the same name as counties—Barre, Newport, Rutland, and St. Albans. The entire state is in the Eastern Time Zone (EST).

REAL ESTATE RECORDS   Most towns/cities will **not** perform real estate searches. Copy fees and certification fees vary. Certified copies are generally very expensive at $6.00 per page total. Deed copies usually cost $2.00 flat.

UCC RECORDS   This has been a **dual filing state** until December 31, 1994. As of January 1, 1995, only consumer goods and real estate related collateral are filed with Town/City Clerks. Most recording offices will perform UCC searches. Use search request form UCC-11. Search fees are usually $10.00 per name, and copy fees vary.

TAX LIEN RECORDS   All federal and state tax liens on personal property and on real property are filed with the Town/City Clerk in the lien/attachment book and indexed in real estate records. Most towns/cities will **not** perform tax lien searches.

OTHER LIENS   Mechanics, local tax, judgment, foreclosure.

Addison County

There is no real estate recording at the county level in Vermont. Determine the town or city in which the property is located.

Addison Town

Town Clerk, 7099 VT Rte 22A, Addison, VT 05491. 802-759-2020. Fax: 802-759-2233.

Albany Town

Town Clerk, P.O. Box 284, Albany, VT 05820-0284. 802-755-6100.

Alburg Town

Town Clerk, P.O. Box 346, Alburg, VT 05440-0346. 802-796-3468. Fax: 802-796-3939.

Andover Town

Town Clerk, 953 Weston-Andover Rd., Andover, VT 05143. 802-875-2765. Fax: 802-875-6647.

Arlington Town

Town Clerk, P.O. Box 304, Arlington, VT 05250. 802-375-2332. Fax: 802-375-6474.

Athens Town

Town Clerk, 56 Brookline Rd., Athens, VT 05143. 802-869-3370.

Bakersfield Town

Town Clerk, Box 203, Bakersfield, VT 05441. 802-827-4495. Fax: 802-527-4495.

Baltimore Town

Town Clerk, 1902 Baltimore Rd., Baltimore, VT 05143. 802-263-5419. Fax: 802-263-9423.

Barnard Town

Town Clerk, P.O. Box 274, Barnard, VT 05031-0274. 802-234-9211.

Barnet Town

Town Clerk, Box 15, Barnet, VT 05821-0015. 802-633-2256. Fax: 802-633-4315.

Barre City

City Clerk, Box 418, Barre, VT 05641. 802-476-0242. Fax: 802-476-0264.

Barre Town

Town Clerk, P.O. Box 124, Websterville, VT 05678-0124. 802-479-9391. Fax: 802-479-9332.

Barton Town

Town Clerk, P.O. Box 657, Barton, VT 05822-1386. 802-525-6222. Fax: 802-525-8856.

Belvidere Town

Town Clerk, RR 1, Box 1062, Belvidere Center, VT 05492. 802-644-2498.

Bennington County

There is no real estate recording at the county level in Vermont. Determine the town or city in which the property is located.

Bennington Town

Town Clerk, 205 South Street, Bennington, VT 05201. 802-442-1043. Fax: 802-442-1068.

Benson Town

Town Clerk, P.O. Box 163, Benson, VT 05731-0163. 802-537-2611. Fax: 802-537-2611.

Berkshire Town

Town Clerk, RFD 1, Box 2560, Enosburg Falls, VT 05450. 802-933-2335.

Berlin Town

Town Clerk, 108 Shed Rd., Berlin, VT 05602. 802-229-9298.

Bethel Town

Town Clerk, RD 2, Box 85, Bethel, VT 05032. 802-234-9722. Fax: 802-234-6840.

Bloomfield Town

Town Clerk, P.O. Box 336, No. Stratford, NH, VT 03590. 802-962-5191. Fax: 802-962-5548.

Bolton Town

Town Clerk, RD 1, Box 445, Waterbury, VT 05676. 802-434-3064. Fax: 802-434-6404.

Bradford Town

Town Clerk, P.O. Box 339, Bradford, VT 05033-0339. 802-222-4727. Fax: 802-222-4728.

Braintree Town

Town Clerk, RD 1, Box 361A, Randolph, VT 05060. 802-728-9787.

Brandon Town

Town Clerk, 49 Center Street, Brandon, VT 05733. 802-247-5721. Fax: 802-247-5481.

Brattleboro Town

Town Clerk, 230 Main Street, Brattleboro, VT 05301-2885. 802-254-4541. Fax: 802-257-2312.

Bridgewater Town

Town Clerk, P.O. Box 14, Bridgewater, VT 05034. 802-672-3334. Fax: 802-672-5395.

Bridport Town

Town Clerk, Box 27, Bridport, VT 05734-0027. 802-758-2483.

Brighton Town

Town Clerk, P.O. Box 377, Island Pond, VT 05846. 802-723-4405. Fax: 802-723-4405.

Bristol Town

Town Clerk, Box 249, Bristol, VT 05443. 802-843-3180. Fax: 802-843-3127.

Brookfield Town

Town Clerk, P.O. Box 463, Brookfield, VT 05036-0463. 802-276-3352. Fax: 802-276-3926.

Brookline Town

Town Clerk, PO Box 403, Brookline, VT 05345. 802-365-4648.

Brownington Town

Town Clerk, 509 Dutton Brook Ln, Orleans, VT 05860. 802-754-8401. Fax: 802-754-8401.

Brunswick Town

Town Clerk, Route 102, RFD 1, Box 470, Guildhall, VT 05905. 802-962-5283.

Burke Town

Town Clerk, P.O. Box 248, West Burke, VT 05871. 802-467-3717. Fax: 802-467-8623.

Burlington City

City Clerk, City Hall, Room 20, 149 Church St., Burlington, VT 05401. 802-865-7135. Fax: 802-865-7014.

Cabot Town

Town Clerk, P.O. Box 36, Cabot, VT 05647-0036. 802-563-2279. Fax: 802-563-2423.

Caledonia County

There is no real estate recording at the county level in Vermont. Determine the town or city in which the property is located.

Calais Town

Town Clerk, 668 West County Rd., Calais, VT 05648. 802-223-5952.

Cambridge Town

Town Clerk, P.O. Box 127, Jeffersonville, VT 05464. 802-644-2251. Fax: 802-644-8348.

Canaan Town

Town Clerk, P.O. Box 159, Canaan, VT 05903-0159. 802-266-3370. Fax: 802-266-7085.

Castleton Town

Town Clerk, P.O. Box 115, Castleton, VT 05735. 802-468-2212. Fax: 802-468-5482.

Cavendish Town

Town Clerk, P.O. Box 126, Cavendish, VT 05142-0126. 802-226-7292. Fax: 802-226-7790.

Charleston Town

Town Clerk, HCR 61 Box 26, West Charleston, VT 05872-7902. 802-895-2814. Fax: 802-895-2814.

Charlotte Town

Town Clerk, P.O. Box 119, Charlotte, VT 05445-0119. 802-425-3071. Fax: 802-425-4241.

Chelsea Town

Town Clerk, P.O. Box 266, Chelsea, VT 05038. 802-685-4460.

Chester Town

Town Clerk, P.O. Box 370, Chester, VT 05143. 802-875-2173. Fax: 802-875-2237.

Chittenden County

There is no real estate recording at the county level in Vermont. Determine the proper town/city in which to record based upon property location.

Chittenden Town

Town Clerk, Holden Road, Town Hall, Chittenden, VT 05737. 802-483-6647.

Clarendon Town

Town Clerk, P.O. Box 30, North Clarendon, VT 05759-0030. 802-775-4274. Fax: 802-775-4274.

Colchester Town

Town Clerk, P.O. Box 55, Colchester, VT 05446. 802-654-0812. Fax: 802-654-0757.

Concord Town

Town Clerk, P.O. Box 317, Concord, VT 05824-0317. 802-695-2220. Fax: 802-695-2220.

Corinth Town

Town Clerk, P.O. Box 461, Corinth, VT 05039. 802-439-5850. Fax: 802-439-5850.

Cornwall Town

Town Clerk, 2629 Route 30, Cornwall, VT 05753-9299. 802-462-2775. Fax: 802-462-2606.

Coventry Town

Town Clerk, P.O. Box 104, Coventry, VT 05825. 802-754-2288. Fax: 802-754-2288.

Craftsbury Town

Town Clerk, Box 55, Craftsbury, VT 05826. 802-586-2823. Fax: 802-586-2823.

Danby Town

Town Clerk, Box 231, Danby, VT 05739-0231. 802-293-5136. Fax: 802-293-5311.

Danville Town

Town Clerk, P.O. Box 183, Danville, VT 05828. 802-684-3352. Fax: 802-684-9606.

Derby Town

Town Clerk, P.O. Box 25, Derby, VT 05829. 802-766-4906. Fax: 802-766-2027.

Dorset Town

Town Clerk, Mad Tom Road, Town Hall, East Dorset, VT 05253. 802-362-1178. Fax: 802-362-5156.

Dover Town

Town Clerk, P.O. Box 527, Dover, VT 05356-0527. 802-464-5100. Fax: 802-464-8721.

Dummerston Town

Town Clerk, 1523 Middle Rd., Dummerston, VT 05346. 802-257-1496. Fax: 802-257-4671.

Duxbury Town

Town Clerk, RD 2, Box 1260, Waterbury, VT 05676. 802-244-6660.

East Haven Town

Town Clerk, P.O. Box 10, East Haven, VT 05837-0010. 802-467-3772.

East Montpelier Town

Town Clerk, P.O. Box 157, East Montpelier, VT 05651-0157. 802-223-3313.

Eden Town

Town Clerk, 71 Old Schoolhouse Rd., Eden Mills, VT 05653. 802-635-2528. Fax: 802-635-1724.

Elmore Town

Town Clerk, P.O. Box 123, Lake Elmore, VT 05657. 802-888-2637.

Enosburg Town

Town Clerk, P.O. Box 465, Enosburg Falls, VT 05450. 802-933-4421. Fax: 802-933-4832.

Essex County

There is no real estate recording at the county level in Vermont. Determine the proper town/city in which to record based on property location.

Essex Town

Town Clerk, 81 Main Street, Essex Junction, VT 05452. 802-879-0413. Fax: 802-878-1353.

Fair Haven Town

Town Clerk, 3 North Park Place, Fair Haven, VT 05743. 802-265-3610. Fax: 802-265-2158.

Fairfax Town

Town Clerk, P.O. Box 27, Fairfax, VT 05454. 802-849-6111.

Fairfield Town

Town Clerk, P.O. Box 5, Fairfield, VT 05455. 802-827-3261.

Fairlee Town

Town Clerk, P.O. Box 95, Fairlee, VT 05045-0095. 802-333-4363. Fax: 802-333-9214.

Fayston Town

Town Clerk, 866 N. Fayston Rd., No. Fayston, VT 05660. 802-496-2454.

Ferrisburgh Town

Town Clerk, P.O. Box 6, Ferrisburgh, VT 05456-0006. 802-877-3429. Fax: 802-877-6757.

Fletcher Town

Town Clerk, RR 1, Box 1550, Cambridge, VT 05444. 802-849-6616. Fax: 802-849-2500.

Franklin County

There is no real estate recording at the county level in Vermont. Determine the proper town/city in which to record based on property location.

Franklin Town

Town Clerk, P.O. Box 82, Franklin, VT 05457-0082. 802-285-2101.

Georgia Town

Town Clerk, RD 2, Box 319, St. Albans, VT 05478. 802-524-3524. Fax: 802-524-9794.

Glover Town

Town Clerk, 51 Bean Hill, Glover, VT 05839. 802-525-6227. Fax: 802-525-6227.

Goshen Town

Town Clerk, 50 Carlisle Hill Rd., Goshen, VT 05733. 802-247-6455.

Grafton Town

Town Clerk, P.O. Box 180, Grafton, VT 05146. 802-843-2419.

Granby Town

Town Clerk, P.O. Box 56, Granby, VT 05840. 802-328-3611. Fax: 802-328-3611.

Grand Isle County

There is no real estate recording at the county level in Vermont. Determine the proper town/city in which to record based on property location.

Grand Isle Town

Town Clerk, 9 Hyde Road, Grand Isle, VT 05458. 802-372-8830. Fax: 802-372-8815.

Granville Town

Town Clerk, P.O. Box 66, Granville, VT 05747-0066. 802-767-4403.

Greensboro Town

Town Clerk, Box 119, Greensboro, VT 05841. 802-533-2911.

Groton Town

Town Clerk, 314 Scott Highway, Groton, VT 05046. 802-584-3276. Fax: 802-584-3276.

Guildhall Town

Town Clerk, P.O. Box 27, Guildhall, VT 05905. 802-676-3797. Fax: 802-676-3518.

Guilford Town

Town Clerk, 236 School Rd., Guilford, VT 05301-8319. 802-254-6857. Fax: 802-257-5764.

Halifax Town

Town Clerk, P.O. Box 45, West Halifax, VT 05358. 802-368-7390.

Hancock Town

Town Clerk, P.O. Box 100, Hancock, VT 05748. 802-767-3660.

Hardwick Town

Town Clerk, Box 523, Hardwick, VT 05843. 802-472-5971. Fax: 802-472-6865.

Hartford Town

Town Clerk, 15 Bridge Street, White River Junction, VT 05001-1920. 802-295-2785.

Hartland Town

Town Clerk, P.O. Box 349, Hartland, VT 05048-0349. 802-436-2444. Fax: 802-436-2444.

Highgate Town

Town Clerk, P.O. Box 67, Highgate Center, VT 05459. 802-868-4697.

Hinesburg Town

Town Clerk, P.O. Box 133, Hinesburg, VT 05461. 802-482-2281. Fax: 802-482-5404.

Holland Town

Town Clerk, 120 School Rd., Derby Line, VT 05830. 802-895-4440. Fax: 802-895-4440.

Hubbardton Town

Town Clerk, RR 1, Box 2828, Fair Haven, VT 05743-9502. 802-273-2951.

Huntington Town

Town Clerk, 4930 Main Rd., Huntington, VT 05462. 802-434-2032.

Hyde Park Town

Town Clerk, P.O. Box 98, Hyde Park, VT 05655-0098. 802-888-2300. Fax: 802-888-6878.

Ira Town

Town Clerk, 808 Route 133, West Rutland, VT 05777. 802-235-2745.

Irasburg Town

Town Clerk, Box 51, Irasburg, VT 05845. 802-754-2242.

Isle La Motte Town

Town Clerk, P.O. Box 250, Isle La Motte, VT 05463. 802-928-3434. Fax: 802-928-3002.

Jamaica Town

Town Clerk, P.O. Box 173, Jamaica, VT 05343. 802-874-4681.

Jay Town

Town Clerk, RFD 2, Box 136, Jay, VT 05859-9820. 802-988-2996.

Jericho Town

Town Clerk, P.O. Box 67, Jericho, VT 05465. 802-899-4936. Fax: 802-899-5549.

Johnson Town
Town Clerk, P.O. Box 383, Johnson, VT 05656. 802-635-2611. Fax: 802-635-9523.

Kirby Town
Town Clerk, Town of Kirby, 346 Town Hall Rd., Lyndonville, VT 05851-9802. 802-626-9386. Fax: 802-626-9386.

Lamoille County
There is no real estate recording at the county level in Vermont. Determine the proper town/city in which to record based on property location.

Landgrove Town
Town Clerk, Box 508, Londonderry, VT 05148. 802-824-3716. Fax: 802-824-3716.

Leicester Town
Town Clerk, 44 Schoolhouse Rd., Leicester, VT 05733. 802-247-5961.

Lemington Town
Town Clerk, 2549 RIver Rd., VT 102, Lemington, VT 05903. 802-277-4814.

Lincoln Town
Town Clerk, 62 Quaker St., Lincoln, VT 05443. 802-453-2980. Fax: 802-453-2975.

Londonderry Town
Town Clerk, P.O. Box 118, South Londonderry, VT 05155-0118. 802-824-3356.

Lowell Town
Town Clerk, P.O. Box 7, Lowell, VT 05847-0007. 802-744-6559. Fax: 802-744-2357.

Ludlow Town
Town Clerk, P.O. Box 307, Ludlow, VT 05149. 802-228-3232. Fax: 802-228-2813.

Lunenburg Town
Town Clerk, P.O. Box 54, Lunenburg, VT 05906. 802-892-5959.

Lyndon Town
Town Clerk, P.O. Box 167, Lyndonville, VT 05851. 802-626-5785. Fax: 802-626-1265.

Maidstone Town
Town Clerk, P.O. Box 118, Maidstone, VT 05905-0118. 802-676-3210. Fax: 802-676-3210.

Manchester Town
Town Clerk, P.O. Box 830, Manchester Center, VT 05255. 802-362-1315. Fax: 802-362-1315.

Marlboro Town
Town Clerk, P.O. Box E, Marlboro, VT 05344-0305. 802-254-2181.

Marshfield Town
Town Clerk, 122 School St., Room 1, Marshfield, VT 05658. 802-426-3305. Fax: 802-426-3045.

Mendon Town
Town Clerk, 34 US Route 4, Mendon, VT 05701. 802-775-1662. Fax: 802-747-4592.

Middlebury Town
Town Clerk, Municipal Building, 94 Main St., Middlebury, VT 05753-1334. 802-388-4041.

Middlesex Town
Town Clerk, 5 Church St., Middlesex, VT 05602. 802-223-5915. Fax: 802-223-0569.

Middletown Springs Town
Town Clerk, P.O. Box 1197, Middletown Springs, VT 05757-1197. 802-235-2220.

Milton Town
Town Clerk, P.O. Box 18, Milton, VT 05468. 802-893-4111. Fax: 802-893-1005.

Monkton Town
Town Clerk, RR 1, Box 2015, North Ferrisburg, VT 05473-9509. 802-453-3800.

Montgomery Town
Town Clerk, P.O. Box 356, Montgomery Center, VT 05471-0356. 802-326-4719. Fax: 802-326-4939.

Montpelier City
City Clerk, 39 Main Street, City Hall, Montpelier, VT 05602. 802-223-9500. Fax: 802-223-9518.

Moretown Town
Town Clerk, P.O. Box 666, Moretown, VT 05660. 802-496-3645.

Morgan Town
Town Clerk, P.O. Box 45, Morgan, VT 05853-0045. 802-895-2927.

Morristown Town
Town Clerk, P.O. Box 748, Morrisville, VT 05661-0748. 802-888-6370. Fax: 802-888-6375.

Mount Holly Town
Town Clerk, P.O. Box 248, Mount Holly, VT 05758. 802-259-2391. Fax: 802-259-2391.

Mount Tabor Town
Town Clerk, P.O. Box 245, Mt. Tabor, VT 05739. 802-293-5282. Fax: 802-293-5287.

New Haven Town
Town Clerk, 78 North St., New Haven, VT 05472. 802-453-3516.

Newark Town
Town Clerk, RFD 1, Box 50C, West Burke, VT 05871. 802-467-3336.

Newbury Town
Town Clerk, P.O. Box 126, Newbury, VT 05051. 802-866-5521.

Newfane Town
Town Clerk, P.O. Box 36, Newfane, VT 05345-0036. 802-365-7772. Fax: 802-365-7692.

Newport City
City Clerk, 222 Main Street, Newport, VT 05855. 802-334-2112. Fax: 802-334-5632.

Newport Town
Town Clerk, P.O. Box 85, Newport Center, VT 05857. 802-334-6442. Fax: 802-334-6442.

North Hero Town
Town Clerk, P.O. Box 38, North Hero, VT 05474-0038. 802-372-6926. Fax: 802-372-3806.

Northfield Town
Town Clerk, 51 South Main Street, Northfield, VT 05663. 802-485-5421. Fax: 802-485-8426.

Norton Town
Town Clerk, P.O. Box 148, Norton, VT 05907. 802-822-9935.

Norwich Town
Town Clerk, P.O. Box 376, Norwich, VT 05055. 802-649-1419. Fax: 802-649-0123.

Orange County
There is no real estate recording at the county level in Vermont. Determine the proper town/city in which to record based on property location.

Orange Town
Town Clerk, P.O. Box 233, East Barre, VT 05649. 802-479-2673. Fax: 802-479-2673.

Orleans County
There is no real estate recording at the county level in Vermont. Determine the proper town/city in which to record based upon property location.

Orwell Town
Town Clerk, P.O. Box 32, Orwell, VT 05760-0032. 802-948-2032.

Panton Town
Town Clerk, P.O. Box 174, Vergennes, VT 05491-0174. 802-475-2333.

Pawlet Town
Town Clerk, P.O. Box 128, Pawlet, VT 05761-0128. 802-325-3309. Fax: 802-325-6109.

Peacham Town
Town Clerk, Box 244, Peacham, VT 05862. 802-592-3218.

Peru Town
Town Clerk, Box 127, Peru, VT 05152. 802-824-3065. Fax: 802-824-3065.

Pittsfield Town
Town Clerk, P.O. Box 556, Pittsfield, VT 05762-0556. 802-746-8170.

Pittsford Town
Town Clerk, P.O. Box 10, Pittsford, VT 5763. 802-483-2931. Fax: 802-483-6612.

Plainfield Town
Town Clerk, P.O. Box 217, Plainfield, VT 5667. 802-454-8461. Fax: 802-454-8461.

Plymouth Town
Town Clerk, 68 Town Office Rd., Plymouth, VT 05056. 802-672-3655. Fax: 802-672-5466.

Pomfret Town
Town Clerk, P.O. Box 286, North Pomfret, VT 05053. 802-457-3861.

Poultney Town
Town Clerk, 9 Main St., Suite 2, Poultney, VT 05764. 802-287-5761.

Pownal Town
Town Clerk, P.O. Box 411, Pownal, VT 05261. 802-823-7757. Fax: 802-823-0116.

Proctor Town
Town Clerk, 45 Main Street, Proctor, VT 05765. 802-459-3333. Fax: 802-459-2356.

Putney Town
Town Clerk, P.O. Box 233, Putney, VT 05346. 802-387-5862.

Randolph Town
Town Clerk, Drawer B, Randolph, VT 05060. 802-728-5682. Fax: 802-728-5818.

Reading Town
Town Clerk, P.O. Box 72, Reading, VT 05062. 802-484-7250. Fax: 802-454-7250.

Readsboro Town
Town Clerk, P.O. Box 246, Readsboro, VT 05350. 802-423-5405. Fax: 802-423-5423.

Richford Town
Town Clerk, P.O. Box 236, Richford, VT 05476-0236. 802-848-7751. Fax: 802-848-7752.

Richmond Town
Town Clerk, P.O. Box 285, Richmond, VT 05477. 802-434-2221. Fax: 802-434-5570.

Ripton Town
Town Clerk, Box 10, Ripton, VT 05766-0010. 802-388-2266.

Rochester Town
Town Clerk, P.O. Box 238, Rochester, VT 05767-0238. 802-767-3631. Fax: 802-767-6028.

Fee & Payment: The fee is $15.00 per item (one party name or case number). Payment may be made by money order, cashier check, personal check. Prepayment is required. Debtor's checks are not accepted. Payee: Clerk, US Bankruptcy Court. Certification fee: $5.00 per document. Copy fee: $.50 per page.

Phone Search: Docket information is available by phone. An automated voice case information service (VCIS) is available. Call VCIS at 800-326-5879 or 804-771-2736.

Mail Search: Always enclose a stamped self addressed envelope.

In Person Search: In person searching is available.

PACER: Sign-up number is 800-676-6856. Access fee is $.60 per minute. Toll-free access: 800-890-2858. Local access: 703-557-6272. Use of PC Anywhere v4.0 suggested. Case records are available back to mid 1989. Records are never purged. New civil records are available online after 1 day.

Electronic Filing: Electronic filing information is available online at http://ecf.vaeb.uscourts.gov

Other Online Access: You can search records using the Internet. Searching is currently free. To search by name - www.vaeb.uscourts.gov/home/SearchNM.html. To search by case number - www.vaeb.uscourts.gov/home/SearchCSNUM.html. More options available from main site.

Norfolk Division PO Box 1938, Norfolk, VA 23501-1938 (Courier Address: Walter E Hoffman US Courthouse, Room 400, 600 Granby St, Norfolk, VA 23510), 757-222-7500.

Counties: Accomack, City of Cape Charles, City of Chesapeake, City of Franklin, Gloucester, City of Hampton, Isle of Wight, James City, Matthews, City of Norfolk, Northampton, City of PoquosonCity of Portsmouth, Southampton, City of Suffolk,City of Virginia Beach, City of Williamsburg, York.

Indexing & Storage: Cases are indexed by debtor as well as by case number. New cases are available in the index 2 days after filing date. A computer index is maintained. Open records are located at this court.

Fee & Payment: The fee is $15.00 per item (one party name or case number). Payment may be made by money order, cashier check, personal check. Prepayment is required. The search fee checks should be made to the clerk. The searcher must use Ikon Management Services for copies. The copy fee checks should be made to Ikon Management Services. Debtor checks are not accepted. Payee: Clerk, US Bankruptcy Court. Certification fee: $5.00 per document. Copy fee: $.50 per page. The fee for copies made by court personnel is $.31 per page.

Phone Search: Call for name, case number, chapter, filing date, judge, attorney for debtor, trustee, Social Security number and date discharged. An automated voice case information service (VCIS) is available. Call VCIS at 800-326-5879 or 804-771-2736.

Mail Search: Always enclose a stamped self addressed envelope.

In Person Search: In person searching is available.

PACER: Sign-up number is 800-676-6856. Access fee is $.60 per minute. New civil records are available online after 7 days.

Electronic Filing: Electronic filing information is available online at http://ecf.vaeb.uscourts.gov

Other Online Access: You can search records using the Internet. Searching is currently free. To search by name - www.vaeb.uscourts.gov/home/SearchNM.html. To search by case number - www.vaeb.uscourts.gov/home/SearchCSNUM.html. More options available from main site.

Richmond Division Office of the clerk, 1100 E Main St, Room 310, Richmond, VA 23219-3515 (Courier Address: 1100 E Main St, Room 301, Richmond, VA 23219), 804-916-2400.

Counties: Amelia, Brunswick, Caroline, Charles City, Chesterfield, City of Colonial Heights, Dinwiddie, City of Emporia, Essex, City of Fredericksburg, Goochland, Greensville, Hanover, Henrico, City of Hopewell, King and Queen, King George, King William,Lancaster, Lunenburg, Mecklenburg, Middlesex, New Kent, Northumberland, Nottoway, City of Petersburg, Powhatan, Prince Edward, Prince George, Richmond, City of Richmond, Spotsylvania, Surry, Sussex, Westmoreland.

Indexing & Storage: Cases are indexed by debtor as well as by case number. New cases are available in the index 1 day after filing date. A computer index is maintained. Open records are located at this court.

Fee & Payment: The fee is $15.00 per item (one party name or case number). Payment may be made by money order, cashier check, personal check. Prepayment is required. The court will not send statements. Debtor checks are not accepted. Dave Jones & Assoc Copy Svc handles search requests. You must fax your request to them at 804-780-0652. They will call you back with the fees. Payee: Clerk, US Bankruptcy Court. Certification fee: $5.00 per document. Copy fee: $.50 per page.

Phone Search: Only docket information is available by phone. An automated voice case information service (VCIS) is available. Call VCIS at 800-326-5879 or.

Mail Search: Always enclose a stamped self addressed envelope.

In Person Search: In person searching is available.

PACER: PACER is not available for this court.

Electronic Filing: Electronic filing information is available online at http://ecf.vaeb.uscourts.gov

Other Online Access: You can search records using the Internet. Searching is currently free. To search by name - www.vaeb.uscourts.gov/home/SearchNM.html. To search by case number - www.vaeb.uscourts.gov/home/SearchCSNUM.html. More options available from main site.

US District Court
Western District of Virginia

Abingdon Division Clerk's Office, PO Box 398, Abingdon, VA 24212 (Courier Address: 180 W Main St, Abingdon, VA 24210), 540-628-5116, Fax: 540-628-1028.

www.vawd.uscourts.gov

Counties: Buchanan, City of Bristol, Russell, Smyth, Tazewell, Washington.

Indexing & Storage: Cases are indexed by defendant and plaintiff as well as by case number. New cases are available in the index immediately after filing date. Both computer and card indexes are maintained. Open records are located at this court.

Fee & Payment: The fee is $15.00 per item (one party name or case number). Payment may be made by money order, cashier check, personal check. Court will bill for searches and copies. Payee: Clerk, US District Court. Certification fee: $5.00 per document. Copy fee: $.50 per page. You are allowed to make your own copies. These copies cost $.10 per page.

Phone Search: Docket information available by phone. An automated voice case information service (VCIS) is not available.

Fax Search: Will accept fax for searches from 1992 to present only.

Mail Search: A stamped self addressed envelope is not required.

In Person Search: In person searching is available.

PACER: Sign-up number is 800-676-6856. Toll-free access: 888-279-7848. Local access: 540-857-5140, 540-857-2290, 540-857-2288. Case records are available back to Mid 1990. Records are never purged. New records are available online after 1 day. PACER is available on the Internet at http://pacer.vawd.uscourts.gov.

Big Stone Gap Division PO Box 490, Big Stone Gap, VA 24219 (Courier Address: 322 Wood Ave E, Room 203, Big Stone Gap, VA 24219), 540-523-3557, Fax: 540-523-6214.

www.vawd.uscourts.gov

Counties: Dickenson, Lee, Scott, Wise, City of Norton.

Indexing & Storage: Cases are indexed by defendant and plaintiff as well as by case number. New cases are available in the index immediately after filing date. The style of the case is needed to conduct a search. A civil action number is very helpful. A computer index is maintained. A microfilm index is also maintained for older cases. Open records are located at this court.

Fee & Payment: The fee is $15.00 per item (one party name or case number). Payment may be made by money order, cashier check, personal check. Payee: Clerk, US District Court. Certification fee: $5.00 per document. Copy fee: $.50 per page. You are allowed to make your own copies. These copies cost $.50 per page.

Phone Search: Only docket information is available by phone. An automated voice case information service (VCIS) is not available.

Mail Search: Always enclose a stamped self addressed envelope.

In Person Search: In person searching is available.

PACER: Sign-up number is 800-676-6856. Toll-free access: 888-279-7848. Local access: 540-857-5140, 540-857-2290, 540-857-2288. Case records are available back to Mid 1990. Records are never purged. New records are available online after 1 day.

Charlottesville Division Clerk, Room 304, 255 W Main St, Charlottesville, VA 22902, 804-296-9284.

www.vawd.uscourts.gov

Counties: Albemarle, Culpeper, Fluvanna, Greene, Louisa, Madison, Nelson, Orange, Rappahannock, City of Charlottesville.

Indexing & Storage: Cases are indexed by defendant and plaintiff as well as by case number. New cases are available in the index immediately after filing date. Both computer and card indexes are maintained. Records are indexed on microfiche from 1981 to 1991, and on card prior to that. Open records are located at this court. District wide searches are available from this court for any information within the district.

Fee & Payment: The fee is $15.00 per item (one party name or case number). Payment may be made by money order, cashier check, personal check. Prepayment is required. Payee: Clerk, US District Court. Certification fee: $5.00 per document. Copy fee: $.50 per page. You are allowed to make your own copies. These copies cost $.50 per page. Court only searches computer index. You may search microfiche index.

Phone Search: Searching is not available by phone.

Mail Search: Always enclose a stamped self addressed envelope.

In Person Search: In person searching is available.

PACER: Sign-up number is 800-676-6856. Toll-free access: 888-279-7848. Local access: 540-857-5140, 540-857-2290, 540-857-2288. Case records are available back to Mid 1990. Records are never purged. New records are available online after 1 day. PACER is available on the Internet at http://pacer.vawd.uscourts.gov.

Danville Division PO Box 52, Danville, VA 24543-0053 (Courier Address: Dan Daniel Post Office Bldg, Room 202, 700 Main St, Danville, VA 24541), 804-793-7147, Fax: 804-793-0284.

www.vawd.uscourts.gov

Counties: Charlotte, Halifax, Henry, Patrick, Pittsylvania, City of Danville, City of Martinsville, City of South Boston.

Indexing & Storage: Cases are indexed by defendant and plaintiff as well as by case number. New cases are available in the index immediately after filing date. Both computer and card indexes are maintained. Open records are located at this court.

Fee & Payment: The fee is $15.00 per item (one party name or case number). Payment may be made by money order, cashier check, personal check. Prepayment is required. Payee: Clerk, US District Court. Certification fee: $5.00 per document. Copy fee: $.50 per page.

Phone Search: If there is an expedited request and the $15.00 search fee is prepaid, the court will call to give the information, and follow with a written response. An automated voice case information service (VCIS) is not available.

Mail Search: A stamped self addressed envelope is not required.

In Person Search: In person searching is available.

PACER: Sign-up number is 800-676-6856. Toll-free access: 888-279-7848. Local access: 540-857-5140, 540-857-2290, 540-857-2288. Case records are available back to Mid 1990. Records are never purged. New records are available online after 1 day. PACER is available on the Internet at http://pacer.vawd.uscourts.gov.

Harrisonburg Division Clerk, PO Box 1207, Harrisonburg, VA 22801 (Courier Address: Post Office Bldg, 116 N Main St, Room 314, Harrisonburg, VA 22801), 540-434-3181.

www.vawd.uscourts.gov

Counties: Augusta, Bath, Clarke, Frederick, Highland, Page, Rockingham, Shenandoah, Warren, City of Harrisonburg, City of Staunton, City of Waynesboro, City of Winchester.

Indexing & Storage: Cases are indexed by defendant and plaintiff as well as by case number. New cases are available in the index 1-2 days after filing date. Both computer and card indexes are maintained. Records are indexed on computer for civil cases from 1991 and criminal cases from 1993. Open records are located at this court. District wide searches are available from this court 1-2 days after it is filed, but the court prefers that searches be conducted where the case is filed.

Fee & Payment: The fee is $15.00 per item (one party name or case number). Payment may be made by money order, cashier check, personal check. Prepayment is required. Payee: Clerk, US District Court. Certification fee: $5.00 per document. Copy fee: $.50 per page.

Phone Search: Limited information available by phone. An automated voice case information service (VCIS) is not available.

Mail Search: A stamped self addressed envelope is not required.

In Person Search: In person searching is available.

PACER: Sign-up number is 800-676-6856. Toll-free access: 888-279-7848. Local access: 540-857-5140, 540-857-2290, 540-857-2288. Case records are available back to Mid 1990. Records are never purged. New records are available online after 1 day. PACER is available on the Internet at http://pacer.vawd.uscourts.gov.

Lynchburg Division Clerk, PO Box 744, Lynchburg, VA 24505 (Courier Address: Room 212, 1100 Main St, Lynchburg, VA 24504), 804-847-5722.

www.vawd.uscourts.gov

Counties: Amherst, Appomattox, Bedford, Buckingham, Campbell, Cumberland, Rockbridge, City of Bedford, City of Buena Vista, City of Lexington, City of Lynchburg.

Indexing & Storage: Cases are indexed by defendant and plaintiff as well as by case number. New cases are available in the index immediately after filing date. Both computer and card indexes are maintained. The computer index goes back to 1989. Open records are located at this court.

Fee & Payment: The fee is $15.00 per item (one party name or case number). Payment may be made by money order, cashier check, personal check. Prepayment is required. Payee: Clerk, US District Court. Certification fee: $5.00 per document. Copy fee: $.50 per page.

Phone Search: Only docket information is available by phone. An automated voice case information service (VCIS) is not available.

Mail Search: A stamped self addressed envelope is not required.

In Person Search: In person searching is available.

PACER: Sign-up number is 800-676-6856. Toll-free access: 888-279-7848. Local access: 540-857-5140, 540-857-2290, 540-857-2288. Case records are available back to Mid 1990. Records are never

purged. New records are available online after 1 day. PACER is available on the Internet at http://pacer.vawd.uscourts.gov.

Roanoke Division Clerk, PO Box 1234, Roanoke, VA 24006 (Courier Address: 210 Franklin Rd SW, Roanoke, VA 24011), 540-857-5100, Fax: 540-857-5110.

www.vawd.uscourts.gov

Counties: Alleghany, Bland, Botetourt, Carroll, Craig, Floyd, Franklin, Giles, Grayson, Montgomery, Pulaski, Roanoke, Wythe, City of Covington, City of Clifton Forge, City of Galax, City of Radford, City of Roanoke, City of Salem.

Indexing & Storage: Cases are indexed by defendant and plaintiff as well as by case number. New cases are available in the index immediately after filing date. Both computer and card indexes are maintained. Records are also indexed on microfiche. The automated in house system is available for records from 1992. Open records are located at this court. District wide searches are available for all records from this court.

Fee & Payment: The fee is $15.00 per item (one party name or case number). Payment may be made by money order, cashier check, personal check. Prepayment is required. Payee: Clerk, US District Court. Certification fee: $5.00 per document. Copy fee: $.50 per page.

Phone Search: If there is an expedited request and the $15.00 search fee is prepaid, the court will call to give the information. However, a written response will follow. An automated voice case information service (VCIS) is not available.

Mail Search: A stamped self addressed envelope is not required.

In Person Search: In person searching is available.

PACER: Sign-up number is 800-676-6856. Toll-free access: 888-279-7848. Local access: 540-857-5140, 540-857-2290, 540-857-2288. Case records are available back to Mid 1990. Records are never purged. New records are available online after 1 day. PACER is available on the Internet at http://pacer.vawd.uscourts.gov.

US Bankruptcy Court

Western District of Virginia

Harrisonburg Division PO Box 1407, Harrisonburg, VA 22801 (Courier Address: 116 N Main St, Harrisonburg, VA 22801), 540-434-8327, Fax: 540-434-9715.

www.vawb.uscourts.gov

Counties: Alleghany, Augusta, Bath, City of Buena Vista, Clarke, City of Clifton Forge, City of Covington, Frederick, City of Harrisonburg, Highland, City of Lexington, Page, Rappahannock, Rockbridge, Rockingham, Shenandoah, City of Staunton, Warren, City of Waynesboro, City of Winchester.

Indexing & Storage: Cases are indexed by debtor as well as by case number. New cases are available in the index immediately after filing date. Both computer and card indexes are maintained. The computer index goes back to 1986. Older cases are on a card index. Open records are located at this court.

Fee & Payment: The fee is $15.00 per item (one party name or case number). Payment may be made by money order, cashier check, business check. Personal checks are not accepted. Prepayment is required. Payee: Clerk, US Bankruptcy Court. Certification fee: $5.00 per document. Copy fee: $.50 per page.

Phone Search: Only docket information is available by phone, and only if it is available from the computer. An automated voice case information service (VCIS) is not available.

Mail Search: Always enclose a stamped self addressed envelope.

In Person Search: In person searching is available.

PACER: Sign-up number is 800-676-6856. Access fee is $.60 per minute. Toll-free access: 800-248-0329. Local access: 540-434-8373. Use of PC Anywhere v4.0 suggested. Case records are available back to March 1986. Records are never purged. New civil records are available online after 1 day.

Lynchburg Division PO Box 6400, Lynchburg, VA 24505 (Courier Address: 1100 Main St, Room 226, Lynchburg, VA 24504), 804-845-0317.

www.vawb.uscourts.gov

Counties: Albemarle, Amherst, Appomattox, Bedford, City of Bedford, Buckingham, Campbell, Charlotte, City of Charlottesville, Culpeper, Cumberland, City of Danville, Fluvanna, Greene, Halifax, Henry, Louisa, City of Lynchburg, Madison, City of Martinsville,Nelson, Orange, Patrick, Pittsylvania, City of South Boston.

Indexing & Storage: Cases are indexed by debtor as well as by case number. New cases are available in the index 24 hours after filing date. A computer index is maintained. The computer index goes back to 1986. Open records are located at this court.

Fee & Payment: The fee is $15.00 per item (one party name or case number). Payment may be made by money order, cashier check, business check. Personal checks are not accepted. Prepayment is required. Payee: Clerk, US Bankruptcy Court. Certification fee: $5.00 per document. Copy fee: $.50 per page.

Phone Search: Only the name, date filed and chapter will be released over the phone. An automated voice case information service (VCIS) is not available.

Mail Search: Always enclose a stamped self addressed envelope.

In Person Search: In person searching is available.

PACER: Sign-up number is 800-676-6856. Access fee is $.60 per minute. Toll-free access: 800-248-2469. Local access: 804-528-9003. Use of PC Anywhere v4.0 suggested. Case records are available back to 1986. New civil records are available online after 1 day.

Roanoke Division PO Box 2390, Roanoke, VA 24010 (Courier Address: Commonwealth Bldg, 210 Church Ave, Roanoke, VA 24011), 540-857-2391, Fax: 540-857-2873.

www.vawb.uscourts.gov

Counties: Bland, Botetourt, City of Bristol, Buchanan, Carroll, Craig, Dickenson, Floyd, Franklin, City of Galax, Giles, Grayson, Lee, Montgomery, City of Norton, Pulaski, City of Radford, Roanoke, City of Roanoke, Russell, City of Salem, Scott, Smyth, Tazewell,Washington, Wise, Wythe.

Indexing & Storage: Cases are indexed by debtor and creditors as well as by case number. New cases are available in the index same day if possible after filing date. A computer index is maintained. Records are indexed numerically (for example: 7-92-00123 = office number, year and 5 digit case number). Open records are located at this court.

Fee & Payment: The fee is $15.00 per item (one party name or case number). Payment may be made by money order, cashier check. Business checks are not accepted. Personal checks are not accepted. Prepayment is required. Only firm checks will be accepted. Payee: Clerk, US Bankruptcy Court. Certification fee: $5.00 per document. Copy fee: $.50 per page.

Phone Search: Only the number of pages of the requested items will be given over the phone.

Mail Search: Always enclose a stamped self addressed envelope.

In Person Search: In person searching is available.

PACER: Sign-up number is 800-676-6856. Access fee is $.60 per minute. Toll-free access: 800-249-9839. Local access: 540-857-2319. Use of PC Anywhere v4.0 suggested. Case records are available back to 1988. Records are never purged. New civil records are available online after 1 day.

Court	Jurisdiction	No. of Courts	How Organized
Circuit Courts*	General	117	31 Circuits
District Courts*	Limited	123	
Combined Courts*		5	

* Profiled in this Sourcebook.

Court	CIVIL								
	Tort	Contract	Real Estate	Min. Claim	Max. Claim	Small Claims	Estate	Eviction	Domestic Relations
Circuit Courts*	X	X	X	$15,000	No Max		X		X
District Courts*	X	X	X	$0	$15,000			X	X

Court	CRIMINAL				
	Felony	Misdemeanor	DWI/DUI	Preliminary Hearing	Juvenile
Circuit Courts*	X				
District Courts*		X	X	X	X

ADMINISTRATION Executive Secretary, Administrative Office of Courts, 100 N 9th St 3rd Fl, Supreme Court Bldg, Richmond, VA, 23219; 804-786-6455, Fax: 804-786-4542. www.courts.state.va.us

COURT STRUCTURE 117 Circuit Courts in 31 districts are the courts of general jurisdiction. There are 123 District Courts of limited juridiction. Please note that a district can comprise a county or a city. Records of civil action from $3000 to $15,000 can be at either the Circuit or District Court as either can have jurisdiction. It is necessary to check both record locations as there is no concurrent database nor index.

The upper limit for civil actions in District Court was raised from $10,000 to $15,000 as of July 1, 1997.

ONLINE ACCESS An online, statewide public access computer system is available, called Law Office Public Access System (LOPAS). The system allows remote access to the court case indexes and abstracts from most of the state's courts. In order to determine which courts are on LOPAS, you must obtain an ID and password (instructions below), and search on the system. A summary list of included courts is not available. Searching is by specific court; there is no combined index.

The system contains opinions from the Supreme Court and the Court of Appeals, as well as criminal and civil case information from Circuit and District Courts. The number of years of information provided varies widely from court to court, depending on when the particular court joined the Courts Automated Information System (CAIS).

The preferred communication software for LOPAS access is PROCOMM+. There are no sign-up or other fees to use LOPAS. Access is granted on a request-by-request basis. Anyone wishing to establish an account or receive information on LOPAS must contact Ken Mittendorf, Director of MIS, Supreme Court of Virginia, 100 N 9th St, Richmond VA 23219 or by phone at 804-786-6455 or Fax at 804-786-4542.

ADDITIONAL INFORMATION In most jurisdictions, the certification fee is $2.00 per document plus copy fee. The copy fee is $.50 per page.

📖 📖 📖 📖 📖 📖

Accomack County

2nd Circuit Court PO Box 126, Accomac, VA 23301; 757-787-5776; Fax: 757-787-1849. Hours: 9AM-5PM (EST). *Felony, Civil Actions Over $15,000, Probate.*

Civil Records: Access: Fax, mail, online, in person. Both court and visitors may perform in person searches. No search fee. Required to search: name, years to search. Civil cases indexed by defendant, plaintiff. Civil records on microfiche and archived from 1663. For information about the statewide online system, LOPAS, see the state introduction. **Criminal Records:** Access: Fax, mail, remote online, in person. Both court and

visitors may perform in person searches. No search fee. Required to search: name, years to search, DOB; also helpful-SSN. Criminal records on microfiche and archived from 1663. For information about the statewide online system, LOPAS, see the state introduction. **General Information:** No juvenile, sealed, probate, tax return or adoption records released. SASE not required. Turnaround time 1-2 days. Copy fee: $.50 per page. Certification fee: No certification fee. Fee payee: Samuel H Cooper Jr, Clerk of Court. Personal checks accepted. Fax notes: $2.00 for first page, $.50 each addl.

2A General District Court PO Box 276, Accomac, VA 23301; 757-787-0920. Hours:

9AM-5PM (EST). *Misdemeanor, Civil Actions Under $15,000, Eviction, Small Claims.*

Civil Records: Access: Phone, mail, online, in person. Both court and visitors may perform in person searches. No search fee. Required to search: name, years to search. Civil cases indexed by defendant. Civil records on computer from 11/88, index cards from 1985. For information about the statewide online system, LOPAS, see the state introduction. **Criminal Records:** Access: Phone, mail, remote online, in person. Both court and visitors may perform in person searches. No search fee. Required to search: name, years to search, DOB; also helpful-SSN. Criminal records on computer from 11/88, index cards from 1985.

For information about the statewide online system, LOPAS, see the state introduction. **General Information:** No juvenile, sealed, adoption records released. Turnaround time 1-3 days. Copy fee: $1.00. Fee for first 2 pages. Add $.50 per page thereafter. Certification fee: No certification fee. Fee payee: Accomack District Court. Personal checks accepted. Credit cards accepted: Visa, Mastercard. Prepayment is required. Public access terminal is available.

Albemarle County

16th Circuit & District Court 501 E Jefferson St, Charlottesville, VA 22902; 804-972-4085; Fax: 804-972-4071. Hours: 8:30AM-4:30PM (EST). *Felony, Misdemeanor, Civil, Eviction, Probate.*

Civil Records: Access: Mail, online, in person. Both court and visitors may perform in person searches. No search fee. Required to search: name, years to search. Civil records on microfiche from 1980 to present and archived from 1700s to 1990. For information about the statewide online system, LOPAS, see the state introduction. **Criminal Records:** Access: Mail, remote online, in person. Both court and visitors may perform in person searches. No search fee. Required to search: name, years to search. Criminal records on microfiche from 1980 to present and archived from 1700s to 1990. For information about the statewide online system, LOPAS, see the state introduction. **General Information:** No juvenile, sealed records released. Turnaround time 7-10 days. Copy fee: $.50 per page. Certification fee: $2.00. Fee payee: Albemarle Clerk of Court. Personal checks accepted. Prepayment is required.

Alexandria City

18th Circuit Court 520 King St. #307, Alexandria, VA 22314; 703-838-4044. Hours: 9AM-5PM (EST). *Felony, Civil Actions Over $15,000, Probate.*

Civil Records: Access: In person only. Court does not conduct in person searches; visitors must perform searches for themselves. Search fee: No civil searches performed by court. Required to search: name, years to search. Civil cases indexed by defendant, plaintiff. Civil records on computer from 1983 to present, microfiche from 1970s to present. **Criminal Records:** Access: In person only. Court does not conduct in person searches; visitors must perform searches for themselves. Search fee: No criminal searches performed by court. Required to search: name, years to search; also helpful-DOB. Criminal records on computer since 7/87. **General Information:** No juvenile, sealed, adoption or expunged records released. Copy fee: $.50 per page. Certification fee: $2.00. Fee payee: Clerk of Court. Only cashiers checks and money orders accepted. Prepayment is required.

18th Judicial District Court 520 King St #201, PO Box 20206, Alexandria, VA 22314; 703-838-4041 (traffic); Civil phone:703-838-4021; Criminal phone:703-838-4021. Hours: 8AM-4PM (EST). *Misdemeanor, Civil Actions Under $15,000, Eviction, Small Claims.*

Civil Records: Access: online, in person. Court does not conduct in person searches; visitors must perform searches for themselves. Search fee: No civil searches performed by court. Required to search: name, years to search. Civil cases indexed by defendant. Civil records on computer from 1989 to present, index cards prior to 1986. For information about the statewide online system, LOPAS, see the state introduction. **Criminal**

Records: Access: Remote online, in person. Court does not conduct in person searches; visitors must perform searches for themselves. Search fee: No criminal searches performed by court. Required to search: name. Criminal records on computer from 1989 to present, index cards prior to 1986. For information about the statewide online system, LOPAS, see the state introduction. **General Information:** No juvenile, sealed records released. No copy fee. Certification fee: No certification. Public access terminal is available.

Alleghany County

25th Circuit Court PO Box 670, Covington, VA 24426; 540-965-1730; Fax: 540-965-1732. Hours: 8:45AM-5PM M-F; 9AM-Noon Sat (EST). *Felony, Civil Actions Over $15,000, Probate.*

www.alleghanycountyclerk.com

Civil Records: Access: online, in person. Court does not conduct in person searches; visitors must perform searches for themselves. Search fee: No civil searches performed by court. Required to search: name. Civil cases indexed by plaintiff. available from 1822, some on microfilm. For information about the statewide online system, LOPAS, see the state introduction. **Criminal Records:** Access: Remote online, in person. Court does not conduct in person searches; visitors must perform searches for themselves. Search fee: No criminal searches performed by court. Required to search: name. available from 1822, some on microfilm. For information about the statewide online system, LOPAS, see the state introduction. **General Information:** No juvenile, adoption or sealed records released. Copy fee: $.50 per page. Certification fee: $2.00. Fee payee: Michael D Wolfe, Clerk of Court. Personal checks accepted. Prepayment is required.

25th General District Court PO Box 139, Covington, VA 24426; 540-965-1720; Fax: 540-965-1722. Hours: 9AM-5PM (EST). *Misdemeanor, Civil Actions Under $15,000, Eviction, Small Claims.*

Civil Records: Access: Fax, mail, online, in person. Both court and visitors may perform in person searches. No search fee. Required to search: name, years to search. Civil cases indexed by defendant, plaintiff. Civil records on computer from 1/90, prior on index cards. For information about the statewide online system, LOPAS, see the state introduction. **Criminal Records:** Access: Fax, mail, remote online, in person. Both court and visitors may perform in person searches. No search fee. Required to search: name, years to search; also helpful-DOB, SSN. Criminal records on computer from 1/90, prior on index cards. For information about the statewide online system, LOPAS, see the state introduction. **General Information:** No juvenile, sealed records released. SASE requested. Turnaround time 1-2 days. Copy fee: $1.00 each for first 2 pages; $.50 each add'l. Certification fee: No certification fee. Personal checks accepted. Credit cards accepted: Visa, Mastercard. Acepted for fines and cost only. Public access terminal is available. Fax notes: No fee to fax results.

Amelia County

11th Circuit Court 16441 Court St, PO Box 237, Amelia, VA 23002; 804-561-2128. Hours: 8:30AM-4:30PM (EST). *Felony, Civil Actions Over $15,000, Probate.*

Civil Records: Access: Mail, online, in person. Both court and visitors may perform in person searches. No search fee. Required to search: name, years to search. Civil cases indexed by defendant,

plaintiff. Civil records on microfiche 1735 to present, indexed on books. For information about the statewide online system, LOPAS, see the state introduction. Will search on telephone request if not busy. **Criminal Records:** Access: Mail, remote online, in person. Both court and visitors may perform in person searches. No search fee. Required to search: name, years to search, DOB; also helpful-SSN. Criminal records on microfiche 1735 to present, indexed on books. For information about the statewide online system, LOPAS, see the state introduction. **General Information:** No juvenile, sealed records released. SASE required. Turnaround time 3-5 days. Copy fee: $.50 per page. Certification fee: $3.00. Fee payee: Amelia County Circuit Court. Personal checks accepted. Prepayment is required.

11th General District Court PO Box 24, Amelia, VA 23002; 804-561-2456; Fax: 804-561-6956. Hours: 8:30AM-4:30PM (EST). *Misdemeanor, Civil Actions Under $15,000, Eviction, Small Claims.*

Civil Records: Access: Mail, online, in person. Both court and visitors may perform in person searches. No search fee. Required to search: name, years to search. Civil cases indexed by defendant, plaintiff. Civil records on computer since 12/20/92, prior records on index cards. For information about the statewide online system, LOPAS, see the state introduction. **Criminal Records:** Access: Mail, remote online, in person. Both court and visitors may perform in person searches. No search fee. Required to search: name, years to search, DOB; also helpful-SSN. Criminal records on computer since 12/20/92, prior records on index cards. For information about the statewide online system, LOPAS, see the state introduction. **General Information:** No juvenile, sealed records released. SASE required. Turnaround time 1-14 days. Copy fee: $1.00 for 1st two pages, $.50 each add'l page. Certification fee: No certification fee. Fee payee: Amelia District Court. Personal checks accepted. Prepayment is required. Public access terminal is available.

Amherst County

24th Circuit Court PO Box 462, Amherst, VA 24521; 804-946-9321; Fax: 804-946-9323. Hours: 8AM-5PM (EST). *Felony, Civil Actions Over $15,000, Probate.*

Civil Records: Access: online, in person. Court does not conduct in person searches; visitors must perform searches for themselves. Search fee: No civil searches performed by court. Required to search: name, years to search. Civil cases indexed by defendant, plaintiff. Civil records on index books from 1761. For information about the statewide online system, LOPAS, see the state introduction. **Criminal Records:** Access: Remote online, in person. Court does not conduct in person searches; visitors must perform searches for themselves. Search fee: No criminal searches performed by court. Required to search: name, years to search, date of offense. Criminal records on index books from 1761. For information about the statewide online system, LOPAS, see the state introduction. **General Information:** No juvenile, sealed or adoption records released. Copy fee: $.50 per page. Certification fee: $2.00. Fee payee: Clerk of Circuit Court. Personal checks accepted. Prepayment is required.

24th General District Court PO Box 513, Amherst, VA 24521; 804-946-9351; Fax: 804-946-9359. Hours: 8AM-4:30PM (EST).

Misdemeanor, Civil Actions Under $15,000, Eviction, Small Claims.

Note: Has handled misdemeanor cases since 1985

Civil Records: Access: online, in person. Court does not conduct in person searches; visitors must perform searches for themselves. Search fee: No civil searches performed by court. Required to search: name, years to search. Civil cases indexed by defendant, plaintiff. Civil records on computer from 1989, cards 10 years prior. For information about the statewide online system, LOPAS, see the state introduction. **Criminal Records:** Access: Remote online, in person. Court does not conduct in person searches; visitors must perform searches for themselves. Search fee: No criminal searches performed by court. Required to search: name, years to search, DOB, SSN. Criminal records on computer from 1989, cards 10 years prior. For information about the statewide online system, LOPAS, see the state introduction. **General Information:** No sealed records released. Copy fee: $.50 per page. Certification fee: $2.00. Personal checks accepted. Credit cards accepted: Visa, Mastercard. Prepayment is required. Public access terminal is available.

Appomattox County

10th Circuit Court PO Box 672, Appomattox, VA 24522; 804-352-5275; Fax: 804-352-2781. Hours: 8:30AM-4:30PM (EST). *Felony, Civil Actions Over $15,000, Probate.*

Civil Records: Access: online, in person. Court does not conduct in person searches; visitors must perform searches for themselves. Search fee: No civil searches performed by court. Required to search: name, years to search. Civil cases indexed by defendant, plaintiff. Civil records on books from 1892 to present. For information about the statewide online system, LOPAS, see the state introduction. **Criminal Records:** Access: Remote online, in person. Court does not conduct in person searches; visitors must perform searches for themselves. Search fee: No criminal searches performed by court. Required to search: name, years to search. Criminal records on books from 1892 to present. For information about the statewide online system, LOPAS, see the state introduction. **General Information:** No juvenile, sealed records released. Copy fee: $.50 per page. Certification fee: No certification fee. Fee payee: Clerk of Circuit Court. Personal checks accepted. Prepayment is required.

10th General District Court PO Box 187, Appomattox, VA 24522; 804-352-5540; Fax: 804-352-0717. Hours: 8:30AM-4:30PM (EST). *Misdemeanor, Civil Actions Under $15,000, Eviction, Small Claims.*

Civil Records: Access: Fax, mail, online, in person. Both court and visitors may perform in person searches. No search fee. Required to search: name, years to search. Civil cases indexed by defendant, plaintiff. Civil records on card file from 1985 to present, prior to 1985 in Circuit Court. For information about the statewide online system, LOPAS, see the state introduction. **Criminal Records:** Access: Fax, mail, remote online, in person. Both court and visitors may perform in person searches. No search fee. Required to search: name, years to search; also helpful-SSN. Criminal records on card file from 1985 to present, prior to 1985 in Circuit Court. For information about the statewide online system, LOPAS, see the state introduction. **General Information:** No juvenile, sealed records released. Turnaround time 1-5 days. Copy fee: $1.00 1st

page; $.50 each add'l. Certification fee: No certification fee. Fee payee: General District Court. Personal checks accepted. Credit cards accepted: Visa, Mastercard. Public access terminal is available. Fax notes: No fee to fax results.

Arlington County

17th Circuit Court 1425 N Courthouse Rd, Arlington, VA 22201; 703-358-7010. Hours: 8AM-5PM (EST). *Felony, Civil Actions Over $15,000, Probate.*

Civil Records: Access: Mail, online, in person. Court does not conduct in person searches; visitors must perform searches for themselves. Search fee: $10.00 per name. Fee is for pre-1987 or lengthy search. Required to search: name, years to search. Civil cases indexed by defendant, plaintiff. Civil records on computer from 1987; prior on books from mid-1930 to present. For information about the statewide online system, LOPAS, see the state introduction. **Criminal Records:** Access: Mail, remote online, in person. Court does not conduct in person searches; visitors must perform searches for themselves. Search fee: $10.00 per name. Fee is for pre 1987 or lengthy search. Required to search: name, years to search. Criminal records on computer from 1987; prior on books from mid-1930 to present. For information about the statewide online system, LOPAS, see the state introduction. **General Information:** No juvenile, adoption or sealed records released. Mail requests not accepted. Turnaround time 1-2 days. Copy fee: $.50 per page. Certification fee: $2.00. Fee payee: Clerk of Court. Personal checks accepted. Prepayment is required. Public access terminal is available. Public Access Terminal Note: Criminal only.

17th General District Court 1425 N Courthouse Rd, Rm 2500, Arlington, VA 22201; 703-228-4590; Fax: 703-228-4593. Hours: 8AM-4PM (EST). *Misdemeanor, Civil Actions Under $15,000, Eviction, Small Claims.*

Civil Records: Access: Phone, mail, online, in person. Both court and visitors may perform in person searches. No search fee. Required to search: name, years to search. Civil cases indexed by defendant. Civil records on computer from 1990, books from early 1970s. For information about the statewide online system, LOPAS, see the state introduction. Phone access limited to 4 requests. **Criminal Records:** Access: Phone, mail, remote online, in person. Both court and visitors may perform in person searches. No search fee. Required to search: name, years to search, DOB, SSN. Criminal records on computer from 1990, books from early 1970s. For information about the statewide online system, LOPAS, see the state introduction. Same as civil. **General Information:** No juvenile, sealed records released. Turnaround time 1-2 days. Copy fee: $.50 per page. Certification fee: $2.00. Fee payee: Clerk of Court. Personal checks accepted. Prepayment is required. Public access terminal is available.

Augusta County

25th Circuit Court PO Box 689, Staunton, VA 24402-0689; 540-245-5321; Fax: 540-245-5318. Hours: 8AM-5PM (EST). *Felony, Civil Actions Over $15,000, Probate.*

Note: Court prefers that searches be done in person. They will only search back to 1987.

Civil Sourcebook: Access: Fax, mail, online, in person. Both court and visitors may perform in person searches. No search fee. Required to search: name, years to search. Civil cases indexed

by defendant, plaintiff. Civil records on computer from 1987 to present, books from 1745 to 1986. For information about the statewide online system, LOPAS, see the state introduction. Phone not available for lengthy search. Mail access limited. **Criminal Records:** Access: Fax, mail, remote online, in person. Both court and visitors may perform in person searches. No search fee. Required to search: name, years to search; also helpful-DOB, SSN. Criminal records go back to 1987 felonies only. For information about the statewide online system, LOPAS, see the state introduction. **General Information:** No juvenile, adoption or sealed records released. SASE required. Turnaround time 1-2 days. Copy fee: $.50 per page. Certification fee: $2.00. Fee payee: Clerk, Augusta County Circuit Court. Personal checks accepted. Public access terminal is available.

25th General District Court 6 E Johnson St, 2nd Floor, Staunton, VA 24401; 540-245-5300; Fax: 540-245-5302. Hours: 8:30AM-4:30PM (EST). *Misdemeanor, Civil Actions Under $15,000, Eviction, Small Claims.*

Civil Records: Access: Mail, online, in person. Both court and visitors may perform in person searches. No search fee. Required to search: name, years to search. Civil cases indexed by defendant, plaintiff. Civil records kept for 10 years on computer, then archived or destroyed. For information about the statewide online system, LOPAS, see the state introduction. **Criminal Records:** Access: Mail, remote online, in person. Both court and visitors may perform in person searches. No search fee. Required to search: name, years to search. Criminal records kept for 10 years on computer, then archived or destroyed. For information about the statewide online system, LOPAS, see the state introduction. **General Information:** No juvenile, sealed records released. SASE requested. Turnaround time 2-3 days. Copy fee: $.50 per page. Certification fee: No certification fee. Fee payee: Augusta General District Court. Personal checks accepted. Credit cards accepted: Visa, Mastercard. Prepayment is required. Public access terminal is available.

Bath County

25th Circuit Court PO Box 180, Warm Springs, VA 24484; 540-839-7226; Fax: 540-839-7222. Hours: 8:30AM-4:30PM (EST). *Felony, Civil Actions Over $15,000, Probate.*

Civil Records: Access: Mail, online, in person. Both court and visitors may perform in person searches. No search fee. Required to search: name, years to search. Civil cases indexed by defendant, plaintiff. Civil records on books from 1791 to present. For information about the statewide online system, LOPAS, see the state introduction. **Criminal Records:** Access: Remote online, in person. Court does not conduct in person searches; visitors must perform searches for themselves. Search fee: No criminal searches performed by court. Required to search: name, years to search; also helpful-DOB, SSN. Criminal records on books from 1791 to present. For information about the statewide online system, LOPAS, see the state introduction. **General Information:** No juvenile, sealed or adoption records released. Turnaround time 1-2 days. Copy fee: $.50 per page. Certification fee: $3.00. Fee payee: Bath County Circuit Court. Personal checks accepted. Prepayment is required.

25th General District Court PO Box 96, Warm Springs, VA 24484; 540-839-7241; Fax:

540-839-7248. Hours: 8:30AM-4:30PM (EST). *Misdemeanor, Civil Actions Under $15,000, Eviction, Small Claims.*

Civil Records: Access: Phone, fax, mail, online, in person. Both court and visitors may perform in person searches. No search fee. Required to search: name, years to search. Civil cases indexed by defendant, plaintiff. Civil records on files from 1985 to present, Prior records in Circuit Court. For information about the statewide online system, LOPAS, see the state introduction. **Criminal Records:** Access: Phone, fax, mail, remote online, in person. Both court and visitors may perform in person searches. No search fee. Required to search: name, years to search, DOB; also helpful-SSN. Criminal records on files from 1985 to present, Prior records in Circuit Court. For information about the statewide online system, LOPAS, see the state introduction. **General Information:** No juvenile, sealed records released. SASE requested. Turnaround time 2 days, will give immediate response on phone if not an extensive search. Copy fee: $.50 per page. Certification fee: No certification fee. Fee payee: Bath County Combined Court. Personal checks accepted. Credit cards accepted: Visa, Mastercard. Public access terminal is available.

Bedford County

Bedford County Circuit Court 1635 Venture Blvd, Bedford, VA 24523; 540-586-7632; Fax: 540-586-6197. Hours: 8:30AM-5PM (EST). *Felony, Civil Actions Over $15,000, Probate.*

Civil Records: Access: online, in person. Court does not conduct in person searches; visitors must perform searches for themselves. Search fee: No civil searches performed by court. Required to search: name, years to search. Civil cases indexed by defendant, plaintiff. Civil records on computer from 1988, index books. For information about the statewide online system, LOPAS, see the state introduction. **Criminal Records:** Access: Remote online, in person. Court does not conduct in person searches; visitors must perform searches for themselves. Search fee: No criminal searches performed by court. Required to search: name, years to search, DOB; also helpful-SSN, race, sex. Criminal records on computer from 1988, index books. For information about the statewide online system, LOPAS, see the state introduction. **General Information:** No juvenile, sealed records released. Copy fee: $.50 per page. Certification fee: $2.00 per page. Fee payee: Bedford Clerk of Court. Personal checks accepted. Prepayment is required. Public access terminal is available.

24th General District Court 1635 Venture Blvd #500, Bedford, VA 24523; 540-586-7637; Fax: 540-586-7684. Hours: 8AM-4PM (EST). *Misdemeanor, Civil Actions Under $15,000, Eviction, Small Claims.*

Civil Records: Access: Mail, online, in person. Court does not conduct in person searches; visitors must perform searches for themselves. Search fee: $5.00 per name. Required to search: name, years to search. Civil cases indexed by defendant. Civil records on computer for ten years. Date of birth or SSN also helpful in searching. For information about the statewide online system, LOPAS, see the state introduction. **Criminal Records:** Access: Mail, remote online, in person. Both court and visitors may perform in person searches. Search fee: $5.00 per name. Required to search: name, years to search; also helpful-DOB, SSN. Criminal records on computer for ten years. Date of birth or SSN also helpful in searching. For information about the statewide online system, LOPAS, see the

state introduction. **General Information:** No sealed records released. SASE required. Turnaround time 1-5 days. Copy fee: $1.00 1st 2 pages, $.50 each additional page. Certification fee: No certification. Fee payee: Bedford General District Court. Personal checks accepted. Credit cards accepted: Visa, Mastercard. Prepayment is required. Public access terminal is available.

Bedford City

Circuit & District Courts

Note: See Bedford County.

Bland County

27th Circuit Court PO Box 295, Bland, VA 24315; 540-688-4562; Fax: 540-688-4562. Hours: 8AM-6PM (EST). *Felony, Civil Actions Over $15,000, Probate.*

Civil Records: Access: Phone, fax, mail, online, in person. Both court and visitors may perform in person searches. Search fee: $10.00 per name. Required to search: name, years to search. Civil cases indexed by defendant, plaintiff. Civil records on books from 1861 to present. For information about the statewide online system, LOPAS, see the state introduction. **Criminal Records:** Access: Phone, fax, mail, remote online, in person. Both court and visitors may perform in person searches. Search fee: $10.00 per name. Required to search: name, years to search, signed release; also helpful-SSN. Criminal records on books from 1861 to present. For information about the statewide online system, LOPAS, see the state introduction. **General Information:** No juvenile, sealed or adoption records released. Turnaround time 2 days. Copy fee: $.50 per page. Certification fee: $2.00. Fee payee: Clerk of Court. Personal checks accepted. Prepayment is required. Fax notes: $1.00 per page.

27th General District Court PO Box 157, Bland, VA 24315; 540-688-4433; Fax: 540-688-4789. Hours: 8AM-5PM (EST). *Misdemeanor, Civil Actions Under $15,000, Eviction, Small Claims.*

Civil Records: Access: Phone, fax, mail, online, in person. Both court and visitors may perform in person searches. No search fee. Required to search: name, years to search. Civil cases indexed by defendant. Civil records on computer from 4/23/92, card index back to 1985. For information about the statewide online system, LOPAS, see the state introduction. Phone access limited to specific cases only. **Criminal Records:** Access: Phone, fax, mail, remote online, in person. Both court and visitors may perform in person searches. No search fee. Required to search: name, years to search; also helpful-DOB, SSN. Criminal records on computer from 4/23/92, card index back to 1985. For information about the statewide online system, LOPAS, see the state introduction. Phone access limited to specific cases only. **General Information:** No juvenile, sealed or adoption records released. SASE requested. Turnaround time 1-2 days. Copy fee: $1.00 1st 2 pages, $.50 each additional page. Certification fee: No certification fee. Fee payee: General District Court. Personal checks accepted. Credit cards accepted: Visa, Mastercard. Public access terminal is available.

Botetourt County

25th Circuit Court PO Box 219, Fincastle, VA 24090; 540-473-8274; Fax: 540-473-8209. Hours: 8:30AM-4:30PM (EST). *Felony, Civil Actions Over $15,000, Probate.*

Civil Records: Access: Mail, online, in person. Both court and visitors may perform in person searches. No search fee. Required to search: name, years to search. Civil cases indexed by defendant, plaintiff. Civil records on computer 7/1/91 to present, books back to 1770. For information about the statewide online system, LOPAS, see the state introduction. **Criminal Records:** Access: Mail, remote online, in person. Both court and visitors may perform in person searches. No search fee. Required to search: name, years to search, DOB, SSN. Criminal records on computer 7/1/91 to present, books back to 1770. For information about the statewide online system, LOPAS, see the state introduction. **General Information:** No juvenile, sealed or adoption records released. SASE required. Turnaround time same day. Copy fee: $.50 per page. Certification fee: $2.00. Fee payee: Clerk of Court. Personal checks accepted. Prepayment is required. Public access terminal is available.

25th General District Court PO Box 205, Fincastle, VA 24090-0205; 540-473-8244; Fax: 540-473-8344. Hours: 8AM-4PM (EST). *Misdemeanor, Civil Actions Under $15,000, Eviction, Small Claims.*

Civil Records: Access: Mail, online, in person. Both court and visitors may perform in person searches. No search fee. Required to search: name, years to search. Civil cases indexed by defendant, plaintiff. Civil records on computer from 1988 to present. Civil records on files back to 1964, others back to 1974. For information about the statewide online system, LOPAS, see the state introduction. **Criminal Records:** Access: Mail, remote online, in person. Both court and visitors may perform in person searches. No search fee. Required to search: name, years to search. Criminal records on computer from 1988 to present. Civil records on files back to 1964, others back to 1974. For information about the statewide online system, LOPAS, see the state introduction. **General Information:** No juvenile, sealed records released. SASE requested. Turnaround time 1-2 days. No copy fee. Certification fee: No certification fee. Fee payee: General District Court. Personal checks accepted. Checks that require verification calls not accepted. Credit cards accepted: Visa, Mastercard. Public access terminal is available.

Bristol City

28th Circuit Court 497 Cumberland St, Bristol, VA 24201; 540-645-7321; Fax: 540-645-7345. Hours: 9AM-5PM (EST). *Felony, Civil Actions Over $15,000, Probate.*

Civil Records: Access: Mail, in person. Both court and visitors may perform in person searches. No search fee. Required to search: name, years to search. Civil cases indexed by defendant, plaintiff. Civil records indexed from 1890 to present. For information about the statewide online system, LOPAS, see the state introduction. **Criminal Records:** Access: In person. Court does not conduct in person searches; visitors must perform searches for themselves. Search fee: No criminal searches performed by court. Required to search: name, years to search. Criminal records indexed from 1890 to present. For information about the statewide online system, LOPAS, see the state introduction. **General Information:** No juvenile, sealed or adoption records released. SASE required. Turnaround time up to 1 week. Copy fee: $.50 per page. Certification fee: $2.00. Fee payee: Clerk of Circuit Court. Personal checks accepted. Prepayment is required.

28th General District Court 497

Cumberland St, Bristol, VA 24201; 540-645-7341; Fax: 540-645-7345. Hours: 8AM-5PM (EST). *Misdemeanor, Civil Actions Under $15,000, Eviction, Small Claims.*

Civil Records: Access: Mail, online, in person. Both court and visitors may perform in person searches. No search fee. Required to search: name, years to search. Civil cases indexed by defendant, plaintiff. Civil records on computer from 1989, card file 1983 to 1988. For information about the statewide online system, LOPAS, see the state introduction. **Criminal Records:** Access: Mail, remote online, in person. Court does not conduct in person searches; visitors must perform searches for themselves. No search fee. Required to search: name, years to search, DOB, SSN. Criminal records on computer from 1989, card file 1983 to 1988. For information about the statewide online system, LOPAS, see the state introduction. **General Information:** No juvenile, sealed records released. SASE requested. Turnaround time 1-2 days. Copy fee: $.50 per page. Certification fee: $2.00. Fee payee: General District Court. Personal checks accepted. Credit cards accepted: Visa, Mastercard. Public access terminal is available.

Brunswick County

6th Circuit Court 216 N Main St,

Lawrenceville, VA 23868; 804-848-2215; Fax: 804-848-4307. Hours: 8:30AM-5PM (EST). *Felony, Civil, Probate.*

Civil Records: Access: online, in person. Court does not conduct in person searches; visitors must perform searches for themselves. Search fee: No civil searches performed by court. Required to search: name, years to search. Civil cases indexed by defendant, plaintiff. Civil records on microfiche and books, on computer since 1996. For information about the statewide online system, LOPAS, see the state introduction. **Criminal Records:** Access: Remote online, in person. Court does not conduct in person searches; visitors must perform searches for themselves. Search fee: No criminal searches performed by court. Required to search: name, years to search. Criminal records on microfiche and books, on computer since 1996. For information about the statewide online system, LOPAS, see the state introduction. **General Information:** No juvenile, sealed or adoption records released. Copy fee: $.50 per page. Certification fee: $2.00. Fee payee: Clerk of Court. Personal checks accepted. Public access terminal is available. Public Access Terminal Note: Available for land records and wills. No case information.

6th General District Court , 202 Main St,

Lawrenceville, VA 23868-0066; 804-848-2315; Fax: 804-848-2550. Hours: 8:30AM-4:30PM (EST). *Misdemeanor, Civil Actions Under $15,000, Eviction, Small Claims.*

Civil Records: Access: Mail, online, in person. Only the court conducts in person searches; visitors may not. No search fee. Required to search: name, years to search. Civil cases indexed by defendant, plaintiff. Civil records computerized since 1987. For information about the statewide online system, LOPAS, see the state introduction. **Criminal Records:** Access: Mail, remote online, in person. Only the court conducts in person searches; visitors may not. Search fee:. Required to search: name, years to search, DOB; also helpful-SSN. Civil records computerized since 1987. For information about the statewide online system, LOPAS, see the state introduction.

General Information: No juvenile, sealed records released. SASE required. Turnaround time 1-2 days. No copy fee. Certification fee: No certification fee. Fee payee: Brunswick Combined District Court. Only cashiers checks and money orders accepted. Public access terminal is available.

Buchanan County

29th Circuit PO Box 929, Grundy, VA 24614;

540-935-6575. Hours: 8:30AM-5PM (EST). *Felony, Misdemeanor, Civil Actions Over $15,000, Probate.*

Civil Records: Access: Phone, mail, online, in person. Both court and visitors may perform in person searches. No search fee. Required to search: name, years to search; also helpful-address. Civil cases indexed by defendant, plaintiff. Civil records on books prior to 1991. For information about the statewide online system, LOPAS, see the state introduction. **Criminal Records:** Access: Phone, mail, remote online, in person. Both court and visitors may perform in person searches. No search fee. Required to search: name, years to search, DOB; also helpful-address, SSN. Criminal records on books prior to 1991. For information about the statewide online system, LOPAS, see the state introduction. **General Information:** No juvenile, sealed records released. Turnaround time 1-2 days. Copy fee: $.50 per page. Certification fee: $2.00. Fee payee: Clerk of Circuit Court. Personal checks accepted. Public access terminal is available.

29th Judicial District Court PO Box 654,

Grundy, VA 24614; 540-935-6526; Fax: 540-935-5479. Hours: 8AM-4PM (EST). *Civil Actions Under $15,000, Eviction, Small Claims.*

Civil Records: Access: Phone, fax, mail, in person. Both court and visitors may perform in person searches. No search fee. Required to search: name; also helpful-years to search. Civil cases indexed by defendant, plaintiff. Civil Records are indexed for 10 years, computerized since 1993. **General Information:** Turnaround time is 1 week. Copy fee: $.50 per page. Certification fee: $2.00. Fee payee: General District Court. Personal checks accepted. Credit cards accepted: Visa, Mastercard. Fax notes: No fee to fax results.

Buckingham County

10th Circuit Court Route 60, PO Box 107,

Buckingham, VA 23921; 804-969-4734; Fax: 804-969-2043. Hours: 8:30AM-4:30PM (EST). *Felony, Civil Actions Over $15,000, Probate.*

Civil Records: Access: Mail, online, in person. Both court and visitors may perform in person searches. No search fee. Required to search: name, years to search. Civil cases indexed by defendant, plaintiff. Civil records on books from 1869 to present. For information about the statewide online system, LOPAS, see the state introduction. Simple requests only by mail. **Criminal Records:** Access: Mail, remote online, in person. Both court and visitors may perform in person searches. No search fee. Required to search: name, years to search; also helpful-DOB. Criminal records on books from 1869 to present. For information about the statewide online system, LOPAS, see the state introduction. **General Information:** No juvenile, sealed or adoption records released. Copy fee: $.50 per page. Certification fee: $2.00. Fee payee: Clerk of Court. Personal checks accepted.

Buckingham General District Court PO

Box 127, Buckingham, VA 23921; 804-969-4755;

Fax: 804-969-1762. Hours: 8:30AM-4:30PM (EST). *Misdemeanor, Civil Actions Under $15,000, Eviction, Small Claims.*

Civil Records: Access: Mail, online, in person. Only the court conducts in person searches; visitors may not. No search fee. Required to search: name, years to search. Civil cases indexed by defendant. Civil records on computer or hard copy from 1993, prior records on index cards. For information about the statewide online system, LOPAS, see the state introduction. **Criminal Records:** Access: Mail, remote online, in person. Only the court conducts in person searches; visitors may not. No search fee. Required to search: name, years to search, DOB, SSN, signed release. Criminal records on computer or hard copy from 1993, prior records on index cards. For information about the statewide online system, LOPAS, see the state introduction. **General Information:** No juvenile, sealed records released. Turnaround time 2 weeks. Copy fee: $.50 per page. Certification fee: $2.00. Fee payee: Buckingham. Personal checks accepted. Credit cards accepted: Visa, Mastercard.

Buena Vista City

25th Circuit & District Court 2039

Sycamore Ave, Buena Vista, VA 24416; 540-261-8627 X626/627; Fax: 540-261-8625. Hours: 8:30AM-5PM (EST). *Felony, Misdemeanor, Civil, Eviction, Probate.*

Civil Records: Access: Mail, online, in person. Both court and visitors may perform in person searches. No search fee. Required to search: name, years to search. Civil cases indexed by defendant, plaintiff. Civil records on manual records 1892 to present. For information about the statewide online system, LOPAS, see the state introduction. **Criminal Records:** Access: Mail, remote online, in person. Both court and visitors may perform in person searches. No search fee. Required to search: name, years to search. Criminal records on manual records 1892 to present. For information about the statewide online system, LOPAS, see the state introduction. **General Information:** No juvenile, sealed records released. SASE required. Turnaround time 1 day. Copy fee: $.50 per page. Certification fee: $3.00. Fee payee: Buena Vista Circuit Court. Personal checks accepted. Prepayment is required. Public access terminal is available. Fax notes: $.50 per page.

Campbell County

24th Circuit Court State RD 501 Village

Hwy, PO Box 7, Rustburg, VA 24588; 804-592-9517. Hours: 8:30AM-4:30PM (EST). *Felony, Civil Actions Over $15,000, Probate.*

Civil Records: Access: Mail, online, in person. Both court and visitors may perform in person searches. No search fee. Required to search: name, years to search. Civil cases indexed by defendant, plaintiff. Civil records on index books. For information about the statewide online system, LOPAS, see the state introduction. **Criminal Records:** Access: Mail, remote online, in person. Both court and visitors may perform in person searches. No search fee. Required to search: name, years to search; also helpful-DOB. Criminal records on index books. For information about the statewide online system, LOPAS, see the state introduction. **General Information:** No juvenile, sealed or adoption records released. SASE required. Turnaround 2-10 days. Copy fee: $.50 per page. Certification fee: $2.00. Fee payee: Clerk of Court. Personal checks accepted.

24th General District Court 1st Floor, New Courthouse Bldg, PO Box 97, Rustburg, VA 24588; 804-332-9546; Fax: 804-332-9694. Hours: 8AM-4PM (EST). *Misdemeanor, Civil Actions Under $15,000, Eviction, Small Claims.*

Civil Records: Access: online, in person. Court does not conduct in person searches; visitors must perform searches for themselves. Search fee: No civil searches performed by court. Required to search: name, years to search. Civil cases indexed by defendant, plaintiff. Civil records on computer for 10 years. For information about the statewide online system, LOPAS, see the state introduction. **Criminal Records:** Access: Remote online, in person. Court does not conduct in person searches; visitors must perform searches for themselves. Search fee: No criminal searches performed by court. Required to search: name, years to search. Criminal records on computer for 10 years. For information about the statewide online system, LOPAS, see the state introduction. **General Information:** Copy fee: $1.00 for 1st 2 copies then $.50 per copy thereafter. Certification fee: No certification fee. Prepayment is required. Public access terminal is available. Public Access Terminal Note: Not available for criminal or civil information.

Caroline County

15th Circuit Court Main St & Courthouse Ln, PO Box 309, Bowling Green, VA 22427-0309; 804-633-5800. Hours: 9AM-5PM (EST). *Felony, Civil Actions Over $15,000, Probate.*

Civil Records: Access: online, in person. Court does not conduct in person searches; visitors must perform searches for themselves. Search fee: No civil searches performed by court. Required to search: name, years to search. Civil cases indexed by defendant, plaintiff. Civil records on books from early 1800s to present. For information about the statewide online system, LOPAS, see the state introduction. **Criminal Records:** Access: Remote online, in person. Court does not conduct in person searches; visitors must perform searches for themselves. Search fee: No criminal searches performed by court. Required to search: name, years to search; also helpful-DOB. Criminal records on books from early 1800s to present. For information about the statewide online system, LOPAS, see the state introduction. **General Information:** No juvenile, sealed, adoption records released. Copy fee: $.50 per page. Certification fee: $2.00. Fee payee: Clerk of Court. Personal checks accepted. Accepted for payment of fines & costs only. Not accepted over the phone. Prepayment is required.

15th General District Court PO Box 511, Bowling Green, VA 22427; 804-633-5720; Fax: 804-633-3033. Hours: 8AM-4PM (EST). *Misdemeanor, Civil Actions Under $15,000, Eviction, Small Claims.*

Civil Records: Access: Mail, online, in person. Both court and visitors may perform in person searches. No search fee. Required to search: name, years to search. Civil cases indexed by defendant, plaintiff. Civil records on computer from 1/92, index cards from 1988. For information about the statewide online system, LOPAS, see the state introduction. **Criminal Records:** Access: Mail, remote online, in person. Both court and visitors may perform in person searches. No search fee. Required to search: name, years to search. Criminal records on computer from 1/92, index cards from 1988. For information about the statewide online system, LOPAS, see the state

introduction. **General Information:** No juvenile, sealed records released. Turnaround time 5 days. Copy fee: $.50 per page. Certification fee: $2.00. Fee payee: Caroline General District Court. Personal checks accepted. Credit cards accepted: Visa, Mastercard. Public access terminal is available.

Carroll County

27th Circuit Court PO Box 218, Hillsville, VA 24343; 540-728-3117. Hours: 8AM-5PM (EST). *Felony, Civil Actions Over $15,000, Probate.*

Civil Records: Access: Mail, online, in person. Both court and visitors may perform in person searches. Search fee: $5.00 per name. Required to search: name, years to search, also helpful- SSN. Civil cases indexed by defendant, plaintiff. Civil records on books from 1842 to present. For information about the statewide online system, LOPAS, see the state introduction. **Criminal Records:** Access: Mail, remote online, in person. Both court and visitors may perform in person searches. Search fee: $5.00 per name. Required to search: name, years to search; also helpful- SSN. Criminal records on books from 1842 to present. For information about the statewide online system, LOPAS, see the state introduction. **General Information:** No juvenile, sealed, adoption records released. SASE requested. Turnaround time 3-5 days. Copy fee: $.50 per page. Certification fee: $2.00. Fee payee: Clerk of Court. Personal checks accepted. Prepayment is required.

Carroll Combined District Court PO Box 698, Hillsville, VA 24343; 540-728-7751; Fax: 540-728-2582. Hours: 8AM-4:30PM (EST). *Misdemeanor, Civil Actions Under $15,000, Eviction, Small Claims.*

Civil Records: Access: online, in person. Court does not conduct in person searches; visitors must perform searches for themselves. Search fee: No civil searches performed by court. Required to search: name, years to search. Civil cases indexed by defendant, plaintiff. Civil records on books from 1800s, on computer from 1988; no plaintiff index prior to computerization. For information about the statewide online system, LOPAS, see the state introduction. **Criminal Records:** Access: Remote online, in person. Court does not conduct in person searches; visitors must perform searches for themselves. Search fee: No criminal searches performed by court. Required to search: name, years to search. Criminal records on books from 1800s, on computer from 1988; no plaintiff index prior to computerization. For information about the statewide online system, LOPAS, see the state introduction. **General Information:** No juvenile, sealed records released. No copy fee. Certification fee: No certification fee. Fee payee: General District Court. Personal checks accepted. Credit cards accepted: Visa, Mastercard. Prepayment is required. Public access terminal is available.

Charles City

9th Circuit Court 10700 Courthouse Rd, PO Box 86, Charles City, VA 23030-0086; 804-829-9212; Fax: 804-829-5647. Hours: 8:30AM-4:30PM (EST). *Felony, Civil Actions Over $15,000, Probate.*

Civil Records: Access: Mail, online, in person. Both court and visitors may perform in person searches. No search fee. Required to search: name, years to search. Civil cases indexed by defendant, plaintiff. Civil records on computer from 1990, on books from 1789. For information about the statewide online system, LOPAS, see the state

introduction. **Criminal Records:** Access: Mail, remote online, in person. Both court and visitors may perform in person searches. No search fee. Required to search: name, years to search, DOB, SSN, signed release. Criminal records on computer from 1990, on books from 1789. For information about the statewide online system, LOPAS, see the state introduction. **General Information:** No juvenile, sealed records released. Turnaround time 2-5 days. Copy fee: $.50 per page. Certification fee: $2.00. Fee payee: Clerk of Circuit Court. Personal checks accepted. Prepayment is required.

9th General District Court Charles City Courthouse, 10700 Courthouse Rd, Charles City, VA 23030; 804-829-9224; Fax: 504-829-5109. Hours: 8:30AM-4PM (EST). *Misdemeanor, Civil Actions Under $15,000, Eviction, Small Claims.*

Civil Records: Access: Mail, online, in person. Both court and visitors may perform in person searches. No search fee. Required to search: name, years to search. Civil cases indexed by defendant, plaintiff. Civil records on computer from 1991, on books from 1700s. For information about the statewide online system, LOPAS, see the state introduction. **Criminal Records:** Access: Mail, remote online, in person. Both court and visitors may perform in person searches. No search fee. Required to search: name, years to search, DOB, SSN. Criminal records on computer from 1991, on books from 1700s. For information about the statewide online system, LOPAS, see the state introduction. **General Information:** No juvenile, sealed records released. Turnaround time 3 days. No copy fee. Certification fee: $2.00. Fee payee: Circuit Court. Personal checks accepted. Prepayment is required. Public access terminal is available.

Charlotte County

10th Circuit Court 115 LeGrande Ave PO Box 38, Charlotte Courthouse, VA 23923; 804-542-5147. Hours: 8:30AM-4:30PM (EST). *Felony, Civil Actions Over $15,000, Probate.*

Civil Records: Access: In person only. Court does not conduct in person searches; visitors must perform searches for themselves. Search fee: No civil searches performed by court. Required to search: name, years to search. Civil cases indexed by defendant, plaintiff. Civil records on books from 1765, in folders by case number. **Criminal Records:** Access: In person only. Court does not conduct in person searches; visitors must perform searches for themselves. Search fee: No criminal searches performed by court. Required to search: name, years to search, DOB. Criminal records on books from 1765, in folders by case number. **General Information:** No juvenile, sealed records released. Copy fee: $.50 per page. Certification fee: $3.00. Fee payee: Clerk of Circuit Court. Personal checks accepted. Prepayment is required.

Charlotte General District Court PO Box 127, Charlotte Courthouse, VA 23923; 804-542-5600; Fax: 804-542-5902. Hours: 8:30AM-4:30PM (EST). *Misdemeanor, Civil Actions Under $15,000, Eviction, Small Claims.*

Civil Records: Access: online, in person. Court does not conduct in person searches; visitors must perform searches for themselves. Search fee: No civil searches performed by court. Required to search: name, years to search. Civil cases indexed by defendant, plaintiff. Civil records on computer since 5/95, on books froom 1988. For information about the statewide online system, LOPAS, see the state introduction. **Criminal Records:** Access: Remote online, in person. Court does not conduct in person searches; visitors must perform searches for themselves. Search fee: No criminal searches performed by court. Required to search: name, years to search, DOB. Criminal records on computer since 5/95, on books froom 1988. For information about the statewide online system, LOPAS, see the state introduction. **General Information:** No juvenile, sealed records released. Copy fee: $.50 per page. Certification fee: No certification fee. Fee payee: Clerk of General District Court. Personal checks accepted. Credit cards accepted: Visa, Mastercard. Visa, MC. Public access terminal is available.

Charlottesville City

16th Judicial Circuit Court 315 E High St, Charlottesville, VA 22902; 804-295-3182. Hours: 8:30AM-4:30PM (EST). *Felony, Civil Actions Over $15,000, Probate.*

Civil Records: Access: online, in person. Court does not conduct in person searches; visitors must perform searches for themselves. Search fee: No civil searches performed by court. Required to search: name, years to search. Civil cases indexed by defendant, plaintiff. Civil records on books from 1888 to present. For information about the statewide online system, LOPAS, see the state introduction. **Criminal Records:** Access: Remote online, in person. Court does not conduct in person searches; visitors must perform searches for themselves. Search fee: No criminal searches performed by court. Required to search: name, years to search; also helpful-DOB. Criminal records on books from 1888 to present. For information about the statewide online system, LOPAS, see the state introduction. **General Information:** No juvenile, sealed or adoption records released. Copy fee: $.50 per page. Certification fee: $2.00. Fee payee: Charlottesville Circuit Court Clerk's Office. Personal checks accepted. No out of state checks accepted. Prepayment is required.

Charlottesville General District Court

606 E Market St, PO Box 2677, Charlottesville, VA 22902; 804-970-3385; Fax: 804-970-3387. Hours: 8:30AM-4:30PM (EST). *Misdemeanor, Civil Actions Under $15,000, Eviction, Small Claims.*

Civil Records: Access: Mail, online, in person. Both court and visitors may perform in person searches. No search fee. Required to search: name, years to search. Civil cases indexed by defendant, plaintiff. Civil records on computer from 1986 to present, on books 1982-1986, records kept for 10 years. For information about the statewide online system, LOPAS, see the state introduction. **Criminal Records:** Access: Mail, remote online, in person. Both court and visitors may perform in person searches. No search fee. Required to search: name, years to search; also helpful-DOB, SSN. Criminal records on computer from 1986 to present, on books 1982-1986, records kept for 10 years. For information about the statewide online system, LOPAS, see the state introduction. **General Information:** No juvenile, sealed, confidential records released. SASE required. Turnaround time 3 days. Copy fee: $1.00 for first page, $.50 each addl. Certification fee: No certification fee. Fee payee: General District Court. Personal checks accepted. Prepayment is required. Public access terminal is available.

Chesapeake City

1st Circuit Court 307 Albemarle Dr, #300A, Chesapeake, VA 23322-5579; 757-382-3000; Fax:

757-382-3034. Hours: 8:30AM-5PM (EST). *Felony, Civil Actions Over $15,000, Probate.*

Civil Records: Access: Mail, online, in person. Court does not conduct in person searches; visitors must perform searches for themselves. Search fee: $5.00 per name. Required to search: name, years to search. Civil cases indexed by defendant, plaintiff. Civil records on books from 1637, on computer from 1990. For information about the statewide online system, LOPAS, see the state introduction. **Criminal Records:** Access: Remote online, in person. Court does not conduct in person searches; visitors must perform searches for themselves. Search fee: No criminal searches performed by court. Required to search: name, years to search, DOB; also helpful-SSN. Criminal records on books from 1637, on computer from 1990. For information about the statewide online system, LOPAS, see the state introduction. **General Information:** No juvenile, sealed records released. SASE required. Turnaround time 1 week. Copy fee: $.50 per page. Certification fee: $2.50. Fee payee: Clerk of Circuit Court. Personal checks accepted. Prepayment is required. Public access terminal is available.

1st General District Court 307 Albenarle Dr #100, Chesapeake, VA 23322;; Civil phone:757-382-3143; Criminal phone:757-382-3143; Fax: 757-382-3171. Hours: 8AM-4PM (EST). *Misdemeanor, Civil Actions Under $15,000, Eviction, Small Claims.*

Note: Indicate division (civil, criminal or traffic) in address

Civil Records: Access: Mail, online, in person. Both court and visitors may perform in person searches. Search fee: $15.00 per name. Required to search: name, years to search. Civil cases indexed by defendant, plaintiff. Civil records on books from 1700. For information about the statewide online system, LOPAS, see the state introduction. Mail access by specific case only. **Criminal Records:** Access: Mail, remote online, in person. Both court and visitors may perform in person searches. No search fee. Required to search: name, years to search, DOB; also helpful-SSN. Criminal records on books from 1700. For information about the statewide online system, LOPAS, see the state introduction. **General Information:** No juvenile, sealed records released. Turnaround time 2-14 days. Copy fee: $1.00 per page. Certification fee: $2.00. Fee payee: General District Court. Personal checks accepted. Credit cards accepted: Visa, Mastercard. Prepayment is required. Public access terminal is available.

Chesterfield County

12th Circuit Court 9500 Courthouse Rd, PO Box 125, Chesterfield, VA 23832; 804-748-1241; Fax: 804-796-5625. Hours: 8:30AM-5PM (EST). *Felony, Civil Actions Over $15,000, Probate.*

www.co.chesterfield.va.us/cc-main.htm

Civil Records: Access: Mail, online, in person. Both court and visitors may perform in person searches. Search fee: $3.00 per name. Required to search: name, years to search. Civil cases indexed by defendant, plaintiff. Civil records on computer from 1988 to present, prior on index books. For information about the statewide online system, LOPAS, see the state introduction. **Criminal Records:** Access: Mail, remote online, in person. Only the court conducts in person searches; visitors may not. Search fee: $3.00 per name. Required to search: name, years to search; also helpful-DOB, SSN. Criminal records on computer from 1988 to present, prior on index books. For

information about the statewide online system, LOPAS, see the state introduction. **General Information:** No juvenile, adoption, sealed records released. SASE required. Turnaround time 1-2 days. Copy fee: $.50 per page. Certification fee: $2.00. Fee payee: Chesterfield Circuit Court. Personal checks accepted. Prepayment is required. Public access terminal is available. Public Access Terminal Note: Civil only.

12th General District Court PO Box 144, Chesterfield, VA 23832; 804-748-1231. Hours: 8AM-4PM (EST). *Misdemeanor, Civil Actions Under $15,000, Eviction, Small Claims.*

Civil Records: Access: Mail, online, in person. Both court and visitors may perform in person searches. No search fee. Required to search: name, years to search. Civil cases indexed by defendant, plaintiff. Civil records on computer from 1986 to present, index books from 1975 to 1986. For information about the statewide online system, LOPAS, see the state introduction. **Criminal Records:** Access: Mail, remote online, in person. Both court and visitors may perform in person searches. No search fee. Required to search: name, years to search, DOB, SSN. Criminal records on computer from 1986 to present, index books from 1975 to 1986. For information about the statewide online system, LOPAS, see the state introduction. **General Information:** No sealed records released. Turnaround time 2 days. Copy fee: $.50 per page. Certification fee: $2.00. Personal checks accepted. Credit cards accepted: Visa, Mastercard. Public access terminal is available.

Clarke County

26th Circuit Court PO Box 189, Berryville, VA 22611; 540-955-5116; Fax: 540-955-0284. Hours: 9AM-5PM (EST). *Felony, Civil Actions Over $15,000, Probate.*

Civil Records: Access: Mail, online, in person. Both court and visitors may perform in person searches. No search fee. Required to search: name, years to search. Civil cases indexed by defendant, plaintiff. Civil records on books from 1920s. For information about the statewide online system, LOPAS, see the state introduction. **Criminal Records:** Access: Remote online, in person. Court does not conduct in person searches; visitors must perform searches for themselves. Search fee: No criminal searches performed by court. Required to search: name, years to search. Criminal records on books from 1920s. For information about the statewide online system, LOPAS, see the state introduction. **General Information:** No juvenile, sealed or adoption records released. No criminal records by mail. SASE requested. Turnaround time 1-2 days. Copy fee: $.50 per page. Certification fee: $.50 per page. Fee payee: Clerk of Court. Personal checks accepted. Prepayment is required.

26th General District Court 104 N Church St (PO Box 612), Berryville, VA 22611; 540-955-5128; Fax: 540-955-1195. Hours: 8:30AM-4:30PM (EST). *Misdemeanor, Civil Actions Under $15,000, Eviction, Small Claims.*

Civil Records: Access: online, in person. Court does not conduct in person searches; visitors must perform searches for themselves. Search fee: No civil searches performed by court. Required to search: name, years to search. Civil cases indexed by defendant, plaintiff. Civil records on computer from 1992, on index cards from 1985 to 1991. For information about the statewide online system, LOPAS, see the state introduction. **Criminal Records:** Access: Remote online, in person. Court does not conduct in person searches; visitors must perform searches for themselves. Search fee: No criminal searches performed by court. Required to search: name, years to search, DOB, SSN, signed release. Criminal records on computer from 1992, on index cards from 1985 to 1991. For information about the statewide online system, LOPAS, see the state introduction. **General Information:** Copy fee: $.50 per page. Certification fee: $2.00. Fee payee: Clarke County General District Court. Personal checks accepted. Personal checks require name and address. Prepayment is required. Public access terminal is available.

Clifton Forge City

25th Circuit Court 547 Main St, PO Box 27, Clifton Forge, VA 24422; 540-863-8536. Hours: 9AM-5PM (EST). *Felony, Civil Actions Over $15,000, Probate.*

Civil Records: Access: Mail, online, in person. Both court and visitors may perform in person searches. No search fee. Required to search: name, years to search. Civil cases indexed by defendant, plaintiff. Civil records on computer since 1994; prior records on index cards from 1906; no plaintiff index prior to 1994. For information about the statewide online system, LOPAS, see the state introduction. **Criminal Records:** Access: Mail, remote online, in person. Both court and visitors may perform in person searches. No search fee. Required to search: name, years to search; also helpful-DOB, SSN. Criminal records on computer since 1994; prior records on index cards from 1906; no plaintiff index prior to 1994. For information about the statewide online system, LOPAS, see the state introduction. **General Information:** No juvenile, sealed, presentencing investigations, probate tax sheet, or adoption records released. Turnaround time 1-2 days. Copy fee: $.50 per page. Certification fee: $2.00. Fee payee: Clerk of Court. Personal checks accepted. Prepayment is required.

25th General District Court 547 Main St, Clifton Forge, VA 24422; 540-863-2510; Fax: 540-863-2543. Hours: 9AM-5PM (EST). *Misdemeanor, Civil Actions Under $15,000, Eviction, Small Claims.*

Civil Records: Access: Mail, online, in person. Both court and visitors may perform in person searches. No search fee. Required to search: name, years to search. Civil cases indexed by defendant, plaintiff. Civil records on computer since 3/94. For information about the statewide online system, LOPAS, see the state introduction. **Criminal Records:** Access: Mail, remote online, in person. Both court and visitors may perform in person searches. No search fee. Required to search: name, years to search; also helpful-DOB, SSN. Criminal records on computer since 3/94. For information about the statewide online system, LOPAS, see the state introduction. **General Information:** No juvenile, sealed records released. Turnaround time 7 days. Copy fee: $.50 per page. Certification fee: $2.00. Fee payee: General District Court. Prepayment required. Public terminal is available.

Colonial Heights City

12th Circuit Court 401 Temple Ave, PO Box 3401, Colonial Heights, VA 23834; 804-520-9364. Hours: 8:30AM-5PM (EST). *Felony, Civil Actions Over $15,000, Probate.*

Civil Records: Access: Mail, online, in person. Both court and visitors may perform in person searches. Search fee: $5.00 per name. Required to search: name, years to search. Civil cases indexed by defendant, plaintiff. Civil records on books from 1961, on computer from 1991. For information about the statewide online system, LOPAS, see the state introduction. **Criminal Records:** Access: Mail, remote online, in person. Both court and visitors may perform in person searches. Search fee: $5.00 per name. Required to search: name, years to search; also helpful-DOB, SSN. Criminal records on books from 1961, on computer from 1991. For information about the statewide online system, LOPAS, see the state introduction. **General Information:** No juvenile, sealed or adoption records released. SASE required. Turnaround time 2 days. Copy fee: $.50 per page. Certification fee: $2.00. Fee payee: Clerk of Circuit Court. Personal checks accepted. Prepayment is required.

12th General District Court 401 Temple Ave, PO Box 279, Colonial Heights, VA 23834; 804-520-9346 (Dial 0); Fax: 804-520-9370. Hours: 8AM-4PM (EST). *Misdemeanor, Civil Actions Under $15,000, Eviction, Small Claims.*

Civil Records: Access: Mail, fax, online, in person. Both court and visitors may perform in person searches. No search fee. Required to search: name, years to search. Civil cases indexed by defendant, plaintiff. Civil records on computer from 1989 to present, index cards from 1985. For information about the statewide online system, LOPAS, see the state introduction. **Criminal Records:** Access: Mail, fax, remote online, in person. Both court and visitors may perform in person searches. No search fee. Required to search: name, years to search, DOB, SSN. Criminal records on computer from 1989 to present, index cards from 1985. For information about the statewide online system, LOPAS, see the state introduction. **General Information:** No juvenile, sealed records released. Turnaround time 1 week. Copy fee: $.50 per page. Certification fee: $2.00. Fee payee: Colonial Heights Combined Court. Personal checks accepted. Credit cards accepted: Visa, Mastercard. Prepayment is required. Public access terminal is available.

Covington City

Circuit & District Courts

Note: See Alleghany County.

Craig County

25th Circuit Court PO Box 185, New Castle, VA 24127-0185; 540-864-6141. Hours: 9AM-5PM (EST). *Felony, Civil Actions Over $15,000, Probate.*

Civil Records: Access: online, in person. Court does not conduct in person searches; visitors must perform searches for themselves. Search fee: No civil searches performed by court. Required to search: name, years to search. Civil cases indexed by defendant. Civil records on books from mid 1800s. For information about the statewide online system, LOPAS, see the state introduction. **Criminal Records:** Access: Remote online, in person. Court does not conduct in person searches; visitors must perform searches for themselves. Search fee: No criminal searches performed by court. Required to search: name, years to search; also helpful-SSN. Criminal records on books from mid 1800s. For information about the statewide online system, LOPAS, see the state introduction. **General Information:** No juvenile, sealed or adoption records released. Copy fee: $.50 per page. Certification fee: $2.00. Fee payee: Clerk of Court. Personal checks accepted. Prepayment is required.

25th General District Court Craig County General District Court, PO Box 232, New Castle,

VA 24127; 540-864-5989. Hours: 8:15AM-4:45PM (EST). *Misdemeanor, Civil Actions Under $15,000, Eviction, Small Claims.*

Civil Records: Access: online, in person. Court does not conduct in person searches; visitors must perform searches for themselves. Search fee: No civil searches performed by court. Required to search: name, years to search. Civil cases indexed by defendant, plaintiff. Civil records in files 10 years back. For information about the statewide online system, LOPAS, see the state introduction. Lengthy searches must be performed in person. **Criminal Records:** Access: Remote online, in person. Court does not conduct in person searches; visitors must perform searches for themselves. Search fee: No criminal searches performed by court. Required to search: name, years to search; also helpful-SSN. Criminal records in files 10 years back. For information about the statewide online system, LOPAS, see the state introduction. Lengthy searches must be performed in person. **General Information:** No juvenile, sealed records released. Copy fee: $.50 for first page, $1.00 each addl. Certification fee: No certification fee. Fee payee: Craig County District Court. Personal checks accepted. Credit cards accepted: Visa, Mastercard. Public access terminal is available.

Culpeper County

16th Circuit Court 135 W Cameron St, Culpeper, VA 22701-3097; 540-727-3438. Hours: 8:30AM-4:30PM (EST). *Felony, Civil Actions Over $15,000, Probate.*

Civil Records: Access: online, in person. Court does not conduct in person searches; visitors must perform searches for themselves. Search fee: No civil searches performed by court. Required to search: name, years to search. Civil cases indexed by defendant, plaintiff. Civil records on computer from 1991, docket books from 1800s. For information about the statewide online system, LOPAS, see the state introduction. **Criminal Records:** Access: Remote online, in person. Court does not conduct in person searches; visitors must perform searches for themselves. Search fee: No criminal searches performed by court. Required to search: name, years to search, signed release. Criminal records on computer from 1991, docket books from 1800s. For information about the statewide online system, LOPAS, see the state introduction. **General Information:** No juvenile, sealed records released. Copy fee: $.50 per page. Certification fee: $2.00. Fee payee: Clerk of Court. Personal checks accepted. Prepayment is required. Public access terminal is available.

16th General District Court 135 W Cameron St, Culpeper, VA 22701; 540-727-3417; Fax: 540-727-3474. Hours: 8:30AM-4:30PM (EST). *Misdemeanor, Civil Actions Under $15,000, Eviction, Small Claims.*

Civil Records: Access: Mail, online, in person. Both court and visitors may perform in person searches. No search fee. Required to search: name, years to search. Civil cases indexed by defendant, plaintiff. Civil records on computer from 1987 to present, prior on index cards. For information about the statewide online system, LOPAS, see the state introduction. **Criminal Records:** Access: Mail, remote online, in person. Both court and visitors may perform in person searches. No search fee. Required to search: name, years to search. Criminal records on computer from 1987 to present, prior on index cards. For information about the statewide online system, LOPAS, see the state introduction. **General Information:** No juvenile, sealed records released. SASE required.

Turnaround time 1-5 days. Copy fee: $.50 per page. Certification fee: No certification fee. Fee payee: General District Court. Personal checks accepted. Prepayment is required. Public access terminal is available.

Cumberland County

10th Circuit Court PO Box 8, Cumberland, VA 23040; 804-492-4442. Hours: 8:30AM-4:30PM (EST). *Felony, Civil Actions Over $15,000, Probate.*

Civil Records: Access: online, in person. Court does not conduct in person searches; visitors must perform searches for themselves. Search fee: No civil searches performed by court. Required to search: name, years to search. Civil cases indexed by defendant, plaintiff. Civil records in files. For information about the statewide online system, LOPAS, see the state introduction. Phone access only available for simple requests. **Criminal Records:** Access: Remote online, in person. Court does not conduct in person searches; visitors must perform searches for themselves. Search fee: No criminal searches performed by court. Required to search: name, years to search. Criminal records in files. For information about the statewide online system, LOPAS, see the state introduction. **General Information:** No juvenile, sealed records released. Copy fee: $.50 per page. Certification fee: No certification. Fee payee: Clerk of Circuit Court. Personal checks accepted. Prepayment is required.

10th General District Court PO Box 24, Cumberland, VA 23040; 804-492-4848; Fax: 804-492-9455. Hours: 8:30AM-4:30PM (EST). *Misdemeanor, Civil Actions Under $15,000, Eviction, Small Claims.*

Civil Records: Access: Phone, fax, mail, online, in person. Only the court conducts in person searches; visitors may not. No search fee. Required to search: name, years to search. Civil cases indexed by defendant, plaintiff. Civil records on books from 1985, on computer from 1993. For information about the statewide online system, LOPAS, see the state introduction. **Criminal Records:** Access: Phone, fax, mail, remote online, in person. Only the court conducts in person searches; visitors may not. No search fee. Required to search: name, years to search; also helpful-DOB, SSN. Criminal records on books from 1985, on computer from 1993. For information about the statewide online system, LOPAS, see the state introduction. **General Information:** No juvenile, sealed records released. SASE required. Turnaround time 2 days. Copy fee: $1.00 per page. Certification fee: No certification fee. Fee payee: Clerk of District Court. Personal checks accepted. Credit cards accepted: Visa, Mastercard.

Danville City

22nd Circuit Court PO Box 3300, Danville, VA 24543; 804-799-5168; Fax: 804-799-6502. Hours: 8:30AM-5PM (EST). *Felony, Civil Actions Over $15,000, Probate.*

Civil Records: Access: online, in person. Court does not conduct in person searches; visitors must perform searches for themselves. Search fee: No civil searches performed by court. Required to search: name, years to search. Civil cases indexed by defendant, plaintiff. Civil records in index books from 1841, judgements on computer since 1990. For information about the statewide online system, LOPAS, see the state introduction. **Criminal Records:** Access: Remote online, in person. Court does not conduct in person searches;

visitors must perform searches for themselves. Search fee: No criminal searches performed by court. Required to search: name, years to search. Criminal records in index books from 1841. Criminal records on computer from 1988. For information about the statewide online system, LOPAS, see the state introduction. **General Information:** No juvenile, sealed or adoption records released. Copy fee: $.50 per page. Certification fee: $2.00. Fee payee: Gerald A Gibson, Clerk. Personal checks accepted. Prepayment is required.

22nd General District Court PO Box 3300, Danville, VA 24543; 804-799-5179; Fax: 804-797-8814. Hours: 8:30AM-4:30PM (EST). *Misdemeanor, Civil Actions Under $15,000, Eviction, Small Claims.*

Civil Records: Access: Phone, fax, mail, online, in person. Both court and visitors may perform in person searches. No search fee. Required to search: name, years to search. Civil cases indexed by defendant, plaintiff. Civil records on computer from 1987 to present. For information about the statewide online system, LOPAS, see the state introduction. **Criminal Records:** Access: Phone, fax, mail, remote online, in person. Both court and visitors may perform in person searches. No search fee. Required to search: name, years to search. Criminal records on computer from 1987 to present. For information about the statewide online system, LOPAS, see the state introduction. **General Information:** No juvenile, sealed records released. SASE requested. Turnaround time 2 days. Copy fee: $1.00 1st 2 pages, $.50 each additional page. Certification fee: No certification fee. Fee payee: General District Court. Personal checks accepted. Credit cards accepted: Visa, Mastercard. Public access terminal is available.

Dickenson County

29th Circuit Court PO Box 190, Clintwood, VA 24228; 540-926-1616; Fax: 540-926-6465. Hours: 8:30AM-4:30PM (EST). *Felony, Civil Actions Over $15,000, Probate.*

Civil Records: Access: Phone, fax, mail, online, in person. Both court and visitors may perform in person searches. No search fee. Required to search: name, years to search. Civil cases indexed by defendant, plaintiff. Civil records on computer from 1989, index book from 1880. For information about the statewide online system, LOPAS, see the state introduction. **Criminal Records:** Access: Phone, fax, mail, remote online, in person. Both court and visitors may perform in person searches. No search fee. Required to search: name, years to search, DOB; also helpful-SSN. Criminal records on computer from 1989, index book from 1880. For information about the statewide online system, LOPAS, see the state introduction. **General Information:** No juvenile, sealed, adoption, confidential records released. SASE requested. Turnaround time 1 week. Copy fee: $.50 per page. Certification fee: $2.00. Fee payee: Joe Tate, Clerk of Circuit Court. Personal checks accepted. Prepayment required. Public terminal is available.

29th General District Court PO Box 128, Clintwood, VA 24228; 540-926-1630; Fax: 540-926-4815. Hours: 8:30AM-4:30PM (EST). *Misdemeanor, Civil Actions Under $15,000, Eviction, Small Claims.*

Civil Records: Access: Phone, mail, in person. Both court and visitors may perform in person searches. No search fee. Required to search: name, years to search. Civil cases indexed by defendant. Civil records on index cards 10 yrs back, on

computer from 5/93. For information about the statewide online system, LOPAS, see the state introduction. **Criminal Records:** Access: Phone, mail, in person. Both court and visitors may perform in person searches. No search fee. Required to search: name, years to search. Criminal records on index cards 10 yrs back, on computer from 5/93. For information about the statewide online system, LOPAS, see the state introduction. **General Information:** No juvenile, sealed records released. SASE requested. Turnaround time 1 week. Copy fee: $.10 per page. Certification fee: No certification fee. Fee payee: Dickenson Combined Court or General District Court. Personal checks accepted. Credit cards accepted: Visa, Mastercard. Public access terminal is available.

Dinwiddie County

11th Circuit Court PO Box 63, Dinwiddie, VA 23841; 804-469-4540. Hours: 8:30AM-4:30PM (EST). *Felony, Civil Actions Over $15,000, Probate.*

Civil Records: Access: Mail, online, in person. Both court and visitors may perform in person searches. No search fee. Required to search: name, years to search; also helpful-address. Civil cases indexed by defendant, plaintiff. Civil records on index cards from 1833; deeds on computer since 1989. For information about the statewide online system, LOPAS, see the state introduction. **Criminal Records:** Access: Mail, remote online, in person. Both court and visitors may perform in person searches. No search fee. Required to search: name, years to search; also helpful-DOB, SSN. Criminal records on index cards from 1833; deeds on computer since 1989. For information about the statewide online system, LOPAS, see the state introduction. **General Information:** No juvenile, sealed or expunged records released. SASE requested. Turnaround time 3 days. Copy fee: $.50 per page. Certification fee: $2.00 plus $.50 per page. Fee payee: Clerk of Court. Personal checks accepted.

11th General District Court PO Box 280, Dinwiddie, VA 23841; 804-469-4533; Fax: 804-469-4412. Hours: 8:30AM-4:30PM (EST). *Misdemeanor, Civil Actions Under $15,000, Eviction, Small Claims.*

Civil Records: Access: Mail, online, in person. Only the court conducts in person searches; visitors may not. No search fee. Required to search: name, years to search. Civil cases indexed by defendant, plaintiff. Civil records on index cards from 1800s, on computer from 1989. For information about the statewide online system, LOPAS, see the state introduction. **Criminal Records:** Access: Mail, remote online, in person. Only the court conducts in person searches; visitors may not. No search fee. Required to search: name, years to search. Criminal records on index cards from 1800s, on computer from 1989. For information about the statewide online system, LOPAS, see the state introduction. **General Information:** No juvenile, sealed records released. SASE required. Turnaround time 3 days. Copy fee: $1.00 per page. Certification fee: $2.00. Fee payee: District Court. Personal checks accepted. Credit cards accepted: Visa, Mastercard. Prepayment is required.

Emporia City

Circuit Court

Note: See Greensville County.

6th General District Court 315 S Main, Emporia, VA 23847; 804-634-5400. Hours: 8:30AM-4:30PM (EST). *Misdemeanor, Civil Actions Under $15,000, Eviction, Small Claims.*

Civil Records: Access: online, in person. Court does not conduct in person searches; visitors must perform searches for themselves. Search fee: No civil searches performed by court. Required to search: name, years to search. Civil cases indexed by defendant, plaintiff. Civil records on computer since 1985. For information about the statewide online system, LOPAS, see the state introduction. **Criminal Records:** Access: Mail, remote online, in person. Only the court conducts in person searches; visitors may not. No search fee. Required to search: name, years to search. Criminal records on computer since 1985. For information about the statewide online system, LOPAS, see the state introduction. **General Information:** No juvenile records released. Turnaround time 1-2 days. No copy fee. Certification fee: No certification fee. Fee payee: City of Emporia. Personal checks accepted. Public access terminal is available.

Essex County

15th Circuit Court PO Box 445, 305 prince St, Tappahannock, VA 22560; 804-443-3541. Hours: 9AM-5PM (EST). *Felony, Civil Actions Over $15,000, Probate.*

Civil Records: Access: In person only. Court does not conduct in person searches; visitors must perform searches for themselves. Search fee: No civil searches performed by court. Required to search: name, years to search. Civil cases indexed by defendant, plaintiff. Civil records on books from 1656. **Criminal Records:** Access: In person only. Court does not conduct in person searches; visitors must perform searches for themselves. Search fee: No criminal searches performed by court. Required to search: name, years to search. Criminal records on books from 1656. **General Information:** No juvenile, sealed records released. Copy fee: $.50 per page. Certification fee: No certification fee. Fee payee: Clerk of Court. Personal checks accepted. Prepayment is required.

15th General District Court PO Box 66, Tappahannock, VA 22560; 804-443-3744; Fax: 804-443-4122. Hours: 8AM-12:30PM, 1-4:30PM (EST). *Misdemeanor, Civil Actions Under $15,000, Eviction, Small Claims.*

Civil Records: Access: Mail, online, in person. Both court and visitors may perform in person searches. No search fee. Required to search: name, years to search. Civil cases indexed by defendant, plaintiff. Civil records on computer from 5/92, prior on index cards. For information about the statewide online system, LOPAS, see the state introduction. **Criminal Records:** Access: Remote online, in person. Court does not conduct in person searches; visitors must perform searches for themselves. Search fee: No criminal searches performed by court. Required to search: name, years to search, DOB, SSN. Criminal records on computer from 5/92, prior on index cards. For information about the statewide online system, LOPAS, see the state introduction. **General Information:** No juvenile, sealed records released. Turnaround time 1-2 days. No copy fee. Certification fee: No certification fee. Fee payee: General District Court. Personal checks accepted. Credit cards accepted: Visa, Mastercard. Prepayment is required. Public access terminal is available.

Fairfax County

19th Circuit Court 4110 Chain Bridge Rd, Fairfax, VA 22030;; Civil phone:703-591-8507; Criminal phone:703-591-8507. Hours: 8AM-4PM (EST). *Felony, Civil Actions Over $15,000, Probate.*

www.co.fairfax.va.us/courts

Civil Records: Access: Mail, in person. Court does not conduct in person searches; visitors must perform searches for themselves. No search fee. Required to search: name, years to search. Civil cases indexed by defendant, plaintiff. Civil records on computer from 1979, index cards from 1940s. **Criminal Records:** Access: Mail, in person. Court does not conduct in person searches; visitors must perform searches for themselves. No search fee. Required to search: name, years to search, DOB; also helpful-SSN. Criminal records on computer from 1979, index cards from 1940s. **General Information:** No juvenile, sealed records released. Copy fee: $.50 per page. Certification fee: $2.00. Fee payee: Fairfax Circuit Court. Personal checks accepted. In-state personal checks accepted. Credit cards accepted: Visa, Mastercard. Prepayment is required. Public access terminal is available.

19th General District Court 4110 Chain Bridge Rd, Fairfax, VA 22030; 703-246-2153; Civil phone:703-246-3012; Criminal phone:703-246-3012; Fax: 703-591-2349. Hours: 8AM-4PM (EST). *Misdemeanor, Civil Actions Under $15,000, Eviction, Small Claims.*

www.co.fairfax.va.us/courts

Note: Traffic division at 703-691-7320

Civil Records: Access: Phone, in person. Court does not conduct in person searches; visitors must perform searches for themselves. Search fee: No civil searches performed by court. Required to search: name, years to search. Civil cases indexed by defendant, plaintiff. Civil records on microfiche for 10 years. **Criminal Records:** Access: Phone, in person. Only the court conducts in person searches; visitors may not. Search fee: No criminal searches performed by court. Required to search: name, years to search; also helpful-DOB, SSN. Criminal records on microfiche for 10 years. **General Information:** No juvenile, sealed records released. Copy fee: $.50 per page. Certification fee: No certification fee. Fee payee: Fairfax General District Court. Personal checks accepted. Prepayment is required.

Fairfax City

Circuit Court

Note: See Fairfax County.

19th General District Court 10455 Armstrong St #304, Fairfax, VA 22030; 703-385-7866; Fax: 703-352-3195. Hours: 8:30AM-4:30PM (EST). *Misdemeanor.*

Note: Find Circuit Court cases and General District civil cases for this city in the Fairfax County listing **Criminal Records:** Access: Mail, in person. Only the court conducts in person searches; visitors may not. No search fee. Required to search: name, years to search; also helpful-SSN. Criminal records on computer and index from 1985. **General Information:** No juvenile or sealed records released. SASE requested. Turnaround time same day. Copy fee: $1.00 for first 2 pages; each add'l page $.50. Certification fee: No certification fee. Fee payee: General District Court. Personal checks accepted. Credit cards accepted: Visa, Mastercard.

Falls Church City

Circuit Court

Note: See Arlington County.

17th District Courts Combined Falls Church District, 300 Park Ave, Falls Church, VA 22046-3305; 703-241-5096 (GDC); Civil phone:703-248-5098; Fax: 703-241-1407. Hours: 8AM-4PM (EST). *Misdemeanor, Civil Actions Under $15,000, Eviction, Small Claims.*

Note: Small claims phone is 703-248-5157; juvenile and domestic relations is 703-248-5099

Civil Records: Access: Fax, mail, online, in person. Only the court conducts in person searches; visitors may not. No search fee. Required to search: name, years to search. Civil cases indexed by defendant, plaintiff. Civil records on computer from 1989, microfiche until 1989. For information about the statewide online system, LOPAS, see the state introduction. **Criminal Records:** Access: Fax, mail, remote online, in person. Only the court conducts in person searches; visitors may not. No search fee. Required to search: name, years to search; also helpful-DOB, SSN. Criminal records on computer from 1989, microfiche until 1989. For information about the statewide online system, LOPAS, see the state introduction. **General Information:** No juvenile, sealed records released. SASE requested. Turnaround time 1-2 days. Copy fee: $.50 per page. Certification fee: No certification fee. Fee payee: Falls Church District Court. Personal checks accepted. Credit cards accepted: Visa, Mastercard. Prepayment is required. Fax notes: No fee to fax results.

Fauquier County

20th Circuit Court 40 Culpeper St, Warrenton, VA 20186-3298; 540-347-8610. Hours: 8AM-4:30PM (EST). *Felony, Civil Actions Over $15,000, Probate.*

http://co.fauquier.va.us/services/ccc/index.html

Civil Records: Access: online, in person. Court does not conduct in person searches; visitors must perform searches for themselves. Search fee: No civil searches performed by court. Required to search: name, years to search. Civil cases indexed by defendant, plaintiff. Civil records on computer from 1988. For information about the statewide online system, LOPAS, see the state introduction. **Criminal Records:** Access: Remote online, in person. Court does not conduct in person searches; visitors must perform searches for themselves. Search fee: No criminal searches performed by court. Required to search: name, years to search. Criminal records on computer from 1988. For information about the statewide online system, LOPAS, see the state introduction. **General Information:** No juvenile, sealed, adoption records released. Copy fee: $.50 per page. Certification fee: $2.00. Fee payee: Clerk of Fauquier Circuit Court. Personal checks accepted. Prepayment is required.

20th General District Court 6 Court St, Warrenton, VA 20186;; Civil phone:540-347-8676; Criminal phone:540-347-8676; Fax: 540-347-5756. Hours: 8:30AM-4:30PM (EST). *Misdemeanor, Civil Actions Under $15,000, Eviction, Small Claims.*

Civil Records: Access: online, in person. Court does not conduct in person searches; visitors must perform searches for themselves. Search fee: No civil searches performed by court. Required to search: name, years to search. Civil cases indexed by defendant, plaintiff. Civil records on computer from 12/86, prior on file cards. For information about the statewide online system, LOPAS, see the state introduction. **Criminal Records:** Access: Remote online, in person. Court does not conduct in person searches; visitors must perform searches for themselves. Search fee: No criminal searches performed by court. Required to search: name, years to search. Criminal records on computer from 12/86, prior on file cards. For information about the statewide online system, LOPAS, see the state introduction. **General Information:** No juvenile, sealed records released. Copy fee: $1.00 1st 2 pages, $.50 each additional page. Certification fee: No certification fee. Fee payee: General District Court. Personal checks accepted. Public access terminal is available.

Floyd County

27th Circuit Court 100 East Main St, #200, Floyd, VA 24091; 540-745-9330. Hours: 8:30AM-4:30PM M-F, 8:30AM-Noon Sat (EST). *Felony, Civil Actions Over $15,000, Probate.*

Civil Records: Access: online, in person. Court does not conduct in person searches; visitors must perform searches for themselves. Search fee: No civil searches performed by court. Required to search: name, years to search. Civil cases indexed by defendant, plaintiff. Civil records on files from 1831. For information about the statewide online system, LOPAS, see the state introduction. **Criminal Records:** Access: Remote online, in person. Court does not conduct in person searches; visitors must perform searches for themselves. Search fee: $5.00 per name. Required to search: name, years to search; also helpful-DOB, SSN. Criminal records on files from 1831. For information about the statewide online system, LOPAS, see the state introduction. **General Information:** No juvenile, sealed records released. Copy fee: $.50 per page. Certification fee: $2.00. Fee payee: Clerk of Circuit Court. Personal checks accepted. Prepayment is required.

27th General District Court 100 East Main St, Floyd, VA 24091-2101; 540-745-9327; Fax: 540-745-9329. Hours: 8AM-4:30PM (EST). *Misdemeanor, Civil Actions Under $15,000, Eviction, Small Claims.*

Civil Records: Access: Phone, fax, mail, online, in person. Both court and visitors may perform in person searches. No search fee. Required to search: name, years to search. Civil cases indexed by defendant, plaintiff. Phone search results may be of limited content. For information about the statewide online system, LOPAS, see the state introduction. **Criminal Records:** Access: Phone, fax mail, remote online, in person. Both court and visitors may perform in person searches. No search fee. Required to search: name, years to search, DOB. Phone seach results may be of limited content. For information about the statewide online system, LOPAS, see the state introduction. **General Information:** No juvenile, sealed records released. SASE required. Turnaround time 1 week. Copy fee: $.50 per page. Certification fee: No certification fee. Fee payee: Clerk of District Court. Prepayment is required. Public access terminal is available.

Fluvanna County

16th Circuit Court PO Box 299, Palmyra, VA 22963; 804-589-8011; Fax: 804-589-6004. Hours: 8:30AM-4:30PM (EST). *Felony, Civil Actions Over $15,000, Probate.*

Civil Records: Access: Mail, online, in person. Both court and visitors may perform in person searches. Search fee: $5.00 per name. Required to search: name, years to search. Civil cases indexed by defendant, plaintiff. Civil records on index books from 1777. For information about the statewide online system, LOPAS, see the state introduction. **Criminal Records:** Access: Mail, remote online, in person. Both court and visitors may perform in person searches. Search fee: $5.00 per name. Required to search: name, years to search, DOB; also helpful-SSN. Civil records on index books from 1777. For information about the statewide online system, LOPAS, see the state introduction. **General Information:** No juvenile or sealed records released. SASE required. Turnaround time same 1-2 days. Copy fee: $.50 per page. Certification fee: $2.00. Fee payee: Clerk of Circuit Court. Personal checks accepted. Prepayment is required.

16th General District Court Fluvanna County Courthouse, PO Box 417, Palmyra, VA 22963; 804-589-8022; Fax: 804-589-6934. Hours: 8:30AM-4:30PM (EST). *Misdemeanor, Civil Actions Under $15,000, Eviction, Small Claims.*

Civil Records: Access: online, in person. Court does not conduct in person searches; visitors must perform searches for themselves. Search fee: No civil searches performed by court. Required to search: name, years to search. Civil cases indexed by defendant, plaintiff. Civil records on computer since 12/91, on books since 1984. For information about the statewide online system, LOPAS, see the state introduction. **Criminal Records:** Access: Remote online, in person. Court does not conduct in person searches; visitors must perform searches for themselves. Search fee: No criminal searches performed by court. Required to search: name, years to search; also helpful-DOB, SSN. Criminal records on computer since 12/91, on books since 1984. For information about the statewide online system, LOPAS, see the state introduction. **General Information:** No juvenile records released. Copy fee: $.50 per page. Certification fee: No certification fee. Fee payee: Fluvanna District Court. Personal checks accepted. Prepayment is required. Public access terminal is available.

Franklin City

5th Circuit Court PO Box 190, Courtland, VA 23837; 757-653-2200. Hours: 8:30AM-5PM (EST). *Felony, Civil Actions Over $15,000, Probate.*

Note: Southampton County serves as the Circuit Court for the city of Franklin

Civil Records: Access: Mail, online, in person. Both court and visitors may perform in person searches. Search fee: $5.00 per name. Required to search: name, years to search. Civil cases indexed by defendant, plaintiff. Civil records on computer since 1989, prior on docket books since 1700s. For information about the statewide online system, LOPAS, see the state introduction. **Criminal Records:** Access: Mail, remote online, in person. Both court and visitors may perform in person searches. Search fee: $5.00 per name. Required to search: name, years to search; also helpful-SSN. Criminal records on computer since 1989, prior on docket books since 1700s. For information about the statewide online system, LOPAS, see the state introduction. **General Information:** No juvenile records released. Turnaround time 2-5 days. Copy fee: $.50. Fee for first 2 pages. Add $.50 per page thereafter. Certification fee: No certification fee. Fee payee: Clerk of the Circuit Court. Personal checks accepted. Credit cards accepted: Visa, Mastercard. Public access terminal is available.

Circuit Court

Note: See Franklin County.

22nd General District Court PO Box 569, Rocky Mount, VA 24151; 540-483-3060; Fax: 540-483-3036. Hours: 8:30AM-4:30PM (EST). *Misdemeanor, Civil Actions Under $15,000, Eviction, Small Claims.*

Civil Records: Access: online, in person. Court does not conduct in person searches; visitors must perform searches for themselves. Search fee: No civil searches performed by court. Required to search: name, years to search. Civil cases indexed by defendant, plaintiff. Civil records file from 1985, index cards from 1985 to 1987, computer from mid-1987. For information about the statewide online system, LOPAS, see the state introduction. **Criminal Records:** Access: Remote online, in person. Court does not conduct in person searches; visitors must perform searches for themselves. Search fee: No criminal searches performed by court. Required to search: name, years to search. Criminal records file from 1985, index cards from 1985 to 1987, computer from mid-1987. For information about the statewide online system, LOPAS, see the state introduction. **General Information:** No juvenile, sealed records released. Copy fee: $.25 per page. Certification fee: No certification fee. Personal checks accepted. Credit cards accepted: Visa, Mastercard. Public access terminal is available.

Frederick County

Circuit Court 5 North Kent St, Winchester, VA 22601; 540-667-5770. Hours: 9AM-5PM *Felony, Misdemeanor, Civil, Eviction, Probate.*

Civil Records: Access: Mail, online, in person. Both court and visitors may perform in person searches. No search fee. Required to search: name, years to search. Civil cases indexed by defendant, plaintiff. Civil records on books from 1970s. For information about the statewide online system, LOPAS, see the state introduction. Mail access limited to simple requests. **Criminal Records:** Access: Remote online, in person. Court does not conduct in person searches; visitors must perform searches for themselves. Search fee: No criminal searches performed by court. Required to search: name, years to search. Criminal records on books from 1970s. For information about the statewide online system, LOPAS, see the state introduction. **General Information:** No juvenile, sealed or adoption records released. Turnaround time 1-2 days. Copy fee: $.50 per page. Certification fee: $2.00. Fee payee: Clerk of Circuit Court. Personal checks accepted. Prepayment is required. Public access terminal is available.

26th District Court 5 North Kent St, Winchester, VA 22601; 540-722-7208; Fax: 540-722-1063. Hours: 8AM-5PM (EST). *Misdemeanor, Civil Actions up to $15,000.*

Civil Records: Access: Phone, fax, mail, in person. Both court and visitors may perform in person searches. No search fee. Required to search: name, years to search. **Criminal Records:** Access: In person only. Court does not conduct in person searches; visitors must perform searches for themselves. Search fee: No criminal searches performed by court. Required to search: name, years to search. **General Information:** Turnaround time 2-4 days. Copy fee: $.50 per page. Certification fee: $.50. Fee payee: Frederick District Court. Personal checks accepted. Prepayment is required. Public access terminal is available.

Rockingham County

26th Circuit Court Courthouse, Harrisonburg, VA 22801;; Civil phone:540-564-3114; Criminal phone:540-564-3114; Fax: 540-564-3127. Hours: 9AM-5PM (EST). *Felony, Civil Actions Over $15,000, Probate.*

Civil Records: Access: online, in person. Court does not conduct in person searches; visitors must perform searches for themselves. Search fee: No civil searches performed by court. Required to search: name, years to search. Civil cases indexed by defendant, plaintiff. Civil records on index cards from the beginning of the county. For information about the statewide online system, LOPAS, see the state introduction. **Criminal Records:** Access: Remote online, in person. Court does not conduct in person searches; visitors must perform searches for themselves. Search fee: No criminal searches performed by court. Required to search: name, years to search. Criminal records on index cards from the beginning of the county. For information about the statewide online system, LOPAS, see the state introduction. **General Information:** No juvenile, sealed records released. Copy fee: $.50 per page. Certification fee: $2.00. Fee payee: Clerk of Circuit Court. Personal checks accepted. Prepayment is required. Public access terminal is available. Public Access Terminal Note: Deeds only.

26th General District Court 53 Court Square, Harrisonburg, VA 22801; 540-564-3130; Civil phone:540-564-3135; Criminal phone:540-564-3135; Fax: 540-564-3096. Hours: 8AM-4PM (EST). *Misdemeanor, Civil Actions Under $15,000, Eviction, Small Claims.*

Civil Records: Access: Phone, mail, online, in person. Both court and visitors may perform in person searches. No search fee. Required to search: name, years to search. Civil cases indexed by defendant, plaintiff. Civil records on computer from 1988, on index cards from 1978, prior at Circuit Court. For information about the statewide online system, LOPAS, see the state introduction. **Criminal Records:** Access: Phone, mail, remote online, in person. Both court and visitors may perform in person searches. No search fee. Required to search: name, years to search, DOB; also helpful-SSN. Criminal records on computer from 1987, on index cards from 1985, prior at Circuit Court. For information about the statewide online system, LOPAS, see the state introduction. **General Information:** No juvenile, sealed, adoption records released. SASE required. Turnaround time up to 1 week. Copy fee: $.50 per page. Certification fee: Cert fee included in copy fee. Fee payee: General District Court. Personal checks accepted. Credit cards accepted: Visa, Mastercard. Prepayment is required. Public access terminal is available.

Russell County

29th Circuit Court PO Box 435, Lebanon, VA 24266; 540-889-8023; Fax: 540-889-8003. Hours: 8:30AM-5PM (6PM M,W,F) (EST). *Felony, Civil Actions Over $15,000, Probate.*

Civil Records: Access: Fax, mail, online, in person. Both court and visitors may perform in person searches. No search fee. Required to search: name, years to search. Civil cases indexed by defendant, plaintiff. Civil records on computer from 1990, archived from 1809. For information about the statewide online system, LOPAS, see the state introduction. Fax access limited to short searches. **Criminal Records:** Access: Fax, mail, remote online, in person. Both court and visitors

may perform in person searches. No search fee. Required to search: name, years to search, signed release. Criminal records on computer from 1990, archived from 1809. For information about the statewide online system, LOPAS, see the state introduction. **General Information:** No juvenile, sealed records released. Turnaround time 1-5 days. Copy fee: $.50 per page. Certification fee: No certification fee. Fee payee: Clerk of Circuit Court. Personal checks accepted. Prepayment is required.

29th General District Court Russell County Courthouse, PO Box 65, Lebanon, VA 24266; 540-889-8051; Fax: 540-889-8091. Hours: 8:30AM-4:30PM (EST). *Misdemeanor, Civil Actions Under $15,000, Eviction, Small Claims.*

Civil Records: Access: Phone, fax, mail, online, in person. Both court and visitors may perform in person searches. No search fee. Required to search: name, years to search. Civil cases indexed by defendant, plaintiff. Civil records on computer from 1990, archived from 1809. For information about the statewide online system, LOPAS, see the state introduction. **Criminal Records:** Access: Phone, fax, mail, remote online, in person. Both court and visitors may perform in person searches. No search fee. Required to search: name, years to search, DOB; also helpful-SSN. Criminal records on computer from 1990, archived from 1809. For information about the statewide online system, LOPAS, see the state introduction. **General Information:** No juvenile, sealed records released. Turnaround time 2-5 days. No copy fee. Certification fee: No certification fee. Fee payee: Clerk of General District Court. Personal checks accepted. Credit cards accepted: Visa, Mastercard. Prepayment is required. Public access terminal is available. Fax notes: No fee to fax results.

Salem City

23rd Circuit Court 2 E Calhoun St, PO Box 891, Salem, VA 24153; 540-375-3067; Fax: 540-375-4039. Hours: 8:30AM-5PM (EST). *Felony, Civil Actions Over $15,000, Probate.*

Civil Records: Access: Mail, online, in person. Both court and visitors may perform in person searches. No search fee. Required to search: name, years to search. Civil cases indexed by defendant, plaintiff. Civil records on computer from 1985, on index books from 1968, prior at Roanoke Circuit Court. For information about the statewide online system, LOPAS, see the state introduction. **Criminal Records:** Access: Remote online, in person. Court does not conduct in person searches; visitors must perform searches for themselves. Search fee: No criminal searches performed by court. Required to search: name, years to search, DOB; also helpful-SSN. Criminal records on computer from 1985, on index books from 1968, prior at Roanoke Circuit Court. For information about the statewide online system, LOPAS, see the state introduction. **General Information:** No juvenile, sealed or adoption records released. SASE required. Turnaround time 2 weeks. Copy fee: $.50 per page. Certification fee: $2.00. Fee payee: Clerk of Circuit Court. Personal checks accepted. Prepayment is required. Public access terminal is available.

23rd General District Court 2 E Calhoun St, Salem, VA 24153; 540-375-3044; Fax: 540-375-4024. Hours: 8AM-4PM (EST). *Misdemeanor, Civil Actions Under $15,000, Eviction, Small Claims.*

Civil Records: Access: online, in person. Court does not conduct in person searches; visitors must perform searches for themselves. Search fee: No

civil searches performed by court. Required to search: name, years to search. Civil cases indexed by defendant, plaintiff. Civil records on computer from 1987, on index cards from 1986, prior records at City of Salem Circuit Court. For information about the statewide online system, LOPAS, see the state introduction. **Criminal Records:** Access: Remote online, in person. Court does not conduct in person searches; visitors must perform searches for themselves. Search fee: No criminal searches performed by court. Required to search: name, years to search, DOB, SSN. Criminal records on computer from 1987, on index cards from 1986, prior records at City of Salem Circuit Court. For information about the statewide online system, LOPAS, see the state introduction. **General Information:** No juvenile, sealed records released. Copy fee: $.50 per page. Certification fee: $2.00. Fee payee: General District Court. Personal checks accepted. Prepayment is required. Public access terminal is available.

Scott County

30th Circuit Court 104 E Jackson St, Suite 2, Gate City, VA 24251; 540-386-3801. Hours: 8:30AM-5PM (EST). *Felony, Civil Actions Over $15,000, Probate.*

Civil Records: Access: Phone, mail, in person. Both court and visitors may perform in person searches. Search fee: $10.00 per name. Required to search: name, years to search. Civil cases indexed by defendant, plaintiff. Civil records on index books back to 1815. For information about the statewide online system, LOPAS, see the state introduction. **Criminal Records:** Access: Mail, in person. Both court and visitors may perform in person searches. Search fee: $10.00 per name. Required to search: name, years to search, DOB; also helpful-SSN. Criminal records on index books back to 1815. For information about the statewide online system, LOPAS, see the state introduction. **General Information:** No juvenile, sealed records released. SASE required. Turnaround time 3-4 days. Copy fee: $.50 per page. Certification fee: $1.50. Fee payee: Mark A. "Bo" Taylor, Clerk. Personal checks accepted. Will bill phone requests.

30th General District Court 104 E Jackson St, Suite 9, Gate City, VA 24251; 540-386-7341. Hours: 8AM-4PM (EST). *Misdemeanor, Civil Actions Under $15,000, Eviction, Small Claims.*

Civil Records: Access: Mail, online, in person. Only the court conducts in person searches; visitors may not. No search fee. Required to search: name, years to search. Civil cases indexed by plaintiff. Civil records on index books, on computer from 1990. For information about the statewide online system, LOPAS, see the state introduction. **Criminal Records:** Access: Mail, remote online, in person. Only the court conducts in person searches; visitors may not. No search fee. Required to search: name, years to search, DOB; also helpful-SSN. Criminal records on index books, on computer from 1990. For information about the statewide online system, LOPAS, see the state introduction. **General Information:** No juvenile, sealed records released. SASE required. Turnaround time up to 1-2 days. Copy fee: $1.00 per page. Certification fee: No certification fee. Fee payee: General District Court. Personal checks accepted. Prepayment is required.

Shenandoah County

26th Circuit Court 112 S Main St, PO Box 406, Woodstock, VA 22664; 540-459-6150; Fax: 540-459-6155. Hours: 9AM-5PM (EST). *Felony, Civil Actions Over $15,000, Probate.*

Civil Records: Access: Mail, online, in person. Both court and visitors may perform in person searches. No search fee. Required to search: name, years to search. Civil cases indexed by defendant, plaintiff. Civil records on computer from 1986, on index cards from 1772. For information about the statewide online system, LOPAS, see the state introduction. Mail access limited to specific cases only. **Criminal Records:** Access: Remote online, in person. Court does not conduct in person searches; visitors must perform searches for themselves. Search fee: No criminal searches performed by court. Required to search: name, years to search, DOB; also helpful-SSN. Criminal records on computer from 1986, on index cards from 1772. For information about the statewide online system, LOPAS, see the state introduction. **General Information:** No juvenile, sealed records released. SASE required. Turnaround time 1-2 days. Copy fee: $.50 per page. Certification fee: $2.00. Fee payee: Clerk of Circuit Court. Personal checks accepted. Prepayment is required.

26th General District Court

103 N Main St, PO Box 189, Woodstock, VA 22664; 540-459-6130; Fax: 540-459-6139. Hours: 8:30AM-4:30PM (EST). *Misdemeanor, Civil Actions Under $15,000, Eviction, Small Claims.*

Civil Records: Access: Mail, online, in person. Court does not conduct in person searches; visitors must perform searches for themselves. Search fee: No civil searches performed by court. Required to search: name, years to search. Civil cases indexed by defendant, plaintiff. Civil records on computer from 1992, on index cards from 1985, prior at Circuit Court. For information about the statewide online system, LOPAS, see the state introduction. **Criminal Records:** Access: Remote online, in person. Court does not conduct in person searches; visitors must perform searches for themselves. No search fee. Required to search: name, years to search, DOB; also helpful-SSN. Criminal records on computer from 1992, on index cards from 1985, prior at Circuit Court. This agency will not do criminal record checks and refer all requesters to the State Police orthe online system. For information about the statewide online system, LOPAS, see the state introduction. **General Information:** No sealed or adoption records relased. Copy fee: $1.00 for first page; $.50 each addl. Certification fee: No certification fee. Fee payee: General District Court. Personal checks accepted. Visa/MC credit cards accepted. Accepted for criminal fines only. Prepayment is required. Public access terminal is available.

Smyth County

28th Circuit Court PO Box 1025, Marion, VA 24354; 540-782-4044; Fax: 540-782-4045. Hours: 9AM-5PM (EST). *Felony, Civil Actions Over $15,000, Probate.*

Civil Records: Access: Mail, online, in person. Both court and visitors may perform in person searches. Search fee: $10.00 per name. Required to search: name, years to search. Civil cases indexed by defendant, plaintiff. Civil records on index cards from 1832, most are computerized since 01/90. For information about the statewide online system, LOPAS, see the state introduction. **Criminal Records:** Access: Mail, remote online, in person. Both court and visitors may perform in person searches. Search fee: $10.00 per name. Required to search: name, years to search; also helpful-DOB, SSN. Criminal records on index cards from 1832, most are computerized since 01/90. For information about the statewide online system, LOPAS, see the state introduction.

General Information: No juvenile, sealed or adoption records released. SASE requested. Turnaround time 1 week. Copy fee: $.50 per page. Certification fee: $2.00. Fee payee: Clerk of Circuit Court. Personal checks accepted. Prepayment is required. Public access terminal is available. Public Access Terminal Note: Not available for criminal or civil information.

28th General District Court

Smythe County Courthouse, Rm 231, 109 W Main St, Marion, VA 24354; 540-782-4047; Fax: 540-782-4048. Hours: 8:30AM-4:30PM (EST). *Misdemeanor, Civil Actions Under $15,000, Eviction, Small Claims.*

Civil Records: Access: Phone, mail, online, in person. Both court and visitors may perform in person searches. No search fee. Required to search: name, years to search; also helpful-address. Civil cases indexed by defendant, plaintiff. Civil records on computer from 7/90, on index cards from 1985, prior records at Circuit Court. For information about the statewide online system, LOPAS, see the state introduction. **Criminal Records:** Access: Phone, mail, remote online, in person. Both court and visitors may perform in person searches. No search fee. Required to search: name, years to search, DOB; also helpful-SSN. Criminal records on computer from 7/90, on index cards from 1985, prior records at Circuit Court. For information about the statewide online system, LOPAS, see the state introduction. **General Information:** No juvenile, sealed records released. Turnaround time 1-2 days. Copy fee: $.50 per page. Certification fee: No certification fee. Fee payee: General District Court. Personal checks accepted. Credit cards accepted: Visa, Mastercard. Prepayment is required. Public access terminal is available.

South Boston City

Circuit & District Courts

Note: See Halifax County.

Southampton County

5th Circuit Court PO Box 190, Courtland, VA 23837; 757-653-2200. Hours: 8:30AM-5PM *Felony, Civil Actions Over $15,000, Probate.*

Civil Records: Access: Mail, online, in person. Both court and visitors may perform in person searches. Search fee: $5.00 per name. Required to search: name, years to search. Civil cases indexed by defendant, plaintiff. Civil records on index books from 1749. For information about the statewide online system, LOPAS, see the state introduction. **Criminal Records:** Access: Mail, remote online, in person. Both court and visitors may perform in person searches. No search fee. Required to search: name, years to search. Criminal records on index books from 1749. For information about the statewide online system, LOPAS, see the state introduction. **General Information:** No juvenile, sealed, adoption records released. Turnaround time 1-5 days. Copy fee: $.50 per page. Certification fee: $2.00. Fee payee: Clerk of Circuit Court. Personal checks accepted. Prepayment is required. Public access terminal is available.

5th General District Court PO Box 347, Courtland, VA 23837; 757-653-2673. Hours: 8:30AM-4:30PM (EST). *Misdemeanor, Civil Actions Under $15,000, Eviction, Small Claims.*

Civil Records: Access: Mail, online, in person. Both court and visitors may perform in person searches. No search fee. Required to search: name, years to search. Civil cases indexed by defendant.

Civil records on index cards and docket books from 1985, prior records at Circuit Court. For information about the statewide online system, LOPAS, see the state introduction. **Criminal Records:** Access: Mail, remote online, in person. Both court and visitors may perform in person searches. No search fee. Required to search: name, years to search, DOB; also helpful-SSN. Criminal records on index cards and docket books from 1985, prior records at Circuit Court. For information about the statewide online system, LOPAS, see the state introduction. **General Information:** No juvenile, sealed, adoption records released. Turnaround time 1-5 days. Copy fee: $1.00 1st 2 pages; $.50 each add'l page. Certification fee: No certification fee. Fee payee: Clerk of General District Court. Personal checks accepted. Credit cards accepted. Prepayment is required. Public access terminal is available.

Spotsylvania County

15th Circuit Court 9113 Courthouse Rd, PO Box 96, Spotsylvania, VA 22553; 540-582-7090; Fax: 540-582-2169. Hours: 8AM-4:30PM (EST). *Felony, Civil Actions Over $15,000, Probate.*

Civil Records: Access: online, in person. Court does not conduct in person searches; visitors must perform searches for themselves. Search fee: No civil searches performed by court. Required to search: name, years to search. Civil cases indexed by defendant, plaintiff. Civil records on computer from 1996, on index books from late 1700s. For information about the statewide online system, LOPAS, see the state introduction. Mail access limited to specific case only. **Criminal Records:** Access: Remote online, in person. Court does not conduct in person searches; visitors must perform searches for themselves. Search fee: No criminal searches performed by court. Required to search: name, years to search, DOB, SSN. Criminal records on computer from 1996, on index books from late 1700s. For information about the statewide online system, LOPAS, see the state introduction. **General Information:** No juvenile, sealed, adoption records released. Copy fee: $.50 per page. Certification fee: $2.00. Fee payee: Clerk of Circuit Court. Personal checks accepted. Prepayment is required. Public access terminal is available.

15th General District Court Judicial Center, PO Box 339, Spotsylvania, VA 22553; 540-582-7110. Hours: 8AM-4PM (EST). *Misdemeanor, Civil Actions Under $15,000, Eviction, Small Claims.*

Civil Records: Access: Mail, online, in person. Both court and visitors may perform in person searches. No search fee. Required to search: name, years to search. Civil cases indexed by defendant, plaintiff. Civil records on computer from 1987, on index cards from 1985 to 1987, prior at Circuit Court. For information about the statewide online system, LOPAS, see the state introduction. **Criminal Records:** Access: Mail, remote online, in person. Both court and visitors may perform in person searches. No search fee. Required to search: name, years to search. Criminal records on computer since 1988. For information about the statewide online system, LOPAS, see the state introduction. **General Information:** No juvenile, sealed records released. Turnaround time 5 days. Copy fee: $.50 per page. Certification fee: $2.00. Fee payee: Clerk of General District Court. Personal checks accepted. Prepayment is required. Public access terminal is available.

Stafford County

15th Circuit Court PO Box 69, Stafford, VA 22554; 540-658-8750. Hours: 8:30AM-4PM (EST). *Felony, Civil Actions Over $15,000, Probate.*

Civil Records: Access: Mail, online, in person. Both court and visitors may perform in person searches. No search fee. Required to search: name, years to search. Civil cases indexed by defendant, plaintiff. Civil records in index books from 1699. For information about the statewide online system, LOPAS, see the state introduction. **Criminal Records:** Access: Mail, remote online, in person. Both court and visitors may perform in person searches. No search fee. Required to search: name, years to search, DOB; also helpful-SSN. Criminal records in index books from 1699. For information about the statewide online system, LOPAS, see the state introduction. **General Information:** No juvenile, sealed records released. Turnaround time up to 10 days. Copy fee: $.50 per page. Certification fee: $2.00. Fee payee: Clerk of Circuit Court. Personal checks accepted. Public access terminal is available.

15th General District Court 1300 Courthouse Rd, PO Box 940, Stafford, VA 22555; 540-658-8763; Fax: 540-720-4834. Hours: 8:AM-4PM (EST). *Misdemeanor, Civil Actions Under $15,000, Eviction, Small Claims.*

Civil Records: Access: Fax, mail, online, in person. Both court and visitors may perform in person searches. No search fee. Required to search: name, years to search. Civil cases indexed by defendant, plaintiff. Civil records on computer since 1986, prior at Circuit Court. For information about the statewide online system, LOPAS, see the state introduction. **Criminal Records:** Access: Fax, mail, remote online, in person. Both court and visitors may perform in person searches. No search fee. Required to search: name, years to search. Criminal records on computer since 1986, prior at Circuit Court. For information about the statewide online system, LOPAS, see the state introduction. **General Information:** No sealed records released. SASE requested. Turnaround time 2-7 days. Copy fee: $.50 per page. Certification fee: No certification fee. Fee payee: Clerk of General District Court. Personal checks accepted. Credit cards accepted: Visa, Mastercard. Prepayment is required. Public access terminal is available. Fax notes: No fee to fax results.

Staunton City

25th Circuit Court PO Box 1286, Staunton, VA 24402-1286; 540-332-3874; Fax: 540-332-3970. Hours: 8:30AM-5PM (EST). *Felony, Civil Actions Over $15,000, Probate.*

Civil Records: Access: online, in person. Court does not conduct in person searches; visitors must perform searches for themselves. Search fee: No civil searches performed by court. Required to search: name, years to search. Civil cases indexed by defendant, plaintiff. Civil records on index books since 1802. For information about the statewide online system, LOPAS, see the state introduction. **Criminal Records:** Access: Remote online, in person. Court does not conduct in person searches; visitors must perform searches for themselves. Search fee: No criminal searches performed by court. Required to search: name, years to search. Criminal records on index books since 1802. For information about the statewide online system, LOPAS, see the state introduction. **General Information:** No juvenile, sealed or adoption records released. Copy fee: $.50 per page. Certification fee: $2.00. Fee payee: Clerk of Circuit Court. Personal checks accepted. Prepayment is required. Public access terminal is available.

25th General District Court 113 E Beverly St, Staunton, VA 24401-4390; 540-332-3878; Fax: 540-332-3985. Hours: 8:30AM-4:30PM (EST). *Misdemeanor, Civil Actions Under $15,000, Eviction, Small Claims.*

Civil Records: Access: Mail, online, in person. Both court and visitors may perform in person searches. No search fee. Required to search: name, years to search; also helpful-address. Civil cases indexed by defendant, plaintiff. Civil records on computer from 11/94, on index cards from 1990, prior at Circuit Court. For information about the statewide online system, LOPAS, see the state introduction. **Criminal Records:** Access: Mail, remote online, in person. Both court and visitors may perform in person searches. No search fee. Required to search: name, years to search, DOB; also helpful-SSN. Criminal records indexed on computer since 1991. For information about the statewide online system, LOPAS, see the state introduction. **General Information:** Turnaround time 1-5 days. Copy fee: $.50 per page. Certification fee: No certification fee. Fee payee: Staunton General District Court. Personal checks accepted. Credit cards accepted: Visa, Mastercard. Credit cards accepted for criminal & traffic cases only. Prepayment is required. Public access terminal is available.

Suffolk City

Suffolk Circuit Court PO Box 1604, Suffolk, VA 23439-1604; 757-923-2251; Fax: 757-934-3490. Hours: 8:30AM-5PM (EST). *Felony, Civil Actions Over $15,000, Probate.*

Civil Records: Access: online, in person. Court does not conduct in person searches; visitors must perform searches for themselves. Search fee: No civil searches performed by court. Required to search: name, years to search. Civil cases indexed by defendant, plaintiff. Civil records on computer from 1989, on index books from 1866. For information about the statewide online system, LOPAS, see the state introduction. **Criminal Records:** Access: Remote online, in person. Court does not conduct in person searches; visitors must perform searches for themselves. Search fee: No criminal searches performed by court. Required to search: name, years to search. Criminal records on computer from 1989, on index books from 1866. For information about the statewide online system, LOPAS, see the state introduction. **General Information:** No juvenile, sealed, adoption records released. Copy fee: $.50 per page. Certification fee: $1.50. Fee payee: Clerk of Circuit Court. Personal checks accepted. Credit cards accepted: Visa, Mastercard. Prepayment is required.

5th General District Court 150 N Main St, PO Box 1648, Suffolk, VA 23434; 757-923-2281; Fax: 757-925-1790. Hours: 8AM-4PM (EST). *Misdemeanor, Civil Actions up to $15,000, Eviction, Small Claims.*

Civil Records: Access: Mail, online, in person. Both court and visitors may perform in person searches. No search fee. Required to search: name, years to search. Civil cases indexed by defendant, plaintiff. Civil records on computer from 1987, prior on index cards. Records destroyed after 10 years. For information about the statewide online system, LOPAS, see the state introduction. **Criminal Records:** Access: Remote online, in person. Court does not conduct in person searches; visitors must perform searches for themselves. Search fee: No criminal searches performed by court. Required to search: name, years to search, DOB; also helpful-SSN. Criminal records on computer from 1987, prior on index cards. For information about the statewide online system, LOPAS, see the state introduction. **General Information:** No juvenile, sealed, adoptions records released. SASE required. Turnaround time 1 week. Copy fee: $.50 per page. Certification fee: No certification fee. Fee payee: Suffolk General District Court. Personal checks accepted. Credit cards accepted: Visa, Mastercard. Prepayment is required. Public access terminal is available.

Surry County

6th Circuit Court 28 Colonial Trail East, PO Box 203, Surry, VA 23883; 757-294-3161; Fax: 757-294-0471. Hours: 9AM-5PM (EST). *Felony, Civil Actions Over $15,000, Probate.*

Civil Records: Access: In person only. Court does not conduct in person searches; visitors must perform searches for themselves. Search fee: No civil searches performed by court. Required to search: name, years to search. Civil cases indexed by defendant, plaintiff. Civil records on cards from 1662. **Criminal Records:** Access: In person only. Court does not conduct in person searches; visitors must perform searches for themselves. Search fee: No criminal searches performed by court. Required to search: name, years to search, DOB; also helpful-SSN. Criminal records on cards from 1662. **General Information:** Juvenile, sealed records not released. Copy fee: $.50 per page. Certification fee: No certification fee. Fee payee: Circuit Clerk. Business checks accepted.

6th General District Court Hwy 10 and School St, PO Box 332, Surry, VA 23883; 757-294-5201; Fax: 757-294-0312. Hours: 8:30AM-4:30PM (EST). *Misdemeanor, Civil Actions Under $15,000, Eviction, Small Claims.*

Civil Records: Access: online, in person. Court does not conduct in person searches; visitors must perform searches for themselves. Search fee: No civil searches performed by court. Required to search: name, years to search. Civil cases indexed by defendant, plaintiff. Civil records on computer since 11/93, on books from 1985, prior at Circuit Court. For information about the statewide online system, LOPAS, see the state introduction. **Criminal Records:** Access: Remote online, in person. Court does not conduct in person searches; visitors must perform searches for themselves. Search fee: No criminal searches performed by court. Required to search: name, years to search, DOB; also helpful-SSN. Criminal records on computer since 11/93, on books from 1985, prior at Circuit Court. For information about the statewide online system, LOPAS, see the state introduction. **General Information:** No juvenile, sealed, adoption records released. No copy fee. Certification fee: No certification fee. Public access terminal is available.

Sussex County

6th Circuit Court PO Box 1337, Sussex, VA 23884; 804-246-5511 X3276; Fax: 804-246-2203. Hours: 9AM-5PM (EST). *Felony, Civil Actions Over $15,000, Probate.*

Civil Records: Access: Mail, online, in person. Only the court conducts in person searches; visitors may not. Search fee: $5.00 per name. Required to search: name, years to search. Civil cases indexed by defendant, plaintiff. Civil records on index books from 1754. For information about the statewide online system, LOPAS, see the state introduction. **Criminal Records:** Access: Mail, remote online, in person. Court does not conduct in person searches; visitors must perform searches for themselves. Search fee: $5.00 per name. Required to search: name, years to search, DOB, SSN, signed release. Criminal records on index books from 1754. For information about the statewide online system, LOPAS, see the state introduction. **General Information:** No juvenile, sealed, adoption, confidential, or probate records released. Turnaround time 1-2 days. Copy fee: $.50 per page. Certification fee: $2.00. Fee payee: Clerk of Circuit Court. Personal checks accepted. Prepayment is required.

6th Judicial District Sussex Court

Sussex Cnty Courthouse 15098 Courthouse Rd Rt 735, PO Box 1315, Sussex, VA 23884; 804-246-5511 X3241; Fax: 804-246-6604. Hours: 8:30AM-4:30PM (EST). *Misdemeanor, Civil Actions Under $15,000, Eviction, Small Claims.*

Civil Records: Access: online, in person. Both court and visitors may perform in person searches. No search fee. Required to search: name, years to search. Civil cases indexed by defendant, plaintiff. Civil records on computer from 9/88, on index cards from 1985, prior in Circuit Court. For information about the statewide online system, LOPAS, see the state introduction. **Criminal Records:** Access: Remote online, in person. Court does not conduct in person searches; visitors must perform searches for themselves. No search fee. Required to search: name, years to search, DOB; also helpful-SSN. Criminal records on computer from 9/88, on index cards from 1985, prior in Circuit Court. For information about the statewide online system, LOPAS, see the state introduction. **General Information:** No juvenile, sealed, adoption records released. Copy fee: $1.00 minimum for first 2 pages, thereafter $.50 per page. Certification fee: No certification fee. Fee payee: Sussex District Court. Personal checks accepted. Credit cards accepted: Visa, Mastercard. Prepayment is required. Public access terminal is available.

Tazewell County

29th Circuit Court PO Box 968, Tazewell, VA 24651-0968; 540-988-7541 X311-312; Fax: 540-988-7501. Hours: 8AM-4:30PM (EST). *Felony, Civil Actions Over $15,000, Probate.*

Civil Records: Access: Mail, online, in person. Both court and visitors may perform in person searches. No search fee. Required to search: name, years to search. Civil cases indexed by defendant, plaintiff. Civil records on index cards from 1800s. For information about the statewide online system, LOPAS, see the state introduction. **Criminal Records:** Access: Mail, remote online, in person. Both court and visitors may perform in person searches. No search fee. Required to search: name, years to search, signed release. Criminal records on computer from 1992. For information about the statewide online system, LOPAS, see the state introduction. **General Information:** No juvenile, sealed records released. Turnaround time 1-3 days. Copy fee: $.50 per page. Certification fee: $2.00. Fee payee: Clerk of Circuit Court. Personal checks accepted. Prepayment is required. Public access terminal is available. Public Access Terminal Note: Deeds, wills, etc.

ᵗʰ General District Court PO Box 566, ˡˡ, VA 24651; 540-988-9057; Fax: 540- Hours: 8AM-4:30PM (EST).

Misdemeanor, Civil Actions Under $15,000, Eviction, Small Claims.

Civil Records: Access: Mail, online, in person. Both court and visitors may perform in person searches. No search fee. Required to search: name, years to search. Civil cases indexed by defendant, plaintiff. Civil records on computer from 1990, prior records to 1985 at Circuit Court. For information about the statewide online system, LOPAS, see the state introduction. Mail access is limited to two searches. **Criminal Records:** Access: Mail, remote online, in person. Both court and visitors may perform in person searches. No search fee. Required to search: name, years to search, DOB; also helpful-SSN. Criminal records on computer from 1990, prior records to 1985 at Circuit Court. For information about the statewide online system, LOPAS, see the state introduction. **General Information:** No juvenile, sealed, adoption records released. SASE requested. Turnaround time 1-3 days. Copy fee: $.50 per page. Certification fee: No certification fee. Fee payee: Clerk of General District Court. Personal checks accepted. Credit cards accepted: Visa, Mastercard. Public access terminal is available.

Virginia Beach City

2nd Circuit Court 2305 Judicial Blvd, Virginia Beach, VA 23456-9002; 757-427-4181; Fax: 757-426-5686. Hours: 8:30AM-5PM (EST). *Felony, Civil Actions Over $15,000, Probate.*

www.virginia-beach.va.us/courts

Civil Records: Access: online, in person. Court does not conduct in person searches; visitors must perform searches for themselves. Search fee: No civil searches performed by court. Required to search: name, years to search. Civil cases indexed by defendant, plaintiff. Civil records on computer from 1986, on files from 1960s. Court will usually only check back 10 years. For information about the statewide online system, LOPAS, see the state introduction. **Criminal Records:** Access: Remote online, in person. Court does not conduct in person searches; visitors must perform searches for themselves. Search fee: No criminal searches performed by court. Required to search: name, years to search, DOB; also helpful-SSN. Criminal records on computer from 1986, on files from 1960s. Court will usually only check back 10 years. For information about the statewide online system, LOPAS, see the state introduction. **General Information:** No juvenile, sealed, presentencing probation report, judges notes or adoption records released. Copy fee: $.50 per page. Certification fee: $2.00. Fee payee: Clerk of Circuit Court. Personal checks accepted. Prepayment required. Public terminal is available.

2nd General District Court 2305 Judicial Blvd, Judicial Center, Virginia Beach, VA 23456-9057; 757-427-8531; Civil phone:757-427-4277; Criminal phone:757-427-4277; Fax: 757-426-5672 Civil; 757-426-5682 Crim. Hours: 8:30AM-4PM (EST). *Misdemeanor, Civil Actions Under $15,000, Eviction, Small Claims.*

Civil Records: Access: Phone, fax, mail, online, in person. Both court and visitors may perform in person searches. Search fee: $10.00 per name. Required to search: name, years to search. Civil cases indexed by defendant, plaintiff. Civil records on computer from 1987, on docket books and cards from 1978. For information about the statewide online system, LOPAS, see the state introduction. **Criminal Records:** Access: Phone, fax, mail, remote online, in person. Both court and visitors may perform in person searches. Search

fee: $10.00 per name. Required to search: name, years to search, DOB; also helpful-SSN. Criminal records on computer from 01/88, records destroyed after 10 years. For information about the statewide online system, LOPAS, see the state introduction. **General Information:** No juvenile, sealed, adoption or mental records released. Turnaround time 3-4 weeks. Copy fee: $.50 per page. Certification fee: No certification fee. Fee payee: Clerk of General District Court. Personal checks accepted. Prepayment is required. Public access terminal is available. Fax notes: No fee to fax results.

Warren County

Circuit Court 1 East Main St, Front Royal, VA 22630; 540-635-2435; Fax: 540-636-3274. Hours: 9AM-5PM (EST). *Felony, Civil Actions Over $15,000, Probate.*

Civil Records: Access: Phone, fax, mail, online, in person. Both court and visitors may perform in person searches. No search fee. Required to search: name, years to search. Civil cases indexed by defendant, plaintiff. Civil records on archives from 1836. For information about the statewide online system, LOPAS, see the state introduction. Phone access limited to specific case only. **Criminal Records:** Access: Phone, fax, mail, remote online, in person. Both court and visitors may perform in person searches. No search fee. Required to search: name, years to search, DOB; also helpful-SSN. Criminal records on archives from 1836. For information about the statewide online system, LOPAS, see the state introduction. **General Information:** No juvenile, sealed, adoption records released. SASE required. Turnaround time 1-2 days. Copy fee: $.50 per page. Certification fee: $2.00. Fee payee: William A Hall, Clerk. Personal checks accepted. Public access terminal is available.

26th General District Court 1 East Main St, Front Royal, VA 22630; 540-635-2335; Fax: 540-636-8233. Hours: 8AM-4:30PM (EST). *Misdemeanor, Civil Actions Under $15,000, Eviction, Small Claims.*

Civil Records: Access: Mail, online, in person. Both court and visitors may perform in person searches. No search fee. Required to search: name, years to search. Civil cases indexed by defendant. Civil records on archives back to 1836, on computer from 1989. For information about the statewide online system, LOPAS, see the state introduction. **Criminal Records:** Access: Mail, remote online, in person. Both court and visitors may perform in person searches. No search fee. Required to search: name, years to search; also helpful-SSN. Criminal records on archives back to 1836, on computer from 1989. For information about the statewide online system, LOPAS, see the state introduction. **General Information:** No juvenile, sealed records released. SASE required. Turnaround time 2-3 days. Copy fee: $.50 per page. Certification fee: No certification fee. Fee payee: General District Court. Personal checks accepted. Credit cards accepted: Visa, Mastercard. Public access terminal is available.

Washington County

Circuit Court of Washington County PO Box 289, Abingdon, VA 24212-0289; 540-676-6224/6226; Fax: 540-676-6218. Hours: 7:30AM-5PM; Recording Hours: 7:30AM-4PM (EST). *Felony, Civil Actions Over $15,000, Probate.*

Civil Records: Access: Mail, online, in person. Both court and visitors may perform in person searches. No search fee. Required to search: name, years to search. Civil cases indexed by defendant, plaintiff. Civil records on archives from 1777, on computer from 1991. For information about the statewide online system, LOPAS, see the state introduction. **Criminal Records:** Access: Remote online, in person. Court does not conduct in person searches; visitors must perform searches for themselves. Search fee: No criminal searches performed by court. Required to search: name, years to search. Criminal records on archives from 1777, on computer from 1991. For information about the statewide online system, LOPAS, see the state introduction. **General Information:** No juvenile, sealed or adoption records released. SASE required. Turnaround time 1 week. Copy fee: $.50 per page. Certification fee: $2.00. Fee payee: Clerk, Circuit Court. Personal checks accepted. Will bill copy fees. Public access terminal is available.

28th General District Court

191 E Main St, Abingdon, VA 24210; 540-676-6279; Fax: 540-676-6293. Hours: 8:30AM-5PM (EST). *Misdemeanor, Civil Actions Under $15,000, Eviction, Small Claims.*

Civil Records: Access: Mail, online, in person. Both court and visitors may perform in person searches. No search fee. Required to search: name, years to search. Civil cases indexed by defendant, plaintiff. Civil records on archives from 1777, on computer from 1987. For information about the statewide online system, LOPAS, see the state introduction. **Criminal Records:** Access: Fax, mail, remote online, in person. Both court and visitors may perform in person searches. No search fee. Required to search: name, years to search. Criminal records on archives from 1777, on computer from 1987. For information about the statewide online system, LOPAS, see the state introduction. **General Information:** No sealed records released. SASE required. Turnaround time 1-2 days. Copy fee: $1.00 for first page, $.50 each addl. Certification fee: $2.00. Fee payee: General District Court. Personal checks accepted. Credit cards accepted: Visa, Mastercard. Prepayment is required. Public access terminal is available.

Waynesboro City

25th Circuit Court 250 S Wayne Ave, PO Box 910, Waynesboro, VA 22980; 540-942-6616; Fax: 540-542-6774. Hours: 8:30AM-5PM (EST). *Felony, Civil Actions Over $15,000, Probate.*

Civil Records: Access: online, in person. Court does not conduct in person searches; visitors must perform searches for themselves. Search fee: No civil searches performed by court. Required to search: name, years to search. Civil cases indexed by defendant, plaintiff. Civil records on computer from 11/88 (some), all on index books from 5/48. For information about the statewide online system, LOPAS, see the state introduction. **Criminal Records:** Access: Remote online, in person. Court does not conduct in person searches; visitors must perform searches for themselves. Search fee: No criminal searches performed by court. Required to search: name, years to search, DOB; also helpful-SSN. Criminal records on computer from 11/88 (some), all on index books from 5/48. For information about the statewide online system, LOPAS, see the state introduction. **General Information:** No juvenile, sealed, adoptions released. Copy fee: $.50 per page. Certification fee: $2.00. Fee payee: Clerk of Circuit Court. Personal checks accepted. Prepayment is required.

25th General District Court-Waynesboro

250 S Wayne, PO Box 1028, Waynesboro, VA 22980; 540-942-6636; Fax: 540-942-6793. Hours: 8:30AM-4:30PM (EST). *Misdemeanor, Civil Actions Under $15,000, Eviction, Small Claims.*

Civil Records: Access: Mail, online, in person. Both court and visitors may perform in person searches. No search fee. Required to search: name, years to search. Civil cases indexed by defendant, plaintiff. Civil records on computer 10 years. For information about the statewide online system, LOPAS, see the state introduction. **Criminal Records:** Access: Mail, remote online, in person. Both court and visitors may perform in person searches. No search fee. Required to search: name, years to search. Criminal records on computer for 10 years. For information about the statewide online system, LOPAS, see the state introduction. **General Information:** Turnaround time up to 1 week. No copy fee. Certification fee: No certification fee. Fee payee: General District. Personal checks accepted. Credit cards accepted: Visa, Mastercard. Public access terminal is available.

Westmoreland County

15th Circuit Court PO Box 307, Montross, VA 22520; 804-493-0108; Fax: 804-493-0393. Hours: 9AM-5PM (EST). *Felony, Civil Actions Over $15,000, Probate.*

Civil Records: Access: online, in person. Court does not conduct in person searches; visitors must perform searches for themselves. Search fee: No civil searches performed by court. Required to search: name, years to search. Civil cases indexed by defendant, plaintiff. Civil records on index books from 1653. For information about the statewide online system, LOPAS, see the state introduction. **Criminal Records:** Access: Remote online, in person. Court does not conduct in person searches; visitors must perform searches for themselves. Search fee: No criminal searches performed by court. Required to search: name, years to search, DOB; also helpful-SSN. Criminal records on index books from 1653. For information about the statewide online system, LOPAS, see the state introduction. **General Information:** No juvenile, sealed, adoption records released. Copy fee: $.50 per page. Certification fee: $3.00. Fee payee: Clerk of Circuit Court. Personal checks accepted. Will bill copy fees.

15th General District Court

PO Box 688, Montross, VA 22520; 804-493-0105. Hours: 8AM-4:30PM (EST). *Misdemeanor, Civil Actions Under $15,000, Small Claims.*

Civil Records: Access: Mail, online, in person. Both court and visitors may perform in person searches. No search fee. Required to search: name, years to search. Civil cases indexed by defendant, plaintiff. Civil records on index books/cards for 10 years. For information about the statewide online system, LOPAS, see the state introduction. **Criminal Records:** Access: Mail, remote online, in person. Both court and visitors may perform in person searches. No search fee. Required to search: name, years to search; also helpful-DOB, SSN. Criminal records on index books/cards for 10 years. For information about the statewide online system, LOPAS, see the state introduction. **General Information:** All records public. SASE required. Turnaround time 1 week. Copy fee: $1.00 for first page, $.50 each addl. Certification fee: No certification fee. Fee payee: General

District Court. Personal checks accepted. Attorney checks accepted. Credit cards accepted: Visa, Mastercard. Prepayment is required. Public access terminal is available.

Williamsburg City

Circuit & District Courts .

Note: See James City County.

Winchester City

26th Circuit Court 5 N Kent St, Winchester, VA 22601; 540-667-5770; Fax: 540-667-6638. Hours: 9AM-5PM (EST). *Felony, Civil Actions Over $15,000, Probate.*

www.winfredclerk.com

Note: The Winchester Court and the Frederick County Court Clerks are housed in the same judicial center. The offices share microfilming and deed indexing systems

Civil Records: Access: online, in person. Court does not conduct in person searches; visitors must perform searches for themselves. Search fee: No civil searches performed by court. Required to search: name, years to search. Civil cases indexed by defendant, plaintiff. Civil records on computer from 1985 to present, on index books from 1790. For information about the statewide online system, LOPAS, see the state introduction. **Criminal Records:** Access: Mail, remote online, in person. Both court and visitors may perform in person searches. No search fee. Required to search: name, years to search; also helpful-DOB, SSN. Criminal records on computer from 1985 to present, on index books from 1790. For information about the statewide online system, LOPAS, see the state introduction. **General Information:** No juvenile, sealed, adoption records released. SASE required. Turnaround time same day. Copy fee: $.50 per page. Certification fee: $2.00. Fee payee: Clerk of Circuit Court. Personal checks accepted. Prepayment is required.

26th General District Court 5 N Kent St, PO Box 526, Winchester, VA 22604; 540-722-7208; Fax: 540-722-1063. Hours: 8AM-4PM (EST). *Misdemeanor, Civil Actions Under $15,000, Eviction, Small Claims.*

Civil Records: Access: Phone, mail, online, in person. Both court and visitors may perform in person searches. No search fee. Required to search: name, years to search. Civil cases indexed by defendant, plaintiff. Civil records on computer from 1987, on index cards from 1985 to 1987, prior at Circuit Court. For information about the statewide online system, LOPAS, see the state introduction. **Criminal Records:** Access: Mail, remote online, in person. Both court and visitors may perform in person searches. No search fee. Required to search: name, years to search, DOB, SSN, signed release. Criminal records on computer from 1987, on index cards from 1985 to 1987, prior at Circuit Court. For information about the statewide online system, LOPAS, see the state introduction. Forms for criminal searches available from State Police. **General Information:** No sealed records released. Turnaround time 1-2 days. Copy fee: $.50 per page. Certification fee: $2.00. Fee payee: Clerk of General District Court. Personal checks accepted. Prepayment is required. Public access terminal is available.

Wise County

30th Circuit Court PO Box 1248, Wise, VA 24293-1248; 540-328-6111; Fax: 540-328-6111. Hours: 8:30AM-5PM (EST). *Felony, Civil Actions Over $15,000, Probate.*

www.courtbar.org

Civil Records: Access: Phone, fax, mail, online, in person. Both court and visitors may perform in person searches. Search fee: $10.00 per name. Required to search: name, years to search; also helpful-address. Civil cases indexed by defendant, plaintiff. Civil records on archives from 1856. For information about the statewide online system, LOPAS, see the state introduction. **Criminal Records:** Access: Phone, fax, mail, remote online, in person. Both court and visitors may perform in person searches. Search fee: $10.00 per name. Required to search: name, years to search, DOB; also helpful-SSN. Criminal records on archives from 1856. For information about the statewide online system, LOPAS, see the state introduction. **General Information:** No juvenile, sealed or adoption records released. Turnaround time 2-3 days. Copy fee: $.50 per page. Certification fee: $2.00 plus copy fee. Fee payee: Clerk of Circuit Court. Personal checks accepted. Prepayment is required. Public access terminal is available.

30th General District Court Wise County Courthouse, PO Box 829, Wise, VA 24293; 540-328-3426; Fax: 540-328-4576. Hours: 8AM-4PM (EST). *Misdemeanor, Civil Actions Under $15,000, Eviction, Small Claims.*

Civil Records: Access: Phone, mail, online, in person. Both court and visitors may perform in person searches. No search fee. Required to search: name, years to search. Civil cases indexed by defendant, plaintiff. For information about the statewide online system, LOPAS, see the state introduction. **Criminal Records:** Access: Phone, mail, remote online, in person. Both court and visitors may perform in person searches. No search fee. Required to search: name, years to search; also helpful-DOB, SSN. For information about the statewide online system, LOPAS, see the state introduction. **General Information:** No juvenile, sealed records released. Turnaround time 5 days. Copy fee: $.50 per page. Certification fee: No certification fee. Fee payee: General District Court. Personal checks accepted. Credit cards accepted. Prepayment is required. Public access terminal is available.

Wythe County

27th Circuit Court 225 S Fourth St, Rm 105, Wytheville, VA 24382; 540-223-6050; Fax: 540-223-6057. Hours: 8:30AM-5PM (EST). *Felony, Civil Actions Over $15,000, Probate.*

Civil Records: Access: Mail, online, in person. Both court and visitors may perform in person searches. No search fee. Required to search: name, years to search. Civil cases indexed by defendant, plaintiff. Civil records on computer from 1989, on index cards/books from 1950s (some back to 1790s). For information about the statewide online system, LOPAS, see the state introduction. **Criminal Records:** Access: Mail, remote online, in person. Both court and visitors may perform in person searches. No search fee. Required to search: name, years to search; also helpful-DOB, SSN. Criminal records on computer from 1989, on index cards/books from 1950s (some back to 1790s). For information about the statewide online system, LOPAS, see the state introduction. **General Information:** No juvenile, sealed or adoption records released. SASE required. Turnaround time 1-2 days. Copy fee: $.50 per page. Certification fee: None. Fee payee: Clerk of Circuit Court. Personal checks accepted. Credit cards accepted: Visa, Mastercard. Prepayment is required.

Wythe General District Court 225 S. Fourth St., # 203, Wytheville, VA 24382-2595; 540-223-6075; Fax: 540-223-6087. Hours: 8AM-4:30PM (EST). *Misdemeanor, Civil Actions Under $15,000, Eviction, Small Claims.*

Civil Records: Access: online, in person. Court does not conduct in person searches; visitors must perform searches for themselves. Search fee: No civil searches performed by court. Required to search: name, years to search. Civil cases indexed by defendant, plaintiff. Civil records on computer from 4/88, on index cards from 1985, prior at Circuit Court. For information about the statewide online system, LOPAS, see the state introduction. **Criminal Records:** Access: Remote online, in person. Court does not conduct in person searches; visitors must perform searches for themselves. Search fee: No criminal searches performed by court. Required to search: name, years to search; also helpful-DOB, SSN. Criminal records on computer from 4/88, on index cards from 1985, prior at Circuit Court. For information about the statewide online system, LOPAS, see the state introduction. **General Information:** Copy fee: $.50 per page. Fee is only applied to requests for excessive amounts of information. Certification fee: No certification fee. Fee payee: General District Court. Personal checks accepted. Credit cards accepted: Visa, Mastercard. Public access terminal is available.

York County

9th Circuit Court PO Box 371, Yorktown, VA 23690; 757-890-3350; Fax: 757-890-3364. Hours: 8:15AM-5PM (EST). *Felony, Civil Actions Over $15,000, Probate.*

Note: Also includes city of poquoson

Civil Records: Access: online, in person. Court does not conduct in person searches; visitors must perform searches for themselves. Search fee: No civil searches performed by court. Required to search: name, years to search. Civil cases indexed by defendant, plaintiff. Civil records on index books from 1633, computerized since 1986. For information about the statewide online system, LOPAS, see the state introduction. **Criminal Records:** Access: Mail, remote online, in person. Both court and visitors may perform in person searches. Search fee: $5.00 per name. Required to search: name, years to search, DOB; also helpful-SSN. Criminal records on index books from 1633, computerized since 1986. For information about the statewide online system, LOPAS, see the state introduction. **General Information:** No juvenile, sealed, adoption records released. SASE required. Turnaround time 1 week. Copy fee: $.50 per page. Certification fee: No certification fee. Fee payee: Clerk of Circuit Court. Personal checks accepted. Prepayment is required. Public access terminal is available.

9th Judicial District Court York County GDC, PO Box 316, Yorktown, VA 23690-0316; 757-890-3450; Fax: 757-890-3459. Hours: 8:30AM-4:30PM (EST). *Misdemeanor, Civil Actions Under $15,000, Eviction, Small Claims.*

Civil Records: Access: Fax, mail, online, in person. Both court and visitors may perform in person searches. No search fee. Required to search: name, years to search. Civil cases indexed by defendant, plaintiff. Civil records on computer from 1990, prior at Circuit Court. For information about the statewide online system, LOPAS, see the state introduction. **Criminal Records:** Access: Fax, mail, remote online, in person. Both court and visitors may perform in person searches. No search fee. Required to search: name, years to search. Criminal records on computer from 1988, prior at Circuit Court. For information about the statewide online system, LOPAS, see the state introduction. **General Information:** No juvenile, sealed, adoption records released. Turnaround time 5 days. Copy fee: $1.00 for first page, $.50 each addl. Certification fee: No certification fee. Public access terminal is available. Fax notes: $1.00 for first page, $.50 each addl.

ORGANIZATION

95 counties and 41 independent cities, 123 recording offices. The recording officer is Clerk of Circuit Court. **Fourteen independent cities share the Clerk of Circuit Court with the county**—Bedford, Emporia (Greenville County), Fairfax, Falls Church (Arlington or Fairfax County), Franklin (Southhampton County), Galax (Carroll County), Harrisonburg (Rockingham County), Lexington (Rockbridge County), Manassas and Manassas Park (Prince William County), Norton (Wise County), Poquoson (York County), South Boston (Halifax County), and Williamsburg (James City County). **Charles City and James City are counties, not cities. The City of Franklin is not in Franklin County, the City of Richmond is not in Richmond County, and the City of Roanoke is not in Roanoke County.** The entire state is in the Eastern Time Zone (EST).

REAL ESTATE RECORDS

Only a few Clerks of Circuit Court will perform real estate searches. Copy fees and certification fees vary. The independent cities may have separate Assessor Offices.

UCC RECORDS

This is a **dual filing state**. Financing statements are filed at the state level and with the Clerk of Circuit Court, except for consumer goods, farm and real estate related collateral, which are filed only with the Clerk of Circuit Court. Some recording offices will perform UCC searches. Use search request form UCC-11. Searches fees and copy fees vary.

TAX LIEN RECORDS

Federal tax liens on personal property of businesses are filed with the State Corporation Commission. Other federal and all state tax liens are filed with the county Clerk of Circuit Court. They are usually filed in a "Judgment Lien Book." Most counties will **not** perform tax lien searches.

OTHER LIENS

Judgment, mechanics, hospital, lis pendens.

Accomack County
County Clerk of the Circuit Court, P.O. Box 126, Accomac, VA 23301-0126. 757-787-5776. Fax: 757-787-1849.

Albemarle County
County Clerk of the Circuit Court, 501 E. Jefferson St., Room 225, Charlottesville, VA 22902-5176. 804-972-4083. Fax: 804-293-0298.

Alexandria City
City Clerk of the Circuit Court, 520 King Street, Room 307, Alexandria, VA 22314. 703-838-4070.

Alleghany County
County Clerk of the Circuit Court, P.O. Box 670, Covington, VA 24426-0670. 540-965-1730. Fax: 540-965-1732.

Amelia County
County Clerk of the Circuit Court, P.O. Box 237, Amelia Court House, VA 23002-0237. 804-561-2128.

Amherst County
County Clerk of the Circuit Court, P.O. Box 462, Amherst, VA 24521. 804-946-9321.

Appomattox County
County Clerk of the Circuit Court, P.O. Box 672, Appomattox, VA 24522. 804-352-5275. Fax: 804-352-2781.

Arlington County
County Clerk of the Circuit Court, 1425 N. Courthouse Rd 6th Floor, Arlington, VA 22201. 703-228-7242.

Augusta County
County Clerk of the Circuit Court, P.O. Box 689, Staunton, VA 24402-0689. 540-245-5321. Fax: 540-245-5318.

Bath County
County Clerk of the Circuit Court, P.O. Box 180, Warm Springs, VA 24484. 540-839-7226.

Bedford City
Bedford County handles recording for this city.

Bedford County
County Clerk of the Circuit Court, P.O. Box 235, Bedford, VA 24523. 540-586-7632.
www.ci.bedford.va.us
Online Access: Property Tax. Records on the City of Bedford (www.ci.bedford.va.us) Property Tax database are available free online at www.ci.bedford.va.us/proptax/lookup.html. County Real Estate records on the

Bedford County Commissioner of the Revenue site are available free online at http://208.206.84.33/realestate2.

Bland County
County Clerk of the Circuit Court, P.O. Box 295, Bland, VA 24315-0295. 540-688-4562. Fax: 540-688-4562.

Botetourt County
County Clerk of the Circuit Court, P.O. Box 219, Fincastle, VA 24090. 540-473-8274.

Bristol City
City Clerk of the Circuit Court, 497 Cumberland Street, Room 210, Bristol, VA 24201. 540-645-7321. Fax: 540-645-7345.

Brunswick County
County Clerk of the Circuit Court, 216 N. Main St., Lawrenceville, VA 23868. 804-848-2215. Fax: 804-848-4307.

Buchanan County
County Clerk of the Circuit Court, P.O. Box 929, Grundy, VA 24614. 540-935-6567. Fax: 540-935-6574.

Buckingham County
County Clerk of the Circuit Court, P.O. Box 107, Buckingham, VA 23921. 804-969-4734. Fax: 804-959-2043.

Buena Vista City
City Clerk of the Circuit Court, 2039 Sycamore Ave., Buena Vista, VA 24416. 540-261-8627. Fax: 540-261-8623.

Campbell County
County Clerk of the Circuit Court, P.O. Box 7, Rustburg, VA 24588. 804-592-9517.

Caroline County
County Clerk of the Circuit Court, P.O. Box 309, Bowling Green, VA 22427-0309. 804-633-5800.

Carroll County
County Clerk of the Circuit Court, P.O. Box 218, Hillsville, VA 24343-0218. 540-728-3117. Fax: 540-728-0255.

Charles City County
County Clerk of the Circuit Court, P.O. Box 86, Charles City, VA 23030-0086. 804-829-9212. Fax: 804-829-5647.

Charlotte County
County Clerk of the Circuit Court, P.O. Box 38, Charlotte Court House, VA 23923. 804-542-5147. Fax: 804-542-4336.

Charlottesville City
City Clerk of the Circuit Court, 315 East High Street, Charlottesville, VA 22902. 804-295-3182.

Chesapeake City
City Clerk of the Circuit Court, P.O. Box 15205, Chesapeake, VA 23328-5205. 757-382-6876. Fax: 757-436-8750.

Chesterfield County
County Clerk of the Circuit Court, P.O. Box 125, Chesterfield, VA 23832-0125. 804-748-1243. Fax: 804-796-5625.

Clarke County
County Clerk of the Circuit Court, P.O. Box 189, Berryville, VA 22611. 540-955-5116. Fax: 540-955-0284.

Clifton Forge City
City Clerk of the Circuit Court, P.O. Box 27, Clifton Forge, VA 24422. 540-863-2508.

Colonial Heights City
City Clerk of the Circuit Court, P.O. Box 3401, Colonial Heights, VA 23834. 804-520-9364.

Covington City
Alleghany County handles recording for this city.

Craig County
County Clerk of the Circuit Court, P.O. Box 185, New Castle, VA 24127-0185. 540-864-6141.

Culpeper County
County Clerk of the Circuit Court, 135 West Cameron St., Room 103, Culpeper, VA 22701. 540-727-3438.

Cumberland County
County Clerk of the Circuit Court, P.O. Box 8, Cumberland, VA 23040. 804-492-4442. Fax: 804-492-4876.

Danville City
City Clerk of the Circuit Court, P.O. Box 3300, Danville, VA 24543. 804-799-5168. Fax: 804-799-6502.
Online Access: Real Estate, Liens. Access to Danville City online records is free; signup is required. Records date back to 1993. The system operates 24 hours daily. Lending agency information is available For information, contact Leigh Ann at 804-799-5168.

Dickenson County
County Clerk of the Circuit Court, P.O. Box 190, Clintwood, VA 24228. 540-926-1616. Fax: 540-926-6465.

Licenses Searchable Online

Architect #26	www.wa.gov/dol/bpd/licquery.htm
Electrical Administrator #12	www.lni.wa.gov/contractors/contractor.asp
Electrical Contractor #12	www.lni.wa.gov/contractors/contractor.asp
Electrician #12	www.lni.wa.gov/contractors/contractor.asp
Engineer #06	www.wa.gov/dol/bpd/pliseng.htm
General Contractor #12	www.lni.wa.gov/contractors/contractor.asp
Insurance Company #25	www.insurance.wa.gov/tableofcontents/annualreptins.htm
Landscape Architect #26	www.wa.gov/dol/bpd/licquery.htm
Liquor Store #19	www.liq.wa.gov/services/storesearch.asp
Optometrist #11	www.arbo.org/nodb2000/licsearch.asp
Plumber #12	www.lni.wa.gov/contractors/contractor.asp
Surveyor #06	www.wa.gov/dol/bpd/plisls.htm

Licensing Quick Finder

Acupuncturist #10	360-586-7759
Alien Bank #07	360-902-8704
Animal Technician #10	360-586-6355
Architect #26	360-664-1388
Athletic Agent #15	360-586-7582
Athletic Announcer #27	360-753-3713
Athletic Inspector #27	360-753-3713
Athletic Judge #27	360-753-3713
Athletic Manager #27	360-753-3713
Athletic Matchmaker #27	360-753-3713
Athletic Physician #27	360-753-3713
Athletic Promoter #27	360-753-3713
Athletic Timekeeper #27	360-753-3713
Attorney #23	206-727-8200
Auction Company #27	360-753-4553
Auctioneer #27	360-753-4553
Audiologist #11	360-753-1817
Bail Bond Agency #15	360-586-4567
Bail Bond Agent #15	360-586-4567
Bank #07	360-902-8704
Barber #18	360-586-6387
Boiler Inspector #13	360-902-5270
Booth Renter #18	360-586-6387
Boxer #27	360-753-3713
Bulk Hauler #14	360-902-3703
Business Opportunities #07	360-902-8760
Cemetery & Funeral-Related Professions #06	360-586-4905
Check Casher & Seller #07	360-902-8703
Chiropractor #10	360-753-0776
Collection Agency #27	360-664-1389
Commercial Applicator #05	877-301-4555
Commercial Fishing #08	360-902-2253
Commercial Marine Pilot #02	206-515-3904
Commercial Operator #05	877-301-4555
Commercial Pest Control Consultant #05	877-301-4555
Commodities #07	360-902-8760
Consumer Loan Company #07	360-902-8703
Cosmetologist #18	360-586-6387
Cosmetology Instructor #18	360-586-6387
Cosmetology School #18	360-586-6387
Counselor #10	360-664-9098
Court Reporter #27	360-753-1061
Credit Union #07	360-902-8701
Crematory #06	360-586-4905
Demonstration & Research Applicator #05	877-301-4555
Dental Hygienist #10	360-586-1867
Dentist #10	360-586-6898
Dietitian #10	360-586-6351
Egg Inspector #04	360-902-1830
Electrical Administrator #12	360-902-5269
Electrical Contractor #12	360-902-5269
Electrician #12	360-902-5269
Embalmer #06	360-586-4905
Emergency Medical Technician #10	360-705-6700

Employment Agency #27	360-664-1389
Engineer #06	360-753-6966
ESA Pathology #20	360-753-6773
Escrow Company & Officers #07	360-902-8703
Esthetician #18	360-586-6387
Firearms Dealer #15	360-753-2803
Franchises #07	360-902-8760
Fruit/Vegetable Inspector #04	360-902-1832
Funeral Director #06	360-586-4905
Funeral Establishment #06	360-586-4905
Gaming #24	360-438-7654
General Contractor #12	360-902-5226
Grain Inspector #06	360-753-1484
Health Care Assistant #10	360-753-1230
Hearing Instrument Fitter/Dispenser #11	360-753-1817
Home Health Care Agency #09	360-705-6611
Horse Racing #22	360-459-6462
Hospital #09	360-705-6611
Hypnotherapist #11	360-586-8584
Insurance Agent #25	360-407-0341
Insurance Broker #25	360-407-0341
Investment Advisors #07	360-902-8760
Kick Boxer #27	360-753-3713
Landscape Architect #26	360-664-1388
Liquor Store #19	360-664-0012
Livestock Brand Recording #03	360-902-1855
Manicurist #18	360-586-6387
Manufactured Home Dealer #14	360-902-3703
Marriage/Family Therapist #10	360-586-4566
Massage Therapist #11	360-586-6351
Medical Doctor #11	360-753-2287
Mental Health Counselor #10	360-586-8584
Midwife #11	360-664-4218
Miscellaneous Vehicle Dealer #14	360-902-3703
Mobile Home Travel Trailer Dealer #14	360-902-3703
Mobile Operator #18	360-586-6387
Mortgage Brokers #07	360-902-8703
Naturopathic Physician #11	360-664-3230
Non Resident Broker #25	360-407-0341
Notary Public #17	360-753-3836
Nurse #11	360-586-1923
Nurse-LPN #11	360-664-4226
Nursing Assistant #11	360-586-1923
Nursing Home #09	360-493-2500
Nursing Home Administrator #11	360-753-3729
Occupational Therapist #11	360-664-8662
Ocularist #11	360-753-3576
Optician #11	360-753-3576
Optometrist #11	360-753-4614
Osteopathic Physician #11	360-586-8438
Pesticide Dealer Manager #05	877-301-4555
Pesticide Operators & Applicator #05	877-301-4555
Pesticide Private Application #05	877-301-4555
Pharmacist #10	360-236-4825
Pharmacy Technician #10	360-236-4825

Physical Therapist #11	360-753-0876
Physician Assistant #11	360-664-3909
Plumber #12	360-902-5207
Podiatrist #11	360-586-8438
Private Commercial Applicator #05	877-301-4555
Private Investigative Agency #15	360-664-9070
Private Investigator, Armed #15	360-664-9070
Private Investigator, Unarmed #15	360-664-9070
Professional Athlete #27	360-753-3713
Program Administrator #20	360-753-6773
Psychologist #11	360-753-2147
Public Accountant-CPA #01	360-753-2585
Public Operator #05	877-301-4555
Public Pest Control Consultant #05	877-301-4555
Radiologic Technologist #11	360-586-6100
Real Estate Appraiser #16	360-753-1062
Real Estate Broker #16	360-753-2262
Real Estate/Sales #16	360-753-2250
Referee #27	360-753-3713
Resident Broker #25	360-407-0341
Resident Corporation #25	360-407-0341
Respiratory Therapist #11	360-586-8437
Salon/Shop #18	360-586-6387
Savings & Loan/Savings Bank #07	306-902-8704
School Counselor #20	360-753-6773
School Nurse #20	360-753-6773
School Occupational Therapist #20	360-753-6773
School Physical Therapist #20	360-753-6773
School Principal #20	360-753-6773
School Psychologist #20	360-753-6773
School Social Worker #20	360-753-6773
School Superintendent #20	360-753-6773
Scrap Processor #14	360-902-3703
Securities Broker/Dealer #07	360-902-8760
Securities Salesperson #07	306-902-8760
Security Guard #15	360-664-9070
Sexual Offender Treatment Provider #11	360-753-2147
Snowmobile Dealer #14	360-902-3703
Social Worker #10	360-586-4566
Speech-Language Pathologist #11	360-753-1817
Sport Fishing #08	360-902-2253
Surveyor #06	360-753-6966
Teacher #21	360-753-6773
Tow Truck Operator #14	360-902-3703
Trainer, Private Investigative #15	360-664-9070
Transporter #14	360-902-3703
Trust Company #07	360-902-8704
Vehicle Dealer Manufacturer #14	360-902-3703
Vessel Dealer #14	360-902-3703
Veterinarian #10	360-586-4566
Veterinary Medical Clerk #10	360-586-4566
Weights & Measures #03	360-902-1857
Wrecker #14	360-902-3703
Wrestler #27	360-753-3713
X-ray Technician #11	360-586-6100

Licensing Agency Information

01 Board of Accountancy, PO Box (PO Box 9131), Olympia, WA 98507-9131; 360-753-2585, Fax: 360-664-9190.

www.cpaboard.wa.gov

02 Board of Pilotage Commissioners, 2911 2nd Ave, Seattle, WA 98121-1012; 206-515-3904, Fax: 206-515-3969.

03 Department of Agriculture, PO Box 42560 (1111 Washington St), Olympia, WA 98504-2560; 360-902-1850, Fax: 360-902-2086.

www.wa.gov/agr

04 Department of Agriculture, PO Box 42560 (PO Box 42560), Olympia, WA 98504-2560; 360-902-2085.

www.agriculture.wa.gov

05 Department of Agriculture, PO Box 42589 (PO Box 42589), Olympia, WA 98504-2589; 360-902-2010, Fax: 360-902-2093.

www.wa.gov/agr/pmd/index.htm

06 Department of Labor, PO Box 9012 (PO Box 9012), Olympia, WA 98507-9012; 360-902-4905, Fax: 360-902-2550.

07 Department of Financial Institutions, PO Box 41200 (PO Box 41200), Olympia, WA 98504-1200; 360-902-8700, Fax: 360-586-5068.

www.wa.gov/dfi

08 Department of Fish & Wildlife, 600 Capitol Way N, Olympia, WA 98501-1091; 360-902-2253, Fax: 360-902-2171.

www.wa.gov/wdfw

09 Department of Health, PO Box 47852 (PO Box 47852), Olympia, WA 98504-7852; 360-705-6611, Fax: 360-705-6654.

www.wa.gov/health

10 Department of Health, PO Box 47860 (PO Box 47860), Olympia, WA 98504-7860; 360-586-5846, Fax: 360-586-4359.

www.doh.wa.gov/Topics/topics.htm#Licensing

11 Department of Health, PO Box 47860 (PO Box 47860), Olympia, WA 98504-7860; 360-753-3576, Fax: 360-586-0745.

www.wa.gov/health

12 Department of Labor & Industries, PO Box 44000 (PO Box 44000), Olympia, WA 98504-4000; 360-902-5800, Fax: 360-902-5292.

www.lni.wa.gov

Direct URL to search licenses: www.lni.wa.gov/contractors/contractor.asp You can search online using name, registration number, uniform business identifier number, and city.

13 Department of Labor & Industries, PO Box 44410 (PO Box 44410), Olympia, WA 98504-4410; 360-902-5270, Fax: 360-902-5292.

www.wa.gov/lni

14 Department of Licensing, PO Box 48001 (1125 Washington St SE), Olympia, WA 98507-9039; 360-902-3703, Fax: 360-586-6703.

www.wa.gov/dol/

15 Department of Licensing, Private Investigator & Security Guard, PO Box 9649 (PO Box 9649), Olympia, WA 98507-9649; 360-664-9070, Fax: 360-753-3747.

16 Department of Licensing, PO Box 9015 (PO Box 9015), Olympia, WA 98507-9015; 360-753-2250, Fax: 360-586-0998.

www.wa.gov/dol/bpd/refront.htm

17 Department of Licensing, Notary Section, PO Box 9027 (PO Box 9027), Olympia, WA 98507-9027; 360-753-3836, Fax: 360-664-2550.

18 Department of Professional Licensing, Cosmetology Division, PO Box 9045 (PO Box 9012, 405 Black Lake Blvd), Olympia, WA 98507-9026; 360-586-6387, Fax: 360-664-2550.

www.wa.gov/dol/bpd/cosfront.htm

19 Liquor Control Board, PO Box 43075 (1025 E Union Ave), Olympia, WA 98504-3075; 360-753-2710.

www.liq.wa.gov

Direct URL to search licenses: www.liq.wa.gov/services/storesearch.asp You can search online using county, city, and store number.

20 Superintendent of Public Instruction, PO Box 47200 (Old Capitol Bldg), Olympia, WA 98504-7200; 360-753-6773, Fax: 360-586-0145.

www.k12.wa.us/cert

21 Teacher Certification, PO Box 47200 (PO Box 47200), Olympia, WA 98504-7200; 360-753-6773, Fax: 360-586-0145.

www.k12.wa.us/cert

22 Horse Racing Commission, 7912 Martin Way, #D, Olympia, WA 98516-5703; 360-459-6462, Fax: 360-459-6461.

www.whrc.wa.gov/licensing/index.htm

23 Bar Association, 2101 4th Ave, 4th Fl, Seattle, WA 98121-2599; 206-727-8200, Fax: 206-727-8320.

www.wsba.org

24 Gambling Commission, PO Box 42400 (PO Box 42400), Olympia, WA 98504-2400; 360-438-7654 x358, Fax: 360-438-7503.

www.wa.gov/gambling/wsgc.htm

25 Insurance Licensing, PO Box 40257 (4224 6th Ave SE, Rowesix Bldg 5), Olympia, WA 98504-0257; 360-407-0341, Fax: 360-438-7629.

www.insurance.wa.gov/

26 Department of Licensing, Architects & Lanscape Architects, Business and Professions Division, PO Box 9045 (PO Box 9045), Olympia, WA 98507-9045; 360-664-1388, Fax: 360-664-2551.

www.wa.gov/dol/bpd/arcfront.htm

Direct URL to search licenses: www.wa.gov/dol/bpd/licquery.htm You can search online using last name or license number

27 Department of Licensing, PO Box 9649 (PO Box 9649), Olympia, WA 98507-9649; 360-753-3713, Fax: 360-664-2550.

www.wa.gov/dol/

The following list indicates the district and division name for each county in the state. If the district or division name of the bankruptcy court is different from the civil/criminal court, it appears in parentheses.

County/Court Cross Reference

Adams	Eastern	Spokane	Lewis	Western	Tacoma
Asotin	Eastern	Spokane	Lincoln	Eastern	Spokane
Benton	Eastern	Spokane	Mason	Western	Tacoma
Chelan	Eastern	Spokane	Okanogan	Eastern	Spokane
Clallam	Western	Tacoma (Seattle)	Pacific	Western	Tacoma
Clark	Western	Tacoma	Pend Oreille	Eastern	Spokane
Columbia	Eastern	Spokane	Pierce	Western	Tacoma
Cowlitz	Western	Tacoma	San Juan	Western	Seattle
Douglas	Eastern	Spokane	Skagit	Western	Seattle
Ferry	Eastern	Spokane	Skamania	Western	Tacoma
Franklin	Eastern	Spokane	Snohomish	Western	Seattle
Garfield	Eastern	Spokane	Spokane	Eastern	Spokane
Grant	Eastern	Spokane	Stevens	Eastern	Spokane
Grays Harbor	Western	Tacoma	Thurston	Western	Tacoma
Island	Western	Seattle	Wahkiakum	Western	Tacoma
Jefferson	Western	Tacoma (Seattle)	Walla Walla	Eastern	Spokane
King	Western	Seattle	Whatcom	Western	Seattle
Kitsap	Western	Tacoma (Seattle)	Whitman	Eastern	Spokane
Kittitas	Eastern	Yakima (Spokane)	Yakima	Eastern	Yakima (Spokane)
Klickitat	Eastern	Yakima (Spokane)			

US District Court

Eastern District of Washington

Spokane Division PO Box 1493, Spokane, WA 99210-1493 (Courier Address: Room 840, W 920 Riverside, Spokane, WA 99201), 509-353-2150.

www.waed.uscourts.gov

Counties: Adams, Asotin, Benton, Chelan, Columbia, Douglas, Ferry, Franklin, Garfield, Grant, Lincoln, Okanogan, Pend Oreille, Spokane, Stevens, Walla Walla, Whitman. Also, some cases from Kittitas, Klickitat and Yakima are heard here.

Indexing & Storage: Cases are indexed by defendant and plaintiff as well as by case number. New cases are available in the index 2-3 days after filing date. A computer index is maintained. Records are also indexed on microfiche. Search must be in Spokane Division for all cases before 1989. Open records are located at this court. Judge McDonald's records are maintained in Yakima (Yakima County). All other cases are kept in the Spokane Division.

Fee & Payment: The fee is $15.00 per item (one party name or case number). Payment may be made by money order, cashier check, personal check. Prepayment is required. Payee: Clerk, US District Court. Certification fee: $5.00 per document. Copy fee: $.50 per page.

Phone Search: Searching is not available by phone.

Mail Search: A stamped self addressed envelope is not required.

In Person Search: In person searching is available.

PACER: Sign-up number is 800-676-6856. Access fee is $.60 per minute. Toll-free access:

888-372-5706. Local access: 509-353-2395. Case records are available back to July 1989. Records are purged every six months. New records are available online after 2-3 days. PACER is available online at http://pacer.waed.uscourts.gov.

Yakima Division PO Box 2706, Yakima, WA 98907 (Courier Address: Room 215, 25 S 3rd St, Yakima, WA 98901), 509-575-5838.

www.waed.uscourts.gov

Counties: Kittitas, Klickitat, Yakima. Cases assigned primarily to Judge McDonald are here. Some cases from Kittitas, Klickitat and Yakima are heard in Spokane.

Indexing & Storage: Cases are indexed by defendant and plaintiff as well as by case number. New cases are available in the index 1 day after filing date. A computer index is maintained. Search must be in Spokane Division for all cases before 1989. Open records are located at this court. Judge McDonald's records are maintained in Yakima. All other cases are kept in the Spokane Division.

Fee & Payment: The fee is $15.00 per item (one party name or case number). Payment may be made by money order, cashier check, business check. Personal checks are not accepted. Prepayment is required. Payee: Clerk, US District Court. Certification fee: $5.00 per document. Copy fee: $.50 per page.

Phone Search: Some docket information is available by phone. An automated voice case information service (VCIS) is not available.

Mail Search: Always enclose a stamped self addressed envelope.

In Person Search: In person searching is available.

PACER: Sign-up number is 800-676-6856. Access fee is $.60 per minute. Toll-free access: 888-372-5706. Local access: 509-353-2395. Case records are available back to July 1989. Records

are purged every six months. New records are available online after 2-3 days. PACER is available online at http://pacer.waed.uscourts.gov.

US Bankruptcy Court

Eastern District of Washington

Spokane Division PO Box 2164, Spokane, WA 99210-2164 (Courier Address: W 904 Riverside, Suite 304, Spokane, WA 99201), 509-353-2404.

www.waeb.uscourts.gov

Counties: Adams, Asotin, Benton, Chelan, Columbia, Douglas, Ferry, Franklin, Garfield, Grant, Kittitas, Klickitat, Lincoln, Okanogan, Pend Oreille, Spokane, Stevens, Walla Walla, Whitman, Yakima.

Indexing & Storage: Cases are indexed by debtor and creditors as well as by case number. New cases are available in the index immediately after filing date. Open records are located at this court.

Fee & Payment: The fee is $15.00 per item (one party name or case number). Payment may be made by money order, cashier check, business check. Personal checks are not accepted. Prepayment is not required for copy requests. Copies will be provided with a bill through the mail. Payee: Clerk, US Bankruptcy Court. Certification fee: $5.00 per document. Copy fee: $.50 per page.

Phone Search: Only docket information is available by phone. An automated voice case information service (VCIS) Press extension 6.

Mail Search: Always enclose a stamped self addressed envelope.

In Person Search: In person searching is available.

PACER: Sign-up number is 800-676-6856. Access fee is $.60 per minute. Toll-free access: 800-314-3430. Local access: 509-353-3289. Use of PC Anywhere V4.0 recommended. Case records are available back to 1986. New civil records are available online after 1 day.

Other Online Access: You can search records on the Internet using RACER. Currently the system is free and requires free registration. Simply visit http://204.227.177.194/wconnect/wc.dll?usbcn_racer~main.

US District Court

Western District of Washington

Seattle Division Clerk of Court, 215 US Courthouse, 1010 5th Ave, Seattle, WA 98104, 206-553-5598.

www.wawd.uscourts.gov

Counties: Island, King, San Juan, Skagit, Snohomish, Whatcom.

Indexing & Storage: Cases are indexed by defendant and plaintiff as well as by case number. New cases are available in the index 10 days after filing date. Both computer and card indexes are maintained. Records are also indexed on microfiche. Open records are located at this court.

Fee & Payment: The fee is $15.00 per item (one party name or case number). Payment may be made by money order, cashier check, personal check. Prepayment is required. Payee: Clerk, US District Court. Certification fee: $5.00 per document. Copy fee: $.50 per page. You are allowed to make your own copies. These copies cost $.25 per page. An outside copy service will make copies for $.11 per page.

Phone Search: Docket information is available by phone for civil cases since 1988 and criminal cases since 1992. An automated voice case information service (VCIS) is not available.

Mail Search: A stamped self addressed envelope is not required.

In Person Search: In person searching is available.

PACER: Sign-up number is 800-676-6856. Access fee is $.60 per minute. Toll-free access: 800-520-8604. Local access: 206-553-6127, 206-553-2288. Case records are available back to 1988. Records are never purged. New civil records are available online after 4 days. New criminal records are available online after 2 days. PACER is available online at http://pacer.wawd.uscourts.gov.

Tacoma Division Clerk's Office, Room 3100, 1717 Pacific Ave, Tacoma, WA 98402-3200, 253-593-6313.

www.wawd.uscourts.gov

Counties: Clallam, Clark, Cowlitz, Grays Harbor, Jefferson, Kitsap, Lewis, Mason, Pacific, Pierce, Skamania, Thurston, Wahkiakum.

Indexing & Storage: Cases are indexed by defendant and plaintiff as well as by case number. New cases are available in the index immediately after filing date. A computer index is maintained. District wide searches are available for information from 1989. Microfiche and card indexes are available for older records. Open records are located at this court.

Fee & Payment: The fee is $15.00 per item (one party name or case number). Payment may be made by money order, cashier check, personal check. Prepayment is required. There is a $25.00 service fee if a check is returned. Payee: Clerk, US District Court. Certification fee: $5.00 per document. Copy fee: $.50 per page.

Phone Search: Only docket information is available by phone. An automated voice case information service (VCIS) is not available.

Mail Search: Always enclose a stamped self addressed envelope.

In Person Search: In person searching is available.

PACER: Sign-up number is 800-676-6856. Access fee is $.60 per minute. Toll-free access: 800-520-8604. Local access: 206-553-6127, 206-553-2288. Case records are available back to 1988. Records are never purged. New civil records are available online after 4 days. New criminal records are available online after 2 days. PACER is available online at http://pacer.wawd.uscourts.gov.

US Bankruptcy Court

Western District of Washington

Seattle Division Clerk of Court, 315 Park Place Bldg, 1200 6th Ave, Seattle, WA 98101, 206-553-7545, Fax: 206-553-0131.

www.wawb.uscourts.gov

Counties: Clallam, Island, Jefferson, King, Kitsap, San Juan, Skagit, Snohomish, Whatcom.

Indexing & Storage: Cases are indexed by debtor and creditors as well as by case number. New cases are available in the index 1 day after filing date. Both computer and card indexes are maintained. Open cases are stored by case number. Closed cases are stored by year closed and then by case number. Open records are located at this court.

Fee & Payment: The fee is $15.00 per item (one party name or case number). Payment may be made by money order, cashier check, personal check. Prepayment is required. Payee: Clerk, US Bankruptcy Court. Certification fee: $5.00 per document. Copy fee: $.50 per page. You are allowed to make your own copies. These copies

cost $.15 per page. An outside copy service is available at $.35 per page.

Phone Search: An automated voice case information service (VCIS) is available. Call VCIS at 888-436-7477 or 206-553-8543.

Fax Search: Will accept fax search request if no copies requested.

Mail Search: Always enclose a stamped self addressed envelope.

In Person Search: In person searching is available.

PACER: Sign-up number is 800-676-6856. Access fee is $.60 per minute. Toll-free access: 800-704-4492. Local access: 206-553-0060, 206-553-0061, 206-553-0062, 206-553-0063, 206-553-0064, 206-553-6127. Case records are available back to June 1995. Records are never purged. New civil records are available online after 2 days. PACER is available on the Internet at http://pacer.wawb.uscourts.gov.

Tacoma Division Suite 2100, 1717 Pacific Ave, Tacoma, WA 98402-3233, 253-593-6310.

www.wawb.uscourts.gov

Counties: Clark, Cowlitz, Grays Harbor, Lewis, Mason, Pacific, Pierce, Skamania, Thurston, Wahkiakum.

Indexing & Storage: Cases are indexed by debtor as well as by case number. New cases are available in the index 1 day after filing date. Records can be searched by debtor's name from 1987 to the present. A computer index is maintained. Open records are located at this court.

Fee & Payment: The fee is $15.00 per item (one party name or case number). Payment may be made by money order, cashier check. Business checks are not accepted. Personal checks are not accepted. Prepayment is required. Attorney checks are accepted. Payee: Clerk, US Bankruptcy Court. Certification fee: $5.00 per document. Copy fee: $.50 per page. You are allowed to make your own copies. These copies cost $.15 per page. An outside copy service is available for $.10 per page.

Phone Search: An automated voice case information service (VCIS) is available. Call VCIS at 888-436-7477 or 206-553-8543.

Mail Search: A stamped self addressed envelope is not required.

In Person Search: In person searching is available.

PACER: Sign-up number is 800-676-6856. Access fee is $.60 per minute. Toll-free access: 800-704-4492. Local access: 206-553-0060, 206-553-0061, 206-553-0062, 206-553-0063, 206-553-0064, 206-553-6127. Case records are available back to June 1995. Records are never purged. New civil records are available online after 2 days. PACER is available on the Internet at http://pacer.wawb.uscourts.gov.

Court	Jurisdiction	No. of Courts	How Organized
Superior Courts*	General	39	29 Districts
District Courts*	Limited	65	39 Counties
Municipal Courts	Municipal	131	131 Cities

* Profiled in this Sourcebook.

Court	CIVIL								
	Tort	Contract	Real Estate	Min. Claim	Max. Claim	Small Claims	Estate	Eviction	Domestic Relations
Superior Courts*	X	X	X	$50,000	No Max		X	X	X
District Courts*	X	X		$0	$50,000	$2500			
Municipal Courts									

Court	CRIMINAL				
	Felony	Misdemeanor	DWI/DUI	Preliminary Hearing	Juvenile
Superior Courts*	X				X
District Courts*		X	X	X	
Municipal Courts		X	X		

ADMINISTRATION
Court Administrator, Temple of Justice, PO Box 41174, Olympia, WA, 98504; 360-357-2121, Fax: 360-357-2127. www.courts.wa.gov

COURT STRUCTURE
District Courts retain civil records for 10 years from date of final disposition, then the records are destroyed. District Courts retain criminal records forever.

Washington has a mandatory arbitration requirement for civil disputes for $35,000 or less. However, either party may request a trial in Superior Court if dissatisfied with the arbitrator's decision.

The limit for civil actions in District Court has been increased from $25,000 to $35,000.

ONLINE ACCESS
Appellate, Superior, and District Court records are available online. The Superior Court Management Information System (SCOMIS), the Appellate Records System (ACORDS) and the District/Municipal Court Information System (DISCIS) are on the Judicial Information System's JIS-Link. Case records available through JIS-Link from 1977 include criminal, civil, domestic, probate, and judgments. JIS-Link is generally available 24-hours daily. Equipment requirements are a PC running Windows or MS-DOS. There is a one-time installation fee of $100.00 per site, and a connect time charge of $25.00 per hour (approximately $.42 per minute). For additional information and/or a registration packet, contact: JISLink Coordinator, Office of the Administrator for the Courts, 1206 S Quince St., PO Box 41170, Olympia WA 98504-1170, 360-357-2407 or visit the web site at www.courts.wa.gov/jislink/

ADDITIONAL INFORMATION
SASE is required in every jurisdiction that responds to written search requests.

📖 📖 📖 📖 📖 📖 📖

Adams County

Superior Court 210 W Broadway (PO Box 187), Ritzville, WA 99169-0187; 509-659-3257; Fax: 509-659-0118. Hours: 8:30AM-Noon, 1-4:30PM (PST). *Felony, Civil, Eviction, Probate.*

Civil Records: Access: Phone, fax, mail, online, in person. Only the court conducts in person searches; visitors may not. Search fee: $20.00 per hour. Required to search: name, years to search; also helpful-address. Civil cases indexed by defendant, plaintiff. Civil records on computer from 1985, archived from 1900s. Index available remotely online (see state introduction). **Criminal Records:** Access: Phone, fax, mail, remote online, in person. Only the court conducts in person searches; visitors may not. Search fee: $20.00 per hour. Required to search: name, years to search;

also helpful-address, DOB, SSN. Criminal records on computer from 1985, archived from 1900s. Index available remotely online (see state introduction). **General Information:** No sealed, juvenile, adoption, paternity, mental health, sex offenders (victims) records released. SASE required. Turnaround time 1 week. Copy fee: $.50 per page. Certification fee: $2.00 plus $1.00 each additional page. Fee payee: Adams County Clerk. Business checks accepted. Prepayment is required. Fax notes: $1.00 per page.

Othello District Court 165 N 1st, Othello, WA 99344; 509-488-3935; Fax: 509-488-3480. Hours: 8:30AM-4:30PM (PST). *Misdemeanor, Civil Actions Under $50,000, Small Claims.*

Civil Records: Access: Phone, fax, mail, online, in person. Only the court conducts in person searches; visitors may not. No search fee.

Required to search: name, years to search; also helpful-address. Civil cases indexed by defendant, plaintiff. Civil records on computer from 1992, on index cards. Index available remotely online (see state introduction). **Criminal Records:** Access: Phone, fax, mail, remote online, in person. Only the court conducts in person searches; visitors may not. No search fee. Required to search: name, years to search; also helpful-address, DOB, SSN. Criminal records on computer from 1992, on index cards. Index available remotely online (see state introduction). **General Information:** No sealed, juvenile, adoption, paternity, mental health, sex offenders (victims) or (sometimes) DUI records released. SASE required. Turnaround time 1-3 days. Copy fee: $2.50 for first page, $1.00 each addl. Certification fee: $2.50 plus $1.00 per page after first. Fee payee: Othello District Court.

Personal checks accepted. Prepayment is required. Fax notes: No fee to fax results.

Ritzville District Court 210 W Broadway, Ritzville, WA 99169; 509-659-1002; Fax: 509-659-0118. Hours: 8:30AM-4:30PM (PST). *Misdemeanor, Civil Actions Under $50,000, Small Claims.*

Civil Records: Access: Fax, mail, online, in person. Only the court conducts in person searches; visitors may not. No search fee. Required to search: name, years to search; also helpful-address. Civil cases indexed by defendant, plaintiff. Civil records on computer from 10/90. Index available remotely online (see state introduction). **Criminal Records:** Access: Fax, mail, remote online, in person. Only the court conducts in person searches; visitors may not. No search fee. Required to search: name, years to search, DOB; also helpful-address, SSN. Criminal records on computer from 10/90. Index available remotely online (see state introduction). **General Information:** No sealed, juvenile, adoption, paternity, mental health, sex offenders (victims) or (sometimes) DUI records released. SASE required. Turnaround time 2 days. Copy fee: $1.00 per page. Certification fee: $5.00. Fee payee: Ritzville District Court. Personal checks accepted. Prepayment is required. Fax notes: No fee to fax results.

Asotin County

Superior Court PO Box 159, Asotin, WA 99402-0159; 509-243-2081; Fax: 509-243-4978. Hours: 9AM-5PM (PST). *Felony, Civil, Eviction, Probate.*

Civil Records: Access: Phone, fax, mail, online, in person. Only the court conducts in person searches; visitors may not. No search fee. Required to search: name, years to search; also helpful-address. Civil cases indexed by defendant, plaintiff. Civil records on computer from mid 1985, on microfiche from 1970s, archived from 1895. Index available remotely online (see state introduction). **Criminal Records:** Access: Phone, fax, mail, remote online, in person. Only the court conducts in person searches; visitors may not. No search fee. Required to search: name, years to search; also helpful-address, DOB, SSN. Criminal records on computer from mid 1985, on microfiche from 1970s, archived from 1895. Index available remotely online (see state introduction). **General Information:** No sealed, juvenile, adoption, paternity, mental health, sex offenders (victims) or (sometimes) DUI records released. SASE required. Turnaround time 1 day. Copy fee: $2.00 for first page, $1.00 each addl. Certification fee: Cert fee included in copy fee. Fee payee: Asotin County Clerk. Personal checks accepted. Prepayment is required.

District Court PO Box 429, Asotin, WA 99402-0429; 509-243-2027; Fax: 509-243-2091. Hours: 8AM-5PM (PST). *Misdemeanor, Civil Actions Under $50,000, Small Claims.*

Civil Records: Access: Fax, mail, online, in person. Only the court conducts in person searches; visitors may not. Search fee: $5.00 per name. Required to search: name, years to search; also helpful-address. Civil cases indexed by defendant, plaintiff. Civil records on computer since 1993; prior records on log books. Index available remotely online (see state introduction). **Criminal Records:** Access: Fax, mail, remote online, in person. Only the court conducts in person searches; visitors may not. Search fee: $5.00 per name. Required to search: name, years

to search; also helpful-address, DOB, SSN. Criminal records on computer from 1989. Index available remotely online (see state introduction). **General Information:** No sealed, juvenile, adoption, paternity, mental health, sex offenders (victims) or (sometimes) DUI records released. SASE required. Turnaround time up to 2 weeks. Copy fee: $.25 per page. Certification fee: $6.00. Fee payee: Asotin County District Court. Personal checks accepted. Prepayment is required. Fax notes: No fee to fax results.

Benton County

Superior Court 7320 W Quinault, Kennewick, WA 99336-7690; 509-735-8388. Hours: 8AM-4PM (PST). *Felony, Civil, Eviction, Probate.*

Civil Records: Access: Fax, mail, in person. Only the court conducts in person searches; visitors may not. Search fee: $20.00 per hour. Required to search: name, years to search; also helpful-address. Civil cases indexed by defendant, plaintiff. Civil records on computer from 1979, pre-1979 on index books. Index available remotely online (see state introduction). **Criminal Records:** Access: Fax, mail, in person. Only the court conducts in person searches; visitors may not. Search fee: $20.00 per hour. Required to search: name, years to search; also helpful-address, DOB, SSN. Criminal records on computer from 1979, pre-1979 on index books. Index available remotely online (see state introduction). **General Information:** No sealed, juvenile, adoption, paternity, mental health, sex offenders (victims). SASE required. Turnaround time 2 days. Copy fee: $.25 per page. Certification fee: $2.00 plus $1.00 per page after first. Fee payee: Benton County Clerk. Personal checks accepted. Prepayment is required. Fax notes: $3.00 for first page, $1.00 each addl.

District Court 7320 W Quinault, Kennewick, WA 99336; 509-735-8476; Fax: 509-736-3069. Hours: 7:30AM-Noon, 1-4:30PM (PST). *Misdemeanor, Civil Actions Under $50,000, Small Claims.*

Civil Records: Access: Mail, online, in person. Both court and visitors may perform in person searches. Search fee: $10.00 per name. Required to search: name, years to search; also helpful-address. Civil cases indexed by defendant, plaintiff. Civil records on computer from 7/91. Index available remotely online (see state introduction). **Criminal Records:** Access: Mail, remote online, in person. Both court and visitors may perform in person searches. Search fee: $10.00 per name. Required to search: name, years to search, DOB; also helpful-address, SSN. Criminal records on computer from 7/91. Index available remotely online (see state introduction). **General Information:** No sealed, juvenile, adoption, paternity, mental health, sex offenders (victims) or (sometimes) DUI records released. SASE requested. Turnaround time 10 days. Copy fee: First 50 copies free, then $.05 each. Certification fee: $5.00. Fee payee: Benton County District Court. Personal checks accepted. Credit cards accepted: Visa, Mastercard. Prepayment is required. Public access terminal is available.

Chelan County

Superior Court 350 Orondo (PO Box 3025), Wenatchee, WA 98807-3025; 509-664-5380; Fax: 509-664-2611. Hours: 9AM-5PM (PST). *Felony, Civil, Eviction, Probate.*

Civil Records: Access: Phone, fax, mail, online, in person. Both court and visitors may perform in person searches. Search fee: $20.00 per hour. Required to search: name, years to search. Civil

cases indexed by defendant, plaintiff. Civil records on computer since 1984; prior on microfilm 1900-1984. Index available remotely online (see state introduction). **Criminal Records:** Access: Phone, fax, mail, remote online, in person. Both court and visitors may perform in person searches. Search fee: $20.00 per hour. Required to search: name, years to search; also helpful-address, DOB, SSN. Criminal records on computer since 1984; prior on microfilm 1900-1984. Index available remotely online (see state introduction). **General Information:** No sealed, juvenile, adoption, paternity, mental health, sex offenders (victims) records released. SASE required. Turnaround time 1 day. Copy fee: $2.00 for first page, $1.00 each addl. Certification fee: The certification fee is included in the copy fee. Fee payee: Chelan County Clerk. Personal checks accepted. Prepayment is required. Public access terminal is available. Fax notes: $3.00 for first page, $1.00 each addl.

Chelan County District Court PO Box 2182, Courthouse 4th Fl, Wenatchee, WA 98807; 509-664-5393; Fax: 509-664-5456. Hours: 8:30AM-4:30PM (PST). *Misdemeanor, Civil Actions Under $50,000, Small Claims.*

Civil Records: Access: Fax, mail, online, in person. Both court and visitors may perform in person searches. Search fee: $15.00 per name. Required to search: name; also helpful-years to search, address. Civil cases indexed by defendant, plaintiff. Civil records on computer from 1984. Records destroyed 10 years after date of last action. Index available remotely online (see state introduction). **Criminal Records:** Access: Fax, mail, remote online, in person. Both court and visitors may perform in person searches. Search fee: $15.00 per name. Required to search: name, DOB, signed release; also helpful-years to search, address, SSN, aliases. Criminal records on computer. Criminal files may be destroyed 5 years after close of case, infractions destroyed 3 years after close. Index available remotely online (see state introduction). **General Information:** No sealed, domestic violence victim info, alcohol/probation evaluation records released. SASE required. Turnaround time 1 week. Copy fee: $2.00 for first page, $1.00 each addl. Certification fee: $5.00. Fee payee: Chelan County District Court. Personal checks accepted. Prepayment is required. Public access terminal is available. Public Access Terminal Note: for cases since 1986 only.

Clallam County

Superior Court 223 E Fourth St, PO Box 863, Port Angeles, WA 98362-3098; 360-417-2333; Fax: 360-417-2495. Hours: 8AM-5PM (PST). *Felony, Civil, Eviction, Probate.*

www.wa.gov/clallam

Civil Records: Access: Phone, mail, in person. Both court and visitors may perform in person searches. Search fee: $20.00 per hour. Required to search: name, years to search; also helpful-address. Civil cases indexed by defendant, plaintiff. Civil records on computer from 10/83, on microfiche from 1914, some records on index cards. **Criminal Records:** Access: Phone, mail, remote online, in person. Both court and visitors may perform in person searches. Search fee: $20.00 per hour. Required to search: name, years to search; also helpful-address, DOB, SSN. Criminal records on computer from 10/83, on microfiche from 1914, some records on index cards. Index available remotely online (see state introduction). **General Information:** No sealed, juvenile, adoption, paternity, mental health, sex offenders (victims) records released. SASE required. Turnaround time 1 week plus. Copy fee: $.10 per page. Certification fee: $2.00 plus $1.00 per page after first. Fee payee: Clerk. Business checks accepted. Prepayment is required. Public access terminal is available.

District Court One
223 E 4th St, Port Angeles, WA 98362; 360-417-2285; Fax: 360-417-2470. Hours: 8AM-5PM. *Misdemeanor, Civil Actions Under $50,000, Small Claims.*

www.wa.gov/clallam/dcourt/index.html

Civil Records: Access: Mail, online, in person. Only the court conducts in person searches; visitors may not. No search fee. Required to search: name, years to search; also helpful-address. Civil cases indexed by defendant, plaintiff. Civil records on computer from 1986, on index cards from 1982-1986. Index available remotely online (see state introduction). **Criminal Records:** Access: Mail, remote online, in person. Only the court conducts in person searches; visitors may not. No search fee. Required to search: name, years to search, DOB; also helpful-address, SSN. Criminal records on computer from 1986, on index cards from 1982-1986. Index available remotely online (see state introduction). **General Information:** No sealed, juvenile, adoption, paternity, mental health, sex offenders (victims) or (sometimes) DUI records released. Turnaround time up to 1 week. Copy fee: $.10 per page. Certification fee: $5.00. Fee is per page. Fee payee: Clallam County Clerk, District Court One. Personal checks accepted. Prepayment is required.

District Court Two
PO Box 1937, Forks, WA 98331; 360-374-6383; Fax: 360-374-2100. Hours: 8AM-5PM (PST). *Misdemeanor, Civil Actions Under $50,000, Small Claims.*

Civil Records: Access: Mail, online, in person. Both court and visitors may perform in person searches. No search fee. Required to search: name, years to search; also helpful-address. Civil cases indexed by defendant, plaintiff. Civil records on computer from 1986, on index cards from 1982-1986. Index available remotely online (see state introduction). **Criminal Records:** Access: Mail, remote online, in person. Only the court conducts in person searches; visitors may not. No search fee. Required to search: name, years to search; also helpful-address, DOB, SSN. Criminal records on computer from 1986, on index cards from 1982-1986. Index available remotely online (see state introduction). **General Information:** No sealed, juvenile, adoption, paternity, mental health, sex offenders (victims) or (sometimes) DUI records released. Turnaround time 1 week. Copy fee: $.15 per page. Certification: $5.00. Fee payee: Clallam County District CourtII. Personal checks accepted.

Clark County

Superior Court 1200 Franklin St, PO Box 5000, Vancouver, WA 98668;; Civil phone:360-397-2292; Criminal phone:360-397-2292. Hours: 8:30AM-4:30PM (PST). *Felony, Civil, Eviction, Probate.*

Civil Records: Access: Phone, mail, online, in person. Both court and visitors may perform in person searches. Search fee: $20.00 per hour. Required to search: name, years to search; also helpful-address. Civil cases indexed by defendant, plaintiff. Civil records on computer from 1979 indexed, on microfiche from 1960, and index books prior to 1979. Index available remotely online (see state introduction). **Criminal Records:** Access: Phone, mail, remote online, in person.

Both court and visitors may perform in person searches. Search fee: $20.00 per hour. Required to search: name, years to search; also helpful-address, DOB, SSN. Criminal records on computer since 1988, prior to 1988 on microfilm. Index available remotely online (see state introduction). **General Information:** No sealed, juvenile, adoption, paternity, mental health, sex offenders (victims). Turnaround time 1-3 days. Copy fee: $2.00 for first page, $1.00 each addl. Certification fee: $2.00. Fee payee: County Clerk. Business checks accepted. Prepayment is required. Public access terminal is available.

District Court
PO Box 9806, Vancouver, WA 98666-5000;; Civil phone:360-397-2411; Criminal phone:360-397-2411; Fax: 360-737-6044. Hours: 8:30AM-4:30PM (PST). *Misdemeanor, Civil Actions Under $50,000, Small Claims.*

Civil Records: Access: Phone, fax, mail, online, in person. Only the court conducts in person searches; visitors may not. No search fee. Required to search: name, years to search; also helpful-address. Civil cases indexed by defendant, plaintiff. Civil records on computer for approximately ten years. Index available remotely online (see state introduction). **Criminal Records:** Access: Phone, fax, mail, remote online, in person. Only the court conducts in person searches; visitors may not. No search fee. Required to search: name, DOB; also helpful-years to search, address, SSN. Criminal records on computer for approximately ten years. Index available remotely online (see state introduction). **General Information:** No sealed, juvenile, adoption, paternity, mental health, sex offenders (victims) or (sometimes) DUI records released. Turnaround time 1 week. Copy fee: $.15 per page. Certification fee: $5.00. Fee payee: Clark County District Court. Personal checks accepted. Prepayment is required. Fax notes: No fee to fax results.

Columbia County

Superior Court 341 E Main St, Dayton, WA 99328; 509-382-4321; Fax: 509-382-4830. Hours: 8:30AM-Noon, 1-4:30PM (PST). *Felony, Civil, Eviction, Probate.*

Civil Records: Access: Phone, fax, mail, online, in person. Only the court conducts in person searches; visitors may not. Search fee: $20.00 per hour. Required to search: name, years to search. Civil cases indexed by defendant, plaintiff. Civil records on computer from 1987, some records on index cards and books, archived from 1900s. Index available remotely online (see state introduction). **Criminal Records:** Access: Phone, fax, mail, remote online, in person. Only the court conducts in person searches; visitors may not. Search fee: $20.00 per hour. Required to search: name, years to search. Criminal records on computer from 1987, some records on index cards and books, archived from 1900s. Index available remotely online (see state introduction). **General Information:** No sealed, juvenile, adoption, paternity, mental health, sex offenders (victims). SASE required. Turnaround time 1 week. Copy fee: $1.00 per page. Certification fee: $2.00 plus $1.00 per page after first. Fee payee: Columbia County Clerk. Personal checks accepted. Prepayment is required.

District Court
341 E Main St, Dayton, WA 99328-1361; 509-382-4812; Fax: 509-382-4830. Hours: 8:30AM-4:30PM (PST). *Misdemeanor, Civil Actions Under $50,000, Small Claims.*

Civil Records: Access: Mail, online, in person. Both court and visitors may perform in person searches. No search fee. Required to search: name, years to search; also helpful-address. Civil cases indexed by plaintiff. Civil records on computer since 05/96; prior on index books. Index available remotely online (see state introduction). **Criminal Records:** Access: Mail, remote online, in person. Both court and visitors may perform in person searches. Search fee: No search fee. Fee for more than 1 case. Required to search: name, years to search, DOB, signed release; also helpful-address, SSN. Criminal records on computer from 1993, on books prior. Index available remotely online (see state introduction). **General Information:** No sealed, juvenile, adoption, paternity, mental health, sex offenders (victims) or (sometimes) DUI records released. SASE required. Turnaround time 7-10 days. Copy fee: $1.00 per page. Certification fee: $5.00 per page. Fee payee: District Court. Personal checks accepted. Prepayment is required.

Cowlitz County

Superior Court 312 SW First Ave, Kelso, WA 98626-1724; 360-577-3016; Fax: 360-577-2323. Hours: 8:30-11:30AM, 12:30-4:30PM (PST). *Felony, Civil, Eviction, Probate.*

www.cowlitzcounty.org/clerk

Civil Records: Access: Phone, fax, mail, online, in person. Both court and visitors may perform in person searches. Search fee: $10.00 per name. Required to search: name, years to search; also helpful-address. Civil cases indexed by defendant, plaintiff. Civil records on computer from 1981, on microfilm through 1985, hard copy files from 1987 to present. Index available remotely online (see state introduction). **Criminal Records:** Access: Phone, fax, mail, remote online, in person. Both court and visitors may perform in person searches. Search fee: $10.00 per name. Required to search: name, years to search; also helpful-address, DOB, SSN. Criminal records on computer from 1981, on microfilm through 1985, hard copy files from 1987 to present. Index available remotely online (see state introduction). **General Information:** No sealed, juvenile, adoption, paternity, mental health records released. SASE required. Turnaround time 2 days. Copy fee: $2.00 for first page, $1.00 each addl. Certification fee: Included in copy fee. Fee payee: Cowlitz County Superior Court Clerk. Business checks accepted. Prepayment is required. Public access terminal is available.

District Court
312 SW First Ave, Kelso, WA 98626-1724; 360-577-3073. Hours: 8:30AM-5PM (PST). *Misdemeanor, Civil Actions Under $50,000, Small Claims.*

Civil Records: Access: Mail, online, in person. Only the court conducts in person searches; visitors may not. No search fee. Required to search: name, years to search; also helpful-address. Civil cases indexed by defendant, plaintiff. Civil records on index cards from 1985. Index available remotely online (see state introduction). **Criminal Records:** Access: Mail, remote online, in person. Only the court conducts in person searches; visitors may not. No search fee. Required to search: name, years to search; also helpful-address, DOB, SSN. Criminal records on index cards from 1985. Index available remotely online (see state introduction). **General Information:** No sealed, adoption, paternity, mental health records released. Turnaround time 2 weeks. Copy fee: $.25 per page. Certification fee: $5.00. Fee payee: District Court. No personal checks accepted. Prepayment is required.

Douglas County

Superior Court PO Box 488, Waterville, WA 98858-0516; 509-745-9063; Fax: 509-745-8027. Hours: 8AM-5PM (PST). *Felony, Civil, Eviction, Probate.*

Note: Clerk is reached at 509-745-8529

Civil Records: Access: Phone, fax, mail, online, in person. Only the court conducts in person searches; visitors may not. Search fee: $20.00 per hour. Required to search: name, years to search; also helpful-address. Civil cases indexed by defendant, plaintiff. Civil records on computer from 1985, archived and on microfiche from 1883, some records on index books. Index available remotely online (see state introduction). **Criminal Records:** Access: Phone, fax, mail, remote online, in person. Only the court conducts in person searches; visitors may not. Search fee: $20.00 per hour. Required to search: name, years to search, DOB; also helpful-address, SSN. Criminal records on computer from 1985, archived and on microfiche from 1883, some records on index books. Index available remotely online (see state introduction). **General Information:** No sealed, juvenile, adoption, paternity, mental health, sex offenders (victims). SASE required. Turnaround time 1 week. Copy fee: $2.00 for first page, $1.00 each addl. Certification fee: $2.00 plus $1.00 per page after first. Fee payee: Douglas County Clerk. Business checks accepted. Prepayment is required. Fax notes: $2.00 for first page, $1.00 each addl.

District Court-Bridgeport 1206 Columbia Ave (PO Box 730), Bridgeport, WA 98813-0730; 509-686-2034; Fax: 509-686-4671. Hours: 8:30AM-4:30PM (PST). *Misdemeanor, Civil Actions Under $50,000, Small Claims.*

Note: If record not found in this court, request forwarded to East Wenatchee (South) court

Civil Records: Access: Fax, mail, online, in person. Only the court conducts in person searches; visitors may not. Search fee: $10.00 per name. Required to search: name, years to search; also helpful-address. Civil cases indexed by defendant. Civil records on computer from 02/95 to present, destroyed after 10 years. Index available remotely online (see state introduction). **Criminal Records:** Access: Fax, mail, remote online, in person. Only the court conducts in person searches; visitors may not. Search fee: $10.00 per name. Required to search: name, years to search; also helpful-address, DOB, SSN. Criminal records on computer since 02/95. Index available remotely online (see state introduction). **General Information:** No sealed, juvenile, adoption, paternity, mental health, sex offenders (victims) or (sometimes) DUI records released. SASE required. Turnaround time 10 days. Copy fee: $1.00 per page. Certification fee: $5.00 per page. Fee payee: Douglas County District Court Bridgeport. Personal checks accepted. Prepayment is required.

District Court-East Wenatchee 110 3rd St NE, East Wenatchee, WA 98802; 509-884-3536; Fax: 509-884-5973. Hours: 8:30AM-4:30PM (PST). *Misdemeanor, Civil Actions Under $50,000, Small Claims.*

Note: If record not found in this court, request forwarded to Bridgeport Branch (North) County District Court

Civil Records: Access: Fax, mail, online, in person. Only the court conducts in person searches; visitors may not. Search fee: $15.00 per hour. Required to search: name, years to search; also helpful-address. Civil cases indexed by defendant, plaintiff. Civil records on index cards from 1982. Index available remotely online (see state introduction). **Criminal Records:** Access: Fax, mail, remote online, in person. Only the court conducts in person searches; visitors may not. Search fee: $15.00 per hour. Required to search: name, years to search; also helpful-address, DOB, SSN. Criminal records on computer back 5 years. Index available remotely online (see state introduction). **General Information:** No sealed, juvenile, adoption, paternity, mental health, sex offenders (victims) or (sometimes) DUI records released. SASE required. Turnaround time 1 week. Copy fee: $1.00 per page. Certification fee: $5.00. Fee payee: Douglas District Court. Personal checks accepted. Prepayment is required. Fax notes: $3.00 for first page, $1.00 each addl. Local faxing only.

Ferry County

Superior Court 350 E Delaware #4, Republic, WA 99166; 509-775-5245. Hours: 8AM-4PM (PST). *Felony, Civil, Probate.*

Civil Records: Access: Phone, mail, online, in person. Both court and visitors may perform in person searches. Search fee: $20.00 per hour. Required to search: name, years to search; also helpful-address. Civil cases indexed by defendant, plaintiff. Civil records on computer since 1987. Index available remotely online (see state introduction). **Criminal Records:** Access: Phone, mail, remote online, in person. Both court and visitors may perform in person searches. Search fee: $20.00 per hour. Required to search: name, years to search; also helpful-address, DOB. Criminal records on computer since 1987. Index available remotely online (see state introduction). **General Information:** No sealed, juvenile, adoption, paternity, mental health or sex offenders (victims). SASE required. Turnaround time 1-4 days. Copy fee: $2.00 for first page, $1.00 each addl. Certification fee: $2.00 plus $1.00 each additional page. Fee payee: Ferry County Clerk. Business checks accepted. Prepayment is required. Public access terminal is available.

District Court 350 E Delaware Ave #6, Republic, WA 99166-9747; 509-775-5244; Fax: 509-775-5221. Hours: 8AM-4PM (PST). *Misdemeanor, Civil Actions Under $50,000, Small Claims.*

Civil Records: Access: Fax, mail, online, in person. Only the court conducts in person searches; visitors may not. No search fee. Required to search: name, years to search; also helpful-address. Civil cases indexed by case number. Civil records on computer since 1995. Index available remotely online (see state introduction). **Criminal Records:** Access: Mail, remote online, in person. Only the court conducts in person searches; visitors may not. No search fee. Required to search: name, years to search, DOB; also helpful-address, SSN. Criminal records on computer since 1995. Index available remotely online (see state introduction). **General Information:** No sealed, juvenile, adoption, paternity, mental health, sex offenders (victims) or (sometimes) DUI records released. SASE required. Turnaround time 1 week. Copy fee: $2.00 for first page, $1.00 each addl. Certification fee: $5.00. Fee payee: Ferry County District Court. Personal checks accepted. Credit cards accepted. Prepayment is required. Fax notes: No fee to fax results.

Franklin County

Superior Court 1016 N 4th St, Pasco, WA 99301; 509-545-3525. Hours: 8:30AM-5PM (PST). *Felony, Civil, Eviction, Probate.*

Civil Records: Access: Mail, online, in person. Only the court conducts in person searches; visitors may not. Search fee: $20.00 per hour. Required to search: name, years to search; also helpful-address. Civil cases indexed by defendant, plaintiff. Civil records on computer from 7/83, on index books, archived from 1900s. Index available remotely online (see state introduction). **Criminal Records:** Access: Mail, remote online, in person. Only the court conducts in person searches; visitors may not. Search fee: $20.00 per hour. Required to search: name, years to search; also helpful-address, DOB, SSN. Criminal records on computer from 7/83, on index books, archived from 1900s. Index available remotely online (see state introduction). **General Information:** No sealed, juvenile, adoption, paternity, mental health, sex offenders (victims). SASE required. Turnaround time 1 week. Copy fee: $2.00 for first page, $1.00 each addl. Certification fee: $2.00 plus $1.00 per page after first. Fee payee: Franklin County Superior Court Clerk. Business checks accepted. Prepayment is required.

District Court 1016 N 4th St, Pasco, WA 99301; 509-545-3593; Fax: 509-545-3588. Hours: 8:30AM-Noon, 1-5PM (PST). *Misdemeanor, Civil Actions Under $50,000, Small Claims.*

Civil Records: Access: Mail, online, in person. Only the court conducts in person searches; visitors may not. Search fee: $10.00 per name. Required to search: name, years to search; also helpful-address. Civil cases indexed by defendant, plaintiff. Civil records on computer from 1993, prior on index cards. Index available remotely online (see state introduction). **Criminal Records:** Access: Mail, remote online, in person. Only the court conducts in person searches; visitors may not. Search fee: $10.00 per name. Required to search: name, years to search, DOB; also helpful-address, SSN. Criminal records on computer from 1987, prior on index cards. Index available remotely online (see state introduction). **General Information:** No sealed, juvenile, adoption, paternity, mental health, sex offenders (victims) or (sometimes) DUI records released. SASE required. Turnaround time 2-3 days. Copy fee: $.25 per page. Certification fee: $5.00. Fee payee: Franklin District Court. Personal checks accepted. Prepayment is required. Public access terminal is available.

Garfield County

Superior Court PO Box 915, Pomeroy, WA 99347-0915; 509-843-3731; Fax: 509-843-1224. Hours: 8:30AM-Noon, 1-5PM (PST). *Felony, Civil, Eviction, Probate.*

www.co.garfield.wa.us

Civil Records: Access: Phone, fax, mail, online, in person. Both court and visitors may perform in person searches. Search fee: $8.00 per hour. Required to search: name, years to search; also helpful-address. Civil cases indexed by defendant, plaintiff. Civil records on docket books, archived from 1882. Index available remotely online (see state introduction). **Criminal Records:** Access: Phone, fax, mail, remote online, in person. Both court and visitors may perform in person searches. Search fee: $8.00 per hour. Required to search: name, years to search; also helpful-address, DOB, SSN. Criminal records on docket books, archived from 1882. Index available remotely online (see state introduction). **General Information:** No sealed, juvenile, adoption, paternity, mental health, sex offenders (victims). SASE requested. Turnaround time 1 week. Copy fee: $1.00 per page. Certification fee: $2.00 plus $1.00 per page after first. Fee payee: Garfield County Clerk. Personal checks accepted. Prepayment is required. Fax notes: $.50 per page.

District Court PO Box 817, Pomeroy, WA 99347-0817; 509-843-1002. Hours: 8:30AM-5PM (PST). *Misdemeanor, Civil Actions Under $50,000, Small Claims.*

Civil Records: Access: Mail, online, in person. Only the court conducts in person searches; visitors may not. Search fee: $3.00 per name. Required to search: name, years to search; also helpful-address. Civil cases indexed by defendant. Civil records on index cards. Index available remotely online (see state introduction). **Criminal Records:** Access: Mail, remote online, in person. Only the court conducts in person searches; visitors may not. Search fee: $3.00 per name. Required to search: name, years to search, DOB; also helpful-address, SSN. Criminal records on index cards. Index available remotely online (see state introduction). **General Information:** No sealed, juvenile, adoption, mental health, sex offenders (victims) or (sometimes) DUI records released. Turnaround time 1 week. Copy fee: $1.00 for first page, $.50 each addl. Certification fee: $5.00. Fee payee: Garfield County District Court. Personal checks accepted. Prepayment is required.

Grant County

Superior Court PO Box 37, Ephrata, WA 98823-0037; 509-754-2011 X448; Fax: 509-754-5638. Hours: 8AM-5PM (PST). *Felony, Civil, Eviction, Probate.*

Civil Records: Access: Phone, mail, online, in person. Both court and visitors may perform in person searches. Search fee: $10.00 per name. Required to search: name, years to search; also helpful-address. Civil cases indexed by defendant, plaintiff. Civil records on computer from 1982, and some on index cards, archived from 1909. Index available remotely online (see state introduction). **Criminal Records:** Access: Phone, mail, remote online, in person. Both court and visitors may perform in person searches. Search fee: $10.00 per name. Required to search: name, years to search; also helpful-address, DOB, SSN. Criminal records on computer from 1982, and some on index cards, archived from 1909. Index available remotely online (see state introduction). **General Information:** No sealed, juvenile, adoption, paternity, mental health, sex offenders (victims) records released. SASE required. Turnaround time 2 weeks. Copy fee: $2.00 for first page, $1.00 each addl. Certification fee: $2.00 plus $1.00 per page after first. Fee payee: Grant County Clerk's Office. Business checks accepted. Prepayment is required. Public access terminal is available.

District Court PO Box 37, Ephrata, WA 98823-0037; 509-754-2011 X318; Fax: 509-754-6099. Hours: 8AM-5PM (PST). *Misdemeanor, Civil Actions Under $50,000, Small Claims.*

Civil Records: Access: Mail, online, in person. Only the court conducts in person searches; visitors may not. Search fee: $20.00 per name. Required to search: name, years to search; also helpful-address. Civil cases indexed by defendant, plaintiff. Civil records on computer from 3/91, on index cards. Index available remotely online (see

state introduction). **Criminal Records:** Access: Mail, remote online, in person. Only the court conducts in person searches; visitors may not. Search fee: $20.00 per name. Required to search: name, years to search, DOB; also helpful-address, SSN. Criminal records on computer from 3/91, on index cards. Index available remotely online (see state introduction). **General Information:** No sealed, probation, juvenile, adoption, paternity, mental health, sex offenders (victims) or (sometimes) DUI records released. Turnaround time up to 30 days. Copy fee: $2.00 for first page, $1.00 each addl. Certification fee: $5.00 per page. Fee payee: Grant County District Court. Personal checks accepted. Prepayment is required.

Grays Harbor County

Superior Court 102 W Broadway, Rm 203, Montesano, WA 98563-3606; 360-249-3842; Fax: 360-249-6381. Hours: 8AM-5PM (PST). *Felony, Civil, Eviction, Probate.*

Civil Records: Access: Phone, fax, mail, online, in person. Both court and visitors may perform in person searches. Search fee: $20.00 per name. No fee for records before 1980. Required to search: name, years to search; also helpful-address. Civil cases indexed by defendant, plaintiff. Civil records on computer from 12/80, on microfiche from 1856, on index cards. Index available remotely online (see state introduction). **Criminal Records:** Access: Phone, fax, mail, remote online, in person. Both court and visitors may perform in person searches. Search fee: $20.00 per name. No fee for records before 1980. Required to search: name, years to search; also helpful-address, DOB, SSN. Criminal records on computer from 12/80, on microfiche from 1856, on index cards. Index available remotely online (see state introduction). **General Information:** No sealed, juvenile, adoption, paternity, mental health, sex offenders (victims). SASE required. Turnaround time 2 days. Copy fee: $2.00 for first page, $1.00 each addl. Certification fee: Included in copy fee. Fee payee: Grays Harbor County Clerk. Business checks accepted. Prepayment is required. Fax notes: No fee to fax results. Fax available in emergency only.

District Court No 1 102 W Broadway, Rm 202, PO Box 647, Montesano, WA 98563-0647; 360-249-3441; Fax: 360-249-6382. Hours: 8AM-Noon, 1-5PM (PST). *Misdemeanor, Civil Actions Under $50,000, Small Claims.*

www.co.gray-harbor.wa.us

Civil Records: Access: Phone, fax, mail, online, in person. Only the court conducts in person searches; visitors may not. No search fee. Required to search: name, years to search; also helpful-address. Civil cases indexed by defendant, plaintiff. Civil records on computer from 4/91, on index cards. Index available remotely online (see state introduction). **Criminal Records:** Access: Phone, fax, mail, remote online, in person. Only the court conducts in person searches; visitors may not. No search fee. Required to search: name, years to search, DOB; also helpful-address, SSN. Criminal records on computer from 4/91, on index cards. Index available remotely online (see state introduction). **General Information:** No sealed, juvenile, adoption, paternity, mental health, sex offenders (victims) records released. SASE required. Turnaround time 1 week. Copy fee: $.25 per page. Certification fee: $5.00. Fee payee: GRays Harbor District Court #1. Personal checks accepted. Prepayment is required.

District Court No 2 PO Box 142, Aberdeen, WA 98520-0035; 360-532-7061; Fax: 360-532-

7704. Hours: 8AM-Noon, 1-5PM (PST). *Misdemeanor, Civil Actions Under $50,000, Small Claims.*

www.co.grays-harbor.wa.us

Civil Records: Access: Phone, fax, mail, online, in person. Only the court conducts in person searches; visitors may not. No search fee. Required to search: name, years to search; also helpful-address. Civil cases indexed by defendant, plaintiff. Civil records on computer from 4/91, on index cards. Index available remotely online (see state introduction). **Criminal Records:** Access: Phone, fax, mail, remote online, in person. Only the court conducts in person searches; visitors may not. No search fee. Required to search: name, years to search, DOB; also helpful-address, SSN. Criminal records on computer from 4/91, on index cards. Index available remotely online (see state introduction). **General Information:** No sealed, juvenile, adoption, paternity, mental health, sex offenders (victims) or (sometimes) DUI records released. SASE required. Turnaround time 1 week. Copy fee: $.25 per page. Certification fee: $5.00. Fee payee: Grays Harbor District Court #2. Personal checks accepted. Prepayment is required. Fax notes: No fee to fax results.

Island County

Superior Court PO Box 5000, Coupeville, WA 98239-5000; 360-679-7359. Hours: 8AM-4:30PM (PST). *Felony, Civil, Eviction, Probate.*

Civil Records: Access: Phone, fax, mail, online, in person. Both court and visitors may perform in person searches. Search fee: $20.00 per hour. Required to search: name, years to search; also helpful-address. Civil cases indexed by defendant, plaintiff. Civil records on computer from 1984, microfiche from 1889. Archived in Bellingham, WA. Index available remotely online (see state introduction). **Criminal Records:** Access: Phone, mail, remote online, in person. Both court and visitors may perform in person searches. Search fee: $20.00 per hour. Required to search: name, years to search; also helpful-address, DOB, SSN. Criminal records on computer from 1984, microfiche from 1889. Archived in Bellingham, WA. Index available remotely online (see state introduction). **General Information:** No sealed, juvenile, adoption, paternity, mental health, sex offenders (victims). SASE required. Turnaround time 1 week. Copy fee: $.25 per page. Certification fee: $2.00 first page and $1.00 each add'l. Fee payee: Island Superior Court. Business checks accepted. Prepayment is required.

District Court 800 S 8th Ave, Oak Harbor, WA 98277; 360-675-5988; Fax: 360-675-8231. Hours: 8AM-4:30PM (PST). *Misdemeanor, Civil Actions Under $50,000, Small Claims.*

Note: Records requests are done as time permits. Bottom of priority list

Civil Records: Access: Fax, mail, online, in person. Both court and visitors may perform in person searches. No search fee. Required to search: name, years to search; also helpful-address. Civil cases indexed by defendant. Civil records on computer from 1991, on index by alpha. Index available remotely online (see state introduction). **Criminal Records:** Access: Fax, mail, remote online, in person. Only the court conducts in person searches; visitors may not. No search fee. Required to search: name, years to search, DOB; also helpful-address, SSN. Criminal records on computer from 1991, on index by alpha. Index available remotely online (see state introduction). **General Information:** No sealed, juvenile, adoption, paternity, mental health, sex offenders (victims) or (sometimes) DUI records released. SASE required. Turnaround time 1-7 days. Copy fee: $.25 per page. Certification fee: $5.00. Fee payee: Island District Court. Personal checks accepted. Prepayment is required. Fax notes: $1.00 per page.

Jefferson County

Superior Court PO Box 1220, Port Townsend, WA 98368-0920; 360-385-9125. Hours: 9AM-5PM (PST). *Felony, Civil, Eviction, Probate.*

Civil Records: Access: Phone, mail, online, in person. Both court and visitors may perform in person searches. Search fee: $8.00 per hour. Required to search: name, years to search. Civil cases indexed by defendant, plaintiff. Civil records on computer from 1983, on microfiche from 1890s. Archive in Bellingham, WA. Index available remotely online (see state introduction). **Criminal Records:** Access: Phone, mail, remote online, in person. Both court and visitors may perform in person searches. Search fee: $8.00 per hour. Required to search: name, years to search; also helpful-DOB. Criminal records on computer from 1983, on microfiche from 1890s. Archive in Bellingham, WA. Index available remotely online (see state introduction). **General Information:** No sealed, juvenile, adoption, paternity, mental health records released. SASE required. Turnaround time 2 days. Copy fee: $1.00 for first page, $.50 each addl. Certification fee: $2.00 plus $1.00 per page after first. Fee payee: County Clerk. Personal checks accepted. Out of state checks not accepted. Prepayment is required.

District Court PO Box 1220, Port Townsend, WA 98368-0920; 360-385-9135; Fax: 360-385-9367. Hours: 8AM-5PM (PST). *Misdemeanor, Civil Actions Under $50,000, Small Claims.*

www.co.jefferson.wa.us

Civil Records: Access: Phone, fax, mail, online, in person. Only the court conducts in person searches; visitors may not. No search fee. Required to search: name, years to search; also helpful-address. Civil cases indexed by defendant. Civil records on DISCIS computer from 1993, on computer from '90-'93, on log books prior to 1990. Physical files kept 10 years from disposition per retention schedule. Index available remotely online (see state introduction). **Criminal Records:** Access: Phone, fax, mail, remote online, in person. Only the court conducts in person searches; visitors may not. No search fee. Required to search: name, DOB; also helpful-years to search, address, SSN. Criminal records on DISCIS computer from 1993, on computer from '90-'93, on log books prior to 1990. Physical files kept 10 years from disposition per retention schedule. Index available remotely online (see state introduction). **General Information:** No sealed, juvenile, adoption, paternity, mental health, sex offenders (victims) records released. SASE required. Turnaround time 1 week. Copy fee: $.15 per page. Certification fee: $6.00. Personal checks accepted. Prepayment is required.

King County

Superior Court 516 Third Ave, E-609 Courthouse, Seattle, WA 98104-2386; 206-296-9300, 800-325-6165 in state. Hours: 8:30AM-4:30AM (PST). *Felony, Civil, Eviction, Probate.*

www.metrokc.gov/kcscc

Civil Records: Access: Mail, online, in person. Both court and visitors may perform in person searches. Search fee: $20.00 per hour. Fee $25.00 minimum including copies. Required to search: name, years to search; also helpful-address. Civil cases indexed by defendant, plaintiff. Civil records on computer since 1979; prior records on microfiche back to 1935. Index available remotely online (see state introduction). **Criminal Records:** Access: Mail, remote online, in person. Both court and visitors may perform in person searches. Search fee: $20.00 per hour. Fee is $25.00 if number of pages unknown. Required to search: name, years to search; also helpful-address, DOB, SSN. Criminal records on computer since 1979; prior records on microfiche back to 1938. Index available remotely online (see state introduction). **General Information:** No sealed, juvenile, adoption, paternity, mental health, sex offenders (victims). SASE required. Turnaround time 2 weeks. Copy fee: $.15 per page. Microfiche Copy Fee: $.25 per page. Certification fee: $2.00 plus $1.00 per page after first. Fee payee: King County Superior Court Clerk. Personal checks accepted. In state personal checks only. Prepayment is required. Public access terminal is available.

District Court (Aukeen Division) 1210 S Central, Kent, WA 98032-7426; 206-296-7740. Hours: 8:30AM-4:30PM (PST). *Misdemeanor, Civil Actions Under $50,000, Small Claims.*

www.metrookc.gov/kcdc

Civil Records: Access: Mail, online, in person. Only the court conducts in person searches; visitors may not. No search fee. Required to search: name, years to search; also helpful-address. Civil cases indexed by defendant, plaintiff. Civil records on computer 5 years back. Index available remotely online (see state introduction). **Criminal Records:** Access: Mail, remote online, in person. Only the court conducts in person searches; visitors may not. No search fee. Required to search: name, years to search, DOB; also helpful-address, SSN. Criminal records on computer 5 years back. Index available remotely online (see state introduction). **General Information:** No sealed, juvenile, adoption, paternity, mental health, sex offenders (victims) or (sometimes) DUI records released. SASE required. Turnaround time 1 day. Copy fee: $.15 per page. Certification fee: $5.00. Fee payee: Aukeen District Court. Personal checks accepted. Credit cards accepted: Visa, Mastercard. Prepayment is required.

District Court (Bellevue Div) 585 112th Ave SE, Bellevue, WA 98004; 206-296-3650; Fax: 206-296-0589. Hours: 8:30AM-4:30PM (PST). *Misdemeanor, Civil Actions Under $50,000, Small Claims.*

Civil Records: Access: Phone, mail, online, in person. Both court and visitors may perform in person searches. No search fee. Required to search: name, years to search; also helpful-address. Civil cases indexed by defendant, plaintiff. Civil records on computer for past 10 years. Index available remotely online (see state introduction). **Criminal Records:** Access: Phone, mail, remote online, in person. Both court and visitors may perform in person searches. No search fee. Required to search: name, years to search, DOB; also helpful-address, SSN. Criminal records on computer from 1987. Criminal records may be removed after 5 years from disposition. Index available remotely online (see state introduction). **General Information:** No sealed, juvenile, adoption, paternity, mental health, sex offenders (victims) or (sometimes) DUI records released. Turnaround time cannot be guaranteed for written requests. Copy fee: $.15 per page. Certification fee: $5.00. Fee payee: KCDC, Bellevue Division. Personal checks accepted. Credit cards accepted: Visa, Mastercard. Prepayment is required.

District Court (Federal Way Division) 33506 10th Pl South, Federal Way, WA 98003-6396; 206-296-7784; Fax: 206-296-0590. Hours: 8:30AM-4:30PM *Misdemeanor, Civil Actions Under $50,000, Small Claims.*

www.metrokc.gov/kcdc

Civil Records: Access: Phone, mail, online, in person. Only the court conducts in person searches; visitors may not. No search fee. Required to search: name, years to search; also helpful-address. Civil cases indexed by defendant, plaintiff. Civil records on computer back 10 years. Index available remotely online (see state introduction). **Criminal Records:** Access: Phone, mail, remote online, in person. Only the court conducts in person searches; visitors may not. No search fee. Required to search: name, years to search, DOB, signed release; also helpful-address. Criminal records on computer back 5 years. Index available remotely online (see state introduction). **General Information:** No sealed, adoption, paternity, mental health, sex offenders (victims) or (sometimes) DUI records released. SASE required. Turnaround time up to 7 days. Copy fee: $.15 per page. Certification fee: $5.00. Fee payee: Federal Way Division King County District Court. Personal checks accepted. Credit cards accepted: Visa, Mastercard. Prepayment is required.

District Court (Issaquah Division) 5415 220th Ave SW, Issaquah, WA 98029-6839; 206-296-7688; Fax: 206-296-0591. Hours: 8:30AM-4:30PM (PST). *Misdemeanor, Civil Actions Under $50,000, Small Claims.*

www.metrokc.gov/kcdc

Civil Records: Access: Mail, online, in person. Only the court conducts in person searches; visitors may not. No search fee. Required to search: name, years to search; also helpful-address. Civil cases indexed by defendant, plaintiff. Civil records on computer back 10 years. Index available remotely online (see state introduction). **Criminal Records:** Access: Mail, remote online, in person. Only the court conducts in person searches; visitors may not. No search fee. Required to search: name, years to search, DOB, signed release; also helpful-address. Criminal records on computer back 5 years. Index available remotely online (see state introduction). **General Information:** No sealed, juvenile, sex offenders (victims) or (sometimes) DUI records released. SASE required. Turnaround time 1-5 days. Copy fee: $.15 per page. Certification fee: $6.00. Fee payee: Issaquah Division. Personal checks accepted. Credit cards accepted: Visa, Mastercard. Prepayment is required.

District Court (Renton Division) 3407 NE 2nd St, Renton, WA 98056-4193; 206-296-3532, 800-325-6165 in state; Fax: 206-296-0593. Hours: 8:30AM-4:30PM (PST). *Misdemeanor, Civil Actions Under $50,000, Small Claims.*

www.metrokc.gov

Civil Records: Access: Phone, fax, mail, online, in person. Only the court conducts in person searches; visitors may not. No search fee. Required to search: name, years to search; also helpful-address. Civil cases indexed by defendant, plaintiff. Civil records on computer back 10 years. Index available remotely online (see state introduction). **Criminal Records:** Access: Phone, fax, mail, remote online, in person. Only the court conducts in person searches; visitors may not. No search fee. Required to search: name, years to search, signed release; also helpful-address, DOB, SSN. Criminal records on computer back 5 years. Index available remotely online (see state introduction). **General Information:** No sealed, juvenile, adoption, paternity, mental health, sex offenders (victims) or (sometimes) DUI records released. SASE requested. Turnaround time 2-3 days. Copy fee: $.15 per page. Certification fee: $5.00. Fee payee: Renton District Court. Personal checks accepted. Credit cards accepted: Visa/MC. Prepayment is required.

District Court (Seattle Division) 516
Third Ave E-327 Courthouse, Seattle, WA 98104-3273; 206-296-3565. Hours: 8:30AM-4:30PM (PST). *Misdemeanor, Civil Actions Under $50,000, Small Claims.*

www.metrokc.gov/kcdc

Civil Records: Access: Mail, online, in person. Both court and visitors may perform in person searches. No search fee. Required to search: name, years to search; also helpful-address. Civil cases indexed by defendant, plaintiff. Civil records on computer from back 10 years. Index available remotely online (see state introduction). **Criminal Records:** Access: Mail, remote online, in person. Both court and visitors may perform in person searches. No search fee. Required to search: name, years to search, DOB, signed release; also helpful-address, SSN. Criminal records on computer from back 10 years. Index available remotely online (see state introduction). **General Information:** No sealed, juvenile, adoption, paternity, mental health, sex offenders (victims), treatment plans or (sometimes) DUI records released. SASE required. Turnaround time 10 days. Copy fee: $.15 per page. Certification fee: $5.00. Fee payee: King County District Court, Seattle. Personal checks accepted. Credit cards accepted: Visa, Mastercard. Prepayment is required. Public access terminal is available. Public Access Terminal Note: 10 minute limit. 90% of info available to public, other 10% can only be searched by court staff.

District Court (Shoreline Division)
18050 Meridian Ave N, Shoreline, WA 98133-4642; 206-296-3679; Fax: 206-296-0594. Hours: 8:30AM-4:30PM (PST). *Misdemeanor, Civil Actions Under $50,000, Small Claims.*

www.metrokc.gov/kcdc

Civil Records: Access: Phone, fax, mail, online, in person. Both court and visitors may perform in person searches. No search fee. Required to search: name, years to search; also helpful-address. Civil cases indexed by defendant, plaintiff. Civil records on computer from 1985. Index available remotely online (see state introduction). **Criminal Records:** Access: Phone, fax, mail, remote online, in person. Both court and visitors may perform in person searches. No search fee. Required to search: name, years to search; also helpful-address, DOB, SSN. Criminal records on computer from 1987. Index available remotely online (see state introduction). **General Information:** No sealed, juvenile, adoption, paternity, mental health, sex offenders (victims) or (sometimes) DUI records released. SASE required. Turnaround time 1 week. Copy fee: $.25 per page. Certification fee: $5.00. Fee payee: King County District Court. Personal checks accepted. Credit cards accepted: Visa, Mastercard. Prepayment is required. Public access terminal is available. Fax notes: No fee to fax results.

District Court (Southwest Division) 601
SW 149th St, Seattle, WA 98166; 206-296-0133; Fax: 206-296-0585. Hours: 8:30AM-4:30PM (PST). *Misdemeanor, Civil Actions Under $50,000, Small Claims.*

Civil Records: Access: Mail, online, in person. Only the court conducts in person searches; visitors may not. No search fee. Required to search: name, years to search; also helpful-address. Civil cases indexed by defendant, plaintiff. Civil records on computer back 10 years. Index available remotely online (see state introduction). **Criminal Records:** Access: Mail, remote online, in person. Only the court conducts in person searches; visitors may not. No search fee. Required to search: name, years to search, DOB, signed release; also helpful-address. Criminal records on computer back 5 years. Index available remotely online (see state introduction). **General Information:** No sealed, juvenile, seax offenders (victims) or (sometimes) DUI records released. SASE requested. Turnaround time 2-4 days. Copy fee: $.15 per page. Certification fee: $5.00. Fee payee: Southwest Division, King County District Court. Personal checks accepted. Credit cards accepted: Visa, Mastercard. Prepayment is required.

District Court (Southwest Division - Vashon) 19021 99th SW (PO Box 111), Vashon, WA 98070-0111; 206-296-3664; Fax: 206-296-0578. Hours: 8:30AM-Noon, 1:15-4:30PM 2nd & 4th F of the month (PST). *Misdemeanor, Civil Actions Under $50,000, Small Claims.*

www.metrokc.gov/kcdc

Civil Records: Access: Fax, mail, online, in person. Only the court conducts in person searches; visitors may not. No search fee. Required to search: name, years to search; also helpful-address. Civil cases indexed by defendant, plaintiff. Civil records on computer back 5 years. Index available remotely online (see state introduction). **Criminal Records:** Access: Fax, mail, remote online, in person. Only the court conducts in person searches; visitors may not. No search fee. Required to search: name, years to search; also helpful-address, DOB, SSN. Criminal records on computer from 1987. Index available remotely online (see state introduction). **General Information:** No sealed, juvenile, adoption, paternity, mental health, sex offenders (victims) or (sometimes) DUI records released. Turnaround time 1 day. Copy fee: $.15 per page. Certification fee: $5.00. Fee payee: Vashon District Court. Personal checks accepted. Prepayment is required. Fax notes: No fee to fax results.

District Court NE Division 8601 160th Ave NE, Redmond, WA 98052-3548; 206-296-3667. Hours: 8:30AM-4:30PM (PST). *Misdemeanor, Civil Actions Under $50,000, Small Claims.*

www.metrokc.gov/kcdc

Civil Records: Access: Mail, online, in person. Both court and visitors may perform in person searches. No search fee. Required to search: name, years to search; also helpful-address. Civil cases indexed by defendant, plaintiff. Civil records on computer back 10 years. Index available remotely online (see state introduction). **Criminal Records:** Access: Mail, remote online, in person. Both court and visitors may perform in person searches. No search fee. Required to search: name, years to search, DOB; also helpful-address. Criminal records on computer back 5 years. Index available remotely online (see state introduction). **General Information:** No sealed, juvenile, adoption, paternity, mental health, sex offenders (victims) or (sometimes) DUI records released. Turnaround

time 1-2 weeks. Copy fee: $.15 per page. Certification fee: $5.00. Fee payee: King County District Court. Personal checks accepted. Credit cards accepted: Visa, Mastercard. Prepayment is required. Public access terminal is available.

Kitsap County

Superior Court 614 Division St, MS34, Port Orchard, WA 98366-4699; 360-337-7164; Fax: 360-337-4927. Hours: 8AM-4:30PM (PST). *Felony, Civil, Eviction, Probate.*

www.wa.gov/kitsap/departments/clerk/index.html

Civil Records: Access: Mail, online, in person. Both court and visitors may perform in person searches. Search fee: $20.00 per hour. Fee is for up to 5 names. Required to search: name, years to search. Civil cases indexed by defendant, plaintiff. Civil records on computer from 1978, on microfiche and archived from 1889. Index available remotely online (see state introduction). **Criminal Records:** Access: Mail, remote online, in person. Both court and visitors may perform in person searches. Search fee: $20.00 per hour. Fee is for up to 5 names. Required to search: name, years to search; also helpful-address, DOB, SSN. Criminal records on computer from 1978, on microfiche and archived from 1889. Index available remotely online (see state introduction). **General Information:** No dependencies, adoption or mental illness records released. SASE required. Turnaround time 2 weeks. Copy fee: $2.00 for first page, $1.00 each addl. Certification fee: Certification fee included in copy fee. Fee payee: Kitsap County Clerk. Personal checks accepted. Out-of state personal checks not accepted. Prepayment is required. Public access terminal is available.

District Court 614 Division St, MS 25, Port Orchard, WA 98366-4614; 360-337-7109; Fax: 360-337-4865. Hours: 8:30AM-4:30PM (PST). *Misdemeanor, Civil Actions Under $50,000, Small Claims.*

Civil Records: Access: Phone, fax, mail, online, in person. Only the court conducts in person searches; visitors may not. No search fee. Required to search: name, years to search; also helpful-address. Civil cases indexed by defendant, plaintiff. Civil records on computer from 6/89, prior in archives. Index available remotely online (see state introduction). **Criminal Records:** Access: Phone, fax, mail, remote online, in person. Only the court conducts in person searches; visitors may not. No search fee. Required to search: name, years to search; also helpful-address, DOB, SSN. Criminal records on computer from 6/89, prior in archives. Index available remotely online (see state introduction). **General Information:** No dependencies, adoption and mental illness records released. Turnaround time 1 week. Copy fee: $.15 per page. Certification fee: $5.00. Fee payee: Kitsap County District Court. Personal checks accepted. Prepayment is required. Fax notes: No fee to fax results. Local faxing only.

District Court North 19050 Jensen Way NE, Poulsbo, WA 98370-0910; 360-337-7109; Fax: 360-337-4865. Hours: 8:30AM-12:15PM; 1:15-4:30PM (PST). *Misdemeanor, Civil Actions Under $50,000, Small Claims.*

Note: The mailing address is 614 Division St, MS-25, ZIP is 98366.

Civil Records: Access: online, in person. Only the court conducts in person searches; visitors may not. No search fee. Required to search: name, years to search. Civil cases indexed by defendant, plaintiff. Civil records on computer back 8 years, on index cards for 10 years. Send all mail requests to Port Orchard District court. Index available remotely online (see state introduction). **Criminal Records:** Access: Remote online, in person. Only the court conducts in person searches; visitors may not. No search fee. Required to search: name, signed release; also helpful-years to search, DOB. Criminal records on computer back 8 years, on index cards for 10 years. Send all mail requests to Port Orchard Distrcit Court. Index available remotely online (see state introduction). **General Information:** No dependencies, adoption and mental illness records released. Copy fee: $.15 per page. Certification fee: $5.00. Fee payee: District Court North, Kitsap County. Only cashiers checks and money orders accepted. Prepayment is required.

Kittitas County

Superior Court 205 W 5th Rm 210, Ellensburg, WA 98926; 509-962-7531; Fax: 509-962-7667. Hours: 9AM-Noon, 1-5PM (PST). *Felony, Misdemeanor, Civil, Eviction, Probate.*

Civil Records: Access: Phone, fax, mail, online, in person. Only the court conducts in person searches; visitors may not. Search fee: $10.00 per name. Required to search: name, years to search; also helpful-address. Civil cases indexed by defendant, plaintiff. Civil records on computer from 1982, on microfiche and archived from 1890. Some records on index cards. Index available remotely online (see state introduction). **Criminal Records:** Access: Phone, fax, mail, remote online, in person. Only the court conducts in person searches; visitors may not. Search fee: $10.00 per name. Required to search: name, years to search; also helpful-address, DOB, SSN. Criminal records on computer from 1982, on microfiche and archived from 1890. Some records on index cards. Index available remotely online (see state introduction). **General Information:** No dependencies, adoption, and mental illness records released. Turnaround time 2 days. Copy fee: $1.00 per page. Certification fee: $2.00. Fee payee: Kittitas County Clerk. Personal checks accepted. Prepayment is required. Fax notes: No fee to fax results. Fax available in emergency only.

District Court Lower Kittitas 205 W 5th, Rm 180, Ellensburg, WA 98926; 509-962-7511. Hours: 9AM-5PM (PST). *Misdemeanor, Civil Actions Under $50,000, Small Claims.*

Civil Records: Access: Mail, online, in person. Only the court conducts in person searches; visitors may not. No search fee. Required to search: name, years to search. Civil cases indexed by defendant, plaintiff. Civil records on computer from 8/91, archived back 10 years, some on index cards. Records retained for 20 years. Index available remotely online (see state introduction). **Criminal Records:** Access: Mail, remote online, in person. Only the court conducts in person searches; visitors may not. No search fee. Required to search: name, years to search, DOB. Criminal records on computer from 8/91, archived back 10 years, some on index cards. Records retained for 20 years. Index available remotely online (see state introduction). **General Information:** No dependencies, adoption, and mental illness records released. SASE required. Turnaround time 7-10 days. Copy fee: $.25 per page. Certification fee: $5.00. Fee payee: Kittitas County District Court. Personal checks accepted. Prepayment is required.

District Court Upper Kittitas 618 E First, Cle Elum, WA 98922; 509-674-5533; Fax: 509-

674-4209. Hours: 8AM-5PM (PST). *Misdemeanor, Civil Actions Under $50,000, Small Claims.*

Civil Records: Access: Fax, mail, online, in person. Only the court conducts in person searches; visitors may not. No search fee. Required to search: name, years to search. Civil cases indexed by defendant, plaintiff. Civil records on computer since 8/91; prior records archived from 1890, some on index cards. Records retained for 10 years. Index available remotely online (see state introduction). **Criminal Records:** Access: Fax, mail, remote online, in person. Only the court conducts in person searches; visitors may not. No search fee. Required to search: name, years to search, DOB; also helpful-SSN. Criminal records on computer since 08/91; prior records archived from 1890, some on index cards. Records retained for 5 years. Index available remotely online (see state introduction). **General Information:** No dependencies, adoption, and mental illness records released. Turnaround time 1 week. Copy fee: $.25 per page. Certification fee: $5.00. Fee payee: UKCDC. Personal checks accepted. Credit cards accepted: Visa, Mastercard. Prepayment is required. Public access terminal is available. Public Access Terminal Note: for records since 1997. Fax notes: No fee to fax results. There is no additional fee for faxing, but same fees as copies or certification fees.

Klickitat County

Superior Court 205 S Columbus, Rm 204, Goldendale, WA 98620; 509-773-5744. Hours: 9AM-5PM (PST). *Felony, Civil, Eviction, Probate.*

Civil Records: Access: Phone, mail, online, in person. Only the court conducts in person searches; visitors may not. Search fee: $8.00 per hour. Required to search: name, years to search; also helpful-address. Civil cases indexed by defendant, plaintiff. Civil records on computer from 9/87. Index available remotely online (see state introduction). **Criminal Records:** Access: Phone, mail, remote online, in person. Only the court conducts in person searches; visitors may not. Search fee: $8.00 per hour. Required to search: name, years to search; also helpful-address, DOB, SSN. Criminal records on computer from 9/87. Index available remotely online (see state introduction). **General Information:** No dependencies, adoption, and mental illness records released. SASE required. Turnaround time 1 week. Copy fee: $2.00 for first page, $1.00 each addl. Certification fee: $2.00 plus $1.00 per page after first. Fee payee: Klickitat County Clerk. Personal checks accepted. Prepayment is required.

East District Court 205 S Columbus, MS-CH11, Goldendale, WA 98620-9290; 509-773-4670. Hours: 8AM-12, 1-5pm (PST). *Misdemeanor, Civil Actions Under $50,000, Small Claims.*

Civil Records: Access: Phone, mail, fax, online, in person. Both court and visitors may perform in person searches. No search fee. Required to search: name, years to search. Civil cases indexed by defendant, plaintiff. Civil records on computer from 4/93, on index cards prior. Retained for 10 years. Index available remotely online (see state introduction). **Criminal Records:** Access: Phone, mail, fax, remote online, in person. Both court and visitors may perform in person searches. No search fee. Required to search: name, years to search, DOB. Criminal records on computer from 4/93, on index cards prior. Retained for 10 years. Index available remotely online (see state introduction).

General Information: No dependencies, adoption, and mental illness records released. SASE required. Turnaround time 1 week. Copy fee: 1st 10 pages free, each additional page $.15. Certification fee: $5.00. Fee payee: East District Court. Personal checks accepted. Prepayment is required.

West District Court PO Box 435, White Salmon, WA 98672-0435; 509-493-1190; Fax: 509-493-4469. Hours: 8AM-5PM (PST). *Misdemeanor, Civil Actions Under $50,000, Small Claims.*

Civil Records: Access: Mail, in person. Only the court conducts in person searches; visitors may not. No search fee. Required to search: name, years to search. Civil cases indexed by defendant, plaintiff. Civil records on computer from 5/93, on docket books. Index available remotely online (see state introduction). **Criminal Records:** Access: Mail, in person. Only the court conducts in person searches; visitors may not. No search fee. Required to search: name, years to search, DOB; also helpful-address. Criminal records on computer from 5/93, on docket books. Index available remotely online (see state introduction). **General Information:** No dependencies, adoption, sealed and mental illness records released. SASE required. Turnaround time 3-5 days. Copy fee: $2.00 for first page, $1.00 each addl. Certification fee: $5.00. Fee payee: West District Court. Personal checks accepted. Prepayment is required.

Lewis County

Superior Court 360 NW North St, MS:CLK 01, Chehalis, WA 98532-1900; 360-740-2704; Fax: 360-748-1639. Hours: 8AM-5PM (PST). *Felony, Misdemeanor, Civil, Eviction, Probate.*

Civil Records: Access: Phone, mail, online, in person. Only the court conducts in person searches; visitors may not. Search fee: $8.00 per hour. Required to search: name, years to search; also helpful-address. Civil cases indexed by defendant, plaintiff. Civil records on computer from 1983, archived from 1900s. Index available remotely online (see state introduction). **Criminal Records:** Access: Phone, mail, remote online, in person. Only the court conducts in person searches; visitors may not. Search fee: $8.00 per hour. Required to search: name, years to search; also helpful-address, DOB, SSN. Criminal records on computer from 1983, archived from 1900s. Index available remotely online (see state introduction). **General Information:** No dependencies, adoption, paternity, and mental illness records released. SASE required. Turnaround time up to 7 days. Copy fee: $2.00 for first page, $1.00 each addl. Certification fee: $2.00. Fee payee: Lewis County Clerk. Personal checks accepted. Prepayment is required.

District Court PO Box 336, Chehalis, WA 98532-0336; 360-740-1203; Fax: 360-740-2779. Hours: 8AM-5PM (PST). *Misdemeanor, Civil Actions Under $50,000, Small Claims.*

Civil Records: Access: Fax, mail, online, in person. Both court and visitors may perform in person searches. No search fee. Required to search: name, years to search. Civil cases indexed by defendant, plaintiff. Civil records on computer from 1983, on index cards. Records retained 10 years. Index available remotely online (see state introduction). **Criminal Records:** Access: Fax, mail, remote online, in person. Both court and visitors may perform in person searches. No search fee. Required to search: name, years to search,

DOB, signed release; also helpful-address, SSN. Criminal records on computer since 1981. Records retained for 5 years. Index available remotely online (see state introduction). **General Information:** No dependencies, adoption, and mental illness records released. SASE required. Turnaround time 1 week. Copy fee: $.25 per page. Certification fee: $5.00. Fee payee: Lewis County District Court. Personal checks accepted. Prepayment required. Fax note: No fee to fax results.

Lincoln County

Superior Court Box 68, Davenport, WA 99122-0396; 509-725-1401; Fax: 509-725-1150. Hours: 8AM-5PM (PST). *Felony, Misdemeanor, Civil, Eviction, Probate.*

Civil Records: Access: Mail, online, in person. Only the court conducts in person searches; visitors may not. Search fee: $20.00 per hour. Required to search: name, years to search; also helpful-address. Civil cases indexed by defendant, plaintiff. Civil records on computer and microfiche from 11/82, archived from 1903. Index available remotely online (see state introduction). **Criminal Records:** Access: Mail, remote online, in person. Only the court conducts in person searches; visitors may not. Search fee: $20.00 per hour. Required to search: name, years to search; also helpful-address, DOB, SSN. Criminal records on computer and microfiche from 11/82, archived from 1903. Index available remotely online (see state introduction). **General Information:** No dependencies, adoption, and mental illness records released. SASE required. Turnaround time same day. Copy fee: $2.00 for first page, $1.00 each addl. Certification fee: $2.00. Fee payee: Lincoln County Clerk. Business checks accepted. Prepayment is required.

District Court PO Box 329, Davenport, WA 99122-0329; 509-725-2281. Hours: 8AM-5PM (PST). *Misdemeanor, Civil Actions Under $50,000, Small Claims.*

Note: This is a small office with limited time allowable for searches

Civil Records: Access: Mail, online, in person. Both court and visitors may perform in person searches. Search fee: $25.00 per hour. Required to search: name, years to search. Civil cases indexed by defendant. Civil records on computer from 6/93, in books from 1985. Retained 10 years. Index available remotely online (see state introduction). **Criminal Records:** Access: Mail, remote online, in person. Only the court conducts in person searches; visitors may not. Search fee: $25.00 per hour. Required to search: name, years to search, DOB. Criminal records on computer from 6/93, in books from 1985. Retained 10 years. Index available remotely online (see state introduction). **General Information:** No dependencies, adoption, and mental illness records released. SASE required. Turnaround time 1 week. Copy fee: $2.00 for first page, $1.00 each addl. Certification fee: $6.00 plus $1.00 per page after first. Fee payee: Lincoln County District Court. Business checks accepted. Prepayment is required.

Mason County

Superior Court PO Box 340, Shelton, WA 98584; 360-427-9670. Hours: 8:30AM-5PM (PST). *Felony, Civil, Eviction, Probate.*

www.co.mason.wa.us

Civil Records: Access: Phone, mail, online, in person. Both court and visitors may perform in person searches. Search fee: $20.00 per hour. Required to search: name, years to search; also

helpful-address. Civil cases indexed by defendant, plaintiff. Civil records on computer from 1982, on microfiche and archived from 1890, on index or docket books prior to 1982. Index available remotely online (see state introduction). **Criminal Records:** Access: Phone, mail, remote online, in person. Both court and visitors may perform in person searches. Search fee: $20.00 per hour. Required to search: name, years to search; also helpful-address, DOB, SSN. Criminal records on computer from 1982, on microfiche and archived from 1890, on index or docket books prior to 1982. Index available remotely online (see state introduction). **General Information:** No dependencies, adoption, and mental illness records released. SASE required. Turnaround time 1 week. Copy fee: $2.00 for first page, $1.00 each addl. Certification fee: $2.00 plus $1.00 per page after first. Fee payee: Mason County Clerk. Business checks accepted. Prepayment is required.

District Court PO Box "O", Shelton, WA 98584-0090; 360-427-9670 X339; Fax: 360-427-7776. Hours: 8:30AM-5PM (PST). *Misdemeanor, Civil Actions Under $50,000, Small Claims.*

Civil Records: Access: Mail, in person. Only the court conducts in person searches; visitors may not. Search fee: $20.00 per name. Fee is for extensive searching. Required to search: name, years to search; also helpful-address. Civil cases indexed by defendant, plaintiff. Civil records on computer from 12/92, prior on index book. Index available remotely online (see state introduction). **Criminal Records:** Access: Mail, in person. Only the court conducts in person searches; visitors may not. Search fee: Will charge $20.00 for extensive search. Required to search: name, years to search, DOB, signed release; also helpful-address, SSN. Criminal records on computer from 12/92, prior on index book. Index available remotely online (see state introduction). **General Information:** No dependencies, adoption, and mental illness records released. SASE required. Turnaround time 1 week. Copy fee: $.15 per page. Certification fee: $5.00. Fee payee: Mason County District Court. Personal checks accepted. Prepayment is required.

Okanogan County

Superior Court PO Box 72, Okanogan, WA 98840; 509-422-7275; Fax: 509-422-7277. Hours: 8AM-5PM (PST). *Felony, Misdemeanor, Civil, Eviction, Probate.*

Civil Records: Access: Phone, fax, mail, online, in person. Both court and visitors may perform in person searches. Search fee: $20.00 per hour. Required to search: name, years to search; also helpful-address. Civil cases indexed by defendant, plaintiff. Civil records on computer from 10/84, on hand-written indexes from 1890. Index available remotely online (see state introduction). **Criminal Records:** Access: Phone, fax, mail, remote online, in person. Both court and visitors may perform in person searches. Search fee: $20.00 per hour. Required to search: name, years to search; also helpful-address, DOB, SSN. Criminal records on computer from 10/84, on hand-written indexes from 1890. Index available remotely online (see state introduction). **General Information:** No dependencies, adoption, and mental illness records released. SASE required. Turnaround time 1-7 days. Copy fee: $1.00 per page. Certification fee: $2.00 plus $1.00 per page after first. Fee payee: Okanogan County Clerk. Personal checks accepted. Prepayment is required.

District Court PO Box 980, Okanogan, WA 98840-0980; 509-422-7170; Fax: 509-422-7174.

Hours: 8AM-5PM (PST). *Misdemeanor, Civil Actions Under $50,000, Small Claims.*

Civil Records: Access: Phone, fax, mail, in person, online. Both court and visitors may perform in person searches. No search fee. Required to search: name, years to search. Civil cases indexed by defendant, plaintiff. Civil records on computer from 8/91, prior on index cards. Index available remotely online (see state introduction). **Criminal Records:** Access: Phone, fax, mail, in person, online. Both court and visitors may perform in person searches. No search fee. Required to search: name, years to search, DOB. Criminal records on computer from 8/91, prior on index cards. Index available remotely online (see state introduction). **General Information:** No dependencies, adoption, alcohol related evaluations, mental illness records released. SASE requested. Turnaround time 7 days. Copy fee: $1.00 for first page, $.50 each addl. Certification fee: $5.00. Fee payee: Okanogan County District Court. Personal checks accepted. Prepayment is required. Fax notes: $1.00 for first page, $.50 each addl.

Pacific County

Superior Court PO Box 67, South Bend, WA 98586; 360-875-9320; Fax: 360-875-9321. Hours: 8AM-4PM M-Th; 8AM-5PM F (PST). *Felony, Civil, Eviction, Probate.*

Civil Records: Access: Phone, mail, online, in person. Both court and visitors may perform in person searches. Search fee: $20.00 per hour if searching before 1984. Required to search: name, years to search. Civil cases indexed by defendant, plaintiff. Civil records on computer from 2/84, archived from 1887, some on docket books. Index available remotely online (see state introduction). **Criminal Records:** Access: Phone, fax, mail, remote online, in person. Both court and visitors may perform in person searches. Search fee: $20.00 per hour if searching before 1984. Required to search: name, years to search. Criminal records on computer from 2/84, archived from 1887, some on docket books. Index available remotely online (see state introduction). **General Information:** No dependencies, adoption, and mental illness records released. Turnaround time varies. Copy fee: $2.00 for first page, $1.00 each addl; Non-certified: $.15 per page. Certification fee: $2.00. Fee payee: Pacific County Clerk. Personal checks accepted. Prepayment is required.

District Court North Box 134, South Bend, WA 98586-0134; 360-875-9354; Fax: 360-875-9362. Hours: 8:30AM-5PM (PST). *Misdemeanor, Civil Actions Under $50,000, Small Claims.*

Civil Records: Access: Phone, fax, mail, online, in person. Both court and visitors may perform in person searches. No search fee. Required to search: name, years to search; also helpful-address. Civil cases indexed by defendant, plaintiff. Civil records on computer from 3/93, prior on index cards. Civil records retained 10 years. Index available remotely online (see state introduction). **Criminal Records:** Access: Phone, fax, mail, remote online, in person. Both court and visitors may perform in person searches. No search fee. Required to search: name, DOB; also helpful-years to search, address, SSN. Criminal Records retained forever, on computer since 03/93. Index available remotely online (see state introduction). **General Information:** No dependencies, adoption, and mental illness records released. SASE required. Turnaround time 1 week. Copy fee: $2.00 for first page, $1.00 each addl. Certification fee: $5.00. Fee payee: North District Court. Personal checks

Indexing & Storage: Cases are indexed by defendant and plaintiff as well as by case number. New cases are available in the index 2 days after filing date. Both computer and card indexes are maintained. The computer index is from 1994 forward. Open records are located at this court.

Fee & Payment: The fee is $15.00 per item (one party name or case number). Payment may be made by money order, cashier check. Business checks are not accepted. Personal checks are not accepted. Prepayment is required. Payee: Clerk, US District Court. Certification fee: $5.00 per document. Copy fee: $.50 per page.

Phone Search: Limited docket information is available by phone. An automated voice case information service (VCIS) is not available.

Mail Search: Always enclose a stamped self addressed envelope.

In Person Search: In person searching is available.

PACER: Sign-up number is 800-676-6856. Access fee is $.60 per minute. Toll-free access: 888-513-7959. Local access: 304-233-7424. Case records are available back to October 1994. Records are purged every 5 years. New records are available online after 1 day. PACER is available on the Internet at http://pacer.wvnd.uscourts.gov.

Wheeling Division Clerk, PO Box 471, Wheeling, WV 26003 (Courier Address: 12th & Chapline Sts, Wheeling, WV 26003), 304-232-0011, Fax: 304-233-2185.

www.wvnd.uscourts.gov

Counties: Brooke, Hancock, Marshall, Ohio, Wetzel.

Indexing & Storage: Cases are indexed by defendant and plaintiff as well as by case number. New cases are available in the index immediately after filing date. Both computer and card indexes are maintained. Civil cases on computer since October 1994, and criminal cases since October 1995. Open records are located at this court. Records have not yet been sent to the Federal Records Center from this office.

Fee & Payment: The fee is $15.00 per item (one party name or case number). Payment may be made by money order, cashier check, personal check. Prepayment is required. Payee: Clerk, US District Court. Certification fee: $5.00 per document. Copy fee: $.50 per page. You are allowed to make your own copies. These copies cost Not Applicable per page.

Phone Search: All information that is not sealed is available for release over the phone. An automated voice case information service (VCIS) is not available.

Mail Search: Always enclose a stamped self addressed envelope.

In Person Search: In person searching is available.

PACER: Sign-up number is 800-676-6856. Access fee is $.60 per minute. Toll-free access: 888-513-7959. Local access: 304-233-7424. Case records are available back to October 1994. Records are purged every 5 years. New records are available online after 1 day. PACER is available on the Internet at http://pacer.wvnd.uscourts.gov.

US Bankruptcy Court

Northern District of West Virginia

Wheeling Division PO Box 70, Wheeling, WV 26003 (Courier Address: 12th & Chapline Sts, Wheeling, WV 26003), 304-233-1655.

www.wvnb.uscourts.gov

Counties: Barbour, Berkeley, Braxton, Brooke, Calhoun, Doddridge, Gilmer, Grant, Hampshire, Hancock, Hardy, Harrison, Jefferson, Lewis, Marion, Marshall, Mineral, Monongalia, Morgan, Ohio, Pendleton, Pleasants, Pocahontas, Preston, Randolph, Ritchie, Taylor,Tucker, Tyler, Upshur, Webster, Wetzel.

Indexing & Storage: Cases are indexed by debtor as well as by case number. New cases are available in the index 24 hours after filing date. A card index is maintained. Open records are located at this court.

Fee & Payment: The fee is $15.00 per item (one party name or case number). Payment may be made by money order, cashier check, personal check. Prepayment is required. Payee: Clerk, US Bankruptcy Court. Certification fee: $5.00 per document. Copy fee: $.50 per page.

Phone Search: Only docket information is available by phone. An automated voice case information service (VCIS) is available.

Mail Search: Always enclose a stamped self addressed envelope.

In Person Search: In person searching is available.

PACER: Sign-up number is 800-676-6856. Access fee is $.60 per minute. Toll-free access: 800-809-3016. Local access: 304-233-2871. Case records are available back to early 1990. Records are never purged. New civil records are available online after 1 day. PACER is available on the Internet at http://pacer.wvnb.uscourts.gov.

US District Court

Southern District of West Virginia

Beckley Division PO Drawer 5009, Beckley, WV 25801 (Courier Address: 400 Neville St, Beckley, WV 25801), 304-253-7481, Fax: 304-253-3252.

www.wvsd.uscourts.gov

Counties: Fayette, Greenbrier, Raleigh, Sumners, Wyoming.

Indexing & Storage: Cases are indexed by defendant and plaintiff as well as by case number. New cases are available in the index immediately after filing date. A card index is maintained. Open records are located at this court.

Fee & Payment: The fee is $15.00 per item (one party name or case number). Payment may be made by money order, cashier check, personal check. Prepayment is required. Payee: Clerk, US District Court. Certification fee: $5.00 per document. Copy fee: $.50 per page. You are allowed to make your own copies. These copies cost $.50 per page.

Phone Search: Only docket information is available by phone. An automated voice case information service (VCIS) is not available.

Fax Search: There is no charge for information on names only.

Mail Search: Always enclose a stamped self addressed envelope.

In Person Search: In person searching is available.

PACER: Sign-up number is 800-676-6856. Access fee is $.60 per minute. Toll-free access: 800-650-2141. Local access: 304-347-5596. Case records are available back to 1991. New records are available online after 1 day. PACER is available online at http://pacer.wvsd.uscourts.gov.

Other Online Access: You can search records online using RACER. Visit http://207.41.17.36/wc.dll?usdc_racer~main.

Bluefield Division Clerk's Office, PO Box 4128, Bluefield, WV 24701 (Courier Address: 601 Federal St, Bluefield, WV 24701), 304-327-9798.

www.wvsd.uscourts.gov

Counties: McDowell, Mercer, Monroe.

Indexing & Storage: Cases are indexed by defendant and plaintiff as well as by case number. New cases are available in the index immediately after filing date. A card index is maintained. Open records are located at this court.

Fee & Payment: The fee is $15.00 per item (one party name or case number). Payment may be made by money order, cashier check, personal check. Prepayment is required. Payee: Clerk, US District Court. Certification fee: $5.00 per document. Copy fee: $.50 per page. You are allowed to make your own copies. These copies cost $.50 per page.

Phone Search: One name may be searched by phone. An automated voice case information service (VCIS) is not available.

Fax Search: Fax requests are accepted.

Mail Search: Always enclose a stamped self addressed envelope.

In Person Search: In person searching is available.

PACER: Sign-up number is 800-676-6856. Access fee is $.60 per minute. Toll-free access: 800-650-2141. Local access: 304-347-5596. Case records are available back to 1991. New records are available online after 1 day. PACER is available on the Internet at http://pacer.wvsd.uscourts.gov.

Other Online Access: You can search records online using RACER. Visit http://207.41.17.36/wc.dll?usdc_racer~main.

Charleston Division PO Box 2546, Charleston, WV 25329 (Courier Address: Room 2201, 500 Quarrier St, Charleston, WV 25301), 304-347-5114.

www.wvsd.uscourts.gov

Counties: Boone, Clay, Jackson, Kanawha, Lincoln, Logan, Mingo, Nicholas, Putnam, Roane.

Indexing & Storage: Cases are indexed by defendant and plaintiff as well as by case number. New cases are available in the index immediately after filing date. Both computer and card indexes are maintained. Open records are located at this court. The fee to retrieve a record that has been sent to the Records Center is $25.00.

Fee & Payment: The fee is $15.00 per item (one party name or case number). Payment may be made by money order, cashier check, personal check. Prepayment is required. Payee: Clerk, US District Court. Certification fee: $5.00 per document. Copy fee: $.50 per page. You are

allowed to make your own copies. These copies cost $.50 per page.

Phone Search: Only docket information is available by phone. An automated voice case information service (VCIS) is not available.

Fax Search: The court plans to accept fax requests beginning in October 1998. Call for more information.

Mail Search: A stamped self addressed envelope is not required.

In Person Search: In person searching is available.

PACER: Sign-up number is 800-676-6856. Access fee is $.60 per minute. Toll-free access: 800-650-2141. Local access: 304-347-5596. Case records are available back to 1991. New records are available online after 1 day. PACER is available online at http://pacer.wvsd.uscourts.gov.

Other Online Access: You can search records online using RACER. Visit http://207.41.17.36/wc.dll?usdc_racer~main.

Huntington Division Clerk of Court, PO Box 1570, Huntington, WV 25716 (Courier Address: Room 101, 845 5th Ave, Huntington, WV 25701), 304-529-5588, Fax: 304-529-5131.

www.wvsd.uscourts.gov

Counties: Cabell, Mason, Wayne.

Indexing & Storage: Cases are indexed by defendant and plaintiff as well as by case number. New cases are available in the index immediately after filing date. Both computer and card indexes are maintained. Open records are located at this court.

Fee & Payment: The fee is $15.00 per item (one party name or case number). Payment may be made by money order, cashier check, personal check. Prepayment is required. Payee: Clerk, US District Court. Certification fee: $5.00 per document. Copy fee: $.50 per page. You are allowed to make your own copies. These copies cost $.50 per page.

Phone Search: Only docket information is available by phone. An automated voice case information service (VCIS) is not available.

Fax Search: Fax requests will be accepted, but for a maximum of 1-2 names.

Mail Search: Always enclose a stamped self addressed envelope.

In Person Search: In person searching is available.

PACER: Sign-up number is 800-676-6856. Access fee is $.60 per minute. Toll-free access: 800-650-2141. Local access: 304-347-5596. Case records are available back to 1991. New records are available online after 1 day. PACER is available online at http://pacer.wvsd.uscourts.gov.

Other Online Access: You can search records online using RACER. Visit http://207.41.17.36/wc.dll?usdc_racer~main.

Parkersburg Division Clerk of Court, PO Box 1526, Parkersburg, WV 26102 (Courier Address: Room 5102, 425 Julianna St, Parkersburg, WV 26101), 304-420-6490, Fax: 304-420-6363.

www.wvsd.uscourts.gov

Counties: Wirt, Wood.

Indexing & Storage: Cases are indexed by defendant and plaintiff as well as by case number. New cases are available in the index immediately after filing date. Both computer and card indexes are maintained. Open records are located at this court.

Fee & Payment: The fee is $15.00 per item (one party name or case number). Payment may be made by money order, cashier check, personal check. Prepayment is required. Payee: Clerk, US District Court. Certification fee: $5.00 per document. Copy fee: $.50 per page. You are allowed to make your own copies. These copies cost $.50 per page.

Phone Search: Only docket information is available by phone. An automated voice case information service (VCIS) is not available.

Fax Search: Fax requests are accepted, but for a maximum of 1-2 names only.

Mail Search: Always enclose a stamped self addressed envelope.

In Person Search: In person searching is available.

PACER: Sign-up number is 800-676-6856. Access fee is $.60 per minute. Toll-free access: 800-650-2141. Local access: 304-347-5596. Case records are available back to 1991. New records are available online after 1 day. PACER is available online at http://pacer.wvsd.uscourts.gov.

Other Online Access: You can search records online using RACER. Visit http://207.41.17.36/wc.dll?usdc_racer~main.

US Bankruptcy Court

Southern District of West Virginia

Charleston Division PO Box 3924, Charleston, WV 25339 (Courier Address: 300 Virginia St E, Room 2400, Charleston, WV 25301), 304-347-3000.

Counties: Boone, Cabell, Clay, Fayette, Greenbrier, Jackson, Kanawha, Lincoln, Logan, Mason, McDowell, Mercer, Mingo, Monroe, Nicholas, Putnam, Raleigh, Roane, Summers, Wayne, Wirt, Wood, Wyoming.

Indexing & Storage: Cases are indexed by debtor as well as by case number. New cases are available in the index 1-2 days after filing date. Both computer and card indexes are maintained. Card index is maintained to December 1, 1988 after which index is on computer. Open records are located at this court.

Fee & Payment: The fee is $15.00 per item (one party name or case number). Payment may be made by money order, cashier check, personal check, Visa or Mastercard. Prepayment is required. Credit cards accepted only from law firms. Payee: Clerk, US Bankruptcy Court. Certification fee: $5.00 per document. Copy fee: $.50 per page.

Phone Search: Only docket information is available by phone. An automated voice case information service (VCIS) is available.

Mail Search: A stamped self addressed envelope is not required.

In Person Search: In person searching is available.

PACER: Sign-up number is 800-676-6856. Access fee is $.60 per minute. Case records are available back to 1988. Records are purged every 6 months. New civil records are available online after 1 day.

Other Online Access: Records are searchable online using RACER. Visit http://207.41.17.36/wconnect/wc.dll?usbc_racer~main.

Court	Jurisdiction	No. of Courts	How Organized
Circuit Courts*	General	55	31 Circuits
Magistrate Courts*	Limited	55	55 Counties
Municipal Courts	Municipal	122	

* Profiled in this Sourcebook.

Court	CIVIL								
	Tort	Contract	Real Estate	Min. Claim	Max. Claim	Small Claims	Estate	Eviction	Domestic Relations
Circuit Courts*	X	X	X	$300	No Max		X		X
Magistrate Courts*	X	X		$0	$5000	$3000		X	X
Municipal Courts									

Court	CRIMINAL				
	Felony	Misdemeanor	DWI/DUI	Preliminary Hearing	Juvenile
Circuit Courts*	X				X
Magistrate Courts*		X	X	X	
Municipal Courts			X		

ADMINISTRATION   Administrative Office, Supreme Court of Appeals, 1900 Kanawha Blvd, 1 E 100 State Capitol, Charleston, WV, 25305; 304-558-0145, Fax: 304-558-1212. www.state.wv.us/wvsca

COURT STRUCTURE   The 55 Circuit Courts are the courts of general jurisdiction. Effective October 1999, a Family Court division was created within the Circuit Court of each county. Probate is handled by the Circuit Court. Records are held at the County Commissioner's Office.

ONLINE ACCESS   There is no statewide online computer system, internal or external. Most courts with a computer system use FORTUNE software; however, no external access is permitted.

ADDITIONAL INFORMATION   There is a statewide requirement that search turnaround times not exceed 10 days. However, most courts do far better than that limit. There is a discrepancy in what courts will and will not release with the decisions resting with the judges and clerks in the various jurisdictions.

Barbour County

Circuit Court 8 N Main St, Philippi, WV 26416; 304-457-3454. Hours: 8:30AM-4:30PM (EST). *Felony, Civil Actions Over $5,000, Probate.*

Note: Probate is handled by the County Clerk at this address

Civil Records: Access: Phone, mail, in person. Both court and visitors may perform in person searches. No search fee. Required to search: name, years to search. Civil cases indexed by defendant, plaintiff. Civil records on microfiche from 1843 to 1980s on index cards back to 1862, on dockets back to 1843. **Criminal Records:** Access: Phone, mail, in person. Both court and visitors may perform in person searches. No search fee. Required to search: name, years to search. Criminal records on microfiche from 1843 to 1980s on index cards back to 1862, on dockets back to 1843. **General Information:** No sealed, juvenile, adoptions, mental health, expunged records released. SASE requested. Turnaround time 1 day. Copy fee: $.50 per page. Certification fee: $1.00. Fee payee: Barbour County Circuit

Clerk. Personal checks accepted. Prepayment is required. Public access terminal is available.

Magistrate Court PO Box 541, Philippi, WV 26416; 304-457-3676; Fax: 304-457-4999. Hours: 8:30AM-4:30PM (EST). *Misdemeanor, Civil Actions Under $5,000, Eviction, Small Claims.*

Civil Records: Both court and visitors may perform in person searches. Search fee:. Phone access limited to one name searched from 8/93 on only. **Criminal Records:** Court does not conduct in person searches; visitors must perform searches for themselves. Search fee: No criminal searches performed by court. Required to search: name, years to search. **General Information:** Turnaround time varies. Fee payee: Magistrate Court. Prepayment is required.

Berkeley County

Circuit Court 110 W King St, Martinsburg, WV 25401-3210; 304-264-1918; Probate phone:304-264-1940. Hours: 9AM-5PM (EST). *Felony, Civil Actions Over $5,000, Probate.*

Note: Probate is handled by Fiduciary Records Clerk, 100 W King St, Room 2, Martinsburg, WV 25401

Civil Records: Access: Fax, mail, in person. Both court and visitors may perform in person searches. No search fee. Required to search: name, years to search. Civil cases indexed by defendant, plaintiff. Civil records on computer from January 1990, on index books from 1800s. **Criminal Records:** Access: In person only. Court does not conduct in person searches; visitors must perform searches for themselves. Search fee: No criminal searches performed by court. Required to search: name, years to search; also helpful-DOB, SSN. Criminal records on computer from January 1990, on index books from 1800s. **General Information:** No sealed, juvenile, adoptions, mental health, guardianship records released. SASE not required. Turnaround time 1 week. Copy fee: $.50 per page. Certification fee: No certification fee. Fee payee: Clerk of Circuit Court. Business checks accepted. Fax notes: $2.00 per page.

Magistrate Court 120 W John St, Martinsburg, WV 25401; 304-264-1956; Fax: 304-263-9154. Hours: 9AM-4PM (EST). *Misdemeanor, Civil Actions Under $5,000, Eviction, Small Claims.*

Civil Records: Both court and visitors may perform in person searches. Search fee:. **Criminal Records:** Both court and visitors may perform in person searches. No search fee. Required to search: name, years to search; also helpful-address, DOB, SSN. **General Information:.** Fee payee: Magistrate Court. Prepayment is required. Public access terminal is available.

Boone County

Circuit Court 200 State St, Madison, WV 25130; 304-369-3925; Probate phone:304-369-7337; Fax: 304-369-7326. Hours: 8AM-4PM *Felony, Civil Actions Over $5,000, Probate.*

Note: Probate is handled by County Clerk, 200 State St, Madison, WV 25130

Civil Records: Access: Phone, fax, mail, in person. Both court and visitors may perform in person searches. No search fee. Required to search: name, years to search. Civil cases indexed by defendant, plaintiff. Civil records on computer from 1986 to present, on index books 1956 to present, on dockets back to 1900. **Criminal Records:** Access: Phone, fax, mail, in person. Both court and visitors may perform in person searches. No search fee. Required to search: name, years to search, signed release. Criminal records on computer from 1986 to present, on index books 1956 to present, on dockets back to 1900. **General Information:** No sealed, juvenile, adoptions, mental health, expunged records released. SASE requested. Turnaround time 1 day. Copy fee: $.50 per page. Certification fee: $.50. Fee payee: Circuit Clerk. Business checks accepted. Prepayment is required. Fax notes: $3.00 per page.

Magistrate Court 200 State St., Madison, WV 25130; 304-369-7364; Fax: 304-369-1932. Hours: 8AM-4PM (EST). *Misdemeanor, Civil Actions Under $5,000, Eviction, Small Claims.*

Civil Records: Both court and visitors may perform in person searches. Search fee:. **Criminal Records:** Court does not conduct in person searches; visitors must perform searches for themselves. Search fee: No criminal searches performed by court. Required to search: name, years to search; also helpful-DOB, SSN. **General Information:** Turnaround time 2-3 weeks. Fee payee: Boone County Magistrate Court. Prepayment is required.

Braxton County

Circuit Court 300 Main St, Sutton, WV 26601; 304-765-2837; Fax: 304-765-2947. Hours: 8AM-4PM (EST). *Felony, Civil Actions Over $5,000, Probate.*

Civil Records: Access: Phone, fax, mail, in person. Both court and visitors may perform in person searches. No search fee. Required to search: name, years to search. Civil cases indexed by defendant, plaintiff. Civil records on microfiche 1806 to 1910, on dockets back to 1810. **Criminal Records:** Access: Phone, fax, mail, in person. Both court and visitors may perform in person searches. No search fee. Required to search: name, years to search, signed release. Criminal records on microfiche 1806 to 1910, on dockets back to 1810. **General Information:** No adoption, juvenile, mental hygiene records released. SASE required. Turnaround time 2-3 days. Copy fee: $.50 per page. Certification fee: No certification fee. Fee payee: JW Morris, Clerk. Personal checks accepted. Prepayment is required. Fax notes: $3.00 for first page, $1.00 each addl.

Magistrate Court 307 Main St, Sutton, WV 26601; 304-765-5678; Fax: 304-765-3756. Hours:

8:30AM-4:30PM (EST). *Misdemeanor, Civil Actions Under $5,000, Eviction, Small Claims.*

Civil Records: Both court and visitors may perform in person searches. Search fee:. **Criminal Records:** Both court and visitors may perform in person searches. No search fee. Required to search: name, years to search, DOB; also helpful-address, SSN. **General Information:** Turnaround time 1-2 weeks. Fee payee: Braxton County Magistrate Court. Prepayment is required.

Brooke County

Circuit Court Brooke County Courthouse, Wellsburg, WV 26070; 304-737-3662; Probate phone:304-737-3661. Hours: 9AM-5PM (EST). *Felony, Civil Actions Over $5,000, Probate.*

Note: Probate is handled by County Clerk, 632 Main St, Courthouse, Wellsburg, WV 26070

Civil Records: Access: Mail, in person. Both court and visitors may perform in person searches. No search fee. Required to search: name; also helpful-years to search. Civil cases indexed by defendant, plaintiff. Civil records on dockets and files from prior to 1960 to present, in boxes back to 1800s. **Criminal Records:** Access: Mail, in person. Both court and visitors may perform in person searches. No search fee. Required to search: name; also helpful-years to search, DOB, SSN. Criminal records on dockets and files from prior to 1960 to present, in boxes back to 1800s. **General Information:** No divorce, juvenile, mental hygiene, adoption records released. Turnaround time same day, unless in archives. Copy fee: $.50 per page. Certification fee: $.50. Fee payee: Brooke County Circuit Clerk. Personal checks accepted. Prepayment is required.

Magistrate Court 632 Main St, Wellsburg, WV 26070; 304-737-1321; Fax: 304-737-1509. Hours: 9AM-4PM (EST). *Misdemeanor, Civil Actions Under $5,000, Eviction, Small Claims.*

Civil Records: Court does not conduct in person searches; visitors must perform searches for themselves. Search fee:. **Criminal Records:** Court does not conduct in person searches; visitors must perform searches for themselves. Search fee: No criminal searches performed by court. Required to search: name; also helpful-DOB, SSN. **General Information:.** Fee payee: Magistrate Court Clerk. Prepayment is required.

Cabell County

Circuit Court PO Box 0545, Huntington, WV 25710-0545; 304-526-8622; Fax: 304-526-8699. Hours: 8:30AM-4:30PM (EST). *Felony, Civil Actions Over $5,000, Probate.*

Civil Records: Access: Mail, in person. Both court and visitors may perform in person searches. Search fee: $5.00 per name. Required to search: name, years to search. Civil cases indexed by defendant, plaintiff. Civil records on computer from 1990 to present. On index books back to 1854. **Criminal Records:** Access: In person only. Court does not conduct in person searches; visitors must perform searches for themselves. Search fee: No criminal searches performed by court. Required to search: name, years to search; also helpful-address, DOB, SSN. Criminal records on computer from 1990 to present. On index books back to 1854. Requests are directed to the state Criminal Investigation Bureau. **General Information:** No sealed, juvenile, adoptions, mental health, guardianship records released. SASE required. Turnaround time 1 day. Copy fee: $.50 per page. Certification fee: No certification fee. Fee payee: Clerk of Circuit Court. Business

checks accepted. Prepayment is required. Public access terminal is available.

Magistrate Court 750 5th Ave, Basement, Rm B 113 Courthouse, Huntington, WV 25701; 304-526-8642; Fax: 304-526-8646. Hours: 8:30AM-4:30PM (EST). *Misdemeanor, Civil Actions Under $5,000, Eviction, Small Claims.*

Civil Records: Court does not conduct in person searches; visitors must perform searches for themselves. Search fee:. **Criminal Records:** Court does not conduct in person searches; visitors must perform searches for themselves. Search fee: No criminal searches performed by court. Required to search: name. **General Information:.** Fee payee: Magistrate Court Clerk. Prepayment is required.

Calhoun County

Circuit Court PO Box 266, Grantsville, WV 26147; 304-354-6910; Fax: 304-354-6910. Hours: 8:30AM-4PM (EST). *Felony, Civil Actions Over $5,000, Probate.*

Civil Records: Access: Phone, fax, mail, in person. Both court and visitors may perform in person searches. No search fee. Required to search: name, years to search. Civil cases indexed by defendant, plaintiff. Civil records on index books from 1800s. **Criminal Records:** Access: Phone, fax, mail, in person. Both court and visitors may perform in person searches. No search fee. Required to search: name, years to search; also helpful-DOB, SSN. Criminal records on dockets from 1900s. **General Information:** No adoption, juvenile, divorce, domestic relations, guardianship/conservatorship records released. Turnaround time same day received. Copy fee: $.50 per page. Certification fee: $1.00. Fee payee: Circuit Clerk. Personal checks accepted. Fax notes: $3.00 for first page, $.50 each addl.

Magistrate Court PO Box 186, Grantsville, WV 26147; 304-354-6698; Fax: 304-354-6698. Hours: 8:30AM-4PM (EST). *Misdemeanor, Civil Actions Under $5,000, Eviction, Small Claims.*

Civil Records: Both court and visitors may perform in person searches. Search fee:. **Criminal Records:** Both court and visitors may perform in person searches. No search fee. Required to search: name; also helpful-years to search, DOB, SSN. **General Information:** Turnaround time 1 week. Fee payee: Magistrate Court. Prepayment is required.

Clay County

Circuit Court PO Box 129, Clay, WV 25043; 304-587-4256; Fax: 304-587-4346. Hours: 8AM-4PM (EST). *Felony, Civil Actions Over $5,000, Probate.*

Civil Records: Access: Phone, fax, mail, in person. Only the court conducts in person searches; visitors may not. No search fee. Required to search: name, years to search, address. Civil cases indexed by defendant, plaintiff. Civil records on docket books and index books back to 1962, microfilm back to 1858. **Criminal Records:** Access: Phone, fax, mail, in person. Only the court conducts in person searches; visitors may not. No search fee. Required to search: name, years to search, address, DOB, SSN. Criminal records on docket books and index books back to 1962, microfilm back to 1858. **General Information:** No juvenile, guardianship, conservatorship or mental health records released. SASE required. Turnaround time 3 days. Copy fee: $.50 per page. Certification fee: No certification fee. Fee payee: Clerk of the Circuit Court. Personal checks accepted. Prepayment is required. Fax notes: $2.00 per page.

Magistrate Court PO Box 393, Clay, WV 25043; 304-587-2131; Fax: 304-587-2727. Hours: 8:30AM-4:30PM (EST). *Misdemeanor, Civil Actions Under $5,000, Eviction, Small Claims.*

Civil Records: Both court and visitors may perform in person searches. Search fee:. **Criminal Records:** Both court and visitors may perform in person searches. No search fee. Required to search: name, offense; also helpful-years to search, DOB, SSN. **General Information:** Turnaround time 5 days. Fee payee: Clay County Magistrate. Prepayment is required.

Doddridge County

Circuit Court 118 E. Court St, West Union, WV 26456; 304-873-2331. Hours: 8:30AM-4PM (EST). *Felony, Civil Actions Over $5,000, Probate.*

Civil Records: Access: Phone, mail, in person. Both court and visitors may perform in person searches. No search fee. Required to search: name, years to search. Civil cases indexed by defendant, plaintiff. Civil records on index books 1960 to present, archived from 1845 to 1960. **Criminal Records:** Access: Phone, mail, in person. Both court and visitors may perform in person searches. No search fee. Required to search: name, years to search. Criminal records in index books and files from 1948. **General Information:** No juvenile, adoption, mental, domestic records released. SASE required. Turnaround time 1-5 days. Copy fee: $.50 per page. Certification fee: No certification fee. Fee payee: Clerk of Circuit Court. Personal checks accepted. Prepayment is required.

Magistrate Court PO Box 207, West Union, WV 26456; 304-873-2694; Fax: 304-873-2643. Hours: 8AM-4PM (EST). *Misdemeanor, Civil Actions Under $5,000, Eviction, Small Claims.*

Civil Records: Both court and visitors may perform in person searches. Search fee:. **Criminal Records:** Both court and visitors may perform in person searches. No search fee. Required to search: name, years to search; also helpful-offense. **General Information:** Turnaround time 5 days. Fee payee: Magistrate Court of Doddridge County. Prepayment is required.

Fayette County

Circuit Court 100 Court St, Fayetteville, WV 25840;; Civil phone:304-574-4249; Criminal phone:304-574-4249; Probate phone:304-574-4226. Hours: 8AM-4PM (EST). *Felony, Civil Actions Over $5,000, Probate.*

Note: Probate is handled by County Clerk, PO Box 569, Fayetteville, WV 25840

Civil Records: Access: Phone, mail, in person. Both court and visitors may perform in person searches. No search fee. Required to search: name; also helpful-years to search. Civil cases indexed by defendant, plaintiff. Civil records on computer since 1995; prior records on file 1850 to present. **Criminal Records:** Access: Mail, in person. Both court and visitors may perform in person searches. No search fee. Required to search: name, years to search; also helpful-DOB, SSN. Criminal records on computer since 1995; prior records on file 1850 to present. **General Information:** No divorce, adoption, mental, juvenile records released. SASE not required. Turnaround time 1 week. Copy fee: $.50 per page. Certification fee: $2.00. Fee payee: Circuit Clerk of Fayette County. Personal checks accepted. Prepayment is required.

Magistrate Court 100 Church St, Fayetteville, WV 25840; 304-574-4279; Fax: 304-574-2458. Hours: 9AM-9PM M-F, 9AM-Noon Sat (EST). *Misdemeanor, Civil Actions Under $5,000, Eviction, Small Claims.*

Civil Records: Court does not conduct in person searches; visitors must perform searches for themselves. Search fee:. **Criminal Records:** Court does not conduct in person searches; visitors must perform searches for themselves. Search fee: No criminal searches performed by court. Required to search: name, years to search. **General Information:** Turnaround time 1 week. Fee payee: Magistrate Court Clerk. Prepayment is required. Public access terminal is available.

Gilmer County

Circuit Court Gilmer County Courthouse, Glenville, WV 26351; 304-462-7241; Fax: 304-462-5134. Hours: 8AM-4PM (EST). *Felony, Civil Actions Over $5,000, Probate.*

Civil Records: Access: Phone, mail, in person. Both court and visitors may perform in person searches. No search fee. Required to search: name, years to search. Civil cases indexed by defendant, plaintiff. Civil records on dockets and files from 1845 to present. **Criminal Records:** Access: Phone, mail, in person. Both court and visitors may perform in person searches. No search fee. Required to search: name, years to search. Criminal records on dockets and files from 1845 to present. **General Information:** No juvenile, mental, confidential records released. SASE not required. Turnaround time 1 day. Copy fee: $.50 per page. Certification fee: No certification fee. Fee payee: Circuit Clerk. Personal checks accepted.

Magistrate Court Courthouse Annex, Glenville, WV 26351; 304-462-7812; Fax: 304-462-8582. Hours: 8:30AM-4PM (EST). *Misdemeanor, Civil Actions Under $5,000, Eviction, Small Claims.*

Civil Records: Both court and visitors may perform in person searches. Search fee:. **Criminal Records:** Both court and visitors may perform in person searches. No search fee. Required to search: name, years to search; also helpful-DOB, SSN. **General Information:** Turnaround time 1-5 days. Fee payee: Gilmer County Magistrate Court. Prepayment is required.

Grant County

Circuit Court 5 Highland Ave, Petersburg, WV 26847; 304-257-4545; Fax: 304-257-2593 (Attn: Circuit Court). Hours: 8:30AM-4:30PM (EST). *Felony, Civil Actions Over $5,000, Probate.*

Civil Records: Access: Phone, fax, mail, in person. Both court and visitors may perform in person searches. No search fee. Required to search: name, years to search; also helpful-address. Civil cases indexed by defendant, plaintiff. Civil records on index cards (current cases only), on index books back to 1866. **Criminal Records:** Access: Phone, fax, mail, in person. Both court and visitors may perform in person searches. No search fee. Required to search: name, years to search, DOB, SSN; also helpful-address. Criminal records on index cards (current cases only), on index books back to 1866. **General Information:** No juvenile, guardianship, adoptions, mental, domestic order records released. SASE required. Turnaround time 1-2 days. Copy fee: $.50 per page. Certification fee: $1.50. Fee payee: Circuit Clerk. Business checks accepted. In-state personal

checks accepted. Prepayment is required. Fax notes: $1.50 for first page, $.75 each addl.

Magistrate Court 5 Highland Ave (PO Box 216), Petersburg, WV 26847; 304-257-4637/1289; Fax: 304-257-9501. Hours: 8:30AM-4:30PM (EST). *Misdemeanor, Civil Actions Under $5,000, Eviction, Small Claims.*

Civil Records: Access: fax, mail. Only the court conducts in person searches; visitors may not. Search fee:. **Criminal Records:** Access: fax, mail. Only the court conducts in person searches; visitors may not. No search fee. Required to search: name, years to search. **General Information:** Turnaround time 1-2 days. Fee payee: Grant County Magistrate Court. Prepayment is required.

Greenbrier County

Circuit Court PO Drawer 751, Lewisburg, WV 24901; 304-647-6626; Fax: 304-647-6666. Hours: 8:30AM-4:30PM (EST). *Felony, Civil Actions Over $5,000, Probate.*

Civil Records: Access: Mail, in person. Both court and visitors may perform in person searches. Search fee: $5.00 per name. Required to search: name, years to search. Civil cases indexed by defendant, plaintiff. Civil records on index books back to 1933 (separated by plaintiff/defendant), on dockets back to 1933. **Criminal Records:** Access: Mail, in person. Both court and visitors may perform in person searches. Search fee: $5.00 per name. Required to search: name, years to search; also helpful-DOB, SSN. Criminal records indexed by general and docket books. **General Information:** No juvenile, adoptions, mental health records released. Turnaround time 1-2 days. Copy fee: $.50 per page. Certification fee: $1.00. Fee payee: Clerk of Circuit Court. Personal checks accepted.

Magistrate Court 200 North Court St, Lewisburg, WV 24901; 304-647-6632; Fax: 304-647-3612. Hours: 8:30AM-4:30PM (EST). *Misdemeanor, Civil Actions Under $5,000, Eviction, Small Claims.*

Civil Records: Both court and visitors may perform in person searches. Search fee:. **Criminal Records:** Both court and visitors may perform in person searches. No search fee. Required to search: name, years to search; also helpful-DOB, SSN. **General Information:** Turnaround time 1-2 days. Fee payee: Greenbrier County Magistrate Court. Prepayment is required.

Hampshire County

Circuit Court PO Box 343, Romney, WV 26757; 304-822-5022; Probate phone:304-822-5112. Hours: 9AM-4PM M-F 5PM-8PM Friday evening (EST). *Felony, Civil Actions Over $5,000, Probate.*

Note: Probate handled by County Clerk, PO Box 806, Romney, WV 26757

Civil Records: Access: Phone, mail, in person. Both court and visitors may perform in person searches. No search fee. Required to search: name, years to search. Civil cases indexed by defendant, plaintiff. Civil records on index files from 1957 to present, on index cards in storage 1885 to 1957. **Criminal Records:** Access: Phone, mail, in person. Both court and visitors may perform in person searches. No search fee. Required to search: name, years to search. Criminal records on index files from 1957 to present, on index cards in storage 1885 to 1957. **General Information:** No juvenile, divorce or adoption records released.

SASE required. Turnaround time 2 days. Copy fee: $.50 per page. Certification fee: $1.50. Fee payee: Clerk of Cicruit Court. Personal checks accepted. Will bill to attorneys.

Magistrate Court 239 W Birch Ln, PO Box 881, Romney, WV 26757; 304-822-4311; Fax: 304-822-3981. Hours: 8:30AM-4PM (EST). *Misdemeanor, Civil Actions Under $5,000, Eviction, Small Claims.*

Civil Records: Both court and visitors may perform in person searches. Search fee:. **Criminal Records:** Both court and visitors may perform in person searches. No search fee. Required to search: name, years to search; also helpful-DOB, SSN. **General Information:** Turnaround time 5 days. Fee payee: Magistrate Court Clerk. Prepayment is required.

Hancock County

Circuit Court PO Box 428, New Cumberland, WV 26047; 304-564-3311; Fax: 304-564-5014. Hours: 8:30AM-4:30PM (EST). *Felony, Civil Actions Over $5,000, Probate.*

Note: Probate can be reached at PO Box 367

Civil Records: Access: Fax, mail, in person. Both court and visitors may perform in person searches. Search fee: $5.00 per name. Required to search: name, years to search; also helpful-address. Civil cases indexed by defendant, plaintiff. Civil records on computer since 1972. **Criminal Records:** Access: Fax, mail, in person. Both court and visitors may perform in person searches. Search fee: $5.00 per name. Required to search: name, years to search, signed release; also helpful-address, DOB, SSN. Criminal records on computer since 1972. **General Information:** No adoption, juvenile, mental hygiene released. SASE required. Turnaround time same day. Copy fee: $.50 per page. Certification fee: $1.50. Fee payee: Clerk of Circuit Court. Personal checks accepted. Public access terminal is available. Fax notes: $2.00 per page.

Magistrate Court 106 Court St, New Cumberland, WV 26047; 304-564-3355; Fax: 304-564-3852. Hours: 8:30-4:30PM M-W, F; 8AM-9PM Th (EST). *Misdemeanor, Civil Actions Under $5,000, Eviction, Small Claims.*

Civil Records: Both court and visitors may perform in person searches. Search fee:. Phone, fax and mail access limited. **Criminal Records:** Both court and visitors may perform in person searches. No search fee. Required to search: name, years to search; also helpful-DOB, SSN. Phone, fax and mail access limited. **General Information:** Turnaround time 1-2 days. Fee payee: Hancock County Magistrate Court. Prepayment is required.

Hardy County

Circuit Court 204 Washington St, RM 237, Moorefield, WV 26836; 304-538-7869; Fax: 304-538-6197. Hours: 9AM-4PM (EST). *Felony, Civil Actions Over $5,000, Probate.*

Civil Records: Access: In person only. Both court and visitors may perform in person searches. No search fee. Required to search: name, years to search. Civil cases indexed by defendant, plaintiff. Civil records on docket books back to 1960 (chrono index in front of book). **Criminal Records:** Access: Phone, in person. Both court and visitors may perform in person searches. No search fee. Required to search: name, years to search, DOB; also helpful-SSN. Criminal records on docket books back to 1960 (chrono index in

front of book). **General Information:** No juvenile, mental, domestic records released. Copy fee: $.50 per page. Certification fee: $1.00. Fee payee: Clerk of Circuit Court. Personal checks accepted. Prepayment is required.

Magistrate Court 204 Washington St, Moorefield, WV 26836; 304-538-6836; Fax: 304-538-2072. Hours: 9AM-4PM (EST). *Misdemeanor, Civil Actions Under $5,000, Eviction, Small Claims.*

Civil Records: Both court and visitors may perform in person searches. Search fee:. **Criminal Records:** Both court and visitors may perform in person searches. No search fee. Required to search: name, years to search; also helpful-DOB, SSN. **General Information:** Turnaround time 1 week, 2 days if on computer. Fee payee: Hardy County Magistrate Court. Prepayment is required. Public access terminal is available.

Harrison County

Circuit Court 301 W. Main, Suite 301, Clarksburg, WV 26301-2967; 304-624-8640; Probate phone:304-624-8673; Fax: 304-624-8710. Hours: 8:30AM-4PM (EST). *Felony, Civil Actions Over $5,000, Probate.*

Note: Probate is handled by County Clerk, 301 W Main St, Courthouse, Clarksburg, WV 26301

Civil Records: Access: In person only. Court does not conduct in person searches; visitors must perform searches for themselves. Search fee: No civil searches performed by court. Required to search: name, years to search. Civil cases indexed by defendant, plaintiff. Civil records on computer from 1990 to present. On index books back to mid-1800s. **Criminal Records:** Access: In person only. Court does not conduct in person searches; visitors must perform searches for themselves. Search fee: No criminal searches performed by court. Required to search: name, years to search; also helpful-DOB, SSN. Criminal records on computer from 1990 to present. On index books back to mid-1800s. **General Information:** No adoption, juvenile, guardianship, mental health records released. Copy fee: $.50 per page. Certification fee: No certification fee. Fee payee: Harrison County Circuit Clerk. Only cashiers checks and money orders accepted. Prepayment is required. Public access terminal is available.

Magistrate Court 306 Washington Ave Rm 222, Clarksburg, WV 26301; 304-624-8645; Fax: 304-624-8740. Hours: 8AM-4PM (EST). *Misdemeanor, Civil Actions Under $5,000, Eviction, Small Claims.*

Civil Records: Both court and visitors may perform in person searches. Search fee:. **Criminal Records:** Both court and visitors may perform in person searches. No search fee. Required to search: name, years to search; also helpful-DOB, SSN. **General Information:** Turnaround time 5 days. Fee payee: Magistrate Court of Harrison County. Prepayment is required.

Jackson County

Circuit Court PO Box 427, Ripley, WV 25271; 304-372-2011 X329; Fax: 304-372-6205. Hours: 9AM-4PM M-F, 9AM-Noon Sat (EST). *Felony, Civil Actions Over $5,000, Probate.*

Civil Records: Access: Phone, mail, in person. Both court and visitors may perform in person searches. No search fee. Required to search: name, years to search. Civil cases indexed by defendant, plaintiff. Civil records on index books back to 1800s. **Criminal Records:** Access: Phone, mail,

in person. Both court and visitors may perform in person searches. No search fee. Required to search: name, years to search; also helpful-DOB, SSN. Criminal records on index books back to 1800s. **General Information:** No juvenile, mental, adoption, domestic records released. SASE required. Turnaround time 1-2 days. Copy fee: $.50 per page. Certification fee: $.50. Fee payee: Clerk of Circuit Court. Only cashiers checks and money orders accepted. Prepayment is required.

Magistrate Court PO Box 368, Ripley, WV 25271; 304-372-2011; Fax: 304-372-7132. Hours: 9AM-4PM (EST). *Misdemeanor, Civil Actions Under $5,000, Eviction, Small Claims.*

Civil Records: Court does not conduct in person searches; visitors must perform searches for themselves. Search fee:. **Criminal Records:** Court does not conduct in person searches; visitors must perform searches for themselves. No search fee. Required to search: name, years to search; also helpful-DOB, SSN.

Jefferson County

Circuit Court PO Box 584, Charles Town, WV 25414; 304-728-3231; Fax: 304-728-3398. Hours: 9AM-5PM (EST). *Felony, Civil Actions Over $5,000.*

Civil Records: Access: In person only. Court does not conduct in person searches; visitors must perform searches for themselves. Search fee: No civil searches performed by court. Required to search: name, years to search. Civil cases indexed by defendant, plaintiff. Civil records on computer from 01/85 to present. On index books 1960 to 1985. On dockets back 1960 back to 1800s in storage. **Criminal Records:** Access: In person only. Court does not conduct in person searches; visitors must perform searches for themselves. Search fee: No criminal searches performed by court. Required to search: name, years to search. Criminal records on computer from 01/85 to present. On index books 1960 to 1985. On dockets back 1960 back to 1800s in storage. **General Information:** No juvenile, mental health records released. Copy fee: $.50 per page. Certification fee: $.50. Fee payee: Circuit Clerk. Personal checks accepted. Prepayment is required. Public access terminal is available.

Magistrate Court PO Box 607, Charles Town, WV 25414; 304-728-3233; Fax: 304-728-3235. Hours: 7:30AM-4:30PM (EST). *Misdemeanor, Civil Actions Under $5,000, Eviction, Small Claims.*

Civil Records: Both court and visitors may perform in person searches. Search fee:. **Criminal Records:** Both court and visitors may perform in person searches. No search fee. Required to search: name; also helpful-years to search, DOB, SSN. **General Information:** Turnaround time 5 days. Fee payee: Magistrate Clerk. Prepayment is required.

Kanawha County

Circuit Court PO Box 2351, Charleston, WV 25328; 304-357-0440; Probate phone:304-357-0130; Fax: 304-357-0473. Hours: 8AM-5PM (EST). *Felony, Civil Actions Over $5,000, Probate.*

Note: Probate is handled by County Clerk, 409 Virginia St East, Charleston, WV 25301

Civil Records: Access: In person only. Court does not conduct in person searches; visitors must perform searches for themselves. Search fee: No civil searches performed by court. Required to

search: name, years to search; also helpful-address. Civil cases indexed by defendant, plaintiff. Civil records on computer from 7/1989 to present. On microfiche back to 1800s. **Criminal Records:** Access: In person only. Court does not conduct in person searches; visitors must perform searches for themselves. Search fee: No criminal searches performed by court. Required to search: name, years to search; also helpful-address, DOB, SSN. Criminal records on computer from 7/1989 to present. On microfiche back to 1800s. **General Information:** No juvenile, neglect, adoption, domestic, guardianship, mental health or conservatorship records released. Copy fee: $.50 per page. Certification fee: No certification fee. Fee payee: Kanawha Circuit Clerk. Business checks accepted. Prepayment is required. Public access terminal is available.

Magistrate Court 111 Court St, Charleston, WV 25333; 304-357-0400; Fax: 304-357-0205. Hours: 8:30AM-4:30PM (EST). *Misdemeanor, Civil Actions Under $5,000, Eviction, Small Claims.*

Civil Records: Both court and visitors may perform in person searches. Search fee:. **Criminal Records:** Both court and visitors may perform in person searches. No search fee. Required to search: name, years to search; also helpful-DOB, SSN. **General Information:** Turnaround time 14 days. Fee payee: Kanawha County Magistrate Court. Prepayment is required.

Lewis County

Circuit Court PO Box 69, Weston, WV 26452; 304-269-8210; Fax: 304-269-8249. Hours: 8:30AM-4:30PM (EST). *Felony, Civil Actions Over $5,000, Probate.*

Civil Records: Access: Phone, fax, mail, in person. Only the court conducts in person searches; visitors may not. No search fee. Required to search: name, years to search. Civil cases indexed by defendant, plaintiff. Civil records on index books 1977 to 1992. No index for chancery books back to 1800s. All active 1992 forward on computer. **Criminal Records:** Access: Phone, fax, mail, in person. Only the court conducts in person searches; visitors may not. No search fee. Required to search: name, years to search; also helpful-SSN. Criminal records on index books 1977 to 1992. No index for chancery books back to 1800s. All active 1992 forward on computer. **General Information:** No adoption, juvenile, domestic records released. SASE not required. Turnaround time 2 days. Copy fee: $.50 per page. Certification fee: $.50. Fee payee: Clerk of Circuit Court. Business checks accepted. Fax notes: $2.00 per page.

Magistrate Court 111 Court St, PO Box 260, Weston, WV 26452; 304-269-8230; Fax: 304-269-8253. Hours: 8:30AM-Noon, 1-4:30PM (EST). *Misdemeanor, Civil Actions Under $5,000, Eviction, Small Claims.*

Civil Records: Both court and visitors may perform in person searches. Search fee:. **Criminal Records:** Both court and visitors may perform in person searches. No search fee. Required to search: name, years to search; also helpful-DOB, SSN. **General Information:** Turnaround time 5 days. Fee payee: Magistrate Court.

Lincoln County

Circuit Court PO Box 338, Hamlin, WV 25523; 304-824-7887; Fax: 304-824-7909. Hours: 9AM-4:30PM (EST). *Felony, Civil Actions Over $5,000, Probate.*

Civil Records: Access: Phone, mail, in person. Both court and visitors may perform in person searches. No search fee. Required to search: name, years to search. Civil cases indexed by defendant, plaintiff. Civil records computerized since 1991, on index books 1971 to present, on docket books back to 1909. **Criminal Records:** Access: Phone, mail, in person. Both court and visitors may perform in person searches. No search fee. Required to search: name, years to search, DOB, SSN; also helpful-address. Criminal records computerized since 1991, on index books 1971 to present, on docket books back to 1909. **General Information:** No juvenile, adoption, divorce or mental hygiene records released. SASE not required. Turnaround time immediate to next day. Copy fee: $.50 per page. Certification fee: No certification fee. Fee payee: Clerk of Circuit Court. Personal checks accepted. Prepayment is required. Public access terminal is available.

Magistrate Court PO Box 573, Hamlin, WV 25523; 304-824-5001 x235; Fax: 304-824-5280. Hours: 9AM-4PM (EST). *Misdemeanor, Civil Actions Under $5,000, Eviction, Small Claims.*

Note: Searches performed by court only on second and fourth Thursday of each month

Civil Records: Only the court conducts in person searches; visitors may not. Search fee:. **Criminal Records:** Only the court conducts in person searches; visitors may not. No search fee. Required to search: name, years to search; also helpful-DOB, SSN. **General Information:** Turnaround time 1-14 days. Fee payee: Magistrate Court.

Logan County

Circuit Court Logan County Courthouse, Rm 311, Logan, WV 25601; 304-792-8550; Fax: 304-792-8555. Hours: 8:30AM-4:30PM (EST). *Felony, Civil Actions Over $5,000, Probate.*

Civil Records: Access: Mail, in person. Both court and visitors may perform in person searches. No search fee. Required to search: name, years to search. Civil cases indexed by defendant, plaintiff. Civil records on index books back to 1800s, on computer from 1995. **Criminal Records:** Access: Mail, in person. Both court and visitors may perform in person searches. No search fee. Required to search: name, years to search. Criminal records on index books back to 1800s, on computer from 1995. **General Information:** No adoptions, juvenile, domestic records released. SASE not required. Turnaround time 1-2 days. Copy fee: $.50 per page. Certification fee: $1.50 plus $.50 per page after first 2. Fee payee: Clerk of Circuit Court. Only cashiers checks and money orders accepted. Will bill to attorneys.

Magistrate Court Logan County Courthouse, 300 Stratton St, Logan, WV 25601; 304-792-8651; Fax: 304-752-0790. Hours: 8:30AM-Noon; 1-4:30PM (EST). *Misdemeanor, Civil Actions Under $5,000, Eviction, Small Claims.*

Civil Records: Both court and visitors may perform in person searches. Search fee:. **Criminal Records:** Both court and visitors may perform in person searches. No search fee. Required to search: name, years to search; also helpful-address, DOB, SSN. **General Information:** Turnaround time 5 days. Fee payee: Magistrate Court.

Marion County

Circuit Court PO Box 1269, Fairmont, WV 26554; 304-367-5360; Fax: 304-367-5374. Hours: 8:30AM-4:30PM (EST). *Felony, Civil Actions Over $3,000.*

Civil Records: Access: Phone, fax, mail, in person. Both court and visitors may perform in person searches. No search fee. Required to search: name, years to search. Civil cases indexed by defendant, plaintiff. Civil records on computer from Jan. 1988 to present. On docket books from 1849 to 1988. **Criminal Records:** Access: In person only. Court does not conduct in person searches; visitors must perform searches for themselves. Search fee: No criminal searches performed by court. Required to search: name, years to search; also helpful-DOB, SSN. Criminal records on computer from Jan. 1988 to present. On docket books from 1849 to 1988. The court refers all written requests to the Dept of Public Safety. **General Information:** No adoptions, juvenile, mental or guardianship records released. SASE not required. Turnaround time 2-3 days. Copy fee: $.50 per page. Certification fee: $.50. Fee payee: Clerk of Circuit Court. Business checks accepted. Prepayment is required. Public access terminal is available. Fax notes: $5.00 for first page, $2.00 each addl. Fax fee: After 10 pages fee is $1.00 per page.

Magistrate Court 200 Jackson St, Fairmont, WV 26554; 304-367-5330; Fax: 304-367-5337. Hours: 8:30AM-4:30PM M-W, F; 8:30AM-9PM Th (EST). *Misdemeanor, Civil Actions Under $5,000, Eviction, Small Claims.*

Civil Records: Only the court conducts in person searches; visitors may not. Search fee:. **Criminal Records:** Only the court conducts in person searches; visitors may not. No search fee. Required to search: name, years to search; also helpful-DOB, SSN. **General Information:** Turnaround time 5-15 days, ASAP for phone requests, time permitting. Copy fee: $.25 per copy. Fee payee: Marion County Magistrate Clerk. Prepayment is required.

Marshall County

Circuit Court Marshall County Courthouse, 7th St, Moundsville, WV 26041; 304-845-2130; Fax: 304-845-3948. Hours: 8:30AM-4:30PM M-Th; 8:30AM-5:30PM F (EST). *Felony, Civil Actions Over $5,000, Probate.*

Civil Records: Access: Fax, mail, in person. Both court and visitors may perform in person searches. No search fee. Required to search: name, years to search. Civil cases indexed by defendant, plaintiff. Civil records on computer since 01/98; prior records on index books and in files from 1836 to present. **Criminal Records:** Access: Fax, mail, in person. Both court and visitors may perform in person searches. No search fee. Required to search: name, years to search; also helpful-DOB, SSN. Criminal records on computer since 01/98; prior records on index books and in files from 1836 to present. **General Information:** No juvenile, mental, adoption, sealed, conservatorship, guardianship or divorce records released. SASE not required. Turnaround time 1-2 days. Copy fee: $.25 per page. Certification fee: $1.00. Fee payee: Clerk of Circuit Court. Personal checks accepted. Will bill to attorneys. Fax notes: $.50 per page.

Mason County

Circuit Court Mason County Courthouse, Point Pleasant, WV 25550; 304-675-4400; Fax: 304-675-7419. Hours: 8:30AM-4:30PM (EST). *Felony, Civil Actions Over $5,000, Probate.*

Civil Records: Access: Phone, fax, mail, in person. Both court and visitors may perform in person searches. No search fee. Required to search: name, years to search. Civil cases indexed by defendant, plaintiff. Civil records on computer. No time limit on open cases. Index books with data back to 1800s. **Criminal Records:** Access: In person only. Court does not conduct in person searches; visitors must perform searches for themselves. Search fee: No criminal searches performed by court. Required to search: name, years to search. Criminal records on computer. No time limit on open cases. Index books with data back to 1800s. **General Information:** No divorce or juvenile records released. SASE not required. Turnaround time 1-2 days. Copy fee: $.50 per page. Certification fee: No certification fee. Fee payee: Circuit Court Clerk. Personal checks accepted. Will bill mail requests.

Magistrate Court Corner of 6th St and Viand, Point Pleasant, WV 25550; 304-675-6840; Fax: 304-675-5949. Hours: 8:30AM-4:30PM (EST). *Misdemeanor, Civil Actions Under $5,000, Eviction, Small Claims.*

Civil Records: Both court and visitors may perform in person searches. Search fee:. **Criminal Records:** Both court and visitors may perform in person searches. No search fee. Required to search: name, years to search. **General Information:** Turnaround time 3-4 days. Fee payee: Mason County Magistrate Court. Prepayment is required.

McDowell County

Circuit Court PO Box 400, Welch, WV 24801; 304-436-8535; Probate phone:304-436-8544. Hours: 9AM-5PM (EST). *Felony, Civil Actions Over $5,000, Probate.*

Note: Probate is handled by Coutny Clerk, 90 Wyoming St, Ste 109, Welch, WV 24801

Civil Records: Access: Mail, in person. Both court and visitors may perform in person searches. No search fee. Required to search: name, years to search. Civil cases indexed by defendant, plaintiff. Civil records on index books back to 1800s. **Criminal Records:** Access: Mail, in person. Both court and visitors may perform in person searches. No search fee. Required to search: name, years to search; also helpful-DOB, SSN. Criminal records on index books back to 1800s. **General Information:** No sealed, juvenile, adoption, mental health, guardianship records released. SASE required. Turnaround time 1 week. Copy fee: $.50 per page. Certification fee: No certification fee. Fee payee: Clerk of Circuit Court. Business checks accepted. Prepayment is required.

Magistrate Court PO Box 447, Welch, WV 24801; 304-436-8587; Fax: 304-436-8575. Hours: 9AM-5PM (EST). *Misdemeanor, Civil Actions Under $5,000, Eviction, Small Claims.*

Civil Records: Court does not conduct in person searches; visitors must perform searches for themselves. Search fee:. **Criminal Records:** Both court and visitors may perform in person searches. No search fee. Required to search: name, years to search; also helpful-DOB, SSN. **General Information:** Turnaround time 5 days. Fee payee: McDowell County Magistrate Court. Prepayment is required.

Mercer County

Circuit Court 1501 W. Main St, Princeton, WV 24740; 304-487-8369; Fax: 304-425-1598. Hours: 8:30AM-4:30PM (EST). *Felony, Civil Actions Over $5,000, Probate.*

Civil Records: Access: Phone, fax, mail, in person. Both court and visitors may perform in person searches. No search fee. Required to search: name, years to search. Civil cases indexed by defendant, plaintiff. Civil records on computer from Oct. 1989 to present. On index books from 1930 to 1989 (Cott System). On index cards back to 1890s. **Criminal Records:** Access: Phone, fax, mail, in person. Both court and visitors may perform in person searches. No search fee. Required to search: name, years to search; also helpful-DOB, SSN. Criminal records on computer from Oct. 1989 to present. On index books from 1930 to 1989 (Cott System). On index cards back to 1890s. **General Information:** No juvenile, adoption, mental health, guardianship or conservatorship records released. Turnaround time 1-2 days. Copy fee: $.50 per page. Certification fee: $.50. Fee payee: Circuit Court Clerk. Business checks accepted. Fax notes: $2.00 per page.

Magistrate Court 120 Scott Street, Princeton, WV 24740; 304-425-7952. Hours: 8:30AM-4:30PM (EST). *Misdemeanor, Civil Actions Under $5,000, Eviction, Small Claims.*

Civil Records: Court does not conduct in person searches; visitors must perform searches for themselves. Search fee:. **Criminal Records:** Court does not conduct in person searches; visitors must perform searches for themselves. Search fee: No criminal searches performed by court. Required to search: name, years to search; also helpful-address, DOB, SSN. **General Information:.** Fee payee: Mercer County Magistrate Court. Prepayment is required.

Mineral County

Circuit Court 150 Armstrong St, Keyser, WV 26726; 304-788-1562; Fax: 304-788-4109. Hours: 8:30AM-5PM (EST). *Felony, Civil Actions Over $5,000, Probate.*

Civil Records: Access: Fax, mail, in person. Both court and visitors may perform in person searches. Search fee: $5.00 per name. Required to search: name, years to search. Civil cases indexed by defendant, plaintiff. Civil records on computer January 1991 to present, on dockets from 1920s. Fax access not guaranteed. **Criminal Records:** Access: Fax, mail, in person. Both court and visitors may perform in person searches. Search fee: $5.00 per name. Required to search: name, years to search; also helpful-DOB, SSN. Criminal records on computer January 1991 to present, on dockets from 1920s. Fax access not guaranteed. **General Information:** No juvenile, adoption, divorce, mental hygiene, conservatorship or guardianship records released. SASE requested. Turnaround time 2-4 days. Copy fee: $.50 per page. Certification fee: No certification fee. Fee payee: Clerk of Circuit Court. Personal checks accepted. Fax notes: No fee to fax results.

Magistrate Court 105 West St, Keyser, WV 26726; 304-788-2625; Fax: 304-788-9835. Hours: 8:30AM-4:30PM (EST). *Misdemeanor, Civil Actions Under $5,000, Eviction, Small Claims.*

Civil Records: Both court and visitors may perform in person searches. Search fee:. **Criminal Records:** Both court and visitors may perform in person searches. No search fee. Required to search: name, years to search; also helpful-DOB,

SSN. **General Information:** Turnaround time 5 days. Fee payee: Magistrate Court. Prepayment is required.

Mingo County

Circuit Court PO Box 435, Williamson, WV 25661; 304-235-0320; Probate phone:304-235-0330. Hours: 8:30AM-4:30PM M-W,F, 8:30AM-6:30PM Th (EST). *Felony, Civil Actions Over $5,000, Probate.*

Note: Probate is handled by County Clerk, 75 E 2nd Ave, Williamson, WV 25661

Civil Records: Access: Mail, in person. Only the court conducts in person searches; visitors may not. Search fee: $10.00 per name. Required to search: name, years to search. Civil cases indexed by defendant, plaintiff. Civil records on computer from 1/1991 to present, civil on index books back to 1960, chancery books back to 1800s (written or in person only). **Criminal Records:** Access: Mail, in person. Only the court conducts in person searches; visitors may not. Search fee: $10.00 per name. Required to search: name, years to search; also helpful-DOB. Criminal records on computer since 1/91, Index books back to 1955. **General Information:** No adoption, mental hygene, juvenile records released. Turnaround time 1-2 days. Copy fee: $.50 per page. Certification fee: $2.00. Fee payee: Mingo County Circuit Clerk. Personal checks accepted. Prepayment is required. Public access terminal is available.

Magistrate Court PO Box 986, Williamson, WV 25661; 304-235-2445; Fax: 304-235-3179. Hours: 8:30AM-4:30PM (EST). *Misdemeanor, Civil Actions Under $5,000, Eviction, Small Claims.*

Civil Records: Access: Phone, mail, in person. Both court and visitors may perform in person searches. Search fee: No search fee. Required to search: name, years to search; also helpful-DOB. **Criminal Records:** Access: Phone, mail, in person. Both court and visitors may perform in person searches. No search fee. Required to search: name, years to search; also helpful-DOB, SSN. **General Information:** Turnaround time 1 week, sooner for phone requests. Copy fee: $.25 per page. Certification fee: $.50 per page. Fee payee: Magistrate Court. Fax notes: Fee to fax is $2.00 per page.

Monongalia County

Circuit Court County Courthouse, 243 High St Rm 110, Morgantown, WV 26505; 304-291-7240; Probate phone:304-291-7230; Fax: 304-291-7273. Hours: 9AM-7PM M; 9AM-5PM T-F (EST). *Felony, Civil Actions Over $5,000, Probate.*

Note: A disclaimer for the Clerk must be included by mail requesters. Probate is handled by County Clerk, 243 High St, Room 123, Morgantown, WV 26505

Civil Records: Access: Mail, in person. Both court and visitors may perform in person searches. Search fee: $5.00 per name. Required to search: name, years to search. Civil cases indexed by defendant, plaintiff. Civil records on computer from 1/90 to present, on index book separated by plaintiff and defendant back to 1865. **Criminal Records:** Access: Mail, in person. Both court and visitors may perform in person searches. Search fee: $5.00 per name. Required to search: name, years to search; also helpful-DOB, SSN. Criminal records on computer from 1/90 to present, on index book separated by plaintiff and defendant back to 1865. **General Information:** No juvenile, divorce, mental hygienie, divorce, adoption, guardianship, conservatorship or domestic records released. SASE required. Turnaround time 1 day. Copy fee: $.50 per page. Certification fee: No certification fee. Fee payee: Circuit Clerk. Business checks accepted. Prepayment is required.

Magistrate Court 265 Spruce St, Morgantown, WV 26505; 304-291-7296; Fax: 304-284-7313. Hours: 8AM-7PM (EST). *Misdemeanor, Civil Actions Under $5,000, Eviction, Small Claims.*

Civil Records: Both court and visitors may perform in person searches. Search fee:. **Criminal Records:** Both court and visitors may perform in person searches. No search fee. Required to search: name, years to search; also helpful-DOB, SSN. **General Information:** Turnaround time 10-14 days. Fee payee: Magistrate Court. Prepayment is required.

Monroe County

Circuit Court PO Box 350, Union, WV 24983-0350; 304-772-4087; Fax: 304-772-5051. Hours: 8AM-4PM (EST). *Felony, Civil Actions Over $5,000.*

Civil Records: Access: Phone, mail, in person. Both court and visitors may perform in person searches. No search fee. Required to search: name, years to search. Civil cases indexed by defendant, plaintiff. Civil records on index books 1799 to present. **Criminal Records:** Access: Phone, mail, in person. Both court and visitors may perform in person searches. No search fee. Required to search: name, years to search; also helpful-DOB, SSN. Criminal records on index books 1799 to present. **General Information:** No juvenile, adoption, divorce records released. SASE requested. Turnaround time 1 week. Copy fee: $.50 per page. Include postage with copy fee. Certification fee: $1.00. Fee payee: Clerk of Circuit Court. Personal checks accepted. Prepayment is required.

Magistrate Court PO Box 4, Union, WV 24983; 304-772-3321/3176; Fax: 304-772-4357. Hours: 8:30AM-4:30PM (EST). *Misdemeanor, Civil Actions Under $5,000, Eviction, Small Claims.*

Civil Records: Both court and visitors may perform in person searches. Search fee:. **Criminal Records:** Both court and visitors may perform in person searches. No search fee. Required to search: name, years to search; also helpful-DOB, SSN. **General Information:** Turnaround time 1-2 days. Fee payee: Monroe County Magistrate Court. Prepayment is required. Fax notes: $2.00.

Morgan County

Circuit Court 202 Fairfax St, Ste 101, Berkeley Springs, WV 25411-1501; 304-258-8554; Fax: 304-258-8557. Hours: 9AM-5PM MTTh, 9AM-1PM Wed, 9AM-7PM Fri (EST). *Felony, Civil Actions Over $5,000, Probate.*

Civil Records: Access: In person only. Court does not conduct in person searches; visitors must perform searches for themselves. Search fee: No civil searches performed by court. Required to search: name, years to search. Civil cases indexed by defendant, plaintiff. Civil records on computer since 1/93, index cards from 1960 to present, in person searching only on index books back to 1800s. **Criminal Records:** Access: In person only. Court does not conduct in person searches; visitors must perform searches for themselves. Search fee: No criminal searches performed by court. Required to search: name, years to search. Criminal records on computer since 1/93, index

cards from 1960 to present, in person searching only on index books back to 1800s. **General Information:** No juvenile, adoption, mental health, divorce records released. Copy fee: $.50 per page. Certification fee: No certification fee. Fee payee: Betty R Moss-Miller, Circuit Clerk. Only cashiers checks and money orders accepted. Will bill to attorneys.

Magistrate Court 202 Fairfax St, Berkeley Springs, WV 25411; 304-258-8631; Fax: 304-258-8639. Hours: 9AM-4:30PM (EST). *Misdemeanor, Civil Actions Under $5,000, Eviction, Small Claims.*

Civil Records: Court does not conduct in person searches; visitors must perform searches for themselves. Search fee:. **Criminal Records:** Court does not conduct in person searches; visitors must perform searches for themselves. Search fee: No criminal searches performed by court. Required to search: name, years to search; also helpful-DOB, SSN. Phone, fax and mail access limited. **General Information:**. Fee payee: Magistrate Court of Morgan County. Prepayment is required.

Nicholas County

Circuit Court 700 Main St, Summersville, WV 26651; 304-872-7810; Probate phone:304-872-7820. Hours: 8:30AM-4:30PM (EST). *Felony, Civil Actions Over $5,000, Probate.*

Note: Probate is handled by County Clerk, 700 Main St, Ste 2, Summersville, WV 26651

Civil Records: Access: Mail, in person. Both court and visitors may perform in person searches. No search fee. Required to search: name, years to search. Civil cases indexed by defendant, plaintiff. Civil records on computer since 1994; prior records on index cards from 1976 to 1994 on dockets back to 1818. **Criminal Records:** Access: Mail, in person. Both court and visitors may perform in person searches. No search fee. Required to search: name, years to search; also helpful-DOB, SSN. Criminal records on computer since 1994; prior records on index cards from 1976 to 1994 on dockets back to 1818. **General Information:** No divorce, juvenile, adoption, mental, guardianship records released. SASE required. Turnaround time 1 week. Copy fee: $.50 per page. Certification fee: No certification fee. Fee payee: Circuit Clerk. Personal checks accepted. Public access terminal is available.

Magistrate Court 511 Church St, Suite 206 2nd Flr, Summersville, WV 26651; 304-872-7829; Fax: 304-872-7888. Hours: 8:30AM-4:30PM (EST). *Misdemeanor, Civil Actions Under $5,000, Eviction, Small Claims.*

Civil Records: Access: Mail. Court does not conduct in person searches; visitors must perform searches for themselves. Search fee:. **Criminal Records:** Access: Mail. Court does not conduct in person searches; visitors must perform searches for themselves. Search fee: No criminal searches performed by court. Required to search: name, years to search; also helpful-DOB, SSN. **General Information:**. Fee payee: Magistrate Court. Public access terminal is available.

Ohio County

Circuit Court 1500 Chapline St, City & County Bldg Rm 403, Wheeling, WV 26003; 304-234-3613; Fax: 304-232-0550. Hours: 8:30AM-5PM (EST). *Felony, Civil Actions Over $5,000, Probate.*

Civil Records: Access: Fax, mail, in person. Both court and visitors may perform in person searches.

Search fee: $5.00 per name. Required to search: name, years to search. Civil cases indexed by defendant, plaintiff. Civil records on computer from Oct 1986 to present, on index books back to 1800s. **Criminal Records:** Access: Fax, mail, in person. Both court and visitors may perform in person searches. Search fee: $5.00 per name. Required to search: name, years to search; also helpful-DOB, SSN. Criminal records on computer from Oct 1986 to present, on index books back to 1800s. **General Information:** No domestic, juvenile, mental, adoption records released. SASE required. Turnaround time 1 week for accounts only. Copy fee: $.50 per page. Certification fee: $1.50. Fee payee: Ohio County Circuit Court. Business checks accepted. Prepayment is required. Public access terminal is available. Fax notes: Fee to fax is $2.00 per page.

Magistrate Court Courthouse Annex, 26 15th St, Wheeling, WV 26003; 304-234-3709; Fax: 304-234-3898. Hours: 8:30AM-4:30PM (EST). *Misdemeanor, Civil Actions Under $5,000, Eviction, Small Claims.*

Civil Records: Both court and visitors may perform in person searches. Search fee:. Phone, fax and mail access limited. **Criminal Records:** Both court and visitors may perform in person searches. No search fee. Required to search: name, years to search; also helpful-DOB, SSN. Phone, fax and mail access limited. **General Information:** Turnaround time 1 week. Fee payee: Ohio County Magistrate Court. Prepayment is required.

Pendleton County

Circuit Court PO Box 846, Franklin, WV 26807; 304-358-7067; Fax: 304-358-2152. Hours: 8:30AM-4PM (EST). *Felony, Civil Actions Over $5,000, Probate.*

Civil Records: Access: Phone, fax, mail, in person. Both court and visitors may perform in person searches. No search fee. Required to search: name, years to search. Civil cases indexed by defendant, plaintiff. Civil records on index books back to 1800s. **Criminal Records:** Access: Phone, fax, mail, in person. Both court and visitors may perform in person searches. No search fee. Required to search: name, years to search; also helpful-DOB, SSN. Criminal records on index books back to 1800s. **General Information:** No juvenile, divorce records released. SASE required. Turnaround time 2-3 days. Copy fee: $.50 per page. Certification fee: No certification fee. Fee payee: Pendleton County Circuit Clerk. Personal checks accepted. Local checks accepted. Fax notes: $2.00 per page.

Magistrate Court PO Box 637, Franklin, WV 26807; 304-358-2343; Fax: 304-358-3870. Hours: 8:30AM-4PM (EST). *Misdemeanor, Civil Actions Under $5,000, Eviction, Small Claims.*

Civil Records: Both court and visitors may perform in person searches. Search fee:. **Criminal Records:** Both court and visitors may perform in person searches. No search fee. Required to search: name, years to search. **General Information:** Turnaround time 3-5 days, will tell phone requesters if request is from 1994-present. Fee payee: Magistrate Court. Prepayment is required.

Pleasants County

Circuit Court 301 Court Lane, Rm 201, St. Mary's, WV 26170; 304-684-3513; Probate phone:304-684-3542; Fax: 304-684-3514. Hours:

Licenses Searchable Online

Accountant #01	http://165.189.238.43/plsql/plsql/Search_Ind_Bdp
Accounting Firm #02	http://165.189.238.43/plsql/plsql/Search_Ent_Bdp
Acupuncturist #04	http://165.189.238.43/plsql/plsql/Search_Ind_Health
Adjustment Service Company #06	www.wdfi.org/fi/lfs/licensee_lists
Aesthetics Establishment #02	http://165.189.238.43/plsql/plsql/Search_Ent_Bdp
Aesthetics Instructor #01	http://165.189.238.43/plsql/plsql/Search_Ind_Bdp
Aesthetics Specialty School #02	http://165.189.238.43/plsql/plsql/Search_Ind_Bdp
Architect #01	http://165.189.238.43/plsql/plsql/Search_Ind_Bdp
Architecural Corp #02	http://165.189.238.43/plsql/plsql/Search_Ent_Bdp
Art Therapist #04	http://165.189.238.43/plsql/plsql/Search_Ind_Health
Auction Company #02	http://165.189.238.43/plsql/plsql/Search_Ent_Bdp
Auctioneer #01	http://165.189.238.43/plsql/plsql/Search_Ind_Bdp
Audiologist #04	http://165.189.238.43/plsql/plsql/Search_Ind_Health
Bank #05	www.wdfi.org/fi/banks/scbanks.htm
Barber #01	http://165.189.238.43/plsql/plsql/Search_Ind_Bdp
Barber/Cosmetology Apprentice #01	http://165.189.238.43/plsql/plsql/Search_Ind_Bdp
Barber/Cosmetology Instructor #01	http://165.189.238.43/plsql/plsql/Search_Ind_Bdp
Barber/Cosmetology Manager #01	http://165.189.238.43/plsql/plsql/Search_Ind_Bdp
Barbering School #02	http://165.189.238.43/plsql/plsql/Search_Ent_Bdp
Boxer #01	http://165.189.238.43/plsql/plsql/Search_Ind_Bdp
Boxing Club (Amateur or Professional) #02	http://165.189.238.43/plsql/plsql/Search_Ent_Bdp
Boxing Show Permit #02	http://165.189.238.43/plsql/plsql/Search_Ent_Bdp
Cemetery Authority #02	http://165.189.238.43/plsql/plsql/Search_Ent_Bdp
Cemetery Preneed Seller #01	http://165.189.238.43/plsql/plsql/Search_Ind_Bdp
Cemetery Salesperson #01	http://165.189.238.43/plsql/plsql/Search_Ind_Bdp
Cemetery Warehouse #02	http://165.189.238.43/plsql/plsql/Search_Ent_Bdp
Charitable Organization #02	http://165.189.238.43/plsql/plsql/Search_Ent_Bdp
Chiropractor #04	http://165.189.238.43/plsql/plsql/Search_Ind_Health
Collection Agency #06	www.wdfi.org/fi/lfs/licensee_lists
Cosmetologist #01	http://165.189.238.43/plsql/plsql/Search_Ind_Bdp
Cosmetology School #02	http://165.189.238.43/plsql/plsql/Search_Ent_Bdp
Credit Service Organization #05	www.wdfi.org/fi/cu/cu.htm
Credit Union #05	www.wdfi.org/fi/cu/cu.htm
Currency Exchange #06	www.wdfi.org/fi/lfs/licensee_lists
Dance Therapist #04	http://165.189.238.43/plsql/plsql/Search_Ind_Health
Debt Collector #06	www.wdfi.org/fi/lfs/licensee_lists
Dental Hygienist #04	http://165.189.238.43/plsql/plsql/Search_Ind_Health
Dentist #04	http://165.189.238.43/plsql/plsql/Search_Ind_Health
Designer of Engineering Systems #01	http://165.189.238.43/plsql/plsql/Search_Ind_Bdp
Dietitian #04	http://165.189.238.43/plsql/plsql/Search_Ind_Health
Drug Distributor #02	http://165.189.238.43/plsql/plsql/Search_Ent_Bdp
Drug Manufacturer #02	http://165.189.238.43/plsql/plsql/Search_Ent_Bdp
Electrologist #01	http://165.189.238.43/plsql/plsql/Search_Ind_Bdp
Electrology Establishment #02	http://165.189.238.43/plsql/plsql/Search_Ent_Bdp
Electrology Instructor #01	http://165.189.238.43/plsql/plsql/Search_Ind_Bdp
Electrology Specialty School #02	http://165.189.238.43/plsql/plsql/Search_Ent_Bdp
Engineer #01	http://165.189.238.43/plsql/plsql/Search_Ind_Bdp
Engineer in Training #01	http://165.189.238.43/plsql/plsql/Search_Ind_Bdp
Engineering Corp #02	http://165.189.238.43/plsql/plsql/Search_Ent_Bdp
Fund Raiser, Professional #01	http://165.189.238.43/plsql/plsql/Search_Ind_Bdp
Fund Raising Counsel #02	http://165.189.238.43/plsql/plsql/Search_Ent_Bdp
Funeral Director #01	http://165.189.238.43/plsql/plsql/Search_Ind_Bdp
Funeral Director Apprentice #01	http://165.189.238.43/plsql/plsql/Search_Ind_Bdp
Funeral Establishment #02	http://165.189.238.43/plsql/plsql/Search_Ent_Bdp
Funeral Preneed Seller #01	http://165.189.238.43/plsql/plsql/Search_Ind_Bdp
General Appraiser (Certified or Licensed) #01	http://165.189.238.43/plsql/plsql/Search_Ind_Bdp
Geologist #01	http://165.189.238.43/plsql/plsql/Search_Ind_Bdp
Geology Firm #02	http://165.189.238.43/plsql/plsql/Search_Ent_Bdp
Hearing Instrument Specialist #04	http://165.189.238.43/plsql/plsql/Search_Ind_Health
Home Inspector #01	http://165.189.238.43/plsql/plsql/Search_Ind_Bdp
Hydrologist #01	http://165.189.238.43/plsql/plsql/Search_Ind_Bdp

Hydrology Firm #02	http://165.189.238.43/plsql/plsql/Search_Ent_Bdp
Insurance Company #06	http://badger.state.wi.us/agencies/oci/dir_ins.htm
Insurance Premium Finance Company #06	www.wdfi.org/fi/lfs/licensee_lists
Interior Designer #01	http://165.189.238.43/plsql/plsql/Search_Ind_Bdp
Investment Advisor #10	www.wdfi.org/fi/securities/licensing/licensee_lists/default.asp
Investment Advisor Representative #10	www.wdfi.org/fi/securities/licensing/licensee_lists/default.asp
Land Surveyor #01	http://165.189.238.43/plsql/plsql/Search_Ind_Bdp
Landscape Architect #01	http://165.189.238.43/plsql/plsql/Search_Ind_Bdp
Loan Company #06	www.wdfi.org/fi/lfs/licensee_lists
Loan Solicitor/Originator #05	www.wdfi.org/fi/mortbank/lists1999/mblistindex1999.htm
Lobbyist #11	http://ethics.state.wi.us/Scripts/Lobbyists2000.asp
Manicuring Establishment #02	http://165.189.238.43/plsql/plsql/Search_Ent_Bdp
Manicuring Instructor #01	http://165.189.238.43/plsql/plsql/Search_Ind_Bdp
Manicuring Specialty School #02	http://165.189.238.43/plsql/plsql/Search_Ent_Bdp
Manicurist #01	http://165.189.238.43/plsql/plsql/Search_Ind_Bdp
Marriage & Family Therapist #04	http://165.189.238.43/plsql/plsql/Search_Ind_Health
Massage Therapist/Bodyworker #04	http://165.189.238.43/plsql/plsql/Search_Ind_Health
Medical Doctor/Surgeon #04	http://165.189.238.43/plsql/plsql/Search_Ind_Health
Mobile Home & RV Dealer #06	www.wdfi.org/fi/lfs/licensee_lists
Mortgage Banker #05	www.wdfi.org/fi/mortbank/lists1999/mblistindex1999.htm
Mortgage Broker #05	www.wdfi.org/fi/mortbank/lists1999/mblistindex1999.htm
Motorcycle Dealer #06	www.wdfi.org/fi/lfs/licensee_lists
Music Therapist #04	http://165.189.238.43/plsql/plsql/Search_Ind_Health
Nurse (Practical or Registered) #04	http://165.189.238.43/plsql/plsql/Search_Ind_Health
Nurse Midwife #04	http://165.189.238.43/plsql/plsql/Search_Ind_Health
Nursing Home Administrator #01	http://165.189.238.43/plsql/plsql/Search_Ind_Bdp
Occupational Therapist #04	http://165.189.238.43/plsql/plsql/Search_Ind_Health
Occupational Therapy Assistant #04	http://165.189.238.43/plsql/plsql/Search_Ind_Health
Optometrist #04	http://165.189.238.43/plsql/plsql/Search_Ind_Health
Pay Day Lender #06	www.wdfi.org/fi/lfs/licensee_lists
Pharmacist #04	http://165.189.238.43/plsql/plsql/Search_Ind_Health
Pharmacy #04	http://165.189.238.43/plsql/plsql/Search_Ind_Health
Physical Therapist #04	http://165.189.238.43/plsql/plsql/Search_Ind_Health
Physician Assistant #04	http://165.189.238.43/plsql/plsql/Search_Ind_Health
Podiatrist #04	http://165.189.238.43/plsql/plsql/Search_Ind_Health
Principal Lobbying Organization #11	http://ethics.state.wi.us/Scripts/OEL2000.asp
Private Detective #01	http://165.189.238.43/plsql/plsql/Search_Ind_Bdp
Private Detective Agency #02	http://165.189.238.43/plsql/plsql/Search_Ent_Bdp
Private Practice of School Psychology #04	http://165.189.238.43/plsql/plsql/Search_Ind_Health
Professional Counselor #04	http://165.189.238.43/plsql/plsql/Search_Ind_Health
Psychologist #04	http://165.189.238.43/plsql/plsql/Search_Ind_Health
Public Accountant #01	http://165.189.238.43/plsql/plsql/Search_Ind_Bdp
Real Estate Appraiser #01	http://165.189.238.43/plsql/plsql/Search_Ind_Bdp
Real Estate Broker #01	http://165.189.238.43/plsql/plsql/Search_Ind_Bdp
Real Estate Business Entity #02	http://165.189.238.43/plsql/plsql/Search_Ent_Bdp
Real Estate Salesperson #01	http://165.189.238.43/plsql/plsql/Search_Ind_Bdp
Residential Appraiser #01	http://165.189.238.43/plsql/plsql/Search_Ind_Bdp
Respiratory Care Practitioner #04	http://165.189.238.43/plsql/plsql/Search_Ind_Health
Sales Finance Company #06	www.wdfi.org/fi/lfs/licensee_lists
Sales Finance Loan Company #06	www.wdfi.org/fi/lfs/licensee_lists
Savings & Loan Sales Finance Company #06	www.wdfi.org/fi/lfs/licensee_lists
Savings Institution #05	www.wdfi.org/fi/si/silist.htm
Securities Agent #10	www.wdfi.org/fi/securities/licensing/licensee_lists/default.asp
Securities Broker/Dealer #10	www.wdfi.org/fi/securities/licensing/licensee_lists/default.asp
Security Guard #01	http://165.189.238.43/plsql/plsql/Search_Ind_Bdp
Seller of Checks #06	www.wdfi.org/fi/lfs/licensee_lists
Social Worker #04	http://165.189.238.43/plsql/plsql/Search_Ind_Health
Soil Science Firm #02	http://165.189.238.43/plsql/plsql/Search_Ent_Bdp
Soil Scientist #01	http://165.189.238.43/plsql/plsql/Search_Ind_Bdp
Speech Pathologist/Audiologist #04	http://165.189.238.43/plsql/plsql/Search_Ind_Health
Time Share Salesperson #01	http://165.189.238.43/plsql/plsql/Search_Ind_Bdp
Veterinarian #04	http://165.189.238.43/plsql/plsql/Search_Ind_Health
Veterinary Technician #04	http://165.189.238.43/plsql/plsql/Search_Ind_Health

Licensing Quick Finder

Accountant #01	608-266-5511 X42
Accounting Firm #02	608-266-5511X43
Acupuncturist #04	608-266-0145
Adjustment Counselor #06	608-261-9555
Adjustment Service Company #06	608-267-3776
Aesthetics Establishment #02	608-266-5511X43
Aesthetics Instructor #01	608-266-5511 X42
Aesthetics Specialty School #02	608-266-5511X43
Architect #01	608-266-5511 X42
Architecural Corp #02	608-266-5511X43
Art Therapist #04	608-266-2811
Asbestos Worker #17	608-267-2297
Attorney #16	608-257-3838
Auction Company #02	608-266-5511X43
Auctioneer #01	608-266-5511X43
Audiologist #04	608-266-0145
Bank #05	608-261-7578
Barber #01	608-266-5511 X42
Barber/Cosmetology Apprentice #01	608-266-5511X43
Barber/Cosmetology Instructor #01	608-266-5511X43
Barber/Cosmetology Manager #01	608-266-5511X43
Barbering School #02	608-266-5511X43
Beer Wholesale #08	608-266-2776
Boxer #01	608-266-5511X442
Boxing Club (Amateur or Professional) #02	608-266-5511X43
Boxing Show Permit #02	608-266-5511X43
Business Tax Registration Certificate #08	608-266-2776
Cemetery Authority #02	608-266-5511X441
Cemetery Preneed Seller #01	608-266-5511X441
Cemetery Salesperson #01	608-266-5511X441
Cemetery Warehouse #02	608-266-5511X441
Charitable Gaming #14	608-270-2555
Charitable Organization #02	608-266-5511X441
Chiropractor #04	608-266-0145
Cigarette & Tabocco Out-of-state Distributor #08	608-266-2776
Cigarette & Tobacco Distributor #08	608-266-2776
Cigarette & Tobacco Jobber #08	608-266-2776
Cigarette & Tobacco Multiple Retailer #08	608-266-2776
Cigarette & Tobacco Vendor #08	608-266-2776
Cigarette & Tobacco Warehouser #08	608-266-2776
Cigarette & Tobacco Wholesaler #08	608-266-2776
Collection Agency #06	608-267-3776
Cosmetologist #01	608-266-5511 X42
Cosmetology School #02	608-266-5511X43
Credit Service Organization #05	608-266-9543
Credit Union #05	608-266-9543
Currency Exchange #06	608-267-3776
Dance Therapist #04	608-266-2811
Debt Collector #06	608-267-3776
Dental Hygienist #04	608-266-2811
Dentist #04	608-266-2811
Designer of Engineering Systems #01	608-266-5511X42
Dietitian #04	608-266-0145
Director of Instruction #15	608-266-1027
Dog Racing #14	608-270-2555
Drug Distributor #02	608-266-5511X43

Drug Manufacturer #02	608-266-5511X43
Electrician #19	608-261-8500
Electrologist #01	608-266-5511X43
Electrology Establishment #02	608-266-5511X43
Electrology Instructor #01	608-266-5511X43
Electrology Specialty School #02	608-266-5511X43
Emergency Medical Technician/Paramdeic #07	608-266-1568
Employee Benefits Plan Administrator #12	608-267-1238
Engineer #01	608-266-5511 X42
Engineer in Training #01	608-266-5511X43
Engineering Corp #02	608-266-5511X43
Excise Tax Permit #08	608-266-2776
Fertilizer #09	608-224-4548
Firearms Permit #02	608-266-5511X43
Fuel Tax Permit #08	608-266-2776
Fund Raiser, Professional #01	608-266-5511X441
Fund Raising Counsel #02	608-266-5511X441
Funeral Director #01	608-266-5511X442
Funeral Director Apprentice #01	608-266-5511X43
Funeral Establishment #02	608-266-5511X43
Funeral Preneed Seller #01	608-266-5511X442
General Appraiser (Certified or Licensed) #01	608-266-5511X43
Geologist #01	608-266-5511 X42
Geology Firm #02	608-266-5511X43
Hearing Instrument Specialist #04	608-266-2811
Home Inspector #01	608-266-5511X43
Hydrologist #01	608-266-5511 X42
Hydrology Firm #02	608-266-5511X43
Indian Gaming Vendor #14	608-270-2555
Insurance Intermediary #12	608-266-8699
Insurance Premium Finance Company #06	608-267-3776
Interior Designer #01	608-266-5511 X43
Investment Advisor #10	608-266-3693
Investment Advisor Representative #10	608-266-3693
Land Surveyor #01	608-266-5511X43
Landfill Operator #18	608-267-6744
Landscape Architect #01	608-266-5511 X42
Liquor (Wholesale) #08	608-266-2776
Loan Company #06	608-267-1708
Loan Solicitor/Originator #05	608-261-7578
Lobbyist #11	608-266-8123
Local Vocational Education Coordinator #15	608-266-1027
Manicuring Establishment #02	608-266-5511X43
Manicuring Instructor #01	608-266-5511X43
Manicuring Specialty School #02	608-266-5511X43
Manicurist #01	608-266-5511X43
Marriage & Family Therapist #04	608-266-0145
Massage Therapist/Bodyworker #04	608-266-2811
Medical Doctor/Surgeon #04	608-266-2811
Mobile Home & RV Dealer #06	608-267-3743
Mortgage Banker #05	608-261-7578
Mortgage Broker #05	608-261-7578
Motorcycle Dealer #06	608-267-3743
Music Therapist #04	608-266-2811
Notary Public #13	608-266-5594
Nurse (Practical or Registered) #04	608-266-0145
Nurse Midwife #04	608-266-0145
Nursing Home Administrator #01	608-266-5511X43

Occupational Therapist #04	608-266-2811
Occupational Therapy Assistant #04	608-266-2811
Optometrist #04	608-266-0145
Osteopathic Physician #04	608-266-2811
Pay Day Lender #06	608-267-1708
Pesticide Applicator #09	608-224-4548
Pesticide Dealer #09	608-224-4548
Pesticide Vet Clinic #09	608-224-4548
Pesticide-Commercial Application Business #09	608-224-4548
Pharmacist #04	608-266-2811
Pharmacy #04	608-266-2811
Physical Therapist #04	608-266-2811
Physician Assistant #04	608-266-2811
Plumber #19	608-261-8500
Podiatrist #04	608-266-2811
Principal Lobbying Organization #11	608-266-8123
Private Detective #01	608-266-5511X43
Private Detective Agency #02	608-266-5511X43
Private Practice of School Psychology #04	608-266-0145
Professional Counselor #04	608-266-0145
Psychologist #04	608-266-0145
Public Accountant #01	608-266-5511 X42
Public Wine Distributor #08	608-266-2776
Racing #14	608-270-2555
Racing Vendor #14	608-270-2555
Real Estate Appraiser #01	608-266-5511 X42
Real Estate Broker #01	608-266-5511X43
Real Estate Business Entity #02	608-266-5511X43
Real Estate Salesperson #01	608-266-5511X43
Residental Appraiser #01	608-266-5511X43
Respiratory Care Practitioner #04	608-266-2811
Sales Finance Company #06	608-267-3743
Sales Finance Loan Company #06	608-267-3743
Sales Witholding Tax Registration #08	608-266-2776
Sanitarian #17	608-266-8018
Savings & Loan Sales Finance Company #06	608-267-3743
Savings Institution #05	608-261-4335
School Business Manager #15	608-266-1027
School Counselor #15	608-266-1027
School Librarian/Media Specialist #15	608-266-1027
School Nurse #15	608-266-1027
School Principal #15	608-266-1027
School Psychologist #15	608-266-1027
School Social Worker #15	608-266-1027
School Superintendent #15	608-266-1027
Securities Agent #10	608-266-3693
Securities Broker/Dealer #10	608-266-3693
Security Guard #01	608-266-5511X43
Seller of Checks #06	608-267-3776
Social Worker #04	608-266-0145
Soil Science Firm #02	608-266-5511X43
Soil Scientist #01	608-266-5511 X42
Speech Pathologist/Audiologist #04	608-266-2811
Teacher #15	608-266-1027
Time Share Salesperson #01	608-266-5511X43
Veterinarian #04	608-266-2811
Veterinary Technician #04	608-266-2811
Viatical Settlement Broker #12	608-266-8699

Licensing Agency Information

01 Department of Regulation and Licensing, Division of Business Professional Licensure & Regulation, PO Box 8935 (1400 E Washington), Madison, WI 53708-8935; 608-266-5511, Fax: 608-267-3816.
http://www.state.wi.us/agencies/drl
Direct URL to search licenses: http://165.189.238.43/plsql/plsql/Search_Ind_Bdp You can search online using name or credential number

02 Bureau of District Licensing & Real Estate, Division of Business Licensure & Regulation, PO Box 8935, (1400 E Washington Ave), Madison, WI 53708; 608-266-5511, Fax: 608-267-3816.
http://badger.state.wi.us/agencies/drl
Direct URL to search licenses: http://165.189.238.43/plsql/plsql/Search_Ent_Bdp You can search online using name or credential number

04 Bureau of Health Services Professions, PO Box 8935 (1400 E Washington Ave), Madison, WI 53708-8935; 608-266-0483, Fax: 608-261-7083.
www.state.wi.us/agencies/drl/
Direct URL to search licenses: http://165.189.238.43/plsql/plsql/Search_Ind_Health You can search online using name or credential number. This Department recommends an internet search; if not, inquire by mail. Phone verifications may not be accepted

05 Department of Financial Institutions, PO Box 7876, Madison, WI 53707-7876; 608-266-1622.
www.wdfi.org Division of Financial Inst. - dfi - offers both a great online list system and telephone system for verifications. This section contains banks, mortgage, and credit union sevices.

06 Department of Financial Institutions, Licensed Financial Services, PO Box 7876, Madison, WI 53707-7876; 608-261-9555, Fax: 608-267-6889.
www.wdfi.org
Direct URL to search licenses: www.wdfi.org/fi/lfs/licensee_lists/ You can search online using generated lists Licensed Financial Services of WS Dept. of Financial Institutiions offers an online list system for verifications.

07 Department of Health & Family Services, Emergency Medical Services & Injury Prevention, PO Box 2659 (1414 E Washington, Rm 227, 53703), Madison, WI 53701-2659; 608-266-1568, Fax: 608-261-6392.
Direct URL to search licenses: www.dhfs.state.wi.us/reg_licens/dohprog/ems/emsindex.htm

08 Department of Revenue, PO Box 8902, Madison, WI 53708-8902; 608-266-2776, Fax: 608-267-1030.
www.dor.state.wi.us

09 Department of Agriculture, Trade & Consumer Protection, Applicator Cert. & Licensing, PO Box 8911 (2811 Agriculture Dr), Madison, WI 53708-8911; 608-224-4548, Fax: 608-224-4656.
http://datcp.state.wi.us/pesticide/pestlic.htm

10 Department of Financial Institutions, Division of Securities, PO Box 1768, Madison, WI 53701; 608-266-3693, Fax: 608-256-1259.
www.wdfi.org/fi/securities/secur.htm
Direct URL to search licenses: www.wdfi.org/fi/securities/licensing/licensee_lists/default.asp You can search online using name, city and state.

11 Ethics Board, 44 E Mifflin St, #601, Madison, WI 53703-2800; 608-266-8123, Fax: 608-264-9309.
http://ethics.state.wi.us
Direct URL to search licenses: http://ethics.state.wi.us/LobbyingRegistrationReports/LobbyingOverview.htm

12 Office of the Commissioner of Insurance, PO Box 7872 (121 E Wilson St, 53702), Madison, WI 53707-7872; 608-266-3585, Fax: 608-264-8115.
http://badger.state.wi.us/agencies/oci/oci_home.htm

13 Office of Secretary of State, PO Box 7848, Madison, WI 53707-7848; 608-266-5594, Fax: 608-266-3159.
http://badger.state.wi.us/agencies/sos

14 Department of Administration, Division of Gamin, PO Box 8979 (2005 W Beltline Hwy, #201), Madison, WI 53713; 608-270-2555, Fax: 608-270-2564.

15 Teacher Education, PO Box 7841, Madison, WI 53707-7841; 608-266-1027, Fax: 608-264-9558.
www.dpi.state.wi.us/dpi/DLSIS/tel/index.html

16 State Bar Association, PO Box 7158, Madison, WI 53707; 608-257-3838, Fax: 608-257-5502.
www.wisbar.org

17 Department of Health & Family Svcs, Occupational Health, 1 W Wilson St, Perry Manor, Madison, WI 53703; 608-267-2297.

18 Department of Natural Resources, 101 S Webster St, PO Box 7921, Madison, WI 53707-7921; 608-267-6744.

19 Department of Commerce, Safety & Buildings, 201 W Washington Ave, PO Box 2689, Madison, WI 53707-2689; 608-261-8500.

The following list indicates the district and division name for each county in the state. If the district or division name of the bankruptcy court is different from the civil/criminal court, it appears in parentheses.

County/Court Cross Reference

County	District	Division
Adams	Western	Madison
Ashland	Western	Madison (Eau Claire)
Barron	Western	Madison (Eau Claire)
Bayfield	Western	Madison (Eau Claire)
Brown	Eastern	Milwaukee
Buffalo	Western	Madison (Eau Claire)
Burnett	Western	Madison (Eau Claire)
Calumet	Eastern	Milwaukee
Chippewa	Western	Madison (Eau Claire)
Clark	Western	Madison (Eau Claire)
Columbia	Western	Madison
Crawford	Western	Madison
Dane	Western	Madison
Dodge	Eastern	Milwaukee
Door	Eastern	Milwaukee
Douglas	Western	Madison (Eau Claire)
Dunn	Western	Madison (Eau Claire)
Eau Claire	Western	Madison (Eau Claire)
Florence	Eastern	Milwaukee
Fond du Lac	Eastern	Milwaukee
Forest	Eastern	Milwaukee
Grant	Western	Madison
Green	Western	Madison
Green Lake	Eastern	Milwaukee
Iowa	Western	Madison
Iron	Western	Madison (Eau Claire)
Jackson	Western	Madison (Eau Claire)
Jefferson	Western	Madison
Juneau	Western	Madison (Eau Claire)
Kenosha	Eastern	Milwaukee
Kewaunee	Eastern	Milwaukee
La Crosse	Western	Madison (Eau Claire)
Lafayette	Western	Madison
Langlade	Eastern	Milwaukee
Lincoln	Western	Madison (Eau Claire)
Manitowoc	Eastern	Milwaukee
Marathon	Western	Madison (Eau Claire)
Marinette	Eastern	Milwaukee
Marquette	Eastern	Milwaukee
Menominee	Eastern	Milwaukee
Milwaukee	Eastern	Milwaukee
Monroe	Western	Madison (Eau Claire)
Oconto	Eastern	Milwaukee
Oneida	Western	Madison (Eau Claire)
Outagamie	Eastern	Milwaukee
Ozaukee	Eastern	Milwaukee
Pepin	Western	Madison (Eau Claire)
Pierce	Western	Madison (Eau Claire)
Polk	Western	Madison (Eau Claire)
Portage	Western	Madison (Eau Claire)
Price	Western	Madison (Eau Claire)
Racine	Eastern	Milwaukee
Richland	Western	Madison
Rock	Western	Madison
Rusk	Western	Madison (Eau Claire)
Sauk	Western	Madison
Sawyer	Western	Madison (Eau Claire)
Shawano	Eastern	Milwaukee
Sheboygan	Eastern	Milwaukee
St. Croix	Western	Madison (Eau Claire)
Taylor	Western	Madison (Eau Claire)
Trempealeau	Western	Madison (Eau Claire)
Vernon	Western	Madison (Eau Claire)
Vilas	Western	Madison (Eau Claire)
Walworth	Eastern	Milwaukee
Washburn	Western	Madison (Eau Claire)
Washington	Eastern	Milwaukee
Waukesha	Eastern	Milwaukee
Waupaca	Eastern	Milwaukee
Waushara	Eastern	Milwaukee
Winnebago	Eastern	Milwaukee
Wood	Western	Madison (Eau Claire)

US District Court

Eastern District of Wisconsin

Milwaukee Division Clerk's Office, Room 362, 517 E Wisconsin Ave, Milwaukee, WI 53202, 414-297-3372.

www.wied.uscourts.gov

Counties: Brown, Calumet, Dodge, Door, Florence, Fond du Lac, Forest, Green Lake, Kenosha, Kewaunee, Langlade, Manitowoc, Marinette, Marquette, Menominee, Milwaukee, Oconto, Outagamie, Ozaukee, Racine, Shawano, Sheboygan, Walworth, Washington, Waukesha, Waupaca, Waushara, Winnebago.

Indexing & Storage: Cases are indexed by defendant and plaintiff as well as by case number. New cases are available in the index immediately after filing date. The computer index for civil cases goes back to 1991 and for criminal cases back to 1993. A computer index is maintained. Open records are located at this court.

Fee & Payment: The fee is $15.00 per item (one party name or case number). Payment may be made by money order, cashier check, personal check. Prepayment is required. Payee: Clerk, US District Court. Certification fee: $5.00 per document. Copy fee: $.50 per page. You are allowed to make your own copies. These copies cost $.25 per page.

Phone Search: Docket information available by phone if you have the case number or party names. An automated voice case information service (VCIS) is not available.

Mail Search: Always enclose a stamped self addressed envelope.

In Person Search: In person searching is available.

PACER: Sign-up number is 800-676-6856. Toll-free access: 877-253-4862. Local access: 414-297-3361. PACER is available on the Internet at http://pacer.wied.uscourts.gov. Case records are available back to 1991. Records are never purged. New records are available online after 1 day. PACER is available on the Internet at http://pacer.wied.uscourts.gov.

US Bankruptcy Court

Eastern District of Wisconsin

Milwaukee Division Room 126, 517 E Wisconsin Ave, Milwaukee, WI 53202, 414-297-3291.

www.wieb.uscourts.gov

Counties: Brown, Calumet, Dodge, Door, Florence, Fond du Lac, Forest, Green Lake,

Kenosha, Kewaunee, Langlade, Manitowoc, Marinette, Marquette, Menominee, Milwaukee, Oconto, Outagamie, Ozaukee, Racine, Shawano, Sheboygan, Walworth, Washington, Waukesha, Waupaca,Waushara, Winnebago.

Indexing & Storage: Cases are indexed by debtor as well as by case number. New cases are available in the index 1-2 days after filing date. The computer index goes back to 1986. A computer index is maintained. Open records are located at this court.

Fee & Payment: The fee is $15.00 per item (one party name or case number). Payment may be made by money order, cashier check, personal check. Prepayment is required. Payee: Clerk, US Bankruptcy Court. Certification fee: $5.00 per document. Copy fee: $.50 per page. You are allowed to make your own copies. These copies cost $.25 per page.

Phone Search: An automated voice case information service (VCIS) is available. Call VCIS at 877-781-7277 or 414-297-3582.

Mail Search: Always enclose a stamped self addressed envelope.

In Person Search: In person searching is available.

PACER: Sign-up number is 800-676-6856. Access fee is $.60 per minute. Toll-free access: 877-467-5537. Local access: 414-297-1400. Case records are available back to 1991. Records are purged aafter case is closed. New civil records are available online after 1-2 days. PACER is available online at http://pacer.wieb.uscourts.gov.

US District Court

Western District of Wisconsin

Madison Division PO Box 432, Madison, WI 53701 (Courier Address: 120 N Henry St, Madison, WI 53703), 608-264-5156.

www.wiw.uscourts.gov

Counties: Adams, Ashland, Barron, Bayfield, Buffalo, Burnett, Chippewa, Clark, Columbia, Crawford, Dane, Douglas, Dunn, Eau Claire, Grant, Green, Iowa, Iron, Jackson, Jefferson, Juneau, La Crosse, Lafayette, Lincoln, Marathon, Monroe, Oneida, Pepin, Pierce, Polk,Portage, Price, Richland, Rock, Rusk, Sauk, Sawyer, St. Croix, Taylor, Trempealeau, Vernon, Vilas, Washburn, Wood.

Indexing & Storage: Cases are indexed by defendant and plaintiff as well as by case number.

New cases are available in the index 24 hours after filing date. A computer index is maintained. Open records are located at this court. District wide searches are available from this court.

Fee & Payment: The fee is $15.00 per item (one party name or case number). Payment may be made by money order, cashier check, personal check. Prepayment is required. Payee: Clerk, US District Court. Certification fee: $5.00 per document. Copy fee: $.50 per page.

Phone Search: Only docket information is available by phone. An automated voice case information service (VCIS) is not available.

Mail Search: Always enclose a stamped self addressed envelope.

In Person Search: In person searching is available.

PACER: Sign-up number is 800-676-6856. Access fee is $.60 per minute. Toll-free access: 800-372-8791. Local access: 608-264-5914. Case records are available back to 1990. Records are never purged. New records are available online after 1 day. PACER is available on the Internet at http://pacer.wiwd.uscourts.gov.

US Bankruptcy Court

Western District of Wisconsin

Eau Claire Division PO Box 5009, Eau Claire, WI 54702 (Courier Address: 500 S Barstow Commons, Eau Claire, WI 54701), 715-839-2980, Fax: 715-839-2996.

www.wiw.uscourts.gov/bankruptcy

Counties: Ashland, Barron, Bayfield, Buffalo, Burnett, Chippewa, Clark, Douglas, Dunn, Eau Claire, Iron, Jackson, Juneau, La Crosse, Lincoln, Marathon, Monroe, Oneida, Pepin, Pierce, Polk, Portage, Price, Rusk, Sawyer, St. Croix, Taylor, Trempealeau, Vernon,Vilas, Washburn, Wood. Division has satellite offices in LaCrosse and Wausau.

Indexing & Storage: Cases are indexed by debtor as well as by case number. New cases are available in the index 1 day after filing date. A computer index is maintained. Open records are located at this court. All division records are maintained here until they are forwarded to the Chicago Federal Records Center.

Fee & Payment: The fee is $15.00 per item (one party name or case number). Payment may be made by money order, cashier check, business check. Personal checks are not accepted.

Prepayment is required. Personal checks are accepted only from attorneys. Payee: Clerk, US Bankruptcy Court. Certification fee: $5.00 per document. Copy fee: $.50 per page.

Phone Search: Only limited docket information is available by phone. An automated voice case information service (VCIS) is available. Call VCIS at 800-743-8247 or 608-264-5035.

Mail Search: A stamped self addressed envelope is not required.

In Person Search: In person searching is available.

PACER: Sign-up number is 800-676-6856. Access fee is $.60 per minute. Toll-free access: 800-373-8708. Local access: 608-264-5630. Case records are available back to April 1991. New civil records are available online after 1 day.

Madison Division PO Box 548, Madison, WI 53701 (Courier Address: Room 340, 120 N Henry St, Madison, WI 53703), 608-264-5178.

www.wiw.uscourts.gov/bankruptcy

Counties: Adams, Columbia, Crawford, Dane, Grant, Green, Iowa, Jefferson, Lafayette, Richland, Rock, Sauk.

Indexing & Storage: Cases are indexed by debtor as well as by case number. New cases are available in the index 24 hours after filing date. A computer index is maintained. Open records are located at this court.

Fee & Payment: The fee is $15.00 per item (one party name or case number). Payment may be made by money order, cashier check, business check. Personal checks are not accepted. Prepayment is required. Payee: Clerk, US Bankruptcy Court. Certification fee: $5.00 per document. Copy fee: $.50 per page.

Phone Search: Only limited docket information is available by phone. An automated voice case information service (VCIS) is available. Call VCIS at 800-743-8247 or 608-264-5035.

Fax Search: Fax requests are accepted.

Mail Search: A stamped self addressed envelope is not required.

In Person Search: In person searching is available.

PACER: Sign-up number is 800-676-6856. Access fee is $.60 per minute. Toll-free access: 800-373-8708. Local access: 608-264-5630. Case records are available back to April 1991. New civil records are available online after 1 day.

Court	Jurisdiction	No. of Courts	How Organized
Circuit Courts*	General	74	69 Circuits
Municipal Courts	Municipal	210	
Probate Courts*	Probate	72	

* Profiled in this Sourcebook.

	CIVIL								
Court	Tort	Contract	Real Estate	Min. Claim	Max. Claim	Small Claims	Estate	Eviction	Domestic Relations
Circuit Courts*	X	X	X	$0	No Max	$5000	X	X	X
Municipal Courts									
Probate Courts*							X		

	CRIMINAL				
Court	Felony	Misdemeanor	DWI/DUI	Preliminary Hearing	Juvenile
Circuit Courts*	X	X	X		X
Municipal Courts			X		
Probate Courts*					

ADMINISTRATION

Director of State Courts, Supreme Court, PO Box 1688, Madison, WI, 53701; 608-266-6828, Fax: 608-267-0980. www.courts.state.wi.us

COURT STRUCTURE

The Circuit Court is the court of general jurisdiction. Probate filing is a function of the Circuit Court; however, each county has a Register in Probate who maintains and manages the probate records. The Register in Probate, also, maintains guardianship and mental health records, most of which are sealed but may be opened for cause with a court order. In some counties, the Register also maintains termination and adoption records, but practices vary widely across the state.

Most Registers in Probate are putting pre-1950 records on microfilm and destroying the hard copies. This is done as "time and workloads permit," so microfilm archiving is not uniform across the state. The small claims limit was raised to $5000 in mid-1995.

ONLINE ACCESS

Wisconsin Circuit Court Access (WCCA) allows users to view circuit court case information at http://ccap.courts.state.wi.us/internetcourtaccess which is the Wisconsin court system web site. Data is available from all counties except Outagamie and Walworth. Searches can be conducted statewide or county by county. WCCA provides detailed information about circuit cases and for civil cases, the program displays judgment and judment party information. WCCA also offers the ability to generate reports. In addition, public access terminals are available at each court. Due to statutory requirements, WCCA users will not be able to view restricted cases. There are probate records for all counties except Outagamie, Milwaukee and Walworth. Portage County offers probate records only online.

ADDITIONAL INFORMATION

The statutory fee schedule for the Circuit Courts is as follows: Search Fee - $5.00 per name; Copy Fee - $1.25 per page; Certification Fee - $5.00. In about half the Circuit Courts, no search fee is charged if the case number is provided. There is normally no search fee charged for in-person searches.

The fee schedule for probate is as follows: Search Fee - $4.00 per name; Certification Fee - $3.00 per document plus copy fee; Copy Fee - $1.00 per page.

Adams County

Circuit Court PO Box 220, Friendship, WI 53934; 608-339-4208; Fax: 608-339-6414. Hours: 8AM-4:30PM (CST). *Felony, Misdemeanor, Civil, Eviction, Small Claims.*

Civil Records: Access: Phone, mail, online, in person. Both court and visitors may perform in person searches. Search fee: $5.00 per name. Required to search: name, years to search. Civil records on computer from 1993, on index cards from 1950, index books from 1950 cross indexed. Historical societies have previous records and indexes. Organized 1848. Civil court records are available free on the Internet at:

http://ccap.courts.state.wi.us/internetcourtaccess.

Criminal Records: Access: Phone, mail, online, in person. Both court and visitors may perform in person searches. Search fee: $5.00 per name. Required to search: name, years to search, DOB. Criminal records on computer from 1993, on index cards from 1950, index books from 1950 cross

indexed. Historical societies have previous records and indexes. Organized 1848. Online access to criminal records is same as civil, see above. **General Information:** No juvenile, paternity, financial, PSI reports released. SASE required. Turnaround time 1-2 days. Copy fee: $1.25 per page. Certification fee: $5.00. Fee payee: Clerk of Court. Personal checks accepted. Prepayment is required. Public access terminal is available.

Register in Probate PO Box 200, Friendship, WI 53934; 608-339-4213; Fax: 608-339-6414. Hours: 8AM-4:30PM (CST). *Probate.*

Ashland County

Circuit Court Courthouse 210 W Main St Rm 307, Ashland, WI 54806; 715-682-7016; Fax: 715-682-7919. Hours: 8AM-Noon, 1-4PM (CST). *Felony, Misdemeanor, Civil, Eviction, Small Claims.*

Civil Records: Access: Phone, fax, mail, online, in person. Both court and visitors may perform in person searches. Search fee: $5.00 per name. Required to search: name, years to search. Civil cases indexed by defendant, plaintiff. Civil records on index cards and index books concurrently from 1960. Orgaiized 1860. Civil court records are available free on the Internet at http://ccap.courts.state.wi.us/internetcourtaccess. **Criminal Records:** Access: Phone, fax, mail, online, in person. Both court and visitors may perform in person searches. Search fee: $5.00 per name. Required to search: name, years to search. Criminal records (some) on computer. Online access to criminal records is same as civil, see above. **General Information:** No juvenile or paternity records released. SASE required. Turnaround time 1-2 days. Copy fee: $1.25 per page. Certification fee: $5.00. Fee payee: Clerk of Court. Personal checks accepted. Local or pre-approved checks accepted. Prepayment is required. Public access terminal is available. Fax notes: $1.25 per page.

Register in Probate Courthouse Rm 203, 201 W Main, Ashland, WI 54806; 715-682-7009. Hours: 8AM-Noon, 1-4PM (CST). *Probate.*

Barron County

Circuit Court Barron County Courthouse, 330 E LaSalle Ave, Barron, WI 54812; 715-537-6265; Fax: 715-537-6269. Hours: 8AM-4:30PM (CST). *Felony, Misdemeanor, Civil, Eviction, Small Claims.*

Civil Records: Access: online, In person. Court does not conduct in person searches; visitors must perform searches for themselves. Search fee: No civil searches performed by court. Required to search: name, years to search. Civil cases indexed by defendant, plaintiff. Civil records on computer, index cards from 1983. Organized 1859. Civil court records are available free on the Internet at http://ccap.courts.state.wi.us/internetcourtaccess. **Criminal Records:** Access: online, in person. Court does not conduct in person searches; visitors must perform searches for themselves. Search fee: No criminal searches performed by court. Required to search: name, years to search. Criminal records on computer, index cards from 1983. Organized 1859. Online access to criminal records is same as civil, see above. **General Information:** No expunged, paternity or sealed records released. Copy fee: $1.25 per page. Certification fee: $5.00. Fee payee: Clerk of Court. Personal checks accepted. Prepayment is required. Public access terminal is available.

Register in Probate Courthouse Rm 218, Barron, WI 54812; 715-537-6261; Fax: 715-537-6277. Hours: 8AM-4PM (CST). *Probate.*

Bayfield County

Circuit Court 117 E 5th, Washburn, WI 54891; 715-373-6108; Fax: 715-373-6153. Hours: 8AM-4PM (CST). *Felony, Misdemeanor, Civil, Eviction, Small Claims.*

Civil Records: Access: Mail, online, in person. Both court and visitors may perform in person searches. Search fee: $5.00 per name. Required to search: name, years to search. Civil cases indexed by defendant, plaintiff. Civil records on computer for all open cases since 1982, on index cards from 1979, index books in archives from 1845 to 1979. Civil court records are available free at http://ccap.courts.state.wi.us/internetcourtaccess. **Criminal Records:** Access: Mail, online, in person. Both court and visitors may perform in person searches. Search fee: $5.00 per name. Required to search: name, years to search, DOB. Criminal records on computer since 1993. Online access to criminal records is same as civil, see above. **General Information:** No sealed records released. SASE required. Turnaround time 1-2 days. Copy fee: $1.25 per page. Certification fee: $5.00. Fee payee: Clerk of Court. Personal checks accepted. Prepayment is required. Public access terminal is available. Fax note: Fee to fax is $2.00.

Register in Probate 117 E 5th, PO Box 86, Washburn, WI 54891; 715-373-6108; Fax: 715-373-6155. Hours: 8AM-4PM (CST). *Probate.*

Brown County

Circuit Court PO Box 23600, Green Bay, WI 54305-3600; 920-448-4161; Fax: 920-448-4156. Hours: 8AM-4:30PM (CST). *Felony, Misdemeanor, Civil, Eviction, Small Claims.*

Civil Records: Access: Mail, online, in person. Both court and visitors may perform in person searches. Search fee: $5.00 per name. Required to search: name, years to search. Civil cases indexed by defendant, plaintiff. Civil records on computer since 1990, on microfiche from 1987-1990, archives from 1962-1990. Crossed on index cards from 1972, index books from 1982. Civil court records are available free on the Internet at http://ccap.courts.state.wi.us/internetcourtaccess. **Criminal Records:** Access: Mail, online, in person. Both court and visitors may perform in person searches. Search fee: $5.00 per name. Required to search: name, years to search, DOB. Criminal records on computer since 1990, on microfiche from 1987-1990, archives from 1962-1990. Crossed on index cards from 1972, index books from 1982. Online access to criminal records is same as civil, see above. **General Information:** No juvenile or paternity records released. SASE required. Turnaround time 10 days. Copy fee: $1.25 per page. Certification fee: $5.00. Fee payee: Brown County Clerk of Court. Personal checks accepted. Prepayment is required. Public access terminal is available.

Register in Probate PO Box 23600, Green Bay, WI 54305-3600; 920-448-4275; Fax: 920-448-6208. Hours: 8AM-Noon, 1-4:30PM (CST). *Probate.*

Buffalo County

Circuit Court 407 S 2nd, PO Box 68, Alma, WI 54610; 608-685-6212; Fax: 608-685-6211. Hours: 8AM-4:30PM (CST). *Felony, Misdemeanor, Civil, Eviction, Small Claims.*

Civil Records: Access: Phone, mail, online, in person. Both court and visitors may perform in person searches. Search fee: $5.00 per name. Required to search: name, years to search. Civil cases indexed by defendant, plaintiff. Civil records on computer from 1994, on index cards from 1979. No civil records available before 1962. Civil court records are available free on the Internet at http://ccap.courts.state.wi.us/internetcourtaccess. **Criminal Records:** Access: Phone, mail, online,

in person. Both court and visitors may perform in person searches. Search fee: $5.00 per name. Required to search: name, years to search. Criminal records on computer from 1994. Felonies retained 50 years; misdemeanors 20 years. No misdemeanors available before 1962. Online access to criminal records is same as civil, see above. **General Information:** No closed records released. SASE required. Turnaround time 1 week. Copy fee: $1.25 per page. Certification fee: $5.00. Fee payee: Buffalo County Clerk of Court. Personal checks accepted. Prepayment is required. Public access terminal is available.

Register in Probate 407 S 2nd, PO Box 68, Alma, WI 54610; 608-685-6202; Fax: 608-685-6213. Hours: 8AM-4:30PM (CST). *Probate.*

Burnett County

Circuit Court 7410 County Road K #115, Siren, WI 54872; 715-349-2147. Hours: 8:30AM-4:30PM (CST). *Felony, Misdemeanor, Civil, Eviction, Small Claims.*

Civil Records: Access: Mail, online, in person. Both court and visitors may perform in person searches. Search fee: $5.00 per name. Required to search: name, years to search. Civil cases indexed by defendant, plaintiff. Civil records on computer from 10/92, on index books from 1800s. Organized 1856. Civil court records are available free online at http://ccap.courts.state.wi.us/internetcourtaccess. **Criminal Records:** Access: Mail, online, in person. Both court and visitors may perform in person searches. Search fee: $5.00 per name. Required to search: name, years to search. Criminal records on computer from 10/92, on index books from 1800s. Organized 1856. Online access to criminal records is same as civil, see above. **General Information:** No paternity, juvenile, sealed or confidential records released. SASE required. Turnaround time 1-2 days. Copy fee: $1.25 per page. Certification fee: $5.00. Fee payee: Clerk of Courts. Personal checks accepted. Prepayment is required. Public access terminal is available.

Register in Probate 7410 County Road K #110, Siren, WI 54872; 715-349-2177; Fax: 715-349-7659. Hours: 8:30AM-4:30PM *Probate.*

Calumet County

Circuit Court 206 Court St, Chilton, WI 53014; 920-849-1414; Fax: 920-849-1483. Hours: 8AM-4:30PM (CST). *Felony, Misdemeanor, Civil, Eviction, Small Claims.*

Civil Records: Access: Mail, online, in person. Both court and visitors may perform in person searches. Search fee: $5.00 per name. Required to search: name, years to search. Civil cases indexed by defendant, plaintiff. Civil records on computer from 1992, index cards from 1978, index books from 1800s. The civil court records are available free online at http://ccap.courts.state.wi.us/internetcourtaccess. **Criminal Records:** Access: Mail, online, in person. Both court and visitors may perform in person searches. Search fee: $5.00 per name. Required to search: name, years to search, DOB. Criminal records on computer from 1992, index cards from 1978, index books from 1800s. Online access to criminal records is same as civil, see above. **General Information:** No juvenile or paternity records released. SASE required. Turnaround time 2 days. Copy fee: $1.25 per page. Certification fee: $5.00. Fee payee: Clerk of Court. Personal checks accepted. Prepayment is required. Public access terminal is available.

Register in Probate 206 Court St, Chilton, WI 53014-1198; 920-849-1455; Fax: 920-849-1483. Hours: 8AM-Noon, 1-4:30PM *Probate.*

Chippewa County

Circuit Court 711 N Bridge St, Chippewa Falls, WI 54729-1879; 715-726-7758; Fax: 715-726-7786. Hours: 8AM-4:30PM (CST). *Felony, Misdemeanor, Civil, Eviction, Small Claims.*

Civil Records: Access: Mail, online, in person. Both court and visitors may perform in person searches. Search fee: $5.00 per name per case type. Required to search: name, years to search; also helpful-address. Civil cases indexed by defendant, plaintiff. Civil records on computer from 1990, index cards from 1979, index books from 1900s. Civil court records are on the Internet at http://ccap.courts.state.wi.us/internetcourtaccess.
Criminal Records: Access: Mail, online, in person. Both court and visitors may perform in person searches. Search fee: $5.00 per name. Required to search: name, years to search, DOB; also helpful-SSN. Criminal records on computer from 1990, index cards from 1979, index books from 1900s. Online access to criminal records is same as civil, see above. **General Information:** Paternity records released only to party or attorney of record, or with written authroization. SASE required. Turnaround time 10 days or less; up to 30 days if pre-1990. Copy fee: $1.25 per page. Certification fee: $5.00. Fee payee: Chippewa County Clerk of Courts. Personal checks accepted. Prepayment is required. Public access terminal is available. Fax note: $2.00 1st page, $1. Each addl.

Register in Probate 711 N Bridge St, Chippewa Falls, WI 54729; 715-726-7737; Fax: 715-726-7786. Hours: 8AM-4:30PM (CST). *Probate.*

Clark County

Circuit Court 517 Court St, Neillsville, WI 54456-1971; 715-743-5181; Fax: 715-743-5154. Hours: 8AM-5PM (CST). *Felony, Misdemeanor, Civil, Eviction, Small Claims.*

Civil Records: Access: Mail, online, in person. Both court and visitors may perform in person searches. Search fee: $5.00 per name. Required to search: name, years to search. Civil cases indexed by defendant, plaintiff. Civil records on computer from 1994, on index cards from 1981, index books from 1900s. Civil court records are available free: http://ccap.courts.state.wi.us/internetcourtaccess.
Criminal Records: Access: Mail, online, in person. Both court and visitors may perform in person searches. Search fee: $5.00 per name. Required to search: name, years to search. Criminal records on computer from 1994, on index cards from 1981, index books from 1900s. Online access to criminal records is same as civil, see above. **General Information:** No sealed or paternity records released. SASE required. Turnaround time 1-2 weeks. Copy fee: $.15 per page. Certification fee: $5.00. Fee payee: Clerk of Court. Personal checks accepted. Prepayment is required.

Register in Probate 517 Court St, Rm 403, Neillsville, WI 54456; 715-743-5172; Fax: 715-743-4350. Hours: 8AM-5PM (CST). *Probate.*

Note: There is a $4.00 search fee.

Columbia County

Circuit Court PO Box 587, Portage, WI 53901; 608-742-2191; Fax: 608-742-9601. Hours: 8AM-4:30PM (CST). *Felony, Misdemeanor, Civil, Eviction, Small Claims.*

Civil Records: Access: Mail, online, in person. Both court and visitors may perform in person searches. Search fee: $5.00 per name. Required to search: name, years to search. Civil cases indexed by defendant, plaintiff. Civil records on computer from 1994, on microfiche to 1960s, concurrent index cards/books from 1940s. Civil court records are available free on the Internet at http://ccap.courts.state.wi.us/internetcourtaccess.
Criminal Records: Access: Mail, online, in person. Both court and visitors may perform in person searches. Search fee: $5.00 per name. Required to search: name, years to search; also helpful-DOB. Criminal records on computer from 1994, on microfiche to 1960s, concurrent index cards/books from 1940s. Online access to criminal records is same as civil, see above. **General Information:** No juvenile or paternity records released. SASE required. Turnaround time 1 week. Copy fee: $1.25 per page. Certification fee: $5.00. Fee payee: Clerk of Court. Personal checks accepted. Prepayment is required. Public access terminal is available.

Register in Probate 400 DeWitt, PO Box 221, Portage, WI 53901; 608-742-9636; Fax: 608-742-9601. Hours: 8AM-4:30PM (CST). *Probate.*

Crawford County

Circuit Court 220 N Beaumont Rd, Prairie Du Chien, WI 53821; 608-326-0211. Hours: 8AM-4:30PM (CST). *Felony, Misdemeanor, Civil, Eviction, Small Claims.*

Civil Records: Access: Mail, online, in person. Both court and visitors may perform in person searches. Search fee: $5.00 per name. Required to search: name, years to search. Civil cases indexed by defendant, plaintiff. Civil records on computer from 1993, on index cards from 1984, index books from 1900. Historical Society has archives. Civil court records are available free on the Internet at http://ccap.courts.state.wi.us/internetcourtaccess.
Criminal Records: Access: Mail, online, in person. Both court and visitors may perform in person searches. Search fee: $5.00 per name. Required to search: name, years to search. Criminal records on computer from 1993, on index cards from 1984, index books from 1900. Historical Society has archives. Online access to criminal records is same as civil, see above. **General Information:** No juvenile, paternity, mental records released. SASE required. Turnaround time 10 working days. Copy fee: $1.25 per page. Certification fee: $5.00. Fee payee: Clerk of Court. Personal checks accepted. Prepayment is required. Public access terminal is available.

Register in Probate 220 N Beaumont Rd, Prairie Du Chien, WI 53821; 608-326-0206; Fax: 608-326-0288. Hours: 8AM-4:30PM *Probate.*

Dane County

Circuit Court 210 Martin Luther King Jr Blvd, Rm GR10, Madison, WI 53709; 608-266-4311; Fax: 608-267-8859. Hours: 7:45AM-4:30PM (CST). *Felony, Misdemeanor, Civil, Eviction, Small Claims.*

Civil Records: Access: Fax, mail, online, in person. Both court and visitors may perform in person searches. Search fee: $5.00 per name. Required to search: name, years to search. Civil cases indexed by defendant, plaintiff. Civil records on computer from 1981, on microfiche from 1976, defendant index books 1848. Civil court records are available free on the Internet at http://ccap.courts.state.wi.us/internetcourtaccess.

Criminal Records: Access: Fax, mail, online, in person. Both court and visitors may perform in person searches. Search fee: $5.00 per name. Required to search: name, years to search; also helpful-DOB. Criminal records on computer from 1983. Online access to criminal records is same as civil, see above. **General Information:** No "confidential records" released. SASE required. Turnaround time 2-3 days. Copy fee: $1.25 per page. Certification fee: $5.00. Fee payee: Dane County Clerk of Courts. Personal checks accepted. Prepayment is required. Public access terminal is available. Fax note: $.50 first page, $.23 each addl.

Register in Probate 210 Martin Luther King Jr Blvd, Rm 305, Madison, WI 53709; 608-266-4331. Hours: 7:45AM-4:30PM *Probate.*

Dodge County

Circuit Court 105 N Main, Juneau, WI 53039; 920-386-3820; Fax: 920-386-3587. Hours: 8AM-4:30PM (CST). *Felony, Misdemeanor, Civil, Eviction, Small Claims.*

Civil Records: Access: Mail, online, in person. Both court and visitors may perform in person searches. Search fee: $5.00 per name. Required to search: name, years to search. Civil cases indexed by defendant, plaintiff. Civil records on computer from 1993, on index cards from 1986, microfiche from 1972, index books from 1900s. Civil court records are available free on the Internet at http://ccap.courts.state.wi.us/internetcourtaccess.
Criminal Records: Access: Mail, online, in person. Both court and visitors may perform in person searches. Search fee: $5.00 per name. Required to search: name, years to search, DOB. Criminal records on computer from 1993, on index cards from 1986, microfiche from 1972, index books from 1900s. Online access to criminal records is same as civil, see above. **General Information:** No juvenile or John Doe records released. SASE required. Turnaround time 1-2 days. Copy fee: $1.25 per page. Certification fee: $5.00. Fee payee: Clerk of Courts. Personal checks accepted. Prepayment is required. Public access terminal is available.

Register in Probate 105 N Main St, Juneau, WI 53039-1056; 920-386-3550; Fax: 920-386-3587. Hours: 8AM-4:30PM (CST). *Probate.*

Note: $4.00 search fee, records computerized since 1992.

Door County

Circuit Court PO Box 670, Sturgeon Bay, WI 54235; 920-746-2205; Fax: 920-746-2520. Hours: 8AM-4:30PM (CST). *Felony, Misdemeanor, Civil, Eviction, Small Claims.*

Civil Records: Access: Mail, online, in person. Both court and visitors may perform in person searches. Search fee: $5.00 per name. Required to search: name, years to search. Civil cases indexed by defendant, plaintiff. Civil records on computer from 4/93, on index cards from 1984, index books from 1900s. Civil court records are available free: http://ccap.courts.state.wi.us/internetcourtaccess.
Criminal Records: Access: Mail, online, in person. Both court and visitors may perform in person searches. Search fee: $5.00 per name. Required to search: name, years to search, DOB. Criminal records on computer from 4/93, on index cards from 1984, index books from 1900s. Online access to criminal records is same as civil, see above. **General Information:** No financial or paternity records released. SASE required. Turnaround time 2-3 days. Copy fee: $1.25 per

page. Certification fee: $5.00. Fee payee: Clerk of Court. Personal checks accepted.

Register in Probate PO Box 670, 421 Nebraska St, Rm C375, Sturgeon Bay, WI 54235-2470; 920-746-2482; Fax: 920-746-2470. Hours: 8AM-4:30PM (CST). *Probate.*

Douglas County

Circuit Court 1313 Belknap, Superior, WI 54880;; Civil phone:715-395-1237; Criminal phone:715-395-1237; Fax: 715-395-1421. Hours: 8AM-4:30PM (CST). *Felony, Misdemeanor, Civil, Eviction, Small Claims.*

Civil Records: Access: Mail, online, in person. Only the court conducts in person searches; visitors may not. Search fee: $5.00 per name. Required to search: name, years to search. Civil cases indexed by defendant, plaintiff. Civil records on computer since 1994; prior records on index cards from 1976, index books from 1900s. Civil court records are available free on the Internet at http://ccap.courts.state.wi.us/internetcourtaccess.
Criminal Records: Access: Mail, online, in person. Only the court conducts in person searches; visitors may not. Search fee: $5.00 per name. Required to search: name, years to search; also helpful-DOB. Criminal records on computer since 1994; prior records on index cards from 1976, index books from 1900s. Online access to criminal records is same as civil, see above.
General Information: No juvenile or paternity records released. SASE required. Turnaround time 1-2 weeks. Copy fee: $1.25 per page. Certification fee: $5.00. Fee payee: Clerk of Courts. Only cashiers checks and money orders accepted. Douglas County personal checks accepted. Prepayment is required. Public access terminal is available.

Register in Probate 1313 Belknap, Superior, WI 54880; 715-395-1229; Fax: 715-395-1421. Hours: 8AM-4:30PM (CST). *Probate.*

Dunn County

Circuit Court Stokke Parkway #1500, Menomonie, WI 54751; 715-232-2611. Hours: 8AM-4:30PM (CST). *Felony, Misdemeanor, Civil, Eviction, Small Claims.*

Civil Records: Access: Mail, online, in person. Both court and visitors may perform in person searches. Search fee: $5.00 per name. Required to search: name, years to search. Civil cases indexed by defendant, plaintiff. Civil records on computer from 1989, index cards from 1977, index books from 1900s, archives from 1970. Civil court records are available free on the Internet at http://ccap.courts.state.wi.us/internetcourtaccess.
Criminal Records: Access: Mail, online, in person. Both court and visitors may perform in person searches. Search fee: $5.00 per name. Required to search: name, years to search, DOB. Criminal records on computer from 1989, index cards from 1977, index books from 1900s, archives from 1970. Online access to criminal records is same as civil, see above. **General Information:** No juvenile, family financial, sealed records released. SASE not required. Turnaround time 2-3 days. Copy fee: $1.25 per page. Certification fee: $5.00. Fee payee: Clerk of Court. Personal checks accepted. Prepayment is required. Public access terminal is available.

Register in Probate 615 Parkway Dr #1300, Menomonie, WI 54751; 715-232-1449; Fax: 715-232-6971. Hours: 8AM-4:30PM (CST). *Probate.*

Eau Claire County

Circuit Court 721 Oxford Ave, Eau Claire, WI 54703; 715-839-4816; Fax: 715-839-4817. Hours: 8AM-5PM (CST). *Felony, Misdemeanor, Civil, Eviction, Small Claims.*

Civil Records: Access: Mail, online, in person. Both court and visitors may perform in person searches. Search fee: $5.00 per name. Required to search: name, years to search. Civil cases indexed by defendant, plaintiff. Civil records on computer from 7/92, on index cards from 1970, index books from 1968. Civil court records are available free: http://ccap.courts.state.wi.us/internetcourtaccess.
Criminal Records: Access: Mail, online, in person. Both court and visitors may perform in person searches. Search fee: $5.00 per name. Required to search: name, years to search, DOB. Criminal records on computer from 7/92, on index cards from 1970, index books from 1968. Online access to criminal records is same as civil, see above. **General Information:** No paternity, financial disclosure, expungement or sealed records released. SASE required. Turnaround time 1-10 days. Copy fee: $1.25 per page. Certification fee: $5.00. Fee payee: Clerk of Court-Eau Claire County. Personal checks accepted. Prepayment is required. Public access terminal is available.

Register in Probate 721 Oxford Ave, Eau Claire, WI 54703; 715-839-4823. Hours: 8AM-5PM (CST). *Probate.*

Florence County

Circuit Court PO Box 410, Florence, WI 54121; 715-528-3205; Fax: 715-528-5470. Hours: 8:30AM-4PM (CST). *Felony, Misdemeanor, Civil, Eviction, Small Claims.*

Civil Records: Access: Mail, online, in person. Both court and visitors may perform in person searches. Search fee: $5.00 per name. Required to search: name, years to search. Civil cases indexed by defendant, plaintiff. Civil records on computer from 1991; prior records on index books from 1900s. Civil court records are available free at http://ccap.courts.state.wi.us/internetcourtaccess.
Criminal Records: Access: Mail, online, in person. Both court and visitors may perform in person searches. Search fee: $5.00 per name. Required to search: name, years to search. Criminal records on computer from 1991; prior records on index books from 1900s. Online access to criminal records is same as civil, see above. **General Information:** No juvenile, mental health, adoption or guardianship records released. SASE required. Turnaround time 2 weeks. Copy fee: $1.25 per page. Certification fee: $5.00. Fee payee: Clerk of Courts. Personal checks accepted. Prepayment is required. Public access terminal is available.

Register in Probate PO Box 410, Florence, WI 54121; 715-528-3205; Fax: 715-528-5470. Hours: 8:30AM-Noon, 1-4PM *Probate.*

Fond du Lac County

Circuit Court PO Box 1355, Fond du Lac, WI 54936-1355; 920-929-3041; Fax: 920-929-3933. Hours: 8AM-4:30PM (CST). *Felony, Misdemeanor, Civil, Eviction, Small Claims.*

Civil Records: Access: Mail, online, in person. Both court and visitors may perform in person searches. Search fee: $5.00 per name. Required to search: name, years to search. Civil cases indexed by defendant, plaintiff. Civil records on computer from 1990, index cards from 1978, microfiche 1836 to 1978, archives prior to 1900s. Old files

destroyed, on microfiche or in Historical Society. Civil court records are on the Internet at http://ccap.courts.state.wi.us/internetcourtaccess.
Criminal Records: Access: Mail, online, in person. Both court and visitors may perform in person searches. Search fee: $5.00 per name. Required to search: name, years to search, DOB. Criminal records on computer from 1990, index cards from 1978, microfiche 1836 to 1978, archives prior to 1900s. Old files destroyed, on microfiche or in Historical Society. Online access to criminal records is same as civil, see above. **General Information:** No juvenile or paternity records released. SASE required. Turnaround time 1-2 days. Copy fee: $1.25 per page. Certification fee: $5.00. Fee payee: Clerk of Circuit Court. Personal checks accepted. Prepayment is required. Public access terminal is available.

Register in Probate PO Box 1355, Fond du Lac, WI 54936-1355; 920-929-3084; Fax: 920-929-7058. Hours: 8AM-Noon, 1-4:30PM (CST). *Probate.*

Forest County

Circuit Court 200 E Madison St, Crandon, WI 54520; 715-478-3323; Fax: 715-478-2430. Hours: 8:30AM-4:30PM (CST). *Felony, Misdemeanor, Civil, Eviction, Small Claims.*

Civil Records: Access: Mail, online, in person. Both court and visitors may perform in person searches. Search fee: $5.00 per name. Required to search: name, years to search. Civil cases indexed by defendant, plaintiff. Civil records on computer from 1994, on index cards from 1979, index books from 1903, Historical Society has books prior to 1903. Civil court records are available free at http://ccap.courts.state.wi.us/internetcourtaccess.
Criminal Records: Access: Mail, online, in person. Both court and visitors may perform in person searches. Search fee: $5.00 per name. Required to search: name, years to search. Criminal records on computer from 1994, on index cards from 1979, index books from 1903, Historical Society has books prior to 1903. Online access to criminal records is same as civil, see above. **General Information:** No juvenile, paternity records released. SASE required. Turnaround time 1-2 days. Certification fee: $5.00. Fee payee: Clerk of Court. Personal checks accepted. Prepayment is required.

Register in Probate 200 E Madison St, Crandon, WI 54520; 715-478-2418; Fax: 715-478-2430. Hours: 8:30AM-4:30PM (CST). *Probate.*

Grant County

Circuit Court PO Box 110, Lancaster, WI 53813; 608-723-2752; Fax: 608-723-7370. Hours: 8AM-4:30PM (CST). *Felony, Misdemeanor, Civil, Eviction, Small Claims.*

Civil Records: Access: Mail, online, in person. Both court and visitors may perform in person searches. No search fee. Required to search: name, years to search. Civil cases indexed by defendant, plaintiff. Civil records on computer from 10/93, on index books from 1900s. Civil court records are available free on the Internet at http://ccap.courts.state.wi.us/internetcourtaccess.
Criminal Records: Access: Mail, online, in person. Only the court conducts in person searches; visitors may not. No search fee. Required to search: name, years to search. Criminal records on computer from 10/93, on index books from 1900s. Online access to criminal records is same as civil, see above. **General**

Information: No juvenile, paternity records released. SASE required. Turnaround time 2 weeks. Copy fee: $1.25 per page. Certification fee: $5.00 plus $1.25 per page. Fee payee: Clerk of Court. Personal checks accepted. Prepayment is required.

Register in Probate 130 W Maple St, Lancaster, WI 53813; 608-723-2697; Fax: 608-723-7370. Hours: 8AM-4:30PM (CST). *Probate.*

Note: $4.00 search fee, records computerized since 1993.

Green County

Circuit Court 1016 16th Ave, Monroe, WI 53566; 608-328-9433; Fax: 608-328-2835. Hours: 8AM-5PM (CST). *Felony, Misdemeanor, Civil, Eviction, Small Claims.*

Civil Records: Access: Mail, online, in person. Both court and visitors may perform in person searches. Search fee: $5.00 per name. Required to search: name, years to search; also helpful-address. Civil cases indexed by defendant, plaintiff. Civil records on index cards from 1984, index books from 1900s. Civil court records available free at http://ccap.courts.state.wi.us/internetcourtaccess.
Criminal Records: Access: Mail, online, in person. Both court and visitors may perform in person searches. Search fee: $5.00 per name. Required to search: name, years to search; also helpful-DOB. Criminal records on index cards from 1984, index books from 1900s. Online access to criminal records is same as civil, see above. **General Information:** No juvenile, paternity or sealed records released. SASE required. Turnaround time 1-2 days. Copy fee: $1.25 per page. Certification fee: $5.00. Fee payee: Clerk of Court. Personal checks accepted. Prepayment is required.

Register in Probate 1016 16th Ave, Monroe, WI 53566; 608-328-9567; Fax: 608-328-2835. Hours: 8AM-12, 1PM-5PM (CST). *Probate.*

Green Lake County

Circuit Court 492 Hill St, PO Box 3188, Green Lake, WI 54941; 920-294-4142; Fax: 920-294-4150. Hours: 8AM-4:30PM (CST). *Felony, Misdemeanor, Civil, Eviction, Small Claims.*

Civil Records: Access: Mail, online, in person. Both court and visitors may perform in person searches. Search fee: $5.00 per name. Required to search: name, years to search. Civil cases indexed by defendant, plaintiff. Civil records on computer from 4/93, on index cards since 1900s. Civil court records are available free on the Internet at http://ccap.courts.state.wi.us/internetcourtaccess.
Criminal Records: Access: Mail, online, in person. Both court and visitors may perform in person searches. Search fee: $5.00 per name. Required to search: name, years to search. Criminal records on computer from 4/93, on index cards since 1900s. Online access to criminal records is same as civil, see above. **General Information:** No paternity or juvenile ordinance records released. SASE required. Turnaround time 1-3 days. Copy fee: $1.25 per page. Certification fee: $5.00. Fee payee: Clerk of Circuit Clerk. Personal checks accepted. Prepayment is required. Public access terminal is available.

Register in Probate 492 Hill St, Green Lake, WI 54941; 920-294-4044; Fax: 920-294-4150. Hours: 8AM-4:30PM (CST). *Probate.*

Iowa County

Circuit Court 222 N Iowa St, Dodgeville, WI 53533; 608-935-0395; Fax: 608-935-0386. Hours: 8:30AM-4:30PM (CST). *Felony, Misdemeanor, Civil, Eviction, Small Claims.*

Civil Records: Access: Mail, online, in person. Both court and visitors may perform in person searches. Search fee: $5.00 per name. Required to search: name, years to search. Civil cases indexed by defendant, plaintiff. Civil records on computer from 1992, index cards from 1987, archives from 1917, index books from 1829. Civil court records are available free on the Internet at http://ccap.courts.state.wi.us/internetcourtaccess.
Criminal Records: Access: Mail, online, in person. Both court and visitors may perform in person searches. Search fee: $5.00 per name. Required to search: name, years to search, DOB. Criminal records on computer from 1992, index cards from 1987, archives from 1917, index books from 1829. Online access to criminal records is same as civil, see above. **General Information:** No adoption, paternity or mental records released. SASE required. Turnaround time same day. Copy fee: $1.25 per page. Certification fee: $5.00. Fee payee: Clerk of Court. Personal checks accepted. Prepayment is required. Public access terminal is available.

Register in Probate 222 N Iowa St, Dodgeville, WI 53533; 608-935-5812; Fax: 608-935-0368. Hours: 8:30AM-Noon, 12;30-4:30PM (CST). *Probate.*

Iron County

Circuit Court 300 Taconite St, Hurley, WI 54534; 715-561-4084; Fax: 715-561-4054. Hours: 8AM-4PM (CST). *Felony, Misdemeanor, Civil, Eviction, Small Claims.*

Civil Records: Access: Phone, mail, online, in person. Both court and visitors may perform in person searches. Search fee: $5.00 per name. Required to search: name, years to search. Civil cases indexed by defendant, plaintiff. Civil records on index cards from 1989, index books from 1920. Phone access for title companies only. Civil court records are available free on the Internet at http://ccap.courts.state.wi.us/internetcourtaccess.
Criminal Records: Access: Mail, online, in person. Both court and visitors may perform in person searches. Search fee: $5.00 per name. Required to search: name, years to search, DOB. Criminal records on index cards from 1989, index books from 1920. Online access to criminal records is same as civil, see above. **General Information:** No juvenile or paternity records released. SASE required. Turnaround time 10 days. Copy fee: $1.25 per page. Certification fee: $5.00. Fee payee: Clerk of Court. Personal checks accepted. Public terminal is available.

Register in Probate 300 Taconite St, Hurley, WI 54534; 715-561-3434; Fax: 715-561-4054. Hours: 8AM-4PM (CST). *Probate.*

Jackson County

Circuit Court 307 Main St, Black River Falls, WI 54615; 715-284-0208; Fax: 715-284-0270. Hours: 8AM-4:30PM (CST). *Felony, Misdemeanor, Civil, Eviction, Small Claims.*

www.co.jackson.wi.us

Civil Records: Access: Mail, online, in person. Both court and visitors may perform in person searches. Search fee: $5.00 per name. Required to search: name, years to search. Civil cases indexed by defendant, plaintiff. Civil records on computer

from 6/92, on index cards from 1979, index books to 1935, files and indexes prior to 1935 destroyed. Civil court records are available free at http://ccap.courts.state.wi.us/internetcourtaccess.
Criminal Records: Access: Mail, online, in person. Both court and visitors may perform in person searches. Search fee: $5.00 per name. Required to search: name, years to search, DOB. Criminal records on computer from 6/92, on index cards from 1979, index books to 1935, files and indexes prior to 1935 destroyed. **General Information:** No juvenile or pre-judgment paternity records released. SASE required. Turnaround time 1-4 days. Copy fee: $1.25 per page. Certification fee: $5.00. Fee payee: Clerk of Court. Personal checks accepted. Prepayment is required.

Register in Probate 307 Main St, Black River Falls, WI 54615; 715-284-0213; Fax: 715-284-0277. Hours: 8AM-4:30PM (CST). *Probate.*

Jefferson County

Circuit Court 320 S Main St, Jefferson, WI 53549; 920-674-7150; Fax: 920-674-7425. Hours: 8AM-4:30PM (CST). *Felony, Misdemeanor, Civil, Eviction, Small Claims.*

Civil Records: Access: Mail, online, in person. Both court and visitors may perform in person searches. Search fee: $5.00 per name. Required to search: name, years to search. Civil cases indexed by defendant, plaintiff. Civil records on computer from 1992, on index cards from 1979, index books from late 1800s. Civil court records are available free online at http://ccap.courts.state.wi.us/internetcourtaccess. **Criminal Records:** Access: Mail, online, in person. Both court and visitors may perform in person searches. Search fee: $5.00 per name. Required to search: name, years to search, DOB. Criminal records on computer from 1992, on index cards from 1979, index books from late 1800s. Online access to criminal records is same as civil, see above. **General Information:** No juvenile or mental health records released. SASE required. Turnaround time 2-3 days. Copy fee: $1.25 per page. Certification fee: $5.00. Fee payee: Clerk of Courts. Personal checks accepted. Prepayment is required.

Register in Probate 320 S Main St, Jefferson, WI 53549; 920-674-7245; Fax: 920-675-0134. Hours: 8AM-4:30PM (CST). *Probate.*

Juneau County

Circuit Court 220 E State St, Mauston, WI 53948; 608-847-9356; Fax: 608-847-9360. Hours: 8AM-Noon, 12:30-4:30PM (CST). *Felony, Misdemeanor, Civil, Eviction, Small Claims.*

Civil Records: Access: Mail, online, in person. Both court and visitors may perform in person searches. Search fee: $5.00 per name. Fee is per case. Required to search: name, years to search. Civil cases indexed by defendant, plaintiff. Civil records on computer from 1988, index cards from 1977, index books from 1900, microfiche from 1856-1900. Civil court records are available free at http://ccap.courts.state.wi.us/internetcourtaccess.
Criminal Records: Access: Mail, online, in person. Both court and visitors may perform in person searches. Search fee: $5.00 per name. Required to search: name, years to search, DOB. Criminal records on computer from 1988, index cards from 1977, index books from 1900, microfiche from 1856-1900. Online access to criminal records is same as civil, see above. **General Information:** No juvenile, confidential family or paternity records released. SASE

required. Turnaround time 1 week. Copy fee: $1.25 per page. Certification fee: $5.00. Fee payee: Juneau County Clerk of Court. Personal checks accepted. Prepayment is required. Public access terminal is available.

Register in Probate 220 E State St Rm 205, Mauston, WI 53948; 608-847-9346; Fax: 608-847-9349. Hours: 8AM-4:30PM *Probate.*

Kenosha County

Circuit Court 912 56th St, Kenosha, WI 53140; 262-653-2664; Fax: 262-653-2435. Hours: 8AM-5PM (CST). *Felony, Misdemeanor, Civil, Eviction, Small Claims.*

Civil Records: Access: Mail, online, in person. Both court and visitors may perform in person searches. Search fee: $5.00 per name. Required to search: name, years to search. Civil cases indexed by defendant, plaintiff. Civil records on computer from 1989, index cards from 1960, microfiche from 1850. Civil court records on the Internet at http://ccap.courts.state.wi.us/internetcourtaccess.
Criminal Records: Access: Mail, online, in person. Both court and visitors may perform in person searches. Search fee: $5.00 per name. Required to search: name, years to search; also helpful-DOB, SSN. Criminal records on computer from 1989, index cards from 1960, microfiche from 1850. Online access to criminal records is same as civil, see above. **General Information:** No juvenile or paternity records released. SASE required. Turnaround time 1-2 days. Copy fee: $1.25 per page. Certification fee: $5.00. Fee payee: Clerk of Court. Personal checks accepted. Prepayment is required. Public access terminal is available.

Register in Probate Courthouse Rm 302, 912 56th St, Kenosha, WI 53140; 262-653-6678; Fax: 262-653-2435. Hours: 8AM-5PM (CST). *Probate.*

Note: $4.00 per search, records indexed on computer (1992) and cards.

Kewaunee County

Circuit Court 613 Dodge St, Kewaunee, WI 54216; 920-388-7144; Fax: 920-388-3139. Hours: 8AM-4:30PM (CST). *Felony, Misdemeanor, Civil, Eviction, Small Claims.*

Civil Records: Access: Phone, mail, online, in person. Both court and visitors may perform in person searches. Search fee: $5.00 per name. Required to search: name, years to search. Civil cases indexed by defendant, plaintiff. Civil records on index cards from 1978, index books from 1852. Civil court records are available free at http://ccap.courts.state.wi.us/internetcourtaccess.
Criminal Records: Access: Phone, mail, online, in person. Both court and visitors may perform in person searches. Search fee: $5.00 per name. Required to search: name, years to search, DOB. Criminal records on index cards from 1978, index books from 1852. Online access to criminal records is same as civil, see above. **General Information:** No paternity records released. SASE required. Turnaround time 1-2 days. Copy fee: $1.25 per page. Certification fee: $5.00. Fee payee: Clerk of Circuit Court. Personal checks accepted. Prepayment is required.

Register in Probate 613 Dodge St, Kewaunee, WI 54216; 920-388-4410; Fax: 920-388-3139. Hours: 8AM-4:30PM (CST). *Probate.*

La Crosse County

Circuit Court 333 Vine St, La Crosse, WI 54601; 608-785-9590/9573; Fax: 608-789-7821. Hours: 8:30AM-5PM (CST). *Felony, Misdemeanor, Civil, Eviction, Small Claims.*

Civil Records: Access: Phone, mail, online, in person. Both court and visitors may perform in person searches. Search fee: $5.00 per name. Required to search: name, years to search. Civil cases indexed by defendant, plaintiff. Civil records on computer from 1992, on index cards from 1983, index books from 1917. Civil court records are available free on the Internet at http://ccap.courts.state.wi.us/internetcourtaccess.
Criminal Records: Access: Phone, mail, online, in person. Both court and visitors may perform in person searches. Search fee: $5.00 per name. Required to search: name, years to search; also helpful-DOB, SSN. Criminal records on computer from 1992, on index cards from 1983, index books from 1917. Online access to criminal records is same as civil, see above. **General Information:** No juvenile, paternity or finances in family records released. SASE required. Turnaround time 1-2 days. Copy fee: $1.25 per page. Fee is for civil copies. Criminal copies $.25 per page. Certification fee: $5.00. Fee payee: Clerk of Courts. Personal checks accepted. Prepayment is required. Public access terminal is available.

Register in Probate 333 Vine St, Rm 1201, La Crosse, WI 54601; 608-785-9882. Hours: 8:30AM-5PM (CST). *Probate.*

Lafayette County

Circuit Court 626 Main St, Darlington, WI 53530; 608-776-4832. Hours: 8AM-4:30PM (CST). *Felony, Misdemeanor, Civil, Eviction, Small Claims.*

Civil Records: Access: Mail, online, in person. Both court and visitors may perform in person searches. Search fee: $5.00 per name. Required to search: name, years to search. Civil cases indexed by defendant. Civil records on index cards from 1973, index books from 1900. Civil court records are available free on the Internet at http://ccap.courts.state.wi.us/internetcourtaccess.
Criminal Records: Access: Mail, online, in person. Both court and visitors may perform in person searches. Search fee: $5.00 per name. Required to search: name, years to search. Criminal records on index cards from 1973, index books from 1900. Online access to criminal records is same as civil, see above. **General Information:** No juvenile records released. SASE required. Turnaround time 2-3 days. Copy fee: $1.25 per page. Certification fee: $5.00. Fee payee: Clerk of Circuit Court. Personal checks accepted. Prepayment is required. Public access terminal is available.

Register in Probate 626 Main St, Darlington, WI 53530; 608-776-4811. Hours: 8AM-4:30PM (CST). *Probate.*

Langlade County

Circuit Court 800 Clermont St, Antigo, WI 54409; 715-627-6215. Hours: 8:30AM-4:30PM (CST). *Felony, Misdemeanor, Civil, Eviction, Small Claims.*

Civil Records: Access: Mail, online, in person. Both court and visitors may perform in person searches. Search fee: $5.00 per name. Required to search: name, years to search. Civil cases indexed by defendant, plaintiff. Civil records on index books from 1905. Civil court records available at

http://ccap.courts.state.wi.us/internetcourtaccess.
Criminal Records: Access: Mail, online, in person. Both court and visitors may perform in person searches. Search fee: $5.00 per name. Required to search: name, years to search. Criminal records on index books from 1905. Online access to criminal records is same as civil, see above. **General Information:** No confidential records released. SASE required. Turnaround time 2-3 days. Copy fee: $1.25 per page. Certification fee: $5.00. Fee payee: Clerk of Court. Personal checks accepted. Prepayment is required.

Register in Probate 800 Clermont St, Antigo, WI 54409; 715-627-6303; Fax: 715-627-6213. Hours: 8:30AM-4:30PM (CST). *Probate.*

Note: There is a $4.00 search fee.

Lincoln County

Circuit Court 1110 E Main St, Merrill, WI 54452; 715-536-0319; Fax: 715-536-6528. Hours: 8:15AM-4:30PM (CST). *Felony, Misdemeanor, Civil, Eviction, Small Claims.*

Civil Records: Access: Mail, online, in person. Both court and visitors may perform in person searches. Search fee: $5.00 per name. Required to search: name, years to search. Civil cases indexed by defendant. Civil records on computer from 1990, index cards from 1982, index books from 1900s. Civil court records are available free at http://ccap.courts.state.wi.us/internetcourtaccess.
Criminal Records: Access: Mail, online, in person. Both court and visitors may perform in person searches. Search fee: $5.00 per name. Required to search: name, years to search; also helpful-DOB, SSN. Criminal records on computer from 1990, index cards from 1982, index books from 1900s. Online access to criminal records is same as civil, see above. **General Information:** No paternity or sealed records released. SASE required. Turnaround time 1-2 days. Copy fee: $1.25 per page. Certification fee: $5.00. Fee payee: Clerk of Court. Personal checks accepted. Local personal checks accepted. Prepayment is required.

Register in Probate 1110 E Main St, Merrill, WI 54452; 715-536-0342; Fax: 715-536-5230. Hours: 8:15AM-Noon, 1-4:30PM *Probate.*

Manitowoc County

Circuit Court PO Box 2000, Manitowoc, WI 54221-2000; 920-683-4030. Hours: 8:30AM-5PM M; 8:30AM-4:30PM T-F (CST). *Felony, Misdemeanor, Civil, Eviction, Small Claims.*

Civil Records: Access: Phone, mail, online, in person. Both court and visitors may perform in person searches. Search fee: $5.00 per name. Required to search: name, years to search. Civil cases indexed by defendant, plaintiff. Civil records on computer from 1993, on index cards from 1962, index books from 1906, Historical Society has prior records. Prior written agreement with court required for phone access. Civil court records are available free on the Internet at http://ccap.courts.state.wi.us/internetcourtaccess.
Criminal Records: Access: Phone, mail, online, in person. Both court and visitors may perform in person searches. Search fee: $5.00 per name. Required to search: name, years to search, DOB. Criminal records on computer from 1993, on index cards from 1962, index books from 1906, Historical Society has prior records. Prior written agreement with court required for phone access. Online access to criminal records is same as civil, see above. **General Information:** No confidential records released. SASE required. Turnaround time

2-3 days. Copy fee: $1.25 per page. Certification fee: $1.25 per page. Fee payee: Clerk of Circuit Court. Personal checks accepted. Prepayment is required. Public access terminal is available.

Register in Probate 1010 S 8th St Rm 116, Manitowoc, WI 54220; 920-683-4016; Fax: 920-683-5182. Hours: 8:30AM-4:30PM *Probate.*

Marathon County

Circuit Court 500 Forest St, Wausau, WI 54403; 715-261-1300; Fax: 715-261-1319 Civ; 261-1280 Crim. Hours: 8AM-5PM (Summer hours 8AM-4:30PM Memorial-Labor Day) *Felony, Misdemeanor, Civil, Eviction, Small Claims.*

Civil Records: Access: Mail, online, in person. Both court and visitors may perform in person searches. Search fee: $5.00 per name. Required to search: name, years to search. Civil cases indexed by defendant, plaintiff. Civil records on computer from 1992, on index cards from 1979, index books from 1900s. All requests must be in writing, using their form if possible. Civil court records are available free on the Internet at http://ccap.courts.state.wi.us/internetcourtaccess.
Criminal Records: Access: Mail, online, in person. Only the court conducts in person searches; visitors may not. Search fee: $5.00 per name. Required to search: name, years to search, DOB. Criminal records on computer from 1992, on index cards from 1979, index books from 1900s. All requests must be in writing, using their form if possible. The DOB of the requester is required. Online access to criminal records is same as civil, see above. **General Information:** No mental health or juvenile records released. SASE required. Turnaround time 1-3 days. Copy fee: $1.25 per page. Certification fee: $5.00. Fee payee: Clerk of Court. Personal checks accepted. Prepayment is required.

Register in Probate 500 Forest St, Wausau, WI 54403; 715-847-5218; Fax: 715-847-5200. Hours: 8AM-5PM (CST). *Probate.*

Marinette County

Circuit Court 1926 Hall Ave, Marinette, WI 54143-1717; 715-732-7450. Hours: 8:30AM-4:30PM (CST). *Felony, Misdemeanor, Civil, Eviction, Small Claims.*

Civil Records: Access: Mail, online, in person. Both court and visitors may perform in person searches. Search fee: $5.00 per name. Required to search: name, years to search. Civil cases indexed by defendant, plaintiff. Civil records on computer from 1989, index cards from 1980, index books from 1906, prior records at Historical Society. Civil court records are available free at http://ccap.courts.state.wi.us/internetcourtaccess.
Criminal Records: Access: Mail, online, in person. Both court and visitors may perform in person searches. Search fee: $5.00 per name. Required to search: name, years to search, DOB. Criminal records on computer from 1989, index cards from 1980, index books from 1906, prior records at Historical Society. Online access to criminal records is same as civil, see above. **General Information:** No paternity records released. SASE required. Turnaround time 2-3 days. Copy fee: $1.25 per page. Certification fee: $5.00. Fee payee: Clerk of Courts. Personal checks accepted. Prepayment is required. Public access terminal is available.

Register in Probate 1926 Hall Ave, Marinette, WI 54143-1717; 715-732-7475; Fax: 715-732-7496. Hours: 8:30AM-Noon, 1-4:30PM (CST). *Probate.*

Marquette County

Circuit Court PO Box 187, Montello, WI 53949; 608-297-9102; Fax: 608-297-9188. Hours: 8AM-Noon, 12:30-4:30PM (CST). *Felony, Misdemeanor, Civil, Eviction, Small Claims.*

Civil Records: Access: Mail, online, in person. Both court and visitors may perform in person searches. Search fee: $5.00 per name. Required to search: name, years to search. Civil cases indexed by defendant, plaintiff. Civil records on index books from 1900s, prior records at Historical Society. Civil court records are available free at http://ccap.courts.state.wi.us/internetcourtaccess.
Criminal Records: Access: Mail, online, in person. Both court and visitors may perform in person searches. Search fee: $5.00 per name. Required to search: name, years to search, DOB. Criminal records on index books from 1900s, prior records at Historical Society. Online access to criminal records is same as civil, see above.
General Information: No adoption, juvenile, paternity, guardianship, mental or termination of parental right records released. SASE not required. Turnaround time 1-2 days. Copy fee: $1.25 per page. Certification fee: $5.00. Fee payee: Clerk of Circuit Court. Personal checks accepted. Prepayment required. Public terminal is available.

Register in Probate 77 W Park St, PO Box 749, Montello, WI 53949; 608-297-9105; Fax: 608-297-9188. Hours: 8AM-4:30PM (CST). *Probate.*

Menominee County

Circuit Court PO Box 279, Keshena, WI 54135; 715-799-3313; Fax: 715-799-1322. Hours: 8AM-4:30PM (CST). *Felony, Misdemeanor, Civil, Eviction, Small Claims.*

Civil Records: Access: Mail, online, in person. Both court and visitors may perform in person searches. Search fee: $5.00 per name. Required to search: name, years to search. Civil cases indexed by defendant, plaintiff. Civil records are indexed by cards, kept in files since 1979. Older records are at the Historical Society. Civil court records are available free on the Internet at http://ccap.courts.state.wi.us/internetcourtaccess.
Criminal Records: Access: Mail, online, in person. Both court and visitors may perform in person searches. Search fee: $5.00 per name. Required to search: name, years to search, DOB. Criminal records are indexed by cards, kept in files since 1979. Older records are at the Historical Society. Online access to criminal records is same as civil, see above. **General Information:** No juvenile, mental, adoption. Turnaround time 3-4 days. Copy fee: $1.25 per page. Certification fee: $5.00. Fee payee: Clerk of Court. Personal checks accepted.

Register in Probate 311 N Main St, Shawano, WI 54166; 715-526-8631; Fax: 715-526-4915. Hours: 8AM-4:30PM (CST). *Probate.*

Note: Tribal probate records only in Keshena (Menominee County); Non-tribal records are in Shawano County.

Milwaukee County

Circuit Court-Civil 901 9th St Rm G-9, Milwaukee, WI 53233; 414-278-4128; Fax: 414-223-1256. Hours: 8AM-4PM (CST). *Civil, Eviction, Small Claims.*

www.co.milwaukee.wi.us/courts/court.htm

Civil Records: Access: Mail, online, in person. Both court and visitors may perform in person searches. Search fee: $5.00 per name. Required to

search: name, years to search. Civil cases indexed by defendant, plaintiff. Civil records on computer from 1985, on microfiche from 1933, prior with County Historical Society. Civil court records are available free on the Internet at http://ccap.courts.state.wi.us/internetcourtaccess.
General Information: No paternity records released. SASE required. Turnaround time 1-2 weeks. Copy fee: $1.25 per page. Certification fee: $5.00. Fee payee: Milwaukee County Clerk of Circuit Court. Personal checks accepted. Prepayment is required. Public access terminal is available.

Circuit Court-Criminal Division 821 W State St, Milwaukee, WI 53233; 414-278-4588, 278-4588 (Misdemeanor); Fax: 414-223-1262. Hours: 8AM-5PM (CST). *Felony, Misdemeanor.*

Note: Address Room 136 for felonies and Room 124 for misdemeanors **Criminal Records:** Access: Fax, mail, online, in person. Both court and visitors may perform in person searches. Search fee: $5.00 per name. Required to search: name, years to search, DOB. Criminal records on computer from 10/86, index books and cards prior. Criminal court records are available free at http://ccap.courts.state.wi.us/internetcourtaccess.
General Information: No sealed records released. SASE required. Turnaround time 4 days. Copy fee: $1.25 per page. Certification fee: $5.00. Fee payee: Clerk of Circuit Court. Personal checks accepted. Prepayment is required. Public access terminal is available. Fax notes: No fee to fax results.

Register in Probate 901 N 9th St Rm 207, Milwaukee, WI 53233; 414-278-4444; Fax: 414-223-1814. Hours: 8AM-4:30PM (CST). *Probate.* Note: probate records are not available online.

Monroe County

Circuit Court 112 S Court St #203, Sparta, WI 54656-1764; 608-269-8745. Hours: 8AM-4:30PM (CST). *Felony, Misdemeanor, Civil, Eviction, Small Claims.*

Civil Records: Access: Fax, mail, online, in person. Both court and visitors may perform in person searches. Search fee: $5.00 per name. Required to search: name, years to search. Civil cases indexed by defendant, plaintiff. Civil records on computer and cards. Civil court records are available free on the internet at http://ccap.courts.state.wi.us/internetcourtaccess.
Criminal Records: Access: Fax, mail, online, in person. Both court and visitors may perform in person searches. Search fee: $5.00 per name. Required to search: name, years to search. Criminal records on computer and cards. Online access to criminal records is same as civil, see above. **General Information:** No paternity, medical or financial records released. SASE required. Turnaround time 1 week. Copy fee: $1.25 per page. Certification fee: $5.00. Fee payee: Clerk of Court. Local checks accepted. Prepayment is required. Public access terminal is available. Fax notes: $1.25 per page. No charge to toll free lines.

Register in Probate 112 S Court, Rm 301, Sparta, WI 54656-1765; 608-269-8701; Fax: 608-269-8950. Hours: 8AM-4:30PM (CST). *Probate.*

Oconto County

Circuit Court 301 Washington St, Oconto, WI 54153; 920-834-6855; Fax: 920-834-6867. Hours: 8AM-4PM (CST). *Felony, Misdemeanor, Civil, Eviction, Small Claims.*

Required to search: name, years to search, address, DOB, SSN, signed release. Criminal records on computer from 6/91, index cards from 1980, index books from 1900s. **General Information:** No expunged records released. SASE required. Turnaround time 10 working days. Copy fee: $1.25 per page. Certification fee: $5.00. Fee payee: Clerk of Court. Business checks accepted. Prepayment is required. Public access terminal is available.

Register in Probate 1516 Church St, Stevens Point, WI 54481; 715-346-1362; Fax: 715-346-1486. Hours: 7:30AM-4:30PM *Probate.* Note: probate records are available free on the Internet at http://ccap.courts.state.wi.us/internetcourtaccess

Price County

Circuit Court Courthouse, 126 Cherry St, Phillips, WI 54555; 715-339-2353; Fax: 715-339-3089. Hours: 8AM-Noon, 1-4:30PM (CST). *Felony, Misdemeanor, Civil, Eviction, Small Claims.*

Civil Records: Access: Mail, online, in person. Both court and visitors may perform in person searches. Search fee: $5.00 per name. Required to search: name, years to search. Civil cases indexed by defendant, plaintiff. Civil records on computer from 1997, prior on index books. Civil court records are available free on the Internet at http://ccap.courts.state.wi.us/internetcourtaccess.
Criminal Records: Access: Mail, online, in person. Both court and visitors may perform in person searches. Search fee: $5.00 per name. Required to search: name, years to search, DOB; also helpful-SSN. Criminal records on computer from 1997, prior on index books. Online access to criminal records is same as civil, see above.
General Information: No confidential records per statute or order released. SASE required. Turnaround time 1-2 days. Copy fee: $1.25 per page. Certification fee: $5.00. Fee payee: Clerk of Circuit Court. Personal checks accepted. Prepayment required. Public terminal is available.

Register in Probate Courthouse, 126 Cherry St, Phillips, WI 54555; 715-339-3078; Fax: 715-339-3089. Hours: 8AM-4:30PM *Probate.*

Racine County

Circuit Court 730 Wisconsin Ave, Racine, WI 53403; 262-636-3333; Fax: 262-636-3341. Hours: 8AM-5PM (CST). *Felony, Misdemeanor, Civil, Eviction, Small Claims, Probate.*

Civil Records: Access: Mail, online, in person. Both court and visitors may perform in person searches. Search fee: $5.00 per name. Required to search: name, years to search. Civil cases indexed by defendant, plaintiff. Civil records on computer from 1990, index cards from 1970, archives prior to 1970. Civil court records are available free at http://ccap.courts.state.wi.us/internetcourtaccess.
Criminal Records: Access: Mail, online, in person. Both court and visitors may perform in person searches. Search fee: $5.00 per name. Required to search: name, years to search, DOB. Criminal records on computer from 1990, index cards from 1970, archives prior to 1970. Online access to criminal records is same as civil, see above. **General Information:** No adoption, juvenile, paternity or mental commitment records released. SASE required. Turnaround time 1-2 weeks. Copy fee: $1.25 per page. Certification fee: $5.00. Fee payee: Clerk of Court. Personal checks accepted. Prepayment required. Public terminal is available.

Register in Probate 730 Wisconsin Ave, Racine, WI 53403; 262-636-3137; Fax: 262-636-3341. Hours: 8AM-5PM (CST). *Probate.*

Richland County

Circuit Court PO Box 655, Richland Center, WI 53581; 608-647-3956; Fax: 608-647-6134. Hours: 8:30AM-4:30PM (CST). *Felony, Misdemeanor, Civil, Eviction, Small Claims.*

Civil Records: Access: Mail, online, in person. Both court and visitors may perform in person searches. Search fee: $5.00 per name. Required to search: name, years to search. Civil cases indexed by defendant, plaintiff. Civil records on index cards from 1982, index books from 1972, archives prior to 1972, on computer from 1993 to present. Civil court records are free on the Internet at http://ccap.courts.state.wi.us/internetcourtaccess.
Criminal Records: Access: Mail, online, in person. Only the court conducts in person searches; visitors may not. Search fee: $5.00 per name. Required to search: name, years to search, DOB. Criminal records on index cards from 1982, index books from 1972, archives prior to 1972, on computer from 1993 to present. Online access to criminal records is same as civil, see above. **General Information:** No juvenile or paternity records released. SASE required. Turnaround time 1 week. Copy fee: $1.25 per page. Certification fee: $5.00. Fee payee: Clerk of Circuit Court. Personal checks accepted. Personal out-of-state checks not accepted. Prepayment is required. Public access terminal is available.

Register in Probate PO Box 427, Richland Center, WI 53581; 608-647-2626; Fax: 608-647-6134. Hours: 8:30AM-Noon, 1-4:30PM (CST). *Probate.*

Rock County

Circuit Court 51 S Main, Janesville, WI 53545; 608-743-2200; Fax: 608-743-2223. Hours: 8AM-5PM (CST). *Felony, Misdemeanor, Civil, Eviction, Small Claims.*

Civil Records: Access: Mail, online, in person. Both court and visitors may perform in person searches. Search fee: $5.00 per name. Required to search: name, years to search. Civil cases indexed by defendant, plaintiff. Civil records on computer from 6/93, on index cards from 6/91, index books from 1940, archives prior to 1940. Civil court records are available free on the Internet at http://ccap.courts.state.wi.us/internetcourtaccess.
Criminal Records: Access: Mail, online, in person. Both court and visitors may perform in person searches. Search fee: $5.00 per name. Required to search: name, years to search, DOB. Criminal records on computer from 6/93, on index cards from 6/91, index books from 1940, archives prior to 1940. Online access to criminal records is same as civil, see above. **General Information:** No juvenile, paternity or sealed records released. SASE required. Turnaround time 2-3 days. Copy fee: $1.25 per page. Certification fee: $5.00. Fee payee: Clerk of Court. Personal checks accepted. Prepayment is required. Public access terminal is available.

Circuit Court - South Janesville Courthouse, 51 S Main St, Janesville, WI 53545; 608-743-2200. Hours: 8AM-5PM (CST). *Felony, Misdemeanor, Civil, Eviction, Small Claims.*

Civil Records: Access: Mail, online, in person. Both court and visitors may perform in person searches. Search fee: $5.00 per name. Required to search: name, years to search. Civil cases indexed by defendant, plaintiff. Civil records on computer

from mid-1993, on index cards from 1970s, index books from 1900s in vault. Civil court records are available free on the Internet at http://ccap.courts.state.wi.us/internetcourtaccess.
Criminal Records: Access: Mail, online, in person. Both court and visitors may perform in person searches. Search fee: $5.00 per name. Required to search: name, years to search, DOB. Criminal records on computer from mid-1993, on index cards from 1970s, index books from 1900s in vault. Online access to criminal records is same as civil, see above. **General Information:** No paternity records released. SASE required. Turnaround time 1 week. Copy fee: $1.25 per page. Certification fee: $5.00. Fee payee: Clerk of Court. Personal checks accepted. Prepayment is required. Public access terminal is available.

Register in Probate 51 S Main, Janesville, WI 53545; 608-757-5635. Hours: 8AM-5PM (CST). *Probate.*

Rusk County

Circuit Court 311 Miner Ave East, #L350, Ladysmith, WI 54848; 715-532-2108. Hours: 8AM-4:30PM (CST). *Felony, Misdemeanor, Civil, Small Claims.*

Civil Records: Access: Mail, online, in person, online. Both court and visitors may perform in person searches. Search fee: $5.00 per name. Required to search: name, years to search. Civil cases indexed by defendant, plaintiff. Civil records on computer from 1992, on index cards from 1978, index books from 1900. Civil court records 1992 to present are available free on the Internet at http://ccap.courts.state.wi.us/internetcourtaccess.
Phone requests are accepted if the case number is known. **Criminal Records:** Access: Mail, online, in person, online. Both court and visitors may perform in person searches. Search fee: $5.00 per name. Required to search: name, years to search; also helpful-DOB. Criminal records on computer from 1992, on index cards from 1978, index books from 1900. Online access to criminal records is same as civil, see above. Phone requests are accepted if the case number is known. **General Information:** No juvenile or paternity records released. SASE required. Turnaround time 5 days. Copy fee: $1.25 per page. Certification fee: $5.00. Fee payee: Clerk of Court. Personal checks accepted. Prepayment is required. Public access terminal is available.

Register in Probate 311 E Miner Ave, Ladysmith, WI 54848; 715-532-2147; Fax: 715-532-2266. Hours: 8AM-4:30PM (CST). *Probate.*

Sauk County

Circuit Court 515 Oak Street, Baraboo, WI 53913; 608-355-3287. Hours: 8AM-4:30PM (CST). *Felony, Misdemeanor, Civil, Eviction, Small Claims.*

Civil Records: Access: Mail, online, in person. Both court and visitors may perform in person searches. Search fee: $5.00 per name. Required to search: name, years to search. Civil cases indexed by defendant, plaintiff. Civil records on computer from 1990, index cards from 1980, index books from 1967. Civil court records are available at http://ccap.courts.state.wi.us/internetcourtaccess.
Criminal Records: Access: Fax, mail, online, in person. Both court and visitors may perform in person searches. Search fee: $5.00 per name. Required to search: name, years to search. Criminal records on computer from 1990, index cards from 1980, index books from 1967. Online access to criminal records is same as civil, see

above. **General Information:** No paternity, juvenile records released. SASE required. Turnaround time 2-3 days. Copy fee: $1.25 per page. Certification fee: $5.00. Fee payee: Clerk of Court. Personal checks accepted. Prepayment is required. Public access terminal is available. Fax notes: $6.25 for first page, $1.25 each addl.

Register in Probate 515 Oak St, Baraboo, WI 53913; 608-355-3226. Hours: 8AM-4:30PM (CST). *Probate.*

Sawyer County

Circuit Court PO Box 508, Hayward, WI 54843; 715-634-4887. Hours: 8AM-4PM (CST). *Felony, Misdemeanor, Civil, Eviction, Small Claims.*

Civil Records: Access: Mail, online, in person. Both court and visitors may perform in person searches. Search fee: $5.00 per name. Required to search: name, years to search. Civil cases indexed by defendant, plaintiff. Civil records on index cards from 7/85, prior on books. Civil court records are available free on the Internet at http://ccap.courts.state.wi.us/internetcourtaccess. **Criminal Records:** Access: Mail, online, in person. Both court and visitors may perform in person searches. Search fee: $5.00 per name. Required to search: name, years to search. Civil records on index cards from 7/85, prior on books. Online access to criminal records is same as civil, see above. **General Information:** No juvenile, probate or paternity records released. SASE required. Turnaround time 1 day. Copy fee: $1.25 per page. Certification fee: $5.00. Fee payee: Clerk of Court. Personal checks accepted. Prepayment is required. Public access terminal is available.

Register in Probate PO Box 447, Hayward, WI 54843; 715-634-7519. Hours: 8AM-4PM (CST). *Probate.*

Shawano County

Circuit Court 311 N Main Rm 206, Shawano, WI 54166; 715-526-9347; Fax: 715-526-4915. Hours: 8AM-4:30PM (CST). *Felony, Misdemeanor, Civil, Eviction, Small Claims.*

Civil Records: Access: Fax, mail, online, in person. Both court and visitors may perform in person searches. Search fee: $5.00 per name. Required to search: name, years to search. Civil cases indexed by defendant, plaintiff. Civil records on computer from 1993, on index books from 1930s, prior in archives. Civil court records are available free on the Internet at http://ccap.courts.state.wi.us/internetcourtaccess. **Criminal Records:** Access: Fax, mail, online, in person. Both court and visitors may perform in person searches. Search fee: $5.00 per name. Required to search: name, years to search, DOB. Criminal records on computer from 1993, on index books from 1930s, prior in archives. Online access to criminal records is same as civil, see above. **General Information:** No juvenile, closed files or mental records released. SASE required. Turnaround time 10-20 days. Copy fee: $1.25 per page. Certification fee: $5.00. Fee payee: Clerk of Court. Personal checks accepted. Public access terminal is available. Fax notes: $1.25 per page, add $2.50 for long distance.

Register in Probate 311 N Main, Shawano, WI 54166; 715-526-8631; Fax: 715-526-4915. Hours: 8AM-4:30PM (CST). *Probate.*

Sheboygan County

Circuit Court 615 N 6th St, Sheboygan, WI 53081; 920-459-3068; Fax: 920-459-3921. Hours: 8AM-5PM (CST). *Felony, Misdemeanor, Civil, Eviction, Small Claims.*

Civil Records: Access: Mail, online, in person. Both court and visitors may perform in person searches. Search fee: $5.00 per name. Required to search: name, years to search; also helpful-address. Civil cases indexed by defendant, plaintiff. Civil records on computer since 1992; prior records on index cards from 1960, index books from 1860s, archives prior to 1971. Civil court records are available free on the Internet at http://ccap.courts.state.wi.us/internetcourtaccess. **Criminal Records:** Access: Mail, online, in person. Both court and visitors may perform in person searches. Search fee: $5.00 per name. Required to search: name, years to search, DOB; also helpful-address. Criminal records on computer since 1992; prior records on index cards from 1960, index books from 1860s, archives prior to 1971. Online access to criminal records is same as civil, see above. **General Information:** No juvenile or paternity records released. SASE required. Turnaround time 2-3 days. Copy fee: $1.25 per page. Certification fee: $5.00. Fee payee: Clerk of Circuit Court. Personal checks accepted. Prepayment is required. Public access terminal is available.

Register in Probate 615 N 6th St, Sheboygan, WI 53081; 920-459-3050 & 459-3202; Fax: 920-459-3921 (Clerk of Courts Office). Hours: 8AM-5PM (CST). *Probate.* Note: There is a $4.00 search fee.

St. Croix County

Circuit Court 1101 Carmichael Rd, Hudson, WI 54016; 715-386-4630. Hours: 8AM-5PM (CST). *Felony, Misdemeanor, Civil, Eviction, Small Claims.*

Civil Records: Access: Mail, online, in person. Both court and visitors may perform in person searches. Search fee: $5.00 per name. Required to search: name, years to search. Civil cases indexed by defendant, plaintiff. Civil records on computer from 10/92, on index cards from 1982, index books from 1900s. Civil court records are available free on the Internet at http://ccap.courts.state.wi.us/internetcourtaccess. **Criminal Records:** Access: Mail, online, in person. Both court and visitors may perform in person searches. Search fee: $5.00 per name. Required to search: name, years to search, DOB. Criminal records on computer from 10/92, on index cards from 1982, index books from 1900s. Online access to criminal records is same as civil, see above. **General Information:** No juvenile forfeitures, paternity, some case specific documents or sealed records released. SASE required. Turnaround time 5-10 days. Copy fee: $1.25 per page. Certification fee: $5.00. Fee payee: Clerk of Court. Personal checks accepted. Prepayment required. Public terminal is available.

Register in Probate 1101 Carmichael Rd, Rm 2242, Hudson, WI 54016; 715-386-4618; Fax: 715-381-4401. Hours: 8AM-5PM (CST). *Probate.*

Taylor County

Circuit Court 224 S 2nd St, Medford, WI 54451-1811; 715-748-1425; Fax: 715-748-2465. Hours: 8:30AM-4:30PM (CST). *Felony, Misdemeanor, Civil, Eviction, Small Claims.*

Civil Records: Access: Mail, online, in person. Both court and visitors may perform in person searches. Search fee: $5.00 per name. Required to search: name, years to search. Civil cases indexed by defendant, plaintiff. Civil records on computer from 1989; prior records index books from 1917. Civil court records are available free at http://ccap.courts.state.wi.us/internetcourtaccess. **Criminal Records:** Access: Mail, online, in person. Both court and visitors may perform in person searches. Search fee: $5.00 per name. Required to search: name, years to search, DOB. Criminal records on computer from 1989; prior records index books from 1917. Online access to criminal records is same as civil, see above. **General Information:** No sealed records released. SASE required. Turnaround time 1-2 days. Copy fee: $1.25 per page. Certification fee: $5.00. Fee payee: Clerk of Circuit Court. Personal checks accepted. Prepayment is required. Public access terminal is available.

Register in Probate 224 S 2nd, Medford, WI 54451; 715-748-1435; Fax: 715-748-2465. Hours: 8:30AM-4:30PM (CST). *Probate.*

Trempealeau County

Circuit Court 36245 Main St, Whitehall, WI 54773; 715-538-2311. Hours: 8AM-4:30PM (CST). *Felony, Misdemeanor, Civil, Eviction, Small Claims.*

www.win.bright.net/~tremphea/circuitcourt.htm

Civil Records: Access: Fax, mail, online, in person. Both court and visitors may perform in person searches. Search fee: $5.00 per name. Required to search: name, years to search. Civil cases indexed by defendant, plaintiff. Civil records on computer from 1993, on index cards from 1987, index books from 1940, archives prior to 1940. Civil court records are available free at http://ccap.courts.state.wi.us/internetcourtaccess. **Criminal Records:** Access: Fax, mail, online, in person. Both court and visitors may perform in person searches. Search fee: $5.00 per name. Required to search: name, years to search, DOB. Criminal records on computer from 1993, on index cards from 1987, index books from 1940, archives prior to 1940. Online access to criminal records is same as civil, see above. **General Information:** No juvenile, paternity or child support records released. SASE required. Turnaround time 2-3 days. Copy fee: $1.25 per page. Certification fee: $5.00. Fee payee: Clerk of Circuit Court. Personal checks accepted. Prepayment is required. Public access terminal available. Fax note: $2.00 per pg.

Register in Probate 36245 Main St, PO Box 67, Whitehall, WI 54773; 715-538-2311 X238; Fax: 715-538-4400. Hours: 8AM-4:30PM (CST). *Probate.*

Vernon County

Circuit Court PO Box 426, Viroqua, WI 54665; 608-637-5340; Fax: 608-637-5554. Hours: 8:30AM-4:30PM (CST). *Felony, Misdemeanor, Civil, Eviction, Small Claims.*

Civil Records: Access: Phone, mail, online, in person. Both court and visitors may perform in person searches. Search fee: $5.00 per name. Required to search: name, years to search. Civil cases indexed by defendant, plaintiff. Civil records on computer since 1992; on index books & cards 1950 to 1992. Civil court records are available at http://ccap.courts.state.wi.us/internetcourtaccess. **Criminal Records:** Access: Phone, mail, online, in person. Both court and visitors may perform in person searches. Search fee: $5.00 per name.

Required to search: name, years to search; also helpful-DOB. Criminal records on computer since 1992; on index books & cards 1950 to 1992. Online access to criminal records is same as civil, see above. **General Information:** No paternity or juvenile records released. SASE required. Turnaround time 2-3 days. Copy fee: $.25 per page. Certification fee: $5.00. Fee payee: Clerk of Court. Personal checks accepted. Will bill to attorneys & credit agencies.

Register in Probate PO Box 448, Viroqua, WI 54665; 608-637-5347; Fax: 608-637-5554. Hours: 8:30AM-4:30PM (CST). *Probate.*

Vilas County

Circuit Court 330 Court St, Eagle River, WI 54521; 715-479-3632; Fax: 715-479-3740. Hours: 8AM-4PM (CST). *Felony, Misdemeanor, Civil, Eviction, Small Claims.*

Civil Records: Access: Mail, online, in person. Both court and visitors may perform in person searches. Search fee: $5.00 per name. Required to search: name, years to search. Civil records on computer from 1992, on index cards from 1978, index books from 1900s. Civil court records are available free on the Internet at http://ccap.courts.state.wi.us/internetcourtaccess. **Criminal Records:** Access: Mail, online, in person. Both court and visitors may perform in person searches. Search fee: $5.00 per name. Required to search: name, years to search, DOB. Criminal records on computer from 1992, on index cards from 1978, index books from 1900s. Online access to criminal records is same as civil, see above. **General Information:** No paternity records released. SASE required. Turnaround time 2 weeks. Copy fee: $1.25 per page. Certification fee: $5.00. Fee payee: Clerk of Circuit Court. Personal checks accepted. Prepayment is required. Public access terminal is available.

Register in Probate 330 Court St, Eagle River, WI 54521; 715-479-3642; Fax: 715-479-3740. Hours: 8AM-4PM (CST). *Probate.*

Walworth County

Circuit Court PO Box 1001, Elkhorn, WI 53121-1001; 262-741-4224; Fax: 262-741-4379. Hours: 8AM-5PM (CST). *Felony, Misdemeanor, Civil, Eviction, Small Claims.*

Civil Records: Access: Mail, in person. Both court and visitors may perform in person searches. Search fee: $5.00 per name. Required to search: name, years to search. Civil cases indexed by defendant, plaintiff. Civil records on computer from 1989, index cards/books from 1836 (organized). **Criminal Records:** Access: Mail, in person. Both court and visitors may perform in person searches. Search fee: $5.00 per name. Required to search: name, years to search, DOB. Criminal records on computer from 1989, index cards/books from 1836 (organized). **General Information:** No sealed records released. SASE required. Turnaround time 1-2 days. Copy fee: $1.25 per page. Certification fee: $5.00. Fee payee: County Clerk of Courts. Business checks accepted. Credit cards accepted: Visa, Mastercard. Credit cards accepted in person only. Prepayment is required. Public access terminal is available.

Register in Probate PO Box 1001, Elkhorn, WI 53121; 262-741-4256; Fax: 262-741-4182. Hours: 8AM-5PM (CST). *Probate.*

Washburn County

Circuit Court PO Box 339, Shell Lake, WI 54871; 715-468-4677; Fax: 715-468-4678. Hours: 8AM-4:30PM (CST). *Felony, Misdemeanor, Civil, Eviction, Small Claims.*

Civil Records: Access: Mail, online, in person. Both court and visitors may perform in person searches. Search fee: $5.00 per name. Required to search: name, years to search. Civil cases indexed by defendant, plaintiff. Civil records on computer since 1993; on index books from 1883. Civil court records are available free on the Internet at http://ccap.courts.state.wi.us/internetcourtaccess. **Criminal Records:** Access: Mail, online, in person. Both court and visitors may perform in person searches. Search fee: $5.00 per name. Required to search: name, years to search; also helpful-DOB. Criminal records on computer since 1993; on index books from 1883. Online access to criminal records is same as civil, see above. **General Information:** No sealed records released. SASE required. Turnaround time 2-3 days. Copy fee: $1.25 per page. Certification fee: $5.00. Fee payee: Clerk of Court. Personal checks accepted. Prepayment is required. Public access terminal is available.

Register in Probate PO Box 316, Shell Lake, WI 54871; 715-468-4688; Fax: 715-468-4678. Hours: 8AM-4:30PM (CST). *Probate.*

Washington County

Circuit Court PO Box 1986, West Bend, WI 53095-7986; 262-335-4341; Fax: 262-335-4776. Hours: 8AM-4:30PM (CST). *Felony, Misdemeanor, Civil, Eviction, Small Claims.*

www.co.washington.wi.us

Civil Records: Access: Mail, online, in person. Both court and visitors may perform in person searches. Search fee: $5.00 per name. Required to search: name, years to search; also helpful-address. Civil cases indexed by defendant, plaintiff. Civil records on computer from 1986, index cards from 1976, index books from 1836. Civil court records are available free on the Internet at http://ccap.courts.state.wi.us/internetcourtaccess. **Criminal Records:** Access: Mail, online, in person. Both court and visitors may perform in person searches. Search fee: $5.00 per name. Required to search: name, years to search, DOB; also helpful-address. Criminal records on computer from 1986, index cards from 1976, index books from 1836. Online access to criminal records is same as civil, see above. **General Information:** No paternity records released prior to adjudication. SASE required. Turnaround time 1 week. Copy fee: $1.25 per page. Certification fee: $5.00. Fee payee: Clerk of Court. Personal checks accepted. Prepayment is required. Public access terminal is available.

Register in Probate PO Box 82, West Bend, WI 53095-0082; 262-335-4334; Fax: 262-306-2224. Hours: 8AM-4:30PM (CST). *Probate.*

Waukesha County

Circuit Court 515 W Moreland Blvd, Waukesha, WI 53188;; Civil phone:262-548-7525; Criminal phone:262-548-7525; Fax: 262-896-8228. Hours: 8AM-4:30PM M,T,Th,F; 7:30AM-5:30PM F (CST). *Felony, Misdemeanor, Civil, Eviction, Small Claims.*

www.co.waukesha.wi.us/departments/courts/index .html

Civil Records: Access: Mail, online, in person. Both court and visitors may perform in person

searches. Search fee: $5.00 per name. Required to search: name, years to search. Civil cases indexed by defendant, plaintiff. Civil records on computer from 1994. The civil court records are available free on the Internet at http://ccap.courts.state.wi.us/internetcourtaccess. **Criminal Records:** Access: Mail, online, in person. Both court and visitors may perform in person searches. Search fee: $5.00 per name. Required to search: name, years to search, DOB. Criminal records on computer from 1994. Online access to criminal records is same as civil, see above. **General Information:** No paternity, mental commitment records released. SASE required. Turnaround time 2-3 days. Copy fee: $1.25 per page. Certification fee: $5.00. Fee payee: Clerk of Circuit Court. Personal checks accepted. Credit cards accepted. Accepted in person only. Prepayment is required. Public access terminal is available.

Register in Probate 515 W Moreland, Rm 375, Waukesha, WI 53188; 262-548-7468. Hours: 8AM-4:30PM M,T,Th,F; 7:30AM-5:30PM W (CST). *Probate.*

Waupaca County

Circuit Court 811 Harding St, Waupaca, WI 54981; 715-258-6460. Hours: 8AM-4PM (CST). *Felony, Misdemeanor, Civil, Eviction, Small Claims.*

Civil Records: Access: Mail, online, in person. Both court and visitors may perform in person searches. Search fee: $5.00 per name. Required to search: name, years to search. Civil cases indexed by defendant, plaintiff. Civil records on computer from 1992. Civil court records are available at http://ccap.courts.state.wi.us/internetcourtaccess. **Criminal Records:** Access: Mail, online, in person. Both court and visitors may perform in person searches. Search fee: $5.00 per name. Required to search: name, years to search. Criminal records on computer from 1992. Online access to criminal records is same as civil, see above. **General Information:** No juvenile, JO, paternity excluding past judgments released. SASE required. Turnaround time 3-4 days. Copy fee: $1.25 per page. Computer document copy fee $.50 per page. Certification fee: $5.00. Fee payee: Clerk of Court. Business checks accepted. Personal in-state checks accepted. Prepayment is required. Public access terminal is available.

Register in Probate 811 Harding St, Waupaca, WI 54981; 715-258-6429; Fax: 715-258-6440. Hours: 8AM-4PM (CST). *Probate.*

Waushara County

Circuit Court PO Box 507, Wautoma, WI 54982; 920-787-0441; Fax: 920-787-0481. Hours: 8AM-4:30PM (CST). *Felony, Misdemeanor, Civil, Eviction, Small Claims.*

Civil Records: Access: Mail, online, in person. Both court and visitors may perform in person searches. Search fee: $5.00 per name. fee only if court does search. Required to search: name, years to search. Civil cases indexed by defendant. Civil records on computer from 1992, index cards from 1978, index books from 1900s. Civil court records are available free on the Internet at http://ccap.courts.state.wi.us/internetcourtaccess. **Criminal Records:** Access: Mail, online, in person. Both court and visitors may perform in person searches. Search fee: $5.00 per name. Fee only id court does search. Required to search: name, years to search, DOB. Criminal records on computer from 1993, prior on cards and books.

Online access to criminal records is same as civil, see above. **General Information:** No paternity records released. SASE required. Turnaround time 1-2 weeks. Copy fee: $1.25 per page. Certification fee: $5.00. Fee payee: Clerk of Court. Personal checks accepted. Personal in-state checks accepted, money orders for out of state requests. Prepayment is required. Public access terminal is available.

Register in Probate PO Box 508, Wautoma, WI 54982; 920-787-0448. Hours: 8AM-4:30PM (CST). *Probate.*

Winnebago County

Circuit Court PO Box 2808, Oshkosh, WI 54903-2808; 920-236-4848; Fax: 920-424-7780. Hours: 8AM-4:30PM (CST). *Felony, Misdemeanor, Civil, Eviction, Small Claims.*

Civil Records: Access: Mail, online, in person. Both court and visitors may perform in person searches. Search fee: $5.00 per name. Required to search: name, years to search. Civil cases indexed by defendant, plaintiff. Civil records are on computer since 1990, prior on books and cards. organized since 1938. Civil court records are available free on the Internet at http://ccap.courts.state.wi.us/internetcourtaccess. **Criminal Records:** Access: Mail, online, in person. Both court and visitors may perform in person searches. Search fee: $5.00 per name. Required to search: name, years to search, DOB. Criminal records are on computer since 1990, prior on books and cards. organized since 1938. Online access to criminal records is same as civil, see above. **General Information:** No juvenile, paternity, financial records released. SASE required. Turnaround time 1 week. Copy fee: $1.25 per page. Certification fee: $5.00. Fee payee: Clerk of Courts. Personal checks accepted.

Register in Probate PO Box 2808, Oshkosh, WI 54903-2808; 920-236-4833; Fax: 920-424-7536. Hours: 8AM-Noon, 1-4:30PM (CST). *Probate.*

Note: Records are open to the pubic, there is a $4.00 search fee.

Wood County

Circuit Court 400 Market St, Po Box 8095, Wisconsin Rapids, WI 54494-958095; 715-421-8490. Hours: 8AM-4:30PM (CST). *Felony, Misdemeanor, Civil, Eviction, Small Claims.*

Civil Records: Access: Mail, online, in person, online. Both court and visitors may perform in person searches. Search fee: $5.00 per name. Required to search: name, years to search. Civil cases indexed by defendant, plaintiff. Civil records on computer from 1983, microfiche from 1856-1980s. Civil court records are available free at http://ccap.courts.state.wi.us/internetcourtaccess. **Criminal Records:** Access: Mail, online, in person, online. Both court and visitors may perform in person searches. Search fee: $5.00 per name. Required to search: name, years to search, DOB. Criminal records on computer from 1980. Online access to criminal records is same as civil, see above. **General Information:** No paternity or sealed records released. SASE required. Turnaround time 2-3 days. Copy fee: $1.25 per page. Certification fee: $5.00. Fee payee: Clerk of Court. Personal checks accepted. Prepayment is required.

Register in Probate Wood County Courthouse, PO Box 8095, Wisconsin Rapids, WI 54495-8095; 715-421-8520; Fax: 715-421-8808. Hours: 8AM-4:30PM (CST). *Probate.*

Note: This court also holds guardianships, juveniles, mentals and adoption records.

ORGANIZATION   72 counties, 72 recording offices. The recording officers are Register of Deeds and Clerk of Court (state tax liens). The entire state is in the Central Time Zone (CST).

REAL ESTATE RECORDS   Registers will **not** perform real estate searches. Copy fees and certification fees vary. Assessor telephone numbers are for local municipalities or for property listing agencies. Counties do not have assessors. Copies usually cost $2.00 for the first page and $1.00 for each additional page. Certification usually costs $.25 per document. The Treasurer maintains property tax records.

UCC RECORDS   Financing statements are filed at the state level, except for consumer goods, farm and real estate related collateral, which are filed only with the Register of Deeds. All recording offices will perform UCC searches, and many will accept a search by phone. Use search request form UCC-11 for mail-in searches. Searches fees are usually $10.00 per debtor name. Copy fees are usually $1.00 per page.

TAX LIEN RECORDS   Federal tax liens on personal property of businesses are filed with the Secretary of State. Other federal tax liens are filed with the county Register of Deeds. State tax liens are filed with the Clerk of Court. Refer to *The Sourcebook of County Court Records* for information about Wisconsin courts. Many Registers will perform federal tax lien searches. Search fees and copy fees vary.

OTHER LIENS   Judgment, mechanics, breeders.

Adams County
County Register of Deeds, P.O. Box 219, Friendship, WI 53934-0219. 608-339-4206.

Ashland County
County Register of Deeds, 201 West Main Street, Room 206, Ashland, WI 54806. 715-682-7008. Fax: 715-682-7032.

Barron County
County Register of Deeds, 330 East LaSalle, Room 201, Barron, WI 54812. 715-537-6210. Fax: 715-537-6277.

Bayfield County
County Register of Deeds, P.O. Box 813, Washburn, WI 54891. 715-373-6119.

Brown County
County Register of Deeds, P.O. Box 23600, Green Bay, WI 54305-3600. 920-448-4468. Fax: 920-448-4449.

Buffalo County
County Register of Deeds, P.O. Box 28, Alma, WI 54610-0028. 608-685-6230. Fax: 608-685-6213.

Burnett County
County Register of Deeds, 7410 County Road K #103, Siren, WI 54872. 715-349-2183.

Calumet County
County Register of Deeds, 206 Court Street, Chilton, WI 53014. 920-849-1441. Fax: 920-849-1469.

Chippewa County
County Register of Deeds, 711 North Bridge Street, Chippewa Falls, WI 54729-1876. 715-726-7994. Fax: 715-726-4582.

Clark County
County Register of Deeds, P.O. Box 384, Neillsville, WI 54456-1989. 715-743-5162. Fax: 715-743-5154.

Columbia County
County Register of Deeds, P.O. Box 133, Portage, WI 53901. 608-742-9677. Fax: 608-742-9602.

Crawford County
County Register of Deeds, 220 North Beaumont Road, Prairie du Chien, WI 53821. 608-326-0219. Fax: 608-326-0220.

Dane County
County Register of Deeds, P.O. Box 1438, Madison, WI 53701. 608-266-4143. Fax: 608-267-3110.
Online Access: Real Estate, Tax Assessor. Property records (except for City of Madison) on the Dane County Main Search page are available free on the Internet at http://216.56.2.131/lio/lis/date_update.idc. Property records on the City of Madison database are

available free on the Internet at www.ci.madison.wi.us/ assessor/property.html.

Dodge County
County Register of Deeds, 127 East Oak Street, Administration Building, Juneau, WI 53039-1391. 920-386-3720. Fax: 920-386-3902.

Door County
County Register of Deeds, P.O. Box 670, Sturgeon Bay, WI 54235-0670. 920-746-2270. Fax: 920-746-2525.

Douglas County
County Register of Deeds, PO Box 847, Superior, WI 54880. 715-395-1463. Fax: 715-395-1553.

Dunn County
County Register of Deeds, 800 Wilson Avenue, Menomonie, WI 54751. 715-232-1228. Fax: 715-232-1324.

Eau Claire County
County Register of Deeds, P.O. Box 718, Eau Claire, WI 54702. 715-839-4745.

Florence County
County Register of Deeds, P.O. Box 410, Florence, WI 54121-0410. 715-528-4252. Fax: 715-528-5470.

Fond du Lac County
County Register of Deeds, P.O. Box 509, Fond du Lac, WI 54935-0509. 920-929-3018.

Forest County
County Register of Deeds, 200 E. Madison Street, Crandon, WI 54520. 715-478-3823.

Grant County
County Register of Deeds, P.O. Box 391, Lancaster, WI 53813-0391. 608-723-2727. Fax: 608-723-7370.

Green County
County Register of Deeds, 1016 16th Avenue, Courthouse, Monroe, WI 53566. 608-328-9439. Fax: 608-328-2835.

Green Lake County
County Register of Deeds, P.O. Box 3188, Green Lake, WI 54941-3188. 920-294-4021. Fax: 920-294-4009.

Iowa County
County Register of Deeds, 222 North Iowa Street, Dodgeville, WI 53533. 608-935-0396. Fax: 608-935-3024.

Iron County
County Register of Deeds, 300 Taconite Street, Hurley, WI 54534. 715-561-2945. Fax: 715-561-2928.

Jackson County
County Register of Deeds, 307 Main, Black River Falls, WI 54615. 715-284-0204. Fax: 715-284-0261.

Jefferson County
County Register of Deeds, P.O. Box 356, Jefferson, WI 53549. 920-674-7235.

Juneau County
County Register of Deeds, P.O. Box 100, Mauston, WI 53948-0100. 608-847-9325. Fax: 608-849-9369.

Kenosha County
County Register of Deeds, 1010 56 St., Kenosha, WI 53140. 262-653-2444. Fax: 262-653-2564.
Online Access: Real Estate, Liens, Vital Records. Access to Kenosha County online records require a $500 set up fee and $6 per hour of use. System operates 24 hours daily and supports baud rates from 14.4-56k. Records date back to 5/1986. Federal tax liens are listed and lending agency info is available For information, contact Joellyn Storz at 262-653-2511.

Kewaunee County
County Register of Deeds, 613 Dodge Street, Kewaunee, WI 54216-1398. 920-388-7126. Fax: 920-388-7195.

La Crosse County
County Register of Deeds, 400 North 4th Street, Room 106, Administrative Center, La Crosse, WI 54601-3200. 608-785-9644. Fax: 608-785-9704.

Lafayette County
County Register of Deeds, P.O. Box 170, Darlington, WI 53530. 608-776-4838. Fax: 608-776-4991.

Langlade County
County Register of Deeds, 800 Clermont Street, Antigo, WI 54409. 715-627-6209. Fax: 715-627-6303.

Lincoln County
County Register of Deeds, 1110 East Main, Courthouse, Merrill, WI 54452. 715-536-0318. Fax: 715-536-0360.

Manitowoc County
County Register of Deeds, P.O. Box 421, Manitowoc, WI 54221-0421. 920-683-4010. Fax: 920-683-2702.
Online Access: Tax Assessor. Records on the Manitowoc's Assessor Database is available free on the Internet at http://206.40.97.36/default.htm.

Marathon County
County Register of Deeds, 500 Forest Street, Courthouse, Wausau, WI 54403-5568. 715-261-1470. Fax: 715-261-1488.

Marinette County
County Register of Deeds, 1926 Hall Avenue, Courthouse, Marinette, WI 54143. 715-732-7550. Fax: 715-732-7532.

Marquette County

County Register of Deeds, P.O. Box 236, Montello, WI 53949-0236. 608-297-9132. Fax: 608-297-7606.

Menominee County

County Register of Deeds, PO Box 279, Keshena, WI 54135-0279. 715-799-3312. Fax: 715-799-1322.

Milwaukee County

County Register of Deeds, 901 North 9th Street, Milwaukee, WI 53233. 414-278-4005. Fax: 414-223-1257.

www.ci.mil.wi.us/citygov

Online Access: Real Estate, Tax Assessor. Records on the City of Milwaukee Assessor database are available at www.ci.mil.wi.us/citygov/assessor/assessments.htm on the Internet, free. Updated daily. Other data includes property sales data and treasurer office.

Monroe County

County Register of Deeds, P.O. Box 195, Sparta, WI 54656. 608-269-8716.

Oconto County

County Register of Deeds, 301 Washington Street, Room 2035, Oconto, WI 54153-1699. 920-834-6807.

Oneida County

County Register of Deeds, P.O. Box 400, Rhinelander, WI 54501. 715-369-6150. Fax: 715-369-6222.

Outagamie County

County Register of Deeds, 410 South Walnut St., CAB 205, Appleton, WI 54911-5999. 920-832-5095. Fax: 920-832-2177.

Ozaukee County

County Register of Deeds, P.O. Box 994, Port Washington, WI 53074-0994. 262-284-8260. Fax: 262-284-8100.

Pepin County

County Register of Deeds, P.O. Box 39, Durand, WI 54736. 715-672-8856. Fax: 715-672-8677.

Pierce County

County Register of Deeds, P.O. Box 267, Ellsworth, WI 54011-0267. 715-273-3531x418. Fax: 715-273-6861.

Polk County

County Register of Deeds, 100 Polk County Plaza, Suite 160, Balsam Lake, WI 54810. 715-485-9249. Fax: 715-485-9202.

Portage County

County Register of Deeds, 1516 Church Street, County-City Building, Stevens Point, WI 54481. 715-346-1428. Fax: 715-345-5361.

Price County

County Register of Deeds, 126 Cherry, Phillips, WI 54555. 715-339-2515.

Racine County

County Register of Deeds, 730 Wisconsin Avenue, Racine, WI 53403. 262-636-3208. Fax: 262-636-3851.

Richland County

County Register of Deeds, P.O. Box 337, Richland Center, WI 53581. 608-647-3011.

Rock County

County Register of Deeds, 51 South Main Street, Janesville, WI 53545. 608-757-5657.

Rusk County

County Register of Deeds, 311 Miner Avenue, Ladysmith, WI 54848-0311. 715-532-2139. Fax: 715-532-2194.

Sauk County

County Register of Deeds, 505 Broadway St., Baraboo, WI 53913. 608-355-3288. Fax: 608-355-3292.

Sawyer County

County Register of Deeds, P.O. Box 686, Hayward, WI 54843-0686. 715-634-4867. Fax: 715-634-6839.

Shawano County

County Register of Deeds, 311 North Main, Shawano, WI 54166. 715-524-2129. Fax: 715-524-5157.

Sheboygan County

County Register of Deeds, 500 New York Ave., 2nd Floor, Sheboygan, WI 53081. 920-459-3023.

St. Croix County

County Register of Deeds, 1101 Carmichael Rd., Hudson, WI 54016. 715-386-4652. Fax: 715-386-4687.

Taylor County

County Register of Deeds, P.O. Box 403, Medford, WI 54451-0403. 715-748-1483.

Trempealeau County

County Register of Deeds, P.O. Box 67, Whitehall, WI 54773. 715-538-2311.

Vernon County

County Register of Deeds, P.O. Box 46, Viroqua, WI 54665. 608-637-3568.

Vilas County

County Register of Deeds, 330 Court St., Eagle River, WI 54521. 715-479-3660. Fax: 715-479-3605.

Walworth County

County Register of Deeds, P.O. Box 995, Elkhorn, WI 53121-0995. 262-741-4214. Fax: 262-741-4221.

Washburn County

County Register of Deeds, P.O. Box 607, Shell Lake, WI 54871. 715-468-4616. Fax: 715-468-4699.

Washington County

County Register of Deeds, P.O. Box 1986, West Bend, WI 53095-7986. 262-335-4318. Fax: 262-335-6866.

Waukesha County

County Register of Deeds, 1320 Pewaukee Rd., Room 110, Waukesha, WI 53188. 262-548-7590.

Waupaca County

County Register of Deeds, P.O. Box 307, Waupaca, WI 54981. 715-258-6250. Fax: 715-258-6212.

Waushara County

County Register of Deeds, P.O. Box 338, Wautoma, WI 54982. 920-787-0444. Fax: 920-787-0425.

Winnebago County

County Register of Deeds, P.O. Box 2808, Oshkosh, WI 54903-2808. 920-236-4883.

Online Access: Tax Assessor. Records on the City of Menasha Tax Roll Information database are available free at http://my.athenet.net/~mencity/search on the Internet.

Wood County

County Register of Deeds, P.O. Box 8095, Wisconsin Rapids, WI 54495. 715-421-8450.

You will usually be able to find the city name in the City/County Cross Reference below. In that case, it is a simple matter to determine the county from the cross reference. However, only the official US Postal Service city names are included in this index. There are an additional 40,000 place names that people use in their addresses. Therefore, we have also included a ZIP/City Cross Reference immediately following the City/County Cross Reference.

If you know the ZIP Code but the city name does not appear in the City/County Cross Reference index, look up the ZIP Code in the ZIP/City Cross Reference, find the city name, then look up the city name in the City/County Cross Reference. For example, you want to know the county for an address of Menands, NY 12204. There is no "Menands" in the City/County Cross Reference. The ZIP/City Cross Reference shows that ZIP Codes 12201-12288 are for the city of Albany. Looking back in the City/County Cross Reference, Albany is in Albany County.

City/County Cross Reference

ABBOTSFORD (54405) Clark(72), Marathon(28)
ABRAMS Oconto
ADAMS Adams
ADELL Sheboygan
AFTON Rock
ALBANY (99999) Green(99), Rock(1)
ALGOMA (54201) Kewaunee(97), Door(3)
ALGOMA Kewaunee
ALLENTON (53002) Washington(99), Dodge(1)
ALMA Buffalo
ALMA CENTER Jackson
ALMENA Barron
ALMOND (54909) Portage(82), Waushara(18)
ALTOONA Eau Claire
AMBERG (99999) Marinette(99), Manitowoc(1)
AMERY Polk
AMHERST Portage
AMHERST JUNCTION Portage
ANIWA (54408) Marathon(58), Shawano(38), Langlade(4)
ANTIGO (54409) Langlade(96), Shawano(2), Marathon(2)
APPLETON (54914) Outagamie(98), Winnebago(2)
APPLETON (54915) Outagamie(67), Calumet(23), Winnebago(11)
APPLETON Outagamie
ARCADIA (54612) Trempealeau(90), Buffalo(10)
ARENA Iowa
ARGONNE Forest
ARGYLE (53504) Lafayette(71), Green(29)
ARKANSAW (54721) Pepin(88), Dunn(7), Pierce(5)
ARKDALE Adams
ARLINGTON (53911) Columbia(90), Dane(10)
ARMSTRONG CREEK (54103) Forest(84), Marinette(15), Florence(1)
ARPIN Wood
ASHIPPUN Dodge
ASHLAND (54806) Ashland(92), Bayfield(8)
ATHELSTANE (54104) Marinette(98), Oconto(1)
ATHENS (54411) Marathon(98), Taylor(2)
AUBURNDALE (54412) Wood(76), Marathon(24)
AUGUSTA Eau Claire
AVALON Rock
AVOCA Iowa
BABCOCK Wood
BAGLEY Grant
BAILEYS HARBOR Door
BALDWIN St. Croix
BALSAM LAKE Polk
BANCROFT (54921) Portage(87), Adams(10), Waushara(3)

BANGOR La Crosse
BARABOO Sauk
BARNEVELD (53507) Iowa(98), Dane(2)
BARRON Barron
BARRONETT (54813) Barron(50), Burnett(30), Washburn(20)
BASSETT Kenosha
BAY CITY Pierce
BAYFIELD Bayfield
BEAR CREEK (54922) Outagamie(53), Waupaca(47)
BEAVER DAM Dodge
BEETOWN Grant
BELDENVILLE Pierce
BELGIUM (53004) Ozaukee(98), Sheboygan(2)
BELLEVILLE (53508) Dane(78), Green(22)
BELMONT Lafayette
BELOIT Rock
BENET LAKE Kenosha
BENOIT Bayfield
BENTON Lafayette
BERLIN (54923) Green Lake(76), Waushara(21), Winnebago(3)
BIG BEND Waukesha
BIG FALLS Waupaca
BIRCHWOOD (54817) Washburn(40), Sawyer(33), Barron(24), Rusk(3)
BIRNAMWOOD (54414) Shawano(82), Marathon(18)
BLACK CREEK (54106) Outagamie(99), Shawano(2)
BLACK EARTH (53515) Dane(99), Iowa(1)
BLACK RIVER FALLS (99999) Jackson(99), Monroe(1)
BLAIR (54616) Trempealeau(96), Jackson(4)
BLANCHARDVILLE (53516) Lafayette(52), Iowa(26), Green(20), Dane(2)
BLENKER Wood
BLOOM CITY Richland
BLOOMER Chippewa
BLOOMINGTON Grant
BLUE MOUNDS (53517) Iowa(51), Dane(49)
BLUE RIVER (53518) Richland(74), Grant(24), Crawford(2)
BONDUEL (54107) Shawano(97), Outagamie(3)
BOSCOBEL (53805) Grant(78), Crawford(22)
BOULDER JUNCTION Vilas
BOWLER Shawano
BOYCEVILLE Dunn
BOYD (54726) Chippewa(66), Eau Claire(34)
BRANCH Manitowoc
BRANDON (53919) Fond du Lac(98), Green Lake(2)
BRANTWOOD Price
BRIGGSVILLE (53920) Marquette(63), Adams(37)

BRILL Barron
BRILLION (54110) Calumet(79), Manitowoc(19), Brown(2)
BRISTOL Kenosha
BRODHEAD (53520) Rock(58), Green(42)
BROKAW Marathon
BROOKFIELD Waukesha
BROOKLYN (53521) Rock(53), Green(25), Dane(22)
BROOKS Adams
BROWNSVILLE (53006) Dodge(75), Fond du Lac(25)
BROWNTOWN (53522) Green(93), Lafayette(7)
BRUCE Rusk
BRULE (54820) Douglas(84), Bayfield(16)
BRUSSELS Door
BRYANT Langlade
BURLINGTON (53105) Racine(58), Walworth(32), Kenosha(9)
BURNETT Dodge
BUTLER Waukesha
BUTTE DES MORTS Winnebago
BUTTERNUT (54514) Price(57), Ashland(38), Iron(6)
BYRON Fond du Lac
CABLE (54821) Bayfield(97), Sawyer(3)
CADOTT (54727) Chippewa(93), Eau Claire(7)
CALEDONIA Racine
CAMBRIA (53923) Columbia(78), Green Lake(22)
CAMBRIDGE (53523) Jefferson(53), Dane(47)
CAMERON Barron
CAMP DOUGLAS (54618) Monroe(51), Juneau(49)
CAMP LAKE Kenosha
CAMPBELLSPORT (53010) Fond du Lac(95), Washington(4)
CAROLINE Shawano
CASCADE (53011) Sheboygan(88), Fond du Lac(12)
CASCO (54205) Kewaunee(98), Door(2)
CASHTON (54619) Monroe(78), Vernon(21), La Crosse(1)
CASSVILLE Grant
CATARACT Monroe
CATAWBA Price
CATO Manitowoc
CAZENOVIA (53924) Richland(99), Sauk(1)
CECIL (54111) Shawano(90), Oconto(10)
CEDAR GROVE (53013) Sheboygan(81), Ozaukee(19)
CEDARBURG (53012) Ozaukee(95), Washington(5)
CENTURIA Polk
CHASEBURG Vernon
CHELSEA Taylor
CHETEK (54728) Barron(90), Rusk(9), Dunn(1)

CHILI (54420) Clark(97), Wood(4)
CHILTON (53014) Calumet(98), Manitowoc(2)
CHIPPEWA FALLS (54729) Chippewa(97), Eau Claire(3)
CHIPPEWA FALLS Chippewa
CLAM LAKE (54517) Ashland(93), Sawyer(7)
CLAYTON (54004) Polk(62), Barron(39)
CLEAR LAKE (54005) Polk(70), St. Croix(11), Barron(10), Dunn(9)
CLEVELAND (53015) Manitowoc(85), Sheboygan(15)
CLINTON (53525) Rock(97), Walworth(3)
CLINTONVILLE (54929) Waupaca(67), Shawano(32), Outagamie(1)
CLYMAN Dodge
COBB Iowa
COCHRANE Buffalo
COLBY (54421) Clark(76), Marathon(25)
COLEMAN (54112) Marinette(76), Oconto(25)
COLFAX (54730) Dunn(79), Chippewa(21)
COLGATE (53017) Washington(71), Waukesha(29)
COLLINS Manitowoc
COLOMA (54930) Waushara(85), Adams(13), Marquette(2)
COLUMBUS (53925) Columbia(83), Dodge(14), Dane(3)
COMBINED LOCKS Outagamie
COMSTOCK (54826) Barron(62), Polk(38)
CONOVER Vilas
CONRATH Rusk
COON VALLEY (54623) La Crosse(51), Vernon(50)
CORNELL Chippewa
CORNUCOPIA Bayfield
COTTAGE GROVE Dane
COUDERAY Sawyer
CRANDON Forest
CRIVITZ (54114) Marinette(91), Oconto(9)
CROSS PLAINS Dane
CUBA CITY (53807) Grant(84), Lafayette(16)
CUDAHY Milwaukee
CUMBERLAND (54829) Barron(91), Polk(9)
CURTISS (54422) Clark(95), Taylor(5)
CUSHING Polk
CUSTER (54423) Portage(98), Marathon(2)
DALE Outagamie
DALLAS Barron
DALTON (53926) Green Lake(79), Marquette(13), Columbia(8)
DANBURY (54830) Burnett(93), Douglas(7)
DANE Dane
DARIEN (53114) Walworth(77), Rock(23)
DARLINGTON Lafayette
DE FOREST (53532) Dane(99), Columbia(1)

DE PERE (54115) Brown(92), Outagamie(8)
DE SOTO (54624) Vernon(82), Crawford(18)
DEER PARK (54007) St. Croix(67), Polk(33)
DEERBROOK Langlade
DEERFIELD Dane
DELAFIELD Waukesha
DELAVAN Walworth
DELLWOOD Adams
DENMARK (54208) Brown(51), Kewaunee(41), Manitowoc(8)
DICKEYVILLE Grant
DODGE Trempealeau
DODGEVILLE Iowa
DORCHESTER (54425) Clark(84), Marathon(10), Taylor(7)
DOUSMAN (53118) Waukesha(96), Jefferson(4)
DOWNING (54734) Dunn(96), St. Croix(4)
DOWNSVILLE Dunn
DOYLESTOWN Columbia
DRESSER Polk
DRUMMOND Bayfield
DUNBAR Marinette
DURAND (54736) Pepin(84), Buffalo(15), Dunn(1)
EAGLE (53119) Waukesha(93), Walworth(5), Jefferson(3)
EAGLE RIVER (54521) Vilas(78), Oneida(20), Forest(2)
EAST ELLSWORTH Pierce
EAST TROY (53120) Walworth(98), Racine(2)
EASTMAN Crawford
EAU CLAIRE (54703) Eau Claire(90), Chippewa(11)
EAU CLAIRE Eau Claire
EAU GALLE (54737) Dunn(96), Pepin(4)
EDEN Fond du Lac
EDGAR Marathon
EDGERTON (53534) Rock(86), Dane(12), Jefferson(1)
EDGEWATER Sawyer
EDMUND Iowa
EGG HARBOR Door
ELAND (54427) Marathon(66), Shawano(34)
ELCHO (54428) Langlade(96), Oneida(4)
ELDERON Marathon
ELDORADO Fond du Lac
ELEVA (54738) Trempealeau(52), Eau Claire(47), Buffalo(2)
ELK MOUND (54739) Dunn(59), Chippewa(41)
ELKHART LAKE (53020) Sheboygan(91), Manitowoc(7), Calumet(3)
ELKHORN Walworth
ELLISON BAY Door
ELLSWORTH Pierce
ELM GROVE Waukesha
ELMWOOD (54740) Pierce(85), Dunn(15)
ELROY (53929) Juneau(73), Monroe(22), Vernon(5)
ELTON Langlade
EMBARRASS Waupaca
EMERALD St. Croix
ENDEAVOR Marquette
EPHRAIM Door
ETTRICK (54627) Trempealeau(92), Jackson(8)
EUREKA Winnebago
EVANSVILLE (53536) Rock(93), Green(7)
EXELAND (54835) Sawyer(89), Rusk(11)
FAIRCHILD (54741) Jackson(53), Eau Claire(47)
FAIRWATER Fond du Lac
FALL CREEK Eau Claire
FALL RIVER (53932) Columbia(94), Dodge(6)

FENCE (54120) Florence(61), Marinette(39)
FENNIMORE Grant
FERRYVILLE (54628) Crawford(96), Vernon(4)
FIFIELD Price
FISH CREEK Door
FLORENCE Florence
FOND DU LAC Fond du Lac
FONTANA Walworth
FOOTVILLE Rock
FOREST JUNCTION Calumet
FORESTVILLE (54213) Door(85), Kewaunee(15)
FORT ATKINSON (53538) Jefferson(97), Rock(3)
FOUNTAIN CITY Buffalo
FOX LAKE Dodge
FOXBORO Douglas
FRANCIS CREEK Manitowoc
FRANKLIN Milwaukee
FRANKSVILLE Racine
FREDERIC (54837) Polk(79), Burnett(21)
FREDONIA (53021) Ozaukee(89), Washington(11)
FREEDOM Outagamie
FREMONT (54940) Waupaca(50), Waushara(33), Winnebago(14), Outagamie(3)
FRIENDSHIP Adams
FRIESLAND Columbia
GALESVILLE Trempealeau
GALLOWAY Marathon
GAYS MILLS Crawford
GENESEE DEPOT Waukesha
GENOA Vernon
GENOA CITY (53128) Walworth(81), Kenosha(19)
GERMANTOWN Washington
GILE Iron
GILLETT (54124) Oconto(93), Menominee(4), Shawano(3)
GILLETT Oconto
GILLETT Shawano
GILMAN (54433) Taylor(80), Chippewa(20)
GILMANTON Buffalo
GLEASON (54435) Lincoln(66), Langlade(34)
GLEN FLORA Rusk
GLEN HAVEN Grant
GLENBEULAH (53023) Sheboygan(97), Fond du Lac(3)
GLENWOOD CITY (54013) St. Croix(96), Dunn(4)
GLIDDEN Ashland
GOODMAN (54125) Marinette(99), Forest(1)
GORDON Douglas
GOTHAM Richland
GRAFTON Ozaukee
GRAND MARSH Adams
GRAND VIEW Bayfield
GRANTON Clark
GRANTSBURG (54840) Burnett(98), Polk(2)
GRATIOT Lafayette
GREEN BAY Brown
GREEN LAKE Green Lake
GREEN VALLEY Shawano
GREENBUSH Sheboygan
GREENDALE Milwaukee
GREENLEAF (54126) Brown(97), Manitowoc(3)
GREENVILLE Outagamie
GREENWOOD Clark
GRESHAM Shawano
GURNEY Iron
HAGER CITY Pierce
HALES CORNERS Milwaukee
HAMMOND St. Croix
HANCOCK (54943) Waushara(82), Adams(18)

HANNIBAL Taylor
HANOVER Rock
HARSHAW Oneida
HARTFORD (53027) Washington(96), Dodge(4)
HARTLAND Waukesha
HATLEY Marathon
HAUGEN Barron
HAWKINS (54530) Rusk(70), Price(29)
HAWTHORNE Douglas
HAYWARD (54843) Sawyer(88), Washburn(12)
HAZEL GREEN (53811) Grant(92), Lafayette(7), Oneida(1)
HAZELHURST Oneida
HEAFFORD JUNCTION Lincoln
HELENVILLE Jefferson
HERBSTER Bayfield
HERTEL Burnett
HEWITT Wood
HIGH BRIDGE Ashland
HIGHLAND (53543) Iowa(93), Grant(7)
HILBERT Calumet
HILLPOINT (53937) Sauk(52), Richland(48)
HILLSBORO (54634) Vernon(71), Richland(28), Juneau(1)
HILLSDALE Barron
HINGHAM Sheboygan
HIXTON Jackson
HOLCOMBE (54745) Chippewa(90), Rusk(10)
HOLLANDALE (53544) Iowa(98), Dane(2)
HOLMEN La Crosse
HONEY CREEK Walworth
HORICON Dodge
HORTONVILLE Outagamie
HUBERTUS Washington
HUDSON St. Croix
HUMBIRD (54746) Clark(76), Jackson(24)
HURLEY Iron
HUSTISFORD Dodge
HUSTLER Juneau
INDEPENDENCE (54747) Trempealeau(86), Buffalo(14)
IOLA (54945) Waupaca(97), Portage(4)
IOLA Waupaca
IRMA Lincoln
IRON BELT Iron
IRON RIDGE Dodge
IRON RIVER Bayfield
IXONIA (53036) Jefferson(70), Dodge(25), Waukesha(5)
JACKSON Washington
JANESVILLE Rock
JEFFERSON Jefferson
JIM FALLS Chippewa
JOHNSON CREEK Jefferson
JUDA Green
JUMP RIVER Taylor
JUNCTION CITY (54443) Portage(95), Marathon(3), Wood(3)
JUNEAU Dodge
KANSASVILLE (53139) Racine(86), Kenosha(14)
KAUKAUNA (54130) Outagamie(95), Brown(3), Calumet(2)
KELLNERSVILLE Manitowoc
KEMPSTER Langlade
KENDALL (54638) Monroe(93), Juneau(4), Vernon(4)
KENNAN Price
KENOSHA Kenosha
KESHENA Menominee
KEWASKUM (53040) Washington(68), Sheboygan(18), Fond du Lac(14)
KEWAUNEE Kewaunee
KIEL (53042) Manitowoc(96), Calumet(4)
KIELER Grant
KIMBERLY Outagamie
KING Waupaca
KINGSTON Green Lake

KNAPP (54749) Dunn(90), St. Croix(10)
KOHLER Sheboygan
KRAKOW (54137) Shawano(80), Oconto(20)
LA CROSSE La Crosse
LA FARGE (54639) Vernon(93), Richland(7)
LA POINTE Ashland
LA VALLE (53941) Sauk(97), Juneau(2), Richland(1)
LAC DU FLAMBEAU (54538) Vilas(89), Oneida(6), Price(5)
LADYSMITH Rusk
LAKE DELTON Sauk
LAKE GENEVA Walworth
LAKE MILLS Jefferson
LAKE NEBAGAMON Douglas
LAKE TOMAHAWK Oneida
LAKEWOOD Oconto
LANCASTER Grant
LAND O LAKES (54540) Vilas(96), Manitowoc(4)
LANNON Waukesha
LAONA Forest
LARSEN Winnebago
LEBANON Dodge
LENA (54139) Oconto(98), Marinette(2)
LEOPOLIS Shawano
LEWIS Polk
LILY Langlade
LIME RIDGE Sauk
LINDEN Iowa
LITTLE CHUTE Outagamie
LITTLE SUAMICO Oconto
LIVINGSTON (53554) Grant(67), Iowa(33)
LODI (53555) Columbia(91), Dane(9)
LOGANVILLE Sauk
LOMIRA (53048) Dodge(98), Fond du Lac(2)
LONE ROCK (53556) Richland(89), Sauk(11)
LONG LAKE (54542) Forest(66), Florence(34)
LOWELL Dodge
LOYAL Clark
LUBLIN (54447) Taylor(98), Clark(2)
LUCK (54853) Polk(94), Burnett(6)
LUXEMBURG (54217) Kewaunee(89), Door(6), Brown(5)
LYNDON STATION (53944) Juneau(87), Sauk(13)
LYNXVILLE Crawford
LYONS Walworth
MADISON Dane
MAIDEN ROCK Pierce
MALONE (53049) Fond du Lac(94), Calumet(6)
MANAWA Waupaca
MANCHESTER Green Lake
MANITOWISH WATERS (54545) Vilas(98), Iron(2)
MANITOWOC Manitowoc
MAPLE Douglas
MAPLEWOOD Door
MARATHON Marathon
MARENGO Ashland
MARIBEL (54227) Manitowoc(99), Brown(1)
MARINETTE Marinette
MARION (54950) Shawano(56), Waupaca(44)
MARKESAN (53946) Green Lake(98), Fond du Lac(2)
MARQUETTE Green Lake
MARSHALL (53559) Dane(98), Jefferson(2)
MARSHALL FIELDS Milwaukee
MARSHFIELD (54449) Wood(93), Marathon(7)
MARSHFIELD Wood
MASON (54856) Bayfield(95), Ashland(5)
MATHER Juneau

MATTOON Shawano
MAUSTON Juneau
MAYVILLE Dodge
MAZOMANIE (53560) Dane(96), Iowa(4)
MC FARLAND Dane
MC NAUGHTON Oneida
MEDFORD Taylor
MEDINA Outagamie
MELLEN Ashland
MELROSE (54642) Jackson(95), La Crosse(3), Trempealeau(2)
MENASHA (54952) Winnebago(90), Calumet(10)
MENOMONEE FALLS Waukesha
MENOMONIE Dunn
MEQUON Ozaukee
MERCER Iron
MERRILL (54452) Lincoln(89), Marathon(11)
MERRILLAN (54754) Jackson(84), Clark(16)
MERRIMAC (53561) Sauk(87), Columbia(13)
MERTON Waukesha
MIDDLETON Dane
MIKANA Barron
MILAN Marathon
MILLADORE (54454) Wood(87), Portage(13)
MILLSTON Jackson
MILLTOWN Polk
MILTON Rock
MILWAUKEE Milwaukee
MINDORO (54644) La Crosse(98), Jackson(3)
MINERAL POINT (53565) Iowa(89), Lafayette(11)
MINOCQUA (54548) Oneida(80), Vilas(20)
MINONG (54859) Washburn(89), Douglas(11)
MISHICOT Manitowoc
MONDOVI (54755) Buffalo(54), Dunn(16), Eau Claire(15), Pepin(14)
MONROE Green
MONTELLO (53949) Marquette(99), Green Lake(1)
MONTFORT (53569) Iowa(50), Grant(50)
MONTICELLO Green
MONTREAL Iron
MORRISONVILLE Dane
MOSINEE (54455) Marathon(98), Portage(3)
MOUNT CALVARY Fond du Lac
MOUNT HOPE Grant
MOUNT HOREB Dane
MOUNT STERLING Crawford
MOUNTAIN Oconto
MUKWONAGO (53149) Waukesha(87), Walworth(12), Racine(1)
MUSCODA (53573) Richland(58), Grant(33), Iowa(9)
MUSKEGO (53150) Waukesha(98), Racine(2)
NASHOTAH Waukesha
NECEDAH Juneau
NEENAH Winnebago
NEILLSVILLE Clark
NEKOOSA (54457) Wood(57), Adams(40), Juneau(3)
NELSON Buffalo
NELSONVILLE Portage
NEOPIT Menominee
NEOSHO Dodge
NESHKORO (54960) Marquette(59), Waushara(35), Green Lake(6)
NEW AUBURN (54757) Chippewa(64), Barron(17), Dunn(13), Rusk(6)
NEW BERLIN Waukesha
NEW FRANKEN Brown
NEW GLARUS (53574) Green(98), Dane(2)

NEW HOLSTEIN (53061) Calumet(96), Fond du Lac(4)
NEW HOLSTEIN Fond du Lac
NEW LISBON Juneau
NEW LONDON (54961) Waupaca(75), Outagamie(25)
NEW MUNSTER Kenosha
NEW RICHMOND (54017) St. Croix(99), Polk(1)
NEWBURG Washington
NEWTON Manitowoc
NIAGARA (54151) Marinette(81), Florence(19)
NICHOLS Outagamie
NORTH FREEDOM Sauk
NORTH LAKE Waukesha
NORTH PRAIRIE Waukesha
NORWALK Monroe
OAK CREEK Milwaukee
OAKDALE Monroe
OAKFIELD (53065) Fond du Lac(91), Dodge(9)
OCONOMOWOC (53066) Waukesha(95), Jefferson(3), Dodge(2)
OCONTO Oconto
OCONTO FALLS (54154) Oconto(97), Shawano(3)
ODANAH Ashland
OGDENSBURG Waupaca
OGEMA Price
OJIBWA Sawyer
OKAUCHEE Waukesha
OMRO Winnebago
ONALASKA La Crosse
ONEIDA (54155) Brown(57), Outagamie(43)
ONTARIO (54651) Vernon(70), Monroe(31)
OOSTBURG Sheboygan
OREGON Dane
ORFORDVILLE Rock
OSCEOLA (54020) Polk(99), St. Croix(1)
OSHKOSH Winnebago
OSSEO (54758) Trempealeau(82), Jackson(9), Eau Claire(9)
OWEN (54460) Clark(97), Taylor(3)
OXFORD (53952) Marquette(51), Adams(49)
PACKWAUKEE Marquette
PALMYRA Jefferson
PARDEEVILLE (53954) Columbia(97), Marquette(3)
PARK FALLS (54552) Price(97), Iron(3)
PATCH GROVE Grant
PEARSON Langlade
PELICAN LAKE (54463) Oneida(97), Langlade(3)
PELL LAKE Walworth
PEMBINE Marinette
PEPIN Pepin
PESHTIGO (54157) Marinette(99), Oconto(1)
PEWAUKEE Waukesha
PHELPS Vilas
PHILLIPS Price
PHLOX Langlade
PICKEREL (54465) Langlade(62), Forest(38)
PICKETT (54964) Winnebago(86), Fond du Lac(15)
PIGEON FALLS Trempealeau
PINE RIVER Waushara
PITTSVILLE (54466) Wood(81), Clark(11), Jackson(8)
PLAIN Sauk
PLAINFIELD (54966) Waushara(85), Portage(13), Adams(2)
PLATTEVILLE (53818) Grant(96), Lafayette(3)
PLEASANT PRAIRIE Kenosha
PLOVER Portage
PLUM CITY (54761) Pierce(98), Dunn(1)
PLYMOUTH Sheboygan

POPLAR Douglas
PORT EDWARDS Wood
PORT WASHINGTON Ozaukee
PORT WING Bayfield
PORTAGE Columbia
PORTERFIELD Marinette
POSKIN Barron
POTOSI Grant
POTTER Calumet
POUND (54161) Marinette(54), Oconto(46)
POWERS LAKE Kenosha
POY SIPPI Waushara
POYNETTE Columbia
PRAIRIE DU CHIEN (53821) Crawford(98), Grant(2)
PRAIRIE DU SAC (53578) Sauk(92), Columbia(8)
PRAIRIE FARM (54762) Barron(90), Dunn(10)
PRENTICE Price
PRESCOTT Pierce
PRESQUE ISLE Vilas
PRINCETON (54968) Green Lake(94), Marquette(6)
PULASKI (54162) Shawano(71), Brown(22), Oconto(7)
RACINE (53403) Racine(98), Kenosha(2)
RACINE Racine
RADISSON Sawyer
RANDOLPH (53956) Dodge(58), Columbia(36), Green Lake(6)
RANDOLPH Columbia
RANDOM LAKE (53075) Sheboygan(94), Ozaukee(5), Washington(1)
READFIELD Waupaca
READSTOWN (54652) Vernon(94), Crawford(6)
REDGRANITE Waushara
REEDSBURG Sauk
REEDSVILLE (54230) Manitowoc(99), Brown(2)
REESEVILLE Dodge
REWEY Iowa
RHINELANDER (54501) Oneida(99), Lincoln(1)
RIB LAKE (54470) Taylor(97), Price(3)
RICE LAKE Barron
RICHFIELD Washington
RICHLAND CENTER Richland
RIDGELAND (54763) Dunn(94), Barron(6)
RIDGEWAY Iowa
RINGLE Marathon
RIO Columbia
RIPON (54971) Fond du Lac(82), Green Lake(14), Winnebago(4)
RIVER FALLS (54022) Pierce(73), St. Croix(28)
ROBERTS St. Croix
ROCHESTER Racine
ROCK FALLS Dunn
ROCK SPRINGS Sauk
ROCKFIELD Washington
ROCKLAND (54653) La Crosse(89), Monroe(11)
ROSENDALE Fond du Lac
ROSHOLT (54473) Portage(80), Marathon(20)
ROTHSCHILD Marathon
ROYALTON Waupaca
RUBICON Dodge
RUDOLPH (54475) Wood(85), Portage(15)
SAINT CLOUD (53079) Fond du Lac(95), Sheboygan(5)
SAINT CROIX FALLS Polk
SAINT FRANCIS Milwaukee
SAINT GERMAIN (54558) Vilas(90), Oneida(10)
SAINT JOSEPH St. Croix
SAINT NAZIANZ Manitowoc
SALEM Kenosha
SAND CREEK Dunn
SARONA (54870) Washburn(96), Barron(4)

SAUK CITY (53583) Sauk(87), Dane(13)
SAUKVILLE Ozaukee
SAXEVILLE Waushara
SAXON (54559) Iron(88), Ashland(12)
SAYNER Vilas
SCANDINAVIA (54977) Waupaca(95), Portage(5)
SCHOFIELD Marathon
SENECA Crawford
SEXTONVILLE Richland
SEYMOUR (54165) Outagamie(96), Shawano(3), Brown(1)
SHARON (53585) Walworth(82), Rock(17), Sauk(2)
SHAWANO Shawano
SHEBOYGAN Sheboygan
SHEBOYGAN FALLS Sheboygan
SHELDON (54766) Rusk(58), Taylor(32), Chippewa(10)
SHELL LAKE (54871) Washburn(69), Burnett(31)
SHERWOOD Calumet
SHIOCTON (54170) Outagamie(90), Shawano(10)
SHULLSBURG Lafayette
SILVER LAKE Kenosha
SINSINAWA Grant
SIREN (54872) Burnett(98), Polk(2)
SISTER BAY Door
SLINGER Washington
SOBIESKI Oconto
SOLDIERS GROVE (54655) Crawford(64), Richland(30), Vernon(6)
SOLON SPRINGS (54873) Douglas(83), Bayfield(17)
SOMERS Kenosha
SOMERSET St. Croix
SOUTH MILWAUKEE Milwaukee
SOUTH RANGE Douglas
SOUTH WAYNE Lafayette
SPARTA Monroe
SPENCER (54479) Marathon(58), Clark(42)
SPOONER (54801) Washburn(87), Burnett(13)
SPRING GREEN (53588) Sauk(67), Iowa(32), Richland(2)
SPRING VALLEY (54767) Pierce(95), St. Croix(4), Dunn(1)
SPRINGBROOK Washburn
SPRINGFIELD Walworth
STANLEY (54768) Chippewa(80), Clark(12), Eau Claire(6), Taylor(2)
STAR LAKE Vilas
STAR PRAIRIE (54026) Polk(64), St. Croix(36)
STETSONVILLE (54480) Taylor(95), Marathon(5)
STEUBEN Crawford
STEVENS POINT Portage
STITZER Grant
STOCKBRIDGE Calumet
STOCKHOLM (54769) Pierce(62), Pepin(39)
STODDARD (54658) Vernon(89), La Crosse(11)
STONE LAKE (54876) Sawyer(63), Washburn(38)
STOUGHTON (53589) Dane(99), Rock(1)
STRATFORD Marathon
STRUM (54770) Trempealeau(74), Eau Claire(26)
STURGEON BAY Door
STURTEVANT (53177) Racine(91), Kenosha(9)
SUAMICO Brown
SULLIVAN Jefferson
SUMMIT LAKE Langlade
SUN PRAIRIE Dane
SUPERIOR Douglas
SURING (54174) Oconto(97), Menominee(3)

SUSSEX Waukesha
TAYLOR (54659) Jackson(90), Trempealeau(10)
THERESA (53091) Dodge(95), Washington(5)
THIENSVILLE Ozaukee
THORP (54771) Clark(93), Taylor(7)
THREE LAKES (54562) Oneida(96), Forest(3)
TIGERTON (54486) Shawano(94), Waupaca(6)
TILLEDA Shawano
TISCH MILLS Manitowoc
TOMAH Monroe
TOMAHAWK (54487) Lincoln(88), Oneida(12)
TONY Rusk
TOWNSEND Oconto
TREGO Washburn
TREMPEALEAU Trempealeau
TREVOR Kenosha
TRIPOLI (54564) Oneida(43), Lincoln(42), Price(16)
TUNNEL CITY Monroe
TURTLE LAKE (54889) Barron(73), Polk(27)
TWIN LAKES Kenosha
TWO RIVERS Manitowoc
UNION CENTER Juneau

UNION GROVE (53182) Racine(92), Kenosha(8)
UNITY (54488) Clark(69), Marathon(31)
UPSON Iron
VALDERS Manitowoc
VAN DYNE (54979) Fond du Lac(88), Winnebago(12)
VERONA Dane
VESPER Wood
VIOLA (54664) Richland(84), Vernon(16)
VIROQUA (54665) Vernon(99), Crawford(1)
WABENO Forest
WALDO Sheboygan
WALES Waukesha
WALWORTH Walworth
WARRENS (54666) Monroe(84), Jackson(15)
WASCOTT Douglas
WASHBURN Bayfield
WASHINGTON ISLAND Door
WATERFORD Racine
WATERLOO (53594) Jefferson(84), Dodge(14), Dane(3)
WATERTOWN Dodge
WATERTOWN Jefferson
WAUKAU Winnebago
WAUKESHA Waukesha
WAUNAKEE Dane

WAUPACA (54981) Waupaca(92), Waushara(5), Portage(4)
WAUPUN (53963) Fond du Lac(51), Dodge(49)
WAUSAU Marathon
WAUSAUKEE Marinette
WAUTOMA (54982) Waushara(97), Marquette(3)
WAUZEKA Crawford
WEBSTER Burnett
WEST BEND Washington
WEST SALEM La Crosse
WESTBORO (54490) Taylor(96), Price(4)
WESTBY Vernon
WESTFIELD (53964) Marquette(97), Waushara(2), Adams(2)
WEYAUWEGA (54983) Waupaca(89), Waushara(11)
WEYERHAEUSER Rusk
WHEELER Dunn
WHITE LAKE (54491) Langlade(91), Oconto(9)
WHITEHALL Trempealeau
WHITELAW Manitowoc
WHITEWATER (53190) Walworth(60), Rock(29), Jefferson(11)
WILD ROSE Waushara
WILLARD Clark
WILLIAMS BAY Walworth
WILMOT Kenosha

WILSON St. Croix
WILTON Monroe
WINDSOR Dane
WINNEBAGO Winnebago
WINNECONNE (54986) Winnebago(96), Waushara(4)
WINTER Sawyer
WISCONSIN DELLS (53965) Columbia(43), Sauk(27), Adams(26), Juneau(5)
WISCONSIN RAPIDS (54494) Wood(93), Portage(7)
WISCONSIN RAPIDS Wood
WITHEE (54498) Clark(92), Taylor(8)
WITTENBERG (54499) Shawano(71), Marathon(28), Portage(1)
WONEWOC (53968) Juneau(66), Sauk(26), Vernon(6), Richland(2)
WOODFORD Lafayette
WOODLAND Dodge
WOODMAN Grant
WOODRUFF (54568) Vilas(66), Oneida(34)
WOODVILLE St. Croix
WOODWORTH Kenosha
WRIGHTSTOWN Brown
WYEVILLE Monroe
WYOCENA Columbia
ZACHOW Shawano
ZENDA Walworth

ZIP/City Cross Reference

ZIP	City	ZIP	City	ZIP	City	ZIP	City
53001-53001	ADELL	53058-53058	NASHOTAH	53126-53126	FRANKSVILLE	53502-53502	ALBANY
53002-53002	ALLENTON	53059-53059	NEOSHO	53127-53127	GENESEE DEPOT	53503-53503	ARENA
53003-53003	ASHIPPUN	53060-53060	NEWBURG	53128-53128	GENOA CITY	53504-53504	ARGYLE
53004-53004	BELGIUM	53061-53062	NEW HOLSTEIN	53129-53129	GREENDALE	53505-53505	AVALON
53005-53005	BROOKFIELD	53063-53063	NEWTON	53130-53130	HALES CORNERS	53506-53506	AVOCA
53006-53006	BROWNSVILLE	53064-53064	NORTH LAKE	53132-53132	FRANKLIN	53507-53507	BARNEVELD
53007-53007	BUTLER	53065-53065	OAKFIELD	53137-53137	HELENVILLE	53508-53508	BELLEVILLE
53008-53008	BROOKFIELD	53066-53066	OCONOMOWOC	53138-53138	HONEY CREEK	53510-53510	BELMONT
53009-53009	BYRON	53069-53069	OKAUCHEE	53139-53139	KANSASVILLE	53511-53512	BELOIT
53010-53010	CAMPBELLSPORT	53070-53070	OOSTBURG	53140-53144	KENOSHA	53515-53515	BLACK EARTH
53011-53011	CASCADE	53072-53072	PEWAUKEE	53146-53146	NEW BERLIN	53516-53516	BLANCHARDVILLE
53012-53012	CEDARBURG	53073-53073	PLYMOUTH	53147-53147	LAKE GENEVA	53517-53517	BLUE MOUNDS
53013-53013	CEDAR GROVE	53074-53074	PORT WASHINGTON	53148-53148	LYONS	53518-53518	BLUE RIVER
53014-53014	CHILTON	53075-53075	RANDOM LAKE	53149-53149	MUKWONAGO	53520-53520	BRODHEAD
53015-53015	CLEVELAND	53076-53076	RICHFIELD	53150-53150	MUSKEGO	53521-53521	BROOKLYN
53016-53016	CLYMAN	53078-53078	RUBICON	53151-53151	NEW BERLIN	53522-53522	BROWNTOWN
53017-53017	COLGATE	53079-53079	SAINT CLOUD	53152-53152	NEW MUNSTER	53523-53523	CAMBRIDGE
53018-53018	DELAFIELD	53080-53080	SAUKVILLE	53153-53153	NORTH PRAIRIE	53525-53525	CLINTON
53019-53019	EDEN	53081-53083	SHEBOYGAN	53154-53154	OAK CREEK	53526-53526	COBB
53020-53020	ELKHART LAKE	53085-53085	SHEBOYGAN FALLS	53156-53156	PALMYRA	53527-53527	COTTAGE GROVE
53021-53021	FREDONIA	53086-53086	SLINGER	53157-53157	PELL LAKE	53528-53528	CROSS PLAINS
53022-53022	GERMANTOWN	53088-53088	STOCKBRIDGE	53158-53158	PLEASANT PRAIRIE	53529-53529	DANE
53023-53023	GLENBEULAH	53089-53089	SUSSEX	53159-53159	POWERS LAKE	53530-53530	DARLINGTON
53024-53024	GRAFTON	53090-53090	WEST BEND	53167-53167	ROCHESTER	53531-53531	DEERFIELD
53026-53026	GREENBUSH	53091-53091	THERESA	53168-53168	SALEM	53532-53532	DE FOREST
53027-53027	HARTFORD	53092-53092	THIENSVILLE	53170-53170	SILVER LAKE	53533-53533	DODGEVILLE
53029-53029	HARTLAND	53093-53093	WALDO	53171-53171	SOMERS	53534-53534	EDGERTON
53031-53031	HINGHAM	53094-53094	WATERTOWN	53172-53172	SOUTH MILWAUKEE	53535-53535	EDMUND
53032-53032	HORICON	53095-53095	WEST BEND	53176-53176	SPRINGFIELD	53536-53536	EVANSVILLE
53033-53033	HUBERTUS	53097-53097	MEQUON	53177-53177	STURTEVANT	53537-53537	FOOTVILLE
53034-53034	HUSTISFORD	53098-53098	WATERTOWN	53178-53178	SULLIVAN	53538-53538	FORT ATKINSON
53035-53035	IRON RIDGE	53099-53099	WOODLAND	53179-53179	TREVOR	53540-53540	GOTHAM
53036-53036	IXONIA	53101-53101	BASSETT	53181-53181	TWIN LAKES	53541-53541	GRATIOT
53037-53037	JACKSON	53102-53102	BENET LAKE	53182-53182	UNION GROVE	53542-53542	HANOVER
53038-53038	JOHNSON CREEK	53103-53103	BIG BEND	53183-53183	WALES	53543-53543	HIGHLAND
53039-53039	JUNEAU	53104-53104	BRISTOL	53184-53184	WALWORTH	53544-53544	HOLLANDALE
53040-53040	KEWASKUM	53105-53105	BURLINGTON	53185-53185	WATERFORD	53545-53547	JANESVILLE
53042-53042	KIEL	53108-53108	CALEDONIA	53186-53188	WAUKESHA	53549-53549	JEFFERSON
53044-53044	KOHLER	53109-53109	CAMP LAKE	53190-53190	WHITEWATER	53550-53550	JUDA
53045-53045	BROOKFIELD	53110-53110	CUDAHY	53191-53191	WILLIAMS BAY	53551-53551	LAKE MILLS
53046-53046	LANNON	53114-53114	DARIEN	53192-53192	WILMOT	53553-53553	LINDEN
53047-53047	LEBANON	53115-53115	DELAVAN	53194-53194	WOODWORTH	53554-53554	LIVINGSTON
53048-53048	LOMIRA	53118-53118	DOUSMAN	53195-53195	ZENDA	53555-53555	LODI
53049-53049	MALONE	53119-53119	EAGLE	53201-53234	MILWAUKEE	53556-53556	LONE ROCK
53050-53050	MAYVILLE	53120-53120	EAST TROY	53235-53235	SAINT FRANCIS	53557-53557	LOWELL
53051-53052	MENOMONEE FALLS	53121-53121	ELKHORN	53237-53295	MILWAUKEE	53558-53558	MC FARLAND
53056-53056	MERTON	53122-53122	ELM GROVE	53401-53408	RACINE	53559-53559	MARSHALL
53057-53057	MOUNT CALVARY	53125-53125	FONTANA	53501-53501	AFTON	53560-53560	MAZOMANIE

Zip Range	City	Zip Range	City	Zip Range	City	Zip Range	City
53561-53561	MERRIMAC	53941-53941	LA VALLE	54149-54149	MOUNTAIN	54430-54430	ELTON
53562-53562	MIDDLETON	53942-53942	LIME RIDGE	54150-54150	NEOPIT	54432-54432	GALLOWAY
53563-53563	MILTON	53943-53943	LOGANVILLE	54151-54151	NIAGARA	54433-54433	GILMAN
53565-53565	MINERAL POINT	53944-53944	LYNDON STATION	54152-54152	NICHOLS	54434-54434	JUMP RIVER
53566-53566	MONROE	53946-53946	MARKESAN	54153-54153	OCONTO	54435-54435	GLEASON
53569-53569	MONTFORT	53947-53947	MARQUETTE	54154-54154	OCONTO FALLS	54436-54436	GRANTON
53570-53570	MONTICELLO	53948-53948	MAUSTON	54155-54155	ONEIDA	54437-54437	GREENWOOD
53571-53571	MORRISONVILLE	53949-53949	MONTELLO	54156-54156	PEMBINE	54439-54439	HANNIBAL
53572-53572	MOUNT HOREB	53950-53950	NEW LISBON	54157-54157	PESHTIGO	54440-54440	HATLEY
53573-53573	MUSCODA	53951-53951	NORTH FREEDOM	54159-54159	PORTERFIELD	54441-54441	HEWITT
53574-53574	NEW GLARUS	53952-53952	OXFORD	54160-54160	POTTER	54442-54442	IRMA
53575-53575	OREGON	53953-53953	PACKWAUKEE	54161-54161	POUND	54443-54443	JUNCTION CITY
53576-53576	ORFORDVILLE	53954-53954	PARDEEVILLE	54162-54162	PULASKI	54444-54444	KEMPSTER
53577-53577	PLAIN	53955-53955	POYNETTE	54165-54165	SEYMOUR	54446-54446	LOYAL
53578-53578	PRAIRIE DU SAC	53956-53957	RANDOLPH	54166-54166	SHAWANO	54447-54447	LUBLIN
53579-53579	REESEVILLE	53959-53959	REEDSBURG	54169-54169	SHERWOOD	54448-54448	MARATHON
53580-53580	REWEY	53960-53960	RIO	54170-54170	SHIOCTON	54449-54449	MARSHFIELD
53581-53581	RICHLAND CENTER	53961-53961	ROCK SPRINGS	54171-54171	SOBIESKI	54450-54450	MATTOON
53582-53582	RIDGEWAY	53962-53962	UNION CENTER	54173-54173	SUAMICO	54451-54451	MEDFORD
53583-53583	SAUK CITY	53963-53963	WAUPUN	54174-54174	SURING	54452-54452	MERRILL
53584-53584	SEXTONVILLE	53964-53964	WESTFIELD	54175-54175	TOWNSEND	54453-54453	MILAN
53585-53585	SHARON	53965-53965	WISCONSIN DELLS	54177-54177	WAUSAUKEE	54454-54454	MILLADORE
53586-53586	SHULLSBURG	53968-53968	WONEWOC	54180-54180	WRIGHTSTOWN	54455-54455	MOSINEE
53587-53587	SOUTH WAYNE	53969-53969	WYOCENA	54182-54182	ZACHOW	54456-54456	NEILLSVILLE
53588-53588	SPRING GREEN	54001-54001	AMERY	54201-54201	ALGOMA	54457-54457	NEKOOSA
53589-53589	STOUGHTON	54002-54002	BALDWIN	54202-54202	BAILEYS HARBOR	54458-54458	NELSONVILLE
53590-53591	SUN PRAIRIE	54003-54003	BELDENVILLE	54203-54203	BRANCH	54459-54459	OGEMA
53593-53593	VERONA	54004-54004	CLAYTON	54204-54204	BRUSSELS	54460-54460	OWEN
53594-53594	WATERLOO	54005-54005	CLEAR LAKE	54205-54205	CASCO	54462-54462	PEARSON
53595-53595	DODGEVILLE	54006-54006	CUSHING	54206-54206	CATO	54463-54463	PELICAN LAKE
53596-53596	SUN PRAIRIE	54007-54007	DEER PARK	54207-54207	COLLINS	54464-54464	PHLOX
53597-53597	WAUNAKEE	54009-54009	DRESSER	54208-54208	DENMARK	54465-54465	PICKEREL
53598-53598	WINDSOR	54010-54010	EAST ELLSWORTH	54209-54209	EGG HARBOR	54466-54466	PITTSVILLE
53599-53599	WOODFORD	54011-54011	ELLSWORTH	54210-54210	ELLISON BAY	54467-54467	PLOVER
53701-53794	MADISON	54012-54012	EMERALD	54211-54211	EPHRAIM	54469-54469	PORT EDWARDS
53801-53801	BAGLEY	54013-54013	GLENWOOD CITY	54212-54212	FISH CREEK	54470-54470	RIB LAKE
53802-53802	BEETOWN	54014-54014	HAGER CITY	54213-54213	FORESTVILLE	54471-54471	RINGLE
53803-53803	BENTON	54015-54015	HAMMOND	54214-54214	FRANCIS CREEK	54472-54472	MARSHFIELD
53804-53804	BLOOMINGTON	54016-54016	HUDSON	54215-54215	KELLNERSVILLE	54473-54473	ROSHOLT
53805-53805	BOSCOBEL	54017-54017	NEW RICHMOND	54216-54216	KEWAUNEE	54474-54474	ROTHSCHILD
53806-53806	CASSVILLE	54020-54020	OSCEOLA	54217-54217	LUXEMBURG	54475-54475	RUDOLPH
53807-53807	CUBA CITY	54021-54021	PRESCOTT	54220-54221	MANITOWOC	54476-54476	SCHOFIELD
53808-53808	DICKEYVILLE	54022-54022	RIVER FALLS	54226-54226	MAPLEWOOD	54479-54479	SPENCER
53809-53809	FENNIMORE	54023-54023	ROBERTS	54227-54227	MARIBEL	54480-54480	STETSONVILLE
53810-53810	GLEN HAVEN	54024-54024	SAINT CROIX FALLS	54228-54228	MISHICOT	54481-54481	STEVENS POINT
53811-53811	HAZEL GREEN	54025-54025	SOMERSET	54229-54229	NEW FRANKEN	54484-54484	STRATFORD
53812-53812	KIELER	54026-54026	STAR PRAIRIE	54230-54230	REEDSVILLE	54485-54485	SUMMIT LAKE
53813-53813	LANCASTER	54027-54027	WILSON	54232-54232	SAINT NAZIANZ	54486-54486	TIGERTON
53816-53816	MOUNT HOPE	54028-54028	WOODVILLE	54234-54234	SISTER BAY	54487-54487	TOMAHAWK
53817-53817	PATCH GROVE	54082-54082	SAINT JOSEPH	54235-54235	STURGEON BAY	54488-54488	UNITY
53818-53818	PLATTEVILLE	54101-54101	ABRAMS	54240-54240	TISCH MILLS	54489-54489	VESPER
53820-53820	POTOSI	54102-54102	AMBERG	54241-54241	TWO RIVERS	54490-54490	WESTBORO
53821-53821	PRAIRIE DU CHIEN	54103-54103	ARMSTRONG CREEK	54245-54245	VALDERS	54491-54491	WHITE LAKE
53824-53824	SINSINAWA	54104-54104	ATHELSTANE	54246-54246	WASHINGTON ISLAND	54492-54492	STEVENS POINT
53825-53825	STITZER	54106-54106	BLACK CREEK	54247-54247	WHITELAW	54493-54493	WILLARD
53826-53826	WAUZEKA	54107-54107	BONDUEL	54301-54344	GREEN BAY	54494-54495	WISCONSIN RAPIDS
53827-53827	WOODMAN	54110-54110	BRILLION	54401-54403	WAUSAU	54498-54498	WITHEE
53901-53901	PORTAGE	54111-54111	CECIL	54404-54404	MARSHFIELD	54499-54499	WITTENBERG
53910-53910	ADAMS	54112-54112	COLEMAN	54405-54405	ABBOTSFORD	54501-54501	RHINELANDER
53911-53911	ARLINGTON	54113-54113	COMBINED LOCKS	54406-54406	AMHERST	54511-54511	ARGONNE
53913-53913	BARABOO	54114-54114	CRIVITZ	54407-54407	AMHERST JUNCTION	54512-54512	BOULDER JUNCTION
53916-53917	BEAVER DAM	54115-54115	DE PERE	54408-54408	ANIWA	54513-54513	BRANTWOOD
53919-53919	BRANDON	54119-54119	DUNBAR	54409-54409	ANTIGO	54514-54514	BUTTERNUT
53920-53920	BRIGGSVILLE	54120-54120	FENCE	54410-54410	ARPIN	54515-54515	CATAWBA
53922-53922	BURNETT	54121-54121	FLORENCE	54411-54411	ATHENS	54517-54517	CLAM LAKE
53923-53923	CAMBRIA	54123-54123	FOREST JUNCTION	54412-54412	AUBURNDALE	54519-54519	CONOVER
53924-53924	CAZENOVIA	54124-54124	GILLETT	54413-54413	BABCOCK	54520-54520	CRANDON
53925-53925	COLUMBUS	54125-54125	GOODMAN	54414-54414	BIRNAMWOOD	54521-54521	EAGLE RIVER
53926-53926	DALTON	54126-54126	GREENLEAF	54415-54415	BLENKER	54524-54524	FIFIELD
53927-53927	DELLWOOD	54127-54127	GREEN VALLEY	54416-54416	BOWLER	54525-54525	GILE
53928-53928	DOYLESTOWN	54128-54128	GRESHAM	54417-54417	BROKAW	54526-54526	GLEN FLORA
53929-53929	ELROY	54129-54129	HILBERT	54418-54418	BRYANT	54527-54527	GLIDDEN
53930-53930	ENDEAVOR	54130-54130	KAUKAUNA	54420-54420	CHILI	54529-54529	HARSHAW
53931-53931	FAIRWATER	54131-54131	FREEDOM	54421-54421	COLBY	54530-54530	HAWKINS
53932-53932	FALL RIVER	54135-54135	KESHENA	54422-54422	CURTISS	54531-54531	HAZELHURST
53933-53933	FOX LAKE	54136-54136	KIMBERLY	54423-54423	CUSTER	54532-54532	HEAFFORD JUNCTION
53934-53934	FRIENDSHIP	54137-54137	KRAKOW	54424-54424	DEERBROOK	54534-54534	HURLEY
53935-53935	FRIESLAND	54138-54138	LAKEWOOD	54425-54425	DORCHESTER	54536-54536	IRON BELT
53936-53936	GRAND MARSH	54139-54139	LENA	54426-54426	EDGAR	54537-54537	KENNAN
53937-53937	HILLPOINT	54140-54140	LITTLE CHUTE	54427-54427	ELAND	54538-54538	LAC DU FLAMBEAU
53939-53939	KINGSTON	54141-54141	LITTLE SUAMICO	54428-54428	ELCHO	54539-54539	LAKE TOMAHAWK
53940-53940	LAKE DELTON	54143-54143	MARINETTE	54429-54429	ELDERON	54540-54540	LAND O LAKES

ZIP	City	ZIP	City	ZIP	City	ZIP	City
54541-54541	LAONA	54654-54654	SENECA	54771-54771	THORP	54889-54889	TURTLE LAKE
54542-54542	LONG LAKE	54655-54655	SOLDIERS GROVE	54772-54772	WHEELER	54890-54890	WASCOTT
54543-54543	MC NAUGHTON	54656-54656	SPARTA	54773-54773	WHITEHALL	54891-54891	WASHBURN
54545-54545	MANITOWISH WATERS	54657-54657	STEUBEN	54774-54774	CHIPPEWA FALLS	54893-54893	WEBSTER
54546-54546	MELLEN	54658-54658	STODDARD	54801-54801	SPOONER	54895-54895	WEYERHAEUSER
54547-54547	MERCER	54659-54659	TAYLOR	54805-54805	ALMENA	54896-54896	WINTER
54548-54548	MINOCQUA	54660-54660	TOMAH	54806-54806	ASHLAND	54901-54906	OSHKOSH
54550-54550	MONTREAL	54661-54661	TREMPEALEAU	54810-54810	BALSAM LAKE	54909-54909	ALMOND
54552-54552	PARK FALLS	54662-54662	TUNNEL CITY	54812-54812	BARRON	54911-54919	APPLETON
54554-54554	PHELPS	54664-54664	VIOLA	54813-54813	BARRONETT	54921-54921	BANCROFT
54555-54555	PHILLIPS	54665-54665	VIROQUA	54814-54814	BAYFIELD	54922-54922	BEAR CREEK
54556-54556	PRENTICE	54666-54666	WARRENS	54816-54816	BENOIT	54923-54923	BERLIN
54557-54557	PRESQUE ISLE	54667-54667	WESTBY	54817-54817	BIRCHWOOD	54926-54926	BIG FALLS
54558-54558	SAINT GERMAIN	54669-54669	WEST SALEM	54818-54818	BRILL	54927-54927	BUTTE DES MORTS
54559-54559	SAXON	54670-54670	WILTON	54819-54819	BRUCE	54928-54928	CAROLINE
54560-54560	SAYNER	54701-54703	EAU CLAIRE	54820-54820	BRULE	54929-54929	CLINTONVILLE
54561-54561	STAR LAKE	54720-54720	ALTOONA	54821-54821	CABLE	54930-54930	COLOMA
54562-54562	THREE LAKES	54721-54721	ARKANSAW	54822-54822	CAMERON	54931-54931	DALE
54563-54563	TONY	54722-54722	AUGUSTA	54824-54824	CENTURIA	54932-54932	ELDORADO
54564-54564	TRIPOLI	54723-54723	BAY CITY	54826-54826	COMSTOCK	54933-54933	EMBARRASS
54565-54565	UPSON	54724-54724	BLOOMER	54827-54827	CORNUCOPIA	54934-54934	EUREKA
54566-54566	WABENO	54725-54725	BOYCEVILLE	54828-54828	COUDERAY	54935-54937	FOND DU LAC
54568-54568	WOODRUFF	54726-54726	BOYD	54829-54829	CUMBERLAND	54940-54940	FREMONT
54601-54603	LA CROSSE	54727-54727	CADOTT	54830-54830	DANBURY	54941-54941	GREEN LAKE
54610-54610	ALMA	54728-54728	CHETEK	54832-54832	DRUMMOND	54942-54942	GREENVILLE
54611-54611	ALMA CENTER	54729-54729	CHIPPEWA FALLS	54834-54834	EDGEWATER	54943-54943	HANCOCK
54612-54612	ARCADIA	54730-54730	COLFAX	54835-54835	EXELAND	54944-54944	HORTONVILLE
54613-54613	ARKDALE	54731-54731	CONRATH	54836-54836	FOXBORO	54945-54945	IOLA
54614-54614	BANGOR	54732-54732	CORNELL	54837-54837	FREDERIC	54946-54946	KING
54615-54615	BLACK RIVER FALLS	54733-54733	DALLAS	54838-54838	GORDON	54947-54947	LARSEN
54616-54616	BLAIR	54734-54734	DOWNING	54839-54839	GRAND VIEW	54948-54948	LEOPOLIS
54618-54618	CAMP DOUGLAS	54735-54735	DOWNSVILLE	54840-54840	GRANTSBURG	54949-54949	MANAWA
54619-54619	CASHTON	54736-54736	DURAND	54841-54841	HAUGEN	54950-54950	MARION
54620-54620	CATARACT	54737-54737	EAU GALLE	54842-54842	HAWTHORNE	54951-54951	MEDINA
54621-54621	CHASEBURG	54738-54738	ELEVA	54843-54843	HAYWARD	54952-54952	MENASHA
54622-54622	COCHRANE	54739-54739	ELK MOUND	54844-54844	HERBSTER	54956-54957	NEENAH
54623-54623	COON VALLEY	54740-54740	ELMWOOD	54845-54845	HERTEL	54960-54960	NESHKORO
54624-54624	DE SOTO	54741-54741	FAIRCHILD	54846-54846	HIGH BRIDGE	54961-54961	NEW LONDON
54625-54625	DODGE	54742-54742	FALL CREEK	54847-54847	IRON RIVER	54962-54962	OGDENSBURG
54626-54626	EASTMAN	54743-54743	GILMANTON	54848-54848	LADYSMITH	54963-54963	OMRO
54627-54627	ETTRICK	54744-54744	HILLSDALE	54849-54849	LAKE NEBAGAMON	54964-54964	PICKETT
54628-54628	FERRYVILLE	54745-54745	HOLCOMBE	54850-54850	LA POINTE	54965-54965	PINE RIVER
54629-54629	FOUNTAIN CITY	54746-54746	HUMBIRD	54851-54851	LEWIS	54966-54966	PLAINFIELD
54630-54630	GALESVILLE	54747-54747	INDEPENDENCE	54853-54853	LUCK	54967-54967	POY SIPPI
54631-54631	GAYS MILLS	54748-54748	JIM FALLS	54854-54854	MAPLE	54968-54968	PRINCETON
54632-54632	GENOA	54749-54749	KNAPP	54855-54855	MARENGO	54969-54969	READFIELD
54634-54634	HILLSBORO	54750-54750	MAIDEN ROCK	54856-54856	MASON	54970-54970	REDGRANITE
54635-54635	HIXTON	54751-54751	MENOMONIE	54857-54857	MIKANA	54971-54971	RIPON
54636-54636	HOLMEN	54754-54754	MERRILLAN	54858-54858	MILLTOWN	54974-54974	ROSENDALE
54637-54637	HUSTLER	54755-54755	MONDOVI	54859-54859	MINONG	54975-54975	ROYALTON
54638-54638	KENDALL	54756-54756	NELSON	54861-54861	ODANAH	54976-54976	SAXEVILLE
54639-54639	LA FARGE	54757-54757	NEW AUBURN	54862-54862	OJIBWA	54977-54977	SCANDINAVIA
54640-54640	LYNXVILLE	54758-54758	OSSEO	54864-54864	POPLAR	54978-54978	TILLEDA
54641-54641	MATHER	54759-54759	PEPIN	54865-54865	PORT WING	54979-54979	VAN DYNE
54642-54642	MELROSE	54760-54760	PIGEON FALLS	54867-54867	RADISSON	54980-54980	WAUKAU
54643-54643	MILLSTON	54761-54761	PLUM CITY	54868-54868	RICE LAKE	54981-54981	WAUPACA
54644-54644	MINDORO	54762-54762	PRAIRIE FARM	54870-54870	SARONA	54982-54982	WAUTOMA
54645-54645	MOUNT STERLING	54763-54763	RIDGELAND	54871-54871	SHELL LAKE	54983-54983	WEYAUWEGA
54646-54646	NECEDAH	54764-54764	ROCK FALLS	54872-54872	SIREN	54984-54984	WILD ROSE
54648-54648	NORWALK	54765-54765	SAND CREEK	54873-54873	SOLON SPRINGS	54985-54985	WINNEBAGO
54649-54649	OAKDALE	54766-54766	SHELDON	54874-54874	SOUTH RANGE	54986-54986	WINNECONNE
54650-54650	ONALASKA	54767-54767	SPRING VALLEY	54875-54875	SPRINGBROOK	54990-54990	IOLA
54651-54651	ONTARIO	54768-54768	STANLEY	54876-54876	STONE LAKE		
54652-54652	READSTOWN	54769-54769	STOCKHOLM	54880-54880	SUPERIOR		
54653-54653	ROCKLAND	54770-54770	STRUM	54888-54888	TREGO		

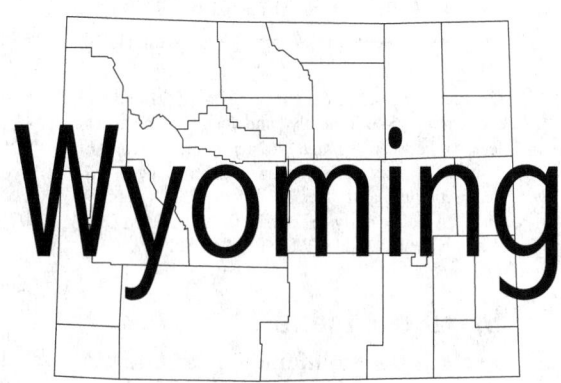

General Help Numbers:

Governor's Office
State Capitol Building, Rm 124   307-777-7434
Cheyenne, WY 82002-0010   Fax 307-632-3909
www.state.wy.us/governor/governor_home.html   8AM-5PM

Attorney General's Office
123 State Capitol   307-777-7841
Cheyenne, WY 82002   Fax 307-777-6869
www.state.wy.us/~ag/index.html   8AM-5PM

State Court Administrator
Supreme Court Bldg   307-777-7480
2301 Capitol Ave   Fax 307-777-3447
Cheyenne, WY 82002   8AM-5PM
www.courts.state.wy.us

State Archives
Archives Division   307-777-7826
Barrett Bldg   Fax 307-777-7044
Cheyenne, WY 82002   8AM-4:45PM M-F
http://commerce.state.wy.us/cr/archives

State Specifics:

Capital:	Cheyenne
	Laramie County
Time Zone:	MST
Number of Counties:	23
Population:	479,602
Web Site:	www.state.wy.us

State Agencies

Criminal Records

Division of Criminal Investigation, Criminal Record Section, 316 W 22nd St, Cheyenne, WY 82002; 307-777-7523, 307-777-7252 (Fax), 8AM to 5PM.

Note: First, obtain a Request for Criminal Record Packet ($15.00) from address above or phone.

Indexing & Storage: Records are available from 1941 on. New records are available for inquiry immediately. Records are indexed on inhouse computer.

Searching: Must have a notarized, signed waiver from the person of record. Must also have a standard 8" x 8" orange fingerprint card (that you must get from this office) with properly rolled fingerprints of person and notarized signature of applicant. Include the following in your request-name, set of fingerprints, date of birth, Social Security Number, number of years to search. Must also fill out waiver from their office that is on the back of the fingerprint card. Major misdemeanors and felonies will indicate arrests as well as convictions. The following data is not released: juvenile records.

Access by: mail, in person.

Fee & Payment: The search fee is $15.00 plus an additional $5.00 if this office must perform the fingerprinting. The fee is only $10.00 if the applicant is part of an organization providing volunteer services. Fee payee: Office of the Attorney General. Prepayment required. Money order, cash or certified checks only. No credit cards accepted.

Mail search: Turnaround time: 2-4 weeks. A self addressed stamped envelope is requested.

In person search: Proper forms are required to be filled out.

Corporation Records
Limited Liability Company Records
Limited Partnership Records
Fictitious Name
Trademarks/Servicemarks

Corporations Division, Secretary of State, State Capitol, Cheyenne, WY 82002; 307-777-7311, 307-777-5339 (Fax), 8AM-5PM.

http://soswy.state.wy.us

Indexing & Storage: Records are available from 1800s on. The records on microfilm are inactive records before 1983. Newer records are on computer. New records are available for inquiry immediately. Records are indexed on microfilm, inhouse computer.

Searching: The Annual Report financial information (Appendix I Worksheet filed with Annual Report) is not released. Include the following in your request-full name of business. In addition to the articles of incorporation, corporation records include the following information: Annual Reports, Officers, Directors, DBAs, Prior (merged) names, Inactive and Reserved names.

Access by: mail, phone, fax, in person, online.

Fee & Payment: Fees are $.50 per page for the first 10 pages and $.15 for each additional page. Certification is $3.00. Fee payee: Secretary of State. They will invoice for copies and certificates. Prepaid accounts are available. Personal checks accepted. No credit cards accepted.

Mail search: Turnaround time: 1-3 days. A self addressed stamped envelope is requested.

Phone search: You may call for information.

Fax search: Turnaround time is 24-48 hours.

In person search: You may request information in person.

Online search: Information is available through the Internet site listed above. You can search by corporate name or even download the whole file. Also, they have 2 pages of excellent searching tips.

Uniform Commercial Code
Federal Tax Liens

UCC Division, Secretary of State, The Capitol, Cheyenne, WY 82002-0020 (Courier: Capitol Bldg, RM 110, Cheyenne, WY 82002); 307-777-5372, 307-777-5988 (Fax), 8AM-5PM.

http://soswy.state.wy.us

Indexing & Storage: Records are available for five years on computer, since the "beginning" on microfiche. Records are indexed on inhouse computer.

Searching: The search includes federal tax liens on businesses. Include the following in your request-debtor name.

Access by: mail, fax, in person, online.

Fee & Payment: The search fee is $5.00. Copies cost $.50 each for the first 10 pages and $.15 for each additional page. Fee payee: Secretary of State. Personal checks accepted. No credit cards accepted.

Mail search: Turnaround time: 7 days. Please include your phone number with all requests.

Fax search: Requests may be faxed in.

In person search: Searching is available in person.

Online search: Fees include a $50 annual registration, $20 monthly, and long distant access fees of between $3 and $6 per hour. A word of caution, if user fails to log off the "clock" still keeps ticking and user is billed! The system is open 24 hours daily except 1:30AM to 5AM Mon through Sunday, and 4PM to 6PM on Sunday.

State Tax Liens

Records not maintained by a state level agency.

Note: There is no state income tax. All other state tax liens are filed at the county level.

Sales Tax Registrations

Revenue Department, Excise Tax Division, Herscher Bldg, 122 W 25th St, Cheyenne, WY 82002; 307-777-5203, 307-777-7722 (Fax), 8AM-5PM.

revenue.state.wy.us

Indexing & Storage: Records are available for at least two years: inactive files are purged every two years.

Searching: This agency will only confirm that the business is registered. They will provide no other information. Include the following in your request-business name. They will also search by tax permit number.

Access by: mail, phone, in person.

Mail search: A self addressed stamped envelope is requested. No fee for mail request.

Phone search: No fee for telephone request.

In person search: No fee for request.

Birth Certificates

Wyoming Department of Health, Vital Records Services, Hathaway Bldg, Cheyenne, WY 82002; 307-777-7591, 307-635-4103 (Fax), 8AM-5PM.

http://wdhfs.state.wy.us/vital_records

Indexing & Storage: Records are available from 1909-present. New records are available for inquiry immediately. Records are indexed on microfilm, inhouse computer.

Searching: Must have a signed release from person of record or parent or guardian. Include the following in your request-full name, names of parents, mother's maiden name, date of birth, place of birth, relationship to person of record. Must include signature on request and copy of photo ID.

Access by: mail, fax, in person.

Fee & Payment: Search fee is $12.00 per name per 5 years searched. Fee includes certification. Use of credit card is an additional $5.00 for expedited service. Fee payee: Vital Records Services. Prepayment required. Personal checks accepted. Credit cards accepted: Mastercard, Visa, AmEx, Discover.

Mail search: Turnaround time: 3-4 working days. No self addressed stamped envelope is required.

Fax search: See expedited services.

In person search: Turnaround time is 15 minutes.

Expedited service: Expedited service is available for fax searches. Turnaround time: next day. Credit card is required ($5.00), records are overnighted for an additional $11.75.

Death Records

Wyoming Department of Health, Vital Records Services, Hathaway Bldg, Cheyenne, WY 82002; 307-777-7591, 307-635-4103 (Fax), 8AM-5PM.

http://wdhfs.state.wy.us/vital_records

Indexing & Storage: Records are available from 1945-present. For prior records, contact the State Archives at 307-777-7826. New records are available for inquiry immediately. Records are indexed on microfilm, inhouse computer.

Searching: Must have a signed release form from immediate family member. The agency will verify information to family member, such as aunts and uncles, but will not release copies. Include the following in your request-full name, date of death, place of death, relationship to person of record, reason for information request. Must include signature and copy of photo ID with request.

Access by: mail, fax, in person.

Fee & Payment: Search fee is $9.00 per name if year is known; fee is $12.00 per name per 5 years if date is unknown. All copies are certified. Use of credit card for expedited service an extra $5.00. Fee payee: Vital Records Services. Prepayment required. Personal checks accepted. Credit cards accepted: Mastercard, Visa, AmEx, Discover.

Mail search: Turnaround time: 3-4 working days. No self addressed stamped envelope is required.

Fax search: See expedited services.

In person search: Turnaround time is 15 minutes.

Expedited service: Expedited service is available for fax searches. Turnaround time: next day. Include credit card fee and funds for overnight delivery.

Marriage Certificates

Wyoming Department of Health, Vital Records Services, Hathaway Bldg, Cheyenne, WY 82002; 307-777-7591, 307-635-4103 (Fax), 8AM-5PM.

http://wdhfs.state.wy.us/vital_records

Indexing & Storage: Records are available from 1941-present. New records are available for inquiry immediately. Records are indexed on microfilm, inhouse computer.

Searching: Must have a signed release from persons of record. Include the following in your request-names of husband and wife, date of marriage, place or county of marriage, relationship to person of record, reason for information request. Signature and copy of photo ID must be included in request.

Access by: mail, fax, in person.

Fee & Payment: The fee is $12.00 per record and an additional $5.00 if a credit card is used fro expedited service. Fee payee: Vital Records Services. Prepayment required. Personal checks accepted. Credit cards accepted: Mastercard, Visa, AmEx, Discover.

Mail search: Turnaround time: 3-4 working days. No self addressed stamped envelope is required.

Fax search: See expedited services.

In person search: Turnaround time is 15 minutes.

Expedited service: Expedited service is available for fax searches. Turnaround time: next day. Include credit card fee and funds for overnight delivery.

Divorce Records

Wyoming Department of Health, Vital Records Services, Hathaway Bldg, Cheyenne, WY 82002; 307-777-7591, 307-635-4103 (Fax), 8AM-5PM.

http://wdhfs.state.wy.us/vital_records

Indexing & Storage: Records are available from 1941-present. New records are available for inquiry immediately. Records are indexed on microfilm, inhouse computer.

Searching: Must have a signed release from person of record. Include the following in your request-names of husband and wife, date of divorce, place of divorce, relationship to person of record. Include copy of photo ID with request.

Access by: mail, phone, fax, in person.

Fee & Payment: Fee is $12.00 per record, add $5.00 if expedited service used. Fee payee: Vital Records Services. Prepayment required. Personal checks accepted. Credit cards accepted: Mastercard, Visa, AmEx, Discover.

Mail search: Turnaround time: 3-4 working days.

Phone search: See expedited service.

Fax search: See expedited services.

In person search: Turnaround time is 30 minutes.

Expedited service: Expedited service is available for fax searches. Turnaround time: next day. Include credit card fee ($5.00) and funds for overnight delivery.

Workers' Compensation Records

Employment Department, Workers Compensation Division, 122 W 25th St, Cheyenne, WY 82002 (Courier: Herschler Bldg, 2nd Floor E, 122 W 25th St, Cheyenne, WY 82002); 307-777-7159, 307-777-5946 (Fax), 8AM-4:30PM.

http://wydoe.state.wy.us/wscd

Indexing & Storage: Records are available from 1987 on computer. Records are on microfiche from 1919-1987. Searches on microfiche must include the date of injury, county of injury, employer and body part affected.

Searching: Only the injured party, employer or legal counsel for either party can obtain records from this agency. Include the following in your request-claimant name, Social Security Number. The only information released is case #, date of injury, body part, employer at time of injury, or other information specifically authorized by claimant.

Access by: mail, fax.

Fee & Payment: No search fee, copy fee is $.25 per copy.

Mail search: Turnaround time: variable. Send release form with request to Gary Lord at address above.No self addressed stamped envelope is required.

Fax search: They will fax results with appropriate request.

Accident Reports

Department of Transportation, Accident Records Section, 5300 Bishop Blvd, Cheyenne, WY 82009-3340; 307-777-4450, 307-777-4250 (Fax), 8AM-5PM.

Note: The agency refers to these reports as "Crash Reports."

Indexing & Storage: Records are available from 1979 on. It takes 3-30 days before new records are available for inquiry.

Searching: Accident reports (done by the officer) are considered open public record reports. Reports compiled by individuals involved are closed. Include the following in your request-date of accident, location of accident, full name, date of birth.

Access by: mail, phone, in person.

Fee & Payment: The fee is $3.00 per record uncertified and $5.00 certified. If the specific year or location is not given, the fee is $25.00. Fee payee: Department of Transportation. Prepayment required. Personal checks accepted. No credit cards accepted.

Mail search: Turnaround time: 1 week to 10 days. A self addressed stamped envelope is requested.

Phone search: Searches may be done by phone, but no copies are sent until payment is received.

In person search: In-person requests are normally processed in a few of minutes.

Driver License Information Driver Records

Wyoming Department of Transportation, Driver Services, 5300 Bishop Blvd, Cheyenne, WY 82009-3340; 307-777-4800, 307-777-4773 (Fax), 8AM-5PM.

http://wydotweb.state.wy.us

Note: Tickets may be obtained from the address above for a fee of $5.00 per citation.

Indexing & Storage: Records are available for 3 years from offense date for moving violations, 5 years from conviction date for DWIs, and 3-5 years based on original charge for suspensions. Accidents are shown only if driver has no insurance. It takes 5-10 days before new records are available for inquiry.

Searching: Companies requesting records must identify themselves and certify the purpose for which the report is to be used and no other purpose. Casual requesters cannot obtain records with personal information unless with signed release from subject. The driver license number or name and DOB is needed when ordering. In addition, a SSN is required when requesting a Commercial Driver License (CDL) record. The following data is not released: medical information.

Access by: mail, in person.

Fee & Payment: The fee is $5.00 per record, $3.00 by tape. Fee payee: Department of Transportation. Prepayment required. Personal checks accepted. No credit cards accepted.

Mail search: Turnaround time: 2 days. A self addressed stamped envelope is requested.

In person search: Normal turnaround time is while you wait. Individual licensees may request a copy of their own record at any field office.

Other access: Magnetic tape retrieval is available at $3.00 per record. The entire driver license file may be purchased for $2,500.

Vehicle Ownership Vehicle Identification

Wyoming Dept. of Transportation, Motor Vehicle Services, 5300 Bishop Blvd, Cheyenne, WY 82009-3340 (Courier: 5300 Bishop Blvd, Cheyenne, WY 82002); 307-777-4709, 307-777-4772 (Fax), 8AM-5PM.

www.wydotweb.state.wy.us

Note: At the web site, click on "Vehicle Services" for detailed WY DOT vehicle information.

Indexing & Storage: Records are available for 40 years on titles and 80 years on registrations. It takes 3-15 days before new records are available for inquiry.

Searching: An opt in provision allows casual requesters to obtain records on subjects who opted in. Requests must be for a legitimate business purpose and requesters must sign a "Privacy Disclosure Agreement." Lien records are not available from the state and must be obtained from the one of the 23 Wyoming county clerk offices.

Access by: mail, in person.

Fee & Payment: The fee is $5.00 per record. Fee payee: Department of Transportation. Prepayment required. Personal checks accepted. No credit cards accepted.

Mail search: Turnaround time: 1 week. No self addressed stamped envelope is required.

In person search: Turnaround time is normally in a few minutes.

Other access: Bulk information is available, customized lists can be obtained. Records cannot be resold once purchased. For more information, call the Info Tech Section at 307-777-4870.

Boat & Vessel Ownership Boat & Vessel Registration

Wyoming Game & Fish Dept, Watercraft Section, 5400 Bishop Blvd, Cheyenne, WY 82006; 307-777-4575, 307-777-4610 (Fax), 8AM-5PM M-F.

gf.state.wy.us

Indexing & Storage: Records are available for the last 3 years. Archives are maintained for years prior to the 3 year period. Records are indexed on computer for the last 2 years. The state does not issue titles. All motorized boats with a 5 HP or larger motor must be registered.

Searching: To search you must provide one of the following: Name, Wyoming #, or Hull Id #.

Access by: mail, phone, fax, in person.

Fee & Payment: There is no search fee.

Mail search: Turnaround time: 2-3 days. Turnaround time is 1 week if archived info is needed.

Phone search: Searching is available by phone.

Fax search: Information can be faxed back.

In person search: No fee for request. Turnaround time is immediate if the file is not archived.

Other access: Printed lists are available, call for further details.

Legislation-Current/Pending Legislation-Passed

Wyoming Legislature, State Capitol, Room 213, Cheyenne, WY 82002; 307-777-7881, 8AM-5PM.

legisweb.state.wy.us

Note: General Session starts on the 2nd Tuesday in January. Budget session starts in February on second Monday.

Indexing & Storage: Records are available for the current session and for past bills, only as introduced. Records are indexed on books (volumes).

Searching: Include the following in your request-bill number, date of debate, topic of bill.

Access by: mail, phone, in person, online.

Fee & Payment: Copies are $.10 a page with a minimum fee of $1.00. Fee payee: Wyoming Legislature. Personal checks accepted. No credit cards accepted.

Mail search: Turnaround time: variable. No self addressed stamped envelope is required.

Phone search: Searching is available by phone.

In person search: Searching is available in person.

Online search: The Internet site contains a wealth of information regarding the legislature and bills.

Voter Registration
Access to Records is Restricted

Secretary of State, Election Division, Wyoming State Capitol, Cheyenne, WY 82002-0020; 307-777-7186, 307-777-7640 (Fax), 8AM-5PM.

http://soswy.state.wy.us

Note: Individual look-ups must be done at the county level. The SSN and DOB are not released. The state will sell all or part of its database, but only for political reasons. Commercial use is not permitted.

GED Certificates

Dept of Education, GED Program, Hathaway Bldg, 2nd Fl, 2300 Capitol Ave, Cheyenne, WY 82002-0050; 307-777-6911, 307-777-6234 (Fax), 8AM-5PM M-F.

www.k12.wy.us/alt_ed.html#GED

Searching: To search, all of the following is required: name, Social Security Number, and date of birth. For transcripts, a signed release is also required.

Access by: mail, fax, in person.

Fee & Payment: There is no fee for verifications or transcripts.

Mail search: Turnaround time: 2 weeks. No self addressed stamped envelope is required.

Fax search: Same criteria as mail searching.

In person search: Turnaround time is typically 10 minutes for verifications, transcripts are mailed.

Hunting License Information Fishing License Information

Game & Fish Department, License Section, 5400 Bishop Blvd, Cheyenne, WY 82006; 307-777-4600 (Licensing Section), 307-777-4679 (Fax), 8AM-5PM.

http://gf.state.wy.us

Note: They have a central database for lottery (big game, moose, big horn sheep, elk, deer & antelope) permits only.

Indexing & Storage: Records are available from 3 years present on computer, 10 years on microfiche.

Searching: Include the following in your request-full name, date of birth, Social Security Number. The following data is not released: Social Security Numbers.

Access by: mail, phone, fax, in person.

Fee & Payment: Fees are incurred if there is extensive searching or lists are involved. Call first. Fee payee: Wyoming Game and Fish. Prepayment required. Money orders and cashier's checks are preferred. No credit cards accepted.

Mail search: Turnaround time: 1-3 days. No self addressed stamped envelope is required.

Phone search: Searching is available by phone.

Fax search: Fax searching available.

In person search: Searching is available in person.

Other access: They have mailing and label lists available. Call (800) 548-9453 for more information.

Licenses Searchable Online

Attorney #09	www.wyomingbar.org/html/search.asp
Bank #23	http://audit.state.wy.us/banking/banks.htm
Collection Agency #24	http://audit.state.wy.us/banking/CAB.htm
Engineer #27	www.wrds.uwyo.edu/wrds/borpe/roster/roster.html
Insurance Agent #08	www.state.wy.us/~insurance
Insurance Claims Adjuster #08	www.state.wy.us/~insurance
Insurance Consultant #08	www.state.wy.us/~insurance
Insurance Service Representatives #08	www.state.wy.us/~insurance
Insurance Solicitor #08	www.state.wy.us/~insurance
Motor Club Agents #08	www.state.wy.us/~insurance
Optometrist #06	www.arbo.org/nodb2000/licsearch.asp
Preneed Agents #08	www.state.wy.us/~insurance
Public Accountant-CPA #29	http://cpaboard.state.wy.us/search.cfm
Public Accountant-CPA Firm #29	http://cpaboard.state.wy.us/search.cfm
Resident Insurance Broker #08	www.state.wy.us/~insurance
Resident Surplus Lines Broker #08	www.state.wy.us/~insurance
Savings & Loan Association #23	http://audit.state.wy.us/banking/fsb.htm
Surveyor #27	www.wrds.uwyo.edu/wrds/borpe/roster/roster.html
Travel & Baggage Agents #08	www.state.wy.us/~insurance

Licensing Quick Finder

Architect #30	307-777-7788
Attorney #09	307-632-9061
Bank #23	307-777-6605
Barber, Barber Shop #02	307-754-5237
Bus Driver #41	307-777-4800
Child Care Facility #22	307-777-6595
Chiropractor #32	307-777-6529
Collection Agency #24	307-777-3497
Cosmetologist #03	307-777-3534
Cosmetologist Instructor #03	307-777-3534
Dental Hygienist #04	307-777-6529
Dentist #04	307-777-6529
Educational Diagnostician #35	307-777-6261
Electrician #26	307-777-7991
Embalmer #05	307-777-7788
Emergency Medical Technician #40	307-777-7955
Engineer #27	307-777-6155
Esthetician #03	307-777-3534
Funeral Director #05	307-777-7788
Geologist #18	307-766-2490
Hearing Aid Specialist #07	307-777-7788
Insurance Agent #08	307-777-7344
Insurance Claims Adjuster #08	307-777-7344
Insurance Consultant #08	307-777-7344
Insurance Service Representatives #08	307-777-7344
Ionizing Radiation Agent #17	307-777-3507
Jockey/Jockey Apprentice #38	307-777-5887
Landscape Architect #30	307-777-7788
Law Enforcement Officer #39	307-777-7718
Lobbyist #36	307-777-7186
Manicurist/Nail Technician #03	307-777-3534
Marriage & Family Therapist #30	307-777-7788
Medical Doctor #10	307-778-7053
Mine Foreman #33	307-362-5222
Mine Inspector/Examiner #33	307-362-5222
Motor Club Agents #08	307-777-7344
Mutuel Employee/Official #38	307-777-5887
Notary Public #36	307-777-5407
Nurse #37	877-626-2681
Nurse-LPN #37	877-626-2681
Nursing Assistant #37	877-626-2681
Nursing Home Administrator #12	307-777-6313
Occupational Therapist #12	307-777-6313
Occupational Therapist Assistant #12	307-777-6313
Optometrist #06	307-777-3507
Outfitter & Guide #13	307-777-5323
Permittee Employee/Official #38	307-777-5887
Pesticide Applicator, Commercial #01	307-777-6569
Pharmacist #14	307-234-0294
Pharmacy Technician #14	307-234-0294
Physical Therapist #15	307-777-3507
Physician Assistant #10	307-778-7053
Podiatrist #19	307-777-3507
Preneed Agents #08	307-777-7344
Professional Counselor #30	307-777-7788
Property Tax Appraiser #25	307-777-5239
Psychiatrist #10	307-778-7053
Psychologist #16	307-777-6529
Public Accountant-CPA #29	307-777-7551
Public Accountant-CPA Firm #29	307-777-7551
Racing #38	307-777-5887
Radiologic Technologist/Technician #17	307-777-3507
Radiopharmaceutical Agent #17	307-778-2068
Real Estate Agent #21	307-777-7142
Real Estate Appraiser #21	307-777-7142
Resident Insurance Broker #08	307-777-7344
Resident Surplus Lines Broker #08	307-777-7344
Risk Retention (Insurance) #08	307-777-7344
Savings & Loan Association #23	307-777-6605
School Counselor #35	307-777-6261
School Librarian #35	307-777-6261
School Principal #35	307-777-6261
School Superintendent #35	307-777-6261
Securities Agent #34	307-777-7370
Securities Broker/Dealer #34	307-777-7370
Social Worker #30	307-777-7788
Solicitor (Insurance) #08	307-777-7344
Speech Pathologist/Audiologist #28	307-777-7788
Surveyor #27	307-777-6155
Teacher #35	307-777-6261
Track Security Employee #38	307-777-5887
Travel & Baggage Agents #08	307-777-7344
Truck Driver #41	307-777-4800
Veterinarian #20	307-777-3507
Water/Waste Water Treatment Plant Operator #42	307-777-7781

Licensing Agency Information

01 Board of Agriculture, 2219 Carey Ave, Cheyenne, WY 82002-0100; 307-777-6569, Fax: 307-777-6593.

02 Board of Barber Examiners, 441 Sunlight Dr, Powell, WY 82435; 307-754-5237.

http://soswy.state.wy.us/director/ag-bd/barber.htm

03 Board of Cosmetology, 2515 Warren Ave, #302, Cheyenne, WY 82002; 307-777-3534, Fax: 307-777-3681.

soswy.state.wy/director/boards.htm

04 Board of Dental Examiners, PO Box 272 (2020 Carey Ave #201), Cheyenne, WY 82002; 307-777-6529, Fax: 307-777-3508.

soswy.state.wy.us/director/ag-bd/dental.htm

05 Board of Embalming, 2020 Carey Ave, #201, Cheyenne, WY 82002; 307-777-7788, Fax: 307-777-3508.

soswy.state.wy.us/director/boards.htm

06 Board of Examiners in Optometry, 2020 Carey Ave, #201, Cheyenne, WY 82002; 307-777-3507, Fax: 307-777-3508.

http://soswy.state.wy.us/director/boards.htm

Direct URL to search licenses: www.arbo.org/nodb2000/licsearch.asp You can search online using national database by name, city or state.

07 Board of Hearing Aid Specialists, 2020 Carey Ave, #201, Cheyenne, WY 82002; 307-777-7788, Fax: 307-777-3508.

soswy.state.wy/director/boards.htm

08 Board of Insurance Agents Examiners, 122 W 25th St, Cheyenne, WY 82002-0040; 307-777-7344, Fax: 307-777-5895.
www.state.wy.us/~insurance.

Direct URL to search licenses: www.state.wy.us/~insurance

09 Board of Law Examiners, PO Box 109 (PO Box 109), Cheyenne, WY 82003; 307-632-9061, Fax: 307-630-3737.
www.wyomingbarg.org

Direct URL to search licenses: www.wyomingbar.org/html/default_search.asp You can search online using name, city, and district.

10 Board of Medicine, 211 W 19th St, 2nd Fl, Cheyenne, WY 82002; 307-778-7053, Fax: 307-778-2069.

http://sosw.state.wy/director/boards.htm

12 Board of Occupational Therapy, 2020 Carey Ave, #201, Cheyenne, WY 82002; 307-777-6313, Fax: 307-777-3508.

http://soswy.state.wy.us/director/boards.htm

13 Board of Outfitters & Professional Guides, 1750 Wland Rd, Cheyenne, WY 82002; 307-777-5323, Fax: 307-777-6715.

http://outfitte.state.wy.us/index.html

14 Board of Pharmacy, 1720 S Poplar St, #4, Casper, WY 82601; 307-234-0294, Fax: 307-234-7226.

http://pharmacyboard.state.wy.us

15 Board of Physical Therapy, 2020 Carey Ave, #201, Cheyenne, WY 82002; 307-777-3507, Fax: 307-777-3508.

http://soswy.state.wy.us/director/boards.htm

16 Board of Psychology, 2020 Carey Ave, #201, Cheyenne, WY 82002; 307-777-6529, Fax: 307-777-3508.

http://soswy.state.wy.us/director/boards.htm

17 Board of Radiologic Technologists, 2020 Carey Ave, #201, Cheyenne, WY 82002; 307-777-3507, Fax: 307-777-3508.

http://soswy.state.wy.us/director/boards.htm

18 Board of Registration for Professional Geologists, PO Box 3008 (PO Box 3008), Laramie, WY 82071-3008; 307-766-2490, Fax: 307-766-2713.

http://soswy.state.wy.us/director/boards.htm

19 Board of Registration in Podiatry, 2020 Carey Ave, #201, Cheyenne, WY 82002; 307-777-3507, Fax: 307-777-3508.

http://soswy.state.wy.us/director/boards.htm

20 Board of Veterinary Medicine, 2020 Carey Ave, #201, Cheyenne, WY 82002; 307-777-3507, Fax: 307-777-3508.

http://soswy.state.wy.us/director/boards.htm

21 Real Estate Appraiser Board, 2020 Carey Ave, #100, Cheyenne, WY 82002; 307-777-7142, Fax: 307-777-3796.

http://soswy.state.wy.us/director/boards.htm

22 Child Care Certification Board, 2300 Capitol Ave, Hathaway Bldg., 3rd Fl, Cheyenne, WY 82002-0490; 307-777-6595, Fax: 307-777-3659.

http://soswy.state.wy.us/director/boards.htm

23 Department of Audit, Division of Banking, 122 W 25th St, Herschler Bldg, 3rd Fl, Cheyenne, WY 82002; 307-777-6605, Fax: 307-777-3555. http://audit.state.wy.us/banking/default.htm

Direct URL to search licenses: http://audit.state.wy.us/banking/Links.htm

24 Department of Audit, Collecting Agency Board, Herschler Bldg, 3rd Fl, Cheyenne, WY 82002; 307-777-3497, Fax: 307-777-3555. http://audit.state.wy.us/banking/CAB.htm

Direct URL to search licenses: http://audit.state.wy.us/banking/CAB.htm You can search online using alphabetical list

25 Department of Revenue, 122 W 25th St, Herschler Bldg, 2nd Fl W, Cheyenne, WY 82002-0110; 307-777-5239.

http://soswy.state.wy.us/director/boards.htm

26 Electrical Board, Herschler Bldg, 1st Fl W, Cheyenne, WY 82002; 307-777-7288, Fax: 307-777-7119.

www.state.wy.us/~fire/electrical.htm

27 Engineers & Professional Land Surveyors, 2424 Pioneer Ave, #400, Cheyenne, WY 82001; 307-777-6155, Fax: 307-777-3403. www.wrds.uwyo.edu/wrds/borpe/borpe.html

Direct URL to search licenses: www.wrds.uwyo.edu/wrds/borpe/roster/roster.html You can search online using name, registration number, branch, city, state, address or corporation

28 Examiners for Speech Pathology & Audiology, 2020 Carey Ave, #201, Cheyenne, WY 82002; 307-777-7788, Fax: 307-777-3508.

http://soswy.state.wy.us/director/boards.htm

29 Board of CPAs, Licensing Boards, 2020 Carey Ave, #100, Cheyenne, WY 82002; 307-777-7551, Fax: 307-777-3796. http://cpaboard.state.wy.us

Direct URL to search licenses: http://cpaboard.state.wy.us/search.cfm You can search online using name, city or state

30 Licensing Boards, 2020 Carey Ave, #201, Cheyenne, WY 82002; 307-777-7788, Fax: 307-777-3508.

http://soswy.state.wy.us/director/boards.htm

32 Licensing Boards - Chiropractic Examiners, 2020 Carey Ave, #201, Cheyenne, WY 82002; 307-777-6529, Fax: 307-777-3508.

http://soswy.state.wy.us/director/boards.htm

33 Mining Council, PO Box 1094 (PO Box 1094), Rock Springs, WY 82901; 307-362-5222, Fax: 307-362-5233.

34 Office of Secretary of State, The Capitol 200 W 24th St, Cheyenne, WY 82002-0020; 307-777-7370, Fax: 307-777-5339.

http://soswy.state.wy.us

35 Professional Teaching Standards Board, 2300 Capitol Ave, Hathaway Bldg, Cheyenne, WY 82002; 307-777-6261, Fax: 307-777-6234.

36 Secretary of State, PO Box (PO Box), Cheyenne, WY 82002-0020; 307-777-7378, Fax: 307-777-5466.

http://soswy.state.wy.us

37 Board of Nursing, 2020 Carey Ave, #110, Cheyenne, WY 82002; 307-777-7601, Fax: 307-777-3519.

http://nursing.state.wy.us

Direct URL to search licenses: http://nursing.state.wy.us/voice/voice.htm You can search online using SSN or license number

38 Pari-Mutuel Commission, 2515 Warren Ave, #301, Cheyenne, WY 82002; 307-777-5887, Fax: 307-777-5700.

39 P.O.S.T. Commission, 1710 Pacific Ave, Cheyenne, WY 82002; 307-777-7718.

40 Office of Emergency Medical Svcs, 2300 Capital Ave, Hathaway Bldg, Cheyenne, WY 82002; 307-777-7955.

41 Driver Svcs, PO Box 1708, 5300 Bishop Blvd, Cheyenne, WY 82003-1708; 307-777-4800.

42 Department of Environmental Quality, Water Wuality Division, 122 W 25th St, Herschler Bldg, Cheyenne, WY 82002; 307-777-7781.

The following list indicates the district and division name for each county in the state. If the district or division name of the bankruptcy court is different from the civil/criminal court, it appears in parentheses.

County/Court Cross Reference

Albany	Cheyenne	Natrona	Cheyenne
Big Horn	Cheyenne	Niobrara	Cheyenne
Campbell	Cheyenne	Park	Cheyenne
Carbon	Cheyenne	Platte	Cheyenne
Converse	Cheyenne	Sheridan	Cheyenne
Crook	Cheyenne	Sublette	Cheyenne
Fremont	Cheyenne	Sweetwater	Cheyenne
Goshen	Cheyenne	Teton	Cheyenne
Hot Springs	Cheyenne	Uinta	Cheyenne
Johnson	Cheyenne	Washakie	Cheyenne
Laramie	Cheyenne	Weston	Cheyenne
Lincoln	Cheyenne		

US District Court

District of Wyoming

Cheyenne Division PO Box 727, Cheyenne, WY 82003 (Courier Address: Room 2131, 2120 Capitol Ave, Cheyenne, WY 82001), 307-772-2145.

www.ck10.uscourts.gov/wyoming/district

Counties: All counties in Wyoming. Some criminal records are held in Casper.

Indexing & Storage: Cases are indexed by defendant and plaintiff as well as by case number. New cases are available in the index 1-2 days after filing date. A computer index is maintained. Records older than 1992 are on microfiche also. Open records are located at this court.

Fee & Payment: The fee is $15.00 per item (one party name or case number). Payment may be made by money order, cashier check, personal check. Prepayment is required. Payee: Clerk, US District Court. Certification fee: $5.00 per document. Copy fee: $.50 per page.

Phone Search: Searching is not available by phone.

Mail Search: A stamped self addressed envelope is not required.

In Person Search: In person searching is available.

PACER: Sign-up number is 800-676-6856. Access fee is $.60 per minute. Toll-free access: 888-417-3560. Local access: 307-772-2808. Case records are available back to 1988. Records are purged once per year. New civil records are available online after 1-2 days. New criminal records are available online after 1 day. PACER is available online at http://pacer.wyd.uscourts.gov.

US Bankruptcy Court

District of Wyoming

Cheyenne Division PO Box 1107, Cheyenne, WY 82003 (Courier Address: 6th Floor, 2120 Capitol Ave, Cheyenne, WY 82001), 307-772-2191.

www.wyb.uscourts.gov

Counties: All counties in Wyoming.

Indexing & Storage: Cases are indexed by debtor as well as by case number. New cases are available in the index 24 hours after filing date. Both computer and card indexes are maintained. Open records are located at this court.

Fee & Payment: The fee is $15.00 per item (one party name or case number). Payment may be made by money order, cashier check, personal check. Prepayment is required. Payee: Clerk, US Bankruptcy Court. Certification fee: $5.00 per document. Copy fee: $.50 per page.

Phone Search: An automated voice case information service (VCIS) is available. Call VCIS at 888-804-5537 or 307-772-2191.

Mail Search: Always enclose a stamped self addressed envelope.

In Person Search: In person searching is available.

PACER: Sign-up number is 800-676-6856. Access fee is $.60 per minute. Toll-free access: 888-804-5536. Local access: 307-772-2036. Case records are available back one year. Records are purged annually. New civil records are available online after 1 day.

Opinions Online: Court opinions are available online at www.wyb.uscourts.gov/opinion_search.htm

Other Online Access: You can search records on the Internet using RACER. Currently the system is free and requires free registration. Simply visit www.wyb.uscourts.gov/wconnect/wc.dll?usbc_racer~main.

Court	Jurisdiction	No. of Courts	How Organized
District Courts*	General	23	9 Districts
Circuit Courts*	Limited	19	16 Counties
Justice of the Peace Courts*	Municipal	7	7 Counties
Municipal Courts	Municipal	80	

* Profiled in this Sourcebook.

Court	CIVIL								
	Tort	Contract	Real Estate	Min. Claim	Max. Claim	Small Claims	Estate	Eviction	Domestic Relations
District Courts*	X	X	X	$3000/ $7000	No Max		X		X
Circuit Courts*	X	X	X	$0	$7000	$3000		X	X
Justice of the Peace Courts*	X	X	X	$0	$3000	$3000			
Municipal Courts									

Court	CRIMINAL				
	Felony	Misdemeanor	DWI/DUI	Preliminary Hearing	Juvenile
District Courts*	X				X
Circuit Courts*		X	X	X	
Justice of the Peace Courts*		X	X	X	
Municipal Courts		X	X		

ADMINISTRATION   Court Administrator, 2301 Capitol Av, Supreme Court Bldg, Cheyenne, WY, 82002; 307-777-7590, Fax: 307-777-3447. www.courts.state.wy.us

COURT STRUCTURE   Some counties have County Courts and others have Justice Courts, thus each county has a District Court and either a County or Justice Court. County Courts handle civil claims up to $7,000 while Justice Courts handle civil claims up to $3,000. The District Courts take cases over the applicable limit in each county, not just over $7,000. Three counties have two county courts each: Fremont, Park, and Sweetwater. Cases may be filed in either of the two courts in those counties, and records requests are referred between the two courts.

The Park and Sublette County Justice Courts were eliminated on January 2, 1995 and were replaced by County Courts, where the prior records are now located.

Probate is handled by the District Court.

ONLINE ACCESS   Wyoming's statewide case management system is for internal use only. Planning is underway for a new case management system that will ultimately allow public access.

📖📖📖📖📖📖

Albany County

2nd Judicial District Court County Courthouse, 525 Grand, Rm 305, Laramie, WY 82070; 307-721-2508. Hours: 9AM-5PM (MST). *Felony, Civil Actions Over $7,000, Probate.*

Civil Records: Access: Phone, mail, in person. Only the court conducts in person searches; visitors may not. No search fee. Required to search: name; also helpful-years to search. Civil cases indexed by defendant, plaintiff. Civil records on computer from 1988, prior records on card index. Limit calls to three names. **Criminal Records:** Access: Mail, in person. Only the court conducts in person searches; visitors may not. Search fee: $5.00 per name. Search results cann be phoned back to a toll-free number only. Required to search: name; also helpful-years to search, DOB, SSN. Criminal records on computer from 1988, prior records on card index. **General Information:** No sex offenses records released, signed release required for child support cases. SASE required. Turnaround time same day. Copy fee: $1.00 for first page, $.50 each addl. Certification fee: No certification fee. Fee payee: Clerk of District Court. Personal checks accepted. Prepayment is required.

Albany Circuit Court County Courthouse, 525 Grand, Rm 105, Laramie, WY 82070; 307-742-5747; Fax: 307-742-5610. Hours: 8AM-5PM (MST). *Misdemeanor, Civil Actions Under $7,000, Eviction, Small Claims.*

Civil Records: Access: Mail, in person. Both court and visitors may perform in person searches. Search fee: $5.00 per name. Required to search: name, years to search. Civil cases indexed by defendant, plaintiff. Civil records on computer from 1993, prior on docket books. **Criminal Records:** Access: Mail, in person. Both court and visitors may perform in person searches. Search fee: $5.00 per name. Required to search: name, years to search, DOB, SSN; also helpful-address. Criminal records on computer from 1989, prior on docket books. **General Information:** No SSN or family violence records released. SASE required. Turnaround time same day. No copy fee. Certification fee: No certification fee. Fee payee:

Albany Circuit Court. Personal checks accepted. In-state checks only. Prepayment is required.

Big Horn County

5th Judicial District Court PO Box 670, Basin, WY 82410; 307-568-2381; Fax: 307-568-2791. Hours: 8AM-Noon, 1-5PM (MST). *Felony, Civil Actions Over $3,000, Probate.*

Civil Records: Access: Fax, mail, in person. Both court and visitors may perform in person searches. Search fee: $5.00 per name. Required to search: name, years to search. Civil cases indexed by defendant, plaintiff. ecords on computer 1989, on microfiche 1982, 1970 to present on cards. **Criminal Records:** Access: Fax, mail, in person. Both court and visitors may perform in person searches. Search fee: $5.00 per name. Required to search: name, years to search. ecords on computer 1989, on microfiche 1982, 1970 to present on cards. **General Information:** Some confidential records not released. SASE required. Turnaround time 24 hours. Copy fee: $1.00 for first page, $.50 each addl. Certification fee: $.50. Fee payee: Clerk of Court. Business checks accepted. Prepayment is required.

Big Horn Circuit Court PO Box 749, Basin, WY 82410; 307-568-2367; Fax: 307-568-2554. Hours: 8AM-5PM (MST). *Misdemeanor, Civil Actions Under $7,000, Small Claims.*

Civil Records: Access: Fax, mail, in person. Both court and visitors may perform in person searches. Search fee: $5.00 per name. Required to search: name, years to search; also helpful-address. Civil cases indexed by defendant. Civil records on microfiche 1985. **Criminal Records:** Access: Fax, mail, in person. Both court and visitors may perform in person searches. Search fee: $5.00 per name. Required to search: name, DOB; also helpful-SSN. Criminal records on computer since 1990, microfiche 1985. **General Information:** No sex or juvenile offenses released. Turnaround time 1 day. Copy fee: $.50 per page. Certification fee: No certification fee. Fee payee: Big Horn Circuit Justice Court. Personal checks accepted. Prepayment is required.

Campbell County

6th Judicial District Court PO Box 817, Gillette, WY 82717; 307-682-3424; Fax: 307-687-6209. Hours: 8AM-5PM (MST). *Felony, Civil Actions Over $7,000, Probate.*

Civil Records: Access: Phone, fax, mail, in person. Both court and visitors may perform in person searches. Search fee: $5.00 per name. Required to search: name, years to search. Civil cases indexed by defendant. Civil records archived from 1913. **Criminal Records:** Access: Phone, fax, mail, in person. Both court and visitors may perform in person searches. Search fee: $5.00 per name. Required to search: name, years to search. Criminal records archived from 1913. **General Information:** Names of victims in sex cases, confidential records not released. SASE not required. Turnaround time 1-2 days. Copy fee: $1.00 for first page, $.50 each addl. Certification fee: No certification fee. Fee payee: Clerk of District Court. Personal checks accepted. Out of state checks not accepted. Prepayment is required. Public access terminal is available. Fax notes: $1.00 per page.

Campbell Circuit Court 500 S Gillette Ave #301, Gillette, WY 82716; 307-682-2190; Fax: 307-687-6214. Hours: 8AM-5PM (MST). *Misdemeanor, Civil Actions Under $7,000, Eviction, Small Claims.*

Civil Records: Access: Mail, in person. Only the court conducts in person searches; visitors may not. Search fee: $5.00 per name. Required to search: name, years to search; also helpful-address. Civil cases indexed by defendant, plaintiff. Civil records on computer since 1983, archives from 1979. **Criminal Records:** Access: Mail, in person. Both court and visitors may perform in person searches. Search fee: $5.00 per name. Required to search: name, years to search, DOB; also helpful-address. Criminal records on computer since 1983, archives from 1979. **General Information:** No sex related cases released. SASE requested. Turnaround time 1-2 days. Copy fee: $1.00 for first page, $.50 each addl. Certification fee: No certification fee. Fee payee: Campbell County Court. Personal checks accepted. Prepayment is required.

Carbon County

2nd Judicial District Court PO Box 67, Rawlins, WY 82301; 307-328-2628; Fax: 307-328-2629. Hours: 8AM-5PM (MST). *Felony, Civil Actions Over $3,000, Probate.*

Civil Records: Access: Phone, fax, mail, in person. Both court and visitors may perform in person searches. No search fee. Required to search: name, years to search; also helpful-address. Civil cases indexed by defendant, plaintiff. Civil records on file from late 1800s, index cards and docket books. **Criminal Records:** Access: Phone, fax, mail, in person. Both court and visitors may perform in person searches. No search fee. Required to search: name, years to search; also helpful-address, DOB, SSN. Criminal records on index cards and docket books. **General Information:** No juvenile or adoption records released. SASE required. Turnaround time 4-5 days. Copy fee: $1.00 for first page, $.50 each addl. Certification fee: No certification fee. Fee payee: Clerk 2nd Judicial District Court, Clerk of Court. Personal checks accepted. Prepayment is required. Fax notes: No fee to fax results. Fax available for 800 numbers only.

Carbon Circuit Court Attn: Chief Clerk, Courthouse, 415 W Pine St, Rawlins, WY 82301; 307-324-6655; Fax: 307-324-9465. Hours: 8AM-5PM (MST). *Misdemeanor, Civil Actions Under $3,000, Eviction, Small Claims.*

Civil Records: Access: Mail, in person. Only the court conducts in person searches; visitors may not. Search fee: $5.00 per name. Required to search: name, years to search; also helpful-address. Civil cases indexed by defendant, plaintiff. Civil records on computer since 3/95. **Criminal Records:** Access: Mail, in person. Both court and visitors may perform in person searches. Search fee: $5.00 per name. Required to search: name, DOB. Criminal records on comoputer since 08/87. **General Information:** Sex related cases not released. SASE required. Turnaround time 1 week. Copy fee: Copy fee for excessive amount of pages is $.25 per page. Certification fee: No certification fee. Fee payee: Carbon County Court. Personal checks accepted. Prepayment is required.

Converse County

8th Judicial District Court Box 189, Douglas, WY 82633; 307-358-3165; Fax: 307-358-6703. Hours: 9AM-5PM (MST). *Felony, Civil Actions Over $7,000, Probate.*

Civil Records: Access: Phone, fax, mail, in person. Both court and visitors may perform in person searches. Search fee: $5.00 per name. Required to search: name, years to search; also helpful-address. Civil cases indexed by defendant, plaintiff. Civil records on card file from 1800.
Criminal Records: Access: Phone, fax, mail, in person. Both court and visitors may perform in person searches. Search fee: $5.00. Required to search: name, years to search; also helpful-address, DOB, SSN. Criminal records on card file from 1800. **General Information:** No juvenile, adoptions or mental cases released. Turnaround time usually same day. Copy fee: $.25 per page. Certification fee: $1.00 plus $.50 each add'l page. Fee payee: Clerk of District Court. Only cashiers checks and money orders accepted. Prepayment is required. Fax notes: $2.00 per page.

Converse Circuit Court 107 N 5th Street #231, PO Box 45, Douglas, WY 82633; 307-358-2196; Fax: 307-358-2501. Hours: 8AM-5PM (MST). *Misdemeanor, Civil Actions Under $7,000, Eviction, Small Claims.*

Civil Records: Access: Mail, in person. Both court and visitors may perform in person searches. Search fee: $5.00 per name. Required to search: name, years to search. Civil cases indexed by defendant, plaintiff. Civil records on computer from 1994, card file prior. **Criminal Records:** Access: Mail, in person. Both court and visitors may perform in person searches. Search fee: $5.00 per name. Required to search: name, years to search; also helpful-address, DOB, SSN. Criminal records on computer from 1990, card file prior. **General Information:** No sealed records released. Turnaround time 1-2 days. Copy fee: $1.00 for first page, $.50 each addl. Certification fee: $2.00. Fee payee: Converse County Court. Personal checks accepted. Prepayment is required. Public access terminal is available.

Crook County

6th Judicial District Court Box 904, Sundance, WY 82729; 307-283-2523; Fax: 307-283-2996. Hours: 8AM-5PM (MST). *Felony, Civil Actions Over $3,000, Probate.*

Civil Records: Access: Mail, in person. Both court and visitors may perform in person searches. Search fee: $5.00 per name. Required to search: name, years to search; also helpful-address. Civil cases indexed by defendant, plaintiff. Civil records on card file from late 1800s. **Criminal Records:** Access: Mail, in person. Both court and visitors may perform in person searches. Search fee: $5.00 per name. Required to search: name, years to search; also helpful-address, DOB, SSN. Criminal records on card file from late 1800s. **General Information:** No sealed records released. SASE required. Turnaround time 2 days. Copy fee: $.25 per page. Certification fee: $1.00. Fee payee: Clerk of District Court. Business checks accepted. Prepayment is required. Fax notes: $1.00 for 1st page, $.50 each add'l.

Justice Court PO Box 117, Sundance, WY 82729; 307-283-2929; Fax: 307-283-1091. Hours: 8AM-5PM (MST). *Misdemeanor, Civil Actions Under $3,000, Small Claims.*

Civil Records: Access: Mail, in person. Only the court conducts in person searches; visitors may not. Search fee: $5.00 per name. Required to search: name, years to search; also helpful-address. Civil cases indexed by defendant, plaintiff. Civil records on cards, archives back to 1977. **Criminal Records:** Access: Mail, in person. Only the court conducts in person searches; visitors may not. Search fee: $5.00 per name. Required to search: name, years to search; also helpful-address, DOB, SSN. Criminal records on computer since 1993. **General Information:** No sex related cases released. SASE required. Turnaround time 2 days.

Copy fee: $3.00 for first page, $1.00 each addl. No certification fee. Fee payee: Crook County Justice Court. Personal checks accepted. Prepayment is required.

Fremont County

9th Judicial District Court PO Box 370, Lander, WY 82520; 307-332-1134; Fax: 307-332-1143. Hours: 8AM-Noon, 1-5PM (MST). *Felony, Civil Actions Over $7,000, Probate.*

Civil Records: Access: Phone, fax, mail, in person. Both court and visitors may perform in person searches. Search fee: $5.00 per name. Required to search: name, years to search; also helpful-address. Civil cases indexed by defendant, plaintiff. Civil records on computer since 1992, in books since 1991, on microfiche since 1939 and on card file from 1898. **Criminal Records:** Access: Phone, fax, mail, in person. Both court and visitors may perform in person searches. Search fee: $5.00 per name. Required to search: name, years to search; also helpful-address, DOB, SSN. Criminal records on computer since 1992, in books since 1991, on microfiche since 1939 and on card file from 1898. **General Information:** No juvenile, involuntary hospitalization or adoption records released. SASE required. Turnaround time same day. Copy fee: $.50 per page. Certification fee: No certification fee. Fee payee: Clerk of District Court. Personal checks accepted. Public access terminal is available. Fax notes: No fee to fax results.

Dubois Circuit Court Box 952, Dubois, WY 82513; 307-455-2920; Fax: 307-455-2132. Hours: 8AM-Noon (MST). *Misdemeanor, Civil Actions Under $7,000, Eviction, Small Claims.*

Note: This is a satellite of the Lander Court

Civil Records: Access: Mail, in person. Both court and visitors may perform in person searches. Search fee: $5.00 per name. Required to search: name, years to search. Civil cases indexed by defendant, plaintiff. Civil records on index. **Criminal Records:** Access: Mail, in person. Both court and visitors may perform in person searches. Search fee: $5.00 per name. Required to search: name, years to search; also helpful-DOB. Criminal records on computer since 12/96; prior records on indexes. **General Information:** No juvenile, sexual data released. SASE required. Turnaround time 2 days. Copy fee: $.10 per page. Certification fee: No certification fee. Fee payee: Fremont County Court. Personal checks accepted. Prepayment is required.

Fremont Circuit Court 450 N. 2nd, Rm 230, Lander, WY 82520; 307-332-3239; Fax: 307-332-1152. Hours: 8AM-5PM (MST). *Misdemeanor, Civil Actions Under $7,000, Eviction, Small Claims.*

Civil Records: Access: Phone, fax, mail, in person. Both court and visitors may perform in person searches. Search fee: $5.00 per name. Required to search: name, years to search; also helpful-address. Civil cases indexed by defendant, plaintiff. Civil records on computer from 1988, archive back to 1979. **Criminal Records:** Access: Phone, fax, mail, in person. Both court and visitors may perform in person searches. Search fee: $5.00 per name. Required to search: name, years to search; also helpful-address, DOB, SSN. Criminal records on computer from 1988, archive back to 1979. **General Information:** No juvenile or sexual data released. SASE required. Turnaround time 2 days. No copy fee. Certification fee: No certification fee. Fee payee: Fremont County Court. Personal checks accepted. In-state checks

only. Prepayment is required. Fax notes: No fee to fax results.

Riverton Circuit Court 818 S Federal Blvd, Riverton, WY 82501; 307-856-7259; Fax: 307-857-3635. Hours: 8AM-5PM (MST). *Misdemeanor, Civil Actions Under $7,000, Eviction, Small Claims.*

Civil Records: Access: Fax, mail, in person. Both court and visitors may perform in person searches. Search fee: $5.00 per name. Required to search: name, years to search. Civil cases indexed by defendant, plaintiff. Civil records are computerized since 1997. **Criminal Records:** Access: Fax, mail, in person. Only the court conducts in person searches; visitors may not. Search fee: $5.00 per name. Required to search: name, years to search, DOB; also helpful-SSN. Criminal records on computer since 1989. **General Information:** No sex released cases released. SASE required. Turnaround time 2 days. No copy fee. Certification fee: No certification fee. Fee payee: Fremont County Court. Personal checks accepted. In state checks only. Prepayment is required. Fax notes: No fee to fax results.

Goshen County

8th Judicial District Court Clerk of District Court, PO Box 818, Torrington, WY 82240; 307-532-2155; Fax: 307-532-8608. Hours: 7:30AM-4PM (MST). *Felony, Civil Actions Over $7,000, Probate.*

Civil Records: Access: Mail, in person. Both court and visitors may perform in person searches. Search fee: $5.00 per name. Required to search: name, years to search; also helpful-address. Civil cases indexed by defendant, plaintiff. Civil records on index file only since 1913. **Criminal Records:** Access: Mail, in person. Both court and visitors may perform in person searches. Search fee: $5.00 per name. Required to search: name, years to search; also helpful-address, DOB, SSN. Criminal records on index file only since 1913. **General Information:** No juvenile records released. SASE required. Turnaround time 3-4 days. Copy fee: $1.00 for first page, $.50 each addl. Certification fee: $.50. Fee payee: Clerk of District Court. Personal checks accepted. In-state checks only. Prepayment is required.

Goshen Circuit Court Drawer BB, Torrington, WY 82240; 307-532-2938; Civil phone:307-532-2938 X251; Criminal phone:307-532-2938 X251; Fax: 307-532-5101. Hours: 7AM-4PM (MST). *Misdemeanor, Civil Actions Under $7,000, Eviction, Small Claims.*

Civil Records: Access: Mail, in person. Both court and visitors may perform in person searches. Search fee: $5.00 per name. Required to search: name, years to search; also helpful-address. Civil cases indexed by defendant. Civil records on computer from 1989, prior archived. **Criminal Records:** Access: Mail, in person. Both court and visitors may perform in person searches. Search fee: $5.00 per name. Required to search: name, years to search; also helpful-address, DOB, SSN. Criminal records on computer from 1989, prior archived. **General Information:** No juvenile records released. SASE required. Turnaround time 3-4 days. Copy fee: $1.00 per page. Certification fee: $5.00. Fee payee: Goshen County Court. Personal checks accepted. Prepayment is required.

Hot Springs County

5th Judicial Circuit Court 415 Arapahoe St, Thermopolis, WY 82443; 307-864-3323; Fax:

307-864-3210. Hours: 8AM-5PM *Felony, Civil Actions Over $3,000, Probate.*

Civil Records: Access: Mail, in person. Both court and visitors may perform in person searches. Search fee: $5.00 per name. Required to search: name, years to search; also helpful-address. Civil cases indexed by defendant, plaintiff. Civil records on card index back to 1900s. **Criminal Records:** Access: Mail, in person. Both court and visitors may perform in person searches. Search fee: $5.00 per name. Required to search: name, years to search, DOB, SSN; also helpful-address. Criminal records on card index back to 1900s. **General Information:** No juvenile, adoption or sexual data released. SASE required. Turnaround time 1 day. Copy fee: $.25 per page. Certification fee: $.50. Fee payee: Clerk of District Court. Personal checks accepted. Prepayment is required.

Hot Springs Circuit Court 417 Arapahoe St, Thermopolis, WY 82443; 307-864-5161; Fax: 307-864-5116. Hours: 8AM-5PM (MST). *Misdemeanor, Civil Actions Under $3,000, Small Claims.*

Civil Records: Access: Mail, in person. Both court and visitors may perform in person searches. No search fee. Required to search: name, years to search. Civil cases indexed by defendant, plaintiff. Civil records on computer from 1990, prior in card file. **Criminal Records:** Access: Mail, in person. Both court and visitors may perform in person searches. No search fee. Required to search: name, years to search. Criminal records on computer from 1990, prior in card file. **General Information:** No closed case records released. SASE required. Turnaround time 2-3 days. No copy fee. Certification fee: No certification fee. Fee payee: Justice Court. Business checks accepted. Prepayment is required.

Johnson County

4th Judicial District Court 76 N Main, Buffalo, WY 82834; 307-684-7271; Fax: 307-684-5146. Hours: 8AM-5PM (MST). *Felony, Civil Actions Over $3,000, Probate.*

Civil Records: Access: Phone, mail, in person. Both court and visitors may perform in person searches. Search fee: $5.00 per name. Required to search: name, years to search; also helpful-address. Civil cases indexed by defendant, plaintiff. Civil records on computer from 1989, card index since 1892. **Criminal Records:** Access: Phone, mail, in person. Both court and visitors may perform in person searches. Search fee: $5.00 per name. Required to search: name, years to search; also helpful-address, DOB, SSN. Criminal records on computer from 1989, card index since 1892. **General Information:** No adoption or juvenile records released. SASE required. Turnaround time 1 week. Copy fee: $.50 per page. Certification fee: $.50. Fee payee: Clerk of District Court. Personal checks accepted. In-state checks only. Prepayment is required.

Justice Court 76 N Main St, Buffalo, WY 82834-1847; 307-684-5720; Fax: 307-684-5585. Hours: 8AM-5PM (MST). *Misdemeanor, Civil Actions Under $3,000, Small Claims.*

Civil Records: Access: Mail, in person. Both court and visitors may perform in person searches. Search fee: $5.00 per name. Required to search: name, years to search; also helpful-address. Civil cases indexed by defendant, plaintiff. Civil records on computer since 1995; prior records on index cards. **Criminal Records:** Access: Mail, in person. Both court and visitors may perform in person searches. Search fee: $5.00 per name.

Required to search: name, years to search, DOB; also helpful-SSN. Criminal records on computer since 05/90, card index back 5 years. **General Information:** No sex cases released. SASE required. Turnaround time 1 week. Copy fee: $1.00 per page. Certification fee: No certification fee. Fee payee: Justice of the Peace. Personal checks accepted. Prepayment is required.

Laramie County

1st Judicial District Court 309 W 20th St, Suite 3205, PO Box 787, Cheyenne, WY 82001; 307-633-4270; Fax: 307-633-4277. Hours: 8AM-5PM (MST). *Felony, Civil Actions Over $7,000, Probate.*

http://webgate.co.laramie.wy.us/dc/dc.html

Civil Records: Access: Phone, fax, mail, in person. Both court and visitors may perform in person searches. Search fee: $5.00 per name. Required to search: name, years to search; also helpful-address. Civil cases indexed by defendant, plaintiff. Civil records on card index to 1890. **Criminal Records:** Access: Phone, fax, mail, in person. Both court and visitors may perform in person searches. Search fee: $5.00 per name. Required to search: name, years to search; also helpful-address, DOB, SSN. Criminal records on card index to 1890. **General Information:** No juvenile or paternity records released. SASE required. Turnaround time 2 days. Copy fee: $1.00 for first page, $.50 each addl. Certification fee: $.50. Fee payee: Laramie County Clerk of District Court. Business checks accepted. Prepayment is required. Public access terminal is available. Fax notes: No fee to fax results. Fax available for 800 numbers only.

Laramie Circuit Court 309 W 20th St Rm 2300, Cheyenne, WY 82001; 307-633-4298; Fax: 307-633-4392. Hours: 8AM-5PM (MST). *Misdemeanor, Civil Actions Under $7,000, Eviction, Small Claims.*

Civil Records: Access: Fax, mail, in person. Both court and visitors may perform in person searches. Search fee: $5.00 per name. Required to search: name, years to search; also helpful-address. Civil cases indexed by defendant, plaintiff. Civil records on computer from 1988, card index from late 1977. **Criminal Records:** Access: Fax, mail, in person. Both court and visitors may perform in person searches. Search fee: $5.00 per name. Required to search: name, years to search; also helpful-address, DOB, SSN. Criminal records on computer from 1988, card index from late 1977. **General Information:** SASE required. Turnaround time 48 hours. Copy fee: $1.00 per page. Certification fee: No certification fee. Fee payee: Laramie Circuit Court. Business checks accepted. In-state checks only. Prepayment is required. Public access terminal is available. Fax notes: $5.00 per document.

Lincoln County

3rd Judicial District Court PO Drawer 510, Kemmerer, WY 83101; 307-877-9056; Fax: 307-877-6263. Hours: 8AM-5PM (MST). *Felony, Civil Actions Over $7,000, Probate.*

Civil Records: Access: Phone, fax, mail, in person. Both court and visitors may perform in person searches. Search fee: $5.00 per name. Required to search: name; also helpful-years to search, address. Civil cases indexed by defendant. Civil records on card index from early 1916. **Criminal Records:** Access: Phone, fax, mail, in person. Both court and visitors may perform in person searches. Search fee: $5.00 per name.

Required to search: name; also helpful-years to search, address, DOB, SSN. Criminal records on card index from early 1916. **General Information:** No juvenile, sexual or PD records released. Turnaround time same day. Copy fee: $1.00 for first page, $.50 each addl. Certification fee: $2.50. Fee payee: 3rd Judicial District Court. Personal checks accepted. Fax notes: $5.00 per document.

Lincoln Circuit Court PO Box 949, Kemmerer, WY 83101; 307-877-4431; Fax: 307-877-4936. Hours: 8AM-5PM (MST). *Misdemeanor, Civil Actions Under $7,000, Eviction, Small Claims.*

Civil Records: Access: Fax, mail, in person. Both court and visitors may perform in person searches. Search fee: $5.00 per name. Required to search: name, years to search. Civil cases indexed by defendant, plaintiff. Civil records on computer from 1/90, on card index from 1984, prior data in archives. All requests must be in writing. **Criminal Records:** Access: Fax, mail, in person. Both court and visitors may perform in person searches. Search fee: $5.00 per name. Required to search: name, years to search, DOB; also helpful-SSN. Criminal records on computer from 10/90, card index from 1984, prior in archives. All requests must be in writing. **General Information:** No sexual or PD records released. SASE requested. Turnaround time same day. Copy fee: $.50 per page. Certification fee: No certification fee. Fee payee: Lincoln County Court. Business checks accepted. Out of state checks not accepted. Prepayment is required. Fax notes: $3.00 per document.

Natrona County

7th Judicial District Court Clerk of District Court, PO Box 2510, Casper, WY 82602; 307-235-9243; Fax: 307-235-9493. Hours: 8AM-5PM (MST). *Felony, Civil Actions Over $7,000, Probate.*

Civil Records: Access: Phone, fax, mail, in person. Both court and visitors may perform in person searches. No search fee. Required to search: name, years to search; also helpful-address. Civil cases indexed by defendant, plaintiff. Civil records on computer, microfiche from 1891. **Criminal Records:** Access: Phone, fax, mail, in person. Both court and visitors may perform in person searches. No search fee. Required to search: name, years to search; also helpful-address, DOB, SSN. Criminal records on computer, microfiche from 1891. **General Information:** No adoption, juvenile, paternity, mental health records released. SASE required. Turnaround time 5 days. Copy fee: $1.00 for first page, $.50 each addl. Certification fee: $.50. Fee payee: Clerk of District Court. Business checks accepted. Prepayment is required. Public access terminal is available. Fax notes: $.30 per page. Fax available to attorneys only.

Natrona Circuit Court PO Box 1339, Casper, WY 82602; 307-235-9266; Fax: 307-235-9331. Hours: 8AM-5PM *Misdemeanor, Civil Actions Under $7,000, Eviction, Small Claims.*

Note: All search requests must be in writing

Civil Records: Access: Phone, fax, mail, in person. Only the court conducts in person searches; visitors may not. Search fee: $5.00 per name. Required to search: name, years to search; also helpful-address. Civil cases indexed by defendant, plaintiff. Civil records on computer from 1994, on microfiche from 1891. **Criminal Records:** Access: Phone, fax, mail, in person.

Only the court conducts in person searches; visitors may not. Search fee: $5.00 per name. Required to search: name, years to search; also helpful-address, DOB, SSN. Criminal records on computer from 1989, microfiche from 1891. **General Information:** No sexual, abuse records released. SASE required. Turnaround time 2 days. Copy fee: $1.00 for first page, $.50 each addl. Certification fee: $1.00. Fee payee: Natrona Circuit Court. Personal checks accepted. Prepayment is required. Fax notes: No fee to fax results. Fax available for 800 numbers only.

Niobrara County

8th Judicial District Court Clerk of District Court, PO Box 1318, Lusk, WY 82225; 307-334-2736; Fax: 307-334-2703. Hours: 8AM-Noon, 1-4PM (MST). *Felony, Civil Actions Over $3,000, Probate.*

Civil Records: Access: In person only. Court does not conduct in person searches; visitors must perform searches for themselves. Search fee: No civil searches performed by court. Required to search: name, years to search; also helpful-address. Civil cases indexed by defendant, plaintiff. Civil records on card index from early 1900. **Criminal Records:** Access: Phone, fax, mail, in person. Both court and visitors may perform in person searches. No search fee. Required to search: name, years to search; also helpful-address, DOB, SSN. Criminal records on card index from early 1900. **General Information:** No juvenile or adoption related released, no PD released. SASE required. Turnaround time 2 days. Copy fee: $1.00 for first page, $.50 each addl. Certification fee: $.50. Fee payee: Niobrara Clerk of District Court. Personal checks accepted. Prepayment is required.

Justice Court PO Box 209, Lusk, WY 82225; 307-334-3845; Fax: 307-334-3846. Hours: 9AM-Noon, 1-5PM (MST). *Misdemeanor, Civil Actions Under $3,000, Small Claims.*

Civil Records: Access: Mail, in person. Both court and visitors may perform in person searches. Search fee: $5.00 per name. Required to search: name, years to search; also helpful-address. Civil cases indexed by plaintiff. Civil records on index cards. **Criminal Records:** Access: Fax, mail, in person. Both court and visitors may perform in person searches. Search fee: $5.00 per name. Required to search: name, years to search, DOB, SSN, signed release; also helpful-address. Criminal records on computer from 1988, prior archived. **General Information:** No juvenile data released. SASE required. Turnaround time 2 days. Copy fee: $.50 per page. Certification fee: $3.00. Fee payee: Niobrara Justice Court. Personal checks accepted. Prepayment is required. Fax notes: $.50 per page.

Park County

5th Judicial District Court Clerk of District Court, PO Box 1960, Cody, WY 82414; 307-527-8690; Fax: 307-527-8676. Hours: 8AM-5PM *Felony, Civil Actions Over $7,000, Probate.*

Civil Records: Access: Phone, fax, mail, in person. Both court and visitors may perform in person searches. Search fee: $5.00 per name. Required to search: name, years to search; also helpful-address. Civil cases indexed by defendant, plaintiff. Civil records on computer from 1989, card index back to 1911. **Criminal Records:** Access: Phone, fax, mail, in person. Both court and visitors may perform in person searches. Search fee: $5.00 per name. Required to search: name, years to search; also helpful-address, DOB, SSN. Criminal records on computer from 1989, card index back to 1911. **General Information:** No juvenile, adoptions or PD released. SASE preferred. Turnaround time same day. Copy fee: $1.00 for first page, $.50 each addl. Fee payee: Clerk of District Court. Personal checks accepted. Prepayment is required. Public access terminal is available. Fax notes: $1.00 per page.

Circuit Court-Cody 1002 Sheridan Ave., Cody, WY 82414; 307-527-8590. Hours: 8AM-5PM (MST). *Misdemeanor, Civil Actions Under $7,000, Eviction, Small Claims.*

Note: On January 2, 1995 this court changed status from a Justice Court to a County Court

Civil Records: Access: Mail, in person. Only the court conducts in person searches; visitors may not. Search fee: $5.00 per name. Required to search: name, years to search; also helpful-address. Civil cases indexed by defendant, plaintiff. Civil records on computer since 08/95. **Criminal Records:** Access: Mail, in person. Only the court conducts in person searches; visitors may not. Search fee: $5.00 per name. Required to search: name, years to search; also helpful-address, DOB, SSN. Criminal records on computer since 1990. **General Information:** No sexual or confidential data released. SASE required. Turnaround time 5 days. Copy fee: $.50 first 10 pages then $.10 thereafter. Certification fee: No certification fee. Fee payee: Park County Court. Business checks accepted. Out of state checks not accepted. Prepayment is required.

Circuit Court-Powell 109 W. 14th, Powell, WY 82435; 307-754-8900. Hours: 8AM-5PM (MST). *Misdemeanor, Civil Actions Under $7,000, Eviction, Small Claims.*

Civil Records: Access: Mail, in person. Only the court conducts in person searches; visitors may not. Search fee: $5.00 per name. Required to search: name, years to search. Civil cases indexed by defendant, plaintiff. Civil records on computer from 1991, rest archived since late 1800. **Criminal Records:** Access: Mail, in person. Only the court conducts in person searches; visitors may not. Search fee: $5.00 per name. Required to search: name, years to search, DOB. Criminal records on computer from 1991, rest archived since late 1800. **General Information:** No sexual, confidential records released. SSE required. Turnaround time 1 week. Copy fee: $.50 per page. Certification fee: No certification fee. Fee payee: Park County Court. Personal checks accepted. Prepayment is required.

Platte County

8th Judicial District Court PO Box 158, Wheatland, WY 82201; 307-322-3857; Fax: 307-322-5402. Hours: 8AM-5PM (MST). *Felony, Civil Actions Over $3,000, Probate.*

Civil Records: Access: Mail, in person. Both court and visitors may perform in person searches. Search fee: $5.00 per name. Required to search: name, years to search; also helpful-address. Civil cases indexed by defendant. Civil records on card file index last 15 yrs, then to archives. **Criminal Records:** Access: Mail, in person. Both court and visitors may perform in person searches. Search fee: $5.00 per name. Required to search: name, years to search; also helpful-address, DOB, SSN. Criminal records on card file index last 15 yrs, then to archives. **General Information:** No juvenile data released. SASE required. Turnaround time same day. Copy fee: $1.00 for first page, $.50 each addl. Certification fee: $.50. Fee payee: Clerk of the Court. Personal checks accepted. Prepayment is required.

Justice Court PO Box 306, Wheatland, WY 82201; 307-322-3441; Fax: 307-322-5402. Hours: 8AM-5PM (MST). *Misdemeanor, Civil Actions Under $3,000, Small Claims.*

Civil Records: Access: Mail, in person. Only the court conducts in person searches; visitors may not. Search fee: $5.00 per name. Required to search: name, years to search; also helpful-address. Civil cases indexed by defendant. Civil records on computer since 11/95; on card index since 1976. **Criminal Records:** Access: Mail, in person. Only the court conducts in person searches; visitors may not. Search fee: $5.00 per name. Required to search: name, years to search; also helpful-address, DOB, SSN. Criminal records on computer from 11/92, card index from 1976. **General Information:** No juvenile data released. SASE required. Turnaround time 2 days. Copy fee: $1.00 for first page, $.50 each addl. No certification fee. Fee payee: Platte County Justice Court. Business checks accepted. Prepayment required.

Sheridan County

4th Judicial District Court 224 S. Main, Suite B-11, Sheridan, WY 82801; 307-674-2960; Fax: 307-674-2909. Hours: 8AM-5PM (MST). *Felony, Civil Actions Over $7,000, Probate.*

Civil Records: Access: Mail, in person. Both court and visitors may perform in person searches. Search fee: $5.00 per name. Required to search: name, years to search. Civil cases indexed by defendant, plaintiff. Civil records archived from 1800s. **Criminal Records:** Access: Mail, in person. Both court and visitors may perform in person searches. Search fee: $5.00 per name. Required to search: name, years to search, DOB, SSN. Criminal records archived from 1800s. **General Information:** No sex related, juvenile or adoption cases released except by judges permission. SASE required. Turnaround time 1 week. Copy fee: $1.00 for first page, $.25 each addl. Certification fee: Cert included in copy fee. Fee payee: Clerk of District Court. Personal checks accepted. Prepayment is required.

Circuit Court 224 S. Main, Suite B-7, Sheridan, WY 82801; 307-674-2940; Fax: 307-674-2944. Hours: 8AM-5PM (MST). *Misdemeanor, Civil Actions Under $7,000, Eviction, Small Claims.*

Civil Records: Access: Mail, in person. Only the court conducts in person searches; visitors may not. Search fee: $5.00 per name. Required to search: name, years to search; also helpful-address. Civil cases indexed by defendant, plaintiff. Civil records on cards from 1983. **Criminal Records:** Access: Mail, in person. Only the court conducts in person searches; visitors may not. Search fee: $5.00 per name. Required to search: name, years to search; also helpful-address, DOB, SSN. Criminal records on computer from 1989, on cards from 1983. **General Information:** Identity of victims not released in sexual assault cases. SASE required. Turnaround time 2-3 days. Copy fee: $1.00 for first page, $.50 each addl. Certification fee: $1.00 per page. Fee payee: Sheridan County Court. Personal checks accepted. Prepayment is required.

Sublette County

9th Judicial District Court PO Box 764, Pinedale, WY 82941-0764; 307-367-4376; Fax: 307-367-6474. Hours: 8AM-5PM (MST). *Felony, Civil Actions Over $7,000, Probate.*

Civil Records: Access: Phone, fax, mail, in person. Both court and visitors may perform in

person searches. No search fee. Required to search: name; also helpful-years to search, address. Civil cases indexed by defendant, plaintiff. Civil records on card file from 1923. **Criminal Records:** Access: Phone, fax, mail, in person. Both court and visitors may perform in person searches. No search fee. Required to search: name, years to search; also helpful-address, DOB, SSN. Criminal records on card file from 1923. **General Information:** No PD or juvenile records released. SASE required. Turnaround time same day. Copy fee: $1.00 for first page, $.50 each addl. Certification fee: No certification fee. Fee payee: Clerk of District Court. Personal checks accepted. Fax notes: $3.00 for first page, $1.00 each addl.

Sublette Circuit Court PO Box 1796, Pinedale, WY 82941; 307-367-2556; Fax: 307-367-2658. Hours: 8AM-5PM (MST). *Misdemeanor, Civil Actions Under $7,000, Eviction, Small Claims.*

Civil Records: Access: Mail, in person. Only the court conducts in person searches; visitors may not. Search fee: $5.00 per name. Required to search: name, years to search; also helpful-address. Civil cases indexed by defendant. DOB helful. **Criminal Records:** Access: Mail, in person. Only the court conducts in person searches; visitors may not. Search fee: $5.00 per name. Required to search: name, years to search, DOB; also helpful-address, SSN. DOB helful. **General Information:** SASE not required. Turnaround time 1 week. Copy fee: $1.00 for first page, $.50 each addl. Certification fee: No certification fee. Fee payee: Circuit Court of Sublette County. Only cashiers checks and money orders accepted. In-state checks only. Prepayment is required.

Sweetwater County

3rd Judicial District Court PO Box 430, Green River, WY 82935; 307-872-6440; Fax: 307-872-6439. Hours: 9AM-5PM (MST). *Felony, Civil Actions Over $7,000, Probate.*

Civil Records: Access: Phone, fax, mail, in person. Both court and visitors may perform in person searches. No search fee. Required to search: name, years to search. Civil cases indexed by defendant, plaintiff. Civil records on computer from 1985, on microfiche from 1960, archived from late 1800. **Criminal Records:** Access: Phone, fax, mail, in person. Both court and visitors may perform in person searches. No search fee. Required to search: name, years to search. Criminal records on computer from 1985, on microfiche from 1960, archived from late 1800. **General Information:** No PD, juvenile, or adoption records released. SASE required. Turnaround time same day. Copy fee: $1.00 for first page, $.50 each addl. Certification fee: No certification fee. Fee payee: Clerk of District Court. Business checks accepted. Prepayment is required. Public access terminal is available. Fax notes: $1.00 for first page, $.50 each addl.

Green River Circuit Court PO Drawer 1720, Green River, WY 82935; 307-872-6460; Fax: 307-872-6375. Hours: 8AM-5PM (MST). *Misdemeanor, Civil Actions Under $7,000, Eviction, Small Claims.*

Civil Records: Access: Mail, in person. Both court and visitors may perform in person searches. Search fee: $5.00 per name. Required to search: name, years to search. Civil cases indexed by defendant, plaintiff. Civil records on computer from 1994, in card file from 1978-1994, archived prior to 1978. **Criminal Records:** Access: Mail, in person. Both court and visitors may perform in person searches. Search fee: $5.00 per name. Required to search: name, years to search, DOB; also helpful-SSN. Criminal Records computerized since 1990, on card file from 1978 to 1990. **General Information:** No sealed, sexual assault records released. Turnaround time same day. Copy fee: $.50 per page. Certification fee: No certification fee. Fee payee: Sweetwater County Court. Business checks accepted. In-state checks only. Prepayment is required.

Sweetwater Circuit Court PO Box 2028, Rock Springs, WY 82902; 307-352-6817; Fax: 307-352-6758. Hours: 8AM-5PM (MST). *Misdemeanor, Civil Actions Under $7,000, Eviction, Small Claims.*

Civil Records: Access: Fax, mail, in person. Only the court conducts in person searches; visitors may not. Search fee: $5.00 per name. Fee includes copy fees. Required to search: name, years to search; also helpful-address. Civil cases indexed by defendant, plaintiff. Civil records on computer from 1995, prior on microfiche, archived to 1981. **Criminal Records:** Access: Fax, mail, in person. Only the court conducts in person searches; visitors may not. Search fee: $5.00 per name. Fee includes copy fees. Required to search: name, years to search; also helpful-address, DOB, SSN. Criminal records on computer from 1989, prior on microfiche, archived to 1981. **General Information:** No sexual assault, sealed records released. SASE required. Turnaround time same day. No copy fee. Certification fee: No certification fee. Fee payee: Sweetwater Circuit Court. Personal checks accepted. Prepayment is required. Fax notes: No fee to fax results.

Teton County

9th Judicial District Court PO Box 4460, Jackson, WY 83001; 307-733-2533; Fax: 307-734-1562. Hours: 8AM-5PM (MST). *Felony, Civil Actions Over $3,000, Probate.*

Note: E-mail record search requests are accepted at clerk-of-district-court@tetonwyo.org

Civil Records: Access: Phone, fax, mail, in person. Both court and visitors may perform in person searches. No search fee. Required to search: name, years to search; also helpful-address. Civil cases indexed by defendant, plaintiff. Civil records on computer since 1990, card index back to 1920s. **Criminal Records:** Access: Phone, fax, mail, in person. Both court and visitors may perform in person searches. No search fee. Required to search: name, years to search; also helpful-address, DOB, SSN. Criminal records on computer since 1990, card index back to 1920s. **General Information:** No juvenile or adoption records released. SASE required. Turnaround time 2 days. Copy fee: $1.00 for first page, $.50 each addl. Certification fee: $.50. Fee payee: Clerk of District Court. Personal checks accepted. Prepayment is required.

Justice Court PO Box 2906, Jackson, WY 83001; 307-733-7713; Fax: 307-733-8694. Hours: 8AM-5PM (MST). *Misdemeanor, Civil Actions Under $3,000, Small Claims.*

Civil Records: Access: Mail, in person. Only the court conducts in person searches; visitors may not. Search fee: $5.00 per name. Required to search: name, years to search. Civil cases indexed by defendant, plaintiff. Civil records on docket books back to 1979. Actual files 5 years. **Criminal Records:** Access: Mail, in person. Only the court conducts in person searches; visitors may not. Search fee: $5.00 per name. Required to search: name, years to search, DOB. Citations on computer from 1991. No citation record older than 5 years. On docket books and files back to 1979. **General Information:** No juvenile, sexual or PD released. SASE required. Turnaround time 3-4 days (longer for pre-1992 criminal records). Copy fee: $1.00 for first page, $.50 each addl. Certification fee: No certification fee. Fee payee: Teton County Justice Court. Personal checks accepted. Prepayment is required.

Uinta County

3rd Judicial District Court PO Drawer 1906, Evanston, WY 82931; 307-783-0320/0401; Fax: 307-783-0400. Hours: 8AM-5PM (MST). *Felony, Civil Actions Over $7,000, Probate.*

Civil Records: Access: Phone, fax, mail, in person. Both court and visitors may perform in person searches. Search fee: $5.00 per name. Required to search: name, years to search; also helpful-address. Civil cases indexed by defendant, plaintiff. Civil records on microfiche from the late 1800s. **Criminal Records:** Access: Phone, fax, mail, in person. Both court and visitors may perform in person searches. Search fee: $5.00 per name. Required to search: name, years to search; also helpful-address, DOB, SSN. Criminal records on microfiche since 1938. **General Information:** Signed release necessary on confidential cases. SASE not required. Turnaround time 1 day. Copy fee: $.25 per page. Certification fee: No certification fee. Fee payee: Clerk of District Court. Personal checks accepted. Will bill copy & fax fees. Fax notes: $1.00 per page.

Uinta Circuit Court 225 9th St, 2nd Fl, Evanston, WY 82931; 307-789-2471; Fax: 307-789-5062. Hours: 8AM-5PM (MST). *Misdemeanor, Civil Actions Under $7,000, Eviction, Small Claims.*

Civil Records: Access: Mail, in person. Only the court conducts in person searches; visitors may not. Search fee: $5.00 per name. Required to search: name, years to search; also helpful-address. Civil cases indexed by defendant. Civil records on computer from 1994, prior on card index. **Criminal Records:** Access: Mail, in person. Only the court conducts in person searches; visitors may not. Search fee: $5.00 per name. Required to search: name, years to search; also helpful-address, DOB, SSN. Criminal records on computer since 1989, prior on index cards. **General Information:** No juvenile records released. SASE requested. Turnaround time 1 week. Copy fee: $1.00 for first page, $.50 each addl. Certification fee: No certification fee. Fee payee: Uinta County Court. Only cashiers checks and money orders accepted. Out of state checks not accepted. Prepayment is required.

Washakie County

5th Judicial District Court PO Box 862, Worland, WY 82401; 307-347-4821; Fax: 307-347-4325. Hours: 8AM-5PM (MST). *Felony, Civil Actions Over $3,000, Probate.*

Civil Records: Access: Phone, fax, mail, in person. Both court and visitors may perform in person searches. Search fee: $5.00 per name. Required to search: name; also helpful-years to search, address. Civil cases indexed by defendant. Civil records on computer from 1985, prior on file index. **Criminal Records:** Access: Phone, fax, mail, in person. Both court and visitors may perform in person searches. Search fee: $5.00 per name. Required to search: name; also helpful-years to search, address, DOB, SSN. Criminal records on computer from 1985, prior on file index. **General Information:** No juvenile, sexual or PD released. SASE required. Turnaround time same day when possible. Copy fee: $1.00 for first page, $.50 each addl. Certification fee: $.50. Fee payee: Clerk of Court. Personal checks accepted. Prepayment is required. Fax notes: $1.00 per page.

Justice Court PO Box 927, Worland, WY 82401; 307-347-2702; Fax: 307-347-4325. Hours: 8AM-5PM (MST). *Misdemeanor, Civil Actions Under $3,000, Small Claims.*

Civil Records: Access: Mail, in person. Search fee: $5.00 per name. Required to search: name, years to search. Civil cases indexed by defendant. Civil records on computer since 1988, on card index from late 1970, prior archived. **Criminal Records:** Access: Mail, in person. Both court and visitors may perform in person searches. Search fee: $5.00 per name. Required to search: name, years to search, DOB; also helpful-SSN. Criminal records on computer since 1988, on card index from late 1970, prior archived. **General Information:** No juvenile or PD released; criminal only. SASE not required. Turnaround time same day. Copy fee: $.25 per document. Certification fee: No certification fee. Fee payee: Justice Court. Personal checks accepted. Prepayment is required.

Weston County

6th Judicial District Court 1 W Main, Newcastle, WY 82701; 307-746-4778; Fax: 307-746-4778. Hours: 8AM-5PM (MST). *Felony, Civil Actions Over $3,000, Probate.*

Civil Records: Access: Phone, fax, mail, in person. Both court and visitors may perform in person searches. No search fee. Required to search: name; also helpful-years to search, address. Civil cases indexed by defendant, plaintiff. Civil records on card index from 1800s. **Criminal Records:** Access: Phone, fax, mail, in person. Both court and visitors may perform in person searches. No search fee. Required to search: name; also helpful-years to search, address, DOB, SSN. Criminal records on card index from 1800s. **General Information:** No juvenile, sexual or PD released. SASE required. Turnaround time same day. Copy fee: $1.00 for first page, $.50 each addl. Certification fee: $.50. Fee payee: Clerk of District Court. Personal checks accepted. Prepayment is required. Fax notes: $2.00 per document.

Justice Court 6 W Warwick, Newcastle, WY 82701; 307-746-3547; Fax: 307-746-3558. Hours: 8:30AM-4:30PM (MST). *Misdemeanor, Civil Actions Under $3,000, Small Claims.*

http://lacountycourts.co.la.ca.us

Civil Records: Access: Mail, in person. Only the court conducts in person searches; visitors may not. No search fee. Required to search: name, years to search; also helpful-address. Civil cases indexed by defendant. Note there is a branch office in Calabasa that handles only traffic (818-222-1148). Online access available at http://webcourt.co.la.ca.us. Court location, case number, and last name are all required to search. Available for civil, small claims, and unlawful detainer records. **Criminal Records:** Access: Fax, mail, in person. Only the court conducts in person searches; visitors may not. No search fee. Required to search: name, years to search, offense, date of offense; also helpful-address, DOB, SSN. **General Information:** No juvenile, sexual data released. SASE required. Turnaround time 2 days or longer. No copy fee. Certification fee: No certification fee. Fee payee: Malibu Superior Court. Business checks accepted. Fax notes: No fee to fax results.

ORGANIZATION 23 counties, 23 recording offices. The recording officer is County Clerk. The entire state is in the Mountain Time Zone (MST).

REAL ESTATE RECORDS County Clerks will **not** perform real estate searches. Copy fees are usually $1.00 per page, and certification fees are usually $2.00 per document. The Assessor maintains property tax records.

UCC RECORDS Financing statements are usually filed with the County Clerk. Accounts receivable and farm products require filing at the state level as well. All recording offices will perform UCC searches. Use search request form UCC-11. Searches fees are usually $10.00 per debtor name. Copy fees vary.

TAX LIEN RECORDS Federal tax liens on personal property of businesses are filed with the Secretary of State. Other federal and all state tax liens are filed with the County Clerk. Most counties will perform tax lien searches. Search fees are usually $10.00 per name.

Albany County
County Clerk, 525 Grand Ave. Room 202, Laramie, WY 82070. 307-721-2547. Fax: 307-721-2544.

Big Horn County
County Clerk, P.O. Box 31, Basin, WY 82410. 307-568-2357. Fax: 307-568-9375.

Campbell County
County Clerk, P.O. Box 3010, Gillette, WY 82717-3010. 307-682-7285. Fax: 307-687-6455.

Carbon County
County Clerk, 415 West Pine, P.O. Box 6, Courthouse, Rawlins, WY 82301. 307-328-2679. Fax: 307-328-2690.

Converse County
County Clerk, P.O. Drawer 990, Douglas, WY 82633-0990. 307-358-2244. Fax: 307-358-4065.

Crook County
County Clerk, P.O. Box 37, Sundance, WY 82729. 307-283-1323. Fax: 307-283-1091.

Fremont County
County Clerk, 450 N. 2nd Street, Courthouse - Room 220, Lander, WY 82520. 307-332-2405. Fax: 307-332-1132.

Goshen County
County Clerk, P.O. Box 160, Torrington, WY 82240. 307-532-4051. Fax: 307-532-7375.

Hot Springs County
County Clerk, 415 Arapahoe Street, Courthouse, Thermopolis, WY 82443-2783. 307-864-3515. Fax: 307-864-5116.

Johnson County
County Clerk, 76 North Main Street, Buffalo, WY 82834. 307-684-7272. Fax: 307-684-2708.

Laramie County
County Clerk, P.O. Box 608, Cheyenne, WY 82003. 307-633-4351. Fax: 307-633-4240.

Lincoln County
County Clerk, P.O. Box 670, Kemmerer, WY 83101-0670. 307-877-9056. Fax: 307-877-3101.

Natrona County
County Clerk, P.O. Box 863, Casper, WY 82602. 307-235-9206. Fax: 307-235-9367.

Niobrara County
County Clerk, P.O. Box 420, Lusk, WY 82225. 307-334-2211. Fax: 307-334-3013.

Park County
County Clerk, Courthouse, 1002 Sheridan Ave., Cody, WY 82414. 307-527-8600. Fax: 307-527-8626.

Platte County
County Clerk, P.O. Drawer 728, Wheatland, WY 82201. 307-322-2315. Fax: 307-322-5402.

Sheridan County
County Clerk, 224 South Main Street, Suite B-2, Sheridan, WY 82801-9998. 307-674-2500. Fax: 307-674-2529.

Sublette County
County Clerk, P.O. Box 250, Pinedale, WY 82941-0250. 307-367-4372. Fax: 307-367-6396.

Sweetwater County
County Clerk, P.O. Box 730, Green River, WY 82935. 307-872-6409. Fax: 307-872-6337.

Teton County
County Clerk, P.O. Box 1727, Jackson, WY 83001. 307-733-4433. Fax: 307-739-8681.

Uinta County
County Clerk, P.O. Box 810, Evanston, WY 82931. www.uintacounty.com/assessor.htm 307-783-0308. Fax: 307-783-0511.

Washakie County
County Clerk, Box 260, Worland, WY 82401-0260. 307-347-3131. Fax: 307-347-9366.

Weston County
County Clerk, One West Main, Newcastle, WY 82701. 307-746-4744. Fax: 307-746-9505.

You will usually be able to find the city name in the City/County Cross Reference below. In that case, it is a simple matter to determine the county from the cross reference. However, only the official US Postal Service city names are included in this index. There are an additional 40,000 place names that people use in their addresses. Therefore, we have also included a ZIP/City Cross Reference immediately following the City/County Cross Reference.

If you know the ZIP Code but the city name does not appear in the City/County Cross Reference index, look up the ZIP Code in the ZIP/City Cross Reference, find the city name, then look up the city name in the City/County Cross Reference. For example, you want to know the county for an address of Menands, NY 12204. There is no "Menands" in the City/County Cross Reference. The ZIP/City Cross Reference shows that ZIP Codes 12201-12288 are for the city of Albany. Looking back in the City/County Cross Reference, Albany is in Albany County.

City/County Cross Reference

AFTON Lincoln
ALADDIN Crook
ALBIN Laramie
ALCOVA Natrona
ALPINE Lincoln
ALVA Crook
ARAPAHOE Fremont
ARMINTO Natrona
ARVADA (82831) Sheridan(40), Campbell(31), Johnson(29)
AUBURN Lincoln
BAGGS Carbon
BAIROIL Sweetwater
BANNER (82832) Sheridan(82), Johnson(18)
BASIN Big Horn
BEDFORD Lincoln
BEULAH Crook
BIG HORN Sheridan
BIG PINEY Sublette
BILL Converse
BONDURANT Sublette
BOSLER Albany
BOULDER Sublette
BUFFALO Johnson
BUFORD Albany
BURLINGTON (82411) Washakie(73), Big Horn(28)
BURNS Laramie
BYRON Big Horn
CARLILE Crook
CARPENTER Laramie
CASPER Carbon
CASPER Natrona
CENTENNIAL Albany
CHEYENNE Laramie
CHUGWATER (82210) Platte(85), Goshen(15)
CLEARMONT Sheridan
CODY Park
COKEVILLE Lincoln
CORA Sublette
COWLEY Big Horn
CROWHEART (82512) Sweetwater(75), Fremont(25)
DANIEL Sublette
DAYTON Sheridan
DEAVER (82421) Big Horn(83), Park(17)
DEVILS TOWER Crook

DIAMONDVILLE Lincoln
DIXON Carbon
DOUGLAS Converse
DUBOIS Fremont
EDGERTON Natrona
ELK MOUNTAIN Carbon
EMBLEM Big Horn
ENCAMPMENT Carbon
ETNA (83118) Lincoln(96), Sweetwater(4)
EVANSTON Uinta
EVANSVILLE Natrona
FAIRVIEW Lincoln
FARSON Sweetwater
FE WARREN AFB Laramie
FORT BRIDGER Uinta
FORT LARAMIE Goshen
FORT WASHAKIE Fremont
FOUR CORNERS Weston
FRANNIE Park
FREEDOM Lincoln
FRONTIER Lincoln
GARRETT Albany
GILLETTE Campbell
GLENDO (82213) Platte(98), Converse(2)
GLENROCK Converse
GRANGER Sweetwater
GRANITE CANON Laramie
GREEN RIVER Sweetwater
GREYBULL Big Horn
GROVER Lincoln
GUERNSEY Platte
HAMILTON DOME Hot Springs
HANNA Carbon
HARTVILLE Platte
HAWK SPRINGS Goshen
HILAND Natrona
HILLSDALE Laramie
HORSE CREEK Laramie
HUDSON Fremont
HULETT Crook
HUNTLEY Goshen
HYATTVILLE Big Horn
IRON MOUNTAIN Laramie
JACKSON Teton
JAY EM Goshen
JEFFREY CITY Fremont
JELM Albany
KAYCEE (82639) Johnson(94), Natrona(7)
KEELINE Niobrara

KELLY Teton
KEMMERER Lincoln
KINNEAR Fremont
KIRBY Hot Springs
LA BARGE Lincoln
LAGRANGE Goshen
LANCE CREEK Niobrara
LANDER Fremont
LARAMIE Albany
LEITER Sheridan
LINCH Johnson
LINGLE Goshen
LITTLE AMERICA Sweetwater
LONETREE Uinta
LOST SPRINGS (82224) Converse(80), Niobrara(20)
LOVELL Big Horn
LUSK Niobrara
LYMAN Uinta
LYSITE Fremont
MANDERSON (82432) Park(78), Big Horn(22)
MANVILLE Niobrara
MC FADDEN Carbon
MC KINNON Sweetwater
MEDICINE BOW (82329) Carbon(67), Albany(33)
MEETEETSE Park
MERIDEN Laramie
MIDWEST Natrona
MILLS Natrona
MOORCROFT (82721) Crook(56), Campbell(44)
MOOSE Teton
MORAN Teton
MOUNTAIN VIEW Uinta
NATRONA Natrona
NEWCASTLE Weston
NODE Niobrara
OPAL Lincoln
OSAGE Weston
OSHOTO (82724) Crook(78), Campbell(22)
OTTO (82434) Washakie(67), Big Horn(33)
PARKMAN Sheridan
PAVILLION Fremont
PINE BLUFFS Laramie
PINEDALE Sublette
POINT OF ROCKS Sweetwater
POWDER RIVER Natrona

POWELL Park
RALSTON Park
RANCHESTER Sheridan
RAWLINS Carbon
RECLUSE Campbell
RELIANCE Sweetwater
RIVERTON Fremont
ROBERTSON Uinta
ROCK RIVER (82083) Albany(50), Carbon(50)
ROCK SPRINGS Sweetwater
ROZET Campbell
SADDLESTRING Johnson
SAINT STEPHENS Fremont
SARATOGA Carbon
SAVERY Carbon
SHAWNEE Converse
SHELL Big Horn
SHERIDAN Sheridan
SHOSHONI Fremont
SINCLAIR Carbon
SMOOT Lincoln
STORY Sheridan
SUNDANCE (82729) Crook(97), Weston(3)
SUPERIOR Sweetwater
TEN SLEEP Washakie
TETON VILLAGE Teton
THAYNE (83127) Lincoln(77), Sweetwater(23)
THERMOPOLIS Hot Springs
TIE SIDING Albany
TORRINGTON Goshen
UPTON (82730) Weston(90), Crook(10)
VAN TASSELL Niobrara
VETERAN Goshen
WALCOTT Carbon
WAMSUTTER Sweetwater
WAPITI Park
WESTON (82731) Campbell(96), Crook(4)
WHEATLAND (82201) Platte(98), Albany(2)
WILSON Teton
WOLF Sheridan
WORLAND Washakie
WRIGHT Campbell
WYARNO Sheridan
YELLOWSTONE NATIONAL PARK Park
YODER Goshen

ZIP/City Cross Reference

82001-82003	CHEYENNE	82058-82058	GARRETT	82084-82084	TIE SIDING	82217-82217	HAWK SPRINGS
82005-82005	FE WARREN AFB	82059-82059	GRANITE CANON	82190-82190	YELLOWSTONE NATIONAL PARK	82218-82218	HUNTLEY
82006-82010	CHEYENNE	82060-82060	HILLSDALE			82219-82219	JAY EM
82050-82050	ALBIN	82061-82061	HORSE CREEK	82201-82201	WHEATLAND	82221-82221	LAGRANGE
82051-82051	BOSLER	82063-82063	JELM	82210-82210	CHUGWATER	82222-82222	LANCE CREEK
82052-82052	BUFORD	82070-82073	LARAMIE	82212-82212	FORT LARAMIE	82223-82223	LINGLE
82053-82053	BURNS	82081-82081	MERIDEN	82213-82213	GLENDO	82224-82224	LOST SPRINGS
82054-82054	CARPENTER	82082-82082	PINE BLUFFS	82214-82214	GUERNSEY	82225-82225	LUSK
82055-82055	CENTENNIAL	82083-82083	ROCK RIVER	82215-82215	HARTVILLE	82227-82227	MANVILLE

82229-82229	SHAWNEE	82440-82440	RALSTON	82714-82714	DEVILS TOWER	82936-82936	LONETREE
82240-82240	TORRINGTON	82441-82441	SHELL	82715-82715	FOUR CORNERS	82937-82937	LYMAN
82242-82242	VAN TASSELL	82442-82442	TEN SLEEP	82716-82718	GILLETTE	82938-82938	MC KINNON
82243-82243	VETERAN	82443-82443	THERMOPOLIS	82720-82720	HULETT	82939-82939	MOUNTAIN VIEW
82244-82244	YODER	82450-82450	WAPITI	82721-82721	MOORCROFT	82941-82941	PINEDALE
82301-82301	RAWLINS	82501-82501	RIVERTON	82723-82723	OSAGE	82942-82942	POINT OF ROCKS
82310-82310	JEFFREY CITY	82510-82510	ARAPAHOE	82725-82725	RECLUSE	82943-82943	RELIANCE
82321-82321	BAGGS	82512-82512	CROWHEART	82727-82727	ROZET	82944-82944	ROBERTSON
82322-82322	BAIROIL	82513-82513	DUBOIS	82729-82729	SUNDANCE	82945-82945	SUPERIOR
82323-82323	DIXON	82514-82514	FORT WASHAKIE	82730-82730	UPTON	83001-83002	JACKSON
82324-82324	ELK MOUNTAIN	82515-82515	HUDSON	82731-82731	WESTON	83011-83011	KELLY
82325-82325	ENCAMPMENT	82516-82516	KINNEAR	82732-82732	WRIGHT	83012-83012	MOOSE
82327-82327	HANNA	82520-82520	LANDER	82801-82801	SHERIDAN	83013-83013	MORAN
82329-82329	MEDICINE BOW	82523-82523	PAVILLION	82831-82831	ARVADA	83014-83014	WILSON
82331-82331	SARATOGA	82524-82524	SAINT STEPHENS	82832-82832	BANNER	83025-83025	TETON VILLAGE
82332-82332	SAVERY	82601-82615	CASPER	82833-82833	BIG HORN	83101-83101	KEMMERER
82334-82334	SINCLAIR	82620-82620	ALCOVA	82834-82834	BUFFALO	83110-83110	AFTON
82335-82335	WALCOTT	82630-82630	ARMINTO	82835-82835	CLEARMONT	83111-83111	AUBURN
82336-82336	WAMSUTTER	82631-82631	BILL	82836-82836	DAYTON	83112-83112	BEDFORD
82401-82401	WORLAND	82633-82633	DOUGLAS	82837-82837	LEITER	83113-83113	BIG PINEY
82410-82410	BASIN	82635-82635	EDGERTON	82838-82838	PARKMAN	83114-83114	COKEVILLE
82411-82411	BURLINGTON	82636-82636	EVANSVILLE	82839-82839	RANCHESTER	83115-83115	DANIEL
82412-82412	BYRON	82637-82637	GLENROCK	82840-82840	SADDLESTRING	83116-83116	DIAMONDVILLE
82414-82414	CODY	82638-82638	HILAND	82842-82842	STORY	83118-83118	ETNA
82420-82420	COWLEY	82639-82639	KAYCEE	82844-82844	WOLF	83119-83119	FAIRVIEW
82421-82421	DEAVER	82640-82640	LINCH	82845-82845	WYARNO	83120-83120	FREEDOM
82422-82422	EMBLEM	82642-82642	LYSITE	82901-82902	ROCK SPRINGS	83121-83121	FRONTIER
82423-82423	FRANNIE	82643-82643	MIDWEST	82922-82922	BONDURANT	83122-83122	GROVER
82426-82426	GREYBULL	82644-82644	MILLS	82923-82923	BOULDER	83123-83123	LA BARGE
82427-82427	HAMILTON DOME	82646-82646	NATRONA	82925-82925	CORA	83124-83124	OPAL
82428-82428	HYATTVILLE	82648-82648	POWDER RIVER	82926-82926	ROCK SPRINGS	83126-83126	SMOOT
82430-82430	KIRBY	82649-82649	SHOSHONI	82929-82929	LITTLE AMERICA	83127-83127	THAYNE
82431-82431	LOVELL	82701-82701	NEWCASTLE	82930-82931	EVANSTON	83128-83128	ALPINE
82432-82432	MANDERSON	82710-82710	ALADDIN	82932-82932	FARSON	83422-83422	DRIGGS
82433-82433	MEETEETSE	82711-82711	ALVA	82933-82933	FORT BRIDGER		
82434-82434	OTTO	82712-82712	BEULAH	82934-82934	GRANGER		
82435-82435	POWELL	82713-82713	CARLILE	82935-82935	GREEN RIVER		

Notes

Notes

Addendum: California - Northern & Southern US District Courts & Bankruptcy Courts

US District Court Northern District of California

San Jose Division Room 2112, 280 S 1st St, San Jose, CA 95113, 408-535-5364. www.cand.uscourts.gov Counties: Alameda, Contra Costa, Del Norte, Humboldt, Lake, Marin, Mendocino, Monterey, Napa, San Benito, San Francisco, San Mateo, Santa Clara, Santa Cruz, Sonoma. **Indexing & Storage:** Cases are indexed by defendant and plaintiff as well as by case number. New cases are available in the index immediately after filing date. Records are stored by case number, however, a case number can be researched by using the plaintiff's or the defendant's name. A computer index is maintained. Records are also indexed on microfiche. Open records are located at this court. **Fee & Payment:** The fee is $15.00 per item (one party name or case number). Payment may be made by money order, cashier check, personal check. Prepayment is required. Payee: Clerk, US District Court. Certification fee: $5.00 per document. Copy fee: $.50 per page. You are allowed to make your own copies. These copies cost Not Applicable per page. Use pay copier for copies. **Phone Search:** Only docket information is available by phone. An automated voice case information service (VCIS) is not available. **Mail Search:** Always enclose a stamped self addressed envelope. **In Person Search:** In person searching is available. **PACER:** Sign-up number is 800-676-6856. Access fee is $.60 per minute. Toll-free access: 888-877-5883. Local access: 415-522-2144. Case records are available back to 1984. Records are purged every six months. New records are available online after 1 day. PACER is available on the Internet at http://pacer.cand.uscourts.gov.

US Bankruptcy Court Northern District of California

Oakland Division PO Box 2070, Oakland, CA 94604 (Courier: Suite 300, 1300 Clay St, Oakland, CA 94612), 510-879-3600. www.canb.uscourts.gov Counties: Alameda, Contra Costa. **Indexing & Storage:** Cases are indexed by debtor as well as by case number. New cases are available in the index 2 days after filing date. Both computer and card indexes are maintained. Open records are located at this court. **Fee & Payment:** The fee is $15.00 per item (one party name or case number). Payment may be made by money order, cashier check, business check. Personal checks are not accepted. Prepayment is required. Payee: Clerk, US Bankruptcy Court. Certification fee: $5.00 per document. Copy fee: $.50 per page. You are allowed to make your own copies. Copies cost $.25 per page. **Phone Search:** An automated voice case information service (VCIS) is available. Call VCIS at 800-570-9819 or 415-705-3160. **Mail Search:** Always enclose a stamped self addressed envelope. **In Person Search:** In person searching is available. **PACER:** Sign-up number is 800-676-6856. Access fee is $.60 per minute. Toll-free access: 888-773-8548. Local access: 415-705-3148, 415-433-0211. Case records are available back to 1993. Records are purged every six months to one year. New civil records are available online after 1 day. You can access PACER via the Internet, using webPACER. For info and software visit www.cacb.uscourts.gov.

San Francisco Division PO Box 7341, San Francisco, CA 94120-7341 (Courier Address: 235 Pine St, San Francisco, CA 94104), 415-268-2300. www.canb.uscourts.gov Counties: San Francisco, San Mateo. **Indexing & Storage:** Cases are indexed by debtor as well as by case number. New cases are available in the index 3-4 working days after filing date. All searches are conducted by a copy service. To reach them, call 415-781-4910. A computer index is maintained. Records are also indexed on microfiche. Open records are located at this court. **Fee & Payment:** The fee is $15.00 per item (one party name or case number). Payment may be made by money order, cashier check, business check. Personal checks are not accepted. Prepayment is required. Payee: Clerk of the Court. Certification fee: $5.00 per document. Copy fee: $.50 per page. You are allowed to make your own copies. These copies cost $.25 per page. **Phone Search:** Only information available from dockets of open cases is released over the phone. An automated voice case information service (VCIS) is available. Call VCIS at 800-570-9819 or 415-705-3160. **Mail Search:** A stamped self addressed envelope is not required. **In Person Search:** In person searching is available. **PACER:** Sign-up number is 800-676-6856. Access fee is $.60 per minute. Toll-free access: 888-773-8548. Local access: 415-705-3148, 415-433-0211. Case records are available back to 1993. Records are purged every six months to one year. New civil records are available online after 1 day. You can access PACER via the Internet, using webPACER. For info and software visit www.cacb.uscourts.gov.

San Jose Division Room 3035, 280 S 1st St, San Jose, CA 95113-3099, 408-535-5118. www.canb.uscourts.gov Counties: Monterey, San Benito, Santa Clara, Santa Cruz. **Indexing & Storage:** Cases are indexed by debtor as well as by case number. New cases are available in the index 1-2 days after filing date. A computer index is maintained. Open records are located at this court. **Fee & Payment:** The fee is $15.00 per item (one party name or case number). Payment may be made by money order, cashier check, business check. Personal checks are not accepted. Prepayment is required. Payee: Clerk, US Bankruptcy Court.

Certification fee: $5.00 per document. Copy fee: at lea per page. **Phone Search:** Only basic information, such as date of filing is released over the phone. An automated voice case information service (VCIS) is available. Call VCIS at 800-570-9819 or 415-705-3160. **Mail Search:** Always enclose a stamped self addressed envelope. **In Person Search:** In person searching is available. **PACER:** Sign-up number is 800-676-6856. Access fee is $.60 per minute. Toll-free access: 888-773-8548. Local access: 415-705-3148, 415-433-0211. Case records are available back to 1993. Records are purged every six months to one year. New civil records are available online after 1 day. You can access PACER via the Internet, using webPACER. For info and software visit www.cacb.uscourts.gov.

Santa Rosa Division 99 South E St, Santa Rosa, CA 95404, 707-525-8539, Fax: 707-579-0374. www.canb.uscourts.gov Counties: Del Norte, Humboldt, Lake, Marin, Mendocino, Napa, Sonoma. **Indexing & Storage:** Cases are indexed by debtor as well as by case number. New cases are available in the index immediately after filing date. A computer index is maintained. Open records are located at this court. **Fee & Payment:** The fee is $15.00 per item (one party name or case number). Payment may be made by money order, cashier check, business check. Personal checks are not accepted. Prepayment is required. This court will not bill. Payee: Clerk - US Bankruptcy Court. Certification fee: $5.00 per document. Copy fee: $.50 per page. You are allowed to make your own copies. These copies cost $.20 per page. This court urges use of their contracted copy service, Attorney's Diversified (707-545-5455). **Phone Search:** Names and accession numbers will be released over the phone. An automated voice case information service (VCIS) is available. Call VCIS at 800-570-9819 or 415-705-3160. **Mail Search:** Always enclose a stamped self addressed envelope. **In Person Search:** In person searching is available. **PACER:** Sign-up number is 800-676-6856. Access fee is $.60 per minute. Toll-free access: 888-773-8548. Local access: 415-705-3148, 415-433-0211. Case records are available back to 1993. Records are purged every six months to one year. New civil records are available online after 1 day. You can access PACER via the Internet, using webPACER. For info and software visit www.cacb.uscourts.gov.

US District Court Southern District of California

San Diego Division Room 4290, 880 Front St, San Diego, CA 92101-8900, 619-557-5600, Fax: 619-557-6684. www.casd.uscourts.gov Counties: Imperial, San Diego. Court also handles some cases from Yuma County, AZ. **Indexing & Storage:** Cases are indexed by defendant and plaintiff as well as by case number. New cases are available in the index 24 hours after filing date. A computer index is maintained. Open records are located at this court. **Fee & Payment:** The fee is $15.00 per item (one party name or case number). Payment may be made by money order, cashier check, personal check. Contract copy service makes copies at $.24 per page. Prepayment is required. Payee: US District Court. Certification fee: $5.00 per document. Copy fee: $.50 per page. **Phone Search:** Searching is not available by phone. **Mail Search:** A stamped self addressed envelope is not required. **In Person Search:** In person searching is available. **PACER:** Sign-up number is 800-676-6856. Access fee is $.60 per minute. Toll-free access: 888-241-9760. Local access: 619-557-7138. Case records are available back to 1990. New records are available online after 1 day. PACER is available on the Internet at http://pacer.casd.uscourts.gov. **Other Online Access:** A computer bulletin board is accessible at 619-557-6779.

US Bankruptcy Court Southern District of California

San Diego Division Office of the clerk, US Courthouse, 325 West "F" St., San Diego, CA 92101, 619-557-5620. www.casb.uscourts.gov Counties: Imperial, San Diego. **Indexing & Storage:** Cases are indexed by debtor as well as by case number. New cases are available in the index 3 days after filing date. A computer index is maintained. Open records are located at this court. **Fee & Payment:** The fee is $15.00 per item (one party name or case number). Payment may be made by money order, cashier check, personal check. Prepayment is required. Payee: Clerk, US Bankruptcy Court. Certification fee: $5.00 per document. Copy fee: $.50 per page. **Phone Search:** Only docket information is available by phone. An automated voice case information service (VCIS) is available. **Fax Search:** The court has contracted Court Copy Ltd to handle copies and fax requests. To make arrangements for a fax transaction, call Court Copy Ltd at 619-234-4425. They will accept credit cards. **Mail Search:** A stamped self addressed envelope is not required. **In Person Search:** In person searching is available. **PACER:** Sign-up number is 800-676-6856. Access fee is $.60 per minute. Toll-free access: 800-870-9972. Local access: 619-557-6875. Case records are available back to 1989. Records are purged every six months. New civil records are available online after 3 days. PACER is available on the Internet at http://pacer.casb.uscourts.gov. **Electronic Filing:** Only law firms and practicioners may file documents electronically. Anyone can search online; however, searches only include those cases which have been filed electronically. Use http://ecf.casb.uscourts.gov/cgi-bin/PublicCaseFiled-Rpt.pl to search. Electronic filing information is available online at http://ecf.casb.uscourts.gov

Notes

Facts on Demand Press

Find It Online

Get the information you need as quickly and easily as a professional researcher. *Find it Online* is a practical, how-to-guide written by a non-techno geek and developed for real people. Learn the difference between search engines and search directories, find people online, cut through government red tape and access the vast amounts of information now available on the Internet.

Alan M. Schlein • 1-889150-20-7 • Pub. Date 2000 • 512 pgs • $19.95

Online Competitive Intelligence

Competitive intelligence on the Internet . . . it's not the wave of the future . . . it's here now! The latest information to keep ahead of the competition is literally at your fingertips. *If* you know where to find it. *Online Competitive Intelligence*, a new title by the nation's leading information professional — Helen P. Burwell, empowers you to find the latest information that major corporations spend thousands of research dollars for — from your own computer.

Helen P. Burwell • 1-889150-08-8 • Pub. Date 2000 • 464 pgs. • $25.95

Public Records Online

How can someone determine which records are available online — who has them and what is available for "free or fee" — without spending time searching endless sources? Use *Public Records Online*. As the only "Master Guide" to online public record searching, *Public Records Online's* second edition details thousands of sites, both government agencies and private sources. This new edition is 80 pages larger, easier to use, and contains:

Facts on Demand Press • 1-889150-21-5 • Pub. Date 2000 • 520 pgs • $20.95

Available at your local bookstore
or online at www.brbpub.com.

Additional Titles and Information

The National Directory of Public Record Providers

ISBN # 1-879792-63-X   Pub. 1/00   Pages 800   Price $59.50

Description: The only "who's who" in the public record industry. Profiles in detail online database vendors and gateways, national and regional search firms, CD-ROM providers, pre-employment and tenant screeners plus over 2,600 hands-on document retrievers. For all states.

The MVR Book

ISBN # 1-879792-61-3   Pub. 1/00   Pages 312   Price $19.95

Description: The national reference detailing — in practical terms — the privacy restrictions, access procedures, regulations, and database systems of all state-held driver and vehicle records. For all states.

The MVR Decoder Digest

ISBN # 1-879792-62-1   Pub 1/00   Pages 320   Price $19.95

Description: The companion to *The MVR Book*. Translates the codes and abbreviations of violations and licensing categories that appear on motor vehicle records. For all states.

The Public Record Research System – CD-ROM

Updated Semi-annually, License fee of $119.00 includes one update.

Description: In-depth reference to over 26,000 sources of public records and public information. Extensive profiles of federal agencies, county recorder offices, state and county courts, state agencies, accredited post-secondary institutions, occupational licensing and business registration agencies, Public Record Retrieval members. Also includes a place name — county — ZIP Code cross reference. Extremely thorough.

BRB Publications, Inc.
PO Box 27869
Tempe, AZ 85285-7869
Phone: 800-929-3811
Fax: 1-800-929-4981

For more information visit www.brbpub.com.